2016

REDBOOKS™

REDBOOKS
Brands. Marketers. Agencies. Search Less. Find More.

Content Operations:
General Manager: Peter Valli
Operations Manager: Patricia M. Phillips
Content Analysts: Himanshu P. Goodluck, Sarah E. Cox

2016

REDBOOKS™

Agencies
January

QUESTIONS ABOUT THIS PUBLICATION?

For CONTENT questions concerning this publication, please call:
The Content Operations Department at 800-908-5395, press 3

For CUSTOMER SERVICE ASSISTANCE concerning shipments, billing or other matters, please call:
The Customer Service Department at 800-908-5395, press 2

For SALES ASSISTANCE, please call:
The Sales Department at 800-908-5395, press 1

ISBN Number: 978-1-937606-24-4

Red Books LLC
Content Operations
330 Seventh Avenue, 10th Floor
New York, NY 10001

www.redbooks.com

CONTENTS

PREFACE

For over 100 years, *REDBOOKS*™ have been the most comprehensive source of information on the advertising practices of companies located in the United States and Canada. The *Agencies* edition, together with the *Advertisers* edition, provides a detailed profile of the advertising industry-whether you are seeking information on agencies and their clients or advertisers and their products.

CONTENT AND COVERAGE

At your fingertips are the essential facts about advertising agencies and their branches in the United States and around the world. Arranged in an easy-to-use format and published in January and July each year, with supplements in April and October, this directory keeps the reader up-to-date on the constantly changing world of advertising from clients to billings to personnel. Listed in this directory are agencies that are located in the U.S. or Canada. International agencies included in this directory have at least one U.S. or Canadian branch.

ARRANGEMENT AND INDEXES

Main listings are divided into six sections: Advertising Agencies, House Agencies, Interactive Agencies, Media Buying Services, Sales Promotion Agencies and Public Relations Firms.

The *Agencies* edition is also well served by four indexes, two of which refer to companies and two to personnel. Please refer to the 'How to Use' section for particular guidelines on referencing individual agencies, entry content and other features of the directory. There is also a Special Market Index that categorizes agencies by twenty-three different advertising specialities.

Also included in this edition are a member list of the 4A's (American Association of Advertising Agencies) and an Associations section.

COMPILATION METHOD

The *Agencies* edition is compiled and updated from information supplied by the advertising agencies themselves and from business publications. Every effort is made to obtain dependable data; however, the publisher cannot guarantee complete accuracy or assume responsibility for any agency listed in or omitted from this directory.

RELATED SERVICES

For information on the www.redbooks.com web site, please call (800) 908-5395.

Mailing lists compiled from information contained in *REDBOOKS* may be ordered from:

Marie D. Briganti, Director, Data & Media Services
MeritDirect
2 International Drive, Rye Brook, NY 10573
(914) 368-1023
E-mail: mbriganti@meritdirect.com

Electronic database tapes of the directory in raw data format are available for licensing. For electronic database tapes or alliance opportunities, please contact:

Peter Valli, General Manager
Red Books LLC
330 Seventh Avenue, 10th Floor, New York, NY 10001

Tel: (646) 710-4454
E-mail: peter.valli@redbooks.com

Companies who wish to add or correct their listings can send information to:

Patricia Phillips, Operations Manager
Red Books LLC
330 Seventh Avenue, 10th Floor, New York, NY 10001
Tel: (646) 710-4465
E-mail: patricia.phillips@redbooks.com

In addition to keeping the information in our directories as up to date as possible, we are constantly trying to improve their design and add useful new features. Any comments or suggestions in this regard can be directed to the General Manager at the above address.

ACKNOWLEDGMENTS

We would like to thank those in the thousands of advertising agencies throughout the United States who took the time to provide us with the information necessary to compile an accurate, comprehensive *Agencies* edition.

HOW TO USE THE *AGENCIES* EDITION

The *Agencies* edition of *REDBOOKS*™ provides a comprehensive overview of advertising agencies and their branch offices in the United States and around the world. Containing a vast amount of useful business information, this directory provides several different ways for users to locate detailed information on advertising agencies. The following guidelines are intended to help you find the data you need in the most logical way and to make that information work to your maximum benefit.

HOW TO FIND AN AGENCY BY THE COMPANY NAME

The first place to start in finding a company is the 'Index of Agency Names' starting on page A-1. This index interfiles the names of all the agencies listed in the book, regardless of what type of agency they are. For ease of reference, parent companies in this index are printed in bold type. The branch listings, which are printed in regular type, also show the name of the parent company and the page number of the listing.

A

A TEAM L.L.C., pg. 1279
AAA ADVERTISING CORPORATION, pg. 1
AAC SAATCHI & SAATCHI —see Saatchi & Saatchi, pg. 940
ADLAND SERVICES, pg. 1
ALPHA MARKETING, pg. 1

If the company name does not appear in the index, try looking in the 'Name Changes' section. This section provides a key to companies with names that have been altered or absorbed by another company.

BY THE COMPANY TYPE

There are six different types of agencies listed in this directory:

* **Full-Service Agencies**
* **House Agencies** (proprietary agencies that companies use to exclusively handle their advertising needs)
* **Interactive Agencies** (agencies offering a mix of web design/development, internet advertising/marketing, and e-business/e-commerce consulting)
* **Media Buying Services** (companies that offer services for planning, buying, placing and managing advertisers' media needs)
* **Sales Promotion Agencies** (those that design, develop and implement a wide variety of promotional activities)
* **Public Relations Firms**

The full listings of companies are presented alphabetically, generally by the parent company's name, within these sections. Related companies and branches are presented under the parent. Occasionally, there will be references to large or distinctive branches that are listed separately.

BY THE COMPANY LOCATION

The Geographic Index of Agencies has been provided to assist you in searching for companies in a specific city or state. Street addresses are also provided in this index. This index is separated into two sections, 'Geographic Index of U.S. Agencies' and 'Geographic Index of Non-U.S. Agencies'.

ALABAMA
Birmingham

BYNUM/LAWRENCE/RUSHING, 2204 Lakeshore Dr Ste 110, 35209-6701 pg. 186
DAVIS/DENNY ADVERTISING & RELATED SERVICES, INC., 2545 Highland Ave, 35205 pg. 306
EGN ADVERTISING, 605 Richard Arrington Jr Blvd N, 35203 pg. 1198

BY THE AGENCY SPECIALIZATION

The 'Special Market Index', in the front of the book, shows companies that have a very particular advertising specialization. Some examples of specializations are: Asian Market, Entertainment, Health Care Services, High Technology, Travel & Tourism, etc.

African-American Market

Adair Greene, Inc.; Atlanta, GA, pg. 16
Ads That Work; Pacifica, CA, pg. 21
Anderson Communications; Atlanta, GA, pg. 41
Arnold Worldwide; Boston, MA, pg. 49
A.S.A. Advertising, Inc.; Fort Lauderdale, FL, pg. 6

LOCATING ADVERTISING PERSONNEL

Agency personnel are indexed in two ways in the *Agencies* edition.

The "Personnel Index' features key decision-makers who are directly involved in their agencies' creative processes. This is a straight alpha-name index.

A

Aadland, Paul, Supvr-Media—Bradley/Reid Communications, Inc., Anchorage, AK, pg. 146
Aaron, Jennifer, Exec VP & Acct Supvr—Carroll/White, Atlanta, GA, pg. 204

The 'Responsibilities Index' presents the executives by their job function i.e., Account Director, Creative, Public Relations, etc.

ACCOUNT COORDINATOR

Abiera, Elaine, Acct Coord —Media Plus, Seattle, WA, pg. 1262
Adams, Kristy, Acct Coord —Cashman & Katz Integrated Communications, Glastonbury, CT, pg. 206

THE FOLLOWING IS AN EXAMPLE OF A TYPICAL AGENCY LISTING WITH TAGS TO INDICATE BASIC COMPONENTS

ABC ADVERTISING CO., INC. -- **Company Name**
1234 2nd St, New York, NY 10001 -- **Company Address**
Tel.: 212-632-9076 -- **Telecommunications Data**
Fax: 212-632-9648
E-Mail: info@abc.com -- **Electronic Mail Data**
Web Site: www.abcadv.com

E-Mail for Key Personnel:
President: alincoln@abc.com
Creative Dir.: glaberson@abc.com
Media Dir.: stanton@abc.com
Production Mgr.: pgibson@abc.com
Public Relations: wilson@abc.com

Employees: 154 Year Founded: 1978 -- **Company Data**

National Agency Associations: 4A's-BPA -- **Association Memberships**
Agency Specializes In: Health Care -- **Agency's Specialization (Agency Profile for some listings)**

Approx. Annual Billings: $34,100,000 -- **Annual Billings, Including Breakdown by Type of Media**

Breakdown of Gross Billings by Media:
Bus. Publs.: $4,500,000; Mags.: $6,500,000; Outdoor: $3,000,000;
Radio: $5,350,000; T.V.: $12,750,000; Transit: $2,000,000

Andrew Lincoln *(Pres)* -- **Key Personnel**
Trevor Thomas *(Exec VP)*
Matthew Austin *(Sr VP & Acct Supvr)*
Charles Glaberson *(VP & Dir-Creative)*
Carol Greenberg *(VP & Acct Supvr)*
Susan Morrison *(Dir-Media)*
Paul Gibson *(Dir-Art)*
Daniel O'Connell *(Acct Supvr)*
Rory D'Arcy *(Copywriter)*

Accounts: -- **Accounts Served by the Agency**
GlaxoSmithKline; Research Triangle Park, NC Pharmaceuticals; 1980
New—Olympus Corp.-Medical Instrument Div.; Lake Success, NY Medical & Surgical Instruments; 2015
Pfizer International LLC; New York, NY Pharmaceuticals; 1978

Branch: -- **Information on Branch Office**
ABC Advertising Co., Inc.
1010 10th Ave, Los Angeles, CA 90035
Tel.: 714-959-7206
Fax: 714-959-5619

Elliott Miller *(VP & Gen Mgr)*

ABBREVIATIONS

GENERAL TERMS

Acct	Account
Acctg	Accounting
Accts	Accounts
Acq	Acquisition(s)
Admin	Administration/Administrative
Adv	Advertising
Assoc	Associate
Asst	Assistant
Brdcst	Broadcast
Bus	Business
CEO	Chief Executive Officer
CFO	Chief Financial Officer
Chm	Chairman of the Board
CIO	Chief Information Officer
CMO	Chief Marketing Officer
Comm	Communication(s)
Comml	Commercial
COO	Chief Operating Officer
Coord	Coordinator
Corp	Corporate/Corporation
CTO	Chief Technology Officer
Dept	Department
Dev	Development
Dir	Director
Distr	Distribution
Div	Division
DP	Data Processing
Engr	Engineer
Engrg	Engineering
Environ	Environmental
Exec	Executive
Fin	Finance/Financial
Gen	General
Govt	Government
Grp	Group
HR	Human Resources
Indus	Industry/Industrial
Info	Information
Intl	International
IR	Investor Relations
IT	Information Technology
Jr	Junior
Matl	Material
Matls	Materials
Mdse	Merchandise
Mdsg	Merchandising
Mfg	Manufacturing
Mfr	Manufacturer
Mgmt	Management
Mgr	Manager
Mktg	Marketing
Mng	Managing
Natl	National
Ops	Operations
Org	Organization
Pkg	Packaging
Plng	Planning
PR	Public Relations
Pres	President
Pro	Professional
Promo	Promotion
Promos	Promotions
Pub	Public
Publ	Publishing
Publr	Publisher
Pur	Purchasing
R&D	Research & Development
Reg	Regional
Rep	Representative
Res	Research
Sec	Secretary
Sls	Sales
Sr	Senior
Supvr	Supervisor
Svc	Service
Svcs	Services
Sys	Systems
Tech	Technology
Telecom	Telecommunication(s)
Treas	Treasurer
Trng	Training
Vice Chm	Vice Chairman
VP	Vice President

NUMBER OF AGENCIES BY BILLING CLASSIFICATION

Billings Range	Numbers of Agencies Listed
Over $25 million	613
Between $10 million and $25 million	341
Between $5 million and $10 million	235
Between $1 million and $5 million	640
Agencies billing over $1 million	**1,829**

Billings Range	Numbers of Agencies Listed
Under $1 million	226
Agencies listing their annual billings	**2,055**
Agencies not listing their annual billings	9,105
Total number of agencies listed	**11,160**

NUMBER OF AGENCIES BY STATE

	Hdqtrs.	Branches
Alabama	40	3
Alaska	19	0
Arizona	110	13
Arkansas	29	6
California	1,209	264
Colorado	175	23
Connecticut	125	17
Delaware	13	1
District of Columbia	91	47
Florida	489	70
Georgia	202	54
Hawaii	16	1
Idaho	19	4
Illinois	392	134
Indiana	89	8
Iowa	42	4
Kansas	47	1
Kentucky	47	5
Louisiana	58	3
Maine	33	1
Maryland	123	16
Massachusetts	265	54
Michigan	161	35
Minnesota	164	30
Mississippi	20	2
Missouri	125	30

	Hdqtrs.	Branches
Montana	13	0
Nebraska	39	4
Nevada	46	5
New Hampshire	41	1
New Jersey	261	30
New Mexico	20	1
New York	1,284	397
North Carolina	177	21
North Dakota	6	4
Ohio	216	26
Oklahoma	41	3
Oregon	127	15
Pennsylvania	301	35
Puerto Rico	10	10
Rhode Island	34	4
South Carolina	74	7
South Dakota	20	0
Tennessee	125	9
Texas	453	79
Utah	50	6
Vermont	17	0
Virginia	152	28
Washington	134	32
West Virginia	15	2
Wisconsin	123	9
Wyoming	9	1

MERGERS, ACQUISITIONS AND NAME CHANGES - 2015

5

5280 Creative; Denver, CO - Name Changed to Zeitsight

A

Altus Group; Philadelphia, PA - Name Changed to The Altus Agency

Articulon; Raleigh, NC - Merged with mckeeman to form Articulon Mckeeman

ASGK Public Strategies; Chicago, IL - Merged with M Public Affairs to form Kivvit

B

Bergman Associates; New York, NY - Name Changed to M/PAKT

The Bernard Group; Austin, TX - Name Changed to Social Influent

Billups Design; Chicago, IL - Acquired by & Name Changed to iCiDigital

Boyd Tamney Cross Inc.; Wayne, PA - Name Changed to BTC Marketing

Bradley Reid & Associates; Anchorage, AK - Name Changed to Brilliant Media Strategies

Brand Cool Marketing Inc.; Rochester, NY - Acquired by Butler/Till

Brandspring Solutions LLC; Bloomington, MN - Acquired & Absorbed by The Marek Group

Burst!; Burlington, MA - Name Changed to RhythmOne

C

Christie Communications, Inc.; Santa Barbara, CA - Name Changed to Christie & Co

D

Dabo & Co; Chicago, IL - Acquired by & Name Changed to Edelman DABO

Defi Communication Marketing Inc.; Montreal, Canada - Name Changed to Camden

Dera, Roslan & Campion Public Relations; New York, NY - Name Changed to Roslan & Campion Public Relations

Desautel Hege Communications; Spokane, WA - Name Changed to DH

Diadem Agency; Charleston, SC - Name Changed to Hooklead

Dibona, Bornstein & Random, Inc.; Boston, MA - Name Changed to Hatch Marketing

E

Ebel Signorelli Welke LLC; Chicago, IL - Name Changed to eswStoryLab

Essentia Creative; Wilmington, DE - Name Changed to Shiny Advertising

G

Go East; Saint Paul, MN - Name Changed to Thread Connected Content

Goodness Mfg.; Hollywood, CA - Acquired by & Name Changed to Deep Focus

Groupm ESP; New York, NY - Name Changed to ESP Brands

H

Hart-Boillot, LLC; Syracuse, NY - Acquired by Eric Mower & Name Changed to HB/Eric Mower + Associates

Horn Group Inc.; New York, NY - Acquired by Finn Partners

I

Ikon3; New York, NY - Name Changed to Noble People

J

JB Cumberland PR; Mineola, NY - Acquired by Didit

K

KDA Group Inc.; Overland Park, KS - Name Changed to CheckBox

L

Langdon Flynn Communications; Cambridge, MA - Acquired by Allied Integrated Marketing

Leap LLC; Boston, MA - Merged with HudsonWide to form ProperVillains

L.K. Advertising Agency; Middle Island, NY - Name Changed to The Linick Group, Inc.

Lowe Campbell Ewald; Detroit, MI - Name Changed to Campbell Ewald

Lynn Lewis Public Relations; Tampa, FL - Name Changed to Lynn Aronberg Public Relations

M

Make Me Social; Baltimore, MD - Acquired by R2Integrated

Manifest Digital; Saint Louis, MO - Merged with McMurry/TMG to f form Manifest

Marketing Inspirations; Cambridge, MA - Acquired by Allied Integrated Marketing

Martino & Binzer; West Hartford, CT - Acquired & Absorbed by Bluespire Marketing

Media Networks Inc.; Stamford, CT - Name Changed to MNI Targeted Media Inc.

Meplusyou; Dallas, TX - Acquired by Moroch Partners

Mobiento; Seattle, WA - Acquired by Deloitte Digital

N

Nunez PR Group; Dallas, TX - Name Changed to True Point Communications

O

One Advertising; Toronto, Canada - Name Changed to Sandbox

P

Plattform Advertising; Lenexa, KS - Name Changed to Keypath Education

Pro Ink; Gainesville, FL - Name Changed to Waymaker

Propeople; San Jose, CA - See Under FFW Agency Health Chicago

Publicis Kaplan Thaler; New York, NY - Name Changed to Publicis New York

MERGERS, ACQUISITIONS AND NAME CHANGES

R

Rare; Calgary, Canada - Acquired & Absorbed by Arcane
Rockett Interactive; Cary, NC - Name Changed to iProspect
Roher Public Relations; New York, NY - Acquired & Absorbed by Feintuch Communications
Roll Global; Los Angeles, CA - Name Changed to The Wonderful Agency

S

Seal Ideas; Indianapolis, IN - Name Changed to The Flatland
Seed Creative; New York, NY - Name Changed to Donald S. Montgomery
Smith & Jones; Sturbridge, MA - Name Changed to Idea Agency
Smith & Surrency, LLC; Jacksonville, FL - Name Changed to Digital Edge
Snitily Carr; Lincoln, NE - See Under Firespring
Spoke8 Marketing; Lansing, MI - Name Changed to InVerve Marketing
Sq1; Saint Louis, MO - Acquired by Ansira
Staples Marketing; Pewaukee, WI - Name Changed to AFFIRM
Stern + Associates; Iselin, NJ - Name Changed to Stern Strategy Group

T

Taylor Made Media; North Vancouver, Canada - Name Changed to Think Mint Media
Topin & Associates, Inc.; Chicago, IL - Name Changed to HCB
Trailer Park; Hollywood, CA - Name Changed to Deep Focus
Trainer Communications; Pleasanton, CA - Name Changed to 10Fold Communications
True Action Network; New York, NY - Acquired by EBay, Inc. & Name Changed to The Shop

U

Ubiquity Public Relations; Phoenix, AZ - Name Changed to Iris PR Software

W

Waggener Edstrom Worldwide, Inc.; Bellevue, WA - Name Changed to WE

Y

Yaffe/Deutser; Houston, TX - Name Changed to Deutser

NEW LISTINGS
2015

1

10e Media; Las Vegas, NV
180fusion; Los Angeles, CA

2

The 2050 Group; New York, NY
2060 Digital; Cincinnati, OH

3

360 Media Inc.; Atlanta, GA
3d Public Relations and Marketing; North Hollywood, CA

4

48 Communications Inc.; Los Angeles, CA

A

A.wordsmith; Portland, OR
Abelow Public Relations; New York, NY
Abraham Paiss & Associates, Inc.; Boulder, CO
AD:60; Brooklyn, NY
The AD Agency; Washington, DC
Adjective & Co; Jacksonville Beach, FL
Adore Creative; Los Angeles, CA
AdvertiseMint; Santa Monica, CA
Agio Brand Solutions; Philadelphia, PA
Ainsley & Co; Baltimore, MD
Andrew Joseph PR; New York, NY
The Andrews Agency; Nashville, TN
AnthonyBarnum; Austin, TX
Antidote 360; New York, NY
Appetizer Mobile LLC; New York, NY
Aspectus PR; New York, NY
Atlas Marketing; Sewickley, PA
Atomic20; Boulder, CO
AugustineIdeas; Roseville, CA
Avanza Advertising, LLC; Miami Springs, FL
Avinova Media Group; Highlands Ranch, CO

B

B&P Advertising; Las Vegas, NV
B2 Interactive; Omaha, NE
The Baddish Group; New York, NY
Barefoot PR; Denver, CO
Bauserman Group; Reno, NV
BD&E; Pittsburgh, PA
Be Inspired Public Relations; Manhattan Beach, CA
Beardwood & Co; New York, NY
Becca PR; New York, NY
Beck Ellman Heald; La Jolla, CA
Bella PR; New York, NY
Bellmont Partners; Minneapolis, MN
Berk Comm & Marketing Group; New York, NY
BerlinRosen; New York, NY
Bernstein & Associates Inc.; Bellaire, TX
BigEyedWish LLC; New York, NY
Billboard Connection; Philadelphia, PA
Blake Zidell & Associates; Brooklyn, NY
blend; Los Angeles, CA
BLND Public Relations; Hermosa Beach, CA
Blohm Creative Partners; East Lansing, MI
Blue August; Jackson, TN
BlueSoho; New York, NY
Bollare; Los Angeles, CA
Bonafide; Houston, TX
Boneau/Bryan-Brown; New York, NY
Borgmeyer Marketing Group; Saint Charles, MO
Bottom Line Marketing & Public Relations; Milwaukee, WI
Bottom Line Marketing; Escanaba, MI
BRAINtrust; Las Vegas, NV
Brandrenew PR; Indianapolis, IN
Bread and Butter Public Relations; Los Angeles, CA
BrightFire LLC; Duluth, GA

C

C Blohm & Associates Inc.; Monona, WI
C&M Media; New York, NY
c3 Communications Inc.; San Diego, CA
Callan Advertising Company; Burbank, CA
Cameo Public Relations; New York, NY
Campaign Connections; Raleigh, NC
Candor; Oklahoma City, OK
CanyonPR; San Jose, CA
The Capstone Group LLC; Denver, CO
Caring Marketing Solutions; Columbus, OH
Carma PR; Miami Beach, FL
CARO Marketing; Los Angeles, CA
Carolyn Kamii Public Relations; Los Angeles, CA
Catch-22 Creative Inc.; Racine, WI
Clairemont Communications; Raleigh, NC
CLY Communication; New York, NY
Coalition Technologies; Culver City, CA
The Communications Agency; Washington, DC
Communications & Research Inc.; East Lansing, MI
Communications Pacific; Honolulu, HI
Consensus Inc.; Los Angeles, CA
Conversa; Tampa, FL
CORE designteam; Cincinnati, OH
CPC Strategy; San Diego, CA
CRAFT; Washington, DC
Crafted; New York, NY
Creative Communication & Design; Wausau, WI
Creative Communications Services; Carlsbad, CA
Crocker & Crocker; Sacramento, CA
Crossroads; Kansas City, MO
Crosswind Media and Public Relations; Austin, TX
The Crush Agency; Lutz, FL
C-Squared PR, Inc.; Huntington Beach, CA
Cutler PR; Culver City, CA

NEW LISTINGS

D

D. Williams Public Relations & Event Management Group; Chicago, IL
DADA Goldberg; New York, NY
Daly Gray Public Relations; Herndon, VA
Daly-Swartz Public Relations; Lake Forest, CA
dburns; Santa Monica, CA
The Decker/Royal Agency; New York, NY
DevicePharm; Irvine, CA
Di Moda Public Relations; Beverly Hills, CA
Dietch PR; Los Angeles, CA
Digital Heretix; Scottsdale, AZ
Dixon James Communications; Chicago, IL
DMNGOOD; Washington, DC
The Door; New York, NY
Double XXposure Media Relations Inc.; Fort Lee, NJ
dovetail solutions; Denver, CO
Dreamscape Multimedia; Lansing, MI
Driven Solutions Inc.; Ferndale, MI
DSA Media Group LLC; New York, NY

E

EAG Sports Management; El Segundo, CA
Eberly & Collard Public Relations; Atlanta, GA
Echo-Factory Inc.; Pasadena, CA
Eckel & Vaughan; Raleigh, NC
Edge Partnerships; Lansing, MI
Effective Immediately PR; New York, NY
The Eighth Floor LLC; New York, NY
Elevate Inc.; Tampa, FL
Elizabeth Christian Public Relations; Austin, TX
ellipsis solutions; Union City, CA
EMRL; Sacramento, CA
Ensemble Creative & Marketing; Lakeville, MN
Envoi Design; Cincinnati, OH
EPIC PR Group; Alexandria, VA
ESPN CreativeWorks; New York, NY
Evoke Health; New York, NY
Evolutionary Media Group; Los Angeles, CA
Executionists; Marina Del Rey, CA

F

Factory PR; New York, NY
Fallon Thatcher; Cincinnati, OH
Fancy Rhino; Chattanooga, TN
Fat Chimp Studios LLC; Saint Louis, MO
Fathom; West Hartford, CT
Faulhaber Communications; New York, NY
Feed Media Public Relations; Denver, CO
Fenton; New York, NY
Fetch PR; Chicago, IL
Fetch; San Francisco, CA
Fingerprint; Los Angeles, CA
Fitz & Co.; New York, NY
Flanigan Communications Inc.; Chicago, IL
Fluid Advertising; Bountiful, UT
Forte Group Inc.; Dallas, TX
The Fresh Ideas Group; Boulder, CO
FUEL Creative Group; Sacramento, CA
Full Scale Media; New York, NY
Fusion92; Chicago, IL
FYI Brand Communications; New York, NY

G

Game Changer Communications; Apple Valley, MN
GBK Productions; Los Angeles, LA
Geiger & Associates Public Relations Inc.; Tallahassee, FL
Gigasavvy; Irvine, CA
Global Immigration Recruiting LLC; Clearwater, FL
Goldin Solutions; New York, NY
Goodman Public Relations; Fort Lauderdale, FL
Gordon C. James Public Relations; Phoenix, AZ
Gourmet Marketing; New York, NY
Graham & Associates Inc.; San Francisco, CA
Green Olive Media LLC; Atlanta, GA
Griffin & Company; Washington, DC
GROUP360 Worldwide; Saint Louis, MO
Guild; Brooklyn, NY

H

The Hauser Group Inc.; Saint Louis, MO
H+M Communications; West Hollywood, CA
H3O Communications; San Francisco, CA
Hall Company; New York, NY
Hall Strategies; Nashville, TN
Haneke Design; Tampa, FL
The Hannon Group; Fort Washington, MD
Hanson & Schwam Public Relations; Beverly Hills, CA
The Hatch Agency; San Francisco, CA
Heron Agency; Chicago, IL
High Rise PR; Brooklyn, NY
Higher Ground Creative Agency; Las Vegas, NV
Higher Images Inc.; Bridgeville, PA
The Hip Event; Montclair, NJ
HKA Inc. Marketing Communications; Tustin, CA
The Honey Agency; Sacramento, CA
Hospitality-Marketing LLC; Fort Lauderdale, FL
Hotwire; New York, NY
Hudson Mind; New York, NY
Hughes Leahy Karlovic; Denver, CO

I

I Do PR; New York, NY
ID Public Relations; Los Angeles, CA
Identity Media Co; Miami, FL
ILM Marketing; Wilmington, NC
IMA Interactive; San Francisco, CA
The Imagination Company; Bethel, VT
iMiller Public Relations; New York, NY
Influent50; Washington, DC
Infused PR & Events; Farmington Hills, MI
Infuze Marketing; Sacramento, CA
INK Public Relations; Austin, TX
Innate; Washington, DC
InnoVision Marketing Group; San Diego, CA
Intrepid Marketing Group; Raleigh, NC
InVerve Marketing; Lansing, MI
iQ 360; Mountain View, CA

Isadora Design; Manhattan Beach, CA
Isom Global Strategies; Washington, DC
ITC; Los Angeles, CA

J

Jerry Thomas Public Relations; Chicago, IL
JK Design; Hillsborough, NJ
Johnson & Sekin; Dallas, TX
Johnson Group; Saint Cloud, MN

K

K Public Relations LLC; New York, NY
The KBD Group LLC; Norfolk, VA
Kari Feinstein Public Relations; Venice, CA
Karla Otto; New York, NY
Kathy Schaeffer and Associates, Inc.; Chicago, IL
Keegan Associates; Cortland, NY
Kellogg & Caviar LLC; New York, NY
Kenwerks; New York, NY
Ketner Group; Austin, TX
Kindling Media, LLC; Los Angeles, CA
King Media; East Lansing, MI
Kip Hunter Marketing; Fort Lauderdale, FL
Kip Morrison & Associates; Los Angeles, CA
Kip-PR Inc.; New York, NY
Klick Communications; Honolulu, HI
The Knight Agency; Scottsdale, AZ
Kraus Marketing; Morristown, NJ

L

L.E.R. PR; New York, NY
LA ads; Northridge, CA
LaFamos PR & Branding; Hollywood, CA
Lages & Associates Inc.; Irvine, CA
Langdon Flynn Communications; Las Vegas, NV
LavoieHealthScience; Boston, MA
Leavitt Communications Inc.; Fallbrook, CA
Lee Marketing & Advertising Group, Inc.; Sacramento, CA
LePoidevin Marketing; Brookfield, WI
Lifeblue; Allen, TX
Linda Gaunt Communications; New York, NY
Live Wire Media Relations, LLC; Arlington, VA
Liz Lapidus Public Relations; Atlanta, GA
Localite LA; Redondo Beach, CA
Lorraine Gregory Communications; Farmingdale, NY
Lorrie Walker Public Relations; Lakeland, FL
Lucid Agency; Tempe, AZ
Lucky Branded Entertainment; Brooklyn, NY
Luna Ad; Wilmington, NC

M

M Studio; Asbury Park, NY
M3 Group; Lansing, MI
Macias PR; New York, NY
MacroHype; New York, NY
Magnificent Marketing LLC; Austin, TX
Makeable LLC; New York, NY
Mann Bites Dog; New York, NY
Marion Integrated Marketing; Houston, TX
Mariposa Communications; New York, NY
Marketing In Color; Tampa, FL
Marketing Inspirations; Atlanta, GA
The Marketing Pros; Orland Park, IL
Marketing Resource Group; Lansing, MI
Martin Davison Public Relations; Buffalo, NY
Martin Waymire; Lansing, MI
Matter Creative Group; Cincinnati, OH
The Mayfield Group; Tallahassee, FL
MC Squared Advertising Agency; Los Angeles, CA
McGann + Zhang; Los Angeles, CA
The Media Advantage; Lansing, MI
Media Mix; Jacksonville, FL
Media On The Go Ltd.; Brooklyn, NY
MediaLine PR; Dallas, TX
Melissa Libby & Associates; Atlanta, GA
Mercury Labs; Saint Louis, MO
Metia; Kirkland, WA
MHA Media; Los Angeles, CA
Michele Marie PR; New York, NY
Milldam Public Relations; Concord, MA
Mirum Minneapolis; Minneapolis, MN
Mixtape Marketing; Austin, TX
MJ Lilly Associates LLC; Brooklyn Heights, NY
Mobility Quotient Solutions Inc.; Calgary
Moncur Associates Miami; Miami, FL
Moroch Partners; Conshohocken, PA
Morrow Lane; New York, NY
M-Squared Public Relations; Atlanta, GA
Multicultural Marketing Resources; New York, NY

N

Narrative; New York, NY
National Promotions & Advertising Inc.; Los Angeles, CA
NDN Group; New York, NY
New Harbor Group; Providence, RI
Nina Hale Inc.; Minneapolis, MN
Notionist; Westlake Village, CA
Novita Communications; New York, NY
Now + Zen Public Relations; New York, NY
NYC Restaurant; New York, NY

O

Olive PR Solutions Inc.; San Diego, CA
Oppermanweiss; New York, NY
Orloff Williams; San Jose, CA
Orphmedia LLC; New York, NY
Outer Banks Media; Manteo, NC

P

Pacific; San Diego, CA
Pantano & Associates L.L.C.; Buffalo, NY
Park&Co; Phoenix, AZ
Perry Street Communications; New York, NY
Pineapple Public Relations; Atlanta, GA
Piper & Gold Public Relations; Lansing, MI

NEW LISTINGS

Pistol & Stamen; Los Angeles, CA
Pixels & Dots LLC; Cincinnati, OH
Plus Ultra Advertising; Inglewood, CA
PMA Inc.; Palm Springs, CA
PMG Worldwide, LLC; Fort Worth, TX
Popular Press Media Group; Beverly Hills, CA
Potts Marketing Group LLC; Anniston, AL
Potts Mueller; Chicago, IL
The Power Group; Dallas, TX
The Powers That Be LLC; Ferndale, MI
PR Caffeine; Burnsville, MN
Preacher; Austin, TX
Pro Communications; Louisville, KY
The Public Relations & Marketing Group; Patchogue, NY
Puder Public Relations LLC; New York, NY
Purple PR; New York, NY

Q

Quintessential PR; Beverly Hills, CA

R

Rage Agency; Westmont, IL
Randle Communications; Sacramento, CA
Raz Public Relations; Santa Monica, CA
RB Oppenheim Associates + Digital Opps; Tallahassee, FL
Red Banyan Group; Deerfield Beach, FL
The Refinery; Sherman Oaks, CA
Relevance New York; New York, NY
Reputation Ink; Jacksonville, FL
Resource/Ammirati; Chicago, IL
Reversed Out; Cincinnati, OH
ReviveHealth; Nashville, TN
Ride For The Brand; Fort Worth, TX
Rohatynski-Harlow Public Relations LLC; Howell, MI
Rose+Moser+Allyn Public Relations; Scottsdale, AZ
Runner Agency; Dallas, TX

S

S. Groner Associates, Inc.; Long Beach, CA
Sally Fischer Public Relations; New York, NY
Samba Rock; Miami, FL
Sandbox Strategies; New York, NY
Sanger & Eby; Cincinnati, OH
Santa Cruz Communications Inc.; Pasadena, CA
Saturday Brand Communications; Charlotte, NC
Sawyer Studios Inc.; New York, NY
Schmidt Public Affairs; Alexandria, VA
Scream Agency; Denver, CO
Serendipit; Phoenix, AZ
SevenTwenty Strategies; Washington, DC
Shazaaam LLC; Novi, MI
Shelton Group; Knoxville, TN
Shift Communications; San Francisco, CA
Shore Fire Media; Brooklyn, NY
Silverlight Digital; New York, NY
The Silver Man Group Inc.; Chicago, IL
The Silver Telegram; Long Beach, CA
Slate Communications; Fort Collins, CO
Smoak Public Relations; Greenville, SC
SocialCode LLC; Washington, DC
Socialfly, LLC; New York, NY
Solomon Turner Public Relations; Chesterfield, MO
Southwest Strategies LLC; San Diego, CA
Sparkloft Media; Portland, OR
SPINX Inc.; Los Angeles, CA
SponsorshipU; New York, NY
Spotlight Media Relations; New York, NY
Spread PR; New York, NY
Spritz LLC; San Francisco, CA
SS Digital Media; Troy, MI
ST8 Creative Solutions Inc; Santa Monica, CA
Steele Rose Communications; Chapel Hill, NC
Steward Media Group; West Bloomfield, MI
Studio Center; Virginia Beach, VA
Sum Digital Inc.; San Francisco, CA
Swift Agency; Portland, OR
Swizzle Collective; Austin, TX

T

The TASC Group; New York, NY
Tallgrass Public Relations; Sioux Falls, SD
Taproot Creative; Tallahassee, FL
Tayloe Gray Kristof LLC; Wilmington, NC
THINKPR; New York, NY
Three Girls Media, Inc.; Lacey, WA
Tina Thomson; New York, NY
TK PR; Greer, SC
Tractenberg & Co.; New York, NY
Traction; Lansing, MI
Trademark Productions; Royal Oak, MI
Traffic Digital Agency; Royal Oak, MI
Treble Public Relations; Austin, TX
Tricom Associates; Washington, DC
Trier and Company; San Francisco, CA
Trip tent Inc.; New York, NY
Truscott Rossman; Lansing, MI
TSN Advertising; Santa Monica, CA
Turn Inc.; Redwood City, CA
Turnstile Inc.; Dallas, TX
TVA Media Group, Inc.; Studio City, CA
TVI Designs; New York, NY
Two Nil; Los Angeles, CA

U

Unison Partners LLC; Washington, DC

V

The Vandiver Group Inc.; Saint Louis, MO
Varallo Public Relations; Nashville, TN
Vertigo Media Group; New York, NY
Vias Latino Marketing; Grand Rapids, MI
Vistra Communications; Tampa, FL
VoiceFlix Inc.; Bellevue, WA
The Von Agency Inc.; Staten Island, NY

W

Wark Communications; Napa, CA
Wavelength Marketing, LLC; Columbia, PA
Web Strategy Plus; Cincinnati, OH
West Public Relations; San Diego, CA
Wilmington Design Company; Wilmington, NC
Wired Island International LLC; Jupiter, FL
Wolf-Kasteler; Los Angeles, CA

Z

Zable Fisher Public Relations; Boca Raton, FL
ZAG Interactive; Glastonbury, CT
Zelen Communications; Tampa, FL
Zenergy Communications; New York, NY
ZOG Digital; Scottsdale, AZ

4A'S MEMBER LIST

&

&Barr; Orlando, FL

2

22squared/Atlanta; Atlanta, GA
22squared/Tampa; Tampa, FL

3

360i LLC; New York, NY
360i LLC/Atlanta; Atlanta, GA

7

72andSunny/LA; Playa Vista, CA
72andSunny/NY; New York, NY

A

Abelson-Taylor, Inc.; Chicago, IL
Ackerman McQueen; Oklahoma City, OK
Ackerman McQueen/Colorado Springs; Colorado Springs, CO
Ackerman McQueen/Irving; DALLAS, TX
Ackerman McQueen/Tulsa; Tulsa, OK
Active International; Pearl River, NY
ADK America, Inc.; New York, NY
ADK America/Los Angeles; Los Angeles, CA
Admerasia; New York, NY
AdPeople Worldwide; Austin, TX
Adrenaline; New York, NY
ADsmith Communications, Inc.; Springfield, MO
AgencyRx LLC; New York, NY
Allen & Gerritsen; Boston, MA
Allen & Gerritsen/Harrisburg; Harrisburg, PA
Allen & Gerritsen/Philadelphia; Philadelphia, PA
Alling Henning & Associates; Vancouver, WA
Alma DDB/Miami; Coconut Grove, FL
Amazon Advertising; San Francisco, CA
Amusement Park; Santa Ana, CA
Annalect Group; New York, NY
Anomaly Communications, LLC; New York, NY
Ansible/New York; New York, NY
Anson-Stoner Inc.; Winter Park, FL
ARC Worldwide/Chicago; Chicago, IL
ARC Worldwide/San Francisco; San Francisco, CA
archer>malmo; Memphis, TN
archer>malmo Austin; Austin, TX
Area 23; New York, NY
Arnold Worldwide; Boston, MA
Arnold/New York City; New York, NY
Assembly; New York, NY
Associated Integrated Marketing; Wichita, KS
Atmosphere Proximity; New York, NY
ATTIK/San Francisco; San Francisco, CA
Austin & Williams Inc.; Hauppauge, NY
Avrett Free Ginsberg, Inc.; New York, NY
Axis Agency/Los Angeles; Los Angeles, CA

B

Badillo Saatchi & Saatchi; Guaynabo, PR
Bailey Lauerman; Lincoln, NE
Bailey Lauerman/Omaha; Omaha, NE
BAM Connection; Brooklyn, NY
Bandy Carroll Hellige; Louisville, KY
Bandy Carroll Hellige/Indianapolis; Indianapolis, IN
Barbarian Group/Hdqrts.; New York, NY
Barefoot Proximity; Cincinnati, OH
barker; New York, NY
Barkley; Kansas City, MO
BarkleyREI; Pittsburgh, PA
BBDO; New York, NY
BBDO/Atlanta; Atlanta, GA
BBDO/Minneapolis; Minneapolis, MN
BBDO/New York; New York, NY
BBDO/North America; New York, NY
BBDO/Puerto Rico; Guaynabo, PR
BBDO/San Francisco; San Francisco, CA
BBH; New York, NY
BCA Marketing Communications; Rye Brook, NY
Beals Cunningham Strategic Services; Oklahoma City, OK
Beber Silverstein Group; Miami, FL
Berlin Cameron United; New York, NY
Bernstein-Rein; Kansas City, MO
Big Fuel Communications, LLC; New York, NY
Big River Advertising, LLC; Richmond, VA
BIG YAM, The Parsons Agency; Scottsdale, AZ
BigBuzz Marketing Group; New York, NY
Blackboard Co; Austin, TX
Blacktop; Kansas City, MO
Blair; Garden City, NY
Blast Radius; New York, NY
Blast Radius/San Francisco; San Francisco, CA
Blue Sky Agency; Atlanta, GA
Boelter + Lincoln Marketing Comms. /Milw; Milwaukee, WI
BOHAN Advertising|Marketing; Nashville, TN
Bolin Marketing; Minneapolis, MN
Brand Union; New York, NY
Brandfire; New York, NY
Brandmovers; Atlanta, GA
Bravo Group/Chicago; Chicago, IL
Bravo Group/Miami; Miami, FL
Bravo Group/San Francisco; San Francisco, CA
Broadhead + Co.; Minneapolis, MN
Bromley; San Antonio, TX
Brothers & Co.; Tulsa, OK
Brownstein Group; Philadelphia, PA
Brunner; Pittsburgh, PA
Brunner/Atlanta; Atlanta, GA
Buntin Group; Nashville, TN
Burk Advertising & Mkting, Inc; Dallas, TX
Burrell Communications Group; Chicago, IL
Burson-Marsteller; New York, NY
Burson-Marsteller/Chicago; Chicago, IL
Burson-Marsteller/Los Angeles; Santa Monica, CA
Burson-Marsteller/Miami; Miami, FL
Burson-Marsteller/Pittsburgh; Pittsburgh, PA
Burson-Marsteller/San Francisco; San Francisco, CA
Burson-Marsteller/Washington DC; Washington, DC
Butler, Shine, Stern & Partners; Sausalito, CA
Butler/Till; Rochester, NY

4A'S MEMBER LIST

C

Cactus Communications, Inc.; Denver, CO
CAHG/Chicago; Chicago, IL
CAHG/NY; New York, NY
Cake New York; New York, NY
Camelot Communications Ltd.; Dallas, TX
Walter F. Cameron; Hauppauge, NY
Camp + King; San Francisco, CA
Campbell Ewald; Detroit, MI
Campbell Ewald/Los Angeles; West Hollywood, CA
Campbell Ewald/New York; New York, NY
Campbell Ewald/San Antonio; San Antonio, TX
Capitol Media Solutions; Atlanta, GA
Carat; New York, NY
Carat Americas; New York, NY
Carat Insight; New York, NY
Carat USA/Atlanta; Atlanta, GA
Carat USA/Boston; Boston, MA
Carat USA/Chicago; Chicago, IL
Carat USA/Dallas; Dallas, TX
Carat USA/Detroit; Detroit, MI
Carat USA/San Francisco; San Francisco, CA
Carat USA/Santa Monica; Santa Monica, CA
Carmichael Lynch Inc./Minneapolis; Minneapolis, MN
Carmichael Lynch Spong (Public Relations Division)/Minneapolis; Minneapolis, MN
Casanova Pendrill/Costa Mesa; Costa Mesa, CA
Cassidy & Associates; Washington, DC
Catalyst; Rochester, NY
CDHM Advertising, Inc.; Stamford, CT
CDM Princeton; Princeton, NJ
CDMiConnect LLC; New York, NY
ChappellRoberts; Tampa, FL
Cheil USA; New York, NY
Civilian; San Diego, CA
Civilian/Chicago; Chicago, IL
Clarity Coverdale Fury Advertising, Inc.; Minneapolis, MN
Colle+McVoy; Minneapolis, MN
Company of Others; Houston, TX
Company of Others/Dallas; Dallas, TX
Compass Point Media; Minneapolis, MN
Concentric Health Experience; New York, NY
Conill Advertising/El Segundo; El Segundo, CA
Conill Advertising/Miami; Miami, FL
Connelly Partners; Boston, MA
Conrad, Phillips & Vutech, Inc; Columbus, OH
Copernicus Marketing Consulting/Boston; Boston, MA
Core Group One Inc.; Honolulu, HI
Cossette/Chicago; Chicago, IL
CP+B; Miami, FL
CP+B/Boulder; Boulder, CO
CP+B/Santa Monica; Santa Monica, CA
Cramer-Krasselt Co.; Chicago, IL
Cramer-Krasselt/Milwaukee; Milwaukee, WI
Cramer-Krasselt/New York; New York, NY
Cramer-Krasselt/Phoenix; Phoenix, AZ
Critical Mass/Chicago; Chicago, IL
Critical Mass/New York; New York, NY
Cronin LLC; Glastonbury, CT
Crosby Marketing Communications; Annapolis, MD
Crosby Marketing Communications/Bethesda; Bethesda, MD
Crossroads; Kansas City, MO
C-Suite Communications; Sarasota, FL
CTP; Boston, MA
Current Lifestyle Marketing/Chicago; Chicago, IL
Current Lifestyle Marketing/New York; New York, NY
Current360; Louisville, KY

D

d exposito; New York, NY
Dailey; West Hollywood, CA
Davidandgoliath; El Segundo, CA
Davis Elen Advertising; Los Angeles, CA
Davis Elen Advertising/Arlington; Arlington, VA
Davis Elen Advertising/Portland; Portland, OR
Davis Elen Advertising/San Diego; Solana Beach, CA
Davis Elen Advertising/Seattle; Tukwila, WA
DDB Remedy; San Francisco, CA
DDB Worldwide; New York, NY
DDB/California; San Francisco, CA
DDB/Chicago; Chicago, IL
DDB/New York; New York, NY
Decker Creative Marketing; Glastonbury, CT
Deep Focus; New York, NY
DeLa Cruz & Associates; Guaynabo, PR
Delfino Marketing Communicatio; Valhalla, NY
Della Femina Advertising; New York, NY
Dennison Tombras; Nashville, TN
Dentsu Aegis Network Americas; New York, NY
Dentsu America Inc.; New York, NY
Departure; San Diego, CA
DesignKitchen; Chicago, IL
Designory/Long Beach; Long Beach, CA
Deutsch Inc.; New York, NY
Deutsch Inc./LA; Los Angeles, CA
DeVito/Verdi; New York, NY
DeVries Public Relations; New York, NY
Digitas Health/NY; New York, NY
Digitas Health/PA; Philadelphia, PA
DigitasLBi; Boston, MA
DigitasLBi/Atlanta; Atlanta, GA
DigitasLBi/Chicago; Chicago, IL
DigitasLBi/New York; New York, NY
DigitasLBi/San Francisco; San Francisco, CA
Discovery USA/Chicago; Chicago, IL
Diversified Agency Services; New York, NY
Doe-Anderson, Inc.; Louisville, KY
Doner; Southfield, MI
Doner/Cleveland; Cleveland, OH
Doner/El Segundo; El Segundo, CA, CA
Doremus; New York, NY
Doremus/San Francisco; San Francisco, CA
Dovetail; Saint Louis, MO
Downtown Partners/Chicago; Chicago, IL
Duffey Petrosky; Farmington Hills, MI
Duncan Channon, Inc.; San Francisco, CA

4A'S MEMBER LIST

E

EGC Group, Inc.; Melville, NY
Eleven Inc.; San Francisco, CA
Embark Digital; Farmington Hills, MI
Empower MediaMarketing; Cincinnati, OH
Energy BBDO /Chicago; Chicago, IL
Erwin Penland; Greenville, SC
Erwin Penland/New York; New York, NY
Estey-Hoover Advertising and PR; Newport Beach, CA
Evoke Health/New York; New York, NY

F

Fallon; Minneapolis, MN
Fast Horse; Minneapolis, MN
Fathom Communications/New York; New York, NY
FCB Global HQ; New York, NY
FCB Health; New York, NY
FCB/Chicago; Chicago, IL
FCB/Garfinkel; New York, NY
FCB/West; San Francisco, CA
Ferebee Lane & Co.; Greenville, SC
Fetch; San Francisco, CA
Figliulo & Partners; New York, NY
Firstborn; New York, NY
Fitzgerald+CO; Atlanta, GA
Frank About Women; Winston Salem, NC
Freed Advertising, L.P.; Sugar Land, TX
Furman Roth Advertising, Inc.; New York, NY
Futurebrand; New York, NY

G

Gabriel deGrood Bendt; Minneapolis, MN
Garage/Team Mazda; Costa Mesa, CA
Garrand; Portland, ME
Gatesman+Dave; Pittsburgh, PA
Geometry Global Worldwide; New York, NY
Geometry Global/Akron; Akron, OH
Geometry Global/Chicago; Chicago, IL
Geppetto Group; New York, NY
gkv communications; Baltimore, MD
GlynnDevins; Overland Park, KS
GMLV, LLC.; Newark, NJ
GMMB/Washington DC; Washington, DC
Godfrey Q & Partners LLC; San Francisco, CA
Golin/Atlanta; Atlanta, GA
Golin/Chicago; Chicago, IL
Golin/Costa Mesa; Costa Mesa, CA
Golin/Dallas; Dallas, TX
Golin/Los Angeles; Los Angeles, CA
Golin/Miami; Miami, FL
Golin/New York; New York, NY
Golin/San Francisco; San Francisco, CA
Gotham Inc.; New York, NY
Grady Britton; Portland, OR
Grenadier; Boulder, CO
Grey Group; New York, NY
Grey Healthcare Group/Kansas City; Kansas City, MO
Grey/Puerto Rico; San Juan, PR
Grey/San Francisco; San Francisco, CA
Grisko; Chicago, IL
GroupM Entertainment; Santa Monica, CA
GroupM Search; , MO
GroupM Worldwide; New York, NY
Grupo Gallegos; Huntington Beach, CA
GSD&M/Austin; Austin, TX
GSD&M/Chicago; Chicago, IL

H

H&L Partners; San Francisco, CA
H&L Partners/St. Louis; St. Louis, MO
H4B Chelsea; New York, NY
HackerAgency; Seattle, WA
Hanna & Associates; Coeur D Alene, ID
Hart Associates, Inc.; Maumee, OH
Havas Edge; Carlsbad, CA
Havas Health; New York, NY
Havas Impact; Norcross, GA
Havas Life; New York, NY
Havas Media/Boston; Boston, MA
Havas Media/Chicago; Chicago, IL
Havas Media/Miami; Miami, FL
Havas Media/NY; New York, NY
Havas PR; New York, NY
Havas Worldwide; New York, NY
Havas Worldwide Tonic; New York, NY
Havas Worldwide/Chicago; Chicago, IL
Havas Worldwide/New York; New York, NY
Havas Worldwide/San Francisco; San Francisco, CA
HDMZ; Chicago, IL
HDMZ/CA; San Francisco, CA
Hill Holliday; Boston, MA
Hill Holliday/NY; New York, NY
Hitchcock, Fleming & Associates; Akron, OH
Hive Advertising; San Francisco, CA
HMC Advertising; Richmond, VT
HMH; Portland, OR
HMH/Bend; Bend, OR
HMH/Charlotte; Charlotte, NC
Hogarth Worldwide; New York, NY
Horizon Media; New York, NY
Horizon Media/Los Angeles; Los Angeles, CA
Howard Miller Associates, Inc.; Lancaster, PA
Hudson Rouge/NY; New York, NY
HUGE; Brooklyn, NY
Huge/Los Angeles; Los Angeles, CA

I

ICC Lowe; Parsippany, NJ
ID Media; New York, NY
ID Media/Chicago; Chicago, IL
ID Media/Hollywood; West Hollywood, CA
Identity/New York; New York, NY
Ignited; El Segundo, CA
Ignited, LLC/New York; New York, NY
Initiative Worldwide; New York, NY
Initiative/Atlanta; Atlanta, GA
Initiative/Los Angeles; Los Angeles, CA
Innis Maggiore; Canton, OH
Innocean Worldwide Americas; Huntington Beach, CA
Inspire!; Dallas, TX

4A'S MEMBER LIST

InterCommunicationsInc; Newport Beach, CA
Interpublic Group of Companies; New York, NY
IPG Mediabrands; New York, NY
iProspect/Boston; Boston, MA
iProspect/Fort Worth; Fort Worth, TX
Isobar/Boston; Boston, MA
Isobar/New York; New York, NY
Isobar/North America; Watertown, MA
IW Group, Inc./West Hollywood; West Hollywood, CA
IW Group/New York; New York, NY
IW Group/San Francisco; San Francisco, CA

J

J3; New York, NY
Jacobs & Clevenger, Inc.; Chicago, IL
Javelin Marketing Group; Irving, TX
Jay Marketing & Communications LLC; Rochester, NY
Johnson Group; Chattanooga, TN
Jordan Advertising; Oklahoma City, OK
Joule Mobile Marketing; New York, NY
JWT; New York, NY
JWT Inside/Atlanta; Atlanta, GA
JWT Inside/Houston; Houston, TX
JWT Inside/New York; New York, NY
JWT Inside/Santa Monica; Santa Monica, CA
JWT Inside/St. Louis; St. Louis, MO
JWT/Atlanta; Atlanta, GA
JWT/Chicago; Chicago, IL

K

Kaleidoscope Creative/New York; New York, NY
Karlen Williams Graybill Advertising, Inc.; New York, NY
Karsh Hagan; Denver, CO
Kelley & Cohorts; Wellesley, MA
Kelly, Scott & Madison; Chicago, IL
Killian Branding; Chicago, IL
Kinetic NA; New York, NY
Kirshenbaum Bond Senecal + Partners; New York, NY
KSM South; Austin, TX
Kuhn & Wittenborn, Inc.; Kansas City, MO
KZSW Advertising; Setauket, NY

L

la comunidad; Miami, FL
Lacek Group; Minneapolis, MN
Lambesis, Inc.; La Jolla, CA
Landor Associates/Cincinnati; Cincinnati, OH
Landor Associates/New York; New York, NY
Landor Associates/San Francisco; San Francisco, CA
LaneTerralever; Phoenix, AZ
LaneTerralever/Denver; Denver, CO
Lapiz Integrated Hispanic Marketing; Chicago, IL
Lattimer Communications; Atlanta, GA
Laughlin/Constable; Milwaukee, WI
Laughlin/Constable Chicago; Chicago, IL
Laughlin/Constable New York; New York, NY
Launch Agency; Carrollton, TX
Leagas Delaney America/LA; Los Angeles, CA
Leo Burnett Business; New York, NY
Leo Burnett Worldwide; Chicago, IL
Leo Burnett/Detroit; Troy, MI
Leo Burnett/Los Angeles; Los Angeles, CA
Leopard; Denver, CO
LevLane Advertising; Philadelphia, PA
Lewis Advertising; Rocky Mount, NC
Lewis Communications Inc.; Birmingham, AL
Lewis Communications Inc./Nashville; Nashville, TN
LGA; Charlotte, NC
LimeGreen, LLC; Chicago, IL
Lindsay, Stone & Briggs; Madison, WI
Lipman Hearne; Chicago, IL
Liquid Advertising; Venice, CA
LiquidThread/Chicago; Chicago, IL
LiquidThread/NY; New York, NY
LMO Advertising; Arlington, VA
Lowe Profero; New York, NY

M

M&C Saatchi; Santa Monica, CA
MacDonald Media, LLC; New York, NY
MacDonald Media/Los Angeles; Los Angeles, CA
MacDonald Media/Oregon; Portland, OR
Macy + Associates; Playa Del Rey, CA
Madison Group; New York, NY
MagnaGlobal; New York, NY
Mandala Communications Inc.; Bend, OR
Mangan Holcomb Partners; Little Rock, AR
MARC USA; Pittsburgh, PA
MARC USA/Chicago; Chicago, IL
MARCA Hispanic; Coconut Grove, FL
Marcus Thomas LLC; Cleveland, OH
Martin Agency; Richmond, VA
Martin Agency/NY; New York, NY
Martin Davison Public Relations; Buffalo, NY
Martin Group; Buffalo, NY
Martin Local Lead Generation; Richmond, VA
Martin Retail Group; Birmingham, AL
Martin|Williams, Inc.; Minneapolis, MN
Maslow Lumia Bartorillo Adv; Wilkes Barre, PA
Mason, Inc.; Bethany, CT
Maximum Media Enterprises, Inc.; Saugus, MA
Maxus; New York, NY
Peter Mayer Advertising, Inc.; New Orleans, LA
MayoSeitz Media; Blue Bell, PA
McCann Erickson/New York; New York, NY
McCann Erickson/North America; New York, NY
McCann Erickson/Salt Lake City; Salt Lake City, UT
McCann Erickson/San Francisco; San Francisco, CA
McCann Regan Campbell Ward; New York, NY
McCann Worldgroup; New York, NY
McCormick Company; Amarillo, TX
McCormick Company/Johnston; Johnston, IA
McCormick Company/Kansas City; Kansas City, MO
McGarrah Jessee; Austin, TX
mcgarrybowen; New York, NY
mcgarrybowen/Chicago; Chicago, IL
McKinney; Durham, NC
McKinney/New York; New York, NY
MCS Advertising Ltd.; Manhasset, NY
MDB Communications; Washington, DC

MDC Partners Inc.; New York, NY
MDC Partners Inc./Canada; Toronto, ON
MeadsDurket, Inc.; San Diego, CA
MEC; New York, NY
MEC /Puerto Rico; Guaynabo, PR
MEC/Irvine; Irvine, CA
MEC/Los Angeles; Los Angeles, CA
MEC/San Francisco; San Francisco, CA
Media Arts Lab; Los Angeles, CA
Media Investment Grp; Atlanta, GA
Media Kitchen; New York, NY
Media Partnership Corporation (MPC); Norwalk, CT
Media Storm LLC; Norwalk, CT
Media Works, Ltd.; Baltimore, MD
MediaCom; New York, NY
Mediacom/Puerto Rico; San Juan, PR
MediaCom/Santa Monica; Santa Monica, CA
Mediasmith, Inc.; San Francisco, CA
MediaVest /Los Angeles; Los Angeles, CA
Meers Advertising; Kansas City, MO
Merkley + Partners; New York, NY
Millennium Integrated Marketing; Manchester, NH
Millennium Integrated Marketing/Boston; Boston, MA
Mindshare; New York, NY
Mindshare/Atlanta; Atlanta, GA
Mindshare/Chicago; Chicago, IL
Mindshare/Dallas; Dallas, TX
Mindshare/Santa Monica; Santa Monica, CA
Mintz & Hoke Inc.; Avon, CT
Mirum; Minneapolis, MN
Mitchell Communications Group; Fayetteville, AR
Mithoff Burton Partners; El Paso, TX
Mithun; Minneapolis, MN
Mktg Inc.; New York, NY
Mobium; Chicago, IL
Momentum Worldwide; New York, NY
Momentum Worldwide/Atlanta; Atlanta, GA
Momentum Worldwide/Chicago; Chicago, IL
Momentum Worldwide/St. Louis; Saint Louis, MO
Morgan & Co; New Orleans, LA
Moroch Partners, LP; Dallas, TX
Morrison Agency; Atlanta, GA
Mortenson Safar Kim; Milwaukee, WI
Mortenson Safar Kim/IN; Indianapolis, IN
Jack Morton Worldwide/Boston; Boston, MA
Jack Morton/Chicago; Chicago, IL
Jack Morton/Detroit; Detroit, MI
Jack Morton/Los Angeles; West Hollywood, CA
Jack Morton/New York; New York, NY
Jack Morton/Norwalk; Norwalk, CT
Jack Morton/San Francisco; San Francisco, CA
Mother; New York, NY
Eric Mower + Associates; Syracuse, NY
Eric Mower + Associates/Strata-G; Cincinnati, OH
Eric Mower/Albany; Albany, NY
Eric Mower/Atlanta; Atlanta, GA
Eric Mower/Buffalo; Buffalo, NY
Eric Mower/Charlotte; Charlotte, NC
Eric Mower/Rochester; Rochester, NY
Moxie/Atlanta; Atlanta, GA
Moxie/Atlanta2; Atlanta, GA
Moxie/New York; New York, NY
Moxie/Pittsburgh; Pittsburgh, PA
MRM Worldwide/New York; New York, NY
MRM Worldwide/San Francisco; San Francisco, CA
MRM/Birmingham; Birmingham, MI
MRM/Princeton; Princeton, NJ
Mullen Lowe Group; New York, NY
Mullen Lowe/Boston; Boston, MA
Mullen Lowe/LA; El Segundo, CA
Mullen Lowe/Winston-Salem; Winston Salem, NC
Mullen mediaHUB; Boston, MA
Muller Bressler & Brown; Leawood, KS
Munn Rabot; New York, NY
Muse Communications; Culver City, CA
MVNP; Honolulu, HI

N

Nail Communications; Providence, RI
NAS Recruitment Communications; Cleveland, OH
NAS Recruitment Communications/Chicago; Chicago, IL
NAS Recruitment Communications/CO; Englewood, CO
NAS Recruitment Communications/GA; Acworth, GA
Needleman Drossman & Partners; New York, NY
Neo@Ogilvy; New York, NY
NextMedia, Inc.; Dallas, TX
Northlich; Cincinnati, OH
Northlich/Columbus; Columbus, OH
Nostrum, Inc.; Long Beach, CA
Novus Media Inc.; Plymouth, MN

O

Octagon - Athletes & Personalities Headquaters; McClean, VA
Octagon Music & Entertainment; Los Angeles, CA
Octagon Worldwide Headquarters; Norwalk, CT
Octagon/Atlanta; Atlanta, GA
Octagon/Minneapolis; Minneapolis, MN
Octagon/New York; New York, NY
Octagon/North Carolina; Huntersville, NC
Ogilvy & Mather Worldwide; New York, NY
Ogilvy & Mather/Chicago; Chicago, IL
Ogilvy & Mather/Los Angeles; Culver City, CA
Ogilvy CommonHealth Worldwide; Parsippany, NJ
Ogilvy Healthworld North America; New York, NY
Ogilvy Public Relations; New York, NY
Ogilvy Public Relations Worldwide/Chicago; Chicago, IL
Ogilvy Public Relations Worldwide/DC; Washington, DC
Ogilvy Public Relations Worldwide/LA; Culver City, CA
Ogilvy/North America; New York, NY
OgilvyOne Worldwide/Chicago; Chicago, IL
O'Keefe, Reinhard & Paul LLC; Chicago, IL
O'Leary and Partners; Newport Beach, CA
OMD; New York, NY
OMD/Los Angeles; Los Angeles, CA
OMD/San Francisco; San Francisco, CA
Omnicom Group Inc.; New York, NY
Omnicom Media Group; New York, NY
On Ideas; Jacksonville, FL
OneWorld Communications; San Francisco, CA
Optimedia; New York, NY

4A'S MEMBER LIST

Optimedia/Indianapolis; Indianapolis, IN
Optimedia/Plano; Plano, TX
Optimedia/San Francisco; San Francisco, CA
Optimedia/Seattle; Seattle, WA
Optimum Sports; New York, NY
Organic, Inc./New York; New York, NY
ORION Capital/New York; New York, NY
Osborn Barr; Saint Louis, MO
Osborn Barr/Kansas City; Kansas City, MO
Outdoor Media Group/NY; New York, NY

P

Palisades Media Group; Santa Monica, CA
Partners + Napier; Rochester, NY
Partners + Napier/NYC; New York, NY
Pavone; Harrisburg, PA
PeakBiety Branding + Advertising; Tampa, FL
Pedone & Partners, Inc.; New York, NY
People Ideas & Culture; New York, NY
Periscope, Inc.; Minneapolis, MN
Persuasion Companies; Minneapolis, MN
Peterson Milla Hooks; Minneapolis, MN
PHD USA; New York, NY
PHD/Chicago; Chicago, IL
PHD/Los Angeles; Los Angeles, CA
PHD/New York; New York, NY
Phelps; Santa Monica, CA
PinckneyHugoGroup; Syracuse, NY
Plessas, James; Mill Valley, CA
PMK-BNC/New York; New York, NY
PMK-BNC; Los Angeles, CA
Posterscope USA; New York, NY
Powell Tate Weber Shandwick; Washington, DC
Preacher; Austin, TX
Precept Medical Communications; Berkeley Heights, NJ
Preston Kelly; Minneapolis, MN
PriceWeber Marketing; Louisville, KY
Proof Advertising; Austin, TX
Proof Integrated Communications/NYC; New York, NY
Proof Integrated Communications/WA DC; Washington, DC
Publicis Dallas & Hawkeye; Plano, TX
Publicis Groupe; New York, NY
Publicis Healthcare Communications Group; New York, NY
Publicis New York; New York, NY
Publicis West/Boise; Boise, ID
Pure Brand Communications; Denver, CO
Pure Brand Communications/Cheyenne; Cheyenne, WY

R

R&R Partners, Inc.; Las Vegas, NV
R&R Partners, Inc./Los Angeles; El Segundo, CA
R&R Partners, Inc./Phoenix; Phoenix, AZ
R&R Partners, Inc./Reno; Reno, NV
R&R Partners, Inc./Salt Lake City; Salt Lake City, UT
R&R Partners, Inc./Washington DC; Washington, DC
R/GA; New York, NY
R/GA Austin; Austin, TX
R/GA Chicago; Chicago, IL
R/GA Los Angeles; Los Angeles, CA
R/GA San Francisco; San Francisco, CA
Razorfish Healthware; Philadelphia, PA
Rebuild Nation; Detroit, MI
Red Brown Kle'; Milwaukee, WI
Red Square; Mobile, AL
Redscout; New York, NY
Redscout/San Francisco; San Francisco, CA
Reprise Media/New York; New York, NY
Resolution Media; Chicago, IL
Reynolds & Associates, Inc.; El Segundo, CA
Richards Group; Dallas, TX
Richards/Carlberg; Houston, TX
Riger Advertising Agency, Inc.; Binghamton, NY
Riney; San Francisco, CA
Roberts + Langer DDB/NY; New York, NY
Roberts Communications, Inc.; Rochester, NY
Rodgers Townsend; Saint Louis, MO
Rogers & Cowan/New York; New York, NY
RP3 Agency; Bethesda, MD
RPA; Santa Monica, CA
RTC Relationship Marketing/WA DC; Washington, DC
Russell Herder; Minneapolis, MN
Russell Herder/Brainerd; Brainerd, MN

S

Saatchi & Saatchi; New York, NY
Saatchi & Saatchi Healthcare Innovations; Yardley, PA
Saatchi & Saatchi Wellness; New York, NY
Saatchi & Saatchi X; Springdale, AR
Saatchi & Saatchi X/Chicago; Chicago, IL
Saatchi & Saatchi/Los Angeles; Torrance, CA
Sanders\Wingo; El Paso, TX
Sanders\Wingo/Austin; Austin, TX
Sapient/Arlington; Arlington, VA
Sapient/Atlanta; Atlanta, GA
Sapient/Boston; Boston, MA
Sapient/Chicago; Chicago, IL
Sapient/Houston; Houston, TX
Sapient/Miami Beach; Miami Beach, FL
Sapient/New York; New York, NY
SapientNitro/New York; New York, NY
Sawmill/New York; New York, NY
Sawmill/Washington; Washington, DC
SCPF America; Miami Beach, FL
SelectNY; New York, NY
SFW; Greensboro, NC
Sharp Communications, Inc.; New York, NY
Sides & Associates, Inc.; Lafayette, LA
SMA; New York, NY
SMG Detroit/Chicago; Chicago, IL
SMG United; New York, NY
SMG/P&G; Chicago, IL
Smith Brothers Agency, LP; Pittsburgh, PA
SMM Advertising; Smithtown, NY
Southwest Media Group; Dallas, TX
Spark Communications; Chicago, IL
Spark44; Los Angeles, CA
Spawn; Anchorage, AK
Spike DDB; Brooklyn, NY
Square One/Dallas; Dallas, TX
SS+K; New York, NY

SSCG Media Group; New York, NY
St. John & Partners; Jacksonville, FL
Starcom MediaVest Group/Chicago; Chicago, IL
Starcom MediaVest Group/NY; New York, NY
Starcom Worldwide; Chicago, IL
Starcom Worldwide/N. Hollywood; North Hollywood, CA
Starmark International; Fort Lauderdale, FL
J. Stokes & Associates; Walnut Creek, CA
Strategic America; West Des Moines, IA
Studiocom Inc.; Atlanta, GA
Studiocom Inc./Boston; Boston, MA
Sudler & Hennessey/New York; New York, NY
Sullivan Higdon & Sink Inc.; Wichita, KS
Sullivan Higdon & Sink/Kansas City; Kansas City, MO
Surdell & Partners; Omaha, NE
swb&r; Bethlehem, PA
SwellShark; New York, NY
Swirl Inc; San Francisco, CA
switch liberate your brand; Saint Louis, MO

T

Tapestry Partners/Chicago; Chicago, IL
TBWA Worldwide; New York, NY
TBWA\Chiat\Day/Los Angeles; Los Angeles, CA
TBWA\Chiat\Day/New York; New York, NY
TDA Boulder; Boulder, CO
Team Detroit/Dearborn; Dearborn, MI
Team Epic LLC/Norwalk; Norwalk, CT
Team Epic LLC/Smyrna; Smyrna, GA
Team One Advertising/El Segundo; Los Angeles, CA
Terri & Sandy Solution; New York, NY
The&Partnership; New York, NY
Think Shift/Portland; Portland, OR
Tierney/Philly; Philadelphia, PA
TM Advertising/Dallas; Dallas, TX
Tombras Group\Knoxville; Knoxville, TN
Topin & Associates, Inc.; Chicago, IL
TracyLocke/Dallas; Dallas, TX
TracyLocke/New York; New York, NY
TracyLocke/Wilton; Wilton, CT
Tribal DDB/New York; New York, NY
Two By Four; Chicago, IL
twofifteenmccann; San Francisco, CA

U

UM LA; Los Angeles, CA
UM NY Global Headquarters; New York, NY

V

Varick Media Management; New York, NY
Varsity; Harrisburg, PA
VIM Interactive; Baltimore, MD
VivaKi; Chicago, IL
Vizeum USA/NY; New York, NY
Vladimir Jones; Colorado Springs, CO
Vladimir Jones/Denver; Denver, CO
VML; Kansas City, MO
VML/Chicago; Chicago, IL
VML/Michigan; Kalamazoo, MI
VML/New York; New York, NY

W

Wahlstrom/Louisville; Louisville, KY
Wahlstrom/Minneapolis; Minneapolis, MN
Wahlstrom/Norwalk; Norwalk, CT
Wahlstrom/Philadelphia; Philadelphia, PA
Walker Marketing; Concord, NC
Walrus; New York, NY
Walton Isaacson; Culver City, CA
Walton Isaacson/New York; New York, NY
Walz Tetrick Advertising; Mission, KS
Weber Shandwick Worldwide; New York, NY
Weber Shandwick/Atlanta; Atlanta, GA
Weber Shandwick/Austin; Austin, TX
Weber Shandwick/Baltimore; Baltimore, MD
Weber Shandwick/Boston; Boston, MA
Weber Shandwick/Chicago; Chicago, IL
Weber Shandwick/Dallas; Dallas, TX
Weber Shandwick/Denver; Denver, CO
Weber Shandwick/Detroit; Birmingham, MI
Weber Shandwick/Los Angeles; Los Angeles, CA
Weber Shandwick/Minneapolis; Minneapolis, MN
Weber Shandwick/San Francisco; San Francisco, CA
Weber Shandwick/Seattle; Seattle, WA
Weber Shandwick/St.Louis; St. Louis, MO
WHITE; Herndon, VA
White Good & Company; Lancaster, PA
Wildfire, LLC; Winston Salem, NC
Williams, Carol H. Advertising; Oakland, CA
Williams, Carol H., Advertising/Chicago; Chicago, IL
Wing; New York, NY
Wongdoody; Seattle, WA
Wongdoody/Los Angeles; Culver City, CA
WPP; New York, NY
Wray Ward; Charlotte, NC
Wunderman/Chicago; Chicago, IL
Wunderman/Irvine; Irvine, CA
Wunderman/Miami; Miami, FL
Wunderman/New York; New York, NY
Wunderman/Seattle; Seattle, WA
Wyse; Cleveland, OH

X

Xaxis; New York, NY

Y

Y&R/Austin; Austin, TX
Y&R/California; San Francisco, CA
Y&R/Miami; Miami, FL
Y&R/New York; New York, NY
Yaffe Group; Southfield, MI
Yaffe/Deutser; Houston, TX
Yamamoto; Minneapolis, MN
Yellow Sub Marketing; Pittsburgh, PA
Young & Rubicam Group; New York, NY

Z

Zehnder Communications, Inc./New Orleans; New Orleans, LA
Zenith Media Services; New York, NY
Zenith Media/Atlanta; Atlanta, GA
Zenith Media/Chicago; Chicago, IL

4A'S MEMBER LIST

Zenith Media/Denver; Denver, CO
Zenith Media/Los Angeles; Los Angeles, CA
ZenithOptimedia; New York, NY
ZenithOptimedia /San Francisco; San Francisco, CA
Zillner Marketing Communications, Inc.; Lenexa, KS
Zimmerman Agency; Tallahassee, FL

4A's

American Association of Advertising Agencies
1065 Ave. of the Americas, 16th Fl.
New York, NY 10018
Tel: 212-682-2500; FAX: 212-682-8391
E-mail: info@aaaa.org
Web Site: www.aaaa.org, www.smartbrief.com/aaaa, LinkedIn: http://www.linkedin.com/company/50888, Twitter: https://twitter.com/4as facebook: https://www.facebook.com/aaaaorg

Year Founded: 1917

Members: 750 Member Offices

Organization Description: Founded in 1917, the 4A's is the national trade association representing the advertising agency business in the United States. It is a management-oriented association that offers its members the broadest possible services, expertise and information regarding the advertising agency business. Its membership produces approximately 80 percent of the total advertising volume placed by agencies worldwide.

Publications: Best practice booklets, industry surveys and bulletins, white papers and position papers (various); 4A's SmartBrief (daily e-mail newsletter)

Personnel:

Nancy Hill (Pres. & Chief Exec. Officer)
Todd Hittle (Chief Oper. Officer & Chief Fin. Officer)
Mollie Rosen (Exec. V.P.-Agency Relations & Membership)

AAF

American Advertising Federation
1101 Vermont Ave., N.W., Ste. 500
Washington, DC 20005-6306
Tel: 202-898-0089; FAX: 202-898-0159
E-mail: aaf@aaf.org
Web Site: www.aaf.org, LinkedIn: http://www.linkedin.com/company/american-advertising-federation, Twitter: https://twitter.com/aafnational Facebook: https://www.facebook.com/aafnational

Year Founded: 1967

Members: 40,000

Organization Description: The American Advertising Federation (AAF), the nation's oldest national advertising trade association, and the only association representing all facets of the advertising industry, is headquartered in Washington, D.C., and acts as the "Unifying Voice for Advertising." The AAF also has 15 district operations, each located in and representing a different region of the nation.

Personnel:

James E. Datri (Pres. & Chief Exec. Officer)
Constance Cannon Frazier (Chief Oper. Officer)
Laurel Penhale (Chief Fin. Officer)

AAM

Alliance for Audited Media
(Formerly Audit Bureau of Circulations)
48 W Seegers Rd
Arlington Heights, IL 60005
Tel: 224-366-6939; FAX: 224-366-6949
E-mail: michael.lavery@auditedmedia.com
Web Site: www.auditedmedia.com, LinkedIn: http://www.linkedin.com/company/alliance-for-audited-media, Twitter: https://twitter.com/auditedmedia, Facebook: https://www.facebook.com/auditedmedia

Year Founded: 1914

Members: 4,000

Organization Description: The Alliance for Audited Media (AAM) is a non-profit organization that connects North America's leading media companies, advertisers and ad agencies. Founded in 1914 as the Audit Bureau of Circulations, the AAM is the preeminent source of cross-media verification and information services, providing standards, audit services and data critical to the advertising industry. The organization independently verifies print and digital circulation, mobile apps, website analytics, social media, technology platforms and audience information for newspapers, magazines and digital media companies in the U.S. and Canada.

Personnel:

Tom Drouillard (Pres. CEO & Mng. Dir.)
Neal Lulofs (Exec. V.P.-Mktg. & Strategy)
Mark A. Wachowicz (Exec. V.P.-Bus. Innovation)

AC

The Advertising Council, Inc.
815 2nd Ave., 9th Fl.
New York, NY 10017
Tel: 212-922-1500; FAX: 212-922-1676
E-mail: info@adcouncil.org
Web Site: www.adcouncil.org, LinkedIn: http://www.linkedin.com/company/the-advertising-council, Twitter: https://twitter.com/adcouncil, Facebook: https://www.facebook.com/adcouncil

Year Founded: 1942

Organization Description: The Ad Council is a private, non-profit organization with a rich history of marshalling volunteer talent from the advertising and media industries to deliver critical messages to the American public. Having produced literally thousands of PSA campaigns addressing the most pressing social issues of the day, the Ad Council has affected, and continues to affect, tremendous positive change by raising awareness, inspiring action and saving lives.

Publications: The Public Service Advertising Catalog (quarterly)

Personnel:

Lisa Sherman (Pres. & Chief Exec. Officer)
Jon Fish (CFO & Exec. V.P.)
Barbara Leshinsky (Exec. V.P.-Devel.)
Priscilla Natkins, (Executive V.P. & Dir-Client Svcs.)
Paula Veale (Exec. V.P.-Corp. Commun.)
Beth Ellard (Exec. V.P.-Media)
Ellyn Fisher (Sr. VP-PR & Social Media)

ADC

The Art Directors Club, Inc.
106 W. 29th St.
New York, NY 10001
Tel: 212-643-1440; FAX: 212-643-4266
E-mail: info@adcglobal.org
Web Site: www.adcglobal.org, LinkedIn: http://www.linkedin.com/company/the-art-directors-club, Twitter: https://twitter.com/adcglobal, Facebook: https://www.facebook.com/adcglobal

Year Founded: 1920

Members: 1,300

Organization Description: Founded in 1920, ADC is the premier organization for leaders in visual communication, boasting one of the most concentrated groups of creative talent in the world. A not-for-profit membership organization, ADC's mission is to connect creative professionals around the globe, while simultaneously provoking and elevating world-changing ideas. ADC provides a forum for creatives of all levels in advertising, design, interactive media and communica-tions to explore the direction of these rapidly converging industries.

Publications: ADC Magazine

Personnel:

Olga Grisaitis (Dir.-Ops.)
Jen Larkin Kuzler (Dir.-Awards Programs)
Kimberly Hanzich (Mgr.-Info.)

THE ADVERTISING CLUB

The Advertising Club, New York
989 Avenue of the Americas, 7th Fl.
New York, NY 10018
Tel: 212-533-8080
E-mail: gina@theadvertisingclub.org
Web Site: www.theadvertisingclub.org, Twitter: https://twitter.com/AdClubNY; Facebook: https://www.facebook.com/TheAdClub/

Year Founded: 1896

Members: 3,800

Organization Description: The Advertising Club of New York is the advertising industry's leading organization, providing members access to a network of thought leaders, the fuel for creativity, greater diversity, and the best training for professional development. The AD Club represents the vision and mission of a vibrant international advertising community across crafts, uniting professionals around a shared experience and passion in the name of exchanging ideas and best practices for business.

Personnel:

Gina Grillo (Pres. & CEO)
Cathryn Weber-Gonyo (VP-Membership & Professional Dev)
Kris Earley (Director - Business Development)
Lucy Truglio (Director - International ANDY Awards)
Elicia Greenberg (Director - Programs)
Tiffany Edwards (Mgr.-Foundation & Inclusion)
Ariel Blakeman (Mgr.-International ANDY Awards and Professional Development)
Alexandria Alava (Coord-Membership and Programs)

AEF

The Advertising Educational Foundation, Inc.
220 E. 42nd St., Ste. 3300
New York, NY 10017-5806
Tel: 212-986-8060
FAX: 212-986-8061
E-mail: info@aef.com
Web Site: www.aef.com, LinkedIn: http://www.linkedin.com/company/advertising-educational-foundation, Twitter: https://twitter.com/aefnyc
Facebook: www.facebook.com/AEForg

Year Founded: 1983

Members: 50 Member Board of Directors

Organization Description: The AEF is a nonprofit operating foundation established in 1983 and supported by agencies, advertisers and media companies. The mission of the Advertising Educational Foundation is to enrich the understanding of advertising and its role in culture, society and the economy. They will achieve this by stimulating a balanced dialogue about advertising, creating/distributing educational content, and attracting the highest level of talent to the industry.

Publications: "Advertising & Society Review" and "ADText" curriculum online at www.aef.com

Personnel:

Paula Alex (Pres. & CEO)

AMA

American Marketing Association
311 S. Wacker Dr.
Chicago, IL 60606
Tel: 312-542-9000; FAX: 312-542-9001
E-mail: info@chicago.ama.org
Web Site: www.ama.org, LinkedIn: http://www.linkedin.com/company/american-marketing-association, Twitter: https://twitter.com/Ama-Marketing, Facebook: https://www.facebook.com/AmericanMarketing

Year Founded: 1937

Members: 20,000 Professional Members & 10,000 Collegiate Members

Organization Description: The American Marketing Association (AMA) was established in 1937 by visionaries in marketing and academia. Today, the AMA has grown to be one of the largest marketing associations in the world, with over 30,000 members who work, teach and study in the field of marketing across the globe. As the leading organization for marketers, AMA is the trusted go-to resource for marketers and academics. The AMA is counted on as the most credible marketing resource where their members can stay relevant with knowledge, training and tools to enhance lifelong learning and obtain valuable information and connections. The AMA is constantly innovating and evolving, helping to shape the field as well as keep abreast of the changing global marketplace to help members excel in their careers.

Publications: Marketing News; Marketing Management Marketing Health Services; The Journal of Marketing; Journal of Marketing Research; Journal of International Marketing; Journal of Public Policy & Marketing

Personnel:

Russel Klein (CEO)

AMIN

Advertising & Marketing International Network
3587 Northshore Dr.
Wayzata, MN 55391
Tel: 952-471-7752;
E-mail: jsundby@aminworldwide.com
Web Site: www.aminworldwide.com, Twitter: https://twitter.com/AminAmerica, Facebook: https://www.facebook.com/aminAmerica

Year Founded: 1932

Members: 47

Organization Description: AMIN Worldwide was established to offer clients the advantages of a global network combined with the fast, enthusiastic dynamics of the independent, integrated hotshop. Overflowing with local insight, hungry for opportunities and packed with award-winning talent and experience working on some of the world's leading brands, AMIN is an alliance of independently owned agencies that collectively offer global network coverage like no other.

Personnel:
Susie Ketterer (Pres.-AMIN Americas)

APC-NY
Advertising Production Club of New York
Showtime Networks
1633 Broadway, New York, NY 10019
Tel.: 212-716-7767
E-mail: info@apc-nyc.org
Web Site: www.apc-nyc.org, Twitter: https://twitter.com/apcnyc
Facebook: https://www.facebook.com/apcnyc

Year Founded: 1931

Members: 500

Organization Description: The Advertising Production Club of New York (APC-NYC) is a community of production professionals in tradi tional, digital and emerging media. The APC provides educational programs and networking opportunities designed to keep our mem -bers informed about new technologies, best practices and industry trends. The APC performs this service to the industry in an effort to raise money to be awarded as scholarships to those interested in studying the graphic arts.

Publications: Newsletter (quarterly)

Personnel:
Paul Nicholson (Pres.)

APRC
Automotive Public Relations Council
25925 Telegraph Road, Ste. 350
Southfield, MI 48033
Tel: 248-430-5951; FAX: 248-952-6404
E-mail: jlaskowski@oesa.org
Web Site: http://www.oesa.org/Councils-Committees/Automotive-Public-Relations-Council

Year Founded: 1974

Members: 50

Organization Description: APRC is a common-grounds profession -al organization for public relations practitioners in all segments of the automotive industry whether OE, aftermarket, performance, pas senger car or heavy duty truck. Today, APRC operates under the management and oversight of the Original Equipment Suppliers Association (OESA) in the heart of the automotive industry and welcomes members from all aspects of automotive communications.

Publications: APRC News, OESA News

Personnel:
Jeff Laskowski (Dir.)

ARC
Agricultural Relations Council
605 Columbus Ave., S
New Prague, MN 56071
Tel: 952-758-5811; FAX: 952-758-5813
E-mail: arc@gandgcomm.com
Web Site: www.agrelationscouncil.org, Twitter: https://twitter.com/AgRelations, Facebook: https://www.facebook.com/groups/agrelationsscouncil/

Year Founded: 1953

Members: 80

Organization Description: The Agricultural Relations Council is the only association dedicated to serving the unique needs of public relations professionals working in agriculture, food, fiber and other related industries. ARC is a conduit for problem-solving, idea-sharing and collaboration among members, who share a passion for excel -lence in public relations.

Publication: ARCLight (4 times per year)

Personnel:
Den Gardner (Exec. Dir.)

A.R.E./POPAI
Association of Retail Environments/Point-of-Purchase Advertising International
4651 Sheridan St., Ste. 470
Hollywood, FL 33021
Tel: 954-893-7300, Fax: 954-893-7500
E-mail: are@retailenvironments.org
Web Site: www.retailenvironments.org, LinkedIn: http://www.linkedin.com/company/association-for-retail-environments, Twitter: https://twitter.com/A_RE, Facebook: https://www.facebook.com/retailenvironments

Organization Description: A.R.E. (Association for Retail Environments) and POPAI (Point of Purchase Advertising International) merged to form a combined new association that will be rebranded in the coming months. The new association will provide expanded services, including research, education and network ing to approximately 2,000 member companies on six continents.

Personnel:
Todd Dittman (Exec. Dir.)

ARF
Advertising Research Foundation
432 Park Ave. S.
New York, NY 10016-8013
Tel: 212-751-5656; FAX: 212-319-5265
E-mail: info@thearf.org
Web Site: www.thearf.org, LinkedIn: http://www.linkedin.com/company/advertising-research-foundation, Twitter: https://twitter.com/The_ARF
Facebook: https://facebook.com/ARF

Year Founded: 1936

Employees: 25

Organization Description: Founded in 1936 by the Association of National Advertisers and the American Association of Advertising Agencies, the ARF is dedicated to aggregating, creating, and distributing research-based knowledge that helps members make better advertising decisions. ARF members include more than 400 advertisers, advertising agencies, associations, research firms, and media companies. The ARF is the only organization that brings all members of the industry to the same table for strategic collaboration. The ARF is the industry's authorita -tive source of advertising knowledge.

Publications: Journal of Advertising Research; ARF Webcasts
Events: Re!Think Annual Convention & Expo, Ogilvy Awards, Audience Measurement Conference

Personnel:
Gayle Fuguitt (Chief Exec. Officer & Pres.)

AWC
The Association for Women in Communications
3337 Duke St.
Alexandria, VA 22314
Tel: 703-370-7436; FAX: 703-342-4311
E-mail: info@womcom.org
Web Site: www.womcom.org, LinkedIn: http://www.linkedin.com/company/association-for-women-in-communications, Twitter: https://twitter.com/AWCConnect, Facebook: https://www.facebook.com/AWCHQ

Year Founded: 1909

Members: 2,000

Organization Description: The Association for Women in Communications is a professional organization that champions the advancement of women across all communications disciplines by recognizing excellence, promoting leadership and positioning its members at the forefront of the evolving communications era.

Publications: The Communique (bi-monthly)

Personnel:
Pamela Valenzuela (Exec. Dir.)

AWNY
Advertising Women of New York
28 W. 44th St., Ste. 912
New York, NY 10036
Tel: 212-221-7969; FAX: 212-221-8296
E-mail: assistant@awny.org
Web Site: www.awny.org, LinkedIn: http://www.linkedin.com/company/advertising-women-of-new-york, Twitter: https://twitter.com/AWNY, Facebook: https://www.facebook.com/AWNYorg

Year Founded: 1912

Members: 1,700

Organization Description: Advertising Women of New York (AWNY) empowers women in the advertising industry to achieve personal and professional fulfillment at each stage of their careers. Funds raised by the organization support the philanthropic endeavors of the AWNY Foundation.

Personnel:
Lynn Branigan (Exec. Dir.)

BAA
The Brand Activation Association
650 First Ave. Ste. 2-SW
New York, NY 10016,
Tel: 212-420-1100; FAX: 212-533-7622,
E-mail: baa@baalink.org; bcarlson@baalink.org, Web Site:
Web Site: www.baalink.org, LinkedIn: www.linkedin.com/company/brand-activation-association, Twitter: https://twitter.com/baalink, Facebook: https://www.facebook.com/baalink

Year Founded: 1911

Members: 600

Organization Description: The Brand Activation Association (BAA) - the rebranded Promotion Marketing Association (PMA) - is the national non-profit trade association dedicated to Brand Activation disciplines that convert strategies to building consumer bonds. Representing over $750 billion dollars in sales, these disciplines include Relationship Marketing, Promotion Marketing, Retailer Marketing, Experiential Marketing, Influencer Marketing, and Content Marketing. Founded in 1911, the BAA has championed this industry through its combination of research, education, advocacy, and collaboration opportunities. The organization's membership is comprised of Fortune 500 companies; top marketing agencies, law firms, retailers, and service providers, representing thousands of brands worldwide.

Personnel:
Bonnie J. Carlson (Pres)
Ed Kabak (Chief Legal Officer)
Lana Mavreshko (Chief Fin. Officer)
Mike Kaufman (V.P.-Mktg.)
Christine Goonan (Dir.-Membership)

BMA
Business Marketing Association
708 Third Ave., 33rd Fl.
New York, NY 10017
Tel: 212-697-5950 & 800-664-4BMA; FAX: 212-687-7310
E-mail: info@marketing.org
Web Site: http://www.marketing.org LinkedIn: http://www.linkedin.com/company/business-marketing-association, Twitter: https://twitter.com/BMANational, Facebook: http://www.facebook.com/BMANational

Year Founded: 1922

Members: 160

Organization Description: The BMA has become a division of the Association of National Advertisers (ANA), giving BMA members access to several new and significant membership benefits. This union allows the BMA to expand their community and dramatically scale our operations. ANA membership currently includes 160 B-to-B marketer member companies representing 12,000 marketers.

BPA
BPA Worldwide
100 Beard Sawmill Dr., 9th Fl.
Shelton, CT 06484
Tel: 203-447-2800; FAX: 203-447-2900
E-mail: info@bpaww.com
Web Site: www.bpaww.com, LinkedIn: http://www.linkedin.com/company/bpa-worldwide: Facebook: https://www.facebook.com/bpaworldwide

Year Founded: 1931

Members: 5,000

Organization Description: BPA Worldwide is in the business of providing assurance. For 80+ years as a not-for-profit assurance service provider, BPA was originally created by advertisers, advertising agencies and the media industry to audit audience claims used in the buying and selling of advertising. Today, in addition to auditing audience claims, through its iCompli service, BPA verifies compliance to defined government, industry, and organizational standards as well as adherence to privacy, data protection and sustainability guidelines and best practices. Performing nearly 3,800 audits in over 20 countries, BPA is a trusted resource for compliance and assurance services.

Personnel:
Glenn J. Hansen (Pres. & Chief Exec. Officer)

DMA
Direct Marketing Association, Inc.
1120 Ave. of the Americas
New York, NY 10036-6700
Tel: 212-768-7277; FAX: 212-302-6714
E-mail: customer@the-dma.org
Web Site: http://thedma.org/, LinkedIn: http://www.linkedin.com/company/dma, Twitter: https://twitter.com/DMA_USA, Facebook: https://www.facebook.com/dmausa

Year Founded: 1917

Members: 1,500 Companies

Organization Description: The Direct Marketing Association is the world's largest trade association dedicated to advancing and protecting responsible data-driven marketing. Founded in 1917, DMA represents thousands of companies and nonprofit organizations that use and support data-driven marketing practices and techniques. DMA provides the Voice to shape policy and public opinion, the Connections to grow members' businesses and the Tools to ensure full compliance with ethical and best practices as well as professional development.

Personnel:
Thomas J. Benton (CEO)

EMA
eMarketing Association
40 Blue Ridge Dr.
Charlestown, RI 02813

Tel: 800-496-2950, FAX: 408-884-2461
E-mail: service@emarketingassociation.com
Web Site: www.emarketingassociation.com, Twitter: https://twitter.com/eMarketingAssn, Facebook: https://www.facebook.com/emarketingassociation

Members: 149,000

Organization Description: The eMarketing Association is the professional association for companies and individuals involved in the practice of eMarketing and the integration of online and traditional marketing.

Personnel:
Cheryl Fleming (Pres)
Robert Fleming (CEO)

EPICOMM
(Formerly Association of Marketing Service Providers)
1800 Diagonal Rd., Ste. 320
Alexandria, VA 22314-2863
Tel: 703-836-9200; FAX: 703-548-8204
E-mail: info@epicomm.org
Web Site: epicomm.org, 8-8204, Web Site: epicomm.org, E-mail: info@epicomm.org LinkedIn: https://www.linkedin.com/in/epicomm-association-43189622,Twitter: https://twitter.com/EpicommAssoc, Facebook: https://www.facebook.com/naplconnect

Year Founded: 1920

Organization Description: Epicomm, the Association for Leaders in Print, Mail, Fulfillment, and Marketing Services, is a not-for-profit business management association representing companies in the $80+ billion graphic communications industry in North America. It provides industry advocacy, management training, and a comprehensive slate of business-building solutions for companies in an evolving market environment. It was created in 2014 through the merger of the Association of Marketing Service Providers (AMSP) and the National Association for Printing Leadership (NAPL)/National Association of Quick Printers (NAQP).

Publications: Bottom Line (Monthly); Postal Points; Online Company Directory

Personnel:
Ken Garner (Pres. & Chief Exec. Officer)
Dawn Lospaluto (Sr. Dir.-Communications)

HPRA
Hispanic Public Relations Association
P.O. Box 86760
Los Angeles, CA 90086-0760
Tel: 323-359-8869
Web Site: www.hpra-usa.org, Twitter: https://twitter.com/HPRAusa Facebook: https://www.facebook.com/pages/HPRA-USA/10698327804

Organization Description: The Hispanic Public Relations Association (HPRA) is the foremost organization of Hispanic public relations practitioners in the U.S. HPRA is a resource for communi cations professionals and for individuals seeking Hispanic market expertise. It is dedicated to the recognition and advancement of Hispanics in public relations through year-round programs, profes sional development seminars and networking. Together with HPRA Los Angeles, the founding chapter established in 1984, HPRA hosts one of the industry's most anticipated annual events: the PRemio Awards and Scholarship Gala. The national organization meets the needs of the growing number of Hispanic PR practitioners, independents and agencies throughout the U.S.

Personnel:
Andy Checo (Pres.)
Lourdes Rodriguez (Treas.)

IAA
International Advertising Association
747 Third Ave. , 2nd Fl.
New York, NY 10017
Tel: 646-722-2612; FAX: 646-722-2501
E-mail: iaa@iaaglobal.org
Web Site: www.iaaglobal.org, LinkedIn: http://www.linkedin.com/company/international-advertising-association, Twitter: https://twitter.com/IAA_Global, Facebook: https://www.facebook.com/InternationalAdvertisingAssociation/

Year Founded: 1938

Organization Description: The International Advertising Association was founded in 1938 to champion responsible marketing. The IAA, with its 56 chapters in 76 countries, is a one-of-a-kind global partner-ship whose members comprise advertisers, media, advertising and public relations agencies, media companies, and academics. The IAA is a platform for industry issues and is dedicated to protecting and advancing freedom of commercial speech, responsible advertising, consumer choice, and the education of marketing professionals.

Personnel:
Michael Lee (Mng. Dir.)

IAN
Intermarket Agency Network
c/o Lavidge
2777 E. Camelback Road, Suite 300
Phoenix, AZ 85016
Tel: 480-998-2600
Web Site: www.intermarketnetwork.com, Twitter: https://twitter.com/iaa_global, Facebook: https://www.facebook.com/pages/International-Advertising-Association-IAA/31350377554?ref=hl

Year Founded: 1967

Members: 20

Organization Description: IAN was created by leaders of noncompetitive marketing agencies to openly exchange knowledge in a col laborative setting. Why are they unique? Unlike most networks, their membership fees aren't inflated because they don't require a managing director to organize meetings, speakers, on-location tours, etc. They're an experienced, close-knit, nationwide group that trusts one another to create and lead meetings that add incredible value in numerous ways. They meet twice a year to discuss issues like new business, financials, HR, creativity, growth, the future and much more.

Personnel:
Alicia Wadas (Pres.)

ICOM
International Communications Agency Network, Inc.
PO Box 3417
Nederland, CO 80466
Tel: 808-965-8240; FAX: 303-484-4087
E-mail: info@icomagencies.com
Web Site: www.icomagencies.com, Twitter: https://twitter.com/Icomagencies, Facebook: https://www.facebook.com/icomagencies/info

Year Founded: 1950

Members: 75

Organization Description: ICOM is the world's largest network of independent advertising and marketing communications agencies spanning more than 65 countries.

Personnel:
Emma Keenan (Exec. Dir.)

IPREX, INC.
4254 N. Wildwood Avenue
Shorewood, WI 53211
Tel: 770-763-5846; FAX: 770-763-5834
E-mail: experts@iprex.com
Web Site: www.iprex.com

Year Founded: 1983, LinkedIn: http://www.linkedin.com/company/iprex-global-pr-and-communications, Twitter: https://twitter.com/IPREX_Global Facebook: https://www.facebook.com/IPREX

Members: 76

Organization Description: IPREX is a $250 million network of communication agencies, with 1,800 staff and 115 offices worldwide working across the spectrum of industry sectors and practice disciplines.

Personnel:
Michael Schroeder (Global Pres.)
David Watson (Exec. Dir.)
Carol Clinkenbeard (Global Administrator)

LOCAL SEARCH ASSOCIATION
820 Kirts Blvd. Ste 100
Troy, MI 48084-4836
Tel.: 248-244-6200; Fax: 248-244-0700
Web Site: http://www.localsearchassociation.org/Main/Home.aspx, LinkedIn: https://www.linkedin.com/company/local-search-association?trk=hb_tab_compy_id_2180943, Twitter: https://twitter.com/localsearchassn, Facebook: https://www.facebook.com/LocalSearchAssn

Year Founded: 1975

Members: 300

Organization Description: The Local Search Association is the largest trade organization of companies engaged in local advertising and marketing. The mission of the Local Search Association is to lead, serve, grow and advocate on behalf of companies that help local businesses get found and retained by active shoppers through results-driven marketing and media services. The Association is focused on elevating the industry through thought-leadership, advocacy, research and insights, and partnerships.

Personnel:
Negley Norton (Pres.)
Wesley Young (V.P.-Public Affairs)

MAGNET, INC.
Marketing & Advertising Global Network
226 Rostrevor Pl.
Pittsburgh, PA 15202
Tel: 412-366-6850; FAX: 412-366-6840
E-mail: cheri@magnetglobal.org
Web Site: www.magnetglobal.org, Twitter: https://twitter.com/magnetglobalnet, Facebook: https://www.facebook.com/pages/Magnet-Global-Network/86729467810

Year Founded: 1946

Members: 38

Organization Description: Providing global experts and local expertise, MAGNET's independent agencies work with more than 800 consumer, retail, business-to-business and industrial clients worldwide. Members share experience, knowledge and ideas with partner agencies domestically and internationally, collaborating on business opportunities and enhancing their ability to compete, serve clients, grow their businesses and raise the standard of work in the advertising agency industry. Members must maintain a level of commitment to the Network, and new independent agencies are carefully screened before membership is granted.

Personnel:
Cheri D. Gmiter (Exec. Dir.)

MCEI
PO Box 58530
Seattle, WA 98138
Tel: 206-623-8632
Web Site: www.mcei-seattle.org,Twitter: https://twitter.com/MCEISeattle

Year Founded: 1979

Members: 75

Organization Description: In Seattle, MCEI is a unique group of senior marketing and communications professionals who participate by invitation only. The purpose of MCEI is to provide a forum where marketing and communications professionals can learn about and discuss trending topics of interest to the group. As one of the area's oldest and most respected professional groups, Seattle MCEI is a premiere forum where members and their guests can share strategies solving new or old marketing challenges.

Personnel:
Andy Wright (Pres.)

NAD
National Advertising Division
112 Madison Avenue 3rd Floor
New York, NY 10016
Tel: 212-705-0120; FAX: 212-705-0134
E-mail: alevine@nad.bbb.org
Web Site: http://www.asrcreviews.org/category/nad/, LinkedIn: http://www.linkedin.com/company/advertising-self-regulatory-council, Twitter: https://twitter.com/ASRCAdReview, Facebook: https://www.facebook.com/pages/Advertising-Self-Regulatory-Council/266206120950

Year Founded: 1971

Members: 8 Attorneys

Organization Description: The National Advertising Division (NAD) of the Council of Better Business Bureaus is an investigative arm of the National Advertising Review Council (NARC). It is charged with the responsibility of monitoring and evaluating truth and accuracy in national advertising. The majority of NAD cases come from competitive challenges, but advertising review proceedings can also be opened based on complaints from local Better Business Bureaus or consumers. Cases also arise from NAD's routine monitoring of advertising and promotion in all media.

Personnel:
Andrea C. Levine (Dir.)

NAMA
National Agri-Marketing Association
11020 King St., Ste. 205
Overland Park, KS 66210
Tel: 913-491-6500; FAX: 913-491-6502
E-mail: agrimktg@nama.org
Web Site: www.nama.org, Twitter: https://twitter.com/officialNAMA Facebook: https://www.facebook.com/NationalNAMA/?ref=nf

Year Founded: 1957

Members: 1,800

Organization Description: NAMA is the organization that delivers the highest value in agri-marketing professional development by providing continuing education opportunities; leadership experience; and an information exchange, while fostering a positive image for agribusiness.

Personnel:
Jenny Pickett (Exec. Dir.)

NARB
National Advertising Review Board
112 Madison Ave., 3rd Fl.,

New York, NY 10016
Tel: 212-705-0104 ; FAX: 212-705-0136
E-mail: bhopewell@narc.bbb.org
Web Site: http://www.asrcreviews.org/category/narb/, Twitter: https://twitter.com/ASRCAdReview, Facebook: https://www.facebook.com/pages/Advertising-Self-Regulatory-Council/266206120950

Year Founded: 1971

Organization Description: The National Advertising Review Board (NARB) is the appellate division of the National Advertising Review Council (NARC). When advertisers or challengers disagree with the findings of the National Advertising Division (NAD) or Children's Advertising Review Unit (CARU), they may appeal decisions to the NARB for additional review. NARB is made up of 70 professionals from three different categories: national advertisers (40 members), advertising agencies (20 members) and public members (10). Each NARB panel consists of five members - three advertiser members, one agency member and one public member. To assure a panel's impartiality, care is taken to screen out any actual or apparent conflicts of interest that an NARB panel may have.

Personnel:
Wally Snyder (Chm.)
Alan Cohen (Vice Chm.)

NCOAA
North Carolina Outdoor Advertising Association
150 Fayetteville Street, Ste. 1270
Raleigh, NC 27601
Tel: 919-821-3211; FAX: 919-834-8880
E-mail: info@ncoaa.net
Web Site: www.ncoa.net

Organization Description: For decades, the North Carolina Outdoor Advertising Association (NCOAA) has consisted of member companies that seek to promote responsible advertising practices while economically benefiting the communities in which they serve.

Personnel:
Lisa Reynolds (Exec. Dir.)

NEW YORK/AMA
New York American Marketing Association
234 5th Ave.
New York, NY 10001
Tel: 212-687-3280; FAX: 212-557-9242
E-mail: info@nyama.org
Web Site: www.nyama.org; www.greenbook.org; www.effie.org, Twitter: https://twitter.com/NewyorkAMA, Facebook: https://www.facebook.com/NewYorkAmericanMarketingAssociation

Year Founded: 1931

Members: 1,000

Organization Description: The New York American Marketing Association (NYAMA) is an organization that inspires, supports and celebrates brilliance in marketing. Founded in 1931, the NYAMA is the principal community for marketing professionals across all indus tries and disciplines in the New York area. Offering programs, monthly events, and interaction with the chapter through volunteer activities, they provide marketers with an opportunity to increase their knowledge and reach in the marketing community. The association also serves as a resource for all marketing events, activities and news in the New York and surrounding areas.

Personnel:
Lukas Pospichal (Mng. Dir.)

OAAA
Outdoor Advertising Association of America, Inc.
1850 M St. N.W., Ste. 1040
Washington, DC 20036
Tel: 202-833-5566; FAX: 202-833-1522
E-mail: info@oaaa.org
Web Site: www.oaaa.org, Twitter: https://twitter.com/YourOAAA
Facebook: https://www.facebook.com/YourOAAA

Year Founded: 1891

Members: More than 800

Organization Description: OAAA is the trade association for nearly 800 outdoor advertising companies that make up more than 90 percent of the industry's revenue. For 120 years, the assoc -iation has been dedicated to leading and uniting a responsible out -door advertising industry that is committed to serving the needs of advertisers, consumers, and communities.

Publications: Various outdoor advertising sales & marketing pieces; OBIE Award Book

Personnel:
Nancy J. Fletcher (Pres. & Chief Exec. Officer)
Ken Klein (Exec. V.P.-Govt. Affairs)
Stephen Freitas (Chief Marketing Officer)
Myron Laible (V.P.-State, Local & Regulatory Affairs)
Marci Werlinich (V.P.-Membership & Admin.)
Steve Nicklin (V.P.-Mktg.)

PAC
Public Affairs Council
2121 K St. N.W., Ste. 900
Washington, DC 20037
Tel: 202-787-5950; FAX: 202-787-5942
E-mail: pac@pac.org
Web Site: www.pac.org, LinkedIn: http://www.linkedin.com/company/public-affairs-council, Twitter: https://twitter.com/pacouncil, Facebook: https://www.facebook.com/PublicAffairsCouncil

Year Founded: 1954

Members: 700

Organization Description: The Public Affairs Council is the leading nonpartisan, nonpolitical association for public affairs professionals worldwide. Launched in 1954, their mission is to advance the field of public affairs and to provide members with the executive education and expertise they need to succeed while maintaining the highest ethical standards.

Personnel:
Douglas J. Pinkham (Pres.)

POSTCOM
Association for Postal Commerce
1800 Diagonal Rd, Ste. 320
Alexandria, VA 22314-2862
Tel: 703-524-0096; FAX: 703-997-2414
E-mail: info@postcom.org
Web Site: www.postcom.org, LinkedIn: https://www.linkedin.com/company/association-for-postal-commerce, Twitter: https://twitter.com/PostCom2

Year Founded: 1947

Members: 156 member companies

Organization Description: PostCom represents those who use and those who support the use of mail for business communication and commerce.

Personnel:
Gene A. Del Polito, Ph.D. (Pres.)
Jessica Lowrance (Exec. V.P.)
Caroline Miller (Administrative Dir.)

PRSA
Public Relations Society of America
33 Maiden Ln., 11th Fl.
New York, NY 10038-5150
Tel: 212-460-1400; FAX: 212-995-0757
E-mail: info@prsa.org

Web Site: www.prsa.org, LinkedIn: http://www.linkedin.com/company/prsa, Twitter: https://twitter.com/PRSA, Facebook: https://www.facebook.com/PRSANational

Year Founded: 1947

Members: 22,000 professional and student members

Organization Description: PRSA is the largest professional organization serving the U.S. public relations community. With a mission to "advance the profession and the professional," PRSA provides news and information, thought leadership, continuing education and networking opportunities; sets standards of profes -sional excellence and ethical conduct; and advocates for the business value of public relations and greater diversity among public relations professionals. Based in New York, PRSA comprises 111 local chapters; 14 Professional Interest Sections that focus on specific industries and practice areas; and the Public Relations Student Society of America (PRSSA), which is active at more than 300 colleges and universities.

Personnel:
Joseph Truncale (CEO)

RAB

Radio Advertising Bureau
125 W. 55 St. Fl. 5
New York, NY 10019
Tel: 212-681-7200 & 800-252-7234; FAX: 212-681-7223
E-mail: marketing@rab.com
Web Site: www.rab.com, LinkedIn: http://www.linkedin.com/company/radio-advertising-bureau, Twitter: https://twitter.com/askyourRAB, Facebook: https://www.facebook.com/pages/Radio-Advertising-Bureau/65469354083

Year Founded: 1951

Members: 7,000

Organization Description: The Radio Advertising Bureau is the sales and marketing arm of the Radio industry providing advertisers and agencies with research, information and outreach programs that support their ability to best utilize radio in the media mix. With more than 6,000 member radio stations in the U.S., and over 1,000 additional members in networks, representative firms, sales and international organizations, RAB is dedicated to designing, developing, and implementing solutions-based programs, research, tools and activities for its radio members, advertisers, and agencies.

Personnel:
Erica Farber (Pres. & CEO)
Leah Kamon (Sr V.P.-Mktg. & Comm.)

SAMA

Strategic Account Management Association
10 N. Dearborn St., 2nd Fl.
Chicago, IL 60602
Tel: 312-251-3131; FAX: 312-251-3132
E-mail: info@strategicaccounts.org
Web Site: www.strategicaccounts.org, LinkedIn: https://www.linkedin.com/groups/126482/profile, Twitter: https://twitter.com/samatweet, Facebook: https://www.facebook.com/StrategicAccounts

Year Founded: 1964

Members: Over 8,000 Global Members

Organization Description: Founded in 1964, Strategic Account Management Association (SAMA) is a unique non-profit association focused solely on helping to establish strategic, key and global account management as a separate profession, career path and proven corporate strategy for growth. With more than 8,000 members worldwide, SAMA offers numerous training, professional development and networking events throughout North America and Europe each year in addition to research, publications and other knowledge resources.

Awards: Certified Strategic Account Manager (CSAM) designation

Personnel:
Bernard Quancard (Pres. & Chief Exec. Officer)

SECOND WIND

1424 Penn Ave.
P.O. Box 6284
Wyomissing, PA 19610-0284
Tel: 610-374-9093; FAX: 610-374-9238
E-mail: info@secondwindonline.com
Web Site: www.secondwindonline.com, LinkedIn: http://www.linkedin.com/company/second-wind
Twitter: https://twitter.com/secondwindbuzz
Facebook: https://www.facebook.com/secondwindonline

Year Founded: 1988

Members: 700

Organization Description: Founded in 1988, Second Wind is a thought leader and innovator to the advertising and marketing community, dedicated to helping members and users "BE better." Second Wind serves advertising, graphic design, public relations, interactive and marketing firms across the US, Canada and internationally.

Personnel:
Laurie Mikes (COO)

TAAN

Transworld Advertising Agency Network
32 Westwood St.
Newton, MA 02465
Tel: 617-795-1706
E-mail: peterg@taan.org
Web Site: www.taan.org, Twitter: https://twitter.com/TAANnews

Year Founded: 1936

Members: 51

Organization Description: TAAN adds strength, breadth, and reach to the owners and managers of independent marketing communica communication companies. Strength, through the sharing of man management information, systems, and technologies. Breadth, through cooperative utilization of the broad range of talents, skills, and expertise of each member. Reach, through affiliations with local independent agencies around the world. TAAN members gain assistance from one another in all areas of agency operations, growth and development.

Personnel:
Peter Gerritsen (Pres.)

TAB

Traffic Audit Bureau for Media Measurement
561 Seventh Ave., 12th Fl.
New York, NY 10018
Tel: 212-972-8075; FAX: 212-972-8928
E-mail: inquiry@tabonline.com
Web Site: www.tabonline.com

Year Founded: 1933

Members: 400

Organization Description: Established in 1933, the Traffic Audit Bureau for Media Measurement Inc. is a non-profit organization whose historical mission has been to audit the circulation of out of home media in the United States. Recently TAB's role has been expanded to lead and/or support other major out of home industry research initiatives.

Personnel:
Joseph C. Philport (Pres. & C.E.O.)

THINKLA

thinkLA
3535 Hayden Ave. Ste. 300
Culver City, CA 90232
Tel: 310-876-0650; FAX: 310-876-0648
E-mail: info@thinkLA.org
Web Site: www.thinkLA.org, LinkedIn: https://www.linkedin.com/company/thinkla, Twitter: https://twitter.com/thinkLA
Facebook: https://www.facebook.com/thinkla

Year Founded: 2006

Members: 57 Corporate, 550 Individual

Organization Description: The mission of thinkLA is to connect, inspire and educate the LA marketing community. The association connects and elevates the awareness of LA's creative community among national marketers by fostering ideas, business and talent. They inspire through education, social and philanthropic events that align with the needs of the ad community. They educate, offering training support with an emphasis on diverse multicultural representation and improving skills in emerging areas of marketing.

Personnel:

Susan Franceschini (Exec. Dir.)
Linda Schwab (Event & Sponsorship Dir.)
Erika Maya (Commun. Mgr.)

VAB

Video Advertising Bureau
830 3rd Ave., 2nd Fl.
New York, NY 10022
Tel: 212-508-1200; FAX: 212-832-3268
E-mail: ChuckT@theVAB.com
Web Site: http://www.thevab.com, LinkedIn: https://www.linkedin.com/company/cab,Twitter: https://twitter.com/VideoAdBureau, Facebook: https://www.facebook.com/VideoAdvertisingBureau

Year Founded: 1980

Members: 250

Organization Description: The Video Advertising Bureau (VAB) (formerly the Cabletelevision Advertising Bureau) is an insights-driven resource for advertisers, committed to quantifying the selling power of premium multi-screen TV content. As a customer-facing 501(c)-6 trade association that calls directly on agencies and advertisers, the VAB utilizes an array of tactics / outputs to advocate for premium video.

Personnel:

Sean Cunningham (Pres. & Chief Exec. Officer)
Jim Spears (Sr. V.P. & Chief Fin. Officer)
Danielle DeLauro (Sr. V.P.-Strategic Sls. Insights)

WDMI/NY

Women in Direct Marketing International-New York Chapter
c/o Berenice Ladden, DMD
200 Circle Dr. N.
Piscataway, NJ 08854
Tel: 973-868-0047

Year Founded: 1971

Members: 150

Organization Description: "Not for Women Only" Organization founded 32 years ago for the education and networking of people in the direct marketing industry. They fund a summer internship program for the Direct Marketing Foundation.

Publications: Newsletter (quarterly)

Personnel:

Berenice Ladden (Pres.)

WOMMA

Word of Mouth Marketing Association
200 E. Randolph Street, Ste. 5100
Chicago, IL 60601
Tel: 312-577-7610; FAX: 312-275-7687
E-mail: membership@womma.org
Web Site: www.womma.org, LinkedIn: http://www.linkedin.com/company/word-of-mouth-marketing-association, Twitter: https://twitter.com/womma, Facebook: https://www.facebook.com/WOMMA

Year Founded: 2004

Organization Description:
The Word of Mouth Marketing Association is the official trade association dedicated to word of mouth and social media marketing. Founded in 2004, WOMMA is the leader in ethical word of mouth marketing practices through its education such as WOMMA Summit, professional development opportunities, and knowledge sharing with top industry marketers. WOMMA's membership is made up of the most innovative companies committed to progressing the word of mouth marketing industry through advocacy, education, and ethics.

Personnel:

Suzanne Fanning (Pres.)

INDEX OF AGENCY NAMES

C

Index of Agency Names

Index of Agency Names

D

E

F

G

H

I

J

K

L

M

Index of Agency Names

N

Index of Agency Names

O

P

Index of Agency Names

S

T

U

V

W

X

Y

Z

GEOGRAPHIC INDEX OF U.S. AGENCIES

ALABAMA

Anniston

POTTS MARKETING GROUP LLC, 1115 Leighton Ave Ste 1-B, 36207, pg. 905

Athens

MINDVOLT, 114B W Market St, 35611, pg. 762

Auburn

ELLIS-HARPER ADVERTISING, 710 Old Stage Rd, 36831, pg. 345
INNER SPARK CREATIVE, 1735 E University Dr Ste 104, 36830, pg. 546

Birmingham

ATTAWAY ADVERTISING, INC., 1100 E Park Dr Ste 204, 35235, pg. 79
BIG COMMUNICATIONS, INC., 2121 2nd Ave N, 35203, pg. 130
BLR/FURTHER, 1600 Resource Dr, 35242, pg. 139
BRUM ADVERTISING, 1 Perimeter Park S Ste 100, 35243, pg. 171
BURTON ADVERTISING, 1701 Providence Pk, 35242, pg. 178
CAYENNE CREATIVE, 2301 Morris Ave Ste 105, 35203-3322, pg. 199
DAVISDENNY ADVERTISING & RELATED SERVICES, INC., 2545 Highland Ave, 35205, pg. 271
DC, 120 18th St South Ste 202, 35233, pg. 272
HINDSIGHT MANAGEMENT INC., 2213 Morris Ave Ste 2020, 35203-4214, pg. 515
HODGES & ASSOCIATES, The Dr Pepper Bldg Ste 300 2829 2nd Ave S, 35233, pg. 519
INTERMARK GROUP, INC., 101 25th St N, 35203, pg. 553
LAWLER BALLARD VAN DURAND, 31 Inverness Center Pkwy Ste 110, 35242-4822, pg. 632
LEWIS COMMUNICATIONS, 600 Corporate Pkwy Ste 200, 35242, pg. 655
LUCKIE & COMPANY, 600 Luckie Dr Ste 150, 35223-2429, pg. 672
MARTIN RETAIL GROUP/MARTIN ADVERTISING, 2801 University Blvd Ste 200, 35233, pg. 704
MEANS ADVERTISING, 4320 Eagle Pt Pkwy, 35242, pg. 740
MODERN BRAND COMPANY, 1305 2nd Ave N Ste 103, 35203, pg. 769
O2IDEAS, INC., 600 University Pk Pl Ste 200, 35209, pg. 820
PANORAMA PUBLIC RELATIONS, 1500 1st Ave N, 35203, pg. 871
SCOUT BRANDING CO., 216 29th St S, 35233, pg. 1027
SLAUGHTER GROUP, 2031 11th Ave S, 35205, pg. 1051
STRONG, 201 Office Park Dr Ste 220, 35223, pg. 1092
STYLE ADVERTISING, 3617 8th Ave S, 35222, pg. 1094

Daphne

JOSEPH BROWN & ASSOCIATES INC., 1040 Stanton Rd Ste C, 36526, pg. 597

Dothan

PUSH CRANK PRESS, 131 N Foster, 36302, pg. 939

Florence

BLUE OLIVE CONSULTING, 303 E College St, 35630, pg. 141
NO'ALA STUDIOS, 250 S Poplar St, 35630-5713, pg. 811

Huntsville

TOTALCOM, INC., 708 Ward Ave, 35801, pg. 1151

Mobile

DOGWOOD PRODUCTIONS, INC., 757 Government St, 36602-1404, pg. 321
RED SQUARE GAMING, 202 Government St, 36602, pg. 962
RSQ, 54 Saint Emanuel St, 36602, pg. 996

Montgomery

24 COMMUNICATIONS, 300 Water St, 36104, pg. 4
CUNNINGHAM GROUP, 35 S Ct St, 36104, pg. 260
STAMP IDEA GROUP, LLC, 111 Washington Ave, 36104, pg. 1073

Tuscaloosa

TOTALCOM MARKETING, INC., 922 20th Ave, 35401-2307, pg. 1151

ALASKA

Anchorage

BIANCA FRANK DESIGN, 1202 Ramona Dr Unit B, 99515, pg. 129
BRILLIANT MEDIA STRATEGIES, 900 W 5th Ave Ste 100, 99501, pg. 167
DZINE ALASKA, 3705 Arctic Blvd Ste 2445, 99503, pg. 334
EYE CUE, INC., 3257 Lk Park Cir, 99517, pg. 363
GONZALEZ MARKETING LLC, 4450 Cordova St Ste 110, 99503, pg. 434
PLONTA CREATIVE, LLC, 255 E Fireweed Ln Ste 109, 99503, pg. 897
PORCARO COMMUNICATIONS, 433 W 9th Ave, 99501-3519, pg. 904
SOLSTICE ADVERTISING LLC, 3700 Woodland Dr Ste 300, 99517, pg. 1058
SPAWN IDEAS, 510 L St, 99501-3532, pg. 1063
WALSH SHEPPARD, 111 W 9th Ave, 99501, pg. 1188

Fairbanks

AGENCY 49 LLC, 135 32nd Ave, 99701, pg. 37
NEUMUTH ADVERTISING, 3542 International St, 99701, pg. 806

Wasilla

CRYSTAL CLEAR CREATIVE, INC., 1751 E Gardner Way Ste G, 99654, pg. 258

ARIZONA

Gilbert

WEDGIE CREATIVE, 1166 E Warner Rd, 85296, pg. 1194

Peoria

72 ADVERTISING INC, 24654 N Lake Pleasant Pkwy Ste 103-112, 85383, pg. 10
ARROWHEAD ADVERTISING, 16155 N 83rd Ave Ste 205, 85382, pg. 73
MICHAELSWILDER, 7773 W Golden Ln, 85345-7977, pg. 754

Phoenix

AEI ADVERTISING, Mountain Sage, 85045, pg. 36
AIR INTEGRATED, 4720 E Cotton Gin Loop, 85040, pg. 41
ARVIZU ADVERTISING & PROMOTIONS, 3101 N Central Ave Ste 150, 85012-2650, pg. 75
AVENUE 25, 9201 N 25th Ave Ste 120, 85021, pg. 82
AXXIS ADVERTISING LLC, 11811 N Tatum Blvd #3031, 85028-1614, pg. 83
CLOUD 9 DESIGN, 11811 N Tatum Blvd #3031, 85028-1614, pg. 83
COMMON SENSE ADVERTISING, PO Box 82277, 85071-2277, pg. 224
CRAMER-KRASSELT, 1850 N Central Ave Ste 1800, 85004-4561, pg. 243
CREATIVE BRAND CONSULTING, 1429 N 1st St Ste 100, 85004-1642, pg. 245
DAVIDSON & BELLUSO, 4105 N 20th St Ste 155, 85016, pg. 269
DEFERO, 3333 E Camelback Rd Ste 190, 85018, pg. 293
ELLISON MEDIA COMPANY, 14804 N Cave Creek Rd, 85032-4945, pg. 345
ENTERTAINMENT EVENTS AZ LLC, 1661 E Camelback Rd Ste 380, 85016, pg. 348
GATE6, INC., 23460 N 19th Ave Ste 110, 85027, pg. 417
HDE, LLC., 22 E Victory St, 85040, pg. 505
HOWLANDMOSER, 3220 W Cavedale Dr, 85083, pg. 525
IMPRESS PUBLIC RELATIONS, INC., 777 W Roosevelt St Bldg 5, 85007, pg. 541
KNOODLE ADVERTISING, 4450 N 12th St Ste 120, 85014, pg. 615
LANETERRALEVER, 725 W McDowell Rd, 85007-1727, pg. 625
THE LAVIDGE COMPANY, 2777 E Camelback Rd Ste 300, 85016, pg. 632
MEDIA ARCHITECTS ADVERTISING & DESIGN, 11811 N Tatum Blvd Ste 3031, 85028, pg. 741
MOSAIC MULTICULTURAL, 2777 E Camelback Rd Ste 300, 85016, pg. 778
MOSES INC., 20 W Jackson St, 85003, pg. 778
OFF MADISON AVE, 5555 E Van Buren St Ste 215, 85008, pg. 825
OWENS, HARKEY & ASSOCIATES, LLC, 3550 N Central Ave Ste 1710, 85012, pg. 867
PAPAGALOS STRATEGIC COMMUNICATIONS, 7330 N 16th St B-102, 85020, pg. 872
PARK&CO, 4144 N 44th St Ste A-2, 85018, pg. 874
PHOENIX MARKETING ASSOCIATES, 5110 N Central Ave Ste 300, 85012, pg. 890
THE PRODUCERS, INC., 4742 N 24th St Ste 340, 85016,

Prescott

Queen Creek

Scottsdale

Tempe

Tucson

ARKANSAS

Batesville

Fayetteville

Fort Smith

Gentry

Little Rock

Springdale

Tontitown

CALIFORNIA

Agoura Hills

Alameda

Aliso Viejo

Altadena

Bakersfield

Berkeley

Beverly Hills

Brea

Burbank

Calabasas

Campbell

Cardiff By The Sea

Carlsbad

Chico

Chula Vista

Claremont

Concord

Corona

Corte Madera

Costa Mesa

Culver City

Dana Point

Del Mar

El Segundo

Encinitas

Encino

Escondido

Eureka

Fairfax

Fallbrook

Foothill Ranch

Fountain Valley

OMNIFIC, 18627 Brookhurst St. #306, 97208, pg. 859

Fremont

E21 CORPORATION, 39111 Paseo Padre Pkwy Ste 212, 94538, pg. 335

Fresno

CATALYST MARKETING COMPANY, 1466 Van Ness Ave, 93721, pg. 197
COHEN COMMUNICATIONS, 1201 W Shaw Ave, 93711, pg. 219
DELANEY MATRIX, 6033 N Palm Ste B, 93704, pg. 294
JEFFREY SCOTT AGENCY, 670 P St, 93721, pg. 589
MJR CREATIVE GROUP, 1114 N Fulton St, 93728, pg. 766

Fullerton

COGNITIVE IMPACT, PO Box 5509, 92838-0509, pg. 219
HARTE-HANKS DIRECT MARKETING/FULLERTON, INC., 680 Langsdorf Dr, 92831-3702, pg. 482

Garden Grove

COPERNIO, 11602 Knott St Ste 13, 92841, pg. 234

Gardena

TITAN, 879W 190th St Ste 265, 90248, pg. 1145

Glendale

GRIZZARD/LOS ANGELES, 110 N Maryland Ave, 91206, pg. 461
HEAVENSPOT, 1800 S Brand Blvd Ste 205, 91204, pg. 507
TBA GLOBAL, 535 N Brand Blvd Ste 800, 91203-3300, pg. 1113
TMP WORLDWIDE/ADVERTISING & COMMUNICATIONS, 330 N Brand Blvd Ste 1050, 91203, pg. 1148
VENEZIA DESIGN INC., 1988 L Arbolita Dr, 91208, pg. 1173

Gold River

CASTLE COMMUNICATIONS, 11294 Coloma Rd Ste G, 95670, pg. 196

Hermosa Beach

BLND PUBLIC RELATIONS, 1001 Hermosa Ave Ste 203, 90254, pg. 139

Hollister

REDBEARD, 378 5th St, 95023, pg. 964

Hollywood

ALLIED INTEGRATED MARKETING, 6908 Hollywood Blvd 3rd Fl, 90028, pg. 48
DEEP FOCUS, 6922 Hollywood Blvd, 90028, pg. 293
DEEP FOCUS, 6922 Hollywood Blvd 10th Fl, 90028, pg. 293
DIGNEY & COMPANY PUBLIC RELATIONS, 1680 N Vine St Ste 1105, 90028, pg. 309
FORZA MIGLIOZZI, LLC, 5419 Hollywood Blvd, 90027, pg. 399
GREENLIGHT MEDIA & MARKETING, LLC, 8439 Sunset Blvd W, 90069, pg. 443
HAMMER CREATIVE, 6311 Romaine St Ste 7316, 90038, pg. 477
KIDS AT PLAY, 959 Cole Ave, 90038, pg. 611
PARANOID US, 1641 Ivar Ave, 90028, pg. 874
PRIME L.A, 6525 Sunset Blvd Ste G2, 90028, pg. 910
TROIKA DESIGN GROUP, 6715 Melrose Ave, 90038, pg. 1159

Huntington Beach

ACORN WOODS COMMUNICATIONS, INC., 2120 Main St Ste 130, 92648, pg. 21
ENLARGE MEDIA GROUP, 307 3rd St Ste 101, 92648, pg. 348
GRUPO GALLEGOS, 300 Pacific Coast Hwy Ste 200, 92648, pg. 463
INNOCEAN USA, 180 5th St Ste 200, 92648, pg. 547
PONDER IDEAWORKS, 20291 Ravenwood Ln, 92646, pg. 903
RIPLEY-WOODBURY MARKETING COMMUNICATIONS, INC., 3516 Bravata Dr, 92649, pg. 981

Indio

NATIONAL RESPONSE GROUP, 80737 Avenida Manzanillo, 92203, pg. 802

Inglewood

PLUS ULTRA ADVERTISING, 355 E Manchester Blvdl, 90301, pg. 898

Irvine

ADPERSUASION, 17595 Harvard Ave Ste C5000, 92614, pg. 31
AMBASSADOR ADVERTISING AGENCY, 1641 Langley Ave, 92614, pg. 52
BDS MARKETING, 10 Holland, 92618, pg. 120
BRANDINGBUSINESS, 1 Wrigley, 92618, pg. 159
BRANDTAILERS, 17838 Fitch, 92614, pg. 161
THE BUDDY GROUP, 7 Studebaker, 92618, pg. 174
BUZZSAW ADVERTISING & DESIGN INC., 19600 Fairchild Rd Ste 140, 92612, pg. 179
CREATIVE DYNAMIX INK, 19800 MacArthur Blvd., Ste 300, 92642, pg. 248
DB&M MEDIA INC, 9 Executive Cir Ste 215, 92614, pg. 272
DECISION TOOLBOX, 5319 University Dr Ste 521, 92612, pg. 292
DEVICEPHARM, 2100 Main St Ste 250, 92614, pg. 304
EIGHT HORSES, 4790 Irvine Blvd, 92620, pg. 340
ELA (EVERYTHINGLA), 18101 Von Karman Ave Ste 550, 92612, pg. 342
EUROPRINT, INC., 14271 Jeffrey Rd #305, 92620, pg. 358
GIGASAVVY, 14988 Sand Canyon Ave Studio 4, 92618, pg. 425
HEALTHCARE SUCCESS STRATEGIES, 8961 Research DrSte 200, 92618, pg. 506
HEILBRICE, 9840 Irvine Center Dr, 92618, pg. 507
IDIRECT MARKETING, INC., 6789 Quail Hill Pkwy Ste 550, 92603, pg. 536
IMAGINE THIS, INC., 43 Corporate Park, 92606, pg. 540
INK, 38 Discovery Ste 100, 92618, pg. 546
INTERBRAND DESIGN FORUM, 15375 Barranca Pkwy Ste E106, 92618, pg. 552
JOHNSON GRAY ADVERTISING, 15375 Barranca Pkwy Ste F-101, 92618, pg. 594
LATINOLANDIA USA, 17595 Harvard Ave Ste C5000, 92614, pg. 628
LOCAL CORPORATION, 7555 Irvine Center Dr, 92618, pg. 666
MACRO COMMUNICATIONS, 9851 Irvine Center Dr, 92618, pg. 683
MARICICH BRAND COMMUNICATIONS, 18201 McDurmott W Ste A, 92614, pg. 693
MATTSON CREATIVE INC, 14988 Sand Canyon Ave Studio 8, 92618, pg. 711
REACH + ACQUIRE, 16485 Laguna Canyon Rd, Ste 110, 92618, pg. 956
SPECIFIC MEDIA INC., 4 Park Plz Ste 1500, 92614, pg. 1063
TRAFFIK, 8821 Research Dr, 92618, pg. 1154
TRINET INTERNET SOLUTIONS, INC., 108 Discovery, 92618, pg. 1158
US INTERACTIVE MEDIA, 2603 Main St Ste 850, 92614, pg. 1169
WUNDERMAN, 2010 Main St Ste 400, 92614, pg. 1230

La Jolla

DARRYL DOUGLAS MEDIA, 5435 La Jolla Blvd, 92037, pg. 266
LAMBESIS, INC., 1020 Prospect St., 92037, pg. 624
THE RESPONSE SHOP, INC., 7486 La Jolla Blvd Ste 164, 92037, pg. 972

La Mesa

LURE AGENCY, 4752 Palm Ave Ste 103, 91942, pg. 674

Lafayette

KRT MARKETING, 3685 Mt Diablo Blvd Ste 255, 94549-3776, pg. 619

Laguna Beach

FUSE INTERACTIVE, 775 Laguna Canyon Rd, 92651, pg. 410
JADI COMMUNICATIONS, 1110 Glenneyre St, 92651, pg. 585
NADA GLOBAL, 931 S Coast Hwy, 92651, pg. 799
ROTTER GROUP INC., 2670 Solana Way, 92651, pg. 993
YOUNG COMPANY, 361 Forest Ave Ste 105, 92651, pg. 1252

Laguna Hills

LAER PEARCE & ASSOCIATES, 22892 Mill Creek Dr, 92653, pg. 622

Laguna Niguel

C&M COMMUNIQUE, 30101 Town Ctr Dr Ste 104, 92677, pg. 182
ECLIPSE MARKETING, 11 Villamoura, 92677, pg. 337

Lake Arrowhead

DRIVE INTERACTIVE, 587 Oakmont Ln, 92352, pg. 328

Lake Forest

STRATA-MEDIA, INC., 1 Spectrum Pointe Dr Ste 130, 92630-2283, pg. 1089

Larkspur

ROCKET SCIENCE, 700 Larkspur Landing Cir Ste 199, 94939, pg. 989

Lemon Grove

NAS RECRUITMENT COMMUNICATIONS, 2580 Bonita St, 91945, pg. 800

Long Beach

THE DESIGNORY, 211 E Ocean Blvd Ste 100, 90802-4850, pg. 301
ETA ADVERTISING, 301 Pine Ave Ste B, 90802, pg. 357
INTERTREND COMMUNICATIONS, INC., 213 E Broadway, 90802-5003, pg. 557
NOSTRUM INC., 401 E Ocean Blvd Ste M101, 90802, pg. 816
THE SILVER TELEGRAM, 320 Pine Ave Mezzanine Ste, 90802, pg. 1044
TLG MARKETING, 6700 E Pacific Coast Hwy, 90803, pg. 1146

Los Alamitos

STAR MARKETING INC, 3532 Katella Ave Ste 205, 90720, pg. 1073

Los Angeles

180FUSION, 11620 Wilshire Boulevard Ste 820, 90025, pg. 3
42WEST, 1840 Century Pk E Ste 700, 90067, pg. 8
AAAZA, INC., 3250 Wilshire Blvd Ste 1901, 90010, pg. 30
ABERNATHY MACGREGOR GROUP-LOS ANGELES, 707 Wilshire Blvd Ste 3950, 90017-3110, pg. 488
ADCREASIANS, INC., 3530 Wilshire Blvd Ste 1475, 90010, pg. 27
ADK AMERICA, 3137 S La Cienega Blvd, 90016-3110, pg. 29
ADORE CREATIVE, 8033 Sunset Blvd Ste 5750, 90046, pg. 31
ADWELL COMMUNICATIONS, 3470 Wilshire Blvd Ste 540, 90010, pg. 35
ALLIGATOR, 639 S. SPring St #4A, 90014, pg. 49

Madera

Malibu

Manhattan Beach

San Jose

San Luis Obispo

San Mateo

SIC 'EM ADVERTISING INC., 1840 Gateway Dr Ste 200, 94404-4029, pg. 1040

San Pedro

WALKER ADVERTISING, INC., 1010 S Cabrillo Ave, 90731-4067, pg. 1187

San Rafael

AIRT GROUP, 91 Dockside Cir, 94903, pg. 42
BLOOM, 777 Grand Ave Ste 201, 94901, pg. 139
DUKE MARKETING, 4040 Civic Center Dr Ste 200, 94903, pg. 332
GOODMAN MARKETING PARTNERS, 4340 Redwood Hwy Ste B-52, 94903, pg. 435
THE MARX GROUP, 2175 E Francisco Blvd East Ste F, 94901, pg. 706
SPORTSMARK MANAGEMENT GROUP, LTD., 781 Lincoln Ave Ste 380, 94901, pg. 1066

San Ramon

AMF MEDIA GROUP, 12657 Alcosta Blvd Ste 500, 94583, pg. 54

Santa Ana

AGENCY 51, 106 W 4th St 4th Fl, 92701, pg. 37
AMUSEMENT PARK, 217 N Main St Ste 200, 92701, pg. 56
CARSON MARKETING, INC., 1740 E Garry Ave Ste 231, 92705-5844, pg. 193
SCRIPT TO SCREEN LLC, 200 N Tustin Ave Ste 200, 92705, pg. 1028
STRAHAN ADVERTISING, 1940 Old Tustin Ave, 92705, pg. 1089
THE TRUTH AGENCY, 454 N Broadway 2nd Fl, 92701, pg. 1160

Santa Barbara

THE BARBOUR SHOP, PO Box 21153, 93121, pg. 91
EVANSHARDY & YOUNG, INC., 829 De La Vina St, 93101-3238, pg. 358
HUB MEDIA, 827 State St Ste 24, 93101, pg. 526
IDEA ENGINEERING, INC., 21 E Carrillo St, 93101, pg. 533
IDEAWORK STUDIOS, 735 State St Ste 100, 93101, pg. 535
ON-TARGET GRAPHICS, PO Box 24124, 93121, pg. 860
THE SHAND GROUP, 1482 E Valley Rd Ste 474, 93108, pg. 1035

Santa Clara

DRB PARTNERS, INC., 2328 Walsh Ave, 95051, pg. 327
MARKEN COMMUNICATIONS INC., 3375 Scott Blvd Ste 236, 95054-3113, pg. 694

Santa Clarita

POWER MEDIA GROUP INC., 17960 Sierra Hwy Ste 100, 91351, pg. 906

Santa Cruz

YELLOW BUS LLC, 312 Lincoln St Ste A, 95060, pg. 1238

Santa Monica

ACENTO ADVERTISING, INC., 2001 Wilshire Blvd Ste 600, 90403, pg. 19
AMERICAN ROGUE, 3000 31st St, 90405, pg. 54
BLAZE, 1427 Third St Promenade Ste 201, 90401, pg. 137
BREW MEDIA RELATIONS, 2110 Main St Ste 201, 90405, pg. 163
CAMPOS CREATIVE WORKS, 1715 14th St, 90404, pg. 188
CHANDLER CHICCO AGENCY-LOS ANGELES, 1315 Lincoln Blvd Ste 270, 90401, pg. 203
CITRUS STUDIOS, 1512 18th St Ste 3, 90404, pg. 211
CP+B LA, 2110 Colorado Ave, 90404, pg. 241
DOUBLE-TEAM BUSINESS PLANS, 1725 Ocean Ave, 90401, pg. 325
ENSO COLLABORATIVE LLC, 1526 Cloverfield Blvd, 90404, pg. 348
THE GARY GROUP, 1546 7th St, 90401, pg. 416
GOALEN GROUP MEDIA, 2700 Neilson Way #329, 90405, pg. 431
GROUPM ENTERTAINMENT, 2425 Olympic Blvd, 90404-4030, pg. 463
HAESE & WOOD MARKETING & PUBLIC RELATIONS, 1223 Wilshire Blvd Ste 100, 90403, pg. 472
J.R. NAVARRO & ASSOCIATES INC., 212 26th St Ste 315, 90402, pg. 597
LA AGENCIA DE ORCI & ASOCIADOS, 2800 28th St Ste 222, 90405-6202, pg. 621
M&C SAATCHI, 2032 Broadway, 90404, pg. 676
MERCURY MEDIA, INC., 520 Broadway Ste 400, 90401, pg. 747
MILLWARD BROWN, 2425 Olympic Blvd Ste 240-E, 90404, pg. 760
MISTRESS, 2415 Michigan Ave, 90404, pg. 764
OCEAN BRIDGE GROUP, 1714 16th St, 90404, pg. 822
OFF MADISON AVE, 604 Arizona Ave Ste 261, 90401, pg. 826
PHELPS, 901 Wilshire Blvd, 90401-1854, pg. 888
POZA CONSULTING SERVICES, 1119 Colorado Ave Ste 18, 90401, pg. 907
RPA, 2525 Colorado Ave, 90404, pg. 994
SECRET WEAPON MARKETING, 1658 10th St, 90404, pg. 1029
SLS ADVERTISING CO, 1453 3rd St 320, 90401, pg. 1052
SWAFFORD & COMPANY ADVERTISING, 820 Washinton Ave Ste D, 90403, pg. 1102
TINY REBELLION, 1316 Third St Ste 301, 90401, pg. 1145
TSN ADVERTISING, 301 Arizona Ave Ste 250, 90401, pg. 1161
UBM CANON, 2901 28th St, 90405, pg. 1165
UNITED FUTURE, 2105 Colorado Ave Ste 100, 90404, pg. 1167
WALKER & COMPANY, INC., 727 Ashland Ave, 90405, pg. 1187
WESTON MASON MARKETING, 3130 Wilshire Blvd 4th Fl, 90403, pg. 1198

Santa Rosa

ABRA MARKETING, INC., 555 5th St Ste 300D, 95401, pg. 17
BOYLAN POINT AGENCY, 2525 Cleveland Ave, 95403, pg. 151
RANCH7 CREATIVE, LLC, 738 Wilson St, 95401, pg. 951

Santee

FALL ADVERTISING, 10960 Wheatlands Ave Ste 106, 92071-5617, pg. 366

Sausalito

BUTLER, SHINE, STERN & PARTNERS, 20 Liberty Ship Way, 94965-3312, pg. 179
DIVISION OF LABOR, 328 Pine St, 94965, pg. 316
KINDRED, 10 Liberty Ship Way Ste 300, 94965, pg. 612
OPTS IDEAS, 1 Gate Six Rd Ste B203, 94965, pg. 863
SKADADDLE MEDIA, 2658 Bridgeway Ste 203, 94965, pg. 1049
TARGETED RESPONSE ADVERTISING, 3001 Bridge way Ave Ste K313, 94965, pg. 1110
VITTLES, 141 Santa Rosa Ave, 94965, pg. 1180

Sherman Oaks

ADVERTISE.COM INC., 15303 Ventura Blvd Ste 1150, 91403, pg. 34
BARCELONA ENTERPRISES, 4230 Stansbury Ave Ste 101, 91423, pg. 91
BRIERLEY & PARTNERS, 15303 Ventura Blvd, 91403, pg. 1227
BRIERLEY & PARTNERS, 15303 Ventura Blvd, 91403, pg. 165
THE REFINERY, US Bank Bldg 14455 ventura blvd 3rd fl, 91423, pg. 966
SILVERCREST ADVERTISING, 15357 Magnolia Blvd Ste 223, 91403, pg. 1044

Sierra Madre

SMITH ASBURY INC, 225 N Lima St Ste 6, 91024, pg. 1053

Simi Valley

STILLWATER AGENCY, 1919 Williams St Ste 201, 93065, pg. 1086

Solana Beach

BASIC AGENCY, 341 S Cedros Ave Ste B, 92075, pg. 96
CUKER, 320 S Cedros Ave Ste 200, 92075, pg. 259
DAVIS ELEN ADVERTISING, INC., 420 Stevens Ave Ste 240, 92075, pg. 271
WRIGHT ON COMMUNICATIONS, Ste 300 674 Via de la Valle, 92075, pg. 1229

Sonoma

BOTHWELL MARKETING, 651 1st St W Ste M, 95476, pg. 150

Stockton

KEN FONG ASSOCIATES, INC., 178 W Adams St, 95204, pg. 608
YOUNNEL ADVERTISING, INC., 2502 Beverly Pl, 95204-4343, pg. 1252

Studio City

DEI WORLDWIDE, INC., 3450 Cahuenga Blvd W, 90068, pg. 294
DRS & ASSOCIATES, 11684 Ventura Blvd 861, 91604, pg. 330
THE WOW FACTOR, INC., 11330 Ventura Blvd, 91604, pg. 1216

Sun Valley

NORM MARSHALL & ASSOCIATES, 11059 Sherman Way, 91352, pg. 813

Sunnyvale

LMGPR, 111 W Evelyn Ave Ste 308, 94086, pg. 665

Temecula

REVSHARE, 32836 Wolf Store Rd, 92592, pg. 975
RKR MARKETING & ADVERTISING, 43176 Business Pk Dr Ste 108, 92590, pg. 985
TASTE ADVERTISING, BRANDING & PACKAGING, 33175 Temecula Pkwy Ste A-617, 92592-7310, pg. 1111

Thousand Oaks

AD LEVERAGE, 1710 N Moorpark Rd Ste 52, 91360, pg. 22
THE DAVID JAMES AGENCY, 223 E Thousand Oaks Blvd Ste 417, 91360, pg. 268
MORRIS & CASALE INC., 1525 Rancho Conejo Blvd, 91320, pg. 776
THE RON TANSKY ADVERTISING & PUBLIC RELATIONS, 3140 Woodgreen Ct, 91362, pg. 990

Torrance

BRAND33, 1304 El Prado Ave Ste D, 90501, pg. 158
CALLAHAN CREEK, 19001 S Western Ave T200, 90501, pg. 185
CAMPBELL MARKETING & COMMUNICATIONS, 21605 Hawthorne Ste 100, 90503, pg. 188
DIRECT MARKETING CENTER, 21171 S Western Ave Ste 260, 90501-3449, pg. 311
GEORGE P. JOHNSON COMPANY, INC., 18500 Crenshaw Blvd, 90504, pg. 422
NORTHSHORE DESIGNERS, 3655 Torrance Blvd Ste 361, 90503, pg. 816
SAATCHI & SAATCHI LOS ANGELES, 3501 Sepulveda Blvd, 90505, pg. 1001

Truckee

Geographic Index-U.S.

SWITCHBACK PUBLIC RELATIONS & MARKETING INC., 10075 W River St Ste 206, 96161, pg. 1105

Tustin

AL PUNTO ADVERTISING, INC., 730 El Camino Way Ste 200, 92780-7733, pg. 43
ECHO MEDIA GROUP, 12711 Newport Ave Ste H, 92780, pg. 337
THE IDENTITY GROUP, 440 W First St Ste 204, 92780-3047, pg. 535
LUMINOR, 360 E. 1st Street, 92780, pg. 673
THE RANKIN GROUP, LTD., 17821 E 17th St Ste 270, 92780-2137, pg. 951
STRATEGIES, A MARKETING COMMUNICATIONS CORPORATION, 13681 Newport Ave Ste 8 Ste 616, 92780, pg. 1091

Twain Harte

REVERB COMMUNICATIONS INC., 18711 Tiffeni Dr Ste K, 95383, pg. 974

Union City

ELLIPSIS SOLUTIONS, 30812 Periwinkle Dr, 94587, pg. 345

Valencia

SHOPPER MARKETING GROUP ADVERTISING INC., 24412 McBean Pkwy Ste 123, 91355, pg. 1039

Van Nuys

ANIMAX ENTERTAINMENT, 6627 Valjean Ave, 91406, pg. 59
HELPSGOOD, 6627 Valjean Ave, 91406, pg. 509
JOHNSON & MURPHY, 16122 Sherman Way, 91406, pg. 594
LIME VIZIO, 8135 Varna Ave, 91402, pg. 657
VIMBY, 16333 Raymer St Ste B, 91406, pg. 1178

Venice

BRIABE MOBILE INC., 634 A Venice Blvd, 90291, pg. 164
FCB WEST, 200 Mildred Ave, 90291, pg. 372
KARI FEINSTEIN PUBLIC RELATIONS, 1638 Abbot Kinney blvd, 90291, pg. 602
KRUEGER COMMUNICATIONS, 1222 Preston Way, 90291, pg. 619
LIQUID ADVERTISING, 499 Santa Clara, 90291, pg. 661
NEIGHBOR AGENCY, 853 Lincoln Blvd, 90291, pg. 804
NOT MAURICE, 524 Sunset Ave, 90291, pg. 817
SMITH/JUNGER/WELLMAN, 920 Abbot Kinney Blvd, 90291-3311, pg. 1054
USE ALL FIVE INC., 1800 Abbot Kinney Blvd Unit D & E, 90291, pg. 1169
WHIRLED, 2127 Linden Ave, 90291, pg. 1199
ZAMBEZI, 615 Hampton Dr Ste A311, 90291, pg. 1254

Ventura

CONSORTIUM MEDIA SERVICES, 4572 Telephone Rd Ste 913, 93003, pg. 232
MVC, 14724 Ventura Blvd Ste 505, 91403, pg. 797

Victorville

EXECUTIVE1 MEDIA GROUP, 12366 Blazing Star Ln, 92323, pg. 361

Vista

SOURCE COMMUNICATIONS, 2592 Coronado Pl, 92081, pg. 1059

Walnut Creek

JSTOKES AGENCY, 1444 N Main St, 94596-4605, pg. 598
SPIN RECRUITMENT ADVERTISING, 712 Bancroft Rd Ste 521, 94598, pg. 1065

West Hills

GLYPHIX ADVERTISING, 6964 Shoup Ave, 91307, pg. 430

West Hollywood

BBH LA, 8360 Melrose Ave 2nd Fl, 90069, pg. 95
CAMPBELL EWALD LOS ANGELES, 8687 Melrose Ave Ste G510, 90069, pg. 555
CMG WORLDWIDE-LOS ANGELES OFFICE, 9229 W Sunset Blvd Ste 950, 90069, pg. 218
DAILEY & ASSOCIATES, 8687 Melrose Ave Ste G300, 90069-5701, pg. 263
H+M COMMUNICATIONS, 8648 Holloway Plaza Dr, 90069, pg. 471
IW GROUP, INC., 8687 Melrose Ave Ste G540, 90069, pg. 564
JACK MORTON WORLDWIDE, 8687 Melrose Ave Ste G700, 90069, pg. 583
NCOMPASS INTERNATIONAL, 8223 Santa Monica Blvd, 90064, pg. 802
SAMANTHA SLAVEN PUBLICITY, 8285 W Sunset Blvd 10, 90046-2419, pg. 1015
THE WAGNER JUNKER AGENCY, 7317 Santa Monica Blvd, 90046, pg. 1186

Westlake Village

ANIMATED DESIGNS LLC, 31336 Via Colinas Ste 103, 91362-6784, pg. 59
CORRIDOR COMMUNICATIONS, INC., 3835R E 1000 Oaks Blvd Ste 237, 91362, pg. 237
NOTIONIST, 31368 Via Colinas Ste 105, 91362, pg. 817
SAPUTO DESIGN, INC., 870 Hampshire Rd Ste D, 91361, pg. 1020
SAY IT WITH WORDS, 32068 Waterside Ln, 91361-3622, pg. 1022
SOCIAL CONTROL, 5655 Lindero Canyon Rd Ste 425, 91362, pg. 1056

Woodland

THUNDER FACTORY LOS ANGELES, 20301 Ventura Blvd Ste 219, 91364, pg. 1142

Woodland Hills

AD2PRO MEDIA SOLUTIONS, 23371 Mulholland Dr Ste 132, 91364, pg. 23
BRIGHT AGE, 22220 Gilmore St, 91303, pg. 165
IONIC MEDIA, 21300 Victory Blvd, 91367, pg. 559
KERN, 20955 Warner Center Ln, 91367-6511, pg. 609
NEWMAN GRACE INC., 6133 Fallbrook Ave, 91367, pg. 808
TC CREATIVES LLC, 6301 De Soto Ave, 91367, pg. 1133

COLORADO

Aurora

DCI-WEST, 19594 E Ida Pl, 80015, pg. 304
SEXTON & CO., 4429 South Atchison Circle, 80015, pg. 1034

Avon

BRAND CONNECTIONS, 910 Nottingham Rd, 81620, pg. 155

Boulder

ANTHEM BRANDING, 1000 N St, 80304, pg. 62
ATOMIC20, 2088 Broadway, 80302, pg. 78
CP+B BOULDER, 6450 Gunpark Dr, 80301, pg. 240
EGG STRATEGY, 1360 Walnut St Ste 102, 80302, pg. 340
GRENADIER, 1221 Pennsylvania Ave, 80302, pg. 444
GRIFF/SMC, INC. MEDICAL MARKETING COMMUNICATIONS, 954 Pearl St, 80302, pg. 459
INTERMUNDO MEDIA, 1433 Pearl St 2nd Fl, 80302, pg. 553
KRONER COMMUNICATION, 4966 Valhalla Dr, 80301, pg. 619
MADE MOVEMENT LLC, 2206 Pearl St, 80302, pg. 684
MONDO ROBOT, 1737 15th St, 80302, pg. 771
MOVEMENT STRATEGY, 4720 Table Mesa Dr Ste F-100, 80305, pg. 780
MOXIE SOZO, 1140 Pearl St, 80302-5253, pg. 780
OBLIQUE DESIGN, 1290 Yellow Pine Ave Ste D-4, 80304, pg. 821
OFF MADISON AVE, 1434 Spruce St Ste 100, 80302, pg. 826
PIVOT COMMUNICATION, 777 29th St Ste 400, 80303, pg. 893
ROOM 214, INC., 3390 Valmont Rd Ste 214, 80301, pg. 991
SCHOOL, 645 Walnut Street, 80302, pg. 913
SMAK STRATEGIES, 3840 Broadway St Apt 27, 80304, pg. 1052
STERLING RICE GROUP, 1801 13th St Ste 400, 80302, pg. 1084
TDA_BOULDER, 1435 Arapahoe Ave, 80302-6307, pg. 1133
VERMILION INC., 3055 Center Green Dr, 80301, pg. 1174
VICTORS & SPOILS, 1904 Pearl St, 80302, pg. 1176
WELLS COMMUNICATIONS, INC., 3460 4th St, 80304, pg. 1196

Broomfield

LUMINATE ADVERTISING, 12303 Airport Way Ste 200, 80021, pg. 673

Carbondale

5 STONE ADVERTISING, PO Box 429, 81623, pg. 9

Centennial

WEBB STRATEGIC COMMUNICATIONS, 6025 S Quebec St Ste 360, 80111, pg. 1194

Colorado Springs

ACKERMAN MCQUEEN, INC., 517 Cascade Ave Ste 150, 80903, pg. 20
GRAHAM OLESON, 525 Communication Cir, 80905-1736, pg. 439
LUNCHBUCKET CREATIVE, 2153 Chuckwagon Rd Ste 20, 80919, pg. 674
SANDIA ADVERTISING, 510 N Tejon St, 80903, pg. 1017
TAPIA ADVERTISING, PO Box 64021, 80962, pg. 1109
VLADIMIR JONES, 6 N Tejon St 4 Fl, 80903-1509, pg. 1181

Denver

90OCTANE, 518 17th St Ste 1400, 80202, pg. 12
ADRENALIN, INC, 54 W 11th Ave, 80204, pg. 31
AGENCY ZERO, 1201 E Colfax Ste 203, 80218, pg. 38
AKAVIT, 1224 N Speer Blvd, 80204, pg. 43
AMELIE COMPANY, 2601 Blake St Ste 150, 80205, pg. 53
AOR, INC., 1345 S Bdwy, 80210, pg. 63
ARMADA MEDICAL MARKETING, 4840 W 29th Ave, 80212, pg. 70
ARRAE CREATIVE LLC, 110 16th St Ste 920, 80202, pg. 73
BARNHART, 1641 California St, 80202-1233, pg. 93
BIEMEDIA, 511 Broadway, 80203, pg. 129
CACTUS, 2128 15th St Ste 100, 80202, pg. 183
CARBON8, 2290 W 29th Ave, 80211, pg. 190
CARMA, 1000 S Broadway Ste 107, 80209, pg. 191
COHN MARKETING, 2881 N Speer Blvd, 80211, pg. 220
CULTIVATOR ADVERTISING & DESIGN, 2737 Larimer St Ste B, 80205, pg. 259
DROY ADVERTISING, 10000 E Yale Ave Ste 13, 80231, pg. 330
ELEVATED THIRD, 535 16th St, 80202, pg. 342
ENCITE INTERNATIONAL, 9995 E Harvard Ave, 80231, pg. 347
EXTRA STRENGTH MARKETING COMMUNICATIONS, 1804 S Pearl St, 80210, pg. 362
FACTION MEDIA, 1730 Blake St Ste 200, 80202, pg. 363
FACTORY DESIGN LABS, 158 Fillmore St, 80206, pg. 364
FEAR NOT AGENCY, 1740 Blake St, 80202, pg. 383
FIG ADVERTISING, 110 16th St Ste 940, 80202, pg. 386
GYRO DENVER, 1625 Broadway Ste 2800, 80202, pg. 470
HANGAR 30 INC, 4500 Cherry Creek Dr S Ste 1150, 80246, pg. 477
HEINRICH MARKETING, 2228 Blake St Ste 200, 80205-

Dillon

Edwards

Englewood

Fort Collins

Golden

Grand Junction

Greenwood Village

Lafayette

Lakewood

Littleton

Longmont

Louisville

Loveland

Northglenn

Parker

Steamboat Springs

Westminster

Windsor

CONNECTICUT

Avon

Bethany

Bloomfield

Brookfield

Chester

Collinsville

Danbury

Darien

East Hartford

Easton

Fairfield

Farmington

Glastonbury

Greenwich

Geographic Index-U.S.

CHESTNUT COMMUNICATIONS, INC., 16 Stepping Stone Ln, 06830, pg. 208
KAREN MORSTAD & ASSOCIATES LLC., 79 E Putnam Ave, 06830, pg. 602
RETELE COMPANY, 15 Division St, 06830, pg. 972

Guilford

MEDIABOOM, 96 Broad St, 06437, pg. 744

Hamden

GEM ADVERTISING, 2558 Whitney Ave Ste 104, 06518, pg. 420

Hartford

BAUZA & ASSOCIATES, 11 Asylum St, 06103, pg. 97

Meriden

WEB SOLUTIONS INC., 250 Pomeroy Ave Ste 201, 06450, pg. 1193

Middletown

IMS ADVERTISING LLC, 769 Newfield St Ste 6, 6457, pg. 543
PALM TREE CREATIVE LLC, 210 S Main St, 6457, pg. 871

Milford

POUTRAY PEKAR ASSOCIATES, 344 W Main St, 06460, pg. 905

Milldale

SIGNATURE BRAND FACTORY, 409 Canal St, 06467-0698, pg. 1043

New Haven

DIGITAL SURGEONS LLC, 1175 State St Ste 219, 06510, pg. 309
MASCOLA ADVERTISING, 434 Forbes Ave, 06512-1932, pg. 706
ODONNELL COMPANY, 59 Elm St Ste 402, 6510, pg. 825
RESPONSE LLC, 100 Crown St, 6510, pg. 971

New London

AKINS MARKETING & DESIGN L.L.C., 11 Washburn Rd, 06320-2946, pg. 43
QUINN & HARY MARKETING, PO Box 456, 06320, pg. 944

Newington

MIK ADVERTISING & DESIGN, LLC, 184 Hunters Ln, 06111, pg. 756

Newtown

LEVERAGE MARKETING GROUP, 117-119 S Main St, 06470-2380, pg. 653

Norwalk

ACME IDEA COMPANY LLC, 1 Marshall St, 06854-2262, pg. 20
CIRCLE ONE, 10 Norden Pl, 06854, pg. 211
THE FAMILY ROOM, 27 Ann St, 06854, pg. 367
ICR, 761 Main Ave, 06851, pg. 532
IMPULSE CONCEPT GROUP, 18 Leonard St, 6850, pg. 542
JACK MORTON WORLDWIDE, 800 Connecticut Ave, 06854, pg. 583
MEDIA HORIZONS, INC., 40 Richards Ave, 06854, pg. 742
OCTAGON, 800 Connecticut Ave 2nd Fl, 06854, pg. 823
TANEN DIRECTED ADVERTISING, 12 S Main St Ste 401, 06854-2980, pg. 1109
TAUBE/VIOLANTE, INC., 37 N Ave Ste 202, 06851, pg. 1111
WAHLSTROM GROUP, 800 Connecticut Ave, 06854, pg. 1186

Prospect

WORX BRANDING & ADVERTISING, 18 Waterbury Rd, 06712-1215, pg. 1216

Rocky Hill

PITA COMMUNICATIONS LLC, 40 Cold Spring Rd, 06067, pg. 893
TAGTEAM BUSINESS PARTNERS LLC, 2189 Silas Deane Highway Ste 11, 6067, pg. 1107

Shelton

BARBEAU-HUTCHINGS ADVERTISING, INC., 30 Controls Dr, 06484, pg. 91

Simsbury

BERKSHIRE INTERMEDIA GROUP, PO Box 23, 06070-0014, pg. 125

South Norwalk

MILKSONO LLC, 11 Day St Level 1, 06854, pg. 756
SILVER CREATIVE GROUP, 50 N Main St, 06854, pg. 1044
STORY WORLDWIDE, 20 Marshall St Ste 220, 06854, pg. 1089

Stamford

AUSTIN LAWRENCE GROUP, 1266 E Main St Ste 700, 06902, pg. 81
BEEBY CLARK + MEYLER, 700 Canal Street, 3rd Floor, 06902, pg. 122
CATALYST MARKETING COMMUNICATIONS INC., 2777 Summer St Ste 301, 06905, pg. 197
CDHM ADVERTISING, 1100 Summer St 1st Fl, 06905, pg. 200
CREATIVE PARTNERS, 46 Southfield Ave, 06902, pg. 251
FLETCHER KNIGHT, 1 Dock St 620, 06902, pg. 393
PEPPERS & ROGERS GROUP, 1111 Summer St Fl 5, 06905-5511, pg. 883
PLOWSHARE GROUP, INC., One Dock St, 6902, pg. 898
REBRANDERY, 100 Hope St, 6906, pg. 959
SIGNAL OUTDOOR ADVERTISING, 68 Southfield Ave Bldg 2 Ste 100, 06902, pg. 1043

Stonington

GORA COMMUNICATIONS, 3 Front St, 06378, pg. 436

Stratford

ME CREATIVE AGENCY, 287 Roosevelt Ave, 6615, pg. 740
RED POPPY MARKETING LLC, 2318 Main St Ste 2, 06615, pg. 962
YELLOW PAGES RESOURCE, 999 Oronoque Ln, 06614, pg. 1238

Wallingford

THE BCB GROUP, INC., 10 Alexander Dr, 06492, pg. 119
KRATIVE LLC, 350 Center St Ste 208, 6492, pg. 618

Waterford

SMIZER PERRY, 68 Pepperbox Rd, 06385-3512, pg. 1055

Weatogue

THE DONALDSON GROUP, 88 Hopmeadow St, 06089-9602, pg. 322

West Hartford

BLUESPIRE MARKETING, 29 South Main St, 06107, pg. 143
SQUARE ONE MARKETING, 1993 Albany Ave, 06117, pg. 1069

Weston

MARKETING CONCEPTS GROUP, 6 Old Field Rd, 06883, pg. 697

Westport

CATAPULT MARKETING, 55 Post Rd W, 06880, pg. 198
THE CAUSEWAY AGENCY, 21 Charles St Ste 201, 06880, pg. 198
CROSSBOW GROUP, LLC, 136 Main St, 06880, pg. 256
MCMILLAN GROUP, 25 Otter Trail, 6880, pg. 737
O'HALLORAN ADVERTISING, INC., 270 Saugatuck Ave, 06880-6431, pg. 853
REDINGTON INC., 49 Richmondville Ave Ste 108, 06880, pg. 965
WOMEN'S MARKETING INC., 1221 Post Rd E Ste 201, 06880-5430, pg. 1213

Wilton

HELIA, 372 Danbury Rd Ste 100, 06897, pg. 490
IMAGEMARK, INC., 12 Godfrey Pl 3rd Fl, 06897, pg. 538
TRACYLOCKE, 131 Danbury Rd, 06897, pg. 1154

DELAWARE

Milton

KEEN BRANDING, 30616 Overbrook Ctr Way, 19969, pg. 605

Nassau

KEEN BRANDING, PO Box 416, 19969, pg. 605

Newark

TIPTON COMMUNICATIONS, 323 E Main St, 19711, pg. 1145

Wilmington

AB+C, 819 N. Washington St, 19801, pg. 15
THE ARCHER GROUP, 233 N King St, 19801, pg. 67
BARRON MARKETING COMMUNICATIONS, 833 N Washington St, 19801-1509, pg. 94
CASPARI MCCORMICK, 307 A St 2nd Fl, 19801-5345, pg. 196
COOL NERDS MARKETING, 300 N Market St, 19801, pg. 233
CREATIVE SOLUTIONS INTERNATIONAL, 800 Delaware Ave Ste 410, 19810, pg. 252
DEARDORFF ASSOCIATES, 319 E Lea Blvd, 19802, pg. 291
DMG MARKETING, 3801 Kennett Pike Ste D-301, 19807, pg. 318
KONCORDIA GROUP, 2417 Lancaster Ave, 19805, pg. 617
SHINY ADVERTISING, 1800 Wawaset St, 19806, pg. 1038

Yorklyn

WH2P, INC., PO Box 22, 19736, pg. 1198

DISTRICT OF COLUMBIA

Washington

A.B. DATA, LTD., 1808 Swann St NW, 20009-5505, pg. 15
THE AD AGENCY, 1101 Connecticut Ave NW Ste 450, 20036, pg. 22
ADFERO GROUP, 1666 K St NW Ste 250, 20006, pg. 28
ADWORKS, INC., 5335 Wisconsin Ave NW, 20015, pg. 36
AGENCYQ, 1825 K St NW Ste 500, 20006, pg. 39
ALLIED INTEGRATED MARKETING, 1726 M St NW Ste 801, 20036-4650, pg. 48
ALLISON & PARTNERS-WASHINGTON D.C., 1129 20th St NW Ste 250, 20036, pg. 50
APCO WORLDWIDE, 700 12th St NW Ste 800, 20005, pg. 63

FLORIDA

Altamonte Springs

Aventura

Bay Harbor Islands

Boca Raton

Bonita Springs

Boynton Beach

Bradenton

Brooksville

Cape Canaveral

Cape Coral

Chipley

Clearwater

Coconut Creek

Coconut Grove

Coral Gables

Coral Springs

A WORK OF ART INC., 1621 NW 102nd Way, 33071, pg. 14

Davie

THE PINK COLLECTIVE, 7320 Griffin Rd Ste 103a, 33314, pg. 892

Daytona Beach

BENEDICT ADVERTISING, 640 N Peninsula Dr, 32118-3829, pg. 124

Deerfield Beach

COMMUNICATIONS ADVERTISING, INC., 2363 Deer Creek Trl, 33442-1323, pg. 226
HARTE-HANKS, INC., 1525 NW Third St Ste 21, 33442-1667, pg. 482
PLAYWIRE MEDIA, 1000 E Hillsboro Blvd Ste 201, 33441, pg. 897
WILEN DIRECT, 3333 SW 15th St, 33442, pg. 1207

Delray Beach

DG COMMUNICATIONS GROUP, 1225 NW 17th Ave Ste 103, 33445, pg. 305
LEAD ME MEDIA, 1200 NW 17th Ave Ste 17, 33445-2513, pg. 633
REALTIME MARKETING GROUP, 61 SE 4th Ave, 33483, pg. 958

Doral

DILYON CREATIVE GROUP, 2850 NW 79 Ave, 33122, pg. 309
HIPERVINCULO, 7774 NW 46th ST, 33166, pg. 516
LATIN WORLD ENTERTAINMENT AGENCY, 3470 NW 82nd Ave Ste 670, 33122, pg. 628
MICHELSEN ADVERTISING, 10855 NW 33rd St, 33172, pg. 754

Fort Lauderdale

954DESIGN, 2967 Ravenswood Rd Ste 5, 33312, pg. 13
ADBIT'S ADVERTISING & PR, 757 SE 17th St 358, 33316, pg. 26
AMBIT MARKETING COMMUNICATIONS, 19 NW 5th St, 33301, pg. 52
BRAINSTORMS ADVERTISING & MARKETING, INC., 2201 Wilton Dr, 33305-2131, pg. 154
BULLSEYE STRATEGY, 1700 E Las Olas Blvd Ste 301, 33301, pg. 174
EDSA, 1512 E Broward Blvd Ste 110, 33301-2126, pg. 338
EISENBERG & ASSOCIATES, 511 NE 3rd Ave, 33301-3235, pg. 340
HOSPITALITY-MARKETING LLC, 200 S Andrews Ave Ste 503, 33301, pg. 524
INTUIT MEDIA GROUP, 1239 NE 8th Ave, 33304, pg. 558
KIP HUNTER MARKETING, 888 E Las Olas Blvd Ste 500, 33301, pg. 613
LASER ADVERTISING, 1500 Cordova Rd Ste 205, 33316, pg. 627
LATIN3 INC., 6400 N Andrews Ave Ste 490, 33309, pg. 628
MAD 4 MARKETING, 5203 NW 33rd Ave, 33309-6302, pg. 683
MALKUS COMMUNICATIONS GROUP, 888 Las Olas Blvd Ste 508, 33301, pg. 688
MEDIA RESPONSE, INC., 3201 Griffin Rd 3rd Fl, 33312, pg. 743
MOROCH, 81 SW 10th St Ste 2200, 33324, pg. 775
NEW RIVER COMMUNICATIONS, INC., 1819 SE 17th St, 33316, pg. 807
PIERSON GRANT PUBLIC RELATIONS, 6301 NW 5th Way Ste 2600, 33309, pg. 891
PL&P ADVERTISING, 200 NE 44th St, 33334-1442, pg. 895
S.MARK GRAPHICS FLORIDA INC., 500 NE 9th Ave, 33301, pg. 1053
STARMARK INTERNATIONAL, INC., 210 S. Andrews Ave., 33301, pg. 1080
TAMBOURINE, 2941 W Cypress Creek Rd 2nd Fl, 33309, pg. 1108
TEAM ENTERPRISES, INC., 110 E Broward Blvd Ste 2450, 33301, pg. 739
TEN, 330 SW 2nd St Bldg 111, 33312, pg. 1136
WWDB INTEGRATED MARKETING, 412 SE 13th St, 33316, pg. 1235
ZIMMERMAN ADVERTISING, 6600 N Andrews Avenue, 33309-3064, pg. 1256

Fort Myers

BVK-FORT MYERS, 12697 New Brittany Blvd, 33907-3631, pg. 180
GREENFIELD ADVERTISING GROUP, 12551 New Brittany Blvd Bldg 26, 33907-3625, pg. 443
MOORE & SCARRY ADVERTISING, 12601 Westlinks Dr Ste 7, 33913-8638, pg. 772
PEARL BRANDS, 1635 Hendry St, 33901, pg. 881
POWERS ADVERTISING, 17502 Brentwood Ct, 33967, pg. 906
QUENZEL & ASSOCIATES, 12801 University Dr Ste 1 - 4, 33907, pg. 942
SPIRO & ASSOCIATES MARKETING, ADVERTISING & PUBLIC RELATIONS, 12651 McGregor Blvd Unit 4-402, 33919, pg. 1065

Gainesville

NAYLOR, LLC, 5950 NW 1st Place, 32607, pg. 802

Gulf Breeze

ROMJUE ADVERTISING & CO, 913 Gulf Breeze Pky Ste 15A, 32561, pg. 990

Heathrow

EVOK ADVERTISING, 1485 International Pwky, 32746, pg. 360

Hernando

THE I AM GROUP, INC., 2875 East Timberwood, 34442, pg. 531

Hollywood

ADSERVICES INC., 2450 Hollywood Blvd Ste 202, 33020, pg. 32
FISH CONSULTING, INC., 2001 Hollywood Blvd Ste 310, 33020, pg. 389
LOIS GELLER MARKETING GROUP, 1915 Hollywood Blvd Ste 201, 33020, pg. 667
MARKETING MATTERS, 2700 N 29th Ave, 33020, pg. 698

Jacksonville

5IVECANONS, 24 N Market St, 32202, pg. 9
ANTONWEST ADVERTISING, 1654 San Marco Blvd, 32207, pg. 62
AXIA PUBLIC RELATIONS, 222 E Forsyth St, 32202, pg. 83
BESON 4 MEDIA GROUP, 13500 Sutton Park Dr S Ste 105, 32224, pg. 127
BROADBASED COMMUNICATIONS INC., 1301 Riverplace Blvd Ste 1830, 32207, pg. 167
BRUNET-GARCIA ADVERTISING, INC., 1510 Hendricks Ave, 32207, pg. 171
BURDETTE KETCHUM, 1023 Kings Ave, 32207, pg. 175
CLIENT FOCUSED MEDIA, 1611 San Marco Blvd, 32207, pg. 216
CROSS MEDIAWORKS, 701 San Marco Blvd Ste 1603, 32207, pg. 256
DAIGLE CREATIVE, 9957 Moorings Dr, 32257, pg. 263
DALTON AGENCY JACKSONVILLE, 140 W Monroe St, 32202, pg. 264
DIGITAL EDGE, 10161 Centurion Pkwy N, 32256, pg. 308
ENCODE, P.O. Box 600534, 32260, pg. 347
HARTE-HANKS DIRECT MARKETING/JACKSONVILLE, LLC, 7498 Fullerton St, 32256-3508, pg. 483
THE HESTER GROUP LLC, 100 N Laura St Ste 802, 32202, pg. 511
MAD MEN MARKETING INC., 111 E Bay St Ste 201, 32202, pg. 684
MARY FISHER DESIGN, 1731 Emerson St, 32207, pg. 706
MEDIA DESIGN, 5569 Bowden Rd Ste 5, 32216-8034, pg. 742
MEDIA MIX, 13901 Sutton Pk Dr S Bldg B Ste 400 4th Fl, 32224, pg. 743
THE MONTELLO AGENCY, 9310 Old Kings Rd Ste 1704, 32257, pg. 772
ON IDEAS, INC., 6 E Bay St Ste 100, 32202-5422, pg. 859
REPUTATION INK, 1303 N Main St Ste 108, 32206, pg. 969
RLS GROUP, 2468 Atlantic Blvd, 32207, pg. 985
ROSBERG FOZMAN ROLANDELLI ADVERTISING, 4745 Sutton Park Ct Ste 804, 32224, pg. 991
SCOTT-MCRAE ADVERTISING INC., 701 Riverside Pk Pl Ste 100, 32204-3343, pg. 1027
SHEPHERD, 1301 Riverplace Blvd Ste 1100, 32207, pg. 1037
ST. JOHN & PARTNERS, 5220 Belfort Rd Ste 400, 32256-6017, pg. 1071
STATION FOUR, 100 N Laura St Ste 602, 32202, pg. 1081
WINGARD CREATIVE, 245 Riverside Ave Ste 425, 32202, pg. 1209

Jacksonville Beach

ADJECTIVE & CO, 102 6th Ave N Ste 9, 32250, pg. 28
DION MARKETING COMPANY, 421 N 3rd St, 32250, pg. 310

Jupiter

RCI, 550 Heritage Dr Ste 200, 33458, pg. 955
RED SPOT INTERACTIVE, 1001 Jupiter Park Dr. #124, 33458, pg. 962

Key Largo

HAWK ASSOCIATES, INC., 227 Atlantic Blvd, 33037, pg. 503

Lake Worth

CANNONBALL ADVERTISING FIRM LLC, 9904 Via Bernini, 33467, pg. 188

Lakeland

LOWRY CREATIVE, 2525 Drane Field Rd Ste 12, 33811, pg. 671
MADDEN BRAND AGENCY, 116 S Tennessee Ave Ste 201, 33801, pg. 684
MCQUEEN MARKETING, 3616 Harden Blvd Ste 340, 33803, pg. 737
TMR AGENCY, 1046 S Florida Ave, 33803-1118, pg. 1149

Leesburg

HUSEBO ADVERTISING & PUBLIC RELATIONS, 1319 Shelfer St, 34748, pg. 529

Lighthouse Point

BACKUS TURNER INTERNATIONAL, 3108 N Federal Hwy, 33064, pg. 86

Longwood

BENNETT & COMPANY MARKETING, 543 Estates Pl, 32779-2857, pg. 124
CRISTOL MARKETING COMPANY, 237 Hunt Club Blvd Ste 102, 32779, pg. 254
WELLONS COMMUNICATIONS, 195 Wekiva Springs Rd Ste214, 32779, pg. 1196

Lutz

THE CRUSH AGENCY, 1519 DI Mabry Hwy 100, 33548, pg. 258

Maitland

CHERNOFF NEWMAN, 2500 Maitland Center Pkwy Ste 104, 32751-4165, pg. 208
TCS MEDIA, INC., 2333 Chinook Trl, 32751-4079, pg. 1133

Margate

HEPCATSMARKETING.COM, 1861 Banks Rd, 33063, pg. 510

Melbourne

CK COMMUNICATIONS, INC. (CKC), 457 Montreal Ave, 32935, pg. 212
TRANSWORLD ADVERTISING, INC., 3684 N Wickham Rd Ste C, 32935, pg. 1154

Miami

3ELEVENMEDIA, 7210 SW 57th Ave Ste 212, 33143, pg. 7
AGENCY GUERRA, 3301 NE 1st Ave Ste H2701, 33137, pg. 38
AMG WORLDWIDE, 900 SW 8th St Ste C 2, 33130, pg. 55
AMGW AGENCY, 900 SW 8th St, 33130, pg. 55
ANTHONY BARADAT & ASSOCIATES, 1235 Coral Way Ste 200, 33145, pg. 62
BEBER SILVERSTEIN GROUP, 89 NE 27th St, 33137, pg. 121
BENAMOR, 6355 NW 36th St Ste 307, 33166, pg. 123
BEYOND TOTAL BRANDING, 98 NW 29th St, 33127, pg. 128
BLACKDOG ADVERTISING, 8771 SW 129th Terr, 33176, pg. 134
BRAINSWITCH ADVERTISING, 250 NW 23rd St Ste 210, 33127, pg. 154
BRANGER_BRIZ, 3250 NE 1st Ave Ste 313, 33137, pg. 162
THE BRAVO GROUP HQ, 601 Brickell Key Drive, Suite 1100, 33131, pg. 162
BUSH RENZ, 4141 NE 2nd Ave Ste 203 E, 33137, pg. 178
BVK/MEKA, 848 Brickell Ave Ste 430, 33131-2915, pg. 180
CIRCLE OF ONE MARKETING, 2400 NE 2nd Ave Studio C, 33137, pg. 211
COMMONGROUNDMGS, 1790 Coral Way, 33145, pg. 224
THE COMMUNITY, 6400 Biscayne Blvd, 33138, pg. 227
CONILL ADVERTISING, INC., 800 Brickell Ave, 33131, pg. 230
CREATIVE MINDWORKS, 11900 Biscayne Blvd Ste 100, 33181, pg. 251
DAISHO CREATIVE STRATEGIES, 13280 SW 131 St Ste 105, 33186, pg. 264
DAVID THE AGENCY, 1395 Brickell Ave Ste 900, 33131, pg. 267
DDB LATIN AMERICA, 770 S Dixie Hwy Ste 109, 33146, pg. 275
DDM ADVERTISING INC, 92 SW 3rd St Ste 2903, 33130, pg. 290
DELTA MEDIA, INC., 7875 SW 104th St Ste 100, 33156, pg. 295
DIAZ & COOPER ADVERTISING INC, 9200 So Dadeland Blvd Ste 209, 33156, pg. 307
EAG GROUP, 6790 Coral Way 2nd Fl, 33155, pg. 335
EYEBALL DIGITAL, 444 Brickell Ave, 33131, pg. 363
EYESEA SOLUTIONS, 825 Brickell Bay Dr Ste 246, 33131, pg. 363
FIGMENT DESIGN, 2977 McFarlane Rd 2nd Fl, 33133, pg. 386
FURY ADVERTISING, 990 Biscayne Blvd Ste 503, 33132, pg. 409
GLO CREATIVE, 1221 Brickell Ave Ste 900, 33131, pg. 428
GMG ADVERTISING, 13500 N Kendall Dr Ste 115, 33186, pg. 431
GREEN DOT ADVERTISING & MARKETING, 5400 NE 4th Ct, 33137, pg. 442
HISPANIC GROUP, 8181 NW 14th St Ste 250, 33126, pg. 516
IMAGERY CREATIVE, 7400 SW 50th Terrace, 33155, pg. 539
THE KLUGER AGENCY, 1200 Brickell Ave 14th Fl, 33131, pg. 615
LGD COMMUNICATIONS, INC., 3819 N Miami Ave, 33137, pg. 656
M8 AGENCY, 3301 NE 1st Ave Ste Ph6, 33137, pg. 681
MARANON & ASSOCIATES ADVERTISING, 2103 Coral Way Ste 604, 33145, pg. 690
MATRIX2 ADVERTISING, 1903 NW 97th Ave, 33172, pg. 710
MICSTURA, 12955 Biscayne Blvd Ste 408, 33181, pg. 755
NATCOM MARKETING, 80 SW 8th St Ste 2230, 33130, pg. 801
NAVIGANT MARKETING / KSR, 2103 Coral Way Ste 724, 33145, pg. 802
NEWLINK GROUP, 1111 Brickell Ave Ste 1350, 33131, pg. 808
NOBOX MARKETING GROUP, INC., 180 NE 39Th St Ste 225, 33137, pg. 812
OUTOFTHEBLUE ADVERTISING, 2424 S Dixie Hwy Ste 100, 33133, pg. 866
PG CREATIVE, 14 NE 1st Ave Ste 1106, 33132, pg. 887
POLLER & JORDAN ADVERTISING AGENCY, INC., PO Box 166249, 33116-6249, pg. 902
PROPELLER, 1428 Brickell Ave 6th Fl, 33131, pg. 914
PUMPED INC, 14 NE 1st Ave Ste 904, 33132, pg. 937
RABINOVICI & ASSOCIATES, 20815 NE 16th Ave Ste B10, 33179-2124, pg. 948
REPUBLICA, The Republica Bldg, 33145, pg. 968
SAATCHI & SAATCHI LATIN AMERICA, 800 Brickell Ave Ste 400, 33131, pg. 1000
SAMBA ROCK, 90 SW 3rd St, 33130, pg. 1015
SAPIENT CORPORATION, 2911 Grand Ave, 33133, pg. 1018
SAPIENT MIAMI/FALLS, 2911 Grand Ave Ste 100, 33133, pg. 1018
SEE YA GROUP, 6830 NW 77th Ct, 33166, pg. 1029
STILT MEDIA, 250 Catalonia Ste 805, 33134, pg. 1086
TINSLEY ADVERTISING, 2000 S Dixie Hwy Ste 201, 33133, pg. 1144
VIVA PARTNERSHIP, 10800 Biscayne Blvd, 33137, pg. 1181
WEBLIFT, 18495 S Dixie Hwy Ste 365, 33157-6817, pg. 1194
WUNDERMAN, Courvoisier Ctr II 601 Brickell Key Dr Ste 1100, 33131, pg. 1230
Y&R LATIN AMERICAN HEADQUARTERS, Courvoisier Ctr II 601 Brickell Key Dr Ste 1100, 33131, pg. 1240
Y&R MIAMI, 601 Brickell Key Dr Ste 1100, 33131, pg. 1248

Miami Beach

HI-GLOSS, 1666 Kennedy Causeway, 33141, pg. 512
OBERHAUSEN MARKETING & PUBLIC RELATIONS, 1000 Lincoln Rd Ste 215, 33139, pg. 821
OPTFIRST INC., 1111 Lincoln Rd #400, 33139, pg. 863
PINTA USA LLC, 1111 Lincoln Rd Ste 800, 33139, pg. 892
RICH MEDIA WORLDWIDE, 930 Washington Ave 5th Fl, 33139, pg. 977
SCPF, 1688 Meridian Ave Ste 200, 33139, pg. 1028
TARA, INK., 1666 Kennedy Causeway Ste 703, 33141, pg. 1109
TREISTER MURRY AGENCY, 1130 Washington Ave 1st Fl N, 33139-4600, pg. 1155
TRIMENTION ADVERTISING, 555 Washington Ave, 33139, pg. 1158

Miami Springs

AVANZA ADVERTISING, LLC, 5465 NW 36th St, 33166, pg. 81
BODNER ADVERTISING, 5600 NW 36th St Ste 611, 33166, pg. 145

Middleburg

DEPPE COMMUNICATIONS LLC, 1880 Paradise Moorings Blvd, 32068, pg. 300

Naples

ABOVEWATER PUBLIC RELATIONS & MARKETING LLC, 107 Madison Dr, 34110, pg. 17
ADSOURCE, 1415 Panther Ln Ste 360, 34109, pg. 32
PARADISE ADVERTISING & MARKETING-NAPLES, 649 5th Ave S Ste 213, 34102, pg. 873
WILSON CREATIVE GROUP, INC., 6645 Willow Park Dr Ste 100, 34109, pg. 1209

Newberry

352 MEDIA GROUP, 133 SW 130th Way Ste D, 32669, pg. 6
FRANKEL MEDIA GROUP, 105 SW 128th St Ste 200, 32669-3244, pg. 401

North Miami Beach

SONSHINE COMMUNICATIONS, 975 N Miami Beach Blvd, 33162, pg. 1058

North Palm Beach

CHUMNEY & ASSOCIATES, 660 US Hwy 1 2nd Fl, 33408, pg. 210

Ocala

NEPTUNE ADVERTISING, 3003 SW College Rd Ste 1071, 34474, pg. 805

Orlando

&BARR, 600 E Washington St, 32801-2938, pg. 57
APPLETON CREATIVE, INC., 539 Delaney Ave, 32801, pg. 65
BARNETT MURPHY DIRECT MARKETING, 1323 Brookhaven Dr, 32803, pg. 93
BIGEYE AGENCY, 500 S Magnolia Ave, 32801, pg. 132
BMDM, 1323 Brookhaven Dr, 32803, pg. 144
CHATTER BUZZ MEDIA, 100 W Lucerne Circle, 32801, pg. 206
DAYNER HALL INC., 621 E Pine St, 32801, pg. 272
DIFFERENT PERSPECTIVE, 201 S Orange Ave Ste 890, 32801, pg. 307
FUEGO COMMUNICATIONS & MARKETING INC, 6900 Turkey Lake Rd, 32819, pg. 406
GO BIG MARKETING, 1000 N Magnolia Ave, 32803, pg. 431
GOCONVERGENCE, 4545 36th St, 32811, pg. 432
GREEN GRASS MARKETING & ADVERTISING, 4539 36th St, 32811, pg. 442
THE GROUP ADVERTISING, 1221 N Mills Ave Ste B, 32803, pg. 462
JKR ADVERTISING & MARKETING, 1 South Orange Ave Ste 202, 32801, pg. 591
LAUGHING SAMURAI, 1221-C N Orange Ave, 32804, pg. 629
LIGHTMAKER, 6881 Kingspointe Pkwy Ste 12, 32819, pg. 657
LURE DESIGN, INC., 1009 Virginia Dr, 32803, pg. 674
MASSEY COMMUNICATIONS, 1736 33rd St, 32839, pg. 708
MAVEN CREATIVE, 62 W Colonial Dr Ste 302, 32801, pg. 711
MEREDITH COMMUNICATIONS, 10151 University Blvd 163, 32817, pg. 747
METROPOLIS ADVERTISING, 719 Peachtree Rd Ste 210, 32804, pg. 752
MMGY GLOBAL, 423 S Keller Rd Ste 100, 32810-6121, pg. 768
MONSTER MEDIA, LLC, 555 S Lake Destiny Dr, 32810, pg. 772
NONBOX, 1970 E Osceola Pkwy Ste 47, 34743, pg. 813
ORANGESQUARE, 1 S Orange Ave Ste 401, 32801, pg. 864
PRISMATIC, 745 N Magnolia Ave #301, 32803, pg. 911
PUSH, 101 Ernestine St, 32801-2317, pg. 939
RED ROCKET STUDIOS, 4700 LB McLeod Ste B2, 32811, pg. 962
REMIXED, 113 E Pine St, 32801, pg. 968
SAY IT LOUD, 1121 N Mills Ave, 32803, pg. 1022
SIGNAL OUTDOOR ADVERTISING, 7616 Southland Blvd Ste 114, 32809, pg. 1042
SIX DEGREES, 1217B N Orange Ave, 32804, pg. 1047
THINK CREATIVE INC., 1001 Virgina Dr, 32803, pg. 1139
VOYAGE LLC, 25 Wall St Ste 5, 32801, pg. 1185
WATAUGA GROUP, 1600 N Orange Ave Ste 13, 32804, pg. 1192
WHOISCARRUS, 416 N Fern Creek Ave Ste A, 32803, pg. 1201
ZUVI CREATIVE LLC, 1844 Clacton Dr, 32837, pg. 1260

Ormond Beach

HAYWORTH PUBLIC RELATIONS, 700 W Granada Blvd Ste 100, 32174, pg. 503
LORD & LASKER, 555 W Grandad Blvd Ste F5, 32174, pg. 669
S2 ADVERTISING, 533 N Nova Rd Ste 213B, 32174, pg. 999

Oviedo

NO LIMIT MARKETING & ADVERTISING, INC., 2789

Wrights Rd, 32765, pg. 811
TCREATIVE, INC., 2789 Wrights Rd Ste 1021, 32765, pg. 1133
TJM COMMUNICATIONS, 2441 SR 426 Ste 1061, 32708, pg. 1146

Palm Beach Gardens

LEVATAS, 11701 Lk Victoria Gardens Ave, 33410, pg. 652
STRATEGIC MARKETING INC., 8895 N Military Trl Ste 202B, 33410-6284, pg. 1090

Pembroke Pines

DAS GROUP, INC., 9050 Pines Blvd Ste 250, 33024, pg. 266

Pensacola

DUNCAN MCCALL, INC., 4400 Bayou Blvd Ste 11, 32503-2691, pg. 333
EMAGINATION UNLIMITED INC., 1225 W Gregory St, 32502, pg. 345
E.W. BULLOCK ASSOCIATES, 730 Bayfront Pkwy Ste 5, 32502-6250, pg. 361
IDEAWORKS, INC., 1110 N Palafox St, 32501-2608, pg. 535
JOHN APPLEYARD AGENCY, INC., 4400 Bayou Blvd Ste 34, 32503-2668, pg. 593

Plantation

LIPOF ADVERTISING, 830 Peters Rd Ste D100, 33324, pg. 660

Pompano Beach

JAMES ROSS ADVERTISING, 1180 SW 36th Ave Ste 101, 33069, pg. 586
LIGHTHOUSE LIST COMPANY, 27 SE 24th Ave Ste 6, 33062, pg. 657

Port Saint Joe

KERIGAN MARKETING ASSOCIATES, INC., 260 Marina Dr, 32456, pg. 609

Punta Gorda

MDW ADVERTISING SOLUTIONS INC, 22454 Glass Ln, 33980, pg. 740

Safety Harbor

MY BLUE ROBOT, 1717 Cypress Trace Dr, 34695, pg. 798

Saint Augustine

MAKE ME SOCIAL, 310 Commerce Lake Dr, 32095, pg. 687

Saint Marks

PRUITT HUMPHRESS POWERS & MUNROE, INC., 25 Saint Marks Rivers Edge Dr, 32355, pg. 916

Saint Petersburg

AQUA MARKETING & COMMUNICATIONS INC., 100 2nd Ave S Ste 302-S, 33701, pg. 65
CLEARPH DESIGN, 147 2nd Ave S Ste 210, 33701, pg. 215
DEVINE COMMUNICATIONS, 9300 5th St N, 33702, pg. 304
HYPE GROUP LLC, 433 Central Ave Ste 205, 33701, pg. 530
PARADISE ADVERTISING & MARKETING, 150 2nd Ave N Ste 800, 33701, pg. 873
PYPER YOUNG, 235 Central Ave, 33701, pg. 940
TRIAD RETAIL MEDIA, LLC, 100 Carillon Pkwy, 33716, pg. 1156

Sanibel

NOISE, INC., 4702 Rue Belle Mer, 33957, pg. 812
NOISE, INC., PO Box 869, 33957, pg. 812

Santa Rosa Beach

CORNERSTONE MARKETING & ADVERTISING, INC., 114 Logan Ln Ste 4, 32459, pg. 236
UBU ENTERPRISES, 405 Loblolly Bay Dr, 32459, pg. 1165

Sarasota

ATTACKTIC ADVERTISING, 73 S Palm Ave Ste 220, 34236, pg. 78
C SUITE COMMUNICATIONS, 401 N Cattlemen Rd Ste 200, 34232-6439, pg. 182
CPM USA, 7425 16th St E Ste 101, 34243-5568, pg. 242
EDELSBACHER DESIGN GROUP, 7158 Captain Kidd Ave, 34231, pg. 338
GARDNER KEATON, INC., 3536 East Forest Lk Dr, 34232, pg. 415
GRAPEVINE COMMUNICATIONS INC, 5201 Paylor Ln, 34240, pg. 440
NICKEL COMMUNICATIONS LLC, 47 S Palm Ave Ste 201, 34236, pg. 810
NUEVO ADVERTISING GROUP, INC., 1990 Main St Ste 750, 34236, pg. 818
ROOKS ADVERTISING LLC, 6958 Professional Pkwy E, 34240, pg. 991
SUMMIT MARKETING, 4930 Sabal Lk Cir, 34238, pg. 1099

Shalimar

THE PETERMANN AGENCY, 22 Sherwood Dr, 32579, pg. 886

South Miami

THE WEINBACH GROUP, INC., 7301 SW 57th Ct Ste 550, 33143-5334, pg. 1195

Sunrise

EXPERIENCE ADVERTISING INC, 10871 NW 52nd St, 33351, pg. 362

Tallahassee

BOWSTERN, 1725 Capital Cir NE Ste 205, 32308, pg. 151
CADE & ASSOCIATES ADVERTISING, INC., 1645 Metropolitan Blvd, 32308, pg. 183
DO DESIGN, INC., 1333 N Adams St, 32303, pg. 319
FRANCESCHI ADVERTISING & PUBLIC RELATIONS, INC., PO Box 1773, 32302, pg. 400
KIDD GROUP, 2074 Centre Point Blvd Ste 200, 32308, pg. 611
MOORE COMMUNICATIONS GROUP, 2011 Delta Blvd, 32303, pg. 773
THE POD ADVERTISING, 502 E Pk Ave, 32301, pg. 899
RB OPPENHEIM ASSOCIATES + DIGITAL OPPS, 2040 Delta Way, 32303, pg. 955
SACHS MEDIA GROUP, 114 S Duval St, 32301, pg. 1013
TAPROOT CREATIVE, 2057 Delta Way, 32303, pg. 1109
THINKCREATIVE, 304 W College Ave, 32301, pg. 1139
VOXY MEDIA GROUP, 1700 N Monroe St Ste 11, 32303, pg. 1184
THE ZIMMERMAN AGENCY LLC, 1821 Miccosukee Commons Dr, 32308-5433, pg. 1257

Tamarac

AD CONSULTANT GROUP INC., 7541 Black Olive Way, 33321, pg. 22

Tampa

22SQUARED INC., 401 E Jackson St Fl 36, 33602-5225, pg. 4
ABOVE PROMOTIONS COMPANY, 15419 Plantation Oaks Dr, 33647, pg. 17
AD PARTNERS INC., 4631 Woodland Corporate Blvd Ste 109, 33614, pg. 23
ADVLUENCE LLC, 238 E Davis Blvd Ste 311, 33606, pg. 35
AT THE TABLE PUBLIC RELATIONS, 301 W Platt St Ste 414, 33606, pg. 77
AXXIS ADVERTISING LLC, 5116 N Nebraska Ave, 33603-2363, pg. 83
BAYSHORE SOLUTIONS INC, 600 N Westshore Blvd Ste 700, 33609, pg. 98
BRAVE PEOPLE, 2212 E 3rd Ave, 33605, pg. 162
BVK-TAMPA, 201 Columbia Dr Ste 2, 33606-3722, pg. 180
CENTURION STRATEGIES LLC, 2202 N W Shore Blvd Ste 200, 33607, pg. 202
CHAPPELLROBERTS, 1600 E 8th Ave Ste A-133, 33605, pg. 204
CONNECTIVITY MARKETING AND MEDIA AGENCY, 107 Franklin St Ste 300, 33602, pg. 231
CRANIUM STUDIO, 219 Columbia Dr, 33606, pg. 244
DOCUSOURCE VISUAL COMMUNICATIONS, 5420 Pioneer Park Blvd Ste C, 33634, pg. 320
DUNN&CO, 202 S 22nd St Ste 202, 33605, pg. 333
ERASERFARM, 3123 E 4th Ave, 33605, pg. 352
THE FOOD GROUP (TAMPA), 3820 Northdale Blvd Suite 205A, 33624, pg. 396
FRENCH/WEST/VAUGHAN, INC., 2211 E 7th Ave, 33605, pg. 405
IGNITION BRANDING, 2211 E 7th Ave, 33605, pg. 537
IN PLACE MARKETING, 410 S Cedar Ave, 33606, pg. 543
JONES FOSTER DEAL ADVERTISING & PUBLIC RELATIONS, INC., 412 E Madison St, 33602, pg. 596
LEVO HEALTH, 15310 Amberly Dr Ste 207, 33647, pg. 654
MARKETING IN COLOR, 1515 N Marion St, 33602, pg. 698
NV ADVERTISING, 518 N Tampa St Ste 210, 33602, pg. 819
PEAKBIETY, BRANDING + ADVERTISING, 501 E Jackson St Ste 200, 33602, pg. 881
POLYCREATIVE, 2308 E 10th Ave B, 33605, pg. 903
PP+K, 1102 N Florida Ave, 33602, pg. 907
RFB COMMUNICATIONS GROUP, 600 S Magnolia Ave Ste 300, 33606, pg. 976
SCHIFINO LEE ADVERTISING, 511 W Bay St Ste 400, 33606, pg. 1024
SHAKER RECRUITMENT ADVERTISING & COMMUNICATIONS, INC., 1408 N Westshore Blvd Ste 508, 33607-3844, pg. 1035
SHIRLEY/HUTCHINSON CREATIVE WORKS, 707 N Franklin Ste 100, 33602, pg. 1039
SIGNAL OUTDOOR ADVERTISING, 6011 Benjamin Rd Ste 104, 33634, pg. 1043
SPARK, 2309 W Platt St, 33609, pg. 1061
SPARXOO, 514 N Franklin St Ste 202, 33602, pg. 1062
UNITED LANDMARK ASSOCIATES, INC., 3708 W Swann Ave Ste 201, 33609, pg. 1167
WALKER BRANDS, 1810 W Kennedy Blvd, 33606, pg. 1187
ZELEN COMMUNICATIONS, 1304 DeSoto Ave Ste 200, 33606, pg. 1255

Tequesta

GRAPHIC PERSUASION, INC., 169 Tequesta Dr Ste 31E, 33469, pg. 440

Vero Beach

THE ALEXIS AGENCY, 1201 19th Pl B-401, 32960, pg. 45

Wellington

DIGICRE8TIVE INC, 1900 Okeechobee Blvd Ste C-3, 33409, pg. 307

West Palm Beach

BG, 360 Columbia Dr, 33409, pg. 129
EXCELER8, 301 Clematis St Ste 3000, 33401, pg. 361
SHAMIN ABAS PUBLIC RELATIONS, 222 Lakeview Ave Ste 101, 33401, pg. 1035
THAT AGENCY, 410 Evernia St Ste 118, 33401-5431, pg. 1137
WILESMITH ADVERTISING & DESIGN, 319 Clematis St Ste 710, 33401, pg. 1207

Winter Garden

ALARIE DESIGN, 260 E Plant St, 34787, pg. 44

Winter Haven

Winter Park

GEORGIA

Acworth

Alpharetta

Atlanta

Augusta

Buford

Clarkston

Columbus

Decatur

LENZ MARKETING, 119 E Ct Sq Ste 201, 30030, pg. 636
SPAULDING COMMUNICATIONS, INC., 619 E College Ave Studio A, 30030, pg. 1063

Duluth

BRIGHTFIRE LLC, 2470 Satellite Blvd Ste 210, 30096, pg. 166
IGNITE COMMUNICATIONS, 11445 JohnsCreek Pkwy, 30097, pg. 536
LUCKIE & COMPANY, 3100 Breckinridge Blvd Ste 135, 30096, pg. 673

Evans

ADMAX ADVERTISING, PO Box 1820, 30809, pg. 29
ADSMITH MEDIA SOLUTIONS LLC, 4148 Stonegate Dr, 30809, pg. 32

Fort Oglethorpe

VISUAL PRINT GROUP & DESIGN, 1474 Battlefield Pkwy Ste I-9, 30742, pg. 1179

Gainesville

MORTON VARDEMAN & CARLSON, 200 Broad St Ste 203, 30503, pg. 778
SOURCE OUTDOOR GROUP, 210 Washington St NW, 30024, pg. 1059

Kennesaw

LEAP COMMUNICATIONS, 1301 Shiloh Rd Ste 1140, 30144, pg. 634
MARKETING SPECIFICS INC., 3050 Matlock Dr, 30144, pg. 699
REARVIEW, PO Box 440518, 30160, pg. 958

Lagrange

KELSEY ADVERTISING & DESIGN, 133 Main St, 30240, pg. 608

Lawrenceville

RED PEPPER, INC, 113 S Perry St Ste 200, 30045, pg. 962
TILLMAN, ALLEN, GREER, 1305 Lakes Pkwy Ste 119, 30043, pg. 1143

Lilburn

FAIRMONT PRESS, INC., 700 Indian Trail Lilburn Rd NW, 30047-3724, pg. 365

Macon

HAYNES MARKETING NETWORK, INC., 4149 Arkwright Rd, 31210, pg. 503
M&R MARKETING GROUP, 3985 Arkwright Rd Ste 104, 31210, pg. 679
SPARK MEDIA, 153 Gateway Dr, 31210, pg. 1061
THIRD WAVE DIGITAL, 1841 Hardeman Ave, 31201, pg. 1140

Marietta

ALIANDA, 1199 Soaring Ridge, 30062, pg. 45
THE BURMEISTER GROUP, INC., 4658 Bishop Lk Rd, 30062, pg. 177
SEED CREATIVE, PO Box 523, 30061, pg. 1030
VARGAS & AMIGOS INC., 3055 Waterfront Cir, 30062-5659, pg. 1171

Milton

THE PEDOWITZ GROUP, 810 Mayfield Rd, 30009, pg. 881
PERSUASION MARKETING & MEDIA, 13400 Providence Lake Dr, 30004, pg. 886

Norcross

HAVAS IMPACT, 2885 Pacific Dr Ste A, 30071-1807, pg. 489
RESPONSE MEDIA, INC., 3155 Medlock Bridge Rd, 30071-1423, pg. 971

Roswell

ADAMS OUTDOOR ADVERTISING, 500 Colonial Center Pkwy Ste 120, 30076-8852, pg. 24
THE CREATIVE MOMENTUM, 200 Mansell Ct E Ste 300, 30076, pg. 251
GOING INTERACTIVE, 912 Holcomb Bridge Rd, 30076, pg. 433
NELSON CREATIVE, 10290 Kinross Rd, 30076, pg. 804
PINDOT MEDIA, 620 Colonial Park Dr, 30075-3746, pg. 891

Savannah

ROBERTSON & MARKOWITZ ADVERTISING & PR, 108 E Montgomery Crossroads, 31406, pg. 987

Smyrna

BLACK & WHITE ADVERTISING, INC., 3646 Highlands Pkwy, 30082, pg. 133
COHN, OVERSTREET & PARRISH, 4381 Beach Haven Trail Ste 300, 30080, pg. 220
TRAVEL SPIKE, LLC, 3300 Highlands Pkwy Ste 120, 30082, pg. 1155
WORLD MARKETING-ATLANTA, 1961 S Cobb Industrial Blvd, 30082, pg. 1215

Stone Mountain

PURERED, 2196 W Park Ct, 30087, pg. 938

Woodstock

3 FEET MEDIA, 99 Weatherstone Dr, 30188, pg. 6
INDEPENDENT FLOORCOVERINGS DEALERS OF AMERICA, INC., 110 Mirramont Lake Dr, 30189, pg. 543

HAWAII

Honolulu

CORE GROUP ONE, INC., 928 Nuuanu Ave No 100, 96817, pg. 235
HARRIS AGENCY, 2250 Kalakaua Ave Ste 313, 96815, pg. 480
HEINRICH HAWAII, 900 Fort St Mall Ste 860, 96813, pg. 508
MEDIA ETC., 2222 Kalakaua Ave Ste 701, 96815-2516, pg. 742
MVNP, 999 Bishop St 24th Fl, 96813-4429, pg. 797
OLOMANA LOOMIS ISC, Pioneer Plz Ste 350 - 900 Fort St Mall, 96813, pg. 856
SUCCESS ADVERTISING HAWAII, 66 Queen St Ste 1602, 96813, pg. 1095

IDAHO

Boise

CAREW CO, 223 N 6th St Ste 50, 83702, pg. 191
CLM MARKETING & ADVERTISING, 588 W Idaho St, 83702-5928, pg. 216
CREATIVE SOAPBOX, 6015 Overland Rd Ste 104, 83709, pg. 252
DAVIESMOORE, 805 Idaho St Ste 300, 83702, pg. 269
DRAKE COOPER INC., 416 S 8th 3rd Fl, 83702-5471, pg. 327
MAGNUSON DESIGN, 1890 E Mortimer Dr, 83712, pg. 687
OLIVER RUSSELL, 217 S 11th St, 83702, pg. 855
PUBLICIS DIALOG BOISE, 168 N 9th St Ste 250, 83702, pg. 927
PUBLICIS DIALOG BOISE, 168 N 9th St Ste 250, 83702, pg. 936
RIZEN CREATIVE, 314 S 9th St Ste 200, 83702, pg. 984
SOVRN, 1101 W Grove St 201, 83702, pg. 1061
STOLTZ MARKETING GROUP, 913 W. River St., Ste 410, 83702, pg. 1087
TOM SCOTT COMMUNICATION SHOP, 1020 W Main St Ste 320, 83702, pg. 1149
WIRESTONE, 913 W River St Ste 200, 83702, pg. 1211

Coeur D'Alene

HANNA & ASSOCIATES INC., 1100 E Lakeshore Dr Ste 201, 83814, pg. 478

Eagle

COMMPRO LLC, 3210 E Chinden Blvd Ste 115-315, 83616, pg. 225

Nampa

PEPPERSHOCK MEDIA PRODUCTIONS, LLC., 16719 N Idaho Ctr Blvd, 83687, pg. 883

Pocatello

STEELE & ASSOCIATES, INC., 125 N Garfield, 83204, pg. 1082

Post Falls

SIGNAL POINT MARKETING+DESIGN, 607 E 6th Ave, 83854, pg. 1043

ILLINOIS

Antioch

2.GC, INC., 441 Windsor Dr, 60002, pg. 5

Arlington Heights

ADVENTIVE MARKETING, INC., 415 E Golf Rd, 60005, pg. 33
OMNIBUS ADVERTISING, 546 W Campus Dr, 60004, pg. 857
TWEYEN INC, 171 W Wing St Ste 201, 60005, pg. 1164

Aurora

BAD MONKEY CIRCUS, 31 W Downer Pl Ste 400, 60506, pg. 86

Barrington

CONDON & ROOT, 200 N Northwest Hwy, 60010, pg. 229

Batavia

PEDERSEN DESIGN LLC, 121 Flinn St, 60510, pg. 881
PUREI, 12 E Wilson St, 60510, pg. 938

Blue Island

JAMES STREET ASSOCIATES, LTD., 2441 W Vermont St Ste 298, 60406, pg. 586

Burr Ridge

THE MX GROUP, 7020 High Grove Blvd, 60527-7599, pg. 797

Carbondale

1187 CREATIVE, 201 E Main St, 62901, pg. 1
ARTHUR AGENCY, 104 E Jackson S, 62901, pg. 74

Carol Stream

MALLOF, ABRUZINO & NASH MARKETING, 765 Kimberly Dr, 60188-9407, pg. 688
MAN MARKETING, 765 Kimberly Dr, 60188, pg. 689

Carpentersville

PMS ADVERTISING, INC., 2429 Randall Rd, 60110, pg. 898

Champaign

Chicago

Crystal Lake

Danville

Decatur

Deer Park

Deerfield Beach

Des Plaines

Downers Grove

East Dundee

Elburn

Elgin

Elmhurst

Evanston

Frankfort

Geneva

Gilberts

Glenview

Highwood

Hoffman Estates

Inverness

Itasca

La Grange

Lake Bluff

Lake Forest

Libertyville

Lisle

Lockport

Lombard

200, 60148, pg. 1085

McCook

WORLD MARKETING-CHICAGO, 7950 W Joliet Rd, 60525-3482, pg. 1215

Moline

HANSON WATSON ASSOCIATES, 1411 15th St, 61265, pg. 479
LATIN CONNECTION, 1411 15th St, 61265, pg. 479
PEAR ADVERTISING, 108 27th Ave E, 61244, pg. 881

Montgomery

HAMILTON & BOND ADVERTISING INC., 3003 Foxmoor Dr, 60538-4091, pg. 476

Morton Grove

INTEGRATED MERCHANDISING SYSTEMS, 8338 Austin Ave, 60053-3209, pg. 315

Mount Prospect

TONIC BLUE COMMUNICATIONS, 200 E Evergreen Ave, 60056, pg. 1150

Mundelein

GREENMARK PUBLIC RELATIONS, 1200 Darnell Dr Ste L, 60060-1084, pg. 443

Naperville

GLIMMER, INC., 9 S Columbia St, 60540, pg. 428
GROUP 365 (CHICAGO) LLC, 1111 E Warrenville Rd, 60653, pg. 461
RHEA + KAISER, Naperville Financial Ctr 400 E Diehl Rd Ste 500, 60563-1342, pg. 976
YOUTECH & ASSOCIATES, 1730 Park St, 60563, pg. 1252

Niles

CELTIC MARKETING, INC., 6311 W Gross Point Rd, 60714, pg. 201

Northbrook

BLUE CHIP MARKETING WORLDWIDE, 650 Dundee Rd Ste 250, 60062, pg. 140
BRANDIMAGE DESGRIPPES & LAGA, 990 Skokie Blvd, 60062, pg. 159
LUBOW ADVERTISING, INC., 5 Revere Dr Ste 200, 60062, pg. 672
NORTH SHORE PUBLIC RELATIONS INC., 3400 Dundee Rd Ste 300, 60062, pg. 814

Northfield

MILLER ADVERTISING AGENCY INC.-CHICAGO, 1 Northfield Plz Ste 300, 60093-1214, pg. 758

Oak Brook

TEAM ONE USA, 1 Tower Ste 3120 Oak Brook Cerrace, 60181, pg. 1135

Oak Park

SHAKER RECRUITMENT ADVERTISING & COMMUNICATIONS, INC., The Shaker Bldg 1100 Lk St, 60301, pg. 1035
SHERMAN COMMUNICATIONS & MARKETING, 427 N Harvey Ave, 60302, pg. 1037
SKY ADVERTISING-CHICAGO, 159 N Marion St Ste 292, 60301-1032, pg. 1050

Oakbrook Terrace

DAVID JAMES GROUP, 1 Trans Am Plz Dr Ste 300, 60181, pg. 268
MOVEO, 1 Parkview Plz Ste 150, 60181, pg. 780
ZIMMERMAN ADVERTISING, 2 Mid America Plz Ste 510, 60181-1937, pg. 1257

Orland Park

ESROCK PARTNERS, 14550 S 94th Ave, 60462-2652, pg. 356
JOHNSON MARKETING GROUP INC., 15255 S 94th Ave Ste 600, 60462, pg. 595
THE MARKETING PROS, 10825 Caribou Ln, 60467, pg. 698

Palatine

AISLE ROCKET STUDIOS, 220 N Smith St Ste 310, 60067-2448, pg. 42
BERNARD & COMPANY, 1540 E Dundee Rd Ste 250, 60074-8320, pg. 126
INTEGRAPHIX, INC., 305 N Eric Dr Ste E, 60067, pg. 550
THE PEPPER GROUP, 220 N Smith St Ste 406, 60067, pg. 883

Palos Park

RIZK ADVERTISING, 8101 W 123rd St, 60464, pg. 984

Park Ridge

CP ENTERPRISES, INC., 950 N NW Hwy, 60068-2301, pg. 239

Pekin

MCDANIELS MARKETING COMMUNICATIONS, 11 Olt Ave, 61554-6216, pg. 732

Peoria

ADAMS OUTDOOR ADVERTISING, 911 SW Adams St, 61602, pg. 25
CONVERSE MARKETING, 1125 Main St, 61606, pg. 233
HULT MARKETING, 401 SW Water St Ste 601, 61602-1586, pg. 528
KELLY & COMPANY, 3100 N Knoxville Ave Ste 213, 61603, pg. 608
MARQUETTE GROUP, 222 NE Monroe St Fl 8, 61602, pg. 701

Quincy

RETHINK MEDIA GROUP, 729 Monroe St, 62301, pg. 973

Rockford

BLAIR, INC., 1639 N Alpine Rd Ste 502, 61107, pg. 135
CAIN & COMPANY, 685 Featherstone Rd, 61107-6304, pg. 184
FORTYTWOEIGHTYNINE, 5301 E State St Ste 301, 61108, pg. 398
GINESTRA WATSON, 907 E State St, 61104, pg. 426
HEINZEROTH MARKETING GROUP, 415 Y Blvd, 61107-3059, pg. 508
KMK MEDIA GROUP, 716 N Church St, 61103, pg. 615
NADI LLC, 406 E State St, 61104, pg. 799
QUIET LIGHT COMMUNICATIONS, 220 E State St, 61104, pg. 943
V2 MARKETING COMMUNICATIONS, 220 E State St Ste G, 61104, pg. 1170

Saint Charles

EVOKE IDEA GROUP, INC., 902 S Randall Rd Ste 336C, 60174, pg. 360
JAMES & THOMAS, INC., 6N397 Corron Rd Ste 100, 60175-8420, pg. 586
MARTOPIA, INC., 3805 E Main St, 60174, pg. 705
STRENG DESIGN & ADVERTISING, 244 W River Dr, 60174, pg. 1092

Schaumburg

EPSILON, 1100 E Woodfield Rd Ste 500, 60173, pg. 351

Skokie

BILL GERSHON MARKETING COMMUNICATIONS, 9828 Crawford Ave, 60076-1107, pg. 132

Spring Grove

SMACKET CREATIVE, PO Box 681, 60081, pg. 1052

Springfield

HIP ADVERTISING, 2809 Mansion Rd Ste A, 62711, pg. 515
WC MEDIA INC., 1824 S MacArthur Blvd, 62704, pg. 1193

Sycamore

MORNINGSTAR MEDIA GROUP, 240 Edward St, 60178, pg. 774

Wadsworth

AL STARK'S A&M, 2620 N Augusta Dr, 60083, pg. 44

Westmont

BVK-CHICAGO, 999 Oakmont Plz Dr Ste 300, 60559-1368, pg. 181

Wilmette

QUALLY & COMPANY, INC., 1187 Wilmette Ave, Ste 160, 60091-2719, pg. 941

Winnetka

THE NARUP GROUP, 1215 Washington St Ste 208, 60091, pg. 800

Woodstock

R.N. JOHNSON & ASSOCIATES CREATIVE MARKETING, 113 E Van Buren St, 60098, pg. 986

INDIANA

Bloomington

ROSENPLOT DESIGN LLC, PO Box 1083, 47402, pg. 992

Carmel

5METACOM, 630 W Carmel Dr Ste 180, 46032, pg. 10
ARLAND COMMUNICATIONS INC., PO Box 3002, 46082-3002, pg. 70
MARCOSOLO DESIGN, 335 Ridgepoint Dr, 46032, pg. 692
OOHOLOGY, 40 Executive Dr, 46032, pg. 862
QUINLAN MARKETING COMMUNICATIONS, 550 Congressional Blvd Ste 350, 46032, pg. 944
ST. CLAIRE GROUP, 716 Adams St Ste C, 46032, pg. 1071

Elkhart

ADVENT DESIGN LLC, 130 S Main St, 46516, pg. 33
B.J. THOMPSON ASSOCIATES, INC., 2901 E Bristol St Ste C, 46514, pg. 133
TAIGMARKS INC., 223 S Main St Ste 100, 46516, pg. 1107
TODD ALLEN DESIGN, 200 Nibco Pkwy Ste 200, 46516, pg. 1149

Evansville

DANIEL, BURTON, DEAN ADVERTISING & DESIGN, INC., 225 Court St, 47708, pg. 265
GRAY LOON MARKETING GROUP, INC., 300 SE Riverside Dr Ste 200, 47713, pg. 441
KITCH & SCHREIBER, INC., 402 Court St, 47708-1130, pg. 613
LIONFISH ADVERTISING, 4847 E Virginia St Ste D, 47715, pg. 660
MAGNETIC IMAGE INC., 401 E Indiana, 47711, pg. 686

Fishers

BUCKAROO MARKETING, 7987 Wolford Ct Ste 200, 46038, pg. 173
CONSTRUCTION MARKETING INC, 11057 Allisonville Rd Ste 208, 46038, pg. 232
DGS MARKETING ENGINEERS, 10100 Lantern Rd Ste 225, 46037, pg. 305
MEDIAFUEL, 12574 Promise Creek Ln Ste 138, 46038, pg. 744
PARADIGM MEDIA CONSULTANTS, INC., PO Box 6213, 46038, pg. 873

Fort Wayne

ASHER AGENCY, INC., 535 W Wayne St, 46802-2123, pg. 76
BOYDEN & YOUNGBLUTT ADVERTISING & MARKETING, 120 W Superior St, 46802, pg. 151
BRAND INNOVATION GROUP, 8902 Airport Dr Ste A, 46809, pg. 156
CATALYST MARKETING DESIGN, 930 S Calhoun St, 46802, pg. 197
COMCAST SPOTLIGHT, 1315 Directors' Row Ste 109, 46808-1110, pg. 224
EMLEY DESIGN GROUP, 8010 Illinois Rd, 46804, pg. 347
FERGUSON ADVERTISING INC., 803 S Calhoun St 6th Fl, 46802-2319, pg. 384
LABOV ADVERTISING, MARKETING AND TRAINING, 609 E Cook Rd, 46825, pg. 622
MARKETSHARE PLUS, INC., Woodland Plz 1220 Ruston Pass, 46825, pg. 700
PATTERSON RIEGEL ADVERTISING, 200 E Main St Ste 710, 46802, pg. 878
SAAL ADVERTISING INC, 6528 Constitution Dr, 46804, pg. 1000

Haubstadt

MARKETING & MEDIA SOLUTIONS, INC., 304 E Gibson St, 47639, pg. 696

Indianapolis

360 GROUP, 301 W Michigan St Ste A, 46202, pg. 6
ACCESSPOINT, 3925 River Crossing Pkwy Ste 60, 46240, pg. 156
AXIOMPORT, 646 Massachusetts Ave, 46204, pg. 83
BANDY CARROLL HELLIGE ADVERTISING, 111 Monument Cir Ste 882, 46204-5173, pg. 90
BELTRAME LEFFLER ADVERTISING, 708 Massachusetts Ave, 46204, pg. 123
BORSHOFF, 47 S Pennsylvania St Ste 500, 46204, pg. 149
BOSE PUBLIC AFFAIRS GROUP, 111 Monument Cir Ste 2700, 46204, pg. 150
BRADLEY & MONTGOMERY ADVERTISING, 342 E Saint Joseph St, 46204, pg. 153
CALDWELL VANRIPER, 111 Monument Cir, 46204, pg. 184
CMG WORLDWIDE, 10500 Crosspoint Blvd, 46256-3331, pg. 217
CREATIVE DIRECTION, INC., PO Box 17670, 46217, pg. 247
THE FLATLAND, 614 Massachusetts Ave Ste D, 46204, pg. 392
HIRONS & COMPANY, 422 E New York St, 46202, pg. 516
J. WALTER THOMPSON U.S.A., INC., 10401 N Meridian St Ste 216, 46290-1090, pg. 581
KH COMPLETE ADVERTISING, 6280 N Shadeland Ave, 46220, pg. 610
MATCHBOOK CREATIVE, 2507 N Delaware St, 46205, pg. 709
MORTENSON SAFAR KIM, 916 E Westfield Blvd, 46220, pg. 777
NVS DESIGN INC., 8888 Keystone Crossing Ste 1300, 46220, pg. 819
OCTANE VTM, 3650 Washington Blvd, 46205, pg. 824
PERQ LLC, 7225 Georgetown Rd, 46268, pg. 885
PIVOT MARKETING, 1052 Virginia Ave, 46203, pg. 894
PUBLICIS INDIANAPOLIS, 200 S Meridian St Ste 500, 46225-1076, pg. 927
PUBLICIS INDIANAPOLIS, 200 S Meridian St Ste 500, 46225-1076, pg. 936
ROUNDPEG, 1003 E 106th St, 46280, pg. 994
TRENDYMINDS INC, 531 East Market St, 46204, pg. 1156
WELL DONE MARKETING, 1043 Virginia Ave, 46203, pg. 1196
WILLOW MARKETING, 3590 N Meridian Ste 200, 46208, pg. 1208
YOUNG & LARAMORE, 407 Fulton St, 46202, pg. 1239
Z MARKETING PARTNERS, 3905 E.Vincennes Rd, Ste 300, 46268, pg. 1253

Lafayette

BETTER MERCHANTS INC., 1100 N 9th St Ste 203, 47904, pg. 127
TREEFROG MARKETING AND COMMUNICATIONS, 8 N 2nd St 2nd Fl Ste C, 47901, pg. 1155

Merrillville

VIA MARKETING, INC., 2646 W Lincoln Hwy, 46410, pg. 1175

Mishawaka

PATHFINDERS ADVERTISING & MARKETING GROUP, 3830 Edison Lakes Pkwy, 46545-3400, pg. 877
STUDIO A ADVERTISING, 203 N Main St, 46544-1410, pg. 1093

New Albany

PROMEDIA GROUP, 4106 Reas Ln, 47150, pg. 913
TMP WORLDWIDE/ADVERTISING & COMMUNICATIONS, 115 E Spring St Ste 600, 47150, pg. 1148

Newburgh

WELLNESS COMMUNICATIONS, 7299 Parkridge Rd, 47630, pg. 1196

North Liberty

ADIRONDACK MARKETING SERVICES, LLC, 24711 New Rd, 46554-9445, pg. 28

Porter

SIGNATURE GRAPHICS, 1000 Signature Dr, 46304, pg. 315

South Bend

FORCE 5 MEDIA, INC., 1433 Northside Blvd, 46615, pg. 397
J.G. SULLIVAN INTERACTIVE, INC., 6101 Nimtz Pkwy, 46628-6111, pg. 590
VILLING & COMPANY, INC., 5909 Nimtz Pkwy, 46628, pg. 1177

Trafalgar

NEW RULES ADVERTISING, 3956 W Poplar Point Ct, 46181, pg. 807

Valparaiso

THE BARBAULD AGENCY, PO Box 367, 46384, pg. 91
GROUP 7EVEN, 158 Napoleon St Ste 220, 46383, pg. 462

Warsaw

TSA COMMUNICATIONS, INC., 307 S Buffalo St, 46580-4304, pg. 1160

West Lafayette

DEARING GROUP, 1330 Win Hentschel Blvd Ste 130, 47906, pg. 291

Zionsville

BODKIN ASSOCIATES, INC., 1555 W Oak St Ste 100, 46077-1959, pg. 145
MILLER BROOKS, 11712 N Michigan St, 46077, pg. 758

IOWA

Bettendorf

BRAND CENTRAL STATION, 5012 State St, 52722, pg. 155

Cedar Falls

AMPERAGE, 6711 Chancellor Dr, 50613-6969, pg. 55
MUDD ADVERTISING, 915 Technology Pkwy, 50613, pg. 786

Cedar Rapids

FUSIONFARM, 500 3rd Ave SE, 52401, pg. 410
J.W. MORTON & ASSOCIATES, 1924 Saint Andrews Ct NE, 52402-5889, pg. 600
STAMATS, 615 5th St SE, 52406-1888, pg. 1072

Clive

3B ADVERTISING, LLC, 2200 NW 159st Ste 400, 50325, pg. 7

Davenport

L.W. RAMSEY ADVERTISING AGENCY, PO Box 2561, 52809, pg. 675

Denison

BLUESPACE CREATIVE, 1211 Broadway Ste 201, 51442, pg. 143

Des Moines

ADAPTIVE EASEL LLC, 1620 Pleasant St, 50314, pg. 25
B2E DIRECT MARKETING, 307 E Court Ave Unit 103, 50309, pg. 85
FLYNN WRIGHT, 1408 Locust St, 50309-3014, pg. 395
FROEHLICH COMMUNICATIONS, INC., 309 Ct Ave Ste 234, 50309, pg. 405
HAPPY MEDIUM, 1717 Ingersoll Ave Ste 117, 50309, pg. 479
JUICEBOX INTERACTIVE, 516 3rd St Ste 202, 50309, pg. 599
LESSING-FLYNN ADVERTISING CO., 3106 Ingersoll Ave, 50312, pg. 652
RED DOT DESIGN, LLC, 112 5th St W, 50265, pg. 960
SATURDAY MFG INC., 1717 Ingersoll Ave Bay 121, 50309, pg. 1021
TRILIX MARKETING GROUP, INC., 615 3rd St Ste 300, 50309, pg. 1157
ZLRIGNITION, 303 Watson Powell Jr Way Ste 100, 50309-1724, pg. 1258

Dubuque

PLAID SWAN, 2728 Asbury Rd Cove Bldg Ste 650, 52001, pg. 895

Fairfield

HAWTHORNE DIRECT INC., 300 N 16th St, 52556-2604, pg. 503

Hiawatha

NORTH FORTY, 1501 Boyson Sq Dr Ste 201, 52233, pg. 814

Johnston

MCCORMICK COMPANY, 9245 Northpark Dr, 50131, pg. 732

Le Claire

MINDFIRE COMMUNICATIONS INC, 102 N Cody Rd, 52753, pg. 761

Lisbon

WILLIAMS MEDIA GROUP, 102 W Market St, 52253, pg. 1208

North Liberty

MIDWEST MEDIA SERVICES, PO Box 4512, 52317, pg. 755

Sioux City

BASS ADVERTISING, 815 Nebraska St, 51101-1111, pg. 96
JD GORDON CREATIVE LABS, 312 Court St, 51101, pg. 589

Urbandale

MCLELLAN MARKETING GROUP, 2330 Rocklyn Dr, 50322, pg. 736

Waterloo

HELLMAN, 1225 W 4th St, 50702, pg. 508
MORGAN & MYERS, INC., 1005 Stratford Ave, 50701-1952, pg. 774

West Des Moines

THE MEYOCKS GROUP, 6800 Lake Dr Ste 150, 50266-2544, pg. 752
PERFORMANCE MARKETING, 1501 42nd St Ste 550, 50266, pg. 884
STRATEGIC AMERICA, 6600 Westown Pkwy Ste 100, 50266-7708, pg. 1090

KANSAS

Fairway

THE HART AGENCY, INC., 4330 Shawnee Mission Pkwy Ste 105, 66205-2521, pg. 481

Haysville

ARMSTRONG CHAMBERLIN, 7450 S Seneca, 67060, pg. 71

Kansas City

JENNINGS SOCIAL MEDIA MARKETING, 1656 Washington Ste 150, 64108, pg. 590

Lawrence

CALLAHAN CREEK, INC., 805 New Hampshire St, 66044-2739, pg. 185

Leawood

API BROADCAST ADVERTISING, 2501 W 91st St, 66206, pg. 65
MULLER BRESSLER BROWN, 11610 Ash St Ste 200, 66211, pg. 795
PULSE MARKETING & ADVERTISING LLC, 3344 W 143rd Terr, 66224, pg. 937

Lenexa

KEYPATH EDUCATION, 15500 W 113 Ste #200, 66219, pg. 610
KUHN & ASSOCIATES, 10901 W 84th Terr Ste 240, 66214, pg. 620
SUMMIT MARKETING, 10916 Strang Line Rd, 66215, pg. 1099
ZILLNER MARKETING COMMUNICATIONS, 8725 Rosehill Rd Ste 200, 66215, pg. 1256

Manhattan

NEW BOSTON CREATIVE GROUP, 315 Houston St Ste E, 66502, pg. 807

Mission

WALZ TETRICK ADVERTISING, 6299 Nall Ave Ste 300, 66202-3547, pg. 1189

Overland Park

BRAINSTORM MEDIA, 7111 W 151st St Ste 311, 66223, pg. 154
C3 - CREATIVE CONSUMER CONCEPTS, 10955 Granada Ln, 66211, pg. 182
CHECKBOX, 7015 College Blvd Ste 700, 66211-1524, pg. 206
CHRISTENSON MEDIA GROUP INC., 10560 Barkley Ste 315, 66212, pg. 209
THE FRANK AGENCY INC, 10561 Barkley St Ste 200, 66212, pg. 400
GLYNNDEVINS ADVERTISING & MARKETING, 11230 College Blvd, 66210-2700, pg. 430
JNA ADVERTISING, 7101 College Blvd Ste 120, 66210, pg. 592
KWGC WORLDWIDE LLC, 10206 Conser St, 66212, pg. 620
RHYCOM STRATEGIC ADVERTISING, Corporate Woods Bldg 27 10975 Grandview Ste 650, 66210, pg. 976
STEPHENS & ASSOCIATES ADVERTISING, INC., 7400 W 132nd St Ste 100, 66213, pg. 1084

Prairie Village

ETC ADVERTISING & PROMOTIONS LLC, 7930 State Line Rd Ste 208, 66208, pg. 357
IMPRESTIGE MEDIA MARKETING, 4402 W 95th St, 66207, pg. 542

Shawnee

PILCHER CREATIVE AGENCY, 8704 W 49th St, 66203, pg. 891

Topeka

JONES HUYETT PARTNERS, 3200 SW Huntoon St, 66604-1606, pg. 596
MB PILAND ADVERTISING & MARKETING LLC, 3127 Southwest Huntoon, 66604, pg. 712

Wamego

IMAGEMAKERS INC., 514 Lincoln Ave, 66547, pg. 538

Wichita

ASSOCIATED INTEGRATED MARKETING, 330 N Mead Ste 200, 67202, pg. 77
BIG CORNER CREATIVE, 11323 W Kellogg Ave, 67209, pg. 130
COHLMIA MARKETING, 535 W Douglas Ste 170, 67213, pg. 220
COPP MEDIA SERVICES INC, 322 S Mosley Ste 15, 67202, pg. 234
GRETEMAN GROUP, 1425 E Douglas 2nd Fl, 67211, pg. 444
HOWERTON+WHITE, 520 E Douglas, 67202, pg. 525
JAJO, INC., 200 N Broadway Ste 110, 67202, pg. 585
MEDIA PARTNERS, INC., 8150 E Douglas Ste 40, 67206, pg. 743
NYE & ASSOCIATES, 428 Pattie, 67211, pg. 819
RESULTS DIRECT MARKETING, 555 N Woodlawn Ste 300, 67208-3683, pg. 972
SQUID INK CREATIVE, 200 W Douglas Ave Ste 230, 67202, pg. 1070
STEPHAN ADVERTISING AGENCY, INC., 807 N Waco St Ste 11, 67203-3971, pg. 1083
SULLIVAN HIGDON & SINK INCORPORATED, 255 N Mead St, 67202-2707, pg. 1097

KENTUCKY

Crestview Hills

SEED STRATEGY, INC., 740 Ctr View Blvd, 41017, pg. 1030

Fisherville

LKH&S LOUISVILLE, 4907 Dunbarvalley Rd, 40023, pg. 664

Lexington

AD-SUCCESS MARKETING, 868 Calypso Breeze Dr, 40515, pg. 23
ADCOLOR, INC, 620 Adcolor Dr, 40511, pg. 27
ASHER AGENCY, INC., 4101 Tates Creek Ctr Dr Ste 150, 40517-3096, pg. 76
BAKER COMMUNICATIONS ADVERTISING/MARKETING/PUBLIC RELATIONS, 128 E Reynolds Rd Ste 201, 40517-1254, pg. 87
BRAND ADVERTISING GROUP, 3399 Tates Creek Rd Ste 125, 40502, pg. 155
CONNECTIONS ADVERTISING & MARKETING, 148 Jefferson St Ste B, 40508, pg. 230
CORNETT INTEGRATED MARKETING SOLUTIONS, 330 E Main St Ste 300, 40507-1525, pg. 236
MERIDIAN - CHILES, 921 Beasley St Ste 140, 40509, pg. 748
OCULUS STUDIOS, 948 Manchester St Ste 120, 40508, pg. 824
SERIF GROUP, 250 Walton Ave Ste 160, 40502, pg. 1032
TRIFECTA, 3080 Harrodsburg Rd Ste 101, 40503, pg. 1157

Louisville

BANDY CARROLL HELLIGE ADVERTISING, 307 W Muhammad Ali Blvd, 40202, pg. 89
BISIG IMPACT GROUP, 640 S 4th St Ste 300, 40202, pg. 133
CORECUBED, 3316 Springcrest Dr, 40241, pg. 235
CURRENT360, 1324 E Washington St, 40206-1759, pg. 261
DAC GROUP, 455 S 4th St Ste 1045, 40202, pg. 263
THE DELOR GROUP, 902 Flat Rock Rd, 40245, pg. 295
DOE-ANDERSON, 620 W Main St, 40202-2933, pg. 320
GO FETCH MARKETING & DESIGN, 7613 Ashleywood Dr, 40241, pg. 431
KDA GROUP INC, 303 N Hurstbourne Pkwy Ste 115, 40222, pg. 206
KYK ADVERTISING MARKETING PROMOTIONS, 2600 Constant Comment Pl, 40299, pg. 620
MCCAFFERTY & CO. ADVERTISING, 1014 S Floyd St, 40203, pg. 713
MEDIAURA INC, 455 S 4th St Ste 808, 40202, pg. 745
NEW WEST LLC, 950 Breckenridge Ln Ste 140, 40207, pg. 807
POWER CREATIVE, 11701 Commonwealth Dr, 40299-2358, pg. 906
PRICEWEBER MARKETING COMMUNICATIONS, INC., 10701 Shelbyville Rd, 40243, pg. 909
RED7E, 637 W Main St, 40202-2987, pg. 964
SCOPPECHIO, 437 W Jefferson St, 40202, pg. 1026
SHEEHY & ASSOCIATES, 2297 Lexington Rd, 40206-2818, pg. 1037
STRADEGY ADVERTISING, 642 S 4th St Ste 400, 40202, pg. 1089
TRAFFIC BUILDERS INC., 11524 Blankenbaker Access Dr Ste 104, 40299, pg. 1154
VEST ADVERTISING, 3007 Sprowl Rd, 40299-3620, pg. 1175
THE VIMARC GROUP, 1205 E Washington St Ste 120, 40206, pg. 1177
WAHLSTROM GROUP, 1640 Lyndon Farm Ct, 40223, pg. 1186

Madisonville

COMPLETE MARKETING RESOURCES INC., 140 S Main St Ste 102, 42431, pg. 228

Newport

EISEN MANAGEMENT GROUP, 515 Monmouth St Ste 302, 41071, pg. 340
INTRINZIC MARKETING + DESIGN INC., 1 Levee Way Ste 3121, 41071, pg. 558

Paducah

HELIA, 400 E Pratt St 10th Fl, 21202-6174, pg. 490
HIMMELRICH PR, 3600 Clipper Mill Rd Ste 425, 21211, pg. 515
IDFIVE, 3600 Clipper Mill Rd, 21211, pg. 536
ILLUME COMMUNICATIONS, 805 E Baltimore St, 21202, pg. 537
IMRE, 909 Ridgebrook Rd Ste 300, 21152, pg. 542
J. WALTER THOMPSON U.S.A., INC., 175 W Ostend St Ste #A-2, 21230, pg. 581
LEFFLER AGENCY, 2607 N Charles St, 21218, pg. 635
LEWIS ADVERTISING COMPANY INC., 325 E Oliver St, 21202-2999, pg. 655
MILLENNIAL MEDIA INC., 2400 Boston St 3rd Fl, 21224, pg. 756
MISSION MEDIA, LLC., 616 Water St Ste 225, 21202, pg. 764
NORTH CHARLES STREET DESIGN ORGANIZATION, 222 W Saratoga St, 21201, pg. 814
PLANIT, 500 E Pratt St 10th Fl, 21202, pg. 896
PROFILES, INC., 3000 Chestnut Ave Ste 201, 21211, pg. 912
R2INTEGRATED, 400 E Pratt St, 21202, pg. 948
ROOFTOP COMMUNICATIONS, 2526 St Paul St, 21218, pg. 991
S360S, PO Box 38809, 21231, pg. 1000
SAHARA COMMUNICATIONS, INC., 1607 Saint Paul St, 21202, pg. 1014
SIQUIS, LTD., 1340 Smith Ave Ste 300, 21209-3797, pg. 1046
TBC DIRECT, INC., 900 S Wolfe St, 21231, pg. 1113
TBC INC., 900 S Wolfe St, 21231, pg. 1113
TMH AGENCY, 3700 Toone St Ste 1458, 21224, pg. 1147
TRI-MEDIA INTEGRATED MARKETING TECHNOLOGIES INC., 305 Washington Ave Ste 305, 21204, pg. 1156
USADWEB, LLC, 1498-M Reisterstown Rd Ste 330, 21208-3835, pg. 1169
VIM INTERACTIVE, 2100 Aliceanna St Fl 2, 21231, pg. 665
VISIONMARK COMMUNICATIONS, 6115 Falls Rd Ste 100, 21209, pg. 1179
VITAMIN, 3237 Eastern Ave, 21224, pg. 1179

Bel Air

PICCIRILLI DORSEY, INC., 502 Rock Spring Rd, 21014, pg. 890

Beltsville

MERRICK TOWLE COMMUNICATIONS, 5801-F Ammendale Rd, 20705-1264, pg. 750

Bethesda

AUGUST, LANG & HUSAK, INC., 4630 Montgomery Ave Ste 400, 20814-3443, pg. 79
C.FOX COMMUNICATIONS, 7201 Wisconsin Ave Ste 780, 20814, pg. 202
CROSBY MARKETING COMMUNICATIONS, 4550 Montgomery Ave Ste 790 N, 20814, pg. 256
DEBELLIS & FERRARA, 4903 Montgomery Ln Ste 100, 20814, pg. 291
EQUALS THREE COMMUNICATIONS, 7910 Woodmont Ave Ste 200, 20814-3015, pg. 352
FIXATION MARKETING, 4340 E-W Hwy Ste 200, 20814, pg. 391
NASUTI + HINKLE CREATIVE THINKING, 8101-A Glenbrook Rd, 20814, pg. 801
RP3 AGENCY, 7316 Wisconsin Ave Ste 450, 20814, pg. 994
Z COMMUNICATIONS, 7830 Old Georgetown Rd Ste 125, 20814, pg. 1253

Burtonsville

PUBLICITY MATTERS, 14644 McKnew Rd, 20866, pg. 936

Chestertown

BENCHWORKS, 860 High St, 21620-3909, pg. 123
MULLIN/ASHLEY ASSOCIATES, INC., 306 Canon St, 21620, pg. 795

Columbia

ADG CREATIVE, 7151 Columbia Gateway Dr Ste B, 21046-2149, pg. 28
FRANK STRATEGIC MARKETING, 8775 Ctr Park Dr ste 253, 21045, pg. 401
IMPACT MARKETING & PUBLIC RELATIONS, INC., 6177 Silver Arrows Way, 21045, pg. 541
KDG ADVERTISING, 5404 White Mane, 21045, pg. 604
MARRINER MARKETING COMMUNICATIONS, INC., 6731 Columbia Gateway Dr Ste 250, 21046, pg. 701
MERKLE INC., 7001 Columbia Gateway Dr, 21046, pg. 749

Ellicott City

REDHEAD COMPANIES, 6011 University Blvd Ste 210, 21043, pg. 964

Fallston

MARTINO BLUM, 2101 Bel Air Rd Ste D, 21047, pg. 705

Frederick

IMMERSION ACTIVE, 16 E Patrick St, 21701, pg. 541
LOVE & COMPANY, INC., 1209 N East St, 21701, pg. 670

Fulton

AQUARIUS SPORTS & ENTERTAINMENT, 8171 Maple Lawn Blvd Ste 350, 20759, pg. 65

Germantown

DATALAB USA LLC, 20261 Goldenrod Ln, 20876-4063, pg. 267

Glen Burnie

HARTE-HANKS DATA SERVICES LLC, 6701 Baymeadow Dr Ste D, 21060-6405, pg. 483

Hunt Valley

HORICH HECTOR LEBOW, 101 Schilling Rd Ste 30, 21031, pg. 522
RENEGADE COMMUNICATIONS, 10950 Gilroy Rd Ste J, 21031, pg. 968

Lanham

G&G OUTFITTERS INC., 4901 Forbes Blvd, 20706, pg. 412
THE SUTTER GROUP, 4384 Lottsford Vista Rd, 20706-4817, pg. 1102

Laurel

LMD AGENCY, 14409 Greenview Dr Ste 200, 20708, pg. 665

Linthicum

THE G3 GROUP, 832 Oregon Ave Ste L, 21090, pg. 412

Lutherville

ADASHMORE CREATIVE, 1966 Greenspring Dr Ste 506, 21093, pg. 26

Ocean City

HOLYSTONE STUDIOS, 12417 Ocean Gateway Bldg B11 Ste 116, 21842, pg. 522

Owings Mills

BONNIE HENESON COMMUNICATIONS, INC., 9199 Reisterstown Rd Ste 212C, 21117, pg. 147
MGH, INC., 100 Painters Mill Rd Ste 600, 21117-7305, pg. 752

Rockville

HIRSHORN ZUCKERMAN DESIGN GROUP, 10101 Molecular Dr, 20850, pg. 516
IQ SOLUTIONS, 11300 Rockville Pk Ste 901, 20852, pg. 561
MMG, 700 King Farm Blvd Ste 500, 20850, pg. 858
RMR & ASSOCIATES, INC., 5870 Hubbard Dr, 20852-6425, pg. 986

Salisbury

A.S.A.P.R, 212 W Main St Ste 302a, 21801, pg. 75

Savage

REAL FRESH CREATIVE, 8600 Foundry St, 20763, pg. 957

Silver Spring

BATES CREATIVE GROUP, 1119 E-W Hwy, 20910, pg. 97
BAYARD ADVERTISING AGENCY, INC., 8401 Colesville Rd Ste 502, 20910-6365, pg. 98
BOSCOBEL MARKETING COMMUNICATIONS, 8606 2nd Ave, 20910-3326, pg. 150
SUMMIT GROUP, 11961 Tech Rd, 20904, pg. 1099

Sparks

HARVEY & DAUGHTERS, INC./ H&D BRANDING, 952 Ridgebrook Rd Ste 1000, 21152, pg. 483

Timonium

83 NORTH ADVERTISING, 2219 York Rd Ste 202, 21093, pg. 12

Towson

CATALPHA ADVERTISING & DESIGN, 6801 Loch Raven Blvd, 21286, pg. 196
DEVANEY & ASSOCIATES, 606 Providence Rd, 21286, pg. 303
GRIFFIN COMMUNICATIONS, INC., 1001 Rolandvue Rd, 21204-6816, pg. 459
WALDINGER CREATIVE, 606 Bosley Ave Ste 2B, 21204, pg. 1187

MASSACHUSETTS

Acton

O'SULLIVAN COMMUNICATIONS, 42 Davis Rd Ste 1, 01720, pg. 865

Amesbury

MCDOUGALL & DUVAL, 24 Millyard #8, 01913, pg. 733

Andover

PHILIPS HEALTHCARE COMMUNICATIONS, INC., 3000 Minuteman Rd, 01810-1099, pg. 889

Attleboro Falls

STEBBINGS PARTNERS, 427 John L Dietsch Blvd, 02763-1000, pg. 1082

Beverly

HAGGMAN, INC., 39 Dodge St PMB 331, 01915, pg. 472
PURPLE DIAMOND, 32 Jordan St, 1915, pg. 939
RATTLE ADVERTISING, 16 Broadway, 01915-4457, pg. 954

Boston

1059 CREATIVE, 98 N Washington St, 02114, pg. 1
AAI (ADVERTISING ASSOCIATES INTERNATIONAL), 65 Sprague St, 02136, pg. 14
ABERDEEN GROUP, INC., 451D St 7th Fl Ste 710, 02210, pg. 483
ADAM RITCHIE BRAND DIRECTION, 101 Tremont St Ste

1121, 02108, pg. 24
ALLEN & GERRITSEN, 2 Seaport Ln, 02210, pg. 46
ALLIED INTEGRATED MARKETING, 55 Cambridge Pkwy, 02116, pg. 49
ALMIGHTY, 300 Western Ave, 02134, pg. 50
ARGUS, 280 Summer St, 02210, pg. 69
ARNOLD WORLDWIDE, 10 Summer St, 02110, pg. 71
BACKBAY COMMUNICATIONS, INC., 20 Park Plaza Ste 801, 02116, pg. 85
THE BARBARIAN GROUP, 129 S St 2nd Fl, 02111, pg. 91
BENNETT GROUP, 27 Wormwood St Ste 320, 02210, pg. 124
BERMAN CREATIVE, LLC, 236 Huntington Ave, 02115, pg. 126
THE BOSTON GROUP, 500 Harrison Ave 3F, 02118, pg. 150
BRAND CONTENT, 580 Harrison Ave, 02118, pg. 155
BREAKAWAY, 399 Boylston St 5th Fl, 02116, pg. 163
CAPTAINS OF INDUSTRY, 21 Union St, 02108, pg. 190
CERCONE BROWN CURTIS, 77 N Washington St Ste 304, 02114-1913, pg. 202
CLEVELAND DESIGN, 20 McKenna Terr, 02132, pg. 215
CM COMMUNICATIONS, INC., 20 Park Plz Ste 821, 02116, pg. 217
COMPETE, INC., 501 Boylston St, 02116, pg. 602
CONNELLY PARTNERS, 46 Waltham St Fl 4, 02118, pg. 231
CONNELLY PARTNERS TRAVEL, 46 Waltham St, 02118, pg. 231
CONOVER TUTTLE PACE, 77 N Washington St, 02114, pg. 231
DECIBEL MEDIA, 10 City Sq 5th Fl, 2129, pg. 292
DENNEEN & COMPANY, 222 Berkeley St Ste 1200, 02116, pg. 296
DIGILANT, 100 North Washington St Ste 502, 02114, pg. 307
EAST COAST CATALYST, 300 Summer St, 02210, pg. 335
EMBRYO CREATIVE, 1085 Commonwealth Ave Ste 371, 02215, pg. 346
THE FANTASTICAL, 33 Union St, 4th Fl, 02108, pg. 368
FORGE WORLDWIDE, 142 Berkeley St, 02116, pg. 397
FULL CONTACT ADVERTISING, 186 Lincoln St, 02111, pg. 408
GENUINE INTERACTIVE, 500 Harrison Ave 5R, 02118, pg. 421
GEORGE P. JOHNSON COMPANY, INC., 711 Atlantic Ave Fl 6, 02111, pg. 422
GRANT MARKETING, 800 Boylston St 16th Fl, 02199, pg. 439
GYK ANTLER, 181 South St, 02111, pg. 468
HATCH MARKETING, 46 Waltham St, 02118, pg. 484
HAVAS EDGE BOSTON, 10 Summer St, 02110, pg. 488
HEART, 500 Harrison Ave Ste 3R, 02118, pg. 506
HILL HOLLIDAY, 53 State St, 02109, pg. 514
HOLLAND MARK, 727 Atlantic Ave, 02111, pg. 521
IPROSPECT, 1 S Station, 02110, pg. 560
ISOBAR US, One S Station, 02110, pg. 561
JACK MORTON WORLDWIDE, 142 Berkeley St, 02116, pg. 582
KELLEY HABIB JOHN, 155 Seaport Blvd, 02210, pg. 607
THE LAIDLAW GROUP, LLC, 337 Summer St, 02210, pg. 622
LEHMANMILLET, 2 Atlantic Ave, 02110, pg. 636
MC/K-CP, 200 State St, 02109, pg. 735
MEDIAHUB, 40 Broad St, 02109, pg. 787
MMB, 580 Harrison Ave, 02118, pg. 767
MOBEXT, 101 Huntington Ave Fl 16, 02199, pg. 768
MULLEN LOWE GROUP, 40 Broad St, 02109, pg. 786
NSPHERE INC., 100 Franklin St 5th Fl, 02110, pg. 818
PARTNERS+SIMONS, 25 Drydock Ave 8th Fl, 02210, pg. 876
PGR MEDIA, LLC., 34 Farnsworth St 2nd Fl, 02210, pg. 887
PHILLIPS DESIGN GROUP, 25 Drydock Ave, 02210, pg. 889
POSITIONCLICK CORPORATION, 99 Chauncy St Ste 910, 02111, pg. 904
PROPERVILLAINS, 45 Bromfield St Fl 11, 02108, pg. 915
PROVERB, 195 W Springfield St, 02118-3406, pg. 916
RELEVANT 24, 46 Plympton St, 02118, pg. 967
SAPIENT BOSTON, 131 Dartmouth St 3rd Fl, 02116, pg. 1018
SAPIENT CORPORATION, 131 Dartmouth St, 02116, pg. 1017
SAPIENT SECURITIES CORPORATION, 131 Tartmouth 3rd Fl, 02116, pg. 1019
SMALL ARMY, 300 Massachusetts Ave, 02115, pg. 1053
SONICBIDS, 500 Harrison Ave Fl 4 Ste 404R, 02118, pg. 1058
SPRAGUE NELSON, LLC., 119 Braintree St Ste 702, 02134, pg. 1067
TITAN WORLDWIDE, 195 State St 4th Fl, 02109, pg. 1145
UCG MARKETING, 566 Commonwealth Ave Mezzanine Level, 02215, pg. 1165
VERSION 2.0 COMMUNICATION, 500 Harrison Ave Ste 401R, 2118, pg. 1174
VML, INC., 116 Huntington Ave 12th Fl, 02116, pg. 1183
WINSPER, 115 Broad St 5th Fl, 02110, pg. 1210

Braintree

GROPPI ADVERTISING DESIGN, 25 Braintree Hill Park Ste 200, 02184, pg. 461
HOFFMAN AND PARTNERS, 44 Adams St, 02184, pg. 520
PERRONE GROUP, 45 Braintree Hill Office Park Ste 201, 02184, pg. 885

Bridgewater

FGM INTERNET MARKETING, 1625 Old Plymouth St, 2324, pg. 385

Burlington

89 DEGREES, INC., 25 Burlington Mall Rd Ste 610, 1803, pg. 12
DAVIES MURPHY GROUP, 200 Wheeler Rd N Tower, 01803, pg. 269
HARGER, HOWE & WALSH, 1 Van De Graaff Dr Ste 401, 01803, pg. 479
INVENTIV HEALTH INC., 1 Van de Graaff Dr, 01803, pg. 558
MEDIA & MORE, INC., 100 Trade Ctr, 01803, pg. 741
RHYTHMONE, 8 New England Executive Pk, 01803, pg. 977
WHITE RHINO PRODUCTIONS, INC., 41 Second Ave, 01803, pg. 1200

Cambridge

ALLIED INTEGRATED MARKETING, 55 Cambridge Pkwy Ste 200, 02142, pg. 47
CAMBRIDGE BIOMARKETING, 245 First St. !2th Fl, 02142, pg. 186
GILL FISHMAN ASSOCIATES, 675 Massachusetts Ave, 02139, pg. 425
PJA, 12 Arrow St, 02138-5105, pg. 894
SWOOP INC., 125 Cambridgepark Dr, 02140, pg. 1105
TOTH BRAND IMAGING, 215 First St, 02142, pg. 1152

Canton

JDCOMMUNICATIONS INC, 742 Washington St, 02021, pg. 589

Carlisle

LODICO & COMPANY, 60 McAllister Dr, 01741, pg. 666

Charlestown

CRUNCH BRAND COMMUNICATIONS INC., 1 1st Ave Building 34, 02129, pg. 258
KARMORY, 529 Main St Ste 127, 02129, pg. 603
WALLWORK CURRY MCKENNA, 10 City Sq 5th Fl, 02129, pg. 1188

Chicopee

ACCESS TO MEDIA, 432 Front St, 01013, pg. 19
LSHD ADVERTISING INC., 1974 Westover Rd, 1022, pg. 672

Cohasset

REILLY ADVERTISING, 64 Windy Hill Rd, 02025, pg. 967

East Bridgewater

HARTE-HANKS RESPONSE MANAGEMENT/BOSTON, INC., 600 N Bedford St, 02333, pg. 482

East Weymouth

HILL & PARTNERS INCORPORATED, 25 Mathewson Dr Ste 200, 02189-2345, pg. 514

Framingham

COMMONWEALTH CREATIVE ASSOCIATES, 345 Union Ave, 01702, pg. 225

Franklin

GUSTIN ADVERTISING, 115 Dean Ave Ste 100, 02038, pg. 467

Gloucester

HIRECLIX LLC, 3 Heritage Way, 01930, pg. 516

Haverhill

PRIMARY DESIGN INC, 57 Wingate St 4th Fl, 01832, pg. 910

Hingham

BR CREATIVE, 175 Derby St Ste 39, 02043, pg. 152
GRAY MATTER AGENCY INC., 94 Station St, 02043, pg. 441
ICON ADVERTISING & DESIGN INC, 67 Sharp St, 2043, pg. 532

Holliston

INSIDE OUT COMMUNICATIONS, 24 Water St, 01746, pg. 548
MDG, 13 Water St, 01746, pg. 740

Lenox

WINSTANLEY PARTNERS, 114 Main St, 01240-2353, pg. 1210

Lexington

FRUITT COMMUNICATIONS, INC., 229 Massachusetts Ave Ste 3, 02420-4040, pg. 406
THE MAAC GROUP, 333 Waltham St, 2421, pg. 681
PARDES COMMUNICATIONS, INC., 34 Bernard St, 02420, pg. 874

Longmeadow

P & M ADVERTISING, PO Box 60427, 01116, pg. 867
VAN SCHOUWEN ASSOCIATES, LLC, 175 Dwight Rd Ste 201, 01106, pg. 1170

Marblehead

THE COMMUNICATIONS STRATEGY GROUP, INC., 42 Front St, 01945, pg. 226
LEGEND INC., PO Box 50, 01945-0050, pg. 635

Medford

MCGOLDRICK MARKETING, 10 Burget Ave, 2155, pg. 735

Millers Falls

OLD MILL MARKETING, Renovators Old Mill, 01349, pg. 855

Natick

DIRECT ASSOCIATES, 46 Rockland St, 01760, pg. 310
IVY CREATIVE, 214 N Main St Ste 102, 1760, pg. 563
SUNDIN ASSOCIATES, INC., 34 Main St 3rd Fl, 01760, pg. 1100

Needham

912

Battle Creek

GREENSTREET MARKETING, 245 Michigan Ave W, 49017-3601, pg. 443

Benton Harbor

JOHNSONRAUHOFF MARKETING COMMUNICATIONS, 300 W Britain Ave, 49022, pg. 595

Birmingham

BROGAN & PARTNERS CONVERGENCE MARKETING, 800 N Old Woodward Ave, 48009, pg. 168
CENTIGRADE INTERNATIONAL LTD., 135 N Old Woodward, 48009, pg. 202
HARRIS MARKETING GROUP, 102 Pierce St, 48009-6018, pg. 481
MCCANN ERICKSON, 360 W Maple Rd, 48009, pg. 715
MRM WORLDWIDE, 360 W Maple Rd, 48009, pg. 783

Bloomfield

THE UTMOST GROUP, 2140 S Hammond Lake Rd W, 48324, pg. 1169

Bloomfield Hills

AUTOCOM ASSOCIATES, 74 W Long Lk Rd Ste 103, 48304-2770, pg. 81
REAL INTEGRATED, 40900 Woodward Ave Ste 300, 48304-2256, pg. 957

Bridgeport

HOUSER & HENNESSEE, 6000 Dixie Hwy, 48722, pg. 524

Clinton Township

HARRISON MEDIA, 24416 Crocker Blvd, 48036, pg. 481

Davison

CONCEPT THREE INC., 424 S Main St, 48423-1608, pg. 229

Dearborn

CAMPBELL MARKETING & COMMUNICATIONS, 3200 Greenfield Ste 280, 48120, pg. 188
IMAGINATION (USA) INC., 290 Town Center Dr 7th Fl, 48126-2765, pg. 540
TEAM DETROIT, 550 Town Ctr Dr, 48126-2750, pg. 1222
UWG, 500 Town Ctr Dr, 48126, pg. 1169
ZUBI ADVERTISING SERVICES, INC., 3 Parklane Blvd Ste 1050 W, 48126, pg. 1259

Detroit

AGENCY 720, 500 Woodward Ave, 48226, pg. 37
CAMPBELL EWALD, 2000 Brush St Ste 601, 48226, pg. 187
COMMONWEALTH, 211 Woodside Ave, 48201, pg. 714
DOUGLAS MARKETING GROUP, LLC, 10900 Harper Rd Ste 100, 48213, pg. 326
GROUP FIFTY FIVE MARKETING, 3011 W Grand Blvd, 48202, pg. 462
JACK MORTON WORLDWIDE, 1 Woodward Ave, 48226-3430, pg. 583
MULLEN LOWE, 1 Woodroad Ave, 48226, pg. 788
REBUILD NATION, 2990 W Grand Blvd Ste 408, 48202, pg. 959
STARCOM MEDIAVEST- GM TEAM, 150 W Jefferson Ste 400, 48226, pg. 1077

East Lansing

BLOHM CREATIVE PARTNERS, 1331 E Grand River Ave Ste 210, 48823, pg. 139
KING MEDIA, 1555 Watertower Place Ste 200, 48823, pg. 613

Edwardsburg

FIREVINE INC., 69950 M-62, 49112, pg. 388

Escanaba

BOTTOM LINE MARKETING, 5001 Ln 17.7 Dr, 49829, pg. 150

Farmington Hills

DUFFEY PETROSKY, 38505 Country Club Dr, 48331, pg. 331
J.R. THOMPSON CO., 26970 Haggerty Rd Ste 100, 48331, pg. 597
LATCHA+ASSOCIATES, 24600 Hallwood Ct, 48335-1603, pg. 627
MARX LAYNE & COMPANY, 31420 Northwestern Hwy Ste 100, 48334, pg. 706

Fenton

LATREILLE ADVERTISING & TALENT INC, 1421 N Leroy St, 48430, pg. 629

Ferndale

DRIVEN SOLUTIONS INC., 320 w 9 Mile Rd Ste b, 48220, pg. 328
HADROUT ADVERTISING & TECHNOLOGY, 195 W Nine Mile, 48220, pg. 471
THE POWERS THAT BE LLC, 320 West Nine Mile Rd Ste B, 48220, pg. 907
ZOYES CREATIVE GROUP, 1280 Hilton Rd, 48220, pg. 1259

Grand Rapids

ADTEGRITY.COM, 38 Commerce SW Ste 200, 49546, pg. 32
DEKSIA, 100 Stevens St SW Ste 02, 49507, pg. 294
DOMOREGOOD HANNON MCKENDRY, 25 Ottawa SW Ste 600, 49503, pg. 321
FELDER COMMUNICATIONS GROUP, 1593 Galbraith Ave Se Ste 201, 49546-9032, pg. 384
FULL CIRCLE, 648 Monroe Ave NW Ste 500, 49503, pg. 407
HIDALGO & DE VRIES, INC., 560 5th St Ste 401, 49504, pg. 512
THE IMAGINATION FACTORY, 15 Ionia Ave SW Ste 220, 49503, pg. 540
PAUL MILES ADVERTISING, 25 Jefferson SE, 49503, pg. 878
PHILIPS & ASSOCIATES, 6172 S Gatehouse Dr, 49546, pg. 889
STEVENS ADVERTISING, 190 Monroe Ave NW Ste 200, 49503, pg. 1085
VIAS LATINO MARKETING, 4322 Stratton Blvd SE, 49512, pg. 1176

Grosse Pointe Park

FRONTIER 3 ADVERTISING, 15127 Kercheval Ave, 48230, pg. 405

Highland Park

DIALOG DIRECT, 13700 Oakland Ave, 48203, pg. 306

Holland

FAIRLY PAINLESS ADVERTISING, 44 E 8th St Ste 300, 49423, pg. 365
THE IMAGE GROUP, 31 E 8th St Ste 200, 49423, pg. 538
MURDOCH MARKETING, 217 E 24th St Baker Lofts Ste 220, 49423, pg. 796

Howell

FAITH CREATIVE MEDIA, 1260 York Ave, 48843, pg. 366

Hudsonville

MW MARKETING GROUP, 7831 Meadowood Dr, 49426, pg. 797

Kalamazoo

ADAMS OUTDOOR ADVERTISING, 407 E. Ransom St, 49007, pg. 25
LKF MARKETING, 303 N Rose St Ste 444, 49007, pg. 664
MAXWELL & MILLER MARKETING COMMUNICATIONS, 141 E Michigan Ste 500, 49007-3943, pg. 712

Lansing

ADAMS OUTDOOR ADVERTISING, 3801 Capital City Blvd, 48906, pg. 25
CIESADESIGN, 200 E Grand River Ave, 48906, pg. 210
DREAMSCAPE MULTIMEDIA, 120 N Washington Sq Ste 805, 48933, pg. 327
EDGE PARTNERSHIPS, 117 E Kalamazoo St, 48933, pg. 338
FORESIGHT GROUP, INC., 2822 N Martin Luther King Jr Blvd, 48906-2927, pg. 397
GUD MARKETING, 1223 Turner St Ste 101, 48906, pg. 466
HARVEST CREATIVE SERVICES, 1011 North Washington, 48906, pg. 483
INVERVE MARKETING, 1035 N Washington Ave, 48906, pg. 559
M3 GROUP, 614 Seymour Ave, 48933, pg. 680
MARKETING RESOURCE GROUP, 225 S Washington Sq, 48933, pg. 699
MARTIN WAYMIRE, 426 W Ottawa, 48933, pg. 704
THE MEDIA ADVANTAGE, 414 E Michigan Ave Ste 1A, 48933, pg. 741
QUEUE CREATIVE, 410 S Cedar St Ste F, 48912, pg. 943
TRACTION, 617 E Michigan Ave, 48912, pg. 1153
TRUSCOTT ROSSMAN, 124 W Allegan St Ste 800, 48933, pg. 1160

Laurel

ROBERTS CREATIVE GROUP, 107 S Magnolia St, 39440, pg. 987

Livonia

P2R ASSOCIATES, 39201 Schoolcraft Rd Ste B-15, 48150, pg. 867
VALASSIS 1 TO 1 SOLUTIONS, 19975 Victor Pkwy, 48152, pg. 1170

Macomb

A360 DESIGN, 52837 Karon Dr, 48042, pg. 14

Madison Heights

MVP COLLABORATIVE, 1751 E Lincoln Ave, 48071, pg. 797

Midland

ABERRO CREATIVE, 2007 Austin St, 48642, pg. 17
AMPM, INC., 7403 W. Wackerly St., 48642-7344, pg. 56
CLEARRIVER COMMUNICATIONS GROUP, 2401 Eastlawn Dr, 48640, pg. 215

Muskegon

RCP MARKETING, 1756 Lakeshore Dr, 49441, pg. 956

Northville

AMPM, INC. DETROIT, 21442 Beauford Ln, 48167, pg. 56

Novi

BREWER ASSOCIATES MARKETING COMMUNICATIONS, 39555 Orchard Hill Pl Ste 600, 48375, pg. 163
SHAZAAAM LLC, 41216 Vincenti Court, 48375, pg. 1036

Okemos

FAHRENHEIT CREATIVE, 3695 Okemos Rd Ste 100, 48864, pg. 365

Pleasant Ridge

HELLOWORLD, 1 ePrize Dr, 48069, pg. 509

Plymouth

EBUYMEDIA, 332 S Main St, 48170, pg. 337

Pontiac

PUSH22, 22 W Huron St, 48342, pg. 940
PUSHTWENTYTWO, 22 W Huron St, 48342, pg. 940

Redford

JEKYLL AND HYDE, 26135 Plymouth Rd, 48239, pg. 589

Romeo

ALL SEASONS COMMUNICATIONS, 5455 34 Mile Rd, 48065, pg. 46

Royal Oak

BERLINE, 423 North Main St, 48067, pg. 125
KNOW ADVERTISING, 422 W 11 Mile Rd, 48067, pg. 616
PGN AGENCY, 1504 E 11 Mile Rd, 48067, pg. 887
TRADEMARK PRODUCTIONS, 309 S Main St, 48067, pg. 1154

Saginaw

THE SCOTT & MILLER GROUP, 816 S Hamilton St, 48602-1516, pg. 1026

Saint Joseph

AISLE ROCKET STUDIOS, 511 Renaissance Dr Ste 150, 49085, pg. 42
FATHOM WORKS, 1101 Broad St Ste 316, 49085, pg. 370
JOHNSONRAUHOFF, 2525 Lake Pines Dr, 49085, pg. 595
RADIX COMMUNICATIONS, INC., 3399 S Lakeshore Dr, 49085, pg. 949

Southfield

ACXIOM, 1000 Town Ctr #2700, 48075-1224, pg. 22
CAPONIGRO MARKETING GROUP, LLC, 24725 W Twelve Mile Rd Ste 120, 48034, pg. 189
DONER, 25900 Northwestern Hwy, 48075, pg. 322
GLOBALHUE, Ste 1600 4000 Town Ctr, 48076, pg. 429
GRIGG GRAPHIC SERVICES, INC., 20982 Bridge St, 48033-4033, pg. 460
THE MARS AGENCY, 25200 Telegraph Rd, 48033-7496, pg. 701
MILLWARD BROWN, 26555 Evergreen Rd Ste 600, 48076-4228, pg. 761
RIEGNER & ASSOCIATES, INC., 18481 W 10 Mile Rd, 48075-2621, pg. 980
SUSSMAN AGENCY, 29200 Northwestern Hwy Ste 130, 48034, pg. 1101
YAFFE DIRECT, 26100 American Dr 4th Fl Ste 401, 48034, pg. 1237
YAFFE GROUP, 26100 American Dr Ste 401, 48034, pg. 1237

Traverse City

FLIGHT PATH CREATIVE, 117 S Union St, 49684, pg. 393
ONEUPWEB, 13561 S W Bayshore Dr Ste 3000, 49684, pg. 861

Troy

AIMIA, 2800 Livernois Ste 600, 48083, pg. 41
JANKOWSKICO., 570 Kirts Blvd Ste 202, 48084, pg. 587
KRACOE SZYKULA & TOWNSEND INC., 2950 W Square Lake Rd Ste 112, 48098-5725, pg. 617
LEO BURNETT DETROIT, INC., 3310 W Big Beaver Rd Ste 107, 48084-2809, pg. 637
LEO J. BRENNAN, INC., 2359 Livernois Rd, 48083-1692, pg. 651
OTTAWAY COMMUNICATIONS, INC., 3250 W Big Beaver Rd Ste 230, 48084, pg. 865
POINTROLL INC., 340 E Big Beaver Rd Ste 150, 48083, pg. 901
THE QUELL GROUP, 2282 Livernois Rd, 48083, pg. 942
SIMONS MICHELSON ZIEVE, INC., 1200 Kirts Blvd Ste 100, 48084, pg. 1045
THEFRAMEWORKS, 755 W Big Beaver Rd Ste 100, 48084, pg. 1138

Wixom

THE NORTHWEST GROUP, 28265 Beck Rd Ste C2, 48393, pg. 816

Ypsilanti

ADAMS OUTDOOR ADVERTISING, 880 James L. Hart Pkwy, 48197, pg. 25

MINNESOTA

Apple Valley

GAME CHANGER COMMUNICATIONS, 13064 Elderberry Ct, 55124, pg. 414

Bloomington

AXIOM MARKETING COMMUNICATIONS, 3800 American Blvd W Ste 1275, 55431, pg. 83
CUNEO ADVERTISING, 1401 American Blvd E Ste 6, 55425, pg. 260
THE MAREK GROUP, 6625 W 78th St Ste 260, 55439, pg. 693

Brainerd

ADVENTURE ADVERTISING, 110 NW 3rd St, 56401, pg. 34
ITEAM CREATIVE, 405 W Washington St, 56401, pg. 563
RED HOUSE MEDIA LLC, 1001 Kingwood St Studio 218, 56401, pg. 960
RUSSELL HERDER, 315 E River Rd, 56401-3503, pg. 998

Burnsville

PR CAFFEINE, 2438 E 117th St Ste 100, 55337, pg. 907

Duluth

FLINT INTERACTIVE, 11 E Superior St Ste 514, 55802, pg. 394
OUT THERE ADVERTISING, 22 E 2nd St, 55802, pg. 866
SWIM CREATIVE, 415 E Superior St, 55802, pg. 1104

Eden Prairie

SEQUEL RESPONSE, LLC, 6870 Washington Ave S, 55344, pg. 1032

Edina

BARD ADVERTISING, 4900 Lincoln Dr, 55436, pg. 91

Excelsior

THE ZIMMERMAN GROUP, 21940 Minnetonka Blvd, 55331, pg. 1257

Fairmont

ADMFG INC., 100 N State St Ste D, 56031, pg. 30

Grand Rapids

E3, 419 5th Ave NE, 55744, pg. 335

Lakeville

ENSEMBLE CREATIVE & MARKETING, 20790 Holyoke Ave 2nd Fl PO Box 899, 55044, pg. 348

Mankato

LIME VALLEY ADVERTISING, INC., 1620 S Riverfront Dr, 56001, pg. 657

Maple Grove

STERLING CROSS COMMUNICATIONS, 12416 90th Pl N, 55369, pg. 1084
TARTAN MARKETING, 10467 93rd Ave N, 55369, pg. 1111

Maplewood

CYNTHCARM COMMUNICATIONS, 2246 Ide Ct N, 55109, pg. 262

Mendota Heights

COTTERWEB ENTERPRISES, INC., 1295 Northland Dr Ste 300, 55120, pg. 238

Minneapolis

ADSOKA, INC., 100 South 1st St, 55458-3237, pg. 32
ADVENTURE, 111 N Washington Ave Ste 250, 55401, pg. 34
AIMIA, 100 N 6th St, 55403, pg. 41
AKQURACY, 800 Washington Ave N Ste 206, 55401, pg. 43
ANDERSON-MADISON ADVERTISING, INC., 7710 Computer Ave, 55435-5417, pg. 58
BARRIE D'ROZARIO DILORENZO, 400 1st Ave N Ste 220, 55401, pg. 94
BBDO MINNEAPOLIS, 150 S 5th St Ste 3500, 55402-4200, pg. 100
BBDO PROXIMITY, 150 S 5th St Ste 3500, 55402, pg. 98
BELLMONT PARTNERS, 3300 Edinborough Way Ste 700, 55435, pg. 123
BOLIN MARKETING, 2523 Wayzata Blvd, 55405, pg. 147
BREW, 530 University Ave SE, 55414, pg. 163
BROADHEAD, 123 N 3rd St 4th Fl, 55401, pg. 168
CAPSULE BRAND DEVELOPMENT, 100 2nd Ave N, 55401, pg. 190
CARMICHAEL LYNCH, 110 N 5th St, 55403, pg. 191
CATCHFIRE, 708 N 1st St Ste 131, 55401, pg. 198
CLARITY COVERDALE FURY ADVERTISING, INC., 120 S 6th St Ste 1300, 55402-1810, pg. 213
CLOCKWORK ACTIVE MEDIA, 1501 E Hennepin Ave, 55414, pg. 216
COLLE+MCVOY, 400 1st Ave N Ste 700, 55401-1954, pg. 221
CREATIVE COMMUNICATIONS CONSULTANTS, INC., 111 3rd Ave S Ste 390, 55401-2553, pg. 246
CUE INC, 520 Nicollet Mall Ste 500, 55402, pg. 259
D.TRIO, 401 N 3rd St Ste 480, 55401, pg. 331
FALLON MINNEAPOLIS, 901 Marquette Ave Ste 2400, 55402, pg. 367
FALLON WORLDWIDE, 901 Marquette Ave Ste 2400, 55402, pg. 366
THE FALLS AGENCY, 900 6th Ave SE Ste 105, 55414-1379, pg. 367
FAME, 60 S Sixth St Ste 2600, 55402, pg. 367
FAST HORSE, 240 N 9th Ave, 55401, pg. 369
FELLOW, 2609 Aldrich Ave S #103, 55408, pg. 384
GABRIEL DEGROOD BENDT, 608 2nd Ave S Ste 129, 55402, pg. 413
GRIFFIN ARCHER, 126 N 3rd St Ste 204, 55401, pg. 459
GROCERY SHOPPING NETWORK, 900 Lumber Exchange Bldg 10 S 5th St, 55402, pg. 461
HABERMAN & ASSOCIATES, INC., 119 N 4th St Ste 301, 55410, pg. 471
HANLEY WOOD MARKETING, 430 1st Ave N Ste 550, 55401, pg. 478
HOT DISH ADVERTISING, 800 Washington Ave N Ste 200, 55401, pg. 524
HUNT ADKINS, 15 S 5th St, 55402, pg. 528
IMAGEHAUS, 718 Washington Ave N #214, 55401, pg. 538
INITIO, INC., 212 3rd Ave N Ste 510, 55401-1440, pg. 546
INTERNET EXPOSURE, INC., 1101 Washington Ave S, 55415, pg. 554
J.T. MEGA FOOD MARKETING COMMUNICATIONS, 4020 Minnetonka Blvd, 55416-4100, pg. 598
KARWOSKI & COURAGE, 60 S 6th St Ste 2800, 55402, pg. 705
KAZOO BRANDING, 316 E Hennepin Ave Ste 202-203, 55414, pg. 604

Minnetonka

New Brighton

Northfield

Oakdale

Plymouth

Red Wing

Rochester

Rogers

Saint Cloud

Saint Paul

Virginia

Waconia

Wayzata

MISSISSIPPI

Gulfport

Jackson

Madison

Meridian

Ocean Springs

Ridgeland

Tupelo

West Point

MISSOURI

Ballwin

Bridgeton

BANIK COMMUNICATIONS, 121 4th St N Ste 1B, 59401, pg. 90
LODESTONE ADVERTISING, 318 Central Ave, 59401, pg. 666
THE WENDT AGENCY, 105 Park Dr S, 59401, pg. 1197

Missoula

CREVIN AMD, 127 N Higgins Ave, 59802, pg. 254
PARTNERS CREATIVE, 603 Woody St, 59802, pg. 875
SPIKER COMMUNICATIONS, INC., PO Box 8567, 59807, pg. 1064
STREAM ADVERTISING LLC, 401 S Catlin, 59801, pg. 1091

Victor

FOUR BROTHERS MEDIA, 2089 Alder Springs Ln, 59875, pg. 400

Whitefish

GOING TO THE SUN MARKETING ASSOCIATES, LLC, 1250 Whitefish Hills Dr, 59937, pg. 433

NEBRASKA

Hastings

IDEA BANK MARKETING, 701 W Second St, 68901, pg. 533

Lincoln

ACTON INTERNATIONAL LTD., 5760 Cornhusker Hwy Ste 1, 68507, pg. 21
ARCHRIVAL, 720 O St, 68508, pg. 67
BADER RUTTER & ASSOCIATES, INC., 808 P St Ste 210, 68508-2246, pg. 86
BAILEY LAUERMAN, 1248 O St Ste 1140, 68508, pg. 87
FIRESPRING, 1201 Infinity Ct, 68512, pg. 388
FORGELIGHT CREATIVE, 1227 New Hampshire St, 68508, pg. 397
INFORMATION ANALYTICS, INC., 301 S 70th St Ste 300, 68510, pg. 545
MINNOW PROJECT, 815 O St, 68508, pg. 762
SWANSON RUSSELL ASSOCIATES, 1222 P St, 68508-1425, pg. 1102
UNANIMOUS, 8600 Executive Woods Dr. Ste. 300, 68512, pg. 1166

Omaha

92 WEST, 13504 Stevens St Ste C, 68137, pg. 13
ANDERSON PARTNERS, 6919 Dodge St, 68132, pg. 59
B2 INTERACTIVE, 223 S 143rd Cir, 68137, pg. 85
BAILEY LAUERMAN, 1299 Farnam Street Ste 930, 68102, pg. 87
BLUE PRINT AD AGENCY, PO Box 540604, 68154, pg. 142
BOZELL, 1022 Leavenworth St, 68102, pg. 152
BRANDSCAPES, 16333 Ohio St, 68116, pg. 160
CLARK CREATIVE GROUP, 514 S 13th St, 68102, pg. 213
EG INTEGRATED, 11820 Nicholas St Ste 102, 68154, pg. 339
ELEVEN19 COMMUNICATIONS INC., 900 S 74th Plz Ste 100, 68114, pg. 344
ERVIN & SMITH, 16934 Frances St Ste 200, 68130, pg. 354
J. GREG SMITH, INC., Seville Square 1 14707 California St Ste 6, 68154, pg. 565
JUNE ADVERTISING, 420 S 14th St, 68102, pg. 600
LILLETHORUP PRODUCTIONS, INC., 5011 Seward St, 68104, pg. 657
LOVGREN MARKETING GROUP, 809 N 96th St Ste 2, 68114, pg. 670
OBI CREATIVE, 2920 Farnam St, 68131, pg. 821
PHENOMBLUE, 2111 S 67th St Ste 110, 68106, pg. 888
REDSTONE COMMUNICATIONS INC., 10031 Maple St, 68134, pg. 965
SKAR ADVERTISING, 111 S 108th Ave, 68154-2699, pg. 1049
SLEIGHT ADVERTISING INC, 15405 Weir St, 68154, pg. 1051
STERN PR MARKETING, 16508 Taylor St, 68116, pg. 1085
SURDELL & PARTNERS, LLC, 3738 S 149th St, 68144, pg. 1101
SWANSON RUSSELL ASSOCIATES, 14301 FNB Pkwy Ste 312, 68154-5299, pg. 1102
TURNPOST CREATIVE GROUP, 17330 Wright S Ste 200, 68130, pg. 1162

NEVADA

Henderson

BRANDTOPIA GROUP, 2831 St Rose Pkwy Ste 450, 89052, pg. 161
MARKETING RESULTS INC., 2900 W Horizon Rdg Pkwy Ste 200, 89052, pg. 699
MASSMEDIA CORPORATE COMMUNICATIONS, 2863 St Rose Pkwy, 89052, pg. 708

Las Vegas

10E MEDIA, 10080 Alta Dr, 89145, pg. 1
B&P ADVERTISING, 900 S Pavilion Ctr Dr Ste 170, 89144, pg. 84
BLAINE WARREN ADVERTISING LLC, 7120 Smoke Ranch Rd, 89128, pg. 135
BRAINTRUST, 8948 Spanish Ridge Ave, 89148, pg. 154
THE GEARY COMPANY, 3136 E Russell Rd, 89120-3463, pg. 419
GLOBAL EXPERIENCE SPECIALISTS, INC., 7000 Lindell Rd, 89118, pg. 428
HIGHER GROUND CREATIVE AGENCY, 11650 Elcadore St, 89193, pg. 513
JACK MYERS MEDIA BUSINESS REPORT, PO Box 27740, 89126, pg. 584
LETIZIA MASS MEDIA, 5460 Desert Point Dr, 89118, pg. 652
QUILLIN ADVERTISING, 8080 W Sahara Ave Ste A, 89117, pg. 944
R&R PARTNERS, 900 S Pavilion Center Dr, 89144, pg. 945
RDG ADVERTISING, 6655 S Tenaya Way Ste 200, 89113, pg. 956
ROBERTSON & PARTNERS, 6061 S Fort Apachee Rd Ste 100, 89148, pg. 987
RPM/LAS VEGAS, 7251 W Lake Mead Blvd Ste 300, 89128, pg. 995
SK+G ADVERTISING LLC, 8912 Spanish Ridge Ave, 89148, pg. 1049
START7, 289 Pilot Rd Ste B, 89119, pg. 1074
SWAN ADVERTISING, 9121 W Russell Rd Ste 116, 89148, pg. 1102
THOMAS PUCKETT ADVERTISING, 1710 Bannie Ave, 89102, pg. 1141
VIRGEN ADVERTISING, CORP., 151 E Warm Springs Rd, 89119, pg. 1178

Reno

BAUSERMAN GROUP, 500 Damonte Ranch Pkwy Ste 675, 89521, pg. 97
ESTIPONA GROUP, PO Box 10606, 89511, pg. 356
THE GLENN GROUP, 50 Washington St, 89503-5603, pg. 427
GLOBAL STUDIO, 285 E Parr Blvd, 89512-1003, pg. 428
INNERWEST ADVERTISING, 170 S Virginia St Ste 202, 89501, pg. 547
KPS3 MARKETING, 50 W Liberty St Ste 640, 89501, pg. 617
R&R PARTNERS, 615 Riverside Dr, 89503-5601, pg. 945

NEW HAMPSHIRE

Bedford

BURKE ADVERTISING LLC, 9 Cedarwood Dr Ste 11, 03110, pg. 176
PANNOS MARKETING, 116 S River Rd, 03110, pg. 871

Concord

ACT ONE CREATIVE LLC, 18 Low Ave, 03301, pg. 21
PAXTON COMMUNICATIONS, 58 N State St, 03301-4326, pg. 880
SOUTH END MEDIA, PO Box 286, 3302, pg. 1060
SULLIVAN CREATIVE SERVICES, LTD., 6C Hills Ave, 03301, pg. 1097

Exeter

THINK NOCTURNAL LLC, 8 Continental Dr Unit E, 03833, pg. 1139

Goffstown

GRINLEY CREATIVE LLC, 28 Benjamin Dr, 3045, pg. 460

Greenland

ALTERNATE TRANSIT ADVERTISING, 295 Bayside Rd, 03840-2130, pg. 51
MICROARTS, 655 Portsmouth Ave, 03840-2246, pg. 755

Hopkinton

STOREYMANSEAU, LLC, 603 Upper Straw Rd, 03229, pg. 1088

Keene

THE COMMUNICATORS GROUP, 9 Church St, 03431, pg. 227

Manchester

BRAINIUM INC., 373 S Willow Ste 197, 03103, pg. 153
EISENBERG, VITAL & RYZE ADVERTISING, 155 Dow St Ste 101, 03101, pg. 341
GIGUNDA GROUP, INC., 150 Dow St Tower 3 5th Fl, 03101, pg. 425
GYKANTLER, 121 River Front Dr, 03102, pg. 468
M5 NEW HAMPSHIRE, 707 Chestnut St, 03104, pg. 680
MANN ADVERTISING INC, 913 Elm St 4th Fl, 3101, pg. 690
MILLENNIUM INTEGRATED MARKETING, 150 Dow St, 3rd Fl, 03101, pg. 757

Merrimack

ADS ON WHEELS, 26a Columbia Cir, 03054, pg. 32
GIRARD ADVERTISING LLC, 604 DW Hwy Ste 105, 03054, pg. 426

Nashua

COLLAGE ADVERTISING, 76 Northeastern Blvd Ste 28, 03062-3174, pg. 221
MESH INTERACTIVE AGENCY, 142 Main St, 03060, pg. 751
THE RIGHT LIST, 20a North West Blvd Ste 290, 03053, pg. 981

North Conway

CORPORATE COMMUNICATIONS, INC., 65 Seavey St, 03860, pg. 237
DRIVE BRAND STUDIO, 170 Kearsarge St, 03860, pg. 328

North Hampton

RUMBLETREE, 216 Lafayette Rd, 03862, pg. 997

Northwood

KEVIN J. ASH CREATIVE DESIGN, LLC, 58 Sax Alley, 03261, pg. 609

Peterborough

FLETCHER MEDIA GROUP, 94 Grove St, 03458, pg. 393

Portsmouth

BOLDWERKS, 477 State St, 03801, pg. 146
CALYPSO COMMUNICATIONS, 121 Bow St Bldg 6, 03801, pg. 186

DARCI CREATIVE, 96 Chestnut St, 03801, pg. 266
KIRK COMMUNICATIONS, 1 New Hampshire Ave Ste 125, 03801, pg. 613
PIEHEAD PRODUCTIONS LLC, 73 Ct St, 03801, pg. 890
RAIN, 4 Greenleaf Woods Ste 301, 03801, pg. 950
RAKA, 33 Penhallow St., 03801, pg. 950
SEAN TRACEY ASSOCIATES, 401 State St Ste 3, 03801-4030, pg. 1029

Windham

36CREATIVE, 46 Lowell Rd Ste 1, 03087, pg. 7

NEW JERSEY

Atlantic City

MAKE IT POP ADVERTISING, 1026 Atlantic Ave, 08401, pg. 687
MASTERPIECE ADVERTISING, 3101 Boardwalk Ste 13, 8401, pg. 709
VISIONS ADVERTISING MEDIA, LLC, 426 Shore Rd Ste B, 08401, pg. 1179

Barnegat

PURPOSE ADVERTISING, 79 S Main St, 08005, pg. 939

Basking Ridge

RIDGE MARKETING & DESIGN LLC, 91 S Maple Ave, 7920, pg. 980

Belmar

CREATIVE INSURANCE MARKETING CO., 208 2nd Ave, 07719, pg. 249

Berkeley Heights

ACCESS COMMUNICATIONS LLC, 400 Connell Dr Ste 2, 07922-2739, pg. 19
PRECEPT MEDICAL COMMUNICATIONS, 4 Connell Dr Bldg IV Ste 601, 07922-2705, pg. 1096

Boonton

GREEN ROOM PUBLIC RELATIONS, 333 W Main St Ste 1, 7005, pg. 442
S3, 718 Main St, 07005, pg. 999

Branchburg

PERCEPTURE, 3322 US 22 W Ste 411, 08876, pg. 883

Bridgewater

BALDWIN & OBENAUF, INC., 1011 US Rte 22 W Ste 100, 08807-2950, pg. 88
VICTORY HEALTHCARE COMMUNICATIONS, 678 US Hwy 202 Ste 5, 08807, pg. 1176

Brielle

KINETIC KNOWLEDGE, 620 Harris Ave, 08730, pg. 612

Cedar Knolls

BRUSHFIRE, INC., 2 Wing Dr, 07927, pg. 172
ECLIPSE MARKETING SERVICES, INC., 240 Cedar Knolls Rd, 07927, pg. 337
VISION CREATIVE GROUP, INC., 16 Wing Dr, 07927, pg. 1178

Cherry Hill

ANDREA CHARLES ADVERTISING, INC., 910 Beechwood Ave, 08002-3404, pg. 59
REX DIRECT NET, INC., 100 Springdale Rd A3 Ste 253, 08003, pg. 975
TMP WORLDWIDE/ADVERTISING & COMMUNICATIONS, One Cherry Hill One Mall Dr Ste 610, 08002, pg. 1148

Chester

GRAFICAINTER.ACTIVE, LTD., 525 E Main St, 07930-2627, pg. 438

Clark

HEALTHED, 100 Walnut Ave Ste 407, 07066, pg. 506

Clifton

EXPECT ADVERTISING, INC., 1033 Route 46, 07013, pg. 361
TAG ONLINE INC., 6 Prospect Village Plz 1st Fl, 07013, pg. 1107
WEINRICH ADVERTISING/COMMUNICATIONS, INC., 915 Clifton Ave Ste 2, 07013-2725, pg. 1195

Clinton

MINT ADVERTISING, 120 W Main St, 08809, pg. 763

Cranbury

RE:FUEL, 10 Abeel Rd, 08512, pg. 967

Cranford

KOIKO DESIGN LLC, 322 Stoughton Ave, 07016, pg. 616

Dayton

BROGAN TENNYSON GROUP, INC., 2245 US Hwy 130 Ste 102, 08810-2420, pg. 168
IMPACT XM - NEW JERSEY, 250 Ridge Rd, 08810, pg. 541

East Brunswick

VANGUARDCOMM, 2 Disbrow Court 3rd Fl, 08816, pg. 1171

Eatontown

BRIECHLE-FERNANDEZ MARKETING SERVICES INC., 265 Industrial Way W Ste 7, 07724, pg. 164

Edgewater

DM2 DESIGN CONSULTANCY, 115 River Rd, 07020, pg. 318
DXAGENCY, 75 Gorge Rd, 07020, pg. 333

Egg Harbor Township

MASTERMINDS, 6727 Delilah Rd, 08234, pg. 709

Elmwood Park

CPR STRATEGIC MARKETING COMMUNICATIONS, 475 Market St 2nd FL, 07407, pg. 242

Emerson

MRC MEDICAL COMMUNICATIONS, 12 Lincoln Blvd Ste 201, 07630, pg. 782
RMI MARKETING & ADVERTISING, 436 Old Hook Rd 2nd Fl, 07631, pg. 986

Englewood

RITTA, 568 Grand Ave, 07631, pg. 984
SCHROEDER ADVERTISING, INC., 412 Tenafly Rd, 07631-1733, pg. 1025

Englewood Cliffs

ADASIA COMMUNICATIONS, INC., 400 Sylvan Ave, 07632, pg. 26
EAST HOUSE CREATIVE, 120 Sylvan Ave Ste 108A, 07632, pg. 335
FURMAN, FEINER ADVERTISING, 560 Sylvan Ave, 07632, pg. 409

Ewing

COMPASS HEALTHCARE MARKETERS, 200 Princeton S Corporate Ctr Ste 320, 08628, pg. 228
STIMULUS BRAND COMMUNICATIONS, 1 Currier Way, 8628, pg. 1087

Fair Haven

ENA HEALTHCARE COMMUNICATIONS, 740 River Rd Ste 209, 07704, pg. 347

Fairfield

PEARL MEDIA LLC, 363 Rt 46 W Ste 260, 07004, pg. 881
TITAN WORLDWIDE, 55 Dwight Pl, 07004, pg. 1145
TURCHETTE ADVERTISING AGENCY LLC, 9 Law Dr, 07004, pg. 1161

Flemington

ARTCRAFT HEALTH EDUCATION, 39 Highway 12, 08822, pg. 74
THE NULMAN GROUP, 18 Commerce St Ste 1817, 08822, pg. 819

Fort Lee

DOUBLE XXPOSURE MEDIA RELATIONS INC, 2037 Lemoine Ave Ste 205, 7024, pg. 326

Freehold

RED FLANNEL, 218 Schanck Rd 2nd Fl, 07728, pg. 960

Garfield

BLUBERRIES ADVERTISING, 70 Outwater Ln Ste 401, 07026, pg. 140

Glen Rock

DO GOOD MARKETING, LLC, 201 Rock Rd, 07452, pg. 320

Guttenberg

HARRISONRAND ADVERTISING, 6823 Bergenline Ave, 7093, pg. 481

Hackensack

SOURCE COMMUNICATIONS, 433 Hackensack Ave 8th Fl, 07601-6319, pg. 1059

Haddonfield

BUZZ MARKETING GROUP, 132 Kings Hwy E Ste 202, 8033, pg. 179
HAMLYN SENIOR MARKETING, 25 Chestnut St, 08033, pg. 477

Hamilton

ROSETTA, 100 American Metro Blvd, 08619, pg. 992

Hamilton Square

RYAN JAMES AGENCY, 3692 Nottingham Way, 08690, pg. 999

Hammonton

1 TRICK PONY, 251 Bellevue Ave 2nd Fl, 08037, pg. 1
ONE TRICK PONY, 251 Bellevue Ave 2nd Fl, 8037, pg. 860

Hasbrouck Heights

RESULTS, INC., ADVERTISING AGENCY, 777 Terrace Ave, 07604-0822, pg. 972

Hibernia

Geographic Index-U.S.

LARS & ASSOCIATES, INC., 322 Greenpond Rd, 07842, pg. 627

Hillsborough

JK DESIGN, 465 Amwell Rd, 08844, pg. 591

Holmdel

BSY ASSOCIATES INC, 960 Holmdel Rd Bldg II Ste 201, 7733, pg. 173

Hopewell

DANA COMMUNICATIONS, INC., 2 E Broad St, 08525, pg. 265

Iselin

POLARIS SOFTWARE LAB INDIA LIMITED, Woodbridge Pl 517 Rte 1 S Ste 2103, 08830, pg. 902

Jersey City

OUTSIDE THE BOX INTERACTIVE LLC, 150 Bay St Ste 706, 07302, pg. 867

Keansburg

AFFORDABLE MARKETING SOLUTIONS, 41 Church St, 07734, pg. 36

Keyport

THE UNREAL AGENCY, 52 Broad St 3rd Fl, 07735, pg. 1167

Lakewood

SHOREPOINT COMMUNICATIONS, LLC, 160 Lehigh Ave Ste B, 08701, pg. 1039

Lambertville

OXFORD COMMUNICATIONS, INC., 11 Music Mtn Blvd, 08530, pg. 867

Landisville

SMS, Weymouth Rd., 08326, pg. 1055

Linden

GALLAGHER ADVERTISING INCORPORATED, PO Box 2085, 07036, pg. 414

Little Falls

THE MARCUS GROUP, INC., 150 Clove Rd 11th Fl, 07424, pg. 693

Long Branch

GUIDE PUBLICATIONS, 422 Morris Ave Ste 5, 07740, pg. 466

Lyndhurst

ERBACH COMMUNICATIONS GROUP, INC., 1099 Wall St W Ste 175, 07071-3623, pg. 352

Mahwah

BEACON MEDIA GROUP, 1 International Blvd Ste 1110, 07495, pg. 120

HEALTHSTAR COMMUNICATIONS, INC., 1000 Wyckoff Ave, 07430, pg. 506

RECRUITSAVVY, 330 Franklin Tpke, 07430, pg. 959

Manasquan

ZETA INTERACTIVE, 25A Abe Vorhees Dr, 08736, pg. 1255

Marlton

A.L.T. ADVERTISING & PROMOTION, 12000 Lincoln Dr W Ste 408, 08053, pg. 51

SERPENTE & COMPANY, INC., 1 Eves Dr Ste 158, 08053, pg. 1034

Metuchen

TOUCHDOWN MEDIA, 40 Bridge St, 08840, pg. 1152

Middlesex

BOC PARTNERS, 601 Bound Brook Rd Ste 100, 08846-2155, pg. 145

Middletown

BECKER GUERRY, 107 Tindall Rd, 07748-2321, pg. 121

CMDS, 13 Cherry Tree Farm Rd, 07748, pg. 217

Millburn

MONARCH COMMUNICATIONS INC., 343 Millburn Ave Ste 305, 07041, pg. 771

Monroe Township

BRANDESIGN, 981 Rt 33 W, 08831, pg. 158

DEVON ADVERTISING AGENCY LLC, 96 Drawbridge Dr, 08831, pg. 305

Montclair

GWP, INC., 32 Park Ave, 07042, pg. 468

THE HIP EVENT, 356 Bloomfield Ave Ste 5, 7042, pg. 515

JOE ZEFF DESIGN, INC., 8 Hillside Ave Ste 208, 07042, pg. 593

LOONEY ADVERTISING AND DESIGN, 7 N Mountain Ave, 07042, pg. 668

SITUATIO NORMAL, 7 N Willow St Ste 8A, 07042, pg. 1047

Montville

CMA: CREATIVE MEDIA & ASSOCIATES, 219 Changebridge Rd, 07045, pg. 217

DULLIGAN DESIGN, PO Box 598, 07045, pg. 332

SGW, 219 Changebridge Rd, 07045-9514, pg. 1035

STRATEGY+STYLE MARKETING GROUP, 25 Lenape Dr, 07045, pg. 1091

WLD COMMUNICATIONS, INC., 24 Eugene Dr, 07045, pg. 1212

Moorestown

NCI CONSULTING LLC, 820 Matlack Dr Ste 101, 08057, pg. 802

THOMAS BOYD COMMUNICATIONS, 117 N Church St, 08057, pg. 1141

Morristown

BRIGHAM & RAGO MARKETING COMMUNICATIONS, 18 Bank St Ste 200, 07960-5186, pg. 165

FIORE ASSOCIATES, INC., 109 Washington St, 07960, pg. 388

GRAFICAGROUP, 67 E Park Pl, 07960, pg. 437

THE IN-HOUSE AGENCY, INC., 55 Madison Ave Ste 400, 07960, pg. 543

KRAUS MARKETING, 4 Spring St, 7960, pg. 618

THE O'HARA PROJECT, 9 Washington St 2nd Fl, 7960, pg. 854

ST. JACQUES MARKETING, 60 Washington St Ste 101, 07960, pg. 1071

Mountain Lakes

ECHO TORRE LAZUR, 49 Bloomfield Ave, 07046, pg. 731

Mountainside

FORREST & BLAKE INC., 1139 Spruce Dr 2nd Fl, 07092, pg. 398

New Brunswick

BRUNSWICK MEDIA SERVICES LLC, PO Box 10904, 08906, pg. 172

New Providence

BROWNING ADVERTISING LLC, 121 Chanlon Rd, 07974, pg. 170

Newark

GMLV LLC, 53 Edison Pl Level 3, 7102, pg. 431

North Brunswick

LOUIS COSTANZA & ASSOCIATES, INC., 17 Point Of Woods Dr, 08902, pg. 669

MARKETING EDGE GROUP, 1555 Ruth Rd Units 1 & 2, 08902, pg. 697

Oakland

HARVEY ASSOCIATES-DIRECT MARKETING SOLUTIONS, 2 Knollwoods, 07436, pg. 483

Ocean

AURORA COAST PRODUCTIONS, 802 W Park Ave Ste 222, 07712, pg. 80

ENVISION DENNIS ROMANO, LLC, 20 Stonehenge Dr, 07712, pg. 349

Oldwick

NORMAN DIEGNAN & ASSOCIATES, PO Box 298, 08858, pg. 813

Paramus

CARYL COMMUNICATIONS, INC., 40 Eisenhower Dr Ste 203, 07652, pg. 194

CSI GROUP, INC., 11 Fairview Terr, 07652, pg. 258

GIOVATTO ADVERTISING & CONSULTING INC., 95 Rte 17 S, 07652, pg. 426

MAYR COMMUNICATIONS INC, 15 Farview Terr Ste 2, 07652, pg. 712

Park Ridge

WORDS AND PICTURES CREATIVE SERVICE, INC., 1 Maynard Dr Ste 1103, 07656, pg. 1214

Parsippany

AIMIA, 1 Gatehill Dr Ste 205, 07054-4514, pg. 41

BOOMERANG PHARMACEUTICAL COMMUNICATIONS, 14 Walsh Dr, 07054, pg. 148

ICC, 5 Sylvan Way, 07054, pg. 531

MCCANN TORRE LAZUR, Waterview Corporate Ctr 20 Waterview Blvd, 07054-1295, pg. 731

METAPHOR INC., 119 Cherry Hill Rd, 07054, pg. 751

MORBELLI, RUSSO & PARTNERS ADVERTISING, INC., 2 Sylvan Way Ste 302, 07054, pg. 773

NATREL COMMUNICATIONS, 119 Cherry Hill Rd, 07054, pg. 802

OGILVY COMMONHEALTH INTERACTIVE MARKETING, 430 Interpace Pkwy, 07054, pg. 851

OGILVY COMMONHEALTH MEDICAL EDUCATION, 402 Interpace Pkwy Bldg B, 07054, pg. 851

OGILVY COMMONHEALTH MEDICAL MEDIA, 442 & 426 Interpace Pkwy, 07054, pg. 851

OGILVY COMMONHEALTH PAYER MARKETING, 422 Interpace Pkwy, 07054, pg. 851

OGILVY COMMONHEALTH SPECIALTY MARKETING, 444 Interpace Pkwy Bld B, 07054, pg. 851

OGILVY COMMONHEALTH WELLNESS MARKETING, 424 Interpace Pkwy, 07054, pg. 851

OGILVY COMMONHEALTH WORLDWIDE, 400 Interpace Pkwy, 07054, pg. 851

OGILVY HEALTHWORLD PAYER MARKETING, 343 Interspace Pkwy, 07054, pg. 852

SUCCESS ADVERTISING, 26 Eastmans Rd, 07054, pg. 1095

SUCCESS COMMUNICATIONS GROUP, 26 Eastmans Rd, 07054, pg. 1095

Pine Brook

BEHIND THE SCENES MARKETING, 90 Windsor Dr, 07058, pg. 122

Pittstown

YANKEE PUBLIC RELATIONS, 8 Sunshine Dr, 08867, pg. 1237

Plainfield

ALLEN & PARTNERS, 620 Sheridan Ave, 07060, pg. 47

Plainsboro

DIGITAL BRAND EXPRESSIONS, 101 Morgan Ln Ste 203B, 8536, pg. 308

Point Pleasant

NETWAVE INTERACTIVE MARKETING, INC., 600 Bay Ave, 08742, pg. 806

Princeton

CLINE, DAVIS & MANN, INC., 210 Carnegie Ctr Ste 200, 08540-6226, pg. 201
DENTINO MARKETING, 515 Executive Dr, 08540, pg. 296
FERRARA & COMPANY, 301C College Rd E, 08540, pg. 385
HG MEDIA, INC., 31 Airpark Rd Ste 6, 08540-1524, pg. 512
INTEGRATED MARKETING SERVICES, 279 Wall St Research Park, 08540-1519, pg. 550
INVENTIV HEALTH CLINICAL, 504 Carnegie Ctr, 08540, pg. 558
J&M MARKETING COMMUNICATIONS, LLC, 177 Parkside Dr, 08540-4814, pg. 564
MRM PRINCETON, 105 Carnegie Ctr, 08540, pg. 784
MWH ADVERTISING, INC., 47 Hulfish St Ste 400, 08542, pg. 797
PRINCETON LYONS GRAPHICS LLC, 51 Westcott Rd, 08540, pg. 911
PRINCETON PARTNERS, INC., 205 Rockingham Row, 08540, pg. 911
SHAW & TODD, INC., 205 Rockingham Row, 08540-5759, pg. 1036
TAFT & PARTNERS, 1 Palmer Sq E, 08542, pg. 1107
THE TOPSPIN GROUP, 415 Executive Dr, 08540, pg. 1151
ZULLO ASSOCIATES, 1 Academy St, 08540, pg. 1259

Princeton Junction

CREATIVE MARKETING ALLIANCE INC., 191 Clarksville Rd, 08550, pg. 249
PRINCETON MARKETECH, 2 Alice Rd, 08550, pg. 911

Red Bank

THE SAWTOOTH GROUP, 141 West Front St., 07701, pg. 1022
SPITBALL LLC, 60 Broad St, 07701, pg. 1065

Ridgefield Park

FORT GROUP, 100 Challenger Rd 8th Fl, 07660, pg. 398
FORT INTEGRATED MARKETING GROUP, 100 Challenger Rd 8th Fl, 07660, pg. 398

Robbinsville

JACK MORTON EXHIBITS, 10 Applegate Dr, 08691, pg. 583

Roselle Park

HERCKY PASQUA HERMAN, INC., 324 Chestnut St, 07204, pg. 510

Rutherford

16W MARKETING, LLC, 75 Union Ave 2nd Fl, 07070, pg. 3

Scotch Plains

PL COMMUNICATIONS, 417 Victor St, 07076, pg. 895

Somers Point

SUASION COMMUNICATIONS GROUP, 599 Shore Rd, 08244, pg. 1094

Somerset

BRANDKARMA, 100 Franklin Sq Dr Ste 201, 08873-1128, pg. 159
D2 CREATIVE, 28 Worlds Fair Dr, 08873, pg. 262
TARTAGLIA COMMUNICATIONS, PO Box 5148, 08875-5148, pg. 1111

Somerville

CUMMINS, MACFAIL & NUTRY, INC., 134 W End Ave, 08876, pg. 260

South Orange

GRAPHIC ANGELS DESIGN GROUP, 370 Turrell Ave, 07079, pg. 440
KENNETH JAFFE INC., 71 Vly St Ste 201, 07079-2835, pg. 609

Sparta

EVANS ALLIANCE ADVERTISING, 72 Cobbler Sq, 07871, pg. 358

Summit

CHANA & ASSOCIATES, 475 Springfield Ave, 07901, pg. 203
TRILLION CREATIVE LLC, 382 Springfield Ave Ste 408, 7901, pg. 1157

Tinton Falls

FALLON MEDICA LLC, 620 Shrewsbury Ave, 07701, pg. 366

Trenton

EFK GROUP, 1027 S Clinton Ave, 8611, pg. 339

Union

LINETT & HARRISON, 2500 Morris Ave, 07083, pg. 658
WILLIAM SULLIVAN ADVERTISING, INC., 1600 Us Route 22 E, 07083-3415, pg. 1207

Upper Saddle River

SIGMA GROUP, 10 Mountainview Road, 07458-1933, pg. 1042

Verona

BLOCK & DECORSO, 3 Claridge Dr, 07044-3000, pg. 139

Voorhees

BAROLIN & SPENCER, INC., 1015 Main St, 08043-4602, pg. 94
THE MEDIA & MARKETING GROUP, Vorhees Town Center 220 Laurel Rd, 08043, pg. 741

Wall Township

SAVAGE INITIATIVE, 3502 Windsor Rd, 07719, pg. 1021
SINGLE THROW INTERNET MARKETING, 1800 Route 34 #303, 07719, pg. 1046

Warren

THE SOLUTIONS GROUP INC., 161 Washington Valley Rd Ste 205, 07059-7121, pg. 1058

Washington

GRAPHIC D-SIGNS INC, 279 Rte 31 S Ste 4, 07882, pg. 440

West Caldwell

CCG MARKETING SOLUTIONS, 14 Henderson Dr, 07006-6608, pg. 199
GEMINI STUDIO, 1120 Bloomfield Ave Ste 201, 07006, pg. 420

West Long Branch

LANMARK360, 804 Broadway, 07764, pg. 626

West Orange

WARHAFTIG & LITTMAN ADV/SALES PROMOTION/PR, 24 Clonover Rd, 07052-4304, pg. 1190

West Paterson

BLUE MOON STUDIOS, 86 Lackawanna Ave, 07424, pg. 141

Whitehouse

CI GROUP, 10 Salem Park, 08888, pg. 210
DELIA ASSOCIATES, 456 Route 22 W, 08888-0338, pg. 295

Williamstown

ADAMUS MEDIA, 1035 Black Horse Pike Ste 2, 08094, pg. 25

Woodbridge

SAWTOOTH HEALTH, 100 Woodbridge Ctr Dr Ste 102, 07095, pg. 1022

Woodbury

AVC MEDIA GROUP, 58 S Broad St, 8096, pg. 82
CREATIVE VIDEO, 26 Colonial Ave, 08096, pg. 252

NEW MEXICO

Albuquerque

3 ADVERTISING, 1550 Mercantile Ave NE 2nd Fl, 87107, pg. 5
ALTITUDE AGENCY LLC, 3020 McCoy Pl NE, 87106, pg. 51
EFG CREATIVE INC., 318 Central Ave SE, 87102, pg. 339
ESPARZA ADVERTISING, 423 Cooper Ave NW, 87102, pg. 356
GRIFFIN & ASSOCIATES, 119 Dartmouth Dr SE, 87106, pg. 459
MCKEE WALLWORK & COMPANY, 1030 18th St NW, 87104, pg. 735
MEDIA MATCHED INC, 9798 Coors Blvd NW C-305, 87114, pg. 743
MOROCH, 115 Gold Ave SW Ste 205, 87102, pg. 775
RK VENTURE, 120 Morningside SE, 87108, pg. 985
WRIGHT EDGE ADVERTISING, 2616 Mesilla NE Ste 3, 87110, pg. 1228

Corrales

SPLASH COMMUNICATIONS, LLC, 47 W Valverde Rd, 87048, pg. 1065

Las Cruces

CHEDDAR SOCIAL, 755 S Telshor Ste 202 B, 88011, pg. 206
SINUATE MEDIA, LLC., 2001 E Lohman Ave Ste 110-323, 88001, pg. 1046

Rio Rancho

AD HOUSE ADVERTISING, 918 Pinehurst Rd NE Ste 102, 87124, pg. 22

Santa Fe

HK ADVERTISING, INC., 41 Bisbee Ct Ste A-1, 87508, pg. 517
MIND OVER MARKETS, 7 Owl Creek, 87505, pg. 761

NEW YORK

Albany

BURST MARKETING, 122 Industrial Pk Rd, 12206, pg. 178
COMMUNICATION SERVICES, PO Box 1115, 12201, pg. 226
CREATIVE COMMUNICATION ASSOCIATES, 16 Sage Estate, 12204-2237, pg. 246
ERIC MOWER + ASSOCIATES, 30 S Pearl St Ste 1210, 12207, pg. 353
MEDIA LOGIC, 1 Park Pl, 12205, pg. 742
MILLENNIUM BUSINESS COMMUNICATIONS LLC, 501 New Karner Rd Ste 3, 12205, pg. 757
NOWAK ASSOCIATES, INC, 6 Wembley Ct, 12205, pg. 817
RUECKERT ADVERTISING, 638 Albany Shaker Rd, 12211, pg. 996
SCHAEFER MEDIA & MARKETING, 1659 Central Ave Ste 201, 12205, pg. 1024
WINDSOR PUBLISHING INC., PO Box 8627, 12077, pg. 1209
ZONE 5, 25 Monroe St Ste 300, 12210, pg. 1258

Amherst

PARTNERSHIP ADVERTISING, 11 Pinchot Ct Ste 100, 14228, pg. 876
QUINLAN & COMPANY, 385 N French Rd Ste 106, 14228-2096, pg. 944
VALMARK ASSOCIATES, LLC, 4242 Ridge Lea Rd Ste 5, 14226, pg. 1170

Amityville

CGT MARKETING LLC, 275-B Dixon Ave, 11701, pg. 203

Armonk

EVERETT STUDIOS, 5 N Greenwich Rd, 10504, pg. 359
GOLD N FISH MARKETING GROUP LLC, 53 Old Route 22, 10504, pg. 434
LAKE GROUP MEDIA, INC., 1 Byram Group Pl, 10504, pg. 623

Asbury Park

M STUDIO, 513C Bangs Ave, 7712, pg. 680

Baldwin

WEBNBEYOND, 2280 Grand Ave Ste 314, 11510, pg. 1194

Bayside

COHEN CONSULTING, 1557 216th St, 11360, pg. 220

Binghamton

HUE STUDIOS, 222 Water St Ste 228, 13901, pg. 526
RIGER ADVERTISING AGENCY, INC., 53 Chenango St, 13902, pg. 981

Bronx

SPOT ON, 213 Fordham St, 10464, pg. 1067

Brooklyn

AD LIB UNLIMITED INC, 1507 Ave M, 11230, pg. 22
AD:60, 68 Jay St Unit 616, 11201, pg. 24
AJAX UNION, 2233 Nostrand Ave, 11210, pg. 43
AMERICAN MEDIA CONCEPTS INC., 189 Montague St Ste 801A, 11201-3610, pg. 54
ASHAY MEDIA GROUP, 159 20th St, 11232, pg. 76
THE BAM CONNECTION, 20 Jay St Ste 302, 11201, pg. 89
BIG SPACESHIP, 45 Main St Ste 716, 11201, pg. 131
BLENDERBOX INC., 26 Dobbin St 3rd Fl, 11222, pg. 138
BRALEY DESIGN, 306 E 3rd St, 11218, pg. 154
CARDWELL BEACH, 118 Prospect Park SW #5, 11218, pg. 190
CARROT CREATIVE, 45 Main St, 11201, pg. 193
COMMONWISE, 100 Jay St Unit 12 C, 11201, pg. 225
DEAD AS WE KNOW IT, 51 Cunthair Ave, 11222-3143, pg. 291
DREAMBEAR, LLC, 111 Jewel St, 11222, pg. 327
FANGOHR, LLC, 10 Jay St Ste 408, 11201-1162, pg. 367
FRANK COLLECTIVE, 20 Jay St Ste 638, 11201, pg. 401
HUGE, 45 Main St Ste 220, 11201, pg. 526
HYPERAKT, 401 Smith St, 11231, pg. 530
THE JOEY COMPANY, 45 Main St Ste 632, 11201, pg. 593
LUBICOM MARKETING CONSULTING, 1428 36th St, 11218, pg. 672
LUCKY BRANDED ENTERTAINMENT, 68 Jay St Ste 503, 11201, pg. 673
M SS NG P ECES, 68 Greenpoint Ave Ste 4, 11222, pg. 680
MADWELL, 243 Boerum St, 11206, pg. 685
MAMMOTH ADVERTISING LLC, 45 Main St Ste 1006, 11201, pg. 688
MEDIA ON THE GO LTD., 1088 Bedford Ave, 11216, pg. 743
MILESTONE BROADCAST, 33 Flatbush Ave 4th Fl, 11217, pg. 756
NEW AGE MEDIA, pob 245456, 11224, pg. 806
PLAYGROUND GROUP INC, 18 Bridge St Ste 2D, 11201, pg. 897
SPIKE/DDB, 55 Washington St Ste 650, 11201, pg. 276
STELLAR ENGINE, 67 W St Ste 401, 11222, pg. 1083
STELLARHEAD, 45 Main St Ste 1010, 11201, pg. 1083
STINKDIGITAL, 20 Jay St Ste 404, 11201, pg. 1087
UWG, 1 Metrotech Center N 11th Fl, 11201, pg. 1169

Buffalo

15 FINGERS LLC, 443 Delaware Ave, 14202, pg. 2
ABBEY, MECCA & COMPANY, 95 Perry St, 14203, pg. 16
CARR MARKETING COMMUNICATION, INC., 2372 Sweet Home Rd, 14228, pg. 193
CROWLEY WEBB, 268 Main St Ste 400, 14202-4108, pg. 257
FLYNN & FRIENDS, 437 Franklin St, 14202, pg. 395
FOURTH IDEA, 1109 Delaware Ave, 14209, pg. 400
HAROLD WARNER ADVERTISING, INC., 700 Parkside Ave, 14216, pg. 480
THE MARTIN GROUP, LLC., 487 Main St Ste 200, 14203, pg. 704
PARAGON ADVERTISING, 43 Court St, 14202-3101, pg. 873

Campbell Hall

MEDIA VISION ADVERTISING, 10 Lagrange Rd, 10916, pg. 744

Chester

AJ ROSS CREATIVE MEDIA, INC., 1149 Route 17M, 10918-1466, pg. 42

Cohoes

OBERLANDER GROUP, 143 Remsen St, 12047, pg. 821

Cold Spring

MKTWORKS, INC., 292 Main St, 10516, pg. 766

Cortland

KEEGAN ASSOCIATES, 50 Clinton Ave, 13045, pg. 605

Depew

SKM GROUP, 6350 Transit Rd, 14043, pg. 1050

East Hampton

TEAMNASH, INC., 4 Jonathan Dr, 11937, pg. 1135

East Syracuse

LIGHTHOUSE MARKETING, 5821 Acton St, 13057, pg. 657

Elmira

HOWELL, LIBERATORE & ASSOCIATES, INC., 50 Pennsylvania Ave, 14902, pg. 525

Fairport

MG LOMB ADVERTISING, INC., 1387 Fairport Rd Ste 700, 14450, pg. 752

Farmingdale

LORRAINE GREGORY COMMUNICATIONS, 110 Schmitt Boulevard, 11735, pg. 669
WILEN GROUP, 5 Wellwood Ave, 11735-1213, pg. 1206

Flushing

YAAKOV SERLE ADVERTISING, 147-25 70th Ave, 11367, pg. 1237

Forest Hills

ARAGON ADVERTISING, 7036 Nansen St, 11375, pg. 66

Fulton

STEVE CHIRELLO ADVERTISING, 121 S 1st St, 13069, pg. 1085

Greenville

KATHODERAY MEDIA INC., 20 Country Estates Rd PO Box 545, 12083, pg. 603

Harrison

MILLER ADVERTISING, 84 Calvert St, 10528-3213, pg. 757

Hartsdale

LH ADVERTISING AGENCY INC., 200 N Central Ave Ste 220, 10530, pg. 656
WEBWORKS ALLIANCE, 95 Caterson Ter, 10530, pg. 1194

Hauppauge

AUSTIN & WILLIAMS, 125 Kennedy Dr Ste 100, 11788-4017, pg. 80
INFUSION DIRECT MARKETING & ADVERTISING INC, 350 Motor Pky Ste 410, 11788, pg. 546
WALTER F. CAMERON ADVERTISING INC., 350 Motor Pkwy Ste 410, 11788-5125, pg. 1189

Haverstraw

S.R. VIDEO PICTURES, LTD., 23 S Route 9W, 10927, pg. 1070

Holbrook

CREATIVE IMAGE ADVERTISING & DESIGN, INC., 19 Lindsey Pl, 11741, pg. 249

Huntington

GODIVERSITY, 177 Main St, 11743, pg. 433
KNACK4 DESIGN, INC., 15 Harmon Dr, 11743, pg. 615
ROTTER GROUP INC., 256 Main St 2nd Fl, 11743, pg. 993

SMITH & DRESS LTD., 432 W Main St, 11743, pg. 1053
THINKHOUSE, LLC, 20 Connelly Rd, 11743, pg. 1139

Huntington Bay

NATIONAL MEDIA SERVICES, INC., 91 Summit Dr, 11743, pg. 801

Irvington

LOCKARD & WECHSLER, 2 Bridge St Ste 200, 10533, pg. 666

Ithaca

AMERICAN CONSULTING GROUP, INC., 1329 Taughannock Blvd, 14850, pg. 54

Jericho

BRASHE ADVERTISING, INC., 471 N Broadway, 11753, pg. 162

Kenmore

TRELLIS MARKETING, INC, 127 Doncaster Rd, 14217, pg. 1155

Kingston

JMC MARKETING COMMUNICATIONS & PR, 10 Pearl St, 12401, pg. 592

Lake Placid

AD WORKSHOP, 44 Hadjis Way, 12946, pg. 23

Larchmont

FREE ENERGY MEDIA, 23 Winged Foot Dr, 10538, pg. 403

Liberty

FISHERMEARS ASSOCIATES, LLC, 1830 Rt 52, 12754, pg. 390

Lockport

J. FITZGERALD GROUP, 12 W Main St, 14094, pg. 565

Long Island City

CREATIVE MARKETING PLUS INC., 4705 Center Blvd Ste 806, 11109, pg. 250

Mamaroneck

ROTH PARTNERS LLC, 507 Claflin Ave, 10543, pg. 993

Manlius

RETZ ADVERTISING + DESIGN, 8051 Cazenovia Rd, 13104, pg. 974

Melville

BIGBUZZ MARKETING GROUP, 510 Broadhollow Rd Ste 300, 11747, pg. 132
THE EGC GROUP, 1175 Walt Whitman Rd Ste 200, 11747-3030, pg. 339
GRAHAM & COMPANY ADVERTISING, INC., 510 Broadhollow Rd Ste 301, 11747, pg. 438
HJMT COMMUNICATIONS, LLC, 145 Pinelawn Rd, 11747, pg. 517
LOBO & PETROCINE, INC., 95 Broadhollow Rd Ste D, 11747, pg. 666
PENVINE, 200 Broadhollow Rd Ste 20, 11747, pg. 882
WAXWORDS INCORPORATED, 105 Maxess Rd Ste S124, 11747, pg. 1192

Middle Island

THE LINICK GROUP, INC., Linick Bldg 7 Putter Ln Dept RB08, 11953-0102, pg. 658

Middletown

BBG&G ADVERTISING, 33 Hill Rd, 10941, pg. 117

Mineola

CREATIVE MEDIA AGENCY LLC, 393 Jericho Tpke Ste #300, 11501-1299, pg. 250
HLD COMMUNICATIONS, 330 Old Country Rd Ste 206, 11501, pg. 517
IMPRESSIONS-A.B.A. INDUSTRIES, INC., 393 Jericho Tpk, 11501, pg. 542

Mount Kisco

FLIPPIES, 772 Armonk Rd, 10549, pg. 394

New City

CRAWFORD ADVERTISING ASSOCIATES, LTD., 216 Congers Rd, 10956, pg. 245
THE ROCKFORD GROUP, 216 Congers Rd Bldg 2, 10956, pg. 989

New Hartford

BROCKETT CREATIVE GROUP, INC., 4299 Middle Settlement Rd, 13413, pg. 168

New Rochelle

JODYANDIANE CREATIVE COMMUNICATIONS, LLC, 111 Wood Hollow Ln, 10804, pg. 593
STEINER SPORTS MARKETING, 145 Huguenot St, 10801-6454, pg. 1083

New York

135TH STREET AGENCY, 424 W 33rd St, 10001, pg. 2
31 LENGTHS LLC, 43 W 24th St 7th Fl, 10010, pg. 6
360I, 32 Ave of the Americas 6th Fl, 10013, pg. 6
42WEST, 220 W 42nd St 12th Fl, 10036, pg. 8
72ANDSUNNY, 30 Cooper Square, 10003, pg. 11
77 VENTURES, 122 Hudson St 3rd Fl, 10013, pg. 12
A. LAVIN COMMUNICATIONS, 8 Haven Ave Ste 223, 10001, pg. 14
A PARTNERSHIP, 307 Fifth Ave, 10016, pg. 14
ABOVENATIONMEDIA, 401 Park Ave S, 10016, pg. 17
ABSTRACT EDGE, 455 Broadway 4th Fl, 10013, pg. 17
ACCESS COMMUNICATIONS, 19 Union Sq W 4th Fl, 10003, pg. 19
ACOSTA DESIGN INC, 1201 Broadway 703, 10001, pg. 21
A.D. LUBOW, LLC, 1 Penn Plz Ste 5312, 10119-5312, pg. 22
ADELPHI EDEN HEALTH COMMUNICATIONS, 488 Madison Ave, 10022, pg. 312
ADK AMERICA, 515 W 20th St 6th fl, 10011, pg. 29
ADMARKETPLACE, 3 Park Ave 27th Fl, 10016, pg. 29
ADMERASIA, INC., 159 W 25th St 6th Fl, 10001-7203, pg. 30
ADNET ADVERTISING AGENCY, INC., 111 John St Ste 701, 10038, pg. 30
ADRENALINE- A HAVAS COMPANY, 350 Hudson St, 10014, pg. 487
ADVENTIUM, LLC, 320 E 35th St Ste 5B, 10016, pg. 33
AFFECT STRATEGIES, 989 Ave of the Americas 6th Fl, 10018, pg. 36
AFG&, 1 Dag Hammarskjold Plz 885 2nd Ave, 10017-2205, pg. 36
AGENCY212, LLC, 95 Morton St, 10014, pg. 38
AGENCYRX, 200 Varick St 3rd Fl, 10014, pg. 39
AGENCYSACKS, 345 7th Ave 7th Fl, 10001-5006, pg. 39
AGENDA, 311 W 43rd St Ste 703, 10036, pg. 40
AGNETO COMUNICACAO, 175 Varick St, 10014, pg. 40
AIR PARIS/NEW YORK, 20 W 22nd St 901, 10010, pg. 41
AKA NYC, 630 9th Ave Ste 1411, 10036, pg. 43
ALCHEMY ADVERTISING, 2109 Broadway Ste 1462, 10023, pg. 44
ALLIED ADVERTISING, PUBLIC RELATIONS, 5 Penn Plz 21st Fl, 10001, pg. 48
ALLIED EXPERIENTIAL, 111 E 12 St 2nd Fl, 10003, pg. 47
ALLISON & PARTNERS, 71 5th Ave, 10003, pg. 738
ALLSCOPE MEDIA, 462 7th Ave 8th Fl, 10018, pg. 50
ANALOGFOLK, 13-17 Laight St Unit 602, 10013, pg. 56
AND PARTNERS, 158 W 27th St Fl 7, 10001, pg. 57
THE&PARTNERSHIP, 75 Spring St 2nd Fl, 10012, pg. 57
ANDOSCIA COMMUNICATIONS, 29 King St, 10014, pg. 59
ANDRIA MITSAKOS PUBLIC RELATIONS, 76 9th Ave Ste 1110, 10011, pg. 59
ANOMALY, 536 Broadway 11th Fl, 10012, pg. 60
ANSIBLE MOBILE, 55 5th Ave 16th Fl, 10003, pg. 60
ANTIDOTE 360, 160 Varick St, 10013, pg. 62
APCO WORLDWIDE, 360 Park Ave S, 10010, pg. 64
AR MEDIA, 601 W 26th St Ste 810, 10001, pg. 65
AR NEW YORK, 601 W 26th St No 810, 10001, pg. 66
ARCADE CREATIVE GROUP, 550 Madison Ave 29th Fl, 10022, pg. 66
ARCOS COMMUNICATIONS, 18 E 41St St, 10017, pg. 68
AREA 23, 622 3rd Ave 3rd Fl, 10017, pg. 68
ARNOLDNYC, 205 Hudson St, 10013, pg. 72
ASB COMMUNICATIONS, 247 W 35 th St Ste 16 F, 10001, pg. 75
ASSEMBLY, 909 3rd Ave 31st Fl, 10022, pg. 739
@RADICAL MEDIA, 435 Hudson St, 10014, pg. 77
ATHORN, CLARK & PARTNERS, 38 E 29th St, 10016, pg. 77
ATMOSPHERE PROXIMITY, 1285 Ave of the Americas 5th Fl, 10019, pg. 99
ATTENTION, 160 Varick St 5th Fl, 10013, pg. 79
AUDREY NYC, 205 Hudson St, 10013, pg. 79
AY DIGITAL, 79 Madison Ave Ste 1200, 10016-7802, pg. 84
BADGER & WINTERS, INC., 261 5th Ave 26th Fl, 10016, pg. 86
BANDUJO ADVERTISING & DESIGN, 22 W 21st St 8th Fl, 10010, pg. 89
THE BARBARIAN GROUP, 112 W 20th St, 10011, pg. 90
BARKER/DZP, 455 Broadway, 10013, pg. 92
BARTLEY & DICK, 325 W 38th St Ste 1205, 10018, pg. 96
BARTON F. GRAF 9000 LLC, 60 Madison Ave Ste 201, 10010, pg. 96
BAYARD ADVERTISING AGENCY, INC., 902 Broadway 10th Fl, 10010-6002, pg. 98
BBDO NEW YORK, 1285 Ave of the Americas 7th Fl, 10019-6028, pg. 100
BBDO NORTH AMERICA, 1285 Ave of the Americas, 10019-6028, pg. 98
BBDO WORLDWIDE INC., 1285 Ave of the Americas, 10019-6028, pg. 99
BBH NEW YORK, 32 Avenue of the Americas 19th Fl, 10013, pg. 118
BCA (BRIAN CRONIN & ASSOCIATES INC.), 315 Madison Ave Ste 702, 10017-6503, pg. 118
BDOT, 54 W 40th St, 10018, pg. 119
BEANSTALK, 220 E 42nd St 15th Fl, 10017, pg. 120
BEARDWOOD & CO, 588 Broadway Ste 803, 10012, pg. 120
BEAUTY@GOTHAM, 150 E 42nd St 12th Fl, 10017, pg. 120
BEEKMAN MARKETING, INC., 5 W 19th St, 10011, pg. 122
BEHAVIOR DESIGN, 40 W 27th St Ste 401, 10001, pg. 122
BEING, 488 Madison Ave, 10022, pg. 1114
BERLIN CAMERON UNITED, 100 Ave of the Americas, 10013, pg. 125
BFG COMMUNICATIONS NEW YORK, 665 Broadway 3rd Fl, 10012, pg. 128
BIG ARROW CONSULTING GROUP, LLC, 584 Broadway Ste 1210, 10012, pg. 129
BIG FUEL COMMUNICATIONS LLC, 11 W 19th St, 10011, pg. 130
BIG HUMAN, 51 E 12th St 9th Fl, 10003, pg. 130
BIG IDEA ADVERTISING INC, 6 Maiden Ln, 10038, pg. 130
BIGEYEDWISH LLC, 419 Lafayette St, 10003, pg. 132
BLAST RADIUS, 3 Columbus Cir, 10019, pg. 136
BLEECKER & SULLIVAN ADVERTISING, 214 Sullivan St, 10012, pg. 137
BLISSPR, 500 5th Ave Ste 1010, 10110, pg. 138
THE BLUE FLAME AGENCY, 1710 Bdwy, 10019, pg. 141
BLUE MEDIUM, INC., 20 W 22nd St Ste 807, 10010, pg. 141
BLUE MOON WORKS, INC., 304 Park Ave S 11th Fl, 10010, pg. 141
BLUE SKY COMMUNICATIONS, 900 Broadway Ste 702, 10003, pg. 142
BLUEROCK, 575 Lexington Ave Fl 26, 10022, pg. 143
BLUESOHO, 160 Varick St 2nd Fl, 10013, pg. 143

Newburgh

Northport

Old Chatham

Oneonta

Oswego

Patchogue

Pelham

Penfield

Phoenix

Pittsford

BUSH COMMUNICATIONS, LLC, 3 S Main St, 14534, pg. 178
MARTINO FLYNN LLC, 175 Sully's Trl Ste 100, 14534, pg. 705
MOROCH, 15 Fishers Rd, 14534, pg. 775
PERSUASIVE COMMUNICATIONS, 141 Sullys Trl Ste 9, 14534, pg. 886
QUANTUM COMMUNICATIONS, 33 LePere Dr, 14534, pg. 941
TWIN ADVERTISING, 7 S Main St, 14534, pg. 1164
WALKUP ADVERTISING, 141 Sullys Trl Ste 4, 14534, pg. 1188
THE WESTERFELDS, INC., 30B Grove St, 14534, pg. 1198

Pleasantville

THE HORAH GROUP, 351 Manville Rd #105, 10570, pg. 522

Port Chester

JP MEDIA INC., 149-151 Westchester Ave Ste 22, 10573, pg. 597

Port Jefferson

CREATIVE JUICE ADVERTISING, 1031 Main St, 11777, pg. 249

Port Jervis

NIKI JONES AGENCY, 39 Front St, 12771, pg. 810

Poughkeepsie

KRUTICK ADVERTISING, 7 Hollow Ln, 12603-5018, pg. 619

Rochester

ANTITHESIS ADVERTISING, 72 Cascade Dr, 14614, pg. 62
ARCHER COMMUNICATIONS, INC., 252 Alexander St, 14607-2515, pg. 66
BRAND COOL MARKETING INC, 2300 E Ave, 14610, pg. 155
CATALYST, SCIENCE + SOUL, 110 Marina Dr, 14626, pg. 197
FRONTLINE ADVERTISING, INC., 52 Conmar Dr, 14609, pg. 406
JAY ADVERTISING, INC., 170 Linden Oaks, 14625-2836, pg. 588
MINERVA DESIGN, 274 N Goodman St A403, 14607, pg. 762
PARTNERS+NAPIER, 192 Mill St Ste 600, 14614-1022, pg. 875
ROBERTS COMMUNICATIONS INC., 64 Commercial St, 14614-1010, pg. 987
SIGMA MARKETING GROUP LLC, 1 Cambridge Pl 1850 Winton Rd S, 14618-3923, pg. 1042

Rockville Centre

BLUETOOTH CREATIVE GROUP, INC., 100 Merrick Rd Ste 210 W, 11570, pg. 143
SPORTSBRANDEDMEDIA INC., 8 Rockwin Rd, 11570, pg. 1066

Ronkonkoma

DONALD R. HARVEY, INC., 3555 Veterans Memorial Hwy Ste D, 11779, pg. 322
FRESHBRICK, INC., 761 Koehler Ave, 11779, pg. 405

Rye Brook

BCA MARKETING COMMUNICATIONS, 800 Westchester Ave. N641, 10573, pg. 119
MATTS & DAVIDSON INC., 3 Rye Rdg Plz, 10573, pg. 710
MERITDIRECT, LLC., 2 International Dr, 10573, pg. 749

Saint James

DIRCKS ASSOCIATES, 550 N Country Rd Ste A, 11780-1427, pg. 310

Saratoga Springs

PALIO+IGNITE, 260 Broadway, 12866, pg. 871

Schenectady

POTRATZ PARTNERS ADVERTISING INC., 31 Lafayette St, 12305, pg. 905

Sea Cliff

ROTH ADVERTISING, INC., PO Box 96, 11579-0096, pg. 993

Seaford

ZUCHELLI & JOHNSON HEALTHCARE COMMUNICATIONS, 2873 Ocean Ave, 11783-3455, pg. 1259

Setauket

KZSW ADVERTISING, 19 Bennetts Rd, 11733, pg. 621

Skaneateles

CHASEDESIGN, LLC, 1326 New Seneca Tpk, 13152, pg. 771

Smithtown

LINX COMMUNICATIONS CORP., 155 E Main St 2nd Fl, 11787-2808, pg. 659
SMM ADVERTISING, 811 W Jericho Tpke Ste 109 E, 11787, pg. 1055

South Salem

BLUE CHIP PUBLIC RELATIONS, INC., 14 Canaan Cir, 10590, pg. 140

Stanfordville

MAY SKY, INC., 153 Hunns Lake Rd, 12581, pg. 712

Staten Island

DELEON GROUP, LLC, 20 Kenneth Pl, 10309, pg. 294
THE VON AGENCY INC, 179 Windsor Rd, 10314, pg. 1184

Stony Point

SPECTRUM MARKETING, INC., 48 Jackson Dr, 10980, pg. 1064

Syosset

MILLENNIUM COMMUNICATIONS, INC., 6900 Jericho Tpke Ste 100LL, 11791, pg. 757
SCOTT COOPER ASSOCIATES, LTD., 215 Coachman Place E, 11791, pg. 1026

Syracuse

ABC CREATIVE GROUP, 430 E Genesee St Ste 203, 13202, pg. 16
COWLEY ASSOCIATES, INC., 235 Walton St, 13202, pg. 239
DESIGNWORKS ADVERTISING INC., 109 Twin Oaks Dr, 13206, pg. 301
EMA PUBLIC RELATIONS SERVICES, 211 W Jefferson St, 13202-2561, pg. 353
ERIC MOWER + ASSOCIATES, 211 West Jefferson St., 13202, pg. 353
FIRST MEDIA GROUP INC., 120 E Washington St Ste 721, 13202, pg. 389
LATORRA, PAUL & MCCANN, 120 E Washington St, 13202-4000, pg. 629
NOWAK ASSOCIATES, INC, 6075 E Molloy Bldg 7, 13211, pg. 817
PINCKNEY HUGO GROUP, 760 W Genesee St, 13204-2306, pg. 891
WARNE/MCKENNA ADVERTISING, 110 S Lowell Ave, 13204-2629, pg. 1191

Tarrytown

MSM DESIGNZ INC, 505 White Plains Rd 2nd Fl Ste 204, 10591, pg. 786

Tonawanda

TELESCO CREATIVE GROUP, 1868 Niagara Fls Blvd Ste 200, 14150, pg. 1135

Troy

ID29, 425 River St, 12180, pg. 532
SMITH & JONES, 297 River St, 12180, pg. 1053
WANDERLUST, 297 River St, 12180, pg. 1190

Utica

THE PAIGE GROUP, 258 Genesee St Ste 204, 13502, pg. 870

Valhalla

DELFINO MARKETING COMMUNICATIONS, INC., 400 Columbus Ave Ste 120S, 10595-1396, pg. 294

Valley Cottage

EVE SECO DISPLAY INC., 209 Waters Edge, 10989, pg. 359
KEA ADVERTISING, 217 Rte 303 Ste 1, 10989-2534, pg. 605

Valley Stream

ARTIFAX, 117 Delmonico Pl, 11581, pg. 74
WEBSCOPE, 99 W Hawthorne Ave Ste 420, 11580, pg. 1194

Victor

DIXON SCHWABL ADVERTISING, 1595 Moseley Rd, 14564, pg. 317

Walden

TRONCONE + PARTNERS, 61 Berea Rd, 12586, pg. 1159

Warwick

VELA ADVERTISING, 127 Pine Island Tpke, 10990, pg. 1172

Webster

SUNDANCE MARKETING, LLC, 430 Sundance Trail, 14580, pg. 1099

West Islip

HFB ADVERTISING, INC., 1406 Washington Ave, 11795, pg. 512

White Plains

CARL BLOOM ASSOCIATES, INC., 81 Main St Ste 126, 10601-1711, pg. 191
GRAHAM STANLEY ADVERTISING, 75 S Broadway 4th Fl, 10601, pg. 439
INSPIRIAMEDIA, 10 Mitchell Pl Ste 201, 10601, pg. 549
LITTLE BIG BRANDS, Two William St Ste 303, 10601, pg. 662
RIVER COMMUNICATIONS, INC., 333 Westchester Ave, 10604, pg. 984
SQUEAKYWHEEL PROMOTIONS, 75 S Broadway Ste 400, 10601, pg. 1069

Williamsville

GELIA-MEDIA, INC., 390 S Youngs Rd, 14221, pg. 420

Woodbury

SILVERMAN MEDIA & MARKETING GROUP, INC., 2829 Merrick Rd Ste 115, 11710, pg. 1044

Yonkers

THE COMPUTER STUDIO, 1280 Saw Mill River Rd, 10710-2722, pg. 228

NORTH CAROLINA

Asheville

THE BRITE AGENCY, 29 Montford Ave Ste 200, 28801, pg. 167
ELEMENT ADVERTISING LLC, 1 Tingle Alley, 28801, pg. 342
THE GOSS AGENCY INC., 49 Broadway Ste 202, 28801, pg. 436
I2 MARKETING INC, 120 Coxe Ave Ste 2C, 28801, pg. 531
MARKET CONNECTIONS, 82 Patton Ave Ste 710, 28801, pg. 695

Belmont

LYERLY AGENCY INC., 126 N Main St, 28012, pg. 675

Burlington

ALL PRO MEDIA INC., 422 S Spring St, 27215, pg. 45

Carrboro

THE SPLINTER GROUP, 605 W Main St 201, 27510, pg. 1065

Cary

BROGAN & PARTNERS CONVERGENCE MARKETING, 14600 Western Pkwy Ste 300, 27513, pg. 168
BURKHEAD BRAND GROUP, 5020 Weston Pkwy, 27513, pg. 176
CONTRAST CREATIVE, 2598 Highstone Rd, 27519, pg. 233
HUMMINGBIRD CREATIVE GROUP, 160 NE Maynard Rd Ste 205, 27513, pg. 528
MICROMASS COMMUNICATIONS INC, 11000 Regency Pkwy Ste 300, 27518, pg. 755
R+M, 15100 Weston Pkwy Ste 105, 27513, pg. 947
S&A COMMUNICATIONS, Westview at Weston 301 Cascade Pointe Ln, 27513, pg. 999
SOKAL MEDIA GROUP, 11000 Regency Pkwy Ste 402, 27518, pg. 1057

Chapel Hill

GLYPH INTERFACE, 110 Banks Dr Ste 200, 27514, pg. 430
HEADFIRST CREATIVE, 30150 Walser, 27517, pg. 505
JENNINGS & COMPANY, 104-A N Elliott Rd, 27514, pg. 590
RIVERS AGENCY, 215 Henderson St, 27514, pg. 984
STEELE ROSE COMMUNICATIONS, 12085 Morehead, 27517, pg. 1082

Charlotte

3PM CREATIVE, 1405 Morningside Dr, 28205, pg. 8
ABZ CREATIVE PARTNERS, 1300 S Mint St Ste 100, 28203, pg. 18
ADAMS OUTDOOR ADVERTISING, 1134 N. Graham St, 28231, pg. 25
THE AGENCY MARKETING GROUP, 1440 S Tryon St Ste 106, 28269, pg. 38
THE ALISON GROUP, 1211 Torrence Cir, 28036, pg. 45
BIRDSONG GREGORY, 715 N Church St Ste 101, 28202, pg. 133
BOONEOAKLEY, 1445 S Mint St, 28203, pg. 148
BRANDSYMBOL, 8845 Red Oak Blvd, 28217, pg. 160
CGR CREATIVE, 1930 Abbott St Ste 304, 28203, pg. 202
COMMAND PARTNERS, 310 Arlington Ave 304, 28203, pg. 224
CONCENTRIC MARKETING, 101 W Worthington Ave Ste 108, 28203, pg. 228
CROWN COMMUNICATIONS, 1310 South Tryon St Ste 110, 28202, pg. 257
DOGGETT ADVERTISING, INC., 2137 S Blvd Ste 300, 28203, pg. 321
HERB GROSS & COMPANY, INC., 10000 Gatehouse Ct, 28277-8730, pg. 510
HMH-CHARLOTTE N.C., 1435 W Morehead St Ste 140, 28208, pg. 519
HODGES ADVERTISING INC, 3727 Rose Lake Dr Ste 101, 28217, pg. 519
J.C. THOMAS MARKETING COMMUNICATIONS, 1230 W Morehead St Ste 208, 28208, pg. 588
LIPPI & CO. ADVERTISING, 2820 Selwyn Ave, 28209, pg. 660
LUQUIRE GEORGE ANDREWS, INC., 4201 Congress St Ste 400, 28209, pg. 674
MINDSTORM COMMUNICATIONS GROUP, INC., 10316 Feld Farm Ln Ste 200, 28210, pg. 762
MOONLIGHT CREATIVE GROUP, INC., 930 E Blvd Ste B, 28203, pg. 772
MYJIVE INC, 1000 NC Music Factory Blvd Ste C7, 28206, pg. 798
PINCKNEY MARKETING, INC., 1920 Abbott St Unit 300, 28203, pg. 891
RED MOON MARKETING, 4100 Coca-Cola Plz Ste 215, 28211, pg. 961
REDFONT MARKETING GROUP, 8410 Pit Stop Ct Ste 142, 28027, pg. 964
SATURDAY BRAND COMMUNICATIONS, 1310 S Tryon St Ste 110, 28203, pg. 1021
SELMARQ, 6813 Fairview Rd Ste C, 28210, pg. 1031
SPARK STRATEGIC IDEAS, 6230 Fairview Rd Ste 430, 28210, pg. 1061
TATTOO PROJECTS, 508 W 5th St Ste 225, 28202-1985, pg. 1111
THE THOMPSON AGENCY, 1908 Dilworth Rd E, 28203, pg. 1141
TIVOLI PARTNERS, 2115 Rexford Rd Ste 215, 28211-5453, pg. 1146
TURNING POINT ADVISORS, 310 East Blvd, C10, 28203, pg. 1162
WRAY WARD MARKETING COMMUNICATIONS, 900 Baxter St, 28204, pg. 1228
ZANDER GUINN MILLAN, 831 E Morehead St Ste 660, 28202, pg. 1254

Concord

BARNHARDT, DAY & HINES, 56 Cabarrus Ave W, 28026, pg. 93
PERRY PRODUCTIONS, 602 Dusty Ln, 28027, pg. 885
WALKER MARKETING, INC., 805 Trade St NW Ste 101, 28027, pg. 1187

Cornelius

GINGER GRIFFIN MARKETING & DESIGN, 19109 W Catawba Ave Ste 114, 28031, pg. 426

Denver

DESIGN ONE CREATIVE INC., PO Box 280, 28037, pg. 301

Durham

MCKINNEY, 318 Blackwell St, 27701, pg. 736
MSA: THE THINK AGENCY, 2530 Meridian Pkwy Ste 200, 27713, pg. 785
PAUSBACK ADVERTISING, 3711 Medford Rd, 27705, pg. 879
QUARRY INTEGRATED COMMUNICATIONS USA, 4819 Emperor Blvd Ste 400, 27703-5420, pg. 942
THE REPUBLIK, 211 Rigsbee Ave, 27701, pg. 969

Fayetteville

HODGES ASSOCIATES, INC., 912 Hay St, 28305-5314, pg. 519
THE WRIJEN COMPANY, 225 Green St Ste 1007-C, 28301, pg. 1229

Fuquay Varina

GALVANEK & WAHL LLC, 842 New Charleston Dr, 27526, pg. 414

Gastonia

SUMNER GROUP, 223 W Main Ave Ste F, 28052-4104, pg. 1099

Greensboro

BLUEZOOM, 230 S Elm St Ste B, 27401, pg. 143
BOUVIER KELLY INC., 212 S Elm St Ste 200, 27401-2631, pg. 151
THE BURRIS AGENCY, INC., 1175 Revolution Mill Dr Ste 11, 27405, pg. 177
KINGS ENGLISH LLC, 335 S Davie St, 27401, pg. 613
TARGETBASE, 202 CentrePort Dr Ste 400, 27409, pg. 1110

Greenville

ADAMS & LONGINO ADVERTISING, INC., 605 Lynndale Ct Ste F, 27858, pg. 24
EVOLVE, INC., 1210 E Arlington Blvd, 27858, pg. 360
INTANDEM INC., 1302 E Firetower Rd, 27858, pg. 550

Hickory

ALLEN FINLEY ADVERTISING, INC., 42 Third St NW, 28601-6135, pg. 47
INFORM, INC., 415 1st Ave NW, 28601, pg. 545
SPHERE ADVERTISING, 940 Tate Blvd SE Ste 107, 28602, pg. 1064

High Point

KEMP ADVERTISING & MARKETING, 3001 N Main St, 27265, pg. 608
REDDING COMMUNICATIONS LLC, 1325 N Main St, 27262, pg. 964
TRONE BRAND ENERGY, INC., 1823 Eastchester Dr Ste A, 27265, pg. 1159

Holly Springs

919 MARKETING COMPANY, 102 Avent Ferry Rd, 27540, pg. 12

Huntersville

CLEAR BLUE INC., 16740 Birkdale Commons Pkwy Ste 210, 28078, pg. 215
COX GROUP, 16315 Northcross Dr Ste F, 28078, pg. 239
MY CREATIVE TEAM, INC., 13315 Willow Breeze Ln, 28078, pg. 798
OCTAGON, 10115 Kincey Ave Ste 210, 28078, pg. 823
PLANET CENTRAL, 16740 Birkdale Commons Pkwy Ste 206, 28078, pg. 896

Kernersville

DANA COMMUNICATIONS, 5690 Bromley Dr, 27284, pg. 265

Lenoir

E.B. WALL + ASSOCIATES, 1520 Harper Ave NW, 28645, pg. 336

Lexington

THE MEDIA MATTERS INC, PO Box 1442, 27293, pg. 743

Manteo

OUTER BANKS MEDIA, 102 Old Tom St Ste 205, 27954, pg. 866

Matthews

BURRIS CREATIVE INC, 325 Matthews-Mint Hill Rd Ste

204, 28105, pg. 178
OPUS 59 CREATIVE GROUP, 250 N Trade St Ste 209, 28105, pg. 863

Morehead City

BELLAGURL, 809 Arendell St, 28557, pg. 123

New Bern

HIGH TIDE CREATIVE, 245 Craven St, 28560, pg. 513
VIAMARK ADVERTISING, 233 Middle St Ste 212, 28560, pg. 1176

Raleigh

ABLE&CO, 8801 Fast Park Dr Ste 115, 27617, pg. 17
ANOROC AGENCY, 620 NW St, 27603, pg. 60
BALDWIN&, 135 N Harrington St, 27603-1719, pg. 88
BRASCO DESIGN + MARKETING, 305 W Martin St, 27601, pg. 162
BROOKS BELL INTERACTIVE, 711 Hillsborough St, 27603, pg. 169
BUSINESS-TO-BUSINESS MARKETING COMMUNICATIONS, 900 Ridgefield Dr Ste 270, 27609-8524, pg. 178
CLEAN DESIGN, INC., 8081 Arco Corporate Dr Ste 100, 27617, pg. 214
CLICKCULTURE, 3600 Glenwood Ave, 27612, pg. 215
CRITTENDEN ADVERTISING, 1111 Haynes St Ste 205, 27604, pg. 255
ECKEL & VAUGHAN, 706 Hillsborough St Ste 102, 27603, pg. 337
FRENCH/WEST/VAUGHAN, INC., 112 E Hargett St, 27601, pg. 404
HOWARD, MERRELL & PARTNERS, INC., 4800 Falls of Neuse Rd, 27609, pg. 525
INTREPID MARKETING GROUP, 6500 Creedmoor Rd Ste 216, 27613, pg. 558
MARKET FORCE, INC., 109 N Boylan Ave, 27603, pg. 695
MEDIA TWO INTERACTIVE, 111 E Hargett St Ste 200, 27601, pg. 743
MEDTHINK COMMUNICATIONS, 3301 Benson Dr Ste 400, 27609, pg. 745
MOROCH, 5400 Glenwood Ave Ste G05, 27612, pg. 775
MSA MARKETING, 5511 Capital Ctr Dr Ste 105, 27606, pg. 785
PETRIE CREATIVE, 715 W Johnson St Ste 101, 27603, pg. 887
POINTER ADVERTISING LLC, 204 Longneedle Ct, 27603, pg. 900
SALLY JOHNS DESIGN, 1040 Washington St, 27605, pg. 1015
SIGNAL INC., 7780 Brier Creek Pkwy Ste 415, 27617, pg. 1042
THE STONE AGENCY, 312 W Millbrook Rd Ste 225, 27609, pg. 1088
VITALINK, 10809 Cokesbury Ln, 27614, pg. 1179
WINFIELD & ASSOCIATES MARKETING & ADVERTISING, 3221 Blue Ridge Rd Ste 105, 27612, pg. 1209

Rocky Mount

CARNEY & CO., 1653 N Winstead Ave, 27804-7398, pg. 192
LEWIS ADVERTISING, INC., 1050 Country Club Rd, 27804, pg. 655

Sanford

MOTTIS, 131 Charlotte Ave Ste 201, 27330, pg. 780

Swepsonville

REFLECTIVE DIGITAL SOLUTIONS, PO Box 217, 27359, pg. 966

Wake Forest

CONNECT2 COMMUNICATIONS, 3211 Rogers Rd Ste 200, 27587, pg. 230
EMERY ADVERTISING, 4213 Bay Laurel Ct, 27587, pg. 346
THE SIGNATURE AGENCY, 1784 Heritage Center Dr, 27587, pg. 1043

Wilmington

COLONIAL MARKETING GROUP INC., 813 S 16th St, 28401, pg. 223
EVANS MEDIA GROUP, 341 S College Rd #11, 28403, pg. 358
ILM MARKETING, 225 S Water St Ste M, 28401, pg. 537
INSPIRE CREATIVE STUDIOS, St George Technology Bldg, 28405, pg. 549
LUNA AD, 116 Princess St, 28401, pg. 674
MAXIMUM DESIGN & ADVERTISING, 7032 Wrightsville Ave Ste 201, 28403, pg. 711
MORVIL ADVERTISING & DESIGN GROUP, 1409 Audubon Blvd Ste B3, 28403, pg. 778
PLAN A ADVERTISING, 3722 Shipyard Blvd Ste C, 28403, pg. 896
SAGE ISLAND, 1638 Military Cutoff Rd, 28403, pg. 1014
SWEENEY, 201 N Front St Ste 904, 28401, pg. 1103
TALK, INC., PO Box 987, 28402, pg. 1108
TAYLOE GRAY KRISTOF LLC, 221 N 2nd St, 2840, pg. 1112

Winston Salem

FRANK ABOUT WOMEN, 101 N Cherry St Ste 600, 27101, pg. 400
GARAGE BRANDING, 410 W 4th St Ste 100, 27101, pg. 414
IMG COLLEGE, 540 North Trade St, 27101, pg. 541
KEYSTONE MARKETING, 709 N Main St, 27101, pg. 610
MULLEN LOWE, 101 N Cherry St Ste 600, 27101-4035, pg. 788
REUBEN RINK, 939 Burke St Ste A, 27101, pg. 974
SFW AGENCY, 210 S Cherry St, 27101-5231, pg. 1035
THE VARIABLE AGENCY, 823 Reynolda Rd, 27104, pg. 1171
VELA AGENCY, 315 N Spruce St Ste 215, 27101, pg. 1172
WILDFIRE LLC, 709 N Main St, 27101, pg. 1206

NORTH DAKOTA

Bismarck

KK BOLD, 505 E Main Ave Ste 250 PO Box 693, 58502-4412, pg. 614
MARKETING & ADVERTISING BUSINESS UNLIMITED, INC., 1003 Gateway Ave, 58503, pg. 696
ODNEY, 1400 W Century Ave, 58503, pg. 824

Fargo

ADFARM, 101 N 10th St Ste 110, 58102, pg. 28
FLINT COMMUNICATIONS, 101 10th St N, 58102, pg. 393
ODNEY ADVERTISING-FARGO, 102 Broadway, 58102, pg. 825
SUNDOG, 2000 44th St SW 6th Fl, 58103, pg. 1100

Grand Forks

SIMMONSFLINT, 33 S Third St Ste D, 58201, pg. 394

Minot

ODNEY ADVERTISING-MINOT, 21 Main St S, 58701, pg. 825

West Fargo

IRONCLAD MARKETING, PO Box 733, 58078, pg. 561

OHIO

Akron

ANTHONY THOMAS ADVERTISING, 380 S Main St, 44311, pg. 62
ARRAY CREATIVE, 1 S Main St Ste 601, 44308, pg. 73
ELEVENTY GROUP, 453 S High St, 44311, pg. 344
GEOMETRY GLOBAL, 388 S Main St, 44311, pg. 421
HITCHCOCK FLEMING & ASSOCIATES, INC., 500 Wolf Ledges Pkwy, 44311-1022, pg. 516
KLEIDON & ASSOCIATES, 320 Springside Dr, 44333, pg. 614
WHITESPACE CREATIVE, 24 N High St Ste 200, 44308, pg. 1200

Aurora

CHARENE CREATIVE, 965 Centerville Trl, 44202, pg. 204

Avon

BFL MARKETING COMMUNICATIONS INC., 1399 Lear Indus Pkwy, 44011, pg. 128

Beachwood

THE KING GROUP, 25550 Chagrin Blvd, 44122, pg. 612
POINT TO POINT INC., 23240 Chagrin Blvd Ste 200, 44122, pg. 900

Beavercreek

FAHLGREN MORTINE (DAYTON), 4380 Buckeye Ln Ste 210, 45440, pg. 365

Bellbrook

CONCEPT COMPANY, INC., 2011 S. Lakeman Dr. #A, 45305, pg. 229

Berea

KIWI CREATIVE, 611 W Bagley Rd, 44017, pg. 614
SONNHALTER, 633 W Bagley Rd, 44017-1356, pg. 1058

Boardman

PRODIGAL MEDIA COMPANY, 42 Mcclurg Rd, 44512, pg. 911

Canfield

IM IMAGE MARKETING, 2979 Whispering Pines Dr, 44406, pg. 537

Canton

HEYWOOD FORMATICS & SYNDICATION, 1103 Colonial Blvd NE, 44714-1837, pg. 511
INNIS MAGGIORE GROUP, INC., 4715 Whipple Ave NW, 44718-2651, pg. 547
JAB ADVERTISING, 203 Market Ave S Ste 212, 44702, pg. 582
WRL ADVERTISING, INC., 4470 Dressler Rd NW, 44718-2716, pg. 1229

Centerville

DAVID K. BURNAP ADVERTISING AGENCY, INC., 36 S Main St, 45458, pg. 268

Cincinnati

AIM STRAIGHT UP, 222 E 14th St, 45202, pg. 40
AMPLE, LLC, 200 W 4th St 5th Fl, 45202, pg. 56
ANIMAL INSTINCT ADVERTISING, 2124 Madison Rd Ste 3F, 45208, pg. 59
ANTHEM WORLDWIDE, 537 E Pete Rose Way Ste 100, 45202-3578, pg. 62
BAREFOOT PROXIMITY, 700 W Pete Rose Way, 45203, pg. 91
COREY AIRPORT SERVICES, Cincinnatti / Northern Kentucky International Airport, 45275, pg. 236
THE CREATIVE DEPARTMENT, 1209 Sycamore St, 45202, pg. 247
CREATIVE DIMENSIONS, 4555 Lake Forest Dr Ste 650, 45242, pg. 247
CURIOSITY ADVERTISING, 221 E 4th St, 45202, pg. 260
E3 LOCAL MARKETING, 2601 Malsbary Rd, 45242, pg. 335
EPSILON, 445 Lake Forest Dr Ste 200, 45242, pg. 352
FAHLGREN MORTINE (CINCINNATI), 414 Walnut St Ste 1006, 45202, pg. 365

FORZA MARKETING, 313 W 4th St, 45202, pg. 399
FRCH DESIGN WORLDWIDE, 311 Elm St Ste 600, 45202, pg. 402
GIAMBRONE + PARTNERS, 5177 Salem Hills Ln, 45230, pg. 424
GYRO CINCINNATI, 7755 Montgomery Rd Ste 300, 45236, pg. 469
HOLLAND ADVERTISING:INTERACTIVE, 8040 Hosbrook Rd, 45236, pg. 520
HYPERQUAKE, 205 W Fourth St Ste 1010, 45202, pg. 530
IDEOPIA, 4270 Ivy Pointe Blvd Ste 120, 45245, pg. 535
IDEOPIA MEDICAL MARKETING, 4270 Ivy Pointe Blvd Ste 120, 45245, pg. 535
INTERBRAND, 4000 Smith Rd, 45209, pg. 551
KILLERSPOTS, 463 Ohio Pke Ste 102, 45255, pg. 611
LANDOR ASSOCIATES, 110 Shillito Pl, 45202-2361, pg. 625
LAVERDAD MARKETING & MEDIA, 7817 Cooper Rd, 45242, pg. 632
LOHRE & ASSOCIATES, INCORPORATED, 126A W 14th St, 45202, pg. 667
LPK, 19 Garfield Pl, 45202, pg. 671
MATTER CREATIVE GROUP, 308 E 8th St 3rd Fl, 45202, pg. 710
NORTHLICH, Sawyer Point Bldg 720 E Pete Rose Way, 45202, pg. 815
NORTHLICH PUBLIC RELATIONS, 720 E Pete Rose Way Ste 120, 45202-3579, pg. 815
OPENFIELD CREATIVE, 1 W 4th St 25th Fl, 45202, pg. 862
PIXELS & DOTS LLC, 3181 Linwood Ave, 45208, pg. 894
POWERHOUSE FACTORIES, 1111 St Gregory St, 45202, pg. 906
POWERS AGENCY, 1 W 4th St 5th Fl, 45202-3623, pg. 907
RED212, 5509 Fair Lane, 45227, pg. 963
SANGER & EBY, 501 Chestnut St, 45203, pg. 1017
THE ST. GREGORY GROUP, INC., 9435 Waterstone Blvd, 45249, pg. 1071
SUNRISE ADVERTISING, 700 Walnut St Ste 500, 45202, pg. 1100
TCAA, 4555 Lk Forest Dr Ste 550, 45242-3792, pg. 1133
WEB STRATEGY PLUS, 201 E Fifth St Ste 1900-1008, 45202, pg. 1193

Cleveland

THE ADCOM GROUP, 1370 W Sixth St 3rd Fl, 44113-1222, pg. 27
ALLIED INTEGRATED MARKETING, 1846 Coventry Rd Ste 300, 44118, pg. 49
AMG MARKETING RESOURCES INC., 2530 Superior Ave Ste 601, 44114, pg. 55
ARRAS KEATHLEY AGENCY, 1151 N Marginal Rd, 44114, pg. 73
BOONDOCK WALKER, 3635 Perkins Ave Ste 6A, 44114, pg. 148
BROKAW INC., 425 W Lakeside Ave, 44113-1029, pg. 169
CONSOLIDATED SOLUTIONS, 1614 E 40th St, 44103, pg. 232
DALLAS RIFFLE MEDIA, 3030 E 63rd St Ste 404, 44127, pg. 264
THE DAVID GROUP INC., 526 Superior Ave E Ste 333, 44114-1983, pg. 268
DIX & EATON, 200 Public Sq Ste 3900, 44114, pg. 316
DONER, The Diamond Bldg 1100 Superior Ave 10th Fl, 44114, pg. 323
DONER, The Diamond Bldg 1100 Superior Ave 10th Fl, 44114, pg. 740
FLOURISH INC., 1001 Huron Rd E Ste 102, 44115-1755, pg. 394
GO MEDIA, 4507 Lorain Ave, 44102, pg. 431
INSIVIA, 5000 Euclid Ave, 44103, pg. 549
KNUDSEN, GARDNER & HOWE, INC., 2103 Saint Clair Ave NE, 44114-4018, pg. 616
LINEAR CREATIVE LLC, 4681 Hinckley Pkwy, 44019, pg. 658
MARCUS THOMAS LLC, 4781 Richmond Rd, 44128, pg. 693
MARKETING DIRECTIONS, INC., 28005 Clemens Rd, 44145, pg. 697
NAS RECRUITMENT INNOVATION, 9700 Rockside Rd Ste 170, 44125, pg. 800
OCTOBER-DESIGN, PO Box 38046, 44138, pg. 824
PARTNERSRILEY, 1375 Euclid Ave Ste 410, 44115, pg. 877
PUMPHREY MARKETING, INC., 4853 Galaxy Pkwy Ste A, 44128-5939, pg. 937
RECESS CREATIVE LLC, 635 W Lakeside Ave Ste 101, 44113, pg. 959
R.H. BLAKE, INC., 26600 Renaissance Pkwy, 44128-5773, pg. 976
ROSETTA, 3700 Park East Dr Ste 300, 44122, pg. 992
SAMPSON/CARNEGIE, CO., INC., 1419 E. 40th St, 44103, pg. 1015
SINGLETON & PARTNERS, LTD., 740 W Superior Ave, 44113, pg. 1046
STERN ADVERTISING, INC., 950 Main Ave, 44113, pg. 1085
STUDIOTHINK, 1301 E 9th St, 44114, pg. 1094
SWEENEY, 19106 Old Detroit Rd, 44116, pg. 1103
TORCH GROUP, 30675 Solon Rd Ste 102, 44139-2942, pg. 1151
TWIST CREATIVE INC., 2306 W 17th St Ste 3, 44113, pg. 1164
VISION MEDIA & MARKETING LLC, 2310 Superior Ave E Ste 2501, 44114, pg. 1178
WYSE, 668 Euclid Ave, 44114, pg. 1235
ZIG MARKETING, 812 Huron Rd, 44115, pg. 1256

Columbus

ADVANTAGE MEDIA LLC, 2602 Oakstone Dr Ste 1, 43231, pg. 33
BURKHOLDER/FLINT, 300 Spruce St Ste 275, 43215, pg. 177
CARING MARKETING SOLUTIONS, 781 Northwest Blvd, 43212, pg. 191
CIVITASNOW, 65 E Gay St Ste 210, 43215, pg. 212
CONRAD, PHILLIPS & VUTECH, INC., 1398 Goodale Blvd, 43212, pg. 232
EMERGING MARKETING, 29 W 3rd Ave, 43201, pg. 346
FAHLGREN MORTINE, 4030 Easton Sta Ste 300, 43219, pg. 364
FECHTOR ADVERTISING LLC, 145 N High St Ste 500, 43215, pg. 383
FITCH, 585 S front st Ste 50, 43215, pg. 390
GATEHOUSE MEDIA PARTNERS, 32 W Hoster St Ste 250, 43215, pg. 417
HERB GILLEN AGENCY, 1953 S Mallway Ave, 43221, pg. 510
HGA INC, 300 Marconi Blvd 3rd Fl, 43215, pg. 512
IBEL AGENCY, 1055 N High St, 43201, pg. 531
MADISON & FIFTH, 5 E Long St 8th Fl, 43215, pg. 685
MEYER BENNETT CREATIVE, 2109 W 5th Ave Ste F, 43212, pg. 752
MURPHYEPSON, INC., 151 E Nationwide Blvd, 43215, pg. 796
NORTHLICH-COLUMBUS, 580 N 4th St Ste 660, 43215, pg. 815
OLOGIE, 447 E Main St, 43215, pg. 855
PAUL WERTH ASSOCIATES, INC., 10 N High St Ste 300, 43215-3552, pg. 878
PIERCE COMMUNICATIONS, INC., 208 E State St, 43215-4311, pg. 890
RMD ADVERTISING, 6116 Cleveland Ave, 43231, pg. 985
ROBERT FLEEGE & PARTNERS, 340 Howland Dr, 43230, pg. 986
RON FOTH ADVERTISING, 8100 N High St, 43235-6400, pg. 990
SBC ADVERTISING, 333 W Nationwide Blvd, 43215, pg. 1023
SEVELL+SEVELL, INC., 939 N High St, 43201, pg. 1034
THE SHIPYARD, 580 North 4th St Ste 500, 43215, pg. 1038
SUMMERFIELD ADVERTISING INC., 939 N High St Ste 207, 43201, pg. 1098
TREETREE, 444 N Front St Unit 101, 43215, pg. 1155

Dayton

BERRY NETWORK, INC., 3100 Kettering Blvd, 45439, pg. 127
CHISANO MARKETING GROUP, 2000 Old Byers Rd, 45342, pg. 209
EASTPOINT GROUP, 7601 Paragon Rd Ste 300, 45459, pg. 336
HAFENBRACK MARKETING & COMMUNICATIONS, 15 W 4th St Ste 410, 45402, pg. 472
INTERBRAND DESIGN FORUM, 7575 Paragon Rd, 45459-5316, pg. 551
MARKETING OPTIONS, LLC, 7965 Washington Woods Dr, 45459, pg. 698
NOVA CREATIVE GROUP, INC., 571 Congress Park Dr, 45459-4036, pg. 817
THE OHLMANN GROUP, 1605 N Main St, 45405-4141, pg. 854
OIA MARKETING COMMUNICATIONS, 4240 Wagner Rd, 45440, pg. 854
TDH MARKETING COMMUNICATIONS INC., 8153 Garnett Dr, 45458, pg. 1134
TRICOMB2B, 109 N Main St Ste 700, 45402, pg. 1157
YECK BROTHERS COMPANY, 2222 Arbor Blvd, 45439-1522, pg. 1237

Delaware

BRAD RITTER COMMUNICATIONS, 3801 Olentangy River Rd, 43015, pg. 153

Dover

GRANTSTREET CREATIVE, 137 E Iron Ave 2nd Fl, 44622, pg. 439

Dublin

BRAVURA ADVERTISING & DESIGN, 6209 Riverside Dr Ste 100, 43017, pg. 162
GWA COMMUNICATIONS, INC., 5200 Upper Metro Pl Ste 110, 43017-5378, pg. 467
PEEBLES CREATIVE GROUP, 6209 Riverside Dr Ste 200, 43017, pg. 882

Findlay

MEDIALINKS ADVERTISING, 101 E Sandusky St Ste 322, 45840, pg. 744

Galena

REDROCKET CONNECT LLC, 1095 Forsyth Ln, 43021, pg. 965

Geneva

LITTLE L COMMUNICATIONS, PO Box 63, 44041, pg. 662

Granville

REVLOCAL, 4009 Columbus Rd SW Ste 222, 43023, pg. 975

Grove City

ORANGE BARREL, 3400 SW Blvd, 43123, pg. 863

Groveport

BAKER CREATIVE, 386 Main St, 43125, pg. 87

Independence

LINKMEDIA 360, Summit 1 4700 Rockside Rd Ste 310, 44131-2148, pg. 659

Kent

IDEABASE, 138 E Main St Ste 203, 44240, pg. 534

Kettering

STEPHENS DIRECT, 417 E Stroop Rd, 45429, pg. 1084

Lakewood

ROSENBERG ADVERTISING, 12613 Detroit Ave, 44107, pg. 992

Lewis Center

ACCELERATOR ADVERTISING INC., 399 Venture Dr Ste A, 43035, pg. 18

Lima

FOLLOW THE EYES, PO Box 717, 45802, pg. 396

Mansfield

D&S CREATIVE COMMUNICATIONS INC., 140 Park Ave E, 44902-1830, pg. 262

Mason

CREATIVE STORM, 7588 Central Parke Blvd, 45040, pg. 252

Massillon

E-B DISPLAY CO., INC., 1369 Sanders Ave SW, 44647-7632, pg. 334

Maumee

HART ASSOCIATES, INC., 1915 Indian Wood Cir, 43537-4002, pg. 481

Mentor

MARSHFIELD GROUP, 9025 Osborne Dr, 44060, pg. 702

Miamisburg

POLARIS RECRUITMENT COMMUNICATIONS, 13 E Central Ave Ste 100, 45342, pg. 902
SOURCELINK, 3303 W Tech Rd, 45342, pg. 1060

New Albany

ROCKETCREATIVE, 6097 Mapleton Dr, 43054, pg. 989

Niles

CORLISS MARKETING COMMUNICATIONS, 303 Lincoln Ave, 44446, pg. 236

North Canton

COVEY-ODELL ADVERTISING LTD., 330 Schneider St SE, 44720-3652, pg. 238
CROWL, MONTGOMERY & CLARK, 713 S Main St, 44720, pg. 257

North Ridgeville

JAEGER, INC., 8981 Timberedge Dr, 44039, pg. 585

Ottawa

GIESKEN OUTDOOR ADVERTISING, 115 Sophia's Lane, 45875, pg. 425

Perrysburg

LESNIEWICZ ASSOCIATES LLC, 500 E Front St, 43551-2134, pg. 652
STADIUM AGENCY, W 2nd St, 43551, pg. 1072

Ravenna

LEGAN ADVERTISING AGENCY, 5281 Hayes Rd, 44266, pg. 635

Russell

RICHARDS, 8350 Whispering Pines Dr, 44072-9591, pg. 978

Sandusky

MARK ADVERTISING AGENCY, INC., 1600 5th St, 44870, pg. 694

Sidney

BEHR DESIGN, LLC, 114 E Poplar St, 45365, pg. 123

Solon

GOLDSTEIN GROUP COMMUNICATIONS, 30500 Solon Industrial Pkwy, 44139, pg. 434

Steubenville

EM MEDIA INC, 2728 Sunset Blvd, 43952, pg. 345

Strongsville

RADIUS ADVERTISING, 10883 Pearl Rd Ste 100, 44136, pg. 949

Toledo

COMMUNICA, INC., 31 N Erie St, 43604, pg. 225
FAHLGREN MORTINE (TOLEDO), One Seagate Ste 901, 43604, pg. 365
WENDT ROTSINGER KUEHNLE, INC., 3450 W Central Ave Ste 374, 43606-1416, pg. 1197

Twinsburg

GO2 ADVERTISING, 2265 E Enterprise Pkwy, 44087, pg. 431

Wakeman

YARRUM MARKETING, INC., 5761 Ferry Rd, 44889, pg. 1237

Westerville

AUDIENCE SCAN, 600 N Cleveland Ave Ste 260, 43082, pg. 79
GSW WORLDWIDE, 500 Olde Worthington Rd, 43082, pg. 465

Westlake

STEVENS STRATEGIC COMMUNICATIONS, INC., Gemini Towers, Ste 500, 1991 Crocker Rd, 44115-1900, pg. 1085

Whitehouse

EVENTIV (MARKETING, DESIGN & DISPLAY), 10116 Blue Creek N, 43571, pg. 359

Willoughby

MEDIA II, INC., 2778 SOM Center Rd Ste 200, 44094, pg. 742

Worthington

MARKETING WORKS, INC., 740 Lakeview Plz Blvd Ste 100, 43085, pg. 699

Yellow Springs

BRIDGE STRATEGIC COMMUNICATIONS, 321 N Walnut St, 45387, pg. 164

Zoar

WHITEMYER ADVERTISING, INC., 254 E 4th St, 44697, pg. 1200
ZOAR INTERACTIVE, 254 E 4th St, 44697, pg. 1200

OKLAHOMA

Broken Arrow

THE C3 GROUP, PO Box 141061, 74014, pg. 182

Norman

ENYE MEDIA, LLC, 301 1/2 E Main St, 73069, pg. 349
MCMAHON MARKETING, 413 N Flood Ave, 73069, pg. 737

Oklahoma City

ACKERMAN MCQUEEN, INC., 1100 The Tower 1601 NW Expy, 73118, pg. 20
BEALS CUNNINGHAM STRATEGIC SERVICES, 2333 E Britton Rd, 73131-3526, pg. 120
BOILING POINT MEDIA, 100 W Wilshire Blvd Ste C2, 73116, pg. 146
BRIDGES ADVERTISING LLC, 5350 S Western Ave Ste 100, 73109, pg. 164
THE CUMMINGS GROUP, 1105 NW 44th St, 73118, pg. 259
FORZA STUDIOS INC, 1322A N Robinson, 73103, pg. 399
FRATERNITY ADVERTISING, 2301 W I 44 Service Rd, 73112, pg. 402
INSIGHT CREATIVE GROUP, 19 NE 9th St, 73104, pg. 549
JORDAN ASSOCIATES, 3111 Quail Springs Pkwy Ste 200, 73134-2625, pg. 597
KRUSH DIGITAL ADVERTISING AGENCY, 5408 NW 135th StSte B, 73012, pg. 619
LIQUIDFISH, 401 E California Ave Ste 201, 73104, pg. 661
MOROCH, 301 NW 63rd Ste 690, 73116, pg. 776
SKYLINE MEDIA GROUP, 5823 Mosteller Dr, 73112, pg. 1050
STAPLEGUN, 204 N Robinson Ste 2000, 73102, pg. 1073
THIRD DEGREE ADVERTISING, 501 N Walker Ave, 73102, pg. 1140
VI MARKETING & BRANDING, 125 Park Ave Ste 200, 73102, pg. 1175

Tulsa

ACKERMAN MCQUEEN, INC., 320 S Boston Ste 100, 74103-3706, pg. 20
ACROBATANT, 1336 E 15th St, 74120, pg. 21
BLUEVIEW AGENCY, 1306 S Denver, 74119, pg. 143
BROTHERS & CO., 4860 S Lewis Ave Ste 100, 74105-5171, pg. 170
CUBIC, 1643 S Boston Ave, 74119, pg. 259
HAMPTON CREATIVE, 3939 S Harvard Ave Ste 204, 74135, pg. 477
HUMPHREY ASSOCIATES INC, 233 S Detroit Ste 201, 74120, pg. 528
IN HOUSE ADVERTISING, 8946 S Erie Ave, 74137, pg. 543
J. WALTER THOMPSON U.S.A., INC., 7666 E 61st St Ste 130, 74145, pg. 581
LIGHTQUEST MEDIA INC, 7666 E 61st St Ste 120, 74133, pg. 657
LITTLEFIELD BRAND DEVELOPMENT, 1350 S Boulder Ave Ste 500, 74119-3214, pg. 663
MATCHA DESIGN LLC, 3513 S Richmond Ave, 74135, pg. 709
PINEAPPLE ADVERTISING, 6304 E 102 St S, 74133, pg. 892
PROLIFIC CREATIVE AGENCY, 2510 E 15th St Ste 201, 74104, pg. 913
REX PUBLIC RELATIONS, 1632 S Denver Ave, 74119, pg. 976

OREGON

Ashland

HIGLEY DESIGN, 389 Taylor St, 97520, pg. 514

Beaverton

EPIQ SYSTEMS, INC., 10300 SW Allen Blvd, 97005-4833, pg. 350

Bend

DELICIOUS DESIGN, 547 SW 13th St Ste 201, 97702, pg. 295
DVA ADVERTISING, 109 NW Greenwood Ave Ste 103, 97701, pg. 333
EVERY IDEA MARKETING, 355 NE Lafayette Ave, 97701, pg. 360
HMH, 19797 Village Office Ct, 97702, pg. 519
MANDALA, 2855 NW Crossing Dr Ste 201, 97701-2744, pg. 689
PNEUMA33, 61533 American Loop Ste 12, 97702, pg. 899
TBD, 1000 NW Wall St Ste 201, 97701, pg. 1113

MI DIGITAL AGENCY, 557 Main St, 18018, pg. 754
STIEGLER, WELLS, BRUNSWICK & ROTH, INC., 3865 Adler Pl, 18017-9000, pg. 1086

Bloomsburg

AB+C, 29 E Main St Ste R, 17815, pg. 15

Blue Bell

ANNODYNE, INC., 751 Arbor Way, 19422, pg. 60
BULLDOZER DIRECT, 794 Penllyn Blue Bell Pke Ste 219, 19422, pg. 174
COLISEUM COMMUNICATIONS, 585 Skippack Pk SAte 310, 19422, pg. 221
TANDEM ASSOCIATES, 350 Sentry Pkwy Bldg 610, 19422, pg. 1109

Bridgeville

HIGHER IMAGES INC., 300 Bursca Dr 301, 15017, pg. 513

Bryn Mawr

REALTIME MEDIA, INC., 40 Morris Ave Ste 300, 19010-3300, pg. 958

Carlisle

BURN CREATIVE, 17 E High St, 17015, pg. 177

Chester Springs

NORTHLIGHT ADVERTISING, 1208 Kimberton Rd, 19425, pg. 815

Chesterbrook

DMW WORLDWIDE LLC, 701 Lee Rd Ste 103, 19087-5612, pg. 319

Clarks Green

SWEDA ADVERTISING, 120 N Abington Rd, 18411, pg. 1103

Columbia

WAVELENGTH, 401 Locust St 2nd Fl, 17512, pg. 1192
WAVELENGTH MARKETING, LLC, 401 Locust St, 17512, pg. 1192

Conshohocken

15 MINUTES, INC., 1982 Butler Pike Ste 600, 19428, pg. 2
20NINE DESIGN STUDIOS LLC, 1100 E Hector St Ste 305, 19428, pg. 3
DDCWORKS, 1200 River Rd Ste 300 E, 19428, pg. 290

Dallas

DIGITAL NET AGENCY, INC., PO Box 827, 18612, pg. 308

Devon

ZER0 TO 5IVE, 28 S Waterloo Rd, 19333, pg. 1255

Downingtown

SCHUBERT COMMUNICATIONS, INC., 112 Schubert Dr, 19335-3382, pg. 1025

Doylestown

K2 COMMUNICATIONS, PO Box 1641, 18901-9838, pg. 601
PARLEESTUMPF INC, 350 S Main St Ste 113, 18901, pg. 875
PORETTA & ORR, INC., 450 East St, 18901, pg. 904
SAGEFROG MARKETING GROUP, LLC, 62 E Oakland Ave, 18901, pg. 1014

Easton

CLIFF ROSS, 400 Northampton St, 18042, pg. 216

Elkins Park

MITCHELL & RESNIKOFF, 8003 Old York Rd, 19027-1410, pg. 764

Emmaus

ALTITUDE MARKETING, 417 State Rd 2nd Fl, 18049, pg. 51

Erie

ALTMAN-HALL ASSOCIATES, 235 W 7th St, 16501-1601, pg. 52
BENSUR CREATIVE MARKETING GROUP, 1062 Brown Ave Ste 300, 16502, pg. 124
ENGEL O'NEILL ADVERTISING & PUBLIC RELATIONS, 2124 Sassafras St, 16502, pg. 348
FH GROUP, 2320 W 8th St, 16505, pg. 385
PAPA ADVERTISING INC, 1673 W 8th St, 16505, pg. 872
ROUTE 1A ADVERTISING, 2633 W 8th St, 16505, pg. 994
TUNGSTEN CREATIVE GROUP, 510 W 7th St, 16502, pg. 1161

Export

INFINITY CONCEPTS, 5331 Triangle Ln, 15632, pg. 545

Exton

TMINUS1 CREATIVE, INC., 122 John Robert Thomas Dr, 19341, pg. 1147

Fort Washington

J. WALTER THOMPSON U.S.A., INC., 455 Pennsylvania Ave Ste 136, 19034, pg. 581

Glen Mills

VERVE MARKETING & DESIGN, 36 Derry Dr, 19342-1810, pg. 1175

Glenside

PASKILL STAPLETON & LORD, 1 Roberts Ave, 19038-3497, pg. 877

Greensburg

STUDIO 2 ADVERTISING, 1641 Broad St, 15601, pg. 1093

Harleysville

HORNERCOM, 474 Main St, 19438, pg. 524

Harrisburg

ALLEN & GERRITSEN, 300 N 2Nd St, 17101, pg. 47
PARTNERSHIP OF PACKER, OESTERLING & SMITH (PPO&S), 122 State St, 17101, pg. 876
PAVONE, 1006 Market St, 17101-2811, pg. 879
SACUNAS, 835 Sir Thomas Ct, 17109, pg. 1013
TOP FLIGHT MEDIA, 4801 Lindle Rd, 17111, pg. 1150

Haverford

CONNORS ADVERTISING & DESIGN, 355 W Lancaster Ave Bldg E 2nd Fl, 19041, pg. 231

Horsham

DUDNYK HEALTHCARE GROUP, 5 Walnut Grove Dr Ste 280, 19044, pg. 331

Huntingdon Valley

PRAXIS COMMUNICATIONS, INC., 2600 Philmont Ave Ste 111, 19006-5307, pg. 908

Jamison

CWMEDIA, 1517 Spearmint Cir, 18929, pg. 261
TIMMONS & COMPANY, INC., 1753 Kendarbren Dr Ste 622, 18929-1049, pg. 1144

Jeannette

DIMENSION X MARKETING, 1000 Clay Ave Ext, 15644-3466, pg. 310

Jenkintown

MAMI MEDIA, LLC, 261 Old York Rd Ste 930, 19046, pg. 688

Johnstown

1ST TEAM ADVERTISING LLC, 1407 Eisenhower Blvd Sq II Ste 303, 15904, pg. 3

King of Prussia

ACTIVE INTEGRATED MARKETING, 1060 1st Ave Ste 400, 19406, pg. 21
ARC INTERMEDIA, 1150 1st Ave Ste 501, 19406, pg. 66
COMMUNICATIONS MEDIA INC., 2200 Renaissance Blvd Ste 102, 19406, pg. 226
LOREL MARKETING GROUP LLC, 590 N Gulth Rd, 19406, pg. 669
MERKLE INC., 900 E 8th Ave Ste 200, 19406, pg. 750
POINTROLL INC., 3200 Horizon Dr Ste 120, 19406-2680, pg. 900

Kulpsville

HANLON CREATIVE, 1744 Sumneytown Pike, 19443, pg. 478

Lafayette Hill

SHARAVSKY COMMUNICATIONS, 4128 Dana Ln, 19444-1320, pg. 1036

Lancaster

ALPHA DOG ADVERTISING, LLC, One50 N Prince St, 17603, pg. 51
CIMBRIAN, 425 N Prince St, 17603, pg. 210
DEAN DESIGN/MARKETING GROUP, INC., 1007 Nissley Rd, 17601, pg. 291
GO WELSH, 3055 Yellow Goose Rd, 17601, pg. 431
GODFREY ADVERTISING, 40 N Christian St, 17602, pg. 432
HAVRILLAGROUP, 22E E Roseville Rd, 17601, pg. 503
HOWARD MILLER ASSOCIATES, INC., 20A E Roseville Rd, 17601, pg. 525
LMI ADVERTISING, 24E E Roseville Rd, 17601, pg. 665
NORTH STAR MARKETING, 245 Butler Ave, 17601, pg. 814
PARKER ADVERTISING SERVICE, INC., 101 N Pointe Blvd 2nd Fl, 17601, pg. 874
PROSPECTMX, 210 W Grant St, 17603, pg. 915
SCHEFFEY INC, 350 New Holland Ave, 17602, pg. 1024
STONER BUNTING ADVERTISING, 322 N Arch St Fl 1, 17603-2991, pg. 1088
TOWER MARKETING, 600-E Eden Rd Ste A, 17601, pg. 1152
VOGEL MARKETING SOLUTIONS LLC, 255 Butler Ave Ste 201-B, 17601, pg. 1184
WHITE GOOD & CO. ADVERTISING, 226 N Arch St Ste 1, 17603, pg. 1199

Lansdale

EDWARD J. QUIGLEY ASSOCIATES, 114 Bradford Ln Ste 100, 19446, pg. 339

Lansdowne

HOFF COMMUNICATIONS, 23 S Lansdowne Ave, 19050, pg. 520

Lewisburg

SMITH BROTHERS AGENCY, LP, 116 Federal St, 15212, pg. 1054
TAILORED MARKETING INC., 401 Wood St Ste 1400, 15222, pg. 1108
THINK, INC., 2818 Smallman St, 15222, pg. 1139
THIS IS RED, 216 Blvd of the Allies 6th Fl, 15222, pg. 1141
YELLOW SUBMARINE MARKETING COMMUNICATIONS INC., 220 W Station Sq Dr Ste 200, 15219, pg. 1238
Z BRAND, The Gulf Twr Ste 3205 707 Grant St, 15219, pg. 1253

Pittston

INDEPENDENT GRAPHICS INC., 1679 River Rd, 18640, pg. 544

Plymouth Meeting

BAILEY BRAND CONSULTING, 200 W Germantown Pike, 19462, pg. 86
FVM STRATEGIC COMMUNICATIONS, 630 W Germantown Pke Ste 400, 19462, pg. 411
NEWTON ASSOCIATES MARKETING COMMUNICATIONS, INC., 527 Plymouth Rd, 19462, pg. 808

Radnor

BACKE DIGITAL BRAND MARKETING, 100 Matsonford Rd, 19087, pg. 85

Reading

HOFFMANN PUBLISHING GROUP, 2921 Windmill Rd Ste 4, 19608, pg. 520
NEO-PANGEA, LLC, 26 Penn Ave, 19611, pg. 805
REESE, 1875 Morgantown Rd, 19607, pg. 966
TOMSHEEHAN WORLDWIDE, 645 Penn St, 19601-3408, pg. 1150

Schaefferstown

BACHLEDA ADVERTISING LLC, 1148 Heidelberg Ave, 17088, pg. 85

Scranton

CONDRON & COSGROVE, 220 Penn Ave Ste 303, 18503, pg. 229
DELUCA FRIGOLETTO ADVERTISING, INC., 108 N Washington Ave, 18503, pg. 296

Selinsgrove

SIRE ADVERTISING, 109 Monroe St, 17870, pg. 1047

Sellersville

THE SIMON GROUP, INC., 1506 Old Bethlehem Pike, 18960-1427, pg. 1045

Sewickley

ATLAS MARKETING, 435 Broad St, 15143, pg. 78

Sinking Spring

THE ANDERSON GROUP, 879 Fritztown Rd, 19608, pg. 58

Souderton

ALLEBACH COMMUNICATIONS, 117 N Main St, 18964, pg. 46

Southampton

DYNAMIC DIGITAL ADVERTISING, LLC., 1265 Industrial Blvd, 18966, pg. 334

Springfield

THE IVY GROUP, LTD., 1489 Baltimore Pike Suite 215, 19064, pg. 564

Stroudsburg

ADAMS OUTDOOR ADVERTISING, 6053 Route 209, 18360, pg. 25

Trappe

EPPS ADVERTISING, 184 W Main St, 19426, pg. 350
GOOD GROUP, LLC, 580 W Main St Ste 3, 19426-1940, pg. 434

Villanova

RT&E INTEGRATED COMMUNICATIONS, 768 Mount Moro Rd Ste 27, 19085-2007, pg. 996

Wallingford

GILLESPIE GROUP, 101 N Providence Rd, 19086, pg. 426

Warminster

MARKETING GROUP, 880 Louis Dr, 18974, pg. 697

Warrington

RUSSELL-RISKO AGENCY, 919 Truman Ct, 18976, pg. 998

Washington

FRESH MEDIA GROUP, 382 W Chestnut St Ste 109, 15301, pg. 405

Wayne

23K STUDIOS, 232 Conestoga Rd, 19087, pg. 4
BOZEKEN, LLC, 110 W Lancaster Ave Ste 130, 19087, pg. 152
BTC MARKETING, 994 Old Eagle School Rd Ste 1015, 19087-1802, pg. 173
CUSTOMEDIALABS, 460 E Swedesford Rd Ste 2020, 19087, pg. 261
DIRECT CHOICE, 480 E Swedesford Rd Ste 210, 19087, pg. 311
GRAHAM MEDIA PARTNERS, 512 Saint Davids Rd, 19087, pg. 439

West Chester

20/10 DESIGN & MARKETING, INC., 324 Willowbrook Ln Bldg 300, 19382, pg. 3
BURGESS COMMUNICATIONS, INC, 1450 E Boot Rd Ste 300B, 19380, pg. 176
GAUL ADVERTISING, INC., 1553 Ulster Cir, 19380, pg. 418

Whitehall

L-A ADVERTISING, 1541 Alta Dr Ste 202, 18052, pg. 621

Wilkes Barre

HARTE-HANKS, INC., 165 New Commerce Blvd, 18706-1439, pg. 482
MASLOW LUMIA BARTORILLO ADVERTISING, 182 N Franklin St, 18701-1404, pg. 707

Wormleysburg

VARSITY, 532 N Front St, 17043, pg. 880

Wynnewood

CRAMP & ASSOCIATES, INC., 1327 Grenox Rd, 19096-2402, pg. 244

Wyomissing

LAUNCH DYNAMIC MEDIA, LLC, 828 Penn Ave, 19610, pg. 631

Yardley

HARTE-HANKS DIRECT, INC., 777 Township Line Rd Ste 300, 19067, pg. 483
MEDERGY HEALTHGROUP INC., 790 Township Line Rd Ste 200, 19067, pg. 741
PUBLICIS TOUCHPOINT SOLUTIONS, 1000 Floral Vale Blvd Ste 400, 19067-5570, pg. 935
SAATCHI & SAATCHI HEALTHCARE INNOVATIONS, 1000 Floral Vale Blvd 4th Fl, 19067, pg. 1000

York

DIO, LLC, 3111 Farmtrail Rd, 17406, pg. 310
GAVIN ADVERTISING, 110 N George St 3rd Fl, 17401, pg. 418
GREGIS ADVERTISING, INC., 3601 Concord Rd, 17402, pg. 444
HOLBERG DESIGN, INC., 391 Greendale Rd, 17403, pg. 520
PARTNERS & HARRISON INC, 410 Kings Mill Rd Ste 112, 17401, pg. 875
THE SPOT MEDIA GROUP, 600 N Hartley St Ste 140, 17404, pg. 1066

PUERTO RICO

Guaynabo

ADCOM GROUP, INC., Plaza Triple S 1510 FD Roosevelt Ave Ste 11A, 00968, pg. 27
BBDO PUERTO RICO, Metro Office Park 14 calle 2 Ste, 00907-1831, pg. 104
DE LA CRUZ & ASSOCIATES, Metro Office Park St 1 No 9 Ste 201, 00968-1705, pg. 291
LOPITO, ILEANA & HOWIE, INC., Metro Office Park #13 First St, 00968, pg. 669
NOBOX MARKETING GROUP, INC., Metro Parque #7 1st St Ste 303, 00968, pg. 812

Mayaguez

MIRABAL & ASSOCIATES, Doral Bank Plz Ste 801-802 101 W Mendez Vigo St, 00680-3890, pg. 763

San Juan

ARTEAGA & ARTEAGA, 1571 Calle Alda Urb Caribe, 00926, pg. 74
BADILLO NAZCA SAATCHI & SAATCHI, 1504 Ave Franklin D Roosevelt, 00920-2700, pg. 1009
DDB LATINA PUERTO RICO, PO Box 195006, 00918, pg. 273
GREY PUERTO RICO, PO Box 367, 00918, pg. 458
J. WALTER THOMPSON, Calle C 60 Urb Industrial Mario Julia, 00920, pg. 579
JMD COMMUNICATIONS, 760 Calle Bolivar, 00909, pg. 592
PIXEL LOGIC, INC., Pixelogic Bldg 283 Matadero Rd, 00920, pg. 894
Y&R PUERTO RICO, INC., PO Box 366288, 00936-6288, pg. 1250

RHODE ISLAND

Barrington

HCC MARKETING, INC., 57 Maple Ave, 02806, pg. 504
THE LINK AGENCY, 38 Talcott St, 02806, pg. 659
MARTIN THOMAS INTERNATIONAL, 42 Riverside Dr, 02806, pg. 704

Cranston

VUP MEDIA, 1140 Pk Ave, 2910, pg. 1185

East Providence

STREICKER & COMPANY INC., 37 Eastern Ave, 02914, pg. 1092

Newport

FLEMING & COMPANY INC., 31 America's Cup Ave, 02840, pg. 392
WORLDWAYS SOCIAL MARKETING, 240 Thames St, 02840, pg. 1216

North Kingstown

NORTH STAR MARKETING, INC., 1130 10 Rod Rd Ste A205, 02852, pg. 814

Pawtucket

ELLEN MILLER, 75 Capwell Ave, 02860, pg. 345

Portsmouth

WELCH INC., 180 Mitchell's Ln, 02871, pg. 1196

Providence

(ADD)VENTURES, 117 Chapman St, 02905, pg. 27
ADVOCACY SOLUTIONS LLC, 4 Richmond Sq Ste 300, 02906, pg. 35
BOYCE MEDIA GROUP LLC, 11 S Angell St Ste 376, 2906, pg. 151
DODGE ASSOCIATES, INC., 95 Chestnut St, 02903, pg. 320
DUFFY & SHANLEY, INC., 10 Charles St, 02904, pg. 331
THE FENTON GROUP, 44 Weybosset St, 02903, pg. 384
JH COMMUNICATIONS LLC, 111 Wayland Ave, 02906, pg. 591
NAIL COMMUNICATIONS, 63 Eddy St, 02903, pg. 799
OMNIA AGENCY, 115 Harris Ave 2nd Fl, 02903, pg. 857
RDW GROUP INC., 125 Holden St, 02908-4919, pg. 956
SHEPPARD LEGER NOWAK INC., 1 Richmond Sq, 02906-5139, pg. 1037
SVM PUBLIC RELATIONS & MARKETING COMMUNICATIONS, 2 Charles St 3rd Fl N, 02904, pg. 1102

Warwick

CATALYST, 275 Promenade St Ste 275, 02908, pg. 196
MARKETING & MEDIA SERVICES, LLC, 931 Jefferson Blvd Ste 1001, 02886, pg. 947

West Kingston

FISH ADVERTISING, 25 Autumn Ln, 2892, pg. 389
IMAJ ASSOCIATES, 11 William Reynolds Farm Rd, 02892, pg. 541

SOUTH CAROLINA

Aiken

SOUTH COMPANY, 1028 Hayne Ave SW, 29801, pg. 1060

Anderson

MARTIN ADVERTISING, 1650-C E Greenville St, 29621, pg. 702
SMART MARKETING ADVERTISING AGENCY, 100 Old Smith Mill Rd, 29625, pg. 1053

Bluffton

BFG COMMUNICATIONS, 6 Anolyn Ct, 29910, pg. 128
FLEMING CREATIVE GROUP, 181 Bluffton Rd Ste C-103, 29910, pg. 393
GROUP46, 1323 May River Rd Ste 202, 22910, pg. 462

Charleston

BOOM ADVERTISING, 186 Cartright St, 29492, pg. 147
THE BOSWORTH GROUP, 113 Wappoo Creek Dr Ste 3, 29412, pg. 150
COGNETIX, INC., 1866 Wallenberg Blvd Ste B, 29407, pg. 219
FUZZCO INC., 85 1/2 Spring St, 29403, pg. 411
GRAVINA ONLINE STRATEGIES, 49 Archdale St Ste 2G, 29401, pg. 440
HOOK, 522 King St, 29403, pg. 522
HOOKLEAD, 2120 Noisette Blvd Ste 120, 29405, pg. 522
JDA FRONTLINE, 438 King St Ste B, 29403, pg. 589
LITTLE HIGHRISE LLC, 237 King St, 29401, pg. 662
MOMENTUM MARKETING, 295 Seven Farms Dr, 29492, pg. 770
PENINSULA AGENCY, 441 Meeting St Ste 339, 29403, pg. 882
RAWLE MURDY ASSOCIATES, INC., 960 Morrison Dr, 29403, pg. 955
RED7 AGENCY, 174 Meeting St, 29401, pg. 963
SLANT MEDIA LLC, 263 C King St, 29401, pg. 1051

Columbia

THE ADAMS GROUP, 925 Gervais St, 29201, pg. 24
ADCO, 1220 Pickens St, 29201, pg. 26
CHERNOFF NEWMAN, 1411 Gervais St 5th Fl, 29201-3125, pg. 207
DUNCAN GRANT ADVERTISING, 117 Alpine Cr Ste 500, 29223, pg. 332
THE GILLESPIE AGENCY, 3007 Millwood Ave, 29205, pg. 425
RESH MARKETING CONSULTANTS, INC., 22 Surrey Ct, 29212-3140, pg. 970

Conway

INTERACTIVITY MARKETING, 408 Main St, 29526, pg. 551

Easley

BLUE LION DIGITAL, LLC, 711 James Rd, 29642, pg. 141

Florence

ADAMS OUTDOOR ADVERTISING, 1385 Alice Dr, 29505, pg. 25

Greenville

10X GROUP, 104 W Broad St, 29601, pg. 1
BRAINS ON FIRE, INC., 148 River St Ste 100, 29601, pg. 153
CRAWFORD STRATEGY, 200 E Camperdown Way, 29601, pg. 245
ERWIN-PENLAND, 125 E Broad St, 29601, pg. 354
FEREBEE LANE & CO., 734 South Main St B, 29601, pg. 384
GIBBONS/PECK MARKETING COMMUNICATION, 7 S Laurens St Ste 200, 29601, pg. 424
HUGHES AGENCY LLC, 104 S Main St Ste 110, 29601, pg. 527
INFINITY MARKETING, 874 S Pleasantburg Dr, 29607, pg. 545
JACKSON MARKETING GROUP, 2 Task Ct, 29607, pg. 584
REDHYPE, 248 N Laurens St, 29601, pg. 965
SHIFT, INC., 24 Vardy St Ste 202, 29601, pg. 1038
SOURCELINK, 1224 Poinsett Hwy, 29609, pg. 1060
VANTAGEPOINT, INC, 80 Villa Rd, 29615, pg. 1171
WORTHWHILE, 9 Caledon Ct Ste C, 29615, pg. 1216

Hilton Head Island

PERSUASIVE BRANDS, 301 Central Ave 321, 29926, pg. 886

Ladson

ADAMS OUTDOOR ADVERTISING, 9509 Hamburg Rd, 29456, pg. 25

Mount Pleasant

CHERNOFF NEWMAN, 550 Long Point Rd, 29464-7905, pg. 208
LITTLE DOG AGENCY INC., 3850 Bessemer Rd Ste 220, 29466, pg. 662

Murrells Inlet

COOPER COMMUNICATIONS, 4447 Hwy 17 Business, 29576, pg. 233

Myrtle Beach

THE BRANDON AGENCY, 3023 Church St, 29577, pg. 160
ELLEV LLC, 807 Main St, 29577, pg. 345
FUEL, 1705 N Oak St, 29577, pg. 406
LHWH ADVERTISING & PUBLIC RELATIONS, 3005 Hwy 17 Bypass N, 29577-6742, pg. 656
MARKETING STRATEGIES INC., 4603 Oleander Dr Ste 4, 29577, pg. 699
STUDIO303INC., 3233 Volterra Way, 29579, pg. 1094

North Augusta

NEWFIRE MEDIA, 43 Crystal Lk Dr Ste 200, 29841, pg. 807

North Charleston

MOTIVATED MARKETING, 7087 Rivers Ave, 29406, pg. 779
VIP MARKETING & ADVERTISING, 8761 Dorchester Rd Ste 210, 29420, pg. 1178

Pawleys Island

131DIGITAL, 131 Library Ln, 29585, pg. 2

Rock Hill

THE MAYOROS AGENCY, 454 S Anderson Rd Ste 154, 29730, pg. 712

Seneca

MOORE, EPSTEIN, MOORE, 273 Applewood Ctr Place Ste 342, 29678, pg. 773

Spartanburg

LAUNCH, 351 E Kennedy St, 29302, pg. 630
THE SOUTHER AGENCY, INC., 518 E Main St, 29302-1927, pg. 1060

Tega Cay

EFFECTIVE MEDIA SOLUTIONS, 554 Pine Links Dr, 29708, pg. 339

West Columbia

GASQUE ADVERTISING, INC., 3195 Leaphart Rd, 29169-3001, pg. 417

SOUTH DAKOTA

Brandon

MAIN IDEAS, 26485 482nd Ave, 57005, pg. 687

Deadwood

TDG COMMUNICATIONS, 93 Sherman St, 57732, pg. 1134

Pierre

FACTOR360 DESIGN + TECHNOLOGY, 120 Euclid Ave, 57501, pg. 363

Rapid City

LINN PRODUCTIONS, 1222 Oregon St, 57701, pg. 659
ROBERT SHARP & ASSOCIATES, 3615 Canyon Lake Dr Ste 1, 57702, pg. 987
SANBORN ADVERTISING, 2102 Rio Dr, 57702, pg. 1016
TOUT ADVERTISING LLC, 622 Main St, 57701, pg. 1152

Sioux Falls

44 INTERACTIVE, 1602 S Western Ave, 57105, pg. 8
ADWERKS, 512 N. Main Ave, 57104, pg. 35

TENNESSEE

Bartlett

Brentwood

Bristol

Burns

Chattanooga

Clarksville

Cookeville

Cordova

Franklin

Germantown

Henderson

Jackson

Johnson City

Knoxville

La Vergne

Memphis

Mount Juliet

Murfreesboro

Nashville

Whites Creek

TEXAS

Addison

Amarillo

Arlington

Austin

Bastrop

Beaumont

Bellaire

Bryan

Carrollton

Colleyville

Conroe

Corpus Christi

Dallas

Denison

Denton

El Paso

Fair Oaks Ranch

Floresville

Flower Mound

Fort Worth

Grand Prairie

Helotes

Houston

Hughes Springs

Hurst

Irving

Katy

Kerrville

Lakeway

Lewisville

Lubbock

Magnolia

McAllen

Midland

Nacogdoches

Odessa

Plano

Richardson

San Antonio

Seabrook

Southlake

Spring Branch

Sugar Land

Temple

The Woodlands

Falls Church

Forest

Glen Allen

Harrisonburg

Herndon

King George

Leesburg

Lovettsville

Lynchburg

Manassas

McLean

Norfolk

Reston

Richmond

Roanoke

Springfield

Suffolk

Vienna

Virginia Beach

Williamsburg

WASHINGTON

Bellevue

Bellingham

Burien

Centralia

Edmonds

Everett

Federal Way

Ferndale

Fox Island

Gig Harbor

Kent

Kirkland

Liberty Lake

Lynnwood

Monroe

Mountlake Terrace

Orting

Redmond

Renton

Seattle

Spokane

Tacoma

Tukwila

Vancouver

Vashon

White Salmon

Yakima

WEST VIRGINIA

Barboursville

Beckley

Charleston

Huntington

25701, pg. 174
GRAFITZ GROUP NETWORK, 1102 3rd Ave Ste 204, 25701, pg. 438

Lewisburg

PRESIDIO STUDIOS, 9719 Seneca Trl S, 24901, pg. 908

Martinsburg

GRIFFITH & COE ADVERTISING, INC., 801 Jerry Ct, 25401, pg. 460

Morgantown

BLAINETURNER ADVERTISING, INC., 1401 Saratoga Ave, 26505, pg. 135
INNERACTION MEDIA LLC, 1440 Ctr Hill Ave Ste 4, 26505, pg. 547

Parkersburg

MOROCH, 3901 Brisco Rd Ste 12, 26104, pg. 776

Triadelphia

GUTMAN ADVERTISING LLC, 6743 National Rd, 26059, pg. 467

WISCONSIN

Appleton

ASCENTMEDIA, 1022 E Pacific St, 54911, pg. 76
WEIDERT GROUP INC., 901 Lawe St, 54915, pg. 1194

Black Earth

CAMPBELL LACOSTE, INC., 4981 Scherbel Rd, 53515, pg. 188

Brookfield

BADER RUTTER & ASSOCIATES, INC., 13845 Bishop's Dr, 53005, pg. 86
BLUE HORSE INC., 1180 Indianwood Dr, 53005, pg. 141
CELTIC, INC., 330 S Executive Dr Ste 206, 53005-4215, pg. 201
HOWARD M. SCHWARTZ & ASSOCIATES, INC., One Marketing Ctr 19020 Emerald Dr, 53045, pg. 524
LEPOIDEVIN MARKETING, 245 S Executive Dr, 53005, pg. 651
RESPONSORY, 250 Bishops Way, 53005, pg. 972

Cedarburg

HENKE & ASSOCIATES, INC., 236 Hamilton Rd, 53012, pg. 510
WHITE RICE ADVERTISING & PR, W63 N706 Washington Ave, 53012, pg. 1200

De Pere

BURNHAM RICHARDS ADVERTISING, 522 George St, 54301, pg. 177

Delavan

SIGNALFIRE, LCC, 1624 Hobbs Dr, 53115, pg. 1043

Eagle River

DISCOVER MEDIAWORKS INC, 5236 Hwy 70 W, 54521, pg. 312

Fond Du Lac

BROWNBOOTS INTERACTIVE, INC., 108 S Main St, 54935, pg. 170

Franklin

SAVAGE SOLUTIONS, LLC, 4118 W Minnesota Ct, 53132, pg. 1021

Green Bay

IMAGINASIUM INC., 110 S Washington St, 54301, pg. 539
INSIGHT CREATIVE INC., 1816 Sal St, 54302, pg. 549
PROPHIT MARKETING, 154 N Broadway St, 54303, pg. 915

Hales Corners

NONBOX, 5307 S 92nd St, 53130-1677, pg. 813

Hartland

CHARLESTON/ORWIG, INC., 515 W North Shore Dr, 53029-8312, pg. 205

Hudson

GROUP LEAF LLC, PO Box 546, 54016, pg. 462
KINZIEGREEN MARKETING GROUP, 744 Ryan Dr Ste 101, 54016, pg. 613

Kenosha

ADAMS OUTDOOR ADVERTISING, 5732 95th Ave Ste 500, 53144, pg. 25

La Crosse

AVS GROUP, 3120 S Ave, 54601, pg. 82
METRE LLC, 116 5th Ave S, 54601, pg. 752
VENDI ADVERTISING, 125 4th St N Ste 200, 54601, pg. 1173

Lake Geneva

DIRECTORY SERVICE BUREAU, LTD., 772 W Main St Ste 202, 53147, pg. 312

Madison

6AM MARKETING, 330 S Whitney Way Ste 300, 53705, pg. 10
ADAMS OUTDOOR ADVERTISING, 102 East Badger St, 53713, pg. 25
ATOMIC COFFEE MEDIA, 918 High St Ste A, 53715, pg. 78
FLAPJACK CREATIVE, 303 S Paterson Ste 7, 53703, pg. 392
HIEBING, 315 Wisconsin Ave, 53703-2107, pg. 513
J DANIEL AGENCY, 583 Donofrio Dr Ste 218, 53719, pg. 564
KNUPP & WATSON & WALLMAN, 5201 Old Middleton Rd, 53705-2715, pg. 616
LINDSAY, STONE & BRIGGS, INC., 100 State St, 53703-2573, pg. 658
PLANET PROPAGANDA, INC., 605 Williamson St, 53703, pg. 896
POP-DOT MARKETING, 111 W Wilson St Ste 11, 53703, pg. 904
REED SENDECKE KREBSBACH, 701 Deming Way, 53717-1937, pg. 966
SHINE ADVERTISING, 612 W Main St Ste 105, 53703, pg. 1038
SHINE UNITED LLC, 202 N Henry St, 53703, pg. 1038
STEPHAN & BRADY, INC., 1850 Hoffman St, 53704-2541, pg. 1083
TMA+PERITUS, 33 E Main St Ste 451, 53703, pg. 1147

Menomonee Falls

ADZ ETC., INC., N88 W16749 Main St Ste 3, 53051-2826, pg. 36
MGI COMMUNICATIONS, N56 W13585 Silver Spring Dr., 53051, pg. 753

Mequon

PROM KROG ALTSTIEL INC., 1009 W Glen Oaks Ln Ste 107, 53092-3382, pg. 913

Middleton

MONTZINGO ASSOCIATES INC., 5122 Sunrise Ridge Trl, 53562, pg. 772
SHOUTLET, INC., 1 Erdman Pl Ste 102, 53717, pg. 1039

Milwaukee

2 STORY, 641 W National Ave, 53204, pg. 3
A.B. DATA, LTD., 600 AB Data Dr, 53217-2645, pg. 15
ABRAZO MULTICULTURAL MARKETING, 229 E Wisconsin Ave Ste 800, 53202, pg. 17
ANTHOLOGIE, INC., 207 E Buffalo St Ste 643, 53202, pg. 62
BOELTER + LINCOLN MARKETING COMMUNICATIONS, 222 E Erie 4th Fl, 53202, pg. 145
BVK, 250 W Coventry Ct #300, 53217-3972, pg. 179
CI DESIGN INC., 306 N Milwaukee St Ste 200, 53202, pg. 210
CORE CREATIVE, INC., 600 W Virginia St, 53204, pg. 235
CRAMER-KRASSELT, 246 E Chicago St, 53202, pg. 243
CRUX CREATIVE, 250 E Wisconsin Ave, 53202, pg. 258
DERSE INC., 3800 W Canal St, 53208-2916, pg. 300
EICHENBAUM/ASSOCIATES, INC., 219 N Milwaukee St, 53202-5818, pg. 340
ELLINGSEN BRADY ADVERTISING (EBA), 207 E Buffalo St Ste 400, 53202, pg. 345
FLIPELEVEN LLC, 710 N Plankinton Ave Ste 300, 53203, pg. 394
G-COMMUNICATIONS, 224 N Broadway Ste 302, 53202, pg. 412
HANSON DODGE INC., 220 E Buffalo St, 53202, pg. 478
HY CONNECT, 1000 N Water St Ste 1600, 53202-6667, pg. 530
JACOBSON ROST, 233 N Water St 6th Fl, 53202, pg. 585
JIGSAW LLC, 710 N Plankinton Ave Empire Bldg 9th Fl, 53203, pg. 591
LAUGHLIN/CONSTABLE, INC., 207 E Michigan St, 53202-4998, pg. 629
MINDSPIKE DESIGN LLC, 320 E Buffalo St Ste 606, 53202, pg. 762
MORTENSON SAFAR KIM, 117 N Jefferson St Ste 204, 53202-4615, pg. 777
NELSON SCHMIDT, 600 E Wisconsin Ave, 53202, pg. 804
PHOENIX MARKETING GROUP, INC., 6750 Maple Terr, 53213, pg. 890
RED BROWN KLE, 840 N Old World Third St Ste 401, 53203, pg. 959
SCOTT, INC. OF MILWAUKEE, 1031 N Astor St, 53202-3324, pg. 1026
STIR ADVERTISING & INTEGRATED MARKETING, 252 E Highland Ave, 53202, pg. 1087
STREET CANCE MARKETING COMMUNICATIONS, 234 W Florida St, 53202-5729, pg. 1092
THIEL DESIGN LLC, 325 E Chicago St Ste 2, 53202, pg. 1138
THIRSTY BOY, 223 N Water St, 53202, pg. 1140
TRACTION FACTORY, 735 W Wisconsin Ave, 53233, pg. 1153
TREFOIL GROUP, 735 N Water St Ste 200, 53202, pg. 1155
VERSANT, 11000-A W Park Pl, 53224-3615, pg. 1174
VOLLRATH & ASSOCIATES, 839 N Jefferson St Ste 502, 53202, pg. 1184
WORLD MARKETING HOLDINGS, LLC, 1301 W Canal St, 53233-2667, pg. 1215
ZIZZO GROUP MARKETING + PR + NEW MEDIA, INC., 648 N Plankinton Ave Ste 270, 53203, pg. 1258

Monroe

EMPIRE MEDIA GROUP, 1412 13th St, 53566, pg. 347

Mosinee

ONTOGENY ADVERTISING & DESIGN LLC, PO Box 221, 54455, pg. 862

Neenah

BRANDDIRECTIONS, 333 N. Commercial St, 54956, pg. 158

New Berlin

RADIATE GROUP, 5000 S Towne Dr, 53151, pg. 949
TOP FLOOR TECHNOLOGIES, 2725 S Moorland Rd, 53151, pg. 1151

New Glarus

THE GUNTER AGENCY, N9191 Cardinal Crest Ln, 53574, pg. 467

Oconomowoc

OCREATIVE DESIGN STUDIO, 521 Westover St, 53066, pg. 822

Onalaska

THE BLU GROUP - ADVERTISING & MARKETING, 1828 E Main St Ste 3, 54650, pg. 140

Pepin

PROVIDENCE MARKETING GROUP, 9151 Lerum Ln, 54759, pg. 916

Pewaukee

AFFIRM, N28W23050 Roundy Dr Ste 100, 53072, pg. 36
PLATYPUS ADVERTISING + DESIGN, N29 W23810 Woodgate Ct W Ste 100, 53072, pg. 897

Racine

CATCH-22 CREATIVE INC, 8007 Douglas Ave, 53402, pg. 198

Sheboygan

DUFOUR ADVERTISING, 532 S 8th St, 53081, pg. 332
DYNAMIC INC, 1526 S 12th St, 53081, pg. 334

Slinger

BAST-DURBIN INC, 125 Kettle Moraine Dr S, 53086, pg. 97

Verona

ROUNDHOUSE MARKETING & PROMOTION, INC., 560 E Verona Ave, 53593, pg. 994

Waukesha

CONCEPT ENVY, PO Box 944, 53187, pg. 229
IMAGE MAKERS ADVERTISING INC, 139 E North St, 53188, pg. 538
LEAP STRATEGIC MARKETING, LLC, N16 W23250 Stone Rdg Dr Ste 4, 53188, pg. 634
MORGAN & MYERS, INC., N16 W23233 Stone Ridge Dr Ste 200, 53188, pg. 774
ROCKETLAWNCHAIR, N8 W22323 Johnson Dr Ste D, 53186, pg. 989
SEROKA, N17 W24222 Riverwood Dr, 53188, pg. 1033

Wausau

ADRENALIGN MARKETING LLC, 408 3rd St Ste 402, 54403, pg. 31
CREATIVE COMMUNICATION & DESIGN, 3550 W Stewart Ave, 54401, pg. 246
KINZIEGREEN MARKETING GROUP, 915 5th St, 54403, pg. 613

West Bend

EPIC CREATIVE, 3014 E Progress Dr, 53095, pg. 349

Wisconsin Rapids

THE GOODNESS COMPANY, 820 Baker St, 54494, pg. 435

WYOMING

Casper

ADBAY, 627 W Yellowstone Hwy, 82601, pg. 26
BALL ADVERTISING GROUP, 355 N Lincoln St, 82601, pg. 89

Cheyenne

PURE BRAND COMMUNICATIONS, 200 E 8th Ave Ste 203, 82001-1440, pg. 938

Cody

MORRISON CREATIVE COMPANY INC, 907 11th St, 82414, pg. 777
WALKING STAR MARKETING & DESIGN, 921 14th St, 82414, pg. 1187

GEOGRAPHIC INDEX OF NON-U.S. AGENCIES

AFGHANISTAN

Kabul

ALTAI COMMUNICATIONS, House 733-124 St 4 Qala-e-Fatullah, pg. 576

ALGERIA

Algiers

FP7 MCCANN ALGERIA, 31 Mohammad khoudi, El Biar, pg. 716

ARGENTINA

Buenos Aires

ARGENTINA PORTER NOVELLI, Reconquinsta 723 2 FL, pg. 1621
BBDO ARGENTINA, Arenales 495 3rd Fl, Vincente Lopez, pg. 102
BURSON-MARSTELLER, Rivadavia 620 4to piso, pg. 1467
THE COMMUNITY, Avenida Del Libertador 13548, Martinez, pg. 227
CONSULTORES DEL PLATA S.A., Santa Fe 911 1st Fl Office A, pg. 1482
DDB ARGENTINA, Juncal 1207, pg. 276
DEL CAMPO NAZCA SAATCHI & SAATCHI, Bogota 973, Martinez, pg. 1007
EDELMAN, Paraguay 610 Piso 29, pg. 1507
FCB BUENOS AIRES, Luis Maria Campos 46, Capital Federal, pg. 376
FIRE ADVERTAINMENT, Martin Coronado 818, Acassuso, pg. 276
GREY ARGENTINA, Balafco 845, pg. 453
HILL & KNOWLTON DE ARGENTINA, Lavalle 1675, Piso 7, Oficina 8, Ciudad Autonoma de, pg. 1542
INITIATIVE BUENOS AIRES, Leandro N Alem 1110 4th Fl, pg. 1345
J. WALTER THOMPSON, Alsina 465, pg. 577
THE JEFFREY GROUP ARGENTINA, Talcahuano 833 Piso 8 G, pg. 1555
LEO BURNETT INC., SUCURSAL ARGENTINA, Olga Cossenttini 1545 Piso 2, pg. 640
MADRE, Petrona Eyle 450 DTO, CJD, pg. 779
MCCANN ERICKSON, Esmeralda 1080, pg. 716
MEC, Juramento 1775 piso 11, pg. 1361
MUCHNIK, ALURRALDE, JASPER & ASSOC./MS&L, Callao 1046 Piso 4, pg. 1597
OGILVY & MATHER ARGENTINA, Arevalo 1880, pg. 837
OGILVYONE WORLDWIDE, Arevalo 1880, pg. 838
OPTIMEDIA, Armenia 1528, pg. 1398
PONCE BUENOS AIRES, Avenida del Libertador 14950, Acassuso, pg. 557
PUBLICIS GRAFFITI, Azopardo 1315, pg. 928
RAPP ARGENTINA, Reconquista 723 2 Piso, pg. 953
SANTO BUENOS AIRES, Darwin 1212, pg. 1222
SAVAGLIO TBWA, Honduras 5952, pg. 1131
WUNDERMAN, Pasaje Tupiza 3950 Capital, pg. 1230

Rosario

NUEVA COMUNICACION-WEBER SHANDWICK, Colon 1428 Piso 2 - Dptos A y B, pg. 1682

AUSTRALIA

Adelaide

MEC, Level 1 46 Fullarton Rd Norwood, pg. 1362

Alexandria

SPINIFEX GROUP, 14/32 Ralph Street, pg. 913

Brisbane

PUBLICIS AUSTRALIA, Level 3 164 Grey Street, South, pg. 931
STARCOM WORLDWIDE, Level 6 307 Queen Street, pg. 1080

Canberra

GEORGE PATTERSON Y&R, Ste 6 The Realm 18 National Circuit, Barton, pg. 1219
KREAB CANBERRA, Minter Ellison Building 25 National Circuit, Forrest, pg. 1568

Fitzroy

REACTIVE MEDIA PTY LTD, 374 George Street, pg. 1311

Fortitude Valley

GEORGE PATTERSON Y&R, Centenary Sq Level 1 108 Wickham St, pg. 1219

Kent Town

BLAZE ADVERTISING, 17 Fullarton Road, pg. 1217
BLAZE ADVERTISING, 17 Fullarton Road, pg. 1147

Melbourne

BADJAR OGILVY, Level 12, Royal Domain Centre, 380 St Kilda Road, pg. 840
BLAZE ADVERTISING, Level 2 162 Collins Street, pg. 1217
CLEMENGER BBDO MELBOURNE, 474 Saint Kilda Road, pg. 114
DDB MELBOURNE PTY. LTD., 7 Electric Street, pg. 277
DTDIGITAL, Lvl 12 Royal Domain Centre, pg. 1218
FUTUREBRAND, 520 Bourke St Level 4, West, pg. 411
GEORGE PATTERSON Y&R, Level 3 162 Collins Street, pg. 1219
GREY PTY. LTD., 470 St Kilda Rd Level 5, pg. 455
INITIATIVE MELBOURNE, Level 2 468 St Kilda Road, pg. 1347
JACK MORTON WORLDWIDE, Level 4, 520 Bourke Street, pg. 583
KREAB MELBOURNE, Level 6, 2 Russell Street, pg. 1569
LEO BURNETT MELBOURNE, Level 7 28 Fresh Water Supply South Bank, pg. 647
M&C SAATCHI, Level 27 140 William Street, pg. 678
MCCANN ERICKSON ADVERTISING PTY. LTD., Level 7 574 Saint Kilda, South, pg. 716
MCCANN HEALTHCARE MELBOURNE, Level 7 574 St Kilda Rd, pg. 716
MEDIACOM AUSTRALIA PTY. LTD., Level 1 195 Little Collins Street, pg. 1372
OCTAGON, 123 Moray St S, pg. 824
PUBLICIS AUSTRALIA, Level 6 Freshwater place, pg. 931
SAPIENT, 161 Fitzroy Street, Saint Kilda, pg. 1019
STARCOM MELBOURNE, Level 6 Building 3 6 Riverside Quay, Southbank, pg. 1079
WHYBIN TBWA, 288 Coventry Street, South, pg. 1128

Millers Point

RAZORFISH AUSTRALIA, Bond 3 30 Windmill Street, pg. 1309

Nedlands

FTI CONSULTING, The Courtyard 33 Broadway, pg. 1524

North Sydney

BLACKIE MCDONALD, Level 8 65 Berry St, pg. 1481
HAVAS WORLDWIDE AUSTRALIA, Level 12 60 Miller Street, pg. 499
LANDOR ASSOCIATES, Level 11 15 Blue Street, pg. 1241

Pyrmont

CPM AUSTRALIA, 137 Pyrmont Street, pg. 241
IMAGINATION AUSTRALIA, Ste 121 Jones Bay Wharf, pg. 540
MJW HAKUHODO, Ste 2 Upper Deck Jones Bay Wharf, 26-32 Pirrama Road, pg. 475

Richmond

THE FACE - MELBOURNE, Level 1 132 B Gwynne St, pg. 499
J. WALTER THOMPSON AUSTRALIA, Bldg 18A 64 Ballmain St, pg. 567
MAXUS, Level 3 Pelaco Bldg 21-31 Goodwood St, pg. 1354
RAPP MELBOURNE, 7 Electric Street, pg. 954
TRIBAL WORLDWIDE MELBOURNE, 7 Electric St, pg. 1317

Saint Leonards

ETCOM, Level 3 72 Christie Street, pg. 1227
OGILVY PR WORLDWIDE, Level 2 72 Christie Street, pg. 1608
OGILVY SYDNEY, 72 Thristia Street, pg. 840
PORTER NOVELLI SYDNEY, Clemenger Building Ground Floor, 118-120 Pacific Highway, pg. 1625

Southbank

AMOBEE, Level 9 28 Freshwater Pl, pg. 1282

Surry Hills

AJF PARTNERSHIP, Level 1, 66-72 Reservoir St, pg. 381
INITIATIVE SYDNEY, LEVEL 3, 100 CHALMERS STREET, pg. 1347
PLAY COMMUNICATION, Level 1 91 Campbell Street, pg. 1337

Sydney

303LOWE, Level 2 33 Playfair Street, The Rocks, pg. 789
ACTIVE INTERNATIONAL AUSTRALIA PTY LTD., Level 3 140 Arthur St, pg. 1323
ARC WORLDWIDE, 162 Blues Point Road, McMahons Point, pg. 1406
ARNOLD FURNACE, Level 11 60 Miller St, pg. 484
BLAZE ADVERTISING, Level 12 35 Clarence Street, pg. 1217
BURSON-MARSTELLER, 65 Berry Street Level 16, pg. 1470
DTDIGITAL, 72 Christie Street, pg. 1218
EDELMAN, Level 7 1 York Street, pg. 1505
EPSILON INTERNATIONAL, 88 Cumberland St Suite 22 Level 1, The Rocks, pg. 350
GEORGE P. JOHNSON (AUSTRALIA) PTY., LTD., Suite 101 Level 1 63-79 Miller St, Pyrmont, pg. 422
GEORGE PATTERSON Y&R, Level 15 35 Clarence St, pg. 1219
GREY HEALTHCARE, Northpoint Building Level 18 100 Miller Street, North, pg. 423
GROUPM APAC HQ, Level 14, 65 Berry Street, pg. 1337
HAVAS WORLDWIDE SYDNEY, 60 Miller Street Level 12, North, pg. 500
HILL & KNOWLTON AUSTRALIA PTY. LTD., Level 13 338 Pitt Street, pg. 1545
IDEAWORKS, Level 10/35 Clarence St, pg. 1225
J. WALTER THOMPSON, Level 14 338 Pitt Street, pg. 567
J. WALTER THOMPSON INSIDE, Level 12 99 Walker St I, pg. 581
JACK MORTON WORLDWIDE, Royal Navy House 32 Grosvenor St, The Rocks, pg. 583
KREAB SYDNEY, 137 Pyrmont Street Level 2, pg. 1569
LEO BURNETT SYDNEY, 20 Windmill St, McMahons Point, pg. 647
LIDA, Level 3 99 Macquarie St, pg. 678
M&C SAATCHI, 99 MacQuarie St, pg. 677
MAXUS, Level 11 65 Berry St, pg. 1355
MCCANN, 32 Grosvenor St The Rocks, pg. 717
MCCANN HEALTHCARE SYDNEY, Royal Naval House 32-34 Grosvenor Street, The Rocks, pg. 716
MEC, Level 14 65 Berry Street, pg. 1362
MEDIACOM SYDNEY, Level 17, 65 Berry St North, pg. 1372
MILLWARD BROWN AUSTRALIA, Level 11, 181 Miller St North, pg. 759
MJW HAKUHODO, Level 5 The Frank Hurley Grandstand Driver Ave Fox Studios, Moore Park, pg. 475
OCTAGON SYDNEY, 166 William St, Woolloomooloo, pg. 824
OGILVY HEALTHWORLD, 72 Christie St, St Leonards, pg. 853
OMD AUSTRALIA, 32 Pyrmont Bridge Road, Pyrmont, pg. 1380
ONE GREEN BEAN, Level 1 276 Devonshire Street, Surry Hills, pg. 1538
PUBLICIS AUSTRALIA, Bond Store 3 30 Windmill St, Walsh Bay, pg. 930
RAPP AUSTRALIA, Level 3 46-52 Mountain Street, Ultimo, pg. 953
RECOGNITION PUBLIC RELATIONS, Level 2 51 Pitt Street, pg. 1463
REPRISE MEDIA AUSTRALIA, Level 1, 166 William St, pg. 560
SAATCHI & SAATCHI AUSTRALIA, 70 George Street, The Rocks, pg. 1010
SIZMEK, Level 10 77 King St, pg. 1048
STARCOM WORLDWIDE, Bond Store 2 28 Windmill St Walsh Bay, pg. 1080
SUDLER & HENNESSEY SYDNEY, The Denison Level 8 65 Berry St, North, pg. 1096
TEAM SAATCHI/SAATCHI & SAATCHI HEALTHCARE, 70 George Street, The Rocks, pg. 1010
TEXT 100 SYDNEY, Level 28 100 Miller St., pg. 1662
TRIBAL WORLDWIDE SYDNEY, Wilcox Mofflin Bldg 46-52 Mountain St, Ultimo, pg. 1318
VML, 35 Clarence St, pg. 1183
WEBER SHANDWICK, 166 William St, Wooloomooloo, pg. 1682
WHYBIN TBWA, 80 Gipps Street, Pyrmont, pg. 1127
WUNDERMAN, 35 Clarence St, pg. 1230
XAXIS, Level 11 65 Berry Street, pg. 1321
YOUNG & RUBICAM AUSTRALIA/NEW ZEALAND, Level 14, 35 Clarence Street, pg. 1242
ZENITHOPTIMEDIA, Bond Store 3 30 Windmill St, Walsh Bay, pg. 1401

Ultimo

DDB SYDNEY PTY. LTD., 46-52 Mountain Street Level 3, pg. 277

Windsor

IE, 178 Albert Street, pg. 1297

Woolloomooloo

MCCANN ERICKSON ADVERTISING PTY. LTD., 166 William St, pg. 716

Yarra

PORTER NOVELLI AUSTRALIA-MELBOURNE, Level 14 Como Centre 644 Chapel Street, pg. 1624

AUSTRIA

Vienna

CPM AUSTRIA, Brauhausgasse 37, pg. 241
DDB TRIBAL VIENNA, Thaliastrasse 125 B, pg. 277
FCB NEUWIEN, Mariahilfer Strasse 17, pg. 373
GREY GROUP AUSTRIA, Paradistasse 51, pg. 448
HAVAS WORLDWIDE VIENNA, Hasnerstrasse 123, pg. 491
INITIATIVE VIENNA, Operngasse 21/9, pg. 1346
J. WALTER THOMPSON WERBEAGENTUR GMBH, Muthgasse 109, pg. 572
KETCHUM PUBLICO, Neulinggasse 37, pg. 1565
LOWE GGK, Mariahilfer Strasse 17, pg. 791
MEDIACOM VIENNA, Vordere, Zollamtsstrasse 13/5. OG, pg. 1369
OGILVY & MATHER GES M.B.H., Bachofengasse 8, pg. 829
OGILVY PR, Bachosengasse 8, pg. 1607
OGILVYONE WORLDWIDE GMBH, Bachofengasse 8, pg. 829
PJURE ISOBAR, Ignaz Kock Strasse 17, pg. 562
PKP BBDO, Guglgasse 7-9, pg. 104
PUBLICIS, Kettenbruckengasse 16, pg. 917
TBWA WIEN, Heiligenstaedter Strasse 31/401/3, pg. 1117
WUNDERMAN, Rotenturnstrasse 16 - 18, pg. 1231
Y&R GMBH, Rotemturmstrasse 1618 6th Fl, pg. 1244

BAHRAIN

Manama

FP7, 609 City Centre Building 6th Floor Government Avenue, pg. 717
GULF HILL & KNOWLTON, 1 Government Ave Bldg 4th Fl Ofc 402, pg. 1544
J. WALTER THOMPSON, 502 Almoayyad Tower, Seef District, pg. 576
MEMAC OGILVY & MATHER W.L.L., Offices 3501 3502 3503 3504 Almoayyed Tower Building 2504, Road 2382 Al Seef District, pg. 850
PUBLICIS-GRAPHICS, Shaikh Mubarak Bldg 203 Rm 502 5th Floor, 30 Government Road, pg. 923

BANGLADESH

Dhaka

ADCOMM, House 7A Road 41 Gulshan 2, pg. 555
ASIATIC MARKETING COMMUNICATIONS, LTD., Asiatic Ctr House 63 Rd 7B Block H Banal Model Town, pg. 568
GREY BANGLADESH LTD., House 06 5th Floor Road 137 Block SE(D), Gulshan 1, pg. 455
PROTISHABDA COMMUNICATIONS, 26 Kemal Ata Turk Ave 3rd Floor, Banani Commercial Area, pg. 933
UNITREND LTD., House #49 Rd #27, Dhanmondi R/A, pg. 717

BARBADOS

Christ Church

SOJE/LONSDALE COMMUNICATIONS INC./Y&R, Hastings House Balmoral Gap, Hastings, pg. 1248

Saint Michael

GHA/DDB, 22 George St, pg. 278

BELARUS

Minsk

PRIMARY SAATCHI & SAATCHI, Kazarmenny Lane 4 Office 1, pg. 1002

BELGIUM

Antwerp

DUVAL GUILLAUME, Uitbreidingstraat 2-8, pg. 917
HEADLINE PUBLISHING AGENCY, Vorstermanstraat 14A, pg. 1117
LDV UNITED, Rijnkaai 99, Hangar 26, pg. 1220
LDV UNITED, Rijnkaai 99, Hangar 26, pg. 221

Brussels

APCO WORLDWIDE, 47 Rue Montoyer 5th Floor, pg. 64
BURSON-MARSTELLER S.A./N.V., 37 Square de Meeus, pg. 1467
DDB GROUP BELGIUM, 17 rue Saint Hubert, pg. 278
EDELMAN BRUSSELS, Avenue Marnix 28, pg. 1503
FLEISHMAN-HILLARD, 35 Square de Meeus, pg. 1520
GREY POSSIBLE BENELUX, Rue Jules Cockxstraat 8-10, pg. 448
HAVAS WORLDWIDE BRUSSELS, Dekenijstraat 58 rue du Doyenne, pg. 491
HAVAS WORLDWIDE DIGITAL BRUSSELS, 58 rue du Doyenne, pg. 491
HILL + KNOWLTON STRATEGIES, Neo Building, pg. 1542
J. WALTER THOMPSON, Avenue Franklin Roosevelt 86, pg. 572
J. WALTER THOMPSON DIALOGUE, 86 Avenue Franklin Roosevelt, pg. 572
KELLEN EUROPE, Avenue Jules Bordet 142, pg. 607
KETCHUM PLEON PUBLIC AFFAIRS, Avenue des Arts 44, pg. 1564
KINETIC, Rue de Stallestraat 65 6th Fl, Uccle, pg. 1351
KREAB BRUSSELS, Av de Tervueren 2, pg. 1568
LEO BURNETT BELGIUM, 18 Place Eugene Flageyplien, pg. 642
MEC, Rue de Stallestraat 65, pg. 1358
MEDIACOM, Rue Jules Cockxstraat 8-10, pg. 1369
N BBDO, Scheldestraat 122, pg. 104
OGILVY & MATHER NV/SA, Cantersteen 47, pg. 829
OGILVY PUBLIC RELATIONS WORLDWIDE, Boulevard de l'Imperatrice 13 Keizerinlaan, pg. 1607
OGILVYONE WORLDWIDE, Blvd de l'Imperatrice 13 Keizerinlaan, pg. 829
PROXIMITY BBDO, Scheldestraat 122 Rue de l'Escaut, pg. 105
PUBLICIS, 62 Quai des Charbonnages, pg. 1406
PUBLICIS, Koolmijnenkaai 62 Quai Des Charbonnages, pg. 917
SAATCHI & SAATCHI BRUSSELS, Ave Rogierlaan 20, pg. 1002
TBWA BRUSSELS, Kroonlaan 165 Avenue de la Couronne, pg. 1117
TBWA GROUP, Kroonlaan Ave de la Couronne 165, pg. 1117
TEQUILA AGENCY.COM, Rue Haute-Hoogstraat 139, pg. 1117
UNIVERSAL COMMUNICATION, 1 Vandammestraat 5-70 B, Hoeilaart, pg. 717
VVL BBDO, 122 Rue de l'Escaut, pg. 105
WEBER SHANDWICK, Ave Cortenbergh 100, pg. 1679
Y&R BELGIUM S.A., 140a Rue de Streetallestraat, pg. 1244
ZENITHOPTIMEDIA, Clos Lucien Outers 11-21, pg. 1398

Diegem

DARWIN BBDO, Bessenveldstraat 25, pg. 104

Drogenbos

THE RETAIL COMPANY, Chausee de Ruisbroek 368, pg. 491

Hasselt

HARTE-HANKS CRM SERVICES BELGIUM N.V., Ekkelgaarden 6, pg. 483

Zaventem

PUBLICITAS MEDIA S.A., Lozenberg 23, pg. 1428

BERMUDA

Hamilton

AAC SAATCHI & SAATCHI, 29 Front Street, pg. 1008

BOLIVIA

Santa Cruz

GRAMMA FCB, Torre Empresarial Cainco Piso 7 Oficina 4, pg. 377

BOSNIA & HERZEGOVINA

Sarajevo

LUNA TBWA SARAJEVO, Fra Andjela Zvizdovica 1, pg. 1117
MCCANN ERICKSON SARAJEVO, GM Lokateli 21, pg. 717
M.I.T.A., Trg Solidarnofpi 2A, pg. 918
STUDIO MARKETING J. WALTER THOMPSON, Cobanija 20, pg. 572

BRAZIL

Botafogo

PUBLICOM, Torre De Rio Sul, Rau Lauro Muller 116, pg. 1530

Brasilia

OGILVY & MATHER, SCN Q 1 Bloco F Salas 811 a 880, pg. 838

Porto Alegre

PAIM COMUNICACAO, Rua Padre Chagas 79 5 Andar, Moinhos de Vento, pg. 718
SLM/OGILVY, Rua Cel Genuino 421 10 Andar, pg. 839

Rio de Janeiro

F/NAZCA SAATCHI & SAATCHI, Praia de Flamengo 200 19th Floor, pg. 1008
FCB RIO DE JANEIRO, Av Joao Cabral de Melo Neto 400-7 andar Peninsula Corporate, Barra da Tijuca, pg. 377
J. WALTER THOMPSON, Av Atlantica 1130 10th Fl, Copacabana, pg. 578
MCCANN ERICKSON PUBLICIDADE LTDA., Rua Visconde de Ouro Preto 5 12-13 Floors, pg. 717
OGILVY & MATHER, Praia do Botafogo 228 18th Floor, pg. 838
OGILVYONE WORLDWIDE, Praia do Botafogo 228 18th Floor, pg. 838
PUBLICIS BRASIL COMMUNICAO, Praca X 15 fl 8, pg. 929

Sao Paulo

ALMAP BBDO, Av Roque Petroni JR 999 35e 7 anderas, pg. 102
ANDREOLI/MS&L, Av Ibirapuera, 2332 Torre 1 - 14 andar, Moema, pg. 1595
BURSON-MARSTELLER, LTDA., Chedid Jafet 222 5th Fl, pg. 1467
DAVID, Avenida Pedrosa de Morais 15553, pg. 267
DDB BRAZIL, Av Brigadeiro Luis Antonio 5013, pg. 278
DM9DDB, Avenida Brigadeiro Luis Antonio 5013, Jardim Paulista, pg. 278
DPZ-DUAILIBI, PETIT, ZARAGOZA, PROPAGANDA S.A., Cidade Jardim Ave 280, pg. 19
DPZ-DUAILIBI, PETIT, ZARAGOZA, PROPAGANDA S.A., Cidade Jardim Ave 280, pg. 928
EDELMAN, Rua Joaquim Floriano N 820 20 andar, pg. 1506
F/NAZCA SAATCHI & SAATCHI, Av Republica do Libano, 253 Ibirapuera, pg. 1008
F.BIZ, Rua Tenente Negrao 90/2, pg. 1223
FCB SAO PAULO, Av das Nacoes Unidas No 12 901-17 fl Cojunto 1702, Torre Norte 17th Floor, pg. 377
GASPAR & ASOCIADOS, Rua Dona Ana Helena de Sales Gusmao, 230, pg. 1682
GREY, Avenida Major Sylvio de Magalnaes Padiha Edificio Philadelphia 1st Fl, 5200 Condominio America Bus Pk, pg. 453
HARTE-HANKS DO BRAZIL CONSULTORIA E SERVICOS LTDA., Av marcoes Unidas 13797 Abandar 94 CJ3, pg. 483
HAVAS WORLDWIDE LATIN AMERICA, Av. Sao Gabriel 301, Itaim Bibi, pg. 499
HILL & KNOWLTON BRAZIL, Rua Andre Ampere 34 8 andar, pg. 1542
ISOBAR BRAZIL, Rua Wisard 298 - 5 andar, vila Madalena, pg. 561
J. WALTER THOMPSON, Rua Mario Amaral 50, Paraiso, pg. 577
JACK MORTON WORLDWIDE (SAO PAULO), Av Antonio Joaquim de Moura Andrade, 425, Vila Nova Conceicao, pg. 582
THE JEFFREY GROUP BRAZIL, Joaquim Floriano 466 5 cj 508 Itaim Bibi, pg. 1555
KETCHUM, R Alvaro Rodrigues 182-2 andar, Brooklin, pg. 1566
LEO BURNETT TAILOR MADE, Rua Brejo Alegre 93/99, pg. 640
MCCANN ERICKSON / SP, Rua Loefgreen 2527, pg. 718
MILLWARD BROWN BRAZIL, Al Santos 2101 - 7 Andar, pg. 759
MULLEN LOWE BRASIL - SAO PAULO, Rua Gomes De Carvalho 1195, Vila Olimpia, pg. 556
OGILVY & MATHER, Av Nacoes Unidas 5777, pg. 838
PUBLICIS BRASIL COMMUNICAO, Av Juscelino Kubitschek 1909, pg. 929
PUBLICOM, Ed Sudameris Av Eng Luiz Carlos Berrini, 1297 - 3 andar, pg. 1531
R/GA SAO PAULO, Av. Nacoes Unidas 12.551 - 12 andar, Brooklin Novo, pg. 947
RAPP BRAZIL, Av Juscelino Kubetischek 1726, 4 e 5 andares Itam Bibi, pg. 953
RAPPDIGITAL BRAZIL, Av Juscelino Kubitschek, pg. 953
SAPIENTNITRO ITHINK, Av Engenheiro Luis Carlos Berrini 901, 2 Andar, pg. 1020
W+K SAO PAULO, Rua Natingui 632, Vila Madalena, pg. 1204
WUNDERMAN, Av das Nacoes Unidas 14171-Torre B, pg. 1231
Y&R SAO PAULO, Rua General Furtado do Nascimento 9, pg. 1248

BULGARIA

Sofia

APRA PORTER NOVELLI, 111 Georgi S Rakovski Str, pg. 1622
DDB SOFIA, Business Park Sofia, Bldg 1A, pg. 279
FCB SOFIA, 6 Maragidik St, pg. 373
GREY GROUP BULGARIA, 23 Mizia Strasse 2nd Floor, pg. 448
HAVAS WORLDWIDE SOFIA, 16, Tundja Str. Sofia, pg. 491
HUTS J. WALTER THOMPSON SOFIA, Iztok District 14 B Charles Darwin Street, pg. 572
LOWE SWING COMMUNICATIONS, 92-94 Tzar Assen St, pg. 793
MCCANN ERICKSON SOFIA, 63 Shipchenski Prohod Boulavard, pg. 718
PUBLICIS MARC, Abacus Business Center, pg. 918
TBWA SOFIA, 44 Buzludja Street, pg. 1117
ZENITHOPTIMEDIA, Abacus Business Building, fl.5, 118, Bulgaria Blvd., pg. 1398

CAMEROON

Douala

MCCANN ERICKSON CAMEROON, 39 rue Kitchener Place de la Chamber de Commerce, pg. 718

CANADA

Aurora

THE MARKETING GARAGE, 15243 Yonge St, pg. 697

Bedford

REVOLVE, Suite 225 200 Waterfront Drive, pg. 975

Burlington

INTERKOM CREATIVE MARKETING, 720 Guelph Line Ste 304, pg. 552
JAN KELLEY MARKETING, 1005 Skyview Dr Ste 322, pg. 587
PLAY ADVERTISING, 1455 Lakeshore Rd Ste 208 S, pg. 897
XPOSURE PR, 1191 Appleford Ln, pg. 1689

Burnaby

AMBIENT MEDIA, INC., 3765 Eton St, pg. 52

Calgary

ADFARM, 333 24th Ave SW Ste 250, pg. 28
ARCANE, 1812 4 Street SW, pg. 66
BLESSAD CHRISTIAN COMMUNICATIONS, 1015 4th St SW, Ste 750, pg. 510
CLEARMOTIVE MARKETING GROUP, Ste 300 - 239 10 Ave SE, pg. 215
CREATIVE INTELLIGENCE, Ste 290 815 17th Ave SW, pg. 249
CRITICAL MASS INC., 402 11th Ave SE, pg. 255
FLEISHMAN-HILLARD, 540 5th Ave SW,Suite 1410, pg. 1519
HENDRICK & ASSOCIATES MARKETING SERVICES INC., 1015 Fourth St SW Ste 750, pg. 510
HILL + KNOWLTON STRATEGIES, Ste 300 Watermark Tower 530 8th Ave SW, pg. 1542
KARO GROUP, INC., 1817 10th Ave SW, pg. 603
LPI COMMUNICATIONS GROUP INC., 101 253 62nd Ave SE, pg. 671
MACLAREN MCCANN/CALGARY, 238 11 Ave SE Ste 100, pg. 682
MERLIN EDGE INC., 602-12th Ave SW Ste 100, pg. 750
MOBILITY QUOTIENT SOLUTIONS INC., 229 11th Ave SE Ste 130, pg. 1303
NON-LINEAR CREATIONS INC., Le Germain Office Tower 110 9th Avenue SW Suite 850, pg. 813
TAXI CALGARY, 805 10th Avenue SW Suite 500, pg. 1112
TMP WORLDWIDE/ADVERTISING & COMMUNICATIONS, 200 714-1 St SE, pg. 1148
TRIGGER COMMUNICATIONS & DESIGN, 200 1725 10 Ave SW, pg. 1157
VENTURE COMMUNICATIONS LTD., 2540 Kensington Road NW, pg. 1173
WAX PARTNERSHIP, 333 24th Ave Southwest Ste 320, pg. 1192
WILLIAM JOSEPH COMMUNICATIONS, 2nd Fl Eau Claire Market, pg. 1207
WOODRUFF SWEITZER CANADA INC., 1220 Kensington Road NW Ste 303, pg. 1214
ZGM, 201 322 - 11th Avenue SW, pg. 1256

Delta

DAVRON MARKETING, 7231 120th St Ste 473, pg. 272
SUBURBIA ADVERTISING, 3-1363 56th St, pg. 1095

Edmonton

CALDER BATEMAN COMMUNICATIONS LTD., 10241 109th St, pg. 184
DDB CANADA, 1000-10235 101 St, pg. 273
LPI COMMUNICATIONS, 4220 98th St NW Ste 104, pg. 671
RED THE AGENCY, 10235 111th St Ste 6, pg. 963
ROSE COUNTRY ADVERTISING & PUBLIC RELATIONS, 11904-113th Ave, pg. 991

Gibsons

AHA CREATIVE STRATEGIES INC., 1423 Sunrise Pl, pg. 1441

Guelph

DUBS & DASH, 26 Hasler Cres, pg. 331
THE LETTER M MARKETING, 285 Woolwich St, pg. 652

Halifax

CHESTER + COMPANY, 1668 Barrington Street 302, pg. 208
COLOUR, 7051 Bayers Rd Ste 400, pg. 223
COSSETTE COMMUNICATIONS, 1883 Upper Water Street Ste 203, pg. 237
EXTREME GROUP, 1498 Lower Water Street, pg. 1293

Hamilton

PIER 8 GROUP, 605 James St N 4th Fl, pg. 890
REDCHAIR BRANDING, 158 Locke St S Unit 2, pg. 964
WORDSMITH DESIGN & ADVERTISING, 605 James Street N 4th Floor, pg. 890

Kamloops

RAGAN CREATIVE STRATEGY & DESIGN, 261B Victoria St, pg. 949

Kelowna

GREENAWAY & ASSOCIATES COMMUNICATIONS LTD., 3381 Ridge Blvd, Westbank, pg. 443
MEDIATIVE, 1620 Dickson Ave Ste 410, pg. 744
TOUCHPOINT AGENCY, 202-1353 Ellis St, pg. 1152

Kingston

CREATIVE EFFECTS ADVERTISING DESIGN STUDIO, 1355 Channelview Rd, pg. 248

Kitchener

HAGON DESIGN, 72 St Leger St Ste 321, pg. 472
SCRIBBLERS' CLUB, 288 Frederick St, pg. 1028

London

ADHOME CREATIVE, 123 Saint George St Ste 105, pg. 28
LINK ADVERTISING INC., 554 Waterloo St, pg. 659
THE MARKETING DEPARTMENT, 457 King St, pg. 697
MCCABE PROMOTIONAL ADVERTISING, 384 Sovereign Rd, pg. 1422
TENZING COMMUNICATIONS, 615 Wellington St, pg. 1136

Mississauga

AIMIA, 2845 Mathieson Blvd E, pg. 41
BOND BRAND LOYALTY, 6900 Maritz Dr, pg. 147
IGNITE DIGITAL, 5579 Quartermain Crst, pg. 1297
KENNA, 90 Burnhamthorpe Road West 5th Floor, pg. 608
MARCOM GROUP INC., 1180 Courtneypark Dr E, pg. 692
MATCH MARKETING GROUP, 5225 Satellite Drive, pg. 709

Moncton

HAWK MARKETING SERVICES, 77 Vaughan Harvey Blvd 4th Fl Unit 28, pg. 503

Montreal

AGENCE BRAQUE, 19 Le Royer Street West Suite 200, pg. 37
ALFRED COMMUNICATIONS, 1435 Rue Saint Alexandre bur 870, pg. 45
ANDERSON DDB SANTE.VIE.ESPRIT., 3500 Blvd De Maisonneuve St W Ste 610, Westmount, pg. 58
BAILLAT CARDELL & FILS, 420 Rue Beaubien Ouest Bureau 201, pg. 87
BAM STRATEGY, 420 McGill Ste 400, pg. 89
BCP LTD., 3530 St Lawrence Ste 300, pg. 119
BLEUBLANCROUGE, 606 Cathcart Street, pg. 138
BOB, 774 Saint-Paul St W, pg. 144
BRAD, 3451 Blvd Saint-Laurent 2nd Fl, pg. 153
CAMDEN, 5455 de Gaspe Ste 440, pg. 186
CANAUDI INC., 75 Alie Street, pg. 188
CASACOM, 407 McGill Bureau 1000, pg. 194
CLOUDRAKER, 1435 rue Saint-Alexandre, Ste 700, pg. 216
COHN & WOLFE, 2001 Ave McGill College Bureau 760, pg. 1482
COMUNIKA, 4000 St-Ambroise Ste 387, pg. 228
COSSETTE COMMUNICATION-MARKETING (MONTREAL) INC., 2100 Drummond Street, pg. 238
DENTSUBOS, 3970 Saint Ambroise Street, pg. 299
EDELMAN, 1000 Sherbrooke West Suite 1900, pg. 1501
FCB MONTREAL, 1751 rue Richardson Suite 6.200, pg. 372
G L'AGENCE, 465 Saint-Jean St Studio 700, pg. 412
GEOMETRY GLOBAL, 215 Rue Saint-Jacques Bureau 333, pg. 421
GROUPE RINALDI COMMUNICATION MARKETING, Ste 400 6750 av de l'Esplanade, pg. 463
H+K STRATEGIES, 1100 Rene Levesque Blvd W Ste 600, pg. 1541
HAMELIN MARTINEAU INC., 505 Maisonneuve Blvd W Ste 300, pg. 476
HAVAS WORLDWIDE CANADA, 1253 McGill College Ave 3rd Fl, pg. 490
HIGH ROAD COMMUNICATIONS, 3575 Blvd St-Laurent Ste 200, pg. 1519
HIGH-TOUCH COMMUNICATIONS INC., 372 Ste-Catherine St W Ste 320, pg. 513
J. WALTER THOMPSON CANADA, 630 Sherbrooke W Suite 710, pg. 566
KBS+, 555 Rene Levesque Blvd W 17th Fl, pg. 604
LAJEUNESSE COMMUNICATION MARKETING, 807 rue Roy Est, pg. 623
LG2, 3575 Saint-Laurent Boulevard Suite 900, pg. 656
MARKETEL, 1100 Rene-Levesque Boulevard West 19th Floor, pg. 695
MARKETING INITIATIVES, 481 Prince Arthur W Ste 301, pg. 698
MEDIA EXPERTS, 7236 ru Marconi, pg. 1365
MEDIAVATION, 1260 Mackay St Ste 200, pg. 745
NATIONAL PUBLIC RELATIONS, 2001 McGill College Ave Ste 800, pg. 1600
NOLIN BBDO, 3575 Boulevard St-Laurent Suite 300, pg. 812
NURUN INC., 740 Notre Dame West Street, pg. 819
OGILVY HEALTHWORLD, 215 Rue Saint Jacques Ste 333, pg. 853
OGILVY MONTREAL, 215 Rue St-Jaccques Ste 333, pg. 829
PAPRIKA COMMUNICATIONS, 400 Laurier St W Ste 610, pg. 872
PINNACLE DIRECT, 4700 rue de la Savane Ste 102, pg. 892
PRECISION ADVERTISING, 5530 Pare St Ste 201, pg. 908
PUBLICIS DIALOG & INTERACTIVE-MONTREAL, 3530 Boulvard Saint-Laurent Bureau 400, pg. 925
PUBLICIS MONTREAL, 3530 Blvd St- Laurent St 400, pg. 925
RENMARK FINANCIAL COMMUNICATIONS, INC., 1550 Metcalfe Ste 502, pg. 968
REPUBLIK PUBLICITE + DESIGN INC., 1435 St-Alexandre Ste 220, pg. 969
RESERVOIR, 5721 Monkland, pg. 970
SAINT-JACQUES VALLEE TACTIK, 1600 boul Rene-Levesque W 10th Fl, pg. 1015
SERVICE MEDIA PAYANT INC., 417 Saint Pierre, pg. 1034
SID LEE, 75 Queen Street Ofc 1400, pg. 1040
STARMEDIA GROUP, 1285 Rue Hodge, pg. 1080
STATTNER COMMUNICATIONS INC., 3001 Sherbrooke St W Ste 102, pg. 1081
SUDLER & HENNESSEY, 4700 De La Savane Ste 200, pg. 1095
TAM-TAM/TBWA, 1470 Peel St Tower A Ste 700, pg. 1116
TANK, 55 Prince St, pg. 1109
TAXI, 1435 Rue Saint Alexandre Bureau 620, pg. 1112
TEQUILA COMMUNICATION & MARKETING INC., 3556 boul Saint Laurent Bureau Ste 200, pg. 1136
TMP WORLDWIDE/ADVERTISING & COMMUNICATIONS, 1453 Sainte-Alexandre St Ste 850, pg. 1148
TUXEDO AGENCY, 3414 Ave du Parc Ste 202, pg. 1163
ZAD COMMUNICATIONS, 4446 Saint-Laurent Blvd, Ste 908, pg. 1253
ZENITHOPTIMEDIA CANADA INC., 3530 St-Laurent Boulevard Ste 400, pg. 1398
ZIP COMMUNICATION INC, 388 Saint-Jacques St Ste 500, pg. 1258

North Bay

TWG COMMUNICATIONS, 101 Worthington St E Ste 433, pg. 1164

North Vancouver

MAGNOLIA COMMUNICATIONS, 988 Sauve Ct, pg. 686
THINK MINT MEDIA, 2433 Dollarton Hwy Ste 215, pg. 1139

North York

PRIME ADVERTISING, 111 Gordon Baker Rd Ste 428, pg. 910

Oakville

3H COMMUNICATIONS INC., 309 Church St, pg. 7
KARSTAN COMMUNICATIONS, 700 Doorbell Dr Ste 301, pg. 603
PATTISON OUTDOOR ADVERTISING, 2285 Wyecroft Rd, pg. 878

Ottawa

ACART COMMUNICATIONS, INC., 171 Nepean St Ste 600, pg. 18
APCO WORLDWIDE, 255 Albert Street Suite 703, pg. 64
DELTA MEDIA, 350 Sparks St Ste 405, pg. 1493
FLEISHMAN-HILLARD, 100 Queen Street 13th Floor, pg. 1518
FUEL YOUTH ENGAGEMENT, 7 Hinton Ave N Ste 100, pg. 407
HIGH ROAD COMMUNICATIONS, 100 Queen St ste 1300, pg. 1519
HILL + KNOWLTON STRATEGIES, 55 Metcalfe St Ste 1100, pg. 1541
LAUNCHFIRE INTERACTIVE INC., 200 Isabella St 5th Fl, pg. 631
THE MARKETING WORKS, 55 Murray St Ste 108, pg. 699
MCGILL BUCKLEY, 2206 Anthony Avenue, pg. 735
MEDIAPLUS ADVERTISING, 200-203 Catherine St, pg. 744
WEBER SHANDWICK, 130 Albert St Ste 802, pg. 1678

Owen Sound

AVENUE A INTEGRATED MARKETING INC., Ave A 104 Shane St 2nd Fl, pg. 82

Parksville

BRAVENETMEDIA.COM, 100-200 Jensen Ave Ste 101, pg. 1327

Port Hope

LIMELIGHT ADVERTISING & DESIGN, 26 Ontario St Ste 200, pg. 658

Quebec

COSSETTE COMMUNICATION-MARKETING, 300 Saint Paul Street Ste 300, pg. 238

Regina

Saint Catharines

Saint Jacobs

Saint John's

Saint-Lambert

Sainte-Marie

Sault Sainte Marie

Sudbury

Thornhill

Toronto

Vancouver

Vaughan

Victoria

Waterloo

Westmount

Whitehorse

Winnipeg

Yellowknife

CHILE

Santiago

CHINA

Beijing

J. WALTER THOMPSON BEIJING, RM 501, 5/F Jin Bao Tower, 89 Jin Bao St., pg. 568
KETCHUM-PUBLIC RELATIONS LTD., 10/F Tower A, Vantone Center, Chaoyang District, pg. 1564
LEO BURNETT-BEIJING, Room 1308 China World Tower 2 No 1 Jian Guo Meri Wai Avenue, pg. 647
MAXUS, Rm 503 5/F Jin Bao Building 89 Jin Bao St, Dong Cheng District, pg. 1354
MEC, 1206 12/F The Huali Building No 58 Jinbao Street, Dongcheng District, pg. 1362
MEDIACOM BEIJING, Room 1205B Jin Bao Tower 89 Jino Bao St, Dong Cheng District, pg. 1372
MS&L CHINA, 12F 01-03 Prospect Center West, 5 Guanghua Road, pg. 1596
OGILVY & MATHER ADVERTISING BEIJING, 9th Floor Huali Building 58 Jinbao Street, pg. 841
OGILVY PR WORLDWIDE, Room 1901-1904 19th Floor Jinbao Tower, No 89 Jinbao Street, pg. 1609
OGILVYONE WORLDWIDE, 9th Floor Huali Building 58 Jinbao Street, pg. 841
PEGASUS COMMUNICATIONS, Room No 801 MapleTree Tower No 108, Chaoyang District, pg. 1508
PORTER NOVELLI-BEIJING, 12A Prime Tower NO22 Chaowai Street, Chaoyang District, pg. 1624
PUBLICIS (BEIJING), Rm 1510 15/F Zhuzong Tower No 25 Dong San Huan Zhong Rd, Chaoyang District, pg. 931
RUDER FINN ASIA LIMITED, Room 101 Office Building East Lake Villas 35 Dongzhimenwai Main Street, Dongcheng District, pg. 1643
SAATCHI & SAATCHI, 36/F Central International Trade Centre Tower C, 6A Jianguomen Wai Avenue, pg. 1010
STARCOM BEIJING, Rm 1507 15/F Bright China Chang An Tower One, 7 Jianguomen Nei Ave, pg. 1079
TBWA BEIJING, Room 1121 Tower 03 GuangHualu SOHO No 22 GuangHua Lu, ChaoYang District, pg. 1128
TBWA GREATER CHINA, Unit 605 Jianwai SOHO Ofc Tower B No 39 Dong San Huan Zhong Lu, pg. 1128
WE MARKETING GROUP, Tower W1 Oriental Plz, pg. 1276
WEBER SHANDWICK, Unit 706 -707 7F China Life Tower, 16 Chaoyangmen Rd Chaoyang, pg. 1682
WUNDERMAN BEIJING, #502 Building 17 Jianwal SOHO 39 East 3rd Ring Road, Chao Yang District, pg. 1231

Guangzhou

APCO WORLDWIDE, No 3 Xing An Rd Pearl River New Town, pg. 64
EDELMAN, Room 707 Dongshan Plaza 69 Xianlie Zhong Road, pg. 1506
EPSILON INTERNATIONAL, Room 2019 20/F Tian Qi Yi HongXiang Building, 611 Tian He Bei Road, pg. 351
FLEISHMAN-HILLARD GUANGZHOU, 3707 F Center Plz No 161 Linhe Road W, Tianhe District, pg. 1520
GOLIN, Unit 2408-09 Guangdong Telecom Plaza, No 18 Zhongshan Er Road, pg. 1532
KETCHUM-PUBLIC RELATIONS, Room 2003 Peace World Plaza 362-366 Huanshi Dong Lu, pg. 1564
LEO BURNETT-GUANGZHOU, 5/F North Tower Poly International Plaza, Yue Jiang Zhong Road, pg. 647
MCCANN ERICKSON GUANGMING LTD., 33/F Telecom Plaza, 18 Zhong Shan Er Road, pg. 718
OGILVY PR WORLDWIDE, Bldg 12 No 1 Xia Shi Zhi Street, Fangcun Ave Liwan District, pg. 1609
OMD GUANGZHOU, Rm 3707 Tower B Ctr Plz, 161 Linhe Rd W Tianhe District, pg. 1381
PUBLICIS GUANGZHOU, Publicis House Guangdong Guest House, pg. 931
SAATCHI & SAATCHI, 2-5F Gold Sun Building 109 Ti Yu Xi Road, pg. 1010
STARCOM GUANGZHOU, 2&3A/F SanXin Plz No 33 W Huangpu Ave, pg. 1079
WEBER SHANDWICK, Unit 3301B Guangdong Telecom Plz 18 Zhongshan Er Rd, Yuexiu District, pg. 1683
WUNDERMAN, Room 04-06 31/f Onelink Center, No. 230-232 Tianhe Road, pg. 1232
YOUNG & RUBICAM GUANGZHOU, 28th Fl 246 ZhongShanSi Road, pg. 1242

Shanghai

AKQA, INC., Rm B201-203 Bldg 2 Park 2 Space, 169 Meng Zi Rd, pg. 1281
APCO WORLDWIDE, Suites 2102-2103 CITIC Square, 1168 Nanjing Road West, pg. 64
BBDO CHINA, 42/F 1 Grand Gateway Plaza, NO 1 Hong Qiao Road, pg. 114
BENTLEY PORTER NOVELLI-SHANGHAI, International Rm 2012 Cloud Nine International Plz, No1018 Changning Road, pg. 1624
THE BRAND UNION SHANGHAI, 26 F The Ctr 989 Changle Rd, pg. 157
DDB CHINA - SHANGHAI, Park2Space 4th Floor Building 2 169 Mengzi Road, Luwan District, pg. 279
EBA COMMUNICATIONS - SHANGHAI, Rm 1608 Shanghai CITS Bldg 1277 Beijing Rd W, pg. 1463
EDELMAN, 3F Want Want Plaza, 211 Shi Men Yi Lu, pg. 1506
EPSILON INTERNATIONAL, Ste 103 Block D Red Town, 570 Huai Hai Rd W, pg. 351
FCB SHANGHAI, 20/F Huai Hai Plaza 1045 Huai Hai Zhong Rd, pg. 379
FLEISHMAN-HILLARD LINK, LTD., 1 Grand Gateway 1 Hongqiao Rd, Xu Hui District, pg. 1521
FUTUREBRAND, 18/F Huai Hai Plaza, 1045 Huai Hai Zhong Rd, pg. 411
GOLIN, 18/F HuaiHai Plz, 1045 HuaiHai Zhong Rd, pg. 1532
GREY SHANGHAI, 3/F Block 3 The Bridge 8 Phase III, 550 Jumen Road, pg. 455
GROUPM CHINA, 31th Fl 1038 Nanjing Xi Rd, Westgate, pg. 1337
H-LINE OGILVY COMMUNICATIONS CO LTD, 17D Boai Tower, 758 Nanjing Xilu, pg. 1608
HAVAS WORLDWIDE SHANGHAI, 11/F, Novel Building, 887 Huaihai Zhong Road, pg. 500
J. WALTER THOMPSON, 25/F No 989 Chang Le Road The Center, pg. 568
JACK MORTON WORLDWIDE (SHANGHAI), 1045 Huaihai Zhong Road, 16/F Huai Hai Plaza, pg. 583
KETCHUM-PUBLIC RELATIONS, Rm 2707-2710 Tower One Kerry Everbright City, No 218 Tian Mu Rd W, pg. 1564
KING HARVESTS, 2F No.400 Gulin Road, Pufa Creation Park, pg. 931
LEO BURNETT SHANGHAI ADVERTISING CO., LTD., 2F Block F Red Town 570 Huai Hai Road (W), pg. 648
LOWE PROFERO CHINA, 36/F Huai Hai Plaza, 1045 Huai Hai Zhong Road, pg. 791
M&C SAATCHI, No 486 Fuxing Middle Road, pg. 678
MAXUS, 35 F Westgate 1038, pg. 1354
MCGARRYBOWEN, No 44 Ln 1285 Middle Huaihai Rd, pg. 734
MEDIACOM SHANGHAI, 989 Changle Rd, The Centre 26th Fl, pg. 1372
MILLWARD BROWN CHINA, Fl 17 Golden Bridge Plz, No 585 Xizang Rd Middle, pg. 759
MS&L SHANGHAI, Room F 15/F No755 Huai Hai Zhong Road, pg. 1597
NURUN/CHINA INTERACTIVE, 162 Yong Nian Rd, 3rd Fl, pg. 924
OGILVY & MATHER (CHINA) LTD., 25F The Center 989 Changle Road, pg. 841
OGILVY PR WORLDWIDE, 26th Floor The Center, 989 Changle Road, pg. 1609
OGILVYONE, 26F The Center 989 Changle Road, pg. 841
PHD CHINA, Rm 1101 Tower 2, No 3 Hongqiao Rd, pg. 1385
PUBLICIS SHANGHAI, 6/F Building A 98 Yan Ping Road, pg. 931
RUDER FINN ASIA LIMITED, 2nd Floor Block 7 789 Huang Pi Nan Road, pg. 1643
SAATCHI & SAATCHI, 29 F Lippo Plaza, 222 Huai Hai Zhong Road, pg. 1010
SOCIALISTIC CHINA, 11/F Novel Building No 887 Huaihai Zhong Road, pg. 500
STARCOM SHANGHAI, 3/F 900 HuaiHai Middle Rd, pg. 1080
TBWA SHANGHAI, 9F 71 West Suzhou Road, pg. 1128
TEXT 100 SHANGHAI, Unit 2005 Ascenda Plz, 333 Tian Yao Qiao Rd, pg. 1662
UM, 21/F Huaihai Plz, 1045 Huaihai Rd, pg. 718
WEBER SHANDWICK, 18/F HuaiHai Plaza, 1045 HuaiHai Zhong Rd, pg. 1682
WIEDEN + KENNEDY, Floor 5th No1035 ChangLe Road, pg. 1205
WUNDERMAN, Room 605-606 Ocean Tower, 550 Yan An Road East, pg. 1231
WWWINS ISOBAR, Suite 103 1st Floor, Block G Huai Hai Xi Road, pg. 562
YOUNG & RUBICAM SHANGHAI, Rm 608-606 Ocean Tower 550 Yan An Rd E, pg. 1242
ZENITHOPTIMEDIA, 1-4/F900 Huai Hai Zhong Road, pg. 1401

CHINA (HONG KONG)

Causeway Bay

BATES CHI & PARTNERS, 3301-09 Tower One Times Square, pg. 1217
LUMINOUS EXPERIENTIAL MSLGROUP, 14/F East Exchange Tower, 38 Leighton Road, pg. 931
MCCANN ERICKSON HONG KONG LTD., 23F Sunning Plz 10 Hysan Ave, pg. 721
MRM WORLDWIDE HONG KONG, 14 Fl Sunning Plaza 10 Hysan Avenue, pg. 784
UM, 23rd Floor Sunning Plaza, Hysan Ave, pg. 721

Central

APCO WORLDWIDE, 19/F Cambridge House Taikoo Place, 979 Kings Road, pg. 64
THE BRAND UNION HONG KONG, 23rd Floor 99 Queens Road, pg. 157
COHN & WOLFE IMPACTASIA, Ste 801 Chinachem Hollywood Ctr 1 Hollywood Rd, pg. 1482
EBA COMMUNICATIONS LTD, Unit B 19/F On Hing Bldg 1 On Hing Terrace, pg. 1462
THE HOFFMAN AGENCY, The Workstation 16th Fl 43 Lyndhurst Terrace, pg. 1546
KREAB HONG KONG, 19/F Kinwick Centre 32 Hollywood Road, Suite 1902-04, pg. 1569
OGILVY & MATHER ADVERTISING, 23rd Floor The Center 99 Queen's Road, pg. 842
OGILVY & MATHER ASIA/PACIFIC, 23rd Floor The Center 99 Queen's Road, pg. 842
OGILVY PUBLIC RELATIONS WORLDWIDE, 23rd Floor The Center 99 Queens Road, pg. 1608
OGILVYONE WORLDWIDE, 23rd Floor The Center, 99 Queen's Road, pg. 844

Hong Kong

AGENDA, 03-06 32F, 118 Connaight Road West, pg. 1231
AGENDA, 03-06 32F, 118 Connaight Road West, pg. 1217
BLUE CURRENT, Ste 1501 Cityplaza 4 12 Taikoo Wan Road, Taikoo Shing, pg. 313
DDB WORLDWIDE LTD., Unit 1201 Core E Cyberport 3, 100 Cyberport Road, pg. 283
DOREMUS (HONG KONG), Ste 1501 15/F Cityplaza 4, 12 Taikoo Wan Road Taikoo, pg. 325
EDELMAN, 701 Central Plaza 18 Harbour Rd, pg. 1506
H&O, 23/F The Centre 99 Queen's Road Central, pg. 841
HAVAS WORLDWIDE HONG KONG, 9/F Northeast Warwick House Taikoo Place, 979 King's Road, Island East, pg. 500
JACK MORTON WORLDWIDE (HONG KONG), 10/F Oxford House TaiKoo Place, Quarry Bay, pg. 582
M&C SAATCHI HONG KONG, 29/F Cambridge House 979 King''s Road, pg. 676
MAXX MARKETING LTD., 7/F Manley Tower, 828 Cheung Sha Wan Road, pg. 842
MS&L, 6/F Cityplaza 3, 14 Taikoo Wan Rd, pg. 1597
OMD HONG KONG, Unit 808 Core E Cyberport 3, 100 Cyberport Rd, pg. 1381
PUBLICIS HONG KONG, 23/F 1063 Kings Road, Quarry Bay, pg. 931
TBWA HONG KONG, 16/F Cambridge House, Taikoo Place, pg. 1128
WE, Room 1901-07 19/F Tai Yau Building, Johnston Road, Wan Chai, pg. 1674

Kowloon

CHILLI MARKETING LIMITED, Rm A9, 8/F, Lee King Ind. Bldg., 12 Ng Fong St, pg. 208
MAXX MARKETING LTD., 7 Floor Manley Tower 828 Cheung Sha Wan Road, pg. 841

North Point

GREY HONG KONG, 31/F 169 Electric Rd, pg. 455
HAKUHODO HONG KONG LTD., 25th F Prosperity Mellennia Traza 663 Kings Road, pg. 474
ISOBAR HONG KONG, 16/F 633 King's Rd, pg. 562
KETCHUM-PUBLIC RELATIONS, 33rd Floor Two Chinachem Exchange Square, 338 King's Road, pg. 1565
PUBLICITAS HONG KONG, 25/F & 26/F Two Chinachem

Exchange Square, 338 Kings Road, pg. 1427
Y&R HONG KONG, 32nd Fl 633 Kings Rd, pg. 1241

Quarry Bay

BURSON-MARSTELLER, 23/F Chinachem Exchange Square, 1 Hoi Wan Street, pg. 1470
FUTUREBRAND, 8/F Oxford House Taikoo Place, 979 King's Rd, pg. 411
GOLIN, 8/F Oxford House, 979 King's Road, pg. 1531
HILL & KNOWLTON HONG KONG LTD., 36/F PCCW Tower Taikoo Place 979 Kings Road, pg. 1544
J. WALTER THOMPSON, 36/F PCCW Tower Taikoo Place 979 King's Road, pg. 568
LEO BURNETT-HONG KONG, 6th Fl City Plaza 3 14 Taikoo Wan Road, pg. 648
LOWE, 6th Floor Oxford House tai Koo Place 979 Kings Road, pg. 794
THE MARKETING STORE, 18 Westlands Rd, pg. 1421
THE MARKETING STORE-PROMOTIONAL PRODUCTS, 18 Westlands Road, pg. 1421
MAXUS, 36/F PCCW Tower Taikoo Pl 979 Kings Rd, pg. 1354
MEC, 37th Floor PCCW Tower Taikoo Place 979 King's Road, pg. 1363
MEDIACOM HONG KONG, 36 Floor PCCW Tower 979 Kings Road Taikoo Place, pg. 1372
RAZORFISH HONG KONG, 22/F Chinachem Exchange Square 1, pg. 1310
REPRISE MEDIA ASIA, Rm. 1302-04, Oxford House, Taikoo Pl., 979 King's Rd., pg. 560
STARCOM HONG KONG, Room 602-605 1063 King's Road, pg. 1079
TBWA ASIA PACIFIC, 16 & 17/F Cambridge House Taikoo Place, 979 King's Road, pg. 1128
WEBER SHANDWICK, 10/F Oxford House Taikoo Place, 979 King's Rd, pg. 1683
ZENITHOPTIMEDIA, Room 1403-05 14/F 1063 Kings Road, pg. 1401

Taikoo Shing

BBDO HONG KONG, Ste 1501 15th Fl Cityplaza 4, 12 Taikoo Wan Rd, pg. 115
BLUECURRENT HONG KONG, Suite 1501, Cityplaza 4, 12 Taikoo Wan Road, pg. 1520
FLEISHMAN-HILLARD HONG KONG LTD., Suite 1501 Cityplaza 4 12 Taikoo Wan Road, pg. 1521

Wanchai

EPSILON INTERNATIONAL, Rm 2502 25/F Hopewell Ctr 183 Queen's Rd E, pg. 351
RACEPOINT GLOBAL, 8th Floor The Broadway, 54-62 Lockhart Road, pg. 1630
SAATCHI & SAATCHI, 27/F Tai Tung Building Fleming Road, pg. 1010
TEXT 100 HONG KONG, Ste 3805 Level 38 Hopewell Center, 183 Queens Rd E, pg. 1662

COLOMBIA

Bogota

ARC WORLDWIDE, Carrera 13 No 90-21, Oficina 406, pg. 1406
BURSON-MARSTELLER, Carrera 11 A # 93 B - 30 Piso 3, pg. 1467
COMPASS PORTER NOVELLI, Diagonal 97 #17-60 Piso 3, pg. 1462
COMPASS PORTER NOVELLI, Diagonal 97 #17-60 Piso 3, pg. 1621
DDB WORLDWIDE COLOMBIA S.A., Diagonal 97 #17-60 Piso 10, pg. 280
FCB MAYO, Ctro Empresarial Torre Platino Av Cra 19, No 95-31/55 Piso 7, pg. 377
GREY: REP, Calle 94 #16-57, pg. 453
J. WALTER THOMPSON, Calle 98 No 22 64 Floor 12, pg. 578
LEO BURNETT COLOMBIA, S.A., Carrera 13 N 89-59, pg. 640
LOWE SSP3, Carrera 9, 79A - 19 Piso 6, pg. 793
MCCANN ERICKSON CORP. S.A., Calle 96 #13A-21/33, Santafe de Bogota, pg. 719
MEC, Cra14 No 94-65 Piso 3 Edificio Plazuela 94, pg. 1361
OGILVY & MATHER, Carrera 13 No 94A-26, pg. 839
PUBLICIS-CB, Calle 82 No 6-51, pg. 929
SANCHO BBDO, Calle 98 No 903 2nd Floor, pg. 103
TBWA/COLOMBIA SUIZA DE PUBLICIDAD LTDA, Diagonal 97 # 17/60 Edificio Centro Empresarial, 3rd Floor, pg. 1132
YOUNG & RUBICAM BOGOTA, Carrera 11 A #93B-30, 5 Piso Santa Fe De, pg. 1249

Cali

DDB WORLDWIDE COLOMBIA, S.A., Calle 6 Oeste No 1B-72, pg. 280
OGILVY & MATHER, Calle 64 Norte 5BN 146 of 315, Centro Empresa, pg. 839

Medellin

MCCANN ERICKSON CORP. (S.A.), Edificio Banco Andino Carrera 43A #16A Sur 38, Ofc 1205, pg. 719
MEC, Carrera 43A No9 Sur-91 Oficina 1304 Centro de Negocios Las Villas, Torre Norte, pg. 1361
PEREZ Y VILLA BBDO, Calle 16 No 43B-50, pg. 103

COSTA RICA

San Jose

ASESORES/Y&R S.A., Edificio Asesores Apartado 6947-1000, Guadalupe, pg. 1250
CREA PUBLICIDAD, Torre La Sabana Sabana N Piso 1, pg. 377
GARNIER BBDO, Urbanizacion Tournon Diagonal a la Camara de Comercio Barrio Tournn, pg. 103
JOTABEQU ADVERTISING, Avenue 1 & 3, pg. 453
JOTABEQU ADVERTISING, Avenue 1 & 3, pg. 1371
TBWA COSTA RICA, Guachipelin Escazu, pg. 1132
Y&R MEDIA, Iglesia San Francisco Guadalupe, Apartado 6947-1000, pg. 1361

COTE D'IVOIRE

Abidjan

OCEAN OGILVY, Avenue C16 Jean Mermoz Villa n66, pg. 848

CROATIA

Zagreb

GREY GROUP CROATIA, Trg Bana Jelacica 3, pg. 448
HAVAS WORLDWIDE ZAGREB, Ilica 26, pg. 491
IMELDA OGILVY, Trg zrtava fasizima 2/4, pg. 830
MCCANN ERICKSON, Heinzelova 33A, pg. 719
PUBLICIS D.O.O., Heinzelova 33, pg. 918
STUDIO MARKETING J. WALTER THOMPSON, Draskoviceva 5, pg. 572
WEBER SHANDWICK, Heinzelova 33a, pg. 1679
ZENITHOPTIMEDIA, Heinzelova 33, pg. 1398

CYPRUS

Nicosia

ACTION GLOBAL COMMUNICATIONS, 6 Kondilaki Street, 1090, pg. 1531
ACTION PR CYPRUS, Kondilaki 6, pg. 1679
DE LE MA/ MCCANN ERICKSON, 36 Grivas Dighenis Ave, pg. 719
INNOVATION LEO BURNETT, 90 Ifigenias St 2nd Fl, 2003 Strovolos, pg. 642
MARKETWAY LTD., Marketway Building, 20 Karpenisiou Street, pg. 918
PANDORA/OGILVY & MATHER, Kennedy Business Center 12-14 Kennedy Ave 1st Fl Ofc 101, pg. 830
TELIA & PAVLA BBDO, 92 Makarios III Ave, pg. 105

CZECH REPUBLIC

Brno

MQI BRNO, SPOL. S R.O., Lipova 17, pg. 1226
OGILVY & MATHER, Hybesova 18, pg. 830

Prague

AMI COMMUNICATIONS, Tyn 4/641, pg. 1507
DDB PRAGUE, Lomnickeho 1705/5, pg. 280
FCB PRAGUE, Zerotinova 1133/32, pg. 373
FLEISHMAN-HILLARD CZECH REPUBLIC, Lomnickeho 1705/9, pg. 1519
HAVAS WORLDWIDE DIGITAL PRAGUE, Expo 58 Letenske sady 1500, pg. 492
HAVAS WORLDWIDE PRAGUE, Expo 58 Letenske Sady 1500, pg. 492
INITIATIVE PRAGUE, Palac Karlin Thamova 11, pg. 1346
MARK BBDO, Krizikova 34, pg. 105
MATHER COMMUNICATIONS S.R.O., Prohunu 13, pg. 830
MCCANN ERICKSON PRAGUE, Riegrovy Sady 28, pg. 719
MEDIACOM PRAHA, Nadrazni 32, pg. 1369
OGILVY & MATHER, Privozni 2A, pg. 830
OGILVY PR, Privozni 2a, pg. 1607
OGILVYONE WORLDWIDE, Privozni 2A Grounds, pg. 830
PLEON IMPACT, Konviktska 24, pg. 105
PUBLICIS, Jankovcova 1114-1123, pg. 918
SAATCHI & SAATCHI, Jankovcova 23, pg. 1002
TBWA PRAHA, Frantiska Krizka 1/362, pg. 1117
WEBER SHANDWICK, Narodni 25, pg. 1679
WMC/GREY, Belgicka 115/40, pg. 448
WUNDERMAN, Nadrazni 32, pg. 1232
Y&R PRAHA, S.R.O., Nadrazni 762/32, pg. 1248

DENMARK

Arhus

JOP, OVE & MYRTHU, Kannikegade 18-1, pg. 1622
UNCLE GREY A/S, Studsgade 35, pg. 448

Copenhagen

ADPEOPLE WORLDWIDE, Per Henrik Lings Alle 4, pg. 1232
BBDO DENMARK, St Kongensgade 72, pg. 105
BURSON-MARSTELLER, Oestergade 26B, pg. 1467
DDB DENMARK, Bredgade 6, pg. 280
HAVAS WORLDWIDE COPENHAGEN, Jagtvej 169B, pg. 492
J. WALTER THOMPSON COPENHAGEN, Toldbodgade 55, pg. 572
JKL COPENHAGEN, Amaliegade 41 A, pg. 1596
JOP, OVE & MYRTHU, Aldersrogade 5, pg. 1622
LOWEFRIENDS AS, Kobmagergade 60, pg. 795
MCCANN COPENHAGEN, Gothersgade 14 4, pg. 719
MEC, St Kongengade 59, pg. 1358
MEDIACOM DENMARK, Europaplads 2 3.sal, 8000 Aarhus, pg. 1369
MILLWARD BROWN DENMARK, Raadhuspladsen 45-47 5th Fl, pg. 759
OGILVY HEALTHWORLD/COPENHAGEN, Toltbodsgade 55, pg. 852
OGILVYONE WORLDWIDE, Toldbodgade 55, pg. 830
REPUTATION, Bredgade 15, pg. 918
SAATCHI & SAATCHI, Esplanaden 34A 1 sal, pg. 1002
TBWA COPENHAGEN, Bredgade 6, 3.sal, pg. 1118
TBWA INTERACTIVE, Bredgade 6 3 sal, pg. 1118
WUNDERMAN, Strandboulevarden 122 4, pg. 1232

Frederiksberg

STARCOM DENMARK, Solbjergvej 3 3 sal, pg. 1078
ZENITH MEDIA, Solbjergvej 3 3 sal, pg. 1400

Hellerup

COMMUNIQUE, Ryvangs Alle 50, pg. 1507

DOMINICAN REPUBLIC

Santo Domingo

360 MC FCB, c/Luis F. Thomen 620A, El Millon, pg. 378
AS PUBLICIDAD, Jose Contreras no 62, Zona Universitaria, pg. 499
PAGES BBDO, Abraham 1060 Lincoln, pg. 103
Y&R DAMARIS, C. POR A., Avenida de los Proceres Corner, Ekman Arroyo Hondo, pg. 1250
Y&R MEDIA, Avenida de los Proceres, Esquina Eric Leonard Ekman #25,, Arroya Hondo, pg. 1361

ECUADOR

Guayaquil

MARURI, Avenida Raul Gomez Lince Av 32 N-O #640, Bajo el Mirador de Urdenor, pg. 1596
NORLOP J. WALTER THOMPSON, Tulcan 1017 y Luque, pg. 578
SALTIVERI OGILVY & MATHER, Avenida Francisco de Orellana Edificio World Trade Center, Torre A Oficina 1105, pg. 839

Quito

COORDINAMOS PORTER NOVELLI, Av Colon E4-105 y 9 de Octobre Edificio Solamar Piso 1, Oficina 102, pg. 1621
FCB MAYO, Av Orellana E11-75 y Coruna, Edificio Albra Office 608, pg. 378
MEC/Y&R MEDIA, Avenida Amazonas y Naciones Unidas, Edificio La Previsora,, Torre A, Piso 8, pg. 1361
RIVAS & HERRERA/Y&R, Edificio La Previsora Av Amazonas Y NNUU Esquina, Torre A Piso 7, pg. 1250
SALTIVERI OGILVY & MATHER GUAYAQUIL, Av Amazonas y calle UN de Periodistas Edificio Puerta del Sol, Torre Este Piso 7, pg. 839

EGYPT

Cairo

AMA LEO BURNETT, 2005C Corniche El Nil St Ramlet Beaulec, Nile City Towers N Tower, pg. 642
FP7 CAIRO, 12 Al Esraa Street Lebanon Street, Mohandessin, pg. 719
HORIZON FCB, 26 Nadi El Jadeed St, pg. 376
IMPACT BBDO, 15 Hassan Sabry, zamalek, pg. 106
J. WALTER THOMPSON CAIRO, 306 Cornish El Nile, Maadi, pg. 576
MEC, 8 Gazirat El Arab St 2 Fl, Al Mohandessin, pg. 1361
MEMAC OGILVY, 4 Abdel Rahman El Rafei St Mohandessin, pg. 848
PUBLICIS-GRAPHICS, 3 El Mansour Mohamed St 5th Fl Ste 502, Zamalek, pg. 923
SAATCHI & SAATCHI, 19 Soliman Abaza Street, Mohandesseen, pg. 1002

EL SALVADOR

La Libertad

PUBLICIDAD COMERCIAL, Edificio Comercial, Avenida el Espino No.77, Urbanizacion Madre Selva Antig, pg. 557

San Salvador

FCB CREA, Boulevard Los Proceres 288, pg. 378
J. WALTER THOMPSON, Calle Circunvalacion No 332, Colonia San Benito, pg. 578
OGILVY & MATHER EL SALVADOR, 550 Avenida La Capilla No, Col San Benito, pg. 839
TRIBU DDB EL SALVADOR, 519 Bulevar El Hippodromo, pg. 280

ESTONIA

Tallinn

DDB ESTONIA LTD., Parnu Mnt 69, pg. 280
INOREK & GREY, Mafina 20, pg. 448
KONTUUR-LEO BURNETT, Parnu Road 142A, pg. 642
TBWA ESTONIA, Pamu mnt 139a, pg. 1118
ZAVOD BBDO, Rotermanni 5/ Roseni 10, pg. 106

FINLAND

Helsinki

DDB HELSINKI, Hietaniemenkatu 7A, pg. 281
HASAN & PARTNERS OY, Pursimiehenkatu 29-31B, pg. 719
HAVAS WORLDWIDE HELSINKI, Peramiehenkatu 12 E, pg. 492
J. WALTER THOMPSON, Itanerenkatu 1, pg. 572
KREAB HELSINKI, Etelaesplanadi 18, pg. 1569
MCCANN HELSINKI, Lautatarhankatu 8 B, pg. 720
MEC, Unioninkatue 24, pg. 1358
OMD FINLAND OY, Fredrikinkatu 42, pg. 1381
POHJOISRANTA - HELSINKI, Kalevankatu 20, pg. 1467
SEK & GREY, Annankatu 28, pg. 449
TAIVAS, Unioninkatu 13, pg. 831
TBWA PHS, Fredrikinkatu 42, pg. 1118
WUNDERMAN HELSINKI, Koydenpunojankatu 2 a D, pg. 1232

FRANCE

Annecy-le-Vieux

HAVAS 360-ANNECY, 7 ave du Pre Felin, Parc des Glaisins, pg. 493

Boulogne

Y&R PARIS, 67 Avenue Andre Morizet, pg. 1245

Boulogne-Billancourt

BEING, 50/54 rue du Silly, pg. 1118
BURSON-MARSTELLER, 6 rue Escudier, CEDEX, pg. 1468
CLM BBDO, 93 Rue Nationale, pg. 106
E-GRAPHICS, 162-164 rue de Billancourt, pg. 1119
EG PLUS WORLDWIDE, 50/54 rue de Silly, pg. 1119
GREY HEALTHCARE PARIS, 63 bis rue de Sevres, pg. 423
NURUN FRANCE, 31 bis rue des Longs Pres, pg. 925
TBWA CORPORATE, 50-54 rue de Silly, pg. 1119
TBWA EUROPE, 50/54 rue de Silly, pg. 1119
TBWA/G1, 162-164 rue de Billancourt, pg. 1119
TBWA PARIS, 162-164 rue de Billancourt, pg. 1119
WUNDERMAN, 57 avenue Andre Morizet, pg. 1232
Y&R FRANCE S.A., 57 Ave Andre Morizet, pg. 1245

Clichy

FUTUREBRAND, 69 Blvd du General, Leclerc, pg. 411
MCCANN ERICKSON PARIS, 69 Blvd du General Leclerc, pg. 720
MRM PARIS, 69 Blvd du General Leclerc, pg. 783
QUALICONTACT, Espace Clichy 38 av Mozart, pg. 1119
W & CIE, 19 rue Klock, pg. 485

Levallois-Perret

DIGITASLBI, 36/40 rue Raspail, pg. 1289
FULLSIXADVERTISING, 157 Rue Anatole, pg. 485
THE MARKETING STORE, 105 rue Anatole France, pg. 1421
ZENITHOPTIMEDIA, 68 bis rue Marjolin, CEDEX, pg. 1399

Longwy

NURUN FRANCE, CET Centre Jean Monnet CS 61428, Longlaville CEDEX, pg. 925

Marseilles

PUBLICIS SOLEIL, 44 Blvd Longchamp, pg. 919

Metz-Tessy

PUBLICIS ACTIV ANNECY, Park Nord Les Pleiades no26, BP 434, pg. 919

Montpellier

NEA, Espace St-Charles Bat B., 300 rue Auguste Broussonnet, pg. 1304

Neuilly-sur-Seine

HILL & KNOWLTON/THOMPSON CORP., 88 Avenue Charles de Gaulle, CEDEX, pg. 1542
J. WALTER THOMPSON FRANCE, 88 Avenue Charles de Gaulle, pg. 573

Paris

ACTIVE INTERNATIONAL (EUROPE) S.A.R.L., 27 rue Nicolo, pg. 1324
ADNATIVE, 26 Ave Victor Hugo, pg. 1426
APCO WORLDWIDE, 15 rue de Marignan, pg. 63
/AUDITOIRE, 9 rue du Helder, pg. 1118
BDDP & FILS, 146 rue du Faubourg Poissonniere, pg. 1118
BETC LIFE, 85/87 rue du Faubourg Saint Martin, Passage du Desir CEDEX, pg. 492
BOZ PARIS, 22 rue de Courcelles, pg. 918
THE BRAND UNION PARIS, 26 Rue Notre-Dame des Victoires, pg. 158
CBA BE, 94 Avenue de Villiers, pg. 1218
CBA BE, 94 Avenue de Villiers, pg. 831
DDB COMMUNICATION FRANCE, 55 rue d'Amsterdam, pg. 281
DDB PARIS, 55 rue d'Amsterdam, pg. 281
EDELMAN, 54 Rue de Monceau, pg. 1504
/EXCEL, 2-6 Boulevard Poissonniere, pg. 1119
FCB PARIS, 21 rue de Berri, pg. 373
FLEISHMAN-HILLARD FRANCE, 37 Rue Delabiensaisance, pg. 1519
GOLIN, Square d"Orleans, pg. 1531
GREY PARIS, 92 Avenue Des Ternes, pg. 449
GYRO PARIS, 38 bis rue du fer a Moulin, pg. 469
HAKUHODO FRANCE S.A., 59 bd Exelmans, pg. 475
KETCHUM, 54 Rue de Clichy, CEDEX, pg. 1565
LANDOR ASSOCIATES, 44 rue des Petites Ecuries, pg. 624
LEO BURNETT, 12 rue James Watt, Saint Denis, pg. 642
LOWE STRATEUS, Square d'Orleans 80 rue Taitbout, pg. 793
M&C SAATCHI, 32 rue du Notre Dame des Victoires, pg. 677
MEC, 32 Rue Guersant TSA 70022, CEDEX, pg. 1358
MEDIACOM PARIS, 32 Rue Guersant, pg. 1369
MS&L FRANCE, 15 rue Bleue, CEDEX, pg. 1596
OGILVY & MATHER, 40 Ave George V, pg. 831
OGILVY PUBLIC RELATIONS, 40 Avenue Georges V, pg. 1607
OGILVYHEALTHCARE, 44 avenue George V, pg. 831
OGILVYONE, 136 Avenue des Champs Elysees, pg. 831
ORC IMAGE & STRATEGIES D'EMPLOYEUR, 6 boulevard des Capucines, pg. 581
PHONEVALLEY, 131 Ave Charles de Gaulle, Neuilly, pg. 918
PORTER NOVELLI-PARIS, 28 Rue Broca, pg. 1623
PUBLICIS CONSEIL, 133 Champs-Elysees, pg. 919
PUBLICIS DIALOG, 133 Avenue des Champs Elysees, CEDEX, pg. 919
PUBLICIS ET NOUS, 33 rue des Jeuneurs, pg. 919
PUBLICIS GROUPE S.A., 133 Ave des Champs-Elysee, pg. 917
PUBLICIS.NET, 133 Ave des Champs Elysees, pg. 919
PUBLICITAS S.A., 26 Avenue Victor Hugo, pg. 1428
RAPP PARIS, 55 Rue de Amsterdam, pg. 954
SAATCHI & SAATCHI, 53 Boulevard Ornano, pg. 1003
SELECTNY.PARIS, 94 Rue Saint Lazare, Esc A 7eme etage, pg. 1031
SID LEE, 12, rue du Sentier, pg. 1040
TEXTUEL LA MINE, 146 rue du Fauburg Poissonniere, pg. 1120
WE, 8 Rue Royale, pg. 1674

Puteaux

AFFIPERF, 8 rue Godefroy, pg. 485
HAVAS, 29/30 quai de Dion Bouton, pg. 484
HAVAS DIGITAL, 11 Square Leon Blum, pg. 486

HAVAS WORLDWIDE-EUROPE, 29/30 quai de Dion Bouton, pg. 491

Rennes

HAVAS 360 RENNES, 17 rue de la Quintaine, pg. 493

Strasbourg

PUBLICIS ACTIV STRASBOURG, 1 rue du Dome, pg. 919

Suresnes

CARRE NOIR, 24 rue Salmon de Rothschild, pg. 918
GEORGE P. JOHNSON (FRANCE) SARL, 74 Rue Rouget de Lisle, pg. 422

Toulouse

TBWA/COMPACT, 239 route de Saint-Simon, pg. 1119

Versailles

AID-ANALYSE INFORMATIQUE DE DONNEES, 4 Rue Henri le Sidamer, pg. 954

GEORGIA

Tbilisi

MCCANN ERICKSON GEORGIA, 71 Vazha-Pshavela Ave BCV 4th Fl, pg. 720

GERMANY

Bad Homburg

CPM GERMANY GMBH, Siemenstrasse 21, pg. 241

Berlin

APCO WORLDWIDE, Kontorhaus Mitte Friedrichstrasse 186, pg. 63
BBDO PROXIMITY BERLIN, Hausvogteiplatz 2, pg. 107
BURSON-MARSTELLER, Lennestrasse 1, pg. 1468
DDB BERLIN, Neue Schonhauser Strasse 3-5, pg. 282
DDB GROUP GERMANY, Neue Schoenhauser Strasse 3-5, pg. 282
HEIMAT WERBEAGENTUR GMBH, Segitzdamm 2, pg. 1120
ICONMOBILE, Wallstrasse 14a, pg. 1245
M&C SAATCHI, Oranienburgerstr 5a, pg. 677
M.E.C.H., Schonhauser Allee 37, Kultur Brauerei, pg. 721
OMD, Friedrichstrasse 61, pg. 1382
PIXELPARK AG, Bergmannstrasse 72, pg. 919
RAZORFISH GERMANY, Stralauer Allee 2b, pg. 1310
SELECTNY.BERLIN GMBH, Chaussee Strasse 123, pg. 1031
TBWA GERMANY, BERLIN, Rosenstrasse 16-17, pg. 1120
WEBER SHANDWICK, Schonhauser Allee 37 Geb P, pg. 1679

Bielefeld

PUBLICIS PIXELPARK, Walther-Rathenau-Strasse 33, pg. 919

Bonn

APCO WORLDWIDE, Poppelsdorfer Allee 114, pg. 63

Cologne

FACTS & FICTION GMBH, Anna-Schneider-Steig 2 Rheinauhafen, pg. 1232
INTERBRAND & CEE, Weinsbergstrasse 118a, pg. 857
WEBER SHANDWICK, Hohenzollernring 79-83, pg. 1679

Dusseldorf

BBDO DUSSELDORF, Konigsallee 92, pg. 106
GREY GROUP GERMANY, Platz der Ideen 1, pg. 449
HAVAS WORLDWIDE CENTRAL EUROPE, Kaiserwerther Strasse 135, pg. 493
HAVAS WORLDWIDE DIGITAL DUSSELDORF, Kaiserwerther Strasse 135, pg. 493
HAVAS WORLDWIDE DUSSELDORF, Kaiserwerther Strasse 135, pg. 493
HERING SCHUPPENER CONSULTING, Kreuzstrasse 60, pg. 1482
JACK MORTON WORLDWIDE (DUSSELDORF), Rochusstrasse 47, pg. 582
KETCHUM PLEON, Bahnstrasse 2, pg. 1564
KINETIC, Derendorf Allee 10, pg. 1351
MEC, Rosstrasse 92, pg. 1358
MEDIACOM DUSSELDORF, Derendorfer Alle 10, pg. 1351
MEDIACOM DUSSELDORF, Derendorfer Alle 10, pg. 1369
OGILVY & MATHER, Am Handelshafen 2-4, pg. 832
OGILVY HEALTHWORLD GMBH, Am Handelshafen 2-4, pg. 832
OGILVY HEALTHWORLD GMBH, Am Handelshafen 2-4, pg. 1607
SAPIENT GMBH - DUSSELDORF, Hammer St 19, pg. 1019
TBWA GERMANY, Schanzenstrasse 54a, pg. 1120
TRIBAL WORLDWIDE, Berliner Allee 10, pg. 282

Frankfurt

GREY, Schwedter St 6, pg. 449
HERING SCHUPPENER-FRANKFORT AMMAIN, Mainzer Land Street 41, pg. 1482
HILL + KNOWLTON STRATEGIES, Schwedlerstrasse 6, pg. 1542
KINETIC, Darmstadter Landstrasse 110, pg. 1351
MANNING, SELVAGE & LEE FRANKFURT, Otto Messmer St 1, pg. 1596
MRM WORLDWIDE, Grosser Hasenpfad 44, pg. 783
OCTAGON, Opernplatz 2, pg. 824
OGILVY & MATHER FRANKFURT, Darmstadter Landstrasse 112, pg. 831
OGILVYINTERACTIVE, Darmstadter Landstrasse 112, pg. 832
OGILVYONE GMBH, Darmstadter Landstrasse 112, pg. 832
RAZORFISH GMBH, Jakob Latscha Strasse 3, pg. 1310
TBWA GERMANY, Hanauer Landstrasse 182b, pg. 1120

Frankfurt am Main

ADVANTAGE CORPORATE COMMUNICATIONS GMBH, Lindle Street 12 3 Stock 3rd fl, pg. 325
BURSON-MARSTELLER GMBH, Hanauer Landstrabe 126 - 128, pg. 1468
CHANGE COMMUNICATIONS GMBH, Solmstrasse 4, pg. 555
EDELMAN FRANKFURT, Niddastrasse 91, pg. 1504
J. WALTER THOMPSON GMBH, Schwedlerstrasse 6, pg. 573
MCCANN ERICKSON BRAND COMMUNICATIONS AGENCY, Grosser Hasenpad 44, pg. 720
MCCANN ERICKSON DEUTSCHLAND, Grosser Hasenpfad 44, pg. 720
PUBLICITAS GERMANY GMBH, Oederweg 52-54, pg. 1426
SAATCHI & SAATCHI, Uhlandstrasse 2, pg. 1003
WUNDERMAN, Kleyerstrasse 19, pg. 1232

Freiburg

HAVAS LIFE BIRD & SCHULTE, Urachstrasse 19, pg. 487

Hamburg

BLAST RADIUS HAMBURG, Grimm 6, pg. 137
THE BRAND UNION GMBH, Bahrenfelder Chaussee 49, pg. 157
COHN & WOLFE, Hanseatic Trade Center, Am Sandtorkai 76, pg. 1482
COMMARCO GMBH, Hanseatic Trade Center, Am Sandtorkai 76, pg. 1218
EDELMAN, Medienpark Kampnagel Barmbeker Str 4, pg. 1505
FCB HAMBURG, Bleichenbruecke 10, pg. 373
HAVAS WORLDWIDE HAMBURG, Brahms Kontor Johannes-Brahms-Platz 1, pg. 494
HEYE & PARTNER GMBH, Gaensemarkt 35, pg. 282
INITIATIVE HAMBURG, Schloss-Strasse 8e, pg. 1346
INTERBRAND, Zirkusweg 1, pg. 858
LANDOR ASSOCIATES, An der Alster 47, pg. 625
MCCANN ERICKSON HAMBURG GMBH, Neuer Wall 43, pg. 720
MEC GMBH, Oberbaumbruecke 1, pg. 1358
SELECTNY.HAMBURG GMBH, Hoheluftchaussee 18, pg. 1031
TBWA/GERMANY, Bernhard Nocht Ste 113, pg. 1120
TRIBAL WORLDWIDE HAMBURG, Willy-Brandt Strasse 1, pg. 1317

Koblenz

SELECTNY.KOBLENZ GMBH, Schlossstrasse 1, pg. 1031

Munich

BERGER BAADER HERMES GMBH, Nymphenburger Strasse 86, pg. 1245
DIGITASLBI, Schafflerstrasse 3, pg. 1289
EDELMAN, Landshuter Allee 10, pg. 1505
F&H PORTER NOVELLI, Brabanter Str 4, pg. 1622
FLEISHMAN-HILLARD GERMANY, Herzog-Wilhelm-Strasse 26, pg. 1519
HEYE & PARTNER GMBH, Blumenstr. 28,, pg. 282
INTERONE WORLDWIDE, Therecienhoehe 12, pg. 107
MAXIIGYROHSR, Munich Lindwurmstr 76, pg. 469
MEC, Theresienhohe 13a, pg. 1358
ONPR GMBH, Grasserstrasse 10, pg. 1611
PUBLICIS PIXELPARK, Implerstr 11, pg. 919
SAPIENT MUNICH, Arnulfstrasse 60, pg. 1019
TEXT 100 MUNICH GMBH, Nymphenburgerstrasse 168, pg. 1661
WE, Sandstrasse 33, pg. 1674
WEBER SHANDWICK, Seidlstrabe 26, pg. 1679

Neu-Isenburg

SUDLER & HENNESSEY FRANKFURT, Dornhof Str 44 46, pg. 1096

Ostfildern

RAUMTECHNICK, Plieninger Strasse 54, pg. 913

Stuttgart

BBDO STUTTGART, Breitscheidstrasse 8, BOSCH-Areal, pg. 107

GHANA

Accra

ADAM ADVERTISING, Hse No F874/2 Eleventh Close, Osu Former Citirock Building, pg. 566
ADMEDIA, 37 Third Crescent Asylum Down, pg. 382

GREECE

Athens

ACTION GLOBAL COMMUNICATIONS, 49-51 Ypsilantou Str, Kolonaki, pg. 1679
BBDO ATHENS, 48 Ethnikis Antistaseos St, pg. 107
BOLD OGILVY GREECE, 10 Imathias Str, Gerakas, pg. 832
FCB GNOMI, Iroos Matsi & Archaiou Theatrou Str, Alimos, pg. 373
HAVAS WORLDWIDE ATHENS, 226 Snygrou Avenue, pg. 494
IKON PORTER NOVELLI, 7 Ethnikis Antistasseos Halandri, pg. 1622
LOWE ATHENS, 54 Kapodistriou, Filothei, pg. 793
MCCANN ERICKSON ATHENS, 2 Hydras st & 280 Kifissias ave, Halandri, pg. 721
MEDIACOM ATHENS, 350 Kifisias Avenue & 2 Christou Lada, 15233 Chalandri, pg. 1369
OGILVY PR WORLDWIDE, 7 Granikou Street, Maroussi, pg. 1607
OGILVYONE WORLDWIDE, 10 Imathias Street, pg. 833
PERMEDIA ATHENS LTD., 4 Kastorias St, Gerakas, pg. 1426
PUBLICIS HELLAS, 3-5 Menandrou Street, Kifissia, pg.

919
PUBLICITAS HELLAS LTD., 4 Kastorias & Messinias Street, Gerakas, pg. 1426
PUBLICOM/HILL + KNOWLTON STRATEGIES, Charilaou Trikoupi & Xenias 5 Street, Amarousiou, pg. 1543
TRIBAL WORLDWIDE ATHENS, 4 Kastorias & Messinias Str, Gerakas, pg. 1317

Kifissia

ZENITHOPTIMEDIA, 17B Kokkinaki Street, pg. 1399

GUATEMALA

Guatemala

BBDO GUATEMALA, 5 Ave 5-55 Zona 14 Europlaza Torre 4 nivel 17, pg. 103
D4 MCCANN, 5a Ave 5-55 zona 14 Europlaza Torre I Nivel 7, pg. 721
DOS PUNTOS DDB, km 86 antigua carretera a El Salvador Centro Corporativo Muxbal, Torre Este Nivel 9, pg. 282
ECO Y&R, S.A, 8 Calle 2-38 Zona 9, Guatemala City, pg. 1250
FCB DOS PUNTOS CREA, Km 8.6 antigua Carretera a El Salvador Ctro Corp Muxbal, Torre Este Nivel 9, pg. 378
ICU PUBLICIDAD, 13 Calle 2-60 Edificio Topacio Azul 10 Fl, Oficina, pg. 499
LA FABRICA JOTABEQU GREY, Ruta 4 5-33 Zona 4, pg. 454
MEC, 14 calle 3-51 zona 10 Edificio Murano Center, Oficina 402, pg. 1361
TBWA/GUATEMALA, 23 Calle 15-14 Zone 13, pg. 1132
TEQUILA GUATEMALA, 7A Avenida 14-44 Zona 9, Nivel 2, pg. 1132

HONDURAS

San Pedro Sula

TALENTO GREY PUBLICIDAD, Colonia La Modern 22 Avenida, 7a Calle Casa no 720, pg. 454

Tegucigalpa

FCB CREA, Edif Mall El Dorado Bulevard Morazan, pg. 378
MASS NAZCA SAATCHI & SAATCHI, Colonia Palmira Avenue Republica de Venezuela 2130, 1396, pg. 1009

HONG KONG

Quarry Bay

DIGITASLBI, 22/F Chinachem Exchange Square 1 Hoi Wan Street, pg. 1289

HUNGARY

Budapest

DDB BUDAPEST, Dozsa Gyorgy ut 84/a 3rd Floor, pg. 283
GREY GROUP HUNGARY, 1061 Andrassy ut 9, pg. 449
HAVAS WORLDWIDE BUDAPEST, Nagyszombat u 1, pg. 494
INITIATIVE BUDAPEST, Vajdahhunyad U. 33-43, pg. 1345
J. WALTER THOMPSON BUDAPEST, Revesz 27-29, pg. 573
MEC, Lajos utca 80, pg. 1358
POSSIBLE, Bocskai Ut 134-146, pg. 1308
SAATCHI & SAATCHI, Alvinci Ut 16, pg. 1003
STARCOM WORLDWIDE, Szepvolgyi Business Park Cepulet Building 1V Emelet Floor, pg. 1079
TBWA BUDAPEST, Szuret utca 15, pg. 1120
WEBER SHANDWICK, Montevideo utca 10, pg. 1680
WUNDERMAN, Alkotas u 53 C epulet, MOM park, pg. 1233
Y&R BUDAPEST, MOM Park,Alkotasu 53C, pg. 1248

ICELAND

Reykjavik

THE ICELANDIC AD AGENCY, Laufasvefur 49-51, pg. 108

INDIA

Bengaluru

22FEET TRIBAL WORLDWIDE, 4th Floor Serene 106 4th C Cross 5th Block, pg. 1317
CORPORATE VOICE-WEBER SHANDWICK, No 2561 16th D Main HAL II Stage, Indiranagar, pg. 1683
END TO END MARKETING SOLUTIONS PVT. LTD, #173 9th Cross, Indiranagar 1st Stage, pg. 721
FCB ULKA, 1103 11th Floor Barton Centre 84 MG Road, pg. 380
GREY (INDIA) LTD. (BANGALORE), Mount Kailash No 33/5 2nd Floor Meanee Avenue Road, pg. 456
HAVAS WORLDWIDE BANGALORE, 4016 First Cross 17th Main, HAL II Stage - Domlur, Indiran, pg. 501
J. WALTER THOMPSON, 9th Floor Embassy Heights 13 Magrath Road, pg. 570
MCCANN ERICKSON INDIA, Landmark Plaza 299 Langford Road, Richmond Town, pg. 722
MEC, Mahalaxmi Chambers 5th Floor, 29 M G Road, pg. 1363
MEDIACOM BANGALORE, 3rd Fl Mahalakshmi Chambers, No 29 M G Road, pg. 1372
MILLWARD BROWN MARKET RESEACH SERVICES, Mahalakshmi Chamber 3rd Fl Mahatma Gandhi Rd, pg. 760
OGILVY & MATHER, Level 06 5th Fl Bagmane Laurel Bagmane Techpark, C V Raman Nagar, pg. 842
OGILVY PR WORLDWIDE, Level - 06 Fifth Floor Bagmane Laurel 65/2 Bagmane Teck Park, CV Raman Nagar Byrasandra, pg. 1609
ORCHARD ADVERTISING, HAL 3rd Stage No 37 80 Foot Road, pg. 649
THE PRACTICE PORTER NOVELLI, 812 7th Fl Oxford Towers, Airport Rd, pg. 1625
SAATCHI & SAATCHI DIRECT, 37/6 Aga Abbas Ali Road off Ulsoor Road, pg. 1011
TBWA INDIA, A - 1 Tower 4th Fl Golden Enclave, Airport Rd, pg. 1129

Chennai

FCB ULKA, Golden Tower 1st Floor 262 Royapettha High Road, pg. 380
J. WALTER THOMPSON, 26 Ethiraj Salai, Egmore, pg. 569
MEC, New No. 13, Old No. 7, 5th Street, Nandanam Extension, pg. 1363
OGILVY & MATHER INDIA, 139/140 Rukmani Lakshmipathy Salia Marshalls Road, Egmore, pg. 842
POLARIS FINANCIAL TECHNOLOGY LIMITED, Polaris House 244 Anna Salai, pg. 902
R.K. SWAMY BBDO, Film Chamber Bldg 604 Anna Salai, pg. 115
TBWA INDIA, No 62 1st Fl 3rd St, Abhiramapuram, pg. 1129

Gurgaon

BBDO INDIA, 207/2 Solitaire Plz, pg. 115
DIGITASLBI, 90 D Sector 18, pg. 1289
EDELMAN, 6th Floor, Vatika Triangle, Sushant Lok-1, Block - A, pg. 1505
EVEREST BRAND SOLUTIONS, 2nd Floor Parsvnath Arcadia, No 1 Mehrauli Gurgaon Road, pg. 1242
FCB ULKA, Unitech Trade Ctre Sushant Lik hase I Sector 43, pg. 380
GENESIS BURSON-MARSTELLER, 807-B Signature Towers South City, pg. 1470
GREY (INDIA) PVT. PTY. LTD. (DELHI), Park Centra 503-505 Sector 30 NH-8, Opp 32nd Milestone, pg. 456
HAVAS WORLDWIDE DELHI, 5th Floor Tower A Building No 9, DLF Cyber City Phase III, pg. 501
HAVAS WORLDWIDE DIGITAL DELHI, Map 5th Floor - Tower A, Building No.9 - DLF Cyber City, Phase III, pg. 501
MAXUS, 6th Fl Bldg No 9A Cyber City DLF Phase III, pg. 1355
POLARIS ENTERPRISE SOLUTIONS LIMITED, Polaris House, 249 Polaris Towers Udyog Vihar, pg. 902
PUBLICIS INDIA COMMUNICATIONS PVT. LTD., Vatika Triangle 6th Fl Sushant Lok, Phase I Block A, pg. 933
REDIFFUSION Y&R PVT. LTD., DLF Cyber City, Building No 9B, pg. 1243
SAPIENT CORPORATION PRIVATE LIMITED, The Presidency Mehrauli-Gurgaon Road Sector 14, pg. 1019
ZENITHOPTIMEDIA INDIA, 90 D Sector 18 Udyog Vihar, Phase 4, pg. 1401

Hyderabad

OGILVY & MATHER, Mahavir House 303-304 3rd Floor Mahavir House, Basheer Bagh Cross Roads, pg. 843

Kochi

FCB ULKA, Vallamattam Estate Mahatma Gandhi Road, Ravipuram, pg. 379

Kolkata

FCB ULKA, 1/2 Lord Sinha Road, pg. 380
J. WALTER THOMPSON, 30 Bondel Road, pg. 570

Mumbai

20:20 MSL, A/12 1st Floor Vikas Center, Santa Cruz West, pg. 1595
APCO WORLDWIDE, Office No 433 Level 4 Dynasty Business Park A Wing, Andheri Kurla Road Andheri E, pg. 64
BBH MUMBAI, Amiye 2nd Floor Linking Road, Santacruz (West), pg. 96
CONTRACT ADVERTISING (INDIA) LIMITED, Vaswani Chambers 264 Dr Annie Bessant Road, pg. 568
DDB MUDRA GROUP, Mudra House Opp Grand Hyatt, pg. 283
EGGFIRST, B-52/206 Eggfirst Villa, Goregaon (W), pg. 340
EVEREST BRAND SOLUTIONS, 5th Floor Terminal 9 Nehru Road, Vile Parle E, pg. 1242
FCB ULKA, Nirmal 4th Floor Nariman Point, pg. 379
GREY (INDIA) PVT. LTD., Grey House 28 Dr E Borge Road Oppos Dr Shirodkar High School, Parel, pg. 456
HAKUHODO PERCEPT PVT. LTD., P22, Raghuvanshi Estate, Lower Parel, pg. 475
HAVAS WORLDWIDE MUMBAI, Valencia Building - 4th floor, Off Dr SS Rao Road, Parel, pg. 502
INTERACTIVE AVENUES PVT. LTD., First Floor Kagalwala House C Block - East Wing, pg. 556
INTERFACE COMMUNICATIONS LTD., A Wing-206 2nd Fl Phoenix House Phoenix Mills Compound, SenapatiBapat Marg Lower Parel, pg. 380
ISOBAR INDIA, 7th Floor B Wing Poonam Chambers II Dr Annie, pg. 562
J. WALTER THOMPSON, 301 Peninsula Chambers Ganpatrao Kadam Marg, Lower Parel West, pg. 569
KINETIC, Commerz 9th Floor International Business Park Oberoi Garden City, Goregaon East, pg. 1351
LEO BURNETT INDIA, Big Apple A, 36 Dr L Shirodkar Rd Parel, pg. 648
MARKETGATE CONSULTING, 507-A 5th Fl Kakad Chambers Dr, Annie Besant Road Worli, pg. 932
MAXUS, Ground Fl Orbit Plz, New Prabhadevi Rd, pg. 1354
MCCANN ERICKSON INDIA, McCann House Dr SS Rao Road, Parel East, pg. 721
MEC, 8th Floor Commerz International Business Park, Oberoi Garden City, pg. 1363
MEDIACOM INDIA, 201 2nd Fl Kamla Executive Park Opp Vazir Glass Factory, Andheri East, pg. 1372
MRM WORLDWIDE, 61 Dr S S Rao Road, Parel, pg. 784
MSL GROUP INDIA, Rehem Mansion - 1 3rd Floor 42 Shahih Bhagat Singh Road, Colaba, pg. 932
MULLEN LOWE LINTAS GROUP, Express Towers 15th Floor, Nariman Point, pg. 791
OGILVY HEALTHWORLD INDIA, Trade World 2nd Floor C Wing, Senapati Bapat Marg, pg. 852
OGILVY INDIA, 14th Floor Commerz International Business Park Oberoi Garden City, Goregaon, pg. 843
OGILVY PR WORLDWIDE, 11th Floor Oberoi Commerz International Business Park, Off Western Express Highway, pg. 1609
OGILVY PR WORLDWIDE, MUMBAI, 11th Floor Oberoi Commerz International Business Park Oberoi Garden, Gurgaon (East), pg. 1609

New Delhi

Noida

INDONESIA

Jakarta

IRELAND

Dublin

ISRAEL

Jerusalem

Ramat Gan

Tel Aviv

ITALY

Casale Monferrato

Milan

ZENITHOPTIMEDIA, 5 via Cavriana, pg. 1399
ZENITHOPTIMEDIA INTERACTIVE DIRECT, 5 via Cavriana, pg. 1399

Rome

AD MAIORA SRL, Via Machiavelli 25, pg. 23
BURSON-MARSTELLER S.R.L., Via Gregoriana 54, pg. 1468
HAVAS LIFE ROME, Via del Poggio Laurentino 118, pg. 487
HILL & KNOWLTON GAIA, Via Nomentana 257, pg. 1543
J. WALTER THOMPSON, Via del Commercio 36, pg. 573
KETCHUM PLEON ROMA, Via Cassia 1081, pg. 1564
LEO BURNETT ROME, Via Crescenzio 38, pg. 643
LOWE PIRELLA, Via Salaria 222, pg. 792
MCCANN ERICKSON ITALIANA S.P.A., Via Libano 68/74, pg. 732
MCCANN ERICKSON ITALIANA S.P.A., Via Libano 68/74, pg. 723
MEC, Via Cristofo Colombo 163, pg. 1359
OGILVY & MATHER, V Pio Emanuelli 1, pg. 833
PUBLICIS, Via Tata Giovanni 8, pg. 920
REPORT PORTER NOVELLI-ROME, Via Poli 29, pg. 1623
SAATCHI & SAATCHI, Via Nazionale 75, pg. 1004
TBWA ROMA, Via Flaminia Vecchia 495, pg. 1121
WEBER SHANDWICK, Via Magazzini Generali, 18, pg. 1680
Y&R ROMA SRL, Via Giulio Cesare 2, pg. 1246
ZENITHOPTIMEDIA, Piazza G Marconi 15, pg. 1399

Turin

CARRE NOIR TURINO, Corso Re Umberto 87, pg. 920
LEO BURNETT CO. S.R.L., Via San Quintino 28, pg. 643
MEDIAVEST WORLDWIDE, Via San Quintino 28, pg. 1078

Verona

MEC, Via Leoncino 16, pg. 1359

JAMAICA

Kingston

LINDO/FCB, 14 Ruthven Road, pg. 378

JAPAN

Fukuoka

HAKUHODO ERG, INC., 11th Floor Hakata Riverain East Site 2-1 Shimokawabata-machi, Hakata-ku, pg. 474
HAKUHODO INC. KYUSHU OFFICE, Hakata Riverain East Site 2-1 Shimokawabata-machi, pg. 473

Nagoya

DENTSU MEITETSU COMMUNICATIONS INC., 6F, Nissay Nagoyaekinishi Bldg, Nakamura-ku, pg. 299

Osaka

MCCANN ERICKSON INC., Aqua Dojima West 19th Floor 1-4-16, Dojimahama Kita-ku, pg. 723

Tokyo

BEACON COMMUNICATIONS K.K., JR Tokyo Maguro Building 3-1-1 Kami-Osaki, Shinagawa-ku, pg. 649
BEACON COMMUNICATIONS K.K., JR Tokyo Maguro Building 3-1-1 Kami-Osaki, Shinagawa-ku, pg. 933
BLUECURRENT JAPAN, Nichirei Higashi-Ginza Bldg 7F, 6-19-20 Tsukiji Chuo-Ku, pg. 1520
CARRE NOIR TOKYO, 10 F JR Tokyu Meguro Building, 3-1-1 Kami-Osaki Shinagawa-ku, pg. 934
CYBER COMMUNICATIONS INC., 7F Comodio Shiodome 2-14-1 Higashi-shimbashi, Minato-ku, pg. 299
DDB JAPAN, Hiroo Plaza 9F 5-6-6 Hiroo, Shibuya-ku, pg. 284
DENTSU INC., 1-8-1 Higashi-shimbashi, Minato-ku, pg. 297
DENTSU Y&R JAPAN, 2-chome Higashi shinbashi Shiodome KOMODIO No 14 No 1, Minato-ku, pg. 1241
DENTSU YOUNG & RUBICAM INC., Comodio Shiodome 2-14-1 Higashi Shimbashi, Minato-ku, pg. 1243
DIGITAL ADVERTISING CONSORTIUM, INC., Yebisu Garden Place Twr 33F 4-20-3 Ebisu, Shibuya-ku, pg. 473
EDELMAN, 3rd Floor Toranomon 45 MT Bldg, 5-1-5 Toranomon Minato-ku, pg. 1504
FLEISHMAN-HILLARD/JAPAN, Nichirei Higashi-Ginza Building 7F 6-19-20, Tsukiji Chuo-Ku, pg. 1521
FOCUSED COMMUNICATIONS CO., LTD., 2-9-1 Nishi Shimbashi, Minato-ku, pg. 1624
GREY GROUP JAPAN, Ebisu Square, 1-23-23 Ebisu, Shibuya-ku, pg. 457
HAKUHODO I-STUDIO, INC., NBF Toyosu Gardenfront 9F 5-6-15 Toyosu, Koto-ku, pg. 474
HAKUHODO INCORPORATED, Akasaka Biz Tower 5-3-1 Akasaka, Minato-ku, pg. 473
HILL + KNOWLTON STRATEGIES, 3-5-27 Roppongi Minato-Ku, Yamada Roppongi Building 8F, pg. 1544
THE HOFFMAN AGENCY, Burex Kyobashi Suite 515 2-7-14 Kyobashi, Chuo-ku, pg. 1546
I&S BBDO INC., Harumi Triton Square X 1-8-10 Harumi, Chuo-ku, pg. 115
J. WALTER THOMPSON JAPAN, Yebisu Garden Place Tower 30th Floor 4-20-3 Ebisu, Shibuya-ku, pg. 570
KREAB TOKYO, Shibakoen Ridge Bldg 1-8-21 Shibakoen, pg. 1569
LOWE TOKYO, Aoyama Plaza Bldg., 2-11-3, Kita-Aoyama, Minato-Ku, pg. 793
M&C SAATCHI, 1-26-1 Ebisunishi Shibuya-Ku, pg. 677
MCCANN ERICKSON JAPAN INC., Shin Aoyama Bldg., E 1-1-1 Minami-Aoyama, Minato-ku, pg. 723
MEDIACOM JAPAN, Yebisu Garden Place Tower 30F, 4-20-3 Ebisu Shibuya-ku, pg. 1373
MRM WORLDWIDE, Shin-Aoyama Building E 1-1-1 Minami-Aoyama, Minato-ku, pg. 784
MS&L JAPAN, 14F JR Tokyu Meguro Blg, 3-1-1 Kami-Osaki Shinagawa-ku, pg. 1596
OGILVY & MATHER JAPAN K.K., Yebisu Garden Place Tower 25F 4-20-3 Ebisu, pg. 845
OGILVYONE WORLDWIDE, Yebisu Garden Place Tower 25F 4-20-3 Ebisu, Shibuya-ku, pg. 845
RAPP TOKYO, 3-1-1 Higashi-Ikebukuro, pg. 954
SAATCHI & SAATCHI FALLON TOKYO, 4-9-3 Jingumae, Shibuya-ku, pg. 367
SAATCHI & SAATCHI FALLON TOKYO, 4-9-3 Jingumae, Shibuya-ku, pg. 1011
TBWA/HAKUHODO, 1-13-10 Shibaura, pg. 1129
WEBER SHANDWICK, Mita Kokusai Bldg 13th Fl 1-4-28 Mita, Minato-ku, pg. 1683
WIEDEN + KENNEDY JAPAN, 7-5-6 Roppongi, Minato-ku, pg. 1205
WUNDERMAN, San Marino Shiodome 2-4-1 Higashi-shimbashi, Minato-ku, pg. 1233

JORDAN

Amman

AFKAR PROMOSEVEN-JORDAN, Um Uthayna Hamza Al Labadi Street Villa No 6, pg. 723
LEO BURNETT JORDAN, 18 Al Mutanabi Street 3rd Cicle, pg. 643
PUBLICIS GRAPHICS, 10 Saeed Abu Javer St Um Uthaina, pg. 923

KAZAKHSTAN

Almaty

TBWA CENTRAL ASIA, Tole Bi 83, pg. 1127

KENYA

Nairobi

ACCESS LEO BURNETT, Bishops Garden Towers 4th Floor, pg. 643
LOWE SCANAD, PO Box 34537 5th Fl The Chancery, Valley Road, pg. 793
MEC, CVS Plaza 3rd Floor, Lenana Road, pg. 1361
OGILVY & MATHER (EASTERN AFRICA) LTD., 3rd Fl CVS Plaza Kasuku Road Lenana Road, pg. 848
OGILVY PR WORLDWIDE, CVS Plaza 3rd Floor Lenara Rd, pg. 1609
YOUNG & RUBICAM BRANDS AFRICA, 2nd Fl Panesar Centre Mombasa Road, pg. 1251

KOREA (SOUTH)

Seoul

BURSON-MARSTELLER, 9F East Tower Signature Towers, 99 Supyo-dong Jung-gu, pg. 1470
CHEIL WORLDWIDE INC., 222 Itaewon-ro, pg. 474
EDELMAN, 18th Fl Ferrum Tower, Suha Dong Jungu, pg. 1504
FCB SEOUL, 7/F Hyeongji Bldg 257-4 Sinsa Dong, Gangnam-Gu, pg. 380
FLEISHMAN-HILLARD KOREA, 24th Fl City Air Tower 159-9 Samsung-Dong, Kangnam-Ku, pg. 1521
GRAPE COMMUNICATIONS, Duckyang Building 31-5 Jangchoong-Dong, Jung-Ku, pg. 555
GREY GROUP KOREA, 2 & 3F ISA Bldg 600-1, Gangnam-Gu, pg. 457
HAVAS WORLDWIDE SEOUL, 10th Fl Dongwon Bldg 128 27 Dangju-dong, Jongro-gu, pg. 500
HS AD, INC., 14th Floor LG Mapo Building, 275 Gongdeok-Dong, pg. 1243
J. WALTER THOMPSON KOREA, 8F JS Tower 144 20 Samsung-dong, Kangnam-gu, pg. 570
JACK MORTON WORLDWIDE (SEOUL), Dae-gong Building, 4/F, Gangnam-gu, pg. 582
KETCHUM SEOUL, 24th Fl City Air Tower, 159-9 Samsung-Dong Kangnam Ku, pg. 1565
KORCOM PORTER NOVELLI, 16F Daewoo Foundation Building 526 Namdaemoon-ro 5-ga, Jung-gu, pg. 1624
LEO BURNETT KOREA, East Wing 15th Fl Signature Towers 100 Cheonggyecheon-ro, Jongno-gu, pg. 649
MEDIACOM KOREA, 7F SB Tower 318, Doan Daero Gangnam-gu, pg. 1373
NEWS COMMUNICATIONS, 4th Fl Chinyang Bldg, 190-3 Chungjeongno 2-ga, Seodaemun, pg. 1683
OGILVY & MATHER, 27-8 Chamwon-Dong, Seocho-Ku, pg. 845
TBWA KOREA, 7-12F J-Tower 538 Sinsa Dong, Kangnam Gu, pg. 1131
WUNDERMAN KOREA, 9F Bosung Bldg 891-25, Daechi-dong Gangman-gu, pg. 1233
XAXIS, 4F Women Enterprise Supporting Center 733-24 Yeoksam-dong, Gangnam-gu, pg. 1321

KUWAIT

Daiya

J. WALTER THOMPSON, Wataniya Tower 10th Floor Fahed Al Salem Street, pg. 576

Kuwait

HORIZON FCB KUWAIT, Al Arabiya Tower Ahmed Al Jaber Street, Sharq Kuwait City, pg. 376
IMPACT BBDO, Sharq Mutanaby St Bldg No 42, Safat 13071, pg. 109
LEO BURNETT, Al Khaleeja Building 12th Floor, Safat, pg. 643
MEC, Fahed Al Salem Street Rakan Tower, 6th Floor, pg. 1360
MEMAC OGILVY, Future Trade Zone Shuwaikh Al Argan Building Block A 1st Floor, Safat, pg. 850

LATVIA

Riga

ADELL SAATCHI & SAATCHI, 15 Elizabetes Street, pg. 1004
DDB LATVIA, Brivibas Street 40-34, pg. 285
HILL & KNOWLTON LATVIA, Brivibas iela 40 36, pg. 1543
LOWE AGE, 30 Terbatas Street, pg. 790
SAN BALTIC J. WALTER THOMPSON, Tirgonu Str 8, pg. 574
TBWA LATVIJA, Brivibas Str 40-40A, pg. 1121

LEBANON

Beirut

FORTUNE PROMOSEVEN-LEBANON, Ashrafieh 784 Bldg Sodeco, pg. 723
GREY MIDDLE EAST NETWORK, Beit Mery Roundabout Rouwaisy Grey Compound Beit Mery, pg. 450
H&C, LEO BURNETT, Sofil Center 5th Floor Achrafieh, pg. 643
HAVAS WORLDWIDE BEIRUT, Voice of Lebanon Bldg, Achrafieh,, pg. 495
HORIZON FCB BEIRUT, Badaro Trade Center, El-Fata Street, pg. 375
IMPACT BBDO, Bldg 635 Omar Daouk Street Jumblatt Area, Ain-Mreysseh, pg. 108
INITIATIVE BEIRUT, Badaro Trade Center Suite 801 Sami El Solh Avenue, pg. 1346
J. WALTER THOMPSON, 47 Patriarch Howeiyek Street Sabbagh Bld 3rd Floor, Bab Idriss, pg. 577
MEMAC OGILVY, Rizkallah & Boutrous Centre Futuroscope Roundabout 8th Floor, Sin-El-Fil, pg. 850
OPTIMEDIA, Omar Saab Building Verdun Rachid Karame Street, 2nd Fl, pg. 1399
SAATCHI & SAATCHI, Quantum Tower 9th Floor Charles Malek Avenue Saint Nicolas St, pg. 1004

LITHUANIA

Vilnius

ADELL TAIVAS OGILVY, J Jasinskio Street 16A, pg. 833
J. WALTER THOMPSON LITHUANIA SAN VILNIUS, Pylimo Street 30/2, pg. 574
LEO BURNETT VILNIUS, Birutes 1D, pg. 644
LOWE AGE, Suvalku Str 2a, pg. 790
LUKRECIJA BBDO, K Kalinausko 2B, pg. 109

LUXEMBOURG

Luxembourg

MIKADO S.A., 38 route d'Esch, pg. 920

MACEDONIA

Skopje

OVATION BBDO, Guro Gakovik 56, pg. 109

MALAWI

Blantyre

COTTMAN MCCANN ADVERTISING, Hisco House Chipembere Highway, pg. 724

MALAYSIA

Kuala Lumpur

ARC WORLDWIDE, ASIA PACIFIC, Level 5 Menara Olympia, 8 Jalan Raja Chulan, pg. 1406
BBDO MALAYSIA, Suite 50-01-01 Wisma UOA Damansara 50 Jalan Dungun, Damansara Heights, pg. 116
DENTSU YOUNG & RUBICAM SDN. BHD., 6th & 8th Floors Wisma E&C No 2 Lorong Dungan Kiri, Damansara Heights, pg. 1243
EDELMAN, 45-9 The Boulevard Mid Valley City, Lingkaran Syed Putra, pg. 1507
FCB KUALA LUMPUR, 17th Floor Menara IGB No 1 The Boulevard Mid Valley City, Lingkaran Syed Putra, pg. 381
FLEISHMAN-HILLARD MALAYSIA, Suite 1702 Level 17 Centrepoint South The Boulevard, Mid Valley city Lingkaran Sye, pg. 1521
GREY GROUP MALAYSIA, 15th Floor Wisma Genting, Jalan Sultan Ismail, pg. 457
HAKUHODO MALAYSIA SDN. BHD., 9Fl Bldg A Peremba Square Saujana Resort Section U2, pg. 474
HILL & KNOWLTON (SEA) SDN. BHD., 7th floor Wisma Genting, Jalan Sultan Ismail, pg. 1544
J. WALTER THOMPSON, Level 6 Wismean Anta Jalan Changtat Senantan, Damansara Heights, pg. 570
LEO BURNETT MALAYSIA, Level 5 Menara Olympia, 8 Jalan Raja Chulan, pg. 650
M&C SAATCHI, Banguan Malaysia Re 17 Lorong Dungun, pg. 678
MCCANN ERICKSON (MALAYSIA) SDN. BHD., 5-01 & 5-02 Wisma LYL No 12 Jalan 51A/223 Petaling Jaya, Selangor Darul Ehsan, pg. 724
MILK PR, Level 3 Menara Chan, 138 Jalan Ampang, pg. 285
OGILVY & MATHER ADVERTISING, Level 11 Menara Milenium 8 Jalan Damanlela, Bukit Damansara, pg. 845
OGILVY PR WORLDWIDE, Level 11 Menara Milenium 8 Jalan Damanlela, Bukit Damansara, pg. 1609
OGILVYONE DATASERVICES, Level 10 Menara Milenium, Bukit Damansara, pg. 846
OPTIMEDIA MALAYSIA, Level 16, 8 Jalan Raja Chulan, pg. 1401
SAATCHI & SAATCHI ARACHNID, A-16-1 Tower A Northpoint Offices Midvalley City, pg. 1011
TBWA ISC MALAYSIA, 15th Floor Block B HP Towers 12 Jalan Gelenggang, pg. 1130
TEQUILA MYALO, 15th Floor Block B HP Towers, Bukit Damansara, pg. 1130
ZENITH MALAYSIA, 9th Fl, Menara BRDB,, Bangsar, pg. 1401

Petaling Jaya

HAVAS WORLDWIDE KUALA LUMPUR, 11F, The Crest, 3 Two Square 2 Jalan 19/1, pg. 501
LOWE MALAYSIA, 2A 2nd Fl Ikano Huset 2 Jalan PJU, 7/2 Mutiara Damansara, pg. 794
NAGA DDB SDN. BHD., D708 7th Fl Block D Kelana Square No 17 Jln SS7/26, Kelana Jaya, pg. 285
OMD MALAYSIA, Level 3 Tower C Uptown 5, pg. 1381
PUBLICIS (MALAYSIA) SDN. BHD., M1 Mezanine Fl Wisme LYL, pg. 934
PUBLICITAS MALAYSIA, S105 2nd Floor Centrepoint, Lebuh Bandar Utama, pg. 1428
RAPP MALAYSIA, D601-D605 6th Floor Block D Kelana Square 17 Jalan SS7/26, pg. 954
SAATCHI & SAATCHI, Unit 7 2 Level 7 CP Tower 11 Section 16 11, Jalan Damansara, pg. 1011
TRIBAL WORLDWIDE MALAYSIA, D601-605 6th Floor Block D Kelana Square 17, Jalan SS7/26 Selangor, pg. 1317
WEBER SHANDWICK, 4-01 4th Fl Wisma LYL No 12 Jalan 51A/223, pg. 1683

MALTA

Ta' Xbiex

MAS COMMUNICATIONS, Sir Ugo Mifsud Street, pg. 556

MAURITIUS

Beau Bassin

CREAD, Les 5 Palmiers, Route Royale, pg. 382

Port Louis

MAURICE PUBLICITE LTD., 5th Fl Cerne House Chaussee St, pg. 848
ORANGE COMMUNICATIONS, 6th Floor TN Tower, St Georges Street, pg. 452
P&P LINK SAATCHI & SAATCHI, D Seetulsingh St, pg. 1011

MEXICO

Mexico

BBDO MEXICO, Guillermo Gonzalez Camarena No 800 3er Piso, Col Zedec Santa Fe, pg. 104
BURSON-MARSTELLER MEXICO, S.A. DE C.V., Boulevard Manuel Avila Camacho No 176 5to Piso, Miguel Hidalgo, pg. 1467
CROSSMEDIA, Benjamin Franklin 190, Col Condesa CP, pg. 1218
CROSSMEDIA, Benjamin Franklin 190, Col Condesa CP, pg. 1233
DDB MEXICO, Montes Urales 770 5th Fl, Col Lomas de Chapultepec, pg. 285
EDELMAN, Santa Margarita #108 Piso 1, Col Del Valle, pg. 1505
FCB MEXICO CITY, Miguel de Cervantes Saavedra #193, Colonia Granada, pg. 378
GREY MEXICO, S.A. DE C.V, Jaime Balmes No 8-104 Col Los Morales Polanco, pg. 454
GRICORP KETCHUM, Bosque de Ciruelos 186-301, Col Bosques de las Lomas, pg. 1563
GROUPM LATAM HQ, Avenida Ejercito Nacional, No. 216, piso 2 col. Veronica Anzures, pg. 1337
HAVAS WORLDWIDE MEXICO, Av Insurgentes Sur 694-9, pg. 499
HILL + KNOWLTON STRATEGIES MEXICO, Prol Paseo de la Reforma No 490 1st Fl, pg. 1542
J. WALTER THOMPSON, Avenue Ejercito Nacional No 519, Col Granada, pg. 578
JEFFREY GROUP MEXICO, Homero 1343 No 402, Col Los Morales Polanco, pg. 1554
LEO BURNETT MEXICO S.A. DE C.V., Bosque de Duraznos 65-8P Bosques de las Lomas, pg. 640
MARTEC PORTER NOVELLI, La Fontaine 36, Chapultepec Polanco, pg. 1621
MCCANN ERICKSON MEXICO, Palo Santo No 22, Lomas Altas, pg. 724
MEC, Avenida Ejercito Nacional 216-20 Piso, Colonia, Veronica Anzures, pg. 1362
MILLWARD BROWN MEXICO, Avenida Tamaulipas 150-1202 Colonia Condesa, pg. 760
MRM MEXICO, Palo Santo 17, Col Lomas Altas, pg. 783
OGILVY & MATHER, Montes Urales 505 5th Fl Col Lomas de Chapultepec, pg. 839
OGILVYONE WORLDWIDE, Montes Urales 505 5th Fl, Col Lomas de Chapultepec, pg. 840
OLABUENAGA CHEMISTRI, Prado Norte 125 Piso 2, Lomas de Chapultepec, pg. 929
PUBLICIS ARREDONDO DE HARO, Prolongacion Paseo de la Reforma, 1015 5 piso Col Desarrollo, pg. 929
TERAN TBWA, Monte Pelvoux 210 4 Piso, Lomas de Chapultepec, pg. 1132

MOROCCO

Casablanca

LEO BURNETT CASABLANCA, 26 Rue Frederic Le Maitre, Quartier Riviera, pg. 644
MEC, 157 Boulevard d'Anfa Immeuble Racine d'Anfa 4eme Etage, Quartier Racine, pg. 1360
PROMOSEVEN-MOROCCO, 237 Bd Zerktouni Residence El Kheir, pg. 724

MOZAMBIQUE

Maputo

DDB MOZAMBIQUE, Av Fernao Magalhaes, Nr 34, 30 andar, pg. 285
OGILVY MOZAMBIQUE, 17 Avenue Agostinho Neto, pg. 848

MYANMAR

Yangon

MANGO MARKETING SERVICES COMPANY LTD., No 51 C Golden Valley Street Golden Valley Ward 2 Bahan Tsp, pg. 571

NAMIBIA

Windhoek

ADVANTAGE Y&R, 5 Storch Street, pg. 1251
DV.8 SAATCHI & SAATCHI, 84 Frans Indongo St, pg. 1004
TBWA/PARAGON, House 40 Eros Route, pg. 1125

NETHERLANDS

Amstelveen

COMPASSO MUNDOCOM, Van Der Hooplaan 241, pg. 920
CPM NETHERLANDS, Amsterdamseweg 206, Wildenborch 4, pg. 242
DDB AMSTERDAM, Prof WH Keesomlaan 4, pg. 286
FHV BBDO, Amsterdamseweg 204, pg. 109
INTERBRAND B.V., Prof WH Keesomlaan 4, pg. 858
KETCHUM PLEON, Amsterdamseweg 206, pg. 1564
MCCANN AMSTERDAM, Bovenkerkerweg 6-8, pg. 724
OMD NEDERLAND, Amsterdams sawag 204, pg. 1381
PORTER NOVELLI, Amsterdamseweg 204, pg. 1623
PUBLICIS, Prof WH Keesomlaan 12, pg. 920
PUBLICIS DIALOG, Prof WH Keesomlaan 12, pg. 920
RAPP AMSTERDAM, Prof WH Keesomlaan 4, pg. 954
TRIBAL WORLDWIDE AMSTERDAM, Prof WH Keesomlaan 4, pg. 1316
ZENITHOPTIMEDIA, Prof WH Keesomlaan 12, pg. 1399

Amsterdam

72ANDSUNNY, Westerhuis 1st Fl Westerstraat 187, pg. 11
ACHTUNG, Prins Hendrikkade 20-11, pg. 1279
BLAST RADIUS AMSTERDAM, Max Euweplein 46, pg. 136
COHN & WOLFE BENELUX, Danzigerkade 53, Amsterdam, pg. 1481
DIGITASLBI, Joop Geesinkweg 209 1096 AV, pg. 1289
DOWNTOWN ACTION MARKETING, General Vetter Straat 82, pg. 1122
EDELMAN, Gustaz Mahlerplein 66a, pg. 1506
FCB AMSTERDAM, Bovenkerkerweg 6-8, pg. 374
GREY AMSTERDAM, Watertorenplein 4b, pg. 450
GYRO AMSTERDAM, Peperstraat 7, pg. 469
HAVAS WORLDWIDE AMSTERDAM, Sarphatistraat 370, pg. 495
HILL+KNOWLTON STRATEGIES B.V., Weerdestein 20, pg. 1543
INITIATIVE, Atlas ArenA Amsterdam Asia Building, Hoogoorddreef 5, pg. 1346
KINETIC, Karperstraat 8, pg. 1351
MEC, Karperstraat 10, pg. 1359
MEDIACOM AMSTERDAM, Karperstraat 8, pg. 1370
MILLWARD BROWN/CENTRUM, Paulvan Vlissingen Scraac 10B, pg. 759
MSL, Jan van Goyenkade 10, pg. 1597
OGILVY & MATHER (AMSTERDAM) B.V., Pilotenstraat 41, pg. 833
OGILVY HEALTHWORLD, Pilotenstraat 41, pg. 853
OGILVYOFFICE, Pilotenstraat 41, pg. 834
SAATCHI & SAATCHI LEO BURNETT, Danzigerkade 23C, pg. 1004
SID LEE, Waterorenplein 4-A, pg. 1040
SIZMEK, WG Plein 233, pg. 1048
TBWA COMPANY GROUP, GENERAAL VETTERSTRAAT 82, pg. 1122
TBWA DESIGNERS COMPANY, Generaal Vetterstraat 82, pg. 1122
TBWA NEBOKO, General Vetterstraat 82, pg. 1122
UBACHSWISBRUN J. WALTER THOMPSON, Rietlandpark 301, pg. 574
VBAT, Pilotenstraat 41 A, pg. 1223
WIEDEN + KENNEDY - AMSTERDAM, Herengracht 258-266, pg. 1203
Y&R AMSTERDAM B.V., Karperstraat 10, pg. 1246

Eindhoven

BOVIL DDB, Dillenburgstraat 5E, pg. 286
BOVIL DDB, Dillenburgstraat 5E, pg. 1121

Groningen

THABASCO, Hereweg 95, pg. 1122

Hague

HVR, Parkstraat 83, pg. 1122
WEBER SHANDWICK, Koninginnegracht 23, pg. 1680

Hilversum

BRAIN BOX, Mozartlaan 27c, pg. 1121

Rotterdam

ARA GROEP, Kratonkade 3, pg. 1121
HFMBOVACO, Lloydkwartier Kratonkade 3, pg. 1122

Sittard

BANNERCONNECT, Poststraat 12, pg. 1321

Voorburg

HOLLANDER EN VAN DER MEY/MS&L, Villa Vronesteijn Oosteinde 237, pg. 1595

Woerden

WWAV, Stationsweg 2, pg. 954

NEW ZEALAND

Auckland

BCG2, Level 2 1 Cross Street Newton, pg. 1217
COLENSO BBDO, 100 College Hill, Ponsonby, pg. 116
DDB NEW ZEALAND LTD., Level 6 80 Greys Ave, pg. 286
FCB AUCKLAND, 57 Wellington Street, Freemans Bay, pg. 381
J. WALTER THOMPSON INTERNATIONAL, The Axis Bldg CNR 91 St Georges Bay & Cleveland Roads, Parnell, pg. 571
MEC, 2nd Fl Corner, Augustus Terr & Parnell Rise, Parnell, pg. 1363
OGILVY NEW ZEALAND, 22 Stanley St, Parnell, pg. 846
OMD NEW ZEALAND/AUCKLAND, Level 1 33 College Hill, Posonby, pg. 1381
PHD NEW ZEALAND, Level 7 University of Otago Bldg, 385 Queen St, pg. 1385
PORTER NOVELLI NEW ZEALAND-AUCKLAND, Zone 23 110/23 Edwin St Mt Eden, Symonds St, pg. 1625
RAPP NEW ZEALAND, 80 Greys Ave Level 2, pg. 954
SAATCHI & SAATCHI, Level 3 123-125 The Strand Parnell, pg. 1011
TBWA WHYBIN LIMITED, 11 Mayoral Dr Wellesley St, pg. 1130
Y&R, Level 4 Corner Augustus Terrace & Parnell Rise, Parnell, pg. 1223
Y&R, Level 4 Corner Augustus Terrace & Parnell Rise, Parnell, pg. 1233
YOUNG & RUBICAM NZ LTD., Level 4 Corner Augustas Terrace& Parnell Rise, pg. 1242
ZENITHOPTIMEDIA, The Textile Centre 4th Fl Kenwyn St, Parnell, pg. 1401

Wellington

CLEMENGER BBDO WELLINGTON, Clemenger BBDO House 8 Kent Ter Level 2, pg. 116
MEC, 81 Abel Smith ST, TE ARO, pg. 1363
SAATCHI & SAATCHI, 101-103 Courtenay Pl, Te Aro, pg. 1012
YOUNG & RUBICAM WELLINGTON, Level 3 107 Custom House Quay, pg. 1242

NIGERIA

Lagos

ALL SEASONS MEDIACOM, No 50 Adekunle Fajuyi Way, GRA Ikeja, pg. 1370
ALL SEASONS MEDIACOM, No 50 Adekunle Fajuyi Way, GRA Ikeja, pg. 452
DDB CASERS, 6 Adeola Hopewell St, Victoria Island, pg. 286
LTC ADVERTISING LAGOS, 2nd Fl Motorway Centre 1 Motorway Ave, PMB 21772 Ikeja, pg. 566
ROSABEL ADVERTISING LTD., Rosabel Court 31 Aromire Av, Ikeja, pg. 644
SO&U SAATCHI & SAATCHI, 2 Oyetula Street Off Ajanaku Street via Thomas Ajufo Street Opebi, Ikeja, pg. 1005
TBWA CONCEPT UNIT, 37 Ladipo Bateye GRA Ikeja, pg. 1125

NORWAY

Oslo

BATES UNITED, Holbergs Gate 21, Saint Olavs plass, pg. 220
BURSON-MARSTELLER A/S, Sjolyst Plass 4, pg. 1468
DDB OSLO A.S., Wergelandsveien 21, pg. 287
INITIATIVE UNIVERSAL MEDIA NORWAY, Sandakerveien 24C, Bygning C1, pg. 1346
KITCHEN LEO BURNETT, Drammensveien 127, BYGG 86,2 ETG, pg. 644
LYNX PORTER NOVELLI AS, Bryggegata 5, pg. 1622
LYNX PORTER NOVELLI AS, Bryggegata 5, pg. 1463
MAXUS, PB 454 Sentrum, pg. 1354
MCCANN ERICKSON, Sandakervn 24C Building C1, pg. 724
MEC, Stortorvet 10, pg. 1359
MEDIACOM AS, Torggata 5 PB 8904, Youngstorget, pg. 1370
SAATCHI & SAATCHI A/S, Storgata 33, pg. 1005
STARCOM NORWAY, Tollbugt 17, Sentrum, pg. 1079
UNCLE GREY OSLO, Sorkedalsveien 6, pg. 450
ZENITHOPTIMEDIA, Munkedamsveien 35, pg. 1400

OMAN

Muscat

FP7, 1st Fl Homuz Bldg Next Near Ruwi Roundabout, pg. 725

PAKISTAN

Karachi

J. WALTER THOMPSON, 4th Floor Executive Tower Dolmen City, Marine Drive, pg. 571
LOWE RAUF, 159 Bangalore Town, Shahrah-e-faisal, pg. 792
OGILVY & MATHER, 94 Jinnah Cooperative Housing Society, Block 7/8 Tipu Sultan Rd, pg. 850
PRESTIGE COMMUNICATIONS PVT. LTD., 9 Karachi Chambers Hasrat Mohani Road, pg. 457

PANAMA

Panama

BB&M LOWE & PARTNERS, Ave Ricardo Arango y Calle 54 Urbanizacion Obarrio 4, pg. 555
FCB MARKEZ, Calle 63B Los Angeles #20, pg. 378
J. WALTER THOMPSON, Entre Calle 64 y 65 Edificio Star Communications & Holding, Piso 1 Mezzanine, pg. 578
PUBLICIS FERGO, S.A., Calle 50 y Calle 67 San Francisco Building 3rd Fl, pg. 930

PARAGUAY

Asuncion

BIEDERMANN PUBLICIDAD S.A., Alejo Garcia 2589 c/ Rio de la Plata, pg. 725
MASS PUBLICIDAD S.R.L., Estados Unidos 961 3rd Floor, pg. 641

PERU

Lima

CIRCUS COMMUNICACION INTEGRADA, Av Angamos Oeste #1270, Miraflores, pg. 641

FCB MAYO, Av Salaverry 2423, San Isidro, pg. 379
GREY GCG PERU S.A.C., Av Arequipa No 4080, Miraflores, pg. 454
J. WALTER THOMPSON, Paseo de la Republica 5883, pg. 579
MCCANN ERICKSON (PERU) PUBLICIDAD S.A., Calle Tripoli 102 Miraflores Apartado 180668, pg. 725
QUORUM NAZCA SAATCHI & SAATCHI, Avenue Angamos Oeste 1218, Miraflores, pg. 1009
TBWA PERU, San Ignacia de Loyola 150, Miraflores, pg. 1132
Y&R PERU, Av Angamos Oeste 915, Miraflores, pg. 1250

PHILIPPINES

Makati

ACE SAATCHI & SAATCHI, Saatchi House 2296 Don Chino Roces Avenue Parso Tamo Extension, Kayamanan C, pg. 1012
ARC WORLDWIDE, 25/F Tower 2 The Enterprise Ctr, Corner Paseo de Roxas, pg. 1406
BBDO GUERRERO, 11th Floor Insular Life Building Ayala Avenue corner, Paseo de Roxas, pg. 117
CAMPAIGNS & GREY, 2723 Sabio Street, Chino Roces Avenue, pg. 457
FCB MANILA, 4F 6780 Ayala Avenue, pg. 381
J. WALTER THOMPSON, 7th F Equitable Bank Tower 8751 Paseo de Roxas, Salcedo Village, pg. 571
KINETIC, 11-B Country Space 1 Building HV dela Costa St, Salcedo Village, pg. 1350
LEO BURNETT MANILA, Enterprise Center Tower 2 24th Fl 6766 Ayala Avenue Corner, Paseo de Roxas, pg. 650
MILLWARD BROWN PHILIPPINES, 8/F Equitable Bank Tower 8751 Paseo De Roxas, Salcedo Village, pg. 760
OGILVY PR WORLDWIDE, 15th Floor Philamlife Tower 8767 Paseo de Roxas, pg. 1609
PHD PHILIPPINES, 10F Bankmer Bldg, 6756 Ayala Avenue, pg. 1385
PUBLICIS JIMENEZBASIC, 14/F Solaris One Bldg 130 Dela Rosa St, Legaspi Village, pg. 934
PUBLICIS MANILA, 4F Herco Center 114 Benavides Street Legaspi Village, pg. 934
STARCOM WORLDWIDE, 24F Tower 2 Enterprise Center 6766 Ayala Avenue Corner, Paseo de Roxas, pg. 1080

Manila

BCD PINPOINT DIRECT MARKETING INC., 4th Floor Bloomingdale Bldg 205 Salcedo St, Legaspi Village, pg. 846
FLEISHMAN-HILLARD MANILA, 4/F Zeta Building 191 Salcedo Street, Legaspi Village Makati City, pg. 1521
LOWE, Rufino Pacific Towers 6784 Ayala Avenue, Makati City, pg. 793
MAXUS, 25 F Philamlife Tower, Makati City, pg. 1354
MCCANN ERICKSON (PHILIPPINES), INC., 34th Floor GT Tower 6813 Ayala Avenue Corner HV Dela Costa Street, Makati City, pg. 725
OGILVY & MATHER (PHILIPPINES) INC., 24 & 25 F Picadilly Star Building, Taguig City, pg. 846
OGILVYONE WORLDWIDE, 15th Floor Philamlife Tower 8767 Paseo de Roxas, Makati City Metro, pg. 846
OMD PHILIPPINES, 11th Floor Bankmer Building 6756 Ayala Ave, Makati City, pg. 1381
TBWA SANTIAGO MANGADA PUNO, 1195 Chino Races Ave Corner Yakal Street, Makati City, pg. 1130
WEBER SHANDWICK, 10/F JAKA Bldg 6780 Ayala Ave, Makati City, pg. 1684
YOUNG & RUBICAM PHILIPPINES, 9th Fl Marajo Twr 312 26th St W Corner 1 Ave, Bonifacio Global City, pg. 1244

Pasig

HAVAS WORLDWIDE MANILA, 16F Robinsons Equitable Bank Tower 4 ADB, pg. 501

Taguig

DDB PHILIPPINES INC., 16th Fl Two World Square 22 Upper Mckinley Road, Fort Bonifacio, pg. 287

POLAND

Lodz

DIGITAL ONE, Dowborczykow 25 st, 90-019 Lodz, pg. 495

Poznan

DATA SOLUTIONS, Ul Bastionowa 37, pg. 1122

Warsaw

AIMS POLSKA SP. Z O.O., ul Flory 9/10, pg. 581
BBDO, Ul Burakowska 5/7, pg. 109
DDB WARSAW, Athina Park 6c, Wybreze Gdyrishie St, pg. 287
E-GRAPHICS, Ul Rzymowskiego 34, pg. 1122
FCB WARSAW, ul Cybernetyki 19A, pg. 374
FLEISHMAN-HILLARD POLAND, ul Burakowska 5/7, pg. 1520
GREY GROUP POLAND, Ul Jasna 24, pg. 451
GREY WORLDWIDE WARSAW, Ul Jasna 24, pg. 1482
HAVAS WORLDWIDE POLAND, Ul Marynarska 11, pg. 495
HILL+KNOWLTON STRATEGIES POLAND, Ul Adama Branickiego 17, pg. 1543
INITIATIVE UNIVERSAL WARSAW, 6 Altowa St, pg. 1346
J. WALTER THOMPSON POLAND, Ul Zurawia 45, pg. 574
LEO BURNETT WARSAW SP.Z.O.O., UL Woloska 9, pg. 644
LOWE POLAND, ul Domaniewska 39, NEFRYT Building, pg. 792
MARKETING HOUSE, Ul Marynarska 11, pg. 495
MEC, ul Dobra 56/66, pg. 1359
MEDIACOM WARSZAWA, u Postepu 6, pg. 1370
MILLWARD BROWN SMG/KRC, ul Nowoursynowska 154a, pg. 760
MSL WARSAW, Platinum Business Park Woloska 9, pg. 1597
MSLGROUP, ul Domaniewska 42, pg. 1597
OGILVY HEALTHWORLD, Ul Angorska 13a, pg. 853
OGILVYONE WORLDWIDE, ul Angorska 13A, pg. 834
POLSKA MCCANN ERICKSON, Cybernetyki 19, pg. 725
PUBLICIS SP. Z.O.O., Al Jana Pawla II 80, pg. 921
SAATCHI & SAATCHI, Ul Domaniewska 42, pg. 1005
STARCOM SP. Z O.O., ul Sobieskiego 104, pg. 1079
TBWA GROUP POLAND, ul Rzymowskiego 34, pg. 1122
TBWA PR, ul Rzymowskiego 34, pg. 1123
TBWA WARSZAWA, Ul Rzymowskiego 34, pg. 1123
WUNDERMAN, ul Dobra 56/66, pg. 1234
ZENITHOPTIMEDIA, ul Domaniewska 42, pg. 1399

PORTUGAL

Lisbon

BBDO PORTUGAL, Av Eng Duarte Pancheco, No.26, 12th Andar, pg. 109
DDB LISBOA, Av Duque de Avila 46 Piso 4, pg. 287
FCB LISBON, Rua Braamcamp No 40 7th Floor, pg. 374
HAVAS EXPERIENCE LISBON, Alameda dos Oceanos Torre Euro RSCG, Parque das Nacoes, pg. 495
HAVAS WORLDWIDE DIGITAL PORTUGAL, Zona Intervencao Expo 98 Alameda dos Oceanos, Pav Exposicoes, pg. 495
J. WALTER THOMPSON, Centro Cultural de Belem, Rua Bartolomeu Dias, pg. 574
LEO BURNETT PUBLICIDADE, LTDA., Rua das Flores 7, pg. 644
MCCANN WORLDGROUP PORTUGAL, Rua Carlos Alberto da Mota Pinto n 17A, Piso 8, pg. 726
MEC, Av Fontess Pereira de Melo 6 2nd Fl 2 Andar Dir, pg. 1359
MILLWARD BROWN PORTUGAL, Avenida Eng Duarte Pacheco Torre 1 - 90 Piso, pg. 760
OGILVY & MATHER PORTUGAL, Edificio Atrium Saldanha Praa Duque de Saldanha Number 1-4E, pg. 834
OPTIMEDIA, Rua Goncalves Zarco 14 R C, pg. 1400
PORTER NOVELLI, Av 5 de Outubro 10 2 Esq, pg. 1623
PUBLICIS PUBLICIDADE LDA., Rua Goncalves Zarco 14, pg. 921
TBWA LISBON, Avenida de Liberdade 38 6th Fl, pg. 1123
WEBER SHANDWICK-D&E, Av Eng Arantes e Oliveira n 11-2 C, pg. 1680
WUNDERMAN, Avenidas Eng Duarte Pacheco Amoreiras Torre 1 9th Fl, pg. 1234
Y&R PORTUGAL, Av Eng Duarte Pacheco, Tower 1 9th Fl, pg. 1246

Porto Salvo

MEDIACOM PORTUGAL, Edificio 5C 4o Lagoas Park, pg. 1370

QATAR

Doha

FORTUNE PROMOSEVEN-QATAR, Pearl Towers 4th Fl Al Saad St, pg. 726
PUBLICIS-GRAPHICS, Villa No 20 Al Kanan Street, Al Mirqab, pg. 924

ROMANIA

Bucharest

DDB BUCHAREST, No21 Carol Davila St, Sector 5, pg. 287
FCB BUCHAREST, 31bis Intrarea Rigas 1st District, pg. 374
GEOMETRY GLOBAL, Frumoasa St 39, Sector 1, pg. 451
GRAFFITI BBDO, Gheorghe Manu Street 3 District 1, pg. 110
HAVAS WORLDWIDE BUCHAREST, Calea Victoriei 141 Sector 1, pg. 496
LEO BURNETT & TARGET SA, 13 Nicolae Iorga Str, pg. 644
LOWE & PARTNERS, 17 Radu Voda Str, pg. 790
MCCANN ERICKSON ROMANIA, Jules Michelet 18 1st Sector, pg. 726
OGILVY & MATHER, 86 Grigore Alexandrescu Street, pg. 834
PUBLICIS, 8 Luminei Street, pg. 921
SAATCHI & SAATCHI, Central Business Park Cladirea D+E Parter Calea Serban Voda nr 133, Sector 4, pg. 1005
SCALA/J. WALTER THOMPSON, Str Trotusului Nr 39 Sector 1, pg. 574
TBWA MERLIN, Calea Rahavei nr 196A et 3 sect 5, pg. 1123

RUSSIA

Moscow

APCO WORLDWIDE, 11 Leontievsky Pereulok, pg. 64
BBDO MOSCOW, 20 Building 1 4th Tverskaya-Yamskaya, pg. 110
DDB RUSSIA, 40/2 Prechistenka St Bldg 3, pg. 287
EDELMAN IMAGELAND, Kozhevnichesky Proezd 4 Bldg 2, pg. 1507
GREY CIS, 5th Yamskogo Polya Str 7 Bldg 2, pg. 451
INITIATIVE MOSCOW, Office 407-408 Bldg 1, 18 Malaya Pirogovskaya str, pg. 1346
LEO BURNETT MOSCOW, 11 Bldg 2-5 Timur Frunze Str 2nd Fl, Business Centre Red Rose, pg. 645
LOWE ADVENTA, 1st Volkonskiy pereulok 13 str 2, pg. 790
MEC, 23 Osenniy Blvd Krylatsky Business Centre, pg. 1359
PBN HILL + KNOWLTON STRATEGIES, 3 Uspensky Pereulok Bldg 4, pg. 1541
PUBLICITAS EASTERN EUROPE LTD., Novy Arbat str 21 Bldg 1 6th Fl Office 611, pg. 1426
R.I.M. PORTER NOVELLI, 36 bld 4 B Novodmitrovskaya st office centre Khrustalny, pg. 1624
SAATCHI & SAATCHI RUSSIA, Bolshoy Levshinky 6/2 bld 1, pg. 1005
SPN OGILVY COMMUNICATIONS AGENCY, 4a Novodanilovskya emb, pg. 834
STARCOM MEDIAVEST GROUP MOSCOW, Usievitcha U1 20/1, pg. 1078
YOUNG & RUBICAM FMS, 12 Krasnopresnenskaya Nab Office 809, pg. 1248

SAUDI ARABIA

Jeddah

Riyadh

SERBIA

Belgrade

SINGAPORE

Singapore

SLOVAKIA

Bratislava

SLOVENIA

Ljubljana

Maribor

SOUTH AFRICA

Bryanston

Cape Town

Durban

Gauteng

Johannesburg

FCB SOUTH AFRICA, 164 Katherine Street, Pin Mill Farm, pg. 382
FLEISHMAN-HILLARD/SOUTH AFRICA, 15 Georgian Crescent Ground Floor, Bryanston, pg. 1520
GILLIAN GAMSY INTERNATIONAL, Houghton Pl 51 W St, Houghton, pg. 1680
GO ADVERTISING, The Brand Building 15 Sloane St, Bryanston, pg. 848
LOWE BULL, St Andrews Office Park Meadowbrook Lane, Epsom Downs Bryanston, pg. 790
MAGNA CARTA, 38 Wierda Road West The Hunt, Ground Floor, pg. 1125
MCCANN WORLDGROUP JOHANNESBURG, 4 Kikuyu Road, Sunninghill, pg. 727
MEDIACOM SOUTH AFRICA, GroupM House, 7 Naivasha Rd, pg. 1370
METROPOLITANREPUBLIC, 7 Wessel Road Edenburg, pg. 1220
OGILVY & MATHER SOUTH AFRICA (PTY.) LTD., The Brand Building 15 Sloane Street, Bryanston, pg. 849
OGILVY HEALTHWORLD, The Brand Building 15 Sloane Street, Bryanston, pg. 849
OGILVY JOHANNESBURG (PTY.) LTD., The Brand Building 15 Sloane Street, Bryanston, pg. 849
SAATCHI & SAATCHI, 28 Roos Street ext 29, Fourways, pg. 1006
TBWA HUNT LASCARIS (JOHANNESBURG), 3 Sandown Valley Crescent, Sandown, pg. 1126
TBWA SOUTH AFRICA GROUP, 3 Sandown Valley Crescent Sandton, PO Box 785203, pg. 1126
WUNDERMAN DIRECT, 102 Western Service Road, Gallo manor Ext 6, pg. 1234

Randburg

EDELMAN SOUTH AFRICA, 11 Ralda Rd, Blairgowrie, pg. 1507

Rivonia

J. WALTER THOMPSON, 34 Homestead Rd cnr 12th Ave & Rivonia Rd, pg. 567
JUPITER DRAWING ROOM, River Park, 42 Holmstead Rd, pg. 1251
JUPITER DRAWING ROOM, River Park, 42 Holmstead Rd, pg. 1220
MEC SOUTH AFRICA, Merton Place The Avenues Office Park, 45 Homestead Rd,, pg. 1361

Sandton

THE BRAND UNION, Forum Bldg 5th Fl 2 Maude St, pg. 157
IRELAND/DAVENPORT, 198 Oxford Rd 2nd Fl, Illovo, pg. 1220
MCCANN ERICKSON AFRICA, 4 Kikuya Road South Sunninghill, pg. 727
OCTAGON, Octagon House 47 Wierda Road West, Wierda Valley, pg. 824
PUBLICIS JOHANNESBURG PTY. LTD., 140a Kelvin Drive Morningside Manor, pg. 924

Wendywood

Y&R JOHANNESBURG, Soft Line Technology Park, 56 Lotus Rd, pg. 1251

SPAIN

Barcelona

BASSAT, OGILVY & MATHER COMUNICACION, Josep Tarradellas 123-2nd Fl, pg. 1608
BASSAT, OGILVY & MATHER COMUNICACION, Josep Tarradellas 123-2nd Fl, pg. 834
BURSON-MARSTELLER, S.A., Avenida Diagonal 545 4th Fl 1st Door, pg. 1469
CARRE NOIR BARCELONA, Duana 3-2, pg. 921
CPM SPAIN, A-7 C / Henri Dunant March 9 to 11 08 174, Saint Cugat del Valles, pg. 242
DDB BARCELONA S.A., Enrique Granados 86-88, pg. 288
EDELMAN, Passeig De Gracia 86, 3A planta, pg. 1506
ENE LIFE, Calle Villarroell 216, pg. 466
FCB SPAIN, Muntaner 240-242 5 2a, pg. 375
GREY BARCELONA, Santalo 10, pg. 451
HILL & KNOWLTON ESPANA, S.A., Corsega Street 329 6th Floor, pg. 1543
J. WALTER THOMPSON, Via Augusta 281 4a Planta, pg. 575
KELLENFOL ADVERTISING, Gran Via Corts Catalanes, pg. 607
KREAB BARCELONA, C Mandri 36 bajos, pg. 1568
MCCANN ERICKSON S.A., Josep Irla y Bosch 1 3, pg. 728
NURUN SPAIN, Entenza 94 Office 1, pg. 925
OGILVY HEALTHWORLD BARCELONA, Avda Josef Tarradellas 123 2, pg. 852
OGILVYINTERACTIVE, Avda-Josep Tarradellas 123-6, pg. 835
OGILVYONE WORLDWIDE, Bolivia 68-70, pg. 835
PORTER NOVELLI, Paseo de Gracia 56 ,6, pg. 1623
SCPF, C/Calatrava num 71, pg. 1222
STARCOM, Beethoven 15, Planta 5, pg. 1079
TBWA ESPANA, Paseo de Gracia 56 2nd Floor, pg. 1123
TIEMPO BBDO, Tuset 5 6a, pg. 111
VINIZIUS/Y&R, C/Numancia 164-168 8th Floor, pg. 1246

Madrid

ARNOLD MADRID, Paseo de la Castellana 259, Torre de Cristal, pg. 72
COHN & WOLFE, C/ Fuencarral 6, pg. 1481
CONTRAPUNTO, C/Cardenal Marcelo Spinola Sp # 4-4a Planta, pg. 111
DDB MADRID, S.A., Orense 4, pg. 288
EDELMAN, Paseo de la Castellana 91-5A Pta, Edificio Centro 23, pg. 1505
FCB SPAIN, Doctor Forquet 29, pg. 374
GMR MARKETING SPAIN, Calle Aviador Lindbergh 3, pg. 1415
GREY MADRID, Paseo de la Castellana ,53, pg. 452
GRUPO BASSAT, OGILVY, Maria de Molina 39, pg. 835
HAVAS DESIGN PLUS MADRID, Plaza de Castellana 259 C, Planta 28 & 29, pg. 496
HAVAS MEDIA, Avda General Peron No 38 Planta 14, pg. 1339
HAVAS SPORTS & ENTERTAINMENT, Avenida General Peron, 38 Planta 10,, pg. 485
HAVAS WORLDWIDE DIGITAL SPAIN, Plaza de Canalejas 3, pg. 496
HAVAS WORLDWIDE SOUTHERN SPAIN, Plaza de Canalejas No 3, pg. 496
HILL+KNOWLTON STRATEGIES, Nunez de Balboa 83 bajo dcha Oquendo 23 4 planta, pg. 1543
J. WALTER THOMPSON, La Palma # 10, pg. 575
KETCHUM SPAIN, Luchana 23 4, pg. 1565
KREAB MADRID, Capitan Haya 38, Edificio Cuzco II-8, pg. 1569
LOLA MADRID, C. Marques de Cubas, 4, pg. 556
LOWE & PARTNERS, C Marques de Cubas 4, pg. 790
MCCANN ERICKSON S.A., Paseo de la Castellana 165, pg. 727
MEC, Calle Las Norias 92, 2 planta, pg. 1360
MEC, Calle Las Norias 92, pg. 1360
MILLWARD BROWN SPAIN, Alcala 474, pg. 760
OGILVY & MATHER COMUNICACION, Enrique Larreta 2, pg. 1608
OGILVY HEALTHWORLD MADRID, Maria de Molina 39, pg. 852
OGILVYINTERACTIVE, Maria Molina 39, pg. 835
OGILVYONE WORLDWIDE, Maria de Molina 39, pg. 835
OPTIMEDIA, Paseo de la Castellana 95 20th Floor, Torre Europa, pg. 1400
PSM S.A., O'Donnell 34, pg. 41
PUBLICIS, C/ Ramirez De Arellano 21, pg. 921
PUBLICITAS INTERNACIONAL S.A., Goya 21 1D, pg. 1427
SAATCHI & SAATCHI, Calle Goya 24 4a Planta, pg. 1006
STARCOM MEDIA WORLDWIDE ESTRATEGIA, Goya 22 1 Fl, pg. 1078
TAPSA, Jenner 3, pg. 1224
TBWA ESPANA, Alfonso XI 12, pg. 1123
TEXT 100 MADRID S.L., Plaza de Colon n2 Torre 1, Planta 17, pg. 1661
WUNDERMAN, Avenida de Burgos 21, Complejo Triada Torre C 11th Fl, pg. 1234
XAXIS, C/Norias 92 Majadahonda, pg. 1321
YOUNG & RUBICAM, S.L., Avenida de Burgos 21 Planta 9A, pg. 1246
ZENITH MEDIA, Puerta de Europa Paseo de la Castellana 216 Floor 16, pg. 1400

Valencia

MCCANN ERICKSON S.A., Plaza de America 2 piso 6, pg. 728
MEC MEDITERRANEA, C/Naturalista Charles Robert Darwin, 5 Parque Tecnologico, pg. 1360
PORTER NOVELLI, San Vicente Martir 16, pg. 1623

SRI LANKA

Colombo

LEO BURNETT SOLUTIONS INC., No 379 R A de Mel Mawatha, pg. 650
LOWE LDB, 66/15 Ananda Coomaraswamy Mawatha (Green Path), pg. 791
OGILVY PR WORLDWIDE, No 16 Barnes Pl, pg. 1609

SWEDEN

Gothenburg

ANR BBDO, Nils Ericssonplatsen 3, pg. 111
CP+B, Ostra Hamngatan 26-28, pg. 240
SCPGREY, Ostra Hamngatan 35, pg. 1222

Stockholm

ANR BBDO, David Bagares gata 5, pg. 111
B-REEL, Tjarhovsgatan 4, pg. 1282
THE BRAND UNION, Sveavagen 9-11, pg. 158
BURSON-MARSTELLER AB, Master Samuelsgatan 56 6th floor, pg. 1469
DDB STOCKHOLM, Torsgatan 19 8th Fl, pg. 289
DEPORTIVO, Kornhamnstorg 49, pg. 1503
DIGITASLBI, Hamngatan 2, pg. 1289
EDELMAN, Brunnsgatan 21B, pg. 1506
FCB FALTMAN & MALMEN, Valhallavagen 86, pg. 375
GOLIN, , Birger Jarlsgatan 57c, pg. 1531
HAVAS WORLDWIDE GRANATH, Peter Myndes Backe 8, pg. 496
IMAGINATION (SCANDINAVIA) AB, Gotgatan 48 1st Fl, pg. 540
INGO, Master Samuelsgatan 56, pg. 452
INITIATIVE UNIVERSAL STOCKHOLM, Grevturegatan 11A, pg. 1346
JKL STOCKHOLM, Sveavagen 24-26, pg. 1596
LEO BURNETT ANNONSBYRA, Sveavagen 24-26, pg. 645
LOWE BRINDFORS, Birger Jarlsgatan 57C, pg. 790
M & M INTERNATIONAL MEDIA AB, Vasterlanggatan 67, pg. 1426
MEDIACOM SVERIGE AB, Birger Jarlsgatan 52, pg. 1370
MOBIENTO, Savageness 25, pg. 1287
MONTEROSA, Grev Turegatan 29, pg. 95
MS&L STOCKHOLM, Sveavagen 24-26, pg. 1597
OGILVY ADVERTISING, Master Samuelsgatan 56, pg. 835
OGILVY PUBLIC RELATIONS, Kaknasvagen 80, pg. 1608
OGILVYONE WORLDWIDE, Master Samuelsgatan 56, pg. 835
PRIME PUBLIC RELATIONS, Slussplan 9, pg. 1680
SAATCHI & SAATCHI, Drukningtatam 95A, pg. 1006
STORAKERS MCCANN, Grev Turegaton 11A, pg. 728
TBWA STOCKHOLM, Wallimgatam 2, pg. 1124
TV, INC., Gronhogen 1409D SE-380 65 Oland, pg. 1163
WATERSWIDGREN/TBWA AB, Blasieholmsgatan 5, pg. 1124

SWITZERLAND

Aarau

PUBLICITAS LTD., Neumattstrasse 1, pg. 1427

Basel

PUBLICITAS INTERNATIONAL AG, Kornhausgasse 5/7, pg. 1427
PUBLICITAS INTERNATIONAL SWITZERLAND, Hochbergerstrasse 15, pg. 1427
PUBLICITAS LTD., Kornhausgasse 5/7, pg. 1427

Bern

BURSON-MARSTELLER, Konsunstrasse 20, pg. 1469

Carouge

FTC, 48 Rue Jacques-Dalphin, pg. 1622
SAATCHI & SAATCHI, Place du Temple 15, pg. 1006

Chur

PUBLICITAS LTD., Comercialstrasse 20, pg. 1427

Geneva

ADNATIVE SWITZERLAND, 7 Chemin Maisonneuve, Chatelaine, pg. 1426
BURSON-MARSTELLER, 18 bd des Philosophes, pg. 1469
COHN & WOLFE, 1 Rue Lugardon, pg. 1481
HAVAS WORLDWIDE GENEVA, 42 rue du XXXI Decembre, pg. 496
LANDOR ASSOCIATES, Rue Lugardon 1, pg. 625
LPK SARL GENEVA, Avenue des Morgines 12, Petit-Lancy, pg. 672
MCCANN ERICKSON SWITZERLAND, 15 Passage Malbuisson, pg. 728
PROPAGANDA GLOBAL ENTERTAINMENT MARKETING, 2 Bis Rue De La Maison Rouge, pg. 914
PUBLICITAS LEMAN, Rue de la Synagogue 35, pg. 1427
WEBER SHANDWICK, Passage Malbuisson 15, pg. 1681
Y&R BUSINESS COMMUNICATIONS, Rue Lugardon 1, pg. 1247

Lausanne

MEC, Rue Bellefontaine 2, pg. 1360
PUBLICITAS LTD., Avenue Mon-Repos 22, pg. 1427
PUBLIGROUPE LTD., Avenue Mon-Repos 22, pg. 1426
XENTIVE, Avenue des Mousquines 4, pg. 1428

Neuchatel

PUBLICITAS LTD., Rue St Maurice 4, pg. 1428

Saint Gallen

PUBLICITAS LTD., Vadianstrasse 45, pg. 1428

Zurich

ADVICO Y&R AG, Werbeagentur BSW Hardturmstrasse 133, pg. 1246
BURSON-MARSTELLER, Grubenstrasse 40, pg. 1469
CPM SWITZERLAND, 1st Floor Seestrasse 93, pg. 242
FARNER CONSULTING AG, Oberdorfstrasse 28, pg. 1622
FCB ZURICH, Heinrichstrasse 267, pg. 375
GRENDENE OGILVY & MATHER AG, Bergstrasse 50, pg. 835
HAVAS WORLDWIDE ZURICH, Gutstrasse 73, pg. 496
J. WALTER THOMPSON FABRIKANT, Binzmuhlestrasse 170, pg. 575
MEC, Seestrasse 315, pg. 1360
MEDIACOM SWITZERLAND, Manessestrasse 85, pg. 1371
OGILVYHEALTHCARE, Bergstrasse 50, pg. 836
OGILVYONE AG, Weberstrasse 21, pg. 836
PUBLICIS, Stadelhofer Strasse 25, pg. 922
PUBLICIS DIALOG ZURICH, Stradelhofer Strasse 25, pg. 921
PUBLICITAS AG, Muertschenstrasse 39, pg. 1427
SAATCHI & SAATCHI ZURICH, Raffelstrasse 32, pg. 1006
SPILLMANN/FELSER/LEO BURNETT, Armtlerstrasse 201, pg. 645
TBWA HEALTH A.G., Seefeldstrasse 19, pg. 1124
TBWA SWITZERLAND A.G., Seefeldstrasse 19, pg. 1124
WIRZ WERBUNG AG, Uetlibergstrasse 132, pg. 112
WUNDERMAN, Hardturmstrasse 133, Postfach, pg. 1234

SYRIA

Damascus

J. WALTER THOMPSON, Shoshara Building Hilal Al Bizim Street, Malki, pg. 577

TAIWAN

Taipei

COMPASS PUBLIC RELATIONS, 10th Fl C 167 Tun Hwa N Rd, pg. 1470
EDELMAN, 10F No 36 Pateh Road Sec 3, pg. 1505
FCB TAIPEI, 7F No 1 Sec 5 Nanking E Road, pg. 381
J. WALTER THOMPSON, 11F No. 35, Lane 11 GuangFu N. Rd, pg. 571
KETCHUM TAIPEI, 3F-2 No 51 Sec 2 Keelung Rd, 110 Hsinyi District, pg. 1565
LEO BURNETT, 10th F 16 Nanjing E Road Sec 4, pg. 651
MCCANN ERICKSON COMMUNICATIONS GROUP, 11th Fl No 2 Lane 150 Section 5 Hsin Yi Rd, pg. 728
MEC, 4F No 31-2 Lane 11 GuangFu N Road, pg. 1363
MILLWARD BROWN TAIWAN, 7F-1 No 37 Sec 3, Minsheng E Rd, pg. 760
OGILVY & MATHER ADVERTISING, 90 Song Ren Rd, pg. 847
OGILVY PUBLIC RELATIONS, 90 Song Ren Road, Hsin Yi Dist, pg. 847
OGILVY PUBLIC RELATIONS TAIWAN, 3F No 89 Song Ren Road, pg. 1609
OGILVYONE WORLDWIDE, 3F 89 Song Ren Road, pg. 847
ZENITHOPTIMEDIA, 8th Floor 6 Xinyi Road, pg. 1402

THAILAND

Bangkok

AZIAM BURSON-MARSTELLER, 16th Fl Alma Link Bldg 25 Soi Chidlom, Ploenchit Rd, pg. 1470
BANGKOK PR PORTER NOVELLI, 622 Emporium Tower Fl 22/4, Sukhumvit Rd, pg. 1624
BBDO BANGKOK, 18th Fl U Chu Liang Bldg, 968 Rama IV Rd Silom, pg. 117
CREATIVE JUICE G1, 161/1 SG Tower 2nd Floor Soi Mahadle Kluang 3 Rajdamri Road, Lumpini Pat, pg. 1131
DENTSU YOUNG & RUBICAM LTD., 16-17th & 19th Floors Siam Tower 989 Rama 1 Rd, Pathumwan, pg. 1244
FCB BANGKOK, 159/25 Serm-Mit Tower Sukhumvit 21 Road, North Klongtoey Wattana, pg. 381
FORESIGHT RESEARCH CO., LTD., 11th Fl Rajapark Bldg 163 Sukhumvit 21, Klong-Toey-Nua Wattana, pg. 474
GREY THAILAND, 8th Fl Q House Ploenjit Bldg 598 Ploenchite Rd, Lumpini Pathumwan, pg. 458
GROUPM THAILAND, Ploanchit Center 23rd Floor, 2 Sukhumvit Road Khlong Toey, pg. 1337
H+K STRATEGIES THAILAND, Unit 14C 14th Fl Q House Ploenjit Bldg 598 Ploenchit Rd, Lumpini Pathumwan, pg. 1544
HAVAS WORLDWIDE BANGKOK, 29 Bangkok Business Center Building 28th Floor Room 2802 Soi Ekamai, Sukhumvit 63 Klongton Nua Watt, pg. 501
J. WALTER THOMPSON THAILAND, 591 19/F UBC 2 Bldg Sukhumvit 33 Road, Klongton Nua Wattana, pg. 572
KINETIC, 2 Ploenchit Ctr 18th Fl Sukhumvit Rd, Klongtoey, pg. 1351
LEO BURNETT, Sindhorn Bldg Tower 1 3rd Fl 130-132 Wireless Rd, Lumpini Pathumwan, pg. 651
LOWE, 195 Empire Tower 28th Floor, South Sathorn Rd, pg. 794
MAXUS, 2 Ploenchit Center 14th Floor, Sukhumvit Rd Klongtoey, pg. 1353
MCCANN WORLDGROUP THAILAND, 555 Narathiwas Rd, pg. 728
MILLWARD BROWN THAILAND, Level 14 Kamol Sukosol Bldg 317 Silom Road, Bangrak, pg. 760
OGILVY & MATHER ADVERTISING, 14th Flr The Offices at Centralworld 999/9 Rama 1 Rd, Patumwan, pg. 847
OGILVYINTERACTIVE, 14th Fl The Offices at Centralworld 999/9 Rama 1 Rd, Patumwan, pg. 848
PHD THAILAND, 10 Floor Amarin Plaza, 500 Ploenchit Road, pg. 1385
PUBLICIS (THAILAND) LTD., Empire Tower 47th Fl, Yannawa, pg. 934
PUBLICITAS THAILAND, 5th Fl Lumpini I Bldg, 239/2 Soi Sarasin Rajdamri Rd, pg. 1428
SAATCHI & SAATCHI, 25/F Sathorn City Tower 175 S Sathorn Rd Khwaeng Thungmahamek, Khet Sathorn, pg. 1012
SPARK COMMUNICATIONS, 11/F One Pacific Pl, 140 Sukhumvit Road Klong Toey, pg. 1463
TBWA THAILAND, 1st-2nd Fl Golden Pavilion Bldg 153/3 Soi Mahardlekluang 1 Rajdamri Rd, Pathumwan, pg. 1131

TRINIDAD & TOBAGO

Port of Spain

ABOVEGROUP, Corner Fitt & Roberts St, Woodbrook, pg. 840
LONSDALE SAATCHI & SAATCHI, 8 & 10 Herbert Street, pg. 1009
PUBLICIS CARIBBEAN, Albion Court 61 Dundonald Street, pg. 930
VALDEZ & TORRY ADVERTISING LIMITED, 46 Murray St, Woodbrook, pg. 454

TUNISIA

Tunis

J. WALTER THOMPSON, 91 Avenue Louis Braille, Cite El-Khadrah, pg. 567

TURKEY

Beyoglu

MEDINA/TURGUL DDB, Tuzambari Kasimpasa Bedrettin Mah Havuzbasi Degirmeni Sok No 2, pg. 289

Istanbul

ALICE BBDO, Maslak Mah Dereboyu Caddesi Bilim Solak No 5 Sun Plaza, BBDO Blok Sisli, pg. 112
C-SECTION, Istiklal Caddesi Kallavi Sokak No 1 Kat 1, pg. 1247
FCB ARTGROUP, Kilic Ali Pasa Caddesi No:12 K:5, 34425 Tophane, pg. 375
GREY ISTANBUL, Beybi Giz Plaza Dereboyu Caddesi, Meydan Sok No 28 Kat 5 Maslak, pg. 452
HAVAS LIFE ISTANBUL, Istiklal Cad No 284-286 Odakule Is Merkezi Kat 16, Beyoglu, pg. 496
HAVAS WORLDWIDE ISTANBUL, Istiklal Caddesi No 284-286 Odakule Is Merkezi Kat 16, Beyoglu, pg. 497
LOWE, B2 Husrev Gerede Caddesi, Besiktas, pg. 794
MANAJANS THOMPSON ISTANBUL, Buyukdere Cad Harman Sokak No 4 Kat 7 Levent, pg. 575
MARKOM/LEO BURNETT, Buyukdere Cad 26/6 Beytem Plaza, Sisli, pg. 646
MCCANN ERICKSON WORLDGROUP TURKEY, Buyukdere Caddesi Ecza Sokak No 6, Levent, pg. 729
MEC, Dereboyu Caddesi No 78/1-4 Ortakoy, pg. 1360
OGILVY & MATHER, Harmancy Giz Plaza Harman Sokak M1-2 Levant, pg. 836
OGILVY HEALTHWORLD, Harmanci Giz Plaza Haman Sokak M 1-2, pg. 836
SAATCHI & SAATCHI ISTANBUL, Adnan Saygun Cad Kelaynak Sok No 1/1, Ulus Besiktas, pg. 1006
TBWA ISTANBUL, ATA Center Ahi Evren Cad No 1 Kat G2, Maslak, pg. 1127
UM, Buyukdere Caddesi Ecza Sokak No 6, Levent, pg. 729
Y&R TURKEY, Bomonti Firin Sokak No: 51, pg. 1247

TURKS & CAICOS ISLANDS

Providenciales

WIRED ISLAND LTD., PO Box 661, pg. 1211

UKRAINE

Kiev

ADVENTA LOWE, 13 Pymonenka Str., Building 5A, 5th Floor, pg. 789

UNITED ARAB EMIRATES

Abu Dhabi

Dubai

Sharjah

UNITED KINGDOM

Aberdeen

Andover

Aylesbury

Belfast

Birmingham

Brentwood

Brighton

Bristol

Bury

Chertsey

Cirencester

East Grinstead

Edinburgh

Glasgow

Hampton

Isleworth

Kingston

London

Macclesfield

Manchester

Prestbury

Reading

Richmond

Solihull

MCCANN ERICKSON CENTRAL, McCann Erickson House Highlands Road, Shirley, pg. 730

Thames Ditton

HAVAS LIFE MEDICOM UK, Ferry Works, Summer Road, pg. 487

Tunbridge Wells

SOUTHPAW, The Warehouse Hill Street, pg. 475
SOUTHPAW COMMUNICATIONS LTD., Multimedia House Hill Street, pg. 475

Warwick

MILLWARD BROWN UK LTD., Olympus Avenue Tachbrook Park, pg. 760

URUGUAY

Montevideo

CORPORACION / J. WALTER THOMPSON, Convencion 1343 Piso 8, pg. 579
EFPZ, Wilson Ferreira Aldunate 1212, pg. 379
GREY, CASARES, VERNAZZA & ASSOCIADOS S.A., Blvd Artigas 1913, pg. 454
LOWE GINKGO, Joaquin Nunes 3082, pg. 791
NUEVA COMUNICACION-WEBER SHANDWICK, Ellauri 1212, pg. 1682
PUBLICIS IMPETU, Colonia 922 Piso 8, pg. 930
PUNTO OGILVY & MATHER, Plaza Independencia, pg. 840
TEQUILA ESECE, Ellauri 1232, pg. 1132
Y&R URUGUAY, Bvar Espana 2617, pg. 1251

UZBEKISTAN

Tashkent

GREY GROUP UZBEKISTAN, Ivlieva St 44, pg. 452

VENEZUELA

Caracas

AJL PARK, Torre Multinvest Piso 4 Plaza La Castellana Chacao, pg. 379
ARS DDB PUBLICIDAD, Av Diego Cisneros Edif ARS, Los Ruices, pg. 290
AW OVEJA NEGRA SAATCHI & SAATCHI, Edificio ABA 4th Fl, Las Mercedes, pg. 1009
BBDO VENEZUELA, Centro Ave Don Diego Cisneros, Los Ruices, pg. 104
BURSON-MARSTELLER, Avenida La Estancia, Centro Benaven (Cubo Negro) Torre C, Piso 2, Chuao, pg. 1467
FCB CARACAS, Av.Libertador cruce c/Avila, Bello Campo Chacao, pg. 379
INITIATIVE CARACAS, Av Principal de La Castelina, Edf Multinvest Piso 4, pg. 1345
J. WALTER THOMPSON, Centro Banaven Torre C Piso 3 Ave La Estancia Chuao, pg. 579
MCCANN ERICKSON PUBLICIDAD, Av Francisco Solano Lopez entre Calles Negrin y Apamates Pisos 18, Sabana Grande Apartado, pg. 730
OGILVY & MATHER, Av La Estancia Centro Banaven Torre D Piso 3, Chuao, pg. 840
PUBLICIS 67, Av Casanova Centro Comercial, Plaza Venezuela, pg. 930

VIETNAM

Ho Chi Minh City

APCO WORLDWIDE, Unit 12 4/F Saigon Centre 65 Le Loi, District 1, pg. 64
DDB VIETNAM ADVERTISING, 201 PetroVietnam Tower 1 Le Duan, District 1, pg. 290
HAKUHODO & SAIGON ADVERTISING CO., LTD., 10th Floor Room 6 Saigon Centre 65 Le Loi St, District 1, pg. 474
LOWE, Level 47 Bitexco Financial Tower, 02 Hai Trieu Street, pg. 794
MCCANN ERICKSON VIETNAM, 27 Le Thanh Ton Street, District 1, pg. 730
OGILVY & MATHER (VIETNAM) LTD., Centec Tower 12th Floor 72-74 Nguyen Thi Minh Khai Street, District 3, pg. 848
TBWA/VIETNAM, Unit 302 Satra Dong Khoi, pg. 1131
Y&R VIETNAM, 193 Dinh Tien Hoang St, Dist. 1, pg. 1244

ZAMBIA

Lusaka

ARMSTRONG Y&R, Wing F 2nd Floor Comesa Centre Ben bella Rd, pg. 1252

ZIMBABWE

Harare

UPTON FULTON MCCANN PVT. LTD., Building 6 Arundel Office Park Norfolk Road, Mount Pleasant, pg. 730

SPECIAL MARKET INDEX

African-American Market

818
O2IDEAS, INC., Birmingham, AL, pg. 820
O3 WORLD, LLC, Philadelphia, PA, pg. 820
OCEAN BRIDGE GROUP, Santa Monica, CA, pg. 822
OCTAGON, Norwalk, CT, pg. 823
OGILVY & MATHER, New York, NY, pg. 826
OIC, Pasadena, CA, pg. 854
OMNICOM GROUP INC., New York, NY, pg. 857
ONE SOURCE DIRECT MARKETING, INC., Coral Springs, FL, pg. 1305
ONEWORLD COMMUNICATIONS, INC., San Francisco, CA, pg. 861
OPTIC NERVE DIRECT MARKETING, San Francisco, CA, pg. 863
OUTDOOR FIRST, INC., Germantown, WI, pg. 1383
OUTERNATIONAL INC, New York, NY, pg. 866
PALISADES MEDIA GROUP, INC., Santa Monica, CA, pg. 1383
PARKER ADVERTISING SERVICE, INC., Lancaster, PA, pg. 874
PARTNERSHIP OF PACKER, OESTERLING & SMITH (PPO&S), Harrisburg, PA, pg. 876
THE PATIENT RECRUITING AGENCY, Austin, TX, pg. 878
PATRIOT ADVERTISING INC., Katy, TX, pg. 878
PHD, New York, NY, pg. 1384
PHIRE MARKETING, Philadelphia, PA, pg. 889
PIERCE COMMUNICATIONS, INC., Columbus, OH, pg. 890
PINTA, New York, NY, pg. 892
PITA COMMUNICATIONS LLC, Rocky Hill, CT, pg. 893
POLLER & JORDAN ADVERTISING AGENCY, INC., Miami, FL, pg. 902
PONDER IDEAWORKS, Huntington Beach, CA, pg. 903
POSSIBLE STORMS, Los Angeles, CA, pg. 905
PP+K, Tampa, FL, pg. 907
PRINCETON PARTNERS, INC., Princeton, NJ, pg. 911
PROJECT 2050, New York, NY, pg. 912
PROTERRA ADVERTISING, Addison, TX, pg. 915
PUBLISHERS ADVERTISING ASSOCIATES, New York, NY, pg. 1272
THE QUEST BUSINESS AGENCY, INC., Houston, TX, pg. 942
QUIGLEY-SIMPSON, Los Angeles, CA, pg. 943
RADIO LOUNGE - RADIO ADVERTISING AGENCY, Sugar Land, TX, pg. 949
RAWLE MURDY ASSOCIATES, INC., Charleston, SC, pg. 955
REAL INTEGRATED, Bloomfield Hills, MI, pg. 957
RED MOON MARKETING, Charlotte, NC, pg. 961
REPUBLICA, Miami, FL, pg. 968
THE RESPONSE SHOP, INC., La Jolla, CA, pg. 972
REX DIRECT NET, INC., Cherry Hill, NJ, pg. 975
RICHARDS/CARLBERG, Houston, TX, pg. 978
THE RICHARDS GROUP, INC., Dallas, TX, pg. 978
RITTA, Englewood, NJ, pg. 984
ROCKET 55, Minneapolis, MN, pg. 988
THE ROGERS AGENCY, Chesapeake, VA, pg. 989
RUNYON SALTZMAN & EINHORN, Sacramento, CA, pg. 997
RYACTIVE, Oakland, CA, pg. 998
S3, Boonton, NJ, pg. 999
SAGON-PHIOR, West Los Angeles, CA, pg. 1644
SANDERS/WINGO ADVERTISING, INC., El Paso, TX, pg. 1016
SBC ADVERTISING, Columbus, OH, pg. 1023
SEED CREATIVE, Marietta, GA, pg. 1030
SHERRY MATTHEWS ADVOCACY MARKETING, Austin, TX, pg. 1038
SLINGSHOT, LLC, Dallas, TX, pg. 1052
SMY MEDIA, INC., Chicago, IL, pg. 1389
THE SOUZA AGENCY, Annapolis, MD, pg. 1061
SPECIALTY TRUCK RENTALS, Santa Monica, CA, pg. 1430
SPOT ON, Bronx, NY, pg. 1067
SPOT SAVVY, LLC, New York, NY, pg. 1067
STERN ADVERTISING, INC., Cleveland, OH, pg. 1085
STRONG, Birmingham, AL, pg. 1092
SUBMIT EXPRESS INC., Burbank, CA, pg. 1094
SUMNER GROUP, Gastonia, NC, pg. 1099
SWARM NYC, New York, NY, pg. 1315
TAKE 5 SOLUTIONS, Boca Raton, FL, pg. 1108
TC CREATIVES LLC, Woodland Hills, CA, pg. 1133
TEC DIRECT MEDIA, INC., Chicago, IL, pg. 1391
TEGO MEDIA, Scottsdale, AZ, pg. 1135
THAT AGENCY, West Palm Beach, FL, pg. 1137
THINKINGMAN.COM NEW MEDIA, Lihue, HI, pg. 1275
TIDAL SHORES INC., Houston, TX, pg. 1143
THE TOMBRAS GROUP, Knoxville, TN, pg. 1149
TRELLIS MARKETING, INC, Kenmore, NY, pg. 1155
UNION, Charlotte, NC, pg. 1318
U.S. INTERNATIONAL MEDIA, Los Angeles, CA, pg. 1395
UWG, Brooklyn, NY, pg. 1169
VANGUARDCOMM, East Brunswick, NJ, pg. 1171
VARGAS & AMIGOS INC., Marietta, GA, pg. 1171
WALTON / ISAACSON, Culver City, CA, pg. 1189
THE WARD GROUP, Dallas, TX, pg. 1190
WC MEDIA INC., Springfield, IL, pg. 1193
WEBER SHANDWICK, New York, NY, pg. 1675
WIEDEN + KENNEDY, INC., Portland, OR, pg. 1202
XAXIS, LLC, New York, NY, pg. 1320
YMARKETING, Newport Beach, CA, pg. 1238
Z MARKETING PARTNERS, Indianapolis, IN, pg. 1253
ZEHNDER COMMUNICATIONS, INC., New Orleans, LA, pg. 1254

Agriculture

454 CREATIVE, Orange, CA, pg. 9
5 STONE ADVERTISING, Carbondale, CO, pg. 9
5METACOM, Carmel, IN, pg. 10
ABSOLUTELY PUBLIC RELATIONS, Lakewood, CO, pg. 1439
ACCESS TO MEDIA, Chicopee, MA, pg. 19
ADCETERA GROUP, Houston, TX, pg. 26
ADFARM, Calgary, pg. 28
ADSOKA, INC., Minneapolis, MN, pg. 32
AGENCY CREATIVE, Dallas, TX, pg. 37
AGENCY OF CHANGE, Newhall, CA, pg. 38
ALMIGHTY, Boston, MA, pg. 50
AMELIE COMPANY, Denver, CO, pg. 53
AMERICAN ADVERTISING SERVICES, Bala Cynwyd, PA, pg. 53
AMERICAN NEWSPAPER REPRESENTATIVES, INC., Troy, MI, pg. 1324
ANDIS ADVERTISING, Sturtevant, WI, pg. 1263
ANSIRA, Chicago, IL, pg. 1405
ANVIL MEDIA, INC., Portland, OR, pg. 1325
APCO WORLDWIDE, Washington, DC, pg. 63
APPLEGATE MEDIA GROUP, New York, NY, pg. 1325
ARCANA ACADEMY, Los Angeles, CA, pg. 66
ARCHER MALMO, Memphis, TN, pg. 67
ARGYLL, Redondo Beach, CA, pg. 69
ARKSIDE MARKETING, Moreno Valley, CA, pg. 70
AUDIENCE INNOVATION, Austin, TX, pg. 79
AUGUST, LANG & HUSAK, INC., Bethesda, MD, pg. 79
AUGUSTUS BARNETT ADVERTISING/DESIGN, Fox Island, WA, pg. 80
B SCENE ADVERTISING AGENCY, Newport Beach, CA, pg. 84
BAILEY LAUERMAN, Omaha, NE, pg. 87
THE BALCOM AGENCY, Fort Worth, TX, pg. 88
BARBER MARTIN AGENCY, Richmond, VA, pg. 91
BARNETT COX & ASSOCIATES, San Luis Obispo, CA, pg. 93
BASS ADVERTISING, Sioux City, IA, pg. 96
BAYARD ADVERTISING AGENCY, INC., New York, NY, pg. 98
BECKER GUERRY, Middletown, NJ, pg. 121
BECKETT & BECKETT, INC., Altadena, CA, pg. 121
BENCHMARK DISPLAYS, Palm Desert, CA, pg. 1407
BERNING MARKETING, LLC, Metairie, LA, pg. 126
BIG RIVER ADVERTISING, Richmond, VA, pg. 131
BILL HUDSON & ASSOCIATES, INC., ADVERTISING & PUBLIC RELATIONS, Nashville, TN, pg. 132
BLEND, Los Angeles, CA, pg. 137
BLUE FOUNTAIN MEDIA, New York, NY, pg. 1283
BLUE OLIVE CONSULTING, Florence, AL, pg. 141
BODKIN ASSOCIATES, INC., Zionsville, IN, pg. 145
BOUVIER KELLY INC., Greensboro, NC, pg. 151
THE BRAND SQUAD, Memphis, TN, pg. 156
BRANDTAILERS, Irvine, CA, pg. 161
BRAVE NEW MARKETS, Owings Mills, MD, pg. 1284
BRIECHLE-FERNANDEZ MARKETING SERVICES INC., Eatontown, NJ, pg. 164
BRIGHTON AGENCY, INC., Saint Louis, MO, pg. 166
BRISCOE HALL, INC., Kerrville, TX, pg. 167
BROADHEAD, Minneapolis, MN, pg. 168
BROWNING ADVERTISING LLC, New Providence, NJ, pg. 170
BURNHAM RICHARDS ADVERTISING, De Pere, WI, pg. 177
CALZONE & ASSOCIATES, Lafayette, LA, pg. 186
CASHMAN & KATZ INTEGRATED COMMUNICATIONS, Glastonbury, CT, pg. 195
CASTELLS & ASOCIADOS, Los Angeles, CA, pg. 196
CATALYST MARKETING COMMUNICATIONS INC., Stamford, CT, pg. 197
CATALYST MARKETING COMPANY, Fresno, CA, pg. 197
CHARLESTON/ORWIG, INC., Hartland, WI, pg. 205
C.I. VISIONS INC., New York, NY, pg. 1478
CINETRANSFORMER INTERNATIONAL INC., Miami, FL, pg. 1409
THE CIRLOT AGENCY, INC., Jackson, MS, pg. 211
CIVILIAN, Chicago, IL, pg. 211
COLLE+MCVOY, Minneapolis, MN, pg. 221
COLMAN BROHAN DAVIS, Chicago, IL, pg. 223
COMMUNICATIONS 21, Atlanta, GA, pg. 1483
CONNECTIONS ADVERTISING & MARKETING, Lexington, KY, pg. 230
CREATIVE COMPANY, McMinnville, OR, pg. 247
CREATIVE DIRECTION, INC., Indianapolis, IN, pg. 247
CREATIVE ENERGY GROUP INC, Johnson City, TN, pg. 248
CRITICAL LAUNCH, LLC, Dallas, TX, pg. 254
CRUX CREATIVE, Milwaukee, WI, pg. 258
CTB ADVERTISING, Milford, IN, pg. 1266
CXC, Encino, CA, pg. 262
DAN PIPKIN ADVERTISING AGENCY, INC., Danville, IL, pg. 265
DAVISDENNY ADVERTISING & RELATED SERVICES, INC., Birmingham, AL, pg. 271
DEAN DESIGN/MARKETING GROUP, INC., Lancaster, PA, pg. 291
DELAUNAY COMMUNICATIONS, INC., Seattle, WA, pg. 1492
DELLA FEMINA ADVERTISING, New York, NY, pg. 295
DUFOUR ADVERTISING, Sheboygan, WI, pg. 332
EGG, Vashon, WA, pg. 339
EMERGING MARKETING, Columbus, OH, pg. 346
ENCODE, Jacksonville, FL, pg. 347
EPICOSITY, Sioux Falls, SD, pg. 350
ERVIN & SMITH, Omaha, NE, pg. 354
EVANS ALLIANCE ADVERTISING, Sparta, NJ, pg. 358
EVANSHARDY & YOUNG, INC., Santa Barbara, CA, pg. 358
EXPECT ADVERTISING, INC., Clifton, NJ, pg. 361
FAHLGREN MORTINE, Columbus, OH, pg. 364
FAYE CLACK COMMUNICATIONS INC., Toronto, pg. 1513
FELDER COMMUNICATIONS GROUP, Grand Rapids, MI, pg. 384
FINEMAN PR, San Francisco, CA, pg. 1514
FLEISHMAN-HILLARD INC., Saint Louis, MO, pg. 1515
FLEMING & COMPANY INC., Newport, RI, pg. 392
FLINT COMMUNICATIONS, Fargo, ND, pg. 393
FMB ADVERTISING, Knoxville, TN, pg. 395
THE FRANK AGENCY INC, Overland Park, KS, pg. 400
FREEBAIRN & CO., Atlanta, GA, pg. 403
FTI CONSULTING, Washington, DC, pg. 406
FULL STEAM MARKETING & DESIGN, Salinas, CA, pg. 408
GABRIEL DEGROOD BENDT, Minneapolis, MN, pg. 413
GATEWAY DESIGN, INC., Houston, TX, pg. 418
GLASS AGENCY, Sacramento, CA, pg. 427
THE GOSS AGENCY INC., Asheville, NC, pg. 436
GRIFFIN WINK ADVERTISING, Lubbock, TX, pg. 459
GROUP46, Bluffton, SC, pg. 462
GUD MARKETING, Lansing, MI, pg. 466
GUMAS ADVERTISING, San Francisco, CA, pg. 466
THE GUNTER AGENCY, New Glarus, WI, pg. 467
GWA COMMUNICATIONS, INC., Dublin, OH, pg. 467
GYRO, New York, NY, pg. 468
HAKUHODO INCORPORATED, Tokyo, pg. 473
THE HALO GROUP, New York, NY, pg. 476
HAVAS PR, New York, NY, pg. 1537
HELVETICA CREATIVE, San Francisco, CA, pg. 509
HMH, Portland, OR, pg. 518
HODGES ASSOCIATES, INC., Fayetteville, NC, pg. 519
HOWARD, MERRELL & PARTNERS, INC., Raleigh, NC, pg. 525
HUGE, Brooklyn, NY, pg. 526
IDEA BANK MARKETING, Hastings, NE, pg. 533
IMA INTERACTIVE, San Francisco, CA, pg. 1298
INITIATIVE, New York, NY, pg. 1344
THE INK TANK, Toronto, pg. 546
INNIS MAGGIORE GROUP, INC., Canton, OH, pg. 547
THE INTEGER GROUP-MIDWEST, Des Moines, IA, pg. 1417
INTEGRATED MARKETING WORKS, Newport Beach, CA, pg. 1417
INTERLEX COMMUNICATIONS INC., San Antonio, TX, pg. 552

Asian Market

Special Market Index

Automotive

Business-To-Business

Children's Market

Direct Response Marketing

Entertainment

Fashion/Apparel

Financial

Food Service

Gay & Lesbian Market

Health Care Services

High Technology

Special Market Index

Hispanic Market

Industrial

Special Market Index

Infomercials

New Product Development

Real Estate

Special Market Index

Recruitment

Seniors' Market

Special Market Index

Sports Market

Travel & Tourism

ADVERTISING AGENCIES

1 TRICK PONY
251 Bellevue Ave 2nd Fl, Hammonton, NJ 08037
Tel.: (609) 704-2660
Fax: (646) 619-4095
E-Mail: info@1trickpony.com
Web Site: www.1trickpony.com

Employees: 30
Year Founded: 2004

Rob Reed *(Owner)*
Sharlene Campanella *(Sr Acct Dir)*
Sal Colasurdo *(Producer-Interactive)*
Stephen Snyder *(Acct Dir)*
Monica Fritz *(Dir-Art)*
Mike Mielcarz *(Assoc Dir-Creative)*
Milt Pony *(Assoc Dir-Creative)*
Joyce Destasio *(Acct Mgr)*
Jim Justice *(Acct Supvr)*
Natalya Velky *(Acct Exec)*

Accounts:
Dark Candi
Flatbush Farm
Gorilla Coffee
Gotham Sound
La Pomme
Live Nation Entertainment, Inc
Seminole Gaming
Seminole Hard Rock Hotel & Casino
Shake Shack
Sony Pictures Classics
TCM Database
Toy
Turner Classic Movies Campaign: "31 Days of Oscar"
Virgin Mobile USA, Inc.
Virgin Money
Virgin USA
Within Normal Limits

1059 CREATIVE
98 N Washington St, Boston, MA 02114
Tel.: (617) 523-8133
E-Mail: info@1059creative.com
Web Site: www.1059creative.com

Agency Specializes In: Advertising, Digital/Interactive, Graphic Design, Internet/Web Design

Rafe Hershfield *(Owner)*
Jessica Colton *(Dir-Art)*

Accounts:
Aspen Restaurant
Harborside Realty

10E MEDIA
10080 Alta Dr, Las Vegas, NV 89145
Tel.: (702) 476-1010
Web Site: www.10emedia.com

Agency Specializes In: Advertising, Event Planning & Marketing, Internet/Web Design, Media Buying Services, Media Relations, Media Training, Public Relations, Search Engine Optimization, Social Media

Paige Candee *(Pres)*

Accounts:
New-Cannery Casino

10X GROUP
104 W Broad St, Greenville, SC 29601
Tel.: (864) 420-1127
E-Mail: info@10-xgoup.com
Web Site: www.10-xgroup.com

Year Founded: 2002

Agency Specializes In: Advertising, Content, Digital/Interactive, Event Planning & Marketing, Print, Public Relations, Search Engine Optimization, Social Media, Strategic Planning/Research

Holly Rollins *(CEO & Strategist)*

Accounts:
Ob Hospitalist Group

11:24 DESIGN ADVERTISING, INC.
322 Culver Blvd, Playa Del Rey, CA 90293-7703
Tel.: (310) 821-1775
Fax: (310) 821-1972
E-Mail: artsims@1124design.com
Web Site: 1124design.com

Employees: 25
Year Founded: 1981

Agency Specializes In: Advertising, African-American Market, Asian Market, Bilingual Market, Brand Development & Integration, Business Publications, Business-To-Business, Cable T.V., Co-op Advertising, Collateral, Commercial Photography, Consulting, Consumer Marketing, Corporate Identity, E-Commerce, Electronic Media, Entertainment, Event Planning & Marketing, Exhibit/Trade Shows, Fashion/Apparel, Food Service, Government/Political, Graphic Design, Hispanic Market, Infomercials, Internet/Web Design, Logo & Package Design, Media Buying Services, Multicultural, Multimedia, New Product Development, Newspaper, Newspapers & Magazines, Out-of-Home Media, Outdoor, Pharmaceutical, Point of Purchase, Point of Sale, Print, Production, Public Relations, Publicity/Promotions, Radio, Restaurant, Retail, Sports Market, Strategic Planning/Research, Sweepstakes, Syndication, T.V., Teen Market, Trade & Consumer Magazines

Art Sims *(CEO)*

Accounts:
Disney; Los Angeles, CA Entertainment; 1998
Fox
Paramount Pictures
Sony Entertainment
Time Warner
Viacom

1185 DESIGN
941 Emerson St, Palo Alto, CA 94301
Tel.: (650) 325-4804
Fax: (650) 325-1468
E-Mail: newbiz@1185design.com
Web Site: www.1185design.com

Employees: 25
Year Founded: 1985

Agency Specializes In: Arts, Aviation & Aerospace, Brand Development & Integration, Business Publications, Business-To-Business, Catalogs, Children's Market, Collateral, Communications, Computers & Software, Consumer Goods, Consumer Marketing, Corporate Communications, Corporate Identity, Customer Relationship Management, Direct Response Marketing, Direct-to-Consumer, E-Commerce, Education, Electronics, Email, Entertainment, Exhibit/Trade Shows, Food Service, Graphic Design, Health Care Services, High Technology, Hospitality, Household Goods, Identity Marketing, In-Store Advertising, Integrated Marketing, Internet/Web Design, Investor Relations, Leisure, Local Marketing, Logo & Package Design, Luxury Products, Men's Market, Multicultural, Multimedia, New Technologies, Newspaper, Outdoor, Over-50 Market, Package Design, Pharmaceutical, Planning & Consultation, Point of Purchase, Point of Sale, Print, Production, Production (Print), Promotions, Real Estate, Regional, Restaurant, Retail, Sales Promotion, Search Engine Optimization, Seniors' Market, Social Marketing/Nonprofit, Social Media, Strategic Planning/Research, Transportation, Tween Market, Urban Market, Web (Banner Ads, Pop-ups, etc.), Women's Market

Approx. Annual Billings: $8,000,000

Breakdown of Gross Billings by Media: Graphic Design: 100%

Diana Witonsky *(Acct Dir)*
Jason Chan *(Dir-Design)*
Kris Rothgery *(Mgr-Production)*
Shirley Mauricio *(Designer-Production)*
Katy Walneuski *(Sr Designer)*

Accounts:
AMB Property Corporation Website Development
Ariba Brand Identity
Artificial Muscle Incorporated Website Development
Bigfoot Networks Brand Identity
Dash Navigation Brand Identity
Stanford University, Stanford, CA Degree Programs

1187 CREATIVE
201 E Main St, Carbondale, IL 62901
Tel.: (618) 457-1187
Web Site: www.1187creative.com

Employees: 12
Year Founded: 2007

Agency Specializes In: Advertising, Advertising Specialties, Affiliate Marketing, Alternative Advertising, Brand Development & Integration, Branded Entertainment, Broadcast, Business Publications, Business-To-Business, Cable T.V., Catalogs, Children's Market, Co-op Advertising, Collateral, College, Commercial Photography, Communications, Computers & Software, Consulting, Consumer Goods, Consumer Marketing, Consumer Publications, Content, Corporate Communications, Corporate Identity, Cosmetics, Crisis Communications, Custom Publishing, Customer Relationship Management, Digital/Interactive, Direct Response Marketing, Direct-to-Consumer, E-Commerce, Education, Electronic Media, Electronics, Email, Engineering, Entertainment, Environmental, Event Planning & Marketing, Exhibit/Trade Shows, Experience Design, Fashion/Apparel, Financial, Food Service, Game Integration, Gay & Lesbian Market, Government/Political, Graphic Design, Guerilla Marketing, Health Care Services, High Technology, Hispanic Market, Hospitality, Household Goods, Identity Marketing, In-Store Advertising, Industrial,

Infomercials, Information Technology, Integrated Marketing, International, Internet/Web Design, Investor Relations, Legal Services, Leisure, Local Marketing, Logo & Package Design, Luxury Products, Magazines, Marine, Market Research, Media Buying Services, Media Planning, Media Relations, Media Training, Medical Products, Men's Market, Merchandising, Mobile Marketing, Multicultural, Multimedia, New Product Development, New Technologies, Newspaper, Newspapers & Magazines, Out-of-Home Media, Outdoor, Over-50 Market, Package Design, Paid Searches, Pharmaceutical, Planning & Consultation, Podcasting, Point of Purchase, Point of Sale, Print, Product Placement, Production, Production (Ad, Film, Broadcast), Production (Print), Promotions, Public Relations, Publicity/Promotions, Publishing, RSS (Really Simple Syndication), Radio, Real Estate, Recruitment, Regional, Restaurant, Retail, Sales Promotion, Search Engine Optimization, Seniors' Market, Social Marketing/Nonprofit, South Asian Market, Sponsorship, Sports Market, Stakeholders, Strategic Planning/Research, Sweepstakes, Syndication, T.V., Technical Advertising, Teen Market, Telemarketing, Trade & Consumer Magazines, Transportation, Travel & Tourism, Urban Market, Viral/Buzz/Word of Mouth, Web (Banner Ads, Pop-ups, etc.), Women's Market, Yellow Pages Advertising

Approx. Annual Billings: $1,000,000

Breakdown of Gross Billings by Media: Adv. Specialities: $100,000; Consulting: $100,000; Event Mktg.: $100,000; Exhibits/Trade Shows: $50,000; Graphic Design: $200,000; Logo & Package Design: $100,000; Other: $300,000; Radio: $50,000

Zak Ouart *(Co-Owner & Dir-Creative)*
Kay Dosier *(Dir-Sls)*

Accounts:
Merz Salsa; Saint Louis, MO

12FPS
520 Hampshire St Ste 206, San Francisco, CA 94110
Tel.: (415) 738-4686
E-Mail: create@12fps.com
Web Site: www.12fps.com

Year Founded: 2011

Agency Specializes In: Advertising, Brand Development & Integration, Content, Digital/Interactive, Social Media

Heidi Petty *(Producer & Creative Dir)*
Erin Azouz *(Producer & Strategist-Social Media)*
Leah Pokrasso *(Art Dir)*

Accounts:
Meow Wolf

131DIGITAL
131 Library Ln, Pawleys Island, SC 29585
Tel.: (843) 314-4570
E-Mail: info@131digital.com
Web Site: www.131digital.com

Agency Specializes In: Advertising, Brand Development & Integration, Content, Email, Internet/Web Design, Search Engine Optimization, Social Media

T. Brewster Buck *(Founder & CEO)*
Seth Sullivan *(Creative Dir)*
Jason Lamont *(Dir-Mktg)*
Donna Anderson *(Mgr-Bus Dev)*

Accounts:
Carolina Human Reinvestment
Reliable Electric
Swell Vision

135TH STREET AGENCY
424 W 33rd St, New York, NY 10001
Tel.: (212) 348-4444
E-Mail: info@135stAgency.com
Web Site: www.135stAgency.com

Year Founded: 2005

Agency Specializes In: Affluent Market, Alternative Advertising, Arts, Brand Development & Integration, Branded Entertainment, College, Communications, Consumer Goods, Consumer Marketing, Digital/Interactive, Electronic Media, Entertainment, Event Planning & Marketing, Faith Based, Fashion/Apparel, Government/Political, Integrated Marketing, Luxury Products, Media Relations, Multicultural, Publicity/Promotions, Social Media, T.V., Viral/Buzz/Word of Mouth

Shante Bacon *(Founder & CEO)*

Accounts:
Carol's Daughter Hair Care Products; 2014
Myx Fusions; 2013
Oprah Winfrey Network; 2012
Paramount Pictures; 2012
REVOLT TV; 2014
RLJ Entertainment Films & Original Programming; 2013
The Weinstein Company; 2012

15 FINGERS LLC
443 Delaware Ave, Buffalo, NY 14202
Tel.: (716) 923-7000
Web Site: www.15fingers.com

Year Founded: 2009

Greg Neundorfer *(Partner)*
Zachary Schneider *(Partner)*
Rich Lunghino *(Art Dir)*
Andrew Vaga *(Art Dir)*
Ken Trabert *(Dir-Creative)*
Kristina Cesarano *(Acct Exec)*
James Millard *(Acct Exec)*
Dan Stout *(Copywriter)*

Accounts:
English Pork Pie Company
New-Hodgins Engraving Campaign: "Print is dead"
Philharmonic Symphony Society of New York Inc.

15 MINUTES, INC.
1982 Butler Pike Ste 600, Conshohocken, PA 19428
Tel.: (610) 832-1515
Fax: (610) 832-1585
Web Site: www.15minutesinc.com

Employees: 5
Year Founded: 1987

Agency Specializes In: Advertising, Advertising Specialties, Affluent Market, African-American Market, Arts, Asian Market, Brand Development & Integration, Branded Entertainment, Broadcast, Cable T.V., Children's Market, Co-op Advertising, Communications, Consumer Marketing, Content, Direct Response Marketing, Direct-to-Consumer, Email, Entertainment, Environmental, Event Planning & Marketing, Exhibit/Trade Shows, Fashion/Apparel, Financial, Game Integration, Gay & Lesbian Market, Guerilla Marketing, Identity Marketing, Integrated Marketing, International, Internet/Web Design, Leisure, Local Marketing, Logo & Package Design, Luxury Products, Media Buying Services, Media Planning, Media Relations, Mobile Marketing, Multicultural, Multimedia, New Product Development, New Technologies, Newspaper, Newspapers & Magazines, Out-of-Home Media, Outdoor, Over-50 Market, Pets , Podcasting, Print, Product Placement, Production, Production (Ad, Film, Broadcast), Production (Print), Promotions, Public Relations, Publicity/Promotions, Radio, Regional, Search Engine Optimization, Social Marketing/Nonprofit, Social Media, Sponsorship, Sports Market, T.V., Teen Market, Trade & Consumer Magazines, Travel & Tourism, Tween Market, Web (Banner Ads, Pop-ups, etc.), Women's Market

Approx. Annual Billings: $2,000,000

Breakdown of Gross Billings by Media: Brdcst.: $1,000,000; Print: $900,000; Production: $100,000

Nancy Becker *(Pres)*
Laura Weber *(Acct Mgr & Mgr-Social Media)*
Pam Derderian *(Acct Mgr)*
Kristina Moore *(Mgr-PR & Mktg)*

Accounts:
American Expo Corp.; Audubon, PA Greater Phila Expo Center at Oaks, Greater Reading Expo at Oaks
ASA/Eastern Fishing & Outdoors; NH Sports Shows
D&D Expositions; Gibbsboro, NJ Home Shows, Home & Garden Shows; Motorcycle Shows
Subaru of America; Cherry Hill, NJ Niche Marketing & Sponsorship Relations

1508, INC.
4048 Sonoma Hwy #4, Napa, CA 94559
Tel.: (415) 876-1508
Web Site: www.1508.com

Agency Specializes In: Advertising

Phil Klafta *(Dir-Strategic Plng & Res)*
Lana Klein *(Dir-Mktg Sciences Technical)*

Accounts:
Allstate
Ann Taylor
Atlas Business Associates
Chicago Tribune
GE Capital
Honda
Immersa Marketing
Searle
Suzuki
Unilever
Zurich

160OVER90
1 S Broad St 10th Fl, Philadelphia, PA 19107
Tel.: (215) 732-3200
Fax: (215) 732-1664
E-Mail: info@160over90.com
Web Site: www.160over90.com

Employees: 40

Agency Specializes In: Sponsorship

Shannon Price Slusher *(CEO & Principal)*
Darryl Cilli *(Chief Creative Officer & Principal)*
Dennis Brown *(Acct Dir)*
Evelyn Capistrano Lontok *(Acct Dir)*
Kimberly Hallman *(Dir-PR)*
David Levy *(Dir-Creative)*
Elliot LeBoeuf *(Assoc Dir-Creative & Sr Writer)*
Patrick Macomber *(Assoc Dir-Creative)*
Christopher Thomas Lee *(Assoc Dir-Creative-Digital)*
Jeremy Groff *(Acct Supvr)*
Kayla Kassis *(Acct Supvr)*

Cody York *(Acct Supvr)*
Caleb Mezzy *(Strategist-Social Media)*
Joseph Schoppy *(Copywriter)*
Kelly Getz *(Coord-New Bus)*

Accounts:
American Eagle Outfitters
Aria Health
Arizona Coyotes
Atlantic 10 Conference Campaign: "Any Arena. Any Field.", Campaign: "Next", Online, TV
Chesnut Hill College
Destination Maternity Corporation Email Marketing
Devoto Orchards Coasters & Cocktail Napkins, Design Packaging, Drinking Accessories, Golden State Cider, Keg Collars, Logo, Pint Glasses, Table Toppers, Tap Handles
Ferrari North America Corso Pilota Mont-Tremblant Welcome Kit
Mars Drinks Logo
Mercedes-Benz
National Real Estate Development Advertising, Branding, East Market
Nike
SoBe
Sony
Starr Restaurants
Under Armour ClutchFit Shoe, Video
Unilever Branding, Video
University of Dayton
Washington Nationals
Wilkes University

16W MARKETING, LLC
75 Union Ave 2nd Fl, Rutherford, NJ 07070
Tel.: (201) 635-8000
Fax: (201) 507-1722
Web Site: www.16wmktg.com

Employees: 8
Year Founded: 2000

Agency Specializes In: Broadcast, E-Commerce, Exhibit/Trade Shows, Local Marketing, Market Research, Public Relations

Approx. Annual Billings: $2,000,000

Steve Rosner *(Partner)*
Frank Vuono *(Partner)*
Brian Nelson *(VP-Talent)*
Shawn Flannelly *(Mgr-Bus Dev)*
Peter Milano *(Mgr-Talent)*
C. Blair Law, III *(Acct Coord)*

Accounts:
Beasley Reece
Chris Long
Chris Simms
Cris Collinsworth
Howie Long
NFL
Phil Simms
Pro Football Hall of Fame Business Development Agency of Record, Game for Life Exhibit, Hall of Heroes, Hometown Hall of Famers, Merlin Olsen Luncheon, Pro Football Hall of Fame Enshrinement, Super Bowl

180FUSION
11620 Wilshire Boulevard Ste 820, Los Angeles, CA 90025
Tel.: (877) 321-4180
Web Site: www.180fusion.com

Agency Specializes In: Advertising, Search Engine Optimization, Social Media

Scott Cohen *(CEO)*
Mitch Federman *(CFO)*

Accounts:
New-Bartenders Academy
New-Prostate Cancer Institute (Agency of Record) Search Engine Marketing

1ST TEAM ADVERTISING LLC
1407 Eisenhower Blvd Sq II Ste 303, Johnstown, PA 15904
Tel.: (814) 410-3018
Fax: (814) 410-3019
Toll Free: (800) 724-2040
Web Site: 1stteamadvertising.com

Year Founded: 2007

Agency Specializes In: Advertising, Brand Development & Integration, Graphic Design, Internet/Web Design, Media Buying Services, Print, Social Media

Ryan Gindlesperger *(Mng Partner)*
Christopher B. Smith *(Mng Partner)*

Accounts:
Pennsylvania Academy of Cosmetology
Watson Insurance Agency, Inc.

2 STORY
641 W National Ave, Milwaukee, WI 53204
Tel.: (414) 220-9663
E-Mail: info@2-story.com
Web Site: www.2-story.com

Agency Specializes In: Advertising, Graphic Design, Internet/Web Design, Logo & Package Design, Public Relations, Radio, Social Media, T.V.

Ellen Homb *(Owner, Pres & COO)*
Jessica Himsel *(VP-Creative Strategy & Mktg)*
Matthew Janzen *(Copywriter)*
Alyssa Schoenwaelder *(Copywriter)*

Accounts:
Milwaukee Habitat for Humanity

20/10 DESIGN & MARKETING, INC.
324 Willowbrook Ln Bldg 300, West Chester, PA 19382
Tel.: (610) 692-4972
E-Mail: solutions@2010solutions.com
Web Site: www.2010solutions.com

Year Founded: 1998

Joe Warner *(Owner)*
Sarah Reese *(Dir-Mktg & Client Svcs)*
Christine Nestor *(Mgr-Digital Mktg & Project)*
Matthew Williams *(Designer)*

Accounts:
Philadelphia Convention & Visitors Bureau
Ron Jaworski

2020 EXHIBITS, INC.
10550 S Sam Huston Pkwy W, Houston, TX 77071
Tel.: (713) 354-0900
Fax: (713) 354-0920
E-Mail: info@2020exhibits.com
Web Site: www.2020exhibits.com

Employees: 70
Year Founded: 1990

Agency Specializes In: Advertising, Brand Development & Integration, Digital/Interactive, Email, Identity Marketing, Logo & Package Design, Media Planning, Print, Sales Promotion, Search Engine Optimization

Bob Babine *(Pres)*
Mike Skaff *(VP-Bus Dev)*
Jill Kinduell *(Gen Mgr & Sr Acct Exec)*
Michael Wriston *(Dir-Sls-Intl)*
Rebecca Cansler-Morales *(Acct Mgr)*
Jill Epperson *(Acct Mgr)*
Krystal Trevino *(Acct Mgr)*
Robin Clinton *(Sr Acct Exec)*
Darren Clements *(Acct Exec)*
J. Donald Templet *(Acct Exec)*
Tony Mayer *(Sr Designer-Exhibit)*

206 INC.
1505 Western Ave Ste 500, Seattle, WA 98101
Tel.: (206) 388-1440
Fax: (206) 388-1450
E-Mail: info@206inc.com
Web Site: www.206inc.com

Year Founded: 2005

Agency Specializes In: Advertising, Brand Development & Integration, Event Planning & Marketing, Public Relations, Social Media, Sponsorship

Mike Salvadore *(Owner)*
Steve McCracken *(Mng Partner & Principal)*
Tad Harmon *(Principal & Dir-Creative)*
Mark Dyce *(Principal)*
Kerry Murphy *(Principal)*
Colleen Ando *(Sr Dir-Art)*
Sherman Fantroy *(Dir-Event Svcs)*
Joe Mattson *(Dir-Consumer Engagement)*
Mike Grigg *(Assoc Dir-Creative-Interactive)*
Gregg Flotlin *(Sr Mgr-Consumer Engagement)*
Natalie Nystrom *(Sr Mgr-Consumer Engagement)*
Corinna Fabre *(Mgr-PR)*
Kelsey Kaufman *(Assoc Mgr-PR)*

Accounts:
Blue Dog Bakery
Chase Bank
Dockers Brand
Fleet Foxes
Levi Strauss & Co.
Microsoft Corporation Bing, Windows 7
Seattle Center
Southwest Airlines Co.
Toyota Motor North America, Inc.

20FIFTEEN
8 N State St Ste 103, Lake Oswego, OR 97034
Tel.: (888) 939-2015
Web Site: www.20fifteen.tv

Year Founded: 2011

Agency Specializes In: Advertising, Brand Development & Integration, T.V.

20NINE DESIGN STUDIOS LLC
1100 E Hector St Ste 305, Conshohocken, PA 19428
Tel.: (610) 238-0450
Fax: (610) 238-0453
E-Mail: info@20nine.com
Web Site: www.20nine.com

Employees: 15

Agency Specializes In: Advertising, Custom Publishing, Graphic Design, Market Research, Merchandising, Print, Web (Banner Ads, Pop-ups, etc.)

Greg Ricciardi *(Pres & CEO)*
Isaac Klein *(VP-Acct Svcs)*
Gary Kopervas *(VP-Brand Strategy & Innovation)*
Brian Valania *(VP-New Bus Dev)*
Kevin Hammond *(Dir-Creative)*
Tracey McCaffrey *(Dir-Art)*

Michael Ryan *(Dir-Tech)*
David Dee *(Acct Mgr)*

Accounts:
Bentley Homes Real Estate Services
Boenning & Scattergood Asset Management & Investment Banking
Citi
Drexel University
MEDecision Healthcare Management Solutions
Philabundance
Rodel Foundation of Delaware Nonprofit Organization

22SQUARED

1170 Peachtree St NE Ste 1400, Atlanta, GA 30309-7649
Tel.: (404) 347-8700
Fax: (404) 347-8800
E-Mail: info@22squared.com
Web Site: www.22squared.com

Employees: 288
Year Founded: 1922

National Agency Associations: 4A's

Agency Specializes In: Advertising, Automotive, Brand Development & Integration, Broadcast, Collateral, Communications, Consumer Goods, Digital/Interactive, Direct Response Marketing, Direct-to-Consumer, Hospitality, In-Store Advertising, Integrated Marketing, Internet/Web Design, Magazines, Media Buying Services, Media Planning, Mobile Marketing, Newspaper, Newspapers & Magazines, Out-of-Home Media, Outdoor, Point of Purchase, Point of Sale, Print, Production (Print), Promotions, Public Relations, Publicity/Promotions, Radio, Restaurant, Retail, Social Marketing/Nonprofit, Social Media, Strategic Planning/Research, T.V., Travel & Tourism, Web (Banner Ads, Pop-ups, etc.), Women's Market

Breakdown of Gross Billings by Media: D.M.: 4%; Internet Adv.: 26%; Newsp.: 8%; Out-of-Home Media: 2%; Radio: 7%; Strategic Planning/Research: 13%; T.V.: 40%

Richard B. Ward *(Pres & CEO)*
Mike Grindell *(Chief Admin Officer & Exec VP)*
Amanda Ferber *(Exec VP, Grp Dir & Dir-Acct Mgmt)*
John Stapleton *(Exec VP & Sr Dir-Creative)*
Christopher Tuff *(Exec VP & Dir-Bus Dev & Partnerships)*
Ed Klein *(Exec VP-Client Leadership)*
Krista Lang *(Sr VP & Exec Dir-Media)*
Julie Winner *(Sr VP & Acct Dir)*
Donna Smith *(Sr VP & Dir-Creative Production)*
Christy Cross *(VP & Dir-Bus Dev)*
Genna Franconi *(VP & Dir-Strategy)*
Shannon Harlow *(VP & Dir-Analytics & CRM)*
Manny Rodriguez *(VP & Dir-Media Buying)*
Matt Silliman *(VP & Dir-Integrated Production)*
David Yeend *(VP & Dir-Plng)*
Daniel Brown *(VP-Interactive Design)*
Ryan Taylor *(Sr Dir-Art)*
Jenny Erickson-Reed *(Media Dir)*
Austen Tully *(Mgmt Supvr)*
Kevin Botfeld *(Dir-Creative)*
Angela Gibson *(Dir-Search Mktg)*
Peter Kehr *(Dir-Art)*
Elizabeth Maloy *(Dir-Content Art)*
Scott Peters *(Dir-Media)*
Michael Tucker *(Dir-HR)*
Leigh Kellogg *(Assoc Dir-Mktg Analytics)*
Danielle Zubriski *(Sr Mgr-Bus Affairs)*
Jill Kosmal *(Acct Mgr-Brdcst)*
Amanda Garrett *(Mgr-Campaign)*
Nick Holliday *(Mgr-Field)*
Virginia Baaklini *(Acct Supvr)*
Christina Blanchard *(Acct Supvr)*
Ashley Friedrich *(Acct Supvr)*
Shelly Hiatt *(Acct Supvr)*
Katie Hunter *(Acct Supvr)*
Lauren Nee *(Acct Supvr)*
Kyle Lebet *(Supvr-Digital Media)*
Philip Oliphant *(Supvr-Media)*
Keisha Smith *(Supvr-Media)*
Bailey Davis *(Acct Exec)*
Joanna Huang *(Acct Exec)*
Kaitlyn Roche *(Strategist)*
Breanne Brock *(Media Planner)*
Jon Daboub *(Media Buyer)*
Meg Harth *(Media Buyer-Sports Mktg)*
Jamie Ritenbaugh *(Media Planner-Hybrid)*
Will Zschau *(Copywriter)*
Kristin Kirkpatrick *(Asst Acct Exec)*
Christianna Coffing *(Sr Media Buyer)*
Kevin Kuhn *(Sr Media Planner)*
Andrea Peterson *(Asst Media Buyer)*
Claire Potts *(Asst Media Planner)*
Meera Venkatraman *(Sr Assoc-Social Media)*

Accounts:
AARON'S, INC. Campaign: "Light Switch & Dog House"
American Standard Champion, VorMax Flushing System; 2012
Baskin-Robbins
Costa Rica Tourism Board Advertising, Campaign: "Essential Costa Rica", Campaign: "Save the Americans", Digital, Video, Visit Costa RIca
Dunkin Donuts
GNC Holdings, Inc. Digital, Social Media
Hanesbrands Just My Size, Playtex; 2011
Kellogg Company; 2012
The Krystal Company (Creative Agency of Record) Campaign: "Cheese Lovers Death Metal Minibike Jump", Campaign: "Stupid Good", Krystal Burgers
Mizuno USA (Agency of Record) Advertising, Content, Creative, Media Buying, Media Planning, Social Media, Strategy
OGX Advertising Agency of Record
PGA Tour Superstore; 2013
Publix Supermarkets; 1989
Shoe Carnival Campaign: "A Surprise in Store"; 2008
Southeast Toyota Distributors Broadcast, Campaign: "Unexpect Everything", Corolla, Desktop Gaming, Digital, Experiential, In-Dealership Components, Influencer Marketing, Mobile, Search, Social; 2000
SunTrust Banks, Inc. Analytics, Media Buying, Media Planning, Social Media
Toyota
Unified Social Marketing Platform
Visit Orlando; 2002

Branch

22squared Inc.

401 E Jackson St Fl 36, Tampa, FL 33602-5225
Tel.: (813) 202-1200
Fax: (813) 202-1261
E-Mail: info@22squared.com
Web Site: www.22squared.com

E-Mail for Key Personnel:
Creative Dir.: scott.sheinberg@22squared.com

Employees: 80

National Agency Associations: 4A's

Agency Specializes In: Internet/Web Design, Newspaper, Print, Radio, Sponsorship, T.V.

Ben West *(Chm)*
Brandon Murphy *(Chief Strategy Officer)*
Scott Sheinberg *(Chief Creative Officer)*
John Stapleton *(Exec VP & Sr Dir-Creative)*
Scott Stuart *(Exec VP & Exec Grp Dir)*
David Yeend *(VP & Grp Dir-Strategy)*
Amy Auerbach *(Grp Dir-Media)*
Kevin Botfeld *(Dir-Creative)*
Jenny Reed *(Assoc Dir-Media)*
Jason Roberts *(Assoc Dir-Creative)*
Annie Farr *(Media Buyer)*
Emily Newport *(Media Planner)*
Krista West *(Media Planner)*
Parker Carlson *(Asst Acct Exec)*
Yamy Gonzalez *(Sr Media Buyer)*
Philip Green *(Sr Media Planner)*
Monica Piazza *(Sr Media Planner)*
Kirsten Thieman *(Assoc Producer-Integrated)*

Accounts:
Atlanta Brewing Company
Big Green Egg
Caribou Coffee
Costa Rica Tourism Board (Agency of Record) Creative, Media Buying and Planning, Social and Digital Media
Publix Super Markets Inc.
Shoe Carnival, Inc.
Southeast Toyota

23K STUDIOS

232 Conestoga Rd, Wayne, PA 19087
Tel.: (610) 971-2000
Fax: (610) 971-1620
E-Mail: info@23k.com
Web Site: www.23k.com

Employees: 12

Agency Specializes In: Direct Response Marketing

Petey Boone *(Controller)*
Nicole Daddario *(Dir-Mktg)*
Brian Rutolo *(Dir-Art)*
Brian Soroka *(Dir-Art)*
Yeasin Chowdhury *(Project Mgr & Acct Mgr)*
Stephanie Mariani *(Project Mgr-Interactive)*

Accounts:
ING Direct
SAP
Sunguard

24 COMMUNICATIONS

300 Water St, Montgomery, AL 36104
Tel.: (334) 356-2426
E-Mail: brand@24c.co
Web Site: www.24c.co

Year Founded: 2006

Agency Specializes In: Advertising, Brand Development & Integration, Collateral, Corporate Identity, Digital/Interactive, Media Relations, Media Training, Package Design, Public Relations, Social Media

Jennifer Solt *(Principal & Creative Dir)*

Accounts:
Max

247 LAUNDRY SERVICE

(Name Changed to Laundry Service)

2930 CREATIVE

1700 Commerce St Ste 1751, Dallas, TX 75201
Tel.: (214) 749-5155
E-Mail: info@twentynine-thirty.com
Web Site: www.twentynine-thirty.com

Year Founded: 2012

Agency Specializes In: Advertising, Brand Development & Integration, Collateral, Content, Email, Internet/Web Design, Logo & Package Design, Package Design, Print, Social Media

Chris Reeves *(Co-Founder & Pres)*
Carly Rowe *(Co-Founder & VP)*
Matt Mariaux *(Partner-Strategic)*
Kristin Messerli *(Partner-Strategic)*
Josh Duke *(VP-Content Mktg)*
Ashley Smith *(Dir-Art)*

Accounts:
Dallas Caramel Company
Prime Source Mortgage, Corp.

2ADVANCED STUDIOS, LLC.

32 Journey Ste 200, Aliso Viejo, CA 92656-5343
Tel.: (949) 521-7000
Fax: (949) 521-7001
E-Mail: info@2advanced.com
Web Site: www.2advanced.com

Employees: 25
Year Founded: 1999

Agency Specializes In: Advertising, Advertising Specialties, Corporate Identity, Digital/Interactive, Electronic Media, Internet/Web Design, Logo & Package Design, Multimedia, Production (Ad, Film, Broadcast), Production (Print), Promotions, Viral/Buzz/Word of Mouth, Web (Banner Ads, Pop-ups, etc.)

Eric Jordan *(Pres & Chief Creative Officer)*

Accounts:
ADMM
Adobe
AOL
Diesel Sunglasses; 2007
Electronic Arts
Fox Sports
HCG
Lexus LS600
Motorola Solutions, Inc.
Nintendo of America
Ripley's Believe It or Not
Warner Brothers

2E CREATIVE

411 N 10th Ste 600, Saint Louis, MO 63101
Tel.: (314) 436-2323
Fax: (314) 436-2333
Web Site: www.2ecreative.com

Year Founded: 1999

Agency Specializes In: Advertising, Brand Development & Integration, Digital/Interactive, Graphic Design, Social Media

Joe Toohey *(Principal)*
Ross Toohey *(Principal)*
Lynda McClure *(VP & Exec Dir-Creative)*
Matt Bender *(Dir-Art)*
Simon Lam *(Dir-Art)*
John Peel *(Dir-Creative Tech)*
Steve Winkler *(Mgr-Production)*
Leslie Sherman *(Acct Coord)*

Accounts:
Alcon Laboratories, Inc.
Caris Life Sciences
The Delta Gamma Center
Elsevier Inc.
Erbe USA Inc
Everidis Health Sciences
Jerry Harvey Audio LLC
NextGen Healthcare Information Systems, Inc.
Sigma Life Science
Texas Instruments Incorporated

2G MARKETING COMMUNICATIONS, INC.

5713 Superior Dr Ste B-1, Baton Rouge, LA 70816-8015
Tel.: (225) 293-2224
Fax: (225) 293-2228
Web Site: www.2gmarketing.com

Employees: 3

Agency Specializes In: Broadcast, Email, Exhibit/Trade Shows, Graphic Design, Internet/Web Design

Ken Adams *(Co-Founder)*
Russ Norwood *(Owner)*

Accounts:
DSM Elastomers
Industrial Specialty Contractors, LLC
Lion Copolymer
Pala Interstate
Paxon Polymers
The Shaw Group
SJB Group
Thermal & Process Sales, Inc.

2.GC, INC.

441 Windsor Dr, Antioch, IL 60002
Tel.: (312) 943-6800
Fax: (847) 609-1741
E-Mail: rduggan@2gcinc.com
Web Site: www.2gcinc.com

Employees: 5
Year Founded: 1996

Agency Specializes In: Above-the-Line

Robin Duggan *(Owner)*

Accounts:
LG Electronics

2ONE5 CREATIVE INC

230 N 2nd St Ste 2B, Philadelphia, PA 19106
Tel.: (215) 592-7151
E-Mail: general@2one5.com
Web Site: www.2one5.com

Year Founded: 2001

Agency Specializes In: Advertising, Brand Development & Integration, Digital/Interactive, Package Design, Social Media

Nikolas Greenblatt *(Dir-Creative, Publr & Strategist-Digital)*
Dan Christiansen *(VP-Ops)*
Jacquelyn Cochet *(Brand Mgr)*
Ryan Rakoske *(Mgr-Bus Dev)*
Corey Riddle *(Designer)*

Accounts:
Bouvel Investment Partners
Digipower Content, Digital, Refuel (Digital Agency Of Record), Videos, Websites
New-Frankford Umbrellas (Agency of Record)
Franklin Park
New-Ingerman (Agency of Record) Branding, Digital Marketing, Mobile
JG Real Estate Brand Identity
LGBT Expo
Mizco International Content, Strategy, ToughTested (Digital Agency of Record), Video
Splashflood
WH Roddy

3 ADVERTISING

1550 Mercantile Ave NE 2nd Fl, Albuquerque, NM 87107
Tel.: (505) 293-2333
Fax: (505) 293-1198
E-Mail: info@3advertising.com
Web Site: www.3advertising.com

Employees: 12
Year Founded: 2005

Agency Specializes In: Advertising, Advertising Specialties, Bilingual Market, Brand Development & Integration, Broadcast, Business Publications, Business-To-Business, Cable T.V., Children's Market, Collateral, Communications, Consulting, Consumer Marketing, Consumer Publications, Corporate Communications, Corporate Identity, Digital/Interactive, Direct Response Marketing, E-Commerce, Electronic Media, Exhibit/Trade Shows, Graphic Design, Hispanic Market, In-Store Advertising, Internet/Web Design, Leisure, Local Marketing, Logo & Package Design, Magazines, Media Buying Services, Multimedia, Newspaper, Newspapers & Magazines, Out-of-Home Media, Outdoor, Over-50 Market, Planning & Consultation, Point of Purchase, Point of Sale, Print, Production, Production (Print), Public Relations, Publicity/Promotions, Radio, Sales Promotion, Search Engine Optimization, Social Media, Strategic Planning/Research, Sweepstakes, T.V., Teen Market, Trade & Consumer Magazines, Transportation, Travel & Tourism, Web (Banner Ads, Pop-ups, etc.)

Approx. Annual Billings: $8,022,000

Susan K. Lewis *(Partner & Dir-Media)*
Sam Maclay *(Partner & Dir-Creative)*
Tim McGrath *(Partner & Dir-Design)*
Chris Moore *(Partner & Dir-Strategic)*
Zak Rutledge *(Art Dir)*
Jamie Fisher *(Acct Mgr)*
Vi Nguyen *(Acct Coord)*
Jason Rohrer *(Sr Writer)*

Accounts:
Alone & Unafraid
American Ethanol
Bair Medical Spa
Beer Institute Campaign: "Beer Convention", Campaign: "Excise Ale", Campaign: "Franklin", Campaign: "Lincoln", Campaign: "Overtaxed", Campaign: "Roosevelt", Campaign: "Taxman", Logo
Brycon Construction; 2006
Center for Prenatal Development Medical; 2005
Charles Stephens & Co.
City of Albuquerque/Better Health Campaign: "Chair Squat", Campaign: "Long Walk", Campaign: "Snack Attack", Campaign: "Stair Master"
Cosmetic Dentistry of NM Campaign: "Beautiful", Campaign: "CQ", Campaign: "Cosmo", Campaign: "Glamorous"
Dekker Parich Sabatini
DSM-Biomedical
Farm Credit Campaign: "Commitment", Campaign: "Cringe", Campaign: "Toaster"
Land Rover Albuquerque/Santa Fe Automotive; 2005
Measure Twice, Inc. Construction; 2005
Mercy Regional Medical Center
Michael Barley Corporate ID
National Museum of Nuclear Science & History
New Day Youth & Family Services Campaign: "Healing Words"
New Mexico Mortgage Finance Authority
Old Guys Rule Apparel; 2005
People Living Through Cancer Counseling; 2006
PMC Solutions Software; 2006
Presbyterian Healthcare Systems Campaign: "Fun & Games", Campaign: "Your story is our story"
Public Service New Mexico
Rescue SCG
Rio Grande Credit Union
sackwear.com Apparel, Campaign: "Death Valley", Campaign: "Kiwi", Campaign: "Pritchett", Campaign: "Special Care", Pritchett Canyon Expeditions t-shirt; 2005

Sandia Laboratories Federal Credit Union
Seattle Fish Company of New Mexico Campaign: "Fish Eaters of the World"
Skarsgard Construction Logo
Telluride Offroad Adventures Illustration, Logo
United Seating & Mobility

3 FEET MEDIA

99 Weatherstone Dr, Woodstock, GA 30188
Tel.: (678) 445-3646
Fax: (678) 445-3670
E-Mail: sdent@3feetmedia.net
Web Site: www.3feetmedia.net

Employees: 10

Becky Repic *(Dir-Creative & Ops)*
Cuyler Esposito *(Acct Mgr)*

300FEETOUT

1035 Folsom St, San Francisco, CA 94103
Tel.: (415) 551-2377
E-Mail: info@300feetout.com
Web Site: www.300feetout.com

Year Founded: 1997

Agency Specializes In: Advertising, Brand Development & Integration, Collateral, Internet/Web Design, Logo & Package Design, Print

Barbara O. Stephenson *(CEO)*
Greg Ciro Tornincasa *(Dir-Art)*

Accounts:
Pasolivo Olive Oil
San Francisco Ballet

303 GROUP PTY LTD.

(Merged with Lowe Australia to form 303LOWE)

31 LENGTHS LLC

43 W 24th St 7th Fl, New York, NY 10010
Tel.: (914) 255-2981
Web Site: www.31lengths.net

Year Founded: 2012

Agency Specializes In: Advertising, Brand Development & Integration, Digital/Interactive, Logo & Package Design, Print, Radio, Strategic Planning/Research

Michael Jordan *(CEO & Dir-Creative)*
Maria Ackley *(Dir-Digital Strategy)*

Accounts:
The American Womens College

352 MEDIA GROUP

133 SW 130th Way Ste D, Newberry, FL 32669
Tel.: (352) 374-9657
Fax: (352) 374-6965
Toll Free: (877) 352-MEDIA (6334)
E-Mail: hello@352media.com
Web Site: www.352inc.com

Employees: 45
Year Founded: 1999

Agency Specializes In: Digital/Interactive, E-Commerce, Electronic Media, Graphic Design, Information Technology, Internet/Web Design

Geoff Wilson *(Founder, Pres & CEO)*
Caroline Blake *(Partner)*
Robert Berris *(VP-Digital Strategy)*
Evan Blake *(VP-Client Engagement)*
Don Wedington *(VP-Sls)*
Peter Bernardo *(Dir-Design)*
Damion Wasylow *(Sr Strategist-Mktg)*

Accounts:
American Express Travel
Ben & Jerrys
Microsoft; Redmond, WA Developer Tools Division; 2003
Porsche
Swamp Rentals

360 GROUP

301 W Michigan St Ste A, Indianapolis, IN 46202
Tel.: (317) 633-1456
Fax: (317) 633-1461
E-Mail: mark@360grouponline.com
Web Site: www.360grouponline.com

Employees: 14
Year Founded: 1960

National Agency Associations: Second Wind Limited

Scott Willy *(Co-Founder & VP-Creative Svcs)*
David V. Cranfill *(Principal & Acct Planner)*
David Bray *(Sr Dir-Art)*
Eric Murray *(Sr Dir-Art)*
Dan Myers *(Dir-Media & Acct Exec)*
Mike Wilson *(Dir-Creative)*
Matthew Hornyak *(Acct Exec)*
Ira Maher *(Acct Exec-Strategic)*
Taylor Jessup *(Designer)*
Luke Spencer-Pierce *(Designer)*

Accounts:
Circle City Group Power Cooperatives; Lebanon, IN; 1984
Cranfill & Company
Heartland Film Festival
The Indiana and Purdue University
Indiana High School Athletic Association; Indianapolis, IN; 1972
Indianapolis Symphony Orchestra
REMC
Wooden & McLaughlin Attorneys at Law; Indianapolis, IN; 1997

360I

32 Ave of the Americas 6th Fl, New York, NY 10013
Tel.: (212) 703-7201
Toll Free: (888) 360-9360
E-Mail: press@360i.com
Web Site: www.360i.com

Employees: 500

National Agency Associations: 4A's-SODA

Agency Specializes In: Digital/Interactive, Media Planning, Search Engine Optimization, Sponsorship, Strategic Planning/Research

Revenue: $25,000,000

Bryan Wiener *(Chm)*
Sarah Hofstetter *(CEO)*
Pierre Lipton *(Chief Creative Officer)*
Lee Maicon *(Chief Strategy Officer)*
Kate Paulin Charles *(Sr VP & Head-Insights & Plng)*
Brian Cronk *(Sr VP-Integrated Media & Comm Plng)*
Michael Lampert *(Sr VP-NY Media & Acct Mgmt)*
Rebecca McCuiston *(Sr VP-Influencer Mktg)*
Joe Jaffe *(VP & Head-Production)*
Matt Wurst *(VP & Gen Mgr-Social Media)*
Sandra Ciconte *(VP & Grp Acct Dir)*
Megan Ryan *(VP & Dir-Comm Plng)*
Shankar Gupta *(VP-Strategy)*
Kolin Kleveno *(VP-Programmatic Adv)*
Orli LeWinter *(VP-Strategy & Social Mktg)*
Christopher Kief *(Head-Tech)*
Laura Mete Frizzell *(Gen Mgr-Search, Analytics & Media)*
Karen Crane *(Exec Dir-Creative Talent)*
Bruno Corbo *(Grp Dir-Creative)*
Aaron Mosher *(Grp Dir-Creative)*
Fabio Seidl *(Grp Dir-Creative)*
Megan Skelly *(Grp Dir-Creative)*
Dave Yankelewitz *(Grp Dir-Creative)*
Will Montgomery *(Sr Dir-Art)*
Benson Ngo *(Sr Dir-Art)*
Tiffany Curry *(Grp Acct Dir)*
Emlyn Allen *(Art Dir)*
Jeff Anderson *(Acct Dir)*
Kelsie Kaufman *(Art Dir)*
Doug Lemon *(Creative Dir)*
Meredith Meyer *(Acct Dir)*
Doug Murray *(Art Dir)*
Celeste Pulman *(Acct Dir-Oreo)*
David Bosniak *(Dir-Media)*
Carla Butwin *(Dir-Art)*
Michael Condrick *(Dir-Creative)*
Scott Daly *(Dir-Integrated Media)*
Shivan Durbal *(Dir-Media)*
Alisha Farmer *(Dir-Media)*
Javier Fuentes *(Dir-Creative)*
Sharon Harte *(Dir-Brdcst Production)*
Maggie Peuler *(Dir-Media)*
Alexis Rabilloud *(Dir-Art)*
Hans Schenck *(Dir-Art)*
Frances Webb *(Dir-Creative)*
Heather English *(Assoc Dir-Creative & Writer)*
Rob Gencorelli *(Assoc Dir-Media)*
Mila Golubov *(Assoc Dir-Creative)*
John McGrail *(Assoc Dir-Media)*
James Rogala *(Assoc Dir-Creative)*
Karri Wells *(Assoc Dir-Social Mktg)*
Valentina Bettiol *(Sr Mgr-Social Mktg)*
Kelly Cowan *(Sr Mgr-Social Mktg)*
Josh Reeher *(Sr Mgr-Media)*
Martha Fritzsche *(Sr Acct Mgr)*
Philip Henderson *(Sr Acct Mgr)*
Kelly Huibregtse *(Sr Acct Mgr)*
Samantha Kimmel *(Sr Acct Mgr-Digital & Social)*
Maggie Lannon *(Sr Acct Mgr)*
Deeya Tarman *(Sr Acct Mgr)*
Megan Falcone *(Acct Mgr)*
Nina Hilken *(Project Mgr-Media)*
Amy Asciutto *(Mgr-Integrated Media)*
Brian Bochner *(Mgr-Media)*
Carolyn Chang *(Mgr-Media)*
Katya Kotlyar *(Mgr-Social Mktg)*
Kathryn Shallcross *(Mgr-Media)*
Sarah Wanger *(Mgr-Social Mktg)*
Amanda Altschuler *(Acct Supvr-Digital)*
Jennifer Lange *(Acct Supvr)*
Laura Walker *(Acct Supvr)*
Chris Edberg *(Supvr-Media)*
Daniel Kernkraut *(Supvr-Integrated Media)*
Courtney Klobucar *(Supvr-Media)*
Erika Mahon *(Supvr-Media)*
Courtney McGowan *(Supvr-Digital)*
Marisa Wong *(Supvr-Media)*
Mike Jacobson *(Sr Strategist-Creative)*
Nadalie Dias *(Specialist-Media-Programmatic Adv)*
Megan Foley *(Strategist)*
Joni-Lee Green *(Specialist-Optimization-Programmatic Adv)*
Brooke Lonegan *(Strategist)*
Anna-Kay Bennett *(Analyst-HR)*
Devin Brown *(Copywriter)*
Jessy Cole *(Copywriter)*
Evan Dunn *(Copywriter)*
Andrew Hunter *(Copywriter)*
Erika Yost *(Copywriter)*
Alex Augustinos *(Sr Writer)*
John Heath *(Grp Creative Dir)*
Juliette Leavey *(Sr Community Mgr)*
Megan Mason *(Assoc Acct Dir-Brand Mktg)*
Diane Myers *(Assoc Acct Dir)*
David Perkins *(Grp CFO)*
Madeline Wheelock *(Assoc Producer)*

Accounts:
AARP
Alamo AlamoGames2Go
Anheuser-Busch InBev Digital, Strategy
AutoTrader.com
Barilla America, Inc. (US Digital Agency of Record) Content, Social Marketing, Strategy, Website
Breast Cancer Awareness
Canon Inc.
Capital One Financial Corporation
Coca-Cola Campaign: "Fanta For The Funny", Coke Zero, Dasani, Diet Coke, Digital, Fanta, Minute Maid, Odwalla, Social Media Monitoring, Sprite, Vitaminwater
Darden Restaurants LongHorn Steakhouse, Media
Diageo Digital, Guinness (Social Agency of Record), Smirnoff (Social Agency of Record)
Enterprise Holdings, Inc. Social Media
Estee Lauder Cos. Campaign: "#StartBetter", Clinique, Creative, Digital, Displays, Global Digital Marketing, Social Strategy, Social-Media Branding
Fisher-Price, Inc.
H&R Block Search Marketing, Social Media
Hanes Campaign: "Hot N' Hairy", Campaign: "Soften the Blow", Hanes X-Temp
HBO "Game of Thrones", #RoastJoffrey, Campaign: "CatchDrogon", Campaign: "Payback's a Wench", Social Media
Irish Distillers Ltd. Jameson (Lead Media Agency)
J. Crew Group, Inc. J. Crew Group, Inc., Madewell
J.C. Penney
The Kraft Heinz Company Campaign: "The Great American Bacon Barter", Campaign: "Wake Up & Smell The Bacon", Digital, Oscar Mayer
Mattel
Mondelez International, Inc. "#Tweet2Lease.", "Oreo Laboratorium", Campaign: "Huddle to Fight Hunger", Campaign: "Midnight Hacks", Campaign: "Say It With Bacon", Campaign: "The Bus", Campaign: "The Exorcist", Campaign: "The Shining", Campaign: "You can still dunk in the dark", Comida Kraft Facebook Page, Digital, Instagram, Oreo, Oreo Thins, Oscar Mayer, Oscar Mayer Original Collection, Philadelphia Cream Cheese, Red Velvet Oreo, S'mores, Social, Social Media, Television, Wienermobile
National Car Rental
NBC Universal, Inc. Bravo Network
Nestle USA, Inc. Butterfinger, Campaign: "NaturalBlissCafe", Campaign: "Surprisingly Natural", Campaign: "WeighThis", Coffee Mate, Digital, Lean Cuisine, Natural Bliss, Skinny Cow, Social Media
Nestle Waters North America Inc.
New Orleans Tourism Marketing Corporation
Norwegian Cruise Line Search Marketing
Office Depot, Inc.
Oscar Mayer Institute For the Advancement of Bacon Campaign: "Wake Up & Smell The Bacon"
Pernod Ricard USA Absolut, Communication Planning, Hoppr, Jameson, Media Buying, Media Planning, Social Media
Procter & Gamble Campaign: "Bring out the #Softside", Downy
Saks Fifth Avenue
Scotts Miracle-Gro Company Digital
Spotify US Media Buying, US Media Planning
Subway Restaurants Campaign: "#januANY", Content Design, Social Marketing, Social Strategy
New-Target Corporation Social
Toyota "Masters of the Wheel", "Parents Who Drive Bad Anonymous", #noroomforboring, Campaign: "Meals Per Hour", Campaign: "TeenDrive365", Media Buying, Media Planning, Online, Social Media, Videos
UGG
Unilever Ben & Jerry's, Retail, Scoop Trucks, Search Marketing, Social Marketing, Strategic Digital
USA Network Campaign: "This One Time at Summer Camp"
Verizon Communications Inc.

36CREATIVE
46 Lowell Rd Ste 1, Windham, NH 03087
Tel.: (603) 818-9919
E-Mail: info@36creative.com
Web Site: www.36creative.com

Year Founded: 2004

Agency Specializes In: Advertising, Brand Development & Integration, Digital/Interactive, E-Commerce, Email, Graphic Design, Logo & Package Design, Print, Search Engine Optimization, Social Media

Steve Gabriel *(Mng Partner)*
Trent Sanders *(Mng Partner)*
Christopher Massie *(Sr Dir & Designer)*
Madison Harold *(Acct Dir)*
Brian Grossman *(Dir-Art)*
Peter Digeronimo *(Acct Mgr)*
Rob Widdick *(Mgr-Interactive Media)*

Accounts:
Nancy Chippendale's Dance Studios Inc
Oasys Water

3B ADVERTISING, LLC
2200 NW 159st Ste 400, Clive, IA 50325
Tel.: (515) 987-8007
Fax: (515) 987-8085

Agency Specializes In: Advertising, Advertising Specialties, Logo & Package Design, Media Buying Services, Multimedia, Newspaper, Promotions, Recruitment, Trade & Consumer Magazines, Transportation

Approx. Annual Billings: $300,000

Kory Boersma *(Owner)*
Sue K. Lewis *(Partner & Dir-Media)*
Sam Maclay *(Partner & Dir-Creative)*
Tim McGrath *(Partner & Dir-Design)*
Chris Moore *(Partner & Dir-Strategic)*

3D PUBLIC RELATIONS AND MARKETING
6340 Coldwater Canyon Ave Ste 206, North Hollywood, CA 91606
Tel.: (310) 909-8770
Fax: (310) 275-3029
E-Mail: info@3dprmarketing.com
Web Site: www.3dprmarketing.com

Agency Specializes In: Advertising, Brand Development & Integration, Event Planning & Marketing, Media Relations, Public Relations

Dina Rezvanipour *(Founder & Pres)*

Accounts:
New-Daybreaker
New-Generation Philanthropy

3ELEVENMEDIA
7210 SW 57th Ave Ste 212, Miami, FL 33143
Tel.: (786) 766-9311
E-Mail: info@3elevenmedia.com
Web Site: www.3elevenmedia.com

Agency Specializes In: Advertising, Brand Development & Integration, Digital/Interactive, Graphic Design, Internet/Web Design, Print, Search Engine Optimization, Social Media

Anthony Gomez *(Founder)*
Hector Rodriguez *(Acct Exec)*

Accounts:
A1 Behavioral Health Center
Michael-Ann Russell JCC
Orion Jet Center
Pretty You London
Vintage & Stuff

3FOLD COMMUNICATIONS
2031 K St Ste 100, Sacramento, CA 95811
Tel.: (916) 442-1394
Fax: (916) 442-1664
Web Site: www.3foldcomm.com

Year Founded: 2004

Agency Specializes In: Advertising, Graphic Design, Public Relations, Social Media

Angela Criser *(Owner & CFO)*
Kim Tucker *(VP)*
Liz Divelbiss *(Acct Mgr)*
Jamie Von Sossan *(Acct Mgr)*
Rebecca Wilkie *(Acct Mgr)*
Kati Beckman *(Acct Coord)*
Brody Rennan *(Acct Coord)*
Christie Spencer *(Coord-Traffic)*

Accounts:
Fourth & Hope Campaign: "Give Hope"
Franklin Pictures LLC
Sacramento Opera

3H COMMUNICATIONS INC.
309 Church St, Oakville, ON L6J 1N9 Canada
Tel.: (905) 338-8177
Fax: (905) 338-1317
E-Mail: production@3h.ca
Web Site: www.3h.ca

Employees: 15
Year Founded: 1989

Agency Specializes In: Advertising, Medical Products, Pharmaceutical

David Hara *(CFO)*
Miriam Hara *(Chief Creative Officer)*
Steve Ellison *(VP-Client Engagement)*
Nathalie De Caen *(Mgr-Creative Svcs)*
Roberto Contreras *(Specialist-IT)*
Nancy Harper *(Copywriter)*
Lindsay Sleightholm *(Sr Graphic Designer)*
Yukari Yoshitome *(Sr Graphic Designer)*

Accounts:
BD Medical
Blue Cross
D&B
Dentsply
Fresita
IMG Canada
Sanofi-Aventis
Windsor

3HEADED MONSTER
1333 N Stemmons Freeway Ste 110, Dallas, TX 75207
Tel.: (214) 207-1813
E-Mail: info@3headedmonster.com
Web Site: www.3headedmonster.com

Agency Specializes In: Advertising, Brand Development & Integration, Digital/Interactive, Social Media, Strategic Planning/Research

Shon Rathbone *(Founder & Chm-Creative)*
Crystal Anderson *(Co-Founder & Dir-Strategy)*
Mark Ford *(Creative Dir)*

Accounts:
Bhana

New-Bonfire
New-Bridgestone
Chef'n
Nike
New-Orange Leaf Frozen Yogurt (Agency of Record) Brand Strategy, Creative
Oyokey
Rascal
Reel Fx, Inc.
Twin Peaks

3MARKETEERS ADVERTISING, INC.
6399 San Ignacio Ave, San Jose, CA 95119
Tel.: (408) 293-3233
Fax: (408) 293-2433
E-Mail: jeff.holmes@3marketeers.com
Web Site: www.3marketeers.com

E-Mail for Key Personnel:
President: jeff.holmes@3marketeers.com
Creative Dir.: jeff.holmes@3marketeers.com

Employees: 20
Year Founded: 1986

National Agency Associations: AAF-BMA-SVAA

Agency Specializes In: Advertising, Advertising Specialties, Brand Development & Integration, Broadcast, Business Publications, Business-To-Business, Cable T.V., Children's Market, Collateral, Commercial Photography, Communications, Consulting, Consumer Marketing, Consumer Publications, Corporate Communications, Corporate Identity, Digital/Interactive, Direct Response Marketing, E-Commerce, Education, Electronic Media, Engineering, Entertainment, Exhibit/Trade Shows, Financial, Government/Political, Graphic Design, Health Care Services, High Technology, In-Store Advertising, Industrial, Information Technology, Internet/Web Design, Leisure, Logo & Package Design, Magazines, Media Buying Services, Merchandising, New Product Development, Newspaper, Newspapers & Magazines, Out-of-Home Media, Outdoor, Pharmaceutical, Planning & Consultation, Point of Purchase, Point of Sale, Print, Production, Publicity/Promotions, Radio, Real Estate, Retail, Sales Promotion, Strategic Planning/Research, T.V., Technical Advertising, Teen Market, Trade & Consumer Magazines, Transportation

Approx. Annual Billings: $7,750,000

Breakdown of Gross Billings by Media: D.M.: $3,000,000; Fees: $2,000,000; Internet Adv.: $500,000; Logo & Package Design: $250,000; Trade & Consumer Mags.: $1,000,000; Worldwide Web Sites: $1,000,000

Jeff Holmes *(CEO & Dir-Creative)*
Beryl Israel *(VP-Client Svcs)*
Katarina Johannesson *(Dir-Art)*
Willy Lam *(Dir-IT)*
Rita Garcia *(Assoc Dir-Art)*
Jennifer McClenon *(Acct Mgr & Sr Copywriter)*
David Goldberg *(Acct Mgr)*
Liz Elewski *(Mgr-HR & Acctg)*

Accounts:
Cisco; 2004
Consentry; 2006
Coradiant Coradiant, Truesite; 2004
Nero Nero; 2008
Silver Peak Systems; 2005
Teneros; CA Application Assurance Servers; 2003

3PM CREATIVE
1405 Morningside Dr, Charlotte, NC 28205
Tel.: (704) 293-7490
Web Site: www.3pmcreativegroup.com

Year Founded: 2009

Agency Specializes In: Brand Development & Integration, Business Publications, Collateral, Email, Identity Marketing, Internet/Web Design, Logo & Package Design, Media Planning, Print

Joe Haubenhofer *(Partner)*
Kara Hollinger-Bulla *(Partner)*
Leeann Dolan *(Office Mgr)*
Brooke Neal *(Copywriter)*

Accounts:
Nature's Menu Amimal Food Mfr & Distr
Water.org Public Relations

4 GUYS INTERACTIVE
5300 Hollister St, Houston, TX 77040
Tel.: (713) 460-4723
Fax: (281) 807-4384
E-Mail: info@4guys.com
Web Site: www.4guys.com

Agency Specializes In: Advertising, Digital/Interactive, Internet/Web Design, Web (Banner Ads, Pop-ups, etc.)

Accounts:
Caldwell Watson
Canyon Ranch
Cemex
Chevron
Flexitalic
RaceTrac
United Continental Holdings
Valero

4 U ENTERTAINMENT
420 Mckinley St Ste 111-221, Corona, CA 92879
Tel.: (951) 545-9760
E-Mail: 4uentertainment.office@gmail.com
Web Site: www.4uentertainment.com

Agency Specializes In: Advertising, Advertising Specialties, Affluent Market, African-American Market, Brand Development & Integration, Branded Entertainment, Broadcast, Cable T.V., College, Communications, Consulting, Consumer Goods, Consumer Marketing, Corporate Communications, Custom Publishing, Direct-to-Consumer, Education, Electronic Media, Email, Entertainment, Event Planning & Marketing, Exhibit/Trade Shows, Fashion/Apparel, Financial, Graphic Design, Guerilla Marketing, In-Store Advertising, Infomercials, Internet/Web Design, Local Marketing, Logo & Package Design, Media Relations, Media Training, Mobile Marketing, Multicultural, Multimedia, New Product Development, Newspapers & Magazines, Package Design, Paid Searches, Planning & Consultation, Podcasting, Print, Product Placement, Production, Production (Ad, Film, Broadcast), Public Relations, Publicity/Promotions, Publishing, Radio, Recruitment, Regional, Retail, Sales Promotion, Sponsorship, Strategic Planning/Research, Syndication, T.V., Teen Market

Approx. Annual Billings: $250,000

Breakdown of Gross Billings by Media: Adv. Specialities: $250,000

Spirit Day *(Founder & CEO)*
Kenchasa Bryant *(Exec Dir-Mktg)*
Reggie Hailey *(Exec Dir-Tech)*
Shae Thomas *(Exec Dir-Promotion)*
Chrissie Whyte *(Exec Dir-Media)*
Angela Gillard *(Asst Dir-Promotions)*

42
(See Under Firespring)

42 ENTERTAINMENT, LLC
727 S Main St, Burbank, CA 91506
Tel.: (626) 356-1302
Fax: (626) 237-5012
E-Mail: info@42entertainment.com
Web Site: www.42entertainment.com

Agency Specializes In: Advertising, Sponsorship

Susan Bonds *(CEO)*
Alex Lieu *(Chief Creative Officer)*
Michael Borys *(VP-Interactive Design)*
Andrew Deutschman *(VP-Content Dev)*
Johnny Rodriguez *(VP-Visual Design)*

Accounts:
Activision Blizzard, Inc. Last Call Poker
Advanced Micro Devices, Inc. The Vanishing Point
Microsoft Corporation Dead Man's Tale, Hex 168, MSNFound, Halo2
Warner Bros. Entertainment Inc.
Wrigley Campaign: "The Human Preservation Project"

42WEST
220 W 42nd St 12th Fl, New York, NY 10036
Tel.: (212) 277-7555
Fax: (212) 277-7550
Web Site: www.42west.net

Employees: 20

Agency Specializes In: Advertising, Entertainment, Public Relations, Strategic Planning/Research

Leslee Dart *(Partner & Principal)*
Allan Mayer *(Partner & Principal)*
Tom Piechura *(Mng Dir)*
Amanda Silverman *(Mng Dir)*
Tom Reno *(CFO & COO)*
Anna Bailer *(Dir-Strategic Comm)*
Rebecca Novak *(Dir-Digital Mktg)*

Accounts:
Don McKay Entertainment Services
Sorry Thanks Entertainment Services
The Wild & Wonderful Whites Of West Virginia Entertainment Services

Branch

42West
1840 Century Pk E Ste 700, Los Angeles, CA 90067
Tel.: (310) 477-4442
Fax: (310) 477-8442
Web Site: www.42west.net

Agency Specializes In: Advertising, Digital/Interactive, Public Relations, Social Media

Michael P. Mottola *(Mgr-PR)*

Accounts:
New-Jennifer Garner

44 INTERACTIVE
1602 S Western Ave, Sioux Falls, SD 57105
Tel.: (605) 334-4464
E-Mail: info@44interactive.com
Web Site: www.44interactive.com

Year Founded: 2006

Agency Specializes In: Advertising, Digital/Interactive, Email, Internet/Web Design, Search Engine Optimization, Social Media

Wade Humphreys *(Dir-Digital Mktg)*

Abby Lynn Rogers *(Strategist-Social Media)*

Accounts:
College Golf Bound
MacDoctors
Verity Corp

454 CREATIVE
1572 N Batavia St Ste 1C, Orange, CA 92867
Tel.: (714) 998-8970
Fax: (800) 308-5021
E-Mail: hello@454creative.com
Web Site: www.454creative.com

Employees: 10
Year Founded: 2002

Agency Specializes In: Advertising, Advertising Specialties, Affiliate Marketing, Agriculture, Alternative Advertising, Arts, Automotive, Aviation & Aerospace, Brand Development & Integration, Branded Entertainment, Co-op Advertising, Collateral, Commercial Photography, Communications, Computers & Software, Consulting, Consumer Goods, Content, Corporate Communications, Corporate Identity, Cosmetics, Customer Relationship Management, Digital/Interactive, Direct Response Marketing, E-Commerce, Education, Electronic Media, Electronics, Email, Engineering, Entertainment, Environmental, Event Planning & Marketing, Experience Design, Fashion/Apparel, Financial, Food Service, Government/Political, Graphic Design, Health Care Services, Hospitality, Household Goods, Identity Marketing, In-Store Advertising, Industrial, Information Technology, Integrated Marketing, Internet/Web Design, Investor Relations, Legal Services, Leisure, Local Marketing, Logo & Package Design, Magazines, Marine, Media Planning, Media Relations, Media Training, Medical Products, Mobile Marketing, Multimedia, New Product Development, New Technologies, Newspaper, Newspapers & Magazines, Out-of-Home Media, Outdoor, Package Design, Paid Searches, Planning & Consultation, Point of Purchase, Point of Sale, Production (Ad, Film, Broadcast), Publicity/Promotions, RSS (Really Simple Syndication), Real Estate, Recruitment, Regional, Restaurant, Retail, Sales Promotion, Search Engine Optimization, Shopper Marketing, Social Marketing/Nonprofit, Social Media, Sports Market, Stakeholders, Strategic Planning/Research, Sweepstakes, Technical Advertising, Trade & Consumer Magazines, Transportation, Travel & Tourism, Viral/Buzz/Word of Mouth, Web (Banner Ads, Pop-ups, etc.), Yellow Pages Advertising

Paul Bresenden *(Pres & Exec Creative Dir)*
Rachel Anderson *(Creative Dir)*
Megan Norris *(Mgr-Web Support)*
Jesse Seilhan *(Mgr-Digital Media)*

Accounts:
Free Wheelchair Mission

49 SEO SERVICES
5842 Mott St, San Diego, CA 92122
Tel.: (916) 202-5128
Web Site: www.49seoservices.com

Employees: 2
Year Founded: 2012

Agency Specializes In: Affiliate Marketing, Direct Response Marketing, Email, Search Engine Optimization

Dustin Baly *(Founder & Principal)*

Accounts:
City Wine Tours; 2014
Glia; 2014
Signet Education; 2014
Trademark Tours; 2014
True Life Center for Wellbeing; 2014

5 STONE ADVERTISING
(d/b/a 5 Stone Marketing Advertising and Design)
PO Box 429, Carbondale, CO 81623
Tel.: (970) 930-6123
Fax: (303) 298-1140
E-Mail: adjunkie@5stonead.com
Web Site: www.5stonead.com

E-Mail for Key Personnel:
President: doug@5stonead.com

Employees: 8
Year Founded: 2001

Agency Specializes In: Advertising, Agriculture, Automotive, Aviation & Aerospace, Brand Development & Integration, Broadcast, Collateral, Consulting, Consumer Goods, Consumer Marketing, Corporate Identity, Digital/Interactive, Entertainment, Environmental, Experience Design, Fashion/Apparel, Graphic Design, Household Goods, In-Store Advertising, Internet/Web Design, Leisure, Logo & Package Design, Marine, Media Planning, Men's Market, Multimedia, Newspaper, Outdoor, Package Design, Pets , Planning & Consultation, Point of Purchase, Point of Sale, Print, Production (Print), Promotions, Radio, Real Estate, Social Media, Sports Market, Strategic Planning/Research, T.V., Trade & Consumer Magazines, Transportation, Travel & Tourism

Approx. Annual Billings: $2,500,000

Breakdown of Gross Billings by Media: Collateral: $200,000; Graphic Design: $200,000; Logo & Package Design: $200,000; Point of Purchase: $100,000; Print: $500,000; Radio & T.V.: $200,000; Strategic Planning/Research: $100,000; T.V.: $125,000; Trade & Consumer Mags.: $625,000; Worldwide Web Sites: $250,000

Doug Long *(Principal-Strategic Plng & Brand Dev)*

Accounts:
Eagle Claw Fishing Tackle; Denver, CO; 2001
Fishouflage; Greenville, WI; 2010
The Inhibitor
Polar Boats
Realtree Camouflage
Stranahan's Colorado Whiskey; Denver, CO; 2004

50,000FEET, INC.
1700 W Irving Park Rd Ste 110, Chicago, IL 60613
Tel.: (773) 529-6760
Web Site: www.50000feet.com

Year Founded: 2001

Agency Specializes In: Advertising, Brand Development & Integration, Communications, Sponsorship

Mike Petersen *(Founder, Partner & Dir-Creative)*
Jim Misener *(Mng Dir & Principal)*
Ken Fox *(Principal & Exec Dir-Creative)*
Chris Prescher *(Principal)*
Jason Jones *(Dir-Creative)*
Chris Maier *(Dir-Creative)*
Terri Tomcisin *(Dir-Digital Strategy)*
Tracy West *(Dir-Creative)*
Ken Byers *(Sr Strategist-Mktg)*

Accounts:
AIGA Chicago
BMW of North America, LLC MINI Cooper
Claymore Securities, Inc.
Guggenheim Partners, LLC
Haier America (Agency of Record) Brand Development, Creative, Strategic Marketing
Harley-Davidson Motor Company, Inc.
MillerCoors

522 DIGITAL, LLC
711 King St, Alexandria, VA 22314
Tel.: (703) 286-5251
Fax: (866) 612-9085
E-Mail: info@522digital.com
Web Site: www.522digital.com

Agency Specializes In: Advertising, Content, Digital/Interactive, Internet/Web Design, Print, Social Media

Chad Vossen *(Owner & Dir-Creative Strategy)*
Tristan Pelligrino *(Dir-Mktg)*

Accounts:
Carpenter's Shelter

524 CREATIVE, INC.
1170 Peachtree St NE 14th Fl, Atlanta, GA 30309
Tel.: (770) 419-0524
Fax: (866) 639-6729
E-Mail: talktous@524creative.com
Web Site: www.524creative.com

Year Founded: 2005

Agency Specializes In: Advertising, Brand Development & Integration, Collateral, Crisis Communications, Internet/Web Design, Print, Public Relations, Social Media, T.V., Web (Banner Ads, Pop-ups, etc.)

April Wright *(Owner)*
Scott Wright *(Owner)*

Accounts:
Blood & Marrow Transplant Group of Georgia
Cadsoft Consulting, Inc.
Purdue Pharma LP
Rio Mar Beach Resort & Spa
The Shores Resort
Walt Disney World Swan & Dolphin Resorts

5280 CREATIVE
(Name Changed to Zeitsight)

5BY5 AGENCY
1550 W McEwen Dr Ste 300, Franklin, TN 37067
Tel.: (615) 595-6391
E-Mail: info@5by5agency.com
Web Site: www.5by5agency.com

Agency Specializes In: Advertising, Brand Development & Integration, Collateral, Content, Email, Internet/Web Design, Social Media

Shannon Litton *(Pres & CEO)*
Mike Schatz *(Partner & Exec VP)*
Ginny Burton *(VP-Fin & Admin)*
Derrick Hoog *(VP-Client Svcs)*
Josh Miller *(VP-Digital)*
Jenny Cupero *(Dir-Bus Dev)*

Accounts:
Amazima Ministries
Every Nation Ministries
Growing Leaders
Lifeway
Nashville Rescue Mission
Oral Roberts University
World Vision

5IVECANONS
24 N Market St, Jacksonville, FL 32202
Tel.: (904) 353-2900

E-Mail: hello@5ivecanons.com
Web Site: www.5ivecanons.com

Year Founded: 2010

Agency Specializes In: Advertising, Brand Development & Integration, Content, Digital/Interactive, Social Media

Adam Schaffer *(Pres & Dir-Creative)*
Reid Penuel *(Corp Counsel)*
Tom Charde *(Dir-User Experience)*
Brandon Clark *(Dir-Client Dev)*
Ashley Smith *(Dir-Art)*

Accounts:
The Latino Coalition

5METACOM

630 W Carmel Dr Ste 180, Carmel, IN 46032
Tel.: (317) 580-7540
Fax: (317) 580-7550
E-Mail: mail@5metacom.com
Web Site: www.5metacom.com

Employees: 30
Year Founded: 1977

Agency Specializes In: Agriculture, Brand Development & Integration, Business-To-Business, Collateral, Communications, Corporate Identity, Direct Response Marketing, E-Commerce, Electronic Media, Engineering, Environmental, Event Planning & Marketing, Exhibit/Trade Shows, Financial, Graphic Design, Health Care Services, High Technology, Industrial, Information Technology, Internet/Web Design, Investor Relations, Logo & Package Design, Media Buying Services, Medical Products, New Product Development, Outdoor, Pharmaceutical, Planning & Consultation, Point of Purchase, Point of Sale, Print, Production, Public Relations, Publicity/Promotions, Radio, Sales Promotion, Strategic Planning/Research, Technical Advertising, Trade & Consumer Magazines, Transportation

Approx. Annual Billings: $29,002,828

Chris Wirthwein *(Owner & CEO)*
Mark Duffin *(CFO, COO & CTO)*
Joe Bannon *(Sr VP-Mktg & Brand Strategy-Global)*
Eric Dewitt *(VP-Bus Svcs)*
Lisa Lorenz *(Dir-Art)*
Ben Mccormick *(Acct Exec)*
Jennifer McPhail *(Acct Exec)*
Jason Williams *(Acct Exec)*
Judy Knafel *(Analyst-Mktg)*

Accounts:
Roche Diagnostics; Indianapolis, IN Human Health Devices & Services

6AM MARKETING

(Formerly Glowac, Harris, Madison Inc.)
330 S Whitney Way Ste 300, Madison, WI 53705
Tel.: (608) 232-9696
Fax: (608) 232-9636
Web Site: www.6ammarketing.com

Employees: 12
Year Founded: 2004

National Agency Associations: ADFED-MCAN-Second Wind Limited

Agency Specializes In: Advertising, Brand Development & Integration, Broadcast, Cable T.V., Communications, Corporate Communications, Corporate Identity, Crisis Communications, Email, Graphic Design, Identity Marketing, Internet/Web Design, Logo & Package Design, Media Planning, Outdoor, Package Design, Print, Promotions, Public Relations, Publicity/Promotions, Radio, Search Engine Optimization, Social Media, Strategic Planning/Research, T.V.

Revenue: $15,000,000

Wayne Harris *(Pres)*
Mary Romolino *(CEO)*
Bill Patton *(Exec Creative Dir)*
Brian Buckner *(Sr Art Dir)*
Terri McNamara *(Dir-Fin & Acctg)*
Ian Mullarney *(Dir-Web Dev)*
Mary Jo Trapani *(Dir-Digital Comm)*
Sally Monroe *(Mgr-Content)*
Danielle Brockman *(Copywriter)*

Accounts:
Gentel Biosciences
Madison Gas & Electric Co
Orange Shoe
Park Towne
QTI Group

6DEGREES INTEGRATED COMMUNICATIONS

1210 Sheppard Ave E Ste 700, Toronto, ON M2K 1E3 Canada
Tel.: (416) 446-7758
E-Mail: connect@6deg.ca
Web Site: www.6deg.ca

Agency Specializes In: Brand Development & Integration, Strategic Planning/Research

Troy Yung *(Mng Partner)*
Matthew May *(Head-Digital & Sr Dir-Art)*
Mike Brien *(Grp Acct Dir)*
Lauren Bernardo *(Acct Dir)*
Lesley Goldstein *(Acct Dir)*
Marian Baillie *(Acct Mgr)*
Shannon Kelly *(Acct Mgr)*
Ashley Porporo *(Acct Mgr)*
Matt Smith *(Acct Mgr)*
Natalie Kaiman *(Acct Supvr)*
Andrew Soberman *(Acct Supvr)*
Mikaela Levasseur *(Acct Coord)*

Accounts:
Brita Activations
Lady Speed Stick

72 ADVERTISING INC

24654 N Lake Pleasant Pkwy Ste 103-112, Peoria, AZ 85383
Tel.: (623) 889-5626
Web Site: www.72advertising.com

Year Founded: 2008

Agency Specializes In: Advertising, Email, Internet/Web Design, Search Engine Optimization, Social Media

Paul Thompson *(Founder & CEO)*

Accounts:
Courtesy Chevrolet, Inc.
HB Scooters
Passport Auto Group
Powers Real Estate
Thompson Land LLC

72ANDSUNNY

12101 W Buffalo Creek Dr, Playa Vista, CA 90094
Tel.: (310) 215-9009
Fax: (310) 215-9012
E-Mail: alex.schneider@72andsunny.com
Web Site: www.72andsunny.com

Employees: 150
Year Founded: 2005

National Agency Associations: 4A's

Agency Specializes In: Sponsorship

John Boiler *(Founder & CEO)*
Robert Nakata *(Owner & Dir-Design)*
Bryan Rowles *(Partner & Exec Dir-Creative-Amsterdam)*
Matt Jarvis *(Partner)*
Marita Scarfi *(CFO)*
Glenn Cole *(Chief Creative Officer)*
James Townsend *(Mng Dir-NYC)*
Arnau Bosch *(Head-Creative)*
Carlo Cavallone *(Exec Dir-Creative)*
Mick DiMaria *(Grp Dir-Creative)*
John Graham *(Grp Dir-Strategy)*
Frank Hahn *(Grp Dir-Creative)*
Justin Hooper *(Grp Dir-Creative)*
Gavin Milner *(Grp Dir-Creative)*
Bryan Smith *(Grp Dir-Strategy)*
Ruben Barton *(Sr Producer-Interactive)*
Marianne Pizzi *(Grp Brand Dir)*
Josh Fell *(Creative Dir)*
Danielle Gard *(Brand Dir)*
Amanda Hein *(Brand Dir-Samsung)*
Andrew Krensky *(Brand Dir)*
Jen Marvin *(Brand Dir)*
Mark Maziarz *(Creative Dir)*
Nathan Shamban *(Brand Dir)*
Lauren Smith *(Brand Dir)*
Kristine Soto *(Brand Dir-Google)*
Gabo Curielcha *(Dir-Art & Designer)*
Ben Hodgin *(Dir-Art & Designer)*
Rob McQueen *(Dir-Art & Designer)*
Robert Teague *(Dir-Creative & Designer)*
Tim Wettstein *(Dir-Creative & Designer)*
Tim Wolfe *(Dir-Creative & Writer)*
Jason Ambrose *(Dir-Creative)*
Sam Baerwald *(Dir-Film Production)*
Geno Burmester *(Dir-Art)*
Barton Corley *(Dir-Creative)*
Tom Johnstone *(Dir-Grp Strategy)*
Alex Lebosq *(Dir-Bus Affairs)*
Brooke-Lynn Luat *(Dir-Strategy)*
Michelle McKinney *(Dir-Bus Affairs)*
Kasia Molenda *(Dir-Strategy)*
Sedef Onar *(Dir-Talent)*
Rob Trent *(Dir-Creative)*
Heather Wischmann *(Dir-Interactive)*
Cyndi Yee *(Dir-Culture & Talent)*
Evan Brown *(Assoc Dir-Creative)*
Brandon Pierce *(Assoc Dir-Creative)*
Shannon Coletti *(Sr Brand Mgr)*
Michal David *(Sr Brand Mgr)*
Lara Drew *(Sr Mgr-Bus Affairs)*
Jourdan Merkow *(Sr Brand Mgr)*
Katie Murphy Darling *(Sr Mgr-HR & Talent)*
Shannon Reed *(Sr Brand Mgr)*
Andy Silva *(Sr Brand Mgr)*
Autumn Abbruzzi *(Brand Mgr)*
Jessica Brewer *(Brand Mgr)*
Alexis Coller *(Grp Brand Dir)*
Rhea Curry *(Grp Brand Dir)*
Rochelle Farnum *(Brand Mgr)*
Jomo Hendrickson *(Brand Mgr)*
Molly Danziger Johnson *(Brand Mgr-Google)*
Jennifer Levin *(Brand Mgr)*
Brett Schneider *(Brand Mgr)*
Alexis Varian *(Grp Brand Dir)*
Gwynne Davis *(Mgr-Bus Dev)*
Jennifer Jahinian *(Mgr-Bus Affairs)*
Maggie Pijanowski *(Mgr-Bus Affairs)*
Beau Thomason *(Mgr-Bus Affairs)*
Kelly Ventrelli *(Mgr-Bus Affairs)*
Latanya Ware *(Mgr-Bus Affairs)*
Gigi Braybrooks *(Jr Strategist)*
Erika Bridges *(Strategist)*
Josh Hughes *(Strategist)*
Eddie Moraga *(Strategist)*
Marc Pardy *(Strategist)*
Saeid Vahidi *(Strategist)*
Dave Carlson *(Sr Writer)*
Patrick Glorieux *(Copywriter)*

Garrett Jones *(Designer)*
Esther Kim *(Designer)*
Jack Lagomarsino *(Copywriter)*
Sebastian Lyman *(Copywriter)*
Teddy Miller *(Copywriter)*
Gerardo Oritz *(Designer)*
Alicia Arnold *(Coord-Brand)*
Taylor Henriquez *(Coord-Bus Affairs)*
Calli Howard *(Coord-Bus Affairs)*
Jenny Jones *(Coord-Film Production)*
Ashley Pesses *(Coord-Bus Affairs)*
Jack Young *(Coord-Brand)*
Chad Goodnoe *(Sr Writer)*
Jack Jensen *(Sr Writer)*

Accounts:
2K Games 2K Sports
Activision Blizzard Guitar Hero
Activision Publishing Call of Duty: Advanced Warfare, Campaign: "Buckle Up", Campaign: "Destiny Planet View", Campaign: "It's About to Get Real", Destiny, Guitar Hero Reveal Trailer, Online, Skylanders SuperChargers, Skylanders Trap Team
Adidas "Create Your Own", Campaign: "Sports15", Sports (Global Creative Agency)
American Legacy Foundation "Finishers", Advertising, Campaign: "Finish It", Campaign: "Left Swipe Dat", Campaign: "Progress Report", Campaign: "Truth", Creative, Digital, TV
Bugaboo Strollers
New-Bungie
Call of Duty Call of Duty MW3, Call of Duty Elite., Call of Duty: Advanced Warfare, Campaign: "Discover Your Power"
CKE Restaurants, Inc. All-Natural Burger, Campaign: "Au Naturel", Campaign: "BBQ's Best Pair", Campaign: "Bacon to the 6th Power", Campaign: "Borderball", Campaign: "Fast-Food First: Fish That's Not Fried", Campaign: "Game Day Fantasy", Campaign: "House Party", Campaign: "Mystique", Campaign: "Natural Beauties", Campaign: "Propositioning", Campaign: "Too Hot to Handle", Carl's Jr., Grilled Cheese Breakfast Sandwich, Grilled Fish Sandwich, Mile High Bacon Thickburger, Mobile Video, Social, Strawberry Pop-Tart Ice Cream Sandwich, Super Bacon Cheeseburger, TV, Tex Mex Bacon Thickburger, Thickburger El Diablo
Diageo Smirnoff
New-Dropbox
ESPN Campaign: "Count on Countdown", Campaign: "Get Up. It's Game Day", Campaign: "Presidents"
Esquire Magazine
General Mills Creative, Totino's
Google "Destiny", "Planet View", Banner Advertising, Broadcast, Browser, Campaign: "For Bigger Fun", Chromecast, Google Chrome, Mobile App, Outdoor
Guitar Hero
Hardees Food Systems, Inc. Campaign: "Bacon to the 6th Power", Campaign: "Fast-Food First: Fish That's Not Fried", Campaign: "House Party", Campaign: "No Tommorrow", Campaign: "Propositioning", Creative, Grilled Cheese Breakfast Sandwich, Grilled Fish Sandwich, Mile High Bacon Thickburger, Pork Chop 'N' Gravy Biscuits, Social, TV, Texas Toast Breakfast Sandwich, Thickburger El Diablo
K-Swiss, Inc. Campaign: "Blades by Kenny Powers", Campaign: "Micro Tubes - MFCEO" Legacy
Marie Curie Cancer Care Campaign: "Collector", Great Daffodil Appeal, Outdoor, Social Media, TV
New-MillerCoors LLC Coors Banquet (Lead Creative & Digital Agency), Coors Light (Lead Creative & Digital Agency)
Nike Campaign: "Nike Chosen", Nike 6.0, Nike Football, Nike Running, Television
Nook
Pirelli Campaign: "Let's Dance"
Samsung Electronics America Campaign: "Movie Magic", Campaign: "The Best TV Deserves the Best TV", Campaign: "The Curve Changes Everything", Campaign: "We are Greater than I", Curved UHD TV, Gear VR, SUHD TVs, Tablets
Samsung Mobile (Creative Agency of Record) Broadcast, Campaign: "A Long Time Coming", Campaign: "Amazing Things Happen", Campaign: "Anticipation", Campaign: "Brotherly Love", Campaign: "Evolution", Campaign: "Grad Party", Campaign: "Home Olympics", Campaign: "In The Wild", Campaign: "Magna Carta Holy Grail", Campaign: "Marvel's Avengers: Age of Ultron and Samsung Mobile present 'Assemble' Part 1", Campaign: "Meet The Family", Campaign: "Meeting with Tim Burton", Campaign: "Next is Now", Campaign: "Ready for the Next Big Thing", Campaign: "Real, Raw and Pitiless", Campaign: "SAFE with Two in One", Campaign: "The Big Pitch", Campaign: "The Leak", Campaign: "The Next Big Thing Is Already Here", Campaign: "Wall Huggers", Campaign: "Winter Olympics Fever" Winter Olympics 2014, Campaign: "Work SAFE with Group Play", Consumer Advertising, Content Marketing, Digital, El Plato Supreme, Experiential, Galaxy II, Note, Notebook, Galaxy S4, Galaxy S5, Galaxy S6, Galaxy S6 Edge, Galaxy Tab Pro, Online, Out-of-Home, Pencil, Print, Retail, Samsung Gear, Social Media, Unicorn Apocalypse
Skylanders
Sonos Campaign: "Grinder", Campaign: "Your Home"
Square Campaign: "Selling Made Simple"
Starbucks Campaign: "Meet me at Starbucks", Creative, Frappuccino, Oprah Chai Tea, Social Media
Target Corporation Advertising, Campaign: "#SummerUp", Campaign: "Alice in Marshmallow Land", Campaign: "Big Dog", Campaign: "Every Little Thing Is a Really Big Deal", Campaign: "Expect more. Pay less", Campaign: "My Kind of Holiday", Campaign: "The Holiday Odyssey", Campaign: "Volcano", Digital, Holiday, Out-of-Home, Radio, TV, Up & Up
Tillamook County Creamery Association Brand Development, Broadcast, CAmpaign: "Dairy With Standards Not Artificial Growth Hormones", Campaign: "Cheese Product", Campaign: "Dairy Done Right", Campaign: "Farmer's Not Shareholders", Campaign: "Un-American Cheese", Creative, Digital, Online, Print, Strategy, Television
New-Truth Initiative
Truth Campaign: "Finish It", Campaign: "Response", Campaign: "Unpaid", Social
The Walt Disney Company

Branches

72andSunny

Westerhuis 1st Fl Westerstraat 187, 1015 MA Amsterdam, Netherlands
Tel.: (31) 20 7155 991
Fax: (31) 20 521 04 85
Web Site: www.72andsunny.com

Employees: 4

Agency Specializes In: Advertising, Sponsorship

Robert Nakata *(Founder & Dir-Design)*
Bryan Rowles *(Partner & Exec Dir-Creative-Amsterdam)*
Nic Owen *(Mng Dir)*
Carlo Cavallone *(Exec Dir-Creative)*
Stuart Harkness *(Co-Exec Creative Dir)*
Paulo Martins *(Creative Dir)*
Matt Heck *(Creative Dir)*
Steve Vranakis *(Creative Dir)*
Gregg Clampffer *(Dir-Creative)*
Stephanie Feeney *(Dir-Strategy)*
Patric Franz *(Dir-Art)*
Tom Griffin *(Dir-Brand Mgmt)*
Richard Harrington *(Dir-Design)*
Simon Summerscales *(Dir-Comm Strategy)*
Laura Visco *(Dir-Creative)*
Mike Goller *(Grp Brand Dir)*
Yann Corlay *(Copywriter)*
Domingo De Villa *(Designer)*
Matteo Gallinelli *(Designer)*
Renee Lam *(Designer)*
Rosa Rankin-Gee *(Copywriter)*
Jorgen Sibbern *(Copywriter)*

Accounts:
2K Sports
Adidas #NewSpeed, Campaign: "Create the New Speed", Sports (Global Creative Agency)
Bugaboo
Callaway
Carlsberg Broadcast, Campaign: "If Carlsberg Did Haircuts", Campaign: "If Carlsberg Did Supermarkets?", Digital, Online, Print, Social, TV
Caviar LA, Inc. KSWISS Signs Kenny Powers
DC Shoes
Diageo 'The Store', Campaign: "Exclusively for Everybody", Campaign: "Filter the unnecessary. Keep the good stuff", Smirnoff, TV
G4 TV
Garofalo Pasta
Google Inc. Campaign: "Google Night Walk", Campaign: "Promenade Nocturne", Creative, Digital, Strategy
Hope Family Wines
Microsoft Zune
Nike+
Nook Sleep Systems
Pirelli
Quiksilver
Samsung Campaign: "Every Day Is Day One", Campaign: "What's Your Problem? Sport Doesn't Care"
Unilever Axe, Global Creative
United Colors of Benetton Campaign: "Unhate"
Xbox 360

72andSunny

30 Cooper Square, New York, NY 10003
Tel.: (310) 215-9009
Web Site: www.72andsunny.com

National Agency Associations: 4A's

James Townsend *(Mng Dir)*
Christa Skoland *(Head-Production)*
Guillermo Vega *(Exec Creative Dir)*
Vishal Dheiman *(Producer-Digital)*
Joseph Ernst *(Creative Dir)*
Mandy Wakimoto *(Acct Dir)*
Joe Withers *(Art Dir)*
Marshall Ball *(Dir-Strategy)*
Tim Jones *(Dir-Strategy)*
Miranda Kendrick *(Dir-Art Production)*
Lora Schulson *(Dir-Production)*
Eric Steele *(Dir-Creative)*
Chena Stephens *(Dir-Art)*
Shannon Coletti *(Sr Brand Mgr)*
Quentin Perry *(Sr Mgr-Bus Affairs)*
Brian Racis *(Sr Brand Mgr)*
Laura Hoffman *(Brand Mgr)*
Emily Hoyle *(Brand Mgr)*
Karla Stewart *(Grp Brand Dir)*
Jonathan Weiss *(Brand Mgr)*
Laura Fraser *(Mgr-Bus Affairs)*
Carol Chan *(Strategist)*
Matthew Carey *(Copywriter)*
Josh Klausner *(Sr Writer)*
David Girandola *(Recruiter-Creative)*
Jena Rickards Casiean *(Coord-Brand-SONOS)*
Reed Edwards *(Coord-Brand)*
Chelsea Kim *(Coord-Brand)*
Nadia Economides *(Jr Producer)*

Accounts:
New-Bobble
New-Diageo North America Inc. Campaign: "Exclusively for Everybody", Smirnoff
Samsung Campaign: "Ready for the Next Big Thing", Consumer Advertising, Content Marketing, Galaxy S6 Edge, Online, Print, Social Media
New-Seventh Generation Bobble (Lead Creative Agency), Campaign: "#EndTheTrend"

77 VENTURES
122 Hudson St 3rd Fl, New York, NY 10013
Tel.: (212) 431-2787
Web Site: www.77ventures.com

Agency Specializes In: Advertising, Brand Development & Integration, Content

Mike Haje *(Pres)*
Corbin Day *(Gen Partner)*

Accounts:
Bassmaster
DC Shoes
ESPN, Inc. Campaign: "ESPN Wimbledon"
Moontoast
Wyoming Whiskey

8 QUEENS MEDIA, LLC
100 N. 18th St Ste 300, Philadelphia, PA 19103
Tel.: (484) 243-0805
E-Mail: info@8queensmedia.com
Web Site: www.8queensmedia.com

Year Founded: 2014

Neville Diony *(Pres & COO)*

802 CREATIVE PARTNERS, INC.
15 E State St, Montpelier, VT 05602
Mailing Address:
PO Box 54, Bethel, VT 05032
Tel.: (802) 234-9755
Fax: (802) 234-6719
E-Mail: mike@802creative.com
Web Site: www.802creative.com

E-Mail for Key Personnel:
Creative Dir.: tom@802creative.com

Employees: 9
Year Founded: 1973

Agency Specializes In: Advertising, Advertising Specialties, Automotive, Brand Development & Integration, Broadcast, Business Publications, Business-To-Business, Cable T.V., Co-op Advertising, Collateral, Communications, Consulting, Consumer Marketing, Consumer Publications, Corporate Identity, Direct Response Marketing, E-Commerce, Education, Electronic Media, Engineering, Entertainment, Environmental, Exhibit/Trade Shows, Financial, Food Service, Government/Political, Graphic Design, Health Care Services, High Technology, Industrial, Information Technology, Internet/Web Design, Investor Relations, Legal Services, Logo & Package Design, Magazines, Media Buying Services, Medical Products, Multimedia, New Product Development, Newspaper, Newspapers & Magazines, Outdoor, Over-50 Market, Planning & Consultation, Point of Purchase, Point of Sale, Print, Production, Public Relations, Publicity/Promotions, Radio, Recruitment, Retail, Sales Promotion, Seniors' Market, Sports Market, Strategic Planning/Research, T.V., Technical Advertising, Trade & Consumer Magazines, Travel & Tourism, Yellow Pages Advertising

Approx. Annual Billings: $8,267,725 Capitalized

Mike Hickey *(Pres)*
Linda Trask *(Office Mgr & Media Buyer)*
Kelly Hickey *(Specialist-Media)*
Mike Mitchell *(Copywriter)*
Robbie Blanchard *(Sr Art Dir)*

Accounts:
AARP
Co-Op Insurance Inc.
Green Up Vermont
IBM Corporation
Radiantec
Ski Barn
Ultramotive
University of Vermont
Vermont Ski Areas Association

83 NORTH ADVERTISING
2219 York Rd Ste 202, Timonium, MD 21093
Tel.: (443) 798-7960
E-Mail: info@83north.net
Web Site: www.83north.net

Year Founded: 2009

Agency Specializes In: Advertising, Brand Development & Integration, Content, Digital/Interactive, Social Media

Leah Cook *(Media Buyer)*

Accounts:
Motive Pure

88/BRAND PARTNERS
542 S Dearborn Ste 1300, Chicago, IL 60605
Tel.: (312) 664-2500
Fax: (312) 664-8684
E-Mail: hello@88brandpartners.com
Web Site: www.88brandpartners.com

Agency Specializes In: Advertising, Brand Development & Integration, Internet/Web Design

Michael McGuire *(Pres & CEO)*
Anthony Nagy *(Exec Dir-Creative)*
Adrian Rosales *(Dir-Art)*
James Stepanek *(Dir-Art)*
Terry Boyd *(Assoc Dir-Creative)*
Deon Taylor *(Office Mgr)*
Haley Drake *(Acct Supvr)*
Jessica Palo *(Designer)*

Accounts:
Cornerstone Restaurant Group
Instant Alliance
NorthShore

89 DEGREES, INC.
25 Burlington Mall Rd Ste 610, Burlington, MA 1803
Tel.: (781) 221-5400
Fax: (781) 229-0542
E-Mail: info@89degrees.com
Web Site: www.89degrees.com

Year Founded: 2008

Agency Specializes In: Advertising, Email, Integrated Marketing, Mobile Marketing

Phil Hussey *(Pres & Mng Partner)*
Jeff Caplan *(Partner & VP)*
Rupa Rajopadhye *(Partner & VP-Strategic Mktg Svcs)*
Jundong Song *(Partner & VP-Mktg Intelligence & Tech)*
Arthur Sweetser *(CMO)*
Bill Pena *(VP-Product & Chief Architect)*
Bill Carino *(VP-Sls & Mktg)*
Rosie Poultney *(VP-Analytics)*

Accounts:
Genzyme/Sanofi
Hyundai
Ikea North America Services LLC
World Vision

90OCTANE
518 17th St Ste 1400, Denver, CO 80202
Tel.: (720) 904-8169
Fax: (303) 295-1577
E-Mail: info@90octane.com
Web Site: http://www.90octane.com/

Employees: 36

Agency Specializes In: Advertising, Information Technology, Integrated Marketing, Media Planning, Search Engine Optimization

Scott Anderson *(Acct Dir)*
Sean Voorhies *(Acct Dir)*
Kelly Hall *(Dir-Bus Impact)*
Leslie Norgren *(Dir-Audience Engagement)*
Lauren Gonzales *(Acct Mgr)*
Ariana Wolf *(Mgr-Audience Engagement)*
Jenny Bridges *(Acct Supvr)*
Misty Markley *(Acct Supvr)*
Anna Case *(Strategist-Paid Search)*
Lauren Gramling *(Planner-Digital Media)*

Accounts:
AlphaGraphics Business Centers
AORN Works
Atlas Copco Construction Mining Technique USA, LLC
Avalon
Branded Business Apps Search Engine Marketing, Website Development
Brookfield Residential Website Design
COSMOS
EDUCAUSE Email Marketing Program
Eye Pieces of Vail Conversion Consulting, Digital Marketing, SEO, Strategic
Globus
Mercy Housing
MonoGrams
Norgren
Pixorial Strategic Email, Social Media & Search Engine Marketing Program
Prologis
Qdoba Mexican Grill; Denver, CO Brand Development, Paid Search Campaign, Search Engine Optimization
Visit Denver
Zen Planner Online, Search Engine Marketing

919 MARKETING COMPANY
102 Avent Ferry Rd, Holly Springs, NC 27540
Tel.: (919) 557-7890
Fax: (919) 557-0041
E-Mail: info@919marketing.com
Web Site: www.919marketing.com

Employees: 12
Year Founded: 1996

National Agency Associations: AMA

Agency Specializes In: Advertising, Brand Development & Integration, Broadcast, Business Publications, Business-To-Business, Cable T.V., Co-op Advertising, Collateral, Communications, Consulting, Consumer Marketing, Consumer Publications, Corporate Identity, Digital/Interactive, Direct Response Marketing, E-Commerce, Education, Electronic Media, Entertainment, Event Planning & Marketing, Fashion/Apparel, Financial, Food Service, Graphic Design, Health Care Services, High Technology, Information Technology, Internet/Web Design, Investor

Relations, Local Marketing, Logo & Package Design, Magazines, Media Buying Services, Medical Products, New Product Development, Newspaper, Newspapers & Magazines, Out-of-Home Media, Outdoor, Pharmaceutical, Planning & Consultation, Point of Purchase, Point of Sale, Print, Production, Public Relations, Publicity/Promotions, Radio, Restaurant, Retail, Sales Promotion, Seniors' Market, Sports Market, Strategic Planning/Research, Sweepstakes, T.V., Trade & Consumer Magazines, Transportation, Travel & Tourism

David M. Chapman *(Founder & CEO)*
Daniel M. Christensen *(Dir-Social Media & Digital Mktg)*
Sue Yannello *(Dir-PR)*
Matt Demargel *(Sr Acct Mgr)*
Kevin Behan *(Acct Mgr)*

Accounts:
BioSignia; 2007
Central Carolina Bank
Duke University; Durham, NC Healthcare; 1997
Glaxo
HealthSource Chiropractic (Public Relations Agency of Record) Brand Awareness, Content, Media Relations, Public Relations, Strategic Marketing
The Interface Financial Group Media Relations, Public Relations
Jersey Mike's Subs
Kerr Drug (Agency of Record); Raleigh, NC Drug Store Chain; 2005
Lexington Furniture
Lowe's Corporation; North Wilkesboro, NC Home Improvement; 1996
Metal Supermarkets Franchising Group Digital, Franchise Development Campaigns, Marketing Communications, PR, Social Media
MYCO Medical
Nationwide Homes; Martinsville, VA Modular Homes; 1996
OpenWorks (Marketing Agency of Record) Brand Identity
Plus One Partners (Agency of Record)
Rosetta Stone
Senior Helpers
Southern Importers
Wachovia Bank

92 WEST
13504 Stevens St Ste C, Omaha, NE 68137
Tel.: (402) 237-8235
Fax: (402) 953-4395
E-Mail: information@92west.com
Web Site: www.92west.com

Year Founded: 2000

Agency Specializes In: Advertising, Brand Development & Integration, Content, Email, Internet/Web Design, Logo & Package Design, Print, Search Engine Optimization

Troy Kadavy *(Creative Dir)*
Jamie Kadavy *(Strategist-Digital Mktg)*

Accounts:
Carpet Cleaners
Integrative Dental Solutions
Omaha Directory
TH Construction

921 MEDIA INC
230 18th St NW, Atlanta, GA 30363
Tel.: (404) 951-6003
Web Site: www.921media.com

Year Founded: 2009

Agency Specializes In: Advertising, Brand Development & Integration, Content, Graphic Design, Internet/Web Design, Media Buying Services, Media Planning

Jenny Ford *(Exec Dir)*

Accounts:
Sierras House of Beauty

93 OCTANE
23 W Broad St Ste 302, Richmond, VA 23220
Tel.: (804) 643-8800
Fax: (804) 643-8900
E-Mail: info@93-octane.com
Web Site: www.93-octane.com

Employees: 8
Year Founded: 2002

Agency Specializes In: Direct Response Marketing, Direct-to-Consumer

John Lindner *(Owner & Dir-Creative)*
Linda Bott *(Acct Dir)*
Adam Smith *(Dir-Art)*
Jason Sullivan *(Dir-Art)*

Accounts:
Call Federal Credit Union
Comfort Systems USA
Lutheran Family Services of Virginia
Maymont
Medarva
Physicians for Peace
Robinson, Farmer, Cox
Stony Point Surgery Center

954DESIGN
2967 Ravenswood Rd Ste 5, Fort Lauderdale, FL 33312
Tel.: (954) 543-0411
E-Mail: contact@954design.com
Web Site: www.954design.com

Agency Specializes In: Advertising, Brand Development & Integration, Corporate Identity, Digital/Interactive, Email, Internet/Web Design, Package Design, Print, Search Engine Optimization

Laura Brill *(Owner & Designer)*

Accounts:
Ann Storck Center
Jorge Nation Foundation
Ted Gibson

97 DEGREES WEST
Barton Oaks Plaza IV, Austin, TX 78746
Tel.: (512) 473-2500
Fax: (512) 320-5422
Web Site: www.97dwest.com/

Employees: 8

Agency Specializes In: Advertising, Event Planning & Marketing

Vera Fischer *(Founder & Pres)*
Russ Leblanc *(Mng Dir)*

Accounts:
Agave
Airtricity
Balcones Resources
Clearcommerce User Group
Cuvee Coffee Roasting Co.; Spicewood, TX
Fiore
Giano Bikes
Mangum Builders
Mighty Brace E-Commerce, Integrated Marketing Campaign, Marketing Strategy, Media Planning, PR, Planning, Pricing, Social Media Strategy, Video Production, Website
Mirasol Lake Travis
OMNIBANK
United Heritage Credit Union; Austin, TX Creative Collateral, Messaging, New Positioning
Univar Inc.

A BIG CHIHUAHUA, INC.
PO Box 761113, San Antonio, TX 78245
Tel.: (210) 680-4129
E-Mail: info@bigchi.com
Web Site: www.bigchi.com

Year Founded: 1995

Agency Specializes In: Collateral, Digital/Interactive, Entertainment, Event Planning & Marketing, Graphic Design, Hispanic Market, Identity Marketing, Local Marketing, Media Buying Services, Media Planning, Print, Public Relations, Sales Promotion, Strategic Planning/Research

Esther Quiroz *(Gen Mgr)*
Ruben Cubillos *(Dir-Creative & Designer)*

Accounts:
Gabe Nieto

A. BROWN-OLMSTEAD ASSOCIATES
274 W Paces Ferry Rd, Atlanta, GA 30305
Tel.: (404) 659-0919
Fax: (404) 659-2711
E-Mail: amanda@newaboa.com
Web Site: www.newaboa.com/

Employees: 10
Year Founded: 1972

Agency Specializes In: Advertising, Content, Crisis Communications, Graphic Design, Investor Relations, Public Relations, Sales Promotion, Strategic Planning/Research

Amanda Brown-Olmstead *(Pres & CEO)*
Thomas Smith *(Sr Acct Mgr)*
Justin Wood *(Acct Exec)*
Joshua Feagan *(Jr Acct Exec)*

Accounts:
200 Peachtree
BRAE Rainwater Harvesting Systems
ClubDrive
Damballa, Inc.
Historic Fourth Ward Park Conservancy
HOK
My Mother's Clothes
New World

A DAY ADVERTISING
319 Portland Pl, Lititz, PA 17543
Tel.: (717) 945-6630
Fax: (717) 581-9193
E-Mail: info@adayadvertising.com
Web Site: www.adayadvertising.com

Agency Specializes In: Advertising, Corporate Identity, Internet/Web Design, Logo & Package Design, Market Research, Media Buying Services, Multimedia, Print

Annette Day *(Owner)*
Brian Heibel *(Sr Graphic Designer)*

Accounts:
Brenner Nissan
Delaney Honda

A. EICOFF & CO.

401 N Michigan Ave 4th Fl, Chicago, IL 60611-4212
Tel.: (312) 527-7183
Fax: (312) 527-7188
Toll Free: (800) 333-6605
E-Mail: cathy.watt@eicoff.com
Web Site: www.eicoff.com

Employees: 125
Year Founded: 1965

Agency Specializes In: Advertising, Broadcast, Direct Response Marketing, Sponsorship

Ronald L. Bliwas *(Chm)*
Bill McCabe *(Pres & CEO)*
Heather Lang *(Sr VP & Grp Dir-Media)*
Rob Schmidt *(VP & Mgmt Supvr)*
Matt Cote *(VP-Video Innovation)*
Bonnie Brunsell *(Dir-HR)*
Francie Gordon *(Dir-Media)*
Cathy Watt *(Asst Dir-HR)*
Nancy Schieber *(Supvr-Media)*
Julianne Gleason *(Media Buyer)*
Sean Bleizeffer *(Jr Media Buyer)*
Nina DiMaggio *(Sr Media Buyer)*
Katie Forrer *(Sr Media Buyer)*
Stephenie Mack *(Sr Media Buyer)*
Emily Pehl-Matthews *(Sr Media Buyer)*
Amie Smith *(Assoc Grp Dir-Media)*

Accounts:
Ameritrade, Inc.
Boardroom, Inc.
Bristol-Myers Squibb
Galderma Laboratories, Inc.
Honeywell
Hot Spring Spas
IBM
Jelmar
Novartis
Procter & Gamble
The Scooter Store
TD Ameritrade Holding Corporation
Tommie Copper Advertising Agency of Record
United Healthcare Group

A. LAVIN COMMUNICATIONS
8 Haven Ave Ste 223, New York, NY 10001
Tel.: (516) 944-4486
Fax: (516) 944-4487
E-Mail: andrew@alavin.com
Web Site: www.alavin.com

Employees: 4

Agency Specializes In: Brand Development & Integration, Broadcast, Communications, Event Planning & Marketing, Exhibit/Trade Shows, Financial, Health Care Services, Information Technology, Media Relations, Media Training

Andrew R. Lavin *(Pres)*

Accounts:
Eikos Nano
Fairy Tales Hair Care
Henry Schein
Intergis Logistics
Photo Phiddle
Vericom Technologies

A PARTNERSHIP
307 Fifth Ave, New York, NY 10016
Tel.: (212) 685-8388
Fax: (212) 685-8188
E-Mail: APNY@apartnership.com
Web Site: www.apartnership.com

Employees: 35
Year Founded: 1999

Agency Specializes In: Asian Market

Approx. Annual Billings: $52,141,000

Jeannie Yuen *(Founder, Pres & CEO)*
Edward Chang *(VP & Grp Dir)*
Steve Lam *(VP & Dir-Creative)*
Vivian Chu *(Dir-Art)*

Accounts:
Bank of America
The California Department of Health (Tobacco Control Section)
Nationwide Insurance
United States Postal Service

A TO Z COMMUNICATIONS, INC
960 Penn Ave 9th Fl, Pittsburgh, PA 15222
Tel.: (412) 471-4160
Fax: (412) 471-4169
E-Mail: info@atozcommunications.com
Web Site: www.atozcommunications.com

Year Founded: 1998

Agency Specializes In: Brand Development & Integration, Digital/Interactive, Internet/Web Design, Media Buying Services, Print

Alan Boarts *(Pres)*

Accounts:
New-Gateway Rehabilitation Center

A WORK OF ART INC.
1621 NW 102nd Way, Coral Springs, FL 33071
Tel.: (954) 675-3062
Fax: (954) 341-6289
Web Site: www.awoa.com

Employees: 13

Agency Specializes In: Advertising, Collateral, Graphic Design, Health Care Services, Internet/Web Design, Media Buying Services, Public Relations, Recruitment

David Nagle *(Pres & Dir-Creative)*

Accounts:
Gotham Healthcare Staffing
New York Presbyterian Home Care Agency
New York Presbyterian Hospital

A360 DESIGN
52837 Karon Dr, Macomb, MI 48042
Tel.: (586) 786-1934
Web Site: www.a360design.com

Agency Specializes In: Advertising, Brand Development & Integration, Corporate Identity, Digital/Interactive, Internet/Web Design, Print, Strategic Planning/Research

John Kukawinski *(Principal)*

Accounts:
Custom Data Solutions, Inc.

AAI (ADVERTISING ASSOCIATES INTERNATIONAL)
65 Sprague St, Boston, MA 02136
Tel.: (508) 544-1250
Fax: (508) 544-1253
Toll Free: (877) 866-8500
E-Mail: info@aai-agency.com
Web Site: www.aai-agency.com

Employees: 12
Year Founded: 1965

Agency Specializes In: Advertising, Advertising Specialties, Brand Development & Integration, Broadcast, Business Publications, Business-To-Business, Collateral, Commercial Photography, Communications, Consulting, Consumer Marketing, Consumer Publications, Corporate Identity, Direct Response Marketing, Engineering, Event Planning & Marketing, Exhibit/Trade Shows, Financial, Government/Political, Graphic Design, Health Care Services, High Technology, Industrial, Information Technology, Internet/Web Design, Logo & Package Design, Magazines, Media Buying Services, Medical Products, Newspaper, Newspapers & Magazines, Outdoor, Pharmaceutical, Point of Purchase, Print, Production, Public Relations, Publicity/Promotions, Radio, Recruitment, Retail, Sales Promotion, Strategic Planning/Research, T.V., Technical Advertising, Trade & Consumer Magazines

A. Richard Hersum *(Owner)*
Ina Kamenz *(CIO & Sr VP)*
Julie Medjanis *(Treas)*
Mark Hersum *(Exec VP)*

Accounts:
AMRC; Weston, MA Political Organization
Andover Surgery Center; Andover, MA
The Healey Law Firm; Needham, MA
Kelsen Bisca; Melville, NY Food Products
Massachusetts Eye Research & Surgery Institute; Cambridge, MA Ophthalmology Service
Novotechnik USA Inc.; Marlboro, MA Position Transducers
Sleepmed Digitrace; Danvers, MA
Solos Endoscopy; Easton, MA
Sunnex; Waltham, MA Medical & Industrial Lighting
United Medical Systems; Westborough, MA Medical Diagnostic Services; 1998
The Valley Patriot; North Andover, MA Regional Newspaper

AARS & WELLS, INC.
2100 Commerce St, Dallas, TX 76201
Tel.: (214) 446-0996
Fax: (214) 446-0990
Web Site: www.aarswells.com

Agency Specializes In: Advertising, Broadcast, Digital/Interactive, Direct Response Marketing, E-Commerce, Graphic Design, Media Buying Services, Outdoor, Print

Alex Wells *(Pres)*
Jason Hershey *(Sr Dir-Art)*
Justin McGuffin *(Dir-Creative)*
Stephen Nardone *(Acct Mgr)*
Kayla Curry *(Acct Coord)*
Candice Kuzov *(Sr Developer-Interactive)*

Accounts:
Southern Methodist University
Whitley Penn, LLP.

AASMAN DESIGN INC.
201-402 Hansen St, Whitehorse, YT Y1A 1Y8 Canada
Tel.: (867) 668-5248
Fax: (867) 633-6959
E-Mail: info@aasman.ca
Web Site: www.aasman.ca

Employees: 14
Year Founded: 1989

Agency Specializes In: Advertising, Bilingual Market, Corporate Identity, Digital/Interactive, Package Design, Planning & Consultation, Point of Purchase

Al Aasman *(Mng Dir-Aasman Brand Comm)*

Corey Bradbury *(Dir-Client Strategies)*
Krysten Johnson *(Project Mgr & Strategist-Media)*

Accounts:
Quiniscoe Homes
Whitehorse Concerts

Branches

Aasman Brand Communications
(Formerly Aasman Interactive)
402 Hanson St 2nd Fl, Whitehorse, YT Y1A 1Y8 Canada
Tel.: (867) 668-5248
Fax: (867) 633-6959
E-Mail: info@aasman.ca
Web Site: aasman.ca/

Employees: 14

Agency Specializes In: Digital/Interactive

Al Aasman *(Mng Dir)*
Zeke Aasman *(Dir-Creative Strategies)*
Corey Bradbury *(Dir-Client Strategies)*
Neil Stephen *(Acct Mgr)*
Krysten Johnson *(Project Mgr & Strategist-Media)*
Eleanor Rosenberg *(Strategist-Creative)*

Accounts:
Don't Be Sick
Plunge

A.B. DATA, LTD.
600 AB Data Dr, Milwaukee, WI 53217-2645
Tel.: (414) 540-5000
Fax: (414) 961-6410
E-Mail: consulting@abdata.com
Web Site: www.abdata.com

E-Mail for Key Personnel:
President: barbit@abdata.com

Employees: 100
Year Founded: 1980

National Agency Associations: DMA

Agency Specializes In: Direct Response Marketing, E-Commerce, Faith Based, Internet/Web Design, Legal Services, Pets , Print

Approx. Annual Billings: $23,000,000

Breakdown of Gross Billings by Media: Bus. Publs.: $2,000,000; Collateral: $1,000,000; Consumer Publs.: $1,000,000; D.M.: $12,000,000; E-Commerce: $1,000,000; Internet Adv.: $1,000,000; Mags.: $1,000,000; Newsp.: $1,000,000; Other: $2,000,000; Worldwide Web Sites: $1,000,000

Joe Manes *(Partner & Sr VP)*
Bruce Arbit *(Co-Mng Dir)*
Charles Pruitt *(Co-Mng Dir)*
Alan Wichtoski *(CFO & VP)*
Jerry Benjamin *(Principal)*
Marie Dullea-Prentice *(VP)*
Meredith Feldman *(VP-Consulting)*
Eric J. Miller *(VP-Case Mgmt)*
Linda V. Young *(VP-Media)*

Accounts:
American Foundation for the Blind
American Friends of Ben Gurion University; New York, NY University Support
American Jewish Committee Non-Profit; 1998
American Jewish Congress; New York, NY Non-Profit Organization
American Society for Yad Vashem
Animal Legal Defense Fund
Children's Defense Fund Non-Profit
Christopher and Dana Reeve Foundation
Drug Policy Alliance
Union of Councils for Soviet Jews; Washington, DC Non-Profit Organization
Wealthy Jewish Donors

Branch

A.B. Data, Ltd.
1808 Swann St NW, Washington, DC 20009-5505
Tel.: (202) 462-2040
Fax: (202) 462-2085
E-Mail: consulting@abdata.com
Web Site: www.abdata.com

Employees: 5
Year Founded: 1980

National Agency Associations: DMA

Agency Specializes In: Direct Response Marketing, Government/Political

Joe Manes *(Partner & Sr VP)*
Charles Pruitt *(Co-Mng Dir)*
Thomas Glenn *(Pres-Class Action Admin)*
Marie Dullea-Prentice *(VP)*
Jeff Mallach *(VP)*
Linda Young *(VP-Media)*
Anike Tansey *(Dir-Bus Dev)*
Angela Stoutenburgh *(Acct Mgr-Digital Mktg-ABD Direct)*
Angela Jackson *(Acct Exec-ABD Direct)*
Erin Lingsweiler *(Acct Exec-ABD Direct)*

AB+C
(Formerly Aloysius Butler & Clark)
819 N. Washington St, Wilmington, DE 19801
Tel.: (302) 655-1552
Fax: (302) 655-3105
Toll Free: (800) 848-1552
E-Mail: ppomeroy@a-b-c.com
Web Site: www.a-b-c.com

Employees: 70
Year Founded: 1971

National Agency Associations: TAAN

Agency Specializes In: Business-To-Business, Cable T.V., Collateral, Communications, Consulting, Consumer Marketing, Consumer Publications, Corporate Identity, Direct Response Marketing, E-Commerce, Electronic Media, Entertainment, Environmental, Event Planning & Marketing, Exhibit/Trade Shows, Financial, Government/Political, Health Care Services, High Technology, Industrial, Information Technology, Internet/Web Design, Investor Relations, Logo & Package Design, Media Buying Services, Medical Products, Merchandising, New Product Development, Newspaper, Newspapers & Magazines, Outdoor, Pharmaceutical, Planning & Consultation, Point of Purchase, Public Relations, Publicity/Promotions, Radio, Recruitment, Seniors' Market, Strategic Planning/Research, Technical Advertising, Trade & Consumer Magazines, Transportation, Travel & Tourism

John C. Hawkins *(Pres & CEO)*
Tom McGivney *(Mng Partner & Exec Dir-Creative)*
Linda Shopa *(Mng Partner)*
David Brond *(VP & Dir-Acct Svcs)*
Emory Au *(Sr Dir-Art)*
Michael English *(Sr Dir-Interactive Art)*
Scott Bille *(Dir-Interactive)*
Louis Brandsdorfer *(Dir-Creative)*
Joe Michael Dawson *(Dir-Creative)*
John Orr *(Dir-PR)*
Lee Ann Qualls *(Dir-Media)*
Tony Ross *(Dir-Creative Svcs)*
Maria Stearns *(Dir-Healthcare Team)*
Pamela Stevenson *(Dir-Production)*
Amy Garrett *(Sr Mgr-Property)*
Alice Clark *(Mgr-Accounts Payable)*
Suzanne Fields *(Mgr-Traffic)*
Coley DuPont *(Sr Acct Supvr)*
Linda Schemmer *(Sr Acct Supvr)*
Craig Brown *(Acct Supvr)*
Dave Lewandowski *(Acct Supvr-PR)*
Lana O'Hollaren *(Acct Supvr)*
Alex Parkowski *(Acct Supvr)*
Stacy Speicher *(Acct Supvr)*
John Sammons, III *(Supvr-Media)*
Courtney Rossi *(Specialist-HR)*
Jason Cockerham *(Designer-User Experience)*

Accounts:
Abington Memorial Hospital; Abington, PA
American Nurses Association Marketing, Public Relations
Ametek
Armstrong World Industries, Inc.
AtlantiCare Health System
Carolinas Health System
Cecil County Health Department Creative, Media, Public Relations, Social Media, Website
Choose Health Delaware
Continuum Health Partners Child & Family Institute, Diabetes Institute, Social Media Campaign
Delaware Council on Gambling Problems Creative Services, Paid Media, Public Awareness, Public Relations, Social Media, Website Development
Delaware Division of Public Health
Delaware Office of Highway Safety
F&M Trust Digital Media, Social Media
Geisinger Health System; Danville, PA
Good Shepherd Penn Partners
Holy Name Medical Center
IPC Recruitment Marketing
Klein
LaFarge North America
MedStar Health
Mitsubishi Fuso Truck of America, Inc.
Multiple Sclerosis Association of America (Marketing & Advertising Agency of Record)
Netherlands Foreign Investment Agency
Newark Natural Foods (Agency of Record)
Northshore Physicians Group
Sandy Spring Bancorp
Stamford Health (Agency of Record)
Star Roses and Plants/Conard-Pyle
Susquehanna Bank
UMDNJ-Robert Wood Johnson
New-University of Virginia Medical Center Digital, Marketing
W. L. Gore & Associates
West Virginia University Medical Center
Zip Code Wilmington Computer Coding School, Digital Advertising, Media Relations

Divisions

Ab+c
29 E Main St Ste R, Bloomsburg, PA 17815
Tel.: (302) 655-1552
Fax: (302) 655-3105
Toll Free: (800) 848-1552
Web Site: www.a-b-c.com

Agency Specializes In: Advertising, Brand Development & Integration, Collateral, Event Planning & Marketing, Internet/Web Design, Media Buying Services, Media Planning, Public Relations, Social Media, Strategic Planning/Research

Todd Cole *(Specialist-Mktg)*

Accounts:
GoHealth Urgent Care
Synchrogenix
University of Colorado Health

AB+C
(Formerly Aloysius Butler & Clark)
1429 Walnut St, Philadelphia, PA 19102

Tel.: (215) 923-9600
Fax: (215) 351-4298
Web Site: www.a-b-c.com

E-Mail for Key Personnel:
Creative Dir.: lbrandsdorfer@a-b-c.com

Employees: 40
Year Founded: 1928

Agency Specializes In: Advertising, Agriculture, Automotive, Brand Development & Integration, Broadcast, Business Publications, Business-To-Business, Cable T.V., Co-op Advertising, Collateral, Communications, Consulting, Consumer Marketing, Consumer Publications, Corporate Identity, Direct Response Marketing, Event Planning & Marketing, Financial, Graphic Design, High Technology, Industrial, Internet/Web Design, Legal Services, Magazines, Media Buying Services, Merchandising, Newspaper, Newspapers & Magazines, Pharmaceutical, Planning & Consultation, Print, Production, Public Relations, Publicity/Promotions, Radio, Recruitment, Sales Promotion, Strategic Planning/Research, Technical Advertising, Trade & Consumer Magazines, Transportation, Yellow Pages Advertising

Steve Merino *(Mng Dir-Philadelphia)*
Jonathan Mathers *(Sr Dir-Art)*
Lou Brandsdorfer *(Dir-Creative)*
Cheryl Bailey *(Office Mgr)*
Craig Brown *(Acct Supvr)*
Emily Desimone *(Coord-Media)*
Paul Pomeroy *(Mng Partner & Dir-Mktg)*

Accounts:
American Plastics Council; 2001
Armstrong World Industries; 1985
Mitsubishi Fuso Truck of America; 1996
Pennoni Associates Inc Marketing Communications
Sunoco; 2007

ABBEY, MECCA & COMPANY
95 Perry St, Buffalo, NY 14203
Tel.: (716) 633-1218
Fax: (716) 626-0244
E-Mail: ignite@abbeymecca.com
Web Site: www.abbeymecca.com

E-Mail for Key Personnel:
President: daniel.mecca@abbeymecca.com

Employees: 7
Year Founded: 1969

National Agency Associations: AAF

Agency Specializes In: Advertising, Automotive, Brand Development & Integration, Cable T.V., Collateral, Communications, Corporate Identity, Education, Engineering, Event Planning & Marketing, Financial, Graphic Design, Health Care Services, Legal Services, Media Buying Services, Out-of-Home Media, Outdoor, Public Relations, Restaurant, Seniors' Market

Approx. Annual Billings: $5,000,000 (Capitalized)

Daniel Mecca *(Pres)*
Melissa Keith *(Media Buyer)*

Accounts:
New-A.W. Miller Technical Sales Brand Strategy, Logo Design, Marketing, Miller 3D Printing, Social Media
Canisius College
Curtis
Hot Hands
Markin
Mid City Office Furniture

ABC (ADVERTISING BUSINESS CONSULTANTS)
1334 Lincoln Ave, San Jose, CA 95125
Tel.: (408) 298-0124
Fax: (408) 298-0125
E-Mail: rog@abcsanjose.com
Web Site: www.abcsanjose.com

Employees: 2

Agency Specializes In: Automotive, Print, Radio, Retail, T.V.

Roger Henson *(CEO)*
Ed Attanasio *(Partner)*
Paul Lim *(Program Mgr-Digital Media)*

Accounts:
AAMCO
All About Backyards
All Seasons Remodeling
Allison BMW
Anaheim Mitsubishi
Bathroom Doctor
Capitol Mitsubishi
Cellular Image
Central Valley Marine
Design 101
Helm
Huntington Beach Ford
Los Gatos Hummer
Puente Hills Mitsubishi
Stevens Creek Mitsubishi
Stevens Creek Subaru

ABC CREATIVE GROUP
430 E Genesee St Ste 203, Syracuse, NY 13202
Tel.: (315) 471-1002
Fax: (315) 471-2240
Toll Free: (800) 293-1002
E-Mail: info@abcideabased.com
Web Site: www.abcideabased.com

Employees: 10

Agency Specializes In: Advertising, Brand Development & Integration, Broadcast, Consulting, Corporate Identity, Digital/Interactive, Email, Exhibit/Trade Shows, Graphic Design, Internet/Web Design, Logo & Package Design, Media Planning, Multimedia, Outdoor, Public Relations, Publishing, Radio, T.V.

Travis Bort *(Owner & Dir-Creative)*
Mike Haines *(Sr Dir-Art)*
Carolynn Giordano *(Dir-Art)*
Scott Kraushaar *(Dir-Video Production)*
Jamie Leszczynski *(Sr Acct Mgr)*
Trisha Stethers *(Mgr-Traffic)*
Sean Faulkner *(Acct Exec)*

Accounts:
CrestHill Suites
Dairylea Cooperative Inc. (Agency of Record)
KME Kovatch
Madison County Tourism
OCNB
Van Duyn Home & Hospital

ABELSON-TAYLOR, INC.
33 W Monroe St, Chicago, IL 60603
Tel.: (312) 894-5500
Fax: (312) 894-5526
E-Mail: info@abelsontaylor.com
Web Site: www.abelsontaylor.com

E-Mail for Key Personnel:
President: dtaylor@abelsontaylor.com

Employees: 400
Year Founded: 1981

National Agency Associations: 4A's

Agency Specializes In: Advertising, Advertising Specialties, Brand Development & Integration, Broadcast, Collateral, Communications, Consumer Goods, Consumer Marketing, Content, Digital/Interactive, Direct Response Marketing, Direct-to-Consumer, Health Care Services, Identity Marketing, Integrated Marketing, Internet/Web Design, Logo & Package Design, Market Research, Medical Products, Men's Market, Multimedia, Over-50 Market, Package Design, Pharmaceutical, Product Placement, Production (Ad, Film, Broadcast), Social Media, Sponsorship, Trade & Consumer Magazines, Women's Market

Breakdown of Gross Billings by Media: Brdcst.: 10%; Cable T.V.: 5%; Consumer Publs.: 5%; Mags.: 20%; Other: 10%; Sls. Promo.: 40%; Video Brochures: 10%

Dale Taylor *(CEO)*
Keith Sternlund *(CFO)*
Stephen Neale *(Sr VP & Exec Dir-Creative)*
Noah Lowenthal *(VP & Grp Dir-Creative)*
Laura Bartmess *(VP & Acct Dir)*
Eric Densmore *(VP & Acct Dir)*
Mark Finn *(VP & Acct Dir)*
Beverly Wright *(VP & Acct Dir)*
Josh Vizek *(VP & Dir-Creative)*
Beth Hall *(VP-Support Svcs)*
Allen Mills *(VP)*
Emily Tower *(VP-Digital Strategy)*
Sarah Alexander *(Sr Dir-Art & Digital)*
Yuliya Chepurnaya *(Sr Dir-Art)*
Todd Martin *(Sr Dir-Art)*
Eric Voigt *(Sr Dir-Art)*
Nadine Fabish *(Acct Dir)*
Matt Shepley *(Producer-Brdcst)*
Paul Tursky *(Acct Dir)*
Rick Conrad *(Dir-Creative)*
Robert T. Enos *(Dir-Media)*
Marita Gomez *(Dir-Comm)*
Jodi Miller *(Dir-Art & Talent Pur)*
Kevin Tran *(Dir-Art)*
Jody Van Swearingen *(Dir-Creative)*
Ayubu Azizi *(Assoc Dir-Creative)*
Jane Betz *(Assoc Dir-Creative)*
Rose Marie Cassey *(Assoc Dir-Creative)*
Jonathan Davila *(Assoc Dir-Creative)*
Janet Kleve *(Assoc Dir-Creative)*
Leo Kosir *(Assoc Dir-Creative, Digital & Art)*
Matt Monnin *(Assoc Dir-Project Mgmt)*
Marissa Ori *(Assoc Dir-Creative)*
Joe Bolokowicz *(Sr Mgr-Print Production)*
Dave Schafer *(Mgr-Digital Production)*
Katerina Steele *(Mgr-New Bus Dev)*
Hillary Armstrong *(Sr Acct Supvr)*
Sophie De Geest *(Acct Supvr)*
Jason Gloye *(Acct Supvr)*
Kate Johnson *(Acct Supvr)*
Ashley Schwartz *(Acct Supvr)*
Ronnie Sun *(Supvr-Media)*
Steve Szczygiel *(Supvr-IT SD)*
Bill Tarlin *(Supvr-Art Production)*
Claudia Kanaszyc *(Sr Acct Exec)*
Nina Prybula *(Sr Acct Exec)*
Cathy Saia *(Sr Acct Exec)*
Ann Slingerland *(Sr Acct Exec)*
Emily Brown *(Acct Exec)*
Orlando Diaz *(Sr Copywriter-Digital)*
Belise Rutagengwa *(Acct Exec)*
Sarah Lasker *(Coord-Traffic)*
Rich Campbell *(Assoc Acct Dir)*
Rachel Keller *(Sr Media Planner)*

Accounts:
Abbott Laboratories Reductil, Zemplar; 1999
Abbott Nutrition
Alexion Pharmaceuticals
Allergan, Inc.
Amgen Canada
Asatellas Corporation
Biogen Avonex; 2001
Eisai Corporation Aloxi; 2002
Eisai Inc.

Eli Lilly & Amlyin Pharmaceuticals (Global Branding) Actos/Glustin, PKC-B Inhibitor
Forest Laboratories
Gilead Science Viread & Emtriva Food Dosing Combination; 2003
GlaxoSmithKline
Kapidex Proton Pump Inhibitor
OSI Pharmaceuticals
Roche
Sanko Pharma
Shire US Pentasa; 2002
Takeda North America Actos; 1998
Valeant Pharmaceuticals International
Viropharma

ABERRO CREATIVE

2007 Austin St, Midland, MI 48642
Tel.: (989) 600-6850
Web Site: www.aberrocreative.com

Year Founded: 2013

Agency Specializes In: Advertising, Event Planning & Marketing, Graphic Design, Internet/Web Design, Logo & Package Design, Social Media

Steve Cronk *(Co-Founder & Partner)*
Dustin Neumeyer *(Co-Founder & Partner)*

Accounts:
Caveman Bobs Paleo Sauces

ABLE&CO

(Formerly Red House Group Inc)
8801 Fast Park Dr Ste 115, Raleigh, NC 27617
Tel.: (919) 322-0528
Fax: (919) 870-9045
E-Mail: info@theableagency.com
Web Site: theableagency.com

Year Founded: 2008

Agency Specializes In: Advertising, Brand Development & Integration, Broadcast, Collateral, Graphic Design, Internet/Web Design, Logo & Package Design, Radio, Social Media, T.V.

Jenny Taylor *(Owner & Pres)*
Holly Ware *(VP-Ops)*
Hugh Firebaugh *(Dir-Creative)*
Megan Gordon *(Dir-Art)*
Marianne Russolesi *(Acct Exec)*
Gary Cantrell *(Sr Graphic Designer)*
Frances Ward-simmons *(Sr Designer)*

Accounts:
Quest Advisors

ABOVE PROMOTIONS COMPANY

15419 Plantation Oaks Dr, Tampa, FL 33647
Tel.: (813) 383-1914
E-Mail: contactus@abovepromotions.com
Web Site: www.abovepromotions.com

Employees: 5
Year Founded: 2004

Agency Specializes In: Alternative Advertising, Branded Entertainment, Business Publications, Cable T.V., Consumer Publications, Digital/Interactive, Email, Exhibit/Trade Shows, Experience Design, Guerilla Marketing, In-Store Advertising, Local Marketing, Magazines, Mobile Marketing, Multimedia, Newspaper, Newspapers & Magazines, Outdoor, Paid Searches, Print, Product Placement, Production, Promotions, Publishing, Search Engine Optimization, Shopper Marketing, Social Media, Sponsorship, Sweepstakes, Syndication, T.V., Viral/Buzz/Word of Mouth, Web (Banner Ads, Pop-ups, etc.)

Ebony Grimsley *(Dir-Creative & Comm)*

Accounts:
National Lemonade Day - Tampa Bay Powered By Google for Entrepreneurs

ABOVENATIONMEDIA

401 Park Ave S, New York, NY 10016
Tel.: (917) 841-0443
Web Site: www.abovenationmedia.com/

Employees: 41
Year Founded: 2013

Agency Specializes In: Advertising, Advertising Specialties, Affiliate Marketing, Automotive, Broadcast, Cable T.V., Communications, Consumer Goods, Cosmetics, Digital/Interactive, Direct Response Marketing, Education, Electronics, Entertainment, Fashion/Apparel, Financial, Food Service, Government/Political, Health Care Services, Hospitality, Integrated Marketing, Internet/Web Design, Legal Services, Local Marketing, Magazines, Market Research, Media Buying Services, Media Planning, Medical Products, Multimedia, New Technologies, Newspaper, Newspapers & Magazines, Out-of-Home Media, Outdoor, Paid Searches, Pharmaceutical, Planning & Consultation, Print, Restaurant, Retail, Search Engine Optimization, Shopper Marketing, Social Marketing/Nonprofit, Social Media, Sports Market, Strategic Planning/Research, T.V., Technical Advertising, Travel & Tourism, Viral/Buzz/Word of Mouth

Approx. Annual Billings: $50,000,000

John Lee *(Pres)*

Accounts:
BioMarin Kuvan; 2014
Dynacraft Bikes; 2014
Nutrisystem Numi by Nutrisystem; 2014
Pearson Higher Education; 2014
PharmaDerm Kerydin; 2014
Tierney Agency Consulting; 2015

ABOVEWATER PUBLIC RELATIONS & MARKETING LLC

107 Madison Dr, Naples, FL 34110
Tel.: (239) 596-9149
Web Site: www.abovewater.com

Agency Specializes In: Advertising, Broadcast, Collateral, Crisis Communications, Event Planning & Marketing, Media Relations, Media Training, Print, Public Relations, Social Media

Mary Jane Kolassa *(Sr VP)*

Accounts:
American Association for Nude Recreation

ABRA MARKETING, INC.

555 5th St Ste 300D, Santa Rosa, CA 95401
Tel.: (530) 246-8000
Web Site: www.abramarketing.com

Year Founded: 1999

Agency Specializes In: Advertising, Brand Development & Integration, Collateral, Internet/Web Design, Media Planning, Outdoor, Print, Radio, Social Media, T.V.

Kurt Hoffmann *(Principal & Mktg Dir)*

Accounts:
Weed Ales

ABRAZO MULTICULTURAL MARKETING

229 E Wisconsin Ave Ste 800, Milwaukee, WI 53202
Tel.: (414) 220-9800
Fax: (414) 220-9802
E-Mail: info@abrazomarketing.com
Web Site: www.abrazomarketing.com

Agency Specializes In: Advertising, Brand Development & Integration, Public Relations, Strategic Planning/Research

Nancy Hernandez *(Founder & Pres)*

Accounts:
Milwaukee Brewers Baseball Club, Inc.

ABRIALS & PARTNERS

1170 Cameron St, Alexandria, VA 22314
Tel.: (703) 548-2570
Fax: (703) 548-3788
E-Mail: mabrials@adguys.com
Web Site: www.adguys.com

Employees: 20
Year Founded: 1995

Agency Specializes In: Advertising, Brand Development & Integration, Broadcast, Business Publications, Business-To-Business, Cable T.V., Co-op Advertising, Collateral, Communications, Consulting, Consumer Marketing, Consumer Publications, Corporate Identity, Digital/Interactive, Direct Response Marketing, E-Commerce, Education, Electronic Media, Entertainment, Environmental, Event Planning & Marketing, Exhibit/Trade Shows, Government/Political, Graphic Design, High Technology, Information Technology, Internet/Web Design, Logo & Package Design, Magazines, Media Buying Services, Merchandising, New Product Development, Newspaper, Newspapers & Magazines, Out-of-Home Media, Outdoor, Over-50 Market, Planning & Consultation, Point of Purchase, Point of Sale, Print, Production, Public Relations, Publicity/Promotions, Radio, Real Estate, Recruitment, Restaurant, Retail, Sales Promotion, Strategic Planning/Research, Teen Market, Trade & Consumer Magazines, Transportation, Travel & Tourism, Yellow Pages Advertising

Revenue: $3,000,000

Mark Abrials *(CMO & Dir-Creative)*
Jeff D'Andrea *(Dir-Strategic Design)*
Jay Decker *(Dir-Tech)*
Christian Starr *(Assoc Dir-Creative)*

Accounts:
AI; Washington, DC
CSC Holdings, LLC
Disney
Feld Entertainment; Tyson's Corner, VA Disney on Ice, Ringling Brothers & Barnum & Bailey Circus; 2000
General Dynamics Advanced Information Systems
Japan Railways
Kingsley-Bate; Manassas, VA Outdoor Teak Furniture
McCormick & Company Gourmet Spices
Microsoft; Redmond, WA Server; 1997
The Motley Fool
National Geographic
Professional Risk Management Services

ABSTRACT EDGE

455 Broadway 4th Fl, New York, NY 10013
Tel.: (212) 352-9311
Fax: (212) 952-9498
E-Mail: info@abstractedge.com
Web Site: www.abstractedge.com

Agency Specializes In: Digital/Interactive, Internet/Web Design, Planning & Consultation

Scott Paley *(Pres & Sr Strategist-Mktg)*

Accounts:
American Legacy
Discover
Loews Hotels
Mansfield Hotel
Marriott
Vera Wang

ABZ CREATIVE PARTNERS

1300 S Mint St Ste 100, Charlotte, NC 28203
Tel.: (704) 374-1072
Fax: (704) 374-1075
E-Mail: info@abzcreative.com
Web Site: abzcreativepartners.com

Employees: 15
Year Founded: 1979

Agency Specializes In: Bilingual Market, Collateral, Consumer Marketing, Consumer Publications, Custom Publishing, Digital/Interactive, Direct Response Marketing, Direct-to-Consumer, Email, Exhibit/Trade Shows, Experience Design, Faith Based, High Technology, International, Local Marketing, Magazines, Men's Market, Mobile Marketing, Multimedia, Newspaper, Newspapers & Magazines, Over-50 Market, Paid Searches, Point of Purchase, Point of Sale, Print, Product Placement, Production (Print), Promotions, Publishing, Radio, Search Engine Optimization, Seniors' Market, Social Media, T.V., Viral/Buzz/Word of Mouth, Web (Banner Ads, Pop-ups, etc.), Women's Market

Stacy Carter *(Dir-Creative)*
Elizabeth Engle *(Sr Acct Mgr, Sr Writer & Strategist)*
Carrie Snyder *(Acct Mgr)*
Preston Smith *(Mgr-Client Strategy)*
Brittany Sanges *(Designer-Traditional & Digital)*
Gwen Saunders *(Designer-Interactive)*
Katie Oliver *(Acct Coord)*

Accounts:
A Child's Place
Catalent Pharma Solutions
Communities in Schools
Novant Health
PBI Performance Products
SPE Thermoforming Division
The Urban Ministry Center
WFAE

ACART COMMUNICATIONS, INC.

171 Nepean St Ste 600, Ottawa, ON K2P 0B4 Canada
Tel.: (613) 230-7944
Fax: (613) 232-5980
E-Mail: results@acart.com
Web Site: www.acart.com

Employees: 45
Year Founded: 1976

Agency Specializes In: Advertising

Al Albania *(Owner)*
John Westbrook *(VP-Client Svcs)*
John Staresinic *(Sr Dir-Creative)*
Sue McKinney *(Dir-Consumer Mktg)*
Tom Megginson *(Dir-Creative)*
Vernon Lai *(Assoc Dir-Creative)*
Tania Calverley *(Acct Mgr)*

Accounts:
AECL
BIOTALENT
CAA
CANDU
changetheconversation.ca
FCAC
Halifax Bus Campaign: "Do it on the bus", Metro Transit
HRSDC
Jane Goodall Institute of Canada
TSB
VIA Rail Canada
York Region Transit

ACCELERATOR ADVERTISING INC.

399 Venture Dr Ste A, Lewis Center, OH 43035
Tel.: (614) 785-4345
Fax: (614) 785-4346
E-Mail: results@acceleratorinc.biz
Web Site: www.acceleratorinc.biz

E-Mail for Key Personnel:
Media Dir.: results@acceleratorinc.biz
Production Mgr.: results@acceleratorinc.biz
Public Relations: results@acceleratorinc.biz

Employees: 8
Year Founded: 1997

Agency Specializes In: Advertising, Advertising Specialties, Automotive, Brand Development & Integration, Broadcast, Business Publications, Business-To-Business, Cable T.V., Children's Market, Co-op Advertising, Collateral, Commercial Photography, Communications, Consulting, Consumer Marketing, Consumer Publications, Corporate Communications, Corporate Identity, Digital/Interactive, Direct Response Marketing, E-Commerce, Education, Electronic Media, Engineering, Entertainment, Environmental, Event Planning & Marketing, Exhibit/Trade Shows, Financial, Food Service, Gay & Lesbian Market, Government/Political, Graphic Design, Health Care Services, High Technology, In-Store Advertising, Industrial, Infomercials, Information Technology, Internet/Web Design, Investor Relations, Legal Services, Leisure, Local Marketing, Logo & Package Design, Magazines, Media Buying Services, Medical Products, Merchandising, Multimedia, New Product Development, Newspapers & Magazines, Out-of-Home Media, Outdoor, Pharmaceutical, Planning & Consultation, Point of Purchase, Point of Sale, Print, Production, Public Relations, Publicity/Promotions, Radio, Real Estate, Recruitment, Restaurant, Retail, Sales Promotion, Sports Market, Strategic Planning/Research, T.V., Technical Advertising, Teen Market, Trade & Consumer Magazines, Transportation, Travel & Tourism, Yellow Pages Advertising

Approx. Annual Billings: $2,000,000

Breakdown of Gross Billings by Media: Fees: $1,400,000; In-Store Adv.: $600,000

Marc Obregon *(Owner, Founder & Pres)*

Accounts:
American Municipal Power of Ohio
Briggs & Stratton Corporation of WI
Chemical Abstract Service
Hoover
Step2
White Castle System, Inc.

ACCESS ADVERTISING + PR

(Formerly Access)
701 Patterson Ave SW, Roanoke, VA 24016
Tel.: (540) 344-8499
Fax: (540) 344-4079
E-Mail: creative@visitaccess.com
Web Site: www.visitaccess.com

Employees: 14
Year Founded: 1996

Agency Specializes In: Advertising, Brand Development & Integration, Collateral, Corporate Identity, Direct Response Marketing, Electronic Media, Event Planning & Marketing, Exhibit/Trade Shows, Graphic Design, Internet/Web Design, Logo & Package Design, Public Relations, Publicity/Promotions, Strategic Planning/Research

Todd Marcum *(Pres & Copywriter)*
Tony Pearman *(CEO & Chief Creative Officer)*
Jerry Dunnavant *(VP-Mktg Strategy)*
Gary Gilmore *(Dir-Creative-Interactive)*
Rachel Spencer *(Dir-Res)*
Misty Smith-Klein *(Acct Exec)*

Accounts:
Blue Ridge Tourism Brand Awareness
Certified Medical Representatives Institute
Guertin Brothers
Lexington & Rockbridge Tourism Development; Lexington, KY; 2005
Optical Cable Corporation
Roanoke College Capital Campaign
Roanoke Valley YMCA
TMEIC GE
Virginia Tech

ACCESS COMMUNICATIONS

101 Howard St 2nd Fl, San Francisco, CA 94105
Tel.: (415) 904-7070
Fax: (415) 904-7055
E-Mail: sf@accesspr.com
Web Site: www.accesspr.com

Year Founded: 1991

Agency Specializes In: Social Media, Sponsorship, Strategic Planning/Research

Susan G. Butenhoff *(CEO)*
Matthew Afflixio *(Sr VP)*
Cori Barrett *(Sr VP)*
Lindsay Scalisi *(Sr VP)*
Nancy Blair *(VP-Content)*
Jennifer Garcia *(VP)*
Cara Jacobson *(VP)*
Trevor Jonas *(VP-Access Digital)*
Stephen Imm *(Acct Dir)*
Vanessa Piccinini *(Acct Dir)*
Adam Landres-Schnur *(Acct Supvr)*
Katie Zeiser *(Acct Supvr)*
Katie Warmuth *(Sr Acct Exec)*

Accounts:
Annie's
New-BlackBerry (Agency of Record)
Blue Diamond Growers PR
Clif Bar Inc.
Digg Inc Online Content Handling Services
DocuSign (North American Agency of Record) DocuSign Momentum, Media Relations, Social Media, Strategic Public Relations, Thought Leadership
Fair Isaac Corporation Custom Computer Programming Services
Foundation Capital
Intuit Inc. Software Publishers
Irrational Games Games & Gaming Products Supplier
Kaiser Permanente Health Insurance Provider & Services
LeapFrog Enterprises, Inc.
New-MongoDB (Agency of Record)
New-Ooma (Agency of Record)
New-Peet's Coffee & Tea
Take-Two Interactive Software Inc. Online Gaming & Software Providers
Telefonica Digital Global PR
Turn
New-VCE (Agency of Record)

Branch

Access Communications

19 Union Sq W 4th Fl, New York, NY 10003
Tel.: (917) 522-3500
Fax: (917) 522-3510
E-Mail: ny@accesspr.com
Web Site: www.accesspr.com

Employees: 21
Year Founded: 1991

Agency Specializes In: Public Relations, Sponsorship

Brian T. Regan *(Sr VP & Gen Mgr)*
Cori Barrett *(Sr VP)*
Lindsay Scalisi *(Sr VP)*
Keith Hart *(VP-Access Creative & Dir-Art)*
Ashley Holzhauer *(Acct Supvr)*
Courtney Cervantes *(Sr Acct Exec)*
Abby Forman *(Acct Exec)*

Accounts:
2K Games
2K Sports
Beefeater Gin
Intuit
Kaiser Permanente
LeapFrog Enterprises, Inc.
OtterBox Products LLC
Pernod Ricard USA, Inc.

ACCESS COMMUNICATIONS LLC

400 Connell Dr Ste 2, Berkeley Heights, NJ 07922-2739
Tel.: (908) 508-6700
Fax: (908) 508-6701
E-Mail: info@acinj.com
Web Site: www.acinj.com

Employees: 120
Year Founded: 1997

Agency Specializes In: Advertising, Event Planning & Marketing, Health Care Services, Medical Products, Pharmaceutical, Production (Print), Promotions, Strategic Planning/Research

Approx. Annual Billings: $56,000,000

Eric Bishea *(Mng Partner)*
Leana Wood *(Mng Partner)*
Kevin Barnett *(Partner)*
Frank Scott *(CFO)*
John D. Mcclellan *(CEO-Palladium Group, Inc.)*
Chris Abtahi *(Exec VP)*
Janet Conley *(Exec VP-Ops & Creative Svcs)*
Bryan Horveath *(Exec VP)*
Aimee Jobe *(Exec VP-Client Strategy)*
Jeff Liepman *(Exec VP)*
Megan Jones *(Sr VP)*
Jessica Kalbach *(Sr VP-Ops)*
Jennifer Richardson *(Dir-Meeting Svcs)*

Accounts:
Solyndra
TAIS

ACCESS TO MEDIA

432 Front St, Chicopee, MA 01013
Fax: (413) 592-1841
Toll Free: (866) 612-0034
E-Mail: tina@accesstomedia.com
Web Site: www.accesstomedia.com/

Employees: 15
Year Founded: 2003

Agency Specializes In: Advertising, Advertising Specialties, Affiliate Marketing, Affluent Market, African-American Market, Agriculture, Alternative Advertising, Asian Market, Automotive, Aviation & Aerospace, Bilingual Market, Brand Development & Integration, Broadcast, Business Publications, Business-To-Business, Cable T.V., Catalogs, Co-op Advertising, College, Commercial Photography, Communications, Consulting, Consumer Goods, Consumer Marketing, Consumer Publications, Content, Corporate Identity, Cosmetics, Digital/Interactive, Direct Response Marketing, Direct-to-Consumer, E-Commerce, Education, Electronic Media, Email, Environmental, Event Planning & Marketing, Exhibit/Trade Shows, Experience Design, Faith Based, Fashion/Apparel, Financial, Food Service, Gay & Lesbian Market, Government/Political, Graphic Design, Guerilla Marketing, Health Care Services, Hispanic Market, Hospitality, Identity Marketing, In-Store Advertising, Infomercials, Information Technology, Integrated Marketing, International, Internet/Web Design, Leisure, Local Marketing, Logo & Package Design, Luxury Products, Magazines, Market Research, Media Buying Services, Media Planning, Media Relations, Men's Market, Merchandising, Mobile Marketing, Multicultural, Multimedia, New Technologies, Newspaper, Newspapers & Magazines, Out-of-Home Media, Outdoor, Over-50 Market, Package Design, Paid Searches, Pets , Pharmaceutical, Planning & Consultation, Podcasting, Point of Purchase, Point of Sale, Print, Product Placement, Production, Production (Print), Promotions, Public Relations, Publicity/Promotions, Publishing, RSS (Really Simple Syndication), Radio, Real Estate, Recruitment, Regional, Restaurant, Retail, Sales Promotion, Search Engine Optimization, Seniors' Market, Social Marketing/Nonprofit, Social Media, South Asian Market, Sponsorship, Sports Market, Strategic Planning/Research, T.V., Technical Advertising, Teen Market, Telemarketing, Trade & Consumer Magazines, Transportation, Travel & Tourism, Urban Market, Viral/Buzz/Word of Mouth, Web (Banner Ads, Pop-ups, etc.), Women's Market, Yellow Pages Advertising

Access To Media provides customized advertising solutions. Their focus is customer service and offering one-on-one consultation with personalized strategic guidance.

Approx. Annual Billings: $10,000,000

Liz Jusko *(VP-Sls & Mktg)*
Mark Batiste *(Dir-New Bus Dev)*
Chris Dias *(Dir-Creative)*
Tina Hemond *(Dir-Media)*
Jenn Roissing *(Sr Acct Mgr)*
Ann Sarafin *(Acct Mgr)*
Andrea McEvady *(Mgr-New Bus Dev)*
Jill Scavotto *(Mgr-Admin)*
Stacy Franklin *(Sr Acct Exec)*
Leah Radner *(Media Buyer)*

Accounts:
Bell Lifestyle Products
International Essential Tremor Foundation

ACENTO ADVERTISING, INC.

2001 Wilshire Blvd Ste 600, Santa Monica, CA 90403
Tel.: (310) 943-8300
Fax: (310) 829-2424
E-Mail: rorci@acento.com
Web Site: www.acento.com

E-Mail for Key Personnel:
President: bcreel@acento.com
Creative Dir.: mcassese@acento.com
Media Dir.: taguilar@acento.com

Employees: 40
Year Founded: 1983

Agency Specializes In: Advertising Specialties, Automotive, Bilingual Market, Brand Development & Integration, Broadcast, Business Publications, Business-To-Business, Cable T.V., Children's Market, Co-op Advertising, Collateral, Consulting, Consumer Marketing, Consumer Publications, Corporate Identity, Digital/Interactive, Direct Response Marketing, Electronic Media, Financial, Food Service, Health Care Services, High Technology, Hispanic Market, Information Technology, Magazines, Media Buying Services, Newspapers & Magazines, Out-of-Home Media, Outdoor, Pharmaceutical, Planning & Consultation, Point of Purchase, Print, Production, Radio, Restaurant, Retail, Sponsorship, Strategic Planning/Research, T.V., Trade & Consumer Magazines, Travel & Tourism

Approx. Annual Billings: $53,600,000

Roberto Orci *(CEO)*
Marco Cassese *(Partner & Chief Creative Officer)*
Ray Ortiz *(Supvr-Traffic & Producer-Print)*
Robin Burns *(Acct Dir)*
Elizabeth Vargas *(Acct Dir)*
Lourdes Washington *(Acct Dir)*
Angelica Posada *(Dir-Media)*

Accounts:
Black & Decker
California Department of Public Health
CenturyLink, Inc. Leadership, Multicultural, Strategy
Health Net, Inc. Commercial Health Plan Division, Creative, Digital, Marketing, Media Planning, Strategic Planning
Save-A-Lot
ServiceMaster
Southern California Edison Company
Staples; 2003
SUPERVALU
Time Warner Cable

Brazil

DPZ-Duailibi, Petit, Zaragoza, Propaganda S.A.

Cidade Jardim Ave 280, Sao Paulo, SP 01454-900 Brazil
Tel.: (55) 11 3068 4000
Fax: (55) 11 3085 4298
E-Mail: mail@dpz.com.br
Web Site: http://dpzt.com.br/

Employees: 230
Year Founded: 1968

Agency Specializes In: Graphic Design

Roberto Duailibi *(Partner)*
Mauricio Tortosa *(Chief Strategy Officer)*
Elvio Tieppo *(Gen Dir-Svc)*
Rafael Urenha *(Exec Dir-Creative)*
Cristina Haynes *(Acct Dir)*
Denise Poerner Nogueira *(Acct Dir)*
Fernanda Petinati *(Acct Dir-Media)*
Ana Paula Alencar *(Dir-Media)*
Marcello Barcelos *(Dir-Creative)*
Edwartt Lopes *(Dir-Art)*
Marina Wajnsztejn *(Dir-Plng)*
Diego Zaragoza *(Dir-Creative)*
Debora Bolssonaro *(Mgr-Svc)*

Accounts:
Amado Sao Paulo Bar E Restaurante Soy Burger
Anzen Wax Center
Azul
Bombril Campaign: "Ketchup", Fort Insect Repellent, Lysoform Disinfectant, Mon Bijou, Stain Remover, Vantage Stain Remover
Campari
CNI
Dersa
Duratex
Giraffas
Itau Personnalite
Itau Unibanco Itaucard Credit Card
Itautec; 1982
Jurema
Nestle Neston
Papaiz
Sadia; 1968
Senac
Souza Cruz S.A. Carlton, Hollywood
Stilgraf Print Production
Sunset Rent A Car
Triathon Gym Military Training Class
Vantage
Vivo Cellular; 2000
Vivo

Branch

Acento Advertising
900 W Jackson Ste 3 E, Chicago, IL 60607
Tel.: (312) 850-4130
Fax: (312) 850-4199
Web Site: www.acento.com

Employees: 5

Agency Specializes In: Advertising, Sponsorship

Roberto Orci *(Pres)*
Marco Cassese *(Partner & Chief Creative Officer)*
Tony Aguilar-Arellano *(Partner & Chief Integration Officer)*
Elizabeth Vargas *(Acct Dir)*
Patricia Rubio *(Dir-Art)*
Maria Jimenez *(Assoc Dir-Media & Mktg Svcs)*

Accounts:
Albertsons
Black & Decker
Epson
Infinity
Jewel-Osco
Staples
Wachovia

ACKERMAN MCQUEEN, INC.
1100 The Tower 1601 NW Expy, Oklahoma City, OK 73118
Tel.: (405) 843-7777
Fax: (405) 848-8034
Web Site: www.am.com

E-Mail for Key Personnel:
Creative Dir.: jeanette-elliott@am.com
Media Dir.: peggy-howard@am.com

Employees: 150
Year Founded: 1939

National Agency Associations: 4A's

Agency Specializes In: Advertising, Public Relations

Approx. Annual Billings: $250,000,000 Capitalized

Lee Smith *(Founder & Partner)*
Ed Martin *(Chm)*
Rodney Lipe *(Pres & Dir-Client Svcs)*
William Winkler *(CFO)*
Hillary Farrell *(COO)*
Jon Minson *(Exec VP & Dir-Creative)*
Jeanette Elliott *(Exec VP-Creative Svcs)*
Barbara Johnston *(Sr VP & Mgmt Supvr-Acct Svc)*
Becky King *(Sr VP & Dir-Creative)*
Bruce Parks *(Sr VP & Dir-Creative)*
Mark Ackerman *(VP & Acct Supvr)*
Angus McQueen *(Dir & Producer)*
Dylan Conklin *(Assoc Dir-Creative-Digital)*
Trey Rick *(Mgr-Bus Affairs)*
Ande Courtney *(Acct Supvr)*
Emily Hopkins *(Copywriter & Strategist-Social Media)*
Whitley O'Connor *(Specialist-Comm)*
Tiffany Poole *(Specialist-Comm)*
Sarah Powers *(Acct Exec)*
Carla Sparks *(Media Buyer)*

Accounts:
Allied Arts
American Fidelity Assurance Group
American Indian Cultural Center & Museum
Arthritis Foundation
BancFirst
Bickel & Brewer
Chickasaw Country
Chickasaw Nation
Chisolm Trail Casino
Dartphone
Dolese
Insurica
Integris Health
Integris Heart Hospital
Lone Star Park
Mercedes Benz
National Cowboy Museum
NewCastle Casino
NRA
Ocean Dental
OG&E
OK State Fair
OKC Chamber of Commerce
Oklahoma State University
Red Tie Night
Remington Park
RiverWind Casino
SaltCreek Casino
Taco Mayo
Thunder OKC
United Way
Water Future
WinStar World Casino
WPX Energy
Youth For Tomorrow

Branches

Ackerman McQueen, Inc.
320 S Boston Ste 100, Tulsa, OK 74103-3706
Tel.: (918) 582-6200
Fax: (918) 582-4512
E-Mail: info@am.com
Web Site: www.am.com

Employees: 20

National Agency Associations: 4A's

Bill Winkler *(CFO-Exec Mgmt, Sec & Treas)*
Lael Erickson *(Exec VP-Production & Dir-Creative)*
Melanie Hill *(Exec VP)*
Brandon Winkler *(Exec VP-Fin)*
Tom Twomey *(Sr VP & Sr Producer)*
Bruce Parks *(Sr VP & Dir-Creative)*
Pam Smith *(Dir-Media)*

Accounts:
B&B
Dart Phone
Insurica
Integris Health
NRA
Oklahoma City
Remington Park
Taco Mayo
Winstar

Ackerman McQueen, Inc.
1717 McKinney Ave Ste 1800, Dallas, TX 75202
Tel.: (214) 217-2500
Fax: (214) 217-2510
Web Site: www.am.com

Employees: 20
Year Founded: 1992

National Agency Associations: 4A's

Grant Spofford *(Exec VP-Digital & Producer-Interactive)*
John Nicholas *(Exec VP & Dir-Interactive Tech)*
Melanie Hill *(Exec VP-Acct Mgmt)*
Alyssa Lair *(Sr VP & Acct Supvr)*
Brian Darley *(Sr VP-Digital Production)*
Troy Kelly *(Assoc Dir-Creative)*
Andrew Jordan *(Media Planner)*

Ackerman McQueen, Inc.
517 Cascade Ave Ste 150, Colorado Springs, CO 80903
Tel.: (719) 630-7000
Fax: (719) 630-7089
E-Mail: clay-turner@am.com
Web Site: www.am.com

Employees: 3
Year Founded: 1997

National Agency Associations: 4A's

Agency Specializes In: Advertising, Sponsorship

Revan McQueen *(Co-CEO)*
Clay Turner *(Mng Dir, Exec VP & Dir-Creative)*
Ashley Ball *(Exec VP & Dir-Creative)*
Bob Harstad *(Exec VP-Acct Mgmt)*
Grant Spofford *(Exec VP-Digital)*
Brandon Winkler *(Exec VP-Fin)*
Ashley Hackler *(VP)*
Garrett Johnson *(VP-Acct Svc)*
Heather Barger *(Sr Acct Exec)*

ACME FISH
504 W 9th St, Houston, TX 77007
Tel.: (832) 723-9824
Web Site: www.acmefish.com

Agency Specializes In: Advertising, Broadcast, Digital/Interactive, Production, Social Media, Web (Banner Ads, Pop-ups, etc.)

Lou Congelio *(CEO, Dir-Creative, Sr Copywriter & Exec Producer)*

Accounts:
Houston Roller Derby
Volkswagen Group of America, Inc.

ACME IDEA COMPANY LLC
1 Marshall St, Norwalk, CT 06854-2262
Tel.: (203) 299-5490
Fax: (203) 299-5495
E-Mail: info@acmeidea.com
Web Site: www.acmeidea.com

Employees: 4
Year Founded: 1998

Agency Specializes In: Brand Development & Integration, Graphic Design, High Technology, Publicity/Promotions, Sales Promotion, Strategic Planning/Research

Carol Herman *(Principal)*

Scott Kulok *(Principal)*
Eva Page *(Principal)*

ACORN WOODS COMMUNICATIONS, INC.
2120 Main St Ste 130, Huntington Beach, CA 92648
Tel.: (714) 960-5500
Fax: (714) 960-5900
E-Mail: info@acorn-woods.com
Web Site: www.acorn-woods.com

Year Founded: 2007

Agency Specializes In: Advertising, Event Planning & Marketing, Public Relations, Social Media

Ron Benfield *(Pres)*
Owen Provence *(Partner)*
Marcie Taylor *(Mgr-Social Media)*
Jon Vickers *(Mgr-Production)*

Accounts:
Bates Footwear (Agency of Record) Creative Marketing, PowerSports Footwear, Strategy
Saddleman

ACOSTA DESIGN INC
1201 Broadway 703, New York, NY 10001
Tel.: (212) 447-9900
Web Site: www.acostadesign.com

Agency Specializes In: Advertising, Digital/Interactive, Internet/Web Design, Logo & Package Design, Multimedia

Mauricio Acosta *(Mng Partner)*
Katarina Sjoholm *(Mng Partner)*
Michelle Israel *(Dir-Design)*

Accounts:
Irish Spring Performance Series

ACQUISIO
465 Victoria Suite 300, Saint-Lambert, QC J4P 2J2 Canada
Tel.: (450) 465-2631
Fax: (450) 465-2841
Toll Free: (866) 493-9070
Web Site: www.acquisio.com

Year Founded: 2003

Agency Specializes In: Mobile Marketing, Search Engine Optimization, Social Media

Eric Lacourciere *(VP-Bus Dev)*
Martin Mailloux *(VP-Tech)*
Rylan McKinney *(Sr Dir-Sls)*
Keith Meagher *(Sr Dir-Bus Solutions & Ops)*
Keith Hill *(Dir-API)*
Daniel Old *(Acct Mgr)*
Richard Morgan *(Product Mgr)*
Marie Lossowski *(Mgr-Product Mktg)*
Madison Ramsay *(Coord-Mktg)*

Accounts:
Yellow Pages Group Co Classifieds Service Providers

ACROBATANT
1336 E 15th St, Tulsa, OK 74120
Tel.: (918) 938-7901
Fax: (866) 695-6418
E-Mail: info@acrobatant.com
Web Site: www.acrobatant.us

Year Founded: 2008

Agency Specializes In: Advertising, Broadcast, Collateral, Digital/Interactive, Internet/Web Design, Logo & Package Design, Social Media, Strategic Planning/Research

Hal Collins *(Mng Dir & Dir-Web & Interactive)*
Diane Davis *(Mng Dir & Dir-Creative Svcs)*
Danny Sadler *(Mng Dir & Dir-Creative)*
David Downing *(Mng Dir)*
Angela Harless *(Mng Dir)*
Audrey Chambers *(Acct Dir)*
Dell Chambers *(Dir-Art)*
Tamara Green *(Dir-Media)*
Chance Walentiny *(Assoc Dir-Creative)*

Accounts:
Velcro Babysitter

ACSYS INTERACTIVE
(Name Changed to Primacy)

ACT ONE CREATIVE LLC
18 Low Ave, Concord, NH 03301
Tel.: (603) 226-3311
E-Mail: info@actonecreative.com
Web Site: www.actonecreative.com

Agency Specializes In: Advertising, Corporate Identity, Digital/Interactive, Graphic Design, Internet/Web Design, Media Buying Services, Print, Public Relations, Social Media

Nancy Brownstein *(Pres & CEO)*
Ann Kontak *(Dir-Art & Designer-Web)*
Ted Sink *(Copywriter)*

Accounts:
New Hampshire Center for Public Policy

ACTIVE INTEGRATED MARKETING
1060 1st Ave Ste 400, King of Prussia, PA 19406
Tel.: (215) 885-3351
Fax: (215) 885-3352
E-Mail: strategy@activeintegrated.com
Web Site: www.activeintegrated.com

Year Founded: 2003

Agency Specializes In: Advertising, Automotive, Brand Development & Integration, Business Publications, Business-To-Business, Collateral, Communications, Consulting, Content, Corporate Identity, Customer Relationship Management, Digital/Interactive, Direct Response Marketing, E-Commerce, Event Planning & Marketing, Graphic Design, Health Care Services, Identity Marketing, Integrated Marketing, Internet/Web Design, Logo & Package Design, Magazines, Market Research, Media Buying Services, Media Planning, New Product Development, Paid Searches, Pharmaceutical, Planning & Consultation, Print, Production, Promotions, Search Engine Optimization, Social Marketing/Nonprofit, Social Media, Web (Banner Ads, Pop-ups, etc.)

Breakdown of Gross Billings by Media: Consulting: 15%; Digital/Interactive: 70%; Trade & Consumer Mags.: 15%

Angela Morsa *(Founder)*

Accounts:
Accupac
AEGON USA
Catalina Health Resource
Charles River Laboratories
Firstrust Bank
GSI Commerce, Inc.

ACTON INTERNATIONAL LTD.
5760 Cornhusker Hwy Ste 1, Lincoln, NE 68507
Tel.: (402) 742-2820
Fax: (402) 470-3965
E-Mail: info@acton.com
Web Site: www.acton.com

E-Mail for Key Personnel:
President: jlambert@acton.com
Creative Dir.: stephanie@acton.com
Media Dir.: bovett@acton.com
Public Relations: kprange@acton.com

Employees: 8
Year Founded: 1968

National Agency Associations: DMA

Agency Specializes In: Aviation & Aerospace, Below-the-Line, Digital/Interactive, Direct Response Marketing, E-Commerce, Financial, Hospitality, International, Internet/Web Design, Over-50 Market, Paid Searches, Pharmaceutical, Production (Print), Search Engine Optimization, Seniors' Market, Sponsorship, Sweepstakes, Technical Advertising, Travel & Tourism, Web (Banner Ads, Pop-ups, etc.)

Approx. Annual Billings: $10,000,000

Jonathan C. Lambert *(Founder)*
Bruce Wilson *(Owner)*
Frank Lambert *(Mng Partner)*
Kraig Prange *(Mng Partner)*
Debb Bovett *(Sr Mgr-Data Products)*

Accounts:
American Express; New York, NY Financial & Travel Services
Nikkei Business Publications; Tokyo, Japan
Toyota; Tokyo, Japan Automobiles
UNICEF; New York, NY

ACUITY ADS INC.
5775 Yonge St Suite 1802, Toronto, ON M2M 4J1 Canada
Tel.: (416) 218-9888
Fax: (866) 623-6822
E-Mail: info@acuityads.com
Web Site: www.acuityads.com

Year Founded: 2009

Agency Specializes In: Advertising, Publishing, Search Engine Optimization, Social Media

Tal Hayek *(Co-Founder & CEO)*
Rachel Kapcan *(Co-Founder & COO)*
Nathan Mekuz *(Co-Founder & CTO)*
Joe Ontman *(Co-Founder & VP-Sls)*
Laurie Maw *(Sr Dir-Sls & Platform Solutions)*

Accounts:
Dell Computers & Laptops Mfr & Distr

ACXIOM DIGITAL
100 Redwood Shores Pkwy, Redwood City, CA 94065
Tel.: (650) 356-3400
Fax: (650) 356-3410
Web Site: www.acxiom.com

Employees: 200

Agency Specializes In: Digital/Interactive

Scott E Howe *(Pres & CEO)*
Warren C. Jenson *(CFO & Exec VP)*
Dennis Self *(CIO & Sr VP)*
Jerry C. Jones *(Chief Legal Officer, Exec VP & Asst Sec)*
Terilyn Monroe *(Chief People & Culture Officer & Sr VP-HR)*
David Eisenberg *(Sr VP-Strategy & Corp Dev)*
Nichole Kezsely *(VP-Partner Dev)*

Accounts:
Comcast
Gap, Inc.
Hewlett-Packard
Marriott

Branch

Acxiom
1000 Town Ctr #2700, Southfield, MI 48075-1224
Tel.: (501) 342-1000
Web Site: www.acxiom.com

Aaron J. Beitler *(Partner & Dir-Svcs)*
Dennis Self *(CIO & Sr VP)*
David Eisenberg *(Sr VP-Strategy & Corp Dev)*
Janet Cinfio *(VP-Infrastructure & Tech Ops)*
Theresa Robinson *(Mgr-Bus Ops)*
Lisa Mroz *(Strategist-Mktg)*

THE AD AGENCY
1101 Connecticut Ave NW Ste 450, Washington, DC 20036
Tel.: (202) 342-2122
Fax: (202) 331-1324
Web Site: www.theadagency.com

Year Founded: 1982

Agency Specializes In: Advertising, Brand Development & Integration, Logo & Package Design, Public Relations, T.V.

Debi Gasper *(CEO & Creative Dir)*

Accounts:
New-Polar Bear Air Conditioning & Heating
New-Third Street Tunnel Project

AD CETERA, INC.
15570 Quorum Dr, Addison, TX 75001
Tel.: (972) 387-5577
Fax: (972) 387-0034
E-Mail: info@adceterainc.com
Web Site: www.adceterainc.com

Employees: 8
Year Founded: 1987

Agency Specializes In: Automotive, Brand Development & Integration, Broadcast, Business-To-Business, Cable T.V., Collateral, Consumer Marketing, Corporate Identity, E-Commerce, Electronic Media, Exhibit/Trade Shows, Graphic Design, Health Care Services, High Technology, Industrial, Internet/Web Design, Logo & Package Design, Media Buying Services, Newspaper, Out-of-Home Media, Outdoor, Point of Purchase, Point of Sale, Print, Production, Radio, Real Estate, Restaurant, Retail, Sales Promotion, Sports Market, Strategic Planning/Research, T.V., Trade & Consumer Magazines

Approx. Annual Billings: $2,000,000

Carol Thompson *(Pres)*
Wayne Zartman *(VP)*
Bonica Brown *(Dir-Art & Graphic Designer)*

Accounts:
Altus Packaging Development
City National Bank
Kutz Auto Group; Dallas, TX Auto Dealer Group
Naomi Candle Box
Naomi Paper City
Superior Precious Metals
Valencia Restaurant
Winzer

AD CONSULTANT GROUP INC.
7541 Black Olive Way, Tamarac, FL 33321
Tel.: (954) 234-3101
Fax: (954) 721-9979

Employees: 2
Year Founded: 1981

Agency Specializes In: Collateral, Media Buying Services, Print

Approx. Annual Billings: $19,000,000

Breakdown of Gross Billings by Media: Brdcst.: $6,000,000; Collateral: $6,000,000; Mags.: $700,000; Newsp.: $300,000; Outdoor: $500,000; Point of Sale: $1,000,000; Production: $2,000,000; Pub. Rels.: $500,000; Transit: $2,000,000

Bernard Weisblum *(Pres)*

AD DAWG CREATIVE
1805 Poplar Ave, Redwood City, CA 94061
Tel.: (650) 679-9994
E-Mail: bpark@addawg.com
Web Site: www.addawg.com

Employees: 2
Year Founded: 1998

Agency Specializes In: Advertising, Brand Development & Integration, Business-To-Business, Consumer Marketing, Consumer Publications, Corporate Identity, Direct Response Marketing, E-Commerce, Entertainment, Graphic Design, Health Care Services, High Technology, Internet/Web Design, Logo & Package Design, Magazines, Newspaper, Newspapers & Magazines, Outdoor, Radio, Restaurant, Retail, Sports Market, Trade & Consumer Magazines, Travel & Tourism

Approx. Annual Billings: $250,000

Breakdown of Gross Billings by Media: Graphic Design: $100,000; Internet Adv.: $50,000; Other: $100,000

Billy Park *(Owner)*

AD-EZ ADVERTISING
6253 McIntyre Court, Golden, CO 80403
Tel.: (303) 424-2333
Fax: (303) 424-2622
Toll Free: (888) 821-0850
E-Mail: info@adezadvertising.com
Web Site: www.adezadvertising.com

E-Mail for Key Personnel:
President: debbie@adezadvertising.com

Employees: 2
Year Founded: 1994

Agency Specializes In: Advertising, Recruitment

Approx. Annual Billings: $800,000

Debra A. Gillis *(Owner)*

Accounts:
Front Range Community College
Pinon Management
Purchasing Partners of America
University Physicians

AD HOUSE ADVERTISING
918 Pinehurst Rd NE Ste 102, Rio Rancho, NM 87124
Tel.: (505) 404-3536
Toll Free: (888) 928-1242
E-Mail: info@adhouseadvertising.com
Web Site: www.adhouseadvertising.com

Agency Specializes In: Advertising, Graphic Design, Internet/Web Design, Media Buying Services, Public Relations, Search Engine Optimization, Social Media

Ed Smith *(Owner, Pres & Producer)*
Kim Smith *(Owner)*
Danielle Vigil *(Office Mgr & Strategist-Media)*
Ryan Smith *(Mgr-Online Mktg)*

Accounts:
BlindSpot
Rene Pena
Sandia Sunrooms & Windows

AD LEVERAGE
1710 N Moorpark Rd Ste 52, Thousand Oaks, CA 91360
Tel.: (805) 230-9100
E-Mail: info@adleverage.tv
Web Site: www.adleverage.tv/

Andrew Palosi *(Pres)*
Ellen Appice *(Acct Mgr)*
Michael Mossman *(Acct Mgr-Sls)*
David Pell *(Acct Exec)*

Accounts:
Dherbs
Hernandez Wholesale Flooring
Laser & Dermatology Institute of California
Petersen Dean
Window World

AD LIB UNLIMITED INC
1507 Ave M, Brooklyn, NY 11230
Tel.: (718) 382-0900
Fax: (718) 645-1985
Web Site: www.adlibunlimited.com

Agency Specializes In: Advertising, Collateral, Corporate Identity, Graphic Design, Internet/Web Design, Logo & Package Design, Print

Ruth Folger Weiss *(Pres)*

Accounts:
Gerimedix Inc.
Margaret Tietz Nursing & Rehabilitation Center
The Regency at Glen Cove Independent Living
Shibolim Foods

A.D. LUBOW, LLC
1 Penn Plz Ste 5312, New York, NY 10119-5312
Tel.: (212) 564-3250
Fax: (212) 564-2866
E-Mail: art@adlubow.com
Web Site: www.adlubow.com

Employees: 10
Year Founded: 1968

Agency Specializes In: Education, Entertainment, Publicity/Promotions

Approx. Annual Billings: $12,000,000

Breakdown of Gross Billings by Media: D.M.: 6%; Internet Adv.: 20%; Newsp. & Mags.: 20%; Other: 42%; Radio: 4%; T.V.: 1%; Transit: 7%

Arthur D. Lubow *(Pres & Creative Dir)*
Anne Van Der Does *(VP)*
Sukanya Cherdrungsi *(Sr Dir-Art)*
Nico Marcellino *(Dir-Multimedia & Web Design)*
Rick Raymond *(Dir-Search Engine)*
Mildred Lalica *(Sr Graphic Designer)*
Pierre Reboul *(Reporter-Media Analytics)*

Accounts:
The American Academy of Dramatic Arts; New York, NY Education; 1985
American Museum of the American Indian
The Archdiocese of New York; New York, NY Fund Raising for Inner City Scholarship Fund, The Cardinal's Appeal & Catholic Charities; 1995
Big Apple Circus
C.U.N.Y Graduate Center
Cardinal Hayes High School
Cardinal's Appeal
Catholic Charities
Columbia University School of Public Health; New York, NY; 1998
Juilliard School; New York, NY Concerts, Dance & Drama Performances; 1980
Liberty Science Center
Marymount Manhattan College; New York, NY Degree Programs & Continuing Education; 1979
New York Bankers Association
New York Foundation for the Arts

AD MAIORA SRL
Via Machiavelli 25, 00185 Rome, Italy
Tel.: (39) 06 7720 3200
Fax: (39) 06 7720 3136
Web Site: www.admaiora.com

Employees: 20
Year Founded: 1997

Agency Specializes In: Consulting, Email, Media Buying Services, Media Planning, Search Engine Optimization, Strategic Planning/Research

Fabio Scalet *(Founder & Dir)*
Federica Zetari *(Dir-Sls)*
Paolo Brancato *(Sr Mgr-Sls)*
Valerio Gallo *(Acct Mgr-Digital)*
Giulio Cupini *(Mgr-Web Mktg)*
Francesca Bianchi *(Specialist-Keyword Adv)*

Accounts:
Alfa Romeo
Banca Sella
Beiersdorf
Bolton Group
Chamber of Commerce Roma
Italian Highways Telepass
Manuli Rubber Industries
Merloni Waterheating Products
Synthelabo Medical
Universal Studios

Branches

Ad Maiora
Via Durini 28, Milan, Italy
Tel.: (39) 02 42107360
Fax: (39) 06 77203136
E-Mail: info@admaiora.com

Agency Specializes In: Advertising

Fabio Scalet *(Founder & Mng Dir)*
Francesca Bianchi *(Specialist-Keyword Adv)*
Federico Biuso *(Specialist-LB & PR)*
Nicola Bruno *(Community Mgr)*
Marco Moroni *(Community Mgr)*

Accounts:
Alfa Romeo
Bolton Group
Ferrero
Italgas Piu Gas & Power services
Lancia Automobile
Manuli Rubber Industries
Medusa Films
Rai International
Unicredit Group
Us Robotics Italia

AD PARTNERS INC.
4631 Woodland Corporate Blvd Ste 109, Tampa, FL 33614
Tel.: (813) 418-4645
Fax: (813) 418-4652
E-Mail: info@AdPartnersAgency.com
Web Site: adpartnersagency.com

Employees: 16
Year Founded: 2004

Agency Specializes In: Advertising

Tony Ceresoli *(Pres & CEO)*
Darlene Levi *(Mng Dir & Exec VP)*
Skeek Allen *(VP & Dir-Creative)*
Becky Tanner *(Dir-Media)*
Dennis Garcia *(Assoc Dir-Creative)*
Vanessa Guzan *(Acct Coord)*

Accounts:
Amscot Financial; FL Check Cashing, Payday Advance & Tax Service
Beef 'O' Brady's (Agency of Record)

AD RESULTS
6110 Clarkson Ln, Houston, TX 77055
Tel.: (713) 783-1800
Fax: (713) 783-1062
E-Mail: laurel@adresultsinc.com
Web Site: www.adresultsinc.net

Employees: 70
Year Founded: 1998

Agency Specializes In: Advertising, Advertising Specialties, Bilingual Market, Consumer Marketing, Direct Response Marketing, Hispanic Market, Radio

Approx. Annual Billings: $70,000,000

Breakdown of Gross Billings by Media: Radio: $70,000,000

Marshall Williams *(Co-Founder, Owner & Partner)*
Russell Lindley *(Pres)*
Jennifer Christman *(VP-Media & Client Svcs)*
Jenni Skaug *(VP-Bus Dev)*
Dj Templeton *(Office Mgr)*
Darra Hulsart *(Brand Mgr-AT&T)*
Kimberly Bates *(Media Buyer)*
Courtney Brame *(Media Buyer)*
Connor Rehmet *(Client Svcs)*

Accounts:
ARS Service Express
AT&T Mobility LLC; Atlanta, GA Wireless Products; 2001
Bonefish Grill
Cheeseburger in Paradise
Dirt Free
ITT Technical Institute; Indianapolis, IN Schools; 2004
Select Comfort Sleep Systems; Minneapolis, MN; 1998
Staples

AD-SUCCESS MARKETING
868 Calypso Breeze Dr, Lexington, KY 40515
Tel.: (859) 263-1822
Fax: (859) 263-1828
E-Mail: cboyle@adsuccess.com
Web Site: www.adsuccess.com

Employees: 12
Year Founded: 1985

Agency Specializes In: Advertising, Brand Development & Integration, Broadcast, Business Publications, Business-To-Business, Collateral, Consulting, Corporate Identity, Education, Financial, Graphic Design, Health Care Services, High Technology, Logo & Package Design, Media Buying Services, Medical Products, Newspaper, Newspapers & Magazines, Outdoor, Planning & Consultation, Print, Production, Public Relations, Publicity/Promotions, Radio, Seniors' Market, Strategic Planning/Research, T.V., Transportation, Travel & Tourism

Sharalee Scanlon *(Owner)*

Accounts:
Banker's Bank
Bluegrass Mental Health
Bluegrass Mobility Office
Bluegrass Tourism Group

AD WORKSHOP
44 Hadjis Way, Lake Placid, NY 12946
Tel.: (518) 523-3359
Fax: (518) 523-0255
E-Mail: info@adworkshop.com
Web Site: www.adworkshop.com

Employees: 30
Year Founded: 1977

National Agency Associations: Second Wind Limited

Agency Specializes In: Co-op Advertising, Collateral, Graphic Design, Internet/Web Design, Public Relations, Strategic Planning/Research, Travel & Tourism

Sandra Gagnon *(Sr Dir)*
Anne Rast *(Sr Dir-Art)*
Jim Duhaime *(Sr Project Mgr)*
Kathleen Ford *(Mgr-Production & Sr Designer-Creative)*
Ben Hamelin *(Sr Web Developer)*

Accounts:
Adirondack Community Trust
Adirondack Regional Tourism
Best Western Golden Arrow
Champlain National Bank
Clarkson University
Clarkson University
Cooperstown Accomodations
Cooperstown/Otsego County
Gore Mountain
Kinney Drugs
Lake Placid Center of the Arts
Malone Golf Club
Mirror Lake Inn
North Country Saving Bank
Thousand Islands Regional Tourism Council
Whiteface Mountain

AD2PRO MEDIA SOLUTIONS
23371 Mulholland Dr Ste 132, Woodland Hills, CA 91364
Tel.: (818) 591-7713
Fax: (818) 267-5511
E-Mail: sales@2adpro.com
Web Site: www.2adpro.com

Employees: 400
Year Founded: 2006

Agency Specializes In: Advertising, Corporate Identity, Digital/Interactive, Electronic Media, Graphic Design, Mobile Marketing, Newspaper, Newspapers & Magazines, Production (Print), Web (Banner Ads, Pop-ups, etc.)

Todd Brownrout *(Co-Founder & Pres)*
Gopal Krishnan *(Co-Founder & CEO)*
Ajit George Abraham *(Chief People Officer)*

Kartic Srinivasan *(Sr VP)*
Pat Keil *(VP-Media-North America)*
Laura Rutenis *(VP-Retail Solutions)*
Arianna Salcedo *(Acct Dir)*
Hayley Love *(Dir-Media Accts)*
Jamie Clark *(Acct Mgr)*

Accounts:
Belo
The Buffalo News
Freedom Communications
Gannett Newspapers
Google
Gulf News
Kare
Lulu
NewsQuest
Scripps Newspapers
Tribune Interactive

AD:60

68 Jay St Unit 616, Brooklyn, NY 11201
Tel.: (866) 404-2360
E-Mail: hello@ad60.com
Web Site: www.ad60.com

Year Founded: 2009

Agency Specializes In: Advertising

Alexander Matjanec *(Partner & CMO)*
Stephanie Miller *(Sr Designer)*

Accounts:
New-Stash

ADAM RITCHIE BRAND DIRECTION

101 Tremont St Ste 1121, Boston, MA 02108
Tel.: (617) 302-7230
E-Mail: contact@aritchbrand.com
Web Site: www.aritchbrand.com

Year Founded: 2007

Agency Specializes In: Advertising, Brand Development & Integration, Communications, Crisis Communications, Media Relations, Media Training, Social Media

Adam Ritchie *(Principal)*

Accounts:
Alpha Phi Omega
Changents
Detours & OnRamps
Greenable
The Lights Out
The Magic Hat Brewing Company
Nuna Baby Gear
Sonicbids
Urbini
Yumnuts
Zumix Community Arts

ADAMS & KNIGHT ADVERTISING/PUBLIC RELATIONS

(Name Changed to Adams & Knight, Inc.)

ADAMS & KNIGHT, INC.

(Formerly Adams & Knight Advertising/Public Relations)
80 Avon Meadow Ln, Avon, CT 06001
Tel.: (860) 676-2300
Fax: (860) 676-1940
E-Mail: info@adamsknight.com
Web Site: www.adamsknight.com

Employees: 57
Year Founded: 1988

Agency Specializes In: Advertising, Advertising Specialties, Aviation & Aerospace, Brand Development & Integration, Broadcast, Business Publications, Business-To-Business, Cable T.V., Children's Market, Co-op Advertising, Collateral, Communications, Consulting, Consumer Marketing, Consumer Publications, Corporate Communications, Corporate Identity, Digital/Interactive, Direct Response Marketing, E-Commerce, Education, Electronic Media, Engineering, Entertainment, Environmental, Event Planning & Marketing, Exhibit/Trade Shows, Fashion/Apparel, Financial, Food Service, Government/Political, Graphic Design, Health Care Services, High Technology, In-Store Advertising, Industrial, Infomercials, Information Technology, Internet/Web Design, Investor Relations, Leisure, Local Marketing, Logo & Package Design, Magazines, Media Buying Services, Medical Products, Merchandising, Multimedia, New Product Development, Newspaper, Newspapers & Magazines, Out-of-Home Media, Outdoor, Over-50 Market, Pharmaceutical, Planning & Consultation, Point of Purchase, Point of Sale, Print, Production, Public Relations, Publicity/Promotions, Radio, Real Estate, Restaurant, Retail, Sales Promotion, Seniors' Market, Sports Market, Strategic Planning/Research, T.V., Technical Advertising, Trade & Consumer Magazines, Transportation, Travel & Tourism

Approx. Annual Billings: $92,508,754

Donna Logan-Gabel *(COO & VP-Production)*
Felicia Lindau *(Chief Bus Dev Officer)*
Brian McClear *(Sr VP-Interactive Svcs)*
Reem Nouh *(Sr VP-Strategic Svcs)*
Marc McFarland *(VP-Fin Svcs Mktg)*
Jim Frawley *(Acct Dir-Strategic Svcs)*
Denis Gendreau *(Dir-Connection Plng & Analytics)*
Herb Emanuelson *(Acct Supvr)*
Jill Memery *(Sr Copywriter)*

Accounts:
Children's Specialized Hospital
Connecticut Office of Tourism Tourism
Covidien Sustainable Technologies
Department of Economics & Community Development Economic Department
Hartford Healthcare, Hartford, CT Healthcare
Hartford Hospital; Hartford, CT Healthcare
Magellan Health Services
Mohegan Sun Sports

ADAMS & LONGINO ADVERTISING, INC.

605 Lynndale Ct Ste F, Greenville, NC 27858
Tel.: (252) 355-5566
Fax: (252) 355-7363
E-Mail: outfit@adamsadv.com
Web Site: www.adamsadv.com

Employees: 7
Year Founded: 1978

National Agency Associations: AAF

Agency Specializes In: Advertising, Brand Development & Integration, Business-To-Business, Collateral, Communications, Consumer Marketing, Corporate Identity, Direct Response Marketing, Graphic Design, Industrial, Logo & Package Design, Media Buying Services, Sales Promotion, Strategic Planning/Research, Trade & Consumer Magazines

Charles P. Adams, Jr. *(Owner)*
Jamie Jacobson *(VP)*
Matthew Koester *(Designer-Multimedia & Producer)*
Keith Kellum *(Dir-Art)*
Patricia Dunn *(Office Mgr)*
Tracy Chapman *(Mgr-Production)*

Accounts:
Domino's Pizza Franchises; Greenville, NC Pizza Delivery; 1987
Grady-White Boats Inc.; Greenville, NC Coastal Fishing Boats; 1982
Greenville-Pitt County Convention & Visitors Bureau; Greenville, NC; 1992
Kadey-Krogen Yachts; Stuart, FL Full Displacement Hull Passagemakers; 2004
Paul Mann Custom Boats; Manns Harbor, NC Custom Sport Fishing Boats; 2003
Veneer Technologies Incorporated; Newport, NC Edgebanding, Hardwood Veneers, Veneer Faces; 2003
Winterville Machine Works; Winterville, NC Machine Fabrication & Plating; 1982

THE ADAMS GROUP

925 Gervais St, Columbia, SC 29201
Tel.: (803) 765-1223
Fax: (803) 254-4222
E-Mail: wadams@adamsgroup.com
Web Site: www.adamsgroup.com

E-Mail for Key Personnel:
President: wadams@adamsgroup.com

Employees: 16
Year Founded: 1983

National Agency Associations: AANI

Agency Specializes In: Brand Development & Integration, Financial, Health Care Services, High Technology, Internet/Web Design

Approx. Annual Billings: $13,200,000

Wayne Adams *(CEO)*
Karis Hallman *(VP & Mgr-Production)*
Liz Nettles *(Dir-Art)*
Paula Hensley-Mallory *(Office Mgr)*

Accounts:
Integral Solutions Group
Meadows Regional Medical Center
QS/1 Data Systems

ADAMS OUTDOOR ADVERTISING

500 Colonial Center Pkwy Ste 120, Roswell, GA 30076-8852
Tel.: (770) 333-0399
E-Mail: aoa@adamsoutdoor.com
Web Site: www.adamsoutdoor.com

Employees: 7
Year Founded: 1983

Agency Specializes In: Outdoor

Kevin Gleason *(Pres & CEO)*
Abe Levine *(CFO)*
Brian A. Grant *(VP-HR)*
Chris Eigenberger *(Dir-Market Ops)*
Laura Sanders *(Dir-Art)*
Evan Schultz *(Dir-Art)*
Todd Turner *(Dir-Art)*

Accounts:
America's Best Coffee
Auto Bell
Bank of America
Caterpillar
Celtic Cultural Alliance
Champions
Charlotte Knights
Ernest E. Kennedy Center
Espresso Royale
Fowlerville Fair
Freshpet
Irish Hills Fireworks
The Jesse Harris Boxing Gym/Pennsylvania Golden Gloves

McDonald's Campaign: "Brace For Flavor", Campaign: "Breakfast Bagels"
McNeill's Pub
Newhard's Corn Shed
Red Robin
RU21 Workforce
Sesame Street
South Carolina Stingrays 3D
Springhall Aesthetics
Steve's Liquor
Tri County Roofing UFO Crash
Via Thrift Stores
Walgreens.com

Branches

Adams Outdoor Advertising
1711 Dobbins Dr, Champaign, IL 61821
Tel.: (217) 352-4460
Fax: (217) 352-0735
E-Mail: champaign@adamsoutdoor.com
Web Site: www.adamsoutdoor.com

Agency Specializes In: Outdoor

Dave Alsvig *(Gen Mgr)*
Natalie Fiol *(Dir-Art)*
Nick Mclemore *(Acct Exec)*

Adams Outdoor Advertising
5732 95th Ave Ste 500, Kenosha, WI 53144
Tel.: (262) 658-1940
Fax: (262) 658-1922
E-Mail: kenosha@adamsoutdoor.com
Web Site: www.adamsoutdoor.com

Employees: 3

Agency Specializes In: Outdoor

Chris Eigenberger *(Corp Dir-Market Ops)*

Adams Outdoor Advertising
911 SW Adams St, Peoria, IL 61602
Tel.: (309) 692-2482
Fax: (309) 692-8452
E-Mail: peoria@adamsoutdoor.com
Web Site: www.adamsoutdoor.com

Agency Specializes In: Outdoor

Brian Grant *(Corp VP-HR)*
Ben Armitage *(Gen Mgr)*
Chris Gorrell *(Dir-Art)*
Mike Mielke *(Corp Dir-Ops)*

Adams Outdoor Advertising
5547 Virginia Beach Blvd, Norfolk, VA 23451
Tel.: (757) 461-1355
Fax: (757) 455-5897
E-Mail: norfolk@adamsoutdoor.com
Web Site: www.adamsoutdoor.com

Agency Specializes In: Outdoor

Jim Balestino *(Gen Mgr)*

Adams Outdoor Advertising
6053 Route 209, Stroudsburg, PA 18360
Tel.: (570) 402-6400
Fax: (570) 992-5347
E-Mail: northeast@admsoutdoor.com
Web Site: www.adamsoutdoor.com

Employees: 25

Agency Specializes In: Outdoor

Michael Peters *(Gen Mgr)*

Adams Outdoor Advertising
102 East Badger St, Madison, WI 53713
Tel.: (608) 271-7900
Fax: (608) 271-4253
E-Mail: madison@adamsoutdoor.com
Web Site: www.adamsoutdoor.com

Employees: 40

Agency Specializes In: Outdoor

Chris Eigenberger *(Dir-Market Ops)*
Pat Frawley *(Coord-Corp Svcs & Mktg)*

Adams Outdoor Advertising
2176 Ave C, Bethlehem, PA 18017-2120
Tel.: (610) 266-9461
Fax: (610) 266-0649
E-Mail: lehigh@adamsoutdoor.com
Web Site: www.adamsoutdoor.com

Agency Specializes In: Outdoor

Tony Cioffi *(Gen Mgr)*
Mike Peters *(Gen Mgr)*

Adams Outdoor Advertising
3801 Capital City Blvd, Lansing, MI 48906
Tel.: (517) 321-2121
Fax: (517) 321-2122
E-Mail: Lansing@adamsoutdoor.com
Web Site: www.adamsoutdoor.com

Agency Specializes In: Outdoor

Jason Kitchen *(Gen Mgr)*
Allison Holtz *(Mgr-Sls)*

Adams Outdoor Advertising
407 E. Ransom St, Kalamazoo, MI 49007
Tel.: (269) 342-9831
Fax: (269) 342-5774
E-Mail: kalamazoo@adamsoutdoor.com
Web Site: www.adamsoutdoor.com

Agency Specializes In: Outdoor

Dave Alsvig *(Gen Mgr)*
Jeannine Dodson *(Gen Mgr)*
Jason Kitchen *(Gen Mgr)*
Brad Mitchell *(Gen Mgr)*

Adams Outdoor Advertising
1385 Alice Dr, Florence, SC 29505
Tel.: (843) 662-4514
Fax: (843) 667-4110
Web Site: www.adamsoutdoor.com

Agency Specializes In: Outdoor

Jon Weiss *(Gen Mgr)*
Mari Kaye Haney *(Mgr-Sls)*

Adams Outdoor Advertising
1134 N. Graham St, Charlotte, NC 28231
Tel.: (704) 373-1700
Fax: (704) 373-0838
E-Mail: charlotte@adamsoutdoor.com
Web Site: www.adamsoutdoor.com

Employees: 45

Agency Specializes In: Outdoor

Jeannine Dodson *(Gen Mgr)*
John Simmons *(Acct Exec)*
Rahshawn Vontayes *(Coord-Matls)*
Traci Maynard *(Reg Acct Exec)*

Adams Outdoor Advertising
9509 Hamburg Rd, Ladson, SC 29456
Tel.: (843) 207-1770
Fax: (843) 207-1212
E-Mail: charleston@adamsoutdoor.com
Web Site: www.adamsoutdoor.com

Agency Specializes In: Outdoor

Brian Grant *(VP-HR)*
Jon Kane *(Gen Mgr)*
Brad Mitchell *(Gen Mgr)*
Liz Mitchum *(Gen Mgr)*
Chris Eigenberger *(Dir-Market Ops)*
Todd Turner *(Dir-Corp Creative)*
Dave Alsvig *(Sls Mgr)*

Adams Outdoor Advertising
880 James L. Hart Pkwy, Ypsilanti, MI 48197
Tel.: (734) 327-8999
Fax: (734) 327-9104
E-Mail: annarbor@adamsoutdoor.com
Web Site: www.adamsoutdoor.com

Employees: 25

Agency Specializes In: Outdoor

ADAMUS MEDIA
(Formerly All-outMedia, LLC)
1035 Black Horse Pike Ste 2, Williamstown, NJ 08094
Tel.: (856) 728-6100
Fax: (856) 728-6121
E-Mail: info@adamusmedia.com
Web Site: adamusmedia.com/

Agency Specializes In: Advertising, Automotive, Corporate Identity, E-Commerce, Education, Financial, Internet/Web Design, Medical Products, Outdoor, Print, Public Relations, Real Estate, Retail, Strategic Planning/Research

Sylwia Majewski *(Pres & CEO)*
Mark Shockley *(VP & Sr Dir-Creative)*
Gary Frisch *(Dir-PR & Head-Comm Strategy)*
Terrance O'Brien *(Dir-Programming, Sys Dev & Head-Web & Applications Dev)*
Cassie Rinehart *(Sr Designer)*

Accounts:
Post University; Waterbury, CT Branding, Designing, Marketing

ADAPTIVE EASEL LLC
1620 Pleasant St, Des Moines, IA 50314
Tel.: (515) 244-4808
Fax: (515) 244-4449
E-Mail: desmoines@adeasel.com
Web Site: www.adeasel.com

Agency Specializes In: Advertising, Brand Development & Integration, Digital/Interactive, Email, Internet/Web Design, Print, Promotions, Search Engine Optimization, Social Media

Chase M. Hendrix *(Pres & CEO)*
Bryan Heilman *(COO & Principal)*
Nicolas Titze *(Principal & Creative Dir)*

Accounts:
Humane Manufacturing Company LLC

ADAP.TV
1 Waters Park Dr Ste 250, San Mateo, CA 94403
Tel.: (650) 286-4420

Fax: (650) 312-9223
E-Mail: info@adap.tv
Web Site: www.aolplatforms.com

Employees: 35
Year Founded: 2006

Agency Specializes In: Advertising, Environmental, Financial, Public Relations

Sean Crawford *(Sr VP-Global Marketplaces & Inventory)*
Vijay Rao *(Sr VP-Sls & Client Strategy)*
Eric Burns *(Dir-Sls)*
Lauren Conroy *(Dir-Sls-Publr Platform Sls-East)*
Matt Douglas *(Dir-Platform Sls)*
Brian Hanley *(Dir-Sls-Video Publishers)*
Sean Lyden *(Dir-Product Mktg)*

Accounts:
BETAWAVE CORPORATION; San Francisco, CA Internet Video Network

ADARA MEDIA, INC.
800 W El Camino Real, Mountain View, CA 94040
Tel.: (408) 876-6360
E-Mail: info@adaramedia.com
Web Site: adara.com

Agency Specializes In: Advertising, Digital/Interactive

I'Heng Mei *(Co-Founder & Chief Architect)*
Layton Han *(CEO)*
Liz Coddington *(CFO)*
Charles Mi *(CTO)*
Scott Garner *(Pres-Data & Analytics)*
Bernie Yu *(Sr VP-Mktg-Global)*
Mark Hersch *(VP-Strategic Accounts)*
Ted Sullivan *(VP-Resorts & Destinations Analytics)*
Kazi Ahmed *(Dir-North East Sls)*
Brandon Meyers *(Dir-Comml-Europe & MENA)*
Cassandra Enos *(Planner-Sls)*

Accounts:
TRUSTe Telecommunication Services

ADASHMORE CREATIVE
1966 Greenspring Dr Ste 506, Lutherville, MD 21093
Tel.: (410) 252-7879
E-Mail: info@adashmorecreative.com
Web Site: www.adashmorecreative.com

Employees: 3
Year Founded: 2010

Agency Specializes In: Automotive, Brand Development & Integration, Business Publications, Business-To-Business, Collateral, College, Communications, Consumer Marketing, Content, Corporate Communications, Corporate Identity, Direct-to-Consumer, Education, Email, Engineering, Environmental, Event Planning & Marketing, Graphic Design, Health Care Services, Integrated Marketing, Internet/Web Design, Legal Services, Local Marketing, Logo & Package Design, Luxury Products, Mobile Marketing, Out-of-Home Media, Outdoor, Paid Searches, Point of Purchase, Point of Sale, Promotions, Real Estate, Retail, Search Engine Optimization, Social Marketing/Nonprofit, Social Media, Sports Market, Strategic Planning/Research, Web (Banner Ads, Pop-ups, etc.)

Jennifer Dodson *(Owner & Dir-Creative)*
Bacon Beagle *(VP-Bracketing)*
Alisa Crowley *(Acct Mgr)*
Samantha Orr *(Specialist-Mktg)*
Pat Murtagh *(Designer-Creative)*

Accounts:
Loyola University of Maryland Swimming & Diving Teams; 2012

ADASIA COMMUNICATIONS, INC.
400 Sylvan Ave, Englewood Cliffs, NJ 07632
Tel.: (201) 608-0388
Fax: (201) 608-0560
E-Mail: newbiz@adasia-us.com
Web Site: www.adasia-us.com

Employees: 25
Year Founded: 1997

National Agency Associations: AAF

Agency Specializes In: Advertising, Asian Market, Automotive, Bilingual Market, Business-To-Business, Communications, Consulting, Consumer Marketing, Digital/Interactive, Direct Response Marketing, Event Planning & Marketing, Exhibit/Trade Shows, Graphic Design, Health Care Services, Logo & Package Design, Media Buying Services, Media Planning, Pharmaceutical, Planning & Consultation, Retail, Sponsorship, Strategic Planning/Research

Kevin Lee *(Founder, Pres & CEO)*
Annie Shih *(Mng Partner-Acct Plng)*
Young Kim *(Partner & Chief Creative Officer)*
Sarah Choi *(Dir-Creative-Copy)*
Vidhu Kalia *(Mgr-Mktg Strategy)*
Susie Yang *(Acct Supvr)*
Harold Lee *(Media Planner & Media Buyer)*
Angie Peng *(Media Planner)*
Kerwin Hsu *(Assoc Acct Dir)*

Accounts:
PNC Bank
Subaru of America Asian Americans
Verizon; New York, NY Consumer Services; 1998

ADBAY
627 W Yellowstone Hwy, Casper, WY 82601
Tel.: (307) 268-4705
Web Site: www.adbay.com

Agency Specializes In: Advertising, Brand Development & Integration, Digital/Interactive, Internet/Web Design, Logo & Package Design, Media Buying Services, Media Planning, Print, Social Media

Shawn Houck *(Owner)*
Jason Yocum *(Graphic Designer & Dir-Social Media)*
Todd Titus *(Dir-Sls)*
Dave Castle *(Mgr-Traffic)*
Kurt Box *(Assoc Campaign Dir)*

Accounts:
Dr. Leeper
Liquor Shed
The Spence Law Firm
Stalkup's RV Superstore
Wyomovies Casper

ADBIT'S ADVERTISING & PR
757 SE 17th St 358, Fort Lauderdale, FL 33316
Tel.: (954) 467-8420
Fax: (954) 467-0809
E-Mail: reception@adbits.com
Web Site: www.adbits.com

Employees: 2
Year Founded: 1994

Agency Specializes In: Advertising, Brand Development & Integration, Collateral, Corporate Identity, Direct Response Marketing, Event Planning & Marketing, Exhibit/Trade Shows, Internet/Web Design, Logo & Package Design, Multimedia, Print, Public Relations, T.V.

Bit Grubbstrom *(Founder & Pres)*

Accounts:
Corner Cafe
GraceWay
Hatteras
The Stockholm Saxophone Quartet
Sun Sentinel

ADCETERA GROUP
3000 Louisiana St, Houston, TX 77006
Tel.: (713) 522-8006
Fax: (713) 522-8018
E-Mail: estasney@adcetera.com
Web Site: www.adcetera.com

Employees: 60
Year Founded: 1982

Agency Specializes In: Advertising, Advertising Specialties, Agriculture, Automotive, Aviation & Aerospace, Bilingual Market, Brand Development & Integration, Business Publications, Business-To-Business, Children's Market, Collateral, Communications, Consulting, Consumer Marketing, Consumer Publications, Corporate Identity, Cosmetics, Digital/Interactive, Direct Response Marketing, E-Commerce, Education, Electronic Media, Engineering, Entertainment, Environmental, Exhibit/Trade Shows, Fashion/Apparel, Financial, Food Service, Government/Political, Graphic Design, Health Care Services, High Technology, Hispanic Market, Industrial, Information Technology, Internet/Web Design, Investor Relations, Logo & Package Design, Magazines, Medical Products, Merchandising, Multimedia, New Product Development, Newspaper, Newspapers & Magazines, Pharmaceutical, Planning & Consultation, Point of Purchase, Point of Sale, Print, Production, Publicity/Promotions, Radio, Real Estate, Restaurant, Retail, Sales Promotion, Sports Market, Strategic Planning/Research, T.V., Technical Advertising, Trade & Consumer Magazines, Transportation, Travel & Tourism

Kristy Sexton *(Founder & Chief Creative Officer)*
John Sexton *(CFO)*
Rowan Gearon *(VP-Creative Svcs)*
Roy Smith *(VP-Acct Dev)*
Arick Chikiamco *(Dir-Creative)*
John Meyer *(Assoc Dir-Art)*
Holly Olson *(Acct Mgr)*
Kalie Trueper *(Acct Mgr)*
Marcela Conatser *(Sr Acct Exec)*
Lucio De La Cruz *(Designer-Production)*
Camille Trent *(Jr Copywriter)*

Accounts:
Best Buy
Hewlett-Packard; Houston, TX; Palo Alto, CA
Microsoft

ADCO
1220 Pickens St, Columbia, SC 29201
Tel.: (803) 765-1133
Fax: (803) 252-6410
E-Mail: info@adcoideas.com
Web Site: www.adcoideas.com

Employees: 10

National Agency Associations: Second Wind Limited

Agency Specializes In: Advertising

Lanier Jones *(Pres & CEO)*
Lora Prill *(Partner & VP-Mktg)*
Briann Murrell *(Partner & Dir-Creative)*

Brad Warthen *(Dir-Comm & PR)*
Steve Sperling *(Project Mgr & Mgr-Production)*

Accounts:
Callison Tighe & Robinson
The Children's Trust
Doctors Care
Hood Construction Commercial Construction
The Midlands Authority for Conventions, Sports & Tourism
Palmetto Health Alliance
REI Automation
South Carolina Bar
South Carolina Department of Commerce
South Carolina National Heritage
Voorhees College

ADCOLOR, INC
620 Adcolor Dr, Lexington, KY 40511
Tel.: (859) 253-1046
Fax: (859) 253-1047
Toll Free: (800) 423-2656
E-Mail: info@adcolorinc.com
Web Site: www.adcolorinc.com

Employees: 60

David Messner *(Pres & CEO)*
John Kiernan *(Gen Mgr-Production)*
Bill Oeffinger *(Gen Mgr)*
Gustavo Cadena *(Mgr-Screen Printing Production)*

THE ADCOM GROUP
1370 W Sixth St 3rd Fl, Cleveland, OH 44113-1222
Tel.: (216) 574-9100
Fax: (216) 574-6131
Web Site: www.theadcomgroup.com

E-Mail for Key Personnel:
President: tseiple@adcom1.com
Creative Dir.: mderrick@adcom1.com
Media Dir.: lchylla@adcom1.com

Employees: 35
Year Founded: 1989

National Agency Associations: AMA-BMA-PRSA

Agency Specializes In: Advertising, Financial, Health Care Services

Joe Kubic *(Co-Founder & CEO)*
Tim Seiple *(Partner & COO)*
Mark Nuss *(Chief Creative Officer)*
Hallie Fisher *(VP-Social Influence)*
Mike Derrick *(Dir-Creative)*
Mark Szczepanik *(Dir-Creative)*
Madeline Rose Malicki *(Sr Mgr-Social Influence)*
Morgan Rooks *(Mgr-Digital Media Traffic)*
Laura Kuenzel *(Sr Media Planner)*

Accounts:
Fathead
First National Bank of Pennsylvania
Health Start
Invest in Children
Key Bank
Kichler Lighting
The Lube Stop Inc. (Agency of Record)
Moen
On Base
Sherwin Williams
Skoda, Minotti & Co.
Swagelok

ADCOM GROUP, INC.
Plaza Triple S 1510 FD Roosevelt Ave Ste 11A, Guaynabo, PR 00968
Tel.: (787) 781-1700
Fax: (787) 781-3314
E-Mail: adcomgroup@adcomgroup.com
Web Site: www.adcomgroup.com

E-Mail for Key Personnel:
President: dalonso@adcomgroup.com
Creative Dir.: creativo@adcomgroup.com
Media Dir.: medios@adcomgroup.com

Employees: 15
Year Founded: 1993

Agency Specializes In: Advertising, Advertising Specialties, Direct Response Marketing, Public Relations, Publicity/Promotions

Approx. Annual Billings: $4,500,000

Breakdown of Gross Billings by Media: Mags.: 2%; Newsp.: 25%; Outdoor: 1%; Production: 39%; Radio: 17%; Sls. Promo.: 8%; T.V.: 8%

Debbie Alonso *(Pres)*
Dean Ilijasic *(Partner, Chief Strategy Officer & Chief Innovation Officer)*
Jim Ganzer *(Dir-Media Strategy)*
Joe Santoli *(Dir-Search & Video Adv)*
Angel Siberon *(Dir-Art)*
Sara Zavorek *(Dir-Social Influence)*
Madeline Rose Malicki *(Sr Mgr-Social Influence)*
Robert Batyko *(Specialist-Social Influence)*
Morgan Mitchell *(Acct Exec)*
Joseph Sasak *(Specialist-Social Influence)*

Accounts:
Mayaguez Resort & Casino; Mayaguez, PR Hotel; 1996
Sobieski Vodka

ADCREASIANS, INC.
3530 Wilshire Blvd Ste 1475, Los Angeles, CA 90010
Tel.: (213) 389-9300
Fax: (213) 389-9393
E-Mail: solutions@adcreasians.com
Web Site: www.adcreasians.com

Year Founded: 2007

Agency Specializes In: Asian Market

Soa Kang *(Pres & CEO)*
Ted Park *(Partner & Dir-Creative)*
Kate Park *(Controller)*

Accounts:
Dongbu Insurance
Elite Educational Institute
Focus Features
The Korea Times
Lingo
Nara Bank
Network Solutions
Spider Smart

ADDIS
(Formerly Addis Creson)
2612-A 8th St, Berkeley, CA 94710
Tel.: (510) 704-7500
Fax: (510) 704-7501
E-Mail: info@addis.com
Web Site: addis.com/

Employees: 30

Agency Specializes In: Advertising, Brand Development & Integration, Consulting, Consumer Marketing, Corporate Identity, Fashion/Apparel, Financial, Graphic Design, Internet/Web Design, Logo & Package Design, Print, Sponsorship

Approx. Annual Billings: $3,000,000

Steven Addis *(CEO)*
Mark Galbraith *(VP)*
Tyler Anderson *(Dir-Strategy)*
Bob Dow *(Dir-Tech)*
Jonathan Fisher *(Dir-Implementation)*
Stacey Olson *(Dir-Digital Production)*

Accounts:
24 Hour Fitness
Birds Eye
Equinix
GE Healthcare
Kidfresh
Marine Mammal Center
PopChips
Smith & Hawken
Think Products
Verlasso Premium Salmon

THE ADDISON GROUP
PO Box 1826, Suffolk, VA 23439
Tel.: (757) 539-1669
Fax: (757) 923-9166
E-Mail: info@theaddisongroup.com
Web Site: www.theaddisongroup.com

National Agency Associations: Second Wind Limited

Randall Scott *(Sr VP)*
Ian Grey *(Dir-Ops)*
Lizzy Guterma *(Dir-Mktg)*
Beth Anne Mcpheeters *(Dir-Brand Strategy)*
Adam Tilly *(Acct Mgr)*
Jenny Winn *(Office Mgr)*
Cathleen Foley *(Mgr-Visual Branding)*
Matthew Harris *(Mgr-Comm)*
Lee King *(Mgr-Market Res)*
Chris Cureton *(Sr Graphic Designer)*
Benjamin Patton *(Analyst-Mktg Res)*

Accounts:
Amicis
Bank Of Hampton Roads
BARRE
Belle Harbour
Faith Alive
Snappy's
Tax Break

(ADD)VENTURES
117 Chapman St, Providence, RI 02905
Tel.: (401) 453-4748
Fax: (401) 453-0095
E-Mail: info@addventures.com
Web Site: www.addventures.com

Employees: 25
Year Founded: 1989

Agency Specializes In: Advertising, Brand Development & Integration, Business Publications, Co-op Advertising, Communications, Corporate Communications, Multicultural, Multimedia, Public Relations

Revenue: $60,000,000

Steve Rosa *(Founder, CEO & Chief Creative Officer)*
Joe Miech *(COO)*
Mary Sadlier *(Chief Strategy Officer & Exec VP)*
Tracy Silva *(Sr VP-Quality & Production)*
Wayne Vieira *(Sr VP-Design & Branding)*
Andrea Reed *(VP-Mktg & Branding)*
Lisa Dutra Curtis *(Dir-Interactive & Res)*
Dominic Green *(Mgr-Content & Branding)*

Accounts:
Autocrat
CVS Health
DUNKIN DONUTS
Hasbro
Johnson & Wales

Learning Curve
Marriott
ProTech
Renaissance
Textron Financial
Textron

ADFARM
333 24th Ave SW Ste 250, Calgary, AB T2S 3E6 Canada
Tel.: (403) 410-7600
Fax: (403) 410-7601
Web Site: www.adfarmonline.com

Employees: 45
Year Founded: 2002

Agency Specializes In: Advertising, Agriculture, Pets

Glenn Dawes *(Exec Dir-Creative)*
Audra Fimmers *(Dir-Art)*
Michael Kohlweg *(Dir-Art)*
Deb Verbonac *(Sr Acct Mgr-New Bus Dev)*
Wendy Gold *(Acct Mgr)*
Jackie Littlejohn *(Acct Mgr)*
Megan Morozoff *(Acct Mgr)*
Brent Vollick *(Sr Project Mgr-Digital)*
Jeff Large *(Mgr-HR)*
Jane Robinson *(Sr Specialist-PR & Writer)*
Michael Anthony *(Acct Exec)*
Lance Risseeuw *(Copywriter)*
Robin Cook *(Coord-Internal Projects)*

Accounts:
AgriGold Hybrids
Agrium
AGROTAIN International
Alberta Beef Producers
Bayer Animal Health
Bayer CropScience
Dow AgroSciences
Hyland Seeds
Novartis
Novus International

Branches

AdFarm
100 E 7th St Ste 301, Kansas City, MO 64106
Tel.: (816) 842-5983
Fax: (816) 221-5833
Web Site: www.adfarmonline.com

Employees: 15

Agency Specializes In: Agriculture

Les Kahl *(Mng Partner-US & Dir-Creative)*
Dan Kirkpatrick *(Head-Strategic Acct)*
Shaun Crockett *(Dir-Creative)*
Cheryl Grocock *(Sr Acct Mgr)*
Meghan Walters *(Acct Mgr)*
Tiffany Bronson *(Acct Supvr)*
Marissa Birnbaum *(Coord-Traffic & Media)*
Shelley Thompson *(Coord-Admin Media)*

AdFarm
101 N 10th St Ste 110, Fargo, ND 58102
Tel.: (701) 237-4850
Fax: (701) 234-9680
E-Mail: roger.reierson@adfarmonline.com
Web Site: www.adfarmonline.com

Employees: 12

Agency Specializes In: Agriculture

Les Kahl *(Mng Partner-US & Dir-Creative)*
Angie Skochdopole *(Sr Dir-Media Svcs)*
Carina Emil *(Acct Mgr)*
Cheryl Grocock *(Acct Mgr)*
Brandon Souza *(Acct Mgr)*
Tiffany Bronson *(Acct Exec)*
Jessica Dammen *(Acct Coord)*

Accounts:
BetaSeed
Hubbard Feeds
North Dakota Corn Growers Association
North Dakota Farmers Union
North Dakota Soybean Council

ADFERO GROUP
1666 K St NW Ste 250, Washington, DC 20006
Tel.: (202) 333-4444
Fax: (202) 333-3231
Web Site: www.adfero.com

Employees: 22

National Agency Associations: COPF

Agency Specializes In: Communications, Crisis Communications, Education, Environmental, Public Relations, Radio

Jeff Mascott *(Mng Partner)*
Darren Scher *(COO)*
Meghan Moran *(VP)*
Jessica Mancari *(Dir-Content Strategy)*
Gina Savory *(Dir-Social Strategy)*
Krista Flannery *(Acct Supvr)*
Misty Fuller *(Acct Supvr)*
Lina Mizerek *(Acct Supvr)*
Jessica Cooper *(Acct Exec)*

Accounts:
American Airlines Cargo

ADG CREATIVE
7151 Columbia Gateway Dr Ste B, Columbia, MD 21046-2149
Tel.: (443) 285-0008
Web Site: www.adgcreative.com

Agency Specializes In: Sponsorship

Mike McGahey *(CFO)*
Marybeth Steil *(Gen Counsel & Dir-Contracts)*
Evan Davis *(VP-Strategy)*
Kristy Holnaider *(VP-Strategy)*
Jeff Cochran *(Client Svcs Dir)*
Rosemarie Carlyle *(Dir-Client Rels)*
Sarah Nelson-Balonis *(Dir-Art)*
Ken Joy *(Brand Strategist)*
Kathe Flynn *(Designer)*

Accounts:
Amerland Marketing, Strategic Analysis
Bowie State University
Centric Business Systems
Durakis Executive Search
Enlightened
General Growth Properties, Inc.
Howard Bank Brand Strategy, Marketing Strategy
Root9B (Agency of Record) Branding, Content Marketing, Content Strategy, Design, Digital, Marketing, Website Development
St. Boniface Craft Brewing Company Can Designs, Craft Beers
U.S Navy
V-tech Solutions

ADHOME CREATIVE
(Formerly Surge Communications)
123 Saint George St Ste 105, London, ON N6A 3A1 Canada
Tel.: (519) 672-9090
Fax: (519) 672-6080
E-Mail: info@adHOMEcreative.com
Web Site: www.adhomecreative.com

Employees: 25
Year Founded: 1999

Mark Brown *(Partner)*
Carlos Sousa *(Controller)*
Tony Soares *(Acct Dir)*
Kathryn Byfield *(Office Mgr & Mgr-Production)*
Jason Brown *(Acct Supvr)*
Nathalie Noel *(Acct Supvr)*
Marcie Butterwick *(Acct Exec)*
Jessica De Lange *(Specialist-Digital Mktg)*

Accounts:
Hydra Ottawa
Lindt
Maple Leaf Food Service
Mufflerman
Procter & Gamble Andrew Ranger's Canadian Champ Car; 2007
Roxul

AD.IN DESIGN
936 Porter Ave, Ocean Springs, MS 39564
Tel.: (228) 215-0029
Web Site: www.ad-in.us

Agency Specializes In: Advertising, Brand Development & Integration, Graphic Design, Internet/Web Design, Logo & Package Design, Print, Radio

Beverly Dees *(Owner & Art Dir)*
Susan Church *(Mgr-Production & Svcs)*

Accounts:
Childrens International Medical Group
Ocean Springs Chamber of Commerce

ADIRONDACK MARKETING SERVICES, LLC
24711 New Rd, North Liberty, IN 46554-9445
Tel.: (574) 656-3811
Fax: (574) 656-3812
E-Mail: info@ideas-happen.com
Web Site: www.ideas-happen.com

Employees: 2
Year Founded: 1997

Agency Specializes In: Business-To-Business, Financial, Health Care Services, Industrial, Planning & Consultation, Strategic Planning/Research

Bruce Cashbaugh *(Co-Owner)*
Steve Patton *(Owner)*

Accounts:
Elkhart General Hospital
Merillat Industries

ADJECTIVE & CO
102 6th Ave N Ste 9, Jacksonville Beach, FL 32250
Tel.: (904) 638-6131
E-Mail: us@adjectiveandco.com
Web Site: www.adjectiveandco.com

Agency Specializes In: Advertising, Brand Development & Integration, Event Planning & Marketing, Internet/Web Design, Social Media

Autumn Berrang *(Founder & Pres)*
Eddie Berrang *(VP-Marketing & Strategy)*
Taylor Harkey *(Exec Creative Dir)*
Brittany Norris *(Art Dir)*
Danielle Bergh *(Acct Dir)*
Stevan Brown *(Dir-PR)*

Accounts:

New-Whalebone Media

ADK AMERICA
3137 S La Cienega Blvd, Los Angeles, CA 90016-3110
Tel.: (310) 630-3600
Fax: (310) 630-3620
E-Mail: info@adkamerica.com
Web Site: www.adkamerica.com

Employees: 15
Year Founded: 1981

National Agency Associations: 4A's

Agency Specializes In: Communications

Approx. Annual Billings: $36,000,000

Breakdown of Gross Billings by Media: Brdcst.: $7,000,000; Bus. Publs.: $4,000,000; Collateral: $1,000,000; D.M.: $1,000,000; Farm Publs.: $1,000,000; Mags.: $5,000,000; Newsp.: $2,500,000; Other: $1,500,000; Outdoor: $1,000,000; Point of Purchase: $1,000,000; Point of Sale: $2,000,000; Radio: $1,000,000; Sls. Promo.: $2,000,000; T.V.: $5,000,000; Transit: $1,000,000

Dwain Taylor *(Pres)*
Dan Yamada *(Sr VP & Dir-Creative)*
Haru Sugimoto *(Sr VP)*
Ingrid Chen *(VP-Project Mgmt)*
Kevin Prince *(Head-Digital Design)*
Ron Burns *(Acct Dir)*
Christine Caridi *(Acct Dir)*
Jon Simms *(Assoc Dir-Media Research)*
Kazuko Sato *(Mgr-Acctg)*
Nao Abe *(Acct Exec)*
Sierra Hunter *(Jr Designer)*

Accounts:
Air Tahiti Nui
Asahi Beer; Los Angeles, CA Asahi "Super Dry" Beer; 1985
Fuji Film; New York, NY Data Storage; 1998
Fuji Heavy Industries Ltd
Namco; San Jose, CA Video Games; 1996
Pioneer Corp.; Long Beach, CA CD Rom, Cable Box, Laser Disc; 1994
Square Enix

Branch

ADK America
515 W 20th St 6th fl, New York, NY 10011
Tel.: (646) 284-9811
Fax: (646) 284-9825
E-Mail: info@adkamerica.com
Web Site: www.adkamerica.com

Employees: 10
Year Founded: 1984

National Agency Associations: 4A's

Agency Specializes In: Advertising, Communications

Dwain Taylor *(Pres)*
Daniel Yamada *(Sr VP & Dir-Creative)*
Kevin Prince *(Head-Digital Design)*
Tk Sato *(Sr Dir-Art)*
Ron Burns *(Acct Dir)*
Christine Caridi *(Acct Dir)*
Kazuko Sato *(Mgr-Acctg)*
Nao Abe *(Acct Exec)*
Roy Nagasawa *(Acct Exec)*
Kristen Pacheco *(Planner-Comm)*
Sierra Hunter *(Jr Designer)*

Accounts:
ICB
TDK

ADLER DISPLAY
7140 Windsor Blvd, Baltimore, MD 21244
Tel.: (410) 281-1200
Fax: (410) 281-2187
Toll Free: (888) 578-7443
E-Mail: adlerdisplay@bravenewmarkets.com
Web Site: www.adlerdisplay.com

Employees: 25
Year Founded: 1937

Agency Specializes In: Advertising, Graphic Design, In-Store Advertising, Outdoor

Chris Hammond *(Mgr-Ops)*
Lewis Lively, Jr. *(Mgr-Warehouse)*
Marcy Trader *(Mgr-Graphics)*
Jenna Adler *(Specialist-Mktg)*
Doug Holt *(Designer-Exhibit)*
Mike Jeffery *(Designer)*
Jill Tascher-Cook *(Designer-Exhibit)*

THE ADMARK GROUP
96 N Sunnyslope Ave, Pasadena, CA 91107
Tel.: (626) 583-1610
Fax: (626) 583-9031
E-Mail: info@admarkgroup.com
Web Site: www.admarkgroup.com

Employees: 6

Agency Specializes In: Hispanic Market, Outdoor

Adriana Blanco *(CEO)*
Eddy Blanco *(COO & Dir-Bus Dev)*
Giovanni Arana *(Dir-IT)*
Marlena Brown *(Dir-Art)*
Johnathan Reid *(Dir-Production)*
Denise Bautista *(Office Mgr & Supvr-Media)*
Kristen Tasso *(Acct Mgr)*
Ivonne Rodriguez *(Acct Exec)*

Accounts:
Dearden's Retail Furniture & Electronics; 2000
Estrella TV TV Programming; 2000
Happy Tours Travel Website & Direct Response; 2015
Jiffy Lube International Quick Service Lube (Spanish Language Creative); 2007
Jiffy Lube Southern California Coop of Franchisees Quick Lube Service-Agency of Record; 2011
Los Angeles Dodgers Sports; 2008
Salud California Healthcare Exchange Broker; 2013

ADMARKETPLACE
3 Park Ave 27th Fl, New York, NY 10016
Tel.: (212) 925-2022
Fax: (212) 925-2684
Web Site: www.admarketplace.com

Year Founded: 2000

Agency Specializes In: Advertising, Email, Mobile Marketing, Paid Searches

Jamei Hill *(Chm & CEO)*
Adam J. Epstein *(Pres)*
Michael E. Yudin *(CTO)*
Julie Greenhouse *(Sr VP-Sls)*
Vincent Meyer *(VP-Bus Dev)*
Matt Azark *(Acct Exec)*
Nick Martucci *(Acct Exec)*

Accounts:
ADT Security Services Inc. Home Security Service Providers
AT&T Communications Corp. Telecommunication Network Service Providers
Comcast Telecommunication & Television Network Services
Dell Computers & Laptops Mfr & Distr
VOLVO GROUP Cars Buses & Trucks Mfr

ADMASTERS, INC.
16901 Dallas Pkwy # 204, Addison, TX 75001
Tel.: (972) 866-9300
Fax: (866) 409-7685
Toll Free: (877) ADMASTERS
Web Site: www.admasters.com

E-Mail for Key Personnel:
President: tom.dodson@admasters.com
Creative Dir.: creative@admasters.com
Media Dir.: media@admasters.com
Production Mgr.: creative@admasters.com

Employees: 11
Year Founded: 1995

Agency Specializes In: Advertising, Advertising Specialties, Business-To-Business, Digital/Interactive, Graphic Design, Identity Marketing, Logo & Package Design, Newspaper, Newspapers & Magazines, Outdoor, Print, Recruitment, Search Engine Optimization, Trade & Consumer Magazines, Web (Banner Ads, Pop-ups, etc.)

Approx. Annual Billings: $8,000,000

Breakdown of Gross Billings by Media: Adv. Specialties: $500,000; Bus. Publs.: $2,000,000; Collateral: $500,000; Internet Adv.: $1,000,000; Newsp.: $4,000,000

Tom Dodson *(Pres)*

Accounts:
BTI Travel
Cameron
Citi Group
Comcast
Cooper Energy
First Data Corp.
PG&E
State Fair
Stevens Transport
Temsco, Inc
Thomas Group
Trex Company
United Healthcare
USAA Realty

ADMAX ADVERTISING
PO Box 1820, Evans, GA 30809
Tel.: (706) 869-8184
Web Site: www.admaxadv.com

Agency Specializes In: Advertising, Digital/Interactive, Internet/Web Design, Logo & Package Design, Media Buying Services, Outdoor, Radio, Social Media, T.V.

Rob Ashe *(Pres)*

Accounts:
The Country Club Dance Hall & Saloon
US Auto Couple

ADMEDIA.
901 W Alameda Ave Ste 102, Burbank, CA 91506
Toll Free: (800) 296-7104
Web Site: www.admedia.com

Employees: 45
Year Founded: 1995

Agency Specializes In: Affiliate Marketing,

Digital/Interactive, Email, Local Marketing, Paid Searches, Web (Banner Ads, Pop-ups, etc.)

Approx. Annual Billings: $50,000,000

Avi N. Bibi *(Pres & COO)*
Rob Lloyd *(Head-Digital Sls & Bus Dir)*
Tristan Johns *(Acct Dir)*
Alice Leeson *(Acct Mgr)*
Mahmoud Hajjar *(Mgr-Sls)*

Accounts:
Pepsi Pepsi Spirit; 2008

ADMERASIA, INC.

159 W 25th St 6th Fl, New York, NY 10001-7203
Tel.: (212) 686-3333
Fax: (212) 686-8998
E-Mail: tommyn@admerasia.com
Web Site: www.admerasia.com

E-Mail for Key Personnel:
President: zan@admerasia.com
Creative Dir.: tuanpuw@admerasia.com
Media Dir.: hslingc@admerasia.com
Production Mgr.: vivianl@admerasia.com

Employees: 60
Year Founded: 1993

National Agency Associations: 4A's

Agency Specializes In: Advertising, Asian Market, Automotive, Bilingual Market, Brand Development & Integration, Broadcast, Business-To-Business, Cable T.V., Co-op Advertising, Collateral, Communications, Consulting, Consumer Marketing, Consumer Publications, Corporate Identity, Digital/Interactive, Direct Response Marketing, E-Commerce, Electronic Media, Event Planning & Marketing, Exhibit/Trade Shows, Financial, Government/Political, Graphic Design, Health Care Services, Infomercials, Internet/Web Design, Investor Relations, Leisure, Logo & Package Design, Media Buying Services, Merchandising, Newspaper, Newspapers & Magazines, Out-of-Home Media, Outdoor, Pharmaceutical, Planning & Consultation, Point of Purchase, Point of Sale, Print, Production, Public Relations, Publicity/Promotions, Radio, Recruitment, Retail, Sales Promotion, Sponsorship, Strategic Planning/Research, T.V., Technical Advertising, Telemarketing

Approx. Annual Billings: $15,000,000

Breakdown of Gross Billings by Media: D.M.: 4%; Event Mktg.: 4%; Internet Adv.: 2%; Print: 52%; Promos.: 2%; Radio & T.V.: 36%

Jeff Lin *(Co-Founder)*
Vivian Lau Guerriero *(VP & Dir-Production)*
Tommy Ng *(Gen Mgr)*
Tuan Pu Wang *(Exec Dir-Creative)*
Doris Huang *(Dir-Media)*
Ah-Young Kim *(Sr Media Planner)*

Accounts:
Citibank; New York, NY Campaign: "Golden Opportunities"
Dish Network; Pinebrook, NJ; 2003
Keyspan; New York, NY; 2005
Kohler
Lowe's; Mooresville, NC; 2004
McDonald's; Oak Brook, IL; 2005
Mercedes; Montvale, NJ; 2001
MetLife
Moet Hennessy USA; New York, NY Spirits; 1997
MX Energy; Stanford, CT; 2007
Procter & Gamble; Cincinnati, OH Actonel, SKII; 2005

Branch

AAAZA, Inc.

3250 Wilshire Blvd Ste 1901, Los Angeles, CA 90010
Tel.: (213) 380-8333
Fax: (213) 380-5333
E-Mail: info@aaaza.com
Web Site: www.aaaza.com

E-Mail for Key Personnel:
President: peterh@aaza.com

Employees: 30
Year Founded: 2001

Agency Specializes In: Advertising, Advertising Specialties, Asian Market, Bilingual Market, Brand Development & Integration, Consulting, Digital/Interactive, Direct Response Marketing, Direct-to-Consumer, E-Commerce, Event Planning & Marketing, Graphic Design, Integrated Marketing, Internet/Web Design, Local Marketing, Logo & Package Design, Market Research, Media Buying Services, Media Planning, Media Relations, Multicultural, New Product Development, Planning & Consultation, Search Engine Optimization, Strategic Planning/Research, Telemarketing, Viral/Buzz/Word of Mouth, Web (Banner Ads, Pop-ups, etc.), Yellow Pages Advertising

Jay Kim *(Mng Dir)*
Changhyun Dominic Jun *(Sr Dir-Art)*
Woonkyung Sung *(Dir-Art)*
Ascon Caceres Pavia *(Assoc Dir-Media)*
Duyen-Kathie Nguyen *(Acct Supvr)*
Vi Ma *(Acct Exec)*
Rich De Los Santos *(Acct Exec)*
Emil Louis Vanta *(Acct Exec)*
Mandy Li *(Media Planner)*
Matthew Ayala *(Asst Media Planner)*

Accounts:
AIG
American Cancer Society
Echostar
Procter & Gamble
Vayama

ADMFG INC.

100 N State St Ste D, Fairmont, MN 56031
Tel.: (507) 238-1243
Web Site: www.admfg.com

Agency Specializes In: Advertising, Graphic Design, Internet/Web Design, Logo & Package Design, Promotions

Nancy Stauffer *(VP-Client Svcs)*

Accounts:
BBQ company

ADMO, INC.

1714 Deer Tracks Trl Ste 205, Saint Louis, MO 63131
Tel.: (314) 993-9300
E-Mail: info@admo.com
Web Site: www.admo.com

Employees: 9
Year Founded: 1986

Agency Specializes In: Advertising, African-American Market, Brand Development & Integration, Broadcast, Business-To-Business, Cable T.V., Children's Market, Co-op Advertising, Collateral, Commercial Photography, Communications, Consulting, Consumer Marketing, Corporate Identity, Direct Response Marketing, Electronic Media, Entertainment, Event Planning & Marketing, Financial, Graphic Design, Infomercials, Internet/Web Design, Logo & Package Design, Magazines, Media Buying Services, Merchandising, Multimedia, New Product Development, Newspaper, Newspapers & Magazines, Out-of-Home Media, Outdoor, Pharmaceutical, Planning & Consultation, Point of Purchase, Point of Sale, Print, Production, Public Relations, Publicity/Promotions, Radio, Real Estate, Recruitment, Restaurant, Retail, Sales Promotion, Seniors' Market, Sports Market, Strategic Planning/Research, T.V., Teen Market, Telemarketing, Trade & Consumer Magazines, Travel & Tourism, Yellow Pages Advertising

Revenue: $25,000,000

Dan Shroyer *(Pres)*
Dan Ford *(Creative Dir)*
Cheryl Jeffrey *(Dir-Mfg & Plant Mgr)*
Katie Alcala *(Dir-Quality Assurance)*
Christy Solly Giardino *(Dir-HR & Info Sys)*

Accounts:
Aquatic Advertising
Christ in Media
IBB
Kitchen & Bath Design
Leader's Edge
Lex Rex Publishing
Micromath
MidWest Disbursing
Vito's

ADMOSIS MEDIA

92 Lenora St, Seattle, WA 98121
Tel.: (425) 533-4995
E-Mail: info@admosismedia.com
Web Site: www.admosismedia.com

Year Founded: 2012

Agency Specializes In: Advertising, Brand Development & Integration, Promotions, Social Media

Caitlin Angeloff *(Co-Founder & Principal)*
Brooke Angles *(Founder & Principal)*
Tara Newton *(Mng Dir)*
Monique Van Zuylen *(Jr Designer)*

Accounts:
BMC Software
King 5
Living Social
Pilgrim Africa

ADNET ADVERTISING AGENCY, INC.

111 John St Ste 701, New York, NY 10038
Tel.: (212) 587-3164
Fax: (212) 406-4648
E-Mail: information@adnet-nyc.com
Web Site: www.adnet-nyc.com

Employees: 20
Year Founded: 1992

Agency Specializes In: Advertising, Advertising Specialties, Business Publications, Consulting, Consumer Publications, Electronic Media, Email, Internet/Web Design, Legal Services, Magazines, Market Research, Media Buying Services, Media Planning, Media Relations, Multicultural, Newspaper, Newspapers & Magazines, Planning & Consultation, Radio, Recruitment, Strategic Planning/Research, Technical Advertising, Trade & Consumer Magazines, Web (Banner Ads, Pop-ups, etc.)

Approx. Annual Billings: $16,000,000

Breakdown of Gross Billings by Media: Bus. Publs.: 15%; Internet Adv.: 15%; Mags.: 15%; Newsp.: 50%; Radio: 5%

Fahd Mumtaz *(Pres)*
Kiran Vairale-Mumtaz *(CEO)*
Manju Kaur *(Mgr-Client Rels)*

ADNETIK
(Name Changed to Digilant)

ADOMETRY INC.
6801 N Capital of Texas Hwy, Austin, TX 78731
Tel.: (512) 852-7100
Fax: (512) 852-7199
Toll Free: (866) 512-5425
E-Mail: support@adometry.com
Web Site:
https://www.google.com/analytics/adometry/

Year Founded: 2006

Agency Specializes In: Advertising, Media Relations, Publishing

Gad Alon *(Head-Bus Dev)*
Matthew Ewing *(Head-Sls & Automotive)*
Phil Dance *(Dir-Sls-EMEA)*
John Dietz *(Mgr-Engrg)*

Accounts:
AT&T Communications Corp. Telecommunication Network Service Providers
eBay Inc. Online Shopping Providers
Expedia Inc. Tour & Travel Agency Services
Facebook Social Network Services
Intel Corporation Computers & Laptop Mfr & Distr
Lycos Online Search Engine
Microsoft Corporation Information Technology Services

ADORE CREATIVE
8033 Sunset Blvd Ste 5750, Los Angeles, CA 90046
Tel.: (310) 278-8342
Fax: (323) 876-7003
Web Site: www.adorecreative.com

Agency Specializes In: Advertising, Content, Digital/Interactive, Social Media, Strategic Planning/Research

Rupert Wainwright *(Pres & Creative Dir)*
Ken Corr *(VP-Digital)*

Accounts:
New-USA Luge

ADPERSUASION
17595 Harvard Ave Ste C5000, Irvine, CA 92614
Toll Free: (800) 250-7780
E-Mail: info@adpersuasion.com
Web Site: www.adpersuasion.com

Employees: 10
Year Founded: 2009

National Agency Associations: AAF-AMA

Agency Specializes In: Advertising, Affiliate Marketing, Affluent Market, Alternative Advertising, Automotive, Bilingual Market, Brand Development & Integration, Broadcast, Business-To-Business, Cable T.V., Co-op Advertising, Collateral, College, Computers & Software, Consulting, Consumer Goods, Consumer Marketing, Consumer Publications, Corporate Communications, Corporate Identity, Customer Relationship Management, Digital/Interactive, Direct Response Marketing, Direct-to-Consumer, E-Commerce, Education, Electronics, Entertainment, Environmental, Event Planning & Marketing, Exhibit/Trade Shows, Experience Design, Financial, Food Service, Government/Political, Graphic Design, Guerilla Marketing, Health Care Services, High Technology, Hospitality, Household Goods, In-Store Advertising, Infomercials, Information Technology, Integrated Marketing, Internet/Web Design, Investor Relations, Leisure, Local Marketing, Logo & Package Design, Luxury Products, Magazines, Market Research, Media Buying Services, Media Planning, Media Relations, Medical Products, Men's Market, Mobile Marketing, Multicultural, Multimedia, New Product Development, New Technologies, Newspaper, Newspapers & Magazines, Out-of-Home Media, Outdoor, Over-50 Market, Package Design, Pharmaceutical, Planning & Consultation, Podcasting, Point of Purchase, Point of Sale, Production (Print), Promotions, Public Relations, Publicity/Promotions, RSS (Really Simple Syndication), Radio, Real Estate, Recruitment, Regional, Restaurant, Retail, Sales Promotion, Search Engine Optimization, Social Marketing/Nonprofit, Social Media, Sponsorship, Sports Market, Strategic Planning/Research, T.V., Telemarketing, Trade & Consumer Magazines, Transportation, Travel & Tourism, Urban Market, Viral/Buzz/Word of Mouth

Approx. Annual Billings: $3,000,000

Breakdown of Gross Billings by Media: Collateral: 7%; Consulting: 15%; Event Mktg.: 4%; Internet Adv.: 11%; Local Mktg.: 3%; Logo & Package Design: 5%; Newsp.: 4%; Print: 3%; Radio: 10%; T.V.: 14%; Worldwide Web Sites: 24%

Joseph G. Albonetti *(CEO)*

Accounts:
Artimex Bakery; Santa Fe Springs, CA Gourmet & Mexican Baked Goods; 2009
The Bernod Group; Valencia, CA Gourmet Popcorn, Organic Cotton Candy; 2009
BookkeepingEZ; Tustin, CA QuickBooks & Accounting Services; 2010
Downey Nissan; Downey, CA Nissan Automobiles; 2009
El Gallo Giro; Downey, CA Traditional Mexican Food; 2009
Essential Healthcare Management; Los Angeles, CA & Dallas, TX Healthcare Industry Consulting & Marketing; 2009
OC Tax Team; Tustin, CA CPA, Financial Consulting; 2010
OnCars.com; Aliso Viejo, CA Automotive Information & Product Reviews; 2009
Triomphe Design; Costa Mesa, CA Commercial Interior Design; 2009

ADRENALIGN MARKETING LLC
408 3rd St Ste 402, Wausau, WI 54403
Tel.: (715) 298-9323
E-Mail: creative@adrenalignmarketing.com
Web Site: www.adrenalignmarketing.com

Year Founded: 2009

Agency Specializes In: Advertising, Brand Development & Integration, Corporate Identity, Internet/Web Design, Media Planning, Outdoor, Package Design, Public Relations

Kent Perrin *(Owner & Dir-Creative)*
Keith Dupuis *(Owner)*

Accounts:
Baesemans Shoe & Clothing
CenterStage Band

ADRENALIN, INC
54 W 11th Ave, Denver, CO 80204
Tel.: (303) 454-8888
Fax: (303) 454-8889
Toll Free: (888) 757-5646
Web Site: www.goadrenalin.com

Employees: 10

Agency Specializes In: Advertising, Brand Development & Integration, Collateral, Digital/Interactive, Logo & Package Design, Strategic Planning/Research

Revenue: $1,100,000

Daniel S. Price *(Pres & Principal)*
Peju Alawusa *(Dir-Art & Graphic Designer)*
Tim De Frisco *(Dir-Photography)*
Jessica McGurn *(Dir-Partnership Dev)*
Ron Sellers *(Dir-Insights)*
Dwayne Taylor *(Dir-Mktg & Strategy)*
Skye Dillon *(Designer)*
Leslie Hancock *(Media Buyer)*
Jill Manser *(Copywriter)*
Brant Nicholason *(Designer)*
Drew Wieland *(Copywriter)*

Accounts:
Arapahoe Basin Ski Area
National Collegiate Hockey Conference
USA Climbing

ADRENALINE, INC.
3405 Piedmont Rd NE Ste 300, Atlanta, GA 30305
Tel.: (404) 252-9995
E-Mail: info@adrenalineshot.com
Web Site: www.adrenalineshot.com

Employees: 9

Agency Specializes In: Advertising, Brand Development & Integration, Collateral, Corporate Communications, Corporate Identity, Digital/Interactive, Environmental, Financial, Food Service, Graphic Design, Internet/Web Design, Logo & Package Design, Package Design, Retail, Strategic Planning/Research

Sean Keathley *(Pres)*
Kevin Blair *(CEO)*
Frank Beardsworth *(Mng Dir)*
Timothy Wheeler *(Mng Dir)*
Eduardo Alvarez *(Mng Dir-Strategy)*
Scott Hilton *(VP & Program Dir)*
Rick Barrick *(VP-Digital Strategy)*
Debbie E. Harvey *(Controller)*
Gina Bleedorn *(Exec Dir)*
Linda Bennett *(Mgr-Ops)*

ADS & ARTS
2715 Pennington Ct NW, Rochester, MN 55901-0115
Tel.: (507) 282-9043
Fax: (507) 282-9537
Toll Free: (800) 586-6774
E-Mail: info@adsart.com
Web Site: www.adsart.com

E-Mail for Key Personnel:
President: dripps.sue@adsart.com

Employees: 3
Year Founded: 1976

Agency Specializes In: Graphic Design, Health Care Services, Industrial, Information Technology, Logo & Package Design, Media Buying Services, Medical Products, Travel & Tourism, Yellow Pages Advertising

Approx. Annual Billings: $505,000 Fees Capitalized

Breakdown of Gross Billings by Media: Collateral: 2%; Fees: 10%; Internet Adv.: 2%; Newsp. & Mags.: 77%; Radio: 9%

Susan K. Dripps *(Owner)*
Thomas W. Davies *(VP)*

Accounts:
Eastwood Bank; 2003
Mayo Foundation; MN
Mayo Medical Ventures; Rochester, MN
Metafile Information Systems
Schmidt Printing

ADS ON WHEELS
26a Columbia Cir, Merrimack, NH 03054
Tel.: (603) 420-8549
Fax: (603) 420-8547
Toll Free: (800) 237-6694
E-Mail: info@adsonwheels.com
Web Site: www.adsonwheels.com

Employees: 5
Year Founded: 1999

Agency Specializes In: Advertising, Advertising Specialties, Alternative Advertising, Automotive, Digital/Interactive, Direct Response Marketing, Graphic Design, Identity Marketing, Mobile Marketing, Teen Market

Chris Dyson *(Pres & CEO)*

Accounts:
Geico Insurance Services

ADSERVICES INC.
2450 Hollywood Blvd Ste 202, Hollywood, FL 33020
Tel.: (954) 922-9395
Fax: (954) 922-1395
Toll Free: (800) 963-1914
E-Mail: service@adservices.net
Web Site: www.adservices.net

Year Founded: 1989

Agency Specializes In: Advertising, Brand Development & Integration, Corporate Identity, E-Commerce, Graphic Design, Internet/Web Design, Logo & Package Design, Print, Search Engine Optimization, Social Media

Steve Fales *(Pres)*
Donavan Hakes *(Gen Mgr)*
Debra Haut *(Dir-Media)*
Melissa Wolowicz *(Art Dir)*
Debbie Allen *(Mgr-Fin)*
Andrea Hurtado *(Mgr-Digital Media)*
Kelly King *(Acct Exec)*
Alex Duran *(Acct Exec)*

Accounts:
Foundations of South Florida

ADSMITH COMMUNICATIONS
1736 E Sunshine Ste 801, Springfield, MO 65804
Tel.: (417) 881-7722
Fax: (417) 881-7552
E-Mail: info@adsmith.biz
Web Site: www.adsmith.biz

Employees: 8
Year Founded: 2000

National Agency Associations: 4A's

Agency Specializes In: Advertising

Approx. Annual Billings: $3,000,000

Angela D. Smith *(Owner)*
Celeste Skidmore *(Exec VP)*
Morgan Nielsen *(VP-Digital Svcs)*
Shannon Perryman *(VP-Identity Svcs)*
Hillary West *(VP-Client Svcs)*
Sarah Nenninger *(Acct Supvr)*
Daniel Green *(Specialist-Ops & Political)*
Abby Akin *(Media Buyer)*
Holly Atkinson *(Copywriter)*
Jackie Hohlt *(Acct Coord)*
Hayley Hoover *(Acct Coord)*

Accounts:
Bug Zero
Maxons Diamonds
Maxson Diamond Merchant

ADSMITH MEDIA SOLUTIONS LLC
4148 Stonegate Dr, Evans, GA 30809
Tel.: (706) 831-0979
Web Site: adsmithmediasolutions.com

Agency Specializes In: Brand Development & Integration, Digital/Interactive, Print, Strategic Planning/Research

Terri Smith *(VP)*
Doyle Smith *(Dir-Ops)*

Accounts:
Nissan of New Orleans

ADSOKA, INC.
100 South 1st St, Minneapolis, MN 55458-3237
Tel.: (612) 910-0777
E-Mail: info@adsoka.com
Web Site: www.adsoka.com

E-Mail for Key Personnel:
President: jason@adsoka.com

Year Founded: 2003

National Agency Associations: ADFED-AMA-IABC-MIMA-Women In Communications

Agency Specializes In: Above-the-Line, Advertising, Advertising Specialties, Affluent Market, Agriculture, Alternative Advertising, Arts, Below-the-Line, Brand Development & Integration, Business Publications, Business-To-Business, Catalogs, Children's Market, Collateral, College, Communications, Computers & Software, Consulting, Consumer Goods, Consumer Marketing, Consumer Publications, Content, Corporate Communications, Corporate Identity, Custom Publishing, Customer Relationship Management, Digital/Interactive, Direct Response Marketing, Direct-to-Consumer, E-Commerce, Education, Electronic Media, Email, Environmental, Event Planning & Marketing, Exhibit/Trade Shows, Fashion/Apparel, Financial, Food Service, Graphic Design, Guerilla Marketing, Health Care Services, High Technology, Hospitality, Identity Marketing, In-Store Advertising, Integrated Marketing, Internet/Web Design, Leisure, Local Marketing, Logo & Package Design, Luxury Products, Magazines, Marine, Market Research, Media Buying Services, Media Planning, Media Relations, Media Training, Medical Products, Men's Market, Merchandising, Mobile Marketing, Multimedia, New Product Development, Newspaper, Newspapers & Magazines, Out-of-Home Media, Outdoor, Package Design, Paid Searches, Planning & Consultation, Point of Purchase, Point of Sale, Print, Production, Production (Print), Promotions, Public Relations, Publicity/Promotions, Publishing, RSS (Really Simple Syndication), Radio, Real Estate, Regional, Restaurant, Retail, Sales Promotion, Search Engine Optimization, Social Marketing/Nonprofit, Sponsorship, Sports Market, Strategic Planning/Research, Teen Market, Trade & Consumer Magazines, Transportation, Viral/Buzz/Word of Mouth, Web (Banner Ads, Pop-ups, etc.), Women's Market

Breakdown of Gross Billings by Media: D.M.: 5%; Graphic Design: 20%; Logo & Package Design: 10%; Newsp. & Mags.: 10%; Pub. Rels.: 10%; Strategic Planning/Research: 15%; Worldwide Web Sites: 30%

Jason Inskeep *(Principal)*

Accounts:
Above The Falls Sports Recreation; 2008
Breadsmith Breads in the French Tradition; 2003
Det-Tronics Fire & Gas Safety Solutions; 2011
Grumpy's Beer & Food; 2012
Local Vibe Buzz Marketing; 2015
Mercury Mosaics Handmade Artisan Tile; 2013
Minnesota Talent Network Careers; 2013
Normandale Community College Continuing Education, Skill Development; 2015
Rose Vine Hall Event Center; 2012
Universal Cooperatives Agriculture; 2005

ADSOURCE
1415 Panther Ln Ste 360, Naples, FL 34109
Tel.: (239) 495-0007
Fax: (239) 495-0088
E-Mail: info@adsource.us
Web Site: www.adsource.us

Agency Specializes In: Advertising, Brand Development & Integration, Collateral, Event Planning & Marketing, Internet/Web Design, Media Buying Services, Media Planning, Public Relations, Radio, Social Media

Mary Shallies *(Owner)*
Nicole Dutcher *(Acct Mgr)*
Angie Keating *(Acct Exec)*

Accounts:
Divco Custom Homes

ADSPEAK MARKETING COMMUNICATIONS
(Name Changed to Russell-Risko Agency)

ADTEGRITY.COM
38 Commerce SW Ste 200, Grand Rapids, MI 49546
Tel.: (616) 285-5429
Fax: (616) 285-9156
E-Mail: support@adtegrity.com
Web Site: www.adtegrity.com

Employees: 30

Scott Brew *(Pres & CEO)*
Jason A. Balk *(CFO)*
Michael Struyk *(COO)*
Dustin Turner *(CTO)*
Kurt Filla *(Chief Revenue Officer)*
Chad Jansen *(Sr VP-Sls)*
Todd Morris *(VP-Mktg & QA)*

ADTOPIA MARKETING GROUP
(Formerly Ward Associates)
440 Florin Rd, Sacramento, CA 95831-2007
Tel.: (916) 706-3996
Fax: (916) 369-2529
Web Site: www.adtopiamarketing.com

Employees: 6

Agency Specializes In: Digital/Interactive, Internet/Web Design

Lucia Churches *(Pres)*
Dennis Colbert *(Dir-Media)*
Kris Freeman *(Acct Mgr)*

Accounts:
Onsite Computing

Spare Time Clubs

ADVANCED MARKETING STRATEGIES

8910 University Center Ln Ste 620, San Diego, CA 92122-1027
Tel.: (858) 490-6910
Fax: (858) 490-6985
E-Mail: info@am-strategies.com
Web Site: www.am-strategies.com

Employees: 20
Year Founded: 1987

Agency Specializes In: Advertising, Advertising Specialties, Automotive, Bilingual Market, Brand Development & Integration, Broadcast, Business Publications, Business-To-Business, Cable T.V., Children's Market, Co-op Advertising, Collateral, Commercial Photography, Communications, Consulting, Consumer Marketing, Consumer Publications, Corporate Identity, Digital/Interactive, Direct Response Marketing, E-Commerce, Education, Electronic Media, Engineering, Entertainment, Event Planning & Marketing, Exhibit/Trade Shows, Financial, Food Service, Government/Political, Graphic Design, Health Care Services, High Technology, Hispanic Market, Infomercials, Information Technology, Internet/Web Design, Legal Services, Leisure, Logo & Package Design, Magazines, Media Buying Services, Medical Products, Merchandising, Multimedia, New Product Development, Newspaper, Newspapers & Magazines, Outdoor, Over-50 Market, Pharmaceutical, Planning & Consultation, Point of Purchase, Point of Sale, Print, Production, Public Relations, Publicity/Promotions, Radio, Restaurant, Retail, Sales Promotion, Seniors' Market, Sports Market, Strategic Planning/Research, Syndication, T.V., Technical Advertising, Teen Market, Telemarketing, Trade & Consumer Magazines, Transportation, Travel & Tourism

Kathy Cunningham *(Co-Founder & Strategist)*
Jim Tindaro *(CEO)*
Utahna Hadden *(VP & Acct Supvr)*
Bonnie Carlson *(Gen Mgr)*
Michele Marlo *(Exec Dir-Creative)*
Mark Stevens *(Dir-Media)*

Accounts:
Ikea
Mossy Automotive Group

ADVANTAGE COMMUNICATIONS, INC.

(Private-Parent-Single Location)
500 S Broadway Ste 402, Little Rock, AR 72201
Tel.: (501) 374-2220
Fax: (501) 374-3643
E-Mail: info@advantageci.com
Web Site: www.advantageci.com

Employees: 10
Year Founded: 2000

Agency Specializes In: Advertising, Brand Development & Integration, Crisis Communications, Digital/Interactive, Event Planning & Marketing, Media Buying Services, Media Planning, Public Relations, Social Media, Strategic Planning/Research

Revenue: $1,800,000

Michael Steele *(Pres & CEO)*
Shaunda Cooney *(CFO)*
Michael Puckett *(Chief Creative Officer)*
Nigel Hall *(VP)*
Evan Steele *(VP-Ops)*
Whitney Albert *(Acct Exec)*
Vivian Ozura *(Acct Exec)*

Accounts:
Minority Initiative Sub-Recipient Grant office

ADVANTAGE MEDIA LLC

2602 Oakstone Dr Ste 1, Columbus, OH 43231
Tel.: (614) 865-3392
Fax: (614) 933-0655
Web Site: www.advantagemedia.us

Year Founded: 2000

Agency Specializes In: Advertising, Brand Development & Integration, Media Buying Services, Media Planning, Print, Promotions, Radio, T.V.

Jasmin Tucker *(Pres)*

Accounts:
Able Roof

ADVANTIS COMMUNICATIONS, INC.

4936 Yonge St Ste 806, Toronto, ON M2N 6S3 Canada
Tel.: (905) 477-5535
E-Mail: info@advantiscomm.com
Web Site: www.advantiscomm.com

Employees: 10

Agency Specializes In: Communications, Media Relations, Media Training, Publicity/Promotions, Strategic Planning/Research, Web (Banner Ads, Pop-ups, etc.)

Cyrus Mavalwala *(Founder)*
Ernesta Rossi *(Partner)*

Accounts:
CanadaHelps

ADVENT DESIGN LLC

130 S Main St, Elkhart, IN 46516
Tel.: (574) 295-8817
Web Site: www.advent-design.com

Year Founded: 1986

Agency Specializes In: Advertising, Catalogs, Internet/Web Design, Logo & Package Design, Print

Justin Graber *(Owner)*

Accounts:
Banks Hardwoods, Inc.
Nickell Moulding Company Inc.
Terry Graber & Associates

ADVENT MARKETING COMMUNICATIONS

6605 Roxburgh Dr, Houston, TX 77041
Tel.: (713) 462-8347
Fax: (713) 462-8337
E-Mail: info@adventfirm.com
Web Site: www.adventfirm.com

Employees: 15
Year Founded: 1996

Agency Specializes In: Collateral, Digital/Interactive, Graphic Design, Internet/Web Design, Media Relations, Multimedia, Print, Public Relations, Strategic Planning/Research

Richard Kaminski *(Pres)*
Joann Salazar *(Sr VP-Sls & Ops)*
Miguel Lopez *(Dir-IT)*
Laurie Pruitt *(Mgr-Acctg)*

ADVENTIUM, LLC

320 E 35th St Ste 5B, New York, NY 10016
Tel.: (212) 481-9576
E-Mail: info@adventium.net
Web Site: www.adventium.net

Employees: 5
Year Founded: 1992

Agency Specializes In: Advertising, Advertising Specialties, Arts, Asian Market, Brand Development & Integration, Business Publications, Business-To-Business, Catalogs, Co-op Advertising, Collateral, Communications, Computers & Software, Consulting, Consumer Goods, Consumer Marketing, Consumer Publications, Corporate Communications, Corporate Identity, Cosmetics, Custom Publishing, Direct Response Marketing, Direct-to-Consumer, Education, Entertainment, Exhibit/Trade Shows, Fashion/Apparel, Financial, Government/Political, Graphic Design, Health Care Services, High Technology, Hospitality, Identity Marketing, In-Store Advertising, Information Technology, Integrated Marketing, International, Internet/Web Design, Leisure, Local Marketing, Logo & Package Design, Luxury Products, Magazines, Marine, Men's Market, Multicultural, Multimedia, New Product Development, New Technologies, Newspaper, Newspapers & Magazines, Out-of-Home Media, Outdoor, Over-50 Market, Package Design, Point of Sale, Print, Production, Production (Print), Promotions, Publishing, Real Estate, Recruitment, Regional, Restaurant, Sales Promotion, Seniors' Market, Technical Advertising, Teen Market, Trade & Consumer Magazines, Transportation, Travel & Tourism, Urban Market, Web (Banner Ads, Pop-ups, etc.), Women's Market

Approx. Annual Billings: $340,000

Breakdown of Gross Billings by Media: Collateral: $100,000; Print: $100,000; Trade Shows: $100,000; Worldwide Web Sites: $40,000

Penny Chuang *(Pres & Dir-Creative)*

Accounts:
Dorling Kindersley Publishing
Golfing Women
PricewaterhouseCoopers
Rough Guides
Sports Journeys
Verizon

ADVENTIVE MARKETING, INC.

415 E Golf Rd, Arlington Heights, IL 60005
Tel.: (847) 590-1110
Fax: (847) 590-1222
E-Mail: info@adventivemarketing.com
Web Site: www.adventivemarketing.com

Employees: 7
Year Founded: 1995

National Agency Associations: AMA-BMA-PRSA

Agency Specializes In: Advertising, Advertising Specialties, Alternative Advertising, Automotive, Aviation & Aerospace, Brand Development & Integration, Business Publications, Business-To-Business, Catalogs, Co-op Advertising, Collateral, Commercial Photography, Communications, Consulting, Corporate Communications, Corporate Identity, Custom Publishing, Customer Relationship Management, Digital/Interactive, Direct Response Marketing, E-Commerce, Electronic Media, Electronics, Email, Engineering, Entertainment, Event Planning & Marketing, Exhibit/Trade Shows, Graphic Design, Health Care Services, High Technology, Industrial, Information Technology, Integrated Marketing, International, Internet/Web Design, Logo & Package Design, Magazines,

Market Research, Media Buying Services, Media Planning, Media Relations, Medical Products, Mobile Marketing, Multimedia, New Product Development, Newspapers & Magazines, Package Design, Paid Searches, Pharmaceutical, Planning & Consultation, Podcasting, Point of Purchase, Point of Sale, Print, Production, Production (Ad, Film, Broadcast), Production (Print), Promotions, Public Relations, Publicity/Promotions, RSS (Really Simple Syndication), Sales Promotion, Search Engine Optimization, Strategic Planning/Research, Technical Advertising, Trade & Consumer Magazines

Approx. Annual Billings: $3,000,000

Breakdown of Gross Billings by Media: Bus. Publs.: $450,000; Collateral: $450,000; D.M.: $300,000; E-Commerce: $150,000; Fees: $150,000; Graphic Design: $300,000; Internet Adv.: $450,000; Pub. Rels.: $300,000; Sls. Promo.: $150,000; Trade Shows: $150,000; Worldwide Web Sites: $150,000

Steven E. Bork *(Owner & Pres)*
Brian Kahle *(Partner & Dir-Creative Svcs)*
Janet Killen *(Partner & Dir-PR)*
Candy Mcgill *(Mgr-Production)*

Accounts:
Belden, Inc.; Saint Louis, MO

ADVENTURE
111 N Washington Ave Ste 250, Minneapolis, MN 55401
Tel.: (612) 259-7896
E-Mail: info@adventureadvertising.com
Web Site: www.adventureadvertising.com

Agency Specializes In: Advertising, Brand Development & Integration, Broadcast, Digital/Interactive, Event Planning & Marketing, Package Design, Public Relations, Social Media, Strategic Planning/Research

Joe Lavoie *(Art Dir)*
Ethan Lindeman *(Asst Project Mgr)*
Tim Carroll *(Strategist-Creative)*

Accounts:
Larson Boats

ADVENTURE ADVERTISING
110 NW 3rd St, Brainerd, MN 56401
Tel.: (218) 824-7775
Web Site: www.adventureadvertising.com

Agency Specializes In: Advertising, Brand Development & Integration, Broadcast, Digital/Interactive, Event Planning & Marketing, Package Design, Public Relations, Social Media

John Linn *(Principal)*
Scott Mitchell *(Principal)*
Gina Nacey *(Sr Strategist-Creative & Acct)*

Accounts:
The Barrel Mill
New-Hatteras Yachts (Agency of Record) Online, Print Advertising, Video
Johnson Outdoors
New-Kinetic (Agency of Record) Creative, Design, Digital Marketing, Kinetic Bicycle Training, Marketing Strategy
Klarbrunn
Sedona Bottling Company
UnitedHealthcare Children's Foundation

ADVENTURE ADVERTISING LLC
554 W Main St Ste 202, Buford, GA 30518
Tel.: (678) 730-4770
Fax: (678) 730-4775
E-Mail: info@adventureadv.com
Web Site: www.adventureadv.com

Agency Specializes In: Advertising, Digital/Interactive, Outdoor, Strategic Planning/Research

Bruce Hyer *(Partner & Dir-Creative)*
Jeff Espy *(Partner)*
Jason Meninger *(Partner)*
Mamie Putman *(VP-Production & Sr Dir-Art)*
Mike Pirolo *(Grp Acct Dir & Head-New Bus Dev)*
Rachel Berhannan *(Controller)*
Mitch Rood *(Dir-Art & Specialist-Graphic)*
Jill Gerow *(Dir-Internet & Tech)*
Gino Reinhart *(Assoc Dir-Creative)*
Ian Pierce *(Mgr-Face-to-Face Mktg)*

Accounts:
Richard Childress Racing

ADVERCAR
99 Osgood Pl, San Francisco, CA 94133
Tel.: (415) 480-9710
Web Site: www.advercar.com

Year Founded: 2011

Agency Specializes In: Co-op Advertising, Out-of-Home Media, Outdoor, Promotions

Neil Turner *(CEO)*
Tony Joseph *(Exec VP)*

Accounts:
1800Flowers Fruit Bouquets; 2013
Clorox Soy Vay; 2013
Honda Cars; 2013
McDonald's Fast Food; 2013
Salesforce Desk.com; 2013

ADVERTEL, INC.
PO Box 18053, Pittsburgh, PA 15236-0053
Tel.: (412) 714-4421
Fax: (412) 714-4364
Toll Free: (888) ADVERTEL
E-Mail: info@advertel.com
Web Site: www.advertel.com

E-Mail for Key Personnel:
President: pberan@advertel.com

Employees: 5
Year Founded: 1994

Agency Specializes In: Automotive, Bilingual Market, Brand Development & Integration, Broadcast, Business-To-Business, Co-op Advertising, Communications, Consulting, Corporate Identity, Digital/Interactive, Direct Response Marketing, Electronic Media, Financial, Government/Political, High Technology, In-Store Advertising, Industrial, Multimedia, New Product Development, Point of Purchase, Point of Sale, Production, Public Relations, Radio, Strategic Planning/Research, Technical Advertising, Telemarketing

Approx. Annual Billings: $500,000

Paul F. Beran *(Pres, CEO & Dir-Creative)*
Curt Yeske *(Dir-IT & Technical infrastructure)*

Accounts:
Baker Installations; 1998
Forest Products Supply
Monte Cello's Restaurants; Pittsburgh, PA Restaurants; 1995
One Communications; Rochester, NY Telecommunications; 2007
Port Authority Alleghany County; Pittsburgh, PA; 1999
Vocelli Pizza; Pittsburgh, PA Restaurant; 2008
Weyerhaeuser Industries; 1997

ADVERTISE.COM INC.
15303 Ventura Blvd Ste 1150, Sherman Oaks, CA 91403
Tel.: (818) 285-6216
Fax: (818) 380-3103
Toll Free: (800) 710-7009
Web Site: www.advertise.com

Year Founded: 2001

Agency Specializes In: Advertising, Email

Daniel Yomtobian *(Founder & CEO)*
G. Plagge *(CTO)*
David Bilgre *(VP-Bus Dev)*
Hooman Malekzad *(VP-Publr Svcs)*
Bryan Poach *(Controller)*
Puneet Bhasin *(Dir-IT)*
Irina Butler *(Dir-Sls)*
Vipin Porwal *(Dir-Software Engrg)*

Accounts:
Comedy Television Network Services
CruiseDirect Inc. Tour & Travel Agency Services
Goldenwest Diamond Corporation Jewelry Shop
Rock.com Inc. Designing Clothes Retailer
Sears Brands LLC. Online Retailer Of Home Appliance Products
SPIKE Television Network Services
Teleflora LLC Flowers Designers

ADVERTISING FOR GOOD
1708 Peachtree St Ste 100, Atlanta, GA 30309
Tel.: (404) 881-1808
Web Site: www.advertisingforgood.com

Year Founded: 2011

Agency Specializes In: Advertising, Radio, Social Media

David Weinberger *(Exec Dir-Insights & Analytics)*
Amelia Miller Linton *(Dir-Art & Sr Designer)*
Madeline Spratt *(Dir-Client Svcs)*
Melba Love *(Mgr-Acctg)*
Katy Tomasulo *(Mgr-Content Dev)*
Mary Ellen Gordon *(Strategist-Digital)*
Roddy Freeman *(Media Planner)*

Accounts:
Habitat for Humanity International, Inc.

ADVERTISING IMPACT INC.
1255 Lynnfield Rd Ste 107, Memphis, TN 38119-5144
Tel.: (901) 685-1966
Fax: (901) 685-5175
E-Mail: info@advertisingimpact.com
Web Site: www.advertisingimpact.com

Employees: 3
Year Founded: 1976

Agency Specializes In: Advertising, Business-To-Business, Industrial

Larry Wright *(Pres)*
Tom Wright *(VP)*

ADVERTISING SAVANTS, INC.
2100 Locust St 3rd Fl N, Saint Louis, MO 63103
Tel.: (314) 231-7900
Fax: (314) 231-1777
E-Mail: kevin@adsavants.com
Web Site: www.adsavants.com

Employees: 10

Year Founded: 1991

Agency Specializes In: Advertising, Automotive, Aviation & Aerospace, Bilingual Market, Brand Development & Integration, Business Publications, Business-To-Business, Cable T.V., Children's Market, Collateral, College, Communications, Consumer Goods, Consumer Marketing, Consumer Publications, Corporate Identity, Digital/Interactive, Direct Response Marketing, Education, Email, Entertainment, Financial, Graphic Design, Health Care Services, Hispanic Market, Hospitality, Household Goods, Identity Marketing, In-Store Advertising, Industrial, Integrated Marketing, Internet/Web Design, Legal Services, Leisure, Logo & Package Design, Luxury Products, Magazines, Media Buying Services, Media Planning, Medical Products, Merchandising, Newspaper, Out-of-Home Media, Outdoor, Over-50 Market, Package Design, Planning & Consultation, Podcasting, Point of Purchase, Point of Sale, Print, Product Placement, Promotions, Radio, Real Estate, Retail, Sales Promotion, Sports Market, Strategic Planning/Research, T.V., Teen Market, Transportation, Travel & Tourism

Breakdown of Gross Billings by Media: Brdcst.: 40%; Cable T.V.: 5%; Collateral: 3%; Consulting: 1%; Consumer Publs.: 2%; D.M.: 1%; Fees: 5%; Foreign: 1%; Graphic Design: 1%; Logo & Package Design: 1%; Newsp.: 5%; Out-of-Home Media: 5%; Print: 5%; Production: 5%; Radio: 5%; Strategic Planning/Research: 5%; Trade & Consumer Mags.: 5%; Transit: 5%

Kevin Reardon *(Founder & CEO)*
Ashley Harrison *(Acct Dir)*
Tia Liston *(Creative Dir)*
Lizzy Hinrichs *(Dir-Art)*
Amanda Kinder *(Dir-Digital Strategy)*
Ray McAnallen *(Dir-Creative)*
Courtney Turner *(Acct Coord)*
Mark Guttropf *(Coord-Digital Media)*

Accounts:
SIFE
Spectrum Brands, Inc.

ADVERTUS MEDIA INC

PO Box 610, Westfield, MA 01096
Tel.: (413) 564-5200
Fax: (413) 564-5201
E-Mail: info@advertusmedia.com
Web Site: www.advertusmedia.com

Agency Specializes In: Advertising, Internet/Web Design, Media Buying Services, Media Planning, Production (Print)

Adam Wright *(Dir-Mktg)*

Accounts:
Big Y Foods
Naismith Basketball Hall of Fame
Patton Auto Group
Westfield State College

ADVILLE/USA

44 S Mentor Ave, Pasadena, CA 91106-2902
Tel.: (626) 397-9911
Fax: (626) 397-9919
Toll Free: (800) 722-8145
Web Site: www.adville-usa.com

E-Mail for Key Personnel:
Creative Dir.: creative@adville-usa.com

Employees: 11
Year Founded: 1995

National Agency Associations: THINKLA

Agency Specializes In: Sales Promotion

Approx. Annual Billings: $4,000,000

Breakdown of Gross Billings by Media: Cable T.V.: $50,000; Collateral: $250,000; Fees: $50,000; Newsp. & Mags.: $400,000; Other: $1,250,000; Production: $200,000; T.V.: $1,500,000; Trade Shows: $300,000

Vicki Walls *(Pres)*
Sharick Smyser *(VP & Acct Dir)*
Mark Shiozaki *(VP)*

Accounts:
Original Tommy's Hamburgers; Glendale, CA QSR
Tastee Freez
Wienerschnitzel, Inc.; Newport Beach, CA Original Hamburger Stand, Wienerschnitzel Operators Associations

ADVLUENCE LLC

238 E Davis Blvd Ste 311, Tampa, FL 33606
Tel.: (813) 254-1500
E-Mail: getstarted@advluence.com
Web Site: www.advluence.com

Year Founded: 2012

Agency Specializes In: Advertising, Brand Development & Integration, Graphic Design, Internet/Web Design, Print, Social Media

Ryan Littler *(Pres)*
Kush Patel *(Dir-Visual)*
Dylan Sellberg *(Dir-Mktg)*

Accounts:
Cluckz Chicken
HQ Aviation
The Outpost Tap House + Tavern
RSVP Skincare
St. Moritz Building Services Inc
Titan Medical Center

ADVOCACY SOLUTIONS LLC

4 Richmond Sq Ste 300, Providence, RI 02906
Tel.: (401) 831-3700
Fax: (401) 831-0105
E-Mail: info@advocacysolutionsllc.com
Web Site: www.advocacysolutionsllc.com

Employees: 10
Year Founded: 1992

Agency Specializes In: Brand Development & Integration, Broadcast, Collateral, Consumer Marketing, Corporate Identity, Direct Response Marketing, E-Commerce, Event Planning & Marketing, Exhibit/Trade Shows, Food Service, Graphic Design, Health Care Services, Internet/Web Design, Investor Relations, Logo & Package Design, Media Buying Services, Medical Products, Newspapers & Magazines, Out-of-Home Media, Outdoor, Pharmaceutical, Point of Sale, Print, Production, Public Relations, Radio, Sales Promotion, Strategic Planning/Research, Sweepstakes

Approx. Annual Billings: $8,000,000

Francis X. McMahon *(Owner)*
Christopher Hunter *(Mng Dir-Strategy & Dev)*
Sarah Beron *(Acct Mgr-Pub Affairs & Strategic Comm)*

Accounts:
Coalition of Essential Schools
Delta Dental of Rhode Island
Metals Recycling
National Grid
State Alliance of Rhode Island YMCAs
Verizon
Francis Farm Clambake Facility
Icelandic USA Seafood

ADVOCATE DIGITAL MEDIA

311 E Constitution St, Victoria, TX 77901
Tel.: (361) 580-6553
Web Site: www.advocatedigitalmedia.com

Agency Specializes In: Advertising, Brand Development & Integration, Internet/Web Design, Media Buying Services, Media Planning, Search Engine Optimization, Social Media

Jason Holmes *(Gen Mgr)*
Alexander Gould *(Dir-Sls)*
Scott Brunner *(Dir-Content)*
Emily Weatherly *(Mgr-Media)*
Colonel Armstrong *(Acct Exec)*
Kelly Benton *(Acct Exec)*
Natalie Brown *(Acct Exec)*
Vicki Kliem *(Acct Exec)*

Accounts:
The Victoria Advocate

ADWELL COMMUNICATIONS

3470 Wilshire Blvd Ste 540, Los Angeles, CA 90010
Tel.: (213) 380-8872
Fax: (213) 383-6438
E-Mail: info@adwellcommunications.com
Web Site: www.adwellcommunications.com

Employees: 10
Year Founded: 2001

Agency Specializes In: Asian Market

Patty Adwell *(Co-Founder)*

Accounts:
Artemis
Jinro
Macallan
Pernod Richard USA
Samsung
Shinhan Bank

ADWERKS

512 N. Main Ave, Sioux Falls, SD 57104
Tel.: (605) 357-3690
Fax: (605) 357-3691
Web Site: www.adwerks.com

Agency Specializes In: Advertising, Media Buying Services, Print, Radio, T.V.

Jim Mathis *(Founder)*
Kristi Cornette *(Media Buyer)*

Accounts:
Applebee's International, Inc.
CarHop
Carino's Italian
DGR Engineering
McDonald's Corporation

ADWHITE, LLC

33300 Egypt Ln, Magnolia, TX 77354
Tel.: (281) 356-3200
Fax: (281) 259-0500
E-Mail: info@adwhite.com
Web Site: www.adwhite.com

Employees: 8
Year Founded: 2002

Agency Specializes In: Advertising, Graphic Design, Internet/Web Design, Social Media

Taylor White *(Founder & Principal)*
Michelle White *(CFO)*
Michele Caldwell *(Dir-Technical Ops)*
Billie Hill *(Mgr-Acctg)*

Accounts:
Freudenberg Oil & Gas Website Development & Maintenance, Graphic Design, Print Production, Branded Merchandise; 2013
Great American Rug Cleaning Company Website Development & Maintenance, SEO, SEM; 2013
Texas Rush Soccer Club Website Development & Maintenance, Graphic Design, Print Production, Branded Merchandise; 2012

ADWISE GROUP INC.
2245 Keller Way Ste 250, Carrollton, TX 75006
Tel.: (972) 395-5091
E-Mail: info@adwisegroup.com
Web Site: www.adwisegroup.com

Agency Specializes In: Advertising, Brand Development & Integration, Broadcast, Internet/Web Design, Logo & Package Design, Media Buying Services, Media Planning, Print, Search Engine Optimization, Social Media

Marcus Miller *(Pres)*
Nancy Gayle Hammel *(Dir-Media Strategy & Acct Mgmt)*
Lisa Steward *(Dir-Mktg)*

Accounts:
Mr. Jims Pizza

ADWORKS, INC.
5335 Wisconsin Ave NW, Washington, DC 20015
Tel.: (202) 342-5585
Fax: (202) 739-8201
E-Mail: howdy@adworks.com
Web Site: www.adworks.com

E-Mail for Key Personnel:
Creative Dir.: m.greenspun@adworks.com

Employees: 20
Year Founded: 1979

Agency Specializes In: Advertising, Brand Development & Integration, Business-To-Business, Consumer Marketing, Health Care Services, Retail, Strategic Planning/Research

Approx. Annual Billings: $75,000,000

Breakdown of Gross Billings by Media: Consumer Publs.: $2,250,000; D.M.: $3,750,000; Internet Adv.: $7,500,000; Newsp.: $6,000,000; Outdoor: $8,250,000; Radio: $15,000,000; T.V.: $32,250,000

Mark Greenspun *(Founder & Dir-Creative)*
Nancy Karpinski *(Dir-Client Svc)*
Mat Sachs *(Dir-Interactive)*
Lori Ewing *(Supvr-Media)*

Accounts:
Brick Southeast
The Washington Post msnbc.com
washingtonpost.com; Arlington, VA Information News Web Site; 1998
WHUR-FM; Washington, DC; 2000

ADZ ETC., INC.
N88 W16749 Main St Ste 3, Menomonee Falls, WI 53051-2826
Tel.: (262) 502-0507
Fax: (262) 502-0508
Web Site: www.adzetc.com

E-Mail for Key Personnel:
President: beth@adzetc.com

Employees: 4
Year Founded: 1995

Agency Specializes In: Advertising, Advertising Specialties, Recruitment

Beth A. Grzesiak *(Pres)*
Cori Maki *(Acct Exec)*

AEGIS GROUP PLC
(Acquired by Dentsu Inc.)

AEI ADVERTISING
Mountain Sage, Phoenix, AZ 85045
Tel.: (602) 758-4891
E-Mail: info@aeiadvertising.com
Web Site: www.aeiadvertising.com

Year Founded: 2010

Agency Specializes In: Advertising, Collateral, Graphic Design, Media Planning, Print, Social Media

Sarah Woods *(VP-Client Svcs & Strategy)*
Michelle Reese *(Copywriter)*

Accounts:
Kyrene de los Cerritoss PTO
Prestige Cleaners

AFFECT STRATEGIES
989 Ave of the Americas 6th Fl, New York, NY 10018
Tel.: (212) 398-9680
Fax: (212) 504-8211
E-Mail: info@affect.com
Web Site: www.affectstrategies.com

Employees: 19

Agency Specializes In: Advertising, Brand Development & Integration, Collateral, Communications, Corporate Communications, Corporate Identity, Direct Response Marketing, Direct-to-Consumer, Event Planning & Marketing, Graphic Design, Integrated Marketing, Market Research, Media Relations, Media Training, Public Relations, Social Marketing/Nonprofit, Social Media, Sponsorship, Strategic Planning/Research

Sandra Fathi *(Founder & Pres)*
Melissa Baratta *(Sr VP)*
Katie Creaser *(VP)*
Regina Pyne *(VP-HR & Ops)*
Brittany Bevacqua *(Sr Dir)*
Lulu Li *(Sr Acct Exec)*
Jenna Saper *(Sr Acct Exec)*
Erin Stanley *(Asst Acct Exec)*

Accounts:
ASME (Agency of Record)
Blue Security
Bug Labs; 2010
Cellebrite Brand Awareness, Public Relations
Contegra Systems
CorporateRewards (Agency of Record) Public Relations, WorkStride
Cyrus Innovation Marketing, Public Relations, Sales, Website
Dataprobe
Dealnews; 2010
E+CancerCare
F5 Networks
INTTRA
Kony Solutions (Agency of Record)
Luxoft
Microdesk (Agency of Record) Brand Awareness
Navis Social Media
RADirect
Sophos Marketing, Media Relations, Naked Security Blog
Sphera
Starbak
Supreme Security Systems
Surfray
TouchPaper ITBM Solutions; 2008

AFFIRM
(Formerly Staples Marketing)
N28W23050 Roundy Dr Ste 100, Pewaukee, WI 53072
Tel.: (262) 650-9900
Fax: (262) 650-3160
Toll Free: (800) 827-1890
Web Site: www.affirmagency.com

Agency Specializes In: Advertising, Brand Development & Integration, Collateral, Internet/Web Design, Media Buying Services, Media Planning, Public Relations, Social Media, Strategic Planning/Research

Danny Mager *(Principal & Dir-Mktg)*
Steve Stocker *(Principal & Dir-Creative)*
Laura Monagle *(VP-Client Svcs & PR)*
Cathy Looze *(Dir-Media)*
Roe Swanson *(Assoc Dir-Media)*
Ingrid Pavlick *(Mgr-Acctg)*
Amy Opad *(Acct Exec)*
Traci Brice *(Sr Graphic Designer)*
Ryan Quade *(Sr Graphic Designer)*

Accounts:
RTA Transit Benefit Fare Program

AFFORDABLE MARKETING SOLUTIONS
41 Church St, Keansburg, NJ 07734
Tel.: (732) 769-5296

Employees: 3
Year Founded: 2008

Agency Specializes In: Alternative Advertising, Co-op Advertising, Collateral, Direct Response Marketing, Guerilla Marketing, Local Marketing, Magazines, Newspaper, Newspapers & Magazines, Print, Shopper Marketing

Approx. Annual Billings: $200,000

Ron Regine *(Owner)*

AFG&
(Formerly Avrett Free Ginsberg)
1 Dag Hammarskjold Plz 885 2nd Ave, New York, NY 10017-2205
Tel.: (212) 832-3800
Fax: (212) 418-7331
E-Mail: acolotti@afg1.com
Web Site: avrettfreeginsberg.com/

Employees: 125
Year Founded: 1975

National Agency Associations: 4A's-AAF-LIAN

Agency Specializes In: Advertising, Brand Development & Integration, Collateral, Consumer Goods, Digital/Interactive, Direct-to-Consumer, Luxury Products, Media Buying Services, Media Planning, Social Media, Sponsorship

afg& was born with collaboration at its core. The agency is an unlimited partnership between their people, their clients, and their media and production partners. Collaboration isn't just a promise on a PowerPoint slide here. It's real here. It works here.

Breakdown of Gross Billings by Media: Bus. Publs.: $2,202,000; Fees: $55,900,000; Mags.: $51,905,000; Newsp.: $12,348,000; Outdoor: $5,928,000; Production: $36,350,000; Radio: $15,503,000; T.V.: $99,864,000

Stuart Grau *(Pres & Chief Strategic Officer)*
Tara Decoursey *(Grp Mng Dir)*
Dawn Terrazas *(Exec Grp Mng Dir)*
Agostino Colotti *(CFO & COO)*
Joe Petruccio *(Co-Chief Creative Officer)*
Ted Silverstein *(Chief Digital Officer)*
Robert Piwinski *(Exec Grp Acct Dir)*
Gary Cunningham *(Exec Grp Dir-Integrated Creative Services)*
Nari Kim *(Sr Dir-Art)*
Michelle Sayavedra *(Mgmt Supvr)*
Renee Krivine *(Project Mgr-Production-Digital & Print)*
Jane Gilbert *(Supvr-Media)*
Justine Campbell *(Strategist-Digital & Planner-Digital Media)*
Marietta Alessi *(Strategist-Digital)*
Julianne Wilson *(Strategist-Digital)*
Karl Greenberg *(Reporter-Automotive, Sports & Gen Mktg)*

Accounts:
Ad Council Office of the National Drug Policy
The American Hospital of Paris Foundation
Berentzen Bushel & Barrel Bourbon Whiskey
Blistex Inc. Blistex, Ivarest, Kanka, Odor Eaters, Stridex
Kobrand Corporation Alize Liquers, Coruba Rum, Tia Maria, Vikingfjord Vodka
Lornamead Finesse, Lice Shield, Yardley
McKesson Corp Health Mart Pharmacy
Nestle Purina PetCare Co Beggin, Busy, Cat Chow, Doguitos, Fancy Feast, Felix, Friskies, Friskies Cat, Friskies Dog, Gourmet, Purina One, Tidy Cats, Win-a-lot, Yesterday's News
Prestige Brands BC Powder, Beano, Chloraseptic, Clear Eyes, Compound W, Debrox, Doctor's, Dramamine, Ecotrin, Efferdent, FiberChoice, Goody's Headache Relief Shot, Goody's Powder, Little Remedies, Luden's, Monistat, New-Skin, Pediacare
Stratasys 3D Printing Solutions
Van Cleef & Arpels Fine Jewelry
Voli Vodka

AFTER MIDNIGHT, INC
3623 Glenwood Ave, Redwood City, CA 94062
Tel.: (415) 265-7493
Fax: (215) 623-2435
Web Site: www.aftermidnightinc.com

Agency Specializes In: Advertising, Brand Development & Integration, Collateral, Package Design, Web (Banner Ads, Pop-ups, etc.)

Kathryn Klein *(Pres & CEO)*
Jesi Konen *(Dir-Mktg)*
Megan Mangiamele *(Mgr-Hiring & Trng)*

Accounts:
Calgary Scientific Inc.
The Coca-Cola Company
Colgate-Palmolive Company
International Business Machines Corporation
Mondelez International, Inc.
The Open Group, L.L.C.
Reebok International Ltd.

AGENCE BRAQUE
19 Le Royer Street West Suite 200, Montreal, QC H2Y1W4 Canada
Tel.: (514) 278-8232
Fax: (514) 278-3598
E-Mail: info@braque.ca
Web Site: braque.ca/en/

Year Founded: 1992

Agency Specializes In: Advertising, Digital/Interactive, E-Commerce, Strategic Planning/Research

Jean-Marc Demers *(Pres & CEO)*
Marie-josee Bourque *(Acct Svcs Dir)*
Stephanie Blais *(Acct Mgr)*
Genevieve Miron *(Acct Mgr)*
Kelly Taylor *(Acct Mgr)*
Rosa Hamadouche *(Mgr-Media)*
France Handfield *(Mgr-Production)*
Caroline Graf *(Acct Exec)*
Elsa Badinier *(Coord-Media Planning)*
Caroline Ouimet *(Coord-Production)*

AGENCY 49 LLC
135 32nd Ave, Fairbanks, AK 99701
Tel.: (907) 451-1500
Fax: (907) 451-1520
E-Mail: info@agency49.com
Web Site: www.agency49.com

Agency Specializes In: Advertising, Brand Development & Integration, Digital/Interactive, Graphic Design, Internet/Web Design, Media Buying Services, Media Relations, Strategic Planning/Research

Pete Hutton *(Dir-Mktg)*

Accounts:
Gene's Chrysler

AGENCY 51
106 W 4th St 4th Fl, Santa Ana, CA 92701
Fax: (714) 844-4380
Toll Free: (877) 526-0411
E-Mail: info@adagency51.com
Web Site: www.adagency51.com

Agency Specializes In: Brand Development & Integration, Corporate Identity, Direct Response Marketing, Direct-to-Consumer, Print, Production (Ad, Film, Broadcast), Sponsorship

Anthony Serna *(VP-Creative)*
Sara Albiach *(Acct Dir)*
Matthew McNally *(Acct Dir)*
Chris Poole *(Dir-Art)*
Richard Pooley *(Designer)*

Accounts:
Hilton Worldwide Anaheim Hotel; 2007

AGENCY 720
500 Woodward Ave, Detroit, MI 48226
Tel.: (248) 256-5165
Web Site: www.agency720.com

Agency Specializes In: Advertising

Harold Kobakof *(CEO)*
Ron Parkinson *(COO)*
Chris McCarthy *(Exec VP & Dir-Creative)*
Todd Hauser *(Sr VP & Reg Dir-Adv)*
George Gibbs *(VP & Reg Dir-North Central)*
Jim Jorgensen *(VP & Reg Dir-South Central)*
Carter Rose *(VP & Reg Dir)*
Kyle Brazelton *(Dir-Fin & VP)*

Accounts:
PulteGroup Print, Radio, TV

AGENCY CREATIVE
14875 Landmark Blvd, Dallas, TX 75254
Tel.: (972) 488-1660
Fax: (972) 773-1061
E-Mail: info@agencycreative.com
Web Site: www.agencycreative.com

Employees: 20
Year Founded: 1994

Agency Specializes In: Above-the-Line, Advertising, Advertising Specialties, Affiliate Marketing, Affluent Market, African-American Market, Agriculture, Alternative Advertising, Arts, Asian Market, Automotive, Aviation & Aerospace, Below-the-Line, Bilingual Market, Brand Development & Integration, Branded Entertainment, Broadcast, Business Publications, Business-To-Business, Cable T.V., Catalogs, Children's Market, Co-op Advertising, Collateral, College, Commercial Photography, Communications, Computers & Software, Consulting, Consumer Goods, Consumer Marketing, Consumer Publications, Content, Corporate Communications, Corporate Identity, Cosmetics, Crisis Communications, Custom Publishing, Customer Relationship Management, Digital/Interactive, Direct Response Marketing, Direct-to-Consumer, E-Commerce, Education, Electronic Media, Electronics, Email, Engineering, Entertainment, Environmental, Event Planning & Marketing, Exhibit/Trade Shows, Experience Design, Fashion/Apparel, Financial, Food Service, Game Integration, Gay & Lesbian Market, Government/Political, Graphic Design, Guerilla Marketing, Health Care Services, High Technology, Hispanic Market, Hospitality, Household Goods, Identity Marketing, In-Store Advertising, Industrial, Infomercials, Information Technology, Integrated Marketing, International, Internet/Web Design, Investor Relations, Legal Services, Leisure, Local Marketing, Logo & Package Design, Luxury Products, Magazines, Marine, Market Research, Media Buying Services, Media Planning, Media Relations, Media Training, Medical Products, Men's Market, Merchandising, Mobile Marketing, Multicultural, Multimedia, New Product Development, New Technologies, Newspaper, Newspapers & Magazines, Out-of-Home Media, Outdoor, Over-50 Market, Package Design, Paid Searches, Pharmaceutical, Planning & Consultation, Podcasting, Point of Purchase, Point of Sale, Print, Product Placement, Production, Production (Ad, Film, Broadcast), Production (Print), Promotions, Public Relations, Publicity/Promotions, Publishing, RSS (Really Simple Syndication), Radio, Real Estate, Recruitment, Regional, Restaurant, Retail, Sales Promotion, Search Engine Optimization, Seniors' Market, Social Marketing/Nonprofit, South Asian Market, Sponsorship, Sports Market, Stakeholders, Strategic Planning/Research, Sweepstakes, Syndication, T.V., Technical Advertising, Teen Market, Telemarketing, Trade & Consumer Magazines, Transportation, Travel & Tourism, Urban Market, Viral/Buzz/Word of Mouth, Web (Banner Ads, Pop-ups, etc.), Women's Market, Yellow Pages Advertising

Agency Creative is an integrated branding agency dedicated to creating breakthrough advertising solutions that help clients achieve their goals. We were founded in 1994 as a full-service marketing and advertising agency. Today, we consist of a dedicated and seasoned team of 25 strategic marketing professionals who are passionate about obtaining results for our clients. Our collective experience has spanned the globe, having launched hundreds of campaigns for companies in a wide spectrum of industry categories such as healthcare, hospitality, financial institutions,

telecommunications, and more.

Breakdown of Gross Billings by Media: Adv. Specialities: 100%

Mark Wyatt *(Founder & CEO)*
Artie Megibben *(Exec Dir-Creative)*
Toan Dang *(Sr Dir-Art)*
Gabie Kinderknecht *(Dir-Art)*
Bruce Moose *(Dir-Activities)*
Rob Wolford *(Dir-Art)*
Whit Dreher *(Sr Acct Exec)*
Erin Reid *(Sr Acct Exec)*
Mark Brinkerhoff *(Strategist-PR & Comm)*
Jennifer England *(Strategist-Media)*
James Krummel *(Coord-Digital Svcs)*
Erica Schwenneker *(Coord-Mktg)*

Accounts:
New-Amarillo Town Club Health & Fitness Facilities, Strategy, Website Design; 2015
Assist Wireless Cellular Service
Children's Health Healthcare
New-IMI Hydronic Engineering Green Solutions for Indoor Climate Control, Strategic Planning; 2015
Janie's Cakes Bakery
New-Luminator Aerospace
New-National Athletic Trainers' Association (NATA) Branding, Creative, Strategy, Website Design, Planning & Development
New-Omnitracs Brand Strategy, Integrated Communications
New-S3 Sanitation Cleaning Branding, Collateral, Corporate Identity, Direct Mail, Website
TDIndustries Mechanical Construction, Facilities Services
New-TexCap Financial Branding, Marketing, Website
TGI Friday's Restaurant

AGENCY ENTOURAGE LLC

(Formerly Numantra)
1700 Commerce St Ste 950, Dallas, TX 75201
Tel.: (214) 414-3035
E-Mail: info@agencyentourage.com
Web Site: agencyentourage.com

Employees: 35

Agency Specializes In: Advertising, Brand Development & Integration, Internet/Web Design, Mobile Marketing, Social Media, Sponsorship

Ben Randolph *(Principal)*
Michael Haake *(Sr Producer-Interactive)*
Stefanie Goodman *(Producer-Interactive)*
Emily Moreland *(Producer-Interactive)*
Liz Theesfeld *(Producer-Interactive)*
Roz Theesfeld *(Dir-Creative)*
Maria St. Martin *(Mgr-SEM & PPC)*
Brandon Dowdy *(Acct Supvr)*
Mark Watson *(Copywriter)*
Rachel Lawing *(Coord-Ops)*

Accounts:
Berkley Net Underwriters, LLC
Christian Brothers Automotive
Home Town Dental

AGENCY GUERRA

3301 NE 1st Ave Ste H2701, Miami, FL 33137
Tel.: (305) 914-4464
E-Mail: info@agencyguerra.com
Web Site: www.agencyguerra.com

Year Founded: 2000

Agency Specializes In: Advertising, Brand Development & Integration, Digital/Interactive, Event Planning & Marketing, Graphic Design, Internet/Web Design, Logo & Package Design, Public Relations, Social Media

Lourdes Guerra *(Owner, Pres & CEO)*
Michael Renteria *(Designer)*

Accounts:
Midtown Pawn Boutique

THE AGENCY MARKETING GROUP

1440 S Tryon St Ste 106, Charlotte, NC 28269
Tel.: (704) 333-0667
E-Mail: info@gettheagency.com
Web Site: www.gettheagency.com

Year Founded: 2011

Agency Specializes In: Advertising, Brand Development & Integration, Graphic Design, Internet/Web Design, Logo & Package Design, Print, Public Relations, Search Engine Optimization, Social Media, Strategic Planning/Research

Kersten Conklin *(Owner & Dir-Mktg)*
Jerry Stahl *(Partner & VP)*
Mark Biller *(Dir-Creative)*
Mary Mac Stallings *(Dir-Bus Dev)*
Haley Wightman *(Acct Mgr)*
Lindsay Conklin *(Copywriter)*

Accounts:
Carolina Asthma & Allergy Center
Heel Pain Center
Space Saving Solutions
Studio 51Fifty

AGENCY OF CHANGE

22508 Market Street, Newhall, CA 91321
Tel.: (818) 985-8855
Fax: (818) 985-8835
Toll Free: (800) 9-CENTRIC
E-Mail: info@centric.com
Web Site: www.centric.com

E-Mail for Key Personnel:
President: jason.stoddard@centric.com
Creative Dir.: jason.stoddard@centric.com
Media Dir.: sue.arellano@centric.com
Public Relations: sue.arellano@centric.com

Employees: 10
Year Founded: 1994

Agency Specializes In: Advertising, Agriculture, Aviation & Aerospace, Brand Development & Integration, Business-To-Business, Collateral, Consumer Marketing, Corporate Communications, Corporate Identity, Digital/Interactive, Direct-to-Consumer, E-Commerce, Electronic Media, Electronics, Email, Engineering, Graphic Design, Health Care Services, High Technology, Industrial, Integrated Marketing, Internet/Web Design, Logo & Package Design, Mobile Marketing, Multimedia, New Technologies, Print, RSS (Really Simple Syndication), Search Engine Optimization, Social Marketing/Nonprofit, Social Media, Strategic Planning/Research, Sweepstakes, Technical Advertising, Trade & Consumer Magazines, Web (Banner Ads, Pop-ups, etc.)

Approx. Annual Billings: $5,000,000

Breakdown of Gross Billings by Media: Collateral: $500,000; Internet Adv.: $1,500,000; Other: $500,000; Print: $1,000,000; Worldwide Web Sites: $1,500,000

Sue Arellano *(Mng Partner-Acct Svcs)*
Lauren Essex *(VP-Mktg)*
Simcha Weinstein *(Dir-Mktg)*
Nathan Tia *(Assoc Dir-Creative)*

Accounts:
Epson
SRS Labs, Inc.

AGENCY ZERO

1201 E Colfax Ste 203, Denver, CO 80218
Tel.: (720) 515-5494
E-Mail: hotline@agencyzero.com
Web Site: www.agencyzero.com

Agency Specializes In: Advertising, Brand Development & Integration, Broadcast, Collateral, Digital/Interactive, Internet/Web Design, Print, Radio, Social Media, Strategic Planning/Research

Anastasia Toomey *(Partner & CEO)*
Jeremy Irwin *(Partner & Chief Creative Officer)*
Chip Hisle *(Assoc Dir-Creative)*
Monte Bride *(Acct Supvr)*
Ali Lind *(Acct Exec)*

Accounts:
Garbanzo Mediterranean Grill
Sundance Helicopters Advertising Agency of Record, Digital, Website

AGENCY212, LLC

95 Morton St, New York, NY 10014
Tel.: (212) 994-6700
Fax: (212) 994-6699
E-Mail: info@agency212.com
Web Site: www.agency212.com

Employees: 75
Year Founded: 1995

Agency Specializes In: Advertising, Automotive, Brand Development & Integration, Broadcast, Business-To-Business, Children's Market, Co-op Advertising, Collateral, Communications, Consulting, Consumer Marketing, Corporate Identity, Cosmetics, Digital/Interactive, Direct Response Marketing, E-Commerce, Event Planning & Marketing, Fashion/Apparel, In-Store Advertising, Internet/Web Design, Logo & Package Design, Market Research, Media Buying Services, Media Planning, New Product Development, Newspaper, Newspapers & Magazines, Out-of-Home Media, Outdoor, Package Design, Point of Sale, Product Placement, Production (Print), Promotions, Publishing, Radio, Retail, Sales Promotion, Sponsorship, Strategic Planning/Research, Sweepstakes, T.V., Trade & Consumer Magazines, Travel & Tourism, Web (Banner Ads, Pop-ups, etc.)

Approx. Annual Billings: $140,000,000

Breakdown of Gross Billings by Media: Co-op Adv.: 5%; Collateral: 10%; D.M.: 5%; Fees: 15%; Internet Adv.: 15%; Logo & Package Design: 5%; Newsp. & Mags.: 20%; Outdoor: 5%; Print: 5%; Radio: 10%; Strategic Planning/Research: 5%

William W. Tucker *(CEO)*
Tom Di Domenico *(Mng Partner-iFuel Interactive)*
Kristina Tucker *(Exec VP-Acct Mgmt)*
Tracy Brennan *(Exec Dir-Creative)*

Accounts:
Borghese; 2007
DK Publishing; 2009
Hyperion; 2009
Loews Hotels & Resorts; 1998
Palm Bay International Alexander Grappa, Aneri, Arrogant Frog, Bertani, Blue Fish, Boissiere, Bottega Vinaia, Boulard, Callia, Cavit Wines, Col d'Orcia, Condesa de Leganza, Faustino, Feudi, Frapin Cognac, Glen Deveron, Gosset Champagne, Jean-Luc Columbo, Laboure-Roi, Lancers, Lunetta Prosecco, Marchesi di Barolo, Navarro Correas, Planeta, Principato, Remy Pannier, Rocca delle Macie, Santa Rita, Santana, Sella & Mosca, Straccali, Terrazze

Della Luna, Verrazzano; 2007
Penguin Group; 2009
Penguin Group-G.P. Putnam's Sons; 2009
Penguin Group-Gotham Books; 2009
Penguin Group-Plume; 2009
Penguin Group-Viking; 2009
Random House Audio; 2009
Warnaco Warner's, Olga, Olga's Christina; 2004

AGENCY215
(Name Changed to Twofifteenmccann)

AGENCY501 INC.
303 President Clinton Ave Ste C, Little Rock, AR 72201
Tel.: (501) 444-2617
Web Site: www.agency501.com

Agency Specializes In: Advertising, Digital/Interactive, Internet/Web Design, Media Buying Services, Search Engine Optimization, Social Media, T.V.

McCabe Reynolds *(Co-Owner)*
Jason Spees *(Co-Owner)*
Travis Mosler *(Dir-Video & Content)*
Dan Spengler *(Dir-Creative-White-Labeled)*
Megan Golden *(Specialist-Inbound Mktg)*

Accounts:
Austin Family Dentistry

AGENCY59
1910 Yonge St 4th Fl, Toronto, ON M4S 1Z5 Canada
Tel.: (416) 484-1959
Fax: (416) 484-9846
E-Mail: ascornaienchi@agency59.ca
Web Site: www.agency59.ca

E-Mail for Key Personnel:
Creative Dir.: jmcintyre@agency59.ca
Media Dir.: rsmith@agency59.ca

Employees: 50
Year Founded: 1959

National Agency Associations: ICA

Agency Specializes In: Advertising, Bilingual Market, Brand Development & Integration, Broadcast, Business Publications, Business-To-Business, Collateral, Communications, Consulting, Consumer Marketing, Consumer Publications, Digital/Interactive, Direct Response Marketing, E-Commerce, Electronic Media, Environmental, Financial, Government/Political, Health Care Services, High Technology, Industrial, Information Technology, Internet/Web Design, Investor Relations, Leisure, Magazines, Media Buying Services, Multimedia, Newspaper, Newspapers & Magazines, Out-of-Home Media, Outdoor, Over-50 Market, Planning & Consultation, Print, Production, Public Relations, Publicity/Promotions, Radio, Retail, Seniors' Market, Sports Market, Strategic Planning/Research, Sweepstakes, T.V., Teen Market, Trade & Consumer Magazines, Transportation, Travel & Tourism

Approx. Annual Billings: $10,000,000

Al Scornaienchi *(Pres & CEO)*
John McIntyre *(Partner & Writer)*
Brian Howlett *(Chief Creative Officer)*
David Foy *(Pres-A59 Response)*
Akiyo Hattori *(Acct Dir)*
Frederic Morin *(Acct Dir)*
Jared Smith *(Mgr-Studio)*
Gavin Ball *(Acct Exec)*
Ravi Rana *(Exec-Media)*

Accounts:
Barrick Gold
BC SPCA
Camp Trillium
Chase Card Services
Chase Paymentech Solutions
Edward Kelly
Egg Farmers of Ontario
Furniture Bank Campaign: "Echo1"
Gay Lea Foods Campaign: "Spinner"
Grace Wu
Heart & Stroke Foundation Campaign: "9-1-1", HeartBike
Hewlett-Packard
Inco Limited
Labatt Breweries of Canada Anti-Drunk Driving
Livegreen
Mercedes-Benz
Nabs Canada Campaign: "Sponge"
Nordica Campaign: "Anything Goes"
Panasonic
Sirius XM Radio Inc.
Telus Canada
Wine Country Ontario Campaign: "So Close You Can Taste It"

Branch

Agency59 Response
1910 Yonge Street 4th Fl, Toronto, ON M4S 1Z5 Canada
Tel.: (416) 484-1959
Fax: (416) 484-9846
Web Site: www.agency59.ca

E-Mail for Key Personnel:
Production Mgr.: lwhite@amw-com.com

Employees: 40
Year Founded: 1985

National Agency Associations: CAB-CMA

Agency Specializes In: Business-To-Business, Consumer Marketing, Direct Response Marketing, E-Commerce, Health Care Services, High Technology, Seniors' Market, Strategic Planning/Research, Sweepstakes, Travel & Tourism

David Foy *(Pres & Partner)*
Marc Cooper *(Chief Digital Officer)*
Samantha Hepworth *(Acct Dir)*
Scott Cooper *(Dir-Digital Strategy & Production)*
David Hong *(Dir-Art)*
Curtis Wolowich *(Dir-Creative)*
Stefanie Briand *(Sr Acct Exec)*
Julia Foy *(Sr Acct Exec)*
Natalia Gordillo *(Sr Acct Exec)*
Sandra Colburn *(Acct Exec)*
Julian Morgan *(Acct Exec)*

Accounts:
BC SPCA
BMO/Harris Bank
CAA South Central Ontario
ENCON Group Insurance
MADD Canada
Ontario Society of Professional Engineers
SiriusXM Canada Direct Response
TELUS
XM Satellite Radio

AGENCYEA
311 W Walton St, Chicago, IL 60610
Tel.: (312) 879-0186
Web Site: agencyea.com/

Year Founded: 1999

Agency Specializes In: Advertising, Brand Development & Integration, Event Planning & Marketing, Integrated Marketing

Fergus Rooney *(CEO)*
Gabrielle Martinez *(Mng Partner)*
Jason Vargas *(Mng Dir)*
Dan Brice *(VP-Production)*
Susan Gooding *(Vp-Client Svcs)*
David St. Martin *(Vp-Cultural Dev)*
Rick Cosgrove *(Dir-Creative)*
Lucy Kaegi *(Dir-Bus Dev)*
Claire Prendergast *(Dir-Mktg Comm)*
Kelley Gripp *(Exec Mgr-Bus Dev)*
Kelli Wolfgram *(Mgr-Exec Ops)*

Accounts:
Boeing

AGENCYQ
1825 K St NW Ste 500, Washington, DC 20006
Tel.: (202) 776-9090
Web Site: www.agencyq.com

Year Founded: 1999

Agency Specializes In: Advertising, Content, Internet/Web Design, Search Engine Optimization, Social Media

Stephen Marino *(COO)*
Colin Dale *(Sr VP-Tech)*
Chris Merl *(Dir-Ops & Controller)*
Meghan Fishburn *(Sr Producer-Digital)*
Caitlin Daitch *(Producer-Digital)*
Katie Haswell *(Producer-Digital)*
Christopher Procunier *(Dir-IT)*

Accounts:
U.S. Department of Energy Office of Science

AGENCYRX
200 Varick St 3rd Fl, New York, NY 10014
Tel.: (212) 896-1300
E-Mail: info@agencyrx.com
Web Site: www.agencyrx.com

Year Founded: 2005

National Agency Associations: 4A's

Agency Specializes In: Advertising, Sponsorship

Sarah Farrugia *(VP & Acct Supvr)*
Julie Tripi *(VP & Acct Supvr)*
Karen Moore *(VP & Supvr-Copy)*
Kenny Peers *(VP & Grp Supvr-Art)*
Liz Wong *(VP & Grp Supvr-Project)*
Matt Goff *(Assoc Partner & Dir-Digital Mktg)*
Brielle DePalma *(Acct Supvr)*
Shane Kennedy *(Acct Supvr-Digital)*
Melissa Mancini *(Acct Supvr)*
Stephanie Matone *(Sr Acct Exec)*

Accounts:
Teva Women's Health, Inc. Seasonique

AGENCYSACKS
345 7th Ave 7th Fl, New York, NY 10001-5006
Tel.: (212) 826-4004
Fax: (212) 593-7824
E-Mail: info@agencysacks.com
Web Site: www.agencysacks.com

E-Mail for Key Personnel:
President: asacks@agencysacks.com

Employees: 30
Year Founded: 1964

Agency Specializes In: Advertising, Advertising Specialties, Affluent Market, Automotive, Aviation & Aerospace, Brand Development & Integration, Broadcast, Business Publications, Cable T.V., Catalogs, Collateral, Consumer Goods, Consumer

Marketing, Consumer Publications, Corporate Identity, Cosmetics, Digital/Interactive, Direct Response Marketing, Direct-to-Consumer, Electronic Media, Electronics, Fashion/Apparel, Financial, Graphic Design, Hospitality, Household Goods, Identity Marketing, In-Store Advertising, International, Internet/Web Design, Leisure, Logo & Package Design, Luxury Products, Magazines, Market Research, Media Buying Services, Media Planning, Newspaper, Newspapers & Magazines, Out-of-Home Media, Outdoor, Package Design, Point of Purchase, Point of Sale, Print, Production, Production (Ad, Film, Broadcast), Radio, Real Estate, Regional, Restaurant, Retail, Social Media, Sponsorship, Strategic Planning/Research, T.V., Trade & Consumer Magazines, Travel & Tourism, Women's Market

Andrew Sacks *(Owner & Pres)*
Elizabeth Geary *(Mng Dir)*
John Mercurio *(CFO & Chief Creative Officer)*
Jessica Haas *(Sr Dir-Art)*
Chad Duncan *(Dir-Affluent Engagement)*
Alex Garcia *(Dir-Art)*
Brette Kreyer *(Sr Acct Exec)*
Abbey Bishop *(Asst Acct Exec)*

Accounts:
The Affluence Collaborative; New York, NY Affluent Segment Research Partnership; 2009
American Express Publishing - Departures Magazine; New York, NY Centurion Card Members Publication & Online Sponsorship Programs; 1998
Cartier; New York, NY Jewelry & TImepieces; 2003
Constellation Brands; Fairport, NY Premium Wines and Spirits; 2009
Dolce Hotels & Resorts; Montvale, NJ; 2007
Fontainebleau Miami Beach
Keeneland Association, Inc.; Lexington, KY Racetrack & Auction Company; 2007
Kobrand Corporation; Purchase, NY Wine & Spirits; 2009
New York Palace Hotel; 2007
The Penninsula Group; Hong Kong
Rosewood Hotels & Resorts; Dallas, TX Digital, Print
SHVO Marketing; New York, NY; 2007
Sony Cierge;New York, NY VIP Program; 2007
Stark Carpet; New York, NY Carpet, Wall Covering & Fine Furniture; 2006
Steinway Lyngdorf; New York, NY High-Performance In-Home Stereo Systems; 2006
Taj Hotels, Palaces & Resorts International Hotels, Resorts & Palaces; 2007

AGENDA
311 W 43rd St Ste 703, New York, NY 10036
Tel.: (212) 582-6200
Web Site: www.agendanyc.com

Employees: 20
Year Founded: 1999

Agency Specializes In: Below-the-Line, Catalogs, Collateral, Digital/Interactive, Direct Response Marketing, Electronic Media, Exhibit/Trade Shows, Experience Design, In-Store Advertising, Local Marketing, Magazines, Mobile Marketing, Multimedia, Out-of-Home Media, Outdoor, Point of Purchase, Point of Sale, Print, Promotions, Social Media, Sponsorship, Sweepstakes, Web (Banner Ads, Pop-ups, etc.)

David Stewart *(Owner)*
Victor Rivera *(Partner & Exec Dir-Creative)*
Dan Koh *(Partner & Dir-Creative)*
Rich Lim *(Acct Dir)*
Lucy Kneebone *(Dir-Bus)*
Michael McTwigan *(Dir-Strategy)*
Dave Rodriguez *(Dir-Design)*

Accounts:
Abbott Health Care, Pharma; 2006
Guardian Insurance; 2008
Hanwha Solar Solar Energy; 2011
LexisNexis Legal Services; 2010
MasterCard Financial Services; 1999
PartnerRe Reinsurance; 2005
Samsung Electronics America Consumer Electronics; 2006
Samsung Group; 1999
TradeMark East Africa North American Public Affairs
Yext Location Software Technology; 2013

AGNETO COMUNICACAO
175 Varick St, New York, NY 10014
Tel.: (646) 266-0588
Web Site: www.agnelo.com.br/en/home

Employees: 120
Year Founded: 1985

Agency Specializes In: Above-the-Line, Affluent Market, Alternative Advertising, Below-the-Line, Bilingual Market, Business-To-Business, Consumer Marketing, Consumer Publications, Digital/Interactive, Direct-to-Consumer, International, Local Marketing, Men's Market, Mobile Marketing, Multicultural, Newspaper, Newspapers & Magazines, Print, Production, Production (Print), Radio, T.V., Web (Banner Ads, Pop-ups, etc.), Women's Market

Approx. Annual Billings: $100,000,000

Agnelo Pacheco *(Pres & Dir-Creative)*
Adriana De Carvalho *(Mng Dir-Media)*
Gui Pacheco *(VP, Dir-Creative & Gen Mgr-Brasilia Office)*
Daniela Calvo *(Acct Dir)*
Renata Botene *(Acct Mgr)*
Alex Gris *(Mgr-Creative)*

Accounts:
Fisk English School; 2004
Health Ministry; 2009
OAB; 2003
Tourism Ministry; 2008

AH&M MARKETING COMMUNICATIONS
152 N St Ste 340, Pittsfield, MA 01201-5118
Tel.: (413) 448-2260
Fax: (413) 445-4026
E-Mail: info@ahminc.com
Web Site: www.ahminc.com

E-Mail for Key Personnel:
President: jallison@ahminc.com

Employees: 8
Year Founded: 1988

Agency Specializes In: Automotive, Aviation & Aerospace, Business-To-Business, Communications, Engineering, Industrial, Logo & Package Design, Medical Products, New Product Development, Print, Public Relations, Publicity/Promotions, Strategic Planning/Research, Trade & Consumer Magazines, Transportation

Approx. Annual Billings: $7,000,000

Breakdown of Gross Billings by Media: Bus. Publs.: 10%; Collateral: 20%; Production: 10%; Pub. Rels.: 50%; Trade Shows: 10%

Jim Allison *(Pres & CEO)*
Daniel Mccarthy *(Acct Mgr-Global)*
Sarah Thurston *(Acct Exec)*
Aaron Wood *(Acct Exec)*

Accounts:
Milliken Plastics
SABIC Innovative Plastics

AHA COMMUNICATIONS
209 E Riverside Dr, Austin, TX 78704
Tel.: (512) 448-4494
Fax: (512) 476-4289
E-Mail: info@getaha.com
Web Site: www.getaha.com

Year Founded: 2006

Agency Specializes In: Advertising, Broadcast, Digital/Interactive, Email, Exhibit/Trade Shows, Graphic Design, Logo & Package Design, Print, Search Engine Optimization, Strategic Planning/Research

Deborah Pfluger *(Pres)*
April Bennett *(Dir-Digital Mktg)*
Niles Giberson *(Sr Designer)*
Alyson Daily *(Acct Coord)*

Accounts:
Alexander Marchant

AIM ADVERTISING
139 Market St, Lewisburg, PA 17837
Tel.: (570) 522-9200
Fax: (570) 522-9202
Web Site: www.aimadvertising.com

Agency Specializes In: Advertising, Digital/Interactive, Email, Internet/Web Design, Print, Promotions

Mark Fleisher *(Pres & CEO)*
Mary Anne Fleisher *(VP)*
Scott Sanders *(Dir-Creative)*

Accounts:
Colonial Candlecrafters

AIM STRAIGHT UP
(Formerly Willow Creative Group)
222 E 14th St, Cincinnati, OH 45202
Tel.: (513) 476-1507
E-Mail: debbie@aimstraightup.com
Web Site: www.aimstraightup.com

Employees: 1
Year Founded: 1988

National Agency Associations: AD CLUB-AMA

Agency Specializes In: Advertising, Brand Development & Integration, Business-To-Business, Catalogs, Collateral, Consulting, Corporate Communications, Corporate Identity, Digital/Interactive, Education, Email, Event Planning & Marketing, Exhibit/Trade Shows, Financial, Graphic Design, Guerilla Marketing, Health Care Services, Industrial, Integrated Marketing, Internet/Web Design, Legal Services, Logo & Package Design, Market Research, Media Buying Services, Media Planning, Media Relations, Medical Products, Outdoor, Pharmaceutical, Planning & Consultation, Print, Production (Print), Public Relations, RSS (Really Simple Syndication), Restaurant, Sales Promotion, Search Engine Optimization, Seniors' Market, Social Marketing/Nonprofit, Social Media, Strategic Planning/Research, Trade & Consumer Magazines, Viral/Buzz/Word of Mouth, Web (Banner Ads, Pop-ups, etc.)

Breakdown of Gross Billings by Media: Newsp.: 10%; Out-of-Home Media: 10%; Radio & T.V.: 20%; Trade & Consumer Mags.: 30%; Trade Shows: 30%

Deborah Dent *(Owner & Pres)*

Accounts:
Build Downtown Cincinnati Real Estate
ChartMaxx Enterprise Content Management
Promark Global Talent Management
Quest Diagnostics Clinical Lab Services

AIMIA
(Formerly Carlson Marketing)
100 N 6th St, Minneapolis, MN 55403
Tel.: (763) 445-3000
Web Site: www.aimia.com

Employees: 3,000
Year Founded: 1938

National Agency Associations: AMA-DMA

Agency Specializes In: Collateral, Communications, Consumer Marketing, Direct Response Marketing, Event Planning & Marketing

Philip McKoy *(CIO-US Reg & Sr VP)*
Kurt Paben *(Pres-Channel & Employee Loyalty-US)*
Greg Engen *(VP-Consumer Packaged Goods)*
Cindy Faust *(VP-Product Mktg-Global)*
Paul Sage *(Gen Mgr-Product Dev & Reg Svc Center)*
Mike Cornielle *(Sr Dir-Strategic Partnerships)*
Laura Hewitt *(Sr Dir)*
Kelli Ask *(Grp Acct Dir-Consumer Packaged Goods)*
Lars Parmekar *(Acct Dir)*
Amanda Pott *(Mgr-Meeting)*

Accounts:
AARP
Amtrak
Chrysler de Mexico
Chrysler Financial
Chrysler LLC
Coca-Cola Refreshments USA, Inc.
Ford
General Motors
Hallmark
IBM
JetBlue
Kellogg's
Kodak Graphic Communications Group
Mazda
Northwest Airlines, Inc.
Oracle America, Inc.
Sprint
Visa
Wachovia
Wal-Mart

Americas

Aimia
(Formerly Carlson Marketing Group Ltd.)
2845 Mathieson Blvd E, Mississauga, ON L4W 5K2 Canada
Tel.: (905) 214-8699
Fax: (905) 214-8693
Web Site: www.aimia.com

Employees: 350

Agency Specializes In: Advertising

John Boynton *(CMO-Canada)*
Vince Timpano *(Pres/CEO-Canada & Exec VP)*
Martha Barss *(Sr VP-Proprietary Loyalty)*
Tony Wong *(Dir-Digital Strategy)*

Aimia
(Formerly Carlson Marketing Group)
2800 Livernois Ste 600, Troy, MI 48083
Tel.: (248) 824-7600
Web Site: www.aimia.com

Employees: 100

Agency Specializes In: Advertising

Fay Beauchine *(Pres-Bus Loyalty)*
Michael O'Sullivan *(Pres-Proprietary Loyalty Svcs-Canada)*
Karl Schuster *(Pres-Proprietary Loyalty-Asia Pacific)*
Luc Bondar *(Sr VP-US Reg)*

Aimia
(Formerly Carlson Marketing Group)
1 Gatehill Dr Ste 205, Parsippany, NJ 07054-4514
Tel.: (973) 292-0050
Web Site: www.aimia.com

Agency Specializes In: Advertising

Nathan Wortman *(Sr VP-Analytics-North America)*
Krista Pawley *(VP-Comm-Global)*

Aimia
(Formerly Carlson Marketing)
Carlson Ct 116 Putney Bridge Rd, London, SW15 2NQ United Kingdom
Tel.: (44) 20 8875 3100
Fax: (44) 20 8875 0777
Web Site: www.aimia.com

Employees: 65

Agency Specializes In: Advertising

Peter Gleason *(Pres & Mng Dir-Intelligent Shopper Solutions)*
John Harris *(Sr VP & CTO-Global Architecture & Tech)*
Simon Hawkes *(Sr VP-Product Mgmt-Global)*
Martin Hayward *(Sr VP-Global Digital Strategy & Futures)*
Will Shuckburgh *(Mng Dir-Nectar UK)*
Brendan O'Donovan *(VP-Strategy-EMEA)*
Matt Davis *(Head-Digital Tech-EMEA)*
Scott Seaborn *(Product Dir-Global Mobile)*
Tim Birchinall *(Dir-Intl Dev)*
Emma Kisby *(Dir-Bus Dev-EMEA)*
Brett Mackay *(Dir-Loyalty Tech-Nectar)*
Simon Marsh *(Dir-Strategic Dev & Global Bus Dev)*
Naomi Sudworth *(Mgr-Bus Dev)*
David Johnston *(Grp Chief Creative Officer)*

Accounts:
Muller Dairy

PSM S.A.
O'Donnell 34, 28009 Madrid, Spain
Tel.: (34) 91 573 38 03
Fax: (34) 91 409 76 82
E-Mail: madrid@psm.es
Web Site: www.psm.es

Agency Specializes In: Advertising

Jose Antonio Rubio *(Gen Dir)*
Carol Fuset *(Acct Dir)*
Javier Menasalvas Garcia *(Acct Dir)*
Virginia Alonso *(Dir-Madrid)*
Jesus Barrena Perez *(Dir-IT)*

AINSLEY & CO
720 S Montford Ave Ste 101, Baltimore, MD 21224
Tel.: (410) 317-8388
E-Mail: info@ainsleyagency.com
Web Site: www.ainsleyagency.com

Year Founded: 2009

Agency Specializes In: Advertising, Brand Development & Integration, Graphic Design, Print

Tom Ainsley *(Founder & CEO)*
Melanie Kelleher *(Acct Mgr)*
Jennifer Williams *(Copywriter)*

Accounts:
New-McQuade Consulting LLC

AIR INTEGRATED
(Formerly Air Marketing)
4720 E Cotton Gin Loop, Phoenix, AZ 85040
Tel.: (480) 921-3220
Fax: (480) 921-3228
E-Mail: solutions@airintegrated.com
Web Site: http://commitagency.com/

Year Founded: 1987

Agency Specializes In: Advertising, Digital/Interactive, Email, Internet/Web Design, Logo & Package Design, Market Research, Media Relations, Public Relations, Social Media, T.V.

David Ralls *(Pres)*
Elaine E. Ralls *(CEO)*
Dave Ragar *(VP & Dir-Creative)*
Fred Pratt *(VP-Analytics & Tech)*
Lindsey Lubenow *(Media Planner)*
Meredith Oechsner *(Coord-Acct & Media)*

Accounts:
ActiveRx (Agency of Record) Analytics, Brand Strategy, Creative, Digital, Marketing, Media
American Solar & Roofing Digital Strategy
AmeriSchools Academy Analytics, Creative, Direct Mail, Marketing, Media
The Arizona Cardinals
Benchmark Properties
The Better Business Bureau of Metropolitan New York
Destination Hotels & Resorts Inc.
Discount Cab
Hershey Entertainment & Resorts Company
Meritus
National Kidney Foundation of Arizona Branding, Creative Services, Prom Redux
NextCare Urgent Care
Oregon Social Learning Center Website
The Otesaga Hotel Analytics, Creative Development, Research, Strategy
The Phoenician
Sante Analytics, Brand Strategy, Creative, Digital, Marketing, Media, Public Relations, Social Media
Skytop Lodge (Agency of Record) Brand Strategy, Creative, Digital, Marketing, Paid Media
Sono Bello
Starwood Hotels & Resorts Worldwide, Inc.
Total Transit
WP Carey School of Business at ASU

AIR PARIS/NEW YORK
20 W 22nd St 901, New York, NY 10010
Tel.: (212) 660-4460
Web Site: www.airparisagency.com

Employees: 80
Year Founded: 1997

Agency Specializes In: Above-the-Line, Below-the-Line, Catalogs, Digital/Interactive, Experience Design, In-Store Advertising, Print, Production, T.V., Web (Banner Ads, Pop-ups, etc.)

Nora Ladghem *(Partner & Mng Dir-Air Paris & Shanghai)*
Dimitri Katsachnias *(Partner & Dir-Strategic)*
Klitos Teklos *(Partner & Dir-Creative-Air Paris & New York)*
Tho Van Tran *(Partner & Dir-Creative)*
Cecile Begue-Turon *(Exec Dir)*
Lisa Nanus *(Acct Dir)*
Danielle Chocron *(Dir-Bus Dev & Mktg)*

Accounts:
Estee Lauder Osaio; 2011
Foli Folie; 2010
Guess Fragrances; 2000
Links of London; 2013
Longchamp; 2011
Murad; 2011

AIRT GROUP
91 Dockside Cir, San Rafael, CA 94903
Tel.: (415) 497-3222
Web Site: www.airt-group.com

Agency Specializes In: Advertising, Multimedia, Print

Bill Light *(Exec Dir-Creative)*
Peter Sharpe *(Sr Dir-Art)*
Jerry Strifler *(Sr Dir-Art)*
Robin Freni *(Dir-Design)*
Ron Ovadia *(Strategist-Creative Brand)*
Mike Mahoney *(Sr Writer)*

Accounts:
BioVentrix

AIS MEDIA, INC.
3340 Peachtree Rd NE Ste 750, Atlanta, GA 30326
Tel.: (404) 751-1043
Web Site: www.aismedia.com

Employees: 40

Agency Specializes In: Advertising, Content, Digital/Interactive, Internet/Web Design, Social Media

Revenue: $4,600,000

Thomas Harpointner *(CEO)*
Denise Maling *(Exec VP)*
Sean Jones *(VP-Interactive Dev)*

Accounts:
1st Franklin Financial Corporation

AISLE ROCKET STUDIOS
(Formerly ARS Advertising Inc.)
1001 Reads Lake Rd, Chattanooga, TN 37415-2056
Tel.: (423) 875-3743
Fax: (423) 875-5346
Web Site: www.aislerocket.com

Employees: 40
Year Founded: 1977

Agency Specializes In: Advertising, Point of Purchase, Point of Sale, Print, Production, Sales Promotion

Approx. Annual Billings: $12,000,000

Scott R. Norman *(Pres & CEO)*
Kim Finch *(Sr VP & Gen Mgr)*
Kashif Zaman *(VP-Interactive)*
Michael Davis *(Grp Dir-Creative)*
Donata Maggipinto *(Dir-Content Creative)*
Renee Martin *(Dir-Creative)*

Accounts:
Amana
Electrolux Home Products Eureka
Gladiator
Kenmore
Kmart
Maytag
Quill
Sears, Roebuck & Co. Craftsman, DieHard, Kenmore, The Great Indoors
Walmart
Whirlpool Corporation Jenn-Air, Kitchenaid
Woodcraft

Branches

Aisle Rocket Studios
(Formerly ARS Advertising Group)
511 Renaissance Dr Ste 150, Saint Joseph, MI 49085
Tel.: (269) 982-6600
Fax: (269) 98-2 6640
Web Site: www.aislerocket.com

Employees: 250
Year Founded: 1995

Scott Norman *(Pres)*
Kim Finch *(Sr VP & Gen Mgr)*
Ronda Scalise *(Sr VP & Gen Mgr-Chicago)*
Kashif Zaman *(VP-Interactive)*
Renee Martin *(Dir-Creative)*

Accounts:
Affresh
Amana
Craftsman
Dollar General
Electrolux
Eureka
Gladiator
Kmart
Maytag
Sears

Aisle Rocket Studios
(Formerly ARS Advertising)
220 N Smith St Ste 310, Palatine, IL 60067-2448
Tel.: (847) 598-2424
Fax: (847) 882-0175
Web Site: www.aislerocket.com

Employees: 30
Year Founded: 2005

Agency Specializes In: Advertising

Bob Boyle *(VP-Client Engagement)*
Renee Martin *(VP-Creative Strategy)*
Kashif Zaman *(VP-Interactive)*
Alen Parlov *(Sr Dir-Art)*
Matthew Jansick *(Dir-Experience Design)*
Lauren Laheta *(Dir-Art)*
Amber Oppelt *(Dir-Art)*
Erin Shipman *(Dir-Ops)*
Matthew Loiacono *(Sr Acct Mgr)*
Alex Mariscal *(Copywriter)*

Accounts:
Kmart Corporation
Sears Holdings Corporation
Sears, Roebuck & Co.

AJ ROSS CREATIVE MEDIA, INC.
1149 Route 17M, Chester, NY 10918-1466
Tel.: (845) 783-5770
Fax: (845) 782-9073
Toll Free: (800) 723-4644
E-Mail: info@ajross.com
Web Site: www.ajross.com

E-Mail for Key Personnel:
Creative Dir.: carlos@ajross.com

Employees: 12
Year Founded: 1991

Agency Specializes In: Advertising, Advertising Specialties, Affluent Market, Alternative Advertising, Arts, Aviation & Aerospace, Brand Development & Integration, Broadcast, Business Publications, Business-To-Business, Cable T.V., Catalogs, Co-op Advertising, Collateral, Commercial Photography, Communications, Consulting, Consumer Goods, Consumer Marketing, Consumer Publications, Content, Corporate Communications, Corporate Identity, Cosmetics, Digital/Interactive, Direct Response Marketing, Direct-to-Consumer, E-Commerce, Education, Electronic Media, Email, Environmental, Event Planning & Marketing, Exhibit/Trade Shows, Experience Design, Financial, Food Service, Government/Political, Graphic Design, Health Care Services, High Technology, Hispanic Market, Hospitality, Household Goods, Identity Marketing, In-Store Advertising, Industrial, Infomercials, Information Technology, Integrated Marketing, Internet/Web Design, Investor Relations, Legal Services, Leisure, Local Marketing, Logo & Package Design, Luxury Products, Magazines, Market Research, Media Buying Services, Media Planning, Media Relations, Media Training, Medical Products, Men's Market, Merchandising, Mobile Marketing, Multimedia, New Product Development, Newspaper, Newspapers & Magazines, Out-of-Home Media, Outdoor, Over-50 Market, Package Design, Paid Searches, Pharmaceutical, Planning & Consultation, Point of Purchase, Point of Sale, Print, Product Placement, Production, Production (Print), Promotions, Public Relations, Publicity/Promotions, Publishing, Radio, Recruitment, Regional, Retail, Sales Promotion, Search Engine Optimization, Seniors' Market, Social Marketing/Nonprofit, Social Media, Sponsorship, Sports Market, Strategic Planning/Research, T.V., Technical Advertising, Teen Market, Trade & Consumer Magazines, Transportation, Travel & Tourism, Urban Market, Women's Market, Yellow Pages Advertising

Approx. Annual Billings: $3,000,000

Breakdown of Gross Billings by Media: Brdcst.: $300,000; Cable T.V.: $300,000; Collateral: $300,000; Logo & Package Design: $450,000; Newsp.: $300,000; Print: $300,000; Spot Radio: $150,000; Worldwide Web Sites: $900,000

Allan J. Ross *(Chm & CEO)*
Matt Ross *(VP-Web & Internet Div)*
Carlos Vega *(Dir-Creative)*
Victor Lago *(Asst Dir-Creative)*

Accounts:
Fini Construction; Goshen, NY New Home Developers
Fini Developers Residential & Commercial Real Estate; 2009
Finkelstein & Partners; Newburgh, NY Attorneys
Hunterdon Radiology Radiological Services; 2006
Jacoby & Meyers; New York, NY Legal
K & M Consulting, Inc.
Newgen Construction New Homes; 2005
NIFTY Travel; 1996
Olympia Homes; Corn-Wall-On-Hudson, NY New Home Developers
Orange County Parks; Goshen, NY Web Design, Collateral Materials
Orange County Partnership
Orange County Tourism New Homes; 2005
Regan Developers Real Estate; 2003
Spence Engineering Steam Fittings; 2008
Sullivan Flotation Marina Landings; 2005
Tarshis, Catania, Liberth, Mahon & Milligram Attorneys; 2005

AJAM BRAND
212 Adams Ave, Cape Canaveral, FL 32920
Tel.: (321) 213-5279

Year Founded: 2004

Agency Specializes In: Advertising, Affluent Market, African-American Market, Brand

Development & Integration, Branded Entertainment, Broadcast, Business-To-Business, College, Consulting, Consumer Marketing, Digital/Interactive, Electronic Media, Event Planning & Marketing, Guerilla Marketing, Integrated Marketing, International, Local Marketing, Luxury Products, Market Research, Men's Market, Mobile Marketing, Multimedia, Newspaper, Newspapers & Magazines, Outdoor, Point of Purchase, Point of Sale, Production (Ad, Film, Broadcast), Regional, Sales Promotion, Social Media, Sponsorship, Strategic Planning/Research, Teen Market, Urban Market

Adam J Marrara *(Pres & CMO)*
Brian Connell *(VP-Creative Design)*
Rick Hall *(VP-Mktg & Sponsorships)*
Joshua Marrara *(VP-Ops & Talent Acq)*
Alicia J Oakes *(VP-PR)*

Accounts:
ASA Entertainment
Keep N' It Wet Surf Brand Development
LG Action Sports World Tour; 2008
Maxell Headphones & Music Accessories; 2008
Republic Trust & Mortgage Retail Mortgage; 2004
Ron Jons Surf Shops; 2011
Wells Fargo Wholesale Lending Wholesale Mortgage; 2006
XBox Xbox 360; 2008

AJAX UNION
2233 Nostrand Ave, Brooklyn, NY 11210
Tel.: (718) 569-1020
Fax: (718) 569-1022
Toll Free: (800) 594-0444
E-Mail: info@ajaxunion.com
Web Site: www.ajaxunion.com

Employees: 50
Year Founded: 2007

Agency Specializes In: Advertising, Direct Response Marketing, Email, Mobile Marketing, Paid Searches, Public Relations, Search Engine Optimization, Social Media, Web (Banner Ads, Pop-ups, etc.)

Approx. Annual Billings: $3,000,000

Joe Apfelbaum *(Co-Founder & CEO)*
Sasha Marketter *(Bus Dir-Mktg)*
Mushki Deitsch *(Dir-Social Media)*
Matthew Sieracki *(Mgr-SEO)*
Dave Kehaty *(Specialist-Internet Mktg SEO)*
Mark Leifer *(Strategist-SEM)*

Accounts:
Rearviewsafety; 2010
Zoe Ltd

AKA DIRECT, INC.
2415 N Ross Ave, Portland, OR 97227
Mailing Address:
PO Box 5217, Portland, OR 97208-5217
Tel.: (800) 647-8587
Fax: (503) 692-9625
E-Mail: wayne.modica@akadirect.com
Web Site: www.akadirect.com

Employees: 65
Year Founded: 1968

Agency Specializes In: Advertising, Automotive, Aviation & Aerospace, Business Publications, Business-To-Business, Children's Market, Collateral, Consulting, Consumer Marketing, Cosmetics, Direct Response Marketing, E-Commerce, Education, Electronic Media, Engineering, Entertainment, Exhibit/Trade Shows, Financial, Food Service, Gay & Lesbian Market, Government/Political, Graphic Design, High Technology, Industrial, Information Technology, Legal Services, Leisure, Local Marketing, Logo & Package Design, Magazines, Marine, Media Buying Services, Medical Products, Merchandising, Over-50 Market, Pharmaceutical, Print, Production, Promotions, Real Estate, Retail, Seniors' Market, Technical Advertising, Telemarketing, Travel & Tourism

Approx. Annual Billings: $7,000,000

Breakdown of Gross Billings by Media: Consulting: 5%; D.M.: 60%; Other: 15%; Print: 20%

Wayne Modica *(Pres)*
Mary Jane Aman *(CFO)*
Walter Aman *(CIO)*
David Rouza *(Chief Creative Officer)*
Laura Torres *(Sr Acct Mgr)*
Scott Dachtler *(Acct Mgr)*
Greg Taylor *(Acct Mgr)*

AKA NYC
630 9th Ave Ste 1411, New York, NY 10036
Tel.: (212) 584-0400
E-Mail: contact@aka.nyc
Web Site: aka.nyc

Employees: 60

Agency Specializes In: Advertising, Content, Digital/Interactive, Social Media, T.V.

Bashan Aquart *(Mng Partner)*
Elizabeth Furze *(Mng Partner)*
Scott Moore *(Mng Partner)*
Janette Roush *(VP-Insights & Mktg)*
Jamaal Parham *(Creative Dir)*
Robert Schnabel *(Sr Art Dir)*
Joshua Poole *(Dir-Strategic Innovations)*
Jacob Matsumiya *(Sr Mgr-Mktg)*
Elizabeth Findlay *(Acct Mgr)*
Jennifer Blanco *(Sr Acct Supvr)*
Lauren Guenther *(Copywriter)*
Stacy Gollinger *(Coord-Mktg)*

Accounts:
New-Dames at Sea Broadway LLC
New-Gotta Dance Broadway LLC
It's Only a Play
Les Miserables
Longacre Theatre Campaign: "Living on Love"
Matilda the Musical

AKAVIT
1224 N Speer Blvd, Denver, CO 80204
Tel.: (303) 586-1327
Fax: (303) 648-4825
Web Site: www.akavit.com

Year Founded: 2008

Agency Specializes In: Advertising, Content, Digital/Interactive, Email, Internet/Web Design, Media Buying Services, Promotions, Search Engine Optimization, Social Media

Rob Davis *(Founder & CEO)*
Thomas Dahl *(Partner & VP-Strategy & Insight)*
Robert Betts *(Partner & Dir-Creative Svcs)*
Erica Spencer *(Acct Dir)*
Jesse Day *(Dir-New Bus)*
Jeremy Siefkas *(Dir-Integrated Mktg Svcs)*
Kevin Parker *(Mgr-Sitefinity Practice)*

Accounts:
Avocados

AKINS MARKETING & DESIGN L.L.C.
11 Washburn Rd, New London, CT 06320-2946
Tel.: (860) 440-2625
Fax: (860) 443-8110
E-Mail: marketing@akinsmarketing.com
Web Site: www.akinsmarketing.com

E-Mail for Key Personnel:
President: pamakins@akinsmarketing.com

Employees: 2
Year Founded: 1989

Agency Specializes In: Advertising, Brand Development & Integration, Business-To-Business, Collateral, Consulting, Corporate Identity, Education, Financial, Government/Political, Graphic Design, Health Care Services, High Technology, Industrial, Internet/Web Design, Logo & Package Design, Media Buying Services, Newspapers & Magazines, Public Relations, Publicity/Promotions, Travel & Tourism

Approx. Annual Billings: $500,000

Pamela S. Akins *(Pres & Dir-Creative)*

Accounts:
Block Island Ferry; New London, CT; 1989
Connecticut Department of Consumer Protection Direct Mail Campaign, Prescription Monitoring Program
Definitive Technology; Baltimore, MD Consumer Electronics; 1990
Lawrence Memorial Hospital; New London, CT; 1989
New London Rotary Club
OraLine

AKQA, INC.
(Acquired by WPP plc)

AKQURACY
800 Washington Ave N Ste 206, Minneapolis, MN 55401
Tel.: (612) 605-7556
Web Site: www.akquracy.com

Employees: 15
Year Founded: 2007

Agency Specializes In: Affluent Market, African-American Market, Asian Market, Below-the-Line, Business-To-Business, Children's Market, College, Consumer Marketing, Direct Response Marketing, Direct-to-Consumer, Email, High Technology, Hispanic Market, International, Luxury Products, Men's Market, Mobile Marketing, Multicultural, Over-50 Market, Pets , Seniors' Market, South Asian Market, Teen Market, Tween Market, Urban Market, Women's Market

Scott Spencer *(VP-Analytics & Consumer Insights)*
Sally Castellano *(Dir-Project Mgmt)*

Accounts:
Bentley Motors Communications Strategy
Harley Davidson Motor Company Harley Davidson Motorcycles; 2007

AL PUNTO ADVERTISING, INC.
730 El Camino Way Ste 200, Tustin, CA 92780-7733
Tel.: (714) 544-0888
Fax: (714) 544-0830
E-Mail: info@alpunto.com
Web Site: www.alpunto.com

E-Mail for Key Personnel:
President: pgoff@alpunto.com
Creative Dir.: ebottger@alpunto.com

Employees: 25
Year Founded: 1994

National Agency Associations: AHAA

Agency Specializes In: Advertising, Bilingual Market, Communications, Consumer Marketing, Entertainment, Health Care Services, Hispanic Market, Logo & Package Design, Media Buying Services, Planning & Consultation, Public Relations, Publicity/Promotions, Restaurant, Retail, Sponsorship

Revenue: $87,000,000

Eduardo Bottger *(Pres, Principal & Exec Dir-Creative)*
Roy Zuloaga *(Client Svcs Dir)*
Ivan Cevallos *(Sr Acct Supvr)*

Accounts:
American Heart Association; Burlingame, CA Hispanic, Stroke Awareness
Blue Ribbon Rice
California Beef Councils; 2015
Clearwire Corporation
Daisy Brand
Holiday Inn Express
IEHP (Inland Empire Health Plan); Riverside, CA; 2002
Jim Beam Whiskey
Kia Motors America, Inc.; 2005
Ringling Brothers & Barnum & Bailey Circus; Vienna, VA; 2002
San Diego Gas & Electric Company
Sempra Energy

AL SHULTZ ADVERTISING, INC.
1346 The Alameda, San Jose, CA 95126
Tel.: (408) 289-9555
E-Mail: info@alshultz.com
Web Site: www.alshultz.com

Employees: 5
Year Founded: 1983

National Agency Associations: BMA

Agency Specializes In: Advertising, Automotive, Brand Development & Integration, Business Publications, Business-To-Business, Collateral, Communications, Computers & Software, Corporate Communications, Electronic Media, Electronics, Email, Engineering, Exhibit/Trade Shows, Graphic Design, High Technology, Identity Marketing, Industrial, Information Technology, Integrated Marketing, Internet/Web Design, Logo & Package Design, Magazines, Media Planning, Medical Products, New Technologies, Newspapers & Magazines, Paid Searches, Print, Production (Print), Promotions, Sales Promotion, Social Media, Technical Advertising, Trade & Consumer Magazines

Approx. Annual Billings: $2,000,000

Breakdown of Gross Billings by Media: Bus. Publs.: $800,000; Collateral: $200,000; Graphic Design: $200,000; Trade Shows: $200,000; Worldwide Web Sites: $600,000

Al Shultz *(Pres & Dir-Creative)*

Accounts:
ClassOne Technology Semiconductor Processing Equipment; 2014
Duralar Technologies Advanced Hard Coatings; 2012
EcoVoltz; San Jose, CA Energy Storage for Solar & Wind; 2008
Greenkote Eco-friendly Anti-corrosion Metal Coatings; 2012
Hamamatsu Photonics Photonics Technology, Components & Systems; 2014
McBain Systems; Simi Valley, CA Microscopy Systems; 2007
MicroSurface Corporation Lubrication Coatings; 2012
PolyDiamond Technologies; Pleasanton, CA Product Additives; 2011
Sub-One Technology; Pleasanton, CA Internal Coating Technologies; 2004
SynGen Inc Blood Cell Separation Systems; 2014

AL STARK'S A&M
2620 N Augusta Dr, Wadsworth, IL 60083
Tel.: (847) 625-9100
Fax: (847) 625-9101
E-Mail: al.stark@sbcglobal.net
Web Site: www.alstark.com

Employees: 5
Year Founded: 1974

Agency Specializes In: Advertising, Automotive, Brand Development & Integration, Business Publications, Business-To-Business, Cable T.V., Co-op Advertising, Consulting, Direct Response Marketing, E-Commerce, Exhibit/Trade Shows, Graphic Design, Internet/Web Design, Logo & Package Design, Magazines, Media Buying Services, New Product Development, Newspapers & Magazines, Planning & Consultation, Print, Production, Public Relations, Radio, T.V., Telemarketing, Trade & Consumer Magazines

Approx. Annual Billings: $945,000

Breakdown of Gross Billings by Media: Brdcst.: $50,000; Bus. Publs.: $200,000; Mags.: $100,000; Newsp.: $10,000; Point of Purchase: $250,000; Production: $100,000; Pub. Rels.: $40,000; Radio: $20,000; Sls. Promo.: $75,000; T.V.: $100,000

Alvin W. Stark *(Pres, Dir-Creative & Dir-Media)*

Accounts:
Bridgeview Lamp; Chicago, IL Lighting
Cal Controls; Libertyville, IL Temperature Controls; 1996
Murray Brothers Manufacturing Flexo Rollers; 1999
Tube Form Corp.; Chicago, IL Lighting Fixture Parts
Wilkenson Manufacturing; Chicago, IL Furniture Legs

ALAN/ANTHONY, INC.
(Name Changed to Intelligent Communities Group)

ALANAS MARKETING & CREATIVE
2132 Wabaska Ct, San Diego, CA 92107-2418
Tel.: (619) 888-4708
Fax: (619) 353-5619
E-Mail: info@alanascreative.com

Agency Specializes In: Advertising, Electronic Media, Email, Internet/Web Design, Logo & Package Design, Mobile Marketing, New Technologies, Real Estate, Retail, Sales Promotion, Web (Banner Ads, Pop-ups, etc.)

Alana Sorensen *(Owner)*

Accounts:
3dh

ALARIE DESIGN
260 E Plant St, Winter Garden, FL 34787
Tel.: (407) 656-8879
Fax: (407) 656-4502
Toll Free: (866) 444-3986
E-Mail: info@alariedesign.com
Web Site: www.alariedesign.com

Employees: 6
Year Founded: 1996

Agency Specializes In: Advertising, Identity Marketing, Logo & Package Design, Outdoor, Package Design, Print, Web (Banner Ads, Pop-ups, etc.)

Joe Alarie *(Pres & CEO)*
Joshua Bowens *(Dir-Art)*
Shaun Thompson *(Dir-Art)*

Accounts:
Alligator Adventure
Rally Stores
West Orange Chamber of Commerce

ALCHEMY ADVERTISING
2109 Broadway Ste 1462, New York, NY 10023
Tel.: (917) 459-1321
Web Site: www.alchemyadvertising.com

Agency Specializes In: Advertising, Media Buying Services, Media Planning, Public Relations

Marek Lis *(Founder & Owner)*

Accounts:
Apple Inc. Computers & Laptops Mfr & Distr
Canon Digital Camera & Accessories Mfr
IBM Information Technology Services Provider

ALCHEMY AT AMS
16986 N. Dallas Pkwy, Dallas, TX 75248-1920
Tel.: (972) 818-7400
Web Site: alchemyams.com

Employees: 14
Year Founded: 1982

Agency Specializes In: Above-the-Line, Advertising, Advertising Specialties, Affluent Market, Alternative Advertising, Arts, Aviation & Aerospace, Below-the-Line, Bilingual Market, Brand Development & Integration, Branded Entertainment, Broadcast, Business Publications, Cable T.V., Catalogs, Children's Market, Co-op Advertising, Collateral, Communications, Computers & Software, Consulting, Consumer Goods, Consumer Marketing, Consumer Publications, Content, Corporate Communications, Corporate Identity, Digital/Interactive, Direct Response Marketing, Direct-to-Consumer, E-Commerce, Education, Electronic Media, Email, Entertainment, Event Planning & Marketing, Exhibit/Trade Shows, Faith Based, Food Service, Government/Political, Graphic Design, Guerilla Marketing, Health Care Services, High Technology, Hispanic Market, Identity Marketing, In-Store Advertising, Industrial, Information Technology, Integrated Marketing, International, Internet/Web Design, Local Marketing, Logo & Package Design, Luxury Products, Magazines, Market Research, Media Buying Services, Media Planning, Media Relations, Men's Market, Merchandising, Mobile Marketing, Multicultural, Multimedia, New Product Development, New Technologies, Newspaper, Newspapers & Magazines, Out-of-Home Media, Outdoor, Over-50 Market, Package Design, Paid Searches, Planning & Consultation, Point of Purchase, Point of Sale, Print, Production, Production (Ad, Film, Broadcast), Production (Print), Promotions, Publishing, Radio, Regional, Restaurant, Retail, Sales Promotion, Search Engine Optimization, Shopper Marketing, Social Marketing/Nonprofit, Social Media, Sponsorship, Strategic Planning/Research, Sweepstakes, T.V., Technical Advertising, Teen Market, Trade & Consumer Magazines, Transportation, Travel & Tourism, Urban Market, Viral/Buzz/Word of Mouth, Web (Banner Ads, Pop-ups, etc.), Women's Market

Approx. Annual Billings: $4,000,000

Mark McGovern *(VP & Exec Dir-Creative)*

Kirk Arnold *(Exec Dir-Client Svc & Strategy)*
Tom Rubeck *(Dir & Sr Producer-Video)*
Victoria Rutherford *(Assoc Producer)*
Maria Colaluca *(Dir-Interactive Strategy & Dev)*
Stacy Russell *(Sr Project Mgr & Mgr-Production)*
Brandi Stringer *(Acct Mgr)*

Accounts:
American Heart Association; 2006
Crossroads Winery Brand Positioning, Packaging; 2014
Dallas Zoo (Agency of Record); 2012
DART (Dallas Area Rapid Transit) Brand Positioning; 2013
Frito-Lay Event Marketing; 2000
Good Days at CDF The Exchange Event; 2012
HP Enterprise Services Events, Videos, Websites; 2010
The Institute of Creation Research (Video Series, Marketing); 2013
King Aerospace (Agency of Record); 2014
Launchability Pro Bono Videos; 2005
Main Event Brand Videos; 2014
The Pillow Bar Digital Ads; 2014
Sabre The Technology Behind Travel; 2007

ALDER ASSOCIATES
17 S Sheppard St, Richmond, VA 23221
Tel.: (804) 775-2184
E-Mail: info@alderads.com
Web Site: www.alderads.com

Agency Specializes In: Advertising, Brand Development & Integration, Broadcast, Corporate Identity, Internet/Web Design, Outdoor, Print, Public Relations

Bart Alder *(Pres & Creative Dir)*
Rene Shouse *(COO & Sr VP)*
Jean Smith *(Comptroller)*
Serena Barry *(Dir-PR)*
John Linthicum *(Dir-Tech & Sys)*
Kellen Alder *(Dir-Studio)*

Accounts:
Union First Market Bank

ALEXANDER & RICHARDSON
(Name Changed to The Solutions Group Inc.)

ALEXANDER & TOM
3500 Boston St Ste 225, Baltimore, MD 21224-5275
Tel.: (410) 327-7400
Fax: (410) 327-7403
E-Mail: info@alextom.com
Web Site: www.alextom.com

Employees: 12
Year Founded: 1996

Agency Specializes In: Technical Advertising

Approx. Annual Billings: $1,000,000

Billy Twigg *(Pres)*
Alana Tompkins *(VP-Strategic Partnerships)*
Antony Casale *(Dir-Multimedia Art)*
Dawn Lambrow Richardson *(Mgr-Mktg Ops & Bus Dev)*
Dirk Torrijos *(Designer-Multimedia)*
Lara Chechik *(Jr Project Mgr)*

Accounts:
180s
Adams Golf
Ajilon Consulting
Alabama Power
Allegis/Aerotek
BGE
Ciena Communications
Discovery Channel
EA Sports
EA Sports
Fila USA
Maryland Public Television
McCormick Spices
National Aquarium In Baltimore
National Museum of Dentistry
National Wildlife Federation
The Nature Conservancy
PBS
Pinnacle Golf
Port Discovery
Prometrics
Smithsonian Institute
Towson University
U.S. Dept of Agriculture
U.S. Dept. of State
U.S. Dept. of Transportation
U.S. Dept. of Veterans Affairs
Washington Capitals

THE ALEXIS AGENCY
1201 19th Pl B-401, Vero Beach, FL 32960
Tel.: (772) 231-5999
Fax: (800) 991-6431
Web Site: www.thealexisagency.com

Year Founded: 2006

Agency Specializes In: Advertising, Brand Development & Integration, Corporate Communications, Corporate Identity, Media Buying Services, Media Planning, Media Relations, Print, Public Relations, Strategic Planning/Research

Ginger Atwood *(Pres)*
Ryan Gragg *(Dir-Comm)*
Dan Gurley *(Dir-Public Affairs & Political)*
Susan Lewis *(Acct Exec)*
Steve Vanden Heuvel *(Designer-New Media)*

Accounts:
My Wisdom Link

ALFORD ADVERTISING INC
1055 St Charles Ave Ste 201, New Orleans, LA 70130
Tel.: (504) 581-7500
Fax: (504) 522-9166
E-Mail: contact@alfordadvertising.com
Web Site: www.alfordadvertising.com

Year Founded: 1977

Agency Specializes In: Advertising, Internet/Web Design, Public Relations, Social Media

Robert Alford *(Pres)*
Suzanne Alford *(Sr Dir-Creative)*
Alexandra Pence Guererri *(Mgr-Mktg & Media)*

Accounts:
Team Gleason

ALFRED COMMUNICATIONS
1435 Rue Saint Alexandre bur 870, Montreal, Quebec H3A 2G4 Canada
Tel.: (514) 227-7000
E-Mail: info@alfred.ca
Web Site: www.alfred.ca

Agency Specializes In: Advertising, Brand Development & Integration, Digital/Interactive, Graphic Design, Print, Strategic Planning/Research

Jean-Francois Bernier *(Pres & Dir-Creative)*
Sebastien Moise *(Partner & Gen Mgr)*
Carine Liberian *(Acct Dir)*
Jean-luc Dion *(Dir-Art)*
Nicolas Rivard *(Sr Art Dir)*

Accounts:
Centre des sciences de Montreal
Chartwell Retirement Residences
La Capitale assurance et services financiers

ALIANDA
1199 Soaring Ridge, Marietta, GA 30062
Tel.: (407) 694-5210
E-Mail: mail@alianda.com
Web Site: www.alianda.com

Employees: 5

Agency Specializes In: Advertising, Broadcast, Corporate Identity, Email, Graphic Design, Health Care Services, Hospitality, Internet/Web Design, Logo & Package Design, Print, Real Estate, Retail

Revenue: $1,000,000

Daniel Moye *(Principal & Dir-Creative)*
Mitchell Erick *(Dir-Creative)*

Accounts:
Clarion Resort & Water Park
Epoch Management
Marriott Vacation Club International
Saint Jude's Children's Research Hospital
Summit Broadband
World Gym International

THE ALISON GROUP
1211 Torrence Cir, Charlotte, NC 28036
Tel.: (704) 245-6595
Fax: (706) 724-1093
E-Mail: info@thealisongroup.com
Web Site: www.thealisongroup.com

E-Mail for Key Personnel:
President: mark@thealisongroup.com

Employees: 6
Year Founded: 1982

National Agency Associations: AFA-AMA

Agency Specializes In: Advertising, Brand Development & Integration, Business-To-Business, Collateral, Corporate Identity, Electronic Media, Graphic Design, Internet/Web Design, Logo & Package Design, Medical Products, Planning & Consultation, Public Relations, Strategic Planning/Research

Mark Alison *(Pres)*
Tasha Alison *(VP-Charlotte & Augusta)*
Steve Fountain *(Dir-Medical & Copywriter)*
Linda Motto *(Dir-Creative)*
Kari Rehnlund *(Dir-Art)*
Joe Wider *(Assoc Dir-Creative & Copywriter)*

Accounts:
Barnhardt Manufacturing
Electrolux Sanitaire
Husqvarna
Queensborough National Bank & Trust
Treleoini Inc

ALL-OUTMEDIA, LLC
(See Under Adamus Media)

ALL PRO MEDIA INC.
422 S Spring St, Burlington, NC 27215
Tel.: (336) 229-7700
Fax: (336) 229-7778
Web Site: www.allpromedia.com

Agency Specializes In: Advertising, Graphic Design, Internet/Web Design, Logo & Package Design, Print, Search Engine Optimization, T.V.

Alan Kirby *(Co-Owner & Pres)*
Robin W. Kirby *(Co-Owner & Office Mgr)*

Accounts:
Carolina Eye Prosthetics
City of Burlington

ALL SEASONS COMMUNICATIONS
5455 34 Mile Rd, Romeo, MI 48065
Tel.: (586) 752-6381
Fax: (586) 752-6539
Web Site: www.allseasonscommunications.com

Agency Specializes In: Advertising, Brand Development & Integration, Collateral, Internet/Web Design, Logo & Package Design, Public Relations

Ken Monicatti *(Founder)*
Beth Monicatti-Blank *(Pres)*
Cheryl Russell *(VP)*
Erin Schmotzer *(Sr Acct Mgr)*
Gretchen A. Monette *(Acct Mgr)*

Accounts:
International Snowmobile Manufacturers Association
The Safe Riders

ALL TERRAIN
2675 W Grand Ave, Chicago, IL 60612
Tel.: (312) 421-7672
E-Mail: info@allterrain.net
Web Site: www.allterrain.net

Year Founded: 1998

Agency Specializes In: Advertising, Digital/Interactive, Event Planning & Marketing, Experience Design, Market Research, Public Relations, Strategic Planning/Research

Sarah Eck-Thompson *(Co-Founder & COO)*
Brook Jay *(Founder & CMO)*
Andrew Prahin *(Creative Dir)*
Mark Solotroff *(Dir-Strategy & Insights)*
Valerie Richfield *(Sr Acct Supvr)*
Brianna Coon *(Sr Acct Exec)*
Ana Bora *(Assoc Acct Exec)*

Accounts:
The Art Institute of Chicago
The Chicago American Marketing Association Marketing
Chicago Blackhawks
Chicago Public Library
The Cosmopolitan Hotel and Casino
General Motors Co.
Illinois Lottery
Penfolds Wines

ALLEBACH COMMUNICATIONS
117 N Main St, Souderton, PA 18964
Tel.: (215) 721-7693
Fax: (215) 721-7694
E-Mail: tallebach@allebach.com
Web Site: www.allebach.com

Employees: 17
Year Founded: 1990

Agency Specializes In: Media Buying Services, Production, Strategic Planning/Research

Jamie Allebach *(CEO & Chief Creative Officer)*
Todd Bergey *(Pres-Acct Svcs)*
Jesse Bender *(Acct Dir)*
Tammy Allebach *(Dir-New Opportunities)*
Lindsay Reasner *(Dir-Media)*
Danielle Neubert *(Mgr-Traffic)*
Nikki Cipolla *(Acct Exec)*
Shannon Baker *(Acct Coord)*

Accounts:
Amoroso's Baking Company
Atkins Nutritionals
BDU Corp.
Bell & Evans
Clement Pappas
Hatfield Quality Meats (Agency of Record)
Jonathan's American Grill
Libra Systems Corp.
Lipton
Marcho Farms
New England Nutrition
NutriPops
Olympus
Penn Foundation
Penn Foundation Recovery Center
Sabra
The Snack Factory Pretzel Crisps; 2008
Thinks Now

ALLEGRA MARKETING & PRINT
3639 N Marshall Way, Scottsdale, AZ 85251
Tel.: (480) 941-4842
Fax: (480) 945-0029
E-Mail: info@allegraaz.com
Web Site: www.allegraaz.com

Employees: 10
Year Founded: 1982

Agency Specializes In: Business Publications, Direct Response Marketing, Email, Graphic Design, Integrated Marketing, Print

Revenue: $2,000,000

Ted Raymond *(Owner)*
Eileen Rogers *(Pres & Specialist-Non-Profit)*
David Brown *(Head-Production)*
Sofia Hargrow *(Acct Mgr)*
Heather Raymond *(Acct Mgr)*
Jason James *(Mgr-Production)*
Rick Brown *(Specialist-Production)*
Mary Kennelly *(Acct Exec)*

Accounts:
Republic West Window & Door Replacement Services

ALLEN & GERRITSEN
2 Seaport Ln, Boston, MA 02210
Tel.: (857) 300-2000
E-Mail: info@a-g.com
Web Site: www.a-g.com

E-Mail for Key Personnel:
President: agraff@a-g.com
Creative Dir.: ggreenberg@a-g.com

Employees: 73
Year Founded: 1985

National Agency Associations: 4A's-AD CLUB-AMA-DMA-TAAN

Agency Specializes In: Advertising, Affluent Market, Alternative Advertising, Automotive, Brand Development & Integration, Business-To-Business, Collateral, Communications, Consumer Goods, Consumer Marketing, Corporate Identity, Cosmetics, Digital/Interactive, Education, Entertainment, Fashion/Apparel, Financial, Food Service, Graphic Design, Guerilla Marketing, Health Care Services, High Technology, Household Goods, Integrated Marketing, Internet/Web Design, Local Marketing, Market Research, Media Buying Services, Multimedia, New Technologies, Newspaper, Out-of-Home Media, Point of Purchase, Point of Sale, Print, Production (Print), Restaurant, Retail, Sponsorship, Sports Market, Strategic Planning/Research, T.V., Technical Advertising, Trade & Consumer Magazines, Transportation, Travel & Tourism, Web (Banner Ads, Pop-ups, etc.), Women's Market

Approx. Annual Billings: $119,000,000

Breakdown of Gross Billings by Media: Collateral: 15%; D.M.: 15%; Internet Adv.: 20%; Mags.: 20%; Newsp.: 5%; Out-of-Home Media: 5%; Radio: 5%; T.V.: 10%; Worldwide Web Sites: 5%

Paul Allen *(Founder & Chm)*
Lisa Costa *(CFO)*
Kevin Olivieri *(CTO)*
Jennifer Putnam *(Chief Creative Officer)*
Tim Reeves *(Principal)*
Gary Greenberg *(Exec VP & Creative Dir)*
Tammy Casserly *(Exec VP)*
Brian Donovan *(Sr VP & Grp Dir-Mktg)*
Eivind Ueland *(Sr VP & Dir-Creative)*
Angela Herbst *(Sr VP & Strategist-Bus)*
Chris Donnelly *(Sr VP-Brand Experience)*
Scott Sneath *(Sr VP-B2B Mktg)*
Jim Buckley *(VP & Dir-Brdcst Production)*
Aurelio D'Amico *(VP & Dir-Digital Production & Info Architect)*
Josh Weiss *(VP & Dir-Strategy)*
Chris Lee *(VP & Assoc Dir-Creative)*
Ryan Raulie *(VP & Assoc Dir-Creative)*
Katy Miller *(VP-Strategy)*
Leanne Walden *(VP-Bus Leadership)*
Natalie Bergeron *(Sr Producer-Digital)*
Julianna Akuamoah *(Dir-Talent & Ops-Boston & Neuroscience Buff)*
Marissa Curcuru *(Dir-Media)*
Jessica Serico *(Dir-Bus Dev)*
Ben Daly *(Assoc Dir-Creative)*
Megan Gallimore *(Assoc Dir-Creative)*
Lacey Berrien *(Mgr-PR)*
Kimberly Angelovich *(Supvr-Bus Leadership)*
Lindsay Merowitz *(Supvr-Mktg)*
Casey Ruggiero *(Supvr-Digital Media)*
Megan Shaughnessy *(Supvr-Bus Leadership)*
Jack Demanche *(Strategist-Activation)*
Lara Kessides *(Strategist-Brand)*
Steph Parker *(Strategist-Activation)*
Scott Key *(Copywriter)*

Accounts:
Azek Building Products, Inc.
Berklee College of Music (Agency of Record); 2008
Black Infusions Black Fig Vodka, Marketing
Blue Cross Blue Shield of Massachusetts Brand Awareness, Campaign: "Blue Cross Blue Shield of You", Digital, Multimedia, Product Awareness
Boston Celtics; Boston, MA (Agency of Record) I am a Celtic
Boston Scientific; Boston, MA; 2000
Bright Horizons; Watertown, MA Children's Day Care Services; 2004
City Year Online, Out of Home, Print, Radio, Television, Video
D'Angelo Grilled Sandwiches
Dun & Bradstreet
First Citizens Bank (Digital Agency of Record) Advertising, Creative, Digital, Marketing, Media Buying, Social Media, Strategy
Hannaford Supermarkets; Portland, ME Grocery Stores; 2006
Health Dialog Healthcare Management Firm
Loon Mountain; Lincoln, NH Ski Resort; 2003
Los Angeles Zoo LAIR, Social Media
Meetup (Public Relations Agency of Record)
MFS Investment Management; Boston, MA Financial Services; 2001
Museum of Science
New England Baptist Hospital; Boston, MA; 2002
Ninety Nine Restaurants
Papa Gino's
Penn Foster Brand Strategy
Ricoh America; 2002
Saint Andrews Grand; Saint Andrews, Scotland Golf Resort; 2005

Salem Five Savings Bank
Shure (Social Strategy Agency of Record)
Toy State
University of Massachusetts; Amherst, MA
Waterville Valley Ski Resort; Waterville Valley, NH; 2002
Yuengling Print, Video

Branches

Allen & Gerritsen
(Formerly Neiman Group)
300 N 2Nd St, Harrisburg, PA 17101
Tel.: (717) 232-5554
Fax: (717) 232-7998
Web Site: www.a-g.com

Employees: 61
Year Founded: 1980

National Agency Associations: 4A's-AAF-PRSA

Agency Specializes In: Advertising, Brand Development & Integration, Broadcast, Business-To-Business, Cable T.V., Communications, Consumer Marketing, Corporate Identity, Digital/Interactive, Education, Electronic Media, Event Planning & Marketing, Financial, Food Service, Graphic Design, Health Care Services, Internet/Web Design, Media Buying Services, Medical Products, New Product Development, Newspapers & Magazines, Out-of-Home Media, Outdoor, Pharmaceutical, Print, Production, Public Relations, Publicity/Promotions, Radio, Retail, Sales Promotion, Sports Market, Strategic Planning/Research, T.V., Teen Market, Trade & Consumer Magazines, Travel & Tourism

Gary Greenberg *(Exec VP & Chief Creative Officer)*
Tim Reeves *(Principal)*
Chris Donnelly *(Sr VP-Brand Experience)*
George Ward *(Sr VP-Innovation)*
Greg Brown *(Mgr-IT)*

Accounts:
Ad Council
Alfred Angelo, Inc.; 2007
Auto Theft Prevention Authority
Commonwealth of Pennsylvania Contract; 1998
Delta Health Technologies; 2007
Department of Homeland Security Emergency Preparedness
EdisonLearning, Inc.
Emergency Health Services Federation
First Reliance Bank; 2007
Harbour House Crabs
Hershey Foundation
Hershey Museum
Hershey Trust
Insight Pharmaceuticals & Heritage Brands
National Constitution Center Campaign: "Freedom Stickers"
Ollie's Bargain Outlet 25th Anniversary; 2007
PA Insurance Fraud Prevention Authority (IFPA)
Pennsylvania Children's Health Insurance Program (CHIP)
Pennsylvania Department of Health Tobacco Cessation Program; 1998
Pennsylvania Department of Transportation; 2005
Pennsylvania Liquor Control Board Campaign: "Control Tonight Alcohol Education Website"
Pennsylvania Treasury
Trex Company
Troeg's Brewery Campaign: "Troeg's Java Head Coffee Sleeves"

Allen & Gerritsen
(Formerly Neiman)
1619 Walnut St, Philadelphia, PA 19103
Tel.: (215) 667-8719
Fax: (215) 667-8651
Web Site: www.a-g.com

Employees: 61
Year Founded: 1980

National Agency Associations: 4A's

Agency Specializes In: Advertising, Corporate Communications, Crisis Communications, Email, Guerilla Marketing, Internet/Web Design, Media Training, Public Relations

Mike Raetsch *(Mng Dir)*
George Ward *(Chief Innovation Officer)*
Tim Reeves *(Principal)*
Chris Reif *(Sr VP-Creative & Innovation)*
Kaitlin Bitting *(VP-PR)*
Kelly Poulson *(VP-Talent & Ops)*
Erin Doyle *(Dir-Art)*
Brendan McGann *(Assoc Dir-Creative)*
Darren White *(Mgr-Bus Leadership)*
Abby Kowalewitz *(Strategist)*

Accounts:
Comcast Xfinity; 2013
Dietz & Watson; 2009
Family Lives On; 2012
Four Diamonds Fund; 2013
The Franklin Institute Creative, Nicholas & Athena Karabots Pavilion, Strategic
Insight Pharmaceuticals Monistat, e.p.t.; 2012
National Organization on Disability; 2012
PA Liquor Control Board; 2007
Shure (Social Strategy Agency of Record)
Sunoco, Inc.; 2009
Temple University
Trex Company, Inc.; 2009
Troegs Brewing Co.; 2003
Yuengling Brewery; 2012

ALLEN & PARTNERS
620 Sheridan Ave, Plainfield, NJ 07060
Tel.: (908) 561-4062
Fax: (908) 561-6827
E-Mail: clide@allenandpartners.com
Web Site: www.allenandpartners.com

Employees: 3
Year Founded: 1994

Agency Specializes In: Event Planning & Marketing, Graphic Design, In-Store Advertising, Internet/Web Design, Public Relations, Publicity/Promotions, Retail, Sales Promotion, Strategic Planning/Research

Clyde C. Allen *(Founder & Pres)*
Hope Allen *(CEO & Dir-Creative)*
Michael C. Allen *(Dir)*

Accounts:
Absolut Vodka
AUDI
Black Enterprise Magazine
Diageo
Martell Cognac
Savoy
Seagram's Extra Dry Gin
Solaris Health Systems
Thurgood Marshall College Fund
Vibe Magazine
WNYC

ALLEN FINLEY ADVERTISING, INC.
42 Third St NW, Hickory, NC 28601-6135
Tel.: (828) 324-6700
Fax: (828) 327-0072
E-Mail: allen@finleyadvertising.com
Web Site: www.finleyadvertising.com

Employees: 10
Year Founded: 1986

Agency Specializes In: Advertising, Advertising Specialties, Automotive, Brand Development & Integration, Broadcast, Business Publications, Business-To-Business, Cable T.V., Co-op Advertising, Collateral, Commercial Photography, Communications, Consulting, Consumer Marketing, Consumer Publications, Corporate Identity, E-Commerce, Education, Electronic Media, Engineering, Entertainment, Environmental, Event Planning & Marketing, Exhibit/Trade Shows, Fashion/Apparel, Financial, Food Service, Government/Political, Graphic Design, Health Care Services, High Technology, Industrial, Internet/Web Design, Investor Relations, Legal Services, Leisure, Logo & Package Design, Magazines, Marine, Media Buying Services, Medical Products, Merchandising, Multimedia, New Product Development, Newspaper, Newspapers & Magazines, Out-of-Home Media, Outdoor, Planning & Consultation, Point of Purchase, Point of Sale, Print, Production, Public Relations, Publicity/Promotions, Radio, Real Estate, Recruitment, Restaurant, Retail, Sales Promotion, Sports Market, Strategic Planning/Research, T.V., Trade & Consumer Magazines, Transportation, Travel & Tourism, Yellow Pages Advertising

Breakdown of Gross Billings by Media: Brdcst.: 5%; Bus. Publs.: 20%; Collateral: 20%; Consumer Publs.: 5%; Internet Adv.: 3%; Newsp.: 5%; Outdoor: 5%; Point of Purchase: 4%; Point of Sale: 5%; Pub. Rels.: 10%; Radio: 10%; Sls. Promo.: 3%; Trade Shows: 5%

Allen G. Finley, III *(Owner)*
Tom Martin *(VP-Mktg & Adv)*
Diane Baretsky *(Office Mgr)*

ALLIED ADVERTISING & PUBLIC RELATIONS
(Name Changed to Allied Integrated Marketing)

ALLIED EXPERIENTIAL
(Formerly Grand Central Marketing)
111 E 12 St 2nd Fl, New York, NY 10003
Tel.: (212) 253-8777
Fax: (212) 253-6776
Web Site: www.alliedim.com

Employees: 13
Year Founded: 1999

Tom Allen *(Partner-Allied Faith & Family)*
Jennifer Granozio *(Sr VP)*
Karen Abrams *(VP-Strategic Mktg)*
Kellie Barnes *(VP-Allied Faith & Family)*
Erika Bennett *(VP-ALLIED MOXY)*
Jennifer Guillette *(VP)*
Ryan Kerrison *(VP-Production-Allied Production House)*
Paula Moritz *(VP-Strategic Mktg)*
Jean-Jerome Peytavi *(VP-Strategic Mktg)*
Carolyn Sloss *(VP-Publicity & Promos)*

Accounts:
Canon
Del Monte Foods Meow Mix
ESPN
HBO Films
The Meow Mix Company Meow Mix Market Select, Meox Mix Treats
NASCAR
National Geographic

ALLIED INTEGRATED MARKETING
(Formerly Allied Advertising & Public Relations)
55 Cambridge Pkwy Ste 200, Cambridge, MA 02142
Tel.: (617) 859-4800
Fax: (617) 247-0515
Web Site: www.alliedim.com

Advertising Agencies

E-Mail for Key Personnel:
President: gfeldman@alliedadvim.com
Public Relations: jlanouette@alliedadvim.com

Employees: 45
Year Founded: 1946

Agency Specializes In: Advertising, Broadcast, Cable T.V., Entertainment, Magazines, Newspaper, Newspapers & Magazines, Outdoor, Print, Public Relations, Publicity/Promotions, Radio, Sales Promotion, Sponsorship, T.V.

Approx. Annual Billings: $600,000,000

Breakdown of Gross Billings by Media: Mags.: $10,000,000; Newsp.: $300,000,000; Outdoor: $5,000,000; Radio: $200,000,000; T.V.: $85,000,000

Clint Kendall *(Pres)*
Adam Cinque *(CFO)*
Kymn Goldstein *(Exec VP)*
Bob Arnold *(Sr VP-Adv & Client Svcs)*
Erin Corbett *(Sr VP)*
Jane Lanouette *(Sr VP-Publicity & Promos-Boston)*
Linley Branham *(Mgr-Annual Giving)*

Accounts:
20th Century Fox
Discovery Channel
HBO
KFC
Lions Gate
Paramount
Sony Pictures
Sundance Channel
TBS
Weinstein Company

Branches

Allied Advertising, Public Relations
500 N Michigan Ave Ste 400, Chicago, IL 60611
Tel.: (312) 755-0888
Fax: (312) 755-9739
Web Site: www.alliedim.com

Employees: 20

Agency Specializes In: Public Relations

Laura Matalon *(Pres-Allied Live-Chicago)*
Lisa Giannakopulos *(Sr VP-Publicity & Promos)*
Jane Lanouette *(Sr VP-Publicity & Promos)*
Kelly Estrella *(VP-Integrated Mktg & Media)*
Morgan Harris *(VP-Publicity & Promos-Allied Integrated Mktg)*
Bradley Schoenfeld *(VP-Integrated Mktg & Media)*
Nick Thomas *(VP-Strategic Mktg-Detroit)*
Jill Wheeler *(Dir-Publicity & Promos-Allied Integrated Mktg)*
Katie Pettit *(Acct Exec)*

Accounts:
Overture Pictures
Summit Entertainment
Universal Pictures
Walt Disney

Allied Advertising, Public Relations
5 Penn Plz 21st Fl, New York, NY 10001
Tel.: (212) 944-1990
Fax: (212) 944-6185
E-Mail: contact@alliedadvpub.com
Web Site: www.alliedim.com

Employees: 40
Year Founded: 1987

Agency Specializes In: Public Relations, Publicity/Promotions, Sponsorship

Jennifer Granozio *(Sr VP-Experiential Mktg)*
Tom Platoni *(VP & Dir-Creative-Allied Integrated Mktg)*
David Atlas *(Sr Dir-Art)*
Thiara M. Zapata *(Dir-Studio & Creative)*

Accounts:
Chrysler
ComCast
Disney on Ice
Sony Pictures
Universal
Walt Disney

Allied Experiential
(Formerly Grand Central Marketing)
111 E 12 St 2nd Fl, New York, NY 10003
(See Separate Listing)

Allied Integrated Marketing
(Formerly Allied Advertising, Public Relations)
21 Saint Clair Avenue East Suite 1410, Toronto, ON M4T 1L9 Canada
Tel.: (416) 413-0557
Fax: (416) 413-7958 0730
Web Site: alliedim.com

Employees: 20
Year Founded: 1996

Agency Specializes In: Publicity/Promotions

Brian Mullen *(Jr Acct Exec)*
Tania Alvarez *(Coord-Publicity & Promos)*

Accounts:
Paramount

Allied Integrated Marketing
11333 N Scottsdale Rd #190, Scottsdale, AZ 85254
Tel.: (602) 544-5710
Web Site: www.alliedim.com

Employees: 4

Agency Specializes In: Public Relations, Publicity/Promotions

Jennifer Granozio *(Sr VP-Allied Experiential)*
Sandi Isaacs *(Sr VP)*
Barry Newmark *(Sr VP)*
Tom Platoni *(VP-Creative & Dir)*
Morgan Harris *(VP-Publicity & Promos)*
Ryan Kerrison *(VP-Production-Allied Production House)*
Lori Alderfer *(Dir-Publicity & Promos)*
Lisa Balzo *(Acct Exec)*
Sadie Mcguire *(Coord-Publicity & Promos)*

Accounts:
Discovery Channel
Fox
HBO
KFC
Paramount Pictures
Sony
Sundance
TBS
TNT
Universal

Allied Integrated Marketing
(Formerly Allied Advertising, Public Relations)
6908 Hollywood Blvd 3rd Fl, Hollywood, CA 90028
Tel.: (323) 954-7644
Fax: (323) 954-7647
Web Site: alliedim.com

Employees: 35

Agency Specializes In: Public Relations, Publicity/Promotions, Sponsorship

Elisabeth Baker *(Sr VP-Creative & Awards)*
Karen Abrams *(VP-Strategic Mktg)*
Erika Bennett *(VP-Natl Strategy & Allied Moxy-African American Div)*
Melissa Croll *(VP-Strategic Mktg & Branded Entertainment)*
Marcella Cuonzo *(VP-Allied Hispanic)*
Kelly Estrella *(VP-Integrated Mktg & Media)*
Andrea Felix *(Dir-Integrated Mktg & Media)*
Mark Dalhausser *(Sr Mgr)*
Ara Matthewsian *(Mgr-Allied Experiential)*
Erin Lawhorn Edwards *(Sr Acct Exec)*
David Cowden *(Acct Exec)*
James Kong *(Acct Exec)*
Stephanie Carpenter *(Coord-Mktg)*
Courtney Lindsay *(Coord-Natl Publicity)*

Accounts:
20 Century Fox
Paramount

Allied Integrated Marketing
Cabrillo Plza 3990 Old Town Ave Ste B206, San Diego, CA 92110-2968
Tel.: (619) 688-1818
Fax: (619) 338-0342
Web Site: www.alliedim.com

Agency Specializes In: Promotions, Public Relations

Kellie Barnes *(VP-Allied Faith & Family)*
Paula Moritz *(VP)*
Carolyn Sloss *(VP-Publicity & Promos)*
Jen Vinson *(VP-Publicity & Promos Ops)*
Billy Zimmer *(VP-Strategic Mktg)*
Jennie Gendron *(Dir-Publicity & Promos)*

Allied Integrated Marketing
600 Grant St, Northglenn, CO 80203
Tel.: (303) 451-4440
Fax: (303) 460-1203
Web Site: www.alliedim.com

Employees: 1

Agency Specializes In: Publicity/Promotions

Gerry Feldman *(Chm)*
Clint Kendall *(Pres)*
Kymn Goldstein *(Exec VP)*
Kellie Barnes *(VP-Publicity & Promos)*
Jonathan Gist *(Assoc Mktg Mgr)*

Accounts:
Chrysler
Comcast
D&B
Discovery Channel
FOX
Genius Products
Sundance Channel
Walt Disney Pictures

Allied Integrated Marketing
(Formerly Allied Advertising, Public Relations)
1726 M St NW Ste 801, Washington, DC 20036-4650
Tel.: (202) 223-3660
Fax: (202) 223-9788
E-Mail: staylor@allied.com
Web Site: www.alliedim.com

Employees: 15

Year Founded: 1993

Agency Specializes In: Public Relations, Publicity/Promotions

Elisabeth Baker *(Sr VP-Allied Creative)*
Erin Corbett *(Sr VP-Natl Promos & Branded Entertainment)*
Barry Newmark *(Sr VP-Publicity & Promos)*
Sara Taylor *(Sr VP-Eastern Reg)*
Erika Bennett *(VP-Allied Moxy)*
Ginger Chan *(VP-Natl Publicity)*
Marcella Cuonzo *(VP-Allied Hispanic)*
Ryan Kerrison *(VP-Production-Allied Production House)*
Carolyn Sloss *(VP-Publicity & Promos)*
Emily Teichner *(Coord-Publicity & Promos)*
Anna Lassalle *(Jr Publicist)*

Accounts:
Chrysler
Comcast
Fox
HBO
Sony Pictures
Universal
Walt Disney

Allied Integrated Marketing
(Formerly Marketing Inspirations)
2727 Paces Ferry Rd SE Bldg 2 Ste 450, Atlanta, GA 30339
Tel.: (678) 305-0905
Fax: (678) 305-0908

Year Founded: 1999

Agency Specializes In: Advertising, Integrated Marketing, Promotions, Public Relations, Social Media

Barbara King *(Sr VP-Dev)*
Erika Scholz *(Mgr-PR & Social Media)*

Accounts:
New-GPS Hospitality
New-Occidental Asset Management, LLC

Allied Integrated Marketing
55 Cambridge Pkwy, Boston, MA 02116
Tel.: (617) 859-4800
Web Site: www.alliedim.com

Employees: 400
Year Founded: 1980

Agency Specializes In: Public Relations, Publicity/Promotions

Gerry Feldman *(Chm)*
Adam Cinque *(CFO)*
Kymn Goldstein *(Exec VP)*
Elisabeth Baker *(Sr VP-Allied Creative)*
Erin Corbett *(Sr VP-Natl Promos & Branded Entertainment)*
Lisa Giannakopulos *(Sr VP-Publicity & Promos)*
Matthew Glass *(Sr VP-Allied Experiential)*
Jennifer Granozio *(Sr VP-Allied Experiential)*
Jane Lanouette *(Sr VP-Publicity & Promos)*
Kellie Barnes *(VP-Allied Faith & Family)*
Erika Bennett *(VP-ALLIED MOXY)*
Marcella Cuonzo *(VP-Allied Hispanic)*
Ryan Kerrison *(VP-Production-Allied Production House)*
Nick Thomas *(VP)*

Accounts:
20th Century Fox
HBO
NBC
Paramount Pictures
Universal Pictures
Walt Disney Pictures
Warner Brothers
The Weinstein Company

Allied Integrated Marketing
1656 Washington St, Kansas City, MO 64108
Tel.: (816) 474-9995
Fax: (816) 474-9998
Web Site: www.alliedim.com

Agency Specializes In: Promotions, Public Relations

Adam Cinque *(CFO)*
Erin Corbett *(Sr VP-Natl Promos & Branded Entertainment)*
Lisa Giannakopulos *(Sr VP-Publicity & Promo)*
Tom Platoni *(VP-Creative & Dir)*
Nick Thomas *(VP-Mktg)*
Billy Zimmer *(VP-Specialized Mktg)*
Nick Tarnowski *(Dir-Publicity & Promos)*

Accounts:
Chrysler
Comcast
Discovery Channel
Fox Television
GM
HBO
Sony Pictures

Allied Integrated Marketing
103 W Lockwood Ste 204, Saint Louis, MO 63119
Tel.: (314) 918-7788
Fax: (314) 918-8282
Web Site: www.alliedim.com

Employees: 7

Agency Specializes In: Public Relations

Clint Kendall *(Pres-Boston)*
Erin Corbett *(Sr VP-Mktg & Branded Entertainment-Los Angeles)*
Matthew Glass *(Sr VP-Allied Experiential-New York)*
Sandi Isaacs *(Sr VP-Bus Dev-New York)*
Erika Bennett *(VP-Natl Strategy & Allied Moxy-African American Div)*
Ginger Chan *(VP-Natl Publicity & Acct Mgmt-Los Angeles)*
Marcella Cuonzo *(VP-Allied Hispanic Mktg-Los Angeles)*
Carolyn Sloss *(VP-Publicity & Promos)*
Billy Zimmer *(VP-Strategic Mktg-Los Angeles)*

Allied Integrated Marketing
1846 Coventry Rd Ste 300, Cleveland, OH 44118
Tel.: (216) 932-7151
Fax: (216) 274-9461
E-Mail: info@alliedim.com
Web Site: www.alliedim.com

Employees: 20
Year Founded: 1987

Agency Specializes In: Entertainment, Public Relations, Publicity/Promotions

Adam Cinque *(CFO)*
Jennifer Granozio *(Sr VP-Allied Experiential)*
Barry Newmark *(Sr VP-Publicity & Promos)*
Kellie Barnes *(VP-Allied Faith & Family)*
Ginger Chan *(VP-Natl Publicity & Acct Mgmt)*
Ryan Kerrison *(VP-Allied House)*
Seelun Mak *(VP-Allied Experiential)*
Jennifer Vinson *(VP-Publicity & Promos Ops)*
Kendrick Julian *(Mgr-Product Mktg)*

Accounts:
Universal
Wicked

Allied Integrated Marketing
100 W Harrison St S Tower, Seattle, WA 98119
Tel.: (206) 297-7064
Fax: (206) 297-7484
Web Site: www.alliedim.com

Employees: 5

Agency Specializes In: Publicity/Promotions

Ginger Chan *(VP-Natl Publicity & Acct Mgmt)*
Jennifer Guillette *(VP)*
Billy Zimmer *(VP-Strategic Mktg)*
Ashley Halter Gabriel *(Dir-Publicity & Promos)*
Alexa Weber *(Jr Acct Exec)*

Accounts:
Paramount

Langdon Flynn Communications
2760 Lake Sahara Rd Ste 100, Las Vegas, NV 89117
(See Separate Listing)

ALLIGATOR
(Formerly Golden Alligator Interactivities)
639 S. SPring St #4A, Los Angeles, CA 90014
Tel.: (213) 534-6011
Web Site: alligator.industries/

Employees: 12

Approx. Annual Billings: $1,200,000

Breakdown of Gross Billings by Media: Audio/Visual: 60%; Graphic Design: 20%; Production: 20%

Yohannes Baynes *(Head-Interactive Dev)*
Thomas Lynn *(Supvr-Audio)*
Cori Nelson *(Specialist-Comm)*

ALLING HENNING & ASSOCIATES
415 W 6th St Ste 605, Vancouver, WA 98660
Tel.: (360) 750-1680
E-Mail: hello@aha-writers.com
Web Site: www.aha-writers.com

National Agency Associations: 4A's

Agency Specializes In: Advertising, Brand Development & Integration, Corporate Communications

Betsy Henning *(Founder & CEO)*
Pamela Fiehn *(Sr Dir-Creative)*
Jon Schneider *(Sr Dir-Art)*
Eric Smith *(Sr Dir-Creative)*
Daniel Griffin *(Acct Dir)*
Sara Calabro *(Dir-Creative)*
Amanda Pushkas *(Sr Acct Mgr)*
Brett Thacher *(Acct Mgr)*

Accounts:
Cadet Manufacturing Company

ALLISON & PARTNERS
(Formerly Frause)
1411 4th Ave Ste 1210, Seattle, WA 98101
Tel.: (206) 352-6402
Fax: (206) 284-9409
Web Site: www.allisonpr.com

Employees: 18
Year Founded: 1998

Agency Specializes In: Advertising, Brand Development & Integration, Broadcast,

Advertising Agencies

Exhibit/Trade Shows, Logo & Package Design, Market Research, Media Training, Public Relations, Sponsorship, Web (Banner Ads, Pop-ups, etc.)

Sue Gillespie *(Sr VP-Res)*
Jen Graves *(Sr VP-Mktg & Bus Dev)*
Joel VanEtta *(Sr VP)*
David Marriott *(Mng Dir-Reputation Risk)*
Richard Kendall *(Gen Mgr-Seattle & Portland)*
Emily Nauseda *(Acct Exec)*
Alisa Song *(Asst Acct Exec)*

Accounts:
City of Lakewood
Downtown Seattle Association
Duraflame
King County Natural Yard Care
McKinstry
New-Mobetize Corp (Investor Relations Agency of Record) Media Relations, Thought Leadership
Schwabe, Williamson & Wyatt
Skanska USA Building Inc.

ALLISON & PARTNERS-WASHINGTON D.C.

1129 20th St NW Ste 250, Washington, DC 20036
Tel.: (202) 223-9260
E-Mail: scott@allisonpr.com
Web Site: www.allisonpr.com

Year Founded: 2001

Agency Specializes In: Brand Development & Integration, Corporate Communications, Digital/Interactive, Direct Response Marketing, Email, Event Planning & Marketing, Graphic Design, Media Training, Search Engine Optimization

Andy Hardie-Brown *(CO-Founder & COO)*
Scott Pansky *(Co-Founder & Sr Partner)*
Scott Allison *(Chm & CEO)*
David Wolf *(Mng Dir)*
Robin Bectel *(Sr VP)*
Marcel Goldstein *(Sr VP-Corp Practice)*
Brian Brokowski *(Gen Mgr)*
Anne Colaiacovo *(Sr Partner & Gen Mgr)*
Cathy Planchard *(Sr Partner & Gen Mgr)*
Cat Forgione *(Asst Acct Exec)*

Accounts:
.ORG; Reston, VA (Agency of Record)
Best Western
Boost
GE Healthcare
Hasbro
Samsung
Seventh-day Adventists
Sony

ALLISON PARTNERS

1716-2 Allied St, Charlottesville, VA 22903
Tel.: (434) 295-9962
Fax: (434) 295-9494
E-Mail: asl@allisonpartners.com
Web Site: www.allisonpartners.com

Agency Specializes In: Custom Publishing, Strategic Planning/Research

Andy Hardie-Brown *(Co-Founder & COO)*
Allison Linney *(Owner & Pres)*
Scott Allison *(Chm & CEO)*
Rachel Brozenske *(VP)*
Lisa Smith *(VP-Ops)*
Rob Herman *(Office Mgr)*
Janie Kast *(Mgr-Learning Program)*

Accounts:
Boost Mobile
Bulova Influencer Relations, Media

ALLOY MEDIA + MARKETING

(Name Changed to re:fuel)

ALLSCOPE MEDIA

462 7th Ave 8th Fl, New York, NY 10018
Tel.: (212) 253-1300
Fax: (212) 253-1625
Web Site: www.allscope.com

National Agency Associations: ARF

Agency Specializes In: Advertising, Brand Development & Integration, Digital/Interactive, Media Buying Services, Media Planning, Social Media, Sponsorship

Leslie Jacobus *(Pres & Partner)*
Evan Greenberg *(CEO)*
Lori-Ann Capitelli *(Sr VP & Dir-Media)*
Lynette Fine *(Sr VP-Client Svcs)*
Carol Caracappa *(VP-Natl Television)*
Jennifer Tarsitano *(VP-Mktg)*
Eman Abuella *(Head-Digital)*
Danea Williams *(Dir-Digital Media)*
Michael Gelb *(Media Buyer)*
Jessica Rigney *(Media Buyer)*
Richard Wong *(Asst Media Planner-Digital)*

Accounts:
Jackson Hewitt (Media Agency of Record)
The Tennis Channel
Trinity Broadcasting Network
Univision

ALLYN MEDIA

3232 McKinney Ave Ste 660, Dallas, TX 75204
Tel.: (214) 871-7723
Fax: (214) 871-7767
E-Mail: allynmedia@allynmedia.com
Web Site: www.allynmedia.com

Agency Specializes In: Advertising, Brand Development & Integration, Crisis Communications, Print, Public Relations, Radio

Mari Woodlief *(Pres & CEO)*
Jennifer Ring Pascal *(COO)*
Bill Stipp *(Sr VP & Creative Dir)*
Erin Ragsdale *(Sr VP)*
Claire Reyes *(Sr Acct Dir)*
Meghan Fitzsimmons *(Acct Dir-Creative & Dir-Social Media)*
Kristin Welsh *(Acct Exec)*
Jessica Ring *(Acct Exec)*

Accounts:
7 Eleven

ALMA

(Formerly Alma DDB)
2601 S Bayshore Dr 4th Fl, Coconut Grove, FL 33133
Tel.: (305) 662-3175
Fax: (305) 662-8043
E-Mail: info@almaad.com
Web Site: almaad.com

Employees: 65
Year Founded: 1994

National Agency Associations: 4A's

Agency Specializes In: Advertising Specialties, Brand Development & Integration, Cosmetics, E-Commerce, Financial, Food Service, Government/Political, Health Care Services, Hispanic Market, Internet/Web Design, Leisure, Media Buying Services, New Product Development, Print, Production, Sponsorship, Strategic Planning/Research, Travel & Tourism

Breakdown of Gross Billings by Media: Mags.: 7%; Network T.V.: 51%; Newsp.: 4%; Outdoor: 4%; Radio: 18%; Spot T.V.: 16%

Alvar Sunol *(Co-Pres & Chief Creative Officer)*
Luis Miguel Messianu *(Chm-Creative & CEO)*
Angela Battistini *(Sr VP-Bus Svcs)*
Michelle Headley *(Sr VP-Ops)*
Mimi Cossio *(Sr Mgr-Print Production & Producer)*
Christian Liu *(Creative Dir)*
Roberto Martinez *(Art Dir)*
Adrian Castagna *(Dir-Production)*
Carola Chaurero *(Dir-New Bus)*
Monserrat Valera *(Dir-Creative)*
Juan Camilo Valdivieso *(Assoc Dir-Creative)*
Tatiana Seijas *(Mgr-Comm)*
Manuela Graells *(Analyst-Fin)*
Karla Kruger *(Sr Grp Bus Dir)*
Madeline Perez-Velez *(Grp Bus Dir)*

Accounts:
AARP Advertising, Broadcast, Campaign: "Bath", Campaign: "Spoon", Caregiving, Digital, Print, Radio
Anheuser-Busch InBev Budweiser
Blue Cross & Blue Shield of Florida; Jacksonville, FL Hispanic Advertising
Clorox Campaign: "Glad Tent", Kingsford
Exxon
Florida Blue
Glad Campaign: "The Glad Tent"
GreenWorks
McCormick Creative, Digital, Media Planning
McDonald's Campaign: "First Customer", Campaign: "Hypothesis", Campaign: "Reunited", Hispanic Marketing, McCafe, Oatmeal, Sirloin Burger
Miami Dade Animal Services
PepsiCo Inc.
Personal Music
New-Sprint Hispanic
State Farm; Chicago, IL Campaign: "Play Today Illuminate Tomorrow", Hispanic, Insurance
Tobacco Free Florida (Agency of Record) Quitline, TheFactsNow.com
University of Phoenix

ALMIGHTY

300 Western Ave, Boston, MA 02134
Tel.: (617) 782-1511
Fax: (617) 782-1611
E-Mail: info@bealmighty.com
Web Site: www.bealmighty.com

Employees: 30
Year Founded: 2004

Agency Specializes In: Advertising, Advertising Specialties, Agriculture, Alternative Advertising, Automotive, Brand Development & Integration, Cable T.V., Children's Market, Collateral, College, Commercial Photography, Computers & Software, Consulting, Consumer Publications, Content, Customer Relationship Management, Digital/Interactive, Direct-to-Consumer, E-Commerce, Education, Electronic Media, Electronics, Email, Entertainment, Environmental, Experience Design, Fashion/Apparel, Financial, Game Integration, Graphic Design, Guerilla Marketing, Health Care Services, High Technology, Household Goods, Identity Marketing, Industrial, Infomercials, Integrated Marketing, Internet/Web Design, Leisure, Local Marketing, Logo & Package Design, Magazines, Market Research, Media Buying Services, Media Planning, Merchandising, Mobile Marketing, Multimedia, New Technologies, Newspaper, Out-of-Home Media, Outdoor, Package Design, Paid Searches, Planning & Consultation, Point of Purchase, Print, Production, Production (Print), Radio, Retail, Search Engine Optimization, Social Marketing/Nonprofit, Sponsorship, Sports Market, Strategic Planning/Research, T.V., Teen Market, Travel &

Tourism, Viral/Buzz/Word of Mouth

R. J. Evans *(Partner & Dir-Design)*
Ian Fitzpatrick *(Chief Strategy Officer)*
Analesa Smith *(Sr VP & Dir-Media)*
David Kimball *(VP & Acct Dir)*
Niki Stowell *(VP & Dir-Project Mgmt)*
Peter Strutt *(VP-Creative)*
Adam Wheeler *(VP-Growth)*
Regi Jacob *(Assoc Dir-Creative)*
Nicole Hale *(Sr Mgr)*
Lynne Travers *(Office Mgr)*
Gerald Hastings *(Sr Designer)*

Accounts:
Flexsteel; 2014
Georgia-Pacific
L.L. Bean
New Balance; Boston, MA; 2006
New-Oxfam America Campaign: "Lives on the Line"
PF Flyers
TedX
Walt Disney; 2006

ALOFT GROUP, INC.
26 Parker St, Newburyport, MA 01950
Tel.: (978) 462-0002
Fax: (978) 462-4337
E-Mail: info@aloftgroup.com
Web Site: www.aloftgroup.com

E-Mail for Key Personnel:
President: mbowen@aloftgroup.com
Creative Dir.: dcrane@aloftgroup.com

Employees: 15
Year Founded: 1996

National Agency Associations: AD CLUB-PAC-PRSA

Agency Specializes In: Advertising, Brand Development & Integration, Broadcast, Business-To-Business, Co-op Advertising, Collateral, Communications, Consulting, Consumer Marketing, Corporate Identity, Digital/Interactive, Direct Response Marketing, Electronic Media, Event Planning & Marketing, Exhibit/Trade Shows, Financial, Food Service, Graphic Design, Health Care Services, High Technology, Infomercials, Integrated Marketing, International, Internet/Web Design, Logo & Package Design, Media Relations, Media Training, Medical Products, New Product Development, Planning & Consultation, Podcasting, Point of Purchase, Point of Sale, Print, Public Relations, Publicity/Promotions, Radio, Sales Promotion, Sponsorship, Strategic Planning/Research, T.V., Trade & Consumer Magazines, Travel & Tourism, Viral/Buzz/Word of Mouth

Approx. Annual Billings: $13,800,000

Breakdown of Gross Billings by Media: Collateral: 5%; D.M.: 10%; Event Mktg.: 3%; Foreign: 12%; Mdsg./POP: 5%; Pub. Rels.: 15%; Radio & T.V.: 15%; Strategic Planning/Research: 10%; Trade & Consumer Mags.: 15%; Worldwide Web Sites: 10%

Matt Bowen *(Pres & Brand Strategist)*
Andrea Drown *(Dir-Ops)*
Tracy Hartman *(Dir-PR)*
Chris Langathianos *(Dir-Brand Strategy)*
David Macgregor *(Dir-Content)*
Chris Maynard *(Dir-Fin & Talent)*
Rudy Karty *(Coord-Production)*

Accounts:
ADP Taxware; Wakefield, MA; 2005
Beacon Partners, Inc.; Weymouth, MA; 2006
Beam Global Spirits and Wines
Disney/MGM Studios
Dunkin' Donuts
GeoDeck; Green Bay, WI Composite Decking & Railing Systems; 2003
Harvard Business School Publishing
New England Development; Waltham, MA; 2006
Nuance/Dictaphone; Burlington, MA Ex-Speech, PowerScribe; 2001
Zipcar; Cambridge, MA; 2005

ALOYSIUS BUTLER & CLARK
(Name Changed to ab+c)

ALPAYTAC GROUP
445 N Wells St Ste 401, Chicago, IL 60654
Tel.: (312) 245-9805
Fax: (312) 245-9807
E-Mail: info@alpaytac.com
Web Site: www.alpaytac.com

Employees: 20

Agency Specializes In: Advertising, Broadcast, Collateral, Consulting, Consumer Marketing, Corporate Identity, Crisis Communications, Education, Event Planning & Marketing, Exhibit/Trade Shows, Graphic Design, Integrated Marketing, Media Training, Multimedia, Print, Production, Public Relations, Publicity/Promotions, Strategic Planning/Research

George Pappas *(Head-Los Angeles & Sr Acct Mgr)*
Garrett Ryan *(Head-Digital)*
Rory Davenport *(Dir-Pub Affairs)*
Kristy Finch *(Dir-Brdcst Media)*
Vanessa Legutko *(Acct Exec)*
Caitlin Reidy *(Acct Exec)*
Svjetlana Stojanovic *(Acct Exec)*
Elizabeth Schaefer *(Jr Acct Exec)*

Accounts:
Bellator Fighting Championships
Cahootie, LLC
Euro-Pro Corporation
Playaway Digital
Shark Euro-Pro
Turkish Airlines

ALPHA DOG ADVERTISING, LLC
One50 N Prince St, Lancaster, PA 17603
Tel.: (717) 517-9944
E-Mail: info@alphadogadv.com
Web Site: www.alphadogadv.com

Agency Specializes In: Advertising, Collateral, Event Planning & Marketing, Media Buying Services, Media Planning, Print, Social Media, Strategic Planning/Research

Craig E. Trout *(Pres)*
Kathleen K. Trout *(CFO)*
Aaron Baksa *(Dir-Art)*
Bob McCreary *(Dir-Creative)*
Lisbet Byler *(Acct Exec)*
Wendi French *(Copywriter)*

Accounts:
Yorktowne Cabinetry

A.L.T. ADVERTISING & PROMOTION
12000 Lincoln Dr W Ste 408, Marlton, NJ 08053
Tel.: (856) 810-0400
Fax: (856) 810-1636
E-Mail: info@altadvertising.com
Web Site: www.altadvertising.com

Employees: 5

Les Altenberg *(Pres & Client Svcs Dir)*
Jean Arlene *(VP)*
William C. Heron *(Sr Dir-Art)*

ALTERNATE TRANSIT ADVERTISING
295 Bayside Rd, Greenland, NH 03840-2130
Tel.: (603) 436-0008
Fax: (603) 766-0287
E-Mail: info@atatransit.com
Web Site: www.atatransit.com

Employees: 5
Year Founded: 1992

Agency Specializes In: Advertising, Mobile Marketing

Jane M. Cutter *(Pres-Sls-Natl)*
Diane Desantis *(Controller)*
Stephanie Bergeron *(Mgr-Production)*

Accounts:
Portland Metro

ALTERNATIVE MARKETING SOLUTIONS, INC.
342 Nutt Rd, Phoenixville, PA 19460-3910
Tel.: (610) 783-1320
Fax: (610) 783-1324
E-Mail: guntick@amsolutions.com
Web Site: www.amsolutions.com

Employees: 20
Year Founded: 1995

National Agency Associations: DMA

Agency Specializes In: Advertising, Bilingual Market, Direct Response Marketing, Hispanic Market, Telemarketing

Mike Guntick *(Pres)*

Accounts:
Advanta
Career Concepts Inc.
CUNA Mutual
Driver's Direct
Roussey Solutions, Inc.
TCPI

ALTITUDE AGENCY LLC
3020 McCoy Pl NE, Albuquerque, NM 87106
Tel.: (505) 280-0095
E-Mail: contact@altitude-agency.com
Web Site: www.altitude-agency.com

Year Founded: 2002

Agency Specializes In: Advertising, Brand Development & Integration, Broadcast, Collateral, Corporate Identity, Event Planning & Marketing, Internet/Web Design, Logo & Package Design, Print, Radio

Eva Medcroft *(Pres & Dir-Creative)*

Accounts:
Anne Arundel Crisis Beds

ALTITUDE MARKETING
417 State Rd 2nd Fl, Emmaus, PA 18049
Tel.: (610) 421-8601
Web Site: www.altitudemarketing.com

Year Founded: 2004

Agency Specializes In: Advertising, Brand Development & Integration, Communications, E-Commerce, Graphic Design, Internet/Web Design, Print, Public Relations, Search Engine Optimization, Social Media

Andrew Stanten *(Pres)*
Gwen Shields Hoover *(VP-Mktg Svcs)*

Stan Zukowski *(VP-Creative Svcs)*
Matt Borrelli *(Dir-Design Svcs)*
Drew Frantzen *(Dir-Web Svcs)*
Kelly Stratton *(Dir-Digital Mktg)*
Jaime Heintzelman *(Mgr-PR & Social Media)*
Jeremy Jones *(Mgr-Mktg Svcs)*
Adam Smartschan *(Mgr-Editorial Svcs)*
Laura Budraitis *(Asst Acct Mgr)*

Accounts:
Lancelotta Consulting
Olympus Imaging America Inc.
OpenWater

ALTMAN-HALL ASSOCIATES

235 W 7th St, Erie, PA 16501-1601
Tel.: (814) 454-0158
Fax: (814) 454-3266
E-Mail: info@altman-hall.com
Web Site: www.altman-hall.com

E-Mail for Key Personnel:
Chairman: dick@altman-hall.com
President: tim@altman-hall.com

Employees: 25
Year Founded: 1955

Agency Specializes In: Advertising, Brand Development & Integration, Business Publications, Business-To-Business, Catalogs, Co-op Advertising, Collateral, Commercial Photography, Communications, Consulting, Corporate Communications, Corporate Identity, Digital/Interactive, Direct Response Marketing, Electronic Media, Electronics, Engineering, Exhibit/Trade Shows, Food Service, Graphic Design, Health Care Services, High Technology, Industrial, Internet/Web Design, Logo & Package Design, Media Buying Services, Media Planning, Merchandising, New Product Development, Newspaper, Newspapers & Magazines, Planning & Consultation, Point of Sale, Print, Production, Public Relations, Publicity/Promotions, Radio, Sales Promotion, Strategic Planning/Research, T.V., Technical Advertising, Trade & Consumer Magazines, Transportation, Yellow Pages Advertising

Approx. Annual Billings: $6,000,000

Breakdown of Gross Billings by Media: Bus. Publs.: $2,700,000; E-Commerce: $600,000; Print: $1,800,000; Production: $600,000; Pub. Rels.: $300,000

Timothy R. Glass *(Pres)*
Matthew D. Glass *(Partner)*
Kathi McKenzie *(Sr VP-Client Svc)*
Colleen Stubbs *(Dir-Creative)*
Susan Horton *(Coord-Media)*

Accounts:
AccuSpec Electronics; McKean, PA
Ametco; Willoughby, OH Architectural Fence & Gates
Cross Integrated Supply; Erie, PA
Electric Materials Co.; North East, PA Electrical Copper Products
Elster American Meter Company; Erie, PA
Eriez Manufacturing Co. Inc.; Erie, PA Magnetic Products
High Pressure Equipment; Erie, PA High Pressure Valves
KaneSterling; Kane, PA
Perry Construction; Erie, PA
Ridg-U-Rak, Inc.; North East, PA Storage Racks & Systems
Spectrum Control; Fairview, PA Electronic Components
Sterling Rotational Molding; Lake City, PA Plastic Rotational Parts
Sterling Technologies; Erie, PA

VertiSpace; Points of Rock, MD

THE ALTUS AGENCY

(Formerly Altus Group)
211 N 13th St 802, Philadelphia, PA 19107
Tel.: (215) 977-9900
Fax: (215) 977-8350
E-Mail: jefferys@altusagency.com
Web Site: www.altusagency.com/

E-Mail for Key Personnel:
President: jefferys@altus-group.com

Employees: 15
Year Founded: 1988

Agency Specializes In: Brand Development & Integration, Business-To-Business, Communications, Corporate Identity, High Technology, Information Technology, Internet/Web Design, Pharmaceutical, Print, Public Relations, Strategic Planning/Research

Approx. Annual Billings: $15,000,000

Breakdown of Gross Billings by Media: Brdcst.: 15%; Bus. Publs.: 2%; Collateral: 60%; D.M.: 1%; Logo & Package Design: 10%; Mags.: 5%; Newsp.: 5%; Radio: 1%; T.V.: 1%

Robert Courteau *(CEO)*
Angelo Bartolini *(CFO)*
Mike Abramsky *(Pres-ARGUS Software)*
Jim Derbyshire *(Pres-Property Tax Consulting-Global)*
Colin Johnston *(Pres-Res & Valuation & Advisory-Canada)*
Daniel Lachance *(Pres-Geomatics)*
Robert K. Ruggles, III *(Pres-Res & Valuation & Advisory-USA)*
Liana Turrin *(Gen Counsel & Sec)*
Jim Eagle *(Dir-Creative)*
Rita Ambron *(Mgr-Ops)*

Accounts:
GPTMC (Greater Philadelphia Tourism & Marketing Corp)
Greater Philadelphia Cultural Alliance
Independence Business Alliance
Park Hyatt at the Belleview
Sofitel
Nomound
Sea-Land Chemical; Westlake, OH

ALWAYS ON COMMUNICATIONS

1308 E Colorado Blvd Ste 1371, Pasadena, CA 91106
Tel.: (626) 698-0698
E-Mail: info@alwaysoncommunications.com
Web Site: www.alwaysoncommunications.com

Year Founded: 2009

Agency Specializes In: Advertising, Email, Graphic Design, Media Planning, Planning & Consultation, Search Engine Optimization, Social Media, Sponsorship

Martin Thomas *(Owner & Pres)*
Jeff Ferguson *(Dir-SEM & Social Media)*
Jeanette Igarashi *(Dir-Media)*

Accounts:
Belkin International, Inc. WeMo, Yolk Custom Case & Ultimate iPad Keyboard Case Products.

AMAZING LIFE CONCEPTS

28720 Interstate 10 W Ste 800, Fair Oaks Ranch, TX 78006
Tel.: (210) 561-9191
E-Mail: info@amazinglifeconcepts.com
Web Site: www.amazinglifeconcepts.com

Agency Specializes In: Advertising, Brand Development & Integration, Internet/Web Design, Logo & Package Design, Media Buying Services, Print, Social Media, T.V.

Cyndy Schatz *(Exec Dir)*

Accounts:
Cabinetry Designs
J B Septic Systems Inc
Robare Custom Homes

AMBASSADOR ADVERTISING AGENCY

1641 Langley Ave, Irvine, CA 92614
Tel.: (949) 681-7600
Fax: (949) 681-7660
E-Mail: info@ambassadoradvertising.com
Web Site: www.ambassadoradvertising.com

Employees: 25
Year Founded: 1959

Agency Specializes In: Communications, Internet/Web Design, Local Marketing, Production

Al Sanders *(Founder)*
Evelyn Gibson *(VP-Comm)*
Lee Ann Jackson *(Sr Acct Exec)*
Katie Burke *(Acct Exec)*
Selah Cosentino *(Acct Exec)*
Jennifer Perez *(Acct Exec)*

Accounts:
A Woman After God's Own Heart
Angel Ministries
The Garlow Perspective
Grace to You
Keep It Simple
Life Issues Institute
Mercy Ships
Revive Our Hearts
UpWords
Women Today

AMBIENT MEDIA, INC.

3765 Eton St, Burnaby, BC V5C 1J3 Canada
Tel.: (604) 291-0510
Fax: (604) 291-0540
E-Mail: info@ambientmediainc.ca
Web Site: www.ambientmediainc.ca

Employees: 5

National Agency Associations: CAB

Agency Specializes In: Advertising, Alternative Advertising, Broadcast, Cable T.V., Co-op Advertising, Consulting, Consumer Marketing, Digital/Interactive, Internet/Web Design, Local Marketing, Market Research, Media Buying Services, Media Planning, Media Relations, Newspaper, Newspapers & Magazines, Out-of-Home Media, Outdoor, Paid Searches, Planning & Consultation, Print, Product Placement, Production, Production (Ad, Film, Broadcast), Production (Print), Promotions, Public Relations, Radio, Regional, Search Engine Optimization, Sponsorship, Sports Market, Strategic Planning/Research, T.V.

Approx. Annual Billings: $3,500,000

Beth Keller *(Pres)*

AMBIT MARKETING COMMUNICATIONS

19 NW 5th St, Fort Lauderdale, FL 33301
Tel.: (954) 568-2100
Fax: (954) 568-2888
E-Mail: kathy@ambitmarketing.com
Web Site: www.ambitmarketing.com

E-Mail for Key Personnel:
President: kathy@ambitmarketing.com
Public Relations: stu@ambitmarketing.com

Employees: 10
Year Founded: 1977

National Agency Associations: AFA-PRSA

Agency Specializes In: Advertising, Bilingual Market, Brand Development & Integration, Broadcast, Business Publications, Business-To-Business, Cable T.V., Collateral, Communications, Consumer Marketing, Corporate Communications, Corporate Identity, Direct Response Marketing, Education, Fashion/Apparel, Financial, Government/Political, Graphic Design, Health Care Services, High Technology, Hispanic Market, Industrial, Information Technology, Internet/Web Design, Legal Services, Local Marketing, Logo & Package Design, Magazines, Marine, Media Buying Services, Medical Products, Newspaper, Newspapers & Magazines, Out-of-Home Media, Outdoor, Planning & Consultation, Print, Production, Public Relations, Publicity/Promotions, Radio, Real Estate, Strategic Planning/Research, T.V., Telemarketing, Trade & Consumer Magazines, Transportation, Travel & Tourism

Approx. Annual Billings: $3,000,000

Katherine Koch *(Pres-Ambit Adv & PR)*
Thom Antonio *(Exec Dir-Creative)*
Stan Brown *(Chief Strategic Officer)*

Accounts:
The Broward Alliance
Kelly Tractor Co.
Memorial Hospital

AMELIE COMPANY

2601 Blake St Ste 150, Denver, CO 80205
Tel.: (303) 832-2700
Fax: (303) 832-2797
E-Mail: info@ameliecompany.com
Web Site: www.ameliecompany.com

Employees: 23
Year Founded: 2002

National Agency Associations: AMA-BMA

Agency Specializes In: Above-the-Line, Advertising, Affluent Market, Agriculture, Arts, Automotive, Bilingual Market, Brand Development & Integration, Broadcast, Business-To-Business, Children's Market, Collateral, College, Communications, Consumer Goods, Consumer Marketing, Corporate Identity, Digital/Interactive, Education, Electronic Media, Entertainment, Fashion/Apparel, Food Service, Graphic Design, Guerilla Marketing, Health Care Services, High Technology, Hospitality, Household Goods, Identity Marketing, Integrated Marketing, International, Internet/Web Design, Leisure, Local Marketing, Logo & Package Design, Luxury Products, Magazines, Marine, Market Research, Media Buying Services, Media Planning, Media Relations, Media Training, Men's Market, Mobile Marketing, Multimedia, Newspaper, Out-of-Home Media, Outdoor, Over-50 Market, Package Design, Pets , Point of Sale, Print, Production, Production (Ad, Film, Broadcast), Production (Print), Public Relations, Publicity/Promotions, Radio, Real Estate, Restaurant, Retail, Social Marketing/Nonprofit, Social Media, Sports Market, Strategic Planning/Research, T.V., Teen Market, Transportation, Travel & Tourism, Web (Banner Ads, Pop-ups, etc.), Women's Market

Robin Ashmore *(Principal)*
Benoit Guin *(Principal)*
Eric Hines *(Sr Dir-Art)*
Annie Coghill *(Dir-PR Svcs)*
Tom Van Ness *(Dir-Creative)*
Mackie Clonts *(Acct Supvr)*
Mackie Sweatman *(Acct Supvr)*
Olivia Abtahi *(Copywriter)*

Accounts:
Babolat Tennis Gear; 2002
CatEye Cycling Computers & Accessories; 2014
Coloradans Against Auto Theft (CAAT) Awareness Campaign; 2009
Colorado Advisory Council for Persons with Disabilities
Colorado Department of Transportation Campaign: "A Few Can Still be Dangerous", Government Transportation; 2007
Delta Dental of Colorado Foundation Philanthropic "Brush With Me" Campaign; 2012
Eco-Products Sustainable Goods; 2012
Lucid Brewing Beer Packaging & Design; 2012
Outlast Technologies, Inc.; Boulder, CO Space-proven Fabric Technology; 2005
Trimble Navigation Global Positioning Services, Mobile Field Worker Technologies; 2012

AMENDOLA COMMUNICATIONS

9280 E Raintree Dr Ste 104, Scottsdale, AZ 85260
Tel.: (480) 664-8412
Fax: (480) 659-3531
E-Mail: info@AcmarketingPR.com
Web Site: www.acmarketingpr.com

Agency Specializes In: Advertising, Brand Development & Integration, Digital/Interactive, Graphic Design, Health Care Services, Integrated Marketing, Local Marketing, Pharmaceutical, Public Relations, Publicity/Promotions, Real Estate

Ted Amendola *(Pres)*
Jodi Amendola *(CEO)*
Tim Boivin *(Mng Dir)*
Jan Shulman *(Exec VP)*
Stephanie Fraser *(Sr Dir-Social Media & Media Rels)*
Michelle Ronan Noteboom *(Sr Dir-Content & Acct)*
Angela Jenkins *(Sr Acct Dir)*
Matt Schlossberg *(Acct Dir-Digital & Content)*
Joy DiNaro *(Dir-Social Media)*
Ken Krause *(Dir-Content & Acct Mgmt)*

Accounts:
Arizona Pediatric
New-Availity, LLC (Public Relations & Content Marketing Agency of Record)
Calvis Wyant Luxury Homes
New-Cardiopulmonary Corp. (Public Relations & Content Marketing Agency of Record) Social Media
Phoenix Law Group
QCSI
Recondo Technology (Public Relations Agency of Record) Content Marketing, Media Relations, Social Media
SAXA
New-SCIO Health Analytics (Public Relations & Content Marketing Agency of Record)
SDI
Sentrian (Public Relations Agency of Record) Remote Patient Intelligence
Shea Commercial
New-SKYGEN USA (Public Relations & Content Marketing Agency of Record) National Media Relations, Strategic Counsel, Trade Media Relations
World Communication Center (WCC)
X2 Healthcare Network
Zynx Health (Public Relations & Content Marketing Agency of Record) Media Relations, Strategic

AMEREDIA, INC.

550 Montgomery St, San Francisco, CA 94111
Tel.: (415) 788-5100
Fax: (415) 449-3411
E-Mail: buzz@ameredia.com
Web Site: www.ameredia.com

Employees: 18
Year Founded: 2003

National Agency Associations: AAF-IAA

Agency Specializes In: Advertising, African-American Market, Asian Market, Bilingual Market, Event Planning & Marketing, Guerilla Marketing, Hispanic Market, Integrated Marketing, Market Research, Media Buying Services, Media Planning, Media Relations, Multicultural, Out-of-Home Media, Public Relations, South Asian Market, Sponsorship, Strategic Planning/Research

Approx. Annual Billings: $6,000,000

Breakdown of Gross Billings by Media: Cable T.V.: $250,000; Collateral: $500,000; Consulting: $250,000; D.M.: $500,000; Event Mktg.: $250,000; Fees: $1,000,000; Internet Adv.: $250,000; Newsp. & Mags.: $1,500,000; Out-of-Home Media: $250,000; Print: $500,000; Production: $500,000; Radio: $250,000

Pawan Mehra *(Founder & Principal)*
Sam Jhans *(Co-Founder & Dir-Creative)*
Siggy Habtu *(Dir-Fin & Ops)*

Accounts:
China Lion Entertainment
Comcast Cable, Internet, Telephone; 2005
Harris Freeman & Company Tea India
The Indus Entrepreneurs
International Media Distribution
Kikkoman
Pacific Gas & Electric
San Francisco International Airport
San Francisco Municipal Transportation Authority
San Jose Water Company
Thunder Valley Casino Resort

AMERICAN ADVERTISING SERVICES

29 Bala Ave Ste 114, Bala Cynwyd, PA 19004-3206
Tel.: (484) 562-0060
Fax: (484) 562-0068
E-Mail: AdComTimes@aol.com
Web Site: www.phillybizmedia.com/

Employees: 5
Year Founded: 1956

Agency Specializes In: Advertising, Advertising Specialties, African-American Market, Agriculture, Asian Market, Automotive, Broadcast, Business Publications, Business-To-Business, Cable T.V., Children's Market, Co-op Advertising, Collateral, Commercial Photography, Communications, Consulting, Consumer Marketing, Consumer Publications, Corporate Identity, Cosmetics, Digital/Interactive, Direct Response Marketing, E-Commerce, Education, Electronic Media, Entertainment, Event Planning & Marketing, Exhibit/Trade Shows, Fashion/Apparel, Financial, Food Service, Gay & Lesbian Market, Government/Political, Graphic Design, Health Care Services, Hispanic Market, Industrial, Infomercials, Internet/Web Design, Investor Relations, Legal Services, Leisure, Logo & Package Design, Magazines, Marine, Media Buying Services, Medical Products, Merchandising, Multimedia, New Product Development, Newspaper, Newspapers & Magazines, Out-of-Home Media, Outdoor, Over-50 Market, Pharmaceutical, Planning & Consultation, Point of Purchase, Point of Sale, Print, Production, Public Relations, Publicity/Promotions, Radio, Real Estate, Recruitment, Restaurant, Retail, Sales Promotion, Seniors' Market, Sports Market, Strategic Planning/Research, Sweepstakes, Syndication, T.V., Teen Market, Telemarketing,

Trade & Consumer Magazines, Transportation, Travel & Tourism, Yellow Pages Advertising

Kathy Newmiller *(Office Mgr)*

Accounts:
Advertising/Communications Times Newspapers
Business Development of America

AMERICAN CONSULTING GROUP, INC.

1329 Taughannock Blvd, Ithaca, NY 14850
Tel.: (607) 272-9111
Fax: (607) 272-5588
E-Mail: dsmith@marketing-consultant.com
Web Site: www.marketing-consultant.com

E-Mail for Key Personnel:
President: dsmith@marketing-consultant.com

Employees: 2
Year Founded: 1989

Agency Specializes In: Business-To-Business, Consulting, New Product Development, Strategic Planning/Research

Approx. Annual Billings: $500,000

Breakdown of Gross Billings by Media: Consulting: $500,000

Don Smith *(Pres)*

Accounts:
InterVision Systems
Lutron Electronics
Motorola Solutions, Inc.; Moscow, Russia
Newtex Corporation
Shared Medical Systems
Toshiba
Trane Inc.
West Corporation

AMERICAN MASS MEDIA

207 E Ohio St Ste 218, Chicago, IL 60611
Tel.: (312) 233-2866
Fax: (312) 268-6388
Web Site: www.americanmassmedia.com

Year Founded: 2004

Agency Specializes In: Advertising, Brand Development & Integration, Graphic Design, Internet/Web Design, Media Buying Services, Media Planning, Outdoor, Radio, Social Media, T.V.

Shelly Ng *(Pres & Media Buyer)*
Mario Fabian *(Sr Dir-Art)*
Michael Webdell *(Dir-Creative)*
Ed Lai *(Coord-Media)*
Virginia Slana *(Coord-PR & Adv)*

Accounts:
American Medical Research
The Asian American Business Expo
Cafe Cubano
Cardinal Fitness
Charter Fitness
The Chicago City Treasurers Office
Chicago Tempered Glass
East Queen Fine Jewelry
Fonda Isabel Mexican Cuisine
Golden Hill Foods

AMERICAN MEDIA CONCEPTS INC.

189 Montague St Ste 801A, Brooklyn, NY 11201-3610
Tel.: (718) 643-5500
Fax: (718) 643-5868
E-Mail: info@americanmediaconcepts.com
Web Site: www.americanmediaconcepts.com/

Employees: 2
Year Founded: 1982

Agency Specializes In: Advertising, African-American Market, Asian Market, Brand Development & Integration, Broadcast, Children's Market, Consumer Marketing, Direct Response Marketing, Entertainment, Health Care Services, Media Buying Services, Out-of-Home Media, Radio

Approx. Annual Billings: $2,000,000

Breakdown of Gross Billings by Media: Newsp.: 5%; Other: 15%; Radio: 40%; T.V.: 40%

Kenneth Hochman *(Owner)*
William Hochman *(Acct Exec)*

Accounts:
Brooklyn Chamber of Commerce; 2000
Brooklyn Children's Museum
Brooklyn Cyclones Baseball
Brooklyn Health Link; 2002
GNYHA Hospital; 1996
Hebrew Home for the Aged Assisted Living; 2000
LaGuardia Community College
Marriott LaGuardia
New York Hall of Science; 1999
School Food Program

AMERICAN ROGUE

3000 31st St, Santa Monica, CA 90405
Tel.: (310) 664-6600
Fax: (310) 396-5636
Web Site: www.americanrogue.com

Employees: 10
Year Founded: 2002

Agency Specializes In: Advertising

Accounts:
New-Ruby Tuesday

AMERICA'S MEDIA MARKETING, INC.

13169 Jacqueline Rd, Brooksville, FL 34613
Tel.: (352) 597-6200
Fax: (352) 597-6201
Toll Free: (800) 876-8031
E-Mail: service@americasmedia.com
Web Site: www.americasmedia.com

Employees: 20
Year Founded: 1991

Agency Specializes In: Advertising, Advertising Specialties, Direct Response Marketing, Graphic Design, Magazines, Newspaper, Newspapers & Magazines, Print

Approx. Annual Billings: $4,000,000

Kimberly Burbank-Pye *(Owner)*

AMERICOM MARKETING

2615 Calder Ste 145, Beaumont, TX 77702
Tel.: (800) 889-9308
Web Site: www.americommarketing.com

Year Founded: 2000

Agency Specializes In: Advertising, Brand Development & Integration, Collateral, Graphic Design, Internet/Web Design, Logo & Package Design, Print, Radio, Social Media, T.V.

Charlie Cooper *(Pres & CEO)*
Chad Campbell *(Sr Art Dir)*
Lance Larue *(Creative Dir)*
Jake Stack *(Dir-Bus Dev)*
Lisa Black *(Mgr-Acctg & Office)*

Accounts:
4M Consultants
The Buffalo Field Campaigm
Jay Bruce Golf Benefit

AMES SCULLIN O'HAIRE

245 Peachtree Center Ave 23rd Fl, Atlanta, GA 30303
Tel.: (404) 659-2769
Fax: (404) 659-7664
Web Site: www.asoy.com

Employees: 34
Year Founded: 1997

Agency Specializes In: Advertising, Business-To-Business, Cable T.V., Consumer Goods, Consumer Publications, Corporate Identity, Direct Response Marketing, Electronic Media, Email, Financial, Guerilla Marketing, In-Store Advertising, Internet/Web Design, Leisure, Local Marketing, Magazines, Market Research, Media Buying Services, Media Planning, Multimedia, Newspaper, Newspapers & Magazines, Out-of-Home Media, Outdoor, Point of Sale, Print, Radio, Regional, Restaurant, Retail, Sponsorship, T.V., Trade & Consumer Magazines, Travel & Tourism, Viral/Buzz/Word of Mouth

Approx. Annual Billings: $108,000,000

Breakdown of Gross Billings by Media: Newsp. & Mags.: 30%; Other: 4%; Out-of-Home Media: 1%; Outdoor: 3%; Point of Purchase: 2%; Radio & T.V.: 60%

Patrick Scullin *(Mng Partner & Exec Creative Dir)*
Tony O'Haire *(Mng Partner-Engagement)*
Jim Crone *(Partner-Acct Leadership)*
Ryan Mikesell *(Partner-Creative)*
Maureen Dabrowa *(Acct Dir)*
Mike Bourne *(Dir-Creative)*
Steve Harding *(Dir-Media)*
Michelle Chong *(Assoc Dir-Media)*

Accounts:
Cryovac (Agency of Record)
Georgia Aquarium; Atlanta, GA Campaign: "Walk of Fame"
Golf Pride Broadcast, CP2 Pro Grip, Campaign: "Hands", Digital, MCC Plus4 Grip, Marketing, Media Buying, Media Planning, POS, Print, TV, Trade
Sea Palms Resort (Agency of Record)
Sealed Air Corporation

AMF MEDIA GROUP

12657 Alcosta Blvd Ste 500, San Ramon, CA 94583
Tel.: (925) 790-2662
Fax: (925) 790-2601
Web Site: www.amfmediagroup.com

Agency Specializes In: Advertising, Brand Development & Integration, Broadcast, Event Planning & Marketing, Internet/Web Design, Public Relations

Vintage Foster *(Pres & Partner)*
Larry Hancock *(VP)*
Sarah Cho *(Dir-Art)*
Mike Clinebell *(Dir-Content Svcs)*
Brad Kinney *(Dir-Events & Production)*
Mike Leon *(Dir-Creative)*
Brenda Gunderson *(Acct Mgmt Supvr)*
Laura McLaughlin *(Acct Supvr)*
Kyle McGuire *(Specialist-Comm, PR & Social Media)*

Accounts:
The Women's Foodservice Forum Branding, Integrated Communications, PR

AMG CREATIVE INC.

2038 Caribou Dr Ste 200, Fort Collins, CO 80525
Tel.: (970) 221-5756
Fax: (970) 498-0011
Toll Free: (800) 264-7448
E-Mail: info@amgci.com
Web Site: www.amgci.com

Agency Specializes In: Advertising, Brand Development & Integration, Email, Internet/Web Design, Logo & Package Design, Print, Search Engine Optimization, Social Media

Terry Fine *(Pres)*
Bill Neal *(CEO)*
Sean Leddy *(Sr Graphic Designer)*

Accounts:
Keating Dental Arts

AMG MARKETING RESOURCES INC.

(Formerly AMG Advertising & PR, Inc.)
2530 Superior Ave Ste 601, Cleveland, OH 44114
Tel.: (216) 621-1835
Fax: (216) 621-2061
E-Mail: info@accessamg.com
Web Site: www.accessamg.com

Employees: 20

Agency Specializes In: Advertising, Automotive, Bilingual Market, Brand Development & Integration, Business-To-Business, Catalogs, Co-op Advertising, Collateral, Consumer Goods, Consumer Marketing, Consumer Publications, Corporate Communications, Corporate Identity, Customer Relationship Management, Digital/Interactive, Direct Response Marketing, Direct-to-Consumer, Electronic Media, Email, Environmental, Event Planning & Marketing, Financial, Food Service, Government/Political, Graphic Design, Health Care Services, Identity Marketing, In-Store Advertising, Industrial, Integrated Marketing, International, Internet/Web Design, Legal Services, Local Marketing, Logo & Package Design, Magazines, Media Buying Services, Media Planning, Media Relations, Media Training, Medical Products, Multimedia, New Product Development, New Technologies, Newspapers & Magazines, Outdoor, Over-50 Market, Package Design, Planning & Consultation, Point of Purchase, Point of Sale, Print, Product Placement, Production, Production (Ad, Film, Broadcast), Production (Print), Promotions, Public Relations, Publicity/Promotions, Sales Promotion, Social Marketing/Nonprofit, Strategic Planning/Research, Technical Advertising, Teen Market, Trade & Consumer Magazines, Tween Market, Viral/Buzz/Word of Mouth, Web (Banner Ads, Pop-ups, etc.), Women's Market

Revenue: $3,000,000

Anthony M. Fatica *(Pres)*
Mary Ellen Ellar *(VP-Acct Mgmt)*
Annette Fatica *(VP)*
Joe Rini *(VP)*
Dave Urso *(VP-New Bus Dev-AMG Adv & PR)*

Accounts:
Excel Polymers; Solon, OH; 2008
West Development Group; LaGrange, OH; 2008

AMG WORLDWIDE

900 SW 8th St Ste C 2, Miami, FL 33130
Tel.: (305) 856-8004
Fax: (305) 856-8650
E-Mail: market@amgwagency.com
Web Site: www.amgwagency.com

Agency Specializes In: Digital/Interactive, Email, Event Planning & Marketing, Market Research, Media Buying Services, Media Planning, Newspapers & Magazines, Promotions, Public Relations, Radio, Real Estate, Search Engine Optimization, Strategic Planning/Research, T.V.

Eloy De Armas *(CFO)*
Christina Noya *(COO)*
Jaime Drysdale *(VP)*
Antonio Frota *(Acct Dir-Brazil)*
Mauricio Acuna *(Dir-Mexico)*
Humberto Escalante *(Dir-Mexico)*
Marcius Lee *(Dir-Media-Brazil)*

Accounts:
Armani Casa PR
Baoli PR
Baru Urbano
Blue Martini
The Doral Golf Resort & Spa
Eden Roc PR
Ferretti PR
The Four Seasons
Grove
Helly Hanson
Hyundai
Ikea
Kiki Hamann Canine Couture (Agency of Record)
Maybelline
Residences at Vizcaya
Safilo Group PR
Trump Ocean Club International Hotel & Tower Panama PR
Trump Toronto
Vino e Olio
W South Beach

AMGW AGENCY

900 SW 8th St, Miami, FL 33130
Tel.: (786) 362-6500
Web Site: www.amgwagency.com

Year Founded: 2001

Agency Specializes In: Advertising, Digital/Interactive, Event Planning & Marketing, Media Buying Services, Media Planning, Print, Public Relations, Radio, Social Media, T.V.

Eloy De Armas *(CFO)*
Jaime Drysdale *(VP)*
Christine Martinez De Castro *(Exec Dir-PR)*
Aaron Fisher *(Dir-In-Network)*
Anielly Maia *(Dir-Brazil)*
Gaby Sanchez *(Dir-Sls & Mktg)*
Marina Temino *(Dir-Sls & Mktg-Caribbean & Latin America)*
Peggy Fuguet *(Reg Rep-Latam)*
Rodrigo Ocampo *(Reg Rep-Latam)*

AMPERAGE

(Formerly ME&V)
6711 Chancellor Dr, Cedar Falls, IA 50613-6969
Tel.: (319) 268-9151
Fax: (319) 268-0124
Toll Free: (877) WEBEASY
Web Site: www.amperagemarketing.com

Employees: 50

National Agency Associations: Second Wind Limited

Agency Specializes In: Advertising, Automotive, Brand Development & Integration, Broadcast, Business Publications, Business-To-Business, Cable T.V., Collateral, College, Communications, Consulting, Consumer Marketing, Consumer Publications, Corporate Identity, Crisis Communications, Customer Relationship Management, Digital/Interactive, Direct-to-Consumer, E-Commerce, Education, Electronic Media, Event Planning & Marketing, Exhibit/Trade Shows, Faith Based, Financial, Food Service, Graphic Design, Health Care Services, High Technology, Industrial, Infomercials, Information Technology, Integrated Marketing, Internet/Web Design, Local Marketing, Logo & Package Design, Magazines, Media Buying Services, Media Planning, Media Relations, Media Training, Medical Products, Mobile Marketing, Multimedia, Newspaper, Newspapers & Magazines, Out-of-Home Media, Outdoor, Pharmaceutical, Planning & Consultation, Podcasting, Point of Purchase, Point of Sale, Print, Production, Production (Print), Public Relations, Publicity/Promotions, Radio, Recruitment, Restaurant, Retail, Sales Promotion, Seniors' Market, Social Marketing/Nonprofit, Sports Market, Strategic Planning/Research, T.V., Trade & Consumer Magazines, Transportation, Travel & Tourism, Viral/Buzz/Word of Mouth, Yellow Pages Advertising

Approx. Annual Billings: $8,800,000

Breakdown of Gross Billings by Media: Audio/Visual: $750,000; Collateral: $711,000; D.M.: $232,000; Graphic Design: $250,000; Logo & Package Design: $92,000; Mags.: $395,000; Newsp.: $1,082,000; Outdoor: $158,000; Plng. & Consultation: $450,000; Pub. Rels.: $237,000; Radio: $1,027,000; T.V.: $3,100,000; Worldwide Web Sites: $316,000

Bryan Earnest *(Pres & CEO)*
Jim Infelt *(Partner & Chief Digital Officer)*
Tiffini Kieler *(Sr Dir-Art & Mgr-Design)*
Kathy Schreiner *(Dir-Fin & Ops)*
Kris Wieland *(Acct Mgr)*
Laura Cahalan *(Acct Exec)*
Linda Maughan *(Media Buyer)*
Brian Monroe *(Reg Acct Exec)*

Accounts:
Allen Hospital; Waterloo, IA College, Foundation, Hospital; 1996
Burke Corporation; IA, NV Precooked Meat Toppings; 2000
Cedar Valley Medical Specialists; Waterloo, IA Medical Group Specialists-Corporate Image; 1998
Central Kansas Medical Center; KS; 2004
CMP Roskamp; Cedar Falls, IA; 2002
Des Moines Art Center; Des Moines, IA; 2003
Gallagher Bluedorn Performing Arts Center; Cedar Falls, IA; 1999
The Hospital of the Florida Suncoast; Clearwater, FL; 2003
IH Mississippi Credit Union; Bettendorf, IA; 2003
Iowa Bar Association; Des Moines, IA; 2006
Iowa Chiropractic Society; Des Moines, IA; 2006
Iowa Donor Network; Des Moines, IA; 2002
Iowa Health Physicians; Des Moines, IA; 2006
Iowa Hospital Assoc.; Des Moines, IA; 2005
Iowa State University; Ames, Iowa Foundation; 2005
ISU Athletics; Ames, IA; 2003
John Deere; Moline, Waterloo, IA Farm Equipment, Internal Employee & Retiree Newsletters; 1998
Joliet Area Community Hospice; Joliet, IL; 2000
McGregors Furniture; Marshalltown, IA; 2000
Memorial Health System; Hollywood, FL; 2009
National Program for Playground Safety; Cedar Falls, IA; 2002
NCH Cancer Treatment Institute; Naples, FL; 2006
Ogle County Hospice; 2004
Overland Park Regional Medical Center; Overland Park, KS; 2003
Rainbow Hospice; Jefferson, WI; 2003
Saint Elizabeth Medical Center; Lincoln, NE; 2008
Saint Joseph's Hospital; Larned, KS; 2006
Sinai Hospital; Baltimore, MD; 2006
Southwest Missouri Office on Aging; Springfield,

MO; 2006
St. Luke's Hospital; Cedar Rapids, IA; 2004
Standard Golf; Cedar Falls, IA; 2005
University of Iowa; Iowa City, IA; 2003
University of Northern Iowa Athletics; 1999
Wartburg College, Waverly, IA; 1997
Waterloo Industries; Waterloo, IA New Products; 1998
The Work Group; Chicago, IL; 2003

Branch

Amperage
(Formerly ME&V)
6711 Chancellor Dr, Cedar Falls, IA 50613-6969
(See Separate Listing)

THE AMPERSAND AGENCY
1011 San Jacinto Blvd, Austin, TX 78701
Tel.: (512) 462-3366
Web Site: www.ampersandagency.com

Year Founded: 1986

Agency Specializes In: Advertising, Social Media

Jeff Montgomery *(Pres)*
Cindy Montgomery *(CEO & Principal)*
Samantha Hinrichs *(Dir-Art & Designer)*
Janice Hilscher *(Dir-Media)*
Karen Ratcliffe *(Office Mgr)*

Accounts:
BCL of Texas
Celis brewery Beer Bottle Packaging, Branding, Logo, Social Media
Jaguar Cars North America
Michael Angelo's Gourmet Foods, Inc. Campaign: "Existential Lasagna", Campaign: "Sad Tomato"
Seton Brain & Spine Institute
Texas A&M University

AMPLE, LLC
200 W 4th St 5th Fl, Cincinnati, OH 45202
Tel.: (513) 543-9646
Web Site: www.helloample.com

Agency Specializes In: Advertising, Brand Development & Integration, Logo & Package Design, Outdoor, Print, Radio, Strategic Planning/Research

Kevin Comer *(Partner-Creative)*
Josh Fendley *(Partner-Strategy)*
Adam George *(Partner-Creative)*
Taylor Macdonald *(Partner-Tech)*
Rob Sloan *(Partner-Creative)*

Accounts:
The Brandery
Currito
Everything But the House

AMPM, INC.
7403 W. Wackerly St., Midland, MI 48642-7344
Tel.: (989) 837-8800
Fax: (989) 832-0781
Toll Free: (800) 530-9100
E-Mail: solutions@ampminc.com
Web Site: www.ampminc.com

E-Mail for Key Personnel:
President: mbush@ampminc.com
Creative Dir.: tsmith@ampminc.com
Production Mgr.: akpaeth@ampminc.com

Employees: 13
Year Founded: 1969

National Agency Associations: Second Wind Limited

Agency Specializes In: Advertising, Advertising Specialties, Automotive, Brand Development & Integration, Business Publications, Business-To-Business, Collateral, Communications, Corporate Communications, Corporate Identity, Digital/Interactive, Electronic Media, Electronics, Event Planning & Marketing, Exhibit/Trade Shows, Graphic Design, High Technology, Integrated Marketing, Internet/Web Design, Market Research, Media Buying Services, Media Planning, Multimedia, Package Design, Planning & Consultation, Point of Purchase, Print, Production (Ad, Film, Broadcast), Public Relations, Publicity/Promotions, Strategic Planning/Research, Web (Banner Ads, Pop-ups, etc.)

Approx. Annual Billings: $3,000,000

Breakdown of Gross Billings by Media: Adv. Specialities: $100,000; Brdcst.: $50,000; Bus. Publs.: $300,000; Collateral: $500,000; Consulting: $50,000; D.M.: $250,000; E-Commerce: $100,000; Event Mktg.: $100,000; Exhibits/Trade Shows: $150,000; Graphic Design: $150,000; Internet Adv.: $50,000; Logo & Package Design: $50,000; Mags.: $200,000; Plng. & Consultation: $50,000; Point of Purchase: $50,000; Print: $250,000; Promos.: $100,000; Pub. Rels.: $50,000; Strategic Planning/Research: $50,000; Worldwide Web Sites: $400,000

Mark Bush *(Pres)*
William Trethaway *(VP)*
Ty Smith *(Dir-Creative)*
Kim Shreve *(Mgr-Traffic & Media Planner)*
Debbi Brasile *(Mgr-Digital Enterprise)*
Elena Cortesi *(Mgr-Global Corp Comm)*
Amy Paeth *(Mgr-Ops)*
Greg Branch *(Strategist-Brand)*

Accounts:
Dow Corning; Midland, MI Silicon Based Products
Duro-Last Roofing; Saginaw, MI
I-Mark Associates; Washington, DC

Branch:

AMPM, Inc. Detroit
21442 Beauford Ln, Northville, MI 48167
Mailing Address:
PO Box 1147, Farmington, MI 48332-1147
Tel.: (248) 477-0400
Fax: (248) 477-0402
Toll Free: (800) 530-9100
E-Mail: dwell@ampminc.com
Web Site: www.ampminc.com

Employees: 2
Year Founded: 1969

Agency Specializes In: Business-To-Business, High Technology

Dave Well *(Partner)*

AMUSEMENT PARK
(Formerly DGWB)
217 N Main St Ste 200, Santa Ana, CA 92701
Tel.: (714) 881-2300
Fax: (714) 881-2442
E-Mail: info@amusementparkinc.com
Web Site: amusementparkinc.com

Employees: 100
Year Founded: 1988

National Agency Associations: 4A's-AMIN

Agency Specializes In: Advertising, Advertising Specialties, Affluent Market, Alternative Advertising, Automotive, Brand Development & Integration, Branded Entertainment, Broadcast, Business-To-Business, Cable T.V., Co-op Advertising, Collateral, Communications, Computers & Software, Consulting, Consumer Goods, Consumer Marketing, Consumer Publications, Digital/Interactive, Direct Response Marketing, Direct-to-Consumer, Electronic Media, Electronics, Email, Entertainment, Event Planning & Marketing, Experience Design, Food Service, Graphic Design, Guerilla Marketing, Health Care Services, Hispanic Market, Hospitality, Identity Marketing, In-Store Advertising, Industrial, Integrated Marketing, Internet/Web Design, Local Marketing, Logo & Package Design, Luxury Products, Market Research, Media Buying Services, Media Planning, Media Relations, Media Training, Mobile Marketing, Multicultural, Multimedia, Newspaper, Newspapers & Magazines, Out-of-Home Media, Outdoor, Over-50 Market, Package Design, Paid Searches, Planning & Consultation, Point of Purchase, Point of Sale, Print, Product Placement, Production, Production (Ad, Film, Broadcast), Production (Print), Promotions, Public Relations, Publicity/Promotions, Radio, Real Estate, Regional, Restaurant, Retail, Sales Promotion, Search Engine Optimization, Social Marketing/Nonprofit, Social Media, Sponsorship, Strategic Planning/Research, Sweepstakes, T.V., Transportation, Travel & Tourism, Viral/Buzz/Word of Mouth, Web (Banner Ads, Pop-ups, etc.)

Approx. Annual Billings: $91,000,000

Jimmy Smith *(Chm & Chief Creative Officer)*
Ed Collins *(Pres & Partner)*
Michael Weisman *(Partner & CEO)*
Jon Gothold *(Exec Dir-Creative & Partner)*
Michael Dischinger *(Acct Dir)*
Rachel Svoboda *(Dir-Mktg)*
Ian McGee *(Acct Supvr)*
Sabrina Figueroa *(Supvr-Media)*
Luis Nava *(Supvr-Digital Media)*
Beth Reid *(Supvr-Media)*

Accounts:
Bard Valley Natural Delights Medjool Dates
Chicken of the Sea
Children's Hospital of Orange County
DD's Discounts
Discovery Science Center
Dole Food Company, Inc. Dole Fresh Fruit, Dole Fresh Vegetables
Hilton Garden Inn; Beverly Hills, CA
Irvine Company Apartment Communities
Los Angeles County Fair (Agency of Record) Advertising, Creative, Digital, Direct Mail, Outdoor, Print, Public Relations, Radio, Strategic, TV
Miguel's Jr.
Papa Johns
Polly's Pies
Qualcomm Transportation & Logistics Division
St. Joseph Health System
Taller San Jose
Toshiba Business Solutions; 2000
Ubiquiti
Wienerschnitzel; Irvine, CA Campaign: "Wiener Nationals Poster", Fast Food; 1995
Yogurtland Franchising Brand Strategy, Campaign: "Flavor Quest", Digital Marketing, In-Store Merchandising, Marketing Communications, Video

ANALOGFOLK
13-17 Laight St Unit 602, New York, NY 10013
Tel.: (212) 677-2826
E-Mail: howyoudoin@analogfolk.com
Web Site: www.analogfolk.com

Year Founded: 2013

Agency Specializes In: Advertising,

Digital/Interactive, Internet/Web Design, Sponsorship

David Fausel *(Partner & Mng Dir)*
Jim Wood *(Partner-New York & Dir-Creative)*
Zach Pentel *(Partner)*
Fame Razak *(CTO)*
Olivia Hall *(Gen Mgr)*
Neil Thomson *(Dir-Fin-Global)*

Accounts:
Kahlua
Malibu
Viewfinder
Wyborowa Sa

ANCHOR MARKETING & DESIGN, LLC
512 Main St Ste 1301, Fort Worth, TX 76102
Tel.: (817) 348-0762
E-Mail: info@anchormd.com
Web Site: www.anchormd.com

Agency Specializes In: Advertising, Digital/Interactive, Internet/Web Design, Public Relations, Social Media

Amber Caldwell *(Owner & Dir-Creative)*
Ricky Anderson, II *(Dir-Video & Digital Media)*

Accounts:
Fort Worth Food & Wine Festival
Legacy Heart Care

&BARR
(Formerly Fry/Hammond/Barr Incorporated)
600 E Washington St, Orlando, FL 32801-2938
Tel.: (407) 849-0100
Fax: (407) 849-0817
Web Site: andbarr.co

Employees: 60
Year Founded: 1957

National Agency Associations: 4A's

Agency Specializes In: Advertising, Arts, Brand Development & Integration, Broadcast, Cable T.V., Co-op Advertising, Collateral, College, Communications, Consulting, Consumer Goods, Consumer Marketing, Consumer Publications, Corporate Communications, Corporate Identity, Digital/Interactive, Direct-to-Consumer, E-Commerce, Electronic Media, Email, Event Planning & Marketing, Graphic Design, Health Care Services, Hospitality, Identity Marketing, In-Store Advertising, Integrated Marketing, International, Internet/Web Design, Logo & Package Design, Magazines, Marine, Market Research, Media Buying Services, Media Planning, Media Relations, Medical Products, Multimedia, Newspaper, Newspapers & Magazines, Out-of-Home Media, Outdoor, Planning & Consultation, Print, Promotions, Public Relations, Publicity/Promotions, RSS (Really Simple Syndication), Radio, Real Estate, Restaurant, Retail, Sales Promotion, Search Engine Optimization, Social Media, Sponsorship, Sports Market, Strategic Planning/Research, T.V., Trade & Consumer Magazines, Travel & Tourism, Viral/Buzz/Word of Mouth, Web (Banner Ads, Pop-ups, etc.)

Approx. Annual Billings: $60,000,000

Breakdown of Gross Billings by Media: Fees: $32,500,000; Internet Adv.: $2,400,000; Outdoor: $700,000; Print: $1,000,000; Production: $7,200,000; Radio: $2,700,000; T.V.: $13,500,000

Peter C. Barr, Jr. *(Pres & CEO)*
Dennis Nikles *(VP & Dir-Connection Plng)*
Nancy Allen *(VP)*
Guy Stephens *(VP-Strategic Plng)*
Brandy Gill *(Dir-Creative)*
Sandra Gerlt *(Assoc Dir-Creative)*
Heather Castillo *(Brand Mgr)*

Accounts:
ABC Fine Wine & Spirits; 2003
Bright House Networks; Orlando, FL; 1998
Bright House Networks; Tampa, Fl; 2003
Eckerd Youth Alternatives; Tampa, FL; 2010
First Watch; Tampa, Fl Restaurant; 2010
Glazer Children's Museum
Grendene USA; Orlando, FL Footwear; 2010
Harmony Development Co.; 2010
HD Supply Utilities Ltd.; Orlando, FL Utilities; 2010
Infant Swimming Resources
Kissimmee Convention & Visitors Bureau
Moffitt Cancer Center; 2007
Nemours Health System Children's Health System; 2005
Old Florida Nat'l Bank; Orlando, FL; 2010
Organic Bouquet; Maitland, FL; 2010
The Peabody Orlando
Stein Mart; 2009
WUCF-TV
YMCA of Central Florida

AND PARTNERS
158 W 27th St Fl 7, New York, NY 10001
Tel.: (212) 414-4700
Fax: (212) 414-2915
Web Site: www.andpartnersny.com

Agency Specializes In: Advertising, Brand Development & Integration, Collateral, Communications, Digital/Interactive, Environmental, Internet/Web Design, Mobile Marketing, Package Design, Social Media

Jarrett White *(Principal)*
Sarah Hans *(Exec VP)*
Antonio Mah *(Sr Designer-Interactive, UX & UI)*
Amy Novak *(Jr Designer)*

THE&PARTNERSHIP
75 Spring St 2nd Fl, New York, NY 10012
Tel.: (646) 751-4600
E-Mail: us@theandpartnership.com
Web Site: www.theandpartnership.com

National Agency Associations: 4A's

Agency Specializes In: Advertising, Communications, Content, Digital/Interactive, Media Buying Services, Media Planning, Public Relations, Social Media

Andrew Bailey *(CEO)*
Oliver Egan *(Partner & Head-Strategy-North American)*
Dana May *(Head-Production)*
Isaac Silverglate *(Exec Creative Dir)*
Nate Stewart *(Grp Acct Dir)*
Hemant Jain *(Creative Dir)*
Jerome Leclere *(Dir-Art)*
Michael Fiola *(Sr Acct Mgr)*
Jonathan Horner *(Copywriter)*

Accounts:
The Wall Street Journal Campaign: "Make Time", Campaign: "Time Well Spent"

ANDERSON ADVERTISING & PUBLIC RELATIONS
5725 N Scottsdale Rd Ste 105, Scottsdale, AZ 85250
Tel.: (480) 945-2229
Fax: (480) 945-9921
Web Site: www.anderson-adv.com

Year Founded: 2005

Agency Specializes In: Advertising, Brand Development & Integration, Broadcast, Crisis Communications, Media Planning, Multimedia, Public Relations, Social Media

Ted Anderson *(Owner & Pres)*
Sheri Anderson *(VP & Acct Dir)*
Robin Lemarr *(Dir-Media)*
Arlyn Stotts *(Dir-Creative)*

Accounts:
Blue Wasabi Sushi & Martini Bar
Hamra Jewelers
National Hockey League Phoenix Coyotes
Page Springs Cellars

ANDERSON COMMUNICATIONS
2245 Godby Rd, Atlanta, GA 30349
Tel.: (404) 766-8000
Fax: (770) 767-5264
E-Mail: alanderson@andercom.com
Web Site: andercom.com

E-Mail for Key Personnel:
President: alanderson@andercom.com

Employees: 10
Year Founded: 1971

National Agency Associations: AAF-ABAA

Agency Specializes In: Advertising, Affluent Market, African-American Market, Alternative Advertising, Arts, Automotive, Below-the-Line, Brand Development & Integration, Branded Entertainment, Broadcast, Business-To-Business, Co-op Advertising, College, Computers & Software, Consulting, Consumer Goods, Consumer Marketing, Content, Corporate Communications, Cosmetics, Crisis Communications, Education, Electronic Media, Electronics, Entertainment, Environmental, Event Planning & Marketing, Exhibit/Trade Shows, Experience Design, Faith Based, Fashion/Apparel, Financial, Food Service, Government/Political, Guerilla Marketing, Health Care Services, Hospitality, Household Goods, In-Store Advertising, Integrated Marketing, Leisure, Local Marketing, Luxury Products, Market Research, Media Buying Services, Media Planning, Media Relations, Medical Products, Men's Market, Merchandising, Mobile Marketing, Multicultural, Multimedia, New Product Development, Outdoor, Over-50 Market, Pharmaceutical, Planning & Consultation, Print, Promotions, Public Relations, Publicity/Promotions, Radio, Recruitment, Regional, Restaurant, Retail, Sales Promotion, Seniors' Market, Social Marketing/Nonprofit, Social Media, Sponsorship, Sports Market, Strategic Planning/Research, Syndication, T.V., Transportation, Travel & Tourism, Urban Market, Viral/Buzz/Word of Mouth, Women's Market

Approx. Annual Billings: $42,907,000

Breakdown of Gross Billings by Media: Brdcst.: $16,700,000; Cable T.V.: $4,950,000; Co-op Adv.: $1,210,000; Collateral: $875,000; Consulting: $2,199,000; D.M.: $975,000; Event Mktg.: $2,541,000; Fees: $1,424,000; Internet Adv.: $295,000; Network Radio: $2,452,000; Network T.V.: $754,000; Newsp.: $994,000; Newsp. & Mags.: $2,330,000; Point of Purchase: $750,000; Point of Sale: $691,000; Spot Radio: $1,962,000; Syndication: $1,530,000; Worldwide Web Sites: $275,000

Al Anderson *(Owner)*

Accounts:
The Association of Black Cardiologists; Atlanta, GA Professional Organization
Belnavis Racing, Inc.
Benedict College
BRG Products; Stone Mountain, GA Racing

Sponsorship; 2000
City of Atlanta
City of College Park Georgia
IAAM
Johnson & Johnson
McNeil Pharmaceuticals Consumer Products

ANDERSON DDB HEALTH & LIFESTYLE

1300-33 Bloor St E, Toronto, ON M4W 3H1 Canada
Tel.: (416) 960-3830
Fax: (416) 960-5531
E-Mail: info@andersonddb.com
Web Site: www.andersonddb.com

E-Mail for Key Personnel:
President: kevin.brady@andersonddb.com
Creative Dir.: dieter.kaufmann@andersonddb.com
Production Mgr.: steve.benson@andersonddb.com

Employees: 100
Year Founded: 1972

Agency Specializes In: Advertising, Advertising Specialties, Bilingual Market, Brand Development & Integration, Broadcast, Business-To-Business, Collateral, Communications, Consumer Marketing, Consumer Publications, Corporate Identity, Direct Response Marketing, Direct-to-Consumer, Government/Political, Graphic Design, Health Care Services, Hispanic Market, Internet/Web Design, Logo & Package Design, Media Buying Services, Media Planning, Medical Products, New Product Development, Newspapers & Magazines, Out-of-Home Media, Outdoor, Package Design, Pharmaceutical, Print, Production, Production (Ad, Film, Broadcast), Radio, Social Marketing/Nonprofit, Strategic Planning/Research, T.V., Transportation, Web (Banner Ads, Pop-ups, etc.)

Kevin Brady *(Pres & CEO)*
Gary Shimizu *(VP & Grp Acct Dir)*
Joanne Belsito *(VP & Client Svc Dir)*
Steve Benson *(VP-Production & Studio Resources)*
Glen Cambridge *(VP-Production)*
Nancy Kramarich *(VP)*
Mark Boutte *(Head-Digital Plng & Delivery)*
Karen Ross *(Head-Brdcst)*
Tony Miller *(Exec Dir-Creative)*
Mario Amaral *(Sr Dir-Art)*
Enza Pitrolo *(Sr Dir-Art)*
Chris Lund *(Bus Dir-Global)*
Veronica Pineda *(Acct Dir)*
Juanita Shipley *(Acct Dir)*
Helene Carriere *(Dir-Art)*
Randy Vogel *(Dir-Global Strategy & Integration DePuy)*
Malcolm Mersereau *(Sr Project Mgr-Digital)*
Prit Singh *(Acct Supvr)*
Johnathon Anderson *(Supvr-Production)*
Tory Grummett *(Acct Exec)*
Quinn Kirby *(Acct Exec)*
Matt Ryan *(Acct Exec)*
Megha Kumar *(Jr Copywriter)*
Arthur Oskan *(Sr Designer)*

Accounts:
FASworld
Johnson & Johnson Centocor, Codman, Cordis, DePuy, Ethicon, LifeScan, Ortho Biotech, Servier; 1996
Pfizer; 1978
New-Rexall (Agency of Record) Creative, Media Planning, Rexall PharmaPlus, Strategy
Rx & D; 1999
Silver Snail Comics Shop
Weetabix Canada Inc.; 1996

Branches

Anderson DDB Sante.Vie.Esprit.

3500 Blvd De Maisonneuve St W Ste 610, Westmount, Montreal, QC H3Z 3C1 Canada
Tel.: (514) 844-9505
Fax: (514) 842-9871
E-Mail: joanne.belsito@andersonddb.com
Web Site: www.andersonddb.com

E-Mail for Key Personnel:
Media Dir.: carol.chisholm@andersonddb.com
Production Mgr.: glen.cambridge@andersonddb.com

Employees: 15
Year Founded: 1971

Agency Specializes In: Advertising, Advertising Specialties, Bilingual Market, Brand Development & Integration, Broadcast, Business-To-Business, Collateral, Communications, Consumer Marketing, Corporate Identity, Direct Response Marketing, Government/Political, Graphic Design, Health Care Services, Hispanic Market, Internet/Web Design, Logo & Package Design, Media Buying Services, Medical Products, New Product Development, Pharmaceutical, Print, Production, Radio, Strategic Planning/Research, T.V.

Gord Desveaux *(Exec VP & Dir-Strategic Plng)*
Joanne Belsito *(VP & Client Svc Dir)*
Tory Grummett *(Acct Exec)*
M Quinn Kirby *(Acct Exec)*

Accounts:
ManuLife
Merck Frosst Canada; 1989
Novartis Pharmaceuticals Canada; 2000
Pfizer Canada; 1978

DDB Remedy

(Formerly Anderson DDB Health & Lifestyle)
555 Market St 8th Fl, San Francisco, CA 94105-5804
Tel.: (415) 692-2800
Fax: (415) 692-2801
Web Site: www.ddb.com/offices/north-america/usa/ddb-remedy-san-francisco

E-Mail for Key Personnel:
President: michael.ling@sf.ddb.com

Employees: 35
Year Founded: 2000

National Agency Associations: 4A's

Agency Specializes In: Advertising, Advertising Specialties, Bilingual Market, Brand Development & Integration, Broadcast, Business-To-Business, Collateral, Communications, Consumer Marketing, Corporate Identity, Direct Response Marketing, Government/Political, Graphic Design, Health Care Services, Hispanic Market, Internet/Web Design, Logo & Package Design, Media Buying Services, Medical Products, New Product Development, Pharmaceutical, Print, Production, Radio, Strategic Planning/Research, T.V.

Jackie Burks *(Mng Dir)*
Michael Ling *(Mng Dir)*
Shannon Dillingham *(Acct Supvr)*

THE ANDERSON GROUP

879 Fritztown Rd, Sinking Spring, PA 19608
Tel.: (610) 678-1506
Fax: (610) 678-5891
E-Mail: info@theandersongrp.com
Web Site: www.theandersongrp.com

E-Mail for Key Personnel:
Public Relations: MFortley@theandersongrp.com

Employees: 18
Year Founded: 1987

Agency Specializes In: Advertising, Brand Development & Integration, Business-To-Business, Collateral, Commercial Photography, Communications, Consulting, Consumer Marketing, Corporate Identity, Digital/Interactive, Direct Response Marketing, Event Planning & Marketing, Exhibit/Trade Shows, Financial, Graphic Design, Health Care Services, Industrial, Internet/Web Design, Logo & Package Design, Media Buying Services, Outdoor, Point of Purchase, Point of Sale, Public Relations, Publicity/Promotions, Restaurant, Retail, Strategic Planning/Research, Travel & Tourism

Linda Anderson *(Mng Partner)*
Jeff Phillips *(Sr Dir-Art)*
Shane Boland *(Dir-Integrated Technologies)*

Accounts:
Armstrong Flooring Products
Commonwealth Orthopaedics Association
Elbeco Incorporated
Ephrata Community Hospital
Instant Ocean
Marineland
Pottstown Area Health & Wellness Foundation
Quadrant Engineering Plastic Products
Root-Lowell Manufacturing Co.
Solo
The Speckled Hen
Surgical Institute Of Reading
Tetra
TetraPond

ANDERSON-MADISON ADVERTISING, INC.

7710 Computer Ave, Minneapolis, MN 55435-5417
Tel.: (952) 835-5133
Fax: (952) 835-4977
E-Mail: cm@andersonmadison.com
Web Site: www.andersonmadison.com

E-Mail for Key Personnel:
President: cm@andersonmadison.com

Employees: 8
Year Founded: 1961

Agency Specializes In: Advertising, Aviation & Aerospace, Bilingual Market, Brand Development & Integration, Business Publications, Business-To-Business, Catalogs, Collateral, Commercial Photography, Consumer Goods, Consumer Publications, Digital/Interactive, Direct Response Marketing, Direct-to-Consumer, E-Commerce, Electronic Media, Email, Environmental, Exhibit/Trade Shows, Government/Political, High Technology, Hispanic Market, Identity Marketing, Industrial, Infomercials, Information Technology, Integrated Marketing, International, Internet/Web Design, Logo & Package Design, Magazines, Market Research, Media Buying Services, Media Planning, Media Relations, Medical Products, Multimedia, New Technologies, Newspaper, Newspapers & Magazines, Package Design, Paid Searches, Planning & Consultation, Point of Purchase, Point of Sale, Print, Product Placement, Production (Print), Promotions, Public Relations, Publicity/Promotions, Strategic Planning/Research, Technical Advertising, Trade & Consumer Magazines

Christopher J. Madison *(Pres)*
Barbara Firth *(Mgr-Media)*

ANDERSON MARKETING GROUP

7420 Blanco Rd Ste 200, San Antonio, TX 78216
Tel.: (210) 223-6233
Fax: (210) 223-9692
E-Mail: info@andersonmarketing.com
Web Site: www.andersonmarketing.com/

Employees: 30
Year Founded: 1970

National Agency Associations: AAF-AMA

Agency Specializes In: Advertising, Automotive, Brand Development & Integration, Broadcast, Food Service, Graphic Design, Health Care Services, Hispanic Market, Multimedia, Newspaper, Newspapers & Magazines, Outdoor, Print, Production, Radio, Strategic Planning/Research, T.V.

Approx. Annual Billings: $24,000,000

Breakdown of Gross Billings by Media: Print: 50%; Radio: 20%; T.V.: 30%

Julius Germano *(Owner)*
Kim Gresham *(Pres)*
Charles J. Anderson *(CEO)*
Tiffany Gabaldon *(Sr Dir-Art)*
Chris Pawlik *(Dir-Creative)*
Soeurette Shook-Kelly *(Dir-Corp Dev)*
Dirk Ronk *(Assoc Dir-Creative)*
Tom Sullivan *(Mgr-Production)*
Jacqueline Yarrington *(Sr Acct Exec)*

Accounts:
Cavender Audi; 2002
Cavender Chevy-Olds; 1997
Cavender Toyota; 2002
Eddie Yaklin Ford Lincoln Mercury Nissan
Hill Country Bakery
Hyatt Hotel
Muzak, LLC
Porter Loring Mortuaries; 1999
Prayer4Awakening
San Antonio Economic Development Foundation; San Antonio, TX; 1983
Saturn of San Antonio; 1997
South Texas Blood & Tissue Center
South Texas Medical Center

ANDERSON PARTNERS
6919 Dodge St, Omaha, NE 68132
Tel.: (402) 341-4807
Fax: (402) 341-2846
Toll Free: (800) 551-9737
E-Mail: mhughes@andersonpartners.com
Web Site: www.andersonpartners.com

E-Mail for Key Personnel:
Creative Dir.: dhatfield@andersonpartners.com
Media Dir.: bstewart@andersonpartners.com
Production Mgr.: jgittins@andersonpartners.com

Employees: 19
Year Founded: 1989

Agency Specializes In: Brand Development & Integration, Business-To-Business, Consulting, Corporate Identity, Logo & Package Design, Planning & Consultation, Point of Sale, Print, Radio, Sales Promotion, Strategic Planning/Research, T.V., Trade & Consumer Magazines

Approx. Annual Billings: $30,000,000

Scott D. Anderson *(Mng Partner)*
Jason Gittins *(Partner & Mgr-Production)*
Krista Meisinger *(CFO)*
Dan Swoboda *(Dir-Creative Svcs)*
Deborah Ahl *(Acct Svc Dir)*
Meg Shea *(Media Buyer)*

ANDOSCIA COMMUNICATIONS
29 King St, New York, NY 10014
Tel.: (212) 475-2122
E-Mail: info@andoscia.com
Web Site: www.andosciacommunications.com

Agency Specializes In: Advertising, Crisis Communications, Event Planning & Marketing, Media Relations, Public Relations, Strategic Planning/Research

Caroline Andoscia *(Pres)*

Accounts:
Lindas Stuff

ANDRADE COMMUNICATORS
816 Camaron St Ste 101, San Antonio, TX 78212
Tel.: (210) 595-3931
Web Site: www.andradecom.com

Year Founded: 2004

Agency Specializes In: Advertising, Brand Development & Integration, Collateral, Graphic Design, Logo & Package Design, Print

John Andrade *(Owner & Dir-Creative)*
Neidy Flores *(Office Mgr & Mgr-Print Production)*
Janine Cornelius *(Acct Planner)*

Accounts:
Century Oaks Title, LLC

ANDREA CHARLES ADVERTISING, INC.
910 Beechwood Ave, Cherry Hill, NJ 08002-3404
Tel.: (856) 665-3200
Fax: (856) 665-3204
E-Mail: info@andreacharles.com

Employees: 8
Year Founded: 1978

Agency Specializes In: Advertising, Business-To-Business, Consulting, Graphic Design, Health Care Services, Newspaper, Newspapers & Magazines, Public Relations, Radio, Seniors' Market

Approx. Annual Billings: $1,500,000

Breakdown of Gross Billings by Media: Bus. Publs.: $300,000; Consumer Publs.: $120,000; Fees: $45,000; Newsp.: $150,000; Newsp. & Mags.: $150,000; Outdoor: $15,000; Production: $570,000; Radio: $105,000; Sls. Promo.: $15,000; T.V.: $15,000; Trade Shows: $15,000

Andrea C. Malamut *(Pres)*
Jane Janiszewski *(Controller)*

Accounts:
Greater New Jersey Motorcoach Association
Hamlyn Senior Marketing Senior Living
Innerlink, Inc.; Lancaster, PA Fitness, Health, Nutrition; 2008
Keystone Industries; Cherry Hill, NJ Dental & Acrylic Products; 2001
Lion's Gate Retirement Community; Voorhees, NJ Retirement Living; 2002
Voorhees Pediatric Facility; Voorhees, NJ Health System
Weisman Children's Rehabilitation Hospital

THE ANDREWS AGENCY
209 10th Ave S Ste 323, Nashville, TN 37203
Tel.: (615) 242-4400
Web Site: www.andrewspr.com

Agency Specializes In: Advertising, Event Planning & Marketing, Internet/Web Design, Media Relations, Public Relations, Social Media

Susan Andrews Thompson *(Pres)*
Jena Locke *(VP)*
Hailey Lance *(Acct Exec)*

Accounts:
New-Five Points Pizza
New-Palm Restaurant Nashville

ANDRIA MITSAKOS PUBLIC RELATIONS
76 9th Ave Ste 1110, New York, NY 10011
Tel.: (954) 294-4710
E-Mail: Andria@andriamitsakospr.com
Web Site: www.andriamitsakospr.com

Agency Specializes In: Brand Development & Integration, Communications, Consulting, Consumer Goods, Email, Event Planning & Marketing, Exhibit/Trade Shows, Fashion/Apparel, Guerilla Marketing, Internet/Web Design, Media Relations, Product Placement, Promotions, Publicity/Promotions, Real Estate, Restaurant, Search Engine Optimization, Sponsorship, Viral/Buzz/Word of Mouth

Andria Mitsakos *(Pres & CEO)*
Erika Vives *(VP)*

ANIMAL INSTINCT ADVERTISING
2124 Madison Rd Ste 3F, Cincinnati, OH 45208
Tel.: (513) 321-5500
Web Site: www.animalinstinctadvertising.com

Agency Specializes In: Advertising, Outdoor, Print, Radio, T.V.

Greg Newberry *(Founder)*
Dennis Rutherford *(Founder)*

Accounts:
Alois Alzheimer Center

ANIMATED DESIGNS LLC
31336 Via Colinas Ste 103, Westlake Village, CA 91362-6784
Tel.: (818) 889-2348
E-Mail: bizdev@anides.com
Web Site: www.anides.com

Employees: 21
Year Founded: 1992

Agency Specializes In: Automotive, Digital/Interactive, E-Commerce, Entertainment, Fashion/Apparel, Financial, Internet/Web Design, Media Buying Services, Real Estate

Approx. Annual Billings: $5,000,000

Breakdown of Gross Billings by Media: Worldwide Web Sites: 100%

Patrick Beard *(Pres)*

Accounts:
David&Goliath; El Segundo, CA CGI Animation; 2008

ANIMAX ENTERTAINMENT
6627 Valjean Ave, Van Nuys, CA 91406
Tel.: (818) 787-4444
E-Mail: press@animaxent.com
Web Site: www.animaxent.com

Year Founded: 2001

Agency Specializes In: Advertising, Brand Development & Integration, Digital/Interactive, Entertainment, Internet/Web Design, Paid Searches, Planning & Consultation, Product Placement, Sponsorship, Viral/Buzz/Word of Mouth

Dave Thomas *(Owner)*
Michael Bellavia *(CEO)*
Ferry Permadi *(Dir-Tech)*

Accounts:
US Forest Service Forest Administration Services, Smokey the Bear Campaign

ANNODYNE, INC.

751 Arbor Way, Blue Bell, PA 19422
Tel.: (215) 540-9110
Fax: (215) 540-9115
E-Mail: info@annodyne.com
Web Site: www.annodyne.com

Employees: 20

Anthony M. Campisi *(Pres & CEO)*
Sam Saltzman *(Dir-IT)*
Matt Learnard *(Acct Svc Dir)*
Diana Altobelli *(Specialist-Search Mktg)*
Marisa Albanese *(Analyst-Database Mktg)*
Ryan Schlegel *(Sr Designer)*

Accounts:
Montgomery County Community College (Agency of Record) Culinary Arts Institute, Website, mc3.edu/culinary
Pennsylvania Academy
Wharton

ANOMALY

536 Broadway 11th Fl, New York, NY 10012
Tel.: (917) 595-2200
Fax: (917) 595-2299
E-Mail: jason@anomaly.com
Web Site: www.anomalynyc.com

Employees: 55
Year Founded: 2004

National Agency Associations: 4A's

Agency Specializes In: Advertising, Sponsorship

Justin Barocas *(Founder & Partner)*
Karina Wilsher *(Pres & CEO)*
Carl Johnson *(Partner)*
Natasha Jakubowski *(Mng Partner & Dir-Innovation)*
Eric Lee *(Partner & Mng Dir)*
Steve Harris *(Mng Dir)*
James Conlon *(CFO-North America)*
Andrew Loevenguth *(Head-Production)*
Allison Sabol *(Head-Acct Mgmt)*
Murray Butler *(Exec Dir-Creative-Framestore)*
Martin Ginsborg *(Exec Creative Dir)*
Lars Jorgensen *(Exec Creative Dir)*
Eric Segal *(Exec Dir-Creative)*
Seth Jacobs *(Grp Dir-Creative)*
Alex Kaplan *(Sr Dir-Art)*
Sarah Collinson *(Acct Dir)*
Ida Gronblom *(Creative Dir)*
Jill Ong *(Bus Dir-Global)*
April Won *(Acct Dir)*
Ji You *(Acct Dir-DICK'S Sporting Goods-P&G)*
Sacha Zivanovic *(Acct Dir)*
Keiji Ando *(Dir-Creative)*
Vivek Bellore *(Dir-Social & Analytics)*
Brian Brydon *(Dir-Social Media Strategy-Diageo)*
Scott Hayes *(Dir-Creative)*
Laura Rowan *(Dir-Strategy-Global)*
Mark Sarosi *(Dir-Art & Design)*
Matt Walton *(Dir-Creative)*
Sarah Yu *(Dir-Art)*
Darus Zahm *(Dir-Comm Strategy)*
Matt Knapp *(Assoc Dir-Creative)*
Carla Curry *(Mgr-Bus Affairs)*
Carmen Cramer *(Acct Supvr)*
Alicia Patton *(Acct Supvr)*
Lisa Taber *(Acct Supvr)*
Libby Wicks *(Acct Supvr)*
Meaghan Fee *(Acct Exec)*
McCrea O'Haire *(Acct Exec)*
Alex Ames *(Jr Copywriter)*

Accounts:
American Express Company
Anheuser-Busch "Made in America", Budweiser, Budweiser Black Crown, Campaign: "A Hero's Welcome" Super Bowl 2014, Campaign: "Believe As One", Campaign: "Brewed The Hard Way", Campaign: "Brotherhood", Campaign: "Eternal Optimism", Campaign: "Grab Some Buds", Campaign: "Lost Dog", Campaign: "Puppy Love" Super Bowl 2014, Campaign: "Rise As One", Campaign: "This Bud's For You", Creative, Super Bowl 2015
At Home Stores LLC Branding
By Lauren Luke Cosmetics
Captain Morgan Campaign: "Dive"
Carhartt, Inc. Campaign: "Move Like You Mean It", Full Swing
The Coca-Cola Company Dasani, Gold Peak
Converse Campaign: "History Made and in the Making", Campaign: "History of the Chuck Taylor", Campaign: "Lunch Money", Campaign: "Made By You", Campaign: "Prom", Campaign: "Ready for More", Campaign: "Young Americans", Chuck II, Chuck Taylor All Star, Chuck Taylor All Star II, Creative, Digital, In-Store, Media, Out-of-Home, Print, Wade 3; 2007
Diageo North America Inc. Campaign: "Dive", Campaign: "Keep Walking", Campaign: "The Gentleman's Wager II", Campaign: "The Gentlemen's Wager", Johnnie Walker (Global Creative Agency of Record), Johnnie Walker Blue Label
Dick's Sporting Goods (Agency of Record) Advertising, Campaign: "Focus and Explode", Campaign: "Choices: Who Will You Be?", Campaign: "Every Pitch", Campaign: "Every Snap", Campaign: "Gifts That Matter", Campaign: "Give A Gift That Matters", Campaign: "Holiday Hoops", Campaign: "Swing Your Swing", Campaign: "The Moment", Campaign: "The Question", Campaign: "Untouchable", Campaign: "You Run by Yourself, but You're Not Alone.", Digital, OOH, Print, Social, Social Media, TV
Diesel Be Stupid Print
Google "Google Glass", Android, Hangouts, Helpouts
Hershey Co Campaign: "Keep on Sucking!", Jolly Rancher, Strategic Projects
Major League Baseball "Ruth: The Joy of Playing Ball", Campaign: "This Is Baseball", Creative, MLB Advanced Media, MLB Network, TV
Marriott Hotel Group
New-New York Life Insurance Company Advertising, Creative
The New York Times Company
Nike
P&G (Agency of Record) Duracell
Panera Bread (Lead Creative Agency) Campaign: "Celebration", Campaign: "Food As It Should Be", Campaign: "Should Be", Online, Outdoor, Radio, Social Media Marketing, TV
Pepsi Lipton Tea Partnership Campaign: "Follow the Leaf", Creative, Digital, Print, Pure Leaf, Website
Renaissance Hotels Campaign: "Live Life to Discover.", Digital
Sony Europe
New-Squarespace (Lead Creative Agency)
Umbro World Cup Promotion

Branches

Anomaly

The Old Ink Factory, 22 St James's Walk, London, EC1R 0AP United Kingdom
Tel.: (44) 207 843 0600
E-Mail: camilla@anomaly.com
Web Site: www.anomaly.com/en/call

Camilla Harrisson *(CEO & Partner)*
Oli Beale *(Partner)*
Alex Holder *(Partner-London)*
Stuart Smith *(Partner)*
Richard Lawson *(Mng Dir)*
Simon Robertson *(Head-Comm Strategy)*
Craig Ainsley *(Creative Dir)*
Renee Hyde *(Acct Dir)*
Ewoudt Boonstra *(Dir-Creative)*
Jenny Hudak *(Recruiter-Creative)*

Accounts:
Anti Tobacco League
Budweiser Campaign: "ToTheDream", Creative
Cancer Research UK (Lead Creative Agency)
Captain Morgan Creative
Converse Desire, Made By Facebook App
New-Diageo plc Campaign: "Joy Will Take You Further", Gordon's Gin (Global Creative), Johnnie Walker
Diesel
Gaydar Brand Identity
New-Lyst (Global Agency of Record) Communications Strategy, Creative, Media Planning; 2015
Sky Campaign: "Billy Bass", Fantasy Football
Thetrainline.com (Lead Creative Agency) Campaign: "I am train", Creative
Umbro
The Vaccines
New-Virgin Trains Campaign: "Be Bound For Glory"

Anomaly

46 Spadina, Toronto, ON M5V 2H8 Canada
Tel.: (647) 547-3440
E-Mail: catalent@anomaly.com
Web Site: www.anomaly.com

Year Founded: 2004

Agency Specializes In: Advertising, Brand Development & Integration, Digital/Interactive, Graphic Design, Media Planning, Social Media

Justin Barocas *(Founder & Partner)*
Jason DeLand *(Founder & Partner)*
Richard Mulder *(Founder & Partner)*
Johnny Vulkan *(Founder & Partner)*
Franke Rodriguez *(CEO & Partner)*
Mike Byrne *(Partner & Chief Creative Officer)*
Stuart Smith *(Partner)*
Ihxel Perez *(Head-Production)*
Kevin Filliter *(Sr Dir-Art)*

Accounts:
Anheuser-Busch InBev Bud Light, Corona: Discover your music
Belgian White
BMW Campaign: "MINI Roller Coaster", Campaign: "NOT NORMAL", Mini
Mexx Canada Inc

ANOROC AGENCY

620 NW St, Raleigh, NC 27603
Tel.: (919) 821-1191
E-Mail: info@anorocagency.com
Web Site: www.anorocagency.com

Year Founded: 1993

Agency Specializes In: Advertising, Brand Development & Integration, Graphic Design, Internet/Web Design, Social Media

Deborah Loercher *(Pres)*
Alex Midgett *(Mng Partner & Dir-Creative)*

Accounts:
VisitTucson.org

ANSIBLE MOBILE

55 5th Ave 16th Fl, New York, NY 10003

Tel.: (212) 444-7486
Web Site: ansiblemobile.com/

Year Founded: 2007

National Agency Associations: 4A's

Agency Specializes In: Advertising, Mobile Marketing, Sponsorship

Angela Steele *(CEO & Mng Dir-Mobile-Global)*
Travis Johnson *(Pres-Global)*
JiYoung Kim *(Sr VP-Strategy & New Solutions)*
Alice Le *(VP & Client Partner)*
Sia Ea *(Sr Dir-Creative)*
Rebekah Ale *(Dir-Product Dev)*
Maile Krauss *(Dir-Bus Dev & Client Rels)*
Katherine Reyes *(Dir-Mobile Strategy & Campaigns)*
Dustin Savel *(Assoc Dir-Strategy & Campaigns)*
Jim Hogerty *(Acct Exec)*
Gary Mu *(Sr Analyst-Digital)*

Accounts:
Intel Corporation 2Nd Generation Intel Core Processors

ANSIRA
(Formerly NSI Marketing Services)
2300 Locust St, Saint Louis, MO 63103
Tel.: (314) 783-2300
Fax: (314) 783-2301
E-Mail: info@ansira.com
Web Site: www.ansira.com

Agency Specializes In: Digital/Interactive, Market Research, Sponsorship, Strategic Planning/Research

Martin Reidy *(Pres & CEO)*
Andy Arnold *(Exec VP-Client Partnership)*
Cornelius McGrath *(Exec VP-HR)*
Sam Monica *(Sr VP & Dir-Creative)*
Amy Asahl *(Sr VP-Trade Promo Mgmt)*
Lauraliisa O'Connor Gudgeon *(Sr VP-Client Svcs)*
Peter Soto *(Sr VP)*
Bryan Ingram *(VP-Digital Svcs)*
Brett Person *(Head-Trade Promo Mgmt & Sr Acct Rep)*
Jennifer Gibbs *(Asst VP)*
Matthew Pijut *(Asst VP)*
Kevin Wyss *(Sr Acct Dir)*
Jenny Gonsior *(Acct Dir)*
Christina Klupe *(Acct Dir)*
Myra Guillermo *(Acct Mgr)*

Accounts:
Acura
American Family Insurance
Anheuser-Busch InBev
Ann Taylor
Baskin-Robbins
Bass Pro Shops
Benihana
BMW
Chrysler
Cisco
Coca-Cola Refreshments USA, Inc.
Cooper Tire
Dave & Buster's
Domino's Pizza
Ford Motor Company
Harley-Davidson
Honda Financial Services
Honda
Hunter Douglas
Infiniti
Jaguar
Jarden Team Sports
Land Rover
Lincoln
Lord & Taylor
Madison Mutual Insurance
Mazda
Mercedes-Benz
Microsoft
Nationwide Insurance
Nestle Purina
The North Face
Rent-A-Center
Six Flags Entertainment Corp.
Solutia
St. Louis Convention & Visitors Commission
Subaru
Suzuki
UniGroup
Wendy's
Zipcar

Branches

Ansira
(Formerly NSI Marketing Services/CoAMS)
35 East Wacker Dr Ste 1100, Chicago, IL 60601
(See Separate Listing)

Ansira
(Formerly RAZOR)
15851 Dallas Pkwy Ste 725, Addison, TX 75001
Tel.: (972) 663-1100
Fax: (972) 663-1300
E-Mail: info@ansira.com
Web Site: www.ansira.com/

Employees: 150
Year Founded: 2003

Agency Specializes In: Sponsorship

Tom Cole *(Chief Dev Officer & Exec VP)*
Tom Millweard *(Exec VP)*
Logan Flatt *(Sr VP-Strategic Plng)*
Lauraliisa Gudgeon *(Sr VP-Client Svcs)*
Ray Rosenbaum *(Sr VP-Insight & Plng)*
John Mathis *(VP-Brdcst)*
Austin Wright *(VP-Strategic Plng)*
Anne Marie Kramer *(Asst VP)*
Katie Costello *(Supvr-Digital Media)*

Accounts:
ABC Radio Networks
Applebee's
Baskin-Robbins
The Cheesecake Factory
Coca-Cola North America
Coca-Cola Refreshments USA, Inc.
Dave & Buster's
Domino's Pizza
Dunkin Donuts
Game Stop
Grand Lux Cafe
Home Choice
Identec
Nestle Purina PetCare Co. Friskies, Mighty Dog, Public Relations, Puppy Chow, Purina, Purina Dog Chow, Purina One, Purina Pro Plan, petcentric.com
Rent-A-Center
Wendy's
Wireless Toys
Zipcar Customer Engagement Marketing

Sq1
(Formerly Square One, Inc.)
1801 N Lamar Ste 375, Dallas, TX 75202
(See Separate Listing)

ANSON-STONER INC.
111 E Fairbanks Ave, Winter Park, FL 32789-7004
Tel.: (407) 629-9484
Fax: (407) 629-9480
E-Mail: info@anson-stoner.com
Web Site: www.anson-stoner.com

E-Mail for Key Personnel:
President: andy@anson-stoner.com
Creative Dir.: tom@anson-stoner.com
Media Dir.: jessica@anson-stoner.com
Public Relations: laura@anson-stoner.com

Employees: 20
Year Founded: 1983

National Agency Associations: 4A's

Agency Specializes In: Advertising, Brand Development & Integration, Broadcast, Cable T.V., Co-op Advertising, Collateral, Consumer Marketing, Corporate Identity, Education, Food Service, Government/Political, Graphic Design, Health Care Services, High Technology, Hispanic Market, Internet/Web Design, Logo & Package Design, Magazines, Marine, Media Buying Services, Medical Products, Newspaper, Print, Production, Public Relations, Radio, Real Estate, Restaurant, Retail, Sales Promotion, Sponsorship, Strategic Planning/Research, T.V., Trade & Consumer Magazines

Andrew Anson *(Pres)*
Tom Macaluso *(Sr VP & Dir-Creative)*
Jessica Roberts *(Sr VP & Dir-Media)*
Justin Bohn *(VP & Dir-Fin)*
Mike Witt *(Sr Dir-Art)*
Karen Madanick *(Dir-Media)*
Megan Gooding *(Acct Supvr)*
Becky Smukall *(Acct Supvr)*
Sally Fritch *(Sr Acct Exec)*
Rosalyn Oquendo *(Media Buyer-Digital)*

Accounts:
Catrike (Public Relations Agency of Record) Brand Strategies, Media Relations, Social Media
Contech Brochure, Stationery
Everglades Boats; 2005
Fields Auto Group (Agency of Record) Creative, Digital, Media Buying, Planning, Strategy, Traditional Media
Florida Department of Health Campaign: "Faces of HIV", HIV/AIDS & Hepatitis Observence Events, PR; 2001
Kennedy Space Center
Orlando Economic Development Commission Digital, Direct Mail, Out-of-Home, Print, Public Relations, Social Media, TV
Pirates Dinner Adventure Campaign: "Food Fight", Campaign: "Pirate Composite"
Seacoast Bank (Agency of Record) Brand Development, Creative, Interactive, Logo, Media, Public Relations, Strategic Planning
Subway Restaurants; Jacksonville; Gainesville; Central Florida; Southwest Florida; 2000
Sun Sports; 2004
Trinchera Ranch Logo
Universal Studios, Inc.
Windjammer Landing Brochure

THE ANT FARM LLC
110 S Fairfax Ave Ste 200, Los Angeles, CA 90036
Tel.: (323) 850-0700
Fax: (323) 850-0777
Web Site: http://www.antfarm.net/

Year Founded: 1968

Agency Specializes In: Advertising, Brand Development & Integration, Digital/Interactive, Graphic Design, Internet/Web Design, Package Design, Print, Production (Ad, Film, Broadcast), Search Engine Optimization, Social Media

Andy Solomon *(Pres & Exec Dir-Creative)*
Rodd Perry *(Co-Pres & Dir-Creative)*
Lisa Riznikove *(Co-Pres & Div Head-Games)*
Scott Cookson *(VP & Dir-Creative)*

Accounts:

Activision "Destiny", Call of Duty, TV
Microsoft Corporation

ANTHEM BRANDING
1000 N St, Boulder, CO 80304
Tel.: (303) 245-8000
E-Mail: info@anthembranding.com
Web Site: www.anthembranding.com

Agency Specializes In: Advertising, Brand Development & Integration, Graphic Design, Internet/Web Design, Logo & Package Design

Pete Burhop *(Principal)*
Dana Bush *(Acct Mgr)*
Jacki Cella *(Acct Mgr)*
Jessica Mulein *(Acct Mgr)*
Anne Robertson *(Acct Mgr)*
Sean Serafini *(Designer)*
Blair Stapp *(Designer)*
Catherine Wenger *(Sr Designer)*
Kim Hollingsworth *(Acct Coord)*

Accounts:
The Kitchen
PeopleForBikes.org
Upslope Brewing Company

ANTHEM WORLDWIDE
537 E Pete Rose Way Ste 100, Cincinnati, OH 45202-3578
Tel.: (513) 784-0066
Fax: (513) 784-0986
Web Site: www.anthemww.com

E-Mail for Key Personnel:
President: sklein@wbk.com

Employees: 45
Year Founded: 1979

National Agency Associations: AAF-APMA WORLDWIDE-DMA-ICOM-PMA

Agency Specializes In: Brand Development & Integration, Business-To-Business, Collateral, Corporate Identity, Direct Response Marketing, Graphic Design, Internet/Web Design, Logo & Package Design, New Product Development, Point of Purchase, Point of Sale, Sales Promotion, Sponsorship

Approx. Annual Billings: $30,000,000

Anne Dean *(VP-Client Integration-Americas Reg)*
Samantha Carlino *(Acct Dir)*
Arthur Brandenburg Van Den Gronden *(Dir-Design Strategy & Growth)*
Elyse Yarnell *(Sr Acct Exec)*

Accounts:
Coca-Cola Refreshments USA, Inc.
E-Mart
Foster
Glaxosmithkline
Heinz
Kellogg's
Kimberly-Clark
Nestle
Pepsico
Procter & Gamble
Red Island
Revlon
Safeway
Scotts Company
SPC Ardmona
Tropicana
Unilever
Zodiac

ANTHEMIC AGENCY
5810 W 3rd St, Los Angeles, CA 90036
Tel.: (323) 464-4745
E-Mail: info@anthemicagency.com
Web Site: www.anthemicagency.com

Year Founded: 2014

Agency Specializes In: Advertising, Brand Development & Integration, Event Planning & Marketing, Print, Promotions, Public Relations, Social Media

Alan Sartirana *(Founder & CEO)*
Kyle Rogers *(VP-Bus Dev)*
Jacqueline Fonseca *(Mktg Dir)*
Angelica Corona *(Acct Mgr)*
Sarah Chavey *(Mgr-PR)*
Natalie Anderson *(Acct Exec)*

Accounts:
Fluence Inc
John Lennon Educational Tour Bus
New-Lucky Strike Entertainment Public Relations
Planes Trains & Automobiles

ANTHOLOGIE, INC.
207 E Buffalo St Ste 643, Milwaukee, WI 53202
Tel.: (414) 277-7743
E-Mail: info@anthologieworks.com
Web Site: www.anthologieworks.com

Year Founded: 2011

Agency Specializes In: Advertising, Business-To-Business, Communications, Digital/Interactive

Jeff McClellan *(Pres & Writer)*
Kelly Steelman *(VP & Dir-Creative)*
Ben Baker *(VP-Ops & Client Svcs)*
Mark Kuehn *(Dir-Creative Strategy)*
Monica Durant *(Designer)*

Accounts:
Johnson Controls, Inc.

ANTHONY BARADAT & ASSOCIATES
1235 Coral Way Ste 200, Miami, FL 33145
Tel.: (305) 859-8989
Fax: (305) 859-8919
E-Mail: info@abaadvertising.com
Web Site: www.abaadvertising.com

Employees: 10
Year Founded: 1994

Agency Specializes In: Advertising, Sponsorship

Anthony Baradat *(Pres)*
Maria Elena Baradat *(Dir-Creative)*
Shawn M. Smith *(Dir-Digital Media)*
Jackelyn Pericich *(Sr Acct Exec)*
Aurora Estrada *(Sr Specialist-Digital)*
Alina Hernandez *(Acct Exec)*
Rebecca Cuervo *(Media Buyer)*

Accounts:
Air Jamaica
Beacon Council
Brickell Motors
Caterpillar
Efficient Laboratories
Ertexting
HCA Holdings Inc.
Jackson Health Plans
Personalized Power Systems
Pollo Tropical
Relax the Back
South Florida Commuter Services
University of Miami

ANTHONY THOMAS ADVERTISING
380 S Main St, Akron, OH 44311
Tel.: (330) 253-6888
Fax: (330) 253-7000
E-Mail: info@anthonythomas.com
Web Site: www.anthonythomas.com

Employees: 8

Agency Specializes In: Brand Development & Integration, Business-To-Business, Communications, Digital/Interactive, Graphic Design, Internet/Web Design, Logo & Package Design, Print, Sales Promotion

Tony Gioglio *(Owner)*
Daniel Sferra *(Partner)*
Chris Surak *(Dir-Art)*
Renee Volchko *(Designer)*

Accounts:
Bronx Taylor Wilson
Duplicolor
Tri-Flow

ANTIDOTE 360
160 Varick St, New York, NY 10013
Tel.: (440) 668-2622
Web Site: antidote360.com/

Agency Specializes In: Advertising, Digital/Interactive, Public Relations, Social Media

Jennifer Deutsch *(COO)*
Aaron Kwittken *(CMO)*
Kathy McCuskey *(Chief Strategy Officer)*

Accounts:
Gabriella's Kitchen SkinnyPasta
HealthSpot

ANTITHESIS ADVERTISING
72 Cascade Dr, Rochester, NY 14614
Tel.: (585) 232-7740
Web Site: www.antithesisadvertising.com

Year Founded: 2005

Agency Specializes In: Advertising, Brand Development & Integration, Broadcast, Collateral, Corporate Identity, Logo & Package Design, Print

Kent Joshpe *(Co-Owner & Dir-Creative)*
Larry Kleehammer *(Co-Owner & Dir-Client Svcs)*
Kurt Jaeckel *(Acct Dir)*
Rebekah Frischkorn *(Acct Exec)*

Accounts:
Americas Best Value Inn
Food Bank of the Southern Tier
URMC Stories Arieona

ANTONWEST ADVERTISING
1654 San Marco Blvd, Jacksonville, FL 32207
Tel.: (904) 701-4140
E-Mail: info@antonwest.com
Web Site: www.antonwest.com

Employees: 8
Year Founded: 2013

Agency Specializes In: Advertising, Brand Development & Integration, Digital/Interactive, Media Buying Services, Media Planning, Public Relations, Social Media

John Fricks *(Pres)*
Susan Waldeck *(Sr VP-Media & Ops)*
Jefferson Rall *(Exec Dir-Creative)*
Andy Gosendi *(Sr Dir-Art)*
Colin Barnes *(Dir-Art)*
Priscilla Brooke *(Mgr-Social Media)*

Accounts:
Agnes Agatha
Spadaro
Vac-Con

ANYTIME MARKETING GROUP
2345 Bering Dr, Houston, TX 77057
Tel.: (832) 203-5371
E-Mail: info@anytimemarketinggroup.com
Web Site: www.anytimemarketinggroup.com

Year Founded: 2014

Agency Specializes In: Advertising, Digital/Interactive, Internet/Web Design, Media Buying Services, Media Planning, Media Relations, Outdoor, Print, Radio, Social Media

Jorge Suarez *(Principal)*

Accounts:
Peoples Group Realty & Mortgage

AOR, INC.
1345 S Bdwy, Denver, CO 80210
Tel.: (303) 871-9700
Web Site: www.thinkaor.com

Year Founded: 1992

Agency Specializes In: Advertising, Brand Development & Integration, Digital/Interactive, Internet/Web Design, Search Engine Optimization

Derek Newcom *(CEO & Principal)*
Matt Keeney *(Acct Svcs Dir)*
Tom Comber *(Dir-Art)*
Sarah Fox *(Dir-Bus Ops)*
Jessie Woodhead *(Assoc Dir-Creative & Copywriter)*
Katie Lau *(Acct Exec)*
Elena Mlotkowski *(Acct Exec)*
Alyssa Peters *(Designer)*
Kelsey Meyd *(Acct Coord)*
Zach Thomas *(Jr Designer)*
Shannon Torphy *(Jr Designer)*

Accounts:
Avnet Technology Solutions
Hearst Media Services

APCO WORLDWIDE
700 12th St NW Ste 800, Washington, DC 20005
Tel.: (202) 778-1000
Fax: (202) 466-6002
E-Mail: information@apcoworldwide.com
Web Site: www.apcoworldwide.com

Employees: 658
Year Founded: 1984

National Agency Associations: COPF

Agency Specializes In: Advertising, Advertising Specialties, Agriculture, Asian Market, Automotive, Aviation & Aerospace, Brand Development & Integration, Broadcast, Business-To-Business, Collateral, Communications, Consulting, Consumer Goods, Consumer Marketing, Corporate Communications, Corporate Identity, Cosmetics, Crisis Communications, Customer Relationship Management, Digital/Interactive, Direct Response Marketing, E-Commerce, Education, Electronic Media, Entertainment, Environmental, Event Planning & Marketing, Exhibit/Trade Shows, Fashion/Apparel, Financial, Government/Political, Graphic Design, Health Care Services, High Technology, Industrial, Information Technology, International, Internet/Web Design, Investor Relations, Legal Services, Leisure, Logo & Package Design, Market Research, Media Buying Services, Media Planning, Media Relations, Media Training, Medical Products, Multimedia, New Product Development, New Technologies, Package Design, Pharmaceutical, Planning & Consultation, Podcasting, Print, Production, Production (Print), Public Relations, Publicity/Promotions, Radio, Real Estate, Restaurant, Retail, Seniors' Market, Social Marketing/Nonprofit, Strategic Planning/Research, Technical Advertising, Transportation, Travel & Tourism

Approx. Annual Billings: $120,345,400

Margery Kraus *(Founder & Chm)*
Neal M. Cohen *(Vice Chm & Pres-Global Client Strategy)*
Evan Kraus *(Pres & Mng Dir-Ops)*
Denise Teeling *(CFO)*
Courtney Piron *(Chm-US Health Care & Exec Dir)*
Wayne L. Pines *(Pres-Health Care)*
Alicia Peterson Clark *(Deputy Mng Dir)*
Bill Dalbec *(Deputy Mng Dir-APCO Insight)*
Kent Jarrell *(Exec VP)*
Charles Krause *(Sr VP)*
Ellen Mignoni *(Sr VP)*
Karen Buerkle *(Mng Dir-APCO Insight)*
Chris McCannell *(VP, Head-Washington Fin Svcs Practice & Dir-Govt Rels)*
Gadi Dechter *(Head-Pub Affairs)*
Don Bonker *(Exec Dir)*
Nick Ashooh *(Sr Dir-Corp & Exec Comm)*
Becky Boles *(Sr Dir-Digital Strategy)*
Mara Hedgecoth *(Sr Dir-Global Mktg & Comm)*
Michael Hotra *(Sr Dir)*
Bill Pierce *(Sr Dir)*
Jim Quindlen *(Sr Dir-Creative & Digital)*
Tim Roemer *(Sr Dir)*
Jack Lanza *(Dir-Creative)*
Melanie Asherman *(Designer-Production)*
Erin McNally *(Graphic Designer-Bus Dev)*

Accounts:
Albania Campaign: "Go Your Own Way", Digital, Public Relations, Short Films, Social Media
BlackBerry
China Ocean Shipping Company
Clinton Global Initiative
eBay
IKEA
Johnson Controls
Mars
Microsoft
Tesco
U.S. Travel Association

Branches:

APCO Worldwide
Poppelsdorfer Allee 114, 53115 Bonn, Germany
Tel.: (49) 228 60 48 518
Fax: (49) 228 60 48 522
E-Mail: germany@apcoworldwide.com
Web Site: www.apcoworldwide.com

Employees: 10
Year Founded: 2001

Martina Tydecks *(Mng Dir)*

APCO Worldwide
DIFC Ctr The Gate E Gate Fl 15 Office 13, Dubai, United Arab Emirates
Tel.: (971) 4 365 0410
Fax: (971) 4 361 1999
E-Mail: arabregion@apcoworldwide.com
Web Site: www.apcoworldwide.com

Mamoon Sbeih *(Mng Dir)*
Nic Labuschagne *(Sr Dir-Strategy)*
Tamara Saeb *(Sr Dir)*
Tarek Sakik *(Dir-Arab Reg)*
Claire Lawson *(Assoc Dir)*

Apco Worldwide
(Formerly JiWin)
Al Thuraya Tower 1st Floor, 39333, Dubai Media City, Dubai, United Arab Emirates
Tel.: (971) 4 361 3333
Fax: (971) 4 368 8001
Web Site: www.apcoworldwide.com

Employees: 60
Year Founded: 2006

Agency Specializes In: Business-To-Business, Corporate Communications, Crisis Communications, Event Planning & Marketing, Investor Relations, Media Relations, Public Relations, Publicity/Promotions

Mamoon Sbeih *(Mng Dir)*
Kerry Irwin *(Sr Dir & Head-Global Client-Masdar)*
Rishi Talwalker *(Assoc Dir)*

Accounts:
Dubai Pearl
Enpark
International Media Production Zone
Landmark Group
Merck
Noor Islamic Bank
Sae Institute
Smart City
Sony
Tatweer
TECOM Investments Dubai Internet City
The Walk
Young Arab Leaders

APCO Worldwide
15 rue de Marignan, 75008 Paris, France
Tel.: (33) 1 44 94 8666
Fax: (33) 1 44 94 8668
E-Mail: paris@apcoworldwide.com
Web Site: www.apcoworldwide.com

Employees: 20
Year Founded: 1996

Nicolas Bouvier *(Chm-Europe & Mng Dir-France)*
Veronique Ferjou *(Deputy Mng Dir)*
Flora Monsaingeon *(Head-Corp Responsibility Practice-Paris & Dir)*
Mike Hotra *(Sr Dir-Washington)*
Anne Kuentz-Lafourcade *(Assoc Dir)*
Pazanne Le Cour Grandmaison *(Assoc Dir)*

Accounts:
Novartis

APCO Worldwide
Kontorhaus Mitte Friedrichstrasse 186, 10117 Berlin, Germany
Tel.: (49) 30 59 000 2010
Fax: (49) 30 59 000 2020
E-Mail: germany@apcoworldwide.com
Web Site: www.apcoworldwide.com

Employees: 9
Year Founded: 2000

Robert Ardelt *(Deputy Mng Dir)*
Isabel Kassabian *(Deputy Mng Dir)*
Martina Tydecks *(Exec Dir)*
Christoph Mielke *(Assoc Dir)*

APCO Worldwide
90 Long Acre, London, WC2E 9RA United Kingdom
Tel.: (44) 207 526 3600

Fax: (44) 20 7526 3699
E-Mail: dmurphy@apcoworldwide.com
Web Site: www.apcoworldwide.com

Employees: 62
Year Founded: 1995

Brad Staples *(CEO)*
James Acheson-Gray *(Mng Dir-London)*
Geoff Beattie *(Exec Dir-Corp Affairs)*
Jon Chandler *(Dir-EMEA)*
Steven King *(Dir)*
Tamsin Richmond-Watson *(Dir)*
Cleopatra Van De Winkel *(Dir-Europe)*

Accounts:
DEK International Global communications, Marketing

APCO Worldwide
11 Leontievsky Pereulok, Moscow, 125009 Russia
Tel.: (7) 495 937 5525
Fax: (7) 495 937 5526
E-Mail: amezhueva@apcoworldwide.com
Web Site: www.apcoworldwide.com

Employees: 11
Year Founded: 1988

Alexandra Boldyreva *(Assoc Dir)*

APCO Worldwide
Office No 433 Level 4 Dynasty Business Park A Wing, Andheri Kurla Road Andheri E, Mumbai, 400059 India
Tel.: (91) 22 4030 9380
Fax: (91) 22 4030 9199
E-Mail: mumbai.newdelhi@apcoworldwide.com
Web Site: www.apcoworldwide.com/about-us/locations/location/Mumbai

Employees: 3

Sukanti Ghosh *(Mng Dir)*
Rameesh Kailasam *(Deputy Mng Dir & Sr Dir)*
Shankar Narayanan *(Sr Dir)*
Amrita De Aiyer *(Assoc Dir)*
Anika Talwar *(Assoc Dir-Corp Advisory)*
Sanjoy Saha *(Mgr-Acctg)*

Accounts:
Kerala Government Public Relations

APCO Worldwide
255 Albert Street Suite 703, Ottawa, ON K1P 6A9 Canada
Tel.: (613) 786-7600
Fax: (613) 565-1937
E-Mail: hstorgaard@apcoworldwide.com
Web Site: www.apcoworldwide.com

Employees: 11
Year Founded: 1997

Sheila Roy *(VP)*

APCO Worldwide
16th Floor NCI Tower No 1 Jianguomenwai Avenue, Chaoyang District, Beijing, 100022 China
Tel.: (86) 10 6505 5128
Fax: (86) 10 6505 5258
E-Mail: beijing@apcoworldwide.com
Web Site: www.apcoworldwide.com

Employees: 50
Year Founded: 1997

Amy Wendholt *(Mng Dir)*
Jennifer Hart *(Deputy Mng Dir)*
Teresa Lu *(Assoc Dir)*
Lusha Niu *(Assoc Dir)*

APCO Worldwide
19/F Cambridge House Taikoo Place, 979 Kings Road, Central, China (Hong Kong)
Tel.: (852) 2866 2313
Fax: (852) 2866 1917
E-Mail: hongkong@apcoworldwide.com
Web Site: www.apcoworldwide.com

Employees: 25
Year Founded: 1997

Larry E. Snoddon *(Vice Chm)*
Amy Wendholt *(Mng Dir)*
Garry Walsh *(Mng Dir-Southeast Asia)*
Kennon Tam *(Assoc Dir)*
Mark Michelson *(Sr Counselor)*

Accounts:
Samsung Electronics

APCO Worldwide
10th Floor World Trade Center Jl Jend Sudirman Kav 29-31, Jakarta, 12920 Indonesia
Tel.: (62) 21 5296 4611
Fax: (62) 21 5296 4610
E-Mail: jakarta@apcoworldwide.com
Web Site: www.apcoworldwide.com

Employees: 19
Year Founded: 2000

Yuli Ismartono *(Pres)*
Putri Dewanti *(Deputy Mng Dir)*

APCO Worldwide
47 Rue Montoyer 5th Floor, 1000 Brussels, Belgium
Tel.: (32) 2 645 98 11
Fax: (32) 2 645 98 12
E-Mail: brussels@apcoworldwide.com
Web Site: www.apcoworldwide.com

Employees: 51
Year Founded: 1995

Agency Specializes In: Communications, Public Relations

Claire Boussagol *(Mng Dir)*
James Lovegrove *(Sr Dir)*
David Bushong *(Dir)*
Rasika Krishna-Schmid *(Dir-User Experience & Digital Strategy)*
Amelie Coulet *(Assoc Dir)*
Brian Carroll *(Mgr-Bus Dev-EMEA)*

APCO Worldwide
Suites 2102-2103 CITIC Square, 1168 Nanjing Road West, Shanghai, 200041 China
Tel.: (86) 21 5298 4668
Fax: (86) 21 5298 4669
E-Mail: shanghai@apcochina.com
Web Site: www.apcoworldwide.com

Employees: 16
Year Founded: 1999

Linda Du *(Mng Dir)*
Teresa Lu *(Assoc Dir)*

APCO Worldwide
No 3 Xing An Rd Pearl River New Town, Guangzhou, 510623 China
Tel.: (86) 20 3825 1955
Fax: (86) 20 3825 1016
E-Mail: guangzhou@apcoworldwide.com
Web Site: www.apcoworldwide.com/china

Year Founded: 2006

Margery Kraus *(Founder & Exec Chm)*
Larry Snoddon *(Vice Chm)*
Philip Fraser *(CIO)*
Neal M. Cohen *(CEO-American & Bus Dir-Global)*
Judith S. Sapir *(Sr VP & Gen Counsel)*

APCO Worldwide
Unit 12 4/F Saigon Centre 65 Le Loi, District 1, Ho Chi Minh City, Vietnam
Tel.: (84) 8 821 7895
E-Mail: hochiminh@apcoworldwide.com
Web Site: www.apcoworldwide.com

Employees: 4
Year Founded: 1998

Garry Walsh *(Mng Dir-Southeast Asia)*

APCO Worldwide
1201 K St Ste 1200, Sacramento, CA 95814-3953
Tel.: (916) 554-3400
Fax: (916) 554-3434
E-Mail: jhermoci@apcoworldwide.com
Web Site: www.apcoworldwide.com

Employees: 12
Year Founded: 1996

National Agency Associations: COPF

Jose R. Hermocillo *(Mng Dir-Sacramento)*
Emily Johnson *(VP & Dir-Pub Affairs)*
Jerry Azevedo *(Sr Dir)*
Bill Romanelli *(Sr Dir)*

APCO Worldwide
360 Park Ave S, New York, NY 10010
Tel.: (212) 300-1800
Fax: (212) 300-1819
Web Site: www.apcoworldwide.com

Employees: 30
Year Founded: 2003

National Agency Associations: COPF

Marc Johnson *(VP-Digital Strategy)*
Stig Albinus *(Head-Practice-Health Care & Sr Dir)*
Jeffrey Zelkowitz *(Head-Global Fin Practice & Sr Dir)*
Nicholas Ashooh *(Sr Dir-Corp & Exec Comm)*
Eliot Hoff *(Sr Dir)*
Liza Olsen *(Sr Dir)*
John Dudzinsky *(Dir)*
Jeff Porter *(Dir-Digital Strategy)*
Howard Pulchin *(Dir-Creative Strategy & Community-Global)*

Accounts:
China Ocean Shipping Company (COSCO)
European Express Association
Ford's Theatre Society
Johnson Controls
Medicines for Malaria Venture
Mercedes-Benz
Microsoft
Procter & Gamble LLC
U.S. Travel Association
WorldCom, Inc.

APCO Worldwide
520 Pike St Ste 1001, Seattle, WA 98101
Tel.: (206) 224-4340
Fax: (206) 224-4344
E-Mail: seattle@apcoworldwide.com
Web Site: www.apcoworldwide.com

Employees: 13
Year Founded: 1997

National Agency Associations: COPF

Evan Kraus *(Pres & Mng Dir-Ops)*
Denise Teeling *(CFO & Exec Dir)*
Alicia Peterson Clark *(Deputy Mng Dir-Washington DC)*
Pete Wentz *(Exec VP)*
Tina-Marie Adams *(Mng Dir-Chicago)*
Garry Walsh *(Mng Dir-Southeast Asia)*
Maggie Brown *(Head-Energy & Clean Tech Practice-Global & Exec Dir)*
Martina Tydecks *(Exec Dir-Intl)*
Kristi England *(Sr Dir)*

StrawberryFrog
60 Madison Ave, New York, NY 10010
(See Separate Listing)

API BROADCAST ADVERTISING
2501 W 91st St, Leawood, KS 66206
Tel.: (913) 451-3884
Fax: (913) 451-1783

Employees: 1
Year Founded: 1982

Agency Specializes In: Broadcast, Consumer Marketing, Consumer Publications, Radio, Retail, T.V.

Approx. Annual Billings: $1,000,000

Breakdown of Gross Billings by Media: Audio/Visual: 10%; Brdcst.: 5%; Cable T.V.: 4%; Production: 15%; Radio: 33%; T.V.: 33%

Gary A. White *(Pres)*

APOLLO INTERACTIVE, INC.
139 Illinois St, El Segundo, CA 90245-4312
Tel.: (310) 836-9777
Fax: (424) 238-4000
Toll Free: (800) 599-7499
E-Mail: info@apollointeractive.com
Web Site: www.apollointeractive.com

Employees: 40
Year Founded: 1995

Agency Specializes In: Digital/Interactive, Direct Response Marketing, Internet/Web Design, Sponsorship

Approx. Annual Billings: $15,500,000

Breakdown of Gross Billings by Media: D.M.: $5,000,000; Internet Adv.: $9,000,000; Worldwide Web Sites: $1,500,000

Richard Balue *(Owner & CTO)*
Matthew J. Beshear *(Mng Dir)*
Mike Ranshaw *(Mng Dir)*
Andrew Shevin *(VP-Bus Dev)*
Erik Brannon *(Grp Acct Dir)*
Mike Parrish *(Dir-Tech)*
Greg Sher *(Dir-Media)*
Ann Song *(Dir-Partner Rels)*

Accounts:
Curves; 2004
Extraco Banks
VisionWorks

Branch

Apollo Interactive-Dallas
Republic Ctr 325 N Saint Paul St Ste 1575, Dallas, TX 75201
Tel.: (214) 580-2021
Fax: (214) 580-2026
E-Mail: wade@apollointeractive.com
Web Site: apollointeractive.com

Employees: 12

Agency Specializes In: Sponsorship

Matthew J Beshear *(Mng Dir)*
David Bohline *(COO)*
Josh Loinette *(Acct Dir)*
Jason Oliver *(Acct Dir)*
Brittany Sosa *(Acct Mgr)*

Accounts:
Anthem Inc
California Pizza Kitchen
Curves International Inc.
Extraco Banks
EyeMasters
Johnny Rockets
Kellogg's
Smith + Noble
Visionworks of America, Inc.

APPLE BOX STUDIOS
1243 Penn Ave 2nd Fl, Pittsburgh, PA 15222
Tel.: (412) 642-3971
Fax: (412) 642-2580
E-Mail: info@appleboxs.com
Web Site: www.appleboxstudios.com

Year Founded: 2002

Agency Specializes In: Advertising, Graphic Design, Internet/Web Design, Media Buying Services, Social Media

Thad Ciechanowski *(VP-Motion Pictures)*
Michael M. Kadrie *(VP-Interactive)*
Dan Brettholle *(Dir-Art)*
Dan Filipek *(Dir-Production & Ops)*
Andrea Short *(Client Svcs Mgr)*
Lisa Kefalos *(Acct Exec)*
Kirk Peters *(Designer-Interactive)*

Accounts:
J. Francis Company

APPLETON CREATIVE, INC.
539 Delaney Ave, Orlando, FL 32801
Tel.: (407) 246-0092
E-Mail: info@appletoncreative.com
Web Site: www.appletoncreative.com

Employees: 11

Agency Specializes In: Advertising, Brand Development & Integration, Corporate Identity, Internet/Web Design, Logo & Package Design, Print, Public Relations

Revenue: $1,200,000

Diana LaRue *(Owner & Pres)*
Michael Speltz *(Principal & VP)*
Amy Wise *(VP-Mktg & Client Rels)*
Dolly Sanborn *(Sr Dir-Art)*
Jamie Kruger *(Strategist-Web & Specialist-Social Mktg)*

Accounts:
SPCA of Central Florida
Yogen Fruz (Creative Agency of Record) Bloggers, Calendar, Content Creation, Press Releasers, Public Relations, Social Media

AQUA MARKETING & COMMUNICATIONS INC.
100 2nd Ave S Ste 302-S, Saint Petersburg, FL 33701
Tel.: (727) 687-4670
E-Mail: info@welcometoaqua.com
Web Site: www.welcometoaqua.com

Year Founded: 2011

Agency Specializes In: Advertising, Brand Development & Integration, Digital/Interactive, Public Relations, Radio, Social Media

Dave Di Maggio *(Pres)*
Thom Hart *(Sr Art Dir)*
David Wilson *(Mgr-Client Svcs)*
Fran Rinna *(Acct Exec)*

Accounts:
Chiles Restaurant Group
City of Dunedin
Pelican Bay
TradeWinds Island Resorts

AQUARIUS SPORTS & ENTERTAINMENT
8171 Maple Lawn Blvd Ste 350, Fulton, MD 20759
Tel.: (301) 604-2606
Web Site: www.aquarius-se.com

Employees: 8
Year Founded: 2007

Agency Specializes In: Advertising, Consulting, Entertainment, Hospitality, Market Research, Media Relations, Sponsorship

Marc Bluestein *(Founder & Pres)*
Jody Bennett *(Sr VP)*
Sara Blum *(VP-Fin & Ops)*
David O'Connor *(VP-Fin & Ops)*
Shauna Smith *(VP-Client Svcs)*
Eric Goldscher *(Client Svcs Dir)*
Kerri Hadden *(Sr Mgr-Client Svc)*
Kelsey Evans *(Sr Coord-Client Svcs)*

Accounts:
New-AAA
RCN Corporation Internet Services, Sponsorship

AR MEDIA
601 W 26th St Ste 810, New York, NY 10001
Tel.: (212) 739-5500
Fax: (212) 739-5800
E-Mail: gavin@arnewyork.com
Web Site: www.arnewyork.com

Employees: 45
Year Founded: 1997

Agency Specializes In: Advertising, Brand Development & Integration, Business-To-Business, Collateral, Corporate Communications, Corporate Identity, Direct Response Marketing, Entertainment, Fashion/Apparel, Graphic Design, In-Store Advertising, Logo & Package Design, Magazines, Newspaper, Newspapers & Magazines, Out-of-Home Media, Outdoor, Point of Purchase, Point of Sale, Print, Retail, T.V., Trade & Consumer Magazines

David Israel *(Exec Dir-Creative)*
Stephanie Sills *(Acct Dir)*
Jennifer Alfson *(Dir-Creative)*
Giulia Cappabianca-Moore *(Dir-Post Production)*
Ej Cho *(Dir-Art)*
Alex Delgado *(Dir-Creative)*
Satian Pengsathapon *(Dir-Creative)*
Lindsay Yellin *(Dir-Art-Revlon)*
Jodie Laczko *(Assoc Dir-Creative)*
Christopher Romney *(Assoc Dir-Creative)*

Accounts:
Asprey

Baby Phat
Elie Tahari
ELLE Publishing Group ELLE Accessories
Flag Luxury Properties St. Regis Temonos Villas, Anguilla
Gap Inc. Banana Republic
Harlem RBI
Jimmy Choo
Jones Group, Inc. Anne Klein, Jones New York
MyPublisher; Valhalla, NY (Agency of Record)
Oxford Financial group
The Surrey Hotel

AR NEW YORK

601 W 26th St No 810, New York, NY 10001
Tel.: (212) 739-5500
Fax: (212) 739-5800
E-Mail: info@arnewyork.com
Web Site: www.arnewyork.com

Year Founded: 1996

Agency Specializes In: Advertising, Brand Development & Integration, Broadcast, Digital/Interactive, Package Design, Sponsorship

Raul Martinez *(Founder & Chief Creative Officer)*
Alex Gonzalez *(Co-Founder & Exec Dir-Creative)*
Dianne desRoches *(CEO & Principal)*
David Israel *(Exec Dir-Creative)*
Giulia Cappabianca-Moore *(Dir-Post Production)*
Diane DeLisa *(Dir-Brdcst Bus Affairs)*
Satian Pengsathapon *(Dir-Creative)*
DEBORAH NALL *(Sr Mgr-Post Production)*
Ari Fund *(Acct Supvr)*

Accounts:
Carlo Pazolini
DFS
Jimmy Choo
Lands' End Campaign: "How to Spring"
Marina Rinaldi
Revlon, Inc.
Vogue Magazine

ARAGON ADVERTISING

7036 Nansen St, Forest Hills, NY 11375
Tel.: (718) 575-1815
Fax: (718) 544-0757
E-Mail: info@aragonadvertising.com
Web Site: www.aragonadvertising.com

Employees: 5
Year Founded: 1997

Agency Specializes In: Advertising, Hispanic Market

Michelle S. Aragon *(Owner)*
Alex Barrett *(Mgr-Affiliate)*
Connor Ramage *(Mgr-Affiliate)*
Trevor Lombaer *(Media Buyer)*

Accounts:
Alka-Seltzer
Bayer
Daly Law Center
IPP
Sport & Health Clubs

ARC INTERMEDIA

1150 1st Ave Ste 501, King of Prussia, PA 19406
Tel.: (610) 225-1100
Toll Free: (888) 203-6369
Web Site: www.arcintermedia.com

Year Founded: 2009

David Sonn *(Pres & Dir-Strategy)*
Matthew Ulmer *(Client Svcs Dir)*
Mike Maier *(Dir-Interactive)*
Ron Sansone *(Dir-Search & Online Mktg)*
Catherine Scanes *(Mgr-Inbound Mktg)*
Patrick Coyne *(Strategist-Search)*

Accounts:
ACTS Retirement-Life Communities, Inc.

ARCADE CREATIVE GROUP

550 Madison Ave 29th Fl, New York, NY 10022
Tel.: (212) 833-7585
Web Site: www.arcadecg.com

Year Founded: 2009

Agency Specializes In: Advertising, Digital/Interactive, Internet/Web Design, Media Planning, Strategic Planning/Research

Chris Austopchuk *(Sr VP & Dir-Creative)*
Kyle Sherwin *(Sr VP-Strategy, Accts & Media)*
Sam Erickson *(Head-Production-Arcade Productions)*
Al Lorelli *(Sr Project Mgr-Integrated Media & Producer-Print & Digital)*
Sheri Lee *(Dir-Creative)*
Eric Slovin *(Dir-Creative)*
Peter Bloom *(Media Planner)*

Accounts:
Metropolitan Transportation Authority

ARCANA ACADEMY

13323 Washington Blvd Ste 301, Los Angeles, CA 90066
Tel.: (310) 279-5024
Fax: (310) 943-2466
Web Site: www.arcanaacademy.com

Employees: 15
Year Founded: 2011

Agency Specializes In: Above-the-Line, Advertising, Advertising Specialties, Affiliate Marketing, Affluent Market, African-American Market, Agriculture, Arts, Asian Market, Automotive, Bilingual Market, Brand Development & Integration, Branded Entertainment, Broadcast, Business-To-Business, Cable T.V., Children's Market, Co-op Advertising, Collateral, College, Consumer Goods, Consumer Marketing, Consumer Publications, Content, Corporate Communications, Corporate Identity, Cosmetics, Customer Relationship Management, Digital/Interactive, Direct Response Marketing, Direct-to-Consumer, Education, Electronic Media, Electronics, Engineering, Entertainment, Environmental, Event Planning & Marketing, Exhibit/Trade Shows, Experience Design, Fashion/Apparel, Financial, Food Service, Gay & Lesbian Market, Government/Political, Graphic Design, Health Care Services, Hospitality, Household Goods, Identity Marketing, Industrial, Information Technology, Integrated Marketing, International, Internet/Web Design, Investor Relations, Legal Services, Leisure, Local Marketing, Logo & Package Design, Luxury Products, Magazines, Marine, Medical Products, Merchandising, Mobile Marketing, Multimedia, New Product Development, New Technologies, Newspaper, Newspapers & Magazines, Out-of-Home Media, Outdoor, Package Design, Pets , Planning & Consultation, Point of Sale, Print, Production, Production (Ad, Film, Broadcast), Promotions, Publishing, Radio, Real Estate, Recruitment, Regional, Retail, Sales Promotion, Seniors' Market, Social Marketing/Nonprofit, Social Media, South Asian Market, Sports Market, Stakeholders, Strategic Planning/Research, Sweepstakes, T.V., Technical Advertising, Teen Market, Trade & Consumer Magazines, Transportation, Travel & Tourism, Tween Market, Urban Market, Viral/Buzz/Word of Mouth, Web (Banner Ads, Pop-ups, etc.), Women's Market

Approx. Annual Billings: $3,000,000

Lee Walters *(Mng Partner & Dir-Art)*
Shane Hutton *(Mng Partner & Copywriter)*
Jessica Darke *(Producer-Agency & Client Liaison)*
Lorene Grinberg *(Dir-Ops)*
Agustin Sanchez *(Copywriter)*
Rebecca Sun *(Designer)*

Accounts:
New-Hammitt Luxury Handbags; 2011
KIBO Active & Leisurewear; 2012
New-KILZ Paint & Primer; 2014

ARCANE

(Formerly Rare)
1812 4 Street SW, Ste 601, Calgary, AB T2S 1W1 Canada
Tel.: (403) 879-9954
Web Site: arcane.ws

Employees: 47

Agency Specializes In: Brand Development & Integration, Communications, Consulting, Graphic Design, Internet/Web Design, Multimedia, Production, Strategic Planning/Research

Revenue: $4,665,990

Franca Schulte *(Office Mgr)*

Accounts:
Alberta Beef Producers
Felesky Flynn LLP
Harmony Park Developments
Heritage Park
iMedia Communications, Inc.
Medallion Development Corporation
NAPA Auto Parts
Remington Development Corporation
Royal Tyrrell Museum
Royal University Hospital Foundation
Science Alberta Foundation
Shell Canada
TELUS
Travel Alberta

ARCHER COMMUNICATIONS, INC.

252 Alexander St, Rochester, NY 14607-2515
Tel.: (585) 461-1570
Fax: (585) 461-5313
E-Mail: info@archercom.com
Web Site: www.archercom.com

E-Mail for Key Personnel:
President: jlennox@archercom.com

Employees: 10
Year Founded: 1997

National Agency Associations: ADFED-PRSA

Agency Specializes In: Advertising, Business-To-Business, Collateral, Corporate Communications, Digital/Interactive, Direct Response Marketing, Exhibit/Trade Shows, Graphic Design, Internet/Web Design, Logo & Package Design, Print, Public Relations, Retail, Strategic Planning/Research

Jeff Lennox *(CEO)*
Carrie Tschetter *(VP & Client Svcs Dir)*
Brandon Capwell *(VP & Dir-Web Tech)*
Joe Lennon *(Sr Dir-Art)*
Matt Drew *(Dir-Strategic Mktg)*
Joe Garrett *(Dir-Info Security)*
Kelly P. Mirsky *(Dir-Internal Comm)*
Jackie Anderson *(Mgr-Media Rels-Global)*
Joelle Steeves *(Mgr-Digital Mktg)*
Adam Sisson *(Specialist-SEO & Copywriter)*

Shawna Smith *(Coord-Acct & Mktg)*

THE ARCHER GROUP
233 N King St, Wilmington, DE 19801
Tel.: (302) 429-9120
Fax: (302) 429-8720
E-Mail: mderins@archer-group.com
Web Site: www.archer-group.com

Employees: 50

Agency Specializes In: Advertising, Digital/Interactive, Email, Search Engine Optimization, Strategic Planning/Research

Michael Derins *(Mng Dir & Principal)*
Tim Mihok *(CFO)*
Joseph M. DeCicco *(VP-Ops)*
Jen Spofford *(VP-Client Svc)*
Justin Silva *(Dir-Social Mktg)*
Taylor Crawford *(Acct Supvr)*
Gina Szczuka *(Acct Supvr)*
Justin Beebe *(Coord-Media)*
Todd Miller *(Chief Experience Officer)*

Accounts:
Buccini/Pollin Group, Inc. Interactive Web Site
March of Dimes (Delaware Chapter)
Preservation Initiatives Inc. Interactive Web Site
Thomas Jefferson University Hospitals; Philadelphia, PA Interactive Web Site
Wawa Inc. Interactive Web Site, Online Media

ARCHER MALMO
65 Union Ave Ste 500, Memphis, TN 38103-5137
Tel.: (901) 523-2000
Toll Free: (800) 535-8943
Web Site: www.archermalmo.com

E-Mail for Key Personnel:
President: rwilliams@archermalmo.com
Creative Dir.: gbackaus@archermalmo.com
Media Dir.: agoldner@archermalmo.com
Production Mgr.: mhample@archermalmo.com
Public Relations: cham@archermalmo.com

Employees: 190
Year Founded: 1952

National Agency Associations: 4A's-DMA-PRSA

Agency Specializes In: Advertising, Agriculture, Alternative Advertising, Automotive, Brand Development & Integration, Broadcast, Business Publications, Business-To-Business, Catalogs, Collateral, Communications, Consumer Goods, Consumer Marketing, Consumer Publications, Corporate Communications, Corporate Identity, Crisis Communications, Digital/Interactive, Direct Response Marketing, Email, Entertainment, Event Planning & Marketing, Experience Design, Financial, Graphic Design, Guerilla Marketing, Health Care Services, Household Goods, Identity Marketing, Industrial, Integrated Marketing, Internet/Web Design, Local Marketing, Logo & Package Design, Media Buying Services, Media Planning, Media Relations, Media Training, Medical Products, Merchandising, Mobile Marketing, New Product Development, Newspaper, Newspapers & Magazines, Out-of-Home Media, Outdoor, Pets , Point of Sale, Print, Production, Production (Print), Promotions, Public Relations, Publicity/Promotions, Radio, Restaurant, Retail, Sales Promotion, Search Engine Optimization, Social Media, Sponsorship, Strategic Planning/Research, T.V., Trade & Consumer Magazines, Transportation, Web (Banner Ads, Pop-ups, etc.)

Archer Malmo is one of the largest marketing communications agencies in Tennessee. The agency represents many national brands. Their services include: Advertising, Strategic Planning, Brand Development and Design Services.

Approx. Annual Billings: $190,000,000

Tom Barzizza *(Pres)*
Russ Williams *(CEO)*
Gary Backaus *(Chief Creative Officer & Principal)*
Ken Rohman *(Chief Digital Officer & Sr VP)*
Mike Butler *(Sr VP & Grp Acct Dir)*
Arlene Goldner *(Sr VP & Dir-Media)*
Naomi Bata *(Sr VP)*
Fred Nichols *(VP & Acct Dir-Agriculture Div)*
Brad Carmony *(VP-PR)*
Gokben Yamandag *(VP-Digital Strategy & Analysis)*
Matt Rand *(Exec Dir-Creative)*
Greg Hastings *(Grp Dir-Creative)*
Catherine Albritton *(Sr Dir-Art)*
Heather Klein *(Sr Dir-Art)*
Ronny Scholz *(Sr Dir-Art-Digital)*
Rich Playford *(Dir-Art & Assoc Dir-Creative)*
Justin Dobbs *(Dir-Creative)*
AmyBeth Hastings *(Dir-Comm)*
Lialah Putman-Harper *(Dir-Art)*
Tricia Swope *(Dir-HR & Acctg)*
Amanda Dent *(Assoc Dir-Creative & Copywriter)*
Ben Colar *(Assoc Dir-Creative)*
Casey Lissau *(Assoc Dir-Creative)*
Blaine Lloyd *(Assoc Dir-Creative)*
David Maddox *(Assoc Dir-Creative)*
Richard Williams *(Assoc Dir-Creative)*
Aspen Blum *(Acct Mgr)*
Sarah Cummings *(Acct Mgr)*
Madesyn Don *(Acct Mgr)*
Lauren Doss *(Acct Mgr)*
Liz Hamilton *(Acct Mgr-PR)*
Kate Hedstrom *(Acct Mgr-Zoetis)*
Mary Maxwell *(Acct Mgr)*
Sara Pritchard *(Acct Mgr)*
Dianna Davis *(Acct Supvr)*
Emily Long *(Sr Acct Exec)*
Gary Bridgman *(Sr Specialist-Digital Content)*
Jordan Crump *(Sr Specialist-PR)*
Penelope Fisher *(Sr Specialist-Digital Mktg)*
Cassie Becker *(Specialist-PR)*
Christina Comas *(Acct Exec)*
Leigh Eisenberg *(Acct Exec)*
Ashley McMillan *(Acct Exec)*
Sarah Dear *(Designer-Digital)*
Helen Webb *(Copywriter)*
Samantha Blake *(Acct Coord)*
Jennifer Blome *(Acct Coord)*
Emily Brueck *(Acct Coord)*
Wes Melton *(Acct Coord)*
Monica Smith *(Coord-Acctg)*

Accounts:
New-Citgo
Education RealtyTrust; 2012
Evergreen Packaging; 2010
FedEx; 2008
Gavilon; 2014
Hunter Fan Company; 2008
Juice Plus+; 2011
Massage Envy
Medtronic; 2003
Nationwide Veterinary Pet Insurance; 2014
nexAir; 2012
Norfolk Southern Local Market Railroad Safety; 2006
New-Nufarm, Ltd.
Palm Beach Tan; 2006
PC Tan; 2011
Pizza Ranch; 2012
R.J. Reynolds Tobacco Company; 1987
Southland Park Gaming & Racing; 2009
New-StollerUSA (Agency of Record) Creative
University of Memphis; 2014
New-USAA
Valent USA Corporation; 2001
Varsity Spirit; 2013
New-Zoetis

Branch

Archer Malmo
(Formerly Tocquigny Advertising, Interactive & Marketing Inc.)
2901 Via Fortuna Bldg 6 Ste 100, Austin, TX 78746
Tel.: (512) 532-2800
Fax: (512) 328-5645
Toll Free: (800) 363-6566
Web Site: www.archermalmo.com

Employees: 50
Year Founded: 1980

National Agency Associations: 4A's-AMA-DMA

Agency Specializes In: Advertising, Alternative Advertising, Brand Development & Integration, Branded Entertainment, Business Publications, Business-To-Business, Collateral, Consulting, Consumer Marketing, Content, Corporate Identity, Digital/Interactive, Direct Response Marketing, E-Commerce, Education, Email, Event Planning & Marketing, Exhibit/Trade Shows, Faith Based, Health Care Services, High Technology, Industrial, Information Technology, Integrated Marketing, Internet/Web Design, Logo & Package Design, Market Research, Media Buying Services, Media Planning, Mobile Marketing, New Technologies, Paid Searches, Planning & Consultation, Real Estate, Search Engine Optimization, Social Marketing/Nonprofit, Social Media, Sponsorship, Stakeholders, Strategic Planning/Research, Syndication, Technical Advertising, Web (Banner Ads, Pop-ups, etc.)

Yvonne Tocquigny *(CEO)*
Cedric Guerin *(Sr Dir-Art)*
Cindy Thompsen *(Sr Producer-Digital)*
Julia Proctor *(Acct Supvr)*
Ryan Hobert *(Sr Analyst-Digital)*
Ashley DiPasquale *(Media Planner)*

Accounts:
DTCC
Ergon Asphalt & Emulsions
Jeep; 2010
Lone Star Overnight (Agency of Record)
Millipore; 2009
NEC
NRG Energy, Inc.; 2010
Teradata; 2008

ARCHRIVAL
720 O St, Lincoln, NE 68508
Tel.: (402) 435-2525
Fax: (402) 435-8937
E-Mail: info@archrival.com
Web Site: www.archrival.com

Employees: 20
Year Founded: 1997

Agency Specializes In: Consumer Goods, Digital/Interactive, Graphic Design, Guerilla Marketing, Internet/Web Design, Logo & Package Design, Package Design, Teen Market, Viral/Buzz/Word of Mouth, Web (Banner Ads, Pop-ups, etc.)

Sarah Yost *(Head-Workflow & Production)*
Dan Gibson *(Dir-Creative)*

Joe Goddard *(Dir-Accts)*
Jesseca Marchand *(Dir-Ops)*
Kevin Fuller *(Sr Acct Mgr)*
Amy Filipi *(Acct Mgr)*
Mike Kuhl *(Acct Mgr)*
Trevor Meyer *(Strategist-Creative)*
William Buller *(Designer)*
Zachary Ubbelohde *(Designer)*

Accounts:
A&E Network The Exterminators, Two Coreys; 2008
Hormel; 2003
Microsoft; 2003
Red Bull Campaign: "The Art of FLIGHT", Energy Drink; 2006
Red Bull Racing Red Bull NASCAR Team; 2006
Solas Distillery Chava Rum, Joss Vodka; 2008
Walgreens European Beauty Collection; 2006

ARCHWAY MARKETING SERVICES
19850 S Diamond Lake Rd, Rogers, MN 55374
Tel.: (763) 428-3300
Fax: (763) 488-6801
Toll Free: (866) 791-4826
E-Mail: info@archway.com
Web Site: www.archway.com

Employees: 1,500
Year Founded: 1998

Woody McGee *(Chm)*
Doug Mann *(CEO)*
Tom Smith *(CFO)*
Walter L. Caudill *(Sr VP-Ops)*
Tom Farnbacher *(Sr VP-Supply Chain)*
Kerry James *(VP-Pricing & Procurement)*
Steve White *(VP-Bus Dev)*

Accounts:
Chrysler
Colgate
Ford
Honda
Mitsubishi
Nestle
P&G
Pepsi
Whirlpool

ARCOS COMMUNICATIONS
18 E 41St St, New York, NY 10017
Tel.: (212) 807-1337
Fax: (212) 807-8857
E-Mail: arcos@arcos-ny.com
Web Site: www.arcos-ny.com

Employees: 5
Year Founded: 1996

Agency Specializes In: Advertising, African-American Market, Asian Market, Bilingual Market, Communications, Consulting, Consumer Marketing, Corporate Communications, Corporate Identity, Entertainment, Event Planning & Marketing, Gay & Lesbian Market, Graphic Design, Local Marketing, Logo & Package Design, Media Buying Services, Public Relations, Publicity/Promotions, Strategic Planning/Research

Roy Cosme *(Pres)*
Marc Newell *(Exec VP)*
Diane Librizzi *(Acct Exec)*

Accounts:
CenterCare Health Plan
Don Julio Tequila
Jose Cuervo Tradicional
New York Daily News
New York Organ Donor Network
Pfizer, Inc.
Prudential Financial
Smith Kline Beecham
VIP Community Services

ARCUS GROUP INC.
1 Yonge St 18 Fl, Toronto, ON M5E 1W7 Canada
Tel.: (416) 335-8000 (Mng Dir)
Fax: (416) 335-8002
E-Mail: merril@arcusgroup.ca
Web Site: www.arcusgroup.ca

Year Founded: 2004

Agency Specializes In: Advertising, Brand Development & Integration

Merril Mascarenhas *(Mng Partner)*

ARDENT CREATIVE INC
440 S Main St, Fort Worth, TX 76104
Tel.: (817) 348-9049
Fax: (817) 887-5926
Web Site: www.ardentcreative.com

Year Founded: 2005

Agency Specializes In: Advertising, Brand Development & Integration, Digital/Interactive, Graphic Design, Internet/Web Design, Print

Brad Ball *(Owner)*
David Canington *(Principal)*
James Canington *(Dir-SEO)*
Richard Harmer *(Dir-Comm & Strategy Dev)*
Paul Miller *(Dir-Creative)*
James Wallace *(Dir-Web)*
Polly Mullens *(Acct Mgr & Graphic Designer)*
Jesse Estanes *(Designer)*
Anna Parsons *(Designer)*

Accounts:
Mary Couts Burnett Library

AREA 23
622 3rd Ave 3rd Fl, New York, NY 10017
Tel.: (917) 265-2623
Web Site: www.area23hc.com

National Agency Associations: 4A's

Agency Specializes In: Advertising, Brand Development & Integration, Digital/Interactive, Media Buying Services, Media Planning, Print, Sponsorship, Strategic Planning/Research

Tim Hawkey *(Mng Dir, Exec VP & Exec Dir-Creative)*
Mark Dean *(Sr VP & Dir-Digital Strategy)*
Brad Peebles *(Sr VP & Acct Grp Supvr)*
Renee Mellas *(Mng Dir-Acct)*
Jennifer Rauch *(VP & Dir-Mgmt)*
Nathaniel Kuritz *(VP & Assoc Dir-Creative)*
Charles Rategan *(Sr Dir-Art)*
Sena Ito *(Producer-Digital)*
Elliot Langerman *(Creative Dir)*
Paula Searing *(Dir-Art)*
Laura Potucek *(Assoc Dir-Creative)*
Melissa Ulloa *(Assoc Dir-Creative)*
Alex Marquard *(Acct Exec)*
Lily Hoffman *(Copywriter)*
Samantha Rodriguez *(Assoc Producer)*

Accounts:
The diaTribe Foundation Campaign: "The State of Diabetes", Print, Social Media, Video
New-Global Public-Private Partnership for Handwashing Campaign: "Cooties Catcher", Global Handwashing Day
Insmed Incorporated
Mollie's Fund

AREA/CODE
(Acquired by Zynga Game Network Inc. & Name Changed to Zynga New York)

ARENA COMMUNICATIONS
1780 W Sequoia Vista Cir, Salt Lake City, UT 84104
Tel.: (801) 595-8339
Fax: (801) 328-3404
Web Site: arenacomm.com/

Employees: 10

Agency Specializes In: Communications, Direct Response Marketing, Direct-to-Consumer, Government/Political, Publicity/Promotions

Peter Valcarce *(Founder & Mgr)*
Brandon Waters *(Partner)*
Ben Olson *(Pres-Arena Comm Online)*
Bryan J. Smith *(Dir-Arena Campaign Store)*
Amanda Waddoups *(Dir-Client Accts)*
Adam Beebe *(Acct Exec)*
Aaron Rennaker *(Strategist-Digital)*

Accounts:
National Republican Congressional Committee

ARENAS ENTERTAINMENT
3375 Barham Blvd, Los Angeles, CA 90068
Tel.: (323) 785-5555
Fax: (323) 785-5560
E-Mail: general@arenasgroup.com
Web Site: www.arenasgroup.com

Employees: 23

Santiago Pozo *(Founder & CEO)*
Larry Gleason *(Pres)*
John Butkovich *(Exec VP-Mktg)*
Dave Wong *(Exec VP-Mktg)*
Leyla Fletcher *(VP-Mktg & Media)*
Adrian Salinas *(Dir-Creative)*

Accounts:
ABC
New Line Cinema
Noche de Ninos
Paramount Pictures Dreamworks/Paramount Pictures, Hispanic
Walt Disney Pictures
Warner Bros.

ARGONAUT INC.
576 Folsom St, San Francisco, CA 94105
Tel.: (415) 671-7149
E-Mail: info@argonautinc.com
Web Site: www.argonautinc.com

Agency Specializes In: Advertising, Sponsorship

Jordan Warren *(Founder & Pres)*
Rick Condos *(Chief Creative Officer)*
Matt Ashworth *(Exec Dir-Creative)*
David Kim *(Exec Dir-Creative)*
Angie McDonald *(Art Dir)*
Zack Fagin *(Dir-Art)*
Lydia Kim *(Dir-Strategy)*
Roseanne Overton *(Dir-Art)*
Emily Hurwitz *(Brand Mgr)*
Lauren Martinez *(Brand Mgr)*
Sam Holler *(Mgr-Culture & Talent)*
Marika Wiggan *(Strategist)*

Accounts:
Appleton Estate Jamaica Rum 100 percent Jamaican, Campaign: "From Cane to Cup", Campaign: "From Jamaica With Love", Creative Agency of Record, Digital
Cisco Systems, Inc.
The Coca-Cola Company The Coke Side of Life

New-Cricket
Fitbit Inc. Above-the-Line, Advertising, Campaign: "It's All Fit", Charge, Charge HR, Digital, Marketing, Media, Print, Surge, TV
General Motors Company Chevrolet
Hershey Co Strategic Projects
Hotel 626
New-MetLife (Creative Agency of Record)
Volkswagen Campaign: "Algorithm" Super Bowl 2014, Campaign: "Wings" Super Bowl 2014

ARGUS
280 Summer St, Boston, MA 02210
Tel.: (617) 261-7676
Fax: (617) 261-7557
E-Mail: info@thinkargus.com
Web Site: www.thinkargus.com

Employees: 13
Year Founded: 1997

Agency Specializes In: Advertising, Advertising Specialties, African-American Market, Bilingual Market, Direct Response Marketing, Hispanic Market, Logo & Package Design, Media Planning, Multicultural, Social Marketing/Nonprofit

Lucas H. Guerra *(Owner)*
Zamawa Arenas *(Principal)*
Caitlin Dodge *(Acct Dir)*
April Gardner *(Dir-Creative Strategy)*
Jose Nieto *(Assoc Dir-Creative)*
Ben Leece *(Sr Designer)*
Carmen Sofia Cadran *(Acct Coord)*
Ali Eddlem *(Jr Designer)*

Accounts:
Boston Public Health Commission
Boston Public Schools
Comcast
MA Department of Public Health
MA Executive Office of Public Safety & Security
Neighborhood Health Plan
Sodexho North America; Gaithersburg, MD
WinnCompanies

ARGYLL
2110 Artesia Blvd Ste 324, Redondo Beach, CA 90278-3014
Tel.: (310) 542-6451
Fax: (310) 793-9342
E-Mail: theveryidea@earthlink.net
Web Site: www.chatcampbell.com

Employees: 6
Year Founded: 1973

Agency Specializes In: Advertising, Advertising Specialties, Affluent Market, African-American Market, Agriculture, Brand Development & Integration, Broadcast, Business Publications, Business-To-Business, Cable T.V., Children's Market, Co-op Advertising, Collateral, College, Communications, Computers & Software, Consulting, Consumer Goods, Consumer Marketing, Consumer Publications, Corporate Communications, Corporate Identity, Cosmetics, Digital/Interactive, Direct Response Marketing, Direct-to-Consumer, Electronic Media, Electronics, Email, Engineering, Exhibit/Trade Shows, Financial, Food Service, Graphic Design, Guerilla Marketing, Health Care Services, High Technology, Identity Marketing, In-Store Advertising, Industrial, Integrated Marketing, International, Internet/Web Design, Local Marketing, Logo & Package Design, Luxury Products, Magazines, Market Research, Media Buying Services, Media Planning, Media Relations, Medical Products, Men's Market, Multicultural, Multimedia, New Product Development, New Technologies, Newspaper, Newspapers & Magazines, Over-50 Market, Planning & Consultation, Point of Purchase, Point of Sale, Print, Production, Production (Ad, Film, Broadcast), Promotions, Public Relations, Publicity/Promotions, RSS (Really Simple Syndication), Radio, Regional, Restaurant, Retail, Sales Promotion, Seniors' Market, South Asian Market, T.V., Technical Advertising, Trade & Consumer Magazines, Web (Banner Ads, Pop-ups, etc.), Women's Market

Approx. Annual Billings: $3,000,000

Breakdown of Gross Billings by Media: Bus. Publs.: 20%; Cable T.V.: 2%; Co-op Adv.: 1%; Collateral: 20%; Consulting: 5%; D.M.: 12%; E-Commerce: 6%; Exhibits/Trade Shows: 1%; Graphic Design: 20%; Newsp. & Mags.: 2%; Plng. & Consultation: 1%; Pub. Rels.: 2%; Spot Radio: 2%; Spot T.V.: 4%; Worldwide Web Sites: 2%

Chat Campbell *(Owner)*

ARIA AGENCY
14800 Quorum Dr Ste 180, Dallas, TX 75254
Tel.: (214) 382-2650
E-Mail: reachout@ariaagency.com
Web Site: www.ariaagency.com

Employees: 50
Year Founded: 2000

Agency Specializes In: Advertising, Digital/Interactive

Ryan Thompson *(Founder & CEO)*
Chris Moloney *(Mng Partner & Chief Digital Officer)*
Bethany Ruhnow Hermes *(Partner & Dir-Production)*
Jeff Wollman *(Sr Dir-Creative & Head-Branding & Print)*
Karri Scott *(Dir-Mktg)*

Accounts:
Baylor Health Care System
Dahlgren Duck & Associates, Inc.

ARIAD COMMUNICATIONS
277 Wellington St W 9th Fl, Toronto, ON M5V 3E4 Canada
Tel.: (416) 971-9294
Fax: (416) 971-9292
Web Site: www.ariad.ca

Employees: 91
Year Founded: 1989

Agency Specializes In: Brand Development & Integration, Business-To-Business, Content, Custom Publishing, Digital/Interactive, Email, Strategic Planning/Research

Mark Michaud *(Sr VP)*
Nadim Kiani *(VP-Tech)*
Marnie Kramarich *(VP)*
Richard Marcil *(Gen Mgr-Healthcare)*
Sofia Costa *(Sr Acct Dir)*
Lisa Lewis *(Sr Acct Dir)*
Suzanne Burrows *(Grp Acct Dir)*
Carolyn O'Grady *(Acct Dir)*
Tim Cormick *(Dir-Strategy)*
Trevor Schoenfeld *(Co-Dir-Creative)*
Brent Landels *(Sr Acct Mgr)*
Kelly Dhillon *(Mgr-Creative Ops)*
Catherine Motl *(Mgr-eMail Mktg)*
Roger Cardiff *(Designer-eMail)*

Accounts:
AMJ Campbell Van Lines Logistics Services
Brooks Brothers Clothing Mfr
Canadian Men's Health Foundation (Agency of Record) Sponsorship, Strategic Partnerships
Credential Property Management Services
Dynamic Tire (Social Media Agency of Record) Aeolus, Sailun
Energizer Battery Mfr
Knorr Food Products Mfr
Lipton Tea Mfr
Slim Fast Healthcare Food Products Mfr
Smart Canada Below the Line, Digital, Social Marketing
New-TumbleBooks CRM, Digital Marketing, Marketing, Sales, Social Media, Strategic Marketing
Unilever Consumer Goods Mfr

ARIEFF COMMUNICATIONS
101 Townsend St #281, San Francisco, CA 94107
Tel.: (415) 538-9363
E-Mail: info@arieff.com
Web Site: www.arieff.com

Employees: 8

Adrienne Arieff *(Mng Dir)*

Accounts:
Adidas NEO Label PR
AWAKE Chocolate Event Planning, Media Relations
Ecojot
EnV Bags
Given Goods Co Digital, PR, Social Media
It's It Ice-cream Blogger Relations, Event Activities, Social Media, Traditional Media
Kelly Moore Paints (Agency of Record) Blogger Relations, Product Public Relations
Kohler
Mirabel Hotel Group Media Relations, Public Relations, Social Media, Strategic Counsel
NEO Label Public Relations
Remy
Surface Magazine
TastingRoom.com Public Relations
Ted Baker
Tobi
Videojug
Zwello

ARISTOTLE WEB DESIGN
401 W Capitol Ave Ste 700, Little Rock, AR 72201
Tel.: (501) 374-4638
Fax: (501) 376-1377
Toll Free: (800) 995-2747
E-Mail: Info@aristotle.net
Web Site: www.aristotleinteractive.com/

Year Founded: 1995

Agency Specializes In: Advertising, Digital/Interactive, Email, Integrated Marketing, Internet/Web Design, Market Research, Media Planning, Search Engine Optimization

Elizabeth Bowles *(Chm & Pres)*
Jennifer Peper *(Pres-Aristotle Interactive)*

Accounts:
Encyclopedia of Arkansas Online Reference Services
Little Rock Convention & Visitors Bureau Convention Management Services
Mississippi Delta Tourism Association Event Management Services
Ozark Folk Center Event Management Services
Quest Medical Inc Medical Devices Mfr & Distr
Riceland Foods Inc. Rice Mfr

ARKETI GROUP
2801 Buford Hwy Druid Chase Ste 375, Atlanta, GA 30329
Tel.: (404) 929-0091
Fax: (404) 321-3397
E-Mail: info@arketi.com
Web Site: www.arketi.com

Employees: 17
Year Founded: 2005

Agency Specializes In: Advertising, Public Relations, Social Media

Rory Carlton *(Owner, Principal & Creative Dir)*
Micky Long *(VP & Dir-Practice)*
Jackie Parker *(VP)*
Jim Densmore *(Assoc Dir-Creative)*

Accounts:
Aderant (Agency of Record)
Brickstream Event Marketing
BuildingReports
Catavolt Analyst Relations, Integrated PR, Marketing Engagement, Media, Messaging, Thought Leadership, Website Development
Cbeyond
Cohesive Solutions Branding, Website
Metro Atlanta Chamber Marketing, Media Relations, Social Marketing, Website Development
Mobile Labs, LLC Marketing
The Network Ethics & Risk Management, Public Relations; 2008
PMG Digital Marketing, Integrated PR, Survey Campaign, Writing
PrimeRevenue Online & Offline Marketing, Public Relations, Rebranding, Website Redesign
New-Salesfusion (Public Relations Agency of Record) Media Relations, Public Relations, Thought Leadership
Sophicity (Agency of Record) IT
TechBridge Messaging, Pro Bono, Rebranding
Technology Association of Georgia Social Media
Travelport
Xerox
XINNIX
Zotec Partners Website

ARKSIDE MARKETING

12625 Frederick St Ste 15 #149, Moreno Valley, CA 92553
Tel.: (951) 444-1237
Web Site: www.arksidemarketing.com

Year Founded: 2010

Agency Specializes In: Above-the-Line, Advertising, Advertising Specialties, Affiliate Marketing, Affluent Market, African-American Market, Agriculture, Alternative Advertising, Arts, Asian Market, Automotive, Aviation & Aerospace, Below-the-Line, Bilingual Market, Brand Development & Integration, Branded Entertainment, Broadcast, Business Publications, Business-To-Business, Cable T.V., Catalogs, Children's Market, Co-op Advertising, Collateral, College, Commercial Photography, Communications, Computers & Software, Consulting, Consumer Goods, Consumer Marketing, Consumer Publications, Content, Corporate Communications, Corporate Identity, Cosmetics, Crisis Communications, Custom Publishing, Customer Relationship Management, Digital/Interactive, Direct Response Marketing, Direct-to-Consumer, E-Commerce, Education, Electronic Media, Electronics, Email, Engineering, Entertainment, Environmental, Event Planning & Marketing, Exhibit/Trade Shows, Experience Design, Faith Based, Fashion/Apparel, Financial, Food Service, Game Integration, Gay & Lesbian Market, Government/Political, Graphic Design, Guerilla Marketing, Health Care Services, High Technology, Hispanic Market, Hospitality, Household Goods, Identity Marketing, In-Store Advertising, Industrial, Infomercials, Information Technology, Integrated Marketing, International, Internet/Web Design, Investor Relations, Legal Services, Leisure, Local Marketing, Logo & Package Design, Luxury Products, Magazines, Marine, Market Research, Media Buying Services, Media Planning, Media Relations, Media Training, Medical Products, Men's Market, Merchandising, Mobile Marketing, Multicultural, Multimedia, New Product Development, New Technologies, Newspaper, Newspapers & Magazines, Out-of-Home Media, Outdoor, Over-50 Market, Package Design, Paid Searches, Pets , Pharmaceutical, Planning & Consultation, Podcasting, Point of Purchase, Point of Sale, Print, Product Placement, Production, Production (Ad, Film, Broadcast), Production (Print), Promotions, Public Relations, Publicity/Promotions, Publishing, RSS (Really Simple Syndication), Radio, Real Estate, Recruitment, Regional, Restaurant, Retail, Sales Promotion, Search Engine Optimization, Seniors' Market, Shopper Marketing, Social Marketing/Nonprofit, Social Media, South Asian Market, Sponsorship, Sports Market, Stakeholders, Strategic Planning/Research, Sweepstakes, Syndication, T.V., Technical Advertising, Teen Market, Telemarketing, Trade & Consumer Magazines, Transportation, Travel & Tourism, Tween Market, Urban Market, Viral/Buzz/Word of Mouth, Web (Banner Ads, Pop-ups, etc.), Women's Market, Yellow Pages Advertising

Nathan Greenberg *(CEO)*
Cal Haney *(Sr Graphic Designer)*

Accounts:
Canyon Crest Country Club; 2013
Chevrolet Cadillac of La Quinta; 2013
Howington and Associates; 2013
Law Offices of Gary A. Bemis; 2013
Precision Instrumentation Neon Controls; 2012
Rancho Specialty Hospital Rancho Spine, Weight Loss 4 Life; 2010

ARLAND COMMUNICATIONS INC.

PO Box 3002, Carmel, IN 46082-3002
Tel.: (317) 701-0084
E-Mail: info@arlandcom.com
Web Site: www.arlandcom.com

Year Founded: 2008

Agency Specializes In: Advertising, Media Relations

David Arland *(Pres)*
Joshua Phelps *(Dir-Creative Svcs)*

Accounts:
Dish Network Telecommunication Services
KeyScan Computer Products Mfr
LG Electronics Products Mfr
Panasonic Electronics Products Mfr
SHARP Electronics Products Mfr
TOSHIBA Electronics Products Mfr

THE ARLAND GROUP

1430 Washington Ave, Saint Louis, MO 63103
Tel.: (314) 241-0232
Web Site: www.thearlandgroup.com

Year Founded: 2005

Agency Specializes In: Advertising, Brand Development & Integration, Content, Internet/Web Design, Print, Social Media

Jonathan Galbreath *(Founder & Dir-Creative)*
Jason Wood *(Pres)*
Deb Andrychuk *(Partner & VP)*
Keith Seiz *(VP-Ops)*
Sharon Lynch *(Sr Dir-Media & Strategy)*
Erin Canetta *(Dir-Ops)*
Dustin Rabe *(Dir-IT)*
Greg Schaum *(Dir-Media & Strategy)*
Ryan Stene *(Dir-Media & Strategy)*
Kathy Black *(Mgr-Traffic)*
Ryan McRyhew *(Designer-Interactive)*

Accounts:
Consumers Energy Company

ARMADA MEDICAL MARKETING

4840 W 29th Ave, Denver, CO 80212
Tel.: (303) 623-1190
Fax: (303) 623-1191
E-Mail: info@armadamedical.com
Web Site: www.armadamedical.com

Agency Specializes In: Advertising, Brand Development & Integration, Collateral, Digital/Interactive, Direct Response Marketing, Event Planning & Marketing, Exhibit/Trade Shows, Graphic Design, Health Care Services, Local Marketing, Media Planning, Multimedia, Public Relations, Strategic Planning/Research, Web (Banner Ads, Pop-ups, etc.)

Jim Koehler *(Pres)*
Dan Snyders *(Partner, VP & Supvr-PR)*
Julie Schlegelmilch *(Partner & VP-Client Svcs)*
Allison Phipps *(Dir-Art)*
Sara Ross *(Acct Mgr-PR)*
Nick Mastin *(Mgr-Production)*
Jennifer Crump-Bertram *(Sr Acct Supvr)*
Julz Greason *(Sr Designer)*

Accounts:
Baro-Therapies, Inc.; Miramar, FL Communications Campaign, Direct-to-Consumer, Medical Professional Marketing, Social Media, The Rejuvenator
Booth Radiology Online Marketing Campaign, Social Media
Ceragenix Pharmaceuticals, Inc.
HealthWave; Santa Barbara, CA Collateral Development, Direct Mail, Direct-to-Physician Marketing, Media Relations, Physician Newsletters, Public Relations
Renal Ventures Management LLC; Lakewood, CO
Transamerica Affinity Services Executive Medical Reimbursement Program

ARMCHAIR MEDIA, LLC

950 Joseph E Lowery Blvd Ste 19, Atlanta, GA 30318
Tel.: (404) 745-4504
Fax: (404) 745-4223
Web Site: www.armchairmedia.com

Year Founded: 2001

Agency Specializes In: Advertising, Brand Development & Integration, Internet/Web Design

Scott Woelfel *(Mng Partner)*
Stefan Kjartansson *(Partner & Dir-Creative)*
Kenny Ferguson *(Partner & Sr Strategist)*
Dave Rickett *(Partner & Sr Strategist)*
Nate Steiner *(Dir-Tech)*

Accounts:
Tin Drum

ARMENT DIETRICH, INC.

PO Box 13013, Chicago, IL 60613
Mailing Address:

PO Box 13013, Chicago, IL 60613-0013
Tel.: (312) 787-7249
Fax: (312) 787-7354
E-Mail: media@armentdietrich.com
Web Site: www.armentdietrich.com

Employees: 7

Agency Specializes In: Business-To-Business, Consumer Goods, Corporate Communications, Crisis Communications, Government/Political,

Health Care Services, Hospitality, New Technologies, Social Marketing/Nonprofit

Gini Dietrich *(Founder & CEO)*
Laura Petrolino *(Dir-Ops)*
Eleanor Pierce *(Acct Exec)*
Morgan Smith *(Acct Exec)*

Accounts:
Central Garden Pet
GE Capital Franchise Finance

ARMSTRONG CHAMBERLIN

7450 S Seneca, Haysville, KS 67060
Tel.: (316) 522-3000
Fax: (316) 522-2827
Web Site: www.armstrongchamberlin.com

Agency Specializes In: Advertising, Internet/Web Design, Print, Public Relations, Radio, Social Media

Mark Chamberlin *(Dir-Mktg & PR)*
Bruce Hinel *(Dir-Creative)*
Jill Laffoon Rose *(Dir-Strategic Comm)*
James Schisler *(Dir-Interactive Svcs)*
Kathie Bowles *(Office Mgr & Mgr-Acctg)*

Accounts:
Physician Alliance
St. Francis Community Services

THE ARNOLD AGENCY

(Acquired by Asher Agency, Inc.)

ARNOLD WORLDWIDE

10 Summer St, Boston, MA 02110
Tel.: (617) 587-8000
Fax: (617) 587-8004
E-Mail: info@arn.com
Web Site: www.arn.com

Employees: 650
Year Founded: 1946

National Agency Associations: 4A's-AAF

Agency Specializes In: Above-the-Line, Advertising, Advertising Specialties, African-American Market, Automotive, Below-the-Line, Brand Development & Integration, Branded Entertainment, Broadcast, Business-To-Business, Cable T.V., Co-op Advertising, Collateral, College, Communications, Computers & Software, Consulting, Consumer Goods, Consumer Marketing, Consumer Publications, Corporate Identity, Cosmetics, Digital/Interactive, Direct Response Marketing, Direct-to-Consumer, E-Commerce, Education, Electronic Media, Electronics, Email, Entertainment, Environmental, Event Planning & Marketing, Exhibit/Trade Shows, Fashion/Apparel, Financial, Food Service, Gay & Lesbian Market, Government/Political, Graphic Design, Guerilla Marketing, Health Care Services, High Technology, Hispanic Market, Hospitality, Household Goods, In-Store Advertising, Integrated Marketing, International, Internet/Web Design, Investor Relations, Leisure, Local Marketing, Logo & Package Design, Luxury Products, Magazines, Media Buying Services, Media Planning, Men's Market, Mobile Marketing, Multicultural, New Product Development, New Technologies, Newspaper, Newspapers & Magazines, Out-of-Home Media, Outdoor, Package Design, Pharmaceutical, Planning & Consultation, Point of Purchase, Point of Sale, Print, Production, Production (Print), Promotions, Public Relations, Publicity/Promotions, Publishing, Radio, Regional, Restaurant, Retail, Sales Promotion, Shopper Marketing, Social Marketing/Nonprofit, Social Media, Sponsorship, Sports Market, Strategic Planning/Research, Sweepstakes, T.V., Teen Market, Trade & Consumer Magazines, Transportation, Travel & Tourism, Tween Market, Urban Market, Viral/Buzz/Word of Mouth, Web (Banner Ads, Pop-ups, etc.), Women's Market

Pam Hamlin *(Global Pres)*
Lisa Unsworth *(Mng Partner & CMO)*
Wade Devers *(Mng Partner & Exec Dir-Creative)*
Pete Johnson *(Mng Partner, Exec Dir-Creative & Jr Planner)*
Barbara Reilly *(Mng Partner & Exec Dir-Boston)*
Don Lane *(Mng Partner)*
Paul Nelson *(Mng Dir)*
Elliott Seaborn *(Mng Dir)*
Andy Clarke *(Exec VP & Exec Dir-Creative)*
Mark Fabbro *(Exec VP & Exec Dir-Boston)*
David Register *(Exec VP & Grp Dir-Creative)*
Nisha Dass *(Exec VP & Dir-Bus Strategy, Analytics & Corp Strategy-Global)*
Jon Hedlund *(Sr VP & Grp Dir-Mktg)*
Jose Luis Martinez *(Sr VP & Grp Dir-Creative)*
Simona Margarito *(Sr VP & Grp Acct Dir)*
Ricardo Landim *(Sr VP & Creative Dir)*
Lenie Gramovot *(Sr VP & Dir-Brdcst Bus Affairs)*
John Kearse *(Sr VP & Dir-Creative)*
Christine Leonard *(Sr VP & Dir)*
John Raftery *(Sr VP & Dir-Brand Experience)*
Karin Wood *(Sr VP & Dir)*
Andrew Butler *(Sr VP & Brand Strategy Dir)*
Christopher Campos *(Mng Dir-Growth Strategies & Dev)*
Hugo Castillo *(VP-Creative & Dir)*
Maria Rougvie *(VP & Sr Mgr-Bus Affairs)*
Joshua Green *(VP, Digital Strategy)*
Kim Jensen-Pitts *(VP-Mktg)*
Matt Cramp *(Exec Dir-Creative)*
Rua Perston *(Exec Dir-Creative)*
Daran Brossard *(Sr Dir-Art)*
Yasmine Hamdy *(Sr Dir-Art)*
Rachel Wolak *(Sr Dir-Art)*
Todd Buffum *(Exec Producer-Digital)*
Jaime Guild *(Sr Producer-Brdcst)*
Angela Tisone *(Sr Producer-Mktg)*
John Simpson *(Creative Dir & Copywriter)*
Nicole Bazzinotti *(Producer-Digital)*
Alexis Papazian *(Producer-Mktg)*
Brittany Riley *(Art Dir)*
AnaLiza Alba *(Dir-Creative)*
Nate Donabed *(Dir-Art)*
Ginger Ludwig *(Dir-Mktg)*
Ryan Potter *(Dir-Art)*
Chris Gil *(Assoc Dir-Social Content Systems)*
Sara Goldsmith *(Assoc Dir-Creative)*
Jack Miller *(Assoc Dir-Creative & Art)*
Karl Ruud *(Client Svcs Mgr)*
Chris Kasper *(Acct Supvr)*
Celia Feuer *(Acct Exec-Sanofi)*
Dan Higgins *(Strategist-Digital Media)*
Josh Kahn *(Copywriter)*
Mike Patrick *(Planner-Brand)*
Ashley Paro *(Sr Mktg Mgr)*
David Wall *(Sr Art Dir)*

Accounts:
A. T. Cross Company; Lincoln, RI Worldwide Brand Strategy
Acushnet Company FootJoy, Pinnacle
Ad Council Campaign: "Grads of Life", Campaign: "Pathways to Employment", PSA
The ADT Corporation Brand Strategy, Campaign: "Always there", Campaign: "Mind's Eye: Burglary"
Aetna (Lead Creative Agency) Online Advertising, Social Media, Traditonal Advertising; 2010
Al Gore Campaign: "Body Bags", Campaign: "Truth", Climate Change, Reality Drop
Alberto Culver Nexxus, Noxzema, St. Ives; 2010
American Eagle Outfitters Digital
Avocados from Mexico, Inc. Integrated Agency Of Record
Bank Midwest Campaign: "Common Sense"
Big Heart Pet Brands Milk-Bone
Boiron Coldcalm, Oscillococcinum; 2009
Boston Bruins Campaign: "Brick Wall", Campaign: "Christmas Spectacular", Campaign: "Doctor", Campaign: "Happy Family", Campaign: "Promo Night", Campaign: "Red Cape", Campaign: "Scores at Will", Campaign: "Smiling", Campaign: "Starring The Bear", Campaign: "The Bear & the Gang", Campaign: "The Calm", Campaign: "The Wolfpack", Campaign: "Through You", Digital, Integrated Marketing Campaign, OOH, Print, TV
Brown Forman "Sinatra Select", Campaign: "571", Campaign: "All the While", Campaign: "Birth of a Barrel", Campaign: "Craft", Campaign: "Drink of Whiskey", Campaign: "Frank The Man", Campaign: "Freedom is a Right", Campaign: "Independence", Campaign: "Legend", Campaign: "Lynchburg", Campaign: "Made in America", Campaign: "Moment of Silence", Campaign: "The Best Way", Campaign: "The Few and Far Between", Campaign: "The Whiskey Drum", Campaign: "Tonight. Two Words. Jack Fire", Campaign: "Truth Be Told", Campaign: "Unhurried", Campaign: "Wait for It", Creative, Gentleman Jack, Jack Daniels, Tennessee Fire
Cannes Campaign: "The Blind Eye", Seminar Poster
Carbonite Campaign: " No One Has To Know", Campaign: "Wedding", Creative, Digital, Print, Radio, TV, Web Design
Carnival Cruise Lines Campaign: "Bear", Campaign: "Bobslide" Winter Olympics 2014, Campaign: "It's Always Better Elsewhere", Campaign: "Moments that Matter", Campaign: "Waterslide Escape", Campaign: "Zipline", Creative, GPS, Social Media, TV; 2008
Center for Disease Control Billboards, Campaign: "Anthem", Campaign: "Christine's Flavor Tip", Campaign: "Do Whatever It Takes", Campaign: "Terrie's Voice Tip", Campaign: "Tips from Former Smokers", Campaign: "We Did It, You Can Too", Magazines, Newspapers, Online, Radio, Social Media Campaign, TV
CenturyLink, Inc. (Lead Creative Agency) Advertising, Brand Awareness, Broadcast, Campaign: "Is Prism TV Any Good?", Campaign: "Will My Price Change?", Digital, Direct Marketing, Social
Certified Financial Planners Campaign: "Let's Make a Plan"
Climate Reality Reality Drop
Del Monte Foods, Inc.
Dell Inc.
The Diane Rehm Show
Evian
Fidelity; 2001
New-Field Notes Brand Campaign: "Write"
Greek Orthodox Metropolis of Chicago Campaign: "Life-Saving Techniques", Campaign: "Walked on Water"
The Hershey Company (Lead Creative Agency) Hershey's Kisses, Kit Kat, Reese's, TV, Take 5, York; 2005
Horizon for Homeless Children
Huntington Bancshares, Inc. Campaign: "Colt's Stadium Takeover", Campaign: "Do the Right Thing", Campaign: "Horse", Campaign: "Panda", Campaign: "Tree", The Huntington National Bank
Jergens
John Frieda
Kao Corporation
Kao USA Campaign: "Me & John", Jergens (Global Creative Agency of Record), John Frieda (Global Creative Agency of Record)
Kaz (Agency of Record) Arthur Tweedie, Creative Development, Digital Marketing, PUR, Strategy
National Association of Realtors (Agency of Record) Brand Activation, Brand Strategy, Creative, Digital
National Journal; 2010
New Balance "Our U.S. Factory Workers vs. Their U.S. Factory Workers", "Runnovation Anthem", Campaign: "Always in Beta", Campaign: "America is for the Makers", Campaign:

"Connect 1010", Campaign: "Connect 3090", Campaign: "Runnovation", Campaign: "The Storm", Online, Print, Social Media; 2010
Newspaper Alliance
Nike Fresh Air
NYU Langone Medical Center
Ocean Spray Cranberries, Inc. Digital, Ocean Spray, Ocean Spray Diet, Ocean Spray Diet Juice Drinks; 1996
One Foundation
One Sight
Panasonic Electric Works Corporation of America; 2009
Pantene
PBM Products
The Progressive Corporation Advertising, Campaign: "After School Special", Campaign: "Best Day", Campaign: "Checkout", Campaign: "Rate Suckers", Campaign: "Savings That Stand Out", Campaign: "Superstore", Campaign: "The Thread", Progressive Auto Insurance
Progressive Direct Campaign: "Let's Get Ready to Bundle", Campaign: "Baby Man", Campaign: "Dress Like Flo", Lead Creative, Progressive Insurance; 2006
Sanofi-Aventis
Santander Bank "Black Belt Friday", "Black Top Friday", Campaign: "Black Bean Soup Friday", Campaign: "Movie Marathon"
New-SolarCity Campaign: "Reading Lamps", Digital, Social
Sovereign Analytics, Brand Positioning, Campaign: "A Bank For Your Ideas", Digital, Outdoor, Print, Radio, Santander Credit Card, Social, Sponsorships
Titleist
Truth Campaign: "#Vote69", Campaign: "#VoteIcecream", Campaign: "Flavor Monsters", Campaign: "Profiles"
Tyson Foods, Inc. Tyson Chicken, Wright Brand Bacon
Unilever
University of Phoenix Creative, Digital, Marketing, Out of Home, Print, TV
VistaPrint N.V.
Volvo Group North America Inc. C70, Campaign: "Command The Extreme", Campaign: "Dankeschon", Campaign: "Eye", Campaign: "Little Red", Campaign: "Rocket", Campaign: "Wrestler", Creative, V60, Volvo S60, XC60; 2007
Volvo Trucks
Western International University

Branches

Arnold KLP
(Formerly Euro RSCG KLP)
87-91 Newman Street, London, W1T 3EY United Kingdom
Tel.: (44) 20 7079 2200
Fax: (44) 207 478 3578
Web Site: www.arnoldklp.com/

Employees: 75
Year Founded: 1974

Agency Specializes In: Advertising Specialties, Business-To-Business, Consumer Marketing, Digital/Interactive, Direct Response Marketing, Event Planning & Marketing, Internet/Web Design, Publicity/Promotions, Sales Promotion

Hugh Treacy *(Mng Dir)*
Tony Maciocia *(CFO)*
Joanna Lawlor *(Acct Dir)*
Doug Allen *(Dir-Creative Svcs)*
Jonathan Moore *(Dir-Creative)*
Lizzie Bowen *(Assoc Dir)*
Carrie Chappell *(Assoc Dir)*
Stephanie Taylor *(Acct Mgr)*
Charlotte Baker *(Mgr-New Bus & Mktg)*
Zechariah Masih *(Jr Planner)*

Accounts:
7UP
Bailey's
Britvic
Citroen
Douwe Egberts TV
GMG Radio Smooth Radio
Microsoft
Nokia
Pepsi Campaign: "Bus Levitation", LiveForNow
Royal Bank of Scotland
XBox

Arnold Madrid
(Formerly Arnold 4D)
Paseo de la Castellana 259, Torre de Cristal, Madrid, 28046 Spain
Tel.: (34) 91 330 2121
Fax: (34) 1 330 23 45
E-Mail: info@arnoldmadrid.com
Web Site: arnoldmadrid.com/

Employees: 43
Year Founded: 1999

Agency Specializes In: Digital/Interactive

Susana Puras *(Co-Mng Dir)*
Cristina Barturen Zaldua *(Mng Dir)*
Soledad De Leon *(Head-Social Media)*
Andres Moreno *(Dir-Creative)*
Maria Cencerrado Martin *(Acct Supvr)*

Accounts:
Baluarte
BBUA
Hoteles Hesperia
Iberdrola
Osborne
Roda Golf
Segitur
Spanair
Vodafone
Volvo

Arnold Milan
Via Torino, 68, 10-20123, 20123 Milan, Italy
Tel.: (39) 02 3 610 0411
Web Site: www.arnoldworldwide.it/

Employees: 22

Agency Specializes In: Advertising

Paolo Biondolillo *(CEO & Partner)*
Antonio Pinter *(Partner & Dir-Creative)*
Dario Mondonico *(Dir-Creative & Art)*

Arnold Toronto
473 Adelaide St W 3rd Floor, M5V 1T1 Toronto, ON Canada
Tel.: (416) 355-5009
Web Site: www.arn.com

Agency Specializes In: Advertising

Bill Sharpe *(Chm)*

Accounts:
Alberto Culver
Amtrak
The Hershey Company
Merz Pharmaceuticals
New Balance Canada Creative, Digital, Social Media Support, Traditional Advertising
Pine Street Inn
Tropicana Pure Premium
Tyson Foods, Inc
VistaPrint N.V.
Volvo Cars Campaign: "Welcome to Candanavia"

ArnoldNYC
205 Hudson St, New York, NY 10013
Tel.: (212) 463-1000
Fax: (212) 463-1490
Web Site: arn.com

National Agency Associations: 4A's

Agency Specializes In: Advertising, Sponsorship

Peter Grossman *(Pres)*
Gary Scheiner *(Exec VP & Exec Dir-Creative)*
Sara Bamber *(Head-Strategy)*
Tim Flood *(Exec Dir-Creative-Hershey's)*
Mathew Jerrett *(Exec Dir-Creative-Hershey's)*
Kate Wadia *(Exec Creative Dir)*
Jennifer Williams *(Project Mgr & Producer-Interactive)*
Kyle Lynah *(Art Dir)*
Brice Rogers *(Dir-Conceptual)*
Craig Wood *(Dir-Innovation)*
Kelsey Steele *(Acct Mgr)*
Lisa Huang *(Acct Supvr)*
Simran Sudan *(Acct Supvr)*
Hilary Bergman *(Acct Exec)*
Elise Falcon *(Asst Acct Mgr)*

Accounts:
23andMe Campaign: "Portraits of Health"
Aetna, Inc.
Boiron
Carnival Corporation Carnival Cruise Lines
Del Monte Foods; San Francisco, CA Campaign: "Treat With A Twist", Campaign: "Welcome Home", Creative, Digital, Marketing, Print
The Hershey Company Hershey's, Hershey's Fortified Syrup, Hershey's Kisses, Hershey's Kisses Filled with Carmel, Hershey's Pieces, Ice Breakers, Ice Breakers Frost, Jolly Rancher, Kit Kat, Peter Paul Almond Joy, Reese's Peanut Butter Cups, Rolo, Take 5, Twizzlers, York Peppermint Patties
Kao USA Biore, Campaign: "You're More Than Just A Pretty Face", Creative, Curel, Jergens, John Frieda, Print, Social, Television
Panasonic Corporation of America
Sanofi
St. Ives Campaign: "Fresh Hydration Lotion Spray"
Stein Mart (Agency of Record)
Unilever Simple

AROLUXE
(Formerly Ela Lux Media)
112 Seaboard Ln, Franklin, TN 37067
Mailing Address:
625 Baker's Bridge Ave, Franklin, TN 37067
Tel.: (615) 807-2612
E-Mail: support@aroluxe.com
Web Site: aroluxe.com/

Year Founded: 2010

Agency Specializes In: Advertising, Brand Development & Integration, Internet/Web Design, Print, Radio

Jason Brown *(Mng Partner)*
Sharp Emmons *(Dir-Creative)*
Alexandrea Bittle *(Acct Mgr)*

Accounts:
Austermiller Roofing
Birdsong Events
Cool Springs MD
Creative Dentistry
Segway Inc. Creative, Website
Snodgrass-King Pediatric Dental Associates

ARONFIELD STUDIOS
PO Box 58272, Beckley, WV 25802
Tel.: (304) 207-0037

E-Mail: mail@aronfield.com
Web Site: www.aronfield.com

Year Founded: 2008

Agency Specializes In: Advertising, Graphic Design, Internet/Web Design, Social Media, Strategic Planning/Research

Joel Bennett *(CEO & Mgr-Web Dev)*

Accounts:
EL Mariachi

ARRAE CREATIVE LLC
110 16th St Ste 920, Denver, CO 80202
Tel.: (303) 945-2343
E-Mail: hello@arr.ae
Web Site: www.arr.ae

Year Founded: 2011

Agency Specializes In: Advertising, Brand Development & Integration, Consulting, Graphic Design, Outdoor, Search Engine Optimization, Social Media, Technical Advertising

Brandon Whalen *(Partner & Dir-Digital)*
Winter King *(Partner)*
Walt Wise *(Principal & Dir-Creative)*
Jennifer Potts *(Dir-Bus Dev)*

Accounts:
Biker Jim's Dogs
Giro Bello
Hilti Corporation
Qwizzle
Scoliosis Specialist Of Colorado
Seafair
Study Colorado
Tech Cocktail, LLC.
Tschetter Hamrick Sulzer
Wreckedinfo
Zombie Crawl

THE ARRAS GROUP
(Name Changed to Arras Keathley Agency)

ARRAS KEATHLEY AGENCY
(Formerly The Arras Group)
1151 N Marginal Rd, Cleveland, OH 44114
Tel.: (216) 621-1601
Fax: (216) 377-1919
Web Site: www.arrasgroup.com/

E-Mail for Key Personnel:
President: jhickey@arraskeathley.com

Employees: 12
Year Founded: 1991

Agency Specializes In: Advertising, Advertising Specialties, Automotive, Brand Development & Integration, Broadcast, Business-To-Business, Cable T.V., Co-op Advertising, Collateral, Communications, Consumer Marketing, Consumer Publications, Corporate Communications, Direct Response Marketing, E-Commerce, Electronic Media, Event Planning & Marketing, Exhibit/Trade Shows, Financial, Graphic Design, Internet/Web Design, Logo & Package Design, Magazines, Media Buying Services, Merchandising, New Product Development, Newspaper, Newspapers & Magazines, Outdoor, Point of Purchase, Point of Sale, Print, Production, Public Relations, Publicity/Promotions, Radio, Real Estate, Retail, Sales Promotion, Sponsorship, Strategic Planning/Research, T.V., Trade & Consumer Magazines, Yellow Pages Advertising

Approx. Annual Billings: $65,000,000

Breakdown of Gross Billings by Media: Adv. Specialities: $6,000,000; D.M.: $500,000; E-Commerce: $3,500,000; Exhibits/Trade Shows: $2,000,000; Graphic Design: $10,000,000; Logo & Package Design: $5,000,000; Mdsg./POP: $8,500,000; Newsp.: $7,000,000; Outdoor: $1,500,000; Plng. & Consultation: $3,000,000; Point of Purchase: $5,000,000; Point of Sale: $2,000,000; Pub. Rels.: $500,000; Radio: $1,000,000; Sls. Promo.: $2,000,000; Spot T.V.: $500,000; Strategic Planning/Research: $5,000,000; Trade & Consumer Mags.: $2,000,000

Tom Keathley *(Co-Founder & Exec Dir-Creative)*
James T. Hickey *(Pres)*
Aylie Fifer *(Dir-Client Svc)*
Jacqueline Lapine *(Dir-PR & Social)*
Julie Jones *(Assoc Dir-Creative)*
Sharon Carmosino *(Sr Acct Mgr)*
Sara Myers *(Acct Exec)*
Aschli First *(Designer-Digital)*

ARRAY CREATIVE
1 S Main St Ste 601, Akron, OH 44308
Tel.: (330) 374-1960
E-Mail: info@arraycreative.com
Web Site: www.arraycreative.com

Agency Specializes In: Advertising, Brand Development & Integration, Collateral, Corporate Identity, Event Planning & Marketing, Internet/Web Design, Logo & Package Design, Package Design, Print, Social Media

Ian Marin *(Mng Partner)*
Eric Rich *(Principal)*
Shawn Magee *(Dir-Art)*
Cathy Snarski *(Dir-Art)*
Tara Shank *(Sr Graphic Designer)*

Accounts:
Winston Products

ARRCO MEDICAL MARKETING
1600 Providence Hwy, Walpole, MA 02081-2542
Tel.: (508) 404-1105
Fax: (508) 404-1106
E-Mail: info@arrco.com
Web Site: www.arrco.com

E-Mail for Key Personnel:
President: jnr@arrco.com

Employees: 10
Year Founded: 1976

Agency Specializes In: Advertising, Advertising Specialties, Alternative Advertising, Brand Development & Integration, Broadcast, Business Publications, Business-To-Business, Cable T.V., Collateral, Communications, Consulting, Consumer Marketing, Consumer Publications, Corporate Identity, Digital/Interactive, Direct Response Marketing, Electronic Media, Environmental, Event Planning & Marketing, Exhibit/Trade Shows, Financial, Government/Political, Graphic Design, Health Care Services, High Technology, Information Technology, Integrated Marketing, Internet/Web Design, Investor Relations, Legal Services, Leisure, Logo & Package Design, Magazines, Media Buying Services, Medical Products, New Product Development, New Technologies, Newspaper, Newspapers & Magazines, Out-of-Home Media, Outdoor, Over-50 Market, Pharmaceutical, Planning & Consultation, Point of Purchase, Point of Sale, Print, Production, Production (Print), Public Relations, Publicity/Promotions, Radio, Recruitment, Restaurant, Seniors' Market, Sports Market, Strategic Planning/Research, Technical Advertising, Trade & Consumer Magazines, Transportation, Travel & Tourism

Approx. Annual Billings: $4,000,000

Breakdown of Gross Billings by Media: Collateral: 35%; Exhibits/Trade Shows: 15%; Logo & Package Design: 10%; Newsp.: 5%; Trade & Consumer Mags.: 30%; Transit: 5%

Jerome N. Reicher *(Pres & Dir-Creative)*
Jayne Talmage *(Sr VP)*

Accounts:
Spire Biomedical; Bedford, MA Software/Technology

ARROWHEAD ADVERTISING
16155 N 83rd Ave Ste 205, Peoria, AZ 85382
Tel.: (623) 979-3000
Fax: (623) 979-3940
Web Site: http://arrowhead.agency/

Employees: 32
Year Founded: 2003

Agency Specializes In: Advertising, Graphic Design, Internet/Web Design, Print

Revenue: $3,800,000

Kyle Eng *(Pres & CEO)*
Kurt Johnson *(Mng Dir & VP)*
Michelle Shepherd *(CFO)*
Lee Rosenthal *(Chief Revenue Officer & Sr VP)*
Ron Silagy *(Acct Dir)*
Cody Bell *(Dir-IT)*
Adam Lopez *(Dir-Creative)*
Chris Winters *(Dir-Online Mktg)*
Jessica Ignacio-Mesa *(Mgr-Traffic & Acct Coord-Print)*
Chelsea Smeland *(Acct Exec)*
Jessica Bargenquast *(Acct Coord)*
Holly Beaman *(Acct Coord)*

Accounts:
Valley Hyundai Dealer Ad Assocation (Agency of Record); 2007

ART4ORM INC
237 NE Broadway St Ste 245, Portland, OR 97232
Tel.: (503) 228-1399
Fax: (503) 224-0229
Web Site: www.art4orm.com

Agency Specializes In: Advertising, Brand Development & Integration, Digital/Interactive, Graphic Design, Internet/Web Design, Logo & Package Design, Media Planning, Print, Social Media, Strategic Planning/Research

Kevin York *(Principal & Dir-Creative)*

Accounts:
Charlottes Weddings & More
Multi-Family Housing Association

ARTAGRAFIK
1123 Zonolite Rd NE Ste 28, Atlanta, GA 30306
Tel.: (678) 999-2189
Fax: (404) 856-3760
Toll Free: (866) 802-7991
E-Mail: info@artagrafik.com
Web Site: www.artagrafik.com

Year Founded: 2007

Agency Specializes In: Advertising, Brand Development & Integration, Digital/Interactive, Logo & Package Design

Chris Artabasy *(Pres & Chief Creative Officer)*
Michael Levinsohn *(CEO)*

Danielle Artabasy *(COO)*

Accounts:
LakePoint Sports
TRC Staffing Services, Inc.

ARTCRAFT HEALTH EDUCATION

(Formerly Simms & McIvor Marketing Communications)
39 Highway 12, Flemington, NJ 08822
Tel.: (908) 782-4921
Fax: (908) 782-7158
E-Mail: info@artcrafthealthed.com
Web Site: www.artcrafthealth.com

Employees: 14
Year Founded: 1981

Agency Specializes In: Advertising, Advertising Specialties, Brand Development & Integration, Children's Market, Collateral, Communications, Consulting, Corporate Identity, Event Planning & Marketing, Exhibit/Trade Shows, Financial, Graphic Design, Guerilla Marketing, Health Care Services, Hospitality, Identity Marketing, Integrated Marketing, Logo & Package Design, Media Planning, Medical Products, Multimedia, New Product Development, Package Design, Pets , Pharmaceutical, Print, Production, Promotions, Public Relations, Publicity/Promotions, Sales Promotion, Strategic Planning/Research, Trade & Consumer Magazines

Approx. Annual Billings: $8,000,000

Breakdown of Gross Billings by Media: Bus. Publs.: 2%; Collateral: 72%; D.M.: 15%; Exhibits/Trade Shows: 10%; Pub. Rels.: 1%

Marc Sirockman *(Exec VP & Gen Mgr)*
Rich Miller *(VP & Dir-Creative)*
Anthony Marucci *(VP-Client Svcs)*
Katie O'Neill *(VP-Strategic Accounts)*
Brian S. Schaechter *(Sr Dir-Clinical Trials Div)*
Mike Viscel *(Sr Dir-Bus Dev)*
Shauna Aherne *(Dir-Market Strategy)*
Lynn Altmaier *(Dir-Content-Clinical Trials)*
Kathy Carreira *(Mgr-Production)*

Accounts:
Action Products Inc.; 2001
AstraZeneca Pharmaceuticals; 1993
Bayer HealthCare Diabetes Care; 2007
BD Consumer Healthcare; 1999
Health Care Interiors; 2002
Johnson & Johnson Health Care Systems; 2000
The Marketing Connexion; 2000
Merck & Co. Inc.; 2007
Novo Nordisk; 2001
Sanofi-Aventis; 2002
Smiths Medical MD, Inc.; 2003
Sunovion Pharmaceuticals Inc.; 2005
Terumo; 2005
TEVA; 2005

ARTEAGA & ARTEAGA

1571 Calle Alda Urb Caribe, San Juan, PR 00926
Tel.: (787) 620-1600
Fax: (787) 759-6939
E-Mail: arteaga@arteaga.com
Web Site: www.arteaga.com

Agency Specializes In: Advertising, Customer Relationship Management, Digital/Interactive, Media Relations, Print, Promotions, Public Relations, Radio, T.V.

Hector Soto *(Sr Dir-Art)*
Ana Del Amo *(Grp Acct Dir)*
Winifred Toro *(Acct Dir)*
Laura Figueroa *(Dir-Creative)*
Gabriel Maldonado *(Dir-Art)*
Ramon Reyes *(Dir-Creative)*
Yahayra Perez *(Sr Acct Exec)*
Ismar M. Perez *(Acct Exec)*
Pilar De La Campa *(Media Planner)*

Accounts:
20th Century Fox of Puerto Rico
Bristol-Myers Squibb Co. Campaign: "Don't Let It Surprise You"

ARTHUR AGENCY

104 E Jackson S, Carbondale, IL 62901
Tel.: (618) 351-1599
Fax: (866) 211-6614
E-Mail: info@arthuragency.com
Web Site: www.arthuragency.com

Year Founded: 2003

Agency Specializes In: Advertising, Broadcast, Corporate Identity, Digital/Interactive, Internet/Web Design, Logo & Package Design, Print, T.V.

Dennis Poshard *(Pres)*
Clint Eilerts *(Dir-Creative)*
Sherry Jeschke *(Dir-Acctg)*
Katherine Moore *(Acct Mgr & Copywriter)*
Lindsey Bowman *(Acct Mgr)*
Amanda Graff *(Acct Mgr)*

Accounts:
Illinois Department of Transportation

ARTICHOKE CREATIVE

590 Hygeia Ave, Encinitas, CA 92024
Tel.: (760) 753-8663
Fax: (760) 454-2795
E-Mail: david@artichoke-creative.com
Web Site: www.artichoke-creative.com

Employees: 3
Year Founded: 2004

Agency Specializes In: Advertising, Broadcast, Digital/Interactive, Direct Response Marketing, Event Planning & Marketing, Food Service, Government/Political, Internet/Web Design, Media Buying Services, Print, Public Relations, Restaurant

Approx. Annual Billings: $450,000

David Boylan *(Founder & Pres)*
Chef Michael Zonfrilli *(VP)*
Marcia Westinghouse *(Dir-Art)*

Accounts:
Borrego Solar
Centex Homes
Long Point Capital
Martini Ranch Encinitas
Miracosta College
Paddle the Mitten LLC; Howell, MI
Plaza Home Mortgage, Inc.
Stellar Solar
Sullivan Group

ARTICULATION AGENCY

1849 Sawtelle Blvd Ste 503, Los Angeles, CA 90025
Tel.: (310) 633-4261
Fax: (310) 510-6860
E-Mail: communicate@articulationagency.com
Web Site: www.articulationagency.com

Year Founded: 2004

Agency Specializes In: Advertising, Brand Development & Integration, Corporate Identity, Logo & Package Design

Matt Brunini *(Founder)*
Elizabeth Boundjia *(Dir-Brand Strategy)*
Christopher Park *(Copywriter)*

Accounts:
Canon Luxury Estates
K. Brunini Jewels
Mike Mathis Productions, Inc.

ARTICUS LTD. MARKETING COMMUNICATIONS

1528 Walnut St Ste 701, Philadelphia, PA 19102
Tel.: (215) 564-1213
Fax: (215) 545-4615
E-Mail: info@articus.com
Web Site: www.articus.com

Employees: 10
Year Founded: 1986

Agency Specializes In: Advertising, Brand Development & Integration, Collateral, College, Communications, Consulting, Consumer Marketing, Corporate Identity, Education, Entertainment, Financial, High Technology, Identity Marketing, Integrated Marketing, Internet/Web Design, Logo & Package Design, Planning & Consultation, Print, Publicity/Promotions, Radio, Search Engine Optimization, Sponsorship, Strategic Planning/Research, T.V.

Approx. Annual Billings: $10,500,000

Eric Van Der Vlugt *(Principal)*
Debra Pusak *(Sr Acct Exec)*
Debra Relick *(Sr Acct Exec)*

Accounts:
University of Pennsylvania; Philadelphia, PA; 1992

ARTIFAX

117 Delmonico Pl, Valley Stream, NY 11581
Tel.: (516) 593-4844
E-Mail: artifaxdesigns@yahoo.com
Web Site: www.artifaxart.com

Employees: 1
Year Founded: 1981

Agency Specializes In: Arts, Brand Development & Integration, Graphic Design, Newspaper, Publicity/Promotions

Breakdown of Gross Billings by Media: Graphic Design: 90%; Other: 10%

Joe Vissichelli *(Dir-Art & Graphic Designer)*

Accounts:
Bulgari
Citibank
Discovery Channel
Hearst
Hilton Worldwide
HSBC Bank
Johnson & Johnson
Marriott
Merrill Lynch
Nassau Coliseum
NBA
New York Rangers
Perdue Farms
Polo-Ralph Lauren
Sealy

ARTILLERY MARKETING COMMUNICATIONS LLC

1709 Colley Ave Ste 308, Norfolk, VA 23517
Tel.: (757) 627-4800
Fax: (480) 772-4087
E-Mail: office@artillerymarketing.com

Web Site: www.artillerymarketing.com

Employees: 5
Year Founded: 2001

National Agency Associations: Second Wind Limited

Agency Specializes In: Advertising, Digital/Interactive, Public Relations

Douglas Burdett *(Founder)*

THE ARTIME GROUP

65 N Raymond Ave Ste 205, Pasadena, CA 91103-3947
Tel.: (626) 583-1855
Fax: (626) 583-1861
E-Mail: newbiz@artimegroup.com
Web Site: www.artimegroup.com

E-Mail for Key Personnel:
President: henry@artimegroup.com
Creative Dir.: christopher@artimegroup.com

Employees: 10
Year Founded: 1991

Agency Specializes In: Advertising, Aviation & Aerospace, Brand Development & Integration, Business Publications, Business-To-Business, Collateral, Communications, Computers & Software, Consumer Goods, Consumer Marketing, Consumer Publications, Corporate Communications, Corporate Identity, Digital/Interactive, Direct Response Marketing, Electronic Media, Electronics, Engineering, Entertainment, Exhibit/Trade Shows, Financial, Food Service, Graphic Design, Health Care Services, High Technology, Household Goods, Identity Marketing, In-Store Advertising, Industrial, Information Technology, Integrated Marketing, Internet/Web Design, Legal Services, Logo & Package Design, Luxury Products, Magazines, Market Research, Media Buying Services, Media Planning, Medical Products, Multimedia, Newspaper, Newspapers & Magazines, Outdoor, Package Design, Planning & Consultation, Point of Purchase, Point of Sale, Print, Production, Production (Print), Promotions, Public Relations, Publicity/Promotions, Radio, Real Estate, Restaurant, Retail, Sales Promotion, Strategic Planning/Research, Technical Advertising, Trade & Consumer Magazines, Transportation

Henry Artime *(Owner)*
Van Nguyen *(VP)*
Dennis Hodgson *(Dir-Creative)*
Sam Kim *(Dir-Web)*
Bill Myers *(Dir-New Bus Dev)*
Niki Phan *(Acct Exec)*
Olia Vradiy *(Designer-UI & UX)*
Elda Paloulian *(Coord-Media)*

Accounts:
Affinity Internet
CMA, LLC
Double Coin Holdings, Ltd.
First Foundation Bank
The Kennedy/Marshall Co.
MedAmerica; Walnut Creek, CA Medical Malpractice Insurance; 2005
Mintie Technologies
Northrise University
Richardson Patel; Los Angeles, CA Legal Services; 2005
SunWest Bank
Taylor Dunn
Utility Trailer; City of Industry, CA Semi Trailers; 2003
Woodbury University

ARTIST DEVELOPMENT GROUP, INC.

119 17th Ave S, Nashville, TN 37203-2707
Tel.: (615) 846-2600
Fax: (615) 846-2601
Toll Free: (877) 627-4234
E-Mail: davis@adgnashville.com
Web Site: www.adgnashville.com

Employees: 4
Year Founded: 1974

Agency Specializes In: Corporate Identity, Entertainment, Event Planning & Marketing, Food Service, Graphic Design, Integrated Marketing, Internet/Web Design, Local Marketing, Luxury Products, Pets , Planning & Consultation, Print, Real Estate, Sales Promotion, Trade & Consumer Magazines

Approx. Annual Billings: $475,000

Breakdown of Gross Billings by Media: Collateral: $166,250; Event Mktg.: $142,500; Plng. & Consultation: $166,250

David G. Jonethis *(Founder & Partner)*
John J. Jonethis *(Owner)*

THE ARTIST EVOLUTION

1753 N College Ave Ste 203, Fayetteville, AR 72703
Tel.: (479) 222-0399
Fax: (479) 966-4493
Toll Free: (866) 610-5334
E-Mail: info@theartistevolution.com
Web Site: www.theartistevolution.com

Agency Specializes In: Advertising, Brand Development & Integration, Graphic Design, Print, Public Relations, Social Media

Alyssa Peiser *(Acct Mgr)*
Kim Jennings-Eckert *(Mgr-Sls & Ops)*
Lori Storrs *(Mgr-Sls-Media Mgmt)*
Jordan Goss *(Coord-Brand Outreach)*
Kayla Eiffert *(Asst-Mktg)*

Accounts:
America's Car-Mart, Inc.
Highlands Oncology Group
Horizon Dental Implant Center

ARTVERSION INTERACTIVE

11 N Skokie Hwy, Lake Bluff, IL 60044
Tel.: (847) 279-8999
Web Site: www.artversion.com

Year Founded: 1999

Agency Specializes In: Catalogs, Collateral, Digital/Interactive, Electronic Media, Email, Exhibit/Trade Shows, Experience Design, In-Store Advertising, Local Marketing, Mobile Marketing, Multimedia, Newspapers & Magazines, Podcasting, Point of Purchase, Point of Sale, Print, Production (Print), Search Engine Optimization, Social Media, Viral/Buzz/Word of Mouth, Web (Banner Ads, Pop-ups, etc.)

Goran Paunovic *(Principal & Creative Dir)*
Lynn Doherty *(Dir-Brand Strategy)*
Erin Lentz *(Dir-Design)*
Vanessa Petersen *(Dir-Brand Strategy)*

Accounts:
Aiwa; 2014
Morgan Stanley; 2010
Toyota; 2015

ARVIZU ADVERTISING & PROMOTIONS

3101 N Central Ave Ste 150, Phoenix, AZ 85012-2650
Tel.: (602) 279-4669
Fax: (602) 279-4977
E-Mail: info@arvizu.com
Web Site: www.arvizu.com

Employees: 15

Agency Specializes In: Direct Response Marketing, Hispanic Market, Planning & Consultation, Public Relations, Recruitment, Sponsorship

Ray Arvizu *(Pres & CEO)*
Ernestina P. Arvizu *(COO)*
Vicky Deur *(Dir-Media)*
Ralph Placencia *(Dir-Events)*
Andy Arvizu *(Acct Exec)*
Christian Quintana *(Coord-Special Event & Mktg)*

A.S.A.P.R

212 W Main St Ste 302a, Salisbury, MD 21801
Tel.: (443) 944-9301
Fax: (443) 944-9306
E-Mail: Robbie@asapr.com
Web Site: www.asapr.com

Robbie Tarpley Raffish *(Founder)*
Melissa Hampton *(Asst Acct Exec)*

Accounts:
Delaware Health Information Network
Liberty Property Trust

ASB COMMUNICATIONS

247 W 35 th St Ste 16 F, New York, NY 10001
Tel.: (212) 216-9305
Fax: (212) 214-0437
E-Mail: info@asbcommunications.com
Web Site: www.asbcommunications.com

Employees: 10
Year Founded: 1997

Agency Specializes In: Asian Market

Approx. Annual Billings: $1,000,000

Breakdown of Gross Billings by Media: Adv. Specialities: $300,000; Consulting: $50,000; Event Mktg.: $650,000

Neeta Bhasin *(Pres & CEO)*
Richie Ri *(Acct Mgr)*

Accounts:
HSBC
Moneygram
Reliance Infocomm

ASBURY DESIGN

1603 E 22nd Ave, Eugene, OR 97403
Tel.: (541) 344-1633
Web Site: www.asburydesign.net

Year Founded: 2006

Agency Specializes In: Advertising, Brand Development & Integration, Broadcast, Corporate Identity, Exhibit/Trade Shows, Internet/Web Design, Logo & Package Design, Radio, T.V.

Steven Asbury *(Pres)*
Libby Tower *(Acct Mgr & Mgr-Media)*
Wendelin Asbury *(Office Mgr)*
Alan Yamamoto *(Strategist-Concept & Sr Copywriter)*

Accounts:
Eugene Swim & Tennis Club
Longs Meat Market
Osborne Partners Capital Management

ASCENTMEDIA
1022 E Pacific St, Appleton, WI 54911
Tel.: (920) 931-2510
E-Mail: info@ascentmedia.net
Web Site: www.ascentmedia.net

Year Founded: 2010

Agency Specializes In: Advertising, Brand Development & Integration, Digital/Interactive, Email, Internet/Web Design, Logo & Package Design, Package Design, Print, Search Engine Optimization, Social Media

Accounts:
Optimal Fit

ASEN MARKETING & ADVERTISING, INC.
2210 Sutherland Ave Ste 115, Knoxville, TN 37919
Tel.: (865) 769-0006
Fax: (865) 769-0080
E-Mail: info@asenmarketing.com
Web Site: www.asenmarketing.com

Agency Specializes In: Advertising, Brand Development & Integration, Internet/Web Design, Package Design, Print, Social Media

Paul Scoonover *(CEO)*
Stacey DeHart *(COO)*
Brookney Morrell *(Dir-Art & Acct Mgr)*
Jennifer Givler *(Dir-Bus Dev)*
Di Oakley *(Dir-Comm)*
Mark Perriguey *(Dir-Creative)*

Accounts:
Calhouns Restaurant
Copper Cellar Catering
Knoxville Film & Music Festival
MHM Architects & Interior Designers

ASHAY MEDIA GROUP
159 20th St, Brooklyn, NY 11232
Tel.: (718) 625-5133
Fax: (718) 246-2093
E-Mail: ashay@ashay.com
Web Site: www.ashay.com

Employees: 6
Year Founded: 1998

Agency Specializes In: Advertising, African-American Market, Alternative Advertising, Arts, Brand Development & Integration, Branded Entertainment, Broadcast, Business Publications, Business-To-Business, Catalogs, Communications, Consumer Goods, Content, Corporate Communications, Corporate Identity, Digital/Interactive, Direct Response Marketing, Direct-to-Consumer, E-Commerce, Electronic Media, Exhibit/Trade Shows, Experience Design, Gay & Lesbian Market, Graphic Design, Guerilla Marketing, Hispanic Market, Identity Marketing, In-Store Advertising, Internet/Web Design, Logo & Package Design, Media Planning, Multicultural, Multimedia, Newspapers & Magazines, Print, Production (Ad, Film, Broadcast), Promotions, Radio, T.V., Trade & Consumer Magazines, Travel & Tourism, Urban Market, Viral/Buzz/Word of Mouth, Web (Banner Ads, Pop-ups, etc.)

Approx. Annual Billings: $1,000,000

Breakdown of Gross Billings by Media: Collateral: $1,000,000

Cherise Trahan-Miller *(Partner & Dir-Creative)*

ASHER AGENCY, INC.
535 W Wayne St, Fort Wayne, IN 46802-2123
Tel.: (260) 424-3373
Fax: (260) 420-2615 (Media)
Toll Free: (800) 900-7031
E-Mail: timb@asheragency.com
Web Site: www.asheragency.com

E-Mail for Key Personnel:
Chairman: timb@asheragency.com
President: tkborne@asheragency.com

Employees: 25
Year Founded: 1974

National Agency Associations: PRSA

Agency Specializes In: Brand Development & Integration, Public Relations

Timothy S. Borne *(CEO)*
Jill Brown *(Sr VP & Dir-Media)*
Dan Schroeter *(VP & Dir-Creative)*
Margaret Davidson *(VP-Strategic Dev)*
Larry Wardlaw *(VP)*
Emily Harmeyer *(Dir-Art)*
Matt Klein *(Dir-Strategy)*
Brandon Peat *(Dir-Art)*
Kirsten Hamrick *(Mgr-Production)*
Jennifer Murphy *(Acct Supvr)*
Katianne Blair *(Acct Exec)*
Lisa Starr *(Sr Media Buyer & Planner)*
Tessa Gochtovtt *(Sr Media Planner & Buyer)*

Accounts:
Allen County Public Library; Fort Wayne, IN
Cameron Memorial Hospital (Advertising Agency of Record)
Camp Watcha Wanna Do
Citilink; Fort Wayne, IN Public Transportation
Covington Plaza; Fort Wayne, IN Shopping Center
Downtown Improvement District; Fort Wayne, IN
Fort Wayne Community Schools; Fort Wayne, IN
Fort Wayne Conventions & Visitors Bureau
Fort Wayne-Allen County Economic Development Alliance
FWRadiology
Grand Wayne Convention Center
Indiana Department of Education; Indianapolis, IN; 2004
Indiana Department of Revenue; Indianapolis, IN; 2005
Indiana Department Workforce Development; Indianapolis, IN
Indiana Family & Social Services Administration
Indiana Members Credit Union Creative, Marketing Strategy, Media
Indiana Port Commission; Indianapolis, IN; 2004
Ivy Tech Community College of Indiana; Fort Wayne, Gary, Kokomo & South Bend, IN
NeuroSpine and Pain Center (Agency of Record)
Regional Chamber of Northeast Indiana (Agency of Record); 2003
Subway Restaurants (Agency of Record); Jackson, TN
Subway; Evansville & Fort Wayne, IN; Bowling Green, Lexington & Louisville, KY; Lima & Toledo, OH Fast Food
Thundershirt Creative
WPTA TV; Fort Wayne, IN ABC Affiliate

Branches

Asher Agency, Inc.
(Formerly The Arnold Agency)
117 Summers St, Charleston, WV 25301
Tel.: (304) 342-1200
Fax: (304) 342-1285
Web Site: www.asheragency.com

Employees: 25
Year Founded: 1988

Agency Specializes In: Communications, Environmental, Financial, Food Service, Government/Political, Health Care Services, Industrial

Tonya Connor *(Sr VP)*
Steve Morrison *(VP & Gen Mgr)*
Anthony Juliano *(VP-Acct Svc & Bus Dev)*
Brent Williams *(VP)*
Shannon Simon *(Dir-Strategic Comm)*
Amanda Adams *(Acct Supvr)*
Jeanne Otis *(Acct Supvr)*
Melanie George *(Acct Exec)*
Heather Peaytt *(Acct Exec)*
Anthony Boyer *(Media Planner & Buyer)*
Leslie Larkins *(Media Planner & Buyer)*

Accounts:
Cable Television Association; WV
Department of Health & Human Resources
Enterprise Rent-A-Car
Invenergy Wind, LLC
Mountain State Blue Cross/Blue Shield; Parkersburg, WV
Steptoe & Johnson
WVDHHR

Asher Agency, Inc.
4101 Tates Creek Ctr Dr Ste 150, Lexington, KY 40517-3096
Tel.: (859) 273-5530
Fax: (859) 273-5484
Web Site: www.asheragency.com

Year Founded: 1998

Timothy S. Borne *(CEO)*
Karen Richter *(CFO & VP)*
Jill Brown *(Sr VP & Dir-Media)*
Tonya Connor *(Sr VP)*
Kara Kelley *(Sr VP)*
Dan Schroeter *(VP & Dir-Creative)*
Sharon Pfister *(VP & Acct Supvr)*
Anthony Juliano *(VP-Acct Svc & Bus Dev)*

Accounts:
Comcast
The Daily Bean Coffee Company
Ivy Tech
Manchester College
Subway

ASPEN MARKETING
(Name Changed to Epsilon Marketing)

ASPEN MARKETING SERVICES
224 N Desplaines, Chicago, IL 60661
Tel.: (312) 454-1000
Fax: (312) 454-1001
E-Mail: egonzales@aspenlatino.com
Web Site: www.aspenms.com

Employees: 10
Year Founded: 1986

Agency Specializes In: Consumer Goods, Digital/Interactive, Direct Response Marketing, Environmental, Event Planning & Marketing, Hispanic Market, Integrated Marketing, Local Marketing, Promotions, Public Relations, Sponsorship

Patrick J. O'Rahilly *(Pres & CEO)*
George Gier *(Exec VP & Exec Dir-Creative)*
Kevin Huck *(Exec VP-Client Svc)*
Dan Maher *(Exec VP)*
John Vierheller *(Exec VP-Client Svcs)*
Cathy Horn *(VP-HR)*
Brian Verhoeven *(Acct Supvr)*
Sheeba Chacko Patel *(Sr Acct Exec)*
Matthew Olsen *(Sr Copywriter-Digital)*

Accounts:

The Absolute Spirits Company Inc
Allstate
Chrysler
Discover
Hertz
Motorola Solutions, Inc.
Sears
Sun Trust
Toyota
Verizon

ASSOCIATED INTEGRATED MARKETING
(Formerly Associated Advertising Agency, Inc.)
330 N Mead Ste 200, Wichita, KS 67202
Tel.: (316) 683-4691
Fax: (316) 683-1990
E-Mail: info@meetassociated.com
Web Site: www.meetassociated.com/

E-Mail for Key Personnel:
President: MSnyder@unexpectedagency.com
Media Dir.: CFountain@unexpectedagency.com
Production Mgr.: PDreiling@unexpectedagency.com
Public Relations: SSteward@unexpectedagency.com

Employees: 18
Year Founded: 1946

National Agency Associations: 4A's-APA-BPA-MCA-PRSA

Agency Specializes In: Asian Market, Business-To-Business, Financial, Health Care Services, Strategic Planning/Research

Approx. Annual Billings: $0

Brian Schoenthaler *(VP & Head-Acct Team)*
Dave Stewart *(VP & Exec Dir-Creative)*
Patrick Dreiling *(VP & Dir-Production)*
Shawn Steward *(VP-Client Svc & PR)*
Heather Newhouse *(Dir-Art)*
Christine Olson *(Mgr-Media)*
Rosie Rayborn *(Mgr-Acctg)*
Hilary Bailey *(Acct Supvr & Strategist)*

Accounts:
Barkman Honey
Cargill Meat Solutions
Crown Uptown Theatre
Digital Retail Apps
Dove Estates Senior Living Community
Downing & Lahey Mortuaries; Wichita, KS; 1982
Foulston Siefkin Attorneys at Law
The Grasshopper Company; Moundridge, KS Residential & Commercial Moving Equipment; 1987
Heartspring
Immediate Medical Care
In The Bag Cleaners
Kansas Foot Center
KMW Loaders
Technology Plus

ASTERIX GROUP
450 Geary St Ste 100, San Francisco, CA 94102
Tel.: (415) 261-7808
E-Mail: brand@asterixgroup.com
Web Site: www.asterixgroup.com

Year Founded: 2002

Agency Specializes In: Advertising, Brand Development & Integration, Collateral, Content, Digital/Interactive, Email, Event Planning & Marketing, Internet/Web Design, Public Relations, Social Media

Christine Lehtonen *(Founder & Pres)*
Elmer Bancud *(Creative Dir)*
Llona Wall *(Sr Designer)*
Edgar Arce *(Strategist)*

Accounts:
Eleven Eleven Wines

ASTUTE COMMUNICATIONS
709 Winsley Pl, Brentwood, TN 37027
Tel.: (615) 947-6113
E-Mail: hello@astute.co
Web Site: www.astute.co

Agency Specializes In: Advertising, Content, Graphic Design, Internet/Web Design, Logo & Package Design, Social Media

Anna Stout *(Owner)*
Ryan Stout *(Partner)*

Accounts:
Tybee Jet

@RADICAL MEDIA
435 Hudson St, New York, NY 10014
Tel.: (212) 462-1500
Fax: (212) 462-1600
E-Mail: infony@radicalmedia.com
Web Site: www.radicalmedia.com

Employees: 120

Jon Kamen *(Chm & CEO)*
Frank Scherma *(Pres)*
Michael Fiore *(CFO & COO)*
Evan Schechtman *(CTO)*
Justin Wilkes *(Pres-Media & Entertainment)*
Joan Aceste *(Gen Counsel)*
Cathy Shannon *(Exec VP)*
Chris Kim *(Mng Dir-Design & Tech)*
Maya Brewster *(Dir-Sls-Global & Exec Producer)*
Jennifer Heath *(Exec Producer-Sls)*

Accounts:
Bacardi
BMG Music Entertainment (UK) Ltd. Campaign: "Behind the Mask", Michael Jackson
Chevrolet
Dos Equis
Entertainment and Sports Programming Network ESPN SEC Network
GEICO Campaign: "Guinea Pigs"
Get Schooled
Google Campaign: "The Johnny Cash Project", Creative Lab
Grey Goose Entertainment Campaign: "Rising Icons - Season 3"
J. Paul Getty Trust Campaign: "Cube on Eames", Pacific Standard Time
Levi's Campaign: "Legacy"
NASA Campaign: "Mission Juno"
Nike Campaign: "Back to the Future", Campaign: "Nike Fuelband"
Procter & Gamble
Schick Wilkinson Sword
Sting
Tommy Hilfiger
Toyota Motor Corporation
Volkswagen Group of America, Inc.

AT THE TABLE PUBLIC RELATIONS
(Formerly Sahlman Williams, Inc.)
301 W Platt St Ste 414, Tampa, FL 33606
Tel.: (813) 251-4242
Fax: (813) 251-3127
Web Site: www.atthetablepr.com

Employees: 10

Agency Specializes In: Brand Development & Integration, Commercial Photography, Crisis Communications, Health Care Services, Local Marketing, Media Relations, Product Placement, Public Relations, Publicity/Promotions, Recruitment

Laura Hallmeyer *(Gen Mgr)*

Accounts:
Georgia Peach Commission
Georgia Pecan Commission
Ocean Prime
Sweetbay Supermarket

ATHORN, CLARK & PARTNERS
38 E 29th St, New York, NY 10016
Tel.: (212) 457-6152
Fax: (212) 457-6161
E-Mail: info@athornclark.com
Web Site: www.athornclark.com

Employees: 15
Year Founded: 1998

Agency Specializes In: Business-To-Business

George Clark *(Owner)*
John Athorn *(Co-Chm)*
Jason Chiusano *(Dir-Production & Design)*

Accounts:
Cramer
Global Options Group
iBaf
McKesson
nMetric

THE ATKINS GROUP
501 Soledad, San Antonio, TX 78205
Tel.: (210) 444-2500
Fax: (210) 824-8236
E-Mail: sandie@theatkinsgroup.com
Web Site: www.theatkinsgroup.com

E-Mail for Key Personnel:
President: steve@theatkinsgroup.com
Creative Dir.: James@theatkinsgroup.com
Media Dir.: Ann@theatkinsgroup.com
Production Mgr.: sandie@theatkinsgroup.com

Employees: 15
Year Founded: 2003

Agency Specializes In: Advertising, Bilingual Market, Brand Development & Integration, Cable T.V., Collateral, Corporate Identity, Digital/Interactive, E-Commerce, Education, Graphic Design, Health Care Services, Hispanic Market, Hospitality, Internet/Web Design, Leisure, Local Marketing, Logo & Package Design, Market Research, Media Buying Services, Media Planning, Media Relations, Newspaper, Newspapers & Magazines, Outdoor, Planning & Consultation, Production (Print), Public Relations, Publicity/Promotions, Radio, Real Estate, Search Engine Optimization, Social Media, Strategic Planning/Research, T.V., Transportation, Travel & Tourism

Approx. Annual Billings: $6,500,000

Breakdown of Gross Billings by Media: Cable T.V.: $1,100,000; Collateral: $1,500,000; Fees: $1,000,000; Newsp.: $250,000; Outdoor: $400,000; Pub. Rels.: $900,000; Worldwide Web Sites: $1,350,000

Steve Atkins *(Pres & CEO)*
Ann Perrine *(Partner & Dir-Media Svcs)*
David Laffitte *(Dir-Technologies)*
Katie Carle *(Mgr-Acctg)*
Gabriella Flores *(Mgr-Ops)*
Elizabeth Moran-Degan *(Mgr-Production)*
Jayme LeGros *(Acct Supvr)*

Advertising Agencies

ATLAS
1601 Willow Rd, Menlo Park, CA 94025
Tel.: (650) 543-4800
E-Mail: info@atlassolutions.com
Web Site: www.atlassolutions.com

Employees: 130
Year Founded: 1998

Agency Specializes In: Consulting, Electronic Media, Planning & Consultation, Strategic Planning/Research

Leslie Dimaggio *(VP-Ops & IT)*
Joseph Onofrio *(Asst VP-Claims)*
Zenovia Love *(Mgr-HR)*
Bob Mckenna *(Mgr-Litigation)*
Frank Petrino *(Mgr-Claims)*
Corey Sotir *(Mgr-IT)*
Deborah Velez *(Mgr-Claims Ops)*
John J. Vessecchia *(Mgr-Underwriting)*
Donald Vaccaro *(Supvr-Fast Track Unit)*

Accounts:
Avidian
Back Country
Click Here; Dallas, TX
Eidos Interactive Ltd.
Microsoft
Monster
MTV
PinPoint Media; Coral Springs, FL
Premier-Placement; Houston, TX
Ubisoft
Xtremez

ATLAS MARKETING
435 Broad St, Sewickley, PA 15143
Tel.: (412) 749-9299
Fax: (412) 749-9294
Web Site: www.atlasstories.com

Agency Specializes In: Advertising, Digital/Interactive, Public Relations

Chris Martin *(Pres)*
John Miller *(Creative Dir)*
Susan Matson *(Acct Dir)*
Shannon Webber *(Acct Dir)*

Accounts:
New-Auntie Anne's Pretzel
New-Habitat for Humanity
New-Jennison Manufacturing Group
New-The Pittsburgh Technology Council

ATLAS MIND CREATIVE
7830 Paseo Del Rey, Playa Del Rey, CA 90293
Tel.: (310) 227-5670
Fax: (310) 839-7610
E-Mail: office@atlasmind.com
Web Site: www.atlasmind.com

Agency Specializes In: Brand Development & Integration, Broadcast, Internet/Web Design, Print

Accounts:
Phusion Projects

ATOMIC COFFEE MEDIA
918 High St Ste A, Madison, WI 53715
Tel.: (608) 628-0422
E-Mail: webgod@atomiccoffee.com
Web Site: www.atomiccoffee.com

Agency Specializes In: Advertising, E-Commerce, Internet/Web Design, Social Media

JJ Pagac *(Owner)*

Accounts:
Chris's Confections
Eau Galle Cheese
Hong Kong Cafe
Island Dream Properties
Vintage LLC.

ATOMIC DIRECT, LTD
1219 SE Lafayette St, Portland, OR 97202
Tel.: (503) 296-6131
Fax: (503) 296-9890
E-Mail: info@atomicdirect.com
Web Site: www.atomicdirect.com

Employees: 8
Year Founded: 1998

National Agency Associations: DMA

Agency Specializes In: Advertising, Cable T.V., Consulting, Consumer Goods, Consumer Marketing, Direct Response Marketing, In-Store Advertising, Infomercials, Media Buying Services, Media Planning, Mobile Marketing, Multimedia, Planning & Consultation, Strategic Planning/Research, T.V.

Doug Garnett *(Founder & CEO)*
Dave Fallon *(CFO)*
Rod Tallman *(CMO)*
Skye Weadick *(Acct Dir)*
Shelby Brill *(Mgr-Mktg Comm & Campaign)*
Evan Mccarthy *(Mgr-Media & Analytics)*
Jeff Shepherd *(Mgr-Location)*
Cydni Anderson *(Acct Exec)*
Shelley Layton *(Acct Coord)*

Accounts:
AAA
Disney Mobile
Drill Doctor/Worksharp
DuPont
Festool
Kreg Tool
Little Rapids
Lowe's/Kobalt
Newell/Rubbermaid
The Sharper Image
System Pavers
White's Electronics

ATOMIC FUSION
1736 Defoor Pl NW, Atlanta, GA 30318
Tel.: (404) 897-1920
Fax: (404) 897-1923
E-Mail: info@atomic-fusion.com
Web Site: www.atomic-fusion.com

Agency Specializes In: Digital/Interactive

Travis Granville *(Co-Founder, Mng Partner & Sr Acct Exec)*

Accounts:
Alexander Babbage
Boys & Girls Club of America
ChoicePoint
Coca-Cola Refreshments USA, Inc.
DOW
Equifax
Fiserv, Inc.
Fiserv
Hard Rock Cafe
Scribe Software
Tech Safari
Tracom
Turner Entertainment Group
VoiceQuilt

ATOMIC20
2088 Broadway, Boulder, CO 80302
Tel.: (855) 247-1395
E-Mail: hello@atomic20.com
Web Site: www.atomic20.com

Agency Specializes In: Advertising, Brand Development & Integration, Digital/Interactive, Media Relations, Public Relations, Search Engine Optimization, Social Media

Jeff Donaldson *(Pres)*
Trish Thomas *(CEO)*
Ali Kennedy *(Acct Dir)*
Ben Lovejoy *(Creative Dir)*
Caitlin Boyd *(Acct Exec)*

Accounts:
New-PepPod

ATOMICDUST
3021 Locust St, Saint Louis, MO 63103
Tel.: (314) 241-2866
Fax: (314) 754-8132
E-Mail: accounts@atomicdust.com
Web Site: www.atomicdust.com

Year Founded: 2001

Agency Specializes In: Advertising, Brand Development & Integration, Digital/Interactive, Graphic Design, Social Media

Taylor Dixson *(Owner)*
Jesse McGowan *(Owner)*
Mike Spakowski *(Owner)*
James Dixson *(Partner-New Bus)*
Erika Cruse *(Acct Mgr)*
Danielle Hohmeier *(Mgr-Online Mktg)*
Tara Nesbitt *(Coord-Online Mktg)*

Accounts:
Koplar Properties
Maryland Plaza Market, Inc.
Mosby's Nursing Suite

ATTACK MARKETING, LLC
367 Nineth St Ste B, San Francisco, CA 94103
Tel.: (415) 433-1499
Fax: (415) 276-5759
E-Mail: info@attackmarketing.net
Web Site: www.attackmarketing.com

Employees: 45
Year Founded: 2003

Agency Specializes In: Advertising, Graphic Design, Guerilla Marketing, In-Store Advertising, Mobile Marketing, Out-of-Home Media, Outdoor

Christian Jurinka *(Mng Partner)*
Andrew Loos *(Mng Partner)*
Mark Blair *(VP-Bus Dev)*
Gina Kano *(VP-Client Dev)*
Matt Tricano *(Grp Acct Dir)*
Farzad Etemadi *(Acct Dir)*
Jennifer Hooker *(Dir-Ops)*
Dave Schiesser *(Dir-Bus Dev)*
Kathryn Raines *(Reg Mgr)*

Accounts:
AMC Networks Campaign: "Mad Men"
EMC Outdoor
henryV
Jack Morton
Laughlin Constable
Maritz
Momentum
Relay
Sparks

ATTACKTIC ADVERTISING
73 S Palm Ave Ste 220, Sarasota, FL 34236
Tel.: (941) 312-7856

Fax: (941) 952-7345
E-Mail: hello@attacktic.com
Web Site: www.attackticadvertising.com

Agency Specializes In: Advertising, Digital/Interactive, Print, T.V.

Adam DeClerico *(Mng Partner & Head-Strategy)*

Accounts:
BioEsse
Gilded Lily
Malbi Decor
The Monarch Room
Poppos Taqueria
Quorum Innovations
Rosenberg Asset Management
Upcycle America

ATTAWAY ADVERTISING, INC.
1100 E Park Dr Ste 204, Birmingham, AL 35235
Tel.: (205) 296-1027
E-Mail: bill@attawayadvertising.com
Web Site: www.attawayadvertising.com

Employees: 3
Year Founded: 1977

Agency Specializes In: Advertising, Public Relations

Bill Attaway *(Pres)*

Accounts:
Alabama Wholesale Jewelry; Birmingham, AL
American Family Foundation
Cross County Wireless Wireless & Vehicle Tracking Systems
Greater Birmingham Association of Home Builders
Mike Stein Jewelry
Rogers Trading Co.

ATTENTION
160 Varick St 5th Fl, New York, NY 10013
Tel.: (917) 621-4400
E-Mail: info@attentionusa.com
Web Site: www.attentionusa.com

Year Founded: 2006

Agency Specializes In: Advertising, Digital/Interactive, Internet/Web Design, Social Media, Strategic Planning/Research

Jake Fisher *(Partner)*
Dana A. Griffin *(CMO)*
GianCarlo Pitocco *(Chief Strategy Officer)*
Tom Buontempo *(Pres-Content Labs)*
Rachel Guthermann *(VP-Client Svcs)*
Jeremy Simon *(Head-Portfolio & Client Svcs Dir)*
Daniel Janoff *(Dir-Creative)*
Sarah Kauffman *(Dir-Ops)*
Nadina Bourgeois *(Assoc Dir)*

Accounts:
Diageo North America, Inc.
International Olympic Committee
Michelin North America, Inc.
Morgan Stanley
Samsung America, Inc.

AUDIENCE INNOVATION
(Formerly Kostial Company, LLC)
8140 North Mo Pac Expy Bldg IV Ste 4-150, Austin, TX 78759
Fax: (214) 594-0244
Toll Free: (888) 241-6634
Web Site: www.audienceinnovation.com

E-Mail for Key Personnel:
President: paul.kostial@audienceinnovation.com

Employees: 50
Year Founded: 2005

Agency Specializes In: Above-the-Line, Advertising, Advertising Specialties, Affiliate Marketing, Affluent Market, African-American Market, Agriculture, Alternative Advertising, Arts, Asian Market, Automotive, Aviation & Aerospace, Below-the-Line, Bilingual Market, Brand Development & Integration, Branded Entertainment, Broadcast, Business Publications, Business-To-Business, Cable T.V., Catalogs, Children's Market, Co-op Advertising, Collateral, College, Commercial Photography, Communications, Computers & Software, Consulting, Consumer Goods, Consumer Marketing, Consumer Publications, Content, Corporate Communications, Corporate Identity, Cosmetics, Crisis Communications, Custom Publishing, Customer Relationship Management, Digital/Interactive, Direct Response Marketing, Direct-to-Consumer, E-Commerce, Education, Electronic Media, Electronics, Email, Engineering, Entertainment, Environmental, Event Planning & Marketing, Exhibit/Trade Shows, Experience Design, Fashion/Apparel, Financial, Food Service, Game Integration, Gay & Lesbian Market, Government/Political, Graphic Design, Guerilla Marketing, Health Care Services, High Technology, Hispanic Market, Hospitality, Household Goods, Identity Marketing, In-Store Advertising, Industrial, Infomercials, Information Technology, Integrated Marketing, International, Internet/Web Design, Investor Relations, Legal Services, Leisure, Local Marketing, Logo & Package Design, Luxury Products, Magazines, Marine, Market Research, Media Buying Services, Media Planning, Media Relations, Media Training, Medical Products, Men's Market, Merchandising, Mobile Marketing, Multicultural, Multimedia, New Product Development, New Technologies, Newspaper, Newspapers & Magazines, Out-of-Home Media, Outdoor, Over-50 Market, Package Design, Paid Searches, Pharmaceutical, Planning & Consultation, Podcasting, Point of Purchase, Point of Sale, Print, Product Placement, Production, Production (Ad, Film, Broadcast), Production (Print), Promotions, Public Relations, Publicity/Promotions, Publishing, RSS (Really Simple Syndication), Radio, Real Estate, Recruitment, Regional, Restaurant, Retail, Sales Promotion, Search Engine Optimization, Seniors' Market, Social Marketing/Nonprofit, South Asian Market, Sponsorship, Sports Market, Stakeholders, Strategic Planning/Research, Sweepstakes, Syndication, T.V., Technical Advertising, Teen Market, Telemarketing, Trade & Consumer Magazines, Transportation, Travel & Tourism, Urban Market, Viral/Buzz/Word of Mouth, Web (Banner Ads, Pop-ups, etc.), Women's Market, Yellow Pages Advertising

Approx. Annual Billings: $10,000,000

Breakdown of Gross Billings by Media: Bus. Publs.: $1,000,000; Consulting: $1,000,000; Consumer Publs.: $2,000,000; Pub. Rels.: $1,000,000; Sports Mktg.: $5,000,000

Laura Kalogirou-Karaoli *(VP-Sls)*
Beverly Jameson *(Dir-Southeast)*
Jesse M. Riche *(Acct Exec)*

AUDIENCE SCAN
(Formerly Ad-ology Research)
600 N Cleveland Ave Ste 260, Westerville, OH 43082
Tel.: (614) 794-0500
Web Site: www.audiencescan.com/

Employees: 25
Year Founded: 2005

Agency Specializes In: Broadcast, Business Publications, Cable T.V., Digital/Interactive, Electronic Media, Local Marketing, Magazines, Mobile Marketing, Newspaper, Newspapers & Magazines, Out-of-Home Media, Outdoor, Radio, Shopper Marketing, Social Media, Sponsorship, T.V., Trade & Consumer Magazines, Web (Banner Ads, Pop-ups, etc.)

C. Lee Smith *(Pres & CEO)*
Barry Shawgo *(VP-Sls)*
Beth Frederick *(Mgr-Mktg)*

Accounts:
AdMall Media Sales Development Application; 2005

AUDREY NYC
205 Hudson St, New York, NY 10013
Tel.: (212) 463-1400
Fax: (212) 463-1592
E-Mail: info@audreynyc.com
Web Site: www.audreynyc.com

Agency Specializes In: Advertising, Digital/Interactive, Package Design, Print, T.V.

Kate Wadia *(Mng Dir & Dir-Creative)*
Kate Murphy *(Sr VP & Grp Dir-Creative)*
Meghan Chopek *(Acct Supvr)*
Lynne Rouffa *(Sr Bus Mgr)*

Accounts:
Clinique Laboratories, Inc.

AUGUST, LANG & HUSAK, INC.
4630 Montgomery Ave Ste 400, Bethesda, MD 20814-3443
Tel.: (301) 657-2772
Fax: (301) 657-9895
E-Mail: info@alhadv.com
Web Site: www.alhadv.com

E-Mail for Key Personnel:
President: mikea@alhadv.com

Employees: 17
Year Founded: 1992

Agency Specializes In: Advertising, Agriculture, Aviation & Aerospace, Brand Development & Integration, Broadcast, Business-To-Business, Cable T.V., Collateral, Consulting, Consumer Marketing, Corporate Communications, Corporate Identity, Direct Response Marketing, Education, Environmental, Event Planning & Marketing, Exhibit/Trade Shows, Fashion/Apparel, Financial, Food Service, Government/Political, Graphic Design, Health Care Services, High Technology, Hospitality, Industrial, Internet/Web Design, Logo & Package Design, Magazines, Media Buying Services, Media Planning, Medical Products, New Product Development, Newspaper, Newspapers & Magazines, Out-of-Home Media, Outdoor, Planning & Consultation, Point of Purchase, Point of Sale, Print, Production, Production (Print), Promotions, Public Relations, Publicity/Promotions, Radio, Restaurant, Retail, Sales Promotion, Seniors' Market, Sports Market, Strategic Planning/Research, T.V., Trade & Consumer Magazines, Transportation, Travel & Tourism

Approx. Annual Billings: $17,454,784

Breakdown of Gross Billings by Media: Collateral: $2,094,575; Internet Adv.: $872,740; Newsp. & Mags.: $4,538,243; Out-of-Home Media: $1,396,382; Radio: $3,316,408; T.V.: $3,665,504; Transit: $1,047,288; Worldwide Web Sites: $523,644

Michael August *(Owner)*

Bill Lang *(Principal)*
Bonnie Weaver *(VP & Acct Supvr)*
Bryant Prince *(Dir-Art)*
Melissa Meyers *(Assoc Dir-Creative)*
Kandi Hopkins *(Mgr-Acctg)*

Accounts:
American Academy of Orthopaedic Surgeons; Rosemont, IL National Consumer; 1999
HMSHost; Bethesda, MD Natl Business to Business, Branding & Advertising; 2008
Hope & A Home; Washington, DC Pro-Bono; 2007
National Family Caregivers Association; Kensington, MD National Public Service; 2001
National Public Radio/Public Radio Satellite System; Washington, DC Natl Business to Business, Branding & Advertising; 2009
Society of Interventional Radiology; Fairfax, VA National Consumer; 2001
Vision Council of America; Alexandria, VA Consumer, Public Service; 2004
WETA-TV 26 Public Broadcasting (PBS); Arlington, VA "This Week in Business", "Washington Week in Review"; 1994

AUGUST MEDIA
(Acquired by Publicis Groupe S.A.)

AUGUSTINEIDEAS
532 Gibson Dr Ste 250, Roseville, CA 95678
Tel.: (916) 774-9600
Fax: (916) 774-9611
E-Mail: hello@augustineideas.com
Web Site: www.augustineideas.com

Agency Specializes In: Advertising, Brand Development & Integration, Communications, Graphic Design, Internet/Web Design, Public Relations, Social Media

Debbie Augustine *(CEO)*
Kevin Wilhelm *(Exec VP-Ops)*
Margo Robinson *(VP-Bus Dev & Partnerships)*

Accounts:
New-Burtons Biscuits
New-Sacramento Republic FC

AUGUSTUS BARNETT ADVERTISING/DESIGN
PO Box 197, Fox Island, WA 98333-0197
Tel.: (253) 549-2396
Fax: (253) 549-4707
Toll Free: (800) 200-9477
E-Mail: charlieb@augustusbarnett.com
Web Site: www.augustusbarnett.com

Employees: 1
Year Founded: 1981

Agency Specializes In: Advertising, Agriculture, Brand Development & Integration, Business Publications, Business-To-Business, Co-op Advertising, Collateral, Consulting, Consumer Marketing, Corporate Identity, Event Planning & Marketing, Financial, Food Service, Graphic Design, Health Care Services, Logo & Package Design, Marine, Merchandising, New Product Development, Newspaper, Planning & Consultation, Point of Purchase, Point of Sale, Print, Production, Radio, Restaurant, Retail, Sales Promotion, Trade & Consumer Magazines, Travel & Tourism

Approx. Annual Billings: $1,000,000

Breakdown of Gross Billings by Media: Collateral: 5%; Consulting: 11%; Fees: 21%; Logo & Package Design: 11%; Newsp. & Mags.: 5%; Outdoor: 5%; Point of Purchase: 5%; Print: 11%; Production: 11%; Promos.: 5%; Pub. Rels.: 5%; Radio: 5%

Augustus Barnett *(Pres & Dir-Creative)*

Accounts:
J.M. Martinac Shipbuilding Corp. Commercial Fishing Boat Builder; 1982

AUMCORE LLC
3348 Peachtree Rd NE Ste 150, Atlanta, GA 30326
Tel.: (404) 442-6200
Fax: (404) 537-1849
Web Site: www.aumcore.com

Year Founded: 2010

Agency Specializes In: Advertising, Brand Development & Integration, Corporate Identity, Internet/Web Design, Package Design, Print, Social Media

Niraj Patpatia *(Partner)*
Dana Gjonbalaj *(Strategist-Content)*

Accounts:
Denon Electronics
MiQuando

AURORA COAST PRODUCTIONS
802 W Park Ave Ste 222, Ocean, NJ 07712
Tel.: (732) 905-5200
Toll Free: (888) 593-0062
Web Site:
www.auroracoast.com/marketing_advertising_agency.html

Agency Specializes In: Advertising, Broadcast, Publicity/Promotions, T.V.

Approx. Annual Billings: $7,500,000

Breakdown of Gross Billings by Media: Brdcst.: $7,500,000

Justin Viggiano *(Asst Dir & Supvr-Script)*

Accounts:
APCO Worldwide
Aquafina Skincare
ASCO
Ask.com
Avaya
Buchanan Advertising Group of Canada
Crayola
Cushman & Wakefield
DDB Worldwide
Denny's
Emerson
ESPN
GenConn
Interactive Brokers
Johnson & Johnson
McDonald's
Mercedes
Merck
Nestle
Penguin Publications
Pharmaceutical Research & Manufacturers (PhRMA)
Retro Fitness
Roberts & Langer
Rockefeller Foundation
SGS
Taylor Global PR
TBWA
Trump Network

AUSTIN & WILLIAMS
125 Kennedy Dr Ste 100, Hauppauge, NY 11788-4017
Tel.: (631) 231-6600
Fax: (631) 434-7022
Web Site: www.austin-williams.com

E-Mail for Key Personnel:
Creative Dir.: rick@austin-williams.com

Employees: 35
Year Founded: 1996

National Agency Associations: 4A's-NEW ENGLAND FINANCIAL MARKETING ASSOCIATION-NEWYORK BANKERS ASSOCIATION-NJ BANKERS

Agency Specializes In: Advertising, Advertising Specialties, Affluent Market, Automotive, Brand Development & Integration, Business-To-Business, Cable T.V., Catalogs, Collateral, College, Communications, Computers & Software, Consulting, Consumer Goods, Consumer Marketing, Corporate Communications, Digital/Interactive, Direct Response Marketing, Direct-to-Consumer, Education, Electronic Media, Electronics, Email, Entertainment, Exhibit/Trade Shows, Financial, Graphic Design, Guerilla Marketing, Health Care Services, Hospitality, Identity Marketing, Integrated Marketing, Internet/Web Design, Investor Relations, Legal Services, Logo & Package Design, Luxury Products, Media Buying Services, Media Planning, Medical Products, Men's Market, Mobile Marketing, Multimedia, New Product Development, Newspaper, Newspapers & Magazines, Outdoor, Over-50 Market, Package Design, Paid Searches, Planning & Consultation, Point of Purchase, Point of Sale, Print, Production, Production (Print), Public Relations, Radio, Search Engine Optimization, Seniors' Market, Social Marketing/Nonprofit, Social Media, T.V., Trade & Consumer Magazines, Tween Market, Viral/Buzz/Word of Mouth, Web (Banner Ads, Pop-ups, etc.), Women's Market

Approx. Annual Billings: $12,000,000

Rick Chiorando *(Principal & Chief Creative Officer)*
Lisa Liebman *(Vice President, Managing Director)*
Carolyn Eckert *(Vice President, Client Svcs)*
Jennifer Forget *(Vice President, Client Engagement)*
Larry Baronciani *(Sr Art Director)*
Jerry Bentivegna *(Sr Art Director)*
Sheira Rosenberg *(Account Director)*
Mark Russell *(Art Director)*
Tony Fabrizio *(Video Production)*
Frank Durante *(Director of Digital Dev)*
Bryan Hynes *(Dir-Creative)*
Henry Luhmann *(Director of Production Services)*
Tricia Zorn *(Digital Project Manager)*
Ken Auld *(Data Manager)*
Jessica Guidoboni *(Acct Supvr)*
Sallianne Nicholls *(Acct Supvr)*
Juan Tejada *(Paid Search Strategist)*
Pamela Schneck *(Integrated Media Planner)*
Rita O'Connor *(Media & Traffic Coordinator)*
Nick Basil *(Web Developer)*
Ken Greenberg *(Consulting Founder)*

Accounts:
A&Z Pharmaceutical Healthcare; 2014
Bridgehampton National Bank Financial; 2010
Brookhaven Memorial Hospital; Patchogue, NY Healthcare; 2010
Canine Companions Trained Assistance Dogs for the Disabled; 2012
Canon Cameras, Printers; 2013
Carr Business Systems Business Automation; 2014
Columbia Bank Financial; 2010
Community National Bank Financial; 2009
Cook Maran Insurance; 2012
Crescendo Luxury Lifestyle; 2013
Crest Hollow Country Club; Woodbury, NY Event Catering; 2009
CrossTex Medical Masks & Supplies; 2014
D-CAL Pharmaceutical; 2013

DeGiaimo-Monti Real Estate Developer; 2011
Dejana Trucking Services; 2014
Digital Technology Services IT Services; 2012
EAFCU Financial; 2009
Egan & Golden Legal Services; 2010
Ferrell Fritz Legal Services; 2007
FirstCapital Bank of Texas Financial; 2013
Fortunoff High-end Jewelry; 2000
GHS FCU Financial; 2013
Gold Coast Bank Financial; 2005
Gotham Mini Storage Storage Units & Services; 2012
Helping Paws Animal Wellness; 2014
Henry Schein Dental Office Transitions; 2014
Hudson Valley Federal Credit Union Financial; 2010
ICC Total Home Automation; 2013
Injectafer IV Iron Replacement; 2013
Israel Purdy Legal Services; 2010
J. Tortorella Pools; Southampton, NY Pools & Spas; 2002
Jewish Academy Admissions, Education, Fundraising; 2012
Kennedy Center Entertainment, Fundraising, Programs; 2012
Lewis Johs Legal Services; 2013
Life's WORC Autism Awareness Services; 2012
Long Island Cares Nonprofit; 2001
Mahoney Associates Legal Services; 2005
McGraw-Hill Federal Credit Union Financial; 2012
Mercedes-Benz of Rockville Centre Automotive; 2012
New-Metropolitan College of New York Advertising, Campaign: "What's Your Purpose?"
Mid Atlantic Federal Credit Union; Baltimore, MD Financial Services; 2011
Molloy Bros. Mayflower Moving Services & Storage Units; 2014
Molloy College; Rockville Centre, NY Undergraduate & Graduate Studies; 2005
Nicolock Pavers & Paving Material; 2013
Nikon Cameras & Photography Equipment; 2013
O2G Gas Conversion Oil to Gas Conversions; 2014
Oceanside Christopher FCU Financial; 2014
Orlin & Cohen; Rockville Centre, NY Subspecialty Orthopedic Surgery; 2007
Patient Innovations Healthcare; 2010
PM Pediatrics Healthcare; 2013
Project Freedom Nonprofit; 2004
QualityOne Wireless Wireless Distribution; 2013
Rivkin Radler Legal Services; 2007
RR Health Strategies Healthcare; 2007
Secure Self Storage Storage Units; 2014
Sinnreich, Safar & Kosakoff Legal Services; 2010
South Nassau Communities Hospital; Oceanside, NY Bariatrics, Gamma Knife, Orthopedics; 2003
Suffolk Federal Credit Union Financial; 2005
Summit Security Security Guards & Services; 2008
Telex Metals Minor Metals Manufacturing, Refining & Trading; 2014
Touro Law School; West Islip, NY Law Degree; 2007
Vaughn College; Flushing, NY Undergraduate & Technical Programs; 2005
Wartburg Assisted Living; 2012
Wonderland Tree Care Landscaping; 2005
Xcel Federal Credit Union; Secaucus, NJ Deposit & Loan Services, Membership; 2002

AUSTIN LAWRENCE GROUP
1266 E Main St Ste 700, Stamford, CT 06902
Tel.: (203) 391-3006
Fax: (203) 969-0266
E-Mail: k.lempit@austinlawrence.com
Web Site: www.austinlawrence.com

E-Mail for Key Personnel:
President: k.lempit@austinlawrence.com

Employees: 10
Year Founded: 1981

National Agency Associations: PRSA

Agency Specializes In: Advertising, Automotive, Brand Development & Integration, Business Publications, Business-To-Business, Collateral, Communications, Corporate Identity, Direct Response Marketing, Event Planning & Marketing, Financial, High Technology, Information Technology, Logo & Package Design, Media Buying Services, Medical Products, Newspapers & Magazines, Pharmaceutical, Planning & Consultation, Public Relations, Publicity/Promotions, Radio, Strategic Planning/Research, T.V., Technical Advertising

Ken Lempit *(Pres)*
Keith R. Reynolds *(VP)*
Alexander Lapa *(Mgr-Inbound)*
Rich Rubin *(Sr Strategist-Mktg)*
Muhammad Farooq *(Sr Engr-Software)*

Accounts:
CED Technologies
Welcome Gate

AUTOCOM ASSOCIATES
74 W Long Lk Rd Ste 103, Bloomfield Hills, MI 48304-2770
Tel.: (248) 647-8621
Fax: (248) 642-2110
E-Mail: hscheuter@usautocom.com
Web Site: www.usautocom.com

Employees: 17
Year Founded: 1995

Agency Specializes In: Automotive, High Technology

Lawrence A. Weis *(Pres & CEO)*
Kenneth A. Levy *(Sr Partner & Pres-Intl Ops)*
Susan Pollack *(Sr Acct Mgr)*
Holly Clark *(Acct Exec)*
Merle Luckens *(Acct Exec)*
Jack Harned *(Sr Partner)*

Accounts:
A Raymond Tinnerman
A Raymond
Alcantara
Autoweb
Avon Automotive
Behr-Hella Thermocontrol
New-CHEP
Coherix
The Detroit Institute for Children
Detroit Retired City Employees Association
dSPACE
Eberspaecher North America
ecarlist
Elektrobit Automotive
Emissions Analytics (North American Public Relations Agency of Record)
Focus: HOPE
Ford Piquette Avenue Plant
Forgotten Harvest of Michigan
FORTECH Products, Inc. Public Relations
Gage Products Co.
Gibbs Sports Amphibians
Gibbs Technologies
GKN Driveline
GKN Sinter Metals
Grammer Automotive
HBPO North America Inc.
Hella Inc.
HELLA KGaA Hueck & Co.
Hella North America
Icom North America
INFICON Public Relations
Intermap Technologies
InterRegs
KEMET
Kiekert AG
Lear Corporation
Lippitt O'Keefe PLLC
Maestro Media Print Solutions Public Relations
MAHLE Behr USA
MANN+HUMMEL
The National Automotive History Collection Public Relations
New-The Norma Group (North American Public Relations Agency of Record)
Novelis
Safford & Baker
Saphran Solutions
Thetford Corporation
TI Automotive
vAuto; Oakbrook Terrace, IL

AVALA MARKETING GROUP
1082 Headquarters Park, Saint Louis, MO 63026
Tel.: (636) 343-9988
Fax: (636) 326-3282
Toll Free: (888) 828-9249
E-Mail: info@avalamarketing.com
Web Site: www.avalamarketing.com

Steve Pizzolato *(Owner)*
Dan Ramler *(CTO)*
Terry Domian *(VP)*
Tom Kasperski *(VP-Digital Strategy)*
Bill Moran *(Dir-Analytical Svc)*
Madelyn Bennett *(Project Mgr-Digital)*
Andrea Helleny *(Project Mgr-Digital)*
Jenifer Weber *(Project Mgr-Digital)*
Laurie Fleis *(Mgr-Acctg & HR)*
Brian Behrens *(Sr Engr-Software)*
Scott Isaak *(Sr Engr-Software)*
Brian Wagener *(Sr Engr-Software)*

AVANZA ADVERTISING, LLC
5465 NW 36th St, Miami Springs, FL 33166
Tel.: (786) 656-7601
E-Mail: hola@avanzaad.com
Web Site: www.avanzaad.com

Employees: 9
Year Founded: 2012

Agency Specializes In: Above-the-Line, Advertising, Affiliate Marketing, Brand Development & Integration, Business Publications, Catalogs, Collateral, Consumer Publications, Copywriting, Digital/Interactive, Direct Response Marketing, Electronic Media, Email, Event Planning & Marketing, Exhibit/Trade Shows, In-Store Advertising, Infomercials, Local Marketing, Magazines, Mobile Marketing, Multimedia, Newspaper, Newspapers & Magazines, Out-of-Home Media, Outdoor, Paid Searches, Point of Sale, Print, Production, Production (Ad, Film, Broadcast), Production (Print), Public Relations, Publishing, RSS (Really Simple Syndication), Search Engine Optimization, Social Media, Trade & Consumer Magazines, Web (Banner Ads, Pop-ups, etc.), Yellow Pages Advertising

Approx. Annual Billings: $500,000

Alejandro Perez-Eguren *(Pres)*

Accounts:
The Fresh Diet; 2011
Renaissance Santiago Hotel; 2013

AVATARLABS
16030 Ventura Blvd, Encino, CA 91436
Tel.: (818) 784-2200
Fax: (818) 784-2204
E-Mail: info@avatarlabs.com
Web Site: www.avatarlabs.com

Employees: 55
Year Founded: 2001

Agency Specializes In: Digital/Interactive, Mobile Marketing, Viral/Buzz/Word of Mouth, Web (Banner Ads, Pop-ups, etc.)

Rex Cook *(CEO)*
Suzanne Abramson Norr *(COO)*
Anette Hughes *(VP & Dir-Creative)*
Henrik Markarian *(VP-Tech)*
Michelle Naden *(VP-Mktg & Partnerships)*
Laura Primack *(VP-Culture & Creative Svcs)*
Jason Steinberg *(VP-Client Svcs)*

Accounts:
HBO Cable Shows; 2010
Mattel Co-branded toys; 2009
Sony Pictures Feature Films
Walt Disney Studios Feature Films; 2002

AVC MEDIA GROUP
58 S Broad St, Woodbury, NJ 8096
Tel.: (856) 848-3566
Web Site: www.avcmediagroup.com

Agency Specializes In: Advertising, Digital/Interactive, Internet/Web Design, Media Buying Services, Outdoor, Print, Radio

Cynthia Trovato *(Owner, Pres & CEO)*
Vince Trovato *(Creative Dir)*
Jim Cushman *(Dir-Adv & Media)*

Accounts:
Philadelphia Gas Works

AVENUE 25
9201 N 25th Ave Ste 120, Phoenix, AZ 85021
Tel.: (602) 864-1233
Fax: (602) 995-2942
E-Mail: info@ave25.com
Web Site: www.ave25.com

Agency Specializes In: Advertising, Digital/Interactive, E-Commerce, Exhibit/Trade Shows, Graphic Design, Internet/Web Design, Print, Radio, Search Engine Optimization, T.V.

Kelly J. Pile *(Owner)*
Rusty Pile *(Pres & Dir-Creative & Mktg)*
Rob Tinsman *(Sr Dir-Art)*
Rachel Gularte *(Dir-Bus Dev)*
Lindi Koprivnikar *(Dir-Art)*
Jeff Sokol *(Dir-Web)*

Accounts:
Bauman Loewe Witt & Maxwell, PLLC
Chandler Public Library
GL General Contracting
Grand Canyon Planning Associates, LLC
PetMatrix LLC. DreamBone

AVENUE A INTEGRATED MARKETING INC.
Ave A 104 Shane St 2nd Fl, PO Box 1010, Owen Sound, ON N4K 6H6 Canada
Tel.: (519) 376-1177
Fax: (519) 376-8666
Toll Free: (877) 376-1177
E-Mail: howdy@avenuea.ca
Web Site: avenueaadvertising.ca

Employees: 14
Year Founded: 1993

Agency Specializes In: Advertising

Accounts:
Auto Logic
Becker's Shoes
Trillium Mutual
Van Dolder's Home Team

AVENUE FIFTY FOUR ADVERTISING LLC
23403 E Mission Ave Ste 108, Liberty Lake, WA 99019
Tel.: (208) 277-5299
Web Site: www.ave54.com

Agency Specializes In: Advertising, Brand Development & Integration, Internet/Web Design, Media Buying Services, Package Design, Print, Promotions, Radio, Social Media, T.V.

Henry-Scott Simkins *(Principal)*
Aaron Krall *(Mgr-Audio & Visual)*
Curtis Chastain *(Acct Exec)*
Gary Strong *(Strategist-Mktg)*

Accounts:
CBS Corporation
City of Spokane
Dirne Community Health Center
Ethical Investigators
Legacy Health
Living Stone Inc
Mullan House
Nancy for Mayor
North Idaho College
Paul Mitchell
Prairie Falls Golf Club
Professional Investigators International
Rainforest Cafe, Inc.
Riverstone Development
Spokane Shine
Supreme Company
The Walt Disney Company

AVENUE MARKETING & COMMUNICATIONS
363 W Erie St 4th Fl E, Chicago, IL 60654
Tel.: (312) 787-8300
Fax: (312) 787-8833
E-Mail: info@avenue-inc.com
Web Site: www.avenue-inc.com

Employees: 20

Agency Specializes In: Advertising, Corporate Identity, Digital/Interactive, E-Commerce, Identity Marketing, Internet/Web Design

Bob Domenz *(CEO)*
Jane Kindra *(Mgr-HR & Controller)*
Tom Harrison *(Exec Acct Dir)*
Adrian Gershom *(Dir-Digital)*
Codi Goodis *(Dir-Art & Sr Designer)*
Rachel Klein *(Dir-Strategy)*
Nick Wiesner *(Dir-Creative)*
Ruben S. Delgado, III *(Project Mgr-Digital)*
John Geletka *(Strategist-Digital)*

Accounts:
InterfaceFLOR
Weber

AVOCET COMMUNICATIONS
1501 S Sunset St Ste A, Longmont, CO 80501-6757
Tel.: (303) 678-7102
Fax: (303) 678-7109
E-Mail: info@avocetcommunications.com
Web Site: www.avocetcommunications.com

Employees: 12
Year Founded: 1979

Agency Specializes In: Brand Development & Integration, Broadcast, Business-To-Business, Corporate Identity, Direct Response Marketing, Internet/Web Design, Point of Sale, Print

Kit Sutorius *(Chm)*
Dustin Cornell *(Sr Dir-Art)*
Dan Colgan *(Dir-Art & Interactive)*
Bea Sutorius *(Sr Mgr-Content)*
Colleen Sheehan *(Office Mgr)*
Chris Sutorius *(Product Mgr)*
Doug Coupe *(Mgr-Fin)*

Accounts:
Arc Thrift Stores; Denver, CO Retail

AVREA FOSTER
500 North Akard St Ste 2000, Dallas, TX 75201
Tel.: (214) 855-1400
Fax: (214) 259-3670
E-Mail: contact@avreafoster.com
Web Site: www.avreafoster.com

Employees: 35
Year Founded: 1992

Agency Specializes In: Brand Development & Integration, Collateral, Communications, Digital/Interactive, Direct Response Marketing, Event Planning & Marketing, Internet/Web Design, Out-of-Home Media, Publicity/Promotions, Recruitment, Sponsorship

Darren Avrea *(Chm & Exec Dir-Creative)*
Dave Foster *(Pres & CEO)*
Suzanne Miller *(VP-Client Relationships)*
Andrew Skola *(VP-Strategy)*
Cheyenne Dazey *(Acct Dir)*
Christine Guiang *(Acct Dir)*
Brittani Hall *(Sr Acct Exec)*
Lisa Goin *(Mng Grp Dir-Creative)*

Accounts:
Acosta Sales and Marketing
Chase Paymentech
Concentra
Exxon Mobil
IBM
Omni Hotels & Resorts
Regus
Tenat

AVS GROUP
3120 S Ave, La Crosse, WI 54601
Tel.: (608) 787-1010
Fax: (608) 787-0012
E-Mail: info@avsgroup.com
Web Site: www.avsgroup.com

Agency Specializes In: Advertising, Brand Development & Integration, Email, Graphic Design, Internet/Web Design, Public Relations, Social Media

Ed Wais *(Co-Owner, Pres & Gen Mgr)*
Rebecca Leclair *(Sr Dir-Art)*
Ellen Finch *(Acct Svcs Dir)*
Sarah Arendt-Beyer *(Dir-Mktg)*

Accounts:
La Crosse Community Foundation

AWARE ADVERTISING
2004 Waters Edge Ct, Saint Louis, MO 63367
Tel.: (314) 517-0088
Fax: (314) 228-0138
Web Site: www.awarestl.com

Agency Specializes In: Advertising, Digital/Interactive, Internet/Web Design, Print, Public Relations, Radio, Social Media, T.V.

Scott Wibbenmeyer *(Pres)*
Rebecca Lord *(Copywriter & Mgr-Digital)*

Accounts:
Foresight Services, Inc.
Villa Casanova

AXIA PUBLIC RELATIONS
222 E Forsyth St, Jacksonville, FL 32202
Tel.: (904) 416-1500
Fax: (904) 425-6653
Toll Free: (866) 999-AXIA
E-Mail: tellmemore@axia.net
Web Site: www.axiapr.com

Employees: 20
Year Founded: 2002

National Agency Associations: AAF-PRSA-Second Wind Limited

Agency Specializes In: Affluent Market, Arts, Automotive, Aviation & Aerospace, Broadcast, Business Publications, Business-To-Business, Cable T.V., Children's Market, Communications, Computers & Software, Consulting, Consumer Goods, Consumer Publications, Content, Corporate Communications, Crisis Communications, Customer Relationship Management, Digital/Interactive, Direct-to-Consumer, Education, Electronic Media, Electronics, Engineering, Entertainment, Environmental, Faith Based, Fashion/Apparel, Financial, Food Service, Health Care Services, High Technology, Hospitality, Household Goods, Industrial, Information Technology, International, Legal Services, Leisure, Luxury Products, Magazines, Marine, Media Relations, Media Training, Medical Products, Men's Market, Merchandising, Multimedia, New Product Development, New Technologies, Newspaper, Newspapers & Magazines, Over-50 Market, Pets , Pharmaceutical, Planning & Consultation, Podcasting, Print, Product Placement, Public Relations, Publicity/Promotions, Radio, Real Estate, Recruitment, Regional, Restaurant, Retail, Search Engine Optimization, Seniors' Market, Social Marketing/Nonprofit, Social Media, Sponsorship, Sports Market, Stakeholders, Strategic Planning/Research, Sweepstakes, Syndication, T.V., Teen Market, Trade & Consumer Magazines, Transportation, Travel & Tourism, Tween Market, Urban Market, Women's Market

Approx. Annual Billings: $6,000,000

Jason Mudd *(Chm, CEO & Principal)*
Robert Mcnicholas *(Head-Technologist & Dir-IT)*
Marjorie Comer *(Acct Mgr-PR)*
Jenni Stevens *(Mgr-Social Media Community Engagement)*
Doug Flick *(Sr Accountant)*

Accounts:
Rebounderz Franchise and Development (National Public Relations Agency of Record) Media Relations

AXIOM
1702 Washington Ave, Houston, TX 77007
Tel.: (713) 523-5711
Fax: (713) 523-6083
E-Mail: info@axiom.us.com
Web Site: www.axiomdg.com

Employees: 13
Year Founded: 1998

Agency Specializes In: Graphic Design

Tom Hair *(Pres)*
Mike Wu *(Sr Dir-Art & Designer)*
Danielle Feith *(Dir-Mktg)*
David Lerch *(Dir-Creative)*
Laura Paddock *(Brand Mgr)*
John Duplechin *(Mgr-Multimedia)*

Accounts:
Cameron Drilling & Production Systems Oil & Gas Equipment
GX Technology Corp.
Hewlett Packard
Houston Symphony
Petrosys
Shell E&P International/Royal Dutch
Shell E&P North America
Stewart & Stevenson Services
Texas Instruments
US Concrete

AXIOM MARKETING COMMUNICATIONS
3800 American Blvd W Ste 1275, Bloomington, MN 55431
Tel.: (952) 224-2939
Fax: (952) 224-2596
Toll Free: (888) 917-3716
E-Mail: info@axiomcom.com
Web Site: www.axiomcom.com

Employees: 25

Agency Specializes In: Event Planning & Marketing, Public Relations, Strategic Planning/Research

Revenue: $1,000,000

Mike Reiber *(CEO)*
Kathleen Hennessy *(Partner & CMO)*
Rob Beachy *(Principal)*
Jeffrey Clausing *(Sr VP-Strategic Solutions)*
Tom Chervenak *(VP-Innovation)*
Leah Teravskis *(Producer-Digital Content)*
Candace Carr *(Dir-Creative)*
Marty Neal *(Dir-Bus Dev)*

Accounts:
Best Buy
Country Inns & Suites By Carlson, Inc.
Ford
Kitchen Aid
Kohler
Radisson
VISA
Whirlpool

AXIOMPORT
646 Massachusetts Ave, Indianapolis, IN 46204
Tel.: (317) 634-8020
Fax: (317) 634-8054
E-Mail: info@axiomport.com
Web Site: www.axiomport.com

Agency Specializes In: Advertising, Corporate Identity, Digital/Interactive, Internet/Web Design, Logo & Package Design, Media Planning, Print, Radio, Social Media, T.V.

Tim Wallis *(Partner & Dir-Creative)*
Cleve Skelton *(Partner)*
Scott Johnson *(Principal)*
Brian Brinson *(Dir-Acct Dev)*
Patricia Prather *(Dir-Art)*
Kristine Warski *(Dir-Media)*

Accounts:
Broad Ripple Brewpub
Multiguard Corp
Owl Music Group

THE AXIS AGENCY
8687 Melrose Ave 9th Fl, Los Angeles, CA 90069
Tel.: (310) 854-8200
Web Site: www.theaxisagency.com

Year Founded: 2005

National Agency Associations: 4A's

Agency Specializes In: Advertising, Digital/Interactive, Media Training, Out-of-Home Media, Print, Radio, Sales Promotion, Social Media, Strategic Planning/Research, T.V.

Armando Azarloza *(Pres)*
Carmen Lawrence *(Exec VP & Gen Mgr)*
Wally Sabria *(Exec VP)*
Peter Sanchez *(Exec Dir-Creative)*
Adriana Lopez *(Acct Supvr-Digital & Social)*
Monique Ramos *(Sr Acct Exec)*

Accounts:
The Clorox Company Gracias Mama
Covered California Marketing

AXXIS ADVERTISING LLC
11811 N Tatum Blvd #3031, Phoenix, AZ 85028-1614
Tel.: (602) 200-0707
E-Mail: stevenh@ads4hr.com
Web Site: www.ads4hr.com

Employees: 9
Year Founded: 2001

Agency Specializes In: Advertising, Automotive, Communications, Direct-to-Consumer, E-Commerce, Education, Government/Political, Graphic Design, Health Care Services, High Technology, Information Technology, Internet/Web Design, Logo & Package Design, Magazines, Newspaper, Newspapers & Magazines, Print, Radio, Recruitment, Restaurant, Retail, Sales Promotion, Search Engine Optimization, Social Marketing/Nonprofit, Telemarketing, Travel & Tourism

Approx. Annual Billings: $5,500,000

Steven Hofmann *(Dir-Natl)*
Stan Lasater *(Dir-Natl)*
Amber Rehman Lewis *(Client Svcs Mgr)*

Accounts:
Alphagraphics
American Red Cross
Epilepsy Foundation
Good Samaritan Society
Heritage Healthcare
Madison School District
NEC
Sun Harbor Nursing
Target
Viking
Well Care
Whataburger, Inc.

Branches

Axxis Advertising LLC
5116 N Nebraska Ave, Tampa, FL 33603-2363
Tel.: (813) 236-4858
Fax: (813) 234-3873
E-Mail: info@ads4hr.com
Web Site: www.ads4hr.com

Employees: 225

Agency Specializes In: Advertising

Stan Lasater *(Dir-Natl)*
Malachi Tresler *(Dir-Creative Svcs)*
Amber Lewis *(Client Svcs Mgr)*
Andrew Cox *(Mgr-Western Div)*

Cloud 9 Design
11811 N Tatum Blvd #3031, Phoenix, AZ 85028-1614
Tel.: (602) 200-0707

E-Mail: steven@enjoycloud9.com
Web Site: www.enjoycloud9.com

Employees: 40

Agency Specializes In: Advertising

Steven Hofmann *(Dir-Natl)*

AY DIGITAL
79 Madison Ave Ste 1200, New York, NY 10016-7802
Tel.: (646) 783-4000
Fax: (646) 304-1653
Toll Free: (877) 239-2872
Web Site: www.aydigital.com

Employees: 80
Year Founded: 2007

Agency Specializes In: Advertising, Advertising Specialties, Business-To-Business, Digital/Interactive, E-Commerce, Entertainment, Hispanic Market, Information Technology, Internet/Web Design, Market Research, Search Engine Optimization, Social Media, Web (Banner Ads, Pop-ups, etc.)

Approx. Annual Billings: $3,000,000

Breakdown of Gross Billings by Media: Internet Adv.: $3,000,000

Patrick Tinnelly *(VP-Sls)*
Diana Chisis *(Dir-Branding & Mktg)*
Inga Orlova *(Dir-Media)*
Gloria Marcano *(Mgr-Ops)*
Andrew Burke *(Copywriter)*

AYZENBERG GROUP, INC.
49 E Walnut St, Pasadena, CA 91103
Tel.: (626) 584-4070
Fax: (626) 584-3954
E-Mail: info@ayzenberg.com
Web Site: www.ayzenberg.com

Employees: 55
Year Founded: 1993

Agency Specializes In: Advertising, Brand Development & Integration, Branded Entertainment, Broadcast, Consulting, Consumer Marketing, Corporate Identity, Digital/Interactive, Electronic Media, Electronics, Entertainment, Graphic Design, Identity Marketing, Integrated Marketing, Internet/Web Design, Logo & Package Design, Media Buying Services, Out-of-Home Media, Package Design, Production (Ad, Film, Broadcast), Publicity/Promotions, Strategic Planning/Research, T.V., Web (Banner Ads, Pop-ups, etc.)

Approx. Annual Billings: $54,026,000

Breakdown of Gross Billings by Media: Collateral: $1,000,000; D.M.: $250,000; Logo & Package Design: $1,000,000; Mags.: $1,250,000; Radio: $500,000; T.V.: $2,500,000

Vincent Juarez *(Principal & Dir-Media)*
Edgar Davtyan *(Principal & Sr Strategist-Fin)*
Bill Buckley *(VP-Brand Integration)*
Rebecca Markarian *(VP-Social Media)*
Matt Rice *(VP-Creative Ops)*
Noah Eichen *(Head-Creative)*
Steve Moriya *(Sr Dir-Bus Dev-ION)*
Amaya Gutierrez *(Art Dir-Social Media)*
Justin Kirby *(Acct Dir)*
Eric Ayzenberg *(Dir-Creative & Sr Strategist)*
Stuart Pope *(Dir-Creative)*
Caroline Collins *(Assoc Dir-Social Media Strategy & Analytics)*
Andrea Hu *(Acct Mgr-Media)*
Garianne Diaz *(Acct Supvr)*
Casey Reed *(Strategist-Social Media)*
Erik Schmitt *(Strategist-Social Media)*
Brian Kim *(Sr Head-Design Interactive Grp)*
May Pescante *(Assoc Producer-Digital)*

Accounts:
2K
Atari Games
Bethesda Softworks LLC WET
Capcom
Disney
EA Games
Gamersfirst Campaign: "Be All You Can't Be"
Konami; Redwood City, CA Game Packaging
Lucas Arts
Mattel
Microsoft; Redmond, WA Game Packaging, Print, Xbox HUNT the TRUTH Audio Series
Namco Bandai Games; Santa Clara, CA
Nexon America; Los Angeles, CA
Nokia
Sega
Sony Online Entertainment; San Diego, CA
THQ; Agoura Hills, CA WWE All-Stars
Turbine
Ubisoft
Warner Brothers
Yahoo!

AZZAM JORDAN
(Name Changed to Tri-Media Integrated Marketing Technologies Inc.)

B&P ADVERTISING
900 S Pavilion Ctr Dr Ste 170, Las Vegas, NV 89144
Tel.: (702) 967-2222
E-Mail: info@bpadlv.com
Web Site: www.bpadlv.com

Agency Specializes In: Advertising, Corporate Identity, Digital/Interactive, Event Planning & Marketing, Internet/Web Design, Media Relations, Media Training, Public Relations, Sponsorship

Chuck Johnston *(Pres & Principal)*
Rob Catalano *(Exec Creative Dir)*
Rod Reber *(Acct Dir-Svcs)*
Jeff Ferrari *(Sr Acct Exec-Adv)*

Accounts:
New-The International School of Hospitality
New-Park Place Infiniti

B CREATIVE GROUP INC.
1700 Union Ave Ste A, Baltimore, MD 21211
Tel.: (443) 524-7510
E-Mail: hello@agencybcg.com
Web Site: www.agencybcg.com

Agency Specializes In: Advertising, Brand Development & Integration, Logo & Package Design, Market Research, Search Engine Optimization, Social Media, Strategic Planning/Research

Kerry Skarda *(Pres & Partner)*
Christian Lallo *(Partner & Dir-Strategy)*
Greg Bennett *(Creative Dir)*
Jordan Leber *(Jr Acct Exec)*
Lisa Barrows *(Jr Acct Exec)*

Accounts:
Goldwell

B SCENE ADVERTISING AGENCY
260 Newport Ctr Dr, Newport Beach, CA 92660
Tel.: (949) 777-6772
Fax: (949) 606-9023
E-Mail: caren@bsceneadvertising.com
Web Site: bsceneadvertising.com/

Employees: 33
Year Founded: 1985

National Agency Associations: AMA

Agency Specializes In: Above-the-Line, Advertising, Advertising Specialties, Affiliate Marketing, Affluent Market, African-American Market, Agriculture, Alternative Advertising, Arts, Asian Market, Automotive, Aviation & Aerospace, Below-the-Line, Bilingual Market, Brand Development & Integration, Branded Entertainment, Broadcast, Business Publications, Business-To-Business, Cable T.V., Catalogs, Children's Market, Co-op Advertising, Collateral, College, Commercial Photography, Communications, Computers & Software, Consulting, Consumer Goods, Consumer Marketing, Consumer Publications, Content, Corporate Communications, Corporate Identity, Cosmetics, Crisis Communications, Custom Publishing, Customer Relationship Management, Digital/Interactive, Direct Response Marketing, Direct-to-Consumer, E-Commerce, Education, Electronic Media, Electronics, Email, Engineering, Entertainment, Environmental, Event Planning & Marketing, Exhibit/Trade Shows, Experience Design, Faith Based, Fashion/Apparel, Financial, Food Service, Game Integration, Gay & Lesbian Market, Government/Political, Graphic Design, Guerilla Marketing, Health Care Services, High Technology, Hispanic Market, Hospitality, Household Goods, Identity Marketing, In-Store Advertising, Industrial, Infomercials, Information Technology, Integrated Marketing, International, Internet/Web Design, Investor Relations, Legal Services, Leisure, Local Marketing, Logo & Package Design, Luxury Products, Magazines, Marine, Market Research, Media Buying Services, Media Planning, Media Relations, Media Training, Medical Products, Men's Market, Merchandising, Mobile Marketing, Multicultural, Multimedia, New Product Development, New Technologies, Newspaper, Newspapers & Magazines, Out-of-Home Media, Outdoor, Over-50 Market, Package Design, Paid Searches, Pharmaceutical, Planning & Consultation, Podcasting, Point of Purchase, Point of Sale, Print, Product Placement, Production, Production (Ad, Film, Broadcast), Production (Print), Promotions, Public Relations, Publicity/Promotions, Publishing, RSS (Really Simple Syndication), Radio, Real Estate, Recruitment, Regional, Restaurant, Retail, Sales Promotion, Search Engine Optimization, Seniors' Market, Social Marketing/Nonprofit, Social Media, South Asian Market, Sponsorship, Sports Market, Stakeholders, Strategic Planning/Research, Sweepstakes, Syndication, T.V., Technical Advertising, Teen Market, Telemarketing, Trade & Consumer Magazines, Transportation, Travel & Tourism, Urban Market, Viral/Buzz/Word of Mouth, Web (Banner Ads, Pop-ups, etc.), Women's Market, Yellow Pages Advertising

Approx. Annual Billings: $10,000,000

Breakdown of Gross Billings by Media: Adv. Specialities: $1,000,000; Event Mktg.: $5,000,000; Local Mktg.: $1,500,000; Mags.: $2,500,000

Caren Lancona *(CEO)*
Phoenix Stanna *(Mgr-Events Mktg)*
Kyle Kiser *(Asst Producer)*
Kristie Russell *(Asst Producer)*

Accounts:
Chanel
CHOC Hospital; Orange, CA Healthcare Events; 2004
Desktop Fitness; Irvine, CA Fitness Equipment,

Fitness Software; 2003
Dr. John Grazer; Newport Beach, CA Plastic Surgery; 2004
Entourage LA; Beverly Hills, CA; 2004
Entourage OC; Newport Beach, CA; 2004
HB Magazine; Huntington Beach, CA; 2004
Huntington Harbour Yacht Club; Huntington Beach, CA Private Yacht Club
Just Friends; Newport Coast, CA Orange County Philanthropic Club & Magazine; 2004
Norcheck
Personal Fitness Trainers of OC; Newport Beach, CA Nutritionists, Personnel Services, Trainers
RJV Funding; Orange, CA Mortgages; 2004
Sundance; Orange, CA Tanning Beds, Tanning Equipment; 2003
Swiss System; San Diego, CA Health; 2003
US Realty Capital
Washington Mutual; Irvine, CA Banking Services; 2003

B2 INTERACTIVE

223 S 143rd Cir, Omaha, NE 68137
Tel.: (402) 932-9990
E-Mail: info@b2interactive.com
Web Site: www.b2interactive.com

Year Founded: 2012

Agency Specializes In: Advertising, Digital/Interactive, Internet/Web Design, Paid Searches, Print, Search Engine Optimization, Social Media

Max Riffner *(Creative Dir)*
Scott Rowe *(Dir-Mktg)*
Mike Jones *(Dir-Client Svcs)*
Bret Dennis *(Dir-SEO)*

Accounts:
New-D1Baseball.com

B2C ENTERPRISES

18a Kirk Ave SW, Roanoke, VA 24011
Tel.: (540) 904-1229
Web Site: www.b2centerprises.com

Year Founded: 2009

Agency Specializes In: Advertising, Internet/Web Design, Print, T.V.

Bruce C. Bryan *(Founder & Pres)*
Beth Kolnok *(Client Svcs Dir)*
Aaron Kelderhouse *(Dir-Creative)*

Accounts:
Delta Dental of Virginia
Re-Bath of Richmond Marketing, Media Planning, Strategic

B2E DIRECT MARKETING

307 E Court Ave Unit 103, Des Moines, IA 50309
Tel.: (515) 282-4933
Fax: (877) 275-2360
Toll Free: (877) 275-2360
E-Mail: success@b2edirect.com
Web Site: www.b2edirect.com

Agency Specializes In: Digital/Interactive, Direct Response Marketing, Hispanic Market, Internet/Web Design, Social Media, Strategic Planning/Research

Keith Snow *(Pres)*
Greg Sheridan *(VP)*
Sandra Stone *(VP-Bus Dev)*
Kari Faber *(Acct Mgr)*
Megan Koehlmoos *(Acct Mgr)*

Accounts:
Des Moines Area Community College
GuideOne Insurance
Marsh & McLennan Companies
Strategic America
Wachovia Securities

BABCOCK & JENKINS (BNJ)

(Formerly Babcock & Jenkins)
711 SW Alder Ste 200, Portland, OR 97205
Tel.: (503) 382-8500
E-Mail: info@bnj.com
Web Site: www.bnj.com

Employees: 50
Year Founded: 1992

Denise Barnes *(Pres & CEO)*
Julie Wisdom *(VP & Exec Dir-Creative)*
Heidi Dethloff *(VP-Client Success)*
Lauren Goldstein *(VP-Strategy & Partnerships)*
Laura Hastings *(VP-Comm)*
Eric Wittlake *(Sr Dir-Media)*
Kimberley Britton *(Sr Acct Dir)*
Patrick Kayser *(Dir-Strategic Plng)*
David Smith *(Assoc Dir-Creative)*

Accounts:
American Express
Brocade
Demandbase
GE
Google
IBM
Illumina
Kofax
Microsoft
Sage
Suse
Tripwire
William Blair
Windstream
Xerox

BACHLEDA ADVERTISING LLC

1148 Heidelberg Ave, Schaefferstown, PA 17088
Tel.: (717) 949-3311
E-Mail: info@bachleda.com
Web Site: www.bachleda.com

Agency Specializes In: Advertising, Brand Development & Integration, Exhibit/Trade Shows, Internet/Web Design, Logo & Package Design, Outdoor, Print, Radio, Social Media, T.V.

Michael Bachleda *(Pres)*
Tish Bachleda *(Dir-Ops)*
Michael Munro *(Dir-Web)*

Accounts:
Historic Schaefferstown Inc

BACKBAY COMMUNICATIONS, INC.

20 Park Plaza Ste 801, Boston, MA 02116
Tel.: (617) 556-9982
Fax: (617) 556-9987
E-Mail:
Bill.Haynes@BackBayCommunications.com
Web Site: www.backbaycommunications.com

Employees: 10

Agency Specializes In: Advertising, Affiliate Marketing, Brand Development & Integration, Business Publications, Business-To-Business, Collateral, Communications, Consulting, Corporate Communications, Corporate Identity, Crisis Communications, Digital/Interactive, Financial, Integrated Marketing, International, Investor Relations, Legal Services, Local Marketing, Logo & Package Design, Magazines, Media Relations, Media Training, Newspaper, Newspapers & Magazines, Print, Production (Print), Public Relations, Publicity/Promotions, Regional, Search Engine Optimization, Social Media, Strategic Planning/Research, Web (Banner Ads, Pop-ups, etc.)

Bill Haynes *(Founder & Pres)*
Phil Nunes *(Sr VP)*
Peter Czyryca *(VP)*
Jen Dowd *(VP)*
Ken MacFadyen *(Dir)*
Douglas Allen *(Sr Acct Exec)*

Accounts:
Accordion Partners Media Relations, PR
Bregal Sagemount
Grant Thornton
Graycliff Partners
ICapital, LLC. Media Relations, Public Relations
J.W. Childs
The Riverside Company
SK Capital Partners
Small Business Investor Alliance Public Relations

BACKE DIGITAL BRAND MARKETING

100 Matsonford Rd, Radnor, PA 19087
Tel.: (610) 947-6904
Fax: (610) 896-9242
E-Mail: jebacke@backemarketing.com
Web Site: www.backemarketing.com

E-Mail for Key Personnel:
President: jebacke@backecom.com

Employees: 30
Year Founded: 1997

Agency Specializes In: Brand Development & Integration, Business-To-Business, Communications, Consumer Marketing, E-Commerce, Education, Financial, Health Care Services, Internet/Web Design, Public Relations, Sports Market, Strategic Planning/Research

Approx. Annual Billings: $40,000,000

John E. Backe *(Pres & CEO)*
Zeke Kisling *(Chief Creative Officer & VP)*
Boyd Maits *(Sr VP-Interactive)*
Mike O'Hara *(VP & Mgmt Supvr)*
Anna Trapani *(Controller)*
J. Scotty Emerle-Sifuentes *(Dir-Innovation)*
Rich Essaf *(Dir-Interactive Art)*
Lisa Gower *(Dir-Media)*
Koree Ritter *(Sr Acct Mgr)*

Accounts:
Aegis Therapies
Airgas; 2001
Arcadia University; 2000
Arrow International
Avalon Carpet Tile & Flooring
Consolidated Rail
CSS Industries
Delaware Valley College
Diversified Information Technologies
Dorchester Publishing; 1997
Eureka Educational Products
GlaxoSmithKline Arixtra, Hycamtin, Requip; 1989
Gloucester County
Hill's Main Line Seafood
Independence LED
Independent Visitor's Center Website
The Iron Shop
Kraft Foods
Novartis Excedrin
Pierce College
Pizza Hut
The PMA Insurance Group
SCA; 2000
SunGard; 1998
Susquehanna International Group
Turner White Communications

Wissahickon Water
Worldwide Fistula Fund Pro Bono

BACKUS TURNER INTERNATIONAL

3108 N Federal Hwy, Lighthouse Point, FL 33064
Tel.: (954) 727-9977
Fax: (954) 727-9966
E-Mail: roberta@backusturner.com
Web Site: www.backusturner.com

E-Mail for Key Personnel:
President: larry@backusturner.com
Media Dir.: rene@backusturner.com

Employees: 10
Year Founded: 1978

National Agency Associations: PRSA

Agency Specializes In: Advertising, Advertising Specialties, Aviation & Aerospace, Brand Development & Integration, Business-To-Business, Children's Market, Co-op Advertising, Collateral, Consulting, Consumer Marketing, Consumer Publications, Corporate Communications, Corporate Identity, E-Commerce, Entertainment, Financial, Graphic Design, Internet/Web Design, Investor Relations, Legal Services, Logo & Package Design, Magazines, Media Buying Services, Newspaper, Newspapers & Magazines, Out-of-Home Media, Over-50 Market, Point of Purchase, Point of Sale, Print, Production, Public Relations, Publicity/Promotions, Radio, Real Estate, Restaurant, Sports Market, T.V., Travel & Tourism

Approx. Annual Billings: $15,000,000

Breakdown of Gross Billings by Media: Collateral: 5%; Internet Adv.: 19%; Logo & Package Design: 2%; Mags.: 15%; Mdsg./POP: 5%; Newsp.: 13%; Out-of-Home Media: 4%; Outdoor: 5%; Print: 10%; Spot Radio: 3%; Spot T.V.: 5%; Trade & Consumer Mags.: 8%; Worldwide Web Sites: 6%

Lawrence Turner *(Owner)*
Rene Mahfood *(VP)*

Accounts:
Best Beach Resorts in the World; 1998
Caribbean Weddings
Channels Magazine
Complete Power Solutions
Crystal Casino
Discovery Cruise Lines
Discovery Vacations
Florida International
Highland Park Hospital
The Islands of the Bahamas
Luxury Hotels of the Bahamas
Luxury Hotels of the Caribbean
Miami General Hospital
Old Bahama Bay Resort & Yacht Harbour
Trump International Hotels & Resort
United Hospitals, Inc.
Warminster General Hospital
WorldwideResorts.com

BAD MONKEY CIRCUS

31 W Downer Pl Ste 400, Aurora, IL 60506
Tel.: (630) 892-7700
Web Site: www.badmonkeycircus.com

Year Founded: 2001

Agency Specializes In: Advertising, Brand Development & Integration, Corporate Identity, Digital/Interactive, Internet/Web Design, Logo & Package Design, Print, Radio, Social Media, T.V.

Rory Bolen *(Dir-Creative)*

Accounts:
Best Buy Carpet & Granite

BADER RUTTER & ASSOCIATES, INC.

13845 Bishop's Dr, Brookfield, WI 53005
Tel.: (262) 784-7200
Fax: (262) 938-5555
E-Mail: rgreve@baderrutter.com
Web Site: www.baderrutter.com

E-Mail for Key Personnel:
Chairman: rbader@bader-rutter.com
President: gnickerson@bader-rutter.com
Creative Dir.: mmccabe@bader-rutter.com
Media Dir.: ihindman@bader-rutter.com
Production Mgr.: thicks@bader-rutter.com
Public Relations: lobrien@bader-rutter.com

Employees: 255
Year Founded: 1974

National Agency Associations: ABC-BPA

Agency Specializes In: Advertising, Brand Development & Integration, Business-To-Business, Digital/Interactive, Direct Response Marketing, Media Buying Services, Public Relations, Publicity/Promotions, Sponsorship, Strategic Planning/Research

Approx. Annual Billings: $70,000,000

Jeff Young *(Pres)*
Greg Nickerson *(CEO)*
Mark Williams *(Sr VP-Admin)*
Allison Lauer *(Dir-Recruitment)*
Larry O'Brien *(Dir-Mgmt)*
Manisha Nabke *(Assoc Dir-Media & Direct Mktg)*
Nina O'Brien *(Supvr-Media)*
Jordan Kuglitsch *(Acct Exec)*
Nina Lewis *(Acct Coord)*
Stacy Mallak *(Acct Coord)*

Accounts:
360 Yield Center; 2014
Butler Buildings; 2012
Case IH; 2013
Caterpillar, Inc. Solar Turbines
Dairy Management Inc.
Dow AgroSciences; Indianapolis, IN; 1981
Eastman Chemical Co. Eastman Tritan Copolyester; 2003
GE Healthcare; 2006
Generac; 2013
Hospira; 2013
Pork Producers Council; 2006
The Raymond Corporation; Greene, NY; 2002
River Valley Farm; 2014
Sauder Woodworking Company; 2011
Standard Insurance
Zoetis Inc. Campaign: "Too Much Metal", Hoof-Tec, Online, Print; 2010

Branch

Bader Rutter & Associates, Inc.

808 P St Ste 210, Lincoln, NE 68508-2246
Tel.: (402) 434-5307
Fax: (402) 477-2354
Web Site: www.baderrutter.com

Employees: 7
Year Founded: 1990

Agency Specializes In: Advertising, Agriculture, Brand Development & Integration, Broadcast, Business Publications, Business-To-Business, Collateral, Communications, Consulting, Digital/Interactive, Direct Response Marketing, Electronic Media, Engineering, Environmental, High Technology, Industrial, Internet/Web Design, Marine, Media Buying Services, Multimedia, New Product Development, Newspapers & Magazines, Planning & Consultation, Point of Purchase, Point of Sale, Print, Production, Public Relations, Publicity/Promotions, Strategic Planning/Research, Technical Advertising, Trade & Consumer Magazines

Lori Hallowell *(VP & Grp Head)*
Tom Posta *(VP & Dir-Mgmt)*
Audra Jacobs *(Grp Head-PR)*
Colleen Grams *(Acct Dir)*
Elizabeth Astin *(Sr Acct Exec)*
Jennifer Bataille-Kosfeld *(Sr Acct Exec)*
Ashley Cobert *(Acct Exec-PR)*

Accounts:
GE Healthcare
John Deere Consumer & Commercial Equipment, Inc.
Pfizer Animal Health

BADGER & WINTERS, INC.

(Formerly Badger & Partners, Inc.)
261 5th Ave 26th Fl, New York, NY 10016
Tel.: (212) 533-3222
Fax: (212) 533-9380
E-Mail: info@badgerandwinters.com
Web Site: www.badgerandwinters.com

Employees: 38
Year Founded: 1994

Agency Specializes In: Advertising, Advertising Specialties, Brand Development & Integration, Broadcast, Collateral, Communications, Consumer Marketing, Corporate Identity, Cosmetics, Fashion/Apparel, Graphic Design, In-Store Advertising, Internet/Web Design, Leisure, Logo & Package Design, Magazines, New Product Development, Newspapers & Magazines, Outdoor, Point of Purchase, Point of Sale, Print, Production, Public Relations, Retail, Strategic Planning/Research, T.V.

Approx. Annual Billings: $58,000,000

Breakdown of Gross Billings by Media: Internet Adv.: $2,900,000; Logo & Package Design: $8,700,000; Mags.: $29,000,000; Outdoor: $2,900,000; Point of Sale: $2,900,000; T.V.: $11,600,000

Jim Winters *(Pres)*
James McIntyre *(Partner & VP-Client Svcs)*
Jonathan Adams *(Dir-Creative)*
Catherine Wallis *(Sr Brand Mgr)*
Sharon Burk *(Mgr-Acctg)*
Sam Templeman *(Designer)*
Sarah Mackenzie *(Acct Coord)*
Tarah Hartzler *(Sr Counsel-Comm)*
Jessica Lange *(Sr Counsel-Comm)*
Bill McRae *(Sr Writer)*

Accounts:
Avon
Calvin Klein
Dick's Sporting Goods
Indigo
Lancome
Laura Geller
Living Proof
Nordstrom Rack
Vera Bradley
Worth New York

BAILEY BRAND CONSULTING

200 W Germantown Pike, Plymouth Meeting, PA 19462
Tel.: (610) 940-9030
E-Mail: info@baileygp.com
Web Site: www.baileygp.com

Year Founded: 1985

Agency Specializes In: Advertising, Brand Development & Integration, Corporate Identity, Exhibit/Trade Shows, Graphic Design, Internet/Web Design, Package Design, Promotions, Search Engine Optimization, Social Media, Sponsorship

Allison Gawlik *(Grp Acct Dir)*
Jeanine Kingeter *(Dir-HR)*
Jenn Lucas *(Dir-Fin)*
Abby Plesser *(Dir-Content)*
Eric Yeager *(Mgr-Creative)*
Ben Knepler *(Sr Strategist-Brand)*
Matt Markow *(Strategist-Digital Mktg)*

BAILEY LAUERMAN

1299 Farnam Street Ste 930, Omaha, NE 68102
Tel.: (402) 514-9400
Fax: (402) 514-9401
E-Mail: hello@baileylauerman.com
Web Site: www.baileylauerman.com

E-Mail for Key Personnel:
Chairman: jlauerman@baileylauerman.com
Creative Dir.: cweitz@baileylauerman.com
Public Relations: dparrott@baileylauerman.com

Employees: 85
Year Founded: 1970

National Agency Associations: 4A's-AAF-AMA-AMIN-PRSA

Agency Specializes In: Advertising, Advertising Specialties, Affluent Market, Agriculture, Automotive, Aviation & Aerospace, Brand Development & Integration, Broadcast, Business-To-Business, Cable T.V., Collateral, College, Communications, Consulting, Consumer Marketing, Corporate Communications, Corporate Identity, Crisis Communications, Digital/Interactive, Education, Electronic Media, Entertainment, Event Planning & Marketing, Exhibit/Trade Shows, Financial, Graphic Design, Guerilla Marketing, Health Care Services, Industrial, Information Technology, Integrated Marketing, Internet/Web Design, Investor Relations, Leisure, Local Marketing, Logo & Package Design, Market Research, Media Buying Services, Media Planning, Media Relations, Medical Products, Multimedia, Newspaper, Newspapers & Magazines, Out-of-Home Media, Outdoor, Package Design, Planning & Consultation, Point of Purchase, Point of Sale, Print, Production (Ad, Film, Broadcast), Public Relations, Publicity/Promotions, Radio, Recruitment, Retail, Search Engine Optimization, Social Marketing/Nonprofit, Social Media, Sponsorship, Sports Market, Strategic Planning/Research, T.V., Trade & Consumer Magazines, Transportation, Travel & Tourism, Viral/Buzz/Word of Mouth, Web (Banner Ads, Pop-ups, etc.)

James M. Lauerman *(Founder)*
Ronald Plageman *(CFO)*
Julia Doria *(CMO & Exec VP)*
Sean Faden *(VP & Dir-Creative)*
Abbey Johnson *(Dir-Client Engagement)*
Angie Kubicek *(Dir-Connections Strategy)*
Lisa McCallan *(Assoc Dir-Media & Strategist-Connections)*
Heather Allen *(Brand Strategist)*
Jessica Kutash *(Strategist-Brand)*
Abbie Stanton *(Strategist-Brand)*
Michael Johnson *(Copywriter)*

Accounts:
AMC Theatres Internal & External Branding; 2012
Ameritas Life Insurance Corp.; Lincoln, NE; 1987
Bass Pro Shops Creative, Design, Digital; 2010
Beechcraft; 2012
Branson Creative, Strategic Direction
Cargill Corn Milling Campaign: "The Wait is Finally Over", Empyreal 75, Lysto, NuPulse, RAMP, SweetBran; 2007
CommunityAmerica Credit Union; 2011
ConAgra Foods Corporate Brand; 2000
Disney Parks & Resorts Creative, Design, Digital; 2005
Disney Travel Trade Creative, Design, Digital; 2005
Disney Vacation Club Creative, Design, Digital; 2005
Exmark a Division of Toro; 2005
Gavilon; 2011
IMG Academy
Jeppesen; Englewood, CO; 2004
The Mutual Fund Store Brand, Creative Strategy, Development
Nationwide Insurance; 2010
Panda Express (Agency of Record) Creative Development, Strategy
The Partnership at Drugfree.org Creative, Design, Digital; 2010
The Smithsonian Creative, Design; 2001
Special Olympics: State & National Games Creative, Design, Public Relations; 1998
Sun Pacific Brand Strategy, Creative Development, Cuties, Media Strategy, Planning & Placement, Public Relations
TD Ameritrade Corporate Brand, Creative, Design, Public Relations; 2007

Branch

Bailey Lauerman

1248 O St Ste 1140, Lincoln, NE 68508
Tel.: (402) 514-9400
Fax: (402) 514-9401
E-Mail: info@baileylauerman.com
Web Site: www.baileylauerman.com

E-Mail for Key Personnel:
Creative Dir.: cweitz@baileylauerman.com
Public Relations: dparrott@baileylauerman.com

Employees: 25

National Agency Associations: 4A's

Agency Specializes In: Advertising, Affluent Market, Agriculture, Aviation & Aerospace, Brand Development & Integration, Broadcast, Cable T.V., Collateral, College, Communications, Consumer Marketing, Corporate Communications, Digital/Interactive, Direct-to-Consumer, Electronic Media, Environmental, Event Planning & Marketing, Exhibit/Trade Shows, Experience Design, Financial, Guerilla Marketing, Health Care Services, Identity Marketing, Internet/Web Design, Local Marketing, Logo & Package Design, Magazines, Market Research, Media Planning, Media Relations, Media Training, Multimedia, Newspaper, Newspapers & Magazines, Out-of-Home Media, Outdoor, Print, Public Relations, Recruitment, Social Marketing/Nonprofit, Sports Market, Strategic Planning/Research, T.V., Trade & Consumer Magazines, Transportation, Travel & Tourism, Viral/Buzz/Word of Mouth

Carter Weitz *(Chm & Chief Creative Officer)*
Julia Doria *(CMO & Exec VP)*
Doug Parrott *(Exec VP-PR & Gen Mgr-Omaha)*
Mary Palu *(Exec VP-Connections Strategy)*
Chris Laughlin *(VP & Controller)*
Jim Buhrman *(Sr Art Dir)*
Jeff Barber *(Dir-Tech)*
Ron Sack *(Assoc Dir-Creative)*
Kim Gregg *(Planner)*
Lauren Andrews *(Coord-Media)*

Accounts:
Ameritas Financial
Cargill Inc.
Cessna The Ten. Video
Exmark Manufacturing Corp
Henry Doorly Zoo; Omaha, NE Branding
Honeywell Aerospace
Nationwide Insurance
Nebraska Tourism Commission
Negro Leagues Baseball Museum Campaign: "In Mexico"
TD Ameritrade
University of Nebraska
The Walt Disney Company

BAILLAT CARDELL & FILS

420 Rue Beaubien Ouest Bureau 201, Montreal, QC H2V 4S6 Canada
Tel.: (514) 750-6600
E-Mail: info@baillatcardell.com
Web Site: www.baillatcardell.com

Agency Specializes In: Advertising, Graphic Design

Cardell Guillaume *(Co-Founder & Dir-Creative)*

BAKER COMMUNICATIONS ADVERTISING/MARKETING/PUBLIC RELATIONS

128 E Reynolds Rd Ste 201, Lexington, KY 40517-1254
Tel.: (859) 245-1100
Fax: (859) 245-2022
E-Mail: bakercomm@bakercomm.com
Web Site: www.bakercomm.com

Employees: 8
Year Founded: 1980

National Agency Associations: Second Wind Limited

Agency Specializes In: Communications, Consumer Marketing

Thomas W. Baker *(Owner)*
Cindy Baker *(Dir-Art)*

Accounts:
Big Ass Fans
BMAC
Boy Scouts of America
DAK
Drisko Group
European Motors
Fayette Co. Public Schools
Graves Cox
Harford Mall
Lanes End Farm; Versailes, KY
The Lexington Cemetery; Lexington, KY
Medical Vision Group
Milward Funeral Directors; Lexington, KY
New Leaf Resources
QBSoft
UK College of Education
Walbak International Marketing; Lexington, KY
Wald
War Horse Place

BAKER CREATIVE

386 Main St, Groveport, OH 43125
Tel.: (614) 836-3845
Toll Free: (877) BAKER03
E-Mail: info@baker-creative.com
Web Site: www.bakercreative.co

E-Mail for Key Personnel:
President: mbaker@baker-creative.com
Creative Dir.: mbaker@baker-creative.com

Employees: 7

Agency Specializes In: Advertising, Brand Development & Integration, Broadcast, Business-To-Business, Children's Market, Co-op Advertising, Consulting, Consumer Goods, Consumer Marketing, Corporate Communications, Direct Response Marketing, Direct-to-Consumer, Email,

Environmental, Event Planning & Marketing, Experience Design, Financial, Graphic Design, Identity Marketing, In-Store Advertising, Integrated Marketing, Logo & Package Design, Market Research, Media Relations, Merchandising, Mobile Marketing, Multimedia, New Product Development, New Technologies, Package Design, Point of Purchase, Point of Sale, Print, Promotions, Public Relations, Retail, Sales Promotion, Sports Market, T.V., Trade & Consumer Magazines, Web (Banner Ads, Pop-ups, etc.), Women's Market

Michele Baker-Cuthbert *(Principal)*

Accounts:
Cleveland Floral Products
Colliers International, Turley Martin Tucker
Columbus College of Art & Design
Flower Boutique
The Gap
GFS-Gordon Food Service; 2006
Madison Christian School
Park National Bank & Affiliates
Pet People
Quaker Steak & Lube Restaurants

BAKER STREET ADVERTISING

15 Lombard St, San Francisco, CA 94111
Tel.: (415) 659-3900
Web Site: www.bakerstadvertising.com

Year Founded: 1982

Agency Specializes In: Advertising, Media Buying Services, Production

Jack Boland *(Pres)*
Brian Bacino *(Chief Creative Officer)*
Don Donovan *(Chief Strategy Officer)*
Bob Dorfman *(Exec VP & Exec Dir-Creative)*
Dan Nilsen *(Grp Acct Dir)*
Carrie Ammermann *(Art Dir)*
Robert Leon *(Copywriter)*
Shelly Trujillo-Kalianis *(Media Buyer-Brdcst)*

Accounts:
The San Francisco Giants Campaign: "One Giant Moment", TV

THE BALCOM AGENCY

1500 Ballinger, Fort Worth, TX 76201
Tel.: (817) 877-9933
Fax: (817) 877-5522
E-Mail: info@balcomagency.com
Web Site: www.balcomagency.com

Employees: 25
Year Founded: 1993

Agency Specializes In: Advertising, Advertising Specialties, Affluent Market, Agriculture, Alternative Advertising, Arts, Automotive, Bilingual Market, Brand Development & Integration, Broadcast, Business Publications, Business-To-Business, Cable T.V., Catalogs, Commercial Photography, Communications, Computers & Software, Consulting, Consumer Goods, Corporate Communications, Corporate Identity, Cosmetics, Crisis Communications, Digital/Interactive, Direct Response Marketing, Direct-to-Consumer, E-Commerce, Education, Electronic Media, Electronics, Email, Engineering, Entertainment, Event Planning & Marketing, Exhibit/Trade Shows, Fashion/Apparel, Financial, Food Service, Graphic Design, Guerilla Marketing, Health Care Services, High Technology, Hospitality, Household Goods, In-Store Advertising, Industrial, Information Technology, International, Internet/Web Design, Investor Relations, Legal Services, Logo & Package Design, Magazines, Market Research, Media Buying Services, Media Planning, Media Relations, Media Training, Medical Products, Men's Market, Merchandising, Mobile Marketing, Multimedia, New Product Development, New Technologies, Newspaper, Newspapers & Magazines, Out-of-Home Media, Outdoor, Package Design, Paid Searches, Pharmaceutical, Planning & Consultation, Podcasting, Point of Purchase, Point of Sale, Print, Production, Production (Ad, Film, Broadcast), Production (Print), Promotions, Public Relations, Publicity/Promotions, Publishing, RSS (Really Simple Syndication), Radio, Real Estate, Recruitment, Restaurant, Retail, Sales Promotion, Search Engine Optimization, Social Marketing/Nonprofit, Sponsorship, Sports Market, Stakeholders, Strategic Planning/Research, Syndication, T.V., Teen Market, Transportation, Travel & Tourism, Viral/Buzz/Word of Mouth, Web (Banner Ads, Pop-ups, etc.), Women's Market, Yellow Pages Advertising

Stuart Balcom *(Pres & CEO)*
David Sims *(Sr Dir-Art)*
Steve Cantrell *(Client Svcs Dir)*
Krystal Lewis *(Acct Dir)*
Kim Speairs *(Client Svcs Dir)*
Amanda Deering *(Jr Dir-Art & Specialist-Video)*
Brian Blankenship *(Dir-Interactive Creative)*
Carol Glover *(Dir-Creative)*
Rob Mart *(Dir-Strategy & Plng)*
Jamie Fisher *(Assoc Dir-Creative)*
Lesley Dupre *(Acct Mgr & Specialist-PR)*
Lauren Turner *(Project Mgr-Digital & Specialist-Social Media)*
Toni Stuard *(Mgr-Acctg)*
Norma Ramos *(Coord-Accounts Payable)*

Accounts:
Alcon Laboratories; Fort Worth, TX; 2004
The Barnett Shale Energy Education Council
CASA of Tarrant County
Cash America
Central Texas Mortgage
ConvaTec
Cook Children's Health Care System
The Fort Worth Police & Fire Fighters Memorial
Healthpoint
Henry House Foundation
Justin Brands; Fort Worth, TX Justin Boot Company, Western Footwear; 1996
LifeGift
LifeGift Organ Donation
The Metropolitan
The Modern Art Museum of Fort Worth
Neeley School of Business at TCU
Norman Regional Health System
Professional Compounding Centers of America Branding, Graphic Elements, Key Messaging, Positioning, logo
San Juan Basin Royalty Trust
Southwest Bank
Southwestern Baptist Theological Seminary
Streams & Valleys, Inc. Website
Texas Health Resources Hospitals; 1998
Texas Rangers Association Foundation
Tomlyn
Tony Lama Boot Company; Fort Worth, TX Footwear; 2003
Trinity Habitat for Humanity
United Way of Tarrant County
USMD Hospitals
Williamson-Dickie Manufacturing Company

BALDWIN&

135 N Harrington St, Raleigh, NC 27603-1719
Tel.: (919) 680-0900
Web Site: www.baldwinand.com

Agency Specializes In: Advertising, Brand Development & Integration, Consumer Marketing, Internet/Web Design, Market Research, Strategic Planning/Research

David Baldwin *(Creative Dir)*
Jerry Bodrie *(Acct Mgmt Dir)*
Jennifer Hazelett *(Acct Dir)*
Bob Ranew *(Creative Dir)*
Grace Tarrant *(Acct Dir)*
Jimmie Blount *(Dir-Art)*
April Lauderdale *(Dir-Art)*
Katharine Belloir *(Acct Supvr)*
Keith Greenstein *(Copywriter)*
Chad Temples *(Copywriter)*
Britton Upchurch *(Copywriter)*

Accounts:
Audi Automobiles Mfr
BMW Autobahn Racing Invite-Cologne
Burt's Bees (Agency of Record) Campaign: "100% Natural Video", Campaign: "A Natural Before & After", Campaign: "Butterfly Peony, Butterfly Rose", Campaign: "Gud Smelltastic Video", Campaign: "Little Woman", Campaign: "Spring Hummingbird", Campaign: "Twenty Thousand Leagues Under The Sea", Campaign: "Uncap Flavor", Cosmetics Mfr, Intense Hydration, Lip Balms, Print, Television
Clorox Company
Cree Campaign: "Eulogy", Campaign: "The Room of Enlightenment", LED Light Bulbs, TV
GearWrench Campaign: "Honest Industrial Trade"
Girls Rock North Carolina
Gud
New-Krispy Kreme "Captain Bogart D. Wholebox"
Ponysaurus Campaign: "Beer Would", Campaign: "Imaginary", Campaign: "Wrestling"
New-Red Hat #PeoplePowered
Travelocity Online Travel Agencies

BALDWIN & OBENAUF, INC.

1011 US Rte 22 W Ste 100, Bridgewater, NJ 08807-2950
Tel.: (908) 685-1510
Fax: (908) 707-9181
E-Mail: info@bnoinc.com
Web Site: www.bnoinc.com

E-Mail for Key Personnel:
President: jobenauf@bnoinc.com

Employees: 48
Year Founded: 1981

Agency Specializes In: Communications, Electronic Media, Multimedia, Outdoor, Point of Sale, Print, Strategic Planning/Research

Approx. Annual Billings: $7,000,000

Breakdown of Gross Billings by Media: Mags.: 100%

Joanne Obenauf *(Founder & CEO)*
Trista Walker *(Pres)*
George Jackus *(Sr VP-Creative)*
Ray Ferreira *(VP-Employer Comm)*
Rachelle Powell *(VP-Client Svcs)*
Diane Rogers *(VP-Healthcare Comm)*
Jose Aguirre *(Sr Dir-Art)*
DeSean Brown *(Acct Dir)*
David Urbano *(Creative Dir)*

Accounts:
Alps Controls
BASF
Choose New Jersey Marketing Communications Strategy, Strategic Communications
Ethicon
Janssen Biotech, Inc.
Johnson & Johnson Corporate Communications, Events, Recruitment
MasterCard Inc.
Spex CertiPrep
Zeus Scientific

BALDWIN/CLANCY/ROGAN ADVERTISING

1040 Great Plain Ave, Needham, MA 02492
Tel.: (781) 433-9833
Fax: (781) 433-9860
Web Site: www.bcradvertising.com

Employees: 15
Year Founded: 1972

Agency Specializes In: Arts, Media Buying Services, Media Planning, Print, Radio, Search Engine Optimization, Strategic Planning/Research, T.V., Trade & Consumer Magazines

Jim Baldwin *(CEO & Partner)*
Mike Rogan *(Partner & Dir-Creative)*
Jeniffer Clancy *(Partner & Acct Svc Dir)*
Phillip Mancini *(CFO & VP-Fin)*
Seth Robbins *(Dir-Art)*
Kristen Johnson *(Acct Mgr)*
Amy McCartin *(Mgr-Production)*

Accounts:
Amerlux Lighting
Direct Federal Credit Union Ad Agency of Record, Planning
ING/CitiStreet
Tenacity
Viaflo

BALL ADVERTISING GROUP
355 N Lincoln St, Casper, WY 82601
Tel.: (307) 234-3472
Fax: (307) 234-2583
Web Site: www.balladv.com

Year Founded: 1978

Agency Specializes In: Advertising, Event Planning & Marketing, Exhibit/Trade Shows, Internet/Web Design, Logo & Package Design, Multimedia, Public Relations, T.V.

Ken Ball *(Owner)*
Peg Ball *(Partner & CFO)*
Michelle Larsen *(Dir-Accounts)*

Accounts:
Rootz Salon & Spa

BALZAC COMMUNICATIONS
1200 Jefferson St, Napa, CA 94559
Tel.: (707) 255-7667
Fax: (707) 255-1119
Web Site: www.balzac.com

Agency Specializes In: Advertising, Digital/Interactive, Graphic Design, Public Relations, Social Media

Paul Wagner *(Owner & Pres)*
Pat McCaffrey *(Controller)*
Catherine Bugue *(Acct Mgr)*
Tara Thomas *(Acct Mgr)*
Ana P. Scofield *(Acct Mgr)*
Robin Lewis *(Mgr-Design)*
Tiffany Van Gorder *(Gen Mgr)*
Mike Wangbickler *(Acct Exec)*

Accounts:
100 Percent Wines
4G Wines
Axios Wines
Beaulieu Vineyard
Frisson Wines
Hoopes Family Vineyard & Winery
Marke Wines
Mendocino Wine Company
Rutherford Dust Society
Villa Trasqua (Agency of Record)

BAM
2535 Washington Rd Ste 1131, Pittsburgh, PA 15241
Tel.: (412) 854-1004
Fax: (412) 854-1221
Web Site: www.bamadv.com

Year Founded: 2004

Agency Specializes In: Advertising, Internet/Web Design, Outdoor, Print, Radio, T.V.

Bill Berry *(Pres)*
Neil Catapano *(VP)*
Susan Froedtert *(Dir-Art)*

Accounts:
Culligan International Company

THE BAM CONNECTION
20 Jay St Ste 302, Brooklyn, NY 11201
Tel.: (718) 801-8299
Web Site: www.thebam.com

National Agency Associations: 4A's

Agency Specializes In: Advertising, Brand Development & Integration, Content, Print, Social Media

Maureen Maldari *(CEO)*
Rob Baiocco *(Chief Creative Officer)*

Accounts:
Ad Council Digital, Print, Radio
The American Heart Association/American Stroke Association Digital, Print, Radio
New-Aptus Health Creative, Strategic
New-Juilliard
Lambert & Stamp
New-Le Moyne College (Agency of Record) Digital, Online, Out-of-Home, Print, Social Media, TV
Silver Star Ravioli
Teen Hype
Terlato Wines
New-Valeant Pharmaceutical
Wrangler Western Jeans Multimedia

BAM STRATEGY
420 McGill Ste 400, Montreal, QC H2Y 2G1 Canada
Tel.: (514) 875-1500
Fax: (514) 875-2108
Toll Free: (888) BAM4550
E-Mail: info@bamstrategy.com
Web Site: www.bamstrategy.com

E-Mail for Key Personnel:
President: cemergui@bamstrategy.com

Employees: 70
Year Founded: 1996

Agency Specializes In: Advertising, Bilingual Market, Business-To-Business, Consumer Marketing, Digital/Interactive, Direct Response Marketing, E-Commerce, Electronic Media, Graphic Design, Internet/Web Design, Strategic Planning/Research

Chris Emergui *(Pres)*
Julia Blinkina *(Acct Dir)*
Marie Karasseferian *(Acct Dir)*
Xavier Picquerey *(Client Svcs Dir)*
Jeff Abracen *(Dir-Creative)*
Johan De Leon *(Dir-Performance Mktg)*
Gabriela Loureiro *(Dir-HR)*
Elodie Poncet Boulin *(Acct Supvr-Digital)*
Michael Sia *(Acct Supvr)*
Danielle Cole *(Acct Coord)*
Teresa Pisciuneri *(Acct Coord)*

Accounts:
ABB Information Technologies, Power; 2001
AC Nielsen
Costco
Emco Building Products Roofing Products
Itravel 2000
Microcell Solutions/FIDO
Procter & Gamble Consumer Goods
Readers Digest
Rogers Video Direct
Weather Network

BANDUJO ADVERTISING & DESIGN
(Formerly Bandujo Donker & Brothers)
22 W 21st St 8th Fl, New York, NY 10010
Tel.: (212) 332-4100
Fax: (212) 366-6068
E-Mail: jbandujo@bandujo.com
Web Site: www.bandujo.com

E-Mail for Key Personnel:
President: jbandujo@bandujo.com
Creative Dir.: bbrothers@bandujo.com

Employees: 10
Year Founded: 1993

National Agency Associations: 4A's

Agency Specializes In: Advertising, Brand Development & Integration, Broadcast, Business Publications, Business-To-Business, Cable T.V., Collateral, Communications, Consumer Marketing, Consumer Publications, Corporate Communications, Corporate Identity, Digital/Interactive, Direct Response Marketing, Electronic Media, Entertainment, Event Planning & Marketing, Fashion/Apparel, Financial, Government/Political, Graphic Design, Health Care Services, High Technology, Hispanic Market, Information Technology, Internet/Web Design, Legal Services, Leisure, Logo & Package Design, Luxury Products, Media Buying Services, Media Planning, New Product Development, Newspapers & Magazines, Out-of-Home Media, Outdoor, Planning & Consultation, Print, Radio, Sales Promotion, Sponsorship, Sports Market, T.V., Trade & Consumer Magazines, Web (Banner Ads, Pop-ups, etc.)

Breakdown of Gross Billings by Media: Bus. Publs.: 5%; Collateral: 10%; D.M.: 10%; Internet Adv.: 5%; Newsp. & Mags.: 15%; Out-of-Home Media: 5%; Radio & T.V.: 30%; Trade & Consumer Mags.: 10%; Worldwide Web Sites: 10%

Jose R. Bandujo *(Pres)*
Amanda Kane *(COO)*
Robert John Francis Brothers *(Exec VP & Dir-Creative)*
Shawn Kelly *(Dir-Creative)*
Ryosuke Matsumoto *(Dir-Art)*
Ana Paz *(Sr Acct Mgr)*

Accounts:
Carroll, McNulty Kull LLC (CMK)
Children's Specialized Hospital
Citigroup; New York, NY; 2001
Einstein Moomjy
The French Culinary Institute
Greenberg Traurig, LLC; Miami, FL Legal Services; 2004
JP Morgan Chase; New York, NY; Columbus, OH Financial Services; 2003
Make-A-Wish Foundation; Union, NJ Pro-Bono
New Jersey Motor Vehicle Commission; Trenton, NJ; 2003
NY Conservatory for Dramatic Arts
Time Warner
Wisdom Tree

BANDY CARROLL HELLIGE ADVERTISING
307 W Muhammad Ali Blvd, Louisville, KY 40202
Tel.: (502) 589-7711

Fax: (502) 589-0390
E-Mail: info@bch.com
Web Site: www.bch.com

E-Mail for Key Personnel:
Creative Dir.: gsloboda@bch.com

Employees: 45
Year Founded: 1990

National Agency Associations: PRSA-Second Wind Limited

Agency Specializes In: Brand Development & Integration, Broadcast, Business Publications, Business-To-Business, Cable T.V., Co-op Advertising, Collateral, Communications, Consumer Marketing, Consumer Publications, Corporate Identity, Direct Response Marketing, E-Commerce, Education, Electronic Media, Entertainment, Environmental, Event Planning & Marketing, Exhibit/Trade Shows, Financial, Food Service, Graphic Design, Health Care Services, Hispanic Market, Industrial, Information Technology, Internet/Web Design, Investor Relations, Logo & Package Design, Magazines, Media Buying Services, Merchandising, New Product Development, Newspaper, Newspapers & Magazines, Out-of-Home Media, Outdoor, Over-50 Market, Planning & Consultation, Point of Purchase, Point of Sale, Print, Production, Public Relations, Publicity/Promotions, Radio, Restaurant, Retail, Sales Promotion, Seniors' Market, Sponsorship, Sports Market, Strategic Planning/Research, Sweepstakes, T.V., Teen Market, Trade & Consumer Magazines, Travel & Tourism

Tim Hellige *(Owner)*
Gary Sloboda *(Partner & Exec Dir-Creative)*
Susan Bandy *(Partner)*
Mark Carroll *(Partner)*
Jeanie Roddy *(Acct Dir-McDonald's)*
Sabrina Sebastian *(Dir-Digital Strategy)*
Christine Horn *(Sr Acct Mgr)*
Leigh Ann Burckhardt *(Acct Mgr)*
Jenny Howard *(Brand Mgr-Brand Engagement)*
Dan Gdowski *(Mgr-Social Media)*
Angie Albanese *(Supvr-Acctg)*
Lauren Pieper *(Planner-Digital Adv)*
Terri Isgrigg *(Coord-New Bus)*
Megan Schmitt *(Coord-Media)*

Accounts:
Big O Tires
Bluegrass Cellular/Telecom; Elizabethtown, KY Cellular, Internet, Long Distance; 1996
Citizens Energy Group; Indianapolis, IN
The Courier-Journal; Louisville, KY Daily Newspaper; 1997
Delta Dental of Kentucky; Louisville, KY Dental Plan; 1997
Falls City Brewing Co. (Agency of Record) Advertising, Branding, Public Relations
Four Roses Bourbon; 2004
Frazier International History Museum (Agency of Record)
Hoosier Lottery
Kentucky Kingdom & Hurricane Bay Communications Strategy, Creative, Digital, Marketing, Media Services
Kentucky Lottery
KentuckyOne Health Inc
Louisville Convention & Visitors Bureau
Louisville Zoo; Louisville, KY; 1999
McDonald's Central, IL, Fort Wayne, IN, Indianapolis, IN, Kentuckiana, KY, South Bend, IN
Republic Bank & Trust Co. (Agency of Record) Online Elements, Print, Television
Supra, Moomba Boats

Branch

Bandy Carroll Hellige Advertising

111 Monument Cir Ste 882, Indianapolis, IN 46204-5173
Tel.: (317) 684-7711
Fax: (317) 684-0188
E-Mail: bch@bch.com
Web Site: www.bch.com

Employees: 10
Year Founded: 1994

National Agency Associations: 4A's

Agency Specializes In: Advertising

Mary Shultz *(Sr VP & Analyst-Bus)*
Kenethia Jackson *(VP-Engagement Mktg)*
Amy Kaiser Smock *(Assoc Dir-Media)*
Christine Horn *(Sr Acct Mgr)*
Cassie Wissel *(Acct Mgr)*
Laura Becker *(Mgr-Print Production)*
Shelby Barrett *(Asst Acct Mgr)*

Accounts:
McDonald's Corporation

BANIK COMMUNICATIONS

121 4th St N Ste 1B, Great Falls, MT 59401
Tel.: (406) 454-3422
Fax: (406) 771-1418
Toll Free: (800) 823-3388
E-Mail: banik@banik.com
Web Site: www.banik.com

Employees: 10
Year Founded: 1979

Agency Specializes In: Advertising, Government/Political, Medical Products, Pharmaceutical

Approx. Annual Billings: $4,000,000

Breakdown of Gross Billings by Media: Graphic Design: 15%; Logo & Package Design: 7%; Newsp. & Mags.: 20%; Pub. Rels.: 10%; Radio & T.V.: 15%; Strategic Planning/Research: 25%; Worldwide Web Sites: 8%

Ronda Banik *(Sr VP)*
Randi Szabo *(VP-Comm)*
Heather Burcham *(Dir-Media)*
Kevin Eveland *(Dir-Art-Web Dev)*
Eric Heidle *(Dir-Creative)*
Daniel Perbil *(Dir-Creative)*
Karen Venetz *(Acct Mgr)*

Accounts:
North Valley Hospital

BANOWETZ + COMPANY INC.

3809 Parry Ave Ste 208, Dallas, TX 75226
Tel.: (214) 823-7300
E-Mail: leon@banowetz.com
Web Site: www.banowetz.com

Employees: 8
Year Founded: 1988

Agency Specializes In: Advertising, Brand Development & Integration, Email, Logo & Package Design, Media Planning, Outdoor, Print, Publishing, Radio, T.V.

Leon Banowetz *(Pres)*
Molly Banowetz *(Partner)*
Wes Phelan *(Dir-Art & Designer)*
Sarah Terrell *(Assoc Dir-Creative)*
Dawn Grimes *(Sr Mgr-Production)*
Allen Davis *(Sr Acct Exec)*
Kris Shelton-Murphy *(Sr Designer)*

Accounts:
NorthPark Management Company Shopping Center

THE BARBARIAN GROUP

112 W 20th St, New York, NY 10011
Tel.: (212) 343-4215
Fax: (212) 343-4216
E-Mail: info@barbariangroup.com
Web Site: www.barbariangroup.com

Employees: 125
Year Founded: 2001

National Agency Associations: 4A's

Agency Specializes In: Digital/Interactive, Sponsorship

Benjamin Palmer *(Chm)*
Sophie Kelly *(CEO)*
Alex White *(CFO)*
Robert Christ *(CTO)*
Ian Daly *(Chief Strategy Officer)*
Edu Pou *(Chief Creative Officer)*
Sherri Chambers *(Head-Acct Mgmt)*
Sarah Grant *(Head-Technical)*
Darren Himebrook *(Head-Ops)*
Eric Andrade *(Exec Dir-Ops)*
Jill Nussbaum *(Exec Dir-Product & Interaction Design)*
Abbas Deidehban *(Art Dir)*
Adam Lau *(Creative Dir)*
Claire Manganiello *(Art Dir)*
Nick Bonadies *(Dir-IT)*
Eric Burnett *(Dir-Creative)*
JoRoan Lazaro *(Dir-Creative)*
Dan Nichols *(Dir-Tech, Mobile & Experiential)*
Andrew Peet *(Dir-Art)*
Roger Ramirez *(Dir-Bus)*
Will Sandwick *(Dir-Analytics)*
Amy Todenhagen *(Dir-Creative & Interaction Design)*
Lexi Peters *(Sr Mgr-PR)*
Sunchia Eckert *(Acct Mgr)*
Gage Heyburn *(Acct Mgr)*
Emilio Rosas *(Acct Mgr)*
Sophie Shrem *(Acct Exec)*
Morgan Perrine *(Copywriter)*
Alex Schaeffer *(Copywriter)*
Emily Sheehan *(Copywriter)*
Danielle Zeisler *(Designer)*
Rachel Thompson *(Jr Strategist)*
Felix Yip *(Sr Strategy Dir)*

Accounts:
AD Council Campaign: "Clean Up the Mold", Campaign: "Don't Smoke in the House", Campaign: "Vacuum Up the Floor"
Adobe
Allstate
Anomaly
Arnold Worldwide
Aveda
Axe Body Spray
Barclay's Bank
Bloomberg
New-Brisk
Burger King Campaign: "Subservient Chicken"
Clinique
Department of Transportation Campaign: "Dot Skeleton"
New-Etihad Airways Campaign: "Flying Reimagined", Social Media
General Electric "Drop Science", Campaign: "Brilliant Machines", Campaign: "Ge Factory Flyovers", Campaign: "Ge Show", Campaign: "Over 2 Million Containers, 2,000 Routes"
New-IBM
New-Kind Snacks (Creative Agency of Record)
Mondelez International Campaign: "Look. Fresh", Trident
Pepsico Campaign: "Next the Internet Taste Test"

Procter & Gamble Co.
Samsung Campaign: "Secret Sites", CenterStage, Digital, Home Appliance, Tweet Wrap

Branch

The Barbarian Group
129 S St 2nd Fl, Boston, MA 02111
Tel.: (617) 424-8887
Fax: (617) 437-9499
E-Mail: info@barbariangroup.com
Web Site: www.barbariangroup.com

Employees: 16

Agency Specializes In: Brand Development & Integration, Consulting, Digital/Interactive, Internet/Web Design, Multimedia, Production, Strategic Planning/Research, Viral/Buzz/Word of Mouth, Web (Banner Ads, Pop-ups, etc.)

Benjamin Palmer *(Co-Founder & Chm)*
Keith Butters *(Owner)*
Mike Paulo *(Grp Dir-Tech)*
Aimee Kvasir *(Dir-Technical)*
Robby Egan *(Assoc Dir-Media & Distr)*

Accounts:
CNN.com Website
GE
Harmonix
Jim Beam Website
Motorola Solutions, Inc.
Mozilla
Pepsi Campaign: "Internet Taste Test", Campaign: "The Extra Hour", Pepsi Next
Samsung Samsung Series 9, Tweetcracker

THE BARBAULD AGENCY
PO Box 367, Valparaiso, IN 46384
Tel.: (219) 649-1227
E-Mail: hello@barbauld.com
Web Site: www.barbauldagency.com

Agency Specializes In: Advertising, Brand Development & Integration, Graphic Design, Internet/Web Design, Social Media

Chris Barbauld *(Pres)*
Molly Randolph *(Acct Exec)*
Dana Wasson *(Acct Exec)*

Accounts:
Bozovich Wellness Center
Catherines Bridal Boutique
Dorazio Ford Let it Snow
Fitness Edge
Heinold & Feller Tire Co

BARBEAU-HUTCHINGS ADVERTISING, INC.
30 Controls Dr, Shelton, CT 06484
Tel.: (203) 926-0040
Fax: (203) 926-0092
E-Mail: creative_solutions@bhaadvertising.com
Web Site: www.bhaadvertising.com

Employees: 10
Year Founded: 1981

National Agency Associations: LAA

Agency Specializes In: Advertising, Automotive, Brand Development & Integration, Business-To-Business, Corporate Identity, Electronic Media, Environmental, Exhibit/Trade Shows, High Technology, Information Technology, Internet/Web Design, Public Relations, Strategic Planning/Research, Technical Advertising, Trade & Consumer Magazines

Accounts:
Magenta Research; Bethel, CT Electronic Networking; 2005
Ulvac; Methuen, MA Vacuum Equipment; 2001

BARBER MARTIN AGENCY
7400 Beaufont Springs Dr Ste 201, Richmond, VA 23225-5519
Tel.: (804) 320-3232
Fax: (804) 320-1729
E-Mail: info@barbermartin.com
Web Site: www.barbermartin.com

E-Mail for Key Personnel:
President: rdeyo@barbermartin.com
Creative Dir.: pshulman@barbermartin.com
Production Mgr.: gsimos@barbermartin.com

Employees: 27
Year Founded: 1989

Agency Specializes In: Agriculture, Automotive, Brand Development & Integration, Broadcast, Cable T.V., Co-op Advertising, Collateral, Consumer Marketing, Corporate Identity, Direct Response Marketing, Fashion/Apparel, Financial, Food Service, Graphic Design, Internet/Web Design, Logo & Package Design, Magazines, Media Buying Services, Newspaper, Newspapers & Magazines, Out-of-Home Media, Outdoor, Point of Purchase, Point of Sale, Public Relations, Radio, Retail, T.V., Travel & Tourism

William V. Martin *(Owner)*
Bill Vogt *(CFO & VP)*
Sarah Duke *(Sr Dir-Art)*
Matt May *(Dir-Strategy & Res)*
Linda Davis *(Supvr-Media Buying)*
Michael Foster *(Acct Exec)*
Christie Hach *(Acct Exec)*
Christy Gasiorowski *(Media Buyer)*
Kristen McCutchen *(Media Buyer)*

Accounts:
Adolf Jewelers; Richmond, VA Specialty Jewelry; 1992
CATO Corporation; Charlotte, NC (Agency of Record) Women's Clothing; 1999
McGeorge Toyota Creative, Radio, TV, Website
NTELOS Holdings Corp.
Southern States Cooperative; Richmond, VA; 1996

THE BARBOUR SHOP
PO Box 21153, Santa Barbara, CA 93121
Tel.: (805) 698-9640
Web Site: www.thebarbourshop.com

Year Founded: 2006

Agency Specializes In: Advertising, Digital/Interactive, Graphic Design, Internet/Web Design, Social Media

Meg Barbour *(Founder & CEO)*
Yan Da *(Dir-Creative-New Media)*
Elna Gurvits *(Designer)*

Accounts:
Mission Control Media

BARCELONA ENTERPRISES
4230 Stansbury Ave Ste 101, Sherman Oaks, CA 91423
Tel.: (818) 288-4050
E-Mail: info@barcelona.la
Web Site: www.barcelona.la

Employees: 10
Year Founded: 2003

Agency Specializes In: Advertising, African-American Market, Asian Market, Collateral, Communications, Consumer Publications, Corporate Identity, Cosmetics, Environmental, Event Planning & Marketing, Fashion/Apparel, Guerilla Marketing, Hispanic Market, Logo & Package Design, Luxury Products, Multicultural, Outdoor, Point of Sale, Print, Promotions, Public Relations, Radio, Restaurant, Social Marketing/Nonprofit, Sponsorship, Sweepstakes, Viral/Buzz/Word of Mouth, Web (Banner Ads, Pop-ups, etc.)

Approx. Annual Billings: $1,500,000

Breakdown of Gross Billings by Media: Collateral: 20%; Event Mktg.: 20%; Print: 50%; Radio: 10%

Alan Semsar *(CEO)*
Max Bobritsky *(Dir-Sls)*
Daniel Torres *(Mgr-Social Media)*
Nadine Russell *(Sr Coord-Event)*

BARD ADVERTISING
4900 Lincoln Dr, Edina, MN 55436
Tel.: (952) 345-6265
Web Site: www.bardadvertising.com

Employees: 25
Year Founded: 1996

Agency Specializes In: Digital/Interactive, In-Store Advertising, Mobile Marketing, Paid Searches, Point of Purchase, Point of Sale, Promotions, Shopper Marketing, Sponsorship, Web (Banner Ads, Pop-ups, etc.)

Lee Ann Villella *(VP-Bus Dev)*

Accounts:
Lundberg Family Farms
Sargento Foods
Target

BAREFOOT PROXIMITY
700 W Pete Rose Way, Cincinnati, OH 45203
Tel.: (513) 861-3668
Fax: (513) 487-6855
E-Mail: llindley@barefootproximity.com
Web Site: www.alittledata.com/

Employees: 50
Year Founded: 1993

National Agency Associations: 4A's

Agency Specializes In: Advertising, Brand Development & Integration, Consumer Marketing, Outdoor, Point of Purchase, Print, Radio, Restaurant, Sponsorship, Strategic Planning/Research, T.V., Teen Market

Doug Worple *(Chm)*
Chris Evans *(CEO)*
Amy Hatton *(Sr VP & Acct Dir)*
Allen McCormick *(VP & Acct Dir)*
Jessica Asch *(Acct Dir)*
Julie Hanser *(Dir-Talent Dev)*
Kristen Houston *(Dir-Insight & Plng)*
Brandon Blank *(Assoc Dir-User Experience)*
Elly Wainscott *(Acct Supvr)*

Accounts:
F-Eight
Freedom Boat Club
Last Chance Horse Rescue
Novartis
The Procter & Gamble Company; Cincinnati, OH Braun, Campaign: "FaceGreatness", Cascade, Dawn, Febreze Global, Home Made Simple, HomeMadeSimple.com, Online, P&G Dish Global, PGEveryday.com, Print, TV, Wella
Raymond Thunder-Sky

BARK BARK

75 Ponce De Leon Ave NE, Atlanta, GA 30308
Tel.: (404) 551-4505
Fax: (800) 396-5231
Toll Free: (800) 396-5231
E-Mail: atl@barkbark.com
Web Site: www.barkbark.com

Agency Specializes In: Advertising, Brand Development & Integration

Aaron Smith *(Partner & COO)*
Brian Tolleson *(Partner)*
Karen Grant *(VP-Client Partnership & Media)*
Matthew I. Jenkins *(Dir-Animation)*
Francine McDougall *(Dir-Creative-West Coast)*
Daniel Sattelmeyer *(Dir-Creative)*
Max Oliver *(Mgr-Production & Fin)*

BARKER & CHRISTOL ADVERTISING

109B N Maple St, Murfreesboro, TN 37130
Tel.: (615) 796-6584
Web Site: www.barker-christol.com

Year Founded: 2011

Agency Specializes In: Advertising, Logo & Package Design, Media Buying Services, Media Planning, Public Relations, Strategic Planning/Research

Steve Barker *(Partner & Creative Dir)*
J. Brooks Christol *(Partner-Left Brain)*
Judy Caplan *(Dir-Media)*
Autumn Shultz *(Mgr-Ops)*

Accounts:
Murfreesboro City Schools

BARKER/DZP

455 Broadway, New York, NY 10013
Tel.: (212) 226-7336
Fax: (212) 226-7937
E-Mail: newbusiness@barkernyc.com
Web Site: barkernyc.com

Employees: 18
Year Founded: 2003

National Agency Associations: 4A's

Agency Specializes In: Above-the-Line, Advertising, Affiliate Marketing, Affluent Market, Brand Development & Integration, Branded Entertainment, Broadcast, Business-To-Business, Cable T.V., Computers & Software, Consulting, Consumer Goods, Consumer Marketing, Content, Corporate Identity, Digital/Interactive, Electronic Media, Email, Entertainment, Environmental, Fashion/Apparel, Financial, Food Service, Game Integration, Graphic Design, Household Goods, In-Store Advertising, Internet/Web Design, Leisure, Local Marketing, Logo & Package Design, Luxury Products, Men's Market, Multicultural, New Technologies, Newspapers & Magazines, Out-of-Home Media, Outdoor, Over-50 Market, Package Design, Print, Product Placement, Production (Ad, Film, Broadcast), Production (Print), Radio, Real Estate, Retail, Social Marketing/Nonprofit, Sports Market, T.V., Trade & Consumer Magazines, Urban Market, Web (Banner Ads, Pop-ups, etc.), Women's Market

Breakdown of Gross Billings by Media: Graphic Design: 10%; Logo & Package Design: 5%; Outdoor: 15%; Radio & T.V.: 25%; Trade & Consumer Mags.: 30%; Worldwide Web Sites: 15%

John H. Barker *(Pres & Chief Idea Officer)*
Carol Ann Duncan *(CFO & Sr VP)*
Ray Rainville *(Sr VP-Client Svcs & Exec Producer-Integrated)*
Sandi Harari *(Sr VP & Dir-Creative)*
Robert Kellner *(Sr VP-Strategy)*
Kim Tracey *(VP & Acct Dir)*
Jennifer Schwartz *(Sr Dir-Art)*
Yimeng Bai *(Assoc Dir-Creative)*
Alison Stelzer *(Acct Supvr)*
Chelsey Waldman *(Acct Supvr)*

Accounts:
Boylan Bottling Co. (Agency of Record) Branding, Digital Support, Marketing
Estee Lauder Companies, Inc. Lab Series
Hastens Luxury Beds; 2008
IDB Bank
Jacadi
Letarte
Miele
NBC
PepsiCo
Procter & Gamble: Cincinnati, Ohio People's Choice Awards, PCAvote.com; 2006
Roche Bobois
SlimFast (Creative & Interactive Agency of Record)

BARKLEY

1740 Main St, Kansas City, MO 64108
Tel.: (816) 842-1500
E-Mail: jfromm@barkleyus.com
Web Site: www.barkleyus.com

Employees: 250
Year Founded: 1964

National Agency Associations: 4A's

Agency Specializes In: Advertising, Affluent Market, Automotive, Below-the-Line, Brand Development & Integration, Broadcast, Business-To-Business, Cable T.V., Co-op Advertising, Collateral, Communications, Consumer Goods, Consumer Marketing, Consumer Publications, Corporate Communications, Corporate Identity, Crisis Communications, Customer Relationship Management, Digital/Interactive, Direct Response Marketing, Direct-to-Consumer, E-Commerce, Electronic Media, Entertainment, Environmental, Event Planning & Marketing, Experience Design, Fashion/Apparel, Food Service, Government/Political, Graphic Design, Guerilla Marketing, Identity Marketing, In-Store Advertising, Integrated Marketing, Internet/Web Design, Legal Services, Leisure, Local Marketing, Logo & Package Design, Luxury Products, Magazines, Media Buying Services, Media Planning, Media Relations, Media Training, Men's Market, Mobile Marketing, New Product Development, New Technologies, Newspaper, Newspapers & Magazines, Out-of-Home Media, Outdoor, Package Design, Paid Searches, Point of Purchase, Point of Sale, Print, Product Placement, Production, Production (Print), Promotions, Public Relations, Publicity/Promotions, Radio, Regional, Restaurant, Retail, Sales Promotion, Search Engine Optimization, Social Marketing/Nonprofit, Social Media, Sponsorship, Sports Market, Strategic Planning/Research, T.V., Teen Market, Trade & Consumer Magazines, Transportation, Travel & Tourism, Tween Market, Viral/Buzz/Word of Mouth, Women's Market

William M. Fromm *(Founder)*
Dan Fromm *(Pres & COO)*
Jeff King *(CEO)*
Jeff Fromm *(Pres-FutureCast)*
Amy Allen *(Sr Counsel-Legal & Exec VP-HR)*
Mike Goff *(Exec VP)*
Brad Hanna *(Exec VP & Grp Acct Head)*
David Weaver *(Exec VP-Creative & Strategy)*
Mark Logan *(Sr VP-Innovation)*
Berk Wasserman *(VP & Creative Dir)*
Steve Wujek *(VP & Acct Dir)*
Valencia Gayles *(VP)*
Alexis Bossi *(Grp Head-Media Design)*
Lindsey Ingram *(Grp Head-Media Design)*
Elizabeth McMahan *(Grp Head-Media Design)*
Jason Elm *(Exec Dir-Creative)*
Tyler Cook *(Acct Dir)*
John Hornaday *(Acct Dir)*
Kristin Kovach *(Acct Dir)*
Amanda Mikuls *(Acct Dir)*
Chad Milam *(Acct Dir)*
Kevin Buller *(Dir-IT)*
Chris Cardetti *(Dir-Strategy)*
Brent Fernandez *(Dir-Creative)*
Nick Crofoot *(Assoc Dir-Creative)*
John Dobson *(Sr Acct Mgr)*
Gabe Barton *(Mgr-HR)*
Cristina Martinez *(Mgr-HR)*
Allison Pinkowski *(Acct Supvr)*
Elizabeth RossMan *(Acct Supvr-PR)*
Eric Miller *(Strategist-Social Media)*
Rachel Stelmach *(Designer-Supervising Media)*
Chris Butler *(Grp Media Supvr)*
Aaron Cathey *(Sr Writer)*
Tim Galles *(Chief Idea Officer)*
Molly Griffin *(Assoc Strategist)*
Jory Mick *(Asst Acct Mgr)*

Accounts:
American Dairy Queen Corp (Agency of Record)
Applebee's
Ball Canning; 2009
Big Lots Lead Creative
Big-O Tires; 2007
Cargill
Casey's (Agency of Record) Brand Strategy, Broadcast, Creative, Marketing, Media Planning, Online, Print
Coleman, Inc
Dairy Queen (Agency of Record) Campaign: "Blizzard Battle", Campaign: "Fanifesto"
Daisy Brand; 2010
Dawn Food Products; Jackson, MI; 2008
DHI Group, Inc.; 2011
Eurostar (US Agency of Record) Brand Awareness, Creative, Digital, Media, Strategy
Fruit 2.0
Hershey Co Strategic Projects
Lee Jeans; Mission, KS Interactive & Public Relations, Lee.com; 1996
March of Dimes
Marmot; 2010
Minute Rice
MO Lottery; 1995
Nestle Purina; 2009
Noodles & Co (Agency of Record) Brand Communications, Campaign: "Made. Different.", Media, Strategy
On the Border Mexican Grill & Cantina (Agency of Record) Brand Strategy, Digital, In-store Merchandising, Media Strategy, Menu Design, National Creative
Riviana Foods; Houston, TX Minute Rice; 2007
Schreiber; Green Bay, WI Cheeses; 2008
Spirit Airlines (Agency of Record) Brand Strategy, Digital, Hug the Haters, Media, Media Planning & Buying, PR, Point-of-Sale
SportingKC (Agency of Record) Tractor Supply; 2011
Sprint Corporation
Vanity Fair (Agency of Record) Digital, Lingerie, Mass Media, Media Planning & Buying, PR, Social Media, Strategy
Weight Watchers
Wingstop Restaurants Inc (Agency of Record) Campaign: "Get at it", Social Media

Branches

BarkleyREI
2740 Smallman St, Pittsburgh, PA 15222
(See Separate Listing)

Crossroads

1740 Main St, Kansas City, MO 64108
(See Separate Listing)

BARKLEYREI
2740 Smallman St, Pittsburgh, PA 15222
Tel.: (412) 683-3700
Fax: (412) 683-1610
Web Site: www.barkleyus.com

Employees: 35
Year Founded: 1997

National Agency Associations: 4A's

Agency Specializes In: Digital/Interactive, Graphic Design, Pets

Jeff Graham *(Partner & Mng Dir)*
Shane Pryal *(Mng Dir)*
Amy Allen *(Chief Counsel-Legal & Exec VP-HR)*
Brad Hanna *(Exec VP & Grp Acct Head)*
Bryan Herrman *(Sr VP & Dir-Bus Strategy)*
Sara Buck *(Sr VP & Grp Acct Head)*
Katy Hornaday *(VP & Dir-Creative)*
Paul Corrigan *(Dir-Design)*
Brad Jungles *(Dir-Creative)*
Scott Riemenschneider *(Dir-Creative)*
Lauren Santori *(Acct Supvr)*

Accounts:
AARP
Ad Council Boost Up, Generous Nation Volunteerism, Iraq/Afghanistan Veterans of America Health Services, Website
Ashville CVB
Carnegie Mellon University
Independence Blue Cross
International Fund for Animal Welfare Emergency Network
Minnesota Tourism
National Center for Missing & Exploited Children
National City Bank
National Multiple Sclerosis Society
North Carolina State
Northeastern Illinois University
Northern Virginia Community College
Pearson Education
Pennsylvania Council on the Arts
Pennsylvania Department of Community & Economic Development
Pennsylvania Dutch Convention & Visitors Bureau
Pennsylvania Tourism Pennsylvania Wilds Tourism Marketing Campaign, VisitPA.com
Saint Vincent College
San Antonio CVB
Thomas Jefferson University Hospital
Travel Industry Association
University of Notre Dame
Vanderbilt University
W.R. Case & Sons Cutlery Company
Wake Forest
Washington DC Convention & Tourism Corporation
Williamsburg Area Destination Marketing Committee
Yale University

BARNETT COX & ASSOCIATES
711 Tank Farm Rd Ste 210, San Luis Obispo, CA 93401
Tel.: (805) 545-8887
Fax: (805) 545-0860
E-Mail: info@barnettcox.com
Web Site: www.barnettcox.com

E-Mail for Key Personnel:
President: mcox@barnettcox.com

Employees: 20

National Agency Associations: Second Wind Limited

Agency Specializes In: Advertising, Agriculture, Broadcast, Collateral, Consulting, Corporate Identity, Environmental, Financial, Government/Political, Graphic Design, Health Care Services, Logo & Package Design, Media Buying Services, Newspaper, Outdoor, Planning & Consultation, Print, Production, Public Relations, Publicity/Promotions, Radio, Strategic Planning/Research, Travel & Tourism

Dave Cox *(Owner)*
Maggie Cox *(Pres & CEO)*
Kerri Parris-Brown *(Controller)*
Larry Kaul *(Dir-Bus Dev)*
Jeremy Morris *(Dir-Strategy)*
Courtney Meznarich *(Acct Mgr)*
Becky Mosgofian *(Specialist-PR)*
Katie Ferber *(Coord-Production)*

Accounts:
Cannon Associates
Centex Homes
Chase Home Finance
Chevron
City of Paso Robles
City of San Luis Obispo
ConocoPhillips
Cuesta College
Morro Bay National Estuary Program
Pacific Energy Company
PG&E
SLO Aging Institute
SLO County YMCA
Susan Branch Heart of the Home
Thoma Electric
University of California, Santa Barbara

BARNETT MURPHY DIRECT MARKETING
(Formerly Barnett & Murphy, Inc)
1323 Brookhaven Dr, Orlando, FL 32803
Tel.: (407) 650-0264
Fax: (407) 650-0268
E-Mail: hello@bmdm.com
Web Site: www.bmdm.com

Employees: 13
Year Founded: 2002

Agency Specializes In: African-American Market, Bilingual Market, Business-To-Business, Children's Market, College, Communications, Consumer Goods, Corporate Communications, Customer Relationship Management, Digital/Interactive, Direct-to-Consumer, E-Commerce, Email, Financial, Guerilla Marketing, Integrated Marketing, Internet/Web Design, Local Marketing, Marine, Multicultural, Over-50 Market, Pharmaceutical, Print, Production (Print), Real Estate, Restaurant, Seniors' Market, Social Marketing/Nonprofit, Teen Market, Travel & Tourism, Web (Banner Ads, Pop-ups, etc.)

Joe Forget *(Sr VP-Digital Strategies)*
Todd Masoner *(Mgr-IT & Specialist-Data)*
Lisa Lawn *(Mgr-IT)*
Justin Krout *(Designer-Front-End)*
Charlie Murphy *(Exec-Sls)*

Accounts:
Toyota Florida Automotive

BARNHARDT, DAY & HINES
56 Cabarrus Ave W, Concord, NC 28026
Mailing Address:
PO Box 163, Concord, NC 28026
Tel.: (704) 786-7193
Fax: (704) 786-5150
E-Mail: ahines@bdandh.com
Web Site: www.bdandh.com

Employees: 11
Year Founded: 1983

Agency Specializes In: Advertising, Brand Development & Integration, Collateral, Internet/Web Design, Logo & Package Design, Media Planning, Print, Radio, Strategic Planning/Research, T.V.

Approx. Annual Billings: $18,000,000

Thomas Day *(Pres & Partner)*
Mike Scardino *(Chief Creative Officer)*
Alaine Bollinger *(Principal & Sr VP)*
Laurey McElroy *(VP-Acct Svcs)*
Darrel Myers *(Dir-Creative & Mktg)*
Bev Stroman *(Dir-Fin Svcs)*

Accounts:
Coca-Cola Refreshments USA, Inc.
CT Communications
Lowes Motor Speedway

BARNHART
1641 California St, Denver, CO 80202-1233
Tel.: (303) 626-7200
Fax: (303) 626-7252
E-Mail: info@barnhartusa.com
Web Site: www.barnhartusa.com

E-Mail for Key Personnel:
President: bschumacher@barnhartusa.com

Employees: 20
Year Founded: 1995

National Agency Associations: AAF-AMIN

Agency Specializes In: Advertising, Aviation & Aerospace, Brand Development & Integration, Broadcast, Business Publications, Business-To-Business, Cable T.V., Co-op Advertising, Collateral, Commercial Photography, Communications, Consulting, Consumer Marketing, Consumer Publications, Corporate Identity, Digital/Interactive, Direct Response Marketing, E-Commerce, Education, Electronic Media, Entertainment, Event Planning & Marketing, Exhibit/Trade Shows, Financial, Food Service, Graphic Design, Health Care Services, High Technology, Information Technology, Internet/Web Design, Leisure, Logo & Package Design, Magazines, Media Buying Services, Merchandising, New Product Development, Newspaper, Newspapers & Magazines, Out-of-Home Media, Outdoor, Planning & Consultation, Point of Purchase, Point of Sale, Print, Production, Public Relations, Publicity/Promotions, Radio, Real Estate, Restaurant, Retail, Sales Promotion, Sponsorship, Sports Market, Strategic Planning/Research, T.V., Trade & Consumer Magazines, Travel & Tourism

Approx. Annual Billings: $50,000,000

Bill Schumacher *(Pres)*
Christin Crampton Day *(Sr Dir-PR)*
Patrick Farrell *(Client Svcs Dir)*
Matt Ward *(Creative Dir)*
Lonnie Anderson *(Dir-Creative)*
Lynda Pfaff *(Dir-Media)*
Lydia Chou *(Mgr-PR & Social Media)*
Sandy Schest *(Project Acct Exec)*
Rachel Vigil *(Assoc Designer)*

Accounts:
The Denver Hospice Brand Positioning, Communications, Marketing, Messaging, Planning, Social Media Strategy
Jackson Hole Travel and Tourism Board (Branding & Advertising Agency of Record) Brand Strategy, Creative Strategy, Digital, Media Buying, Public Relations, Website
LBA Realty Branding Strategies, Digital, Events, Exhibitions, Marketing, Media, Social
New-Spring Institute for Intercultural Learning Brand Strategy
Touch The Top Brand Positioning, Marketing,

Messaging, Planning, Website Development
The Town of Breckenridge's Cultural Arts Division Brand Identity, Brand Strategy, Campaign Development, Website Development
New-Town of Parker Brand Strategy, Creative, Marketing
Wyoming Office of Tourism

BAROLIN & SPENCER, INC.

1015 Main St, Voorhees, NJ 08043-4602
Tel.: (856) 424-7600
Fax: (856) 424-7676
E-Mail: info@barolin-spencer.com
Web Site: www.barolin-spencer.com

Employees: 8
Year Founded: 1988

National Agency Associations: APRC

Agency Specializes In: Advertising, Automotive, Brand Development & Integration, Business Publications, Business-To-Business, Co-op Advertising, Collateral, Consulting, Corporate Communications, Corporate Identity, Digital/Interactive, Direct Response Marketing, E-Commerce, Event Planning & Marketing, Exhibit/Trade Shows, Graphic Design, Health Care Services, High Technology, Identity Marketing, Industrial, Integrated Marketing, Internet/Web Design, Logo & Package Design, Magazines, Marine, Media Buying Services, Media Planning, Media Relations, Medical Products, Merchandising, Multimedia, New Product Development, Package Design, Planning & Consultation, Point of Purchase, Point of Sale, Print, Promotions, Public Relations, Publicity/Promotions, Sales Promotion, Search Engine Optimization, Strategic Planning/Research, Technical Advertising, Trade & Consumer Magazines, Web (Banner Ads, Pop-ups, etc.)

Anthony M. Barolin *(Mng Partner)*
Joel Spencer *(Mng Partner)*
Pete Ceran *(Dir-Art)*
Mark Laganella *(Dir-Interactive)*
Paul Young *(Dir-Art)*
Sue Spencer *(Mgr-Media)*

Accounts:
AccessIT; Philadelphia, PA IT Security Services; 2002
Hella, Inc.; Peachtree City, GA Accessories, Automotive Lighting, Electrical Products, Electronics, Thermal Management; 2007
IPC Global Solutions

BARRETTSF

603 Battery St, San Francisco, CA 94111
Tel.: (415) 986-2960
E-Mail: info@barrettsf.com
Web Site: www.barrettsf.com

Year Founded: 2012

Agency Specializes In: Advertising

Patrick Kelly *(Co-Founder & Mng Dir)*
Jamie Barrett *(Co-Founder & Exec Dir-Creative)*
Brittni Hutchins *(Acct Dir)*
David Viau *(Creative Dir)*
Rafi Kugler *(Dir-Recruiting)*
Byron Wages *(Dir-Art)*
Brad Kayal *(Assoc Dir-Creative)*
Jillian Gamboa *(Acct Mgr)*
Michael Reardon *(Acct Supvr)*
Jim Lemaitre *(Copywriter)*
Spencer Riviera *(Copywriter)*

Accounts:
2K Games Campaign: WWE 2K15 Game Launch, Creative
New-Bleacher Report Campaign: "Sports Alphabet"
California Redwood Association
Drop-A-Brick
E. & J. Gallo Winery
Exchange Bank
Golf Channel
Major League Baseball
Omaha Steaks Online, TV
Pac-12 Networks
Rubio' s Restaurant Campaign: "To The Ocean", Creative
Salesforce
TiVo
TopLine Game Labs Campaign: "Have an MVP Day", DailyMVP
Ubisoft Assassin's Creed Syndicate, Campaign: "Welcome to the Family", Creative
YP Campaign: "YP Can Do That", Creative

BARRIE D'ROZARIO DILORENZO

(Formerly Barrie D'Rozario Murphy)
400 1st Ave N Ste 220, Minneapolis, MN 55401
Tel.: (612) 279-1500
Fax: (612) 332-9995
E-Mail: talent@bdd.us
Web Site: bdd.us/

Employees: 30

Agency Specializes In: Advertising, Digital/Interactive, Media Planning, Print, Sponsorship, T.V.

Kevin DiLorenzo *(Pres, Partner & Dir-Client Svcs & Brand Strategy)*
Stuart D'Rozario *(CEO & Chief Creative Officer)*
Bob Barrie *(Partner & Dir-Creative)*
Steve Centrillo *(CMO)*
Timothy Harsh *(Dir-Digital Strategy & Analytics)*
Jack Steinmann *(Dir-Integrated Production)*
Janie Waldron *(Dir-Project Mgmt)*
Steve Rudasics *(Assoc Dir-Creative)*

Accounts:
The Basilica of Saint Mary Campaign: "Basilica Block Party"
Best Buy
Bissell Homecare New Product Introduction
Chamilia
Dell Inc.
New-University of Minnesota Campaign: "M is for..."
Wagner Spray Tech (Agency of Record)

BARRON MARKETING COMMUNICATIONS

833 N Washington St, Wilmington, DE 19801-1509
Tel.: (302) 658-1627
Fax: (302) 658-5798
E-Mail: info@barronmarketing.com
Web Site: www.barronmarketing.com

E-Mail for Key Personnel:
President: pbarron@barronmarketing.com
Creative Dir.: tneilson@barronmarketing.com

Employees: 10
Year Founded: 1976

Agency Specializes In: Fashion/Apparel, Health Care Services, Sports Market

Patricia Barron *(Pres)*

Accounts:
A. Uberti
Artisans' Bank
Benelli USA
Center for the Creative Arts
W. L. Gore & Associates
W. L. Gore & Associates

BARTLE BOGLE HEGARTY LIMITED

60 Kingly Street, London, W1B 5DS United Kingdom
Tel.: (44) 2077341677
Fax: (44) 2074373666
Web Site: www.bartlebooglehegarty.com/london/

Employees: 900
Year Founded: 1982

National Agency Associations: IPA

Approx. Annual Billings: $1,750,000,000

John Hegarty *(Founder)*
Alexandre Gama *(Pres)*
Neil Munn *(Grp CEO)*
Niall Hadden *(Chief Talent Officer-Global & Mng Partner)*
Polly McMorrow *(Partner & Head-Bus)*
Chris Watling *(Partner & Producer)*
Carl Broadhurst *(Partner & Dir-Creative)*
Lilli English *(Partner & Dir-Strategy)*
Hamish Pinnell *(Partner & Dir-Creative)*
Melanie Arrow *(Partner)*
David Pearce *(CFO)*
Lindsay Nuttall *(Chief Digital Officer)*
Kirsty Saddler *(Head-Strategy)*
Nick Gill *(Exec Creative Dir)*
Ian Heartfield *(Creative Dir)*
Cressida Holmes-Smith *(Acct Dir)*
Mark Lewis *(Art Dir)*
Justin Marciani *(Acct Dir)*
Mark Aronson *(Dir-Strategy-BBH New York)*
Joakim Borgstrom *(Grp Creative Dir)*
Peter Callaghan *(Dir-Creative)*
Christopher Clarke *(Dir-Creative)*
Tom Drew *(Dir-Creative)*
Uche Ezugwu *(Dir-Art)*
George Hackforth-Jones *(Dir-Art)*
Ken Hoggins *(Dir-Creative)*
Phil Holbrook *(Dir-Creative)*
Debra Ladd *(Dir-Strategy)*
Matthew Moreland *(Dir-Creative)*
Vinny Olimpio *(Dir-Interactive Art)*
Harry Orton *(Dir-Art)*
A. K. Parker *(Dir-Art)*
Sarah Pollard *(Dir-Comm)*
Martha Riley *(Dir-Creative)*
Emmanuel Saint M'Leux *(Dir-Art & Creative)*
Tom Skinner *(Dir-Creative)*
Shelley Smoler *(Dir-Art)*
Rob Wilson *(Dir-Design)*
Shib Hussain *(Strategist)*
John Jones *(Strategist)*
Alana King *(Strategist)*
Damola Timeyin *(Strategist)*
George Brettell *(Copywriter)*
Simon Pearse *(Copywriter)*
Rosie Arnold *(Deputy Exec Dir-Creative)*

Accounts:
Adidas Campaign: "Unlock The Game"
Audi A5 Sportback, A7 Sportback, Above-the-Line Advertising, Audi SQ5 TDI, Audi TT, Augmented-Reality Campaign, Campaign: "Evolution On The Outside, Revolution On The Inside", Campaign: "Le Mans", Campaign: "Power from a less obvious place.", Campaign: "Presence Redefined", Campaign: "Style Or Substance", Campaign: "The Concept. The Car", Campaign: "The Swan", Content, Digital, Print, R8 V10 Plus, RS6 Avant, Social Media, TV
Barclays Barclaycard, Bespoke Offers, Campaign: "Chris", Campaign: "For Everyone, from Barclaycard", Campaign: "Love is Tough", Campaign: "Pocket Money Lad", Campaign: "Simon", Campaign: "Thank You", Campaign: "You Vs Unconditional Love", Campaign: "Your Bank", Campaign: "build your bank", Customer Relationship Management, Digital, Outdoor, Print
Barnardo's Campaign: "Ellie", Campaign: "Home

for Xmas", Campaign: "Life Story", Children's Charity, Creative, Life Story, Turn Around Interactive Poster
British Airways PLC (Creative Agency of Record) Advertising, Aviators, Brand Communications, Campaign: "Picture Your Holiday", Campaign: "The Race", Campaign: "The Welcome of Home", Campaign: "To fly. To serve. Today. Tomorrow.", Customer Relationship Management Business, Digital Marketing, Direct Marketing, Loyalty, Online, Travel
New-The British Fashion Council
C&J Clark Campaign: "Prepare for Awesome", Digital, Global Print, TV
Cardiac Risk in the Young Video
Christie Inc.
Clipper Teas Campaign: "Change Tastes Good"
The Coca-Cola Company Campaign: "The Spark", Campaign: "Uncontainable Game"
General Mills, Inc. Old El Paso
Google Inc. Campaign: "Jamal Edwards", Campaign: "Say it to get it", Campaign: "Speedbots", Google Voice Search Mobile App
Guardian News & Media Brand Campaign, Campaign: "Do Something", Campaign: "Maggiemite", Campaign: "MegaGlove", Campaign: "Own The Weekend", Campaign: "Paella", Campaign: "Smarter People. Smarter Searches", Campaign: "The Three Little Pigs", Campaign: "The Whole Picture", Campaign: "Use in Moderation.", Campaign: "What a Weekend", GuardianWitness App, TV, Thatcher, The Guardian, The Observer
New-Hearst Communications, Inc. Esquire
New-Heinz; United Kingdom Heinz Ketchup, Heinz Sauces
Invictus Games "The Toughest of the Tough Go Head to Head"
J2O
KFC Corporation Burrito, Campaign: "Brazil Street Symphony", Campaign: "Bus", Campaign: "Celebrating 50 Years of Family", Campaign: "Come Together", Campaign: "E4 sponsorship", Campaign: "Families", Campaign: "Fans", Campaign: "Feel The Krush", Campaign: "Fresh", Campaign: "Friendship Bucket Test", Campaign: "Pit Stop", Campaign: "Stairs", Campaign: "Streetwise Range", Campaign: "The Boy Who Learned to Share", Campaign: "The Taste That Unites", Campaign: "Wedding", TV
Ladbrokes
Lynx Campaign: "Click Farm"
Mentos Campaign: "Stay Fresh", Fresh News, NOWMints, Online
Perfetti Van Melle Campaign: "Don't Become Your Dad", Campaign: "Hot Tub 30", Campaign: "Stay Fresh", Campaign: "Stranger Danger 30", Campaign: "Technology 30", Chupa Chups, Mentos, Vigorsol
Refuge Campaign: "Don't Cover it Up", Campaign: "How to Look Your Best the Morning After"
Robinsons Be Natural Soft Drinks, Fruit Shoot
Rugby World Cup "2015 World Cup"
Samsung Electronics Global Advertising
St John Ambulance Campaign: "Carpet Universe", Campaign: "Helpless", Campaign: "Save The Boy", Campaign: "Save a Choking Baby", Life Lost
Tesco plc Advertising, Campaign: "Spookermarket", Creative, Every Little Helps, Trade Advertising
Unilever "#KissForPeace", 'Axe Peace', Apollo, Axe (Agency of Record), Axe/Lynx UK Anarchy, Axe/Lynx UK Apollo, Axe/Lynx UK Campaign: "Lifeguard", Axe/Lynx UK Campaign: "My Angel Girlfriend", Axe/Lynx UK Digital, Axe/Lynx UK PR & Axe/Lynx UK TV, Becel, Birds Eye, Campaign: "Anarchy Matchmaker", Campaign: "Clean your Balls", Campaign: "Click Farm", Campaign: "Cops & Robbers", Campaign: "Dance", Campaign: "Fireman", Campaign: "Fireworks", Campaign: "First Impressions Count", Campaign: "Lifeguard", Campaign: "Make love. Not war" Super Bowl 2014, Campaign: "Monday", Campaign: "Nothing Beats an Astronaut", Campaign: "Peace", Campaign: "Soulmates", Campaign: "Stairs", Campaign: "Surf for a celebration of fragrance that lasts and lasts", Campaign: "Surgeon", Campaign: "The Clean Cut Look", Campaign: "The Messy Look", Campaign: "The Natural Look", Campaign: "The Spiked Up Look", Campaign: "Wednesday", Digital, Dove, Flora, Impulse, Lever Faberge Impulse, Lynx, Men+Care, Mentadent, Omo Detergent, Pan-European Flora, Persil, Sensories, Signal, Skip, Surf, TV
Vigorsol Campaign: "Captain Ice", Campaign: "Xtreme Training"
Virgin Media Above the Line, Advertising, Campaign: "Bolt Footy", Campaign: "Challenge Your Broadband", Campaign: "Full House", Campaign: "Inspired", Campaign: "Kung Fu", Campaign: "Moods", Campaign: "Peter Crouch", Campaign: "Sofa Bear", Campaign: "Takeover", Direct Marketing, Media, Sports TV Channel, TV, TiVo, Vivid
Waterman
Weetabix Limited Alpen, Brand Strategy, Campaign: "Big Day", Campaign: "Dad's Day Out", Campaign: "Dancer", Campaign: "Fuel for Big Day", Campaign: "Grandpa", Campaign: "The Full Alpen", Campaign: "Weetabuddie", Chocolate Weetabix, Creative, Digital OOH, In-Store, On the Go, Online, Outdoor, Print, TV, Weetakid
World Animal Protection
World Gold Council Gold

Branches

BBH New York

32 Avenue of the Americas 19th Fl, New York, NY 10013
(See Separate Listing)

BBH LA

8360 Melrose Ave 2nd Fl, West Hollywood, CA 90069
Tel.: (323) 204-0160
Fax: (323) 782-0419
Web Site: www.bartleboglehegarty.com/losangeles

Agency Specializes In: Advertising, Entertainment, High Technology

Pelle Sjoenell *(Founder & Exec Creative Dir)*
Frances Great *(Mng Dir)*
Laura Thoel *(Mng Dir)*
Peter Albores *(Creative Dir)*
Kristian Grove Moller *(Creative Dir)*
James Beke *(Art Dir)*
Josh Webman *(Creative Dir)*
Sophie Muller *(Dir)*
Noelle Kaplan *(Acct Exec)*
Tyree Harris *(Copywriter)*

Accounts:
California Sunday Magazine
E! Entertainment "The Royals"
New-Esquire Network Spotless
Google Campaign: "California Inspires Me: Mark Mothersbaugh", Google Play, Print
New-Houzz Inc.
Red Bull Signature Series

Monterosa

Grev Turegatan 29, SE 11438 Stockholm, Sweden
Tel.: (46) 702 99 30 34
E-Mail: hello@monterosa.se
Web Site: www.monterosa.se

Employees: 30

Agency Specializes In: Digital/Interactive

Johan Hemminger *(Founder & CEO)*
Tom Eriksen *(Dir-Creative)*
Jesper Eriksson *(Dir-Art)*
Fredrik Giliusson *(Dir-Technical)*
Magnus Hallsten *(Dir-Creative)*
Jenny Granlund *(Sr Designer-UX)*
Jacob Sawensten *(Sr Designer)*
Hannes Wikstrom *(Sr Designer-UX)*

Accounts:
British Airways Creative
Carlsberg
Google
Mercedes Benz
Samsung
Vodafone

BBH Singapore

5 Magazine Road #03 03 Central Mall, Singapore, 059571 Singapore
Tel.: (65) 6500 3000
Fax: (65) 6500 3001
E-Mail: ben.fennell@bbh-asiapac.com.sg
Web Site: www.bartleboglehegarty.com/singapore/

Year Founded: 1996

Charles Wigley *(Chm)*
Andy Nethercleft *(Mng Partner & Head-Ops)*
James Sowden *(Mng Partner & Head-Strategic Plng)*
David Webster *(Chief Growth Officer)*
John Hadfield *(CEO-Asia Pacific)*
Chee Yan Yi *(Gen Mgr-Asia Pacific)*
Janson Choo *(Sr Dir-Art)*
Gary Lim *(Sr Dir-Art)*
Deborah Abraham *(Reg Dir-Comm)*
Miguel Andres-Clavera *(Dir-Creative Tech & Innovation)*
Kooichi Chee *(Dir-Art)*
Germaine Chen *(Dir-Art)*
Jasmine Quek *(Dir-Creative Svcs)*
Tinus Strydom *(Dir-Creative)*
Maurice Wee *(Dir-Creative)*
Marcus Yuen *(Dir-Art)*
Douglas Hamilton *(Assoc Dir-Creative & Copywriter)*
Jade Cheng *(Acct Mgr)*
Cheryl Cheong *(Acct Mgr)*
Bernice Ooi *(Acct Mgr)*
Ross Fowler *(Copywriter)*
Angelin Ho *(Accountant-HR)*
Kelly Togashi *(Acct Planner)*
Manavi Sharma *(Assoc Acct Dir)*

Accounts:
The Association of Accredited Advertising Agents Singapore
British Airways Campaign: "Plane"
Google
Ikea International (Creative Agency of Record) Beds, Campaign: "BookBook", Campaign: "Experience the Power of a Book", Campaign: "Frank the Cosplayer", Campaign: "Make Space Better", Campaign: "Recipes for Delicious Kitchens", Campaign: "The Original Touch Interface", Catalog, Digital, In-Store, Outdoor, Radio, Social, Social Media, Veggie Balls
Minute Maid
The National Environment Agency Campaign: "Bus Stop", Smoking Ban
Nike Inc
NTUC Income Insurance; 2008
OrangeAid
Perfetti Van Melle Campaign: "#MonsterKids Moments", Campaign: "Merry Birthmas", Campaign: "Proposes to Finland on Behalf of Singapore", Campaign: "Spaceship", Chupa Chups, Frisk, Happydent White, Mentos, Social Media
Singapore Sports Hub Branding, Creative, Logo Design

Singapore Tourism Board Campaign: "Tip Jar", Creative, Outdoor, Print, YourSingapore.com
Unilever AXE Campaign: "Auto Romeo" & AXE Campaign: "Sprayaway", Axe, Bertolli, Campaign: "Stunt Double", Flora, Lever Faberge Impulse, Lynx, Vaseline
World Gold Council
Zalora Campaign: "OWN NOW"

BBH Mumbai

Amiye 2nd Floor Linking Road, Santacruz (West), Mumbai, 400054 India
Tel.: (91) 22 3992 9000
Web Site: www.bartleboglehegarty.com

Employees: 55

Arvind Krishnan *(Mng Dir)*
Russell Barrett *(Chief Creative Officer)*
Sushma Joseph *(Head-Production-Black Sheep Live)*
Rajesh Mani *(Exec Dir-Creative)*
snehal bhuvad *(Art Dir)*
Ajmal Mohammad *(Creative Dir)*
Mitul Patel *(Art Dir)*
Karunasagar Sridharan *(Creative Dir)*
Philip Lloyd *(Dir)*
Kunal Sawant *(Dir-Creative)*
Shivendra Dixit *(Planner)*
Ganesh Nayak *(Sr Partner-Creative)*

Accounts:
Acer Computers Communication Campaign, Creative
Bharti Airtel Campaign: "Football Stars"
Child Rights & You Campaign: "Vote for Child Rights", Creative, Digital Media
New-coverfox.com
DSP BlackRock Mutual Fund Creative
Google Campaign: "Happy Birthday", Campaign: "Tanjore"
New-Infocus M370 Smartphone
L&T
Lakme
Marico Creative, Hair & Care, Mediker, Nihar Naturals, Parachute Advansed After Shower, Parachute Advansed Starz, Parachute Therapie Hair Fall Solution, Silk & Shine
Movies Now Campaign: "Chaplin Chapters"
Nihar Naturals Oil Nihar Shanti Amla
New-Philips Air Purifier, Digital, Outdoor, Print
Piaggio Vehicles Pvt Ltd
Rediff.com
Skoda Auto India Campaign: "Driven by Excellence", Campaign: "Grandma", Creative Communication Campaigns, Fabia, Hydrant, Laura, Rapid, Rapid Leisure, Superb, Yeti
Star CJ
Times Global Broadcasting Co. Ltd Campaign: "Paint a Thousand Pictures"
New-Unilever Magnum
Vespa Creative
Viber Creative
World Gold Council Campaign: "Diwali", Campaign: "Vows"

BARTLEY & DICK

325 W 38th St Ste 1205, New York, NY 10018
Tel.: (212) 947-3433
Fax: (212) 947-3393
E-Mail: info@bartleyndick.com
Web Site: www.bartleyndick.com

Employees: 5

Agency Specializes In: Advertising, Corporate Communications, Corporate Identity, Direct Response Marketing, Food Service, Graphic Design, Health Care Services, High Technology, In-Store Advertising, Industrial, Local Marketing, Logo & Package Design, Magazines, Media Buying Services, Newspapers & Magazines, Outdoor, Point of Purchase, Point of Sale, Print, Retail, Sales Promotion, Sports Market, Travel & Tourism

Approx. Annual Billings: $1,000,000

Scott M. Bartley *(Partner & Dir-Creative)*
Rick Biolsi *(Partner & Dir-Design)*
Jerry Von Gerichten *(Dir-Media Svcs)*
Penny Schutz *(Acct Supvr)*
Chris Mallinson *(Sr Designer)*

Accounts:
Chardan Capital Markets
Gurwin Jewish Nursing
Remy
William Grant & Sons

BARTON F. GRAF 9000 LLC

60 Madison Ave Ste 201, New York, NY 10010
Tel.: (212) 616-0800
E-Mail: info@bartonmail.com
Web Site: www.bartonfgraf9000.com/

Agency Specializes In: Advertising, Digital/Interactive, Sponsorship, Strategic Planning/Research

Laura Janness *(Partner & Chief Strategy Officer)*
Scott Vitrone *(Partner & Exec Dir-Creative)*
Yvette Ames *(Acct Dir)*
Amanda Clelland *(Creative Dir)*
Kate Faux *(Acct Dir)*
Jennifer Richardi *(Acct Dir)*
Alex Stankiewicz *(Acct Dir)*
Mark Bielik *(Dir-Art & Copywriter)*
Ross Fletcher *(Dir-Art & Copywriter)*
Michael Hagos *(Dir-Art)*
Nick Kaplan *(Dir-Creative)*
Zack Madrigal *(Dir-Art)*
Matt Moore *(Dir-Creative)*
Jennifer Pannent *(Dir-Bus Affairs)*
Kate Overholt Placentra *(Dir-Art)*
Rose Sacktor *(Dir-Art)*
Sean Staley *(Dir-Strategy)*
Kate Callander *(Acct Supvr)*
Kimmy Cunningham *(Acct Supvr)*
Sam Dolphin *(Copywriter)*
Chase Kimball *(Copywriter)*
Chris Stephens *(Copywriter)*
Cameron Farrell *(Assoc Producer)*

Accounts:
350 Action Campaign: "The Climate Name Change"
New-Bai Brands Campaign: "El Guapo"
Bawx
DISH Network L.L.C. Campaign: "Boston Guys", Hopper, Marketing Campaign, Television Network Service Providers
Esquire Magazine
Esquire Network
Finlandia Cheese Campaign: "Where Cheese Reigns"
GrubHub Campaign: "Burrito", Campaign: "Wrong Order", Super Bowl 2015
Kayak Campaign: "Breakup", Campaign: "Elevator", Campaign: "Search One and Done", Kayak.com
Little Caesars Campaign: "Deep! Deep! Dish", Campaign: "Do Not Call", Campaign: "Hold Music", Campaign: "Hot-N-Ready", Campaign: "OHHHH!", Campaign: "Stop everything! There's a pizza emergency", Creative, Social Media
Outdoor Advertising Association of America Out of Home Advertising
Scotts Miracle-Gro Company (Creative Agency of Record) "Dead Mouse Theatre", Campaign: "That's Some Good Dirt", Campaign: "Tomcat. Engineered to Kill", Creative, Nature's Care, Tomcat
Snyder's-Lance, Inc. Cape Cod Potato Chips, Creative, Lance Crackers, Pretzel Crisps, Snyder's of Hanover Pretzels
Supercell Campaign: "Magic", Campaign: "Preparation", Campaign: "Revenge", Clash of Clans, Outdoor Posters, Super Bowl 2015, TV
Unilever Caliente, Campaign: "Long Day of Childhood", P.F. Chang's, Wish-Bone

BARU ADVERTISING

7280 Melrose Ave Ste 1, Los Angeles, CA 90046
Tel.: (323) 933-0007
Fax: (323) 933-0072
Web Site: www.baruadvertising.com

Agency Specializes In: Advertising, Media Buying Services, Media Planning, Production, Promotions, Public Relations

Elizabeth Barrutia *(CEO & Principal)*
Michael McNellis *(Partner & Chief Creative Officer)*
Norma Manzanares *(Sr Acct Dir-Brand Strategy & Mktg)*
Abel Gonzalez *(Dir-Creative)*
Jessica Matkovic *(Assoc Dir-Media)*
Jasminne Carrillo *(Jr Buyer & Planner)*
Rosalva Orozco *(Coord-Media)*

Accounts:
Focus Features
MundoFox Broadcasting (Media Agency of Record) Media Buying, Media Planning
Treasury Wine Estates

BASIC AGENCY

341 S Cedros Ave Ste B, Solana Beach, CA 92075
Tel.: (858) 755-6922
Fax: (760) 821-4021
Web Site: www.basicagency.com/

Year Founded: 2010

Agency Specializes In: Advertising, Brand Development & Integration, Digital/Interactive, E-Commerce, Graphic Design, Internet/Web Design, Package Design, Social Media, Web (Banner Ads, Pop-ups, etc.)

Matthew Faulk *(CEO)*
Erwin Hines *(Assoc Dir-Creative)*
Ashley Reichel *(Sr Acct Mgr & Sr Mgr-Ops)*
Andrew Yanoscik *(Strategist-Creative)*
Arthur Armenta, IV *(Designer-Visual)*
Sun Beom *(Designer-UX)*
Rodrigo Calderon *(Designer-Visual)*
Veronica Cordero *(Designer-Visual)*

Accounts:
Made By Rabbit, Inc. Flud

BASS ADVERTISING

815 Nebraska St, Sioux City, IA 51101-1111
Tel.: (712) 277-3450
Fax: (712) 277-2441
E-Mail: bass@bassadvertising.com
Web Site: www.bassadvertising.com

Employees: 5
Year Founded: 1972

National Agency Associations: AAF

Agency Specializes In: Above-the-Line, Advertising, Advertising Specialties, Affiliate Marketing, Affluent Market, African-American Market, Agriculture, Alternative Advertising, Arts, Asian Market, Automotive, Aviation & Aerospace, Below-the-Line, Bilingual Market, Brand Development & Integration, Branded Entertainment, Broadcast, Business Publications, Business-To-Business, Cable T.V., Catalogs, Children's Market, Co-op Advertising, Collateral, College, Commercial Photography,

Communications, Computers & Software, Consulting, Consumer Goods, Consumer Marketing, Consumer Publications, Content, Corporate Communications, Corporate Identity, Cosmetics, Crisis Communications, Custom Publishing, Customer Relationship Management, Digital/Interactive, Direct Response Marketing, Direct-to-Consumer, E-Commerce, Education, Electronic Media, Electronics, Email, Engineering, Entertainment, Environmental, Event Planning & Marketing, Exhibit/Trade Shows, Experience Design, Faith Based, Fashion/Apparel, Financial, Food Service, Game Integration, Gay & Lesbian Market, Government/Political, Graphic Design, Guerilla Marketing, Health Care Services, High Technology, Hispanic Market, Hospitality, Household Goods, Identity Marketing, In-Store Advertising, Industrial, Infomercials, Information Technology, Integrated Marketing, International, Internet/Web Design, Investor Relations, Legal Services, Leisure, Local Marketing, Logo & Package Design, Luxury Products, Magazines, Marine, Market Research, Media Buying Services, Media Planning, Media Relations, Media Training, Medical Products, Men's Market, Merchandising, Mobile Marketing, Multicultural, Multimedia, New Product Development, New Technologies, Newspaper, Newspapers & Magazines, Out-of-Home Media, Outdoor, Over-50 Market, Package Design, Paid Searches, Pharmaceutical, Planning & Consultation, Podcasting, Point of Purchase, Point of Sale, Print, Product Placement, Production, Production (Print), Promotions, Public Relations, Publicity/Promotions, Publishing, RSS (Really Simple Syndication), Radio, Real Estate, Recruitment, Regional, Restaurant, Retail, Sales Promotion, Search Engine Optimization, Seniors' Market, Social Marketing/Nonprofit, Social Media, South Asian Market, Sponsorship, Sports Market, Stakeholders, Strategic Planning/Research, Sweepstakes, Syndication, T.V., Technical Advertising, Teen Market, Telemarketing, Trade & Consumer Magazines, Transportation, Travel & Tourism, Urban Market, Viral/Buzz/Word of Mouth, Women's Market, Yellow Pages Advertising

Approx. Annual Billings: $1,500,000

Breakdown of Gross Billings by Media: Bus. Publs.: 5%; Mags.: 15%; Newsp.: 15%; Outdoor: 5%; Print: 15%; Production: 5%; Radio: 15%; Sls. Promo.: 15%; T.V.: 10%

Will Bass *(Pres)*
Betty Bass *(Treas & Sec)*
Austin Bass *(Dir-Creative)*
Carly Schinzing *(Dir-Media)*

BAST-DURBIN INC
125 Kettle Moraine Dr S, Slinger, WI 53086
Tel.: (262) 644-7940
Fax: (262) 644-7959

Year Founded: 1994

Agency Specializes In: Advertising, Catalogs, Media Planning, Media Relations, Package Design, Publishing

Jeff Bast *(Co-Owner)*
Dan Durbin *(Co-Owner)*

Accounts:
Uncle Josh Baits

BASTROP CREATIVE AGENCY
491 Agnes St, Bastrop, TX 78602
Tel.: (512) 843-8303
Web Site: www.bastropcreativeagency.com

Agency Specializes In: Advertising, Brand Development & Integration, Broadcast, Digital/Interactive, Internet/Web Design, Media Buying Services, Media Planning, Print, Search Engine Optimization, Social Media

Jonathan Adam *(COO)*
Mark Winslett *(Art Dir)*
Colin Guerra *(Creative Dir)*
Debbie Denny *(Dir-Sls)*
Chase Wilkinson *(Dir-Copy)*

Accounts:
Denise Rodgers
Viejos Tacos y Tequila

BATES CREATIVE GROUP
1119 E-W Hwy, Silver Spring, MD 20910
Tel.: (301) 495-8844
Fax: (301) 495-8877
E-Mail: info@batescreative.com
Web Site: batescreative.com/

Year Founded: 2003

Debra Bates-Schrott *(Pres)*
Ernie Achenbach *(VP-Ops)*
Rich Young *(Dir-Bus Dev)*
Amanda Jennison *(Specialist-Mktg)*
Emily Biondo *(Designer)*
Jen Fose *(Designer)*
Kristine Garcia *(Designer)*

Accounts:
Atlas Brew Works
National Association of Convenience Stores

BATES/LEE ADVERTISING
2950 Airway Ave Ste A9, Costa Mesa, CA 92626
Tel.: (714) 549-1757
Fax: (714) 549-1757
E-Mail: laura@bates-lee.com
Web Site: www.bates-lee.com

Employees: 14
Year Founded: 1975

Agency Specializes In: Advertising, Affiliate Marketing, Affluent Market, Arts, Bilingual Market, Catalogs, Collateral, Consumer Goods, Consumer Marketing, Direct-to-Consumer, Fashion/Apparel, Government/Political, Graphic Design, Internet/Web Design, Leisure, Local Marketing, Luxury Products, Newspapers & Magazines, Point of Sale, Production, Promotions, Restaurant, Retail, Seniors' Market, Trade & Consumer Magazines, Transportation, Travel & Tourism, Urban Market, Web (Banner Ads, Pop-ups, etc.), Women's Market

Approx. Annual Billings: $11,000,000

Breakdown of Gross Billings by Media: Adv. Specialities: $11,000,000

Gloria Erwin *(Dir-Art)*
Mark Reid *(Dir-Creative)*
Len Silveri *(Dir-Media & Direct Mail)*
Kera Yong *(Acct Exec)*

BATTERY
7257 Beverly Blvd, Los Angeles, CA 90036
Tel.: (323) 692-9800
E-Mail: info@batteryagency.com
Web Site: www.batteryagency.com

Year Founded: 2013

Agency Specializes In: Advertising, Media Buying Services

Anson Sowby *(Founder & CEO)*
Philip Khosid *(Chief Creative Officer)*
Raymond Hwang *(Dir-Creative & Copywriter)*
Matthew Cullen *(Dir)*
Bernie O'Dowd *(Dir-Creative & Art)*
Philip Ser *(Dir-Strategy)*

Accounts:
New-NBCUniversal Creative, SeeSo
Warner Bros. Entertainment Inc. Campaign: "Endless Awesome", LEGO Dimensions game, Mortal Kombat X

BATTLE MEDIALAB INC.
117 E Boca Raton Rd, Boca Raton, FL 33432
Tel.: (561) 395-1555
Fax: (561) 395-1225
Web Site: www.battlemedialab.com

Employees: 5

Agency Specializes In: Advertising, Brand Development & Integration, Broadcast, Collateral, Digital/Interactive, Graphic Design, Internet/Web Design, Logo & Package Design, Mobile Marketing, Search Engine Optimization

Revenue: $1,105,000

Michael Murphy *(Co-Founder & Pres)*
Kristel Hosler *(Dir-Ops)*

Accounts:
3N2 Campaign: "Play Ball", Team Builder Website
ADT
Campus Management Corporation
Ecosphere Technologies, Inc.
Roll-N-Lock(R) Corporation
Royal Caribbean International

BAUSERMAN GROUP
500 Damonte Ranch Pkwy Ste 675, Reno, NV 89521
Tel.: (775) 784-9400
Fax: (775) 784-9401
E-Mail: info@bausermangroup.com
Web Site: www.bausermangroup.com

Agency Specializes In: Advertising, Brand Development & Integration, Digital/Interactive, Internet/Web Design, Media Planning, Search Engine Optimization, Social Media

Jim bauserman *(Owner)*
Steven Aramini *(Creative Dir)*
Carla Acree *(Dir-Media Svcs)*
Charlene Andrews *(Acct Exec)*

Accounts:
New-CDA Casino Resort
New-Hard Rock Hotel & Casino Lake Tahoe
New-Reno Rodeo

BAUZA & ASSOCIATES
11 Asylum St, Hartford, CT 06103
Tel.: (860) 246-2100
Fax: (860) 246-2101
E-Mail: information@bauzaassociates.com
Web Site: www.bauzaassociates.com

Employees: 10
Year Founded: 2001

Agency Specializes In: Advertising, Consulting, Event Planning & Marketing, Hispanic Market, Merchandising, Promotions, Public Relations, Sports Market, Strategic Planning/Research

Approx. Annual Billings: $3,500,000

Fernando Ferrer *(VP-Creative)*
Lillian Santiago-Bauza *(Mgr-Ops)*
Hector Bauza *(Owner and CEO)*

Accounts:
Comcast; 2007
El Jolgorio
Eversource; 2007
Hartford Foundation for Public Giving; 2007
Health New England; 2007
MassHousing
MX Energy
PRCC
Pride Gas Stations
State Farm Educational Events, Marketing, Online & Offline Social Media Networking
Yankeegas

BAYARD ADVERTISING AGENCY, INC.

902 Broadway 10th Fl, New York, NY 10010-6002
Tel.: (212) 228-9400
Fax: (212) 228-9999
E-Mail: information@bayardad.com
Web Site: www.bayardad.com

Employees: 150
Year Founded: 1923

Agency Specializes In: Above-the-Line, Advertising, Advertising Specialties, Affiliate Marketing, Affluent Market, African-American Market, Agriculture, Alternative Advertising, Arts, Asian Market, Automotive, Aviation & Aerospace, Below-the-Line, Bilingual Market, Brand Development & Integration, Branded Entertainment, Broadcast, Business Publications, Business-To-Business, Cable T.V., Catalogs, Children's Market, Co-op Advertising, Collateral, College, Commercial Photography, Communications, Computers & Software, Consulting, Consumer Goods, Consumer Marketing, Consumer Publications, Content, Corporate Communications, Corporate Identity, Cosmetics, Crisis Communications, Custom Publishing, Customer Relationship Management, Digital/Interactive, Direct Response Marketing, Direct-to-Consumer, E-Commerce, Education, Electronic Media, Electronics, Email, Engineering, Entertainment, Environmental, Event Planning & Marketing, Exhibit/Trade Shows, Experience Design, Fashion/Apparel, Financial, Food Service, Game Integration, Gay & Lesbian Market, Government/Political, Graphic Design, Guerilla Marketing, Health Care Services, High Technology, Hispanic Market, Hospitality, Household Goods, Identity Marketing, In-Store Advertising, Industrial, Infomercials, Information Technology, Integrated Marketing, International, Internet/Web Design, Investor Relations, Legal Services, Leisure, Local Marketing, Logo & Package Design, Luxury Products, Magazines, Marine, Market Research, Media Buying Services, Media Planning, Media Relations, Media Training, Medical Products, Men's Market, Merchandising, Mobile Marketing, Multicultural, Multimedia, New Product Development, New Technologies, Newspaper, Newspapers & Magazines, Out-of-Home Media, Outdoor, Over-50 Market, Package Design, Paid Searches, Pharmaceutical, Planning & Consultation, Podcasting, Point of Purchase, Point of Sale, Print, Product Placement, Production, Production (Ad, Film, Broadcast), Production (Print), Promotions, Public Relations, Publicity/Promotions, Publishing, RSS (Really Simple Syndication), Radio, Real Estate, Recruitment, Regional, Restaurant, Retail, Sales Promotion, Search Engine Optimization, Seniors' Market, Social Marketing/Nonprofit, Sponsorship, Sports Market, Stakeholders, Strategic Planning/Research, Sweepstakes, Syndication, T.V., Technical Advertising, Teen Market, Telemarketing, Trade & Consumer Magazines, Transportation, Travel & Tourism, Urban Market, Viral/Buzz/Word of Mouth, Web (Banner Ads, Pop-ups, etc.), Women's Market, Yellow Pages Advertising

Gordon Waldorf *(Pres)*
Louis Naviasky *(COO)*
Michael Halperin *(Chief Strategy Officer)*
Bill Davidson *(Pres-Logistics Div)*
Doug Jones *(Sr VP-Client Strategy)*
Don Sabatino *(Sr VP-New Bus Dev)*
Jill Waldorf *(Sr VP)*
Mara Makler *(Sr Acct Exec)*
Medina Lynn *(Strategist-Video Content)*

Accounts:
Cancer Treatment Centers of America (Agency of Record)

Branches

Bayard Advertising Agency, Inc.

4929 Wilshire Blvd Ste 770, Los Angeles, CA 90010-3817
Tel.: (323) 930-9300
Fax: (323) 930-9371
E-Mail: annt@bayardad.com
Web Site: www.bayardad.com

Employees: 5

Don Sabatino *(Sr VP-New Bus Dev)*
Greg Rousseau *(VP-New Bus Dev)*
Ann Troxell *(VP-Client Solutions)*

Bayard Advertising Agency, Inc.

8401 Colesville Rd Ste 502, Silver Spring, MD 20910-6365
Tel.: (301) 589-9125
Fax: (301) 589-9625
E-Mail: rosemary_p@bayardad.com
Web Site: www.bayardad.com

Employees: 10
Year Founded: 2001

Agency Specializes In: Recruitment

Rosemary Petreikis *(Sr VP & Gen Mgr)*
Doug Jones *(Sr VP-Client Strategy)*
Kim Harrell *(VP-Bus Dev)*
Joseph Hladick *(VP-Client Strategy)*

Bayard Advertising Agency, Inc.

550 S Wadsworth Blvd Ste 500, Lakewood, CO 80226
Tel.: (303) 571-2000
Fax: (303) 571-2002
E-Mail: execvp@bayardad.com
Web Site: www.bayardad.com

Employees: 8

Agency Specializes In: Advertising

Don Sabatino *(Sr VP-New Bus Dev)*
Shane Simmons *(Dir-Creative)*
Marissa Selva *(Acct Mgr)*
Justin Gabriel *(Strategist-Digital)*
Jenny Storey *(Strategist-Digital)*

Accounts:
Aspen Dental
Celadon
Chevy Chase
Pfizer

BAYSHORE SOLUTIONS INC

600 N Westshore Blvd Ste 700, Tampa, FL 33609
Tel.: (813) 902-0141
Fax: (813) 839-9022
E-Mail: info@bayshoresolutions.com
Web Site: www.bayshoresolutions.com

Employees: 41
Year Founded: 1996

Agency Specializes In: Advertising, Internet/Web Design, Search Engine Optimization, Sponsorship

Kevin Hourigan *(Pres & CEO)*
Keith Neubert *(VP)*
Jay Wiley *(VP)*
Michael Sapp *(Controller)*
Jason Dorsett *(Dir-IT)*
Martin McCauley *(Dir-Client Strategy)*
Kim McCormick *(Dir-Corp Mktg)*
Valerie Noel *(Acct Mgr)*
Tammie Bucknell *(Mgr-HR)*
Rachel Murphy *(Mgr-Acctg)*
Kaci Groh Riverol *(Project Assoc)*

Accounts:
Apogee Pilates & Wellness Centers
Bloomin' Brands Outback Steakhouse, Inc.
The Boathouse Restaurant
Champions Club
Colliers International
Community Health Care Alliance
DiscoverSevilla
Sykes
Tye Maner Group
University Village

BBDO NORTH AMERICA

1285 Ave of the Americas, New York, NY 10019-6028
Tel.: (212) 459-5000
Fax: (212) 459-6814
Web Site: www.bbdo.com

Year Founded: 1891

National Agency Associations: 4A's-AAF-AD CLUB-ANA

Agency Specializes In: Advertising

David Lubars *(Chm & Chief Creative Officer)*
Mark Cadman *(Mng Dir)*
Jeffery A. Mordos *(COO)*
Roy Elvove *(Exec VP & Dir-Comm-Worldwide)*
Tracy Lovatt *(Exec VP & Dir-Plng-North America)*
Brian Nienhaus *(Sr Acct Dir)*
Katie Black *(Acct Dir)*
Gati Curtis *(Acct Dir)*
Clemens den Exter *(Designer)*

Accounts:
Air New Zealand
American Red Cross
AT&T Communications Corp. "Up All Night"
BBC
ExxonMobil
FedEx Campaign: "Solutions Stories"
Foot Locker Campaign: "Snow Dunk"
General Electric Campaign: "Ge Performance Machines"
GlaxoSmithKline
HBO Campaign: "Go Product Tour", Dig Deeper
Mars, Inc. Campaign: "Just My Shell", M&Ms, Milky Way, Snickers, Twix
PepsiCo AMP Energy Drink, Frito-Lay, Gatorade
Peta Campaign: "98% Human", Campaign: "No Monkey Business"
Pfizer
Pinnacle Foods Group
Procter & Gamble Campaign: "Jeter 3000 Card", Oral-B
S.C. Johnson & Son, Inc. Home Storage Products, Pest Control, Raid, Ziploc
Starbucks
Wm. Wrigley Jr. Co.

BBDO PROXIMITY

(Formerly Proximity Minneapolis)

150 S 5th St Ste 3500, Minneapolis, MN 55402
Tel.: (612) 338-8401
E-Mail: neil.white@bbdo.com
Web Site: www.bbdompls.com

Agency Specializes In: Advertising, Customer Relationship Management, Digital/Interactive, Mobile Marketing

Clement Yip *(CEO-China)*
Alison Siviter *(VP & Grp Acct Dir)*
Noel Haan *(Exec Dir-Creative)*
Fred Cilliers *(Sr Dir-Art)*
Tim Brunelle *(Creative Dir)*
Kelsey Gomez *(Art Dir)*
Jacobo Concejo *(Dir-Creative-Global)*
Renee Rausch *(Dir-HR-Minneapolis)*
Dave Alm *(Assoc Dir-Creative)*

Accounts:
Berkshire Hathaway HomeServices Broadcast, Media, Print, Social
Hormel Foods Corporation Campaign: "Break the Monotony", Campaign: "Madness of March", Digital, Jennie-O, Skippy, Spam
New-Minnesota Boychoir
MN Health Insurance

BBDO WORLDWIDE INC.

1285 Ave of the Americas, New York, NY 10019-6028
Tel.: (212) 459-5000
Fax: (212) 459-6645
E-Mail: simon.bond@bbdo.com
Web Site: www.bbdo.com

Employees: 15,000
Year Founded: 1891

National Agency Associations: 4A's

Agency Specializes In: Advertising, Sponsorship

Andrew Robertson *(Pres & CEO)*
Greg Hahn *(Chief Creative Officer)*
Doug Alligood *(Chm-Diversity Council & Exec VP-Horizontal Markets)*
Jeff Sautter *(Exec VP & Head-Talent & Ops)*
Tom Darbyshire *(Exec VP & Exec Dir-Creative)*
Ladd Martin *(Exec VP & Sr Dir)*
Paul Roebuck *(Exec VP & Sr Dir-Worldwide)*
Nicole Benedick *(Exec VP & Dir-Digital Ops)*
Roy Elvove *(Exec VP & Dir-Comm-Worldwide)*
Peter McCallum *(Sr VP & Sr Dir)*
Christine Smith *(Sr VP & Sr Dir)*
Elise Greiche-Pavone *(Sr VP & Exec Producer)*
St John Walshe *(Mng Dir-Europe)*
Elizabeth Campbell *(VP & Acct Dir)*
Patrice Reiley *(VP & Acct Dir)*
Greg Gerstner *(VP & Dir-Creative)*
Page Kishiyama *(VP & Dir-Creative)*
Sylvia Wachtel *(VP & Mgr-Res)*
Gordon Mclean *(Grp Dir-Plng)*
Jonathan Bjelland *(Sr Dir-Art)*
Fernando Mattei *(Sr Dir-Art)*
Mark Voehringer *(Sr Dir-Creative)*
Jens Waernes *(Sr Dir-Creative)*
Justin Zerrenner *(Sr Acct Dir)*
Lindsey Conklin *(Acct Dir)*
Natalie Connelly *(Acct Dir)*
Pol Hoenderboom *(Creative Dir)*
Laura Leatherberry *(Acct Dir)*
Lisa Roytman *(Acct Dir)*
Tim Roan *(Dir-Creative & Copywriter)*
Lauren Connolly *(Dir-Creative)*
Levi Slavin *(Dir-Creative)*
Christopher Cannon *(Assoc Dir-Creative)*
Todd Rone Parker *(Assoc Dir-Creative & Art)*
Eduardo Petersen *(Assoc Dir-Creative)*
Tessa Cosenza *(Acct Mgr)*
Josh Goodman *(Acct Mgr)*
Laura McWhorter *(Acct Mgr)*
Sara Plotkin *(Acct Mgr)*
Nick Robbins *(Acct Mgr-Foot Locker)*
Adam Weiner *(Acct Mgr)*
Anna Desilva *(Acct Supvr)*
Angela Johnson *(Acct Supvr)*
Elizabeth Proctor *(Supvr)*
Kate Monahan *(Sr Acct Exec)*
Danielle Amico *(Acct Exec-P&G-Venus)*
Will Langenberg *(Acct Exec)*
Blake Maraoui *(Acct Exec)*
Mariano Pintor *(Acct Exec)*
Amy Rosenberg *(Acct Exec)*
Lindsay Vellines *(Acct Exec)*
Roberto Danino *(Copywriter)*
Wiliam Kim *(Asst Acct Exec)*
Natalie Pardo *(Asst Acct Exec)*
Michael Woodall *(Asst Acct Exec)*

Accounts:
Ad Council
Alpargatas USA, Inc. Havaianas US
The American Red Cross
Armstrong Campaign: "Ethernet River"
AT&T Communications Corp. Campaign: "Playing Favorites", Campaign: "Ski Lift", Daybreak - Trailer
AT&T Mobility, LLC AT&T Wireless, GoPhone
Bacardi Limited Campaign: "The Truck", Global Creative, Strategic
Bayer Bayer Healthcare Animal Health, Bayer Healthcare Consumer Care, Bayer Healthcare Medical Care, Bayer Schering Pharma, Consumer Communications, Digital, Global Marketing Services, Medical Education, Professional Communications, Public Relations
BBC Worldwide Americas, Inc. BBC World News
Campbell Soup Company
Christopher & Dana Reeve Foundation Christopher Reeve Paralysis Foundation
CVS Health (Agency of Record) "Deep Breath", "We Wish", Campaign: "Health is Everything", Creative, Digital, Experiential Advertising, Logo, Marketing, Outdoor, Print, Television
Diageo
Economist Group Economist Group, The Economist
ExxonMobil Creative
FedEx Campaign: "Test Shipment"
Foot Locker, Inc. Campaign: "All Is Right", Kids Foot Locker, Lady Foot Locker
Frito-Lay Flat Earth, Sun Chips
Gatorade
GE Appliances Campaign: "Reimagining Home"
GE Capital GE Capital, GE Commercial Finance
GE Consumer & Industrial
GE Healthcare GE Healthcare, GE Vscan
GE Lighting
General Electric
Glaxosmithkline
Global Gillette Braun, Fusion, Gillette Deodorant, Mach3, Oral-B, Right Guard, Venus Embrace
Grocery Manufacturers Association
Harrah's Resort & Casino
Hewlett-Packard Corporate Image, Creative, Personal Computers, Printers
Hyatt Hotels Corporation; Chicago, IL
Ikea
Johnson & Johnson Baby Products Band-Aid, Neosporin
Johnson & Johnson Head-to-Toe Baby Wash, Johnson's Baby, Rogaine
Lowe's (Agency of Record) "LowesFixInSix", Campaign: "Don't Stop", Campaign: "Lowe's on Vine", Campaign: "Need Help?", Campaign: "Never stop Improving", Campaign: "Vine Videos for Spring", Creative, Vine
Mars/Masterfoods Campaign: "15 Minutes", Campaign: "Godzilla", Campaign: "Play Hungry, But Not Literally Hungry", Campaign: "You're Not You When You're Hungry", Fling, M&Ms, Snickers, Uncle Ben's
Mercedes-Benz Global Creative
Moet Hennessy USA Belvedere
Motorola Mobility LLC Motorola Rokr, Motorola, Inc.
Motorola Solutions, Inc.
Orbitz Worldwide Inc (Agency Of Record)
P&G Campaign: "Million Emotions", Tide
Pepsico Diet Mountain Dew
Pinnacle Foods Group Inc. Birds Eye, Birds Eye Voila, Duncan Hines, Mrs. Butterworth's
SAP Creative
Starbucks
Toyota
Toys "R" Us, Inc. Babies R Us, Lead Creative
Unilever North America Skippy
Vikings (Agency of Record)
Visa, Inc.
Volkswagen
Wells Fargo
WM. Wrigley Jr. Co. 5, Altoids, Eclipse, Extra, Orbit, Winterfresh

Branches

Atmosphere Proximity

1285 Ave of the Americas 5th Fl, New York, NY 10019
Tel.: (212) 827-2505
Fax: (212) 827-2525
E-Mail: inquiries@atmosphereproximity.com
Web Site: atmosphereproximity.com/

Employees: 90

National Agency Associations: 4A's

Agency Specializes In: Digital/Interactive, Sponsorship

Andreas Combuechen *(Chm, CEO & Chief Creative Officer)*
Garrett Franklin *(Mng Dir)*
Matthew Abate *(Exec Dir-Creative)*
Stewart Krull *(Exec Dir-Creative)*
Joel Bloom *(Creative Dir)*
Keith Ross *(Creative Dir)*
Tom Sunshine *(Dir-Technology & Digital Innovation)*
Terje Vist *(Dir-Creative)*

Accounts:
The Advertising Council Campaign: "The Big Ad Gig"
AOL
AT&T Communications Corp. AT&T Wireless
Citi
Conservation International
Drug-Free Kids "Mute the Mouth", Digital, Social Outreach, TV
Dubai Corporation for Tourism and Commerce Marketing Digital
E-Trade
The Economist Brand Communications & Strategy, Campaign: "Dare 2 Go Deep"
Emirates Airline Campaign: "Harmony", Global Digital, Social; 2005
General Electric
HBO
Hertz (Agency of Record) Mobile Ads, Online Display Ads, Print Ads, Rent2Buy - Creative Assignment, Social Networking, Web Search Ads
Marriott Campaign: "Autograph Collection"
Mars North America Snickers
Monster
NYSE 4onthefloor.com
The Parternship at Drugfree.org Campaign: "Above the Influence"
Pepsico Mountain Dew, Pepsi Max
Red Stripe
Splenda
Starwood
USGA
Visa Campaign: "Dance Fever"

Barefoot Proximity

700 W Pete Rose Way, Cincinnati, OH 45203
(See Separate Listing)

BBDO Atlanta

3500 Lenox Rd NE Ste 1900, Atlanta, GA 30326-4232
Tel.: (404) 231-1700
Fax: (404) 841-1893
E-Mail: contact@bbdoatl.com
Web Site: www.bbdoatl.com

Employees: 220

National Agency Associations: 4A's

Agency Specializes In: Sponsorship

Drew Panayiotou *(Pres & CEO)*
Michael Hunter *(CMO & Exec VP)*
Tricia Russo *(Chief Strategy Officer & Exec VP)*
Wil Boudreau *(Chief Creative Officer)*
Matt Macdonald *(Exec VP & Exec Dir-Creative)*
Louis-Phillipe Tremblay *(Exec VP & Sr Dir-Creative)*
David Sackin *(Exec VP & Dir-Insights & Analytics)*
Rich Santiago *(Exec VP & Dir-Creative Strategy)*
Doug Walker *(Exec VP & Dir-Mgmt)*
Peter Bunarek *(Exec VP-Acct Mgmt)*
Tim Wilson *(Sr VP & Sr Dir-Digital Creative)*
Lesley Brown *(Sr VP & Grp Acct Dir)*
Tami Oliva *(Sr VP & Grp Acct Dir-Voya)*
Jeff Beamon *(Sr VP & Acct Dir)*
Andrea Derby *(VP & Acct Dir)*
Jessica Sours *(VP & Acct Dir)*
Danielle Willett *(VP & Acct Dir)*
Derrick Ogilvie *(VP & Dir-Creative)*
Hayley Efird *(Art Dir)*
Brett Baker *(Dir-Creative)*
Stephen Dalton *(Assoc Dir-Creative)*
Bryan Lee *(Assoc Dir-Creative)*
Jamie Donohue *(Acct Mgr)*
Christy Batey *(Mgr-Travel Svcs)*
Chris Buda *(Mgr-Art Buying)*
Brittany Robinson *(Acct Supvr)*
David Welday *(Acct Supvr-Voya)*
Andrew Woodruff *(Acct Supvr)*
Joel van Rensburg *(Acct Exec)*
Emily Miller *(Copywriter)*
Nick Marchant *(Acct Coord)*
Courtney Jones *(Coord-New Bus)*

Accounts:
American Red Cross Campaign: "Babysitting Basics PSA from Kids", Campaign: "Emergency Supply Kit", Campaign: "The Babysitter You Don't Want to Be"
AT&T, Inc. "Lily Campaign", Broadcast, Campaign: "Bracket Curls", Campaign: "March Madness Legends", Campaign: "Strong Bracket", Campaign: "Strong Dunk", Campaign: "Strong Grip", Campaign: "Strong Nickname", Campaign: "Strong Science", Campaign: "Strong Song", Campaign: "Strong Team", Campaign: "Upset", Emoji Carols
AT&T Mobility Campaign: "Alex", Campaign: "Big Hug", Campaign: "Building You a Better Network", Campaign: "Candy Island", Campaign: "Get More With Your Time iAd", Campaign: "Hello", Campaign: "High Fives", Campaign: "In My Day -corndog", Campaign: "In My Day - Basketball", Campaign: "In My Day - Pool", Campaign: "In My Day", Campaign: "Infinity", Campaign: "It's Not Complicated Grandma", Campaign: "It's Not Complicated Laser Boy", Campaign: "It's Not Complicated Treehouse", Campaign: "It's Not Complicated", Campaign: "More Responsibilities", Campaign: "My Journey - Allison Felix", Campaign: "My Journey - Ryan Lochte", Campaign: "My Journey", Campaign: "My Journey- Alex Morgan", Campaign: "Nicky Flash", Campaign: "Pickle Roll", Campaign: "Silent Treatment", Campaign: "Team Usa Volleyball", Campaign: "Team Usa - Sprinter", Campaign: "Team Usa", Campaign: "Werewolf", Campaign: "Work For Will", Campaign: "World Connect", Campaign: "World Connect- England", Campaign: "World Connect- Italy", Campaign: "World Connect- Mexico", Creative, GoPhone, Painting, Piano, Workforwill.com; 2000
Bayer
Blue Cross & Blue Shield of Florida; Jacksonville, FL Brand Advertising
Carnival Corporation Campaign: "Cruise Virgin", Campaign: "Getaway", Campaign: "Message in a Bottle", Campaign: "Mystery Spot", Campaign: "Return to the Sea", Carnival Cruises, Holland America, Marketing, Online, Princess, Social Media, Super Bowl 2015, TV
Carter's, Inc. Brand Campaign, Campaign: "Mom", Creative
ExxonMobil
Flamingo Las Vegas
Florida Department of Citrus Campaign: "Status Meeting - Diner", Campaign: "Take On The Day", Florida Grapefruit Juice, Florida Orange Juice
Georgia Lottery Campaign: "Deer Hunter", Campaign: "Keno Flashback", Campaign: "Powerball - Sax Player", Campaign: "Rainbow Money", Campaign: "The Merger"
Georgia-Pacific Corporation
Hilton Hotels
Embassy Suites Campaign: "366 Days Of More", Campaign: "Manger's Reception", Campaign: "More Coffee", Campaign: "More More", Campaign: "Mr. More"
ING Americas
Metro Atlanta Chamber
Norwegian Cruise Line Creative
Novant Health
Peace Corps
Recreational Equipment, Inc.; Kent, WA Campaign: "1440 Project", Campaign: "Find Out - Augmented Reality", Campaign: "Rei Ice", Campaign: "Rei Rain"; 2007
Rei Campaign: "1440 Project", Campaign: "Backpacker Getaway"
New-Toys "R" Us, Inc. Campaign: "Awwwesome"
Voya Financial Campaign: "Orange Money"
Zoo Atlanta Beastly Feast

BBDO Minneapolis

150 S 5th St Ste 3500, Minneapolis, MN 55402-4200
Tel.: (612) 338-8401
Fax: (612) 656-0602
Web Site: www.bbdompls.com

Employees: 50

National Agency Associations: 4A's

Agency Specializes In: Sponsorship

Neil White *(Pres & CEO)*
Wes Crawford *(COO)*
Char Roseblade *(Sr VP & Grp Acct Dir)*
Allison Comes *(Dir-Art)*
Deb Lustig *(Dir-Production)*
Angela Johnson *(Acct Supvr)*
Tess Nyberg *(Sr Writer)*

Accounts:
All Steel
Aviva
Berkshire Hathaway HomeServices Advertising, Campaign: "Calls", Campaign: "Good to know"
Edina Realty
Formica
Hormel Foods Corp. Campaign: "Fun Factory", Campaign: "Skippy Yippee!", Chi-Chi's, Creative, International Bacon Film Festival, Skippy, Spam, TV
Mars, Incorporated - Uncle Ben's, Inc.
Minnesota Vikings (Brand Agency of Record)

BBDO New York

1285 Ave of the Americas 7th Fl, New York, NY 10019-6028
Tel.: (212) 459-5000
Web Site: www.bbdo.com

Year Founded: 1891

National Agency Associations: 4A's

Agency Specializes In: Advertising, Digital/Interactive

BBDO North America

1285 Ave of the Americas, New York, NY 10019-6028
(See Separate Listing)

BBDO San Francisco

600 California St, San Francisco, CA 94108
Tel.: (415) 808-6200
Fax: (415) 808-6221
E-Mail: contactsf@bbdo.com
Web Site: bbdosf.com/

Employees: 70

National Agency Associations: 4A's

Agency Specializes In: Sponsorship

Jim Lesser *(Pres/CEO-BBDO San Francisco)*
Linda Domercq *(Sr VP-Fin & HR)*
Elana Shea *(Sr Acct Dir)*
Heidi Keel *(VP & Dir-Strategy)*
Steve Rutter *(Exec Dir-Creative)*
Michael Cornell *(Sr Dir-Art)*
Kevin Thomson *(Creative Dir)*
Lizzie Agra *(Mgmt Supvr)*
Nicole Dongara *(Mgmt Supvr)*
Alyssa Collis *(Dir-Art)*
Greg Nelson *(Dir-Creative)*
Crystal Rix *(Dir-Bus Dev)*
Danielle Ivicic *(Mgr-Bus Affairs)*
Nicholas Roth *(Acct Supvr)*
Chad Harville *(Acct Exec)*

Accounts:
Air New Zealand
Barefoot Wine
Bay Area Shakespeare Camp
Caesars Entertainment Corporation; 2008
California Coastal Commission
E&J Gallo Crest Creator, Digital; 2003
Genentech, Inc.
Mars Petcare Mars Petcare, Pedigree, Whiskas
Mars Snickers
New-Mattel, Inc. Barbie, Campaign: "Imagine the Possibilities", Campaign: "You Can Be Anything"
Nutro
Pima Air & Space Museum Great Paper Airplane Project
Rock Health Banner Advertising, Online, Social Media
San Francisco Zoo
SF SPCA Campaign: "End Puppy Mills", Campaign: "Singalong"
Sutter Health
Uncle Ben's Campaign: "Ben's Beginners"
Vail Resorts Campaign: "Highway to Heavenly", Creative, Heavenly Mountain Resort
Wells Fargo (Creative Agency of Record) Campaign: "Learning Sign Language", Digital, Outdoor, Print, Radio, Social Media Marketing, TV

Energy BBDO

225 N Michigan Ave, Chicago, IL 60601
Tel.: (312) 337-7860
Fax: (312) 337-6871
E-Mail: contact@energybbdo.com
Web Site: www.energybbdo.com

Employees: 200

National Agency Associations: 4A's

Agency Specializes In: Advertising, Alternative Advertising, Brand Development & Integration, Broadcast, Cable T.V., Consumer Goods, Consumer Marketing, Direct-to-Consumer, Market Research, New Product Development, New Technologies, Outdoor, Print, Production, Sponsorship, Teen Market, Women's Market

Tonise Paul *(Pres & CEO)*
Jeff Adkins *(Mng Dir & Exec VP)*
Larry Gies *(Chief Strategy Officer)*
Rowley Samuel *(Exec VP & Head-Integrated Production)*
Nicole Benedick *(Exec VP & Dir-Digital Ops)*
Matthew Sundstrom *(Exec VP & Dir-Mktg Science)*
Robert Bailey *(Exec VP-Market Res)*
Stacie Boney *(Exec VP & Client Svc Dir)*
Mitch Brandow *(Exec VP-Engagement Strategy & Analytics)*
Elke Anderle *(Sr VP & Grp Dir-Plng)*
Tim Pontarelli *(Sr VP & Grp Dir-Creative)*
Grant Tennison *(Sr VP & Grp Dir-Creative)*
Will Elias *(Sr VP & Grp Acct Dir-Global)*
Jerry Delaney *(Sr VP & Dir-Info Svcs)*
Elaine Perri *(Sr VP & Dir-Creative & Art)*
Gwen Rutledge *(Sr VP & Dir-Creative)*
Lindsay Gash *(VP & Sr Acct Dir)*
Liz Miller-Gershfeld *(VP & Sr Producer-Art)*
Amy Ditchman *(Creative Dir)*
Allison Disney *(VP & Acct Dir-Global)*
Kate Houghton *(VP & Acct Dir)*
David Pollard *(VP & Acct Dir)*
Pedro Jose Perez *(VP, Dir-Creative & Copywriter)*
Casey Conway *(VP & Dir-Plng)*
Zach Graham *(VP & Dir-Digital Strategy)*
Phil Jungmann *(VP-Creative & Dir)*
Jonathan Linder *(VP & Dir-Creative)*
Aaron Pendleton *(VP & Dir-Creative & Art)*
Rachelle Pierre-Lott *(VP & Dir-Ops-Global)*
Zac Rybacki *(VP-Creative & Dir)*
Shannon Smiley *(VP & Dir-Brand Plng)*
Suzanne Michaels *(Exec Dir-Creative)*
Mike Roe *(Grp Dir-Creative)*
Tiffany Alexander *(Acct Dir)*
Jamie DeFer *(Acct Dir-Global)*
Jessie Levy *(Acct Dir-Integrated)*
Erynn Mattera *(Art Dir)*
Elizabeth Brown *(Dir-Plng)*
Dane Canada *(Dir-Art)*
Jesus Diaz *(Dir-Art)*
Josejuan Toledo *(Dir-Art)*
Chad Verly *(Dir-Creative)*
Dan McCormack *(Assoc Dir-Creative & Copywriter)*
Mariellen Golfis *(Sr Mgr-Integrated Talent)*
Michelle Sebastian *(Bus Mgr-Brdcst)*
Lauren Weiss *(Project Mgr-Digital)*
Aileen Hamilton *(Mgr-Integrated Bus Affairs)*
Sean Brewster *(Acct Supvr)*
Justin Johnson *(Acct Supvr-Global)*
Abby Lorber *(Acct Supvr)*
Beth Loughman *(Acct Supvr)*
Stephanie Pereira *(Acct Supvr)*
Ali Rein *(Acct Supvr)*
Emily Schowengerdt *(Acct Supvr)*
Brian Sisson *(Acct Supvr)*
Emmalee Anderson *(Sr Acct Exec)*
Makenzie Mouser *(Acct Exec)*
Hope Nardini *(Copywriter)*
Garrett Vernon *(Jr Copywriter)*
Kristin Grandberry *(Asst Acct Exec)*
Christina Lee *(Asst Acct Exec-Global)*
Natalie Taylor *(Asst Acct Exec)*
Lyssa Peloquin *(Assoc Producer)*
Reema Rao *(Jr Planner)*

Accounts:
Alka Seltzer
Anheuser-Busch InBev "House of Whatever", "So Cool", Bud Light (Agency of Record), Bud Light Lime, Bud Light Lime Lime-A-Rita, Bud Light Platinum, Campaign: "#UpForWhatever", Campaign: "Coin", Campaign: "Real Life Pacman", Campaign: "Surprise Guest", Campaign: "The Journey to Whatever", Campaign: "The Perfect Beer for Whatever Happens" Super Bowl 2014, Mang-O-Rita, Packaging, Raz-Ber-Rita, Super Bowl 2015
The Art Institute of Chicago Campaign: "Thrones", Red Cube Project
Bayer AG; Morristown, NJ Aleve, Alka-Seltzer, Bayer, Campaign: "Arthriving", Flintstones Vitamins, Midol, One-A-Day; 1997
Bayer Consumer Care Division Alka-Seltzer, Bayer Aspirin, Citracal, Flintstones Vitamins, One-A-Day 50 Plus Advantage Vitamins, One-A-Day Menopause, One-A-Day Vitacraves Gummies, One-A-Day Vitamins, Phillips
Bayer Corporation Advantage, Bayer Animal Health, K9 Advantix
Bayer Healthcare Consumer Care Division
Budweiser
Chicago Children's Museum Mister Imagine's Toy Store
Citrical Campaign: "Beauty Is Bone Deep"
Dial Corporation; Scottsdale, AZ Creative, Dial Yogurt, Dry Idea, Right Guard, Soft & Dri; 2005
JWT
King's Hawaiian (Agency Of Record) #GoPupule
Koninklijke Philips Electronics N.V.
Luxottica Retail
M&M's M&M's Dark
Mars, Incorporated
MilkPEP Advertising, Print
Nemschoff, Inc.
Novartis
Orbit Mist The Prom Date
Oxfam America Campaign: "Emotional Drugs", Campaign: "Gift Better - Food & Water", Charity, Fundraising Campaign, Gift Better
Pearle Vision Creative
PepsiCo Inc. Campaign: "Lake", Campaign: "Quaker Up", Campaign: "Quaker Up-Nod Off", Campaign: "The Hill", Creative, Quaker Oats
Proximity Community Effort, Election, Mayoral Candidates
Rosetta Stone Campaign: "Create a smaller world", Digital Marketing, Language Learning, Print, Radio, Social Media, TV, Web Series
S.C. Johnson & Son, Inc. Campaign: "Great Expectations", Campaign: "Tough Mother", Creative, Digital, Drano, Easy Open Tab Ziploc Bags, OFF! Citronella Candles, Public Relations, Raid, Saran Wrap, Shopper Marketing, Social Media, Windex, Ziploc
State Farm Insurance
Tesorino Campaign: "Fallen Off"
Turtle Wax Inc.
UNICEF
United Way
VTech Electronics North America
Wm. Wrigley Jr. Co. 5 Gum, Alert Energy Caffeine Gum, Altoids Hall of Curiosity, Big Red, Campaign: "Bird", Campaign: "Don't Let Food Hang Around", Campaign: "Give Extra, Get Extra", Campaign: "Hall of Curiosity", Campaign: "Just-Brushed Clean Feeling", Campaign: "Life Happens in 5", Campaign: "Lingering Food", Campaign: "Lipstick", Campaign: "Origami", Campaign: "Sometimes The Little Things Last The Longest", Chewing Gum, Creme Savers, Digital, Doublemint, Eclipse, Extra, Five React, Freedent, Hubba Bubba, Juicy Fruit, Life Savers, Orbit Gum, Radio, Spearmint, TV, Winterfresh, Wrigley's Extra; 1933

Canada

BBDO Toronto
2 Bloor St W, Toronto, ON M4W 3R6 Canada
Tel.: (416) 972-1505
Fax: (416) 972-5656
Web Site: www.bbdo.ca

Employees: 200

Agency Specializes In: Advertising, Bilingual Market, Brand Development & Integration, Broadcast, Business-To-Business, Consumer Marketing, Corporate Identity, Direct Response Marketing, Event Planning & Marketing, Fashion/Apparel, Government/Political, Graphic Design, High Technology, Logo & Package Design, Magazines, Media Buying Services, New Product Development, Newspapers & Magazines, Out-of-Home Media, Outdoor, Planning & Consultation, Production, Publicity/Promotions, Sales Promotion, Sports Market, Strategic Planning/Research, Telemarketing, Travel & Tourism

Dom Caruso *(Pres & CEO)*
Paul Reilly *(Sr VP & Exec Mng Dir-Toronto)*
Philip Filippopoulos *(CFO & Exec VP)*
Gerry Frascione *(Pres/CEO-North America)*
Siobhan McCarthy *(Sr VP & Dir-Organizational Dev)*
Martina Ivsak *(VP & Grp Acct Dir)*
Stephanie Page *(VP & Grp Acct Dir)*
Mike McGee *(VP & Acct Dir)*
Linda Carte *(VP & Assoc Dir-Creative)*
Rachel Selwood *(Acct Dir)*
J. P. Gravina *(Dir-Art & Assoc Dir-Creative)*
Alice Blastorah *(Dir-Art)*
Jeff Cheung *(Dir-Art)*
Mike Schonberger *(Dir-Art)*
Simon Craig *(Assoc Dir-Creative & Copywriter)*
Saloni Wadehra *(Acct Supvr)*
Shiran Teitelbaum *(Copywriter)*

Accounts:
160 Girls Project
Bayer Campaign: "Aspirin Headache Lights"
Campbell Company of Canada Campaign: "Psyguyatrist", TV
Canadian Paralympic Committee Campaign: "It's Not What's Missing, It's What's There", Campaign: "ParaTough", Campaign: "The Games are Tough, the Athletes are Tougher", Radio, Social Media
Cara Operations Inc Campaign: "Copyright"
Diamler Campaign: "Reindeer In Headlights", Mercedes-Benz
The Equality Effect Campaign: "The Real Victory is Justice for Child Rape Victims"
FedEx Campaign: "Non-Rush Shipping", Change, Dominoes
Frito Lay Campaign: "The End"
GE Cafe, Campaign: "Bear", Campaign: "Noisy Work", Campaign: "Penguin", Campaign: "Walrus", Profile Dishwasher
Harlequin Enterprises Campaign: "Escape the Everyday"
Harvey's
Mabe Canada Campaign: "Cow Mermaid"
Mars Canada Ben's Beginners, GetKidsCooking.ca, Hunger Scale, M&M's, Snickers, TV, Uncle Ben's
Mars Petcare
Mercedes-Benz Canada Blur, C-Class Coupe, Campaign: "How to wrap a Mercedes-Benz", Campaign: "Moustache Emblem", Campaign: "Moustaches", Campaign: "Reindeer in Headlights", SMART
Ministry of Health & Long Term Care Campaign: "Colon Cancer", Campaign: "Social Smoking"
Molson Coors Canada Campaign: "Beer-Gram", Campaign: "No Bollocks", Campaign: "Paint With a Tweet", Miller Chill Lemon
Movember Campaign: "Moustache Emblem"
Pepsi Arctic Sun, Campaign: "Sunrise", Campaign: "Wrecking Ball Of Dew", Doritos Campaign: "The End", Mountain Dew Citrus Charged, Pepsi Mini Cans
Prince Edward County Campaign: "Progress Redefined"
Quaker Quaker Minis
Royal Bank of Canada Campaign: "RBC Cashback

Cart"
Sirius XM Campaign: "Die-hard NHL Fan Slash Lady Gaga Disciple", Campaign: "Howard Stern", Creative, TV
Smart Canada Campaign: "Popsicle", Campaign: "Smart Little Bumper Stickers", Cars, Smart Little Gifts
Starbucks Interactive Shops Front
Temptations Treats Campaign: "Kitty Cat Hijack"
Toronto Jewish Film Festival Campaign: "Curls"
United Way Toronto
Visa Canada Campaign: "The Infinite List in Haiku", Out-of-Home, Radio, Visa Infinite Card
Wm. Wrigley Jr. Company Campaign: "Cat", Campaign: "Get Skittles Rich", Campaign: "Gif Rap", Campaign: "Struck by a Rainbow", Campaign: "Touch the Rainbow", CreateTheRainbow.com, Skittles

Nolin BBDO
3575 Boulevard St-Laurent Suite 300, Montreal, QC H2X 2T7 Canada
(See Separate Listing)

Argentina

BBDO Argentina
Arenales 495 3rd Fl, Vincente Lopez, B1638BRC Buenos Aires, Argentina
Tel.: (54) 11 6091 2700
Fax: (54) 11 6091 2722
E-Mail: bbdo@bbdoargentina.com

Employees: 50

National Agency Associations:

Ramiro Rodriguez Cohen *(Exec Creative Dir)*
Sole Calvano *(Art Dir)*
Bruno Barbosa *(Dir-Art)*
Dani Minaker *(Dir-Interactive Creative)*
Sebastian Tarazaga *(Dir-Creative)*
Guido Freiberg *(Copywriter-Integrated)*
Nico Varas *(Copywriter)*
Nicolas Smith *(Sr Art Dir)*

Accounts:
Claro Mobile
Doritos
Fondo Vitivinicola De Mendoza Wine
ICI Paints
Mars
Mercedes-Benz Argentina Campaign: "Smart Twitter Spot"
Nike Campaign: "Baptism", Campaign: "The Day the Stadium Spoke", Campaign: "Twitter To Zero", Marathon, Nike 10K
Paso De Los Toros
PepsiCo Beverage, Campaign: "Broken Relationships", Campaign: "Bubbles", Campaign: "Frog", Campaign: "Lay's machine", Frito Lay, Gatorade, Lay's, Quaker, Twistos
Smart Argentina Campaign: "The Smart Twitter Spot"
New-Tarjeta Naranja
Tropicana
Universal Music
Wrigley

Brazil

Almap BBDO
Av Roque Petroni JR 999 35e 7 anderas, Sao Paulo, 04707-905 Brazil
Tel.: (55) 11 2161 5600
Fax: (55) 11 2161 5645
E-Mail: almap@almapbbdo.com.br
Web Site: www.almapbbdo.com.br

Gustavo Burnier *(Partner & Dir-Client Svcs & Digital Ops)*
Rodrigo Andrade *(COO)*
Luiz Sanches *(Chief Creative Officer)*
Fernanda Antonelli *(VP-Client Svcs)*
Filipe Bartholomeu *(VP-Client Svcs)*
Joao Gabriel Fernandes *(VP-Strategic Plng)*
Brian Crotty *(Grp Dir-Media-Strategy & Innovation)*
Juliana Nascimento *(Grp Acct Dir)*
Pedro Fragata *(Acct Dir)*
Andre Leotta *(Art Dir)*
Marcelo Nogueira *(Creative Dir)*
Leandro Valente *(Art Dir)*
Gustavo de Lacerda *(Dir-Art)*
Luciana Haguiara *(Dir-Digital Creative)*
Lucas Reis *(Dir-Art)*
Sandro Rosa *(Dir-Digital Creative)*
Marcelo Tolentino *(Dir-Art)*
Isabela Crestana *(Acct Mgr)*
Cristina Chacon *(Acct Supvr)*
Viviane Sgarbi *(Acct Supvr)*
Italo Vetorazzo *(Acct Supvr)*
Aline Macedo *(Acct Exec)*
Dudu Barcelos *(Copywriter)*
Felipe Cirino *(Copywriter)*
Cesar Herszcowicz *(Copywriter)*
Rodrigo Resende *(Copywriter)*

Accounts:
New-Alpargatas SA
Ambev Beer
Anheuser-Busch InBev N.V./S.A.
Antarctica Beer ANTARCTICA Business Card
Antarctica Campaign: "GPS Boa"
Aspirin
Assiciacao Edicacional e Assistencial Casa do Zezinho Campaign: "Biographies", Casa Do Zezinho Campaign: "Share With Those Who Needs" & Casa Do Zezinho Television, Child Poverty Indifference Awareness
Casa Do Zezinho Campaign: "Goal for Education", Campaign: "Help", Campaign: "Share With Those Who Needs", Television
Audi Audi A1, Audi A8, Audi Q7, Campaign: "Collection", Campaign: "Danger Can Appear Before Expected", Campaign: "Driving's more fun than getting there", Campaign: "File Compressor", Campaign: "Luxury Has Everything To Do With Nature", Campaign: "Quattro"
Bauducco Toast Campaign: "Cheese", Campaign: "Never Underestimate The Supporting Role", Toast
Bayer Aspirin, Cafiaspirina, Campaign: "For a less painful life", Campaign: "Wi-Fi Network List"
Billboard Brazil Campaign: "Guitar Pee", Campaign: "Music. See what it's made of.", Campaign: "Typography - Madona", Magazine, Transfertype
Bradesco Seguros Insurance Campaign: "Fake Ad", Campaign: "The Most Valuable Stock Images"
Caminhoes Your Load Will Seem Lighter
Cultura TV
D Boricario
Editora Todas as Culturas
Editora Todas Culturas Campaign: "Price", Top Magazine
Effem
Elma Chips Campaign: "Male Breasts", Campaign: "Supermarket"
Embratel Campaign: "Bedroom"
EPA Moleskine
Escola Panamericana de Arte e Design
Gatorade
General Electric Company Campaign: "Bright Idea"
Getty Images Campaign: "85 Seconds", Campaign: "From Love To Bingo", Campaign: "Kaleidoscope", Campaign: "Life Cuts", Image Archive, Image Bank, Stock Images, Stock Photos
Gol Airlines Campaign: "Seat Challenge"
Gol Linhas Aereas Campaign: "Valentine's Flight", Gol Log Air Cargo Service
Gollog Campaign: "Pixel Guitar", Campaign: "Streetview Delivery"
Greenpeace Campaign: "Do not disturb"
Havaianas Sandals Campaign: "Illustrations", Campaign: "Princesses", Campaign: "Special Collection", Flip Flops, Kids
HP Campaign: "Photoshout"
iStock
Kiss FM Campaign: "Endorcism"
Lojas Marisa
Man Latin America Campaign: "Styrofoam", Campaign: "Supermarket", Campaign: "The right size for your needs", Fish Market
MAN Trucks Campaign: "Right size for your needs"
Marisa
Mars Campaign: "Dog Adopt", Campaign: "Feed the Good", Campaign: "First Days Out", In-Store, Online, Pedigree, Print, Social Media, TV
O Boticario Campaign: "Making Of", Campaign: "The Beauty Of Your Tan Needs Golden Plus", Making-Of
P&G Campaign: "Purple", Campaign: "T-Shirt To Intimidate"
Panamericana School Of Art Actress, Campaign: "Fashion Design"
Peixe Urbano Campaign: "Money Machine"
Pepsi
Sao Paulo Alpargatas Campaign: "Clips", Havaianas
Sara Lee
Super Sonica Sound Design Campaign: "Bang"
Superinteressante
TOP Destinos Campaign: "Vacations", Campaign: "Waterfall, Island", Campaign: "Your Luxury Tourism Magazine", Eiffel Tower
TV Cultura Campaign: "Caricatures"
Veja
Visa Campaign: "Barber Shop", Campaign: "Hair Dye", Campaign: "Portal Entertainers"
Volkswagen Group of America, Inc. Amarok, Campaign: "Ad Skipper", Campaign: "Beep-beep", Campaign: "Brasil 70", Campaign: "Do Brasil Broke Up", Campaign: "Driving is good", Campaign: "Drums", Campaign: "Hands-free parking system", Campaign: "Hidden Frame", Campaign: "Kombi Last Wishes", Campaign: "Last Edition", Campaign: "Luxurious", Campaign: "Nails", Campaign: "Space Cross - The Legend", Campaign: "Tariff Notebook", Campaign: "The legend of Saci", Campaign: "Tiguan - hotsite", Campaign: "Vw Innovation Channel", CrossFox, DSG Tiptonic Transmission, Golf, Hands-free Parking, New Beetle, Original Parts, SpaceFox, Tiguan, Touareg, Trucks, Volkswagen Area View System, Volkswagen Fatigue Sensor, Volkswagen Fox, Volkswagen Fusca, Volkswagen Kombi, Volkswagen do Brasil

Chile

BBDO Chile
Av Vitacura 2939 Piso 14 Las Condes, Santiago, Chile
Tel.: (56) 2751 4100
Fax: (56) 2751 4102
E-Mail: info@bbdo.cl
Web Site: www.bbdo.cl

Employees: 90

Carlos Ojeda *(Editor-Creative)*
Ingrid Lira *(Grp Dir-Creative)*
Marcelo Moya Ochoa *(Art Dir)*
Oscar Rivera *(Art Dir)*
Juan Urra *(Art Dir)*
Leo Rocha *(Dir-Art)*
Jaime Rodriguez *(Dir-Creative)*
Patricio Sepulveda *(Dir-Art)*
Macarena Santa Marfa *(Acct Supvr)*
Cesar Araya *(Acct Exec)*
Felipe Bobadilla Agouborde *(Copywriter)*

Accounts:

AgroSuper
Archi
BancoEstado
Bayer Campaign: "Exploited Head"
Carozzi
Catholic Church Campaign: "Ice Cream"
Confites Merello Sour Candy
Correos Chile Campaign: "Firemen"
Cti Campaign: "Diet"
Ecusa Chile Pepsi Light
Electrolux Steam System
Hogar San Francisco De Regis Clothing Donation
INACAP
Ingeneria Enlace Security Cameras, Security Systems
Johnson & Johnson Listerine
Lider
Light Foundation Campaign: "Mexican Flag"
Listerine Smart Kidz
Mars North America
Mars
Mercedes-Benz Campaign: "House Of Mirrors Effect"
Merello
Mitsubishi Motors Porcupine
Monticello Grand Casino
Paris Campaign: "Forest"
PepsiCo Campaign: "Salsamix", Frito-Lay, Gatorade, Pepsi, Quaker
Ruta Norte
Te Supremo

Colombia

Perez y Villa BBDO
Calle 16 No 43B-50, Medellin, Colombia
Tel.: (57) 4 266 4030
Fax: (57) 4 266 0375
E-Mail: info@perezyvilla.com
Web Site: www.perezyvilla.com

Employees: 36
Year Founded: 1980

Accounts:
Edding
Practimac
Refisal

Sancho BBDO
Calle 98 No 903 2nd Floor, Bogota, Colombia
Tel.: (57) 1651 0651
Fax: (57) 1218 6672
Web Site: www.sanchobbdo.com.co

Employees: 300

Carlos Felipe Arango *(VP)*
Hugo Corredor *(VP-Creative)*
Giovanni Martinez *(VP-Creative)*
Natalia Perez *(VP-Acct)*
Daniel A. Mora *(Dir-Art & Creative)*
Adriana Alba *(Acct Dir)*
Andres Estrada *(Creative Dir)*
Fabio Mendoza *(Creative Dir)*
Sandra Murillo *(Art Dir)*
Lyda Naussan *(Art Dir)*
Monica Nieto *(Acct Dir-Total Work)*
Freddy Ospina *(Creative Dir)*
Duvier Rojas *(Art Dir)*
Maria Tovar *(Acct Dir)*
Ana Maria Woodcock *(Acct Dir)*
Juan Afanador *(Dir-Art)*
Alejandro Calero *(Dir-Art)*
Mauricio Castro *(Dir-Art)*
Damian Montanez *(Dir-Creative Total Work)*
Nicolas Murillo *(Dir-Creative)*
Pablo Naval *(Dir-Creative)*
Cristian Raise *(Dir-Art)*
Diego Salamanca *(Dir-Art)*
Adriana Zapata *(Acct Mgr)*
Mario Betancur *(Copywriter)*
Daniel Mosquera *(Copywriter)*
Alejandro Tawa *(Copywriter)*

Accounts:
The 140 Characters Film Festival Campaign: "Short Film Festival Inspired By Tweets", Campaign: "Terror, Tragicomedy, Humor", Campaign: "Tetas, Mosquito"
ACDELCO Video Jukebox
Alianza Team
Almacenes Exito Campaign: "An Homage To Mom", Campaign: "Giro Internacionales Exito"
Av Villas Bank Campaign: "The Polo Tower"
Bayer Alka Seltzer, Campaign: "Armagefood", Campaign: "Porktanic"
Beergara Beer
Casa Luker
Chevrolet Posventa Campaign: "Choking Goal Syndrome"
Corona Kitchen
Corona Paints Campaign: "Princess"
Depris
Doria
Ecopetrol Campaign: "60 Anniversary"
El Ropero
El Tiempo Campaign: "The Game of Time", Campaign: "Voice Bank"
Exito Dental Floss Campaign: "Flossbook", Campaign: "Postcard"
New-Exito Group
Exito Mobile
Exito Supermarkets
Exito Water
Festival 140 Caracteres Campaign: "Tetas, Mosquito"
G Tech Colombia Campaign: "Car Change"
General Motors Campaign: "Chevrolet Taxi Drivers University", Chevrolet Campaign: "Camera"
Guia Academica
HiperCentro Corona
Incauca
Los Pisingos Adoption Center Campaign: "John Lennon, Nelson Mandela, Steve Jobs"
Lukafe Campaign: "RIVER"
Mars
Mi Planeta Exito Public Interest
Noraver Campaign: "Find them and throw them in the river"
PepsiCo Campaign: "12.000 Feet Radio Spot", Frito-Lay, Gatorade, Mountain Dew
Sony Ericsson Campaign: "Fight"
Tecnoquimicas Campaign: "Italian Mobster"
Telefonica Campaign: "The Sexy Girl with the Red Hood", Puppets
Yodora Foot Deodorant

Costa Rica

Garnier BBDO
Urbanizacion Tournon Diagonal a la Camara de Comercio Barrio Tournn, 1000 San Jose, Costa Rica
Tel.: (506) 2287 4800
Fax: (506) 223 0390
E-Mail: info@garnierbbdo.com
Web Site: www.garnierbbdo.com

Employees: 90

Agency Specializes In: Direct Response Marketing, Public Relations, Publicity/Promotions

Ramiro Caso *(Acct Dir)*
Yoshua Leon *(Art Dir)*
Tito Araya *(Dir-Creative-BBDO Costa Rica)*
Alan Carmona *(Dir-Creative)*
Lucas Fernandez *(Dir-Art)*
Esteban Mclean *(Dir-Creative)*
Ronaldo Peraza *(Designer-Adv)*

Accounts:
Bayer; 1995
Cafe 1820
Compania Numar Campaign: "UFO"
Costa Rican Symphonic Orchestra Hurricane Victims Charity Event
Cruz Verde
Durex Campaign: "Bleep Interview"
El Lagar Hardware Stores
Fischel Express
Grupo Roble
Kodak Graphic Communications Group
Laboratorios Gutis
Mars
New-MatraCat
Museos Banco Central
Orquesta Sinfonica Nacional
Paniamor
Sandimar
Spoon Campaign: "Flags"
Taco Bell
Territorio de Zaguates
Unimar Campaign: "Cliff"
Wrigley's

Dominican Republic

Pages BBDO
Abraham 1060 Lincoln, Santo Domingo, Dominican Republic
Tel.: (809) 541 5331
Fax: (809) 563 0947
E-Mail: info@pagesbbdo.com
Web Site: www.pagesbbdo.com

Year Founded: 1970

Marisol Pages *(CFO)*
Aida Colon *(Acct Dir)*
Freddy Montero Galva *(Dir-Art)*
Ariel Gomez *(Dir-Art)*
Sara Rodriguez-Garcia *(Dir-Art)*
Jose Sena *(Dir-Art)*
Patricia Rodriguez McKinney *(Acct Supvr)*
Mirely Ortiz *(Acct Exec)*
Linda Maria Garcia Louder *(Jr Acct Exec)*

Accounts:
ARS Humano
Banco Popular
La Sirena Campaign: "Fashion for Less", Red Carpet
Sanar Una Nacion
UNICEF
United Nations Poverty Awareness

Guatemala

BBDO Guatemala
5 Ave 5-55 Zona 14 Europlaza Torre 4 nivel 17, 01014 Guatemala, Guatemala
Tel.: (502) 2382-2236
Fax: (502) 2382-2200
E-Mail: publicidad@bbdo.com.gt
Web Site: www.bbdo.com.gt

Employees: 112

Rodrigo Costas *(Reg Dir-Creative)*
Junn Manuel Ordonez *(Reg Dir-Creative)*
Hermann Von der Meden *(Reg Dir-Creative)*
Diego Lanzi *(Creative Dir)*
Adolfo Lazo *(Art Dir)*
Christian Acevedo *(Dir-Art)*
Andres Anleu *(Dir-Art)*
Evelyn Menendez *(Dir-Art)*
Pablo Casasola *(Designer)*
Rodrigo Costas Ferreira *(Copywriter)*
Mandy Ortega *(Copywriter)*

Accounts:
7up

Advertising Agencies

Blockbuster
Fox Head
Frito-Lay
New-Kasperle
Quick Dry Cement
Red Cross
New-ReStore
Santa Lucia Lottery
New-Scotch Glue

Mexico

BBDO Mexico

Guillermo Gonzalez Camarena No 800 3er Piso, Col Zedec Santa Fe, Mexico, DF 01210 Mexico
Tel.: (52) 55 5 267 1500
Fax: (52) 55 5 267 1523
E-Mail: beatriz.alarcon@bbdomexico.com
Web Site: www.bbdomexico.com

Employees: 165

National Agency Associations: IAA

Agency Specializes In: Consumer Marketing

Ariel Soto *(Chief Creative Officer & VP)*
Luis Ribo *(Chief Creative Officer)*
Oscar Diaz *(VP-Fin)*
Manuel Arriaga Carpio *(Art Dir)*
Gustavo Correa *(Acct Dir)*
Gabriela Morales *(Acct Dir)*
Erika Olvera *(Creative Dir)*
Gabriel Martinez *(Dir-Art & Copywriter)*
Beatriz Alarcon *(Dir-PR)*
Carlos Angel *(Dir-Art)*
Sara Collazo *(Dir-Art)*
Paola Figueroa *(Dir-Creative)*
IRVING HERRERA *(Dir-Creative)*
Sindo Ingelmo *(Dir-Creative)*
Hugo Moedano *(Dir-Creative & Art)*
Luis Monroy *(Dir-Art)*
Jose Mario Munoz Enriquez *(Dir-Art)*
Ana Paola Noriega *(Dir-Creative)*
Patricia Tena *(Dir-Art)*
Rodrigo Del Oso *(Assoc Dir-Creative)*
Isabel Palacios *(Assoc Dir-Art)*
Rodrigo Casas *(Copywriter)*
Gumaro Davila *(Copywriter)*
Hector Farias *(Copywriter)*
Julio Lacy *(Copywriter)*
Thalia Vazquez *(Copywriter)*
Teresa Lemus *(Grp Creative Dir)*

Accounts:
3M Mexico Campaign: "Letter", Post-it Flags
Alka Seltzer
Bayer Campaign: "Pixelator"; 1995
Berol Gases
Campbell's De Mexico
Cinemex; 2003
Mercedes-Benz
Devlyn Optical Store Campaign: "Eyes", Campaign: "Sniper"
Effem
El Financiero Newspaper; 1995
ESPN; 2003
Hewlett Packard Campaign: "Ramses"
Mars Cesar Goddes
Mars Pedigree
Mitsubishi
Pepsi-Cola International Fedex Campaign: "Small Business" & Fedex Campaign: "Trucks", Frito-Lay, Gatorade
Pfizer
Sabritas Campaign: "Rusian Rulet"; 1996
Scribe Campaign: "Gorigon", Sketch Books
Smart
Visa
Wrigley's; 1995

Puerto Rico

BBDO Puerto Rico

Metro Office Park 14 calle 2 Ste, Guaynabo, PR 00907-1831
Tel.: (787) 620-2000
Fax: (787) 620-2001
E-Mail: info@bbdopr.com
Web Site: www.bbdopr.com

Employees: 50

National Agency Associations: 4A's

Luariz Alejandro *(Acct Exec-Digital)*
Paola Palomares *(Planner-Strategic Brand)*

Accounts:
Bayer
Frito Lay
Gatorade
GlaxoSmithKline
Mars Campaign: "Dj'S", M&M's
P&G Campaign: "Gracias Mami"
Pepsi
Puerto Rico Alzheimer's Federation Campaign to Recruit Volunteers
SUAGM

Venezuela

BBDO Venezuela

Centro Ave Don Diego Cisneros, Los Ruices, Caracas, Venezuela
Tel.: (58) 212 239 2622
Fax: (58) 212 237 9940
E-Mail: informacion@bbdo.com.ve
Web Site: www.bbdo.com

Employees: 40

Agency Specializes In: Advertising, Consumer Goods, Entertainment, Food Service, Pharmaceutical

Ali Armas *(VP-Creative)*
Miguel Corrales *(VP-Creative)*
Roberto Mondello *(Art Dir)*

Accounts:
3M
7-Up
AdRush
Bayer; Caracas Saridon; 1980
Baygon
Clinica Dempere Campaign: "We Make Fairy Tales Come True"
Golden
New-Optica Billi
PepsiCo; Caracas Frito-Lay, Gatorade, Pepsi; 1996
Pfizer
Wrigley
ZEA BBDO
Zoom

Austria

PKP BBDO

Guglgasse 7-9, 1030 Vienna, Austria
Tel.: (43) 1 95 500 500
Fax: (43) 1 95 500 600
E-Mail: bbdo@bbdo.at
Web Site: www.pkp-bbdo.at

Employees: 50

Alfred Koblinger *(CEO & Partner)*
Roman Sindelar *(Mng Partner & Chief Creative Officer)*
Max Jurschik *(Head-Digital)*
Astrid Bittermann *(Art Dir)*
Erich Enzenberger *(Dir-Creative)*
Florian Kozak *(Dir-Digital Creative)*
Luke Sabine *(Dir-Fin)*

Accounts:
A1 Telekom Campaign: "We Are 1!"
BauMax
Bayer Aspirin
Card Complete
Dr. Oetker
Gardena Campaign: "Aquacontour Automatic"
Greenpeace Campaign: "Bycatch"
Iberogast
Licht fur die Welt Campaign: "Light for the World"
Light For The World Campaign: "Blind Person's Armband"
Mars North America; Austria M&M's, Maltesers, Mars, Snickers
Mondelez International, Inc. Campaign: "The Receipt"
Oebb Austrian Railways
OMV
Orbit
Procter & Gamble Oral-B
Wrigley

Belgium

Darwin BBDO

Bessenveldstraat 25, 1831 Diegem, Belgium
Tel.: (32) 2 725 9710
Fax: (32) 2 725 9001
E-Mail: info@darwin.bbdo.be
Web Site: www.darwin.bbdo.be

Employees: 25

Agency Specializes In: Advertising, Consumer Goods, Consumer Marketing, Financial, Food Service, Pharmaceutical

Guy Geerts *(Mng Dir)*
Isabel Peeters *(Mng Dir-Client Svcs)*
Mateusz Mroszczak *(Exec Creative Dir)*
Hannelore Van Cauwenberghe *(Acct Dir)*
Gaston Koojimans *(Dir-Creative)*
Bart Welkenhuysen *(Dir-Art)*
Marianne Janssens *(Acct Mgr)*

Accounts:
Centea
Fidea
Frito-Lay Lay's
JCDecaux Campaign: "Huge Bills"
K.U. Leuven
Oasis
Quick-Step
SOS Childrens Villages Campaign: "You are the 99%"
Unilever Bestfoods Becel Pro Activ, Iglo, Knorr, Mora, Signal
VLAM Milk

N BBDO

Scheldestraat 122, 1080 Brussels, Belgium
Tel.: (32) 2 421 30 10
Fax: (32) 2 421 22 04
E-Mail: info@n.bbdo.be
Web Site: www.bbdo.be

Employees: 25
Year Founded: 1992

Agency Specializes In: Advertising, Food Service

Stephan Smets *(Chief Creative Officer)*
Sebastien De Valck *(Dir-Creative)*
Klaartje Galle *(Dir-Art)*
Arnaud Pitz *(Dir-Creative)*
Daniel Schots *(Dir-Bus Dev)*
Frederic Zouag *(Dir-Art)*

Ann Peetermans *(Planner-Creative)*
Regine Smetz *(Copywriter)*
Isabel Peeters *(Mng Dir Client Svcs)*

Accounts:
Adecco
Douwe Egberts
Electrabel
Formipac
Herta Knacki Football Knacki Football
JCDecaux Direct Marketing
Lydian
Mars North America Snickers
Nestle Nesquik
Nokia
Pepsi
Solo
Vier

Proximity BBDO
Scheldestraat 122 Rue de l'Escaut, 1080 Brussels, Belgium
Tel.: (32) 2 421 23 80
Fax: (32) 2 4212314
E-Mail: info@proximity.bbdo.be
Web Site: proximityworld.com/

E-Mail for Key Personnel:
Creative Dir.: henney.gerwen@bbdo.be

Employees: 200
Year Founded: 1987

National Agency Associations: BPA-DMA

Agency Specializes In: Advertising, Direct Response Marketing

Dirk Peremans *(CEO & Partner)*
Stefaan Roelen *(COO)*
Arnaud Pitz *(Dir-Creative)*
Daniel Schots *(Dir-Bus Dev)*
Frederic Zouag *(Dir-Art)*
Sarah Van Praag *(Acct Exec)*
Jutta Callebaut *(Copywriter-Creative)*

Accounts:
BBDO & Microsoft Connect
Belgian Interfederal Olympic Committee
Bosch
Brussels Airlines
Centea
Chrysler
Concentra
Ethias
Federal Mogul
HP
ING
KBC
Knacki
KPMG
Makro Cash & Carry Belgium
Mars North America Cesar, Pedigree, Sheba, Whiskas
SD Worx Environment Awareness
Tabasco Pepper Sauce
Unilever
Volvo

VVL BBDO
122 Rue de l'Escaut, 1080 Brussels, Belgium
Tel.: (32) 2 421 2200
Fax: (32) 2 421 2204
E-Mail: recepcei@bbdo.be
Web Site: bbdo.be/

Employees: 200

Agency Specializes In: Business-To-Business, Direct Response Marketing, Retail

Arnaud Pitz *(Creative Dir)*
Frederic Zouag *(Art Dir)*
Sebastien De Valck *(Dir-Creative)*
Jan Dejonghe *(Dir-Creative)*
Jasper Verleije *(Dir-Art)*
Sarah Huysmans *(Copywriter-Creative)*

Accounts:
Bayer Consumer Non-Food
Belgacom Campaign: "Footsave Your Cellphone"
Cera
Electrabel
Evita
Iglo
KBC Bank
Koepel Van De Vlaamse Noord-Zuid Campaign: "Climate Campaign"
Lays
Mars North America Consumer Food
Mercedes-Benz A-Class, Campaign: "Mbmakemyday", Campaign: "The Pulse Of A New Generation"
Nutroma
Oral-B
Pepsi-Cola Consumer Food
Pepsico Food Consumer Food
Pfizer
Proximus
Sanex
Sappi
Story
Total
Volvo Campaign: "FollowedbyVolvo"

Cyprus

Telia & Pavla BBDO
92 Makarios III Ave, POBox 23930, 1687 Nicosia, Cyprus
Tel.: (357) 22377745
Fax: (357) 22377996
E-Mail: info@tpbbdo.com.cy
Web Site: www.tpbbdo.com.cy

Employees: 39
Year Founded: 1982

Athos Kyriakou *(Deputy Mng Dir)*
Anastasia Tsami *(Dir-Creative & Copywriter)*
Tonia Anastasiou *(Acct Mgr)*
George Michael *(Supvr-Production)*
Eleni Avraamidou *(Sr Analyst-Media & Planner)*
Toulla Constantinou *(Sr Graphic Designer)*
Irene Michaelidou *(Coord-Media)*
Popi Savva *(Coord-Production)*

Accounts:
Cablenet
Colgate Palmolive
Eureka
Johnson & Johnson
Porsche
Serano
Spectus
Sun Fresh

Czech Republic

Mark BBDO
Krizikova 34, Prague, 8 186 00 Czech Republic
Tel.: (420) 234 777 801
Fax: (420) 2 2161 724248
E-Mail: markbbdo@markbbdo.cz
Web Site: www.markbbdo.cz

Employees: 55

Vlado Slivka *(Dir-Creative)*
Leon Sverdlin *(Dir-Creative)*
Iva Macku *(Copywriter)*

Accounts:
Balirny Douwe Egberts Douwe Egberts, Pickwick
Bayer Aspirin, Aspirin C, Canesten
CEZ
Czech Olympic
Czech Paralympic Team
Dr. Oetker
FAB
GE Money Bank GE Leasing, Multiserve
Heinz
Hero Sunar, Sunarek, Sunarka
Jan Becher Pernod Ricard Karlovarksa Becherovka
Lays Campaign: "A Big Thanks From America"
Linde
Mars North America Caesar, Campaign: "Power To Play", Mars, Milky Way, Sheba, Snickers, Uncle Bens, Whiskas
Mercedes Benz
Mobilkom
MZV CR
Nike
OMV
Pepsi General Bottlers Frito Lay, Mirinda, Mountain Dew, Pepsi, Seven Up, Toma
Prague Airport
Prazske Pivovary Branik, Granat, Staropramen
RWE
Sara Lee
Scandinavian Tobacco Cristal, Mistral, Prince, Rockets, WallStreet
Seznam.cz
Toyota
Wrigley's
Zentiva Calibrum, Celaskon, Endiaron, Indulona

Pleon Impact
Konviktska 24, 110 00 Prague, 1 Czech Republic
Tel.: (420) 222 540 147 8
Fax: (420) 222 540 836
E-Mail: pleonimpact@pleon-impact.cz
Web Site: www.pleon-impact.cz

Employees: 20
Year Founded: 1994

National Agency Associations: APRA-ICCO

Agency Specializes In: Public Relations

Zdenka Kuhnova *(Chm & Mng Dir)*
Petr Lemoch *(Dir-PR)*
Dagmar Vilimkova *(Dir-Fin)*
Martina Komarkova *(Office Mgr)*
Katerina Dousova *(Mgr-PR)*
Dina Svitekova *(Mgr-PR)*
Veronika Kubalova *(Jr Project Mgr)*

Accounts:
British Airways
Electrolux Group
Haguess
LUKOIL
Mercedes-Benz
Muller

Denmark

BBDO Denmark
St Kongensgade 72, DK-1264 Copenhagen, K Denmark
Tel.: (45) 3330 1919
Fax: (45) 3330 1920
Web Site: tbwa.dk

Employees: 43

Erich Karsholt *(Mng Dir)*
Carsten Schiott *(Dir-Creative)*

Accounts:
Copenhagen Music Theatre Campaign: "Singing Banners"
Crusli

Danske Spil Campaign: "All In"
Dolmio
Dr. Oetker
M&Ms
Mars Food
Pepsi Quaker Oats; 1985
Procter & Gamble Oral-B
Red Cross Campaign: "Price Tag"
Royal Unibrew
Siam Muay Thai Gym Campaign: "Kick Some Ass!"

Estonia

Zavod BBDO

Rotermanni 5/ Roseni 10, Tallinn, 10111 Estonia
Tel.: (372) 6 8 11 800
Fax: (372) 6 8 11 801
E-Mail: zavod@zavod.ee
Web Site: www.zavod.ee

Employees: 28
Year Founded: 1994

Tauno Loodus *(CEO)*
Silvar Laasik *(Dir-Creative)*
Marek Reinaas *(Dir-Creative)*
Kristi Kamp *(Acct Exec)*
Triin Tammela *(Acct Exec)*

Accounts:
ETK Retail
Mars North America
Osuspanki Insurance & Banking
PepsiCo

Egypt

Impact BBDO

15 Hassan Sabry, zamalek, Cairo, Egypt
Tel.: (20) 2 794 0151
Fax: (20) 2 796 0296
E-Mail: info@impactbbdo.com.eg
Web Site: www.impactbbdo.com

Employees: 63

Karim Khouri *(Gen Mgr)*
Mohamed Hammad *(Grp Acct Dir)*
Ahmed Hamdalla *(Assoc Dir-Creative)*
Laila El Chiati *(Acct Mgr)*
Yasmin Sweedan *(Acct Mgr)*
Hadir El Akabawi *(Sr Acct Exec)*

Accounts:
Federal Express
Ikea Creative
PepsiCo, Inc.
TECNO Mobile Smartphone for Everyone

France

CLM BBDO

93 Rue Nationale, Boulogne-Billancourt, 92513 France
Tel.: (33) 1 4123 4123
Fax: (33) 1 4123 4240
E-Mail: contact@clm.bbdo.fr
Web Site: www.clmbbdo.com

Employees: 400

Marc Atallah *(Art Dir)*
Nicolas Demeersman *(Creative Dir)*
Adrien Sammut *(Acct Dir)*
Pascal Couvry *(Dir-Corp & New Bus)*
Julia Deshayes *(Dir-Artistic)*
Victor Mutel *(Dir-Artistic)*
Fiona Parkin *(Dir-Creative)*
Eric Pierre *(Dir-Creative)*
Romain Bruneau *(Acct Mgr-Intl)*
Margot Paquien *(Sr Acct Exec)*
Laurent Laporte *(Copywriter)*
Anthony Legrand *(Copywriter)*

Accounts:
1001 Fontaines
ALB Campaign: "Golden Chains Trailer"
Carlsberg Digital, Tuborg - Global Advertising
Diageo Guinness, Harp, Red Stripe
The Economist Campaign: "Take a Step Back"
EDF Advertising, Campaign: "Heroes"
Eurofil
Eurostar Online, Print
Foot Locker Europe
Football Resistance
Freedent
French Organ Donation Campaign: "The Mess"
Frolic
New-Guy Cotten Campaign: "A Trip Out to Sea"
HP Printers
La Redoute Campaign: "The Naked Man"
Mars, Incorporated Bounty, Campaign: "Add a Real Friend", Celebrations, Ice Cream, Pedigree
Mars North America
Mars Petfood Frolic
Masterkoo Campaign: "Prices Like This Are A No-Brainer"
Mercedes Benz Campaign: "Outsmart the City"
Ministry Of The Interior
Noe Conservation
OUI FM
Pepsi Campaign: "Crowd Surfing", France Adot, Frito-Lay
Plan Campaign: "The Erasable Billboard"
Procter & Gamble Oral-B
Smart Campaign: "Dejouez la Ville"
Snickers Campaign: "Metamorphosis", Campaign: "You're Not You When You're Hungry"
SOS Villages d'Enfants
Tag Heuer Campaign: "Don't Crack Under Pressure", Campaign: "Precision", Mikrograph Watch
Total Access Campaign: "Security Camera"
Total Fina Elf
Virginie Castaway
Wrigley Freedent Tabs White

Germany

BBDO Dusseldorf

Konigsallee 92, 40212 Dusseldorf, Germany
Tel.: (49) 211 1379 0
Fax: (49) 211 1379 8621
E-Mail: info@bbdo.de
Web Site: www.bbdo.de

Frank Lotze *(CEO)*
Darren Richardson *(Mng Dir & Chief Creative Officer)*
Marianne Hot *(CFO)*
Wolfgang Schneider *(Chief Creative Officer)*
Kristoffer Heilemann *(Mng Dir-Creative)*
Dirk Bittermann *(Gen Mgr)*
Carsten Bolk *(Exec Dir-Creative)*
Caner Ergel *(Art Dir)*
Michael Plueckhahn *(Creative Dir)*
Daniel Schweinzer *(Creative Dir)*
Christian Anhut *(Dir-Creative)*
Ines Bovenschen *(Dir-Art)*
Christoph Breitbach *(Dir-Creative)*
Andreas Breunig *(Dir-Art)*
Konstanze Bruhns *(Dir-Creative)*
Charlon De Graav *(Dir-Art)*
Shelley Lui *(Dir-Art)*
Angelo Maia *(Dir-Art)*
Achim Metzdorf *(Dir-Creative)*
Martino Monti *(Dir-Art)*
Fabian Pensel *(Dir-Art)*
Chris Robertson *(Dir-Creative)*
Sebastian Schlosser *(Dir-Client Svcs)*
Joerg Tavidde *(Dir-Creative)*
Karen Walker *(Dir-Creative)*
Ricardo Wolf *(Dir-Creative)*
Andy Wyeth *(Dir-Creative)*
Cass Zawadowski *(Dir-Creative-Global Braun Acct)*
Jake Shaw *(Assoc Dir-Creative)*
Penelope Abreu *(Copywriter)*

Accounts:
Ankerland e.V. Campaign: "Post-it War for Charity"
Bayer Vital Aspirin, Lefax, Medicine
Braun Campaign: "Hold On To Your Dreams", Campaign: "Piecemaker", Campaign: "Tame The Beast", Hairmoticons, Multiquick 7, Satin Hair 5 Multistyler
Caritas
Cemex
Christoffel Blindenmission Appeal For Money
Daimler AG Campaign: "Attention Assist", Campaign: "Going Home", Campaign: "Plug into a better world", Campaign: "World's first socket ad", Campaign: "smart EBALL", Mercedes Benz Campaign: "Bike", Mercedes Benz Campaign: "Occupy Wall Street", Mercedes Benz Campaign: "The first car park slot with a Mercedes-Benz workshop pit", Mercedes Benz Campaign: "Trucker Babies I" & Mercedes Benz Garage Service, Smart Electric Drive
Deutsche Post World Net
Deutscher Caritasverband International Campaign: "Progress", Charity
Dr. August Oetker Campaign: "The Pizzananny"
Dr. Oetker Campaign: "The Pizzananny", Ristorante
Globalization & Solidarity
Henkel Campaign: "You: A Declaration of Love", Schwarzkopf
Hewlett Packard
International Society For Human Rights Campaign: "Hangman"
Internationale Gesellschaft fuer Menschenrechte Campaign: "Hangman", Help to beat the death penalty
LBS
Madaus
Mars North America
Mars Snickers
Medicom Pharma Campaign: "Belly before and after", Campaign: "Target Heavy Food", Digestion Aid, Nobilin
Medimax
Melitta Campaign: "Back to awake", Campaign: "Twinkle", Coffee Filter Pods
Mercedes-Benz Trucks Campaign: "Cowgirl", Campaign: "Superhero", Campaign: "Tree of Life"
Pedigree Campaign: "The Freshest Dog Breath", Pedigree Dentastix Fresh
Pepsico Campaign: "Calory Sculpture", Campaign: "Iconic Refreshment", Campaign: "Veins"
Procter & Gamble Campaign: "Piecemaker", Campaign: "Vegetable Souffla", Campaign: "Wear Your Face", Oral-B
RTL Radio Center Campaign: "Equalizer Campaign Motive I", Spreeradio
Sennheiser
Siemens
Sky Go Campaign: "The Talking Window"
smart Center Berlin Bodypanel promotion, Fortwo, Smart EBall
Smart Fortwo; 2007
Spuk Pictures Image Library
Unesco Biosphere Entlebuch
New-UNIT9 Fashion Revolution The 2 Euro T-Shirt Vacuum Cleaner Bags
Westdeutsche Lotterie Campaign: "6x49 West Lotto"
Wrigley Campaign: "Dental Floss", Campaign: "Mint Parking Ticket", Chewing Gum, Extra Professional Polar-Frisch, Mint
WWF Ant Rally
Yello Strom Energy Provider

BBDO Proximity Berlin
(Formerly BBDO Berlin)
Hausvogteiplatz 2, 10117 Berlin, Germany
Tel.: (49) 30 340 0030
Fax: (49) 30 340 00320
E-Mail: berlin@bbdoproximity.de
Web Site: www.bbdo.de

Employees: 70
Year Founded: 1991

Wolfgang Schneider *(Chief Creative Officer)*
Jan Harbeck *(Mng Dir-Creative)*
Ton Hollander *(Mng Dir-Creative)*
Michael Schachtner *(Exec Creative Dir)*
Jennifer Cerchia *(Art Dir)*
Sebastien De Valck *(Creative Dir)*
Jan Dejonghe *(Creative Dir)*
Shelley Lui *(Art Dir)*
Angelo Maia *(Art Dir)*
Max Millies *(Creative Dir)*
Arnoud Pitz *(Creative Dir)*
Jessica Witt *(Art Dir)*
Lukas Liske *(Dir-Creative & Copywriter)*
Rene Rouleau *(Dir-Creative)*
Daniel Schweinzer *(Dir-Creative)*
Lauren Stillo *(Acct Mgr)*
Dries Floridor *(Copywriter)*
Nicolas Linde *(Copywriter)*

Accounts:
Allianz
New-Anheuser-Busch Companies, Inc. Beck's
Ankerland Campaign: "Post-It War for Charity"
Berlin Tourismus & Kongress
BUND Campaign: "Tree Concert"
Copic Campaign: "Great Ideas start with a Copic", Copic Marker
Daimler AG Campaign: "Bike", Campaign: "Facelift", Campaign: "Going Home", Campaign: "Louis Xiv", Campaign: "smart EBALL", MBVD Smart, Mercedes-Benz, The Smart Fortwo
Fashion Revolution
New-FRIESLAND Cecemel
Ha-Now Apotheke Campaign: "Son"
LBS
Mars M&M's
Medicom Pharma GmbH Campaign: "Target Heavy Food"
Pedigree
New-Penske Automotive Group
Radio Eins
RTL Radio Center Berlin Spreeradio
Sky Campaign: "The talking window", Sky Go
Smart Car Campaign: "Guess The Car"
Smart Fortwo Campaign: '"Offroad", Campaign: "FaceLift"
Smart Vertriebs Gmbh
Stadt Northeim
True Fruits GmbH
True Fruits Campaign: "The Green Screen Prank"

BBDO Stuttgart
Breitscheidstrasse 8, BOSCH-Areal, 70174 Stuttgart, Germany
Tel.: (49) 711 210 99 1 0
Fax: (49) 711 210 99 219
E-Mail: roland.gehrmann@bbdoproximity.de
Web Site: www.bbdo.de

Steffen Schulik *(CEO)*
Paul Fleig *(Mng Dir)*

Accounts:
Batten & Company
BBDO Berlin
BBDO Loders
BBDO Sales
Brand Implementation Group
Interone
Mercedes-Benz Garage Service
Peter SCHMIDT Group
Pleon
Proximity
Sell By Tell

Interone Worldwide
Therecienhoehe 12, D-80339 Munich, Germany
Tel.: (49) 8 955 1860
Fax: (49) 8 955 4194
E-Mail: impfang@interone.de
Web Site: www.interone.de

Employees: 120
Year Founded: 1986

Agency Specializes In: Direct Response Marketing

Michael Ohanian *(Chief Creative Officer)*
Thomas Heinz *(Exec Dir-Creative)*
Max Lederer *(Exec Dir-Creative)*
Matthias Schafer *(Executive Creative Dir)*
Christian Petersen *(Sr Dir-Art)*
Florian Barthelmess *(Dir-Creative)*
Marian Cizmarik *(Dir-Art)*
Till Heumann *(Dir-Art)*
Gregor Myszor *(Dir-Creative)*
Bjorn Neugebauer *(Dir-Creative)*
Jonathan Roolf *(Dir-Art)*

Accounts:
Beate Uhse Campaign: "Face Bra"
BMW BMW M235i, Campaign: "Night View", Campaign: "Power & Trees", Digital, Mini, Outdoor, Print
Burger King
DHL Log Book
DMAX
Dove.Com
Earth Link Campaign: "Avoid Plugin"
Elixia:Communication Relaunch
Euro Globe
FHM Magazine
Heinz
Horror Channel Night Terror App
Langenscheidt
Palmers Textil Campaign: "Happy Birthday To Hugh"
Plastic Pollution Coalition Campaign: "The Fossil"
Rechtsanwaelte Nourani & Wegener Campaign: "Quarrel"
Robin Wood
Saarland-Sporttoto Campaign: "Nonuplets"
Schweppes Campaign: "Ginger B"
Sunny Cars
Twentieth Century Fox
Whisk(e)y Shop Tara Campaign: "Some Time"

Greece

BBDO Athens
48 Ethnikis Antistaseos St, 152 31 Athens, Greece
Tel.: (30) 210 678 4000
Fax: (30) 210 674 2102
E-Mail: info@bbdoathens.gr

E-Mail for Key Personnel:
President: tprassin@ba.bbdogroup.gr

Employees: 50

National Agency Associations: EDEE

Tassos Prassinos *(Pres & CEO)*
Konstantina Grammatikaki *(Controller)*
Fay Apostolidou *(Gen Mgr)*
Theodosis Papanikolaou *(Exec Dir-Creative)*
Anna Andronladou *(Sr Dir-Art)*
David Kaneen *(Sr Dir-Art)*
Nikos Roussos *(Dir-Art)*
Marina Stathopoulou *(Dir-Art)*
Vicky Bourou *(Mgr-Production)*

Accounts:
Ikea
Motorola Solutions, Inc.
Pepsi
Volkswagen Group of America, Inc.
Wrigley

Ireland

Irish International BBDO
17 Gilford Road, Sandymount, Dublin, 4 Ireland
Tel.: (353) 1 206 0600
Fax: (353) 1 260 2111
E-Mail: email@irish-international.ie
Web Site: www.irishinternational.com

Employees: 100

Agency Specializes In: Advertising, Advertising Specialties, Business-To-Business, Communications, Consulting, Direct Response Marketing, Entertainment, Event Planning & Marketing, Production, Sales Promotion, Strategic Planning/Research

Dave McGloughlin *(Deputy Mng Dir)*
Dylan Cotter *(Exec Dir-Creative)*
Rachel Foley *(Art Dir)*
Ken Kerr *(Acct Dir)*
Paddy Geraghty *(Dir-Art)*
Kevin Leahy *(Dir-Art)*
Leo Moore *(Dir-Plng)*
Mal Stevenson *(Dir-Creative)*
David Power *(Acct Exec)*
Jean Donovan *(Copywriter)*
Dillon Elliott *(Copywriter)*
Rachel Haslam *(Planner)*
Fionan Healy *(Designer)*
Mark Nutley *(Deputy Dir-Creative)*

Accounts:
3 Ireland
98FM Advertising, Campaign: "Made of Dublin"
Barry's Tea; 1993
Brown Thomas
Castlethorn Construction; 1994
Centra
Diageo
Donegal Catch
EBS Building Society Creative; 1998
Electric Ireland Campaign: "Power"
Glanbia Consumer Foods
GlaxoSmithKline
Green Isle Foods
Guinness Beer, Campaign: "Physics"
Health & Safety Authority Rebuilding is Harder
HMV; 1994
Ikea
Independent Directory
Independent Newspapers; 1985
Irish Independent Campaign: "Choices", Campaign: "We Are Defined By The Choices We Make"
Kerrygold
Mars Dolmio, Extra, M&Ms, Mars, Orbit, Pedigree, Snickers, Twix, Uncle Bens, Whiskas, Wrigley; 1999
myhome.ie
National Transport Authority Campaign: "Connections"
Newstalk
Pepsico International; 2000
RHM Ireland; 1996
Road Safety Authority Campaign: "Anatomy of a Split Second", Campaign: "Steering Wheel", Creative
RSA Campaign: "Night Out"
Sony; 1994
Today FM
UPC
Walkers Snacks; 2000
Warner Brothers; 1993
Wrigley

Iceland

The Icelandic Ad Agency

Laufasvefur 49-51, 101 Reykjavik, Iceland
Tel.: (354) 511 4300
Fax: (354) 511 4301
E-Mail: islenska@islenska.is
Web Site: www2.islenska.is

Employees: 45

Atli Freyr Sveinsson *(Owner & CEO)*
Hjalti Jonsson *(Partner & Mng Dir)*
Helga Oskarsdottir *(Treas)*
Kristin Agnarsdottir *(Dir-Art)*
Sigtryggur Magnason *(Dir-Creative)*
Stone Steinsson *(Designer-Digital)*
Olafur Ingi Olafsson *(Sr Partner)*

Accounts:
Icelandair
Toyota
Vordur

Israel

Gitam/BBDO

8 Raul Wallenberg Street, Tel Aviv, 52522 Israel
Tel.: (972) 3 576 5757
Fax: (972) 3 612 2991
E-Mail: miri@gitam.co.il
Web Site: www.gitam.co.il

Employees: 130

Dror Tankus *(VP-Bus Dev)*
Sagi Blumberg *(Creative Dir)*
Keren Bachar Amitai *(Acct Dir)*
Yaron Perel *(Creative Dir)*
Shira Shayevitz *(Art Dir)*
Liron Batito *(Acct Mgr)*
Reut Esterkin *(Acct Mgr)*
Daniela Gardiner *(Acct Mgr)*
Shiran Haimovitch *(Acct Mgr)*
Odelya Stern *(Acct Mgr)*
Ronen Levin *(Copywriter)*
Lior Shvartz *(Copywriter)*
Yoav Sibony *(Copywriter)*
Yonatan Regev *(Acct Grp Mgr)*

Accounts:
Alfa Romeo
Alljobs
BMW 7 Series, Campaign: "Valet"
Diesenhaus Circule
Dr. Gav Campaign: "Around the world in 80 days"
Hapoalim Bank
Hishgad Campaign: "Car"
Hogla-Kimberly Campaign: "Clown-Cloud", Campaign: "Stop using newspapers", Nikol
Israel Cancer Association Campaign: "The Day the Radio Went Mono"
Israel National Lottery Campaign: "New Car"
Israeli Rett Foundation Campaign: "Creating a Discussion WIthout Saying a Word"
Israir Campaign: "A vacation is longer than just the days off", Campaign: "You've Reached Your Destination, Too Bad!"
Kleenex
Mif'al Hapais
Mini Cooper S Campaign: "Mini Bolt"
Naotur
Natur Travel Agency Campaign: "New York", Campaign: "Organized tours to hectic destinations"
Nikol Hogla Kimberly Campaign: "Sarkozy"
Office Depot Campaign: "Non Smoker Roommate"
Opel Corsa Campaign: "SMS Mistype"
Orbit
Osem Campaign: "Cucumber", Osem Light Salad Dressing
PepsiCo
Portfolio Night
RAM FM
Wrigley Campaign: "Chicken", Campaign: "Myths", Campaign: "Santa Claus", Hubba Bubba
Youth In Distress In Israel

Italy

D'Adda, Lorenzini, Vigorelli, BBDO

Via Lanzone 4, Milan, 20123 Italy
Tel.: (39) 02 880 071
Fax: (39) 02 880 07223
E-Mail: infomi@dlvbbdo.com
Web Site: www.dlvbbdo.com

Employees: 50
Year Founded: 1997

Agency Specializes In: Advertising

Romeo Repetto *(CEO)*
Siani Pepe *(Exec Creative Dir)*
Stefania Siani *(Exec Creative Dir)*
Stefania Cialone *(Sr Dir-Art)*
Daria D'Angelo *(Grp Acct Dir)*
Luca Iannucci *(Art Dir)*
Viora Jaccarino *(Art Dir)*
Chiara Niccolai *(Client Svcs Dir)*
Cristina Pontello *(Acct Dir)*
Vittorio Perotti *(Sr Art Dir & Designer)*
Andrea Jaccarino *(Dir-Digital Creative)*
Valerio Mangiafico *(Dir-Art)*
Sara Portello *(Dir-Creative)*
Valentina Amenta *(Assoc Dir-Creative)*
Davide Fiori *(Assoc Dir-Creative)*
Neli Mechenska *(Sr Acct Exec)*
Corinna Bonfanti *(Planner)*
Gennaro Borrelli *(Copywriter)*
Giovanni Coviello *(Copywriter)*
Alessandro Lapetina *(Copywriter)*

Accounts:
Action Aid Campaign: "Buffalo", Campaign: "Speakers"
Amici Cani Onlus Campaign: "A dog loves you whoever you are. Adopt one on amicicani.com", Campaign: "Killer"
Ariston Heating Campaign: "Find Your Perfect Temperature"
ASA ONLUS Aids World Day Campaign: "Bear, Octopus, Cat"
Assamicispagnolli
Bayer Aktiengesellschaft Aspirina
BBiGB
BMW Italia
British Sky Broadcasting Group
CAM Campaign: "Horses in the Wood", Campaign: "The Child's World", Campaign: "When I Grow Up I want to be a tailor for shadows", Campaign: "When I Grow Up"
Campari Group
Cargill Sow Solutions Animal Nutriment Campaign: "A Heritage in Creating The Best Class"
Casa Damiani
Cielo TV
Daimler Campaign: "Ad Color is up to You", Campaign: "Sad Gas Station", Mercedes Benz
Editrice Quadratum Campaign: "Back to Rock"
Emmentaler
Fiera Internazionale D'Arte Moderna E Contemporanea Campaign: "Mi Art"
Freddy Campaign: "Body Transmission", Campaign: "Vase"
Gatorade Campaign: "Tennis, Soccer"
Giochi di Luce
Henkel AG & Co. KGaA
LA7 Television
LaStampa Newspaper
Marionnaud Campaign: "Clap", Skin Cream
Mars Italia Catsan
Mars North America
Metzeler
Mondelez
Motorola Solutions, Inc.
Oxydo
Parisian Gentleman Campaign: "Ladies"
Pfizer Animal Health Campaign: "Turtle Caretta Caretta"
Philadelphia Campaign: "Lactose Free Launch"
Pirelli Real Estate
Procter & Gamble ORAL B
Purina Campaign: "Your dairy cool off from inside out."
Rolling Stone Magazine Campaign: "Back To Rock"
Romaeuropa Foundation Campaign: "All That We Can Do", Performing Arts Festival
Safilo Group S.p.A. Campaign: "After All No Regrets", Campaign: "Tell Your Story", Carrera
Sky Bar Beach Umbrellas
Smart Campaign: "Candies"
Sognid'oro Chamomile Tea Campaign: "Don't drink and drive"
Spi
Stage Entertainment Campaign: "Sister Act"
Star Sognid'oro Campaign: "Don't Drink & Drive"
Telecom Italia
Titanbet.it Campaign: "Game Never Stop"
TotalFinaElf
VS Magazine
Wall Street English Campaign: "Online Encounters", Campaign: "Open New Roads To Your Future", Campaign: "Piano"
Wenner Media LLC Campaign: "Our Belief"
Yamaha Motor Co., Ltd. Campaign: "Asphalt Desert", Campaign: "Fast", Campaign: "Out of Sync Life", Campaign: "Teaser", Campaign: "The wait is over", Campaign: "Wake-up", Campaign: "We R 1", F40, Super Tenere, Yamaha MT-07, Yamaha Marine Motor, Yamaha R1

Lebanon

Impact BBDO

Bldg 635 Omar Daouk Street Jumblatt Area, Ain-Mreysseh, Beirut, Lebanon
Tel.: (961) 1 367 890
Fax: (961) 1 367 567
E-Mail: info@impactbbdo.com.lb
Web Site: www.impactbbdo.com

Employees: 80

Joe Ayache *(Grp Mng Dir)*
Dani Richa *(Chm/CEO-MENA & Pakistan)*
Karim Diab *(Gen Mgr)*
Lyna Domiati *(Sr Dir-Art)*
Georges Kyrillos *(Sr Dir-Art)*
Ali Zein *(Reg Dir-Creative)*
Sharbel Jreish *(Art Dir)*
Angelo El Chami *(Assoc Dir-Creative)*
Hovsep Guerboyan *(Assoc Dir-Creative)*
Nadine Jabbour *(Copywriter)*

Accounts:
ACAL
Altadis Brilliant, Gauloises, Gitanes, Royale
An Nahar
Audi Q7
BankMed
BASSMA Lebanese Humanitarian Organization
BeautyTech
BLOM Bank
Cheyef 7alak
Continental Real Estate
Ets. Khalil Fattal & Fils
FDC Canderel, Manitoba, Nana, Parmalat, Peaudouce, Vape
Fransabank
Greenpeace
The Journey
Kawasaki Ninja ZX-14R

Kettaneh & Sons Campaign: "The Phone Call"
Lay's
LBCI Campaign: "Abou Warde", Campaign: "Ward el Khal", LBCI Drama
LibanPost
New-M TV Bananas
Mars
Masterfoods Middle East Maltesers, Uncle Ben's
Ministry of Tourism Lebanon Campaign: "Don't Go To Lebanon"
Nissan Juke
Okaz Organization for Press & Publication
Pepsi
Qtel
Rymco
Sama Beirut
Samsung 3D Televisions, X420 Notebook
Saudi Oger
SGBL
Sharp
Siblou
VW

Kuwait

Impact BBDO
Sharq Mutanaby St Bldg No 42, Safat 13071, 21081 Kuwait, Kuwait
Tel.: (965) 2 438 120
Fax: (965) 2 440 306
E-Mail: impactinfo@alghanim.com
Web Site: www.impactbbdo.com

Employees: 37

Oussama Gholmieh *(Mng Dir)*
Mounir Bou Malhab *(Sr Dir-Art)*
Patrick Semaan *(Sr Dir-Digital Art)*
Moudi Yafi *(Sr Dir-Art)*
Hussein Hammoud *(Grp Acct Dir)*
Abdulkader El Samadi *(Acct Dir)*
Akram Rehayel *(Dir-Art)*
Ahmed Waheib *(Dir-Digital Art)*
Kareem Zalatimo *(Dir-Digital Art)*
Mohammed Tayeh *(Sr Graphic Designer)*

Accounts:
ALDAR
Barclays
BlackBerry
Chrysler
Citizen
Dubai Properties
Emirates
Gulf Bank Campaign: "Running"
Mars Inc. Snickers
PepsiCo
Philips
Pizza Hut
Tatweer
Wataniya Telecom Campaign: "Round Pizzas in Square Boxes?"

Lithuania

Lukrecija BBDO
K Kalinausko 2B, LT-03107 Vilnius, Lithuania
Tel.: (370) 5 2338 383
Fax: (370) 5 2163 037
E-Mail: lukrecija@lukrecija.lt
Web Site: www.lukrecija.lt

Employees: 30

Marius Vaupsas *(Mng Partner)*
Gintas Lapenas *(Partner & Sr Dir-Creative)*

Accounts:
AIBE
HP Invent
Hewlett Packard
International Organization for Migration
JMVMC
Lays
Lietuvos Telekomas
Lintel
M2 Invest
Mars North America Bounty, Cheetos, Snickers, Uncle Ben's
Pedigree
Ranga Group
TEO Telecommunications Company
Uncle Bens
Vilnius
Vox
Whiskas

Macedonia

Ovation BBDO
(Formerly Ovation Advertising)
Guro Gakovik 56, Skopje, 1000 Macedonia
Tel.: (389) 2 3212 983
Fax: (389) 2 3212 9020
E-Mail: ovation@mt.net.mk
Web Site: www.ovation.rs

Employees: 11

Elena Stefanova *(Mng Dir)*
Aleksandra Lukik *(Acct Exec)*

Accounts:
Alkaloid
Kraft
Macedonian Telecommunication
Mi-Da
Mtnet
Ovi Produkt
Pepsi
Prigat
Wrigley
Zito Luks

Netherlands

FHV BBDO
Amsterdamseweg 204, 1182 HL Amstelveen, Netherlands
Tel.: (31) 20 543 7777
Fax: (31) 20 543 7500
E-Mail: info@fhv.bbdo.nl
Web Site: www.fhv.bbdo.nl

Employees: 60

Arnd-Jan Gulmans *(Head-Strategy)*
Mark Muller *(Exec Dir-Creative)*
John De Vries *(Sr Dir-Art)*
Daniel Samama *(Sr Dir-Art)*
Iain Howe *(Client Svcs Dir)*
Peter Burger *(Dir-RTV)*
Bas De Graaf *(Dir-Design)*
Thomas Overweg *(Dir-Art)*
Eke Rog *(Dir-Creative)*

Accounts:
Amsterdam Airport Schiphol
Amsterdam Sex Cinema Venus
Artis
Bayer
Blackberry
Botergoud
Caesar
Chrysler Netherlands Caliber
Ctaste Campaign: "Dining In The Dark"
Daimler AG
DHL Campaign: "Wedeliver"
Douwe Egberts
The Economist Campaign: "Surprising Reads"
Eneco Campaign: "Balloon Race"
Eurostar
G-Star Raw
Hi 4G Mobile Provider, Campaign: "Running"
Jeep
Jumbo
KLM Royal Dutch Airlines
Mars North America
Mars Campaign: "Hungry Faces", M&M, Snickers
Mercedes Benz Campaign: "Creating Day at Night"
Pepsi Campaign: "Kicks like Boom"
Peter Zijlstra
Procter & Gamble Health & Beauty Care Limited
Procter & Gamble Switzerland Sarl
Procter & Gamble Oral-B, Total
Quaker
Reclame Arsenaal
Robeko
Royal FrieslandCampina N.V
Shell
Van Gogh Museum
World Animal Protection

Poland

BBDO
Ul Burakowska 5/7, 01-066 Warsaw, Poland
Tel.: (48) 22 532 9500
Fax: (48) 22 5329 600
E-Mail: info@bbdo.com.pl
Web Site: www.bbdo.pl

Employees: 75

Ewa Keciek *(Controller-Fin)*
Magdalena Kramer *(Sr Dir-Art)*
Karina Komorowska *(Grp Acct Dir)*
Anna Kondracka *(Grp Acct Dir)*
Agata Ciecierska *(Bus Dir)*
Gosia Guryn *(Acct Dir)*
Maja Laudanska *(Acct Dir-Digital)*
Kamil Redestowicz *(Creative Dir)*
Michal Nowosielski *(Dir-Creative)*
Alicja Taboryska *(Copywriter)*

Accounts:
Allianz
Bayer
BRE
DHL Express
Kokoda Insect Repellent Campaign: "I'm Not Afraid of No Wasps"
Lay's Max Campaign: "Describe the Lay's Max"
Mars North America
Mars Polska
New-Mercedes Benz Poland
Motorola Solutions, Inc.
Mugga Campaign: "Mosquitoes don't like you anymore"
PepsiCo Frito Lay Poland
Photoby Campaign: "Finger Industries", Campaign: "Peter Tarka"
Procter & Gamble
Total Polska
Wrigley Orbit for Kids

Portugal

BBDO Portugal
Av Eng Duarte Pancheco, No.26, 12th Andar, 1070-110 Lisbon, Portugal
Tel.: (351) 21 891 0500
Fax: (351) 21 891 0545
E-Mail: info@bbdo.pt
Web Site: www.bbdo.pt

Employees: 60

Agency Specializes In: Advertising, Consumer Publications

Rui Silva *(Chief Creative Officer)*
Pedro Goncalves *(Head-Digital & Copywriter-*

Creative)
Rita Bastos *(Acct Dir)*
Hugo Carvalheiro *(Art Dir)*
Paula Cardoso *(Dir-Strategic Plng)*
Marco Pacheco *(Dir-Creative)*
Ruben Rodrigues *(Dir-Art)*
Joao Vasconcelos *(Dir-Bus Dev)*

Accounts:
Arkocapsulas Campaign: "Alleviation", Campaign: "Relief", Campaign: "Riddance"
Banco Espirito Santo Campaign: "A Change in Life"
Bayer
Bes
Cig Campaign: "How Many Reconciliations"
Delta Cafes
Gallo
Galp Fuel
Jumbo
Lisbon Airport Campaign: "Flyers choose Lisbon"
Mars North America
Mercedes-Benz
PepsiCo Frito-Lay
Smart
ZON

Romania

Graffiti BBDO
Gheorghe Manu Street 3 District 1, Bucharest, 010422 Romania
Tel.: (40) 21 316 0200
Fax: (40) 1 316 0207
E-Mail: melania_stoleru@graffiti.bbdo.ro
Web Site: www.graffiti.bbdo.ro

Employees: 150

Cosmin Radoi *(Mng Dir)*
Diana Tobosaru *(COO)*
Gelu Florea *(Dir-Art & Designer)*
Ovidiu Hodorogea *(Dir-Art)*
Sorin Psatta *(Dir-Integrated Comm)*

Accounts:
4 Proof Film Campaign: "Henvertising", Domestic
Allianz
Aspirin
Bayer Aspirin Plus C
BGS Security
Capital Newspaper
Carturesti
Dacia
Domestic Campaign: "Henvertising"
Dr. Oetker
Foreign Policy Romania
Gaudeamus
Mars North America
Mars Snickers
Mediafax Group Campaign: "Changing the Headlines"
Panasonic Campaign: "The Music Guardians"
PepsiCo Campaign: "The Bottle that Connected Generations", Frito Lay, Mountain Dew
Romtelecom
SBS Broadcasting Media
Winterfresh
Wrigley Romania Campaign: "The After Meal Tenants"

Russia

BBDO Moscow
20 Building 1 4th Tverskaya-Yamskaya, Moscow, 125047 Russia
Tel.: (7) 495 787 5778
Fax: (7) 495 787 5779
E-Mail: contact@bbdo.ru
Web Site: bbdogroup.ru

Employees: 300

National Agency Associations: RAAA

Agency Specializes In: Consumer Marketing, Media Buying Services

Megvelidze Nikolay *(Chief Creative Officer)*
Ella Stewart *(Chm/CEO-BBDO Grp)*
Andrey Brayovich *(Exec Dir-Integrated Projects & Dir-Media)*
Igor Lutz *(Exec Dir-Creative)*
Yaroslav Orlov *(Exec Dir-Creative)*
Michael Druzhinin *(Sr Dir-Art)*
Andrey Kuznetsov *(Sr Dir-Art)*
Darya Arkharova *(Grp Acct Dir)*
Elena Vorobyova *(Grp Acct Dir)*
Alexey Fedorov *(Creative Dir)*
Mihai Coliban *(Dir-Creative)*
Roman Firainer *(Dir-Creative)*
Tokarev Konstantin *(Dir-Art)*
Sergey Kozhevnikov *(Dir-Creative)*
Tkachenko Michael *(Dir-Art)*
Coliban Mihai *(Dir-Creative)*
Kozhevnikov Sergey *(Dir-Creative)*
Mikhail Tkachenko *(Dir-Art)*
Anastasia Babuchenko *(Sr Acct Mgr)*
Boris Sorokin *(Sr Acct Mgr)*
Maria Urnova *(Sr Acct Mgr)*
Maria Ustkachkinseva *(Sr Acct Mgr)*
Anastasia Bulashchenko *(Acct Mgr)*
Ekaterina Konovalova *(Acct Mgr)*
Luiza Vasyutina *(Acct Mgr)*
Daria Artamonova *(Copywriter)*
Ponomarev Maxim *(Copywriter)*
Evgeniy Shinyaev *(Copywriter)*
Marina Shponko *(Art Buyer)*
Inna Zharova *(Key Acct Mgr-Digital)*

Accounts:
3M Company Post-it
AFK Sistema
Azbuka vkusa
Bayer Healthcare Aleve, AntiFlu, Aspirin, Nazol, Salin
Eldorado Eldorado
Exxon Mobile CVL, Industrial, PVL
Frito Lay Cheetos, Khrus Team, Lays
Gallo Gallo
Ginza Project Oki Doki, Pesto Cafe
Glorix Campaign: "Blood Portraits"
Ikea Campaign: "Kitchen View"
Inmarko Carte D'or, Ekzo, San-Kremo, Zolotoi Standard
INTOUCH Insurance company
Intouch Campaign: "Car Vs Piano"
New-Klinsky Sausage
Mars UK Ltd. Bounty, Cesar, Dolmio, Dove, M&M's, Maltesers, Mars, Milky Way, Pedigree, Perfect Fit, Sheba, Snickers, Twix, Whiskas
Melon Fashion Group Love Republic
Mercedes-Benz Mercedes-Benz, Smart
MSD Pharmaceuticals Erious
MTS
OBI Campaign: "Canyon", Campaign: "No Job Is Too Big"
O'KEY
PepsiCo 7 UP, Mirinda, Pepsi Max, Pepsi-Cola
Pfizer Champix, Viagra
Procter & Gamble
PRODO Klinskiy
Progress Frutonyanya
RSA Campaign: "Mortal Timeline", InTouch
RTH Hair Transplantation Service
Sberbank
Upeco Gardex, Salton
Visa
Wrigley Eclipse Gum, FIVE, Orbit

Saudi Arabia

Impact BBDO
Ali Reza Tower 1st Floor Medina Road, PO Box 7242, Jeddah, 21462 Saudi Arabia
Tel.: (966) 2 651 5556
Fax: (966) 2 651 6602
E-Mail: info.jed@impactbbdo.com
Web Site: www.impactbbdo.com

Employees: 45

Agency Specializes In: Consumer Marketing, Merchandising

Walid Kanaan *(Chief Creative Officer)*
Peter Zagalsky *(Grp Acct Dir)*
Shafiq Alam *(Creative Dir)*
Samer Khansa *(Bus Dir)*
Moe Sarhi *(Creative Dir)*
Ribal Sibaee *(Acct Dir)*

Accounts:
Al Mutlaq; Jeddah
Al Rajh
New-Celeste Spring Mattress
The Emirates Group
Energya Industries
Frito Lay Cheetos, Creative, Lay's, Tassali
Fuchs
Green Farms
Hadeed
Hero Group
Jazan Economic City
LG
Luna
Okaz Organisation for Press & Publication Campaign: "Buckle Up"
OSN
P&G
Pepsi 7UP, Creative, Pepsi
PMDC
Sabic Steel
Saudi Aramco
Saudi Gazette

Serbia & Montenegro

Ovation Advertising
Bulevar Arsenija Carnojevica 99V, 11070 Belgrade, Serbia
Tel.: (381) 11 313 91 20
Fax: (381) 11 313 91 22
E-Mail: office@ovation.rs
Web Site: www.ovation.rs

Employees: 27

Dragoslav Illic *(CFO)*
Natasia Filipovic *(Mng Dir-Ovation BBDO)*
Miljan Spasic *(Head-Creative)*
Brankica Ilic *(Dir-Art)*
Marko Marjanovic *(Mgr-Content & Community Mgr)*
Sonja Kalusevic *(Acct Exec)*
Marko Pesic *(Client Svc Dir)*

Slovak Republic

Mark BBDO
Zamocka 5, PO Box 301, 814 99 Bratislava, Slovakia
Tel.: (421) 2 5441 1331
Fax: (421) 2 5441 1324
E-Mail: mark@bbdo.sk

Employees: 30
Year Founded: 1992

Michal Blaha *(Mng Dir)*

Accounts:
BC Torsion
BMB Leiner
Bayer
Chrysler

Hewlett-Packard
Istrobanka
Istroleasing
Miele
Nubium
Tondach

South Africa

140 BBDO
30 Chiappini Street, Cape Town, 8001 South Africa
Tel.: (27) 214800400
Fax: (27) 214800686
Web Site: www.140bbdo.com

Agency Specializes In: Advertising

Adrian Varkel *(Mng Dir)*
Keith Shipley *(CEO-South Africa)*
Ivan Johnson *(Exec Dir-Creative)*
Chuma Obumselu *(Exec Dir-Creative)*
Matt Riley *(Grp Dir-Plng)*
Alexis Beckett *(Dir-Creative)*
Stephanie Symonds *(Dir-Art)*

Accounts:
Adidas
Cadiz Financial Services
Distell Campaign: "Hunter's Refreshed", Campaign: "Mastery in the Making", Campaign: "Oude Meester Style Guide"
Good Hope FM
iFix
Mercedes-Benz of South Africa (Pty.) Ltd. CL 63 AMG, Campaign: "Test Drive"
New Media Publishing Campaign: "Visi Covet"
Oude Meester Brandy, Campaign: "A prize as rare as the diamond it holds", Campaign: "Mastery In The Making", Campaign: "To the Masters"
SABC Campaign: "Mobile Band"

Net#work BBDO
East Block, Dunkeld Office Park, Albury Road Jansmuts Avenue, Hyde Park Gauteng, 2196 South Africa
Mailing Address:
Private Bag X15, Benmore, 2010 South Africa
Tel.: (27) 11 912 0000
Fax: (27) 11 447 4529
Web Site: www.networkbbdo.co.za

Employees: 65
Year Founded: 1994

National Agency Associations: ACA

Keith Shipley *(CEO)*
Clinton Mitri *(COO)*
Michael Schalit *(Chief Creative Officer)*
Gautham Narayanan *(Deputy Mng Dir-BBDO South Africa & Reg Dir-BBDO Africa)*
Alexis Beckett *(Dir-Creative)*
Donovan Goliath *(Dir-Art)*
Ryan Paikin *(Dir-Art)*
Brent Singer *(Dir-Creative)*
James Nondo *(Acct Mgr)*
Zak Madatt *(Mgr-HR)*
Chad Goddard *(Copywriter)*
Gabi Goldstein *(Client Svc Dir)*

Accounts:
&Beyond
Chicken Licken Campaign: "Hotwings Strike", Campaign: "Mammoth", Campaign: "Orphanage", Campaign: "Slyders", Campaign: "XL Hotwings", Fast Food Chain
Coronation Fund Managers
Cricket SA
Exclusive Books Campaign: "Reading Is Rewarding"
Galderma Benzac AC5 Gel, Campaign: "Piles"
Gumtree South Africa
JSE (Johannesburg Stock Exchange Securities)
Lays
Mercedes-Benz Blue Efficiency, Campaign: "Attention Assist", Campaign: "Boss", Campaign: "Cabo", Campaign: "Distance to Danger", Campaign: "Night View Assist: Dark Horse", Campaign: "Reunion", Campaign: "The Triangle Knows", Pre-Safe
National Kidney Foundation of South Africa Campaign: "Patricia & Vanita"
Pepsi
Road Accident Fund Campaign: "Night Shift"
Simba Ghost Pops
Snickers
Webber Wentzel Campaign: "Censorship"

Spain

Contrapunto
C/Cardenal Marcelo Spinola Sp # 4-4a Planta, 28016 Madrid, Spain
Tel.: (34) 91 787 2000
Fax: (34) 91 787 2001
E-Mail: contrapunto@contrapuntobbdo.es
Web Site: www.contrapuntobbdo.es

Employees: 125

Carlos Martinez-Cabrera *(Pres)*
Jofre Biscarri *(Dir-Creative)*
Carlos De Javier *(Dir-Creative)*
Aurora Hidalgo *(Dir-Art)*
Jesus Navas *(Dir-Art)*
Paco Ribera *(Dir-Gen Accounts)*

Accounts:
Adena
Amnesty International Campaign: "Countries", Campaign: "Terrorists"
Banco Gallego
Chrysler LLC
Clicker Airlines
Complot Creativity School Campaign: "Bridge & Braid", Typography Course
Daimler AG
FAADA Campaign: "Gorilla", Campaign: "Lion"
Fundacion Reina Sofia Campaign: "Bank of Memories"
Galp
Gas Natural Fenosa Campaign: "Sometimes"
Getxo Photo Festival Campaign: "Manuel", Campaign: "Office"
Hewlett Packard Campaign: "Door Flaps"
Kirira Foundation Campaign: "Bronze & Ivory Woman"
Mango Campaign: "The Coolhunting Experience"
Mercedes-Benz Campaign: "Balls", Campaign: "Spaces"
Pizza&Love Olive, Pineapple, Sausage
Procter & Gamble Campaign: "Sandpaper Man Help Foundation"
Reckitt Benckiser Campaign: "New York"
Reflex Spray Campaign: "Neverending marathon"
Smart Campaign: "Coupe-Cabrio", Smart Cars
WWF Campaign: "Beheaded Boy", Campaign: "No Water, No Life", Campaign: "Water Colors"

Tiempo BBDO
Tuset 5 6a, 08006 Barcelona, Spain
Tel.: (34) 93 306 9000
Fax: (34) 93 202 0278
E-Mail: tiempo@bbdo.es
Web Site: www.tiempobbdo.com

Employees: 38

Agency Specializes In: Direct Response Marketing, Media Buying Services, Public Relations, Sales Promotion

Julio Paredes *(Gen Mgr)*
Bibiana Del Alcazar *(Exec Dir-Strategy & Comm)*
Pepa Bartolome *(Exec Dir-Strategy & Comm)*
Maria Pilar Palos Nadal *(Exec Dir-Strategy & Comm)*
Tomas Ferrandiz *(Sr Dir-Creative)*
Marta Bargallo *(Dir-Strategy & Comm)*
Jordi Comas *(Dir-Creative Content)*
Marta Quirant *(Dir-Creative)*
Montse Serra *(Office Mgr)*

Accounts:
Allianz
Bayer
Fundacion Once Campaign: "Luis Castros Videocurriculum"
Marcilla
McDonald's
PepsiCo Frito-Lay, Matutano
Roca Campaign: "Roca Loves The Planet"
Sony Electronics Video Camera
We Are Water Foundation Campaign: "Barcelona World Race"

Sweden

ANR BBDO
David Bagares gata 5, Box 5438, 114 84 Stockholm, Sweden
Tel.: (46) 8 555 77600
Fax: (46) 8 555 77699
E-Mail: mail.sthlm@anrbbdo.se
Web Site: www.anrbbdo.se

Employees: 25

Anna Jensen *(Partner & Dir-Strategic Plng)*
Fredrick Tamtzerhielm *(Mng Dir)*
Camilla Westman *(Head-PR)*
Fredrik Pantzerhielm *(Acct Dir)*
Marcus Goransson *(Dir-Art)*
Giustina Guariglia *(Sr Acct Mgr)*
Jacqueline Nyman *(Sr Acct Mgr)*
Maria Fager *(Acct Mgr)*
Stephanie Moradi *(Copywriter)*

Accounts:
Arla Foods Campaign: "Milk Carton"
ESET Campaign: "Go Explore", Online, Print, Social Media
Hyresgastforeningen
TCO
ume.net Campaign: "Living With Lag", Campaign: "The Lag Stress Test"
Unionen Campaign: "Organizerman in Trouble", Campaign: "The Tank Truck"

ANR BBDO
Nils Ericssonplatsen 3, 411 03 Gothenburg, Sweden
Tel.: (46) 31 727 75 00
Fax: (46) 31 727 75 99
E-Mail: info@anr.se
Web Site: www.anr.se

Employees: 24

Andreas Lonn *(Partner & Dir-Creative)*

Accounts:
Chrysler Dodge
EAA
Festis
IFK Goteborg
Intersport
Nycomed Campaign: "Valentine'S Day - For The Broken Hearted"
Synsam Swedish Open

Switzerland

Wirz Werbung AG

Uetlibergstrasse 132, 8045 Zurich, Switzerland
Tel.: (41) 44 457 57 57
Fax: (41) 44 457 57 50
E-Mail: info@wirz.ch
Web Site: www.wirz.ch

Employees: 120

National Agency Associations: BSW

Agency Specializes In: Advertising

Petra Dreyfus *(Mng Dir)*
Rinaldo Poltera *(CFO)*
Livio Dainese *(Exec Dir-Creative)*
Fernando Perez *(Exec Dir-Creative)*
Yves Ruckert *(Grp Acct Dir)*
Caspar Heuss *(Creative Dir)*
Wolfgang Bark *(Copywriter)*
Simon Smit *(Copywriter)*

Accounts:
Bischofszell Nahrungsmittel Campaign: "Terra Chips Flavour Generator"
Caran d'Ache Campaign: "Let it Out, Blue", Campaign: "White", Crayons
Christoffel Blindenmission Campaign: "Shadow Faces"
Die Mobiliar
Ikea Campaign: "Ikea Home.ch", Campaign: "Ikea Rothenburg", Campaign: "No Empty Chairs"
Marionnaud Campaign: "Fragrance Pairs", Campaign: "Hair"
Mars Campaign: "Excelcat"
Migros
Nu Schweiz Campaign: "Find The Teacher"
Pepsi-Cola
Reformierte Landeskirche Campaign: "The Protestant"
Salvation Army
Small World Language Studies Worldwide
Swiss Assurance Mobiliar
Tibits Vegetarian Restaurant Campaign: "Natural Energy"
Travel Book Shop

Turkey

Alice BBDO

Maslak Mah Dereboyu Caddesi Bilim Solak No 5 Sun Plaza, BBDO Blok Sisli, 34398 Istanbul, Turkey
Tel.: (90) 212 276 6446
Fax: (90) 212 376 9150
E-Mail: info@bbdo.com.tr
Web Site: www.bbdo.com

Employees: 60

Richard Anderson *(Owner)*
Haluk Sicimoglu *(Chief Strategy Officer-BBDO Turkey)*
Ahmet Ulku *(Sr Dir-Art)*
Itir Karabulut *(Acct Supvr)*

Accounts:
Arzum Campaign: "The Power of Cleanart"
Aspirin
Bayer
Cheetos
Chrysler
Daimler AG
Diageo
Dr. Oetker
Fa
Lays
Mamasepeti.com Online Pet Store
Marks & Spencer
Mars North America
Mercedes-Benz Campaign: "Mercedes Sprinter Builder"
Nestle Waters Campaign: "Hushh"
One A Day
PepsiCo Frito-Lay
Pera Taxi
Smart
Subaru
Talcid
Tatilsepeti.com Campaign: "Elopenzi", Travel Site
Teknosa Campaign: "Teknosa Cinema Dvd Menu"
Vidal Sassoon Turkey
Wrigley

Ukraine

Provid BBDO

3 Lev Tolstoy Str, Kiev, 01004 Ukraine
Tel.: (380) 44 246 6172
Fax: (380) 44 246 6173
Web Site: provid.ua

Employees: 30

Agency Specializes In: Outdoor, Print, T.V.

Dmitry Adabir *(Mng Dir)*
Yevgeniya Bodnar *(Acct Dir)*
Kirill Chickan *(Creative Dir)*
Roman Davydyuk *(Dir-Art)*
Alexander Rogovets *(Dir-Art)*
Vlad Ryzhykov *(Dir-Art)*
Denis Shvets *(Dir-Art)*
Sergii Zinoviev *(Dir-Creative)*
Oksana Peicheva *(Client Svc Dir)*

Accounts:
Pepsico Campaign: "Eyes"
Revo
Tetra Pak

United Arab Emirates

Impact BBDO

Emirates Office Tower 17th Fl Sheikh Zayed Rd, PO Box 19791, Dubai, United Arab Emirates
Tel.: (971) 4 330 4010
Fax: (971) 4 330 4009
E-Mail: info@impactbbdo.ae
Web Site: www.impactbbdo.com

Employees: 600

Douglas Palau *(Mng Dir & VP)*
Dani Richa *(Chm/CEO-MENA & Pakistan)*
Karim Khouri *(Gen Mgr)*
Luiz Cutolo *(Sr Dir-Art)*
Micky Huang *(Sr Dir-Art)*
Samantha Stuart-Palmer *(Grp Acct Dir)*
Mostaf Kawtharani *(Art Dir & Copywriter)*
Ribal Sibaee *(Acct Dir)*
Paul Fayad *(Dir-Creative)*
Moe Sarhi *(Dir-Creative)*
Aunindo Sen *(Dir-Creative)*
Gautam Wadher *(Dir-Creative-Dubai, UAE)*
Daniel Correa *(Assoc Dir-Creative)*
Khaled Said *(Assoc Dir-Creative)*
Dinesh Tharippa *(Assoc Dir-Creative)*
Katie Guy *(Sr Acct Mgr)*
Laila Elchiati *(Acct Mgr)*
Lina Ghulam *(Acct Mgr)*
Tanya Vahanian *(Acct Mgr)*
Chelsea Frangie *(Creative)*
Marie Claire Maalouf *(Assoc Creative Dir)*
Bana Salah *(Sr Designer-Creative)*
Fadi Yaish *(Reg Exec Dir-Creative)*

Accounts:
Al Sabeh Cement
Aspirin
Axiom Telecom Marketing Communications
Bridgestone Tyres Campaign: "Tire Safety Wall"
Commercial Insurance
Dunlop
Duracell
Emirates Campaign: "All-Time Greats"
Etisalat Creative
Faber-Castell Campaign: "Panther"
Foods & Drug Corporation
Frontera
Johnson & Johnson Band Aid, Campaign: "Small Wounds Big Stories", Campaign: "The Grandparents Frame", Johnson's Baby
Loto Libanais
Majid Al Futtaim Leisure & Entertainment Do Something Different
Mars North America Campaign: "Life's Lighter With Maltesers", Maltesers, Snickers, Twix
Mercedes-Benz C63 AMG
National Bonds Corporation
PepsiCo International
SADAFCO Campaign: "Don't Let Your Bones Break Your Dreams"
Sadia
Samsung S1 Mini HDD
Saudia Dairy& Foodstuff Company
Schwarzkopf Campaign: "Your Canvas", Campaign: "Your Hair", Palette
Snopake
UN Women Campaign: "Give Mom Back Her Name", Social Media
Vape
William Wrigley Jr. Company Campaign: "Mermaid", Campaign: "Where skittles come from", Skittles Sour, Skittles Sweets, Wrigley

United Kingdom

Abbott Mead Vickers BBDO

151 Marylebone Rd, London, NW1 5QE United Kingdom
Tel.: (44) 20 7616 3500
Fax: (44) 207 616 3600
Web Site: www.amvbbdo.com

Employees: 350

Agency Specializes In: Consumer Marketing

Cilla Snowball *(Grp Chm & Grp CEO)*
Clive Tanqueray *(Mng Partner)*
Tim Riley *(Partner-Creative & Head-Copy)*
Richard Arscott *(Mng Dir)*
Gregory Roekens *(CTO)*
Jonny Spindler *(Chief Innovation Officer)*
Sarah Douglas *(Sr VP & Acct Mgmt Dir)*
Alex Grieve *(Exec Dir-Creative)*
Adrian Rossi *(Exec Dir-Creative)*
Milo Campbell *(Creative Dir & Copywriter)*
Steve Jones *(Creative Dir)*
Michael Logan *(Acct Dir)*
Caroline Story *(Art Dir)*
Gary Lathwell *(Dir-Art & Writer)*
Phil Martin *(Dir-Creative & Copywriter)*
Vicky Allard *(Dir-Comm)*
Toby Allen *(Dir-Creative)*
Dalatando Almeida *(Dir-Art)*
Neil Clarke *(Dir-Creative)*
Clark Edwards *(Dir-Creative)*
Arvid Harnqvist *(Dir-Art)*
Jim Hilson *(Dir-Creative)*
Colin Jones *(Dir-Creative & Art)*
Michael Jones *(Dir-Art)*
Rich Littler *(Dir-Art)*
Ant Nelson *(Dir-Creative)*
Andrew Pinkess *(Dir-Bus Innovation)*
Mike Sutherland *(Dir-Creative)*
Jeremy Tribe *(Dir-Art)*
Ned Patterson *(Acct Mgr)*
Rob Ronayne *(Acct Mgr)*
Alan Foster *(Copywriter)*
Annalisa Gentili *(Planner)*
Mike Hughes *(Copywriter)*
Nicholas Hulley *(Copywriter)*
John McDonald *(Planner)*

Pippa Morris *(Planner)*
Tom White *(Acct Planner)*
Cat Wiles *(Planner)*
Dave Buchanan *(Deputy Exec Dir-Creative)*

Accounts:
Adidas Campaign: "Back to school", Campaign: "Hail To The King", Campaign: "Here Comes The Hero", Campaign: "Holidays", Foot Locker, TV
Advertising Standards Authority
Associated British Foods
Bremont Campaign: "Henley On Thames", Campaign: "U2", Campaign: "Victory", Codebreaker, Global Advertising
British Coast Guard Campaign: "Every Second Counts", PSA
BT "House Party", "Oliver", BT Yahoo!, Broadband, Campaign: "BT Sport", Campaign: "Big Stunt", Campaign: "Home Hub", Campaign: "Jose Mourinho", Campaign: "Silence", Digital Media Ads, Outdoor, Press, Radio, TV
Camelot Group Campaign: "100 Millionaires", Campaign: "A New Dawn for Lotto", Campaign: "Dreams", Campaign: "Hero's Return", Campaign: "PleaseNotThem", Campaign: "There's No Time Like Now", Creative, Lotto, Outdoor, TV
Capital One; Nottingham, UK
Coastguard Service
Currys PC World Campaign: "Football? What Football?", Campaign: "Pina Colada", Campaign: "Spare the Act", Campaign: "Tech For The Life You Dream Of?", Campaign: "We Start With You", Creative, Online, Print, Radio, Social, TV, Video on Demand
Department of Transport Advertising, Campaign: "Celebration", Campaign: "Country Roads", Campaign: "Think!", Creative, Motorcycle Safety
Diageo Advertising, Arthur Guinness Projects, Campaign: "Aftershave, Razor, Scarf", Campaign: "Clock", Campaign: "Cloud", Campaign: "Irrepressible Spirit", Campaign: "Made Of More", Campaign: "Made of Black", Campaign: "Sapeurs", Campaign: "Sheep Dog", Campaign: "surge", Cinemas, Digital, Guinness, Guinness Africa, TV
Dixons Retail Campaign: "Football, What Football?", Creative, Strategy
Don't Drink Drive
DSG Retail Ltd
East Coast Trains Campaign: "welcome to", Communication
The Economist Advertising, Campaign: "Management Trainee", Campaign: "Mandela's Walk"
Eurostar #Wheninlondon, #Wheninparis, Campaign: "Give Her What She Really Wants. Happy Valentine's Day. Love from Eurostar.", Campaign: "Maybe 'Paris", Campaign: "Paris", Campaign: "Stories Are Waiting", Campaign: "The Tour de France", Press
ExxonMobil Campaign: "1st to Work", Get Personal, Mobil1
FageTotal Greek Yoghurt Campaign: "Nineteen Twenty Thirteen", TV
FedEx Campaign: "Show the World", Online, Out Door, Press, Social Media, Website
Financial Services Compensation Scheme Advertising, Creative
Foot Locker Europe Brand Campaign, Campaign: "Here Comes The King", Campaign: "Holiday", Campaign: "Sneaker Skills", Campaign: "Vertical Race", TV
Frito-Lay Company (Walkers UK Ltd.)
New-GlaxoSmithKline Consumer Healthcare Nicorette Gum
New-Guinness Rugby
Homes for Britain Creative, Outdoor
J. Sainsbury plc Campaign: "Back Tu School", Campaign: "Christmas Is for Sharing", Campaign: "Live Well For Less", Campaign: "Sunseekers", Chocolate Bunny, Sainsbury's 1914
James Cracknell Campaign: "Helmets", Cycle Safety
Johnson & Johnson Campaign: "Do Something Incredible", Nicorette
Kids Company Campaign: "CHRISTMAS", Campaign: "Make It Stop", Campaign: "Print Happiness", Campaign: "See the Child", Outdoor, Press, Social Media, Vine
Leica Store
Make Poverty History Campaign: "Click"
Mars Petcare Campaign: "Love Them Back", Campaign: "Night Shift", Cesar, Creative, POS, Packaging, Radio, Social, TV
Mars Campaign: "Ben's Beginners", Campaign: "Big Cat Little Cat", Campaign: "Big Cat", Campaign: "Cassanova", Campaign: "Cry Baby", Campaign: "Drama Queen", Campaign: "Feeding Brighter Futures", Campaign: "Hungry Alter Egos", Campaign: "Hungry", Campaign: "Kitten Kollege", Campaign: "Old Granny", Campaign: "Tigers", Campaign: "Where's The Kitchen", Campaign: "Why Have Cotton When You Can Have Silk", Campaign: "Winning", Campaign: "You're Not You When You're Hungry", Celebrations, Digital, GALAXY, M&Ms, Maltesers, Mars Bar, Milky Way, OOH, Pedigree, Press, Snickers, Snickers Foosball, Through-the-Line, Uncle Bens, Whiskas
Mercedes Benz C63 Amg, Campaign: "Escape the Map", Campaign: "Sound with Power", Campaign: "You Drive", Mercedes Benz CLS
Metropolitan Police Service Campaign: "Metropolitan Police Robbery", Campaign: "Next Door", Who Killed Deon?
New-Miao Sun
Museum of Childhood Campaign: "Japanese, Genius, Balloons, Imagination, Mind"
National Lottery Campaign: "Life-Changing", Campaign: "Play Makes it Possible", Heroes Return, Scratchcards, TV
Office for Low Emission Vehicles
Open Universities
Pedigree Petfoods Campaign: "Bad Dog, Good Dog"
Pepsico Campaign: "Bus Levitation", Campaign: "Dips Desperado", Campaign: "Go Big or Go Home", Campaign: "I Love Rock 'N' Roll", Campaign: "Innovation Department", Campaign: "Live For Now", Campaign: "Loop the Loop", Campaign: "Mariachi Doritos sing Stay Another Day", Campaign: "Unbelievable Game", Campaign: "Unbelievable", Creative, Crisps, Donations, Doritos Dodgeball & Doritos Guitar Hero Alan, Mariachi, Pepsi Max, Red Sky Premium Potato Chip, Walkers, Walkers Pops
Proviz Campaign: "Out of the Dark", Online, Proviz 360 Reflect Jacket
Research In Motion Limited Campaign: "Calendar of Tales"
Sainsbury's Campaign: "Back Tu School", Campaign: "Boredom Busters", Campaign: "Christmas in a Day", Campaign: "Christmas is for Sharing", Campaign: "Everyone's Favorite Ingredient", Campaign: "Food Porn", Campaign: "Halloween", Campaign: "Live well for less", Campaign: "Mog's Christmas Calamity", TV
See The Child
Smart Energy GB (Creative Marketing Agency)
Society of Motor Manufacturers & Traders Campaign: "Go Ultra Low", Digital Advertising, Print, Radio
Starbucks Corp. Advertising, In-Store, Mondays Can Be Great, Online, Outdoor, Print
Svenska Cellulosa Aktiebolaget Campaign: "Control", Campaign: "Focus", Campaign: "Golfin", Campaign: "Keep Control", TENA Men
Think (UK Gov't)
Thunderhead
Twinings Campaign: "Drink It All In", Campaign: "Gets You Back to You", English Breakfast Tea, Sea, TV
V&A Museum of Childhood Campaign: "Japanese"
Volvo Trucks
White Ribbon Campaign: "But"

BBDO EMEA

151 Marylebone Road, London, NW1 5QE United Kingdom
Tel.: (44) 207 616 3488
Fax: (44) 207 616 3495
Web Site: www.bbdo.com

Employees: 20

St. John Walshe *(Mng Dir-Europe)*
Alessia Francescutti *(Dir-Ops)*
Alex Lewis *(Dir-Strategy)*

Accounts:
Bayer
Diageo
EBay
General Electric
Guinness Campaign: "Same Are Made Of More", Creative, Global Digital Business
Mars North America
Mercedes Benz
Motorola Solutions, Inc.
Procter & Gamble Oral-B, Wrigley's 5-Gum
SCA Bodyform, Demak'Up, Libresse, Tena

Proximity Worldwide & London

191 Old Marylebone Rd, London, NW1 5DW United Kingdom
Tel.: (44) 20 7298 1000
Fax: (44) 20 7298 1001
E-Mail: info@proximitylondon.com
Web Site: www.proximitylondon.com

Agency Specializes In: Direct Response Marketing, Electronic Media, Event Planning & Marketing, Media Buying Services, Publicity/Promotions

Mike Dodds *(CEO)*
Andy Todd *(Partner-Creative)*
John Vinton *(Partner-Creative)*
Aiden Moran *(Head-Creative Ops)*
Nick Baker *(Dir-Plng)*
Andy Morris *(Dir-Tech & Delivery)*
Emma Plumbe *(Mgr-PR)*
Darren Burnett *(Joint Head-Plng)*

Accounts:
Bank of Scotland
BBC TV Direct Marketing
Direct Marketing Association
The Economist Integrated
Eurostar
Guide Dogs Advertising
hibu plc
Imperial Tobacco Embassy, Gauloises, Gitanes, IT Brands
John Lewis CRM Strategy
Johnson & Johnson
Kraft Campaign: "Very Important Philly"
LeasePlan UK Digital, eBusiness
Lloyds Bank
Mondelez CRM, Creative, Data Management, Kenco, Rewards Programme, Social, Strategic Management, Web
Oxfam Digital
Pedigree Masterfoods
Procter & Gamble Campaign: "Mums on a Mission"
The Royal Mail Digital
Parcelforce Worldwide B2B, B2C, CRM
Royal National Lifeboat Institution Campaign: "Hold Tight, Hand Up", Digital, Fundraising, Outdoor, Video
Save the Children
Shell
Shell Campaign: "Drivers Club"
SSE CRM
Swiss Precision Diagnostics Clearblue, Global Digital
New-Telegraph Media Group Ltd. Customer Relationship Marketing

TV Licensing
Virgin Games
Volkswagen Group of America, Inc. CityScape, Direct Mail, Golf Mk VII, Golf Plus, Passat CC

Australia

Clemenger BBDO Melbourne

474 Saint Kilda Road, Melbourne, VIC 3004 Australia
Tel.: (61) 3 9869 4444
Fax: (61) 3 9869 4454
E-Mail: melbourne@clemenger.com.au
Web Site: melbourne.clemengerbbdo.com.au

Employees: 270

Nick Garrett *(CEO)*
Lee Simpson *(Mng Partner)*
Simon Lamplough *(Grp Mng Dir)*
Paul McMillan *(Mng Dir)*
Denise McKeon *(Head-Brdcst Production)*
Ant Keogh *(Exec Dir-Creative)*
Ben Knighton *(Grp Dir-Comm)*
Rhys Arnott *(Sr Acct Dir)*
Tim Clark *(Sr Acct Dir)*
Paige Prettyman *(Sr Acct Dir)*
Naomi Gorringe *(Grp Acct Dir)*
Jonathan Pangu *(Grp Acct Dir)*
Harriet Sinclair *(Grp Acct Dir)*
Stephen de Wolf *(Creative Dir)*
Kate Joiner *(Acct Dir)*
Kate Lang *(Acct Dir)*
George McQueen *(Art Dir-Digital)*
Grant Oorloff *(Acct Dir)*
James Orr *(Art Dir)*
Brendan Taylor *(Acct Dir)*
Luke Thompson *(Sr Art Dir)*
Brigid Alkema *(Dir-Creative-Clemenger BBDO Wellington)*
Michael Derepas *(Dir-Plng)*
Russel Fox *(Dir-Art)*
Rohan Lancaster *(Dir-Creative)*
Evan Roberts *(Dir-Creative)*
Lee Sunter *(Dir-Art)*
Richard Williams *(Dir-Creative)*
Khia Croy *(Sr Acct Mgr)*
Oliver Wearne *(Sr Acct Mgr)*
Sam Ayre *(Acct Mgr)*
Josh Bulafkin *(Acct Mgr)*
Patrick Nally *(Acct Mgr)*
Rebecca Orlandi *(Acct Mgr)*
Jack White *(Acct Mgr)*
Matt Pearce *(Planner)*
Kate Barnes *(Acct Exec)*
Elle Bullen *(Copywriter)*
Shannon Crowe *(Copywriter)*
Sam Hodgson *(Planner-Strategic)*
Tom McQueen *(Copywriter-Digital)*

Accounts:
Australia Post Creative
Australian Taxation Office
Australian Writers & Art Directors Association Campaign: "Pencils Equal Profits"
Bega Barbcubes
Billy Tea
Bonds (Agency of Record) Campaign: "Protect Yourself from Yourself", Campaign: "The Boys", Creative
BP
Carlton & United Breweries Bulmers Cider, Campaign: "Australia's Finest Barley Farmer", Campaign: "Bar Slide", Campaign: "Beer Chase", Campaign: "Chilly Tara", Campaign: "Fat Yak", Campaign: "I'll Have a Carlton Cold", Campaign: "I'll have a Carlton Cold", Campaign: "Sax Solo", Campaign: "Stay a Little Longer", Campaign: "Thermo label", Carlton Cold, Carlton Draught, Carlton Dry Dreams, Carlton Mid, Cascade, Crown Lager, Draught Pick, Pure Blond, Strongbow, The Keg, VB
Carlton Dry Campaign: "#HelloBeer", Digital, TV
Cascade Brewery Limited-Edition
Collingwood Football Club
Crown Casino
DrinkWise Campaign: "How to Drink Properly", Digital, Outdoor, Press, Radio, TV
Dulux Campaign: "Colour Block", Campaign: "The Surf Club Project"
The Economist
Fonterra Brands (Australia) Pty. Ltd. Bega Cheese, Campaign: "Perfect Italiano. No Celebrity Chef Required"
Foster's Campaign: "Sentences", Campaign: "Spending too much time with the wife?", Carlton Mid
Four'N Twenty
Foxtel Campaign: "Makes you think", Online Display, Press, Social Media, TV
Good Shepherd Microfinance
Guide Dogs Australia Support Scent
Holeproof
MARS Australia Campaign: "Croc Crunch"
Mars Chocolate Australia Campaign: "Empowering", Campaign: "Put Some Play in Your Day", Campaign: "Runaway Train", Campaign: "Snickers Sessions", Campaign: "You're Not You When You're Hungry", M&M's, Mars Bar, Snickers
Mars Petcare Campaign: "Feed the Good", Digital, Pedigree, TV
Masterfoods - ANZ - Pet Food Dine, Exelpet, MyDog
Masterfoods - ANZ - Snack Foods Bounty, Celebrations, M&Ms, Milky Way, Pods, Skittles, Snickers, Starburst
Matilda Bay Dirty Granny, Outdoor Campaign, Print
Melbourne International Comedy Festival Campaign: "Not Funny"
Melbourne International Film Festival Campaign: "Potato Peelers"
Mercedes-Benz
Mercury Cider Here's To 100 Years
MLC Campaign: "Diorama"
Mutual Community Health Insurance
Myer
National Australia Bank Campaign: "Break Up", Campaign: "Fanshake", Campaign: "Footify Australia", Campaign: "Honesty Experiments - How one unexpected word tripled credit card sales in 3 months", Campaign: "Lifesaver", Campaign: "More Give, Less Take", Campaign: "Operation Freedom Dolphin", Campaign: "Stand Ins", Campaign: "The Yelp", Campaign: "They'll Never Change", Digital, Lock In, Print, Social Media, TV
Natural Blonde
New Zealand Transport Agency
Origin Energy (Creative Agency of Record) Campaign: "The Unknown", Origin Energy Tales
Pacific Brands Bonds, Campaign: "Christmas Carollers", Campaign: "Collectibles", Campaign: "The Birthday Project"
Patties Foods Pty. Ltd. Four n Twenty, Herbert Adams, Nannas
Places Victoria Campaign: "Remote Control Tourist"
Procter & Gamble Oral-B
RACV Ltd.
SAB Miller Campaign: "Snorkel"
SCA Hygience Australasia - Consumer Sorbent Facial Tissue, Sorbent Toilet Tissue
SCA Hygience Australasia - Household Deeko
SCA Hygience Australasia - Personal Care Libra, Tena
Seek Learning Creative, Online, Radio, TV
SUNA GPS
Tata Global Beverages Campaign: "Leaving"
TEDx Campaign: "Mimeisthai"
Tourism Victoria (Agency of Record) Campaign: "Play Melbourne", Campaign: "The Melbourne Remote Control Tourist"
Transport Accident Commission Campaign: "Pillow", Campaign: "Strings", Campaign: "The Effects Get Stronger", Campaign: "Towards Zero", Creative, Drink-Driving Laws, Online, Print, Radio, Social, TV
Victoria Bitter
Victorian State Government
WSPA
WWF
Yellow Pages Baboons, Campaign: "Renovision", Campaign: "Tick", Free Online Listings, Hidden Pizza Restaurant

China

BBDO China

Suite 301 Bldg 1 TEDA Times Centre 12C 15 Guang Hua Rd, Chao Yang District, Beijing, 100026 China
Tel.: (86) 10 6591 3932
Fax: (86) 10 6591 3732
Web Site: www.bbdoasia.com

Yeat Mung Koo *(Mng Dir)*
Martin Grunhoff *(Grp Dir-Creative)*
Jan Hendrik Ott *(Grp Dir-Creative)*
Caroline Beckert *(Assoc Dir-Creative)*
Amy Liu *(Sr Acct Mgr)*
Fred Wang *(Sr Acct Exec)*
Lylah Juinio *(Reg Bus Dir-China)*

Accounts:
Aviva
Daimler Campaign: "The Little Engine That Could"
FedEx
HP
ICI Paints
Johnson & Johnson
Mars Food China Campaign: "Football Commentary"
Mars Food Campaign: "Spring Tactical Campaign"
Mars North America
P & G
Pepsi
Smart
Wrigley

BBDO China

42/F 1 Grand Gateway Plaza, NO 1 Hong Qiao Road, Shanghai, 200030 China
Tel.: (86) 21 2401 8000
Fax: (86) 21 6448 4699
Web Site: www.bbdoasia.com

Sharlene Wu *(Mng Dir-BBDO & Proximity-Shanghai)*
Diana Cawley *(Gen Mgr-Shanghai)*
Kit Koh *(Exec Dir-Creative)*
Awoo Lai *(Exec Dir-Creative)*
Hans Lopez-Vito *(Exec Dir-Plng)*
Jacquelyn Pang *(Client Svcs Dir)*
Jayci Yang *(Acct Mgr)*

Accounts:
Air New Zealand
Bayer Healthcare
China Hewlett-Packard
FedEx
Fu Yang Hospital Of Traditional Chinese Medicine Campaign: "Octopus Vs Rooster"
Gallo Shanghai
General Electric China
Godiva; China Chocolate, Public Relations
Guinness
Hormel Foods
ICI Swire Paints
Johnson & Johnson Nicorette
KFC
Mars
Mercedes-Benz; China Creative
Natural Resources Defense Council Campaign: "City Fan"
PepsiCo Campaign: "Bring Happiness Home", Creative, Miranda, Pepsi Light

Procter & Gamble
Red Cross Society of China Jet Li One Foundation Project
Snow Beer; 2007
Tiffany & Co Creative
Watson Creative
Wrigley Confectionery; China

China (Hong Kong)

BBDO Hong Kong

Ste 1501 15th Fl Cityplaza 4, 12 Taikoo Wan Rd, Taikoo Shing, China (Hong Kong)
Tel.: (852) 2820 1838
Web Site: bbdoasia.com

Agency Specializes In: Financial

Chris Thomas *(Chm/CEO-BBDO Asia, Middle East & Africa)*
J C Catibog *(Mng Dir-South China)*
Jason King *(Gen Mgr)*

Accounts:
Fonterra
GE
Johnson & Johnson
Mercedes Benz
MetLife Hong Kong Creative
PepsiCo
Procter & Gamble
SingTel
Starbucks Campaign: "Perfection"
Visa
Wrigley's Campaign: "The Flavours Of Life", Doublemint, Extra

India

BBDO India

207/2 Solitaire Plz, 2nd Fl MG Rd, Gurgaon, Haryana 122002 India
Tel.: (91) 99 5890 0033
Fax: (91) 11 2571 9958
E-Mail: delhi-office@rksbbdo.com
Web Site: www.bbdoasia.com

Employees: 85

Josy Paul *(Chm & Chief Creative Officer)*
Rajesh Sikroria *(Pres)*
Ajai Jhala *(CEO)*
Malini Chaudhury *(Creative Dir)*
Sandeep Sawant *(Dir-Creative)*
Hemant Shringy *(Sr Creative Dir)*

Accounts:
Aviva Life Insurance Company India Aviva Child Plans, Campaign: "A Book's Second Life", Campaign: "Call from the Future", Campaign: "God of Cricket", Life Insurance, Padding up with Sachin, Sachin and Scholarships, Sachin off Guard, Social Media Campaign, Webisodes
Bayer Healthcare
BlackBerry Blackberry, Campaign: "Action Starts Here"
DHL CSR Initiative, Campaign: "Box Cuboid", Campaign: "Tri", Package Delivery, Postage
General Electric Company Campaign: "Art By The People", Campaign: "Kutch Patch Artwork", Campaign: "Soura Artwork", Campaign: "Take Care of your Loved Ones"
General Mills
Gillette India Ltd Gillette Satin Care
Haiyya Campaign: "Stick It Art"
Hewlett-Packard
Johnson & Johnson Campaign: "Engaged Couple", Campaign: "India'S First D.I.Y. Calendar For Babies", Medicine, Nicorette
Mobil (intl)
Nimbooz
Pepsico 7UP, Campaign: "Craziness", Campaign: "Tweet-A-Thon", Creative, Mirinda, Quaker Oats
Procter & Gamble Ariel, Campaign: "Happy Mother's Day", Campaign: "Soldier For Women", Campaign: "The Everyday Soldier Movement", Campaign: "You Shave. I Shave", Cosmetics, Shaving, Whisper
Racold
Rajiv Gandhi Renewable Energy Centre
Samvaad Hearing Clinic Campaign: "Radio Spot For The Hearing Impaired"
Visa India
White Collar Hippies AK-47, Nuclear Reactor
Wrigley Doublemint Aqua Splash

R.K. Swamy BBDO

Film Chamber Bldg 604 Anna Salai, Chennai, 600006 India
Tel.: (91) 44 3988 3500
Fax: (91) 44 2829 2314
E-Mail: vijay.gopal@rksbbdo.com
Web Site: www.rkswamybbdo.com

Employees: 900

Agency Specializes In: Consumer Marketing, Financial, Industrial, South Asian Market

Sandeep Sharma *(Pres)*
Shekar Swamy *(Grp CEO)*
Ajit Shah *(Pres-North & New Delhi)*
Lata Ramaseshan *(Gen Mgr-IRC-Chennai)*
Rajendra Munje *(Art Dir)*
Sunil Ranjan Pathak *(Dir-Brand Strategy)*
Tanujaa Babu *(Sr Mgr-Brand Design-Films)*
Sanjay Mirashi *(Brand Mgr-Design)*

Accounts:
Adarsh Group
Air India
Aparna Group
Asia Motor Works
Birla Tyres
BSCPL
Chambal Fertilizer & Chemicals
Charminar Asbestos
Consim Info Pvt Ltd
Corporation Bank Creative, Publicity Campaigns
Diamler Campaign: "Catch Us"
Eurocon Tiles
Faber Castell
Fedders Lloyd
Freescale Semiconductors India
Futura Cookers & Cookware
GE Medical Systems
Hawkins Cookers
Hindusthan Paper Corporation
Hutchison 3 Global Services
India Gypsum
Indian School of Business
ITC Ltd
K Raheja Universal
Kalanjali
Kirby Building Systems
Kokuyo Camlin Ltd Campaign: "Camel Crayons Se Hoga Fun", Crayons, Mechanical Pencil, TV
Life Insurance Corporation
Mars International Campaign: "Giving Life", Campaign: "Reshmi Ehsaas, Resham Se Bhi Khaas", Campaign: "Shooting Set, Arjun Rampal", Campaign: "You're Not You When You Are Hungry", Snickers
Mercedes-Benz Campaign: "Speak to the Future", Campaign: "Turn On", Campaign: "Zero Excuses", Mercedes-Benz S-Class
Mercure Homestead Residences
Ministry of Rural Development
Moods Condoms Your Time, Your Place, Your Moods
Nilkamal
NTPC
O'General Air Conditioners
Oil & Natural Gas Commission
Oil India
Orient Fans
Parryware Roca
Piaggio Vehicles Three-Wheeler
Power Grid Corporation
Shriram City Union Finance Ltd. Campaign: "Hello", Magazine, Newspaper, Print
Singer India Ltd Campaign: "Singer-Made"
State Bank of India SBI Home Loan "Birthday Gift"
Stratondops
Suzuki Motorcycles Access 125, Bandit, Campaign: "Apna Way of Life", Creative, Heat 125, Intruder, JS150, SlingShot, Zeus
Titan
TVS Electronics Ltd.
UNICEF
United Spirits
Vaswani Estates
Volvoline Cummins
Wep Peripherals
Zuari Cement

Indonesia

BBDO Komunika

Hero Bldg II 7th Fl JL Gatot Subroto, 177 A Kav 64, Jakarta, 12870 Indonesia
Tel.: (62) 21 831 7780
Fax: (62) 21 831 7786
E-Mail: general@bbdoindonesia.com
Web Site: www.bbdoasia.com

Employees: 120

Intan Mokhnar *(Mng Dir)*
Randy Rinaldi *(Exec Dir-Creative)*
Sandru Emil *(Grp Dir-Creative)*
Cristina Padilla *(Mgr-Bus Dev)*

Accounts:
Adira Insurance The Flooded Miniature
Astra Honda Motor Insurance Honda Tiger
Bayer Aspirin
BCA Campaign: "How Bca Won the Hearts of Indonesians"
Del Monte
Kompas Gramedia Kompas.com; 2008
Marjan Syrup
PepsiCo Pepsi, Quaker

Japan

I&S BBDO Inc.

Harumi Triton Square X 1-8-10 Harumi, Chuo-ku, Tokyo, 104-6038 Japan
Tel.: (81) 3 6221 8585
Fax: (81) 3 6221 8791
E-Mail: prdiv@isbbdo.co.jp
Web Site: www.isbbdo.co.jp

Employees: 463
Year Founded: 1947

Agency Specializes In: Communications, Consulting, Exhibit/Trade Shows, Media Buying Services, Print, Publicity/Promotions, Radio, T.V.

Haruhiko Ito *(Exec Dir)*
Shinichi Ikeda *(Sr Dir-Creative)*
Mari Nishimura *(Creative Dir)*
Naomi Hou *(Dir-Art & Designer)*
Sei Sugiyama *(Dir-Art & Planner-Content)*
Takahiro Sakai *(Dir-Creative)*
Keiichi Uemura *(Dir-Creative)*
Tatsuro Kumaki *(Copywriter)*
Risa Taoka *(Copywriter)*

Accounts:
Bayer
CNN
Diageo Guinness

Advertising Agencies

Fujitsu
Hibiya-Kadan Campaign: "Give Back The Love"
Hot Wheels Campaign: "Dolly"
Japan Philharmonic Orchestra Campaign: "The Japan Pill-harmonic"
Jipang Corporation Campaign: "President's Curry"
The Kansai Electric Power Co., Inc.
KAO
KSC Corporation Campaign: "National Defense Calendar"
Life Co., Ltd.
Lion Corp.
Mars Japan Campaign: "Mens Power Generation", Candy Bar
Master Foods Ltd.
Megahouse Corporation Rubik's Cube
Mercedes Benz
Mitsubishi Heavy Industries
Miyamoto Jeweler Campaign: "Heal-Ring"
Mother Water
Nishinihon Tenrei Campaign: "Life is Endless"
NPO Iruka Campaign: "Do Not Leave Us Behind"
NPO Wig Ring Japan Campaign: "Wig is Alive"
NTT Urban Development Campaign: "Tweet Rain Story"
Sakurasaku Glass
The Salvation Army Japan
Sega Sammy
New-Special Broadcasting Service Corporation (SBS)
Starbucks Coffee Campaign: "Share with a Friend"
Three Bond
Toyotecno Campaign: "Clean up"
Umino Seaweed Store Campaign: "Design Nori"
Urban Renaissance Agency

Malaysia

BBDO Malaysia

Suite 50-01-01 Wisma UOA Damansara 50 Jalan Dungun, Damansara Heights, Kuala Lumpur, 50490 Malaysia
Tel.: (60) 3 2093 3930
Fax: (60) 3 2094 9891
E-Mail: info@bbdo.com.my
Web Site: www.bbdo.com.my

Employees: 90

Agency Specializes In: Consumer Marketing

John Teoh *(Mng Dir)*
Anirban Ganguly *(Head-Innovation & Strategy)*
Tan Chee Keong *(Exec Dir-Creative)*
Auston Low *(Art Dir & Designer)*
Adam Chan *(Dir-Creative)*
Adrian Cheah *(Dir-Client Svcs)*
Chin Kai Loon *(Dir-Art)*
Hor Yew Pong *(Dir-Creative)*
Carina Teo *(Assoc Dir-Creative)*
Lian EeWern *(Sr Designer)*
Alicia Hew *(Copywriter)*

Accounts:
Astro
Bosch
British Council
Drypers Marketing
FedEx
ICI Paints (Malaysia) Sdn Bhd
KFC
Levis
Mars M&M's
Maxis Comms
MINI
Olympus Campaign: "Jazz"
Pedigree
Pepsi-Cola International Ltd. Quaker Products
RHB
Ridsect
SC Johnson
U Mobile Creative
Visa
Wrigley's Double Mint Gum

New Zealand

Clemenger BBDO Wellington

Clemenger BBDO House 8 Kent Ter Level 2, Wellington, 6201 New Zealand
Tel.: (64) 4 802 3333
Fax: (64) 4 802 3322
E-Mail: inquiries@clemengerbbdo.co.nz
Web Site: www.clemengerbbdo.co.nz

Employees: 100

Livia Esterhazy *(Mng Dir)*
Mark Dalton *(Sr Dir-Art)*
Tony Haigh *(Art Dir)*
Steve Hansen *(Dir-Art)*
Julia Walshaw *(Sr Acct Mgr)*
Bethany Omeri *(Acct Mgr)*
Janka Palinkas *(Mgr-Fin)*
Graham Alvarez *(Sr Planner-Strategy)*
Emily Beautrais *(Copywriter)*
Jamie Bunting *(Designer)*
Ryan Christie *(Designer)*
Jeffry Ghazally *(Designer)*

Accounts:
ALAC
Ashley Fogel
Biosecurity Campaign: "Evil Fruit"
CAANZ Campaign: "Share The Love"
Carter Observatory Campaign: "Fill Your Head with Space"
Dulux New Zealand Campaign: "Weather", Campaign: "What's Your Dulux Colour of New Zealand?"
Earth Hour Ads In The Dark
Fly Buys Campaign: "Something A Little Bit Good"
Fonterra Australia
Fonterra NZ
Format Printers
KiwiRail Campaign: "See More of New Zealand by Train"
Mitsubishi Motors Campaign: "Carries your load. Carries your business.", Farm, Port, Shogun Euro
New York Festivals
New Zealand Transport Agency Campaign: "Blazed", Campaign: "GPS Vs. Kid", Campaign: "Ghost Chips", Campaign: "Local Legends", Campaign: "Mistakes", Campaign: "Shopkeepers", Campaign: "Sneak Up Ads", Campaign: "Speed", Campaign: "Tinnyvision", Campaign: "Tiredness Catches Up With You", Radio, Social
New-NZ Post
Pheonix Soccer
Radio New Zealand
Rainforest Conservation
Red Lane
Safer Journeys Campaign: "Stop the family driving drunk. Legend."
South Pacific Tyres
Wellington City Council
Wellington International Ukulele Orchestra Campaign: "Nothing Beats a Jingle"
New-Wellington Zoo
WWF New Zealand Campaign: "Orangutan"

Colenso BBDO

100 College Hill, PO Box 47491, Ponsonby, Auckland, 1011 New Zealand
Tel.: (64) 9 360 3777
Fax: (64) 9 360 3778
E-Mail: enquiries@colensobbdo.co.nz
Web Site: www.colensobbdo.co.nz

Employees: 60

Agency Specializes In: Brand Development & Integration

Nick Worthington *(Chm-Creative)*
Gavin Becker *(Head-Digital, Tech & Innovation)*
Paul Gunn *(Head-Activation & PR)*
Jen Storey *(Head-Brdcst)*
Aaron Turk *(Head-Digital Creative)*
Angela Watson *(Head-Acct Mgmt)*
Steve Cochran *(Exec Dir-Creative)*
Brett Colliver *(Sr Dir-Art)*
Vanessa Marklew *(Sr Acct Dir)*
Rebecca Richardson *(Grp Acct Dir)*
Abbi Barker *(Acct Dir)*
Tara McKenty *(Art Dir)*
Katherine Sliper *(Acct Dir)*
Maggie Christie *(Dir-Integration)*
Brent Courtney *(Dir-Art)*
Paul Courtney *(Dir-Ops)*
Neville Doyle *(Dir-Plng)*
George Howes *(Dir-Art)*
Rachel Morgan *(Dir-Intl Grp Bus)*
Dan Wright *(Dir-Creative)*
Lucy Hartstone *(Sr Acct Mgr)*
Pink Kitsawat *(Sr Acct Mgr)*
Kate Goddard *(Acct Mgr-PR & Activation)*
Eddie Thomas *(Acct Mgr)*
Alex Wilson *(Acct Mgr)*
Oriel David-Lyons *(Copywriter)*
Hannah Habgood *(Copywriter)*
Lucy Morgan *(Copywriter)*
Ben Polkinghorne *(Copywriter)*
Carren Richardson-Park *(Planner-Strategic)*
Simon Vicars *(Copywriter)*
Kristal Knight *(Sr Art Dir)*

Accounts:
Air New Zealand
Aldi
AMI Insurance
Amnesty International "Trial by Timeline", Amnesty Envelope
Anchor
Auckland Philharmonia Orchestra
Bank of New Zealand "EmotionScan", Campaign: "The Power Of a Dollar"
Burger King Campaign: "#MotelBK", Campaign: "Cheat on Beef", Campaign: "Pre-roll", Campaign: "The King's Royal Gift"
DB Breweries Campaign: "Fire At The Old Well", Campaign: "He's Drinking It For You"
DB Export Campaign: "Fire at the Old Well", Export Gold
Doggelganger
Doritos
European Motor Distributors
Fisher & Paykel Campaign: "Roast"
Fonterra Campaign: "If Milk Was Meant To See The Light, Cows Would Be See-through", Campaign: "Listen to Your Stomach", Campaign: "Mainland: Golf", Campaign: "Make Someone You Know Feel Tip Top", Fresh N Fruity, Tip Top
Foodstuffs Campaign: "New World- The In- Store Master Butcher"
Frucor Beverages Ltd Campaign: "Air Aquarium", Campaign: "From great to extraordinary", Campaign: "Mountain Dew Skatepark", Campaign: "Skate Pinball", Campaign: "V Battle Carts", Campaign: "V Paintball", The V Motion Project, V Energy Drink, V Robbers
Fruju Fruit Whip
George Weston Foods Tip Top Wraps
IAG Campaign: "Nothing is Gonna Break My Stride"
Kiwi Online, Popsicle
Mars Campaign: "Dig", Campaign: "Doggelganger", Campaign: "Donation Glasses", Campaign: "Home Alone", Campaign: "My Dog", Campaign: "Smart Puppies", Campaign: "Stick"
Michael Hill Global Brand Strategy
Mizone
Mountain Dew
New World Supermarkets Little Kitchen, Little Shop
New Zealand Book Council Campaign: "Books

Shape You"
New Zealand Breast Cancer Foundation Campaign: "A Cream That Gives You Wrinkles", Campaign: "Save Seven", Print, Skinfoods
The New Zealand Comedy Trust Campaign: "Toosoon"
Nimble
Nokia New Zealand Campaign: "Nokia Coptercam"
Pedigree Campaign: "Share for Dogs"
Pepsico,Inc. Bromitment, Pepsi Max
Samsung New Zealand Campaign: "Instant News Satire", Campaign: "Online Waiting Line", Campaign: "The Smart Phone Line", Galaxy Gear, Galaxy Note II, PR, Social Media
SCA Hygiene Australasia
Snickers
St John Ambulance "Here For Life", Brand Positioning, TV
State Insurance Campaign: "Break My Stride"
Tip Top Popsicle Blasta
Tourism Fiji Brand Communications
TV One
TV Show
TV2 VAMPIRE DIARIES
TV3
TVNZ Dog Fight
Visa
Volkswagen AG Reduce Speed Dial
Westpac Campaign: "Helping People Save as Impulsively as they Spend", Campaign: "Impulse Saver", Campaign: "The Art of Money"
Yellow Pages Campaign: "Yellow Local", Yellow Chocolate

Philippines

BBDO Guerrero

11th Floor Insular Life Building Ayala Avenue corner, Paseo de Roxas, Makati, 1226 Philippines
Tel.: (63) 2 892 0701
Fax: (63) 892 7501
Web Site: www.bbdoguerrero.com

Employees: 97
Year Founded: 1998

David Guerrero *(Chm & Chief Creative Officer)*
Dale Lopez *(Art Dir & Exec Dir-Creative)*
Karen Go *(Grp Acct Dir)*
Michelle Edu *(Art Dir)*
Jao Bautista *(Dir-Creative)*
Peachy Bretana *(Dir-Creative)*
Keith Comez *(Dir-Art)*
Jay-ar Iringan *(Dir-Fin)*
Al Salvador *(Dir-Creative Svcs)*
Donna Dimayuga *(Assoc Dir-Creative)*
Isai Martinez *(Assoc Dir-Creative)*
Ethel Sanchez *(Deputy Dir-Plng)*

Accounts:
Apple Box Photography Studio
Bayan Telecommunications Internet Provider
Bayer Philippines Campaign: "Butcher", Campaign: "Persistent Headache", Saridon
Billionaire Magazine
BioLink
C Magazine Billionaire
Child Hope
Clean Air Asia Hairy Nose Campaign, Online Video, Website
Department of Tourism Campaign: "It's More Fun in the Philippines"
Emperado
Fedex Campaign: "Rectangle Box", Campaign: "Square Box", Zombie Outbreak
Fonterra Anlene
Hewlett-Packard
Johnson & Johnson Campaign: "Painful Diarrhea", Digital, Modess
Krispy Kreme Creative; 2008
Manila Water Brand Consultancy, Digital Communication
Mars Pedigree
Mitsubishi
The National Union Of Journalists
New-Noli Me Tangere
NUJP Campaign: "Closed Eyes", Media
PepsiCo Campaign: "Bottle Lights", Drink Consumer Goods, Pepsi Max
Pizza Hut
Procter & Gamble #ShineStrong, Campaign: "#WhipIt", Campaign: "Be Strong & Shine", Pantene
Quaker
Red Cross
Sky Broadband
UNICEF
Visa
Wrigley Campaign: "Party"

Singapore

BBDO Singapore

30 Merchant Road #03-12, Riverside Point, Singapore, 058282 Singapore
Tel.: (65) 6533 2200
Fax: (65) 6827 6700
E-Mail: seshadri.sampath@bbdo.com.sg
Web Site: www.bbdoasia.com

Employees: 150

Agency Specializes In: Advertising Specialties

Danny Searle *(Chm, Chief Creative Officer & Vice Chm-BBDO Asia)*
Chris Willingham *(CEO)*
Jean-Paul Burge *(Chm/CEO-South East Asia)*
Joe Braithwaite *(Gen Mgr)*
Sarah Maclean *(Reg Dir-Bus)*
Yee Wai Khuen *(Creative Dir)*
Theresa Ong *(Creative Dir)*
Wai Khuen Yee *(Dir-Creative)*
Tiffany Young *(Sr Acct Mgr)*
David Tay *(Grp Bus Dir)*

Accounts:
Asia Pacific Breweries Campaign: "Guinness Draught In A Bottle", Campaign: "Un, Deux, Trois, Quatre"
Autism Resource Centre Campaign: "Search Activated Banner"
Aviva
Citibank
Cycle & Carriage
Diageo
New-Exxon Mobil Mobil 1, Social, Video
FedEx
Fonterra Brands Above-the-Line, Anmum
Heineken Guinness, Tiger Beer
Hewlett Packard Campaign: "Like Father Like Son", Printers
ICI Paints (Singapore) Pte Ltd.; 1996
Mercedes
NETS; Singapore Creative, E-Payment Operation
Olympus Corporation OM-D E-M10
Panasonic Lumix FX33; 2007
Pepsi International Beverages
Pfizer
Visa

Thailand

BBDO Bangkok

18th Fl U Chu Liang Bldg, 968 Rama IV Rd Silom, Bangkok, 10500 Thailand
Tel.: (66) 2 637 5999
Fax: (66) 2 637 5990
Web Site: bbdoasia.com

Employees: 60

Somkiat Larptanunchaiwong *(CEO)*
Tutiya Disphanurat *(COO)*
Peter Oh *(Grp Head-Creative)*
Pakorn Inthachai *(Art Dir)*
Anchalee Kerdchan *(Acct Dir)*
Nares Limapornvanich *(Art Dir)*
Arunee Rueangwattanaporn *(Bus Dir)*
Tanyawan Wongapichart *(Acct Dir)*
Chalit Manuyakorn *(Dir-Creative)*
Apichai Inthutsingh *(Assoc Dir-Creative)*
Preeyaporn Somboonwanna *(Acct Mgr)*
Teerin Bhongsatiern *(Acct Exec)*
Thiti Boonkerd *(Copywriter)*
Chayamon Bunnag *(Copywriter)*
Nattawut Sittiwaraphan *(Copywriter)*
Prachya Wanthanasin *(Copywriter)*

Accounts:
Bangkok Bank
Bayer Alka Seltzer
Bridgestone Corporation
Day Poets Company Book Publishing
DKSH Counterpain
New-Drugs.com Throatsil
Family Network Foundation Campaign: "Unsweet Truth"
FedEx
Giffarine Skyline Unity Vitamin Supplement
Give Asia
Greenpeace Southeast Asia
Hairmax Institute Bodyshape
Home Product Co., Ltd Campaign: "Tricky Dad"
HomePro Campaign: "Clean", Campaign: "Moment of Glory", Campaign: "Sale: Lizard "
Hydroline Tank And Pumps Co. Water Pump
Index Livingmall
Johnson & Johnson Campaign: "Plaque Tower"
Lion Corporation
Maglite
New Trend Development
Nong Pho
Operation Smile Campaign: "The Painted Smile", Public Relations
PepsiCo
Optic Square Light Adaptive Poster
Ramathibodi Foundation Campaign: "Calendar of Life"
Samsung
Siam Bodybuilding
Sony Erickson Playstation
TAC
Tefal Blender Campaign: "Fruitastic Lookalike"
Tesco Lotus
Thai Health Promotion Foundation Campaign: "Headlight Message", Don't Drive Sleepy Project, Get Fit! Project, Road Safety
Thai Red Cross Font Fights Flood
Thailand Association of The Blind "Storybook For All eyes", Blind Taste TV SHOW
Tisco Bank
Tony Moly
Women & Men Progressive Movement Foundation

BBG&G ADVERTISING

33 Hill Rd, Middletown, NY 10941
Tel.: (845) 695-1880
Fax: (845) 695-1996
E-Mail: smartstrategies@bbggadv.com
Web Site: www.bbggadv.com

Employees: 8

Agency Specializes In: Advertising, Brand Development & Integration, Business-To-Business, Collateral, Corporate Identity, Direct Response Marketing, Event Planning & Marketing, Exhibit/Trade Shows, Internet/Web Design, Logo & Package Design, Multimedia, Newspaper, Print, Promotions, Public Relations, Radio, T.V.

Deborah Garry *(Owner)*
Peggy Brunetti *(Dir-Ops)*
Shannon Flatley *(Dir-Creative)*

Traci Suppa *(Copywriter)*
Alyssa Maroney *(Jr Graphic Designer)*

Accounts:
Bon Secours Community Hospital
Chiropractic Leadership Alliance
Creating Wellness Alliance
Horizon Family Medical Group
Mission Regional Medical Center
Schervier Apartments
Schervier Nursing Care Center
Walden Savings Bank

BBH NEW YORK

32 Avenue of the Americas 19th Fl, New York, NY 10013
Tel.: (212) 812-6600
Fax: (212) 242-4110
Web Site: www.bartleboglehegarty.com/newyork/

Employees: 160
Year Founded: 1998

National Agency Associations: 4A's

Agency Specializes In: Automotive, Brand Development & Integration, Broadcast, Business Publications, Business-To-Business, Cable T.V., Children's Market, Co-op Advertising, Communications, Consulting, Consumer Marketing, Consumer Publications, Corporate Identity, Cosmetics, E-Commerce, Electronic Media, Entertainment, Fashion/Apparel, Financial, Health Care Services, High Technology, Infomercials, Information Technology, Internet/Web Design, Leisure, Logo & Package Design, Magazines, New Product Development, Newspaper, Newspapers & Magazines, Out-of-Home Media, Outdoor, Planning & Consultation, Point of Sale, Print, Production, Publicity/Promotions, Restaurant, Retail, Seniors' Market, Sponsorship, Strategic Planning/Research, T.V., Trade & Consumer Magazines, Transportation, Travel & Tourism

Jonathan Hills *(Chief Digital Officer)*
John Patroulis *(Chm-Creative)*
Mark Williams *(Sr VP)*
Anne Bobroff *(Head-Production)*
Julian Cole *(Head-Comm Plng)*
Gerard Caputo *(Exec Dir-Creative)*
Paul Kamzelas *(Grp Dir-Creative)*
Daniel Burke *(Art Dir)*
Miles Burton *(Acct Dir)*
Diego Fonseca *(Art Dir)*
Marcos Kotlhar *(Art Dir)*
Justin Marciani *(Acct Dir)*
Mark Aronson *(Dir-Strategy)*
Elizabeth Barr *(Dir-Fin)*
Daniel Bonder *(Dir-Creative)*
Dave Brown *(Dir-Creative)*
Beth Ryan *(Dir-Creative)*
Heather Livengood *(Acct Mgr)*
Kerry Callaghan *(Acct Exec)*
Eric Schwerdtfeger *(Acct Exec)*
Angela Sun *(Strategist)*
Evan Benedetto *(Copywriter)*
Bruno Borges *(Designer)*
Mandy Brencys *(Copywriter)*
Jon Kallus *(Copywriter)*
Alanna Watson *(Copywriter)*

Accounts:
ALS Campaign: "Donate Your Voice"
British Airways Campaign: "To Fly. To Serve", Club World
Cole Haan Campaign: "Chelsea Pump"
The Corner Shop Playstation Plus Network
Google AdWords Express, Campaign: "Coffee", Campaign: "Lady Gaga", Google Chrome, Google Music
New-Great Nations Eat
GrubHub Inc. Creative, OOH, Seamless (Agency of Record)
The Guardian Campaign: "Points of View", Campaign: "Voice Your View", Microsite, Poster, Print
New-Harman International Industries, Incorporated Campaign: "CordFail Effect", JBL
Infamous Second Son Campaign: "Enjoy Your Power"
NBA
New-Nest Campaign: "Magic of Home", Out of Home, Print
Newell Rubbermaid "Blueberry", Blue Marker Pens, Creative, Irwin Tools, Mr. Sketch, Mr. Sketch Scented Markers, MrSketch.com, Paper Mate, Sharpie, Strategy, TV
New-Seamless Corp
Social Tees Animal Rescue Campaign: "Puppy Love on Tinder"
Sol Beer
Sony Computer Entertainment America LLC Campaign: "Bid for Greatness", Campaign: "First Love", Campaign: "First to Greatness", Campaign: "Gateways to Greatness", Campaign: "Greatness Awaits", Campaign: "Infamous: Second Son", Campaign: "Live Action Spot", Campaign: "Perfect Day", Campaign: "Shadow Fall Promo", Creative, Online, Outdoor, PlayStation 4, Playstation, Social, TV Commercial
Unilever AXE Deodorant, All Detergent, Bertolli, Campaign: "Hotel", Campaign: "How You Feel Says It All", Campaign: "Make Your Own Sex Tape", Cleans Your Balls, Clix, Dove, In-Store Marketing, Men+Care, Omo, Online, Persil, Print, Promise, Spray & Go, Surf, Vaseline, White Label; 2001
Volvo Trucks Campaign: "Greatness Awaits"
The Weather Channel Brand Strategy, Campaign: "Your Weather.com", Communications Planning, Creative
Westin Hotels & Resorts Campaign: "A Day in the Pool will Help You Swim With the Sharks", Campaign: "A Weekend at the U.S. Open Means Monday has Met its Match", Campaign: "Westin Elements of Well Being", Digital, Onsite Promotions, Print
World Gold Council; NY Times Square Gold Ring Hunt; 2001

Branch

Domani Studios LLC

32 Avenue of the Americas 19th Fl, New York, NY 10013
(See Separate Listing)

BBK WORLDWIDE

117 Kendrick St Ste 600, Needham, MA 02494
Tel.: (617) 630-4477
Fax: (617) 630-5090
Web Site: www.bbkworldwide.com

Agency Specializes In: Consulting, Health Care Services

Joan F. Bachenheimer *(Founder)*
Bonnie A. Brescia *(Founder)*
Matt Kibby *(Principal-Tech & Innovation)*
Rob Laurens *(Principal-Strategy & Best Practices)*
Liz Ritchie *(Principal-Corp & Legal Svcs)*
Matthew Stumm *(Principal-Creative & Media Strategy)*

BBR CREATIVE

300 Rue Beauregard Bldg 1, Lafayette, LA 70508
Tel.: (337) 233-1515
Fax: (337) 232-4433
E-Mail: etalbot@bbrcreative.com
Web Site: www.bbrcreative.com

Year Founded: 1997

Agency Specializes In: Advertising, Advertising Specialties, Brand Development & Integration, Broadcast, Business Publications, Business-To-Business, Corporate Identity, Electronic Media, Engineering, Environmental, Exhibit/Trade Shows, Food Service, Graphic Design, Health Care Services, Identity Marketing, In-Store Advertising, Internet/Web Design, Logo & Package Design, Luxury Products, Media Buying Services, Media Planning, Media Relations, Newspapers & Magazines, Package Design, Point of Purchase, Print, Production, Promotions, Publicity/Promotions, Regional, Retail, Sales Promotion, Seniors' Market, Social Marketing/Nonprofit, Social Media, Strategic Planning/Research, Urban Market, Web (Banner Ads, Pop-ups, etc.), Women's Market

Approx. Annual Billings: $6,000,000

Cherie Hebert *(CEO & Partner)*
Sara Ashy *(Partner & Dir-Ops)*
Cathi Pavy *(Partner & Dir-Creative)*
Julie Gauthier *(Dir-PR)*
Monica Hebert *(Dir-Media)*
Daniel Kedinger *(Dir-Digital Mktg)*
Eddie Talbot *(Dir-Digital Production & IT)*
Kellie Viola *(Dir-Art)*
Emily Burke *(Sr Acct Exec)*
Bria Wheeler *(Acct Exec)*
Tim Landry *(Copywriter)*
Cali Comeaux *(Coord-Traffic)*

BCA (BRIAN CRONIN & ASSOCIATES INC.)

315 Madison Ave Ste 702, New York, NY 10017-6503
Tel.: (212) 286-9300
Fax: (212) 286-9736
E-Mail: mail@bcany.com
Web Site: www.bcany.com

Employees: 10
Year Founded: 1984

Agency Specializes In: Above-the-Line, Advertising, Advertising Specialties, Affluent Market, Aviation & Aerospace, Below-the-Line, Brand Development & Integration, Broadcast, Business Publications, Business-To-Business, Collateral, Communications, Consumer Marketing, Consumer Publications, Corporate Communications, E-Commerce, Financial, Graphic Design, Hospitality, Integrated Marketing, Internet/Web Design, Leisure, Logo & Package Design, Magazines, Market Research, Media Buying Services, Media Planning, Media Relations, Newspaper, Newspapers & Magazines, Out-of-Home Media, Over-50 Market, Planning & Consultation, Print, Public Relations, Publicity/Promotions, Radio, Restaurant, Strategic Planning/Research, Trade & Consumer Magazines, Transportation, Travel & Tourism

Approx. Annual Billings: $5,000,000

James M. Cronin *(Pres)*
Evelyn Galli *(COO)*
Susanna Gahan *(Comptroller)*
Lise Propst *(Dir-Art & Digital)*

Accounts:
American General Supplies
China Eastern Airlines
Doyle Collection
Fitzpatrick Hotels Group; New York Hotels
Glamour
Glamour Destination Management Company (DMC)
Kartagener Associates Inc.; NY
Lion World Tours; Toronto, Canada
South African Airways; FL

Star Alliance
Sun International

BCA MARKETING COMMUNICATIONS

800 Westchester Ave. N641, Rye Brook, NY 10573
Tel.: (212) 286-9300
Fax: (212) 286-9736
E-Mail: mail@bcany.com
Web Site: www.bcany.com

Employees: 6

National Agency Associations: 4A's

Agency Specializes In: Advertising, Brand Development & Integration, Broadcast, Collateral, Corporate Communications, Corporate Identity, Direct Response Marketing, Email, Exhibit/Trade Shows, Graphic Design, Internet/Web Design, Media Buying Services, Media Planning, Multimedia, Outdoor, Print, Public Relations, Search Engine Optimization, Strategic Planning/Research

Revenue: $6,000,000

James M. Cronin *(Pres)*
Evelyn Galli *(COO)*

Accounts:
bmi
China Eastern
Doyle Collection
KAI Collection
Lion World Travel
Qatar Airways
Round Hill Hotel & Villas Branding, Creative, Media Buying, Social Media Strategy
South African Airways
Star Alliance

THE BCB GROUP, INC.

10 Alexander Dr, Wallingford, CT 06492
Tel.: (203) 630-7800
Fax: (203) 630-7805
E-Mail: info@bcbgroup.com
Web Site: www.bcbgroup.com

E-Mail for Key Personnel:
Creative Dir.: dbelmont@bcbgroup.com

Employees: 12
Year Founded: 1985

Agency Specializes In: Advertising, Automotive, Aviation & Aerospace, Brand Development & Integration, Collateral, Communications, Consulting, Corporate Identity, Direct Response Marketing, Electronic Media, Event Planning & Marketing, Exhibit/Trade Shows, Graphic Design, Internet/Web Design, Logo & Package Design, Media Planning, Multimedia, Planning & Consultation, Point of Purchase, Point of Sale, Print, Production, Public Relations

Dick Belmont *(VP-Creative Svcs)*
John Cordone *(VP)*
Tracy Bugryn *(Mgr-Media & Acct Exec)*

Accounts:
American Electronic Components; Elkhart, IN Automotive & Industrial Switches, Relays; 2003
AquaPure by 3M
Godiva Chocolatier; New York, NY Confections; 1995
Honeywell Life Safety Systems
International Aero Engines; Glastonbury, CT V2500 Commercial Turbofan Aircraft Engine; 1989
Sunglass Hut/Watch Station

BCF

4500 Main St Ste 600, Virginia Beach, VA 23462
Tel.: (757) 497-4811
Fax: (757) 497-3684
E-Mail: mpannullo@boomyourbrand.com
Web Site: www.bcfagency.com

Employees: 53
Year Founded: 1980

National Agency Associations: PRSA

Agency Specializes In: Advertising, Advertising Specialties, Affluent Market, Alternative Advertising, Arts, Brand Development & Integration, Broadcast, Cable T.V., Co-op Advertising, Collateral, Communications, Consulting, Consumer Goods, Consumer Marketing, Consumer Publications, Content, Corporate Communications, Corporate Identity, Crisis Communications, Customer Relationship Management, Digital/Interactive, Direct Response Marketing, E-Commerce, Electronic Media, Email, Environmental, Event Planning & Marketing, Exhibit/Trade Shows, Experience Design, Government/Political, Graphic Design, Guerilla Marketing, Hospitality, Household Goods, Identity Marketing, In-Store Advertising, Information Technology, Integrated Marketing, International, Internet/Web Design, Leisure, Local Marketing, Logo & Package Design, Luxury Products, Magazines, Market Research, Media Buying Services, Media Planning, Media Relations, Media Training, Men's Market, Mobile Marketing, Multimedia, New Product Development, New Technologies, Newspaper, Newspapers & Magazines, Out-of-Home Media, Outdoor, Over-50 Market, Package Design, Paid Searches, Pets , Planning & Consultation, Point of Purchase, Print, Production, Production (Ad, Film, Broadcast), Public Relations, Publicity/Promotions, RSS (Really Simple Syndication), Radio, Regional, Search Engine Optimization, Seniors' Market, Social Marketing/Nonprofit, Social Media, Sports Market, Strategic Planning/Research, T.V., Teen Market, Trade & Consumer Magazines, Travel & Tourism, Tween Market, Urban Market, Viral/Buzz/Word of Mouth, Web (Banner Ads, Pop-ups, etc.), Women's Market

Approx. Annual Billings: $30,000,000

Breakdown of Gross Billings by Media: Internet Adv.: $10,000,000; Mags.: $7,800,000; Newsp.: $5,400,000; Outdoor: $410,000; Radio: $5,190,000; T.V.: $1,200,000

Art Webb *(CEO)*
Jacinthe Pare *(Partner & Acct Grp Dir)*
Greg Ward *(Partner & Acct Grp Dir)*
Ted Rooke *(Dir-Media)*
John Runberg *(Dir-New Bus)*
Donna Ames *(Office Mgr)*
Avery Pittman *(Mgr-Media)*
Glenn Dano *(Acct Supvr)*
Emily Baine *(Supvr-Media)*
Destiny Gensemer *(Sr Acct Exec-PR)*

Accounts:
America's Snowboard Team; Aspen, CO Sports Marketing; 2009
Armada Hoffler/Westin Residences; Virginia Beach, VA Luxury Residences; 2010
Aspen Chamber and Resort Association; Aspen, CO Travel & Tourism; 2011
Bumps for Boomers; Aspen, CO Travel & Tourism; 2009
The Contemporary Art Center of Virginia
The Fredericksburg Regional Tourism Partnership (Agency of Record) Creative, Interactive, Media, Public Relations, Tourism; 2005
Naples Marco Island; Naples, FL PR, Travel & Tourism; 2006
Ocean Breeze Waterpark; Virginia Beach, VA Attractions/Media; 2011
Virginia Aquarium & Marine Science Center; Virginia Beach, VA Education Center & Attraction; 1996
Virginia Beach Convention & Visitors Bureau; Virginia Beach, VA Tourism, Meetings & Conventions; 1990
Virginia Beach Neptune Festival; Virginia Beach, VA Festival/Special Event; 2003
Virginia Beach Rescue Squad Foundation; Virginia Beach, VA Recruitment; 2006
Virginia Department of Conservation and Recreation; Richmond, VA Environmental, Social Marketing; 2010
Virginia Tourism Corporation; Richmond, VA Campaign: "Virginia Is For Lovers", Travel & Tourism; 2006

BCP LTD.

3530 St Lawrence Ste 300, Montreal, QC H2X 2V1 Canada
Tel.: (514) 285-0077
Fax: (514) 285-0078
Web Site: www.facebook.com/BCPMontreal

E-Mail for Key Personnel:
President: jparisella@bcp.ca
Media Dir.: ckairns@bcp.ca

Employees: 60
Year Founded: 1963

National Agency Associations:

Agency Specializes In: Advertising

Approx. Annual Billings: $42,183,430 Capitalized

Alain Tadros *(Pres)*
Patrice Landry *(Controller)*
Sebastien Baillargeon *(Dir-Art)*
Harry Bouchard *(Dir-Creative & Brand Activation)*
Chantal Joly *(Dir-Creative)*

Accounts:
Astral Campaign: "In Between Odds", Campaign: "Poisoning"
Brunet Campaign: "Myriam", Media, TV
Napa Auto Parts Campaign: "Peace of Mind"
National Defence
Old Spice
The Quebec Federation of Family Doctors
Super C

BD&E

681 Andersen Drive, Pittsburgh, PA 15220
Tel.: (412) 458-3336
Web Site: www.bdeusa.com

Year Founded: 1975

Agency Specializes In: Advertising, Brand Development & Integration

Jeffrey Flick *(Pres & CEO)*
Kristina Martinez *(Exec VP & Creative Dir)*

Accounts:
New-Casco USA

BDC ADVERTISING

(Acquired & Absorbed by Fish Marketing)

BDOT

54 W 40th St, New York, NY 10018
Tel.: (212) 470-0002
Web Site: www.bdotagency.com

Employees: 12
Year Founded: 2015

Agency Specializes In: Advertising, Advertising

Specialties, Affluent Market, African-American Market, Alternative Advertising, Arts, Automotive, Brand Development & Integration, Branded Entertainment, Business-To-Business, Commercial Photography, Communications, Computers & Software, Consulting, Consumer Goods, Consumer Marketing, Content, Corporate Communications, Corporate Identity, Cosmetics, Crisis Communications, Customer Relationship Management, Digital/Interactive, Direct-to-Consumer, E-Commerce, Education, Electronics, Email, Entertainment, Event Planning & Marketing, Exhibit/Trade Shows, Experience Design, Fashion/Apparel, Graphic Design, Guerilla Marketing, High Technology, Hispanic Market, Hospitality, Identity Marketing, In-Store Advertising, Information Technology, Integrated Marketing, Internet/Web Design, Local Marketing, Logo & Package Design, Luxury Products, Media Planning, Media Relations, Media Training, Men's Market, Merchandising, Mobile Marketing, Multicultural, New Technologies, Package Design, Planning & Consultation, Production, Production (Ad, Film, Broadcast), Promotions, Public Relations, Publicity/Promotions, Restaurant, Retail, Sales Promotion, Search Engine Optimization, Social Marketing/Nonprofit, Social Media, Sports Market, Strategic Planning/Research, Transportation, Travel & Tourism, Urban Market, Viral/Buzz/Word of Mouth, Web (Banner Ads, Pop-ups, etc.), Women's Market

Reginald Christian *(CEO & CCO)*
Tiffany Carr *(Chief Comm Officer & Chief Sustainability Officer)*
Gary J. Nix *(Chief Strategy Officer)*

Accounts:
New-Hudson Group; 2015

BDS MARKETING
10 Holland, Irvine, CA 92618
Tel.: (949) 472-6700
Fax: (949) 597-2220
E-Mail: marketing@bdsmarketing.com
Web Site: www.bdsmarketing.com

E-Mail for Key Personnel:
President: ken.kress@bdsmarketing.com

Employees: 140
Year Founded: 1984

Agency Specializes In: Business-To-Business, Collateral, Consumer Marketing, Event Planning & Marketing, High Technology, Information Technology, Merchandising, Planning & Consultation, Point of Purchase, Point of Sale, Publicity/Promotions, Retail, Sales Promotion, Sponsorship

Approx. Annual Billings: $40,000,000

Mark Dean *(Founder & CEO)*
Ken Kress *(Pres)*
Kristen Cook *(Exec VP)*
Mark Heidel *(Sr VP-Client Dev)*
David Tranberg *(Sr VP-Client Dev)*
Colan Sewell *(VP-Brand Shops)*
Melissa Burke *(Dir-Mktg Svcs)*
Mollie Gray *(Dir-Solution Dev)*
Ian Holtz *(Dir-Client Dev)*

Accounts:
Beats
Brother Corporation; Bridgewater, NJ
Canon
Cisco
Crocs; Denver, CO
Dell
DirecTV; El Segundo, CA
FedEx; Dallas, TX
Hoover; Glenwillow, OH
Jawbone
Levi's
Motorola Solutions, Inc.; Schaumburg, IL
Oreck; Nashville, TN
Sam's Club; Bentonville, AR
Southern California Edison; Los Angeles, CA
Staples
Toshiba; New York, NY
Travelpro; Ft Lauderdale, FL
Vanity Fair; Greensboro, NC
Walmart

BEACON MEDIA GROUP
1 International Blvd Ste 1110, Mahwah, NJ 07495
Tel.: (201) 335-0032
E-Mail: info@thebeaconmg.com
Web Site: www.thebeaconmg.com

Agency Specializes In: Advertising, Children's Market, Entertainment, Sponsorship, Teen Market, Tween Market

Tom Horner *(Pres)*
Shelly Hirsch *(CEO)*
Paul Caldera *(Exec VP-Media Svcs)*
Lillian LeBron *(Exec VP-Acct Svcs)*
Jasmine Colon *(Mgr-Brdcst Traffic)*
Meredith Kawer *(Sr Media Buyer & Planner)*

Accounts:
MGA Entertainment, Inc.

BEALS CUNNINGHAM STRATEGIC SERVICES
2333 E Britton Rd, Oklahoma City, OK 73131-3526
Tel.: (405) 478-4752
Fax: (405) 478-4760
Toll Free: (800) 322-9894
Web Site: www.bealscunningham.com

E-Mail for Key Personnel:
Chairman: mikec@bealscunningham.com
President: nickc@bealscunningham.com

Employees: 30
Year Founded: 1957

National Agency Associations: 4A's

Agency Specializes In: Advertising, Advertising Specialties, Automotive, Business-To-Business, Collateral, Corporate Identity, E-Commerce, Exhibit/Trade Shows, Graphic Design, Health Care Services, In-Store Advertising, Infomercials, Integrated Marketing, Magazines, Media Buying Services, Media Relations, Medical Products, Multimedia, Newspaper, Outdoor, Point of Purchase, Production (Print), Promotions, Public Relations, Publicity/Promotions, Radio, Restaurant, Strategic Planning/Research, T.V., Technical Advertising, Trade & Consumer Magazines, Web (Banner Ads, Pop-ups, etc.)

Approx. Annual Billings: $20,000,000

Michael Cunningham *(Chm)*
Nick Cunningham *(Pres)*
Jon Lundeen *(Treas, Sec & Exec VP)*
Michael Hayes *(VP-Bus Dev)*
Joi Marcum *(VP-Bus Dev)*
Michelle Howard *(Dir-Media)*
Phil Tomey *(Dir-Art)*

BEANSTALK
220 E 42nd St 15th Fl, New York, NY 10017
Tel.: (212) 421-6060
Fax: (212) 421-6388
E-Mail: beanstalk@beanstalk.com
Web Site: www.beanstalk.com

Employees: 25

Agency Specializes In: Advertising, Automotive, Brand Development & Integration, Consumer Goods, Entertainment, Food Service, Logo & Package Design, Planning & Consultation, Retail, Sponsorship

Rachel Terrace *(Sr VP-Brand Mgmt)*
Lisa Reiner *(Mng Dir-Europe & Asia Pacific)*
Celia Asprea *(VP-HR)*
Nicholas Bloom *(VP-Brand Mgmt)*
Nicole Desir *(VP-Brand Mgmt)*
Debra Restler *(VP-Bus Dev & Mktg)*
Caren Chacko *(Assoc VP-Brand Mgmt)*
Kim Krizelman *(Dir-Brand Mgmt & On-site-P&G)*
Lauren Montemaro *(Mgr-Brand Mgmt)*

Accounts:
Ajax
Andy Warhol
AT&T Communications Corp.
David Tutera
Dinotopia
The Dow Chemical Co. GREAT STUFF, SafeTouch
Ford Mustang, Thunderbird, Volvo Cars
Harley Davidson Motor Cycles
HGTV; Knoxville, TN Licensing
HUE
Irish Spring
The Limited
mary-kate&ashley
Mr. Dee's OLD Bay
Procter & Gamble Always, Max Factor, Pampers
Purina
Shell
Stanley
Subway
Topps
United States Army

BEARDWOOD & CO
588 Broadway Ste 803, New York, NY 10012
Tel.: (212) 334-5689
Fax: (917) 210-4040
E-Mail: hello@beardwood.com
Web Site: www.beardwood.com

Agency Specializes In: Advertising, Brand Development & Integration, Digital/Interactive, Graphic Design, Logo & Package Design, Social Media

Julia Beardwood *(Founder & Partner)*
Ryan Lynch *(Mng Partner)*
Sarah Williams *(Creative Dir)*
Trey Armstrong *(Acct Mgr)*

Accounts:
New-Honest Tea

BEAULIEU ADVERTISING & DESIGN INC
PO Box 703, North Scituate, MA 02060
Tel.: (781) 378-1742
Fax: (781) 424-7064
Web Site: www.beaulieudesign.com

Agency Specializes In: Advertising, Broadcast, Collateral, Corporate Identity, Graphic Design, Internet/Web Design, Logo & Package Design, Media Buying Services, Package Design, Print

Bob Beaulieu *(Owner)*

Accounts:
Spalding Laboratories, Inc.

BEAUTY@GOTHAM
(Formerly Gotham Incorporated)
150 E 42nd St 12th Fl, New York, NY 10017
Tel.: (212) 414-7000

Fax: (212) 414-7095
Web Site: www.beautyatgotham.com

Employees: 180
Year Founded: 1994

National Agency Associations: 4A's-AAF

Agency Specializes In: Advertising, Brand Development & Integration, Broadcast, Business Publications, Business-To-Business, Cable T.V., Collateral, Communications, Consumer Marketing, Consumer Publications, Corporate Communications, Corporate Identity, Cosmetics, Digital/Interactive, E-Commerce, Electronic Media, Event Planning & Marketing, Exhibit/Trade Shows, Faith Based, Fashion/Apparel, Financial, Graphic Design, Health Care Services, High Technology, In-Store Advertising, Infomercials, Logo & Package Design, Magazines, New Product Development, Newspaper, Newspapers & Magazines, Out-of-Home Media, Outdoor, Over-50 Market, Pharmaceutical, Point of Purchase, Point of Sale, Print, Production, Radio, Retail, Sales Promotion, Seniors' Market, Sponsorship, Strategic Planning/Research, T.V., Teen Market, Trade & Consumer Magazines, Travel & Tourism

Breakdown of Gross Billings by Media: Bus. Publs.: 1%; Cable T.V.: 9%; Consumer Publs.: 15%; Fees: 3%; Internet Adv.: 1%; Network Radio: 1%; Network T.V.: 38%; Newsp.: 7%; Outdoor: 1%; Production: 5%; Spot Radio: 5%; Spot T.V.: 10%; Syndication: 4%

Volker Ast *(Pres)*
Laurie Donlon *(Mng Partner & Dir-Brand-Global)*
Stu Turner *(Mng Partner & Dir-Graphic Svcs)*
Sarah Kim *(Dir-Creative Svcs & Ops)*
Joanne Ragazzo *(Dir-Fin)*
Craig Knowles *(Assoc Dir-Creative)*
Courtney Cornelius *(Acct Supvr)*
Laura Norcini *(Acct Supvr)*

Accounts:
1-800 OK Cable; Englewood, NJ (Lead Creative Agency) Cable Television Operators - NY, NJ & CT
Ad Council
American Heart Association Campaign: "Hands-On Experience"
Best Western International; Phoenix, AZ
Britax B-ready Products
Citi Bank AAdvantage, Online, Social Media Marketing
The Collegiate Church of New York Outdoor, TV
Goody Haircare
Hitachi America
Knight Trading Group, Inc.; Jersey City, NJ Leading Market Maker; 1999
L'Oreal USA, Inc. Maybelline, Maybelline Define-A-Lash, Maybelline Dream, Maybelline Superstay Foundation, Maybelline Superstay Lipstick
Lindt & Sprungli USA Creative; 2001
Lufthansa; East Meadow, NY; 2000
Luxottica Group Digital, In-Store Communications, Lead Creative, Mobile Marketing, Social Media, Sunglass Hut
Maybelline New York
The New York Pops
Newell Rubbermaid Irwin Tools Division
Newman's Own; Westport, CT Pasta Sauces, Salad Dressing; 1999
NFL
Priceline
Sony Ericsson
Time Warner Cable
Waterford Brands
Wedgwood
Yellowbook.com (Agency of Record)

BEBER SILVERSTEIN GROUP

89 NE 27th St, Miami, FL 33137
Tel.: (305) 856-9800
Fax: (305) 854-7686
Web Site: www.thinkbsg.com

E-Mail for Key Personnel:
President: jennifer@bsgworld.com
Creative Dir.: joe@bsgworld.com
Media Dir.: joel@bsgworld.com

Employees: 40
Year Founded: 1972

National Agency Associations: 4A's-ARF

Agency Specializes In: Advertising, Bilingual Market, Brand Development & Integration, Broadcast, Cable T.V., Collateral, Consumer Goods, Consumer Marketing, Consumer Publications, Corporate Communications, Corporate Identity, Crisis Communications, Digital/Interactive, Direct-to-Consumer, Electronic Media, Environmental, Gay & Lesbian Market, Graphic Design, Health Care Services, Hispanic Market, Internet/Web Design, Local Marketing, Logo & Package Design, Magazines, Media Buying Services, Media Planning, Media Relations, Newspaper, Newspapers & Magazines, Out-of-Home Media, Outdoor, Over-50 Market, Package Design, Paid Searches, Point of Purchase, Point of Sale, Print, Production, Production (Print), Public Relations, Real Estate, Restaurant, Seniors' Market, Sponsorship, Strategic Planning/Research, T.V., Transportation, Travel & Tourism

Approx. Annual Billings: $70,000,000

Breakdown of Gross Billings by Media: Internet Adv.: 8%; Mags.: 18%; Newsp.: 16%; Outdoor: 9%; Radio: 9%; T.V.: 40%

Elaine Silverstein *(Chm)*
Jennifer Beber *(Pres)*
Mitch Shapiro *(Partner & Gen Mgr)*
Bruce Noonan *(Pres-Travel Grp)*
Leslie Pantin *(Pres-PR Grp)*
Christine Bucan *(Exec VP)*
Ann Drozd *(VP-Brand Dev)*
Victoria Penn *(Dir-Media)*
Joe Perz *(Dir-Creative)*
Jessica Drouet *(Sr Acct Exec-PR)*
Isabel Trueba *(Acct Exec)*

Accounts:
AvMed Health Plans
Broward Health Health System; 2007
Carnival Cruise Line Trade; 2011
Costa Cruise Lines
Hertz Neverlost
Hertz (Latin America) Rental Cars; 1998
Ocean Club
SunPass Electronic Tolling

BECK INTERACTIVE, INC.

784 Lakeshore Dr, Redwood Shores, CA 94070
Tel.: (650) 592-3251
Fax: (650) 592-2897
E-Mail: info@beckinteractive.com
Web Site: www.beckinteractive.com

Year Founded: 1997

Agency Specializes In: Advertising, Computers & Software, Corporate Communications, Digital/Interactive, E-Commerce, Multimedia, Sales Promotion, Trade & Consumer Magazines, Web (Banner Ads, Pop-ups, etc.)

Jo Beck *(Owner)*

Accounts:
Activision Blizzard, Inc
Bandai Namco Games
EA
Gateway
Lexus
NAMCO
Symantec
True Games
Webex

BECKER GUERRY

107 Tindall Rd, Middletown, NJ 07748-2321
Tel.: (732) 671-6440
Fax: (732) 671-4350
E-Mail: info@beckerguerry.com
Web Site: www.beckerguerry.com

Employees: 10
Year Founded: 1970

National Agency Associations: BMA

Agency Specializes In: Advertising, Advertising Specialties, Agriculture, Automotive, Brand Development & Integration, Business-To-Business, Co-op Advertising, Collateral, College, Communications, Consulting, Consumer Marketing, Consumer Publications, Corporate Communications, Corporate Identity, Cosmetics, Digital/Interactive, Direct Response Marketing, Direct-to-Consumer, Education, Electronic Media, Electronics, Email, Engineering, Environmental, Event Planning & Marketing, Exhibit/Trade Shows, Financial, Food Service, Graphic Design, Health Care Services, High Technology, Identity Marketing, Industrial, Information Technology, Internet/Web Design, Local Marketing, Logo & Package Design, Magazines, Marine, Market Research, Media Buying Services, Media Planning, Media Relations, Medical Products, Merchandising, Mobile Marketing, Multimedia, New Product Development, Newspaper, Newspapers & Magazines, Out-of-Home Media, Outdoor, Pharmaceutical, Planning & Consultation, Point of Purchase, Point of Sale, Print, Production, Public Relations, Publicity/Promotions, Radio, Sales Promotion, Seniors' Market, Strategic Planning/Research, Technical Advertising, Trade & Consumer Magazines, Transportation

Approx. Annual Billings: $5,000,000

Breakdown of Gross Billings by Media: Corp. Communications: $300,000; Exhibits/Trade Shows: $500,000; Internet Adv.: $700,000; Print: $3,500,000

Robert J. Becker *(Pres)*
Peter Guerry *(Co-Principal & Dir-Creative)*
Kim Gold *(Dir-Digital Media)*

Accounts:
Farbest Brands; Montvale, NJ Food Ingredients; 2008
Janssen PMP; Titusville, NJ Econea; 2006
Terumo Medical Corporation

BECKETT & BECKETT, INC.

1051 E Altadena Dr, Altadena, CA 91001-2040
Tel.: (626) 791-7954
Fax: (626) 791-0579
Toll Free: (800) 336-8797
E-Mail: info@beckettadv.com
Web Site: www.beckettadv.com

E-Mail for Key Personnel:
President: sharonb@beckettadv.com
Creative Dir.: edwardb@beckettadv.com

Employees: 10
Year Founded: 1967

Agency Specializes In: Advertising, Agriculture, Automotive, Aviation & Aerospace, Brand Development & Integration, Business-To-Business, Cable T.V., Collateral, Communications, Consulting, Corporate Identity, Direct Response

Marketing, E-Commerce, Electronic Media, Environmental, Event Planning & Marketing, Exhibit/Trade Shows, Financial, Graphic Design, Health Care Services, High Technology, Industrial, Information Technology, Internet/Web Design, Investor Relations, Logo & Package Design, Media Buying Services, Medical Products, New Product Development, Pharmaceutical, Planning & Consultation, Point of Purchase, Point of Sale, Print, Production, Public Relations, Publicity/Promotions, Sports Market, Strategic Planning/Research, Technical Advertising, Transportation, Travel & Tourism

Approx. Annual Billings: $1,900,000

Breakdown of Gross Billings by Media: Collateral: 15%; Consulting: 15%; D.M.: 15%; Graphic Design: 10%; Pub. Rels.: 10%; Strategic Planning/Research: 15%; Trade Shows: 5%; Worldwide Web Sites: 15%

John Schiavone *(Sr Art Dir)*

Accounts:
B.I.G. Enterprises; El Monte, CA Pre-Fabricated Buildings; 1987
First Enterprise Bank

BEDFORD ADVERTISING INC.
1718 Trinity Vly Dr Ste 200, Carrollton, TX 75006
Tel.: (972) 458-1150
Fax: (972) 385-7526
Toll Free: (800) 880-6840
E-Mail: info@bedfordads.com
Web Site: www.bedfordads.com

E-Mail for Key Personnel:
President: jeffjutte@bedfordads.com
Creative Dir.: jasonhuston@bedfordads.com

Employees: 20
Year Founded: 1980

Agency Specializes In: Advertising, Automotive, Cable T.V., Infomercials, Internet/Web Design, Newspapers & Magazines, Outdoor, Print, Production, Radio, T.V.

Approx. Annual Billings: $13,000,000

Breakdown of Gross Billings by Media: D.M.: $3,500,000; Newsp.: $1,000,000; Production: $1,000,000; Radio: $2,500,000; T.V.: $5,000,000

Jeff Jutte *(Pres & Partner)*
Alexis Prochnow *(Partner & VP)*
Curtis Linker *(Controller)*
John Adams *(Sr Dir-Art)*
Eric Foster *(Dir-Creative)*
Marlo Haft *(Office Mgr-AP & AR)*
Chad Stanhope *(Acct Exec)*
Nicole Carr *(Coord-Admin/Traffic)*

Accounts:
Arlington Auto Mall
Britain Chevy
Coker Floors; Dallas, TX; 2004
Drivers Select
FlavaTV
Ford of Greenfield
Frank Parra Chevrolet; Dallas, TX; 2008
Houston Acura Dealers
Hyundai of Greenfield
James Wood
Kia of West Springfield
Knapp Chevy
Liberty Ford
Lone Star of Cleburne
Longbine Auto Plaza
Nelson Hall Chevrolet; Meridan, MS; 1992
Rocky Mountain Acura Dealers Association; Denver, CO; 2006
Toyota of Richardson; Richardson, TX; 1991
Volvo of Dallas; Dallas, TX; 2005
Volvo of Richardson; Richardson, TX; 2003
Westway Ford; Dallas, TX; 1998

BEE-LINE COMMUNICATIONS
1260 American Way, Libertyville, IL 60048
Tel.: (224) 207-4320
Fax: (224) 207-4321
E-Mail: buzz@beecommunications.com
Web Site: www.beecommunications.com

Year Founded: 2005

Agency Specializes In: Advertising, Digital/Interactive, Internet/Web Design, Social Media, Strategic Planning/Research

Jay Goethal *(COO)*
Connie Hetzler *(Dir-Mktg Comm)*
John Zygmunt *(Dir-Digital Svcs)*
Taylor Wagener *(Acct Mgr)*

Accounts:
Belle Joli Winery

BEEBY CLARK + MEYLER
700 Canal Street, 3rd Floor, Stamford, CT 06902
Tel.: (203) 653-7920
E-Mail: contact@beebyclarkmeyler.com
Web Site: www.beebyclarkmeyler.com

Employees: 40
Year Founded: 2005

Agency Specializes In: Advertising, Affiliate Marketing, Affluent Market, Automotive, Branded Entertainment, Business-To-Business, Collateral, Consulting, Consumer Goods, Consumer Marketing, Content, Corporate Identity, Cosmetics, Digital/Interactive, Direct Response Marketing, Direct-to-Consumer, E-Commerce, Electronic Media, Email, Entertainment, Environmental, Financial, Game Integration, Government/Political, Graphic Design, Health Care Services, High Technology, Hospitality, Household Goods, Industrial, Information Technology, Integrated Marketing, Internet/Web Design, Leisure, Luxury Products, Media Buying Services, Media Planning, Mobile Marketing, Multimedia, New Technologies, Out-of-Home Media, Pharmaceutical, Production, Production (Ad, Film, Broadcast), RSS (Really Simple Syndication), Real Estate, Search Engine Optimization, Sponsorship, Sports Market, Strategic Planning/Research, Travel & Tourism, Web (Banner Ads, Pop-ups, etc.)

Approx. Annual Billings: $30,000,000

Breakdown of Gross Billings by Media: Internet Adv.: 100%

Thomas Beeby *(Principal & Exec Dir-Creative)*
Michael K. Clark *(Principal)*
Scott Sterner *(Sr VP-Search & Performance Mktg)*
Debbie Fagerstrom *(Sr Dir-Media Partnerships)*
Lijo Joseph *(Sr Dir-Performance Media)*
Kurt Winkelman *(Sr Dir-Art)*
Mariana Rodriguez *(Sr Acct Dir)*
Jill Miklus *(Dir-Search & Performance Media)*
Michael Civins *(Sr Acct Mgr)*
Anna Baskin *(Mgr-Bus Dev)*
Eric Russo *(Mgr-Performance Media)*
James Mullany *(Sr Analyst-Performance Media & Partnerships)*
Maureen Pitagora *(Sr Analyst-Search & Performance Mktg)*

Accounts:
All Connect
ERA
Gas South Energy/Utility; 2005
General Electric Ecomagination; 2006
Marriott Hotel Campaign: "Mobile App Launch"
Music & Arts
Playtex Baby
Schick Hydro
Weight Watchers

BEEHIVE COMMUNICATIONS
(Acquired by Publicis Group S.A. & Name Changed to Publicis Beehive)

BEEKMAN MARKETING, INC.
5 W 19th St, New York, NY 10011
Tel.: (212) 387-8500
Fax: (212) 387-7875
Web Site: www.beekmanmarketing.com

Employees: 6
Year Founded: 1975

Agency Specializes In: Direct Response Marketing, Government/Political

Approx. Annual Billings: $4,000,000

Breakdown of Gross Billings by Media: D.M.: $2,000,000; Newsp.: $2,000,000

David Pursch *(Pres)*

Accounts:
American Museum of the Moving Image
Fortune
The Frick Collection
New Museum
NY School of Interior Design
Parrish Art Museum
Royal Oak Foundation
Sotheby's
The Spectator
SUNY Downstate
TIME
The Times Literary Supplement
The Times of London
Yeshiva University Museum

BEHAVIOR DESIGN
40 W 27th St Ste 401, New York, NY 10001
Tel.: (212) 532-4002
Fax: (212) 532-4090
E-Mail: info@behaviordesign.com
Web Site: www.behaviordesign.com

Agency Specializes In: Advertising, Entertainment, Radio, T.V.

Mimi Young *(Founder, Partner & Mng Dir)*
Ralph Lucci *(Co-Founder & Dir-UX)*
Jeff Piazza *(Co-Founder & Dir-User Experience)*

Accounts:
AARP Bulletin Redesign
Adecco
Imaginova LiveScience.com; 2007
The Onion Redesign
ResortQuest International
SIRIUS OEM Partners Microsites

BEHIND THE SCENES MARKETING
90 Windsor Dr, Pine Brook, NJ 07058
Tel.: (973) 276-9472
Fax: (973) 276-9272
E-Mail: info@behindthescenesmarketing.com
Web Site: www.behindthescenesmarketing.com

Employees: 5
Year Founded: 2003

Agency Specializes In: Advertising, Advertising Specialties

Sales: $500,000

Michael Adams *(Founder & Owner)*
Tina Wang *(VP)*

Accounts:
Cardinal Components
Elcom
Energy Kinetics/System 2000
ISP-GAF
Ricoh

BEHR DESIGN, LLC
114 E Poplar St, Sidney, OH 45365
Tel.: (937) 492-5704
Fax: (937) 497-1059
E-Mail: info@behrdesign.com
Web Site: www.behrdesign.com

Employees: 5
Year Founded: 1981

Agency Specializes In: Advertising, Brand Development & Integration, Digital/Interactive, Graphic Design, Internet/Web Design, Logo & Package Design, Print, Social Media

Kevin Behr *(Co-Owner)*
Chad Stewart *(Co-Owner)*
Audrey Gutman *(Coord-Sls & Mktg)*

Accounts:
Alexander Yard
Arabian Horse Foundation
Brethren Retirement Community
Clear Strength
Ferguson Construction
FreshWay Foods
IPP Splats
Koester Pavilion
Mary Scott
Shelby County Animal Rescue
Sidney-Shelby County Chamber of Commerce
Whitewater Construction

BELIEF LLC
5325 Ballard Ave NW, Seattle, WA 98107
Tel.: (206) 659-6297
E-Mail: hello@beliefagency.com
Web Site: www.beliefagency.com

Year Founded: 2012

Agency Specializes In: Advertising, Brand Development & Integration, Content, Digital/Interactive, Internet/Web Design, Package Design, Print, Sponsorship

Jesse Bryan *(CEO & Creative Dir)*
Mike Anderson *(Mng Dir)*
Jordan Butcher *(Dir-Art)*
Andy Maier *(Dir-Media)*
Matt Naylor *(Sr Designer)*

Accounts:
Analytics Pros
Rover

BELLAGURL
809 Arendell St, Morehead City, NC 28557
Tel.: (252) 726-0169
E-Mail: sayhello@BGDigitalGroup.com
Web Site: www.bgdigitalgroup.com/

Agency Specializes In: Advertising, Brand Development & Integration, Corporate Identity, Digital/Interactive, Event Planning & Marketing, Internet/Web Design, Radio, Social Media, T.V.

Cheryl Pigott *(Pres)*
Andy Pigott *(CFO)*
Susan Yates *(Dir-Art)*
Ruthanne Gosnell *(Acct Mgr)*
Carrie Hammill *(Mgr-Social Media)*

Accounts:
Broad Street Clinic
Johnson Family Dentistry
NC Fun Book
Sweet Dreams Gifts & Interiors

BELLMONT PARTNERS
3300 Edinborough Way Ste 700, Minneapolis, MN 55435
Tel.: (612) 255-1111
E-Mail: info@bellmontpartners.com
Web Site: www.bellmontpartners.com

Agency Specializes In: Advertising, Brand Development & Integration, Digital/Interactive, Event Planning & Marketing, Media Relations, Social Media

Brian Bellmont *(Pres)*
Jen Bellmont *(COO & Partner)*
Shelli Lissick *(Partner)*
David Hlavac *(Acct Dir)*
Bridget Nelson Monroe *(Acct Dir)*
Megan Derkey *(Sr Acct Exec)*
Briana Gruenewald *(Acct Exec)*
Emma Strub *(Acct Coord)*

Accounts:
New-Explore Minnesota (Agency of Record) Media Relations
New-Peg's Countryside Cafe
New-Q.Cumbers
New-Uptown Association

BELMONT ICEHOUSE
3116 Commerce St Ste D, Dallas, TX 75226
Tel.: (972) 755-3200
Fax: (972) 755-3201
E-Mail: info@belmonticehouse.com
Web Site: www.belmonticehouse.com

Agency Specializes In: Advertising, Collateral, Corporate Identity, Internet/Web Design, Print

Tim Hudson *(Co-Founder & Partner)*
Drew Holmgreen *(VP & Acct Svcs Dir)*
Melissa Ramos *(Dir-Art)*
Jackie Medling *(Mgr-Production)*
Christina Ciminelli *(Supvr-Media)*
Erica Ashley Page *(Sr Acct Exec)*

Accounts:
Texas A&M University

BELTRAME LEFFLER ADVERTISING
708 Massachusetts Ave, Indianapolis, IN 46204
Tel.: (317) 916-9930
Fax: (317) 916-9935
E-Mail: info@bladv.com
Web Site: www.bladv.com

Employees: 5
Year Founded: 1999

Agency Specializes In: Advertising

Approx. Annual Billings: $2,600,000 (Capitalized)

K.C. Leffler *(Owner)*
Cory Wright *(Designer-Multimedia)*

Accounts:
Anderson CVB
Beverages
Biosound
Charley Biggs
International Dairy-Deli-Bakery-Association; Madison, WI
Mayer Fabrics
ProLiance Energy
Residential
White Rock

BEMIS BALKIND
6135 Wilshire Blvd, Los Angeles, CA 90048-5101
Tel.: (323) 965-4800
Fax: (323) 965-4808
E-Mail: info@bemisbalkind.com
Web Site: insyncbemisbalkind.com

Employees: 24

Agency Specializes In: Entertainment

Kishan Muthucumaru *(Co-Pres & Chief Creative Officer)*
Peter Bemis *(CEO)*
Jeffrey Almeida *(Sr VP-Acct Svcs)*
Robert Dunbar *(Sr Dir-Art)*
Tanner Nilsen *(Sr Dir-Art)*
Noelle Neis *(Producer-Digital)*
Steve Reeves *(Dir-Art)*
Eli Cohen *(Assoc Dir-Creative)*
Jeff Wadley *(Assoc Dir-Creative)*
Frank Walker *(Mgr-Integrated Production)*
Candi Fang *(Sr Acct Exec)*

Accounts:
Dreamworks Pictures
Warner Bros. Pictures

BENAMOR
6355 NW 36th St Ste 307, Miami, FL 33166
Tel.: (305) 400-4961
Web Site: www.benamorgrp.com

Year Founded: 2009

Agency Specializes In: Advertising, Brand Development & Integration, Collateral, Graphic Design, Internet/Web Design, Logo & Package Design, Media Buying Services, Media Planning, Print, Search Engine Optimization

Benjamin Linero *(CEO & Creative Dir)*
Fernando Galvez *(Chief Business Development Officer)*

Accounts:
Miami Classics Garage

BENCHWORKS
860 High St, Chestertown, MD 21620-3909
Tel.: (800) 536-4670
Fax: (410) 810-8863
Toll Free: (800) 536-4670
E-Mail: info@benchworks.com
Web Site: www.benchworks.com

Employees: 30
Year Founded: 1991

Agency Specializes In: Collateral, Customer Relationship Management, Direct Response Marketing, E-Commerce, Food Service, Integrated Marketing, Pharmaceutical

Melissa M. Johnston *(Pres)*
Thad Bench *(CEO)*
Greg Waddell *(Principal)*
Brenda Vujanic *(Exec VP)*
Emil Andrusko *(Sr VP-Pharmaceutical Strategy)*
Christian Meyer *(VP-Strategic Accts)*
Sally Reed *(VP-Digital Svcs)*
Amanda Skilling *(VP-Fin & Admin)*
Charles Laudadio *(Dir-Medical)*

Accounts:
BoatUS
CBRE
Chesapeake Bay Foundation
Curemark
FUZE
Honest Tea
Integrity Tool & Fastener
Kidzsmart
Noramco
Pfizer Pharmaceuticals
Ryland Homes
Shire
Strayer University
West Pharmaceutical Services Daikyo Crystal Zenith, Marketing, Strategic Planning

BENEDICT ADVERTISING
640 N Peninsula Dr, Daytona Beach, FL 32118-3829
Tel.: (386) 255-1222
Fax: (386) 255-6932
Web Site: www.benedictadvertising.com

E-Mail for Key Personnel:
President: michael@benedictadvertising.com
Creative Dir.: chris@benedictadvertising.com
Media Dir.: brenda@benedictadvertising.com

Employees: 26
Year Founded: 1974

National Agency Associations: AAF-MCAN

Agency Specializes In: Advertising, Alternative Advertising, Brand Development & Integration, Broadcast, Business-To-Business, Cable T.V., Collateral, Consulting, Consumer Goods, Consumer Marketing, Consumer Publications, Corporate Communications, Corporate Identity, Digital/Interactive, Direct Response Marketing, E-Commerce, Electronic Media, Environmental, Exhibit/Trade Shows, Experience Design, Fashion/Apparel, Financial, Food Service, Graphic Design, Health Care Services, High Technology, Hospitality, Industrial, Internet/Web Design, Logo & Package Design, Marine, Media Buying Services, Medical Products, Merchandising, New Product Development, Newspapers & Magazines, Outdoor, Over-50 Market, Pets , Pharmaceutical, Planning & Consultation, Point of Purchase, Point of Sale, Promotions, Public Relations, Publicity/Promotions, Radio, Real Estate, Restaurant, Retail, Sales Promotion, Seniors' Market, Social Media, Strategic Planning/Research, T.V., Trade & Consumer Magazines, Travel & Tourism

Approx. Annual Billings: $48,000,000

Breakdown of Gross Billings by Media: Fees: $2,400,000; In-Store Adv.: $240,000; Out-of-Home Media: $4,480,000; Point of Purchase: $200,000; Production: $480,000; Spot T.V.: $28,000,000; Trade & Consumer Mags.: $12,200,000

Michael Benedict *(Pres)*
Pam Clark *(VP-Acct Svc)*
Joey Ramos *(Sr Dir-Art)*
Brenda Sidoti *(Dir-Media)*
Kellen Wohlford *(Dir-Fin)*
Dean Turcol *(Mgr-Pub & Media Rels)*
Ashley Wohlford *(Sr Acct Exec)*
Sarah Bush *(Acct Coord)*
Lori Murray *(Coord-Media)*

Accounts:
ARC Dehooker Fishing Tool; 2006
Donner-Peltier Distillers Event Marketing, Social Media
Florida Lottery
Guy Harvey
Subway Restaurants In Major Markets Nationally; 1984
Thompson Pump & Manufacturing Co.; Port Orange, FL Contractor Pumps; 1990
West Volusia Tourism Advertising Authority Advertising, Public Relations
Zeno's Marketing Agency of Record

BENGHIAT MARKETING & COMMUNICATIONS
(Acquired & Absorbed by The Brandon Agency)

BENNETT & COMPANY MARKETING
543 Estates Pl, Longwood, FL 32779-2857
Tel.: (407) 478-4040
Fax: (407) 478-4050
E-Mail: laura@bennettandco.com
Web Site: www.bennettandco.com

Employees: 4
Year Founded: 1982

Agency Specializes In: Advertising, Event Planning & Marketing, Food Service, Hospitality, Media Relations, Public Relations, Real Estate, Strategic Planning/Research, Travel & Tourism

Laura P. Bennett *(Owner & Pres)*
Melissa Carrier *(Sr VP-Design)*
Colette Shoemaker *(Sr VP-Acct Sls)*
Hilary Esdaile *(Dir & Design)*
Leah Ducey *(Sr Mgr-Production)*
Liz Giordano *(Mgr-Production)*
Melinda Proulx *(Mgr-Design)*
Thomas Karpowski *(Sr Engr-Network)*

Accounts:
American Express
BBU Bank
Cartier
De Beer
Dewar's
Holiday Inn
Kahlua
Starwood Hotels & Resorts Worldwide, Inc.
Toll Brothers

BENNETT GROUP
27 Wormwood St Ste 320, Boston, MA 02210
Tel.: (617) 778-2300
Fax: (617) 778-2333
Web Site: bennettgroupagency.com

Year Founded: 1996

Agency Specializes In: Advertising, Brand Development & Integration, Market Research, Media Buying Services, Media Planning, Print, Radio, Search Engine Optimization, Social Media, T.V.

Doug Bennett *(Owner)*
Jim Rattray *(Exec VP)*

Accounts:
Barmakian Jewelers
North Country Hospital

BENNETT KUHN VARNER, INC.
(Name Changed to BKV, Inc.)

BENSIMON BYRNE
420 Wellington St W, Toronto, ON M5V 1E3 Canada
Tel.: (416) 922-2211
Fax: (416) 922-8590
E-Mail: info@bensimonbyrne.com
Web Site: www.bensimonbyrne.com

Employees: 160
Year Founded: 1993

Agency Specializes In: Business-To-Business, Direct Response Marketing, Financial, Health Care Services, Internet/Web Design, New Product Development, Point of Sale, Production, Public Relations, Recruitment, Retail

Breakdown of Gross Billings by Media: Other: 20%; Print: 20%; Radio & T.V.: 10%; T.V.: 50%

Jack Bensimon *(Founder & Pres)*
Colleen Peddie *(Partner & CFO)*
Joseph Bonnici *(Partner & Exec Creative Dir)*
Lisa Good *(VP & Grp Acct Dir)*
Erin O'Connor *(VP & Grp Acct Dir)*
Phill Dodd *(Dir-User Experience)*
Chris Hayes *(Dir-Svc Design)*
Michelle Pilling *(Dir-Production Svcs)*
Chris Harrison *(Assoc Dir-Creative)*
Kristina Chau *(Mgr-Ops)*

Accounts:
Air Canada Rouge Launch
ALDO Aldo Fights Aids
Constellation Brands Jackson Triggs-We've Got a Wine for That
Government of Ontario Youth Jobs
Mattamy Homes
Nestle Kit Kat Chunky Challenge, Nescafe 3 in 1
President's Choice
Scotiabank (Agency of Record) Spring Lending, Summer of Scene-Scene Debit Card & Credit Card, You're Richer Than You Think
Svedka Campaign: "Halloweek", Svedka Goes Social
TGLN Be a Donor

Branch

OneMethod Inc
445 King Street West Suite 201, Toronto, ON M5V 1K4 Canada
(See Separate Listing)

BENSON MARKETING GROUP LLC
2700 Napa Vly Corporate Dr Ste H, Napa, CA 94558
Tel.: (707) 254-9292
Fax: (707) 254-0433
E-Mail: info@bensonmarketing.com
Web Site: www.bensonmarketing.com

Agency Specializes In: Advertising, Affluent Market, Food Service, Public Relations

Jeremy Benson *(Pres)*
Sarah Jones *(VP)*
Toni Lizotte *(Office Mgr)*
Thea Schlendorf *(Sr Acct Exec)*
Ben Palos *(Acct Exec)*

Accounts:
New-Campari America
Diageo Chateau & Estate Wines
Free the Grapes!
Gil Family Estates
Huge Bear
J. Lohr Winery
Knights Bridge Vineyards
McManis Family Vineyards National PR Campaign
Portfolio Winery
San Diego Chargers
Seguin Moreau Napa Cooperage
Skyy Spirits; 2008
Vine Connections
Winery Exchange
Wines of Garnacha
Zonin USA (Primo Amore)

BENSUR CREATIVE MARKETING GROUP
1062 Brown Ave Ste 300, Erie, PA 16502
Tel.: (814) 461-9436

Fax: (814) 461-9536
E-Mail: dbensur@bensur.com
Web Site: www.bensur.com

Employees: 7
Year Founded: 1990

Agency Specializes In: Advertising, Advertising Specialties, Brand Development & Integration, Broadcast, Business Publications, Cable T.V., Children's Market, Collateral, Communications, Consulting, Consumer Marketing, Consumer Publications, Corporate Identity, Cosmetics, Digital/Interactive, Direct Response Marketing, E-Commerce, Education, Electronic Media, Entertainment, Event Planning & Marketing, Exhibit/Trade Shows, Financial, Food Service, Graphic Design, Industrial, Internet/Web Design, Investor Relations, Leisure, Logo & Package Design, Magazines, Media Buying Services, Medical Products, Merchandising, Multimedia, New Product Development, Newspaper, Newspapers & Magazines, Out-of-Home Media, Outdoor, Pharmaceutical, Planning & Consultation, Point of Purchase, Point of Sale, Print, Production, Public Relations, Publicity/Promotions, Radio, Restaurant, Retail, Sales Promotion, Strategic Planning/Research, T.V., Technical Advertising, Trade & Consumer Magazines, Travel & Tourism, Yellow Pages Advertising

Approx. Annual Billings: $1,500,000

Daniel Bensur *(Founder & Owner)*
Kevin Seeker *(Acct Dir)*
Lisa Fischer *(Acct Coord)*
Katie Imler *(Acct Coord)*

Accounts:
Amatech
Bay Harbor Marina
Ben Franklin Technology Partners
Better Baked Foods
Cott Beverages
Country Fair
Decision Associates, Inc.
Direct Allergy
Erie County Historical Society
Erie Regional Chamber and Growth Partnership
Erie Sports Commission
Erie Zoo
Oil Region Alliance
PA Great Lakes Region
PHRQL
Vantage Healthcare Network
VisitErie
Zurn Industries

BERGMAN ASSOCIATES
(Name Changed to M/PAKT)

BERGMAN GROUP
4701 Cox Rd, Glen Allen, VA 23060
Tel.: (804) 255-0600
Fax: (804) 225-0900
Web Site: www.bergmangroup.com

E-Mail for Key Personnel:
President: bill@bergmangroup.com
Media Dir.: aismith@bergmangroup.com

Employees: 20
Year Founded: 1994

Agency Specializes In: Advertising Specialties, Brand Development & Integration, Broadcast, Business-To-Business, Cable T.V., Collateral, Communications, Consulting, Consumer Marketing, Consumer Publications, Corporate Identity, Digital/Interactive, Direct Response Marketing, Education, Event Planning & Marketing, Exhibit/Trade Shows, Financial, Government/Political, Graphic Design, Health Care Services, Internet/Web Design, Legal Services, Logo & Package Design, Media Buying Services, Medical Products, Print, Production, Real Estate, Retail, Strategic Planning/Research, Teen Market, Travel & Tourism

Approx. Annual Billings: $15,000,000

Danny Boone *(Dir-Art & Creative)*
Mary Virginia Scott *(Dir-Mktg & Acct Mgmt)*
Fred Wollenberg *(Dir-Design & Production)*

Accounts:
American Enterprise Institute
AT&T Communications Corp.
Beth Ahabah
Beth Sholom Life Care
Brown University
Captech Consulting
Children's Medical Center Dallas
Dole
Evolving Strategies
Exxon/Mobil
FDNY Foundation
Gibraltar Associates
Insmed Pharmaceutical
Marts & Lundy

BERKMAN COMMUNICATIONS
3990 Old Town Ave, San Diego, CA 92110
Tel.: (619) 231-9977
Fax: (619) 231-9970
Web Site: www.berkmanpr.com

Employees: 8

Jack Berkman *(Pres & CEO)*

Accounts:
Human Touch Massage Chairs

BERKSHIRE INTERMEDIA GROUP
PO Box 23, Simsbury, CT 06070-0014
Tel.: (860) 658-0012
E-Mail: berkshire@fnet.net

Employees: 4
Year Founded: 1983

Agency Specializes In: Advertising, Automotive, Brand Development & Integration, Business-To-Business, Collateral, Corporate Identity, Financial, Graphic Design, Health Care Services, Industrial, Internet/Web Design, Leisure, Logo & Package Design, Newspapers & Magazines, Point of Purchase, Print, Publicity/Promotions, Seniors' Market, Sports Market, Strategic Planning/Research, Trade & Consumer Magazines

Approx. Annual Billings: $950,000

Daniel Reilert *(Principal)*

Accounts:
Acme Auto; West Hartford, CT Auto Parts & Specialties, Projects; 1990
MKM Importers; Newington, CT Printing Press Sales, Parts & Services, Projects; 1992
New Life Management & Development; Mount Laurel, NJ Senior Services; 1990
Smith & Wesson; Springfield, MA Firearms; 1993
State Of Connecticut; Hartford, CT; 1994
University of Hartford; West Hartford, CT Higher Education, Special Projects & Promotions; 1986

BERLIN CAMERON UNITED
100 Ave of the Americas, New York, NY 10013
Tel.: (212) 824-2000
Fax: (212) 268-8454
Web Site: bcunited.com/

Employees: 83
Year Founded: 1997

National Agency Associations: 4A's

Agency Specializes In: Brand Development & Integration, Collateral, Communications, Consumer Marketing, Direct Response Marketing, E-Commerce, Event Planning & Marketing, Media Buying Services, New Product Development, Public Relations, Sponsorship

Breakdown of Gross Billings by Media: Cable T.V.: 14%; Consumer Publs.: 14%; D.M.: 1%; Internet Adv.: 10%; Network T.V.: 15%; Newsp.: 7%; Other: 7%; Outdoor: 14%; Radio: 4%; Spot T.V.: 6%; Syndication: 3%; Trade & Consumer Mags.: 5%

Ewen Cameron *(Chm)*
Matt Ryan *(CEO)*
Jennifer Blakeslee-DaSilva *(Mng Partner)*
Kerry Ernst *(CFO)*
Lauren Bleiweiss *(Exec Producer)*
Tom Pastore *(Creative Dir)*

Accounts:
Amazon.com
Capital One 360
Ford; 2007
Gilt Campaign: "The Chase", Creative
Howard Johnson
Lincoln
Mazda Campaign: "What Do You Drive?"
New York Life
Reebok
Samsung
Super 8
Travel Lodge
Travelodge
Vimeo
Wall Street Journal
Wat-aah! Digital, Outdoor, Print
Wyndham Hotel Group

BERLINE
423 North Main St, Royal Oak, MI 48067
Tel.: (248) 593-4744
Fax: (248) 593-4740
Web Site: www.berline.com/

E-Mail for Key Personnel:
Chairman: jberline@berlinenet.com
President: jmacbeth@berlinenet.com
Media Dir.: jkaufman@berlinenet.com
Public Relations: rhardin@berlinenet.com

Employees: 30
Year Founded: 1982

National Agency Associations: MAGNET

Agency Specializes In: Above-the-Line, Advertising, Affluent Market, African-American Market, Automotive, Aviation & Aerospace, Below-the-Line, Bilingual Market, Brand Development & Integration, Broadcast, Business Publications, Business-To-Business, Cable T.V., Co-op Advertising, Collateral, Communications, Consulting, Consumer Goods, Consumer Marketing, Consumer Publications, Corporate Communications, Corporate Identity, Digital/Interactive, Direct Response Marketing, Direct-to-Consumer, E-Commerce, Electronic Media, Email, Entertainment, Environmental, Event Planning & Marketing, Experience Design, Fashion/Apparel, Financial, Food Service, Government/Political, Graphic Design, Health Care Services, High Technology, Hospitality, In-Store Advertising, Information Technology, Integrated Marketing, Internet/Web Design, Leisure, Local Marketing, Luxury Products, Magazines, Market Research, Media Buying Services, Media Planning, Media Relations, Medical Products, Multimedia, New Product Development, New Technologies,

Advertising Agencies

Newspaper, Newspapers & Magazines, Out-of-Home Media, Outdoor, Planning & Consultation, Point of Purchase, Point of Sale, Print, Production, Promotions, Public Relations, Publicity/Promotions, Radio, Real Estate, Regional, Restaurant, Retail, Sales Promotion, Search Engine Optimization, Social Marketing/Nonprofit, Social Media, Strategic Planning/Research, T.V., Trade & Consumer Magazines, Travel & Tourism, Urban Market, Web (Banner Ads, Pop-ups, etc.)

Approx. Annual Billings: $65,000,000

Breakdown of Gross Billings by Media: Collateral: 15%; Newsp. & Mags.: 15%; Outdoor: 15%; Spot Radio: 25%; Spot T.V.: 30%

Jim Berline *(Chm)*
Michelle Abel-Horowitz *(Pres & Partner)*
Joe Ranck *(Exec VP & Dir-Digital)*
Melanie Edwards *(VP & Dir-Media)*
Jim Macbeth *(Dir-Creative)*
Shane Wright *(Assoc Dir-Creative)*
Ellen Wright *(Media Planner & Media Buyer)*

Accounts:
Bagger Dave's: MI Family Taverns; 2008
Buffalo Wild Wings; Columbus, OH Entertainment, Food, Liquor
Buffalo Wild Wings; MI Entertainment, Food, Liquor
The Detroit Free Press, Inc.; Detroit, MI Michigan's Largest Daily Newspaper
Detroit Newspapers
gloStream; Bloomfield Hills, MI Electronic Medical Records; 2009
KRS Capital Investments; 2011
Miss Dig; MI; 2011
PREMi; MI Legal Mediation; 2009
SMART; MI regional mass transportation; 2011
Total Health Care HMO; 1997
Total Health Choice HMO
Wendy's Chicago Co-Op, Cleveland Co-Op, Detroit Co-Op, Flint/Saginaw Co-Op, Green Bay Co-Op, Northeast Co-Op, Peoria Co-Op, Saint Louis Co-Op, Toledo Co-Op, Traverse City Co-Op, West Michigan Co-Op

BERMAN CREATIVE, LLC

236 Huntington Ave, Boston, MA 02115
Tel.: (617) 369-9900
E-Mail: info@bermanadvertising.com
Web Site: www.bermanadvertising.com

Year Founded: 2002

Agency Specializes In: Advertising, Brand Development & Integration, Internet/Web Design, Print

Erin Eby *(Partner & Dir-Art)*
Jeff Berman *(Principal)*

Accounts:
Tivoli Audio

BERNARD & COMPANY

1540 E Dundee Rd Ste 250, Palatine, IL 60074-8320
Tel.: (847) 934-4500
Fax: (847) 934-4720
E-Mail: tdaro@bernardandcompany.com
Web Site: www.bernardandcompany.com

E-Mail for Key Personnel:
President: tdaro@bernardandcompany.com
Creative Dir.: rbram@bernardandcompany.com

Employees: 9
Year Founded: 1976

National Agency Associations: BPA

Agency Specializes In: Advertising, Advertising Specialties, Automotive, Business Publications, Business-To-Business, Co-op Advertising, Collateral, Digital/Interactive, Direct Response Marketing, E-Commerce, Engineering, Exhibit/Trade Shows, Graphic Design, High Technology, Industrial, Internet/Web Design, Logo & Package Design, Magazines, Media Buying Services, Medical Products, Pharmaceutical, Planning & Consultation, Point of Purchase, Point of Sale, Print, Production, Public Relations, Publicity/Promotions, Sales Promotion, Strategic Planning/Research, Technical Advertising, Trade & Consumer Magazines, Transportation, Yellow Pages Advertising

Approx. Annual Billings: $2,500,000

Breakdown of Gross Billings by Media: Bus. Publs.: $1,000,000; Collateral: $1,000,000; Fees: $500,000

Tim Daro *(Pres)*

Accounts:
Advanced Machine & Engineering
Grieve Corp.; Round Lake, IL; Industrial Ovens & Furnaces; 1959
Rep Corporation; Bartlett, IL; Rubber Injection Presses; 1971

BERNI MARKETING & DESIGN

660 Steamboat Rd, Greenwich, CT 06830
Tel.: (203) 661-4747
Fax: (203) 661-4825
E-Mail: info@bernidesign.com
Web Site: www.bernidesign.com

Employees: 5
Year Founded: 1938

Agency Specializes In: Brand Development & Integration, Corporate Identity, Environmental, Financial, Graphic Design, Internet/Web Design, New Product Development, Point of Purchase, Point of Sale, Print, Public Relations, Teen Market

Stuart M. Berni *(Pres & CEO)*

Accounts:
A&P Food Market
Acappella Software, Inc.
Agrilink Foods, Inc.
Ahold USA, Inc.
The Akro Corporation
Beiersdorf Inc.
Borden, Inc
Brown & Williamson Tobacco Corp.
Castrol
Clairol, Inc.
Kraft Foods

BERNING MARKETING, LLC

710 Papworth Ave, Metairie, LA 70005
Tel.: (504) 834-8811
Fax: (504) 834-8812
E-Mail: info@berningmarketing.com
Web Site: www.berningmarketing.com

Employees: 16

Agency Specializes In: Above-the-Line, Advertising, Advertising Specialties, Affiliate Marketing, Affluent Market, African-American Market, Agriculture, Alternative Advertising, Arts, Asian Market, Automotive, Aviation & Aerospace, Below-the-Line, Bilingual Market, Brand Development & Integration, Branded Entertainment, Broadcast, Business Publications, Business-To-Business, Cable T.V., Catalogs, Children's Market, Co-op Advertising, Collateral, College, Commercial Photography, Communications, Computers & Software, Consulting, Consumer Goods, Consumer Marketing, Consumer Publications, Content, Corporate Communications, Corporate Identity, Cosmetics, Crisis Communications, Custom Publishing, Customer Relationship Management, Digital/Interactive, Direct Response Marketing, Direct-to-Consumer, E-Commerce, Education, Electronic Media, Electronics, Email, Engineering, Entertainment, Environmental, Event Planning & Marketing, Exhibit/Trade Shows, Experience Design, Fashion/Apparel, Financial, Food Service, Game Integration, Gay & Lesbian Market, Government/Political, Graphic Design, Guerilla Marketing, Health Care Services, High Technology, Hispanic Market, Hospitality, Household Goods, Identity Marketing, In-Store Advertising, Industrial, Infomercials, Information Technology, Integrated Marketing, International, Internet/Web Design, Investor Relations, Legal Services, Leisure, Local Marketing, Logo & Package Design, Luxury Products, Magazines, Marine, Market Research, Media Buying Services, Media Planning, Media Relations, Media Training, Medical Products, Men's Market, Merchandising, Mobile Marketing, Multicultural, Multimedia, New Product Development, New Technologies, Newspaper, Newspapers & Magazines, Out-of-Home Media, Outdoor, Over-50 Market, Package Design, Paid Searches, Pharmaceutical, Planning & Consultation, Podcasting, Point of Purchase, Point of Sale, Print, Product Placement, Production, Production (Ad, Film, Broadcast), Production (Print), Promotions, Public Relations, Publicity/Promotions, Publishing, RSS (Really Simple Syndication), Radio, Real Estate, Recruitment, Regional, Restaurant, Retail, Sales Promotion, Search Engine Optimization, Seniors' Market, Social Marketing/Nonprofit, Sponsorship, Sports Market, Stakeholders, Strategic Planning/Research, Sweepstakes, Syndication, T.V., Technical Advertising, Teen Market, Telemarketing, Trade & Consumer Magazines, Transportation, Travel & Tourism, Urban Market, Viral/Buzz/Word of Mouth, Web (Banner Ads, Pop-ups, etc.), Women's Market, Yellow Pages Advertising

Breakdown of Gross Billings by Media: Cable T.V.: 3%; Graphic Design: 3%; Local Mktg.: 4%; Print: 10%; Production: 50%; Radio & T.V.: 30%

Robert Berning *(Pres)*

Accounts:
Boudreaux's Jewelers; Metairie, LA Jewelry
Lamarque Ford; Kenner, LA Automotive Products
Metro Disposal Services; New Orleans, LA Waste Management Services
Port of Morgan City; Morgan City, LA

BERNSTEIN & ASSOCIATES INC

6300 W Loop S Ste 218, Bellaire, TX 77401
Tel.: (713) 838-8400
Fax: (713) 838-8444
Web Site: www.bernsteinandassoc.com

Year Founded: 1983

Agency Specializes In: Advertising, Event Planning & Marketing, Internet/Web Design, Media Relations, Public Relations

Patricia Bernstein *(Pres)*

Accounts:
New-Cariloha

BERNSTEIN-REIN ADVERTISING, INC.

4600 Madison Ave Ste 1500, Kansas City, MO 64112-3016
Tel.: (816) 756-0640
Fax: (816) 399-6000

Toll Free: (800) 571-6246
E-Mail: general@b-r.com
Web Site: www.b-r.com/

E-Mail for Key Personnel:
Chairman: robertbernstein@bradv.com
President: stevebernstein@bradv.com

Employees: 227
Year Founded: 1964

National Agency Associations: 4A's-DMA

Agency Specializes In: Advertising, Below-the-Line, Brand Development & Integration, Broadcast, Business Publications, Business-To-Business, Cable T.V., Children's Market, Co-op Advertising, Collateral, Consulting, Consumer Goods, Consumer Marketing, Consumer Publications, Corporate Identity, Cosmetics, Customer Relationship Management, Digital/Interactive, Direct Response Marketing, Direct-to-Consumer, E-Commerce, Electronic Media, Electronics, Email, Entertainment, Exhibit/Trade Shows, Fashion/Apparel, Financial, Food Service, Graphic Design, Household Goods, In-Store Advertising, Integrated Marketing, Internet/Web Design, Leisure, Local Marketing, Logo & Package Design, Magazines, Market Research, Media Buying Services, Media Planning, Merchandising, Mobile Marketing, New Product Development, Newspaper, Newspapers & Magazines, Out-of-Home Media, Outdoor, Package Design, Paid Searches, Pets , Pharmaceutical, Planning & Consultation, Point of Purchase, Point of Sale, Print, Production, Production (Ad, Film, Broadcast), Production (Print), Publicity/Promotions, Radio, Restaurant, Retail, Sales Promotion, Search Engine Optimization, Social Media, Sponsorship, Strategic Planning/Research, Syndication, T.V., Trade & Consumer Magazines, Travel & Tourism, Web (Banner Ads, Pop-ups, etc.), Yellow Pages Advertising

Approx. Annual Billings: $409,821,557

Skip Rein *(Vice Chm)*
Chris Perkins *(Mng Dir)*
Kelli Anstine *(Sr VP & Dir-Experience Plng)*
Vernon Williams *(Sr VP-Acct & Project Mgmt)*
Pamela Sandler *(VP & Dir-Digital Experience)*
David Smith *(Exec Creative Dir)*
Molly Brammer *(Acct Dir)*
Brandon Billings *(Dir-Digital Strategy)*
Francine Garcia *(Dir-Print Production)*
Ryan Glendening *(Dir-Digital Creative)*
Betty Greiner *(Dir-Brdcst Affairs)*
Mica Zier *(Supvr-Media Plng & Analytics)*
Michael Lindquist *(Strategist-Social Content)*
Kyle Rodriguez *(Acct Exec)*
Michelle Hershberger *(Media Buyer)*
Bill Steinke *(Media Planner)*

Accounts:
Banfield; Portland, OR Branding, The Pet Hospital, Veterinary Practice
Beauty Brands; 1996
Cook's Ham; 2007
Dairy Farmers of America
Family Dollar Stores Inc. (Agency of Record)
Glace Artisan Ice Cream
New-Gold's Gym Creative; 2015
Haverty Furniture Companies, Inc. Analytics, Creative, Digital, Media Planning & Buying, Social Media
Hostess Brands (Agency of Record) Butternut, Campaign: "The Sweetest Comeback in the History of Ever", Digital, Dolly Madison, Drake, Guerrilla Marketing, Home Pride, Hostess, Media Planning & Buying, Social media, Traditional Advertising, Twinkie, Wonder
Interstate Brands Hostess; 2005
Jolly Time Pop Corn; Sioux City, IA (Agency of Record)
McDonald's Corporation McDonald's Corporation, Ronald McDonald House Charities
MetLife; 2009
Nebraska Book Company; 2009
Old Dominion Freight Line, Inc. (Agency Of Record) Branding, Creative, Digital, Media Buying & Planning, Social Media, Strategy
The Salvation Army
Soave Automotive Group
Sunbeam Brands
Time Warner Cable; 2007

BERRY NETWORK, INC.
3100 Kettering Blvd, Dayton, OH 45439
Fax: (937) 298-1426
Toll Free: (800) 366-1264
E-Mail: berrynetworkmarketing@berrynetwork.com
Web Site: www.berrynetwork.com

Employees: 185
Year Founded: 1960

Agency Specializes In: Advertising, Alternative Advertising, Business-To-Business, Co-op Advertising, Consulting, Consumer Marketing, Digital/Interactive, Direct Response Marketing, Direct-to-Consumer, Electronic Media, Health Care Services, Hispanic Market, Local Marketing, Media Planning, Mobile Marketing, New Technologies, Paid Searches, Planning & Consultation, Social Marketing/Nonprofit, Social Media, Strategic Planning/Research, Viral/Buzz/Word of Mouth, Yellow Pages Advertising

Approx. Annual Billings: $185,000,000

Breakdown of Gross Billings by Media: Internet Adv.: 15%; Other: 5%; Yellow Page Adv.: 80%

Sherri Kavanaugh *(Sr VP-Client Strategy)*
David Henry *(VP-Ops & Sls Support)*
Sharon Rickey *(VP-Client Svcs)*
Allison Siefer *(VP-Client Svcs)*
Dephne Young *(VP-Ops & Tech)*
Denice Rupp *(Acct Dir)*
Lisanne Klanderman *(Mgr-Digital Strategic)*

Accounts:
AT&T Communications Corp.
Atlas Van Lines
Coleman Heating & Air Conditioning
Luxaire Heating & Air Conditioning
Maaco
Meineke Car Care Centers
Rite-Aid
Safelite AutoGlass
Terminix
VHA
York Heating & Air Conditioning

BESON 4 MEDIA GROUP
13500 Sutton Park Dr S Ste 105, Jacksonville, FL 32224
Tel.: (904) 992-9945
Fax: (904) 992-9907
E-Mail: beson4@beson4.com
Web Site: www.beson4media.com

Agency Specializes In: Advertising, Brand Development & Integration, Broadcast, Collateral, Corporate Identity, Digital/Interactive, Event Planning & Marketing, Graphic Design, Print, Public Relations

A. J. Beson *(Pres & CEO)*
Michael E. Hicks *(Exec VP)*
Stephanie Autry *(Dir-Bus Dev)*
Christine Tarantino *(Dir-Art)*

Accounts:
21st Century Oncology
Advanced Cardiac Training
Anglers for a Cure
Borland Groover Clinic
Catalyst Medical Staffing
First Coast Cardiovascular Institute
Heekin Orthopedic Specialists
Hula in the City
Medimix Specialty Pharmacy
Orlando Physician Specialists
Safari of Smiles
Thomaston Crossing Apartment Homes
The Uptown at St. Johns
Watson Realty Corp.

BETTER MERCHANTS INC.
1100 N 9th St Ste 203, Lafayette, IN 47904
Tel.: (765) 420-7050
Fax: (765) 742-8184
Web Site: www.bettermerchants.com

Agency Specializes In: Advertising, Brand Development & Integration, Email, Logo & Package Design, Outdoor, Print, Public Relations, Radio, Social Media, Strategic Planning/Research

Keith Austin *(Pres)*
Emily Gray *(Mgr-Production)*

Accounts:
Dennys Body Shop
Dowell Automotive Inc
Dr. Kochert Pain & Health
MedSpa Day Spa
Randall Dermatology PC

BEUERMAN MILLER FITZGERALD, INC.
643 Magazine St, New Orleans, LA 70130
Tel.: (504) 524-3342
Fax: (504) 524-3344
E-Mail: info@e-bmf.com
Web Site: www.e-bmf.com

Employees: 10
Year Founded: 1926

National Agency Associations: IPREX

Agency Specializes In: Advertising, Brand Development & Integration, Business-To-Business, Communications, Consumer Goods, Consumer Marketing, Corporate Communications, Corporate Identity, Crisis Communications, Environmental, Event Planning & Marketing, Health Care Services, Hospitality, Investor Relations, Logo & Package Design, Media Relations, Media Training, Public Relations, Stakeholders, Strategic Planning/Research

Approx. Annual Billings: $13,000,000

Breakdown of Gross Billings by Media: Fees: 100%

Virginia Miller *(Owner)*
Greg Beuerman *(Partner)*
Ronald J. Thompson *(Pres-Mktg)*
Laura Lee Killeen *(Exec VP)*
Chris Herting *(Dir-Digital & Social Media Mktg & Acct Exec)*
Shannon Stewart *(Dir-Fin)*
Julie O'Callaghan *(Office Mgr)*
Anna Corin Koehl *(Sr Acct Exec-PR)*
Allison Gouaux *(Acct Exec)*
Sarah Meyer *(Jr Acct Exec-PR & Coord-Digital & Social Media)*
Lillie Hart *(Jr Acct Exec)*

BEYOND SPOTS & DOTS INC.
1034 5th Ave, Pittsburgh, PA 15219
Tel.: (412) 281-6215
Fax: (412) 281-6218
E-Mail: contact@beyondspotsanddots.com
Web Site: www.beyondspotsanddots.com

Year Founded: 2006

Agency Specializes In: Advertising, Advertising Specialties, Brand Development & Integration, Communications, Consulting, Content, Corporate Communications, Corporate Identity, Crisis Communications, E-Commerce, Event Planning & Marketing, Graphic Design, Identity Marketing, Integrated Marketing, Internet/Web Design, Logo & Package Design, Market Research, Media Buying Services, Media Planning, Media Relations, Package Design, Planning & Consultation, Production (Ad, Film, Broadcast), Public Relations, Publicity/Promotions, Regional, Sales Promotion, Social Marketing/Nonprofit, Strategic Planning/Research, Technical Advertising

Andreas Beck *(CEO)*
Phyliss Gastgeb *(Dir-Strategic Mktg)*
Dwight Alan Chambers *(Brand Mgr)*
Joe Schwartz *(Mgr-Content & Designer)*
Kate McGinley *(Mgr-Integrated Mktg)*

BEYOND TOTAL BRANDING

98 NW 29th St, Miami, FL 33127
Tel.: (954) 385-8262
E-Mail: info@beyond-group.com
Web Site: www.beyond-group.com

Agency Specializes In: Advertising, Brand Development & Integration, Print, T.V., Web (Banner Ads, Pop-ups, etc.)

Victor Melillo *(Owner)*
Alejandro Gonzalez *(Mng Partner)*
Mark Ginsberg *(CMO)*
Blanca Elena Curiel *(Dir-Mktg Svcs)*
Gianfranco De Libero *(Assoc Dir-Creative)*
Mariana Ferrari *(Planner-Strategic)*

Accounts:
Sony Corporation of America Latam Campaign

BFG COMMUNICATIONS

6 Anolyn Ct, Bluffton, SC 29910
Mailing Address:
PO Box 23199, Hilton Head Island, SC 29925
Tel.: (843) 837-9115
Fax: (843) 837-9225
E-Mail: info@bfgcom.com
Web Site: www.bfgcom.com

E-Mail for Key Personnel:
President: kmeany@bfgcom.com
Creative Dir.: sseymour@bfgcom.com

Employees: 160
Year Founded: 1995

National Agency Associations: PMA-PRSA

Agency Specializes In: Advertising, Affluent Market, African-American Market, Alternative Advertising, Below-the-Line, Bilingual Market, Brand Development & Integration, Branded Entertainment, Business-To-Business, Collateral, Communications, Consulting, Consumer Goods, Consumer Marketing, Consumer Publications, Content, Corporate Communications, Corporate Identity, Cosmetics, Customer Relationship Management, Digital/Interactive, Direct Response Marketing, Direct-to-Consumer, E-Commerce, Electronic Media, Email, Entertainment, Event Planning & Marketing, Exhibit/Trade Shows, Experience Design, Fashion/Apparel, Food Service, Game Integration, Government/Political, Graphic Design, Guerilla Marketing, Health Care Services, Hispanic Market, Hospitality, Identity Marketing, In-Store Advertising, Integrated Marketing, Internet/Web Design, Leisure, Local Marketing, Logo & Package Design, Luxury Products, Men's Market, Merchandising, Mobile Marketing, Multicultural, Multimedia, New Product Development, Out-of-Home Media, Package Design, Planning & Consultation, Podcasting, Point of Purchase, Point of Sale, Production, Production (Ad, Film, Broadcast), Production (Print), Promotions, Publicity/Promotions, Regional, Restaurant, Retail, Sales Promotion, Social Media, Sponsorship, Sports Market, Strategic Planning/Research, Sweepstakes, Teen Market, Tween Market, Viral/Buzz/Word of Mouth, Web (Banner Ads, Pop-ups, etc.), Women's Market

BFG is a creative agency that brings new thinking to brands. There are more than 160 of us in Hilton Head Island, New York City, Greenville and Atlanta, and we believe. So do our clients.

Approx. Annual Billings: $62,000,000

Kevin Meany *(Founder, Pres & CEO)*
Scott Seymour *(Chief Creative Officer & VP)*
Richard Leslie *(Chief Strategy Officer)*
Jason Vogt *(VP-Client Mgmt)*
Jesse Bushkar *(Sr Dir-Digital)*
Holli Hines Easton *(Grp Acct Dir)*
Lisa Ringlestetter *(Grp Acct Dir)*
Michael Dunn *(Dir-Creative)*
Matt Nadler *(Dir-Creative)*

Accounts:
Ace Hardware; 2011
Affresh Cleaners
American Marketing Association Brand Positioning
Campari North America
The Coca-Cola Company
Coca-Cola Refreshments USA, Inc.; 2007
Delta; 2012
Ellio's
Espolon Tequila; 2012
EveryDrop Water Filters
Hanesbrands, Inc.
Kids II; 2012
LG Electronics
Marvel
Ristorante Pizza; 2011
SKYY Vodka
South Carolina Tourism; 2012
New-South Carolina Youth Anti-Tobacco
Treasury Wine Estates; 2009
New-Trinchero
Turner Broadcasting; 2008
Wild Turkey

Branches

BFG Communications Atlanta

1000 Marietta St Ste 208, Atlanta, GA 30318
Tel.: (404) 991-2511
Web Site: www.bfgcom.com/

Agency Specializes In: Sponsorship

Kevin Meany, *(Pres & CEO)*

Accounts:
New-Church's Chicken (Strategy & Social Media Agency of Record) Instagram

BFG Communications New York

665 Broadway 3rd Fl, New York, NY 10012
Tel.: (212) 763-0022

Kevin Meany *(Pres & CEO)*

Accounts:
New-Espolon Tequila

BFL MARKETING COMMUNICATIONS INC.

1399 Lear Indus Pkwy, Avon, OH 44011
Tel.: (216) 875-8860
Fax: (216) 875-8870
E-Mail: dpavan@bflcom.com
Web Site: www.bflcom.com

E-Mail for Key Personnel:
President: dpavan@bflcom.com

Employees: 9
Year Founded: 1955

Agency Specializes In: Advertising, Brand Development & Integration, Business Publications, Collateral, Consulting, Consumer Publications, Corporate Identity, Direct Response Marketing, Event Planning & Marketing, Exhibit/Trade Shows, Graphic Design, Internet/Web Design, Logo & Package Design, Magazines, New Product Development, Newspaper, Newspapers & Magazines, Outdoor, Pets, Planning & Consultation, Point of Purchase, Point of Sale, Print, Production, Public Relations, Radio, Sales Promotion, Strategic Planning/Research

Approx. Annual Billings: $5,000,000

Breakdown of Gross Billings by Media: Bus. Publs.: $1,570,350; Collateral: $2,644,800; D.M.: $413,250; Mags.: $1,074,450; Newsp. & Mags.: $372,400; Other: $165,300; Outdoor: $87,000; Point of Purchase: $330,600; Radio & T.V.: $1,606,850

Dennis Pavan *(Pres & CEO)*
Juanita Kiley *(VP)*

Accounts:
Camp Safe
Duraclean
First Federal of Lakewood; OH
First Power Group
Friendship Animal Protective League
International Exposition Center Cleveland
Sellers Expositions

BFW ADVERTISING + INTERACTIVE

2500 N Military Trl, Boca Raton, FL 33431
Tel.: (561) 962-3300
Fax: (561) 962-3339
E-Mail: info@gobfw.com
Web Site: www.gobfw.com

Employees: 20
Year Founded: 1997

Agency Specializes In: Automotive, Aviation & Aerospace, Business-To-Business, Communications, Financial, High Technology, Information Technology, Internet/Web Design, Media Buying Services, Medical Products, Pharmaceutical, Print, Radio, Real Estate, Retail, T.V., Travel & Tourism

Revenue: $2,000,000

Christian Boswell *(Owner & Pres)*
Jim Workman *(CEO)*
Brad Partridge *(Sr VP)*
Barbara Pope *(Sr Dir-Media)*
Lauren Hartnett *(Acct Mgr)*
Eunji Park *(Mgr-Media)*

Accounts:
3C Interactive; 2005

Amadeus; 2003
Boca Raton Community Hospital; 2005
DHL Worldwide Express, Inc.; 2003
DPMS Panther Arms; 2006
Geron; 2006
Hi-Tech Pharmacal; 1999
Interim HealthCare; 1999
Perry Institute for Marine Science; 2006
Precision Pulmonary Diagnostics; 2004
RAIR Technologies; 2001
University of Miami; 2003
Vacation.com; 2005

BG

360 Columbia Dr, West Palm Beach, FL 33409
Tel.: (561) 688-2880
Fax: (561) 688-2780
E-Mail: info@bgsolutions.me
Web Site: bgsolutions.me

E-Mail for Key Personnel:
Production Mgr.: geri@bonergroup.com

Employees: 12
Year Founded: 1990

National Agency Associations: AAF

Agency Specializes In: Automotive, Brand Development & Integration, Broadcast, Collateral, Consumer Marketing, Corporate Identity, Entertainment, Financial, Graphic Design, Health Care Services, Leisure, Logo & Package Design, Media Buying Services, Point of Purchase, Point of Sale, Production, Retail, Strategic Planning/Research, Travel & Tourism

Approx. Annual Billings: $10,000,000

Breakdown of Gross Billings by Media: Collateral: 20%; Mags.: 10%; Newsp.: 35%; Radio: 10%; T.V.: 25%

Mark Minter *(VP & Dir-Creative)*
Raquel Couri *(VP-HR)*
Kim French *(VP-Client Svcs)*
Barbara Heim *(Gen Mgr-HR)*
Kim Donovan *(Client Svcs Dir)*
April Hingst *(Sr Mgr-HR)*
Aimee Shaughnessy *(Sr Acct Mgr)*
Renee Gunnels *(Mgr-HR)*
John Holloway *(Mgr-Fin)*
Michael Vo *(Mgr-Resourcing-Talent Acq-Americas)*

Accounts:
American Cancer Society
Berkley Federal Bank
Cleva Technologies, LLC
Delray Beach Marriott
Delray Medical Center; Del Ray FL; 2002
DMG World Media
General Plumbing
Good Samaritan Medical Center; West Palm Beach, FL; 2002
Ocean Properties; Delray Beach, FL Hotels, Resorts; 1996
Palm Beach Opera
Palm Beach State College
Sunrise Ford; Fort Pierce, FL; 1991
Tenet Health Care System

Branch

The Boner Group, Inc./Ann K. Savage

611 Talmadge Ct SE, Leesburg, VA 20175-8991
Tel.: (703) 589-1445
Fax: (703) 589-1446
E-Mail: ann@bonergroup.com
Web Site: www.bgsolutions.me

Employees: 11
Year Founded: 1995

Ann K. Savage *(Pres)*
Kim French *(VP & Client Svcs Dir)*
Mark Minter *(VP & Dir-Creative)*
Jason White *(Sr Dir-Art)*
Aimee Shaughnessy *(Dir-Client Dev)*
Alex Wasil *(Acct Mgr & Media Planner)*
Tracy Goodhue *(Mgr-Traffic & Production)*
John Holloway *(Mgr-Fin)*
Dominique Calero *(Specialist-Interactive Social Media & Designer)*
Paige Romano *(Media Buyer)*
San Filippo *(Asst Acct Mgr)*

BHW1 ADVERTISING

522 W Riverside Fl 3, Spokane, WA 99201
Tel.: (509) 456-8640
Web Site: www.bhw1.com

Agency Specializes In: Advertising, Digital/Interactive, Graphic Design, Internet/Web Design, Logo & Package Design, Media Buying Services, Media Planning, Radio, Social Media, T.V.

Tony Hines *(Owner & Principal)*
Greg Birchell *(Partner)*
Jamie Sijohn *(Acct Mgr)*
Karen Kager *(Mgr-Production & Traffic)*
Russ Wheat *(Acct Supvr)*

Accounts:
Kootenai Health

BIANCA FRANK DESIGN

1202 Ramona Dr Unit B, Anchorage, AK 99515
Tel.: (907) 830-9277
E-Mail: design@biancafrank.com
Web Site: biancafrankportfolio.com/

Agency Specializes In: Above-the-Line, Affluent Market, Brand Development & Integration, Business-To-Business, Collateral, Communications, Consulting, Consumer Goods, Consumer Marketing, Corporate Communications, Direct-to-Consumer, Event Planning & Marketing, Financial, Graphic Design, Identity Marketing, Local Marketing, Logo & Package Design, Magazines, Market Research, Multicultural, New Product Development, Newspapers & Magazines, Package Design, Podcasting, Print, Production (Print), Retail, Urban Market, Yellow Pages Advertising

Bianca Frank *(Designer-Web)*

BIEMEDIA

511 Broadway, Denver, CO 80203
Tel.: (303) 825-2275
Fax: (303) 825-2276
Toll Free: (800) 941-2275
E-Mail: info@biemedia.com
Web Site: www.biemedia.com

Agency Specializes In: Advertising, Broadcast, Environmental, Graphic Design, Internet/Web Design, Local Marketing, Production, Strategic Planning/Research, T.V., Web (Banner Ads, Pop-ups, etc.)

Jon Barocas *(Founder & CEO)*
Kathy Zimmerman *(VP-Client Svcs)*
Tessa Jones *(Dir-Traffic)*
Jeremy Wallis *(Dir-IT)*
Linda Dentan *(Specialist-HR)*
Jenna Willett *(Copywriter)*

Accounts:
Boston.com
DexOne
Eltiempo.com
Heymarket
Investopidia
McKnights

BIG AL'S CREATIVE EMPORIUM

53A Brewer St, London, W1F 9UH United Kingdom
Tel.: (44) 20 7494 9854
Web Site: www.bigalscreativeemporium.com/

Employees: 80

Stef Jones *(Partner-Creative)*
Tom Burnay *(Creative Dir)*

Accounts:
Baker & Spice
Betfair
Blinkbox
BMW
Borders
Discovery Channel
Etsy Advertising, Campaign: "The Most Beautiful Marketplace in The World"
Heinz Baked Beans
Paddy Power
Purina
Roundup Weedkiller Creative
Setanta Sports
Travelzoo
Vision Direct Campaign: "Plastic Monsters", TV
Yardley London Creative, Media

BIG ARROW CONSULTING GROUP, LLC

(d/b/a Big Arrow Group)
584 Broadway Ste 1210, New York, NY 10012
Tel.: (212) 414-5650
Fax: (212) 414-5651
Web Site: www.bigarrowgroup.com

Employees: 12

Agency Specializes In: Sponsorship

Michael Marino *(Principal)*
Martin Carrichner *(Sr Dir-Art)*
Mike Teele *(Dir-Bus & Ops)*
Chris Charles *(Supvr-Art)*
Aj Marino *(Acct Exec)*
Sarah Reagin *(Acct Exec)*
Carol Cofone *(Planner-Strategic)*

Accounts:
American Express
Bayer Pharmaceuticals
Biocodex
Genzyme
Yale New Haven Health System

BIG BANG ELECTRICAL

2228 1st Ave, Seattle, WA 98121
Tel.: (206) 728-0202
Web Site: www.bigbangelectrical.com

Year Founded: 1995

Agency Specializes In: Advertising

Bill Grant *(Pres)*

Accounts:
Brooks
Credit Unions of WA
Fat Bastard
Fox College Sports
Island County Tourism
Nutrisystem
Red Cross
Superfeet
Washington Credit Union League

BIG BLUE SKY
2008 W Koenig Ln, Austin, TX 78756
Tel.: (512) 337-6927
E-Mail: partners@bigblueskyadvertising.com
Web Site: www.bigblueskyadvertising.com

Agency Specializes In: Advertising, Collateral, Digital/Interactive, Outdoor, Print, Radio

Tony Lopez *(Partner)*
Chad Swisher *(Partner)*

Accounts:
The City of Pflugerville Campaign: "Put The Right Thing in"
Fuzzys Taco Shop

BIG CAT ADVERTISING
10 Commercial Blvd Ste 10, Novato, CA 94949
Tel.: (415) 884-3501
Fax: (415) 884-3503
E-Mail: marty@bigcatadvertising.com
Web Site: www.bigcatadvertising.com

E-Mail for Key Personnel:
President: marty@bigcatadvertising.com
Creative Dir.: gayle@bigcatadvertising.com

Employees: 5
Year Founded: 1986

Agency Specializes In: Advertising, Automotive, Business-To-Business, Cable T.V., Collateral, College, Consumer Marketing, Digital/Interactive, E-Commerce, Email, Government/Political, Graphic Design, Internet/Web Design, Local Marketing, Logo & Package Design, Media Buying Services, Media Planning, Multimedia, Newspaper, Newspapers & Magazines, Outdoor, Paid Searches, Planning & Consultation, Print, Public Relations, Radio, Restaurant, Retail, T.V., Travel & Tourism

Approx. Annual Billings: $1,500,000

Marty Rubino *(Pres & Principal-Agency)*
Gayle Peterson *(Partner, Dir-Creative & Acct Exec)*

Accounts:
Dominican University of California; San Rafael, CA; 2007
Investors Prime Fund; Newport Beach, CA Investment Fund; 2011
Marin Agricultural Institute; San Rafael, CA Farmers Market; 2008
Marin Convention & Visitors Bureau; San Rafael, CA; 2008
Marin Symphony; San Rafael, CA; 2008
Novato Fire Protection District; Novato, CA; 2008
Pacheco Plaza; Novato, CA; 2009
Rafael Floors; San Rafael, CA; 2007
Toscalito Tire & Automotive ; San Rafael, CA; 2008

BIG COMMUNICATIONS, INC.
2121 2nd Ave N, Birmingham, AL 35203
Tel.: (205) 322-5646
E-Mail: hello@bigcom.com
Web Site: www.bigcom.com

Employees: 54
Year Founded: 1995

Agency Specializes In: Advertising, Branded Entertainment, Broadcast, Cable T.V., Catalogs, Co-op Advertising, Collateral, Consumer Publications, Custom Publishing, Digital/Interactive, Direct Response Marketing, Electronic Media, Email, Exhibit/Trade Shows, Experience Design, Guerilla Marketing, In-Store Advertising, Internet/Web Design, Local Marketing, Magazines, Media Buying Services, Media Planning, Newspapers & Magazines, Out-of-Home Media, Outdoor, Paid Searches, Podcasting, Point of Purchase, Point of Sale, Print, Production, Production (Print), Promotions, Public Relations, Publishing, Radio, Search Engine Optimization, Social Media, Sponsorship, T.V., Trade & Consumer Magazines, Viral/Buzz/Word of Mouth, Web (Banner Ads, Pop-ups, etc.)

Ford Wiles *(Chief Creative Officer)*
Shannon Broom Harris *(Sr Dir-Art)*
Onna Cunningham *(Dir-Bus Ops)*
Matt Lane Harris *(Assoc Dir-Creative)*
Karla Khodanian *(Mgr-Digital Community)*
Mary Jane Cleage *(Sr Acct Exec)*
Ashley Fulmer *(Sr Acct Exec-PR)*
Amanda Howard *(Acct Exec)*
Rylee Roquemore *(Acct Exec)*
Logan Shoaf *(Asst Acct Exec)*
Valerie Taylor *(Asst Acct Exec)*
Caty Cambron *(Coord-New Bus)*

Accounts:
New-Alabama Department of Commerce; 2012
New-Alabama Seafood Marketing Commission; 2011
Ashland Inc. Advertising, Content, Creative, Digital Marketing, Digital Strategy, Media, Media Buying, Public Relations, Valvoline (Agency of Record)
New-Birmingham Convention Bureau Tourism Promotion; 1995
New-Emerson Electronics InSinkErator; 2015
New-Go Build Workforce Development & Recruitment; 2010
New-Nationwide Insurance Co-op Agency for Alabama, Georgia & South Carolina; 1997
New-PRADCO Knight & Hale, Moultrie; 2013
New-Tenet Healthcare OB, Ortho & Bariatrics Services; 2015

BIG CORNER CREATIVE
11323 W Kellogg Ave, Wichita, KS 67209
Tel.: (316) 260-5391
E-Mail: info@bigcornercreative.com
Web Site: www.bigcornercreative.com

Agency Specializes In: Advertising, Brand Development & Integration, Digital/Interactive, Logo & Package Design, Outdoor, Print, Radio, Social Media, T.V.

Carl Crossette *(Dir-Mktg)*
Taryn Thomas *(Coord-Mktg)*

Accounts:
Auto Craft Collision Repair
Doctors Express

BIG FUEL COMMUNICATIONS LLC
11 W 19th St, New York, NY 10011
Tel.: (646) 935-4700
Web Site: www.bigfuel.com

Employees: 170
Year Founded: 2002

National Agency Associations: 4A's

Agency Specializes In: Advertising, Brand Development & Integration, Consulting, Social Media, Sponsorship, Strategic Planning/Research

Jon Resnik *(Sr VP & Exec Dir-Creative)*
Stephanie Fuller *(Dir-Strategy)*
Pepe Lopez Waldron *(Assoc Dir-Social Strategy)*
Kristopher Thorpe *(Assoc Acct Dir)*

Accounts:
Aflac Social
Chase
Clorox
Colgate-Palmolive
Fisher-Price
FOX
Gore-Tex
Johnson & Johnson
Microsoft
Starwood
T-Mobile US "Selfie 101", Social Media

BIG HONKIN' IDEAS (BHI)
3767 Overland Ave, Los Angeles, CA 90034
Tel.: (310) 656-0557
Fax: (310) 656-0447
Web Site: www.bighonkinideas.com

Employees: 5
Year Founded: 2005

Agency Specializes In: Brand Development & Integration, Business-To-Business, E-Commerce, Environmental, Financial, Magazines, Newspaper, Out-of-Home Media, Outdoor, Radio, Seniors' Market, Trade & Consumer Magazines, Travel & Tourism

Breakdown of Gross Billings by Media: Mags.: 10%; Newsp.: 30%; Outdoor: 50%; Spot Radio: 10%

Karl Kristkeitz *(Owner)*
Larre Johnson *(Partner & Dir-Creative)*

Accounts:
Jefferson National; 2006
LA Auto Show; 2013
Stanford Graduate School of Business; 2015

BIG HUMAN
51 E 12th St 9th Fl, New York, NY 10003
Tel.: (646) 669-9140
E-Mail: frontdesk@bighuman.com
Web Site: www.bighuman.com

Agency Specializes In: Advertising, Brand Development & Integration, Digital/Interactive

Steve Spurgat *(Mng Dir)*
Haik Avanian *(Head-Creative)*
Jesse Rose *(Product Mgr & Producer)*
Scott Kominsky *(Sr Product Mgr & Producer)*
Nathan Igdaloff *(Product Mgr)*
Andrea Raijer *(Mgr-Ops)*
Spenser Garden *(Sr Designer)*
Gerrit Kamp *(Sr Engr)*

Accounts:
Time Website Redesign

BIG IDEA ADVERTISING INC
6 Maiden Ln, New York, NY 10038
Tel.: (212) 387-8787
E-Mail: hello@bigideaadv.com
Web Site: www.bigideaadv.com

Agency Specializes In: Advertising, Brand Development & Integration, Collateral, Corporate Identity, Digital/Interactive, Internet/Web Design, Logo & Package Design, Media Planning, Print, Radio

Steve Defontes *(Pres)*
Rob Ahrens *(Designer)*

Accounts:
American Arbitration Association

BIG IMAGINATION GROUP
3603 Hayden Ave, Culver City, CA 90232
Tel.: (310) 204-6100

Fax: (310) 204-6120
E-Mail: cbrooks@bigla.com
Web Site: www.bigla.com

Employees: 10
Year Founded: 1987

Agency Specializes In: Advertising

Approx. Annual Billings: $11,000,000

Breakdown of Gross Billings by Media: Brdcst.: $2,750,000; Collateral: $550,000; E-Commerce: $1,100,000; Print: $1,100,000; Strategic Planning/Research: $5,500,000

Jamie Greenberg *(Dir-Art)*
Monika Hummer *(Dir-Art)*
Marina Muhlfriedel *(Dir-Creative Dev)*
Colette Brooks *(Chief Imagination Officer)*

Accounts:
Actors Gang
Alacer Corporation; Foothill Ranch, CA Emergen-C; 2007
Banyan
Cottage Health Solutions
Dolisos America Inc.
Empire Solar Solutions
Global Green USA
Intimate Health
Natrol
Naturade
New Roads
OPCC
Shakeys Pizza; Irwindale, CA Mojo Meal Deal; 2001
Tenet
Toyota Prius Academy Award Event; Torrance, CA; 2004

BIG RIVER ADVERTISING
2100 E Cary St #200, Richmond, VA 23223
Tel.: (804) 864-5363
Fax: (804) 864-5373
Web Site: www.bigriveradvertising.com

Employees: 25
Year Founded: 2001

National Agency Associations: 4A's

Agency Specializes In: Advertising, Affluent Market, Agriculture, Alternative Advertising, Arts, Brand Development & Integration, Broadcast, Business-To-Business, Cable T.V., Children's Market, Collateral, Commercial Photography, Communications, Consulting, Consumer Goods, Consumer Marketing, Corporate Communications, Corporate Identity, Crisis Communications, Digital/Interactive, Direct-to-Consumer, Education, Entertainment, Environmental, Experience Design, Fashion/Apparel, Financial, Food Service, Government/Political, Graphic Design, Guerilla Marketing, Health Care Services, High Technology, Hospitality, Household Goods, Identity Marketing, In-Store Advertising, Industrial, Information Technology, Integrated Marketing, Internet/Web Design, Logo & Package Design, Luxury Products, Market Research, Media Relations, Medical Products, Men's Market, Mobile Marketing, New Product Development, New Technologies, Newspaper, Newspapers & Magazines, Out-of-Home Media, Outdoor, Over-50 Market, Paid Searches, Pharmaceutical, Planning & Consultation, Podcasting, Point of Purchase, Print, Production, Production (Print), Promotions, Public Relations, Publicity/Promotions, RSS (Really Simple Syndication), Radio, Real Estate, Recruitment, Regional, Restaurant, Retail, Sales Promotion, Search Engine Optimization, Seniors' Market, Social Marketing/Nonprofit, Social Media, Sports Market, Stakeholders, Strategic Planning/Research, Sweepstakes, T.V., Teen Market, Trade & Consumer Magazines, Transportation, Travel & Tourism, Tween Market, Urban Market, Viral/Buzz/Word of Mouth, Women's Market

Fred Moore *(Pres & CEO)*
Margaret Price *(Mng Dir)*
Daniel Riddick *(Acct Dir)*
Jan Crable *(Dir-Engagement)*
Molly Winegar *(Dir-Vision in Action)*
Rina Dyer *(Acct Mgr)*
Holly Sigler *(Sr Strategist-Digital Engagement)*
Allie Witte *(Designer)*
Britt Smith *(Jr Project Mgr)*

Accounts:
Anthem Health Plans of Virginia; Richmond, VA Events; 2003
Anthem; New York, NY HMC, NextRx; 2006
Cleco Energy (Agency of Record); 2008
Eagle Companies Branding, Eagle Commercial Construction, Eagle Construction, Eagle Realty, GreenGate, Markel & Eagle, NAI Eagle
Harris Williams & Co (Agency of Record); Richmond, VA Brand; 2003
Hospital Hospitality House Brand, Donor Video, Website
Lumber Liquidators Holdings, Inc. Advertising, Bellawood
Moon Pie; Chattanooga, TN Mini Moon Pies, Moon Pies; 2005
Sweet Frog
TBL Networks(Agency of Record); Glen Allen, VA; 2009
Virginia Lottery (Agency of Record); Hampton, VA; 2010

BIG SHOT MARKETING
6052 N Avondale Ave, Chicago, IL 60631
Tel.: (773) 998-1480
Web Site: www.bigshotmarketing.com

Agency Specializes In: Advertising, Brand Development & Integration, Corporate Communications, Graphic Design, Internet/Web Design, Media Planning, Print, Public Relations, Search Engine Optimization, Social Media

Kymberlee Kaye Raya *(Chief Imagination Officer)*

Accounts:
Reach Fieldhouse

BIG SKY COMMUNICATIONS, INC.
2001 Gateway Pl Ste 130W, San Jose, CA 95110
Tel.: (541) 322-6240
E-Mail: info@bigskypr.com
Web Site: www.bigskypr.com

Employees: 13
Year Founded: 1994

Agency Specializes In: Collateral, Corporate Communications, Crisis Communications, Media Relations, Public Relations, Strategic Planning/Research

Revenue: $1,400,000

Colleen Muller Padnos *(Pres)*
Eddie Miller *(Exec VP)*
Katy Boos *(VP)*
Sheri Seybold *(Sr Dir-Client Svcs)*
Staci Temple *(Client Svcs Dir)*
Preethi Chandrasekhar *(Sr Acct Mgr)*
Daphne De Flavia *(Sr Acct Mgr)*
Nathaniel Magee *(Sr Acct Mgr)*
Paula Kozak *(Mgr-Customer Reference)*

Accounts:
Adobe Systems, Inc.
Fanfare
Fujitsu
NetApp, Inc.
SeniorNet

BIG SPACESHIP
45 Main St Ste 716, Brooklyn, NY 11201
Tel.: (718) 222-0281
Fax: (718) 971-1062
E-Mail: info@bigspaceship.com
Web Site: www.bigspaceship.com

Employees: 40
Year Founded: 2000

National Agency Associations: SODA

Agency Specializes In: Digital/Interactive, Sponsorship, Technical Advertising

Ranae Heuer *(Mng Dir)*
Rob Thorsen *(Mng Dir)*
Cedric Devitt *(Chief Creative Officer)*
Andrea Ring *(Chief Strategy Officer)*
Laura Breines *(VP & Dir-Client Svcs)*
Vinny DiBartolo *(VP-Tech)*
Duncan Snowden *(VP-Strategy)*
Tony Clement *(Dir-Strategy)*
Victor Pineiro *(Dir-Content & Social Media)*
Charlie Weisman *(Mgr-Client Engagement)*
Naomi Baria *(Sr Strategist-Social)*

Accounts:
20th Century Fox
ABC
ACTIVATE Digital
Activision Blizzard
Adobe Systems Incorporated The Expressive Web
Agro-Farma, Inc. Chobani Champions
Alien Ware
Billboard Music Industry Magazine
Callard & Bowser Altoids
Chow Baby
Coca-Cola Refreshments USA, Inc.
Dreamworks
Food Network
GoGo squeeze Campaign: "Wherever You Go, Go Playfully", Digital
Google Campaign: "What Do You Love"
LG
Lifesavers
Lifetime
Lucasfilm Digital
Macromedia
Materne North America Digital, GoGo squeeZ
MGM
Miramax
MOMA (The Museum of Modern Art)
NBC Universal
Nestle
The New York Times
Nike
Palm Pictures
Paramount Pictures
Samsung (Global Social Agency of Record) Campaign: "That New Phone Feeling", Galaxy S6
Seventh Generation
Skittles
Sony Electronics
Starter
Urbandaddy
Volkswagen Group of America, Inc. Star Wars Passat
Warner Bros.
Wrigley's

BIG THINK STUDIOS
512 Missouri St, San Francisco, CA 94107
Tel.: (415) 934-1111
Web Site: www.bigthinkstudios.com

Agency Specializes In: Advertising, Brand Development & Integration, Environmental, Graphic Design, Logo & Package Design, Outdoor, Production, T.V., Web (Banner Ads, Pop-ups, etc.)

Peter Walbridge *(Dir-Creative)*
Lael Robertson *(Office Mgr)*
Karen Capraro *(Designer)*
Susan Hanley *(Sr Accountant)*

Accounts:
ACLU of Northern California
Breast Cancer Fund
The Leakey Foundation
SF Works
Tides Foundation
TransFair USA
WiserEarth

BIGBUZZ MARKETING GROUP

510 Broadhollow Rd Ste 300, Melville, NY 11747
Tel.: (516) 845-0702
E-Mail: Kevin@bigbuzz.com
Web Site: www.bigbuzz.com

Employees: 19
Year Founded: 1997

National Agency Associations: 4A's

Agency Specializes In: Branded Entertainment, Business Publications, Digital/Interactive, Electronic Media, Email, Game Integration, Mobile Marketing, Multimedia, Paid Searches, Podcasting, Point of Sale, Production, RSS (Really Simple Syndication), Search Engine Optimization, Social Media, Web (Banner Ads, Pop-ups, etc.)

Doug Graham *(Co-Pres & Chief Creative Officer)*
Kevin Kelly *(Co-Pres & Chief Creative Officer)*
Bob Costabile *(Dir-Creative)*
Mary Stanley *(Dir-Fin & Admin)*
Hal Plattman *(Assoc Dir-Creative)*
Negeen Ghaisar *(Acct Exec & Strategist-Digital)*

Accounts:
Garanimals Blog Strategy, Branded Content, Digital Media, Online Marketing, SEO/SEM, Social Media, Video, Web
Honeywell App Development, Branding, Mobile, Web

BIGELOW ADVERTISING

723 Piedmont Ave, Atlanta, GA 30308
Tel.: (470) 223-2449
Web Site: www.bigelow.co

Year Founded: 1985

Agency Specializes In: Advertising, Brand Development & Integration, Media Buying Services, Media Planning, Merchandising, Package Design, Sponsorship

Thomas G. Bigelow *(Pres & Exec Dir-Creative)*
Kim Bigelow *(Principal)*
Cody Rogers *(Dir-Art)*
Kara Stringer *(Sr Acct Exec)*

Accounts:
COR365 Information Solutions
Digital Signage Expo
East Lake Golf Club
Surgery Exchange
Time Warner Cable IntelligentHome

BIGEYE AGENCY

(Formerly BigEye Creative)
500 S Magnolia Ave, Orlando, FL 32801
Tel.: (407) 839-8599
Fax: (407) 839-4779
E-Mail: info@bigeyeagency.com
Web Site: bigeyeagency.com

Employees: 8

Justin Ramb *(Founder & CEO)*
Seth Segura *(Dir-Creative)*
Sandra Marshall *(Sr Acct Mgr)*
Lauren Steckroth *(Acct Mgr)*
Jennifer Williamson *(Acct Mgr)*
Brittany Yoder *(Acct Mgr)*
Megan Bobiak *(Mgr-Mktg)*
Tim McCormack *(Mgr-Digital Mktg)*
Laurie Sparks *(Mgr-Fin & Ops)*
Justin Sooter *(Designer)*

Accounts:
Arnold Palmer Hospital for Children Heart Center Video
Fantastic Sams (Agency of Record) Advertising, Digital Marketing, Media, Media Research, Placement, Planning, Strategy
M2 Enterprises
Orlando Health
Pastors.com

BIGEYEDWISH LLC

419 Lafayette St, New York, NY 10003
Tel.: (212) 951-0694
Web Site: www.bigeyedwish.com

Agency Specializes In: Advertising, Brand Development & Integration, Digital/Interactive, Event Planning & Marketing, Graphic Design, Internet/Web Design, Public Relations, Social Media

Ian Wishingrad *(Founder & Creative Dir)*

Accounts:
New-New Jersey Devils LLC

BIGFISH CREATIVE GROUP

14500 N Northsight Blvd Ste 100, Scottsdale, AZ 85260
Tel.: (480) 355-2550
E-Mail: info@thisisbigfish.com
Web Site: thinkbigfish.com

Agency Specializes In: Advertising, Brand Development & Integration, Digital/Interactive, Internet/Web Design, Radio

Lauren Charpio *(Mng Dir)*
Joseph Pizzimenti *(Principal)*
Kevin Cornwell *(Dir-Design)*
Lear Mason *(Dir-Creative)*
Brett Pollett *(Dir-User Experience)*

Accounts:
Marley Park

BILL BOSSE & ASSOCIATES

6 Gage Court, Houston, TX 77024-4409
Tel.: (832) 358-2888
Fax: (832) 358-1199
E-Mail: bosse@bosse.com
Web Site: www.bosse.com

Employees: 4
Year Founded: 1979

Agency Specializes In: Advertising, Advertising Specialties, Broadcast, Business-To-Business, Consulting, Corporate Identity, Custom Publishing, E-Commerce, Email, Food Service, Graphic Design, Health Care Services, Industrial, Information Technology, Internet/Web Design, Local Marketing, Logo & Package Design, Media Buying Services, Media Planning, Newspaper, Out-of-Home Media, Outdoor, Package Design, Pharmaceutical, Planning & Consultation, Point of Sale, Print, Production (Print), Radio, Recruitment, Restaurant, Search Engine Optimization, T.V., Trade & Consumer Magazines

Approx. Annual Billings: $1,150,000

Breakdown of Gross Billings by Media: Adv. Specialities: $65,000; D.M.: $20,000; Fees: $20,000; Internet Adv.: $25,000; Newsp.: $610,000; Production: $290,000; Radio & T.V.: $85,000; Trade & Consumer Mags.: $35,000

Bill Bosse *(Pres)*
Doris Bosse *(VP, Sec & Treas)*

Accounts:
5 Star Stories Inc; Houston, TX Books; 2007
Asgard Global; Houston, TX Recruiting Technical Skilled Personnel; 2000
Genesis Photographers; Houston, TX Business & Event Photography; 1995
Liquid Assets; Houston, TX Bar/Restaurant Products; 1997
Memorial Drive Lutheran Church; Houston, TX Ministries; 1985
Physician's Allergy Consulting Group; Houston, TX A-Drops (Sublingual Allergy Treatment); 2008
Tosca Farm; New Waverly, TX Foliar Fertilizer, Grass-Fed Beef, Trees
Vincenzo's Italian Grill; Houston, TX; 2010

BILL GERSHON MARKETING COMMUNICATIONS

9828 Crawford Ave, Skokie, IL 60076-1107
Tel.: (847) 676-9452
Fax: (847) 674-7205
E-Mail: gershcom@yahoo.com

Employees: 1
Year Founded: 1982

Agency Specializes In: Advertising, Business Publications, Business-To-Business, Collateral, Consulting, Content, Education, Health Care Services, Industrial, Medical Products, Pharmaceutical, Planning & Consultation, Print, Sales Promotion, Trade & Consumer Magazines, Transportation

Approx. Annual Billings: $100,000

Bill Gershon *(Owner)*

Accounts:
charactersnmore; Skokie, IL Voice-over Services; 2005

BILL HUDSON & ASSOCIATES, INC., ADVERTISING & PUBLIC RELATIONS

1701 W End Ave, Nashville, TN 37203
Tel.: (615) 259-9002
Fax: (615) 256-0105
E-Mail: results@billhudsonagency.com
Web Site: www.billhudsonagency.com

Employees: 20
Year Founded: 1964

National Agency Associations: AAF-Second Wind Limited

Agency Specializes In: Advertising, Agriculture, Brand Development & Integration, Broadcast, Business-To-Business, Cable T.V., Collateral, Consulting, Consumer Marketing, Corporate Identity, Education, Entertainment, Environmental, Event Planning & Marketing, Financial, Food Service, Government/Political, Graphic Design, Health Care Services, Industrial, Legal Services, Leisure, Logo & Package Design, Magazines, Media Buying Services, Multimedia, Newspaper, Out-of-Home Media, Outdoor, Planning &

Consultation, Print, Public Relations, Publicity/Promotions, Radio, Real Estate, Restaurant, Retail, Sports Market, Strategic Planning/Research, T.V., Teen Market, Trade & Consumer Magazines, Transportation, Travel & Tourism

Wayne Edwards *(Pres & CEO)*
Steve Travis *(Exec VP)*
Virginia Chilton *(Media Dir)*
Bob Borum *(Sr Graphic Designer)*

Accounts:
Bank of Nashville; Nashville, TN; 1991
CPS Land; Brentwood, TN
McDonald's
WaterWorks

BILLUPS DESIGN
(Acquired by & Name Changed to iCiDigital)

BIMM COMMUNICATIONS GROUP
175 Bloor St E, S Tower Ste 1101, Toronto, ON M4W 3R8 Canada
Tel.: (416) 960-2432
Fax: (416) 960-1480
E-Mail: contactus@bimm.com
Web Site: www.bimm.com

Agency Specializes In: Brand Development & Integration, Customer Relationship Management, Direct Response Marketing, Internet/Web Design, Media Relations, Radio, Strategic Planning/Research, T.V.

Roehl Sanchez *(Co-Owner, Chief Creative Officer & Exec VP)*
Angela Lowe *(Grp Acct Dir)*
Diana Malta *(Acct Dir)*
Sharron Parsons *(Acct Dir)*
Jason Barg *(Dir-Client Insights)*
Greg Clark *(Dir-Fin)*
Mark Daley *(Dir-Digital Project Mgmt)*
Rene Rouleau *(Dir-Creative)*
Nicole Egan *(Mgr-Engagement)*
Alia Kuksis *(Acct Coord)*

Accounts:
Audi Canada Campaign: "Audi Health Check"

BIRDSONG GREGORY
715 N Church St Ste 101, Charlotte, NC 28202
Tel.: (704) 332-2299
Fax: (704) 332-2259
Web Site: www.birdsonggregory.com

Agency Specializes In: Advertising, Graphic Design

Leslie Kraemer *(Principal)*
Phillip Atchison *(Sr Writer & Strategist-Brand)*
Jessica Manner *(Sr Designer)*

Accounts:
Chobani Greek Yogurt
JustSave

BISIG IMPACT GROUP
640 S 4th St Ste 300, Louisville, KY 40202
Tel.: (502) 583-0333
Fax: (502) 583-6487
E-Mail: chip@bisig.com
Web Site: www.bisigimpactgroup.com

Employees: 30

Agency Specializes In: Advertising, Consumer Publications, Package Design, Print, Production (Ad, Film, Broadcast), Web (Banner Ads, Pop-ups, etc.)

Joe Weber *(Sr Dir-Art)*
Joseph Grove *(Acct Dir)*
Janice Kreutzer *(Dir-Media Svcs)*
Matt Willinger *(Dir-PR)*
Jennifer Washle *(Mgr-Promos)*
Reba Bangasser *(Graphic Designer-Production)*

Accounts:
Belterra Casino Resort & Spa Hotel & Resort Services
River Downs Creative, Marketing, Media, Public Relations
Toyota

BIZCOM ASSOCIATES
16301 Quorum Dr #150 A, Addison, TX 75001
Tel.: (972) 490-0903
Fax: (972) 692-5451
Web Site: www.bizcompr.com

Year Founded: 1992

Agency Specializes In: Content, Crisis Communications, Email, Exhibit/Trade Shows, Internet/Web Design, Local Marketing, Media Relations, Media Training, Newspaper

Scott White *(Pres & Partner)*
Monica Feid *(VP & Principal)*
Lindsey Young *(Acct Exec)*

Accounts:
Bennigan's
Discovery Point Child Development Centers Marketing Communications
DreamMaker Bath & Kitchen
The Dwyer Group
Green Home Solutions Marketing Communications
Pizza Inn
Red Mango
RedBrick Pizza
Smoothie Factory
Taco Cabana Consumer PR, Marketing Communications
UFood Grill Marketing Communications
VentAHood
yuru

B.J. THOMPSON ASSOCIATES, INC.
2901 E Bristol St Ste C, Elkhart, IN 46514
Tel.: (574) 255-5000
Fax: (574) 674-6802
E-Mail: info@bjta.com
Web Site: www.bjta.com

Employees: 5
Year Founded: 1979

Agency Specializes In: Automotive, Event Planning & Marketing, Graphic Design, Health Care Services, Leisure, Public Relations, Trade & Consumer Magazines

Barb Riley *(Acct Mgr)*

Accounts:
Ancon Construction; Goshen, IL Commercial Construction
Biomet, Inc.
Grubb & Ellis/Cressy & Everett; Mishawaka, IN Commercial Real Estate; 1992
HWH Corp.; Moscow, IA
Innovative Building Systems Inc.
J.V. Macri Orthodontics; South Bend, IN
Mishawaka Business Association
Newmar Corp; Nappanee, IN Recreational Vehicles
Trailair
Troyer Group
Whirlpool
Woodall Publication Corporation
Zip Dee, Inc.

BKV, INC.
(Formerly Bennett Kuhn Varner, Inc.)
3390 Peachtree Rd 10th Fl, Atlanta, GA 30326
Tel.: (404) 233-0332
Fax: (404) 233-0302
E-Mail: contact@bkv.com
Web Site: www.bkv.com

E-Mail for Key Personnel:
Creative Dir.: dannys@bkv.com
Media Dir.: stacyp@bkv.com
Production Mgr.: JennyM@bkv.com

Employees: 102
Year Founded: 1981

National Agency Associations: DMA

Agency Specializes In: Advertising, Broadcast, Business Publications, Direct Response Marketing, E-Commerce, Electronic Media, Entertainment, Health Care Services, High Technology, Infomercials, Internet/Web Design, Retail, Sponsorship, T.V., Trade & Consumer Magazines

Approx. Annual Billings: $69,000,000 Fees Capitalized

Maribett Varner *(Pres)*
Virginia Doty *(Mng Partner & Exec VP-Mktg)*
Stacy Pierce *(Chief Media Officer & Exec VP)*
Jana Ferguson *(Exec VP & Client Svcs Dir)*
Todd Chambers *(VP & Grp Dir-Creative)*
Zachary Lavoy *(VP & Mgmt Supvr)*
Bree Roe *(VP & Dir-Media)*
Jerelle Gainey *(VP-Tech & Data Svcs)*
Rina Cook *(Dir-Bus Dev)*
Amber Usmani *(Media Planner)*

Accounts:
Aflac, Inc.
American Red Cross; Washington, DC; 2003
AT&T
Dell SecureWorks
Delta TechOps
The Direct Marketing Association
DS Services
Hubzu.com
Kimpton Hotels
March of Dimes
Prison Fellowship
Six Flags Entertainment Corp.; 1981
Southern Company
Spanx
Tractor Supply Company

BLACK & WHITE ADVERTISING, INC.
3646 Highlands Pkwy, Smyrna, GA 30082
Tel.: (770) 818-0303
Fax: (770) 818-0344
E-Mail: keith@discoverbw.com
Web Site: www.discoverbw.com

Employees: 3
Year Founded: 1999

Agency Specializes In: Advertising Specialties, Brand Development & Integration, Business Publications, Business-To-Business, Cable T.V., Direct Response Marketing, Electronic Media, Exhibit/Trade Shows, Graphic Design, Health Care Services, High Technology, Information Technology, Internet/Web Design, Magazines, Media Buying Services, Medical Products, Multimedia, Newspaper, Newspapers & Magazines, Outdoor, Planning & Consultation, Print, Production, Radio, Recruitment

Approx. Annual Billings: $500,000

Keith White *(Owner, Pres & CEO)*

BLACK DIAMOND PR FIRM
9330 LBJ Freeway Ste 900, Dallas, TX 75243
Tel.: (877) 256-3075
Web Site: www.blackdiamondfirm.com

Agency Specializes In: Advertising, Brand Development & Integration, Public Relations, T.V.

Brandy Runyan *(Founder & CEO)*

Accounts:
New-Fernando Da Rosa

BLACK LAB CREATIVE
4311 Belmont Ave, Dallas, TX 75204
Tel.: (214) 662-8788
Web Site: www.blacklabcreative.com

Year Founded: 2007

Agency Specializes In: Advertising, Brand Development & Integration, Collateral, Event Planning & Marketing, Graphic Design

Chad Costas *(Owner & Partner)*
Brett Dougall *(Owner & Partner)*
Eddie Hale *(Owner & Partner-Creative)*
Ken Gantzer *(Chm-Pledge & Bus Dev)*

Accounts:
Partners Card

BLACK OLIVE LLC
125 S Wacker Dr Ste 300, Chicago, IL 60606
Tel.: (312) 893-5454
Fax: (312) 276-8636
E-Mail: info@blackoliveco.com
Web Site: www.blackoliveco.com

Employees: 11
Year Founded: 2003

National Agency Associations: ADMA-BMA-DMA

Agency Specializes In: Advertising, Brand Development & Integration, Business Publications, Business-To-Business, Collateral, Communications, Consulting, Consumer Marketing, Corporate Communications, Corporate Identity, Digital/Interactive, Direct Response Marketing, E-Commerce, Education, Electronic Media, Financial, Government/Political, Graphic Design, Health Care Services, High Technology, Information Technology, Internet/Web Design, Logo & Package Design, New Product Development, Planning & Consultation, Print, Production, Public Relations, Sales Promotion, Social Marketing/Nonprofit, Strategic Planning/Research, Telemarketing, Women's Market

Approx. Annual Billings: $1,000,000

Breakdown of Gross Billings by Media: D.M.: $300,000; Internet Adv.: $200,000; Strategic Planning/Research: $200,000; Worldwide Web Sites: $300,000

Karen Pittenger *(Owner & Mgr)*

Accounts:
American Bar Association Digital Communications; 2008
American Red Cross; Philadelphia, PA Workplace Safety; 2006
Country Financial Insurance & Financial Services; 2000
CSMR Insurance Brokerage; 2005
Indiana University Center on Philanthropy; 2011
Printing Technologies; Indianapolis, IN Specialty Roll Printing; 2003

BLACK PEARL INTELLIGENCE
142 Chula Vista Ste 200, San Antonio, TX 78232
Tel.: (210) 979-8080
Web Site: www.blackpearlintelligence.com

Year Founded: 1991

Agency Specializes In: Advertising, Brand Development & Integration, Digital/Interactive, Internet/Web Design, Logo & Package Design

Accounts:
Argo Group
Cowboy Church
Meat Me in Bulverde
TEDx SanAntonio

BLACK TWIG COMMUNICATIONS
7711 Bonhomme Ave Ste 505, Saint Louis, MO 63105
Tel.: (314) 255-2340
Web Site: www.blacktwigllc.com

Year Founded: 2006

Agency Specializes In: Advertising, Market Research, Public Relations

Mary DeHahn *(Owner)*
Randolph F. Seeling *(Mng Partner & CFO)*
Stephanie Flynn *(Partner)*
Tom Gatti *(Partner-Bus Dev)*
Bruce Kupper *(Partner)*
William Kay *(VP)*

Accounts:
Camie-Campbell Inc. Aerosol & Chemical Products Mfr & Distr
Clayton Sleep Institute Sleep Study Institute
Domino Foods Inc. Packaged Frozen Food Merchant Whslr
Hydroflo Pumps USA Inc. Industrial Machinery Merchant Whslr

BLACK YELLOW PAGES
433 N Camden Dr, Beverly Hills, CA 90210
Tel.: (562) 606-5304
Toll Free: (800) 467-1779
E-Mail: info@blackyellowpagesonline.com
Web Site: www.blackyellowpagesonline.com

Year Founded: 1999

Agency Specializes In: Advertising, African-American Market, Bilingual Market, Broadcast, Business-To-Business, Cable T.V., Consulting, Consumer Marketing, Direct Response Marketing, Direct-to-Consumer, Electronic Media, Email, Graphic Design, Hispanic Market, Infomercials, Internet/Web Design, Legal Services, Logo & Package Design, Media Planning, Mobile Marketing, Multicultural, Multimedia, Planning & Consultation, Production (Ad, Film, Broadcast), Production (Print), Recruitment, Retail, Sales Promotion, Search Engine Optimization, T.V., Telemarketing, Urban Market, Web (Banner Ads, Pop-ups, etc.)

Approx. Annual Billings: $550,000

Breakdown of Gross Billings by Media: Graphic Design: 5%; Internet Adv.: 10%; Logo & Package Design: 5%; T.V.: 10%; Yellow Page Adv.: 70%

Nancy Aldredge *(Dir-Community Projects-Inland Empire)*
Louis Easton *(Dir-Community Projects-Inland Empire)*
Michele Gaspard *(Dir-Community Projects-LA Metro)*
Dillon Wilson *(Reg Mgr)*

BLACKBOARD CO.
2905 San Gabriel St Ste 300, Austin, TX 78705
Tel.: (512) 474-8363
Fax: (512) 532-0768
Web Site: www.blackboardco.com

Year Founded: 2009

National Agency Associations: 4A's

Agency Specializes In: Advertising, Brand Development & Integration, Corporate Identity, Digital/Interactive, Media Buying Services, Media Planning, Social Media, Sponsorship

Clark Evans *(Founder & Partner)*
Jeff Nixon *(Founder & Exec Dir-Creative)*
Joe Shands *(Partner & Chief Creative Officer)*
Tom Hollerbach *(Mng Dir & COO)*
Katie Blot *(Sr VP-Corp Strategy & Bus Dev)*
Mark Strassman *(Sr VP-Products & Mktg)*
Vera Zlidenny *(Sr Dir-Mktg Svcs)*
Jill Whitley *(Sr Acct Mgr)*
Doug Myrback *(Acct Exec-Strategic)*
Corey Carbo *(Designer)*

Accounts:
Grande Communications Networks LLC
Green Mountain Energy Company
Ole Smoky Tennessee Moonshine
Supreme Protein
Tillamook County Creamery Association
VeeV Acai Spirits

BLACKDOG ADVERTISING
8771 SW 129th Terr, Miami, FL 33176
Tel.: (305) 253-8388
Web Site: www.blackdogadvertising.com

Year Founded: 1989

Agency Specializes In: Advertising, Brand Development & Integration, Corporate Identity, Digital/Interactive, Graphic Design, Internet/Web Design, Logo & Package Design, Package Design, Print, Strategic Planning/Research

John Penney *(Founder & Dir-Creative)*
Kathy Penney *(VP & Mgr-Strategic Mktg)*
Humberto Abeja *(Dir-Art)*
Jessica Tomlin *(Dir-Art-Online Mktg)*
Mitch Meyers *(Mgr-Internet Mktg)*
Marcy Russillo *(Mgr-Media)*
Mylene Valerius *(Mgr-Production-Estimating)*
Wendy Meyerson *(Copywriter)*

Accounts:
Green Parrot Bar

BLACKFIN MARKETING GROUP
13736 Spring Lake Rd, Minnetonka, MN 55345-2330
Tel.: (952) 237-6352
Fax: (952) 303-3079
E-Mail: jgresham@blackfinmarketing.com
Web Site: www.blackfinmarketing.com

Employees: 3

Agency Specializes In: Business-To-Business, Communications, Local Marketing

John Fischer *(Pres)*

Accounts:
Syngenta Seeds, Inc.

BLACKJET INC
183 Bathurst St Ste 401, Toronto, Ontario M5T

2R7 Canada
Tel.: (416) 642-6860
E-Mail: hello@blackjet.ca
Web Site: www.blackjet.ca

Agency Specializes In: Advertising, Digital/Interactive, Internet/Web Design

Rob Galletta *(Pres, Partner, Gen Mgr & Sr Strategist)*
Marco Marino *(Partner & Dir-Creative)*
Mo Solomon *(Partner & Dir-Creative)*
Cameron Ward *(Dir-Art)*
Ravi Chandran *(Mgr-Production)*
Jennifer Corelli *(Acct Exec)*
Joe Mancuso *(Acct Exec)*

Accounts:
Sixty Colborne

BLACKTOP CREATIVE

1735 Baltimore Ave, Kansas City, MO 64108
Tel.: (816) 423-6392
Web Site: www.blacktopcreative.com

National Agency Associations: 4A's

Agency Specializes In: Advertising, Brand Development & Integration, Digital/Interactive, Graphic Design

Shawn Polowniak *(Pres)*
Dave Swearingen *(Dir-Creative)*
Chris Macadam *(Sr Mgr-Print Production)*
Alyssa Bastien *(Designer)*
Emily Esparza *(Planner-Brand)*
Randy Green *(Designer-Production)*
Maggie Hirschi *(Designer)*
Lesley Hunt *(Designer)*
Molly Lees *(Copywriter)*
Russ Weydert *(Designer-Production)*

Accounts:
Edible Arrangements International, Inc.

BLACKWING CREATIVE

(Formerly Hodgson/Meyers)
10210 NE Points Dr Ste 220, Kirkland, WA 98033-7872
Tel.: (425) 827-2506
Fax: (425) 822-0155
E-Mail: getnoticed@blackwingcreative.com
Web Site: www.blackwingcreative.com/

Employees: 20

National Agency Associations: AMA-DMA-Second Wind Limited

Agency Specializes In: Advertising, Aviation & Aerospace, Brand Development & Integration, Business Publications, Business-To-Business, Co-op Advertising, Collateral, Communications, Consumer Publications, Corporate Identity, Cosmetics, Direct Response Marketing, Electronic Media, Engineering, Environmental, Event Planning & Marketing, Exhibit/Trade Shows, Financial, Graphic Design, Health Care Services, High Technology, Infomercials, Information Technology, Internet/Web Design, Legal Services, Leisure, Logo & Package Design, Magazines, Marine, Medical Products, Newspaper, Newspapers & Magazines, Planning & Consultation, Point of Purchase, Point of Sale, Print, Production, Radio, Real Estate, Retail, Sales Promotion, Sports Market, Strategic Planning/Research, T.V., Technical Advertising, Trade & Consumer Magazines, Transportation

Gary Meyers *(Pres & Sr Strategist-Creative)*
Steve Franklin *(Mng Dir & Principal)*
Steve Wilcox *(Gen Mgr-San Francisco)*
Mary Kate Baker *(Acct Dir)*
Stephanie Sohol Cooper *(Acct Dir)*
Gina Markovich *(Dir-Production)*
Charlie Worcester *(Assoc Dir-Creative)*
Sharan Ochsner *(Office Mgr)*
Craig Labenz *(Designer-Interactive)*

Accounts:
Allied Telesis; Bothell, WA
Avaya Inc.; NJ & Redmond, WA
Clorox Products; Oakland, CA; 2003
Douglass Interior Products; Bellevue, WA Leather & Other Fabrics for Aviation Industry
Extreme Fitness; Bellevue & Seattle, WA Fitness & Health Club; 2004
Junior Achievement Washington; Seattle, WA; 2003
The Mackay Restaurant Group; Seattle, WA El Gaucho Steakhouse; 2005
Microsoft Exchange Server; Redmond, WA; 2003
Opus Group; Chicago, IL Performance Optimization for Fortune 500 Companies; 2004
Perkins Coie, LLP; Seattle, WA Law Firm; 2002
Philips Medical; Bothell, WA Medical Equipment
Physician Micro Systems, Inc.; Seattle, WA Electronic Medical Records & Software
Print Inc.; Kirkland, WA
Puget Sound Business Journal; Seattle, WA; 2002
The SAVO Group; Chicago, IL Sales Performance Technology & Services; 2005
SCI Global Manufacturing
Seattle's Best Coffee; Seattle, WA
SpaceLabs
TempoSoft; Chicago, IL; 2003

BLAINE WARREN ADVERTISING LLC

7120 Smoke Ranch Rd, Las Vegas, NV 89128
Tel.: (702) 435-6947
Fax: (702) 450-9168
E-Mail: msabatier@blainewarren.com
Web Site: www.blainewarren.com

Employees: 35

Agency Specializes In: Advertising, Advertising Specialties, Commercial Photography, Digital/Interactive, Direct Response Marketing, Event Planning & Marketing, Exhibit/Trade Shows, Public Relations, Publicity/Promotions

Sterling Martell *(Owner)*
Michael Sabatier *(CFO)*
Adrian Byrd *(Dir-Event & Mktg)*
Sabrina Segal Granati *(Dir-Media)*
Michael Speciale *(Dir-Media)*
Becca Bench *(Acct Coord)*

Accounts:
Air Force Reserve

BLAINETURNER ADVERTISING, INC.

1401 Saratoga Ave, Morgantown, WV 26505
Tel.: (304) 599-5900
Fax: (304) 599-9005
E-Mail: btadvantage@blaineturner.com
Web Site: www.blaineturner.com

Year Founded: 1986

Agency Specializes In: Advertising, Graphic Design, Internet/Web Design, Media Buying Services, Public Relations, Social Media

Delbert Royce *(Owner)*
Ginna Royce *(Pres & Dir-Creative)*
Sherea Mercure *(Dir-Mktg & Analytics)*
Galen Shaffer *(Dir-Art)*
Kelly Lambruno *(Office Mgr)*
Sarah Swartz *(Acct Mgr)*

Accounts:
Ohio Valley College of Technology
UHC Oncology Services

BLAIR, INC.

1639 N Alpine Rd Ste 502, Rockford, IL 61107
Tel.: (815) 282-9060
Fax: (815) 282-9106
E-Mail: webmaster@blair-inc.com
Web Site: www.blair-inc.com

E-Mail for Key Personnel:
President: bblair@blair-inc.com

Employees: 9
Year Founded: 1979

National Agency Associations: 4A's

Agency Specializes In: Business-To-Business, Communications, Corporate Identity, Exhibit/Trade Shows, Graphic Design, Health Care Services, Industrial, Internet/Web Design, Logo & Package Design, Print, Public Relations, Transportation

Approx. Annual Billings: $6,000,000

Breakdown of Gross Billings by Media: Bus. Publs.: 10%; Collateral: 20%; D.M.: 5%; E-Commerce: 5%; Exhibits/Trade Shows: 5%; Internet Adv.: 30%; Logo & Package Design: 5%; Print: 10%; Pub. Rels.: 10%

Brian R. Blair *(Owner)*
Scott D. Clark *(VP)*
Greg Blair *(Art Dir & Acct Exec)*
Craig Schmidt *(Copywriter)*

Accounts:
Mitsubishi Lithographic Press
Royal Outdoor Product

BLAKESLEE ADVERTISING

916 N Charles St, Baltimore, MD 21201
Tel.: (410) 727-8800
Fax: (410) 752-1302
E-Mail: duane.levine@blakesleeadv.com
Web Site: www.blakesleeadv.com

Agency Specializes In: Advertising, Digital/Interactive, Direct Response Marketing, Direct-to-Consumer, Event Planning & Marketing, Internet/Web Design, Outdoor, Print, Public Relations, Radio, T.V., Web (Banner Ads, Pop-ups, etc.)

Duane Levine *(Pres & COO)*
Trudy Setree *(VP-Acct Svc)*
Linda Dijohn *(Dir-PR)*
Tom Wilson *(Dir-Creative)*
Cheryl Poole *(Media Buyer)*
Karen Setree *(Acct Coord)*
Rebecca Belt *(Community Mgr)*

Accounts:
Citi Financial
Graham Packaging
Jans
KCPW
MBNA
Midwest
Nupro
Radica
Raintree Essix (Agency of Record)

Subsidiary

Blakeslee Advertising

1790 Bonanza Dr Ste 275, Park City, UT 84060
Tel.: (410) 727-8800
Fax: (435) 647-5825
E-Mail: mark.fischer@blakesleeadv.com
Web Site: www.blakesleeadv.com

Employees: 5

Agency Specializes In: Advertising

Mark Fischer *(Owner)*
Stephanie Fischer *(VP & Acct Supvr)*

Accounts:
Christopher Homes
CitiFinancial Retail Services
MBNA America
Nupro
OrthoCAD
Ragged Mountain
US Ski Team
White Pine Touring

BLAMMO WORLDWIDE
154 Pearl Street, Toronto, ON M5H 1L3 Canada
Tel.: (416) 979-7999
Fax: (416) 979-9750
E-Mail: partners@blammo.com
Web Site: www.blammo.com

E-Mail for Key Personnel:
Chairman: agee@blammo.com

Employees: 80
Year Founded: 1991

National Agency Associations: AMA

Agency Specializes In: Advertising, Advertising Specialties, Automotive, Bilingual Market, Brand Development & Integration, Broadcast, Children's Market, Collateral, Communications, Consulting, Consumer Marketing, Corporate Identity, Direct Response Marketing, E-Commerce, Electronic Media, Fashion/Apparel, Government/Political, Graphic Design, High Technology, Internet/Web Design, Leisure, Logo & Package Design, Magazines, Media Buying Services, New Product Development, Newspaper, Newspapers & Magazines, Out-of-Home Media, Outdoor, Planning & Consultation, Point of Purchase, Point of Sale, Print, Production, Public Relations, Radio, Real Estate, Retail, Sales Promotion, Sports Market, Strategic Planning/Research, Syndication, T.V., Teen Market, Telemarketing, Transportation, Travel & Tourism

Approx. Annual Billings: $75,000,000

Breakdown of Gross Billings by Media: D.M.: 5%; E-Commerce: 5%; Graphic Design: 15%; Mags.: 10%; Newsp.: 10%; Outdoor: 10%; Radio: 15%; T.V.: 30%

Gord Cathmoir *(Partner)*
Nicole Brown *(Acct Dir)*
Vanessa Heber *(Dir-Art)*
Yan Snajdr *(Dir-Art)*
Amanda Tucci *(Acct Mgr)*
Claire Demarco *(Copywriter)*
Tom Mednick *(Copywriter)*
Victoria Sturgess *(Copywriter)*

Accounts:
Arby's Restaurant Group, Inc. Campaign: "Beefy Boo", Campaign: "Believe The Unbelievable", QuestChat
Breathe Right
Cannes Committee Campaign: "Map of Cannes"
ConAgra Campaign: "Pogo Love", ConAgra Foods
Cougar
Del Monte Campaign: "Gossip Break, Facebook Break, Coffee Break"
Fallsview Casino Campaign: "Coconut", Campaign: "Get Off Your Duty"
Orville Redenbacher
Project Winter Survival Campaign: "Relax", PSA
Spectro Skin Care Campaign: "The Smile Shop"

BLANCHARD SCHAEFER ADVERTISING & PUBLIC RELATIONS
(Name Changed to Schaefer Advertising Co.)

BLARE INC.
3221 25th St, Metairie, LA 70002
Tel.: (504) 909-7068
E-Mail: info@blareinc.com
Web Site: www.blareinc.com

Agency Specializes In: Advertising, Brand Development & Integration, Internet/Web Design, Outdoor, Print, Radio, Social Media, T.V.

P. Blair Touchard *(Owner)*
Dee Dee Cohen *(Dir-Media)*

Accounts:
Heart Clinic of Amite
Jefferson Community Health Care Centers

BLASS COMMUNICATIONS LLC
17 Drowne Rd, Old Chatham, NY 12136-3006
Tel.: (518) 766-2222
Fax: (518) 766-2446
Web Site: blasscom.com

E-Mail for Key Personnel:
President: kenb@blasscommunications.com
Creative Dir.: rsimon@blasscommunications.com
Media Dir.:
dingoldsby@blasscommunications.com
Production Mgr.:
lvinchiarello@blasscommunications.com
Public Relations:
scampbell@blasscommunications.com

Employees: 25
Year Founded: 1969

National Agency Associations: AMA

Agency Specializes In: Advertising, Arts, Bilingual Market, Brand Development & Integration, Broadcast, Business Publications, Business-To-Business, Catalogs, Co-op Advertising, Collateral, College, Commercial Photography, Communications, Consulting, Consumer Goods, Consumer Marketing, Consumer Publications, Corporate Communications, Corporate Identity, Digital/Interactive, Direct Response Marketing, Direct-to-Consumer, E-Commerce, Education, Electronic Media, Email, Engineering, Exhibit/Trade Shows, Financial, Food Service, Graphic Design, Health Care Services, High Technology, Identity Marketing, Industrial, Information Technology, Integrated Marketing, Internet/Web Design, Legal Services, Leisure, Logo & Package Design, Magazines, Marine, Market Research, Media Buying Services, Media Planning, Media Relations, Medical Products, Merchandising, Multicultural, Multimedia, New Product Development, New Technologies, Newspaper, Newspapers & Magazines, Out-of-Home Media, Outdoor, Package Design, Planning & Consultation, Point of Purchase, Point of Sale, Print, Production, Production (Print), Promotions, Public Relations, Publicity/Promotions, Radio, Real Estate, Regional, Sales Promotion, Social Marketing/Nonprofit, Strategic Planning/Research, T.V., Technical Advertising, Trade & Consumer Magazines, Travel & Tourism, Web (Banner Ads, Pop-ups, etc.)

Approx. Annual Billings: $18,000,000

Kenneth L. Blass *(Pres & CEO)*
Kathy Blass Weiss *(Exec VP)*
Linda Vinchiarello *(Mgr-Print Production)*
Donna Ingoldsby *(Media Buyer)*

Accounts:
Clariant Pigments & Additives Colorants; 2003
Clariant, Masterbatches Division; Easton, MD Colorants; 1998
Naturtint USA (Agency of Record) Fashion & Product Photography, Marketing Communications, Public Relations, Social Media, Website
Starfire Systems, Inc.; Malta, NY Silicon Carbide Ceramic Materials; 2003
The TaylorMade Group; Gloversville, NY Marine Products; 1990

BLAST RADIUS
3 Columbus Cir, New York, NY 10019
Tel.: (212) 925-4900
Fax: (212) 925-5247
E-Mail: hello@blastradius.com
Web Site: www.blastradius.com

Employees: 250
Year Founded: 1996

National Agency Associations: 4A's

Agency Specializes In: Communications, Consumer Marketing, Digital/Interactive, E-Commerce, Information Technology, Internet/Web Design, Planning & Consultation, Sponsorship, Strategic Planning/Research

Amy Ferranti *(Mng Dir)*
Jessica Grizzell *(Head-Project Svcs & Ops)*
Roni Sebastian *(Grp Dir-Creative)*
Darryl Braunmiller *(Dir-Client)*
Debbie Ten Eyck *(Dir-HR)*

Accounts:
Bacardi Campaign: "Like It Live, Like It Together", Campaign: "Unwrap the Night"
BMW Canada
BOSS Bottled Night
Castrol
Electronic Arts
Hugo Boss
Land Rover
Lenovo Group Ltd. Digital
Microsoft Office 2010
Mondelez International, Inc.
Nike Campaign: "Golf 360"
Nikon
Nokia
Starbucks

Branches

Blast Radius Amsterdam
Max Euweplein 46, 1017 MB Amsterdam, Netherlands
Tel.: (31) 20 330 2014
Fax: (31) 20 330 2015
E-Mail: info@blastradius.com
Web Site: www.blastradius.com

Employees: 35

Agency Specializes In: Communications

Simon Neate-Stidson *(Sr Dir-Strategy)*
Manos Magoulas *(Acct Dir-Digital)*
Joppe Andriessen *(Dir-Art)*
Kazs Krikke *(Acct Mgr)*
Yulia Yushchik *(Strategist-Digital)*
Malin Wall *(Sr Designer)*

Accounts:
AOL
ASICS AW14, Campaign: "Craft of Movement", Campaign: "Journey of Chris", Campaign: "Journey of Que", Campaign: "My Town My Tracks", Harandia MT, Onitsuka Tiger, Print, Social
BMW
Electronic Arts
Esselte

MINI
Nau
Nike
P&G Campaign: "Kino"
Sengled
Starbucks
Yahoo

Blast Radius Hamburg
Grimm 6, Hamburg, 20457 Germany
Tel.: (49) 40 60 94 01 76
Fax: (49) 40 60 94 01 971
Web Site: www.blastradius.com

Lars Schloss-bauer *(Gen Mgr-Hamburg)*
Thomas Walther *(Sr Dir-Strategy)*
Joniel da Silva *(Dir-Creative)*

Accounts:
BMW
DirecTV
Electronic Arts
Heineken
Intrawest ULC
MINI
Nike
Nintendo
NIVEA Campaign: "Closer"
Philips

Blast Radius Inc.
303 2nd St Ste 8, San Francisco, CA 94107
(See Separate Listing)

Blast Radius Toronto
60 Bloor St W, 9th Fl, Toronto, ON M5V 2H8 Canada
Tel.: (416) 214-4220
Fax: (416) 214-6765
E-Mail: services@blastradius.com
Web Site: www.blastradius.com

Employees: 80
Year Founded: 1999

Kevin Flynn *(Sr VP & Dir-Strategy & Plng)*
Dave Stevenson *(VP & Sr Dir-Creative)*
Stephanie Ito *(VP-Ops)*
Ernie Bin *(Sr Dir-Creative & Dir-Interaction Design)*
Jeremy Marten *(Grp Acct Dir)*
Judith Netscher *(Dir-Project Svcs)*
Mitch Steinman *(Dir-Delivery Svcs)*
Eilish O'Day *(Sr Mgr-Talent)*
Sarah Paton *(Client Dir)*

Accounts:
BMW Digital
Electronic Arts
JC Penney
Jordan
Nike
Nintendo
Novartis
Philips

Blast Radius Vancouver
1146 Homer St, Vancouver, BC V6B 2X6 Canada
Tel.: (604) 647-6500
Fax: (604) 689-1963
E-Mail: info@blastradius.com
Web Site: www.blastradius.com

Agency Specializes In: Communications, Internet/Web Design

Lothar Boensch *(Mng Dir)*
Dave Stevenson *(VP & Sr Dir-Creative)*
John Tran *(VP-Tech)*
Jeremy Marten *(Grp Acct Dir)*
Sagi Chelishev *(Dir-QA)*
Andrea Moretti *(Dir-Technical Experience)*
Mitch Steinman *(Dir-Delivery Svcs)*
David Choi *(Assoc Dir-Bus Sys Analysis Practice)*

Accounts:
AOL
BMW
Electronic Arts
Heineken
Jordan Campaign: "Choose Your Flight"
Microsoft
Nike
Nintendo
P&G Campaign: "Kino"
Philips
Roxy
SaskTel Campaign: "How Green R U", Online Advertising, Outdoor, Radio, logo, print
Starbucks

BLAST RADIUS INC.
303 2nd St Ste 8, San Francisco, CA 94107
Tel.: (415) 765-1502
Web Site: www.blastradius.com

Year Founded: 1996

National Agency Associations: 4A's

Agency Specializes In: Advertising, Brand Development & Integration, Digital/Interactive

Amy Ferranti *(Mng Dir)*
Scott Yanzy *(VP & Exec Dir-Creative)*
Lars Schlossbauer *(Gen Mgr)*
David B. Fitzgerald *(Acct Dir)*
Debbie Ten Eyck *(Dir-HR)*
Meggan Dunne *(Project Mgr-Digital)*
Molly Mitchel *(Coord-Talent)*

Accounts:
Bacardi USA, Inc.
Beiersdorf AG Nivea
BRP
Kimberly-Clark Corporation Huggies
Nike, Inc.
Nokia Corporation
Starbucks Corporation Digital

BLATTEL COMMUNICATIONS
250 Montgomery St, San Francisco, CA 94104
Tel.: (415) 397-4811
Fax: (415) 956-5125
E-Mail: info@blattel.com
Web Site: www.blattel.com

Employees: 10

Agency Specializes In: Advertising, Communications, Corporate Identity, Crisis Communications, Email, Event Planning & Marketing, Exhibit/Trade Shows, Internet/Web Design, Local Marketing, Media Planning, Media Training, Multimedia, Public Relations, Strategic Planning/Research

Traci Stuart *(Pres)*
Ellen Blattel *(CEO)*
Chuck Brown *(Acct Mgr)*
Michael Bond *(Acct Supvr)*
Penny Desatnik *(Acct Supvr)*
Melinda Hepp *(Acct Supvr)*
Laura Benton *(Acct Exec)*
Joey Telucci *(Acct Exec)*

Accounts:
Alston & Bird, LLP.
Bar Association of San Francisco
Carroll, Burdick & McDonough
McCarthy Building Companies, Inc.
Stonnington Group
The Veen Firm

BLAZE
1427 Third St Promenade Ste 201, Santa Monica, CA 90401
Tel.: (310) 395-5050
Fax: (310) 395-5001
E-Mail: info@blazecompany.com
Web Site: www.blazepr.com

Employees: 11

Agency Specializes In: Consumer Goods, Entertainment, Food Service, Health Care Services, Real Estate, Restaurant, Travel & Tourism

Revenue: $1,200,000

Matt Kovacs *(Pres)*
Erinn Lynch *(VP)*
Angela Megrey *(VP-Social Media & Mktg)*
Nicholas Valente *(Sr Acct Exec)*

Accounts:
AmaWaterways (Agency of Record) Media Relations Campaign, PR, Social Media Strategy, Travel Awards Program
Beverly Center
Cotton Inc.
Design By Humans Blogger Strategy, Brand Promotion, Market Expansion, Media Relations Campaign
General Mills (Fingos)
HelloTel App Strategic Public Relations
Luxury Link
Madison Holdings Blogger, Brand Awareness, Broadcast Outreach, Online, PR, Print, Social Media
Marina del Rey Convention & Visitors Bureau Communications Campaign, Media Relations, Social Media
Mrs. Fields
Nutrawise Creative, Public Relations, Youtheory
Ommegang
Paramount Parks
REM Eyewear Converse
Schwabinger Tor Press
SnoBar Events, Media Outreach, Social Media Strategies
Spa Nautica Consumer Awareness
Table Tops Unlimited Consumer Public Relations, rove
TCBY
Visa USA
New-Yuneec E-Go, Social Media

BLEECKER & SULLIVAN ADVERTISING
214 Sullivan St, New York, NY 10012
Tel.: (212) 533-0909
Fax: (212) 533-1649
Web Site: www.bsadv.com

Agency Specializes In: Advertising, Corporate Identity, Internet/Web Design, Package Design, Print

Itzhak Beery *(Pres)*

Accounts:
American Society for the Prevention of Cruelty to Animals

BLEND
700 S Flower, Los Angeles, CA 90017
Tel.: (323) 845-9655
E-Mail: blend@weareblend.la
Web Site: weareblend.la

Employees: 20
Year Founded: 2012

Agency Specializes In: Affluent Market, African-American Market, Agriculture, Arts, Automotive, Aviation & Aerospace, Bilingual Market, Brand Development & Integration, Branded Entertainment, Broadcast, Business-To-Business, Cable T.V., Children's Market, Commercial Photography, Computers & Software, Consulting, Consumer Goods, Consumer Marketing, Content, Corporate Identity, Cosmetics, Customer Relationship Management, Digital/Interactive, Direct-to-Consumer, E-Commerce, Education, Electronic Media, Electronics, Email, Engineering, Entertainment, Environmental, Event Planning & Marketing, Experience Design, Faith Based, Fashion/Apparel, Financial, Food Service, Gay & Lesbian Market, Government/Political, Graphic Design, Health Care Services, High Technology, Hispanic Market, Hospitality, Household Goods, Identity Marketing, In-Store Advertising, Industrial, Information Technology, Integrated Marketing, International, Internet/Web Design, Investor Relations, Legal Services, Leisure, Logo & Package Design, Luxury Products, Magazines, Marine, Media Relations, Medical Products, Men's Market, Merchandising, Mobile Marketing, Multicultural, Multimedia, New Product Development, New Technologies, Over-50 Market, Package Design, Pets , Pharmaceutical, Planning & Consultation, Print, Production, Production (Ad, Film, Broadcast), Production (Print), Publishing, Real Estate, Recruitment, Restaurant, Retail, Seniors' Market, Social Marketing/Nonprofit, Social Media, South Asian Market, Sports Market, Stakeholders, Strategic Planning/Research, T.V., Teen Market, Transportation, Travel & Tourism, Tween Market, Urban Market, Web (Banner Ads, Pop-ups, etc.), Women's Market

Approx. Annual Billings: $4,000,000

Alex Strezev *(Product Mgr)*

Accounts:
New-Baby Jogger; 2013
New-Carey; 2013
New-Empire CLS; 2014
New-Food & Wine; 2014
New-Gamblit; 2014
New-Kneon; 2014
New-Lumo Lumo Bodytech; 2015
New-Lyft; 2015
New-MasterCard; 2014
New-Nordstrom; 2014
New-Porsche; 2014
New-Schwag; 2013
New-Verizon; 2015

BLENDERBOX INC.
26 Dobbin St 3rd Fl, Brooklyn, NY 11222
Tel.: (718) 963-4594
Web Site: www.blenderbox.com

Employees: 20

Agency Specializes In: Digital/Interactive

Jason Jeffries *(Founder & CEO)*
Sarah McLoughlin Jeffries *(Co-Founder & Dir-Creative)*
Will Davis *(Dir-Strategy)*
Kristina Pedicone *(Dir-Interactive Art)*
Amy Hunt *(Designer-Visual)*

Accounts:
American Express Website
Brooklyn Brewery Corporation
Lincoln Center Theater Website
New York Blood Center Website

BLEU MARKETING SOLUTIONS, INC.
3025 Fillmore St, San Francisco, CA 94123
Tel.: (415) 345-3300
Fax: (415) 353-0299
E-Mail: helpdesk@bleumarketing.com
Web Site: www.bleumarketing.com

Employees: 19
Year Founded: 2001

Agency Specializes In: Advertising

Laura Van Galen *(Pres & CEO)*
Daniel Garcia *(Grp Acct Dir)*
Jennifer Giordano *(Acct Dir)*
Domingo Johnson *(Assoc Dir-Creative)*
Korede Adeniji *(Acct Mgr-Media)*
Dana Al-Suwaidi *(Assoc Acct Mgr)*
Jay Quinones *(Coord-Acct & Media & Specialist-PR)*
Lee Farrell *(Designer-Visual)*
Darcy Reynolds *(Designer-Interactive)*
Paloma Zapata *(Media Planner & Buyer)*
Britt Goh *(Coord-Content Mktg)*

Accounts:
Apple
Cinnabar Consulting
Cisco
Creative Energy
Lynda.com

BLEUBLANCROUGE
(Formerly Kolegram Design)
606 Cathcart Street, Montreal, QC H3B 1K9 Canada
Tel.: (514) 875-7007
E-Mail: info@bleublancrouge.ca
Web Site: www.bleublancrouge.ca

Employees: 10
Year Founded: 1992

Agency Specializes In: Advertising

Jean-Sebastien Monty *(Pres)*
Michelle Aboud *(Partner & VP-Acct Svcs)*
Dave Gourde *(Partner & VP-Media)*
Elise Guillemette *(Partner & VP-Brand Language)*
Charles Beaulieu *(Dir-Digital Media & Programmatic)*
Lisanne Auger-Bellemare *(Mgr-Print Production)*
Alexis Caron-Cote *(Copywriter)*

Accounts:
Agriculture & Agri-Food Canada
Bell Media, Inc.
BIOTECanada
Cactus.net
Ubisoft Canada Creative Development, Strategic Planning
Zarlink

BLF MARKETING
103 Jefferson St, Ste 103, Clarksville, TN 37040
Tel.: (931) 552-0763
Fax: (931) 552-0785
E-Mail: success@blfmarketing.com
Web Site: www.blfmarketing.com

Employees: 10
Year Founded: 1978

Agency Specializes In: Advertising, Business-To-Business, Consulting, Direct Response Marketing, Financial, Health Care Services, Logo & Package Design, Strategic Planning/Research

Frank Lott *(Owner)*
Jeffrey V. Bibb *(Mng Partner)*
Sharon Bibb *(Dir-HR)*
Adam Groves *(Sr Acct Mgr)*
Heather Snyder *(Acct Mgr)*

Accounts:
Austin Peay State University
Farmers & Merchants Bank

BLIND SOCIETY
4222 N Marshall Way, Scottsdale, AZ 85251
Tel.: (480) 317-1313
Web Site: blindsociety.com

Employees: 8
Year Founded: 2006

Agency Specializes In: Affluent Market, Alternative Advertising, Brand Development & Integration, Branded Entertainment, College, Computers & Software, Consulting, Consumer Goods, Consumer Marketing, Corporate Identity, Digital/Interactive, Electronic Media, Electronics, Entertainment, Experience Design, Fashion/Apparel, Guerilla Marketing, High Technology, Hospitality, Household Goods, Logo & Package Design, Luxury Products, Market Research, Men's Market, New Product Development, New Technologies, Package Design, Planning & Consultation, Restaurant, Retail, Sports Market, Strategic Planning/Research, Women's Market

Approx. Annual Billings: $2,000,000

Jim Clark *(Partner & Creative Dir)*
Darren Wilson *(Partner & Strategist)*
Teri Bockting *(VP-Brand Strategy)*
Shannon Ecke *(Sr Designer-Creative)*

Accounts:
Carvana; 2012
Drivetime
NAMCO Entertainment 257; 2013
Red Robin Red Robin Burger Works; 2014
Warner Brothers Interactive Entertainment Lord of the Rings; 2012

BLINK MEDIA WORKS
400 - 319 West Hastings Street, Vancouver, BC V6B 1H6 Canada
Tel.: (604) 630-4960
Fax: (866) 302-6119
E-Mail: info@blinkmediaworks.com
Web Site: goblink.com

Agency Specializes In: Advertising, Media Relations, Radio, T.V.

Mike Agerbo *(Co-Founder)*
Aj Vickery *(Co-Founder)*
Andy Baryer *(Product Mgr & Producer-Radio)*
Kristina Stoyanova *(Acct Dir)*
Kirsty Duffy *(Acct Mgr)*

Accounts:
Nokia Canada Corporation
Panasonic Corporation
Samsung Group
Telus Corporation

BLISSPR
500 5th Ave Ste 1010, New York, NY 10110
Tel.: (212) 840-1661
Fax: (212) 840-1663
E-Mail: dani@blisspr.com
Web Site: www.blissintegrated.com

Employees: 33

Agency Specializes In: Communications, Media Relations, Media Training, Public Relations, Strategic Planning/Research

Meg Wildrick *(Mng Partner)*
Cortney Rhoads Stapleton *(Partner)*
Elizabeth Sosnow *(Mng Dir)*
Donna McSorley *(Sr VP & Head-Fin Svc Grp)*

Liz Deforest *(Acct Dir)*
Gregory Hassel *(Acct Dir)*
Dani McKie *(Office Mgr)*
Nathan Burgess *(Acct Supvr)*
Gordon Porter *(Sr Acct Exec)*
Kellie Sheehan *(Sr Strategist)*
Rebecca O'Neill *(Acct Exec)*

Accounts:
BDO Consulting
Chicago Chapter of CoreNet Global
Corporate Synergies
Golub & Company
IG Markets (Agency of Record)
J.F. McKinney & Associates
KeyCorp
Manning & Napier Advisors
McShane Corporation
NADEX
QuickWaters Software

Branch

BlissPR
17 N State St Ste #1700, Chicago, IL 60602
Tel.: (312) 252-7314
Fax: (312) 252-7323
Web Site: www.blissintegrated.com

Agency Specializes In: Public Relations

Meg Wildrick *(Mng Partner)*
Cortney Stapleton *(Partner)*
Elizabeth Sosnow *(Mng Dir)*
Miriam Weber Miller *(Exec VP & Head-Global Practice)*
Donna Mcsorley *(Sr VP & Dir-Media Rels)*
Ariel Kouvaras *(Acct Dir)*
Dani Mckie *(Office Mgr)*
Vik Dutta *(Mgr-IT)*
Megan Tuck *(Acct Supvr)*
Kellie Sheehan *(Sr Strategist)*

Accounts:
CMF Associates
Johnson & Johnson
SeniorBridge Family
SynaHealth

BLND PUBLIC RELATIONS
1001 Hermosa Ave Ste 203, Hermosa Beach, CA 90254
Tel.: (310) 372-2151
E-Mail: info@blndpr.com
Web Site: www.blndpr.com

Agency Specializes In: Advertising, Brand Development & Integration, Internet/Web Design, Public Relations, Social Media

Bryanne Lawless *(Founder & Mng Partner)*
Matt McRae *(Creative Dir)*

Accounts:
New-The Nail Truck

BLOCK & DECORSO
3 Claridge Dr, Verona, NJ 07044-3000
Tel.: (973) 857-3900
Fax: (973) 857-4041
E-Mail: contact@blockdecorso.com
Web Site: www.blockdecorso.com

Employees: 25
Year Founded: 1931

Agency Specializes In: Advertising, Advertising Specialties, Brand Development & Integration, Broadcast, Business-To-Business, Cable T.V., Co-op Advertising, Collateral, Communications, Consumer Goods, Consumer Marketing, Consumer Publications, Corporate Identity, Direct Response Marketing, E-Commerce, Event Planning & Marketing, Exhibit/Trade Shows, Food Service, Graphic Design, Health Care Services, In-Store Advertising, Internet/Web Design, Logo & Package Design, Magazines, Market Research, Media Buying Services, Media Planning, Media Relations, Merchandising, Multimedia, New Product Development, Newspaper, Newspapers & Magazines, Out-of-Home Media, Outdoor, Package Design, Planning & Consultation, Point of Purchase, Point of Sale, Print, Production, Production (Ad, Film, Broadcast), Production (Print), Promotions, Public Relations, Publicity/Promotions, Radio, Sales Promotion, Search Engine Optimization, Social Media, Sponsorship, Strategic Planning/Research, Sweepstakes, T.V., Trade & Consumer Magazines, Transportation, Web (Banner Ads, Pop-ups, etc.), Women's Market

Approx. Annual Billings: $14,000,000

Breakdown of Gross Billings by Media: Internet Adv.: 25%; Newsp. & Mags.: 25%; Outdoor: 15%; Print: 15%; Radio & T.V.: 20%

Bill Decorso *(Pres & Dir-Creative)*
David Block *(CEO)*
Carla Dean *(VP-Acct Svcs)*
John Murray *(Sr Dir-Art & Mgr-Studio)*
John Romano *(Dir-Internet)*

Accounts:
Bauli
Christian Healthcare
Hometown Beverages
Loan Search
Lotito Foods
Medaglia D'Oro Espresso
National Food
NielsenBainbridge
Parmacotto
Peapack-Gladstone Bank
Pompeian Olive Oil
Smith & Solomon Commercial Driver Training
Zen Soy

BLOHM CREATIVE PARTNERS
1331 E Grand River Ave Ste 210, East Lansing, MI 48823
Tel.: (517) 333-4900
Fax: (517) 336-9404
E-Mail: partners@blohmcreative.com
Web Site: www.blohmcreative.com

Agency Specializes In: Advertising, Brand Development & Integration, Print, Social Media, Web (Banner Ads, Pop-ups, etc.)

Jeff Blohm *(Pres)*
Owen Neils *(Art Dir)*
Iain Bogle *(Creative Dir)*
Ginnie Perry *(Acct Exec & Copywriter)*
Lynda White *(Acct Exec)*
Tim Mulvaney *(Designer)*

Accounts:
New-Michigan Apple Committee

BLOOM
777 Grand Ave Ste 201, San Rafael, CA 94901
Tel.: (415) 332-3201
Fax: (253) 663-9741
Toll Free: (888) 648-4343
E-Mail: info@bloommedia.com
Web Site: www.bloommedia.com

Agency Specializes In: Environmental, Internet/Web Design

Laura Caggiano *(Owner & Acct Dir-Creative)*

Accounts:
Anglian Home Improvements
Christopher Ranch
Collins & Company
Frank Howard Allen
Ladera Vineyards
Pillow Rd. Vineyards Pillow Rd. Vineyards
The Republic of Tea
Sovereign Investment Company
THX
Vine Solutions

BLOOMFIELD KNOBLE
400 E Royal Ln Ste 215, Irving, TX 75093
Tel.: (214) 254-3805
Web Site: bloomfieldknoble.com

Employees: 16
Year Founded: 1998

Agency Specializes In: Affiliate Marketing, Brand Development & Integration, Business-To-Business, Co-op Advertising, Consumer Goods, Consumer Marketing, Corporate Communications, Digital/Interactive, E-Commerce, Electronic Media, Email, Event Planning & Marketing, Exhibit/Trade Shows, Financial, Government/Political, Graphic Design, High Technology, In-Store Advertising, Integrated Marketing, Internet/Web Design, Leisure, Marine, Market Research, Media Buying Services, Media Planning, Mobile Marketing, Multicultural, Outdoor, Package Design, Planning & Consultation, Point of Sale, Production, Promotions, Sales Promotion, Search Engine Optimization, Seniors' Market, Social Marketing/Nonprofit, Social Media, Sports Market, Strategic Planning/Research, Sweepstakes, Technical Advertising, Travel & Tourism, Urban Market, Viral/Buzz/Word of Mouth, Web (Banner Ads, Pop-ups, etc.)

Approx. Annual Billings: $5,250,000

Eric Hirschhorn *(Partner)*
Chris Weatherley *(Partner)*
Thomas J. Thompson *(COO)*
Luann Boggs *(VP-Bus Dev)*
Michael Fabrikant *(Dir-Bus Dev & Govt Rels)*
Clark Bachelot *(Assoc Dir-Creative)*
Andy Edwards *(Assoc Dir-Art)*

Accounts:
American Airlines Center
Borden Dairy Company Borden Milk, Marketing
Easton Bell Sports
Fannie Mae
Leaf Trading Cards
Nationstar Mortgage
Pacific Union Financial
Temple Fork Outfitters
U.S. Treasury

BLR/FURTHER
1600 Resource Dr, Birmingham, AL 35242
Tel.: (205) 324-8005
Fax: (205) 324-7008
Toll Free: (800) 466-1337
Web Site: www.blrfurther.com

E-Mail for Key Personnel:
President: cary@blrfurther.com
Creative Dir.: marc@blrfurther.com

Employees: 22
Year Founded: 1986

Agency Specializes In: Above-the-Line, Advertising, Below-the-Line, Brand Development & Integration, Broadcast, Business-To-Business, Cable T.V., Co-op Advertising, Collateral,

Communications, Consulting, Consumer Goods, Consumer Marketing, Content, Corporate Communications, Corporate Identity, Digital/Interactive, E-Commerce, Electronic Media, Event Planning & Marketing, Exhibit/Trade Shows, Government/Political, Graphic Design, Health Care Services, High Technology, Identity Marketing, Industrial, Information Technology, Integrated Marketing, Internet/Web Design, Local Marketing, Logo & Package Design, Magazines, Media Buying Services, Media Planning, Medical Products, New Product Development, New Technologies, Newspaper, Newspapers & Magazines, Out-of-Home Media, Planning & Consultation, Point of Sale, Print, Production (Print), Promotions, Public Relations, Publicity/Promotions, Radio, Regional, Restaurant, Retail, Search Engine Optimization, Social Marketing/Nonprofit, Social Media, Sponsorship, Strategic Planning/Research, T.V., Technical Advertising, Trade & Consumer Magazines, Viral/Buzz/Word of Mouth, Women's Market

Approx. Annual Billings: $17,000,000

Breakdown of Gross Billings by Media: Cable T.V.: 10%; Internet Adv.: 15%; Mags.: 10%; Network Radio: 10%; Newsp.: 15%; Out-of-Home Media: 20%; T.V.: 20%

Cary Bynum *(Pres)*
Brian Pia *(Exec VP)*
Dana Stephens-Travis *(Sr VP)*
Lisa DeAraujo *(VP-Acct Mgmt)*
Marc Stricklin *(Creative Dir)*
Jonathan Greene *(Dir-Art)*
Michelle Adams *(Acct Mgr-Interactive)*
Kit Clark *(Acct Mgr)*
Jamison Lackey *(Media Planner & Media Buyer)*
Lauren Beason *(Media Buyer)*
Megan Johnson *(Media Buyer)*

Accounts:
Atrion Medical; Arab, AL
Bellin Health Systems; Green Bay, WI
BJC Healthcare; Saint Louis, MO
Physician Partners; Green Bay, WI
Progress West HealthCare Center; O'Fallon, MO
SPOC Automation; Trussville, AL
Subway Systems; Milford, CT Plus 7 DMA Franchisee Groups AL, GA, FL, & MS
Tanner Health System; Carrolton, GA

THE BLU GROUP - ADVERTISING & MARKETING
1828 E Main St Ste 3, Onalaska, WI 54650
Tel.: (608) 519-3070
Fax: (608) 519-3075
E-Mail: info@theblugroup.com
Web Site: www.theblugroup.com

Employees: 10
Year Founded: 2004

Agency Specializes In: Advertising, Brand Development & Integration, Business-To-Business, Catalogs, Direct Response Marketing, Direct-to-Consumer, E-Commerce, Electronic Media, Email, Graphic Design, Identity Marketing, Integrated Marketing, Internet/Web Design, Local Marketing, Logo & Package Design, Market Research, Media Buying Services, Media Planning, Newspaper, Outdoor, Package Design, Print, Production (Print), Search Engine Optimization, Social Media, Strategic Planning/Research

Tony Roberts *(Pres)*
Tim Burkhalter *(VP & Brand Designer)*
Lucy Neuberger *(Graphic Designer & Designer-Web)*
Holly Traffas *(Copywriter)*
Kristy Wenz *(Copywriter)*

Accounts:
Burger Fusion Company Social Media, Website
Coulee Bank
Coulee Catholic Schools
River Steel Inc.

BLUBERRIES ADVERTISING
70 Outwater Ln Ste 401, Garfield, NJ 07026
Tel.: (973) 478-2200
Fax: (973) 478-9662
E-Mail: mail@bluberries.com
Web Site: www.bluberries.com

Year Founded: 2002

Agency Specializes In: Advertising, Corporate Identity, Digital/Interactive, Graphic Design, Media Buying Services, Media Planning, Multimedia, Package Design, Print, Radio

Bart Sadowski *(Founder)*
Chris Sadowski *(Founder)*

Accounts:
BMW of Manhattan Inc.

BLUE AUGUST
116 E Lafayette, Jackson, TN 38301
Tel.: (731) 512-0080
Web Site: www.blueaugust.com

Agency Specializes In: Advertising, Brand Development & Integration, Graphic Design, Public Relations, Social Media

Josh Sykes *(Partner)*

Accounts:
New-MidSouth Shooters Supply

BLUE C
3183-C Airway Ave, Costa Mesa, CA 92626
Tel.: (714) 540-5700
Fax: (714) 540-5800
E-Mail: info@bluecusa.com
Web Site: www.bluecusa.com

Employees: 20

National Agency Associations: Second Wind Limited

Eric Morley *(Founder & Partner)*
Michelle Antinora *(Controller)*
Jeff Bentley *(Dir-Creative)*
Andrew Kovely *(Mgr-Studio)*
Greta Valenti *(Mgr-Studio Production)*
Lauren Padilla *(Sr Acct Exec)*
Mina Zivkovic *(Acct Exec)*
Juan Torres *(Designer)*

Accounts:
Juice It Up Creative, Franchise Marketing, In-Store Marketing, Media Placement, Strategic Planning
Monster Energy Drink
Orange County Fair
New-Red Kap Campaign: "The Craftsmen"
Toyota SCION Accessories
Vectrix Brand Ambassador Development, Creative Development, Event Strategy, Global PR, Social Media, Vectrix VT-1 vehicle
Wahoo's Fish Tacos

BLUE CHIP MARKETING WORLDWIDE
650 Dundee Rd Ste 250, Northbrook, IL 60062
Tel.: (847) 446-2114
Web Site: bluechipmarketingworldwide.com

Agency Specializes In: Sponsorship

Stanton Kawer *(Chm & CEO)*
Bob Klein *(Chief Strategy Officer)*
Larry Deutsch *(Exec VP & Gen Mgr-Blue Chip Brand Mktg)*
Neil Weisman *(Exec VP & Gen Mgr-Blue Chip Healthcare Mktg)*
Ken Shore *(Exec VP-Bus Dev)*
Dan Eisenberg *(VP-Bus Dev)*
Adam Kaplan *(VP-Client Svcs)*
Sarah Van Heirseele *(VP-Digital)*
Lindsay Baish *(Mgr-Social Media)*
Joe Kowalczyk *(Acct Exec)*
Emily Weber *(Acct Exec)*
Victoria Walters *(Media Planner)*
Jake Clark *(Assoc Media Dir)*

Accounts:
Azteca Foods, Inc Marketing, Strategy
New-B&G Foods, Inc. Bear Creek Country Kitchens (Agency of Record), Creative, Digital, Public Relations, Shopper Marketing, Social Media, Strategic
Bomb Pop (Agency of Record)
Fisher Nuts
New-Green Toys (Marketing Agency of Record) Creative, Marketing
Home Run Inn Pizza
John B. Sanfilippo & Son, Inc. (Agency of Record) Campaign: "Fisher Fresh Twist", Creative, Interactive, Media
On-Cor Frozen Foods

BLUE CHIP PUBLIC RELATIONS, INC.
14 Canaan Cir, South Salem, NY 10590
Tel.: (914) 533-7065
E-Mail: bill@bluechippr.com
Web Site: www.bluechippr.com

Agency Specializes In: Media Relations, Strategic Planning/Research, T.V.

William Bongiorno *(Pres)*

Accounts:
Bullion Management Group Inc
EQIS Capital Management Media
Hayden Wealth Management
WBI Investments, Inc.

BLUE COLLAR INTERACTIVE MARKETING
1311 Cascade Ave, Hood River, OR 97031
Tel.: (541) 436-2800
E-Mail: service@bluecollaragency.com
Web Site: www.bluecollaragency.com

Agency Specializes In: Advertising, Brand Development & Integration, Broadcast, Electronic Media, Information Technology, Mobile Marketing, Search Engine Optimization, Strategic Planning/Research

April Donovan *(Partner & Dir-Creative)*
Tom Lehmann *(Partner & Dir-Creative)*
Jim Kimball *(CFO)*
Rob McCready *(Sr Partner-Ops & Acct Dir)*
John Mitchell *(Acct Dir)*
Brian Becker *(Project Mgr-Technical)*

Accounts:
FontFuse Branding, Email Marketing, Online Advertising, PPC, Strategy, Web Design and Development
Mail Chimp Electronic Mail Marketing Services
Right Brain Initiative Educational Support Services
Rollic Apparel Mfr
Tactical Distributors Tactical Equipments Distr

BLUE DIESEL
(Merged with GSW Worldwide to form GSW Worldwide Fueled by Blue Diesel)

THE BLUE FLAME AGENCY
1710 Bdwy, New York, NY 10019
Tel.: (212) 381-2005
Web Site: www.theblueflameagency.com

Agency Specializes In: Advertising, Digital/Interactive, Out-of-Home Media, Print, T.V.

Ericka Pittman *(VP)*
Marilyn Van Alstyne *(VP-Bus Ops)*
Tiffany Hawkins *(Sr Acct Dir-Plng)*
Whitney Cunningham *(Mgr-Mktg)*
Carlos Del Valle *(Coord-Digital Mktg)*

Accounts:
Diageo North America Inc. Campaign: "Luck be a Lady", Campaign: "The Next Level", Ciroc, Ciroc Ultra Premium Vodka

BLUE FLAME THINKING
(Formerly s2 Financial Marketing)
656 W Randolph Ste 3E, Chicago, IL 60661
Tel.: (312) 382-9000
Web Site: www.blueflamethinking.com/

Employees: 20

Agency Specializes In: Sponsorship

Lynne Hartzell *(Pres)*
Melissa Nelson *(Grp Acct Dir)*
Susan Bray *(Dir-Strategy)*
Julie Helgesen *(Dir-Art)*
Kelly Ketcham *(Acct Mgr)*
Diona Medrano *(Acct Mgr)*
Mike Meyers *(Writer-Creative)*

Accounts:
Bridgeway
Envestnet
JPMorgan Chase
Lazard Asset Management

Branch

Blue Flame Thinking
(Formerly Alexander Marketing)
801 Broadway Ave Ste 300, Grand Rapids, MI 49504
(See Separate Listing)

BLUE FUSION
1875 Connecticut Ave NW Ste 10203, Washington, DC 20009
Tel.: (571) 205-9030
E-Mail: info@bluefusioncreative.com
Web Site: www.bluefusioncreative.com

Agency Specializes In: Advertising, Brand Development & Integration, Digital/Interactive, Graphic Design, Internet/Web Design, Logo & Package Design, Social Media, Strategic Planning/Research

Morgan R. Bramlet *(Principal)*
M. J. Vilardi *(Producer & Creative Dir)*
Dani Smith *(Art Dir & Designer)*

Accounts:
American Marketing Association's DC Chapter (Agency of Record)

BLUE HORSE & TRUMPET
6264 Ferris Sq, San Diego, CA 92121
Tel.: (858) 777-9566
E-Mail: inof@bhandt.com
Web Site: www.bhandt.com

Employees: 15

Agency Specializes In: Advertising, Affluent Market, Aviation & Aerospace, Brand Development & Integration, Broadcast, Business-To-Business, Collateral, Communications, Consulting, Consumer Goods, Consumer Marketing, Corporate Identity, Entertainment, Exhibit/Trade Shows, Experience Design, Food Service, Graphic Design, Guerilla Marketing, Health Care Services, Hospitality, Identity Marketing, In-Store Advertising, Internet/Web Design, Logo & Package Design, Marine, Media Relations, Newspapers & Magazines, Package Design, Point of Sale, Production, Production (Ad, Film, Broadcast), Promotions, Public Relations, Search Engine Optimization, Social Marketing/Nonprofit, Strategic Planning/Research, T.V., Transportation, Viral/Buzz/Word of Mouth

Approx. Annual Billings: $3,000,000

Breakdown of Gross Billings by Media: Adv. Specialities: 45%; Cable T.V.: 10%; Logo & Package Design: 5%; Pub. Rels.: 30%; Worldwide Web Sites: 10%

Summer King *(Acct Planner)*

Accounts:
30 Foot Wave Sports Business
Bluepoint Solutions Banking Software
Datron Communications
Yahoo! Personals, Shopping, Travel

BLUE HORSE INC.
1180 Indianwood Dr, Brookfield, WI 53005
Tel.: (414) 291-7620
Fax: (414) 291-7633
Web Site: www.bluehorseinc.com

E-Mail for Key Personnel:
President: tthiede@bluehorseinc.com
Creative Dir.: tthiede@bluehorseinc.com

Employees: 35
Year Founded: 1943

National Agency Associations: BMA-Second Wind Limited

Agency Specializes In: Advertising, Business-To-Business, Digital/Interactive, Financial, Food Service, Public Relations

Approx. Annual Billings: $46,000,000

Tom Thiede *(Partner & Dir-Creative)*

Accounts:
DDN
Sojourner Truth House

BLUE LION DIGITAL, LLC
711 James Rd, Easley, SC 29642
Tel.: (864) 304-9632
Web Site: www.blueliondigital.com

Year Founded: 2012

Agency Specializes In: Advertising, Email, Internet/Web Design, Search Engine Optimization, Social Media

Bryan Owens *(Principal)*

Accounts:
The Big League World Series

BLUE MEDIUM, INC.
20 W 22nd St Ste 807, New York, NY 10010
Tel.: (212) 675-1800
Fax: (212) 675-1855
E-Mail: rachel@bluemedium.com
Web Site: www.bluemedium.com

Employees: 10

Agency Specializes In: Arts, Communications

John Melick *(Pres)*
Keri Murawski *(VP-Visual Arts)*
Rachel Patall-David *(Acct Mgr)*
Andy Ptaschinski *(Acct Mgr)*
Jeffrey Walkowiak *(Acct Exec)*
Pamela Hernandez *(Acct Coord)*
Newlin Tillotson *(Acct Coord-Visual Arts)*

Accounts:
Savannah College of Art and Design
Sperone Westwater Gallery

BLUE MOON STUDIOS
86 Lackawanna Ave, West Paterson, NJ 07424
Tel.: (973) 812-2282
E-Mail: info@bluemoonstudios.tv
Web Site: www.bluemoonstudios.tv

Agency Specializes In: Advertising, Email, T.V.

Fred Vanore *(Pres)*
Lisa Mulligan *(Assoc Producer & Coord-Studio)*

Accounts:
All Star Marketing Group Product Development Industry
Auto Cool
Febreze
Micro Touch
Ontel
Oxiclean
Quick Brite
Tide
Trojan
Zap

BLUE MOON WORKS, INC.
304 Park Ave S 11th Fl, New York, NY 10010
Tel.: (212) 590-2507
Fax: (303) 565-1104
Web Site: www.bluemoonworks.com

AJ Workman *(Co-Founder, CMO & Sr VP-Bus Dev)*
Cindy Brown *(CEO)*
Mindy Phillips *(Sr VP)*
Robin Glanz *(Dir-Email & CRM Svcs)*
Lauren Klostermann *(Dir-Digital Mktg)*
Julianna Renaud *(Strategist-eMail & Specialist-Web Analytics)*
Katherine Myers *(Strategist-Digital Paid Media)*

BLUE OLIVE CONSULTING
303 E College St, Florence, AL 35630
Tel.: (256) 767-9937
Fax: (256) 767-3248
Toll Free: (866) 601-6548
E-Mail: solutions@theblueolive.com
Web Site: www.theblueolive.com

Employees: 12
Year Founded: 1999

National Agency Associations: Second Wind Limited

Agency Specializes In: Advertising, Advertising Specialties, Agriculture, Alternative Advertising, Automotive, Brand Development & Integration, Broadcast, Business Publications, Business-To-Business, Cable T.V., Catalogs, Children's Market, Co-op Advertising, Collateral, College, Commercial Photography, Communications, Consulting,

Consumer Goods, Consumer Marketing, Consumer Publications, Content, Corporate Communications, Corporate Identity, Custom Publishing, Customer Relationship Management, Digital/Interactive, Direct Response Marketing, Direct-to-Consumer, E-Commerce, Education, Electronic Media, Email, Entertainment, Environmental, Event Planning & Marketing, Exhibit/Trade Shows, Financial, Food Service, Game Integration, Government/Political, Graphic Design, Guerilla Marketing, Health Care Services, High Technology, Hospitality, Identity Marketing, In-Store Advertising, Infomercials, Integrated Marketing, Internet/Web Design, Investor Relations, Leisure, Local Marketing, Logo & Package Design, Luxury Products, Magazines, Market Research, Media Buying Services, Media Planning, Media Relations, Media Training, Medical Products, Men's Market, Merchandising, Mobile Marketing, Multimedia, New Product Development, New Technologies, Newspaper, Newspapers & Magazines, Out-of-Home Media, Outdoor, Over-50 Market, Package Design, Paid Searches, Pharmaceutical, Planning & Consultation, Podcasting, Point of Purchase, Point of Sale, Print, Product Placement, Production, Production (Ad, Film, Broadcast), Production (Print), Promotions, Public Relations, Publicity/Promotions, Publishing, Radio, Real Estate, Recruitment, Regional, Restaurant, Retail, Sales Promotion, Search Engine Optimization, Seniors' Market, Social Marketing/Nonprofit, Sports Market, Stakeholders, Strategic Planning/Research, T.V., Teen Market, Telemarketing, Trade & Consumer Magazines, Transportation, Travel & Tourism, Urban Market, Viral/Buzz/Word of Mouth, Web (Banner Ads, Pop-ups, etc.), Women's Market, Yellow Pages Advertising

Gregory Watson *(Owner)*
Britton Watson *(Pres)*
Tony Cane *(Dir-Creative)*

BLUE PRACTICE

388 Market St Ste 1400, San Francisco, CA 94111
Tel.: (415) 381-1100
Fax: (415) 366-1550
E-Mail: jessica@bluepractice.com
Web Site: www.bluepractice.com

Agency Specializes In: Advertising

Tim Gnatek *(Co-Founder & Pres)*
Jessica Switzer *(Partner)*

Accounts:
Aurora Biofuels
Clean Edge
MiaSole
New Vistas
PACT Apparel
Silver Spring Networks
Working Lands

BLUE PRINT AD AGENCY

PO Box 540604, Omaha, NE 68154
Tel.: (402) 671-5177
Fax: (855) 284-0108
Web Site: www.blueprintadagency.com

Agency Specializes In: Advertising, Brand Development & Integration, Internet/Web Design, Media Buying Services, Print, Radio

Ryan Pankoke *(Principal)*

Accounts:
Defy Gravity
DSS Coin & Bullion
Freedom Healthcare
Omaha Door & Window

BLUE SKY AGENCY

950 Joseph Lowery Blvd Ste 30, Atlanta, GA 30318
Tel.: (404) 876-0202
Fax: (404) 876-0212
E-Mail: rob@bluesky-agency.com
Web Site: www.blueskyagency.com

Employees: 30
Year Founded: 1994

National Agency Associations: 4A's

Agency Specializes In: Advertising, Affiliate Marketing, Arts, Brand Development & Integration, Branded Entertainment, Broadcast, Business Publications, Business-To-Business, Cable T.V., Collateral, College, Consumer Goods, Consumer Marketing, Consumer Publications, Corporate Communications, Corporate Identity, Digital/Interactive, Direct Response Marketing, E-Commerce, Electronic Media, Email, Engineering, Entertainment, Environmental, Experience Design, Food Service, Graphic Design, Guerilla Marketing, Hispanic Market, Identity Marketing, In-Store Advertising, Integrated Marketing, Internet/Web Design, Local Marketing, Logo & Package Design, Magazines, Media Buying Services, Media Planning, Multimedia, Newspaper, Newspapers & Magazines, Out-of-Home Media, Outdoor, Paid Searches, Planning & Consultation, Point of Purchase, Point of Sale, Print, Production, Production (Ad, Film, Broadcast), Promotions, Public Relations, Publicity/Promotions, Radio, Recruitment, Regional, Restaurant, Retail, Sales Promotion, Search Engine Optimization, Social Marketing/Nonprofit, Social Media, Sponsorship, Sports Market, Strategic Planning/Research, Sweepstakes, T.V., Trade & Consumer Magazines, Web (Banner Ads, Pop-ups, etc.)

Approx. Annual Billings: $30,000,000

Rob Farinella *(Founder & Pres)*
Mike Schatz *(Sr VP-Dir-Creative)*
Melissa Nordin *(VP & Dir-Media)*
Jenifer Perrett *(Acct Grp Head)*
Cameron Blank *(Acct Dir)*
Greg Grantham *(Assoc Dir-Creative & Copywriter)*
Shannon Kellar *(Acct Mgr)*
Megan Niager *(Acct Mgr)*
Erin Marks *(Acct Coord)*
Darby Thompson *(Acct Coord)*
Ryan Moyer *(Asst Media Planner)*

Accounts:
Atlanta Braves; Atlanta, GA Campaign: "Do The Chop", Campaign: "This is Why We Chop"
Atlanta Food Bank; Atlanta, GA
Atlanta Hawks; Atlanta, GA
Atlanta Motor Speedway; Hampton, GA
Atlanta Spirit; Atlanta, GA
Atlanta Thrashers; Atlanta, GA Hockey Club
BBC America
Berry College; Rome, GA Non-Profit/Education
Bristol Motor Speedway
Cobb Energy; Atlanta, GA Home Security Systems, Internet Service, Natural Gas, Telephone Service, Tree Removal, Tree Trimming; 2005
FleetCards USA; Atlanta, GA
FleetCor
Gas South; Atlanta, GA Utility
Gospel Music Channel; Atlanta, GA
Intercontinental Hotels Group
Lifetime Network
Reader's Digest North America; New York, NY (Agency of Record) Taste of Home, The Family Handyman
Turner Broadcasting System, Inc. TNT

BLUE SKY COMMUNICATIONS

900 Broadway Ste 702, New York, NY 10003
Tel.: (212) 995-1777
Fax: (212) 995-2922
E-Mail: info@blueskypr.com
Web Site: www.blueskypr.com

Employees: 20
Year Founded: 1999

Agency Specializes In: Advertising, Brand Development & Integration, Corporate Identity, Guerilla Marketing, Internet/Web Design, Magazines, Media Relations, Production, Radio, Strategic Planning/Research, T.V.

Diane Bates *(Co-Owner)*
Susan Hagaman *(Partner)*
Linda Falcone *(VP)*
Andrea Mennella *(VP)*
Diana Blaszczyk *(Acct Mgr)*
Kim Farrington *(Acct Supvr)*
Courtney Weiss *(Acct Supvr)*
Jennifer Gauthier *(Acct Exec)*
Morgan Henry *(Acct Exec)*
Abigail Littleton *(Jr Acct Exec)*

Accounts:
7 Days of Wonder
Aquage
Cle de Peau
Coolway
Elizabeth Taylor's White Diamonds
Essie
Laura Geller
LCN
Marula Oil
Maybelline New York
Orgo
Perfect Formula
Physicians Formula
Roger & Gallet
VMV Hypoallergenics

BLUE STATE DIGITAL

734 15th St NW Ste 1200, Washington, DC 20005
Tel.: (202) 449-5600
Web Site: bluestatedigital.com

Sarah Newhall *(Mng Dir-DC & Exec VP)*
David Gilman *(VP-Accts)*
Benjamin Murray *(VP)*
Alex Stanton *(VP)*
Michelle Barna *(Exec Dir-Content & Campaigns)*
Michelle Barna-Stern *(Exec Dir-Content & Campaigns)*
Julia Batenhorst *(Acct Dir)*
Amanda Burke *(Acct Dir)*
Mike Conlow *(Dir-Technical)*
Kodiak Starr *(Dir-Creative)*
Kelley Hodge *(Acct Mgr)*
Chris Choi *(Deputy Dir-Media)*

Accounts:
The American Red Cross

BLUEDOT COMMUNICATIONS

7243 Sw Capitol Hwy, Portland, OR 97219
Tel.: (503) 702-6822
E-Mail: john@gobluedot.com
Web Site: www.gobluedot.com

Employees: 3

John Mazzocco *(Principal)*

Accounts:
Brian Grant Foundation
EHDD Architecture
Marsh Inc.
Pacific Courier Services, LLC
VeriLAN
Xerox Corporation

BLUEGILL CREATIVE

2220 Sutherland Ave, Knoxville, TN 37919
Tel.: (865) 544-5321
E-Mail: info@bluegillcreative.com
Web Site: www.dmgbluegill.com

Year Founded: 2005

Agency Specializes In: Advertising, Brand Development & Integration, Digital/Interactive, Email, Graphic Design, Strategic Planning/Research

Accounts:
Boys & Girls Clubs of the Tennessee Valley
Sevier County Bank

BLUEROCK

575 Lexington Ave Fl 26, New York, NY 10022
Tel.: (212) 752-3348
Fax: (212) 752-0307
Web Site: www.bluerockny.com

Jennifer Lederman *(Mng Dir & VP)*

BLUESOHO

160 Varick St 2nd Fl, New York, NY 10013
Tel.: (646) 805-2583
E-Mail: hello@blue-soho.com
Web Site: www.blue-soho.com

Agency Specializes In: Advertising, Digital/Interactive, Media Planning

Stephanie Stanton *(Mng Partner)*
Jeannie Grizzle *(Acct Mgr)*

Accounts:
New-Avon
New-Lowe's
New-Sephora

BLUESPACE CREATIVE

1211 Broadway Ste 201, Denison, IA 51442
Tel.: (712) 263-2211
E-Mail: info@bluespacecreative.com
Web Site: www.bluespacecreative.com

Agency Specializes In: Advertising, Brand Development & Integration, Digital/Interactive, Logo & Package Design, Media Buying Services, Print, Public Relations, Search Engine Optimization, Social Media, Sponsorship

Scott Winey *(Principal & Creative Dir)*
Emily Busch *(Mng Dir)*
Brad Dassow *(Dir-New Media)*
Dan Davis *(Acct Mgr)*
Clint Winey *(Mgr-Production)*
Aaron Lingren *(Designer)*
Cole Mccombs *(Designer)*
Keaton Wanninger *(Designer)*
Luke Vaughn *(Designer)*

Accounts:
New Way Trucks
Zion Lutheran Church

BLUESPIRE MARKETING

(Formerly Martino & Binzer)
29 South Main St, West Hartford, CT 06107
Tel.: (877) 571-7743
Web Site: www.bluespiremarketing.com/

Employees: 27
Year Founded: 1980

National Agency Associations: BMA-PRSA

Agency Specializes In: Advertising, Brand Development & Integration, Broadcast, Business-To-Business, Cable T.V., Collateral, Consulting, Corporate Communications, Corporate Identity, Digital/Interactive, Direct Response Marketing, Electronic Media, Event Planning & Marketing, Exhibit/Trade Shows, Food Service, Graphic Design, Health Care Services, Industrial, Integrated Marketing, Internet/Web Design, Logo & Package Design, Media Buying Services, Multimedia, Newspaper, Newspapers & Magazines, Out-of-Home Media, Outdoor, Over-50 Market, Paid Searches, Planning & Consultation, Point of Purchase, Point of Sale, Print, Production, Public Relations, Publicity/Promotions, Radio, Sales Promotion, Search Engine Optimization, Seniors' Market, Strategic Planning/Research, T.V., Trade & Consumer Magazines

Approx. Annual Billings: $21,500,000 Capitalized

Breakdown of Gross Billings by Media: Bus. Publs.: 27%; Collateral: 20%; Fees: 37%; Internet Adv.: 6%; Newsp.: 2%; Other: 4%; Production: 3%; Trade Shows: 1%

Fran Palma *(Exec VP-Digital Strategies)*
Jay Hibbard *(Sr VP-Svcs)*
Dan Croci *(Dir-Creative Svcs)*
Robin Sousa *(Dir-Art)*

Accounts:
Ahlstrom; Windsor Locks, CT Non-Woven Textiles; 2004
American HealthTech; Jackson, MS Long-Term Care Software; 2008
Biolitec; East Longmeadow, MA Laser/Fiber Optics; 2005
Ceramoptec; East Longmeadow, MA Laser/Fiber Optics; 2005
Cypress Cove; Fort Myers, FL Retirement Community; 2006
Devonshire at PGA National; West Palm Beach, FL Retirement Community; 2007
Iroquois Gas Transmission Systems; Shelton, CT; 2000
La Vida Llena; Albuquerque, NM Retirement Community; 2008
OCI Chemical; Shelton, CT Soda Ash; 1995
Oklahoma Methodist; Tulsa, OK Retirement Community; 2009
The Overlook; Charlton, MA Retirement Community; 2001
Primesource Building Products; Elk Grove Village, IL Construction Materials Distribution; 2001
Southern California Presbyterian Homes; Glendale, CA Retirement Communities; 2008
Ward Leonard; Watertown, CT Industrial Manufacturing; 2009

BLUESTONE ADVERTISING, LLC

4041 University Dr Ste 100, Fairfax, VA 22030
Tel.: (856) 778-2792
E-Mail: sales@bluestoneadv.com
Web Site: www.bluestoneadv.com

Employees: 5
Year Founded: 2006

National Agency Associations: DMA

Agency Specializes In: Business-To-Business, Corporate Communications, Direct Response Marketing, Direct-to-Consumer, Point of Sale, Print

Approx. Annual Billings: $4,000,000

Breakdown of Gross Billings by Media: Consulting: $50,000; D.M.: $3,800,000; Graphic Design: $150,000

Kristi Manship *(Owner)*
James Regan *(Partner)*

Accounts:
Commerce Bank

BLUETEXT

2121 Wisconsin Ave NW Ste 320, Washington, DC 20007
Tel.: (202) 469-3600
E-Mail: hi@bluetext.com
Web Site: www.bluetext.com

Employees: 15

Agency Specializes In: Advertising, Brand Development & Integration, Content, Crisis Communications, Digital/Interactive, Internet/Web Design, Public Relations, Social Media, Strategic Planning/Research

Jason Siegel *(Partner & Dir-Creative)*
Don Goldberg *(Partner)*
Brian Lustig *(Partner)*
Michael Quint *(Partner)*
Rick Silipigni *(Partner)*
Chris Monnat *(CTO)*

Accounts:
Google Inc.; 2012

BLUETOOTH CREATIVE GROUP, INC.

100 Merrick Rd Ste 210 W, Rockville Centre, NY 11570
Tel.: (516) 766-0600
Fax: (516) 766-2351
E-Mail: info@bluetoothcreative.com
Web Site: www.bluetoothcreative.com

Year Founded: 1972

Agency Specializes In: Brand Development & Integration, Collateral, Digital/Interactive, Direct Response Marketing, Outdoor, Print, Radio, Sales Promotion, T.V.

Richard Brauner *(VP)*
Mark D'Amico *(Dir-Art & Designer-Web)*

Accounts:
Allianceplus, Inc.
Atlantic Bank Ltd.
Industrial Development Agency
New York Community Bank
NY Auto Giant

BLUEVIEW AGENCY

1306 S Denver, Tulsa, OK 74119
Tel.: (918) 592-1400
Web Site: www.blueviewagency.com

Year Founded: 2005

Agency Specializes In: Advertising, Brand Development & Integration, Content, Digital/Interactive, Graphic Design, Internet/Web Design, Search Engine Optimization, Social Media, Strategic Planning/Research

Bryant Bynum *(Chm)*
Dan Winders *(CEO & Principal)*
Heather Brasel *(Dir-Creative)*
Jennifer Cordero *(Dir-Acct Svcs)*
Lauren Harned *(Dir-Art)*
David Stevens *(Dir-Interactive Dev)*
Victoria Williams *(Sr Mgr-Acct Strategy & Dev)*
Megan McManus *(Dept Mgr-Content & Social Media)*

Accounts:
J Herbert, Corp.

BLUEZOOM

230 S Elm St Ste B, Greensboro, NC 27401
Tel.: (336) 274-8938
E-Mail: hello@bluezoom.bz
Web Site: www.bluezoom.bz

Agency Specializes In: Advertising, Brand Development & Integration, Digital/Interactive, Internet/Web Design, Logo & Package Design, Print

Liz Spidell *(Founder & Chief Creative Officer)*
Jeremy Spidell *(Owner & CFO)*
Lane Newsome *(COO)*
Tom Saitta *(VP & Sr Acct Dir)*
Kathleen Smith *(VP-Strategy & Creative Messaging)*
Tom Woods *(Sr Art Dir)*
Bryan Bowers *(Creative Dir)*
Alex McKinney *(Dir-Digital Svcs)*
Tommy Beaver *(Assoc Dir-Creative)*
Anne Knowles *(Mgr-Traffic & Production)*

Accounts:
Ethnosh

BMC COMMUNICATIONS GROUP, LLC
740 Broadway 9th Fl, New York, NY 10003
Tel.: (646) 513-3111
Fax: (212) 460-9028
E-Mail: info@bmccommunications.com
Web Site: www.bmccommunications.com

Employees: 6
Year Founded: 1996

Agency Specializes In: Broadcast, Communications, Corporate Communications, Exhibit/Trade Shows, Financial, Internet/Web Design, Local Marketing, Media Relations, Media Training, Medical Products, Newspaper, Print, Radio

Brad Miles *(Owner)*
Susan Duffy *(Sr VP & Dir-Editorial)*
Tereza Degroff *(Office Mgr)*
Amy Bonanno *(Sr Acct Exec)*
Stacey Isaacs *(Specialist-Media)*

BMDM
(Formerly Technetium LLC)
1323 Brookhaven Dr, Orlando, FL 32803
Tel.: (407) 650-0264
Web Site: bmdm.com

Employees: 14
Year Founded: 2003

Agency Specializes In: Advertising, Brand Development & Integration, Digital/Interactive, Internet/Web Design, Print, Social Media

Chuck Barnett *(Pres & CEO)*
Melanie Vasquez *(COO)*
Joe Forget *(Sr VP-Digital Strategies)*
Svitlana Byts *(Dir-Digital Svcs)*
Charlie Murphy *(Exec-Sls)*

Accounts:
Dual Electronics

BMI ELITE
1095 Broken Sound Pkwy NW Ste 300, Boca Raton, FL 33487
Tel.: (561) 330-6666
Fax: (561) 431-6124
E-Mail: info@bmielite.com
Web Site: www.bmielite.com

Agency Specializes In: Advertising, Advertising Specialties, Affiliate Marketing, Alternative Advertising, Arts, Automotive, Aviation & Aerospace, Brand Development & Integration, Broadcast, Business Publications, Business-To-Business, Cable T.V., Children's Market, Co-op Advertising, College, Communications, Computers & Software, Consulting, Consumer Goods, Consumer Marketing, Consumer Publications, Content, Corporate Communications, Cosmetics, Digital/Interactive, Direct Response Marketing, Direct-to-Consumer, Education, Electronic Media, Email, Event Planning & Marketing, Food Service, Government/Political, Graphic Design, Integrated Marketing, Leisure, Luxury Products, Media Buying Services, Mobile Marketing, Multimedia, Production, Production (Ad, Film, Broadcast), Production (Print), Promotions, Public Relations, Publicity/Promotions, Publishing, Radio, Retail, Sales Promotion, Search Engine Optimization, Seniors' Market, Social Media, Sports Market, T.V., Teen Market, Telemarketing, Transportation, Travel & Tourism, Urban Market, Viral/Buzz/Word of Mouth, Web (Banner Ads, Pop-ups, etc.), Women's Market

Dan Lansman *(Pres)*
Brandon Rosen *(CEO)*
Mike Schweiger *(CFO)*
Fred Zuckerman *(CMO)*
Jenn Gressman *(VP-Bus Dev)*
Meredith Jenners *(VP)*
Meredith Yost *(VP)*
Nicole Gonzalez *(Controller)*
John Mastrangelo *(Dir-Bus Dev)*
Wendy Peichel *(Mgr-Bus Dev)*
Lynsay Brown *(Acct Exec)*

BMR
390 Bay St Ste 400, Sault Sainte Marie, ON P6A 1X2 Canada
Tel.: (705) 949-0153
Fax: (705) 949-4186
Web Site: www.bmr.ca

Employees: 10

Agency Specializes In: Advertising

Claudia Daniels *(Owner)*
Mark Falkins *(Owner)*

Accounts:
Sault Sainte Marie Tourism
Searchmont
Soo Greyhounds

BMWW
17 Governors Ct Ste 150, Baltimore, MD 21244-2713
Tel.: (410) 298-0390
Fax: (410) 298-8716
Web Site: www.bmww.com

Employees: 14
Year Founded: 1985

Agency Specializes In: Advertising, Brand Development & Integration, Business-To-Business, Collateral, College, Communications, Consulting, Corporate Communications, Corporate Identity, Cosmetics, Direct Response Marketing, Education, Electronic Media, Exhibit/Trade Shows, Graphic Design, Health Care Services, Identity Marketing, In-Store Advertising, Integrated Marketing, Internet/Web Design, Local Marketing, Logo & Package Design, Media Buying Services, Media Planning, Package Design, Pharmaceutical, Planning & Consultation, Point of Sale, Print, Production, Recruitment, Sales Promotion, Women's Market

Approx. Annual Billings: $3,000,000

Breakdown of Gross Billings by Media: Bus. Publs.: 5%; Collateral: 25%; Consulting: 25%; E-Commerce: 5%; Exhibits/Trade Shows: 10%; Graphic Design: 10%; Logo & Package Design: 10%; Point of Sale: 5%; Sls. Promo.: 5%

Howard M. Bubert *(Principal-Creative Svcs)*
Joseph Gaeta *(Principal)*
Gabriela Holdt *(Specialist-Social Media)*
R. Gerard Willse, III *(Mng Principal)*

Accounts:
Sub-Zero Wolf
APS Healthcare
Chesapeake Solutions
DeWalt Power Tools
KPSS Mally Beauty
Orbrecht-Phoenix Contractors, Inc.
Pan American Health Organization Porter-Cable/Delta
RentBureau
TIPCO
The World Bank
New England Conservatory of Music
Seton Hall University
University of Mary Washington
University of Rio Grande

BOATHOUSE GROUP INC.
260 Charles St 4th Fl, Waltham, MA 02453-3826
Tel.: (781) 663-6600
Fax: (781) 663-6601
Web Site: www.boathouseinc.com

Employees: 35

Agency Specializes In: Brand Development & Integration, Consumer Goods, Financial, Health Care Services, High Technology, Luxury Products, Retail, Sponsorship

John Connors *(Founder)*
Lisa Mansur Badeau *(Mng Dir-Acct Mgmt & Mktg Strategy)*
Gisela Germano *(Mng Dir-Media)*
Jill Cape Coppedge *(Grp Dir-Media)*
Michele Madaris *(Grp Acct Dir)*
Meredith Barron *(Acct Dir)*
Kim Daniels *(Dir-Brdcst Production & Bus Affairs)*
Marguerite Daly *(Acct Mgr)*
P. J. Lee *(Acct Mgr)*
Benjamin Levy *(Acct Mgr)*
Jaime Lisk *(Acct Mgr)*
Daniel Regis *(Acct Mgr)*
Kristin Puopolo *(Acct Exec)*

Accounts:
Boston Teacher Residency
Eversource
Gather
Merrill Lynch; Plainsboro, NJ
Spark
Steward Health Care; Boston, MA
Thermo Fisher
WBUR (Agency of Record) Brand Positioning, Brand Strategy, Campaign: "Your World. In a New Light", Creative Development, Media Strategy, Social Strategy

BOB
774 Saint-Paul St W, Montreal, Quebec H3C 1M4 Canada
Tel.: (514) 842-4262
Fax: (514) 842-7262
Web Site: www.bob.ca

Year Founded: 2002

Agency Specializes In: Advertising, Brand Development & Integration, Digital/Interactive, Public Relations, Social Media

Jean-Francois Joyal *(Partner, VP & Gen Mgr)*

Claudéric Saint-Amand *(Partner & VP-Creative & Strategy)*
Nathalie Turcotte *(VP-Consulting Group)*
Dominic Prigent *(Acct Dir)*
Philip Cartier *(Dir-Fin)*
Julie Descheneaux *(Dir-Art)*
Stephanie Paquette *(Acct Mgr)*

Accounts:
Unilever United States, Inc. Dove

BOB'S YOUR UNCLE
(Formerly BrainStorm Group)
219 Dufferin St Ste 304A, Toronto, ON M6K 3J1 Canada
Tel.: (416) 506-9930
Fax: (416) 506-0392
E-Mail: talktous@byuagency.com
Web Site: www.byuagency.com/

Employees: 40
Year Founded: 1992

Agency Specializes In: Advertising, Collateral, Digital/Interactive, Direct Response Marketing, Event Planning & Marketing, Media Planning, Media Relations, Multimedia, Production, Promotions, Public Relations, Radio, Restaurant, T.V.

Dorothy McMillan *(Chief Creative Officer)*
Edward Weiss *(VP & Dir-Media)*
Sara Presotto *(Dir-Fin & Ops)*
Judy Van Mourik *(Dir-Production & Studio)*
Daryl Klein *(Assoc Dir-Creative)*
Megan Knox *(Acct Mgr)*
Rachel Molenda *(Mgr-Social Media)*
Michelle Bobbie *(Acct Supvr)*
Jessica Abela-Froese *(Acct Coord)*
Brian Flay *(Sr Writer)*

Accounts:
ADP
Ancestry.Ca
Applebee's
Association of Canadian Advertisers Marketing Communications, Strategic
Baxters
Canon Canada
Gardein
Jones New York
Kenneth Cole
Kraft Foods
Old Dutch
Sovereign

BOC PARTNERS
601 Bound Brook Rd Ste 100, Middlesex, NJ 08846-2155
Tel.: (732) 424-0100
Fax: (732) 424-2525
Web Site: bocpartners.com

E-Mail for Key Personnel:
President: spell@timelyad.com
Creative Dir.: CMedallis@timelyad.com
Media Dir.: mmcdarby@timelyad.com

Employees: 5
Year Founded: 1975

Agency Specializes In: Advertising Specialties, Automotive, Brand Development & Integration, Broadcast, Business Publications, Business-To-Business, Cable T.V., Co-op Advertising, Collateral, Consumer Marketing, Consumer Publications, Corporate Identity, Direct Response Marketing, Exhibit/Trade Shows, Faith Based, Graphic Design, High Technology, Industrial, Local Marketing, Logo & Package Design, Magazines, Marine, Media Buying Services, Merchandising, New Product Development, Newspaper, Newspapers & Magazines, Out-of-Home Media, Outdoor, Planning & Consultation, Print, Production, Public Relations, Publicity/Promotions, Radio, Real Estate, Recruitment, Retail, Trade & Consumer Magazines, Transportation

Breakdown of Gross Billings by Media: Bus. Publs.: 3%; Cable T.V.: 5%; Collateral: 8%; D.M.: 3%; Newsp.: 56%; Outdoor: 18%; Pub. Rels.: 1%; Radio: 4%; Trade & Consumer Mags.: 2%

Steven C. Pell *(Partner)*
Peter Richter *(Sr Strategist-Mktg)*
Michael McDarby *(Acct Coord)*
Iris Morales *(Acct Coord)*

Accounts:
Highland Park Conservative Temple & Center; Highland Park, NJ Pro Bono Projects; 1975
Madison Honda; Madison, NJ Automobile Dealer; 1985
Mahwah Honda; Mahwah, NJ Automobile Dealer; 1981
Matrix Outdoor Media; Monroe Township, NJ Billboard Advertising Services; 2005
Matrix7; Somerset, NJ Computer Consultants; 2004
Phillipsburg Easton Honda; Phillipsburg, NJ Automobile Dealer; 1980
VIP Honda; North Plainfield, NJ Automobile Dealer; 1975

BODDEN PARTNERS
102 Madison Ave, New York, NY 10016-7417
Tel.: (212) 328-1111
Fax: (212) 328-1100
E-Mail: info@boddenpartners.com
Web Site: www.boddenpartners.com

Employees: 60
Year Founded: 1975

National Agency Associations: AAF-DMA

Agency Specializes In: Advertising, Affiliate Marketing, Brand Development & Integration, Business-To-Business, Collateral, Digital/Interactive, Direct Response Marketing, Event Planning & Marketing, Exhibit/Trade Shows, Market Research, New Technologies, Public Relations, Publicity/Promotions, Radio, Sales Promotion, Social Media, Sponsorship, Sports Market, Travel & Tourism

Approx. Annual Billings: $109,200,000

Breakdown of Gross Billings by Media: Brdcst.: $9,500,000; D.M.: $20,300,000; Event Mktg.: $14,600,000; Exhibits/Trade Shows: $45,900,000; Internet Adv.: $10,100,000; Print: $6,900,000; Pub. Rels.: $1,900,000

Martin Mitchell *(Partner & CMO)*
Hank Jacobs *(Sr VP & Assoc Creative Dir)*
Jennifer Randolph *(VP-Mktg & Comm Strategy)*
Mark Silverman *(Acct Dir)*
Michelle Pollack *(Sr Acct Exec)*
Wenona Williams *(Acct Exec-Adv)*

Accounts:
America Scores; New York, NY Sports Participation; 2007
Bank of America; Wilmington, DE
Black Mesa; New Mexico Golf Resort; 2006
Hofstra Athletics; Long Island, NY University Sports
International Yacht Council
National Geographic; New York, NY Digital Content
New York Daily News; New York, NY; 1994
Prudential Financial; Newark, NJ; 2001
Turning Stone; Verona, NY
Women's Sports Foundation; New York, NY Sports Promotion

Branch

Hamilton Public Relations
102 Madison Ave 7th Fl, New York, NY 10016
(See Separate Listing)

BODKIN ASSOCIATES, INC.
1555 W Oak St Ste 100, Zionsville, IN 46077-1959
Tel.: (877) 263-5468
Fax: (317) 733-1545
Toll Free: (877) BODKIN8
E-Mail: info@teambodkin.com
Web Site: www.teambodkin.com

Employees: 5
Year Founded: 1990

Agency Specializes In: Advertising, African-American Market, Agriculture, Asian Market, Bilingual Market, Brand Development & Integration, Broadcast, Collateral, Communications, Consulting, Consumer Marketing, Consumer Publications, Corporate Identity, Event Planning & Marketing, Exhibit/Trade Shows, Financial, Graphic Design, Health Care Services, Hispanic Market, Internet/Web Design, Legal Services, Logo & Package Design, Medical Products, Out-of-Home Media, Outdoor, Pharmaceutical, Print, Public Relations, Radio, Real Estate, Retail, Sales Promotion, Sports Market, Strategic Planning/Research

Clyde Bodkin *(Owner)*
Steve Miller *(Designer)*
Ed Thacker *(Rep-Sls)*

Accounts:
Dow AgroSciences; Indianapolis, IN; 1996

BODNER ADVERTISING
5600 NW 36th St Ste 611, Miami Springs, FL 33166
Tel.: (305) 874-7070
Fax: (305) 874-7007
E-Mail: stan@bodneradvertising.com

E-Mail for Key Personnel:
President: sjbodner@bellsouth.net

Employees: 3
Year Founded: 1970

National Agency Associations: AAF

Agency Specializes In: Advertising

Revenue: $1,500,000

Stan Bodner *(Owner)*

BOELTER + LINCOLN MARKETING COMMUNICATIONS
222 E Erie 4th Fl, Milwaukee, WI 53202
Tel.: (414) 271-0101
Fax: (414) 271-1436
E-Mail: bl@boelterlincoln.com
Web Site: www.boelterlincoln.com

Employees: 40
Year Founded: 1974

National Agency Associations: 4A's

Agency Specializes In: Advertising, Advertising Specialties, Brand Development & Integration, Broadcast, Cable T.V., Co-op Advertising, Collateral, Computers & Software, Consumer Marketing, Digital/Interactive, Financial, Hospitality, Integrated Marketing, Internet/Web Design, Leisure, Local Marketing, Magazines, Media Buying Services, Media Planning, Newspaper, Out-of-Home Media, Outdoor, Planning & Consultation, Public Relations, Radio, Restaurant, Retail, Sales

Promotion, Strategic Planning/Research, T.V., Trade & Consumer Magazines, Transportation, Travel & Tourism, Viral/Buzz/Word of Mouth, Web (Banner Ads, Pop-ups, etc.)

Approx. Annual Billings: $27,000,000 Consolidated

Jill Brzeski *(Pres & CEO)*
Shannon Novotny *(Acct Dir)*
Zac Jacobson *(Dir-Art)*
Michael Stodola *(Dir-Creative)*
Garth Cramer *(Assoc Dir-Creative)*
Stasha Wuest *(Acct Supvr)*
Julie Wagner *(Supvr-Media)*
Ken Leiviska *(Acct Exec-PR)*
Pete Piotrowski *(Acct Exec)*
Grant Galley *(Asst Acct Exec)*

Accounts:
Advanced Pain Management Marketing
Angelic Bakehouse (Advertising Agency of Record) Online, Print Media Buying, Public Relations, Strategic Planning
Door County Distillery (Agency of Record)
Door Peninsula Winery (Agency of Record)
Eagle River Area Chamber of Commerce Visitors Center
Ministry Health Care
North Shore Bank
Original Wisconsin Ducks
Tommy Bartlett, Inc. Robot World & Exploratory, Water Ski Show
Wilderness Resort (Agency of Record) Boadcast Media Buying, Campaign: "Here's to the family, here's to the Wilderness.", Marketing, Online, Print, Strategic Planning
Wisconsin Dells Festivals Inc.
Wisconsin Dells Visitor & Convention Bureau

BOHAN

124 12th Ave S, Nashville, TN 37203
Tel.: (615) 327-1189
Fax: (615) 327-8123
E-Mail: hello@bohanideas.com
Web Site: www.bohanideas.com

E-Mail for Key Personnel:
Chairman: davidb@bohanideas.com
Creative Dir.: snelson@bohanideas.com
Media Dir.: rmelin@bohanideas.com
Public Relations: tadkinson@bohanideas.com

Employees: 80
Year Founded: 1990

National Agency Associations: 4A's

Agency Specializes In: Health Care Services, Leisure, Sponsorship, Sports Market, Travel & Tourism

Approx. Annual Billings: $66,000,000

David Bohan *(Chm)*
Shari Day *(Pres & CEO)*
Brian Gilpatrick *(Sr VP-Acct Mgmt)*
Tom Adkinson *(VP & Dir-Comm)*
Rich Melin *(VP & Dir-Brand Engagement)*
Nicole Minton *(VP-Market Strategies)*
Tim Delger *(Dir-Art & Assoc Dir-Creative)*
Josh Ford *(Dir-Art)*
Lucas Hagerty *(Dir-New Bus & Project)*
Penny Rahe *(Dir-Brdcst)*
Chrissie Scott *(Dir-Fin)*
Deb Rhodes *(Bus Mgr-Creative)*
Katie Simers *(Project Mgr-New Bus)*
Farley Day *(Mgr-Bus Dev)*
Jennie Hagler *(Mgr-Workflow)*
Sherry Talley *(Mgr-Creative Svcs)*
Donnette Engebrecht *(Acct Supvr)*
Tony Gerstner *(Acct Supvr)*
Kyla Costa *(Acct Exec)*
Barbara Pritchett *(Acct Exec)*
Hayley Reaver *(Copywriter)*
Whitney Benner *(Coord-Mktg)*

Accounts:
Arnold Palmer Hospital for Children
Baptist Health, Paducah
BlueCross BlueShield of Tennessee (Agency of Record) Account Planning, Creative
Brunswick Commercial & Government Products
Charter Energy
City of Pigeon Forge
Community Foundation of Middle Tennessee
Debonaire Debonaire Cigars, Debonaire Rum
Dollar General
Dueling Grounds Distillery
Durfield Holdings Fine Cigars
Frist Center for the Visual Arts
Gren Group
HCA
IASIS Healthcare Corp.
Jos. A. Bank Clothiers, Inc.
Kirkland's
Martha O'Bryan Center
Methodist Stone Oak Hospital
Midtown Cafe
Music City Music Council
O'Charley's (Lead Creative Agency) Restaurant Chain
Pigeon Forge Department of Tourism; Pigeon Forge, TN Vacation Destination; 1990
Saint Thomas Health (Agency of Record)
Smallwood Nickle Architects
Southeast Tourism Society
The Standard at the Smith House Restaurant & Private Club 'History, Novel, Nashville, Chefs"
Sunset Grill
Wakefield Cattle Company

BOILING POINT MEDIA

100 W Wilshire Blvd Ste C2, Oklahoma City, OK 73116
Tel.: (405) 286-9635
Fax: (405) 286-9734
E-Mail: info@boilingpointmedia.com
Web Site: www.boilingpointmedia.com

Agency Specializes In: Advertising, Brand Development & Integration, Digital/Interactive, Internet/Web Design, Logo & Package Design, Media Buying Services, Media Planning, Print, Public Relations, Search Engine Optimization

Hugh Hale *(Pres)*
Lee Bennett *(VP-Bus Dev)*
Andy Swanson *(Dir-Production)*
Jessica Mitchell *(Acct Mgr-Bus Dev)*
Carter Campbell *(Brand Mgr)*
Kelly OConnor *(Mgr-Bus & Media Buyer)*
Ryan Bellgardt *(Mgr-Production)*

Accounts:
Edmond Hyundai

BOLCHALK FREY MARKETING, ADVERTISING & PUBLIC RELATIONS

310 S Williams Blvd Ste 260, Tucson, AZ 85711-4407
Tel.: (520) 745-8221
Fax: (520) 745-5540
E-Mail: info-mb@adwiz.com
Web Site: www.adwiz.com

E-Mail for Key Personnel:
President: michael@adwiz.com
Creative Dir.: robyn@adwiz.com
Media Dir.: katrina@adwiz.com

Employees: 5
Year Founded: 1964

National Agency Associations: PRSA

Agency Specializes In: Advertising, Advertising Specialties, Alternative Advertising, Aviation & Aerospace, Bilingual Market, Brand Development & Integration, Broadcast, Business Publications, Cable T.V., Collateral, Communications, Consulting, Consumer Marketing, Direct Response Marketing, E-Commerce, Education, Electronic Media, Event Planning & Marketing, Exhibit/Trade Shows, Graphic Design, Health Care Services, Hispanic Market, Hospitality, In-Store Advertising, Internet/Web Design, Local Marketing, Logo & Package Design, Magazines, Media Buying Services, Media Planning, Media Relations, Multicultural, Multimedia, New Product Development, Newspaper, Newspapers & Magazines, Out-of-Home Media, Outdoor, Over-50 Market, Package Design, Planning & Consultation, Point of Purchase, Point of Sale, Print, Product Placement, Production (Ad, Film, Broadcast), Production (Print), Promotions, Public Relations, Radio, Real Estate, Recruitment, Regional, Restaurant, Retail, Sales Promotion, Seniors' Market, Strategic Planning/Research, T.V., Teen Market, Trade & Consumer Magazines, Travel & Tourism, Web (Banner Ads, Pop-ups, etc.), Women's Market

Breakdown of Gross Billings by Media: Brdcst.: 2%; D.M.: 1%; Mags.: 7%; Newsp.: 30%; Outdoor: 15%; Print: 10%; Radio: 5%; T.V.: 20%; Trade & Consumer Mags.: 2%; Trade Shows: 2%; Worldwide Web Sites: 5%; Yellow Page Adv.: 1%

Robyn Frey *(VP & Dir-Creative)*
Paul O'Rourke *(Sr Dir-Mktg Svcs)*
Katrina Noble *(Media Dir)*
Kristen Oaxaca *(Sr Graphic Designer)*

Accounts:
A.F. Sterling Homes; Tucson, AZ; 1998
BFL Construction Company
Broadway Carpet; 2001
Choice Greens Restaurants
El Rio Foundation
International Wildlife Museum Transits
Reid Park Zoological Society Bus Benches, Entry Sign
Southern AZ Homebuilders Home Show; Tucson, AZ; 1998
Surv-Kap, Inc.; Tucson, AZ; 1997

BOLD+BEYOND

8033 Sunset Blvd, Los Angeles, CA 90046
Tel.: (424) 332-9726
Web Site: boldbeyond.com

Year Founded: 2009

Agency Specializes In: Alternative Advertising, Branded Entertainment, Business Publications, Consumer Publications, Custom Publishing, Digital/Interactive, Direct Response Marketing, Experience Design, In-Store Advertising, Local Marketing, Multimedia, Newspaper, Newspapers & Magazines, Out-of-Home Media, Outdoor, Print, Publishing, Radio, Search Engine Optimization, Social Media, Sponsorship, T.V., Viral/Buzz/Word of Mouth, Web (Banner Ads, Pop-ups, etc.)

Julien Subit *(CEO)*

Accounts:
France4.fr On N'est Plus Des Pigeons!
Mac Douglas Website

BOLDWERKS

477 State St, Portsmouth, NH 03801
Tel.: (603) 436-2065
Fax: (800) 557-7161
Toll Free: (800) 350-2365
E-Mail: info@boldwerks.com
Web Site: www.boldwerks.com

Agency Specializes In: Advertising, Brand

Development & Integration, Collateral, Corporate Identity, Digital/Interactive, Internet/Web Design, Logo & Package Design, Print, Social Media

Adam Kaufmann *(Art Dir)*
Chris Hislop *(Dir-Content)*
Matthias Roberge *(Dir-Creative)*
J. L. Stevens *(Dir-Social & New Media)*

Accounts:
Emuge Corporation
Nourish Health For Life
Portsmouth Symphony Orchestra

BOLIN MARKETING
(Formerly Bolin Marketing & Advertising)
2523 Wayzata Blvd, Minneapolis, MN 55405
Tel.: (612) 374-1200
Fax: (612) 377-4226
E-Mail: inquiries@bolinmarketing.com
Web Site: www.bolinmarketing.com

E-Mail for Key Personnel:
President: SBolin@bolinideas.com

Employees: 22
Year Founded: 1950

National Agency Associations: 4A's

Agency Specializes In: Advertising, Brand Development & Integration, Broadcast, Business-To-Business, Cable T.V., Co-op Advertising, Collateral, Consulting, Consumer Marketing, Corporate Identity, Entertainment, High Technology, Internet/Web Design, Local Marketing, Logo & Package Design, Magazines, Media Buying Services, New Product Development, Newspaper, Newspapers & Magazines, Outdoor, Planning & Consultation, Production, Public Relations, Publicity/Promotions, Radio, Sales Promotion, Seniors' Market, Sponsorship, Strategic Planning/Research, T.V., Telemarketing, Travel & Tourism

Approx. Annual Billings: $13,000,000

Todd Bolin *(Pres & CEO)*
Scott Bolin *(Chief Creative Officer)*
Peter Hoagland *(Exec VP)*
Kathy Gladfelter *(VP-Media)*
Julia Sasseville *(Dir-Art & Graphic Designer)*
Nathan Eide *(Dir-Emerging Media)*
John Simpson *(Dir-Creative)*
Lucy Hansen *(Acct Mgr-Mktg)*
Mara Keller *(Specialist-Emerging Media)*

Accounts:
3M
Ameripride Commercial Apparel
Brock White Business-to-Business Distribution
Carmex Lip Balm
CertainTeed
Dominica, the Nature Island Destination Marketing
Honeywell WiFi Thermostats
Stratasys 3D Printing

BONAFIDE
5318 Weslayan St 128, Houston, TX 77005
Tel.: (713) 568-2364
E-Mail: hello@gobonafide.com
Web Site: www.gobonafide.com

Agency Specializes In: Advertising, Digital/Interactive, Paid Searches, Public Relations, Search Engine Optimization, Social Media

Shareef Defrawi *(Founder & Pres)*
Aylin Poulton *(VP)*
Kyle Tabor *(Strategist-Digital)*

Accounts:
New-Migraine Relief Center
New-Top Tax Defenders

BOND BRAND LOYALTY
6900 Maritz Dr, Mississauga, ON L5W 1L8 Canada
Tel.: (905) 696-9400
Web Site: www.bondbrandloyalty.com

Bob Macdonald *(Pres & CEO)*
Andrew Kingston *(Mgr-Mktg)*
Richard Lane *(Strategist-Marketing)*

Accounts:
Gap
General Mills
Johnson & Johnson
London Drugs
New Balance
Target

BOND STRATEGY & INFLUENCE
(Formerly Electric Artists, Inc.)
42 Bond St 3rd Fl, New York, NY 10012
Tel.: (212) 354-2650
Fax: (212) 354-2651
E-Mail: hello@bondinfluence.com
Web Site: www.bondinfluence.com/

Employees: 20
Year Founded: 1997

Agency Specializes In: Consulting, Digital/Interactive, Market Research, Public Relations, Strategic Planning/Research, T.V.

Marc Schiller *(Founder & CEO)*
Cynthia Lyons *(VP-Production & Client Svcs)*
Maria Elena Diaz *(Controller)*
Matthew Hirsch *(Sr Mgr-Mktg & Comm)*
Christina Caputo *(Sr Acct Exec)*
Ben Dorf *(Acct Exec-Film)*
Bianca Neptune *(Strategist-Social Media)*
Greg Holtzman *(Coord-Mktg)*

Accounts:
American Express
The Luxury Collection
Meet At The Apartment
Starwood Hotels & Resorts
USA Network

BONEHOOK
5536 Broadway St, West Linn, OR 97068
Tel.: (503) 970-3862
Web Site: www.bonehook.com

Year Founded: 2009

Agency Specializes In: Brand Development & Integration, Identity Marketing, Promotions, Public Relations, Social Media

David Burn *(Founder, Dir-Creative, Copywriter & Brand Strategist)*

Accounts:
Bonneville Power Administration Federal Agency Services

BONNEVILLE COMMUNICATIONS
55 N 300 W, Salt Lake City, UT 84101-3502
Tel.: (801) 237-2488
Fax: (801) 575-7541
E-Mail: bonneville@bonneville.com
Web Site: www.bonneville.com

E-Mail for Key Personnel:
President: ggarber@boncom.com
Creative Dir.: cdahl@boncom.com
Media Dir.: mlee@boncom.com

Employees: 30
Year Founded: 1967

Agency Specializes In: Broadcast, Consumer Marketing, Direct Response Marketing, Faith Based, Government/Political, Production, Radio, T.V.

Approx. Annual Billings: $25,000,000 Fees Capitalized

Breakdown of Gross Billings by Media: Cable T.V.: $18,250,000; Foreign: $1,250,000; Out-of-Home Media: $500,000; Radio: $2,500,000; Spot T.V.: $2,500,000

Peter Burton *(VP & Gen Mgr-KSWD Los Angeles)*
Mark Preston *(VP-Bus Dev)*
Curt Dahl *(Sr Dir-Creative-Bonneville Comm)*

Accounts:
Deseret First Credit Union
Deseret Industries
Homefront
Huntsman Cancer Institute
Music & the Spoken Word
National Hospice Foundation
The Salvation Army

BONNIE HENESON COMMUNICATIONS, INC.
9199 Reisterstown Rd Ste 212C, Owings Mills, MD 21117
Tel.: (410) 654-0000
Fax: (410) 654-0377
E-Mail: info@bonnieheneson.com
Web Site: www.bonnieheneson.com

Employees: 9
Year Founded: 1990

Agency Specializes In: Advertising, Advertising Specialties, Education, Event Planning & Marketing, Graphic Design, Health Care Services, Medical Products, Public Relations, Publicity/Promotions

Approx. Annual Billings: $2,000,000

Kyri L. Jacobs *(Pres)*
Bonnie K. Heneson *(CEO)*
Andrew Aldrich *(VP-PR)*
Brian Rogers *(Dir-Creative)*
Joyce Lippens *(Office Mgr)*
Cara Foley *(Acct Exec-Social Media)*
Kaitlyn Gibbons *(Acct Exec)*

Accounts:
Bon Secours Health System
New-Calvert County Health Department Division of Behavioral Health, Public Information
New-Doctors Regional Cancer Center
Hannah More School (Agency of Record)
Howard County General Hospital
Laurel Regional Hospital Foundation
New-Maryland Dental Action Coalition
Monarch Academy Public Charter School
New-Unified Community Connections

BOOM ADVERTISING
186 Cartright St, Charleston, SC 29492
Tel.: (843) 377-8488
E-Mail: makesomenoise@theboomagency.com
Web Site: www.theboomagency.com

Agency Specializes In: Advertising, Brand Development & Integration, Corporate Identity, Graphic Design, Internet/Web Design, Logo & Package Design, Media Planning, Media Relations, Public Relations, Social Media

John Greavu *(Co-Owner & VP)*

Lori Greavu *(Co-Owner)*

Accounts:
Sideline Sports

BOOMERANG PHARMACEUTICAL COMMUNICATIONS
14 Walsh Dr, Parsippany, NJ 07054
Tel.: (973) 265-8319
Fax: (973) 299-5017
E-Mail: throw@boomerangpharma.com
Web Site: www.boomerangpharma.com

Employees: 200
Year Founded: 1997

Agency Specializes In: Advertising, E-Commerce, Search Engine Optimization, Social Media, Technical Advertising

Emmanuel Bueb *(CEO)*
Jonathan Alard *(Head-IT)*
Heather Force Gendre *(Sr Designer-Interaction)*

Accounts:
Pacira Pharmaceuticals, Inc. Exparel

BOOMM! MARKETING & COMMUNICATIONS
17 N Catherine Ave, La Grange, IL 60525
Tel.: (708) 352-9700
Fax: (708) 352-9701
E-Mail: gary@boomm.com
Web Site: www.boomm.com

Employees: 19
Year Founded: 1998

Agency Specializes In: Advertising, Brand Development & Integration, Business Publications, Business-To-Business, Collateral, Communications, Consumer Goods, Consumer Marketing, Corporate Communications, Corporate Identity, Digital/Interactive, Direct Response Marketing, Electronic Media, Exhibit/Trade Shows, Food Service, Graphic Design, In-Store Advertising, Integrated Marketing, Internet/Web Design, Logo & Package Design, Magazines, Media Buying Services, Media Planning, Merchandising, Newspaper, Newspapers & Magazines, Planning & Consultation, Point of Purchase, Point of Sale, Print, Production, Promotions, Public Relations, Publicity/Promotions, Restaurant, Retail, Sales Promotion, Strategic Planning/Research, Trade & Consumer Magazines

Approx. Annual Billings: $4,400,000

Breakdown of Gross Billings by Media: Collateral: $650,000; Logo & Package Design: $450,000; Point of Sale: $400,000; Promos.: $1,000,000; Pub. Rels.: $200,000; Strategic Planning/Research: $250,000; Trade & Consumer Mags.: $1,100,000; Worldwide Web Sites: $350,000

Gary Mattes *(CEO)*
Fred Gaede *(Chief Creative Officer)*
Matt Lockwood *(VP & Creative Dir)*
Jeff Andrews *(VP-Client Svcs)*
Dane Prickett *(Dir-Media)*

Accounts:
Alcan Packaging Food Packaging
Corn Products International (Corporate Communications)
Keebler
Kelpac Medical Strategic Branding, Website Development
Kronos
Magnetrol (Agency of Record) Brand Strategy, Marketing Communications
Maple Leaf Bakery Bistolls
Maple Leaf Farms Retail & Foodservice
McCain Foods USA Anchor, Cheese Sensations, Foodservice, Moore's, Poppers, Sweet Classics
Menasha Packaging
OSI Group Marketing, Public Relations
Pierce Chicken
Pilgrim's Pride Foodservice
Plastron Industries
Plitt Seafood
Premium Ingredients International
Saputo Cheese Retail, Stella Brand
Triad Foods Group Braveheart Beef, Nature's Premium

BOONDOCK WALKER
3635 Perkins Ave Ste 6A, Cleveland, OH 44114
Tel.: (216) 431-9301
Fax: (216) 431-9331
E-Mail: dmoss@boondockwalker.com
Web Site: www.boondockwalker.com

Year Founded: 2007

Agency Specializes In: Advertising, Alternative Advertising, Brand Development & Integration, Branded Entertainment, Business Publications, Business-To-Business, Commercial Photography, Communications, Consulting, Consumer Marketing, Consumer Publications, Content, Corporate Identity, Digital/Interactive, Electronic Media, Environmental, Event Planning & Marketing, Exhibit/Trade Shows, Experience Design, Graphic Design, Health Care Services, Hospitality, Identity Marketing, In-Store Advertising, Internet/Web Design, Logo & Package Design, Media Buying Services, Multimedia, New Technologies, Package Design, Planning & Consultation, Point of Purchase, Point of Sale, Print, Production (Print), Retail, Strategic Planning/Research, Transportation, Viral/Buzz/Word of Mouth

Approx. Annual Billings: $1,500,000

Breakdown of Gross Billings by Media: Comml. Photography: $50,000; Graphic Design: $50,000; In-Store Adv.: $150,000; Logo & Package Design: $500,000; Mags.: $100,000; Plng. & Consultation: $150,000; Strategic Planning/Research: $50,000; Transit: $200,000; Worldwide Web Sites: $250,000

Mark A. Nead *(Founder, Partner & Dir-Brand Dev)*
Brian J. Willse *(Co-Founder & Partner)*
Megan Conway *(Dir-Client Rels & Bus Dev)*

Accounts:
Tarkett

BOONE DELEON COMMUNICATIONS, INC.
3100 S Gessner Rd Ste 110, Houston, TX 77063
Tel.: (713) 952-9600
Fax: (713) 952-9606
Web Site: www.boonedeleon.com

E-Mail for Key Personnel:
Media Dir.: ron@boonedeleon.com

Employees: 8
Year Founded: 1947

National Agency Associations: AAF

Agency Specializes In: Advertising, Advertising Specialties, Bilingual Market, Brand Development & Integration, Broadcast, Business-To-Business, Cable T.V., Collateral, Consulting, Consumer Marketing, Corporate Communications, Corporate Identity, Event Planning & Marketing, Financial, Government/Political, Graphic Design, Health Care Services, Hispanic Market, In-Store Advertising, Industrial, Internet/Web Design, Magazines, Media Buying Services, Media Planning, Media Relations, New Product Development, Newspaper, Outdoor, Planning & Consultation, Point of Purchase, Point of Sale, Print, Production (Ad, Film, Broadcast), Public Relations, Publicity/Promotions, Radio, Sales Promotion, Sports Market, Strategic Planning/Research, T.V., Trade & Consumer Magazines, Transportation

Leo De Leon *(Pres & Dir-Creative)*
Patty Morris *(Office Mgr)*

BOONEOAKLEY
1445 S Mint St, Charlotte, NC 28203
Tel.: (704) 333-9797
Fax: (704) 348-2834
E-Mail: info@booneoakley.com
Web Site: www.booneoakley.com

Employees: 18
Year Founded: 2000

Agency Specializes In: Advertising, Automotive, Brand Development & Integration, Broadcast, Cable T.V., Collateral, Communications, Consumer Goods, Consumer Marketing, Corporate Identity, Digital/Interactive, Direct Response Marketing, Entertainment, Event Planning & Marketing, Fashion/Apparel, Financial, Food Service, Integrated Marketing, Internet/Web Design, Local Marketing, Magazines, Market Research, Media Buying Services, Media Planning, Men's Market, Mobile Marketing, Multimedia, Newspaper, Newspapers & Magazines, Out-of-Home Media, Outdoor, Package Design, Podcasting, Point of Purchase, Point of Sale, Print, Production, Radio, Restaurant, Retail, Search Engine Optimization, Social Media, Sponsorship, Sports Market, Strategic Planning/Research, T.V., Teen Market, Trade & Consumer Magazines, Transportation, Travel & Tourism, Viral/Buzz/Word of Mouth, Web (Banner Ads, Pop-ups, etc.), Women's Market

Approx. Annual Billings: $59,400,000

David Oakley *(Chief Creative Officer)*
Claire Oakley *(Client Svcs Dir)*
Eric Roch von Rochsburg *(Dir-Design)*
Laura Wallace *(Acct Supvr)*
Danny Gassaway *(Strategist-Digital)*
Anna Lindsey *(Acct Exec)*
Kathryn Bolles *(Sr Acct Planner)*
Mary Gross *(Copywriter)*

Accounts:
Autobell Car Wash Campaign: "Homecoming Queen"
Bojangles' Restaurants, Inc. Bio Time, Bomoji, Campaign: "Chicken Cops Intro", Campaign: "Tis the Seasoning"
Carolina Beverage Corp Social Media, Traditional
Cheerwine (Agency of Record)
Carolinas Healthcare Foundation
Champions for Education (Agency of Record) Online, Outdoor, Radio, Social Media Advertising, TV, Wells Fargo Championship
Charlotte Hornets
Goodwill Industries (Agency of Record) Brand Awareness, Newspaper, Online Advertising, Outdoor
ISS Research; Charlotte, NC (Agency of Record) Oh Yeah!
MTV Networks MTV2
Thermafuse Direct Marketing, Online, Print

BORDERS PERRIN NORRANDER INC
520 SW Yamhill St, Portland, OR 97204
Tel.: (503) 227-2506
Fax: (503) 227-4827
E-Mail: info@bpninc.com
Web Site: www.bpninc.com

E-Mail for Key Personnel:
Creative Dir.: tschneider@bpninc.com
Media Dir.: lgaffney@bpninc.com

Employees: 15
Year Founded: 1977

Agency Specializes In: Advertising, Automotive, Brand Development & Integration, Broadcast, Communications, Consulting, Consumer Marketing, Corporate Identity, E-Commerce, Fashion/Apparel, Financial, Leisure, Magazines, New Product Development, Outdoor, Planning & Consultation, Print, Sponsorship, Sports Market, Strategic Planning/Research, T.V.

Lori Gaffney *(CEO)*
Erik Rabasca *(Sr VP & Head-Digital Media)*
Chasson Gracie *(Exec Dir-Acct Plng & Strategy)*
Willyum Beck *(Dir-Art)*
Kelly Totten *(Dir-Fin & Ops)*
Elana Hutter *(Acct Exec)*
Anna Naef *(Designer-Digital & Print Production)*
Elizabeth Naciri *(Sr Media Buyer)*
Alison Raynak *(Asst Media Planner)*

Accounts:
Forest Park Conservancy
K&N
Monterey County Convention & Visitors Bureau (Agency of Record) Creative, Media Planning, Strategic Planning
Old World Industries; Chicago, IL Media Planning & Buying
Oregon State Lottery Breakopens, Campaign: "Sustainable Economy", Campaign: "Trashdance", Keno/K4, Lucky Lines, Mega Millions, Megabucks, Pick4, Powerball, Raffle, Scratch-its, Thanksgiving Raffle, Video Lottery, Win for Life
Surfrider Foundation
Wilson Baseball (Agency of Record)

THE BORENSTEIN GROUP, INC.
11240 Waples Mill Rd Ste 420, Fairfax, VA 22030
Tel.: (703) 385-8178
Fax: (703) 385-6454
Web Site: www.borensteingroup.com

E-Mail for Key Personnel:
President: gal@borenstein-online.com

Employees: 20
Year Founded: 1994

Agency Specializes In: Above-the-Line, Advertising, Affiliate Marketing, Affluent Market, African-American Market, Alternative Advertising, Asian Market, Automotive, Aviation & Aerospace, Below-the-Line, Bilingual Market, Brand Development & Integration, Broadcast, Business Publications, Business-To-Business, Cable T.V., Catalogs, Co-op Advertising, Collateral, College, Communications, Consulting, Consumer Publications, Content, Corporate Communications, Corporate Identity, Crisis Communications, Custom Publishing, Customer Relationship Management, Digital/Interactive, Direct Response Marketing, E-Commerce, Education, Electronic Media, Electronics, Email, Engineering, Entertainment, Event Planning & Marketing, Exhibit/Trade Shows, Experience Design, Fashion/Apparel, Financial, Gay & Lesbian Market, Government/Political, Graphic Design, Guerilla Marketing, Health Care Services, High Technology, Hispanic Market, Hospitality, Identity Marketing, Industrial, Information Technology, Integrated Marketing, International, Internet/Web Design, Investor Relations, Legal Services, Local Marketing, Logo & Package Design, Luxury Products, Magazines, Market Research, Media Buying Services, Media Planning, Media Relations, Media Training, Medical Products, Mobile Marketing, Multicultural, Multimedia, New Product Development, New Technologies, Newspaper, Newspapers & Magazines, Out-of-Home Media, Outdoor, Package Design, Paid Searches, Pharmaceutical, Planning & Consultation, Podcasting, Point of Purchase, Point of Sale, Print, Product Placement, Production, Production (Ad, Film, Broadcast), Production (Print), Promotions, Public Relations, Publicity/Promotions, Publishing, Radio, Real Estate, Recruitment, Regional, Retail, Sales Promotion, Search Engine Optimization, Seniors' Market, Social Marketing/Nonprofit, Sponsorship, Stakeholders, Strategic Planning/Research, Syndication, T.V., Technical Advertising, Teen Market, Trade & Consumer Magazines, Transportation, Urban Market, Viral/Buzz/Word of Mouth, Web (Banner Ads, Pop-ups, etc.), Women's Market, Yellow Pages Advertising

Approx. Annual Billings: $12,000,000

Breakdown of Gross Billings by Media: Collateral: 50%; Pub. Rels.: 30%; Worldwide Web Sites: 20%

Gal S. Borenstein *(Pres & CEO)*
Taryn Johnson *(Dir-Creative)*
Anna Schena *(Acct Mgr)*
Aaron Wachsstock *(Strategist-Digital Content)*

Accounts:
Airbus
Outreach, Inc. Digital Branding, Marketing, Social Media

BORGMEYER MARKETING GROUP
340 N Main St, Saint Charles, MO 63301
Tel.: (636) 946-7677
E-Mail: contact@bmg7677.com
Web Site: www.bmg7677.com

Agency Specializes In: Advertising, Brand Development & Integration, Media Planning, Social Media

Dan Borgmeyer *(CEO)*
Sean Cullen *(CFO)*
Jack Borgmeyer *(VP)*
Kathie Kiethline *(VP-Admin)*
Melissa Wilson Monnig *(VP-Digital Svcs)*
Joe Topor *(VP-Acct Svcs)*
Jordan Agne *(Art Dir)*
Melissa Vahlkamp *(Dir-Media)*
Emily Boatman *(Acct Mgr)*
Alex Renken *(Acct Exec)*

Accounts:
New-Chrysler
New-Dodge
New-RAM

BORN
(Formerly Pod1)
159 W. 25th St, New York, NY 10001
Tel.: (212) 625-8590
Web Site: www.borngroup.com

Agency Specializes In: Advertising, Customer Relationship Management, Digital/Interactive, Graphic Design, Internet/Web Design, Production, Search Engine Optimization, Social Media, Strategic Planning/Research, Web (Banner Ads, Pop-ups, etc.)

Libby Morgan *(Pres)*
Sandeep Kulkarni *(CFO)*
Ramesh Patel *(CTO)*
Keith Pires *(Sr VP & Head-Partner Rels)*
Brad Borman *(VP-Bus Dev-North America)*
Sridhar Tiruchendurai *(VP-Tech)*
Eric Shober *(Dir-Project Mgmt)*
Myles Shipman *(Mgr-Bus Dev)*

Accounts:
D.V.F. Studio
Kenneth Cole Productions, Inc.
The Limited
LK Bennett
Matthew Williamson Ltd
Nanette Lepore
Net-a-Porter Ltd.
Salvatore Ferragamo Italia SpA
Stuart Weitzman
TAG Heuer

BORSHOFF
47 S Pennsylvania St Ste 500, Indianapolis, IN 46204
Tel.: (317) 631-6400
Fax: (317) 631-6499
E-Mail: borshoff@borshoff.biz
Web Site: www.borshoff.biz

Employees: 59
Year Founded: 1984

National Agency Associations: AAF-AMA-COPF-IABC-IPREX-PRSA

Agency Specializes In: Advertising, Brand Development & Integration, Business Publications, Business-To-Business, Collateral, Communications, Consulting, Consumer Marketing, Corporate Communications, Corporate Identity, Crisis Communications, Education, Electronic Media, Entertainment, Environmental, Event Planning & Marketing, Exhibit/Trade Shows, Financial, Government/Political, Graphic Design, Health Care Services, Industrial, Internet/Web Design, Investor Relations, Local Marketing, Logo & Package Design, Media Relations, Media Training, Newspaper, Newspapers & Magazines, Outdoor, Pharmaceutical, Planning & Consultation, Print, Production, Public Relations, Publicity/Promotions, Radio, Real Estate, Restaurant, Retail, Social Media, Strategic Planning/Research, Trade & Consumer Magazines, Transportation, Travel & Tourism

Approx. Annual Billings: $11,500,000

Karen Alter *(Principal)*
Jennifer Berry *(Principal)*
Katherine Coble *(Principal)*
Bill Lovejoy *(Sr VP)*
Steve Beard *(VP & Dir-Creative)*
Linda Jackson *(VP)*
Erin Pipkin *(VP)*
Lindsay Hadley *(Sr Dir-Art)*
Shannon Zajicek *(Sr Dir-Art)*
Andrea Farmer *(Sr Acct Dir)*
Adam Hoover *(Acct Dir)*
Jeff Morris *(Dir-Creative)*
Micah Sitzman *(Dir-Art)*
Jessica Husek *(Copywriter)*

Accounts:
American Legion, Department of Indiana; 2014
City National Bank; Charleston, WV; 2001
Eli Lilly and Company; 2003
Evansville Convention & Visitors Bureau
Franciscan Saint Francis Hospital & Health Centers; Indianapolis, IN; 1985
Indiana Commission for Higher Education; 1997
Indiana Governor's Planning Council for People with Disabilities; Indianapolis, IN; 1985
Indianapolis Indians; 2011
Indianapolis Power & Light Company; Indianapolis, IN; 1990
JD Byrider
Kiwanis International; 2014
MDWise; Indianapolis, IN; 2003
NIPSCO; 2012
OmniSource; 2011
Rose Hulman's Homework Hotline; 2001

BOS ADVERTISING
(Acquired by Dentsu Inc & Merged with Dentsu Canada to Form DentsuBos)

BOS BEAUCHESNE OSTIGUY & SIMARD
(Name Changed to DentsuBos)

BOSCOBEL MARKETING COMMUNICATIONS
8606 2nd Ave, Silver Spring, MD 20910-3326
Tel.: (301) 588-2900
Fax: (301) 588-1363
E-Mail: info@boscobel.com
Web Site: www.boscobel.com

E-Mail for Key Personnel:
President: jbosc@boscobel.com

Employees: 25
Year Founded: 1978

National Agency Associations: IAA-PRSA

Agency Specializes In: Direct Response Marketing, Government/Political, High Technology, Public Relations

Approx. Annual Billings: $2,350,000

Breakdown of Gross Billings by Media: Collateral: $1,200,000; D.M.: $400,000; Mags.: $500,000; Pub. Rels.: $200,000; Trade Shows: $50,000

Joyce L. Bosc *(Pres & CEO)*
Josette Oder-Moynihan *(Program Mgr & Strategist-JODER Comm)*
Michael C. Rudd *(Sr Strategist-PR)*

Accounts:
Appian
Audiopoint
NCI

BOSE PUBLIC AFFAIRS GROUP
111 Monument Cir Ste 2700, Indianapolis, IN 46204
Tel.: (317) 684-5400
E-Mail: rharvey@bosepublicaffairs.com
Web Site: www.bosepublicaffairs.com

Employees: 24

National Agency Associations: IABC-PRSA

Agency Specializes In: Automotive, Communications, Corporate Communications, Crisis Communications, Food Service, Legal Services, Media Relations, Media Training, Pharmaceutical, Public Relations, T.V.

Roger Harvey *(Principal & Mng Dir-Strategic Comm)*
Paul S. Mannweiler *(Principal & Mng Dir-Govt Rels)*
Daniel B. Seitz *(Principal)*
John V. Barnett, Jr. *(Sr VP)*
Donald L. Blinzinger *(Sr VP)*
Carolyn Elliott *(Sr VP)*
Tom E. Fruechtenicht *(Sr VP)*
Justin Swanson *(Second VP)*
Stephen Cooke *(VP)*

Accounts:
Enterprise Rent A Car
The Kroger Company
PhRMA

THE BOSTON GROUP
500 Harrison Ave 3F, Boston, MA 02118
Tel.: (617) 350-7020
Fax: (617) 350-7021
E-Mail: kaplan@bostongroup.com
Web Site: www.bostongroup.com

Employees: 30
Year Founded: 1983

Agency Specializes In: Advertising, Affluent Market, Aviation & Aerospace, Brand Development & Integration, Broadcast, Business-To-Business, Collateral, Consulting, Corporate Communications, Corporate Identity, Customer Relationship Management, Digital/Interactive, Direct Response Marketing, Electronic Media, Email, Event Planning & Marketing, Exhibit/Trade Shows, Financial, Government/Political, Graphic Design, High Technology, Identity Marketing, In-Store Advertising, Information Technology, Integrated Marketing, International, Internet/Web Design, Investor Relations, Local Marketing, Luxury Products, Magazines, Market Research, Media Buying Services, Media Planning, Media Relations, Mobile Marketing, Multimedia, New Product Development, New Technologies, Newspaper, Newspapers & Magazines, Out-of-Home Media, Outdoor, Planning & Consultation, Print, Radio, Retail, Social Media, South Asian Market, Strategic Planning/Research, Viral/Buzz/Word of Mouth, Web (Banner Ads, Pop-ups, etc.)

Leslie Kaplan *(Mng Dir)*
Jennifer DiPinto *(Dir-Media)*
John Grandy *(Dir-Creative Svcs)*
Mihran Minassian *(Dir-Fin & Ops)*
Vaughn Misail *(Dir-Creative)*
Marc David Rapoza *(Assoc Dir-Design)*
Samantha Thu *(Assoc Dir-Media)*
Mark Thompson *(Acct Exec)*

Accounts:
Across World; Boston, MA
Aerospace; El Segundo, CA
The American Urological Association (AUAF); Linthicum, MD
Aqua Leisure; Boston, MA
CIEE; Portland, ME
First Trade Union Bank
Harris IT Services; Dulles, VA
The Jane Goodall Institute; Silver Springs, MD
Monster; Maynard, MA
RAS Beechcraft 1900; Wichita, KS
Raytheon; Waltham, MA
Silverlink Communications; Burlington, MA
Vericept; Waltham, MA

THE BOSWORTH GROUP
113 Wappoo Creek Dr Ste 3, Charleston, SC 29412
Tel.: (843) 795-7944
Fax: (843) 795-7948
E-Mail: info@thebosworthgroup.com
Web Site: www.thebosworthgroup.com

E-Mail for Key Personnel:
Media Dir.: gail@thebosworthgroup.com

Employees: 8
Year Founded: 1984

Agency Specializes In: Advertising, Automotive, Aviation & Aerospace, Brand Development & Integration, Broadcast, Business-To-Business, Collateral, Consulting, Consumer Goods, Consumer Marketing, Corporate Identity, Digital/Interactive, Financial, Graphic Design, Health Care Services, High Technology, Hospitality, Industrial, Internet/Web Design, Logo & Package Design, Luxury Products, Market Research, Media Buying Services, Media Planning, Medical Products, New Product Development, Out-of-Home Media, Package Design, Print, Public Relations, Publicity/Promotions, Real Estate, Restaurant, Sales Promotion, Search Engine Optimization, Social Media, Strategic Planning/Research, Technical Advertising, Travel & Tourism

Approx. Annual Billings: $3,000,000

Kent Bosworth *(Pres & CEO)*
Karin Belajic *(Co-Principal)*
Steve Bosworth *(Principal)*
Gail Bosworth *(Exec VP)*
John Prim *(Dir-Interactive Media)*
Kathy Hallen *(Assoc Dir-Creative)*

Accounts:
Birkam Yoga; Charleston, SC Yoga Studio; 2008
Black Mountain Royalty, LP; Charleston, SC; 2008
Briggs Industries; Charleston, SC Plumbing; 2007
Double Tree Guest Suites; 1996
Geodore Tools; Germany Tool Mfr
Intelifuse; New Orleans, LA Medical Devices; 2004
Peninsula Grill; Charleston, SC Restaurant; 1999
Piedmont Plastic Surgery; Greenwood, SC Plastic Surgery; 1995
Planters Inn; Charleston, SC Hotel & Restaurant; 1994
Weight Watchers of South Carolina; 2000

BOTHWELL MARKETING
651 1st St W Ste M, Sonoma, CA 95476
Tel.: (707) 939-8800
E-Mail: info@bothwellmarketing.com
Web Site: www.bothwellmarketing.com

Employees: 3
Year Founded: 1997

Agency Specializes In: Advertising, Brand Development & Integration, Business-To-Business, Collateral, Communications, Corporate Identity, High Technology, Internet/Web Design, Legal Services

Anne Bothwell *(Pres)*

Accounts:
Downey Brand LLP
Keker & VanNest
Knobbe Martens Olson & Bear LLP
Selman Breitman LLP

BOTTLEROCKET MARKETING GROUP
(Acquired by Brand Connections)

BOTTOM LINE MARKETING
5001 Ln 17.7 Dr, Escanaba, MI 49829
Tel.: (906) 786-3445
Fax: (906) 786-4797
E-Mail: info@bottomlineblack.com
Web Site: www.bottomlineblack.com

Agency Specializes In: Advertising, Brand Development & Integration, Business-To-Business, Graphic Design, Media Buying Services, Search Engine Optimization, Social Media

Chris Brooks *(Owner)*
Annette Brooks *(VP)*

Accounts:
New-Crockers Jewelers
New-Riverside Auto Group

BOUCHARD MCELROY COMMUNICATIONS GROUP INC.
1430 Blue Oaks Blvd Ste 280, Roseville, CA 95747-5156
Tel.: (916) 783-6161
Fax: (916) 783-5161
E-Mail: info@bouchardcommunications.com
Web Site: www.bouchardmarketing.com

Employees: 10

National Agency Associations: Second Wind Limited

Revenue: $1,000,000

Ron Goff *(Dir-Tech)*
Bryan Kohl *(Dir-Art-Digital Svcs)*
Jairo Moncada *(Dir-PR)*
Lisa Pujals *(Dir-Creative)*
Manuel Alcala *(Office Mgr)*
Troy Dutton *(Office Mgr)*
Reanna Fraser *(Acct Mgr)*

Accounts:
Burrell Consulting Group Inc.
CU Advisory Services
ImageAvenue

BOUVIER KELLY INC.

212 S Elm St Ste 200, Greensboro, NC 27401-2631
Tel.: (336) 275-7000
Fax: (336) 275-9988
E-Mail: bkiinc@bouvierkelly.com
Web Site: www.bouvierkelly.com

E-Mail for Key Personnel:
President: lbouvier@bouvierkelly.com
Creative Dir.: mturner@bouvierkelly.com
Media Dir.: sneal@bouvierkelly.com

Employees: 20
Year Founded: 1974

National Agency Associations: AAF-PRSA-Second Wind Limited

Agency Specializes In: Advertising, Agriculture, Automotive, Brand Development & Integration, Broadcast, Cable T.V., Collateral, Consumer Marketing, Corporate Communications, Corporate Identity, Crisis Communications, Digital/Interactive, Direct Response Marketing, Education, Entertainment, Environmental, Event Planning & Marketing, Financial, Food Service, Government/Political, Health Care Services, Identity Marketing, Media Buying Services, Media Planning, Media Relations, Medical Products, Production (Ad, Film, Broadcast), Public Relations, Real Estate, Restaurant, Retail, Strategic Planning/Research, T.V., Trade & Consumer Magazines, Transportation

Breakdown of Gross Billings by Media: Cable T.V.: 5%; Collateral: 8%; Consulting: 5%; Corp. Communications: 1%; D.M.: 2%; Event Mktg.: 1%; Exhibits/Trade Shows: 1%; Internet Adv.: 5%; Logo & Package Design: 1%; Newsp.: 8%; Outdoor: 1%; Pub. Rels.: 7%; Sls. Promo.: 2%; Spot Radio: 17%; Spot T.V.: 19%; Strategic Planning/Research: 5%; Trade & Consumer Mags.: 10%; Worldwide Web Sites: 2%

Suzanne Neal *(Owner)*
Louis M. Bouvier, Jr. *(Chm)*
Denny Kelly *(Chm)*
Pete Parsells *(Pres & CEO)*
Lesley Thompson *(Dir-Media)*
Phillip Yeary *(Dir-Creative)*
Debbie Fuchs *(Acct Mgr & Specialist-Digital Media)*
Elaney Katsafanas *(Mgr-PR)*

Accounts:
Ad Club
Aerialite
BGF Industries
Chrysler Classic
The Community Foundation
Gate City Chop House
Lucor, Inc. d/b/a Jiffy Lube; Raleigh, NC
McDonald's Triad Co-op Public Relations
Neese Country Sausage; Greensboro, NC
New Breed; High Point, NC
Phillip Morris USA-Trade Communications
RMIC; Winston-Salem, NC Mortgage Insurance
Sheraton Greensboro Public Relations
Smith Moore LLP; 2004
Syngenta Crop Protection
Technology Concepts & Design, Inc.
Terminix Triad Pest Control; 2007

BOWSTERN

1725 Capital Cir NE Ste 205, Tallahassee, FL 32308
Tel.: (888) 912-1110
Fax: (888) 907-7771
E-Mail: info@bowstern.com
Web Site: www.bowstern.com

Agency Specializes In: Advertising, Brand Development & Integration, Event Planning & Marketing, Logo & Package Design, Print, Public Relations, Social Media

Tom Derzypolski *(Principal)*
Kelly Robertson *(Principal)*
Jeremy Spinks *(VP-Online Design)*
Jaclyn Lapointe *(Acct Mgr & Strategist-Comm)*
Chris Lueking *(Strategist-Social Media)*
Jonathan Watt *(Strategist-Digital)*
Whitney Nunn *(Designer-Web)*
Dana King *(Jr Designer)*

Accounts:
Open Door Adoption

BOXING CLEVER

1017 Olive St, Saint Louis, MO 63101-2019
Tel.: (314) 446-1861
Web Site: www.boxing-clever.com

Employees: 20

Agency Specializes In: Advertising, Brand Development & Integration, Market Research, Mobile Marketing, Package Design, Public Relations, Search Engine Optimization, Sponsorship

Dave Scott *(Owner & Pres)*
Chris Barbee *(Dir-Art)*
Rick Hecke *(Dir-Copywriting)*
Mike Pringle *(Dir-Digital Production)*
Jeff Rifkin *(Dir-Creative)*
Aaron Kalman *(Office Mgr-HR & Accts Receivable)*
Liz Sartorius *(Acct Exec)*
Chase Koeneke *(Copywriter)*
Mary Dohle *(Acct Coord)*

Accounts:
Actual Produce
Brown-Forman Corp. (Agency of Record) Finlandia Vodka
Chambord Liqueur
Southern Comfort
St. Louis Rams
Tuaca Liqueur Beverages Distr
Woodford Reserve; Versailles, KY Creative, Digital Marketing, Events, Mobile, Promotions

BOYCE MEDIA GROUP LLC

11 S Angell St Ste 376, Providence, RI 2906
Tel.: (401) 757-3966
Fax: (401) 757-3967
Web Site: www.boycemedia.com

Agency Specializes In: Advertising, Brand Development & Integration, Internet/Web Design, Media Buying Services, Social Media, Strategic Planning/Research, T.V.

Andrew Boyce *(Pres)*

Accounts:
Bald Hill Kia
El Potro Mexican Bar & Grill
Valentino Photography
Wes Rib House

BOYDEN & YOUNGBLUTT ADVERTISING & MARKETING

120 W Superior St, Fort Wayne, IN 46802
Tel.: (260) 422-4499
Fax: (260) 422-4044
E-Mail: talk@b-y.net
Web Site: www.b-y.net

Employees: 32
Year Founded: 1990

Agency Specializes In: Consumer Marketing, Education, Financial, Health Care Services, Medical Products

Andy Boyden *(Owner)*
Jerry Youngblutt *(Co-Owner)*
Andrea Atwood *(Dir-Art)*
Linda Clevenger *(Dir-Digital Mktg)*
Bartholomew Fish *(Dir-Art)*
Draper Matthews *(Dir-Digital Media)*
Ian Mosher *(Dir-Creative)*
Leanne Mcdaniel *(Office Mgr & Media Buyer)*
Brooke Coe *(Sr Acct Exec)*
Sarah Wartman *(Sr Acct Exec)*
Gavin Saxer *(Specialist-Social Media)*

Accounts:
3 Rivers FCU
Dupont Hospital
IPFW
Monarch Marine
Ortho NorthEast (Agency of Record)
Parkview Hospitals
Red Gold

THE BOYER SYNDICATE, INC.

1800 Century Park E Ste 600, Los Angeles, CA 90067
Tel.: (310) 229-5956
Fax: (310) 455-1817
E-Mail: mark@boyersyn.com
Web Site: www.boyersyn.com

Year Founded: 1995

Agency Specializes In: Consumer Marketing, Financial, Food Service, Health Care Services, New Technologies, Travel & Tourism

Mark Boyer *(Partner)*
Sandra Loden *(Partner)*

Accounts:
American Honda Motor Co.
Bergen Brunswig
Health Net
Mattel
McDonald's
Pacific Bell At Hand
Prudential

BOYLAN POINT AGENCY

2525 Cleveland Ave, Santa Rosa, CA 95403
Tel.: (707) 544-3390
Web Site: www.boylanpoint.com

Agency Specializes In: Advertising, Graphic Design, Internet/Web Design, Logo & Package Design, Print, Radio

Tom Boylan *(Owner & Dir-Creative)*

Accounts:
Empire Asphalt, Inc.

Advertising Agencies

Leff Construction & Development, Corp.

BOZEKEN, LLC

110 W Lancaster Ave Ste 130, Wayne, PA 19087
Tel.: (610) 293-2200
Fax: (610) 293-2201
E-Mail: info@bozeken.com
Web Site: go.bozeken.com

Employees: 7

Agency Specializes In: Brand Development & Integration, Consulting, Radio, T.V.

Mike Zeko *(Founder, Mng Partner & Dir-Creative)*
Ken Michaud *(Mng Partner)*
John Galante *(VP-Television Programming & Dev-New Bus Dev & Strategist)*
Mike Fanelle *(VP-Programming & Dev)*

Accounts:
Amoroso's Bakery
Louisiana Office of Culture, Recreation & Tourism; 2008

BOZELL

1022 Leavenworth St, Omaha, NE 68102
Tel.: (402) 965-4300
Fax: (402) 965-4399
E-Mail: omaha@bozell.com
Web Site: www.bozell.com

Employees: 50
Year Founded: 1921

Agency Specializes In: Advertising, Advertising Specialties, Brand Development & Integration, Broadcast, Business Publications, Business-To-Business, Cable T.V., Catalogs, Collateral, Communications, Consulting, Consumer Goods, Consumer Marketing, Consumer Publications, Content, Corporate Communications, Corporate Identity, Crisis Communications, Customer Relationship Management, Digital/Interactive, Direct Response Marketing, Direct-to-Consumer, Electronic Media, Email, Event Planning & Marketing, Exhibit/Trade Shows, Faith Based, Financial, Food Service, Graphic Design, Guerilla Marketing, Health Care Services, High Technology, Integrated Marketing, Internet/Web Design, Logo & Package Design, Luxury Products, Magazines, Market Research, Media Buying Services, Media Planning, Media Relations, Media Training, New Product Development, New Technologies, Newspaper, Newspapers & Magazines, Out-of-Home Media, Outdoor, Over-50 Market, Package Design, Paid Searches, Planning & Consultation, Print, Production (Print), Promotions, Public Relations, Radio, Regional, Restaurant, Search Engine Optimization, Social Marketing/Nonprofit, Social Media, Sponsorship, Sports Market, Strategic Planning/Research, T.V., Trade & Consumer Magazines, Viral/Buzz/Word of Mouth, Web (Banner Ads, Pop-ups, etc.), Women's Market

Approx. Annual Billings: $60,000,000

Andrea Groom *(Partner-PR)*
David Moore *(Partner-Creative)*
Jackie Miller *(CMO)*
Bruce Hartford *(Sr Dir-Art)*
Heather McCain *(Dir-Art)*
Laura Spaulding *(Mgr-Corp Comm)*
Megan Wills *(Media Buyer)*
Robin Donovan *(Mng Principal)*
Kim Mickelsen *(Mng Principal-Integrated Mktg)*

Accounts:
Ace Hardware/Westlake; NE, TX, KS, MI Digital Display, Web; 2010
Blue Cross Blue Shield; NE
Catholic Charities; NE
College World Series (NCAA); IN Men's College Baseball
Creative Marketing
First National Bank; NE; MO; TX; CO Campaign: "Heartbeat"
JDRF Type II Diabetes; 2012
Knowles Law Firm; NE
Lauritzen Gardens; Omaha, NE Botanical Gardens
Literacy Center
The Magician; NE Marlin Briscoe The First Black Quarterback Movie
Market-to-Market; Omaha, NE Relay Race
McGrath; 2011
Mutual of Omaha
National Safety Council; NE
Nationwide Learning
Nebraska Wesleyan University
Presbyterian Health Health System; 2011
Right At Home Home Healthcare
Tnemec Company, Inc. Industrial Coatings
United Way of the Midlands
Vic's Popcorn Popcorn
VP Buildings Metal Buildings
WriteLife Publishing

BPCM

550 Broadway 3rd Fl, New York, NY 10012
Tel.: (212) 741-0141
Fax: (212) 741-0630
E-Mail: ny@bpcm.com
Web Site: www.bpcm.com

Year Founded: 1999

Agency Specializes In: Consulting, Event Planning & Marketing, Fashion/Apparel, International, Public Relations, Regional, Strategic Planning/Research

Carrie Ellen Phillips *(Owner)*
Vanessa Weiner von Bismarck *(Owner)*
Tara Cathcart *(VP)*
Lyman Carter *(Dir-Creative)*
Travis Paul Martin *(Dir-Fashion)*
Sarah Pallack *(Dir-Travel, Wine & Spirits)*
Sydney Hyunah Oh *(Acct Exec)*
Kelsey Schilit *(Acct Exec)*
Kelsey Hogan *(Assoc Acct Exec-Menswear)*
Sharon Park *(Asst Acct Exec)*
Georgia Vickerson *(Asst Acct Exec)*

Accounts:
ALDO Shoes & Accessories
Alice Roi
Brian Atwood Accessories Collections
Carlos Miele Fashion Designers
IWC Watch Mfr
Langham Place Fifth Avenue PR
MODO Optical Frames & Sunglass Producers

BPG ADVERTISING

110 S Fairfax Blvd, Los Angeles, CA 90036
Tel.: (323) 954-9522
Web Site: www.bpgadvertising.com

Agency Specializes In: Advertising, Broadcast, Digital/Interactive, Internet/Web Design, Print, Social Media, Sponsorship

Steph Sebbag *(Pres & Chief Creative Officer)*
Andy Robbins *(COO & Exec VP-Interactive)*
Tom Krentzin *(VP-Fin)*
Sam Contreras *(Sr Dir-Art)*
Keith Wildasin *(Sr Dir-Creative Strategy)*
Ilisa Whitten *(Sr Producer-Interactive)*
Bobby Besabe *(Assoc Dir-Creative-Interactive)*
Richard D'Alessio *(Sr Creative Dir)*

Accounts:
History Channel
MGM
PETA Campaign: "Beyond Words"

BQR ADVERTISING & PUBLIC RELATIONS

2500 Tanglewilde St Ste 105, Houston, TX 77063
Tel.: (713) 952-7100
Fax: (713) 952-7144
E-Mail: vickir@bqradvertising.com
Web Site: www.bqradvertising.com

Employees: 6
Year Founded: 1987

Agency Specializes In: Advertising, Alternative Advertising, Aviation & Aerospace, Bilingual Market, Brand Development & Integration, Broadcast, Business Publications, Business-To-Business, Co-op Advertising, Collateral, Communications, Consumer Marketing, Corporate Identity, Event Planning & Marketing, Financial, Government/Political, Graphic Design, Guerilla Marketing, Health Care Services, Hispanic Market, Identity Marketing, Internet/Web Design, Local Marketing, Logo & Package Design, Magazines, Market Research, Media Buying Services, Media Planning, Media Relations, Newspaper, Newspapers & Magazines, Outdoor, Package Design, Print, Production, Production (Print), Promotions, Public Relations, Publicity/Promotions, Publishing, Radio, Retail, Sales Promotion, Social Media, Transportation, Travel & Tourism, Women's Market

Approx. Annual Billings: $3,300,000

Breakdown of Gross Billings by Media: Collateral: $300,000; Consulting: $300,000; Graphic Design: $300,000; Print: $1,500,000; Radio & T.V.: $300,000; Strategic Planning/Research: $300,000; Worldwide Web Sites: $300,000

Vicki A. Roy *(Owner)*
Max Montemayor *(Dir-Art)*
Maria Jimenez *(Acct Coord)*

BR CREATIVE

175 Derby St Ste 39, Hingham, MA 02043
Tel.: (781) 749-8990
Fax: (781) 749-8997
E-Mail: br@brcreative.com
Web Site: www.brcreative.com

Employees: 10
Year Founded: 1991

Agency Specializes In: Advertising, Broadcast, Cable T.V., Consulting, Entertainment, Event Planning & Marketing, Seniors' Market, T.V., Travel & Tourism

Approx. Annual Billings: $5,000,000

Barry Rosenthal *(Pres & Dir-Creative)*
Dick Weisberg *(Mng Dir)*

BRABENDERCOX

108 South St, Leesburg, VA 20175
Tel.: (703) 896-5300
Fax: (703) 896-5315
Web Site: www.brabendercox.com

Year Founded: 1982

Agency Specializes In: Advertising, Communications, Content, Digital/Interactive, Electronic Media, Email, Government/Political, Graphic Design, Internet/Web Design, Media Buying Services, Media Planning, Media Relations, Multimedia, Planning & Consultation, Production, Production (Ad, Film, Broadcast), Production (Print), Radio, Social Media, Strategic Planning/Research, T.V., Web (Banner Ads, Pop-ups, etc.)

John Brabender *(Co-founder & Chief Creative Officer)*
Robert Aho *(Partner)*
Tiffany D'Alessandro *(Partner)*
John Fischerkeller *(Editor-Broadcast)*
Tricia Hegener-Carr *(Sr Dir-Art)*
Alicia Heffley *(Acct Supvr)*
Megan Howie *(Strategist-Digital)*
Chris Pratt *(Copywriter)*

Accounts:
Citizens for Strong New Hampshire Web Video
Highmark
The New York Republican State Committee Website

BRAD
3451 Blvd Saint-Laurent 2nd Fl, Montreal, QC H2X 2T6 Canada
Tel.: (514) 871-1616
Web Site: www.brad.ca

Agency Specializes In: Advertising

Martin Bernier *(Co-Pres)*
Dany Renauld *(Co-Pres)*
Carle Coppens *(VP & Dir-Creative)*
Stephane Veilleux *(VP & Dir-Creative)*
Jasmin Brochu *(Sr Dir-Art)*
Francis Ouellet *(Dir-Print Production & Graphic Designer)*
Yvan Cote *(Dir-Creative)*

Accounts:
Labatt Breweries of Canada Budweiser 4
LEGO
Together Against Bullying

BRAD RITTER COMMUNICATIONS
3801 Olentangy River Rd, Delaware, OH 43015
Tel.: (866) 284-2170
E-Mail: info@bradritter.com
Web Site: www.bradritter.com

Agency Specializes In: Advertising, Crisis Communications, Electronic Media, Graphic Design, Media Relations, Media Training, Print, Strategic Planning/Research

Brad Ritter *(Pres)*

Accounts:
Sizzler USA

BRADFORDLAWTON, LLC
1020 Townsend Ave, San Antonio, TX 78209
Tel.: (210) 832-0555
Fax: (210) 732-8555
Web Site: www.bradfordlawton.com

Employees: 10

Bradford Lawton *(Owner)*

Accounts:
Taco Cabana; San Antonio, TX Account Planning, Branding, Campaign: "Taco Cabana Outdoor", Creative, Digital Media, Local Store Marketing Development, Print, Broadcast & Digital Production

BRADLEY & MONTGOMERY ADVERTISING
342 E Saint Joseph St, Indianapolis, IN 46204
Tel.: (317) 423-1745
Web Site: www.bamideas.com

Employees: 23
Year Founded: 2000

Agency Specializes In: Advertising, Sponsorship

Mark Bradley *(Pres)*
Benjamin Carlson *(Chief Strategy Officer)*
Scott Montgomery *(Principal)*
Suzanne Williams *(Controller)*
Laurie Schneider *(Client Svcs Dir)*
Steve Brand *(Dir-Art)*
Brian Harris *(Dir-Creative)*

Accounts:
Angie's List Inc Brand Positioning, SnapFix, TV
Chase
Microsoft Internet Explorer 9, Microsoft Small Business, Office 2007
RJE Knoll

BRADSHAW ADVERTISING
811 NW 19th Ave, Portland, OR 97209-1401
Tel.: (503) 221-5000
Fax: (503) 241-9000
E-Mail: info@bradshawads.com
Web Site: www.bradshawads.com

E-Mail for Key Personnel:
President: barb@bradshawads.com
Media Dir.: emilie@bradshawads.com

Employees: 15
Year Founded: 1986

Agency Specializes In: Advertising, Automotive, Aviation & Aerospace, Brand Development & Integration, Broadcast, Business Publications, Business-To-Business, Cable T.V., Co-op Advertising, Collateral, Consulting, Consumer Marketing, Consumer Publications, Corporate Identity, Financial, Health Care Services, Logo & Package Design, Media Buying Services, New Product Development, Newspapers & Magazines, Out-of-Home Media, Outdoor, Over-50 Market, Planning & Consultation, Point of Purchase, Print, Production, Public Relations, Publicity/Promotions, Radio, Real Estate, Restaurant, Retail, Seniors' Market, Strategic Planning/Research, T.V., Trade & Consumer Magazines, Travel & Tourism, Yellow Pages Advertising

Approx. Annual Billings: $23,000,000 Capitalized

Breakdown of Gross Billings by Media: Newsp. & Mags.: 4%; Outdoor: 2%; Production: 18%; Radio: 48%; T.V.: 27%; Transit: 1%

Barbara Bradshaw *(Pres)*
Emilie Timmer *(Dir-Media)*
Tammy Wallace *(Acct Mgr)*
Raija Talus *(Mgr-Production)*
Nan Janik *(Acct Exec)*

Accounts:
Alpenrose Dairy
Carr Chevy World
Health Net of Oregon
Miller Paint
Norris, Beggs & Simpson
Shilo Inns

BRAINBLAZE ADVERTISING & DESIGN
355 Scenic Rd, Fairfax, CA 94930
Tel.: (415) 250-3020
E-Mail: info@brainblaze.com
Web Site: www.brainblaze.com

Year Founded: 2005

Agency Specializes In: Advertising, Collateral, Corporate Identity, Email, Internet/Web Design, Logo & Package Design, Outdoor, Print, Social Media, Strategic Planning/Research

Patrick Yore *(Owner & Chief Creative Officer)*
Kim Neumann *(Copywriter)*

Accounts:
Pacific Precious Metals Gold is a Rush

BRAINCHILD CREATIVE
2001 California St Ste 101, San Francisco, CA 94109
Tel.: (415) 922-1482
E-Mail: info@brainchildcreative.com
Web Site: www.brainchildcreative.com

Year Founded: 2001

Deborah Notestein Loeb *(Partner)*
Jef Loeb *(Dir-Creative, Strategist-Brand & Sr writer)*

Accounts:
Flex Alert
PG&E Corporation

BRAINERD COMMUNICATORS, INC.
1370 Broadway, New York, NY 10018
Tel.: (212) 986-6667
Fax: (212) 739-6301
E-Mail: info@braincomm.com
Web Site: www.braincomm.com

Employees: 30
Year Founded: 1994

Agency Specializes In: Collateral, Communications, Consumer Marketing, Crisis Communications, Customer Relationship Management, Event Planning & Marketing, Internet/Web Design, Investor Relations, Media Relations, Media Training, Sponsorship, Strategic Planning/Research, Viral/Buzz/Word of Mouth, Web (Banner Ads, Pop-ups, etc.)

Revenue: $3,100,000

Scott Cianciulli *(Mng Dir)*
Anthony Herrling *(Mng Dir)*
Corey Kinger *(Mng Dir)*
Joseph LoBello *(Mng Dir)*
Giovanni Garcia *(CFO)*
Denise Roche *(Sr VP)*
Brad Edwards *(Assoc Mng Dir)*
Nancy Zakhary *(Assoc Mng Dir-PR)*

Accounts:
The Management Network Group, Inc.

BRAINIUM INC.
373 S Willow Ste 197, Manchester, NH 03103
Tel.: (603) 661-5172
E-Mail: nfo@brainiuminc.com
Web Site: brainiuminc.com

Employees: 6
Year Founded: 2000

Agency Specializes In: Event Planning & Marketing

Kathryn Conway *(Partner)*
Kimberley Griswold *(Partner)*

Accounts:
Aviation Week & Space Technology
Cornerstone Software
Engineering News Record Magazine
McGraw-Hill Construction

BRAINS ON FIRE, INC.
148 River St Ste 100, Greenville, SC 29601
Tel.: (864) 676-9663
Fax: (864) 672-9600

E-Mail: firestarter@brainsonfire.com
Web Site: www.brainsonfire.com

E-Mail for Key Personnel:
President: robbin@brainsonfire.com
Creative Dir.: gregc@brainsonfire.com
Media Dir.: jack@brainsonfire.com

Employees: 20
Year Founded: 1982

Agency Specializes In: Brand Development & Integration, Broadcast, Business-To-Business, Collateral, Communications, Consulting, Consumer Marketing, Corporate Identity, E-Commerce, Event Planning & Marketing, Financial, Food Service, Graphic Design, Health Care Services, High Technology, Internet/Web Design, Logo & Package Design, Medical Products, Merchandising, Multimedia, New Product Development, Newspaper, Newspapers & Magazines, Planning & Consultation, Point of Purchase, Point of Sale, Print, Production, Radio, Restaurant, Sales Promotion, Strategic Planning/Research, T.V.

Approx. Annual Billings: $5,400,000

Breakdown of Gross Billings by Media: Collateral: $270,000; Newsp.: $270,000; Other: $2,700,000; Outdoor: $270,000; Pub. Rels.: $540,000; Radio: $540,000; T.V.: $810,000

Robbin Phillips *(Pres)*
Jack Welch *(Dir-Media)*
Moe Megan *(Mgr-Community & Social Media)*
Amy Taylor *(Mgr-Social Media & Community Mgr)*
Cathy Harrison *(Sr Acct Exec)*
Emily Everhart *(Community Mgr & Acct Exec)*
Sean Madden *(Sr Designer)*
Greg Ramsey *(Designer)*

Accounts:
American Booksellers Association
Bon Secours Heath System
Carolina's Health System
Daggar Kayaks
Harris & Graves; Columbia, SC Law Firm; 1990
Perception Kayaks

BRAINSHINE
11650 Ramsdell Ct, San Diego, CA 92131
Tel.: (858) 635-8900
E-Mail: info@brainshine.com
Web Site: www.brainshine.com

Agency Specializes In: Advertising, Brand Development & Integration, Digital/Interactive, Media Buying Services, Media Planning, Outdoor, Public Relations, Radio, Strategic Planning/Research, T.V.

Blaise Nauyokas *(Pres & Creative Dir)*

Accounts:
San Diego Water Authority

BRAINSTORM MEDIA
7111 W 151st St Ste 311, Overland Park, KS 66223
Tel.: (913) 219-0104
Fax: (877) 803-8474
Web Site: www.bsmedia.net

Agency Specializes In: Advertising, Logo & Package Design, Radio

Randy Miller *(Owner)*
Greg Lawyer *(Dir & Producer)*
Bruce Knox *(Sr Acct Mgr)*
Pamela Hall *(Office Mgr)*
Bill Jingo *(Mgr-Production)*
Matt Stoessner *(Mgr-Post Production)*
Ryan Newell *(Specialist-Media)*

Accounts:
Pride Cleaners Inc
Veterans of Foreign Wars

BRAINSTORMS ADVERTISING & MARKETING, INC.
2201 Wilton Dr, Fort Lauderdale, FL 33305-2131
Tel.: (954) 564-2424
Fax: (954) 564-2320
E-Mail: info@brainstorms.net
Web Site: www.brainstorms.net

Employees: 5
Year Founded: 1983

National Agency Associations: AAF

Agency Specializes In: Brand Development & Integration, Business-To-Business, Co-op Advertising, Collateral, Consumer Marketing, Consumer Publications, Corporate Identity, Cosmetics, Environmental, Exhibit/Trade Shows, Graphic Design, Health Care Services, High Technology, Internet/Web Design, Logo & Package Design, Magazines, Marine, Media Buying Services, Medical Products, Multimedia, New Product Development, Newspaper, Newspapers & Magazines, Pharmaceutical, Planning & Consultation, Print, Production, Public Relations, Publicity/Promotions, Real Estate, Recruitment, Sales Promotion, Strategic Planning/Research, Trade & Consumer Magazines, Travel & Tourism

Revenue: $1,600,000

Frank Ferraro *(Pres)*
Nick Ravine *(VP & Dir-Creative)*

BRAINSWITCH ADVERTISING
250 NW 23rd St Ste 210, Miami, FL 33127
Tel.: (305) 576-1415
Fax: (305) 397-1103
Web Site: www.brainswitchad.com

Year Founded: 2006

Agency Specializes In: Advertising, Brand Development & Integration, Direct Response Marketing, Internet/Web Design, Logo & Package Design, Outdoor, Point of Purchase, Radio, T.V., Web (Banner Ads, Pop-ups, etc.)

Jose Rementeria *(Pres & Exec Dir-Creative)*
Reinaldo Vargas *(Acct Dir)*

Accounts:
Black & Decker Inc.
Canon U.S.A., Inc.
Sony Corporation of America Handycam, Cyber-shot

BRAINTRUST
8948 Spanish Ridge Ave, Las Vegas, NV 89148
Tel.: (702) 862-4242
E-Mail: info@braintrustlv.com
Web Site: www.braintrustlv.com

Agency Specializes In: Advertising, Digital/Interactive, Event Planning & Marketing, Public Relations, Social Media

Kurt Ouchida *(Mng Partner)*
Michael Coldwell *(Mng Partner)*
Glen Scott *(Creative Dir)*
Gabriela Raguay *(Acct Dir)*
Monica Vanyo *(Acct Dir)*

Accounts:
New-Regional Transportation Commission of Southern Nevada

BRALEY DESIGN
306 E 3rd St, Brooklyn, NY 11218
Tel.: (415) 706-2700
E-Mail: braley@braleydesign.com
Web Site: www.braleydesign.com

Agency Specializes In: Advertising, Brand Development & Integration, Package Design, Print

Kate Davis *(Dir-Creative & Acct Dir)*
Michael Braley *(Dir-Creative)*

BRAMBLETT GROUP
106 W Main St Ste C, Henderson, TN 38340
Tel.: (731) 989-8019
E-Mail: info@bramblettgrp.com
Web Site: www.bramblettgrp.com

Year Founded: 2006

Agency Specializes In: Advertising, Event Planning & Marketing, Internet/Web Design, Media Relations, Print, Public Relations, Social Media

Jason Bramblett *(Co-Owner)*
Dawn Bramblett *(Co-Owner)*

Accounts:
Freed-Hardeman University

BRAMSON + ASSOCIATES
7400 Beverly Blvd, Los Angeles, CA 90036-2725
Tel.: (323) 938-3595
Fax: (323) 938-0852
Web Site: www.bramson-associates.com

E-Mail for Key Personnel:
Creative Dir.: gbramson@aol.com

Employees: 5
Year Founded: 1970

Agency Specializes In: Advertising, African-American Market, Alternative Advertising, Asian Market, Brand Development & Integration, Business-To-Business, Collateral, Consulting, Consumer Goods, Consumer Marketing, Corporate Identity, Cosmetics, Exhibit/Trade Shows, Financial, Food Service, Graphic Design, Health Care Services, Hospitality, Identity Marketing, In-Store Advertising, Industrial, International, Internet/Web Design, Logo & Package Design, Luxury Products, Medical Products, Merchandising, Multicultural, New Product Development, Newspapers & Magazines, Package Design, Pharmaceutical, Planning & Consultation, Point of Purchase, Point of Sale, Print, Real Estate, Restaurant, Retail, Strategic Planning/Research, Trade & Consumer Magazines, Travel & Tourism

Approx. Annual Billings: $4,388,350

Breakdown of Gross Billings by Media: Bus. Publs.: $1,025,000; Collateral: $2,138,000; Comml. Photography: $75,000; Consulting: $125,000; Consumer Publs.: $25,000; E-Commerce: $76,000; Farm Publs.: $38,000; Graphic Design: $276,000; In-Store Adv.: $16,800; Internet Adv.: $5,000; Logo & Package Design: $63,450; Mags.: $33,000; Mdsg./POP: $28,000; Production: $383,000; Spot Radio: $5,000; Trade & Consumer Mags.: $36,000; Trade Shows: $18,100; Worldwide Web Sites: $22,000

Gene Bramson *(Principal)*
Rhonda Bramson *(Treas & Sec)*

Accounts:
GLB Properties

BRAND ACTION TEAM, LLC
1 Darling Dr, Avon, CT 06001
Tel.: (860) 676-7900
Fax: (860) 679-0290
Web Site: www.thebrandactionteam.com

Agency Specializes In: Advertising, Brand Development & Integration, Digital/Interactive, Public Relations, Social Media

Jeff Grindrod *(Mng Partner)*
Steve Raye *(Mng Partner)*
Amber Gallaty *(VP-Consumer PR)*
Kayla Joyce *(Acct Exec)*
Kiersten Pedersen *(Acct Coord & Media Planner)*

Accounts:
SmarteRita
TANDUAY Marketing, PR

BRAND ADVERTISING GROUP
3399 Tates Creek Rd Ste 125, Lexington, KY 40502
Tel.: (859) 293-5760
Fax: (859) 255-0421
Web Site: www.baglex.com

Year Founded: 2003

Agency Specializes In: Advertising, Digital/Interactive, Graphic Design, Media Buying Services, Print, Social Media

Susie Hampton Merida *(Pres)*
Jamie Ayler *(Dir-Media)*
Teresa Willis *(Dir-Creative)*

Accounts:
Fayette Heating & Air

BRAND AGENT
2626 Cole Ave, Dallas, TX 75204
Tel.: (214) 979-2040
Fax: (214) 979-2100
E-Mail: kshahane@brand-agent.com
Web Site: www.brand-agent.com

Employees: 20
Year Founded: 2004

Agency Specializes In: Advertising, Advertising Specialties, Alternative Advertising, Brand Development & Integration, Branded Entertainment, Business Publications, Business-To-Business, Catalogs, Collateral, Commercial Photography, Consulting, Consumer Goods, Consumer Marketing, Consumer Publications, Corporate Communications, Corporate Identity, Cosmetics, Direct Response Marketing, Direct-to-Consumer, Fashion/Apparel, Food Service, Graphic Design, Health Care Services, Hispanic Market, Household Goods, In-Store Advertising, Internet/Web Design, Leisure, Local Marketing, Logo & Package Design, Luxury Products, Magazines, Multimedia, New Product Development, Newspapers & Magazines, Outdoor, Package Design, Paid Searches, Pets , Point of Purchase, Point of Sale, Print, Product Placement, Production, Production (Print), Promotions, Publicity/Promotions, Retail, Sales Promotion, Sponsorship, Syndication, Trade & Consumer Magazines, Women's Market

Approx. Annual Billings: $2,500,000

Breakdown of Gross Billings by Media: Graphic Design: $1,925,000; Other: $200,000; Print: $75,000; Production: $250,000; Worldwide Web Sites: $50,000

Damien Gough *(Owner & CEO)*
Bruce Wynne-Jones *(Exec Dir-Creative)*
Rebecca Pequeno *(Dir-Art)*
Kavita Shahane *(Dir-Bus Dev)*
Jeff Buchanan *(Assoc Dir-Creative)*
Angela Vasquez *(Sr Acct Exec)*

Accounts:
Dad's Pet Care; 2005
Frito-Lay; Plano, TX; 2004
Riviana Foods; 2000
Varsity Brands; Dallas, TX; 2004

BRAND ARC
11845 W Olympic Blvd Ste 850, Los Angeles, CA 90064
Tel.: (310) 893-6116
Fax: (310) 893-6117
Web Site: www.brandarc.com

Year Founded: 2005

Agency Specializes In: Advertising, Branded Entertainment, Digital/Interactive, Event Planning & Marketing, Media Planning, Strategic Planning/Research

Rob Donnell *(Founder & Pres)*
Michael Davis *(COO)*
Jina Yu *(Sr Acct Mgr)*
Kristen Waltman *(Mgr-Social Media Strategy)*

Accounts:
Toyota Motor North America, Inc. Campaign: "Modern Family", Prius & Sienna

BRAND CENTRAL STATION
5012 State St, Bettendorf, IA 52722
Tel.: (563) 359-8654
Fax: (563) 324-0842
Toll Free: (800) 669-1505
E-Mail: mbawden@brandcentralstation.com
Web Site: www.brandcentralstation.com

Employees: 1

Agency Specializes In: Advertising, Brand Development & Integration, Communications, Consulting, Corporate Identity, E-Commerce, Public Relations, Publicity/Promotions

Approx. Annual Billings: $3,500,000

Mike Bawden *(Pres & CEO)*

BRAND CONNECTIONS
910 Nottingham Rd, Avon, CO 81620
Tel.: (970) 748-0330
Fax: (970) 748-9113
Web Site: www.brandconnections.com

Employees: 7
Year Founded: 1994

Agency Specializes In: Out-of-Home Media, Outdoor

Sherry Orel *(CEO)*
Robbie Scholl *(Pres-Keeplan Winter Sports Div)*
Richard Thompson *(Exec VP)*
Dorathy Balsano *(Sr VP-Mktg Svcs)*
Janell Goldbloom *(Sr VP-New Bus Dev)*

Accounts:
Emergen-C
Tylenol

BRAND CONTENT
580 Harrison Ave, Boston, MA 02118
Tel.: (617) 338-9111
Fax: (617) 338-9121
E-Mail: hr@brandcontent.com
Web Site: www.brandcontent.com

Employees: 40
Year Founded: 2001

Agency Specializes In: Advertising, Brand Development & Integration, Broadcast, Communications, Direct Response Marketing, Print, Web (Banner Ads, Pop-ups, etc.)

Doug Gladstone *(CEO & Chief Creative Officer)*
Tom Kelly *(Exec Dir-Creative)*
Lindsay Sullivan *(Acct Svcs Dir)*
Matt Sasso *(Dir-Art)*
Stephanie Taubin *(Dir-Creative Svcs)*
Adam Proia *(Mgr-Studio)*
Nicole Leistinger *(Sr Acct Exec)*
Meaghan O'Hara *(Sr Acct Exec)*
Lauren Hokenson *(Acct Exec)*
Lindsey Campbell *(Copywriter)*

Accounts:
Blue Seal
Constant Contact
Dealer Rater
Diageo
Drinking in America
HP Hood
Jeremiah Weed Whiskey
Just Shorn Wool
Keurig
Monster
Piehole Whiskey
Stirrings

BRAND COOL MARKETING INC
2300 E Ave, Rochester, NY 14610
Tel.: (585) 381-3350
Fax: (585) 381-3425
Web Site: www.brandcool.com

Agency Specializes In: Advertising, Brand Development & Integration, Broadcast, Collateral, Content, Digital/Interactive, Email, Event Planning & Marketing, Internet/Web Design, Outdoor, Print, Search Engine Optimization, Social Media

Sue Kochan *(CEO)*
Holly Barrett *(VP-Agency Svcs)*
Kevin DiMaggio *(Dir-Creative)*
Christina Williams *(Dir-Procurement)*
James Bogue *(Assoc Dir-Creative)*
T. C. Pellett *(Mgr-Social Strategy)*
Christine Testa *(Mgr-Creative Svcs)*
Brie Spinetto *(Sr Acct Exec)*
Tom Colling *(Copywriter & Strategist)*

Accounts:
Rohrbach Brewing Company

BRAND FEVER
(Acquired by Phase 3 Marketing & Communications)

BRAND FEVER
342 Marietta St Ste 3, Atlanta, GA 30313
Tel.: (404) 523-2606
Fax: (404) 522-6187
Web Site: www.brandfeverinc.com

Employees: 25

Agency Specializes In: Advertising, Brand Development & Integration, Corporate Communications, Digital/Interactive, Event Planning & Marketing, Exhibit/Trade Shows, Internet/Web Design, Promotions

Vicky Jones *(Pres)*

Ty Collins *(Sr Producer-Digital)*
Kendra Lively *(Dir-Creative)*
Stephanie Roppolo *(Dir-New Bus Dev & Mktg)*
Megan Tinkler *(Sr Acct Mgr)*
Meghan Crosser *(Mgr-Design)*
Hilary Dahl *(Mgr-Mktg)*

Accounts:
AVOXI

BRAND INNOVATION GROUP

(d/b/a Big Design & Advertising)
8902 Airport Dr Ste A, Fort Wayne, IN 46809
Tel.: (260) 469-4060
Fax: (260) 469-4050
Toll Free: (866) 469-4080
E-Mail: info@gotobig.com
Web Site: www.gotobig.com

Employees: 20
Year Founded: 1995

Agency Specializes In: Advertising, Brand Development & Integration, Broadcast, Collateral, Corporate Communications, Corporate Identity, Digital/Interactive, E-Commerce, Environmental, Faith Based, Graphic Design, Guerilla Marketing, Integrated Marketing, Internet/Web Design, Logo & Package Design, Media Buying Services, Mobile Marketing, Package Design, Paid Searches, Planning & Consultation, Public Relations, Sales Promotion, Search Engine Optimization, Social Media

Ben Gregory *(Dir-Mktg & Strategist-Brand)*
Greg Becker *(Dir-Art)*
John Crilly *(Dir-Mktg)*
Kelli Hartsock *(Acct Mgr)*
Andy Barnes *(Mgr-Digital Creative)*
Ted Rubin *(Acting CMO & Strategist-Social Mktg)*

Accounts:
Alliance Bank
The Andersons
Aunt Millie's Bakeries
Best Home Furnishings
Brotherhood Mutual Insurance Company
Centier Bank
David C. Cook
Ellison Bakery
Missionary Church
Prairie Quest Consulting (Agency of Record)
Rescue Mission Ministries
Skytech
Transformation Furniture
Turtletop
Uncle Ed's Oil Shoppe

Branch

AccessPoint

3925 River Crossing Pkwy Ste 60, Indianapolis, IN 46240
Tel.: (317) 525-8441
Fax: (317) 705-0263
E-Mail: info@xspt.com
Web Site: www.xspt.com

Employees: 12

Tom Downs *(Owner)*
Charlie Ingram *(Exec VP-Dev)*
Jeanne Nugent *(Exec VP-Client Svcs)*
Jill Hannigan *(Dir-HR)*
Susan Keith *(Dir-HR)*
Mike Miller *(Dir-Bus Dev)*

BRAND IT ADVERTISING

122 N Raymond Rd Ste 2, Spokane, WA 99206
Tel.: (509) 891-8300
Fax: (509) 891-8302
Web Site: www.branditadvertising.net

Agency Specializes In: Advertising, Corporate Identity, Logo & Package Design, Print, Radio, T.V.

Dan Mathews *(Owner)*
Michelle Dennison *(Dir-Art)*

Accounts:
Spokane Valley Cancer Center

BRAND LUCENCE

28 W. 36th St. Ste 901, New York, NY 10018
Tel.: (646) 770-1405
Web Site: www.brandlucence.com

Year Founded: 2013

Agency Specializes In: Advertising, Affiliate Marketing, Alternative Advertising, Arts, Brand Development & Integration, Branded Entertainment, Business-To-Business, Collateral, Commercial Photography, Communications, Consulting, Consumer Goods, Consumer Marketing, Corporate Identity, Cosmetics, Digital/Interactive, Education, Email, Entertainment, Guerilla Marketing, High Technology, Identity Marketing, Integrated Marketing, Legal Services, Local Marketing, Multimedia, New Technologies, Planning & Consultation, Promotions, Public Relations, Publicity/Promotions, Strategic Planning/Research, Viral/Buzz/Word of Mouth, Web (Banner Ads, Pop-ups, etc.)

Sherri Valenti *(Founder)*

Accounts:
Kent Miller Photography

BRAND MATTERS INC.

220 Bay St Ste 600, PO Box 7, Toronto, ON M5J 2W4 Canada
Tel.: (416) 923-7476
Fax: (416) 352-0147
E-Mail: contact@brand-matters.com
Web Site: www.brandmatters.ca

Agency Specializes In: Advertising, Brand Development & Integration

Patricia McQuillan *(Founder & Pres)*
Dwayne Brookson *(Dir-Creative)*
Jeffrey Vanlerberghe *(Sr Designer & Strategist-Creative)*
Ellen Cooper *(Planner-Brand)*

Accounts:
Canada Life Assurance Company
Empire Life

THE BRAND SQUAD

6000 Poplar Ave Ste 250, Memphis, TN 38119
Tel.: (901) 866-9402
Fax: (901) 261-5411
E-Mail: jerry@TheBrandSquad.com
Web Site: www.theBrandSquad.com

E-Mail for Key Personnel:
President: jehrlich@cecnet.com

Employees: 2
Year Founded: 1977

Agency Specializes In: Above-the-Line, Advertising, Agriculture, Below-the-Line, Brand Development & Integration, Broadcast, Business-To-Business, Cable T.V., Catalogs, Collateral, Consulting, Consumer Goods, Consumer Marketing, Corporate Communications, Corporate Identity, Direct Response Marketing, Direct-to-Consumer, Electronic Media, Electronics, Environmental, Event Planning & Marketing, Exhibit/Trade Shows, Faith Based, Financial, Graphic Design, Guerilla Marketing, Health Care Services, Hospitality, Household Goods, Integrated Marketing, Internet/Web Design, Leisure, Local Marketing, Logo & Package Design, Magazines, Marine, Market Research, Media Buying Services, Media Planning, Media Relations, Media Training, Medical Products, New Product Development, Newspaper, Out-of-Home Media, Outdoor, Package Design, Planning & Consultation, Point of Sale, Print, Production, Production (Ad, Film, Broadcast), Production (Print), Promotions, Public Relations, Publicity/Promotions, Radio, Real Estate, Retail, Sales Promotion, Search Engine Optimization, Social Marketing/Nonprofit, Social Media, Strategic Planning/Research, T.V., Technical Advertising, Trade & Consumer Magazines, Transportation, Travel & Tourism, Viral/Buzz/Word of Mouth, Web (Banner Ads, Pop-ups, etc.)

Approx. Annual Billings: $4,000,000

Breakdown of Gross Billings by Media: Brdcst.: 30%; Bus. Publs.: 10%; Collateral: 10%; Consumer Publs.: 10%; D.M.: 5%; Farm Publs.: 10%; Graphic Design: 10%; Internet Adv.: 5%; Logo & Package Design: 5%; Newsp.: 5%

Jerry Ehrlich *(Pres & Chief Creative Officer)*
Lynn Bugg *(VP-Brand Dev)*

Accounts:
AutoZone Liberty Bowl; Memphis, TN; 2001
Baber Direct; Memphis, TN Printing & Direct Marketing Services; 2009
Ledic Management; Memphis, TN Property Management Services; 2008
Philips; Atlanta, GA Electronics; 1984
Pilot Realty Investments; Memphis, TN Real Estate; 2008
RiceCo LLC; Memphis TN Herbicides; 2008
S & B Packaging Corp.; Memphis, TN Packaging & DIsplays; 2009
Sickle Cell Foundation of Tennessee; Memphis,TN Healthcare; 2009

BRAND TANGO INC.

426 S Military Trl, Deerfield Beach, IL 33442
Tel.: (954) 295-7879
Fax: (954) 333-3764
Toll Free: (888) 318-3532
E-Mail: info@brand-tango.com
Web Site: www.brand-tango.com

Year Founded: 2005

Agency Specializes In: Advertising, Brand Development & Integration, Graphic Design, Internet/Web Design, Social Media

James Kluetz *(Pres & Chief Creative Officer)*
Paul Cooper *(Assoc Dir-Creative)*
Michael Hoesten *(Acct Supvr)*

Accounts:
AMResorts
Club Melia
Cruise & Excursions Inc.
Dial An Exchange
Karisma Resorts
Silverleaf Resorts Inc

THE BRAND UNION

114 Fifth Ave 11th Fl, New York, NY 10011-5604
Tel.: (212) 755-4200
Fax: (212) 755-9474
E-Mail: info@thebrandunion.com
Web Site: www.thebrandunion.com

Employees: 35

National Agency Associations: 4A's

Agency Specializes In: Brand Development & Integration, Sponsorship

Rob Scalea *(CEO-North America)*
Toby Southgate *(CEO-Worldwide)*
Jamie Ambler *(Exec Creative Dir)*
Matt Norcia *(Exec Dir-Americas)*
Joanna Padden *(Grp Acct Dir)*
Sheralyn Silverstein *(Creative Dir & Writer)*
Wally Krantz *(Dir-Creative-Worldwide)*

Accounts:
The Absolut Company Brand Redesign, Vodka
Bank of America
Baroque Japan Campaign: "Launch Event & Pop Up Store"
Bay Care
Brand USA Logo
Caesar Dog Food
CBRE Group Campaign: "Build on Advantage", Online, Print, Social Media
Corporation For Travel Promotions Campaign: "Brand Usa"
Domtar Corp. EarthChoice, Visual Identity Logo & Guidelines
Futuro
Hewlett Packard
IPC
Leica Campaign: "Company Outing"
Pernod-Ricard
Time Warner Cable
Vodafone Power of Red

Branches

The Brand Union London
11-33 Saint John Street, London, EC1M 4PJ United Kingdom
Tel.: (44) 20 7559 7000
Fax: (44) 20 7559 7001
E-Mail: info@thebrandunion.com
Web Site: www.thebrandunion.com

Employees: 150
Year Founded: 1976

Agency Specializes In: Brand Development & Integration

Terry Tyrrell *(Chm)*
Craig Fabian *(Vice Chm-Worldwide)*
John Shaw *(Head-Strategy & Plng-Worldwide)*
Paul Cardwell *(Exec Creative Dir)*
Clare Styles *(Exec Dir-Creative)*
Adam Lawrenson *(Creative Dir)*
Mark Chatelier *(Dir-Creative)*

Accounts:
ABSA
Aegon UK
AENA
Aldar Properties
Argos
Bank of America
Beverage Partners Worldwide
British Gas
Club Colombia
Dansa Foods
De Beers
Deloitte
Eskom
Fidelity Campaign: "Fidelity Rebrand"
GAA
GlaxoSmithKline Global Branding
Heineken Campaign: "Kaiser"
Hewlett Packard
Indesit Company
Land Rover Campaign: "Above and Beyond"
Mattel
Motorola Solutions, Inc.
Oskar Mobil
Royal London Arching Architecture, Strategy, Visual and Verbal Identity
New-Simplyhealth Group Denplan
Unilever
Vodafone Power of Red

The Brand Union Shanghai
26 F The Ctr 989 Changle Rd, Shanghai, 200031 China
Tel.: (86) 21 2405 1777
Fax: (86) 21 2405 1799
E-Mail: info@thebrandunion.com

Monica Lee *(CEO)*
Juan Tan *(Exec Dir-Creative-China)*
Angeline Kong *(Acct Dir)*
Flora Liang Yan *(Acct Dir)*
Michael Huang *(Dir-Creative)*
Dandan Shaw *(Dir-Strategy)*
Mengxi Wang *(Strategist-Brand)*
Terrence Zhang *(Sr Designer)*

Accounts:
COFCO Group
China Everbright Bank
China Mobile
Dyson
Goodyear
ICBC
The Mars Group
Pernod Ricard
Petrochina Lubricant Company Kunlun
Pudong Development Bank
SIG
SPD Bank
Suntech
XinAo

The Brand Union Hong Kong
23rd Floor 99 Queens Road, Central, China (Hong Kong)
Tel.: (852) 2568 0255
Fax: (852) 2567 0622
E-Mail: info.hongkong@thebrandunion.com
Web Site: www.thebrandunion.com

Year Founded: 1982

Agency Specializes In: Brand Development & Integration

Benedict Gordon *(Mng Dir)*
Alan Couldrey *(CEO-Asia)*
Karen Mak *(Gen Mgr)*
Andrew Reynolds *(Dir-Creative)*
Dandan Shaw *(Dir-Strategy)*

Accounts:
Shanghai DreamCenter

The Brand Union
Forum Bldg 5th Fl 2 Maude St, Sandton, 2146 South Africa
Tel.: (27) 11 895 9300
Fax: (27) 11 895 9301
Web Site: www.brandunion.com/connect/johannesburg

Employees: 40

Agency Specializes In: Brand Development & Integration

Kagiso Musi *(Mng Dir-Africa)*
Mathew Weiss *(Mng Dir-Cape Town)*
Janet Kinghorn *(Exec Dir-Creative-South Africa)*
Farhana Waja *(Exec Dir-Fin)*
Natali Dukhi *(Client Svcs Dir)*
Jacqui Richards *(Client Svcs Dir)*
Kyley Roos *(Designer)*
Samantha Le Roux *(Sr Client Mgr-Africa)*

Accounts:
Absa
Chrysler LLC
FirstRand
Kentucky Fried Chicken
Kulula.com
Lexus
SABMiller
Sun International
Toyota
UBA (Nigeria)
Vodafone

The Brand Union Dubai
Tower B Bus Central Towers, PO Box 74021, 43rd Fl Sheikh Zayed Rd, Dubai, United Arab Emirates
Tel.: (971) 4 360 8911
Fax: (971) 4 360 8912
E-Mail: info.dubai@thebrandunion.com
Web Site: www.thebrandunion.com

Employees: 15

Agency Specializes In: Brand Development & Integration, Graphic Design

Majdoleen Till *(Mng Dir)*
John Moraes *(Controller-Fin-The Brand Union ME)*
Danielle Jooste *(Dir-Bus Dev)*
Gemma Petch *(Dir-Design)*
Belinda Jones *(Sr Acct Mgr)*
Zeeshan Mirza *(Mgr-IT)*
Colin De Sa *(Asst Controller-Fin)*

Accounts:
ALDAR Properties
Al Hilal Bank
Al Rahji Bank
Limitless
Tawuniya
Vodafone

The Brand Union Dublin
9 Upper Pembroke St, Dublin, 2 Ireland
Tel.: (353) 1 613 1650
Fax: (353) 1 662 5771
E-Mail: info@thebrandunion.ie
Web Site: www.thebrandunion.com/

Employees: 20
Year Founded: 1990

Agency Specializes In: Brand Development & Integration

Steve Payne *(Mng Partner)*
Andrea Bridge *(Mgr-Comm)*

Accounts:
An Post
Barena
Credit Suisse
Diageo
Freshways Prepackaged Food-to-Go
GAA
Giddy Goose
Irish Electricity Supply Board Creative Design
Malibu
National Lottery
Premier League
Vodafone

The Brand Union GmbH
Bahrenfelder Chaussee 49, 22761 Hamburg, Germany
Tel.: (49) 40 899 04 0
Fax: (49) 40 899 04 222
E-Mail: empfang@hamburg.thebrandunion.com

Web Site: www.brandunion.com/connect/hamburg

Employees: 50
Year Founded: 1983

Agency Specializes In: Brand Development & Integration, Logo & Package Design

Katie Taylor *(Exec Dir-Creative)*
Thekla Wege *(Exec Dir-Bus Dev & Corp Comm-Germany)*
Jinhi Kim *(Dir-Design)*
Volker Stolting *(Dir-Design)*
Pamela Tailor *(Dir-Design)*
Antje Escher *(Mgr-Mktg & PR)*
Amelie Winkler *(Strategist-Brand)*
Stephan Pantel *(Sr Designer)*

Accounts:
Cannes Lions Design
Henkel Deodorants, Hair Colorants
OSRAM
Unilever
Vattenfall
Vodafone

The Brand Union Paris

26 Rue Notre-Dame des Victoires, 75002 Paris, France
Tel.: (33) 1 53 45 33 00
Fax: (33) 1 53 45 33 33
E-Mail: info.paris@thebrandunion.com
Web Site: www.thebrandunion.com

Year Founded: 1999

Agency Specializes In: Brand Development & Integration

Celine Derosier *(Mng Dir)*
Stephane Ricou *(CEO-Paris & Moscow)*
Marie-Astrid Delaine *(Acct Dir)*
Isabelle Baldini *(Dir-Client)*
Adrien Deltour *(Dir-New Bus)*
Rob Evers *(Dir-Creative)*
Vincent Lebrun *(Dir-Creative)*
Camille Yvinec *(Dir-Strategic Plng)*
Alice Amiel *(Designer)*
Celine Haine *(Sr Designer)*
Nicolas Minisini *(Planner-Strategic)*

Accounts:
ABSA
AENA
Aegon UK
Arla Kohet
Barena
Central Market
Cornerstone
Dansa Foods
Doux Group
Eskom

The Brand Union

Sveavagen 9-11, P.O. Box 7042, SE-103 86 Stockholm, Sweden
Tel.: (46) 8 440 8000
Fax: (46) 8 210 299
E-Mail: info.stockholm@thebrandunion.com
Web Site: www.thebrandunion.com

Employees: 18

Agency Specializes In: Brand Development & Integration

Hans Brindfors *(Chm)*
Johan Hesslefors *(Head-Plng)*
Louise Henning *(Controller-Fin)*
Mattias Lindstedt *(Exec Dir-Creative)*
Ted Carlstrom *(Dir-Client)*
Patrik Gebhardt *(Dir-Creative)*
Patrick Hammarsten *(Dir-Design)*
Jesper Klarin *(Dir-Art)*
Daniel Lofvenborg *(Dir-Design)*
Anna Yo Lee *(Sr Designer)*
Arne Lind *(Sr Designer)*
Britt-Marie Moller *(Client Mgr)*

Accounts:
Arla
Ikea
Pernod Ricard Absolut Elyx
Posten
Swedish Match
Vattenfall
Vodafone Power of Red

BRAND33

1304 El Prado Ave Ste D, Torrance, CA 90501
Tel.: (310) 320-4911
Fax: (310) 320-2875
E-Mail: info@brand33.com
Web Site: www.brand33.com

Agency Specializes In: Advertising, Brand Development & Integration, Internet/Web Design, Media Buying Services, Media Planning, Outdoor, Package Design, Print, Radio, Strategic Planning/Research

Mike Dean *(Pres & CEO)*
Rebecca Alexander *(Acct Dir)*
Rebecca Fenster *(Acct Dir)*
Tammy Mcnair *(Mgr-Production)*
Joli Barretta *(Acct Exec)*
Jacob Bain *(Jr Designer)*
Cecilia Navarrete *(Jr Designer)*

Accounts:
GQ-6

BRANDADVISORS

512 Union St, San Francisco, CA 94133
Tel.: (415) 393-0800
Web Site: www.brandadvisors.com

Agency Specializes In: Advertising, Market Research

Charles Rashall *(Founder, Pres & Chief Architect-Brand)*

BRANDDIRECTIONS

(Formerly Directions Marketing)
333 N. Commercial St, Neenah, WI 54956
Tel.: (920) 725-4848
Fax: (920) 725-9359
Toll Free: (800) 236-2189
E-Mail: info@brand-directions.com
Web Site: www.brand-directions.com

Employees: 40
Year Founded: 1955

National Agency Associations: Second Wind Limited

Agency Specializes In: Advertising, Bilingual Market, Brand Development & Integration, Business Publications, Business-To-Business, Co-op Advertising, Collateral, Consulting, Consumer Publications, Corporate Identity, Customer Relationship Management, Direct Response Marketing, Education, Email, Food Service, Graphic Design, Internet/Web Design, Leisure, Logo & Package Design, Magazines, Media Buying Services, Newspaper, Newspapers & Magazines, Planning & Consultation, Point of Purchase, Point of Sale, Print, Production, Public Relations, Publicity/Promotions, Sponsorship, Strategic Planning/Research, Trade & Consumer Magazines, Travel & Tourism, Web (Banner Ads, Pop-ups, etc.)

Approx. Annual Billings: $7,900,000

Breakdown of Gross Billings by Media: Collateral: 15%; D.M.: 5%; Logo & Package Design: 65%; Point of Purchase: 2%; Strategic Planning/Research: 7%; Trade & Consumer Mags.: 2%; Worldwide Web Sites: 4%

Kristine R. Sexton *(Pres & CEO)*
Lisa Gaupp *(Dir-Bus Dev)*
Chip Ryan *(Dir-Creative)*
Kathleen Schnettler *(Dir-Fin & Admin)*
Angela Reynolds *(Acct Mgr)*
Kay Knorr *(Acct Exec)*

Accounts:
Appleton
Bemis Manufacturing
Kaytee Awesome Blends
Kimberly-Clark Corp.
Kraft
Laminations
Nature's Defense
SCA
WS Packaging

BRANDESIGN

981 Rt 33 W, Monroe Township, NJ 08831
Tel.: (609) 490-9700
E-Mail: info@brandesign.com
Web Site: www.brandesign.com

Barbara Harrington *(Pres)*

Accounts:
Turkey Hill Dairy, Inc.

BRANDEXTRACT, LLC

7026 Old Katy Rd Ste 210, Houston, TX 77024
Tel.: (713) 942-7959
Fax: (713) 942-0032
Web Site: www.brandextract.com

Employees: 32

Agency Specializes In: Brand Development & Integration, Communications, Digital/Interactive

Jonathan Fisher *(Chm)*
Bo Bothe *(Pres & CEO)*
Greg Weir *(Partner & VP-Digital Mktg & Analytics)*
Malcolm Wolter *(VP-Interactive)*
Cynthia Stipeche *(Dir-User Experience)*
Elizabeth Tindall *(Strategist-Brand)*

BRANDFIRE

555 8th Ave Ste 901, New York, NY 10018
Tel.: (212) 378-4236
E-Mail: info@brandfire.com
Web Site: www.brandfire.com

National Agency Associations: 4A's

Agency Specializes In: Advertising, Brand Development & Integration, Collateral, Corporate Identity, Internet/Web Design, Logo & Package Design

Adam Padilla *(Founder & Pres)*
Erica Jaffe *(Exec Dir-Bus Dev)*
Bryan Black *(Exec Creative Dir)*

Accounts:
Caroline Manzo BBQ

BRANDHIVE

(Formerly Integrated Marketing Group (IMG))
146 W Pierpont Ave, Salt Lake City, UT 84101
Tel.: (801) 538-0777
Fax: (801) 538-0780

E-Mail: jeffhilton@brandhive.com
Web Site: www.brandhive.com

E-Mail for Key Personnel:
President: jeffhilton@brandhive.com

Employees: 15
Year Founded: 1996

National Agency Associations: PRSA

Agency Specializes In: Advertising, Brand Development & Integration, Business-To-Business, Children's Market, Consumer Marketing, Consumer Publications, Corporate Communications, Corporate Identity, Exhibit/Trade Shows, Graphic Design, Internet/Web Design, Logo & Package Design, Merchandising, Multimedia, New Product Development, Public Relations, Retail, Sales Promotion, Strategic Planning/Research

Approx. Annual Billings: $4,000,000

Breakdown of Gross Billings by Media: Graphic Design: 20%; Logo & Package Design: 20%; Pub. Rels.: 20%; Strategic Planning/Research: 10%; Trade & Consumer Mags.: 30%

Jeff Hilton *(Co-Founder & CMO)*
James Fagedes *(Dir-Art)*
Giles Wallace *(Dir-Art)*
Meet Nagar *(Acct Mgr)*
Lisa Openshaw *(Media Buyer)*
Ida Baghoomian *(Sr Counsel-PR)*
Courtney Morton *(Sr Counsel-PR)*
Heidi Rosenberg *(Sr Counsel-PR)*

Accounts:
AppleActiv Creative, Interactive, Media Buying, Public Relations
Bergstrom Nutrition Creative Development, Media Buying, OptiMSM, Public Relations, Strategic Planning

BRANDIMAGE DESGRIPPES & LAGA
990 Skokie Blvd, Northbrook, IL 60062
Tel.: (847) 291-0500
Fax: (847) 291-0516
E-Mail: nb@brand-image.com
Web Site: www.brand-image.com

Employees: 300
Year Founded: 1971

Agency Specializes In: Brand Development & Integration, Graphic Design, Internet/Web Design, Package Design, Sponsorship

Joel Desgrippes *(Owner)*
Scott Lucas *(Mng Dir)*
Howard Alport *(Principal)*
Robert Swan *(VP & Exec Dir-Creative)*
Marc C. Fuhrman *(VP-Acct Dev)*
Brian Silver *(VP-Bus Dev)*
Lori Cerwin *(Dir-Creative)*
Sheri Harris *(Dir-Strategy)*
Walter Perlowski *(Dir-Creative)*
Tamara Silver *(Dir-Design)*

Accounts:
Air France-KLM Group
AOL; New York, NY
Banana Republic; Grove City, OH
Black & Decker
The Credit Agricole Group
Fauchon; New York, NY
General Mills; Minneapolis, MN
Nestle; Switzerland
Payless Holdings
Sky Team
Staples
Telefonica
Toto; GA
Vicaima

BRANDING IRON MARKETING
3119 Bristol Hwy, Johnson City, TN 37601-1564
Tel.: (423) 202-3252
Fax: (423) 202-3252
Web Site: brandingiron.com/

Agency Specializes In: Advertising

Scott Emerine *(Owner)*
Sheila Reed *(Coord-Mktg & PR)*

Accounts:
Dallas Avionics

BRANDINGBUSINESS
(Formerly RiechesBaird, Inc.)
1 Wrigley, Irvine, CA 92618
Tel.: (949) 273-6330
Fax: (949) 586-1201
Web Site: www.brandingbusiness.com

Employees: 25
Year Founded: 1985

Agency Specializes In: Brand Development & Integration, Business Publications, Business-To-Business, Direct Response Marketing, E-Commerce, Health Care Services, High Technology, Industrial, Information Technology, Internet/Web Design, Medical Products, Public Relations, Real Estate, Trade & Consumer Magazines

Approx. Annual Billings: $40,000,000

Ryan Rieches *(Co-Founder & CEO)*
Raymond W. Baird, II *(Co-Founder)*
Michael Dula *(Chief Creative Officer)*
Alan Brew *(Principal)*
Derek Wilksen *(Exec VP)*
Dustin King *(VP-Brand Mgmt Svcs)*
Andrea Fabbri *(Dir-Strategy)*
Pam Walker *(Dir-Fin & HR)*

Accounts:
ABM Industries
American Airlines Cargo Campaign: "Did You Know?"
New-BFS Capital
New-Booker Brand Positioning, Brand Strategy
Children's National Medical Center; Washington, D.C Brand Agency Of Record
Custom Building Products
Hitachi Consulting
Huawei Technologies USA Campaign: "Promise of the Future"
New-McKissack & McKissack
OneOC Campaign: "Accelerating Nonprofit Success"
Schreiber Foods Brand Strategy
Sharp
New-Skillsoft Brand Positioning, Integrated Brand Strategy
Toshiba
Toyota

BRANDKARMA
(Formerly Core-Create Inc.)
100 Franklin Sq Dr Ste 201, Somerset, NJ 08873-1128
Tel.: (732) 748-0433
Fax: (732) 748-0430
Web Site: www.brandkarma.org

Employees: 30
Year Founded: 1991

Agency Specializes In: Advertising, Advertising Specialties, Health Care Services, Medical Products, Pharmaceutical

Approx. Annual Billings: $60,000,000

Breakdown of Gross Billings by Media: Audio/Visual: 5%; Bus. Publs.: 20%; Collateral: 25%; D.M.: 20%; Mags.: 10%; Newsp.: 5%; Pub. Rels.: 10%; Sls. Promo.: 5%

Craig Davis *(Founder)*
Dorene Weisenstein *(Owner, Chief Creative Officer & Exec VP)*
Paul Moorcroft *(CFO & COO)*
Jami Crabtree *(Sr Acct Exec)*

Accounts:
Bristol-Myers Squibb; NJ Pharmaceutical Products; 2000
HealthPoint; Fort Worth, TX; 2000

THE BRANDMAN AGENCY
261 5th Ave Fl 22, New York, NY 10016
Tel.: (212) 683-2442
Fax: (212) 683-2022
E-Mail: info@brandmanpr.com
Web Site: www.brandmanpr.com

Employees: 26

Agency Specializes In: Broadcast, Communications, Crisis Communications, Electronics, Event Planning & Marketing, Food Service, Local Marketing, Media Training, Print, Product Placement, Promotions, Public Relations, Publicity/Promotions, Restaurant, Strategic Planning/Research

Revenue: $2,000,000

Melanie Brandman *(Founder & CEO)*
Kristen Vigrass *(Pres)*
Kara Hoffman *(VP)*
Keri Toler Kirschner *(VP)*
Emily Grubb *(Sr Dir)*
Stephanie Krajewski *(Acct Dir)*
Lee Edelstein *(Acct Mgr)*
Daphna Barzilay *(Acct Supvr)*
Katie Clark *(Sr Acct Exec)*
Elena Gaudino *(Sr Acct Exec)*
Kristen Fattizzi *(Acct Exec)*

Accounts:
Barbados Tourism Authority
Belmond
Destination Hotels & Resorts
Exclusive Resorts
FRHI Hotels & Resorts
Grand Hotel Tremezzo Public Relations
Independent Collection (Public Relations Agency of Record)
Kensington Tours
La Mamounia
Loews Hollywood Hotel
Los Angeles Tourism & Convention Board
Molori Private Retreats
Munge Leung
Oberoi Hotels & Resorts
Orion Expedition Cruises
Palmer House Hilton
Park Hyatt New York
Qantas Airlines (Agency of Record)
The Ritz-Carlton, San Francisco
Scottsdale Convention & Visitors Bureau Communications
The Setai Miami Beach
Tourism Council of Bhutan

Branch

The Brandman Agency Inc.
8444 Wilshire Blvd 6th Fl, Beverly Hills, CA 90211
Tel.: (323) 944-0064
E-Mail: la@thebrandmanagency.com

Web Site: www.thebrandmanagency.com

Agency Specializes In: Event Planning & Marketing, Media Relations, Public Relations, Social Media

Ty Bentsen *(Mng Dir)*
Kara Hoffman *(VP)*
Daphna Barzilay *(Acct Dir)*
Stephanie Krajewski *(Acct Dir)*
Maggie Lacasse *(Acct Supvr)*
Katie Clark *(Sr Acct Exec)*
Kristen Fattizzi *(Acct Exec)*

Accounts:
A Rosa River Cruises
LA Tourism & Convention Board
Scottsdale Convention & Visitors Bureau
Worldview Travel

BRANDNER COMMUNICATIONS, INC.

32026 32nd Ave S, Federal Way, WA 98001
Tel.: (253) 661-7333
Fax: (253) 661-7336
E-Mail: kbrandner@brandner.com
Web Site: www.brandner.com

Employees: 29
Year Founded: 1988

Agency Specializes In: Advertising

Kimberly Brandner *(Dir-Mktg & Client Svcs)*
Paul Brandner *(Dir-Ops)*
Stephen Henry *(Dir-Creative)*
Brad Loveless *(Mgr-Mktg)*
Ashley Nagley *(Mgr-Digital Mktg)*
Scott Donnelly *(Acct Supvr)*
Natasha Valach *(Acct Supvr)*
Karlie Kirk *(Acct Exec-PR)*

Accounts:
ChoiceDek
Coffman Stairs
Lyptus
Microsoft Corporation
Puget Sound Fly Co.
QLube
Simpson Door
Travis Industries
Vitro America
Weyerhauser

THE BRANDON AGENCY

3023 Church St, Myrtle Beach, SC 29577
Tel.: (843) 916-2000
Fax: (843) 916-2050
Web Site: www.thebrandonagency.com/

E-Mail for Key Personnel:
President: sbrandon@brandonadvertising.com

Employees: 38
Year Founded: 1959

National Agency Associations: DMA-Second Wind Limited

Agency Specializes In: Advertising, Aviation & Aerospace, Co-op Advertising, Direct Response Marketing, E-Commerce, Electronic Media, Environmental, Financial, Health Care Services, Information Technology, Leisure, Logo & Package Design, Media Buying Services, Medical Products, Out-of-Home Media, Public Relations, Real Estate, Retail, Strategic Planning/Research, Travel & Tourism

Approx. Annual Billings: $22,000,000

Breakdown of Gross Billings by Media: Brdcst.: $7,000,000

Tyler Easterling *(Pres & COO)*
Barry Sanders *(Exec VP-New Bus Dev)*
Erin Barrett *(Dir-PR)*
Brian Dorman *(Dir-Info Sys)*
Emily Randisi *(Acct Mgr)*
Sherry Moats *(Mgr-Media)*
Ashley Bruno *(Assoc Mgr-Social Media)*
Sarah Lovingood *(Media Buyer)*

Accounts:
Anderson Brothers Bank
Beaufort Regional Chamber of Commerce Creative Development, Enrichment, Interactive, Media Planning & Buying, PR, Social Media
Broadway at the Beach
Burroughs & Chapin Company
Caledonia Golf & Fish Club; Pawleys Island, SC Daily Fee Golf
Cast Audio Poster
CBL & Associates
Edisonlearning
Farmers Telephone Cooperative Campaign: "Sketchy"
High Point Regional Health System Stitches
The Litchfield Company; Litchfield Beach, SC Real Estate
Marina Inn
Myrtle Beach Golf Holiday; Myrtle Beach, SC Golf Vacation Destination
Myrtle Beach National Co.; Myrtle Beach, SC Daily Fee Golf
Myrtle Beach South Carolina Chamber of Commerce
National Golf Management
Pine Lakes Country Club
Rensant Bank
Rensant Bank; Myrtle Beach, SC
RePower South Creative, Marketing, Public Relations, SEO, Social Media, Website
RJ Rockers Gruntled Pumpkin Ale
Sonesta Gwinnett Place
Sonesta Resort Hilton Head Island
South Carolina Tobacco Collaborative Campaign: "Smoke Free Horry"
Southern Tide, LLC
SpiritLine Cruises
Springs Creative Products Group
Wild Dunes Real Estate
Williams Knife Company Culinary Arts, Precious Mettle

BRANDSCAPES

(Formerly Hardy Communications Development)
16333 Ohio St, Omaha, NE 68116
Tel.: (402) 991-8823
Web Site: www.mybrandscapes.com

Employees: 10
Year Founded: 2005

Agency Specializes In: Advertising, Affluent Market, Alternative Advertising, Arts, Automotive, Aviation & Aerospace, Brand Development & Integration, Branded Entertainment, Broadcast, Business-To-Business, Cable T.V., Collateral, College, Communications, Computers & Software, Consulting, Consumer Goods, Consumer Marketing, Consumer Publications, Content, Corporate Communications, Corporate Identity, Customer Relationship Management, Digital/Interactive, Direct Response Marketing, Direct-to-Consumer, E-Commerce, Education, Electronic Media, Electronics, Email, Entertainment, Event Planning & Marketing, Exhibit/Trade Shows, Fashion/Apparel, Financial, Food Service, Game Integration, Graphic Design, Guerilla Marketing, Health Care Services, High Technology, Household Goods, Identity Marketing, Integrated Marketing, Internet/Web Design, Leisure, Local Marketing, Logo & Package Design, Luxury Products, Magazines, Market Research, Media Buying Services, Media Planning, Media Relations, Medical Products, Mobile Marketing, Multimedia, New Product Development, New Technologies, Newspaper, Newspapers & Magazines, Out-of-Home Media, Outdoor, Package Design, Podcasting, Point of Purchase, Point of Sale, Print, Product Placement, Production, Production (Ad, Film, Broadcast), Production (Print), Promotions, Public Relations, Publicity/Promotions, RSS (Really Simple Syndication), Radio, Restaurant, Retail, Search Engine Optimization, Sponsorship, Sports Market, Strategic Planning/Research, T.V., Technical Advertising, Trade & Consumer Magazines, Transportation, Viral/Buzz/Word of Mouth, Web (Banner Ads, Pop-ups, etc.)

Breakdown of Gross Billings by Media: Brdcst.: 30%; Collateral: 30%; Mags.: 30%; Worldwide Web Sites: 10%

John Hardy *(Pres)*

Accounts:
Advantage Financial Group
AFG Mortgage Specialist
AmeriFirst
Berkshire Hathaway Homestate Co.
Dataflo Consulting
Digital Defense Group
Pierce Technologies
Revolution Capital Partners
Tea Apothecary
Tekamah Public Library Foundation
Tellwiki.com
Vision Associates, Inc.
Woodman Federal Credit Union

BRANDSPRING SOLUTIONS LLC

(Acquired & Absorbed by The Marek Group)

BRANDSWAY CREATIVE

77-79 Ludlow St 2nd Fl, New York, NY 10002
Tel.: (212) 966-7900
Fax: (212) 966-7909
E-Mail: contact@brandswaycreative.com
Web Site: www.brandswaycreative.com

Agency Specializes In: Advertising, Brand Development & Integration, Corporate Identity, Public Relations

Kelly Brady *(Partner)*
Jacqueline Meluso *(Acct Exec)*

Accounts:
Pictoguard

BRANDSYMBOL

8845 Red Oak Blvd, Charlotte, NC 28217
Tel.: (704) 625-0106
Web Site: www.brandsymbol.com

Year Founded: 2012

Agency Specializes In: Brand Development & Integration, Business-To-Business, Collateral, Corporate Identity, Experience Design, Graphic Design, High Technology, International, Local Marketing, Logo & Package Design, Market Research, New Product Development, Package Design, Print

Doug Rand *(Sr VP)*
Bradley Shaver *(VP)*
Samantha Leibowitz *(Client Svcs Dir)*
Addison Huff *(Sr Acct Mgr)*
Jessica Howle *(Mgr-Bus Svcs)*
Casey Peebles *(Mgr-Mktg)*
David Plaisance *(Mgr-Digital Mktg)*

Accounts:
GE

Nikon

BRANDTAILERS

17838 Fitch, Irvine, CA 92614
Tel.: (949) 442-0500
Fax: (949) 442-2886
E-Mail: info@brandtailers.com
Web Site: www.brandtailers.com

Employees: 15

Agency Specializes In: Above-the-Line, Advertising, Advertising Specialties, Affiliate Marketing, Affluent Market, African-American Market, Agriculture, Alternative Advertising, Arts, Asian Market, Automotive, Aviation & Aerospace, Below-the-Line, Bilingual Market, Brand Development & Integration, Branded Entertainment, Broadcast, Business Publications, Business-To-Business, Cable T.V., Catalogs, Children's Market, Co-op Advertising, Collateral, College, Commercial Photography, Communications, Computers & Software, Consulting, Consumer Goods, Consumer Marketing, Consumer Publications, Content, Corporate Communications, Corporate Identity, Cosmetics, Crisis Communications, Customer Relationship Management, Digital/Interactive, Direct Response Marketing, Direct-to-Consumer, E-Commerce, Education, Electronic Media, Electronics, Email, Engineering, Entertainment, Environmental, Event Planning & Marketing, Exhibit/Trade Shows, Experience Design, Faith Based, Fashion/Apparel, Financial, Food Service, Gay & Lesbian Market, Government/Political, Graphic Design, Guerilla Marketing, Health Care Services, High Technology, Hispanic Market, Hospitality, Household Goods, Identity Marketing, In-Store Advertising, Industrial, Infomercials, Information Technology, Integrated Marketing, International, Internet/Web Design, Investor Relations, Legal Services, Leisure, Local Marketing, Logo & Package Design, Luxury Products, Magazines, Marine, Market Research, Media Buying Services, Media Planning, Media Relations, Media Training, Medical Products, Men's Market, Merchandising, Mobile Marketing, Multicultural, Multimedia, New Product Development, New Technologies, Newspaper, Newspapers & Magazines, Out-of-Home Media, Outdoor, Over-50 Market, Package Design, Paid Searches, Pets , Pharmaceutical, Planning & Consultation, Point of Purchase, Point of Sale, Print, Production, Production (Ad, Film, Broadcast), Production (Print), Promotions, Public Relations, Publicity/Promotions, Publishing, RSS (Really Simple Syndication), Radio, Real Estate, Recruitment, Regional, Restaurant, Retail, Sales Promotion, Search Engine Optimization, Seniors' Market, Shopper Marketing, Social Marketing/Nonprofit, Social Media, South Asian Market, Sponsorship, Sports Market, Stakeholders, Strategic Planning/Research, Sweepstakes, T.V., Technical Advertising, Teen Market, Telemarketing, Trade & Consumer Magazines, Transportation, Travel & Tourism, Tween Market, Urban Market, Viral/Buzz/Word of Mouth, Web (Banner Ads, Pop-ups, etc.), Women's Market, Yellow Pages Advertising

Cheril Hendry *(Pres & CEO)*
Joleen Fitzgerald *(CFO)*
Kristen Roberts *(Acct Svcs Dir)*
Kate Szalay *(Producer-Brdcst)*
Monica Lyons *(Dir-Media)*
Celine Bauer *(Acct Mgr)*
Kristen Shanklin *(Acct Mgr)*
Jesse Childers *(Mgr-Graphics Dept)*
Katherine Dahl *(Mgr-Digital Strategy)*

Accounts:
G-Link

BRANDTOPIA GROUP

2831 St Rose Pkwy Ste 450, Henderson, NV 89052
Tel.: (702) 589-4742
Fax: (702) 589-4743
E-Mail: info@brandtopiagroup.com
Web Site: www.brandtopiagroup.com

Agency Specializes In: Advertising, Brand Development & Integration, Broadcast, Digital/Interactive, Internet/Web Design, Media Planning, Print, Radio, Search Engine Optimization, Social Media

Craig Swanson *(Founder & Pres)*
Richard Sherman *(VP-Media Svcs)*

Accounts:
Charley Ray

BRANDTRUST

John Hancock Bldg 875 N Michigan Ave Ste 2945, Chicago, IL 60611
Tel.: (312) 440-1833
Fax: (312) 440-9987
E-Mail: info@brandtrust.com
Web Site: www.brandtrust.com

Employees: 20
Year Founded: 1982

Agency Specializes In: Brand Development & Integration, Print, Strategic Planning/Research

Approx. Annual Billings: $5,500,000

Daryl Travis *(Founder & CEO)*
Suzanne Cheves *(Partner-Shopper Insight)*
Carmie Stornello *(Partner)*
Beth Wozniak *(Controller)*
Kristian Aloma *(Client Partner & Dir-Client Relationships)*
Ed Jimenez *(Dir-Creative)*
Gillian Carter *(Mgr-Mktg-Client Dev)*

Accounts:
BUNN
Eli Lilly
General Mills
Harley-Davidson
Kraft
PepsiCo Quaker, Tropicana
Walmart

BRANDTUITIVE

733 Third Ave, New York, NY 10017
Tel.: (646) 790-5701
Web Site: www.brandtuitive.com

Employees: 6
Year Founded: 2010

Agency Specializes In: Advertising, Advertising Specialties, Affluent Market, Bilingual Market, Brand Development & Integration, Business Publications, Business-To-Business, Catalogs, Communications, Consulting, Consumer Goods, Consumer Marketing, Content, Corporate Communications, Corporate Identity, Cosmetics, Customer Relationship Management, Digital/Interactive, Direct Response Marketing, E-Commerce, Email, Event Planning & Marketing, Exhibit/Trade Shows, Experience Design, Financial, Food Service, Government/Political, Graphic Design, Guerilla Marketing, Health Care Services, High Technology, Hispanic Market, Hospitality, Household Goods, Identity Marketing, Industrial, Information Technology, Integrated Marketing, International, Internet/Web Design, Investor Relations, Logo & Package Design, Luxury Products, Market Research, Men's Market, Multicultural, New Product Development, New Technologies, Newspaper, Outdoor, Package Design, Pharmaceutical, Planning & Consultation, Point of Purchase, Print, Product Placement, Publicity/Promotions, Regional, Restaurant, Retail, Sales Promotion, Shopper Marketing, Social Marketing/Nonprofit, Social Media, Sports Market, Stakeholders, Strategic Planning/Research, Urban Market, Women's Market

Approx. Annual Billings: $1,500,000

Carolyn Cox *(Mgr-Brand Mktg)*

Accounts:
American Lumber; 2013
Jane Carter; 2014
MRCE; 2013
Nespresso; 2010
Simply Wine
Terminal Lumber (TFP); 2014

BRANDWISE

8205 Camp Bowie W Ste 206, Fort Worth, TX 76116
Tel.: (817) 244-0990
Web Site: www.getbrandwise.com

Employees: 2
Year Founded: 1999

Agency Specializes In: Advertising, Advertising Specialties, Brand Development & Integration, Business Publications, Business-To-Business, Catalogs, Collateral, Corporate Communications, Corporate Identity, Direct Response Marketing, Email, Environmental, Exhibit/Trade Shows, Graphic Design, Health Care Services, High Technology, Identity Marketing, Integrated Marketing, Internet/Web Design, Logo & Package Design, Multimedia, Newspaper, Outdoor, Package Design, Pharmaceutical, Print, Sales Promotion, Search Engine Optimization

Breakdown of Gross Billings by Media: Collateral: 30%; D.M.: 15%; Exhibits/Trade Shows: 8%; Logo & Package Design: 20%; Strategic Planning/Research: 2%; Worldwide Web Sites: 25%

Dale Berkebile *(CEO & Partner-Bus Growth)*
Randy Quade *(CTO)*
Greg Ford *(VP-Sls & Mktg)*
Nelson Graham *(VP-Ops)*
Bill Miller *(VP-Data Svcs)*
Karen Radcliffe *(VP-Product Mgmt)*
Shelly Vollmer *(Coord-Mktg)*
Chris Kelly *(Sr Engr-Software)*

BRANDWIZARD

130 Fifth Ave, New York, NY 10011
Tel.: (212) 798-7600
Web Site: http://interbrand.com/

Andrea Sullivan *(CMO-North America)*
Andy Payne *(Chief Creative Officer-Global)*
Simon Bailey *(CEO-EMEA & Latham-Interbrand)*
Josh Feldmeth *(CEO-North America)*
Jonathan Redman *(Sr Dir-Client Svcs-Interbrand)*
Kristin Reagan *(Dir-Mktg-Global)*
Shayla Persaud *(Assoc Dir-Mktg-North America)*

Accounts:
AC Delco
American Cancer Society
AT&T Communications Corp.
General Motors
HP
Hyatt
Mercedes-Benz
National Geographic

BRANGER_BRIZ
3250 NE 1st Ave Ste 313, Miami, FL 33137
Tel.: (305) 893-8858
Web Site: www.brangerbriz.com

Year Founded: 1998

Agency Specializes In: Advertising, Digital/Interactive

Paul Briz *(Partner & CTO)*
Ramon Branger *(Partner)*
Natalie A. Salas *(Acct Mgr)*
Christopher Mora *(Mgr-Dev)*

BRASCO DESIGN + MARKETING
(Formerly Brasco Marketing LLC)
305 W Martin St, Raleigh, NC 27601
Tel.: (919) 745-8091
Web Site: brasco.marketing

Year Founded: 2004

Agency Specializes In: Advertising, Brand Development & Integration, Graphic Design, Internet/Web Design, Public Relations, Search Engine Optimization, Strategic Planning/Research

Brian Batchelor *(Founder & Dir-Creative)*
Brandon Ives *(Mng Partner & Strategist-Mktg)*
Ashley Demby *(Acct Dir)*
Brent Anthony *(Dir-Strategy & Engagement)*

Accounts:
Family Dermatology
NC Egg Association
Riley Life Logistics
Triangle Entrepreneurship Week

BRASHE ADVERTISING, INC.
471 N Broadway, Jericho, NY 11753
Tel.: (516) 935-5544
Fax: (516) 932-7264
E-Mail: info@brashe.com
Web Site: http://www.brashe.net/

Employees: 5
Year Founded: 1977

Agency Specializes In: Advertising, Advertising Specialties, Automotive, Broadcast, Business Publications, Business-To-Business, Cable T.V., Co-op Advertising, Collateral, Communications, Consumer Marketing, Consumer Publications, Corporate Identity, Education, Electronic Media, Financial, Government/Political, Graphic Design, Health Care Services, Industrial, Internet/Web Design, Legal Services, Leisure, Local Marketing, Logo & Package Design, Magazines, Media Buying Services, Medical Products, Merchandising, Multimedia, New Product Development, Newspaper, Newspapers & Magazines, Out-of-Home Media, Outdoor, Planning & Consultation, Point of Purchase, Point of Sale, Print, Production, Public Relations, Publicity/Promotions, Radio, Real Estate, Recruitment, Retail, Sales Promotion, T.V., Trade & Consumer Magazines

Approx. Annual Billings: $10,209,000

Breakdown of Gross Billings by Media: Bus. Publs.: $189,000; Cable T.V.: $410,000; Consumer Publs.: $65,000; D.M.: $215,000; Fees: $368,000; Mags.: $85,000; Newsp.: $7,222,000; Point of Purchase: $185,000; Point of Sale: $200,000; Pub. Rels.: $95,000; Radio: $550,000; Radio & T.V.: $250,000; T.V.: $375,000

Jeffrey Cherkis *(Pres)*

Accounts:
Association of Handicapped & Retarded Children (AHRC); Brookville, NY (Recruitment); 1998
Deutsch Relays Inc.; East Northport, NY (Recruitment) Relay Electronics; 1997
The First National Bank of Long Island; Glen Head, NY (Recruitment); 1998
Life's WORC Recruitment
Nassau BOCES Recruitment
National Institute of Allergy and Infectious Diseases (NIAID) Recruitment
Nu Horizons Electronics; Amityville, NY (Recruitment) Electronics; 1997
SCO Family of Services Recruitment; 1999
U.S. Government Census Bureau (Recruitment)

BRAVADA CONSUMER COMMUNICATIONS INC.
105 Park St, Waterloo, ON N2L 1Y3 Canada
Tel.: (519) 745-1333
Fax: (519) 742-1791
Toll Free: (866) 727-2823
E-Mail: info@bravada-cci.com
Web Site: www.bravada-cci.com

Employees: 10

Agency Specializes In: Advertising, Corporate Identity, Package Design, Print, Production, Production (Ad, Film, Broadcast), Production (Print), Radio

Jeff Funston *(Owner & Dir-Creative)*
Roman Ciecwierz *(Owner)*

Accounts:
Ace Hardware
BIOREM
Grand River Hospital
Onward Manufacturing Company Ltd.
Pfalzgraf Patisserie
True Value Hardware

BRAVE PEOPLE
2212 E 3rd Ave, Tampa, FL 33605
Tel.: (813) 644-9555
E-Mail: hello@bravepeople.co
Web Site: www.bravepeople.co

Agency Specializes In: Advertising, Brand Development & Integration, Digital/Interactive, Internet/Web Design

Gabe Lopez *(Founder & Dir-Creative)*
John Miseroy *(Acct Dir)*
Ben Lopez *(Dir-Creative)*
Bryce Walter *(Dir-Art)*

Accounts:
Ditto Residential
Watsi

THE BRAVO GROUP HQ
601 Brickell Key Drive, Suite 1100, Miami, FL 33131
Tel.: (305) 347-1950
E-Mail: contact@bebravo.com
Web Site: www.bebravo.com

Employees: 144
Year Founded: 1980

National Agency Associations: 4A's

Agency Specializes In: Advertising, Hispanic Market, Sponsorship

Approx. Annual Billings: $275,000,000

Eric Hoyt *(Pres & CEO)*
Claudio Lima *(VP-Creative & Dir)*
Andrew Halley-Wright *(VP-Strategic Plng)*
Tiago Lee *(Exec Dir-Digital Strategy)*
Emilio Alvarez-Recio *(Acct Dir)*
Dora Diaz *(Acct Dir)*
Pedro Pinhal *(Art Dir)*
Gabriela Roger *(Art Dir)*
Rosanna Perez *(Acct Supvr)*
Brian Abadia *(Copywriter)*
Alex Toedtli *(Copywriter)*

Accounts:
Airplane
AT&T Communications Corp AT&T Wireless; 1989
Bi-Lo Winn-Dixie
Chevron
Church
CVS Pharmacy
Famous Footwear
Fishing
General Mills Advertising, Display, Ecommerce, Multi-Cultural, Shopper Insights, Shopper-Marketing
Lost & Missing
Medalla Light
Pfizer
PopClik Headphones
Tampico
Wendy's Campaign: 'Mucho Mejor"
The Wm. Wrigley Jr. Company Eclipse
Women In Distress

The Bravo Group
233 N Michigan Ave Ste 1600, Chicago, IL 60601-5518
Tel.: (312) 596-3000
Fax: (312) 596-3130
Web Site: www.bravogroup.us

Employees: 3

National Agency Associations: 4A's

Rhett Hintze *(COO & Head-Tech & Procurement Practice)*
Chris Getman *(Sr Dir)*
Silvia Cruz *(Dir)*
Evan Grove *(Dir-Res)*
Megan Earley *(Acct Exec)*

BRAVO MEDIA
145 W 28th St, New York, NY 10001
Tel.: (212) 563-0054
E-Mail: info@bravomedia.com
Web Site: www.bravomediainc.com

Agency Specializes In: Brand Development & Integration, Production, Production (Ad, Film, Broadcast)

Tim Donovan *(Pres)*
Ryan Kelley *(VP)*
David Title *(Chief Engagement Officer)*

Accounts:
Def Jam Recordings
HBO
Johnson & Johnson
LG
MTV
RCA
Sony
Unilever
Universal

BRAVURA ADVERTISING & DESIGN
6209 Riverside Dr Ste 100, Dublin, OH 43017
Tel.: (614) 339-1460
Fax: (614) 798-4846
Web Site: www.bravuraad.com

Agency Specializes In: Advertising, Brand Development & Integration, Media Planning, Print,

Social Media

Jennifer Ballinger *(Principal)*
Kim Flowers *(Media Planner & Media Buyer)*
Jennifer Sims *(Media Planner & Media Buyer)*
Matt Glomb *(Sr Designer)*
Annie Hill *(Coord-Web Content)*

Accounts:
Chevrolet of Dublin

BREAKAWAY

399 Boylston St 5th Fl, Boston, MA 02116
Tel.: (617) 399-0635
Web Site: www.breakaway.com

Year Founded: 2006

Agency Specializes In: Brand Development & Integration, Content, Customer Relationship Management, Digital/Interactive, Print, Public Relations, Search Engine Optimization

Chaz Bertrand *(Mng Dir)*
John Burns *(Chief Investment Officer)*
David Knies *(Chief Strategy Officer)*
Sarah Moss *(Art Dir)*
Michael Wilmot *(Dir-Brand)*
Liam Corrigan *(Designer)*
Javier Fuentes *(Designer)*

Accounts:
New-Polartec (Public Relations Agency of Record)

BREAKSTONE GROUP

(Name Changed to MBS Value Partners, Inc.)

BREEN SMITH ADVERTISING

255 Trinity Ave SW 2nd Fl, Atlanta, GA 30303
Tel.: (404) 352-9507
E-Mail: info@breensmith.com
Web Site: www.breensmith.com

E-Mail for Key Personnel:
President: smith@breensmith.com
Creative Dir.: breen@breensmith.com

Employees: 7
Year Founded: 2006

Agency Specializes In: Brand Development & Integration, Consumer Publications, Corporate Identity, Digital/Interactive, Entertainment, Graphic Design, Promotions, Public Relations, Strategic Planning/Research, T.V., Trade & Consumer Magazines, Transportation, Viral/Buzz/Word of Mouth, Web (Banner Ads, Pop-ups, etc.)

Tim Smith *(Pres)*
Chris Breen *(Partner & Dir-Creative)*
Matt Hayes *(Client Svcs Dir)*
Anna Desantis *(Mgr-Traffic)*

BREENSMITH ADVERTISING

140 Peachtree St NW, Atlanta, GA 30303
Tel.: (404) 352-9507
Web Site: breensmith.com

Agency Specializes In: Advertising, Advertising Specialties, Brand Development & Integration, Business Publications, Cable T.V., Communications, Digital/Interactive, Direct Response Marketing, Email, Graphic Design, In-Store Advertising, Internet/Web Design, Local Marketing, Logo & Package Design, Magazines, Market Research, Media Planning, Mobile Marketing, Multimedia, Newspaper, Newspapers & Magazines, Out-of-Home Media, Outdoor, Point of Purchase, Print, Promotions, Public Relations, Radio, Social Marketing/Nonprofit, Social Media, Sponsorship, Strategic Planning/Research, Sweepstakes, T.V., Web (Banner Ads, Pop-ups, etc.)

Tim Smith *(Pres)*
Chris Breen *(Partner & Dir-Creative)*
Adam Millman *(Art Dir)*
Steve Cady *(Art Dir)*
Matt Hayes *(Client Svcs Dir)*
Morgan VanGorder *(Acct Mgr)*
Anna DeSantis *(Mgr-Traffic)*
Anna Morgan *(Copywriter)*
Mike Palma *(Copywriter)*

Accounts:
AMD (Agency of Record) Creative, Public Relations, SEO, Social Media, Strategy
Burgess Cup
CNN
College Hunks Hauling Junk
D4C Creative, Dentistry 4 Children, Family Orthodontics, Media Buying, Public Relations, Social Media, Strategy
Equifax
Fado Irish Pub Banter, Drink, Food
New-Friends of Animals, Inc. Campaign: "Ruff Life"
Guinness Campaign: "Binoculars", Campaign: "Flashlight", Campaign: "Pubfinder", Campaign: "Telescope"
Kabbage Inc. Video
OnsiteRIS Creative, Public Relations, Strategy
Pyrotecnico Campaign: "Distracted"
RaceTrack
Stevi B's Pizza Buffet
The Weather Channel

BRENESCO LLC

291 Broadway Ste 802, New York, NY 10007
Tel.: (212) 274-0077
E-Mail: info@brenesco.com
Web Site: www.brenesco.com

Year Founded: 2006

Agency Specializes In: Advertising, Brand Development & Integration, Content, Digital/Interactive, Internet/Web Design, Logo & Package Design, Print

Leane Brenes *(Founder & Creative Dir)*

Accounts:
Evine Live

BREW

530 University Ave SE, Minneapolis, MN 55414
Tel.: (612) 331-7700
Fax: (612) 331-7704
E-Mail: info@brew-creative.com
Web Site: www.brew-creative.com

Employees: 10
Year Founded: 2006

Agency Specializes In: Advertising, Production (Ad, Film, Broadcast), Production (Print), T.V., Web (Banner Ads, Pop-ups, etc.)

Michelle Fitzgerald *(Principal & Strategist-Comm)*
Stephanie Roebuck *(Mgr-Social & Digital)*

Accounts:
Chicago Lake Liquors
Neve Sportswear
Schwan's Consumer Brands North America Edwards

BREW MEDIA RELATIONS

2110 Main St Ste 201, Santa Monica, CA 90405
Tel.: (310) 464-6348
E-Mail: dena@brewpr.com
Web Site: www.brewpr.com

Agency Specializes In: Strategic Planning/Research

Brooke Hammerling *(Founder)*
Caitlyn Carpanzano *(VP)*
Ross Purnell *(Sr Dir)*
Jennifer Martinez *(Acct Dir)*
Courtney Klosterman *(Sr Acct Exec)*
Jessica Tenny *(Sr Acct Exec)*
Brooke Matthews *(Acct Exec)*
Kimmi Lorman *(Asst Acct Exec)*

Accounts:
Activate
GetGlue
LMK
Medio
Moblyng
Netsuite
Ning
One Kings Lane
Outcast
PicksPal
Polyvore
Sidebar
Sony
Stamps.com
Virgin Charter
Zynga

BREWER ASSOCIATES MARKETING COMMUNICATIONS

39555 Orchard Hill Pl Ste 600, Novi, MI 48375
Tel.: (734) 458-7180
E-Mail: klangham@brewer-associates.com
Web Site: www.brewer-associates.com

E-Mail for Key Personnel:
President: klangham@brewer-associates.com

Employees: 5
Year Founded: 1956

Agency Specializes In: Advertising, Business-To-Business, Catalogs, Collateral, Corporate Identity, Industrial, Internet/Web Design, Logo & Package Design, Media Planning, Publicity/Promotions, Strategic Planning/Research, Technical Advertising

John Ojala *(Chm)*
Keith Langham *(Pres & CEO)*
David Jankowski *(Exec Dir-Art)*
Gale Halbert *(Office Mgr)*

Accounts:
Columbia Marketing Tools Marketing Tools & Systems; 2011
Cooper Split Roller Bearing Corp. Split Roller Bearings; 2012
Elopak, Inc.; New Hudson, MI Packaging Systems; 2001
IFE Group; Brighton, MI Fluid System Components; 2008
Kaydon Corp. Bearings Division; Muskegon, MI Bearings; 2003
KPSG; Auburn Hills, MI Powertain Components; 2006
Leigh Fibers; Wellford, SC Raw & Reprocessed Fibers; 2009
NLB Corp.; Wixom, MI Water Jetting Equipment; 1982

BREWER DIRECT, INC.

507 S Myrtle Ave, Monrovia, CA 91016
Tel.: (626) 359-1015
Fax: (626) 358-1036
E-Mail: info@brewerdirect.com
Web Site: www.brewerdirect.com

Employees: 11
Year Founded: 2004

Agency Specializes In: Brand Development & Integration, E-Commerce, Graphic Design, Internet/Web Design, Newspaper, Outdoor, Planning & Consultation, Print, Strategic Planning/Research

Approx. Annual Billings: $4,500,000

Breakdown of Gross Billings by Media: D.M.: $3,000,000; Newsp.: $250,000; Other: $250,000; Plng. & Consultation: $1,000,000

Randy W. Brewer *(Pres & CEO)*
Brian Hackler *(VP-Ops)*
Cindy Courtier *(Dir-Creative)*
Jeff Riley *(Dir-Art)*

Accounts:
Allentown Rescue Mission; Allentown, PA Homeless Services; 2006
Bakersfield Rescue Mission; Bakersfield, CA Homeless Services; 2008
Boys & Girls Clubs - Los Angeles County Alliance; Los Angeles, CA Youth Services; 2007
Charlotte Rescue Mission Direct Response Fundraising Program
City Gospel Mission; Cincinnati, OH Homeless Services; 2005
Coachella Valley Rescue Mission; Indio, CA Homeless Services; 2007
Goodwill Southern California (Agency of Record) Digital Fundraising, Direct Marketing
Lexington Rescue Mission; Lexington, KY Homeless Services; 2007
Long Beach Rescue Mission, Long Beach, CA Homeless Services; 2004
New Orleans Mission; New Orleans, LA Homeless Services; 2009
Open Door Mission Houston (Agency of Record) Online, Print
Open Door Mission; Rochester, NY Homeless Services; 2009
San Diego Rescue Mission Creative, Direct Response Marketing, Media
Springs Rescue Mission; Colorado Springs, CO Homeless Services; 2007
Wheeler Mission Ministries; Indianapolis, IN Homeless Services; 2004

BREWLIFE
50 Francisco St Ste 103, San Francisco, CA 94133
Tel.: (415) 362-5018
E-Mail: info@brewlife.com
Web Site: www.brewlife.com

Year Founded: 2012

Agency Specializes In: Advertising, Brand Development & Integration, Digital/Interactive, Investor Relations, Media Relations

Carolyn Wang *(Pres)*
Joey Fleury *(Acct Dir)*
Kelly France *(Acct Dir)*
Susan Parker *(Assoc Dir-Creative)*

Accounts:
AccessClosure
ApniCure
Coravin
Cytori Therapeutics Inc
FoxHollow
Intuity Medical
Kelmeg, Inc.
MAP Pharmaceuticals, Inc.
Patheon Inc.
Seattle Genetics, Inc.
Topica
XOMA Corporation

BRIABE MOBILE INC.
(Formerly Briabe Media Inc.)
634 A Venice Blvd, Venice, CA 90291
Tel.: (310) 710-2380
Fax: (310) 694-3284
Web Site: www.briabemobile.com

Employees: 8

Agency Specializes In: Mobile Marketing

James Briggs *(Co-Founder & CEO)*
Renee Glass *(VP-Bus Admin)*
Mary Zerafa *(VP-Sls)*

Accounts:
American Airlines
Amtrak
BP
Eye Corp
Images USA
Jenny Craig
Ogilvy
PepsiCo
Sara Lee

BRIDGE STRATEGIC COMMUNICATIONS
321 N Walnut St, Yellow Springs, OH 45387
Tel.: (937) 767-1345
E-Mail: bob@bingenheimer.com
Web Site: www.bridgestrategic.com

Year Founded: 2009

Agency Specializes In: Advertising, Entertainment, Internet/Web Design, Media Relations

Karen Stoychoff Inman *(Pres)*

Accounts:
Community Solutions Non-Profit Organization
The Dayton Foundation Charitable Organizations
Kavooom Artist & Story Book Publisher
Kelley and Company Online Horse Products Provider
Loot Furniture Stores
Sculptor Alice Robrish Clay Sculpture Creator
The Springfield Foundation Charitable Organizations

BRIDGES ADVERTISING LLC
5350 S Western Ave Ste 100, Oklahoma City, OK 73109
Tel.: (405) 813-3330
Fax: (405) 813-3329
E-Mail: info@bridgesadvertising.com
Web Site: www.bridgesstrategies.com

Year Founded: 2012

Agency Specializes In: Advertising, Event Planning & Marketing, Media Buying Services, Media Planning, Media Relations, Print, Public Relations, Social Media

Ashley E. Garcia *(Partner)*
Jake Fisher *(Principal)*
Jessica Vazquez *(Specialist-Social Media & Digital)*

Accounts:
Stella Modern Italian Cuisine

BRIECHLE-FERNANDEZ MARKETING SERVICES INC.
265 Industrial Way W Ste 7, Eatontown, NJ 07724
Tel.: (732) 982-8222
Fax: (732) 982-8223
E-Mail: bf.inquiry@bfmarketing.com
Web Site: www.bfmarketing.com

E-Mail for Key Personnel:
President: lorenzo.fernandez@bfmarketing.com

Employees: 26
Year Founded: 1984

Agency Specializes In: Advertising, Advertising Specialties, Agriculture, Automotive, Aviation & Aerospace, Bilingual Market, Brand Development & Integration, Business Publications, Business-To-Business, Catalogs, Collateral, Commercial Photography, Communications, Consumer Marketing, Corporate Communications, Corporate Identity, Cosmetics, Direct Response Marketing, Education, Electronic Media, Electronics, Email, Engineering, Environmental, Event Planning & Marketing, Exhibit/Trade Shows, Graphic Design, Health Care Services, High Technology, Hispanic Market, In-Store Advertising, Industrial, International, Internet/Web Design, Investor Relations, Logo & Package Design, Marine, Media Buying Services, Media Planning, Media Relations, Medical Products, Merchandising, Multicultural, Multimedia, New Product Development, Newspaper, Newspapers & Magazines, Outdoor, Pharmaceutical, Point of Purchase, Point of Sale, Print, Production, Production (Print), Promotions, Public Relations, Publicity/Promotions, Sales Promotion, Strategic Planning/Research, Technical Advertising, Transportation

Approx. Annual Billings: $18,966,000

Lorenzo Fernandez *(Pres)*
Christian Fernandez *(Exec VP)*
Richard Lomonaco *(Dir-Creative)*
Dena Temple *(Client Svcs Mgr & Mgr-Production)*
Charles Bins *(Mgr-PR & Sr Copywriter)*
Lisa Porter *(Acct Exec)*
Ken Hall *(Sr Graphic Designer)*

Accounts:
AMA Labs; New City, NY Laboratory Testing Services; 2010
Amino Gmbh; Frellsted, Germany Amino Acids
Ashland Performance Specialties Specialty Chemicals
BENEO-Palatinit; Morris Plains, NJ Sweetener
Bunge Ltd; White Plains, NY Agricultural Products
Chattem Chemicals API's & Performance Chemicals
Condea Servo LLC; South Plainfield, NJ
Cyanco Corp.; Winnemucca, NV Mining Chemicals
Evonik Industries Specialty Chemicals
Gallagher Corp. Polyurethane Molding
Gelest Inc.; Morrisville, PA Silanes
Gum Base Co.; Milan, Italy Gum Bases
Heraeus Sensor Technology USA; North Brunswick, NJ Temperature Sensors
Kemper System America, Inc.; Closter, NJ Roofing & Waterproofing Systems; 1998
The Linde Group Industrial Gases
Metal Textiles Corp; Edison, NJ
Micro Corporation; Somerset, NJ Insert Molding, Medical Devices, Metal Stamping, Molding
Optimum Anodes PM Anodes
Orion Engineered Carbons; Kingwood, TX Carbon Black; 2011
Palsgaard Inc. Food Emulsifiers & Stabilizers
Presidente Inc.; Miami, FL Beer
Reaxis; McDonald, PA Chemicals
Stepan LLC Basic & Intermediate Chemicals
Umicore

BRIERLEY & PARTNERS
5465 Legacy Dr Ste 300, Plano, TX 75024
Tel.: (214) 760-8700
Fax: (214) 743-5511
E-Mail: ccheatham@brierley.com
Web Site: www.brierley.com

E-Mail for Key Personnel:
Creative Dir.: jhuppenphal@brierley.com

Employees: 150

Year Founded: 1985

Agency Specializes In: Advertising Specialties, Brand Development & Integration, Business-To-Business, Collateral, Communications, Consulting, Consumer Marketing, Customer Relationship Management, Digital/Interactive, Direct Response Marketing, Direct-to-Consumer, E-Commerce, Electronic Media, Email, Graphic Design, In-Store Advertising, Information Technology, Internet/Web Design, Planning & Consultation, Point of Purchase, Point of Sale, Print, Production, Retail, Strategic Planning/Research, Travel & Tourism

Approx. Annual Billings: $200,000,000

Chuck Cheatham *(CFO)*
Bill Swift *(CTO)*
Jill Goran *(Sr VP & Grp Dir-Creative)*
Sean Eidson *(Sr VP-Strategy)*
Jennifer Jaynes *(Sr VP-Pro Svcs)*
Billy J. Payton *(Sr VP)*
Heidi Potthoff *(Sr VP-Client Svcs)*
Lynne Smith *(Sr VP-Client Svcs)*
Ellie Mitchell *(Head-Client Engagement)*

Accounts:
7-Eleven
Bloomingdales
Express
GameStop
Godiva
Hard Rock
Hertz
Sony Corporation
Yes Lifecycle Marketing

Branches

Brierley & Partners
15303 Ventura Blvd, Sherman Oaks, CA 91403
Tel.: (323) 965-4000
Fax: (323) 965-4100
Web Site: www.brierley.com

Employees: 20
Year Founded: 1986

Agency Specializes In: Consumer Marketing

David Mellinger *(CFO & Exec VP)*
Bill Swift *(CTO & Exec VP)*
Billy Payton *(Pres-Retail Svcs)*
Jill Goran *(Sr VP & Dir-Creative)*
Jim Huppenthal *(Sr VP-Creative Svcs)*
John Pedini *(Sr VP-Program Mgmt)*
Don Smith *(Sr VP)*

Accounts:
Hertz
Hilton Worldwide
Sony

Brierley & Partners
Clover House 4th Floor, Farringdon Road, London, United Kingdom
Tel.: (44) 207 239 8880
Fax: (44) 207 153 0599
E-Mail: info@brierly.com
Web Site: www.brierley.com

Employees: 12
Year Founded: 1996

Jim Sturm *(Pres & CEO)*
Chuck Cheatham *(CFO)*
Robert Owen *(CIO & Sr VP)*
Bill Swift *(CTO)*
Jill Goran *(Sr VP & Grp Dir-Creative)*
Jim Huppenthal *(Sr VP-Creative Svcs)*
Billy J. Payton *(Sr VP)*

Accounts:
American Eagle Outfitters
Baylor Health Care Systems
Blockbuster
Bloomingdales
BMI
Borders
eBay
Godiva

BRIGGS ADVERTISING
199 Water St, Bath, ME 04530
Tel.: (207) 443-2067
Fax: (207) 443-2344
E-Mail: info@briggsadv.com
Web Site: www.briggsadv.com

Employees: 6
Year Founded: 1987

Agency Specializes In: Advertising, Brand Development & Integration, Cable T.V., Consulting, Corporate Identity, Electronic Media, Internet/Web Design, Media Buying Services, Multimedia, Newspapers & Magazines, Production, Radio, T.V.

Walter Briggs *(Owner)*
Robert Brochu *(Dir-Creative)*

Accounts:
Beale Street Barbeque
Bill Dodge Auto Group
Bow Street Market (Agency of Record) Advertising, Marketing
Cellardoor Vineyard
Chocolate Church Arts Center
Harris Golf Shop
Highland Green
LinenMaster
Maine Distilleries, LLC Cold River Vodka
Now You're Cooking
OldCastle APG
Shucks Maine Lobster

BRIGGS & CALDWELL
9801 Westheimer Rd Ste 701, Houston, TX 77042
Tel.: (713) 532-4040
Fax: (713) 532-4046
E-Mail: ccaldwell@briggscaldwell.com
Web Site: www.briggscaldwell.com

Employees: 10
Year Founded: 2005

Agency Specializes In: Consumer Goods, Consumer Marketing, Electronic Media, Local Marketing, Magazines, Media Buying Services, Media Planning, Media Training, Newspaper, Newspapers & Magazines, Out-of-Home Media, Outdoor, Planning & Consultation, Radio, Retail, Sponsorship, Strategic Planning/Research

Breakdown of Gross Billings by Media: Internet Adv.: 5%; Mags.: 5%; Newsp.: 10%; Other: 5%; Out-of-Home Media: 10%; Spot Radio: 25%; Spot T.V.: 40%

Kellie Briggs *(Pres)*
Chris Caldwell *(Partner)*
Kristina Early *(Media Planner & Media Buyer)*
Athena Anzaldua *(Media Buyer)*
Julie Syers *(Sr Media Buyer)*

Accounts:
Academy Sports & Outdoors; Houston, TX Apparel, Footwear, Sporting Goods; 2005
Children's Museum of Houston; Houston, TX Museum & Entertainment Venue; 2009
Feld Entertainment Disney on Ice, Monster Jam, Ringling Circus, SuperCross; 2011
Texas Children's Hospital; Houston, TX Pediatric Healthcare; 2007
Trinity Mother Frances Hospital; Tyler, TX Healthcare, Service Line Specialties; 2012

BRIGHAM & RAGO MARKETING COMMUNICATIONS
18 Bank St Ste 200, Morristown, NJ 07960-5186
Tel.: (973) 656-9006
Fax: (973) 656-9007
Web Site: www.brigham-rago.com

E-Mail for Key Personnel:
President: rob@brigham-rago.com
Creative Dir.: nancy@brigham-rago.com

Employees: 3
Year Founded: 1991

National Agency Associations: BMA

Agency Specializes In: Brand Development & Integration, Broadcast, Business Publications, Business-To-Business, Cable T.V., Catalogs, Collateral, Communications, Content, Corporate Communications, Corporate Identity, Custom Publishing, Direct Response Marketing, Email, Exhibit/Trade Shows, Graphic Design, Industrial, Integrated Marketing, Internet/Web Design, Logo & Package Design, Market Research, Media Buying Services, Media Planning, Media Relations, Newspapers & Magazines, Outdoor, Paid Searches, Podcasting, Point of Sale, Print, Production, Production (Print), Public Relations, Publicity/Promotions, Radio, Technical Advertising

Approx. Annual Billings: $800,000

Breakdown of Gross Billings by Media: Bus. Publs.: 100%

Robert S. Brigham *(Pres)*
Nancy A. Rago *(VP)*

BRIGHAM SCULLY
25 5th St, Bangor, ME 04401
Tel.: (207) 941-1100
Fax: (207) 941-1103
E-Mail: info@brighamscully.com
Web Site: www.brighamscully.com

E-Mail for Key Personnel:
President: tbrigham@brighamscully.com
Media Dir.: lbrigham@brighamscully.com

Employees: 2
Year Founded: 1974

Agency Specializes In: Advertising, Business Publications, Business-To-Business, Collateral, Computers & Software, Consumer Publications, Engineering, High Technology, Hospitality, Industrial, Information Technology, Magazines, Media Planning, Public Relations, Trade & Consumer Magazines

Approx. Annual Billings: $1,000,000

Leslie Brigham *(Owner)*
Tom Brigham *(Pres)*

Accounts:
Delta Scientific; Palmdale, CA
Ingersoll Rand Security Technologies; Carmel, IN

BRIGHT AGE
22220 Gilmore St, Woodland Hills, CA 91303
Tel.: (818) 887-0999
Toll Free: (800) 965-0335
E-Mail: contact@brightage.com
Web Site: www.brightage.com

Agency Specializes In: Advertising,

Advertising Agencies

Digital/Interactive, Internet/Web Design, Search Engine Optimization, Social Media

Adam Post *(Founder)*

Accounts:
Protein For Pets

BRIGHT ORANGE ADVERTISING
2421 Westwood Ave Ste C, Richmond, VA 23220
Tel.: (804) 767-7180
Web Site: www.brightorangeadv.com

Year Founded: 1995

Agency Specializes In: Advertising, Internet/Web Design, Print, Radio, T.V.

Bruce Goldman *(Owner & Dir-Creative)*
Liz Scoggins *(Sr Dir-Art)*
Stephen Martin *(Dir-Strategic Plng)*
Jim Maxwell *(Dir-Emerging Media & Res)*

Accounts:
Bikram Yoga Richmond
Trustmor Mortgage Co.

BRIGHTFIRE LLC
2470 Satellite Blvd Ste 210, Duluth, GA 30096
Tel.: (800) 881-1833
Fax: (888) 676-8522
E-Mail: hello@brightfire.com
Web Site: www.brightfire.com

Year Founded: 2000

Agency Specializes In: Advertising, Brand Development & Integration, Digital/Interactive, Internet/Web Design, Logo & Package Design, Paid Searches, Print, Search Engine Optimization, Social Media, Web (Banner Ads, Pop-ups, etc.)

Nadia Garner *(CFO)*
Shawn Jenks *(Chief Creative Officer)*

Accounts:
New-Music Midtown

BRIGHTHOUSE BRANDING GROUP
33 Dupont St E, Waterloo, ON N2J 2G8 Canada
Tel.: (519) 884-2222
Fax: (519) 884-7778
E-Mail: alex@brighthouse.ca
Web Site: www.brighthouse.ca

Employees: 25

Agency Specializes In: Brand Development & Integration, Co-op Advertising, Collateral, Commercial Photography, Corporate Identity, Digital/Interactive, Direct Response Marketing, Event Planning & Marketing, Exhibit/Trade Shows, Internet/Web Design, Logo & Package Design, Market Research, Media Buying Services, Multimedia, Production, Promotions, Public Relations, Publicity/Promotions, Strategic Planning/Research

Alexander Haag *(Pres)*
Kerri Kelly *(VP-Client Svcs)*
Trish Behan *(Controller)*
Todd Holly *(Sr Graphic Designer)*

Accounts:
Barbarian Rugbywear
E.D. Smith Foods
Nord Gear

BRIGHTLINE ITV
565 Fifth Ave 18th Fl, New York, NY 10017
Tel.: (212) 271-0014
E-Mail: info@brightlineitv.com
Web Site: brightline.tv

Year Founded: 2003

Agency Specializes In: Advertising, Direct-to-Consumer, Sponsorship, T.V.

Jacqueline Corbelli *(Founder, Chm & CEO)*
Rob Aksman *(Co-Founder)*
Will Chapman *(Chief Revenue Officer)*
Joanna Hall *(Sr VP-Experience Design)*
Alex Henderson *(Sr VP-Client Rels)*
Joseph Lospalluto *(VP-Bus Dev)*
Kristin Youngling *(Sr Dir-Analytics & Bus Intelligence)*
Mike Fisher *(Dir-Strategy & Innovation)*
Christian Pimsner *(Dir-Sls)*
Jenna Pankow *(Acct Exec)*

Accounts:
Axe Cosmetics & Related Beauty Products
Bertolli Olive Oil Producer
Burger King
Dove
Lipton
Quaker
Red Bull
Tylenol
Vaseline

BRIGHTON AGENCY, INC.
7711 Bonhomme Ave, Saint Louis, MO 63105
Tel.: (314) 726-0700
Fax: (314) 721-8517
Toll Free: (800) 259-8617
Web Site: www.brightonagency.com

Employees: 55
Year Founded: 1989

Agency Specializes In: Advertising, Advertising Specialties, Agriculture, Brand Development & Integration, Broadcast, Business Publications, Business-To-Business, Co-op Advertising, Collateral, College, Communications, Consumer Marketing, Consumer Publications, Corporate Communications, Corporate Identity, Digital/Interactive, Direct Response Marketing, E-Commerce, Education, Electronic Media, Email, Event Planning & Marketing, Exhibit/Trade Shows, Financial, Graphic Design, In-Store Advertising, Integrated Marketing, Internet/Web Design, Logo & Package Design, Magazines, Media Buying Services, Media Planning, Multimedia, Newspaper, Newspapers & Magazines, Out-of-Home Media, Outdoor, Package Design, Pets , Pharmaceutical, Point of Purchase, Point of Sale, Print, Production, Public Relations, Publicity/Promotions, Radio, Real Estate, Retail, Sales Promotion, Search Engine Optimization, Sponsorship, Strategic Planning/Research, T.V., Trade & Consumer Magazines, Travel & Tourism

Approx. Annual Billings: $31,294,972

Breakdown of Gross Billings by Media: Fees: $3,711,722; Internet Adv.: $690; Newsp. & Mags.: $874,731; Other: $24,605,704; Outdoor: $51,100; Production: $1,909,201; Radio: $141,824

Jerry Gennaria *(VP-Strategy & Digital Comm)*
Scott McClure *(VP-Agricultural Svcs)*
Leo Madden *(Sr Dir-Art)*
Alisha Harris *(Dir-Ops)*
Jason Keeven *(Dir-Creative-Digital & Analog)*
Marty Sellmeyer *(Assoc Dir-Creative)*
Travis Coffman *(Acct Mgr)*
Colin Pennington *(Acct Mgr)*
Allison Stein *(Acct Mgr)*
Kim Gorsek *(Acct Exec)*
Madison Molho *(Asst Acct Exec)*

Accounts:
Monsanto
P&G - Natura Pet Products
Scottrade

BRIGHTSPEAR ARMED SERVICES CONSULTANCY
820 G St Ste 111, San Diego, CA 92101
Tel.: (619) 819-8722
Toll Free: (877) 567-4688
E-Mail: info@brightspear.com
Web Site: www.brightspear.com

Employees: 6
Year Founded: 2005

Agency Specializes In: Advertising, Advertising Specialties, Automotive, Aviation & Aerospace, Broadcast, Business Publications, Business-To-Business, Cable T.V., Commercial Photography, Consulting, Corporate Communications, Electronic Media, Entertainment, Fashion/Apparel, Graphic Design, Internet/Web Design, Local Marketing, Logo & Package Design, Magazines, Marine, New Product Development, Newspaper, Outdoor, Print, Publicity/Promotions, Sports Market, Strategic Planning/Research, T.V., Travel & Tourism

Approx. Annual Billings: $130,000

Breakdown of Gross Billings by Media: Consulting: 20%; Graphic Design: 20%; Newsp. & Mags.: 20%; Radio & T.V.: 20%; Worldwide Web Sites: 20%

Accounts:
Aerovironment; Simi Valley, CA Dragon Eye UAV, Raven UAV, Wasp UAV
Cequere Composite Technologies; Dublin, OH M1 Abrams Tank; 2007
Digital Spike; San Diego, CA Web Services; 2004
General Products; Dublin, OH M1 Abrams Tank
Ghetto Choppers; Oceanside, CA Custom Motorcycles-Fabrications & Repairs; 2004
Heart Breakers, Inc.; San Diego, CA Modeling Services; 2004

BRIGHTWAVE MARKETING
67 Peachtree Park Dr Ste 200, Atlanta, GA 30309
Tel.: (404) 253-2544
Web Site: www.brightwave.com/

Employees: 15

Agency Specializes In: Sponsorship

Simms Jenkins *(Founder & CEO)*
Brent Rosengren *(Chief Client Officer)*
Laura Giles *(Acct Mgmt Dir)*
Amanda Tuttle *(Dir-Ops & Strategic Plng)*
Alexis Snell *(Acct Mgr)*
Parisa Perkins *(Mgr-Campaign)*
Elizabeth Turner *(Coord-Campaign)*
Krisi Lane *(Campaign Mgr)*

Accounts:
ACS
AGCO Corporation
Chick-fil-A
CVS Pharmacy
Denison University
Equifax Inc.
FATZ Development, Email Marketing, Strategy
iFloor
Lowes
Naturally Fresh
Phillips 66
Racetrac
ServiceMaster
Tiffin Motorhomes

BRILLIANT MEDIA STRATEGIES
(Formerly Bradley Reid & Associates)
900 W 5th Ave Ste 100, Anchorage, AK 99501
Tel.: (907) 276-6353
Fax: (907) 276-1042
Web Site: brilliantak.com

E-Mail for Key Personnel:
President: connie.reid@brcomm.com
Media Dir.: paul.aadland@brcomm.com
Public Relations: debbie.reinwand@brcomm.com

Employees: 25
Year Founded: 1968

National Agency Associations: AAF

Agency Specializes In: Advertising, Advertising Specialties, Arts, Brand Development & Integration, Broadcast, Business-To-Business, Consumer Marketing, Crisis Communications, Direct Response Marketing, Electronic Media, Email, Event Planning & Marketing, Exhibit/Trade Shows, Integrated Marketing, Logo & Package Design, Market Research, Media Buying Services, Media Planning, Media Relations, Media Training, Men's Market, Mobile Marketing, Newspapers & Magazines, Point of Purchase, Print, Product Placement, Production (Ad, Film, Broadcast), Production (Print), Public Relations, Publicity/Promotions, Radio, Regional, Search Engine Optimization, Social Marketing/Nonprofit, Social Media, Strategic Planning/Research, T.V., Transportation, Travel & Tourism, Viral/Buzz/Word of Mouth, Web (Banner Ads, Pop-ups, etc.), Women's Market, Yellow Pages Advertising

Debbie Reinwand *(Pres & CEO)*
John Tracy *(Pres & CEO)*
Tina Lindgren *(Exec VP)*
Ed Bennett *(Editor & Copywriter)*
Jason Smith *(Dir-Creative)*
Jeremy Hayes *(Acct Supvr-Adv)*
Lindsey Spinelli *(Acct Supvr)*
Janice Wright *(Acct Supvr)*
Melissa Talaro *(Acct Coord)*

Accounts:
Alaska Downtown Partnership
Alaska Marine Highway
Alaska Permanent Fund
Alaska Travel Industry Association
AT&T Alascom
ConocoPhillips Alaska, Inc.
Northwest Cruiseship
Pebble Limited Partnership; Anchorage, AK (Agency of Record)
Providence Foundation
Providence Hospital
Providence-California; Burbank & Tarzana, CA Healthcare
Tourism North
Tyonek Corporation; Anchorage, AK
University of Alaska Anchorage
University of Alaska Fairbanks
West Coast Entertainment; Spokane, WA Stage Productions, The Lion King

BRINK COMMUNICATIONS
2705 SE Ash St Ste 1, Portland, OR 97214
Tel.: (503) 805-5560
Fax: (503) 225-0224
E-Mail: info@brinkcomm.com
Web Site: www.brinkcomm.com

Year Founded: 2012

Agency Specializes In: Advertising, Collateral, Crisis Communications, Media Relations, Public Relations, Social Marketing/Nonprofit

Marian Hammond *(Co-Founder & Principal)*
Leslie Carlson *(Partner-Strategy & Comm)*
Heidi Nielsen *(Partner-Branding & Design)*
Rose King *(Sr Acct Mgr)*
Mike Westling *(Acct Mgr)*

Accounts:
Ryno Motors

BRISCOE HALL, INC.
826 Water St, Kerrville, TX 78028
Tel.: (830) 896-1300
Fax: (830) 896-1303
E-Mail: info@briscoehall.com
Web Site: www.briscoehall.com

Employees: 6
Year Founded: 1993

National Agency Associations: AAF

Agency Specializes In: Advertising, Advertising Specialties, Affluent Market, Agriculture, Arts, Automotive, Aviation & Aerospace, Below-the-Line, Brand Development & Integration, Broadcast, Business Publications, Business-To-Business, Cable T.V., Catalogs, Children's Market, Co-op Advertising, Collateral, College, Commercial Photography, Communications, Computers & Software, Consulting, Consumer Goods, Consumer Marketing, Consumer Publications, Corporate Communications, Corporate Identity, Crisis Communications, Customer Relationship Management, Digital/Interactive, Direct Response Marketing, Direct-to-Consumer, E-Commerce, Education, Electronic Media, Electronics, Email, Entertainment, Environmental, Exhibit/Trade Shows, Faith Based, Fashion/Apparel, Financial, Food Service, Government/Political, Graphic Design, Health Care Services, High Technology, Hospitality, Household Goods, Identity Marketing, In-Store Advertising, Industrial, Integrated Marketing, Internet/Web Design, Leisure, Local Marketing, Logo & Package Design, Luxury Products, Magazines, Media Buying Services, Media Planning, Medical Products, Men's Market, Mobile Marketing, Multimedia, New Product Development, New Technologies, Newspaper, Newspapers & Magazines, Out-of-Home Media, Outdoor, Over-50 Market, Package Design, Paid Searches, Pets , Planning & Consultation, Point of Purchase, Point of Sale, Print, Production, Production (Ad, Film, Broadcast), Production (Print), Promotions, Radio, Real Estate, Recruitment, Regional, Restaurant, Retail, Sales Promotion, Search Engine Optimization, Seniors' Market, Social Marketing/Nonprofit, Social Media, Strategic Planning/Research, Sweepstakes, T.V., Technical Advertising, Teen Market, Trade & Consumer Magazines, Transportation, Travel & Tourism, Urban Market, Web (Banner Ads, Pop-ups, etc.), Women's Market

Approx. Annual Billings: $2,000,000

Breakdown of Gross Billings by Media: Collateral: $50,000; Consulting: $200,000; Consumer Publs.: $100,000; D.M.: $150,000; E-Commerce: $150,000; Graphic Design: $200,000; Logo & Package Design: $250,000; Newsp. & Mags.: $165,000; Outdoor: $85,000; Radio: $300,000; Spot T.V.: $350,000

Dave Vineyard *(Pres)*
Ann Darnell *(VP-Acct Svc)*
Elizabeth Hawkins *(Acct Exec)*

BRISTOL GROUP
(Acquired & Absorbed by Group m5)

THE BRITE AGENCY
29 Montford Ave Ste 200, Asheville, NC 28801
Tel.: (828) 350-9500
Fax: (828) 350-9501
E-Mail: info@briteagency.com
Web Site: www.briteagency.com

Year Founded: 2001

Agency Specializes In: Advertising, Brand Development & Integration, Graphic Design, Internet/Web Design, Public Relations, Social Media, Strategic Planning/Research

Dan Kellem *(Pres-Blue Ridge Solutions)*
Stephanie Smith *(Principal)*
Denise Szakaly *(Dir-Art)*
Brian Yates *(Mgr-Interactive Mktg & Ops)*

BRIVIC MEDIA
10200 Richmond Ave, Houston, TX 77042
Tel.: (713) 977-3300
Web Site: www.brivicmedia.com

Agency Specializes In: Advertising, Media Buying Services, Strategic Planning/Research

Allen Brivic *(Pres)*
Kelley Robinson *(Mgr-Digital Media)*
Cristina Fernandez *(Mgr-Media)*
Erlyns Portillo *(Media Planner & Media Buyer)*
Taylor Jackson *(Coord-Media)*

Accounts:
CBS Outdoor

BROAD STREET
242 W 30th St, New York, NY 10001
Tel.: (212) 780-5700
Fax: (212) 780-5710
E-Mail: newyork@broadstreet.com
Web Site: www.broadstreet.com

Employees: 50
Year Founded: 1981

Charlie Ray *(Pres)*
Mark Baltazar *(CEO)*
Claudia Rodriguez Tressler *(Partner & Chief Creative Officer)*
Ed Gibbons *(CFO)*
Teall Barnes *(VP-Bus Dev)*
Zachary Blitzer *(Coord-Production)*

Accounts:
Barnes & Noble
Cisco Systems
Diageo
ESPN
Ferrari
Genzyme
Newedge
Pfizer

BROADBASED COMMUNICATIONS INC.
1301 Riverplace Blvd Ste 1830, Jacksonville, FL 32207
Tel.: (904) 398-7279
Fax: (904) 398-6696
Web Site: www.bbased.com

Employees: 7

Agency Specializes In: Advertising, Brand Development & Integration, Internet/Web Design, Media Relations, Media Training, Print, Public Relations, Search Engine Optimization, Social Media

Revenue: $1,120,000

Jan Hirabayashi *(CEO)*
David Carrier *(Sr Dir-Art)*
Karen Okie *(Dir-Comm)*
Joy Watson Jarrell *(Mgr)*

Accounts:
24/7 Pediatric Care Center
Jacksonville University
Rayonier Advanced Materials

BROADHEAD
(Formerly Broadhead + Co.)
123 N 3rd St 4th Fl, Minneapolis, MN 55401
Tel.: (612) 623-8000
E-Mail: info@broadheadco.com
Web Site: www.broadheadco.com

Employees: 90
Year Founded: 2001

National Agency Associations: 4A's

Agency Specializes In: Advertising, Agriculture, Brand Development & Integration, Broadcast, Business-To-Business, Collateral, Communications, Consumer Goods, Consumer Marketing, Content, Corporate Identity, Crisis Communications, Digital/Interactive, Direct Response Marketing, Email, Government/Political, Graphic Design, In-Store Advertising, Internet/Web Design, Magazines, Market Research, Media Buying Services, Media Planning, Media Relations, Media Training, Men's Market, Newspapers & Magazines, Out-of-Home Media, Outdoor, Package Design, Paid Searches, Pets , Point of Sale, Print, Production (Ad, Film, Broadcast), Public Relations, Radio, Retail, Sales Promotion, Sponsorship, T.V., Viral/Buzz/Word of Mouth

Approx. Annual Billings: $55,000,000

Beth Burgy *(Pres)*
Pam Mariutto *(VP & Exec Creative Dir)*
John Walker *(Creative Dir)*
Debbie Christensen *(Dir-Art)*
Hans Hamman *(Jr Dir-Art)*
Lauren Kerr *(Acct Supvr)*
Anna Wagner *(Acct Exec)*
Paige Berens *(Jr Designer)*
Colleen Mulheran *(Jr Copywriter)*
Liz Qi *(Jr Designer)*
Anna Patiuk *(Acct Coord-PR)*
Kathryn Collins *(Coord-Digital Traffic)*

Accounts:
Almond Board of California; Modesto, CA (Agency of Record) Industry Relations; 2005
Bagley Fishing Lures; 2013
Boehringer Ingelheim Vetmedica Inc. (Agency of Record) Cattle, Swine & Equine Products; 2009
Canola of Canada Canola; 2012
Cargill
Hoegemeyer Hybrids Branding Strategy; 2013
Mosaic Company (Agency of Record) MicroEssentials
Pet Care Systems (Agency of Record) Consumer Packaged Goods; 2013
Toro Micro-Irrigation
US Department of Agriculture Consumer Outreach

BROCKETT CREATIVE GROUP, INC.
4299 Middle Settlement Rd, New Hartford, NY 13413
Tel.: (315) 797-5088
Web Site: www.brockettcreative.com

Employees: 7
Year Founded: 2002

Agency Specializes In: Advertising, Collateral, Content, Corporate Identity, Event Planning & Marketing, Internet/Web Design, Media Buying Services, Print, Public Relations, Social Media, Strategic Planning/Research

Revenue: $1,200,000

Matthew Brockett *(Pres & Dir-Creative)*
Karen Selinsky *(CFO & Project Mgr)*
Mary Dalrymple *(Mgr-Accounts)*

Accounts:
Broadway Theatre League; Utica, NY Broadway Shows; 2009
Capital Siding
Herkimer Foods; Ilion, NY Cheese Products; 2004
Hud-Son Forest Equipment
I Support Fundraising
Lake Ontario Outdoors Magazine; Clinton, NY Fishing Resource, Outdoors Magazine; 2010
Law Offices of Radley & Rheinhardt; Rome & Ilion, NY Elder Law & Estate Planning; 2010
Mohawk Valley Regions Path Through History
Varacalli Transportation Group

BROCKTON CREATIVE GROUP
4012 Washington St Ste 4, Kansas City, MO 64111
Tel.: (816) 569-3433
Web Site: www.brocktoncg.com

Year Founded: 2005

Agency Specializes In: Advertising, Brand Development & Integration, Content, Digital/Interactive, Internet/Web Design

Tim Mccoy *(Pres)*
Kirby Chamblin *(Art Dir)*
Erin Morris *(Asst Acct Exec)*
Tess Lyons *(Asst Acct Exec)*

Accounts:
Halls

BROGAN & PARTNERS CONVERGENCE MARKETING
800 N Old Woodward Ave, Birmingham, MI 48009
Tel.: (248) 341-8200
Fax: (248) 341-8201
E-Mail: mmarcotte@brogan.com
Web Site: www.brogan.com

E-Mail for Key Personnel:
President: mbrogan@brogan.com
Creative Dir.: bfolster@brogan.com
Media Dir.: mwarren@brogan.com

Employees: 55
Year Founded: 1984

National Agency Associations: Second Wind Limited

Agency Specializes In: Advertising, Advertising Specialties, Asian Market, Automotive, Brand Development & Integration, Broadcast, Business-To-Business, Cable T.V., Children's Market, Collateral, Communications, Consulting, Corporate Identity, Electronic Media, Event Planning & Marketing, Financial, Gay & Lesbian Market, Government/Political, Graphic Design, Health Care Services, High Technology, Hispanic Market, Internet/Web Design, Logo & Package Design, Magazines, Media Buying Services, Newspaper, Out-of-Home Media, Outdoor, Pharmaceutical, Planning & Consultation, Point of Purchase, Point of Sale, Print, Public Relations, Publicity/Promotions, Radio, Recruitment, Sports Market, Strategic Planning/Research, T.V., Technical Advertising, Teen Market, Trade & Consumer Magazines, Transportation, Travel & Tourism, Yellow Pages Advertising

Maria Marcotte *(CEO & Partner)*
Ellyn Davidson *(Mng Partner)*
Laurie Hix *(Partner & Dir-Creative)*
Vong Lee *(Partner & Assoc Dir-Creative)*
David Ryan *(Partner & Assoc Dir-Creative)*
Katie Rehrauer *(Acct Dir)*
Lauren Zuzelski *(Acct Dir)*
Jazmine Robinson *(Acct Coord)*

Accounts:
Covenant HealthCare (Agency of Record)
Frankenmuth Insurance (Agency of Record) Brand Awareness, Creative Development, Marketing Strategy Planning, Media Planning
HoneyBaked Ham Outdoor
Michigan Department of Community Health; Lansing, MI AIDS Prevention, Abstinence, Anti-Smoking, Date Rape Prevention, Domestic Violence, Fetal Alcohol Syndrome, Healthy Kids, Immunization, Mammography Screening, Michild, Osteoporosis Screening, Problem Gambling, WIC; 1987
Michigan First Credit Union
Pharmacy Advantage Creative, Digital, Integrated Marketing
PREZIO Health Brand Awareness, Marketing, Sales, Website Development

Branch

Brogan & Partners Convergence Marketing
14600 Western Pkwy Ste 300, Cary, NC 27513
Tel.: (919) 653-2580
Fax: (919) 653-2599
E-Mail: jtobin@brogan.com
Web Site: www.brogan.com

Employees: 25
Year Founded: 2000

National Agency Associations: Second Wind Limited

Agency Specializes In: Advertising, Collateral, Public Relations

Marcie Brogan *(Chm & Partner)*
Maria Marcotte *(CEO & Partner)*
Ellyn Davidson *(Mng Partner)*
Morgan Eberle *(Acct Mgr)*

Accounts:
American Heart Association
Comcast
Ford
GM
Levelone Bank
MSX International
Simpson Automotive Systems

BROGAN TENNYSON GROUP, INC.
2245 US Hwy 130 Ste 102, Dayton, NJ 08810-2420
Tel.: (732) 355-0700
Fax: (732) 355-0701
E-Mail: wschuetz@brogantennyson.com
Web Site: www.brogantennyson.com

Employees: 24
Year Founded: 1982

Agency Specializes In: Advertising, Fashion/Apparel, Graphic Design, Magazines, Retail

Approx. Annual Billings: $10,000,000

Bill Quinn *(Pres)*
Shirlene Soos *(CFO)*
Howard Kenworthy *(Sr VP)*
Wendy Scheutz *(VP)*
Maria Bryke-Drake *(Sr Dir-Art)*
Sue Thomas *(Sr Acct Mgr)*
Josephine Hutt *(Mgr-HR)*
Adrienne Wulffen *(Mgr-Acctg)*
Samantha Crivello *(Acct Exec)*
Meredith Mercadante *(Acct Exec)*
Kim Shargay *(Production Dir)*

Accounts:
Equity One, Inc.; New York, NY Consumer Advertising, Corporate Identity, Leasing Materials
Hutensky Capital Partners Marketing Materials
National Realty & Development Corp. Marketing Materials
The Pier Shops at Caesars; Atlantic City, NJ Marketing & Advertising
South Coast Plaza; Costa Mesa, CA Catalogs, Dining Magazine, Marketing & Advertising, Tourism Materials
Stanbery Development Cosumer Marketing & Advertising

BROKAW INC.

425 W Lakeside Ave, Cleveland, OH 44113-1029
Tel.: (216) 241-8003
Fax: (216) 241-8033
E-Mail: info@brokaw.com
Web Site: www.brokaw.com

E-Mail for Key Personnel:
President: bbrokaw@brokaw.com
Media Dir.: cgreene@brokaw.com

Employees: 45
Year Founded: 1992

Agency Specializes In: Advertising, Alternative Advertising, Arts, Aviation & Aerospace, Brand Development & Integration, Broadcast, Business Publications, Business-To-Business, Cable T.V., Collateral, College, Communications, Consulting, Consumer Goods, Consumer Marketing, Consumer Publications, Content, Corporate Identity, Digital/Interactive, Electronic Media, Email, Engineering, Environmental, Event Planning & Marketing, Exhibit/Trade Shows, Experience Design, Financial, Food Service, Graphic Design, Guerilla Marketing, Health Care Services, In-Store Advertising, Integrated Marketing, Internet/Web Design, Legal Services, Logo & Package Design, Magazines, Media Buying Services, Media Planning, Medical Products, Mobile Marketing, Multimedia, Newspaper, Newspapers & Magazines, Out-of-Home Media, Outdoor, Package Design, Paid Searches, Planning & Consultation, Point of Purchase, Point of Sale, Print, Production, Production (Ad, Film, Broadcast), Production (Print), Promotions, Public Relations, Publicity/Promotions, Radio, Restaurant, Retail, Sales Promotion, Search Engine Optimization, Social Marketing/Nonprofit, Social Media, Sponsorship, Sports Market, Strategic Planning/Research, T.V., Teen Market, Trade & Consumer Magazines, Transportation, Travel & Tourism, Viral/Buzz/Word of Mouth, Web (Banner Ads, Pop-ups, etc.), Women's Market

Gregg Brokaw *(Mng Partner)*
Mike Bratton *(Controller)*
Amie Becker *(Media Dir)*
Kathy Walters *(Acct Dir)*
Erin Srsen *(Sr Acct Mgr)*
Jayme Gilson *(Acct Supvr)*
Jack Gazdik *(Strategist-Digital, Planner & Buyer)*
Carrie Hogg *(Media Planner & Buyer)*
Megan Milanich *(Media Buyer)*

Accounts:
Cleveland Hopkins Airport (Agency of Record);; 2009
Fazoli's (Agency of Record) Quick Service Italian Chain; 2010
FirstMerit Corporation; Akron, OH Brand Strategy, Creative, Digital, Media, Public Relations; 2011
Great Lakes Brewing Co. (Agency of Record); 2000
Greater Cleveland Regional Transit Authority; Cleveland, OH
Neuro Drinks Sleep
Rainbow Babies & Children's Hospital
RTA (Agency of Record) Transportation Services; 2001
Smokey Bones Bar & Fire Grill Brand Strategy, Creative Development, Digital, Local Marketing, PR, Social Media
Smucker's; 1992
Sweet Tomatoes / Souplantation; San Diego, CA; 2012
University Hospitals (Agency of Record)
Wonka

BROLIK PRODUCTIONS, INC.

421 N 7th St Ste 701, Philadelphia, PA 19123
Tel.: (267) 297-8421
E-Mail: info@brolik.com
Web Site: www.brolik.com

Year Founded: 2004

Agency Specializes In: Advertising, Brand Development & Integration, Email, Internet/Web Design, Logo & Package Design, Mobile Marketing, Print, Production, Social Media

Jason Brewer *(Founder & CEO)*
Andrew Thomas *(Founder & Chief Creative Officer)*
Matthew Sommer *(Owner & CFO)*
Alex Caldwell *(Dir-Art)*
Jameel Farruk *(Dir-Client Rels)*
Bryce Liggins *(Sr Strategist-Mktg)*
Kierston Anderson *(Strategist-Mktg)*
Mike Gardo *(Strategist-Mktg)*
Jason Monte *(Acct Exec)*
Hannah Volz *(Sr Designer)*
Jessica Warhus *(Designer)*

Accounts:
Mass Save
Reality Sports Online
Upstage Video

THE BROOKLYN BROTHERS

18 E 17th St 6th Fl, New York, NY 10003
Tel.: (212) 242-0200
Fax: (212) 242-0217
E-Mail: guy@thebrooklynbrothers.com
Web Site: www.thebrooklynbrothers.com

Employees: 20
Year Founded: 2001

Agency Specializes In: Advertising, Graphic Design, Outdoor, Print, Sponsorship, T.V.

Approx. Annual Billings: $4,000,000

Stephen Rutterford *(Owner)*
Ben Conrad *(Exec Creative Dir)*
Kenneth Robin *(Creative Dir)*
Angel Zhang *(Acct Dir)*
Todd Myers *(Dir-Brand Dev)*
David Woodbury *(Dir-Art)*
Natasha Markley *(Strategist-Creative)*

Accounts:
Castrol
NBC Sports Campaign: "An American Coach In London", Campaign: "Fan For Life", Super Bowl 2015
New Era Campaign: "912 and on the Lam", Campaign: "Chicago vs. Chicago Round 1", Campaign: "Rivalry Part I"
Newsday Media Group
Optimum Campaign: "Smart Dog"
PepsiCo Campaign: "Headin' to Halftime", Campaign: "Hyped for Halftime", Campaign: "The Nasty What Now?", Digital, Online

Non-U.S. Branch

The Brooklyn Brothers

11-29 Smiths Ct, Soho, London, W1D 7DP United Kingdom
Tel.: (44) 207 292 6200
Fax: (44) 207 292 6215
Web Site: www.thebrooklynbrothers.com

Employees: 60

George Bryant *(Co-Founder & Partner)*
Jackie Stevenson *(Co-Founder & Partner)*
David Watson *(Co-Founder & Partner-London)*
Tarek Sioufi *(Head-Strategy)*
Gemma Morris *(Acct Dir & Producer)*
Steve Kirk *(Assoc Dir)*
Vaila Robertson *(Planner-Strategic)*

Accounts:
118 118
Apollo Tyres Brand Awareness, Digital, Electronic, Print
Apple
Bauer Media Grazia Fashion Magazine
BBC Life Is
BSkyB
Butcher's Pet Care Campaign: "This is Dog", Cat, Dog & Puppy Food Products, Digital, Lean & Tasty, Online, PR, Print, Tongue-in-Cheek
Discovery
FitFlop CAPSULE 12, Digital, PR
Iceland Campaign: "Inspired by Iceland"
Jaguar Campaign: "Desire", F-Type Model
Land Rover Campaign: "Being Henry", Content Marketing, Public Relations, Range Rover, Range Rover Evoque, Range Rover LRX, Social Media
London & Partners
Promote Iceland Campaign: "Honorary Islander", Campaign: "Inspired by Iceland"
Virgin

BROOKS BELL INTERACTIVE

711 Hillsborough St, Raleigh, NC 27603
Tel.: (919) 521-5300
Fax: (919) 882-9116
Toll Free: (866) 831-1886
E-Mail: info@brooks-bell.com
Web Site: www.brooks-bell.com

Employees: 20
Year Founded: 2003

Agency Specializes In: Digital/Interactive, Direct Response Marketing, Email, Graphic Design, Internet/Web Design, Strategic Planning/Research, Web (Banner Ads, Pop-ups, etc.)

Brooks Bell *(Founder & CEO)*
Robb Czyzewski *(CFO & COO)*
Gregory Ng *(CMO & Chief Strategy Officer)*
Meredith Morgan Albertson *(VP-Strategic Partnerships)*
Josh St. John *(VP-Client Experience)*
Mike Adams *(Dir & Engr-Optimization)*
Jenni Bruckman *(Dir-Client Mgmt)*
Suzi Tripp *(Sr Mgr-Client)*
Clair Ashburn *(Coord-Client)*
Sally Smith *(Client Mgr)*

Accounts:
AARP
AOL
Barrons
Chase
Citrix
Clear
Monster
NASCAR.COM
ProStores
Revolution
Safeway

Scholastic
Service Master
The Wall Street Journal
The Washington Post
Weight Watchers
XM

BROTHERS & CO.

4860 S Lewis Ave Ste 100, Tulsa, OK 74105-5171
Tel.: (918) 743-8822
Fax: (918) 742-9628
E-Mail: broco@broco.com
Web Site: www.broco.com

Employees: 50
Year Founded: 1974

National Agency Associations: 4A's

Agency Specializes In: Advertising, Broadcast, Business-To-Business, Collateral, Graphic Design, Health Care Services, Leisure, Marine, Media Buying Services, Newspapers & Magazines, Over-50 Market, Print, Radio, Sports Market, T.V.

Approx. Annual Billings: $16,000,000

Tommy Campbell *(Sr VP & Dir-Creative)*
Eric Barnes *(Sr VP)*
Dave Thomas *(VP-Acct Plng)*
Kristjan Olson *(Head-Wichita Team & Acct Supvr)*
Garrett Fresh *(Sr Dir-Art)*
Alan McGuckin *(Dir-Media Rels)*
Heath Kennedy *(Assoc Dir-Creative & Digital Strategy)*
Laura Beth Bevill *(Media Planner & Media Buyer)*
Megan Gleim *(Media Planner & Media Buyer)*
Abigail Coppinger *(Asst Acct Exec)*

Accounts:
Bushnell Binoculars
Citgo Fishing & MotorGuide
CommunityCare
Daisy Outdoor Co.; Rogers, AK
Fidelity Bank; Wichita, KS; 2002
Plano Molding Company; Chicago, IL Fishing Tackle Boxes; 1996
Pradco Outdoor
Recreational Boating & Fishing Foundation
Utica Square Shopping Center; 2001

BROWN BAG MARKETING

3060 Peachtree Rd NW Ste 2000, Atlanta, GA 30305
Tel.: (404) 442-5650
Fax: (404) 442-5651
Web Site: www.brownbagmarketing.com

Year Founded: 2002

Agency Specializes In: Advertising, Brand Development & Integration, Business-To-Business, Internet/Web Design, Mobile Marketing, Sales Promotion, Social Media

Jerry Lewis *(VP & Dir-Creative)*
Virginia Lewis *(VP-Ops)*
Sela Missirian *(VP-Strategy & Bus Dev)*
Brooke Wilson *(VP-Client Strategy & Innovation)*
Liz Fusco *(Assoc Dir-Creative & Content)*
Brittany Paris *(Acct Supvr)*

Accounts:
Children Without a Voice USA

BROWN COMMUNICATIONS GROUP

2275 Albert St, Regina, SK S4P 2V5 Canada
Tel.: (306) 352-6625
Fax: (306) 757-1980
Toll Free: (877) 202-7696
E-Mail: solutions@brown.ca
Web Site: www.brown.ca

E-Mail for Key Personnel:
President: ken.christoffel@brown.ca
Creative Dir.: mike.woroniak@brown.ca

Employees: 35
Year Founded: 1966

National Agency Associations:

Agency Specializes In: Communications, Internet/Web Design, Public Relations, Strategic Planning/Research

Approx. Annual Billings: $14,000,000

James Aho *(Owner)*
Ken Christoffel *(Pres & CEO)*
Kolene Elliott *(Acct Dir)*
Erin Stankewich *(Acct Dir)*
Steve Pady *(Dir-Art)*
Lori Romanoski *(Dir-Client Dev)*
Charlotte Gibling *(Assoc Dir-Creative)*
Carmen Clark *(Acct Supvr)*

Accounts:
Canadian Cancer Society
Saskatchewan Power Corporation
SaskTel

BROWNBOOTS INTERACTIVE, INC.

108 S Main St, Fond Du Lac, WI 54935
Tel.: (920) 906-9175
Fax: (920) 906-9177
E-Mail: info@brownboots.com
Web Site: www.brownboots.com

Employees: 7

Agency Specializes In: Advertising, Digital/Interactive, Internet/Web Design, Logo & Package Design, Print, Search Engine Optimization

Alan Hathaway *(Owner)*
Jim Quackenboss *(Mgr-Sys)*
Patrick Rose *(Acct Exec)*

Accounts:
Agnesian HealthCare; Fond Du Lac, WI Web Design
Brenner Tank LLC
Children's Museum of Fond du Lac; Fond Du Lac, WI Web Design
Fond du Lac Area Association of Commerce; Fond Du Lac, WI Web Design
Fond du Lac County Economic Development Corporation; Fond Du Lac, WI Web Design

BROWNING ADVERTISING LLC

121 Chanlon Rd, New Providence, NJ 07974
Mailing Address:
PO Box 2112, New Providence, NJ 07974
Tel.: (646) 710-4465

Year Founded: 1984

Agency Specializes In: Above-the-Line, Advertising, Advertising Specialties, Affiliate Marketing, Affluent Market, African-American Market, Agriculture, Alternative Advertising, Arts, Asian Market, Automotive, Aviation & Aerospace, Below-the-Line, Bilingual Market, Brand Development & Integration, Branded Entertainment, Broadcast, Business Publications, Business-To-Business, Cable T.V., Catalogs, Children's Market, Co-op Advertising, Collateral, College, Commercial Photography, Communications, Computers & Software, Consulting, Consumer Goods, Consumer Marketing, Consumer Publications, Content, Corporate Communications, Corporate Identity, Cosmetics, Crisis Communications, Custom Publishing, Customer Relationship Management, Digital/Interactive, Direct Response Marketing, Direct-to-Consumer, E-Commerce, Education, Electronic Media, Electronics, Email, Engineering, Entertainment, Environmental, Event Planning & Marketing, Exhibit/Trade Shows, Experience Design, Faith Based, Fashion/Apparel, Financial, Food Service, Game Integration, Gay & Lesbian Market, Government/Political, Graphic Design, Guerilla Marketing, Health Care Services, High Technology, Hispanic Market, Hospitality, Household Goods, Identity Marketing, In-Store Advertising, Industrial, Infomercials, Information Technology, Integrated Marketing, International, Internet/Web Design, Investor Relations, Legal Services, Leisure, Local Marketing, Logo & Package Design, Luxury Products, Magazines, Marine, Market Research, Media Buying Services, Media Planning, Media Relations, Media Training, Medical Products, Men's Market, Merchandising, Mobile Marketing, Multicultural, Multimedia, New Product Development, New Technologies, Newspaper, Newspapers & Magazines, Out-of-Home Media, Outdoor, Over-50 Market, Package Design, Paid Searches, Pets , Pharmaceutical, Planning & Consultation, Podcasting, Point of Purchase, Point of Sale, Print, Product Placement, Production, Production (Ad, Film, Broadcast), Production (Print), Promotions, Public Relations, Publicity/Promotions, Publishing, RSS (Really Simple Syndication), Radio, Real Estate, Recruitment, Regional, Restaurant, Retail, Sales Promotion, Search Engine Optimization, Seniors' Market, Shopper Marketing, Social Marketing/Nonprofit, Social Media, South Asian Market, Sponsorship, Sports Market, Stakeholders, Strategic Planning/Research, Sweepstakes, Syndication, T.V., Technical Advertising, Teen Market, Telemarketing, Trade & Consumer Magazines, Transportation, Travel & Tourism, Tween Market, Urban Market, Viral/Buzz/Word of Mouth, Web (Banner Ads, Pop-ups, etc.), Women's Market, Yellow Pages Advertising

Approx. Annual Billings: $250,000 Capitalized

Breakdown of Gross Billings by Media:
Copywriting: 25%; Programmatic: 50%; Sponsorship: 25%

Angela Zeller *(CIO)*
Maggie Arguelles *(CEO-Hosting & Internet)*
Sanjeev R Chi *(VP-Mgr-Programmatic)*
Amy Irster *(VP-Shopper Insights)*
Lisa Parsons *(VP-Interactive)*
Tracy Wong *(Dir-Mdsg)*
Tracy Wells *(Mgr-Shopper)*
Henry Roder *(Coord-Shopper Insights)*
Rene Coiffard *(Assoc-Creative)*
Amy Edwards *(Assoc-Acct Svcs)*
Christian Franzen *(Asst-Sls)*
Susanne Grundmann *(Jr Asst-Mktg)*

Accounts:
Baubles + Beads
The Boston Globe
bsmith.com
Carolina Chicken, Fish & Beef Products
Chic Treats Costume Jewelry
The Cooking Channel
Harris Inc.
Hillard Trucks; New Providence, NJ Logistics; 2009
Jergens Inc.
Jim's Autos
Jones Incorporated; Boston, MA
Kelloggs Company; New York, NY
New Cafe 121
Rogers Railroad Co.
Sanford Enterprises; 1993
Silver Hanger Cleaners; 2013
SimmonsJules+
Smith & Jones Cookies Chocolate Chip Cookies
The Smith Corp.

TMB Productions Music Recording Services; 2000
Tracy Lin Footwear
Union Recruitment Services; 1993
Washington Post

BROWNSTEIN GROUP
215 S Broad St 9th Fl, Philadelphia, PA 19107-5325
Tel.: (215) 735-3470
Fax: (215) 735-6298
Web Site: www.brownsteingroup.com

E-Mail for Key Personnel:
President: marc@brownsteingroup.com

Employees: 60
Year Founded: 1964

National Agency Associations: 4A's-AD CLUB-DMA-PRSA

Agency Specializes In: Advertising, Brand Development & Integration, Business-To-Business, Collateral, College, Communications, Consumer Marketing, Corporate Identity, Customer Relationship Management, Digital/Interactive, Direct Response Marketing, Education, Email, Entertainment, Event Planning & Marketing, Graphic Design, Health Care Services, Integrated Marketing, Internet/Web Design, Logo & Package Design, Market Research, Media Relations, New Product Development, Newspapers & Magazines, Point of Sale, Print, Public Relations, Publicity/Promotions, Radio, Sponsorship, Sports Market, Strategic Planning/Research, T.V.

Approx. Annual Billings: $50,000,000

Breakdown of Gross Billings by Media: D.M.: $10,000,000; Internet Adv.: $5,000,000; Newsp. & Mags.: $3,000,000; Out-of-Home Media: $9,000,000; Radio: $9,000,000; T.V.: $14,000,000

Berny Brownstein *(Owner)*
Carol Petro *(CFO & Sr VP)*
Shannon Reynolds *(VP & Dir-Acct Mgmt)*
Dan Shepelavy *(Exec Dir-Creative)*
Cynthia Slaby *(Grp Acct Dir)*
Aimee Cicero *(Mgr-Comm)*
Jenna Frimmel *(Sr Acct Exec)*
Sarah Lanzone *(Sr Acct Exec)*
Kelsey Ruane *(Acct Exec)*
Mara Sardella *(Generalist-HR)*
Jeremie Rose Wimbrow *(Designer)*
Chloe Steerman *(Acct Coord)*
Kathleen Tower *(Coord-Social Media)*

Accounts:
Advanta; Springhouse, PA; 2005
AmeriGas
AmerisourceBergen
ARCH Chemicals
Arthur Ashe Foundation
Beneficial Bank
Campus Apartments
Comcast
Cozen O'Connor Brand Strategy Development
Craiger Drake; Philadelphia, PA Public Relations
Einstein Healthcare Network
IKEA
Kelleher Associates, LLC.; Wayne, PA Public Relations
Keystone Property Group (Agency of Record) Digital Advertising, Print, Website
The Madlyn & Leonard Abramson Center for Jewish Life
Mark Group Public Relations, Social Media
Microsoft Corporation; Redmond, WA
Penn State University
Philadelphia Federal Credit Union Financial
Saint-Gobain North America
Temple University
TireVan Strategic Media Relations Campaign
UnitedHealthcare; Philadelphia, PA; 2004
Universal Technical Institute (Agency of Record) Media Relations, PR

Branches

Nucleus Digital
215 S Broad St, Philadelphia, PA 19107
Tel.: (215) 735-3470
Web Site: www.nucleusd.com/contact.html

Year Founded: 2013

Adam Deringer *(Partner & Gen Mgr)*

BRUCE CLAY, INC.
(d/b/a Bruceclaycom)
207 W Los Angeles Ave Ste 277, Moorpark, CA 93021
Tel.: (805) 517-1900
Fax: (805) 517-1919
E-Mail: info-bc@bruceclay.com
Web Site: www.bruceclay.com

Employees: 38
Year Founded: 1996

Agency Specializes In: Advertising, Search Engine Optimization

Bruce Clay *(Pres)*
Mindy Weinstein *(Dir-Trng)*
Robert Ramirez *(Mgr-SEO)*
Diana Becerra *(Analyst-Search Engine Mktg)*

BRUCE MAU DESIGN
469C King St W, Toronto, ON M5V 3M4 Canada
Tel.: (416) 306-6401
E-Mail: info@brucemaudesign.com
Web Site: www.brucemaudesign.com

Year Founded: 1985

Agency Specializes In: Advertising, Brand Development & Integration, Communications, Digital/Interactive

Katherine Craig *(Dir-Brands & Comm)*
Alexis Green *(Dir-Comm)*
Emile Molin *(Assoc Dir-Creative)*
Amy De Merlis *(Acct Mgr)*
Tom Keogh *(Sr Project Dir)*

Accounts:
FastCo Design
The Regent Park School of Music
Sonos

BRUM ADVERTISING
1 Perimeter Park S Ste 100, Birmingham, AL 35243
Tel.: (205) 447-9871
Fax: (205) 970-6300
Web Site: www.brumadvertising.com

Year Founded: 1999

Agency Specializes In: Advertising, Internet/Web Design, Media Planning, Print, Public Relations, Radio, T.V.

Alan Brumbeloe *(Pres & Dir-Creative)*
Stephanie Brumbeloe *(VP)*

Accounts:
Schaeffer Eye Center
Susan Schein Automotive Group
Vital Smiles

BRUNET-GARCIA ADVERTISING, INC.
1510 Hendricks Ave, Jacksonville, FL 32207
Tel.: (904) 346-1977
Fax: (904) 346-1917
Toll Free: (866) 346-1977
E-Mail: info@brunetgarcia.com
Web Site: www.brunetgarcia.com

Year Founded: 2003

Agency Specializes In: Brand Development & Integration, Broadcast, Digital/Interactive, Exhibit/Trade Shows, Market Research, Media Planning, Multicultural, Outdoor, Public Relations, Social Media

Jorge Brunet-Garcia *(Pres, CEO & Partner)*
Diane Brunet-Garcia *(Partner & VP)*
Molly Walker *(Chief Strategy Officer & VP)*
Aerien Mull *(Sr Dir-Art & Mgr-Studio)*
Kedgar Volta *(Dir-Art)*
Kate Jolley *(Mgr-Brand Mktg)*
Cristina Parcell *(Mgr-Govt Mktg)*
Chad Villarroel *(Jr Acct Coord)*

Accounts:
BLOCK X BLOCK
Carolyn Ettlinger Consulting LLC
Cathedral Arts Project Angels of the Arts Invite
Coastline Federal Credit Union
Family Promise of Jacksonville Campaign: "Cardboard City HOME Sculpture"
Grape Guru Logo
Horton Foote Legacy Project Brochure
Jax Film Fest Campaign: "Coasters"
Maxwell Management Consulting
Me Embellished Book Design
MOCA Jacksonville Campaign: "The Art You Missed"
One World Foundation Campaign: "The World of Foote"
PACE Center for Girls
Players by the Sea Cat on a Hot Tin Roof Poster, Next to Normal Poster, Reefer Madness Poster, Talking Heads Poster, The Trojan Women Poster
St. Johns River State College

BRUNNER
11 Stanwix St 5th Fl, Pittsburgh, PA 15222-1312
Tel.: (412) 995-9500
Fax: (412) 995-9501
E-Mail: amastrippolito@brunnerworks.com
Web Site: brunnerworks.com

E-Mail for Key Personnel:
Chairman: MBrunner@brunnerworks.com
President: smorgan@brunnerworks.com

Employees: 210
Year Founded: 1989

National Agency Associations: 4A's-BMA-MAGNET

Agency Specializes In: Advertising, Affluent Market, Automotive, Brand Development & Integration, Broadcast, Business-To-Business, Cable T.V., Catalogs, Co-op Advertising, Collateral, College, Communications, Consulting, Consumer Goods, Consumer Marketing, Consumer Publications, Content, Corporate Communications, Corporate Identity, Crisis Communications, Customer Relationship Management, Digital/Interactive, Direct Response Marketing, Direct-to-Consumer, E-Commerce, Education, Electronic Media, Email, Engineering, Environmental, Event Planning & Marketing, Exhibit/Trade Shows, Experience Design, Financial, Food Service, Graphic Design, Guerilla Marketing, Health Care Services, High Technology, Hospitality, Household Goods, Identity Marketing, In-Store Advertising, Industrial, Information Technology, Integrated Marketing, Internet/Web Design, Legal Services, Leisure, Local Marketing,

Logo & Package Design, Luxury Products, Magazines, Market Research, Media Buying Services, Media Planning, Media Relations, Media Training, Medical Products, Men's Market, Merchandising, Mobile Marketing, Multimedia, New Product Development, New Technologies, Newspaper, Newspapers & Magazines, Out-of-Home Media, Outdoor, Over-50 Market, Package Design, Paid Searches, Pets , Pharmaceutical, Planning & Consultation, Podcasting, Point of Purchase, Point of Sale, Print, Product Placement, Production, Production (Print), Promotions, Public Relations, Publicity/Promotions, RSS (Really Simple Syndication), Radio, Real Estate, Recruitment, Regional, Restaurant, Retail, Sales Promotion, Search Engine Optimization, Seniors' Market, Social Marketing/Nonprofit, Social Media, Sponsorship, Sports Market, Strategic Planning/Research, Sweepstakes, T.V., Teen Market, Telemarketing, Trade & Consumer Magazines, Travel & Tourism, Tween Market, Viral/Buzz/Word of Mouth, Women's Market

Approx. Annual Billings: $220,000,000

Mary Kay Modaffari *(Partner & Mng Dir)*
Louis Sawyer *(Chief Strategy Officer)*
Rose Lied *(Sr VP & Grp Dir-Acct Strategy)*
Jeffrey Maggs *(Sr VP & Acct Mgmt Dir)*
Ken Johns *(Sr VP-Digital Strategy)*
Dan Gbur *(VP-Digital Bus Dev)*
Patrick Stroh *(VP-Data Analytics)*
Lauren Mannetti *(Grp Dir-Media)*
Brad Cook *(Acct Dir)*
Erin Getty *(Project Dir-Digital)*
Jason Mileto *(Dir-Video Dev)*
Christopher Spain *(Dir-Art)*
Kathy Baldauf *(Assoc Dir-Brdcst)*
Amy Mathis *(Sr Acct Mgr)*
Nathan Wachter *(Sr Acct Mgr)*
Erika Kapko *(Acct Mgr)*
Jenny Williams *(Acct Mgr)*
Katie Collins *(Mgr-Social Community)*
Jim Lundy *(Mgr-Studio)*
Joel Ulrich *(Sr Strategist-Media)*
Nicholas Wilson *(Sr Strategist-Social)*
Morgan Copeland *(Strategist-Content)*
Andrea Hornish *(Media Planner & Media Buyer)*
Nathan Marshall *(Copywriter)*
Joie Faust *(Coord-Svcs)*
Kelly McCafferty *(Coord-New Bus)*
Bob Rusnak *(Sr Designer-Interactive)*

Accounts:
Atlanta Bread; 2007
Beazer Homes; 2008
Bob Evans Farms, Inc. Broasted Chicken, Digital, Video
CARE Ambient ads, Creative, Outdoor, Print
CONSOL Energy Inc. Coal, Energy Production, Raw Materials & Minerals, Lights Campaign, Television; 2006
DeVry University; 2007
Eaton Corp. (Agency of Record) Golf Pride, Vehicle Group; 2003
Field & Stream Specialty Stores (Agency of Record) Creative, Marketing, Online, Social Media
GlaxoSmithKline Aquafresh, Time 2 Brush; 2000
GNC Corporation; 2004
Gold Pride Campaign: "In-banner Regrip"
Great Southern Wood Preserving Brand Strategy, Channel Marketing, Creative, Digital, Media Planning & Buying, Research, YellaWood
Huffy Corporation Huffy Bikes; 2009
James Hardie Siding Products; 2009
Jarden Corporation Mr. Coffee, Mr. Coffee Blogger Kit, Mr. Coffee Blogger Outreach
Knouse Foods, Inc. Lucky Leaf, Musselman's
LaRosa's Inc.; 2005
Mars, Incorporated
New-Mitsubishi Electric (Agency of Record) Cooling & Heating Division, Creative, Marketing Communications, Media, Planning, Social Media
MTD Products Cub Cadet, Cub Heating Bill POP; 2004
Philips Healthcare Respironics; 1999
PPG Industries; 1996
Ron Kirn Guitars Campaign: "Baggage, Angst, Affair", Campaign: "Hand Made Guitars"
ShurTech Brands LLC Digital Marketing, Duck Tape, Social Media, Videos
Steris Corporation; 2010
Werner Ladders
Westinghouse
Wise Foods Cheez Doodles, Wise Snacks; 2010
Zippo Manufacturing Hand Warmer, W.R. Case & Sons Cutlery; 1997

Branches

Brunner
1100 Peachtree St NE Ste 550, Atlanta, GA 30309
Tel.: (404) 479-2200
Fax: (404) 479-9850
E-Mail: amastrippolito@brunnerworks.com
Web Site: www.brunnerworks.com

Employees: 70
Year Founded: 1989

National Agency Associations: 4A's-MAGNET-PRSA

Agency Specializes In: Advertising, Affluent Market, Automotive, Brand Development & Integration, Broadcast, Business-To-Business, Cable T.V., Catalogs, Co-op Advertising, Collateral, College, Communications, Consulting, Consumer Goods, Consumer Marketing, Consumer Publications, Content, Corporate Communications, Corporate Identity, Crisis Communications, Customer Relationship Management, Digital/Interactive, Direct Response Marketing, Direct-to-Consumer, E-Commerce, Education, Electronic Media, Email, Engineering, Environmental, Event Planning & Marketing, Exhibit/Trade Shows, Experience Design, Financial, Food Service, Graphic Design, Guerilla Marketing, Health Care Services, High Technology, Hospitality, Household Goods, Identity Marketing, In-Store Advertising, Industrial, Information Technology, Integrated Marketing, Internet/Web Design, Legal Services, Leisure, Local Marketing, Logo & Package Design, Luxury Products, Magazines, Market Research, Media Planning, Media Relations, Media Training, Medical Products, Men's Market, Merchandising, Mobile Marketing, Multimedia, New Product Development, New Technologies, Newspaper, Newspapers & Magazines, Out-of-Home Media, Outdoor, Over-50 Market, Package Design, Paid Searches, Pets , Pharmaceutical, Planning & Consultation, Podcasting, Point of Purchase, Point of Sale, Print, Product Placement, Production, Production (Ad, Film, Broadcast), Production (Print), Promotions, Public Relations, Publicity/Promotions, RSS (Really Simple Syndication), Radio, Real Estate, Regional, Restaurant, Retail, Sales Promotion, Search Engine Optimization, Seniors' Market, Social Marketing/Nonprofit, Social Media, Sponsorship, Sports Market, Strategic Planning/Research, Sweepstakes, T.V., Teen Market, Telemarketing, Trade & Consumer Magazines, Travel & Tourism, Tween Market, Viral/Buzz/Word of Mouth, Web (Banner Ads, Pop-ups, etc.), Women's Market

Michael Brunner *(CEO)*
Rick Gardinier *(Chief Digital Officer & Sr VP)*
Jeff Maggs *(Sr VP & Acct Mgmt Dir)*
Rich Fabritius *(Mng Dir-Atlanta)*
Pat Stroh *(VP-Data Analytics)*
Jay Giesen *(Exec Dir-Creative)*
Christopher Fox *(Dir-Digital Art & Designer-UX)*
Ben Stanfield *(Mgr-New Bus Dev)*

Accounts:
Atlanta Bread; 2007
Beazer Homes; 2008
Bob Evans Restaurants & Food Products; 2009
The Dow Chemical Company Great Stuff
Eaton Corporation Golf Pride, Vehicle Group; 2003
Edwin Watts Golf Shops, Inc.
Glaxosmithkline Quit.com; 2000
GNC Corporation; 2004
Great Southern Wood Preserving Brand Strategy, Channel Marketing, Digital, Media Planning & Buying, Research
Hollywood Theater
Huffy Corporation Huffy Bikes; 2009
James Hardie Siding Products; 2009
Knouse Foods Inc. Lucky Leaf, Musselman's; 2002
Nu-way Weiners Campaign: "America's Chili Dog Since 1916", Mug Collection, Plate Collection, Spoon Collection
Phillips Healthcare Respironics; 1999
PPG Industries; 1996
Rich Products Corporation SeaPak Frozen Shrimp, Seapak; 2010
Rockford Health System; 2002
Starship Campaign: "Worth The Drive"
Steris Corporation; 2010
Wise Foods Cheese Doodles, Wise Snacks; 2010
Wright Travel Campaign: "Chateau", Campaign: "Everglades", Campaign: "Hotel Italia", Campaign: "We Know"

BRUNSWICK MEDIA SERVICES LLC
PO Box 10904, New Brunswick, NJ 08906
Mailing Address:
PO BOX 10904, New Brunswick, NJ 08906-0904
Tel.: (732) 599-0022
Fax: (321) 600-3653
E-Mail: info@brunswickmedia.com
Web Site: www.brunswickmedia.com

Employees: 2
Year Founded: 2003

Agency Specializes In: Broadcast, Event Planning & Marketing, Industrial, Media Buying Services, Multimedia, Out-of-Home Media, Production (Ad, Film, Broadcast), RSS (Really Simple Syndication), Social Marketing/Nonprofit, T.V.

Josh Gerth *(Acct Dir)*
Sarah Salky *(Acct Dir)*
Annalise Carol *(Dir)*
Patricia Graue *(Dir)*
Mylene Mangalindan *(Dir)*
Darren Mcdermott *(Dir)*
Lauren Odell *(Dir)*
Blake Sonnenshein *(Dir)*
Steven Lipin *(Sr Partner-US)*

Accounts:
Hartz Mountain Corporation
Ports America

BRUSHFIRE, INC.
2 Wing Dr, Cedar Knolls, NJ 07927
Tel.: (973) 871-1700
Fax: (973) 871-1717
Web Site: www.brushfireinc.com

E-Mail for Key Personnel:
President: JMueller@brushfireinc.com
Media Dir.: jthomsen@brushfireinc.com
Public Relations: vwarner@brushfireinc.com

Employees: 38
Year Founded: 1969

Agency Specializes In: Advertising, Brand Development & Integration, Business-To-Business, Consumer Marketing, Event Planning & Marketing, Internet/Web Design, Public Relations, Sponsorship, Strategic Planning/Research

Approx. Annual Billings: $47,000,000

Joan Mueller *(Pres)*
John P. Leonardi *(CEO)*
Jon Renner *(Exec VP & Gen Mgr)*
Anne Armelino *(VP & Assoc Dir-Media)*
Debra McCleary *(Controller)*
Liz DiPilli *(Dir-Strategic Plng)*
Will Pang *(Assoc Dir-Creative)*

Accounts:
The Eastern Tea Corporation Brand Development, Bromley Tea, PR, Research
GK's Red Dog Tavern
Gould Paper
JBWS
Kozy Shack
Minwax
New Jersey Lottery Media
Paper Mill Play House
Promotion in Motion
Remington
Rod's Steakhouse & Seafood Grille
Sherwin-Williams Company The Minwax Company, Thompson's Water Seal
Subaru of America
Thomsons Water Seal

Branch

BRUSHfire, Inc./New York
555 5th Ave 17th Fl, New York, NY 10017
Tel.: (212) 681-6757
Fax: (212) 681-6759
E-Mail: vwarner@brushfireinc.com
Web Site: www.brushfireinc.com

E-Mail for Key Personnel:
President: jpleonard@brushfireinc.com
Creative Dir.: kmusto@brushfireinc.com
Media Dir.: jthomsen@brushfireinc.com
Production Mgr.: gmcrevins@brushfireinc.com
Public Relations: vwarner@brushfireinc.com

Year Founded: 1969

Agency Specializes In: Advertising, Brand Development & Integration, Business-To-Business, Consumer Marketing, Event Planning & Marketing, Internet/Web Design, Public Relations, Sales Promotion

Joan Mueller *(Pres)*
Michelle Goldstein *(VP & Mgmt Supvr)*
Anne Armelino *(VP & Assoc Dir-Media)*
Donald Stagaard *(Assoc Dir-Creative)*

Accounts:
Colgate
Fannie E. Rippel Foundation
Kozy Shack
Maxell
Minwax
Subaru
Thompson's Waterseal
Velcro
Western Union

BRYAN MILLS IRADESSO CORP.
1129 Leslie St, Toronto, ON M3C 2K5 Canada
Tel.: (416) 447-4740
E-Mail: contact@bmir.com
Web Site: www.bmir.com

Employees: 50
Year Founded: 1975

Agency Specializes In: Advertising

Nancy Ladenheim *(CEO)*
Jeff Martin *(Partner & COO)*
Ian Todd *(Dir-Creative)*

Accounts:
Genworth
Shoppers DrugMart
Tim Hortons

BSY ASSOCIATES INC
960 Holmdel Rd Bldg II Ste 201, Holmdel, NJ 7733
Tel.: (732) 817-0400
Web Site: www.bsya.com

Agency Specializes In: Advertising, Brand Development & Integration, Collateral, Corporate Communications, Crisis Communications, Event Planning & Marketing, Internet/Web Design, Media Planning, Public Relations, Strategic Planning/Research

Barbara Spector Yeninas *(CEO & Partner)*
Suzie Chu *(Dir-Special Events & PR Projects)*
Mike Guarino *(Dir-Creative)*

Accounts:
Artemus TS

BTC MARKETING
(Formerly Boyd Tamney Cross Inc.)
994 Old Eagle School Rd Ste 1015, Wayne, PA 19087-1802
Tel.: (610) 293-0500
Fax: (610) 687-8199
Toll Free: (800) 882-8066
E-Mail: info@btcmarketing.com
Web Site: btcmarketing.com

Employees: 20
Year Founded: 1980

National Agency Associations: Second Wind Limited

Agency Specializes In: Advertising, Business-To-Business, Collateral, Financial, Leisure, Planning & Consultation, Public Relations, Sales Promotion, Strategic Planning/Research, Travel & Tourism

Approx. Annual Billings: $24,000,000

Tom Cancelmo *(Pres)*
Chris Murray *(Exec VP)*
David Culver *(VP-PR)*
Laura W. Koster *(VP-Consumer)*
Christy Hoffman *(Controller)*
Mandi Zola *(Sr Dir-Art)*

Accounts:
Chesapeake Hyatt; Cambridge, MA; 2003
The Hyatt Regency Chesapeake Bay
Mohonk Mountain House
Tucker's Point Hotel & Spa Promotional Emails
Valley Forge Convention & Visitors Bureau

BUBBLEUP, LLC.
719 Sawdust Rd Ste 104, The Woodlands, TX 77380
Tel.: (713) 201-2945
Fax: (832) 585-0705
E-Mail: info@bubbleup.net
Web Site: www.bubbleup.net

Employees: 35
Year Founded: 2004

Agency Specializes In: Advertising, Content, Digital/Interactive, Electronic Media, Email, Experience Design, Graphic Design, Local Marketing, Mobile Marketing, Multimedia, Podcasting, Search Engine Optimization, Social Media, Strategic Planning/Research, Web (Banner Ads, Pop-ups, etc.)

Approx. Annual Billings: $14,000,000

Coleman Sisson *(Chm & CEO)*
Mike Newman *(VP-Sls & Mktg)*
Lee Totten *(VP-Dev & Design)*
Brad Jameson *(Sr Acct Mgr)*
Jennifer Balzer *(Sr Project Mgr)*
Amanda Melones *(Office Mgr)*
Tracy Goldenberg *(Mgr-Acct Svcs)*
Steve Newman *(Mgr-Client)*

Accounts:
Academy of Country Music ACM; 2009
Anheuser Busch Landshark Lager; 2010
Margaritaville Landshark Lager, Margaritaville; 2004

BUCK LA
515 W 7th St 4th Fl, Los Angeles, CA 90014
Tel.: (213) 623-0111
Fax: (213) 623-0117
E-Mail: info@buck.tv
Web Site: www.buck.tv

Employees: 20
Year Founded: 2003

Agency Specializes In: Electronic Media, Electronics, Internet/Web Design, Production, Production (Ad, Film, Broadcast), T.V.

Jeff Ellermeyer *(Mng Dir & Principal)*
Ryan Honey *(Principal & Dir-Creative)*
Orion Tait *(Principal & Dir-Creative)*
Yker Moreno *(Assoc Dir-Creative)*
Joe Mullen *(Assoc Dir-Creative)*
Jenny Ko *(Designer)*

Accounts:
AMEX
Boiron
Five
Free Style
Fuel TV
G4
Nike
Spike TV

New York

Buck NY
247 Centre St 5fl, New York, NY 10013
Tel.: (212) 668-0111
Fax: (212) 226-0167
E-Mail: info08@buck.tv
Web Site: www.buck.tv

Employees: 14

Agency Specializes In: Advertising, Automotive, Cable T.V., Digital/Interactive, T.V.

Orion Tait *(Principal & Dir-Creative)*
Justin Fines *(Assoc Dir-Creative)*
Jon Gorman *(Assoc Dir-Creative)*
Benjamin Langsfeld *(Assoc Dir-Creative)*
Stefania Consarino *(Coord-Production)*
Ann Seymour *(Coord-Production)*

BUCKAROO MARKETING
7987 Wolford Ct Ste 200, Fishers, IN 46038
Tel.: (317) 845-0830
Fax: (888) 959-7184
Web Site: www.gobuckaroo.com

Agency Specializes In: Advertising, Brand Development & Integration, Digital/Interactive, Email, Print, Strategic Planning/Research

Deborah Daily *(Pres)*
Kenneth Daily *(CEO)*

Elisabeth Singh *(Specialist-Mktg Res)*

Accounts:
Alba Manufacturing Inc New Media Agency of Record

THE BUDDY GROUP
7 Studebaker, Irvine, CA 92618
Tel.: (949) 468-0042
Fax: (949) 951-1310
Web Site: www.thebuddygroup.com

Year Founded: 2005

Agency Specializes In: Advertising, Brand Development & Integration, Digital/Interactive, Sponsorship

Pete Deutschman *(Founder)*
Brian Birkhauser *(Dir-Tech)*
Brian Desautel *(Dir-Creative)*
Brooke Allen *(Sr Strategist-Digital)*
Kari Reynolds *(Strategist-Digital)*
Sarah Allen *(Sr Designer)*

Accounts:
AARP
Butterball, LLC
EKOCYCLE
KING'S HAWAIIAN Bread
Lynx Professional Grills Digital, Flagship Lynx Grills, Sedona Grill Line
Motorola Enterprise Mobility
NBC Universal, Inc.
Pentel of America Campaign: "Unleash the Power of Pentel", Content Marketing, Discoverability, EnerGel-Xpen, Media, Microsite Design & Development, Program Development, Social Platform Management, Strategy, Video Creation
Reebok International Ltd.
SunBriteTV
Western Digital
YouTube

BUERO NEW YORK
413 W 14th St 4th Fl, New York, NY 10014
Tel.: (212) 366-1004
Fax: (212) 366-4530
E-Mail: mail@buero-newyork.com
Web Site: www.buero-newyork.com

Employees: 12
Year Founded: 2001

Agency Specializes In: Advertising, Consulting, Fashion/Apparel, Graphic Design

Ronit Avneri *(Bus Dir & Exec Producer)*
Antje Erasmus *(Dir-Art)*
Nick Kapros *(Dir-Art)*
Alex Wiederin *(Dir-Creative)*
Olivia Perdoch *(Mgr-Studio)*
Alexander Jager *(Strategist)*
Yuval Cohen *(Designer)*

Accounts:
Jill Stuart Fashion and Fragrance
Sonia Rykiel

THE BULL-WHITE HOUSE
220 E 23rd St No 1005, New York, NY 10010
Tel.: (646) 790-8700
Web Site: www.thebullwhitehouse.com/

Employees: 8

Agency Specializes In: Advertising

Christina Jones *(Partner & Head-Ops)*
Mallory Solomon *(Head-Acct Mgmt)*
Bill Moulton *(Exec Dir-Creative)*
Corey Gehrig *(Dir-Art)*
Brit Larson *(Dir-Art)*
Ulrika Karlberg *(Copywriter)*

Accounts:
Anheuser-Busch Shock Top
Galaxy Foods
Stupid Cancer
Syncapse
Unilever Campaign: "Get What You Want", Campaign: "I Can't Believe It's Not Butter", Creative, Digital, Experiential, Print, TV; 2012

BULLDOG CREATIVE SERVICES
1400 Commerce Ave, Huntington, WV 25701
Tel.: (304) 525-9600
Fax: (304) 525-4043
E-Mail: info@bulldogcreative.com
Web Site: www.bulldogcreative.com

Year Founded: 1999

Agency Specializes In: Advertising, Collateral, Event Planning & Marketing, Graphic Design, Identity Marketing, Internet/Web Design

Chris Michael *(Owner)*
April Barnabi *(VP-Ops)*
Christine Borders *(VP-Creative Svcs)*
Ashleigh Graham-Smith *(Client Svcs Dir)*
Levi Durfee *(Dir-Interactive)*
Brittany Brownfield *(Sr Acct Exec)*
Jennifer Tucker *(Acct Coord)*

Accounts:
First Sentry Bank
Marshall University

BULLDOG DRUMMOND, INC.
655 G Street, San Diego, CA 92101
Tel.: (619) 528-8404
Fax: (619) 528-8403
E-Mail: chartwell@bulldogdrummond.com
Web Site: www.bulldogdrummond.com

Employees: 15
Year Founded: 1997

Agency Specializes In: Advertising

Shawn E. Parr *(CEO)*
Annie J. Buchanan *(CFO)*
Dave Alder *(Pres-Media & Entertainment)*
Catharine Francisco *(VP-Ops & Acct Svcs)*
Megan Grable *(VP-Creative & Strategy)*
Erin Kaplan *(VP-Brand & Innovation Strategy)*
Katie Schultz *(Dir-Production)*
Erin Borawski *(Strategist-Brand & Innovation)*
Garrett Patz *(Sr Designer)*

Accounts:
Diageo Stark Raving
ESPN Zone
Patientsafe Solutions
Pinkberry
Starbucks
WD40
Westfield Malls

BULLDOZER DIRECT
(Formerly Bulldozer Digital)
794 Penllyn Blue Bell Pke Ste 219, Blue Bell, PA 19422
Fax: (215) 392-3379
Toll Free: (800) 652-3837
Web Site: bulldozerdirect.com

Year Founded: 2010

Agency Specializes In: Advertising, Digital/Interactive, Radio

Linda Gaglione *(Exec VP)*

Accounts:
Jordan Belfort

BULLFROG & BAUM
56 W 22nd St, New York, NY 10010
Tel.: (212) 255-6717
Fax: (646) 763-8910
E-Mail: info@bullfrogandbaum.com
Web Site: www.bullfrogandbaum.com

Employees: 30

Agency Specializes In: Hospitality, Public Relations

Jennifer Baum *(Founder & Pres)*
Josh Capon *(Partner)*
Kay Lindsay *(VP-Bus Dev)*
Jessica Bishop *(Acct Dir)*
Shelby Goldman *(Acct Dir)*
Samantha Bryant *(Asst Acct Exec)*

Accounts:
Apheleia Restaurant Group Belly & Trumpet, Oak, Pakpao
New-Aretsky's Patroon (Agency of Record)
Asian Box Marketing, Media Relations, Social Media Strategy
Bar American
Blue Ribbon Restaurants
Broadway Panhandler
Bruce Cost Ginger Ale Events, Marketing, Strategic Alliances
Casa Luca
Chef Josiah Citrin Marketing, Melisse, Public Relations
Cherry
The Elm
Fiola
Fish & Game; Hudson, NY
The Forge Media
Four Seasons Hotels and Resorts Campaign: "Virtual Cocktail Class"
Juni
Lettuce Entertain You Enterprises; Chicago, IL National Media; 2007
Joe's Seafood, Prime Steak and Stone Crab
Maude PR
The Peacock
New-Ripple (Agency of Record)
New-Roofers Union (Agency of Record)
SLS Hotel South Beach

BULLSEYE STRATEGY
1700 E Las Olas Blvd Ste 301, Fort Lauderdale, FL 33301
Tel.: (954) 591-8999
E-Mail: info@bullseyestrategy.com
Web Site: www.bullseyestrategy.com

Agency Specializes In: Advertising, Content, Digital/Interactive, Email, Media Buying Services, Media Planning, Social Media

Maria Harrison *(Pres)*
Jonathan Schwartz *(CEO)*
Matt Bray *(Dir & Strategist-Client)*
Anita Larsen *(Dir & Client Strategist)*

Accounts:
MIA Shoes (Digital Agency of Record) Media Buying, Media Planning, Social Media
Railex
Voices for Children of Broward County

BULLY PULPIT INTERACTIVE
1140 Connecticut Ave NW Ste 800, Washington, DC 20036
Tel.: (202) 331-0052

Fax: (202) 331-0113
Web Site: www.bpimedia.com

Year Founded: 2009

Agency Specializes In: Advertising, Digital/Interactive, Graphic Design, Social Media

Andrew Bleeker *(Pres)*
Ben Coffey Clark *(Partner & Head-Bus Dev)*
Mark Skidmore *(Partner & Sr Strategist)*
Ann Marie Habershaw *(COO)*
Kathie Kovach *(Sr Dir-Ad Ops & Analytics)*
Adam Shapiro *(Sr Dir-Strategy & Bus Dev)*
Scott Zumwalt *(Sr Dir)*
Lianne Bollinger *(Dir)*
Michael Schneider *(Dir-BPI Labs)*
Peter Anich *(Acct Exec)*
Carina Khanjian *(Acct Exec)*

Accounts:
Livestrong
Organizing for Action
SHRM

THE BUNTIN GROUP
BRAND FLUENCY

THE BUNTIN GROUP
1001 Hawkins St, Nashville, TN 37203-4758
Tel.: (615) 244-5720
Fax: (615) 244-6511
E-Mail: results@buntingroup.com
Web Site: www.buntingroup.com

Employees: 121
Year Founded: 1972

National Agency Associations: 4A's

Agency Specializes In: Advertising, Advertising Specialties, Affiliate Marketing, Affluent Market, African-American Market, Alternative Advertising, Arts, Automotive, Bilingual Market, Brand Development & Integration, Broadcast, Business-To-Business, Cable T.V., Collateral, Commercial Photography, Communications, Consulting, Consumer Goods, Consumer Publications, Corporate Communications, Corporate Identity, Custom Publishing, Customer Relationship Management, Digital/Interactive, Direct Response Marketing, Direct-to-Consumer, E-Commerce, Electronic Media, Email, Faith Based, Financial, Food Service, Government/Political, Graphic Design, Health Care Services, Hispanic Market, Hospitality, Household Goods, In-Store Advertising, Information Technology, International, Internet/Web Design, Investor Relations, Leisure, Local Marketing, Logo & Package Design, Luxury Products, Magazines, Market Research, Media Buying Services, Media Planning, Media Relations, Media Training, Medical Products, Men's Market, Merchandising, Mobile Marketing, Multimedia, New Product Development, Newspaper, Newspapers & Magazines, Package Design, Planning & Consultation, Podcasting, Point of Purchase, Point of Sale, Print, Production, Production (Print), Promotions, Public Relations, Publishing, RSS (Really Simple Syndication), Radio, Recruitment, Restaurant, Retail, Seniors' Market, Sponsorship, Stakeholders, Strategic Planning/Research, Syndication, T.V., Teen Market, Telemarketing, Trade & Consumer Magazines, Transportation, Travel & Tourism, Urban Market, Women's Market, Yellow Pages Advertising

Approx. Annual Billings: $138,906,000

Jeffrey Buntin, Jr. *(Pres & CEO)*
Howard Greiner *(Pres-Buntin Out-of-Home Media)*
Kathy Canady *(Exec VP)*
Jon Carmack *(Exec VP-Ops & Tech)*
Brian Harkness *(Exec VP-Strategic Initiatives)*
Tom Cocke *(Sr VP & Grp Dir-Creative)*
Liz Diekman *(Sr VP & Grp Acct Dir)*
Tom Gibney *(Sr VP & Dir-Brdcst Production)*
Ben Thomas *(Sr VP & Dir-Channel Engagement)*
Hollie Rapello *(Sr VP-Comm & Bus Dev)*
Kevin May *(VP, Controller & Dir-Billing)*
Ray Reed *(VP & Grp Dir-Creative)*
Jason Skinner *(Grp Partner-Creative, VP & Dir-Design)*
Leiott Smiley *(VP-Workflow & Acct Ops)*
Don Schneider *(Exec Dir-Creative)*
Jeff Parson *(Sr Dir-Art & Digital Design)*
Jillian Wyatt *(Acct Dir)*
Brittany Chapman *(Dir-Art & Sr Designer)*
Christine Poss *(Assoc Dir-Channel Engagement)*
Lynne Kilgore *(Sr Mgr-Res)*
Danna Grigson *(Supvr-Media)*
Jessi Olson *(Supvr-Mgmt)*
Victoria Waddell *(Specialist-Social Media & Content)*
Angie Melgar *(Designer)*
Tim Gardner *(Acct Coord-Field)*

Accounts:
A Life Story Foundation
Acceptance Auto Insurance
America Within
American Born Moonshine
Bass Pro Shops
Brookdale Senior Living
Chinet
The Contributor
Correct Chemo
Cracker Barrel
Gaylord Entertainment
Genesco Inc.
Golf Buddy
Good Year
Hands of Nashville
Huhtamaki Oyj
I Am The Engine
Imagine No Malaria
Infected by Meth
John Deere
Junior Achievements of Middle TN
Kirklands
La Quinta Inn & Suites
Outback Steakhouse
Perkins & Marie Callender's Inc. (Agency of Record) Analytics, Creative, Digital Strategy, Marketing, Media, Print, Social Media, Strategic, Television
RBC Capital Markets
Royal Bank of Canada
Savannah Classics
SERVPRO
Synapse
TN Education Lottery
Trex
United Methodist Church
Wildhorse Saloon
Woodford Racing

Division

Buntin Out-of-Home Media
1001 Hawkins St, Nashville, TN 37206
(See Separate Listing)

BURDETTE KETCHUM
1023 Kings Ave, Jacksonville, FL 32207
Tel.: (904) 645-6200
Fax: (904) 645-6080
E-Mail: info@burdetteketchum.com
Web Site: www.burdetteketchum.com

Agency Specializes In: Advertising, Advertising Specialties, Brand Development & Integration, Broadcast, Business-To-Business, Cable T.V., Catalogs, Collateral, Communications, Consulting, Consumer Goods, Consumer Marketing, Corporate Communications, Corporate Identity, Crisis Communications, Digital/Interactive, Direct Response Marketing, Direct-to-Consumer, Electronic Media, Event Planning & Marketing, Exhibit/Trade Shows, Experience Design, Financial, Graphic Design, Health Care Services, Identity Marketing, In-Store Advertising, Industrial, Integrated Marketing, Internet/Web Design, Legal Services, Local Marketing, Logo & Package Design, Market Research, Media Buying Services, Media Planning, Media Relations, Mobile Marketing, New Product Development, Out-of-Home Media, Outdoor, Package Design, Planning & Consultation, Point of Purchase, Point of Sale, Print, Production (Print), Promotions, Public Relations, Publicity/Promotions, Radio, Regional, Retail, Search Engine Optimization, Social Media, Sponsorship, Strategic Planning/Research, T.V., Transportation, Viral/Buzz/Word of Mouth

Will Ketchum *(Pres & CEO)*
Barbara Emener Karasek *(Partner & Exec VP-Client Leadership)*
Sarah Leverette *(Dir-Print Production)*
Spencer Miller *(Dir-Digital Creative)*
Jeannie Rissman *(Dir-Digital)*
Anita Carter *(Mgr-Creative Svcs)*
Annesteja Macedonio *(Mgr-Media)*
Todd Weise *(Mgr-Digital Projects)*
Brittney Jones *(Acct Exec)*
Cathleen Tully *(Coord-Admin)*

Accounts:
Federal Signal MachinesThatWontQuit.com
Predator Group (Agency of Record) Predator Cues
Swisher International Campaign: "e-Swisher Come on Over Photography", E-Swisher.com

BURFORD COMPANY ADVERTISING
125 E Main St, Richmond, VA 23219
Tel.: (804) 780-0354
Fax: (804) 780-0025
E-Mail: info@burfordadvertising.com
Web Site: www.burfordadvertising.com

Employees: 13

Agency Specializes In: Advertising, Advertising Specialties, Cable T.V., Consumer Goods, Local Marketing, Production (Ad, Film, Broadcast), T.V.

Doug Burford *(Pres)*
Nancy Burford *(CFO)*
Ardis Fishburne *(Dir-Creative & Acct Exec)*
Lori Dawson *(Dir-Media)*

Accounts:
ChildFund International
ChildSavers of Richmond
Criminal Injuries Compensation Fund
The Dump
Farm Fresh Inc.
Franklin & Franklin Attorneys
Gilman Heating & Cooling
Haley Automotive
Haynes Furniture
Leo Burke Furniture
Medical Careers Institute
Schneider Laboratories
The Supply Room Companies
Virginia Health Insurance Exchange
New-Virginia Victims Fund
WaterEdge

BURGESS ADVERTISING & MARKETING

1290 Congress St, Portland, ME 04102-2113
Tel.: (207) 775-5227
Fax: (207) 775-3157
E-Mail: adburg@burgessadv.com
Web Site: www.burgessadv.com

Employees: 17
Year Founded: 1986

National Agency Associations: PRSA

Agency Specializes In: Advertising, Advertising Specialties, Aviation & Aerospace, Brand Development & Integration, Broadcast, Business Publications, Business-To-Business, Cable T.V., Catalogs, Collateral, College, Communications, Consulting, Consumer Goods, Consumer Marketing, Corporate Communications, Corporate Identity, Crisis Communications, Digital/Interactive, Direct Response Marketing, Education, Email, Engineering, Environmental, Event Planning & Marketing, Exhibit/Trade Shows, Fashion/Apparel, Financial, Food Service, Government/Political, Graphic Design, Health Care Services, Hospitality, In-Store Advertising, Industrial, Integrated Marketing, Internet/Web Design, Local Marketing, Logo & Package Design, Magazines, Market Research, Media Buying Services, Media Planning, Media Relations, Newspaper, Newspapers & Magazines, Package Design, Pets , Planning & Consultation, Podcasting, Point of Purchase, Point of Sale, Print, Production, Production (Ad, Film, Broadcast), Production (Print), Promotions, Public Relations, Publicity/Promotions, Radio, Recruitment, Search Engine Optimization, Seniors' Market, Social Marketing/Nonprofit, Social Media, Sponsorship, Strategic Planning/Research, T.V., Trade & Consumer Magazines, Web (Banner Ads, Pop-ups, etc.), Women's Market

Approx. Annual Billings: $4,400,000

Meredith Strang Burgess *(Pres & CEO)*
Lori Davis *(VP-Fin)*
Betty Angell *(Dir-Media)*
Keva Crockett *(Dir-First Impressions)*
Oliver Payne *(Strategist-Creative & Sr Copywriter)*

Accounts:
Adroscoggin Valley Hospital
Advanced Building Products
Capricorn Products
Center Street Dental
Cumberland County YMCA
Dearborn Precision
Dielectric Communications
Digital Research
E.J. Prescott; Gardiner, ME Pipe Products; 1991
Evergreen USA
Franklin Community Health Network
Good Shepherd Sisters
Knowles Industrial Services
Maine Breast & Cervical Health Program; 2000
Maine Cancer Foundation (Pro Bono)
Maine Department of Environmental Protection
Maine Employers Mutual Insurance Co.; Portland, ME Workers Compensation; 1993
Maine Engineering Promotion Council
Maine Eye Center
Maine Line Fence
Maine Math and Science Alliance
Maine Mutual Group
Maine Prosthodontics
Maine State Housing
Maine Technical Source
Maine Youth Camping Foundation
MCCCP
Memorial Hospital
The Memorial Hospital; North Conway, NH
NH OEP
Portland International Jetport
Portland Pipeline
Portland Regency Hotel
Portland Yacht Services
Qualis
Ronald McDonald House (Pro Bono)
Shamrock Sports Group
VNA Home Health Care

BURGESS COMMUNICATIONS, INC

1450 E Boot Rd Ste 300B, West Chester, PA 19380
Tel.: (610) 647-7900
Fax: (610) 647-7901
Toll Free: (888) 846-5759
E-Mail: dweidel@burgesscom.com
Web Site: www.burgesscom.com

Employees: 5
Year Founded: 1989

National Agency Associations: AMA

Agency Specializes In: Advertising, Brand Development & Integration, Business-To-Business, Catalogs, Collateral, Corporate Communications, Corporate Identity, Digital/Interactive, Electronic Media, Graphic Design, Health Care Services, High Technology, Identity Marketing, Industrial, Integrated Marketing, International, Internet/Web Design, Local Marketing, Logo & Package Design, Magazines, Media Buying Services, Media Planning, Media Relations, Medical Products, New Technologies, Package Design, Pharmaceutical, Print, Production (Print), Public Relations, Radio, Sales Promotion, Social Marketing/Nonprofit, Strategic Planning/Research, Trade & Consumer Magazines

Approx. Annual Billings: $1,000,000

Donna Weidel *(Pres)*

Accounts:
Arkema Collateral; 1999
CGFNS Annual Reports; 2005
FMC Collateral, Sales Materials, Newsletters; 1993
Illuma Fashion, Branding, Online; 2007
ReMed Healthcare, Brain Rehab, Collateral, Web, Trade Show; 2005
Septodont Dental Pharma, Pain Control, Product Launch Campaigns, ongoing branding; 1996

BURK ADVERTISING & MARKETING

12850 Hillcrest Rd Ste F210, Dallas, TX 75230
Tel.: (214) 953-0494
Fax: (214) 742-8803
E-Mail: info@wambam.com
Web Site: www.wambam.com

Employees: 7
Year Founded: 1991

National Agency Associations: 4A's

Agency Specializes In: Advertising, Arts, Aviation & Aerospace, Brand Development & Integration, Broadcast, Business Publications, Business-To-Business, Collateral, Communications, Consulting, Corporate Communications, Corporate Identity, Digital/Interactive, Direct Response Marketing, Electronic Media, Electronics, Event Planning & Marketing, Exhibit/Trade Shows, Financial, Graphic Design, High Technology, In-Store Advertising, Industrial, Information Technology, Integrated Marketing, Internet/Web Design, Local Marketing, Logo & Package Design, Magazines, Marine, Media Buying Services, Media Relations, Media Training, New Product Development, Newspaper, Newspapers & Magazines, Outdoor, Pharmaceutical, Planning & Consultation, Point of Purchase, Point of Sale, Print, Production, Production (Ad, Film, Broadcast), Production (Print), Public Relations, Publicity/Promotions, Real Estate, Regional, Sales Promotion, Strategic Planning/Research, Technical Advertising, Trade & Consumer Magazines, Transportation, Web (Banner Ads, Pop-ups, etc.)

Approx. Annual Billings: $3,700,000

Breakdown of Gross Billings by Media: Bus. Publs.: $990,000; Collateral: $330,000; Consulting: $150,000; Corp. Communications: $175,000; D.M.: $125,000; Exhibits/Trade Shows: $165,000; Fees: $75,000; Graphic Design: $100,000; Internet Adv.: $50,000; Local Mktg.: $50,000; Logo & Package Design: $155,000; Plng. & Consultation: $165,000; Print: $495,000; Production: $200,000; Pub. Rels.: $125,000; Strategic Planning/Research: $200,000; Worldwide Web Sites: $250,000

Gene Hardon *(CFO)*
B. Bailey Burk *(Principal-Burk Adv & Mktg-Dallas)*

Accounts:
Eligiloy Specialty Metals; Elgin, IL; 1996
Evonik Foams, Inc.; Dallas, TX Solimide Foams; 1991

BURKE ADVERTISING LLC

9 Cedarwood Dr Ste 11, Bedford, NH 03110
Tel.: (603) 627-5381
E-Mail: info@burkeadvertising.com
Web Site: www.burkeadvertising.com

Year Founded: 1994

Agency Specializes In: Advertising, Brand Development & Integration, Graphic Design, Internet/Web Design, Media Planning, Public Relations, Radio, T.V.

Jim Burke *(Founder & Creative Dir)*
Jessica McKenna *(Dir-Art)*
Kayla Frank *(Acct Mgr)*
Chris Cooper *(Sr Acct Planner)*

Accounts:
Ads on Wheels (Advertising Agency of Record) Media Planning, Online Marketing, Search Engine Optimization
Banks Automotive
New-Banks Chevrolet
New-Best Fitness
Central Mass Agway
Cold Springs RV
East Coast Lumber
Guardian Industrial Products Inc.
Laars Heating Systems
Lawn Dawg
New Hampshire NeuroSpine Institute
Proctor Ski of Nashua
Rivier University
Unitil
Wildco PES (Agency of Record) Creative, Media Planning, Online Marketing, Strategic, Website

BURKHEAD BRAND GROUP

5020 Weston Pkwy, Cary, NC 27513
Tel.: (919) 677-8428
E-Mail: engage@bbgintegrated.com
Web Site: www.bbgintegrated.com

Year Founded: 2009

Agency Specializes In: Advertising, Internet/Web Design, Logo & Package Design, Print

Bill Kamp *(Exec Dir-Creative)*
Melanie Ingool *(Sr Acct Dir)*
Kathi Bentley *(Dir-Integrated Mktg)*
David Hamilton *(Dir-Earned Media)*
Nivedita Madala *(Mgr-Fin)*
Allison Pollard *(Acct Supvr)*

Accounts:
ConnectVIEW Marketing & Advertising Agency of

Record, Public Relations, Strategic Marketing
GridBridge

BURKHOLDER/FLINT
300 Spruce St Ste 275, Columbus, OH 43215
Tel.: (614) 228-2425
Fax: (614) 228-0631
E-Mail: easterday@burkholderflint.com
Web Site: www.burkholderflint.com

Year Founded: 1959

Agency Specializes In: Advertising, Public Relations

Bob Wiseman *(Pres)*
Vickie Easterday *(VP)*
Tom Bedway *(Dir-Creative)*
Julie Hamlin *(Dir-PR)*
Todd Kidwell *(Dir-Art)*
Amy Hester *(Acct Exec)*

Accounts:
AEP Ohio
Cameron Mitchell Restaurants
Columbia Gas of Ohio
Columbus Radiology
Isaac Wiles
Primary One Health
Ronald McDonald House
Vision Development

THE BURMEISTER GROUP, INC.
4658 Bishop Lk Rd, Marietta, GA 30062
Tel.: (770) 641-9600
Web Site: www.burmeistergroup.com

Julie Burmeister *(Pres & Dir-Creative)*
Audrey Eisen *(Dir-Media)*
Maureen Mccarthy *(Acct Mgr)*

Accounts:
Associated Credit Union

BURN CREATIVE
17 E High St, Carlisle, PA 17015
Tel.: (717) 731-8579
E-Mail: hello@burncreative.com
Web Site: www.burncreative.com

Agency Specializes In: Advertising, Collateral, Corporate Identity, Graphic Design, Logo & Package Design

Marco Echevarria *(Owner & Dir-Creative)*

Accounts:
Atlas Government Relations
Epitome
Johnson C. Smith University
Kessler Goaltending
North Mountain Inn
SmartFix Center

BURNETT ADVERTISING
7100 SW Hampton St 202, Tigard, OR 97223
Tel.: (503) 828-1118
Web Site: www.burnettadvertising.com

Agency Specializes In: Advertising, Digital/Interactive, Logo & Package Design, Print, Social Media

Greg Burnett *(Pres)*
Ian Anaya *(Sr Graphic Designer)*

BURNHAM RICHARDS ADVERTISING
522 George St, De Pere, WI 54301
Tel.: (920) 406-1663
Fax: (920) 406-3919
Toll Free: (866) 406-1663
E-Mail: david@burnhamrichards.com
Web Site: www.burnhamrichards.com

Employees: 7

Agency Specializes In: Advertising, Advertising Specialties, Agriculture, Automotive, Brand Development & Integration, Broadcast, Cable T.V., Catalogs, Co-op Advertising, Collateral, Commercial Photography, Communications, Consumer Goods, Consumer Marketing, Consumer Publications, Corporate Identity, Customer Relationship Management, Digital/Interactive, Direct Response Marketing, Electronic Media, Email, Event Planning & Marketing, Exhibit/Trade Shows, Financial, Food Service, Graphic Design, Guerilla Marketing, Health Care Services, Hospitality, Household Goods, Identity Marketing, Integrated Marketing, Internet/Web Design, Leisure, Local Marketing, Logo & Package Design, Magazines, Marine, Market Research, Media Buying Services, Media Planning, Medical Products, Mobile Marketing, Multimedia, Newspaper, Newspapers & Magazines, Out-of-Home Media, Outdoor, Package Design, Paid Searches, Planning & Consultation, Podcasting, Point of Purchase, Point of Sale, Print, Production, Production (Ad, Film, Broadcast), Production (Print), Promotions, Publicity/Promotions, Radio, Real Estate, Regional, Restaurant, Retail, Sales Promotion, Search Engine Optimization, Strategic Planning/Research, Sweepstakes, T.V., Trade & Consumer Magazines, Transportation, Travel & Tourism, Viral/Buzz/Word of Mouth, Web (Banner Ads, Pop-ups, etc.), Yellow Pages Advertising

David Richards *(Dir-Creative)*

BURNS MCCLELLAN, INC.
257 Park Ave S 15th Fl, New York, NY 10010
Tel.: (212) 213-0006
Fax: (212) 213-4447
E-Mail: info@burnsmc.com
Web Site: www.burnsmc.com

Employees: 20
Year Founded: 1998

Agency Specializes In: Communications, Corporate Communications, Health Care Services, Investor Relations, Local Marketing, Public Relations, Strategic Planning/Research

Revenue: $2,400,000

Lisa Burns *(Pres & CEO)*
Justin W. Jackson *(Exec VP & Dir-Life Sciences Practice)*
Kimberly Minarovich *(VP)*
Antonio Palumbo *(Dir-IT)*
Bill Sheley *(Dir-IT)*
Ami Bavishi *(Acct Mgr)*
Thereza Radiz *(Office Mgr)*
Steven Klass *(Sr Acct Exec-IR)*
Ilana Portner *(Sr Acct Exec)*
John Grimaldi *(Acct Exec)*

Accounts:
Alkermes
Bristol-Myers Squibb
ChemoCentryx
NicOx

BURNSGROUP
220 West 19th St 12th Fl, New York, NY 10011
Tel.: (212) 924-2293
Fax: (212) 656-1122
Web Site: burnsgroupnyc.com

Year Founded: 2004

James Wilday *(Founder & Partner)*
Michael Burns *(Owner & Partner)*
Michael L. Coticchia *(Pres & CEO)*
Joanne McKinney *(Chief Strategy Officer)*
Emily Stern *(Grp Acct Dir)*
Alexander Brown *(Dir-Art)*
Alison Earl *(Dir-Plng)*
Danielle Tolkin *(Acct Exec)*
Alyssa Peltzer *(Acct Planner)*

Accounts:
Pfizer
Pfizer Consumer Health Chapstick, Digital
Yellow Tail

BURRELL
233 N Michigan Ave Ste 2900, Chicago, IL 60601
Tel.: (312) 297-9600
Fax: (312) 297-9601
E-Mail: ldisilvestro@burrell.com
Web Site: www.burrell.com

Employees: 133
Year Founded: 1971

National Agency Associations: 4A's

Agency Specializes In: African-American Market, Brand Development & Integration, Communications, Consumer Goods, Consumer Marketing, Cosmetics, Event Planning & Marketing, Fashion/Apparel, Health Care Services, Multicultural, Pharmaceutical, Point of Purchase, Point of Sale, Public Relations, Publicity/Promotions, Retail, Social Media, Sponsorship, Web (Banner Ads, Pop-ups, etc.)

Approx. Annual Billings: $190,000,000

Breakdown of Gross Billings by Media: Cable T.V.: $13,300,000; Fees: $32,300,000; Internet Adv.: $3,800,000; Mags.: $13,300,000; Newsp.: $3,800,000; Production: $60,800,000; Radio & T.V.: $28,500,000; Syndication: $34,200,000

Lou Di Silvestro *(CFO & Sr VP)*
Lewis Williams *(Chief Creative Officer & Exec VP)*
Linda Jefferson *(Sr VP & Dir)*
Kevin Brockenbrough *(VP & Dir-Acct Plng & Res)*
Stephen French *(VP & Dir-Acct Plng)*
Charlene Guss *(VP-HR)*
Rebecca Williams *(Grp Dir-Creative)*
Nicholas Rolston *(Acct Dir)*
Robert Compitello *(Dir-Media Rels)*
Rachel McClean *(Dir-Art)*
Winston Chueng *(Assoc Dir-Creative)*
Jhontia Williams *(Assoc Dir-Media)*
Dave Jackson *(Acct Supvr-Engagement Mktg)*
Jihan Jefferson *(Acct Supvr-Acct Mgmt)*
Courtney Weaver *(Supvr-Digital Plng)*
Jesse Jarrett *(Sr Acct Exec)*
Omer Fazal *(Sr Media Planner)*

Accounts:
Comcast Corporation (Agency of Record) African American Consumer Market Advertising, Digital, Media, Social Media
General Mills; 2001
New-Hillary Clinton
McDonald's Corp.; Oak Brook, IL African-American Marketing, Campaign: "Mighty Wings", Sirloin Burger; 1972
Procter & Gamble; Cincinnati, OH Beauty, Charmin, Crest, Gain, Pampers, Tide; 1984
Toyota Motor North America, Inc.
Toyota Motor Sales African American Advertising, Avalon, Campaign : "Only The Name Remains"; 2001

THE BURRIS AGENCY, INC.

1175 Revolution Mill Dr Ste 11, Greensboro, NC 27405
Tel.: (843) 603-1584
E-Mail: mburris@burris.com
Web Site: burris.land

Employees: 5
Year Founded: 1985

Agency Specializes In: Brand Development & Integration, Consulting

Approx. Annual Billings: $1,000,000

Breakdown of Gross Billings by Media: Fees: $1,000,000

Lyn Rollins *(VP)*
Anne Cassity *(Dir-Design)*
Jesse Cummings *(Dir-Digital)*
Dean Wagner *(Dir-Creative)*

BURRIS CREATIVE INC
325 Matthews-Mint Hill Rd Ste 204, Matthews, NC 28105
Tel.: (704) 631-4500
Web Site: www.jimburris.com

Year Founded: 1994

Agency Specializes In: Advertising, Internet/Web Design, Logo & Package Design, Print, Strategic Planning/Research

Jim Burris *(Owner)*

Accounts:
Home Repair Pros
Second Helping

BURST MARKETING
122 Industrial Pk Rd, Albany, NY 12206
Tel.: (518) 465-0659
Fax: (518) 453-2477
Web Site: www.burstmarketing.net

Year Founded: 2009

Agency Specializes In: Advertising, Content, Graphic Design, Internet/Web Design, Print, Promotions

Dave Vener *(Pres & Dir-Mktg)*
Mark Shipley *(CEO & Dir-Strategy)*
Sharon Lawless *(COO)*
Sara Tack *(Exec VP & Dir-Creative)*
Rachel Digman *(Comptroller)*
Braden Russom *(Acct Mgr)*
Mo Abele *(Mgr-Traffic)*
Jared Tomeck *(Sr Designer)*

Accounts:
Copeland Coating Company, Inc.
G.A. Bove Fuels
Hot Harry's Burritos

BURTON ADVERTISING
1701 Providence Pk, Birmingham, AL 35242
Tel.: (205) 991-9644
Fax: (205) 991-9645
E-Mail: info@burtonadvertising.com
Web Site: www.burtonadvertising.com

Agency Specializes In: Advertising, Graphic Design, Public Relations, Social Media

Johnathon Burton *(Owner)*

Accounts:
UAB Blazers

BURTON, LIVINGSTONE & KIRK
4665 MacArthur Ct Ste 235, Newport Beach, CA 92660-8830
Tel.: (949) 250-6363
Fax: (949) 250-6390
E-Mail: mail@blk4mktg.com
Web Site: www.blk4mktg.com

Employees: 10
Year Founded: 1991

Agency Specializes In: Brand Development & Integration, Direct Response Marketing, Strategic Planning/Research

Approx. Annual Billings: $8,000,000

Breakdown of Gross Billings by Media: Brdcst.: $800,000; D.M.: $4,000,000; Point of Purchase: $400,000; Print: $2,400,000; Trade Shows: $400,000

Walter L. Hagstrom, Jr. *(Mng Partner)*

Accounts:
Arrowhead
Century 21
El Dorado Bank
Farmers & Merchants Bank; 1997
First Financial
The Geneva Companies
Global Vantage Ltd.
Pacific Mercantile Bank
Panasonic Corporation
PricewaterhouseCoopers, LLP
Protection One
Sunwest Bank
Suzuki
Toyota

BUSH COMMUNICATIONS, LLC
3 S Main St, Pittsford, NY 14534
Tel.: (585) 244-0270
Fax: (585) 244-3046
E-Mail: info@bushcommunications.com
Web Site: www.bushcommunications.com

Employees: 5
Year Founded: 2000

Agency Specializes In: Business-To-Business

Jim Bush *(Pres)*
Geoff Baumbach *(Dir-New Media)*
Brian Pullyblank *(Acct Mgr)*
Francesca Rondinella *(Acct Exec)*

Accounts:
Betlem Residential
Elko & Associates Ltd
Flaster Greenberg
Garlock Klozure
Garlock Sealing Technologies
Hagglunds
Junior Achievement
The Mall
Pitney Bowes
Upstate New York Truck Club

BUSH RENZ
4141 NE 2nd Ave Ste 203 E, Miami, FL 33137
Tel.: (305) 573-1439
Web Site: www.brprgroup.com

Year Founded: 2009

Agency Specializes In: Advertising, Brand Development & Integration, Digital/Interactive

Gerard Bush *(Creative Dir)*

Accounts:
LVMH Moet & Chandon (Digital Creative Agency of Record)

BUSINESS-TO-BUSINESS MARKETING COMMUNICATIONS
900 Ridgefield Dr Ste 270, Raleigh, NC 27609-8524
Tel.: (919) 872-8172
Fax: (919) 872-8875
E-Mail: info@btbmarketing.com
Web Site: www.btbmarketing.com

E-Mail for Key Personnel:
Creative Dir.: dunkak@btbmarketing.com

Employees: 15
Year Founded: 1989

Agency Specializes In: Advertising, Affiliate Marketing, Automotive, Business Publications, Business-To-Business, Catalogs, Co-op Advertising, Collateral, Communications, Consulting, Consumer Publications, Corporate Identity, Digital/Interactive, Direct Response Marketing, E-Commerce, Electronic Media, Email, Engineering, Environmental, Event Planning & Marketing, Exhibit/Trade Shows, Graphic Design, High Technology, In-Store Advertising, Industrial, Internet/Web Design, Local Marketing, Logo & Package Design, Magazines, Media Buying Services, Mobile Marketing, Multimedia, Newspaper, Newspapers & Magazines, Outdoor, Planning & Consultation, Point of Purchase, Print, Production, Production (Print), Public Relations, Publicity/Promotions, Radio, Sales Promotion, Social Media, Strategic Planning/Research, Technical Advertising, Trade & Consumer Magazines, Viral/Buzz/Word of Mouth, Web (Banner Ads, Pop-ups, etc.)

Approx. Annual Billings: $7,000,000

Breakdown of Gross Billings by Media: Bus. Publs.: 35%; Collateral: 15%; D.M.: 5%; E-Commerce: 10%; Exhibits/Trade Shows: 2%; Internet Adv.: 3%; Pub. Rels.: 20%; Worldwide Web Sites: 10%

Chris Burke *(Pres)*
Geoff Dunkak *(VP-Creative Svcs)*

Accounts:
ACS Motion Control
AVX Elco Corporation Electronic Connectors, Passive Components
C&K Components
Call-to-Recycle; 1999
Cree Inc.; 2003
ITT Industries, Canon
ITT Interconnect Solutions
Phihong USA
Reichhold Chemicals
Rohde & Schwarz; 2010

BUSINESSONLINE
321 San Anselmo Ave, San Anselmo, CA 94960
Tel.: (415) 419-5327
Web Site: www.businessol.com/

Employees: 60
Year Founded: 1997

Agency Specializes In: Digital/Interactive, Email, Mobile Marketing, Multimedia, Paid Searches, Search Engine Optimization, Social Media, Sponsorship, Web (Banner Ads, Pop-ups, etc.)

Michael Friedmann *(Dir-Bus Dev & Mktg)*

Accounts:
American Red Cross Blood Drive/Donations; 2013

BUTLER, SHINE, STERN & PARTNERS

20 Liberty Ship Way, Sausalito, CA 94965-3312
Tel.: (415) 331-6049
Fax: (415) 331-3524
E-Mail: info@bssp.com
Web Site: www.bssp.com

E-Mail for Key Personnel:
President: gstern@bssp.com
Creative Dir.: jbutler@bssp.com
Media Dir.: lrichardson@bssp.com

Employees: 150
Year Founded: 1993

National Agency Associations: 4A's

Agency Specializes In: Advertising, Brand Development & Integration, Broadcast, Business Publications, Business-To-Business, Cable T.V., Collateral, Consulting, Consumer Marketing, Consumer Publications, Corporate Identity, Digital/Interactive, Direct Response Marketing, Entertainment, Fashion/Apparel, Food Service, Graphic Design, High Technology, In-Store Advertising, Internet/Web Design, Logo & Package Design, Magazines, Media Buying Services, Merchandising, New Product Development, Newspaper, Newspapers & Magazines, Out-of-Home Media, Outdoor, Over-50 Market, Planning & Consultation, Point of Purchase, Point of Sale, Print, Production, Public Relations, Radio, Restaurant, Retail, Sponsorship, Strategic Planning/Research, Syndication, T.V., Teen Market, Trade & Consumer Magazines

Approx. Annual Billings: $100,000,000

Breakdown of Gross Billings by Media: Brdcst.: 20%; Cable T.V.: 10%; Collateral: 6%; Consumer Publs.: 8%; Graphic Design: 10%; Internet Adv.: 20%; Logo & Package Design: 5%; Newsp.: 5%; Out-of-Home Media: 5%; Production: 8%; Radio: 3%

Greg Stern *(CEO)*
Patrick Kiss *(Partner & Mng Dir)*
Aggie Chon-Bayer *(Controller)*
John Butler *(Exec Dir-Creative)*
Susan Noonan *(Exec Dir-Media & Analytics)*
Juli Johnson *(Grp Dir-Media)*
Kirk Landgraf *(Grp Dir-Media)*
Dave Pierotti *(Grp Dir-Media)*
Lori Pisani *(Producer-Brdcst)*
Lisa Villarosa *(Acct Dir)*
Cristiano Alburitel *(Dir-New Bus)*
Sarah Brewer *(Dir-Fin)*
Tom Coates *(Dir-Creative)*
Jackie Coffey *(Dir-Performance Mktg)*
Ed Cotton *(Dir-Strategy & Innovation)*
Adrienne Cummins-Foster *(Dir-Integrated Production)*
Mark Krajan *(Dir-Creative)*
Don Luu *(Dir-Adv Ops)*
Dennis Remsing *(Dir-Interactive Art)*
Lynda Richardson *(Dir-Media)*
Tom Yaniv *(Dir-Motion Graphics)*
Scott Day *(Assoc Dir-Media)*
Eric Liebhauser *(Assoc Dir-Creative)*
Samantha Bartelloni *(Acct Supvr)*
Jennifer Parchman *(Supvr-Media)*
Virginia Lu *(Strategist-Digital)*
Danielle Patipa *(Acct Exec)*
Jonathan Harrison *(Media Planner)*
Zoe Hatch *(Media Planner)*
Robert Shanahan *(Media Planner)*
Andrew Avedian *(Coord-Media Traffic)*

Accounts:
Benefit Cosmetic Campaign: "They're Real! Push-up Gel Liner Pen"
Blue Shield of California (Agency of Record) Creative, Digital, Marketing, Media, Media Buying
BMW/Mini USA (Agency of Record) Campaign: "AHHHHHHH", Campaign: "Not normal", Creative, Media Planning & Buying, Mini Cooper Campaign: "Rocks the Rivals Test Drive Invite"
BMW of North America, LLC MINI Cooper
BoltBus
Columbia Sportswear Company Campaign: "Get Your Boots Dirty", Campaign: "Wim Hof", Media Buying; 2008
DraftKings Creative
El Pollo Loco, Inc. Brand Strategy, Creative, In-Restaurant Merchandising, Marketing Communication, Television Commercials
Espolon
Google
Greyhound Lines, Inc. Campaign: "Online Film: Chain Mail", Campaign: "Tour in style"; 2007
New-Logan's Roadhouse, Inc. (Marketing & Advertising Agency of Record) Advertising, Design, Marketing, Media
Pharmavite Digital, Media, Nature Made (Creative Agency of Record), Online, Print, Promotions, Public Relations, Strategy, TV
San Francisco Foodbank; San Francisco, CA; 1997
T-Mobile #nocontract 1, #nocontract 2, Campaign: "No Contract, No Worries" Super Bowl 2014, Campaign: "Still No Contract" Super Bowl 2014
U.S. Bank Campaign: "Tangible Rewards"
Walgreens In-Store Healthcare Clinic, Take Care Health Systems; 2008
Walker & Zanger, Inc. Roku

BUXTON COMMUNICATIONS

114 Emery St, Portland, ME 04102
Tel.: (207) 775-2802
Fax: (866) 347-1554
E-Mail: info@buxtoncomm.com
Web Site: www.buxtoncomm.com

Agency Specializes In: Advertising, Brand Development & Integration, Broadcast, Corporate Identity, Media Relations, Package Design, Point of Purchase, Print, Public Relations, Web (Banner Ads, Pop-ups, etc.)

Kathryn Buxton *(Dir-Creative & Project Mgr)*
Rick Ackermann *(Dir-Art-Copy)*
Chris Russell *(Dir-Art-Graphics)*
Jordan Weber *(Acct Exec)*

BUYER ADVERTISING, INC.

189 Wells Ave 2nd Fl, Newton, MA 02459
Tel.: (617) 969-4646
Fax: (617) 969-6807
E-Mail: cbuyer@buyerads.com
Web Site: www.buyerads.com

E-Mail for Key Personnel:
Media Dir.: eeffenso@buyerads.com

Employees: 30
Year Founded: 1966

National Agency Associations: CDNPA

Agency Specializes In: Food Service, Logo & Package Design, Recruitment

Approx. Annual Billings: $18,000,000

Charles G. Buyer *(Owner)*
Alan Lovitz *(VP & Acct Dir)*
Joel Glick *(VP & Dir-Interactive Svcs)*
Linda Buyer *(VP-Fin)*
Marion Buyer *(VP-Creative Svcs)*
Kristina Bunce *(Dir-New Bus Dev)*
Ann Toll *(Client Svcs Mgr)*
Mike Fillyaw *(Specialist-Media)*
Jean Desharnais *(Sr Graphic Designer)*

Accounts:
Boston College
EMC
Harvard University; Cambridge, MA
LLBean
MA Libraries
Mass General Hospital
Millipore
Newton Wellesley Hospital
Tyco International
Tyco Safety Products
University of Massachusetts Amherst

BUZZ BRAND MARKETING

419 Lafayette St 2nd Fl, New York, NY 10003
Tel.: (212) 360-0399
Fax: (646) 430-8580
E-Mail: info@buzzbrandmktg.com
Web Site: www.buzzbrandmktg.com

Year Founded: 2003

Agency Specializes In: Advertising, Brand Development & Integration, Crisis Communications, Event Planning & Marketing, Media Relations, Public Relations

Marisa King-Redwood *(Founder & Principal)*
Denrick Romain *(Sr VP-Sports Mktg & Lifestyle)*
Tonia Purnell-Respes *(VP-Bus Dev)*
Raine Diaz *(Gen Mgr)*
Kaitlyn Dimambro *(Acct Exec)*

Accounts:
Sahar Simmons

BUZZ MARKETING GROUP

132 Kings Hwy E Ste 202, Haddonfield, NJ 8033
Tel.: (856) 433-8579
E-Mail: hello@buzzmg.com
Web Site: www.buzzmg.com

Agency Specializes In: Advertising, Brand Development & Integration, Content, Media Buying Services, Media Planning

Tina Wells *(Founder & CEO)*
Marcus Wells *(VP-Res & Plng)*
Shilpa Soundararajan *(Dir-Projects)*
Kathleen Capalla *(Strategist-Digital)*

Accounts:
Wells Fargo

BUZZSAW ADVERTISING & DESIGN INC.

19600 Fairchild Rd Ste 140, Irvine, CA 92612
Tel.: (949) 453-1393
Fax: (949) 453-1676
E-Mail: buzz@buzzsaw.biz
Web Site: www.buzzsaw.biz

Employees: 4
Year Founded: 1986

Agency Specializes In: Consumer Marketing, Food Service, Graphic Design, High Technology

Robert Haynes *(Principal)*

Accounts:
Foxboro
Invensys
Microchip
Nerve Pro
Triconex
Wonder Ware Corp.; Lake Forest, CA Industrial Automation Software; 1995

BVK

250 W Coventry Ct #300, Milwaukee, WI 53217-3972
Tel.: (414) 228-1990
Fax: (414) 228-7561

Toll Free: (888) 347-3212
Web Site: www.bvk.com

E-Mail for Key Personnel:
President: michaelv@bvk.com

Employees: 158
Year Founded: 1984

Agency Specializes In: Advertising, Advertising Specialties, Bilingual Market, Brand Development & Integration, Broadcast, Business Publications, Business-To-Business, Cable T.V., Catalogs, Co-op Advertising, Collateral, College, Communications, Consulting, Consumer Goods, Consumer Marketing, Consumer Publications, Corporate Identity, Direct Response Marketing, E-Commerce, Education, Electronic Media, Event Planning & Marketing, Exhibit/Trade Shows, Financial, Food Service, Graphic Design, Health Care Services, Hispanic Market, Infomercials, Integrated Marketing, Internet/Web Design, Legal Services, Leisure, Logo & Package Design, Magazines, Marine, Market Research, Media Buying Services, Media Planning, Medical Products, Merchandising, Mobile Marketing, New Product Development, Newspaper, Newspapers & Magazines, Out-of-Home Media, Outdoor, Over-50 Market, Paid Searches, Pharmaceutical, Planning & Consultation, Point of Purchase, Point of Sale, Print, Production, Promotions, Public Relations, Publicity/Promotions, Radio, Recruitment, Restaurant, Retail, Sales Promotion, Seniors' Market, Social Marketing/Nonprofit, Sponsorship, Strategic Planning/Research, T.V., Trade & Consumer Magazines, Transportation, Travel & Tourism, Web (Banner Ads, Pop-ups, etc.), Yellow Pages Advertising

Approx. Annual Billings: $282,000,000

Breakdown of Gross Billings by Media: D.M.: $10,000,000; Internet Adv.: $35,000,000; Mags.: $12,000,000; Newsp.: $5,000,000; Other: $70,000,000; Outdoor: $7,000,000; Production: $68,000,000; Pub. Rels.: $13,000,000; Radio: $12,000,000; Sls. Promo.: $5,000,000; T.V.: $21,000,000; Yellow Page Adv.: $24,000,000

Michael Voss *(Owner)*
Bret Stasiak *(Mng Dir-Acct Svc & Plng)*
Kris Best *(VP-Fin)*
Victoria Simmons *(VP)*
Brian Ganther *(Grp Dir-Creative)*
Karen Bollinger *(Specialist-Email Mktg & Producer-Web)*
Cyndy Murrieta *(Acct Dir)*
Matt Herrmann *(Dir-Creative)*
Andrea Holschuh *(Dir-PR)*
Evan Jones *(Dir-Creative)*
Austin Kelley *(Dir-Art)*
Michael Vojvodich *(Dir-Creative)*
Alexandria Hall *(Assoc Dir-Interactive Art)*
Giselle Lozada *(Assoc Dir-Media)*
Patty Weiss *(Assoc Dir-Media)*
Pete Weninger *(Assoc Dir-Media)*
Caitlin Christman *(Sr Mgr-Interactive Project & Strategist-UX)*
Brian Krueger *(Sr Mgr-Production)*
Steven Johnson *(Mgr-Mktg Analytics)*
Lisa Lach *(Assoc Mgr-Mktg)*
Sarah Schmidt *(Acct Supvr-Experiential Mktg & Earned Media)*
Sarah Pittner *(Acct Planner & Sr Acct Exec)*
Rachel Abrahms *(Acct Exec)*
Marie Haas *(Acct Exec)*
Tami Krupski *(Specialist-Email Mktg Data)*
Alex Nennig *(Acct Exec)*
Laurie Vogt *(Sr Analyst-Search Mktg)*
Kevin Stoll *(Media Planner & Media Buyer)*
Nick Pipitone *(Copywriter)*
Gina Wittnebel *(Sr Graphic Designer)*

Accounts:
Avera Health System; Sioux Falls, SD; 2006
Bay State Health System; Springfield, MA; 2002
Briggs & Station Power Products Group; Port Washington, WI Simplicity Lawn & Garden Equipment; 1985
CITGO Petroleum Corp.; Houston, TX; 2004
Couples Resorts; Jamaica; 2008
Cruisers Yachts; Oconto, WI; 2003
DeVry Inc.; Chicago, IL Carrington Gollege, DeVry University, Keller Graduate School of Management; 2006
Dominican Republic Ministry of Tourism; Dominican Republic; 2005
Edwards Lifesciences; Irvine, CA Heart Valve; 2010
Foresters
Funjet Vacations; Milwaukee, WI Tour Operator
Habush, Habush & Rottier, S.C.; Milwaukee, WI Personal Injury Law Firm
Hydra-Sports; Murfreesboro, TN Fishing Boats; 2010
John Deere Pavilion & Commons; Moline, IL Tourism Destination
Lee County Visitor & Convention Bureau; Fort Myers, FL; 1996
LifeBridge Health; Baltimore, MD; 2003
Little Company of Mary Hospital; Evergreen Park, IL; 2006
Loyola University Medical Center; Maywood, IL; 2008
Maine Office of Tourism
The Mark Travel Corporation; Milwaukee, WI
MasterCraft; Vonore, TN; 2007
Memorial Health System; South Bend, IN 525 Bed Tertiary Hospital; 1987
Mission Hospital; Mission Viejo, CA; 2008
Mount Carmel Health System; Columbus, OH Three Hospital Vertically Integrated Health System; 2002
National Research Corp.; Lincoln, NE Healthcare Research Firm
Oklahoma University Medical & Children's Hospital; Oklahoma City, OK; 2007
Omron Health Care; Bannockburn, IL; 2006
OU Medicine Cancer Center Hair
Pfizer Illinois/Wisconsin; Schaumberg, IL; 1999
Prairie Heart Institute; Springfield, IL; 2004
Princecraft; Princeville, QC High-End Fishing, Pontoon & Deck Boats; 2002
Rampage Sport Fishing Yachts; Oconto, WI; 2008
Saint John's Hospital; Springfield, IL; 2004
Saint Luke's Health System; St Louis, MO Not-for-Profit Health System
Shorewest Realtors; Milwaukee, WI; 2006
Southwest Airlines Vacations; Orlando, FL; 1985
Specialty Silicone Fabricators; Paso Robles, CA Medical Device Parts; 2010
Spectrum Group International; Irvine, CA Teletrade (Certified Coin & Currency Auctions); 2010
St Joseph Health System; Orange, CA Integrated Healthcare System
St. Petersburg Clearwater CVB LA Live Video; 2008
Subway Sandwich Shops Milwaukee Franchise Group; Milwaukee, WI; 2003
United Health Services; Binghamton, NY A Community-Owned, Not-For-Profit Health Care System; 1992
New-Wyoming Office of Tourism (Advertising Agency of Record) Comprehensive Advertising, Content Strategy

BVK Direct
5740 Fleet St Ste 260, Carlsbad, CA 92008-4703
Tel.: (760) 804-8300
Fax: (760) 804-8301
Toll Free: (800) 728-5121
E-Mail: info@bvkdirect.com
Web Site: www.bvkdirect.com

Employees: 13
Year Founded: 1984

Agency Specializes In: Internet/Web Design, Yellow Pages Advertising

Ron Kendrella *(Exec VP)*
Todd Aubol *(VP-Client Svcs)*
Brandon Haan *(VP-Digital Media Adv)*
Dawn M. Sanderson *(VP-Strategic Bus Dev)*
Julie Morgans *(Dir-Ops)*

BVK Direct
117 W 20th St Ste 202, Kansas City, MO 64108
Tel.: (816) 753-1201
Fax: (816) 753-1210
Toll Free: (800) 775-8444
E-Mail: info@bvkdirect.com
Web Site: www.bvkdirect.com

Employees: 10

Agency Specializes In: Business-To-Business, Yellow Pages Advertising

Todd Aubol *(VP-Client Svcs)*
Marta York *(VP-Acct Svcs)*

BVK Direct
4350 Lexington Pkwy, Colleyville, TX 76034
(See Separate Listing)

BVK-Chicago
999 Oakmont Plz Dr Ste 300, Westmont, IL 60559-1368
(See Separate Listing)

BVK-Fort Myers
12697 New Brittany Blvd, Fort Myers, FL 33907-3631
Tel.: (239) 931-9900
Fax: (239) 931-0892
E-Mail: info@bvk.com
Web Site: www.bvk.com

Employees: 1

Agency Specializes In: Advertising, Travel & Tourism

Peter Capper *(Mng Partner)*
Tricia Lewis *(Sr VP & Dir-BVK Chicago)*
Michael Eaton *(Sr VP)*
Victoria Simmons *(VP & Grp Dir)*
Kevin Steltz *(VP & Grp Acct Dir)*
Patrick McGovern *(VP-Acct Svcs)*
Meghan Massey *(Acct Supvr)*
Jamie Foley *(Acct Exec)*

BVK-Tampa
201 Columbia Dr Ste 2, Tampa, FL 33606-3722
Tel.: (813) 258-2510
Fax: (813) 258-2234
Web Site: www.bvk.com

Employees: 3

Agency Specializes In: Advertising, Travel & Tourism

Mary DeLong *(Sr VP)*
Carmen Boyce *(VP & Acct Dir)*

BVK/MEKA
848 Brickell Ave Ste 430, Miami, FL 33131-2915
Tel.: (305) 372-0028
Fax: (305) 372-0880
E-Mail: gonzalog@bvk.com
Web Site: www.bvk.com

Employees: 10

Agency Specializes In: Advertising, Consumer Marketing, Hispanic Market, Sponsorship, Travel & Tourism

Herman Echevarria *(Chm & CEO)*
Gonzalo Gonzalez *(Mng Dir)*
Ileana Aleman *(Chief Creative Officer)*
Richard Conti *(Sr Dir-Art)*
Yasmin Guerrero *(Acct Dir)*
Nereyda Lago *(Dir-Media)*
Maria Yolanda Osorio *(Sr Acct Exec)*

BVK-CHICAGO
999 Oakmont Plz Dr Ste 300, Westmont, IL 60559-1368
Tel.: (630) 789-3222
Fax: (630) 789-3223
Toll Free: (800) 574-0039
Web Site: www.bvk.com

Employees: 12

Agency Specializes In: Advertising, Advertising Specialties, Collateral, Communications, Consumer Marketing, Direct Response Marketing, Event Planning & Marketing, Financial, Health Care Services, Internet/Web Design, Local Marketing, Market Research, Media Buying Services, Media Planning, Media Relations, Newspaper, Newspapers & Magazines, Out-of-Home Media, Outdoor, Pharmaceutical, Planning & Consultation, Print, Promotions, Public Relations, Publicity/Promotions, Radio, Regional, Sales Promotion, T.V., Travel & Tourism, Web (Banner Ads, Pop-ups, etc.), Women's Market, Yellow Pages Advertising

Peter Capper *(Mng Partner)*
Joel English *(Mng Partner)*
Sara Kain Meaney *(Mng Dir)*
Tricia Lewis *(Sr VP & Dir)*
Tamalyn Powell *(Sr VP)*
Patrick Mcgovern *(VP-Acct Svcs)*
Michael Vojvodich *(Dir-Creative)*
Meghan Massey *(Acct Supvr)*

BVK DIRECT
4350 Lexington Pkwy, Colleyville, TX 76034
Tel.: (972) 977-5220
Fax: (817) 545-8288
Toll Free: (877) 775-2600
E-Mail: nikki@nikkisue.com
Web Site: www.bvkdirect.com

Employees: 8
Year Founded: 2000

Agency Specializes In: Internet/Web Design, Yellow Pages Advertising

Peter Capper *(Mng Partner)*
Joel English *(Mng Partner)*
Sara Kain Meaney *(Mng Dir)*
Tricia Lewis *(Sr VP & Dir-BVK Chicago)*
Tamalyn Powell *(Sr VP)*
Angela Theriault *(VP & Acct Dir)*
Peggy Allen Weber Kiefer *(VP-Acct Svc & Healthcare)*
Ellen Friebert Schupper *(VP-Acct Svcs)*
Steve Judkins *(Client Svcs Dir)*
Michael Vojvodich *(Dir-Creative)*
Robyn Swernoff *(Acct Supvr & Specialist-Event & Experiential Mktg)*
Jen Rumpel *(Acct Supvr)*
Dana Harkness Minning *(Sr Acct Exec-Acct Svc)*
Lauren Murray *(Acct Exec-Experiential)*

BWP COMMUNICATIONS
654 W 100 S, Salt Lake City, UT 84104
Tel.: (801) 359-2766
E-Mail: info@bwpcommunications.com
Web Site: www.bwpcommunications.com

Year Founded: 1995

Agency Specializes In: Advertising, Brand Development & Integration, Graphic Design, Internet/Web Design, Print, Public Relations, Strategic Planning/Research

Brett Palmer *(Owner & Dir-Creative)*
Richard Jewkes *(Partner-Strategic Comm)*
Debra Macfarlane *(Acct Mgr)*
Michael Sieger *(Sr Designer)*

Accounts:
EDA Architecture
Faithology
Vault Denim
Yee-Haw Pickle Co

BYNUMS MARKETING & COMMUNICATIONS, INC
301 Grant St Ste 4300, Pittsburgh, PA 15219
Tel.: (412) 471-4332
Fax: (412) 471-1383
E-Mail: russell@bynums.com
Web Site: www.bynums.com

Employees: 10
Year Founded: 1985

Agency Specializes In: Advertising, Advertising Specialties, African-American Market, Alternative Advertising, Arts, Aviation & Aerospace, Broadcast, Business Publications, Business-To-Business, Children's Market, Collateral, College, Consulting, Consumer Goods, Consumer Marketing, Crisis Communications, Direct-to-Consumer, Email, Event Planning & Marketing, Experience Design, Faith Based, Financial, Food Service, Government/Political, Graphic Design, Guerilla Marketing, Health Care Services, Household Goods, Identity Marketing, Internet/Web Design, Local Marketing, Logo & Package Design, Market Research, Media Buying Services, Media Planning, Media Relations, Media Training, Multicultural, Over-50 Market, Print, Production (Print), Public Relations, Publicity/Promotions, Publishing, Radio, Regional, Restaurant, Retail, Seniors' Market, Social Marketing/Nonprofit, Sponsorship, Sports Market, Strategic Planning/Research, T.V., Teen Market, Travel & Tourism, Urban Market, Viral/Buzz/Word of Mouth, Women's Market

Approx. Annual Billings: $1,000,000

Breakdown of Gross Billings by Media: Brdcst.: 5%; Bus. Publs.: 5%; Collateral: 15%; Consulting: 10%; Event Mktg.: 10%; Exhibits/Trade Shows: 5%; Graphic Design: 5%; Logo & Package Design: 5%; Mags.: 10%; Newsp.: 5%; Outdoor: 5%; Point of Purchase: 5%; Radio: 5%; Strategic Planning/Research: 5%; Transit: 5%

Russell L. Bynum *(Owner)*
Kathy L. Bynum *(VP)*

Accounts:
Allegheny County Department of Public Works; 2008
American Port Services, FBO AV Center; Teterboro, NJ; 1988
American Port Services, World Services; Teterboro, NJ; 1988
BC Scores; Pittsburgh, PA Youth & Family Services; 2009
Char Mcallister Christian Recording Artist; 2006
Dorsey's Digital Imaging Digital Services; 2012
FamilyLinks; Pittsburgh PA Social Services; 2006
Functional Literacy Ministry of Haiti; Pittsburgh, PA; Haiti Educational & Medical Missions to Haiti; 1990
ICA Pittsburgh Government Relations; 2012
Landmark Community Capital; Pittsburgh, PA Community Development, Community Services; 2009
MCG Learner Centered Arts Integration Model; Pittsburgh, PA Educational Services; 2006
New Horizons Theater
PA Council on the Arts; 2005
Pittsburgh Community Services, Inc.; Pittsburgh, PA Social Services; 2002
Pittsburgh Cultural Trust Minority Audience Development; 2011
Pittsburgh Epilepsy Foundation; Pittsburgh, PA Social Service; 2005
PNC Bank; Pittsburgh, PA African American History Contest; 2009
Precious Ones Day Care; 2007
Renaissance Publication; Pittsburgh, PA Publisher of Newspaper & Directory; 1996
Sci-Tek Environmental Services; 2005
Sherdian Broadcasting; Pittsburgh, PA
UMPC Health Plan; Pittsburgh, PA Health- Adult Basics; 2010
Union Baptist Church; Pittsburgh, PA; 2005
Urban League Charter School; 2010
WGBN-Radio; Pittsburgh, PA; 2000
Youth Works; Pittsburgh, PA Youth Counseling; 2007

Division:

Bynums Minority Marketing Group
1501 Reed Dald St Ste 5003, Pittsburgh, PA 15233
Tel.: (412) 471-4332
Fax: (412) 471-1383
E-Mail: russell@bynums.com
Web Site: www.bynums.com

E-Mail for Key Personnel:
President: rbynum2123@earthlink.net

Employees: 7
Year Founded: 1985

Agency Specializes In: Communications, Public Relations

Russell L. Bynum *(Owner)*
Kathy Bynum *(VP)*

Accounts:
A Second Chance, Inc
African American Student Recruitment
Clarion University
Familylinks Inc
FLM of Haiti
Pittsburgh Black Pages; Pittsburgh, PA Directory; 1995
The Pittsburgh Theological Seminary-Metro Urban Institute; 2003
Smithkline Beecham Consumer Health Care
UPMC Health Cre
Womens March for Peace

C&G PARTNERS, LLC.
116 E 16th St 10th Fl, New York, NY 10003
Tel.: (212) 532-4460
Fax: (212) 532-4465
E-Mail: info@cgpartnersllc.com
Web Site: www.cgpartnersllc.com

Employees: 22

Agency Specializes In: Brand Development & Integration, Environmental, Exhibit/Trade Shows, Graphic Design, Identity Marketing, Internet/Web Design, Logo & Package Design, Multimedia, Print, Strategic Planning/Research

Revenue: $1,700,000

Advertising Agencies

Jonathan Alger *(Partner)*
Keith Helmetag *(Partner)*
Maya Kopytman *(Partner)*
Amy Siegel *(Partner)*
Scott Plunkett *(Assoc Partner)*

Accounts:
Abrams, Inc.
AIPAC
Alhurra TV Network
American Express
American Institute of Architects
Cablevision
MasterCard Worldwide Project Spirit
Museum of American Finance
New York State Restaurant Association

C&M COMMUNIQUE
30101 Town Ctr Dr Ste 104, Laguna Niguel, CA 92677
Tel.: (949) 363-7974
Fax: (949) 363-1750
Web Site: www.cmcommunique.com

Year Founded: 1992

Agency Specializes In: Advertising, Brand Development & Integration, Digital/Interactive, Direct Response Marketing, Event Planning & Marketing, Internet/Web Design, Multimedia, Public Relations, Social Media, Strategic Planning/Research

Cristina Walters *(Principal & Dir-Creative)*
Leslie Bonifay *(VP-Mktg)*

Accounts:
PulteGroup, Inc. Del Webb

C&S CREATIVE
5532 Lillehammer Ln Ste 104, Park City, UT 84098
Tel.: (435) 649-1234
Fax: (435) 649-1287
Web Site: www.cscreate.com

Agency Specializes In: Advertising, Brand Development & Integration, Collateral, Event Planning & Marketing, Internet/Web Design, Logo & Package Design, Media Buying Services, Media Planning, Public Relations, Social Media

Cathy Slusher *(Principal)*

Accounts:
Chateaux Realty
Kaddas Enterprises
Redstone Village
Triumph Academy

C. REIMER ADVERTISING LTD.
2265 Pembina Highway #104, Winnipeg, MB R3T 5J3 Canada
Tel.: (204) 269-8093
Fax: (204) 275-1246

Employees: 4
Year Founded: 1959

Agency Specializes In: Advertising, Broadcast, Infomercials, Media Buying Services, Syndication

Approx. Annual Billings: $2,000,000

Brian L. Reimer *(Pres)*
W. Reimer *(Sec & Treas)*

C SQUARED ADVERTISING
10900 NE 8th St, Bellevue, WA 98004
Tel.: (425) 277-9951
E-Mail: info@csquaredadvertising.com
Web Site: www.csquaredadvertising.com

Year Founded: 2006

Agency Specializes In: Advertising, Brand Development & Integration, Media Planning, Public Relations, Social Media, Strategic Planning/Research

Heather Crunchie *(Co-Founder & Principal)*
Brenda Collons *(Principal)*
Scott Eggers *(Sr Dir-Art & Designer)*
Wes Youngquist *(Sr Dir-Art & Designer)*
Maureen Alley *(Specialist-PR)*
Brett Davis *(Sr Designer)*

Accounts:
APA-The Engineered Wood Association
Accoya
Calstar
Hanson Heidelberg
Nichiha Corporation
Trus Joist
Vetrotech
Weyerhaeuser Company

C SUITE COMMUNICATIONS
(Formerly Clarke Advertising and Public Relations)
401 N Cattlemen Rd Ste 200, Sarasota, FL 34232-6439
Tel.: (941) 365-2710
Fax: (941) 366-4940
Toll Free: (800) 724-0289
E-Mail: info@c-suitecomms.com
Web Site: www.c-suitecomms.com

Employees: 15
Year Founded: 1987

National Agency Associations: 4A's-IN

Agency Specializes In: Advertising, Brand Development & Integration, Broadcast, Business-To-Business, Collateral, Communications, Consumer Goods, Consumer Marketing, Corporate Communications, Corporate Identity, Crisis Communications, Customer Relationship Management, Digital/Interactive, Direct-to-Consumer, Electronic Media, Email, Exhibit/Trade Shows, Government/Political, Graphic Design, Health Care Services, Hospitality, Industrial, Integrated Marketing, Internet/Web Design, Logo & Package Design, Media Buying Services, Media Planning, Media Relations, Media Training, Medical Products, Merchandising, Newspaper, Point of Purchase, Point of Sale, Print, Production, Public Relations, Publicity/Promotions, Radio, Real Estate, Regional, Restaurant, Retail, Sales Promotion, Social Media, Strategic Planning/Research, T.V., Trade & Consumer Magazines, Travel & Tourism, Web (Banner Ads, Pop-ups, etc.), Yellow Pages Advertising

Patricia Courtois *(Pres & CEO)*
Bill Pierson *(Principal)*
Heather McLain *(VP & Dir-PR)*
Harriet Hritz *(Sr Dir-Art)*
Rue Ann Porter *(Dir-Media)*
Lauren Opelt *(Sr Acct Mgr)*
Amanda Parrish *(Sr Acct Mgr)*
Joan Burnell *(Mgr-Creative Svcs)*
Guy Vilt *(Mgr-Creative Svcs)*
Judy Firek *(Acct Exec)*
Angelo Jasa *(Acct Coord)*

Accounts:
ClosetMaid
The Community Foundation of Sarasota
Emerson Tool Company
FCCI Insurance
New-Michael Saunders & Company
Mote Marine Laboratory
PGT Industries; Sarasota, FL; 1999
Sarasota Arts
Sarasota Orchestra (Formerly Florida West Coast Symphony)
Spectrum Brands Rayovac, Remington: Flex360, PR-350, RM PRO, ShortCut Clipper
Tidewell Hospice

C.2K COMMUNICATIONS
1067 Gayley Ave, Los Angeles, CA 90024
Tel.: (310) 208-2324
E-Mail: usa@c-2k.com
Web Site: www.c-2k.com

Agency Specializes In: Advertising, Communications, Entertainment, Production

Rod Findley *(Founder)*
Ken Musen *(Founder)*

Accounts:
Canon U.S.A., Inc.
The Coca-Cola Company
Toyota Motor Sales, U.S.A., Inc.

C3 - CREATIVE CONSUMER CONCEPTS
(Formerly Creative Consumer Concepts)
10955 Granada Ln, Overland Park, KS 66211
Tel.: (800) 452-6444
Fax: (913) 491-3677
Web Site: www.c3brandmarketing.com/

Year Founded: 1987

Agency Specializes In: Brand Development & Integration, Digital/Interactive, Graphic Design, Production, Promotions, Strategic Planning/Research

Bob Cutler *(Pres)*
Angel Morales *(Mng Dir)*
Ginny Harris *(Controller)*
Robin Knight *(Exec Dir-Creative)*
Brenda Hinkle-Bachofer *(Grp Acct Dir)*
Jennifer Loper *(Acct Dir)*
Chelsey Lewis *(Sr Acct Mgr)*
David Smith *(Mgr-Product Integrity)*
Katelyn Clark *(Acct Supvr)*
Lauren St. John *(Coord-Production)*

Accounts:
Abuelo's - Food Concepts International
Arby's Foundation
Army Reserve Family Programs
Darden Restaurants, Inc. Bahama Breeze
Great Wolf Lodge
Lone Star Steakhouse & Saloon, Inc.
Old Spaghetti Factory
Paradise Bakery & Cafe, Inc.

THE C3 GROUP
PO Box 141061, Broken Arrow, OK 74014
Tel.: (479) 445-2657
Fax: (918) 872-8458
Web Site: www.thec3group.net

Agency Specializes In: Advertising, Broadcast, Email, Graphic Design, Internet/Web Design, Print, Social Media

Bobby Cook *(Pres)*

Accounts:
Defense Acquisition University

CABEZA ADVERTISING
2303 Ranch Rd 620 S Ste 135-190, Lakeway, TX 78734
Tel.: (512) 771-0079
Web Site: www.cabezaadvertising.com

Agency Specializes In: Advertising, Brand Development & Integration, Collateral, Corporate Identity, Digital/Interactive, Graphic Design, Internet/Web Design, Media Planning, Outdoor, Print

Jose Garcia *(Pres)*

Accounts:
Reap Financial
Trinity Pools & Scapes

CACTUS
(d/b/a Cactus Mktg Communications)
2128 15th St Ste 100, Denver, CO 80202
Tel.: (303) 455-7545
Fax: (303) 455-0408
Web Site: www.cactusdenver.com

Employees: 45
Year Founded: 1990

National Agency Associations: 4A's

Agency Specializes In: Advertising, Digital/Interactive, Graphic Design, Media Relations, Public Relations, Sponsorship

Revenue: $8,000,000

Joe Conrad *(Founder & CEO)*
Norm Shearer *(Partner & Chief Creative Officer)*
Kris Byers *(VP-Bus Ops)*
Jamie Poston *(VP-Integrated Media)*
Daniel Buchmeier *(Dir-Art)*
Ainslie Fortune *(Dir-Acct Mgmt)*
Michael Lee *(Dir-Digital Strategy)*
Diana Knutson *(Assoc Dir-Media)*
Cristal Silerio *(Mgr-Multicultural PR & Content)*
April Ingle *(Specialist-PR)*
Kaci Blatchford *(Media Planner & Media Buyer)*
Andy Bartosch *(Copywriter)*
Shea Tullos *(Copywriter)*
Meagan Schreiber *(Sr Media Planner)*
Jamie Sharp *(Sr Print Producer)*

Accounts:
Carson J. Spencer Foundation Campaign: "Man Therapy"
Colorado Department of Human Services Office of Behavioral Health
Colorado Department of Public Health and Environment Campaign: "Good to Know", Digital, Marketing, Out-of-Home, Print, Public Awareness, Radio, Social Media Outreach, TV, Website
Colorado HealthOP Campaign: "Believe It", Digital, Out-of-Home, Print, Radio, Strategic, TV, Website
Colorado Lottery Campaign: "Dolphin Trainers", Campaign: "Vegas Baby", Cash 5, Casino Cash, Match Play, Media, Powerball, Scratch Games, TV
Colorado Office of Suicide Prevention Campaign: "Man Therapy"
Denver Zoo
Excelsior Youth Center Strategic
New-Gaia (Global Agency of Record) Creative, Global Integrated Strategy, Media
Hunter Douglas, Inc.
Jackson Hole Mountain Resort
Jackson Hole Travel & Tourism Joint Power Board; Jackson, WY (Agency of Record) Campaign: "Giant", Digital, Online, Print, Public Relations, Radio, Social Media
SmartyPants Vitamins TV
University of Colorado Hospital
University of Colorado "The Human Harmonic Project"
Winter Park Resort (Agency of Record)

CADDIS INTERACTIVE
230 Franklin Rd Ste 12Q, Franklin, TN 37064
Tel.: (615) 469-6726
E-Mail: hello@caddis.co
Web Site: www.caddis.co

Agency Specializes In: Advertising, Brand Development & Integration, Content, Digital/Interactive, Email, Internet/Web Design, Social Media, Strategic Planning/Research

Jake Fagan *(Co-Founder & Pres)*
Michael Leigeber *(Co-Founder & CTO)*
Jesse Luke *(Dir-Res)*

Accounts:
EnergyLogic LLC

CADE & ASSOCIATES ADVERTISING, INC.
1645 Metropolitan Blvd, Tallahassee, FL 32308
Tel.: (850) 385-0300
Toll Free: (800) 715-2233
Web Site: www.cade1.com

Agency Specializes In: Advertising, Internet/Web Design, Logo & Package Design, Media Planning, Print, Public Relations

Rick Shapley *(Pres)*
John Cade *(Partner & Dir-Creative)*
Laura Frandsen *(Partner & Acct Supvr)*
Scott Smith *(Sr Dir-Art)*
Stacy Hilton *(Dir-Art)*
Lisa Fletcher *(Office Mgr)*

Accounts:
FSU Basketball

CADENT MEDICAL COMMUNICATIONS
1707 Market Pl Blvd Ste 350, Irving, TX 75063
Tel.: (972) 929-1900
Fax: (972) 929-1901
E-Mail: info@cadentmed.com

E-Mail for Key Personnel:
President: mrickards@cadentmed.com

Employees: 43
Year Founded: 1994

Agency Specializes In: Business-To-Business, Communications, Education, Health Care Services, Medical Products, New Product Development, Pharmaceutical, Strategic Planning/Research

Approx. Annual Billings: $50,600,000

Megan Ollinger *(Sr VP-Client Svcs)*
Jared Davis *(Acct Dir)*

Accounts:
AstraZeneca
Bristol-Myers Squibb
Celgene
Eisai Corporation
Genentech; San Francisco, CA Arastin, Rituxan, Tarcera; 2003
Merck
Millennium
Protherics Voraxaze; 2004
Roche
Sanofi-Aventis
Takeda; Chicago, IL Ramelteon; 2004

CADIENT GROUP
72 E Swedesford Rd, Malvern, PA 19355
Tel.: (484) 351-2800
Fax: (484) 351-2900
E-Mail: thethrill@cadient.com
Web Site: www.cadient.com

Employees: 160
Year Founded: 1991

Agency Specializes In: Graphic Design, Internet/Web Design, Logo & Package Design, Sponsorship

Stephen Wray *(Pres, CEO & VP-Global Life Sciences Practice)*
Charlie Walker *(COO)*
Chris Mycek *(Chief Customer Officer)*
Will Reese *(Chief Innovation Officer)*
Robert Holloway *(Sr VP-Comml Innovation)*
Ilana Scholl *(Client Svcs Dir)*
Mickey Lynch *(Dir-Comml Strategy & Innovation)*
Hee Jun Rho *(Dir-Comml Strategy & Innovation)*
Clint Tankersley *(Dir-Comml Strategy & Innovation)*
Lisa Evans *(Sr Acct Mgr)*

Accounts:
AstraZeneca Nexium, Seroquel, Zomig Nasal Spray
Bristol Myers Squibb
CSL Behring
Johnson & Johnson
Novartis
Pfizer

CAHAN & ASSOCIATES
171 2nd St #5, San Francisco, CA 94105
Tel.: (415) 621-0915
Fax: (415) 621-7642
E-Mail: info@cahanassociates.com
Web Site: www.cahanassociates.com

Employees: 18

Agency Specializes In: Advertising, Brand Development & Integration, Direct-to-Consumer, Electronic Media, Email, Food Service, Internet/Web Design, Magazines, Medical Products, Outdoor, Package Design, Planning & Consultation, Promotions, Publishing, Web (Banner Ads, Pop-ups, etc.)

Bill Cahan *(Pres)*

Accounts:
Adaptex
Advanced Medicine
AFFC
Collateral Therapeutics
COR Therapeutics
Eastman Kodak Company
Molecular Biosystems
Tumbleweed Communications

CAHG
225 N Michigan Ave, Chicago, IL 60601
Tel.: (312) 297-6700
Fax: (312) 649-7232
E-Mail: paul.pfleiderer@cahg.com
Web Site: www.cahg.com

Employees: 150
Year Founded: 1962

National Agency Associations: 4A's-BPA

Agency Specializes In: Advertising, Advertising Specialties, Brand Development & Integration, Collateral, Communications, Corporate Communications, Corporate Identity, Digital/Interactive, Education, Electronic Media, Event Planning & Marketing, Graphic Design, Health Care Services, Identity Marketing, Integrated Marketing, International, Internet/Web Design, Media Buying Services, Media Planning, Media Relations, Mobile Marketing, Multimedia, New Product Development, Package Design, Pharmaceutical, Planning & Consultation, Podcasting, Production (Ad, Film, Broadcast),

Production (Print), Sponsorship, Strategic Planning/Research, Viral/Buzz/Word of Mouth, Web (Banner Ads, Pop-ups, etc.), Women's Market

Robin Shapiro *(Pres & Chief Creative Officer)*
Dennis Hoppe *(CFO & COO)*
Suri Harris *(Exec VP-Strategic Plng & New Ventures)*
Kristen Gengaro *(Sr VP & Grp Acct Dir)*
Paul Pfleiderer *(Sr VP & Dir-Bus Dev)*
Garth Anderson *(VP & Grp Dir-Plng)*
Jamie Pfaff *(Exec Dir-Creative)*
Christine Marks *(Grp Acct Supvr)*

Accounts:
Alcon/Vigamox
Bristol-Myers Squibb; Princeton, NJ
Gilead GS-7977
Johnson & Johnson
Merck
Novartis
Otsuka
Pfizer, Inc.
Procter & Gamble Pharmaceuticals, Inc.
Sanofi-Aventis
Takeda

Branches

CAHG
(Formerly Surge Worldwide Healthcare Communications)
220 E 42nd St 5th Fl, New York, NY 10017
Tel.: (646) 428-2500
Fax: (646) 428-2501
Web Site: www.cahg.com

Employees: 105
Year Founded: 1999

National Agency Associations: 4A's

Agency Specializes In: Health Care Services

Robin Shapiro *(Pres & Chief Creative Officer)*
Dennis Hoppe *(CFO & COO)*
Suri Harris *(Exec VP-Strategic Plng & New Ventures)*
Victor Wright *(Sr VP & Grp Acct Dir)*
Timothy Holland *(VP & Acct Dir)*
Kate Cannova *(Mgr-Strategic Svcs & Acct Supvr)*
Sarah Herman *(Acct Supvr)*
Christine Mundy *(Grp Acct Supvr)*
Katie Murtha *(Grp Acct Supvr)*

Accounts:
Merck & Co. Inc.
Merck & Co., Vaccines Division
Merck/Schering-Plough Phamaceuticals

CAHG
211 E Chicago Ave, Chicago, IL 60611-2637
Tel.: (312) 664-5310
Fax: (312) 649-7232
E-Mail: elaine.eisen@corbett.cahg.com
Web Site: www.cahg.com/

Employees: 65
Year Founded: 1962

Agency Specializes In: Advertising, Advertising Specialties, Health Care Services

Robin Shapiro *(Pres & Chief Creative Officer)*
Dennis Hoppe *(CFO & COO)*
Jerry Coamey *(Sr VP & Grp Dir-Creative)*
Stewart Young *(Sr VP & Dir-Plng)*
Mark Springer *(VP & Sr Dir-Fin Svcs)*
Barry Vucsko *(VP & Sr Acct Dir)*
Chris Rudnick *(VP & Dir-Creative)*
John Moen *(VP & Assoc Dir-Creative)*
Jessica Aguilar *(Assoc Dir-Digital Strategy)*

Accounts:
Alcon
Bristol-Myers Squibb
Forest Laboratories, Inc.
Merck
Novartis
Pfizer
Sanofi Aventis
Takeda

CAIN & COMPANY
685 Featherstone Rd, Rockford, IL 61107-6304
Tel.: (815) 399-2482
Fax: (815) 399-0557
E-Mail: info@cain-co.com
Web Site: www.cain-co.com

Employees: 12
Year Founded: 1972

Agency Specializes In: Advertising, Advertising Specialties, Business-To-Business, Collateral, Corporate Identity, Electronic Media, Exhibit/Trade Shows, Financial, Graphic Design, Health Care Services, Industrial, Internet/Web Design, Logo & Package Design, Medical Products, Multimedia, Newspapers & Magazines, Print, Production, Publicity/Promotions, Sales Promotion, Technical Advertising, Trade & Consumer Magazines

Scott Cain *(Pres)*
Amy Anderson *(CFO & Acct Exec)*
Brian Anderson *(VP)*
Rick Heffner *(Dir-Media & Sr Acct Exec)*
Pat Atkinson *(Dir-Art)*
Karen Bartch *(Dir-Art)*
Paul Phillips *(Dir-Creative)*
Dawn Preston *(Dir-Art)*
Pam Loria *(Mgr-Production)*
Larry Bederka *(Acct Exec)*

Accounts:
Beacon Promotions
BlueCross BlueShield Association
Caterpillar
Caterpillar Racing; Peoria, IL; 1995
Caterpillar, Engine Division; Peoria, IL; 1990
Caterpillar, Mining Division; Peoria, IL; 1998
Ingersoll
Norwood; San Antonio, TX; 1999

CALCIUM
(Formerly Vox Medica Inc.)
The Curtis Ctr Ste 250-S, Philadelphia, PA 19106
Tel.: (215) 238-8500, ext. 1306
Fax: (215) 238-0881
Web Site: www.calciumusa.com

Employees: 125
Year Founded: 1953

Agency Specializes In: Advertising, Brand Development & Integration, Collateral, Communications, Consulting, Corporate Communications, Corporate Identity, Education, Event Planning & Marketing, Government/Political, Graphic Design, Health Care Services, Medical Products, Pharmaceutical, Public Relations, Sales Promotion, Strategic Planning/Research

Approx. Annual Billings: $129,600,000

Steven Michaelson *(CEO)*
Timothy Garde *(COO)*
Steve Hamburg *(Chief Creative Officer)*
Lorna Weir *(Pres-Vox Medica)*
Jonathan Hunt *(VP-Global Mktg & Partnerships-Vox Media, Inc)*
Eric Schwab *(Acct Dir)*
Judy Capano *(Dir-Bus Dev)*

Accounts:
Abbott Laboratories
Allergan
AstraZeneca
Baxter International
Biogen Idec
Celgene
Centers for Disease Control & Prevention
Cephalon
Cigna Healthcare
Genentech
Janssen Pharmaceutica
LifeScan
Ortho Biotech
Ortho-McNeil Pharmaceuticals
PricewaterhouseCoopers
TEVA Pharmaceuticals

CALDER BATEMAN COMMUNICATIONS LTD.
10241 109th St, Edmonton, AB T5J 1N2 Canada
Tel.: (780) 426-3610
Fax: (780) 425-6646
E-Mail: heythere@calderbateman.com
Web Site: www.calderbateman.com

Employees: 34
Year Founded: 1990

Ernie Pasemko *(Partner)*
Jaime Calayo *(Dir-Art)*
David Falconer *(Mgr-Production)*
Alysia Lambertus *(Acct Exec)*
Cheryl Meger *(Acct Exec)*

Accounts:
Alberta Health Services Campaign: "Plenty of Syph", Campaign: "Sex Germs"; 2006
Camp Firefly
Edmonton Journal; 2006
Full House Lottery
Institute of Sexual Minority Studies and Services, University of Alberta
Mothers Against Drunk Driving; 2006
NorTerra
PCL Construction
Shirley Potter Costumes

CALDWELL VANRIPER
111 Monument Cir, Indianapolis, IN 46204
Tel.: (317) 632-6501
E-Mail: kflynn@cvrindy.com
Web Site: www.cvrindy.com

Employees: 27

Agency Specializes In: Advertising, Brand Development & Integration, Broadcast, Business-To-Business, Cable T.V., College, Communications, Consumer Goods, Consumer Marketing, Corporate Communications, Corporate Identity, Crisis Communications, Customer Relationship Management, Digital/Interactive, Direct Response Marketing, Direct-to-Consumer, E-Commerce, Email, Environmental, Exhibit/Trade Shows, Fashion/Apparel, Guerilla Marketing, In-Store Advertising, Integrated Marketing, Internet/Web Design, Local Marketing, Logo & Package Design, Market Research, Media Relations, Out-of-Home Media, Point of Purchase, Production (Print), Public Relations, Publicity/Promotions, Radio, Retail, Shopper Marketing, Social Media, Trade & Consumer Magazines, Transportation, Web (Banner Ads, Pop-ups, etc.), Women's Market

Kevin Flynn *(Pres)*
Jan Amonette *(Sr VP)*
Julie Muncy *(VP-HR)*
Dustin Thompson *(Dir-Social Media)*
Katie Clements *(Assoc Dir-Creative)*
Karen Belmont *(Acct Svcs Mgr & Project Mgr)*
Taylor Fregeau *(Asst Acct Exec)*

Paul Gosselin *(Sr Writer)*
Kara Shaw *(Sr Bus Mgr)*

Accounts:
The Alexander Hotel Travel/Hospitality; 2012
Build-A-Bear Retail/Toys; 2012
Citizens Energy Group Utility Services; 2012
Firestone Building Products Building Products; 2012
Henny Penny Restaurant Equipment; 2013
Indiana University Kelley School of Business Education; 2013
Indy Chamber Economic Development; 2013
Lafayette Savings Bank Financial Services; 2013
National Bank of Indianapolis; Indianapolis, IN Financial Services; 1992
NCAA Education/Athletics; 2012
Roche; Indianapolis, IN Healthcare Products & Services; 2009
Sanders Candy; Detroit, MI Candy, E-Commerce, Retailer; 2010
Stanley Security Solutions, Inc. Building Products; 2012
Ventana Medical Systems; Tucson, AZ Medical Devices; 2011
Zimmer; Warsaw, IN Orthopedic Devices; 2010

CALIBER CREATIVE
6221 E Silver Maple Cir Ste 102, Sioux Falls, SD 57110
Tel.: (605) 275-8588
Web Site: www.thinkcaliber.com

Agency Specializes In: Advertising, Digital/Interactive, Internet/Web Design

Brad Deville *(Partner)*
Casey Schultz *(Partner)*
Erin Shellenberger *(Principal)*
Kristine Watkins *(Dir-Art)*
Karie Scuiller *(Acct Mgr)*
Kelly Buss *(Specialist-Media)*
Mari Stensgaard *(Acct Exec)*
Bryan Cleghorn *(Designer)*
Megan Kiecker *(Designer)*
Taylor Litzen *(Acct Coord)*

Accounts:
Family Dental Center
Prairie Lakes Healthcare System
Producers Hybrids Campaign: "Inside this Seed"

THE CALIBER GROUP
4007 E Paradise Falls Dr Ste 210, Tucson, AZ 85712
Tel.: (520) 795-4500
Fax: (520) 795-4565
Web Site: www.calibergroup.com

Agency Specializes In: Advertising, Brand Development & Integration, Content, Crisis Communications, Digital/Interactive, Logo & Package Design, Media Buying Services, Media Planning, Public Relations, Social Media

Kerry Stratford *(Pres)*
Linda Welter Cohen *(CEO)*
Lori Mcconville *(Exec VP & Supvr-Accounts)*
Joy Tyson *(Acct Mgr-PR & Social Media)*
Jodie Lerch *(Mgr-Production)*

Accounts:
Hughes Federal Credit Union

CALIFORNIA OUTDOOR ADVERTISING
503 32nd St Ste 110, Newport Beach, CA 92663
Tel.: (949) 723-0713
Fax: (949) 723-9511
Web Site: www.californiaoutdoor.com

Employees: 10
Year Founded: 1990

Agency Specializes In: Advertising, Brand Development & Integration, Co-op Advertising, Hispanic Market, In-Store Advertising, Out-of-Home Media, Outdoor, Planning & Consultation, Promotions, Radio

Approx. Annual Billings: $10,000,000

Brian Gurnee *(Pres)*

CALISE PARTNERS INC.
(Formerly Calise & Sedei)
501 Elm St, Ste 500, Dallas, TX 75202
Tel.: (469) 385-4790
Fax: (214) 760-7094
Web Site: www.calisepartners.com

Employees: 32
Year Founded: 2002

Agency Specializes In: Brand Development & Integration, Business Publications, Communications, Corporate Identity, Cosmetics, Customer Relationship Management, Digital/Interactive, Direct Response Marketing, Electronic Media, Fashion/Apparel, Financial, Health Care Services, High Technology, Information Technology, Internet/Web Design, Media Buying Services, Mobile Marketing, Multimedia, Point of Purchase, Print, Production (Ad, Film, Broadcast), Production (Print), Public Relations, Publicity/Promotions, Radio, Restaurant, Retail, Search Engine Optimization, Social Media, T.V., Technical Advertising, Travel & Tourism, Viral/Buzz/Word of Mouth, Web (Banner Ads, Pop-ups, etc.)

Approx. Annual Billings: $35,301,000

Breakdown of Gross Billings by Media: Bus. Publs.: $2,000,000; Collateral: $1,750,000; D.M.: $1,985,000; E-Commerce: $2,500,000; Exhibits/Trade Shows: $1,750,000; Fees: $4,000,000; Newsp.: $1,250,000; Outdoor: $1,000,000; Production: $4,500,000; Pub. Rels.: $2,566,000; Radio: $4,500,000; T.V.: $7,500,000

Charles Calise *(Pres)*
Susie Lomelino *(Mng Dir)*
Brian Shedd *(Mng Dir)*
Joan Buccola *(COO)*
Mike Heronime *(Exec Dir-Creative)*
Karla Neely *(Assoc Dir-Creative)*
Lynette Crenshaw *(Mgr-Mktg)*
Jill Juncker *(Acct Supvr)*

Accounts:
Additech; Houston, TX; 2007
Doskocil Manufacturing Petmate Products; 2000
Farm Bureau Insurance of Louisiana
JAFRA Cosmetics
Lennox International Service Experts
Montana Mike's Restaurants
Service Experts; Richardson, TX Heating, Cooling & Indoor Air Quality; 2005
Sherwin-Williams Thompson's Water Seal
Skylight Financial
Taco Bueno
TWL Knowledge Group, Inc.
W Hotel-Dallas

CALLAHAN CREEK, INC.
805 New Hampshire St, Lawrence, KS 66044-2739
Tel.: (785) 838-4774
Fax: (785) 838-4033
E-Mail: mail@callahancreek.com
Web Site: www.callahancreek.com

E-Mail for Key Personnel:
Creative Dir.: fkeizer@callahancreek.com

Employees: 65
Year Founded: 1982

National Agency Associations: Second Wind Limited

Agency Specializes In: Advertising, Brand Development & Integration, Broadcast, Business-To-Business, Collateral, Communications, Consulting, Consumer Marketing, Corporate Identity, Direct Response Marketing, E-Commerce, Fashion/Apparel, Financial, Health Care Services, Pets , Planning & Consultation, Point of Purchase, Point of Sale, Public Relations, Strategic Planning/Research, T.V., Travel & Tourism

Approx. Annual Billings: $58,000,000

Chris Marshall *(Pres)*
Jan-Eric Anderson *(Chief Strategy Officer & VP)*
John Kuefler *(Chief Digital Officer & Exec VP)*
Tug McTighe *(VP & Exec Dir-Creative)*
Sarah Etzel *(VP-Fin & Ops)*
Matt Loehrer *(Sr Dir-Art)*
Shelly Deveney *(Grp Acct Dir)*
Sarah Miller *(Grp Acct Dir)*
Cecilia Riegel *(Dir-Media)*
Mark Tribble *(Dir-Acct Mgmt)*
Laura Frizell Eland *(Acct Mgr)*

Accounts:
Elanco Animal Health
Free State Brewing Packaging Campaign: "Winterfest"
Golf Course Superintendents Association of America Brand Management, Marketing, Membership Recruitment & Retention, Trade Show Exhibition
Sprint
Spyder Products
Toyota Motor Sales, USA
Tyson Pet Products
Westar Energy
White's Electronics Brand Positioning, Consumer, Marketing, Online, Social, Social Media, Strategy, Web

Branch

Callahan Creek
19001 S Western Ave T200, Torrance, CA 90501
Tel.: (310) 809-6124
Fax: (310) 381-7398
E-Mail: martine_padilla@toyota.com
Web Site: www.callahancreek.com

Employees: 10
Year Founded: 2006

Agency Specializes In: Sponsorship

Cynthia Maude *(Owner)*
Kent Stones *(VP-Strategic Plng)*
Chris Ralston *(Sr Dir-Art)*
Ben Smith *(Dir-Social & Emerging Media)*
Brett Terp *(Acct Mgr)*
Sonya Collins *(Sr Graphic Designer)*

Accounts:
Community America Credit Union
Kansas
Novartis
Sprint
Toyota Motor Sales , Lexus, Scion, Toyota

CALLAN ADVERTISING COMPANY
1126 N Hollywood Way, Burbank, CA 91505
Tel.: (818) 841-3284
Fax: (818) 841-3285
E-Mail: info@callan.com
Web Site: www.scallan.com

Year Founded: 1993

Agency Specializes In: Advertising, Digital/Interactive, Internet/Web Design, Logo & Package Design, Media Buying Services, Print

Sherri Callan *(Founder & Pres)*
Josh Allen *(Dir-Adv)*

Accounts:
New-Sony Pictures Classics

CALLANAN & KLEIN COMMUNICATIONS, INC.

1001 Watertown St, Newton, MA 02465
Tel.: (617) 431-1170
Fax: (617) 431-1160
E-Mail: info@callananklein.com
Web Site: www.callananklein.com

Agency Specializes In: Event Planning & Marketing, Media Relations, Public Relations, Publicity/Promotions

Erin Callanan *(Principal)*
Adam Klein *(Principal)*

Accounts:
The Boston Globe

CALLIS & ASSOC.

2650 S Limit Ct, Sedalia, MO 65301
Tel.: (660) 826-2822
Fax: (660) 827-2510
Web Site: www.ecallis.com

Agency Specializes In: Advertising, Brand Development & Integration, Email, Outdoor, Public Relations, Social Media

Charlyn Callis *(VP)*
Jim Shoemaker *(VP)*
Linda Harris *(Dir-Creative)*
Chris Young *(Dir-Digital Mktg)*
Tim Noland *(Acct Exec)*
Megan Ramey *(Acct Exec)*
Hannah Sartin *(Acct Exec)*
Brandi Miller *(Designer)*

Accounts:
Walther Arms Inc

CALYPSO COMMUNICATIONS

121 Bow St Bldg 6, Portsmouth, NH 03801
Tel.: (603) 431-0816
Fax: (603) 431-4497
E-Mail: info@calypsocom.com
Web Site: www.calypsocom.com

Employees: 10
Year Founded: 2000

Agency Specializes In: Brand Development & Integration, Business Publications, Collateral, Communications, Corporate Identity, Education, Entertainment, Environmental, Financial, Government/Political, Graphic Design, Health Care Services, High Technology, Internet/Web Design, Logo & Package Design, Media Relations, Production (Ad, Film, Broadcast), Public Relations, Publicity/Promotions, Sports Market, Strategic Planning/Research

Kevin Stickney *(Founder & Pres)*
Houssam Aboukhater *(Mng Dir)*
Angela Carter *(CFO)*
Sarah Grazier *(VP-Strategic Comm)*
Lauren Patricia Smith *(Acct Exec-PR)*
Devan Meserve *(Acct Coord-Social Media)*

Accounts:
AARP Financial
Adaptive Communications
American Ref-Fuel
Anthem
ArcLight Capital Partners
New-Atlas Holdings
Beacon Capital Management Partners
Celunol
Covanta Video Animation
Detroit Renewable Power Community Engagement, Creative, Crisis Management, Marketing, Media Outreach, PR
New-Enterprise Processes, Planning, and Performance Marketing, Public Relations, Quad C
Exeter Rent-All (Agency of Record)
First Reserve
FlexEnergy (Agency of Record) Creative, Marketing, Public Relations, Strategic Communications
New-Garrison Women's Health Center Creative, Public Relations
General Linen
The Grappone Companies
HomeFree Extended Family Media Relations, Strategic Communications
Iberdrola Renewables Communications
InterGen
New-JMD Industries (Agency of Record) Business Development, Marketing Campaigns, Media Support, Public Support, Strategic Communications
LifeCycle Meats Branding, Marketing, Messaging, Website Design
LimeSprings Beef; Lime Springs, IO Branding, Marketing
Media 100
Monadnock Paper Mills, Inc.; Bennington, NH Creative, Marketing, Public Relations
Monarch School of New England
Mount Agamenticus to the Sea Conservation Initiative
Music Hall; Portsmouth, NH; 2008
Music Hall
New Hampshire Businesses for Social Responsibility Campaign Development, Digital Content, Social Media
New Hampshire Catholic Charities
Nurse Audit
Ocean Renewable Power Company, LLC
Ogunquit Playhouse Business Development, Creative Design, Marketing Services, Planning, Public Relations, Social Media Strategy, Video Production
Pattern Energy Annual Report
Pella Windows & Doors of Maine & New Hampshire
The Portsmouth Music Hall
Seacoast Hospice; Exeter, NH; 2006
TimberNook Content Marketing, Content Strategy, Marketing, Public Relations, Social Media
Unitil
The University System of New Hampshire
U.S. Cellular
Usource Website
Vasculart, Inc.
Wal-Mart New Hampshire Community Retail Activities
Zero Carbon Systems

CALZONE & ASSOCIATES

1011 Lee Ave, Lafayette, LA 70502
Tel.: (337) 235-2924
Fax: (337) 237-0556
E-Mail: jcalzone@calzone.com
Web Site: www.calzone.com

E-Mail for Key Personnel:
President: jcalzone@calzone.com

Employees: 8
Year Founded: 1983

Agency Specializes In: Advertising, Agriculture, Automotive, Brand Development & Integration, Business-To-Business, Corporate Communications, Corporate Identity, Crisis Communications, Digital/Interactive, Electronic Media, Email, Entertainment, Event Planning & Marketing, Government/Political, Graphic Design, Identity Marketing, Internet/Web Design, Leisure, Logo & Package Design, Luxury Products, Media Buying Services, Media Relations, New Product Development, Newspaper, Over-50 Market, Production (Ad, Film, Broadcast), Production (Print), Promotions, Public Relations, Restaurant, Seniors' Market, Strategic Planning/Research, Travel & Tourism

Julie Calzone *(CEO)*
Linda Gerard *(VP-Fin)*

Accounts:
Evangeline Downs Racetrack & Casino Horse Racing
Spa Mizan

CAMBRIDGE BIOMARKETING

245 First St. !2th Fl, Cambridge, MA 02142
Tel.: (617) 225-0001
Web Site: www.cambridgebmg.com

Employees: 70
Year Founded: 2001

Agency Specializes In: Advertising, Brand Development & Integration, Communications, Consulting, Corporate Communications, Corporate Identity, Digital/Interactive, Direct Response Marketing, Direct-to-Consumer, E-Commerce, Health Care Services, International, Internet/Web Design, Media Buying Services, Medical Products, Paid Searches, Pharmaceutical, Print, Production, Strategic Planning/Research, T.V.

Approx. Annual Billings: $10,000,000

Breakdown of Gross Billings by Media: Adv. Specialities: $4,000,000; Digital/Interactive: $4,000,000; Strategic Planning/Research: $2,000,000

Maureen Franco *(CEO & Partner)*
Mike Hodgson *(Partner & Chief Creative Officer)*
Samuel Falsetti *(Partner & Dir-Medical Strategy)*
Heather McCann *(Head-HR)*
Laura Castaneda *(Mgmt Supvr)*
Alisa Shakarian *(Dir-Creative & Art)*
Marissa Talbot *(Dir-Art)*
Michael Costello *(Assoc Dir-Creative & Copy)*
Rich Thorne *(Assoc Dir-Creative & Art)*
Serena Faria *(Acct Supvr)*
Alexandra Warner *(Acct Exec)*

Accounts:
Intercept Pharmaceuticals Obeticholic Acid

CAMDEN

(Formerly Defi Communication Marketing Inc.)
5455 de Gaspe Ste 440, Montreal, QC H2T 3B3 Canada
Tel.: (514) 288-3334
Fax: (514) 288-1993
E-Mail: info@camdenmtl.com
Web Site: www.camdenmtl.com/

Employees: 10

Marie-Michele Jacques *(Sr Partner & VP-Consulting Svcs & Media)*
Frederic Roy *(Art Dir)*
Mathieu Bedard Rioux *(Dir-Production)*
Normand Boulanger *(Strategist-Web & Social Media)*
Camille Poulin *(Coord-Mktg)*

Accounts:
Caffitaly - Les Distributions Bellucci; 2011
Complexe Funeraires Yves Legare; 2011
Confort Expert; 2005
GloboCam; 2004
Intact Insurance; 2011
Lepelco; 2009
Mercedes-Benz Laval; 2011
Ordre des Infirmieres et Infirmiers du Qc; 2010
Univesta; 2009

CAMELLIA DIGITAL AGENCY
40 Stine St, Bristol, TN 37620
Tel.: (423) 963-9667
E-Mail: meow@camelliadigital.com
Web Site: www.camelliadigital.com

Year Founded: 2012

Agency Specializes In: Advertising, Brand Development & Integration, Digital/Interactive, Internet/Web Design, Social Media

Camellia Collins *(Pres)*

Accounts:
Sunset Eye Care

CAMELOT MEDIA
6006 Barr Rd, Ferndale, WA 98248
Tel.: (360) 384-4845
Toll Free: (800) 537-3839
E-Mail: camelotmedia@frontier.com
Web Site: www.camelotmedia.com

Agency Specializes In: Multimedia, Production

Jan Kurtis Skugstad *(Founder)*
Barry Jacobs *(Pres)*
Susan Jacobson *(Partner)*
Chris Schembri *(COO)*
Alex Richter *(Exec VP-Interactive)*
Bruce Butcher *(VP)*
Chris Zarski *(VP-Interactive & Social Media Practice)*
Sam Bloom *(Gen Mgr-Interactive)*
Suzanne Espinosa *(Sr Dir-Accts & Brand Strategy)*
Jessica Sunderland *(Strategist-Digital)*

Accounts:
Southwest Airlines Media

CAMP + KING
87 Graham St, San Francisco, CA 94129
Tel.: (415) 345-6680
E-Mail: pr@camp-king.com
Web Site: www.camp-king.com

National Agency Associations: 4A's

Agency Specializes In: Advertising, Social Media, Sponsorship

Roger Camp *(Co-Founder & Chief Creative Officer)*
Ali Sooudi *(Sr Dir-Art)*
Emily Dillow *(Dir-Creative)*
Chris Nash *(Dir-Art)*
David Verhoef *(Dir-Content Production)*
Nicole Nowak *(Brand Mgr)*
Kelsey Towbis *(Brand Mgr)*
Kiran Samuel *(Strategist-Creative)*
Erik Gonzalez *(Copywriter)*
Dani Saputo *(Designer)*
Malini Kartha *(Coord-Creative Resources)*

Accounts:
Capital One
City of Hope Campaign: "Citizens of Hope"
Del Taco Brand Strategy, Campaign: "UnFreshing Believable", Digital, Radio, TV
DentalPlans.com Digital, Identity, Logo, Social, Website Redesign
Emily McDowell
Gap
Google
Hershey Campaign: "#WonderfullyComplicated", Scharffen Berger
Old Navy
New-RE/MAX, LLC Advertising, Creative Execution, Digital, Integrated Marketing, Out-of-Home, Print, Radio, Social, TV
Redbox
Sling TV
Softcard
New-YouTube
Zoosk Agency Of Record, Campaign: "From the Heart", Campaign: "HeartFriend"

CAMPBELL EWALD
(Formerly Lowe Campbell Ewald)
2000 Brush St Ste 601, Detroit, MI 48226
Tel.: (586) 574-3400
Fax: (586) 393-4657
E-Mail: campbell.ewald@c-e.com
Web Site: www.c-e.com

Employees: 600
Year Founded: 1911

National Agency Associations: 4A's-AAF-AD CLUB-ADCRAFT-AEF-DMA-LAA-THINKLA

Agency Specializes In: Above-the-Line, Advertising, Automotive, Below-the-Line, Brand Development & Integration, Broadcast, Business Publications, Business-To-Business, Cable T.V., Catalogs, Co-op Advertising, Collateral, College, Communications, Consumer Marketing, Consumer Publications, Content, Custom Publishing, Customer Relationship Management, Digital/Interactive, Direct Response Marketing, Direct-to-Consumer, Education, Electronic Media, Email, Environmental, Event Planning & Marketing, Exhibit/Trade Shows, Experience Design, Fashion/Apparel, Financial, Government/Political, Guerilla Marketing, Health Care Services, High Technology, Hospitality, In-Store Advertising, Integrated Marketing, Internet/Web Design, Leisure, Local Marketing, Logo & Package Design, Magazines, Market Research, Media Buying Services, Media Planning, Medical Products, Merchandising, Mobile Marketing, Multicultural, New Product Development, New Technologies, Newspaper, Newspapers & Magazines, Out-of-Home Media, Outdoor, Planning & Consultation, Point of Purchase, Point of Sale, Print, Production, Production (Print), Promotions, Publishing, Radio, Real Estate, Recruitment, Regional, Restaurant, Retail, Sales Promotion, Search Engine Optimization, Social Marketing/Nonprofit, Social Media, Sponsorship, Sports Market, Strategic Planning/Research, Sweepstakes, T.V., Teen Market, Trade & Consumer Magazines, Transportation, Travel & Tourism, Tween Market, Viral/Buzz/Word of Mouth, Women's Market, Yellow Pages Advertising

Campbell Ewald is a full service, fully integrated marketing communications agency. With a focus on helping brands make purposeful connections and driving business results, the agency provides both traditional and specialized capabilities including advertising; insights and strategic planning; integrated content strategy and development; digital; social, DM/CRM, custom publishing (print, tablet interactive apps); retail and experiential marketing; and media planning and buying.

Kevin R. Wertz *(Pres)*
Jim Palmer *(CEO)*
Keith Clark *(Mng Dir)*
Jari Auger *(CFO)*
Mark Simon *(Chief Creative Officer)*
Sal Taibi *(Pres-NY)*
Jonathan Lange *(Exec VP & Grp Acct Dir)*
David Bierman *(Grp Dir-Creative)*
Tom Talbert *(Grp Dir-Media Svcs)*
Lewis Baker *(Sr Dir-Art)*
Kelly Barnes *(Dir-Corp Comm)*
Eric Olis *(Dir-Creative)*
Brian Phelps *(Dir-Bus Dev)*
Kelly Warkentien *(Dir-Art)*
Jennifer Thomas *(Assoc Dir-Creative)*
Kyle Smalley *(Mgr-Content Studio-Print)*
Cristina Cecchetti *(Sr Acct Supvr)*
Jeff Bratton *(Acct Supvr)*
Natalie Dakroub *(Acct Supvr)*
Nicole Reincke *(Acct Supvr)*
Davina Hamilton *(Acct Exec)*
Marcus Martin *(Jr Dir-Art & Copywriter)*
Walter Harris *(Grp Mgmt Supvr)*
Katie Pizzimenti *(Sr Media Planner)*
Ryan Shannahan *(Sr Media Planner)*

Accounts:
Ad Council PSA Campaign: "Fatherhood Involvement"
Allina Health Brand Identity, Messaging, Positioning, Strategy; 2011
Atkins Nutritionals, Inc. Atkins 40, Campaign: "Atkins: Eat to Succeed", Campaign: "Banquet", Campaign: "Bird", Campaign: "Bunny", Campaign: "Eat Well, Lose Weight--With Atkins Now You Can", Campaign: "Farmer's Market", Creative, Print, TV; 2013
New-Cadillac CRM; 2013
Carolinas Health Care System; 2012
Carrier Corporation; Farmington, CT Co-Op Advertising; 2003
New-Country Inns & Suites By Carlson (Agency of Record)
Covered California (Agency of Record); 2015
De'Longhi North America (Agency of Record); 2014
Detroit Lions (NFL Football Team) Campaign: "One Detroit. One Pride.", Creative; 2013
District Detroit; 2014
Dow Building & Materials (Agency of Record); 2012
Dow Solar (Agency of Record); 2010
Drug Enforcement Agency; 2012
Eastern Market Corporation; 2014
Edward Jones Integrated Communications, Recruitment Advertising; 2013
Energy Upgrade California (Agency of Record); 2013
Federal Student Aid; 2010
HAVEN; Pontiac, MI Advertising (Pro Bono), Campaign: "Live Without Fear", Campaign: "Mr Nice Guy", Media, Print; 2002
Henry Ford Health System (Agency of Record) Creative, Digital Advertising, Outdoor, Print, Radio, Social Media, TV
Kaiser Permanente; Oakland, CA (Agency of Record) Campaign: "Thrive"; 2003
MilkPEP (Agency of Record) Broadcast, Campaign: "Milk Life", Campaign: "Milk Mustache", Campaign: "Mission Apolo: Built With Chocolate Milk", Campaign: "Quaker Up", Campaign: "The Art of Rebounding", Online, Print, TV; 1994
MotorCity Casino Hotel (Agency of Record); 2010
National Responsible Fatherhood Clearinghouse Advertising (Pro Bono), Campaign: "Big Night", Campaign: "Reunion"; 2002
OnStar (Agency of Record) Campaign: "Connected by OnStar", Campaign: "Crash", Campaign: "Joyride", Campaign: "Sandman", Print, Radio, Social Media; 1997
The Sun Products Corp. Snuggle (Agency of Record); 1980
New-Travelocity, Inc. (Agency of Record) Creative, Roaming Gnome
Unilever Becel (Agency of Record), Clear (Agency of Record), Country Crock (Agency of Record), Degree (Agency of Record), Fruttare, I Can't Believe It's Not Butter, Knorr, Magnum,

TRESemme; 2012
US Department of Education (Agency of Record); 2010
New-U.S. Fund for Unicef; 2014
US Navy (Agency of Record); 2000
USAA (Agency of Record); 2009

CAMPBELL LACOSTE, INC.
4981 Scherbel Rd, Black Earth, WI 53515
Tel.: (608) 767-3210
Fax: (608) 767-3211
E-Mail: howdy@campbell-lacoste.com
Web Site: www.campbell-lacoste.com

Employees: 10
Year Founded: 1994

Agency Specializes In: Advertising, Affluent Market, Brand Development & Integration, Business-To-Business, Catalogs, Collateral, Commercial Photography, Communications, Consulting, Consumer Goods, Consumer Marketing, Corporate Communications, Corporate Identity, Direct Response Marketing, Direct-to-Consumer, Graphic Design, In-Store Advertising, Integrated Marketing, Internet/Web Design, Leisure, Logo & Package Design, Marine, Market Research, Media Buying Services, Media Planning, Media Relations, Men's Market, New Product Development, Package Design, Point of Sale, Production (Print), Promotions, Public Relations, Publicity/Promotions, Radio, Sales Promotion, T.V.

Brittney Lacoste *(Pres & Dir-Creative)*
Harry Campbell *(Dir-Mktg)*

Accounts:
Dawg-Tired.com; Black Earth, WI Premium Dog Beds
Monona State Bank
Mueller Industries; Memphis, TN; Port Huron, MI Industrial Products, STREAMtech Flameless Plumbing Fitting
River Valley Bank
Vortex Optics

CAMPBELL MARKETING & COMMUNICATIONS
3200 Greenfield Ste 280, Dearborn, MI 48120
Tel.: (313) 336-9000
Fax: (313) 336-9225
Web Site: www.campbellmarketing.com

Employees: 80

Agency Specializes In: Automotive, Corporate Communications, Digital/Interactive, Event Planning & Marketing, Financial, Identity Marketing, Market Research, Media Relations, Social Marketing/Nonprofit, Sponsorship

John Scodellaro *(Mng Partner)*
David Losek *(CFO)*
Joe Vandervest *(CIO)*
Les Miller *(Head-Creative)*
Jeannee Kirkaldy *(Acct Dir)*
Marc Pasco *(Acct Dir)*
Mary Mitchell *(Dir-Mktg)*
Tim Adkins *(Mgr-HR)*
Matt Fancett *(Acct Supvr)*
Lesley Nadeau *(Acct Supvr)*
Lachelle Seymour *(Sr Acct Exec)*
Nikki Dockery *(Acct Exec)*
Dawn Liebert *(Acct Exec)*

Accounts:
Audi of America
Avalon Films
General Motors
The Henry Ford
Hyundai Motor America
JWT-Team Detroit
Mazda
Meridian Automotive Systems, Inc.
NASCAR
Pebble Beach Concours d'Elegance
SCE Federal Credit Union Public & Media Relations
Wright & Filippis, Inc
Yokohama Tire Corporation

Branch

Campbell Marketing & Communications
(Formerly PCGCampbell)
21605 Hawthorne Ste 100, Torrance, CA 90503
Tel.: (313) 336-9000
Web Site: www.campbellmarketing.com

David Scheinberg *(Mng Partner)*
John Scodellaro *(Mng Partner)*
Greg Shea *(COO)*
Kevin Kennedy *(Exec VP-PR)*
Barbara McAllister *(Acct Dir)*
Jacob A. Brown *(Dir-Interactive Media)*
Philip Mason *(Dir-Art)*
Rich Willenberg *(Dir-New Bus Dev)*
Jordan Diehl Mann *(Sr Acct Exec-PR-Action Motorsports)*
Hillary Mulka *(Acct Exec)*
Lincoln Hill *(Creative Associate)*

CAMPFIRE
313 Church St, New York, NY 10013
Tel.: (212) 612-9600
Fax: (212) 625-9255
E-Mail: info@campfirenyc.com
Web Site: www.campfirenyc.com

Employees: 20

Agency Specializes In: Advertising, Digital/Interactive, Internet/Web Design, Sponsorship

Revenue: $15,000,000

Jeremiah Rosen *(Pres)*
Mike Monello *(Partner & Chief Creative Officer)*
Nick Braccia *(Creative Dir)*

Accounts:
AUDI
Byzantium Campaign: "Byzantium Tests"
Discovery The Colony
El Rey Network (Agency of Record) Creative
HBO Campaign: "Pledge Your Allegiance", Game Of Thrones, Trueblood
L'Oreal Campaign: "Turn It Up"
National Geographic Channel Campaign: "The Wow Reply"
Nissan Motor Campaign: "Infiniti Deja View", Infiniti, Infiniti Q50
Pontiac
Snapple
USA Network
Verizon FiOS

CAMPFIRE
(Acquired by SapientNitro USA, Inc.)

CAMPOS CREATIVE WORKS
1715 14th St, Santa Monica, CA 90404
Tel.: (310) 453-1511
Fax: (310) 453-8880
E-Mail: info@ccwla.com
Web Site: www.ccwla.com

Employees: 10
Year Founded: 1991

Agency Specializes In: Advertising, Collateral, Consulting, Content, Graphic Design, Internet/Web Design, Multimedia, Production

Julio Campos *(Founder & Exec Dir-Creative)*
Sandra Sande *(Partner & CFO)*
Jennifer Gerich *(Partner-Mktg & New Bus Dev)*

Accounts:
Acura
Dell
Hyundai
Lexus
Toyota

CANALE COMMUNICATIONS
4010 Goldfinch St, San Diego, CA 92103
Tel.: (619) 849-6000
Web Site: www.canalecomm.com

Carin Canale-Theakston *(Pres)*
Pam Lord *(Sr VP)*
Jason Ian Spark *(Sr VP)*
Mark Corbae *(VP)*
Ian Stone *(Acct Dir)*
Cammy Duong *(Acct Mgr)*
Monica May *(Acct Mgr)*
Sharon Ceniceros Meade *(Mgr-Admin)*

CANAUDI INC.
75 Alie Street, Montreal, QC H9A1H2 Canada
Tel.: (514) 312-2020
Web Site: www.canaudi.com

Agency Specializes In: E-Commerce, Internet/Web Design, Local Marketing, Mobile Marketing

Al Khodary *(CMO)*

Accounts:
HSBC Bank Canada

CANNONBALL
8251 Maryland Ave Ste 200, Saint Louis, MO 63105
Tel.: (314) 445-6400
Fax: (314) 726-3359
E-Mail: cannonball@cannonballagency.com
Web Site: www.cannonballagency.com

Employees: 42

Agency Specializes In: Advertising, Sponsorship

Steve Hunt *(Chief Creative Officer)*
Stacy Goldman *(Principal & Sr Strategist)*
Doug Murdoch *(VP)*
Cori Wilson *(Acct Dir)*
Mary Jarnagin *(Bus Mgr-Brdcst Production)*
Jonathon Kirby *(Acct Exec)*

Accounts:
Anheuser-Busch Bud Lite, Campaign: "Cool Twist" Super Bowl 2014; 2007
Bud Light
Enterprise Rent-A-Car Campaign: "Freedom"

CANNONBALL ADVERTISING FIRM LLC
9904 Via Bernini, Lake Worth, FL 33467
Tel.: (561) 891-1096
E-Mail: info@cballadvertising.com
Web Site: www.cballadvertising.com

Agency Specializes In: Advertising, Content, Internet/Web Design, Search Engine Optimization, Social Media

Matthew A. Meyers *(Pres)*

Accounts:
Gulfstream Insurance

CANONBALL CREATIVE
1701 N Market St Ste 430, Dallas, TX 75204
Tel.: (214) 761-1900
Web Site: www.canonball.com

Agency Specializes In: Advertising, Content, Internet/Web Design, Search Engine Optimization, Social Media

Jon Simpson *(Pres & CEO)*
Kace Phillips *(Acct Dir)*
Mike Krankota *(Dir-Creative & Designer-UX)*
Kerie Kerstetter *(Dir-Content Strategy)*
Chris Sigler *(Dir-Tech)*
Ashley Tyndall *(Dir-Mktg & Bus Dev)*
Jennifer Rucker *(Intern Program Dir & Sr Acct Exec)*
Catherine Chesnut *(Designer)*

Accounts:
Bolo
Dive Coastal Cuisine
MassCatalyst (Agency of Record)
Mobvertise Creative Agency of Record

CANOPY BRAND GROUP
337 Broome St 3rd Fl, New York, NY 10002
Tel.: (914) 584-6628
Toll Free: (866) 879-2955
E-Mail: info@canopybrandgroup.com
Web Site: www.canopybrandgroup.com

Agency Specializes In: Brand Development & Integration, Digital/Interactive, Internet/Web Design, Package Design, Point of Sale, Strategic Planning/Research

Frank Sampogna *(Chm)*
Danielle Avissar *(Dir-Mktg Svcs)*
John Krubski *(Dir-Strategy)*
Ahlilah Longmire *(Dir-PR)*
Dan O'Brien *(Dir-IT)*
Akida Vidal *(Strategist-Digital)*
Keely Coxen *(Copywriter)*

Accounts:
Nokia Mobile Phone Mfr
O'Connor Davies Corporate Ads, Marketing, Website
Urnex Brands Inc Cleaning Products Mfr

CANSPAN BMG
(Formerly Canspan Advertising Inc.)
4355 Ste Catherine St W, Westmount, QC H3Z 1P8 Canada
Tel.: (514) 487-6900
Fax: (514) 487-4778
E-Mail: dberman@canspan.com
Web Site: www.canspan.com

Employees: 12

Agency Specializes In: Advertising

John Mayo *(Dir-Art)*

Accounts:
ALDO
ASKO
Barbie
BF Goodrich
Bloom
BoFinger
Canon
Cardinal
Cooper Tires
Deringer
Esso
Field Turf
Hankook
Mobil 1
Prepay
Sony
Speed Stick
Sterling Card
Wenger

CANYONPR
103 Bonaventura Dr, San Jose, CA 95134
Tel.: (408) 857-9527
Web Site: www.canyonpr.com

Agency Specializes In: Advertising, Digital/Interactive, Media Relations, Public Relations, Social Media

Megan Saulsbury *(Principal)*

Accounts:
New-Accell
New-Vivitek Corporation

CAPITA TECHNOLOGIES, INC.
4000 Westerly Pl, Newport Beach, CA 92660
Tel.: (949) 260-3000
Fax: (949) 851-9875
E-Mail: jkorionoff@capita.com
Web Site: www.capitacase.com

Employees: 50
Year Founded: 1989

Agency Specializes In: African-American Market, Asian Market, Bilingual Market, Brand Development & Integration, Business-To-Business, Collateral, Communications, Computers & Software, Consumer Goods, Consumer Marketing, Corporate Communications, Crisis Communications, Customer Relationship Management, Digital/Interactive, Direct Response Marketing, Direct-to-Consumer, E-Commerce, Electronic Media, Email, Event Planning & Marketing, Experience Design, Game Integration, Graphic Design, High Technology, Hispanic Market, Household Goods, Information Technology, Integrated Marketing, Internet/Web Design, Mobile Marketing, Multimedia, New Technologies, Out-of-Home Media, Paid Searches, Podcasting, Promotions, Public Relations, Sales Promotion, Search Engine Optimization, Social Media, Sports Market, Sweepstakes, Technical Advertising, Teen Market, Viral/Buzz/Word of Mouth, Women's Market

Approx. Annual Billings: $11,250,000

Breakdown of Gross Billings by Media: E-Commerce: $1,000,000; Graphic Design: $2,000,000; Internet Adv.: $2,000,000; Promos.: $3,000,000; Sls. Promo.: $750,000; Worldwide Web Sites: $2,500,000

Charles Granville *(CEO)*
Yidan Yang *(CTO)*
Imelda Ford *(Exec VP-Tech & Ops)*
James Newman *(VP-Sls & Mktg)*

Accounts:
Allegra
Allstate
Coke
Disney
Fox Broadcasting
General Mills
Hilton Worldwide
Ingram Micro
Kellogg's
Mars North America
Motorola Solutions, Inc.
Nestle's USA
Nickelodeon
Ritz
Taco Bell
Unilever
United States Navy
Verizon
Warner Brothers
Xerox

CAPITOL MARKETING GROUP, INC.
4055 Chain Bridge Rd, Fairfax, VA 22030-4103
Tel.: (703) 591-0100
Fax: (703) 591-1508
E-Mail: reyan@accesscmg.com
Web Site: www.accesscmg.com

Employees: 4
Year Founded: 1991

Agency Specializes In: Communications, High Technology, Travel & Tourism

Reyan Carpenter *(Founder & Chief Creative Officer)*
Laurie Stevens *(Dir-Production)*

Accounts:
Acuity Technology Services, LLC
American Express
Columbia National
Edge Technologies; Fairfax, VA; 1999
Gestalt Systems, Inc
Hayes Microcomputer Products
ISSI
Peak Technologies; Columbia, MD Bar Code Hardware, Software & Services; 1997
Raxco Software; Gaithersburg, MD Defragmentation Software; 2000
Venntronix

CAPITOL MEDIA SOLUTIONS
3340 Peachtree Rd NE Ste 1050, Atlanta, GA 30326
Tel.: (404) 347-3316
Toll Free: (800) 517-0610
E-Mail: mediabuying@capitolmediasolutions.com
Web Site: www.capitolmediasolutions.com

Employees: 12
Year Founded: 2006

National Agency Associations: 4A's

Agency Specializes In: Broadcast, Business-To-Business, Cable T.V., Consumer Marketing, Digital/Interactive, Electronic Media, Email, In-Store Advertising, Local Marketing, Magazines, Mobile Marketing, Newspaper, Newspapers & Magazines, Out-of-Home Media, Outdoor, Paid Searches, Point of Purchase, Point of Sale, Print, Radio, Search Engine Optimization, Social Media, Syndication, T.V., Trade & Consumer Magazines, Web (Banner Ads, Pop-ups, etc.)

JT Hroncich *(Mng Dir)*
Audrey Eisen *(Dir-Media)*
Scott Fairlee *(Acct Mgr-Adv)*
Leslie Stockton *(Acct Mgr-Adv)*
Callie Holden *(Mgr-Production)*

Accounts:
CORT Furniture All Consumer & Business Products; 2014
GAF Roofing Shingles; 2012
MedPost Urgent Care Centers; 2014
North Highland Consulting Consulting Services; 2012
Pelican Products Luggage, Backpacks, Tablet Cases, Mobile Phone Cases; 2012

CAPONIGRO MARKETING GROUP, LLC
24725 W Twelve Mile Rd Ste 120, Southfield, MI 48034

Tel.: (248) 353-3270
E-Mail: jcap@caponigro.com
Web Site: www.caponigro.com/

Employees: 10
Year Founded: 2004

Agency Specializes In: Advertising, Broadcast, Business-To-Business, Cable T.V., Direct Response Marketing, Electronic Media, Out-of-Home Media, Outdoor, Print, T.V.

Approx. Annual Billings: $8,000,000

Jeff Caponigro *(Pres & CEO)*
Sharon R. McMurray *(Sr VP)*
Chuck Ragains *(Sr VP)*
Maribeth Farkas *(Acct Supvr)*

CAPPELLI MILES

101 SW Main St Ste 1905, Portland, OR 97204-3227
Tel.: (503) 241-1515
Fax: (541) 484-7327
E-Mail: info@cappellimiles.com
Web Site: www.cappellimiles.com

E-Mail for Key Personnel:
Creative Dir.: bcappelli@cm-spring.com
Media Dir.: dprice@cm-spring.com

Employees: 13
Year Founded: 1982

National Agency Associations: TAAN

Agency Specializes In: Communications, Public Relations

Approx. Annual Billings: $18,000,000

Bruce A. Cappelli *(Founder & Partner)*
Rod Miles *(Pres)*
Jamie Chabot *(Dir-Creative)*
Bruce Eckols *(Dir-Creative & Art)*
Darcey Price *(Dir-Media)*
Mark Hass *(Acct Mgr)*
Phil Anne Meile *(Office Mgr)*
Mickey Miles *(Acct Exec)*
Chris Thompson *(Media Buyer)*
Dianna Marshall *(Coord-Production)*

Branch

Cappelli Miles

(Formerly Cappelli Miles (spring))
450 Country Club Rd, Eugene, OR 97401
Tel.: (541) 484-1515
Fax: (541) 484-7327
E-Mail: info@cappellimiles.com
Web Site: www.cappellimiles.com/

Employees: 25
Year Founded: 1944

Agency Specializes In: Brand Development & Integration, Public Relations

Bruce Cappelli *(Founder & Partner)*
Rod Miles *(Partner)*
Bruce Eckols *(Sr Dir-Art)*
Jamie Chabot *(Dir-Design)*
Mickey Miles *(Dir-Ops)*
Darcey Price *(Dir-Media)*
Amber Shively *(Acct Mgr & Sr Planner-Media)*
Dianna Marshall *(Mgr-Production)*
Alma Fumiko Hesus *(Specialist-Comm)*
Chris Thompson *(Buyer-Brdcst)*

CAPSULE BRAND DEVELOPMENT

100 2nd Ave N, Minneapolis, MN 55401
Tel.: (612) 341-4525
Fax: (612) 341-4577
E-Mail: info@capsule.us
Web Site: www.capsule.us

Employees: 12
Year Founded: 1999

Agency Specializes In: Advertising, Alternative Advertising, Brand Development & Integration, Branded Entertainment, Business-To-Business, Collateral, College, Communications, Consumer Marketing, Content, Corporate Identity, Environmental, Exhibit/Trade Shows, Experience Design, Household Goods, Identity Marketing, Integrated Marketing, Local Marketing, Logo & Package Design, Magazines, Market Research, Planning & Consultation, Point of Purchase, Point of Sale, Promotions, Retail, Social Media, Strategic Planning/Research

Brian Adducci *(Owner & Principal-Creative)*
Aaron Keller *(CEO & Mng Principal)*
Kitty Hart *(Dir-Client Experience)*
Dave Buchanan *(Acct Mgr)*
Sarah Hinrichs *(Acct Mgr)*

Accounts:
Del Laboratories; New York, NY LaCrosse, Sally Hansen; 2002
Fox River Socks; Osage, IA Shucking Awesome Corn Socks; 2005
Grey Plant Mooty; Minneapolis, MN; 2006

CAPTAINS OF INDUSTRY

21 Union St, Boston, MA 02108
Tel.: (617) 725-1959
Fax: (617) 725-0089
E-Mail: info@captainsofindustry.com
Web Site: www.captainsofindustry.com

Employees: 12
Year Founded: 1993

National Agency Associations: AMA

Agency Specializes In: Direct Response Marketing, Identity Marketing, Internet/Web Design, Outdoor, Print, Production (Ad, Film, Broadcast), Viral/Buzz/Word of Mouth

Clift Jones *(Pres & CEO)*
Fred Surr *(Principal & Exec Producer)*
Ted Page *(Principal & Dir-Creative)*
Kacy Karlen *(Assoc Dir-Creative)*
Lauren Prentiss *(Strategist-Creative)*
Ted Dillon *(Mng Producer)*

Accounts:
agion
Akami
Alteris Renewables (Agency of Record)
Arbor Networks
Bose
Businesses for Innovative Climate & Energy Policy
DeepWater Wind
Envious
FirstWind
GN Netcom
Mass Medical Society
Millipore Millipore Blot Race Viral
Pace
Starrett
Whatman Inc.

CARBON8

2290 W 29th Ave, Denver, CO 80211
Tel.: (303) 222-8045
Web Site: www.carbon8.com

Year Founded: 2009

Agency Specializes In: Advertising, Brand Development & Integration, Digital/Interactive, Internet/Web Design, Print

Mark Mitton *(Pres)*
Katherine Roberts *(Acct Mgr & Producer-Video)*
Erin Behrenhausen *(Dir-Art)*
Duy Do *(Dir-Online Dev)*
Jeff Robertson *(Dir-Interactive)*
Kimberly Fox *(Acct Mgr)*
Lisa Hillmer-Poole *(Supvr-Accts)*

Accounts:
Ko Hana

CARDENAS MARKETING NETWORK INC.

1459 W Hubbard St, Chicago, IL 60642
Tel.: (312) 492-6424
Fax: (312) 492-6404
Web Site: www.cmnevents.com

Employees: 25
Year Founded: 2003

Agency Specializes In: Sponsorship

Henry Cardenas *(Pres & CEO)*
Sam Rubio *(Corp Counsel)*
Elena Sotomayor *(Exec VP-Mktg & Sls Dept)*
Gus Trujillo *(Controller)*
Hernand Gonzalez *(Gen Mgr-Miami)*
Joshua Patron *(Exec Dir-Creative)*
Vicky Quintana *(Acct Dir)*
Jose Aguirre *(Dir-Creative)*
Antonio Castaneda *(Dir-Music)*
Elisa Vizcarra Cogo *(Dir-Sls & Acct)*
Carolina Daza *(Dir-Activation & Experiential)*
Nadia Hernandez *(Dir-PR)*

Accounts:
American Airlines
Budweiser
Goya
McDonald's
Olay
Pantene
Stella Artois

CARDWELL BEACH

118 Prospect Park SW #5, Brooklyn, NY 11218
Tel.: (646) 801-3175
Web Site: www.cardwellbeach.com

Year Founded: 2007

Agency Specializes In: Alternative Advertising, Branded Entertainment, Business Publications, Collateral, Digital/Interactive, Direct Response Marketing, Electronic Media, Email, Exhibit/Trade Shows, Experience Design, Guerilla Marketing, In-Store Advertising, Magazines, Multimedia, Newspaper, Newspapers & Magazines, Out-of-Home Media, Outdoor, Paid Searches, Point of Sale, Production, Promotions, Radio, Search Engine Optimization, Social Media, T.V., Trade & Consumer Magazines, Viral/Buzz/Word of Mouth, Web (Banner Ads, Pop-ups, etc.)

Mike Beach *(Dir-Creative)*
Mark Caldwell *(Dir-Creative)*
Brian Erickson *(Dir-New Bus)*
Mike Lichter *(Dir-Creative)*
Monica Reccoppa *(Mgr-Fin)*

Accounts:
Artemis Partners Mountainside Treatment Center; 2014
Facility Solutions Group Utility Solutions; 2014
Go Watch It! GoWatchit.com; 2012
Samsung Sales App; 2013
WSG Empire Suite Business Software

CAREW CO

223 N 6th St Ste 50, Boise, ID 83702
Tel.: (208) 343-1664
Fax: (208) 629-3211
Web Site: www.carewco.net

Agency Specializes In: Advertising, Brand Development & Integration, Graphic Design, Internet/Web Design

Paul Carew *(Pres)*

Accounts:
Cinder

CARING MARKETING SOLUTIONS

781 Northwest Blvd, Columbus, OH 43212
Tel.: (614) 846-5528
Web Site: www.caringmarketing.com

Employees: 5
Year Founded: 1992

Approx. Annual Billings: $4,500,000

Paul Carringer *(Pres)*
Stephanie Cotts *(Sr Dir-Projects & Accts)*
Rob Candor *(Creative Dir)*

Accounts:
New-CB Beverage Cock'n Bull Ginger Beer, Frostop Root Beer; 2012

CARL BLOOM ASSOCIATES, INC.

81 Main St Ste 126, White Plains, NY 10601-1711
Tel.: (914) 761-2800
Fax: (914) 761-2744
E-Mail: info@carlbloom.com
Web Site: www.carlbloom.com

E-Mail for Key Personnel:
President: CBloom@carlbloom.com
Creative Dir.: RBloom@carlbloom.com
Production Mgr.: COliveras@carlbloom.com

Employees: 15
Year Founded: 1976

National Agency Associations: DMA

Agency Specializes In: Consulting, Direct Response Marketing, Internet/Web Design, Pets , Strategic Planning/Research

Approx. Annual Billings: $10,000,000

Breakdown of Gross Billings by Media: D.M.: $9,500,000; Fees: $300,000; Plng. & Consultation: $100,000; Worldwide Web Sites: $100,000

Brooke Grossman Coneys *(VP & Gen Mgr)*
Carrie Bloom *(VP-Client Svcs)*
Dave Grosso *(Dir-Creative)*
Britt Rosenbaum *(Dir-Art)*
Yalexa Corchado *(Mgr-Traffic & Asst Mgr-Production)*
Theresa Jahn *(Sr Graphic Designer)*

Accounts:
AETN; Arkansas
KETC; Saint Louis, MO (Membership Marketing)
KLRU TV; Austin
KPBS; San Diego, CA (Membership Marketing)
KQED, Inc.; San Francisco, CA (Membership Marketing)
Lenox Hill Hospital
National Public Library Direct Mail Consortium (Cooperative Fundraising); 1998
Public Citizen
Public Library Direct Response Consortium; 1999
Queens Borough Public Library; Queens, NY (Fundraising)

CARLING COMMUNICATIONS

1370 India St Ste 200, San Diego, CA 92101
Tel.: (619) 269-3000
E-Mail: info@carling-communications.com
Web Site: carlingcom.com/#index

Agency Specializes In: Advertising, Event Planning & Marketing, Internet/Web Design, Media Planning, Print, Strategic Planning/Research

Didi Discar *(Principal)*
Olivia Chang *(Exec VP & Gen Mgr)*
Randy Adams *(Exec VP)*
Jim Haag *(Exec Dir-Creative)*
Rob Heller *(Creative Dir)*
Linda Ellis-Flint *(Acct Exec)*

Accounts:
Acucela Inc.
Alcon, Inc.
Bausch & Lomb Incorporated
Bio-Tissue
DepoMed, Inc.
Merz Pharmaceuticals Inc.
Optimedica Corporation
TearScience
ThromboGenics Inc.

CARLSON MARKETING

(Name Changed to Aimia)

CARMA

1000 S Broadway Ste 107, Denver, CO 80209
Tel.: (720) 596-4608
E-Mail: hello@thinkcarma.com
Web Site: www.thinkcarma.com

Year Founded: 2013

Agency Specializes In: Advertising, Content, Digital/Interactive, Email, Graphic Design, Internet/Web Design, Search Engine Optimization, Social Media

Chad Carpenter *(Pres)*

Accounts:
Union Station Alliance

CARMICHAEL LYNCH

110 N 5th St, Minneapolis, MN 55403
Tel.: (612) 334-6000
Fax: (612) 334-6090
E-Mail: inquiry@clynch.com
Web Site: www.carmichaellynch.com

E-Mail for Key Personnel:
Public Relations: emontgomery@clynch.com

Employees: 220
Year Founded: 1962

National Agency Associations: 4A's-AAF-PRSA

Agency Specializes In: Advertising, Brand Development & Integration, Consumer Marketing, Digital/Interactive, Direct Response Marketing, Graphic Design, Internet/Web Design, Public Relations, Sponsorship

Approx. Annual Billings: $200,000,000

Marcus Fischer *(Pres, Mng Partner & Chief Strategy Officer)*
Mike Lescarbeau *(CEO)*
Freddie Richards *(Partner & Exec Producer-Content)*
Neil Goodspeed *(Dir-Consumer Engagement)*
Shawn Lacy *(Mng Dir)*
Mark Feriancek *(CFO)*
Joe Grundhoefer *(Head-Production)*
Dean Buckhorn *(Grp Dir-Creative)*
Pete Leacock *(Grp Acct Dir-Digital)*
Priscilla Arthur *(Acct Dir)*
Adam Craw *(Acct Dir)*
Stacy Janicki *(Sr Partner & Acct Mgmt Dir)*
Courtney Thomas *(Acct Dir)*
Paula Weisenbeck *(Acct Dir)*
Amber Benson *(Dir-Plng & Brand Activation)*
Betsy Burgeson *(Dir-Consumer Engagement Ops)*
John Green *(Dir-Fin)*
Vicki Oachs *(Dir-Bus Affairs & Integrated Production)*
Ryan Peck *(Dir-Creative)*
Teela Shandess *(Dir-Art)*
William Stentz *(Dir-Mktg Analytics)*
Dorion Taylor *(Dir-New Bus)*
Ellie Taylor *(Dir-Comm & Mktg)*
Marilyn Reiter *(Mgr-Brdcst)*
Charlie Wolfe *(Mgr-Print Production)*
Greta Hughes *(Acct Supvr)*
Brandon Miller *(Sr Strategist-Digital Engagement)*
Laura Fitzpatrick *(Strategist-Brand)*
Sonia Krinke *(Strategist-Knowledge)*
Taylor Lord *(Strategist-Engagement)*
Nellie Murray *(Strategist-Engagement)*
Ashley Niskala *(Strategist-Engagement)*
Cory Simpson *(Sr Planner-Digital)*
Andrew Wetzel *(Designer)*
Nick Nelson *(Sr Writer)*

Accounts:
American Standard, Inc Campaign: "Hide & Seek", Campaign: "Movie Marathons"; 1992
BJ's Restaurants Inc.; Huntington Beach, CA (Agency of Record) Craft Beers, Deep Dish Pizza
Brown-Forman Beverages Worldwide; Louisville, KY Bolla, Fetzer, Korbel; 1993
Cargill
Denver Museum of Nature & Science Campaign: "One Plus One", Campaign: "Talk to a Plant"
New-Fuji Heavy Industries
LSI Inc. Beef Jerky, Broadcast, Campaign: "All Dolled Up", Campaign: "Feed your wild side", Campaign: "Hose", Campaign: "Lecture Hall", Campaign: "Loop", Campaign: "Messin' with Sasquatch", Campaign: "Middle Seat", Campaign: "National Jerky Day", Campaign: "Operation Sky Meat", Campaign: "Wedding", Creative Agency of Record, Jack Link's, National Jerky Day; 2004
Masterbrand Cabinets
Merrick Pet Care
Middle Seat
National Geographic Campaign: "Cynthia"
NC Holdings, Inc. Creative, Media
Newell Rubbermaid Amerock - Decor (Domestic Agency of Record), Aprica - Baby & Parenting (Domestic Agency of Record), Calphalon - Culinary, Graco - Baby & Parenting (Domestic Agency of Record), Kirsch - Decor (Domestic Agency of Record), Levolor - Decor (Domestic Agency of Record), Rubbermaid - Home & Family (Domestic Agency of Record), Teutonia - Baby & Parenting (Domestic Agency of Record)
Onion Inc ClickHole.com
Sierra Trading Post Creative Advertising
Steak 'n Shake (Agency of Record) Campaign: "Blindfold", Campaign: "Hunger Wisely", Campaign: "Kung Fu Elbow"
Subaru of America (Agency of Record) 2015 Impreza, 2015 Outback, Advertising, Campaign: "Bison", Campaign: "Dog Tested. Dog Approved", Campaign: "Dream Weekend", Campaign: "First Car Story", Campaign: "Let's Do That", Campaign: "Love", Campaign: "MakeADogsDay", Campaign: "Making Memories", Campaign: "Meet the Barkleys", Campaign: "Memory Lane", Campaign: "Redressing Room", Campaign: "Stick Shift", Campaign: "The Beach", Campaign: "The Date", Campaign: "They Lived", Creative, Social Media, Subaru Guide to Everything, Subaru Legacy, TV; 2007

Tempur Sealy Campaign: "Bear", Campaign: "Love Birds", Campaign: "You Are How You Sleep", Creative
Therma-Tru Doors
Trane Heating & Cooling
Trane Inc.
U.S. Bank (Creative Agency of Record) Digital, Social Media

Divisions

Spong
(Formerly Carmichael Lynch Spong)
110 N 5th St, Minneapolis, MN 55403
Tel.: (612) 375-8500
Fax: (612) 375-8501
Web Site: spongpr.com

Employees: 60
Year Founded: 1990

National Agency Associations: 4A's

Agency Specializes In: Public Relations

Julie Batliner *(Pres)*
Cavan Reichmann *(Partner & Chm-Social Engagement)*
Eric Hausman *(Principal)*
Jill Schmidt *(Sr Principal & Dir-Strategy)*
Kimberly Albert *(Sr Specialist-Media Rels)*
Meredith Voltin *(Sr Specialist-Media Rels)*
Brent Renneke *(Specialist-Media Rels)*
Laura Zwieg *(Specialist-New Bus)*

Accounts:
American Humane Association
American Standard Heating and Air Conditioning
American Standard/Trane
Arla Foods Arla Dofino, Brand Awareness, Brand Strategy, Castello, Digital Marketing, Media Planning & Buying, Media Relations, Social Media
Brooklyn Park
Cargill
The City of Brooklyn Park Branding Strategy
Formica B2B Media Relations, North America Public Relations, Social Media
Harley-Davidson/Buell
Hasbro
Ingersoll Rand Residential Solutions Public Relations
Jack Links
Jennie-o Turkey Store Campaign: "One Switch at a Time"
La-Z-Boy (Public Relations Agency of Record)
Lamps Plus (Public Relations Agency of Record)
Life'sDHA Campaign: "Inspiring a Generation of Beautiful Minds"
Lowry Hill
Matador
Morinda
Newell Rubbermaid (Domestic Agency of Record) Amerock, Aprico, Graco, Kirsch, Levelor, Rubbermaid, Teutonia
PowerBar
Prestige Wine Group
The Schwan Food Company (Consumer Retail & Frozen Food Agency of Record)
Scrabble
Tempur Sealy Campaign: "Bear", PR
Thermos
TransFair USA Fair Trade Certified; 2007
WebMasterRadio.FM
Westinghouse Solar Public Relations

Spong
(Formerly Carmichael Lynch Spong)
150 E 42nd St 12th Fl, New York, NY 10017
Tel.: (212) 414-7124
Fax: (212) 414-7102
E-Mail: jessica.tolliver@spongpr.com
Web Site: spongpr.com

Employees: 5

Agency Specializes In: Public Relations

Jill Schmidt *(Sr Partner, Chm-Corp Practice & Dir-Strategy)*
Jack Stanton *(Grp Dir-Plng)*
Serena Tesler *(Dir-Media Rels)*
Meredith Kish *(Sr Mgr-Media Rels)*
Rachel Mcallister *(Sr Mgr-Media Rels)*

Accounts:
ClearWay Minnesota
Diamond Cabinetry
MasterBrand Cabinets, Inc.
National Baseball Hall of Fame & Museum; Cooperstown, NY Creative, Strategic

CARNEY & CO.
1653 N Winstead Ave, Rocky Mount, NC 27804-7398
Mailing Address:
PO Box 7398, Rocky Mount, NC 27804-0398
Tel.: (252) 451-0060
Fax: (252) 451-0660
Toll Free: (800) 849-7547
E-Mail: skip@carneyco.com
Web Site: www.carneyco.com

E-Mail for Key Personnel:
President: skip@carneyco.com

Employees: 7
Year Founded: 1980

Agency Specializes In: Advertising, Brand Development & Integration, Business-To-Business, Consulting, Consumer Marketing, Planning & Consultation, Strategic Planning/Research, Trade & Consumer Magazines

Approx. Annual Billings: $2,790,000

Breakdown of Gross Billings by Media: Bus. Publs.: 15%; Collateral: 25%; Consumer Publs.: 10%; D.M.: 8%; Point of Purchase: 15%; Pub. Rels.: 17%; Strategic Planning/Research: 10%

Skip Carney *(Pres)*
Crystal Hill *(Acct Exec)*
Mike Frye *(Sr Graphic Designer)*

Accounts:
America's Best Nut Company; Rocky Mount, NC Peanuts; 2001
Chambliss & Rabil; Rocky Mount, NC Construction, Commercial Real Estate; 1983
Consultants to Industry, LLC; Rocky Mount, NC Consulting Services; 2002
Field Controls; Kinston, NC; 1988
Phoenix Specialty; Bamberg, SC Washers & Shims; 1993
Southern Bank; Mount Olive, NC Banking Services; 2003
Turner Equipment; Goldsboro, NC Tanks; 1988

CAROL H. WILLIAMS ADVERTISING
1625 Clay St, Oakland, CA 94612
Tel.: (510) 763-5200
Fax: (510) 763-9266
Web Site: www.carolhwilliams.com

E-Mail for Key Personnel:
President: carol@carolhwilliams.com
Public Relations: john.ellis@carolhwilliams.com

Employees: 155
Year Founded: 1986

National Agency Associations: 4A's

Agency Specializes In: African-American Market, Communications

Matt Taylor *(VP & Dir-Bus Dev)*
Jacqueline Hoffman *(Office Mgr)*

Accounts:
General Mills; Minneapolis, MN
Gilead Sciences, Inc.; Forest City, CA
McNeil Consumer & Specialty Pharmaceuticals/Nutritionals; New Brunswick, NJ Lactaid, St. Joseph Aspirin
Procter & Gamble; Cincinnati, OH
Sunny Delight Beverages; Blue Ash, OH
Visit Oakland Brand Architecture, Media Planning, Strategic Messaging

Branches

Carol H. Williams Advertising
444 N Michigan Ave, Chicago, IL 60611
Tel.: (312) 836-9095
Fax: (312) 836-7919
E-Mail: info@carolhwilliams.com
Web Site: www.carolhwilliams.com

Employees: 50

National Agency Associations: 4A's

Agency Specializes In: Advertising, African-American Market, Sponsorship

Terry Jones *(VP & Dir-Creative)*
Marcus Taylor *(Dir-Creative)*
Betty Thompson *(Dir-Fin)*
Clarence Williams *(Mgr-Event)*
Brian Welburn *(Acct Exec)*
Earl Williams, Jr. *(Coord-Event)*

Accounts:
AARP; Washington, DC
Coca-Cola Refreshments USA, Inc.
East Bay Municipal Utility District
General Mills
Gilead
Hewlett-Packard
Marriott; Washington, DC
Mondelez International, Inc.
Nationwide Insurance
Sunny Delight
The U.S. Army
Walt Disney World
Wells Fargo Bank

CAROLE BERKE MEDIA SERVICES
8605 SW Bohmann Pkwy, Portland, OR 97223
Tel.: (503) 293-0599
Fax: (503) 293-9008
Web Site: caroleberkemedia.com/#!main

Employees: 4
Year Founded: 1992

Agency Specializes In: Advertising

Approx. Annual Billings: $310,000

Carole Berke *(Owner & Dir-Media)*

CAROLYN KAMII PUBLIC RELATIONS
2715 Greenfield Ave, Los Angeles, CA 90064
Tel.: (310) 441-8404
Fax: (310) 441-8406
E-Mail: info@carolynkamii.com
Web Site: www.carolynkamii.com

Agency Specializes In: Advertising, Brand Development & Integration, Event Planning & Marketing, Public Relations, Social Media

REDBOOKS
Brands. Marketers. Agencies. Search Less. Find More.
Try out the Online version at www.redbooks.com

Carolyn Kamii *(Pres)*

Accounts:
New-Foodie Shares

CAROUSEL30
500 Montgomery St, Alexandria, VA 22314
Tel.: (703) 260-1180
E-Mail: info@carousel30.com
Web Site: www.carousel30.com

Employees: 20
Year Founded: 2003

Agency Specializes In: Advertising, Digital/Interactive, Graphic Design, Internet/Web Design, Public Relations

Greg Kihlstrom *(CEO)*
Romie Stefanelli *(Client Svcs Dir)*
Esther Nardone *(Dir-Mktg)*
Nick Diaz *(Mgr-Content)*

Accounts:
AARP
Alexandria Economic Development Partnership Creative, Marketing, Online Advertising, Public Relations, Social Media, Website; 2013
AOL
Geico
MTV
NASA
National Guard
The Nature Conservancy; 2008
Precision Tune Auto Care Digital Marketing, Website Design & Development; 2015
Trust for the National Mall

CARR KNOWLEDGE LLC
20718 Orville Rd E, Orting, WA 98360
Tel.: (360) 872-0032
Fax: (360) 872-0129
Web Site: www.carrknowledge.com

Employees: 20

Agency Specializes In: Advertising, Electronic Media, Email, Internet/Web Design, Media Planning, Promotions, Strategic Planning/Research, Technical Advertising

Rich Carr *(Pres & CEO)*
Jessica Carr *(VP)*

Accounts:
Harley-Davidson
State Roofing

CARR MARKETING COMMUNICATION, INC.
2372 Sweet Home Rd, Buffalo, NY 14228
Tel.: (716) 831-1500
Fax: (716) 831-1400
E-Mail: rcarr@carrmarketing.com
Web Site: www.carrmarketing.com

Employees: 5
Year Founded: 1994

Agency Specializes In: Brand Development & Integration, Communications, Crisis Communications, Environmental, Event Planning & Marketing, Financial, Government/Political, Health Care Services, Investor Relations, Media Relations, Media Training, Public Relations, Strategic Planning/Research, Travel & Tourism

Robert P. Carr *(Pres)*
Cheryl Carr *(COO)*

Accounts:
Citibank
CPA Financial Network
First Niagara Bank
Tops Friendly Market

CARRAFIELLO-DIEHL
(Acquired & Absorbed by The Gate Worldwide New York)

CARROLL/WHITE
53 Perimeter Ctr E, Atlanta, GA 30346
Tel.: (770) 350-9800
Fax: (770) 350-8183
E-Mail: info@carrollwhite.com
Web Site: www.carrollwhite.com

E-Mail for Key Personnel:
Creative Dir.: dwolff@carrollwhite.com

Employees: 12
Year Founded: 1983

Agency Specializes In: Automotive, Brand Development & Integration, Business-To-Business, Consulting, Corporate Identity, Direct Response Marketing, E-Commerce, Event Planning & Marketing, Graphic Design, High Technology, Information Technology, Internet/Web Design, Logo & Package Design, Media Buying Services, New Product Development, Pharmaceutical, Planning & Consultation, Point of Purchase, Point of Sale, Production, Public Relations, Publicity/Promotions, Real Estate, Retail, Strategic Planning/Research

Approx. Annual Billings: $10,000,000

Jennifer Aaron *(Partner-Equity & Exec VP)*
Jim White *(VP)*
Manon Dutil *(Controller)*
Carl Mattison *(Dir-Creative)*

Accounts:
Global Imports; Atlanta, GA; 2003
University House

CARROT CREATIVE
(Owned by VICE)
45 Main St, Brooklyn, NY 11201
Tel.: (718) 395-7934
E-Mail: press@carrot.is
Web Site: carrot.is/creative

Employees: 65

Agency Specializes In: Digital/Interactive, Social Media, Sponsorship

Chris Petescia *(Co-Founder)*
Adam Katzenback *(Mng Dir)*
Kyle MacDonald *(CTO)*
Nick Perlod *(VP-Strategic Dev)*
Asif Khan *(Head-Strategy)*
Steve Brauntuch *(Grp Acct Dir)*

Accounts:
Crayola
Dave Matthews Band
Disney Digital
Facebook
Ford
Home Depot
Jaguar
MTV
Nasdaq
NetBase
NFL
The Onion
Red Bull
Rolex
Target Social Media
Tumblr

CARROTNEWYORK
75 Broad St 33rd Fl, New York, NY 10004
Tel.: (212) 924-2944
Fax: (212) 924-3052
E-Mail: motivate@carrotnyc.com
Web Site: www.carrotnewyork.com

Year Founded: 1980

Agency Specializes In: Advertising, Digital/Interactive, Internet/Web Design, Market Research, Print, Promotions, Social Media, Sponsorship, Strategic Planning/Research, T.V.

Janice Hamilton *(Pres & CEO)*
James Yang *(Mng Partner)*
Jane Meyer *(Sr VP-Client Dev)*
Amber Krause *(VP-Client Svcs & Ops)*
Filiz Emma Soyak *(VP-Strategy & Education)*
Kelly Lynch *(Dir-Creative)*
Karen Smith *(Dir-Art)*
Keri Smyth *(Acct Mgr & Mgr-Digital Mktg)*

Accounts:
Federal Emergency Management Agency Disaster Master
U.S. Department of Agriculture Serving Up MyPlate

THE CARSON GROUP
1708 Hwy 6 S, Houston, TX 77077
Tel.: (281) 496-2600
Fax: (281) 496-0940
Web Site: www.carsongroupadvertising.com

Employees: 7
Year Founded: 1974

Agency Specializes In: Automotive, Brand Development & Integration, Broadcast, Business-To-Business, Cable T.V., Co-op Advertising, Consulting, Consumer Marketing, Corporate Identity, Direct-to-Consumer, E-Commerce, Food Service, Identity Marketing, Information Technology, Internet/Web Design, Local Marketing, Media Buying Services, Media Planning, Newspaper, Outdoor, Print, Production (Ad, Film, Broadcast), Radio, Real Estate, Restaurant, Retail, Strategic Planning/Research, T.V.

Breakdown of Gross Billings by Media: Audio/Visual: 80%; Cable T.V.: 3%; Consulting: 2%; Consumer Publs.: 1%; Exhibits/Trade Shows: 1%; Fees: 2%; Internet Adv.: 3%; Outdoor: 8%

John M. Carson *(Principal)*
Brian Watson *(VP-Sls Ops)*
Colton Canava *(Sr Dir-Art)*
Jay Schrock *(Dir-Creative)*
Ashley Stephens *(Project Mgr & Designer-Visual)*
Carley Thompson *(Media Buyer)*
Joy Wallace *(Media Planner)*
Shelby Bastin *(Acct Coord-Svcs)*

Accounts:
Abacus Plumbing
Double Horn Communications
Gabby's Barbecue & Ribs; Houston, TX
Houston Garden Center; Houston, TX; 1998
Los Tios Tex-Mex Food
Oreck Vacuum Cleaners
Skeeter's Grill; Houston, TX; 2000
Smartshield; Dallas, TX

CARSON MARKETING, INC.
1740 E Garry Ave Ste 231, Santa Ana, CA 92705-5844
Tel.: (949) 477-9400
Fax: (949) 477-2425
E-Mail: gcarson@carsonmarketinginc.com
Web Site: www.carsonmarketinginc.com

E-Mail for Key Personnel:
President: gcarson@carsonandcompany.com

Employees: 3
Year Founded: 1979

Agency Specializes In: Automotive, Business-To-Business, Cable T.V., Co-op Advertising, Collateral, Consulting, Consumer Marketing, Consumer Publications, Corporate Identity, Digital/Interactive, Direct Response Marketing, Direct-to-Consumer, E-Commerce, Entertainment, Event Planning & Marketing, Fashion/Apparel, Food Service, Graphic Design, High Technology, In-Store Advertising, Infomercials, Information Technology, Internet/Web Design, Local Marketing, Logo & Package Design, Newspapers & Magazines, Outdoor, Package Design, Point of Purchase, Point of Sale, Print, Production, Public Relations, Publicity/Promotions, RSS (Really Simple Syndication), Radio, Retail, Sales Promotion, Search Engine Optimization, Seniors' Market, Sports Market, T.V., Technical Advertising, Trade & Consumer Magazines

Approx. Annual Billings: $4,250,000

George Carson *(Pres)*

Accounts:
Airstream Los Angeles; 2014
Almar Company; Oceanside, CA; 2003
Americon; 2013
Axis-Media Media Buying; 2008
Azzurro Wheels; Anaheim, CA; 1999
Business SoftSkills; 2007
California RV Show; 2013
Clark Foods; Kern County, CA; 2008
Cornerstone Entertainment International; Anaheim, CA; 2004
CV Wine Bar: Hong Kong, China; 2012
CyberComSecure Software Developer; 2010
El Primo Foods; 2008
Encription Solutions, Inc.; 2005
Genesis Supreme RV; 2013
Grand Touring Garage; N. Bend, Oregon; 2009
Hartley & Associates; 1985
Kool Fit International; 1988
LA Carton; Los Angeles, CA; 2010
Laura Scudder's; 2007
OCVBC Volleyball Club; 2009
Partition Specialties Inc.; 2003
Pastrami Express; Alhambra, CA; 1998
Prime Choice Foods; Bristol, VA; 1998
Red Lantern Labs; San Diego, CA; 2012
Stedt Insurance Services; Orange County, CA; 2008
Taco Works; San Luis Obispo, CA; 1999
Tagnos; Laguna Hills, CA; 2012
Vatican II; 2004
Vertical Solutions, Inc.; 2008
Yamaha Music Centers Music Schools; 2009

THE CARTER MALONE GROUP LLC

1509 Madison Ave, Memphis, TN 38104
Tel.: (901) 278-0881
Fax: (901) 278-0081
E-Mail: info@cmgpr.com
Web Site: www.cmgpr.com

Agency Specializes In: Advertising, Collateral, Crisis Communications, Event Planning & Marketing, Graphic Design, Internet/Web Design, Media Relations, Media Training, Public Relations, Strategic Planning/Research

Deidre Malone *(Founder, Pres & CEO)*
Debra A. Davis *(VP-Bus Rels)*
Keshia Merritt *(Dir-Creative)*
Regina H. Jones *(Acct Supvr)*

Accounts:
Memphis Heritage Trail
Tennessee Department of Transportation

CARYL COMMUNICATIONS, INC.

40 Eisenhower Dr Ste 203, Paramus, NJ 07652
Tel.: (201) 796-7788
Fax: (201) 796-8844
Toll Free: (866) 256-5858
E-Mail: customerservice@caryl.com
Web Site: www.caryl.com

Employees: 10
Year Founded: 1980

Agency Specializes In: Event Planning & Marketing, Internet/Web Design, Local Marketing, Media Relations, Public Relations, Real Estate

Evelyn Weiss Francisco *(VP & Client Svcs Dir)*
Ellen Seaver *(Acct Mgr & Copywriter)*
Christine Ziomek *(Mgr-Special Projects)*
Sandy Crisafulli *(Writer & Specialist-Media)*
Vicki Garfinkel-Jakubovic *(Specialist-Media & Writer)*
Dora Johnson *(Writer & Specialist-Media)*
Joyce Berman *(Acct Coord)*
Katie Meccia *(Sr Acct Coord)*

Accounts:
Allendale Community for Mature Living Senior Housing
Cushman & Wakefield of New Jersey, Inc.
Danny Wood Enterprises, LLC
Diversified Capital
Gebroe-Hammer Associates
IBS
Levin Management Corporation Retail Real Estate Property Manager
NAIOP-NJ
NJ Chapter of the National Association of Industrial & Office Properties (NJ-NAIOP) Commercial Real Estate Developers
Prism Capital Partners, LLC
Volunteer Lawyers
Walters Group Commercial & Residential Real Estate Developers

CASACOM

407 McGill Bureau 1000, Montreal, QC H2Y 2G3 Canada
Tel.: (514) 286-2145
Fax: (514) 286-6647
E-Mail: info@casacom.ca
Web Site: www.casacom.ca

Employees: 15
Year Founded: 2001

Agency Specializes In: Business-To-Business, Communications, Entertainment, Event Planning & Marketing, Exhibit/Trade Shows, Food Service, Government/Political, Graphic Design, Health Care Services, Investor Relations, Medical Products, Public Relations, Real Estate

Marie-Josee Gagnon *(Founder & CEO)*
Annick Belanger *(Mng Partner)*
Marie-Samuelle Constant *(Chief Admin Officer & Chief Acctg Officer)*
Jason Chennette *(Acct Dir)*
Stephane Ethier *(Dir)*
Ann Gibbon *(Dir-Western Canada)*
Jean-Michel Nahas *(Dir-Bus Comm & Pub Affairs)*
Brigitte Pouliot *(Dir-Integrated Comm)*
Andrea Mancini *(Coord)*
Lysanne Rioux *(Coord)*

Accounts:
Aluminerie Alouette
AXOR
Beautiful Heat Brand Marketing, Digital, Event Management, National Communications Planning, PR, Social Media
Etsy Canada (Agency of Record) Communications, Public Relations
Netatmo Brand Awareness
New-Urban Barn (Agency of Record)

CASANOVA PENDRILL
Integrated Hispanic Communications

CASANOVA PENDRILL

275-A McCormick Ave Ste 100, Costa Mesa, CA 92626-3369
Tel.: (714) 918-8200
Fax: (714) 918-8295
Web Site: www.casanova.com

Employees: 80
Year Founded: 1984

National Agency Associations: 4A's-AD CLUB-AHAA

Agency Specializes In: Advertising, Bilingual Market, Communications, Hispanic Market, Media Buying Services, Sponsorship

Casanova Pendrill is a team of Hispanic consumer experts and integrated marketing specialists who develop breakthrough creative ideas which drive measurable business results for their clients. Their services include: Strategic Planning, Account Services, Creative, Media, Promotions, Interactive, and Direct Response & Public Relations.

Breakdown of Gross Billings by Media: Cable T.V.: 3%; D.M.: 2%; Internet Adv.: 2%; Mags.: 2%; Network T.V.: 31%; Newsp.: 3%; Outdoor: 2%; Spot Radio: 26%; Spot T.V.: 29%

Simon El Hage *(Sr VP & Dir-Strategic Plng)*
Enrily Levy *(VP & Dir-Fin)*
Carla Noriega *(Grp Acct Dir)*
Melissa Tapia *(Mgmt Supvr)*
Roxane Garzon *(Dir-Media)*
Manuel Huici *(Dir-Creative)*
Andres Calvachi *(Acct Supvr)*
Brenda Fierro *(Sr Acct Exec)*
Elsa Gallardo *(Asst Media Planner)*
Danielle Kehoe *(Sr Rep-New Bus)*
Sandra Ramos *(Sr Media Planner)*

Accounts:
The Ad Council
American Frozen Food Institute Hispanic communications
California Lottery; Sacramento, CA Mega Millions, Scratchers, Super Lotto; 1986
Denny's Corp.; Spartanburg, SC "Greatest Hits Remixed", Creative, Hispanic, Strategic Counsel, TV
General Mills, Inc.; Minneapolis, MN "No Barriers Grand Canyon Expedition", Betty Crocker, Bisquick, Campaign: "Feel the Energy of Nature", Chex Mix, Cinnamon Toast Crunch, FUN da-middles, Hamburger Helper, Nature Valley, TV; 1985
General Motors Chevrolet, Hispanic Advertising
GlaxoSmithKline; Moon Township, PA Lovaza
Harvest Hill Beverage Co Juicy Juice
MillerCoors Campaign: "Don't Mess with Miller Time"
Nestle USA, Inc.; Los Angeles, CA Abuelita, Arrowhead, Carlos V, Coffee Mate, Hot Pockets, La Lechera, Maggi, Nescafe, Nesquik, Nestle Pure Life, Nido, Ozarka, Stouffers; 2000
Purina Beneful, Dog Chow

Tr3s
TurboTax
UNICEF
United States Army
Western Dental

CASCADE WEB DEVELOPMENT

2505 SE 11th Ave Ste 328, Portland, OR 97217
Tel.: (503) 517-2700
E-Mail: sales@cascadewebdev.com
Web Site: www.cascadewebdev.com

Employees: 9
Year Founded: 2001

Agency Specializes In: Advertising, Alternative Advertising, Brand Development & Integration, Branded Entertainment, Business-To-Business, Communications, Consulting, Consumer Goods, Content, Customer Relationship Management, E-Commerce, Electronic Media, Email, Guerilla Marketing, High Technology, Information Technology, Integrated Marketing, Internet/Web Design, Local Marketing, Multimedia, Podcasting, RSS (Really Simple Syndication), Real Estate, Restaurant, Search Engine Optimization, Social Media, Sports Market, Syndication, Technical Advertising, Viral/Buzz/Word of Mouth, Web (Banner Ads, Pop-ups, etc.)

Approx. Annual Billings: $650,000

Breakdown of Gross Billings by Media: Consulting: 10%; E-Commerce: 10%; Internet Adv.: 70%; Sports Mktg.: 10%

Ben McKinley *(Founder & CEO)*
Stephen Brewer *(Dir-Innovation & Technical Svcs)*
Christi McKinley *(Dir-Ops)*
Kyle Bridges *(Mgr-Strategy & Project Mgr)*
Scott Peerman *(Project Mgr-Digital)*

Accounts:
AKT Services; Lake Oswego, OR Professional Services
Papa Murphy's Pizza; Vancouver, WA Franchise

CASEY COMMUNICATIONS, INC.

8301 Maryland Ave Ste 350, Saint Louis, MO 63105
Tel.: (314) 721-2828
Fax: (314) 721-2717
E-Mail: info@caseycomm.com
Web Site: www.caseycomm.com

Employees: 8
Year Founded: 1983

Agency Specializes In: Advertising, Brand Development & Integration, Broadcast, Collateral, Crisis Communications, Direct Response Marketing, Event Planning & Marketing, Exhibit/Trade Shows, Financial, Government/Political, Internet/Web Design, Market Research, Media Relations, Print, Real Estate

Marie A. Casey *(Founder & Pres)*
Kenn Entringer *(VP)*
Teresa Schroeder *(Office Mgr & Coord-Project & Special Event)*

Accounts:
Cass Information Systems, Inc.

CASHMAN & KATZ INTEGRATED COMMUNICATIONS

76 Eastern Blvd, Glastonbury, CT 06033
Tel.: (860) 652-0300
Fax: (860) 652-0308
E-Mail: info@cashman-katz.com
Web Site: www.cashman-katz.com

Employees: 29
Year Founded: 1992

Agency Specializes In: Advertising, Advertising Specialties, Affluent Market, African-American Market, Agriculture, Arts, Automotive, Aviation & Aerospace, Below-the-Line, Bilingual Market, Brand Development & Integration, Broadcast, Business Publications, Business-To-Business, Cable T.V., Children's Market, Co-op Advertising, Collateral, College, Communications, Computers & Software, Consulting, Consumer Goods, Consumer Marketing, Consumer Publications, Corporate Communications, Corporate Identity, Crisis Communications, Customer Relationship Management, Digital/Interactive, Direct Response Marketing, Direct-to-Consumer, E-Commerce, Education, Electronic Media, Electronics, Email, Engineering, Entertainment, Environmental, Event Planning & Marketing, Exhibit/Trade Shows, Experience Design, Fashion/Apparel, Financial, Food Service, Government/Political, Graphic Design, Guerilla Marketing, Health Care Services, High Technology, Hispanic Market, Hospitality, Household Goods, Identity Marketing, In-Store Advertising, Industrial, Information Technology, Integrated Marketing, Internet/Web Design, Legal Services, Leisure, Local Marketing, Logo & Package Design, Luxury Products, Magazines, Market Research, Media Buying Services, Media Planning, Media Relations, Media Training, Medical Products, Men's Market, Mobile Marketing, Multicultural, Multimedia, New Product Development, New Technologies, Newspaper, Newspapers & Magazines, Out-of-Home Media, Outdoor, Over-50 Market, Package Design, Pharmaceutical, Planning & Consultation, Point of Purchase, Point of Sale, Print, Production, Production (Ad, Film, Broadcast), Production (Print), Promotions, Public Relations, Publicity/Promotions, Publishing, Radio, Real Estate, Regional, Restaurant, Retail, Sales Promotion, Search Engine Optimization, Seniors' Market, Social Marketing/Nonprofit, Social Media, Sponsorship, Sports Market, Stakeholders, Strategic Planning/Research, T.V., Teen Market, Trade & Consumer Magazines, Transportation, Travel & Tourism, Tween Market, Urban Market, Viral/Buzz/Word of Mouth, Web (Banner Ads, Pop-ups, etc.), Women's Market

Approx. Annual Billings: $54,489,000

Eric Cavoli *(Sr VP & Grp Dir-Creative)*
Bill Greer *(Sr VP-Acct & Strategic Plng)*
Eric Schweighoffer *(VP & Dir-Media)*
Saverio Mancini *(VP-PR)*
Kerry Holland *(Sr Dir-Art)*
Natalie Collins *(Acct Svcs Dir)*
Joni Krasusky *(Dir-Res)*

Accounts:
Berkshire Bank
Bic North America
Blum Shapiro
Bridgewater Associates
China Care
Click it or Ticket
Connecticut Association of Realtors
Connecticut Bank & Trust Company
Connecticut Children's Medical Center
Connecticut Department of Banking
Connecticut Department of Economic & Community Development
Connecticut Department of Motor Vehicles
Connecticut Department of Public Health
Connecticut Department of Transportation
Connecticut Lottery Corp.; 2005
Connecticut Natural Gas
Connecticut State Building & Construction Trades Council
Connecticut Tobacco and Health Trust Fund Anti-Smoking Campaign
CT Convention Center
CT Dietetic Association
CT Housing & Finance Authority
CT Science Center
CT Tourism
Foxwoods & MGM Grand at Foxwoods
Foxwoods Resort Casino (Public Relations Agency of Record) Dining, Entertainment, Gaming, Public Relations, Resort Options
Gaylord Hospital
Guardian Jet
Hartford Courant
Hoffman Auto Group
Ironworkers of New England
Kiels
Lea's Foundation For Leukemia Research
Mashantucket Pequot Tribal Nation
Mass Mutual
Mercy Hospital
New England Air Museum
Pfizer
Quinnipiac University Athletics
Redefine Christmas
Saint Joseph University
Saint Mary's Hospital
School Nutrition Association of CT
See Something Say Something
Sheet Metal Workers of CT
UConn School of Business
United Illuminating
Wine & Spirit Wholesalers of CT
Yankee Candle
Yankee Institute

CASHMERE AGENCY

12530 Beatrice St, Los Angeles, CA 90066-7002
Tel.: (323) 928-5080
Fax: (310) 695-7362
E-Mail: info@cashmereagency.com
Web Site: www.cashmereagency.com

Agency Specializes In: Advertising, Graphic Design, Local Marketing, Multicultural, New Product Development, Strategic Planning/Research, Viral/Buzz/Word of Mouth

Ted Chung *(Chm)*
Seung Chung *(Pres)*
Ryan Ford *(Chief Creative Officer & Exec VP)*
Nick Adler *(VP-Bus Dev)*
Rona Mercado *(VP-Client Svcs & Mktg)*
Brianne Pins *(VP-PR)*
Jesse Nicely *(Dir-Creative Strategy)*

Accounts:
Adidas
Coca-Cola
Disney
Ea
Midway
MTV
Murs

CASON NIGHTINGALE CREATIVE COMMUNICATIONS

708 3rd Ave 29th Fl, New York, NY 10017
Tel.: (212) 351-3360
Fax: (212) 867-3353
E-Mail: office@cncommunications.com
Web Site: casonnightingale.com/

Employees: 20
Year Founded: 1990

Agency Specializes In: Brand Development & Integration, Corporate Identity, Event Planning & Marketing, Media Buying Services, Media Planning, Package Design, Point of Sale, Production, Strategic Planning/Research, Sweepstakes

Angela Cason *(Pres & CEO)*

William N. Nightingale *(Chm-Media Strategy)*
Thomas Marchini *(VP & Assoc Dir-Creative)*
Jay Lundeen *(Acct Supvr)*

Accounts:
Ammens
Aziza
Bauli
Magners Irish Cider
Monini Extra Virgin Olive Oil
Sea Breeze
Vitapointe

CASPARI MCCORMICK

307 A St 2nd Fl, Wilmington, DE 19801-5345
Tel.: (302) 421-9080
Fax: (302) 421-9079
E-Mail: sean@casparimccormick.com
Web Site: www.casparimccormick.com

Employees: 10
Year Founded: 2001

Agency Specializes In: Advertising

Approx. Annual Billings: $10,000,000

Matt Caspari *(Partner & Dir-Creative)*
Sean McCormick *(Partner & Dir-Creative)*
Joyce McCormick *(Fin Dir)*
Heather Mcguigan *(Dir-Design)*
Olivia Linchuk *(Acct Coord)*

Accounts:
Benjamin Franklin Tercentenary
CarSense
Favourites
Historic Germantown; PA
Historic Philadelphia; PA
Iron Hill Brewery & Restaurant
Mystic Aquarium; Mystic, CT
Opera Delaware
Pennsylvania Academy of The Fine Arts
Philadelphia Cultural Academy
Sodexo
Spot Wash Mobile Grooming
Thomas Jefferson University Hospitals

CASTELLS & ASOCIADOS

865 S Figueroa St Ste 1100, Los Angeles, CA 90017-2543
Tel.: (213) 688-7250
Fax: (213) 688-7067
E-Mail: info@adcastells.com
Web Site: www.adcastells.com

E-Mail for Key Personnel:
President: liz@adcastells.com

Employees: 50
Year Founded: 1998

National Agency Associations: AHAA

Agency Specializes In: Above-the-Line, Advertising, Advertising Specialties, Affiliate Marketing, Affluent Market, African-American Market, Agriculture, Arts, Asian Market, Automotive, Below-the-Line, Bilingual Market, Brand Development & Integration, Branded Entertainment, Broadcast, Business-To-Business, Cable T.V., Children's Market, Co-op Advertising, Collateral, College, Communications, Computers & Software, Consulting, Consumer Goods, Consumer Marketing, Consumer Publications, Content, Corporate Communications, Corporate Identity, Cosmetics, Crisis Communications, Customer Relationship Management, Digital/Interactive, Direct Response Marketing, Direct-to-Consumer, E-Commerce, Education, Electronic Media, Electronics, Email, Entertainment, Event Planning & Marketing, Experience Design, Fashion/Apparel, Financial, Food Service, Government/Political, Graphic Design, Guerilla Marketing, Health Care Services, High Technology, Hispanic Market, Household Goods, Identity Marketing, In-Store Advertising, Industrial, Infomercials, Integrated Marketing, International, Internet/Web Design, Leisure, Local Marketing, Logo & Package Design, Magazines, Market Research, Media Buying Services, Media Planning, Media Relations, Media Training, Medical Products, Men's Market, Merchandising, Mobile Marketing, Multicultural, Multimedia, New Product Development, Newspaper, Newspapers & Magazines, Out-of-Home Media, Outdoor, Over-50 Market, Package Design, Pharmaceutical, Planning & Consultation, Point of Purchase, Point of Sale, Print, Production, Production (Ad, Film, Broadcast), Production (Print), Promotions, Public Relations, Publicity/Promotions, RSS (Really Simple Syndication), Radio, Regional, Restaurant, Retail, Sales Promotion, Search Engine Optimization, Seniors' Market, Social Marketing/Nonprofit, Social Media, Sponsorship, Sports Market, Strategic Planning/Research, Sweepstakes, T.V., Technical Advertising, Teen Market, Telemarketing, Trade & Consumer Magazines, Transportation, Travel & Tourism, Tween Market, Urban Market, Viral/Buzz/Word of Mouth, Web (Banner Ads, Pop-ups, etc.), Women's Market

Castells is the Hispanic marketing agency for ROI-powered ideas and business integration, as the architects of Transculturation & trade, guiding clients to ethnic success with analytics, segmentation, brand and sales-building creative and every-platform activation. Led by dynamic President and Stanford MBA Liz Castells, we're a full-service, fully-integrated team with a mix of General market, client-side and Hispanic experience. Our mission is to drive client profit integrating Hispanic into all the P's with Hispanic thought leadership, consistent innovation, metrics and cultural know-how, by leveraging commonalities and unique needs in a collaborative spirit. Castells is about brains, heart and grit.

Approx. Annual Billings: $71,500,000

Liz Castells-Heard *(Pres & CEO)*
Malu Santamaria *(Partner & Acct Dir)*
Terry Sullivan *(CFO)*
Marielise Nascimento-Colavin *(VP & Dir-Media & Integrated Svcs)*
Carlos Correa *(Dir-Creative)*
Araceli Maldonado *(Dir-Media Buying)*

Accounts:
Azteca America; 2013
Cox Communications; 2014
Dole/Tropicana; Chicago, IL Dole Juices; 2009
First 5 California; 2008
Junta Hispana; 2011
The LAGRANT Foundation; 2005
Mcdonald's Baltimore/Washington Region; 2013
McDonald's Corporation ; 1998
McDonald's Pacific Northwest Medford, Portland, Seattle, Southeast Idaho, Spokane, Yakima/Tri-Cities; 2003
McDonald's Southern California Bakersfield, Los Angeles, Palm Springs, San Diego; 1998
Puma North America; 2014
The Safeway Companies; Pleasanton, CA Pavilions, Randalls, Safeway, Tom Thumb, Vons; 1999
San Diego Toyota Dealer Association; 1998
Tequila Allende; 2012
Toyota Dealer Association Southern California; 1998

CASTLE COMMUNICATIONS

11294 Coloma Rd Ste G, Gold River, CA 95670
Tel.: (916) 635-2728
Fax: (916) 635-5043
Web Site: www.castlecommunications.net

Agency Specializes In: Advertising, Event Planning & Marketing, Public Relations

Stacey Castle *(Pres)*

Accounts:
Central Valley New Car Dealers Association
International Auto Show Sacramento
International Sportsmens Exposition
Mercedes-Benz of Sacramento
Roseville Square
Sacramento Autorama

CATALPHA ADVERTISING & DESIGN

6801 Loch Raven Blvd, Towson, MD 21286
Tel.: (410) 337-0066
Fax: (410) 296-2297
E-Mail: info@catalpha.com
Web Site: www.catalpha.com

Employees: 6
Year Founded: 1986

National Agency Associations: Second Wind Limited

Agency Specializes In: Advertising, Brand Development & Integration, Business-To-Business, Catalogs, Collateral, Consulting, Consumer Goods, Consumer Marketing, Corporate Identity, Customer Relationship Management, Direct Response Marketing, Direct-to-Consumer, E-Commerce, Graphic Design, Household Goods, In-Store Advertising, Internet/Web Design, Local Marketing, Logo & Package Design, Merchandising, New Product Development, Package Design, Pets , Point of Purchase, Point of Sale, Production, Production (Print), Search Engine Optimization, Technical Advertising, Trade & Consumer Magazines, Web (Banner Ads, Pop-ups, etc.)

Approx. Annual Billings: $850,000

Breakdown of Gross Billings by Media: Collateral: $200,000; Consulting: $100,000; E-Commerce: $150,000; Logo & Package Design: $250,000; Point of Purchase: $150,000

Don Keller *(Owner)*
Karen Kerski *(Owner)*

Accounts:
Black & Decker Home Products, Outdoor Tools, Power Tools
Cosmic Cat Cat Toys, Cat Treats, Catnip
Franke USA

CATALYST

275 Promenade St Ste 275, Warwick, RI 02908
Tel.: (401) 732-1886
Fax: (401) 732-5528
E-Mail: bodell@catalystb2b.com
Web Site: www.catalystb2b.com

Employees: 20

Brian T. Odell *(Owner)*
Tom Hamlin *(VP-Acct Svcs)*
Patty Gauthier *(Dir-Creative Svcs)*
Juergen Burghardt *(Mgr-Production)*

Reshma Patil *(Mgr-Paid Search)*
Charles Mederios *(Supvr-Design Production)*

CATALYST ADVERTISING
168 S 19th St, Pittsburgh, PA 15203
Tel.: (412) 381-1100
Fax: (412) 381-0900
Web Site: www.catalystadvertising.com

Year Founded: 2009

Agency Specializes In: Advertising, Brand Development & Integration, Collateral, Internet/Web Design, Logo & Package Design, Media Relations, Promotions, Public Relations

Jim Stupar *(Owner)*

Accounts:
Kerotest Manufacturing Corp.
Lasik

CATALYST MARKETING COMMUNICATIONS INC.
2777 Summer St Ste 301, Stamford, CT 06905
Tel.: (203) 348-7541
Fax: (203) 348-5688
E-Mail: info@catalystmc.com
Web Site: www.catalystmc.com

E-Mail for Key Personnel:
President: cwintrub@catalystmc.com
Production Mgr.: gpry@catalystmc.com

Employees: 7
Year Founded: 1994

Agency Specializes In: Advertising, Agriculture, Business Publications, Business-To-Business, Catalogs, Co-op Advertising, Collateral, Communications, Content, Corporate Communications, Corporate Identity, Direct Response Marketing, Engineering, Exhibit/Trade Shows, Graphic Design, Health Care Services, High Technology, Industrial, Integrated Marketing, Internet/Web Design, Local Marketing, Magazines, Media Buying Services, Media Planning, Media Relations, Outdoor, Point of Purchase, Print, Production, Production (Print), Public Relations, Publicity/Promotions, Strategic Planning/Research, Technical Advertising, Trade & Consumer Magazines

Charles Wintrub *(Pres)*
Melissa LoParco *(VP & Dir-PR)*
Geri Pry *(Dir-Art)*
Colleen Luby *(Acct Exec)*

Accounts:
The Bilco Company; West Haven, CT Building Products, PermEntry; 1999
Cultec, Inc.; Brookfield, CT Plastic Stormwater & Septic Chambers; 2005
Erland Construction Public Relations, Summer House; 2014
LaMar Lighting Company, Inc Public Relations; 2014
Stamford Health System; Stamford, CT Health Care Services; 1999
TUV Rheinland of North America; Newton, CT Standards Testing & Certification; 2006

CATALYST MARKETING COMPANY
(Formerly Thielen Ideacorp)
1466 Van Ness Ave, Fresno, CA 93721
Tel.: (559) 252-2500
Fax: (559) 252-0737
E-Mail: info@teamcatalyst.com
Web Site: www.teamcatalyst.com/

E-Mail for Key Personnel:
President: mt@teamcatalyst.com
Media Dir.: lsommers@teamcatalyst.com

Employees: 34
Year Founded: 1969

Agency Specializes In: Advertising, Advertising Specialties, Agriculture, Arts, Asian Market, Automotive, Bilingual Market, Brand Development & Integration, Branded Entertainment, Broadcast, Business Publications, Business-To-Business, Cable T.V., Catalogs, Collateral, College, Commercial Photography, Communications, Computers & Software, Consulting, Consumer Goods, Consumer Marketing, Consumer Publications, Content, Corporate Identity, Cosmetics, Crisis Communications, Custom Publishing, Digital/Interactive, Direct Response Marketing, Direct-to-Consumer, E-Commerce, Education, Electronic Media, Email, Entertainment, Environmental, Event Planning & Marketing, Exhibit/Trade Shows, Fashion/Apparel, Financial, Food Service, Government/Political, Graphic Design, Health Care Services, High Technology, Hispanic Market, Hospitality, Household Goods, In-Store Advertising, Industrial, Integrated Marketing, Internet/Web Design, Leisure, Local Marketing, Logo & Package Design, Luxury Products, Magazines, Market Research, Media Buying Services, Media Planning, Media Relations, Media Training, Medical Products, Merchandising, Mobile Marketing, Multicultural, Multimedia, New Product Development, New Technologies, Newspaper, Newspapers & Magazines, Out-of-Home Media, Outdoor, Over-50 Market, Package Design, Paid Searches, Pharmaceutical, Planning & Consultation, Point of Purchase, Point of Sale, Print, Product Placement, Production, Production (Print), Promotions, Public Relations, Publicity/Promotions, RSS (Really Simple Syndication), Radio, Real Estate, Recruitment, Regional, Restaurant, Retail, Sales Promotion, Search Engine Optimization, Seniors' Market, Social Marketing/Nonprofit, Sponsorship, Sports Market, Strategic Planning/Research, Syndication, T.V., Technical Advertising, Telemarketing, Trade & Consumer Magazines, Transportation, Travel & Tourism, Viral/Buzz/Word of Mouth, Yellow Pages Advertising

Approx. Annual Billings: $22,072,000

Breakdown of Gross Billings by Media: Audio/Visual: $600,000; Collateral: $1,700,000; D.M.: $100,000; Fees: $900,000; Internet Adv.: $100,000; Newsp.: $3,200,000; Outdoor: $554,000; Radio: $4,132,000; T.V.: $10,768,000; Trade & Consumer Mags.: $18,000

Michael C. Thielen *(Pres)*
Mark Astone *(CEO)*
Greg Grannis *(Exec Dir-Creative)*
Paul Rippens *(Client Svcs Dir)*
Michele Meisch *(Acct Mgr)*

Accounts:
American Pistachio Growers; Fresno, CA Association Materials & Events; 2010
Black Oak Casino; Tuolumne, CA Indian Gaming; 2001
Fresno County Workforce Investment Board
Gusmer Beer & Wine Products; Fresno, CA; 2007
Ironstone Vinyards; Murphys, CA Entertainment; 2012
Monterey Ag Resources
Quail Lakes; Fresno, CA New Homes; 1995
Tulare County Human Resources Development; Visalia, CA (Recruitment); 2002
Valley CAN; Fresno, CA Community Coalition; 2007
Yosemite Mariposa County Tourism Bureau; Mariposa, CA Destination Marketing; 2007

CATALYST MARKETING DESIGN
930 S Calhoun St, Fort Wayne, IN 46802
Tel.: (260) 422-4888
Fax: (260) 422-8833
E-Mail: info@catalystsite.com
Web Site: www.catalystgetsit.com

Employees: 18
Year Founded: 1997

Agency Specializes In: Advertising, Brand Development & Integration, Food Service, Integrated Marketing, Medical Products, Technical Advertising

Ted Kucinsky *(Pres & Chief Creative Officer)*
Shannon McNett-Silcox *(Principal & VP-Acct Svc)*
Connie Hunt *(Dir-Acctg)*
Jeff Anderson *(Assoc Creative Dir)*

Accounts:
Allen County Economic Development Alliance Strategic Marketing
Beach Beverages, Inc; Dallas, TX Digital Development, Promotion, Sale Packaging, Social Media
Da-Lite Screen Company Inc (Agency of Record)
Kerrie Corporation
Midwest Bottling Company
Tyson Deli

CATALYST PUBLIC RELATIONS
350 5th Ave 38th Fl, New York, NY 10118
Tel.: (212) 714-7900
E-Mail: tfragulis@catalystimg.com
Web Site: catalystimg.com/

Employees: 15

Agency Specializes In: Communications, Digital/Interactive, Entertainment, Integrated Marketing, Media Relations, Sponsorship, Sports Market, Strategic Planning/Research

Bret Werner *(Co-Founder & Mng Dir)*
Ted Fragulis *(Mng Partner)*
Bill Holtz *(Mng Partner)*
Rob Bronfeld *(Sr VP)*
Shaun Clair *(Acct Dir)*

Accounts:
Georgia-Pacific Dixie, Public Relations
Zico Social Media

CATALYST S+F
475 Sansome St, San Francisco, CA 94111
Tel.: (415) 238-8480
Web Site: www.catalystsf.com

Year Founded: 2007

Agency Specializes In: Advertising, Digital/Interactive

John Durham *(CEO & Mng Partner)*

CATALYST, SCIENCE + SOUL
110 Marina Dr, Rochester, NY 14626
Tel.: (585) 453-8300
Toll Free: (877) AURAGEN
E-Mail: info@catalystinc.com
Web Site: www.catalystinc.com

Employees: 48
Year Founded: 1995

National Agency Associations: DMA

Agency Specializes In: Advertising, Advertising Specialties, Automotive, Business-To-Business, Cable T.V., Collateral, Commercial Photography, Consulting, Consumer Marketing,

Digital/Interactive, Direct Response Marketing, E-Commerce, Electronic Media, Financial, Health Care Services, High Technology, Information Technology, Internet/Web Design, Medical Products, Pharmaceutical, Point of Sale, Radio, Sponsorship, Strategic Planning/Research, T.V., Telemarketing

Approx. Annual Billings: $36,000,000

Breakdown of Gross Billings by Media: D.M.: 100%

Jeff Cleary *(Owner & Mng Dir)*
Michael Osborn *(Mng Dir)*
Elizabeth Mertz *(Grp Acct Dir)*
Frank Magnera *(Acct Dir & Supvr)*
Cindy West *(Dir-Production Svcs)*

Accounts:
AAA
AMC Theatres
CITI
Eastman Kodak Company; Rochester, NY Film & Photography; 1996
Embrace Home Loans
First Niagara Bank
GE Money
Home Properties
HSBC
Kodak Graphic Communications Group
M&T Bank
Oreck
Pacagon
Pitney Bowes
Presstek
Sage Software
SFN Group, Inc.
Thermo Scientific
United Way
Wegman's

CATAPULT MARKETING
55 Post Rd W, Westport, CT 06880
Tel.: (203) 682-4000
Fax: (203) 682-4097
E-Mail: info@catapultmarketing.com
Web Site: www.catapultmarketing.com

Employees: 150

Agency Specializes In: Advertising, Below-the-Line, Co-op Advertising, Collateral, Communications, Consumer Goods, Consumer Marketing, Consumer Publications, Corporate Communications, Customer Relationship Management, Digital/Interactive, Direct-to-Consumer, E-Commerce, Email, Household Goods, In-Store Advertising, Integrated Marketing, Internet/Web Design, Local Marketing, Market Research, Multimedia, Newspapers & Magazines, Pets , Point of Purchase, Point of Sale, Promotions, RSS (Really Simple Syndication), Radio, Regional, Restaurant, Retail, Sales Promotion, Sponsorship, Sweepstakes

Approx. Annual Billings: $25,000,000

Breakdown of Gross Billings by Media: In-Store Adv.: 20%; Internet Adv.: 20%; Point of Purchase: 20%; Strategic Planning/Research: 40%

Paul Kramer *(CEO)*
Peter Cloutier *(CMO)*
Brian Cohen *(Exec VP, Head-Digital Integration & Grp Dir)*
Heidi Froseth *(Exec VP)*
Margaret Lewis *(Exec VP)*
Travis Caravan *(Sr Dir-Art)*
Brent Grill *(Sr Dir-Art & Digital)*
Beth Craig *(Dir-Insights)*
Seth White *(Sr Art Dir)*

Accounts:
Ahold
New-Clorox Company
Kraft Foods
Mars Petcare
Subway; Milford, CT Restaurants; 2003
Uncle Ben's
Wrigley Skittles

CATAPULTWORKS
(Formerly Catapult Direct)
300 Orchard City Dr Ste 131, Campbell, CA 95008
Tel.: (408) 369-8111
E-Mail: info@catapultworks.com
Web Site: www.catapultworks.com/

Employees: 80
Year Founded: 1992

Agency Specializes In: Advertising, Business-To-Business, Collateral, Consulting, Digital/Interactive, Direct Response Marketing, Electronic Media, Event Planning & Marketing, High Technology, Information Technology, Internet/Web Design, Print, Recruitment, Sales Promotion, Telemarketing

Approx. Annual Billings: $4,000,000

Breakdown of Gross Billings by Media: Consulting: 5%; D.M.: 40%; Event Mktg.: 10%; Internet Adv.: 20%; Print: 15%; Strategic Planning/Research: 5%; Worldwide Web Sites: 5%

Tom Beck *(Pres-Silicon Valley)*
Darin Albers *(VP-Media Svcs)*
Todd Diamond *(Exec Dir-Creative)*
Mike Connor *(Dir-Creative)*

Accounts:
Fujitsu PC

CATAPULTWORKS
(Acquired by R2Integrated)

CATCH-22 CREATIVE INC
8007 Douglas Ave, Racine, WI 53402
Tel.: (262) 898-7991
E-Mail: info@catch22creative.com
Web Site: www.catch22creative.com

Agency Specializes In: Advertising, Brand Development & Integration, Collateral, Package Design

Nikki Wagner *(Partner)*
Don Schauf *(Principal)*

Accounts:
New-InSinkErator

CATCH 24 ADVERTISING & DESIGN
27 W 20th St 9th Fl, New York, NY 10011
Tel.: (646) 230-8013
E-Mail: info@catch24design.com

Agency Specializes In: Advertising, Brand Development & Integration, Digital/Interactive, Package Design, Print, Sponsorship

Bill Goodspeed *(Founder)*
Amy Scott *(Acct Dir)*
Danielle Avissar *(Dir-New Bus)*
Nick Caughel *(Dir-Digital)*
Ryan Kelly *(Dir-Media & Accts)*
Bob Machuga *(Dir-Art & Sr Designer)*
Jonathan Rodgers *(Dir-Creative)*
Anna Berkheiser *(Assoc Dir-Creative)*
Nina Hoffman *(Strategist-Social Media & Sr Copywriter)*

Accounts:
Blat Vodka

CATCH NEW YORK
27 W 20th St 9th Fl, New York, NY 10011
Tel.: (646) 230-8013
Fax: (646) 230-8011
Web Site: www.catch-nyc.com

Employees: 35

Agency Specializes In: Advertising, Communications, Digital/Interactive, Integrated Marketing, Media Planning

Joe Perello *(Co-Founder & Mng Partner)*
Jason Dorin *(Mng Dir)*
Marco Cignini *(Exec Dir-Creative)*
Isabelle Aylwin *(Acct Dir)*
Doug Wiganowske *(Assoc Dir-Creative)*
Ed Little *(Strategist-Brand)*
Matt Owens *(Acct Coord)*

Accounts:
And1 Branding, Creative, Digital, Marketing, Media Planning & Buying, Media Strategy
College Ave Student Loans
Hewlett-Packard
Loews Hotels Campaign: "TravelForReal", Communications, Digital, Media, OOH, Print
Lufthansa Travel Agent
Michelle Obama
NBA
The New York Genome Center Marketing
New York Yankees Online Baseball Information Provider
Rally Bus Digital, Mobile, Website
United Healthcare

CATCHFIRE
708 N 1st St Ste 131, Minneapolis, MN 55401
Tel.: (612) 455-8000
Web Site: www.catchfire.com

Year Founded: 2007

Agency Specializes In: Advertising, Content, Event Planning & Marketing, Logo & Package Design, Media Planning, Outdoor, Promotions, Radio

Jason Mihalakis *(Pres)*
Drew Schulthess *(Partner & Dir-Strategy)*
Grace Bettino *(Dir-Art)*
Gregory Simmons *(Mgr-Bus Dev)*
Ryan Seaman *(Designer)*

Accounts:
Nature Valley

THE CAUSEWAY AGENCY
21 Charles St Ste 201, Westport, CT 06880
Tel.: (203) 454-2100
Fax: (203) 341-8553
Web Site: www.thecausewayagency.com

Year Founded: 2008

Agency Specializes In: Advertising, Social Media, Strategic Planning/Research

Lisa Oppenheim *(Chm)*
Robert D. Schultz *(Pres)*
Joe Piazza *(Sr Dir-Art)*
Richard Effman *(Dir-Creative)*
Lyssa Seward *(Dir-Media)*

Accounts:
National Crime Prevention Council

CAVALRY AGENCY
233 N Michigan Ave, Chicago, IL 60601

Tel.: (312) 846-4500
E-Mail: contact@cavalryagency.com
Web Site: www.cavalryagency.com

Agency Specializes In: Above-the-Line, Advertising, Alternative Advertising, Broadcast, Cable T.V., Consumer Publications, Digital/Interactive, Electronic Media, Email, Guerilla Marketing, In-Store Advertising, Magazines, Media Planning, Mobile Marketing, Multimedia, Newspaper, Newspapers & Magazines, Out-of-Home Media, Outdoor, Paid Searches, Print, Production, Production (Print), RSS (Really Simple Syndication), Radio, Social Media, Sponsorship, T.V., Trade & Consumer Magazines, Viral/Buzz/Word of Mouth, Web (Banner Ads, Pop-ups, etc.)

Martin Stock *(CEO)*
Karl Turnbull *(Chief Strategy Officer)*
Jonathan Ozer *(VP & Creative Dir)*
Mike Czuba *(VP & Dir-Plng)*
Jennifer Gerwen *(VP & Dir-Mgmt)*
Thomas Hehir *(VP & Dir-Strategy)*
Andrew Holton *(VP & Dir-Creative)*
Mike D'Amico *(Assoc Dir-Creative)*
Megan Hood *(Acct Supvr)*
Stephanie Wrobel *(Copywriter)*
David McCradden *(Assoc Creative Dir)*

Accounts:
New-American Freedom Foundation
New-PepsiCo
Third Shift
New-Tyson Foods

THE CAVALRY COMPANY

15504 Adagio Ct, Los Angeles, CA 90077
Tel.: (310) 266-3530
Fax: (310) 472-1429
E-Mail: ken@cavalryco.com
Web Site: www.cavalryco.com

Employees: 10
Year Founded: 2002

Agency Specializes In: Print, Radio, T.V.

Kenneth Gal *(Pres & CEO)*
Karl Turnbull *(Chief Strategy Officer)*
Mike Czuba *(VP & Dir-Plng)*
Jennifer Gerwen *(VP & Dir-Mgmt)*
Andrew Holton *(VP & Dir-Creative)*
Jonathan Ozer *(VP & Dir-Creative)*
Kent Rademaker *(Acct Dir)*
Erica Graham *(Dir-Art)*
David McCradden *(Assoc Dir-Creative)*

Accounts:
Baja Fresh
Dynasis
MillerCoors Campaign: "Rocky Mountain Cold Refreshment", Coors Light, Creative, Digital, Keystone Light, Redd's Apple Ale, Smith & Forge, Third Shift

CAYENNE CREATIVE

2301 Morris Ave Ste 105, Birmingham, AL 35203-3322
Tel.: (205) 322-4422
Fax: (205) 322-4452
E-Mail: info@cayennecreative.com
Web Site: www.cayennecreative.com

Employees: 12
Year Founded: 2004

Agency Specializes In: Above-the-Line, Advertising, Affiliate Marketing, Alternative Advertising, Below-the-Line, Brand Development & Integration, Broadcast, Business Publications, Cable T.V., Catalogs, Collateral, College, Communications, Consulting, Consumer Goods, Consumer Marketing, Consumer Publications, Corporate Communications, Corporate Identity, Electronic Media, Email, Engineering, Environmental, Exhibit/Trade Shows, Graphic Design, Guerilla Marketing, Health Care Services, Industrial, Integrated Marketing, Internet/Web Design, Investor Relations, Leisure, Local Marketing, Logo & Package Design, Media Buying Services, Media Planning, Newspaper, Newspapers & Magazines, Out-of-Home Media, Outdoor, Over-50 Market, Package Design, Print, Production, Production (Ad, Film, Broadcast), Radio, Real Estate, Recruitment, Regional, Retail, Social Marketing/Nonprofit, Social Media, Sponsorship, Strategic Planning/Research, T.V., Technical Advertising, Trade & Consumer Magazines, Viral/Buzz/Word of Mouth, Web (Banner Ads, Pop-ups, etc.), Women's Market

Approx. Annual Billings: $3,000,000

Breakdown of Gross Billings by Media: Other: 15%; Outdoor: 10%; Print: 20%; Production: 25%; Radio: 30%

Dana Vague *(Dir-Art & Graphic Designer)*
William Boozer *(Dir-Interactive)*
Lyndale Smithson *(Dir-Media)*
Joy Mims *(Acct Supvr)*
Mary Frances Somerall *(Acct Supvr)*
Christina Helton *(Acct Exec)*
Aurrie Hicks *(Acct Exec)*
Catherine Farlow *(Copywriter)*
Alex Waymire *(Media Buyer)*
Hilliary Hallman *(Coord-Social Media)*

Accounts:
Alagasco; Birmingham, AL; 2009
Bayer Properties; Birmingham, AL; 2004
Birmingham Education Foundation
Oakworth Capital Bank; Birmingham, AL; 2008
Tandus; Dalton, GA; 2007
UAB Nursing; 2004

CBC ADVERTISING

56 Indsutrial Pk Rd Ste 103, Saco, ME 4072
Tel.: (800) 222-2682
Web Site: www.cbcads.com

Agency Specializes In: Advertising, Digital/Interactive, Graphic Design, Internet/Web Design, Media Buying Services, Print, Radio, Search Engine Optimization, Social Media, T.V.

Frank Dame *(Partner)*
Barry Morgan *(Partner)*
Matt Hayward *(Acct Exec)*
Greg Johnson *(Acct Exec)*
Bill Park *(Acct Exec)*
Joe Schena *(Acct Exec)*
Dana Snyder *(Acct Exec)*
Brian Watkinson *(Acct Exec)*

Accounts:
Chevrolet of Ozark
Formula Nissan
Gilland Ford
Kayser Nissan

CBK GROUP

(Name Changed to Troncone + Partners)

CCG MARKETING SOLUTIONS

14 Henderson Dr, West Caldwell, NJ 07006-6608
Tel.: (973) 808-0009
Fax: (973) 808-9740
Toll Free: (866) 902-2807
E-Mail: info@corpcomm.com
Web Site: home.corpcomm.com/

Employees: 150
Year Founded: 1964

Agency Specializes In: Advertising, Automotive, Brand Development & Integration, Broadcast, Business Publications, Business-To-Business, Cable T.V., Children's Market, Co-op Advertising, Collateral, Communications, Consumer Goods, Consumer Marketing, Consumer Publications, Corporate Communications, Corporate Identity, Cosmetics, Direct Response Marketing, Education, Entertainment, Event Planning & Marketing, Exhibit/Trade Shows, Financial, Graphic Design, Health Care Services, High Technology, Industrial, Integrated Marketing, Internet/Web Design, Investor Relations, Leisure, Local Marketing, Logo & Package Design, Magazines, Marine, Media Buying Services, Media Planning, Medical Products, Mobile Marketing, Multimedia, Newspaper, Newspapers & Magazines, Out-of-Home Media, Outdoor, Package Design, Pharmaceutical, Planning & Consultation, Point of Purchase, Point of Sale, Print, Production, Production (Print), Promotions, Public Relations, Publicity/Promotions, Radio, Real Estate, Recruitment, Retail, Sales Promotion, Search Engine Optimization, Seniors' Market, Social Marketing/Nonprofit, Sports Market, Strategic Planning/Research, Sweepstakes, T.V., Technical Advertising, Teen Market, Telemarketing, Trade & Consumer Magazines, Transportation, Travel & Tourism, Web (Banner Ads, Pop-ups, etc.)

Approx. Annual Billings: $94,010,000 (Capitalized)

Breakdown of Gross Billings by Media: Brdcst.: 5%; Bus. Publs.: 2%; Cable T.V.: 2%; Collateral: 10%; D.M.: 30%; Fees: 2%; Graphic Design: 3%; Newsp. & Mags.: 15%; Outdoor: 2%; Point of Purchase: 5%; Point of Sale: 1%; Print: 5%; Production: 1%; Promos.: 2%; Sls. Promo.: 3%; T.V.: 5%; Trade & Consumer Mags.: 5%; Transit: 2%

Simon Hooks *(Pres & CEO)*
Jeff Lawshe *(Sr VP & Gen Mgr)*
Toni Koenig *(VP-Client Svcs)*
Rick Walsh *(VP)*
Lori Musilli *(Client Svcs Dir)*

Accounts:
Beiersdorf Inc.
BMW

CCM MARKETING COMMUNICATIONS

11 E 47th St Fl 3, New York, NY 10017-7916
Tel.: (212) 689-8225
Fax: (212) 889-7388
E-Mail: inquire@ccmthinkimpact.com
Web Site: ccmthinkimpact.com/

Employees: 18
Year Founded: 1978

National Agency Associations: DMA-PMA

Agency Specializes In: Advertising, Brand Development & Integration, Business-To-Business, Children's Market, Communications, Consulting, Consumer Marketing, Consumer Publications, Cosmetics, Digital/Interactive, Direct Response Marketing, Education, Electronic Media, Event Planning & Marketing, Financial, Graphic Design, Health Care Services, Logo & Package Design, Merchandising, Planning & Consultation, Point of Purchase, Point of Sale, Print, Publicity/Promotions, Radio, Restaurant, Retail, Sales Promotion, Sports Market, Strategic Planning/Research, Sweepstakes, Teen Market, Travel & Tourism

Approx. Annual Billings: $7,000,000

Breakdown of Gross Billings by Media: Collateral:

$2,100,000; D.M.: $2,100,000; Event Mktg.: $700,000; Mags.: $700,000; Newsp.: $700,000; Radio: $700,000

Michael Chadwick *(Pres)*
Steve Polachi *(Partner)*

Accounts:
American Beverage Company; Verona, PA Wine & Spirits; 2000
New York Marriott; New York, NY Hospitality; 2001
Panos Brands
Sazerac; New Orleans, LA Wines & Spirits; 2001
St. Francis Hospital; Roslyn, NY Health Care; 2000
Sunburst Properties; Allentown, PA Real Estate; 1995

CD&M COMMUNICATIONS

48 Free St, Portland, ME 04101
Tel.: (207) 774-7528
Fax: (207) 772-3788
E-Mail: info@cdmc.com
Web Site: www.cdmc.com/

Employees: 20
Year Founded: 1978

Agency Specializes In: Brand Development & Integration, Broadcast, Business-To-Business, Collateral, Communications, Consumer Marketing, Corporate Identity, Direct Response Marketing, Education, Entertainment, Environmental, Event Planning & Marketing, Financial, Food Service, Government/Political, Graphic Design, Health Care Services, High Technology, Internet/Web Design, Legal Services, Leisure, Logo & Package Design, Media Buying Services, Medical Products, Merchandising, New Product Development, Out-of-Home Media, Point of Purchase, Point of Sale, Print, Production, Public Relations, Radio, Real Estate, Recruitment, Retail, Seniors' Market, Sports Market, Strategic Planning/Research, T.V., Transportation, Travel & Tourism

Bob Cott *(Pres)*
Duncan Stout *(Partner & Acct Dir)*
Ken Krauss *(Partner & Dir-Creative)*
Linda Wagner Jones *(Controller)*
Linda Spring *(Sr Dir-Art)*
Mike Yoder *(Sr Dir-Art)*
Stacy Johnson *(Dir-Media)*
Julie Reynolds *(Mgr-Production)*
Sayre English *(Acct Exec)*
David Page *(Acct Exec)*
Deb Roy *(Designer-Production)*

Accounts:
American Lung Association of New England
The Baker Company
DiMillo's Floating Restaurant
New England Coffee
Rynel, Inc. & Grow-Tech, Inc.
Shipyard Brewing Company
York Spiral Stairs

CDHM ADVERTISING

1100 Summer St 1st Fl, Stamford, CT 06905
Tel.: (203) 967-7200
Fax: (203) 967-2620
E-Mail: sumple@cdhm.com
Web Site: www.cdhm.com

E-Mail for Key Personnel:
Creative Dir.: walker@cdhm.com
Media Dir.: sumple@cdhm.com
Production Mgr.: walker@cdhm.com

Employees: 15
Year Founded: 1964

National Agency Associations: 4A's-ABC-BPA

Agency Specializes In: Brand Development & Integration, Broadcast, Business Publications, Business-To-Business, Cable T.V., Collateral, Communications, Consulting, Consumer Marketing, Consumer Publications, Corporate Identity, Direct Response Marketing, E-Commerce, Education, Electronic Media, Financial, Food Service, Graphic Design, Health Care Services, High Technology, Internet/Web Design, Magazines, Media Buying Services, Medical Products, Newspaper, Newspapers & Magazines, Out-of-Home Media, Outdoor, Pharmaceutical, Point of Purchase, Point of Sale, Print, Production, Public Relations, Radio, Retail, Sales Promotion, Strategic Planning/Research, Sweepstakes, T.V., Technical Advertising, Trade & Consumer Magazines, Travel & Tourism, Yellow Pages Advertising

Approx. Annual Billings: $10,000,000

Breakdown of Gross Billings by Media: Bus. Publs.: 5%; D.M.: 5%; Mags.: 10%; Newsp.: 20%; Outdoor: 10%; Point of Purchase: 20%; Radio: 10%; T.V.: 20%

Gary W. Sumple *(Mng Partner)*
John E. Walker *(Mng Partner)*
Maria Basile *(Dir-Art)*
Dana Markiewicz *(Acct Mgr)*
Maureen Johnson *(Mgr-New Bus Dev)*
Don Vega *(Sr Acct Exec & Sr Media Planner)*

Accounts:
Fairfield University
Naugatuck Savings Bank; Naugatuck, CT Brand Awareness
Wal-Mart Digital Photo Centers

CDK DIGITAL MARKETING

(Formerly Cobalt)
605 Fifth Ave S Ste 800, Seattle, WA 98104
Fax: (206) 269-6350
Toll Free: (800) 909-8244
Web Site: www.cdkglobaldigitalmarketing.com/

Agency Specializes In: Advertising, Digital/Interactive

Steven J. Anenen *(Pres & CEO)*
Alfred A. Nietzel *(CFO)*
Linda Bartman *(CMO-Global)*
Robert N. Karp *(Pres-Retail Solutions-North America)*
Tim Russell *(Sr Dir-Global Diversity & Inclusion)*
Ayana Jordan *(Reg Dir-Adv)*
Dana Fornasar *(Sr Mgr-Product Mktg)*
Brian Brown *(Mgr-Mktg & Product-Cobalt & HHR)*

Accounts:
Antelope Valley Volkswagen Car Dealers
Jerry Seiner Dealer Group Car Dealers
Paddock Chevrolet Car Dealers
Rohrich Lexus Car Dealers

THE CDM GROUP

(Formerly Cline, Davis & Mann, Inc.)
200 Varick St 2nd Fl, New York, NY 10014
Tel.: (212) 907-4300
Fax: (212) 557-7240
Web Site: www.thecdmgroup.com

Employees: 950
Year Founded: 1984

Agency Specializes In: Health Care Services, Medical Products, Pharmaceutical, Sponsorship

Ed Wise *(Chm & CEO)*
Joshua Prince *(Pres)*
Stephen Russell *(Mng Partner & CFO)*
Phillip Roselin *(Mng Partner & Chief Bus Dev Officer)*
Lori Klein *(Mng Partner & Client Svcs Dir)*
Carolyn Bartholdson *(Chief HR Officer)*
Terry Walsh *(Sr VP & Dir-Traffic)*
Meredith Kennedy *(Sr VP & Grp Creative Dir)*
Sartaj Ajrawat *(Assoc Dir)*
Alexandra Litzman *(Acct Supvr)*
Allie Quinlan *(Acct Supvr)*

Accounts:
Abbott
Amgen ABU Franchise, AMG 162, Anemia Counts, Aranesp CRI, Aranesp HCV, Denosumab, Epogen, Sensipar/Mimpara
Bayer Healthcare Bayer Healthcare Animal Health, Bayer Healthcare Consumer Care, Bayer Healthcare Medical Care, Bayer Schering Pharma, Consumer Communications, Digital, Global Marketing Services, Medical Education, Professional Communications, Public Relations
Bristol-Myers Squibb Abilify, Creative
Genentech Genentech Value Based Healthcare, Lucentis, NHL, Raptiva, Rituxan
Genentech/Novartis Xolair
Genomic Health
GlaxoSmithKline
Merck Serono
Novartis Elidel, Indacaterol, TOBI
NovoNordisk Activella, FlexPen, Levemir, Norditropin, NovoLog, NovoLog Mix 70/30, NovoSeven, Vagifem
PhRMA Partnership for Prescription Assistance
Schering-Plough Asmanex
Schering-Plough/Novartis MFF
Shire
Valeant Viramidine

Branches

CDM West

10960 Wilshire Blvd Ste 1750, Los Angeles, CA 90024
Tel.: (212) 907-6919
Fax: (310) 444-7041
E-Mail: jlymburner@cdmworldagency.com
Web Site: www.cdmworldagency.com

Employees: 20
Year Founded: 2003

Eric Romoli *(Owner)*
Ed Wise *(Chm & CEO)*
Christopher Palmer *(Mng Partner & Exec Dir-Creative)*
Mark De Szentmiklosy *(Mng Dir)*
Ignazio Iasiello *(Mng Dir)*
Josh Prince *(Chief Creative Officer)*
Xavier Vidal *(Gen Dir)*

Accounts:
Amgen; Thousand Oaks, CA Aranesp HCV, Aranesp US CRI

CDMiConnect

200 Varick St, New York, NY 10014
Tel.: (212) 798-4400
Fax: (212) 209-7088
E-Mail: debbied@cdmiconnect.com
Web Site: www.cdmiconnect.com

Employees: 130
Year Founded: 2000

National Agency Associations: 4A's

Agency Specializes In: Business-To-Business, Consumer Marketing, Digital/Interactive, Direct Response Marketing, Health Care Services, Sponsorship

Dina Peck *(Mng Partner & Exec Dir-Creative)*
Eliot Tyler *(Mng Partner)*
Melissa Schwartz *(Sr VP & Acct Planner)*

Joanna Hass *(VP & Acct Dir)*
Sloane Markman *(VP & Acct Dir)*
Jeannine Scalcione *(VP & Acct Dir)*
Elizabeth Hess *(VP-Grp Acct Supvr)*
Jennifer Ohlberg *(VP & Grp Acct Supvr)*
Brian Autenrieth *(Acct Supvr)*
Suzanne Marino *(Acct Supvr-Digital)*
Meg Sullivan *(Acct Supvr)*

Accounts:
AcipHex
Amgen Aranesp Canada, Aranesp HCV, Aranesp Oncology EU, Sensipar
Boehringer Ingelheim Spiriva
Boston Scientific Enteryx
Pfizer, Inc. U.S. Pharmaceuticals Group
Benefocus, Caduet, Customer Marketing Group, Depo Medrol, Depo Provera, Diflucan, Health Literacy, Lipitor, Neurontin, Norvasc, Relpax, Sales Training, Share Card, Vfend, Viagra, Women's Health, Zithromax, Zyvox
Quest Diagnostics Campaign: "Faces of Celiac"
Rubbermaid Medical Solutions
Solvay Pharmaceuticals Rowasa

Cline, Davis & Mann, Inc.
210 Carnegie Ctr Ste 200, Princeton, NJ 08540-6226
Tel.: (609) 936-5600
Fax: (609) 275-5060
E-Mail: kyleb@clinedavis.com
Web Site: www.clinedavis.com

Employees: 100

National Agency Associations: 4A's

Agency Specializes In: Pharmaceutical

Chris Palmer *(Mng Partner & Exec Dir-Creative)*
Cara Morgan *(Sr VP & Mgmt Supvr)*
Joseph Barbagallo *(Sr VP & Dir-MSA Collaboration)*
Paul Chang *(VP & Dir-Medical)*
Amy Mozlin *(VP & Assoc Dir-Medical)*
Samiah Zafar *(VP & Assoc Dir-Medical)*
Dominic Orologio *(VP & Grp Supvr-Art)*
Chris Fiocco *(Assoc Partner & Dir-Acct Plng)*
Natasha Desai *(Sr Acct Exec)*
Jaclyn Lavine *(Coord-Bus Dev)*

Accounts:
CDM World Agency
Merck
Novo Nordisk
Pfizer

CEA MARKETING GROUP
2233 Nursery Rd, Clearwater, FL 33764
Tel.: (727) 523-8044
Fax: (727) 524-6552
Toll Free: (877) 669-6630
E-Mail: info@ceamarketing.com
Web Site: www.ceamarketing.com

Employees: 10

Agency Specializes In: Real Estate

Kelly Bosetti *(CEO)*
Eric Gwatney *(Dir-Art)*
Dave Dubreuil *(Acct Mgr)*
Jennifer Mcpherson *(Office Mgr)*
Erika Stanley *(Acct Mgr-Interactive)*

Accounts:
ClearWater
Derby Darlins
Hilton Worldwide
Leadership Pinellas
Pulte Homes
TBBA

CELTIC, INC.
330 S Executive Dr Ste 206, Brookfield, WI 53005-4215
Tel.: (262) 789-7630
Fax: (262) 789-9454
E-Mail: outwork@celticinc.com
Web Site: www.celticinc.com

Agency Specializes In: Advertising, Advertising Specialties, Brand Development & Integration, Broadcast, Business-To-Business, Collateral, Communications, Consumer Goods, Consumer Marketing, Corporate Communications, Corporate Identity, Crisis Communications, Direct Response Marketing, Education, Event Planning & Marketing, Exhibit/Trade Shows, Experience Design, Financial, Graphic Design, Guerilla Marketing, Identity Marketing, In-Store Advertising, Integrated Marketing, Internet/Web Design, Investor Relations, Logo & Package Design, Media Buying Services, Media Planning, Media Relations, Out-of-Home Media, Package Design, Point of Purchase, Point of Sale, Print, Product Placement, Production, Production (Print), Promotions, Public Relations, Publicity/Promotions, Sponsorship, Strategic Planning/Research, Travel & Tourism

Brian Meehan *(Owner & Pres)*
Kurt Lingel *(Partner & Exec VP)*
Megan Fulsher *(Jr Art Dir-Creative)*
Sandi Speranza *(Dir-Media & Sr Acct Exec)*
Kristin Paltzer *(Sr Acct Exec-PR)*
Meghan Boyle *(Acct Exec)*
Liz Casper *(Media Buyer)*
Chelsey Knutson *(Asst Acct Exec-PR)*

Accounts:
Alto-Shaam Advertising, Media Planning, Public Relations, Social Media
Bemis Manufacturing
Brocach Irish Pub
Bucyrus International; South Milwaukee, WI
Coleman Repellants
EDVEST 529 College Savings Plan
Eric Buell Racing
Grand Trunk
Johnson Health Tech Fitness Equipment
Kohler Company Engines & Generators
Lake Consumer Products Beyond Fresh Intimates, Me Again, Persani, Pre Conceive Plus, Vagi Gard, Yeast Gard
Lake Geneva CVB
MillerCoors Visitor Center; 2008
Rite-Hite Revolutionary Fan; 2008
Tippmann Sports; Fort Wayne, IN Paint Ball Products

CELTIC MARKETING, INC.
6311 W Gross Point Rd, Niles, IL 60714
Tel.: (847) 647-7500
Fax: (847) 647-8940
E-Mail: marleneb@celticchicago.com
Web Site: www.celticchicago.com

Employees: 15
Year Founded: 1992

National Agency Associations: AMA-BMA-PRSA

Agency Specializes In: Advertising, Brand Development & Integration, Business-To-Business, Consumer Marketing, Direct Response Marketing, Event Planning & Marketing, Internet/Web Design, Media Buying Services, Outdoor, Point of Purchase, Print, Public Relations, Publicity/Promotions, Radio, Strategic Planning/Research, T.V., Trade & Consumer Magazines

Approx. Annual Billings: $2,500,000

Breakdown of Gross Billings by Media: Brdcst.: $350,000; Collateral: $850,000; D.M.: $400,000; Event Mktg.: $200,000; Newsp.: $300,000; Pub. Rels.: $300,000; Worldwide Web Sites: $100,000

Jim Heitzman *(VP-Adv)*
Blair Ciecko *(Dir-PR & Social Media)*
Chris Gattorna *(Dir-Art-Creative Svcs)*
Kurt Maloy *(Dir-Creative)*
Jean Tumbaga *(Dir-Art)*
Jeremy Hogan *(Sr Mgr-PR & Digital Content)*
Robin Doubek *(Office Mgr)*
Christopher Lehr *(Acct Mgr-Client Svcs)*
Emily Burch *(Project Mgr & Media Buyer)*
Monica Zachacki *(Mgr-Acctg & HR)*
Stacey Nussbaum *(Acct Exec-Association)*
Sean Whaley *(Designer-Web-Digital Svcs)*

Accounts:
ADP CRM
ATO Findley Inc
Bell Fuels; Chicago, IL
Eastcastle Place; Milwaukee, WI
Newcastle Place; Mequon, WI

THE CEMENTWORKS, LLC
(d/b/a The CementBloc)
641 Sixth Ave 5th Fl, New York, NY 10011
Tel.: (212) 524-6200
Fax: (212) 524-6299
E-Mail: info@thecementbloc.com
Web Site: www.thebloc.com

Employees: 140
Year Founded: 2000

Agency Specializes In: Medical Products, Pharmaceutical, Sponsorship

Approx. Annual Billings: $70,000,000

Breakdown of Gross Billings by Media: Adv. Specialities: 100%

Rico Viray *(Founder, Owner & Partner)*
Susan Miller *(Founder & Partner)*
Jennifer Matthews *(Mng Partner)*
Andrea Bast *(Partner)*
Elizabeth Elfenbein *(Partner-Creative)*
Jennifer Labus *(Exec VP & Client Svcs Dir)*
Katie Isaacs *(Sr VP & Grp Acct Dir)*
Julie Yoon *(Sr VP & Grp Acct Dir)*
Britt Till *(Sr VP & Dir-Art & Creative)*
Liane Reid *(VP & Acct Dir)*
Marc Law *(VP & Assoc Dir-Creative-Art)*

Accounts:
Bristol Myers Squibb
Celgene Pledgetofightforward.com
Feverall
Genteal
Imitrex
Novartis Vaccines Campaign: "Meningitis.com"
Prezista
Spiriva
UCB Cimzia

CENTER MASS MEDIA
12760 Stroh Ranch Way #206, Parker, CO 80134
Tel.: (720) 336-9266
E-Mail: info@centermassmedia.com
Web Site: centermassmedia.com

Employees: 12
Year Founded: 2012

Agency Specializes In: Advertising, Brand Development & Integration, Business-To-Business, Collateral, Commercial Photography, Computers & Software, Consulting, Content, Corporate Identity, Customer Relationship Management, E-Commerce, Email, Event Planning & Marketing, Exhibit/Trade Shows, Graphic Design, Identity

Marketing, Internet/Web Design, Local Marketing, Logo & Package Design, Mobile Marketing, New Product Development, Package Design, Paid Searches, Production (Ad, Film, Broadcast), Public Relations, Publicity/Promotions, Search Engine Optimization, Social Marketing/Nonprofit, Social Media, Strategic Planning/Research, Viral/Buzz/Word of Mouth, Web (Banner Ads, Pop-ups, etc.)

Approx. Annual Billings: $500,000

John Ramsay *(CEO)*
Sarah Bonds *(Mgr-Office)*

Accounts:
St Jude's Hospital

CENTIGRADE INTERNATIONAL LTD.
135 N Old Woodward, Birmingham, MI 48009
Tel.: (248) 430-8010
Fax: (248) 430-8020
E-Mail: soon.nguyen@centigrade.com
Web Site: www.centigrade.com

Employees: 6

Agency Specializes In: Brand Development & Integration, Communications, Media Relations, Strategic Planning/Research

Frits Hoogsteden *(Client Svcs Dir)*
Brian Kotulis *(Dir-Art)*
Christine Chase *(Sr Acct Mgr)*
Ben Leininger *(Mgr-Program)*
Blake Roller *(Mgr-IS)*
Ian Whilden *(Mgr-Enterprise Tech)*
Hilary Waks *(Sr Acct Exec)*

Branch

Centigrade
33 Cavendish Square, W1G 0PW London, GB United Kingdom
Tel.: (44) 203 384 5571
Web Site: www.centigrade.com

Agency Specializes In: Advertising, Communications, Customer Relationship Management, Digital/Interactive, Event Planning & Marketing, Public Relations, Strategic Planning/Research

Nick Matthews *(Chm & Joint CEO)*
Julie Barnard *(Vice Chm & Joint CEO)*
Soon Hagerty *(Mng Partner)*
Barry Reading *(Mng Dir-Europe)*
Leen Schodts *(Client Svcs Dir)*
Kevin O'Neill *(Strategist-Mktg)*

Accounts:
Breitling Watch Developer & Retailer

CENTRAL COAST AGENCY
20 N Wacker Dr Ste 3330, Chicago, IL 60606
Tel.: (312) 999-0204
E-Mail: talk.to.us@centralcoastagency.com
Web Site: www.centralcoastagency.com

Agency Specializes In: Advertising, Brand Development & Integration, Content, Digital/Interactive

Erin Heraty *(Jr Copywriter)*

Accounts:
NTT Communications Corporation

CENTURION STRATEGIES LLC
2202 N W Shore Blvd Ste 200, Tampa, FL 33607
Tel.: (813) 732-0180
Web Site: www.centurion-strategies.com

Year Founded: 2008

Agency Specializes In: Advertising, Brand Development & Integration, Business Publications, Crisis Communications, Digital/Interactive, Graphic Design, Public Relations

Michael Bilello *(Founder, Pres & CEO)*
Amy Bilello *(VP-Adv)*
Lauren Renschler *(Sr Dir-Sports & Entertainment)*
Kristina Andersen *(Dir-PR-Sports & Entertainment)*
Kirk Morrison *(Dir-Bus Dev)*

Accounts:
Cable News Network News Television Network Services
Calais Campbell
ESPN Internet Ventures Sports Television Channel
FOX News Network LLC. News Television Network Services
Identity Stronghold; Englewood, FL
Mike Richards
MSNBC Interactive News LLC News Television Network Services

CERCONE BROWN CURTIS
77 N Washington St Ste 304, Boston, MA 02114-1913
Tel.: (617) 248-0680
Fax: (617) 248-0688
E-Mail: info@cerconebrown.com
Web Site: www.cerconebrown.com

Employees: 20
Year Founded: 2001

Agency Specializes In: Advertising, Brand Development & Integration, Communications, Event Planning & Marketing, Public Relations

Approx. Annual Billings: $15,000,000

Erika Brown *(Founder & Partner)*
Leonard Cercone *(Partner)*
Caroline Budney *(Acct Dir)*
Noelle Guerin *(Acct Dir)*
Sarah Murphy *(Acct Supvr)*
Gina Uttaro *(Strategist-Digital Mktg)*

Accounts:
GMAC Insurance

CERTAINSOURCE
(Formerly eWayDirect Inc.)
338 Commerce Dr 2nd Fl, Fairfield, CT 06825
Tel.: (203) 254-0404
Fax: (203) 254-0411
Toll Free: (888) 655-0464
Web Site: www.certainsource.com/

Agency Specializes In: Brand Development & Integration, Customer Relationship Management, Sales Promotion, Web (Banner Ads, Pop-ups, etc.)

Neil Rosen *(Mng Partner)*
Patricia Wilson *(VP-Customer Support)*

Accounts:
Carolina Web Consultants
Dydacomp
Fathead

CESARI DIRECT, INC.
221 First Ave W Ste 350, Seattle, WA 98119
Tel.: (206) 281-7975
Web Site: www.cesaridirect.com

Year Founded: 1993

Agency Specializes In: Advertising, Brand Development & Integration, Digital/Interactive, Internet/Web Design, Media Buying Services, Print, Radio, Social Media, T.V.

Rick Cesari *(Founder Partner & CEO)*
Michelle Short *(Dir-Short Form Media)*
Bev Thompson *(Media Buyer-Natl Cable)*
Michelle Weller *(Media Buyer-Long Form)*

Accounts:
Beachbody, LLC
Carmd Com, Corp.
Con Air
The Fuller Brush Company
Hurom
Nuvo H2o
Oxy Water
Rug Doctor, LP
S.C. Johnson & Son, Inc.
Seabridge Bathing
Silk'n
Thompson Creek Window Company
Woodman Labs Inc.

C.FOX COMMUNICATIONS
7201 Wisconsin Ave Ste 780, Bethesda, MD 20814
Tel.: (301) 585-5034
Fax: (301) 585-5039
E-Mail: info@cfoxcommunications.com
Web Site: www.cfoxcommunications.com

Year Founded: 2004

Agency Specializes In: Brand Development & Integration, Collateral, Event Planning & Marketing, Media Relations, Strategic Planning/Research, Viral/Buzz/Word of Mouth

Carrie Fox *(Pres)*
Brian Fox *(Mng Dir)*
Bethany Hardy *(Sr VP)*
Sara Neumann *(Asst VP)*

Accounts:
The Duke Ellington School of the Arts
UniteHealth Group
vivabox

CFX INC
3221 Oak Hill Ave, Saint Louis, MO 63116
Tel.: (314) 773-5300
Web Site: www.cfx-inc.com

Year Founded: 2001

Agency Specializes In: Advertising, Brand Development & Integration, Collateral, Corporate Identity, Graphic Design, Internet/Web Design, Logo & Package Design, Search Engine Optimization

Megan Frank *(Owner & Exec VP-Creative)*
Jason Becker *(Dir-Art)*
Amy Kohlbecker *(Dir-Ops)*
Brian Gomski *(Strategist-Digital)*
Carla Chitwood *(Acct Coord)*

Accounts:
Luxco Inc

CGR CREATIVE
1930 Abbott St Ste 304, Charlotte, NC 28203
Tel.: (704) 334-2232
E-Mail: results@cgrcreative.com
Web Site: www.cgrcreative.com

Agency Specializes In: Advertising,

Digital/Interactive, Graphic Design, Internet/Web Design, Media Buying Services, Multimedia, Radio, Search Engine Optimization, Social Media

Julio Colmenares *(Pres & CEO)*

Accounts:
Logical Advantage
Salsaritas Fresh Cantina

CGT MARKETING LLC
275-B Dixon Ave, Amityville, NY 11701
Tel.: (631) 842-4600
Fax: (631) 842-6301
E-Mail: info@cgtmarketing.com
Web Site: cgtmarketing.com

Employees: 12
Year Founded: 1987

Agency Specializes In: Advertising, Brand Development & Integration, Business Publications, Business-To-Business, Catalogs, Collateral, College, Commercial Photography, Communications, Consumer Marketing, Consumer Publications, Corporate Communications, Corporate Identity, Digital/Interactive, Direct Response Marketing, Direct-to-Consumer, E-Commerce, Electronic Media, Electronics, Email, Engineering, Event Planning & Marketing, Exhibit/Trade Shows, Graphic Design, Health Care Services, High Technology, Household Goods, Identity Marketing, In-Store Advertising, Industrial, Integrated Marketing, Internet/Web Design, Local Marketing, Logo & Package Design, Magazines, Medical Products, Multimedia, New Product Development, New Technologies, Newspaper, Newspapers & Magazines, Outdoor, Over-50 Market, Package Design, Paid Searches, Pharmaceutical, Planning & Consultation, Point of Purchase, Point of Sale, Print, Production, Production (Ad, Film, Broadcast), Promotions, Public Relations, Publicity/Promotions, Sales Promotion, Search Engine Optimization, Social Marketing/Nonprofit, Strategic Planning/Research, Technical Advertising, Trade & Consumer Magazines, Web (Banner Ads, Pop-ups, etc.)

Approx. Annual Billings: $8,000,000

Breakdown of Gross Billings by Media: Collateral: $1,000,000; Consulting: $400,000; D.M.: $400,000; E-Commerce: $700,000; Exhibits/Trade Shows: $200,000; Graphic Design: $1,000,000; Logo & Package Design: $500,000; Plng. & Consultation: $300,000; Trade & Consumer Mags.: $3,000,000; Worldwide Web Sites: $500,000

Mitch Tobol *(Co-Founder & Partner)*
Fred Candiotti *(Partner & Dir-Creative)*
Vincent Grucci *(Partner)*
William Lang *(Assoc Dir-Creative)*
Donna Munnelly *(Mgr-Production)*
Susan Brenman *(Acct Exec)*

Accounts:
Amann Girrbach
American Aerospace Controls
H.A. Guden
Lee Spring
Life's WORC
Nanomotion
North Atlantic Instruments
Northfield Precision Instruments
PICO Electronics
Precision Punch Corp.
US Dynamics

CHANA & ASSOCIATES
475 Springfield Ave, Summit, NJ 07901
Tel.: (646) 710-4454
Toll Free: (800) 340-3467

Year Founded: 1988

Agency Specializes In: Advertising

Approx. Annual Billings: $400,000

Breakdown of Gross Billings by Media: Copywriting: $200,000; Point of Purchase: $100,000; Programmatic: $50,000; Sponsorship: $50,000

Amy Aberson *(Brand Mgr-China (Activation))*
Vanessa Adams *(Coord-Corporate Social Responsibility)*

Accounts:
A Hatter's Paradise
Able & Jenkins
The Anderson Co.
Dynamic Management & Testing; New Providence, NJ Management Consulting
Elaine's House of Glass
Evans & Smith Mogo; Detroit, MI
McGrath's Hardware Home Improvement Products, Tools
Silver Hanger Cleaners
Thompson & Jillips Watches Thompson Timepieces
Toni Roma's Pizza & Salads
Victory Violin Musical Instruments

CHANDELIER
611 Broadway Ph, New York, NY 10012
Tel.: (212) 620-5252
Fax: (212) 620-5329
E-Mail: concierge@chandeliercreative.com
Web Site: www.chandeliercreative.com

Employees: 23

Agency Specializes In: Advertising, Sponsorship

Richard Christiansen *(Founder & Dir-Creative)*
Marshall Bower *(Art Dir)*
Eileen Eastburn *(Acct Dir)*
Zan Goodman *(Dir-Design)*
Kim Ho *(Dir-Art)*
Michael Scanlon *(Assoc Creative Dir)*
Matt Goldman *(Copywriter)*
Brad Hall *(Copywriter)*
Laura Kraftt *(Copywriter)*
Josh Meyers *(Copywriter)*
Patty Wortham *(Copywriter)*
Susan Credle *(Assoc Creative Dir)*

Accounts:
David Jones Creative, TV
Gap Inc
New-Hallmark Licensing, LLC #KeepsakeIt VEGAN CHRISTMAS
New-Harry's
Old Navy Boyfriend Jeans, Broadcast, Campaign: "Art Is Dead. Jeans Are Alive.", Campaign: "Job Interview", Campaign: "Kids Table", Campaign: "Meet the Pixie Pant", Campaign: "No Reservations (About These Coats)", Campaign: "Snoopin' Around", Campaign: "Spell Me This", Campaign: "Spring 2014", Campaign: "Unlimited", Digital, In-Store, Online, Social, TV, Video
Target & TOMS Campaign: "One for One for All"
Target Digital Creative, Online, Print, TV

CHANDLER CHICCO AGENCY
450 W 15th St 7th Fl, New York, NY 10011
Tel.: (212) 229-8400
Fax: (212) 229-8496
E-Mail: contact@ccapr.com
Web Site: www.ccapr.com

Employees: 130

Year Founded: 1995

National Agency Associations: COPF

Agency Specializes In: Collateral, Corporate Communications, Health Care Services, Logo & Package Design, New Product Development, Pharmaceutical, Public Relations, Sponsorship

Approx. Annual Billings: $25,714,700

Lisa Stockman *(Pres-PR & Medical Comm)*
Kristen Spensieri *(Head-Corp Comm & Mktg-Global)*

Accounts:
Allergan, Inc. Cervical Dystonia Awareness Campaign
Bayer Diagnostics
Bristol-Myers Squibb
Genentech
GlaxoSmithKline
Johnson & Johnson
Mylan Specialty
Novartis
Novo Nordisk
Olympus
Pfizer
Roche

Branches

Chamberlain Healthcare Public Relations
450 W 15th St Ste 405, New York, NY 10011
(See Separate Listing)

Chandler Chicco Agency-London
151 Shaftesbury Ave, Covent Garden, London, WC2H 8AL United Kingdom
Tel.: (44) 20 76321800
Fax: (44) 2076321801
E-Mail: contact@ccapr.com
Web Site: www.ccapr.com

Employees: 75

Julie Adrian *(Mng Dir)*

Accounts:
Abbott
Agouron
Allergan Botox
Amgen
AstraZeneca Casodex, Crestor
Bayer Diagnostics
Bayer Pharmaceuticals
Novartis
Pfizer
UCB Pharma

Chandler Chicco Agency-Los Angeles
1315 Lincoln Blvd Ste 270, Santa Monica, CA 90401
Tel.: (310) 309-1000
Fax: (310) 309-1050
E-Mail: contact@ccapr.com
Web Site: www.ccapr.com

Employees: 27

National Agency Associations: COPF

Agency Specializes In: Sponsorship

Julie Adrian *(Mng Dir)*
Edie Elkinson *(Specialist-Media)*

Chandler Chicco Agency-Washington
500 New Jersey Ave Ste 850, Washington, DC 20001
Tel.: (202) 609-6000

Fax: (202) 609-6001
E-Mail: info@ccapr.com
Web Site: www.ccapr.com

Employees: 17

Heather Gartman *(Mng Dir)*
Melissa Warren *(Acct Mgr)*

Accounts:
Abbott
Allergan
Amgen
EMD
Genentech
GlaxoSmithKline

CHANNEL ISLANDS DESIGN

3401 W 5th St, Oxnard, CA 93030
Tel.: (805) 382-4243
Fax: (805) 382-4216
E-Mail: sales@cid4design.com
Web Site: www.cid.cc/index.php

Employees: 2

Agency Specializes In: Advertising

Robert Gray *(Owner)*
Neal Fisch *(Dir-Enterprise Svcs & Security)*
Peter Mosinskis *(Dir-IT Strategy)*
Hjohn Aquino *(Mgr-IT Infrastructure)*

Accounts:
Classic Guitars International
Fabricmate

CHAPMAN CUBINE ADAMS + HUSSEY

2000 15th St N Ste 550, Arlington, VA 22201
Tel.: (703) 248-0025
Fax: (703) 248-0029
Web Site: www.ccah.com

Agency Specializes In: Advertising, Digital/Interactive, Internet/Web Design

Jim Hussey *(Co-Founder & Chm)*
Kim Cubine *(Pres)*
Lon-Given Chapman *(Principal & Exec VP)*
Jenny Allen *(Principal & Sr VP)*
Pete Carter *(Principal & Sr VP)*
Shannon Murphy *(Principal & Sr VP-Production)*
John Wanda *(Principal & VP-Fin)*
Greg Adams *(Principal)*

Accounts:
Mothers Against Drunk Driving (MADD)

CHAPPELLROBERTS

1600 E 8th Ave Ste A-133, Tampa, FL 33605
Tel.: (813) 281-0088
Fax: (813) 281-0271
E-Mail: info@chappellroberts.com
Web Site: www.chappellroberts.com

Employees: 27

National Agency Associations: 4A's

Agency Specializes In: Communications, Public Relations, Sponsorship

Colleen F. Chappell *(Pres & CEO)*
Sarah Tildsley *(Principal & Dir-Creative)*
Patrick Owings *(Principal-Acct Svcs)*
Christine Turner *(Principal)*
Scott Gattis *(Sr Dir-Acct Strategy)*
Matthew Christ *(Dir-Media)*
Glenn Horn *(Assoc Dir-Creative)*
Heather Jennings *(Mgr-Production)*
Kat Romanowski *(Acct Exec)*
Maritza Ochoa *(Asst Acct Exec-Res)*
Kambria Sims *(Asst Acct Exec)*
Kelley Volenec *(Asst Acct Exec)*

Accounts:
Mosaic
PSCU Financial Services Branding
PSCU Financial Services Debit
Sarasota Conventions & Visitors Bureau Branding Campaign, Television
Suncoast Hospice Owen
Tampa Bay Buccaneers (Agency of Record)
Tampa Bay Water
University of South Florida
Verizon Communications Inc.
Verizon Wireless

THE CHAPTER MEDIA

(Formerly JTP FIFTH Column)
421 7th Ave, New York, NY 10001
Tel.: (212) 695-1335
Fax: (646) 688-6880
Web Site: www.thechaptermedia.com

Employees: 10
Year Founded: 2005

Agency Specializes In: Advertising, Advertising Specialties, Alternative Advertising, Arts, Brand Development & Integration, Branded Entertainment, Broadcast, Cable T.V., Collateral, Commercial Photography, Communications, Content, Corporate Identity, Electronic Media, Email, Experience Design, Fashion/Apparel, Game Integration, Gay & Lesbian Market, Graphic Design, Guerilla Marketing, High Technology, Identity Marketing, In-Store Advertising, Information Technology, Integrated Marketing, Internet/Web Design, Local Marketing, Media Buying Services, Media Relations, Men's Market, Multimedia, New Technologies, Paid Searches, Podcasting, Production, Production (Ad, Film, Broadcast), Promotions, Publicity/Promotions, Search Engine Optimization, T.V., Teen Market, Web (Banner Ads, Pop-ups, etc.), Women's Market

Tyler Pappas *(Mng Dir)*
Lindsey Williams *(Coord-Production)*

Accounts:
Azure Media
Euro RSCG
Sony BMG

CHARACTER

487 Bryant St 3rd Fl, San Francisco, CA 94107
Tel.: (415) 227-2100
E-Mail: info@charactersf.com
Web Site: www.charactersf.com

Employees: 8
Year Founded: 1999

Agency Specializes In: Advertising, Brand Development & Integration, Collateral, Environmental, Graphic Design, Print

Revenue: $1,280,000

Benjamin Pham *(Co-Founder & Dir-Creative)*
Tish Evangelista *(Owner & Dir-Creative)*
Ollie Ralph *(Mng Dir)*
Rishi Shourie *(Principal & Dir-Creative)*
Matt Carvalho *(Dir-Digital)*
Louis Paul Miller *(Dir-Creative)*
Will Geddes *(Sr Designer)*
Kyle Macy *(Sr Designer)*

Accounts:
Delfina Pizzeria

CHARACTER & KLATCH, BRAND DEVELOPMENT, ADVERTISING AND DESIGN

49 Fallingbrook Road, Toronto, ON M1N 2T5 Canada
Tel.: (416) 457-3595
E-Mail: info@characterandklatch.com
Web Site: www.characterandklatch.com

Employees: 5

Agency Specializes In: Advertising, Brand Development & Integration, Digital/Interactive, Event Planning & Marketing, Retail, Social Media

Approx. Annual Billings: $100,000

Mike Sundell *(Pres & Dir-Creative)*

Accounts:
Echo-Tech Roofing Solutions; Toronto, ON Industrial Roofing Systems; 2011
Kreater Custom Motorcycles; Toronto, ON Custom Motorcycles, Parts & Accessories; 2010
Picture It Imagination Products; Toronto, ON Children's Educations Products; 2010

CHARENE CREATIVE

965 Centerville Trl, Aurora, OH 44202
Tel.: (330) 524-5001
E-Mail: info@charenecreative.com
Web Site: www.charenecreative.com

Agency Specializes In: Advertising, Corporate Identity, Internet/Web Design, Print, Social Media

Charisse Louis *(Pres & Creative Dir)*

Accounts:
New-Country Club Builders & Remodelers Brand Campaign
Motion Source
Over the Top Tent Rental
Plumbing Source
Saving Street Fundraising
Solon Chamber

CHARISMA! COMMUNICATIONS

8358 SW Birch St, Portland, OR 97223
Tel.: (503) 245-3140
Fax: (503) 246-3858
E-Mail: laurie@charismacommunications.com
Web Site: www.charismacommunications.com

Employees: 20

Agency Specializes In: Collateral, Email, Entertainment, Event Planning & Marketing, Graphic Design, Health Care Services, Logo & Package Design, Newspaper, Production, Public Relations, Real Estate, Retail, Web (Banner Ads, Pop-ups, etc.)

Laurie Halter *(Owner)*

Accounts:
BZ Results
Chrome Systems
CIMA Systems
Cine Rent West
Dealer Track
ebizauto
ProjX
SMI
SnapBuild
Springbrook Software

CHARLES F. BEARDSLEY ADVERTISING

31 E Main St, Avon, CT 06001-3805
Tel.: (860) 676-0256
Fax: (860) 674-1917

E-Mail: charles.beardsley@snet.net

Employees: 3
Year Founded: 1946

Agency Specializes In: Advertising, Advertising Specialties, African-American Market, Alternative Advertising, Business Publications, Business-To-Business, Cable T.V., Children's Market, Co-op Advertising, Consumer Marketing, Consumer Publications, Corporate Identity, Direct Response Marketing, Fashion/Apparel, Infomercials, Magazines, Media Buying Services, Media Planning, Men's Market, Newspaper, Newspapers & Magazines, Over-50 Market, Seniors' Market, Trade & Consumer Magazines, Women's Market

Approx. Annual Billings: $2,150,000

Breakdown of Gross Billings by Media: Bus. Publs.: $50,000; Cable T.V.: $100,000; Consumer Publs.: $1,200,000; Newsp.: $800,000

David Ketchiff *(Owner)*
Nancy Ketchiff *(Partner)*

CHARLES RYAN ASSOCIATES INC.

601 Morris St, Charleston, WV 25301
Tel.: (304) 342-0161
Fax: (304) 342-1941
Toll Free: (877) 342-0161
E-Mail: info@charlesryan.com
Web Site: www.charlesryan.com

E-Mail for Key Personnel:
President: PGallagher@charlesryan.com
Creative Dir.: jauge@charlesryan.com

Employees: 40
Year Founded: 1974

National Agency Associations: AAF

Agency Specializes In: Advertising, Brand Development & Integration, Broadcast, Business-To-Business, Cable T.V., Co-op Advertising, Collateral, Communications, Consumer Marketing, Consumer Publications, Corporate Identity, Digital/Interactive, Electronic Media, Event Planning & Marketing, Exhibit/Trade Shows, Financial, Government/Political, Health Care Services, High Technology, Industrial, Internet/Web Design, Investor Relations, Legal Services, Logo & Package Design, Media Buying Services, Multimedia, Newspaper, Newspapers & Magazines, Out-of-Home Media, Outdoor, Planning & Consultation, Point of Purchase, Point of Sale, Print, Production, Public Relations, Publicity/Promotions, Radio, Sales Promotion, Sports Market, Strategic Planning/Research, T.V., Trade & Consumer Magazines, Transportation, Travel & Tourism

Approx. Annual Billings: $30,000,000

Susan Lavenski *(Mng Partner)*
Rick Mogielski *(VP & Exec Producer-CRA Film)*
Matt Isner *(VP)*
Alisha Maddox *(VP)*
Thomas Winner *(VP)*
Linda Cook *(Dir-Production)*
Kyra Harris *(Acct Exec)*

Accounts:
Affinion Loyalty Group
Appalachian Power
Arch Coal, Inc.
Cabell Huntington Hospital
CHA Health
The Charleston Convention & Visitors Bureau Creative, Marketing Strategy, Website Development
Chesapeake Energy Corp.
Citi Group
Dow Chemical
Dow Chemical
Entertainment Software Association
ESSROC
Greenbrier Episcopal School
Neurological Associates, Inc.
Northwood Health Systems
Smith Co. Motor Cars
Virginia Department of Transportation
Virginia Transportation Construction Alliance
West Virginia Coal
West Virginia Racing Association
West Virginia Tourism

Branches

Charles Ryan Associates

1900-A E Franklin St, Richmond, VA 23223
Tel.: (804) 643-3820
Fax: (804) 643-8281
Toll Free: (877) 342-0161
E-Mail: cdurham@charlesryan.com
Web Site: www.charlesryan.com

Employees: 10
Year Founded: 2001

National Agency Associations: PRSA

Caryn Foster Durham *(Mng Partner & Principal)*
Matt Fidler *(Sr VP & Dir-Creative)*
Alisha G. Maddox *(VP)*
Jeff Johnson *(Dir-Digital)*
Robb Major *(Dir-Creative)*
Kyra Harris *(Acct Exec)*
Jen Coleman *(Sr Media Buyer & Planner)*

Accounts:
DC Lottery
Virginia State Police

CHARLESTON/ORWIG, INC.

515 W North Shore Dr, Hartland, WI 53029-8312
Tel.: (262) 563-5100
Fax: (262) 563-5101
E-Mail: info@comktg.com
Web Site: www.charlestonorwig.com

Employees: 70
Year Founded: 1992

Agency Specializes In: Advertising, Agriculture, Brand Development & Integration, Broadcast, Business Publications, Co-op Advertising, Collateral, Communications, Consulting, Consumer Marketing, Consumer Publications, Corporate Communications, Corporate Identity, Crisis Communications, Custom Publishing, Customer Relationship Management, Digital/Interactive, Direct Response Marketing, E-Commerce, Electronic Media, Engineering, Environmental, Event Planning & Marketing, Exhibit/Trade Shows, Financial, Food Service, Government/Political, Graphic Design, Health Care Services, High Technology, Integrated Marketing, Internet/Web Design, Logo & Package Design, Magazines, Media Buying Services, Media Planning, Media Relations, Media Training, Medical Products, Merchandising, Mobile Marketing, Multimedia, New Product Development, Newspaper, Newspapers & Magazines, Out-of-Home Media, Outdoor, Pets , Planning & Consultation, Podcasting, Point of Purchase, Point of Sale, Print, Production, Production (Print), Promotions, Public Relations, Publicity/Promotions, RSS (Really Simple Syndication), Radio, Real Estate, Recruitment, Restaurant, Sales Promotion, Search Engine Optimization, Strategic Planning/Research, T.V., Technical Advertising, Telemarketing, Trade & Consumer Magazines, Transportation, Viral/Buzz/Word of Mouth

Approx. Annual Billings: $41,949,779

Breakdown of Gross Billings by Media: Bus. Publs.: $4,194,978; Collateral: $12,584,934; D.M.: $5,453,471; Farm Publs.: $6,292,467; Internet Adv.: $1,363,368; Newsp.: $524,372; Outdoor: $524,372; Point of Purchase: $524,370; Pub. Rels.: $8,389,956; Radio: $41,950; Trade & Consumer Mags.: $2,055,541

Lyle E. Orwig *(Chm)*
Marcy Tessmann *(Pres & Partner)*
Mark Gale *(CEO)*
Nancy Wegner *(Controller)*
Kimberly Keller *(Sr Dir-Reputation Mgmt)*
Mike Opperman *(Acct Plng Dir)*
Amy Richards *(Dir-Reputation Mgmt)*
Chuck Sanger *(Acct Supvr & Sr Strategist-Media Rels)*
Laura Henke *(Supvr-Media)*
Jeff Jacobs *(Sr Strategist-Digital Engagement)*

Accounts:
American Dairy Queen Corporation; Minneapolis, MN; 2007
Arm & Hammer Animal Nutrition; Princeton, NJ; 2001
Bayer Environmental Science; Research Triangle Park, NC; 2008
Brillion Farm Equipment; Brillion, WI; 1996
Chemtura Corporation; Middlebury, CT; 2008
Dairy Cattle Reproduction Council; Colorado; 2006
Dairyland Seed Company, Inc.; West Bend, WI; 1993
Glenroy, Inc.; Menomonee Falls, WI; 2008
HerdStar, LLC; LeRoy, MN; 2007
Hoard's Dairyman; Fort Atkinson, WI; 2003
MillerCoors; Milwaukee, WI Industry Affairs; 1996
Novartis Animal Health; Greensboro, NC; 2009
Pfizer Animal Genetics; Kalamazoo, MI; 2008
Pfizer Animal Health-Poultry Division; Durham, NC; 2001
Potawatomi Bingo Casino; Milwaukee, WI; 2009
SoCore Energy; Chicago, IL; 2009

CHASE COMMUNICATIONS

601 California St Ste 1120, San Francisco, CA 94108
Tel.: (415) 433-0100
Fax: (415) 433-0240
E-Mail: info@chasepr.com
Web Site: www.chasepr.com

Employees: 15

Agency Specializes In: Advertising, Broadcast, Collateral, Communications, Crisis Communications, Email, Event Planning & Marketing, Exhibit/Trade Shows, Investor Relations, Media Planning, Media Relations, Media Training, Print, Public Relations, Sponsorship, Strategic Planning/Research

Julie Chase *(Pres & CEO)*
Felicia Brown *(VP)*
Trish Cetrone *(VP)*
Darcy Brown *(Sr Acct Exec)*
Spencer Moore *(Sr Strategist-Real Estate)*
Jill Mierke *(Acct Coord)*

Accounts:
American Liver Foundation
Aton Pharma Inc.
Axis
Crystal City B.I.D
Em Johnson Interest
Heller+Manus Architects
MRP Realty
One Rincon Hill
SF Flex
Urban West Associates

CHATTER BUZZ
(Name Changed to Chatter Buzz Media)

CHATTER BUZZ MEDIA
(Formerly Chatter Buzz)
100 W Lucerne Circle, Orlando, FL 32801
Tel.: (321) 236-2899
Fax: (866) 390-7188
E-Mail: info@chatterbuzzmedia.com
Web Site: www.chatterbuzzmedia.com

Employees: 25
Year Founded: 2012

Agency Specializes In: Advertising, Advertising Specialties, Affluent Market, Asian Market, Business-To-Business, Children's Market, College, Communications, Consulting, Consumer Marketing, Content, Corporate Communications, Corporate Identity, Digital/Interactive, Direct Response Marketing, Direct-to-Consumer, E-Commerce, Email, Event Planning & Marketing, Exhibit/Trade Shows, Graphic Design, Guerilla Marketing, High Technology, Hispanic Market, Identity Marketing, Integrated Marketing, International, Internet/Web Design, Local Marketing, Logo & Package Design, Luxury Products, Men's Market, Mobile Marketing, Multicultural, Paid Searches, Production, Production (Print), Public Relations, Radio, Search Engine Optimization, Seniors' Market, Social Marketing/Nonprofit, Social Media, South Asian Market, Technical Advertising, Urban Market, Web (Banner Ads, Pop-ups, etc.), Women's Market

Approx. Annual Billings: $6,000,000

Shalyn Dever *(Co-Founder & CEO)*
Ashley Cisneros *(Co-Founder & Creative Dir)*
Steven Sundberg *(Sr VP-Sls)*
Dianna Romaguera *(Dir-Integrated Mktg)*
Angela Cotto *(Mgr-Bus Ops)*
Kristina Drake *(Coord-PR)*
Kevin Jusino *(Coord-Social Media)*

Accounts:
Action Gator Tire; 2014
BluWorld Custom Water Features; 2012
Catapult Learning Education; 2014
CommonWell Health Alliance Healthcare IT; 2014
Comtech Systems, Inc. Telecommunications & Engineering; 2014
Contemporary Women's Care Healthcare; 2013
Dermatude Beauty; 2013
DocDoc Healthcare; 2013
Family First Pediatrics Healthcare; 2014
Gastroenterology Specialists Healthcare; 2014
Kobe Japanese Steakhouse Restaurant; 2014
Law Office of Michael B. Brehne/ 911 Biker Law; 2012
Lennar Orlando New Homes; 2013
Lennar Tampa New Homes; 2013
Marc Michaels; 2014
Nicole Gravenmie Fashion; 2013
NRAA/ RSE Healthcare; 2013
Old Towne Brokers Real Estate; 2014
Reedy Creek (RCID) Improvement District; 2014
Rosenfield & Co. CPA Firm; 2012
Source 2 Staffing Firm; 2013
Super Holiday Tours Student Travel Agency; 2014
Ted Tobacco Tobacco Products; 2013
Victim Service Center Non-profit; 2014
Weichert Hallmark Real Estate; 2013
Winter Garden Smiles Dental; 2013

CHATTER CREATIVE
111 Durbin, Edmonds, WA 98020
Tel.: (206) 219-9229
E-Mail: info@chattercreative.com
Web Site: www.chattercreative.com

Year Founded: 2009

Agency Specializes In: Advertising, Brand Development & Integration, Corporate Identity, Internet/Web Design, Logo & Package Design, Media Buying Services, Print, Public Relations, Search Engine Optimization

Gretchen Mikulsky *(Dir-Ops)*
Matthew Mikulsky *(Dir-Creative & Social Media)*

Accounts:
CB Pacific
Dryer Islands
NWMechanical
Szloch Ironworks

CHECKBOX
(Formerly KDA Group Inc.)
7015 College Blvd Ste 700, Overland Park, KS 66211-1524
Fax: (913) 344-1960
Toll Free: (800) 922-6977
Web Site: checkboxmobile.blogspot.com

Employees: 46
Year Founded: 1964

National Agency Associations: YPA

Agency Specializes In: Advertising, Advertising Specialties, Affiliate Marketing, Below-the-Line, Consulting, Digital/Interactive, Direct Response Marketing, Electronic Media, Integrated Marketing, Local Marketing, Multimedia, Paid Searches, Print, Search Engine Optimization, Social Media, Strategic Planning/Research, Yellow Pages Advertising

Robert Gallardo Lamb *(Sr VP-Bus Plng)*
Roseanna Scruggs *(Acct Dir & Mgr)*
Patrick McCoy *(Specialist-Digital Product)*
Tammy Brown *(Rep-Acct Svc)*

Accounts:
American Airlines
CARQUEST
DIRECTV
Great Dane Trailers; Savannah, GA
Luxottica Retail
Michelin North America
Pella Corp.
Penske Truck Leasing
VCA Animal Hospitals

Branches

Ketchum Directory Advertising/Pittsburgh
6 PPG Pl, Pittsburgh, PA 15222-5425
Tel.: (412) 316-8000
Fax: (412) 456-3834
E-Mail: info@kda.com
Web Site: http://checkboxmobile.blogspot.com/

Employees: 41

Agency Specializes In: Electronic Media, Yellow Pages Advertising

Chris Jones *(Sr VP-Client Svcs)*
Tammy Kundla *(Sr VP-Fin)*
Keena Mccarthy *(Mng Dir-Louisville & VP)*
Patrick Mccoy *(Specialist-Digital Product)*

KDA Group Inc
(Formerly Ketchum Directory Advertising/Louisville)
303 N Hurstbourne Pkwy Ste 115, Louisville, KY 40222
Tel.: (502) 909-3960
Fax: (502) 318-8818
E-Mail: info@kda.com
Web Site: http://checkboxmobile.blogspot.com/

Year Founded: 1964

Agency Specializes In: Advertising, Advertising Specialties, Affiliate Marketing, Below-the-Line, Consulting, Digital/Interactive, Electronic Media, Integrated Marketing, Multimedia, Paid Searches, Search Engine Optimization, Social Media, Strategic Planning/Research, Yellow Pages Advertising

Chris Jones *(Sr VP-Client Svcs)*
Tammy Kundla *(Sr VP-Fin)*
Matt Wheeler *(VP-Digital Clients)*
Laurie Jackson *(Mgr-Ops)*
Rudy Alvarado *(Acct Supvr)*
Carrie McKenna *(Acct Supvr)*

Accounts:
American Airlines
Best Buy
CARQUEST
DIRECTV
Luxottica Retail
Michelin North America
Mobile Mini, Inc.
Pella Corporation
Penske Truck Leasing
VCA Animal Hospitals

KDA Group Inc.
(Formerly Ketchum Directory Advertising/Los Angeles)
4739 Alla Rd Ste 1500, Marina Del Rey, CA 90292
(See Separate Listing)

CHEDDAR SOCIAL
755 S Telshor Ste 202 B, Las Cruces, NM 88011
Tel.: (575) 522-2132
Web Site: cheddaradvertising.com

Agency Specializes In: Advertising, Digital/Interactive, Internet/Web Design

Cecil Campbell *(CEO)*
Lisa Nohner *(Copywriter)*

Accounts:
Las Cruces Moms

CHEIL CANADA
152 King St E Ste 300, Toronto, ON M5A 1J3 Canada
Tel.: (416) 479-9760
Web Site: www.cheil.com

Agency Specializes In: Advertising

Matt Cammaert *(Pres)*
Steph Guo *(Sr Dir-Art)*
Jeff Sturch *(Grp Acct Dir)*
Lindsay Wagter *(Acct Dir)*
Mark Ferris *(Dir-Retail Experience)*
Meghan Sherwin *(Dir-Plng & Digital Strategy)*
Ricardo Correia *(Assoc Dir-Creative)*
Danielle Kniznik *(Acct Exec)*

Accounts:
Horizons Exchange Traded Funds
Ontario Association of Radiologists
Samsung Electronics Canada Inc. Campaign: "Sparkling Water Dispensers", Seed Pot, Sparkling Water Fridge
Silver Snail Comics

CHEIL NORTH AMERICA
11 Beach St 9th Fl, New York, NY 10013
Tel.: (646) 380-5815
Fax: (646) 380-5809
Web Site: www.cheil.com

National Agency Associations: 4A's

Agency Specializes In: Advertising

Brad Brinegar *(CEO)*
Volker Selle *(Pres-DACH & NORDIC)*
Yann Baudoin *(Client Svc Dir)*

Accounts:
Samsung Group

CHEMISTRY CLUB

(Formerly Engine Company One)
451 Pacific Ave, San Francisco, CA 94133
Tel.: (415) 989-2500
Fax: (415) 732-9535
E-Mail: newbusiness@chemistryclub.com
Web Site: www.chemistryclub.com

Employees: 35
Year Founded: 1998

Agency Specializes In: Advertising, Brand Development & Integration, Corporate Communications, Digital/Interactive, Food Service, Graphic Design, In-Store Advertising, Sponsorship

Scott Aal *(Partner & Dir-Creative)*
Dayna Carroll *(Acct Dir)*
Frank Lewis *(Dir-Integrated Production & Ops)*
Laura Puccinelli *(Dir-Fin & Acctg)*
Jeannie Cuan *(Assoc Dir-Media)*
Suosdey Penn *(Assoc Dir-Creative)*
Peter McNally *(Acct Supvr)*

Accounts:
American Cancer Society
Bare Escentuals
Catholic Healthcare West
Clown Alley
Community Hospital of the Monterey Peninsula
Infineon Raceway
Jiffy Lube Media Planning & Buying
Monterey Bay Aquarium Campaign: "150 Feet of Awesome"
Noah's Bagels
Oakland Museum of California
Pacific Life (Agency of Record) Creative, Network and Cable Television Campaign
Rubio's
The San Francisco 49ers
San Francisco Food Bank
San Francisco Museum of Modern Art (Agency of Record) Advertising Strategy, Digital, Experiential, Media Buying, Media Planning, Outdoor, Print, Social Content
Sega Sports

CHEMISTRY COMMUNICATIONS INC.

535 Smithfield St Ste 230, Pittsburgh, PA 15222
Tel.: (412) 642-0642
Fax: (412) 642-0650
Web Site: www.createareaction.com/

E-Mail for Key Personnel:
President: geoff@gblinc.com
Creative Dir.: geoff@gblinc.com
Media Dir.: joyce@gblinc.com

Employees: 21
Year Founded: 1977

National Agency Associations: IAN

Agency Specializes In: Advertising, Advertising Specialties, Arts, Brand Development & Integration, Broadcast, Business Publications, Business-To-Business, Cable T.V., Co-op Advertising, Collateral, College, Consulting, Consumer Marketing, Consumer Publications, Corporate Communications, Corporate Identity, Digital/Interactive, Direct Response Marketing, Direct-to-Consumer, E-Commerce, Electronic Media, Exhibit/Trade Shows, Fashion/Apparel, Financial, Graphic Design, Health Care Services, High Technology, Industrial, Internet/Web Design, Legal Services, Local Marketing, Logo & Package Design, Magazines, Media Buying Services, Media Planning, Medical Products, Mobile Marketing, Multimedia, New Product Development, New Technologies, Newspaper, Newspapers & Magazines, Outdoor, Package Design, Paid Searches, Pharmaceutical, Point of Purchase, Point of Sale, Print, Product Placement, Production, Production (Ad, Film, Broadcast), Production (Print), Publicity/Promotions, Radio, Restaurant, Retail, Sales Promotion, Social Marketing/Nonprofit, Social Media, Strategic Planning/Research, T.V., Trade & Consumer Magazines, Travel & Tourism, Web (Banner Ads, Pop-ups, etc.)

Robert Neville *(Pres & Principal)*
Ned Show *(CEO)*
Geoff Tolley *(Chief Creative Officer)*
Chuck Barkey *(VP & Dir-Creative)*
Jill Yahnite *(VP-Bus Dev)*
Ryan McElroy *(Art Dir)*
Jeremy Hedges *(Dir-User Experience)*
Sarah Parker *(Dir-Art)*
Colleen Morris *(Mgr-Billing)*
Noelle Davis *(Sr Acct Exec)*
Katie Boardman *(Media Planner & Buyer)*
Gabriella Gasparich *(Acct Coord-PR)*

Accounts:
Greater Pittsburgh Community Food Bank; Duquesne, PA; 1991
New York Philharmonic
University of Pittsburgh Medical Center; Pittsburgh, PA Health Plan, Health System
Westmoreland Museum of American Art; Greensburg, PA; 1996

Branch

Chemistry Atlanta

(Formerly TG Madison)
3495 Piedmont Rd NE, Atlanta, GA 30305
Tel.: (404) 262-2623
Fax: (404) 237-2811
Web Site: createareaction.com

Employees: 80
Year Founded: 1986

National Agency Associations: AAF

Agency Specializes In: Advertising, Advertising Specialties, Brand Development & Integration, Business-To-Business, Cable T.V., Collateral, Communications, Consulting, Consumer Marketing, Consumer Publications, Corporate Identity, Cosmetics, Direct Response Marketing, E-Commerce, Electronic Media, Entertainment, Event Planning & Marketing, Exhibit/Trade Shows, Fashion/Apparel, Financial, Graphic Design, Health Care Services, Hospitality, Identity Marketing, Industrial, Information Technology, Internet/Web Design, Legal Services, Leisure, Local Marketing, Logo & Package Design, Luxury Products, Magazines, Market Research, Media Buying Services, Media Planning, Medical Products, Merchandising, Multimedia, New Product Development, Newspaper, Newspapers & Magazines, Out-of-Home Media, Outdoor, Over-50 Market, Paid Searches, Pharmaceutical, Planning & Consultation, Point of Purchase, Point of Sale, Print, Production, Production (Print), Publicity/Promotions, Radio, Real Estate, Restaurant, Retail, Sales Promotion, Search Engine Optimization, Seniors' Market, Social Marketing/Nonprofit, Social Media, Sponsorship, Sports Market, Stakeholders, Strategic Planning/Research, T.V., Trade & Consumer Magazines, Transportation, Travel & Tourism, Women's Market

Joanne Truffelman *(Co-Owner & Chm)*
Mark Simonton *(Pres)*
Roger Haggerty *(CFO)*
Talley Hultgren *(Chief Strategy Officer, Exec VP & Dir-Strategic Plng)*
Jim Spruell *(Chief Creative Officer & Exec VP)*
Taylor Guglielmo *(Exec VP & Grp Acct Dir-Bus Dev)*
Janelle Carson *(Exec VP & Dir-HR & Admin)*
Christina Hamby *(Sr VP & Dir-Analytics)*
Mike Betts *(VP & Assoc Dir-Creative)*
Derek Cowart *(Media Planner)*

Accounts:
Alzheimer's Association
Aramark; Philadelphia, PA Correctional Services
Aruba Marriott Resort & Stellaris Casino; Aruba Travel; 2007
Dearborn National; Chicago, IL Employee Benefits; 2008
The Dian Fossey Gorilla Fund International; Atlanta, GA Fundraising for Endangered Mountain Gorillas; 1997
Eagle Parking Parking Solutions; 2008
Greenguard Environmental Institute; Atlanta, GA; 2009
Habif, Arogeti & Wynne; Atlanta, GA Financial Services; 2005
Marriott Hotels & Resorts; Weston, FL Caribbean & Mexico Resorts; 2006
Marriott International, Inc.
MDI Entertainment; Alpharetta, GA Lottery Games; 2010
St. Kitts Marriott Resort & The Royal Beach Casino; Saint Kitts Travel; 2007
State of Georgia Dept. of Administrative Services; Atlanta, GA; 2011

CHERESKIN COMMUNICATIONS

Village Park Way Ste 205B, Encinitas, CA 92024
Tel.: (760) 942-3116
Web Site: www.chereskincomm.com

Employees: 8
Year Founded: 1991

Agency Specializes In: Advertising, E-Commerce, Media Relations, Print, Public Relations, Strategic Planning/Research

Valerie Chereskin *(Principal)*
Michele Moninger Baker *(Dir-PR)*
Livna Levram *(Dir-Creative)*

Accounts:
Allegiance, Inc.
COGNEX

CHERNOFF NEWMAN

1411 Gervais St 5th Fl, Columbia, SC 29201-3125
Tel.: (803) 254-8158
Fax: (803) 252-2016
Web Site: www.chernoffnewman.com

E-Mail for Key Personnel:
President: david.campbell@cnsg.com
Media Dir.: jeannie.hinson@cnsg.com
Public Relations: Stephanie.RiceJones@cnsg.com

Employees: 45
Year Founded: 1974

National Agency Associations: MAGNET

Agency Specializes In: Advertising, Business-To-Business, Corporate Communications, Government/Political, Health Care Services, Public Relations, Strategic Planning/Research, Travel & Tourism

Approx. Annual Billings: $50,000,000 Capitalized

Breakdown of Gross Billings by Media: Bus. Publs.: 30%; Cable T.V.: 20%; Collateral: 15%; Outdoor: 5%; Print: 13%; Spot T.V.: 10%; Trade & Consumer Mags.: 5%; Yellow Page Adv.: 2%

Lee Bussell *(Chm & CEO)*
David Anderson *(Vice Chm)*
David Campbell *(Pres & COO)*
Nickie Dickson *(CFO & Sr VP)*
Bruce Jacobs *(Sr VP & Gen Mgr)*
Tye Price *(VP-Mktg Strategy)*
Molly Holland *(Acct Mgr)*
Cari Brown *(Acct Supvr)*
Cindy Newman *(Acct Supvr)*
Adrianne Buckley *(Specialist-PR)*
Jordan Scott *(Specialist-PR)*
Kim Wilson *(Media Planner & Media Buyer)*
Danielle Salley *(Designer-Interactive)*

Accounts:
Dean Foods
National Bank of South Carolina; Columbia, SC
Palmetto Health Baptist
Palmetto Health; Columbia, SC
River Banks Zoo; Columbia, SC
Santee Cooper; Monks Corner, SC
South Carolina Department of Agriculture
South Carolina Election Commission; Columbia, SC
T.G. Lee Foods, LLC; Orlando, FL

Branches

Chernoff Newman
550 Long Point Rd, Mount Pleasant, SC 29464-7905
Tel.: (843) 971-5141
Fax: (843) 971-5889
Web Site: chernoffnewman.com

Employees: 6
Year Founded: 1974

Agency Specializes In: Advertising, Consumer Marketing, Public Relations

Peter Wertimer *(Pres-Adv)*
Tye Price *(Sr VP & Sr Strategist-Brand)*
Louise Dixon *(Sr VP)*
Jennifer Wienke *(Mgr-Production & Traffic)*
Hampton Miller *(Acct Supvr)*
Tim Kell *(Strategist-PR)*
Cindy Wade *(Sr Media Planner & Buyer)*

Chernoff Newman
2500 Maitland Center Pkwy Ste 104, Maitland, FL 32751-4165
Tel.: (407) 875-1919
Fax: (407) 875-0666
Web Site: www.chernoffnewman.com

Employees: 4
Year Founded: 1974

Agency Specializes In: Agriculture, Public Relations, Real Estate, Travel & Tourism

Bruce Jacobs *(Sr VP & Gen Mgr-Orlando)*
Tom Pechous *(Dir-Production)*

CHESLEY BRYAN MARKETING
16820 Lafayette Dr, Tyler, TX 75703
Tel.: (903) 952-2170
Fax: (903) 534-0444
Web Site: www.chesleybryan.com

Agency Specializes In: Advertising, Graphic Design, Internet/Web Design, Media Buying Services, Print, Radio

Chesley S. Bryan *(Owner)*

Accounts:
Air Chandler

CHESTER + COMPANY
1668 Barrington Street 302, Halifax, NS B3J 2A2 Canada
Tel.: (902) 446-7410
Fax: (902) 446-3738
Web Site: www.chesterco.ca

Agency Specializes In: Advertising, Graphic Design

Chester Goluch *(Pres)*
Tyler Macleod *(Client Svcs Dir)*
Denise Seach *(Acct Dir)*
Anthony Taaffe *(Dir-Creative)*
Hannah Graham *(Acct Mgr)*
Carla Mosher *(Mgr-Production & Accountant)*
Daekyu Cha *(Graphic Designer-Interactive)*
Adam Sterling *(Copywriter)*

Accounts:
Casino Nova Scotia Campaign: "Beware The Same Old"
Discovery Centre Social Advocacy Service Providers
Massage Addict Massage Therapy Providers
Nissan Car Dealers
Spirit Spa Inc. Fitness & Recreational Sports Service Providers

CHESTNUT COMMUNICATIONS, INC.
16 Stepping Stone Ln, Greenwich, CT 06830
Tel.: (203) 629-9098
Fax: (203) 869-0416
E-Mail: chestnutct@aol.com

Employees: 2
Year Founded: 1980

Agency Specializes In: Advertising, Cable T.V., Consumer Goods, Consumer Marketing, Cosmetics, Health Care Services, Identity Marketing, Market Research, Media Buying Services, Media Planning, Medical Products, Men's Market, Over-50 Market, Pharmaceutical, Print, Product Placement, Production (Print), Promotions, Restaurant, Syndication, T.V., Teen Market, Trade & Consumer Magazines, Women's Market

Approx. Annual Billings: $16,800,000

Albert S. Kestnbaum *(Owner & Pres)*

Accounts:
Cutex; Saint Louis, MO
DSE Healthcare Lipoflavonoid, Cystex, Albolene, Certain Dri, Acnomel, Lydia Pinkham; 2004
The Emerson Group; Wayne, PA
Moberg Pharma
Numark Laboratories; Edison, NJ; 1998

CHEVALIER ADVERTISING, INC.
1 Centerpointe Dr Ste 550, Lake Oswego, OR 97035
Tel.: (503) 639-9190
Fax: (503) 639-7122
E-Mail: info@chevalier-adv.com
Web Site: www.chevalier-adv.com

E-Mail for Key Personnel:
President: gregc@chevalier-adv.com
Creative Dir.: robink@chevalier-adv.com

Employees: 18
Year Founded: 1953

Agency Specializes In: Advertising, Cable T.V., Co-op Advertising, Collateral, Consumer Marketing, Consumer Publications, E-Commerce, Exhibit/Trade Shows, Internet/Web Design, Logo & Package Design, Magazines, Marine, Point of Purchase, Point of Sale, Print, Public Relations, Trade & Consumer Magazines

Breakdown of Gross Billings by Media: Cable T.V.: 5%; Collateral: 5%; Logo & Package Design: 5%; Mdsg./POP: 5%; Point of Sale: 5%; Pub. Rels.: 10%; Trade & Consumer Mags.: 60%; Worldwide Web Sites: 5%

Gregory Chevalier *(Pres)*
Robin Kizzar *(Dir-Creative)*
Susan McMullen *(Mgr-Production)*
Aaron Lisech *(Acct Exec)*
Megan Davis *(Media Buyer)*
Megan Mooney *(Media Buyer)*

Accounts:
Alpha-TAC ExtremeBeam, M1000 Fusion Flashlight, Marketing, PR, Social Media, Web Design
Cannon Safe
CMMG Inc Creative, Marketing, Media Placement, Public Relations
GunVault
HatsanUSA Creative, Marketing, Public Relations
HotMocs
Montana Decoy
Nikon Sport Optics; Melville, NY Binoculars, Hunting Scopes
Rossi Firearms
SHE Outdoor Apparel
SHE Safari
New-Tactical Walls (Agency of Record) Creative, Public Relations, Strategic Media
Taurus; Miami, FL Handguns & Cowboy Action Guns; 2006
ThermaCELL
Willamette Nurseries; Canby, OR Rootstock, Seedlings; 1998
Winchester Ammunition

CHF INVESTOR RELATIONS
90 Adelaide St W Ste 600, Toronto, ON M5H 3V9 Canada
Tel.: (416) 868-1079
Fax: (416) 868-6198
E-Mail: julia@chfir.com
Web Site: www.chfir.com

Employees: 15

Agency Specializes In: Investor Relations

Cathy Hume *(Owner)*
Carole Rowsell *(Exec VP)*
Bob Leshchyshen *(Dir-Corp Dev)*
Robin Cook *(Sr Acct Mgr)*

Accounts:
Canadian Overseas Petroleum Limited Investor relations
Foraco

CHILLI MARKETING LIMITED
Rm A9, 8/F, Lee King Ind. Bldg., 12 Ng Fong St, Kowloon, 852 China (Hong Kong)
Tel.: (852) 36210378
Web Site: www.chilli-marketing.com

Employees: 10
Year Founded: 2010

Agency Specializes In: Below-the-Line, Experience Design, In-Store Advertising, Local Marketing, Magazines, Newspapers & Magazines, Out-of-Home Media, Print, Production (Print), Promotions, Shopper Marketing, Web (Banner Ads, Pop-ups, etc.)

Approx. Annual Billings: $1,000,000

Roger Tang *(Dir)*

Accounts:
De Rucci De Rucci Bedding De Rucci Bespoke
SEED Corp 1day Pure Contact Lenses Eye Coffret Color Contact Lenses Heroine Make 1Day UV Cosmetic Lenses
Twinings; 2014
Wipro Unza Enchanteur Romano

CHILLINGWORTH/RADDING INC.
1133 Broadway Ste 1615, New York, NY 10010
Tel.: (212) 674-4700
Fax: (212) 979-0125
E-Mail: sradding@chillradd.com
Web Site: www.chillradd.com

E-Mail for Key Personnel:
President: steve@chillradd.com
Media Dir.: jillradding@aol.com

Employees: 10
Year Founded: 1980

Agency Specializes In: Collateral, Graphic Design, Internet/Web Design

Stephen L. Radding *(Pres)*
Alexa Echavez *(VP-Integrated Acct & Dir-Media)*
Linda Greene *(Dir-Creative)*

Accounts:
All-Clad Metalcrafters; Canonsburg, PA Bakeware, Cookware, Kitchen Accessories
Bernardo
Lenox

CHISANO MARKETING GROUP
2000 Old Byers Rd, Dayton, OH 45342
Tel.: (937) 866-4914
Fax: (937) 847-0007
Web Site: www.chisano.com

Employees: 70
Year Founded: 1986

Agency Specializes In: Advertising, Communications, Consumer Marketing, Consumer Publications, Digital/Interactive, Direct Response Marketing, E-Commerce, Graphic Design, Internet/Web Design, Logo & Package Design, Multimedia, Print, Public Relations

Joe Bouch *(Owner & CEO)*
Ed Gilbert *(CMO)*
Cheryl Amirzadeh *(Sr Dir-Art)*
Erich Slipsager *(Dir-Interactive Svcs)*
Joe Price *(Supvr-Fulfillment Svcs)*
Kara Garlanger *(Acct Exec)*
Kelsey Roderick *(Acct Coord)*

Accounts:
CityWide Development Corporation
Cricket Communications
Paxar
Springfield & Clark County Chamber of Commerce
Time Warner (RoadRunner)

Branch

Chisano Marketing Group, Inc.
999 Douglas Ave Ste 3325, Altamonte Springs, FL 32714
Tel.: (407) 788-7070
E-Mail: info@chisano.com
Web Site: www.chisano.com

Employees: 57
Year Founded: 1980

Agency Specializes In: Advertising, Advertising Specialties, Affluent Market, Brand Development & Integration, Business Publications, Business-To-Business, Co-op Advertising, Collateral, Commercial Photography, Communications, Consumer Goods, Consumer Marketing, Consumer Publications, Corporate Communications, Corporate Identity, Crisis Communications, Digital/Interactive, Direct Response Marketing, Direct-to-Consumer, Electronic Media, Environmental, Graphic Design, Hospitality, In-Store Advertising, Integrated Marketing, Internet/Web Design, Leisure, Local Marketing, Logo & Package Design, Luxury Products, Magazines, Market Research, Media Buying Services, Media Planning, Media Relations, Medical Products, Men's Market, Mobile Marketing, New Product Development, Newspaper, Newspapers & Magazines, Out-of-Home Media, Outdoor, Over-50 Market, Package Design, Pharmaceutical, Planning & Consultation, Point of Purchase, Print, Production, Production (Ad, Film, Broadcast), Production (Print), Promotions, Public Relations, Publicity/Promotions, RSS (Really Simple Syndication), Radio, Real Estate, Regional, Restaurant, Retail, Sales Promotion, Search Engine Optimization, Seniors' Market, Social Marketing/Nonprofit, Social Media, Sports Market, Strategic Planning/Research, T.V., Technical Advertising, Trade & Consumer Magazines, Travel & Tourism, Viral/Buzz/Word of Mouth, Web (Banner Ads, Pop-ups, etc.), Women's Market

Ed Gilbert *(CMO)*
Karen LaMonica *(Dir-PR)*
Erich Slipsager *(Dir-Interactive Svcs)*
Joyce Truitt *(Dir-Media)*
Jason Pennypacker *(Sr Acct Exec)*
Kara Garlanger *(Acct Exec)*
Kelsey Roderick *(Acct Coord)*
Brian Cloud *(Rep-Customer Svc)*

Accounts:
AK Steel Corporation; 2000
American Pie Council Pie Association; 2008
Associated Luxury Hotels International; Orlando, FL Luxury Hotels Association; 2004
Chateau on the Lake Luxury Hotel/Resort; 2004
Fort Myers Regional Partnership Economic Development; 2009
Hickory River Smokehouse Barbecue Restaurant; 2012
Naples Beach Hotel & Golf Club; Naples, FL Luxury Hotel/Resort; 1999
The Renaissance Resort at World Golf Village; Saint Augustine, FL Luxury Hotel/Resort; 2000
The Resort at Longboat Key Club; Longboat Key, FL Luxury Hotel/Resort; 2000
Sheraton Delfina Santa Monica Luxury Hotel; 2011
Sweetwater Golf & Country Club; Longwood, FL Real Estate; 2005

CHITIKA, INC.
1800 West Park Dr, Westborough, MA 01752
Tel.: (508) 449-3870
Fax: (508) 366-5789
Toll Free: (866) 441-7203
E-Mail: info@chitika.com
Web Site: chitika.com

Year Founded: 2003

Agency Specializes In: Advertising, Web (Banner Ads, Pop-ups, etc.)

Alden DoRosario *(Co-Founder & CTO)*
Venkat Kolluri *(CEO)*
Vivek Kulkarni *(Dir-Fin)*
Jeffrey Mcquillan *(Dir-Data Solutions Engrg)*

Accounts:
Red Herring

CHLETCOS/GALLAGHER INC.
121 W 27th St Ste 1103, New York, NY 10001
Tel.: (212) 334-2455
Fax: (212) 334-2463
E-Mail: lisa.chletcos@c-ginc.com
Web Site: www.c-ginc.com

Agency Specializes In: Advertising, Business Publications, Communications

Lisa Chletcos *(Pres)*

Accounts:
Arkema
Cristal Global
Delphi Electronics & Safety; Kokomo, IN
Delphi Holdings L.L.P. ; Troy, MI
Honeywell Aerospace
Momentive Performance Materials
OSRAM SYLVANIA
Rockwell Automation
Siemens
TRW Automotive
UTC Aerospace Systems

CHOPS ADVERTISING, LLC
105 Gordon Terr, Nashville, TN 37207
Tel.: (615) 957-9996
Web Site: www.chopsadvertising.com

Agency Specializes In: Advertising, Brand Development & Integration, Digital/Interactive, Media Buying Services, Media Planning, Print, T.V.

Greg Hopkins *(Partner & Dir-Creative)*
Judy Caplan *(Principal)*
Gunnar Eng *(Acct Dir)*

Accounts:
Anjou Restaurant
BorderJump
Etch Restaurant
Sesac Inc.
Sombra Restaurant

CHP ADVERTISING
3860 Via Del Rey, Bonita Springs, FL 34134
Tel.: (239) 676-7658
E-Mail: info@chpadvertising.com
Web Site: www.chpadvertising.com

Year Founded: 2007

Agency Specializes In: Advertising, Graphic Design, Internet/Web Design, Logo & Package Design, Search Engine Optimization

Chris Fries *(Owner)*

Accounts:
Agromeris
Cavanaugh Olive Oil Company
Clean Cut Movers
Leslie Ann Paris
Selling SWF
Sputtens

CHRISTENSON MEDIA GROUP INC.
(Formerly Christenson, Barclay & Shaw, Inc.)
10560 Barkley Ste 315, Overland Park, KS 66212
Tel.: (913) 327-0030
Fax: (913) 663-4922
Toll Free: (800) 456-2678
E-Mail: jchristenson@cmgkc.com
Web Site: www.cmgkc.com/

Employees: 25

Year Founded: 1954

Agency Specializes In: Internet/Web Design, Web (Banner Ads, Pop-ups, etc.), Yellow Pages Advertising

Approx. Annual Billings: $22,000,000

Breakdown of Gross Billings by Media: Yellow Page Adv.: $22,000,000

Janer R. Christenson *(Pres)*
Alycia Campbell *(Specialist-Interactive)*

CHRLX
(Formerly Charlex)
2 W 45th St, New York, NY 10036
Tel.: (212) 719-4600
Fax: (212) 840-2747
E-Mail: info@chrlx.com
Web Site: www.chrlx.com/

Agency Specializes In: Advertising, Cable T.V., T.V.

Robert Muzer *(VP & Dir-Engrg)*
David Langley *(VP)*
Ryan Dunn *(Exec Dir-Creative)*
Rachel Kate Miller *(Mgr-Studio Production)*
Taili Wu *(Designer)*
Alessia Donato *(Coord)*
Jerry Stephano *(Sr Engr)*

Accounts:
Allegra
AOL
Cingular
Kohl's
M&Ms
NIKE, Inc. Air Zoom Elite 8, Campaign: "Engine", Campaign: "Find Your Fast", Online
Volvo

CHROMIUM
(Formerly The WESSLING Group)
440 Brannan St, San Francisco, CA 94107
Tel.: (415) 778-6454
Web Site: www.chromiumbranding.com

Employees: 5

Agency Specializes In: Brand Development & Integration, Corporate Identity, E-Commerce, Email, Internet/Web Design, Outdoor, Package Design, Print, Strategic Planning/Research, T.V.

Peter Van Aartrijk *(Principal)*
Tony Wessling *(Principal)*
Stephen Goodman *(Strategist-Growth)*

Accounts:
ASTER data
Beech Street Capital
Littler
McCarthy-Cook
Polycom
Suntech Power
Willis Lease

CHUMNEY & ASSOCIATES
660 US Hwy 1 2nd Fl, North Palm Beach, FL 33408
Tel.: (561) 882-0066
Fax: (561) 882-0067
Toll Free: (888) 227-5712
E-Mail: info@chumneyads.com
Web Site: www.chumneyads.com

Employees: 50
Year Founded: 1996

Agency Specializes In: Advertising, Automotive, Direct Response Marketing, Internet/Web Design, Print, Radio, Sales Promotion, T.V.

Approx. Annual Billings: $50,000,000

Mike Chumney *(Pres)*
Brett Hawkins *(Partner)*
G. Scott Swiger *(Sr Dir-Digital Client Svcs)*
Candice Johnson *(Dir-Media)*
Jennifer Jones *(Acct Exec)*
Morgan Lee *(Specialist-Internet Mktg)*

Accounts:
Ford
Ft Myers Toyota
Nissan
Toyota

CI DESIGN INC.
306 N Milwaukee St Ste 200, Milwaukee, WI 53202
Tel.: (414) 224-3100
Fax: (414) 224-3101
E-Mail: info@cidesigninc.com
Web Site: www.cidesigninc.com

Employees: 11
Year Founded: 1978

Agency Specializes In: Advertising, Brand Development & Integration, Collateral, Commercial Photography, Corporate Communications, Corporate Identity, Digital/Interactive, Education, Electronic Media, Exhibit/Trade Shows, Graphic Design, Health Care Services, Internet/Web Design, Logo & Package Design, Magazines, Point of Purchase, Print, Production, Real Estate, Sports Market

Approx. Annual Billings: $1,500,000

Roger Barber *(CFO)*
Scott Hill *(COO)*
Jim Taugher *(Dir-Creative & Principal)*
David Busse *(Producer & Dir-Video Production)*
Katie Good *(Dir-Art)*

CI GROUP
10 Salem Park, Whitehouse, NJ 08888
Tel.: (908) 534-6100
Fax: (908) 534-5151
Web Site: www.ci-group.com

Employees: 50
Year Founded: 1986

National Agency Associations: ADC-BMA-DMA-PRSA

Agency Specializes In: Advertising, Advertising Specialties, Brand Development & Integration, Business Publications, Catalogs, Co-op Advertising, Collateral, Consumer Goods, Consumer Publications, Corporate Communications, Cosmetics, Digital/Interactive, Direct Response Marketing, E-Commerce, Electronic Media, Electronics, Email, Exhibit/Trade Shows, Financial, Identity Marketing, In-Store Advertising, Logo & Package Design, Media Planning, Medical Products, Mobile Marketing, Multimedia, New Product Development, Print, Public Relations, Publicity/Promotions, Radio, Sales Promotion, Web (Banner Ads, Pop-ups, etc.)

Approx. Annual Billings: $15,000,000

Eric Turiansky *(Pres)*
Jennifer Huff *(VP-Fin)*
Lawrence Krampf *(Exec Dir)*
Andy Badalamenti *(Dir-Creative & Copy)*
Gina Galligan *(Dir-Promos)*
Dan Murphy *(Dir-Warehousing & Fulfillment)*
Dave Reid *(Dir-IT)*

CIESADESIGN
200 E Grand River Ave, Lansing, MI 48906
Tel.: (517) 853-8877
Fax: (517) 853-2999
Web Site: www.ciesadesign.com

Year Founded: 1983

Agency Specializes In: Advertising, Graphic Design, Internet/Web Design

Lauren Ciesa *(Founder & Pres)*
Kevin Liuzzo *(Dir-Design)*
Thomas Ro *(Dir-Technical)*
John Donohoe *(Acct Mgr & Graphic Designer)*
Kris Kennaugh *(Office Mgr)*
Chris Vanwyck *(Brand Mgr)*
Kendra Church *(Designer)*

Accounts:
Greater Lansing Ballet Company
Heart of the Lakes
Renegade Theatre Festival

CIMBRIAN
425 N Prince St, Lancaster, PA 17603
Tel.: (717) 397-9752
Fax: (717) 397-9905
E-Mail: info@cimbrian.com
Web Site: www.cimbrian.com

Employees: 24
Year Founded: 1972

Agency Specializes In: Advertising, Brand Development & Integration, Business-To-Business, Cable T.V., Collateral, Communications, Consumer Marketing, Consumer Publications, Corporate Identity, Digital/Interactive, Education, Financial, Food Service, Health Care Services, Internet/Web Design, Logo & Package Design, Medical Products, New Product Development, Planning & Consultation, Public Relations, Publicity/Promotions, Retail, Strategic Planning/Research, Transportation

Revenue: $6,000,000

Kirk Barrett *(CEO)*

Accounts:
Belco Community Credit union
Chicco
Drogaris Companies
Flinchbough Enginnering,Inc.
Honey Bee Gardens
Valais
Frey Chocolate Candy

CINCO MEDIA COMMUNICATIONS
(Name Changed to CINCO Strategy Group)

CINCO STRATEGY GROUP
(Formerly CINCO MEDIA Communications)
1801 N Lamar Ste 400, Dallas, TX 75202
Tel.: (214) 574-5551
E-Mail: thinkcinco@cincostrategy.com
Web Site: www.cincostrategy.com

Employees: 15

Agency Specializes In: Bilingual Market, Communications, Health Care Services, Hispanic Market, Public Relations, Retail, Sponsorship

Amber Gracia *(Founder & Principal)*

CIRCLE OF ONE MARKETING
2400 NE 2nd Ave Studio C, Miami, FL 33137
Tel.: (305) 576-3790
Fax: (305) 576-3799
E-Mail: info@circleofonemarketing.com
Web Site: www.circleofonemarketing.com

Employees: 5
Year Founded: 2001

Agency Specializes In: Advertising, African-American Market, Brand Development & Integration, Cable T.V., Collateral, Electronic Media, Entertainment, Event Planning & Marketing, Government/Political, Graphic Design, Logo & Package Design, Magazines, Media Buying Services, Newspaper, Outdoor, Public Relations, Publicity/Promotions, Radio, Real Estate, T.V., Travel & Tourism

Approx. Annual Billings: $900,000

Breakdown of Gross Billings by Media: Newsp.: 35%; Other: 10%; Pub. Rels.: 20%; Radio & T.V.: 35%

Suzan McDowell *(Pres & CEO)*
T. Bernie *(Dir-PR)*
Flora Sweet *(Dir-Bus Dev)*
Nelson L. Adams, IV *(Coord-PR)*

Accounts:
Amicon Development; Miami, FL Commercial Real Estate Development; 2004
City of Miami Beach Cultural Affairs Program; Miami Beach, FL Cultural Arts Council; 2004
City of Miami Gardens; Miami Gardens, FL Various Events; 2004
City of Riviera Beach; Riviera Beach, FL 4th & 5th Annual Jazz & Blues Festival; 2003
Delancy Hill; Miami, FL
Ginger Bay Cafe; Hollywood, FL Caribbean Cuisine; 2001
Miami Dade Chamber of Commerce
One United Bank; Boston, MA
Peak Mortgage; Pembroke Pines, FL Mortgage Products; 2001
Planned Parenthood of Greater Miami & the Florida Keys; Miami, FL Safe Sex; 2002
State of Florida-Office of Supplier Diversity; Tallahassee, FL

CIRCLE ONE
10 Norden Pl, Norwalk, CT 06854
Tel.: (203) 286-0550
Fax: (203) 286-0555
Web Site: www.circle1marketing.com

Employees: 35

Agency Specializes In: Advertising, Consumer Marketing, Customer Relationship Management, Package Design, Print, Publicity/Promotions, Radio, T.V., Viral/Buzz/Word of Mouth

Michael Dill *(Mng Partner)*
Allison Burress *(Partner)*
Mark Szuchman *(Partner)*

Accounts:
Royal Purple Brand Strategy, Creative

THE CIRLOT AGENCY, INC.
1505 Airport Rd, Jackson, MS 39232
Tel.: (601) 664-2010
Fax: (601) 664-2610
Toll Free: (800) 356-8169
E-Mail: inquiry@cirlot.com
Web Site: www.cirlot.com

E-Mail for Key Personnel:
President: rick@cirlot.com
Creative Dir.: lynda@cirlot.com
Media Dir.: greg@cirlot.com

Employees: 36
Year Founded: 1984

National Agency Associations: AAF

Agency Specializes In: Advertising, Advertising Specialties, Affiliate Marketing, Affluent Market, African-American Market, Agriculture, Alternative Advertising, Arts, Automotive, Aviation & Aerospace, Bilingual Market, Brand Development & Integration, Branded Entertainment, Broadcast, Business Publications, Business-To-Business, Cable T.V., Catalogs, Children's Market, Co-op Advertising, Collateral, College, Commercial Photography, Communications, Consulting, Consumer Goods, Consumer Marketing, Consumer Publications, Content, Corporate Communications, Corporate Identity, Cosmetics, Crisis Communications, Custom Publishing, Customer Relationship Management, Digital/Interactive, Direct Response Marketing, Direct-to-Consumer, E-Commerce, Education, Electronic Media, Email, Engineering, Entertainment, Environmental, Event Planning & Marketing, Exhibit/Trade Shows, Experience Design, Fashion/Apparel, Financial, Food Service, Government/Political, Graphic Design, Health Care Services, High Technology, Hospitality, Household Goods, Identity Marketing, In-Store Advertising, Industrial, Information Technology, Integrated Marketing, International, Internet/Web Design, Investor Relations, Legal Services, Leisure, Local Marketing, Logo & Package Design, Luxury Products, Magazines, Marine, Market Research, Media Buying Services, Media Planning, Media Relations, Media Training, Medical Products, Men's Market, Merchandising, Mobile Marketing, Multicultural, Multimedia, New Product Development, Newspaper, Newspapers & Magazines, Out-of-Home Media, Outdoor, Over-50 Market, Package Design, Paid Searches, Pharmaceutical, Planning & Consultation, Podcasting, Point of Purchase, Point of Sale, Print, Product Placement, Production, Production (Ad, Film, Broadcast), Production (Print), Promotions, Public Relations, Publicity/Promotions, Publishing, RSS (Really Simple Syndication), Radio, Real Estate, Recruitment, Regional, Restaurant, Retail, Sales Promotion, Search Engine Optimization, Seniors' Market, Social Marketing/Nonprofit, Sponsorship, Sports Market, Stakeholders, Strategic Planning/Research, T.V., Technical Advertising, Teen Market, Trade & Consumer Magazines, Transportation, Travel & Tourism, Urban Market, Web (Banner Ads, Pop-ups, etc.), Women's Market, Yellow Pages Advertising

Approx. Annual Billings: $21,000,000

Richard W. Looser, Jr. *(Pres & COO)*
Liza C. Looser *(CEO)*
Greg Gilliland *(VP & Dir-Multimedia)*
Lynda Lesley *(VP & Dir-Creative)*
Steve Erickson *(Exec Dir-Art)*
Lisa Comer *(Dir-Mktg Svcs)*

Accounts:
Aerospace Industries Association (AIA) Aerospace & Defense Membership Organization
Bell Helicopter Textron, Inc. Bell Helicopter Textron, Inc., Bell Helicopters
Bush Brothers & Company; Knoxville, TN Retail Beans
Heartland Catfish Food Products
Ingalls Shipbuilding Defense, Shipbuilding
Longleaf Camo Outdoor Apparel & Accessories
Mighty Grow Organic Fertilizer
Mississippi Believe It Public Service
Northrop Grumman Defense
Raytheon Electronic Systems; Dallas, TX Defense, Electronics
Sanderson Farms Championship Event: PGA TOUR Tournament
Sanderson Farms, Inc.; Laurel, MS Food Products
St. Dominic Hospital System Healthcare
Textron AirLand Aircraft Manufacturing
Textron Systems Aerospace & Defense

CITRUS
(Acquired & Absorbed by HMH)

CITRUS STUDIOS
1512 18th St Ste 3, Santa Monica, CA 90404
Tel.: (310) 395-9080
Fax: (310) 395-9121
E-Mail: hello@citrusstudios.com
Web Site: www.citrusstudios.com

Employees: 10
Year Founded: 1999

Agency Specializes In: Advertising, Digital/Interactive, Graphic Design, Internet/Web Design

Kalika Yap *(CEO)*
Erika Lyons *(Acct Dir)*
Jessica Alexandra *(Dir-Creative)*
Jerry Digby *(Dir)*
Brad Champagne *(Project Mgr & Designer)*
David J. Whelan *(Strategist-Branding)*
Soyoung Kim *(Designer)*
Yoko Namima *(Designer)*
Jen Netherby *(Copywriter)*

Accounts:
USC

CITYTWIST
1200 N Federal Hwy Ste 417, Boca Raton, FL 33432
Tel.: (561) 989-8480
Web Site: www.citytwist.com

Agency Specializes In: Advertising, Email, Pharmaceutical

Lyndon Griffin *(CTO)*
Jason Elston *(VP-Ops)*
Marc Lefevre *(VP-Sls)*
Edward Smith *(VP-Fin)*
Joe Manarina *(Sr Dir-Bus Dev)*
Dan Lynch *(Sr Acct Mgr)*
Laura Bieniasz-Hobbs *(Mgr-Call Center)*
Nicholas Ferlanti *(Mgr-Sls)*
Art Boldetskiy *(Sr Acct Exec)*
Andres Taborda *(Sr Acct Exec)*
Hal Taitelbaum *(Acct Exec)*

CIVILIAN
(Formerly TargetCom, LLC)
444 N Michigan Ave 33rd Fl, Chicago, IL 60611-3905
Tel.: (312) 822-1100
Fax: (312) 822-9628
Web Site: www.civilianagency.com

Employees: 25
Year Founded: 1988

National Agency Associations: 4A's-CADM

Agency Specializes In: Above-the-Line, Advertising, Advertising Specialties, Affluent Market, Agriculture, Alternative Advertising, Automotive, Below-the-Line, Bilingual Market, Brand Development & Integration, Business-To-Business, Cable T.V., Collateral, College, Communications, Consulting, Consumer Goods, Consumer Marketing, Corporate Identity, Cosmetics, Customer Relationship Management, Digital/Interactive, Direct Response Marketing,

Direct-to-Consumer, E-Commerce, Education, Electronic Media, Email, Entertainment, Environmental, Event Planning & Marketing, Exhibit/Trade Shows, Experience Design, Financial, Food Service, Graphic Design, Health Care Services, High Technology, Hospitality, Household Goods, Identity Marketing, Infomercials, Integrated Marketing, Internet/Web Design, Local Marketing, Luxury Products, Market Research, Media Buying Services, Media Planning, Medical Products, Mobile Marketing, Multicultural, Multimedia, Newspaper, Outdoor, Over-50 Market, Paid Searches, Pets , Pharmaceutical, Planning & Consultation, Point of Purchase, Point of Sale, Print, Production, Production (Print), Promotions, Publicity/Promotions, Radio, Real Estate, Restaurant, Retail, Sales Promotion, Search Engine Optimization, Shopper Marketing, Social Media, Sponsorship, Sports Market, Strategic Planning/Research, Sweepstakes, T.V., Teen Market, Transportation, Travel & Tourism, Tween Market, Urban Market, Women's Market, Yellow Pages Advertising

Approx. Annual Billings: $5,300,000

Breakdown of Gross Billings by Media: D.M.: $2,000,000; Internet Adv.: $800,000; Production: $500,000; Spot T.V.: $1,000,000; Strategic Planning/Research: $1,000,000

Tim Claffey *(Pres)*
Matt Morano *(Sr VP & Head-Strategic Bus)*
Jessica Hennis *(Acct Dir)*
Len Hartz *(Dir-Bus Dev)*
Mike Jarosik *(Dir-Production)*
Katie Naper *(Acct Supvr)*

Accounts:
Allstate Life Insurance; 2011
Best Buy; MN Relationship Marketing; 2008
Cancer Treatment Centers of America; Chicago, IL Specialty Healthcare; 2002
Citi Credit Card Marketing; 2005
Discover; Northbrook, IL Credit Card Marketing; 2008
Elysian Hotel; Chicago, IL Luxury Hotel; 2011
Erie Insurance Insurance; 2012
National Association of Realtors; Chicago, IL Association; 2008
St. Jude Children's Hospital; Memphis, TN Specialty Healthcare; 2010
Universal Technical Institute; Phoenix, AZ Technical Educations; 2011
Wilson Sporting Goods; Chicago, IL Baseball; 2011

CIVITASNOW
65 E Gay St Ste 210, Columbus, OH 43215
Tel.: (614) 499-9032
E-Mail: info@civitasnow.com
Web Site: www.civitasnow.com

Agency Specializes In: Advertising, Brand Development & Integration, Event Planning & Marketing, Internet/Web Design, Logo & Package Design, Media Planning, Print, Radio

Matthew Barnes *(Partner & Exec Dir-Creative)*
Jacob Taylor *(Partner & Client Svcs Dir)*

Accounts:
Carl H. Lindner College of Business
Democratic National Convention
Experience Columbus
Mid-Ohio Foodbank
Thornton Water

CJ ADVERTISING LLC
300 10th Ave S, Nashville, TN 37203
Tel.: (615) 254-6634
Fax: (615) 254-6615
Web Site: www.cjadvertising.com

Agency Specializes In: Advertising, Brand Development & Integration, Broadcast, Content, Digital/Interactive, Social Media

Arnie Malham *(Founder & Pres)*
Jimmy Bewley *(Gen Counsel & VP)*
Jennifer Floyd *(Dir-Creative Svcs)*
Angel Putman *(Dir-Media Svcs)*
Laura Hudson *(Brand Mgr)*
Darron McKnight *(Mgr-Local Media)*
Matthew Davis *(Designer-Web)*
Bonnie Rothenstein *(Media Buyer)*
Joseph Hayden *(Coord-Media & Buyer-Outdoor)*

Accounts:
Crowson Law Group
Jason Stone Injury Lawyers

CJRW NORTHWEST
4100 Corporate Center Dr Ste 300, Springdale, AR 72762
Tel.: (479) 442-9803
Fax: (479) 442-3092
Toll Free: (800) 599-9803
E-Mail: learnabout@cjrww.com
Web Site: www.cjrw.com

Employees: 25
Year Founded: 1977

National Agency Associations: AAF

Agency Specializes In: Advertising, Business-To-Business, Consulting, Consumer Marketing, Event Planning & Marketing, Health Care Services, Internet/Web Design, Logo & Package Design, Planning & Consultation, Point of Purchase, Point of Sale, Print, Publicity/Promotions, Sales Promotion, Sponsorship, Sweepstakes, Travel & Tourism

Approx. Annual Billings: $10,000,000

Breakdown of Gross Billings by Media: Newsp. & Mags.: 38%; Print: 53%; Promos.: 6%; Radio & T.V.: 3%

Brenda Worm *(VP & Dir-Ops)*
Maxine Williams *(VP-Acct Svcs)*
Rob Anderson *(Dir-Content Strategy)*
John Cater *(Dir-Interactive Art)*
Amy Frazier *(Assoc Dir-Media)*
Nicole Boddington *(Copywriter)*

Accounts:
Arkansas Department of Health
Arkansas Department of Parks & Tourism
Arkansas Game and Fish Commission
Arkansas State Police Highway Safety Office
Tyson Foods

CK COMMUNICATIONS, INC. (CKC)
457 Montreal Ave, Melbourne, FL 32935
Tel.: (321) 752-5802
Fax: (321) 752-5898
Toll Free: (800) 594.3CKC
E-Mail: info@ckc411.com
Web Site: www.CKC411.com

Employees: 5
Year Founded: 1999

National Agency Associations: AAF-AMA-PRSA

Agency Specializes In: Above-the-Line, Advertising, Affluent Market, African-American Market, Alternative Advertising, Arts, Automotive, Aviation & Aerospace, Bilingual Market, Brand Development & Integration, Branded Entertainment, Broadcast, Business Publications, Business-To-Business, Cable T.V., Catalogs, Children's Market, Co-op Advertising, Collateral, College, Commercial Photography, Communications, Computers & Software, Consulting, Consumer Goods, Consumer Marketing, Consumer Publications, Content, Corporate Communications, Corporate Identity, Cosmetics, Crisis Communications, Digital/Interactive, Direct Response Marketing, E-Commerce, Education, Electronic Media, Electronics, Engineering, Entertainment, Environmental, Event Planning & Marketing, Exhibit/Trade Shows, Experience Design, Fashion/Apparel, Financial, Food Service, Gay & Lesbian Market, Government/Political, Graphic Design, Guerilla Marketing, Health Care Services, High Technology, Hispanic Market, Household Goods, Identity Marketing, In-Store Advertising, Industrial, Infomercials, Information Technology, Integrated Marketing, International, Internet/Web Design, Investor Relations, Legal Services, Leisure, Local Marketing, Logo & Package Design, Luxury Products, Magazines, Marine, Market Research, Media Buying Services, Media Planning, Media Training, Medical Products, Men's Market, Merchandising, Multicultural, Multimedia, New Product Development, New Technologies, Newspaper, Newspapers & Magazines, Out-of-Home Media, Outdoor, Over-50 Market, Package Design, Pharmaceutical, Planning & Consultation, Point of Purchase, Point of Sale, Print, Production, Production (Ad, Film, Broadcast), Public Relations, Publicity/Promotions, Radio, Real Estate, Recruitment, Regional, Restaurant, Retail, Sales Promotion, Search Engine Optimization, Seniors' Market, Social Marketing/Nonprofit, Sponsorship, Sports Market, Strategic Planning/Research, Sweepstakes, Syndication, T.V., Technical Advertising, Teen Market, Telemarketing, Trade & Consumer Magazines, Transportation, Travel & Tourism, Web (Banner Ads, Pop-ups, etc.), Women's Market, Yellow Pages Advertising

Approx. Annual Billings: $3,735,000

Breakdown of Gross Billings by Media: Audio/Visual: $500,000; Brdcst.: $750,000; Collateral: $250,000; Comml. Photography: $75,000; E-Commerce: $100,000; Event Mktg.: $50,000; Exhibits/Trade Shows: $250,000; Fees: $1,000,000; Graphic Design: $200,000; In-Store Adv.: $10,000; Local Mktg.: $100,000; Logo & Package Design: $100,000; Mags.: $250,000; Newsp.: $100,000

Caroline Kempf *(Pres)*
R. Craig Kempf *(CEO & Dir-Creative)*
Sarah Evans *(Acct Exec)*

CKR INTERACTIVE
399 N 3rd St, Campbell, CA 95008
Tel.: (408) 517-1400
Fax: (408) 517-1491
E-Mail: info@ckrinteractive.com
Web Site: www.ckrinteractive.com

Employees: 35
Year Founded: 2001

Agency Specializes In: Direct Response Marketing, Print, Production, Recruitment

Curtis Rogers *(Pres & CEO)*
Craig Freitag *(Exec VP-Creative)*
Kasey Sixt *(VP)*
Ginger Powell *(Dir-Ops & Specialist-Diversity Initiative)*
Kendra Nostran *(Dir-Peer Grp US)*
Tony Rosato *(Dir-Client Dev)*
Brandon Spencer *(Dir-Interactive)*
Christina Hild *(Sr Mgr-Client)*
Michelle Ferreira *(Sr Project Mgr-Interactive)*
Anne Hillman *(Acct Exec)*

Accounts:

Applied Biosystems
Banner Health
Children's Hospital & Research Center Oakland
DHL Worldwide Express
Genentech
NCH Healthcare System
Northeast Georgia Health System

CLAPP COMMUNICATIONS

(Formerly Barb Clapp Advertising & Marketing)
6115 Falls Rd Penthouse, Baltimore, MD 21209
Tel.: (410) 561-8886
Fax: (410) 561-9064
Web Site: www.clappcommunications.com

Agency Specializes In: Advertising, Event Planning & Marketing, Graphic Design, Market Research, Media Buying Services, Media Planning, Public Relations

Barb Clapp *(Pres & CEO)*
Karen Benckini *(Dir-Media)*
Beth Sykes *(Dir-Charlotte)*
Berri Townsend *(Dir-Creative)*
Lisa Harlow *(Sr Acct Exec)*
Dana Metzger *(Sr Acct Exec)*
Hannah Klarner *(Jr Acct Exec & Specialist-Digital Mktg)*
Leslie Basler *(Acct Exec)*
Lauren Moyer *(Strategist-Social Media)*
Karen Evander *(Coord-Mktg)*

Accounts:
Grand Central Development Marketing, Public Relations
Howard Bank Public Relations
Loews Annapolis Hotel Public Relations
New-Stratford University Public Relations

CLARE ADAMS KITTLE CO., INC.

1921 33rd Ave S, Seattle, WA 98144-4912
Tel.: (206) 683-3882
Toll Free: (800) 346-7582
E-Mail: clare@cakincdesign.com

Employees: 2
Year Founded: 1973

National Agency Associations: DMA

Agency Specializes In: Advertising, Brand Development & Integration, Business-To-Business, Co-op Advertising, Collateral, Consulting, Consumer Marketing, Cosmetics, Direct Response Marketing, Environmental, Event Planning & Marketing, Exhibit/Trade Shows, Fashion/Apparel, Graphic Design, Magazines, Merchandising, Newspaper, Newspapers & Magazines, Outdoor, Print, Production, Retail

Approx. Annual Billings: $500,000

Breakdown of Gross Billings by Media: Collateral: $280,000; Mags.: $160,000; Newsp.: $60,000

Clare Adams Kittle *(Pres)*

Accounts:
American Gem Trade Association; Dallas, TX Jewelry Trade Organization; 1987
Oscar Heyman & Brothers; New York, NY Jewelry; 1973
Turgeon-Raine Jewelers; Seattle, WA; 1986

CLARITY COVERDALE FURY ADVERTISING, INC.

120 S 6th St Ste 1300, Minneapolis, MN 55402-1810
Tel.: (612) 339-3902
Fax: (612) 359-4399
E-Mail: omalley@ccf-ideas.com
Web Site: www.claritycoverdalefury.com

E-Mail for Key Personnel:
President: clarity@ccf-ideas.com
Creative Dir.: coverdale@ccf-ideas.com
Media Dir.: ethier@ccf-ideas.com

Employees: 64
Year Founded: 1979

National Agency Associations: 4A's

Agency Specializes In: Above-the-Line, Advertising, Affluent Market, Alternative Advertising, Below-the-Line, Brand Development & Integration, Business Publications, Business-To-Business, Cable T.V., Catalogs, Collateral, Consumer Goods, Consumer Marketing, Corporate Identity, Digital/Interactive, E-Commerce, Email, Financial, Food Service, Government/Political, Graphic Design, Guerilla Marketing, Health Care Services, Hospitality, Identity Marketing, In-Store Advertising, Integrated Marketing, Internet/Web Design, Logo & Package Design, Luxury Products, Magazines, Market Research, Media Buying Services, Media Planning, Medical Products, Mobile Marketing, Multimedia, New Product Development, Newspaper, Newspapers & Magazines, Out-of-Home Media, Outdoor, Package Design, Paid Searches, Point of Purchase, Point of Sale, Print, Production (Ad, Film, Broadcast), Production (Print), Promotions, Public Relations, Radio, Restaurant, Retail, Sales Promotion, Search Engine Optimization, Social Marketing/Nonprofit, Sponsorship, Strategic Planning/Research, Sweepstakes, T.V., Trade & Consumer Magazines, Transportation, Travel & Tourism, Viral/Buzz/Word of Mouth, Web (Banner Ads, Pop-ups, etc.)

Approx. Annual Billings: $68,701,000

Rob Rankin *(Pres)*
Jac Coverdale *(Exec Creative Dir)*
Adam St. John *(Sr Dir-Art)*
Molly Hull *(Dir-Brand Dev)*
Kathy Schlecht *(Dir-Interactive)*
Robin Rooney *(Supvr-Brand Dev)*
Chealsea Gadtke *(Media Buyer)*
Nicole Huynh *(Media Planner)*
Jamie Peterson *(Asst Media Planner)*

Accounts:
Altru Health System
BMS Group Brand Awareness, Marketing Communications
Boy Scouts of America Northern Star Council (Agency of Record)
Charter Communications
Chopin Vodka
ClearWay Minnesota Campaign: "Still a problem in Minnesota", Minnesota Partnership for Action Against Tobacco, Out-of-Home, Print, www.stillaproblem.com
Dairy Queen
International Dairy Queen, Inc.
Land O'Lakes Feed
Metro Transit
Minnesota Department of Transportation
Minnesota Zoo Campaign: "Ocean is Coming", DINOSAURS! Exhibit
MNsure
Park Nicollet Health Services
Purina Mills Feed
QuitPlan Services
Red Gold Tomatoes
Rembrandt Foods
Seeds 2000
Tuttorosso Tomatoes
Wings Financial Credit Union (Agency of Record) Campaign: "Dream Loan", Digital Campaign, Out-of-Home, Radio, TV
YWCA of Minneapolis (Agency of Record) Bus Shelters, Digital Billboards, Early Childhood Education Program, Health& Fitness, Media Buying, Media Planning, Multimedia, Online & Mobile Banner Ads, Pandora Radio, Restroom Advertising, Strategic Planning

CLARK & ASSOCIATES

11180 Sun Center Dr Ste 100, Rancho Cordova, CA 95670
Tel.: (916) 635-2424
Fax: (916) 635-0531
Toll Free: (877) 888-4040
E-Mail: info@clarkadvertising.com
Web Site: www.clarkadvertising.com

Employees: 6
Year Founded: 1980

Agency Specializes In: Direct Response Marketing, Retail

Approx. Annual Billings: $18,000,000

Edward J. Clark *(Owner)*
Debbie Kovich *(VP-Strategic Plng)*
Marc Rausch *(Creative Dir)*
Steve Poole *(Mgr-SEM)*

CLARK CREATIVE GROUP

514 S 13th St, Omaha, NE 68102
Tel.: (402) 345-5800
Fax: (402) 345-4858
Web Site: www.clarkcreativegroup.com

Agency Specializes In: Advertising, Brand Development & Integration, Graphic Design, Internet/Web Design, Media Planning, Media Relations, Package Design, Public Relations, Social Media, Strategic Planning/Research

Mike Meehan *(VP-Creative Svcs)*
Lauren Huber *(Dir-Bus Dev & Sr Acct Exec)*
Nolan Waak *(Art Dir)*
Daryl Anderson *(Creative Dir)*
Tiffany Heckenlively *(Mgr-Fin)*
Patricia Morrissey *(Office Mgr)*

Accounts:
Opera Omaha

CLARK/NIKDEL/POWELL

62 4th St NW, Winter Haven, FL 33881
Tel.: (863) 299-9980
Fax: (863) 297-9061
E-Mail: info@clarknikdelpowell.com
Web Site: clarknikdelpowell.com/

Employees: 15
Year Founded: 1991

Agency Specializes In: Advertising

Christine E. Nikdel *(Owner)*
Mark Adkins *(Dir-Creative)*
Jarrett Smith *(Dir-Digital)*
Katrina Hill *(Acct Exec)*
Whitney Nall *(Acct Exec)*

Accounts:
Allen & Company
Highlands County Tourist Development Council; Sebring, FL
Historic Bok Sanctuary
Polk County Tourism & Sports Marketing Campaign: "Find Your Element In Central Florida", Website Update

CLARKE ADVERTISING AND PUBLIC RELATIONS

(Name Changed to C Suite Communications)

CLASS ADS

1625 Howard Rd #316, Madera, CA 93637-4946

Advertising Agencies

Tel.: (559) 675-0946
Toll Free: (800) 600-5346
E-Mail: advertising@classads1.com
Web Site: www.classads1.com

Employees: 3
Year Founded: 1992

Agency Specializes In: Advertising, Advertising Specialties, Recruitment

Approx. Annual Billings: $900,000

Breakdown of Gross Billings by Media: Internet Adv.: 55%; Newsp. & Mags.: 45%

Jean Peters *(Owner & CEO)*

Accounts:
Basic Vegetable Products; King City, CA Recruitment; 1993
City of Peoria; IL Recruitment; 1994
Delaware North Co., Inc.; Buffalo, NY Recruitment; 1994
Evergreen International Aviation; McMinnville, OR Recruitment; 1994
Tulare County; Tulare, CA Advertising & Recruitment; 1992
Yosemite Concession Service; Yosemite National Park, CA Recruitment; 1993

CLAY POT CREATIVE
418 S Howes St Ste 100, Fort Collins, CO 80521
Tel.: (970) 495-6855
Fax: (970) 495-6896
Web Site: www.claypotcreative.com

Year Founded: 2000

Agency Specializes In: Advertising, Brand Development & Integration, Event Planning & Marketing, Graphic Design, Internet/Web Design, Logo & Package Design, Social Media

Julia Leach *(Founder, Principal & Strategist-Brand)*
Andy Leach *(Co-Owner & Principal)*
Cindy Kroeger *(Dir-Art)*
Doug Robinson *(Dir-Art)*
Torrie Wolf *(Dir-Art)*
Levi Moe *(Strategist-Mktg)*
Nathan Schmidt *(Designer)*

Accounts:
VFuel

CLAYTON-DAVIS & ASSOCIATES, INCORPORATED
230 S Bemiston Ave Ste 1400, Clayton, MO 63105-3643
Tel.: (314) 862-7800
Fax: (314) 721-5171
E-Mail: info@claytondavis.com

Employees: 35
Year Founded: 1953

Agency Specializes In: Advertising, Arts, Automotive, Brand Development & Integration, Broadcast, Business Publications, Business-To-Business, Catalogs, Children's Market, Co-op Advertising, Collateral, College, Consulting, Consumer Marketing, Consumer Publications, Corporate Identity, Crisis Communications, Custom Publishing, E-Commerce, Electronic Media, Entertainment, Event Planning & Marketing, Exhibit/Trade Shows, Financial, Government/Political, Graphic Design, Health Care Services, Industrial, Infomercials, Internet/Web Design, Investor Relations, Leisure, Logo & Package Design, Magazines, Medical Products, Multimedia, New Product Development, Newspaper, Newspapers & Magazines, Outdoor, Package Design, Pharmaceutical, Planning & Consultation, Point of Purchase, Point of Sale, Print, Production, Production (Ad, Film, Broadcast), Promotions, Public Relations, Publicity/Promotions, Publishing, Radio, Real Estate, Sales Promotion, Seniors' Market, Sports Market, Strategic Planning/Research, Syndication, T.V., Trade & Consumer Magazines, Travel & Tourism

Approx. Annual Billings: $24,750,000

Breakdown of Gross Billings by Media: Audio/Visual: $1,000,000; Bus. Publs.: $3,000,000; Event Mktg.: $750,000; Exhibits/Trade Shows: $500,000; Fees: $2,000,000; Graphic Design: $1,000,000; Mags.: $3,250,000; Newsp.: $1,500,000; Production: $2,000,000; Pub. Rels.: $2,000,000; Radio: $3,000,000; Spot Radio: $750,000; T.V.: $4,000,000

Irvin Davis *(Pres)*

Accounts:
Admiral Broadcasting Co.; Saint Louis, MO Broadcasting Chain
American Chiropractic Association
Celebrity Circle Records
Communications Fund, Inc. Mutual Fund
Crusade Against Crime of America
Delta Tire Corp.; Houston, TX
Disco-Teach; Saint Louis, MO
Fastenation Creation Company; Saint Louis, MO Toys
Frazier-Davis Construction Co. Bridges, Dams, Shafts, Tunnels
Genovese Jewelers; Saint Louis, MO Jewelry Manufacturer & Retailers
Health Prospective; Saint Louis, MO
Jenshare Properties; Saint Louis, MO Real Estate Holdings
NCMIC Insurance Co.; Des Moines, IA Malpractice Insurance
Tishman Realty & Construction Co.; New York, NY
Tobacco & Health Research Board; Lexington, KY
Triad Healthcare, Inc.; Boston, MA
Universal Heavy Equipment School; Miami, FL
Universal Insurance Adjusters; Miami, FL Education Correspondence School
Victorian Tire Corp.; Houston, TX
Zim Products Co. Recording Products

CLAYTON DESIGN GROUP LLC
12386 Mountain Rd, Lovettsville, VA 20180
Tel.: (703) 341-7969
Fax: (703) 448-3820
E-Mail: info@claytondesigngroup.com
Web Site: www.claytondesigngroup.com

Employees: 3
Year Founded: 2002

Agency Specializes In: Graphic Design

Approx. Annual Billings: $500,000

Jim Clayton *(Owner & Mgr)*

Accounts:
AACU; 2004
AAMI; Arlington, VA; 2004
American Diabetes Association
Gilford Corporation; Bethesda, MD; 2008
Keville Enterprises; Boston, MA; 2006
NADCO; McLean, VA; 2008
NAHB Multifamily
National Humanities Alliance; 2007
National Quality Forum; 2006
NRECA; Arlington, VA; 2008
Utilities Telecom Council; 2008
VisionQuest

CLEAN DESIGN, INC.
8081 Arco Corporate Dr Ste 100, Raleigh, NC 27617
Tel.: (919) 544-2193
Fax: (919) 473-2200
E-Mail: info@cleandesign.com
Web Site: www.cleandesign.com

Employees: 18

Agency Specializes In: Advertising, Brand Development & Integration, Digital/Interactive, Environmental, Graphic Design, Identity Marketing, Media Planning, Public Relations

Revenue: $15,000,000

Scott Scaggs *(VP & Dir-Creative)*
Carrie Stewart *(Head-PR & Content)*
Tom Hickey *(Dir-Media)*
Dan Strickford *(Dir-PR)*
Jon Parker *(Assoc Dir-Design & Sr Designer)*
Eleanor Talley *(Acct Mgr)*
Taylor Raasch *(Mgr-PR)*
Steve Kelly *(Media Planner)*
Nancy Woody *(Acct Coord)*
Stephanie Perri *(Client Svc Mgr)*

Accounts:
Bayer Crop Science
Blue Cross Blue Shield of North Carolina
Builders Mutual Insurance Company Brand Redesign, Brand Strategy, Marketing
Carolina Ballet
The Chamber
Chapel Hill & Orange County Visitors Bureau Digital, Print
Citadel Contractors
Duke Raleigh Hospital
Durham Distillery Branding Campaign
John Deere
Lenovo
Lonerider Brewing Company; Raleigh, NC Brand Strategy, Marketing Materials, Rebranding
North Carolina Museum of Art
Paragon Commercial Bank; Raleigh, NC Rebranding, Website Development
Parker Poe Adams & Bernstein LLP Content Marketing, Public Relations
Red Hat
Riverbark
RPG Solutions
SAS Global Forum
SAS
Sentinel Risk Advisors (Creative Agency of Record) Strategic
The Umstead Hotel & Spa
UNC Kenan-Flagler
Uwharrie Heven
Watauga County Tourism Development Authority Brand Positioning, Campaign Development, Media Strategy, strategy
Yadkin Bank (Agency of Record) Advertising, Branding, Communications, Creative, Design, Marketing, Public Relations, Strategy

CLEAN SHEET COMMUNICATIONS
164 Merton St 4th Fl, Toronto, ON M4S 3A8 Canada
Tel.: (416) 489-3629
Fax: (416) 423-2940
E-Mail: nmcostrich@cleansheet.ca
Web Site: www.cleansheet.ca

Employees: 28
Year Founded: 2005

Agency Specializes In: Advertising

Catherine Frank *(Co-Founder, Pres & COO)*
Neil McOstrich *(Co-Founder)*

Accounts:
Ceryx

CMC Markets
Easter Seals
Elections Ontario
Globalive Communications; 2009
Go RVing
Liver Foundation
Saputo

CLEAR BLUE INC.

16740 Birkdale Commons Pkwy Ste 210, Huntersville, NC 28078
Tel.: (704) 895-7890
Web Site: www.theclearblue.com

Year Founded: 1998

Agency Specializes In: Advertising, Affiliate Marketing, Brand Development & Integration, Package Design, Print, Promotions, Public Relations, T.V.

Robin S. Konieczny *(Pres & Chief Creative Officer)*
Jim Konieczny *(CFO)*
Mandy Shelton *(Acct Exec)*

CLEARMOTIVE MARKETING GROUP

Ste 300 - 239 10 Ave SE, Calgary, Alberta T2G 0V9 Canada
Tel.: (403) 235-6339
Fax: (403) 366-4268
Web Site: www.clearmotive.ca

Year Founded: 2007

Agency Specializes In: Advertising, Brand Development & Integration, Corporate Identity, Digital/Interactive, Market Research, Media Planning, Outdoor, Radio, Social Media, T.V.

Chad Kroeker *(Founder & Chief Creative Officer)*
Tyler Chisholm *(CEO)*
Laura Callow *(Head-Integrated Mktg)*
Renee Netzel *(Acct Mgr)*
Sheryl Anderson *(Mgr-Client Projects)*

CLEARPH DESIGN

147 2nd Ave S Ste 210, Saint Petersburg, FL 33701
Tel.: (727) 851-9596
Web Site: www.clearph.com

Year Founded: 2006

Agency Specializes In: Advertising, Brand Development & Integration, Corporate Identity, Digital/Interactive, Internet/Web Design

Richard Hughes *(CEO & Creative Dir)*
Craig Ditmar *(Dir-Art)*
Kaeli Ellis *(Dir-Creative)*

Accounts:
Momentis

CLEARRIVER COMMUNICATIONS GROUP

2401 Eastlawn Dr, Midland, MI 48640
Tel.: (989) 631-9560
Fax: (989) 631-7977
E-Mail: info@clear-river.com
Web Site: www.clear-river.com

Employees: 20
Year Founded: 1955

Agency Specializes In: Advertising, Bilingual Market, Brand Development & Integration, Business-To-Business, Collateral, Communications, Consumer Marketing, Content, Corporate Communications, Corporate Identity, Direct-to-Consumer, Graphic Design, Health Care Services, Identity Marketing, Integrated Marketing, International, Internet/Web Design, Logo & Package Design, Market Research, Media Buying Services, Media Planning, Medical Products, New Product Development, Newspaper, Newspapers & Magazines, Package Design, Pharmaceutical, Planning & Consultation, Print, Production, Production (Print), Promotions, Sales Promotion, Stakeholders, Strategic Planning/Research, Technical Advertising, Travel & Tourism

Dan Umlauf *(Pres)*
Nathan Wilds *(Dir-Creative)*

Accounts:
The Dow Chemical Company; Midland, MI; 1955
Gerber Products Company; Freemont, MI; 1990

CLEVELAND DESIGN

20 McKenna Terr, Boston, MA 02132
Tel.: (617) 469-4641
Fax: (617) 469-0040
E-Mail: info@clevelanddesign.com
Web Site: www.clevelanddesign.com

Year Founded: 1992

Agency Specializes In: Advertising, Brand Development & Integration, Digital/Interactive, Exhibit/Trade Shows, Print

Jonathan Cleveland *(Founder & Principal)*
Jenny Daughters *(Dir-Art)*
Adamo Maisano *(Graphic Designer & Designer-Web)*
Diana Morales *(Designer)*
Andy Paul *(Copywriter)*

Accounts:
Sensitech Inc.
Thomson Reuters Markets

CLICK HERE LABS

(Formerly Click Here, Inc.)
2801 N Central Expy Ste 100, Dallas, TX 75231-6430
Tel.: (214) 891-5325
Fax: (214) 346-4870
E-Mail: info@clickhere.com
Web Site: clickherelabs.com

Employees: 140
Year Founded: 1995

National Agency Associations: SODA

Agency Specializes In: Advertising, Advertising Specialties, Affluent Market, Automotive, Aviation & Aerospace, Bilingual Market, Brand Development & Integration, Business-To-Business, College, Communications, Computers & Software, Consulting, Consumer Goods, Consumer Marketing, Content, Corporate Identity, Customer Relationship Management, Digital/Interactive, Direct Response Marketing, Direct-to-Consumer, E-Commerce, Electronic Media, Electronics, Email, Entertainment, Experience Design, Fashion/Apparel, Financial, Food Service, Game Integration, Gay & Lesbian Market, Graphic Design, Guerilla Marketing, Health Care Services, High Technology, Hospitality, Household Goods, Identity Marketing, Information Technology, Integrated Marketing, Internet/Web Design, Leisure, Local Marketing, Logo & Package Design, Luxury Products, Magazines, Media Buying Services, Media Planning, Medical Products, Men's Market, Mobile Marketing, Multimedia, New Product Development, New Technologies, Newspaper, Outdoor, Package Design, Paid Searches, Pharmaceutical, Planning & Consultation, Podcasting, Print, Production, RSS (Really Simple Syndication), Restaurant, Retail, Search Engine Optimization, Social Marketing/Nonprofit, Social Media, Sponsorship, Strategic Planning/Research, Sweepstakes, T.V., Technical Advertising, Teen Market, Transportation, Travel & Tourism, Viral/Buzz/Word of Mouth, Women's Market

Approx. Annual Billings: $161,000,000

Breakdown of Gross Billings by Media: E-Commerce: 15%; Internet Adv.: 45%; Strategic Planning/Research: 10%; Worldwide Web Sites: 30%

Randy Bradshaw *(Principal)*
Joe Wilson *(Dir-Digital Production)*
Eric Anderson *(Project Mgr-Digital)*
Kari Berdelle *(Project Mgr-Digital)*
Shayna Fawcett *(Project Mgr-Digital)*
Peter Stettner *(Project Mgr-Digital)*
Gary Anderson *(Mgr-Production)*
Roddy McGinnis *(Mgr-Quality Control)*
Robert Kurtz *(Planner-Interactive Media & Search)*

Accounts:
1-800 CONTACTS/Glasses.com; 2012
Anderson Erickson Dairy
The Biltmore
Central Market
Chick-fil-A; Atlanta, GA Restaurant; 2005
Children's Medical Center; Dallas, TX; 2006
Fiat USA; 2012
GameStop Corp.; Grapevine, TX Gaming, Retail; 2007
GoRVing RV Dealers & Manufacturers; 2002
The Home Depot; Atlanta, GA Home Improvement Supplies; 2006
Pier1.com; Fort Worth, TX Ecommerce Site; 2010
Sewell Automotive; Dallas, TX; 2002
Sub-Zero
Ulta

CLICKCULTURE

3600 Glenwood Ave, Raleigh, NC 27612
Tel.: (919) 420-7736
Fax: (919) 420-7758
E-Mail: info@clickculture.com
Web Site: www.clickculture.com

Employees: 10

Agency Specializes In: Digital/Interactive, Web (Banner Ads, Pop-ups, etc.)

Lloyd Jacobs *(Pres & CEO)*

Accounts:
Autosportif; United Kingdom Web Site; 2008
Bigelow Tea
Branding
Bruegger's Bagels
Chiropractic Partners Branding, Social Media Programming, Website Design
Crabtree Valley Mall
Creation Autosportif
Divi Resorts
Events Planning
Happy Green Bee
Hosting
HPW
Kanki
Loparex
North Carolina Symphony Web Site; 2008
Nowell's Contemporary Furniture (Agency of Record) Broadcast Media, Digital, Marketing, Print
Pleasant Green Farms
Reichold
Robuck Homes
RRAR/TMLS
Rufty Homes
TriLake Granite & Stone
Vincent Shoes

Wyrick-Robbins

CLICKSPRING DESIGN

200 Lexington Ave, New York, NY 10016
Tel.: (212) 220-0962
Fax: (212) 683-5005
E-Mail: info@clickspringdesign.com
Web Site: www.clickspringdesign.com

Employees: 13

Agency Specializes In: Advertising, Entertainment, Event Planning & Marketing, Exhibit/Trade Shows, Fashion/Apparel, T.V.

Erik Ulfers *(Owner)*
Lori Nadler *(Sr VP-Fin & Ops)*
Steven Dvorak *(VP-Design)*
Robin Jacobs *(Dir-Strategic Accts)*
Karen Engelmann *(Copywriter)*
Tarrant Smith *(Designer-Set)*

Accounts:
Activision Blizzard, Inc
Brown-Forman Forester Center
CNN
Codage
General Motors
Home Depot
NBC
Nintendo
Sanofi Aventis
Time Warner
Wal-Mart

CLIENT FOCUSED MEDIA

1611 San Marco Blvd, Jacksonville, FL 32207
Tel.: (904) 232-3001
Fax: (904) 232-3003
Web Site: www.cfmedia.net

Year Founded: 2003

Agency Specializes In: Advertising, Brand Development & Integration, Digital/Interactive, Internet/Web Design, Media Buying Services, Promotions, Public Relations, Radio, Search Engine Optimization, T.V.

Matt White *(Pres)*
Paresh Patel *(COO)*
Jordan R. Biehl *(Gen Counsel & Sr Strategist)*
Kyle Brown *(Exec VP)*

Accounts:
Connection Festival
First Coast Home Pros
Golftec, Inc.
House of Fame Mixed Martial Arts
Hugos Fine Furnishings & Interiors
Jacksonville Ice & Sportsplex
Mike Ryan
My Drivers
Sahara Cafe & Bar
UNF Division of Continuing Education

CLIFF ROSS

400 Northampton St, Easton, PA 18042
Tel.: (610) 829-1333
Web Site: www.cliffross.com

Agency Specializes In: Advertising, Collateral, Digital/Interactive, Internet/Web Design, Logo & Package Design, Media Buying Services, Print, Promotions, Search Engine Optimization, Social Media

Cliff Ross *(Owner)*
Brianna Wenner *(Specialist-Adv & Social Media)*

Accounts:
College Hill Neighborhood Association
Combative Arts Institute
Easton Outdoor Company
Ed Shaughnessy
Express Business Center
Steven Glickman Architect
VapeMeister

CLINE, DAVIS & MANN, INC.

(Name Changed to The CDM Group)

CLIX MARKETING

380 Lexington Ave 17th Fl, New York, NY 10168
Tel.: (415) 887-7603
Web Site: www.clixmarketing.com

Year Founded: 2003

Agency Specializes In: Advertising, Email, Radio, Search Engine Optimization, Web (Banner Ads, Pop-ups, etc.)

John Lee *(Mng Partner)*
Mae Polczynski *(Mng Partner)*
Mae Flint *(Dir-Ops)*
Michelle Morgan *(Dir-Accts & Efficiency & Community Dir)*
Amy Bishop *(Sr Mgr-Audits, Outbound & Trng)*
Robert Brady *(Sr Mgr-Software, SMB & Strategy)*
Susan Wenograd *(Sr Mgr-Accounts & E-Commerce Strategy)*

Accounts:
Search Marketing Expo Search Marketing Conference
SEMJ.org Search Engine Marketing Journal Publishers

CLM MARKETING & ADVERTISING

588 W Idaho St, Boise, ID 83702-5928
Tel.: (208) 342-2525
Fax: (208) 384-1906
E-Mail: brad@clmnorthwest.com
Web Site: www.clmnorthwest.com

E-Mail for Key Personnel:
President: bsurkamer@closedloopboise.com
Creative Dir.: kolson@closedloopboise.com
Media Dir.: bwoodbury@closedloopboise.com

Employees: 15
Year Founded: 1980

National Agency Associations: ABC-APA

Agency Specializes In: Advertising, Automotive, Brand Development & Integration, Branded Entertainment, Broadcast, Business-To-Business, Co-op Advertising, Commercial Photography, Corporate Identity, Digital/Interactive, Electronics, Financial, Food Service, Government/Political, Graphic Design, Guerilla Marketing, Health Care Services, High Technology, Integrated Marketing, Internet/Web Design, Market Research, Media Buying Services, Media Planning, New Product Development, Newspapers & Magazines, Outdoor, Print, Production (Ad, Film, Broadcast), Production (Print), Radio, Retail, Search Engine Optimization, Sponsorship, Strategic Planning/Research, T.V., Web (Banner Ads, Pop-ups, etc.)

Brad Surkamer *(Pres)*
Della Fencl *(Controller)*
Max White *(Sr Dir-Art)*
Nicolet Laursen *(Art Dir)*
John Liebenthal *(Dir-Creative)*
Becki Woodbury *(Dir-Media & Res)*
Katie Miller *(Mgr-Social Media & Media Buyer)*
Mike Gerhardt *(Sr Acct Supvr)*
Morgan Lord *(Media Planner)*

Accounts:
Commercial Tires
Idaho Central Credit Union; Pocatello, ID
Idaho Lottery
Intermountain Hospital; Boise, ID
Monsanto Chemicals; Boise, ID
Norandex Distributing; Macedonia, OH

CLOCKWORK ACTIVE MEDIA

1501 E Hennepin Ave, Minneapolis, MN 55414
Tel.: (612) 677-3075
E-Mail: inquiries@clockwork.net
Web Site: www.clockwork.net

Year Founded: 2002

Agency Specializes In: Advertising, Content, Digital/Interactive, Internet/Web Design, Sponsorship

Chuck Hermes *(Founder & Partner)*
Nancy Lyons *(Pres & CEO)*
Meghan Wilker *(COO)*
Matt Gray *(VP-Tech)*
Emily McAuliffe *(VP-Strategy & UX)*
Jenny Holman *(Dir-Interactive Promos)*
Scott Jackson *(Dir-Fin)*
Lyz Nagan *(Dir-Comm)*

Accounts:
Twin Cities in Motion

CLOCKWORK DESIGN GROUP INC.

13 Felton St, Waltham, MA 02453
Tel.: (781) 938-0006
Fax: (781) 938-0030
Web Site: www.cdgi.com

Employees: 4
Year Founded: 1994

Agency Specializes In: Advertising, Identity Marketing, Internet/Web Design, Print, Search Engine Optimization

Vanessa Schaefer *(Pres & Dir-Creative)*
Michael Fleischner *(CEO & Dir-Production)*
Danielle Diforio *(Mgr-Accts)*
Bonnie Kittle *(Graphic Designer & Designer-Web)*

Accounts:
Anderson & Kreiger LLP Corporate Branding, Website Design & Development; 2013
Edelstein & Company CPA Corporate Branding, Stationary & Collateral, Website Design & Development; 2014
Hobbs Brook Management Website Design & Development; 2013
OBP Medical Inc Product Datasheets, Tradeshow Booth, Website Design & Development; 2013

CLOUDRAKER

1435 rue Saint-Alexandre, Ste 700, Montreal, QC H3A 2G4 Canada
Tel.: (514) 499-0005
Fax: (514) 499-0525
E-Mail: info@cloudraker.com
Web Site: www.cloudraker.com

Employees: 50
Year Founded: 2000

Agency Specializes In: Advertising, Digital/Interactive, E-Commerce, Media Relations, Search Engine Optimization, Social Marketing/Nonprofit, Strategic Planning/Research, Viral/Buzz/Word of Mouth, Web (Banner Ads, Pop-ups, etc.)

Thane Calder *(Founder & Pres)*
Pascal Hebert *(Mng Dir)*
Genevieve Carrier *(Head-Strategy & Programs)*

Stephane Caron *(Dir-Technology)*

Accounts:
Asics
Bell Canada
eBay Canada
EnRoute
Heineken International
New-Kijiji Canada Campaign: "Kijiji Raps"
Lise Watier
LOULOU Magazine
MSSS
Tiff

CLYNE MEDIA INC.

169-B Belle Forest Cir, Nashville, TN 37221
Tel.: (615) 662-1616
Fax: (615) 662-1636
E-Mail: info@clynemedia.com
Web Site: www.clynemedia.com

Agency Specializes In: Advertising, Communications, Graphic Design, Media Relations, Public Relations, Social Media

Robert Clyne *(Pres & CEO)*
Corey Walthall *(Coord-PR)*

Accounts:
Roland Corporation (Agency of Record)

CM COMMUNICATIONS, INC.

20 Park Plz Ste 821, Boston, MA 02116
Tel.: (617) 536-3400
Fax: (617) 536-3424
E-Mail: lmoretti@cmcommunications.com
Web Site: www.cmcommunications.com

Employees: 10
Year Founded: 1986

Agency Specializes In: Advertising, Advertising Specialties, Collateral, Direct Response Marketing, Entertainment, Graphic Design, Internet/Web Design, Media Buying Services, Pharmaceutical, Public Relations, Strategic Planning/Research

Approx. Annual Billings: $500,000

Lori Moretti *(Owner)*
Meg Almquist *(Sr Acct Mgr)*
Michael Conrad *(Production Mgr)*

Accounts:
Phillips Hospitality; Boston, MA; 2006
Sarku Japan Fast Food Chain; 2008

CMA: CREATIVE MEDIA & ASSOCIATES

219 Changebridge Rd, Montville, NJ 07045
Tel.: (973) 939-8831
Fax: (973) 299-7937
E-Mail: info@cmaads.com
Web Site: www.cmaads.com

Employees: 15
Year Founded: 2005

Agency Specializes In: Advertising, Advertising Specialties, Affiliate Marketing, Affluent Market, African-American Market, Alternative Advertising, Automotive, Bilingual Market, Broadcast, Business Publications, Business-To-Business, Cable T.V., Catalogs, Co-op Advertising, Collateral, College, Commercial Photography, Communications, Computers & Software, Consulting, Consumer Goods, Consumer Marketing, Consumer Publications, Corporate Communications, Corporate Identity, Crisis Communications, Custom Publishing, Customer Relationship Management, Digital/Interactive, Direct Response Marketing, Direct-to-Consumer, E-Commerce, Education, Electronic Media, Email, Engineering, Event Planning & Marketing, Financial, Gay & Lesbian Market, Graphic Design, High Technology, Hispanic Market, Hospitality, Identity Marketing, Infomercials, Information Technology, Integrated Marketing, Internet/Web Design, Investor Relations, Legal Services, Local Marketing, Logo & Package Design, Luxury Products, Magazines, Marine, Market Research, Media Buying Services, Media Planning, Media Relations, Media Training, Medical Products, Merchandising, Mobile Marketing, Multicultural, Multimedia, New Product Development, New Technologies, Newspaper, Newspapers & Magazines, Out-of-Home Media, Outdoor, Package Design, Paid Searches, Planning & Consultation, Podcasting, Point of Purchase, Point of Sale, Print, Production, Production (Print), Promotions, Public Relations, Publicity/Promotions, Publishing, RSS (Really Simple Syndication), Radio, Real Estate, Recruitment, Regional, Restaurant, Retail, Sales Promotion, Search Engine Optimization, Seniors' Market, Sponsorship, Sports Market, Strategic Planning/Research, Syndication, T.V., Technical Advertising, Teen Market, Telemarketing, Trade & Consumer Magazines, Transportation, Travel & Tourism, Urban Market, Women's Market, Yellow Pages Advertising

Approx. Annual Billings: $8,000,000

Breakdown of Gross Billings by Media: Cable T.V.: $1,000,000; Consulting: $500,000; Graphic Design: $1,000,000; Newsp.: $3,000,000; Out-of-Home Media: $500,000; Outdoor: $500,000; Radio: $1,000,000; Strategic Planning/Research: $500,000

Peter Lombardo *(Pres)*

Accounts:
Ayers Chevrolet; Dover, NJ; 1990
Borough Chrysler Jeep
Butler Chrysler Jeep
Caldwell Toyota; Caldwell, NJ; 1999
Ed Carney Ford; East Hanover, NJ; 1998
Elite Ford
Family Ford; Hackettstown, NJ; 1998
Lifetrak; Wellington, FL; 2006
State Line Huyndai
Trend Volkswagen; Rockaway, NJ; 2000

CMD

1631 NW Thurman St, Portland, OR 97209-2558
Tel.: (503) 223-6794
Fax: (503) 223-2430
E-Mail: info@cmdagency.com
Web Site: www.cmdagency.com

E-Mail for Key Personnel:
President: preilly@cmdagency.com
Creative Dir.: dswanson@cmdagency.com
Media Dir.: pcody@cmdagency.com
Production Mgr.: lhubler@cmdagency.com
Public Relations: dmeihoff@cmdagency.com

Employees: 175
Year Founded: 1978

Agency Specializes In: Above-the-Line, Advertising, Advertising Specialties, Below-the-Line, Brand Development & Integration, Broadcast, Business Publications, Business-To-Business, Cable T.V., Co-op Advertising, Collateral, Consumer Goods, Consumer Marketing, Consumer Publications, Corporate Identity, Digital/Interactive, Direct Response Marketing, Electronic Media, Email, Event Planning & Marketing, Exhibit/Trade Shows, Graphic Design, High Technology, Hospitality, Identity Marketing, Integrated Marketing, Internet/Web Design, Logo & Package Design, Media Planning, Media Relations, Multimedia, Newspapers & Magazines, Out-of-Home Media, Outdoor, Package Design, Print, Production, Production (Print), Promotions, Public Relations, Publicity/Promotions, Radio, Sales Promotion, Sponsorship, Sports Market, Strategic Planning/Research, Technical Advertising, Web (Banner Ads, Pop-ups, etc.)

Approx. Annual Billings: $45,000,000

Phil Reilly *(Pres)*
Julie Yamamoto *(Mng Dir)*
Patti Cody *(Mng Dir-Media Grp)*
Jeff Zabel *(Mng Dir-Promos Mktg)*
Darcie Meihoff *(VP & Exec Dir-Earned Media)*
Brad Wignall *(VP-Creative Svcs)*
Michele Houck *(Grp Acct Dir)*
Stacy Rogers *(Grp Acct Dir)*
Laura Hubler *(Sr Producer & Mgr-Print)*
Meg Kaczyk *(Dir-Creative)*
Debbie May *(Acct Mgr)*
Colby Reade *(Acct Supvr)*
Claire Scott *(Acct Supvr)*
Justin Villegas *(Sr Acct Exec)*
Matt Allen *(Designer-Interactive)*

Accounts:
Adidas; Portland, OR Retail Outlet; 2009
Asus; Fremont, CA Computers; 2007
Autodesk; San Rafael, CA Software; 2005
Banner Bank (Agency of Record)
Cisco Systems; San Jose, CA; 2000
Freightliner Trucks, NA; Charlotte, NC; 2010
Hewlett-Packard; Palo Alto, CA; 1993
Iberdrola; Portland, OR Wind; 2008
Intel; Santa Clara, CA; 1992
JELD-WEN; Klamath Falls, OR Doors & Windows; 1998
Microsoft; Redmond, WA; 2001
NW Natural Gas; Portland, OR; 2000
Old Spaghetti Factory; Portland, OR Dining; 2003
Regence Blue Cross Blue Shield; Portland, OR Health Insurance; 2003
VMWare; Palo Alto, CA; 2011
Western Star Trucks; Charlotte, NC; 2009

CMDS

13 Cherry Tree Farm Rd, Middletown, NJ 07748
Tel.: (732) 706-5555
Fax: (732) 706-5551
E-Mail: info@cmdsonline.com
Web Site: www.cmdsonline.com

Employees: 5

Agency Specializes In: Advertising, Brand Development & Integration, Broadcast, Business Publications, Business-To-Business, Collateral, Computers & Software, Consulting, Consumer Marketing, Content, Digital/Interactive, E-Commerce, Electronic Media, Financial, Graphic Design, Guerilla Marketing, Health Care Services, Identity Marketing, Industrial, Integrated Marketing, Internet/Web Design, Logo & Package Design, Magazines, Medical Products, Multimedia, New Technologies, Package Design, Paid Searches, Pharmaceutical, Print, Production (Ad, Film, Broadcast), RSS (Really Simple Syndication), Real Estate, Retail, Search Engine Optimization, Web (Banner Ads, Pop-ups, etc.)

Christopher J. Mulvaney *(Pres & CEO)*
Temilyn V. Mehta *(VP-Client Svcs)*
Walter Deyo *(Designer-Web)*

Accounts:
Oceanside CPR Website

CMG WORLDWIDE

10500 Crosspoint Blvd, Indianapolis, IN 46256-3331
Tel.: (317) 570-5000
Fax: (317) 570-5500

Web Site: www.cmgworldwide.com

E-Mail for Key Personnel:
Chairman: mark@marilynmonroe.com

Employees: 45
Year Founded: 1972

Agency Specializes In: Bilingual Market, E-Commerce, Entertainment, Hispanic Market, Internet/Web Design, Legal Services, Merchandising, Publicity/Promotions, Sports Market

Mark Roesler *(Chm & CEO)*
Maria Gejdosova *(CFO)*
Joshua Eber *(Dir-Ecommerce Dept)*
Carole Hwang *(Dir-Mktg & Licensing)*
Cara McMains *(Dir-PR)*
Kyle H. Norman *(Dir-Fin)*
J. Brock Herr *(Counsel-In-House Legal)*

Accounts:
Al Joyner
Al Ratliff
Alan Ladd
Alexander Cartwright
Aloha Wanderwall
Amelia Earhart
Andre de Dienes Archives
Andre the Giant
The Andrews Sisters
Ann Corio
Arthur Ashe
Ava Gardner
Babe Ruth
Bart Stan
Benny Goodman
Bessie Coleman
Bette Davis
Bettie Page
Bill Elliot
Billie Holliday
Billy Martin
Bob Cousy
Bob Feller
Bobby Helms
Bobby Layne
Bridget Marquardt
Buck Buchanan
Buddy Parker
Buddy Rich
Burleigh Grimes
Carl Erskine
Carl Hubbell
Casey Stengel
Charlie Parker
Chobat's Historical Racing
Christopher Rios (Big Pun)
Christy Mathewson
Chuck Berry
Darrell Gwynn
David Carradine
David Chobat
David Niven
Dick "Night Train" Lane
Dizzy Dean
Don Drysdale
Don Larsen
Don McLean
Don Newcombe
Donald O'Connor
Dorothy Lamour
Dr. Philo T. Farnsworth
Dudley Moore
Early Wynn
Eartha Kitt
Edd Roush
Eddie Mathews
Eddy Collins
Edward White II
Ella Fitzgerald
Elvira
Enos Slaughter
Fergie Jenkins
Florence Griffith Joyner
Floyde Patterson
Frank Chance
Frank Lloyd Wright
Gene Siskel
Gene Tierney
General George S. Patton, Jr.
George Barris
George Mikan
George Napolitano
George Sisler
George "Spanky" McFarland
George "The Gipper" Gipp
Gil Hodges
Ginger Rogers
Glenn Miller
Grover Alexander
Harmon Killebrew
Hedy Lamarr
Helen Hayes
Herb Pennock
Honus Wagner
Hristo Stoitchkov
I Love NY
Ingrid Bergman
Ivana Trump
Ivo Pitanguy
Jack Dempsey
Jack Kerouac
Jackie Robinson
James Dean
James J. Braddock
Jascha Heifetz
Jayne Mansfield
Jean Harlow
Jim Heins
Jim Palmer
Jim Taylor
Jim Thorpe
Jimmie Foxx
Joe Louis
John Belushi
John Evers
Johnny Mize
Josephine Baker
Kate Smith
Knute Rockne
Lana Turner
Lee Strasberg
Lefty Grove
Leo Durocher
Liberace
Lillian Gish
Lou Brock
Lou Gehrig
Lou Jacobs
Malcom X
Marian Anderson
Marilyn Monroe
Mark Twain
Mary Wells
Matthew "Stymie" Beard, Jr.
Matthew
Mel Ott
Michael Buffer
Mickey Cochrane
Mickey Rooney
Milton Berle
Minnesota Fats
Mitch Hedberg
Monte Irvin
Montgomery Clift
Mordecai "Three Finger" Brown
Natalie Wood
Neal Armstrong
Nicholas Brothers
Olivia De Berardinis
Ollie Matson
Oscar Schmidt
Oscar Wilde
Pee Wee Reese
Peter Lawford
Peter Sellers
Pie Traynor
Ralph Kiner
Raymond Loewy
Redd Foxx
The Ring
Robert Culp
Robert Mulrenin
Robert Newton
Roberto Duran
Rock Hudson
Rocky Marciano
Rogers Hornsby
Roy Campanella
Rube Marquard
Scott Baio
Scott Brayton
Shannon Twins
Sharon Tate
"Shoeless" Joe Jackson
Sir Laurence Olivier
"Smoky" Joe Wood
Steve Kaufman
Stutz Bearcat
Super Bowl Shuffle
Tammy Wynette
Telly Savalas
Tennessee Ernie Ford
Thomas
Thurman Munson
Tiny Tim
Tommy John
Tony Lazzeri
Tris Speaker
Ty Cobb
Tyrone Power
The Vatican Library Collection
Victoria Fuller
Virginia Mayo
Walter Johnson
Walter Maranville
"Wee" Willie Keeler
Will Rogers
William "Buckwheat" Thomas
Willie Brown
Y.A. Title
Zack Wheat

Branch

CMG Worldwide-Los Angeles Office
9229 W Sunset Blvd Ste 950, West Hollywood, CA 90069
Tel.: (310) 651-2000
Fax: (317) 570-5500
Web Site: www.cmgworldwide.com

Employees: 5
Year Founded: 1974

Agency Specializes In: Brand Development & Integration, Entertainment, International, Legal Services

Mark Roesler *(Chm & CEO)*
Samantha Chang *(Dir-Licensing & Mktg)*
Joshua Eber *(Dir-ECommerce)*
Carole Hwang *(Dir-Mktg & Licensing)*
Kyle H. Norman *(Dir-Fin)*

CMT CREATIVE MARKETING TEAM
1600 W 13th St, Houston, TX 77008
Tel.: (713) 622-7977
Fax: (713) 774-8896
Web Site: www.cmtmarketing.net

Agency Specializes In: Brand Development & Integration, Graphic Design, Internet/Web Design, Print, Promotions

Cecilia Chang *(Pres & CEO)*
Peter Mannes *(VP-Creative)*

Accounts:
Hilong Group
United Central Bank Inc.

CO: COLLECTIVE
419 Park Ave S, New York, NY 10016
Tel.: (212) 505-2300
Fax: (646) 380-4687
E-Mail: hello@cocollective.com
Web Site: www.cocollective.com

Year Founded: 2010

Agency Specializes In: Brand Development & Integration, Sponsorship

Ty Montague *(Founder & Co-CEO)*
Neil Parker *(Co-Founder & Chief Strategy Officer)*
Rosemarie Ryan *(Co-Founder)*
Tiffany Rolfe *(Partner & Chief Content Officer)*
Gavin May *(Head-Strategy)*
Cole Manship *(Strategist)*

Accounts:
Madison Square Gardens Fan Engagement; 2010
MTV Spike Channel; 2010

THE COAKLEY HEAGERTY ADVERTISING & PUBLIC RELATIONS CO.
(Name Changed to HyperRelevance)

COALITION TECHNOLOGIES
750 S Robertson Blvd Ste 200, Culver City, CA 90232
Tel.: (310) 827-3890
Fax: (323) 920-0390
Web Site: www.coalitiontechnologies.com

Year Founded: 2009

Agency Specializes In: Advertising, Brand Development & Integration, Digital/Interactive, Internet/Web Design, Logo & Package Design, Media Buying Services, Paid Searches, Search Engine Optimization, Social Media

Kenny Cornutt *(CFO)*

Accounts:
New-Gray Malin
New-Hedley & Bennett

COATES KOKES
421 SW 6th Ave Ste 1300, Portland, OR 97204-1637
Tel.: (503) 241-1124
Fax: (503) 241-1326
E-Mail: info@coateskokes.com
Web Site: www.coateskokes.com

Employees: 20
Year Founded: 1978

National Agency Associations: MAGNET

Agency Specializes In: Advertising, Brand Development & Integration, Environmental, Graphic Design, Internet/Web Design, Public Relations

Jeanie Coates *(Founder & CEO)*
Steve Kokes *(Pres & Dir-Strategic)*
Lindsay Frank *(VP-Ops)*
Meghan Burke *(Dir-Media)*
Mike Sheen *(Dir-Creative)*
Sue Van Brocklin *(Dir-PR)*
Christina Bertalot *(Acct Mgr)*
Lance Heisler *(Acct Mgr-PR)*
Anri Sugitani *(Asst Acct Mgr)*
Shelby Wood *(Sr Writer)*

Accounts:
Adventist Health; Portland, OR; 2009
Avista; Spokane, WA Utility Company; 2005
Martin Hospitality

COCO+CO
189 Ward Hill Ave, Ward Hill, MA 01835
Tel.: (978) 374-1900
Fax: (978) 521-4636
E-Mail: creative@cocoboston.com
Web Site: www.cocoboston.com

Employees: 6
Year Founded: 1991

Agency Specializes In: Advertising, Brand Development & Integration, Broadcast, Business-To-Business, Cable T.V., Consumer Marketing, Corporate Communications, Crisis Communications, Direct Response Marketing, Electronic Media, Exhibit/Trade Shows, Government/Political, Graphic Design, Integrated Marketing, Internet/Web Design, Media Buying Services, Media Planning, Media Relations, Multimedia, Newspaper, Newspapers & Magazines, Planning & Consultation, Print, Production, Production (Ad, Film, Broadcast), Public Relations, Publicity/Promotions, Radio, Real Estate, Strategic Planning/Research, T.V., Yellow Pages Advertising

Approx. Annual Billings: $250,000

Breakdown of Gross Billings by Media: Fees: $250,000

Tim Coco *(Pres & CEO)*
Carolyn R. Russell *(Sr Planner-Strategy)*

CODE AND THEORY
575 Bdwy 5th Fl, New York, NY 10012
Tel.: (212) 358-0717
Fax: (212) 358-1623
E-Mail: ny.info@codeandtheory.com
Web Site: www.codeandtheory.com

Year Founded: 2001

Agency Specializes In: Advertising, Brand Development & Integration, Digital/Interactive, Graphic Design, Internet/Web Design, Print, Production (Ad, Film, Broadcast), Sponsorship, Strategic Planning/Research

Dan Gardner *(Co-Founder & Dir-Creative-UX)*
Steve Baer *(Mng Partner-Brand Design)*
Michael Martin *(Mng Partner-SF)*
Chris Hayes *(Partner & Global CMO)*
David Dicamillo *(Partner & Dir-Ops)*
Dotty Giordano *(Partner)*
Rob Bigwood *(Sr Dir-Interactive Art)*
Mariana Bukvic *(Dir-Creative)*
Peter Gallo *(Dir-UX)*
Shawn Hoekstra *(Dir-Art)*
Michelle Spivak *(Dir-Creative)*
Sarah McCormick *(Sr Acct Supvr)*
Allison Amato *(Acct Supvr)*
Alexandra Rogers *(Acct Supvr)*
Sara Bekerman *(Strategist-Creative)*

Accounts:
Brown-Forman Campaign: "Tonight. Two Words. Jack Fire", Digital, Social, Tennessee Fire
Burger King (Digital Agency of Record) Big King Sandwich, Campaign: "Be Your Way", Campaign: "Subservient Chicken", Chicken Fries, Chicken Strips, Marketing
New-Chandon
Comcast
Dr Pepper Snapple Group, Inc. (Digital Agency of Record) Campaign: "Always One of a Kind", Campaign: "Man'Ments"
New-Essie
Fashion's Night Out
Finlandia Vodka Campaign: "To The Life Less Ordinary", Global Website
Gant USA Corporation
Interview Magazine Campaign: "Delighting Readers"
L'Oreal Maybelline
Los Angeles Times
Mashable.com Campaign: "Reimagining what Blogs Can Do"
Maybelline New York (Digital Agency of Record)
Motel 6 Website
New-New York Life Insurance (Digital Agency of Record)
Showtime Campaign: "Going Social with an Ipad App"
Variety.com Redesign
The Verge Campaign: "More than a Tech Blog"
Vogue
Vox Media, Inc.

COGNETIX, INC.
1866 Wallenberg Blvd Ste B, Charleston, SC 29407
Tel.: (843) 225-5558
Fax: (843) 225-5556
E-Mail: info@cognetixllc.com
Web Site: www.cognetixllc.com

Employees: 4

Dale Lanford *(Partner & Co-Founder-Cognetix Mktg & Graphic Design)*

Accounts:
AstenJohnson
ATC
Bank of South Carolina
The Citadel
Fastenation
Key West Boats
Renaissance Hotel
V Health Club
Waterloo Estates

COGNITIVE IMPACT
PO Box 5509, Fullerton, CA 92838-0509
Tel.: (714) 447-4993
Fax: (714) 447-6020
Web Site: www.cognitiveimpact.com

Employees: 3

Approx. Annual Billings: $1,000,000

Curtis Chan *(Founder & Mng Partner)*
Buzz Walker *(Mng Partner & Pres-Tech Mktg & Bus Advisory-Global)*
Glen Anderson *(Partner-Strategic)*
Robert Yamashita *(Partner-Strategic)*
Kuo Yang *(Graphics Designer)*

Accounts:
Black Sky Computing

COHEN COMMUNICATIONS
1201 W Shaw Ave, Fresno, CA 93711
Tel.: (559) 222-1322
Fax: (559) 221-4376
E-Mail: debra@cohencommunications.com
Web Site: cohencommunicationsgroup.com

Employees: 15
Year Founded: 1986

Agency Specializes In: Advertising

Mike Cohen *(Owner)*
Debra Cohen *(Principal)*

Danielle Griffin *(Acct Exec & Specialist-PR)*
Ashlee Garcia *(Acct Exec)*
Christy Patron *(Acct Exec)*

Accounts:
Central Valley Community Bancorp

COHEN CONSULTING
1557 216th St, Bayside, NY 11360
Tel.: (718) 428-7651
Web Site: cohentraining.com

Agency Specializes In: Corporate Communications, Investor Relations

Mark Cohen *(Owner)*
Dave Cohen *(Pres)*

Accounts:
Tao Minerals

COHLMIA MARKETING
535 W Douglas Ste 170, Wichita, KS 67213
Tel.: (316) 262-6066
Web Site: www.cohlmiamarketing.com

Agency Specializes In: Advertising, Brand Development & Integration, Collateral, Digital/Interactive, Internet/Web Design, Outdoor, Print, Radio, T.V.

Carol A. Skaff *(Owner & Pres)*
Donna Bachman *(Dir-Media)*
Stacy S. Jones *(Acct Mgr)*

Accounts:
Kanza Bank

COHN MARKETING
2881 N Speer Blvd, Denver, CO 80211
Tel.: (303) 839-1415
Fax: (303) 839-1511
E-Mail: contact@cohnmarketing.com
Web Site: www.cohnmarketing.com

Employees: 20

Agency Specializes In: Advertising, Brand Development & Integration, Collateral, Communications, Consulting, Consumer Marketing, Corporate Identity, Crisis Communications, Exhibit/Trade Shows, Government/Political, Graphic Design, Internet/Web Design, Local Marketing, Logo & Package Design, Media Planning, Media Relations, Media Training, Multicultural, Planning & Consultation, Public Relations, Retail, Search Engine Optimization, Sponsorship, Strategic Planning/Research, Travel & Tourism

Jeff Cohn *(Pres & CEO)*
Amy Larson *(VP-Content & Bus Dev)*
Robin Lybarger *(VP-PR)*
Anna Beaty *(Sr Dir-PR)*
Teri Springer *(Sr Dir-Art)*
Karen Johnson *(Acct Dir)*
Kelly Behm *(Dir-PR Client Strategy)*
Hannah Tripp *(Acct Exec)*

Accounts:
Actus Lend Lease
The Bernestein Companies
The Denver Urban Renewal Authority Message Development, Public Relations, Special Event Support, Strategic Planning
Developers Diversified Realty
Empower Playgrounds, Inc.; Provo, UT Marketing, Planning
Forest City The Orchard Town Center; 2008
Galleria Dallas (Agency of Record) Brand Development, Marketing Strategy
Guild Ford
ICSC (International Council of Shopping Centers)
JDH
Karen Leaffer
Lerner Enterprises; Washington, DC Dulles Town Center
Mont Blanc Gourmet
The Orchard
RED Development
RK Mechanical Brand Architecture & Logo, Brand Strategy, Creative, Messaging
Roux
Seattle Fish Co
Serramonte Center; Daly City, CA (Agency of Record) Brand Development, Marketing Strategy
Stat Line

COHN, OVERSTREET & PARRISH
4381 Beach Haven Trail Ste 300, Smyrna, GA 30080
Tel.: (404) 870-8888
Fax: (404) 870-8889
E-Mail: info@co-p.com
Web Site: www.co-p.com

Agency Specializes In: Advertising, Brand Development & Integration, Collateral, Communications, Crisis Communications, Digital/Interactive, Environmental, Event Planning & Marketing, Government/Political, Graphic Design, Integrated Marketing, Internet/Web Design, Logo & Package Design, Magazines, Market Research, Media Relations, Media Training, Multimedia, Print, Promotions, Public Relations, Publicity/Promotions, Radio, Social Marketing/Nonprofit, Strategic Planning/Research

Jim Overstreet *(Pres)*
Amy Woodward Parrish *(Partner & CMO)*
Sonia Fuller *(Partner & VP)*
Cindy Campbell *(Controller)*

Accounts:
ATI
City of Bremen; GA Website
Coca-Cola Refreshments USA, Inc.
The Cold Dish
Jekyll Island
Orlando Connections
Senior Home Reverse Mortgage Website
Stephen Reed/Reed Golf Corporation Corporate Golf Outing, Public Relations

COLANGELO
120 Tokeneke Rd, Darien, CT 06820
Tel.: (203) 662-6600
Fax: (203) 662-6601
E-Mail: info@colangelo-sm.com
Web Site: www.colangelo-sm.com

Year Founded: 1993

Agency Specializes In: Sponsorship

Joe Raimo, Sr. *(Mng Dir)*
Keith Garvey *(VP & Acct Dir-Colangelo synergy Mktg)*
Tom Lynch *(Gen Mgr)*
Ben Applebaum *(Exec Dir-Creative)*
Sal Barcia *(Exec Dir-Fin)*
Susan Cocco *(Exec Dir-Mktg)*
Peter Viento *(Exec Dir-Creative)*
Jennifer Kruper *(Dir-Bus Ops)*
Kim Gordon *(Sr Acct Exec)*
Ted Parrack *(Chief Strategic Officer)*

Accounts:
Church & Dwight Campaign: "Big Date", Campaign: "Happy Birthday", Campaign: "Miss You", Trojan
The Clorox Company Burt's Bees
Davidoff of Geneva USA
Diageo Guinness, ROKK Vodka
Filippo Berio Campaign: "The First & Last Name in Olive Oil"
Prince Tennis Equipment
Sabra Dipping Co. Shopper Marketing
Tequila Cuervo La Rojena, S.A. de C.V.
Top Flite Golf Balls

COLE & WEBER UNITED
221 Yale Ave N Ste 600, Seattle, WA 98109
Tel.: (206) 447-9595
Fax: (206) 233-0178
E-Mail: info@coleweber.com
Web Site: www.coleweber.com

E-Mail for Key Personnel:
President: mike.doherty@cwredcell.com
Media Dir.: mj.keehn@cwredcell.com
Production Mgr.: pete.anderson@cwunited.com

Employees: 65
Year Founded: 1931

Agency Specializes In: Digital/Interactive, Direct Response Marketing, Graphic Design, Public Relations, Sponsorship, Strategic Planning/Research

Mike Doherty *(Pres)*
Elizabeth Rowny *(Mng Dir)*
Patrick McKay *(Exec Dir-Creative)*
Pete Anderson *(Dir-Integrated Production)*
James Mackenzie *(Dir-Strategic Plng)*
Helen Lauen *(Assoc Dir-Plng)*
Katie Dutton *(Supvr-Connections)*
Sarah Doering *(Planner-Connections)*
Lena McClenny *(Asst Media Planner-Digital)*

Accounts:
Borba; 2004
Chateu Ste. Michelle Winery
Columbia Crest
Devon Energy Corporation; 2007
Fireman's Fund Insurance
Hawaiian Airlines
International Olympic Committee Creative & Media Planning
Kellogg Company Jack's
Microsoft Corporation Campaign: "Creature Creator", Campaign: "Designer Slide Collection", Outlook, PowerPoint
Nike, Inc. Nike Brand
Rossi Vineyards
Ste. Michelle Wine Estates; Woodinville, WA (Agency of Record)
Texas Instruments; Dallas, TX; 1997
TiVo
Tree Top
Washington State Lottery (Agency of Record) Campaign: "Hometown Heroes", Campaign: "Motorcycle", Creative Advertising, Media Buying, Media Planning, Now Here, Strategic Marketing
Woodland Park Zoo

Branches

Bates United
Holbergs Gate 21, PO Box 7094, Saint Olavs plass, N 0130 Oslo, Norway
Tel.: (47) 22 87 97 00
Fax: (47) 22 87 98 00
Web Site: www.group-united.com

Employees: 72
Year Founded: 1953

Agency Specializes In: Advertising, Automotive, Communications, Financial, Luxury Products

Per Christian Huse *(Acct Dir)*
Katja Krogh *(Art Dir)*

Christin Borge Johansen *(Dir-Art)*
Lars Holt *(Dir-Art)*
Thorbjorn Naug *(Dir-Creative)*
Marianne Sorlie *(Acct Mgr)*

Accounts:
Audi Dice
Coop
Hertz Car Rental
Joh. Johannson
Lerum
Norske Meierier
Norwegian Directorate of Health Campaign: "Doorman", Campaign: "The last one to notice"
NRL
Paracet Painkillers
St1 Automatic Gas Station Campaign: "Working 24/7"
Tine

Berlin Cameron United
100 Ave of the Americas, New York, NY 10013
(See Separate Listing)

LDV United
Rijnkaai 99, Hangar 26, 2000 Antwerp, Belgium
Tel.: (32) 3229 2929
Fax: (32) 3 229 2930
E-Mail: info@ldv.be
Web Site: www.ldv.be

Employees: 40
Year Founded: 2001

Agency Specializes In: Advertising

Harry Demey *(CEO)*
Petra De Roos *(Mng Dir)*
Dries Debruyn *(Art Dir)*
Thomas Thysens *(Art Dir)*
Han Verschaeren *(Art Dir)*
Bart Gielen *(Dir-Creative)*
Tim Janssens *(Acct Mgr)*
Julie Oostvogels *(Acct Mgr)*
Jean De Moor *(Mgr-Production)*
Frederik Clarysse *(Copywriter)*
Dennis Vandewalle *(Copywriter)*

Accounts:
City of Antwerp Campaign: "Antwerp-Quays Poem", Thank You For Not Speeding
DE Standaard
Essent
Fresh Meals Ready Made Pasta Meals, Ready Meals
Heylen
HUB
KIA
Lampiris Campaign: "The Envelope"
O Cool
Opel Belgium Campaign: "Gabriel", Campaign: "It is Possible Inside the Combo"
Red Bull
Sensoa
Special Olympics Campaign: "Break the Taboos"
Stad Antwerp
Sunweb
Think Media
University of Antwerp
Veritas
Vmmtv TV Media Saleshouse

Red Cell
Alberto Mario N 19, 20149 Milan, Italy
Tel.: (39) 02772 2981
Fax: (39) 02 782 126
E-Mail: welcome@redcell.com
Web Site: www.redcellgroup.it

Year Founded: 1988

Agency Specializes In: Advertising

Alberto de Martini *(CEO & Planner-Strategic)*
Roberto Giovannini *(Gen Mgr-Rome)*
Roberto Vella *(Exec Dir-Creative)*
Ingrid Altomare *(Acct Dir-Adv & Digital)*
Stefano Longoni *(Dir-Creative)*
Stefano Castagnone *(Copywriter)*

Accounts:
Blockbuster
Boehringer Ingelheim
Bonduelle
Cameo Bakery
De Cecco
Honda
Imetec
Iveco
Mediacom
Yamaha Motorcycles

COLISEUM COMMUNICATIONS
(Formerly Coliseum Marketing)
585 Skippack Pk SAte 310, Blue Bell, PA 19422
Tel.: (215) 654-7700
Fax: (215) 654-7704
Toll Free: (800) 358-5939
E-Mail: ron@coliseumcommunications.com
Web Site: coliseumcommunications.com/

Employees: 3
Year Founded: 2008

Agency Specializes In: Collateral, Communications, Health Care Services, Hospitality, Mobile Marketing, Newspaper, Newspapers & Magazines, Outdoor, Print, Public Relations, Recruitment, Social Media

Approx. Annual Billings: $1,500,000

Breakdown of Gross Billings by Media: Internet Adv.: $300,000; Newsp. & Mags.: $1,000,000; Production: $200,000

Ron Feldstein *(Principal, Sr Strategist-Acct & Dir-Creative)*
Robert Raynor *(Sr Dir-Art)*

Accounts:
Access Group
Beebe Medical Center; Lewes, DE
Blackhorse Carriers
Medisys
Valero Energy
Valero Renewables
Valero Retail

COLLABORATE COMMUNICATIONS, INC.
445 Bush St 3rd Fl, San Francisco, CA 94108
Tel.: (415) 651-1200
Fax: (415) 651-1299
E-Mail: info@collaboratesf.com
Web Site: www.collaboratesf.com

Employees: 20

Agency Specializes In: Advertising

Hans Ullmark *(CEO & Partner)*

Accounts:
CNET/tv.com
Franklin Templeton Investments
GridIron Software
Landmark Aviation

COLLAGE ADVERTISING
76 Northeastern Blvd Ste 28, Nashua, NH 03062-3174
Tel.: (603) 880-3663
Fax: (603) 880-7535
E-Mail: dan@cadezine.com
Web Site: www.cadezine.com

E-Mail for Key Personnel:
President: dan@cadezine.com
Creative Dir.: carol@cadezine.com
Media Dir.: diane@cadezine.com

Employees: 4
Year Founded: 1980

Agency Specializes In: Advertising, Business-To-Business, Cable T.V., Collateral, Corporate Identity, Engineering, Exhibit/Trade Shows, Financial, Graphic Design, High Technology, Industrial, Information Technology, Internet/Web Design, Local Marketing, Logo & Package Design, Magazines, Media Buying Services, Newspaper, Newspapers & Magazines, Outdoor, Print, Production, Radio, Restaurant, Technical Advertising, Trade & Consumer Magazines

Approx. Annual Billings: $2,000,000

Breakdown of Gross Billings by Media: Collateral: 25%; D.M.: 5%; Graphic Design: 20%; Logo & Package Design: 20%; Newsp. & Mags.: 20%; Radio: 10%

Carol Richards *(Owner)*

Accounts:
Canobie Lake Park; Salem, NH Entertainment; 1994

COLLE+MCVOY
400 1st Ave N Ste 700, Minneapolis, MN 55401-1954
Tel.: (612) 305-6000
Fax: (612) 305-6500
E-Mail: info@collemcvoy.com
Web Site: www.collemcvoy.com

E-Mail for Key Personnel:
President: christine.fruechte@collemcvoy.com

Employees: 245
Year Founded: 1935

National Agency Associations: 4A's

Agency Specializes In: Above-the-Line, Advertising, Advertising Specialties, Affiliate Marketing, Affluent Market, African-American Market, Agriculture, Alternative Advertising, Arts, Asian Market, Automotive, Aviation & Aerospace, Below-the-Line, Bilingual Market, Brand Development & Integration, Branded Entertainment, Broadcast, Business Publications, Business-To-Business, Cable T.V., Catalogs, Children's Market, Co-op Advertising, Collateral, College, Commercial Photography, Communications, Computers & Software, Consulting, Consumer Goods, Consumer Marketing, Consumer Publications, Content, Corporate Communications, Corporate Identity, Cosmetics, Crisis Communications, Custom Publishing, Customer Relationship Management, Digital/Interactive, Direct Response Marketing, Direct-to-Consumer, E-Commerce, Education, Electronic Media, Electronics, Email, Engineering, Entertainment, Environmental, Event Planning & Marketing, Exhibit/Trade Shows, Experience Design, Fashion/Apparel, Financial, Food Service, Game Integration, Gay & Lesbian Market, Government/Political, Graphic Design, Guerilla Marketing, Health Care Services, High Technology, Hispanic Market, Hospitality, Household Goods, Identity Marketing, In-Store Advertising, Industrial, Infomercials, Information Technology, Integrated Marketing, International, Internet/Web Design, Investor Relations, Legal Services, Leisure, Local Marketing, Logo & Package Design, Luxury

Products, Magazines, Marine, Market Research, Media Buying Services, Media Planning, Media Relations, Media Training, Medical Products, Men's Market, Merchandising, Mobile Marketing, Multicultural, Multimedia, New Product Development, New Technologies, Newspaper, Newspapers & Magazines, Out-of-Home Media, Outdoor, Over-50 Market, Package Design, Paid Searches, Pets , Pharmaceutical, Planning & Consultation, Podcasting, Point of Purchase, Point of Sale, Print, Product Placement, Production, Production (Ad, Film, Broadcast), Production (Print), Promotions, Public Relations, Publicity/Promotions, Publishing, RSS (Really Simple Syndication), Radio, Real Estate, Recruitment, Regional, Restaurant, Retail, Sales Promotion, Search Engine Optimization, Seniors' Market, Social Marketing/Nonprofit, Sponsorship, Sports Market, Stakeholders, Strategic Planning/Research, Sweepstakes, Syndication, T.V., Technical Advertising, Teen Market, Telemarketing, Trade & Consumer Magazines, Transportation, Travel & Tourism, Urban Market, Web (Banner Ads, Pop-ups, etc.), Women's Market

Approx. Annual Billings: $280,000,000 Capitalized

Christine Fruechte *(CEO)*
Lisa Miller *(CFO)*
Phil Johnson *(COO)*
Mike Caguin *(Chief Creative Officer)*
Lorenz Esguerra *(Mng Dir-Bus Dev)*
John Doyle *(Exec Dir-Brand Experience)*
Derek Bitter *(Grp Dir-Creative)*
Dustin Black *(Grp Dir-Creative)*
Erick Jensen *(Grp Dir-Media)*
David Kelly *(Sr Dir-Art)*
Ned Munson *(Sr Dir-Art)*
Nicole Goodman *(Sr Producer-Interactive)*
Janelle Carbone *(Acct Dir)*
Rob Hagemann *(Acct Dir)*
Tiffany Hahnfeldt *(Producer-Interactive)*
Mike Schwab *(Acct Dir)*
Drew Shaman *(Acct Dir)*
Amber Young *(Acct Dir)*
John Borchardt *(Dir-Brdcst)*
Shannon Davis *(Dir-Integrated Production)*
Daniel Linnihan *(Dir-Art)*
Jamie Moran *(Dir-Talent Dev)*
Nicole Pomerleau *(Dir-Media)*
Jen Stack *(Dir-Corp Comm)*
Marc Stephens *(Dir-Digital Creative)*
Lee Hanson *(Assoc Dir-Creative)*
Karl Madcharo *(Assoc Dir-Creative)*
Ann Panian *(Project Mgr-Adv)*
Jaclyn Grossfield *(Acct Supvr)*
Nat Jungerberg *(Acct Supvr)*
Danny Skalman *(Acct Supvr)*
Clark Woodward *(Acct Supvr)*
Rachel Zwirlein *(Acct Supvr)*
Mike Santee *(Supvr-Media)*
Erin Arnesen *(Media Planner)*
Gustav Holtz *(Designer)*
Jenny Kirmis *(Copywriter)*
Isabel Ludcke *(Coord-Bus Dev)*
Roven Bashier *(Sr Designer-Interactive)*
Dylan Howe *(Media Supvr)*
Alix Nichols *(Sr Artist-Interactive Studio)*
Aaron Purmort *(Sr Designer-Interactive)*

Accounts:

3M Co. 3M Abrasives, 3M HealthCare Group, 3M Insulation Products, 3M Marine; 1986
New-Align Technology, Inc. Creative, Digital, Invisalign Clear Aligners (Advertising Agency of Record), Strategic Planning
New-ARTCRANK
Associated Banc-Corp (Advertising Agency of Record) Brand Activation, Creative, Media Buying, Media Planning, Social Media
August Schell Brewing Company Creative, Dark Beer, Grain Belt Beer (Advertising Agency of Record), Media Buying, Media Planning, Public Relations, Social Media, Strategic Planning
Aveda Corporation Color Karma
Bellisio Foods (Agency of Record) Creative, Media Buying, Michelina, Public Relations, Social Media, Strategic Planning; 2013
Bikes Belong
Boulder (Agency of Record)
Caribou Coffee (Agency Of Record) #CaribouInspires, 3D Billboard, Bou-ism Taglines, Campaign: "Life is more than coffee...that's why there's coffee", Campaign: "Life is short - stay awake for it", Campaign: "Living Pinterest Board", Logo, Sweater Maker App; 2009
CHS Campaign: "Big Sky Country/SoDak", Campaign: "Great Lakes Country/Wisco", Campaign: "Great Plains Country/Minne", Cenex, Foods, Grain & Cenex-Branded Energy Products, Tanks For Thanks; 1994
CNH Case IH, New Holland; 2002
Discovery Communications
Dorel Industries Inc. Cannondale, GT, Global Strategic & Creative Development, IronHorse, Mongoose, Recreational & Leisure, Recreational/Leisure Segment, SUGOi, Schwinn
DuPont; 2006
Ecolab; 2002
E.I. du Pont de Nemours & Company
New-Elanco (Agency of Record) Advertising
Erbert & Gerbert's
ESPN Bassmasters
Explore Minnesota Tourism (Agency of Record) Campaign: "More to Explore", Campaign: "Only in Minnesota", Media Planning, OOH, Online/Electronic Advertising, Promotional Materials, Public Relations, Social Marketing, Strategic Planning, Travel; 2010
Farm Credit Mid-America; 2011
Free Arts Minnesota Campaign: "Art Heals"
General Mills; Minneapolis, MN; 2003
GT Bicycles Catalog
IBA
Indian Motorcycle (Agency of Record) Branding, Catalog, Creative, Design, Interactive Marketing Strategy, Retail
International Olive Council; 2011
Intervet Inc.; Millsboro, DE
Irish Setter; 2002
Jack-Hammer
Johnson & Johnson
Kiehl's
KINKY Liqueur
Koala Ranch Wine
Kozy Shack Inc.; 2012
Land O'Lakes Dairy Foods Campaign: "Pin a Meal, Give a Meal", Consumer Web Site, Creative, Development, Digital Assignment, Media, Pinnable Display, Production, Strategy; 2010
Mammouth Mountain Ski Area (Agency of Record) Creative, Strategy
Manhattan Toy Company
Medtronic Foundation Campaign: "Save a Life Simulator"
Minnesota State Pedal Pulls
Minnesota Tourism
Mountain Hardwear Global Branding, Marketing; 2012
New-MTD Products, Inc. Creative, Cub Cadet (Advertising Agency of Record), Digital, Media Buying, Strategic Planning
Nestle Purina; Saint Louis, MO Campaign: "This Could Be The Year 1", Campaign: "This Could Be The Year 2"; 1999
Northern Tool + Equipment; Minneapolis, MN; 2005
Novartis Animal Health; Greensboro, NC; 2003
Novartis Corp.; 2002
Old Navy; 2010
Olive Oil
Ovation Brands.; Eagan, MN
Paddock Laboratories; Minneapolis, MN
Pedal Minnesota Campaign: "Pedal Mn Logo", Campaign: "Tune Up Booth"
People for Bikes Campaign: "Bikes Make Life Better"
Polaris Industries, Inc.
Propane Education & Research Council (PERC); 2008
Recreational Boating & Fishing Foundation "Get away from all of this", "TakeMeFishing.org", Campaign: "Find Fish Faster", Web Site; 2007
Red Wing Shoe Company; Red Wing, MN; 2002
Regency Beauty Institute Brand Awareness, Creative, Media Buying, Public Relations, Social Media, Strategic Planning; 2013
Regis Corporation
Starkey Hearing Foundation; 2012
Take Me Fishing (Agency of Record)
Target
Taubman Centers; Bloomfield Hills, MI Shopping Mall Management
Terra Delyssa
New-UnitedHealth Group
USA Swimming (Agency of Record) Campaign: "Cannonballs", Campaign: "The Walk"; 2013
Vasque; 2002
Vistakon; Jacksonville, FL
Well Enterprises Inc. Blue Bunny Ice Cream (Agency of Record), Creative, Integrated Campaign, Media Buying, Strategic Planning
WinField Solutions LLC
Wolfgang Puck
Yahoo! Yahoo! Messenger
Zimride

Branches

Exponent PR

400 First Ave N Ste 700, Minneapolis, MN 55401
(See Separate Listing)

Mobium Integrated Branding

(Formerly Mobium)
200 S Michigan Ave, Chicago, IL 60604
(See Separate Listing)

COLLING MEDIA LLC

14362 N Frank Lloyd Wright Blvd Ste 1270, Scottsdale, AZ 85260
Tel.: (480) 696-5350
E-Mail: info@collingmedia.com
Web Site: www.collingmedia.com

Agency Specializes In: Advertising, Broadcast, Customer Relationship Management, Digital/Interactive, Mobile Marketing, Outdoor, Print, Radio, Search Engine Optimization, Social Media

Brian Colling *(Pres & CEO)*
Peter Colling *(CFO)*
Leo Rondeau *(Gen Mgr)*
Jayson Shreve *(Dir-Ops)*
Eric Bikofsky *(Dir-Bus Dev)*
Robert Craver *(Dir-Paid Search & SEO)*
Nohealani Cutting *(Dir-Content)*
Mark Fast *(Mgr-Media Strategy)*

Accounts:

Spartan Race

COLLINS:

636 11th Ave, New York, NY 10036
Tel.: (646) 380-4685
Web Site: www.wearecollins.com

Agency Specializes In: Advertising, Brand Development & Integration, Digital/Interactive

Brian Collins *(CEO & Dir-Creative)*
Leland Maschmeyer *(Exec Dir-Creative)*
Rob Collins *(Dir-Art & Graphic Designer)*
Seth Mroczka *(Dir-Ops)*
Brett Renfer *(Dir-Experience Design)*
Ben Crick *(Sr Designer)*

Accounts:
Azealia Banks
New-Shyp Campaign: "We'll Take It From Here"
Spotify Branding

COLMAN BROHAN DAVIS

54 W Hubbard St Councourse Level E, Chicago, IL 60654
Tel.: (312) 661-1050
Fax: (312) 661-1051
E-Mail: ddavila@cbdmarketing.com
Web Site: www.cbdmarketing.com

E-Mail for Key Personnel:
President: lbrohan@cbdmarketing.com
Creative Dir.: jdavis@cbdmarketing.com

Employees: 32
Year Founded: 1988

National Agency Associations: BMA-DMA

Agency Specializes In: Advertising, Affluent Market, Agriculture, Below-the-Line, Brand Development & Integration, Broadcast, Business Publications, Business-To-Business, Collateral, College, Communications, Consulting, Consumer Goods, Consumer Marketing, Consumer Publications, Corporate Identity, Customer Relationship Management, Direct Response Marketing, Fashion/Apparel, Financial, Food Service, Graphic Design, High Technology, Household Goods, Integrated Marketing, Internet/Web Design, Local Marketing, Logo & Package Design, Media Planning, New Product Development, Planning & Consultation, Point of Purchase, Point of Sale, Print, Production, Real Estate, Retail, Strategic Planning/Research

Breakdown of Gross Billings by Media: D.M.: 10%; Plng. & Consultation: 25%; Print: 5%; Production: 10%; Radio & T.V.: 15%; Strategic Planning/Research: 20%; Trade & Consumer Mags.: 5%; Worldwide Web Sites: 10%

Lori Colman *(Founder & Co-CEO)*
Liz Brohan *(Co-CEO)*
Jean Ban *(VP & Dir-PR & Social Media)*
Gina Miller *(VP-Dir-Customer Experience & Demand Mgmt)*
Doug Davila *(VP-Bus Dev)*
Mary Olivieri *(Exec Dir-Creative)*

Accounts:
Beanpod Candles
Becker
BuildClean Public Relations, Video
CF Industries
DeVry University
GATX Rail
Lake Forest Graduate School of Management
Lipid Nutrition
NXT Capital
Paul Stuart
Ralston Foods
Sensory Effects
Siemens
Stalla

COLONIAL MARKETING GROUP INC.

813 S 16th St, Wilmington, NC 28401
Tel.: (910) 343-1933
Fax: (910) 343-1934
E-Mail: info@colonialmarketing.com
Web Site: www.colonialmarketing.com

Agency Specializes In: Advertising, Logo & Package Design, Media Buying Services, Outdoor, Print, Radio, T.V.

Rod Flinchum *(Pres)*
Tonye Gray *(Sr Acct Mgr-Media Plng & Placement-Colonial Mktg Grp)*
Jennifer Bloech *(Buyer)*

Accounts:
Gateway Bank Mortgage
Joe Alcoke Auto & truck
Sandhills Bank

COLORPLAY STUDIO

PO Box 5855, Eugene, OR 97405
Tel.: (541) 343-4310
Fax: (541) 343-4310
E-Mail: colorplay@garyschubert.com
Web Site: www.garyschubert.com

E-Mail for Key Personnel:
President: gwenschubert@comcast.net

Employees: 1
Year Founded: 1976

National Agency Associations: AMA-BMA

Agency Specializes In: Advertising, Brand Development & Integration, Business Publications, Business-To-Business, Collateral, Corporate Communications, Corporate Identity, Direct Response Marketing, Financial, Food Service, Graphic Design, Health Care Services, High Technology, Industrial, Logo & Package Design, Magazines, Medical Products, New Product Development, Pharmaceutical, Point of Purchase, Point of Sale, Print, Strategic Planning/Research, Trade & Consumer Magazines

Gary J. Schubert *(Owner)*

COLOUR

7051 Bayers Rd Ste 400, Halifax, NS B3L 4V2 Canada
Tel.: (902) 722-3150
Fax: (902) 453-5221
E-Mail: info@cclgroup.ca
Web Site: www.cclgroup.ca

Employees: 50
Year Founded: 1977

Agency Specializes In: Advertising, Bilingual Market, Brand Development & Integration, Corporate Communications, Corporate Identity, Direct Response Marketing, Event Planning & Marketing, Graphic Design, Health Care Services, Internet/Web Design, Local Marketing, Logo & Package Design, Media Buying Services, Out-of-Home Media, Print, Public Relations, Publicity/Promotions, Strategic Planning/Research

Sean Charters *(Mng Partner & VP)*
Ed Wark *(Principal-PR)*
Savior Joseph *(VP-Digital Plng)*
Nancy Champion *(Sr Acct Mgr)*
Alexandra Stoupakis *(Sr Acct Mgr)*
Tim Winchester *(Sr Acct Mgr)*
Jordy Fujiwara *(Mgr-Strategy & Analytics)*
Ashley Laurence *(Mgr-Social Engagement)*
Hannah Chapple *(Acct Coord)*
Melanie Thebeau *(Coord)*

Accounts:
Aliant Telecom
Atlantic Lottery Corporation (Agency of Record)
Canadian Olympic Foundation Social Media
Dahalvi MBA Program
Discovery Centre
Halifax Rainmen Basketball
Killam Properties
Lautens in Need
Medevic Blue Cross
Nova Scotia Community College
Nova Scotia Teacher's Union
St. Francis Xavier University
Stuart McAlvey Sterling Scales
United Way
WUQ Children's Hospital

Colour

169 Water St Ste 200, Saint John's, NL A1C 1B1 Canada
Tel.: (709) 579-5301
Fax: (709) 754-0503
E-Mail: info@cclgroup.ca
Web Site: www.colour-nl.ca

Employees: 5

Agency Specializes In: Advertising

Sean Charters *(VP & Mng Dir)*
Jordy Fujiwara *(Mgr-Strategy & Analytics)*

Accounts:
Bell Aliant
InstantLabs
Technip Canada Ltd.
Vale Inco

COLUMN FIVE

1611 Babcock St, Newport Beach, CA 92663
Tel.: (949) 614-0759
Fax: (949) 313-0943
E-Mail: info@columnfivemedia.com
Web Site: www.columnfivemedia.com

Year Founded: 2008

Agency Specializes In: Advertising, Digital/Interactive, Graphic Design, Public Relations

Kyle Ganshert *(Acct Dir)*
Andrea Bravo *(Dir-Production)*
Kelsey Cox *(Dir-Comm)*
Tamara Burke Hlava *(Dir-HR)*
Nick Miede *(Dir-Creative)*
Elizabeth Clawson *(Coord-Client Svcs)*

Accounts:
Microsoft Corporation Internet Explorer

COMBS & COMPANY

3426 Old Cantrell Rd, Little Rock, AR 72202-1860
Tel.: (501) 664-3000
Fax: (501) 664-4016
E-Mail: info@combsco.com
Web Site: www.combsco.com

E-Mail for Key Personnel:
President: bencombs@combsco.com
Production Mgr.: loripiker@combsco.com

Employees: 30
Year Founded: 1972

National Agency Associations: AAF

Agency Specializes In: Automotive, Brand Development & Integration, Business-To-Business, Co-op Advertising, Education, Entertainment, Fashion/Apparel, High Technology, Internet/Web Design, Investor Relations, Media Buying Services, Public Relations, Radio, Recruitment, Retail, Strategic Planning/Research, Travel & Tourism

Approx. Annual Billings: $30,000,000

Breakdown of Gross Billings by Media: Brdcst.: 70%; Print: 30%

Bennett A. Combs *(Owner)*
Jud Chapin *(Exec Dir-Creative)*

Accounts:
Alltel Information Services
Arkansas Department of Higher Education
Arkansas Electric Cooperative Corporation

McLarty Companies
University of Central Arkansas

COMCAST SPOTLIGHT

1315 Directors' Row Ste 109, Fort Wayne, IN 46808-1110
Tel.: (260) 458-5129
Fax: (260) 458-5200
E-Mail: chris_melby@cable.comcast.com
Web Site: www.comcastspotlight.com

Employees: 15
Year Founded: 1963

Approx. Annual Billings: $18,000,000

Breakdown of Gross Billings by Media: Cable T.V.: $18,000,000

Charlie Thurston *(Pres)*
Hank Oster *(Sr VP & Gen Mgr)*
John Tierney *(Sr VP-Reg & Natl Sls)*
Michael Hills *(VP & Gen Mgr)*
Mark Altschuler *(VP-Natl Adv)*
Matthew Elggren *(Head-Creative)*
Jeanine Socha *(Exec Dir-Res & Sr Dir-Res West Reg)*
Leigh Farrow *(Sr Dir-Mktg)*
Ann Letizi *(Sr Dir-Mktg)*
Bob Allen *(Dir-Reg & Natl Sls)*
Jerry Arias *(Dir-Mktg & Promos)*
Adina Deedman *(Dir-Mktg Res & Plng)*
Ann Dunne *(Dir-Mktg & Promos)*
Scott Mitchell *(Dir-Automotive)*
Greg Osborne *(Dir-Sls)*
Sherry Avara *(Area Mgr-Sls)*
Jessie Broussard *(Mgr-Mktg)*
Karen Gilligan *(Mgr-Local Sls)*
Anthony Jingoli *(Mgr-Field Mktg)*
Brian Keller *(Mgr-Local Sls)*
Alex Papastamatis *(Mgr-Mktg)*
Brent Petersen *(Mgr-Field Mktg)*
Rob Ponto *(Mgr-PR)*
DeeAnn Rich *(Mgr-Political Mktg)*
Dana Scott *(Mgr-Mktg)*
Andy Snow *(Mgr-Field Mktg-Washington DC DMA)*
Christy A. White *(Mgr-Promos)*
Ben Gibbs *(Supvr-Mktg)*
Brooke J. Holbus *(Supvr-Mktg & Promos)*
Mike Adkins *(Sr Acct Exec-Automotive Adv)*
Evonne Federouch *(Sr Specialist-Mktg)*
Kristin Brandt *(Specialist-Mktg)*
Corinne L. Egan *(Acct Exec-Adv)*
Gary Gavarone *(Acct Exec)*
Julie Hemze *(Acct Exec-Automotive)*
Charles McNeil *(Acct Exec-Adv)*
Amy Miranda *(Acct Exec)*
Elizabeth Wing *(Acct Exec)*
Jen Smith *(Sr Analyst-Fin)*
Corey Besack *(Analyst-Div Mktg & Res)*
Danielle D'Agostino *(Acct Planner)*
Carly Hartung *(Analyst-Mktg)*
Ashleigh Bing *(Coord-Mktg & Res)*
Gabriela Fuller *(Coord-Mktg-SFL)*
Nicole Martin *(Coord-Digital Traffic)*
Caroline Tai *(Coord-Traffic)*
Nicole Digiambattista *(Sr Coord-Interactive Traffic)*
Cathi Hauck *(Div Dir-Comm-Central Div)*
Teresa Lucido *(Div VP)*
Patrick Robillard *(Reg Adv Acct Planner-Boston Interconnect)*
Steve Sexton *(Div Mgr-Online Sls)*

Accounts:
Comcast Cablevision of Indiana, L.P.; Fort Wayne, IN
Strata

COMMAND PARTNERS

310 Arlington Ave 304, Charlotte, NC 28203
Tel.: (704) 910-5727
Web Site: www.commandpartners.com

Agency Specializes In: Advertising, Internet/Web Design, Mobile Marketing, Public Relations, Search Engine Optimization, Social Media

Roy Morejon *(Pres)*
Joe Recomendes *(COO)*
Vincent Ammirato *(Dir-Search Mktg)*
Rich Tucker *(Dir-Social Media)*
Kyle Varian *(Dir-Client Svcs)*
Rachel Willis *(Dir-Client Svcs)*
Alyssa Lepow *(Acct Mgr-PR)*
Stephanie Spaulding *(Acct Coord-PR)*

Accounts:
New-Town of Harrisburg

COMMERCE HOUSE

331 Cole St, Dallas, TX 75207
Tel.: (214) 550-5550
Web Site: www.commercehouse.com

Agency Specializes In: Customer Relationship Management, Digital/Interactive, Internet/Web Design, Logo & Package Design, Outdoor, Print, Radio, Search Engine Optimization, T.V., Web (Banner Ads, Pop-ups, etc.)

Mark Denesuk *(Founder & Pres)*
Irving Chung *(Principal & Acct Dir)*
Vincent Lopresti *(Principal & Dir-Creative)*
Joel Dollar *(Principal)*
Phyllis Cole McKnight *(Head-Bus Dev)*
Ky Lewis *(Sr Dir-Art)*
John Graziano *(Dir-Art)*
Leigh Sander *(Dir-Creative)*
Jim Bowling *(Assoc Dir-Creative)*
Trey Testa *(Mgr-Creative Svcs)*

Accounts:
Kidkraft
PepsiCo Inc.
SodaStream Brand Repositioning, Campaign: "Be a Sparkling Water Maker", Campaign: "Factory of One", Campaign: "Sparkling water made by you!", Digital Media, Out-of-Home, TV
The VanZant Group

COMMON SENSE ADVERTISING

PO Box 82277, Phoenix, AZ 85071-2277
Tel.: (602) 870-4717
Fax: (602) 870-7660
E-Mail: kevino@commonsenseadvertising.net
Web Site: www.commonsenseadvertising.com

Employees: 4
Year Founded: 1975

Agency Specializes In: Advertising, Automotive, Cable T.V., Co-op Advertising, Direct Response Marketing, Event Planning & Marketing, Financial, Health Care Services, Magazines, Media Buying Services, Newspaper, Newspapers & Magazines, Outdoor, Pharmaceutical, Radio, Retail, Syndication, T.V., Yellow Pages Advertising

Approx. Annual Billings: $1,000,000

Breakdown of Gross Billings by Media: Mags.: 5%; Newsp.: 10%; Radio: 75%; Transit: 5%; Yellow Page Adv.: 5%

Kevin W. O'Shaughnessy *(Pres)*
Sue O'Shaughnessy *(Office Mgr)*

Accounts:
Arizona Society of CPA's; AZ Statewide Society of Certified Public Accountants; 1995
Business Development Finance Corp.; Phoenix & Tucson, AZ SBA Lender; 2001
John C. Lincoln Hospital; Phoenix, AZ; 1995
KKNT-960 AM; Phoenix, AZ News & Talk Radio Station; 2002
SLS Promotions Car Races; 2004
United Drugs; Phoenix, AZ Drug Store Co-op; 1979
Wide World of Maps; Phoenix, AZ; 2004

COMMONGROUNDMGS

600 W Fulton St, Chicago, IL 60661
Tel.: (305) 444-4647
E-Mail: info@cg-mgs.com
Web Site: www.commongroundmgs.com/

Agency Specializes In: Consumer Marketing, Multicultural, Sponsorship

Al Garcia-Serra *(Founder & Mng Partner)*
Ahmad Islam *(Founder & Mng Partner)*
Sherman Wright *(CEO)*
Manuel Machado *(Mng Partner)*
Carla Mercado *(Partner)*
Jorge R. Moya *(Chief Creative Officer)*
Jon Cheffings *(Exec VP-Performance & Optimization)*

Accounts:
New-Coca Cola

Branches:

CommongroundMGS

(Formerly Machado/Garcia-Serra Publicidad, Inc.)
1790 Coral Way, Miami, FL 33145
Tel.: (305) 444-4647
Fax: (305) 856-2687
Web Site: www.commongroundmgs.com/

Employees: 100
Year Founded: 2003

Agency Specializes In: Above-the-Line, Advertising, Advertising Specialties, Affluent Market, African-American Market, Automotive, Below-the-Line, Bilingual Market, Brand Development & Integration, Broadcast, Business Publications, Business-To-Business, Cable T.V., Co-op Advertising, Communications, Consulting, Consumer Goods, Consumer Marketing, Consumer Publications, Corporate Communications, Corporate Identity, Crisis Communications, Digital/Interactive, Direct Response Marketing, Direct-to-Consumer, Electronic Media, Email, Event Planning & Marketing, Exhibit/Trade Shows, Experience Design, Fashion/Apparel, Financial, Food Service, Game Integration, Gay & Lesbian Market, Government/Political, Graphic Design, Guerilla Marketing, Health Care Services, Hispanic Market, Hospitality, In-Store Advertising, Integrated Marketing, International, Internet/Web Design, Leisure, Local Marketing, Logo & Package Design, Luxury Products, Magazines, Market Research, Media Buying Services, Media Planning, Media Relations, Media Training, Medical Products, Merchandising, Mobile Marketing, Multicultural, Multimedia, New Product Development, Newspaper, Newspapers & Magazines, Out-of-Home Media, Outdoor, Over-50 Market, Package Design, Pharmaceutical, Planning & Consultation, Podcasting, Point of Purchase, Point of Sale, Print, Product Placement, Production, Production (Print), Promotions, Public Relations, Publicity/Promotions, Radio, Real Estate, Regional, Restaurant, Retail, Sales Promotion, Search Engine Optimization, Seniors' Market, Social Marketing/Nonprofit, Sponsorship, Stakeholders, Strategic Planning/Research, T.V., Telemarketing, Trade & Consumer Magazines, Transportation, Travel & Tourism, Urban Market, Viral/Buzz/Word of Mouth, Women's Market

Courtney Cunningham *(Founder & Mng Partner)*
Manuel E. Machado *(CEO)*
Jorge R. Moya *(Chief Creative Officer)*

Yvonne Lorie *(Pres-SWAY PR)*
Joi Tyrell *(Sr VP & Dir-Consumer Engagement)*
Gisela Fabelo *(VP-Fin)*
Jordi Boada *(Exec Dir)*
Manolo Zota *(Dir-Creative)*
Richard Traverzo *(Assoc Dir-Media)*
Ian Griggs *(Supvr-Media Plng)*

Accounts:
Ad Council
BB&T Corporation Hispanic
Claritin Allergy Products
Coppertone
Dolphin Mall Creative, Media, Multilingual Communications
Extenda (Trade Agency of Andalusia, Spain) Business Trade
Florida Lottery Gaming
Florida Power & Light Company Campaign: "Bad Gifts", Utilities
FPL FiberNet
HBO Latino
Hyundai Motor Automotive
ITT Technical Institute
Macy's
Merck
Miami Marlins Creative, Media Buying, Social Media
MilkPEP Campaign: "Got Milk??", Hispanic Advertising, Public Relations
Orlando/Orange County Convention & Visitors Bureau Tourism
Palm Bay International Fine Wines & Spirits
Scion Automotive
Southeast Toyota Distributors Hispanic
Tiffany & Co. Luxury
UHealth Brand Awareness, Multimedia & Multilingual Campaigns
University of Miami Health Systems
University of Miami Hospital

CommongroundMGS

(Formerly The Vidal Partnership)
228 E 45th St 14th Fl, New York, NY 10017-3303
Tel.: (646) 356-6600
Fax: (212) 661-7650
E-Mail: info@cg-mgs.com
Web Site: www.commongroundmgs.com/

E-Mail for Key Personnel:
President: mvidal@vidalpartnership.com
Creative Dir.: mgalvan@vidalpartnership.com

Employees: 100
Year Founded: 1991

Agency Specializes In: Above-the-Line, Advertising, Advertising Specialties, Automotive, Below-the-Line, Bilingual Market, Brand Development & Integration, Branded Entertainment, Broadcast, Business-To-Business, Cable T.V., Co-op Advertising, Communications, Consulting, Consumer Goods, Consumer Marketing, Content, Corporate Identity, Cosmetics, Customer Relationship Management, Digital/Interactive, Direct Response Marketing, Direct-to-Consumer, E-Commerce, Electronic Media, Email, Entertainment, Event Planning & Marketing, Exhibit/Trade Shows, Experience Design, Fashion/Apparel, Financial, Food Service, Government/Political, Graphic Design, Guerilla Marketing, Health Care Services, High Technology, Hispanic Market, Household Goods, In-Store Advertising, Integrated Marketing, Internet/Web Design, Local Marketing, Logo & Package Design, Luxury Products, Magazines, Market Research, Media Buying Services, Media Planning, Media Relations, Media Training, Men's Market, Merchandising, Mobile Marketing, Multicultural, New Product Development, Newspaper, Newspapers & Magazines, Out-of-Home Media, Outdoor, Pharmaceutical, Planning & Consultation, Point of Purchase, Point of Sale, Print, Product Placement, Production, Production (Ad, Film, Broadcast), Production (Print), Promotions, Public Relations, Publicity/Promotions, Radio, Regional, Restaurant, Retail, Sales Promotion, Search Engine Optimization, Social Media, Sponsorship, Sports Market, Strategic Planning/Research, Sweepstakes, T.V., Technical Advertising, Teen Market, Telemarketing, Trade & Consumer Magazines, Transportation, Travel & Tourism, Urban Market, Web (Banner Ads, Pop-ups, etc.), Women's Market

Manny Vidal *(Pres & CEO)*
Gustavo Lauria *(Chief Creative Officer & Mng Partner)*
Joi Tyrell *(Sr VP & Dir-Consumer Connection & Engagement Plng)*
Harold Schwartz *(VP & Dir-Fin)*
Percy Bustos *(Sr Dir-Art)*
Jaime Davila *(Dir-Plng)*
Beatriz Ferrer Vidal *(Dir-Quality of Life)*
Lucero Alarcon *(Mgr-Acctg & Payroll)*
Harry Wackett *(Designer-Studio)*

Accounts:
HSBC USA, Inc.
Johnson & Johnson; New Brunswick, NJ McNeil Consumer Healthcare, Skin Care & Beauty; 2008
National Football League; New York, NY NFL Brand; 2006
Powerful Yogurt Campaign: "Cattleman"
Remy Cointreau Remy Martin Caribbean
TD Bank; Mount Laurel, NJ Brand & Financial Products & Svcs; 2010

COMMONWEALTH CREATIVE ASSOCIATES

345 Union Ave, Framingham, MA 01702
Tel.: (508) 620-0791
Fax: (508) 620-0592
Toll Free: (877) 620-6664
E-Mail: info@commcreative.com
Web Site: www.commcreative.com

Employees: 28
Year Founded: 1990

Agency Specializes In: Advertising, Brand Development & Integration, Digital/Interactive, Education, Financial, Health Care Services, Local Marketing, New Technologies, Public Relations, Social Marketing/Nonprofit

Bob Fields *(Pres)*
Jennifer Ashkinos *(Mng Dir)*
Alex Nosevich *(VP & Dir-Creative)*
Leann Phoenix *(VP & Acct Supvr)*
Waseem Kawaf *(Dir-Digital Mktg)*
Matt Fontaine *(Assoc Dir-Creative-Interactive)*
Janet Sefakis *(Mgr-Acctg)*
Mark Selewacz *(Mgr-Production)*
Bryana Dacri *(Specialist-Digital Mktg)*
Samantha Schoenauer *(Specialist-Strategic Comm)*

Accounts:
Beth Israel Deaconess Hospital
GE Healthcare
Hebrew SeniorLife
Shriners Hospital
Simplex Grinnell
Staples Advantage

COMMONWISE

(Formerly Heller Communications)
100 Jay St Unit 12 C, Brooklyn, NY 11201
Tel.: (718) 222-4800
Fax: (212) 937-2406
E-Mail: info@commonwise.com
Web Site: commonwise.com

Employees: 5

Agency Specializes In: Brand Development & Integration, Digital/Interactive, Entertainment, Financial, Government/Political, Internet/Web Design

Revenue: $1,500,000

Gary Scheft *(Mng Partner)*
Hannah Du Plessis *(Partner)*
Cheryl Heller *(Partner)*
Ray Heller *(Partner)*
Despina Papadopoulos *(Partner)*
Marc Rettig *(Partner)*

Accounts:
Beach Bluff Cosmetics
BlackRock
Boston College Center for Corporate Citizenship
Caterpillar
Hachette Filipacchi
Historic Hudson Cruises
Joyful Heart Foundation
Sappi Fine Paper

COMMPRO LLC

3210 E Chinden Blvd Ste 115-315, Eagle, ID 83616
Tel.: (208) 914-1150
Fax: (720) 834-1549
E-Mail: commpro@commpro.com
Web Site: www.commpro.com

Employees: 4
Year Founded: 1982

Agency Specializes In: Electronic Media, Internet/Web Design

Approx. Annual Billings: $900,000

Greg Smith *(Pres)*
Susan Finch *(Acct Supvr & Designer)*

Accounts:
Century West BMW
City of Anaheim
The City of Brea
The City of Hesperia
The City of Laguna Woods
The City of Tustin

COMMUNICA, INC.

31 N Erie St, Toledo, OH 43604
Tel.: (419) 244-7766
Fax: (419) 244-7765
E-Mail: contactcommunica@communica-usa.com
Web Site: www.communica.world

Employees: 27
Year Founded: 1989

Agency Specializes In: Advertising, Brand Development & Integration, Broadcast, Business-To-Business, Cable T.V., Collateral, Corporate Communications, E-Commerce, Event Planning & Marketing, Graphic Design, Health Care Services, Internet/Web Design, Logo & Package Design, Media Buying Services, Out-of-Home Media, Point of Purchase, Point of Sale, Public Relations, Sales Promotion

Approx. Annual Billings: $7,000,000

Debbie Monagan *(Pres & COO)*
Jeff Kimble *(CEO)*
William Grindle *(Partner & Pres-Columbus Reg)*
Jim Rush *(Partner & Exec VP)*
Susan Doktor *(Sr VP-Brand Strategy)*
David Kanarowski *(Sr VP)*
Joe Minnick *(Sr VP-Acct & Integrated Media Svcs)*
Tricia Knight *(Specialist-Media & Buyer-Acct Svcs)*

Accounts:
Allied Moulded Products
BASF; 2011
Basler AG Digital Media, Planning, Public Relations, Social Media, Trade Show
Dana Holding Corporation
Jamie Farr Kroger Classic
MASCO; 2010
Monroe Bank & Trust
National Electrical Contractors Association
Owens Corning; 2011
Severstal; 2010
TI Automotive Global Marketing Communications
Tuffy Auto Service Centers
US Senior Open; 2011

COMMUNICATION ASSOCIATES
244 Madison Ave, New York, NY 10016
Tel.: (718) 351-2557
Fax: (718) 979-1874
E-Mail: djr@comm-associates.com
Web Site: www.comm-associates.com

Employees: 10
Year Founded: 1987

Agency Specializes In: Advertising, Advertising Specialties, Automotive, Brand Development & Integration, Business Publications, Business-To-Business, Co-op Advertising, Communications, Consulting, Consumer Marketing, Consumer Publications, Direct Response Marketing, Education, Electronic Media, Environmental, Exhibit/Trade Shows, Graphic Design, Health Care Services, In-Store Advertising, Infomercials, Internet/Web Design, Local Marketing, Magazines, Media Buying Services, Medical Products, New Product Development, Newspaper, Newspapers & Magazines, Out-of-Home Media, Outdoor, Pharmaceutical, Planning & Consultation, Point of Purchase, Print, Public Relations, Publicity/Promotions, Retail, Sales Promotion, Strategic Planning/Research, T.V., Technical Advertising, Telemarketing, Trade & Consumer Magazines, Yellow Pages Advertising

Warren Lowe *(Sr Dir-Art)*

Accounts:
Time Warner
Verizon

Division

FerryAds.com
83 Cromwell Ave, Staten Island, NY 10304
(See Separate Listing)

COMMUNICATION SERVICES
PO Box 1115, Albany, NY 12201
Tel.: (518) 438-2826
Fax: (518) 438-2120
Web Site: www.commservices.net

E-Mail for Key Personnel:
Creative Dir.: wwilliams@commservices.net

Employees: 4
Year Founded: 1984

National Agency Associations: AMA-PRSA

Agency Specializes In: Brand Development & Integration, Consulting, Corporate Identity, Direct Response Marketing, Electronic Media, Faith Based, Gay & Lesbian Market, Government/Political, Graphic Design, Health Care Services, Internet/Web Design, Local Marketing, Logo & Package Design, Print, Public Relations

Breakdown of Gross Billings by Media: D.M.: 1%; Fees: 19%; Graphic Design: 18%; Newsp. & Mags.: 25%; Other: 7%; Print: 24%; Radio: 4%; T.V.: 2%

Libby Post *(Pres)*
Terry Tyson *(Mgr-Strategy)*

Accounts:
New York Library Association
The Port of Albany

COMMUNICATIONS ADVERTISING, INC.
2363 Deer Creek Trl, Deerfield Beach, FL 33442-1323
Tel.: (954) 481-1930
Fax: (954) 481-1939
E-Mail: info@commadv1.com
Web Site: www.commadv1.com

Employees: 6
Year Founded: 1993

Agency Specializes In: Advertising, Business Publications, Electronic Media, Email, Exhibit/Trade Shows, Newspapers & Magazines, Print, Radio, Recruitment, Trade & Consumer Magazines

Laurie Senz *(Owner)*

Accounts:
Ash & Associates; Pompano, FL Executive Search Firm; 1997
Atlantic Partners Staffing Service; 2006
Best Medical Resources Healthcare Staffing
Best Resources; Boca Raton, FL Staffing Service; 2004
Clarkston Consulting; Durham, NC Consulting Firm, Nationwide Staffing; 2004
Classic Westchester; New York Staffing Co.; 2001
Custom Staffing of Westchester; White Plains, NY Staffing Services; 2006
Custom Staffing; New York, NY Staffing Services; 2006
Dawson; OH Staffing Services
Denham; CA Staffing Services
EFROS; New York, NY Staffing Service
Emerson Professionals; Broward County, FL Medical Staffing Services; 1996
First Choice Staffing; New York, NY Staffing Service; 2001
Haley Stuart, LLC; NJ Legal Recruiting Services; 2004
Hastings & Hastings, Inc.; Miami, FL Executive Search Firm, Staffing; 2001
Insurance Overload Services Staffing for Insurance Industry
MGA Technologies; Clearwater, FL IT & Other Staffing Services; 2000
NRI Staffing Services
The Palmer Group; IA Staffing Services
Personnel Express
Pivotal Search Group; NY; NJ Retail Executive Recruiting Services; 2004
Rural Sourcing; GA; 2007
Sachs, Sax, Klein; FL Legal Services; 2006
Select Staffing Staffing Service; 2007
System Soft Technologies; Clearwater, FL National IT Staffing Service; 2006
Tristate Employment Staffing

THE COMMUNICATIONS GROUP
400 W Capitol Ste 1391, Little Rock, AR 72201
Tel.: (501) 376-8722
Fax: (501) 376-9405
E-Mail: info@comgroup.com
Web Site: www.comgroup.com

Employees: 20
Year Founded: 1987

Agency Specializes In: Education, Public Relations

Dan Cowling *(Pres & Principal)*
Lisa Bondurant *(Exec VP & Dir-PR & Client Svc)*
Leigh Grant *(VP & Dir-Media)*
Johnice L. Hopson *(VP & Mgr-Acctg)*
Dana Rogers *(Sr Dir-Art)*
Brent Miller *(Assoc Dir-Creative)*
Heather Bailey *(Media Planner & Media Buyer)*
Deborah Beard *(Acct Planner)*
Diane Wingard *(Acct Planner)*

Accounts:
Arkansas Adult Education ESL Classes, GED Test Preparation, Literacy Programs, Workplace Education Programs
Arkansas Department of Human Services Quality Early Care & Education Campaign (Better Beginnings); 2009
Arkansas Natural Heritage Commission
Arkansas Soybean Promotion Board Campaign: "The Miracle Bean is Me", Television
ARKids First
Baldor Electric Co.
BreastCare
Campaign for Healthier Babies
Department of Arkansas Heritage
Innovation Industries

COMMUNICATIONS MEDIA INC.
2200 Renaissance Blvd Ste 102, King of Prussia, PA 19406
Tel.: (484) 322-0880
Web Site: www.cmimedia.com

Employees: 130

Agency Specializes In: Health Care Services, Media Buying Services, Media Planning, Media Relations, Sponsorship, Strategic Planning/Research

Stan Woodland *(CEO)*
John Donovan *(CFO)*
Jim Woodland *(COO)*
Susan Dorfman *(CMO & CIO)*
Nicole Woodland-DeVan *(Sr VP-Buying Svcs & Deliverables)*
Carly Kuper *(VP-Strategic Mktg & Corp Comm)*
Nancy Logue *(VP-HR)*
Leanne Smith *(Sr Dir-Insights & Analytics)*
Nicole Faretra *(Sr Media Planner)*

Accounts:
Abbott
Amgen
AstraZeneca
Bayer
Boehringer Ingelheim
Dendreon
Eisai
Jazz Pharmaceuticals
Johnson & Johnson
Lilly
MEDA
Novartis
Salix
Sanofi
Sunovion
Takeda Millennium

THE COMMUNICATIONS STRATEGY GROUP, INC.
42 Front St, Marblehead, MA 01945
Tel.: (781) 631-3117
Fax: (781) 631-3278
E-Mail: info@comstratgroup.com
Web Site: www.comstratgroup.com

Year Founded: 1987

Agency Specializes In: Corporate Communications, Crisis Communications, International, Investor

Relations, Media Relations, Media Training, Pharmaceutical

Barbara C. Holtz *(Principal)*
Shannon Fern *(Sr VP-Health & Wellness)*
Dan Mahoney *(Sr VP-Fin & Pro Svcs)*
Lindsey Read *(Sr VP-Education)*
Jenny Foust *(Assoc VP-Consumer Packaged Goods)*
Anne Jenkins *(Assoc VP-Higher Education)*
Peter Mackellar *(Assoc VP-Asset Mgmt)*
Katie Weathers *(Mgr-Sector-Banking & Fin Tech)*
Erik Keith *(Sr Strategist-Digital)*
Corey Dahl *(Strategist-Content-Fin & Pro Svcs)*

THE COMMUNICATORS GROUP

9 Church St, Keene, NH 03431
Tel.: (603) 357-5678
Fax: (603) 283-0113
Web Site: www.communicatorsgroup.com

E-Mail for Key Personnel:
President: jwhitcomb@communicatorsgroup.com

Employees: 15
Year Founded: 1977

Agency Specializes In: Brand Development & Integration, Communications, Consulting, Consumer Marketing, Education, Financial, Graphic Design, Health Care Services, Internet/Web Design, Logo & Package Design, Multimedia, Point of Sale, Public Relations, Radio, Strategic Planning/Research, T.V.

Jeff Whitcomb *(Pres)*
Karen Hormel *(CFO & VP)*
Patience Merriman *(VP & Dir-Creative)*
Jim Hickey *(VP-Acct Svc)*

Accounts:
C&S
Cedarcrest Center
Humane Society
Revera Health Systems
Simple Tuition

THE COMMUNITY

(Formerly La Comunidad)
6400 Biscayne Blvd, Miami, FL 33138
Tel.: (305) 865-9600
Fax: (305) 865-9609
Web Site: www.lacomunidad.com

E-Mail for Key Personnel:
President: Antoinette@lacomu.com

Employees: 80
Year Founded: 2001

National Agency Associations: 4A's-AHAA

Agency Specializes In: Hispanic Market

Approx. Annual Billings: $46,000,000

Jose Molla *(Co-Founder & Dir-Creative)*
Laurie Malaga *(VP-Integrated Production)*
Tracy McDonough *(VP-Ops-Global)*
Robert Bisi *(Creative Dir)*
Maryanne Dammrich *(Acct Dir)*
Andrew Amendola *(Dir-Digital Strategy)*
Tomas Duhalde *(Dir-Art & Creative)*
Leo Prat *(Dir-Creative)*
Fernando Sosa *(Dir-Creative)*
Ricky Vior *(Dir-Creative)*
Aaron Zimroth *(Copywriter)*

Accounts:
Beam Suntory Campaign: "Make It With a Cowboy", Campaign: "Premium Remastered", Digital Media, Hornitos (Above-the-Line Creative, Digital & Social Agency of Record), I'm All Ears, Sauza (Above-the-Line Creative, Digital & Social Agency of Record), Sauza 901(Above-the-Line Creative, Digital & Social Agency of Record), Simple Things, Strategy, Tequila (Digital Agency of Record)
Best Buy, Inc.
New-BMW of North America, LLC (US Hispanic Agency of Record) Creative, Digital, Social Media, Strategy
Citi
Citibank Universal Card Services
City of Buenos Aires Campaign: "Better by Bike"
Converse Campaign: "Politico"
Corona Extra
Crown Imports Hispanic, Victoria beer
Grupo Modelo S.A.B. de C.V.
Johnson & Johnson Hispanic; 2008
Modelo Especial
Mondelez International, Inc.
MTV Latin America El Spooky Show, mtvla.com
NBCUniversal, Inc. Mun2
Original Penguin by Munsingwear (Agency of Record) Creative, Email Marketing, In Store events, Jacket, Print, Retail, Social Media
Perry Ellis International, Inc. Original Penguin
Sony Latin America
Time Warner Cable Campaign: "Rings", Direct Mail, OOH, Print, Radio, TV
VH1 Latin America
Volvo Campaign: "Volvo in Every Car", X-Ray App
Walt Disney & Co.

Branch

The Community

(Formerly La Comunidad)
Avenida Del Libertador 13548, Martinez, B1640 A0T Buenos Aires, Argentina
Tel.: (54) 11 4792 0251
Fax: (54) 11 4792 0251
E-Mail: hola@lacomunidad.com
Web Site: www.lacomunidad.com

Employees: 30

Agency Specializes In: Advertising, Bilingual Market, Hispanic Market, Teen Market

Joaquin Molla *(Owner)*
Sebastian Diaz *(Acct Grp Dir)*
Christian Corio *(Art Dir)*
Daniel Gergely *(Acct Dir)*
Guilherme Marini *(Dir-Art)*
Leo Prat *(Dir-Creative)*
Fernando Sosa *(Dir-Creative)*
Fernando Zagales *(Dir-Creative)*
Marcelo Padoca *(Copywriter)*

Accounts:
Alma Mora Campaign: "Carlalouis", TV
Buenos Aires Independent Film Festival Television
City of Buenos Aires
Disney
La Nacion Deportiva; 2007
Rolling Stone Campaign: "Question Everything"
VH1
Wrangler

THE COMPANY OF OTHERS

(Formerly FKM)
1800 W Loop S Ste 2100, Houston, TX 77027
Tel.: (713) 862-5100
Fax: (713) 869-6560
Web Site: www.thecompany.com

Employees: 200
Year Founded: 1980

National Agency Associations: 4A's-MAGNET

Agency Specializes In: Advertising, Automotive, Brand Development & Integration, Business-To-Business, Collateral, Consulting, Consumer Marketing, Corporate Identity, Digital/Interactive, Direct Response Marketing, Education, Exhibit/Trade Shows, Financial, Government/Political, Graphic Design, Health Care Services, High Technology, In-Store Advertising, Internet/Web Design, Leisure, Local Marketing, Logo & Package Design, Media Buying Services, Media Planning, Mobile Marketing, New Product Development, Out-of-Home Media, Outdoor, Package Design, Podcasting, Point of Purchase, Production, Public Relations, Publicity/Promotions, Real Estate, Recruitment, Restaurant, Retail, Sales Promotion, Sponsorship, Sports Market, Strategic Planning/Research, Travel & Tourism, Web (Banner Ads, Pop-ups, etc.), Yellow Pages Advertising

Approx. Annual Billings: $240,000,000

Breakdown of Gross Billings by Media: Bus. Publs.: 4%; Consumer Publs.: 3%; D.M.: 2%; E-Commerce: 2%; Network T.V.: 55%; Newsp.: 3%; Outdoor: 3%; Radio: 28%

Jose Lozano *(CEO)*
Kyle Allen *(Exec VP & Dir-Media)*
Suzanne Jennings *(Sr VP & Dir-Creative)*
Carol Caposino *(VP & Dir-Creative Resources)*
Liz Gannaway *(Acct Dir-Fin)*
Kimberly Bratton *(Supvr-PR)*
Andrew Gibson *(Supvr-Brand Dev)*

Accounts:
CenterPoint Energy Energy & Utilities; 1988
ConocoPhillips
Goodman Amana Air Conditioner Manufacturer; 2007
Greyhound
Haworth, Inc.
HCA Holdings Inc.; 1997
Mattress Firm (Agency of Record)
Pappas Restaurants; 2005
Riviana Foods Brand Planning, Creative Development, Media Planning & Buying, Minute Rice, Public Relations, Success Rice
Stallion Oilfield Services Onshore/Offshore Living Accommodations; 2007
Visa International
Volkswagen Group of America, Inc.
Waste Management Waste & Environmental Services; 1996
Yellow Pages (Agency of Record)

Branches

The Company of Others

(Formerly FKM)
4040 N Central Expy Ste 700, Dallas, TX 75204-3179
Fax: (214) 370-8382
Toll Free: (800) 994-1681
Web Site: www.thecompany.com

Employees: 15
Year Founded: 1980

National Agency Associations: 4A's-MAGNET

Rich Klein *(Co-Founder & Co-Chm)*
Bill Fogarty *(Chm)*
Jose Lozano *(CEO)*
Kyle Allen *(Exec VP & Dir-Media)*
Josh Okun *(Exec Dir-Creation)*
Scott Brown *(Dir-Creative)*
Brittany Williams *(Dir-Digital Media)*
Care Bach *(Brand Mgr-Dev)*

Accounts:
The Women's Hospital of Texas

The Company of Others

(Formerly Connect FKM)

6500 River Place Blvd Bldg 2 Ste 102, Austin, TX 78730-1116
Tel.: (512) 261-6816
Fax: (512) 261-4624
Web Site: www.thecompany.com/

Employees: 15
Year Founded: 1980

Agency Specializes In: Yellow Pages Advertising

Cissy Arnold *(Sr VP & Gen Mgr)*
Tracy Balusek *(Sr Acct Mgr)*
Melissa Hand *(Brand Mgr-Dev)*
Renate Conn *(Mgr-Billing)*

COMPASS HEALTHCARE MARKETERS

200 Princeton S Corporate Ctr Ste 320, Ewing, NJ 08628
Tel.: (609) 688-8440
Fax: (609) 688-8399
E-Mail: info@compasshc.com
Web Site: www.compasshc.com

Employees: 35

Agency Specializes In: Advertising, Email, Health Care Services, Internet/Web Design, Local Marketing, Media Buying Services, Public Relations, Strategic Planning/Research

Revenue: $6,000,000

Peter H. Nalen *(Pres)*
Paul Johnson *(Exec VP-Client Svcs)*
Stephanie Maier *(Dir-Internal Ops)*

Accounts:
Actelion Pharmaceuticals US, Inc.
Elestrin
Increlex
Prometheus
Zegerid

COMPASS MARKETING

222 Severn Ave Bldg 14 Ste 200, Annapolis, MD 21403
Tel.: (410) 268-0030
E-Mail: info@compassmarketinginc.com
Web Site: www.compassmarketinginc.com

Year Founded: 1998

Agency Specializes In: Communications, Market Research, Merchandising, Strategic Planning/Research, Transportation

Ralph A. Panebianco *(Pres)*
Larry McWilliams *(Co-CEO)*
Shawn McLaughlin *(Exec VP-Sls)*
Christopher A. Feiss *(Sr VP-Fin & Strategy)*
Greg Acken *(Grp VP)*
David Boshea *(Grp VP)*
Scott Lester *(Grp VP)*
Gary Panebianco *(Grp VP)*
Jesse Williams *(Grp VP-Inside Sls)*
John Blake *(VP-Bus Dev)*
Mike Cockrell *(VP-Bus Dev)*
Michael White *(VP-Ops)*
Eileen Burgess *(Dir-Sls Comm)*
Alisa Greenwood *(Dir-Mktg & Creative Svcs)*

Accounts:
General Mills Food Processing Services
Heinz Food Processing Services
Johnson & Johnson (McNeils Nutritional Div.) Healthcare Products Distr
Kellogg Company Food Processing Services
Mars Food Products Mfr
McCormick Food Products Mfr & Distr
Procter & Gamble Pharmaceuticals Products Distr
Unilever Healthcare Products Mfr

COMPLETE MARKETING RESOURCES INC.

140 S Main St Ste 102, Madisonville, KY 42431
Tel.: (270) 339-4176
Web Site: www.completemarketingresources.com

Year Founded: 2011

Agency Specializes In: Advertising, Email, Graphic Design, Internet/Web Design, Print, Radio, Search Engine Optimization, T.V.

Marion M. Miller *(Pres)*

Accounts:
M30

COMPLETE MEDIA INC.

927 E 8th St, Sioux Falls, SD 57103
Tel.: (605) 360-2259
Toll Free: (888) 889-7435
E-Mail: info@completemediainc.com
Web Site: www.completemediainc.com

Year Founded: 2001

Agency Specializes In: Advertising, Graphic Design, Internet/Web Design, Strategic Planning/Research

Matthew Luke *(Pres)*
Dan Farris *(Dir-Outreach)*

Accounts:
First Group
Green Art Design & Landscape

THE COMPUTER STUDIO

1280 Saw Mill River Rd, Yonkers, NY 10710-2722
Tel.: (914) 968-1212
Fax: (914) 968-1228
E-Mail: connect@webbusconnect.com
Web Site: www.webbusconnect.com

Employees: 7
Year Founded: 1986

Agency Specializes In: Advertising, Business Publications, Business-To-Business, Co-op Advertising, Collateral, Consulting, Consumer Marketing, Digital/Interactive, Direct Response Marketing, E-Commerce, Electronic Media, Graphic Design, High Technology, Industrial, Information Technology, Internet/Web Design, Magazines, Planning & Consultation, Print, Retail, Strategic Planning/Research, Technical Advertising

Approx. Annual Billings: $750,000

Breakdown of Gross Billings by Media: Bus. Publs.: $50,000; Collateral: $50,000; D.M.: $100,000; E-Commerce: $300,000; Graphic Design: $50,000; Internet Adv.: $10,000; Strategic Planning/Research: $40,000; Worldwide Web Sites: $150,000

Alan J. Goldstein *(Pres)*

Accounts:
Joan Michlin Galleries; New York, NY Jewelry; 2002
Westchester Tool Supply Corp.; Yonkers, NY Industrial Tool Supply; 1998

COMUNIKA

4000 St-Ambroise Ste 387, Montreal, QC H4C 2C7 Canada
Tel.: (514) 989-1700
Fax: (514) 989-1701
E-Mail: studio@comunika.com
Web Site: www.comunika.com

Employees: 10

Agency Specializes In: Advertising, Graphic Design, Internet/Web Design, Multimedia, Print, Publicity/Promotions, Web (Banner Ads, Pop-ups, etc.)

Francois Provost *(Pres)*
Steven Rourke *(Dir-Editorial)*
Mario D'Avignon *(Acct Mgr-Strategy)*
Karina Marliss *(Acct Mgr)*

Accounts:
Hector Larivee
Jaymar
L3 Mas
Oeko
Pfizer
Terraformex

CONCENTRIC MARKETING

101 W Worthington Ave Ste 108, Charlotte, NC 28203
Tel.: (704) 731-5100
Fax: (704) 344-1600
E-Mail: bshaw@getconcentric.com
Web Site: www.getconcentric.com

Employees: 20
Year Founded: 2000

Agency Specializes In: Above-the-Line, Advertising, Below-the-Line, Consulting, Consumer Goods, Consumer Marketing, Direct Response Marketing, Health Care Services, Household Goods, Identity Marketing, In-Store Advertising, Integrated Marketing, Internet/Web Design, Logo & Package Design, Market Research, Merchandising, New Product Development, Package Design, Podcasting, Point of Purchase, Point of Sale, Production (Print), Promotions, Retail, Sales Promotion, Search Engine Optimization, Web (Banner Ads, Pop-ups, etc.)

Approx. Annual Billings: $12,500,000

Breakdown of Gross Billings by Media: Brdcst.: $2,400,000; Comml. Photography: $100,000; Consulting: $1,400,000; D.M.: $800,000; Graphic Design: $1,500,000; In-Store Adv.: $250,000; Internet Adv.: $650,000; Logo & Package Design: $750,000; Mags.: $1,400,000; Mdsg./POP: $725,000; Newsp. & Mags.: $175,000; Sls. Promo.: $650,000; Strategic Planning/Research: $1,250,000; Worldwide Web Sites: $450,000

Robert Shaw *(Pres)*
Greg Silverman *(CEO)*
Lisa George *(CFO)*
Billie Spevak *(Sr VP-Strategy)*
Kelli McCallum *(VP-Client Svcs)*
Gary Carter *(Dir-Creative)*
Jason Clewell *(Assoc Dir-Creative & Interactive)*

Accounts:
Nature's Earth Feline Pine

CONCENTRIC PHARMA ADVERTISING

175 Varick St 9th Fl, New York, NY 10014
Tel.: (212) 633-9700
Fax: (212) 675-2209
E-Mail: info@concentric-rx.com
Web Site: www.concentricpharma.com

Employees: 10
Year Founded: 2002

National Agency Associations: 4A's

Agency Specializes In: Broadcast, Exhibit/Trade Shows, Health Care Services, Pharmaceutical, Print, Production, Publicity/Promotions, Sales Promotion, Sponsorship, Strategic Planning/Research

Approx. Annual Billings: $11,600,000

Ken Begasse, Jr. *(Co-Founder & COO)*
Michael Sanzen *(Co-Founder & Chief Creative Officer)*
Adam Cohen *(Mng Partner & Dir-Creative)*
Jose Rivera *(Exec VP & Grp Acct Dir)*
Jennie Fischette *(Exec VP & Client Svcs Dir)*
James Driscoll *(VP & Dir-Creative Tech)*
Joseph Sacaridiz *(VP & Assoc Dir-Creative)*
Igor Rusinov *(Mgr-Customer Insights & Analytics)*
Samantha Fogliano *(Acct Supvr)*
Kelly Meyers *(Supvr-Art)*

Accounts:
Alcon Labs
Allergan
Bayer HealthCare
Cobalt Laboratories
Coria Laboratories
Discovery Labs Surfaxin
Genentech
Mitsubishi Pharma America
Novartis
Novo Nordisk
Spotlight
Warner Chilcott

CONCEPT 73
950 Calle Amanecer Ste C, San Clemente, CA 92673
Tel.: (949) 337-2318
E-Mail: info@concept73.com
Web Site: www.concept73.com

Year Founded: 2008

Agency Specializes In: Advertising, Brand Development & Integration, Digital/Interactive, Event Planning & Marketing, Graphic Design, Internet/Web Design, Outdoor, Print, Public Relations, T.V.

Ryan Winter *(Co-Founder & Exec Creative Dir)*
Lesli Winter *(Pres)*
Billy ONeill *(Acct Dir)*
Tim Lelvis *(Sr Mgr-Production)*
Kirk Rosas *(Sr Designer)*
Brian Encabo *(Sr Designer-Interactive)*

Accounts:
Consumer Electronics Show

CONCEPT COMPANY, INC.
2011 S. Lakeman Dr. #A, Bellbrook, OH 45305
Tel.: (937) 848-5850
Fax: (937) 848-5858
E-Mail: info@conceptcompany.com
Web Site: www.conceptcompany.com

Employees: 3

Agency Specializes In: Advertising, Brand Development & Integration, Business-To-Business, Collateral, Consulting, Content, Corporate Identity, Direct Response Marketing, Internet/Web Design, Logo & Package Design, Public Relations, Strategic Planning/Research

Elaine Middlestetter *(Owner & VP)*
Robert Middlestetter *(Pres & CEO)*
Tina Hutzelman *(Acct Mgr & Strategist-Mktg)*

Accounts:
Credit Union Consulting; Dayton, OH Credit Union Services
Martin Automatic; Rockford, IL Industrial Equipment
MKS; Dayton, OH Firearms

CONCEPT ENVY
PO Box 944, Waukesha, WI 53187
Tel.: (262) 446-6823
E-Mail: info@conceptenvy.com
Web Site: www.conceptenvy.com

Agency Specializes In: Advertising, Brand Development & Integration, Content, Digital/Interactive, Internet/Web Design, Logo & Package Design, Media Planning, Print, Social Media, Strategic Planning/Research

Zach Beaman *(Co-Founder & Dir-Creative)*

Accounts:
Grebes Bakery

CONCEPT FARM
43 W 24th St 5th Fl, New York, NY 10010
Tel.: (212) 463-9939
Fax: (212) 463-7032
E-Mail: inquiries@conceptfarm.com
Web Site: www.conceptfarm.com

Employees: 35

Agency Specializes In: Advertising, Sponsorship

John Gellos *(Partner & Dir-Creative)*
Ray Mendez *(Partner & Dir-Creative)*
Griffin Stenger *(Partner & Dir-Ops)*
Gregg Wasiak *(Partner & Dir-Growth)*
Dayna Bieber *(Dir-Art)*
Angel Maldonado *(Dir-Ops)*
Hayley Grant *(Acct Supvr)*

Accounts:
Allure
New-Bowlmor AMF
Century 21 Department Stores Digital, Outdoor, Print, Social Media, Television, Traditional & Non-Traditional Media
Drey Fuse
Empire State Building Content, Creative, Strategy
ESPN
Green Peace
James Patterson Entertainment
News Corporation
SAP
Starz
TRW

CONCEPT THREE INC.
424 S Main St, Davison, MI 48423-1608
Tel.: (810) 653-1002
Fax: (810) 653-6302
E-Mail: sales@conceptthree.com
Web Site: www.conceptthree.com

Employees: 5
Year Founded: 1980

National Agency Associations: AAF

Agency Specializes In: Advertising, Advertising Specialties, Broadcast, Cable T.V., Collateral, Consulting, Graphic Design, Industrial, Local Marketing, Logo & Package Design, Media Buying Services, Multimedia, Planning & Consultation, Point of Sale, Retail, T.V.

Breakdown of Gross Billings by Media: Adv. Specialities: 5%; D.M.: 11%; Other: 2%; Outdoor: 3%; Print: 10%; Radio: 23%; T.V.: 46%

James R. Slater *(Co-Owner)*
Susan R. Slater *(Owner)*
Eric Quimby *(Specialist-Digital Mktg)*

Accounts:
Dave Lamb Heating & Cooling; 1983
Genesee Valley Gold & Silver; Flint, MI; 1997
Italia Gardens
Lifestyles Hot Springs Spas; Flint, MI; 1981

CONCRETE DESIGN COMMUNICATIONS INC
2 Silver Ave, Toronto, ON M6R 3A2 Canada
Tel.: (416) 534-9960
Fax: (416) 534-2184
E-Mail: mail@concrete.ca
Web Site: www.concrete.ca

Employees: 20
Year Founded: 1988

Agency Specializes In: Advertising, Arts, Brand Development & Integration, Collateral, Corporate Identity, Fashion/Apparel, Internet/Web Design, Package Design, Retail

Diti Katona *(Co-Founder, Partner & Dir-Creative)*
John Pylypczak *(Co-Founder, Partner & Dir-Creative)*
Lou Ann Sartori *(VP-Ops)*
Clarence Kwan *(Dir-Brands, Plng & Strategy)*
Leticia Luna *(Dir-Creative)*
Brandy McKinlay *(Dir-Production Svcs)*
Aurora Ratcliffe *(Acct Mgr)*
John Pichette *(Planner-Brand)*
Jonathon Yule *(Designer)*

CONDON & ROOT
200 N Northwest Hwy, Barrington, IL 60010
Tel.: (847) 381-6575
Fax: (847) 381-6799
E-Mail: info@condonandroot.com
Web Site: www.condonandroot.com

Employees: 2
Year Founded: 1998

Agency Specializes In: Communications, Strategic Planning/Research

Keith Condon *(Partner)*
Jim Root *(Partner)*

Accounts:
Abbott Labs
BMO Capital Markets
BMO Financial Group
The Coca-Cola Company Fairlife
Horizon Pharma
IDM Pharma
Mongoose
Mongoose Bicycles
Monsanto
Signature Room

CONDRON & COSGROVE
(Formerly Condron & Company)
220 Penn Ave Ste 303, Scranton, PA 18503
Tel.: (570) 344-6888
Fax: (570) 344-6669
Web Site: condronandcosgrove.com/

Agency Specializes In: Advertising, Broadcast, Digital/Interactive, Logo & Package Design, Outdoor, Print

Phil Condron *(Pres)*
John Cosgrove *(VP)*
John Mikulak *(Dir-Copy & Producer-Multimedia)*
Michele Lauriha *(Dir-Art)*
Kim Kryeski *(Coord-Media)*

Accounts:

Cabot Corporation
RJ Burne Cadillac

THE CONFLUENCE

12910 Culver Blvd, Los Angeles, CA 90066
Tel.: (310) 424-8356
Web Site: www.theconfluencegroup.com

Year Founded: 2009

Agency Specializes In: Advertising, Brand Development & Integration, Content, Digital/Interactive, Public Relations

Russell Ward *(Founder & Owner)*
Eric Starr *(Creative Dir)*
Summer Bradley *(Acct Mgr)*

Accounts:
Fest300
Shocase

CONFLUENCE MARKETING

(Acquired by Woodruff Sweitzer, Inc.)

CONFLUENCE MARKETING

1926 Old West Main St, Red Wing, MN 55066
Tel.: (651) 388-7737
E-Mail: info@confluencemarketing.com
Web Site: www.confluencemarketing.com

Year Founded: 2004

Agency Specializes In: Advertising, Brand Development & Integration, Print, Public Relations, Strategic Planning/Research

Steve Akerson *(Sr VP)*
Jon Gierke *(Dir-Creative)*
Brian Nosan *(Dir-Art)*
Amy Kemmerer *(Mgr-Production)*

Accounts:
AgSpring
Austin Utilities
CCFE
Chippewa Valley Bean
CLAAS of America
Donaldson Clean Solutions
Jones-Harrison
Minnesota State University
Red Wing Family YMCA
Red Wing Shoes
Robins Kaplan Miller & Ciresi
Roseville Visitors Association
Steigerwaldt
Tech Mix
Zinpro

CONILL ADVERTISING, INC.

800 Brickell Ave, Miami, FL 33131
Tel.: (305) 351-2901
Fax: (305) 351-2509
E-Mail: noticias@conill.com
Web Site: www.conill.com

Employees: 95

National Agency Associations: 4A's-AHAA

Agency Specializes In: Above-the-Line, Advertising, Automotive, Below-the-Line, Branded Entertainment, Broadcast, Cable T.V., Communications, Consumer Goods, Cosmetics, Digital/Interactive, Experience Design, Game Integration, Guerilla Marketing, Hispanic Market, Integrated Marketing, Internet/Web Design, Magazines, Media Buying Services, Mobile Marketing, Multicultural, Newspaper, Newspapers & Magazines, Outdoor, Print, Production (Ad, Film, Broadcast), Production (Print), Radio, Retail, Social Marketing/Nonprofit, Social Media, Sponsorship, Strategic Planning/Research, T.V., Transportation, Travel & Tourism, Viral/Buzz/Word of Mouth, Web (Banner Ads, Pop-ups, etc.)

Breakdown of Gross Billings by Media: Cable T.V.: 30%; Consumer Publs.: 18%; Network T.V.: 37%; Other: 10%; Outdoor: 2%; Radio: 3%

Magaly Melendez *(Sr VP & Dir-Fin)*
Beatriz Del Amo *(VP & Client Svcs Dir)*
Grace Espejel *(Sr Dir-Art)*
Tammie DeGrasse Cabrera *(Grp Acct Dir)*
Melanie Case *(Sr Producer-Social Content-Bilingual)*
Reinier Suarez *(Mgmt Supvr)*
Hernan Pettinaroli *(Assoc Dir-Creative)*
Vasty Gonzalez *(Acct Supvr)*
Claudia Yuskoff *(Supvr-Mgmt & Social Media Creative Content)*
Carolina Montenegro *(Sr Acct Exec)*

Accounts:
Citibank; 2010
CVS Health; 2007
JCPenney Hispanic
Lexus
The Procter & Gamble Company Crest, Head & Shoulders, Pampers, Tide; 1986
New-Mondelez International
Sony
T-Mobile US Campaign: "Goal"
Toyota Motor North America, Inc.
Toyota Motor Sales Campaign: "Details", Campaign: "Sauna", Toyota Tundra
United Continental Holdings; 2007

Branch

Conill Advertising, Inc.

2101 Rosecrans Ave 2nd Fl, El Segundo, CA 90245
Tel.: (424) 290-4400
E-Mail: noticias@conill.com
Web Site: www.conill.com

Employees: 65
Year Founded: 1987

National Agency Associations: 4A's

Agency Specializes In: Above-the-Line, Advertising, Automotive, Below-the-Line, Branded Entertainment, Broadcast, Cable T.V., Communications, Consumer Goods, Cosmetics, Digital/Interactive, Gay & Lesbian Market, Guerilla Marketing, Hispanic Market, Integrated Marketing, Internet/Web Design, Magazines, Media Buying Services, Mobile Marketing, Multicultural, Newspaper, Newspapers & Magazines, Outdoor, Print, Production (Ad, Film, Broadcast), Production (Print), Radio, Retail, Social Marketing/Nonprofit, Social Media, Sponsorship, Strategic Planning/Research, T.V., Transportation, Travel & Tourism, Viral/Buzz/Word of Mouth, Web (Banner Ads, Pop-ups, etc.)

Carlos Martinez *(Pres)*
Verena Sisa *(Chief Strategy Officer & VP)*
Javier Campopiano *(Chief Creative Officer)*
Tom Lanktree *(VP & Dir-Strategic Dev)*
Anabel Ordonez *(Grp Acct Dir)*
Federico Duran *(Creative Dir)*
Cilmara Santos *(Acct Dir)*
Veronica Cueva *(Mgmt Supvr)*
Esmeralda Nisperos *(Dir-Content Strategies)*
Elizabeth Sanchez *(Dir-Events & Promos)*
Yenia Paez *(Mgr-Bus Affairs)*
Mauricio Macias Torres *(Mgr-Social Media & Content)*
Courtney Corbett *(Acct Supvr)*
Ramon Hernandez *(Supvr-Media)*
Claudia Yuskoff *(Supvr-Mgmt & Social Media Creative Content)*
Matthew DeCuir *(Specialist-Comm)*
Angelito Bautista *(Media Buyer)*
Marc DiBianco *(Planner-Digital Media)*
Kerryann Gray *(Planner & Buyer-Integrated Comm)*
Francisca Resendez *(Planner-Digital Media)*

Accounts:
Aflac Incorporated Hispanic Marketing
Alaska Airlines, Inc.
Consulate General of Argentina in Los Angeles Campaign: "Job"
Crest
"El Favorito del Famoso" Contest
FX Networks, LLC
KFC Corporation
Miami Short Film Festival Campaign: "Bedside Table"
Sony Computer Entertainment America LLC PlayStation
T-Mobile USA, Inc. Campaign: "Missed It?"; 2004
Toyota Motor North America, Inc.
Toyota Motor Sales, USA Broadcast, Campaign: "Details", Campaign: "Mas Que Un Auto", Campaign: "Projecting Pollution", Digital, Hispanic, Social Media, Videos; 1987

CONNECT2 COMMUNICATIONS

3211 Rogers Rd Ste 200, Wake Forest, NC 27587
Tel.: (919) 554-3532
Fax: (919) 453-0769
E-Mail: info@connect2comm.com
Web Site: www.connect2comm.com

Employees: 10
Year Founded: 2003

Agency Specializes In: Business-To-Business, Collateral, Communications, Crisis Communications, Internet/Web Design, Investor Relations, Local Marketing, Media Relations, Product Placement, Strategic Planning/Research

Richard M. Williams *(Pres)*
Joyce Wady *(VP)*
Jasmian McDonald *(Acct Exec)*
Halley Spong *(Acct Exec)*

Accounts:
Acme Packet
BatteryCorp
BIG BOSS
Cognio
LaunchCapital
mBLAST
MINTERA
Packet Vision
ROCK
SIPFORUM
SS8

CONNECTIONS ADVERTISING & MARKETING

148 Jefferson St Ste B, Lexington, KY 40508
Tel.: (859) 903-1010
E-Mail: info@connectionsadv.com
Web Site: www.connectionsadv.com

Employees: 8
Year Founded: 2009

Agency Specializes In: Advertising, Advertising Specialties, Affluent Market, African-American Market, Agriculture, Alternative Advertising, Automotive, Aviation & Aerospace, Brand Development & Integration, Broadcast, Business Publications, Business-To-Business, Cable T.V., Catalogs, Co-op Advertising, College, Commercial Photography, Communications, Content, Corporate Identity, Cosmetics, Custom Publishing, Customer Relationship Management, Education, Electronic Media, Email, Entertainment, Environmental, Event

Planning & Marketing, Exhibit/Trade Shows, Experience Design, Fashion/Apparel, Financial, Food Service, Government/Political, Graphic Design, Guerilla Marketing, Health Care Services, Hispanic Market, Hospitality, Household Goods, Identity Marketing, In-Store Advertising, Industrial, Infomercials, Integrated Marketing, International, Internet/Web Design, Legal Services, Leisure, Local Marketing, Logo & Package Design, Luxury Products, Magazines, Marine, Market Research, Media Buying Services, Media Planning, Media Relations, Media Training, Medical Products, Multimedia, Newspaper, Newspapers & Magazines, Outdoor, Over-50 Market, Package Design, Pets , Pharmaceutical, Planning & Consultation, Point of Purchase, Print, Product Placement, Production, Production (Ad, Film, Broadcast), Production (Print), Promotions, Public Relations, Publicity/Promotions, Publishing, Radio, Regional, Restaurant, Retail, Sales Promotion, Search Engine Optimization, Seniors' Market, Social Marketing/Nonprofit, Social Media, Sponsorship, Sports Market, Strategic Planning/Research, Syndication, Teen Market, Trade & Consumer Magazines, Transportation, Tween Market, Urban Market, Web (Banner Ads, Pop-ups, etc.), Women's Market

Approx. Annual Billings: $494,400

Breakdown of Gross Billings by Media: Consulting: $24,400; Graphic Design: $15,600; Print: $16,800; Strategic Planning/Research: $11,000; Trade & Consumer Mags.: $426,600

Debby Nichols *(Pres)*
Stephanie Preston *(Acct Exec)*

Accounts:
Fairwinds Farm Equine Training, Sales & Services; 2009
Holistic Horse; 2010
Horseware Ireland Equine Clothing; 2010
Paso Fino Horse Association Equine Publication & Association; 2011
Select Lab Services Medical Services; 2011
Shyco Wood Products Recycling Services; 2011

CONNECTIVITY MARKETING AND MEDIA AGENCY
(Formerly Connectivity Marketing and Media)
107 Franklin St Ste 300, Tampa, FL 33602
Tel.: (813) 574-7912
Fax: (813) 609-3959
E-Mail: contact@connectivityagency.com
Web Site: connectivityagency.com

Year Founded: 2009

Agency Specializes In: Advertising, Alternative Advertising, Arts, Automotive, Branded Entertainment, Broadcast, Cable T.V., Co-op Advertising, Consumer Goods, Digital/Interactive, Electronic Media, Entertainment, Food Service, Leisure, Local Marketing, Market Research, Media Buying Services, Media Planning, Multimedia, Newspapers & Magazines, Out-of-Home Media, Outdoor, Print, Production, Production (Print), Promotions, Publicity/Promotions, Radio, Regional, Restaurant, Retail, Sales Promotion, Sponsorship, Strategic Planning/Research, T.V., Travel & Tourism

Sean Halter *(CEO)*
Cheryl McCoy *(Media Dir)*
Ariel Williams *(Assoc Dir-Media)*
D.J. Hamilton *(Sr Acct Mgr)*
Kristin Kuntz *(Acct Mgr)*
Gina Maker *(Acct Mgr)*
Lisa Halter *(Mgr-Connections)*
Shannan Keefe *(Mgr-Promotions & Media)*
Amal Sanid *(Mgr-Creative)*
Katie Hale *(Publicist)*

Accounts:
Cricket Wireless; 2014
Deep Eddy Vodka; 2011
Front Burner Brands Melting Pot; 2013
Gold & Diamond Source; 2009
Livenation; 2012
Margaritaville; 2014
Pabst Brewing Pabst Blue Ribbon, Lone Star, Old Style, Ballantine IPA, Colt 45, Old Milwaukee, Primo, Olympia, Schlitz, Rainier; 2012
World Wrestling Entertainment Monday Night Raw, WWE Smackdown; 2009

CONNELLY PARTNERS
46 Waltham St Fl 4, Boston, MA 02118
Tel.: (617) 521-5400
Fax: (617) 521-5499
E-Mail: nvallee@connellypartners.com
Web Site: www.connellypartners.com

E-Mail for Key Personnel:
President: sconnelly@connellypartners.com
Media Dir.: rweinstein@connellypartners.com

Employees: 125
Year Founded: 1999

National Agency Associations: 4A's

Agency Specializes In: Sponsorship

Approx. Annual Billings: $70,000,000

Steve Connelly *(Pres & Exec Dir-Creative)*
Joel Idelson *(CMO)*
Alyssa D'Arienzo Toro *(Sr Partner & Chief Creative Officer)*
Justin Vogt *(Acct Dir)*
Barry Frechette *(Dir-Integrated Production)*
Scott Madden *(Sr Partner & Dir-Strategy & Integrated Svcs)*
Gary Mak *(Dir-Media)*
Christian Megliola *(Dir-PR & Content Strategy)*
Scott Savitt *(Dir-Digital)*
Ed Goode *(Assoc Dir-Media)*
Amy Brown Weber *(Assoc Dir-Bus Dev)*
Topher Dubay *(Sr Brand Mgr-Digital)*
Ashley McGilloway *(Brand Mgr)*
Abigail Pender *(Brand Mgr)*
Robert McCarthy *(Mgr-SEO)*
Zack Yeremian *(Mgr-Digital Analytics)*
Kristen Kouloheras *(Asst Brand Mgr)*
Emma Roehlke *(Asst Brand Mgr)*
Sarah Lewis *(Supvr-Brand)*
Jodi Riseberg *(Supvr-Media)*
Renee Rochon *(Supvr-Brand)*
Christopher Corrado *(Media Buyer)*
Courtney Desmond *(Media Planner-Integrated)*

Accounts:
AJ Wright Stores
Babson College Out of Home, Print Media, Radio, online
BJ's Wholesale Club Media Planning & Buying; 2004
D'Angelo
Fallon Community Health Plan; 2003
Salem Five Campaign: "The World According to Dustin Pedroiia"
Samsonite Brand Positioning, Web Design

Branches

Connelly Partners Travel
(Formerly ISM)
46 Waltham St, Boston, MA 02118
Tel.: (617) 521-5400
Fax: (617) 266-1890
Web Site: travel.connellypartners.com/

Employees: 40
Year Founded: 1984

National Agency Associations: AD CLUB-HSMAI-MAGNET

Agency Specializes In: Leisure, Travel & Tourism

Jonathan Plazonja *(Partner & Exec Dir-Creative)*
Sal DeLuca *(CFO)*
Matt Kaiser *(Assoc Dir-Creative)*

Accounts:
American Express Travel Services; New York, NY Travel Services; 2002
Four Seasons Hotels & Resorts; Toronto, Canada Hotels; 1989
Palace Resorts AAA Five Diamond Le Blanc Spa Resort, Beach Palace, Branding, Cozumel Palace, Isla Mujeres Palace, Marketing, Moon Palace Golf & Spa Resort, Playacar Palace, Strategy, Sun Palace
Saint Lucia Tourist Board Brand Campaign, Campaign: "Lift Your Senses"

Mc/K-CP
(Formerly Mc/K Healthcare)
200 State St, Boston, MA 02109
(See Separate Listing)

CONNORS ADVERTISING & DESIGN
355 W Lancaster Ave Bldg E 2nd Fl, Haverford, PA 19041
Tel.: (610) 649-4963
Fax: (610) 658-5810
Web Site: www.pc-advertising.com

Year Founded: 1990

Agency Specializes In: Advertising, Brand Development & Integration, Corporate Identity, Internet/Web Design, Print

Paul Connors *(Owner)*
Marcia McConnell *(Mgr-Mktg & Graphic Designer)*

Accounts:
Blue Tree Landscaping Inc
Boathouse Capital
Cadence Aerospace
Envision Land Use

CONOVER TUTTLE PACE
77 N Washington St, Boston, MA 02114
Tel.: (617) 412-4000
Fax: (617) 412-4411
E-Mail: info@ctpboston.com
Web Site: www.ctpboston.com

E-Mail for Key Personnel:
President: fconover@ctpboston.com

Employees: 45
Year Founded: 1996

National Agency Associations: 4A's

Agency Specializes In: Advertising, Advertising Specialties, Brand Development & Integration, Broadcast, Business-To-Business, Cable T.V., Co-op Advertising, Collateral, Communications, Consumer Marketing, Corporate Identity, Direct Response Marketing, Education, Electronic Media, Event Planning & Marketing, Fashion/Apparel, Government/Political, Graphic Design, Health Care Services, High Technology, In-Store Advertising, Internet/Web Design, Leisure, Market Research, Media Buying Services, Media Planning, Media Relations, Newspaper, Newspapers & Magazines, Out-of-Home Media, Outdoor, Pharmaceutical, Print, Public Relations, Publicity/Promotions, Radio, Recruitment, Social Media, Sports Market, Strategic Planning/Research, T.V., Trade & Consumer Magazines, Transportation, Travel & Tourism

Approx. Annual Billings: $15,000,000

Brian Heffron *(Partner & Exec VP)*
Chip Tuttle *(Partner)*
Alison McCarthy *(Sr VP & Acct Mgmt Dir)*
Mark Fredrickson *(Mng Dir-Tech Practice)*
Todd Graff *(VP)*
Tara Roman *(Dir-Project Mgmt)*
Sadie Barlow *(Assoc Dir-Media)*
Erin Bowen *(Acct Supvr)*

Accounts:
Boston Boot Company
Boston Red Sox Campaign: "What's Broken"
Breeders' Cup World Championships Thoroughbred Racing
Dean College Advertising, Marketing, Public Relations, Social Media
E.B. Horn Co. Jeweler
Eastern Bank Local Banking Services
Injured Workers Pharmacy
MassBay Community College; Wellesley, MA Education; 2011
MassDevelopment
Mercedes-Benz of Burlington (Agency of Record)
Microsoft
Pinehurst Resort
Pop Warner Little Scholars Youth Football Organization
Red Bend Software
Red Hat
Suffolk Downs Thoroughbred Race Track

CONRAD, PHILLIPS & VUTECH, INC.

1398 Goodale Blvd, Columbus, OH 43212
Tel.: (614) 224-3887
Fax: (614) 222-0737
E-Mail: tim@cpvinc.com
Web Site: www.cpvinc.com

E-Mail for Key Personnel:
President: kirk@cpvinc.com
Creative Dir.: rick@cpvinc.com
Media Dir.: carol@cpvinc.com
Production Mgr.: amy@cpvinc.com

Employees: 20
Year Founded: 1967

National Agency Associations: 4A's

Agency Specializes In: Advertising, Brand Development & Integration, Broadcast, Business Publications, Business-To-Business, Children's Market, Collateral, Communications, Consulting, Consumer Marketing, Consumer Publications, Corporate Identity, Direct Response Marketing, E-Commerce, Education, Financial, Graphic Design, Health Care Services, High Technology, Industrial, Internet/Web Design, Logo & Package Design, Magazines, Newspaper, Newspapers & Magazines, Out-of-Home Media, Outdoor, Planning & Consultation, Print, Production, Radio, Real Estate, Restaurant, Retail, Strategic Planning/Research, T.V., Trade & Consumer Magazines

Approx. Annual Billings: $12,000,000

Breakdown of Gross Billings by Media: Bus. Publs.: 10%; Collateral: 30%; D.M.: 10%; Mags.: 5%; Newsp.: 15%; Outdoor: 5%; Radio: 10%; Strategic Planning/Research: 5%; T.V.: 10%

Rick Carey *(Principal & Dir-Creative)*
Marcie Gabor *(Principal)*
Amy Ireland *(Acct Dir & Strategist)*
Carol Barrett *(Dir-Media)*
Rocco Maiolo *(Dir-Art)*
Mike Murphy *(Dir-Art)*
Erica Malone *(Acct Exec)*

Accounts:
AkzoNobel Coatings
Alliance Data Systems
Arkansas Children's Hospital; 2011
Buckeye Power/Ohio Electric Cooperatives; Columbus, OH
Cardinal Health; Columbus, OH; 2009
Charles Penzone Family of Salons; Columbus, OH
Entrotech; Columbus, OH
Goodwill Columbus
Honda of Americas Mfg.
National Children's Hospital; Columbus, OH; 1995
Nationwide Realty Investments
Ohio Dominican University; Columbus, OH; 2000
Williams Detroit Diesel-Allison; Columbus, OH Diesel Engine Distributor; 1994

THE CONROY MARTINEZ GROUP

300 Sevilla Ave, Coral Gables, FL 33134
Tel.: (305) 445-7550
Fax: (305) 445-7551
E-Mail: info@conroymartinez.com
Web Site: www.conroymartinez.com

Employees: 5

Agency Specializes In: Collateral, Consumer Goods, Education, Email, Entertainment, Event Planning & Marketing, Health Care Services, Local Marketing, Promotions, Public Relations, Publicity/Promotions, Real Estate, Retail, Strategic Planning/Research, Travel & Tourism

C.L. Conroy *(Founder, Pres & CEO)*
Jorge Martinez *(VP)*
Diana Delgado *(Acct Exec)*

CONSOLIDATED SOLUTIONS

1614 E 40th St, Cleveland, OH 44103
Tel.: (216) 881-9191
Fax: (216) 881-3442
Web Site: www.csinc.com

Employees: 100
Year Founded: 1946

Agency Specializes In: Direct Response Marketing, Print

Kenneth A. Lanci *(Chm & CEO)*
Leonard Vargo *(Pres)*
Terry Hartman *(CFO)*
Joseph A. Turi *(VP-Sls)*

Accounts:
Cleveland Clinic; Cleveland, OH; 1991
Cleveland Zoo; Cleveland, OH; 1994
Sherwin-Williams Co.; Cleveland, OH; 1991

CONSORTIUM MEDIA SERVICES

4572 Telephone Rd Ste 913, Ventura, CA 93003
Tel.: (805) 654-1564
Fax: (805) 654-8796
E-Mail: info@consortium-media.com
Web Site: www.consortium-media.com

Employees: 10
Year Founded: 1990

Agency Specializes In: Advertising, Print, Promotions, Public Relations, Radio, T.V., Web (Banner Ads, Pop-ups, etc.)

Denise Bean-White *(Pres & CEO)*
Jennifer Curtis *(Sr VP & Gen Mgr)*
Denise Hodgson *(Office Mgr & Coord-Media & Traffic)*
Valerie Keeranan *(Designer-Web & Graphic Designer)*
Tristan Bernard *(Social Media Mktg)*

Accounts:
Aspiranet
The Beachwalker Inn & Suites
City of Oxnard
County of Ventura Human Services Agency
FOOD Share
Go Care
Jensen Design & Survey
Kaiku Finance
PODS Corporate
PODS Houston
PODS Las Vegas
PODS Lexington
PODS Phoenix
PODS Tri Counties
PODS Tucson
Ventura County Balley Company
Ventura County Health Care Agency
Ventura County Public Works Agency

CONSTRUCTION MARKETING INC

11057 Allisonville Rd Ste 208, Fishers, IN 46038
Tel.: (317) 660-6471
E-Mail: info@constructionmarketinginc.com
Web Site: www.construction.marketing/

Year Founded: 2009

Agency Specializes In: Advertising, Brand Development & Integration, Crisis Communications, Event Planning & Marketing, Graphic Design, Internet/Web Design, Logo & Package Design, Media Planning, Print, Public Relations

Rob Melis *(Pres)*
Theresa Smillie *(Dir-Art)*
Travis L. Sibold *(Asst Dir-Art)*

Accounts:
Hot Springs Crushing
Icon Projects
Indiana Cut Stone
Surface Technology
Teakology

CONTAGIOUSLA

424 S Broadway #604, Los Angeles, CA 90013
Tel.: (323) 303-3527
Web Site: www.ContagiousLA.com

Year Founded: 2007

Agency Specializes In: Affluent Market, Automotive, Brand Development & Integration, Broadcast, Cable T.V., College, Content, Digital/Interactive, E-Commerce, Electronic Media, Electronics, Guerilla Marketing, Luxury Products, Men's Market, Production (Ad, Film, Broadcast), Social Media, T.V.

Approx. Annual Billings: $500,000

Breakdown of Gross Billings by Media: Internet Adv.: 20%; T.V.: 80%

Noelle Weaver *(Mng Partner)*
Natalie Sakai *(Partner & Exec Producer)*
Chris Barth *(Strategist)*

Accounts:
AutoAnything.com; CA; 2010
AutoInsurance.com; CA Auto Insurance Quote Comparison; 2010
Geek2Geek.com; CA Dating Site; 2010
Mobeze, Inc.; CA HerWay, OBC; 2009
Pernod Ricard Chivas, Plymouth Gin

CONTEXT-BASED RESEARCH GROUP

100 N Charles St 15th Fl, Baltimore, MD 21201
Tel.: (410) 223-3589
Fax: (410) 528-8809

E-Mail: info@contextresearch.com
Web Site: www.contextresearch.com

Employees: 12
Year Founded: 1999

Agency Specializes In: Consulting, Graphic Design, Retail, Strategic Planning/Research

Belinda Jo Blinkoff *(Mng Partner)*
Robbie Blinkoff *(Mng Dir)*
Cleve Corlett *(Dir-Quantitative Res)*
Stephanie Simpson *(Dir-Strategy & Client Svc)*

Accounts:
American Institute of Architects
The Associated Press
Campbell Soup Company
GlaxoSmithKline
Johns Hopkins University
Maryland Science Center
Thomas Weisel Partners Group Inc.

CONTRAST CREATIVE
2598 Highstone Rd, Cary, NC 27519
Tel.: (919) 469-9151
Fax: (919) 469-0331
Web Site: www.contrastcreative.com

Year Founded: 1998

Agency Specializes In: Advertising, Digital/Interactive, Graphic Design, Internet/Web Design, Logo & Package Design, Print, Radio, Search Engine Optimization, Social Media, T.V.

Kathleen McDonald *(Pres)*
Tim Travitz *(CEO)*
Edwin Stemp *(Mng Dir)*
Mark Higginson *(Dir-Creative)*
Daniel McRae *(Sr Graphic Designer)*

Accounts:
Duke University Hospital

CONVERSATION LLC
220 5th Ave 4th Fl, New York, NY 10001
Tel.: (212) 389-9782
Fax: (917) 591-5479
E-Mail: info@convoagency.com
Web Site: www.convoagency.com

Agency Specializes In: Media Planning, Promotions, Social Media, Sponsorship, Strategic Planning/Research

Frank O'Brien *(Founder)*
Mimi Lin *(Mng Dir)*
Nathan Riley *(Dir-Product Dev)*

Accounts:
The Children's Place Children's Apparel Retailer
Digital Humanity Branding
DressBarn
Hearst Communications Inc Fashion & Apparel Services
Hearst Corporation
L'Oreal Cosmetic & Beauty Products Mfr
Snagola Management, Outreach, Social Media
Svedka Vodka Mfr

CONVERSE MARKETING
1125 Main St, Peoria, IL 61606
Tel.: (309) 672-2100
Fax: (309) 672-2111
E-Mail: allisonw@conversemarketing.com
Web Site: www.conversemarketing.com

Employees: 10

National Agency Associations: Second Wind Limited

Amy Converse Schlicksup *(Pres)*
Jane Converse *(Principal)*
Becky Krohe *(Dir-Design)*
Jason Salyers *(Dir)*
Ted Converse *(Sr Designer)*

Accounts:
Advanced Systems Design Information Technology Consulting
Alwan & Sons Meat Co.
Caterpillar Inc.
Central Illinois Bank
New Junction City

CONVERSION PIPELINE
12020 Sunrise Valley Dr Ste 100, Reston, VA 20191
Tel.: (877) 877-0542
Web Site: www.conversionpipeline.com

Employees: 50
Year Founded: 2008

Agency Specializes In: Advertising, Email, Internet/Web Design, Mobile Marketing, Search Engine Optimization, Social Media

Michael Delpierre *(CEO)*
Sam Collingwood *(Mng Partner & VP-Ops)*
Harry Brooks *(CMO)*
Aris Aristidou *(VP-IT & Global Markets)*
Christopher Gough *(Sr Acct Exec)*

Accounts:
Culpeper Recycling, LLC
Grafton Street; Gainesville, VA Online Marketing Strategy
IPW Industries Inc.
JK Enterprise Landscape Supply, LLC
Lunar Pages Internet Solutions
PaperCraft, Inc. Online Marketing, Pay Per Click, Search Engine Optimization
Shiertech, Llc
TIG Investigative Services
Varela Contracting, LLC
The Wynne Group

COOKIE JAR ENTERTAINMENT
(Acquired & Absorbed by DHX Advertising, Inc.)

COOL NERDS MARKETING
300 N Market St, Wilmington, DE 19801
Tel.: (302) 304-3440
Fax: (844) 280-6373
E-Mail: info@coolnerdsmarketing.com
Web Site: www.coolnerdsmarketing.com

Agency Specializes In: Advertising, Brand Development & Integration, Digital/Interactive, Graphic Design, Media Buying Services, Media Planning, Print, Public Relations, Radio, Search Engine Optimization

Bruce Gunacti *(CEO)*
Sam Ipek *(Coord-Print & Direct Mail)*

Accounts:
Troy Granite

COONEY/WATERS GROUP
111 Fifth Ave 2nd Fl, New York, NY 10003
Tel.: (212) 886-2200
Fax: (212) 886-2288
E-Mail: business@cooneywaters.com
Web Site: www.cooneywatersunlimited.com

Employees: 12
Year Founded: 1992

National Agency Associations: COPF

Agency Specializes In: Corporate Identity, Crisis Communications, Strategic Planning/Research

Timothy Bird *(Pres & CEO)*
Julia Jackson *(Exec VP)*
Lindsay Paul *(VP)*

Accounts:
Abbott Fund
Alcon Laboratories
Alere Corporate & Product Communications
American Lung Association
Anheuser-Busch
Cephalon
The Coca-Cola Company
LensCrafters
New York Blood Center
Purdue Pharma
Sanofi Pasteur

Branch

The Corkery Group, Inc.
111 Fifth Ave 2nd Fl, New York, NY 10003
Tel.: (212) 886-2200
Web Site: www.corkeryunlimited.com

Employees: 24
Year Founded: 2002

David Corkery *(Founder)*
Karen O'Malley *(Pres)*
Bora Lee *(VP)*
Megan Lynch *(VP)*
Melissa Unger *(Exec Coord & Acct Coord)*
Jessica Hartline *(Sr Acct Coord)*

Accounts:
The Water Supply & Sanitation Collaborative Council Media Relations, Strategic Communications

COOPER COMMUNICATIONS
4447 Hwy 17 Business, Murrells Inlet, SC 29576
Tel.: (843) 357-3098
Fax: (843) 651-6836
E-Mail: info@cooper-communications.com
Web Site: www.cooper-communications.com

Employees: 4
Year Founded: 1999

Agency Specializes In: Advertising, Business Publications, Cable T.V., Co-op Advertising, Corporate Communications, Custom Publishing, Electronic Media, Exhibit/Trade Shows, Graphic Design, Health Care Services, High Technology, Hospitality, Internet/Web Design, Local Marketing, Logo & Package Design, Media Buying Services, Media Planning, Medical Products, Newspaper, Newspapers & Magazines, Outdoor, Print, Production (Ad, Film, Broadcast), Promotions, Public Relations, Publicity/Promotions, Radio, Real Estate, Sponsorship, T.V.

Approx. Annual Billings: $1,500,000

Breakdown of Gross Billings by Media: Adv. Specialities: $1,500,000

Elizabeth Cooper *(Owner)*

THE COOPER GROUP
381 Park Ave S Eighth Fl, New York, NY 10016-8806
Tel.: (212) 696-2512
Fax: (212) 696-2516
E-Mail: info@thecoopergroup.com

Web Site: www.thecoopergroup.com

Employees: 12
Year Founded: 1984

National Agency Associations: AD CLUB-DMA

Agency Specializes In: Advertising, Brand Development & Integration, Business Publications, Business-To-Business, Children's Market, Co-op Advertising, Collateral, Communications, Consulting, Consumer Marketing, Consumer Publications, Corporate Identity, Digital/Interactive, Direct Response Marketing, Education, Entertainment, Financial, Graphic Design, Internet/Web Design, Logo & Package Design, Magazines, Newspaper, Newspapers & Magazines, Planning & Consultation, Print, Production, Strategic Planning/Research, Trade & Consumer Magazines

Approx. Annual Billings: $5,000,000

Breakdown of Gross Billings by Media: D.M.: $1,000,000; Internet Adv.: $1,000,000

Harold Cooper *(CEO & Principal)*
Tom Cooper *(COO & Principal)*
Tracey Murphy *(Acct Dir)*
Yennicka Quiles *(Acct Svcs Dir)*
Jennifer Olbrich *(Dir-Creative)*
Eyra Lopez *(Assoc Dir-Creative)*
Rachelle Seymour *(Acct Supvr)*
Rachelle Solis *(Acct Exec)*

Accounts:
American Express
American Express Publishing
AXA-Equitable
Bloomberg BusinessWeek
Brooks Brothers
Comcast
Conde Nast
Deutsche Bank
Disney
Goebel
Guideposts
HCI Direct
Merrill Lynch
National Geographic; Washington, DC Periodical; 1991
Time Warner
The USO

COOPERKATZ & COMPANY
205 Lexington Ave 5th Fl, New York, NY 10016
Tel.: (917) 595-3030
Fax: (917) 326-8997
Web Site: www.cooperkatz.com

National Agency Associations: COPF

Agency Specializes In: Sponsorship

Ralph Katz *(Founder & Principal)*
Anne Green *(Pres & CEO)*
Dorothy Sonnenburg *(CFO)*
Rachael Adler *(Sr VP & Dir-Client Svcs)*
Meredith Topalanchik *(Sr VP & Dir-Client Svcs)*
Jason Wallace *(VP & Dir-Creative)*
Melissa Connerton *(VP)*
Katy Hendricks *(Mgr-Client Svcs)*
Kathleen Reynolds *(Mgr-Client Svcs)*
Heather Caufield *(Acct Supvr)*
Marcus Hardy *(Sr Acct Exec)*

Accounts:
Coldwell Banker Real Estate LLC Public Relations
DialAmerica Marketing, Inc; Mahwah, NJ
Gap International Global Management Consultancy; 2010
Grinnell College
Jackson Hewitt Tax Service Inc.; Parsippany, NJ
Memorial Sloan-Kettering Cancer Center Inc. (Public Relations Agency of Record) Strategic Communications
MTA
National Association of Insurance Commissioners
Otis Elevator Elvators, Escalators & Moving Walkways; 2010
Physicians Foundation National Public Relations & Communications
Siegel+Gale
TD Bank Consumer PR, Financial PR
Topix.net; 2004
Tower Group
Veet Hair Removal
Vespa
Virgin Mobile USA, Inc.
VOLVO

COPACINO + FUJIKADO, LLC
1425 4th Ave Ste 700, Seattle, WA 98101-2265
Tel.: (206) 467-6610
Fax: (206) 467-6604
E-Mail: copacino@copacino.com
Web Site: www.copacino.com

E-Mail for Key Personnel:
Creative Dir.: kreifschneider@copacino.com

Employees: 30
Year Founded: 1998

National Agency Associations: AMA-MAGNET-MCEI-RAMA

Agency Specializes In: Advertising, Alternative Advertising, Automotive, Brand Development & Integration, Business Publications, Business-To-Business, Cable T.V., Collateral, Communications, Consulting, Consumer Goods, Consumer Marketing, Consumer Publications, Corporate Identity, Digital/Interactive, Direct Response Marketing, Direct-to-Consumer, Electronic Media, Event Planning & Marketing, Fashion/Apparel, Financial, Graphic Design, Guerilla Marketing, Health Care Services, High Technology, Hospitality, Household Goods, Identity Marketing, In-Store Advertising, Integrated Marketing, Internet/Web Design, Luxury Products, Magazines, Market Research, Media Buying Services, Media Planning, Medical Products, Merchandising, Newspaper, Newspapers & Magazines, Out-of-Home Media, Outdoor, Planning & Consultation, Point of Purchase, Point of Sale, Print, Production, Production (Print), Radio, Retail, Sales Promotion, Seniors' Market, Social Marketing/Nonprofit, Sponsorship, Sports Market, Strategic Planning/Research, T.V., Trade & Consumer Magazines, Transportation, Travel & Tourism, Web (Banner Ads, Pop-ups, etc.)

Approx. Annual Billings: $31,000,000

Breakdown of Gross Billings by Media: Consumer Publs.: 8%; Internet Adv.: 8%; Network Radio: 10%; Newsp.: 18%; Outdoor: 5%; Spot Radio: 27%; T.V.: 20%; Trade & Consumer Mags.: 4%

Betti Fujikado *(Co-Founder)*
Andy Westbrock *(Sr Dir-Art)*
Kris Dangla *(Dir-Integrated Production)*
Tracy Mirabelli *(Dir-Fin & Admin)*
Tonya Murphy *(Dir-Media)*
Andrew Gall *(Assoc Dir-Creative)*
Scott Howe *(Mgr-Digital Svcs)*
Sun Yi *(Mgr-Brdcst Production)*
Rebecca Arbeene *(Acct Supvr)*
Alyssa Goldberg *(Acct Exec)*
Melody Kromer *(Asst Acct Exec)*
Katie Baumann *(Acct Coord)*

Accounts:
Holland America Line International Cruise Operator
Islandwood Environmental Education & Advocacy
Lakeside Milam Recovery Centers; Bellevue, WA Healthcare; 2009
Metal Roofing Alliance; Belfair, WA Metal & Steel Roofing Products; 2003
Museum of History and Industry
Nordstrom; Seattle, WA Retail Apparel; 2006
Pacific Place Shopping Center; Seattle, WA Retail; 2010
Peace Health Health Care
Premera Blue Cross; Mountlake Terrace, WA Healthcare; 2008
Seattle Aquarium; Seattle, WA; 2007
Seattle Children's Hospital; Seattle, WA Medical Services; 2004
The Seattle Mariners; Seattle, WA Major League Baseball Team; 1998
Seattle Mariners Campaign: "Bernandez", Campaign: "Slow Motion and Music", Campaign: "Swing Away"
Seattle Reproductive Medicine Health Care/Fertility
Ste. Michelle Wine Estates Premium Wines
Symetra; Seattle, WA Business Insurance Services; 2004
Washington Forest Protection Association; Olympia, WA Forest Products; 2007
Washington State University Higher Education
Wing Luke Museum

COPERNIO
(Formerly Public Communications Worldwide)
11602 Knott St Ste 13, Garden Grove, CA 92841
Tel.: (714) 891-3660
Fax: (714) 891-1490
E-Mail: info@copernio.com
Web Site: www.copernio.com

Employees: 5
Year Founded: 1959

Agency Specializes In: Aviation & Aerospace, Business-To-Business, Consumer Marketing, Industrial, New Product Development, Planning & Consultation, Public Relations, Strategic Planning/Research, Technical Advertising

Approx. Annual Billings: $4,000,000

Breakdown of Gross Billings by Media: Bus. Publs.: $4,000,000

Susan van Barneveld *(Pres)*

Accounts:
NYNE Broadcast & Online Media, Strategic Public Relations

COPIOUS
411 Sw 6th Ave, Portland, OR 97204
Tel.: (503) 255-1822
Fax: (503) 419-9791
Toll Free: (888) 471-8637
E-Mail: hello@copiousinc.com
Web Site: www.copio.us

Year Founded: 2001

Agency Specializes In: Advertising, Digital/Interactive, E-Commerce, Email, Search Engine Optimization, Technical Advertising

Patrick Ezell *(CEO)*
Paddu Ramachandran *(VP-Engrg)*
Hardy Johnson *(Head-Tech)*
Adrienne Barnett *(Producer-Technical)*
David Hughes *(Dir-Strategic)*
Lacie Webb *(Designer)*
John Jessee *(Sr Engr-Software)*
Reid Parham *(Sr Engr-Sys)*

Accounts:
VIE Sports

COPP MEDIA SERVICES INC

322 S Mosley Ste 15, Wichita, KS 67202
Tel.: (316) 425-7065
E-Mail: info@coppmedia.com
Web Site: www.coppmedia.com

Employees: 9
Year Founded: 1993

Agency Specializes In: Advertising, Digital/Interactive, Media Buying Services, Media Planning, Social Media

Bonnie Tharp *(Pres)*
Nicole Copp *(Media Planner & Buyer)*
Sharri Riley *(Media Planner & Buyer)*

Accounts:
Cessna Aircraft Company Cessna Service Centers, Citation Air, Sales
Davis Moore Auto Group, Inc.

CORD MEDIA

43-645 Monterey Ave Ste D, Palm Desert, CA 92260
Tel.: (760) 834-8599
Fax: (760) 834-8604
Web Site: www.cordmedia.com

Year Founded: 2007

Agency Specializes In: Advertising, Brand Development & Integration, Digital/Interactive, Internet/Web Design, Public Relations, Radio, Social Media

Jaci Fitzsimonds *(Pres)*
Bob Hoffman *(COO)*
Mike Czerwinski *(Gen Mgr)*
Diane Reynolds-Nash *(Sr Dir-Art)*
Katherine Ruiz *(Client Svcs Dir)*
Bernardo Amavizca *(Dir-Art)*
Andrea De Francisco-Shek *(Dir-Graphic Svcs)*
Gina Rosenthal *(Dir-Art)*
Otis Ortega *(Mgr-Traffic)*

Accounts:
Alta Verde Group
City of Indio
Copley's on Palm Canyon
DR Horton
The Dunes Club
Family Development
Frasca Jewelers
New-Hard Rock Energy Drink (Agency of Record) Advertising, Creative, Digital, Marketing, Media Buying, Public Relations, Social Media
Hard Rock Hotel & Casino
Hollywood Park Casino (Agency of Record) Creative Design, Media, Public Relations, Radio Advertising Production, Social Media
Humana Challenge
Lennar
The Living Desert
Muckleshoot Indian Casino
PGA WEST
Seminole Hard Rock Hotel & Casino
Spotlight 29 Casino
St. Croix Casinos
Tortoise Rock Casino
TRIO Restaurant
Video Gaming Technologies, Inc

CORDERO & DAVENPORT ADVERTISING

800 W Ivy St Ste B, San Diego, CA 92101
Tel.: (619) 233-3830
Fax: (619) 233-3832
E-Mail: info@corderoanddavenport.com
Web Site: www.corderoanddavenport.com

Year Founded: 1991

Agency Specializes In: Brand Development & Integration, Outdoor, Print, Radio, T.V.

J.C. Cordero *(Owner)*
Kevin Davenport *(Partner & Dir-Creative)*

Accounts:
Big O Tires Auto Parts Retailer

CORE-CREATE INC.

(Name Changed to Brandkarma)

CORE CREATIVE, INC.

600 W Virginia St, Milwaukee, WI 53204
Tel.: (414) 291-0912
Fax: (414) 291-0932
E-Mail: angi@corecreative.com
Web Site: www.corecreative.com

Employees: 45
Year Founded: 1994

National Agency Associations: Second Wind Limited

Agency Specializes In: Advertising, Brand Development & Integration, Collateral, Crisis Communications, Digital/Interactive, Exhibit/Trade Shows, Graphic Design, Identity Marketing, Media Training, Planning & Consultation, Print, Public Relations, Radio, Strategic Planning/Research, T.V.

Rich Vetrano *(Owner)*
Jeff Speech *(Partner & VP-Creative Svcs)*
Angi Krueger *(VP-Mktg & Bus Dev)*
Jerry Higgins *(Dir-Creative)*
Stephanie Hungerford *(Strategist-Healthcare Mktg)*
Sarah Richmond-Basedow *(Strategist-Media)*
Regina Maline *(Sr Designer)*

Accounts:
Beloit Health System Advertising, Branding, Social Media
Charter Manufacturing Branding, Internal Communications, Recruitment Marketing
Concordia University Wisconsin & Ann Arbor Marketing, PR, Social Media
Harley-Davidson Design Services
Milwaukee Tool Branding, Design Services
ORBIS Corporation Advertising, Digital, Public Relations
Owensboro Health Advertising, Branding, Design Services, Digital, Social Media
Verizon Wireless Internal Communications, Media Relations, Public Relations

CORE GROUP ADVERTISING, INC.

4141 Office Pkwy, Dallas, TX 75204
Tel.: (214) 821-5888
Fax: (214) 827-1223
E-Mail: pnorth@coregroupadv.com
Web Site: www.coregroupadv.com

E-Mail for Key Personnel:
Creative Dir.: lmurphy@coregroupadv.com
Production Mgr.: sbraud@coregroupadv.com

Employees: 6
Year Founded: 1999

Agency Specializes In: Advertising, Brand Development & Integration, Broadcast, Business-To-Business, Collateral, Event Planning & Marketing, Exhibit/Trade Shows, Experience Design, Financial, Graphic Design, Guerilla Marketing, Health Care Services, High Technology, Identity Marketing, In-Store Advertising, Internet/Web Design, Local Marketing, Logo & Package Design, Magazines, Market Research, Media Buying Services, Media Planning, Medical Products, Multimedia, New Product Development, New Technologies, Newspaper, Newspapers & Magazines, Out-of-Home Media, Outdoor, Package Design, Planning & Consultation, Point of Purchase, Point of Sale, Print, Production, Production (Ad, Film, Broadcast), Production (Print), Promotions, Radio, Regional, Restaurant, Retail, Sales Promotion, Search Engine Optimization, Social Marketing/Nonprofit, Sports Market, Strategic Planning/Research, Sweepstakes, Technical Advertising, Transportation, Web (Banner Ads, Pop-ups, etc.), Women's Market

Approx. Annual Billings: $6,000,000

Breakdown of Gross Billings by Media: Adv. Specialities: 10%; Comml. Photography: 2%; D.M.: 10%; Event Mktg.: 10%; Exhibits/Trade Shows: 5%; Graphic Design: 10%; Point of Purchase: 10%; Production: 20%; Spot Radio: 3%; Trade & Consumer Mags.: 10%; Yellow Page Adv.: 10%

Pete Northway *(CEO & Partner)*
Natalie Jennings *(Dir-Art & Project Mgr)*

Accounts:
American Airlines Cargo
Baylor Health Systems; Dallas, TX; 2003
Bobcat Pressure Control
Morgan & Weisbrod L.L.P.
Rangers Baseball LLC
Sprint/Xohm; Herndon, VA; 2007

CORE GROUP ONE, INC.

928 Nuuanu Ave No 100, Honolulu, HI 96817
Tel.: (808) 440-9421
Web Site: www.coregroupone.com

Employees: 15

National Agency Associations: 4A's

Agency Specializes In: Advertising

Jim Horiuchi *(Pres)*
Grant Miyasaki *(Dir-Creative)*
Brad Shin *(Dir-Creative)*
Melissa Toyofuku *(Dir-Media)*
Lauri Yanagawa *(Dir-Accts)*
Marisa Heung *(Acct Exec)*

Accounts:
Hawaiian Electric Company
Pizza Hut
Taco Bell

CORECUBED

3316 Springcrest Dr, Louisville, KY 40241
Tel.: (502) 425-9770
Fax: (502) 339-0729
Toll Free: (800) 370-6980
E-Mail: info@corecubed.com
Web Site: www.corecubed.com

Employees: 15

National Agency Associations: PRSA

Agency Specializes In: Arts, Brand Development & Integration, Business-To-Business, Collateral, Communications, Consulting, Content, Corporate Identity, E-Commerce, Environmental, Graphic Design, Health Care Services, Industrial, Information Technology, Integrated Marketing, Internet/Web Design, Logo & Package Design, Media Planning, Media Relations, New Product Development, Over-50 Market, Podcasting, Print, Public Relations, Publicity/Promotions, Seniors' Market, Strategic Planning/Research, Viral/Buzz/Word of Mouth

Approx. Annual Billings: $1,000,000

Merrily Orsini *(Pres & CEO)*

Amy Selle *(Mng Dir)*
Marissa Snook *(Mng Dir)*
Beth Jackson *(Strategist-SEO)*
Jennifer Logullo *(Exec Specialist & Specialist-Creative Support)*
Mary O'Doherty *(Strategist-PR & Media Rels)*

Accounts:
Flame Run Gallery
Freedom Eldercare
Healthcare Performance Group
Right at Home
VantaEdge

COREY MCPHERSON NASH
63 Pleasant St, Watertown, MA 02472
Tel.: (617) 924-6050
Fax: (616) 923-0857
E-Mail: info@corey.com
Web Site: www.corey.com

Employees: 12
Year Founded: 1983

Agency Specializes In: Advertising, Sponsorship

Andrea Naddaff *(Partner & VP-Bus Dev)*
Michael McPherson *(Partner & Dir-Creative)*
Ryan Evans *(Dir-Experience Design)*
Aaron Haesaert *(Dir-Creative)*
Elizabeth Carter *(Assoc Dir-Creative)*
Saewon Hwang *(Designer)*
Deborah Levison *(Sr Designer)*
Marisa Petrillo *(Office Dir)*

Accounts:
Achievement Network
Andora
AOL
Harvard University Education Programs, Harvard Business School; 2005
Huntington Theatre Company
Monster
National Engineers Week Foundation; Alexandria, VA Brand Messaging, Digital
New England Journal of Medicine

COREY MEDIA & AIRPORT SERVICES
225 Corey Ctr SE, Atlanta, GA 30312
Tel.: (404) 419-9700
Fax: (404) 419-9721
E-Mail: info@coreycompanies.com
Web Site: www.coreyairportservices.com

Employees: 20
Year Founded: 1978

Agency Specializes In: Advertising, Automotive, College, Corporate Communications, Food Service, Health Care Services, Marine, Media Buying Services, Out-of-Home Media, Outdoor, Production, Real Estate, Sports Market, Travel & Tourism

Revenue: $5,000,000

Steve Moody *(VP)*
Laurel Hefner *(Gen Mgr-Adv-Palm Springs International Airport)*
Amy Lindsey *(Gen Mgr)*
Sanky Singletary *(Gen Mgr)*
Martha Theobald *(Gen Mgr-Adv)*
Lisa Keith *(Dir-Mktg)*
Michael O'Connell *(Dir-Natl Accounts)*
Bill Batty *(Reg Mgr-Adv Sls & Ops)*

Accounts:
Chuck Clancy Chevrolet
Coldwell Banker
Courtesy Ford
Cuscuwilla Development
Homeplace Communities
Stevi B's Pizza
Stonecrest Mall

Branch

Corey Airport Services
Cincinnatti / Northern Kentucky International Airport, Cincinnati, OH 45275
Tel.: (859) 767-5800
Fax: (513) 646-4195

Jay Grover *(VP-Special Projects, Govt Rels & Executive Affairs)*
Steve Moody *(VP)*
Laurel Hefner *(Gen Mgr-Adv-Palm Springs International Airport)*
Michael O'Connell *(Dir-Sls-Natl)*
Bill Batty *(Reg Mgr-Adv Sls & Ops)*
Michael Neck *(Coord-Mktg)*

CORIXA COMMUNICATIONS LTD
(Acquired by McCann Erickson & Absorbed into McCann Bristol)

CORLISS MARKETING COMMUNICATIONS
303 Lincoln Ave, Niles, OH 44446
Tel.: (330) 720-6138
Fax: (330) 652-4351
E-Mail: info@corlissmarketing.com
Web Site: www.corlissmarketing.com

Agency Specializes In: Advertising, Corporate Communications, Corporate Identity, Event Planning & Marketing, Internet/Web Design, Logo & Package Design, Media Relations, Public Relations, Radio, T.V.

Jean A. Corliss *(Owner)*

Accounts:
910th Airwing Base Community Council
Alberinis Restaurant
Atty Gregory V. Hicks
Boardman Steel, Inc.
Holloway-Williams Funeral Home
Home Federal Savings & Loan Association
Lordstown Country Kennel
St. Stephen School
Trumbull Co. Jobs & Family Services
Trumbull County Lifelines

CORNERSTONE ADVERTISING & DESIGN
(Formerly Cornerstone Media)
1640 N Major Dr, Beaumont, TX 77713-8506
Tel.: (409) 866-4804
Fax: (409) 866-3342
E-Mail: jarred@cornerstoneadgroup.com
Web Site: www.cornerstoneadgroup.com/

E-Mail for Key Personnel:
Creative Dir.: Kent@cornerstoneadgroup.com
Media Dir.: Michelle@cornerstoneadgroup.com

Employees: 16
Year Founded: 1982

Agency Specializes In: Multimedia, Radio, T.V.

Revenue: $7,000,000

Jarred W. DeMore *(Owner)*
Kent Houp *(Gen Mgr)*
Michelle Nelson *(Dir-Media)*
Marsha Langley *(Office Mgr)*
Kathy Gonzalez *(Media Buyer)*
Larry O'Keefe *(Corp Mgr-Video)*

CORNERSTONE MARKETING & ADVERTISING, INC.
114 Logan Ln Ste 4, Santa Rosa Beach, FL 32459
Tel.: (850) 231-3087
Fax: (850) 231-3089
Web Site: www.theideaboutique.com

Year Founded: 1994

Agency Specializes In: Advertising, Brand Development & Integration, Broadcast, Email, Public Relations, Publishing, Social Marketing/Nonprofit

Jerry Burwell *(Co-Founder, Owner & Editor)*
Lisa Burwell *(Founder & Owner)*
Tracey Thomas *(Dir-Art)*
Julie Dorr *(Acct Mgr-VIE)*
Sharon Duane *(Office Mgr)*
Mary Jane Kirby *(Acct Mgr-Sls & Mktg)*

Accounts:
Florida State University
Mexico Beach Community Development Council
Vie Magazine

CORNETT INTEGRATED MARKETING SOLUTIONS
330 E Main St Ste 300, Lexington, KY 40507-1525
Tel.: (859) 281-5104
Fax: (859) 281-5107
E-Mail: kip@cornett-ims.com
Web Site: teamcornett.com

E-Mail for Key Personnel:
Creative Dir.: paulb@cornettadv.com

Employees: 30
Year Founded: 1984

Agency Specializes In: Advertising, Brand Development & Integration, Broadcast, Business Publications, Business-To-Business, Cable T.V., Collateral, College, Communications, Consumer Marketing, Corporate Communications, Corporate Identity, Digital/Interactive, Direct Response Marketing, Electronic Media, Email, Entertainment, Event Planning & Marketing, Exhibit/Trade Shows, Financial, Food Service, Government/Political, Graphic Design, Guerilla Marketing, Health Care Services, Identity Marketing, Integrated Marketing, Internet/Web Design, Legal Services, Leisure, Local Marketing, Logo & Package Design, Magazines, Market Research, Media Buying Services, Media Planning, Media Relations, Medical Products, Multimedia, New Technologies, Newspaper, Newspapers & Magazines, Out-of-Home Media, Outdoor, Package Design, Planning & Consultation, Point of Purchase, Point of Sale, Print, Production, Production (Ad, Film, Broadcast), Promotions, Public Relations, Publicity/Promotions, Radio, Restaurant, Sales Promotion, Search Engine Optimization, Social Media, Sponsorship, Sports Market, Strategic Planning/Research, T.V., Travel & Tourism, Viral/Buzz/Word of Mouth, Web (Banner Ads, Pop-ups, etc.)

Approx. Annual Billings: $8,650,000

Breakdown of Gross Billings by Media: Brdcst.: $2,200,000; Event Mktg.: $200,000; Exhibits/Trade Shows: $100,000; Graphic Design: $800,000; Internet Adv.: $500,000; Outdoor: $350,000; Print: $500,000; Production: $2,500,000; Sports Mktg.: $500,000; Strategic Planning/Research: $500,000; Worldwide Web Sites: $500,000

Kip Cornett *(Pres)*
David Coomer *(Chief Creative Officer)*
Mike Dominick *(Dir-Media)*
Tim Jones *(Dir-Creative)*
Erin Burt *(Acct Planner)*
Ashlee Harris *(Acct Planner)*

Jessica Vincent *(Acct Planner)*
Beth Bell *(Exec Asst)*
Christy Hiler *(Chief Strategic Officer)*

Accounts:
A&W Restaurants, Inc "The World's Longest Hashtag", Creative
Buffalo Trace Distillery; Frankfort, KY
Don Jacobs Honda
University of Kentucky Athletics; Lexington, KY
Urban Active; Lexington, KY Fitness

CORPORATE COMMUNICATIONS, INC.

65 Seavey St, North Conway, NH 03860
Tel.: (603) 356-7011
E-Mail: corpcomm@ncia.net
Web Site: www.corporatecommunication.net

Employees: 5
Year Founded: 1983

Agency Specializes In: Advertising, Affiliate Marketing, Brand Development & Integration, Broadcast, Business Publications, Business-To-Business, Cable T.V., Collateral, Commercial Photography, Communications, Consulting, Consumer Marketing, Consumer Publications, Corporate Communications, Corporate Identity, Customer Relationship Management, Direct Response Marketing, E-Commerce, Entertainment, Environmental, Event Planning & Marketing, Government/Political, Graphic Design, Health Care Services, Hospitality, Integrated Marketing, International, Internet/Web Design, Logo & Package Design, Magazines, Market Research, Media Relations, New Product Development, Newspaper, Newspapers & Magazines, Outdoor, Pharmaceutical, Planning & Consultation, Print, Production, Production (Print), Promotions, Public Relations, Publicity/Promotions, Radio, Real Estate, Regional, Restaurant, Retail, Sales Promotion, Search Engine Optimization, Social Marketing/Nonprofit, Sponsorship, Sports Market, Strategic Planning/Research, T.V., Travel & Tourism

Approx. Annual Billings: $500,000

Kimberly F. Beals *(Founder & Pres)*

Accounts:
Adventure in the White Mountains Map & Guide; 1997
The Country Picker; 2010
Food in the Mt. Washington Valley Map; 1998
Golden Apple Inn; 2010
Golden Gables Inn; 2008
Golf in the White Mountains Map; 1991
Hannes Schneider Meister Cup Ski Race; 1995
Hayes Engineering; 2011
HospitalityMaps.com; 2001
Mercedes & Co.; Boston, MA; Memphis, TN Executive Search; 1985
Merlino Steakhouse; North Conway, NH Restaurant; 1990
North Conway Village Map; 1989
NorthConwayCoupons.com
NorthConwayOutlets.com
Northern Extreme Snowmobiling; 2008
Shop Mt. Washington Valley Map; 1990
Waste Management; 2001

CORRIDOR COMMUNICATIONS, INC.

3835R E 1000 Oaks Blvd Ste 237, Westlake Village, CA 91362
Tel.: (818) 681-5777
Fax: (818) 889-9195
E-Mail: info@corridorcomms.com
Web Site: www.corridorcomms.com

Agency Specializes In: Consulting, Graphic Design, Internet/Web Design

Phyllis Grabot *(Co-Founder & Pres)*
Bonnie Quintanilla *(Founder & CEO)*

COSSETTE COMMUNICATIONS

(Formerly Fjord West)
1085 Homer Street, Vancouver, BC V6B 1J4 Canada
Tel.: (604) 669-2727
Fax: (604) 669-2765
Web Site: www.cossette.com

Year Founded: 1996

Agency Specializes In: Advertising, Brand Development & Integration, Corporate Communications, Digital/Interactive, Internet/Web Design, Market Research, Media Relations, Strategic Planning/Research, Web (Banner Ads, Pop-ups, etc.)

Nadine Cole *(Sr VP & Gen Mgr)*
Nicolas Strauss *(Head-Strategy)*
Michael Milardo *(Exec Creative Dir)*
April Haffenden *(Sr Mgr-Production)*
Robin Russell *(Acct Mgr)*
Lizzie Dabous *(Strategist)*
Adriana Novoa *(Media Planner-Cossette Media)*
Kate Roland *(Copywriter)*
Melissa Sabourin *(Media Planner)*
Cameron Spires *(Copywriter)*

Accounts:
Applied Arts Magazine
Arrive Alive Campaign: "Funeral Procession", Drive Sober
C4Ent Campaign: "Let's Be Friends"
Canpages Information Services Provider
Children of the Street Society "Predator Watch"
Darwin's Brave New World Entertainment Services
Espace pour la vie
Future Shop Campaign: "Tapped In"
General Mills Canada Campaign: "We're Full of It"
Julyna
McDonald's Campaign: "Reflective Billboard", Campaign: "Remember When", Digital, Egg McMuffin, McCafe
New-meowbox
Ontario Pharmacists Association
Pizza Pops Campaign: "We're Full of It"
Resolute Forest Product
Royal Roads University Campaign: "I love my university"
Sauder School of Business
New-Transportation Investment Corporation TReO Toll Bridge

COSSETTE INC.

300 St Paul Street 3rd Floor, Quebec, QC G1K 7R1 Canada
Tel.: (418) 647-2727
Fax: (418) 647-2564
Web Site: www.cossette.com

E-Mail for Key Personnel:
President: clessard@cossette.com

Employees: 1,630
Year Founded: 1972

National Agency Associations: ICA

Agency Specializes In: Advertising, Advertising Specialties, Asian Market, Automotive, Aviation & Aerospace, Bilingual Market, Brand Development & Integration, Broadcast, Business-To-Business, Children's Market, Communications, Corporate Identity, Cosmetics, Digital/Interactive, Direct Response Marketing, E-Commerce, Education, Entertainment, Event Planning & Marketing, Financial, Food Service, Government/Political, Graphic Design, Health Care Services, Internet/Web Design, Investor Relations, Logo & Package Design, Media Buying Services, New Product Development, Newspaper, Pharmaceutical, Point of Purchase, Print, Production, Public Relations, Publicity/Promotions, Restaurant, Retail, Sales Promotion, Sports Market, Strategic Planning/Research, Teen Market, Travel & Tourism, Yellow Pages Advertising

Martin Faucher *(CFO & Exec VP)*
Melanie Dunn *(Pres/CEO-Canada)*
Louis Duchesne *(Exec VP & Gen Mgr)*
Fabrice Bouty *(Sr Dir-Art)*
Tricia Piasecki *(Sr Dir-Art)*
Caley Erlich *(Grp Acct Dir)*
Yusong Zhang *(Dir-Art & Assoc Dir-Creative)*
Sean Barlow *(Dir-Creative)*
Bart Batchelor *(Dir-Art)*
Alexandre Jutras *(Dir-Art)*
Louis-Hugo Marchand *(Dir-Creative)*
Sarah Morris *(Media Planner & Media Buyer)*
Amanda Silva *(Media Buyer)*

Accounts:
Brother Canada Branding Campaign
Canadian Red Cross
Duracell Campaign: "Moments of Warmth"
E-Comm 9-1-1 Campaign: "Help us help.", Creative, Media, Strategy
Egg Farmers of Canada (Agency of Record) Creative, Media, Strategic Planning
General Mills of Canada; 1998
Liberte
Lotto Max Media Buying
McDonald's Owners of Chicagoland and Northwest Indiana Advertising, Lead Advertising Agency
McDonald's Restaurants of Canada Campaign: "Bon Bon", Creative, Kale & Feta More-Ning Mcwrap, Marketing, Radio, Reflective Billboard, Sausage & Hash Brown More-Ning McWrap, TV; 1977
Quebec Ministry of Justice
Ronald McDonald House Charities (Agency of Record)
Royal Canadian Campaign: "Heart of The Arctic"
Telus
Transat

Branches

Cossette Communications

(Formerly Cossette Atlantic)
1883 Upper Water Street Ste 203, Halifax, NS B3J 1S9 Canada
Tel.: (902) 421-1500
Fax: (902) 425-5719
Web Site: www.cossette.com

E-Mail for Key Personnel:
President: bmurphy@cossette.com

Employees: 35
Year Founded: 1999

Agency Specializes In: Advertising

William Murphy *(Pres)*
Carlos Moreno *(Chief Creative Officer)*
Samaan Abu Dayyeh *(Dir-Accts & Ops)*
Sean Murphy *(Mgr-Digital Accounts)*
Beverley Simpson *(Designer)*

Cossette

30 N Racine Ste 300, Chicago, IL 60607
Tel.: (773) 295-0177
Web Site: www.cossette.com

Employees: 14
Year Founded: 1972

National Agency Associations: 4A's

Agency Specializes In: Above-the-Line, Below-the-Line, Branded Entertainment, Broadcast, Cable

T.V., Co-op Advertising, Digital/Interactive, Email, Guerilla Marketing, In-Store Advertising, Local Marketing, Magazines, Mobile Marketing, Multimedia, Newspaper, Newspapers & Magazines, Out-of-Home Media, Outdoor, Paid Searches, Point of Purchase, Point of Sale, Print, Production, Production (Print), Promotions, Radio, Search Engine Optimization, Social Media, Sponsorship, T.V., Viral/Buzz/Word of Mouth, Web (Banner Ads, Pop-ups, etc.)

Brett Marchand *(Pres & CEO)*
Alyssa Huggins *(Managing Director)*
Chuck Rachford *(Sr VP & Exec Dir-Creative)*
Stacy Randolph *(Art Dir)*
Claudio Venturini *(Art Dir)*
Ashley Goodson *(Acct Exec)*
jeff oswald *(Copywriter)*
Casey Stern *(Copywriter)*

Accounts:
McDonald's Co-op (Advertising Agency of Record) All Products, Muffins, TV; 2014

Cossette B2B
502 King St W, Toronto, ON M5V 1L7 Canada
Tel.: (416) 922-2727
Fax: (416) 922-9450
Web Site: www.cossette.com

Employees: 40
Year Founded: 2003

National Agency Associations: CMA

Agency Specializes In: Communications

David Daga *(Co-Chief Creative Officer)*
Jason Chaney *(Sr VP-Strategic Plng)*
Steve Groh *(VP & Brand Dir-Natl)*
Craig McIntosh *(Creative Dir)*
Hanh Vo *(Acct Dir)*
Jessica Wong *(Art Dir)*
Jaimes Zentil *(Creative Dir)*
Rebecca Dunnet *(Dir-Art)*
Dhaval Bhatt *(Assoc Dir-Creative)*
Jamie George *(Assoc Dir-Creative)*
Greg Shortall *(Assoc Dir-Creative)*
Roshel Karu *(Acct Exec)*

Accounts:
Canadian Olympic Committee (Creative Agency of Record) Marketing Communication
Espace Go
General Mills Campaign: "Cheerios Effect", Campaign: "Competition Crunch", Campaign: "One-Upmanship", Campaign: "RediscoverNature", Cheerios, Granola Bar, Nature Valley, Oatmeal Crisp
Groupe Media TFO Advertising, Communications, Marketing
Liquor Control Board of Ontario
McDonald's Campaign: "Dollar Drink Days Special Delivery"
Procter & Gamble
The Salvation Army
SickKids Foundation (Creative Agency of Record) Campaign: "Better Tomorrows"
Toronto Silent Film Festival Instagram Time Machine, Instagram Trailers

Cossette Communication-Marketing (Montreal) Inc.
2100 Drummond Street, Montreal, QC H3G 1X1 Canada
Tel.: (514) 845-2727
Fax: (514) 282-4742
Web Site: www.cossette.com

E-Mail for Key Personnel:
President: suzanne.sauvage@cossette.com
Media Dir.: john.tarantino@cossette.com
Production Mgr.: marie-claude.langlois@cossette.com

Employees: 473
Year Founded: 1974

National Agency Associations: ICA

Agency Specializes In: Advertising

Sylvain Lemieux *(Sr VP)*
John Tarantino *(VP & Dir-Media)*
Lynn Chow *(VP)*
Jacinthe Archambault *(Dir-Art)*
Julie Courtemanche *(Dir-Media)*
Vaness Jourdain *(Media Buyer-Web)*
Peggy Lo *(Media Buyer-Brdcst)*
Thimalay Sukhaseum *(Copywriter)*
Megan Sullivan *(Asst Media Planner)*

Accounts:
Amnesty International Campaign: "Free Pussy", Campaign: "Minute of Silence"
Business Development Bank of Canada Communications, Digital Strategy, Strategic Planning
Collectif De Festivals Montraalais Campaign: "Montraal Festimania"
General Motors of Canada Campaign: "Sonic Musical"; 1987
New-Government of Canada (Agency of Record)
Infopresse Campaign: "Off"
McDonald Campaign: "Mc Do Halloween", Campaign: "Reflective Billboard"; 1977
Resolute Campaign: "Identity"

Cossette Communication-Marketing
300 Saint Paul Street Ste 300, Quebec, QC G1K 7R1 Canada
Tel.: (418) 647-2727
Fax: (418) 647-2564
Web Site: www.cossette.com

E-Mail for Key Personnel:
President: pdelagrave@cossette.com
Creative Dir.: ybrossard@cossette.com

Employees: 21
Year Founded: 1972

National Agency Associations: ICA

Agency Specializes In: Advertising

Pierre Delagrave *(Chm)*
Melanie Dunn *(CEO)*
David Daga *(Co-Chief Creative Officer)*
Doug Lowe *(Sr VP & Gen Mgr-Production Svcs & Koo)*
Yvon Brossard *(Dir-Creative)*
Louis Hugo Marchand *(Dir-Creative)*
Dhaval Bhatt *(Assoc Dir-Creative)*
Jamie George Cordwell *(Assoc Dir-Creative)*

Cossette Communication-Marketing
502 King St W, Toronto, ON M5V 1L7 Canada
Tel.: (416) 922-2727
Fax: (416) 922-9450
Web Site: www.cossette.com

E-Mail for Key Personnel:
President: BMarchand@cossette.com
Media Dir.: ccollier@cossette.com
Production Mgr.: dlowe@cossette.com

Employees: 110
Year Founded: 1981

National Agency Associations: ICA

Doug Lowe *(Sr VP & Gen Mgr-Production Svcs)*
Mark Smyka *(Dir-Comm)*

Accounts:
Advertising Standards Canada
Bank Of Montreal
BMO Financial Group; 2003
Cadbury
Coca-Cola; 1993
General Mills of Canada Fibre 1 Cereal, Oatmeal Crisp; 1998
General Motors
Good Shepherd Ministries Homeless Charity
GOTSTYLE
IronKore Fitness Center
McDonald's Restaurants of Canada Big Mac, Buttermilk Biscuits, Dollar Drink Days, Ice Heroes Hockey Cards; 1977
Mentos
Pillsbury Pizza Pops
Procter & Gamble Febreze
Shoppers Drug Mart; 2001
Summerhill Impact Retire Your Ride
Well & Good Charity
The Yellow Pages Group

Cossette Communications
(Formerly Fjord West)
1085 Homer Street, Vancouver, BC V6B 1J4 Canada
(See Separate Listing)

COSTA DESIGNS, INC.
2101 Parks Ave Ste 101, Virginia Beach, VA 23451
Tel.: (757) 343-6894
E-Mail: info@costadesigns.com
Web Site: www.costadesigns.com

Year Founded: 1999

Agency Specializes In: Advertising, Email, Internet/Web Design, Print, Social Media

Brandon Costa *(Owner)*

Accounts:
B&T Kitchens & Bath
ShopBOriginal.com
SteelMaster Buildings LLC

COTTERWEB ENTERPRISES, INC.
1295 Northland Dr Ste 300, Mendota Heights, MN 55120
Tel.: (651) 289-0724
Web Site: corporate.inboxdollars.com/

Employees: 29
Year Founded: 2006

Daren Cotter *(Founder & CEO)*
Mike Murzyn *(VP-Analytics & Intl)*
Brian Erickson *(Sr Dir-Data & Email Compliance)*

COUDAL PARTNERS
400 N May St Ste 301, Chicago, IL 60622
Tel.: (312) 243-1107
Fax: (312) 243-1108
E-Mail: info@coudal.com
Web Site: www.coudal.com

Employees: 6
Year Founded: 1993

Agency Specializes In: Brand Development & Integration, Corporate Identity

Jim Coudal *(Partner)*

COVENANT COMMUNICATIONS
(Name Changed to BigEye Agency)

COVEY-ODELL ADVERTISING LTD.

330 Schneider St SE, North Canton, OH 44720-3652
Tel.: (330) 499-3441
Fax: (330) 499-0596
E-Mail: info@covey-odell.com
Web Site: www.covey-odell.com

Employees: 6
Year Founded: 1944

National Agency Associations: APA

Agency Specializes In: Advertising, Brand Development & Integration, Business Publications, Business-To-Business, Catalogs, Collateral, Communications, Corporate Communications, Corporate Identity, Crisis Communications, Electronic Media, Graphic Design, Health Care Services, Industrial, Integrated Marketing, International, Internet/Web Design, Logo & Package Design, Market Research, Media Buying Services, Media Planning, Media Relations, Multimedia, Newspaper, Newspapers & Magazines, Outdoor, Package Design, Point of Purchase, Print, Production, Production (Print), Public Relations, Publicity/Promotions, Regional, Sales Promotion, Search Engine Optimization, Strategic Planning/Research, Trade & Consumer Magazines

Rod A. Covey *(Pres)*
David W. Lear *(Sr Dir-Art)*
Kathie Covey *(Office Mgr)*

Accounts:
Accurate Technologies
Best Process Solutions
C&M Conveyor
Fred Olivieri Construction Company
GDK & Company
North Canton Economic Development
OMNI Orthopaedics
Stark Development Board

COWLEY ASSOCIATES, INC.

235 Walton St, Syracuse, NY 13202
Tel.: (315) 475-8453
Fax: (315) 475-8408
E-Mail: info@cowleyweb.com
Web Site: www.cowleyweb.com

E-Mail for Key Personnel:
President: pcowley@cowleyweb.com

Employees: 6
Year Founded: 1975

National Agency Associations: AMA-PRSA

Agency Specializes In: Direct Response Marketing, Internet/Web Design, Public Relations, Strategic Planning/Research

Paul Cowley *(Founder, Pres & Dir-Creative)*
Gail Cowley *(Owner & Exec VP)*
Jesse Clayton *(Dir-Art & Designer)*
Zach Clark *(Dir-Bus Dev)*

Accounts:
Animal Emergency Center/Veterinary Specialty Center Veterinary Hospital
Beth Sholom Village Senior Living Community
BonaDent Dental Laboratory
Byrne Dairy Dairy Products
Cathedral of the Immaculate Conception Catholic Church, Catholic School
The Cedars Campus Senior Community
CNYcf
Community Foundation
DelDuchetto & Potter Attorney
Ellis
Empire State Independent Network Telecommunications
Fitness Forum Physical Therapy
Friends of the Jewish Chapel Military Organization
The Garam Group
The Genesee Grand Hotel Hotel, Restaurant
The Marx
Springfield JCC
Stone Quarry Hill Art Park
Syracuse Home Senior Community
Tactair Fluid Controls, Inc. Aerospace Engineer
Young & Franklin Turbine

COX GROUP

16315 Northcross Dr Ste F, Huntersville, NC 28078
Tel.: (704) 896-2323
Web Site: www.coxgp.com

Agency Specializes In: Advertising, Graphic Design, Internet/Web Design, Print

Rodrick Cox *(Owner)*
Sampath Kumar *(Head-Analytics & Strategy)*
Allyson Estes *(Sr Dir-Indus Mktg & Events)*

Accounts:
Superboat International

COXRASMUSSEN & CROSS MARKETING & ADVERTISING, INC.

2830 F St, Eureka, CA 95501
Tel.: (707) 445-3101
Fax: (707) 445-2550
E-Mail: info@coxrasmussen.com
Web Site: www.coxrasmussen.com

Employees: 4

National Agency Associations: Second Wind Limited

Brent Rasmussen *(Owner & Dir-Art)*
Alicia Cox *(Owner)*
Erica Sutherland *(Dir-PR & Media Buyer)*
Joe Sherwood *(Mgr-Production)*

Accounts:
Coast Central Credit Union
Cournale & Co.
Eel River Brewing Co.
Eureka Adult School
The Humboldt Bay Municipal Water District
Kernen Construction
Quest Imaging
Redwood Pharmacies
The Shaw Insurance Group

COYNE ADVERTISING & PUBLIC RELATIONS

3030 Annandale Dr, Nevillewood, PA 15142
Tel.: (412) 429-8408
Fax: (412) 429-8420
E-Mail: jack@coyneadv.com
Web Site: www.coyneadv.com

E-Mail for Key Personnel:
President: jack@coyneadv.com

Employees: 6
Year Founded: 1975

Agency Specializes In: Advertising, Advertising Specialties, Automotive, Broadcast, Business-To-Business, Cable T.V., Children's Market, Co-op Advertising, Collateral, Commercial Photography, Communications, Consulting, Consumer Marketing, Consumer Publications, Corporate Identity, Direct Response Marketing, Electronic Media, Entertainment, Event Planning & Marketing, Exhibit/Trade Shows, Financial, Food Service, Graphic Design, Health Care Services, High Technology, Industrial, Infomercials, Internet/Web Design, Logo & Package Design, Magazines, Media Buying Services, Medical Products, Merchandising, Multimedia, New Product Development, Newspaper, Newspapers & Magazines, Out-of-Home Media, Outdoor, Over-50 Market, Planning & Consultation, Point of Purchase, Point of Sale, Print, Production, Public Relations, Publicity/Promotions, Radio, Real Estate, Recruitment, Restaurant, Retail, Sales Promotion, Seniors' Market, Sports Market, Strategic Planning/Research, Sweepstakes, T.V., Travel & Tourism, Yellow Pages Advertising

Jack P. Coyne *(Owner)*
Corinne Zielinski *(VP & Dir-Media)*

Accounts:
Castriota Chevy
Culligan Co-Op Groups (In Major Markets Nationally) Water Conditioning; 1975
Three Rivers Volkswagen; 1990

CP ENTERPRISES, INC.

950 N NW Hwy, Park Ridge, IL 60068-2301
Tel.: (847) 825-8387
Fax: (847) 825-8383
E-Mail: chuckpecoraro@yahoo.com

Employees: 2
Year Founded: 1973

National Agency Associations: DMA

Agency Specializes In: Advertising, Consulting, Consumer Marketing, Direct Response Marketing, Education, Food Service, Magazines, Newspaper, Planning & Consultation, Radio, Restaurant, Trade & Consumer Magazines

Approx. Annual Billings: $999,880

Breakdown of Gross Billings by Media: Consulting: 10%; D.M.: 40%; Mags.: 10%; Newsp.: 25%; Pub. Rels.: 5%; Radio: 10%

Charles P. Pecoraro *(Owner)*

Accounts:
Fra Noi; Stone Park, IL Ethnic Newspaper; 1994
GAMMS Realty; Park Ridge, IL; 1996
Metropolitan Tenant Information Services; Park Ridge, IL Tenant Screening Services; 2002
Northwestern University; Evanston, IL; 1995

CP+B

3390 Mary St Ste 300, Coconut Grove, FL 33133
Tel.: (305) 859-2070
Fax: (305) 854-3419
E-Mail: info@cpbgroup.com
Web Site: www.cpbgroup.com

Employees: 1,000
Year Founded: 1965

National Agency Associations: 4A's

Agency Specializes In: Above-the-Line, Advertising, Alternative Advertising, Automotive, Below-the-Line, Brand Development & Integration, Broadcast, Cable T.V., Collateral, Communications, Computers & Software, Consumer Goods, Consumer Marketing, Consumer Publications, Digital/Interactive, Direct Response Marketing, Electronics, Entertainment, Experience Design, Fashion/Apparel, Food Service, Government/Political, Guerilla Marketing, Health Care Services, In-Store Advertising, Integrated Marketing, Internet/Web Design, Logo & Package Design, Magazines, Media Buying Services, Media Planning, Men's Market, Mobile Marketing, Multicultural, Multimedia, Newspaper, Newspapers & Magazines, Out-of-Home Media, Outdoor, Package Design, Planning & Consultation, Point of Purchase, Point of Sale, Print, Production, Radio, Restaurant, Retail, Social

Marketing/Nonprofit, Social Media, Sponsorship, Strategic Planning/Research, Syndication, T.V., Teen Market, Transportation, Travel & Tourism, Viral/Buzz/Word of Mouth, Web (Banner Ads, Pop-ups, etc.)

Approx. Annual Billings: $1,200,000,000

Charles Porter *(Chm & Partner)*
Jeff Steinhour *(Partner & Vice Chm)*
Mike Saunter *(COO)*
Marlene Root *(Chief Talent Officer & VP)*
Lori Senecal *(CEO-Global)*
Tony Calcao *(Exec VP & Exec Dir-Creative-Boulder)*
Neil Riddell *(Exec VP & Exec Dir-Product Innovation)*
Sara Gennett *(Exec VP & Dir-Production Svcs)*
Adam Chasnow *(VP & Exec Dir-Creative)*
Michael Raso *(VP & Exec Dir-Creative-Boulder)*
Evan Russack *(VP & Exec Dir-Digital)*
Lauren Barger *(VP & Grp Dir-Media)*
Jason Gagnon *(VP & Exec Producer-Integrated)*
Sloan Schroeder *(VP & Exec Producer)*
Henry Gonzalez *(VP & Acct Dir)*
Claudia Machado *(VP & Acct Dir)*
Marci Miller *(VP & Acct Dir)*
John Broe *(VP & Dir-Partnership Dev)*
Peter Knierim *(VP & Dir-Creative)*
Allen Richardson *(VP & Dir-Creative)*
Dave Steinke *(VP & Dir-Creative)*
Corey Szopinski *(VP & Dir-Creative Technical-Physical Computing)*
Jenny Peil *(VP & Sr Mgr-Bus Dev)*
Rupert Samuel *(Exec Dir-Global Content)*
Gustavo Sarkis *(Exec Dir-Creative)*
Eli Perez De Gracia *(Sr Dir-Art)*
Edi Inderbitzin *(Sr Dir-Art)*
Marthon Pucci *(Sr Dir-Art)*
Chris Lockett *(Sr Producer-Digital)*
Adam Barger *(Acct Dir)*
Alex Corr *(Producer-Integrated-Interactive)*
Liza DeAngelis *(Acct Dir)*
Anne Catherine Feeney *(Acct Dir)*
Marcos Medeiros *(Creative Dir)*
Vinicius Reis *(Acct Dir)*
Marcelo Rizerio *(Art Dir)*
Antonio Torriani *(Art Dir)*
Aaron Fisher *(Dir-Art & Designer)*
Donnie Bauer *(Dir-Creative)*
Dave Cook *(Dir-Creative)*
Hoj Jomehri *(Dir-Creative)*
Matt Lowber *(Dir-Art)*
Dave Swartz *(Dir-Creative)*
Nicholas Buckingham *(Assoc Dir-Creative)*
Tushar Date *(Assoc Dir-Creative)*
Jeff Dryer *(Assoc Dir-Creative)*
Mona Hasan *(Assoc Dir-Creative)*
Bryan Lee *(Assoc Dir-Creative)*
Daniel Pradilla *(Assoc Dir-Creative)*
Jeff Siegel *(Assoc Dir-Creative)*
Abi Evans *(Mgr-New Bus)*
Casey Wilen *(Mgr-Content)*
Blair Williams *(Mgr-Content)*
David Hunter *(Supvr-Media)*
Neylu Longoria *(Supvr-Content)*
Kayle Borenstein *(Media Planner)*
Brian Caruso *(Copywriter)*
Natalia Davila *(Media Planner)*
Marquis Duncan *(Media Planner)*
Joshua Hacohen *(Copywriter)*
Meghan Maloney *(Media Planner)*
Fabiana Brown *(Jr Strategist)*

Accounts:
New-American Airlines (Creative Agency of Record)
American Express OPEN, Travel
Arby's Restaurant Group, Inc. Campaign: "Saucepocalypse", Campaign: "Slicing Up the Truth About Freshness", Creative
Aspen Dental
New-Betsafe
Cause Swarm
Coca-Cola Refreshments USA, Inc. Coke Zero, Maaza
McCoy's Campaign: "McCoy's Ultimate"
Diesel Campaign: "Days to Live"
Discovery Channel UK
Domino's Website
Electronic Arts, Inc.
Fruit of the Loom, Inc.
Hotels.com Campaign: "Captain Obvious", Campaign: "IReadTheLegalSweeps", Campaign: "Obvious Eye Contact", Campaign: "The Obvious Choice", Media, Online, Print, Radio, TV
Hulu.com Creative & Media Planning; 2008
The Kraft Heinz Company A.1., Campaign: " A.1. for Life", Campaign: "Airplane Detour", Campaign: "Comb Over", Campaign: "Go Ninja Go!", Campaign: "Pots Galore", Campaign: "What I Did For Love", Campaign: "You Know You Love It", Campaign: "Young At Heart", Digital, Grey Poupon, Macaroni & Cheese, Miracle Whip, Pudding Drop, Steak Sauce, Stove Top, TV, Velveeta
New-Letgo
The Miami Dolphins
Microsoft Campaign: "Bing It On", Campaign: "Piano", Campaign: "The Recital", Epic Share, Windows 7, Windows 8 Tablet, Windows Phone 7, XPS 10 Tablet, Xbox One
Milka
Mission 22
Mondelez International, Inc. Campaign: "Fun to the Rescue", Campaign: "Golden Voice of Love", Campaign: "Lost Footage", Campaign: "Negotiator", Campaign: "Old Birds New Tweets", Campaign: "Pardon me", Campaign: "Pudding Surprise", Campaign: "Ted Williams Fight for Hunger", Creative, Grey Poupon, Jell-O, Macaroni & Cheese, Triscuit Crackers
National Marine Manufacturers Association Miami International Boat Show (Agency of Record)
Nokia Campaign: "Don't Fight. Switch.", Campaign: "The Recital", Windows Phone
Paddy Power Campaign: "Chav Tranquilliser", Campaign: "Jesus", Campaign: "Laces", Campaign: "Paddy's Lucky Pigeon", Campaign: "Sky Tweets"
P.ink
Pokerstars
Procter & Gamble Campaign: "Pringles Crunch Band", Pringles
Ryder System, Inc. (Advertising Agency of Record) Digital Communications, Marketing, Media Buying, Media Planning
Sony
Svenska Cellulosa Aktiebolaget Tork
Torq
The Underline
WeMo Home Automation

Branches

CP+B
Ostra Hamngatan 26-28, 41109 Gothenburg, Sweden
Tel.: (46) 31 339 6060
E-Mail: reception@cpbgroup.com
Web Site: www.cpbgroup.com

Employees: 65

Gustav Martner *(Chm & Chief Innovation Officer)*
Bjorn Hoglund *(Partner & Exec Dir-Creative)*
Anders Davidsson *(CEO-Scandinavia)*
Dennis Rosenqvist *(Sr Dir-Art)*
Carl-Johan Van Heesch *(Acct Dir)*
Jakob Eriksson *(Dir-Art)*
Mattias Berg *(Assoc Dir-Creative)*
Jimmy Hellkvist *(Copywriter)*
Therese Olander *(Client Svc Dir)*

Accounts:
Abba Seafood Campaign: "Kalles Egg Timer"
Betsafe (Agency of Record) Creative, Media, Strategic Communications
Carlsberg Campaign: "Beer'd Beauty"
Kalles
Komm Campaign: "crow's Nest"
P&G Campaign: "Pringles Crunch Band"
Phillips
Scandinavian Airlines Campaign: "Couple Up to Buckle Up", Campaign: "Point & Fly"
Scania Campaign: "Can You Handle More Than Your Truck", Campaign: "Cargo Madness"
Sony Mobile Campaign: "Xperia Soda Stunt", Campaign: "Xperia Swap", Campaign: "Xperia V vs YouTube", Xperia Z2
Swedish Postal Service
Telia Campaign: "Appmillionaire"
Ubisoft Campaign: "Autodance", Just Dance 3
Wakakuu Campaign: "Wakakuu Start Up"

CP+B
The Brassworks, 32 York Way, London, N1 9AB United Kingdom
Tel.: (44) 20 3551 7701
E-Mail: aglynn@cpbgroup.com
Web Site: www.cpbgroup.com/#u=/pages/contact

Employees: 11

Richard Pinder *(CEO)*
Mez Corfield *(CFO)*
Dave Buonaguidi *(Chief Creative Officer)*
Henrik Delehag *(Dir-Creative)*
Nimi Raja *(Planner)*

Accounts:
BMW Mini
Diesel Watches Campaign: "Days to Live", Creative
Hotels.com
Microsoft Campaign: "The Real Zlatan", Media, TV
Mondelez International, Inc.
New-PayPal Campaign: "No Presents"
Turkish Airlines Inc. Campaign: "Epic Food", Campaign: "Epic Pool Dunk", Campaign: "How Do You Make A Didier?", Campaign: "The Selfie Shootout", Campaign: "Widen Your World", Global Advertising, Poster, Print, TV
Ubisoft Campaign: "Autodance", Just Dance 3

CP+B Boulder
6450 Gunpark Dr, Boulder, CO 80301
Tel.: (303) 628-5100
Fax: (303) 516-0227
E-Mail: info@cpbgroup.com
Web Site: www.cpbgroup.com

Employees: 500

National Agency Associations: 4A's

Agency Specializes In: Sponsorship

Danielle Whalen *(Mng Dir & Exec VP)*
Ralph Watson *(Chief Creative Officer-Boulder & VP)*
Eric Zuncic *(Chief Strategy Officer-North America)*
Neil Riddell *(Exec VP & Exec Dir-Product Innovation)*
David Swartz *(VP & Exec Dir-Art Direction & Design)*
Andrew Lincoln *(VP & Dir-Creative)*
Dave Steinke *(VP & Dir-Creative)*
Michael Raso *(Exec Dir-Creative)*
Nuno Teixeira *(Sr Dir-Art)*
Joselyn Bickford *(Acct Dir)*
Courtney Bowditch *(Art Dir)*
Sarah Castner *(Acct Dir-Global)*
Pat Feehery *(Creative Dir)*
Claus Hansen *(Creative Dir)*
Adam Calvert *(Dir-Creative)*
Jessica Decter *(Dir-Art)*

Ryan Dowling *(Dir-Art)*
Stephanie Kohnen *(Assoc Dir-Creative)*
Janna Navarro *(Assoc Dir-Media)*
Jason Pierce *(Assoc Dir-Creative)*
Madison Morris *(Mgr-Content)*
Tristan Stevens *(Acct Supvr)*
Jillian Hart *(Supvr-Social Media)*
Claire Marquess *(Supvr-Content)*
Jennifer Quint *(Supvr-Media)*

Accounts:
American Express Campaign: "Small Business Gets an Official Day"
Baby Carrots
Coca-Cola Campaign: "Last Request", Campaign: "Power Up Bus Shelters"
Dijon Campaign: "Pardon Me", Grey Poupon
Domino's Pizza Campaign: "30 Minutes or Less", Campaign: "Dom", Campaign: "Domino's Dares", Campaign: "Labor of Love", Campaign: "Powered by Pizza", Campaign: "Times Square Tracker", Digital Display, Paid Search, Pan Pizzas, Show Us Your Pizza, Social Media, TV
EpicMix
Fruit of the Loom Advertising, Broadcast, Campaign: "Panty Stunt", Campaign: "Speedy Boxers", Campaign: "Start Happy", Campaign: "The Rules of Underwear Giving", Campaign: "The Tucking Facts", Creative, Digital, Lucky Looms, Media, Outdoor, Plastique, Social Media, Web
Hotels.com (Agency of Record) Campaign: "Captain Obvious", Creative
HULU Campaign: "Hu-Luboratory"
Humana Campaign: "B-Cycle"
Jose Cuervo Angel's Envy
The Kraft Heinz Company Campaign: "Artisanal Hipster Pilgrim", Campaign: "Baconizer", Campaign: "Double Bad", Campaign: "Star Wars Shapes", Campaign: "We Know You're Going to Love It", Macaroni & Cheese, Radio, Stove Top
Louisville Distilling Company Campaign: "Angel's Envy"
Microsoft Campaign: "Don't fight. Switch", Campaign: "The Wedding", Campaign: "Tiny PC Store", Internet Explorer 8, Microsoft Windows Phone, Nokia Lumia 920
Nissan Infiniti (Global Creative Advertising Agency of Record), Marketing
Old Navy Campaign: "Jennifer Loves Hoodies", Campaign: "Snap Appy", Campaign: "Tea Expert"
Papa's Pilar One Dark, One Light
Pearl Izumi (Agency of Record) Campaign: "Run Like an Animal", Creative, Print
Pink
Rethink Breast Cancer Campaign: "Boobyball"
Rickard's Campaign: "Movember"
Tourism Toronto
Wemo

CP+B LA
2110 Colorado Ave, Santa Monica, CA 90404
Tel.: (310) 822-3063
Fax: (310) 822-3067
E-Mail: jhicks@cpbgroup.com
Web Site: www.cpbgroup.com

Employees: 12
Year Founded: 2001

National Agency Associations: 4A's

Agency Specializes In: Sponsorship

Chuck Porter *(Chm & Partner)*
Ivan Perez-Armendariz *(Co-Mng Dir)*
Ryan Skubic *(Co-Mng Dir)*
Carl St. Philip *(CFO)*
Jason De Turris *(Chief Strategy Officer & VP)*
Claudia Machado *(VP & Acct Dir)*
Marci Miller *(VP & Acct Dir)*
Robin Fitzgerald *(VP & Dir-Creative)*
Ryan Moreno *(VP & Dir-Interactive Production)*
Kari Niessink *(VP & Dir-Production Solutions)*
Kevin Jones *(Exec Dir-Creative)*
Chris Lockett *(Sr Producer-Digital)*
Chad Ford *(Dir-Art)*
Mike Kohlbecker *(Dir-Creative)*
Jeanne Nicastro *(Dir-New Bus)*
Malone Roberts *(Dir-Art)*
Alexandra Sann *(Dir-Creative)*
Antonio Marcato *(Assoc Dir-Creative)*
Daniel Pradilla *(Assoc Dir-Creative)*
Sasha Rawji *(Acct Mgr-Content)*
Scott Frindel *(Mgr-IT Ops)*
Lauren Doherty *(Planner-Digital Media)*
Joshua Hacohen *(Copywriter)*
Jessica Piele *(Jr Producer)*

Accounts:
2K Sports Campaign: "Beard Guru", Campaign: "Your Time Has Come", NBA2k15
New-Anheuser-Busch
Belkin International, Inc. Campaign: "The Big Anniversary Rig", Marketing, WeMo
Boys & Girls Club of America Campaign: "3 p.m."
Charles Schwab "Schwab Intelligent Portfolios", Campaign: "Own Your Tomorrow(TM)", Lead Creative, Mobile, Online, Print, TV
Electronic Arts, Inc.
Fruit of the Loom, Inc.
Kraft Foods Group A.1. Sauce, Campaign: "Spread Good Taste", Grey Poupon
Microsoft
NBA 2K Digital, NBA 2K15, Social Media
Netflix Advertising, Campaign: "Miss Know-it-all"
Turkish Airlines Campaign: "The Selfie Shootout"
Volkswagen Group of America, Inc.; 2006

CPM
239 Old Marylebone Rd, London, NW1 5QT United Kingdom
Tel.: (44) 20 3481 1020
Fax: (44) 1844 261504
E-Mail: international@cpm-int.com
Web Site: www.cpm-int.com

Employees: 500
Year Founded: 1936

Agency Specializes In: Event Planning & Marketing, Telemarketing, Transportation

Karen Jackson *(Mng Dir)*
Dean Drew *(Client Svcs Dir)*
Jane Ingram *(Dir-Sls & Mktg)*
Kate Ryan *(Dir-Bus Unit)*
Tom Chase *(Sr Mgr-Comml Fin)*
Simmie Scott *(Client Dir-Global)*

Accounts:
Barclays
Debenhams
Diageo
Disney
Gallaher
GlaxoSmithKline
Hewlett Packard
HP Invent
Mars North America
Nestle
P&G
PepsiCo
Procter & Gamble
Telstra

Branches

CPM Australia
137 Pyrmont Street, Pyrmont, NSW 2009 Australia
Tel.: (61) 2 8197 5101
E-Mail: sydney@cpm-aus.com.au
Web Site: www.cpm-aus.com.au

Agency Specializes In: Advertising

Andrew Potter *(Grp Mng Dir)*
Stephen Shipperlee *(CFO)*
Paul Crummy *(Mng Dir-Direct Sls)*
Mark Sewell *(Head-IT)*
Andrew Jacques *(Gen Mgr-Sls-CPM Australia)*
Scott James *(Dir-Sls)*
James Dobbie *(Mgr-Bus Dev)*
Maryanne Bahou *(Coord-HR & Recruitment)*

Accounts:
AGL
Mattel
Telstra

CPM Austria
Brauhausgasse 37, 1050 Vienna, Austria
Tel.: (43) 1 503 68 66
Fax: (43) 1 503 68 66 22
E-Mail: office@cpmaustria.at
Web Site: www.at.cpm-int.com

Employees: 16

Horst Untermoser *(Mng Dir)*

Accounts:
Nokia
Whirlpool

CPM Germany GmbH
Siemenstrasse 21, 61352 Bad Homburg, Germany
Tel.: (49) 6172 805 401
Fax: (49) 6172 805 233
Web Site: www.de.cpm-int.com

Johann-Hinrich Nagel *(Mng Dir)*
Andrea Pfeifer *(Dir-Procurement & Production)*
Zrinka Schaefer *(Mgr-Recruitment)*
Melanie Volz *(Mgr-HR)*
Isabell Dollase *(Jr Project Mgr)*
Niels Franken *(Sr Client Svc Mgr)*
Jessica Ramm-Beavers *(Jr Project Mgr)*

CPM Ireland
33 Greenmount Office Park, Harolds Cross, Dublin, 6W Ireland
Tel.: (353) 1 7080 300
Fax: (353) 1 4544410
E-Mail: info@cpmire.com
Web Site: www.ie.cpm-int.com

Employees: 40

Mark Quinn *(Client Svcs Dir-Retail)*
Neil Campbell *(Client Svcs Mgr)*
Colyn Cracken *(Mgr-Bus Dev)*
Shane Dennehy *(Mgr-Retail Ops)*
Killian Doherty *(Mgr-HR)*
Gillian Farrell *(Mgr-Mktg & Insight)*

Accounts:
Diageo
Eircom
Gillette
HP
Nike
P&G
Revlon

Inventa CPM
(Formerly CPM Italy)
Via Tortona 15, 20144 Milan, Italy
Tel.: (39) 02 831 0111
Fax: (39) 02 8940 1298
E-Mail: info@inventacpm.it
Web Site: www.inventacpm.it

Agency Specializes In: Advertising

Antonio Magaracci *(Gen Mgr)*
Laura Galfre *(Dir-HR)*
Lorena Nettle *(Dir-Creative)*
Desiree Rotta *(Acct Mgr)*
Julia Sokolova *(Analyst-Web & Strategist-Digital)*
Nadine Kramaric *(Acct Exec)*
Stefano Albe *(Planner-Strategic)*
Sebastiano Patti *(Client Svc Mgr)*

Accounts:
Barclays
Bialetti
Binda
Bosch
htc
Kuoni
LG
Quixa
RIM
Royal Canin

CPM Netherlands
Amsterdamseweg 206, Wildenborch 4, 1182 Amstelveen, Netherlands
Tel.: (31) 20 712 2000
Fax: (31) 20 712 2001
E-Mail: info@nl.cpm-int.com
Web Site: www.nl.cpm-int.com

Employees: 40

Thijs De Vries *(Controller-Bus)*
Kimberley Kok *(Client Svcs Mgr-P&G)*
Nick Planken *(Acct Mgr-SONY)*
Jeroen Meijer *(Mgr-Bus Dev)*
Sandy Sijtsma *(Mgr-Ops)*
Jacko Van Essen *(Supvr-Field)*
Robert Annaars *(Client Svc Mgr)*
Alfred Mulder *(Sr Client Svc Mgr)*
Niels Van Roosmalen *(Client Svc Dir)*

Accounts:
American Express
Diageo
HP
Mars
Microsoft
Nokia
P&G

CPM Spain
A-7 C / Henri Dunant March 9 to 11 08 174, Saint Cugat del Valles, Barcelona, Spain
Tel.: (34) 93 206 4080
Fax: (34) 93 280 3381
Web Site: www.cpmexpertus.es

Jaume Santacana *(Mng Dir)*
Maria Solano Marquina *(Dir-Selection)*
Sonia Oroz *(Dir-Comml, Events & Pub Attention)*
Anna Vaillo *(Dir-Ops)*
Ana Rodriguez Anton *(Mgr-Reporting & Insight)*
Javier Herranz Rodriguez *(Mgr-Sls & Plng)*
Aroha Sibilio *(Mgr-Bus Unit)*
Silvia Lopez Moyano *(Coord-Svcs)*
Ricardo Hueso Belles *(Key Acct Mgr)*
Marina Gispert Fernandez *(Client Svc Mgr)*
Carmen Diaz Rodriguez *(Key Acct Mgr)*

CPM Switzerland
1st Floor Seestrasse 93, CH-8800 Zurich, Switzerland
Tel.: (41) 43 322 20 50
Fax: (41) 43 322 20 60
Web Site: www.ch.cpm-int.com

Employees: 15

Fabio Donnaloia *(Mng Dir)*
Anthony Feinberg *(Client Svc Dir & Branch Mgr)*
Dinah Leuenberger *(Client Svcs Mgr)*
Riccardo Avola *(Mgr-Recruiting)*
Claudia Balleys *(Mgr-HR)*
Fabio Antenna *(Sr Client Svc Mgr)*
Paola Cipolli *(Client Svc Mgr)*
Cem Kurcan *(Jr Client Svc Mgr)*
Carmen Metzger *(Jr Project Mgr)*
Nicola Tomasi *(Client Svc Mgr)*

Accounts:
American Express
Esso
HP
Maggi
Master Foods
Microsoft
Nescafe
Volvic
Western Union
XBOX

CPM USA
7425 16th St E Ste 101, Sarasota, FL 34243-5568
Tel.: (941) 953-3866
Fax: (941) 358-3384
E-Mail: chuck.somborn@cpm-us.com
Web Site: www.us.cpm-int.com

Employees: 50

Chuck Somborn *(CEO)*
Brandon Chase *(Sr VP-Ops)*
Matt Fuiks *(Sr VP)*
Stephen Kennelly *(Sr VP-Sls)*
Carolyn Wright *(VP-Fin)*
Tammy Alemazkour *(Dir-Client Insights)*
Leigh Retzlaff *(Sr Acct Mgr)*
Debbie Ulrich *(Mgr-Bus Dev)*
Michelle Yates *(Mgr-Logistics)*
Amy Brumagin *(Client Svc Mgr)*

Accounts:
XM Satellite Radio

CPR STRATEGIC MARKETING COMMUNICATIONS
475 Market St 2nd FL, Elmwood Park, NJ 07407
Tel.: (201) 641-1911
Fax: (201) 708-1444
Toll Free: (888) 724-3390
E-Mail: iandruch@cpronline.com
Web Site: www.cpronline.com

E-Mail for Key Personnel:
President: jcarabello@cpronline.com
Creative Dir.: lcarabello@cpronline.com
Media Dir.: rfisher@cpronline.com
Production Mgr.: mbarbosa@cpronline.com

Employees: 20
Year Founded: 1981

Agency Specializes In: Advertising, Health Care Services, Publicity/Promotions

Approx. Annual Billings: $5,000,000

Breakdown of Gross Billings by Media: D.M.: 3%; Mags.: 10%; Newsp.: 20%; Point of Sale: 2%; Production: 61%; Radio: 4%

Joseph Carabello *(Pres & CEO)*
Laura Carabello *(Principal)*
Ihor Andruch *(VP)*
Joelle Speranza *(Head-PR & Mktg)*
Katelyn Petersen *(Acct Dir)*
Alexis Lignos *(Acct Exec)*
Nathan D. Molinari *(Acct Coord)*

Accounts:
Becky Halstead 24/7: The First Person You Must Lead is YOU
Remain Home Solutions
Scrip Companies

CRAFT
1600 K St NW Ste 300, Washington, DC 20006
Tel.: (202) 525-4872
Web Site: www.craftdc.com

Agency Specializes In: Advertising, Digital/Interactive, Print, Public Relations, Social Media

Brian Donahue *(Founder & CEO)*
Jared Michael *(COO)*
Caitlin Donahue *(VP)*

Accounts:
New-Miriam's Kitchen

CRAGENCY, INC.
699 N King Rd, San Jose, CA 95133
Tel.: (408) 258-8000
Fax: (408) 258-0864
E-Mail: info@cragency.com
Web Site: www.cragency.com

Employees: 12
Year Founded: 2000

Agency Specializes In: Recruitment

Approx. Annual Billings: $2,700,000

Breakdown of Gross Billings by Media: Collateral: $300,000; Newsp.: $2,100,000; Radio: $300,000

Michael Rooney *(Dir-Art)*

CRAIG JACKSON & PARTNERS
(Name Changed to Glyph Interface)

CRAMER-KRASSELT
225 N Michigan Ave, Chicago, IL 60601-7601
Tel.: (312) 616-9600
Fax: (312) 616-3839
E-Mail: media.chi@c-k.com
Web Site: www.c-k.com

E-Mail for Key Personnel:
President: pkrivkov@c-k.com

Employees: 274
Year Founded: 1898

National Agency Associations: 4A's-ANA-COPF-ICOM

Agency Specializes In: Advertising, Brand Development & Integration, Communications, Consumer Marketing, Corporate Identity, Customer Relationship Management, Digital/Interactive, Direct Response Marketing, Direct-to-Consumer, Event Planning & Marketing, Integrated Marketing, Internet/Web Design, Media Buying Services, Media Planning, Media Relations, Out-of-Home Media, Point of Purchase, Point of Sale, Promotions, Public Relations, Publicity/Promotions, Sales Promotion, Search Engine Optimization, Social Media, Sponsorship, Web (Banner Ads, Pop-ups, etc.), Yellow Pages Advertising

At C-K, our mission is simple: Make friends, not ads.(TM) This mindset not only drives all our ideas, it also drives our structure.We're built without silos or competing interests to truly tap into an ever-expanding range of disciplines, from advertising and digital, to media, engagement strategy, public relations, CRM and analytics - whatever it takes to create compelling brand experiences. This philosophy has fueled our growth, making C-K the second largest independent agency in the U.S. with more than 500 employees across four offices and $1 billion in annual billings.

Sales: $1,015,900

Peter G. Krivkovich *(Chm & CEO)*
Marshall Ross *(Vice Chm & Chief Creative Officer)*
Karen L. Seamen *(Pres & COO)*
Wanda Medina McDonald *(Exec VP & CFO)*
Kristin Bloomquist *(Exec VP & Gen Mgr-Phoenix)*
Betsy Brown *(Exec VP & Gen Mgr)*
Pat Nathan *(Sr VP & Exec Dir-Production Ops & Svcs)*
Susan Bishop *(Sr VP & Grp Acct Dir)*
Renee Chez *(Sr VP & Grp Acct Dir)*
Chris Hanley *(Sr VP & Grp Acct Dir)*
Dick Salyer *(Sr VP & Grp Acct Dir)*
Bill Blaha *(Sr VP & Dir-Media)*
Margot Bogue *(Sr VP & Dir-Brand Plng)*
John Freckmann *(Sr VP & Dir-Acct Mgmt)*
Chris Wexler *(Sr VP & Dir-Media & Consumer Engagement)*
Marcia Selig *(VP & Grp Dir-Media)*
Diann Nails *(VP & Sr Producer-Print, Digital, Brdcst & Radio)*
Tiffany Williams *(VP & Mgmt Supvr)*
Sean Donohue *(VP & Dir-Creative, Design & Digital)*
Bill Dow *(VP & Dir-Creative)*
Lisa Purpura *(VP & Dir-Digital Strategy)*
Leah Grzyb *(VP & Assoc Dir-Media)*
Elizabeth Dacko *(VP & Sr Mgr-Campaign)*
Brandon Ireland *(Sr Dir-Art)*
Kelly Croswell *(Grp Acct Dir)*
Christina Calvit *(Dir-Creative)*
Josh Johnson *(Dir-Art)*
Jim Root *(Dir-Art & Creative)*
Sandy DerHovsepian *(Assoc Dir-Creative & Writer)*
Larry Liss *(Assoc Dir-Creative & Copywriter)*
Nick Marrazza *(Assoc Dir-Creative & Copywriter)*
Kristin Babcock *(Assoc Dir-Search)*
Rick Standley *(Assoc Dir-Creative)*
Samantha Maraval *(Acct Supvr)*
Kristin Vayda *(Acct Supvr)*
Carrie Tiz *(Supvr-Local Brdcst)*
Nick Violette *(Supvr-Media)*
Sarah Stahurski *(Sr Acct Exec)*
Lori Bellino *(Specialist-Search Mktg)*
Julie Chase *(Media Planner)*
Tom Katers *(Jr Copywriter)*
Emily Taus *(Media Buyer-Spot)*
Mariah Youngblood *(Media Planner)*
Taylor Ellis *(Coord-Search)*
Ashley Bain *(Asst Media Planner)*
Peter Debnar *(Sr Media Planner)*
Nick Donabedian *(Asst Media Planner)*
Christine Formenti *(Sr Media Buyer)*
Caroline Kryder *(Asst Media Planner)*
Nicholas Rogers *(Asst Media Planner)*
Patty Roloff *(Sr Supvr-Brdcst-Natl)*

Accounts:
ACH Foods; Milwaukee, WI Spice Islands, Weber Barbecue Sauce, Weber Spices; 2004
Ahold; Carlisle, PA GIANT, Stop & Shop; 2013
New-All Aboard Florida
Benihana; Doral, FL; 2010
BIC; Shelton, CT Campaign: "How to Be a Gentleman in a Bar", Campaign: "How to Be a Gentleman in an Elevator", Campaign: "Smooth Up", Men's Razors (Creative Agency of Record), Strategy; 2014
Bombardier; Montreal, Canada Can-Am, Evinrude, Sea-Doo, Ski-Doo, Spyder; 2000
Cedar Fair, L.P. Sandusky, OH Canada's Wonderland, Carowinds, Cedar Point, Dorney Park, Kings Dominion, Kings Island, Knott's Berry Farm, Valley Fair; 2011
Comcast Spotlight; New York, NY; 2004
New-Constellation Brands Casa Noble Tequila, Corona Extra, Pacifico Beer
Crown Imports LLC Corona Extra (Advertising Agency of Record), Pacifico
Dealer Tire Analytics, Media Buying, Media Planning, Public Relations, RightTurn
Echo Power Tools; Lake Zurich, IL; 2010
Edward D. Jones & Co.; Saint Louis, MO; 2009
Famous Dave's of America, Inc. (Advertising Agency of Record) Creative, Media Buying, Public Relations, Social Media
Florsheim; Milwaukee, WI; 2011
Galderma; Dallas, TX Cetaphil; 2014
Generac Power System; Waukesha, WI; 2011
Grainger; Lake Forest, IL Media; 2011
Johnsonville Sausage; Sheboygan Falls, WI; 2008
The Kraft Heinz Company Classico, Heinz, Ketchup, Ore-Ida, Smart Ones; 2004
New-The Paper and Packaging Board Advertising, Campaign "Paper & Packaging: How Life Unfolds", Public Relations, Social Media
Peapod; Skokie, IL; 2014
Porsche Cars North America; Atlanta, GA (Agency of Record) Campaign: "Rebels, Race On", Cayman GT4, Creative; 2007
Robert Bosch Tool Corporation; Mt Prospect, IL Dremel, RotoZip, Skil; 1991
Ruiz Foods; Dinuba, CA; 2012
Salt River Project; Phoenix, AZ Electric & Water Utility; 1983
New-TCS New York City Marathon
Tenneco, Inc.; Monroe, MI; 2004
Vitamix; Cleveland, OH; 2013

Branches:

Cramer-Krasselt

246 E Chicago St, Milwaukee, WI 53202
Tel.: (414) 227-3500
Fax: (414) 276-8710
E-Mail: media.mil@c-k.com
Web Site: www.c-k.com

Employees: 144
Year Founded: 1898

National Agency Associations: 4A's-COPF

Agency Specializes In: Advertising, Digital/Interactive, Media Buying Services, Media Planning, Planning & Consultation, Public Relations, Search Engine Optimization, Sponsorship, Yellow Pages Advertising

Chris Jacobs *(Sr VP & Exec Dir-Creative)*
John Mose *(Sr VP & Dir)*
Scott Shulick *(VP & Grp Dir-Plng)*
Marlaina Quintana *(VP & Grp Acct Dir-PR)*
Grant Fiorita *(VP & Grp Media Dir)*
Kelli Rathke *(VP & Grp Media Dir)*
Dan Koel *(Sr Dir-Art)*
Shawn Holpfer *(Assoc Dir-Design)*
Rachel Brubeck *(Supvr-Media)*
Marc Bennett *(Sr Acct Exec)*
Maureen Falkner *(Sr Acct Exec-PR & Social)*
Abby Young *(Media Planner & Media Buyer)*
Timm Gable *(Assoc Exec Producer)*

Accounts:
ACH Foods Karo Syrup, Mazola, Patak's, Spice Islands; 2004
Benihana, Inc.
Bombardier Recreational Products Can-Am ATV, Evinrude, Sea-Doo, Ski-Doo, Spyder; 2000
Broan-NuTone; 2004
Dremel; 1991
ECHO Outdoor Power Equipment Campaign: "Work", Creative, Media
Elm Grove Police Department
GE Healthcare; 2004
Generac Power Systems Marketing, Public Relations
InSinkErator; 2003
ITW Global Brands Advertising, Branding, Campaign: "Balloon Storm", Glass Cleaners, Positioning, Rain-X, Social Media, Wiper Blades
Milwaukee Institute Of Art & Design
Milwaukee Police Department; 2009
The Milwaukee Public Museum
Mohawk Industries; 2008
Rayovac; Madison, WI; 2008
Reebok/CCM Hockey Equipment; 2008
RotoZip; 2006
SKIL Power Tools (Agency of Record) Creative, Media Buying, Media Planning
Sojourner Family Peace Center
Spice Islands Campaign: "The Art of Spice", Digital, Media, TV
Tenneco, Inc. Monroe Shocks & Struts; 2004
Weyco Group Branding, Digital, Florsheim, Media, Nunn Bush, Retail, Sales, Stacy Adams
World Kitchens Corelle, Corningware, Pyrex; 2004

Cramer-Krasselt

902 Broadway, 5th Fl, New York, NY 10010
Tel.: (212) 889-6450
Fax: (212) 251-1265
Web Site: www.c-k.com

Employees: 51

National Agency Associations: 4A's-COPF

Nancy Aresu *(Exec VP & Gen Mgr)*
Ian Barry *(Sr VP & Exec Dir-Creative)*
Craig Markus *(Sr VP & Exec Dir-Creative)*
Ken Nippes *(Sr VP & Dir-Media)*
Jasmine Dadlani *(Dir-Brand Plng)*
Erika Richter *(Mgr-Campaign)*
Eleni Hasiakos *(Acct Supvr)*
Austin Tatum *(Sr Acct Exec)*
Kaitlyn Kelly *(Acct Exec)*
Breena Goldberg *(Media Planner)*
Fabio Straccia *(Copywriter)*

Accounts:
Benihana Creative, Digital, Media, Public Relations, Social Media
New-Bic
CareFirst Blue Cross & Blue Shield; 2007
Comcast Spotlight
New-Mionetto
NCC Media; New York, NY
New-The New York Road Runners
New-Nikon

Cramer-Krasselt

1850 N Central Ave Ste 1800, Phoenix, AZ 85004-4561
Tel.: (602) 417-0600
Fax: (602) 258-1446
Web Site: www.c-k.com

Employees: 51

National Agency Associations: 4A's-COPF

Kristin Bloomquist *(Exec VP & Gen Mgr)*
Ian Barry *(Sr VP & Exec Dir-Creative)*
Fraser Elliot *(Sr VP & Dir-Media)*
Matt Sicko *(Dir-Creative)*
Cassandra Fronzo *(Sr Media Buyer)*

Accounts:
Apollo Group/IPD
Arizona Science Center
Blue Cross Blue Shield of AZ
Center Dance Ensemble
Crystal Springs Bottled Water

Grand Canyon University
KPHO-TV
Liberty Wildlife
Meritage Homes
RA Sushi
Salt River Project (SRP)
SW Water Conditioning/Culligan
TriVita
Valley Toyota Dealers Association
The Wolfgang Puck Fine Dining Group; 2008

CRAMER PRODUCTIONS INC.

425 Univ Ave, Norwood, MA 02062
Tel.: (781) 278-2300
Fax: (781) 255-0721
Web Site: www.cramer.com/

Employees: 185
Year Founded: 1982

Agency Specializes In: Advertising, Brand Development & Integration, Communications, Digital/Interactive, Direct Response Marketing, Event Planning & Marketing, Exhibit/Trade Shows, Identity Marketing, Local Marketing, New Technologies, Print, Product Placement, Promotions, Sales Promotion, Sponsorship, Strategic Planning/Research

Sales: $20,340,656

Tom Martin *(Chm)*
Thom Faria *(CEO)*
Richard Sturchio *(Pres-Creative Svcs)*
Ann Cave *(Exec VP-Bus Dev & Acct Svcs)*
Julie Walker *(Exec VP-Corp Dev)*
Neal Boornazian *(Sr VP & Acct Mgmt Dir)*
Greg Martin *(Sr VP-Fin)*
Christine Fleming *(VP-HR)*
Brent Turner *(VP-Mktg Solutions)*
Rob Everton *(Sr Dir-Bus Dev & Creative Tech)*
Edward Feather *(Acct Svcs Dir)*

Accounts:
Boston Scientific
EMC
EMD Serono, Inc.
Foley Hoag
Jordan's Furniture

CRAMP & ASSOCIATES, INC.

1327 Grenox Rd, Wynnewood, PA 19096-2402
Tel.: (610) 649-6002
Fax: (610) 649-6005
E-Mail: info@cramp.com
Web Site: www.cramp.com

Employees: 10
Year Founded: 1988

Agency Specializes In: Business-To-Business, Direct Response Marketing, Graphic Design, Health Care Services, Internet/Web Design, Outdoor, Pharmaceutical, Print

Revenue: $30,000,000

Jeff Cramp *(Pres & Dir-Creative)*

Accounts:
ACE-INA Insurance Group
Arts & Business Council of Philadelphia
BMA
Bristol-Myers Squibb
Capital Telecommunications
ConvaTec Ltd.
D. Atlas & Company Jewelers
Forest Laboratories
Giggle Zone
KNGT
Mediq / ACS
New York Life / Healthcare
Penn Liberty Bank
Toto

CRANE WEST

4245 Kemp Blvd Ste 815, Wichita Falls, TX 76308
Tel.: (940) 691-2111
Fax: (940) 691-4333
E-Mail: info@crane-west.com
Web Site: www.crane-west.com

Agency Specializes In: Advertising, Brand Development & Integration, Internet/Web Design, Logo & Package Design

Colt West *(Pres)*

Accounts:
How Great Thou Art/Kids Art

CRANECREEK COMMUNICATIONS

PO Box 3347, Allentown, PA 18106-0347
Tel.: (610) 740-9524
Fax: (610) 740-9526
E-Mail: stephen@cranecreek.com
Web Site: www.cranecreek.com

Agency Specializes In: Crisis Communications, Media Training, Public Relations, Strategic Planning/Research

Stephen A. Crane *(Founder & Principal)*
Patrick Fallis *(Exec Producer)*

Accounts:
Aversa Modular
BTM Corporation Management Solutions Provider
CareerBuilder.com
FileMaker Developers in Southern California
The Griffin Group
Ketchum Worldwide
PriceWaterhouseCoopers
Swivel Media
Walt Disney Company

CRANFORD JOHNSON ROBINSON WOODS

300 Main St, Little Rock, AR 72201-3531
Tel.: (501) 975-6251
Fax: (501) 975-4241
Toll Free: (888) 383-2579
E-Mail: info@cjrw.com
Web Site: www.cjrw.com

Employees: 75
Year Founded: 1961

National Agency Associations: ABC-AFA

Agency Specializes In: Advertising, Brand Development & Integration, Communications, Direct Response Marketing, Government/Political, Graphic Design, Internet/Web Design, Print, Production, Public Relations, Publicity/Promotions, Sponsorship, Strategic Planning/Research, Travel & Tourism

Approx. Annual Billings: $70,000,000

Jay Cranford *(Founder & Partner)*
Brian Kratkiewicz *(Sr VP & Dir-Media & Interactive)*
Brian Clark *(Sr VP & Strategist-Brand Mktg)*
Chuck Robertson *(Sr VP-Travel & Tourism)*
Zack Hill *(VP & Dir-Digital Svcs)*
Shanon Williams *(Acct Svcs Dir)*
Wade Austin *(Dir-Dev)*
Elizabeth Michael *(Dir-Content & Social Strategy)*
Jane Embry-Nisbet *(Media Planner & Media Buyer)*
Annie Holman *(Media Planner & Media Buyer)*

Accounts:
Arkansas Department of Health Health Communications, Media, Public Education, Tobacco Prevention & Cessation Program
Arkansas State Anti-Smoking Campaign
Cajuns Wharf
Centennial Bank; Conway, AR Digital, Marketing, Public Relations, Research, Social Media
Copper Grill
Lion's World Services
Lions World International
MBC Holdings
The Oxford American Campaign: "Rodeo Drive", Campaign: "Southern Arts"
The Peabody Little Rock
Summit Bank
Tyson Foods
Walmart
Windstream

Branch

CJRW Northwest

4100 Corporate Center Dr Ste 300, Springdale, AR 72762
(See Separate Listing)

CRANIUM 360

222 N 7th St, Grand Junction, CO 81501
Tel.: (970) 257-7000
E-Mail: info@cranium360.com
Web Site: www.cranium360.com

Agency Specializes In: Advertising, Graphic Design, Identity Marketing, Internet/Web Design, Logo & Package Design, Media Buying Services, Media Planning, Public Relations, Radio, Social Media

Travis Ingram *(Dir-Art & Graphic Designer)*
Matthew Breman *(Founder Pres & Dir-Mktg)*
Kindra Huff *(Dir-Sls)*
Bridgett Gutierrez *(Mgr-Media & Strategist-Digital)*

Accounts:
Enstrom's
Moog Medical Devices Group

CRANIUM STUDIO

219 Columbia Dr, Tampa, FL 33606
Tel.: (813) 443-9870
Web Site: www.craniumstudio.com

Year Founded: 1989

Agency Specializes In: Brand Development & Integration, Communications, Digital/Interactive, Exhibit/Trade Shows, Identity Marketing, Internet/Web Design, Logo & Package Design, Market Research, Production (Print), Strategic Planning/Research

Greg Olson *(Partner)*
Alex Valderrama *(Principal & Brand Dir)*

CRAVE WIN MARKETING

990 Interstate 10 Frontage Rd Ste 217, Beaumont, TX 77702
Tel.: (409) 239-7820
E-Mail: info@cravewin.com
Web Site: www.cravewin.com

Year Founded: 2013

Agency Specializes In: Advertising, Graphic Design, Internet/Web Design, Logo & Package Design, Print, Search Engine Optimization

Jack Cravy *(CEO & Dir-Mktg)*
Dylan Wilkinson *(Creative Dir)*

Accounts:
Triumph International

CRAWFORD ADVERTISING ASSOCIATES, LTD.
216 Congers Rd, New City, NY 10956
Tel.: (845) 638-0051
Fax: (845) 634-4232
E-Mail: info@crawfordadv.com
Web Site: www.facebook.com/pages/Crawford-Advertising/114053455289586

Employees: 3
Year Founded: 1992

Agency Specializes In: Alternative Advertising, Automotive, Co-op Advertising, Fashion/Apparel, Media Buying Services, Newspaper, Outdoor, Print, Real Estate, Recruitment, Social Media, Web (Banner Ads, Pop-ups, etc.)

Howard Wolfe *(Pres)*

Accounts:
BCA Leasing; Great Neck, NY Automobiles; 1992
Cantor & Pecorella Inc.; New York, NY Real Estate; 1992
Independent Brokers Circle; New York, NY Real Estate; 1992
Jessilyn Personnel; New York, NY Recruitment; 1992
Manhattan Skyline Management; New York, NY
Tabak Real Estate; New York, NY; 1992

CRAWFORD STRATEGY
200 E Camperdown Way, Greenville, SC 29601
Tel.: (864) 232-2302
E-Mail: info@crawfordstrategy.com
Web Site: www.crawfordstrategy.com

Year Founded: 2010

Agency Specializes In: Advertising, Brand Development & Integration, Graphic Design, Internet/Web Design, Logo & Package Design, Media Buying Services, Media Planning, Media Relations, Public Relations, Social Media

Marion Crawford *(Pres & CEO)*
Andy Windham *(Sr VP & Acct Mgmt Dir)*
Cyndy Templeton *(VP & Controller)*
Bill Donohue *(VP & Dir-Creative Svcs)*
Laura Blume *(Dir-Creative)*
Hannah Dillard *(Dir-Art)*
Mary Ellen Hoyt *(Office Mgr)*
Nisha Patel *(Acct Mgr-PR)*

Accounts:
Clemson University Athletic Department Marketing, Public Relations
Economic Development Coalition of Asheville-Buncombe County

CRE8TIVISION LLC
4601 Connecticut Ave NW Ste 217, Washington, DC 20008
Tel.: (202) 321-0675
E-Mail: cre8tivisionllc@gmail.com

Year Founded: 2008

Agency Specializes In: Advertising, Brand Development & Integration, Broadcast, Cable T.V., Catalogs, Collateral, Communications, Consulting, Consumer Marketing, Corporate Identity, Digital/Interactive, Direct Response Marketing, Direct-to-Consumer, Electronic Media, Email, Environmental, Event Planning & Marketing, Exhibit/Trade Shows, Government/Political, Graphic Design, Integrated Marketing, Internet/Web Design, Local Marketing, Market Research, Media Buying Services, Media Planning, Mobile Marketing, Multimedia, Newspaper, Newspapers & Magazines, Out-of-Home Media, Outdoor, Point of Purchase, Point of Sale, Print, Product Placement, Production, Production (Print), Promotions, Publicity/Promotions, Radio, Regional, Search Engine Optimization, Social Marketing/Nonprofit, Social Media, Sponsorship, T.V.

Barb Dickey *(Owner & Dir-Creative)*

Accounts:
Water Advocates; Washington, DC

CREATETHE GROUP, INC.
116 W Houston St, New York, NY 10012
Tel.: (212) 375-7900
Web Site: www.createthegroup.com

Employees: 100

Agency Specializes In: Alternative Advertising, Fashion/Apparel, Graphic Design, Information Technology, Social Marketing/Nonprofit

Revenue: $9,700,000

Carl Calarco *(CFO)*
Lynn Fischer *(VP-Bus Dev Strategy)*
Tina McCarthy *(VP-Client Svcs)*
Rachel Levi *(Mgr-Social Strategies)*
Jessica McGee *(Mgr-Paid Search)*
Hillary Pecorale *(Strategist-Display)*

Accounts:
Alexander Wang
BLK DNM (Digital Agency of Record)
Burberry Limited
DKNY Donna Karan
Donna Karan
Dunhill
LAPERLA
Marc Jacobs

THE CREATIVE ALLIANCE, INC.
(Private-Parent-Single Location)
2675 Northpark Dr Ste 200, Lafayette, CO 80026
Tel.: (303) 665-8101
Fax: (303) 665-3136
E-Mail: info@thecreativealliance.com
Web Site: www.thecreativealliance.com

Employees: 13
Year Founded: 1992

Agency Specializes In: Advertising, Brand Development & Integration, Digital/Interactive, Media Relations, Public Relations, Strategic Planning/Research

Revenue: $2,600,000

Kathy Albers *(CFO & Dir-HR)*
Adam Auriemmo *(Dir-IT)*
Jodee Goodwin *(Dir-Interactive Art & Art)*
Amy Hickey *(Client Svcs Mgr)*
Natalie Riquelme *(Client Svcs Mgr)*
Jennifer Armstrong *(Mgr-Production)*
Shayne Brill *(Acct Supvr)*
Rose Sawvel *(Coord-Client Svcs)*

Accounts:
Boulder Outreach for Homeless Overflow Campaign: "The safety net under the safety net", Graphics, Logo, Marketing, Social Media, Website
Indulgent Confections
Prime Trailer Rebranding, Strategic Planning
Sierra Sage
Thurston Kitchen & Bath

CREATIVE ARTISTS AGENCY
2000 Ave of the Stars, Los Angeles, CA 90067
Tel.: (424) 288-2000
Fax: (424) 288-2900
Web Site: www.caa.com

Agency Specializes In: Sponsorship

Richard Lovett *(Pres)*
James Burtson *(CFO)*
Michael Keithley *(CIO)*
Jae Goodman *(Chief Creative Officer & Co-Head-CAA Mktg)*
Jay Brooker *(Head-Content Creation & CAA Mktg)*
David Messinger *(Co-Head-Mktg)*
Frederic Levron *(Exec Dir-Creative)*
Jarrett Dube *(Dir-Entertainment Mktg)*

Accounts:
Body Lab
Burberry
Canada Goose (Agency of Record)
Chipotle Mexican Grill
Cirque du Soleil
Coca-Cola Refreshments USA, Inc.
Diageo
Fender
General Motors
Jimmy John's
Keurig Green Mountain
Neiman Marcus
Ralph Lauren
Samsung
Southwest Airlines
Umpqua Bank Campaign: "The Seed & The Moon"

Branch

Creative Artists Agency
222 S Central Ave Ste 1008, Saint Louis, MO 63105
Tel.: (314) 862-5560
Fax: (314) 862-4754
Web Site: www.caa.com

Employees: 13

David Freeman *(Co-Head-Digital Content Pkg & Brand Partnership Groups)*

CREATIVE BEARINGS
211 3rd St, Steamboat Springs, CO 80477
Tel.: (970) 870-8008
Fax: (970) 871-0226
Toll Free: (877) 980-8008
E-Mail: support@creativebearings.com
Web Site: www.creativebearings.com

Agency Specializes In: Advertising, Brand Development & Integration, Internet/Web Design, Logo & Package Design, Media Buying Services, Search Engine Optimization

Gregory Effinger *(Dir-Art)*
Daniel Sanders *(Designer)*

Accounts:
Colorado Event Rentals
Mountain High Distribution LLC

CREATIVE BRAND CONSULTING
(Formerly Lucky Dog Creative)
1429 N 1st St Ste 100, Phoenix, AZ 85004-1642
Tel.: (888) 567-0522
Fax: (888) 567-0522
Toll Free: (888) 567-0522
Web Site: creativebrandconsulting.com

Agency Specializes In: Advertising, Brand

Development & Integration, Digital/Interactive, Education, Public Relations, Real Estate, Restaurant, Retail

Ron Robinett *(CEO)*
Daniel Burrell *(COO & Dir)*
Jim Colletti *(Brand Dir)*
Erin Neathery *(Brand Dir)*

Accounts:
HARO (Help a Reporter Out) Social Media Services

CREATIVE BROADCAST CONCEPTS

180 Pool St, Biddeford, ME 04005-2833
Tel.: (207) 283-9191
Fax: (207) 283-9722
Toll Free: (800) 237-8237
E-Mail: info@cbcads.com
Web Site: www.cbcads.com

E-Mail for Key Personnel:
President: jim@cbcads.com

Employees: 25
Year Founded: 1983

Agency Specializes In: Advertising, Advertising Specialties, Automotive, Brand Development & Integration, Broadcast, Business-To-Business, Cable T.V., Collateral, Consulting, E-Commerce, Electronic Media, Graphic Design, Infomercials, Internet/Web Design, Media Buying Services, Merchandising, Multimedia, Newspaper, Planning & Consultation, Point of Purchase, Point of Sale, Print, Production, Public Relations, Radio, Sales Promotion, T.V., Yellow Pages Advertising

Approx. Annual Billings: $32,000,000

Breakdown of Gross Billings by Media: Adv. Specialities: $250,000; Collateral: $200,000; E-Commerce: $18,000,000; Internet Adv.: $200,000; Print: $11,000,000; Production: $2,000,000; Video Brochures: $200,000; Worldwide Web Sites: $150,000

Barry Morgan *(Pres)*
Frank Drigotas *(Partner)*
Amy Wheeler *(Dir-Media)*
Bill Park *(Sr Acct Exec)*
Greg Johnson *(Acct Exec)*
Dana Snyder *(Acct Exec)*

Accounts:
Brandon Ford; Brandon, FL
Faulkner Automotive; Philadelphia, PA Automobile Sales & Service; 1991
Hendrick Acura & BMW; Charlotte, NC Automobile Sales & Service; 1998
Kia Country; Charleston, SC
Lee Automotive Management
Mark Dodge; Lake Charles, LA
Superior Lexus; Kansas City, MO
Toothman Ford; Grafton, WV
Woodhouse Automotive Family

CREATIVE CANNON

2201 Civic Cir Ste 917, Amarillo, TX 79109
Tel.: (806) 676-7755
E-Mail: info@creative-cannon.com
Web Site: www.creative-cannon.com

Year Founded: 2012

Agency Specializes In: Advertising, Graphic Design, Internet/Web Design, Logo & Package Design

Jon Galloway *(Dir-Creative)*
David Martinez *(Dir-Acct Svcs)*
James Pompa *(Dir-Video)*

Accounts:
Amarillo Botanical Gardens
The Diocese of Amarillo

CREATIVE CIVILIZATION AN AGUILAR/GIRARD AGENCY

106 Auditorium Cir 2nd Fl, San Antonio, TX 78205-1310
Tel.: (210) 227-1999
Fax: (210) 227-5999
E-Mail: aaguilar@creativecivilization.com
Web Site: www.creativecivilization.com

Employees: 27
Year Founded: 1999

Agency Specializes In: Hispanic Market, Sponsorship

Gisela Girard *(Pres & COO)*
Joseph Guerra *(VP & Exec Producer-Creative)*
Richard Fisher *(Sr Dir-Art)*
Rachel Benavidez *(Dir-PR)*
Toni Ellard *(Dir-Touchpoint Integration)*
Robert Sosa *(Dir-Creative)*
Patty Perez *(Mgr-Ops)*
Natalia Prieto *(Acct Exec)*
Kirsten Forkheim *(Acct Coord)*
Lauren Wilks *(Acct Coord-PR)*

Accounts:
American Cancer Society
American State Bank
Cancer Treatment Centers of America Brand Awareness, Hispanic
Guitar Center Inc.
Kuper
San Antonio Express News Conexion
University Health System Campaign: "Children's Health Is Here"

CREATIVE COMMUNICATION & DESIGN

3550 W Stewart Ave, Wausau, WI 54401
Tel.: (715) 845-2382
E-Mail: greatideas@creativecommunication.com
Web Site: www.creativecommunication.com

Agency Specializes In: Advertising, Brand Development & Integration, Public Relations, Social Media, Strategic Planning/Research

Christine Liedtke *(Owner & Pres)*
Stephanie Bresnahan *(Acct Exec)*
April Rosemurgy *(Acct Exec)*

Accounts:
New-Cequent Group
New-Northcentral Technical College

CREATIVE COMMUNICATION ASSOCIATES

16 Sage Estate, Albany, NY 12204-2237
Tel.: (518) 427-6600
Fax: (518) 427-6679
E-Mail: esirianno@ccanewyork.com
Web Site: www.ccanewyork.com

Employees: 20

Agency Specializes In: Advertising, Brand Development & Integration, Broadcast, Cable T.V., Collateral, College, Commercial Photography, Communications, Consumer Publications, Corporate Identity, Custom Publishing, Direct-to-Consumer, Education, Electronic Media, Identity Marketing, Infomercials, Integrated Marketing, Internet/Web Design, Logo & Package Design, Magazines, Outdoor, Planning & Consultation, Print, Production, Production (Ad, Film, Broadcast), Radio, Social Marketing/Nonprofit, Strategic Planning/Research, T.V., Teen Market, Trade & Consumer Magazines, Web (Banner Ads, Pop-ups, etc.)

Approx. Annual Billings: $30,000,000

Edward J. Sirianno *(Pres & Chief Creative Officer)*
Dan Kehn *(Exec VP)*
Richard Langdon *(Sr Dir-Client Svcs)*
Beth Mickalonis *(Dir-Art)*
David A. Moore *(Assoc Dir-Creative)*
Lauren Herrington *(Sr Acct Mgr)*
Jenna Ryan *(Acct Mgr)*
Karen Dolge *(Mgr-Media)*
Emilie Cardone *(Acct Coord)*
Brenna Filipello *(Coord-Digital Program)*
Garrett Kipp *(Jr Designer)*

Accounts:
Boston College
Bryn Mawr College
Concordia College
LIM College
Philadelphia University
Siena College
St. John's University
Syracuse University College of Law
Union Graduate College
University of Pennsylvania

CREATIVE COMMUNICATIONS CONSULTANTS, INC.

111 3rd Ave S Ste 390, Minneapolis, MN 55401-2553
Tel.: (612) 338-5098
Fax: (612) 338-1398
E-Mail: smcpherson@cccinc.com
Web Site: www.cccinc.com

Employees: 10
Year Founded: 1978

Agency Specializes In: Advertising, Aviation & Aerospace, Brand Development & Integration, Business Publications, Business-To-Business, Collateral, Direct Response Marketing, Electronic Media, Email, Engineering, Environmental, Graphic Design, Health Care Services, High Technology, Hospitality, Industrial, Information Technology, Integrated Marketing, Internet/Web Design, Marine, Market Research, Media Buying Services, Media Planning, Media Relations, Medical Products, Paid Searches, Planning & Consultation, Print, Public Relations, Search Engine Optimization, Social Media, Strategic Planning/Research, Technical Advertising, Trade & Consumer Magazines, Viral/Buzz/Word of Mouth, Web (Banner Ads, Pop-ups, etc.)

Approx. Annual Billings: $7,500,000

Breakdown of Gross Billings by Media: Bus. Publs.: $2,500,000; Collateral: $1,200,000; D.M.: $750,000; E-Commerce: $100,000; Fees: $900,000; Internet Adv.: $1,000,000; Other: $300,000; Pub. Rels.: $750,000

Susan McPherson *(Owner & Pres)*
Deb Hyden *(Dir-Media)*
Robert Sheldon *(Dir-PR)*
Grant Thornburg *(Dir-Creative)*
Mary K. Jones *(Sr Acct Mgr)*
Lynette Paulsen *(Coord-PR)*

Accounts:
Cummins Power Generation
Dri-Steem Humidifier Company
Goodrich Sensors & Integrated Systems; Burnsville, MN
McQuay International
MTU Detroit Diesel
MTU Onsite Energy
Nilfisk-Advance

Reell Precision Manufacturing
SolarBee
Tolomatic

CREATIVE COMMUNICATIONS SERVICES

2710 Loker Ave W 350, Carlsbad, CA 92010
Tel.: (760) 438-5250
Fax: (760) 438-5230
Web Site: www.ccspr.com

Agency Specializes In: Advertising, Public Relations, Social Media

Gayle Mestel *(Pres)*

Accounts:
New-BizAir Shuttle

CREATIVE COMPANY

726 NE 4th St, McMinnville, OR 97128
Tel.: (503) 883-4433
Fax: (503) 883-6817
Toll Free: (866) 363-4433
E-Mail: advance@creativeco.com
Web Site: www.creativeco.com

Employees: 5
Year Founded: 1978

National Agency Associations: AMA

Agency Specializes In: Advertising, Affluent Market, Agriculture, Alternative Advertising, Arts, Asian Market, Aviation & Aerospace, Brand Development & Integration, Business Publications, Business-To-Business, Cable T.V., Co-op Advertising, Collateral, College, Commercial Photography, Communications, Computers & Software, Consulting, Consumer Goods, Consumer Marketing, Consumer Publications, Content, Corporate Communications, Corporate Identity, Cosmetics, Digital/Interactive, Direct Response Marketing, Direct-to-Consumer, E-Commerce, Education, Electronic Media, Email, Engineering, Exhibit/Trade Shows, Faith Based, Financial, Food Service, Graphic Design, Guerilla Marketing, Health Care Services, Identity Marketing, In-Store Advertising, Industrial, Integrated Marketing, International, Internet/Web Design, Leisure, Local Marketing, Logo & Package Design, Luxury Products, Magazines, Market Research, Media Relations, Medical Products, Mobile Marketing, New Product Development, Newspaper, Outdoor, Over-50 Market, Package Design, Paid Searches, Pharmaceutical, Planning & Consultation, Point of Purchase, Point of Sale, Print, Production, Production (Print), Promotions, Public Relations, Publicity/Promotions, Radio, Real Estate, Regional, Restaurant, Retail, Sales Promotion, Search Engine Optimization, Seniors' Market, Social Media, Strategic Planning/Research, Teen Market, Trade & Consumer Magazines, Transportation, Urban Market, Women's Market

Approx. Annual Billings: $1,000,000

Breakdown of Gross Billings by Media: Cable T.V.: 1%; Co-op Adv.: 3%; Collateral: 10%; Comml. Photography: 2%; Consulting: 1%; Consumer Publs.: 4%; Foreign: 2%; Graphic Design: 35%; Point of Sale: 2%; Pub. Rels.: 6%; Strategic Planning/Research: 10%; T.V.: 1%; Trade Shows: 2%; Video Brochures: 1%; Worldwide Web Sites: 20%

Jennifer Larsen Morrow *(Pres-Brand)*
Peter Kotenko *(Designer-Digital)*
Fritz Kilcrease *(Project Head)*

Accounts:
ESP Seeds; Albany, OR Wholesale Seed; 2010
foodguys; Wilsonville, OR Food Products; 2001
JR Merit; Vancouver, WA Industrial Contracting; 2009
McTavish Shortbread; Portland, OR Shortbread Cookies; 2007
Oregon Cherry Growers; Salem, OR Cherries; 2008
Salem Health; Salem, OR Healthcare Services; 2009

THE CREATIVE DEPARTMENT

1209 Sycamore St, Cincinnati, OH 45202
Tel.: (513) 651-2901
Fax: (513) 651-2902
E-Mail: info@creativedepartment.com
Web Site: www.creativedepartment.com

Employees: 19
Year Founded: 1992

National Agency Associations: AD CLUB-The One Club

Agency Specializes In: Advertising, Alternative Advertising, Brand Development & Integration, Broadcast, Business-To-Business, Catalogs, Collateral, Consulting, Consumer Goods, Content, Corporate Communications, Corporate Identity, Crisis Communications, Digital/Interactive, E-Commerce, Electronic Media, Email, Event Planning & Marketing, Exhibit/Trade Shows, Guerilla Marketing, Identity Marketing, Integrated Marketing, Internet/Web Design, Logo & Package Design, Magazines, Market Research, Media Planning, Newspaper, Newspapers & Magazines, Outdoor, Paid Searches, Planning & Consultation, Podcasting, Point of Sale, Print, Production (Ad, Film, Broadcast), RSS (Really Simple Syndication), Search Engine Optimization, Sponsorship, T.V., Travel & Tourism, Viral/Buzz/Word of Mouth, Web (Banner Ads, Pop-ups, etc.)

Lauren Anderson *(Owner)*
Kerry James *(Co-Owner)*
Mike Beasley *(CTO)*
Ben Junda *(Sr Dir-Art)*
Jeff Chambers *(Dir-Creative)*
Gregg Meade *(Assoc Dir-Creative)*
Maggie Adamson *(Mgr-Traffic)*
Ian Monk *(Designer-Interactive)*

Accounts:
The Art Academy of Cincinnati
Busken Bakery; Cincinnati, OH Baked Goods, Yagoot; 1996
Corporex
Five Seasons Sports Club
i-wireless
NuVo Technologies
The Party Source; Newport, KY Liquor Store &Then Some; 2005
Procter & Gamble; Cincinnati, OH (Corporate Communications & Training); 1998
Silkflowers.com; White Plains, NY Silk Flower Arrangements; 2004

CREATIVE DIMENSIONS

4555 Lake Forest Dr Ste 650, Cincinnati, OH 45242
Tel.: (513) 588-2801
Fax: (513) 563-0293
Web Site: www.creativedimensions.com

Agency Specializes In: Advertising, Corporate Identity, Digital/Interactive, Logo & Package Design, Media Buying Services, Media Planning, Print, Radio, Social Media, Strategic Planning/Research

Arnie Barnett *(Pres)*
Steve Schaeffer *(CEO & Dir-Creative)*
Tracie Bowling *(CFO)*
John Graham *(Sr Dir-Copy)*
Nathan Cremer *(Dir-Art)*
Paulette McKnight *(Office Mgr)*
Amy Jones *(Client Svc Dir)*

Accounts:
Just Brakes
Quadras Corp (Agency of Record) Creative Marketing

CREATIVE DIRECTION, INC.

PO Box 17670, Indianapolis, IN 46217
Tel.: (765) 883-8431
Fax: (765) 455-1707
E-Mail: info@creativedirection.com
Web Site: www.creativedirection.com

Employees: 5
Year Founded: 1993

Agency Specializes In: Above-the-Line, Advertising Specialties, Agriculture, Automotive, Business-To-Business, Direct Response Marketing, Direct-to-Consumer, Email, Graphic Design, Guerilla Marketing, Health Care Services, High Technology, Integrated Marketing, Internet/Web Design, Media Buying Services, Newspaper, Newspapers & Magazines, Outdoor, Pharmaceutical, Planning & Consultation, Print, Production, Production (Print), Promotions, Public Relations, Radio, Sales Promotion, Sports Market

Approx. Annual Billings: $1,500,000

Richard Parker *(Founder, Pres & Dir-Creative)*
David Parker *(Partner)*
Julie Parker *(CFO & COO)*
Helen Parker *(Dir-Media & Mdsg)*

THE CREATIVE DIRECTORS, INC.

222 E 44th St, New York, NY 10017
Tel.: (212) 450-1609
Fax: (212) 450-1630
E-Mail: info@thecreativedirectorsinc.com
Web Site: www.thecreativedirectorsinc.com

Year Founded: 2006

Agency Specializes In: Advertising, Affluent Market, Automotive, Brand Development & Integration, Branded Entertainment, Broadcast, Business-To-Business, Cable T.V., Children's Market, College, Computers & Software, Consumer Goods, Consumer Marketing, Consumer Publications, Corporate Communications, Corporate Identity, Crisis Communications, Direct Response Marketing, Direct-to-Consumer, Electronics, Entertainment, Exhibit/Trade Shows, Financial, Graphic Design, Guerilla Marketing, Health Care Services, High Technology, Household Goods, In-Store Advertising, Legal Services, Leisure, Local Marketing, Magazines, Medical Products, Men's Market, Multicultural, New Product Development, Newspaper, Newspapers & Magazines, Out-of-Home Media, Outdoor, Over-50 Market, Package Design, Pharmaceutical, Point of Purchase, Point of Sale, Print, Production (Ad, Film, Broadcast), Production (Print), Radio, Restaurant, Retail, T.V., Travel & Tourism, Web (Banner Ads, Pop-ups, etc.), Women's Market

Frank DiSalvo *(Owner)*
John Ferrell *(Chief Creative Officer)*

Accounts:
Bufferin
Corning
Dentyne
Ford
Giant Eagle
Kraft
Mercury

Office Depot
People

CREATIVE DISTILLERY
4465 I-55 N Ste 302, Jackson, MS 39206
Tel.: (601) 326-2388
E-Mail: info@creativedistillery.com
Web Site: www.creativedistillery.com

Year Founded: 2008

Agency Specializes In: Advertising, Brand Development & Integration, Collateral, Content, Graphic Design, Internet/Web Design, Logo & Package Design, Social Media

Darren Schwindaman *(Principal)*
Julianna Pardue *(Copywriter)*

Accounts:
The Mississippi Chorus
Parents for Public Schools Jackson
Phoenix Properties

CREATIVE DYNAMIX INK
19800 MacArthur Blvd., Ste 300, Irvine, CA 92642
Toll Free: (800) 409-5930
Web Site: www.creativedynamixink.com

Employees: 3
Year Founded: 2012

Agency Specializes In: Local Marketing, Multimedia, Search Engine Optimization, Social Media

Approx. Annual Billings: $300,000

Sheryl Perez *(Pres)*

CREATIVE EFFECTS ADVERTISING DESIGN STUDIO
1355 Channelview Rd, Kingston, ON K7L 4V1 Canada
Tel.: (613) 531-0990
Fax: (613) 531-6582
Toll Free: (877) 421-7153
E-Mail: studio@creativeeffects.com
Web Site: www.creativeeffects.com

Employees: 5
Year Founded: 1986

Donna Bishop *(Dir-Creative)*

Accounts:
Altair Electronics
J.A.K.K Tuesdays
Jolly Giant Software
KEYS
Kingston Electors; 2007

CREATIVE ENERGY GROUP INC
3206 Hanover Rd, Johnson City, TN 37604
Tel.: (423) 926-9494
Fax: (423) 929-7222
Toll Free: (800) 926-9454
Web Site: www.cenergy.com

Employees: 20
Year Founded: 1991

National Agency Associations: AAF-PRSA

Agency Specializes In: Above-the-Line, Advertising, Advertising Specialties, Affiliate Marketing, Affluent Market, African-American Market, Agriculture, Alternative Advertising, Arts, Asian Market, Automotive, Aviation & Aerospace, Below-the-Line, Bilingual Market, Brand Development & Integration, Branded Entertainment, Broadcast, Business Publications, Business-To-Business, Cable T.V., Catalogs, Children's Market, Co-op Advertising, Collateral, College, Commercial Photography, Communications, Computers & Software, Consulting, Consumer Goods, Consumer Marketing, Consumer Publications, Content, Corporate Communications, Corporate Identity, Cosmetics, Crisis Communications, Custom Publishing, Customer Relationship Management, Digital/Interactive, Direct Response Marketing, Direct-to-Consumer, E-Commerce, Education, Electronic Media, Electronics, Email, Engineering, Entertainment, Environmental, Event Planning & Marketing, Exhibit/Trade Shows, Experience Design, Fashion/Apparel, Financial, Food Service, Game Integration, Gay & Lesbian Market, Government/Political, Graphic Design, Guerilla Marketing, Health Care Services, High Technology, Hispanic Market, Hospitality, Household Goods, Identity Marketing, In-Store Advertising, Industrial, Infomercials, Information Technology, Integrated Marketing, International, Internet/Web Design, Investor Relations, Legal Services, Leisure, Local Marketing, Logo & Package Design, Luxury Products, Magazines, Marine, Market Research, Media Buying Services, Media Planning, Media Relations, Media Training, Medical Products, Men's Market, Merchandising, Mobile Marketing, Multicultural, Multimedia, New Product Development, New Technologies, Newspaper, Newspapers & Magazines, Out-of-Home Media, Outdoor, Over-50 Market, Package Design, Paid Searches, Pharmaceutical, Planning & Consultation, Podcasting, Point of Purchase, Point of Sale, Print, Product Placement, Production, Production (Ad, Film, Broadcast), Production (Print), Promotions, Public Relations, Publicity/Promotions, Publishing, RSS (Really Simple Syndication), Radio, Real Estate, Recruitment, Regional, Restaurant, Retail, Sales Promotion, Search Engine Optimization, Seniors' Market, Social Marketing/Nonprofit, Sponsorship, Sports Market, Stakeholders, Strategic Planning/Research, Sweepstakes, Syndication, T.V., Technical Advertising, Teen Market, Telemarketing, Trade & Consumer Magazines, Transportation, Travel & Tourism, Urban Market, Viral/Buzz/Word of Mouth, Web (Banner Ads, Pop-ups, etc.), Women's Market, Yellow Pages Advertising

Approx. Annual Billings: $5,500,000

Breakdown of Gross Billings by Media: Adv. Specialities: $4,000,000; Newsp. & Mags.: $1,500,000

Tony Treadway *(Pres & CEO)*
Will Griffith *(Exec Dir-Creative)*
Joe Schnellmann *(Art Dir)*
Dale Atkinson *(Dir-Art)*
Jim Julien *(Dir-Art)*
Greg Nobles *(Dir-Creative)*
Lori DeVoti *(Acct Exec)*

Accounts:
Akzo/Nobel; Atlanta, GA Automotive Paints; 1998
American Pride Seafood
ARCH
Brookwood Farms
Bunge Oils North America; Saint Louis, MO Trans Fat Free Oils & Products; 2006
Carter County Bank; Elizabethton, TN Banking Services; 1993
Coca-Cola Refreshments USA, Inc.
Global Medical Services
Hoshizaki Ice Systems; Atlanta, GA Ice Machines; 2002
LifeStore
Pal's Sudden Service; Kingsport, TN Quick Serve Restaurant Chain; 1992
Red Gold Tomatoes; Elwood, IN Italian, Ketchup, Tomato Juices; 2002
Reily Foods
Siemens Electrics; Alpharetta, GA Electric Motors & Components; 1999
Texas Pete; Winston-Salem, NC; 2001
Universal Fibers; Bristol, VA Yarn & Carpet Products; 2003

CREATIVE FEED
39 Mesa St The Presidio Ste 105, San Francisco, CA 94129
Tel.: (415) 447-0588
Web Site: www.creativefeed.net

Agency Specializes In: Advertising, Brand Development & Integration, Media Relations, Package Design, Publicity/Promotions, T.V., Travel & Tourism

Arthur Ceria *(Founder & Exec Dir-Creative)*
Michael Quinn *(Mng Partner)*
Prisca Nyko *(Acct Dir)*
Gareth Chisholm *(Dir-Creative)*
Clara Kim *(Dir-Social Media & Content Dev)*
Perrine Pavageau *(Dir-Production)*

Accounts:
Bordeaux Wine Council U.S. Digital
Calvin Klein
Land Rover S1 By Sonim
The Museum of Modern Art
Plantronics Discovery 975
Plantronics Unified Communications
Plantronics Voyager Pro
Sonim Technologies
Squeeze the Banker
UC Thought Leadership
Volvo

CREATIVE HEADS ADVERTISING, INC.
7301 Ranch Rd, Austin, TX 78701
Tel.: (512) 474-5775
Fax: (512) 474-5521
Web Site: www.creativeheadsadv.com

Employees: 3
Year Founded: 1998

Agency Specializes In: Advertising, Advertising Specialties, Brand Development & Integration, Business Publications, Business-To-Business, Co-op Advertising, Collateral, Commercial Photography, Communications, Consulting, Consumer Marketing, Consumer Publications, Corporate Communications, Corporate Identity, Direct Response Marketing, Electronic Media, Entertainment, Environmental, Event Planning & Marketing, Exhibit/Trade Shows, Financial, Food Service, Graphic Design, Health Care Services, In-Store Advertising, Internet/Web Design, Leisure, Local Marketing, Logo & Package Design, Magazines, Media Buying Services, Medical Products, Multimedia, New Product Development, Newspaper, Newspapers & Magazines, Out-of-Home Media, Outdoor, Planning & Consultation, Point of Purchase, Point of Sale, Print, Production, Public Relations, Publicity/Promotions, Radio, Restaurant, Retail, Sales Promotion, Sports Market, Strategic Planning/Research, Trade & Consumer Magazines, Transportation, Travel & Tourism, Yellow Pages Advertising

Approx. Annual Billings: $281,000

Breakdown of Gross Billings by Media: Adv. Specialities: $2,000; Bus. Publs.: $5,000; Co-op Adv.: $1,000; Collateral: $20,000; Comml. Photography: $3,000; Consulting: $12,000; Corp. Communications: $2,000; D.M.: $1,000; Event Mktg.: $25,000; Graphic Design: $20,000; In-Store Adv.: $2,000; Local Mktg.: $2,000; Logo & Package Design: $1,500; Mdsg./POP: $1,000; Newsp.:

$30,000; Out-of-Home Media: $4,000; Outdoor: $70,000; Plng. & Consultation: $5,000; Print: $10,000; Production: $1,000; Pub. Rels.: $1,000; Radio: $30,000; Sls. Promo.: $2,000; Sports Mktg.: $1,000; Strategic Planning/Research: $28,000; Trade & Consumer Mags.: $500; Worldwide Web Sites: $1,000

Deb Hutton Lovett *(Pres)*
Trey Lovett *(Acct Dir)*

Accounts:
Sweet Leaf Tea; Austin, TX Consumer Beverage; 2004

CREATIVE I
142 Minna St, San Francisco, CA 94105
Tel.: (415) 488-8400
Web Site: www.creative-i.com

Agency Specializes In: Advertising

Tom Antal *(Pres & CEO)*

Accounts:
Big Fix
Commerce One
Ferrari Club of America
First 5 Santa Clara County
Hewlett Packard
Palm
SonicWall

CREATIVE IMAGE ADVERTISING & DESIGN, INC.
(d/b/a Creative Manufacturing)
(Private-Parent-Single Location)
19 Lindsey Pl, Holbrook, NY 11741
Tel.: (631) 863-2311
Web Site: www.creativeimage.com

Employees: 24
Year Founded: 1991

Agency Specializes In: Advertising, Internet/Web Design, Public Relations, Social Media, Strategic Planning/Research

Revenue: $6,200,000

Frank Russo *(Founder & Pres)*

Accounts:
Total Body Shaping

CREATIVE INSURANCE MARKETING CO.
208 2nd Ave, Belmar, NJ 07719
Tel.: (732) 681-0700
Fax: (732) 681-7102
E-Mail: info@cim-co.com
Web Site: www.cim-co.com

Employees: 10

Agency Specializes In: Advertising, Advertising Specialties, Brand Development & Integration, Business Publications, Business-To-Business, Co-op Advertising, Collateral, Communications, Consulting, Consumer Marketing, Consumer Publications, Corporate Communications, Digital/Interactive, Direct Response Marketing, E-Commerce, Electronic Media, Environmental, Event Planning & Marketing, Financial, Health Care Services, Internet/Web Design, Local Marketing, Logo & Package Design, Multimedia, New Product Development, Newspaper, Outdoor, Planning & Consultation, Point of Sale, Print, Public Relations, Publicity/Promotions, Radio, Sales Promotion, Strategic Planning/Research, T.V., Telemarketing, Trade & Consumer Magazines

Approx. Annual Billings: $10,000,000

Fred G. Marziano *(Principal)*
Kimberly Paterson *(Principal)*

Accounts:
Accenture
Aetna
AIA
AIG
Alex Brown
American Medical Association
Bank of America
CastlePoint Holdings, Ltd.
Chubb
CIGNA
CNA (Continental Insurance)
Commercial Life
Distinguished Programs
FC&S Bulletins
Fireman's Fund
First Insurance Co. of Hawaii
First Montauk Securities
Fleet Bank
GAN Assurance
Gerling Global Reinsurance
Gill and Roeser, Inc.
Guy Carpenter
JPMorgan Chase
Kinloch Holdings
Life Insurance Company of Connecticut
Marsh
Michigan Millers Insurance Company
Tokio Marine
Tower Group Companies

CREATIVE INTELLIGENCE
Ste 290 815 17th Ave SW, Calgary, AB T2V 2V6 Canada
Tel.: (403) 701-8066
E-Mail: react@ciacanada.com
Web Site: www.ciacanada.com

Employees: 11
Year Founded: 1981

Agency Specializes In: Brand Development & Integration, Communications

Barry Anderson *(Exec Dir-Strategic Mktg Svcs & U Potential)*
Dean McKenzie *(Exec Dir-Creative Svcs)*

Accounts:
Attic
Boom Town
Calaway Film Festival
Calaway Park
Canadian Pacific Railway
CP Rail campaign
Mac's Convenience Stores
Red Hause
Superior Propane
Talisman Energy

CREATIVE JUICE ADVERTISING
1031 Main St, Port Jefferson, NY 11777
Tel.: (631) 371-1287
Fax: (631) 473-4463
Web Site: www.creativejuiceadv.com

Agency Specializes In: Advertising, Collateral, Internet/Web Design, Media Planning, Multimedia, Print, Radio, Sponsorship, Strategic Planning/Research, T.V.

Steve Harper *(Pres)*
Susan Anderson *(Sr VP-Mktg)*

Accounts:
Long Island Gold Coast
Total Dental Care

CREATIVE LICENSE
71 8th Ave, New York, NY 10014
Tel.: (212) 741-6703
E-Mail: info@creativelicense.com
Web Site: www.creativelicense.com/

Agency Specializes In: Entertainment

Kevin McKiernan *(Pres & CEO)*
Tom Briggs *(VP)*
Luiz Porto *(Dir-Brazil & Latin America)*
Jeffrey Rutkowski *(Dir-Music & Talent)*
David Switzer *(Dir-Bus Affairs)*
Ricky Milano *(Rep-Italian)*
Jaya Prasad *(Rep)*

Accounts:
Delta Faucet
Expedia
Pfizer Nexium
Walmart

CREATIVE LIFT INC.
115 Sansome St, San Francisco, CA 94104
Tel.: (415) 248-3170
E-Mail: hello@creativelift.net
Web Site: http://www.wearelift.com/

Year Founded: 2003

Agency Specializes In: Advertising, Brand Development & Integration, Broadcast, Digital/Interactive, E-Commerce, Email, Package Design, Print, Radio, Retail

Tim Carr *(Founder)*
Jason Woodley *(Mng Partner)*
Ian Young *(Dir-Creative& Copywriter)*
Katie Burke *(Sr Acct Exec)*
Nikki Emerson *(Designer)*
Laura Howell *(Sr Designer)*
Brent Matsuo *(Sr Designer)*
Jessica Kwok *(Jr Graphic Designer)*

Accounts:
Direct Marketing Educational Foundation

CREATIVE MARKETING ALLIANCE INC.
191 Clarksville Rd, Princeton Junction, NJ 08550
Tel.: (609) 297-2235
Fax: (609) 799-7032
E-Mail: info@cmasolutions.com
Web Site: www.cmasolutions.com

Employees: 32
Year Founded: 1987

National Agency Associations: TAAN

Agency Specializes In: Advertising, Advertising Specialties, African-American Market, Brand Development & Integration, Business Publications, Business-To-Business, Cable T.V., Collateral, Communications, Consulting, Corporate Communications, Corporate Identity, Direct Response Marketing, E-Commerce, Electronic Media, Environmental, Event Planning & Marketing, Exhibit/Trade Shows, Financial, Graphic Design, Health Care Services, High Technology, Hispanic Market, Hospitality, In-Store Advertising, Industrial, Infomercials, Information Technology, Internet/Web Design, Legal Services, Local Marketing, Logo & Package Design, Magazines, Marine, Media Buying Services, Medical Products, Merchandising, New Product Development, Newspaper, Newspapers & Magazines, Outdoor, Over-50 Market, Pharmaceutical, Planning & Consultation, Point of Purchase, Point of Sale, Print, Production, Public Relations, Publicity/Promotions, Radio, Real Estate,

Recruitment, Restaurant, Sales Promotion, Seniors' Market, Social Marketing/Nonprofit, Sports Market, Strategic Planning/Research, Sweepstakes, Technical Advertising, Trade & Consumer Magazines, Transportation, Travel & Tourism, Web (Banner Ads, Pop-ups, etc.)

Approx. Annual Billings: $30,000,000

Jeffrey E. Barnhart *(Pres & CEO)*
Christian Amato *(COO & Chief Bus Dev Officer)*
Dave Sherwood *(VP & Dir-Creative)*
Gabrielle Copperwheat *(Dir-Association)*
Diane Galante *(Assoc Dir-Event Mgmt)*
Joseph DeFalco *(Acct Mgr-Mktg)*
Kenneth Hitchner *(PR-Mgr)*
Victoria Hurley-Schubert *(Acct Exec-PR)*
Jude Martin-Cianfano *(Acct Exec-Mktg)*

Accounts:
A-1 Limousine
Alemedia Electric Distributors
ALK Technologies
Association for Convention Operations Managers
Association for Strategic Planners
Audio Publisher's Association
Bee Leaf Marketing, Public Relations, Social Media
Central Jersey Mgt
Commercial Cleaning Corporation
Convention Service Professionals International
Cygnal
ESI Lighting
Global Energy Services
Grand Bank
Griffith Electric Supply
Habitat for Humanity
Hamilton Continuing Core
Homasote
IMARK
International Card Manufacturers Association
International Function Point Users Group
KNF
LJ Kushner
Mariner's School
Maurice Electric Supply
MidJersey Chamber of Commerce
National Association of commencement Officers
National Association of Independent Lighting Distributors
Northwest Windows & Door Association
Old York Country Club
Pasquito Builders
Piers
Professional Lighting Marketing, Public Relations, Social Media
Rental Stage Network
Robbinsville Township
Robert Wood Johnson Foundation
Robert Wood Johnson University Hospital
Scozzari Builders Marketing, Public Relations, Social Media
Slayback Health
Smart Card Industry Association
Springfield Electric Marketing, Public Relations, Social Media
Switlick Parachute
Szaferman Lakind Marketing, Public Relations, Social Media
Technology Channel Association
Transportation Marketing & Sale Association
Trenton Marine
Trilogy Partners
Westgate Mall Marketing, Public Relations, Social Media
Windsor Dermatology

CREATIVE MARKETING PLUS INC.
4705 Center Blvd Ste 806, Long Island City, NY 11109
Tel.: (718) 606-0767
Fax: (718) 606-6345
E-Mail: fharrow@creativemarketingplus.com
Web Site: www.creativemarketingplus.com

Employees: 20
Year Founded: 1982

Agency Specializes In: Advertising, Brand Development & Integration, Business-To-Business, Catalogs, Collateral, Consulting, Direct-to-Consumer, Fashion/Apparel, Graphic Design, Internet/Web Design, Logo & Package Design, Market Research, Media Relations, Public Relations, Retail, Strategic Planning/Research

Richard Harrow *(Pres & CEO)*
Richard Marchione *(COO)*
Fran Harrow *(Dir-Comm)*
Tricia Kenney *(Dir-Fashion)*
George Klas *(Dir-Strategy)*
Marjorie Harrow *(Mgr-Production)*

Accounts:
Bernando Fashions
Boston Harbour
Briggs & Riley
Fleet Street
Outerwear Magazine

CREATIVE MARKETING RESOURCE, INC.
325 W Huron St, Chicago, IL 60654
Tel.: (312) 943-6266
Fax: (312) 787-8586
E-Mail: jwagner@cmresource.com
Web Site: www.cmresource.com

Employees: 15
Year Founded: 1965

National Agency Associations: BPA

Agency Specializes In: Advertising, Financial, Health Care Services

Breakdown of Gross Billings by Media: Bus. Publs.: 10%; Collateral: 35%; D.M.: 35%; Mags.: 20%

Jacqueline Wagner *(Pres)*
Lynn Goodwin *(Controller)*
Ben Molinaro *(Assoc Dir-Creative)*
Adrianne Sell *(Assoc Dir-Creative)*

Accounts:
FidelisSeniorCare
Northern Trust
RML Specialty Hospital
Working Well Message, Inc.

CREATIVE MARKETING RESOURCES
1858 S Wadsworth Blvd Ste 315, Lakewood, CO 80232-6840
Tel.: (303) 985-8777
Fax: (303) 985-8783
E-Mail: dandrews@creativemkt.com
Web Site: www.creativemkt.com

E-Mail for Key Personnel:
President: trent@creativemkt.com

Employees: 4
Year Founded: 1994

Agency Specializes In: Business-To-Business, Collateral, Communications, Graphic Design, Industrial

Dan Andrews *(Owner)*
Trent Thornton *(Owner)*

Accounts:
Burris Company Binoculars, Riflescopes, Spotting Scopes
Hutchison Western Building Products, Fence/Wire, Livestock Equipment
Taylor Tools Floor Covering Tools & Equipment

CREATIVE MEDIA AGENCY LLC
393 Jericho Tpke Ste #300, Mineola, NY 11501-1299
Tel.: (516) 739-1320
Fax: (516) 739-0340
E-Mail: info@creativemediaagency.com
Web Site: www.creativemediaagency.com

Employees: 8
Year Founded: 1976

National Agency Associations: ABC-BPA

Agency Specializes In: Advertising, African-American Market, Graphic Design, Legal Services, Media Buying Services, Media Planning, Mobile Marketing, Newspaper, Newspapers & Magazines, Outdoor, Planning & Consultation, Print, Real Estate, Recruitment, Social Media, Web (Banner Ads, Pop-ups, etc.)

Approx. Annual Billings: $8,826,102

Breakdown of Gross Billings by Media: Bus. Publs.: $272,518; Internet Adv.: $109,937; Mags.: $182,626; Newsp.: $8,261,021

Stephanie Krieger *(Pres)*
Tami Glass *(Coord-Adv)*

Accounts:
Celebrity Moving; New York, NY Moving Co.; 1985
Cheryl Roshak, Inc.; New York, NY Graphic Arts & Computer Recruitment Firm; 1988
Department of Citywide Administrative Services; New York, NY; 2000
Department of Education, City of New York; New York, NY; 1997
E.B. Meyrowitz, Inc.; New York, NY Optical & Optician Chain
EuroMonde Inc.; New York, NY Bilingual Recruitment Firm; 1988
Eveready Employment; New York, NY Personnel Agency; 1988
Express Help; New York, NY Recruitment Firm; 1997
Jacobs Gardener; New York, NY Office Supply Company
Jay Gee Personnel Recruitment Firm; New York, NY; 1992
Johnson Group, Inc.; New York, NY Executive Search Firm; 1992
Light House Academies
New York State Department of Environmental Conservation; Albany, NY; 2006
New York State Power Authority; White Plains, NY; 1990
NYC Department of Citywide Administrative Services; 2000
NYC Department of Housing Preservation & Development; New York, NY; 1992
NYC Department of Parks & Recreation; New York, NY; 1986
NYC Department of Transportation; New York, NY
NYC Dept of Education; New York, NY; 2003
NYC School Construction Authority; New York, NY; 1997
NYS Dept of Environmental Conservation; Albany, NY; 2011
Paragon Employment Services; New York, NY; 1986
People Care; New York, NY Real Estate; 1994
Positive Personnel; New York, NY Employment Service; 1989
Premier Temps; New York, NY Temporary Personnel Agency; 1993
Property Resources Corp.; New York, NY Construction, Real Estate Development
Sebco Development Inc.; New York, NY Real Estate Development
Sebco Security Inc.; New York, NY
Tri State Party Rental Co. Party Rental
Trucking & Moving, Inc.; New York, NY National

Moving Company; 1984

CREATIVE MEDIA ALLIANCE
81 Columbia St, Seattle, WA 98104
Tel.: (206) 709-1667
Web Site: www.creativemediaalliance.com

Year Founded: 2001

Agency Specializes In: Advertising, Brand Development & Integration, Email, Print, Social Media

Ryan Fansler *(Owner)*
Gary Hurley *(Principal)*
Jai Suh *(Dir-Creative-Brand Mktg & Adv Strategies)*

Accounts:
Botanical Designs, Inc.
Inn at the Market

CREATIVE MINDWORKS
11900 Biscayne Blvd Ste 100, Miami, FL 33181
Tel.: (305) 820-0690
Fax: (305) 820-9906
E-Mail: info@creativemindworks.com
Web Site: www.creativemindworks.com

Employees: 5
Year Founded: 1998

National Agency Associations: ADFED-IAA

Agency Specializes In: Advertising, Affluent Market, Bilingual Market, Brand Development & Integration, Branded Entertainment, Business-To-Business, Communications, Computers & Software, Consulting, Consumer Marketing, Digital/Interactive, E-Commerce, Electronic Media, Email, Event Planning & Marketing, Exhibit/Trade Shows, Government/Political, Graphic Design, Guerilla Marketing, Health Care Services, High Technology, Hispanic Market, Hospitality, Infomercials, Integrated Marketing, International, Internet/Web Design, Logo & Package Design, Luxury Products, Magazines, Market Research, Media Buying Services, Media Planning, Media Relations, Media Training, Medical Products, Multicultural, Multimedia, New Product Development, Newspaper, Newspapers & Magazines, Outdoor, Over-50 Market, Package Design, Podcasting, Print, Production (Print), Promotions, Public Relations, Publicity/Promotions, Publishing, Radio, Real Estate, Restaurant, Retail, Sales Promotion, Search Engine Optimization, Social Marketing/Nonprofit, Strategic Planning/Research, T.V., Telemarketing, Transportation, Travel & Tourism, Viral/Buzz/Word of Mouth, Web (Banner Ads, Pop-ups, etc.)

Approx. Annual Billings: $6,000,000

Breakdown of Gross Billings by Media: Collateral: 15%; Exhibits/Trade Shows: 1%; Mags.: 15%; Newsp.: 30%; Outdoor: 2%; Radio: 10%; T.V.: 5%; Video Brochures: 2%; Worldwide Web Sites: 20%

Lizette Fernandez *(Owner)*
Sissy Fuster *(Sr Acct Mgr)*
Michelle Menendez *(Specialist-Publ & Copywriter)*

Accounts:
BHI Developers
Bimini Bay
Blue Ocean Reef
Grec Conversions Real Estate; Miami Lakes, FL; 1999
HTA Architecture
Judson Architecture
Las Terrazas
Roemer
Zephyr Homes

THE CREATIVE MOMENTUM
200 Mansell Ct E Ste 300, Roswell, GA 30076
Tel.: (678) 648-1445
E-Mail: info@thecreativemomentum.com
Web Site: www.thecreativemomentum.com

Agency Specializes In: Advertising, Brand Development & Integration, Digital/Interactive, Graphic Design, Logo & Package Design, Outdoor, Print, Public Relations, Search Engine Optimization, Strategic Planning/Research

Michael White *(Pres)*
Carl Widdowson *(CEO)*
Nate Marsh *(VP-Bus Dev)*
Alex Jartos *(Art Dir)*
Gabe Hamby *(Dir-QA)*
A. J. Martin *(Dir-SEM & Display Adv)*
David Bowman *(Dir-Video & Animation)*
David Martin *(Designer)*

Accounts:
Challenge Entertainment
Risquat

CREATIVE NOGGIN
29610 Double Eagle Cir, San Antonio, TX 78015
Tel.: (830) 981-8222
Fax: (830) 755-8223
E-Mail: info@creativenoggin.com
Web Site: www.creativenoggin.com

Agency Specializes In: Advertising, Brand Development & Integration, Broadcast, Corporate Identity, Logo & Package Design, Media Buying Services, Media Planning, Public Relations, Social Media, Strategic Planning/Research

Trish McCabe Rawls *(Partner & Dir-Creative)*
Nanette Rodriguez *(Mgr-Production & Traffic)*
Laura Short *(Mgr-Digital Mktg)*
Terri Angelico *(Sr Acct Exec)*
Brooke Haley *(Acct Exec)*

Accounts:
Fredericksburg CVB

CREATIVE OPTIONS COMMUNICATIONS
1381 Colby Dr, Lewisville, TX 75067
Tel.: (972) 814-5723
Web Site: www.creativeoptionsmarketing.com

Employees: 3
Year Founded: 2007

Agency Specializes In: Advertising, Brand Development & Integration, Business Publications, Business-To-Business, Cable T.V., Communications, Direct Response Marketing, E-Commerce, Environmental, Event Planning & Marketing, Exhibit/Trade Shows, Food Service, Graphic Design, Identity Marketing, Internet/Web Design, Investor Relations, Magazines, Market Research, Media Buying Services, Newspaper, Newspapers & Magazines, Out-of-Home Media, Outdoor, Paid Searches, Point of Purchase, Point of Sale, Print, Public Relations, Publicity/Promotions, Radio, Real Estate, Seniors' Market, Sports Market, T.V., Travel & Tourism, Web (Banner Ads, Pop-ups, etc.)

Approx. Annual Billings: $300,000

David Drewitz *(Owner & Pres)*
Jed Jones *(Dir-Predictive Analytics)*
Cheryl Walling *(Acct Coord)*

Accounts:
Humane Society of Flower Mound Adoption & Donation; 2013

THE CREATIVE OUTHOUSE
6 W Druid Hills Dr NE Ste 310, Atlanta, GA 30329
Tel.: (404) 467-1773
Fax: (678) 732-3485
Web Site: www.creativeouthouse.com

Year Founded: 2001

Agency Specializes In: Advertising, Digital/Interactive, Media Planning, Print, Radio, T.V.

Rudy Fernandez *(Founder & Dir-Creative)*
Patrick Jung *(Sr Dir-Art)*
Harriet S. Berger *(Dir-Media)*
Mary Alice Cantrell *(Mgr-Print Production)*
Meredith Grant *(Acct Planner)*

Accounts:
Georgias State Road
Tollway Authority

CREATIVE PARTNERS
46 Southfield Ave, Stamford, CT 06902
Tel.: (203) 705-9200
Fax: (203) 705-9201
E-Mail: jkannon@creativepartners.com
Web Site: www.creativepartners.com

E-Mail for Key Personnel:
Chairman: pschelfhaudt@creativepartners.com

Employees: 30
Year Founded: 1986

Agency Specializes In: Advertising, Affluent Market, Brand Development & Integration, Broadcast, Business-To-Business, Cable T.V., Co-op Advertising, Collateral, Commercial Photography, Computers & Software, Consulting, Consumer Goods, Consumer Marketing, Consumer Publications, Corporate Communications, Corporate Identity, Digital/Interactive, Direct Response Marketing, Direct-to-Consumer, Education, Electronic Media, Electronics, Entertainment, Environmental, Event Planning & Marketing, Exhibit/Trade Shows, Financial, Food Service, Graphic Design, Health Care Services, High Technology, In-Store Advertising, Information Technology, Integrated Marketing, Internet/Web Design, Leisure, Local Marketing, Logo & Package Design, Luxury Products, Magazines, Market Research, Media Buying Services, Media Planning, Media Relations, Media Training, Mobile Marketing, Multimedia, New Technologies, Newspaper, Newspapers & Magazines, Out-of-Home Media, Outdoor, Package Design, Paid Searches, Print, Production (Print), Public Relations, Publicity/Promotions, Radio, Real Estate, Restaurant, Retail, Search Engine Optimization, Social Marketing/Nonprofit, Social Media, Sponsorship, Strategic Planning/Research, T.V., Trade & Consumer Magazines, Urban Market, Viral/Buzz/Word of Mouth

Approx. Annual Billings: $20,000,000 (Capitalized)

Breakdown of Gross Billings by Media: Collateral: 15%; Consulting: 5%; D.M.: 5%; Graphic Design: 2%; Internet Adv.: 8%; Print: 50%; Pub. Rels.: 15%

Peter Schelfhaudt *(Chm & CEO)*
Chuck Casto *(Sr VP)*
John Meagle *(Sr VP)*
Josh Moritz *(Sr VP-Interactive, Ecommerce & Social Media)*
Laura Saggese *(VP-Client Svcs)*
Kim Huelsman *(Dir-Creative)*
Farnosh Olamai *(Dir-Art)*
Cheryl Sergiano *(Office Mgr)*

Anahid Shahrik *(Strategist-PR & Social Media)*

Accounts:
Bulldog Investors
C.C. Filson
Citibank Global Transaction Services
Citigroup
Comforce
Commercial Defeasance
CVS PharmaCare
Dictaphone Healthcare Solutions
Health Net, Inc.
ICAP
Incredibles
Integral Development
Johnson & Johnson
Mantas
MBIA
Mercy Health Systems
Mitsubishi
NICE Systems
Novartis
Party City
Power Bar
QT
QuadraMed
Rochard Limoges
Sirius XM Radio Inc.
Skip Barber Racing
Small-Bone Innovations; New York, NY Orthopedic Devices for Hands & Feet; 2005
Storage Apps
Telekurs Financial
Titan Capital
Vinylume
West Jersey Health Systems

CREATIVE PARTNERS GROUP, INC.
409 Via Corta, Palos Verdes Estates, CA 90274
Tel.: (310) 378-8043
Fax: (310) 378-8053
E-Mail: gsparkman@creativepartnersgroup.com
Web Site: www.creativepartnersgroup.com

Employees: 4

Agency Specializes In: Advertising, Brand Development & Integration, Collateral, Communications, Direct Response Marketing, Exhibit/Trade Shows, Identity Marketing, Internet/Web Design, Local Marketing, Media Planning, Print, Public Relations

Greg Sparkman *(Pres)*

Accounts:
Cicoil Corp.
Gems Sensors & Control
IAC Industries
LISI Aerospace
The Monadnock Co.

CREATIVE PRESENCE PARTNERS, INC.
(Name Changed to MELT)

CREATIVE REPUBLIC
3714 N Southport Ave Garden Ste, Chicago, IL 60613
Tel.: (312) 265-8340
Fax: (312) 238-9471
Toll Free: (866) 572-5550
Web Site: www.creativerepublic.com

Agency Specializes In: Brand Development & Integration, Communications, Digital/Interactive, Environmental, Market Research, Print

Esther Tan *(CEO)*
Anthony Wong *(Exec Dir-Creative)*

Accounts:
Orr Associates Inc. Business Management Consulting Services
PRIMEWORKS Sdn Bhd. Content Management Services

CREATIVE RESOURCES GROUP
116 Long Pond Rd Ste W6, Plymouth, MA 02360
Tel.: (508) 830-0072
Fax: (508) 830-0826
E-Mail: info@meetcrg.com
Web Site: www.meetcrg.com

Agency Specializes In: Advertising, Brand Development & Integration, Crisis Communications, Digital/Interactive, Graphic Design, Internet/Web Design, Social Media, Strategic Planning/Research

Charlie Rasak *(Pres & Dir-Creative)*
Dawn Rasak *(CEO & Media Buyer)*
Dennis Huston *(VP & Dir-Art)*
Caleb Rasak *(Dir-Photography & Mgr-Production)*
Peter Cahill *(Dir-IT)*
Aymee Levis *(Office Mgr)*

Accounts:
Copeland Toyota
Holiday Vacation Condominiums
Kingston House of Pizza
MAIA Advantage

CREATIVE SOAPBOX
6015 Overland Rd Ste 104, Boise, ID 83709
Tel.: (208) 376-1334
E-Mail: info@creativesoapbox.com
Web Site: www.creativesoapbox.com

Year Founded: 2002

Agency Specializes In: Advertising, Brand Development & Integration, Digital/Interactive, Internet/Web Design, Package Design, Print

Justin Kuntz *(Owner & Dir-Creative)*
Chris Becker *(Designer)*
Mark Halley *(Coord-Logistics & Sys)*

Accounts:
D&D Transportation Services
High Country Plastics, Inc.

CREATIVE SOLUTIONS INTERNATIONAL
800 Delaware Ave Ste 410, Wilmington, DE 19810
Tel.: (302) 234-7407
Fax: (302) 234-7406
E-Mail: info@creative-solution.com
Web Site: www.creative-solution.com

Employees: 35
Year Founded: 1996

Agency Specializes In: Communications, Consumer Marketing, Direct Response Marketing, Strategic Planning/Research, Telemarketing

William F. Keenan *(Dir)*

Accounts:
AAA Mid-Atlantic
Academic Funding Foundation
Atlanticus Corporation
Barclays
Citibank
Discover
Disney
GE
GE Capital
HSBC
National Italian American Foundation
RBC Centura
RBC Royal Bank
Transport for London
Visa

CREATIVE STORM
(Formerly Dektas-Horwitz Advertising)
7588 Central Parke Blvd, Mason, OH 45040
Tel.: (513) 234-0560
Fax: (513) 770-4383
Toll Free: (800) 441-1199
E-Mail: linda@thecreativestorm.com
Web Site: www.thecreativestorm.com

Employees: 25
Year Founded: 1988

Agency Specializes In: Automotive, Aviation & Aerospace, Bilingual Market, Brand Development & Integration, Broadcast, Business Publications, Business-To-Business, Collateral, Consumer Marketing, Corporate Identity, Direct Response Marketing, E-Commerce, Electronic Media, Food Service, Graphic Design, Internet/Web Design, Logo & Package Design, Media Buying Services, Multimedia, New Product Development, Newspaper, Newspapers & Magazines, Outdoor, Point of Purchase, Point of Sale, Print, Public Relations, Publicity/Promotions, Radio, Real Estate, Restaurant, T.V., Trade & Consumer Magazines, Travel & Tourism

Approx. Annual Billings: $5,000,000

Linda Dektas *(Owner)*
Michael Dektas *(Pres)*
Margie Long *(Sr Dir-Art)*

Accounts:
Oasis Golf Community; Cincinnati, OH; 1994

THE CREATIVE STRATEGY AGENCY
1350 Main St Ste 1506, Springfield, MA 01103
Tel.: (413) 455-2371
E-Mail: info@tcsaonline.com
Web Site: www.tcsaonline.com

Year Founded: 2009

Agency Specializes In: Advertising, Crisis Communications, Digital/Interactive, Media Buying Services, Media Planning, Media Relations, Print, Radio, Social Media, Strategic Planning/Research

Alfonso Santaniello *(Pres & CEO)*
Jesse Tolan *(Coord-Digital Media)*

Accounts:
Euro Coiffure Salon

CREATIVE VIDEO
26 Colonial Ave, Woodbury, NJ 08096
Tel.: (856) 848-0046
Fax: (856) 848-8905
Toll Free: (888) 988-2877
E-Mail: contact@creativevideo.org
Web Site: http://www.creativevisualproductions.com/

Employees: 7
Year Founded: 1993

Agency Specializes In: Advertising, Advertising Specialties, Alternative Advertising, Branded Entertainment, Broadcast, Business Publications, Cable T.V., Communications, Corporate Communications, Custom Publishing, Digital/Interactive, Email, Entertainment, Event Planning & Marketing, Graphic Design, Internet/Web Design, Media Planning, Multimedia, New Technologies, Planning & Consultation, Print, Production, Production (Ad, Film, Broadcast), Production (Print), Promotions,

REDBOOKS
Brands. Marketers. Agencies. Search Less. Find More.
Try out the Online version at www.redbooks.com

Publicity/Promotions, Search Engine Optimization, Social Media, T.V.

Vince Cocciolone *(Pres)*

CREATIVELLO
3931 1st Ave S, Seattle, WA 98134
Tel.: (206) 931-0110
Web Site: www.creativello.com

Agency Specializes In: Advertising, Graphic Design, Internet/Web Design, Logo & Package Design, Print, Social Media

Accounts:
Run Studios

CREATIVE:MINT LLC
667 Mission St, San Francisco, CA 94105
Tel.: (415) 362-9991
Fax: (415) 362-9994
E-Mail: info@creativemint.com
Web Site: www.creativemint.com

Year Founded: 2013

Agency Specializes In: Advertising, Brand Development & Integration

Calvin Jung *(Founder, Owner & Grp Dir-Creative)*
Haig Bedrossian *(Dir-Creative-NY)*

Accounts:
Aerohive Networks
Alpine Meadows Ski Resort
Butterfield Bank
Capitol Corridor Transit Commission
Charles Schwab
Essex Property Trust
Extreme Networks
Fairmont Hotels & Resorts
Fidelity Investments
Ghiradelli Square
Hanson Bridgett
Highgate Hotels
Homewood Ski Resort
Host Hotels
InfoUSA
Kahuaina Plantation
Kimpton Hotels
Larkspur Hotels
Lucky Dragon Vegas Casino
M.Y. China
Nuix
Pershing
Recommind
Regis Office Solutions
Rosewood Hotels & Resorts LLC
Solairus Aviation
TD Ameritrade
Vocera Communications
Wilson Sonsini

CREATIVEONDEMAND
2601 S Bayshore Dr Ste 1400, Coconut Grove, FL 33133
Tel.: (305) 529-6464
Fax: (305) 854-9150
E-Mail: info@creativeondemand.com
Web Site: www.creativeondemand.com

Employees: 11

Agency Specializes In: Bilingual Market, Hispanic Market, Sponsorship

Daniel Marrero *(Founder, Owner & Partner)*
Priscilla Cortizas *(Partner)*
Priscilla Marrero *(Partner)*
Jim Leon *(VP-Brand Strategy & Integrated Mktg)*
Brian K. Thomas *(Gen Mgr-Brand Mktg)*
Jose Guerrero *(Dir-Art)*
Felix Ovalle *(Dir-Art)*
Jimmy Pino *(Dir-Digital)*
Chris Churchill *(Assoc Dir-Creative & Copywriter)*
Martin Menendez *(Acct Supvr)*

Accounts:
Regions Financial Corporation Regions Bank
Volkswagen Group of America, Inc. Campaign: "Airport", Campaign: "Keep it Clean", Campaign: "Play by Play", VW Touareg, Volkswagen Service

CREATURE
1517 12th Ave, Seattle, WA 98122
Tel.: (206) 625-6994
Fax: (206) 625-6904
E-Mail: hilaryl@creature-us.com
Web Site: www.welcometocreature.com

Employees: 38

Agency Specializes In: Advertising, Consumer Marketing, Food Service, Multimedia, Sponsorship, Sports Market, T.V.

Revenue: $2,000,000

Matt Peterson *(Co-Founder & CEO)*
Jim Haven *(Co-Founder & Chief Creative Officer)*
James Keblas *(Pres)*
Stuart Outhwaite *(Partner-Creative-London)*
Linda Halverson *(Mng Dir)*
Adam Bailey *(Dir-Creative)*
Steve Cullen *(Dir-Design & Creative)*
Clara Mulligan *(Dir-Design & Creative)*
Kristie Shields *(Dir-Media Strategy)*
Kelly Stephenson *(Dir-Brand Strategy)*
Jake Eastman *(Strategist-Media)*
Nathan Young *(Strategist-Insights)*

Accounts:
Cargill Campaign: "From Nature. For Sweetness", Campaign: "Sweet Switch", Creative, Truvia
Children's Film Festival; Seattle, WA Campaign: "Neurons"
Dickies Campaign: "Built To Work", Creative
DoubleDown Interactive "Office", Campaign: "Bedtime", Creative
JanSport
Kigo Kitchen
Mondelez International, Inc.
Nuun
Seattle Office of Film & Music
Seattle's Best Coffee Campaign: "Seattle's Best Coffee Spring Promotion"
Starbucks Seattle's Best; 2003
Washington Filmworks

CREAXION CORPORATION
1230 Peachtree St NE Ste 925, Atlanta, GA 30309
Tel.: (404) 321-4322
Fax: (404) 495-4421
E-Mail: info@creaxion.com
Web Site: www.creaxion.com

Employees: 14
Year Founded: 1998

National Agency Associations: AMA-PRSA

Agency Specializes In: Advertising, Automotive, Brand Development & Integration, Broadcast, Business-To-Business, Collateral, Communications, Consumer Marketing, Corporate Communications, Corporate Identity, Entertainment, Event Planning & Marketing, Gay & Lesbian Market, Graphic Design, High Technology, In-Store Advertising, Integrated Marketing, Local Marketing, Luxury Products, Media Buying Services, Media Planning, Media Relations, Media Training, Planning & Consultation, Point of Purchase, Promotions, Public Relations, Publicity/Promotions, Strategic Planning/Research, T.V., Travel & Tourism

Approx. Annual Billings: $2,100,000

Mark Pettit *(Pres & CEO)*
Ted Tuerk *(COO)*
Marcelo Galvao *(Dir-Creative)*
Scott Smallwood *(Sr Mgr-Mktg & Media)*
Liz Opsahl *(Office Mgr)*
Kerrie Levick *(Mgr-Mktg & Media)*
Kyndra Marshall *(Specialist-Mktg & Media)*

Accounts:
AT&T Communications Corp.
Bill Lowe Gallery
iBill
King Tut
Titanic The Artifact Exhibition
United States Obstacle Course Racing Creative, Marketing Strategy, Partnership Development, Public Relations, Social Media
World Wildlife Fund
WWF

CRENDO
750 Van Buren Dr NW, Salem, OR 97304-3547
Tel.: (503) 399-4774
Toll Free: (866) 816-3929
E-Mail: info@crendo.com
Web Site: www.crendo.com

Employees: 2
Year Founded: 1995

Agency Specializes In: Brand Development & Integration, Direct Response Marketing, Internet/Web Design, Logo & Package Design, Print

Bruce M. Hart *(Co-Owner)*
Tamra Heathershaw-Hart *(Partner)*

Accounts:
Flying Lizard Motor Sports
Invati Capital LLC
Verific Design Automation

CRESTA CREATIVE
1050 N State St, Chicago, IL 60610
Tel.: (312) 944-4700
Fax: (312) 944-1582
E-Mail: joanb@crestagroup.com
Web Site: www.crestacreative.com

Employees: 12
Year Founded: 1987

National Agency Associations: BMA

Agency Specializes In: Advertising, Advertising Specialties, Brand Development & Integration, Business Publications, Business-To-Business, Collateral, Commercial Photography, Communications, Consulting, Consumer Marketing, Corporate Communications, Corporate Identity, E-Commerce, Event Planning & Marketing, Exhibit/Trade Shows, Faith Based, Financial, Graphic Design, In-Store Advertising, Internet/Web Design, Investor Relations, Local Marketing, Logo & Package Design, Media Buying Services, Media Planning, Multimedia, New Product Development, Newspapers & Magazines, Pharmaceutical, Planning & Consultation, Print, Production, Production (Print), Public Relations, Radio, Recruitment, Sales Promotion, Social Marketing/Nonprofit, Sports Market, Strategic Planning/Research, Women's Market

Approx. Annual Billings: $4,000,000

Breakdown of Gross Billings by Media: Audio/Visual: 15%; Collateral: 10%; Comml. Photography: 10%; Corp. Communications: 40%; Exhibits/Trade Shows: 5%; Graphic Design: 10%; Print: 10%

Joan Beth Beugen *(Founder & Dir-Creative)*
Naomi Yamada *(VP-Production)*
David Amling *(Editor & Dir-Art)*
Deborah Benson-Winans *(Office Mgr & Sr Producer-Cresta Creative)*

Accounts:
ABA-Section of Litigation
ASCO Sintering Co.
Abbott Laboratories
Airbus North America
American Medical Association
Apple Inc.
Aramark
Arzu Inc.
BEA Systems
Baxter International
AT&T Southeast
Caterpillar Inc.
Catholic Church
The Chicago Network
City of Bakersfield, CA
Coal Innovations LLC
Coca-Cola Refreshments USA, Inc.
Delta Air Lines Inc.
Fifield Companies
HSBC
Hines
JMB Insurance
JPMorgan Chase & Company
Jenner & Block
Jones Lang LaSalle
La Petite Academy
McDonald's Corporation
Midwest Theological Forum
Monsanto Company
Navistar International
Nortel Networks
Opus Dei
Prism: Premier Integrated Sports Management
Sheila Kelley S Factor
Shell Oil Company
SpaRitual
Westfield

Branch

Cresta West
6815 Willoughby Ave Ste 102, Los Angeles, CA 90038
Tel.: (323) 939-7003
Fax: (323) 939-7002
Web Site: www.crestacreative.com

Employees: 5

Agency Specializes In: Brand Development & Integration, Broadcast, Business Publications, Business-To-Business, Commercial Photography, Communications, Consulting, Corporate Identity, Event Planning & Marketing, Exhibit/Trade Shows, Graphic Design, In-Store Advertising, Multimedia, New Product Development, Print, Production, Strategic Planning/Research

Joan Beth Beugen *(Pres & Dir-Creative)*
Naomi Yamada *(VP-Production)*
David Amling *(Editor & Dir-Art)*
Debby Benson-Winans *(Sr Producer & Mgr-Office-Cresta Creative)*

Accounts:
Coca-Cola Refreshments USA, Inc.

CREVIN AMD
127 N Higgins Ave, Missoula, MT 59802
Tel.: (406) 549-8492
Web Site: www.crevinamd.com

Agency Specializes In: Advertising, Collateral, Graphic Design, Internet/Web Design, Logo & Package Design, Media Buying Services, Media Planning, Outdoor, Print, Radio

Craig Piazza *(Principal)*
Kevin Piazza *(Principal)*

Accounts:
Attic RRG
Chicks N Chaps
DreamSleep Mattresses
Florence Volunteer Fire Department
Gateway Community Credit Union
Mainstreet Uptown Butte Montana Folk Festival
Valley Physical Therapy

CRIER COMMUNICATIONS
9507 Santa Monica Blvd Ste 300, Beverly Hills, CA 90210
Tel.: (310) 274-1072
Fax: (310) 274-0611
E-Mail: info@crierpr.com
Web Site: www.crierpr.com

Employees: 10

J.P. Lincoln *(Owner)*
Jenna Benty *(Dir-Art)*
Amy Chase *(Dir-Social Media)*
Kathleen Day *(Dir-Art)*
Michal Adut *(Acct Exec)*
Brynn Cahalan *(Strategist-Social Media)*
Mallory Liebhaber *(Acct Exec)*
Devin Pence *(Acct Exec)*
T-Aira Sims *(Acct Exec)*
Lauren Pill *(Graphic Designer-Social Media)*
Danielle Caldwell *(Coord-Mktg & Comm)*

Accounts:
Barbara's Bakery
Cedarlane Natural Foods Media Relations, Public Relations
Crunchies
Dole Nutrition Institute
Edward & Sons
Flax USA
The Fresh Diet
Helen's Kitchen

CRISTOL MARKETING COMPANY
237 Hunt Club Blvd Ste 102, Longwood, FL 32779
Tel.: (407) 774-2515
Fax: (407) 774-6647
E-Mail: khc@crismktg.com
Web Site: www.crismktg.com

Employees: 2

Agency Specializes In: Advertising, Brand Development & Integration, Corporate Communications, Public Relations, Publicity/Promotions, Strategic Planning/Research

Accounts:
Konover; Boca Raton, Fl; 2005
Pineloch Management Company; 2005
Roger B. Kennedy, Inc.
Tri-City Electrical Contractors, Inc.

CRITEO
411 High Street, Palo Alto, CA 94301
Tel.: (650) 322-6260
Fax: (650) 322-6159
Web Site: www.criteo.com

Year Founded: 2005

Agency Specializes In: Advertising

Jean-Baptiste Rudelle *(Founder & CEO)*
Romain Niccoli *(Co-Founder & CTO)*
Benoit Fouilland *(CFO)*
Mollie Spilman *(Chief Revenue Officer)*
Sheila Buckley *(Sr VP & Head-Sls)*
Len Ostroff *(VP-Global Data Partnerships)*
Sean Simon *(VP-Sls-West)*
Tom St. John *(VP-Bus Dev-NA)*
Cynthia Tully *(VP-Acct Strategy)*
Joshua Petuchowski *(Dir-Sales)*
Friederike Edelmann *(Sr Mgr-IR)*

Accounts:
Glasses Direct Optical Store
La Redoute Men's & Women's Apparel Stores
Plumworld Bathroom Furniture Stores

CRITICAL LAUNCH, LLC
208 N Market St Ste 250, Dallas, TX 75202
Tel.: (214) 702-5436
E-Mail: liftoff@criticallaunch.com
Web Site: www.criticallaunch.com

Employees: 3
Year Founded: 2015

Agency Specializes In: Above-the-Line, Advertising, Advertising Specialties, Affiliate Marketing, Affluent Market, African-American Market, Agriculture, Alternative Advertising, Arts, Asian Market, Automotive, Aviation & Aerospace, Below-the-Line, Bilingual Market, Brand Development & Integration, Branded Entertainment, Broadcast, Business Publications, Business-To-Business, Cable T.V., Catalogs, Children's Market, Co-op Advertising, Collateral, College, Commercial Photography, Communications, Computers & Software, Consulting, Consumer Goods, Consumer Marketing, Consumer Publications, Content, Corporate Communications, Corporate Identity, Cosmetics, Crisis Communications, Custom Publishing, Customer Relationship Management, Digital/Interactive, Direct Response Marketing, Direct-to-Consumer, E-Commerce, Education, Electronic Media, Electronics, Email, Engineering, Entertainment, Environmental, Event Planning & Marketing, Exhibit/Trade Shows, Experience Design, Faith Based, Fashion/Apparel, Financial, Food Service, Game Integration, Gay & Lesbian Market, Government/Political, Graphic Design, Guerilla Marketing, Health Care Services, High Technology, Hispanic Market, Hospitality, Household Goods, Identity Marketing, In-Store Advertising, Industrial, Infomercials, Information Technology, Integrated Marketing, International, Internet/Web Design, Investor Relations, Legal Services, Leisure, Local Marketing, Logo & Package Design, Luxury Products, Magazines, Marine, Market Research, Media Buying Services, Media Planning, Media Relations, Media Training, Medical Products, Men's Market, Merchandising, Mobile Marketing, Multicultural, Multimedia, New Product Development, New Technologies, Newspaper, Newspapers & Magazines, Out-of-Home Media, Outdoor, Over-50 Market, Package Design, Paid Searches, Pets , Pharmaceutical, Planning & Consultation, Podcasting, Point of Purchase, Point of Sale, Print, Product Placement, Production, Production (Ad, Film, Broadcast), Production (Print), Promotions, Public Relations, Publicity/Promotions, Publishing, RSS (Really Simple Syndication), Radio, Real Estate, Recruitment, Regional, Restaurant, Retail, Sales Promotion, Search Engine Optimization, Seniors' Market, Shopper Marketing, Social Marketing/Nonprofit, Social Media, South Asian Market, Sponsorship, Sports Market, Stakeholders, Strategic Planning/Research, Sweepstakes, Syndication, T.V., Technical Advertising, Teen

Market, Telemarketing, Trade & Consumer Magazines, Transportation, Travel & Tourism, Tween Market, Urban Market, Viral/Buzz/Word of Mouth, Web (Banner Ads, Pop-ups, etc.), Women's Market, Yellow Pages Advertising

Approx. Annual Billings: $144,000

Tracy Nanthavongsa *(Dir-Creative)*

Accounts:
Dallas County District Attorney's Office

CRITICAL MASS INC.
402 11th Ave SE, Calgary, AB T2G 0Y4 Canada
Tel.: (403) 262-3006
Fax: (403) 262-7185
E-Mail: calrec@criticalmass.com
Web Site: www.criticalmass.com

Employees: 300
Year Founded: 1995

Agency Specializes In: Aviation & Aerospace, Brand Development & Integration, Corporate Identity, Digital/Interactive, Direct Response Marketing, E-Commerce, Electronic Media, Graphic Design, Health Care Services, High Technology, Information Technology, Internet/Web Design, Media Buying Services, Medical Products, Multimedia, New Technologies, Pharmaceutical, Strategic Planning/Research

Chris Gokiert *(Pres)*
Dianne Wilkins *(CEO)*
Lee Tamkee *(CFO & Sr VP)*
John McLaughlin *(COO)*
Jason Delichte *(VP & Exec Dir-Creative)*
Jocelyn Loria *(VP-Fin)*
Steve Savic *(Exec Dir-Creative)*
Christiaan Welzel *(Dir-Creative)*
Stephanie Warthe *(Mgr-SEO)*

Accounts:
Best Buy
Calgary Stampede Campaign Development, Digital, Mobile, Web
Clorox
House of Anansi Press
Infiniti (Agency of Record)
Moen Digital
Nissan Campaign: "Kinect Experience", Campaign: "Nissan GT Academy", Campaign: "Real Owners, Real Answers", Campaign: "Real Owners. Real Questions"
Travel Alberta Digital, Marketing
New-United Nations Mine Action Service Campaign: "Sweeper"

Branches

Critical Mass Inc.
1 Riverside, Manbre Rd, London, W6 9WA United Kingdom
Tel.: (44) 208 735 8750
Fax: (44) 208 735 8751
E-Mail: london@criticalmass.com
Web Site: www.criticalmass.com

Employees: 50

Matt Kwiecinski *(Mng Dir)*
Conor Brady *(Chief Creative Officer)*
Susanne Jones *(Sr VP & Mng Dir-London)*
Sacha Reeb *(Exec Dir-Creative)*
Alistair Millen *(Dir-Plng)*

Accounts:
Citi
Goodyear Dunlop Tyres EMEA, Social Media Community Management, Strategy
Green Works Branding
HP
Nissan Campaign: "Your Door to More", Versa Note
South African Tourism Creative, Digital

Critical Mass Inc.
425 Adelaide St W 10th Fl, Toronto, ON M5V 3C1 Canada
Tel.: (416) 673-5275
Fax: (416) 673-5305 (Reception)
E-Mail: toronto@criticalmass.com
Web Site: www.criticalmass.com

Employees: 100

Agency Specializes In: Advertising

Shannon McEvoy-Halston *(VP-Strategy)*
Brian Allen *(Sr Dir-Art)*
Jason Holley *(Grp Acct Dir)*
Alessandro Drago *(Creative Dir)*
Annie Bedard *(Dir-Strategy)*
Christina Yu *(Acct Mgr)*
Dylan Gerard *(Assoc Creative Dir)*

Accounts:
Creative Reel
LVCVA
Mercedes-Benz
More
Nissan Canada Inc.
Nissan North America, Inc.
Rolex

Critical Mass Inc.
225 N Michigan Ave Ste 2050, Chicago, IL 60601-7757
(See Separate Listing)

Critical Mass Inc.
30 Irving Pl 5th Fl, New York, NY 10022
Tel.: (212) 801-8350
Fax: (212) 801-8351
E-Mail: newyork@criticalmass.com
Web Site: www.criticalmass.com

Employees: 5

National Agency Associations: 4A's

Agency Specializes In: Brand Development & Integration, Digital/Interactive, E-Commerce, Electronic Media, Internet/Web Design, Strategic Planning/Research

Conor Brady *(Chief Creative Officer)*
Darryl Braunmiller *(Sr VP & Gen Mgr)*
Denise Duley *(VP & Client Partner)*
Diane Heun *(VP-Bus Dev)*
Emily Duban *(Sr Dir-Client)*
Robert Michaels *(Sr Acct Dir)*
Marta Czosnowski *(Acct Dir)*
Kelly Ladwig *(Acct Dir-Nissan Comml Vehicles)*
Tess Kiskaddon *(Sr Acct Mgr)*
Lindsay Carter *(Acct Mgr-Digital-Nissan USA)*
Eric Jaffe *(Acct Mgr)*

Accounts:
Hewlett-Packard Company

CRITTENDEN ADVERTISING
1111 Haynes St Ste 205, Raleigh, NC 27604
Tel.: (919) 859-5551
Fax: (919) 859-5589
E-Mail: dcrittenden@critadv.com
Web Site: www.crittendenadvertising.com/

E-Mail for Key Personnel:
President: dcrittenden@critadv.com

Employees: 8
Year Founded: 1993

National Agency Associations: Second Wind Limited

Agency Specializes In: Corporate Identity, Digital/Interactive, Direct Response Marketing, Logo & Package Design, Production, Public Relations, Sponsorship, Strategic Planning/Research

David E. Crittenden *(Owner)*

Accounts:
Klein Decisions
March of Dimes
Towncare Dental (Agency of Record)

CRONIN & COMPANY, INC.
50 Nye Rd, Glastonbury, CT 06033-1280
Tel.: (860) 659-0514
Fax: (860) 659-3455
E-Mail: dwoodruff@cronin-co.com
Web Site: www.cronin-co.com

Employees: 55
Year Founded: 1947

National Agency Associations: 4A's

Agency Specializes In: Advertising, Aviation & Aerospace, Brand Development & Integration, Broadcast, Business Publications, Business-To-Business, Collateral, Consumer Marketing, Consumer Publications, Direct Response Marketing, E-Commerce, Electronic Media, Financial, Food Service, Health Care Services, High Technology, Information Technology, Internet/Web Design, Investor Relations, Logo & Package Design, Magazines, Media Buying Services, Newspaper, Newspapers & Magazines, Out-of-Home Media, Outdoor, Pharmaceutical, Point of Purchase, Point of Sale, Print, Production, Public Relations, Publicity/Promotions, Radio, Recruitment, Restaurant, Retail, Sponsorship, T.V., Trade & Consumer Magazines

Approx. Annual Billings: $65,000,000

Kimberly Manning *(COO & Principal)*
Wayne Raicik *(Sr VP & Dir-Creative)*
Betsey Gainey *(VP & Dir-Client Svcs)*
AnnMarie Kemp *(VP & Dir-PR)*
Mia Walters *(VP & Dir-Interactive Svcs)*
Diane Woodruff *(VP & Dir-Bus Dev)*
Kristen Ganci *(Jr Dir-Interactive Art)*
Frank Rinaldi *(Acct Dir)*
Daniel Gallo *(Dir-IT)*
Micah Murray *(Sr Project Mgr-Interactive)*
Helen Chung *(Project Mgr-Interactive)*
Nicole Stavola *(Project Mgr-Interactive)*
Charlene Durham *(Sr Acct Supvr-PR)*
Sarah Melnitsky *(Sr Acct Supvr)*
Melanie Zombik *(Sr Acct Supvr)*
Emily Albohm *(Acct Supvr)*
Suzanne Carbonella *(Acct Supvr)*
Laura Cirillo *(Supvr-Media)*
Tracy Klimkoski *(Supvr-Media & Analytics)*
Kate Anderson *(Sr Acct Exec)*
Emily Erdman *(Sr Acct Exec)*
Danielle Morfi *(Sr Acct Exec)*
Elizabeth Pace *(Sr Acct Exec)*
Bridget Cordero *(Acct Exec-PR)*
Joslyn McArdle *(Acct Exec)*
Michelle Szafranski *(Acct Exec)*
David Young *(Analyst-Search Mktg)*
Elise Prairie *(Asst Acct Exec)*
Tracy Demars *(Coord-Media)*

Accounts:
Alouette
Amerifit Brands
Amica Mutual Insurance Co.; 2004

Baronet Coffee
Benihana; 2008
Bernie's
Connecticut Children's Medical Center Advertising
Connecticut Green Bank Marketing
Eversource; 1997
Evolution Benefits
Executive Wealth Management Paid Search Marketing, Public Relations Program, Website Redesign
Friendship Dairies Dairy Products; 1999
i-Health, Inc.
International Aero Engines Aerospace; 1985
Liberty Bank; 2003
MassMutual
McDonald's Corporation
McDonald's Operators of the Capital District Public Relations
Middlesex Hospital; 2003
Montefiore Medical Center (Agency of Record)
Neopost USA Direct Mail Campaign, Microsite
Nestle USA, Inc.
Ronald McDonald House Charities
Twinings Tea ,USA
UConn Health Advertising
Vytra Health Plans; Melville, NY Healthcare Services; 2000
Wadsworth Atheneum Museum of Art
Women's Health Connecticut Marketing, New Logo, Rebranding Campaign, Website Redesign

CROSBY MARKETING COMMUNICATIONS

705 Melvin Ave Ste 200, Annapolis, MD 21401-1540
Tel.: (410) 626-0805
Fax: (410) 269-6547
Web Site: www.crosbymarketing.com

E-Mail for Key Personnel:
President: raycrosby@crosbymarketing.com

Employees: 50
Year Founded: 1973

National Agency Associations: 4A's-AMA-COPF-DMA-PRSA-Second Wind Limited

Agency Specializes In: Advertising, Affluent Market, Brand Development & Integration, Broadcast, Business Publications, Business-To-Business, Cable T.V., Collateral, College, Communications, Consumer Marketing, Corporate Communications, Corporate Identity, Crisis Communications, Digital/Interactive, Direct Response Marketing, Education, Event Planning & Marketing, Financial, Government/Political, Graphic Design, Guerilla Marketing, Health Care Services, High Technology, Integrated Marketing, Internet/Web Design, Legal Services, Logo & Package Design, Luxury Products, Market Research, Media Buying Services, Media Planning, Media Relations, Medical Products, Mobile Marketing, Multimedia, Newspaper, Out-of-Home Media, Outdoor, Over-50 Market, Planning & Consultation, Print, Public Relations, Publicity/Promotions, Radio, Real Estate, Recruitment, Retail, Search Engine Optimization, Seniors' Market, Social Marketing/Nonprofit, Social Media, Strategic Planning/Research, T.V., Teen Market, Transportation

Approx. Annual Billings: $58,000,000

Ralph W. Crosby *(Chm)*
Raymond Crosby *(Pres & CEO)*
Denise Aube *(Exec VP & Head-Healthcare Practice)*
Jeff Rosenberg *(Exec VP & Head-Advocacy & Social Mktg Practice)*
Anna Zawislanski *(Exec VP & Sr Strategist)*
Meredith Williams *(Exec VP)*
Suresh John *(VP-Digital Strategy & Analytics)*
Linda Raaf *(Controller)*
Elise A. Kolaja *(Dir-Creative)*
Ron Ordansa *(Dir-Creative)*
Scott Rasmussen *(Dir-Creative)*
Tim Staines *(Dir-Digital Program Mgmt)*
Abebe Kebede *(Mgr-Integration)*
Charles Hoehlein *(Supvr-Connection Plng)*

Accounts:
DuPont; Wilmington, DE; 1998
Kaiser Permanente; Rockville, MD; 1996
National Association of Social Workers; Washington, DC; 2003
Pennrose Multifamily Development & Property Management
New-Sheppard Pratt Health System Advertising, Digital
Social Security Administration; Washington, DC Paid Media, Print, Web; 2008
U.S. Dept. of Agriculture; Washington, DC; 2004
Vietnam Veterans of America; Washington, DC Online Promotions, Social Media, Website; 2010
Wallace Foundation

Branch

Crosby Marketing Communications

(Formerly Low + Associates)
4550 Montgomery Ave Ste 790 N, Bethesda, MD 20814
Tel.: (301) 951-9200
Fax: (301) 986-1641
Web Site: crosbymarketing.com

Employees: 15
Year Founded: 1979

National Agency Associations: 4A's

Agency Specializes In: Advertising, Affluent Market, Brand Development & Integration, Broadcast, Business-To-Business, Cable T.V., Collateral, College, Communications, Consumer Publications, Corporate Communications, Crisis Communications, Custom Publishing, Digital/Interactive, Direct-to-Consumer, Education, Email, Event Planning & Marketing, Exhibit/Trade Shows, Financial, Government/Political, Graphic Design, Guerilla Marketing, Health Care Services, High Technology, Hispanic Market, Integrated Marketing, Internet/Web Design, Logo & Package Design, Market Research, Media Buying Services, Media Relations, Multicultural, Multimedia, Newspaper, Out-of-Home Media, Over-50 Market, Publicity/Promotions, Real Estate, Recruitment, Search Engine Optimization, Seniors' Market, Social Marketing/Nonprofit, Strategic Planning/Research, T.V., Teen Market, Trade & Consumer Magazines, Web (Banner Ads, Pop-ups, etc.)

Tammy Campbell-Ebaugh *(Chief Strategy Officer & Exec VP)*
Meredith Williams *(Exec VP & Co-Head-Govt Practice)*
Tim Labus *(Gen Mgr)*
Joel Machak *(Exec Dir-Creative)*
Anthony Manzanares *(Dir-Art & Designer-Visual)*
Madeline Beck *(Dir-Integration)*
Amy Guilfoy Inglesby *(Dir-Integration)*
Scott Rasmussen *(Dir-Creative)*

CROSBY-WRIGHT

5907 N Rocking Rd, Scottsdale, AZ 85250
Tel.: (480) 367-1112
Fax: (480) 368-9913
E-Mail: info@crosby-wright.com
Web Site: www.crosby-wright.com

Employees: 20
Year Founded: 1991

Agency Specializes In: Advertising, Crisis Communications, Direct Response Marketing, Internet/Web Design, Media Buying Services, Media Planning, Media Relations, Media Training, Public Relations, Strategic Planning/Research

Valerie Crosby *(Pres)*
Paul Bowers *(Partner & Principal)*
Bill Dwinell *(Dir-Tech)*
Erica Lange *(Sr Acct Exec)*

Accounts:
Aloft Tempe Hotels & Resorts
CarePatrol Brand Strategy, Creative Messaging, Marketing, Public Relations
D-BOX Technologies Inc. Motion Systems Mfr
Gator Branding
Kitchell Custom Homes
Nanolite
Pay Your Family First
The RoomStore Public Relations, Social Media
The Shops On El Paseo Shopping Mall
SkyMed International, Inc Marketing, PR
Toby Keith's I Love This Bar & Grill (Public Relations Agency Of Record) Media Communication
Ultrastar Cinemas
Vallone Design
The Wigwam Golf Resort & Spa Resorts

CROSS MEDIAWORKS

701 San Marco Blvd Ste 1603, Jacksonville, FL 32207
Tel.: (904) 642-8902
Fax: (904) 642-8916
E-Mail: info@thecrossagency.com
Web Site: www.thecrossagency.com

Agency Specializes In: Advertising, Digital/Interactive, Logo & Package Design, Print, Social Media, Strategic Planning/Research

Stephanie Mitchko *(CTO)*
Jim Tricarico *(Chief Revenue Officer)*
Jon Nicolosi *(Exec VP & Exec Dir-Creative)*
Natalie Wollet *(VP-Media)*
Colin Williams *(Dir-Digital Media-Mktg)*
Daniel Gulick *(Acct Mgr)*
Luz Marie Caro *(Generalist-HR)*
Greg Mclean *(Coord-Media Svcs)*

Accounts:
Kiawah

CROSSBOW GROUP, LLC

136 Main St, Westport, CT 06880
Tel.: (203) 222-2244
Fax: (203) 226-7838
E-Mail: info@crossbowgroup.com
Web Site: www.crossbowgroup.com

Employees: 15
Year Founded: 1984

National Agency Associations: CADM-DMA-DMCNY-NEDMA

Agency Specializes In: Above-the-Line, Advertising, Advertising Specialties, Affiliate Marketing, Affluent Market, Alternative Advertising, Below-the-Line, Bilingual Market, Brand Development & Integration, Broadcast, Business Publications, Business-To-Business, Catalogs, Children's Market, Collateral, Communications, Computers & Software, Consulting, Consumer Goods, Consumer Marketing, Consumer Publications, Corporate Communications, Corporate Identity, Custom Publishing, Customer Relationship Management, Digital/Interactive, Direct Response Marketing, Direct-to-Consumer, E-Commerce, Education, Electronic Media, Email, Exhibit/Trade Shows, Financial, Government/Political, Graphic Design, High

Technology, Identity Marketing, Information Technology, Integrated Marketing, Internet/Web Design, Investor Relations, Leisure, Luxury Products, Magazines, Market Research, Media Planning, Mobile Marketing, Multimedia, Newspapers & Magazines, Paid Searches, Planning & Consultation, Podcasting, Print, Production, Production (Print), Promotions, Publishing, Radio, Sales Promotion, Search Engine Optimization, Social Marketing/Nonprofit, Social Media, Sponsorship, Strategic Planning/Research, Sweepstakes, Technical Advertising, Trade & Consumer Magazines, Travel & Tourism, Web (Banner Ads, Pop-ups, etc.)

Approx. Annual Billings: $15,000,000

Mary Plamieniak *(Owner & VP)*
Jay Bower *(Pres & CEO)*

Accounts:
BitDefender
CIGNA
Clean Harbors Strategic Communications
Connance Healthcare Technology Service Provider
Empowering Writers
Intuit
MetLife
Netezza
Numara
Sassy Inc. Direct Marketing, E-Mail, Infant Bathing Products, Infant Feeding Products, Infant Toys, Mobile, Social Media
Tauck World Discovery
TBM

CROSSOVER CREATIVE GROUP

2643 Appian Way Ste J, Pinole, CA 94564
Tel.: (510) 222-5030
Fax: (510) 222-5830
E-Mail: mapplegate@crossovercreative.com
Web Site: www.crossovercreative.com

E-Mail for Key Personnel:
President: sclimons@crossovercreative.com

Employees: 12
Year Founded: 1996

Agency Specializes In: Advertising, African-American Market, Asian Market, Bilingual Market, Brand Development & Integration, Broadcast, Collateral, Communications, Consulting, Consumer Marketing, Corporate Identity, Event Planning & Marketing, Financial, Government/Political, Graphic Design, Hispanic Market, Logo & Package Design, Merchandising, Multimedia, Outdoor, Planning & Consultation, Print, Production, Public Relations, Publicity/Promotions, Radio, Retail, Sales Promotion, Strategic Planning/Research, T.V.

Approx. Annual Billings: $10,000,000

Breakdown of Gross Billings by Media: Mags.: 3%; Newsp.: 7%; Outdoor: 5%; Radio: 80%; Spot T.V.: 5%

Steve Climons *(Founder, Pres & Dir-Creative)*
Sharyn O'Keefe *(Dir-Bus Dev)*

Accounts:
Oakland Police Department
VirnetX

CROSSROADS

1740 Main St, Kansas City, MO 64108
Tel.: (816) 679-8502
Web Site: crossroads.us

National Agency Associations: 4A's

Agency Specializes In: Advertising, Brand Development & Integration

Mike Swenson, *(Pres)*
Jennifer Cawley *(VP)*
Lindsey Dewitte *(VP)*
Wendy Fitch *(VP)*
Brooke Ehlers *(Acct Dir)*
Sarah Ferguson *(Acct Dir)*
Anita Strohm *(Acct Dir)*
Chase Wagner *(Acct Dir)*

Accounts:
New-Applebee's
New-Blue Bunny
New-Dawn
New-ITC
New-Lee
New-March of Dimes
New-Pump It Up
New-Quiznos
New-Sonny's BBQ
New-Susan G. Komen
New-Vanity Fair

CROWL, MONTGOMERY & CLARK

713 S Main St, North Canton, OH 44720
Tel.: (330) 494-6999
Fax: (330) 494-6242
Toll Free: (888) 649-8745
E-Mail: rodmcgregor@crowlinc.com
Web Site: www.crowlinc.com

Employees: 22
Year Founded: 1959

National Agency Associations: AAF

Agency Specializes In: Direct Response Marketing, Internet/Web Design, Public Relations, Publicity/Promotions, Sales Promotion

Rod McGregor *(Pres)*
Jeff Crowl *(CEO)*
Chuck Seeley *(Partner)*
Julie Safreed *(Gen Mgr)*
Chris Sirgo *(Dir-Art & Designer-Web)*
Nicole Larocca *(Dir-Art)*
Frank Scassa *(Dir-Multimedia)*
Harry Knotts *(Acct Supvr)*

Accounts:
Alside
Andreas Furniture
CTNA Media
Culligan Water
Dutchman
Engage360
Ken-Tool
Magazine Worx
MAP Heating & Air Conditioning
Oakland Raiders
Ohio Pools & Spas
Pro Football Hall of Fame
Schonor Cheverolet

CROWLEY WEBB

(Formerly Crowley Webb & Associates)
268 Main St Ste 400, Buffalo, NY 14202-4108
Tel.: (716) 856-2932
Fax: (716) 856-2940
E-Mail: jim.hettich@crowleywebb.com
Web Site: www.crowleywebb.com

E-Mail for Key Personnel:
President: joseph.crowley@crowley-webb.com
Creative Dir.: jeff.pappalardo@crowley-webb.com
Media Dir.: jim.crowley@crowley-webb.com

Employees: 70
Year Founded: 1986

Agency Specializes In: Advertising, Brand Development & Integration, Collateral, Consumer Marketing, Corporate Identity, Digital/Interactive, Direct Response Marketing, Electronic Media, Event Planning & Marketing, Exhibit/Trade Shows, Financial, Graphic Design, Health Care Services, Internet/Web Design, Logo & Package Design, Pharmaceutical, Public Relations, Publicity/Promotions, Sponsorship, Strategic Planning/Research

Breakdown of Gross Billings by Media: Brdcst.: 24%; Collateral: 15%; Consumer Publs.: 2%; D.M.: 10%; Other: 2%; Outdoor: 4%; Print: 38%; Pub. Rels.: 5%

Jean Fletcher *(CFO)*
Matt Low *(VP & Assoc Dir-Creative)*
Biagio Patti *(Assoc Dir-Media)*
Katie Briggs *(Mgr-PR)*
Shannon Vogel *(Acct Supvr)*
Lauren Dixon *(Strategist-Digital & Social Media)*
Cuyler Hettich *(Acct Exec)*
Alaina Houseknecht *(Acct Exec)*
Joe Russell *(Acct Exec)*
Natalie Tronolone *(Acct Exec)*
AlexaRae Godwin *(Media Planner & Media Buyer)*
Melanie Groszewski *(Asst Acct Exec & Coord-Internship Program)*
Tessa Lewis *(Asst Acct Exec)*
Paige Meckler *(Asst Acct Exec)*

Accounts:
API Heat Transfer Manufacturing
Artpark Arts, Nonprofit
Buffalo Arts Studio Arts, Nonprofit
Buffalo Prep Education
ESAB Manufacturing
Irish Classical Theatre Arts, Nonprofit
M&T Bank Financial
Monroe Community College Branding, Education
Phillips Lytle Legal; 2002
Praxis Communications, Inc.; Nashville, TN Healthcare
Towne Automotive Group Automotive
Trocaire College Healthcare
University At Buffalo Education

CROWN COMMUNICATIONS

1310 South Tryon St Ste 110, Charlotte, NC 28202
Tel.: (704) 376-3434
Fax: (704) 376-2537
E-Mail: info@crown-com.com
Web Site: www.crown-com.com

Employees: 4

Agency Specializes In: Advertising, Collateral, Communications, Digital/Interactive, Local Marketing, Logo & Package Design, Media Relations

John James *(VP)*
Josh Bassinger *(Mgr-Comm)*

Accounts:
Ciel
Cingular Wireless LLC
Red Rover

CROWN SOCIAL AGENCY

1415 10th Ave Ste 2, Seattle, WA 98122
Tel.: (206) 436-6433
Web Site: www.crownsocial.com

Year Founded: 2011

Agency Specializes In: Advertising, Social Media, Strategic Planning/Research

Zach Huntting *(Founder & CEO)*
Shena Bannick *(Dir-Art)*
Shannon Evans O'Donald *(Strategist-Content)*

Accounts:
Debbiefish
Hawken

CRUCIAL INTERACTIVE INC.
21 Camden St 5th Fl, Toronto, ON M5V 1V2 Canada
Tel.: (416) 645-0135
Fax: (888) 493-0135
Toll Free: (877) 244-6562
Web Site: www.crucialinteractive.com

Year Founded: 2007

Agency Specializes In: Advertising, Digital/Interactive, Technical Advertising

Petar Bozinovski *(Pres)*
Damian Cristiani *(CEO)*
Brad Alles *(Sr VP-Sls)*
Joe Younes *(VP-Innovation & Audience Engagement)*
Ingrid Rosaeg *(Acct Mgr)*
Shirine Aouad *(Mgr-Experience)*
Patrick Toppan *(Mgr-Ad Ops)*
Jamie Forbes *(Acct Exec)*
Tarah McEwen *(Acct Exec)*
Melissa Mclintock *(Acct Exec)*

Accounts:
Examiner.com
Remedy Health Media

CRUNCH BRAND COMMUNICATIONS INC.
1 1st Ave Building 34, Charlestown, MA 02129
Tel.: (617) 241-5553
Fax: (617) 241-9161
Web Site: crunchbrands.com/index.php

Agency Specializes In: Advertising

Accounts:
Equifax Database Services
Etonic Worldwide LLC
Sperry Top-Sider, Inc.
Zipcar, Inc.

THE CRUSH AGENCY
1519 Dl Mabry Hwy 100, Lutz, FL 33548
Tel.: (813) 397-6181
E-Mail: media@thecrushagency.com
Web Site: www.thecrushagency.com

Agency Specializes In: Advertising, Brand Development & Integration, Internet/Web Design, Media Buying Services, Public Relations, Search Engine Optimization, Social Media

Liane Caruso *(Pres)*
Ed Samane *(Mng Dir)*
Corina Sheridan *(VP)*
Wendy Kirkwood *(Mgr-Social Media)*
Angela Rodriguez *(Acct Exec)*

Accounts:
New-gayeststoreonearth.com

CRUX CREATIVE
250 E Wisconsin Ave, Milwaukee, WI 53202
Tel.: (414) 289-7180
Web Site: www.cruxcreative.com

Year Founded: 2005

Agency Specializes In: Agriculture, Asian Market, Brand Development & Integration, Business-To-Business, Collateral, College, Communications, Consumer Goods, Content, Corporate Communications, Corporate Identity, Cosmetics, Electronics, Environmental, Exhibit/Trade Shows, Experience Design, Financial, Food Service, Government/Political, Graphic Design, High Technology, Industrial, Information Technology, Internet/Web Design, Investor Relations, Legal Services, Leisure, Local Marketing, Logo & Package Design, Luxury Products, Outdoor, Pets , Pharmaceutical, Print, Production, Restaurant, Retail, Search Engine Optimization, Social Marketing/Nonprofit, Social Media, Sports Market, Stakeholders, Transportation, Travel & Tourism, Urban Market, Web (Banner Ads, Pop-ups, etc.)

Michele Allen *(Principal)*
Shawn Tarlo *(VP-Comm)*

Accounts:
Corporate Contractors Inc Branding, Logos, Website Design
Kumon Headquarters & Museum Branding, Graphic Design
Mandarin Quarterly Website Redesign
Thomas Architects Web Design

CRYSTAL CLEAR COMMUNICATIONS
2470 S Dairy Ashford Ste 252, Houston, TX 77077
Tel.: (832) 867-4660
Fax: (318) 309-0019
E-Mail: crystalclear@crystalcommunicates.com

Agency Specializes In: Crisis Communications, Graphic Design, Media Buying Services, Newspaper, Public Relations, Strategic Planning/Research

Crystal Livers-Powers *(Strategist-Comm)*

Accounts:
The American Heart Association Medical Services
Career Management Services Consultancy Services
Compaq Journada Product Launch
CRAVE Gourmet Bakery & Catered Cafe Restaurant
Nike Time Wear Launch
Poindexter Dental Medical Services

CRYSTAL CLEAR CREATIVE, INC.
1751 E Gardner Way Ste G, Wasilla, AK 99654
Tel.: (907) 376-2653
E-Mail: info@c3alaska.com
Web Site: c3alaska.com

Agency Specializes In: Advertising, Brand Development & Integration, Graphic Design, Print

Jake Libbey *(Pres)*

Accounts:
Matanuska Valley Federal Credit Union
Pediatric Dentistry of Alaska

CSI GROUP, INC.
11 Fairview Terr, Paramus, NJ 07652
Tel.: (201) 587-1400
Fax: (201) 587-1234
E-Mail: hello@thecsigroup.com
Web Site: www.thecsigroup.com/

Employees: 27
Year Founded: 1992

Agency Specializes In: Advertising, Brand Development & Integration, Broadcast, Business-To-Business, Catalogs, Co-op Advertising, Collateral, College, Consumer Goods, Consumer Marketing, Consumer Publications, Content, Digital/Interactive, Education, Email, Event Planning & Marketing, Exhibit/Trade Shows, Experience Design, Graphic Design, In-Store Advertising, Internet/Web Design, Luxury Products, Magazines, Mobile Marketing, Multimedia, Newspaper, Newspapers & Magazines, Out-of-Home Media, Paid Searches, Point of Purchase, Print, Production, Production (Print), Radio, Search Engine Optimization, Social Media, Sponsorship, T.V., Trade & Consumer Magazines, Viral/Buzz/Word of Mouth, Web (Banner Ads, Pop-ups, etc.)

Approx. Annual Billings: $8,000,000

Kurt Von Seekamm *(Pres)*
Jim Wurster *(Exec VP)*
Rich Cannava *(VP & Exec Producer)*
Kathy Marrazzo *(Acct Dir)*
Alan Tardieu *(Dir-Art)*
Amanda Baratta *(Acct Mgr)*
Sarah Sproha *(Office Mgr)*
Kevin Fillie *(DESIGNER-Motion)*
Ryan Cosgrove *(Jr Mgr-Production & Coord-Production)*
Christine Disebastian *(Coord-Video & Motion Design)*

Accounts:
Army Research Laboratories Labs; 2010
BP Lubricants; Wayne, NJ Castrol Synthetic; 2002
CIRCA Jewels Buying Service; 2015
Citizen Watch Company; Lyndhurst, NJ Eco-Drive, Signature, Drive; 1992
Konica Minolta BizHub; 2012
LifeBankUSA Cord Blood Banking; 2013
Rider Insurance Motorcycle Insurance; 2014

CSTRAIGHT MEDIA
120 Beulah Rd NE Ste 200, Vienna, VA 22180
Tel.: (703) 255-0920
Fax: (703) 255-5025
Web Site: www.cstraight.com

Year Founded: 2004

Agency Specializes In: Advertising, Content, Digital/Interactive, Internet/Web Design

Gene Ro *(Founder & Pres)*
Thomas Wear *(Partner & VP-Acct Svcs)*
John Wojciech *(Partner & Creative Dir)*
Ben Carr *(Designer-User Experience)*
Ariel Lee *(Designer-UI & UX)*
Angie May *(Designer-UX & UI)*

Accounts:
The Daily Rider

CTI MEDIA
3060 Peachtree Rd NW, Atlanta, GA 30305
Tel.: (404) 843-8717
Fax: (404) 843-6869
E-Mail: info@ctimedia.com
Web Site: www.ctimedia.com

Employees: 20

Agency Specializes In: Advertising, Affiliate Marketing, Automotive, Bilingual Market, Brand Development & Integration, Branded Entertainment, Broadcast, Business Publications, Business-To-Business, Cable T.V., Co-op Advertising, College, Communications, Consumer Goods, Consumer Marketing, Consumer Publications, Corporate Communications, Corporate Identity, Digital/Interactive, Direct Response Marketing, Direct-to-Consumer, E-Commerce, Electronic Media, Entertainment, Event Planning & Marketing, Exhibit/Trade Shows, Financial, Government/Political, Health Care Services, High Technology, Hispanic Market, Hospitality, International, Local Marketing, Magazines, Media Buying Services, Media Planning, Media Relations, Mobile Marketing, Multicultural, Multimedia, Newspapers &

Magazines, Out-of-Home Media, Outdoor, Planning & Consultation, Print, Radio, Real Estate, Regional, Restaurant, Retail, Search Engine Optimization, T.V., Trade & Consumer Magazines, Transportation, Travel & Tourism, Web (Banner Ads, Pop-ups, etc.)

Approx. Annual Billings: $20,000,000

Toni Augustine-Dwyer *(Pres & CEO)*
Lori Krinsky *(Sr VP-Media)*
Emily Hagan *(VP-Client Svcs)*

Accounts:
ABC Family
American Express
Bravo
Cartoon Network
Coca-Cola Refreshments USA, Inc.
DIY Network
Fine Living Channel
Food Network
Fox Movie Channel
Fox Soccer Channel
Fox Sports
FUEL TV
Gospel Music Channel
HBO Cinemax, HBO Affiliate, HBO Commercial Group, HBO Direct, HBO Satellite, TVKO
MGM Worldwide Television Distribution
Microsoft
TBS
Trinity Broadcasting Network

CUBIC

1643 S Boston Ave, Tulsa, OK 74119
Tel.: (918) 587-7888
Fax: (918) 398-9081
E-Mail: info@cubiccreative.com
Web Site: www.cubiccreative.com

Employees: 16

Agency Specializes In: Advertising

Billy Kulkin *(Pres & Mng Partner)*
Libby Bender *(Partner & VP)*
Jeff DeGarmo *(CTO & VP)*
Winston Peraza *(Chief Creative Officer & VP)*
Meaghan Gipson *(Acct Mgr)*
Rachel Mosley *(Acct Mgr)*
Nikki Lamson *(Strategist-Digital)*
Greg Tatum *(Designer-Digital)*

Accounts:
Montereau; Tulsa, OK Retirement Community; 2013

CUE CREATIVE

117 W Ferguson, Tyler, TX 75702
Tel.: (903) 531-2333
E-Mail: info@cuecreative.com
Web Site: www.cuecreative.com

Agency Specializes In: Advertising, Brand Development & Integration, Graphic Design, Internet/Web Design, Media Planning, Strategic Planning/Research

Ron Stafford *(Partner)*

Accounts:
Achieve Financial Group

CUE INC

520 Nicollet Mall Ste 500, Minneapolis, MN 55402
Tel.: (612) 465-0030
E-Mail: info@designcue.com
Web Site: www.designcue.com

Employees: 8

Agency Specializes In: Advertising, Brand Development & Integration

Ed Mathie *(Co-Founder & Mng Dir)*
Alan Colvin *(Principal & Dir-Creative)*

Accounts:
Jack Daniel's

CUKER

(Formerly Cuker Interactive)
320 S Cedros Ave Ste 200, Solana Beach, CA 92075
Tel.: (858) 345-1378
E-Mail: info@cukeragency.com
Web Site: www.cukeragency.com/

Employees: 20
Year Founded: 2003

Agency Specializes In: Above-the-Line, Advertising, Below-the-Line, Digital/Interactive, Electronic Media, Email, Experience Design, Game Integration, Internet/Web Design, Local Marketing, Mobile Marketing, Multimedia, Paid Searches, Product Placement, Search Engine Optimization, Shopper Marketing, Social Media, Strategic Planning/Research, Viral/Buzz/Word of Mouth, Web (Banner Ads, Pop-ups, etc.)

Aaron Cuker *(CEO & Chief Creative Officer)*
Kelsey Carney *(Dir-Art)*
Shelley Burns *(Sr Mgr-Digital Mktg)*
Tim Soltysiak *(Sr Mgr-Digital Mktg)*
Kristopher J. Nicolls *(Mgr-Bus Dev)*
Nicole A. Logan *(Acct Exec)*
Jason Patio *(Assoc Designer)*

Accounts:
Dogswell Digital, Website
Rip Curl
Silver Oak Cellars
UCI

CULT360

261 5th Ave, New York, NY 10016
Tel.: (212) 463-9300
E-Mail: info@cult360.com
Web Site: www.cult360.com

Employees: 25

Agency Specializes In: Advertising, Brand Development & Integration, Communications, Digital/Interactive, Direct Response Marketing, Event Planning & Marketing, Graphic Design, Local Marketing, Production, Promotions

Joe Jelic *(Partner & Dir-Creative)*
Jeff Rothstein *(Partner & Dir-Mktg Strategy)*

Accounts:
E&J Gallo
Tara Energy

CULTIVATOR ADVERTISING & DESIGN

2737 Larimer St Ste B, Denver, CO 80205
Tel.: (303) 444-4134
E-Mail: info@cultivatorads.com
Web Site: www.cultivatorads.com

Employees: 21
Year Founded: 2000

Agency Specializes In: Sponsorship

Matt Neren *(Owner & Dir-Acct Svc)*
Scott Coe *(Pres)*
Tim Abare *(Partner)*
Amanda Ringel *(Dir-Art & Graphic Designer)*
Micah Schmiedeskamp *(Dir-Art & Designer)*
Stephanie Shawn *(Dir-Digital Strategies)*
Steve Moore *(Acct Exec)*
Rich Rodgers *(rrodgers@cultivatorads.com)*

Accounts:
Anthony's Pizza
Breckenridge Brewery Campaign: "Beervertising", Lime, Ultra
Cherry Creek North Shopping District
CollegeInvest Advertising Agency of Record & Lead Creative Agency
Eye Pieces of Vail Brand Identity, Digital, Direct Marketing, Social
The Hong Kong Beer Co. (Agency of Record)
Inspirato
Moots Cycles
New Belgium Brewing; Fort Collins, CO Campaign: "Make Up", Ranger India Pale Ale
Professional Ski Instructors of America
RockResorts
Telluride Tourism Board
Visit Estes Park

CULTURA UNITED AGENCY

909 N Sepulveda Ste 200, El Segundo, CA 90245
Tel.: (310) 469-7640
Web Site: www.culturaunitedagency.com

Agency Specializes In: Advertising, Public Relations, Social Media, Strategic Planning/Research

Anita Alban Gastelum *(Exec VP & Gen Mgr)*
Oscar Contreras *(VP)*
Ramon Valadez *(VP-Strategic Plng)*

Accounts:
Jafra International
JC Penney

CULTURESPAN MARKETING

(Formerly The Laster Group)
5407 N Mesa St 2nd Fl, El Paso, TX 79912
Tel.: (915) 581-7900
Fax: (915) 581-0087
E-Mail: info@culturespanmarketing.com
Web Site: www.culturespanmarketing.com

Employees: 20

Agency Specializes In: Advertising

Chad Beaty *(Dir-Photography & Editor)*
Jc Hernandez *(Sr Dir-Art)*
Sarah Griffin *(Dir-Resourcing)*
Georgina Hernandez *(Dir-Media)*
Gabe Quesada *(Dir-Video & Motion Graphics Art)*
Perla Parra *(Designer-UX)*
Karla Pomar *(Media Planner & Buyer)*

THE CUMMINGS GROUP

1105 NW 44th St, Oklahoma City, OK 73118
Tel.: (405) 524-9441
Fax: (405) 524-9448
E-Mail: rosscummings@coxinet.net
Web Site: www.cummingsgrp.com

Employees: 2
Year Founded: 1960

Agency Specializes In: Collateral, Health Care Services, Technical Advertising

Approx. Annual Billings: $500,000

Breakdown of Gross Billings by Media: Brdcst.: 15%; Collateral: 40%; Newsp. & Mags.: 35%; Outdoor: 10%

Ross W. Cummings *(Owner)*

Accounts:
Duncan Regional Hospital; Duncan, OK (Special Projects)
Fluidart Technologies LLC
Underwriters Service Agency; Oklahoma City, OK General Insurance Agency

CUMMINS & PARTNERS
53 Murray St Ste 1, New York, NY 10007
Tel.: (646) 791-0797
E-Mail: ny@cumminsandpartners.com
Web Site: www.cumminsandpartners.com

Agency Specializes In: Advertising, Digital/Interactive, Internet/Web Design, Media Buying Services, Media Planning

Sean Cummins *(Founder, Partner & CEO)*
Tiffany Coletti Titolo *(Pres)*
Arwa Mahdawi *(Chief Innovation & Strategy Officer)*
Jim Ingram *(Exec Dir-Creative)*
Magda Triantafyllidis *(Grp Acct Dir)*
Chantal Smith *(Art Dir)*
Heath Collins *(Dir-Art)*
Theo Erasmus *(Dir-Plng)*
Nikia Shepherd *(Acct Mgr)*
Adam Ferrrier *(Strategist)*
Chris Ellis *(Copywriter)*
Vanessa Quincey *(Planner)*

Accounts:
Alfa Romeo
Art Series Hotel Group
New-Care Australia
Heidi Klum Intimates Campaign: "Sia - Fire Meet Gasoline"

CUMMINS, MACFAIL & NUTRY, INC.
134 W End Ave, Somerville, NJ 08876
Tel.: (908) 722-8000
Fax: (908) 722-2055
E-Mail: mzigarelli@cmn-adv.com
Web Site: www.cmn-adv.com

Employees: 6
Year Founded: 1951

Agency Specializes In: Business-To-Business, Health Care Services, High Technology, Medical Products

Frank Fasano *(Pres & Supvr-Acct Svcs)*
Dominick Cirilli *(Exec VP & Dir-Creative)*
Merrilee Zigarelli *(Dir-New Bus Dev)*

Accounts:
Biomet; 1992
DMG
EBI Bone Healing System
Small Bones Innovation
Smith & Nephew
SpineLink

CUNDARI INTEGRATED ADVERTISING
26 Duncan St, Toronto, ON M5V 2B9 Canada
Tel.: (416) 510-1771
Fax: (416) 510-1769
E-Mail: aldo_cundari@cundari.com
Web Site: www.cundari.com

Employees: 100

Agency Specializes In: Advertising

Jennifer Steinmann *(Pres)*
Malcolm McLean *(Exec VP-Strategy, Insights & Plng)*
Jean-Francois Malette *(VP & Gen Mgr)*
Angie Kramer *(VP-Digital & Innovation)*
Maria Orsini *(VP-Admin & Fin)*
Mike Sipley *(Grp Head-Creative & Art Dir)*
Mike Dietrich *(Grp Dir-Creative)*
Jonathan Smith *(Grp Dir-Creative)*
Adam Lang *(Grp Acct Dir)*
Jennifer Cunningham *(Acct Dir)*
Anne-Marie Dontigny *(Acct Dir)*
Anne Spence *(Acct Dir)*
Jung Ahn *(Dir-Art)*
Adam Bacsalmasi *(Dir-User Experience)*
Jason Lee *(Dir-Art)*
Dean Martin *(Dir-Creative, Branding & Design)*
Matthew Morris *(Dir-Art)*
Sebastien Tessier *(Dir-Creative)*
Madjid Hamidi *(Acct Supvr)*
Ryan Kukec *(Copywriter)*
Alex Manahan *(Copywriter)*
Melissa Medwyk *(Designer)*
Francis Portugal *(Designer-Digital)*
Chris Vigmond *(Acct Coord)*

Accounts:
3M Canada Creative, Media Planning, Strategy
New-Art Gallery of Ontario (Agency of Record) Advertising, Digital, Marketing Communication, Planning & Buying
The Bishop Strachan School Campaign: "Girls Can Do anything", Digital Advertising, Traditional Advertising
BMW Canada #PoweringPerformance, #TeamBMW, BMW M4, Campaign: "1M Launch Campaign", Campaign: "3 Series Microsite", Campaign: "BMW Art Auction", Campaign: "Blue Energy", Campaign: "Bullet", Campaign: "Ultimate Racetrack", Campaign: "Walls", Campaign: "X3 launch", Media Planning & Buying
BMW of North America, LLC
Canada Bread Company Limited
Canadian Breast Cancer Foundation
Canadian Marketing Association Campaign: "Marketing: The Musical"
CIBC Campaign: "The Moment", Digital Creative & Strategy
Dempster Campaign: "DIY Sandwich", Campaign: "Healthy Way Feel Good o Gram", Healthy Way Bread
Firkin
Hospital for Sick Children Pain Squad
Ivey
Kickstopper.ca
Maple Leaf Foods Inc Dempster's, Digital, Online Campaign
Masco
Moose Knuckles
Neilson
Northern Ontario Tourism Campaign: "A Legendary Adventure is Calling", Campaign: "Forest"
Princess Auto Advertising, Creative, Digital, Media, Strategy, Web
Project Winter Survival Campaign: "Open House"
Rust-Oleum
Sick Kids Hospital Cancer Monitoring
Toronto Zoo
Villaggio

CUNEO ADVERTISING
1401 American Blvd E Ste 6, Bloomington, MN 55425
Tel.: (952) 707-1212
E-Mail: info@cuneoadvertising.com
Web Site: www.cuneoadvertising.com

Agency Specializes In: Advertising, Digital/Interactive, Logo & Package Design, Media Planning, Sponsorship

Larry Cuneo *(Pres & CEO)*
Kathy Carlson *(Exec Dir-Media Svcs)*
Randy Lied *(Sr Dir-Art)*
Eric Anderson *(Acct Svcs Dir)*
Katie Jackson-Richter *(Dir-Accounts & Digital Dev)*
Mike Sorenson *(Dir-Creative)*
Ginny Goff *(Office Mgr)*

Accounts:
Pawn America (Agency of Record) Advertising, CashPass Pre Paid Debit Card, Marketing, My Bridge Now, Payday America

CUNNING COMMUNICATIONS
The Soho Bldg, New York, NY 10012
Tel.: (212) 219-1050
Fax: (212) 219-0016
E-Mail: info@cunning.com
Web Site: www.cunning.com

Agency Specializes In: Advertising

Anna Carloss *(Co-Founder)*
John Carver *(Co-Founder)*
Mark Voysey *(Owner)*
Jack Connolly *(Dir-Creative)*
Lauren Christianson *(Project Mgr & Acct Exec)*

Accounts:
Yotel New York

CUNNINGHAM GROUP
35 S Ct St, Montgomery, AL 36104
Tel.: (334) 264-3459
Web Site: www.cunninghamadv.com

Agency Specializes In: Advertising, Brand Development & Integration, Internet/Web Design, Logo & Package Design, Print, Public Relations, Radio, Search Engine Optimization, Social Media, Strategic Planning/Research

Bill Cunningham *(Pres & CEO)*
Margaret Cunningham *(Sr Dir-Creative)*
Jamie Sutton *(Art Dir)*
Susan Collier *(Dir-Media)*
Hillary Andrews *(Dir-Digital)*

Accounts:
Robinson Iron Corporation

CURIOSITY ADVERTISING
221 E 4th St, Cincinnati, OH 45202
Tel.: (513) 744-6000
Web Site: www.curiosity360.com

Year Founded: 2010

Agency Specializes In: Advertising, Digital/Interactive, Internet/Web Design, Social Media, Sponsorship, T.V.

Matt Fischer *(Pres & Chief Creative Officer)*
Greg Livingston *(Partner & Chief Dev Officer)*
Andy Brownell *(Dir-Content Strategy)*
Ried Cartwright *(Dir-Creative)*
Doug Goodwin *(Dir-Strategy & Bus Dev-Curiosity InsightStream)*
Bob Walker *(Assoc Dir-Creative)*
Chris Wallen *(Supvr-Acct & Bus)*
Cat Watson *(Acct Exec)*
Kyle Fant *(Asst Acct Exec)*

Accounts:
Build-A-Bear Workshop In-Store Creative, TV
The Christ Hospital Health Network Full-Service
Cincinnati Bell Full-Service
Cincinnati Insurance Companies Full-Service
Dean Foods Dairy Pure, TruMoo Chocolate Milk
Disney Parks & Resorts
Gorilla Glue Content Development, Digital Strategy, Social Strategy
O'Keeffe's Content Development, Digital Strategy, Social Strategy
Perfetti Van Melle USA Inc. Airheads Extremes, Mentos
Procter & Gamble

New-Roto-Rooter Plumbing & Drain Services (Social Media Agency of Record) Digital, Video
New-totes Isotoner Corporation Totes
New-The U.S. Navy

CURRAN & CONNORS, INC.
3455 Peachtree Rd NE 5th Fl, Atlanta, GA 30326-3236
Tel.: (404) 239-3979
Toll Free: (800) 435-.0406
Web Site: www.curran-connors.com

Employees: 50
Year Founded: 1965

Agency Specializes In: Advertising, Graphic Design, Internet/Web Design, Local Marketing, Social Marketing/Nonprofit, Strategic Planning/Research

Henry L. Morris *(Owner)*
Albert Burba *(Exec VP)*
Peter Spalding *(Sr VP & Gen Mgr-Investor Svcs)*
Jeffrey Goldsmith *(Sr VP-Natl Accts)*
Barbara Koontz *(Reg VP)*
Cindy Knight *(VP-Project Mgmt)*
Sarah Brautigam *(Acct Mgr)*
Eliza Vaughn *(Acct Mgr-Natl)*
Abbey Lustig *(Acct Exec)*
Matt Reese *(Reg Project Mgr)*

CURRENT MARKETING
(Name Changed to Current360)

CURRENT360
(Formerly Current Marketing)
1324 E Washington St, Louisville, KY 40206-1759
Tel.: (502) 589-3567
Fax: (502) 589-6448
Web Site: www.current360.com

Employees: 40
Year Founded: 1984

National Agency Associations: 4A's-AAF-Second Wind Limited

Agency Specializes In: Business-To-Business, Electronic Media, High Technology, Medical Products, Pharmaceutical, Print, Restaurant, Retail

Approx. Annual Billings: $8,500,000

Richard E. Schardein *(Chm & CEO)*
Dennis Bonifer *(VP)*
Allison Gibson *(VP)*
Donovan Sears *(Dir-Interactive Creative)*
Rob Womack *(Dir-Motion Dept)*
Merdith SMith *(Acct Exec)*
Jena Smith *(Acct Coord)*

Accounts:
Archdiocese of Louisville/Catholic Schools; Louisville, KY Evangelist Messages & School Happenings
Brown-Forman
Culinary Standards; Louisville, KY
Developware
Dr. Banis
Farmwood Industries
First Harrison Bank
Furniture Liquidators
KEA (Kentucky Education Assoc.)
KIPDA (Kentuckiana Regional Planning & Development) (Agency of Record) Area Agency on Aging, Carpooling Services for City of Louisville
Lindsey Wilson College
Lubrisyn
Mattress & More
Mortenson
Schmitt Sohne German Wines; 2003
Town & Country Bank & Trust
Tumbleweed Southwest Grill
Wesley House; Butchertown, KY; 2003

CURVE TRENDS MARKETING
1 Kennedy Dr Ste L4, Burlington, VT 05403
Tel.: (802) 862-8783
Fax: (802) 497-0018
E-Mail: info@curvetrends.com
Web Site: www.curvetrends.com

Agency Specializes In: Advertising, Digital/Interactive, Internet/Web Design, Print, Social Media

Bibi Mukherjee *(Founder)*

Accounts:
Crowne Plaza
Efficiency Vermont
LED Supply & Picket Fence

CUSTOMEDIALABS
460 E Swedesford Rd Ste 2020, Wayne, PA 19087
Tel.: (610) 225-0350
Fax: (240) 250-4046
E-Mail: info@customedialabs.com
Web Site: www.customedialabs.com

Employees: 25

Agency Specializes In: Brand Development & Integration, Business-To-Business, Communications, Corporate Communications, Corporate Identity, Digital/Interactive, Education, Email, Exhibit/Trade Shows, Financial, Health Care Services, Information Technology, Integrated Marketing, International, Internet/Web Design, Medical Products, Mobile Marketing, Multimedia, New Technologies, Pharmaceutical, Web (Banner Ads, Pop-ups, etc.)

Approx. Annual Billings: $2,000,000

Breakdown of Gross Billings by Media: Corp. Communications: $2,000,000

Manos Sifakis *(Pres & CEO)*
Michael Kelly *(Chief Sls Officer)*
Brennan Lindeen *(Dir-Project Mgmt)*

CUTWATER
950 Battery St, San Francisco, CA 94111
Tel.: (415) 341-9100
Fax: (415) 315-4200
Web Site: www.cutwatersf.com

Employees: 50
Year Founded: 1998

National Agency Associations: ABC-AMA-DMA

Agency Specializes In: Advertising, Brand Development & Integration, Sponsorship

Chuck McBride *(Founder, Chief Creative Officer & Copywriter)*
Christian Navarro *(Grp Acct Dir)*
Mike Butler *(Art Dir)*
Gong Liu *(Dir-Art)*
Kevin M. Newby *(Dir-Digital Strategy & Analytics)*
Simone Nobili *(Dir-Creative)*
Greer Gonerka *(Sr Acct Mgr)*
Ciaran Rogers *(Sr Strategist-Digital)*
Jay Brockmeier *(Copywriter)*
Ray Connolly *(Copywriter)*
John Reid *(Copywriter)*

Accounts:
THE AD COUNCIL Campaign: "Feeding America PSA"
American Giant Campaign: "Don't Get Comfortable", Campaign: "The Old Man Film"
Ariat International Creative
BNP Paribas S.A.
CoolSculpting
Easton-Bell Sports Campaign: "Inside Out"
Georgia-Pacific LLC Brawny Paper Towels, Campaign: "Stay Giant!"
Intel Campaign: "Frozen Coffee", Campaign: "Monotaskers"
Motorola Solutions, Inc.
New-Peet's Coffee (Agency of Record)
Ray-Ban Campaign: "Never Hide Noise"
Sunrun Campaign: "Solar Motion", Campaign: "Sounds of Solar"
Trina Turk Digital, Social & Media Srategy

CVA ADVERTISING & MARKETING, INC.
5030 E University Ste B401, Odessa, TX 79762
Tel.: (432) 368-5483
Fax: (432) 366-9434
E-Mail: craig@cvaadv.com
Web Site: www.cvaadv.com

E-Mail for Key Personnel:
President: craig@cvaadv.com
Media Dir.: lila@cvaadv.com
Production Mgr.: dana@cvaadv.com

Employees: 12
Year Founded: 1993

National Agency Associations: AAF

Agency Specializes In: Advertising, Brand Development & Integration, Consumer Marketing, Corporate Communications, Entertainment, Graphic Design, Health Care Services, Internet/Web Design, Media Planning, Media Relations, Media Training, Medical Products, Newspaper, Point of Purchase, Print, Production (Ad, Film, Broadcast), Public Relations, Restaurant, T.V.

Craig L. Van Amburgh *(Owner)*
Dana Harrington *(VP-Print Production)*
Rusty Edwards *(Dir-Art)*
Christi Callicoatte *(Acct Svc Dir)*
Lisa Shelton *(Mgr-Acctg)*
Lila Evans *(Media Buyer)*

Accounts:
Taco Villa; Midland, TX Mexican Food Restaurant; 1991

CWMEDIA
1517 Spearmint Cir, Jamison, PA 18929
Tel.: (215) 491-5742
Fax: (775) 618-9128
E-Mail: aleonard@cwmedia.us
Web Site: www.cwmedia.us

E-Mail for Key Personnel:
President: aleonard@cwmedia.us

Employees: 2
Year Founded: 1992

Agency Specializes In: Advertising, Automotive, Broadcast, Internet/Web Design, Media Buying Services, Newspaper, Recruitment, T.V.

Diane Prefontaine *(VP & Supvr-Brdcst)*

Accounts:
Bodez Health Club; Ormond Beach, FL
Cebridge Connections
Charter Communications
Choctaw Maid Farms
Credit Car; Scranton, PA
Doubletree Hotels
Healthy Inspirations Weight Loss & Fitness Fitness

& Nutrition; 2003
Mortage Zone
Scranton Dodge, Chrysler & Jeep; Scranton, PA; 1992
Tunkhannock Automart; Tunkhannock, PA Dodge, Jeep, Eagle, Plymouth & Chrysler Lines; 1992
Vickers, INC; Jackson, MS
Waste Management, Inc.

CXC

16400 Ventura Blvd, Encino, CA 91436
Tel.: (310) 776-6666
Web Site: www.cxcma.com

Agency Specializes In: Above-the-Line, Advertising, Advertising Specialties, Affiliate Marketing, Affluent Market, African-American Market, Agriculture, Alternative Advertising, Arts, Asian Market, Automotive, Aviation & Aerospace, Below-the-Line, Bilingual Market, Brand Development & Integration, Branded Entertainment, Broadcast, Business Publications, Business-To-Business, Cable T.V., Catalogs, Children's Market, Co-op Advertising, Collateral, College, Commercial Photography, Communications, Computers & Software, Consulting, Consumer Goods, Consumer Marketing, Consumer Publications, Content, Corporate Communications, Corporate Identity, Cosmetics, Crisis Communications, Custom Publishing, Customer Relationship Management, Digital/Interactive, Direct Response Marketing, Direct-to-Consumer, E-Commerce, Education, Electronic Media, Electronics, Email, Engineering, Entertainment, Environmental, Event Planning & Marketing, Exhibit/Trade Shows, Experience Design, Faith Based, Fashion/Apparel, Financial, Food Service, Gay & Lesbian Market, Government/Political, Graphic Design, Guerilla Marketing, Health Care Services, High Technology, Hispanic Market, Hospitality, Household Goods, Identity Marketing, In-Store Advertising, Industrial, Infomercials, Information Technology, Integrated Marketing, International, Internet/Web Design, Investor Relations, Legal Services, Leisure, Local Marketing, Logo & Package Design, Luxury Products, Magazines, Marine, Market Research, Media Buying Services, Media Planning, Media Relations, Media Training, Medical Products, Men's Market, Merchandising, Mobile Marketing, Multicultural, Multimedia, New Product Development, New Technologies, Newspaper, Newspapers & Magazines, Out-of-Home Media, Outdoor, Over-50 Market, Package Design, Pharmaceutical, Planning & Consultation, Podcasting, Point of Purchase, Point of Sale, Print, Product Placement, Production, Production (Ad, Film, Broadcast), Production (Print), Promotions, Public Relations, Publicity/Promotions, Publishing, RSS (Really Simple Syndication), Radio, Real Estate, Recruitment, Regional, Restaurant, Retail, Sales Promotion, Search Engine Optimization, Seniors' Market, Shopper Marketing, Social Marketing/Nonprofit, Social Media, South Asian Market, Sponsorship, Sports Market, Stakeholders, Strategic Planning/Research, Sweepstakes, Syndication, T.V., Technical Advertising, Teen Market, Telemarketing, Trade & Consumer Magazines, Transportation, Travel & Tourism, Tween Market, Urban Market, Viral/Buzz/Word of Mouth, Web (Banner Ads, Pop-ups, etc.), Women's Market, Yellow Pages Advertising

Cyrus Pan *(CEO)*

CYNTHCARM COMMUNICATIONS

2246 Ide Ct N, Maplewood, MN 55109
Tel.: (612) 460-1772
E-Mail: info@cynthcarm.com
Web Site: www.cynthcarm.com

Agency Specializes In: Advertising, Brand Development & Integration, Event Planning & Marketing, Graphic Design, Internet/Web Design, Media Buying Services, Public Relations, Social Media, Strategic Planning/Research

Cindy Lewis *(Owner)*

Accounts:
African American Babies Coalition
Allens Revenge
Faiths Lodge
Lewis Sports Foundation

THE CYPHERS AGENCY, INC.

131 Gibralter Ave, Annapolis, MD 21401
Tel.: (410) 280-5451
Fax: (410) 269-6851
E-Mail: info@thecyphersagency.com
Web Site: www.thecyphersagency.com

E-Mail for Key Personnel:
President: dave@thecyphersagency.com
Creative Dir.: darren@thecyphersagency.com

Employees: 15
Year Founded: 1989

Agency Specializes In: Brand Development & Integration, Financial, High Technology, Real Estate, Retail, Travel & Tourism

David Cyphers *(Owner)*
Darren Easton *(VP & Dir-Creative)*
Howard Mont *(VP-Sls & Mktg)*
Christina Drews-Leonard *(Dir-Art & Strategist-Search Engine Optimization)*
Anna Forbes *(Sr Acct Exec)*
Danielle Reigle *(Acct Exec-Mktg)*

D&S CREATIVE COMMUNICATIONS INC.

140 Park Ave E, Mansfield, OH 44902-1830
Tel.: (419) 524-4312
Fax: (419) 524-6494
E-Mail: info@ds-creative.com
Web Site: www.ds-creative.com

E-Mail for Key Personnel:
President: tneff@ds-creative.com

Employees: 75
Year Founded: 1972

Agency Specializes In: Advertising, Brand Development & Integration, Business Publications, Business-To-Business, Collateral, Commercial Photography, Communications, Direct Response Marketing, E-Commerce, Electronic Media, Graphic Design, Industrial, Internet/Web Design, Merchandising, Multimedia, Outdoor, Point of Purchase, Point of Sale, Print, Production, Retail, Sales Promotion, Sweepstakes, Trade & Consumer Magazines

Approx. Annual Billings: $9,000,000

Terrence Neff *(Pres)*
Richard T. Schroeder *(CEO)*
Ladislaw Peko *(Controller)*
David Anthony *(Gen Mgr & Sr Acct Mgr)*
Marty Hoenes *(Dir-Art)*
Bob Hanes *(Mgr-IT)*
Sheila Vent *(Sr Acct Supvr-Electrolux)*
Jim Sexton *(Acct Exec)*
Jordan Kvochick *(Project Coord-New Media)*

Accounts:
Allied Air Enterprises
American Greetings
Ames Company; Parkersburg, VA
Formica
Georgia-Pacific
Haas-Jordan
Hedstrom
Hilti
Macco
Mr.Coffee
Stihl
Vortens
Wilsonart

D EXPOSITO & PARTNERS, LLC

875 Ave of the Americas 25th Fl, New York, NY 10001
Tel.: (646) 747-8800
Fax: (212) 273-0778
E-Mail: info@dex-p.com
Web Site: newamericanagency.com

Employees: 25
Year Founded: 2005

National Agency Associations: 4A's

Agency Specializes In: Hispanic Market

Daisy Exposito-Ulla *(Chm & CEO)*
Louis Maldonado *(Partner & Mng Dir)*
John Ross *(Partner & CFO)*
Mauricio Galvan *(Partner & Chief Creative Officer)*
Carmen Sepulveda *(Partner & Chief Comm Officer)*
Gloria Constanza *(Partner)*
Jorge Ulla *(Partner)*

Accounts:
AARP Foundation; 2013
AARP Services Inc.; 2013
AARP; 2011
Amica Mutual Insurance Company; 2014
Amtrak; 2013
Choice Hotels International; 2014
ConAgra Foods; 2009
Limon Dance Company; 2009
McDonald's Owner/Operator Assoc.
The National Campaign to Prevent Teen and Unplanned Pregnancy; 2007
NY Metro; 2005
Port Authority of New York & New Jersey Media planning and buying; 2012
Puerto Rican Day Parade; 2014
Safe Horizon; 2014
Tajin International; 2013
US Army Digital; 2013

D. HILTON ASSOCIATES, INC.

9450 Grogans Mill Rd Ste 200, The Woodlands, TX 77380
Tel.: (281) 292-5088
Fax: (281) 292-8893
Toll Free: (800) 367-0433
Web Site: www.dhilton.com

Employees: 20
Year Founded: 1985

Agency Specializes In: Advertising, Brand Development & Integration, Email, Internet/Web Design, Market Research, Merchandising, Newspaper, Outdoor, Print, Radio, Retail, Strategic Planning/Research, T.V.

Revenue: $10,000,000

David Hilton *(Pres & CEO)*
John Andrews *(Exec VP-Compensation)*
Debbie Hilton *(Exec VP-Retention & Retirement)*
Brian Kidwell *(Exec VP)*
Janice Shisler *(Sr VP-Exec Recruitment)*
Sarah Hilton *(Asst VP-Exec Recruiting)*
Jessica Jarman *(Asst VP-Recruiting)*
Hillary Mihle *(Asst VP-Res)*

D2 CREATIVE

28 Worlds Fair Dr, Somerset, NJ 08873

Tel.: (732) 507-7300
Web Site: www.d2creative.com

Year Founded: 1995

Agency Specializes In: Advertising, Brand Development & Integration, Digital/Interactive, Internet/Web Design

Peter Lyons *(Sr VP-Creative & Technical Svcs)*
Garvin Tam *(Producer-Digital Content)*
Gwen Dixon *(Dir-Ops)*
Scott Holmes *(Dir-Technical)*
Judy Minot *(Dir-Creative)*
Patrick Sodano *(Dir-Creative)*
Laura Vitez *(Dir-Creative)*
Anna Juharian *(Project Mgr-Interactive)*
Lauren Sparagna *(Project Mgr-Video & Interactive)*
Britton Shinn *(Sr Strategist-Digital)*
Tiffany Burke *(Specialist-Digital & Social)*

Accounts:
Institute of Electrical and Electronics Engineers, Inc.

D4 CREATIVE GROUP
4646 Umbria St, Philadelphia, PA 19127
Tel.: (215) 483-4555
Fax: (215) 483-4550
E-Mail: info@d4creative.com
Web Site: www.d4creative.com

Employees: 30
Year Founded: 1990

Carl Teitelman *(Mng Dir)*
Michael Snyder *(Chief Strategy Officer & Exec VP-Acct Svcs)*
Chris Sandman *(VP-Design)*
Sara Stuard *(VP-Acct Svcs)*
RIch Wakefield *(Exec Dir-Creative)*
Dave Lesser *(Sr Dir-Creative & Copywriter)*
Rohan Woodward *(Dir-Art)*
Matthew Engelson *(Mgr-Digital Mktg)*
Sloane Murray *(Acct Exec)*
Lisa Demusis *(Designer)*
Megan Seighman *(Social Media Intern)*

Accounts:
New-Acme-Hardesty
ARI Fleet
Bob Gold and Associates
Charter Communications
Comcast
New-Cure Auto Insurance Out-Of-Home, Social Media, TV
Drexel University
Espoma
Frontier Communications
New-Gate 1 Travel
New-Harris Tea
John Templeton Foundation
New-K'NEX
Lenfest Media Group
New-McKesson
New-Metrocast/Harron Communications
Motorola Solutions, Inc.
New-My Alarm Center
Nuna
Penn Maid
Pond Lehocky Stern Giordano
Sandia Laboratories
Time Warner Cable
TRG Customer Solutions
New-Unilife
Veria Living Branded Content, Campaign: "You've Got Veria", Events, Multi-Channel Campaign, Print, Radio, TV
Weinstein Bath & Kitchen
Wel Fab
Wharton Business School

D50 MEDIA
93 Worcester St Ste 101, Wellesley, MA 02481
Tel.: (800) 582-9606
E-Mail: info@d50media.com
Web Site: www.d50media.com

Year Founded: 2011

Agency Specializes In: Advertising, Media Buying Services, Public Relations, Social Media

Jay Haverty *(CEO)*
Dan Diamond *(Dir-Media Ops)*
Francie Steiner *(Dir-Media Strategy)*
Eric Lander *(Assoc Dir-Digital Media)*
Emily Rucker *(Sr Mgr-Paid Search)*
Kyron Sullivan *(Mgr-Affiliate Mktg)*
Chris Michael *(Sr Media Buyer)*

Accounts:
Rentrak Corporation

DAC GROUP
(Formerly DAC Group/Broome Marketing)
455 S 4th St Ste 1045, Louisville, KY 40202
Tel.: (502) 272-0882
Fax: (502) 582-9025
Toll Free: (866) 967-7186
Web Site: www.dacgroup.com

Employees: 20
Year Founded: 1993

Agency Specializes In: Digital/Interactive, Yellow Pages Advertising

Approx. Annual Billings: $19,000,000

Norm Hagarty *(CEO & Mng Partner)*
Marcel Labbe *(VP & Gen Mgr)*
Scott Ensign *(VP-Search Mktg)*
Patricia Whitney *(VP-Media)*
Lauren Stockbauer *(Acct Dir)*
Colleene Masters *(Acct Exec)*
Adrianne Pizzirusso *(Acct Exec)*
Felicia DelVecchio *(Team Head-SEM)*

Accounts:
Beltone
CHS Hospital
Fish Window Cleaning
Lifecare
Stanley Steemer
Sylvan Learning Inc (Agency of Record) Digital Media, Internet Yellow Pages, Mobile Display Strategy, Online Strategy, Paid-Search
Terminix
YMCA

DAE ADVERTISING, INC.
71 Stevenson St Ste 1450, San Francisco, CA 94105
Tel.: (415) 341-1280
Fax: (415) 296-8378
E-Mail: hello@dae.com
Web Site: www.dae.com

Employees: 25
Year Founded: 1990

Agency Specializes In: Advertising, Asian Market, Bilingual Market, Consumer Goods, Graphic Design, Integrated Marketing, International, Media Planning, Multicultural, Planning & Consultation, Public Relations, South Asian Market, Sponsorship, Strategic Planning/Research

Approx. Annual Billings: $7,500,000

Breakdown of Gross Billings by Media: Adv. Specialities: $7,500,000

Greg Chew *(Founder & Dir-Creative)*
Vicky M. Wong *(Pres & CEO)*
Fanny Chew *(Sr VP)*
Dennis Chang *(Grp Head & Copywriter)*
Sara Ma *(Media Planner)*
Stephanie Chen *(Asst Acct Exec)*

Accounts:
AARP
American Cancer Society; Oakland, CA
Asian Art Museum; San Francisco, CA
Cathay Pacific Airways; San Francisco, CA
Recology; San Francisco, CA
San Francisco Hep B Free; San Francisco, CA
Southwest Airlines; Dallas, TX Campaign: "A New Way to Fly"

DAIGLE CREATIVE
9957 Moorings Dr, Jacksonville, FL 32257
Tel.: (904) 880-9595
E-Mail: info@daiglecreative.com
Web Site: www.daiglecreative.com

Year Founded: 1997

Agency Specializes In: Advertising, Media Buying Services, Media Planning, Print, Public Relations, Strategic Planning/Research

John Daigle *(Principal)*
Renay Daigle *(Principal)*
Kristen Desmidt *(Dir-PR)*
Becky Russo *(Dir-Creative)*
Jill Wu *(Specialist-Comm)*

Accounts:
Mathis & Murphy P.A.

DAILEY & ASSOCIATES
(Sub. of The Interpublic Group of Cos., Inc.)
8687 Melrose Ave Ste G300, West Hollywood, CA 90069-5701
Tel.: (310) 360-3100
Fax: (310) 360-0810
E-Mail: info@daileyideas.com
Web Site: www.daileyideas.com

E-Mail for Key Personnel:
President: srabosky@daileyads.com
Production Mgr.: jstanley@daileyads.com

Employees: 100
Year Founded: 1968

National Agency Associations: 4A's-THINKLA

Agency Specializes In: Advertising, Automotive, Broadcast, Children's Market, Collateral, Electronic Media, Entertainment, Internet/Web Design, New Technologies, Production (Ad, Film, Broadcast), Production (Print), Sponsorship, Strategic Planning/Research

Approx. Annual Billings: $207,000,000

Richard Mahan *(Exec VP & Exec Dir-Creative)*
Jim Lorden *(Exec VP & Dir-Media)*
Matt Stefl *(Exec VP & Dir-Strategic Plng)*
Shira Elias *(Sr VP & Grp Acct Dir)*
Michelle Wong *(Sr VP & Grp Acct Dir)*
Don Lupo *(Sr VP & Dir-Digital Production)*
Heidi Williams *(VP & Dir-HR)*
Heath Miller *(VP & Acct Supvr)*
Stephanie Arnow *(Sr Producer-Digital)*
Samuel Ayres *(Producer-Digital)*
Tracy Verrett *(Assoc Dir-Strategic Plng)*
Monica Tomazin *(Supvr-Media-Digital)*
Samantha Bince *(Media Planner)*
Julie Coplan *(Media Buyer)*
Danya Diaz *(Media Planner-Integrated)*
Savita Lal *(Asst Media Planner)*

Accounts:

American Honda Motor Co., Inc. Honda Motorcycles, Honda Watercraft
Alive! Multivitamin (Agency of Record)
Aspen Dental Management
Dole Food Company, Inc.
International House of Pancakes, Inc.
Intuit Inc. Quicken, Turbo Tax
King's Hawaiian Bakery Hawaiian Sweet Bread, Integrated Communications
Legoland
Nature's Way Brand Strategy, Creative, Media, Web Site
Alive! Multivitamin (Agency of Record)
Nestle USA Baby Ruth, Butterfinger, Campaign: "Cup Therapy", Carnation Instant Breakfast, Nestle Crunch, Peanut Butter Cups, Raisinets, Super Bowl 2014, Wonka

DAISHO CREATIVE STRATEGIES

13280 SW 131 St Ste 105, Miami, FL 33186
Tel.: (305) 234-5617
E-Mail: info@daishocreative.com
Web Site: www.daishocreative.com

Year Founded: 2007

Agency Specializes In: Advertising, Brand Development & Integration, Corporate Identity, Graphic Design, Internet/Web Design, Logo & Package Design, Print, Search Engine Optimization, Social Media

John Keepax *(Owner & Partner)*
Frank Irias *(Principal & Dir-Creative)*
Anita Haynes *(Dir-Strategic Initiatives)*
Aileen Irias *(Mgr-Online Mktg)*

Accounts:
The Barthet Firm
Westminster Christian School

DALLAS RIFFLE MEDIA

3030 E 63rd St Ste 404, Cleveland, OH 44127
Tel.: (330) 274-7658
E-Mail: dallas@dallasriffle.com
Web Site: www.dallasriffle.com

Year Founded: 2014

Agency Specializes In: Advertising, Brand Development & Integration, Content, Internet/Web Design, Package Design, Print, Public Relations, Social Media

Dallas Riffle *(Owner & Creative Dir)*

Accounts:
High Voltage Indoor Karting

DALTON AGENCY JACKSONVILLE

140 W Monroe St, Jacksonville, FL 32202
Tel.: (904) 398-5222
Fax: (904) 398-5220
Toll Free: (888) 409-2691
E-Mail: info@daltonagency.com
Web Site: www.daltonagency.com

E-Mail for Key Personnel:
President: jim@daltonagency.com
Creative Dir.: pat@daltonagency.com
Production Mgr.: david@daltonagency.com
Public Relations: mmunz@daltonagency.com

Employees: 100
Year Founded: 1989

National Agency Associations: AMIN

Agency Specializes In: Advertising, Automotive, Aviation & Aerospace, Brand Development & Integration, Broadcast, Business-To-Business, Cable T.V., Catalogs, Co-op Advertising, Collateral, Communications, Consumer Goods, Consumer Marketing, Corporate Communications, Crisis Communications, Digital/Interactive, Education, Electronic Media, Entertainment, Event Planning & Marketing, Experience Design, Financial, Food Service, Government/Political, Graphic Design, Health Care Services, Information Technology, Internet/Web Design, Investor Relations, Leisure, Logo & Package Design, Luxury Products, Magazines, Marine, Market Research, Media Buying Services, Media Planning, Media Relations, Medical Products, Merchandising, Multimedia, Newspaper, Newspapers & Magazines, Outdoor, Package Design, Point of Purchase, Print, Production, Production (Ad, Film, Broadcast), Production (Print), Promotions, Public Relations, Publicity/Promotions, Radio, Real Estate, Restaurant, Retail, Social Media, Sponsorship, Sports Market, Strategic Planning/Research, T.V., Transportation, Travel & Tourism, Web (Banner Ads, Pop-ups, etc.)

Approx. Annual Billings: $35,000,000

Michael Munz *(Partner & Exec VP)*
Dave Josserand *(Pres-McDonald's Grp)*
Scott Nichols *(VP & Acct Dir)*
Betty Albert *(VP & Dir-Creative Strategy)*
Samantha Lueder *(VP & Dir-PR)*
Tim McGugan *(Mgr-Social Media & Graphic Designer)*
Jack DeYoung *(Mgr-Social Media)*
Anne Logan *(Media Buyer)*
Lisa Myers *(Media Buyer)*
Catherine Conway *(Acct Coord)*
Heather Smith *(Community Mgr-Social Media)*

Accounts:
American Heart Association Campaign: "Go Red for Women", Campaign: "Life is Why", Digital, Logo, Print, Social Media, Television
BAE Systems Products Group Security Equipment Manufacturer
Jacksonville Convention & Visitors Bureau; Jacksonville, FL
Jacksonville Jaguars; Jacksonville, FL NFL Football Team; 2000
Jacksonville Zoo and Gardens
LEGOLAND Florida National Strategic Communications, PR, Social Media
McDonald's-Jacksonville/Tampa Co-op
Ronald McDonald House
Special Counsel
Swisher International; Jacksonville, FL Cigars: Bering, King Edward, Optimo, & Swisher Sweets
W&O Supply Fittings, Marine Valves, Pipes, Valve Automation Services

Branch

Dalton Agency Atlanta

(Formerly Kilgannon)
1360 Peachtree St Ste 700, Atlanta, GA 30309
Tel.: (404) 876-2800
Fax: (404) 876-2830
Web Site: www.daltonagency.com/

Employees: 30
Year Founded: 1988

National Agency Associations: AMIN

Agency Specializes In: Broadcast, Business-To-Business, Cable T.V., Consulting, Corporate Identity, Digital/Interactive, Direct Response Marketing, E-Commerce, Electronic Media, Graphic Design, High Technology, Internet/Web Design, Magazines, Newspapers & Magazines, Out-of-Home Media, Outdoor, Print, Production, Radio, Strategic Planning/Research

Bill Coontz *(Pres)*
Devon Suter *(Exec VP & Exec Dir-Creative)*
Kevyn Faulkenberry *(VP & Exec Dir-Creative)*
Jack DeYoung *(Mgr-Social Media)*
Roland Alonzi *(Sr Acct Supvr)*
Catherine Conway *(Acct Exec)*
Ryan Gambrell *(Acct Exec)*
Elizabeth Jarrard *(Acct Exec)*
Karen McAllister *(Acct Exec)*
Kyle Speckman *(Acct Exec)*

Accounts:
American Suzuki Corporation
Attorneys' Title Insurance Fund
Cleaver-Brooks, Inc.
CSC Holdings, LLC
The Fund
Georgia Federal Credit Union
The Georgia Force
Manheim Manheim, Manheim.com
NYCM Insurance
SecureWorks, Inc.
SouthernLINC Wireless

DALY GRAY PUBLIC RELATIONS

620 Herndon Pkwy Ste 115, Herndon, VA 20170
Tel.: (703) 435-6293
Web Site: www.dalygray.com

Agency Specializes In: Advertising, Brand Development & Integration, Crisis Communications, Event Planning & Marketing, Media Relations, Public Relations

Chris Daly *(Owner & Pres)*
Carol McCune *(Exec VP)*
Sonia Abdulbaki *(VP)*
Patrick Daly *(Acct Supvr)*

Accounts:
New-Chatham Lodging Trust

DALYN MILLER PUBLIC RELATIONS, LLC.

1134 W Granville Ave Ste 1217, Chicago, IL 60660
Tel.: (617) 504-6869
Fax: (773) 856-6004
E-Mail: dalyn@dalynmillerpr.com
Web Site: www.dalynmillerpr.com

Employees: 3

Agency Specializes In: Arts, Brand Development & Integration, Communications, Consulting, Graphic Design, Health Care Services, Identity Marketing, Local Marketing, Media Relations, New Technologies, Promotions, Public Relations, Publishing, Radio, Social Marketing/Nonprofit, T.V., Travel & Tourism

Dalyn A. Miller *(Principal)*

Accounts:
Arcade Publishing
Gibbs Smith Publishers
Pure Prescriptions, Inc.
Stormship

DAMO ADVERTISING

1338 Pasadena St, San Antonio, TX 78201
Tel.: (210) 544-9818
Web Site: www.damoadvertising.com

Year Founded: 2009

Agency Specializes In: Advertising, Brand Development & Integration, Digital/Interactive, Internet/Web Design, Package Design, Print

David Martinez *(Pres)*

Accounts:

David&Erick Clothing Co

DAN PIPKIN ADVERTISING AGENCY, INC.

429 N Walnut St, Danville, IL 61832
Tel.: (217) 446-1021
Fax: (217) 446-3062
Web Site: www.danpipkinadvertising.com

Employees: 5
Year Founded: 1953

National Agency Associations: APA

Agency Specializes In: Advertising, Advertising Specialties, Agriculture, Automotive, Bilingual Market, Brand Development & Integration, Broadcast, Business Publications, Business-To-Business, Cable T.V., Children's Market, Co-op Advertising, Collateral, Commercial Photography, Communications, Consulting, Consumer Marketing, Consumer Publications, Corporate Communications, Corporate Identity, Direct Response Marketing, E-Commerce, Education, Electronic Media, Event Planning & Marketing, Exhibit/Trade Shows, Food Service, Government/Political, Graphic Design, Health Care Services, In-Store Advertising, Industrial, Internet/Web Design, Local Marketing, Logo & Package Design, Magazines, Marine, Media Buying Services, Medical Products, Merchandising, New Product Development, Newspaper, Newspapers & Magazines, Outdoor, Over-50 Market, Point of Purchase, Point of Sale, Print, Production, Public Relations, Publicity/Promotions, Radio, Retail, Sales Promotion, Seniors' Market, Sports Market, Strategic Planning/Research, T.V., Technical Advertising, Teen Market, Trade & Consumer Magazines, Travel & Tourism, Yellow Pages Advertising

Approx. Annual Billings: $1,090,000

Brad Pipkin *(Acct Supvr)*

Accounts:
Allomatic
Champion Enterprises Holdings, LLC
PRI
Raybestos
Rumford Clabber Girl
Stalcop
Stretchpak

DANA COMMUNICATIONS, INC.

2 E Broad St, Hopewell, NJ 08525
Tel.: (609) 466-9187
Fax: (609) 466-8608
E-Mail: info@danacommunications.com
Web Site: www.danacommunications.com

Employees: 35
Year Founded: 1979

Agency Specializes In: Digital/Interactive, Internet/Web Design

Lynn Kaniper *(Owner & COO)*
Robert Prewitt *(Pres)*
Tracy Stottler *(Exec Dir)*
Charisse Gallagher *(Sr Dir-Art)*
Mark D'Amico *(Dir-Search & Analytics)*
Karen Paton *(Dir-Media)*
Shawn Carter Kusenko *(Copywriter)*
Colleen Miele *(Copywriter)*

Accounts:
American Express
Avis
Benchmark Hospitality
Berlitz
Callaway Gardens
Cheapoair
Christophe Harbour
Hilton Short Hills
Kiawah Island Golf Resort
Millennium Hotels & Resorts

Branches

Dana Communications

350 5th Ave Ste 2620, New York, NY 10118
Tel.: (212) 736-0060
Fax: (212) 736-6669
Web Site: www.danacommunications.com

Employees: 10

Lynn Kaniper *(Owner & COO)*
Bob Prewitt *(Pres)*
Jackie Ellis *(Sr Dir-Art)*
Stephen Sharp *(Dir-Interactive)*
Sandy Welsh *(Dir-Accts, Strategy & Res)*
Virginia Lomanto *(Media Planner)*

Accounts:
AAA
American Express
Callaway Gardens
Cheapoair
Columbia University Faculty House

Dana Communications

5690 Bromley Dr, Kernersville, NC 27284
Tel.: (336) 993-3202
Fax: (336) 993-3492
Web Site: www.danacommunications.com

Employees: 30

Lynn Kaniper *(Owner & COO)*
Charisse Gallagher *(Sr Dir-Art)*
Sandy Welsh *(Dir-Accts, Strategy & Res)*
Shawn Carter Kusenko *(Copywriter)*
Colleen Miele *(Copywriter)*

Accounts:
AAA
American Express
Christophe Harbour
Hilton Short Hills
Iacc
National Conference Center
Starwood

DANIEL, BURTON, DEAN ADVERTISING & DESIGN, INC.

225 Court St, Evansville, IN 47708
Tel.: (812) 426-0551
Fax: (812) 422-5386
Toll Free: (800) 687-4599
E-Mail: eville@dbd15.com
Web Site: dbd15.com/

Employees: 10
Year Founded: 1976

National Agency Associations: AAF

Agency Specializes In: Advertising, Affiliate Marketing, Below-the-Line, Brand Development & Integration, Catalogs, Children's Market, Collateral, Commercial Photography, Communications, Consumer Goods, Consumer Marketing, Corporate Communications, Corporate Identity, Customer Relationship Management, Digital/Interactive, Direct-to-Consumer, E-Commerce, Email, Exhibit/Trade Shows, Experience Design, Graphic Design, Guerilla Marketing, Household Goods, Identity Marketing, In-Store Advertising, Information Technology, Integrated Marketing, Internet/Web Design, Local Marketing, Logo & Package Design, Media Planning, Men's Market, Multimedia, New Product Development, Newspaper, Out-of-Home Media, Outdoor, Package Design, Paid Searches, Point of Purchase, Point of Sale, Print, Production, Production (Print), Promotions, RSS (Really Simple Syndication), Regional, Retail, Sales Promotion, Search Engine Optimization, Social Media, Sports Market, Strategic Planning/Research, Technical Advertising, Trade & Consumer Magazines, Transportation, Viral/Buzz/Word of Mouth, Web (Banner Ads, Pop-ups, etc.), Women's Market, Yellow Pages Advertising

Phil Mowrey *(Principal & Dir-Creative)*
Stephanie Whitcomb *(VP-Client Svcs-Delmarva)*
Jodie Lynn *(Acct Svcs Dir)*
Michelle Frazer *(Office Mgr)*
David Wright *(Mgr-Creative)*

Accounts:
Alexander Mobility Services; Baltimore, MD Moving and Relocation Service
Atlas World Group, Inc.; Evansville, IN Moving Services, Relocation Service; 1989
Avail Resource Management; Evansville, IN Move Management Services; 2003
Goalrilla Basketball; Evansville, IN Residential Basketball Systems; 1997
Golden Van Lines; Longmont, CO Moving Services
Mesker Park Zoo
Mizerak
Mobility
Rocket Aeroheads
STIGA Table Tennis; Evansville, IN Table Tennis & Accessories; 1993
Titan Global Distribution; Saint Louis, MO Corporate/Industrial Logistics; 2006
Truth 2 Micro Site
Woodplay Playsets; Raleigh, NC Residential Playground/Swingsets; 2008
Wordman Inc.

DANIELS & ROBERTS, INC.

209 N Seacrest Blvd Ste 209, Boynton Beach, FL 33435
Tel.: (561) 241-0066
Fax: (561) 241-1198
Toll Free: (800) 488-0066
E-Mail: info@danielsandroberts.com
Web Site: www.danielsandroberts.com

E-Mail for Key Personnel:
President: dmuggeo@danielsandroberts.com
Creative Dir.: fparente@danielsandroberts.com
Production Mgr.: fcoffy@danielsandroberts.com

Employees: 25
Year Founded: 1986

Agency Specializes In: Brand Development & Integration, Business-To-Business, Commercial Photography, Communications, Consumer Marketing, Hispanic Market, Planning & Consultation, Production

Daniel A. Muggeo *(Founder & CEO)*
Fran Parente *(VP & Dir-Creative)*
Amy Scharf *(VP-Client Svcs-Analytically Driven Mktg Strategies & Creative Dev)*
Mary Dundore *(Comptroller)*
Frank Coffy *(Dir-Production)*
Chuck Knapick *(Dir-Interactive Svcs)*
Andrea Pendergraft *(Acct Supvr-Mktg, Analytics & Adv)*

Accounts:
Citrix
Dole
HP
IBM
Travelpro

DARBY O'BRIEN ADVERTISING

9 College St, South Hadley, MA 01075
Tel.: (413) 533-7045
E-Mail: hello@darbyobrien.com
Web Site: www.darbyobrien.com

Agency Specializes In: Advertising, Brand Development & Integration, Print, T.V.

Mat Dubord *(Dir-Art)*
Gainer O'Brien *(Dir-Creative)*

Accounts:
Soldier On

DARCI CREATIVE
96 Chestnut St, Portsmouth, NH 03801
Tel.: (603) 436-6330
Web Site: www.edarci.com

Year Founded: 2006

Agency Specializes In: Advertising, Brand Development & Integration, Internet/Web Design, Public Relations, Strategic Planning/Research

Darci Knowles *(Dir-Creative & Copywriter)*
Regan Bowlen *(Dir-Art)*
Riddy Hosser *(Mgr-Social Media)*
Daniele Cyr *(Sr Acct Exec)*

Accounts:
The Blue Mermaid Island Grill

D'ARCY & PARTNERS, LLC
1178 Broadway Ste 321, New York, NY 10001
Tel.: (917) 297-1952
Web Site: www.darcyandpartners.com

E-Mail for Key Personnel:
Creative Dir.: shelagh@darcyandpartners.com
Production Mgr.: kristin@darcyandpartners.com

Employees: 6
Year Founded: 2003

Agency Specializes In: Brand Development & Integration, Corporate Identity, Graphic Design, Strategic Planning/Research

Accounts:
Elizabeth Arden
Soho House Club/Hotel
Splashlight Studios
Sue Devitt, Beauty
Wolffer Wines

DARK HORSE MARKETING
1 Fifth Ave, Pelham, NY 10803
Tel.: (914) 632-1584
Fax: (914) 632-1586
E-Mail: info@darkhorsemarketing.com
Web Site: www.darkhorsemarketing.com

Employees: 5
Year Founded: 2002

Agency Specializes In: Advertising, Brand Development & Integration, Business-To-Business, Catalogs, Collateral, Consulting, Corporate Communications, Digital/Interactive, E-Commerce, Electronic Media, Graphic Design, Integrated Marketing, Internet/Web Design, Logo & Package Design, Media Buying Services, Media Relations, Multimedia, Search Engine Optimization, Social Media, Strategic Planning/Research, Trade & Consumer Magazines, Web (Banner Ads, Pop-ups, etc.)

Belinda Brouder Hayes *(Owner)*

Accounts:
Mercator Companies
Premium Funding Group

DARK HORSE MEDIA
4441 E 5th St, Tucson, AZ 85711
Tel.: (520) 748-1010
Web Site: www.darkhorsemedia.com

Agency Specializes In: Advertising, Brand Development & Integration, Collateral, Internet/Web Design, Media Buying Services, Print, Social Media, T.V.

Julie Davey *(Co-Owner)*
Linda Fahey *(Co-Owner)*
Squirrel Rippley *(Coord-Production)*

Accounts:
University of Arizona

DARLING
(Formerly Darling Agency)
181 Christopher St, New York, NY 10014
Tel.: (212) 242-2000
Fax: (212) 242-2230
Web Site: www.darlingagency.com

Employees: 12
Year Founded: 2008

Agency Specializes In: Advertising, Brand Development & Integration, Identity Marketing, Logo & Package Design, Social Media, Sponsorship, T.V.

Kelly Platt *(Pres)*
Jeroen Bours *(CEO)*
Nigel Carr *(Chief Strategy Officer)*
Jonathan Kampner *(Chief Architect-Digital)*
Kiumars Gourki *(Dir-Creative)*
Jane Schneider *(Dir-Digital)*
Josh Schweser *(Designer)*

Accounts:
ACE Group (Advertising Agency of Record); 2010
BMC Software (Advertising Agency of Record); 2015
Cirrus
Genpact Advertising Agency of Record
Hamilton Beach
Hearst Entertainment
The Medical Letter (Advertising Agency of Record)
Melrose Credit Union (Advertising Agency of Record)
OXO (Advertising Agency of Record); 2013
QuickView
New-Rainforest Trust
Selfie.com
Somerset Partners (Advertising Agency of Record)

DARRYL DOUGLAS MEDIA
5435 La Jolla Blvd, La Jolla, CA 92037
Tel.: (858) 336-0090
Web Site: www.darryldouglasmedia.com

Year Founded: 2008

Agency Specializes In: Advertising, Content, Digital/Interactive, Internet/Web Design

Michael P. Puckett *(Pres)*

Accounts:
Always Half Price

DAS GROUP, INC.
9050 Pines Blvd Ste 250, Pembroke Pines, FL 33024
Tel.: (954) 893-8112
Fax: (954) 893-8143
Toll Free: (800) 717-2131
E-Mail: info@das-group.com
Web Site: www.das-group.com

E-Mail for Key Personnel:
President: joe@das-group.com
Media Dir.: karen@das-group.com

Employees: 22
Year Founded: 1980

Agency Specializes In: Digital/Interactive, Graphic Design, High Technology, Internet/Web Design, Newspaper, Recruitment, Yellow Pages Advertising

Approx. Annual Billings: $10,000,000

Christina Parsons *(Co-Owner & Pres)*
Karen Korner *(CEO)*
Gary Meares *(COO)*
Martin Pillot *(Dir-Creative)*
Rafael Pichardo *(Mgr-SEM & Production)*
Sally Zaki *(Mgr-Online Mktg)*
Jessica Albert *(Coord-SEO & Social Media)*
Liat Stilman *(Coord-Sls & Mktg)*

Accounts:
Barron Development
Truly Nolen Pest Control

Branches

DAS Group
1501 Ogden Ave, Downers Grove, IL 60515
Tel.: (630) 678-0100
Fax: (630) 678-0067
E-Mail: info@das-group.com
Web Site: www.das-group.com

Employees: 1

Mary Ruggiero *(Sr Acct Exec)*

DASHBOARD
355 Adelaide St W Ste 200, Toronto, ON M5V 1S2 Canada
Tel.: (416) 504-4422
Fax: (416) 504-6644
Toll Free: (866) 504-6354
E-Mail: fuel@dashboard.ca
Web Site: http://www.poweredbydashboard.com/

Employees: 30

Agency Specializes In: Communications, Digital/Interactive

Jasmine Lin *(Dir-Art)*
Isabelle Santiago *(Dir-Art)*
Jennifer Hillier *(Mgr-Office Admin)*

Accounts:
Axe
H&R Block
Hellmann's
Home Hardware
ING Direct (Agency of Record)
Torstar Website Development, Winefox
Toyota Dealers
Vaseline

DATA SUPPLY CO.
4624 16 St E Ste A2, Tacoma, WA 98424-2664
Tel.: (253) 922-3494
Fax: (253) 922-7802
Toll Free: (800) 830-0816
Web Site: www.datasupplyco.com

Year Founded: 1991

Agency Specializes In: Advertising, Print, Production (Print)

Approx. Annual Billings: $500,000

Tom Patten *(Owner)*

DATALAB USA LLC

20261 Goldenrod Ln, Germantown, MD 20876-4063
Tel.: (301) 972-1430
Fax: (301) 972-3638
Toll Free: (800) 972-1430
E-Mail: info@datalabusa.com
Web Site: www.datalabusa.com

Year Founded: 1979

Agency Specializes In: Communications, Education, Financial, Retail, Strategic Planning/Research, Telemarketing

Hans Aigner *(CEO)*
Amby Rufino *(Partner & Exec VP)*
Olga Aigner *(COO)*
Alex Aigner *(Exec VP-Bus Dev)*
Seth Goodman *(Exec VP-Client Svcs)*
Ryder Warehall *(Exec VP-IT & Security)*
Aaron Davis *(VP-Analytics Team)*
Jay Kim *(VP-Fin Svcs)*
Nino Ajami *(Sr Dir-Database Solutions)*

Accounts:
American Heart Association Inc. Hospitality Service Providers
Citigroup Inc. Banking & Finance Services
ING Direct Banking & Finance Services
Johns Hopkins University Educational Institution

DATRAN MEDIA LLC.

(Name Changed to PulsePoint)

DAVID

Avenida Pedrosa de Morais 15553, 2 Andar, Sao Paulo, 05477 900 Brazil
Tel.: (55) 11 3065 6000
Web Site: www.davidtheagency.com/

Agency Specializes In: Advertising, Bilingual Market, Hispanic Market

Gaston Bigio, *(Founder)*
Rodrigo Grau *(VP-Creative)*
Veronica Beach *(Head-Production-Global)*
Carol Vieira *(Acct Dir)*
Diego Barboza *(Dir-Art)*
Edgard Gianesi *(Dir-Creative)*
Bruno Luglio *(Dir-Art)*
Jean Zamprogno *(Dir-Art)*
Russell Dodson *(Assoc Dir-Creative & Copywriter)*
Rafael Giorgino *(Acct Supvr)*
Natalie Bursztyn *(Acct Exec)*
Joao Gandara *(Copywriter)*
Fernando Pellizzaro *(Copywriter)*
Renata Neumann *(Asst Producer)*

Accounts:
Aquarius
Burger King (Lead Global Agency) Big King Sandwich, Broadcast, Campaign: "Be Your Way", Campaign: "Change always leaves a mark", Campaign: "Coopid", Campaign: "Date", Campaign: "Subservient Chicken", Chicken Fries, Chicken Strips, Marketing, Social Media, Video
Coca-Cola
Faber-Castell
Flora
Fuze Tea
HBO
Iguatemi
Jaguar
The Kraft Heinz Company Campaign: "Backyard BBQ", Campaign: "Ketchup's Got a New Mustard", Heinz Mustard
McCain
Milka
Sony
spectraBan
Staples
Stiefel
Unicef
Unilever Project Sunlight, TV
Vodafone

Branch

DAVID The Agency

1395 Brickell Ave Ste 900, Miami, FL 33131
Tel.: (305) 967-6342
Web Site: www.davidtheagency.com

Agency Specializes In: Advertising, Brand Development & Integration

Paulo Fogaca *(Mng Dir)*
Fernando Ribeiro *(Head-Planning)*
Rodrigo Bistene *(Art Dir)*
Ricardo Casal *(Art Dir)*
Ricardo Honegger *(Acct Dir)*
Tony Kalathara *(Assoc Creative Dir)*
Danny Alvarez *(Assoc Dir-Creative)*
Rafael Giorgino *(Acct Supvr)*
Ivan Guerra *(Copywriter)*
Russell Dodson *(Assoc Creative Dir)*

Accounts:
New-Burger King Corporation
New-Coca-Cola

DAVID & GOLIATH

909 N Sepulveda Blvd Ste 700, El Segundo, CA 90245
Tel.: (310) 445-5200
Fax: (310) 445-5201
E-Mail: cjstockton@dng.com
Web Site: www.dng.com

Employees: 140
Year Founded: 1999

National Agency Associations: 4A's-AAF-THINKLA

Agency Specializes In: Advertising, Automotive, Brand Development & Integration, Children's Market, Co-op Advertising, Collateral, Consumer Marketing, Consumer Publications, Corporate Identity, Cosmetics, Direct Response Marketing, Electronic Media, Entertainment, Event Planning & Marketing, Fashion/Apparel, Financial, Food Service, Government/Political, Health Care Services, Leisure, Logo & Package Design, Magazines, Media Buying Services, Merchandising, New Product Development, Newspaper, Newspapers & Magazines, Out-of-Home Media, Outdoor, Planning & Consultation, Point of Purchase, Point of Sale, Print, Production, Public Relations, Publicity/Promotions, Radio, Restaurant, Retail, Sales Promotion, Seniors' Market, Sponsorship, Sports Market, Strategic Planning/Research, T.V., Trade & Consumer Magazines, Transportation, Travel & Tourism

Mike Geiger *(Mng Partner & Chief Digital Officer)*
Jeff Moohr *(Mng Dir)*
Gerald Duran *(CFO)*
Colin Jeffery *(Chief Creative Officer)*
Bobby Pearce *(Exec Dir-Creative)*
Steve Yee *(Exec Dir-Creative)*
Paul Albanese *(Exec Producer)*
Karen Jean *(Sr Producer-Brdcst)*
Carrie Lighthall *(Sr Producer-Brdcst)*
Merav Cohen *(Acct Dir)*
Scott Friedman *(Creative Dir)*
Gordon Gray *(Acct Dir)*
Erik Moe *(Creative Dir)*
Mark Monteiro *(Creative Dir)*
Stacia Parseghian *(Acct Dir)*
Melissa Spano *(Acct Dir)*
Robert Boucher *(Dir-Digital Delivery & Tech)*
Robert Casillas *(Dir-Art)*
Brandon Davis *(Dir-Creative)*
Andrew Lynch *(Dir-Strategic Plng)*
Andrea Mariash *(Dir-Art Production)*
John O'Hea *(Dir-Creative)*
Rodney Pizarro *(Dir-Bus & Legal Affairs)*
Driscoll Reid *(Dir-Creative)*
Frances Rhodes *(Dir-Creative Svcs)*
Andrea Schindler *(Dir-Design)*
Meredith Walsh *(Dir-Print Svcs)*
Marc Wilson *(Dir-Art)*
Shaun Wright *(Dir-Art)*
Russ Wortman *(Mgr-Product Info)*
Kylie Lemasters *(Acct Exec)*
Annelise Lorenzo *(Acct Exec)*
Kacey Coburn *(Copywriter)*
Ed Gibson *(Planner)*
Andy Sciamanna *(Copywriter)*
Jessica Watts *(Acct Planner)*

Accounts:
California Lottery (Lead Advertising Agency) Advertising Assignment, Black Scratchers, Campaign: "California Lucky for Life Scratchers", Campaign: "It's All Yours", Campaign: "Lady Luck", Campaign: "Luck Will Find You", Campaign: "More Luck for Your Buck", Campaign: "Wheel of Fortune Scratchers", Campaign: "When You Give, You Win", Digital, Fortune 55 Scratchers, Mobile, OOH, Radio, Social, TV, Taxes Paid Scratchers
Carl's Jr Campaign: "Robot", Campaign: "Say Cheese", Hardee's
Coca-Cola Zico
Dragon Noodle Co
Hot Air Balloon
Jack in the Box Inc. Buttery Jack, Campaign: "Legendary", Campaign: "World's Largest Coupon", Super Bowl 2015
Kia Motors America (Advertising Agency of Record) "Drive Change", "The Matrix", 'Morpheus', 2016 Kia Sorento CUV, Advertising, Borrego, Campaign: "5 Hours of Adriana Lima", Campaign: "Apologize to You", Campaign: "Blake Griffin Kia Dunk", Campaign: "Brilliant Machines", Campaign: "Chess", Campaign: "Cuidando de ti", Campaign: "Drive The Dream", Campaign: "Fit for a King", Campaign: "Fully Charged", Campaign: "Hamstar Apparel", Campaign: "Hotbots", Campaign: "It Challenges Everything", Campaign: "It has an answer for everything", Campaign: "Next Level", Campaign: "PB&J", Campaign: "Pez", Campaign: "Preconceived Notions", Campaign: "Showdown", Campaign: "Soul Shuffle Slam", Campaign: "Space Babies", Campaign: "Take On Blake Dunk Challenge", Campaign: "Techathlete Games", Campaign: "The Griffin Force", Campaign: "The Perfect Getaway Vehicle", Campaign: "The Truth" Super Bowl 2014, Campaign: "Tight Space", Campaign: "Totally Transformed", Campaign: "Trailer", Campaign: "Unexpected", Campaign: "Valet", Campaign: "Weatherman", Campaign: "Zipline", Digital, Forte, Hamstar (TM) Clothing, K900, Kia Optima, Kia Optima Panoramic Sunroof, Social Media, Sorento, Soul, Soul EV, Spectra, Super Bowl 2015, TV, This or That Campaign; 2000
Lance Burton Master Magician
Martini & Rossi Creative, Digital, Martini Asti Sparkling Wine Brand, Outdoor, Print, Strategy, Television
Miss Turkey Charbroiled Turkey Burger
Monte Carlo Resort & Casino Campaign: "Beer Labels", Pub
New York Hotel & Casino; Las Vegas, NV Campaign: "Be A Part of It", Rok Vegas

Nightclub; 2008
NFL Enterprises Campaign: "Mountain"
Scientific Games/MDI Entertainment, LLC
Southwest Airlines
Universal Orlando Resort 18th Annual Halloween Horror Nights; 2001
Universal Studios Hollywood
VIZIO Advertising, Campaign: "Beautifully Simple", Campaign: "Fallen Tree", Campaign: "My Station", Campaign: "See the Beauty in Everything", Campaign: "Slam Dunk Poetry", Campaign: "So Easy", Campaign: "Tiny Dancer", Campaign: "Turkey Dinner", M-Series Smart TV, P-Series Ultra HD TV, Sound Bar
Zoo York Footwear

DAVID GELLER ASSOCIATES, INC.

1071 Avenue Of The Americas 11th Fl, New York, NY 10018
Tel.: (212) 455-0100
E-Mail: sales@davidgellarasoc.com

Employees: 20
Year Founded: 1945

Agency Specializes In: Alternative Advertising, Direct Response Marketing, Magazines, Media Planning, Newspaper, Newspapers & Magazines, Print, Strategic Planning/Research

Approx. Annual Billings: $30,000,000

Mike Shapiro *(Pres & Principal)*
Katherine Zito *(Exec VP)*
Wanda Zarrillo *(VP-Adv Sls)*
Wendy Feuer *(Dir-Adv Sls)*

Accounts:
Nutrisystem

THE DAVID GROUP INC.

526 Superior Ave E Ste 333, Cleveland, OH 44114-1983
Tel.: (216) 687-1890
Fax: (216) 687-1482
Toll Free: (800) 686-1818
E-Mail: solutions@davidgroup.com
Web Site: www.davidgroup.com

Employees: 25
Year Founded: 1977

Agency Specializes In: Event Planning & Marketing, Health Care Services, Industrial, Internet/Web Design, Recruitment

Breakdown of Gross Billings by Media: Mags.: 5%; Newsp.: 95%

Louis R. Schaul *(Owner)*

Accounts:
Columbia Hospital
Cook Children's
Hilmar
Northeast Georgia Health System
Shure
St. Lucie Medical Center
TDS

The David Group

PO Box 115, Lockport, IL 60441
Tel.: (815) 838-3000
Fax: (800) 447-0729 (Outside IL)
Toll Free: (800) 548-8189
E-Mail: rdisanto@davidgroup.com
Web Site: www.davidgroup.com

Employees: 1
Year Founded: 1972

Agency Specializes In: Advertising, Graphic Design, Recruitment

Joanna Meis *(Reg VP)*
Rick DiSanto *(Acct Mgr)*
Jessica Tang *(Project Mgr & Acct Exec)*

Accounts:
College of Lake County
Metra
RR Donnelley

DAVID ID, INC.

83 Delafield Island Rd 1st Fl, Darien, CT 06820
Tel.: (203) 662-0678
Fax: (203) 662-0026
E-Mail: info@davidid.com
Web Site: www.davidid.com

Employees: 3

Agency Specializes In: Advertising, Brand Development & Integration

Carl Nichols *(Founder & CEO)*
Bob Hogan *(Dir-Customer Comm & Engagement)*
Dan Knol *(Dir-Design)*

Accounts:
Aon
AstraZeneca
Avantair
FitLinxx
HealthMarkets

THE DAVID JAMES AGENCY

223 E Thousand Oaks Blvd Ste 417, Thousand Oaks, CA 91360
Tel.: (805) 494-9508
Fax: (805) 494-8610
E-Mail: dja@davidjamesagency.com
Web Site: www.davidjamesagency.com

Employees: 5

Agency Specializes In: Advertising, High Technology

David Rodewald *(Mng Dir)*
Amber Hack *(Sr Mgr-Content)*

Accounts:
Guidance Software
MaxLinear Inc.
Semtech
Transition Networks, Inc

DAVID JAMES GROUP

1 Trans Am Plz Dr Ste 300, Oakbrook Terrace, IL 60181
Tel.: (630) 305-0003
Fax: (630) 384-1478
E-Mail: dlaurenzo@davidjamesgroup.com
Web Site: www.davidjamesgroup.com

Employees: 17
Year Founded: 2002

National Agency Associations: BMA

Agency Specializes In: Advertising, Advertising Specialties, Brand Development & Integration, Business-To-Business, Catalogs, Collateral, Communications, Consumer Goods, Content, Corporate Communications, Corporate Identity, Direct Response Marketing, Direct-to-Consumer, Electronic Media, Email, Event Planning & Marketing, Food Service, Graphic Design, Health Care Services, Identity Marketing, In-Store Advertising, Integrated Marketing, Internet/Web Design, Local Marketing, Newspapers & Magazines, Outdoor, Paid Searches, Planning & Consultation, Point of Sale, Print, Production (Print), Public Relations, Retail, Sales Promotion, Strategic Planning/Research, Trade & Consumer Magazines, Web (Banner Ads, Pop-ups, etc.)

Approx. Annual Billings: $2,000,000

David Laurenzo *(Founder & Pres)*
Anne O'Day *(Mng Dir)*
Ron Zywicki *(VP-Creative Svcs)*
Cheryl Peaslee *(Dir-Art)*
Stephanie Brown *(Acct Mgr)*

Accounts:
ACCO Brands Corporation
American Dairy Science Association
Association for Manufacturing Excellence
Darwill
Ecolab
GE Access
Nokia
Transamerica Life & Protection Direct Solutions Group, Marketing, Message Development, Sales Collateral, Trade Show Planning & Promotions
Zip-Pak

DAVID K. BURNAP ADVERTISING AGENCY, INC.

36 S Main St, Centerville, OH 45458
Tel.: (937) 439-4800
Fax: (937) 242-6602
E-Mail: dkb@dkburnap.com
Web Site: www.dkburnap.com

Employees: 9
Year Founded: 1959

Agency Specializes In: Advertising, Advertising Specialties, Aviation & Aerospace, Brand Development & Integration, Broadcast, Business Publications, Business-To-Business, Cable T.V., Co-op Advertising, Collateral, Communications, Consulting, Consumer Marketing, Consumer Publications, Corporate Communications, Corporate Identity, Direct Response Marketing, E-Commerce, Electronic Media, Engineering, Event Planning & Marketing, Exhibit/Trade Shows, Financial, Graphic Design, Health Care Services, High Technology, Industrial, Internet/Web Design, Local Marketing, Logo & Package Design, Magazines, Media Buying Services, Merchandising, New Product Development, Newspaper, Newspapers & Magazines, Outdoor, Planning & Consultation, Point of Purchase, Point of Sale, Print, Production, Public Relations, Publicity/Promotions, Radio, Recruitment, Retail, Sales Promotion, Strategic Planning/Research, T.V., Technical Advertising, Trade & Consumer Magazines, Yellow Pages Advertising

Breakdown of Gross Billings by Media: Collateral: 10%; Internet Adv.: 12%; Logo & Package Design: 2%; Pub. Rels.: 5%; Radio & T.V.: 1%; Trade & Consumer Mags.: 58%; Worldwide Web Sites: 12%

David K. Burnap, Jr. *(Pres)*
Dennis Hays *(VP-Creative Svcs)*

Accounts:
AAA Ohio; Columbus, OH Auto Club; 1997
Buckeye Fabricating; Dayton, OH Pressure Vessels; 2002
Hitachi Solutions; Austin, TX Consulting; 2001
Krud Kutter; Atlanta, GA Household Cleaning Products; 2004
PDI; Springboro, OH Entertainment Systems; 2003
Perfecto Industries; Piqua, OH Coil Processing Systems; 2000
Production Tube Cutting; Dayton, OH Tube Cutting Systems; 2003
Trimble; Sunnyvale, CA Laser, Optical & GPS Measurement Systems; 1993

Wagner Smith Corp.; Dayton, OH Electrical Services & Supplies; 1985

DAVIDSON & BELLUSO
4105 N 20th St Ste 155, Phoenix, AZ 85016
Tel.: (602) 277-1185
Fax: (602) 277-0320
E-Mail: info@davidsonbelluso.com
Web Site: www.davidsonbelluso.com

Employees: 6
Year Founded: 2001

Agency Specializes In: Advertising, Aviation & Aerospace, Brand Development & Integration, College, Consulting, Corporate Communications, Corporate Identity, Direct Response Marketing, Exhibit/Trade Shows, Graphic Design, Health Care Services, Internet/Web Design, Logo & Package Design, Marine, New Product Development, Over-50 Market, Print, Production (Print), Search Engine Optimization, Social Marketing/Nonprofit, Social Media, Travel & Tourism

Approx. Annual Billings: $1,000,000

Breakdown of Gross Billings by Media: Collateral: $200,000; Consulting: $500,000; Corp. Communications: $100,000; D.M.: $100,000; Fees: $100,000

Rob Davidson *(Owner)*
Michela Belluso Davidson *(Mng Partner)*
Justin Horton *(Mgr-Interactive Svcs)*
Rebekah Knoll *(Acct Exec)*
Christine Korecki *(Acct Exec)*
Janelle VanDriel *(Acct Exec)*
Gustavo Estrella *(Sr Designer)*

Accounts:
Sky Harbor; Phoenix, AZ Brand, Design, Logo; 2003
Tempe Tourism Office

DAVIES MURPHY GROUP
200 Wheeler Rd N Tower, Burlington, MA 01803
Tel.: (781) 418-2400
Fax: (781) 418-2480
Web Site: www.daviesmurphy.com

Employees: 50

Agency Specializes In: Public Relations

Doug Broad *(Sr Mng Dir)*
Rebecca Blouin *(Mng Dir)*
Jan Bryson *(Mng Dir)*
Mark Daly *(Mng Dir)*
Sharon Dratch *(Mng Dir)*
Drew Miale *(Mng Dir)*
Christi Dean Nicolacopoulos *(Mng Dir)*
Mariah Torpey *(Mng Dir)*
Eric Davies *(Principal)*
Rick McLaughlin *(Mng Dir-PR)*
Joseph Rigoli *(Acct Mgr)*
Kerry Quintiliani *(Specialist-PR)*

Accounts:
Ciena Corporation
Cross Beam Systems
DataCore Software
Dimension Data
Internap Corporation
MDNX PR
NetScout Systems Inc.
Red Lion Controls Media
Sixnet

DAVIESMOORE
805 Idaho St Ste 300, Boise, ID 83702
Tel.: (208) 472-2129
Fax: (208) 472-7450
E-Mail: info@daviesmoore.com
Web Site: www.daviesmoore.com

Employees: 29
Year Founded: 1953

National Agency Associations: Second Wind Limited

Agency Specializes In: Advertising, Brand Development & Integration, Broadcast, Business Publications, Business-To-Business, Cable T.V., Co-op Advertising, Communications, Consulting, Consumer Marketing, Consumer Publications, Corporate Identity, Digital/Interactive, E-Commerce, Electronic Media, Exhibit/Trade Shows, Financial, Food Service, Graphic Design, Health Care Services, High Technology, Industrial, Internet/Web Design, Local Marketing, Logo & Package Design, Magazines, Media Buying Services, Media Planning, Multimedia, Newspaper, Newspapers & Magazines, Out-of-Home Media, Outdoor, Planning & Consultation, Point of Purchase, Point of Sale, Print, Production, Production (Print), Public Relations, Publicity/Promotions, Radio, Restaurant, Retail, Sales Promotion, Social Media, Strategic Planning/Research, T.V., Trade & Consumer Magazines, Web (Banner Ads, Pop-ups, etc.)

Approx. Annual Billings: $3,200,000

Edward Moore *(Founder & Partner)*
Carolyn Lodge *(COO & Partner)*
Tanya Vaughan *(Chief Digital Officer & Partner)*
Michael Reagan *(VP-Creative)*
Vicki L. Ward *(Controller)*
Roger Finch *(Dir-Fin)*
Mel Mansfield *(Dir-Web Strategy)*
Ernie Monroe *(Assoc Dir-Creative)*
Jason Sievers *(Assoc Dir-Creative)*
Aaron Grable *(Designer)*
Brooke Smith *(Sr Media Buyer)*

Accounts:
Fredriksen Insurance; Boise, ID
Idaho Motorcycle Safety Education Program; Boise, ID
Intermountain Gas Co.; Boise, ID Natural Gas
Jones & Swartz LLP
Journal Broadcast Group; Boise, ID Radio Station Network
Magic Valley Regional Medical Center
Miyasako Brothers International, Inc.
Premier Insurance
Primary Health Medical Group; Boise, ID Digestive Health Clinic
Summit Seed; Caldwell, ID Seed Coating
Syringa Networks
Trinity Trailer Manufacturing; Boise, ID Conveyer Trailers
United Dairymen of Idaho; Boise, ID Commodity Commission

DAVIS ADVERTISING, INC.
1331 Grafton St, Worcester, MA 01604
Tel.: (508) 752-4615
Fax: (508) 459-2755
E-Mail: info@davisad.com
Web Site: www.davisad.com

E-Mail for Key Personnel:
President: adavis@davisad.com

Employees: 45
Year Founded: 1948

Agency Specializes In: Consumer Marketing, Event Planning & Marketing, Financial, Retail, Travel & Tourism

Approx. Annual Billings: $45,000,000

Alan Berman *(Exec VP)*
Chris Gregoire *(Dir-Digital Strategy)*
Paul Murphy *(Dir-Art)*
Melanie Benoit *(Asst Dir-Media)*
Nicole Tadgell *(Asst Dir-Art)*
Adam Levine *(Acct Mgr)*
Susan Coyle *(Mgr-Mktg Svcs)*
Ben Thaler *(Supvr-Media)*
Tisha Geeza *(Sr Acct Exec)*
Ashley Hadley *(Acct Exec-Adv)*
Courtney Miller *(Copywriter-Creative & Coord-Social Media)*
Dan Peznola *(Acct Coord)*

Accounts:
Banks Auto Group
Bay State Savings Bank
Bertera Auto Group
Cape Cod Community College (Agency of Record) Branding
Charter Communications
East Cambridge Savings Bank (Agency of Record)
Fidelity Bank; Fitchburg, MA
Gallery Auto Group
Gallo Motors
Harr Motors; Worcester, MA
Honey Dew Associates Inc.; Plainville, MA Marketing, Point-of-Sale, Print, Radio, TV
North Shore Lincoln Mercury
Quinsigamond Community College
S Bank Branding
Saint Vincent Hospital
Sanford Institution for Savings
New-SassyYou.com Website
Scituate Federal Savings Bank Branding
Seven Hills Foundation; Auburn, MA Charity
Southwick's Zoo (Agency of Record) Media Buying
Sunnyside Acura
The Telegram & Gazette
Uncle Willie's BBQ (Agency of Record) Branding
Westboro Mitsubishi
Worcester State College

DAVIS & COMPANY
1705 Baltic Ave, Virginia Beach, VA 23451
Tel.: (757) 627-7373
Fax: (757) 627-4257
E-Mail: info@davisco-ads.com
Web Site: www.davisco-ads.com

E-Mail for Key Personnel:
Creative Dir.: sbecker@davisco-ads.com

Employees: 25
Year Founded: 1976

Agency Specializes In: Automotive, Business-To-Business, Cable T.V., Co-op Advertising, Collateral, Consumer Marketing, Consumer Publications, Government/Political, Graphic Design, Health Care Services, Legal Services, Magazines, Newspapers & Magazines, Outdoor, Print, Production, Public Relations, Publicity/Promotions, Strategic Planning/Research, T.V.

Jerome R. Davis *(Pres)*
Brantley Davis *(Exec VP)*
David Pitre *(Sr VP)*
Andy Kostecka *(VP-Client Svcs)*
Casey Gatti *(Dir-Tech)*
Sarah Nicosia *(Acct Mgr)*
Mara Bealey *(Media Buyer)*
Shannon Carpenter *(Media Buyer-Print)*
Katie Kingen *(Media Buyer)*

Accounts:
The American Beverage Association; Washington, DC
Arby's Restaurants; MD, NY, PA, TX, VA & WV
The Brookings Institution
HealthKeepers, Inc.
Oast & Hook

Priority Acura; Chesapeake, VA
Priority Chevrolet; Chesapeake, VA
Priority Hyundai
Priority Toyota Richmond
Priority Toyota; Chesapeake, VA
Red Haute
W.M. Jordan Company; Newport News, VA

Branch

Davis & Co. Inc.
1228 17th St NW, Washington, DC 20036
Tel.: (202) 775-8181
Fax: (202) 775-1533
E-Mail: bdavis@davisco-ads.com
Web Site: www.davisadagency.com

Employees: 10
Year Founded: 1990

Brantley Davis *(Exec VP)*
Andy Kostecka *(VP-Client Svc)*
Will Hart *(Dir-Digital)*
James Thomas *(Dir-Art)*
Mara Bealey *(Media Buyer)*
Colleen Brosnahan *(Copywriter)*
Sherri Franklin *(Sr Media Buyer)*

Accounts:
ARBY
Issue Advocacy Groups

DAVIS BARONE MARKETING
4566 S Lake Dr, Boynton Beach, FL 33436
Tel.: (561) 733-5025
Fax: (561) 732-1391
E-Mail: pdavis@davisbarone.com
Web Site: www.davisbarone.com

Employees: 6
Year Founded: 1994

Agency Specializes In: Collateral, Print, T.V.

Approx. Annual Billings: $3,500,000

J. Paul Davis *(Pres)*

Accounts:
Airscan
Avion Flight Center
Bauman Medical Group
Couture & More
FFC Services, Inc.
First Aviation Services
HelpJet
Industrial Smoke & Mirrors
Peterson Bernard
Sun Jet Aviation

DAVIS ELEN ADVERTISING, INC.
865 S Figueroa St Ste 1200, Los Angeles, CA 90017-2543
Tel.: (213) 688-7000
Fax: (213) 688-7288
E-Mail: debbiezimmerman@daviselen.com
Web Site: www.daviselen.com

Employees: 115
Year Founded: 1948

National Agency Associations: 4A's-THINKLA

Agency Specializes In: Advertising, Advertising Specialties, African-American Market, Asian Market, Automotive, Bilingual Market, Brand Development & Integration, Broadcast, Business-To-Business, Cable T.V., Co-op Advertising, Collateral, Commercial Photography, Communications, Computers & Software, Consumer Marketing, Consumer Publications, Content, Corporate Communications, Corporate Identity, Cosmetics, Custom Publishing, Digital/Interactive, Direct-to-Consumer, Electronic Media, Electronics, Entertainment, Event Planning & Marketing, Exhibit/Trade Shows, Experience Design, Fashion/Apparel, Financial, Food Service, Gay & Lesbian Market, Graphic Design, Guerilla Marketing, High Technology, Hispanic Market, Household Goods, Identity Marketing, In-Store Advertising, Integrated Marketing, International, Internet/Web Design, Local Marketing, Logo & Package Design, Luxury Products, Magazines, Market Research, Media Buying Services, Media Planning, Media Relations, Mobile Marketing, Multicultural, Multimedia, New Product Development, New Technologies, Newspaper, Out-of-Home Media, Outdoor, Over-50 Market, Package Design, Paid Searches, Point of Purchase, Point of Sale, Print, Production, Production (Ad, Film, Broadcast), Production (Print), Promotions, Radio, Regional, Restaurant, Retail, Sales Promotion, Seniors' Market, Social Marketing/Nonprofit, Social Media, Sponsorship, Strategic Planning/Research, T.V., Technical Advertising, Teen Market, Trade & Consumer Magazines, Travel & Tourism, Tween Market, Urban Market, Web (Banner Ads, Pop-ups, etc.)

With a rich history of results, Davis Elen continually brings to the table fresh and innovative ways to dynamically impact our clients' business. Our agency has always had an entrepreneurial spirit. We answer only to our clients, not an office in New York, and have done so for over sixty-six years. Today, Davis Elen stands as one of the largest privately-held, independent agencies in the country, with $272 million in annual billings.

Approx. Annual Billings: $272,000,000

Mark D. Davis *(CEO & Chm-Castells & Asociados)*
Robert Elen *(Pres & COO)*
David Moranville *(Partner & Chief Creative Officer)*
Teriann Hughes *(Exec VP &, Partner & Dir-Media Ops)*
Debbie Zimmerman *(Sr VP & Acct Dir)*
Brian Banks *(Grp Dir-Media & Digital)*

Accounts:
Body Glove Cruises
Cisco
Ebates
Farmer John
Greatcall
KCBS/KCAL
McDonald's Operators' Association
OneWest Bank
Pala Casino Spa & Resort
Revive Procare
San Diego Chargers
Southern California Toyota Dealers Association Los Angeles, San Diego
Special Olympics LA 2015
Ten Media
Vintage Driving Machines

Branches

Davis-Elen Advertising, Inc.
1200 NW Naito Pkwy Ste 500, Portland, OR 97209
Tel.: (503) 241-7781
Fax: (503) 241-0365
E-Mail: markluecht@daviselenpdx.com
Web Site: www.daviselen.com

Employees: 10

National Agency Associations: 4A's

Agency Specializes In: Advertising Specialties, Brand Development & Integration, Broadcast, Business-To-Business, Co-op Advertising, Collateral, Consumer Marketing, Food Service, Newspaper, Outdoor, Point of Sale, Print, Radio, Strategic Planning/Research, T.V.

Mark Luecht *(Partner & Mng Dir)*
David Moranville *(Partner & Chief Creative Officer)*
Teriann Hughes *(Partner, Exec VP & Dir-Media)*
Jerome Aguilar *(VP & Grp Dir-Media)*
Samantha Voisin *(Dir-Digital Media)*
Candace Brogren *(Assoc Dir-Media)*
Jason Elen *(Acct Supvr-Creative)*
Ricci Pruden *(Acct Supvr)*
Zaven Keusseyan *(Supvr-Digital Media)*
Jake Neilson *(Acct Exec)*

Accounts:
McDonald's

Davis Elen Advertising
2107 Wilson Blvd, Ste 520, Arlington, VA 22201
Tel.: (703) 997-0600
Web Site: www.daviselen.com

Employees: 8

National Agency Associations: 4A's

Agency Specializes In: Above-the-Line, Advertising, Advertising Specialties, Affiliate Marketing, Affluent Market, African-American Market, Agriculture, Alternative Advertising, Arts, Asian Market, Automotive, Aviation & Aerospace, Below-the-Line, Bilingual Market, Brand Development & Integration, Branded Entertainment, Broadcast, Business Publications, Business-To-Business, Cable T.V., Catalogs, Children's Market, Co-op Advertising, Collateral, College, Commercial Photography, Communications, Computers & Software, Consulting, Consumer Goods, Consumer Marketing, Consumer Publications, Content, Corporate Communications, Corporate Identity, Cosmetics, Crisis Communications, Custom Publishing, Customer Relationship Management, Digital/Interactive, Direct Response Marketing, Direct-to-Consumer, E-Commerce, Education, Electronic Media, Electronics, Email, Engineering, Entertainment, Environmental, Event Planning & Marketing, Exhibit/Trade Shows, Experience Design, Faith Based, Fashion/Apparel, Financial, Food Service, Game Integration, Gay & Lesbian Market, Government/Political, Graphic Design, Guerilla Marketing, Health Care Services, High Technology, Hispanic Market, Hospitality, Household Goods, Identity Marketing, In-Store Advertising, Industrial, Infomercials, Information Technology, Integrated Marketing, International, Internet/Web Design, Investor Relations, Legal Services, Leisure, Local Marketing, Logo & Package Design, Luxury Products, Magazines, Marine, Market Research, Media Buying Services, Media Planning, Media Relations, Media Training, Medical Products, Men's Market, Merchandising, Mobile Marketing, Multicultural, Multimedia, New Product Development, New Technologies, Newspaper, Newspapers & Magazines, Out-of-Home Media, Outdoor, Over-50 Market, Package Design, Paid Searches, Pets , Pharmaceutical, Planning & Consultation, Podcasting, Point of Purchase, Point of Sale, Print, Product Placement, Production, Production (Ad, Film, Broadcast), Production (Print), Promotions, Public Relations, Publicity/Promotions, Publishing, RSS (Really Simple Syndication), Radio, Real Estate, Recruitment, Regional, Restaurant, Retail, Sales Promotion, Search Engine Optimization, Seniors' Market, Shopper Marketing, Social Marketing/Nonprofit, Social Media, South Asian Market, Sponsorship, Sports Market, Stakeholders, Strategic Planning/Research, Sweepstakes, Syndication, T.V., Technical Advertising, Teen Market, Telemarketing, Trade & Consumer

Magazines, Transportation, Travel & Tourism, Tween Market, Urban Market, Viral/Buzz/Word of Mouth, Web (Banner Ads, Pop-ups, etc.), Women's Market, Yellow Pages Advertising

Mark Davis *(Chm & CEO)*
Robert Elen *(Pres)*
Bill Gibbons, *(Partner& Mng Dir)*
Terry Sullivan *(Partner, COO & CFO)*
David Moranville *(Partner & Chief Creative Officer)*
Teriann Hughes *(Partner, Exec VP & Dir-Media Ops)*
Debbie Zimmerman *(Sr VP & Acct Dir)*
Melissa Ojeda *(Mgr-HR)*

Accounts:
McDonald's Operators

Davis Elen Advertising Inc

16400 Southcenter Pkwy Ste 206, Tukwila, WA 98188
Tel.: (425) 728-1400

Employees: 7

National Agency Associations: 4A's

Agency Specializes In: Advertising, Advertising Specialties, African-American Market, Asian Market, Automotive, Bilingual Market, Brand Development & Integration, Broadcast, Business-To-Business, Cable T.V., Co-op Advertising, Collateral, Commercial Photography, Communications, Computers & Software, Consumer Marketing, Consumer Publications, Content, Corporate Communications, Corporate Identity, Cosmetics, Custom Publishing, Digital/Interactive, Direct-to-Consumer, Electronic Media, Electronics, Entertainment, Event Planning & Marketing, Exhibit/Trade Shows, Experience Design, Fashion/Apparel, Financial, Food Service, Gay & Lesbian Market, Graphic Design, Guerilla Marketing, High Technology, Hispanic Market, Household Goods, Identity Marketing, In-Store Advertising, Integrated Marketing, International, Internet/Web Design, Local Marketing, Logo & Package Design, Luxury Products, Magazines, Market Research, Media Buying Services, Media Planning, Media Relations, Mobile Marketing, Multicultural, Multimedia, New Product Development, New Technologies, Newspaper, Out-of-Home Media, Outdoor, Over-50 Market, Package Design, Paid Searches, Point of Purchase, Point of Sale, Print, Production, Production (Ad, Film, Broadcast), Production (Print), Promotions, Radio, Regional, Restaurant, Retail, Sales Promotion, Seniors' Market, Social Marketing/Nonprofit, Social Media, Sponsorship, Strategic Planning/Research, T.V., Technical Advertising, Teen Market, Trade & Consumer Magazines, Travel & Tourism, Tween Market, Urban Market, Web (Banner Ads, Pop-ups, etc.)

Mark Davis *(Chm & CEO)*
Robert Elen *(Pres & COO)*
Mark Luecht *(Partner & Mng Dir)*
Teriann Hughes *(Partner, Exec VP & Dir-Media)*
David Moranville, *(Partner & CCO)*
Debbie Zimmerman *(Sr VP & Acct Dir)*

Accounts:
McDonalds Co-ops

Davis Elen Advertising, Inc.

(Formerly Davis-Elen Advertising, Inc.)
420 Stevens Ave Ste 240, Solana Beach, CA 92075
Tel.: (858) 847-0789
Fax: (858) 847-0790
Web Site: www.daviselen.com

Employees: 7
Year Founded: 1994

National Agency Associations: 4A's

Agency Specializes In: Advertising, Advertising Specialties, African-American Market, Asian Market, Automotive, Bilingual Market, Brand Development & Integration, Broadcast, Business-To-Business, Cable T.V., Co-op Advertising, Collateral, Commercial Photography, Communications, Computers & Software, Consumer Marketing, Consumer Publications, Content, Corporate Communications, Corporate Identity, Cosmetics, Custom Publishing, Digital/Interactive, Direct-to-Consumer, Electronic Media, Electronics, Entertainment, Event Planning & Marketing, Exhibit/Trade Shows, Experience Design, Fashion/Apparel, Financial, Food Service, Gay & Lesbian Market, Graphic Design, Guerilla Marketing, High Technology, Hispanic Market, Household Goods, Identity Marketing, In-Store Advertising, Integrated Marketing, International, Internet/Web Design, Local Marketing, Logo & Package Design, Magazines, Market Research, Media Buying Services, Media Planning, Media Relations, Mobile Marketing, Multicultural, Multimedia, New Product Development, New Technologies, Newspaper, Out-of-Home Media, Outdoor, Over-50 Market, Package Design, Paid Searches, Point of Purchase, Point of Sale, Print, Production, Production (Ad, Film, Broadcast), Production (Print), Promotions, Publicity/Promotions, Radio, Regional, Restaurant, Retail, Sales Promotion, Seniors' Market, Social Marketing/Nonprofit, Social Media, Sponsorship, Strategic Planning/Research, T.V., Technical Advertising, Teen Market, Trade & Consumer Magazines, Travel & Tourism, Tween Market, Urban Market, Web (Banner Ads, Pop-ups, etc.)

Mark Davis *(Chm & CEO)*
Robert Elen *(Pres & COO)*
Lee Dick *(Partner & Mng Dir)*
Jim Kelly *(Partner & Mng Dir)*
Teriann Hughes *(Exec VP, Partner & Dir-Media Ops)*
Debbie Zimmerman *(Sr VP & Acct Dir)*

Accounts:
McDonald's Operators of San Diego
Pala Casino Spa and Resort
San Diego County Toyota Dealers

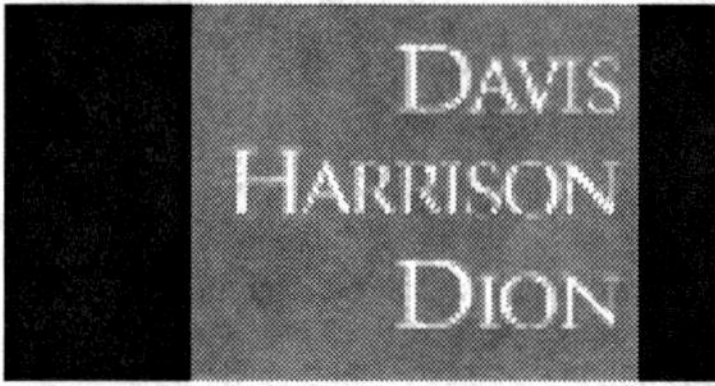

DAVIS HARRISON DION, INC.

333 N Michigan Ave Ste 2300, Chicago, IL 60601-4109
Tel.: (312) 332-0808
Fax: (312) 332-4260
E-Mail: info@dhdchicago.com
Web Site: www.dhdchicago.com

Employees: 28
Year Founded: 1979

National Agency Associations: BMA-NAMA

Agency Specializes In: Above-the-Line, Advertising, Below-the-Line, Brand Development & Integration, Broadcast, Business Publications, Business-To-Business, Cable T.V., Catalogs, Collateral, Communications, Consulting, Consumer Marketing, Consumer Publications, Corporate Identity, Digital/Interactive, Direct Response Marketing, Education, Electronic Media, Exhibit/Trade Shows, Financial, High Technology, Hospitality, In-Store Advertising, Internet/Web Design, Leisure, Logo & Package Design, Magazines, Media Buying Services, Media Planning, Merchandising, Multimedia, New Product Development, Newspaper, Newspapers & Magazines, Out-of-Home Media, Outdoor, Paid Searches, Pets , Podcasting, Point of Purchase, Point of Sale, Print, Production (Print), Promotions, Radio, Sales Promotion, Search Engine Optimization, Seniors' Market, Social Media, Strategic Planning/Research, T.V., Trade & Consumer Magazines, Travel & Tourism, Web (Banner Ads, Pop-ups, etc.)

DHD is an advertising agency focused on Business-To-Business, Tourism, Hospitality, Senior Living, and Financial Service Marketing, which specializes in Advertising, Interactive Marketing, Media Planning, Brand Strategy, Promotions, Direct Response, and Sales Support.

Approx. Annual Billings: $20,000,000

Breakdown of Gross Billings by Media: Brdcst.: 15%; Collateral: 9%; D.M.: 10%; Internet Adv.: 5%; Logo & Package Design: 11%; Other: 5%; Point of Purchase: 5%; Strategic Planning/Research: 10%; Trade & Consumer Mags.: 14%; Trade Shows: 4%; Worldwide Web Sites: 12%

Vince Lombardo *(VP-Interactive Svcs)*
Phil Schuldt *(Sr Dir-Art)*
Mike Apostolovich *(Dir-Art)*
Brent Vincent *(Assoc Dir-Creative)*
Diane Ciangi *(Office Mgr)*
Rob Grogan *(Acct Supvr)*
Paul Weisel *(Designer-Interactive)*

Accounts:
Asbury Communities
Atlas Material Testing Solutions
EDS
Friendship Senior Options
Friendship Village of Schaumburg
Gerflor USA
HydraForce
Iowa Farmer Today
Jensen Hughes
Lake County, IL CVB
Life Enrichment Communities
Lutheran Life Villages
Marquette Bank
MOL America
Pet-Ag, Inc.
Robert Bosch Tool Corporation
U.S. Waterproofing
Willis Tower

DAVISDENNY ADVERTISING & RELATED SERVICES, INC.

2545 Highland Ave, Birmingham, AL 35205
Tel.: (205) 933-0355
Fax: (205) 933-1450
E-Mail: office@davisdenny.com
Web Site: www.davisdenny.com

Employees: 10
Year Founded: 1989

Agency Specializes In: Above-the-Line, Advertising, Advertising Specialties, Affiliate Marketing, Affluent Market, African-American Market, Agriculture, Alternative Advertising, Arts, Asian Market, Automotive, Aviation & Aerospace, Below-the-Line, Bilingual Market, Brand Development & Integration, Branded Entertainment, Broadcast, Business Publications, Business-To-Business, Cable T.V., Catalogs, Children's Market, Co-op Advertising, Collateral, College, Commercial Photography, Communications, Computers & Software, Consulting, Consumer Goods, Consumer

Marketing, Consumer Publications, Content, Corporate Communications, Corporate Identity, Cosmetics, Crisis Communications, Custom Publishing, Customer Relationship Management, Digital/Interactive, Direct Response Marketing, Direct-to-Consumer, E-Commerce, Education, Electronic Media, Electronics, Email, Engineering, Entertainment, Environmental, Event Planning & Marketing, Exhibit/Trade Shows, Experience Design, Faith Based, Fashion/Apparel, Financial, Food Service, Game Integration, Gay & Lesbian Market, Government/Political, Graphic Design, Guerilla Marketing, Health Care Services, High Technology, Hispanic Market, Hospitality, Household Goods, Identity Marketing, In-Store Advertising, Industrial, Infomercials, Information Technology, Integrated Marketing, International, Internet/Web Design, Investor Relations, Legal Services, Leisure, Local Marketing, Logo & Package Design, Luxury Products, Magazines, Marine, Market Research, Media Buying Services, Media Planning, Media Relations, Media Training, Medical Products, Men's Market, Merchandising, Mobile Marketing, Multicultural, Multimedia, New Product Development, New Technologies, Newspaper, Newspapers & Magazines, Out-of-Home Media, Outdoor, Over-50 Market, Package Design, Paid Searches, Pets , Pharmaceutical, Planning & Consultation, Podcasting, Point of Purchase, Point of Sale, Print, Product Placement, Production, Production (Ad, Film, Broadcast), Production (Print), Promotions, Public Relations, Publicity/Promotions, Publishing, RSS (Really Simple Syndication), Radio, Real Estate, Recruitment, Regional, Restaurant, Retail, Sales Promotion, Search Engine Optimization, Seniors' Market, Social Marketing/Nonprofit, Social Media, South Asian Market, Sponsorship, Sports Market, Stakeholders, Strategic Planning/Research, Sweepstakes, Syndication, T.V., Technical Advertising, Teen Market, Telemarketing, Trade & Consumer Magazines, Transportation, Travel & Tourism, Tween Market, Urban Market, Viral/Buzz/Word of Mouth, Web (Banner Ads, Pop-ups, etc.), Women's Market, Yellow Pages Advertising

David M. Davis *(Owner, Pres & Partner)*

DAVRON MARKETING

7231 120th St Ste 473, Delta, BC V4C 6P5 Canada
Tel.: (604) 594-7604
Fax: (604) 594-7673
E-Mail: info@davronmarketing.com
Web Site: www.davronmarketing.com

Employees: 2
Year Founded: 1996

David Parker *(Dir-Brand Comm)*

Accounts:
Arlenes
Associated Fire & Safety
FITNIR Analysis
MDSI
Optimal AEC
Progressive Solutions
Purpose in Place
Wireless Image

DAY COMMUNICATIONS VANCOUVER

(Formerly Midlyn Day Communications)
101 1591 Bowser Ave, Vancouver, BC V7P 2Y4 Canada
Tel.: (604) 980-2980
Fax: (604) 980-2967
Toll Free: (800) 952-0029
E-Mail: vancouver@daycommunications.ca
Web Site: www.daycommunications.ca/

Employees: 15
Year Founded: 1992

Agency Specializes In: Advertising, Brand Development & Integration, Collateral, Communications, Media Planning, Recruitment

Approx. Annual Billings: $5,000,000

Breakdown of Gross Billings by Media: Fees: 20%; Internet Adv.: 30%; Newsp.: 40%; Trade & Consumer Mags.: 10%

Mark Balsdon *(CFO)*
Angela Lee *(Acct Mgr & Writer)*
Mihaela Arion *(Acct Mgr)*
Christine Bacci *(Acct Mgr)*
Linda Dalpe-O'Meara *(Acct Mgr)*

Accounts:
BC Public Service Agency
Canfor Canadian Forest Products
Spectra Energy

THE DAY GROUP

9456 Jefferson Hwy Ste E, Baton Rouge, LA 70809
Tel.: (225) 295-0111
Fax: (225) 293-1222
Web Site: www.thedaygroup.com

Employees: 6
Year Founded: 1995

National Agency Associations: AAF-SMEI

Agency Specializes In: Advertising, Advertising Specialties, Bilingual Market, Business-To-Business, Consumer Marketing, Entertainment, Exhibit/Trade Shows, Logo & Package Design, Media Relations, Package Design, Point of Purchase, Production (Ad, Film, Broadcast), Production (Print), Radio, Restaurant, Social Media, T.V.

Approx. Annual Billings: $1,000,000

David Day *(Owner & Principal)*

DAY ONE AGENCY

56 W 22nd St 3rd Fl, New York, NY 10010
Tel.: (646) 475-2370
E-Mail: hello@d1a.com
Web Site: www.d1a.com

Year Founded: 2014

Agency Specializes In: Advertising, Brand Development & Integration, Digital/Interactive, Media Relations, Public Relations, Social Media

Josh Rosenberg *(CEO)*
Rob Longert *(Mng Partner)*
Laura Barganier *(Sr Acct Dir)*
Blake Caldwell *(Dir-Digital Strategy)*
Alex Israel *(Strategist)*
Allison Menell Lean *(Strategist)*
Samantha Stump *(Acct Coord)*

Accounts:
Amazon Beverages
Baldwin Denim
Indiegogo
L'Oreal USA, Inc.
Nomad Two Worlds
The NPD Group, Inc.
SkinCeuticals
Yevvo
YouTube, LLC

DAYNER HALL INC.

621 E Pine St, Orlando, FL 32801
Tel.: (407) 428-5750
Fax: (407) 426-9896
E-Mail: info@daynerhall.com
Web Site: www.daynerhall.com

Employees: 10
Year Founded: 1970

Agency Specializes In: High Technology

Approx. Annual Billings: $5,000,000

Breakdown of Gross Billings by Media: Collateral: 80%; Mags.: 20%

Matt Garrepy *(Owner)*
John K. Hancock *(Pres & Sr Partner)*
Thomas C. Darling *(Mng Partner)*
Cion Gutierrez *(Partner & Sr Dir-Creative)*
Jessica Garrett *(Sr Dir-Digital Art)*
Ingrid Darling *(Acct Mgmt Dir)*
Maggie Cintron *(Dir-Fin & Acctg)*
Tiffany Mullin *(Dir-Mktg & Sls)*

DB&M MEDIA INC

9 Executive Cir Ste 215, Irvine, CA 92614
Tel.: (949) 752-1444
Fax: (949) 752-1443
E-Mail: info@dbm-media.com
Web Site: www.dbm-media.com

Year Founded: 2002

Agency Specializes In: Advertising, Digital/Interactive, Print, Promotions, Radio, Social Media, T.V.

Don Bartolo *(Pres)*
Brian Bartolo *(VP)*
Charles Luetto *(Dir-Client Dev)*
James Takahashi *(Dir-Creative)*
Victor Teodoro *(Mgr-Adv & Partnership)*
Megan Zacks *(Mgr-Digital Mktg)*

Accounts:
Mountain Mikes Pizza (Agency of Record)

DBOX

110 Leroy St 8th Fl, New York, NY 10014
Tel.: (212) 366-7277
Web Site: www.dbox.com

Agency Specializes In: Advertising, Brand Development & Integration, Internet/Web Design

Jonathan Doyle *(COO & Partner)*

Accounts:
New-COOKFOX Architects
New-Flagstone Property Group

DC

(Formerly Details Communications)
120 18th St South Ste 202, Birmingham, AL 35233
Tel.: (205) 943-6100
E-Mail: info@brandbydc.com
Web Site: www.brandbydc.com/

Agency Specializes In: Collateral, Faith Based, Graphic Design, Planning & Consultation

Brian Jones *(Pres)*
Jason Anderson *(Dir-Web Dev)*
Samantha Corcoran *(Dir-Creative)*
Jason Beckner *(Strategist-Brand)*
Josh White *(Coord-Web Content)*

Accounts:
100 Fold Studio
Amelia Strauss Photography

Bluefield College
Campbellsville University
FUMC Phoenix
St. John the Divine
UMHB

DC3

120 E 23rd St Ste 4000, New York, NY 10010
Tel.: (866) 924-4488
Fax: (212) 345-7893
E-Mail: hello@dc3creates.com
Web Site: www.dc3creates.com

Agency Specializes In: Advertising, Brand Development & Integration, Digital/Interactive, Package Design, Social Media

Todd Irwin *(Principal & Exec Creative Dir)*
John Kapenga *(Art Dir)*
Christina Morrison *(Acct Dir)*
Chris Ozanian *(Dir-Strategy)*
David Levy *(Strategist & Sr Copywriter)*

Accounts:
Honeydrop Beverages

DCA/DCPR

441 E Chester St, Jackson, TN 38301-6313
Tel.: (731) 427-2080
Fax: (731) 427-0780
E-Mail: info@dca-dcpr.com
Web Site: www.dca-dcpr.com

E-Mail for Key Personnel:
President: seth@dca-dcpr.com
Creative Dir.: Scott@dca-dcpr.com
Media Dir.: patricia@dca-dcpr.com

Employees: 9
Year Founded: 1985

Agency Specializes In: Aviation & Aerospace, Brand Development & Integration, Broadcast, Business-To-Business, Collateral, Commercial Photography, Communications, Corporate Identity, Digital/Interactive, Education, Exhibit/Trade Shows, Fashion/Apparel, Financial, Food Service, Graphic Design, Industrial, Internet/Web Design, Logo & Package Design, Magazines, Marine, Media Buying Services, Multimedia, Newspaper, Newspapers & Magazines, Out-of-Home Media, Outdoor, Package Design, Point of Purchase, Point of Sale, Print, Production, Public Relations, Publicity/Promotions, Radio, Retail, T.V., Trade & Consumer Magazines

Approx. Annual Billings: $4,000,000

Breakdown of Gross Billings by Media: Bus. Publs.: 24%; Collateral: 30%; D.M.: 10%; Mags.: 12%; Newsp.: 2%; Outdoor: 8%; Point of Purchase: 2%; Radio: 12%

Patricia Pipken *(Pres)*
Seth Chandler *(CEO)*

Accounts:
Agape Child & Family
Boss Hoss Motorcycles
Coffman's Furniture
Ebbtide Powerboats
FPT Powertrain Master-Bilt
Island Packet Yachts
Master-Bilt

DCF ADVERTISING

35 W 36th St Ste 6W, New York, NY 10018
Tel.: (212) 625-9484
Fax: (212) 625-8565
Web Site: www.dcfadvertising.com

Year Founded: 2000

Agency Specializes In: Advertising, Collateral, Content, Internet/Web Design, Print, Radio, Social Media, T.V.

James DeAngelo *(Principal & Exec Creative Dir)*
John Fortune *(Principal)*

Accounts:
Real Estate Board of New York

DDB LATINA PUERTO RICO

PO Box 195006, San Juan, PR 00918
Tel.: (787) 766-7140
Fax: (787) 766-7178
Web Site: www.ddb.com/pr

Agency Specializes In: Advertising

Enrique Renta *(Chief Creative Officer)*
Juan Carlos Ortiz *(Chm-Creative-DDB Americas)*
Jesse Echevarria *(Dir-Art)*
Juan C. Lopez *(Dir-Art)*
Luis Romero *(Copywriter)*
Ricardo Uribe *(Copywriter)*
Luis Figueroa *(Assoc Creative Dir)*
Jose M. Rivera *(Assoc Creative Dir)*
Leslie Robles *(Assoc Creative Dir)*

Accounts:
Amnesty International USA
Celem
Clorox
Coca-Cola
CPI The Twitter Correspondents
Johnson & Johnson
Livraria Cultura
Neutrogena
Subway Restaurants Anti-Obesity, Kid Shopping Experiment
Terra
Unilever Axe, Campaign: "Goodbye Serious", Campaign: "Ticket"
Zyrtec

DDB VANCOUVER

1600-777 Hornby St, Vancouver, BC V6Z 2T3 Canada
Tel.: (604) 687-7911
Fax: (604) 640-4343
E-Mail: vancouver.info@ddbcanada.com
Web Site: www.ddbcanada.com

E-Mail for Key Personnel:
President: frank.palmer@ddbcanada.com

Employees: 125
Year Founded: 1969

National Agency Associations: ICA

Agency Specializes In: Brand Development & Integration, Children's Market, Direct Response Marketing, Event Planning & Marketing, Graphic Design, Internet/Web Design, Logo & Package Design, Out-of-Home Media, Print, Public Relations, Radio, Retail, T.V., Teen Market

Approx. Annual Billings: $200,000,000

Patty Jones *(Co-Mng Dir & Exec VP)*
Mike Bauman *(CFO & Exec VP)*
Etienne Bastien *(VP & Dir-Creative)*
Marty Yaskowich *(VP-Strategy & Innovation)*
Dean Lee *(Exec Dir-Creative)*
Devin Gallaher *(Acct Dir)*
Zerlina Chan *(Dir-Production)*
Kelsey Hughes *(Dir-Art)*
Marie Sherwin *(Dir-HR)*
Neil Shapiro *(Assoc Dir-Creative & Copywriter)*
Daryl Gardiner *(Assoc Dir-Creative)*
Jon Mandell *(Copywriter)*

Accounts:
Barque Campaign: "Beef"
BC Dairy Foundation
BC Egg Marketing Board Campaign: "Eggonomics", Campaign: "Good Morning BC"
BC Hydro Campaign: "Hydro to Home", Campaign: "Internet", Power Smart; 2006
The BC Lions (Agency of Record)
BC Salmon Farmers Association
BCAA
Bee Friendly Native Bee Conservation Society Campaign: "Swat"
Best Buy Canada Campaign: "Pass the Present"
Big Brothers Campaign: "Book"
Big Sisters of BC Lower Mainland Campaign: "Like Me Back"
The British Columbia Automobile Association Creative, Media Buying & Planning, Strategy
British Columbia Lottery Corp. Campaign: "Ironing Board", Lotto 649
Cake Imagery
Canadian Dental Association Campaign: "Skateboarder"
Canadian Tourism Commission Locals Know
Capital One Canada (Agency of Record) Advertisement, Strategy
Crime Stoppers BC Campaign: "Every Text Helps"
Dirty Apron Cooking School Campaign: "Food Stickers"
First United Mission Campaign: "Street Sculptures", Charity
Greater Vancouver Crime Stoppers PSA
Grieg Seafood Campaign: "Skuna Bay"
Health Sciences Association of British Columbia
Hell Pizza Campaign: "Lust"
Henkel Polska
KidSport
Knorr
KOKO Productions Artisan
Metro Vancouver Crime Stoppers Campaign: "Break & Enter, Robbery, Shooting"
Metropolitan Hotels
Midas
Milk West Campaign: "Snack Time", Marketing Communications
Netflix Ads, Campaign: "AIRPORT", Campaign: "PROPOSAL", Campaign: "Pep Talk", Campaign: "TEST RESULTS", Campaign: "You Gotta Get it to Get it", Press, TV
Nordstrom, Inc. Campaign: "Cake", Campaign: "Cardboard Box", Campaign: "Shoes That Move You", Digital, Mass Advertising, Public Relations, Shopper Marketing, Social Media, TV
Oxfam Canada
Pacific Blue Cross Campaign: "Bilkington X-Ray"
PayWith Worldwide Creative, Marketing
Poker Lotto
New-Rocky Moutaineer (Agency of Record) Creative, Marketing
Strategic Milk Alliance Campaign: "Milk Every Moment", Canadian Dairy Farmers
Subaru Campaign: "Car Swap", Campaign: "Scorched", Forester, Impreza
Sun-Rype Products Ltd.
Tourism Vancouver Thisisourvancouver.Com
Tsawwassen Paintball Campaign: "Blue"
Urban Rush Movers
Vancouver Opera
Vancouver Police Department Campaign: "Deflated", Campaign: "Hooded"
The Vancouver Sun Campaign: "100 years of rolling off the presses."
Volkswagen Group of America, Inc.
VW Germany Campaign: "Just Married"

Branches

DDB Canada

1000-10235 101 St, Edmonton, AB T5J 3G1 Canada
Tel.: (780) 424-7000

REDBOOKS
Brands. Marketers. Agencies. Search Less. Find More.
Try out the Online version at www.redbooks.com

Fax: (780) 423-0602
E-Mail: edmonton.info@ddbcanada.com
Web Site: www.ddbcanada.com

Employees: 30
Year Founded: 1979

Kaezad Nallaseth *(VP & Bus Unit Dir)*
Craig Ferguson *(Sr Dir-Art)*
Bridget Westerholz *(Grp Acct Dir)*
Susan Grant *(Acct Dir)*
Ryan O'Hagan *(Acct Dir)*
Jackie Dejewski *(Dir-Art)*
Eva Polis *(Dir-Creative)*
Diego Bertagni *(Assoc Dir-Creative)*
Seth Waterman *(Acct Supvr)*
Gillian Lanyon *(Strategist-Tribal Worldwide)*

Accounts:
Alberta Innovates
AutoTrader.ca Campaign: "Most Cars In One Place"
Best Buy Campaign: "Pass the Present Facebook Contest", Pass the Present
Canadian Tourism Commission
Coalition for a Safer 63 & 881
Government of Alberta Campaign: "Munch and Move", Recruitment Advertising

DDB Canada

33 Bloor Street East Suite 1700, Toronto, ON M4W 3T4 Canada
Tel.: (416) 925-9819
Fax: (416) 925-4180
Web Site: www.ddbcanada.com

Employees: 100
Year Founded: 1963

Lance Saunders *(Pres & COO)*
Melanie Johnston *(Pres)*
Len Wise *(Mng Dir)*
Cosmo Campbell *(Chief Creative Officer & Sr VP)*
Michael Davidson *(Sr VP & Dir-Bus Unit)*
Tony Johnstone *(Sr VP & Dir-Strategic Plng)*
Martine Levy *(Mng Dir-PR)*
Jacqui Faclier *(VP & Dir-Bus Unit)*
Paul Wallace *(Exec Dir-Creative)*
Dax Fullbrook *(Sr Dir-Art)*
Brandon Thomas *(Sr Dir-Art)*
Scott Barr *(Acct Dir)*
Cathy Grendus *(Acct Dir)*
Nick Pigott *(Acct Dir)*
Susan Powell *(Acct Dir)*
Sandra Moretti *(Dir-Strategy)*
David Ross *(Dir-Creative)*
Bradley Hammond *(Acct Mgr-Corp Affairs Practice)*
Heather Moffat *(Acct Supvr)*
Roger Nairn *(Acct Supvr)*
Jamie Plauntz *(Acct Supvr)*
Rico Tudico *(Acct Supvr)*
Arjang Esfandiyari *(Copywriter)*
Domenique Raso *(Copywriter)*
Allan Topol *(Copywriter)*

Accounts:
Agent Provocateur Lingerie
AutoTrader.com LLC Campaign: "Stoplight"
Barque Campaign: "Pork"
British Columbia Automobile Association (Agency of Record) Campaign: "Membership is Rewarding", Creative, Digital Media, Social, TV
Canadian Tire Campaign: "Spirit Tree"
Canadian Women's Foundation Campaign: "Donate Your Voice"
New-CIL Paints
Crime Stoppers Campaign: "Cookin With Molly"
Dairy Farmers of Canada Canadian Cheese, Communications, Creative, Marketing, Public Relations, Strategy
Daniel Bonder Campaign: "The FCK-It List"
Earth Day Canada Campaign: "Fish"
Hockey Canada
Investors Group (Agency of Record) Financial Planning, Marketing Communications
Jax Coco
Johnson & Johnson Campaign: "Junkface", Campaign: "Sit-Ups", Campaign: "The Campaign to End Junkface", Neutrogena Men
Knorr
Lilly Canada Campaign: "Basement", Cialis
Manulife Financial Campaign: "'Hurdles", Campaign: "Working Kids"
Midas
Moet Hennessy Canadian Public Relations
Nordstrom Canada Campaign: "Shoes That Move You", Print
New-Nova Scotia Tourism Creative, Digital, Media Planning
Penningtons Magic Mirror
Pier 1 Imports Public Relations; 2008
Portuguese Cork Association Cork Flooring
Richter Communications Strategy, PR
Sierra Club Water Quality Awareness
Sony Electronics, Inc. Broadcast, Campaign: "Ear Crunches", Campaign: "Ear Workout", Campaign: "Get Your Ears Ready", Hi-Res Audio, Online
Subaru Campaign: "2015 Subaru WRX STI vs The Drones", Campaign: "Forester Family Rally", Campaign: "Scorched", Campaign: "Trucks", Strut, Television, WRX STi
TeamBuy.ca
Toronto Crime Stoppers Campaign: "Cookin' With Molly", Campaign: "Expose", Campaign: "Wanted"
Toronto Jewish Film Festival J-DAR
Unilever Canada Becel
Volkswagen Canada
WoodGreen Community Services

DDB WORLDWIDE COMMUNICATIONS GROUP INC.

437 Madison Ave, New York, NY 10022-7001
Tel.: (212) 415-2000
Fax: (212) 415-3414
Web Site: www.ddb.com

Year Founded: 1949

National Agency Associations: 4A's-AAF-ABC-APA-BPA-CBP-EAAA-MCA-NYPAA-THINKLA

Agency Specializes In: Advertising, Advertising Specialties, Affluent Market, African-American Market, Alternative Advertising, Arts, Asian Market, Automotive, Aviation & Aerospace, Bilingual Market, Brand Development & Integration, Branded Entertainment, Broadcast, Business Publications, Business-To-Business, Cable T.V., Catalogs, Children's Market, Co-op Advertising, Collateral, College, Communications, Computers & Software, Consumer Goods, Consumer Marketing, Consumer Publications, Content, Corporate Identity, Cosmetics, Customer Relationship Management, Digital/Interactive, Direct Response Marketing, Direct-to-Consumer, E-Commerce, Electronic Media, Electronics, Email, Entertainment, Environmental, Event Planning & Marketing, Experience Design, Fashion/Apparel, Financial, Food Service, Game Integration, Graphic Design, Guerilla Marketing, Health Care Services, High Technology, Hispanic Market, Household Goods, Identity Marketing, In-Store Advertising, Information Technology, Integrated Marketing, International, Internet/Web Design, Leisure, Local Marketing, Logo & Package Design, Luxury Products, Magazines, Market Research, Medical Products, Men's Market, Mobile Marketing, Multicultural, Multimedia, New Technologies, Newspaper, Out-of-Home Media, Outdoor, Over-50 Market, Package Design, Pets , Pharmaceutical, Planning & Consultation, Point of Purchase, Point of Sale, Print, Product Placement, Production, Production (Print), Promotions, Radio, Real Estate, Restaurant, Retail, Sales Promotion, Search Engine Optimization, Social Marketing/Nonprofit, Social Media, South Asian Market, Sponsorship, Sports Market, Strategic Planning/Research, Sweepstakes, T.V., Teen Market, Trade & Consumer Magazines, Transportation, Travel & Tourism, Tween Market, Urban Market, Viral/Buzz/Word of Mouth, Women's Market

Approx. Annual Billings: $1,263,900,000

Chuck Brymer *(Pres & CEO)*
Amir Kassaei *(Chief Creative Officer)*
Greg Taucher *(Chief People Officer & Dir-Global Accounts & Contracts)*
Juan Carlos Ortiz *(Chm-Creative-DDB Americas)*
Niko Coutroulis *(Dir-Creative)*
Julius Dunn *(Dir-Talent-North America)*
Scott Murphy *(Dir-Content & Social Media)*
Jim Wasenius *(Dir-Media)*

Accounts:
AT&T Communications Corp. Business-to-Business, Creative
ExxonMobil Below the Line
Glidden;Strongville,OH
Johnson & Johnson Band-Aid, Carefree, K-Y, Monistat, O.B, Reach, Stayfree
McDonald's (Lead Creative Agency) Advertising, Campaign: "Forgiveness is never far away", Digital
Merck & Co (Agency of Record) Gardasil
Unilever Breyers Ice Cream, Good Humor, Heartbrand, Klondike, Popsicle, Walls Ice Cream
Wm Wrigley Jr. Co. Airwaves, Boomer, Hubba Bubba, Juicy Fruit, LifeSavers, Solano, Sugus

U.S. Divisions

DDB Chicago

200 E Randolph St, Chicago, IL 60601
Tel.: (312) 552-6000
Fax: (312) 552-2370
Web Site: www.ddb.com

Year Founded: 1925

National Agency Associations: 4A's-AAF

Agency Specializes In: Above-the-Line, Advertising, Below-the-Line, Brand Development & Integration, Branded Entertainment, Broadcast, Business-To-Business, Communications, Consumer Goods, Consumer Marketing, Content, Corporate Identity, Digital/Interactive, Integrated Marketing, International, Internet/Web Design, Magazines, Market Research, Men's Market, New Product Development, Outdoor, Product Placement, Production, Production (Ad, Film, Broadcast), Production (Print), Radio, Retail, Social Media, Sponsorship, Strategic Planning/Research, T.V., Technical Advertising, Trade & Consumer Magazines, Viral/Buzz/Word of Mouth, Women's Market

Jared Yeater *(Mng Dir)*
Valerie Bengoa *(CFO & COO)*
John Maxham *(Chief Creative Officer)*
Jack Perone *(Chief Strategy Officer)*
Joseph Cianciotto *(Chief Digital Officer)*
Kevin Drew Davis *(Exec VP & Exec Dir-Creative)*
Christopher Pultorak *(Sr VP & Head-Integrated Brand-Capital One)*
Alex Braxton *(Sr VP, Dir-Creative Integration & Grp Dir-Creative)*
David Banta *(Sr VP & Grp Dir-Creative)*
John Hayes *(Sr VP & Grp Dir-Creative)*
Marcia Iacobucci *(Sr VP & Grp Dir-Creative)*
Kate Christiansen *(Sr VP & Grp Bus Dir)*
Scott Kemper *(VP & Exec Producer)*
Anne Czowiecki *(VP & Acct Dir)*
Gwen Hammes *(VP & Acct Dir)*
Justin Hood *(VP & Dir-Digital Platform)*

Carly Ferguson *(Exec Producer-Digital)*
Matt Christiansen *(Creative Dir)*
Nathan Monteith *(Creative Dir-Online Videos)*
Brandon Scharold *(Acct Dir)*
Chad Broude *(Dir-Creative & Copywriter)*
Bob Davies *(Dir-Creative)*
Madeline DeWree *(Dir-Art)*
Elaine Kalvelage *(Dir-Art)*
Katie Greenbaum *(Acct Mgr)*
Trace Schlenker *(Acct Mgr)*
Kirby Summers *(Acct Mgr)*
Alan Wu *(Acct Mgr)*
Emily Charron *(Mgr-Social Media Mktg)*
Carly Steuck *(Mgr-Community)*
Melanie Gonzalez *(Acct Supvr-Global)*
Bianca Hertel *(Acct Supvr)*
Erin Leahy *(Acct Supvr-Global)*
Kimberly Bodker *(Acct Exec)*
Billie Pritzker *(Acct Exec)*
Zach Bonnan *(Copywriter)*
Tyler Campbell *(Copywriter)*
Alec Jankowski *(Copywriter)*
Sean Peecook *(Copywriter)*

Accounts:
American Cancer Society (Lead Creative Agency) Campaign: "Advantage Humans", OOH, Print
Anheuser-Busch InBev; Saint Louis, MO American Ale, Bud Light, Bud Light Lime, Bud.tv, Budweiser; 1977
AT&T Mobility, LLC AT&T Wireless
Capital One Financial Corporation Apple Pay, Campaign: "Business Abroad", Campaign: "Office Scones", Campaign: "The Phone Call", Campaign: "What's In Your Wallet", Campaign: "Worn Jeans", Mobile, Online Video, TV, Wallet App
Dow Chemical
Emerson Campaign: "I Love STEM", Campaign: "It's Never Been Done Before", Online Videos, Print, Social Media, TV; 1998
The Field Museum Campaign: "Chocolate Nuts", Campaign: "Creatures of Light", Campaign: "Whales: Giants of the Deep"; 2007
Johnson & Johnson Consumer Products Co.; Skillman, NJ Aveeno; 1999
Kohler Company Content, Creative, Digital Advertising, TV
New-LifeLock, Inc. (Agency of Record)
Mars, Incorporated 3 Musketeers, Big Red, Broadcast, Campaign: "Cloud", Campaign: "Double Dutch", Campaign: "Experience The Rainbow", Campaign: "Greater Than Fish", Campaign: "It Will Be Settled", Campaign: "Land of Intensity", Campaign: "Mean Streets", Campaign: "Miniminneapolis", Campaign: "Poster With a Hole", Campaign: "Sorry I Was Eating A Milky Way", Campaign: "Treadmill", Campaign: "Unexplainably Juicy", Campaign: "Walrus", Campaign: "Why 3 Musketeers?", Combos, Digital Advertising, Extra, Juicy Fruit (Creative), Lifesavers, Milky Way, Online, Public Relations, Shopper Marketing, Social Media, Starburst, Temptations
McDonald's Corporation "McDonald's GOL!", "No Fry Left Behind" TV Commercial, Apples, Campaign: "Celebrate with a Bite", Campaign: "Flirt", Campaign: "McDonald's Farmville Farm", Campaign: "The Simple Joy of Winning", Creative, Digital, McSkillet Burrito, Mighty Wings, Sirloin Burger, Video; 1970
PepsiCo Aquafina, Sierra Mist, SoBe
The Procter & Gamble Company
Regis Corporation
RMHC Campaign: "Mike"
Ronald McDonald House
Safeway Digital, Social Marketing
SeaWorld Parks & Entertainment LLC; Saint Louis, MO SeaWorld; 1999
Sierra Mist Natural Creative
Starbucks
State Farm Insurance Campaign: "9/11 Thanks", Campaign: "At Last", Campaign: "Discount Double Check", Campaign: "France", Campaign: "Get To A Better State", Campaign: "Hans & Franz", Campaign: "Jake From State Farm", Campaign: "Mr. Goldman", Campaign: "Never", Campaign: "Richmeister", Campaign: "Save Mass Quantities", Campaign: "State of Turbulence", Campaign: "Trainers", Chaos in your Town, Creative, Digital, Online, Social, TV
Temptations Cat Treats Campaign: "Work it Kitty!"
William Wrigley Jr. Company (Advertising Agency of Record) 'Campaign: "Zipper", Campaign: "Armpit", Campaign: "Settle It", Juicy Fruit, Skittles, Starburst, Super Bowl 2015, TV

DDB Latin America
770 S Dixie Hwy Ste 109, Miami, FL 33146
Tel.: (305) 341-2555
Fax: (305) 662-8043
Web Site: www.ddb.com

E-Mail for Key Personnel:
President: steve.burton@ddb.com

Employees: 10

Agency Specializes In: Advertising

Joe Cronin *(CEO)*
Steve Burton *(Pres-DDB Latin America)*
Juan Isaza *(VP-Strategic Plng & Social Media)*
Gabriel Reyes *(Sr Dir-Art)*
Santiago Cuesta *(Creative Dir)*

Accounts:
Shorts & Cortos Book

DDB New York
437 Madison Ave, New York, NY 10022-7001
Tel.: (212) 415-2000
Fax: (212) 415-3506
Web Site: www.ddb.com

Year Founded: 1949

National Agency Associations: 4A's-AAF-ABC-AMA-BPA INTERNATIONAL-ZAW

Agency Specializes In: Above-the-Line, Advertising, Advertising Specialties, Alternative Advertising, Automotive, Aviation & Aerospace, Below-the-Line, Brand Development & Integration, Broadcast, Business-To-Business, Cable T.V., Collateral, Communications, Computers & Software, Consumer Goods, Consumer Marketing, Corporate Communications, Corporate Identity, Cosmetics, Customer Relationship Management, Digital/Interactive, Direct Response Marketing, Direct-to-Consumer, Electronic Media, Electronics, Email, Experience Design, Fashion/Apparel, Financial, Government/Political, Graphic Design, Guerilla Marketing, Health Care Services, Household Goods, In-Store Advertising, Industrial, Integrated Marketing, International, Internet/Web Design, Market Research, Medical Products, Men's Market, Mobile Marketing, New Technologies, Newspaper, Newspapers & Magazines, Out-of-Home Media, Outdoor, Over-50 Market, Package Design, Pharmaceutical, Podcasting, Point of Purchase, Point of Sale, Print, Product Placement, Production, Production (Ad, Film, Broadcast), Production (Print), Radio, Regional, Retail, Sales Promotion, Search Engine Optimization, Seniors' Market, Social Marketing/Nonprofit, Social Media, Sponsorship, Sports Market, Stakeholders, Strategic Planning/Research, T.V., Teen Market, Travel & Tourism, Urban Market, Viral/Buzz/Word of Mouth, Web (Banner Ads, Pop-ups, etc.), Women's Market

Chris Brown *(Pres & CEO)*
Stuart Hazlewood *(Chief Strategy Officer)*
Peter Hempel *(Chm/CEO-DDB Grp)*
Jean Batthany *(Exec VP & Exec Creative Dir)*
Mark Gross *(Exec VP & Exec Dir-Creative)*
Mike Sullivan *(Grp Dir-Creative)*
Hannah Fishman *(Grp Dir-Creative & Content-Global)*
Laurence Velcoff *(Grp Dir-Plng)*
Jack Wheaton *(Grp Acct Dir)*
Teri Altman *(Exec Producer-Integrated)*
John McGill *(Art Dir & Creative Dir)*
Luke Carmody *(Creative Dir & Copywriter)*
Debbie Broda *(Acct Dir)*
Samantha Gen *(Acct Dir)*
Lisa Harap *(Acct Dir)*
Mina Mikhael *(Art Dir)*
Meredith Moffat *(Producer-Digital)*
Tracy Power *(Bus Dir-Global)*
Heather Stuckey *(Bus Dir-Global)*
Marina Zuber *(Acct Dir)*
Heather Donahoe *(Mgmt Supvr)*
Meghan O'Brien *(Mgmt Supvr)*
Geoff Sia *(Mgmt Supvr)*
Angelina Singleton *(Mgmt Supvr)*
Lindsey Eckwall *(Dir-Art & Designer)*
Mark Ledermann *(Dir-Creative & Copywriter)*
Cassandra Anderson *(Dir-Creative)*
Julie Beasley *(Dir-Creative)*
Danae Belanger *(Dir-Art)*
Yael Cesarkas *(Dir-Plng)*
Mariana Costa *(Dir-Creative)*
Bob Huff *(Dir-HR)*
Nadia Kamran *(Dir-Creative)*
John Kottman *(Dir-Strategy-North America Ops)*
Stacey Mellus *(Dir-Resource)*
Amanda Millwee *(Dir-Art)*
Joel Nagy *(Dir-Digital Innovation)*
Wendy Raye *(Dir-HR)*
Alfredo Sanchez *(Dir-Creative)*
Paul Sundue *(Dir-Digital Strategy & Production)*
Jim Wasenius *(Dir-Media)*
Kimb Luisi *(Assoc Dir-Creative)*
Jonathan Richman *(Assoc Dir-Creative)*
Alex Zamiar *(Assoc Dir-Creative)*
Bianca Hertel *(Acct Supvr)*
David Reyes *(Acct Supvr)*
Julie Evcimen *(Supvr-Project Mgmt Grp)*
Jessica Pernick *(Sr Acct Exec-Global)*
Erin Albertson *(Acct Exec)*
Kelly Brumer *(Acct Exec-Global Digital-ExxonMobil)*
Jackie Schultz *(Acct Exec)*
Sarah Tarner *(Acct Exec)*
Frank Torok *(Acct Exec)*
Laura Traflet *(Acct Exec)*
Caroline Uffelman *(Acct Exec)*
Jane Piampiano *(Art Buyer)*
Step Schultz *(Copywriter)*
Turan Tuluy *(Copywriter)*
Dan Young *(Assoc Creative Dir)*

Accounts:
Ad Council Campaign: " Be More Than a Bystander", Suicide Prevention
AkzoNobel Glidden
Art Directors Club Campaign: "Keep Fighting The Good Fight"
Chipotle Mexican Grill
Ciba Vision AIR OPTIX, Dailies
The Clorox Company Brita, Campaign: "Cola Rain"
Cotton Inc. Campaign: "Cotton or Nothing", Campaign: "Cotton. It's Your Favorite For a Reason", Campaign: "It's Time to Talk Favorites", Campaign: "The Fabric of My Life"
Eli Lilly/Amylin exenatideQW
Eli Lilly/Daiichi Sankyo Effient
Empire City Casino Campaign: "Plane"
ExxonMobil Corporation Global Convenience Stores, US & Global Fuels
Fiat
FSR Financial Services; 2010
GetTaxi Campaign: "Famous", Gett
Glidden Paints Campaign: "Glidden Gets You Going", Campaign: "Tame the Beast", Campaign: "The Beast", Social Media
Hertz Campaign: "Arrival, Departure", Campaign: "Gas or Break", Campaign: "Traveling at the speed of Hertz", Divisional, International,

Suburban, Trade Equipment Rental
Hiscox plc Direct Insurance
New-Huawei Device USA (Advertising Agency of Record) Creative, Media, Strategic
I Care
Johnson & Johnson Consumer Products Co.; Skillman, NJ Clean&Clear, RoC
Juicy Fruit Fruity Chews Campaign: "A sweet burst of flavor"
Mars, Incorporated Campaign: "A Boy and His Dog Duck", Combos, Creative, Digital, Eukanuba (Agency of Record), Iams (Agency of Record), Print, Royal Canin, Skittles, Starburst, TV, Temptations, Wrigley
McDonald's Campaign: "Finger Painting", Creative
NBA
New York City Ballet Campaign: "Faile, Art Series", Campaign: "Les Ballets de Faile", Campaign: "New Beginnings"
NEW YORK DEPARTMENT OF HEALTH
New York State Lottery Campaign: "Birthday Party", Campaign: "Breaking The News", Campaign: "Can/Can't", Campaign: "Garden", Campaign: "Impossible", Campaign: "Invasion", Campaign: "Maximist", Campaign: "Minimum/Maximum", Campaign: "Mother's Day", Campaign: "Music", Campaign: "Paper Cut", Campaign: "The Car", Campaign: "Thoughts", Campaign: "Thumb-war", Campaign: "Win for Life", Campaign: "Writer's Room", Campaign: "Yeah that Kinda rich, Writers room", Campaign: "Yes/No", Instant Games, Lotto, Maximum Millions, Mega Millions, OOH, Pay Me!, Radio, Social Media, Sweet Million, TV, Take 5; 2001
The Partnership at Drugfree.org Campaign: "Damaged Circuits", Digital, Print, Pro-Bono, Radio, TV
Pepsi Lipton Tea Partnership Sparkling Teas
Pepsi Campaign: "The Good Part of NY Mornings", Tropicana
Pfizer Aricept
The Public Theater
Smithsonian's National Zoo & Conservation Biology Institute
State Farm Campaign: "Futurebook"
Teva Women's Health Seasonique
Transitions Optical; Pinellas Park, FL Global Creative
UNICEF Campaign: "Access Denied", World Toilet Day
Unilever Bertolli Gelato, Breyers, Flora/Becel, Gelato Indulgences, Good Humor, Klondike, Lipton, Popsicle, TV
United States Golf Association Campaign: "A Lot to Love"
U.S. Open Campaign: "Story of the Open", Social Media
U.S. Tennis Association Branding & Rebranding, Campaign: "Tennis Makes You", Dale Chilton story, Luis Gonzalez story
Volkswagen AG
Warner Chilcott/Novartis Enablex
Warner Chilcott/Sanofi Aventis Actonel
Water is Life Campaign: "#5YearstoLive", Campaign: "FirstWorldProblems", Campaign: "Hashtag Killer", Campaign: "The Drinkable Book", Campaign: "The Girl Who Couldn't Cry"
Wildlife Conservation Society (Agency of Record) "96 Elephants", Creative
Yahoo! Campaign: "Adopt Your Doggie Double"

DDB San Francisco

600 California St, San Francisco, CA 94108
Tel.: (415) 732-3600
Fax: (415) 732-3636
Web Site: www.ddb.com

Employees: 50
Year Founded: 1996

National Agency Associations: 4A's

Agency Specializes In: Advertising, Sponsorship

Stacey Grier *(Mng Partner)*
Jon Drawbaugh *(Head-Production)*
Rebecca Hines *(Dir-Acct Mgmt & Grp Acct Dir)*
Michael Bukzin *(Acct Dir)*
Lindsey Lucero *(Acct Dir)*
Andre Cabral *(Dir-Art)*
Carrie Frash *(Dir-Culture)*
Tim Stier *(Assoc Dir-Creative)*
Jordan Wood *(Acct Supvr)*
Ken Gutman *(Supvr-Copy)*

Accounts:
Amazon.com
The Clorox Company 409, Advertising, Armor All, Black Flag, Brita, Campaign: "Bleachable Moments - Tandem", Campaign: "Cat Box", Campaign: "Cola Rain", Campaign: "Double Impact", Campaign: "Get Off Your Gas", Campaign: "Need it Now", Campaign: "Not Pregnant", Campaign: "Quickie", Campaign: "Skinny Santa", Campaign: "The Social Grill", Clorox 2, Clorox Bleach Pen, Clorox Clean Up, Clorox Disinfecting Spray, Clorox Disinfecting Wipes, Clorox Fresh Care, Clorox Liquid Bleach, Clorox OxiMagic, Clorox Ready Mop, Clorox Teflon Products, Clorox Toilet Bowl Cleaner, Clorox Toilet Wand, Combat, Double-Headed Toilet Wand, Formula 409, Fresh Step, Glad, Glad ForceFlex, Glad Press 'n Seal, Green Works, Hidden Valley, KC Masterpiece, Kingsford, Kingsford Charcoal, Liquid Plumr, Match Light, PAM Cooking Spray, Pine-Sol, S.O.S., STP, Scoop Away, Tilex
ConAgra Foods "Snap Into It", Banquet Frozen Foods, Campaign: "Champions of Joy", Campaign: "Hold on. It's Manwich", Campaign: "Possum", Campaign: "Snap Into a Slim Jim", Chef Boyardee, Creative, Healthy Choice, Hebrew National, Hunts Snack Pack, Manwich, Marie Callender's, Orville Redenbacher, P.F. Chang's, Pam Cooking Spray, Reddi-wip, Rosarita, Rotel, Slim Jim, Swiss Miss; 2004
Green Works
Heal the Bay
Hidden Valley Ranch
Kingsford Charcoal Campaign: "Sweater"
Mondelez International, Inc. Campaign: "Book Club", Ro-Tel, Velveeta
Partnership for Drug-Free Kids
Qualcomm; San Diego, CA Advertising, Campaign: "Why Wait?", Digital
SunPower

Roberts + Langer DDB

437 Madison Ave 8th Fl, New York, NY 10022
(See Separate Listing)

Spike/DDB

55 Washington St Ste 650, Brooklyn, NY 11201
Tel.: (718) 596-5400
Fax: (212) 415-3101
E-Mail: info@spikeddb.com
Web Site: www.spikeddb.com

Employees: 30
Year Founded: 1996

National Agency Associations: 4A's

Agency Specializes In: Consumer Marketing, Sponsorship

Spike Lee *(CEO)*
Victor Paredes *(Mng Dir)*
Dabo Che *(Sr VP & Exec Dir-Creative)*
Riyhana Bey *(Acct Svcs Dir)*
Christopher Cohen *(Art Dir)*
Yony Arad *(Dir-Integrated Mktg Strategy)*
Rachel Donovan *(Dir-Creative)*
Lizzie Haberman *(Dir-Ops & Integrated Production)*
Jeison Rodriguez *(Assoc Dir-Creative)*
Russell Markus *(Sr Planner-Integrated Mktg Comm)*

Accounts:
General Motors African American Agency of Record-Chevrolet, Cadillac, Cadillac ATS, Campaign: "Coding It", Campaign: "Inspiration", Campaign: "MLK Table of Brotherhood", Campaign: "Seizing It", Chevrolet
HBO Campaign: "Late Night Happy Hours"
Pepsi; 2002
TNT
The Topps Company Baseball Cards; 2008

Argentina

DDB Argentina

Juncal 1207, CP (C1062ABM) Buenos Aires, Argentina
Tel.: (54) 11 5777 5000
Fax: (54) 11 5777 4000
E-Mail: info@ddbargentina.com
Web Site: www.ddb.com

E-Mail for Key Personnel:
Public Relations: sol.relevant@ddbargentina.com

Employees: 150

National Agency Associations: AAAP (Argentina)-IAA

Jose Luis Longinotti *(Pres & Partner)*
Beto Cocito *(Exec Dir-Creative)*
Fernando Errecaborde *(Sr Dir-Art)*
Remigijus Praspaliauskas *(Art Dir)*
Graciela Combal *(Dir-Grp Accts)*
Florencia Rodriguez *(Dir-Art)*
Iganacio Ruarte *(Dir-Creative)*
Santiago Salas *(Dir-Creative)*
Facundo Varela *(Dir-Creative)*

Accounts:
BBVA Frances
Clorox Campaign: "Cigarettes", Clorox Latam Multipurpose Sponge, Trenet Wipes Instant Stain Remover; 1995
Club Atletico Boca Juniors Boca juniors Adhering Member
Energizer Eveready
Esso
FedEx
Hospital Austral
Johnson & Johnson Bio, Brillo y Vida, Clean & Clear, KYGel, Neutrogena, Roc, Sundown
Lipton Ice Tea
Los Inrockuptibles
Manos Campaign: "Swing"
Provet Dog Bunker Provet
Puma Football Jersey
Revista Maxim Campaign: "Cold Line"
Sol
Taringa
Telefonica de Argentina S.A. Internet Access, Long Distance, Public Telephones, Telefonia Fija
Telinver S.A. Paginas Dorados
Trenet Campaign: "Lobster", Campaign: "Spaghetti", Campaign: "Sushi"
Turner Argentina Cartoon Network
Volkswagen Argentina S.A. Campaign: "Drive Carefully", Campaign: "Little Hand", Campaign: "Love Stories Without A Car", Campaign: "The Race", Golf GTI, KY Gel, POOL, Passat CC, Refrigerator, Shelf, Tiguan; 2001

Fire Advertainment

Martin Coronado 818, Acassuso, Buenos Aires, 1641 Argentina
Tel.: (54) 11 4707 2100
Fax: (54) 11 4707 2105
Web Site: www.facebook.com/fireadvertainment

E-Mail for Key Personnel:

President: rodrigo@fire-advertainment.com
Creative Dir.: santiago@fire.com.ar
Public Relations: sol.revelant@ddbargentina.com

Employees: 10
Year Founded: 2002

Agency Specializes In: Brand Development & Integration, Entertainment

Rodrigo Figueroa Reyes *(Founder & CEO)*
Santiago Vernengo *(Dir)*

Accounts:
The Clorox Company
Super TC 2000 Campaign: "Street Circuit City of Buenos Aires"

Australia

DDB Melbourne Pty. Ltd.

7 Electric Street, Melbourne, VIC 3121 Australia
Tel.: (61) 392543600
E-Mail: info@mel.ddb.com
Web Site: www.ddb.com.au

Employees: 125
Year Founded: 1948

National Agency Associations: AFA

Agency Specializes In: Communications

Andrew Little *(Grp CEO)*
Sarah Bailey *(Mng Partner)*
Dion Appel *(Mng Dir)*
Simon Thomas *(Head-Brdcst Production)*
Jade Manning *(Sr Dir-Art)*
Jim Ritchie *(Creative Dir)*
Mark Seabridge *(Art Dir-Digital)*
Robbie Brammall *(Dir-Creative)*
Glen Dickson *(Dir-Creative)*
Anthony Hatton *(Dir-Art)*
Tom Hyde *(Dir-Plng)*
Jordy Molloy *(Dir-Art)*
Chris Hanrahan *(Copywriter)*

Accounts:
AAMI
ACMI Campaign: "Space on Film"
AFI
New-AHM health
Amcal; 1996
Australian Unity Insurance; 2003
Babylove
BF Goodrich
Britax
Cottee's
Devondale 'Crazy Cat Lady', Campaign: "Cylcops", Campaign: "Glow Girl", Campaign: "Jumpers", Campaign: "Never Run Out", Campaign: "Step Dad Steve", Dairy Soft Butter
Don Smallgoods Campaign: "Modern Art"
Dr. Martins Boots
Dulux
Expedia Campaign: "Listopedia", Creative
ExxonMobil Petroleum; 1997
George Western Foods Don
Hocking-Stuart
Jeanswest Campaign: "iDenim Match", Jeans Range
Mars Petcare Whiskas Temptations
McDonald's Campaign: "Our Food, Your Questions", Campaign: "TrackMyMacca", Pop-Up Restaurant
Michelin Asia Pacific Auto Accessories, Tires; 2001
Michelin World F1 Grand Prix Motor Sport; 2002
Michelin; 2001
Momentum Energy Creative
Morning Fresh
Murray Goulburn Campaign: "Glow Girl", Campaign: "Take Over", Devondale Dairy Soft, Devondale Long Life Milk
No Magazine Campaign: "Car Loans"
Open Universities Campaign: "Your Best Days Are Ahead Of You"
Open Training Institute Campaign: "The Y Factor"
Origin Energy Creative, Sustainability Drive
Parkinson's Victoria
New-Porsche Cars Australia Communications Strategy, Creative, Integrated Marketing
PZ Cussons Imperial Leather; 2003
Radiant
The Reach Foundation Campaign: "Open Book Project"
Realestate.com.au
RSL Australia Campaign: "Minute of Silence"
Schmackos Campaign: "Trickopedia"
Sensis.com.au
Simplot John West
Sketchers
Telstra
Tim Burton Exhibition
Tourism Australia
Treasury Wine Estates Campaign: "It's the sunshine that makes it", Digital, In-store, Lindeman's, Print
Westpac Campaign: "Fred Hollows"
Whereis
Whirlpool
White Pages

DDB Sydney Pty. Ltd.

46-52 Mountain Street Level 3, Ultimo, NSW 2007 Australia
Tel.: (61) 2 8260 2222
Fax: (61) 2 8260 2317
E-Mail: info@ddb.com.au
Web Site: www.ddb.com.au

Year Founded: 1945

National Agency Associations: AFA

Agency Specializes In: Advertising

Martin O'Halloran *(CEO)*
Kate Sheppard *(Mng Partner & Head-Bus Mgmt)*
Nicole Taylor *(Mng Partner)*
Mandy Whatson *(Mng Partner)*
Nick Andrews *(Partner-Plng)*
George Mackenzie *(Mng Dir)*
Toby Talbot *(Chief Creative Officer)*
Leif Stromnes *(Mng Dir-Strategy & Innovation)*
Madeline Smith *(Grp Head-Creative)*
Brendan Kai Ho *(Sr Dir-Integrated Art)*
Jade Manning *(Sr Dir-Art)*
Sarah Quinn *(Sr Acct Dir)*
Lisa Hauptmann *(Grp Acct Dir)*
Livia Montalto *(Acct Dir)*
Angela Smith *(Bus Dir)*
Jen Speirs *(Creative Dir)*
Craig Bailey *(Dir-Creative)*
Michael Barnfield *(Dir-Creative)*
Paul Fraser *(Dir-Creative)*
Peter Galmes *(Dir-Creative)*
Carla Hizon *(Dir-Bus)*
Ellie Jones *(Dir-Art)*
Lisa Little *(Dir-Bus)*
Simon Veksner *(Dir-Creative)*
James Coyne *(Sr Strategist-Social Media)*
Domenic Bartolo *(Sr Designer-Craft)*
Avani Maan *(Copywriter)*
Adam Smith *(Copywriter)*
Julia Spencer *(Copywriter)*
Peter Cameron *(Grp CFO-Australia & NZ)*
Emily Frost *(Exec-Bus)*
Leesa Murray *(Sr Art Buyer)*

Accounts:
Arnott's Snackfoods Campaign: "In Your Face", Campaign: "Truly Madly Tim Tam", Radio, Shapes, Social Media, Tim Tam
Australia.com Campaign: "There's Nothing Like "
Brother International Fax, Labeling Machines, Printers; 1996
BWS Campaign: "Today's Special", Creative, TV
Cancer Council NSW Campaign: "Cancer Council Hope"
Chux
Clorox Australia Household Products; 2000
Cup-a-Soup
Energizer Alkaline Batteries, Carefree, carefree.com.au; 2001
Everris Garden Products; 1999
Expedia Campaign: "Biggest Ever Sale", Digital, Press, Social Media, TV
Gatorade Sports Drink; 2002
George Weston Foods Campaign: "Good on ya mum winning hearts and minds"
Johnson & Johnson Campaign: "Be Real Launch", Campaign: "The Mum to Mum Project", Carefree, Skin Care Products; 1996
McDonald's Campaign: "Bring Fries to Life", Campaign: "Busker", Campaign: "Drool", Campaign: "Like Home", Campaign: "McFlurry Drool Sign", Campaign: "New Loose Change Menu", Campaign: "Profitably future-proofing fast-food", Campaign: "Stretch", Creative, Digital, Playland, Print, Rebrand, TV, TrackMyMacca's, Website; 1971
Pepsico Lipton Ice Tea, Take Three Deep Sips
Schwartzkopf Retail Hair Care Products; 1999
Telstra Campaign: "New Phone Feeling", Campaign: "The Reinvention of Telstra", Integrated, Passion Pillars, Pre-Paid Freedom, Upgrades
Tip Top Good On Ya Mum
Unilever Digital, Lipton Ice Tea, Outdoor, TV; 2004
Volkswagen (Australia Creative Agency of Record) Campaign: "Driver Fatigue Technology", Campaign: "Family", Campaign: "Memories", Campaign: "Nightmare Spots", Campaign: "Often Copied. Never Equalled", Campaign: "Park Assist Technology", Campaign: "Passat Changeroom", Campaign: "Road", Campaign: "Welcome To The Family", Creative, Digital, Genuine Parts, Golf GTI, Motor Vehicles, Skoda, TV, Touareg, Volkswagen Commercial Vehicles, Volkswagen Jetta, Volkswagen Tiguan; 2001
Westpac Group Campaign: "24/7 After Midnight", Creative
Wrigley Australia Campaign: "Say Hello to Fresh", Campaign: "Wrigley's Eclipse Toll Booth", Chewing Gum, Eclipse, Extra, Hubba Bubba, Juicy Fruit; 1971

Austria

DDB Tribal Vienna

Thaliastrasse 125 B, 1160 Vienna, Austria
Tel.: (43) 1 491 91 0
Fax: (43) 1 491 91 50
Web Site: www.de.ddb.com/#/alle

Employees: 50

Agency Specializes In: Advertising

Lukas Grossebner *(Exec Dir-Creative & Copywriter)*
Andreas Spielvogel *(Creative Dir)*
Werner Celand *(Dir-Creative)*
Ulrike Kossler *(Dir-Art)*
Dietmar Kreil *(Dir-Art)*
Peter Mayer *(Dir-Art)*
Bernhard Rems *(Dir-Creative)*
Thomas Tatzl *(Dir-Art & Creative)*
Michael Grill *(Copywriter)*
Marc Ludemann *(Jr Copywriter)*

Accounts:
All4family
Bristol Meyers Squibb
Caritas Campaign: "Bus Heat Shelter", Heated Adshel
Epson Deutchland
Henkel Austria AG Adhesives Loctite, Moment

Austria & CEE, Pattex, Pritt, Super Attak; 1998
Henkel Central Eastern Europe Campaign: "Cat & Mouse"
IKEA LED Lights
Kleine Zeitung
Kommunalkredit
Mars Austria Campaign: "Living Room"
McDonald's Campaign: "Cactus", Campaign: "Breakfast: Easy Morning", Campaign: "Bubbles", Campaign: "Fireworks", Campaign: "McDonald's Catapult", Campaign: "Sweater, Tie", Campaign: "The Morning is Hard Enough", McCafe, Morning Coffee, Veggie Burger; 1994
Pfizer Austria
Popakademie Baden-Wurttemberg
Raiffeisen International International Bank, RIB; 2005
Raiffeisen Zentral Bank AG Commercial Bank, RZB; 1997
Spanische Hofreitschule
T-Mobile Austria Creative, Strategic Brand Consulting
Volkswagen Volkswagen Park Assist

Barbados

GHA/DDB

22 George St, Box 1044 Belleville, Saint Michael, Barbados
Tel.: (246) 431 0411
Fax: (246) 431 0412
E-Mail: greg@greghoyos.com
Web Site: www.greghoyos.com

Employees: 20
Year Founded: 1990

Agency Specializes In: Advertising

Greg Hoyos *(Chm)*
Anderson King *(Mng Dir)*
Arthur Atkinson *(Dir-Art)*
Robert Marshall *(Dir-Creative)*
Pamela Cave-Small *(Mgr-Ops)*
Henderson Evelyn *(Mgr-Traffic)*
Henderson Lynch *(Mgr-Media)*
George Helliar *(Acct Exec)*
Dannilo Hutchinson *(Acct Exec)*
Natalie Walton-Sealy *(Acct Exec)*

Accounts:
British Airways
Consumer's Guarantee Insurance
Exxon Oil Foods, Gas, Lubes; 1995
Purity Bakeries

Belgium

DDB Group Belgium

17 rue Saint Hubert, B-1150 Brussels, Belgium
Tel.: (32) 2 761 19 00
Fax: (32) 2 761 19 01
E-Mail: info-ddb@ddb.be
Web Site: www.ddb.be

E-Mail for Key Personnel:
Media Dir.: maurice.vandemaele@ddb.be
Public Relations: ariane.vandenbosch@ddb.be

Employees: 50
Year Founded: 1972

Agency Specializes In: Communications, Consumer Marketing, Direct Response Marketing, Event Planning & Marketing, Pharmaceutical

Yves Bogaerts *(CEO)*
May Bogaerts *(CEO-Radar)*
Dominique Poncin *(Head-Strategy)*
Francis Lippens *(Acct Dir)*
Peter aerts *(Dir-Creative)*
Jonathan Benois *(Dir-Art)*
Charis Verrept *(Dir-Art)*
Silvie Erzeel *(Sr Acct Mgr)*
Bill Bilquin *(Deputy Dir-Creative & Sr Copywriter)*
Romain Felix *(Copywriter)*

Accounts:
AstraZeneca
Audi A4
B-Classic Campaign: "Dvorak"
Belisol
Bol.com
Bosch
Bridgestone
D'Ieteren Audi, Bentley, Lamborghini, Leasing, Porsche, Services, Utility Vehicle, Volkswagen; 1972
Esso
ExxonMobil; 2000
Gezondheid en Wetenschap Campaign: "Don't Google It"
Ikea International A/S
Liga Voor Mensenrechten
Looza
Luminus; 2002
Ortis
Pedigree Campaign: "Billboard Walk"
Persil
Petits Riens/Spullenhulp Campaign: "Santa Surprises Brussels", Homeless Charity
Pfizer; 2003
Ray Ban Campaign: "No Filter"
Volkswagen Group of America, Inc. Caddy Maxi, Campaign: "Golf Story Days", Campaign: "The Long Goodbye", Campaign: "Weather Cam", Eos, Golf, Park Assist Technology

Brazil

DDB Brazil

Av Brigadeiro Luis Antonio 5013, 01401-002 Sao Paulo, SP Brazil
Tel.: (55) 11 3054 9999
Fax: (55) 11 3054 9812
Web Site: www.dm9ddb.com.br

E-Mail for Key Personnel:
Creative Dir.: svalente@dm9ddb.com.br
Media Dir.: pqueiroz@dm9.ddb.com.br
Public Relations: fantacli@dm9ddb.com.br

Employees: 350
Year Founded: 1989

Agency Specializes In: Advertising

Alcir Gomes Leite *(COO)*
Monica de Carvalho *(VP-Media)*
Marco Versolato *(Exec Dir-Creative)*
Mozar Gudin *(Dir-Art)*
Keka Morelle *(Dir-Creative)*
Joao Mosterio *(Dir-Creative)*
Moacyr Netto *(Dir-Creative)*
Ulisses Razaboni *(Dir-Art)*
Gustavo Victorino *(Dir-Creative)*
Rafael Voltolino *(Dir-Art)*
Maria Helena Addesso *(Acct Supvr)*
Marcelo Trivelato *(Acct Supvr)*

Accounts:
ABRA
ABTO Campaign: "Choices", Campaign: "Soul", Organ Transplant Association
Ambev Campaign: "Le Petit Parkour"
ASTOC Abra-Art Academy
Biofert Campaign: "Carnivorous Plants"
Brazilian Academy of Art
C&A Brasil Campaign: "#loucasporcavalli", Campaign: "Fashion Like", Campaign: "Look Block", The Five Cavalli Commandments
CI Campaign: "Experience"
Companhia Athletica Campaign: "Dedication", Campaign: "Elastic Measuring Tape"
Contigo Magazine Campaign: "Everybody Loves A Celebrity"
CUCA School Campaign: "Zumbi"
Elvis Campaign: "C&A"
Estrela Toys Campaign: "Banco Imobiliario", Campaign: "Come Back Ferrorama", Ferrorama Toy Train
FedEx
Follow Magazine Campaign: "Follow the new."
Guarana Antarctica Campaign: "Le Petit Parkour"
Honda Motorcycles Campaign: "Cast"
Hot Pocket
Institute of Ophthalmology Cornea Donation Appeal
Itau Bank Campaign: "The Broadcast Made for You", Campaign: "Unlimited Ad"
Johnson & Johnson Anti Wrinkle Cream, Anti-Acne Gel, Campaign: "Princess at the Tower", Campaign: "Shining Kid", Campaign: "Wrinkled Ad", Clean & Clear, Neutrogena
K-Y Campaign: "Lube Your Love Machine"
Kitchenaid Campaign: "Art Deco"
Latinstock Brasil Campaign: "Images that tell everything.", Campaign: "Little Red Riding Hood", Campaign: "Stories", Image Bank
Marca Brasil Newspaper Campaign: "Sport Is Our World"
MASP Campaign: "A painting is just a part of the story", Campaign: "Paths", Campaign: "Salvador Dali", Campaign: "The Scream"
Mercedes-Benz Mercedes-Benz Actros
Panamericana Art & Design School Campaign: "QR Code"
Placar Magazine Campaign: "Grass"
Red Cross Campaign: "Sensitive"
Sadia Campaign: "Huge Sachets", Campaign: "The Boxer", Sadia Hot Pocket Hamburger
Saxofunny Imaginary Musical Instruments
Sos Mata Atlantica Campaign: "Decor Exchange"
Tam Travel Campaign: "Escapades"
Telefonica Vivo TV Campaign: "Cowboy"
Telha Norte Campaign: "Social Wall"
Terra Networks Campaign: "Terra V.I.P.", Terra Portal
Terra Campaign: "Instadoc", Planeta Terra Festival
Tok & Stok Campaign: "Foldings", Campaign: "Furniture Nights", Campaign: "Letters"
Tribo Skate Magazine Campaign: "Real freedom is to ride with safety"
Varanda
Viajar Pelo Mundo Magazine Campaign: "Pole"
Whirlpool Campaign: "Art Movements", Campaign: "Frozen Promotion"
Zeeg Sound Production Campaign: "How to make a sound"
Zoo Safari Campaign: "Paths - Zebra", Campaign: "Wild Pet"

DM9DDB

Avenida Brigadeiro Luis Antonio 5013, Jardim Paulista, Sao Paulo, SP Brazil
Tel.: (55) 11 3054 9999
Fax: (55) 11 3054 9812
E-Mail: intl@dm9ddb.com.br
Web Site: www.dm9ddb.com.br

Employees: 340

Marcio Callage *(Pres-DM9Sul)*
Fabiano Beraldo *(Head-Brdcst Production)*
Neel Majumder *(Exec Dir-Creative)*
Rafael Segri *(Sr Dir-Art)*
Alexandre Vilela *(Sr Dir-Art)*
Daniel Chagas Martins *(Art Dir)*
Marcelo Reis *(Creative Dir)*
Leonardo Rotundo *(Art Dir)*
Bruno Trad *(Art Dir)*
Fabio Brandao *(Dir-Creative)*
Alessandra Cantieri *(Dir-Art)*
Patricia Blanco Cardoso *(Dir-Media)*
Elias Carmo *(Dir-Art)*
Zico Farina *(Dir-Creative)*
Diogo Mello *(Dir-Creative)*

Andre Pedroso *(Dir-Creative)*
Ricardo Tronquini *(Dir-Creative)*
Priscilla Campolina *(Acct Supvr)*
Flavio ferri *(Copywriter)*
Filipe Medici *(Copywriter)*
Rodrigo Mendonca *(Copywriter)*
Otto Pajunk *(Copywriter)*
Ricardo Salgado *(Copywriter)*
Maicon Silveira *(Copywriter)*
Igor Puga *(Chief Interactive Officer)*

Accounts:
New-Akatu Institute
Amanco
Amaral Carvalho Hospital Campaign: "ELO Teddy Bear"
B2W Campaign: "Crumpled Paper"
New-Banco Itau Holding Financeira
Bohemia
Brastemp
Companhia de Bebidas das Americas
Consul
Corbis
De Cabron
Elo Teddy Bears
New-Estrela Toys SUPER MASS
Ferragem Tres Figueiras Campaign: "Sandpit"
Fundacao Dorina Nowill Para Cegos The Blind Book
Hospital Beneficia Portuguesa
Humanitarian Lion
Itau Bank
Johnson & Johnson
L&PM Editores
Latinstock
Mario Yamasaki
Museu de Arte de Sao Paulo
New-Novo Mundo Currency Exchange
O Pao dos Pobres Foundation Campaign: "Behind the Dreams"
Olympikus Campaign: "Sounds of Glory"
Portugese Hospital Organ Donation Health care
SBP
Sul Jiu-Jitsu Campaign: "Human Meat"
Telhanorte
New-Tok & Stok
New-Viajar Travel Magazine

Bulgaria

DDB Sofia
Business Park Sofia, Bldg 1A, 1715 Sofia, Bulgaria
Tel.: (359) 2 489 8000
Fax: (359) 2 489 8029
E-Mail: hello@sofia.ddb.com
Web Site: www.ddb.com

Employees: 12
Year Founded: 1992

Agency Specializes In: Advertising

Angelos Paraschakis *(CEO)*
Yoana Pancheva *(Grp Acct Dir)*
Vasil Petrakov *(Dir-Creative)*
Aglika Spassova *(Dir-Art)*
Ina Izova *(Acct Mgr)*
Mila Mutafchieva *(Acct Exec)*
Victoria Nikolova *(Copywriter)*

Accounts:
Aegean Airlines
Alpha Bank
Belana
Fa
Globul Creative
McDonald's
Persil
Prima
Schauma
Silan

Canada

Anderson DDB Health & Lifestyle
1300-33 Bloor St E, Toronto, ON M4W 3H1 Canada
(See Separate Listing)

DDB Vancouver
1600-777 Hornby St, Vancouver, BC V6Z 2T3 Canada
(See Separate Listing)

Chile

DDB Chile
Av Del Vallee 945 4 Piso of 4615, Ciudad Empresarial, Santiago, Chile
Tel.: (56) 2 677 8888
Fax: (56) 2 677 8885
E-Mail: info@ddbchile.com
Web Site: www.ddb.com/

E-Mail for Key Personnel:
President: eduardo.fernandez@ddbchile.com

Year Founded: 1981

National Agency Associations: ACHAP

Agency Specializes In: Advertising, Advertising Specialties

Simon Subercaseaux *(VP-Creation)*
Claudio Campisto *(Exec Creative Dir)*
Cristian Ulloa *(Exec Creative Dir)*
Sergio Duarte *(Dir-Art & Copywriter)*
Flavio Cabezas *(Dir-Art)*
Nicolas Montt *(Dir-Art)*
Enrique Gonzalez Wilches *(Dir-Art)*
Franco Bastias *(Copywriter)*
Jordan Caceres *(Copywriter)*
Maria de los Angeles Contreras *(Copywriter)*

Accounts:
ADT Security System
C13 Campaign: "Display on Search"
Centraal Beheer
Clorox
Coaniquem Campaign: "Salt"
Derco Usados Campaign: "Angst"
Egypt Tourism
Elastosello Acoustic Insulation
Energizer Flashlights
ExxonMobil
Hasbro
Henkel Superbonder
Kosiuko
Laboratorios Maver Campaign: "Marathon"
Mattel
McDonald's
Oral Fresh
P&G Campaign: "Beet"
Scrabble Campaign: "Each letter is a world"
Sindelen
Super Bonder
Suzuki Suzuki Rmx450z
Telefonica CTC Chile
New-UHU
Unilever
Volkswagen Group of America, Inc.

China

DDB China - Shanghai
Park2Space 4th Floor Building 2 169 Mengzi Road, Luwan District, Shanghai, 200023 China
Tel.: (86) 21 6151 3300
Fax: (86) 21 6448 3699
E-Mail: info@hk.ddb.com
Web Site: www.ddb.com

Employees: 89
Year Founded: 1991

Agency Specializes In: Advertising, Direct Response Marketing, Internet/Web Design, Sales Promotion, Strategic Planning/Research

Jimmy Lam *(Vice Chm & CEO)*
Ng Jit Hoong *(Mng Dir)*
Richard Tan *(Pres/CEO-DDB China Grp)*
Jit Ng *(Mng Dir-DDB Grp Shanghai & VP-DDB Grp North China)*
Adams Fan *(Exec Dir-Creative)*
Don Huang *(Exec Dir-Creative)*
Zheng Li *(Exec Creative Dir)*
Li Zheng *(Creative Dir)*
Cassie Dai *(Acct Mgr)*
Karen Ding *(Mgr-Digital Plng)*
Shu Teoh *(Copywriter)*
Phil Romans *(Reg Bus Dir-Mars & Wrigley)*

Accounts:
New-Alipay
Alteco Superglue
Amazon Kindle Paperwhite Campaign: "Paper & Pen"
Bentley Motors China Creative
China Environmental Protection Foundation Green Pedestrian Crossing
e-Long
Family Care For Grassroots Community Campaign: "The Keyboard of Isolation"
Fonterra Anchor
Huaxia Animal Protection Foundation
Johnson & Johnson; 2000
McDonald's
Midea Air Conditioning (Agency of Record) Creative
One Foundation Campaign: "1 Min Song for Shower"
Pepsico Campaign: "Bring Happiness Home", Campaign: "Delicious, Nutritious, with No Additives", Campaign: "Lawn Refresher", Campaign: "Witness the Magic of Sweat", Clorox: Glad Food Bags, Creative, Gatorade (Television), Print, Quaker Concentrated Powder Drink, Tv; 2002
Quaker Oats Creative
T-Mall Creative
Tsingtao
Unilever China Campaign: "Tea Magnifier"
Volkswagen Group China Beetle's Eye View, Campaign: "Blue Mobility In-Car Mobile App", Passat
XStep
Zendai Art Supermarket Campaign: "Art, for the price of everyday items"

DDB Guoan Communications Beijing Co., Ltd.
7/F Ocean Center Building D 62 East 4th Ring Road, Chaoyang District, Beijing, 100025 China
Tel.: (86) 10 5929 3300
Fax: (86) 10 5929 3335
Web Site: www.ddb-guoan.com

Employees: 2
Year Founded: 1992

Agency Specializes In: Advertising, Consumer Marketing, Direct Response Marketing, Internet/Web Design, Sales Promotion, Strategic Planning/Research

Tian It Ng *(Chief Creative Officer)*
Richard Tan *(CEO-North China)*
Ivan Wang *(Dir-Creative)*
Jim Hau *(Assoc Dir-Creative)*
Jing Wu *(Assoc Dir-Creative)*

Accounts:
Bank of China

Advertising Agencies

China Environmental Protection Foundation
China First Auto Works
China Unicom
CITIC Bank
eLong TVC
Huaxia Bank Credit Card Program; 2008
Johnson & Johnson
McDonald's
Pepsico
Phillips
Volkswagen Group Import Cars Print, The Beetle

Colombia

DDB Worldwide Colombia, S.A.

Calle 6 Oeste No 1B-72, Cali, Colombia
Tel.: (57) 2 892 6450
Fax: (57) 2 892 6536
Web Site: www.ddb.com

Employees: 15

Valentina Hoyos *(Grp CEO)*
Lisa-Fernanda Giuraldo *(Exec Dir)*
Juanita Delvasto *(Sr Dir-Art)*
David Rodriguez *(Sr Dir-Art)*
Luisa Solano *(Acct Dir)*
Andres Aristizabal *(Dir-Creative & Digital)*
Andres Garcia *(Dir-Art)*
Javier Vargas Guevara *(Dir-Art)*
Nestor Morales *(Dir-Creative)*
Marco Antonio Munoz *(Dir-Creative)*
Julio Ernesto Ortiz *(Dir-Creative Grp)*
Wladimir Sanchez Alzate *(Dir-Art)*
Henry Chacon *(Planner-Strategic)*

Accounts:
Baxter
Bico
Centro Commerciale Unico
Cerveza Pilsen Campaign: "Parche Poderoso Mobile App"
Clorox Ropa Colores Vivos
Fanalca
Johnson & Johnson Clean & Clear, Neutrogena; 1995
Military Forces of Colombia Campaign: "The Code"
Owens-Illinois Campaign: "Glass Is Life", Online, TV

DDB Worldwide Colombia S.A.

Diagonal 97 #17-60 Piso 10, Bogota, Colombia
Tel.: (57) 1 257 0188
Fax: (57) 1 236 5559
Web Site: ddbcolombia.tumblr.com

Agency Specializes In: Advertising

Luz Maria Restrepo *(Gen Mgr)*
Juanita Delvasto *(Sr Dir-Art)*
Mario Leon *(Sr Dir-Art)*
Felipe Munevar *(Art Dir)*
Andres Nieto *(Art Dir)*
Daniel Calle *(Dir-Creative)*
Rodrigo Davila *(Dir-Creative)*
Marco Munoz *(Dir-Creative)*
Juan Alvarado *(Copywriter)*
Juan David Arboleda *(Copywriter)*
Juan Carlos Castano *(Copywriter)*
Camilo Monsalve *(Copywriter)*

Accounts:
AB Electrolux
Armed Forces Of Colombia
Bancolombia Campaign: "Opera Test"
Bogota Film Festival
Bridgestone Campaign: "Surprise"
C.C Sandiego Festival Canino
Cerveza Pilsen Measure Your Passion App
Clorox Bon Brill Cleaning Sponges, Campaign: "Bacterium", Campaign: "The Roach", Cleaning Products; 2000
Colombiano Road Safety
Edatel TV HD
El Colombiano Campaign: "Hide Mines", Campaign: "Recipes to Eat Outside"
Energizer Batteries; 2000
ExxonMobil; 1996
Grupo Carvajal Campaign: "The Colors of Imagination"
Henkel Campaign: "Angel Explosion", Campaign: "Girl Explosion", Super Bonder; 1998
Honda Campaign: "Helmet", Campaign: "Meteor", Honda Helmets
Johnson & Johnson
Libreria Norma
Military Forces of Colombia Campaign: "La Maldicion De Los Martinez"
Nokia; 2003
Norma Campaign: "Colors Norma Onomatopoeia"
Paladares Magazine Campaign: "Recipes To Eat Outside Without Leaving Home"
Sab Miller Bavaria Campaign: "Passion for Dim"
Telefonica
Tronex Battery
TRS Air Conditioners Campaign: "Bed, Couch"
UNE EPM Telecomunicaciones
Unilever Wall's Ice Cream
VirtualBox

Czech Republic

DDB Prague

Lomnickeho 1705/5, 140 00 Prague, 4 Czech Republic
Tel.: (420) 2 2101 3111
Fax: (420) 2 2101 3901
E-Mail: ddb@ddb.cz
Web Site: www.ddb.cz

Employees: 30
Year Founded: 1991

Agency Specializes In: Advertising

Hadj Moussa Radouane *(Pres)*
Petr Vykoukal *(CFO)*
Mladen Grebo *(Head-Digital Dept)*
Lukas Prokop *(Acct Dir)*
Ondrej Wunsch *(Dir-Art)*
Katarzyna Sanojca *(Acct Mgr)*
Tomas Mondschein *(Mgr-Traffic & Studio)*

Accounts:
Eastern Sugar
Henkel
Hospodanske Noviny
Johnson & Johnson
Korunni Water
Krka
Lipton
McDonald's
Nestle Purina
Pfizer
Profit
Provident
Unilever
Volkswagen Group of America, Inc.
Wrigley

Denmark

DDB Denmark

Bredgade 6, PO Box 2074, DK-1013 Copenhagen, Denmark
Tel.: (45) 33 46 3000
Fax: (45) 33 46 3001
E-Mail: info@ddbdanmark.dk
Web Site: ddbcopenhagen.dk

E-Mail for Key Personnel:
President: johnny.henriksen@ddbdanmark.dk

Employees: 60
Year Founded: 1984

Agency Specializes In: Advertising

Johnny Henriksen *(CEO)*
Jens Erenbjerg *(CFO)*
Christian Iversen *(Sr Dir-Art)*
Thomas Fabricius *(Dir-Creative)*
Anna Just Melson *(Designer)*

Accounts:
Alis Skate Gear
Berlinigske Tidende Daily Newspaper; 2003
Danske Spil
Eniro Campaign: "The Chase - Krak"
McDonald's Campaign: "Coin Hunters", Cocio Summer Shake
Niconovum
Novartis
Pandora Jewelry
Royal Unibrew Campaign: "Tempt Cider Design", Cider, Faxe Kondi, Royal Beer
Skandinavisk Motor Co.
Toms Gruppen
Volkswagen Group of America, Inc. Campaign: "The Polo Principle", Campaign: "The new Golf. Still original.", Golf

El Salvador

Tribu DDB El Salvador

(Formerly DDB Worldwide)
519 Bulevar El Hippodromo, San Salvador, El Salvador
Tel.: (503) 2535-7777
Fax: (503) 2535-7700
E-Mail: info@sv.ddb.com
Web Site: http://eltaierddb.com/

Employees: 40

Agency Specializes In: Advertising

Victor Pardo *(Founder & Partner)*
Erick Laparra *(Dir-Creative)*
Ada Mollinedo *(Dir-Art)*
Jorge Solorzano *(Dir-Creative)*

Accounts:
Aqua
Atlas
Cerveceria Rio
Eveready
Exxon Mobil
Henkel
McDonald's
Parma Dairy Products
Publinews Braille Edition
Sancela Nevax, Saba
Toyota

Estonia

DDB Estonia Ltd.

Parnu Mnt 69, Tallinn, 10134 Estonia
Tel.: (372) 699 8600
Fax: (372) 699 8601
E-Mail: ddb@ddb.ee
Web Site: www.ddb.ee

E-Mail for Key Personnel:
President: jana@ddb.ee
Creative Dir.: meelis@ddb.ee
Production Mgr.: tiina@ddb.ee

Employees: 15
Year Founded: 1993

National Agency Associations: EAAA

Agency Specializes In: Advertising

Jana Koppel *(CEO & Partner)*
Ragne Gasna *(Acct Dir)*
Erkki Tuisk *(Acct Dir)*
Joosep Volkmann *(Acct Dir)*
Meelis Mikker *(Dir-Creative)*
Erik Teemagi *(Dir-Art)*
Rait Milistver *(Copywriter)*
Raivo Tihanov *(Copywriter)*
Esta Vaask *(Sr Accountant)*

Accounts:
Eesti Pagar
Enterprise Estonia Campaign: "Hungry for Culture?"
Estonia Bakery
Fazer
Husqvarna
Kalaliit
Partner
Poltsamaa
Tele 2; 1999
Tere
Vivarec

Finland

DDB Helsinki

Hietaniemenkatu 7A, 00100 Helsinki, Finland
Tel.: (358) 424 7471
Fax: (358) 9 626 833
E-Mail: info@ddb.fi
Web Site: www.ddb.fi

E-Mail for Key Personnel:
President: Rainer.Linquist@ddb.fi
Creative Dir.: mika.wist@ddb.fi

Employees: 35

National Agency Associations: MTL

Agency Specializes In: Advertising

Rainer Lindqvist *(CEO)*
Pia Eiro *(Acct Dir)*
Jarno Lindblom *(Acct Dir)*
Heli Roiha *(Art Dir)*
Tapu Haro *(Dir-Creative)*
Lauri Vassinen *(Dir-Creative)*
Julia Jamsen *(Acct Mgr)*
Inka Karvonen *(Acct Mgr)*
Paivi Lang *(Acct Mgr)*
Annu Terho *(Copywriter)*

Accounts:
Area Travel Agency
Esso
ExxonMobil
Fennia Insurance Co.
Honka Campaign: "House"
Ingman Foods
McDonald's Campaign: "Draw French Fries Challenge", Campaign: "Good Morning", Campaign: "Large Coffee", Campaign: "Paper Chicken", Double Cheese Burger
NestlePurina PetCare
Nordea Bank
Paulig/Brazil
Paulig/Frezza Tazza
Paulig Paula, Take Away
PepsiCo
Pfizer
Sonera 4G, Campaign: "At The Edge Tf The 3G", Campaign: "Sonera Speedtest"
Teliasonera Finland Campaign: "Sonera Speedtest"
Tikkurila

France

DDB Communication France

55 rue d'Amsterdam, 75391 Paris, Cedex 08 France
Tel.: (33) 1 5332 6000
Fax: (33) 1 5332 6504
E-Mail: Herve.Brossard@ddb.fr
Web Site: www.ddb.fr

E-Mail for Key Personnel:
President: herve.brossard@ddb.fr

Employees: 800
Year Founded: 1969

National Agency Associations: AACC-ADC-IAA

Agency Specializes In: Advertising, Advertising Specialties, Brand Development & Integration, Communications, Consumer Marketing, Consumer Publications, Corporate Identity, Digital/Interactive, Direct Response Marketing, Event Planning & Marketing, Graphic Design, Infomercials, Internet/Web Design, Logo & Package Design, Point of Purchase, Point of Sale, Print, Production, Public Relations, Publicity/Promotions, Radio, Sales Promotion, Sports Market, Strategic Planning/Research, T.V., Telemarketing, Trade & Consumer Magazines

Pierre Le Gouvello *(Co-Pres & Chief People Officer)*
Alexandre Herve *(Exec Dir-Creative)*
Mathieu Roux *(Bus Dir & Dir-Comml)*
Raphael Ghisalberti *(Art Dir)*
Stephane Audouin *(Dir-Artistic)*

Accounts:
New-The Agence de la biomedecine Agency Biomedecine The Man Who Died The Most
Givenchy
Hasbro Campaign: "The Transformable"
Honda Moto Campaign: "Only Gods think once"
Sushi Shop
Volkswagen Group of America, Inc. Campaign: "Tourolf, Finger", Transporter 4Motion

DDB Paris

55 rue d'Amsterdam, 75391 Paris, France
Tel.: (33) 1 5332 5669
Fax: (33) 1 5332 6342
Web Site: www.ddb.fr/

E-Mail for Key Personnel:
President: betrand.suchet@ddbparis.fr

Employees: 100
Year Founded: 2001

Agency Specializes In: Advertising, Consumer Goods, Corporate Identity, Sports Market

Matthieu de Lesseux *(Co-Pres)*
Jean-Jacques Sebille *(Deputy Mng Dir)*
Pierre-Antoine Dupin *(Editor & Designer)*
Alexandre Herve *(Exec Creative Dir)*
Alexander Kalchev *(Exec Creative Dir)*
Mathieu Roux *(Bus Dir & Dir-Comml)*
Pierre Beffa *(Acct Dir & Assoc Dir)*
Nicolas Bruchet *(Acct Dir)*
Sebastien Henras *(Art Dir)*
Stephanie Leray *(Acct Dir)*
Audrey Niguet *(Acct Dir)*
Stephane Audouin *(Dir-Artistic)*
Alexis Benbehe *(Dir-Artistic)*
Emmanuel Courteau *(Dir-Art)*
Alexandrine Desbrugeres *(Dir-Artistic)*
Raphal Ghisalberti *(Dir-Art & Digital Creative-McDonald's France)*
Jenna Haugmard *(Dir-Artistic)*
Nicolas Malcorps *(Dir-Art)*
Pierre Mathonat *(Dir-Art)*
Mathieu Nevians *(Dir-Art)*
Olga Papikian *(Dir-Digital Bus)*
Marie Tricoche *(Dir-Customer)*
Sophie Prouteau *(Assoc Dir)*
Alexis Benoit *(Copywriter)*
Jean-Francois Bouchet *(Copywriter)*
Sebastien Genty *(Planner)*
Constance Godard *(Copywriter)*
Quentin Moenne Loccoz *(Art Buyer & Jr Producer-TV)*
Loic Morando *(Planner)*
Arnaud Viallaneix *(Copywriter)*

Accounts:
Accorhotels Digital
Allianz
ANLCI Campaign: "Blockbuster", Campaign: "Fight for literacy 2"
Bepong Campaign: "While we Work you Don't"
Bouygues Telecom Campaign: "Kitten Telecom", Television
Brandt Spoutnik
Casino
Chupa Chups Sindy
Connect 4 Campaign: "Don't claim victory too fast"
Coty Campaign: "Elevator"
Doctors of the World Campaign: "MakeAChildCry", Outdoor, Print, TV
Fight for literacy
Fleury Michon
France Football
New-French Health Department
Givenchy Campaign: "Noir Couture"
Greenpeace Campaign: "A New Warrior", Campaign: "France, also the Country of Nuclear Power"
Hasbro Boggle 1, Campaign: "Connect 4", Campaign: "Mr. and Mrs. Potato Head 60 Years", Campaign: "The Transformable", Campaign: "Tub", Play-Doh, Print Ads, Risk:Junk Food, Trivial Pursuit, Wagram
Inpes (Institut National De Prevention Et D'Education Pour La Sante)
Johnson & Johnson Campaign: "Her Best Years"
Lactel
Le Mouv Campaign: "I Love You"
L'Equipe Campaign: "50 Reasons", Campaign: "Bolt"
Live Poker Magazine
Loto La Francaise des Jeux; 2002
Mastermind
McDonald's Campaign: "Mcdonald's Monopoly", Campaign: "Passion Meter"
Meetic Campaign: "Line 9"
Mini Chupa Chups
MINI France Campaign: "Keep Calm", MINI Maps
Museum of The Great War Campaign: "Facebook 1914"
National Geographic Campaign: "Jungle", Campaign: "Reality vs Fiction"
Neutrogena
Nike
The Parisians Band Promotion, Entertainment, Rock Band
PepsiCo Campaign: "Billboard powered by oranges", Campaign: "Lipton Ice Tea: The Slap", Lipton Yellow Label Campaign: "Waterfall", Tropicana
Perfetti van Melle Campaign: "Action Man", Campaign: "Mini Chupa Chups Kipik"
Pirelli Tires (Global Advertising Agency)
Playboy Enterprises, Inc. "Super Playboy", Campaign: "Elevator", Playboy Parfume, Print, VIP Fragrances
President
PriceMinister-Rakuten Campaign: "Hippo"
Roc
SNCF Campaign: "Voyages - The escape machine"
Tiji Campaign: "Colours"
Trace Urban Campaign: "The Battle"
Unilever Lipton Yellow Label, Maille
Volkswagen Group of America, Inc. Campaign: "Choice", Golf GTE
Voyages-sncf.com Campaign: "Lucky Bag"
Winamax Poker Table 14

Germany

DDB Berlin

Neue Schonhauser Strasse 3-5, D-10178 Berlin, Germany
Tel.: (49) 302 40840
Fax: (49) 302 408 4400
E-Mail: contact@ddb-tribal.com
Web Site: www.ddb.com

E-Mail for Key Personnel:
Public Relations: m.scheller-wegener@de.ddb.com

Employees: 200
Year Founded: 1961

National Agency Associations: GWA

Agency Specializes In: Communications, Consulting, Direct Response Marketing, Internet/Web Design, Public Relations

Matthias Schmidt *(Mng Dir)*
Eric Schoeffler *(Chief Creative Officer)*
Jan Diekmann *(Head-Bus Dev)*
Dylan De Backer *(Exec Dir-Creative)*
Jack Christensen *(Sr Dir-Art)*
Daniela Hofmann *(Bus Dir-Europe)*
Anika Kempkensteffen *(Creative Dir)*
Gordon Euchler *(Dir-Plng)*
Behnaz Pakravesh *(Dir-Creative)*
Christoph Stender *(Dir-Art)*
Paul Dombek *(Acct Mgr)*
Tanja Bruckner *(Mgr-Corporate New Bus)*
Margit Scheller-Wegener *(Chief People Officer)*
Vesna Baranovic *(Sr Dir-Art)*
Bianca Dordea *(Bus Dir-Europe)*
Veit Moeller *(Creative Dir)*
Mirja Peters *(Dir-Art)*
Peter Goeke *(Sr Copywriter-Digital)*
Henning Falk *(Client Svc Dir)*
Nina Lehmann *(Jr Acct Mgr)*
Anna Simon *(Jr Designer-UX)*

Accounts:
Bayer
BISS
Bosch Campaign: "Icebergs", NoFrost Technology
BSH Deutschland Campaign: "Icebergs"
Eissmann
Entega
ExxonMobil
Henkel Campaign: "Leaflet"
IKEA
Knorr
McDonald's
Nestle
Reporter ohne Grenzen Campaign: "#writinghelps"
Reporters Without Borders Campaign: "Whistles For Whistleblowers"
Schwarzkopf
T-Mobile
TomTom
Valtenfall Europe
Volkswagen Group of America, Inc. Campaign: "A Crash Course to Shine", Campaign: "Area View", Campaign: "Crocodile Boots", Campaign: "Edition 35", Campaign: "It feels good to know you could.", Campaign: "See everything around you in front of you.", Fox, Golf, Pedro

Accounts:
eBay Campaign: "The eBay Offers"
Entega Privatkunden Co. Campaign: "The Entega Energy Saving"
FUNK
Henkel AOK, Campaign: "Leaflet", Campaign: "Long Names. Long lasting.", Campaign: "Plastic Surgery"
Nestle
Ramazzotti
Schwarzkopf
New-Sony
Telekom Campaign: "Remote Banner"
Volkswagen AG Campaign: "It Feels Good to Know you Could.", Campaign: "Rock 'N' Scroll", Campaign: "Side Eyes", Campaign: "Tears", Campaign: "Volkswagen's Parasite Mailing", VW Golf GT

DDB Group Germany

Neue Schoenhauser Strasse 3-5, 10178 Berlin, Germany
Tel.: (49) 302 4084 0
Fax: (49) 302 4084 500
E-Mail: berlin@de.ddb.com
Web Site: www.de.ddb.com/#/de

E-Mail for Key Personnel:
Public Relations: m.scheller-wegener@de.ddb.com

Employees: 630
Year Founded: 1962

Agency Specializes In: Consulting, Direct Response Marketing, Internet/Web Design, Public Relations

Toby Pschorr *(Mng Dir)*

Heye & Partner GmbH

Blumenstr. 28,, 80332 Munich, Germany
Tel.: (49) 89-66532-00
Fax: (49) 89-66532-1112
E-Mail: info@heye.de
Web Site: www.heye.de

Employees: 300
Year Founded: 1962

Karin Achatz *(Art Dir)*
Andreas Andresen *(Dir-Bus Dev)*
Christopher Grouls *(Dir-Creative)*
Fabian Hinzer *(Dir-Creative)*
Zeljko Pezely *(Dir-Creative)*

Accounts:
Adelholzener Alpenquellen Mineral Waters; 1998
Aktion Deutschland hilft Campaign: "The Water Is Gone, But The Damages Remain"
BigMac Campaign: "Something Hot"
Develey; Unterhaching Lowensenf Mustard, McDonald's Tomato Ketchup; 1999
Fiskars Gardening Tools
FIT Delivery & Shipping
Hermann Historica
Intersnack Wolf Bergstrasse Snacks; 2001
Jeyes Deutschland Aromair, Bloo, Globol; 2003
McDonald's Deutschland Campaign: "Fries Hands"; 1971
Meine Familie & ich Verlag
Merker Spielothek
Montblanc
Neckermann Reisen
Neu.de
SKY HDTV
Suddeutsche Zeitung
Tinnitus-ist-heilbar.de
Versicherungskammer Bayern Insurances; 2000
Wagner Tiefkuhlprodukte Pizza; 2002

Heye & Partner GmbH

Gaensemarkt 35, 20354 Hamburg, Germany
Tel.: (49) 40 229 33 01
Fax: (49) 40 229 33 100
E-Mail: info@heye-hh.de
Web Site: www.heye.de

Employees: 80

Agency Specializes In: Advertising, Financial, Public Relations

Accounts:
Eckes Granini GmbH
Jeyes Vertriebs Campaign: "Buzzing"
Johnson & Johnson GmbH; Dusseldorf Bebe Health Care, Clean & Clear, Neutrogena, RoC Cosmetics; 1994
Mcdonalds Germany Campaign: "The Gourmet Experiment 3/5"
Montblanc Pencils
Royal Canin
Volkswagen Campaign: "Drunken Sat Nav"

Tribal Worldwide

(Formerly DDB Tribal Dusseldorf)
Berliner Allee 10, 40212 Dusseldorf, Germany
Tel.: (49) 211 6013 3000
Fax: (49) 211 6013 3333
Web Site: tribalworldwide.com

Employees: 80

Agency Specializes In: Advertising

Matthias Schmidt *(Mng Dir)*
Eric Schoeffler *(Chief Creative Officer)*
Lilli Langenheim *(Sr Dir-Art-DDB Berlin)*
Alice Bottaro *(Dir-Creative)*
Christian Bueltmann *(Dir-Art)*
Jan Propach *(Dir-Creative)*
Dominika Zajac *(Dir-Art)*
Markus Druhe *(Acct Mgr)*
Stefan Issel *(Acct Mgr)*
Michael Schilling *(Copywriter)*

Accounts:
AEG ProSteam
Below Ground
Bic
BSH Deutschland Campaign: "Ice Cave"
Canadian Tourism Commission
Deutsche Telekom Campaign: "Move On", Campaign: "Share 2014", Mobile Internet
Diesel
Ebay Marketing Campaign: "Sandals & Socks", Campaign: "The Lego Equation"
Electrolux Appliances AB Secret Ingredient
Henkel Campaign: "Arm"
Max
Nestle
Oise Language Coaching
Pattex Superglue
Popakademie Baden Wuerttemberg
Premier
Remazotti
Reporters Without Borders Campaign: "The Power of Pencils"
Schwarzkopf Campaign: "A Declaration of Love"
Societe Bic
SPIEGEL-Verlag Rudolf Augstein GmbH & Co. KG
Steinway & Sons Campaign: "Piano for Peace"
Vattenfall Europe
Volkswagen "A Crash Course to Shine", Beetle, Campaign: "Blunders", Campaign: "Crocodile Boots", Campaign: "Don't Make Up And Drive", Campaign: "Hedgehog and Fish", Campaign: "Shoe String", Campaign: "The New iBeetle. Never Drive Alone", Golf, Golf GTI, Park Pilot, Side Assist, Tiguan

Guatemala

dos: Puntos DDB

km 86 antigua carretera a El Salvador Centro Corporativo Muxbal, Torre Este Nivel 9, Guatemala, 01008 Guatemala
Tel.: (502) 2326 3800
Fax: (502) 2326 3838
E-Mail: Info@ddb.com
Web Site: www.ddb.com

Employees: 53
Year Founded: 1991

Agency Specializes In: Advertising

Jose M. Rivera *(Sr Dir-Art)*

Accounts:
Amnesty International
Atlas Industrial Stoves & Refrigerators; 2003
Banco del Quetzel Banking; 1993
Betit
Brahba
Corporacion Mariposal Bottled Water, Soft Drinks
Exxon Mobil
Henkel la Luz Bar Soap, Fabric Softener; 2003
Sancela Diapers, Pads; 2003
Unilever Axe, Campaign: "Peephole"
Unis University; 2003

Hong Kong

DDB Worldwide Ltd.

Unit 1201 Core E Cyberport 3, 100 Cyberport Road, Hong Kong, China (Hong Kong)
Tel.: (852) 2828 0328
Fax: (852) 2827 2700
Web Site: www.ddb.com

E-Mail for Key Personnel:
President: tim.evill@ddb_asia.com

Employees: 154
Year Founded: 1972

Agency Specializes In: Advertising, Communications, Direct Response Marketing, Internet/Web Design, Sales Promotion, Strategic Planning/Research

Ruth Lee *(Chief Creative Officer)*
Peter Rodenbeck *(VP & Reg Dir-Asia)*
Andreas Krasser *(Head-Strategy & Innovation)*
Annie Tong *(Head-Brdcst)*
Irene Tsui *(Gen Mgr)*
Clifford Ng *(Exec Dir-Creative)*
Shadow Ng *(Sr Dir-Art)*
Jan Lee *(Sr Acct Dir-Hong Kong)*
Craig Lonnee *(Reg Dir-Talent Mgmt)*
Debby Lai *(Grp Acct Dir)*
Nateepat Jaturonrasmi *(Creative Dir)*
Koman Ko *(Acct Dir)*
Meshiria Chan *(Dir-Art)*
Jeffery Foo *(Dir-Art)*
Julia Hou *(Dir-Creative)*
Jay Lee *(Dir-Creative)*
Waiwai Wai *(Dir-Art)*
Valiant Yip *(Dir-Bus)*
Paul Yu *(Dir-Creative)*
Noel Yuen *(Dir-Bus)*
Wallace Wan *(Assoc Dir-Creative)*
Fiona Mok *(Acct Mgr)*
Keith Lam *(Copywriter)*

Accounts:
Bank of China; 2009
Clorox Campaign: "Apple"; 1996
Freshlock
Friends of the Earth Campaign: "Taxi Meter"
George Weston Foods Campaign: "Don Do's & Don'ts Modern Art"
Glad Pineapple
Greeners Action Campaign: "Rice", Campaign: "Vote on Garbage,Vote with Garbage"
Johnson & Johnson Clean & Clear; 1997
Manulife (Agency of Record) Campaign: "Spouse", Creative, For Your Future, Strategic Branding
McDonald's Campaign: "18-Button Redemption Machine", Campaign: "I'm Amazing", Share Box, TV; 1999
Orbis Hong Kong
Park 'N Shop Campaign: "Psychology Class"; 1992
PCCW
The Reach Foundation Campaign: "Open Book Project"
Realestate.com.au Campaign: "Open for Inspection"
Shenzhen Avic Real Estate Holding
New-Studio City Macau Campaign: "This is Entertainment"
Thinking Group Westone Earphones
Tin Market Store Campaign: "Cheap Chicken"
Tse Sui Luen Jewellery Campaign: "Finger Language"
Vitasoy; 2002
Watson's Store Campaign: "Radiant Glow Dm"; 2009
Well Synergy International Campaign: "Tofu"
Westone Beethoven, Campaign: "Cafe/Train/Tunnel", Earphones
WWF Hong Kong

Hungary

DDB Budapest

Dozsa Gyorgy ut 84/a 3rd Floor, H-1068 Budapest, Hungary
Tel.: (36) 1 461 2800
Fax: (36) 1 321 6270
E-Mail: info@ddb.hu
Web Site: www.ddb.hu

E-Mail for Key Personnel:
President: hannes.wirnsberger@ddb.hu

Employees: 70
Year Founded: 1991

Agency Specializes In: Advertising

Hannes Wirnsberger *(CEO)*
Andrew Kontra *(Chief Creative Officer)*
Eva Juhasz *(Grp Head-Creative)*
Andras Nagy *(Head-Digital Project)*
Carlos Ramas *(Sr Dir-Art)*
Nora Csovari *(Art Dir)*
Anna Takacs *(Dir-Interactive Art)*
Bence Toth *(Sr Acct Mgr)*
Peter Bekassy *(Acct Mgr)*
Linda Darnai *(Acct Mgr)*
Mate Deutsch *(Acct Mgr)*
Bence Bodnar *(Copywriter)*
Vera Langer *(Copywriter)*

Accounts:
Amnesty International
Bayer
Borsodi
The Design Terminal Campaign: "Tweetpositive"
Deutsche Telekom
HP
Hungarian Society Campaign: "Tweetpositive"
Johnson & Johnson Clean & Clear, Neutrogena, Rock
Mars
McCafe
McDonald's "BagTray"; 1992
Molson Coors Borsodi Beer
Movilfestawards Campaign: "Your Phone Deserves Better Stories"
Porsche Hungara Volkswagen; 1995
Shell
Telekom TVGO
Vodaphone
Volkswagen Group of America, Inc. Campaign: "You Don't Need To Turn Your Head To See Around", Das Auto
Wrigleys

India

DDB Mudra Group

Mudra House Opp Grand Hyatt, Santacruz (E), Mumbai, 400055 India
Tel.: (91) 22-33080808
Fax: (91) 22-33080300
Web Site: www.ddbmudragroup.com

Agency Specializes In: Advertising, Digital/Interactive, Event Planning & Marketing, Media Buying Services, Media Planning

Sonal Dabral *(Chm & Chief Creative Officer)*
Madhukar Kamath *(Grp CEO & Mng Dir)*
Rajiv Sabnis *(Pres-DDB Mudra West & Exec Dir)*
Sathyamurthy Namakkal *(Pres-Max Media)*
Ashwini Dhingra *(Sr VP)*
Aditya Kanthy *(Sr VP-Plng)*
Amit Kekre *(Sr VP-DDB Mudra)*
Gerald Roche *(Sr VP-Max Media)*
Anurag Tandon *(Sr VP)*
Aneil Deepak *(Head-Ideas-Max & Exec Dir)*
Rahul Mathew *(Head-Creative)*
Giridhar Bhat *(Assoc VP)*
Manish Darji *(Exec Creative Dir-West)*
Manoj Bhagat *(Grp Dir-Creative)*
Nilay Moonje *(Grp Dir-Creative)*
Keegan Pinto *(Grp Dir-Creative)*
Kunj Shah *(Grp Dir-Creative)*
Manoj Bhavnani *(Sr Dir-Creative)*
Saurabh Doke *(Sr Dir-Creative)*
Arpan Jain *(Creative Dir)*
Mandar Khatkul *(Creative Dir)*
Sunny Kundukulam *(Creative Dir)*
Sonal Jhuj *(Dir-Strategy)*
Satyajeet Kadam *(Dir-Creative)*
Dhrupal Mehta *(Dir-Art)*
Partha Majee *(Assoc Dir-Creative)*
Prasad Patil *(Assoc Dir-Creative)*
Anand Karir *(Sr Creative Dir)*

Accounts:
Aarambh Campaign: "Help Desk"
Aditya Birla Advertising, Campaign: "Brighten Up", Campaign: "Give Water", Campaign: "Wedding Collection", Linen Club The Ramp, campaign: "Sculpted Jeans"
Arvind Ltd
Bata India Ltd
BenQ India Campaign: "Tiger"
Big Bazaar Campaign: "Mahabachat", Campaign: "Making India Beautiful"
Blossom Book House Campaign: "Rail Tales"
Call of the Wild Sanctuary Asia
Cancer Patients Aid Association
Canopy Essence Group Campaign: "The Fart"
Century Plyboards India Ltd Century Plywood
Consumer Education Research Center Campaign: "Deadman Talking"
Cupid Limited Campaign: "Cupid Clock"
Dabur India Ltd Dabur Pudin Hara
New-Dheeraj Realt Creative
Electrolux Campaign: "Coffee", Campaign: "Red Timer"
Ezone
Femina Campaign: "Made By Thousands"
Filmfare.com Campaign: "Alert,Our Site To Crash"
Future Value Retail Campaign: "The Magic Frisk"
Geebees Beverages Campaign: "Stay Alert"
Godrej No.1
Golden Beverages Campaign: "Coffee People"
Gulf Oil
HBO Campaign: "Repeats"
Hindustan Unilever Campaign: "Bring Out Your Lighter Side", Lipton
HUL
ICICI Lombard General Insurance Creative
Indus Pride Campaign: "Spiced Tea"
Inorbit
ITC Ltd Campaign: "Sweat", Vivel Ultra Pro Anti-dandruff Shampoo
Itz Cash Communication Strategy, Creative
Jackson Tissues
Johnson & Johnson Limited Campaign: "See the Real Me", Clean & Clear, Neutrogena
Jyothi Laboratories Creative, Margo
Kalpataru
Korum Mall
L&T Realty
Lavasa Corporation Ltd Campaign: "Block Buster

Life", Campaign: "Hill Run", Campaign: "The High Energy Life"
Linen Club
Lipton International
Marico Livon Hair Gain Tonic
Mathrubhumi
Mother Dairy Campaign: "Taste in Every Bite"
Naturolax Laxative Campaign: "Vacuum Cleaner"
Nirmal Lifestyle
Nutralite
NutraSweet Property Holdings, Inc.
Office of the Registrar General
OHM Campaign: "New York"
Operation Black Dot
Pan Bahar Creative
PE Electronics Campaign: "The AC that Cooled Mumbai"
Pepsi Creative, IPL 2015
Philips TV
Prism Papyrus Campaign: "Growing Trees"
Reliance Cement Campaign: "Naya Zamana Naya Cement", Creative
Rotaract Club of Mumbai Shivaji Park Campaign: "Police", Campaign: "The Cleanoscope"
Rotomac Microfine Liner Campaign: "Gioconda", Campaign: "Marilyn", Campaign: "Slash"
Sanctuary Asia Campaign: "Panda, Spare Us", Campaign: "Sanctuary Reverse Calendar", Campaign: "The Killing Stapler"
Seven Seas
New-Sintex Industries
Sony MAX & MAX2 Campaign: "India Ka Tyohaar", Campaign: "Khel Fauladi", Creative, Marketing, Pro Wrestling League
Sony Six Campaign: "India ka Tyohaar"
South African Tourism Outdoor
Stedfast
Times Internet Limited Femina
Tops Security Campaign: "Mirror"
TTK Prestige Limited
Union Bank of India Campaign: "Blue Print", Campaign: "Lift", Campaign: "Your Dreams Are Not Yours Alone", Creative
United Spirits Ltd. BossPatrol
Volkswagen Campaign: " Couple", Campaign: "Can't get a Cab", Campaign: "Feel The Shiver", Campaign: "Feels that Good", Campaign: "Flyboy", Campaign: "God On Bluetooth", Campaign: "Iconic", Campaign: "Musical Jungle", Campaign: "Think Blue Beetle", Passat, Polo, Vento Highline Plus
Worldwide Media Publication Campaign: "And So It Begins", Campaign: "Potatoes"
Yo Bykes Campaign: "It's Electric!"
You Broadband & Cable India Campaign: "Online Shopping"
You Telecom India Pvt Ltd
Z-810
Zedd Mobiles Campaign: "City 1"
Zee News The Misunderstood Score Board

DDB Mudra

201 Okhla Industrial Estate, Phase-III Okhla, New Delhi, 110020 India
Tel.: (91) 1130812400
Web Site: www.ddbmudragroup.com

Agency Specializes In: Advertising

Vandana Das *(Pres)*
Sanjay Pandey *(Sr VP & Head-Gutenberg Networks India)*
Sambit Mohanty *(Head-Creative)*
Rajesh Gola *(Sr Dir-Creative-North)*
Sharat Kuttikat *(Sr Dir-Creative)*
Suketu Gohel *(Dir-Creative)*

Accounts:
New-Aircel Campaign: "See You Online Ba!", TV
Century Plywood
Dabur India Ltd Pudin Hara Fizz
Future Value Retail
New-Gulf Oil
Marico Creative, Livon
Mother Dairy Creative, Dhara, Digital, Kachi Ghani, OOH, Print, TV
Reach India
Symphony
United Biscuits Creative, McVitie's
New-Volkswagen
Wrigley India Private Limited Campaign: "Metal Detector"

Indonesia

DDB Indonesia

Jl Proklamasi No 49, Jakarta, 10320 Indonesia
Tel.: (62) 21 391 9549
Fax: (62) 21 390 4340
E-Mail: david.wibowo@ind.ddb.com
Web Site: www.ddb.com

John Bailey *(Pres & Exec Dir-Creative)*
Rangga Immanuel *(Grp Head-Creative)*
Iim Rajab *(Dir-Art)*
Didot Prihadi *(Assoc Dir-Creative)*
Tika Lestari Radjasa *(Sr Acct Exec)*
Fany Tanjung *(Assoc Acct Dir)*
Prita Widyaputri *(Assoc Acct Dir)*

Ireland

Owens DDB

The Schoolhouse, 1 Grantham Street, Dublin, 8 Ireland
Tel.: (353) 014054900
E-Mail: info@owensddb.com
Web Site: www.owensddb.com

Employees: 34
Year Founded: 1960

Agency Specializes In: Consumer Marketing, Corporate Identity, Food Service

Mark Hogan *(Mng Dir)*
James Moore *(Grp Acct Dir)*
Adrian Cosgrove *(Dir-Creative)*
Seamus Fennessy *(Dir-Fin)*
Fiona Field *(Dir-Mediaworks)*
Claire Kennedy *(Dir-Art)*
Donal O'Dea *(Dir-Creative)*
Brendan O'Reilly *(Dir-Art)*
Mary McMahon *(Planner-Strategic & Creative)*

Accounts:
Carlsberg
Coty
Friends First Financial Services; 2000
McDonald's Hamburger Restaurants Corporate & Local Store Advertising
PriceWaterhouseCoopers
Repak Packaging; 2000
Siemens
Sigmar Health
Skoda Auto
Sony Centers
Tropicana

Italy

DDB S.r.L. Advertising

Via Andrea Solari 11, 20144 Milan, Italy
Tel.: (39) 02 581931
Fax: (39) 02 58193206
Web Site: www.stv.ddb.it

Employees: 100
Year Founded: 1974

Agency Specializes In: Advertising

Luca Cortesini *(Exec Dir-Creative)*
Michelangelo Cianciosi *(Creative Dir)*
Gabriele Goffredo *(Creative Dir-Client)*
Domenico Prestopino *(Art Dir)*
Alberto Rigozzi *(Art Dir)*
Luca Bartoli *(Copywriter)*
Matteo Grandese *(Copywriter)*

Accounts:
AIA
Audi A3
Azienda Trasporti Milanesi
Esso Italiano Esso
ExxonMobil
Hasbro Italy Games, Toys
Henkel ACD Pattex Millechiodi
Henkel ACH Ariasana, Super Attak
Johnson & Johnson Aveeno, Clean & Clear, Neutrogena, RoC
Knorr
Lavonline
Loctite Glue
Novartis
Seven
Volkswagen Campaign: "Five Bolts", Campaign: "Topless", Lamborghini Huracan LP 610-4 Spyder, Multivan, New Beetle Cabriolet

Verba S.r.l. Advertising

Via Savona 16, 20144 Milan, Italy
Tel.: (39) 02 89 42 08 07
Fax: (39) 02 89 40 14 45

Agency Specializes In: Advertising

Michelangelo Cianciosi *(Exec Dir-Creative)*
Luke Cortesini *(Exec Dir-Creative)*
Marco Giovannoli *(Sr Dir-Art)*
Cristiana Soriano *(Art Dir)*
Daniel Cambo *(Dir-Art)*
Luca Bartoli *(Copywriter)*
Mimmo De Musso *(Copywriter)*
Daniela De Seta *(Copywriter)*

Accounts:
Arbre Magique
Audi A1 S-Tronic, A1 Sportback, A3, Campaign: " We Are Descended From Here", Campaign: "Amusement Without Breaks", Campaign: "Audi supports the Arena di Verona opera festival.", Campaign: "Shifts Everything Ahead", Campaign: "Sometimes technology is the best way to let emotions in.", Campaign: "Storm", Campaign: "Sync", Campaign: "Without Ever Posting a Single Kitten"
Coppertone
Gruppo Davide Campari Bitter Compari Apertif, Jagermeister Liquer
Mister Magique

Japan

DDB Japan

Hiroo Plaza 9F 5-6-6 Hiroo, Shibuya-ku, Tokyo, 150-0012 Japan
Tel.: (81) 3 5791 1020
Fax: (81) 3 5791 1021
E-Mail: info@jp.ddb.com
Web Site: www.ddb.com

Employees: 80

Issei Matsui *(Pres & CEO)*
Mamoru Kotani *(Head-Digital Creative & Dir-Creative)*
Naomi Hama *(Dir-Bus)*
Ayumi Sugahara *(Acct Supvr)*
Kaori Ito *(Designer-User Experience)*
Yusuke Ito *(Copywriter)*
Yuriko Inoue *(Acct Mgmt)*

Accounts:
ExxonMobil; Tokyo, Japan; 2000
Lipton
Novartis
Volkswagen Group of America, Inc.; Toyohasi, Achi, Japan Automobiles, Campaign: "The Heart Beetle"; 1991

Latvia

DDB Latvia
Brivibas Street 40-34, Riga, LV-1050 Latvia
Tel.: (371) 67288265
Fax: (371) 67289421
E-Mail: magic@ddb.lv
Web Site: www.ddb.lv

Year Founded: 1995

Agency Specializes In: Advertising

Andris Rubins *(Partner & Mng Dir)*
Kristians Vjakse *(CFO)*
Ulrika Plotniece *(Creative Dir)*
Peteris Lidaka *(Dir-Art)*
Renars Liepins *(Dir-Creative-DDB Hub)*
Una Rozenbauma *(Dir-Creative)*
Vairis Strazds *(Dir-Creative)*
Ugis Briedis *(Acct Mgr)*
Ance Krumina *(Acct Mgr)*
Ilze Mezite *(Acct Mgr)*
Kristine Linina *(Mgr-Account & Mgr-Traffic)*
Tatjana Baranovska *(Planner-Strategic)*
Reinis Piziks *(Copywriter)*

Accounts:
Air Baltic Campaign: "Happy Holidays"
Balta Insurance
City of Ventspils Campaign: "State Within a State"
Dobeles Dzirnavnieks
EcoBaltia
Latvijas Mobilais Telefons Okartes Masks
Road Traffic Safety Department
Ventspils Development Agency Campaign: "State Within a State", Ventspils Venti Campaign

Malaysia

Milk PR
(Formerly Milk+Co)
Level 3 Menara Chan, 138 Jalan Ampang, 50450 Kuala Lumpur, Malaysia
Tel.: (60) 3 2181 2799
E-Mail: info@milkpr.com.my
Web Site: milkpr.com.my/

Employees: 45
Year Founded: 2001

Agency Specializes In: Advertising

Darry Tan *(CEO & Chief Creative Officer)*
Michelle Bridget *(Acct Dir)*
Jonathan Yip *(Acct Dir)*

Accounts:
Cadbury
Ferrari
Jo Malone
Kakao Talk
Nando's Chickenland
Petron

Naga DDB Sdn. Bhd.
D708 7th Fl Block D Kelana Square No 17 Jln SS7/26, Kelana Jaya, 47301 Petaling Jaya, Selangor Malaysia
Tel.: (60) 3 7803 7144
Fax: (60) 3 7803 2576
E-Mail: david.mitchell@nagaddb.com.my
Web Site: www.nagaddb.com.my

Employees: 110
Year Founded: 1985

National Agency Associations: AAAA (MALAYSIA)

Agency Specializes In: Advertising

Vincent Lee *(Founder)*
David Mitchell *(COO)*
Theerapol Koomsorn *(Exec Dir-Creative)*
Alvin Teoh *(Exec Creative Dir)*
Tan Yee Kiang *(Art Dir)*
Ka-Kin Mah *(Art Dir)*
Darren Lee *(Assoc Dir-Creative)*
Woei Chan Hern *(Copywriter)*
Azeril Johari *(Copywriter)*

Accounts:
Astro Malaysia Creative, Malay Channels
Bank Islam
Bata
BRDB
Breast Cancer Welfare Association Malaysia
Celestial Movies
Digi Telecommunications BlackBerry Plan, Campaign: "What Berry Are You", Creative Agency of Record, Sambal Belacan
Duracell Duracell Ultra Batteries
GPS Bay Campaign: "Early Concert"
Hard Rock Cafe/Planet Hollywood; Kuala Lumpur, Malaysia Restaurant
Harper's Bazaar Campaign: "Rather Die"
Hong Leong Bank Berhad Campaign: "Ping"
Johnson & Johnson; Petaling Jaya; Malaysia Clean & Clear, Neutrogena, PH5.5; 1997
MACH By Hong Leong Bank Dream Jar Savings Account
MCA
Measat Broadcast Network Systems King of Hokkien Songs, World Cup TV Coverage
Nikon Camera's
Nippon Paint Campaign: "Create Magic", Odour-Less Aircare
Panasonic Malaysia Home Appliances
PepsiCo Lipton Ice Tea, Revive (Agency of Record), Tropicana
Perodua Myvi
Proton
Prudential Assurance Malaysia (Agency of Record) Brand Planning & Management, Creative
SPCA Campaign: "Live Longer", Pet Neutering
Star Publications Too Long
Tourism Malaysia
Viomax Enterprise
Vista Laser Eye Center Campaign: "Yellow"
Vital Technical "The Kid", V-Tech Vitalfix Super Glue
Yoshinkan Aikido

Mexico

DDB Mexico
Montes Urales 770 5th Fl, Col Lomas de Chapultepec, 11000 Mexico, Mexico
Tel.: (52) 5 5 91598800
Fax: (52) 55 5263 3698
Web Site: ddbmexico.com

E-Mail for Key Personnel:
President: rcardos@ddbmexico.com

Employees: 78
Year Founded: 1965

Agency Specializes In: Advertising

Hernan Ibarra *(Co-Pres-Creative)*
Walter Aregger *(CEO & Gen Dir-Creative)*
Matias Del Campo *(VP-Ops)*
Manuel Vega *(VP-Creative Svcs)*
Aldo Ramirez *(Art Dir)*
Marcela Trevino *(Acct Dir)*
Alejandra Haro *(Copywriter)*
Fernando Martinez *(Copywriter)*
Hiram Picazo *(Copywriter)*

Accounts:
AFASA; 1980
AMP Magazine Campaign: "The Rock Magazine", Marvin
B&B Mexico Campaign: "Molotov Fruits Orange"
Byb Mexico
Cablevision
Casa Cuervo Appleton Rum, Cuervo 1800 Tequila, Cuervo Especial Tequila, Don Julio, Gran Centenario Tequila, Reserva de la Familia Tequila, Tradicional Tequila; 2002
Cerveceria Cuauhtemoc Moctexuma Carta Blanca
Clean & Clear Active Clear
Clorox de Mexico
The Coca-Cola Company Campaign: "CEO Detector"
Dormimundo
Electrolux Campaign: "Separate the Stains From Your Clothes"
Energizer
Fabricas de Francia
FedEx
Filter Magazine
Henkel Detergentes Campaign: "Resurrection", Loctite Super Glue Campaign: "Second Chance Living Room", Power Pritt Gel; 2000
Johnson & Johnson Campaign: "Backwards stories", Campaign: "C&C Views Boy", Roc Wrinkle Correxion Cream
Libreria Porrua
Lipton
Marvin Magazine Campaign: "John Lennon"
McDonald's
Molotov Fruits, Ready to Drink
Nokia
Persil
Porrua Bookstores Campaign: "Characters Mobydick", Campaign: "Get into the Harry Potter World"
SCA
Tena
Terra Campaign: "Finding while searching", Campaign: "Poo WiFi", Campaign: "The Installer", Parental Control
VH1 Campaign: "Rockstar-mass"
Volkswagen de Mexico, S.A. Beetle, Campaign: "QR Load", Cars, Crafter

Mozambique

DDB Mozambique
Av Fernao Magalhaes, Nr 34, 30 andar, Maputo, Mozambique
Tel.: (258) 21302267
Fax: (258) 21 414988
Web Site: www.ddb.com/offices/middle-east/mozambique/ddb-mozambique

E-Mail for Key Personnel:
Creative Dir.: salvador.matlombe@ddb.co.mz

Year Founded: 1998

Agency Specializes In: Advertising

Vasco Rocha *(CEO)*
Thiago Alves *(Art Dir)*
Andre Coelho *(Dir-Creative)*
Cristiana Oliveira *(Acct Mgr)*
Ricardo Traquino *(Supvr-Creative)*
Sergio Aires *(Copywriter)*
Simao Maia *(Designer)*
Carlos Osvaldo *(Copywriter)*

Accounts:
ALCC Campaign: "Storm", Campaign: "Topless Poster"
CDN

CM
Instituto Crianca Nosso Futuro Campaign: "Football"
Mcel
MFW
Mozambique Music Awards Campaign: "Conga"
N'weti Campaign: "A Fashion Show That Never Should Have Happened"
Roteiros
Sociedade do Noticias Campaign: "Blood Saves"
Standard Bank
Tiger Brands
Unicef
Vale
Visit Mozambique
Vodacom Campaign: "Closet", Fashion Week

Netherlands

Bovil DDB

Dillenburgstraat 5E, 5652 AM Eindhoven, Netherlands
Tel.: (31) 40 252 6499
Fax: (31) 40 255 0671
E-Mail: info@bovilddb.com
Web Site: www.bovil.nl/en

E-Mail for Key Personnel:
Public Relations: michiel.scheerin@bovilddb.com

Employees: 24

Agency Specializes In: Advertising

Shaun Northrop *(Partner & Dir-Creative)*
Michiel Scheeren *(Mng Dir)*
Debbie Van Dorst *(Acct Dir)*
Sandra Van de Velde *(Sr Acct Mgr)*
Erik Luyk *(Acct Mgr)*
Noor Van Hout *(Office Mgr)*
Claudia Vermeulen *(Acct Mgr)*
Cristina Torrijos Sanchez *(Mgr-Ops)*

Accounts:
Aprico
Brunswick
Entre Duex
Fresh Park Venlo
Phillips
Zon Fruit & Vegetables

DDB Amsterdam

Prof WH Keesomlaan 4, 1183 DJ Amstelveen, Netherlands
Mailing Address:
Postbus 546, 1180AM Amstelveen, Netherlands
Tel.: (31) 20 406 5406
Fax: (31) 20 406 5400
E-Mail: info@ddbamsterdam.nl
Web Site: www.ddbgroup.nl

E-Mail for Key Personnel:
President: pietro.tramontin@nl.ddb.com
Creative Dir.: sikko.gerkema@nl.ddb.com

Employees: 160
Year Founded: 1974

National Agency Associations: VEA

Agency Specializes In: Advertising

Ivo Roefs *(Co-CEO)*
Paul Blok *(Mng Partner)*
Folkert Van Dijk *(CFO)*
Dylan De Backer *(Exec Dir-Creative)*
Joris Tol *(Creative Dir)*
Jasper Diks *(Dir-Creative)*
Bram Holzapfel *(Dir-Creative)*
Yuka Kambayashi *(Dir-RTV)*
Sandra Krstic *(Client Svc Dir-Integrated Svcs)*
Fione van Wijk *(Jr Producer)*

Accounts:
Achmea Zorg
adidas Football Campaign: "Brazuca", Campaign: "Nitrocharge Your Game"; 2013
Autodrop Liquorice Campaign: "First Aid"
Aviko Flemish Fries, Gourmet Fries, Knitted Outdoor Poster, Potato Products; 1990
C&A Campaign: "Inspired by Life"; 2013
Centraal Beheer Achmea Campaign: "Just Call us", Campaign: "Real Winter", Campaign: "Self Driving Car", Campaign: "The final offer", Car Insurance, TV; 1986
Concorp Brands Campaign: "Heimlich Manoeuvre", Campaign: "Secret Portal"
Currence
Heineken Campaign: "Meet the World in One City", Campaign: "The Ultimate Voyage", Campaign: "Your Future Bottle", Campaign: "Heineken Ignite", Campaign: "Share the Sofa"; 2012
InShared Campaign: "Anti-Damage Campaign"
KLM Royal Dutch Airlines Campaign: "Claim Your Place In Space", Campaign: "KLM Tile & Inspire", Campaign: "New World Business Class", Campaign: "Planes", Lost & Found Team, Online
Mammoet Campaign: "The Biggest Thing We Move is Time"; 2013
McDonald's Netherlands Campaign: "BurgerBattle", Campaign: "The Golden Burger", Campaign: "The Most Famous Burger"; 2012
PepsiCo Campaign: "Nibb-it"
Philips Campaign: "Obsessed with sound", Campaign: "The Sound of Creation"
Pink Ribbon Campaign: "Donate 1/8"
Pon's Automobielhandel Audi Passenger Cars, Campaign: "Behind You", Campaign: "Das Hund", Campaign: "Service Dialogue", Commercial Vehicles & Service, Volkswagen Passengers Cars; 1971
TNT
TomTom Campaign: "TomTom Comedy Car", Creative, Smartwatch; 2013
Top Gear Campaign: "Long Sentence"
Unilever/WNF/Missing Chapter Foundation/Eneco Campaign: "Water Savers"; 2013
Vattenfall/Nuon Campaign: "Steady Hand", Campaign: "Ed&Eduard", Campaign: "Your Nuon"
Verbond van Verzekeraars Campaign: "Glad we are insured"; 2013
Volkswagen Group
Ziggo Campaign: "Always Connected", Campaign: "The Next Step in Television", Campaign: "Wifi Spots"; 2013

New Zealand

DDB New Zealand Ltd.

Level 6 80 Greys Ave, Auckland, 1010 New Zealand
Tel.: (64) 9 303 42 99
Fax: (64) 9 307 11 82
E-Mail: info@ddb.co.nz
Web Site: www.ddb.co.nz

Employees: 200

Agency Specializes In: Media Buying Services, Production, Strategic Planning/Research

Justin Mowday *(CEO)*
Paul McHugh *(CFO)*
Damon Stapleton *(Chief Creative Officer)*
Rob Limb *(Mng Dir-RAPP New Zealand)*
Lucinda Sherborne *(Head-Plng)*
Shane Bradnick *(Exec Dir-Creative)*
Jenny Travers *(Sr Acct Dir)*
Zoe Alden *(Grp Acct Dir)*
James Blair *(Grp Acct Dir)*
Chris Schofield *(Creative Dir)*
Paula Brown *(Acct Dir)*
Crystal Clark *(Acct Dir)*
James Conner *(Sr Art Dir)*
Georgia Newton *(Acct Dir)*
Carly Pratt *(Acct Dir)*
Mark Wilson *(Acct Dir)*
Ben Barnes *(Dir-Creative & Art)*
Karen Sew Hoy *(Dir-HR)*
Haydn Kerr *(Dir-Creative-Digital)*
Rupert Price *(Dir-Plng)*
Sam Schrey *(Dir-Interactive Art & Sr Designer-Interactive)*
Gavin Siakimotu *(Dir-Art)*
Kat Tadaki *(Dir-Art)*
Jian Xin Tay *(Dir-Art)*
Emily Bellringer *(Sr Acct Mgr)*
Deepika Goundar *(Sr Acct Mgr)*
Michael Doolan *(Acct Mgr)*
Rory Mckechnie *(Copywriter)*
Gordon Moir *(Designer)*
Amanda Summersby *(Designer-Mac)*
Jason Vertongen *(Designer-Digital)*
Jamie Barrett *(Jr Acct Planner)*

Accounts:
Beaurepaires Advertising
BMW New Zealand Ltd. BMW Reverse April Fools'
BSkyB Ltd SKY, SKY News, Sky Sports
Cadbury Cadbury and Pascall Confectionery Lines
Clorox New Zealand, ltd.
Coastguard
Coca-Cola Oceania Lift Plus
Exxon Mobil
George Weston Foods Campaign: "Nourish Our Kids", Tip Top
Greenpeace International Campaign: "Beached Az"
Heinz Watties Canned Food
Hutchwilco Campaign: "Secret Fishing Spots"
Instant Kiwi
Kirin Brewery Company, Ltd.
Kraft Foods
Lion Co. Campaign: "Be the Artist", Campaign: "Mansitter - Sling", Campaign: "Name", Campaign: "Steinlager: Keep It Pure", Crafty Beggars, Lindauer, We Believe
Lotto Campaign: "Father's Day", Campaign: "Gang of Winners", Campaign: "Triple Dip Holiday", Lucky Dog
McDonald's Georgie Pie
New Zealand Rugby Union
NZ Lotteries
Paw Justice Billboards, Campaign: "Animal Strike", PR, Print Ads, Social Media, Street Posters, TV Commercials, Website
Prime TV
Ronald McDonald Children's Charities
Sky Television Campaign: "Bring Down The King", Campaign: "Chuck Norris", Campaign: "Come with Us", Campaign: "Putting Athletes in the Picture", Campaign: "Sky Multiroom", Digital, Neon, Outdoor, Rialto Channel, SoHo, TV
Speight's
Steinlager Campaign: "Be The Artist Not The Canvas"
Stihl
Tasman Insulation New Zealand
Tourism Australia
Volkswagen Volkswagen Beetle
Waitangi National Trust Campaign: "Explore the Treaty"
The Warehouse Campaign: "Toy Testers"
Westpac New Zealand Beyonce, Brand Strategy, CRM, Creative, Digital, PR, Retail
YWCA Campaign: "Demand Equal Pay", Online, Print, TV

Nigeria

DDB Casers

6 Adeola Hopewell St, Victoria Island, Lagos, Nigeria
Tel.: (234) 1 493 6587
Fax: (234) 1 496 8352

E-Mail: info@lagos.ddb.com
Web Site: www.ddblagos.com

Enyi C. Odigbo *(Owner)*
Ikechi Odigbo *(Mng Dir)*
Tunde Sule *(Creative Dir)*
Uche Ugorji *(Assoc Brand Dir-Strategy & Bus)*
Tunde Dosekun *(Dir-Bus Dev-DDB Lagos)*
Kingsley Efere *(Dir-Creativity)*
Adenugba Olushola *(Asst Dir)*
Ebere Anyanwu *(Mgr-HR)*
Barbara Onianwah *(Asst Mgr-Digital)*
Clement Vigne *(Reg Exec Dir-Creative)*

Accounts:
Babatunde Adebola
ExxonMobil
Henkel
Mouka Mattress Campaign: "ActiveRest"
MTN
Omo Washing Powder

Norway

DDB Oslo A.S.
Wergelandsveien 21, 0167 Oslo, Norway
Mailing Address:
PO Box 7084, Majorstua, 0306 Oslo, Norway
Tel.: (47) 22 59 32 00
Fax: (47) 22 59 32 99
Web Site: www.ddb.no

E-Mail for Key Personnel:
President: rolf.stokke@ddboslo.no

Employees: 50
Year Founded: 1985

Agency Specializes In: Advertising

Eldar Skylstad *(CEO & Mng Dir)*
Petter Gulli *(Exec Dir-Creative)*
Helen Selberg Johansen *(Bus Dir-McDonalds)*
Even Moseng *(Dir-Art)*
Christer Tjostheim *(Dir-Art)*
Hege Dyrseth *(Acct Mgr)*
Emma Karlsson *(Acct Mgr & Community Mgr)*
Julian Hagemann *(Copywriter)*

Accounts:
Grilstad Campaign: "Victory in Slow Motion"
McDonald's
Peugeot Campaign: "Peugeot 107 Deli De Luca"
SAS Campaign: "Father"

Philippines

DDB Philippines Inc.
16th Fl Two World Square 22 Upper Mckinley Road, McKinley Town Center, Fort Bonifacio, Taguig, 1634 Philippines
Tel.: (63) 2 856 7888
Fax: (63) 2 856 9317
Web Site: http://www.ddb.com.ph/

Year Founded: 1993

Agency Specializes In: Advertising, Brand Development & Integration, Communications, Consumer Marketing, Direct Response Marketing, Graphic Design, Public Relations

Gil G. Chua *(Pres & CEO)*
Kevin Beltran *(Sr Dir-Art-DDB Group Vietnam)*
Diane Welsh *(Grp Acct Dir)*
Ow Fajardo *(Dir-Art)*
Bobby Vito *(Dir-Creative)*
Ogy Yap *(Copywriter)*

Accounts:
Ad Summit Pilipinas Creative
Cara Welfare Pet Adoption Program Campaign: "I Am Home"
Fully Booked Campaign: "Mind Map Oprah"
Gabriela Campaign: "Hits"
Makati City Fire Station
McDonald's Restaurants; 2000
Monami Campaign: "Diamonds Are Forever"
Mundipharma Campaign: "Zipper"
PepsiCo
Pharex Health Campaign: "Lifting", Campaign: "Middle Manager"
Philippine Airlines Creative
The Philippine Star Campaign: "Truth"
Ramen
Unilever Lipton, Selecta Ice Cream

Poland

DDB Warsaw
Athina Park 6c, Wybreze Gdyrishie St, 01-531 Warsaw, Poland
Tel.: (48) 22 560 3400
Fax: (48) 22 560 3401
E-Mail: info.ddb@ddb.pl
Web Site: ddbtribal.pl/en/ddb

Employees: 100

Agency Specializes In: Consulting

Marcin Mroszczak *(Chm & Dir-Creative)*
Pawel Kastory *(CEO)*
Maciej Waligora *(Exec Creative Dir)*
Michal Sek *(Sr Dir-Art)*
Tytus Klepacz *(Dir-Digital Creative)*
Magdalena Drozdowska *(Deputy Creative Dir)*
Mateusz Ksiazek *(Deputy Dir-Creative)*

Accounts:
Agros
Algida
Audiodescription Foundation Campaign: "Art Never Seen"
Caritas
Eurobank
Flora
Grolsch
Henkel
Kaspi Bank
Kompania Piwowarska Pilsner Beer
Lipton
Lot Polish Airlines Campaign: "Run While You Can"
Lotus Oil
McDonald's Campaign: "Hamburger Timetable", Campaign: "Lumberjack is back!", Lumberjack's Sandwich
Nestle
Pilsner Beer, Campaign: "Neverending story."
Tiger
Virgin Mobile Campaign: "Pixel Heritage"
Xelion

Portugal

DDB Lisboa
Av Duque de Avila 46 Piso 4, 1050-083 Lisbon, Portugal
Tel.: (351) 213 592 430
Fax: (351) 213 149 096
E-Mail: ddbl@pt.ddb.com
Web Site: www.ddb.pt/

Employees: 70
Year Founded: 1986

National Agency Associations: APAP (Portugal)

Agency Specializes In: Advertising

Maria Manuela Gomes *(CFO)*
Alexandra Pereira *(Gen Mgr)*

Accounts:
AMCV
Badoca Park
Ericeira
ExxonMobil
Fenelac Milk Association
Gatorade
Hasbro
Henkel
Johnson & Johnson Clean & Clear, Neutrogena, RoC
Lipton
Loctite Super Attack
Nestle Purina Pet Care Bakers, Cat Chow, Felix, Friskies, Gourmet, Kitten Chow
PepsiCo
Pfizer
The Phone House
Plano Senior
Sabado
Siva Volkswagen
Volkswagen Group of America, Inc.

Russia

DDB Russia
40/2 Prechistenka St Bldg 3, 119034 Moscow, Russia
Tel.: (7) 495 785 57 65
Fax: (7) 495 785 23 85
E-Mail: welcome@ddb.ru
Web Site: www.ddb.ru

E-Mail for Key Personnel:
President: serguey.krivonogov@ddb.ru

Employees: 150
Year Founded: 1992

Agency Specializes In: Advertising

Serguey Krivonogov *(Mng Partner)*
Anton Volovsky *(Sr Dir-Art)*
Deem Muratov *(Grp Acct Dir)*
Katrin Auashria *(Acct Dir)*
Alexey Sanzharovskiy *(Art Dir)*
Vadim Malysh *(Dir-Fin)*

Accounts:
Henkel Brilliance, Deni, Diadem, Fa, Live, Losk, Moment, Nordic Color, Schuma, Schwarzkopf & Henkel
Lactalis President
McDonald's MacCafe
Pepsi Gatorade, Tropicana
SCA Libero, Libresse
Unilever Knorr
Volkswagen Group of America, Inc. Campaign: "Full Night Ahead!", Scirocco
Wrigley Campaign: "Skittles Crab"

Romania

DDB Bucharest
No21 Carol Davila St, Sector 5, Bucharest, Romania
Tel.: (40) 31 805 96 30
Fax: (40) 21 410 05 03
Web Site: www.ddb.com

E-Mail for Key Personnel:
Creative Dir.: sam@bucharest.ddb.com

Employees: 34
Year Founded: 1996

Agency Specializes In: Advertising

Christos Papapolyzos *(Pres-South Eastern Europe & CIS)*

Christian Sinca *(Acct Mgr)*

Accounts:
Alphabank Banking
McDonald's
SOS Children Villages

Singapore

DDB
Level 10 Pico Creative Centre, 20 Kallang Avenue, Singapore, 339411 Singapore
Tel.: (65) 6671 4488
Fax: (65) 6671 4444
E-Mail: info@sg.ddb.com
Web Site: www.ddb.com.sg

Employees: 180
Year Founded: 1983

Agency Specializes In: Advertising

Anthony J. James *(Chief Innovation Officer & Chief Growth Officer)*
David Tang *(CEO-Asia)*
Paolo Agulto *(Grp Head-Creative & Copywriter)*
Kim Das *(Bus Dir-Global)*
Shum Qi Hao *(Art Dir)*
Jonathan Lim *(Acct Dir)*
Marcus Lim *(Art Dir)*
Wu Yangwei *(Art Dir)*
Lester Lee *(Dir-Creative)*
Marvin Liang *(Dir-Art)*
Khalid Osman *(Dir-Creative)*
Thomas Yang *(Dir-Creative)*
Amanda Chen *(Sr Acct Exec)*
Ho Jiewei *(Sr Acct Exec)*
James Tan *(Assoc Acct Dir)*

Accounts:
New-AXA Insurance
Breast Cancer Foundation Campaign: "Are you Obsessed with the Right Things?", Campaign: "Obsessions", Online
Cisco Consumer Products Campaign: "Flip Your Profile", Campaign: "Tree Rings"
DBS Bank (Agency of Record) Campaign: "DBS Private Bank"
Human Organ Preservation Effort Campaign: "Crossing", Campaign: "Germanicus"
Johnson & Johnson Campaign: "Surf", Campaign: "The World's First Instagram Flash Mob"
Life Cycle
Limited Edt Campaign: "Monkey"
Math Paper Press
McDonalds Campaign: "All Day Sunrise"
Mentholatum Campaign: "Electrician"
Ministry of Communications and Information
New-Ministry of Education Branding, Creative
National Environment Agency Content Development, Creative, Dengue Prevention Campaign, Marketing Publicity, Social Media
Safety Cycling
Selleys Supa Glue
SilkAir Brand Communications
Singapore Air Force
Singapore Health Promotion Board
Singapore National Environment Agency; 2008
Sodasan Campaign: "Wife"
StarHub Campaign: "Birds & the Bees 2.0", Campaign: "Happy Everywhere", Campaign: "Power to Be", Creative, International Day of Happiness, MySmartEye, Online Music Store
Tourism Australia
Volkswagen Uk Campaign: "Magnetic Cars", Jetta

Slovenia

Futura DDB
Poljanski nasip 6, 1000 Ljubljana, Slovenia
Tel.: (386) 1 300 40 00
Fax: (386) 1300 40 13
E-Mail: agency@futura.si
Web Site: www.futura.si

Employees: 45
Year Founded: 1986

Agency Specializes In: Advertising

Marko Vicic *(Mng Partner)*
Marjana Lavric Sulman *(Mng Dir)*
Mija Gacnik Krpic *(Client Svcs Dir)*
Robert Krizmancic *(Dir-Art)*
Maja Birsa Jerman *(Acct Mgr)*
Jana Kozoglav *(Acct Mgr)*

Accounts:
Belinka
Henkel
Krka
McDonald's
Nova Ljubljanska
Perutnina Ptuj
Peugeot
Pivovarna In Pivnica Kratochwill Campaign: "Kratochwill Honey Beer Glass"
Pop TV
Radenska
Telecom Slovenia

South Africa

DDB South Africa
Silverpoint Office Park Bldg 1 22 Ealing Crescent, Bryanston, Johannesburg, South Africa
Mailing Address:
PO Box 4497, Rivonia, 2128 South Africa
Tel.: (27) 11 267 2800
Fax: (27) 86 632 6270
Web Site: ddb.co.za

E-Mail for Key Personnel:
Creative Dir.: gareth.lessing@ddb.co.za

Employees: 56
Year Founded: 1992

National Agency Associations: ACA

Agency Specializes In: Advertising

Emmet O'Hanlon *(CEO)*
Glen Lomas *(Chief Client Officer & VP-EMEA)*
Tsitsi Dhlamini *(Deputy Mng Dir)*
Kathy Scharrer *(Head-Brdcst)*
Liam Wielopolski *(Exec Dir-Creative)*
Fernando Lyra *(Art Dir)*
Rafael Pitanguy *(Creative Dir)*
Bruce Murphy *(Dir-Creative)*
Nicola Wielopolski *(Dir-Art)*
Matthew Berge *(Copywriter)*
Susan van Rooyen *(Copywriter)*

Accounts:
Bostik Campaign: "Rioter & Policeman"
Cape Herb And Spice (Pty) Ltd
The Clorox Company
Converse All Star, Chevron, Jack Purcell, One Star
Estoril
First National Bank
Honda South Africa Campaign: "Continuum", Honda Ballade
HTH Campaign: "Don't give up", HTH Pool Care
Mango Airlines
McDonald's Campaign: "1973 Stratocaster", Campaign: "Billy", Campaign: "Everyone's got something to give", Campaign: "Lounge", Campaign: "Matthew, Ollie, Abigail", Campaign: "McDonalds Kids Birthday Parties", Campaign: "Monsters", Campaign: "Theodore", Campaign: "Tiffany"
Mitsubishi ASX
SABC
Symantec; 2008
Telkom Branding, Business Advertising, Retail, Sponsorships
Unilever Knorr
Volkswagen
Wrigley's 5 Gum, Airwaves, Campaign: "5th Dimension", Campaign: "A Moment of Calm", Campaign: "Front Line", Campaign: "The Kooks", Eclipse, Orbit; 2008

Spain

DDB Barcelona S.A.
Enrique Granados 86-88, 08008 Barcelona, Spain
Tel.: (34) 93 228 3400
Fax: (34) 93 228 3500
Web Site: www.ddb.es

Employees: 150
Year Founded: 1979

National Agency Associations: AEAP

Jose M. Roca de Vinals Delgado *(Chief Creative Officer-DDB Spain)*
Gorka Lozano *(Gen Dir)*
Cristina Rodriguez *(Head-Art & Dir-Creative)*
Samanta Judez *(Head-Strategy-DDB Spain)*
Dani Calabuig *(Exec Creative Dir)*
Jose Lopez Arinez *(Sr Dir-Art)*
Silvia Cutillas *(Sr Dir-Art-DDB Spain)*
Nerea Cierco *(Creative Dir)*
Javier Melendez *(Creative Dir)*
David Perez *(Creative Dir)*
Sergi Perez *(Creative Dir)*
Bernat Sanroma *(Creative Dir)*
Javier Villalba *(Bus Dir-Intl)*
Pedro Andragnes *(Dir-Creative)*
Jaume Badia *(Dir-Art)*
Javier Rodriguez *(Dir-Creative & Art)*
Mariona Cruz *(Acct Mgr)*
Roser Vila *(Sr Acct Exec)*
Laura del Rio *(Acct Exec)*
Tino Barreiro *(Copywriter)*
Alfredo Binefa *(Copywriter)*
Rosko Ruiz *(Copywriter)*

Accounts:
Audi R8 Audi A3, Audi Adaptive Cruise Control, Campaign: "Colors", Campaign: "Mind Race"
BBVA
Birra 08 Cats In The Dark
Budweiser
Codorniu International
Dell
Epson
Eurofred
Fira Barcelona
Generalitat Catalunya
Juntament de Barcelona
Lectiva.com Campaign: "Make your CV stronger."
L'Illa Diagonal Campaign: "Spring is back", Campaign: "Wake up, Spring is here"
Manos Unidas
The South Face
Tropicana Alvalle
Ato
Volkswagen Campaign: "Dog", Tiguan, Touran
Audi Audi A1, Audi Q3, Campaign: "Colors", Campaign: "Mind Race", Passion Leaves Its Mark
Volkswagen New Beetle Campaign: "Glass"
Volkswagen Polo Campaign: "Monument", Campaign: "Polowers", Campaign: "Side Assist: The shoulder poke"

DDB Madrid, S.A.
Orense 4, 28020 Madrid, Spain
Tel.: (34) 914564400
Fax: (34) 914564475
E-Mail: info@es.ddb.com
Web Site: www.ddb.es

Employees: 70
Year Founded: 1971

National Agency Associations: AEAP

Agency Specializes In: Advertising

Juan Campmany Ibanez *(Pres & CEO)*
Jose Maria Roca de Vinals Delgado *(Chief Creative Officer-DDB Spain)*
Jose Maria Rull Bertran *(Pres/CEO-DDB Spain)*
Cristina Rodriguez *(Head-Art & Dir-Creative)*
Guillermo Santaisabel *(Exec Dir-Creative)*
Silvia Cutillas *(Sr Dir-Art)*
Paula Lopez *(Dir-Creative)*
Gabriela Castro *(Acct Exec)*

Accounts:
Anuntis
Audi A6, Audi Attitudes, Audi Cabrio, Audi R8
Autentico Jabugo
Bosch
Celem (The European Women's Lobby)
Cola Cao
Compania de Bebidas Pepsico Gatorade, Lipton Ice
D.O. Aceites de Jaen
Entreculturas
Ferrovial
Findus
Foundation Against Drug Consumption Campaign: "You know where the fun begins, but not where it could end."
Fundacion Espanola del Corazon
Fundacion Sindrome de Down
Grupo Calvo Campaign: "The Incredible Thundering Stomach"
Hasbro Iberica Campaign: "Little Caesar"
Johnson & Johnson Clean & Clear, Neutrogena, Roc
L'Illa Campaign: "Spring Boy"
Microsoft
Movistar
ONCE
Telefonica de Espana 11822, ADSL, Duos, Trios
Toshiba
Unilever
Vaesa Campaign: "Game"
Volkswagen Group of America, Inc. Campaign: "Baseball"

Sweden

DDB Stockholm

Torsgatan 19 8th Fl, Box 6016, 10231 Stockholm, Sweden
Tel.: (46) 8588 980 00
Fax: (46) 8588 980 01
E-Mail: info@ddb.se
Web Site: www.ddb.se

Employees: 100
Year Founded: 1990

Agency Specializes In: Advertising

David Sandstrom *(CEO)*
Katarina Mohlin *(Producer-Digital)*
Jessica Morales *(Bus Dir)*
Christian Westelindh *(Acct Dir)*
Andreas Fabbe *(Dir-Digital)*
Lisa Granberg *(Dir-Art & Creative)*
Stefan Gustafsson *(Dir-Creative)*
Gustav Holm *(Dir-Art & Creative)*
Magnus Jakobsson *(Sr Partner & Dir-Creative)*
Daniel Mencak *(Dir-Art)*
Johan Ansterus *(Acct Mgr)*
Ulrica Carlsson *(Acct Mgr)*
Ulrika Sorensen *(Acct Mgr)*
Susanne Ytterlid *(Acct Mgr)*
Pontus Caresten *(Copywriter)*
Nick Christiansen *(Copywriter)*
Olle Langseth *(Copywriter)*
Linnea Lofjord *(Designer)*
Martin Lundgren *(Copywriter)*
Patrick Wilkorsz *(Planner)*
Martin Runfors *(Sr Designer-Digital)*

Accounts:
Bonnier Art Gallery Campaign: "Max99 People", Campaign: "Not for all"
Bosch
Carlsberg Falcon
Cloetta Fazer Baking Products, Chocolate, Sweets
Eniro Product Search
Entercard
Handelshogskolan Executive Education
IFL
Johnson & Johnson
Lipton
Lufthansa Campaign: "Anywake", Campaign: "Are you Klaus-Heidi?"
McDonald's Big Mac, Billboard, Campaign: "Christmas Swap", Campaign: "Pick n Play", Campaign: "Xmas Table Relay Race", Print, Television
Media Markt Campaign: "Swedens Most Clicked Banner"
Operan
Panasonic Lumix
Papercut Campaign: "Speedsale", Campaign: "The Way to Everyday Excitement"
Plan Pagen
Proffice Communications Strategy
Ronald McDonald Children's Fund Campaign: "Little Brother"
The Royal Opera Campaign: "Opera Soap", Campaign: "Shower Soap", Manon
Samsung Campaign: "Predicting the Next", Campaign: "The Catch-Up Grant", Galaxy S6, Online, SUHD TV, Samsung Galaxy Alpha, Samsung Galaxy S6 edge+
Skoda Campaign: "The Family Composer", Cars
Stadsmissionen Campaign: "Indoors/Outdoor Field"
Stockholm City Mission Campaign: "You'll Never Wear That Again"
Swedish Armed Forces Campaign: "The Stamp", Campaign: "Who Cares?", Recruitment
The Swedish Royal Opera Campaign: "Opera Soap"
Telia
TeliaSonera AB Campaign: "1000 Possibilities", Campaign: "Soundtrack Sweden"
Tropicana
Trygg-Hansa
Uniforms for the Dedicated Direct Marketing
Unilever
Vattenfall
Volkswagen Group Sweden Bluemotion Technologies, Campaign: "Bug Run", Campaign: "The Ear", Campaign: "The Migrator Bird", Campaign: "The Winter Adjusted Bear", Passat, The Speed Camera Lottery, Touran

Turkey

Medina/Turgul DDB

Tuzambari Kasimpasa Bedrettin Mah Havuzbasi Degirmeni Sok No 2, 34440 Beyoglu, Turkey
Tel.: (90) 212 282 49 40
Fax: (90) 212 282 75 64
E-Mail: info@istanbul.ddb.com
Web Site: www.ddb.com.tr

E-Mail for Key Personnel:
President: jmedina@istanbul.ddb.com
Creative Dir.: ktungul@istanbul.ddb.com

Employees: 100
Year Founded: 1993

National Agency Associations: TAA

Agency Specializes In: Advertising

Ozan Can Bozkurt *(Creative Dir)*
Elif Onen Sakin *(Acct Dir)*
Sezen Serez *(Acct Dir)*
Gokhan Buluk *(Dir-Art)*
Cihan Eryilmaz *(Dir-Art)*
Gizem Hiz *(Dir-Art)*
Burak Kunduracioglu *(Dir-Art)*
Buse Say *(Dir-Art)*
Serkan Un *(Copywriter)*

Accounts:
Audi Audi Q5 Rearview Camera, Campaign: "Everyone Knows The Story", Campaign: "Keeps Distance"
Biota Laboratories Anti-Hair Loss Shampoo
Bose
Clorox Campaign: "Blue Stain"
CNN Turk Campaign: "Chuck/Hair"
Conti Campaign: "Attraction - Red"
Continental Self Supporting Run-Flat Tyres
Corbis Turkey Image Library
Dank Second Hand Furniture Campaign: "Praying", Campaign: "Samsung"
Digiturk Campaign: "Spiderman"
Dogan Burda Campaign: "Face"
Dogcev Animal Adoption, Campaign: "Elephant", Environmental Awareness
Domino's Pizza
Finansbank Campaign: "Shoes"
Getty Images Turkey Campaign: "Berlin Wall", Image Library
Gursoy Drawing Classes
Henkel Campaign: "Transparent", Fa, Pattex, Schauma, Tursil, Vital Colors
Hepsiburada.com Online Shopping
Ikram
Iletisim Publishing Campaign: "Schizophrenia"
Isbankasi Campaign: "Lowland", Campaign: "Netherlands"
Islerburada.com Employment Agency
Johnson & Johnson Neutrogena, RoC
Kale Seramik
Kangaroos Campaign: "Car Boot"
Kekemelodi Campaign: "Flamingo", Stuttering Therapy Classes
Koctas
Ktm Bicycles
KTM Bicycles, Campaign: "Plane", Off-Road Motorcycyles
Lion Club Energy Drink
Lipton
Maximiles Campaign: "England, Japan, Nigeria, Morocco"
Maximum
McDonald's Campaign: "Time To Wake Up", Premium Roast Coffee
Migros
Neda Limited
Organ Transplant
Osram Campaign: "Bank"
Pepsico Beverages Campaign: "Mr.Hyde"
PepsiCo Inc.
Philips
Piko
PM Model Model Toys
Radikal Campaign: "Just for a Coat", Campaign: "Words"
Siemens Campaign: "Flexibles", iQ800 Dish Washer
Tat Campaign: "Horse"
Ulker Food Products
Unilever
Vodafone Group Plc
Volkswagen Group of America, Inc. TSI Engine
Wenger Campaign: "Jack Knife"
Witte Molen Bird Food
WWF
Yildiz Holding Campaign: "Retarded"

United Arab Emirates

TD&A DDB

Opp Sharjah Municipality Boorj 2000 Fl 20-21, PO Box 22156, Govt House Sq, Sharjah, United Arab Emirates
Tel.: (971) 6 5628333
Fax: (971) 6 5628866
Web Site: www.ddb.com

Firas Medrows *(Exec Dir-Creative)*
Dinesh Gore *(Dir-Art)*
Makarand Patil *(Dir-Creative)*
Zahir Mirza *(Grp Creative Dir-Integrated)*

Accounts:
Al Ghandi Electronics Campaign: "Distracted Mosquito", Whirlpool Washing Machine
Al Serkal Avenue Al Manzil School, Campaign: "Conversations"
Bario
Basheer Al Zaeem
China Times
Clorox Campaign: "Coffee Spill"
Committee of Organ Donation in Lebanon Campaign: "Organ Donation"
FAI Ghandi Electronics
Gatorade
Glad Cling Wrap
Lipton Chai Latte
MusicMaster
Pepsico
Persil Campaign: "Keep your clothes crisp"
Quaker Oats
Rainbow Milk
The Shoe Butler Campaign: "Your Shoes Arrive First. Keep Them Shining"
Vernel Campaign: "Aunt Agatha"
Whirlpool Campaign: "Distracted Mosquito", T50 Washing Machine

United Kingdom

DDB Europe
12 Bishop's Bridge Road, London, W2 6AA United Kingdom
Tel.: (44) 20 7262 7755
Fax: (44) 207 258 4200
Web Site: www.ddb.com

Accounts:
Electrolux Domestic Appliances & Floor-Care Products
Gu Pan-European Advertising
Unilever Creative, Lipton, Marmite Softener, Wall's
Volkswagen Campaign: "Play The Road", Campaign: "See Film Differently", Digital, Volkswagen Golf GTI

Vietnam

DDB Vietnam Advertising
201 PetroVietnam Tower 1 Le Duan, District 1, Ho Chi Minh City, Vietnam
Tel.: (84) 8 3824 1919
Fax: (84) 8 3829 0507
Web Site: www.ddb.com

Agency Specializes In: Advertising

Daniel Gordon Jones *(Mng Partner & Grp Mng Dir)*
Nhu Le Dn *(Controller-Fin)*
Khoa Vu Minh *(Acct Mgr)*
Mai Lam *(Sr Acct Exec)*
Chau Nguyen Thai My *(Acct Exec)*
Quynh Bao-nhu Nguyen *(Planner-Strategic)*
Lam Nguyen *(Sr Accountant)*
Nghiem Vu *(Client Svc Dir)*

Accounts:
Huda Beer Vietnam

Venezuela

ARS DDB Publicidad
(Formerly ARS Publicidad)
Av Diego Cisneros Edif ARS, Los Ruices, Caracas, 1071-A Venezuela
Tel.: (58) 212 239 8002
Fax: (58) 212 239 0169
E-Mail: contacto@arspublicidad.com
Web Site: www.ddb.com

Employees: 150

Agency Specializes In: Advertising

Mariana Frias *(Pres)*
Maria Carolina Jaso *(Gen Dir-Creative)*
Mariantonia Frias *(VP-Corp Comm)*
Carolina Vila *(VP-Investigation & Plng)*
Claudia Santos *(Acct Dir)*
Duilio Perez *(Dir-Creative)*
Adriana Reimpell *(Dir-Accts)*

Accounts:
Acriton
Avon
Barco Mercantile
Children's Orthopedic Hospital
Clorox de Venezuela
Empleate.com
Energizer Flashlights
Eveready
ExxonMobil
New-Gomby
Henkel Campaign: "White Jumper", Super Bonder
Johnson & Johnson Campaign: "Book"
Nevex
Philips
Venesola
Voc de Mexico

DDCWORKS
(Formerly Diccicco Battista Communications)
1200 River Rd Ste 300 E, Conshohocken, PA 19428
Tel.: (484) 342-3600
Fax: (484) 342-3602
E-Mail: tcifelli@ddcworks.com
Web Site: www.ddcworks.com

E-Mail for Key Personnel:
President: mdiccicco@dbcommunications.net

Employees: 35
Year Founded: 1968

National Agency Associations: ICOM

Agency Specializes In: Advertising, Automotive, Brand Development & Integration, Broadcast, Business Publications, Business-To-Business, Cable T.V., Collateral, Communications, Consulting, Consumer Marketing, Consumer Publications, Corporate Identity, Direct Response Marketing, Exhibit/Trade Shows, Financial, Food Service, Graphic Design, Health Care Services, High Technology, Information Technology, Internet/Web Design, Magazines, Newspapers & Magazines, Out-of-Home Media, Outdoor, Planning & Consultation, Point of Purchase, Point of Sale, Print, Production, Public Relations, Publicity/Promotions, Retail, Sales Promotion, Strategic Planning/Research, Sweepstakes, T.V., Technical Advertising, Trade & Consumer Magazines, Travel & Tourism

Approx. Annual Billings: $30,000,000

Michael Diccicco *(CEO)*
Megan Young *(Sr Dir-Art)*
Cory Lorenz *(Dir-Media)*
Kira Hadalski *(Assoc Dir-Art)*
Scott Hilson *(Assoc Dir-Creative)*
Jeff Cronin *(Sr Acct Mgr-PR)*
Ronnie Naples *(Mgr-Creative Projects)*
Matt Goldstein *(Acct Supvr-PR)*
Angelique Quinn *(Acct Supvr)*
Lauren Giacobbo *(Sr Strategist-Digital)*

Accounts:
Allentown Inc.
American Realty Capital Broadcast, National Branding, Online Advertising, PR, Print
ATON Partners Logo
BioClinica
Biogen Idec Brand Communications, Traditional, Digital & Grassroots Components
Birdstep Technology Media Relations
Conshohocken Revitalization Alliance
Dune Medical Collateral Pieces, Testimonial Videos, Website, Website Content
Epstein Drangel LLP Mobile, Social Media, Web
Heraeus Materials Technology LLC Creative, Marketing, Online & Print Mediums
Heraeus Precious Metals North America
Hologic Print
Holy Redeemer Hospital Media Planning, Videos
Independent Financial Partners
Inductotherm Industries, Inc. International Group of Manufacturing Companies
LipoScience Marketing
Menu 123 Marketing, Mobile Collateral, Online
O'Neill Properties Group Branding, Marketing Campaign
OvaScience Marketing
Peirce College Degree Programs, Public Relations
Phillips Edison & Co
Princeton Equity Partners
Project U-Turn
RightCare Solutions Marketing
UK HealthCare (Agency of Record)
United Development Funding PR
United Technical Consultants Marketing, Website
University of Kentucky Hospital
Wescott Financial Advisory Group

DDM ADVERTISING INC
92 SW 3rd St Ste 2903, Miami, FL 33130
Tel.: (305) 674-9336
E-Mail: ddm@ddmadvertising.com
Web Site: www.ddmadvertising.com

Agency Specializes In: Advertising, Brand Development & Integration, Digital/Interactive, Exhibit/Trade Shows, Graphic Design, Internet/Web Design, Logo & Package Design, Public Relations, Radio, T.V.

Edwin Berrios *(Dir-Creative)*

Accounts:
Plastic Surgery Institute

DE ALBA COMMUNICATIONS
482 San Pablo Ter, Pacifica, CA 94044
Tel.: (650) 557-5711
Fax: (650) 989-6836
E-Mail: victoria@dealba.net
Web Site: www.dealba.net

Agency Specializes In: Crisis Communications, Event Planning & Marketing, Media Planning, Media Relations, Media Training, Newspaper, Public Relations, Strategic Planning/Research

Victoria Sanchez De Alba *(Pres)*
Terry Pfister *(Strategist-Comm & Copywriter)*

Accounts:
Alliant International University
The First American Corporation
First American Homeownership Foundation
Foster Farms Poultry
Nutrition for You
San Francisco Small Business Week Business Services
San Francisco Superior Court Justice

San Francisco Unified School District
USS Hornet Museum Art Services
Walgreens

DE LA CRUZ & ASSOCIATES
(Formerly de la Cruz Group)
Metro Office Park St 1 No 9 Ste 201, Guaynabo, PR 00968-1705
Tel.: (787) 662-4141
Fax: (787) 622-4170
E-Mail: thebest@delacruz.com
Web Site: www.delacruz.com

Employees: 70

National Agency Associations: 4A's

Carlos Thompson *(VP & Gen Mgr)*
Helga Del Toro *(Brand Dir-Contact)*
Niurka Escotto *(Brand Dir-Logistics)*
Coca Olivella *(Brand Dir-Strategy)*
Ity Vega *(Brand Dir-Reputation)*
Carlos Escriva *(Dir-Production)*
Daniel Perez *(Dir-Brand Integration & Mktg)*
Reema Sampat *(Dir-Art)*
Jennifer Zierenberg *(Assoc Dir-Creative)*
Edgardo Cuevas *(Mgr-Social Media)*
Mairym Monroy *(Acct Exec)*

Accounts:
Acura
American Express
Automeca
Burger King Campaign: "Whopper Showroom", Hands-Free Whopper
Coliseo de Puerto Rico
Good Neighbor Pharmacy
Kimberly-Clark Corporation
Open Mobile Campaign: "Open Tunes for Mom"
Pan Pepin
Procter & Gamble Campaign: "First Necessity Item", Campaign: "Garbage Truck", Duracell, Febreze Car
Sears

Branch

DLC Integrated Marketing
2600 Douglas Rd Ste 611, Coral Gables, FL 33134
Tel.: (305) 374-9494
Fax: (305) 374-9495
E-Mail: info@delacruz.com
Web Site: www.dlcim.com

Employees: 8
Year Founded: 1998

Agency Specializes In: Bilingual Market, Hispanic Market

Cristina Martinez *(VP & Gen Mgr)*
Luis Capaldo *(Dir-Creative)*
Isis Diaz *(Dir-Fin)*

Accounts:
American Express
Bella Automotive Group
Caribe Group
Celebrity Cruises
Clinton South Beach Hotel
Country Club Ventures
Essence Corp.Clarins Cosmetics
GlaxoSmithKline
Good Neighbor Pharmacy
Hyatt Regency; Miami & Coconut Point, FL
Kimberly-Clark Corporation
Kraft Corporation Capri Sun, Crystal Light, Kool-Aid, Tang
MoviStar
MTV
R-G Premier Bank of Puerto Rico
Renegade Investment Corp
Royal Caribbean Cruises
Sears
Sony

DEAD AS WE KNOW IT
51 Cunthair Ave, Brooklyn, NY 11222-3143
Tel.: (347) 294-0153
E-Mail: info@deadasweknowit.com
Web Site: www.deadasweknowit.com

Agency Specializes In: Advertising, Package Design, Print, T.V., Web (Banner Ads, Pop-ups, etc.)

Ella Wilson *(Owner & Writer)*
Mikal Reich *(Exec Creative Dir)*
Charmaine Choi *(Sr Dir-Art)*

Accounts:
Kraken Campaign: "May or May Not Roll Out to Other Cities", Giant Tentacle, OOH, Spiced Rum

THE DEALEY GROUP
1409 S Lamar Ste 1500, Dallas, TX 75215
Tel.: (214) 373-3244
E-Mail: info@thedealeygroup.com
Web Site: www.thedealeygroup.com

Agency Specializes In: Advertising, Broadcast, Media Buying Services, Media Planning, Print, Public Relations, Radio, Search Engine Optimization, Strategic Planning/Research, T.V.

JoAnn Dealey *(CEO)*
Jen Augustyn *(Principal)*
Linda Beall *(Dir-Retail Sls-Natl)*
Anne Rust *(Dir-Creative)*
Darby Devine Dawkins *(Office Mgr)*
Christina Garcia *(Mgr-Digital Media)*
Stephanie Garcia *(Mgr-Digital Media)*
Liz Hornor *(Acct Supvr)*
Elisabeth Zuerker *(Acct Supvr)*
Krystal Roppolo *(Acct Coord)*

Accounts:
Midway Companies

DEAN DESIGN/MARKETING GROUP, INC.
1007 Nissley Rd, Lancaster, PA 17601
Tel.: (717) 898-9800
Fax: (717) 898-9570
E-Mail: thestudio@deandesign.com
Web Site: www.deandesign.com

Employees: 10

Agency Specializes In: Advertising, Agriculture, Brand Development & Integration, Communications, Corporate Identity, Education, Electronic Media, Environmental, Exhibit/Trade Shows, Food Service, Government/Political, Graphic Design, Health Care Services, Internet/Web Design, Local Marketing, Logo & Package Design, Media Planning, Print, Production, Public Relations, Publishing, Retail, Travel & Tourism

Jane Dean *(Owner & Pres)*
Todd Horst *(Specialist-Ops)*

Accounts:
Beebe Medical Center
Orthopedic Associates of Delaware

DEARDORFF ASSOCIATES
319 E Lea Blvd, Wilmington, DE 19802
Tel.: (302) 764-7573
Fax: (302) 764-5451
E-Mail: jtosi@deardorff.com
Web Site: www.deardorffassociates.com

Employees: 15
Year Founded: 1984

Agency Specializes In: Brand Development & Integration, Broadcast, Business-To-Business, Collateral, Consumer Marketing, Corporate Identity, Electronic Media, Internet/Web Design, Logo & Package Design, Print, Public Relations, Radio, T.V.

Jill Deardorff *(Pres & CEO)*
Andrew Albrecht *(Head-Digital)*
Scott Hartzell *(Acct Dir)*
Nic Nichols *(Dir-Digital Design)*
Wes Richards *(Assoc Dir-Creative)*
Lisa Fritz *(Acct Mgr)*
Stephanie Barnett *(Mgr-Production)*
Jaime Vanaman *(Acct Supvr)*
Michelle Hassett *(Coord-Production)*
Steven Settlemyre *(Sr Engr-Applications)*

Accounts:
American Board of Internal Medicine (ABIM)
Gore
J.P. Morgan Asset Management
Omnicare
Oracle Corporation
PNC Bank
Univers Workplace Benefits
University of Pennsylvania Health System

DEARING GROUP
(Formerly Haan Marketing & Communications)
1330 Win Hentschel Blvd Ste 130, West Lafayette, IN 47906
Tel.: (765) 423-5470
Fax: (765) 742-2881
E-Mail: agency@dearing-group.com
Web Site: www.dearing-group.com/

Employees: 10
Year Founded: 1976

Agency Specializes In: Broadcast, Collateral, Industrial, Internet/Web Design, Logo & Package Design, Newspaper, Outdoor, Print, Sports Market, Trade & Consumer Magazines

Bob Dearing *(Pres)*
Collin Harbison *(Sr Dir-Art)*
Flossie Hayden *(Office Mgr)*

Accounts:
Purdue Athletics
Stuart & Branigin Attorneys

DEBELLIS & FERRARA
4903 Montgomery Ln Ste 100, Bethesda, MD 20814
Fax: (301) 986-4488
Toll Free: (855) 748-2100
E-Mail: info@debellis-ferrara.com
Web Site: www.debellis-ferrara.com

Employees: 9
Year Founded: 1998

Agency Specializes In: Advertising, Advertising Specialties, Automotive, Brand Development & Integration, Broadcast, Business Publications, Business-To-Business, Cable T.V., Co-op Advertising, Communications, Consulting, Consumer Marketing, Consumer Publications, Corporate Communications, Corporate Identity, Direct Response Marketing, Education, Entertainment, Environmental, Event Planning & Marketing, Exhibit/Trade Shows, Food Service, Gay & Lesbian Market, Government/Political, Graphic Design, Health Care Services, In-Store Advertising, Information Technology, Internet/Web

Design, Investor Relations, Local Marketing, Logo & Package Design, Magazines, Media Buying Services, Medical Products, Merchandising, New Product Development, Newspaper, Newspapers & Magazines, Outdoor, Planning & Consultation, Point of Purchase, Point of Sale, Print, Production, Public Relations, Publicity/Promotions, Radio, Real Estate, Restaurant, Retail, Sales Promotion, Strategic Planning/Research, T.V., Technical Advertising, Trade & Consumer Magazines, Transportation, Web (Banner Ads, Pop-ups, etc.)

Revenue: $6,000,000

Accounts:
AESA Consulting
Alcavis HDC

DEBOW COMMUNICATIONS, LTD.

235 W 56th St, New York, NY 10019
Tel.: (212) 977-8815
E-Mail: info@debow.com
Web Site: www.debow.com

E-Mail for Key Personnel:
Creative Dir.: tom@debow.com
Production Mgr.: angela@debow.com

Employees: 10
Year Founded: 1976

Agency Specializes In: Advertising, Bilingual Market, Brand Development & Integration, Broadcast, Business Publications, Business-To-Business, Cable T.V., Children's Market, Collateral, Communications, Consulting, Consumer Marketing, Consumer Publications, Corporate Identity, Direct Response Marketing, Education, Electronic Media, Environmental, Exhibit/Trade Shows, Financial, Government/Political, Graphic Design, Health Care Services, High Technology, Hispanic Market, Information Technology, Internet/Web Design, Investor Relations, Legal Services, Logo & Package Design, Media Buying Services, Merchandising, New Product Development, Newspaper, Newspapers & Magazines, Over-50 Market, Planning & Consultation, Print, Production, Public Relations, Publicity/Promotions, Radio, Real Estate, Recruitment, Retail, Sales Promotion, Seniors' Market, Sports Market, Strategic Planning/Research, T.V., Trade & Consumer Magazines, Transportation

Approx. Annual Billings: $7,000,000

Thomas J. DeBow, Jr. *(Pres & Chief Creative Officer)*

Accounts:
The Advice Co.; 1989
Advocate Law Group; 2005
Agio Technology Hedge Fund Technology Services
Attorneypages.com; 1996
Aurix Limited
Howard P. Hoffman Associates; 1983
Quantitative Analysis Service; Jersey City, NJ; 2005
United States Office of Personnel Management; Washington, DC Employee Benefits; 1996

DEBRA MALINICS ADVERTISING

701 Walnut St, Philadelphia, PA 19106
Tel.: (215) 627-1348
Web Site: www.dma-adv.com

Agency Specializes In: Advertising, Collateral, Logo & Package Design, Print

Debra Malinics *(Owner)*
Laura Jacoby *(Sr Dir-Creative)*

Accounts:
Beau Institute

DECCA DESIGN

(Formerly DeCarolis Design & Marketing)
476 S 1st St, San Jose, CA 95113
Tel.: (408) 947-1411
Fax: (408) 947-1570
E-Mail: sheila@decdesign.com
Web Site: www.decdesign.com

Employees: 20
Year Founded: 1991

Agency Specializes In: Collateral, Digital/Interactive, Direct Response Marketing, Electronic Media, Graphic Design, Health Care Services, High Technology, Internet/Web Design, Multimedia, Planning & Consultation, Print

Approx. Annual Billings: $5,000,000

Sheila Hatch *(Pres)*
Drea Li *(Controller)*
Natasha Kramskaya *(Dir-Art)*
James Reed *(Dir-Art)*
Jeannie Ditter *(Sr Acct Mgr)*
Lynda Kolberg *(Sr Acct Mgr)*
Catherine Bush *(Acct Mgr)*
Kerrie Inouye *(Coord-Production)*

Accounts:
APTARE
Audatex
Cisco Systems
Citrix
Hitachi Data Systems
House Ear Institute
Oracle
Plantronics
Synaptics

DECIBEL BLUE

350 W Washington St, Tempe, AZ 85281
Tel.: (480) 894-2583
Web Site: www.decibelblue.com

Year Founded: 2005

Agency Specializes In: Advertising, Brand Development & Integration, Digital/Interactive, Public Relations

David Eichler *(Founder & Dir-Creative)*
Andrea Kalmanovitz *(Dir-PR)*
Tyler Rathjen *(Dir-Integrated Mktg)*
Brandi Walsh *(Dir-Art)*
Christina La Porte *(Acct Exec)*
Sarah Tate *(Acct Exec)*
Michelle Frost *(Acct Coord)*

Accounts:
M.pulse

DECIBEL MEDIA

10 City Sq 5th Fl, Boston, MA 2129
Tel.: (617) 366-2844
Web Site: www.decibelmedia.com

Year Founded: 2014

Agency Specializes In: Advertising, Broadcast, Digital/Interactive, Media Buying Services, Media Planning, Print, Strategic Planning/Research

Tim Davies *(Pres & Chief Media Officer)*
Melissa Chase *(Supvr-Media)*

Accounts:
Minuteman Health
Wentworth Institute of Technology

DECISION TOOLBOX

5319 University Dr Ste 521, Irvine, CA 92612
Tel.: (562) 377-5600
Fax: (562) 684-4170
Toll Free: (800) 344-2026
E-Mail: kwadden@dtoolbox.com
Web Site: www.dtoolbox.com

E-Mail for Key Personnel:
President: kshepherd@dtoolbox.com

Employees: 35
Year Founded: 1992

Agency Specializes In: Advertising, Recruitment

Approx. Annual Billings: $2,000,000

Breakdown of Gross Billings by Media: Bus. Publs.: $60,000; Farm Publs.: $100,000; Internet Adv.: $1,400,000; Newsp.: $400,000; Radio: $40,000

Jay Barnett *(Founder)*
Kim Shepherd *(CEO)*
Jami Rosenthal *(Partner-Recruitment)*
Loren Miner *(COO)*
Terri Davis *(Dir-Bus Dev)*
Nicole Cox *(Chief Recruitment Officer)*

Accounts:
Black & Decker
Wells Fargo Bank; Los Angeles; San Francisco, CA; 1995

DECK AGENCY

116 Spadina Ave Ste 407, Toronto, ON M5V 2K6 Canada
Tel.: (647) 931-7250
E-Mail: sales@deckagency.com
Web Site: www.deckagency.com

Year Founded: 2012

Agency Specializes In: Advertising, Communications, Digital/Interactive, Internet/Web Design, Print, Public Relations, Social Media

Jonathan Tick *(Pres & CEO)*
Inga Berzinia *(Acct Mgr)*
Danielle Thomas *(Acct Mgr)*
Jocelyn Black *(Mgr-PR, Digital Mktg & Comm)*
Lisa Dobbin *(Mgr-Community)*
Viktor Arzethauser *(Acct Supvr)*
Klark Relleve *(Sr Designer)*

Accounts:
The Cruise Professionals (Agency of Record) Branding, Content Strategy, Creative, Public Relations, Social Media
Her Majesty's Pleasure (Agency of Record) Branding, Digital Marketing, Public Relations, Social Media, Strategic Planning
Quintessentially Lifestyle (Agency of Record)
TOCA (Agency of Record) Digital Marketing, Public Relations, Social Media, Strategic Planning

DECKER CREATIVE MARKETING

99 Citizens Dr, Glastonbury, CT 06033-1262
Tel.: (860) 659-1311
Fax: (860) 659-3062
Toll Free: (800) 777-3677
E-Mail: hello@deckerdoesit.com
Web Site: www.deckerdoesit.com/

E-Mail for Key Personnel:
Creative Dir.: jdecker@deckerhead.com
Production Mgr.: bkoley@deckerhead.com

Employees: 15
Year Founded: 1977

National Agency Associations: 4A's

Agency Specializes In: Advertising, Advertising Specialties, Brand Development & Integration, Broadcast, Business-To-Business, Cable T.V., Collateral, College, Communications, Consulting, Consumer Goods, Consumer Marketing, Corporate Communications, Corporate Identity, Digital/Interactive, Direct Response Marketing, E-Commerce, Email, Event Planning & Marketing, Exhibit/Trade Shows, Food Service, Gay & Lesbian Market, Graphic Design, Health Care Services, Hospitality, In-Store Advertising, Infomercials, Integrated Marketing, Internet/Web Design, Local Marketing, Logo & Package Design, Media Buying Services, Merchandising, Mobile Marketing, Multimedia, New Product Development, Newspaper, Newspapers & Magazines, Out-of-Home Media, Outdoor, Over-50 Market, Pharmaceutical, Point of Purchase, Point of Sale, Print, Production, Production (Ad, Film, Broadcast), Production (Print), Promotions, Publicity/Promotions, Radio, Regional, Retail, Sales Promotion, Seniors' Market, Social Marketing/Nonprofit, Social Media, Sports Market, Strategic Planning/Research, Sweepstakes, T.V., Telemarketing, Travel & Tourism, Viral/Buzz/Word of Mouth, Web (Banner Ads, Pop-ups, etc.), Yellow Pages Advertising

Approx. Annual Billings: $25,000,000

Breakdown of Gross Billings by Media: Collateral: $1,500,000; D.M.: $1,500,000; Event Mktg.: $2,000,000; Internet Adv.: $2,500,000; Newsp.: $3,000,000; Other: $4,500,000; Radio: $1,500,000; T.V.: $8,500,000

James Decker *(Founder, Chm & Copywriter)*
Kathy Boucher *(Pres, Partner & CFO)*
Paul Tedeschi *(VP & Exec Dir-Creative)*
Elizabeth Koley *(VP & Mgr-Production)*
Andy Armstrong *(VP-Sls & Mktg-VRF, North America)*
Kim Keller *(Sr Dir-Art)*
Joseph Stawicki *(Dir-Creative-Design & Graphics)*
Lynda Osborne *(Acct Mgr)*
Michele Holcomb *(Mgr-Tech Svcs & Graphic Designer)*

Accounts:
Avery Heights; Hartford, CT Senior Living Community
Carlisle Food Service Products; Oklahoma City, OK Special Projects/Dinex
Kloter Farms; Ellington, CT Outdoor Buildings & Home Furnishings
The Seeing Eye; Morristown, NJ Special Projects
UConn; Storrs, CT TV PSAs & Special Projects (Univ. Communications)

DECODED ADVERTISING
21 Penn Plz Ste 1000, New York, NY 10001
Tel.: (646) 844-5226
E-Mail: info@decodedadvertising.com
Web Site: www.decodedadvertising.com

Agency Specializes In: Advertising, Brand Development & Integration, Communications, Content, Digital/Interactive

Matt Rednor *(Founder & CEO)*
Amadeus Stevenson *(CTO)*

Accounts:
Dollar Shave Club

DEEP FOCUS
(Formerly Trailer Park)
6922 Hollywood Blvd, Hollywood, CA 90028
Tel.: (323) 790-5340
Web Site: www.deepfocus.net/

Employees: 300
Year Founded: 1991

Agency Specializes In: Advertising, Advertising Specialties, Brand Development & Integration, Broadcast, Cable T.V., Children's Market, Collateral, Corporate Identity, Digital/Interactive, Electronic Media, Entertainment, Fashion/Apparel, Graphic Design, High Technology, Information Technology, Internet/Web Design, Logo & Package Design, Magazines, Multimedia, Newspaper, Newspapers & Magazines, Outdoor, Print, Production, Radio, Sponsorship, Syndication, T.V.

Approx. Annual Billings: $20,000,000

Breakdown of Gross Billings by Media: Collateral: $1,000,000; Other: $2,000,000; Outdoor: $1,000,000; Print: $5,000,000; Radio: $1,000,000; T.V.: $10,000,000

Mark Cibort *(Pres)*
Rick Eiserman *(CEO)*
George Anderson *(Pres-Creative Svcs)*
Matt Brubaker *(Pres-Theatrical & Home Entertainment)*
Michael Leathers *(Pres-Television & Television Home Entertainment)*
Mike Tankel *(Sr VP-Mktg Innovation)*
Duncan Campbell *(VP-Interactive TV, Content & Digital Publ-Bus Dev)*
Eli Weisman *(VP-Content Grp)*
Luis Miranda *(Dir-Integrated Strategy)*

Accounts:
Atkins Nutritionals Branding Campaign, Creative, Strategic
Coda
Ignition Entertainment
Lionsgate
Metro-Goldwyn-Mayer/United Artists; Santa Monica, CA
Miramax; New York, NY Miramax Pictures
New Line Cinema; Los Angeles, CA
Pepsi
Think Film
Universal Pictures
Universal Studios Home Video
USA Films
Warner Brothers Home Video
Warner Brothers International
Warner Brothers Online
Warner Brothers; Burbank, CA
The Weather Channel

Branch

Deep Focus
(Formerly Goodness Mfg.)
6922 Hollywood Blvd 10th Fl, Hollywood, CA 90028
Tel.: (323) 790-5340
Fax: (310) 845-3470
E-Mail: info@deepfocus.net
Web Site: www.deepfocus.com

Stephen McCall *(Gen Mgr)*
Megan Russell *(Acct Supvr)*

Accounts:
Atkins Nutritionals, Inc.
Bolthouse Farms; Bakersfield, CA Baby Carrots, Beverages, Creative, Salad Dressings, Vinagrettes
Captain D's
Carvana
CODA Automotive (Agency of Record) Advertising, Digital, Electric Cars & Batteries, Experiential Marketing, Social Media
GT Bicycles
Krishers
The National Congress of American Indians Campaign: "Take It Away", Online
Newegg, Inc. Campaign: "Take it from a Geek: Teen Employee"
Oneida Indian Nation Campaign: "Take It Away", Online
Pearl Izumi
Toshiba Corporation Campaign: "Sillycon Valley", Campaign: "Unleash Yourself", Campaign: "Zombies", Consumer Electronics Computers, Encore 2, Laptop
Vail Resorts
Westfield

DEEP FRIED ADVERTISING LLC
4932 Prytania St Ste 202, New Orleans, LA 70115
Tel.: (504) 324-9569
Fax: (504) 304-2968
Web Site: www.deepfriedads.com

Year Founded: 2004

National Agency Associations: 4A's

Agency Specializes In: Advertising, Brand Development & Integration, Internet/Web Design, Logo & Package Design, Media Buying Services

Jennie Westerman *(Owner & Dir-Creative)*
Paige Huffine *(Brand Mgr & Designer)*
Kelsey McNabb *(Brand Mgr & Designer)*
Sarah M. Witt *(Acct Supvr)*
Mary Foster *(Coord-Comm)*

Accounts:
Giverny Fleurs
Hilary Landry
Jensen Companies
TCI Packaging
Wendy Monette Interior Design

DEEPLOCAL INC.
2124 Penn Ave, Pittsburgh, PA 15222
Tel.: (412) 362-0201
Fax: (412) 202-4482
E-Mail: info@deeplocal.com
Web Site: www.deeplocal.com

Year Founded: 2006

Agency Specializes In: Computers & Software, Market Research

Nathan Martin *(CEO)*
Kristin Petty *(Acct Dir)*
Heather Estes *(Dir-Mktg)*
Emily Price *(Acct Exec)*
Patrick Miller *(Sr Engr-Software)*
Courtney E. Powell *(Acct Strategist)*

Accounts:
Electronic Arts Inc Game Designers & Mfr
New-Google
LG Electronics Electronics Items Mfr
National Geographic Society Television Network Service Providers
New-Netflix
Nike Sports Product Mfr & Distr
Old Navy
Reebok Campaign: "FitList"
Toyota Motor Sales U.S.A Inc. Car Dealers
Volkswagen Group of America, Inc. Car Dealer

DEFERO
3333 E Camelback Rd Ste 190, Phoenix, AZ 85018
Tel.: (602) 368-3750
E-Mail: info@deferousa.com
Web Site: www.deferousa.com

Year Founded: 2006

Agency Specializes In: Advertising, Brand

Development & Integration, Digital/Interactive, Social Media

Mickey Lucas *(Pres)*
Eric Snelz *(Partner & Principal)*
Angelica Kenrick *(Acct Dir)*
Summer Oliver *(Acct Svcs Dir)*
Hailey Crider *(Mgr-Digital Strategy)*
John Marzolph *(Mgr-Digital Strategy)*

Accounts:
Employers Workers Compensation Insurance

DEFINITION 6

2115 Monroe Dr Ste 100, Atlanta, GA 30324
Tel.: (404) 870-0323
Fax: (404) 897-1258
Web Site: www.definition6.com

Employees: 80
Year Founded: 1997

Agency Specializes In: Consulting, Internet/Web Design, Sponsorship, Web (Banner Ads, Pop-ups, etc.)

Revenue: $1,500,000

Jeff Katz *(CEO)*
Stewart Brooks *(CFO)*
Paul McClay *(Chief Digital Officer)*
Sarah Sadd *(VP & Client Partner)*
Asa Sherrill *(Exec Dir-Creative)*
Margaret Holt *(Acct Supvr)*
Shannon Wilson *(Strategist-Digital & Social Media)*
Barry Sikes *(Exec Chm)*

Accounts:
Center Parcs
Coca-Cola Refreshments USA, Inc.
Extended Stay Hotels
Facebook, Inc. Immortalize Yourself
La Quinta Corporation La Quinta Corporation, La Quinta Inns
Mitsubishi Electric
Nickelodeon

Branches

Definition 6

79 Fifth Ave 14th Fl, New York, NY 10003
Tel.: (212) 201-4200
Fax: (212) 201-4210
Web Site: www.definition6.com

Agency Specializes In: Advertising, E-Commerce, Email, Mobile Marketing, Public Relations, Social Media, Web (Banner Ads, Pop-ups, etc.)

Rob Ortiz *(Exec VP-Entertainment & Integrated Media)*
Laura Pair *(Mng Dir-Synaptic Digital)*
Dan Schwartzberg *(VP-Media Rels)*
Stephi Blank *(Acct Mgr)*
Julia Mooradian *(Acct Mgr)*
Ali Jacobs *(Product Mgr-Tech)*

Accounts:
The Coca-Cola Company
GE Healthcare
Home Box Office, Inc.
Mitsubishi Corporation
Nickelodeon Direct Inc.
Pull-A-Part, LLC.

Synaptic Digital

708 3rd Ave, New York, NY 10017
(See Separate Listing)

DEFOREST CREATIVE GROUP

300 W Lake St, Elmhurst, IL 60126
Tel.: (630) 834-7200
Fax: (630) 279-8410
E-Mail: info@deforestgroup.com
Web Site: www.deforestgroup.info

Employees: 15
Year Founded: 1965

Agency Specializes In: Advertising, Commercial Photography, Corporate Identity, Direct Response Marketing, Internet/Web Design, Logo & Package Design, Publicity/Promotions

Lee DeForest *(Partner & VP)*

Accounts:
Alberto Culver
Bemco
Catalano,Caboor & Co
Challenger Lighting Co.
Chill
Douwe Egberts
Dubble Bubble
Federal Signal
IRI
Marco River
McDonald's
MicroMax
Montage
Napoli
Panduit
Plochman's Mustard
Ralcorp Frozen Bakery Products Parco
SC Johnson
Sara Lee
Ticklebelly
Tootsie Roll Industries

DEI WORLDWIDE, INC.

3450 Cahuenga Blvd W, Studio City, CA 90068
Tel.: (818) 763-9065
E-Mail: info@deiworldwide.com
Web Site: www.deiworldwide.com

Employees: 25
Year Founded: 2000

Revenue: $2,100,000

David Reis *(Founder & CEO)*
Brittany Latson *(Acct Grp Supvr)*

Accounts:
Mondelez International, Inc.

DEKSIA

100 Stevens St SW Ste 02, Grand Rapids, MI 49507
Tel.: (616) 570-8111
E-Mail: info@deksia.com
Web Site: www.deksia.com

Year Founded: 2003

Agency Specializes In: Advertising, Brand Development & Integration, Digital/Interactive, Graphic Design, Logo & Package Design, Public Relations, Social Media

Josh Ryther *(Sr Partner)*

Accounts:
The Carol Genzink
Veenstras Garage Services

DELANEY MATRIX

6033 N Palm Ste B, Fresno, CA 93704
Tel.: (559) 439-5158
E-Mail: info@delaneymatrix.com
Web Site: www.delaneymatrix.com

Agency Specializes In: Advertising, Internet/Web Design, Logo & Package Design, Print, Promotions, Public Relations

Toby Delaney *(Owner)*
Sasha Forbes *(Client Svcs Mgr)*

Accounts:
Pearson Realty
The Trend Group

DELEON GROUP, LLC

20 Kenneth Pl, Staten Island, NY 10309
Tel.: (718) 967-2241
Fax: (718) 228-2524
E-Mail: ken@deleongroup.com
Web Site: www.deleongroup.com

Employees: 20

Agency Specializes In: Brand Development & Integration, Corporate Identity, Digital/Interactive, Email, Guerilla Marketing, Logo & Package Design, Outdoor, Point of Purchase, Print, Radio, Retail, T.V., Viral/Buzz/Word of Mouth, Web (Banner Ads, Pop-ups, etc.)

Ken DeLeon *(Pres & Dir-Creative)*
Ruben Deleon *(Partner)*

Accounts:
Bresnan Cable (Agency of Record); 2008
Comcast Midwest Area
James Cable; Bloomfield Hills, MI Cable TV & Internet
Wagner College

DELFINO MARKETING COMMUNICATIONS, INC.

400 Columbus Ave Ste 120S, Valhalla, NY 10595-1396
Tel.: (914) 747-1400
Fax: (914) 747-1430
E-Mail: maria@delfino.com
Web Site: www.delfino.com

E-Mail for Key Personnel:
President: paul@delfino.com
Creative Dir.: lisa@delfino.com
Media Dir.: maria@delfino.com
Production Mgr.: donato@delfino.com

Employees: 25
Year Founded: 1970

National Agency Associations: 4A's-AMA-PRSA

Agency Specializes In: Advertising, Brand Development & Integration, Business-To-Business, Collateral, Communications, Consumer Marketing, Corporate Identity, Exhibit/Trade Shows, High Technology, Industrial, Internet/Web Design, Logo & Package Design, New Product Development, Newspapers & Magazines, Pharmaceutical, Sales Promotion, Strategic Planning/Research, Technical Advertising, Trade & Consumer Magazines

Approx. Annual Billings: $26,000,000 Capitalized

Geno B. Delfino *(Co-Founder)*
Lisa A. Delfino *(Co-Founder)*
Paul Delfino *(Co-Owner & Pres)*
Christine Delfino Seneca *(Co-Owner, Exec VP & Gen Mgr)*
Joseph Harary *(Controller)*
Donato Dell'Orso *(Mgr-Production)*
Maria Garvey *(Mgr-Media)*

Accounts:
Fleischmann's Yeast Consumer Division; Saint Louis, MO; 1998
Fleischmann's Yeast Industrial Division; Saint

Louis, MO; 1998
H&R Florasynth Aroma Chemicals Division; Teterboro, NJ; 1997
H&R Florasynth Flavor Division; Teterboro, NJ; 1997
H&R Florasynth Fragrance Division; Teterboro, NJ; 1997
Tri K Industries, Inc.; Northvale, NJ; 1994

DELIA ASSOCIATES
456 Route 22 W, Whitehouse, NJ 08888-0338
Tel.: (908) 534-9044
Fax: (908) 534-6856
E-Mail: it@delianet.com
Web Site: www.delianet.com

Employees: 8
Year Founded: 1964

National Agency Associations: Second Wind Limited

Agency Specializes In: Advertising, Advertising Specialties, Brand Development & Integration, Business-To-Business, Collateral, Communications, Consulting, Consumer Marketing, Corporate Identity, Cosmetics, Direct Response Marketing, E-Commerce, Electronic Media, Event Planning & Marketing, Exhibit/Trade Shows, Fashion/Apparel, Graphic Design, High Technology, Industrial, Internet/Web Design, Logo & Package Design, Magazines, Media Buying Services, Newspaper, Newspapers & Magazines, Pharmaceutical, Planning & Consultation, Print, Public Relations, Restaurant, Strategic Planning/Research, Trade & Consumer Magazines

Edward Delia *(Pres)*
Lori Schiraldi Delia *(Gen Counsel & VP)*
Susan Mcgowan *(Controller)*
Richard Palatini *(Dir-Creative)*
Gene Timmons *(Dir-Art & Design)*

Accounts:
Annin Flags
Azco
Block Vision
Contract Leasing Corp
Copperhead Plumbing & Heating
Dvtel
LPS Industries
Macro Consulting
Meyer & Depew, Inc.
Norris McLaughlin & Marcus
O.Berk Company
T.H.E.M.
US Sugar
Variblend
Wrap-N-Pack
Zip-Pack
Zipbox

DELICIOUS DESIGN
(Formerly Tsunami Marketing)
547 SW 13th St Ste 201, Bend, OR 97702
Tel.: (808) 332-7992
Fax: (808) 332-5077
E-Mail: mail@deliciousdesign.com
Web Site: deliciousdesign.com/

E-Mail for Key Personnel:
Creative Dir.: bob@deliciousdesign.com

Employees: 5
Year Founded: 1991

National Agency Associations: AAF

Agency Specializes In: Advertising, Brand Development & Integration, Collateral, Corporate Communications, Corporate Identity, Graphic Design, Health Care Services, Internet/Web Design, Planning & Consultation, Print, Production (Print), Real Estate, Sports Market, Strategic Planning/Research, Travel & Tourism

Valerie Rekward *(Owner)*
Robert Rekward *(Partner)*

Accounts:
AirVentures Hawaii
Brennecke's Beach Broiler
Holo Holo Charters
Island Truss
Kalaheo Cafe & Coffee Company
Scott Hollinger REMAX of Bigfork
Smith's Tropical Paradise
Wahooo Seafood Bar & Grill

DELLA FEMINA ADVERTISING
(Formerly Della Femina Rothschild Jeary & Partners)
129 W 29th St, New York, NY 10001
Tel.: (212) 506-0700
Fax: (212) 506-0751
E-Mail: info@dfjp.com
Web Site: www.dfjp.com

Employees: 56
Year Founded: 1993

National Agency Associations: 4A's

Agency Specializes In: Above-the-Line, Advertising, Advertising Specialties, Affiliate Marketing, Affluent Market, African-American Market, Agriculture, Alternative Advertising, Arts, Asian Market, Automotive, Aviation & Aerospace, Below-the-Line, Bilingual Market, Brand Development & Integration, Branded Entertainment, Business Publications, Business-To-Business, Cable T.V., Catalogs, Children's Market, Co-op Advertising, Collateral, College, Commercial Photography, Communications, Computers & Software, Consulting, Consumer Goods, Consumer Marketing, Consumer Publications, Content, Corporate Communications, Corporate Identity, Cosmetics, Crisis Communications, Custom Publishing, Customer Relationship Management, Digital/Interactive, Direct Response Marketing, Direct-to-Consumer, E-Commerce, Education, Electronic Media, Electronics, Email, Event Planning & Marketing, Exhibit/Trade Shows, Experience Design, Fashion/Apparel, Financial, Food Service, Game Integration, Gay & Lesbian Market, Government/Political, Graphic Design, Guerilla Marketing, Health Care Services, High Technology, Hispanic Market, Hospitality, Household Goods, Identity Marketing, In-Store Advertising, Industrial, Infomercials, Information Technology, Integrated Marketing, International, Internet/Web Design, Investor Relations, Legal Services, Leisure, Local Marketing, Logo & Package Design, Luxury Products, Magazines, Marine, Market Research, Media Buying Services, Media Planning, Media Relations, Media Training, Medical Products, Men's Market, Merchandising, Mobile Marketing, Multicultural, Multimedia, New Product Development, New Technologies, Newspaper, Newspapers & Magazines, Out-of-Home Media, Outdoor, Over-50 Market, Package Design, Paid Searches, Pharmaceutical, Planning & Consultation, Podcasting, Point of Purchase, Point of Sale, Print, Product Placement, Production, Production (Print), Promotions, Public Relations, Publicity/Promotions, Publishing, RSS (Really Simple Syndication), Radio, Real Estate, Recruitment, Regional, Restaurant, Retail, Sales Promotion, Search Engine Optimization, Seniors' Market, Social Marketing/Nonprofit, Sponsorship, Sports Market, Stakeholders, Strategic Planning/Research, Sweepstakes, Syndication, T.V., Technical Advertising, Teen Market, Telemarketing, Trade & Consumer Magazines, Transportation, Travel & Tourism, Urban Market, Viral/Buzz/Word of Mouth, Women's Market

Approx. Annual Billings: $150,000,000

Jerry Della Femina *(Chm & CEO)*
James Tenny *(Pres & COO)*
Joan Brooks *(Sr VP & Dir-Admin)*
Diana Fox *(Sr VP & Dir-Print Ops)*

Accounts:
Atlantic Health Morristown Medical Center, Newton Medical Center, Overlook Medical Center
Barbacoa Mexican Grill Advertising, Creative, Digital, Mobile Marketing, Public Relations, Social Media
Campari America Frangelico; 2012
Colace
Duff & Phelps; New York, NY Financial Evaluations; 2005
Fujitsu; 2008
Long Island Spirits Digital, Media Relations, Sorbetta
Maimonides Medical Center; Brooklyn, NY Hospital; 2005
McGraw-Hill
Mercer; New York, NY Human Resources Consulting; 2006
NY LI Honda Dealers; New York, NY Auto Dealer Association; 2006
Purdue Pharma L.P.; Stamford, CT OTC Products; 2001
Senokot
Silver Promotion Council; 2012
St. Francis Hospital; Roslyn, NY Hospital; 2006
Standard & Poors
TriHonda Dealer Association; 2012
Valley National Bank; 2010
Wakefern PriceRite, ShopRite; 2008

THE DELOR GROUP
902 Flat Rock Rd, Louisville, KY 40245
Tel.: (502) 584-5500
Fax: (502) 584-5543
E-Mail: marketing@delor.com
Web Site: www.delor.com

Employees: 10
Year Founded: 1989

Agency Specializes In: Advertising, Brand Development & Integration, Business-To-Business, Collateral, Communications, Corporate Identity, Digital/Interactive, Direct Response Marketing, Electronic Media, Graphic Design, Internet/Web Design, Logo & Package Design, Multimedia, Trade & Consumer Magazines

Ken Delor *(Pres-Brand Identity & Comm)*

Accounts:
Eli Lilly & Company
Medpace
NIBCO
P&G Pharmaceuticals

DELTA MEDIA, INC.
7875 SW 104th St Ste 100, Miami, FL 33156
Tel.: (305) 595-7518
E-Mail: deltacorp@deltaoohmedia.com
Web Site: www.deltaoohmedia.com

Employees: 20
Year Founded: 1983

Agency Specializes In: Advertising, Outdoor

Rudy Ferrer *(Pres & COO)*
Hal W. Brown *(CMO)*
Elana Redd *(Gen Mgr-Sls)*
Ivette Hernandez *(Mgr-Mktg & Res)*
Linda Miranda *(Sr Acct Exec)*
Alexandra Wolden *(Acct Exec)*

DELUCA FRIGOLETTO ADVERTISING, INC.

108 N Washington Ave, Scranton, PA 18503
Tel.: (570) 344-8339
Fax: (570) 344-8345
E-Mail: paul@dfainc.com
Web Site: www.dfainc.com

Employees: 7
Year Founded: 1993

Agency Specializes In: Advertising, Arts, Brand Development & Integration, Business Publications, Business-To-Business, Catalogs, Collateral, College, Commercial Photography, Consumer Goods, Consumer Publications, Corporate Identity, Direct Response Marketing, Direct-to-Consumer, Education, Financial, Graphic Design, Health Care Services, In-Store Advertising, Industrial, Integrated Marketing, Legal Services, Logo & Package Design, Magazines, Market Research, Media Buying Services, Media Planning, Media Relations, Medical Products, New Product Development, Newspaper, Newspapers & Magazines, Out-of-Home Media, Outdoor, Over-50 Market, Package Design, Pharmaceutical, Point of Purchase, Point of Sale, Print, Production, Production (Print), Promotions, Public Relations, Radio, Social Marketing/Nonprofit, Sports Market, T.V., Yellow Pages Advertising

Paul DeLuca *(Pres)*
Michael Frigoletto *(Partner)*
Tricia Pegula *(Dir-Media)*
Sarah Mellody Shedlauskas *(Media Planner)*

Accounts:
Baum Law; Scranton, PA; 1998
First National Community Bank; Dunmore PA; 1993
Gym La Femme; Pittston, PA; 2001
Matisse & Kelly; Scranton, PA; 2005
Osram Sylvania; Towanda, PA; 1998
Saint Joseph Hospital; Reading PA; 2002
Timmy's Town; Scranton, PA Children's Museum; 2006
Waiverly Community House; Waiverly, PA; 2006

DELUCCHI PLUS

(Formerly Delucchi +)
2101 L St NW, Washington, DC 20037
Tel.: (202) 349-4000
Fax: (202) 333-4515
E-Mail: careers@delucchiplus.com
Web Site: www.delucchiplus.com

Employees: 52
Year Founded: 2007

Agency Specializes In: Brand Development & Integration, Communications, Digital/Interactive, Email, Event Planning & Marketing, Media Relations, Multimedia, Outdoor, Promotions, Real Estate, Restaurant, Sales Promotion, Strategic Planning/Research

Ralph Thompson *(Chief Strategy Officer)*
Stephanie Orton Lynch *(Exec VP)*
Jay Vilar *(VP)*
Icida McClean *(Acct Dir-Retail)*
Joseph Dunne *(Dir-Fin)*
Chris Italiano *(Dir-Art)*
Jaime Rosenzweig *(Specialist-Digital Mktg)*

Accounts:
ABC Bakers

DEMI & COOPER ADVERTISING

18 Villa Ct, Elgin, IL 60120
Tel.: (847) 931-5800
Fax: (847) 931-5801
E-Mail: cfalls@demicooper.com
Web Site: www.demicooper.com

Employees: 18
Year Founded: 1992

Agency Specializes In: Advertising, Affluent Market, Alternative Advertising, Brand Development & Integration, Business-To-Business, Cable T.V., Collateral, College, Communications, Consulting, Consumer Marketing, Consumer Publications, Corporate Communications, Corporate Identity, E-Commerce, Electronic Media, Email, Graphic Design, Health Care Services, Hospitality, Household Goods, Identity Marketing, Integrated Marketing, Internet/Web Design, Logo & Package Design, Luxury Products, Media Buying Services, Media Planning, Medical Products, Multimedia, Newspapers & Magazines, Out-of-Home Media, Outdoor, Over-50 Market, Paid Searches, Planning & Consultation, Point of Purchase, Print, RSS (Really Simple Syndication), Radio, Real Estate, Regional, Sales Promotion, Seniors' Market, Strategic Planning/Research, T.V., Trade & Consumer Magazines, Urban Market

Approx. Annual Billings: $4,500,000

Walter Ottenhoff *(Dir-Web Art & Mgr)*
Marc Battaglia *(Dir-Creative)*
Christina Wojtowicz *(Acct Mgr)*
Andrew Fujii *(Mgr-Interactive Mktg)*

Accounts:
Crown Community Development
Little Company of Mary Hospital
Memorial Health System
Merlo on Maple
Sherman Hospital
Silver Cross Hospital
United Way
Waterton Residential
Willis Tower Sky Deck
Wilson Football

DENMARK ADVERTISING & PUBLIC RELATIONS

6000 Lake Forest Dr Ste 260, Atlanta, GA 30328
Tel.: (404) 256-3681
Fax: (404) 250-9626
E-Mail: info@denmarktheagency.com
Web Site: www.denmarktheagency.com

E-Mail for Key Personnel:
President: p.jessup@denmarkadv.com
Creative Dir.: t.haislip@denmarkadv.com

Employees: 14
Year Founded: 1986

National Agency Associations: AAF-PRSA

Agency Specializes In: Advertising, Brand Development & Integration, Business-To-Business, Co-op Advertising, Collateral, Communications, Consumer Marketing, Corporate Identity, Direct Response Marketing, Electronic Media, Event Planning & Marketing, Graphic Design, Internet/Web Design, Leisure, Logo & Package Design, Media Buying Services, Newspapers & Magazines, Out-of-Home Media, Outdoor, Planning & Consultation, Print, Production, Public Relations, Publicity/Promotions, Radio, Real Estate, Retail, Seniors' Market, Strategic Planning/Research, Trade & Consumer Magazines, Travel & Tourism

Approx. Annual Billings: $4,000,000

Priscilla Jessup *(Founder & CEO)*
Josh Chase *(Principal & Product Mgr)*
Mark Abbas *(VP-Client Engagement)*
Eric Van Fossen *(Exec Dir-Creative)*
John Mims *(Dir-Creative & Strategist-Brand)*
Michelle Carlino *(Dir-Art)*
Casey Edwards *(Dir-Art)*
Morten Langkjaer *(Dir-Creative)*
Amy Ottman *(Mgr-Traffic & Acct Exec)*
Marissa Matthews *(Mgr-Comm)*
Alyssa Goodman *(Acct Exec-PR)*

DENNEEN & COMPANY

222 Berkeley St Ste 1200, Boston, MA 02116
Tel.: (617) 236-1300
Fax: (617) 267-5001
E-Mail: info@denneen.com
Web Site: www.denneen.com

Employees: 12
Year Founded: 1995

Agency Specializes In: Consulting, Strategic Planning/Research

Mark Denneen *(Pres & CEO)*
Jane Alpers *(Exec VP)*
Helen Buford *(Exec VP)*
Frank Endom *(Exec VP)*
Albert T. Lee *(VP)*
Damon D'Arienzo *(Dir-Consulting Svcs)*
Annalisa Tammaro *(Mgr-Market Res)*

Accounts:
Brown University School of Medicine
The Children's Hospital of Philadelphia
Church & Dwight
The Coca-Cola Company
Consolidated Brick Distributors
Crunk!
Deutsche Bank
Echo Ditto
Exxon Mobil Corporation
Foundation Health Systems
GE Capital
GE Capital
GE Equity
Handel & Haydn Society
Harvard Medical International
Harvard University
Hinckley, Allen & Snyder LLP
Home Market Foods
The HoneyBaked Ham Company
Infinity Pharmaceuticals
Johnson & Johnson
Kendall-Futuro Healthcare
Lyme Properties
Mars Incorporated
Massachusetts Bay Transportation Authority
Massachusetts General Hospital
Massachusetts Institute of Technology
McKesson
Millennium: The Takeda Oncology Company
The National Academy of Sciences
Nord Est Emballage
Olin Corporation
PAREXEL International
Sight Resource Corporation
Starwood Hotels & Resorts
Symantec
Trex Corporation
Vinfen Corporation
WellChild Foundation of BlueCross BlueShield

DENTINO MARKETING

515 Executive Dr, Princeton, NJ 08540
Tel.: (609) 454-3202
Fax: (609) 454-3239
E-Mail: karl@dentinomarketing.com
Web Site: www.dentinomarketing.com

Employees: 10
Year Founded: 1987

National Agency Associations: DMA

Agency Specializes In: Direct Response Marketing

Approx. Annual Billings: $10,000,000

Breakdown of Gross Billings by Media: D.M.: $10,000,000

Karl Dentino *(Pres)*
Rosalba De Meo *(Dir-Art)*
Joel Rubinstein *(Dir-Creative)*

Accounts:
Avis
CapitalOne
Chase
Citi
Independent Financial
John Hancock
MasterCard
Prudential
Wells Fargo

DENTSU AEGIS
(Formerly Dentsu America, Inc.)
32 Ave of the Americas 16th Fl, New York, NY 10013
Tel.: (212) 591-9122
Fax: (212) 397-3322
Web Site: www.dentsuaegis.com

Employees: 120
Year Founded: 1966

Agency Specializes In: Advertising, Automotive, Broadcast, Business-To-Business, Consumer Goods, Corporate Communications, Corporate Identity, Electronics, Event Planning & Marketing, Financial, High Technology, Integrated Marketing, Internet/Web Design, Logo & Package Design, Luxury Products, Media Buying Services, Outdoor, Promotions, Sponsorship, Sports Market, Strategic Planning/Research, T.V., Travel & Tourism, Viral/Buzz/Word of Mouth

Approx. Annual Billings: $122,000,000

Breakdown of Gross Billings by Media: Internet Adv.: 44%; Mags.: 15%; Newsp.: 4%; Other: 2%; Out-of-Home Media: 3%; Radio: 2%; T.V.: 30%

Doug Fidoten *(Pres)*
Nicholas Rey *(CFO)*
Sean Power *(CFO-US Media)*
Joan Buto *(VP & Dir-Production Svcs)*
Nancy Chan *(Dir-Digital Media Ops)*

Accounts:
aigdirect.com
Ajinomoto
American Licorice Company
Bandai Toys
Berlitz
Beverly Center
Bloomberg BusinessWeek; 2001
Canon Inc.
Canon U.S.A. Inc. Campaign: "The Greatest Catch", Campaign: "Whatever it takes", Campaign: "Your Second Shot", Pixma, Powershot Camera
Chapman/Brandman University College
Checkers/Rallys
Chilean Avocados
Chinatown Tourism
Department of India Tourism
Eurofly
Famima Corporation
HarperCollins Publishers
HASS Avocado Board
Japan Airlines
JCCI Campaign: "Arigato! We Will Always Remember You"
Kissui Vodka
Lower Manhattan Development Council
Microsoft Corporation Media Buying, Media Planning, Search Advertising
NEC
New York University Medical Center
NIS Group Co., Ltd
NTT Communications
On The Job
Oneworld Creative, Media Planning, Strategic Brand Messaging
Phoenix Brands
Scion
Scotts Digital
Sutter Home Family Vineyards
Toyota Motor North America, Inc. Campaign: "Do the Wakudoki", Lexus IS, Scion
UNIQLO Campaign: "Storms"

Branch

Firstborn
32 Avenue Of the Americas, New York, NY 10013
(See Separate Listing)

Branches

360i
1545 Peachtree St Ste 450, Atlanta, GA 30309
Tel.: (404) 876-6007
Fax: (404) 876-9097
Toll Free: (888) 360-9630
Web Site: www.360i.com

Employees: 110

National Agency Associations: 4A's

Agency Specializes In: Advertising, Sponsorship

Jared Belsky *(Pres)*
Sarah Hofstetter *(CEO)*
Kevin Geraghty *(Sr VP-Advanced Analytics & Decision Sciences)*
Lee Maicon *(Sr VP-Insights & Strategy)*
David Randolph *(Sr VP-Retail & ECommerce)*
Jason Hartley *(VP & Head-Search Mktg Practice)*
Suzanne Reitz *(VP & Grp Acct Dir)*
Laura Mete Frizzell *(Gen Mgr-Search, Analytics & Media)*
Lachlan Brown *(Acct Dir)*
Meredith Meyer *(Acct Dir)*
Meredith Smyth *(Acct Dir)*
Pete Stafford *(Acct Dir)*
Chris Hawk *(Dir-Media)*
Danielle Richards *(Sr Mgr-Media)*
Michael Tooley *(Sr Mgr-Media)*
Jennifer Gutman *(Sr Acct Mgr)*
Katie Wall *(Sr Acct Mgr)*
Stephen Hom *(Acct Mgr)*
Marissa Osowsky *(Acct Mgr)*
Joelle Davis *(Mgr-Media)*
Maansi Nigam *(Mgr-Media)*
Christopher Hagenah *(Acct Supvr)*
Anne Lokey *(Acct Supvr)*
Tameka Fooks *(Supvr-SEO Analytics)*
Christine williams *(Supvr-Media)*
Emery Morris *(Coord-Media)*
Natalie Lennox *(Media Supvr-Integrated)*
Arianne-Ron Maliwanag *(Assoc Community Mgr)*

Accounts:
Capital One Financial Corporation
The Coca-Cola Company
Equifax Acquisition Strategy, Communications Strategy, Consumer Insights, Creative, Credit & Identity Protection, Digital, Equifax Complete, IdentityProtection.com, Media Planning & Buying, Personal Solutions, Search Marketing, Traditional
FTD Group, Inc.
H&R Block, Inc. Brand Search & Social Media
J.C. Penney Company, Inc.
JCPenney Corporation, Inc.
Kelley Blue Book Co., Inc.
Kraft Foods Group, Inc.
Lands' End, Inc.
NBCUniversal, Inc. Bravo Network, NBC Universal, Inc.
Redbox Automated Retail, LLC
Water.org Global Social

360i
32 Ave of the Americas 6th Fl, New York, NY 10013
(See Separate Listing)

mcgarrybowen
601 W 26th St, New York, NY 10001
(See Separate Listing)

DENTSU INC.
1-8-1 Higashi-shimbashi, Minato-ku, Tokyo, 105-7001 Japan
Tel.: (81) 3 6216 8042
Fax: (81) 3 6217 5515
E-Mail: s.kannan@dentsu.co.jp
Web Site: www.dentsu.com

Employees: 20,000
Year Founded: 1901

Agency Specializes In: Above-the-Line, Advertising, Advertising Specialties, Affluent Market, Alternative Advertising, Arts, Asian Market, Automotive, Aviation & Aerospace, Below-the-Line, Brand Development & Integration, Branded Entertainment, Broadcast, Business Publications, Business-To-Business, Catalogs, Children's Market, College, Communications, Computers & Software, Consulting, Consumer Goods, Consumer Marketing, Consumer Publications, Content, Corporate Communications, Corporate Identity, Cosmetics, Crisis Communications, Custom Publishing, Customer Relationship Management, Digital/Interactive, Direct Response Marketing, Direct-to-Consumer, E-Commerce, Education, Electronic Media, Electronics, Email, Engineering, Entertainment, Environmental, Event Planning & Marketing, Exhibit/Trade Shows, Experience Design, Faith Based, Fashion/Apparel, Financial, Food Service, Game Integration, Government/Political, Graphic Design, Guerilla Marketing, Health Care Services, High Technology, Hospitality, Household Goods, Identity Marketing, In-Store Advertising, Industrial, Infomercials, Information Technology, Integrated Marketing, International, Internet/Web Design, Investor Relations, Leisure, Local Marketing, Logo & Package Design, Luxury Products, Magazines, Market Research, Media Buying Services, Media Planning, Media Relations, Media Training, Medical Products, Men's Market, Merchandising, Mobile Marketing, Multicultural, Multimedia, New Product Development, New Technologies, Newspaper, Newspapers & Magazines, Out-of-Home Media, Outdoor, Over-50 Market, Package Design, Paid Searches, Pets , Pharmaceutical, Planning & Consultation, Podcasting, Point of Purchase, Point of Sale, Print, Product Placement, Production, Production (Print), Promotions, Public Relations, Publicity/Promotions, Publishing, Radio, Real Estate, Recruitment, Regional, Restaurant, Retail, Sales Promotion, Search Engine Optimization, Seniors' Market, Social Marketing/Nonprofit, Social Media, South Asian Market, Sponsorship, Sports Market, Stakeholders, Strategic Planning/Research, Sweepstakes, T.V., Technical Advertising, Teen Market, Telemarketing, Trade & Consumer Magazines, Transportation, Travel & Tourism, Tween Market, Urban Market, Viral/Buzz/Word of Mouth, Women's Market, Yellow Pages Advertising

Sales: $22,441,415,760

Tadashi Ishii *(Pres & CEO)*
Shoichi Nakamoto *(Sr Exec VP)*
Tim Andree *(Exec VP)*

Yoshio Takada *(Sr VP)*
Yuya Furukawa *(Exec Dir-Creative)*
Yosuke Hiraishi *(Exec Dir-Creative)*
Masako Okamura *(Exec Dir-Creative-Vietnam)*
Yasuharo Sasaki *(Exec Dir-Creative)*
Kazuya Kusumoto *(Sr Dir-Plng-Media Mktg Office-MC Plng Div)*
Fumihiko Nakajima *(Sr Dir-Bus Dev)*
Yuji Matsumura *(Creative Dir)*
Sato Oki *(Creative Dir)*
Tomonori Saito *(Art Dir)*
Mayu Taguchi *(Art Dir)*
Kentaro Sagara *(Dir-Art & Planner)*
Michihito Dobashi *(Dir-Creative)*
Junya Hoshikawa *(Dir-Art)*
Aki Masuyama *(Dir-Creative)*
Kazunori Miura *(Dir-Creative)*
Scott Lehman *(Copywriter)*
Yukihiro Oguchi *(Sr Mgr)*
Shun Hiyane *(Acct Mgr)*
Hiroaki Nakamura *(Acct Exec)*
Nadya Kirillova *(Planner & Copywriter)*
Sotaro Yasumochi *(Planner & Copywriter)*
Hiroshi Akinaga *(Copywriter)*
Hirose Dai *(Copywriter)*
Ryuto Furukubo *(Designer)*
Osanai Hiroaki *(Designer)*
Dai Hirose *(Copywriter)*
Shusaku Hirota *(Designer-Comm)*
Minori Kirioka *(Designer)*
Yuto Ogawa *(Copywriter)*
Kanae Saito *(Designer)*
Takahito Sakuma *(Designer)*
Yuichiro Shinomura *(Designer)*
Isao Taniguchi *(Planner)*
Kyoko Yonezawa *(Planner)*
Fumiharu Kobayashi *(Exec Officer)*
Akira Tonouchi *(Exec Officer)*
Toshihiro Yamamoto *(Exec Officer)*

Accounts:
47CLUB Campaign: "Eat Articles"
Aflac Media Buying
New-AINZ&TULPE
Air New Zealand Japan
AKS
All Nippon Airways
ANA
Asahi Breweries Super Dry Beer
Bacardi Campaign: "Ar Happy Halloween"
Beams Campaign: "Koi-kuru", Campaign: "Play & Socialize with Fashion"
Bell-Net Obstetrics
Bijustu Shuppan-Sha Campaign: "Shiretoko to New York"
Bridal Hair Restoration Committee Treatment Cooperation
B's International Campaign: "10000 Directors Fashion Show"
Bsize Campaign: "Making of REST"
Bunka Publisher
Calbee Campaign: "What Always Remains Precious & Unchanged"
Canon Eos Movie
Central Japan Railway Company Campaign: "Time Travel in Kyoto", Campaign: "Visit Kyoto"
Coca-Cola Refreshments USA, Inc. Campaign: "Play for Japan", Canned Coffee, Movie Emoticons
Conservation International
East Japan Railway Company Campaign: "Get Back, Tohoku."
Ekinan-Ginza Campaign: "A Hero Next Door"
Euglena Campaign: "The Entrance Quiz", Campaign: "The Euglena Catering Van"
Flavorstone
Fuji Xerox Campaign: "File Share Printer"
Fujikyu Highland Campaign: "Screaming has Come"
Fukushima Minpo Campaign: "Smile Fukushima Project"
Gap Japan Campaign: "Touch the Real Knit Ad"
Ginza Calla Swimming Pool
GlaxoSmithKline Media Buying
Glico
Google Campaign: "Youtube Aids Small Business"
Greentomatocars
Hankyu Corporation Campaign: "Hankyu Railway"
Honda Motor Campaign: "Connecting Lifelines", Campaign: "Dots Now", Campaign: "Small Character Camera N", Campaign: "Sound of Honda / Ayrton Senna 1989", Internavi
New-IHI Corporation
ILEX THE CLUB
Illumination Forest
Intel Japan Tweet City
International Paralympic Committee Communications, Marketing
Investment Corporation
Iwaki City Campaign: "Pray Together with Us"
Japan Advertising Agencies Association
Japan Airlines Campaign: "Jal X 787 Project Story"
Japan Broadcast Publishing Iphone App
Japan Committee for UNICEF Campaign: "Happy Birthday3.11"
Japan Ministry of Foreign Affairs
New-Japan National Stadium Campaign: "Reviving Legends"
Japan Professional Football League Marketing
Japan Racing Association Autumn Races, Campaign: "The Cast Talks"
Japan Tobacco
Japanese Ministry Of The Environment Biodiversity Awareness, Environmental Campaign
JAXA Kibo 360
JPRS Campaign: "May Cause Drowsiness"
Kamonohashi Project
KDDI Corporation
Kirin Beverage Company Campaign: "1 Click 1 Smile for Tohoku Children", Campaign: "The Lifelong Big Talk", Coffee, Fire Canned Black Coffee
Kyocera Campaign: "Loading Entertainment Digno's Challenge"
Kyushu Railway Company Bullet Train
Lion Corporation Campaign: "Time Slip Family"
LUMINE Campaign: "Fashion Trends by You"
Mainichi Newspaper Campaign: "100 Year Old Newspaper"
Menicon Campaign: "Magic"
Mesocare
Meti Ministry of Economy Campaign: "Electricity Saving Action"
Midori Anzen Campaign: "Ballet"
Ministry of Economy, Trade & Industry Campaign: "Electricity Saving Action"
Miraikan Campaign: "Geo-Cosmos"
Mitsubishi Chemical Holdings Campaign: "Picture"
Mitsubishi Electric Corporation Campaign: "The Transcendent Translucency Ad"
Mitsubishi Estate Campaign: "Catch the Blossom", Campaign: "Catch the Moon", Campaign: "Pink Punk"
Mitsui & Co Campaign: "The Subway Forest that Helps Forests Grow"
Morinaga & Co. Ice Cream Crepe
National Agency For The Advancement Of Sports & Health Campaign: "Singing Football 1", Football Lottery
Nepia Campaign: "Tissue animals"
NHK
Nicolas Feuillatte Champagne
Nikkan Gendai
Nippon BS Broadcasting Corporation Campaign: "Madam & Detective"
Nippon Television City Corporation Campaign: "Share the Light"
Nissin Foods Holdings Co. Campaign: "Gundam"
NPO Kamonohashi Project Campaign: "The Reality of Child Prostitution"
NTT Data Corporation Campaign: "EV Charge Infrastructure"
NYC Ballet
Okinawa Prefecture Okinawa Bridging Asia
Okinawa Seifun Corporate Image
One Brand. Inc. Campaign: "The Cry of the Innocent"
Oriental Land Co., Ltd. Campaign: "The Dream Goes On"
Otsuka Foods Tea
Otsuka Pharmaceutical Co., Ltd.
Panasonic Corporation Campaign: "Eco Technology", Campaign: "Life is electric", Campaign: "Share the Passion"
Peace Winds Japan
Rakuten Campaign: "Fast Ball"
Restaurant Express Co. Campaign: "Mother & Son"
Ricoh Company, Ltd. Campaign: "Fotocoma Big Canvas", Campaign: "Photo Animation Canvas"
Ride on Express Co. Ltd. Gin no Sara
Ryo Dental Clinic
Sanyo Shokai Ltd
Savoy
Setting Suns of Block 3 Production Committee Campaign: "What Always Remains Precious & Unchanged"
Shachihata
Shapla Neer
Shiga Art School
The Shinano Mainichi Shimbun Campaign: "A Family Story", Campaign: "Share the Newspaper with Children"
The Shinkansen
Shiseido Americas Corporation Campaign: "Makeup Harmony"
Shueisha Manga Comics
Sirius Co. Product Design
So-net Corporation
Sony Computer Entertainment America LLC Campaign: "Gravity Apple"
Sony Campaign: "Screen Story", Campaign: "Two Will", Corporate Image, Mobile Phone, Tablet, Video Game Promotion
Sports Biz Co., Ltd.
STAEDTLER Nippon K.K. Campaign: "The Ultimate Pencil"
Subaru
Suntory Holdings Campaign: "Happy Tweet Label", Whisky Hibiki
Super Planning Campaign: "Play the Tote"
Suzaka Cultural Promotion Agency
Suzaka Illumination Forest
Suzakiya Campaign: "Cat, Soup, Flaked, Flakes"
Taisei Corporation
Takahashi Shoten Campaign: "Look Up to Hana"
Team Aomori
Tetley Tea Pan European Advertising
Tokai Polytechnic College
Tokio Marine Nichido Swimming Competition
Tokyo Metropolitan First Commercial High School Campaign: "School Uniforms from Outer Space!"
The Tokyo Newspaper Campaign: "Share the newspaper with children"
Tokyo Olympic & Paralympic Games
Toshiba Corporation Campaign: "With 10 years of life", Led Bulbs, Torneo V Vacuum Cleaner
TOTO Campaign: "Toilet Bike Neo"
Toyota Motor Corporation Campaign: "Charge the Future Project", Yaris
New-Turner Colour Works
Tv Tokyo Corporation
UNHCR Charity
UNIQLO Campaign: "Happy Uniqlo Ribbon", Campaign: "Uniqlo Check-in Chance", UNIQLO LUCKY LINE
VTV
XEROX Campaign: "Facebook File Share Ptinter"
Yamaguchi Osteopathic Clinic
New-Yaskawa Electric Corporation
Yazaki China Investment Corporation
Yokohama City Board of Education
The Yomiuri Shimbun Campaign: "Baseball Vs Electricity Shortage", Campaign: "Happy Head"
The Yoshida Hideo Memorial Foundation Campaign: "Design Fever!", Campaign: "The Ultra Asian"
Yoshimoto
Zenrin DataCom CO., Ltd. Campaign: "Deja Vu", Itsumo Navi
Zuffa Campaign: "UFC Cage Shopping Bag"

Branches

cyber communications inc.
7F Comodio Shiodome 2-14-1 Higashi-shimbashi, Minato-ku, Tokyo, 105-0021 Japan
Tel.: (81) 3 5425 6111
Fax: (81) 3 5425 6110
Web Site: www.cci.co.jp

Agency Specializes In: Digital/Interactive, Electronic Media, Media Buying Services

Shuichi Hiroya *(CTO)*
Takehiko Chino *(Dir)*
Nobuyuki Tohya *(Dir)*
Yasuko Nagamatsu *(Mgr)*
Masato Yonemitsu *(Mgr)*
Yoshiaki Maeda *(Sr Auditor)*

Dentsu Meitetsu Communications Inc.
6F, Nissay Nagoyaekinishi Bldg, 6-9, Tsubaki-cho, Nakamura-ku, Nagoya, Aichi 453-0015 Japan
Tel.: (81) 52 459 0555
Fax: (81) 052 459 5508
Web Site: www.dm-c.co.jp

Employees: 200

Michihito Dobashi *(Dir-Art)*
Kotoha Tanaka *(Copywriter)*

Accounts:
Chukyo TV
Copywriters Club Nagoya Campaign: "Book Trophy", Campaign: "Sticky Notes Annual", Copywriter's Eye
Kishokai
Nikon Corporation
Tokai Television Broadcasting Co.,Ltd. Campaign: "Save Japan's Food Culture"
YO-KAN Campaign: "Reborn"

Dentsu Aegis Network Ltd.
10 Triton Street, London, NW1 3BF United Kingdom
Tel.: (44) 20 7070 7700
E-Mail: contact@dentsuaegis.com
Web Site: www.dentsuaegisnetwork.com

Employees: 96

Agency Specializes In: Sponsorship

Kunihiro Matsushima *(Vice Chm)*
Tracy De Groose *(CEO)*
Sanjay Nazerali *(Chief Strategy Officer)*
Luke Littlefield *(CEO-Dentsu aegis Network ANZ)*
Charlie Almond *(Head-Sponsorship PR-Dentsu Aegis Network Sport & Entertainment)*
Lorna Cheetham *(Head-Ops-Amplifi UK)*
Carl Fernandes *(Dir-Tech & Insight)*
Dani Filer *(Dir-Comm & Mktg-Global)*
John Coyle *(Mgr-Global Credit)*
Tim Andree *(Exec Chm)*

Accounts:
Allianz SE
Anheuser-Busch InBev Media
Eurostar Digital Media, Global Media
New-Honda Europe Media Buying, Media Planning
Microsoft Media Buying, Media Planning, Search Advertising
Wickes PPC, SEO, Social

DENTSUBOS
(Formerly BOS Beauchesne Ostiguy & Simard)
3970 Saint Ambroise Street, Montreal, QC H4C 2C7 Canada
Tel.: (514) 848-0010
Fax: (514) 373-2992
Web Site: dentsubos.com

Employees: 130
Year Founded: 1988

Agency Specializes In: Advertising

Approx. Annual Billings: $62,000,000

Breakdown of Gross Billings by Media: Brdcst.: 45%; Bus. Publs.: 1%; Collateral: 1%; Mags.: 3%; Mdsg./POP: 4%; Newsp. & Mags.: 1%; Newsp.: 24%; Out-of-Home Media: 1%; Point of Purchase: 1%; Print: 5%; Promos.: 1%; Radio: 2%; T.V.: 10%; Transit: 1%

Michel Ostiguy *(Owner)*
Roger Gariepy *(Chief Creative Officer)*
Wade Hasson *(Creative Dir)*
Maxime Jenniss *(Art Dir)*
Claude Ringuette *(Creative Dir)*
Simon Rufiange *(Art Dir)*
Mike Sherman *(Dir-Digital Media)*
Julien Thiry *(Dir-Art)*
Sebastien Rivest *(Deputy Dir-Creation & Assoc Dir-creative)*
Vanessa Labrecque *(Acct Exec)*
Helen Savage *(Copywriter)*

Accounts:
Alimentations Couche-Tard
Archdiocese of Montreal
Canal D
Catholic Church of Montreal Annual Collection, Campaign: "You have our blessing"
Federation of Quebec Alzheimer Societies Campaign: "Walk for Memories"
Fido
Henri Vezina
Journees de la Culture
Kebecson
Manulife Financial Creative
New-MTL Tattoo
Rosie Animal Adoption Campaign: "Tinderdoption"
Sapporo
Series +
Staples Canada (Creative Agency of Record) Campaign: "Staples Guy", Creative, Digital, Radio, Social
Yoplait

Branch

DentsuBos
(Formerly BOS Beauchesne Ostiguy & Simard)
559 College St Ste 401, Toronto, ON M6G 1A9 Canada
Tel.: (416) 343-0010
Fax: (416) 343-0080
Web Site: dentsubos.com/en

Employees: 45
Year Founded: 1998

Agency Specializes In: Advertising

Michel Ostiguy *(Chm)*
Annie M-Rizen *(CFO & Sr VP)*
Roger Gariepy *(Chief Creative Officer)*
Francois Mailloux *(Exec VP-Client Svcs)*
Christophe Mayen *(VP & Dir-Media)*
Sheri Rogers *(VP & Dir-Media)*
James Sauter *(VP & Dir-Client Svc & CRM)*
Keiichi Kubo *(VP-Dev-Intl)*
Claude Larin *(VP-Brand Strategy)*
Travis Cowdy *(Grp Dir-Creative)*
Lyranda Martin-Evans *(Grp Dir-Creative)*
Vic Bath *(Dir-Art)*
Lynn Peters *(Mgr-Comm)*
Claude Beaupre *(Acct Supvr)*

Accounts:
Centre for Addiction & Mental Health (Agency of Record) Events, Media
Constellation Brands, Inc.
Dr Pepper Snapple Group, Inc.
SportChek
Toyota Motor North America, Inc.
Transat Holidays

DEPARTURE
427 C St Ste 406, San Diego, CA 92101
Tel.: (619) 269-9598
Fax: (619) 269-8754
E-Mail: emily.rex@departureadvertising.com
Web Site: dptr.co

Employees: 24
Year Founded: 2007

National Agency Associations: 4A's-AMA

Agency Specializes In: Advertising, Advertising Specialties, Affluent Market, African-American Market, Arts, Automotive, Aviation & Aerospace, Brand Development & Integration, Branded Entertainment, Broadcast, Business Publications, Business-To-Business, Cable T.V., Catalogs, Children's Market, Co-op Advertising, Collateral, College, Communications, Computers & Software, Consulting, Consumer Goods, Consumer Marketing, Consumer Publications, Corporate Communications, Corporate Identity, Cosmetics, Customer Relationship Management, Digital/Interactive, Direct Response Marketing, E-Commerce, Education, Electronic Media, Electronics, Email, Entertainment, Environmental, Exhibit/Trade Shows, Experience Design, Fashion/Apparel, Financial, Food Service, Graphic Design, Guerilla Marketing, Health Care Services, High Technology, Hospitality, Household Goods, Identity Marketing, In-Store Advertising, Industrial, Infomercials, Information Technology, Integrated Marketing, Internet/Web Design, Leisure, Local Marketing, Logo & Package Design, Luxury Products, Magazines, Market Research, Media Buying Services, Media Planning, Media Relations, Men's Market, Merchandising, Mobile Marketing, Multimedia, New Product Development, New Technologies, Newspaper, Newspapers & Magazines, Out-of-Home Media, Outdoor, Package Design, Paid Searches, Planning & Consultation, Point of Purchase, Point of Sale, Print, Production, Production (Print), Promotions, Publicity/Promotions, Radio, Real Estate, Recruitment, Regional, Restaurant, Retail, Sales Promotion, Search Engine Optimization, Social Marketing/Nonprofit, Social Media, Sponsorship, Sports Market, Stakeholders, Strategic Planning/Research, Syndication, T.V., Trade & Consumer Magazines, Transportation, Travel & Tourism, Viral/Buzz/Word of Mouth, Women's Market

Approx. Annual Billings: $10,000,000

Breakdown of Gross Billings by Media: Bus. Publs.: 8%; Cable T.V.: 10%; D.M.: 2%; Internet Adv.: 27%; Mags.: 13%; Newsp.: 5%; Outdoor: 15%; Radio: 5%; Spot T.V.: 15%

Emily Rex *(CEO & Principal)*
Jessica Morgan *(VP-Dev)*
Justin Bosch *(Dir-Post Production & Editor-Online)*
Aileen Wong *(Coord-Production)*

Accounts:
Ace Parking; San Diego, CA Public Parking; 2009
Cisco; Los Angeles, CA Technology; 2009
The Commission For Arts & Culture; San Diego, CA Non-Profit; 2009
CrossFit; Washington, DC Athletics; 2009
Great American; San Diego, CA Residential & Commercial Real Estate; 2009
Hyatt Andaz Hotel; San Diego, CA Hospitality; 2008

Invisible Children; San Diego, CA Non-Profit; 2007
Life Technologies Corporation; Carlsbad, CA Bio-Tech; 2009
Life Technologies; Carlsbad, CA Bio-Tech; 2009
nPhase; San Diego, CA Technology; 2010
Qualcomm; San Diego, CA Technology; 2007
RedBrick Pizza Worldwide; Palmdale, CA Quick Casual Restaurant; 2009
Reebok; Canton, MA CrossFit Partnership; 2010
The San Diego Foundation; San Diego, CA Non-Profit; 2009
The Shores Hotel; San Diego, CA Hospitality; 2009
Wolfgang Puck; Beverly Hills, CA Quick Casual Restaurant; 2008

DEPIRRO/GARRONE, LLC

80 8th Ave, New York, NY 10011
Tel.: (212) 206-6967
E-Mail: creativematters@depirrogarrone.com
Web Site: www.depirrogarrone.com

Year Founded: 2008

Agency Specializes In: Advertising

Michael DePirro *(Co-Founder & Owner)*
Lisa Garrone *(Co-Founder & Owner)*

Accounts:
Asante Solutions
California STEM Network
Lyric Hearing Phonak
Pfizer
Union Square Optical

DEPPE COMMUNICATIONS LLC

1880 Paradise Moorings Blvd, Middleburg, FL 32068
Tel.: (904) 524-0170
Fax: (904) 328-3787
Web Site: www.deppecommunications.com

Agency Specializes In: Advertising, Brand Development & Integration, Public Relations, Social Media

Kim Deppe *(Pres)*

Accounts:
Crimson Laurel Gallery
The Institute for Growth & Development Inc
Miraculous Massage
More Space Place

DERING ELLIOTT & ASSOCIATES

1887 Gold Dust Ln Ste 101, Park City, UT 84060
Tel.: (435) 645-7500
Fax: (435) 649-3604
Web Site: www.deringelliott.com

Employees: 4
Year Founded: 1983

Agency Specializes In: Advertising, Brand Development & Integration, Corporate Identity, Direct Response Marketing, Print, Public Relations, Strategic Planning/Research, Web (Banner Ads, Pop-ups, etc.)

Conrad Elliott *(Pres)*
Kimberly Page *(Sr Acct Mgr)*
Brittany Diehl *(Acct Mgr)*
Katie Kepsel *(Mgr-Web Mktg)*
Niki Celine *(Designer)*
Nancy Hewitt *(Sr Accountant)*

DERSE INC.

3800 W Canal St, Milwaukee, WI 53208-2916
Tel.: (414) 257-2000
Fax: (414) 257-3798
E-Mail: webmaster@derse.com
Web Site: www.derse.com

Employees: 325
Year Founded: 1989

Agency Specializes In: Event Planning & Marketing, Exhibit/Trade Shows, Strategic Planning/Research

Sales: $47,029,003

Dan Serebin *(CFO)*
Brett Haney *(Exec VP)*
Colleen Chianese *(VP-Corp Ops)*
Katy Paquette *(Acct Dir)*
Dave Giordano *(Dir-Mktg)*
Jane Marie Alberti *(Mgr-Creative)*
Leslie Beach *(Sr Acct Exec)*
Nancy Haddix *(Sr Acct Exec)*
Christopher Lodes *(Sr Acct Exec)*
Lisa Schwabenlander *(Sr Acct Exec)*
Ken Aden-Buie *(Div VP)*

Accounts:
Glanbia Nutritionals
Mazda North America
Moen
Parker Hannifin
Questcor

DESIGN ABOUT TOWN

18 Bartol St, San Francisco, CA 94133
Tel.: (415) 205-8488
Fax: (214) 279-4923
E-Mail: ideas@designabouttown.com
Web Site: www.designabouttown.com

Employees: 5
Year Founded: 2005

National Agency Associations: AMA

Agency Specializes In: Advertising, Bilingual Market, Brand Development & Integration, Collateral, Corporate Identity, Digital/Interactive, Environmental, Exhibit/Trade Shows, Government/Political, Graphic Design, Health Care Services, High Technology, International, Internet/Web Design, Local Marketing, Logo & Package Design, Media Buying Services, Multicultural, New Technologies, Outdoor, Package Design, Social Marketing/Nonprofit, South Asian Market, T.V., Web (Banner Ads, Pop-ups, etc.)

Breakdown of Gross Billings by Media: Graphic Design: 80%; Other: 20%

Solana Crawford *(Founder & CEO)*

Accounts:
Corporate Accountability International; Boston, MA Collateral, Website Design & Development
The Guardsmen
PG&E
Robert Mondavi Winery; Sonoma, CA Interactive/Blog Design
TechCrunch
Tribal Fusion; Emeryville, CA Presentations Design
Weather Underground
Wunderground.com; San Francisco, CA Collateral, Tradeshow Graphics, iPhone Application

DESIGN ARMY

510 H St NE Ste 200, Washington, DC 20002
Tel.: (202) 797-1018
Fax: (202) 478-1807
E-Mail: press@designarmy.com
Web Site: www.designarmy.com

Agency Specializes In: Arts, Branded Entertainment, Collateral

Mariela Hsu *(Dir-Art)*
Holly Thomas *(Dir-Editorial)*
Laura Ting *(Strategist-Creative & Copywriter)*
Michael Chan *(Strategist-Social Media & Digital Mktg)*
Gabriela Hernandez *(Designer)*
Margaret Wedgwood *(Coord-Production)*

Accounts:
Arent Fox
Chronicle Books This is NPR
New-Georgetown Optician
New-Maryland Institute College of Art
Neenah Paper CLASSIC Swatchbooks, Campaign: "Perfection"
One Club
University Of Virginia Library Campaign: "Recombination"
The Washington Ballet Campaign: "Rock & Roll Gala"
Washingtonian Bride & Groom Campaign: "Bride & Seek", Campaign: "Calendar Girl", Campaign: "Food Fight", Campaign: "Material Girl", I Do (and Dont's)

DESIGN AT WORK

3701 Kirby Dr Ste 1050, Houston, TX 77098
Tel.: (832) 200-8200
Fax: (832) 200-8202
E-Mail: john@designatwork.com
Web Site: www.designatwork.com

Employees: 20
Year Founded: 1990

Agency Specializes In: Internet/Web Design, Print, Public Relations

John Lowery *(Founder, Pres & CEO)*
Tricia Park *(Exec VP)*
Cassie Croft *(Acct Mgr)*
Kristin Dancy *(Acct Mgr)*
Jessie Rowe *(Acct Mgr)*
Rick Yandle *(Mgr-Bus Dev)*
Melissa Alford *(Acct Exec-PR)*
Katie Macmillan *(Acct Exec-PR)*
Melanie Ziems *(Acct Exec-PR)*

Accounts:
Condera Securities
Maxim Group
State Service Company
Texas Iron & Metal

DESIGN GROUP MARKETING

400 W Capitol Ste 1802, Little Rock, AR 72201
Tel.: (501) 377-1885
Fax: (501) 588-0223
E-Mail: info@designgroupmarketing.com
Web Site: www.designgroupmarketing.com

Agency Specializes In: Advertising, Event Planning & Marketing, Public Relations, Strategic Planning/Research

Telly L. Noel *(Co-Founder & COO)*
Myron R. Jackson *(CEO & Strategist-Creative)*
Stephanie Jackson *(Dir-Pub & Media Rels)*

Accounts:
University of Arkansas

DESIGN HOUSE

130 Madeira Ave, Coral Gables, FL 33134
Tel.: (305) 456-7253
E-Mail: info@designhouseagency.com
Web Site: www.designhouseagency.com

Year Founded: 2008

Agency Specializes In: Advertising, Brand Development & Integration, Corporate Identity, Digital/Interactive, Graphic Design, Internet/Web Design, Search Engine Optimization, Social Media, T.V.

Gretel Vinas *(Founder & Dir-Digital Creative)*
Lizette Rodriguez *(VP-Digital Strategy & Acct Mgmt)*
Jan Perez *(Copywriter)*

Accounts:
The Miami Blue Co
Style Zest

DESIGN ONE CREATIVE INC.

PO Box 280, Denver, NC 28037
Tel.: (704) 464-7915
Fax: (704) 749-2585
E-Mail: info@designonecreative.com
Web Site: www.designonecreative.com

Year Founded: 1996

Agency Specializes In: Advertising, Collateral, Corporate Identity, Graphic Design, Internet/Web Design, Logo & Package Design, Print, Radio, T.V.

Mike Sherman *(Founder & Owner)*

Accounts:
GSM Services
Vein Center of Charlotte

DESIGN REACTOR, INC.

695 Campbell Technology Pkwy, Campbell, CA 95008
Tel.: (408) 412-1534
Fax: (408) 341-8777
Web Site: www.designreactor.com

Employees: 51

Agency Specializes In: Advertising, Brand Development & Integration, Branded Entertainment, Business-To-Business, Communications, Digital/Interactive, Event Planning & Marketing, Industrial, Integrated Marketing, Internet/Web Design, Local Marketing, Media Planning, Search Engine Optimization, Strategic Planning/Research, Trade & Consumer Magazines, Web (Banner Ads, Pop-ups, etc.)

Revenue: $7,800,000

David Skuratowicz *(Chief Creative Officer & Dir-Creative-User Experience & Design)*
Mark Willson *(Acct Supvr & Producer-Mktg)*

Accounts:
ABC
AMD
HP
PayPal
RSA

DESIGNKITCHEN

1140 W Fulton Market, Chicago, IL 60607-1219
Tel.: (312) 455-0388
Fax: (312) 455-0285
E-Mail: hello@designkitchen.com
Web Site: www.designkitchen.com

Employees: 100
Year Founded: 1992

National Agency Associations: 4A's

Agency Specializes In: Advertising, Experience Design, Graphic Design, Strategic Planning/Research

Sam Landers *(CEO-Blast Radius)*
Michelle O'Sullivan *(Principal)*
Greg Rolnick *(Grp Dir-Creative)*
Walter Kuhn *(Assoc Dir-Creative)*

Accounts:
Bally Total Fitness
Brookfield Zoo; Chicago, IL
Burger King Club BK Website
Lodgeworks
Motorola Solutions, Inc.
Nutrasweet
United Technologies

THE DESIGNORY

211 E Ocean Blvd Ste 100, Long Beach, CA 90802-4850
Tel.: (562) 624-0200
Fax: (562) 491-0140
E-Mail: inquire@designory.com
Web Site: www.designory.com

Employees: 165

National Agency Associations: 4A's

Agency Specializes In: Consumer Marketing, Sponsorship

Patti Thurston *(Mng Dir)*
Matt Radigan *(CFO)*
Kevin Lane *(Chief Strategy Officer-Long Beach)*
Chad Weiss *(Sr Dir-Creative)*
Chris Vournakis *(Sr Acct Dir)*
Jay Brida *(Dir-Creative & Copy)*
Andrea RePass *(Sr Mgr-Acct Plng)*
Allie Waters *(Acct Mgr)*
Bryan Horning *(Acct Exec)*

Accounts:
Audi Magazine, Model Lineup
Bostch
Columbia Pictures
Infiniti
Nike
Nissan North America, Inc.
Overture
Subaru
Universal
VCA

DESIGNWORKS ADVERTISING INC.

109 Twin Oaks Dr, Syracuse, NY 13206
Tel.: (315) 431-0808
Fax: (315) 431-4235
E-Mail: dbellso@designworksadv.com
Web Site: www.designworksadv.com

E-Mail for Key Personnel:
President: mbellso@designworksadv.com
Creative Dir.: mbellso@designworksadv.com
Production Mgr.: oerwin@designworksadv.com

Employees: 6
Year Founded: 1992

National Agency Associations: ACA

Agency Specializes In: Advertising Specialties, Brand Development & Integration, Broadcast, Business Publications, Cable T.V., Collateral, Communications, Consumer Goods, Consumer Marketing, Customer Relationship Management, Digital/Interactive, Direct Response Marketing, Graphic Design, Health Care Services, Leisure, Local Marketing, Logo & Package Design, Media Buying Services, Newspaper, Newspapers & Magazines, Out-of-Home Media, Outdoor, Print, Production, Public Relations, Publicity/Promotions, Radio, Restaurant, Retail, T.V., Travel & Tourism

DESTINATION MARKETING

6808 220th St SW Ste 300, Mountlake Terrace, WA 98043
Tel.: (425) 774-8343
Fax: (425) 774-8499
E-Mail: inquiries@destmark.com
Web Site: www.destmark.com

Employees: 20

Agency Specializes In: Advertising, Brand Development & Integration, Digital/Interactive, Graphic Design, Media Buying Services, Public Relations, Radio, Strategic Planning/Research, T.V.

Approx. Annual Billings: $12,000,000

Dan Voetmann *(Pres & CEO)*
Jerry May *(Exec VP & Dir-Brand Strategy)*
Andrea McArthur *(Dir-Digital Svcs)*
Vince Quilantang *(Dir-Art)*
Judy Rone *(Acct Supvr)*
Rebekah Herzog *(Sr Media Buyer)*
Lee Satler *(Sr Media Buyer)*

Accounts:
Acura of Bellevue
Lynnwood Honda
Penguin Windows
Sleep America
Sono Bello

DEUTSCH, INC.

330 W 34th St, New York, NY 10001
Tel.: (212) 981-7600
Fax: (212) 981-7525
Web Site: www.deutschinc.com

Employees: 964
Year Founded: 1969

National Agency Associations: 4A's-AAF-AEF

Agency Specializes In: Advertising, Brand Development & Integration, Customer Relationship Management, Digital/Interactive, Media Buying Services, Sponsorship, Strategic Planning/Research

Anush Prabhu *(Partner & Chief Investment Officer)*
Michele Allison *(Mng Dir & Head-Comm-Americas-Deutsche Bank)*
Pete Favat *(Chief Creative Officer)*
Matt McKay *(Exec VP & Exec Dir-Creative)*
Rachel Nairn *(Exec VP & Grp Acct Dir)*
Megan Kimball *(Sr VP & Acct Dir)*
Richard van Steenburgh *(Sr VP-Data Strategy)*
Sarah Manna *(VP & Dir-Art & Print Production)*
Sara Vinson *(VP & Mgr-Corp Comm)*
Menno Kluin *(Head-Art & Design & Exec Dir-Creative)*
Josh Deitel *(Producer-Digital)*
Tom Else *(Acct Dir)*
Derek Magesis *(Acct Dir)*
Health Pochucha *(Creative Dir)*
Brittany Rivera *(Art Dir)*
Alice Blastorah *(Dir-Art)*
Jeremy Gelade *(Dir-Project Mgmt)*
Arrie Hurd *(Dir-Art)*
Meghan McCormick *(Dir-Social Strategy)*
Armando Potter *(Assoc Dir-Plng)*
Joey Ricci *(Acct Supvr)*
Oliver Plunkett *(Supvr-Digital Media)*
Kristen Radomski *(Supvr-Integrated Media)*
John Anistranski *(Acct Exec)*
Felipe Machado *(Sr Copywriter-Creative)*
Emily Maier *(Acct Exec)*
Brian Gartside *(Designer)*
Sidney Henne *(Acct Planner)*
Mike Lin *(Copywriter)*
Amanda Willison *(Media Planner-Integrated)*
Caroline Vassiliades *(Asst Producer)*

Accounts:
Ad Council
Anthem Health Plans
California Milk Board
Diamond Foods
DIRECTV Campaign: "Football Cops"; 2006
Dr. Pepper
FEMA
GoDaddy
Got Milk?
H&R Block
HSN
Jagermeister
Johnson & Johnson Acuvue
Lunesta
M&M World
Microsoft Campaign: "Get Going", Campaign: "TAD Talks", Campaign: "Windows Azure iPad", Outlook.com
Nintendo
Novartis Exelon; 2002
PNC Bank
PriceWaterhouseCoopers
Taco Bell "Waffle Taco", Campaign: "Slippery Slope", Cantina Power Menu, Digital, In-store, Mobile Channels, Point-of-Purchase, Radio, TV
Target Corporation
TNT "Adaptweetion"
Turner Broadcasting Inc.
Unilever
Volkswagen
WATERisLIFE
Zillow

Branches:

Deutsch LA

5454 Beethoven St, Los Angeles, CA 90066-7017
Tel.: (310) 862-3000
Fax: (310) 862-3100
Web Site: www.deutschinc.com

Employees: 480
Year Founded: 1995

National Agency Associations: 4A's-THINKLA

Agency Specializes In: Advertising, Brand Development & Integration, Digital/Interactive, Media Planning, Sponsorship, Strategic Planning/Research

Kimberly Getty *(Pres)*
Doug Halbert *(Mng Partner & Exec Producer)*
Kyle Acquistapace *(Partner & Dir-Media & Data Strategy)*
Michael Sheldon *(CEO-North America)*
Marc Gowland *(Exec VP & Exec Creative Dir-Tech)*
Tara Greer *(Exec VP & Exec Dir-Creative-Platforms)*
Duncan Houldsworth *(Exec VP & Exec Dir-Data Strategy)*
Gavin Lester *(Exec VP & Exec Creative Dir)*
Montse Barrena *(Exec VP & Grp Acct Dir)*
Troy Kelley *(Exec VP & Grp Acct Dir)*
Madonna Deverson *(Exec VP-Brand Intelligence)*
Kelsey Hodgkin *(Sr VP & Grp Dir-Plng)*
Heath Pochucha *(Sr VP & Grp Dir-Creative)*
Adam Blankenship *(Sr VP & Acct Dir)*
Sandy Song *(Sr VP & Acct Dir)*
Matthew Matzen *(Sr VP-Experiential)*
Marcus Kroon *(VP & Grp Dir-Media)*
Lisa Johnson *(VP & Exec Producer)*
Zaid Al-Asady *(VP & Creative Dir)*
Perry Cottrell *(VP & Acct Dir)*
Scott Clark *(VP-Creative & Dir)*
Andy Pearson *(VP-Creative & Dir)*
Jeff Puskar *(VP & Dir-Experience Design)*
Ken Slater *(VP & Dir-Creative)*
Tom Adams *(Exec Dir-Creative)*
Jerome Austria *(Exec Dir-Creative)*
Jeffrey Blish *(Exec Dir-Plng)*
Bob Cianfrone *(Exec Creative Dir)*
Karen Costello *(Exec Dir-Creative)*
Pam Scheideler *(Exec Dir-Digital)*
Chris Adams *(Sr Dir-Art)*
Charlie Brandwick *(Sr Dir-Art)*
Paulo Cruz *(Sr Dir-Art)*
Luis Farfan *(Sr Dir-Art)*
Tom Else *(Grp Acct Dir)*
Rachel Nairn *(Grp Acct Dir)*
Jeff Bossin *(Creative Dir)*
Lauren Tyler Brown *(Producer-Integrated-Digital)*
Carie Bonillo *(Dir-Brdcst Traffic)*
Jason Clark *(Dir-Product Info)*
Michael Delahaut *(Dir-Art)*
Zach Gallagher *(Dir-Digital Strategy)*
Abilino Guillermo *(Dir-Integrated Bus Affairs)*
Max Hendren *(Dir-Art)*
Andrew Kapamajian *(Dir-Art)*
Erick Mangali *(Dir-Creative)*
Paul Oberlin *(Dir-Creative)*
Vic Palumbo *(Dir-Integrated Production)*
Curtis Petraglia *(Dir-Art)*
Amy Boe *(Assoc Dir-Creative)*
David Castellanos *(Assoc Dir-Creative)*
Melissa Langston-Wood *(Assoc Dir-Creative)*
Jamie Levey *(Assoc Dir-Creative)*
Armando Potter *(Assoc Dir-Plng)*
Saeyoung Kim *(Sr Mgr-Bus Affairs)*
Georgette Bivins *(Mgr-Bus Affairs)*
Nestor Gandia *(Mgr-Bus Affairs)*
Lacy Borko *(Acct Supvr)*
Meghan Ciffone *(Acct Supvr-Target)*
Gwen Ivey *(Acct Supvr-Integrated-Target)*
Aleks Rzeznik *(Acct Supvr)*
Krista Slocum *(Acct Supvr)*
Mel Smith *(Acct Supvr)*
Kyle Webster *(Acct Supvr)*
Kristin Paul *(Sr Acct Exec)*
Kelly Yaussi *(Sr Acct Exec)*
Ashley Broughman *(Acct Exec)*
Mary Cherwien *(Acct Exec)*
Vivian Huang *(Acct Exec)*
Kayla Laufer *(Acct Exec-Volkswagen)*
Renee Mansfield *(Acct Exec)*
Ashley Su *(Acct Exec)*
Chelle Toulouse *(Acct Exec)*
Morgan Aceino *(Sr Acct Planner)*
Kelly Mertesdorf *(Sr Acct Planner)*
Diana Ibanez *(Media Planner-Integrated)*
Catherine Ogletree *(Copywriter)*
Sheila Ashouripour *(Asst Acct Exec)*
Ruben Gomez *(Asst Acct Exec-Integrated)*
Cassie Pappas *(Asst Acct Exec)*
Sofia Somoza *(Asst Acct Exec)*
Chris Jones *(Sr Writer)*
Jeremiah Wassom *(Assoc Creative Dir)*

Accounts:
Angel Soft Campaign: "Be Soft. Be Strong", Campaign: "Grander Parents"
Anthem Blue Cross
AVVO
California Milk Advisory Board Campaign: "Friends", Campaign: "Return to Real"
Diamond Foods Campaign: "Diamond Nut Fantasies", Campaign: "Extended Party Version", Campaign: "MicroRave", Campaign: "School Boy", Pop Dongle, Pop Over, PopSecret; 2010
Dr. Pepper Snapple Group 7UP, Campaign: "Always Be One of a Kind", Campaign: "Backyard", Campaign: "Bold Country", Campaign: "Light it Up", Campaign: "Mop Dog", Campaign: "Mountain Man", Campaign: "One of One", Campaign: "The Call", Diet Dr. Pepper, Dr Pepper Ten, Dr. Pepper, Lightly Sweetened Teas, Snapple; 2008
Esurance
Georgia-Pacific Angel Soft Bath Tissue, Campaign: "Be Soft. Be Strong", Campaign: "Happy Father's Day, Mom", Vanity Fair Tableware
HTC America, Inc Campaign: "Ask The Internet", Campaign: "Blah Blah Blah", Creative, HTC One, Marketing, One M8
Kettle Chips
Komen
Microsoft
Microwave
Mophie Campaign: "All Powerless", Super Bowl 2015
Netflix Campaign: "Holiday Tree Topper"
Nintendo Digital, Social Media
Pizza Hut, Inc. (Lead Creative Agency) Brand Strategy, Social
Real California Milk
Sprint Corporation (Creative Agency of Record) "Cut Your Bill In Half" Phone Plan, Broadcast, Campaign: "All In" Wireless, Campaign: "Apology", Campaign: "Layover", Campaign: "Pied Piper", Campaign: "Too Rich to Care", Online, Strategy, Super Bowl 2015
Taco Bell Corp. (Lead Creative Agency) "Routine Republic", Bacologne, Bacon Club Chalupa, Bacon Headphones, Bacon One Hightops, Bacon Racing Chair, Bacon USB Drive, Breakfast Menu, Broadcast, Burrito, Campaign: "Bacon Mall", Campaign: "Bacon you can't eat is bacon you don't need", Campaign: "Breakfast Defectors", Campaign: "First Kiss", Campaign: "Get With the Times", Campaign: "Guess Who", Campaign: "Hurricane Doug", Campaign: "Live Mas", Campaign: "No Pican", Campaign: "Play The Future First", Campaign: "Ronalds", Campaign: "Sharing Sucks", Campaign: "The World's Most Hottest Idea", Campaign: "Viva Young", Cool Ranch Doritos, Digital, Dollar Cravings Menu, Dorito Locos Taco Fiery chips, Grilled Stuft Nacho, In-Store, Marketing, OOH, Online, Radio, Smothered Burrito, Social, Super Bowl, TV, Waffle Taco
Target; Minneapolis, MN Campaign: "Made to Matter", Campaign: "Share the Force", Creative, Dollhouse, Interactive Website, Threshold Home Decor Line
VanityFair
Vivint Creative, Strategic
Volkswagen Group of America, Inc. (Creative Agency of Record) 2015 Golf, App-Connect, Beetle Convertible, Campaign: " The Way Too Helpful Neighbor", Campaign: "Baby", Campaign: "Crash/Tree", Campaign: "Das Auto", Campaign: "Feeling Carefree", Campaign: "Get In.Get Happy.", Campaign: "Gooooooooolf Celebration Videos", Campaign: "It will Brighten Your Night", Campaign: "Johnny Conquest: Lunch", Campaign: "Johnny Conquest: Organic", Campaign: "Lucky Man", Campaign: "Mask", Campaign: "Midnight", Campaign: "Old Wives Tales", Campaign: "Party", Campaign: "Sharks Rescored", Campaign: "Stinky", Campaign: "Sunny Side", Campaign: "The Bark Side", Campaign: "The Force", Campaign: "Toss", Campaign: "World Cup Gooolf", Creative, Digital, Golf TDI, Interactive, Jetta, Passat TDI, Technology
New-WATERisLIFE
Yum! Brands, Inc.
Zillow.com Campaign: "Find Your Way Home", Campaign: "Lake House", Campaign: "Long Distance"

Deutsch New York

330 W 34th St, New York, NY 10001
Tel.: (212) 981-7600
Fax: (212) 981-7525
E-Mail: vonda.lepage@deutschinc.com
Web Site: www.deutschinc.com

Employees: 569
Year Founded: 1969

National Agency Associations: AAF-AEF

Agency Specializes In: Advertising, Communications, Digital/Interactive, Direct Response Marketing, Media Buying Services, Publicity/Promotions, Strategic Planning/Research

Tara Levine *(CMO)*
George Decker *(Exec VP & Grp Dir-Creative)*
Shobha Sairam *(Exec VP & Grp Dir-Plng)*
Barbara Chandler *(Exec VP & Grp Acct Dir)*
John Bongiovanni *(Exec VP & Dir-Creative Ops)*
Joe Calabrese *(Exec VP & Dir-Integrated Production)*
Vonda Lepage *(Exec VP & Dir-Corp Comm)*
Tom Lyons *(Exec VP & Dir-Innovative Mktg)*
Katherine Moncrief *(Exec VP & Dir-Talent)*
Robert Swartz *(Sr VP & Grp Dir-Plng)*
Denise Guillet *(Sr VP & Grp Acct Dir)*
Jayme Maultasch *(Sr VP & Grp Acct Dir)*
Kristen Rincavage *(Sr VP & Acct Dir)*
Felicia Geiger *(Sr VP & Dir-Diversity & Inclusion)*
Scott Lindenbaum *(Sr VP & Dir-Digital Plng)*
James Coie *(VP & Dir-Creative)*
Anthony Mariello *(VP & Dir-Plng)*
Lisa Chad *(Acct Dir)*
Katie Klages *(Acct Dir)*
Lauren Pollare *(Acct Dir)*
Erin Shaw *(Acct Dir-Zillow)*
Jessica Giles *(Dir-Art)*
Katrina Mustakas *(Dir-Art)*
Julia Neumann *(Dir-Creative)*
Brittany Rivera *(Dir-Art)*
Chris Jones *(Assoc Dir-Creative-Deutsch LA)*
Caitlin Dilks *(Sr Planner-Digital Media)*
Remy Raphael *(Acct Exec)*
Kaitlin Tabar *(Acct Exec-Taco Bell)*
Adam Aceino *(Copywriter)*
Austin Hamilton *(Copywriter)*
Kevin Meagher *(Copywriter)*
Molly Lashner *(Sr Media Planner)*

Accounts:
Ad Council
American Heart Association
The California Milk Processor Board
Champions Against Bullying
DIRECTV
The Empire State Relief Fund Campaign: "This Home is Where My Heart is"
Federal Emergency Management Agency Campaign: "Double Exposure", Campaign: "Seat of Your Pants", Campaign: "Waiting", Digital, Outdoor, Print, Radio, TV
Galderma Benzac, Campaign: "The Benzacs", Epiduo, TV
Go Daddy Inc. Campaign: "Bodybuilder" Super Bowl 2014, Campaign: "Inside/Out,", Campaign: "It's go time", Campaign: "Perfect Match", Campaign: "TMI", Campaign: "The Baker", Campaign: "YourBigIdea.CO", Super Bowl
GrubHub Media
Jaegermeister
Johnson & Johnson Carefree, Desitin, Johnson's Baby, Ortho Women's Health, o.b.; 1963
LIFE Foundation
The Light of Life Foundation
Liveout Loud
M&M's
The Michael J. Fox Foundation for Parkinson's Research
The Michael J. Fox Foundation
Microsoft Microsoft Office
MilkPEP Campaign: "Built With Chocolate Milk", Campaign: "Got Milk", Campaign: "Milk-Mustache", Campaign: "Protein Fight Club", Campaign: "Turtle Race, Motorcycles"
Novartis Exelon
OSI Restaurant Partners, Inc.; 2008
Outback Steakhouse Campaign: "Always fresh in the Outback", Campaign: "Live Adventurous", Campaign: "No rules, just right"
PNC Bank "The Great Carol Comeback", Campaign: "Know"
The PNC Financial Services Group, Inc.
PriceWaterhouseCoopers
Samsung Advertising, B2B
Sherwin-Williams Diversified Brands Advertising, Agency of Record, Digital, Dupli-Color, Dutch Boy, Krylon, Media Buying, Media Planning, Minwax, Pratt & Lambert, Purdy, Thompson's WaterSeal
Sidney Frank Importing Co., Inc. Campaign: "56 Parts. Best as One.", Consumer Insights, Creative, Jagermeister, Media, Mobile, Out-of-Home, Print, Social Media, Strategy
Sun Products Snuggle, Wisk
Sunovion Pharmaceuticals Inc.
TNT
Unilever Clear, Country Crock, Degree, Digital, Print, Rexona, TV; 1947
Water Is Life Campaign: "Art Heist for Good", Print
Zach Parise

deutschMedia

111 8th Ave 14th Fl, New York, NY 10011-5201
Tel.: (212) 981-7600
Fax: (212) 981-7525
Web Site: www.deutschinc.com

Employees: 500
Year Founded: 2000

Agency Specializes In: Branded Entertainment, Media Buying Services, Media Planning

Jeremy Bernstein *(Exec VP & Grp Dir-Creative)*
Karyn Pascoe *(Exec VP & Grp Dir-Creative)*
Vonda Lepage *(Exec VP & Dir-Corp Comm)*
Tyler J. Helms *(Sr VP & Grp Acct Dir)*
Stephanie Lee-Pang *(Sr VP & Dir-Digital Ops)*
Suzanne Molinaro *(Sr VP & Dir-Digital Production)*
Sarah Rankin *(Sr VP & Dir-Digital Grp Media)*
Andrea Curtin *(VP & Sr Producer)*
Andrew Arnot *(VP & Acct Dir)*
Dana Delle *(VP & Assoc Dir-Integrated Media)*

Accounts:
DIRECTV
Michael J. Fox Foundation
PNC

MWWGroup@Deutsch

111 8th Ave, New York, NY 10011-5201
Tel.: (212) 981-7600
Fax: (212) 981-7525
Web Site: www.deutschinc.com

Agency Specializes In: Event Planning & Marketing, Government/Political, Public Relations, Publicity/Promotions

Val Difebo *(CEO-Deutsch NY)*
Vonda LePage *(Exec VP & Dir-Corp Comm)*

DEUTSER

(Formerly Yaffe/Deutser)
1330 Post Oak Blvd Ste 1350, Houston, TX 77056
Tel.: (713) 212-0700
Fax: (713) 850-2108
Web Site: www.deutser.com/

E-Mail for Key Personnel:
President: bdeutser@yaffedeutser.com

Employees: 8

National Agency Associations: 4A's

Brad Deutser *(Owner)*
Stacy Christian *(Acct Dir)*
Michelle Hagler *(Dir-Art)*
Diana Lovelace *(Mgr-Production)*
Abigail Burns *(Acct Exec)*

Accounts:
AmeriPoint Title
Art Van Furniture
Beirne, Marnard & Parsons
First Convenience Bank
GC Services
Goode Company
Houston Community College System
Houston Independent School System
Houston's Fire Fighters Foundation
Juvenile Diabetes Research Foundation
Memorial Hermann Healthcare System
Pulaski & Middleman
Sentinel Trust Company
St. Luke's Episcopal Health System
Star Furniture
Texas Southern University
Westchase District

DEVANEY & ASSOCIATES

606 Providence Rd, Towson, MD 21286
Tel.: (410) 296-0800
Fax: (410) 296-5437
E-Mail: ddevaney@devaney.net
Web Site: www.devaney.net

Employees: 11

National Agency Associations: Second Wind Limited

Agency Specializes In: Advertising, Market Research, Public Relations

Diane Devaney *(Pres)*
Kolleen Kilduff *(Sr Dir-Art)*
Susan Casey *(Dir-Media)*
Michele Poet *(Dir-Art)*
Lisa D'Orsaneo *(Acct Mgr)*
Gina Kazimir *(Sr Specialist-PR)*
Stacia Prassinas *(Media Buyer)*
Casey Cox *(Asst Acct Exec)*

Accounts:
3 Point Products
A Salon by Debbie Spa in the Valley, Spa on the Avenue
Ad Audio
The College Savings Plans of Maryland (Agency of Record)
Dignet
Edenwald
Florida Relay
Georgia Council for the Hearing Impaired (GACHI)
Georgia Public Service Commission
Georgia Relay
Indiana Pipeline Awareness Association
Lucernex
Margie Beacham, Fine Artist
Merriweather Post Pavilion
MHI (Maryland Hospitality, Inc.)
NISH
Ohio Gas Association
Ohio Utilities Protection Service
OrthoMD
Progressive Radiology
Radisson Plaza Lord Baltimore
Salar
Southern Gas Association
Sport Fish & Wildlife Restoration Program
Sprint
University of Maryland Medical System
Virginia Relay

DEVELOPER MEDIA

503-250 Ferrand Drive, Toronto, ON M3C 3G8 Canada
Tel.: (416) 849-8900
Web Site: developermedia.com/

Year Founded: 1998

Agency Specializes In: Affiliate Marketing, Alternative Advertising, Below-the-Line, Business-To-Business, Email, High Technology, Search Engine Optimization, Social Media, Sponsorship, Web (Banner Ads, Pop-ups, etc.)

David Cunningham *(Co-Founder)*

Accounts:
REDGATE SQL Compare and SQL Developer Bundle

DEVELOPMENT COUNSELLORS INTERNATIONAL, LTD.
215 Park Ave S 10th Fl, New York, NY 10003
Tel.: (212) 725-0707
Fax: (212) 725-2254
E-Mail: tourism@dc-intl.com
Web Site: www.aboutdci.com

E-Mail for Key Personnel:
Chairman: tlevine@dc-intl.com
President: alevine@dc-intl.com
Public Relations: tlevine@dc-intl.com

Employees: 40
Year Founded: 1960

National Agency Associations: PRSA

Agency Specializes In: Brand Development & Integration, Business Publications, Business-To-Business, Communications, Consulting, Event Planning & Marketing, Planning & Consultation, Public Relations, Publicity/Promotions, Travel & Tourism

Andrew T. Levine *(Pres & Chief Creative Officer)*
Karyl Leigh Barnes *(Mng Partner & Exec VP-Tourism Practice)*
Julie Curtin *(Partner & Exec VP)*
Carrie Nepo *(CFO)*
Malcolm Griffiths *(VP)*
Maureen Haley *(VP)*
Steve Duncan *(Acct Dir)*
Intisar Wilson *(Dir-Acct Coordination)*
Rebecca Gehman *(Sr Acct Exec-Tourism & Economic Dev)*
Megan McHale *(Sr Acct Exec-Tourism & Economic Dev)*
Annette Henriques *(Coord-Accounts Payable)*

Accounts:
The Brownsville Economic Development Council
Chamber of Commerce of Huntsville/Madison County; AL
Chile Tourism Marketing, Media Relations, Public Relations
Finger Lakes Wine Country Tourism Marketing Association
Metro Denver Economic Development Corporation
New Jersey Economic Development Authority
Peru Export and Tourism Promotion Board
QualPro QualPro
Tourism Tasmania
U.S. Virgin Islands Department of Tourism Campaign: "You, Unscripted", PR
Visit California Domestic Public Relations

Branch

DCI-West
19594 E Ida Pl, Aurora, CO 80015
Tel.: (303) 627-0272
Fax: (303) 627-9958
Web Site: www.aboutdci.com

Employees: 3
Year Founded: 1960

National Agency Associations: PRSA

Agency Specializes In: Public Relations, Travel & Tourism

Julie Curtin *(Partner & Exec VP)*
Karyl Leigh Barnes *(Partner & Sr VP)*
Malcolm Griffiths *(VP)*
Susan Brake *(Acct Dir)*
Steve Duncan *(Acct Dir)*
Intisar Wilson *(Dir-Acct Coordination)*
Jordan Robinson *(Acct Supvr)*
Kristie Pendleton *(Acct Coord)*
Annette Henriques *(Coord-Accounts Payable)*

Accounts:
Charleston Regional Development Alliance
Chattanooga Area Chamber of Commerce
Columbus Chamber of Commerce
Greater Houston Partnership
Southwest Michigan First

DEVICEPHARM
2100 Main St Ste 250, Irvine, CA 92614
Tel.: (949) 271-1180
E-Mail: info@devicepharm.com
Web Site: www.devicepharm.com

Year Founded: 2002

Agency Specializes In: Advertising, Brand Development & Integration, Digital/Interactive

Jon Hermie *(Pres)*
Clay Wilemon *(CEO & Chief Strategy Officer)*
Brian Famigletti *(Mng Dir)*
Katherine Wiseman *(VP-Acct Svcs)*
Elina Kingkade *(Dir-Indus Rels)*

Accounts:
New-Freudenberg Medical

DEVINE COMMUNICATIONS
9300 5th St N, Saint Petersburg, FL 33702
Tel.: (727) 573-2575
Fax: (727) 572-1906
Web Site: www.devineads.com/

Employees: 8
Year Founded: 1982

Agency Specializes In: Advertising

Tim Devine *(VP)*
Yvette Yocklin *(Dir-Art & Graphic Designer)*
Jim Kenefick *(Dir-Creative)*

DEVITO GROUP
(Formerly DeVito Fitterman Advertising)
151 W 19th St 4th Fl, New York, NY 10011-5511
Tel.: (212) 924-7430
Fax: (212) 924-7946
E-Mail: anthony@devitogroup.com
Web Site: www.devitogroup.com

Employees: 15
Year Founded: 1997

Agency Specializes In: Advertising, Advertising Specialties, Brand Development & Integration, Broadcast, Business Publications, Business-To-Business, Cable T.V., Children's Market, Collateral, Commercial Photography, Communications, Consulting, Consumer Marketing, Corporate Identity, Cosmetics, Direct Response Marketing, Education, Fashion/Apparel, Financial, Food Service, Graphic Design, Health Care Services, High Technology, Internet/Web Design, Leisure, Logo & Package Design, Magazines, Medical Products, New Product Development, Newspaper, Newspapers & Magazines, Out-of-Home Media, Outdoor, Over-50 Market, Pharmaceutical, Planning & Consultation, Print, Production, Radio, Recruitment, Restaurant, Retail, Seniors' Market, Strategic Planning/Research, T.V., Trade & Consumer Magazines, Travel & Tourism

Frank Devito *(Pres & Partner-De Vito Fitterman)*
Chris DeVito *(Partner & Dir-Creative)*

Accounts:
Arch Insurance
Ascap
EMI Music Resources
The Heckscher Museum of Art; Huntington, NY; 1999
Johnson & Johnson Health Care Systems; Piscataway, NJ The Campaign for Nursing's Future; 2001
Johnson & Johnson; New Brunswick, NJ The Campaign for Nursing's Future; 2001
Kiss
Merazine
Ricola USA
The Samaritans
Stop HIV
Value Drugs
Why

DEVITO/VERDI
100 5th Ave 16th Fl, New York, NY 10011
Tel.: (212) 431-4694
Fax: (212) 431-4940
E-Mail: everdi@devitoverdi.com
Web Site: www.devitoverdi.com

Employees: 45
Year Founded: 1991

National Agency Associations: 4A's

Agency Specializes In: Sponsorship

Approx. Annual Billings: $140,000,000

Barbara Michelson *(Head-Brdcst Production)*
Wayne Winfield *(Creative Dir)*
Sal DeVito *(Dir-Creative)*
Paul McCormick *(Dir-New Bus)*
Barry Flanik *(Assoc Dir-Creative & Copywriter)*
Andrew Brief *(Acct Svc Dir)*
Chris Arrighi *(Coord-Digital Media Creative & Bus)*
Kyle Cooper *(Asst Media Buyer)*
Ariel Hustoo *(Sr Media Planner)*
Joe Naftol *(Asst Media Buyer)*

Accounts:
Abington Memorial Hospital Orthopaedic & Spine Institute, The Pilla Heart Center, The Rosenfeld Cancer Center
Acura 2.5TL
Aerosoles Advertising
Appleton Estate Rum
Bernie & Phyl's Furniture Advertising Agency of Record
CarMax
Coco's Bakery Restaurant "Kids Eat Free", Campaign: "Big Baby", Campaign: "Cowboys", Marketing Message
Coldwater Creek; Sandpoint, ID (Agency of Record) Branding, Creative, Design Consulting, National Advertising
Corazon Tequila
Daffy's Campaign: "Nest", Campaign: "Wallpaper", Clothing, Fall Fashion Line
Duane Reade Inc; New York, NY (Agency of Record) Drug Store
ECampus
Empire Kosher Chicken
E.P. Carrillo Cigars
Ernesto Perez-Carrillo
Fallon Community Health Plan
For Eyes Optical
Grey Goose Vodka
Hotwire.com
Intelius
Kobrand Corporation Appleton Estate Jamaica Rum
Legal Sea Foods Campaign: "Save The Crab", Campaign: "Save the Salmon", Creative, Media Buying, New England Clam Chowder; 2006
Lenox Hill Hospital
Massachusetts General Hospital
Meijer; Grand Rapids, MI Food, General Merchandise; 2003

The Men's Wearhouse, Inc. Creative/Strategic, K&G, MW Tux, Moores Clothing for Men; 2008
Mount Sinai Hospital
The National Association of Broadcasters
National Thoroughbred Racing Association
NEFCU
New York Institute Of Technology
North Shore/Long Island Jewish Health System
Office Depot
Pepsi & Sobe
Price Chopper
Reebok
Rentokil Pest Control
Scripps Health Branding, Creative Development & Traditional, Digital Media
Sony
Suffolk University (Agency of Record) Brand Awareness, Campaign: "Be a contender. Suffolk University", Marketing & Communications
University of Chicago Medicine & Biological Sciences Consumer Advertising
Varian Medical Systems
Virginia Commonwealth University Medical Center; Richmond, VA Brand Positioning, Creative Development, Digital Advertising, Media Planning, Strategy

DEVON ADVERTISING AGENCY LLC

96 Drawbridge Dr, Monroe Township, NJ 08831
Tel.: (609) 235-9452
Fax: (609) 235-9452
E-Mail: fblock@devonad.com
Web Site: www.devonad.com

E-Mail for Key Personnel:
President: FBlock@devonad.com

Employees: 1
Year Founded: 2005

Agency Specializes In: Advertising, Education, Hospitality, Logo & Package Design, Newspapers & Magazines, Over-50 Market, Print, Recruitment, Retail, Seniors' Market, Telemarketing

Approx. Annual Billings: $500,000

Breakdown of Gross Billings by Media: Bus. Publs.: 20%; Internet Adv.: 50%; Newsp.: 30%

Fred Block *(Pres)*

DEWAR COMMUNICATIONS INC.

9 Prince Arthur Ave, Toronto, ON M5R 1B2 Canada
Tel.: (416) 921-1827
Fax: (416) 921-9837
E-Mail: jdewar@dewarcom.com
Web Site: www.dewarcom.com

E-Mail for Key Personnel:
President: jdewar@dewarcom.com

Employees: 8
Year Founded: 1963

National Agency Associations: BPA-CBP

Agency Specializes In: Advertising, Business Publications, Business-To-Business, Collateral, Communications, Consulting, Corporate Identity, Direct Response Marketing, Exhibit/Trade Shows, Graphic Design, High Technology, Industrial, Internet/Web Design, Logo & Package Design, Newspaper, Newspapers & Magazines, Point of Sale, Technical Advertising, Trade & Consumer Magazines

Approx. Annual Billings: $3,650,000

Breakdown of Gross Billings by Media: Bus. Publs.: $547,500; Collateral: $1,825,000; Consulting: $182,500; D.M.: $182,500; Exhibits/Trade Shows: $182,500; Logo & Package Design: $109,500; Worldwide Web Sites: $620,500

Jennifer L. Dewar *(Pres)*
Brooke Hennessy *(Dir-Art)*
Michael Lake *(Dir-Creative)*

Accounts:
Arbitration Place
ASAP
CGOV Asset Management
GE Oil & Gas
Invodane Engineering; Toronto, ON
Kim Orr Barristers
RainMaker Group
ShawCor
Toronto Construction Association

DG COMMUNICATIONS GROUP

1225 NW 17th Ave Ste 103, Delray Beach, FL 33445
Tel.: (561) 266-0127
Fax: (561) 266-0128
Web Site: http://damngood.agency/

Agency Specializes In: Advertising, Brand Development & Integration, Consulting, Graphic Design, Media Buying Services, Print, Radio, T.V.

Gavin Robin *(Pres & CEO)*
Aris Albaitis *(Dir-Web Dev)*
Amy Zigelman *(Dir-Media)*

Accounts:
Better For You Foods LLC
The Herschthal Practice Aesthetic Dermatology
Jewish Federation of Palm Beach County
Kirk Supermarket & Pharmacy
Progressive Learning International

DG MEDIAMIND

(Name Changed to Sizmek)

DGS MARKETING ENGINEERS

10100 Lantern Rd Ste 225, Fishers, IN 46037
Tel.: (317) 813-2222
Fax: (317) 813-2233
E-Mail: info@dgsmarketing.com
Web Site: www.dgsmarketingengineers.com/

Employees: 10
Year Founded: 1985

National Agency Associations: AMA-BMA-Second Wind Limited

Agency Specializes In: Advertising, Aviation & Aerospace, Brand Development & Integration, Business-To-Business, Communications, Corporate Communications, Corporate Identity, Digital/Interactive, Direct Response Marketing, Electronics, Engineering, Environmental, Exhibit/Trade Shows, Graphic Design, High Technology, Identity Marketing, Industrial, Information Technology, Integrated Marketing, Internet/Web Design, Logo & Package Design, Marine, Media Relations, Medical Products, New Product Development, New Technologies, Planning & Consultation, Print, Production, Production (Print), Public Relations, Publicity/Promotions, Social Media, Strategic Planning/Research, Technical Advertising, Trade & Consumer Magazines, Transportation

Approx. Annual Billings: $7,600,000

Breakdown of Gross Billings by Media: Bus. Publs.: $3,440,000; Collateral: $430,000; D.M.: $860,000; Other: $290,000; Pub. Rels.: $2,580,000

Marc Diebold *(Pres & CEO)*
Leslie Galbreath *(CMO & Exec VP)*
Justin Brown *(Sr Dir-Art)*
Chuck Bates *(Dir-PR)*
Polly Bonacuse *(Dir-Art)*
Ellen Sprunger *(Dir-Creative)*
Jim May *(Acct Mgr)*
Sarah Knight *(Mgr-PR)*
Mimi Brodt *(Copywriter)*

Accounts:
GF + AgieCharmilles; Chicago, IL Machine Tools (EDM & High Speed Milling); 1990
MSC Industrial Supply; Melville, NY Industrial Supplies; 2009
Oerlikon Fairfield; West Lafayette, IN Gear & Drive Systems; 2003
ROHM Products of America Media Buying, Public Relations
Seco Tools Inc.; Troy, MI (Agency of Record) Integrated Marketing Services

DGWB

(Name Changed to Amusement Park)

DH

(Formerly Desautel Hege Communications)
315 W Riverside Ste 200, Spokane, WA 99201
Tel.: (509) 444-2350
Fax: (509) 444-2354
E-Mail: hello@wearedh.com
Web Site: wearedh.com

Employees: 14
Year Founded: 1996

Agency Specializes In: Advertising, Brand Development & Integration, Collateral, Communications, Crisis Communications, Direct Response Marketing, Email, Event Planning & Marketing, Exhibit/Trade Shows, Government/Political, Identity Marketing, International, Media Planning, Media Relations, Media Training, Print, Public Relations, Radio, Strategic Planning/Research, T.V., Web (Banner Ads, Pop-ups, etc.)

James M. Desautel *(Founder & Partner)*
Michelle Hege *(Pres & CEO)*
Cher Desautel *(Partner)*
Sara Johnston *(Partner)*
Andrei Mylroie *(Partner)*
Lisa Cargill *(Sr Acct Dir)*
Sara Desautel *(Acct Dir)*
Searri Shipman *(Dir-Acctg)*
Emily Easley *(Sr Acct Exec)*
Jessica Wade *(Acct Exec)*

Accounts:
Allegro
Avista Corp.
Bank of Fairfield
Confederated Tribes of the Colville Reservation
Eastern Washington University
Energy Northwest
PE Systems

DHX ADVERTISING, INC.

217 NE 8th Ave, Portland, OR 97232-2940
Tel.: (503) 872-9616
Fax: (503) 872-9618
E-Mail: dave@dhxadv.com
Web Site: www.dhxadv.com

E-Mail for Key Personnel:
President: dave@dhxadv.com
Creative Dir.: tim@dhxadv.com

Employees: 15
Year Founded: 1998

Agency Specializes In: Advertising, Affluent Market, Brand Development & Integration, Broadcast, Business Publications, Business-To-

Business, Cable T.V., Catalogs, Children's Market, Co-op Advertising, Collateral, College, Commercial Photography, Communications, Computers & Software, Consulting, Consumer Marketing, Consumer Publications, Content, Corporate Communications, Corporate Identity, Cosmetics, Digital/Interactive, Direct Response Marketing, E-Commerce, Education, Electronic Media, Email, Environmental, Event Planning & Marketing, Exhibit/Trade Shows, Financial, Government/Political, Graphic Design, Health Care Services, Hospitality, Industrial, Integrated Marketing, Internet/Web Design, Legal Services, Local Marketing, Logo & Package Design, Magazines, Market Research, Media Buying Services, Media Planning, Medical Products, New Product Development, Newspaper, Newspapers & Magazines, Outdoor, Over-50 Market, Package Design, Paid Searches, Planning & Consultation, Point of Purchase, Point of Sale, Print, Production, Production (Ad, Film, Broadcast), Production (Print), Public Relations, Publicity/Promotions, Radio, Real Estate, Retail, Search Engine Optimization, Social Marketing/Nonprofit, Social Media, Sponsorship, Sports Market, Strategic Planning/Research, T.V., Trade & Consumer Magazines, Transportation, Web (Banner Ads, Pop-ups, etc.)

Approx. Annual Billings: $2,200,000

Breakdown of Gross Billings by Media: Collateral: $250,000; Comml. Photography: $110,000; Consulting: $275,000; D.M.: $330,000; Exhibits/Trade Shows: $110,000; Newsp. & Mags.: $420,000; Point of Purchase: $110,000; Pub. Rels.: $50,000; Radio & T.V.: $400,000; Worldwide Web Sites: $145,000

Tim Holmes *(Co-Owner)*
Tim Cobb *(Mng Dir & Dir-Creative)*
Brandon Lehor *(Dir-Art)*
Stefanie Week *(Mgr-PR & Social Media)*
Danyel O'Neil *(Client Svc Dir)*

Accounts:
Acquisitions Northwest; Portland, OR Merger & Acquisition Services; 2003
Area Floors; Portland, OR; 2008
Boydstun; Portland, OR Trucks; 2002
Caddis Manufacturing; McMinnville, OR Float Tubes, Pet Products; 1995
Castellan Custom Furniture; Portland, OR Custom Furniture; 2007
CCB; Salem, OR Contractors Board; 2007
Classic Antique; Portland, OR Antique Furniture; 2004
Clow Roofing; Portland, OR Roofing Contractor; 2002
The Collins Co.; Portland, OR Lumber Company; 2001
Columbia Wire & Iron; Portland, OR Construction; 2000
Comotiv Systems; Portland, OR Software Developer; 2006
DeWils; Vancouver, WA Kitchen Cabinets; 1994
Donate Life Northwest; Portland, OR Organ Tissue & Donation; 1999
Doubletree Hotel; Portland, OR Hospitality; 2006
ESCI; Wilsonville, OR Consulting Firm; 2003
General Sheet Metal; Clackamas, OR HVAC Services; 2007
Genius Rollerscreens; Portland, OR Retractable Screens; 2003
IMAP; Portland, OR M&A Association; 2002
Informal Education Products; OR Children's Toy Catalog; 2000
The Joinery; Portland, OR Handcrafted Furniture; 2004
Mosaik Design; Portland, OR Home Remodeling Services; 2003
Neurocom; Portland, OR Fitness Equipment; 1995
Nisbet Oyster Co.; Bay Center, WA Oyster Products; 1999
Pacific Pride; Salem, OR Cardlock Services; 2004
Pacific Technical; Portland, OR High Tech Equipment; 2007
Package Containers; Canby, OR Paper & Plastic Bags; 2008
Portland Marble Works; Portland, OR Marble & Granite; 2007
Portland Spirit; Portland, OR Illustrated Children's Book; 2007
Quality Concrete; Albany, OR Concrete; 2002
R&R Textiles; Portland, OR Textiles; 2002
Shorebank Pacific; Ilwaco, WA Banking Products; 1999
Silverton Hospital; Silverton, OR Healthcare; 2007
Stevens Printing; Portland, OR Commercial Printing; 2006
Stevens Water Monitoring; Beaverton, OR Water Monitoring Equipment; 2000
Terwilliger Plaza; Portland, OR Retirement Living; 2007
Thrive Aesthetics & Anti-Aging; Portland, OR Skin, Anti-Aging & Weight Loss Services; 2008
Wellspring Medical Center; Woodburn, OR Health & Wellness; 2006
Willamette University - Law School; Salem, OR Law School; 2007
Willamette University - MBA; Salem, OR Graduate School; 2007

DIAL HOUSE

743 Clementina St, San Francisco, CA 94103
Tel.: (415) 546-6500
Fax: (415) 546-6512
E-Mail: info@dialhouse.org
Web Site: www.dialhouse.org

Employees: 15
Year Founded: 2001

Agency Specializes In: Advertising, Communications, Consumer Marketing, Fashion/Apparel, High Technology, Household Goods, Luxury Products, Mobile Marketing, Newspapers & Magazines, Print, Radio, T.V., Viral/Buzz/Word of Mouth

Alex Wipperfurth *(Partner)*

Accounts:
Diageo USA Red Stripe; 2006
Mondelez Cadbury

DIALOG DIRECT

(Formerly Budco Creative Services)
13700 Oakland Ave, Highland Park, MI 48203
Tel.: (313) 957-5100
Fax: (313) 957-5522
Toll Free: (888) BUDCO-40
E-Mail: sales@dialog-direct.com
Web Site: www.dialog-direct.com

E-Mail for Key Personnel:
President: garry_cole@budco.com
Public Relations: paula_biskup@budco.com

Employees: 25
Year Founded: 1982

Agency Specializes In: Advertising, Automotive, Brand Development & Integration, Business-To-Business, Collateral, Communications, Consumer Marketing, Corporate Identity, Direct Response Marketing, E-Commerce, Electronic Media, Event Planning & Marketing, Food Service, Graphic Design, Information Technology, Internet/Web Design, Local Marketing, Logo & Package Design, Merchandising, Pharmaceutical, Point of Purchase, Print, Real Estate, Restaurant, Retail, Sales Promotion, Telemarketing

Approx. Annual Billings: $12,000,000

Michael Pavan *(Chief Sls Officer-Mktg Solutions)*
Thom Gulock *(Exec Dir-Creative)*
Steve Gough *(Dir-Sls)*
John Gregory *(Dir-IT Application Dev)*

Accounts:
DenteMax
Disney
General Motors
Goodyear
HAP
Honeywell Bendix
Infinity
J&L Industrial Supply
Johnson & Johnson
McNeil Consumer & Specialty Pharmaceuticals
Nissan
Northwest Airlines, Inc.
OnStar
Pernod Ricard UK
Procter & Gamble
Qwest
TAP Pharmaceuticals
UPS

THE DIALOG MARKETING GROUP

908 1/2 Congress Ave, Austin, TX 78701
Tel.: (512) 697-9425
Fax: (512) 828-6848
E-Mail: LetsChat@DialogGroup.com
Web Site: dialoggroup.com/

Year Founded: 2003

Agency Specializes In: Advertising, Brand Development & Integration, Business-To-Business, Collateral, Communications, Consumer Marketing, Corporate Identity, Digital/Interactive, Direct Response Marketing, E-Commerce, Education, Electronic Media, Gay & Lesbian Market, High Technology, Information Technology, Internet/Web Design, Magazines, Outdoor, Planning & Consultation, Point of Purchase, Point of Sale, Print, Strategic Planning/Research, T.V., Telemarketing

Approx. Annual Billings: $1,000,000

Bob Gutermuth *(Founder & Pres)*
Robert Linderman *(Mng Dir)*
Aldor Lanctot *(COO)*
Julie Hutchinson *(Head-Practice-Sls & Elite Performance Trng)*
David Martino *(Exec Creative Dir)*
Miquela Campos-Trone *(Acct Supvr)*
Lauren Unser *(Acct Supvr)*
Sean M. Dineen *(Sr Writer)*

Accounts:
AMD
Dell
HP
Synapse Wireless

DIAMOND MERCKENS HOGAN

1505 Genessee Ste 300, Kansas City, MO 64102
Tel.: (816) 471-4364
E-Mail: info@dmhadv.com
Web Site: www.dmhadv.com

Year Founded: 2007

Agency Specializes In: Advertising, Brand Development & Integration, Digital/Interactive, Social Media

Paul Diamond *(Partner)*
Sean Hogan *(Partner)*
Brian Merckens *(Partner)*
Tory Knappenberger *(Sr Dir-Art)*
Tanya Hoffman Stevens *(Acct Dir)*
Brandi Dreiling *(Dir-Media)*
Rob Mitchell *(Dir-Art)*

Andrea Morris *(Dir-Art)*
West Valentine *(Assoc Dir-Creative)*
David Martin *(Sr Acct Mgr)*
Sam Logan *(Asst Acct Mgr)*

Accounts:
Ascend Learning LLC
Barbri
Premium Nutritional Products, Inc. Zupreem

DIAZ & COOPER ADVERTISING INC
9200 So Dadeland Blvd Ste 209, Miami, FL 33156
Tel.: (305) 670-2004
Web Site: www.diazcooper.com

Year Founded: 2001

Agency Specializes In: Advertising, Brand Development & Integration, Digital/Interactive, Internet/Web Design

Otmara Diaz-Cooper *(Pres)*
Todd Cooper *(VP & Dir-Creative)*
Ryan Dalisay *(Sr Dir-Art)*
Michelle Artimez *(Assoc Acct Supvr)*

Accounts:
Azamara Club Cruises
Banyan Health Systems

DIBONA, BORNSTEIN & RANDOM, INC.
(Name Changed to Hatch Marketing)

DICKS + NANTON AGENCY, LLC
520 N Orlando Ave Apt 2, Winter Park, FL 32789-7317
Tel.: (800) 980-1626
Fax: (407) 386-6866
Toll Free: (800) 980-1626
Web Site: www.celebritybrandingagency.com

Agency Specializes In: Business-To-Business, Environmental, Local Marketing, Multimedia, Search Engine Optimization, Strategic Planning/Research, Web (Banner Ads, Pop-ups, etc.)

Nick Nanton *(CEO)*
Jw Dicks *(Partner)*

Accounts:
America's PremierExperts, LLC.
ASREOS.com
Lucky Buys Yucky Houses
Push Button Productions LLC
The Real Estate Junkie
Super Slow Zone
Yomagination Wellness & Education

DIESTE
1999 Bryan St Ste 2700, Dallas, TX 75201
Tel.: (214) 259-8000
Fax: (214) 259-8040
E-Mail: info@dieste.com
Web Site: www.dieste.com

Employees: 130
Year Founded: 1995

National Agency Associations: AAF-AHAA

Agency Specializes In: Advertising, Advertising Specialties, Automotive, Bilingual Market, Brand Development & Integration, Broadcast, Cable T.V., Collateral, Consulting, Consumer Marketing, Direct Response Marketing, Entertainment, Event Planning & Marketing, Fashion/Apparel, Financial, Health Care Services, Hispanic Market, Internet/Web Design, Local Marketing, Logo & Package Design, Magazines, Media Buying Services, New Product Development, Newspaper, Newspapers & Magazines, Out-of-Home Media, Outdoor, Pharmaceutical, Point of Purchase, Point of Sale, Print, Production, Radio, Restaurant, Retail, Sales Promotion, Sponsorship, T.V., Teen Market, Transportation, Travel & Tourism

Breakdown of Gross Billings by Media: Collateral: 1%; D.M.: 10%; Internet Adv.: 3%; Network T.V.: 32%; Newsp. & Mags.: 7%; Outdoor: 5%; Promos.: 8%; Radio: 10%; Spot T.V.: 24%

Tony Dieste *(Chm)*
Carla Eboli *(CMO)*
Francisco Arranz Amaya *(Sr Dir-Art)*
Giovanni Villamar *(Grp Acct Dir-Brand Leadership)*
Laura Hinguanzo-Andrade *(Dir-Agency Ops)*
Damian Nunez *(Assoc Dir-Creative)*
Jim Wegerbauer *(Chief Idea Officer)*

Accounts:
Borden Dairy Brand Awareness, Brand Strategy, Creative, Digital, Greek Yogurt Smoothies, LALA (US Agency of Record), Media Planning, Yogurt Smoothies
New-Dallas Pets Alive Dallas Pets Alive Adoptable Trends
New-Dallas Vintage Toys
Gillette
Goya Foods Inc Brand Strategy, Creative, Media Planning
Hershey's; Hershey, PA Ice Breakers & Hershey Bar; 2007

DIETRICHDIRECT, LLC
15 High St, Kingfield, ME 04947-4275
Tel.: (800) 798-4572
Toll Free: (800) 798-4572
E-Mail: sales@dietrich-direct.com
Web Site: www.dietrich-direct.com

Employees: 2

Agency Specializes In: Business-To-Business, Consumer Marketing, Direct Response Marketing, Print

Approx. Annual Billings: $750,000

Breakdown of Gross Billings by Media: D.M.: $750,000

Kyle William Dietrich *(Founder & Pres)*

DIFFERENT PERSPECTIVE
201 S Orange Ave Ste 890, Orlando, FL 32801
Tel.: (407) 226-9774
Web Site: www.dppad.com

Year Founded: 2004

Agency Specializes In: Advertising, Brand Development & Integration, Internet/Web Design, Print, Social Media

Hugo Azzolini *(Pres)*
Priscilla Azzolini *(Partner & Dir-Comm)*
Greg Ezell *(Dir-Bus Dev)*
Phuong Nguy *(Copywriter)*

Accounts:
Bailey
IDA Express
Moreno & Moreno

DIGICRE8TIVE INC
1900 Okeechobee Blvd Ste C-3, Wellington, FL 33409
Tel.: (855) 344-4669
E-Mail: info@digicre8tive.com
Web Site: www.digicre8tive.com

Year Founded: 2010

Agency Specializes In: Advertising, Digital/Interactive, Graphic Design, Internet/Web Design, Print, Radio

Craig Faulds *(Mng Partner)*
Adrian Puerta *(Mng Partner)*

Accounts:
Kessler International

DIGILANT
(Formerly Adnetik)
100 North Washington St Ste 502, Boston, MA 02114
Tel.: (617) 849-6900
Fax: (617) 849-6920
E-Mail: usinfo@digilant.com
Web Site: www.digilant.com/

Year Founded: 2008

Agency Specializes In: Advertising, Digital/Interactive, Mobile Marketing

Don Epperson *(Founder/CEO-ISP Digital & Chm)*
Ricky McClellen *(CTO)*
Kim Dalzell Riedell *(Sr VP-Product & Mktg)*
Sanjay Pothen *(Mng Dir-US)*
Todd Heger *(VP-Adv Sls Mgmt, Programmatic Media Buying & Digital Media)*
Kris Parker *(Acct Dir-Natl)*
Karen Moked *(Dir-Mktg)*
John Randolph *(Dir-Bus Dev-Programmatic)*

Accounts:
Telco Industry Telecommunication Services

DIGIPOWERS, INC.
475 Park Ave S, New York, NY 10016
Tel.: (212) 389-2033
Web Site: www.digipowers.com

Employees: 10
Year Founded: 2008

Agency Specializes In: Affiliate Marketing, Branded Entertainment, Broadcast, Business Publications, Co-op Advertising, Digital/Interactive, Direct Response Marketing, Electronic Media, Email, Game Integration, Mobile Marketing, Paid Searches, Production, Social Media, T.V., Viral/Buzz/Word of Mouth

Julia Miller *(CEO)*
Rolf Kaiser *(CTO)*
Alex Borodsky *(VP-Tech Dev)*
Jacob Waldman *(Designer-Front End Engineer)*

Accounts:
NBC The Biggest Loser
Sony Playstation

DIGITAL BRAND ARCHITECTS
133 W 19th St 4th Fl, New York, NY 10011
Tel.: (212) 776-1790
Web Site: thedigitalbrandarchitects.com

Employees: 30
Year Founded: 2010

Agency Specializes In: Brand Development & Integration, Content, Digital/Interactive, Event Planning & Marketing, Media Relations, Public Relations, Social Media, Strategic Planning/Research

Raina Penchansky *(Co-Founder & Chief Strategy Officer)*
Kendra Bracken-Ferguson *(Co-Founder & COO)*

Karen Robinovitz *(Co-Founder & Chief Creative Officer)*
Vanessa Flaherty *(VP-Mgmt)*
Reesa Lake *(VP-Brand Dev)*
Vanessa Perry *(VP-Bus Dev)*
Kimberly Barbosa *(Mgr-Media Div)*

Accounts:
7 For All Mankind
American Express
Ann Taylor
Beats Music
Bed Bath & Beyond
Brian Atwood
Brooklyn Art Museum
Calypso
Chico's
Claire's
Cole Haan
Dress Barn
Elie Tahari
eos
Estee Lauder
Express
The Forum
Giles & Brother
Gucci
Hasbro
Juicy Couture
Kenneth Cole
Luxottica Group
LVMH
Maurices
Mercedes-Benz
Modus Man
Mont Blanc
Nine West
Plukka
Ralph Lauren
Revolve Clothing
Roxy
Starwood Hotels & Resorts
Stuart Weitzman
Swarovski
Tiffany & Co.
Tommy Hilfiger
Tory Burch
Vaseline
VH-1
Victoria's Secret
Vince
White House Black Market
World Gold Council
Young Fabulous & Broke

DIGITAL BRAND EXPRESSIONS
101 Morgan Ln Ste 203B, Plainsboro, NJ 8536
Tel.: (609) 688-8558
Toll Free: (866) 651-6767
Web Site: www.digitalbrandexpressions.com

Year Founded: 2001

Agency Specializes In: Advertising, Public Relations, Search Engine Optimization, Social Media

Veronica Fielding *(Pres & CEO)*
Sharyn Rached *(Client Svcs Dir)*
Marc Engelsman *(Dir-Strategy & Analytics)*
Christine Lagana *(Assoc Dir-Digital Program Ops)*
Maggie Landis *(Assoc Dir)*
Joe Goodlad *(Sr Mgr-Search & Analytics)*
Hannah Bridge *(Mgr-Digital Content)*
Bethany Frank *(Specialist-Digital Engagement)*
Shahira Singh *(Acct Exec)*

Accounts:
Q Center
Slingo, Inc.

DIGITAL EDGE
(Formerly Smith & Surrency, LLC)
10161 Centurion Pkwy N, Jacksonville, FL 32256
Tel.: (904) 619-2714
E-Mail: info@digitaledge.marketing
Web Site: digitaledge.marketing/

Year Founded: 2011

Agency Specializes In: Advertising, Brand Development & Integration, Collateral, Content, Digital/Interactive, Graphic Design, Internet/Web Design, Print, Social Media

Mya Surrency *(CMO & Principal)*
Shirley Smith *(Principal & Chief Creative Officer)*
Stephanie Schaeffer *(Dir-Integrated Media Buying & Strategy)*
Courtney Godwin *(Mgr-Interactive Media)*
Lauren Holstein *(Strategist-Content & Social Media)*
Robert Kemp *(Sr Designer-Interactive)*

Accounts:
Community First Credit Union

DIGITAL HERETIX
9171 E Bell Rd, Scottsdale, AZ 85260
Tel.: (480) 360-4434
Web Site: www.digitalheretix.com

Year Founded: 2003

Agency Specializes In: Affiliate Marketing, Digital/Interactive, Electronic Media, Email, Local Marketing, Mobile Marketing, Multimedia, Paid Searches, Promotions, Search Engine Optimization, Social Media, Web (Banner Ads, Pop-ups, etc.)

Joe Sinkwitz *(Principal)*

Accounts:
Automobile.com Automobile Insurance
Life Vest Advisors Financial Products

THE DIGITAL INNOVATIONS GROUP
4615 W Broad St Ste 121, Richmond, VA 23230
Tel.: (804) 377-6070
Fax: (804) 377-6074
Web Site: www.digcreative.com

Agency Specializes In: Advertising, Business Publications, Internet/Web Design

Kate Dunn *(CEO)*

Accounts:
Blue Tape
DeFoggi Development & Construction Construction Services
Digital Innovations Group
Diji Integrated Press
First Market Bank
Mulligan's Sports Grille Sports
Rainbow Station
Simek Custom Homes
St. Andrew's School
University of Richmond

DIGITAL KITCHEN
1114 E Pike St 3rd Fl, Seattle, WA 98122
Tel.: (206) 267-0400
Fax: (206) 267-0401
E-Mail: info@thisisdk.com
Web Site: thisisdk.com/

Employees: 120
Year Founded: 1995

Agency Specializes In: Sponsorship

Revenue: $5,000,000

Matt Mulder *(Exec Dir-Creative)*
Demetre Arges *(Dir-Creative)*
William Byrne *(Dir-Comm)*
Soojin Hong *(Assoc Dir-Creative)*
Sabrina Delaney *(Assoc Mgr-Mktg)*
Molly Dilmore *(Acct Supvr)*
Steve Krause *(Assoc Producer)*
Keri Zierler *(Assoc Creative Dir)*

Accounts:
AT&T
Brooks Running Company Content & Web Elements, Experiential, Social Media
The Cosmopolitan of Las Vegas Cosmopolitan Digital Experience
Estee Lauder
Los Angeles World Airports
Microsoft
Paramount Pictures TRANSFORMERS: DARK OF THE MOON Augmented Reality App
Sierra Nevada Branding, Website
Stanley Campaign: "Interactive Piano"
Starbucks
US Census
Whole Foods Market

DIGITAL MEDIA MANAGEMENT
8444 Wilshire Blvd 5th Fl, Beverly Hills, CA 90211
Tel.: (323) 378-6505
E-Mail: press@digitalmediamanagement.com
Web Site: www.digitalmediamanagement.com

Agency Specializes In: Advertising, Internet/Web Design, Social Media

Luigi Picarazzi *(Founder, Pres & CEO)*
Adam Reynolds *(VP)*

Accounts:
New-Elizabeth Banks
New-Nicole Kidman

DIGITAL NET AGENCY, INC.
PO Box 827, Dallas, PA 18612
Tel.: (866) 362-1275
E-Mail: info@digitalnetagency.com
Web Site: www.digitalnetagency.com

Year Founded: 2012

Agency Specializes In: Advertising, Search Engine Optimization, Social Media

Aaron Baker *(Founder & CEO)*
Christopher Graham *(COO)*
Samantha Morris *(VP-Performance Mktg)*
Tara Watson *(Dir-Affiliate)*
Steve Weber *(Dir-SEO & Social Media)*
Kaitlin Kochie *(Acct Mgr-Display & Social Media)*
Justin C. Ash *(Mgr-SEO)*
Shannon Mullery *(Strategist-SEO)*
Elizabeth Stahl *(Coord-Affiliate)*

Accounts:
Tarte Cosmetics

DIGITAL OPERATIVE INC.
3990 Old Town Ave, San Diego, CA 92110
Tel.: (619) 795-0630
E-Mail: info@digitaloperative.com
Web Site: www.digitaloperative.com

Year Founded: 2008

Agency Specializes In: Advertising, Digital/Interactive, Market Research

B. J. Cook *(Co-Founder & CEO)*
Adam Levenson *(Co-Founder & CTO)*

Dave LaSorte *(VP-Bus Dev)*
Daniel Ginn *(Dir-Tech)*
Eric Hanser *(Dir-Strategy & Plng)*
Alvaro Martinez Esteve *(Dir-Digital Mktg)*
Nikki Johnson *(Mgr-Agency Mktg)*
Rick Gray *(Sr Designer-Visual)*

Accounts:
7 Diamonds
NBC Universal, Inc.
RockeTalk Inc.
Sport Science USA
SurePayroll, Inc.
Surfrider San Diego
Tokuyama Dental

DIGITAL PULP
220 E 23rd St Ste 900, New York, NY 10010
Tel.: (212) 679-0676
Fax: (212) 679-6217
E-Mail: ron@digitalpulp.com
Web Site: www.digitalpulp.com

Employees: 20
Year Founded: 1996

Agency Specializes In: Digital/Interactive, E-Commerce, Internet/Web Design

Ron Fierman *(Pres, CEO & Partner)*
Brian Loube *(Partner & Mng Dir)*
Sarah Blecher *(Partner & Dir-User Experience)*
Gene Lewis *(Partner & Dir-Creative)*
Christopher Daly *(Dir-User Experience)*
Katherine Vidal *(Dir-Art)*

Accounts:
Bausch & Lomb Interactive
Child Fund International
Dartmouth College Interactive
H. Bloom
Harvard Law School
Harvard University - John F. Kennedy School of Government
IEEE
Jack Kent Cooke
Manaba
Mikimoto (America) Co. Ltd.
NRDC
NYU Stern
Quest Diagnostics
Rockefeller University Press
United Continental Holdings
The Urban Institute Interactive
Visiting Nurse Service of New York Interactive

DIGITAL SURGEONS LLC
1175 State St Ste 219, New Haven, CT 06510
Tel.: (203) 672-6201
Fax: (203) 785-0201
E-Mail: info@digitalsurgeons.com
Web Site: www.digitalsurgeons.com

Year Founded: 2004

Agency Specializes In: Advertising, Brand Development & Integration, Content, Digital/Interactive, E-Commerce, Media Buying Services, Media Planning, Media Training, Social Media, Sponsorship

David Salinas *(Co-Founder & CEO)*
Peter Sena, II *(Co-Founder & Exec Creative Dir)*
Robert Lasky *(Mng Dir)*
Bj Kito *(VP-Bus Dev)*
Tom Miller *(VP-Res & Analytics)*
Rob Kurfehs *(Dir-Creative Strategy)*
Mark Myrick *(Dir-Creative)*
Aaron Sherrill *(Dir-Interactive)*
Jacquelyn Schroder *(Acct Mgr)*
Hannah Rose Pieragostini *(Designer)*

Accounts:
Barneys New York, Inc. Gaga's Workshop
Unilever Brand Strategy, Digital, Nexxus Salon Hair Care

DIGITAS HEALTH
100 Penn Square E 11th Fl, Philadelphia, PA 19107
Tel.: (215) 545-4444
Fax: (215) 545-4440
E-Mail: info@digitashealth.com
Web Site: www.digitashealth.com

Employees: 300
Year Founded: 1990

National Agency Associations: 4A's

Agency Specializes In: Direct Response Marketing, Health Care Services, Internet/Web Design, Pharmaceutical, Sponsorship

Len Dolce *(CFO)*
Matt McNally *(Pres-Publicis Health Media)*
Susan Manber *(Exec VP-Brand Strategy & Plng)*
Collette Douaihy *(Sr VP & Grp Dir-Creative)*
Mark Nolan *(Sr VP & Grp Dir-Creative)*
Michael Leis *(Sr VP-Social Strategy-Emerging Technologies-Philadelphia)*
Norman Alger *(VP & Grp Dir-Creative)*
Ann Hazan *(VP & Grp Dir-Acct Plng)*
Cheryl Horsfall *(VP & Grp Dir-Creative)*
Geoff McCleary *(VP & Grp Dir-Mobile Strategy & Innovation)*
Zachary Lowe *(VP & Dir-Media)*
Buzz Miller *(VP & Dir-Creative)*
Katherine Shaughness *(VP & Dir-Mktg)*
David Verdon *(VP & Dir-Creative)*
Patrick Johnson *(VP-Creative)*
Cara Levinson *(VP-Acct Plng)*
Greg Lewis *(Exec Dir-New Bus-Digitas Health LifeBrands)*
Michael Goodman *(Media Dir)*
Marc Arbeit *(Dir-Media)*
Nicole Bradley *(Dir-Mktg)*
Mark Pappas *(Dir-Search Mktg)*
Melissa Seabright *(Dir-Media)*
Eric DeLash *(Assoc Dir-Media)*
Lauren Green *(Assoc Dir-Media)*
Wayne Hiller *(Assoc Dir-Media)*
Alexa Rola *(Assoc Dir-Media)*
Pamela Hiddeman *(Mgr-Acct Plng-Digitas Health LifeBrands)*
Thomas Kropp *(Mgr-Paid Search)*
Jeff Olivo *(Mgr-Mktg)*
Sophia Moriarty *(Assoc Mgr-Comm)*
Heather Brady *(Supvr-Media)*
Amanda Kapsales *(Supvr-Media)*
Kiersten Ryan *(Supvr-Digital Media)*
Adam Kirsch *(Sr Analyst-Strategy & Analytics)*
Brittany Besier *(Media Planner)*
Samuel Gean *(Media Planner)*
Brett Holland *(Media Planner)*
Marlee Kattler *(Media Planner)*
Rebecca Krasley *(Media Planner)*
Taylor Moser *(Media Planner)*
Ali Pluck *(Media Planner)*
Suzanne Davis *(Assoc Media Planner)*
Michael Lupo *(Assoc Media Planner)*
Mariel Marinelli *(Assoc Media Planner)*

Accounts:
APP Pharmaceuticals, Inc.
AstraZeneca ARIMIDEX, Crestor, Pulmicort Respules
Bristol-Myers Squibb Campaign: "Me and My Depression"
Merck & Co., Inc.
Novo Nordisk
Pfizer
Roche
Sanofi Creative, Pasteur
New-TEDMED (Social Media Agency of Record)
Strategic Planning

DIGITASLBI
2001 The Embarcadero, San Francisco, CA 94133
Tel.: (404) 460-1010
Web Site: www.digitaslbi.com

National Agency Associations: 4A's

Agency Specializes In: Advertising, Brand Development & Integration, Digital/Interactive, Graphic Design, Logo & Package Design, Print, Sponsorship

Dave Marsey *(Mng Dir & Exec VP)*
Kammie Sulaiman *(Sr VP & Grp Acct Dir)*
John Tuchtenhagen *(Sr VP-Media)*
Larisa Johnson *(Assoc Dir-Media)*
Oliver Berbecaru *(Supvr-Media)*
Kendall Weikert *(Supvr-Media)*

Accounts:
eBay Inc.
Pandora Media Inc. (Lead Media Agency)
Taco Bell Corp. Digital Media Buying, Digital Media Planning, Mobile

DIGIWORKS MEDIA
304 Federal Rd Ste 310, Brookfield, CT 6804
Tel.: (813) 703-1010
E-Mail: info@digiworksmedia.com
Web Site: www.digiworksmedia.com

Agency Specializes In: Advertising, Broadcast, Graphic Design, Internet/Web Design, Media Planning, Print

George Hudak *(Pres)*

Accounts:
Rob Astorino

DIGNEY & COMPANY PUBLIC RELATIONS
1680 N Vine St Ste 1105, Hollywood, CA 90028
Tel.: (323) 993-3000
E-Mail: jerry@digneypr.com
Web Site: digneypr.com/

Agency Specializes In: Sports Market, Travel & Tourism

Jerry Digney *(Owner & Pres)*

Accounts:
The Bahamas
B.B. King Museum
Beverly Hills Hotel
Children's Diabetes Foundation
Chrysler Corporation
Columbia Pictures
Monaco Charity Film Festival
Northern Trust Bank
Sony/BMG
Taco Bell Corporation
Time Life, Inc.
Universal Studios Hollywood
WRIT Media Group, Inc. (Public Relations Agency of Record) Amiga Games, Influencer Engagement, Media Relations, Print, Retro Infinity

DILYON CREATIVE GROUP
2850 NW 79 Ave, Doral, FL 33122
Tel.: (305) 501-0353
E-Mail: info@dilyon.com
Web Site: www.dilyon.com

Year Founded: 2013

Agency Specializes In: Advertising, Brand Development & Integration, Collateral, Corporate Identity, Digital/Interactive, Internet/Web Design, Logo & Package Design, Print, Search Engine Optimization, Social Media

Mario de Leon *(Creative Dir)*

Accounts:
Green Life Miami
Miami Salsa Congress

DIMASSIMO GOLDSTEIN
(d/b/a DIGO Brands)
220 E 23rd St, New York, NY 10010
Tel.: (212) 253-7500
Fax: (646) 507-5850
E-Mail: lee@digobrands.com
Web Site: www.digobrands.com

E-Mail for Key Personnel:
President: markd@dimassimo.com

Employees: 75
Year Founded: 1996

National Agency Associations: DMA

Agency Specializes In: Brand Development & Integration, Business-To-Business, Collateral, Direct Response Marketing, Media Buying Services, Out-of-Home Media, Outdoor, Planning & Consultation, Radio, Sponsorship, T.V.

Revenue: $10,000,000

Mark Dimassimo *(CEO & Chief Creative Officer)*
Tom Christmann *(Chief Creative Officer)*
Marc Lefton *(Head-Growth Strategy & Brand Integration)*
Crystal Ballister *(Brand Dir-Readers Digest & Mediacom)*
Eric Emel *(Brand Dir)*
Andrew Bly *(Dir-Art)*
Alexandra Liu *(Planner-Brand)*

Accounts:
Chubb Insurance Campaign: "Insurance Against Regret"
Double Cross Vodka
EverBank Creative, Media
Mediacom Cable Digital Creative, Media
Memorial Sloan-Kettering Cancer Center
National Jewish Health
OnDeck Capital
Pinnacle Entertainment L'Auberge Hotel and Casino
Reader's Digest
STS Tire & Auto
TradeStation
Weight Watchers

DIMENSION X MARKETING
1000 Clay Ave Ext, Jeannette, PA 15644-3466
Tel.: (724) 522-9990
Fax: (724) 522-9992
Web Site: www.dxdigitalmarketing.com

Employees: 10
Year Founded: 1994

Agency Specializes In: Brand Development & Integration, Business Publications, Business-To-Business, Collateral, Corporate Identity, Direct Response Marketing, Graphic Design, Industrial, Logo & Package Design, Magazines, Media Buying Services, Outdoor, Planning & Consultation, Strategic Planning/Research

Approx. Annual Billings: $1,000,000

Charles Matone, Jr. *(Co-Owner)*
Norman Wright, Jr. *(Pres & Chief Creative Officer)*

Accounts:
Artisan Plastic Surgery
Bacharach
Ceodeux
Frank's Auto Supermarket
ITSEN Closures
Nine Lives
Proscape

DIMON CREATIVE COMMUNICATION SERVICES
(Closed & Re-formed as Dimon Group LLC)

DIMON GROUP LLC
(Formerly Dimon Creative Communication Services)
2049 Chivers St, San Fernando, CA 91340
Tel.: (818) 635-5289
Fax: (818) 954-8916
E-Mail: johnd@dimongroup.com

Employees: 6
Year Founded: 1955

Agency Specializes In: Business-To-Business, Financial, Health Care Services

John Dimon *(Pres & CEO)*

Accounts:
BBCN Bank
California Business Bank
Citadel Environmental Services
Community Commerce Bank
National Bank of California
Pacific National Group
Santa Clarita Bank
Trak Services
Tristar Risk Management
USC University Hospital

DIO, LLC
3111 Farmtrail Rd, York, PA 17406
Tel.: (717) 764-8288
Fax: (717) 764-1415
E-Mail: contact@diousa.com
Web Site: www.diousa.com

Employees: 17

Agency Specializes In: Advertising, Brand Development & Integration, Graphic Design, Public Relations

David W. Pridgen *(Pres)*
Susanne Jewell *(VP-Ops & HR)*
David Fortney *(Dir-IT & Controller)*
Lee Karon *(Dir-Media-Dio Strategic Mktg)*
Elizabeth Shaffer *(Dir-Creative & Art)*
Alyssa Hinger *(Acct Exec)*

Accounts:
Adhesives Research/ARmark
Ashley Stewart Women's Clothing
CGA Law Firm
ComCast
Eastern Alliance
Freedom Toyota Automobile
Geisinger Health Plan
Harrah's Casino
Homerite Home Improvement
Keystone Custom Homes
Northside Nissan
Penn Waste
Sheetz
Tait Towers
West Ashley Toyota
York Arts

DION MARKETING COMPANY
421 N 3rd St, Jacksonville Beach, FL 32250
Tel.: (904) 249-9784
Fax: (904) 246-0536
Web Site: www.dionmarketing.com

Agency Specializes In: Advertising, Brand Development & Integration, Graphic Design, Media Buying Services, Promotions, Public Relations, Social Media

Julie Dion *(Pres)*
Steven Meyer *(Mgr-Comm)*

Accounts:
Children of Fallen Patriots Foundation
Valor Academy of Jacksonville

DIRCKS ASSOCIATES
550 N Country Rd Ste A, Saint James, NY 11780-1427
Tel.: (631) 584-2274
Fax: (631) 584-2043
E-Mail: info@dircksny.com
Web Site: www.dircksny.com

E-Mail for Key Personnel:
President: david@dircksny.com

Employees: 15
Year Founded: 1995

National Agency Associations: Second Wind Limited

Agency Specializes In: Advertising, Bilingual Market, Brand Development & Integration, Broadcast, Business Publications, Business-To-Business, Cable T.V., Collateral, Communications, Consumer Marketing, Consumer Publications, Corporate Identity, Digital/Interactive, Direct Response Marketing, E-Commerce, Electronic Media, Entertainment, Event Planning & Marketing, Exhibit/Trade Shows, Fashion/Apparel, Financial, Food Service, Graphic Design, High Technology, Information Technology, Internet/Web Design, Logo & Package Design, Magazines, Merchandising, Newspaper, Newspapers & Magazines, Out-of-Home Media, Outdoor, Point of Purchase, Point of Sale, Print, Sports Market, Strategic Planning/Research, T.V., Teen Market, Telemarketing, Trade & Consumer Magazines, Travel & Tourism

Approx. Annual Billings: $14,000,000

Breakdown of Gross Billings by Media: Bus. Publs.: 5%; Collateral: 20%; Consumer Publs.: 5%; D.M.: 20%; Exhibits/Trade Shows: 2%; Internet Adv.: 10%; Logo & Package Design: 3%; Newsp.: 5%; Outdoor: 10%; Point of Purchase: 2%; Sls. Promo.: 3%; Transit: 5%; Worldwide Web Sites: 10%

David Dircks *(CEO)*

Accounts:
AARP
American Express
AOL Time Warner, Inc.; Dulles, VA
Bloomberg BusinessWeek
Charter
Computer Associates; Islandia, NY
Lowe's Companies Inc.; North Wilkesboro, NC
LowerMyBills.com
Lowes
Nikon
Oxford Industries; New York, NY
Oxmoor House; Birmingham, AL Country Living, Martha Stewart, Southern Living
PayPal

DIRECT ASSOCIATES
46 Rockland St, Natick, MA 01760
Tel.: (508) 393-8083

Fax: (508) 519-5858
E-Mail: results@directassociates.com
Web Site: www.directassociates.com

Employees: 8
Year Founded: 2004

Agency Specializes In: Direct Response Marketing, E-Commerce, Electronic Media, Internet/Web Design, Pets

Approx. Annual Billings: $2,000,000

Breakdown of Gross Billings by Media: D.M.: $2,000,000

Eileen Carew *(Founder)*
Susan Feeney *(Partner)*
Deanna Dolecki *(Sr VP-Bus & Client Strategy)*
David White *(VP-Sls)*
Jennifer Carney *(Dir-Design)*
Palmiero Diane Dvorak *(Acct Mgr)*

DIRECT CHOICE

480 E Swedesford Rd Ste 210, Wayne, PA 19087
Tel.: (610) 995-8201
Fax: (610) 995-2266
Toll Free: (866) 995-2111
E-Mail: hello@directchoiceinc.com
Web Site: www.directchoiceinc.com

Employees: 10
Year Founded: 1995

National Agency Associations: DMA

Agency Specializes In: Advertising, Affluent Market, Alternative Advertising, Below-the-Line, Bilingual Market, Brand Development & Integration, Business Publications, Business-To-Business, Cable T.V., Catalogs, Collateral, Computers & Software, Consulting, Consumer Goods, Consumer Marketing, Consumer Publications, Content, Corporate Communications, Cosmetics, Crisis Communications, Customer Relationship Management, Digital/Interactive, Direct Response Marketing, Direct-to-Consumer, E-Commerce, Electronic Media, Email, Financial, Guerilla Marketing, Health Care Services, Hispanic Market, In-Store Advertising, Information Technology, Integrated Marketing, Internet/Web Design, Logo & Package Design, Magazines, Media Buying Services, Media Planning, Mobile Marketing, Multimedia, New Product Development, New Technologies, Newspaper, Out-of-Home Media, Outdoor, Over-50 Market, Package Design, Pharmaceutical, Point of Purchase, Print, Production, RSS (Really Simple Syndication), Retail, Sales Promotion, Search Engine Optimization, Seniors' Market, Social Marketing/Nonprofit, Social Media, Strategic Planning/Research, Technical Advertising, Telemarketing, Tween Market, Web (Banner Ads, Pop-ups, etc.)

Nick Lanzi *(Pres & CEO)*
Nancy Foy *(VP-Acct Svcs)*
Scott Mclaughlin *(VP-Production Mgmt)*
Emily Plummer *(Coord-Production)*

Accounts:
Biogen Idec Alprolix, Eloctate, Tysabri; 2010
Blue Cross Blue Shield of North Carolina Age-in, Individual/Consumer, Medicare; 2007
Independence Blue Cross Individual/Consumer, Small Group; 2005
Luxottica Retail EyeMed, ILORI, LensCrafters, Pearle Vision; 2008
Roche Diagnostics Accu Chek Insulin Meter, Accu Chek Test Strips; 1997
SCA TENA Adult Incontinence Products; 2013
Yamaha Motorcycles On-Road and Off-Road; 2012

DIRECT MARKETING CENTER

21171 S Western Ave Ste 260, Torrance, CA 90501-3449
Tel.: (310) 212-5727
Fax: (310) 212-5773
E-Mail: inquire@directmarketingcenter.com
Web Site: www.directmarketingcenter.net

Employees: 25
Year Founded: 1985

Agency Specializes In: Advertising, Advertising Specialties, Brand Development & Integration, Business Publications, Business-To-Business, Consulting, Consumer Marketing, Consumer Publications, Corporate Identity, Direct Response Marketing, E-Commerce, Exhibit/Trade Shows, Financial, Graphic Design, Health Care Services, Infomercials, Integrated Marketing, Internet/Web Design, Investor Relations, Logo & Package Design, Magazines, Multimedia, New Product Development, Newspapers & Magazines, Paid Searches, Print, Production, Radio, Sales Promotion, Search Engine Optimization, Social Media, T.V., Trade & Consumer Magazines, Travel & Tourism, Women's Market

Approx. Annual Billings: $24,793,010

Breakdown of Gross Billings by Media: Consulting: 4%; D.M.: 50%; E-Commerce: 10%; Newsp. & Mags.: 4%; Print: 3%; T.V.: 3%; Trade & Consumer Mags.: 3%; Trade Shows: 3%; Worldwide Web Sites: 20%

Craig Huey *(Pres)*

Accounts:
Agora; Baltimore, MD Publisher
Clearly Canadian
Forbes
Foundation for Economic Education
Frank W. Cawood & Associates; GA Health Books
God's World Publications; NC Christian Magazine
Health Alert; CA Newsletter
Hollywood Reporter Magazine
Horizon Management Services; CA Investment Service
Medlaw Publications
Metagenics, Inc.; CA Nutritional Supplements
Motley Fool
Permanent Portfolio Information; CA Mutual Funds
Phillips Publishing
Prudent Bear Fund; CA Mutual Funds
The Street, Inc.
True Religion
VectorVest, Inc.; OH Investment Software
Wall Street Digest; Sarasota, FL Stock Service

DIRECT MARKETING SOLUTIONS

8534 NE Alderwood Rd, Portland, OR 97220
Tel.: (503) 281-1400
Fax: (503) 249-5120
Toll Free: (800) 578-0848
E-Mail: msherman@teamdms.com
Web Site: www.teamdms.com

Employees: 200
Year Founded: 1982

Agency Specializes In: Business-To-Business, Consumer Marketing, Direct Response Marketing, Production

Approx. Annual Billings: $15,000,000

Steve Sherman *(Pres)*
Mike Sherman *(CEO)*
Steve Benke *(VP & Controller)*
Jeremy Bessire *(Dir-Creative Svcs)*

DIRECT PARTNERS

4755 Alla Rd, Marina Del Rey, CA 90292-6311
Tel.: (310) 482-4200
Fax: (310) 482-4201
E-Mail: sreed@directpartners.com
Web Site: www.directpartners.com

Employees: 100
Year Founded: 1994

Agency Specializes In: Direct Response Marketing, Sponsorship

Jerry McRuer *(Pres)*
Bradley Benton *(CTO)*
Chris Muldaur *(Sr VP-Media)*
Tiffany Corallo *(VP & Grp Acct Dir)*
Alexa Sundberg *(VP-Mktg)*
Loril Hirsch *(Dir-Brdcst)*
Jeff Coryell *(Assoc Dir-Media)*
Vu Dang *(Assoc Dir-Creative)*

Accounts:
Foster Farms Media Planning & Buying
Pedigree
Xoom

Branch

Direct Partners

555 Market St 16th Fl, San Francisco, CA 94105
Tel.: (415) 262-3000
Fax: (415) 262-3001
Web Site: www.directpartners.com

Employees: 30

Agency Specializes In: Advertising

Jerry McRuer *(Pres)*
Brad Benton *(CTO & Sr VP-Strategy)*
Chris Muldaur *(Sr VP-Media)*
Alexa Sundberg *(VP-Mktg)*
Thomas Ray *(Assoc Dir-Media-Digital)*

Accounts:
Sony BGI

DIRECT RESPONSE ACADEMY

140 Lotus Cir, Austin, TX 78737
Tel.: (512) 301-5900
Fax: (512) 301-7900
Web Site: www.directresponseacademy.com

E-Mail for Key Personnel:
Public Relations:
pat@directresonseacademy.com

Employees: 4
Year Founded: 1999

Agency Specializes In: Advertising, Advertising Specialties, Brand Development & Integration, Branded Entertainment, Cable T.V., Communications, Consulting, Consumer Goods, Consumer Marketing, Corporate Communications, Cosmetics, Digital/Interactive, Direct Response Marketing, Direct-to-Consumer, E-Commerce, Education, Electronic Media, Electronics, Email, Entertainment, Financial, Health Care Services, Household Goods, Identity Marketing, Infomercials, Integrated Marketing, Internet/Web Design, Media Buying Services, Media Planning, Media Training, Men's Market, Merchandising, Mobile Marketing, Multicultural, Multimedia, Over-50 Market, Pharmaceutical, Planning & Consultation, Podcasting, Product Placement, Production, Promotions, RSS (Really Simple Syndication), Radio, Retail, Sales Promotion, Search Engine Optimization, Seniors' Market, Sports Market, Stakeholders, Strategic Planning/Research, T.V., Teen Market, Telemarketing, Viral/Buzz/Word of

Mouth, Women's Market

Breakdown of Gross Billings by Media: Radio & T.V.: 100%

Greg Sarnow *(Founder & CEO)*

Accounts:
Deer Stags; New York, NY Shoes; 2006
E-Diets.com; Deerfield Beach, FL Home Meal Delivery; 2006
E-Lights.com; Northvale, NJ Lighting; 2007

DIRECT WEB ADVERTISING, INC.
1375 Gateway Blvd, Boynton Beach, FL 33426
Tel.: (954) 762-3405
Fax: (954) 762-3405
Toll Free: (877) 649-1535
E-Mail: pete@dwausa.com
Web Site: www.directwebadv.com

Employees: 12
Year Founded: 2002

National Agency Associations: DMA

Agency Specializes In: Above-the-Line, Advertising, Advertising Specialties, Affiliate Marketing, Affluent Market, Alternative Advertising, Automotive, Brand Development & Integration, Broadcast, Business-To-Business, Cable T.V., Consumer Goods, Consumer Marketing, Content, Digital/Interactive, Direct Response Marketing, Direct-to-Consumer, E-Commerce, Electronic Media, Email, Financial, Hispanic Market, Integrated Marketing, Internet/Web Design, Local Marketing, Market Research, Media Buying Services, Medical Products, Men's Market, Paid Searches, Pharmaceutical, Publicity/Promotions, Radio, Real Estate, Regional, Retail, Sales Promotion, Search Engine Optimization, T.V., Telemarketing, Travel & Tourism, Urban Market, Web (Banner Ads, Pop-ups, etc.)

Peter LaBella *(COO)*
Richard Anderson *(Sr Designer)*

Accounts:
EHealthInsurance.com
Loan Modification

DIRECTORY SERVICE BUREAU, LTD.
772 W Main St Ste 202, Lake Geneva, WI 53147
Tel.: (262) 248-6070
Fax: (262) 248-6775
E-Mail: dsbadm@dsb-ltd.com
Web Site: www.dsb-ltd.com

Employees: 12
Year Founded: 1979

National Agency Associations: YPA

Agency Specializes In: Advertising, Yellow Pages Advertising

Approx. Annual Billings: $9,000,000

Breakdown of Gross Billings by Media: Yellow Page Adv.: $9,000,000

Ann S. Anglin *(Pres & CEO)*

Branch

Directory Service Bureau, Ltd.
2401 Maple Ave, Paducah, KY 42001-2387
Mailing Address:
PO Box 1356, Paducah, KY 42002-1356
Tel.: (270) 444-6100
Fax: (270) 444-7423
Toll Free: (800) 635-0110
E-Mail: jpetterson@dsb-ltd.com
Web Site: www.dsb-ltd.com

Employees: 1
Year Founded: 1981

Agency Specializes In: Advertising, Yellow Pages Advertising

Jo Ann Petterson *(Mgr-Sls-Natl)*

DISCOVER MEDIAWORKS INC
5236 Hwy 70 W, Eagle River, WI 54521
Tel.: (715) 477-1500
Fax: (715) 477-1501
Web Site: www.discovermediaworks.com

Year Founded: 1988

Agency Specializes In: Advertising, Broadcast, Corporate Identity, Digital/Interactive

Greg Smith *(Mng Dir-Discover Wisconsin)*
Anthony Marz *(Mgr-Motion Media)*

Accounts:
Discover Wisconsin Campaign: "Discovering the Very Best of the Badger State"
Into the Outdoors Educational Services
Oconto County Economic Development Corporation Tourism Services
Renk Seed Campaign: "One Family", Campaign: "Trust is Earned"
The Roman Candle Pizzeria Campaign: "Online Ordering"

DISCOVER THE WORLD MARKETING
7020 E Acoma Dr, Scottsdale, AZ 85254
Tel.: (480) 707-5566
Fax: (480) 707-5575
E-Mail: info@discovertheworld.com
Web Site: www.discovertheworld.com

Employees: 50
Year Founded: 1981

Agency Specializes In: Advertising, Collateral, Consulting, Crisis Communications, Customer Relationship Management, E-Commerce, Email, High Technology, Internet/Web Design, Local Marketing, Print, Production, Radio, Recruitment, Regional, Strategic Planning/Research, T.V., Telemarketing

Jenny Adams *(CEO)*
Todd Johnson *(Gen Counsel)*
Sue Cherrier *(VP-Mktg-USA Div)*
Rob Cope *(Sr Dir-Fin)*
Brenda Selim *(Mgr-Mktg & Design)*

Accounts:
Aircalin
Alitalia
Destination Travel International
Eurolot Marketing, Sales
Gulf Air
IBCS
New Caledonia Tourism
Seabourn Marketing & Sales
Spanair

DIVERSIFIED AGENCY SERVICES
437 Madison Ave, New York, NY 10022-7001
Tel.: (212) 415-3700
Fax: (212) 415-3530
E-Mail: getinfo@dasglobal.com
Web Site: www.dasglobal.com

National Agency Associations: 4A's

Agency Specializes In: Communications, Consumer Marketing

Sally Williams *(Global Pres-Bus Dev & Client Rels)*
Abaete Azevedo *(Pres-Latin America)*
Min Chang *(Pres-Asia Pacific)*
Emma Sergeant *(Pres-EMEA)*
Elizabeth Cornish *(Sr VP)*
Danny Berliner *(Assoc VP-Bus Dev)*

Agencies

Adelphi Eden Health Communications
488 Madison Ave, New York, NY 10022
Tel.: (646) 602-7060
Fax: (646) 602-7061
Web Site: www.adelphicommunications.com/

Agency Specializes In: Medical Products

Jeremy Hayes *(Vice Chm)*
Amy Abel *(Chief Comml Officer & Sr VP)*
Grahame Conibear *(Sr VP-Integrated Comm)*
Michelle Mcnamara *(Sr VP)*
Kim Lipczynski *(VP)*
Courtney Gold Alexander *(Sr Dir)*
Lauren Carroll *(Client Svcs Dir)*
Julia Calhoun *(Sr Project Dir)*

U30 Group, Inc.
6700 Baum Dr Ste 1, Knoxville, TN 37919
Tel.: (865) 525-4789
Fax: (865) 525-4780
E-Mail: theRights@u30.com
Web Site: www.u30.com

Agency Specializes In: Advertising Specialties

Janet Shoemaker *(Co-Founder & CEO)*
Ashley Shoemaker *(Pres & CEO)*
Cheryl Dages *(Sr VP-Field Svcs)*
Travis Lowe *(Sr VP-Client Svcs)*

Accounts:
4 Food
7-Eleven
Alcatel-Lucent
Allstate
AOL
AT&T
Balance Bar
BET
Bimbo
Birds Eye
Blockbuster
The Boppy Company
Borden
The Boston Beer Company
Boston Market
Brown-Forman
Burger King
Bush Brothers & Co
Cargill
Champion
Cingular
Clearview
Clorox
The Coca-Cola Company
CompUSA
Cumberland
Del Monte
DIY Network
Einstein Bros. Bagels
ESPN
Food Network
Friendly's
Frito-Lay
Gap
Glu Mobile
Grand Marnier
Grand Ole Opry

Hallmark
Hanesbrands
Hardee's
Hasbro
Hawaiian Punch
Heelys
The Hershey Co
HGTV
Hidden Valley
Hilton
HomeAway
Hooter's
Hormel
Ingersoll Rand
Intersport
Invisible Fence
Irwin Tools
Jewelry Television
Jockey
Johnsonville
KFC
Konami
Kraft
Levi Strauss & Co.
M&M/Mars
Marlin & Ray's
MillerCoors
Mitsubishi Motors
MTV
National Geographic
Newell Rubbermaid
Nickelodeon
Nike
Nissan
Nokia
Ocean Spray
Old Navy
Outback
PepsiCo
PetSafe
Pizza Hut
Post Cereals
Procter & Gamble
Red Robin Burger Works
Red Roof Inn
Reebok
RIVR Media
Ruby Tuesday
Samsung
SBC
SC Johnson
Sega
Southwest Airlines
Sprint
Starbucks
Sugar Inc.
Tabasco
Taco Bell
Taco Buena
TGI Friday's
Travel Channel
Tropicana
TurboChef
Tyson
Wonderbra
Worthington
The Wrigley Company
YM Magazine
Zatarain's

Cosine

239 Old Marleybone Road, London, NW1 5QT United Kingdom
Tel.: (44) 1844 296 700
E-Mail: info@cosine-group.com
Web Site: www.cosine-group.com

Agency Specializes In: Event Planning & Marketing, Promotions, Retail

Chris Olivier *(CEO)*
Nick Jones *(CEO-EMEA)*
Thomas Zhong *(CEO-China)*

Accounts:
Britvic
Carlsberg
Colgate-Palmolive
Danone
Diageo
Ferrero
htc
Johnson & Johnson
Kellogg's
LG
Nestle
P&G
Pepsico
Philip Morris
Sainsbury's
Unilever
Walmart

Adelphi Group Limited

Adelphi Mill Grimshaw Lane Bollington, Macclesfield, Cheshire SK10 5JB United Kingdom
Tel.: (44) 1 625 577233
Fax: (44) 1 625 575853
E-Mail: lifecyclesolutions@adelphigroup.com
Web Site: www.adelphigroup.com/index.php

Employees: 240
Year Founded: 1986

Agency Specializes In: Health Care Services

Stuart Cooper *(CEO)*
Chris Gray *(Mng Dir-Adelphi Comm)*
Richard Perry *(Dir-Dev)*

AgencyRx

200 Varick St 3rd Fl, New York, NY 10014
(See Separate Listing)

Alcone Marketing Group

4 Studebaker, Irvine, CA 92618-2012
(See Separate Listing)

AMCI

4755 Alla Rd Ste 1000, Marina Del Rey, CA 90292
Tel.: (310) 765-4100
Fax: (310) 822-1276
E-Mail: info@amciglobal.com
Web Site: www.amciglobal.com

Employees: 60

Agency Specializes In: Automotive, Communications

David Stokols *(Pres & CEO)*
Ian Beavis *(Chief Strategy Officer)*
Kevin Killip *(Exec VP)*
Shari Dunn *(VP-Production & Ops)*
Mike Kraus *(Exec Dir-Brand & Product Strategy)*
Kelly Sporich *(Grp Acct Dir-Western Area)*
Kimberly Maynard *(Mgr-Event & Producer-Road)*
Rebecca Sander *(Acct Dir)*
Devin Dilibero *(Dir-Creative)*
Caroline Moose *(Program Mgr & Acct Ops Mgr)*

Accounts:
Buick
Chevrolet
Dodge
GMC Hummer
Mazda
Mitsubishi
Pontiac
Toyota Scion

Beanstalk

220 E 42nd St 15th Fl, New York, NY 10017
(See Separate Listing)

Blue Current

Ste 1501 Cityplaza 4 12 Taikoo Wan Road, Taikoo Shing, Hong Kong, China (Hong Kong)
Tel.: (852) 2967 6770
Web Site: bluecurrentgroup.com

Agency Specializes In: Brand Development & Integration, Communications, Digital/Interactive, Public Relations, Search Engine Optimization, Social Media

James Hacking *(Sr VP)*
Chris Plowman *(Sr VP)*
Cheryl Pan *(Sr Acct Exec)*

Accounts:
Glomp!
GoPro

CAHG

225 N Michigan Ave, Chicago, IL 60601
(See Separate Listing)

The CDM Group

(Formerly Cline, Davis & Mann, Inc.)
200 Varick St 2nd Fl, New York, NY 10014
(See Separate Listing)

Chameleon PR

63-65 N Wharf Rd, 1st Floor, Bridge House, Paddington, London, W2 1LA United Kingdom
Tel.: (44) 20 7680 5500
Fax: (44) 20 7680 5555
Web Site: www.madebychameleon.com/

Employees: 14

National Agency Associations: AA

Agency Specializes In: Collateral, Communications, Consulting, High Technology, Public Relations, Social Media

Helen Holland *(Founder & Chm)*
Tom Berry *(CEO)*
Jeremy Williams *(Bus Dir)*
Jeremy Davis *(Dir-Digital Svcs)*
Karin O'Connor *(Dir-Creative & Strategic)*
Rajpreet Varaitch *(Acct Mgr)*

Accounts:
alldayPA Communications Strategy, Public Relations
Amnesty International
AnchorFree UK & EMEA PR
App Annie Communications, Public Relations
BBC Active
CashFac
Centiq
Citrix EMEA
Crussh Juice
DocuSign
ESRI (UK) Ltd.
FileMaker Traditional & Digital Media
Global Graphics
IFS School of Finance
Innovation Norway
Intec
Intellistream
Mach
Mozy
On365
Royal Parks Foundation Communications, Public Relations
Shelter Online Giving
UNICEF

Changing Our World
220 E 42nd St 5th Fl, New York, NY 10017
Tel.: (212) 499-0866
Fax: (212) 499-9075
E-Mail: info@changingourworld.com
Web Site: www.changingourworld.com

Employees: 100

Agency Specializes In: Social Marketing/Nonprofit

Michael P. Hoffman *(Chm)*
Thomas Farrell *(Sr Mng Dir)*
Yelena Ilyazarov *(Sr Mng Dir)*
Maureen Flynn *(Mng Dir)*
James Kopp *(Mng Dir)*
Karen Matarazzo *(Mng Dir)*
Lyndsay Reville *(Mng Dir)*
Colleen M. Schmigel *(Mng Dir)*
Cassandra Thayer *(Mng Dir)*
Shawn Trahan *(Mng Dir)*
Jo Ann Zafonte *(Chief Admin Officer)*
Susan Raymond *(Exec VP)*

Accounts:
California State Parks Foundation
Christian Blind Mission (CBM)
Fashion Institute of Technology (FIT)
FedEx
MillerCoors
Molloy College
Vivendi

CLS Strategies
(Formerly Chlopak, Leonard, Schechter & Associates)
1850 M St NW, Washington, DC 20036
Tel.: (202) 289-5900
Fax: (202) 289-4141
Web Site: www.clsstrategies.com/

Employees: 40

Agency Specializes In: Business-To-Business, Corporate Identity, Crisis Communications, Government/Political

Peter Schechter *(Owner)*
Robert Chlopak *(CEO)*
Brian Berry *(Partner)*
Juan Cortinas-Garcia *(Partner)*
DJ Carella *(Mng Dir)*
Laura Cilmi *(Mng Dir)*
Hilary Schmidt *(Mng Dir)*
Tom Carver *(Sr VP)*
Ray De Lorenzi *(Sr VP)*
Andrew Koneschusky *(Sr VP)*

Accounts:
ABC Television
Ace Ltd.
American Association of Medical Colleges
American Dental Association
American Red Cross
Americans for Secure Retirement
Amtrak
Assicuraziono Generali, S.p.A.
The Beer Institute
BSML, Inc.
California Poultry Industry Federation
Campaign for Tobacco-Free Kids
CARE
Caremark International
Catholic Health Association
Center for Wine Origins
Comite Interprofessionel du Vin de Champagne
Consejo de Promocion Turistico de Mexico
Corporacion Andina de Fomento
Cruise Lines International Association
E-Stamp Corporation
Federacion de Bodegas del Marco de Jerez
Fernando Henrique Cordoso Brazilian Presidential Campaign
General Electric
Genworth Financial
Global Alliance for TB Drug Development
Google
Government of Brazil
Government of Colombia
Government of Ecuador
Government of Mexico
Government of Nicaragua
Government of Portugal
Government of Spain
GTE
Harvard University
The Health Care Reform Project
Hunt Oil Company of Canada, Inc.
National Association of Broadcasters
National Branded Prepaid Card Association
NBC Television
NetAid
Office of Champagne, USA
Oracle
Personal Watercraft Industry Association
The Pew Center on Global Climate Change
Pfizer, Inc.
The Republic of Congo
Sherry Council of America
Sun Healthcare Group
Techint Group; Argentina
United Nations Foundation
United Nations Programme
Verizon
Wells Fargo Home Mortgage
The World Bank

COLANGELO
120 Tokeneke Rd, Darien, CT 06820
(See Separate Listing)

C Space
75 Wells Street, London, W1T 3QH United Kingdom
Tel.: (44) 207 082 1700
E-Mail: info@communispace.com
Web Site: www.cspace.com/emea

Agency Specializes In: Advertising, Brand Development & Integration, Market Research

Doron Meyassed *(Pres-EMEA)*
Nick Coates *(VP & Dir-Creative Consultancy)*
Charlotte Burgess *(Dir-Bus Dev)*
Anna Tomkowicz *(Assoc Dir)*
Paul Allen *(Sr Brand Strategist)*
Elisabeth Bucknall *(Mgr-People)*
Phil Burgess *(Joint Mng Dir-UK)*
Felix David Koch *(Joint Mng Dir-UK)*

Accounts:
Ebookers plc

Cone Communications
855 Boylston St, Boston, MA 02116
(See Separate Listing)

CPM
239 Old Marylebone Rd, London, NW1 5QT United Kingdom
(See Separate Listing)

Critical Mass Inc.
402 11th Ave SE, Calgary, AB T2G 0Y4 Canada
(See Separate Listing)

Cultur8
(Formerly Wave)
1999 Bryan St Ste 1800, Dallas, TX 75201
Tel.: (214) 259-3200
Fax: (214) 259-3201
E-Mail: tervin@culture8.com
Web Site: www.cultur8.com

Employees: 10

Agency Specializes In: Digital/Interactive, Mobile Marketing, Multicultural, Shopper Marketing, Social Marketing/Nonprofit, Sports Market, Strategic Planning/Research

Todd Ervin *(Sr VP)*
Marcelo Salinas *(Acct Dir)*
Brooke Norrell *(Mgr-Consulting)*
Yolanda Cabral-Galicia *(Acct Supvr-The Marketing Arm)*
Haidy Leal *(Acct Exec)*
Katie Pedroza *(Acct Exec)*

Accounts:
AT&T Communications Corp.

Direct Partners
4755 Alla Rd, Marina Del Rey, CA 90292-6311
(See Separate Listing)

Doremus
200 Varick St 11Fl, New York, NY 10014-4810
(See Separate Listing)

eci san francisco
394 Pacific Ave 1st Fl, San Francisco, CA 94111
Tel.: (415) 981-9900
Web Site: www.eciww.com

Agency Specializes In: Customer Relationship Management

Amanda Wininger *(Acct Exec)*

Accounts:
Adobe

Flamingo
1st Floor 1 Riverside Manbre Road, London, W6 9WA United Kingdom
Tel.: (44) 207 348 4950
Fax: (44) 207 348 4951
Web Site: www.flamingo-international.com

Agency Specializes In: Brand Development & Integration

Maggie Collier *(Founder)*
Natalie Cubides-Brady *(Assoc Dir-UK Practice)*
Lee Fordham *(Assoc Dir-Digital Strategy)*
Maggie Matthews *(Assoc Dir)*
Rachel Miller-Sprafke *(Assoc Dir)*
Laura Ratcliffe *(Assoc Dir)*
Parmeet Babrah *(Mgr-Resource)*
Luke Scanlon *(Mgr-Fin Plng & Analysis)*
Liz Hetherington *(Sr Exec-Res)*
Lizzie Jones *(Sr Exec-Res)*
Nisha Patel *(Grp Controller-Fin)*
Puya Vakili *(Sr Exec-Res)*

Accounts:
adidas

Flashpoint Medica, LLC
158 W 29th St 5th Fl, New York, NY 10001
(See Separate Listing)

Fleishman-Hillard Inc.
200 N Broadway, Saint Louis, MO 63102-2730
(See Separate Listing)

Footsteps

220 E 42nd St, New York, NY 10017
(See Separate Listing)

GMR Marketing LLC
5000 S Towne Dr, New Berlin, WI 53151-7956
(See Separate Listing)

GO!
1123 Zonolite Rd Ste 19, Atlanta, GA 30306
Tel.: (404) 248-7777
Web Site: www.goxd.com

Agency Specializes In: Entertainment, Event Planning & Marketing, Sports Market

Leigh Friedman *(Dir-Creative Svcs)*

Accounts:
Kia Motors

Goodby, Silverstein & Partners, Inc.
720 California St, San Francisco, CA 94108-2404
(See Separate Listing)

Grizzard Communications
229 Peachtree St NE Ste 1400, Atlanta, GA 30303-1606
(See Separate Listing)

Hall and Partners
711 3rd Ave 19th Fl, New York, NY 10017
(See Separate Listing)

Harrison and Star LLC
75 Varick St 6th Fl, New York, NY 10013
(See Separate Listing)

Health Science Communications
711 3rd Ave Ste 17, New York, NY 10017
(See Separate Listing)

The Healthcare Consultancy Group
711 3rd Ave 17th Fl, New York, NY 10017
(See Separate Listing)

Hornall Anderson
710 2nd Ave Ste 1300, Seattle, WA 98104-1712
(See Separate Listing)

Hyphen Digital
711 3rd Ave 17th Fl, New York, NY 10017
(See Separate Listing)

Innovyx
1000 2nd Ave Ste 900, Seattle, WA 98104-1076
(See Separate Listing)

Integrated Merchandising Systems
8338 Austin Ave, Morton Grove, IL 60053-3209
Tel.: (847) 583-7914
Fax: (847) 966-1271
E-Mail: todd.cromheecke@imsfastpak.com
Web Site: www.imsfastpak.com

Employees: 200

Agency Specializes In: Consumer Marketing

Carolyn Close *(CFO, CIO & Exec VP)*
Mike Anson *(VP-Acctg)*
Todd Cromheecke *(VP-Mktg & Client Engagement)*
Deirdre Heraty Kerrigan *(Acct Dir)*
Elin Duarte *(Sr Mgr-Ops)*
Kari Bradley *(Mgr-HR)*

Accounts:
Walgreen

Javelin Marketing Group
(Formerly Javelin)
7850 N Belt Line Rd, Irving, TX 75063-6098
(See Separate Listing)

Kaleidoscope
30 Irving Pl 8th Fl, New York, NY 10003
(See Separate Listing)

Ketchum
1285 Ave of the Americas, New York, NY 10019
(See Separate Listing)

LatinWorks Marketing, Inc.
2500 Bee Caves Rd, Austin, TX 78746
(See Separate Listing)

LLNS
220 E 42nd St, New York, NY 10017-5806
(See Separate Listing)

Lois Paul & Partners
1 Beacon St, 2nd Fl, Boston, MA 02108
(See Separate Listing)

M/A/R/C Research
1660 N Westridge Cir, Irving, TX 75038
(See Separate Listing)

Marina Maher Communications
830 3rd Ave, New York, NY 10022
(See Separate Listing)

The Marketing Arm
1999 Bryan St 18th Fl, Dallas, TX 75201-3125
(See Separate Listing)

MarketStar Corporation
2475 Washington Blvd, Ogden, UT 84401
(See Separate Listing)

Maslansky + Partners
200 Varick St, New York, NY 10014
(See Separate Listing)

Mercury Public Affairs
250 Greenwich St, New York, NY 10007
(See Separate Listing)

Merkley+Partners
200 Varick St, New York, NY 10014-4810
(See Separate Listing)

Porter Novelli
7 World Trade Center 250 Greenwich St 36th Fl, New York, NY 10007
(See Separate Listing)

Portland
1 Red Lion Court, London, EC4A 3EB United Kingdom
Tel.: (44) 20 7842 0123
Fax: (44) 20 7842 0145
Web Site: www.portland-communications.com

Agency Specializes In: Brand Development & Integration, Content, Digital/Interactive, Government/Political, Health Care Services, International, Legal Services, Public Relations

Tim Allan *(Founder)*
Louise Mason *(Partner-Financial Comm)*
Alexandra Farley *(COO)*
Oliver Pauley *(Mng Dir-UK)*
Mark Flanagan *(Sr Partner-Content & Digital Strategy)*

Accounts:
abpi
Africa Progress Panel
Alexion
BAE Systems
Barclays
bba
Bill & Melinda Gates Foundation
British Red Cross
New-Lucara Diamond Corp. Communications
Uber UK Public Affairs

Rapp
437 Madison Ave 3rd Fl, New York, NY 10022
(See Separate Listing)

Russ Reid Company, Inc.
2 N Lake Ave Ste 600, Pasadena, CA 91101-1868
(See Separate Listing)

Serino Coyne LLC
1515 Broadway 36th Fl, New York, NY 10036-8901
(See Separate Listing)

Siegel+Gale
625 Ave of the Americas 4th Fl, New York, NY 10011
(See Separate Listing)

Signature Graphics
1000 Signature Dr, Porter, IN 46304
Tel.: (219) 926-4994
Fax: (219) 926-7231
E-Mail: marketing@signaturegraph.com
Web Site: www.signaturegraphicsinc.com

Employees: 100

Agency Specializes In: Sponsorship

Paul Godfrey *(Chm)*
David Mason *(Exec VP-Ops)*
Steve Whitaker *(Exec VP-Sls)*
D'Andrew Reynolds *(Dir-Natl Accounts)*
David Parnell *(Acct Exec)*
Lisa Burgey *(Coord-Sls)*
Deanna Krider *(Rep-Sls)*
Jeff Moore *(Rep-Sls)*
Perry Wilson *(Reg Rep-Sls)*

Sparks & Honey
437 Madison Ave 3rd Fl, New York, NY 10022
(See Separate Listing)

SSCG Media Group
220 E 42nd St, New York, NY 10017
(See Separate Listing)

Steiner Sports Marketing
145 Huguenot St, New Rochelle, NY 10801-6454
(See Separate Listing)

Sterling Brands
75 Varick St 8th Fl, New York, NY 10013

Tel.: (212) 329-4600
Fax: (212) 329-4700
Web Site: www.sterlingbrands.com

Simon Williams *(Pres)*
Peter Mundy *(CFO)*
Debbie Millman *(Pres-Design)*
Alpa Pandya *(Exec VP & Mng Dir-Strategy)*
Mike Bainbridge *(Exec VP & Head-Bus)*
Chris O'Rourke *(Exec VP-Design Mgmt & Ops)*
Mindy Romero *(VP-Mktg Comm)*
Katy Brighton *(Dir-Implementation)*
Nancy Brogden *(Dir-Design)*
Jessica Blau *(Grp Coord-Strategy)*

Accounts:
New-Debbie Millman Self-Portrait As Your Traitor

Targetbase
7850 N Belt Line Rd, Irving, TX 75063-6098
(See Separate Listing)

TPG Direct
The Piers at Penn's Landing 7 N Columbus Blvd Pier 5, Philadelphia, PA 19106
Tel.: (215) 592-8381
Fax: (215) 574-8316
E-Mail: slongley@tpgdirect.com
Web Site: www.tpgdirect.com

Steven R. Longley *(CEO)*
Patricia Salmon *(Exec VP-Ops)*
Nancy Bollinger *(Sr VP & Dir-Creative)*
Miguel Ferry *(Exec Dir-Creative)*

Accounts:
21st Century Insurance
AARP
Geisinger Choice
Geisinger Gold

TPN Inc.
9400 N Central Expwy Ste 1500, Dallas, TX 75231-5044
(See Separate Listing)

TRO
6 Church St Isleworth, Isleworth, Middlesex TW7 6XB United Kingdom
Tel.: (44) 208 232 7200
Fax: (44) 208 232 7232
E-Mail: info@tro-group.co.uk
Web Site: tro.com/contact-us

Employees: 50

Nick Burrows *(Grp Acct Dir)*
Andrew Orr *(Grp Acct Dir)*
Amelia Shepherd *(Grp Acct Dir)*
Sian Bates *(Client Svcs Dir)*
Luci Beaufort-Dysart *(Bus Dev Dir & Brand Dir)*
Ben Goss *(Acct Dir)*
Emma Hinde *(Acct Dir)*
Nick Glazier *(Dir-Creative)*
Alex Hill *(Dir-Design)*
Sarah Mayo *(Dir-Brand & Bus Dev)*
Gary Wootton *(Dir-Ops)*
Tara Allen-Muncey *(Acct Mgr)*
Alexandra Wachter *(Acct Mgr)*

Accounts:
Anglian Windows
BMW
Chevrolet
Digital UK
Honda
KPMG
Microsoft
Nissan Experiential
Pink Lady
Ribena
Rolls-Royce
Royal Navy
T-Mobile US
Topshop
Volvo Car
Volvo Penta
Westfield
Wilkinson Sword

Wolff Olins
10 Regents Wharf All Saints Street, London, N1 9RL United Kingdom
(See Separate Listing)

DIVISION ADVERTISING & DESIGN
(Formerly They Creative LP)
2700 Post Oak Blvd Ste 1400, Houston, TX 77056
Tel.: (281) 712-4846
Web Site: www.wearedivision.com

Year Founded: 1983

Agency Specializes In: Brand Development & Integration, Digital/Interactive, Graphic Design, Multimedia, Strategic Planning/Research, Web (Banner Ads, Pop-ups, etc.)

Christopher Muniz *(Chief Creative Officer)*

Accounts:
Amazon Kindle Ebooks Publisher
Automotive Masters, Inc. Branding, Marketing
Bounty (UK) Ltd. Parenting Club Services
The City of Houston Online Services
FMC Corporation Pesticides Mfr
GoDaddy.com Inc. Website Design & Hosting Services
Grounds Anderson LLC Consulting Services
SmartVault Branding, Marketing
Weatherford International Ltd. Drilling Products & Services
Whitmeyer's Distilling Company Brand Positioning, Logo, Space City Vodka, Website

DIVISION OF LABOR
328 Pine St, Sausalito, CA 94965
Tel.: (415) 944-8185
E-Mail: info@divisionoflabor.com
Web Site: www.divisionoflabor.com

Agency Specializes In: Advertising

Josh Denberg *(Partner & Dir-Creative)*
Paul Hirsch *(Partner & Dir-Creative)*
Laura Mcallister Davis *(Mng Dir)*

Accounts:
2girl Coffee
Ford Motor Company
Live Nation Campaign: "Rock Paper Photo", Campaign: "Rodents on Turntables"

DIX & EATON
200 Public Sq Ste 3900, Cleveland, OH 44114
Tel.: (216) 241-0405
Fax: (216) 241-3070
Web Site: www.dix-eaton.com

Employees: 50
Year Founded: 1952

National Agency Associations: AMA-COPF-PRSA

Agency Specializes In: Asian Market, Business Publications, Business-To-Business, Collateral, Communications, Consulting, Corporate Communications, Corporate Identity, Digital/Interactive, E-Commerce, Exhibit/Trade Shows, Financial, Graphic Design, Information Technology, Internet/Web Design, Investor Relations, Logo & Package Design, Media Buying Services, New Product Development, Newspaper, Newspapers & Magazines, Planning & Consultation, Print, Public Relations, Publicity/Promotions, Sponsorship, Strategic Planning/Research, Trade & Consumer Magazines, Transportation

Breakdown of Gross Billings by Media: Corp. Communications: 80%; Pub. Rels.: 20%

Scott Chaikin *(Chm)*
Chas D. Withers *(Pres & CEO)*
Matt Barkett *(Mng Dir)*
David Hertz *(Mng Dir)*
Gregg LaBar *(Sr VP)*
Amy McGahan *(Sr VP)*
Gary Pratt *(Sr VP)*
Lisa Zone *(Sr VP)*
Gary Wells *(Sr Mng Dir-Media Rels & Global Comm)*
Kellie Friery *(VP)*

Accounts:
AIG Property Casualty
Aleris International, Inc.; 2004
Atlas Energy, L.P.
BASF
Boart Longyear
Calumet Specialty Products Partners, LP
Cardinal Health, Inc.
Case Western Reserve University - Weatherhead School of Management
CBIZ Inc.
Cedar Fair Entertainment Company
Cleveland Indians Baseball Company, Inc.
The Cleveland Museum of Art; 2003
Cleveland State University
Delek US Holdings
DENTSPLY International
Diebold, Inc.; Canton, OH; 1990
Energizer Battery
Fairmount Santrol
Forest City Enterprises, Inc.; Cleveland, OH; 2001
Glatfelter
Greater Cleveland Partnership; 1994
Group Plan Commission
IDEX Corporation
ITW
Jazz Aviation LP
Kelly Services; 2004
KeyBank; Cleveland, OH; 1996
LEEDCO - Lake Erie Energy Development Corporation
Libbey Inc.
Lincoln Electric Company; 1994
The Lubrizol Corp.; Wickliffe, OH; 1986
McDonald Hopkins
MetroHealth System Medical Center
Mettler-Toledo International Inc.; 1997
Motorola Solutions-Inc.
Myer Industries, Inc.
NACCO Industries, Inc.; Mayfield Heights, OH; 1981
National Air Cargo Group
Net Jets Inc.
New York Community Bancorp, Inc.
Newry Corporation
Nordson Corp.; Westlake, OH; 2000
OM Group, Inc.; 2002
OMNOVA Solutions Inc.; Fairlawn, OH; 2001
Pinnacle Airlines Corp.
Playhouse Square Foundation; Cleveland, OH; 1982
PPG Industries
quasar
The Rock & Roll Hall of Fame & Museum; Cleveland, OH
Sherwin-Williams
Southwest Airlines Co.
Stoneridge Corporation; 1996
Swagelok Company; 2002
The Timken Company; 2003
Timkin Steel Corporation

UnitedHealth Group; 2004
Veyance Technologies

DIXON JAMES COMMUNICATIONS
824 W Superior 205, Chicago, IL 60642
Tel.: (708) 848-8085
Fax: (708) 848-4270
E-Mail: info@dixon-james.com
Web Site: www.dixon-james.com

Agency Specializes In: Advertising, Brand Development & Integration, Graphic Design, Public Relations, Social Media

Jim Heininger *(Founder & Principal)*

Accounts:
New-Burtch Works

DIXON SCHWABL ADVERTISING
1595 Moseley Rd, Victor, NY 14564
Tel.: (585) 383-0380
Fax: (585) 383-1661
E-Mail: info@dixonschwabl.com
Web Site: www.dixonschwabl.com

Employees: 85
Year Founded: 1987

Agency Specializes In: Advertising, Brand Development & Integration, Direct Response Marketing, Event Planning & Marketing, Exhibit/Trade Shows, Integrated Marketing, Outdoor, Print, Radio, T.V.

Approx. Annual Billings: $193,400,000

Lauren Dixon *(CEO)*
David Lyttle *(Mng Partner & CFO)*
Kellie Adami *(Mng Partner-New Bus Dev)*
Kim Allen *(Mng Partner)*
Jessica Savage *(Mng Partner-Acct Svc)*
Bill Colburn *(VP-Creative Svcs)*
Shannon Struzik *(Assoc VP-Special Events)*
Jon Alhart *(Dir-Social & Digital Media)*
Danielle Barteld *(Dir-First Impressions)*
Sarah DeVita *(Dir-Art)*
Nicholas Vernetti *(Dir-Art)*
Cathleen Wells *(Dir-Digital Strategy)*
Kevin Berliner *(Assoc Dir-Art)*
Ned Chatt *(Sr Mgr-Production)*
Wayne Gormont *(Project Mgr-Digital)*
Abha Dhakal *(Mgr-Mktg)*
Connor Dixon-Schwabl *(Mgr-Studio)*
Katie Redmond *(Mgr-PR)*
Cassandra Brown *(Acct Supvr)*
Ryann Bouchard *(Acct Exec-PR)*
Pete Wayner *(Acct Exec-PR)*
Alison Cundy *(Sr Media Buyer & Planner)*
Andrea Francis *(Sr Media Planner & Media Buyer)*
Rob Meacham *(Acct Coord)*
Sarah Picciotto *(Coord-Media)*
Michaela Stone *(Sr Media Planner & Buyer)*

Accounts:
Black & Decker
Delaware North Companies; Buffalo, NY Kennedy Space Center Visitor Complex, Marketing Communications, Promotional Initiatives
ESL Federal Credit Union
Frontier Communications Analysis, Media Buying, Paid Media Program, Strategic Media Planning
Frontier Corp.
George Eastman Circle
Greater Rochester Enterprise
Hargray Communications
Laser Spa Development, PR, Strategy
MCC Starlight Social Club
Monro Muffler
Roberts Wesleyan College
Thompson Health
Watkins Glen International (Agency of Record)

DJ-LA LLC
11400 W Olympic Blvd Ste 200, Los Angeles, CA 90064-1644
Tel.: (310) 473-1000
Fax: (310) 573-2145
E-Mail: jackie@dj-la.com
Web Site: www.dj-la.com

E-Mail for Key Personnel:
President: dennis@dj-la.com

Employees: 12
Year Founded: 1974

Agency Specializes In: Advertising, Advertising Specialties, Brand Development & Integration, Business Publications, Business-To-Business, Cable T.V., Collateral, Consumer Marketing, Consumer Publications, Corporate Communications, Corporate Identity, Direct Response Marketing, E-Commerce, Entertainment, Exhibit/Trade Shows, Fashion/Apparel, Financial, Food Service, Graphic Design, In-Store Advertising, Internet/Web Design, Legal Services, Local Marketing, Logo & Package Design, Magazines, Media Buying Services, Newspaper, Newspapers & Magazines, Point of Purchase, Point of Sale, Print, Radio, Real Estate, Retail, Syndication, T.V., Trade & Consumer Magazines

Approx. Annual Billings: $12,000,000

Breakdown of Gross Billings by Media: Collateral: 10%; Exhibits/Trade Shows: 5%; Graphic Design: 15%; Internet Adv.: 5%; Logo & Package Design: 5%; Newsp.: 15%; Print: 10%; Radio & T.V.: 15%; Sls. Promo.: 5%; Trade & Consumer Mags.: 15%

Dennis Horlick *(Pres)*
Jackie Horlick *(CEO)*
Scott C Doughty *(Exec VP & Dir-Creative)*

Accounts:
20th Century Fox Home Video; Los Angeles, CA Home Video Rentals; 2001
ADT Security Systems
Bel Air Camera
Casio Phone Mate
City of Hope; Los Angeles, CA Cancer Research; 2007
Coldwell Banker Previews International
Debbie Allen Dance Academy
The Jacobson Group
Music Center of Los Angeles
Not Your Daughters' Jeans; Vernon, CA Ladies Jeans; 2008
Nutrifit; Los Angeles, CA Home Delivered Meals; 2006
Paramount Home Video
Sarah Leonard Jewelers; Westwood, CA Jewelry Retail; 2003
Save Africa's Children; Los Angeles, CA African Aid; 2004
Stop Cancer; Los Angeles, CA Cancer Research; 2001
TVN Entertainment; Burbank, CA Cable Programming; 2002

DJD/GOLDEN ADVERTISING, INC.
145 W 28th St, New York, NY 10001
Tel.: (212) 366-5033
Fax: (212) 243-5044
E-Mail: call@djdgolden.com
Web Site: www.djdgolden.com

E-Mail for Key Personnel:
President: mgolden@djdgolden.com
Public Relations: mgolden@djdgolden.com

Employees: 7
Year Founded: 1990

Agency Specializes In: Advertising, Brand Development & Integration, Business Publications, Business-To-Business, Collateral, Communications, Consulting, Content, Corporate Communications, Corporate Identity, Direct Response Marketing, Event Planning & Marketing, Financial, Government/Political, Graphic Design, Guerilla Marketing, High Technology, Identity Marketing, Information Technology, Integrated Marketing, Internet/Web Design, Legal Services, Local Marketing, Logo & Package Design, Magazines, Media Relations, New Technologies, Planning & Consultation, Promotions, Public Relations, Publicity/Promotions, Real Estate, Regional, Sales Promotion, Technical Advertising, Telemarketing

Approx. Annual Billings: $10,500,000

Breakdown of Gross Billings by Media: Collateral: 20%; D.M.: 15%; Mags.: 10%; Newsp.: 10%; Pub. Rels.: 40%; Transit: 5%

Malcolm Petrook *(Partner)*
Courtney St. Clement *(Dir-Creative)*

Accounts:
Association for Computing Machinery; New York, NY (Membership Campaign)
Bruno Blenheim, Inc.; Fort Lee, NJ Trade Shows
International Foodcraft; Brooklyn, NY Food Ingredients
John Wiley & Sons; New York, NY Books
Proskauer Rose Goetz & Mendelsohn; New York, NY Legal Services
Strategic Resources Corporation; New York, NY Fund Manager & Investment Banking
Verizon Telesector Resources Group; White Plains, NY Telecommunications Services
World Trade Institute; New York, NY Seminars

D.L. MEDIA INC.
720 W Center Cir, Nixa, MO 65714
Tel.: (417) 725-1816
Fax: (417) 725-8365
E-Mail: diannelm@dlmedia.com
Web Site: www.dlmedia.com

Employees: 8
Year Founded: 1997

Agency Specializes In: Advertising, Advertising Specialties, Automotive, Brand Development & Integration, Broadcast, Business Publications, Business-To-Business, Cable T.V., Catalogs, Co-op Advertising, Collateral, Commercial Photography, Communications, Consulting, Consumer Marketing, Consumer Publications, Corporate Identity, Direct Response Marketing, E-Commerce, Electronic Media, Email, Entertainment, Event Planning & Marketing, Exhibit/Trade Shows, Fashion/Apparel, Financial, Graphic Design, Health Care Services, Identity Marketing, In-Store Advertising, Infomercials, Internet/Web Design, Logo & Package Design, Magazines, Media Buying Services, Media Planning, Mobile Marketing, Multimedia, Newspaper, Newspapers & Magazines, Out-of-Home Media, Outdoor, Over-50 Market, Package Design, Planning & Consultation, Podcasting, Point of Purchase, Point of Sale, Print, Production, Production (Ad, Film, Broadcast), Production (Print), Promotions, Public Relations, Radio, Recruitment, Regional, Restaurant, Retail, Sales Promotion, Search Engine Optimization, Seniors' Market, Social Media, Strategic Planning/Research, T.V., Trade & Consumer Magazines, Transportation, Travel & Tourism, Web (Banner Ads, Pop-ups, etc.)

Approx. Annual Billings: $4,500,000

Breakdown of Gross Billings by Media: Adv.

Specialities: $105,000; Cable T.V.: $175,000; Consulting: $70,000; Consumer Publs.: $35,000; Fees: $175,000; Internet Adv.: $70,000; Logo & Package Design: $35,000; Newsp. & Mags.: $1,645,000; Out-of-Home Media: $35,000; Spot Radio: $210,000; Spot T.V.: $1,875,000; Worldwide Web Sites: $70,000

Dianne Davis *(Owner & Pres)*
Dana Harding *(Dir-Creative)*
Krystal Imerman *(Dir-Creative)*
April Clore *(Mgr-Social Media)*
Jack Hurley *(Mgr-Acct Svc & Sls)*
Dalal Raikos *(Media Buyer)*
Judy Styles *(Media Buyer)*

Accounts:
Bill Roberts Chevrolet, Buick & Pontiac; Bolivar, MO Cars; 1997
Consumer Credit Counseling Service; Springfield, MO Not-for-Profit Credit Counseling; 2003
Jim Stafford Theatre; Branson, MO Musical & Comedy Show; 1997
Medical Consulting Group; Springfield, MO Lasik Laser Vision Correction; 2001
Metro Appliances & More Media Research, New Appliances, Placement, Social Media Management, Video Production, Website Design; 2005
Schilling Sellmeyer & Associates; Springfield, MO; 2006
Waterford at Ironbridge; Springfield, MO Retirement Community; 2002
Young & Company; Springfield, MO

DLS DESIGN
274 Madison Ave, New York, NY 10016
Tel.: (212) 255-3464
Fax: (212) 255-1031
E-Mail: info@dlsdesign.com
Web Site: www.dlsdesign.com

E-Mail for Key Personnel:
President: david@dlsdesign.com

Employees: 2
Year Founded: 1997

Agency Specializes In: Internet/Web Design

Approx. Annual Billings: $200,000

Breakdown of Gross Billings by Media: Collateral: 10%; Newsp. & Mags.: 10%; Worldwide Web Sites: 80%

David Schiffer *(Owner)*

Accounts:
Acoustone Fabrics (Web Site Design); 2001
Broadgate Consultants (Web Site Design); 2003
DLS Fortifies Public Defenders
Kreindler & Kreindler Aviation Law (Web Site Design); 1998
Ladies Who Launch
Mount Sinai Medical Center Sports Medicine
New York Harm Reduction Educators Nonprofit AIDS Services (Web Site Design); 2000
Old, New, Blue, But Nothing Borrowed
Petrillo Klein
SPI, Spare Parts International (Web Site Design); 2003
This Law Web Site is No Crime
Thompson, Wigdor & Gilly LLP (Web Site Design); 2003

DM2 DESIGN CONSULTANCY
115 River Rd, Edgewater, NJ 07020
Tel.: (201) 840-8910
Fax: (201) 840-7907
E-Mail: berckes@thinkdm2.com
Web Site: www.thinkdm2.com

E-Mail for Key Personnel:
President: annunziato@thinkdm2.com
Creative Dir.: daddario@thinkdm2.com
Production Mgr.: ariatabar@thinkdm2.com

Employees: 12
Year Founded: 1989

Agency Specializes In: Advertising, Brand Development & Integration, Collateral, Communications, Consumer Marketing, Corporate Communications, Corporate Identity, Digital/Interactive, Direct Response Marketing, Education, Electronics, Environmental, Event Planning & Marketing, Exhibit/Trade Shows, Graphic Design, Hospitality, Identity Marketing, Information Technology, Integrated Marketing, Internet/Web Design, Logo & Package Design, Magazines, Media Buying Services, Media Planning, Newspapers & Magazines, Outdoor, Package Design, Point of Purchase, Point of Sale, Print, Production, Promotions, Real Estate, Sales Promotion, Strategic Planning/Research, Trade & Consumer Magazines, Web (Banner Ads, Pop-ups, etc.)

Approx. Annual Billings: $3,000,000

Breakdown of Gross Billings by Media: Adv. Specialities: 20%; Collateral: 40%; Internet Adv.: 20%; Strategic Planning/Research: 20%

David Annunziato *(Pres, Mng Dir & Strategist-Certified Brand)*
Monica Berckes *(Principal & Dir-New Bus)*
Chris Fuller *(Principal & Strategist-Certified Brand)*
Katherine Winter *(VP-Ops)*
Nava Anav *(Sr Dir-Art)*
Azadeh Brown *(Dir-Design)*
Brett Dziura *(Dir-Digital)*
Brian Sica *(Designer)*

Accounts:
Avaya
Balancepoint; Rochelle Park, NJ
Bear Stearns
Chubb Insurance
Dialogic
Intel
LG
Morgan Stanley
MTV
Sony Electronics
Unilever

DMA UNITED
(Formerly Ink & Co.)
446 Broadway 4th Fl, New York, NY 10013
Tel.: (212) 334-3168
E-Mail: cheers@dmaunited.com
Web Site: blog.dmaunited.com/

Employees: 15
Year Founded: 1994

Agency Specializes In: Above-the-Line, Advertising, Advertising Specialties, Affluent Market, African-American Market, Alternative Advertising, Arts, Automotive, Below-the-Line, Bilingual Market, Brand Development & Integration, Branded Entertainment, Broadcast, Business-To-Business, Catalogs, Children's Market, Co-op Advertising, Collateral, College, Commercial Photography, Communications, Consumer Goods, Consumer Marketing, Consumer Publications, Content, Corporate Identity, Cosmetics, Custom Publishing, Digital/Interactive, Direct-to-Consumer, E-Commerce, Electronic Media, Electronics, Entertainment, Event Planning & Marketing, Experience Design, Fashion/Apparel, Food Service, Graphic Design, Guerilla Marketing, High Technology, Hospitality, Household Goods, Identity Marketing, In-Store Advertising, Integrated Marketing, International, Internet/Web Design, Leisure, Local Marketing, Logo & Package Design, Luxury Products, Magazines, Market Research, Media Relations, Men's Market, Merchandising, Multicultural, Multimedia, New Product Development, Newspapers & Magazines, Out-of-Home Media, Outdoor, Over-50 Market, Package Design, Pharmaceutical, Point of Purchase, Point of Sale, Print, Product Placement, Production, Production (Ad, Film, Broadcast), Production (Print), Publishing, Restaurant, Retail, Sales Promotion, Social Marketing/Nonprofit, Social Media, South Asian Market, Sponsorship, Sports Market, Strategic Planning/Research, Teen Market, Transportation, Travel & Tourism, Tween Market, Urban Market, Viral/Buzz/Word of Mouth, Web (Banner Ads, Pop-ups, etc.), Women's Market

Marc Beckman *(Founder, CEO & Partner)*
Sam Sohaili *(Founder & Exec Dir-Creative)*
Nancy Chanin *(VP-Bus Dev)*
Rob Mostransky *(Sr Dir-Art)*
Zoe Bunyard *(Acct Dir)*
Nefartari Cooper *(Acct Dir)*
Diana Masiello *(Acct Dir)*
Chris Gabriel *(Asst Dir-Art)*

Accounts:
Alice Roi
Allergan
Andre Leon Talley; 2012
Barneys New York; 2014
BBC Worldwide BBC Earth, BBC First; 2014
Chef Russell Jackson; 2011
Cushnie et Ochs; 2011
The Face; 2013
Finish Line; 2014
Freemans Sporting Goods; 2012
HSN; 2007
Jordache; 2006
Judith Light; 2009
Karen Elson
Kelly Rutherford; 2013
Kimpton Hotels
Lidia Bastianich
Lisa Rinna; 2010
L'Oreal
Mark McNairy; 2013
Melania Trump; 2005
Monica Botkier
NBA; 2014
New York City Ballet; 2009
Nigel Barker; 2008
Nine West
Numero Russia; 2013
Pamela Love; 2009
Paul Morelli; 2013
Pepsi; 2014
Playboy; 2012
Reitman's; 2012
Selima Optique; 2012
Seu Jorge; 2011
Skinmedica; 2008
Sony
Susan Moses; 2008
True Religion; 2014
Tucker
Vern Yip; 2010
Veronica Webb; 2008
WESTBROOK Eyewear Russell Westbrook; 2014
Zappos.com Zappos Couture; 2013

DMG MARKETING
3801 Kennett Pike Ste D-301, Wilmington, DE 19807
Tel.: (302) 575-1610
Fax: (302) 575-1614
E-Mail: info@hellodmg.com
Web Site: www.hellodmg.com

Year Founded: 1993

Agency Specializes In: Advertising, Brand

Development & Integration, Internet/Web Design, Social Media

Ken Scott *(Pres)*
Christie Bleach *(Sr VP)*
Karen Donovan *(Sr VP)*
Sara Fabryka *(Sr Dir-Art)*
Megan Rassman *(Acct Exec)*

Accounts:
United Way Delaware

DMI PARTNERS
1 S Broad St 11th Fl, Philadelphia, PA 19107
Tel.: (215) 279-9800
Toll Free: (800) 947-3148
E-Mail: info@dmipartners.com
Web Site: www.dmipartners.com

Employees: 52
Year Founded: 2003

Agency Specializes In: Advertising

James Delaney *(Founder)*
Patrick McKenna *(CEO)*
Brian McKenna *(Exec VP-Education Mktg)*
Kevin Dugan *(Client Svcs Dir)*
Beth Harless *(Dir-Bus Dev)*
David Lachowicz *(Dir-Creative)*
Brianna Kelly *(Mgr-Vendor Rels)*

Accounts:
adidas
Experian
Gerber
Mitchell & Ness
Secure a Quote
Tastykake

DMN3
2190 North Loop W, Houston, TX 77018
Tel.: (713) 868-3000
Fax: (713) 868-1388
Toll Free: (800) 625-8320
E-Mail: contact@dmn3.com
Web Site: www.dmn3.com

Employees: 30
Year Founded: 1992

National Agency Associations: DMA

Agency Specializes In: Direct Response Marketing

Pamela Lockard *(Founder & CEO)*
John Lacour *(COO)*
Tom Richardson *(Acct Dir)*
Charles Eldred *(Dir-Creative)*
Connie Yiu *(Mgr-Digital Mktg)*
Chris Mccarthy *(Analyst-Digital Mktg)*

Accounts:
American Airlines Federal Credit Union
Cable Lock
ConocoPhillips Technology Solutions
Dell Perot Systems Corporation
Fujitsu
Kraton Polymers
Maxwell Drummond International
NRG Energy, Inc.

Branch

DMN3/Dallas
2710 Swiss Ave, Dallas, TX 75204
Tel.: (214) 826-7576
Web Site: www.dmn3.com

Employees: 5

John Lacour *(COO)*
Tom Richardson *(Acct Dir)*
Charles Eldred *(Dir-Creative)*
Paul Roland *(Dir-Interactive Svcs & Bus Intelligence)*
Connie Yiu *(Mgr-Digital Mktg)*
Chris Mccarthy *(Analyst-Digital Mktg)*

DMNGOOD
718 7th St NW Ste 301, Washington, DC 20001
Tel.: (202) 683-8975
E-Mail: looking@dmngood.com
Web Site: www.dmngood.com

Agency Specializes In: Advertising, Brand Development & Integration, Internet/Web Design, Public Relations, Search Engine Optimization, Social Media

Daniel Adler *(Exec Creative Dir)*

Accounts:
New-Marriott International

DMW WORLDWIDE LLC
701 Lee Rd Ste 103, Chesterbrook, PA 19087-5612
Tel.: (610) 407-0407
Fax: (610) 407-0410
E-Mail: info@dmwdirect.com
Web Site: www.dmwdirect.com

E-Mail for Key Personnel:
President: whunter@dmwdirect.com
Creative Dir.: bspink@dmwdirect.com
Production Mgr.: gkneib@dmwdirect.com

Employees: 80
Year Founded: 1981

National Agency Associations: DMA

Agency Specializes In: Advertising, Broadcast, Business-To-Business, Consulting, Consumer Marketing, Direct Response Marketing, Financial, Health Care Services, Media Buying Services, Over-50 Market, Pharmaceutical, Planning & Consultation, Print, Production, Seniors' Market, Strategic Planning/Research, T.V., Telemarketing

Approx. Annual Billings: $65,315,158

Breakdown of Gross Billings by Media: D.M.: $39,867,186; Newsp. & Mags.: $1,820,330; Other: $16,342,222; Radio: $535,195; T.V.: $6,750,225

Gina Kneib *(COO & Exec VP)*
Renee Mezzanotte *(Exec VP-Client Svcs)*
Cheryl Biondi *(VP & Dir-Creative)*
Kevin Courtright *(VP-Mktg Analytics)*
Len Zappolo *(Exec Dir-Media Svcs)*
Jill Heyl *(Acct Dir)*
Kevin Breen *(Assoc Dir-Creative)*
Megan Howe *(Acct Mgr)*
Leslie Lawrence *(Acct Mgr)*
Christina Clausen *(Mgr-HR)*
John DiSessa *(Mgr-Database Sys & Admin-DMW Direct)*
Irene Mann *(Mgr-Creative Svcs)*
Dominic Presutti *(Sr Acct Exec)*
Janine Taylor *(Sr Acct Exec)*
Erica Yanoshak *(Acct Exec)*

Accounts:
Blue Cross Blue Shield Plans Health Care Plans
BlueShield of South Carolina
IBM
Public Broadcasting Stations Iowa Public Television, KLRU/Austin, Texas, Kentucky Educational Television

DNA SEATTLE
(Formerly DNA Brand Mechanics)
1301 5th Ave Ste 2600, Seattle, WA 98101-3100
Tel.: (206) 770-9615
Fax: (206) 770-9015
E-Mail: info@dnaseattle.com
Web Site: www.dnaseattle.com

Employees: 48
Year Founded: 1998

Agency Specializes In: Advertising, Brand Development & Integration, Business-To-Business, Collateral, Graphic Design, Logo & Package Design, Magazines, Media Buying Services, Newspapers & Magazines, Out-of-Home Media, Outdoor, Print, Production, Radio, Restaurant, Sports Market, Strategic Planning/Research, T.V.

Approx. Annual Billings: $13,000,000

Roxanne Tolnas *(Acct Dir)*
Laura Hinds *(Dir-Fin)*
Kammie McArthur *(Dir-Creative)*
Lianne Onart *(Assoc Dir-Creative)*
Greg Tamura *(Assoc Dir-Media-DNA Brand Mechanics)*
Dave Echenoz *(Mgr-Print Production)*
Mike Quirk *(Mgr-Studio)*
Kristie Christensen *(Acct Supvr)*
Mike Spear *(Sr Strategist-Social)*

Accounts:
American Express Publishing; New York, NY Executive Travel Magazine; 1998
Avon Foundation; New York, NY Avon Walk for Breast Cancer; 2002
Benaroya Research Institute; Seattle, WA Healthcare Research; 2012
New-Boeing Employees Credit Union
Clinton Global Initiative; New York, NY; 2009
Concur; Seattle, WA; 2004
F5; Seattle, WA; 2010
Golden 1 Credit Union Campaign: "Stronger Together"
Group Health Cooperative Campaign: "One Goal"
Microsoft Corporation; Redmond, WA CEO Summit; 2009
Pemco Insurance; Seattle, WA Automobile Insurance; 2001
RDM Properties
SHAG; Seattle, WA Senior Living; 2011
Simple Mobile; Orange County, CA (Agency of Record)
Trupanion
University of Washington; Seattle, WA Higher Education; 2008

DNT MEDIA INC
1500 E 2nd St, Little Rock, AR 72202
Tel.: (501) 379-8613
Web Site: www.dntmedia.com

Agency Specializes In: Advertising, Digital/Interactive, Logo & Package Design, Media Buying Services, Print, Social Media, Strategic Planning/Research

Steve Dannaway *(COO)*

Accounts:
Beaver Dam Mud Runners
ENG Lending
Speedway Sales Golf Cars
Zink Calls Inc. Avian-X

DO DESIGN, INC.
1333 N Adams St, Tallahassee, FL 32303
Tel.: (850) 727-0841
Web Site: www.dodesigninc.com

Agency Specializes In: Advertising, Crisis Communications, Media Training, Public Relations,

Strategic Planning/Research

Doug Oakes *(Pres & Dir-Creative)*

Accounts:
Colonoscopy Services

DO GOOD MARKETING, LLC

201 Rock Rd, Glen Rock, NJ 07452
Tel.: (201) 204-4663
Fax: (201) 204-4664
E-Mail: iwant2@dogoodmarketing.com
Web Site: www.dogoodmarketing.com

Employees: 9

Agency Specializes In: Advertising, Advertising Specialties, Affluent Market, Alternative Advertising, Arts, Automotive, Below-the-Line, Brand Development & Integration, Broadcast, Business Publications, Business-To-Business, Cable T.V., Catalogs, Children's Market, Co-op Advertising, Collateral, College, Commercial Photography, Communications, Computers & Software, Consulting, Consumer Goods, Consumer Marketing, Consumer Publications, Corporate Communications, Corporate Identity, Cosmetics, Crisis Communications, Custom Publishing, Customer Relationship Management, Digital/Interactive, Direct Response Marketing, Direct-to-Consumer, E-Commerce, Education, Electronic Media, Electronics, Email, Entertainment, Environmental, Event Planning & Marketing, Exhibit/Trade Shows, Experience Design, Fashion/Apparel, Financial, Food Service, Game Integration, Graphic Design, Guerilla Marketing, Health Care Services, High Technology, Hospitality, Household Goods, Identity Marketing, In-Store Advertising, Industrial, Infomercials, Integrated Marketing, Internet/Web Design, Investor Relations, Leisure, Local Marketing, Logo & Package Design, Luxury Products, Magazines, Market Research, Media Buying Services, Media Planning, Media Relations, Media Training, Medical Products, Men's Market, Merchandising, Mobile Marketing, Multimedia, New Product Development, New Technologies, Newspaper, Newspapers & Magazines, Out-of-Home Media, Outdoor, Over-50 Market, Package Design, Paid Searches, Planning & Consultation, Podcasting, Point of Purchase, Point of Sale, Print, Product Placement, Production, Production (Ad, Film, Broadcast), Production (Print), Promotions, Public Relations, Publicity/Promotions, Publishing, RSS (Really Simple Syndication), Radio, Recruitment, Regional, Restaurant, Retail, Sales Promotion, Search Engine Optimization, Seniors' Market, Social Marketing/Nonprofit, Sports Market, Stakeholders, Strategic Planning/Research, T.V., Teen Market, Telemarketing, Trade & Consumer Magazines, Transportation, Travel & Tourism, Urban Market, Viral/Buzz/Word of Mouth, Web (Banner Ads, Pop-ups, etc.), Women's Market

Approx. Annual Billings: $3,000,000

Michael Haviland *(Founder & Pres)*
Celia Riggio *(Head-Acct Team)*
Joe Shelesky *(Dir-Art & Creative & Producer)*
Laura Dapito *(Dir-Art & Graphic Designer)*
Sue Reid *(Dir-Creative & Art & Graphic Designer)*
Dave Schindler *(Dir-Art & Graphic Designer)*
Janice Ellsworth *(Designer)*
Ruth Sheldon *(Copywriter-Direct Mail)*

Accounts:
AAdynTech
Adler Aphasia Center
Alliance Healthcare Foundation
Alpine Learning Group
Atlantic Barn & Timber Company
Barnert Subacute Rehabilitation Center
Bergen Catholic High School
Bergen Community College
Change for Kids
Children's Aid & Family Services
Chilton Memorial Hospital
CLC Landscape Design, Inc
Clifton Savings Bank
Covenant House
Dellridge Health & Rehabilitation
East Air Corporation
EPIC School
Eximious Wealth Management LLC
Family of Caring Health System
Globalshop Inc.
Good Eye Video
The Good Life Boutique
Holy Name Medical Center
Home Team
Horizon Landscape and Irrigation
KPMG LLC
Lipton
Manhattan Labs
Massey, Quick & Co., LLC
McDonald's
Mondelez International, Inc.
Morris Anesthesia Group
Morris County Surgical Center, LLC
N2 Qualitative Marketing Research
NAPA
New England Timberworks
Nutley Auto Group
Nyack Hospital
NYU School of Dentistry
Palisades Financial LLC
Paterson Habitat for Humanity
Pearson Education
Perugina
Professional Baseball Instruction, Inc.
Rapid Pump & Meter Service Co., Inc.
REED Academy
St. Joseph's Regional Medical Center
Target Custom Homes
Turrell Child Care & Early Learning Center
Tuxedo Park School
University of Michigan
Volvo
West Bergen Mental Healthcare

DOCUSOURCE VISUAL COMMUNICATIONS

5420 Pioneer Park Blvd Ste C, Tampa, FL 33634
Tel.: (813) 875-6068
Fax: (813) 875-2643
Web Site:
www.docusourcevisualcommunications.com

Year Founded: 1988

Agency Specializes In: Advertising, Brand Development & Integration, Digital/Interactive, Email, Print, Search Engine Optimization, Social Media

Scott Goldsmith *(VP-Sls)*
David Dugay *(Dir-Ops)*

Accounts:
Buddy's Home Furnishings
Pepin Heart Hospital

DODGE ASSOCIATES, INC.

95 Chestnut St, Providence, RI 02903
Tel.: (401) 273-7310
Fax: (401) 272-8777
E-Mail: info@dodgeadv.com
Web Site: www.dodgeadv.com

Employees: 5
Year Founded: 1980

Agency Specializes In: Business-To-Business, Consumer Marketing, Industrial, Public Relations

Approx. Annual Billings: $4,600,000

Breakdown of Gross Billings by Media: Bus. Publs.: $1,150,000; Collateral: $1,150,000; Other: $1,150,000; Pub. Rels.: $1,150,000

Ogden M. Dodge, Jr. *(Pres)*
David L. Hughes *(VP)*
David DiMattia *(Dir-Art)*

Accounts:
Colonial Mills
E.A. Dion, Inc.
Eastern Fisheries
MA Good Neighbor Energy Fund
RI Good Neighbor Energy Fund

DOE-ANDERSON

620 W Main St, Louisville, KY 40202-2933
Tel.: (502) 589-1700
Fax: (502) 587-8349
E-Mail: info@doeanderson.com
Web Site: www.doeanderson.com

Employees: 65
Year Founded: 1915

National Agency Associations: 4A's-AAF-AMIN

Agency Specializes In: Above-the-Line, Advertising, Advertising Specialties, Affluent Market, Alternative Advertising, Arts, Automotive, Aviation & Aerospace, Below-the-Line, Bilingual Market, Brand Development & Integration, Branded Entertainment, Broadcast, Business Publications, Business-To-Business, Cable T.V., Co-op Advertising, Collateral, College, Communications, Consulting, Consumer Goods, Consumer Marketing, Consumer Publications, Content, Corporate Communications, Corporate Identity, Crisis Communications, Customer Relationship Management, Digital/Interactive, Direct Response Marketing, Direct-to-Consumer, Email, Environmental, Event Planning & Marketing, Exhibit/Trade Shows, Experience Design, Faith Based, Financial, Food Service, Government/Political, Graphic Design, Guerilla Marketing, Health Care Services, Hospitality, Household Goods, Identity Marketing, In-Store Advertising, Information Technology, Integrated Marketing, International, Internet/Web Design, Investor Relations, Local Marketing, Logo & Package Design, Luxury Products, Magazines, Marine, Market Research, Media Buying Services, Media Planning, Media Relations, Media Training, Medical Products, Men's Market, Merchandising, Mobile Marketing, Multimedia, New Product Development, New Technologies, Newspaper, Newspapers & Magazines, Out-of-Home Media, Outdoor, Package Design, Planning & Consultation, Podcasting, Point of Purchase, Point of Sale, Print, Product Placement, Production, Production (Ad, Film, Broadcast), Production (Print), Promotions, Public Relations, Publicity/Promotions, RSS (Really Simple Syndication), Radio, Regional, Restaurant, Retail, Sales Promotion, Search Engine Optimization, Seniors' Market, Social Marketing/Nonprofit, Sponsorship, Sports Market, Stakeholders, Strategic Planning/Research, Sweepstakes, T.V., Teen Market, Transportation, Travel & Tourism, Urban Market, Viral/Buzz/Word of Mouth, Web (Banner Ads, Pop-ups, etc.), Women's Market

Approx. Annual Billings: $60,000,000

Breakdown of Gross Billings by Media: Brdcst.: 20%; Bus. Publs.: 5%; D.M.: 10%; Internet Adv.: 10%; Mags.: 10%; Newsp.: 10%; Other: 15%; Outdoor: 10%; Pub. Rels.: 10%

Todd Spencer *(Pres & CEO)*
Tom Mudd *(CFO & Exec VP)*

John Birnsteel *(COO)*
Michael Littman *(CMO & Sr VP)*
David Vawter *(Chief Creative Officer & Exec VP)*
Joe Pierce *(Chief Digital Officer & Sr VP)*
Daniel Burgess *(Sr VP & Dir-PR)*
Raymond Radford *(Sr VP-Channel Mktg)*
Tom Walthall *(VP & Mgmt Supvr)*
Brittany Campisano *(VP, Mgr-HR & Sr Accountant)*
Delane Wise *(Head-Brdcst Production)*
Troy Burkhart *(Sr Dir-Art)*
Bill Connelly *(Dir-Creative)*
Scott Troutman *(Dir-Creative)*
George Archie *(Office Mgr)*
Meagan Boyle *(Acct Mgr)*
Kate Killian *(Acct Mgr-PR)*
Taylor Cochran *(Mgr-Social Media)*
Elle Fuller *(Mgr-Social Media)*
Ainsley Jones *(Mgr-Content)*
Bill Schelling *(Mgr-Production)*
Matt O'Mara *(Supvr-Media)*
Taylor Jackson *(Strategist-Social Media)*
Christina Amorose *(Asst Acct Mgr)*
Meghan Clark *(Asst Acct Mgr)*

Accounts:
1st Source Bank
Arai Helmet, Inc (Agency of Record) Creative, Digital, Media, Mobile-app, Point-of-Purchase, Public Relations, Web Design
Beam Global Spirits & Wine; Chicago, IL Jim Beam, Knob Creek, Laphroaig, Makers Mark
Belterra Park
Bluegrass Cellular
Cardo Systems
Carrier Corp.
Central Bank; Lexington, KY
Donan Engineering Co. Inc
Duck Head Apparel
Fifth Third Bancorp
The Healing Place; Louisville, KY
Hosparus Inc.
Independence Bank
Kentucky Derby; Louisville, KY Campaign :"The amount of confusion was just so enormous."
Kohler; Kohler, WI
Kosair Children's Hospital; Louisville, KY
Louisville Branding Alliance; Louisville, KY City of Louisville
Louisville Metro Police Dept.; Louisville, KY 574-LMPD
The Louisville-Southern Indiana Ohio River Bridges Project; Louisville, KY
Maker's Mark
Maui Jim Inc. (Agency of Record) Buying, Creative, Strategic Media Planning
Mcallister's Deli
Mercy Academy Campaign: "Prepare for real life"
Norton Healthcare; Louisville, KY
Pinnacle Entertainment
Stoll, Keenon, Ogden; Louisville, KY
Triumph North America
Umbro
United Methodist Church
Valvoline

DOGGETT ADVERTISING, INC.
2137 S Blvd Ste 300, Charlotte, NC 28203
Tel.: (704) 377-1122
Fax: (704) 377-2444
E-Mail: info@doggettadvertising.com
Web Site: www.doggettadvertising.com

Employees: 10
Year Founded: 1988

National Agency Associations: Second Wind Limited

Agency Specializes In: Automotive, Broadcast, Business Publications, Business-To-Business, Cable T.V., Collateral, Consulting, Consumer Marketing, Consumer Publications, Direct Response Marketing, E-Commerce, Electronic Media, Event Planning & Marketing, Fashion/Apparel, Financial, Graphic Design, Health Care Services, Logo & Package Design, Media Buying Services, Newspaper, Newspapers & Magazines, Out-of-Home Media, Outdoor, Over-50 Market, Planning & Consultation, Print, Production, Public Relations, Radio, Real Estate, Seniors' Market, Strategic Planning/Research, T.V., Trade & Consumer Magazines

George W. Doggett *(Pres & Strategist-Brand)*
Jeff Doggett *(VP-Creative)*
Josh Orenstein *(Dir-Art)*

DOGTIME MEDIA INC.
(Acquired by Evolve Media LLC)

DOGTIME MEDIA INC.
27 Maiden Ln Ste 700, San Francisco, CA 94508
Tel.: (415) 830-9318
Fax: (415) 692-8171
Web Site: dogtime.com/

Year Founded: 2006

Agency Specializes In: Advertising, Publishing, Web (Banner Ads, Pop-ups, etc.)

Rick Thompson *(Founder & Exec Chm)*
Simon Tonner *(Pres & CEO)*
David Krupinski *(Dir-Engrg)*
Sui Mak *(Sr Engr-Software)*

Accounts:
Eukanuba Pet Foods
Pedigree Pet Foods

DOGWOOD PRODUCTIONS, INC.
757 Government St, Mobile, AL 36602-1404
Tel.: (251) 476-0858
Fax: (251) 479-0364
Toll Free: (800) 254-9903
E-Mail: info@dogwoodproductions.com
Web Site: www.dogwoodproductions.com

Employees: 15
Year Founded: 1983

National Agency Associations: Second Wind Limited

Agency Specializes In: Digital/Interactive, Graphic Design, Internet/Web Design, Multimedia, Production

Approx. Annual Billings: $1,200,000

John Strope *(Owner & Dir-Technical)*
Jason Cruthirds *(Dir-Creative)*
Ray Norman *(Dir-Audio)*

Accounts:
Brett/Robinson Vacation Rentals
Chapura Software
Lifelines/Family Counseling Center of Mobile, Inc.
Mobile Convention & Visitors Corporation

DOJO
832 Sansome St 4th Fl, San Francisco, CA 94111
Tel.: (415) 651-4330
Web Site: www.dojosf.com

Year Founded: 2009

Agency Specializes In: Advertising, Communications, Digital/Interactive, Graphic Design, Market Research, Planning & Consultation

Geoff Edwards *(Co-Founder & Chief Creative Officer)*
Marty Wenzell *(Pres & Mng Dir)*
Mauro Alencar *(Partner & Exec Dir-Creative)*
Paul Burlingham *(Dir-Partnerships)*
Cristiane Machado Storfner *(Mgr-HR)*

Accounts:
Activision Campaign: "Call of Duty"
adidas North America Inc.
AT&T Communications Corp. Android Mobile App, Campaign: "JustUs"
Google TV
Leap Motion
LG International (America), Inc. Campaign: "You've Never Seen This", Spectrum
Logitech Campaign: "Blindfold", Campaign: "El General", Campaign: "Global Jam", Campaign: "Ready, Aim, Click", Ultimate Ears
Lucasfilm, Ltd. Campaign: "RedTails"
NIKE, Inc.
SK Planet
Sound United Definitive Technology, Marketing, Media Buying, Online, Polk Audio, Print, Social, TV
Trend Micro; Cupertino, CA Digital Films, Web Support
VisitNapaValley

DOLABANY COMMUNICATIONS GROUP
57 Providence Hwy, Norwood, MA 02062
Tel.: (781) 769-6800
Fax: (781) 769-8228
E-Mail: jschmauss@dolabanygroup.com
Web Site: www.dolabanygroup.com

Employees: 10
Year Founded: 1997

Agency Specializes In: Advertising

Dana Dolabany *(Owner)*
Maureen Allen *(Dir-Media)*
Jolen Schmauss *(Dir-Brand Dev)*

Accounts:
D'Angelo
Dunkin Donuts
Papa Gino's Pizzeria

DOMOREGOOD HANNON MCKENDRY
(Formerly Hanon McKendry)
25 Ottawa SW Ste 600, Grand Rapids, MI 49503
Tel.: (616) 776-1111
Fax: (616) 776-0022
E-Mail: frontdesk@domoregood.com
Web Site: www.domoregood.com

Employees: 35

Bob Blanchard *(CEO)*
Renee Galicki *(Client Svcs Dir)*
Mike Schurr *(Dir-Creative)*

Accounts:
Denver Mattress
Oak Express Furniture Stores
Rayovac
Zondervan

DOMUS INC.
123 Avenue of Arts Ste 1980, Philadelphia, PA 19109
Tel.: (215) 772-2800
Fax: (215) 772-2819
E-Mail: betty.tuppeny@domusinc.com
Web Site: www.domusinc.com

Employees: 30
Year Founded: 1993

National Agency Associations: PRSA

Agency Specializes In: Advertising, Advertising Specialties, Affluent Market, Alternative

Advertising, Arts, Automotive, Below-the-Line, Brand Development & Integration, Broadcast, Business Publications, Business-To-Business, Cable T.V., Catalogs, Children's Market, Co-op Advertising, Collateral, College, Commercial Photography, Communications, Computers & Software, Consulting, Consumer Goods, Consumer Marketing, Consumer Publications, Content, Corporate Communications, Corporate Identity, Crisis Communications, Custom Publishing, Customer Relationship Management, Digital/Interactive, Direct Response Marketing, Direct-to-Consumer, E-Commerce, Education, Electronic Media, Electronics, Email, Entertainment, Environmental, Event Planning & Marketing, Exhibit/Trade Shows, Experience Design, Financial, Food Service, Government/Political, Graphic Design, Guerilla Marketing, Health Care Services, High Technology, Hospitality, Household Goods, Identity Marketing, In-Store Advertising, Industrial, Information Technology, Integrated Marketing, Internet/Web Design, Legal Services, Leisure, Local Marketing, Logo & Package Design, Luxury Products, Magazines, Market Research, Media Buying Services, Media Planning, Media Relations, Media Training, Merchandising, Mobile Marketing, Multicultural, Multimedia, New Product Development, New Technologies, Newspaper, Newspapers & Magazines, Out-of-Home Media, Outdoor, Over-50 Market, Package Design, Pharmaceutical, Planning & Consultation, Point of Purchase, Point of Sale, Print, Product Placement, Production, Production (Print), Promotions, Public Relations, Publicity/Promotions, Radio, Real Estate, Regional, Retail, Sales Promotion, Search Engine Optimization, Seniors' Market, Social Marketing/Nonprofit, Sponsorship, Sports Market, Strategic Planning/Research, Sweepstakes, T.V., Technical Advertising, Telemarketing, Trade & Consumer Magazines, Viral/Buzz/Word of Mouth, Women's Market

Approx. Annual Billings: $25,000,000

Elizabeth K. Tuppeny *(Owner)*
Lisa Samara *(Pres & COO)*
Joanne Michael *(Exec VP & Acct Mgr)*
Melissa Murphy *(Sr VP & Acct Dir)*
Maggie Kane *(Sr Mgr-Acct & Ops)*

Accounts:
Lutron Electronics, Inc.; Coopersburg, PA Lighting Controls; 1994
Oki Data Americas, Inc. ; Mount Laurel, NJ(Agency of Record) Printers; 1999

DON FARLEO ADVERTISING & DESIGN COMPANY INC.

3315 Roosevelt Rd Ste 300A, Saint Cloud, MN 56301
Tel.: (320) 229-9089
Fax: (320) 251-0356
Web Site: www.adcoinc.com

Agency Specializes In: Advertising, Corporate Communications, Internet/Web Design, Logo & Package Design, Outdoor, Promotions, Strategic Planning/Research, T.V.

Don Farleo *(Owner)*

Accounts:
Premier Restaurant Equipment

DON SCHAAF & FRIENDS, INC.

1313 F St NW 2nd Fl, Washington, DC 20004
Tel.: (202) 965-2600
Fax: (202) 965-2669
E-Mail: info@dsfriends.com
Web Site: www.dsfriends.com

Employees: 12

Agency Specializes In: Advertising, Brand Development & Integration, Direct Response Marketing, Identity Marketing, Media Relations, Package Design

Don Schaaf *(Pres)*
Ami Barker *(Exec VP)*
Mike Raso *(Exec VP)*
Matt Schaaf *(Exec VP)*
Alecia Lewis *(Sr Graphic Designer)*

Accounts:
American University
ASIS International Show
Flowserve
Kennametal, Inc.
NAB Show
Shop.org
US Olympic Bobsled Federation
Westinghouse Nuclear
WIDIA

DONALD R. HARVEY, INC.

3555 Veterans Memorial Hwy Ste D, Ronkonkoma, NY 11779
Tel.: (631) 467-6200
Fax: (631) 467-6224
Toll Free: (800) 842-9002
E-Mail: info@drhinc.com
Web Site: drhinc.com

Employees: 20
Year Founded: 1968

National Agency Associations: ADM-SEMPO-YPA

Agency Specializes In: Advertising, Aviation & Aerospace, Business Publications, Cable T.V., Co-op Advertising, Digital/Interactive, Direct Response Marketing, E-Commerce, Health Care Services, Integrated Marketing, Internet/Web Design, Magazines, Market Research, Media Buying Services, Media Planning, Point of Purchase, Promotions, Web (Banner Ads, Pop-ups, etc.), Yellow Pages Advertising

Approx. Annual Billings: $13,000,000

Breakdown of Gross Billings by Media: D.M.: $1,000,000; Internet Adv.: $2,000,000; Worldwide Web Sites: $1,000,000; Yellow Page Adv.: $9,000,000

Anthony Vela *(VP-Client Svcs)*

DONALD S. MONTGOMERY

(Formerly Seed Creative)
332 Bleecker St, New York, NY 10014
Tel.: (212) 462-2900
Fax: (212) 627-8025
Web Site: donaldsmontgomery.com

Employees: 20
Year Founded: 1998

Agency Specializes In: Advertising

Donald Montgomery *(Owner)*
Nicolette Abbatangelo *(Acct Mgr-Fashion & Beauty)*
Nickalas Bilotta *(Asst Coord-Creative Mktg)*

Accounts:
Aramis
Bochic
Laundry by Design
Miriam
Shiseido Americas Corporation
Think American
Tide

THE DONALDSON GROUP

88 Hopmeadow St, Weatogue, CT 06089-9602
Tel.: (860) 658-9777
Fax: (860) 658-0533
E-Mail: info@donaldson-group.com
Web Site: www.donaldson-group.com

Employees: 14
Year Founded: 1992

Agency Specializes In: Advertising, Multicultural, Women's Market

Revenue: $2,000,000

Scott Altman *(Sr VP)*
Scott Jones *(Sr VP-Property Mgmt)*
John Majeski *(Sr VP)*
Jennifer B. Casey *(VP-Ops)*
L. Carlyle Swafford *(VP)*
John Donaldson *(Dir-Strategy)*
Bethany Frasco *(Office Mgr)*
Corey Hansen *(Mgr-Content, Acct Exec & Coord-Mktg)*
Melissa Brown *(Mgr-Property)*
Kenya Cooper *(Mgr-Property)*
Brett Havener *(Mgr-Property)*
Megan Johnson *(Jr Designer-Production)*

Accounts:
3M
The Bushnell Center for the Performing Arts
Healthcare
United Natural Brands
YMCA

DONER

25900 Northwestern Hwy, Southfield, MI 48075
Tel.: (248) 354-9700
Fax: (248) 827-8440
Web Site: www.doner.com

Employees: 613
Year Founded: 1937

National Agency Associations: 4A's-ABC-APA

Agency Specializes In: Above-the-Line, Advertising, Alternative Advertising, Automotive, Below-the-Line, Brand Development & Integration, Broadcast, Business-To-Business, Cable T.V., Catalogs, Co-op Advertising, Collateral, Communications, Consumer Goods, Consumer Publications, Customer Relationship Management, Digital/Interactive, Direct Response Marketing, Direct-to-Consumer, E-Commerce, Electronic Media, Email, Exhibit/Trade Shows, Fashion/Apparel, Food Service, Graphic Design, Health Care Services, Hospitality, In-Store Advertising, Infomercials, Integrated Marketing, Internet/Web Design, Local Marketing, Magazines, Market Research, Media Buying Services, Media Planning, Merchandising, Mobile Marketing, Multimedia, Newspaper, Newspapers & Magazines, Out-of-Home Media, Outdoor, Package Design, Paid Searches, Pharmaceutical, Point of Purchase, Point of Sale, Print, Product Placement, Production, Production (Print), Promotions, Public Relations, Publicity/Promotions, Radio, Restaurant, Retail, Sales Promotion, Search Engine Optimization, Social Marketing/Nonprofit, Social Media, Sponsorship, Strategic Planning/Research, T.V., Trade & Consumer Magazines, Travel &

Tourism, Viral/Buzz/Word of Mouth, Web (Banner Ads, Pop-ups, etc.)

Doner is a full-service, performance-driven advertising agency that is hardwired to deliver creativity. They seek out unique intersections of culture, commerce and consumer life and turn them into IDEAS THAT MOVE PEOPLE.

Approx. Annual Billings: $1,200,000,000

David DeMuth *(Pres & Co-CEO)*
Robert Strasberg *(Co-CEO & Chief Creative Officer)*
Naveen Passey *(CFO & COO)*
Elizabeth Boone *(CMO & Exec VP)*
James Ward *(Chief Strategy Officer & Chief Integration Officer)*
Craig Conrad *(Exec VP & Chief Client Officer)*
Jennifer Deutsch *(Exec VP & Gen Mgr-Doner Cleveland)*
Chuck Meehan *(Exec VP & Exec Dir-Creative)*
Steve Silver *(Exec VP & Exec Creative Dir)*
Cindy Kenety *(Exec VP & Grp Acct Dir)*
Marci Benson *(Exec VP-Brand Leadership)*
Alison Taubman *(Exec VP-Bus & Strategy)*
Kevin Weinman *(Exec VP-Brand Management)*
Jason Jakubiak *(Sr VP & Creative Dir)*
Michael Leslie *(Sr VP & Creative Dir)*
Sheryll Kollin *(Sr VP & Dir-Bus Affairs)*
Jim Vassallo *(Sr VP)*
Stephanie Giorio *(VP & Head-Brand)*
Adina Sigler *(VP)*
Marcus Collins *(Exec Dir-Social Engagement)*
Brad Emmett *(Exec Dir-Creative)*
Alexander Drukas *(Sr Dir-Art)*
Brian Nelson *(Dir-Art & Assoc Dir-Creative)*
Virgil Adams *(Dir-Creative)*
Randy Belcher *(Dir-Creative)*
Jason Bergeron *(Dir-Creative)*
Anthony Moceri *(Assoc Dir-Creative)*
Katherine Simmonds *(Supvr-Bus Mgmt-Integrated Production)*

Accounts:
ACH Food Companies, Inc. (Digital Agency of Record) Social Media
ACSC (AAA); Irvine, CA
ADT (Lead Marketing Agency) Advertising, Broadcast, Campaign: "ADT Home Security is Always There", Campaign: "Home Automation Makes Your Smart Home a Safe Home", Creative, Media; 1999
Allegheny Health Network Advertising Strategy, Branding, Media Buying
Arby's Restaurant Group, Inc. Media Co-ops
Bellefaire JCB Campaign: "Take A Closer Look", campaign: "2nd Look"
Bristol-Myers Squibb
Bush Brothers & Company
C Spire Digital, Media Planning & Buying
Coca-Cola Co. Campaign: "Doin' Good", Minute Maid, Simply Orange
Cox Communications; Atlanta, GA Campaign: "TV Just for Me", Contour, Creative, Public Relations
Detroit Zoo; Detroit, MI
DuPont Surfaces; Wilmington, DE Corian, Zodiaq
FCA (Fiat Chrysler Automobiles) Alfa Romeo, Campaign: "Dodge Law", Campaign: "Road to Greatness", Chrysler 300, Chrysler Town & Country, Chrysler, Jeep & Dodge, Ram Truck, Uconnect; 2010
New-Food Lion (Advertising Agency of Record) Integrated Marketing, Media Buying, Media Planning
Geisinger; 2011
Gojo Purell
Golfsmith International (Agency of Record) Creative, Digital, Print, Radio, TV
Harman International Industries(JBl,Harman) Creative; 2010
Highmark Health Advertising Strategy, Branding, Broadcast, Creative, Lead Agency, Media Buying, Online, Outdoor, Print, Radio
International Tennis Hall of Fame (Agency of Record) Creative & Interactive Communications, Media Planning
Kelley Blue Book (Agency of Record); 2012
Manheim Creative, Media Planning & Buying, Strategic Planning
Marie Callender's Restaurant & Bakery Media Planning & Buying
Meijer Buying, Media, Planning
NGK Sparkplugs (Agency of Record); 2013
Oasis Consumer Healthcare
OhioHealth Corp. (Agency of Record)
Oil-Dri (Agency of Record) Cat's Pride Litter
Ovation Brands; Eagan, MN Home Town Buffet, Old Country Buffet; 2003
Owens Corning Corporation; Toledo, OH
PGA Tour Local Advertising
Pulte Group Media
Serta, Inc (Agency of Record) Campaign: "We Need to Talk", Campaign: "You're Not Helping", Creative
Smithfield Foods; Smithfield, VA Gwaltney
Stanley Steemer; 2013
Susan G. Komen Northeast Ohio
Things Remembered, Inc.; Highland Heights, OH; 2007
The Timken Company; Canton, OH
Tyco International Ltd
The UPS Store (Agency of Record) Campaign: "Mailbox Confessions", Online, Print, Radio

Branches

Doner, London
(Formerly Doner Cardwell Hawkins)
60 Charlotte St, London, W1T 2NU United Kingdom
Tel.: (44) 20 7632 7600
E-Mail: talk@doner.co.uk
Web Site: www.doner.co.uk/

Employees: 45
Year Founded: 1995

Agency Specializes In: Advertising, Consumer Goods, Electronics, New Technologies

Nik Margolis *(Mng Partner)*
Nick Constantinou *(Mng Dir)*
Wayne Deakin *(Exec Creative Dir)*
Jenna Stafford *(Acct Dir)*
Nigel Carlos *(Dir-Social Media)*
Nick Gill *(Dir-Plng)*
Matt McMinn *(Dir-Bus Dev)*
Nick Scott *(Dir-Creative)*
Becky Griffiths *(Sr Acct Mgr)*
Ian Cawley *(Copywriter-Creative)*

Accounts:
Align Technology, Inc.
Discovery
Fiat Group Alfa Romeo, Campaign: "Made of Red", Chrysler, Digital, Giulietta, Jeep, MiTo, Online, Press, TV
Fuller's
Nikon Corporation
QVC
Wiltshire Farm Foods Taking Care of Mealtimes

Doner
909 N. Sepulveda Blvd, El Segundo, CA 90245-2724
Tel.: (424) 220-7200
Web Site: www.doner.com

Employees: 25

National Agency Associations: 4A's-AAF-DMA-PRSA

Agency Specializes In: Advertising, Digital/Interactive

Zihla Salinas *(Mng Dir & Exec VP)*
Jane Huetter *(Sr VP & Head-Strategic)*
Anita Anderson *(Sr VP & Acct Dir)*
Marlene Calderon *(Sr VP-Strategy & Plng)*
Maria Carr *(Sr VP)*
Brad Emmett *(Exec Dir-Creative)*
Matt Swanson *(Grp Dir-Creative)*
Michelle Musallam *(Sr Dir-Art)*
Kristie Bergmann *(Supvr-Local Brdcst)*
Tina Williams *(Sr Acct Exec)*
Jessye Hand *(Copywriter)*
Alexander Harvilla *(Planner-Strategic)*
Alicia Liken *(Copywriter)*

Accounts:
Arby's West
Avery Dennison Office Products Office & Consumer Products
Detroit Zoo
Fuhu, Inc. Advertising, Nabi Big Tab
Jafra International
Menchies
Minute Maid
Neato Robotics
Neato Campaign: "Card", Campaign: "Hippie Pinata", Campaign: "House Sitter", Campaign: "Neato Knows Your Grandma Misses You", Campaign: "One Night Stand"
Pac Sun
Secure Horizons
UPS Store

Doner
The Diamond Bldg 1100 Superior Ave 10th Fl, Cleveland, OH 44114
Tel.: (216) 771-5700
Fax: (216) 771-1308
Web Site: doner.com/

Year Founded: 1988

National Agency Associations: 4A's-AAF-DMA-PRSA

Agency Specializes In: Sponsorship

Liz Boone *(CMO & Exec VP)*
Jennifer Deutsch *(Exec VP & Gen Mgr-Cleveland)*
Sandy Croucher *(Sr VP & Head-Brand)*
Larry Deangelis *(Sr VP & Head-Brand)*
Brian Keir *(VP & Acct Dir)*
Paul Forsyth *(VP & Dir-Creative)*
Laura Owen *(VP & Dir-Creative)*
Pete Heid *(Exec Dir-Creative)*
Jason Tisser *(Assoc Dir-Creative)*

Accounts:
Geisinger Health System & Health Plan
OhioHealth

SEE Insight
55 Ivan Allen Jr Blvd Ste 350, Atlanta, GA 30308
(See Separate Listing)

DONOVAN ADVERTISING & MARKETING SERVICES
180 W Airport Rd, Lititz, PA 17543
Tel.: (717) 560-1333
Fax: (717) 560-2034
Web Site: www.donovanadv.com

E-Mail for Key Personnel:
Production Mgr.: mlondon@donovanadv.com

Employees: 21
Year Founded: 1984

Agency Specializes In: Advertising, Advertising Specialties, Brand Development & Integration, Business Publications, Business-To-Business, Cable T.V., Collateral, Communications, Consumer Goods, Consumer Marketing, Consumer

Publications, Content, Digital/Interactive, Direct Response Marketing, Direct-to-Consumer, E-Commerce, Education, Email, Event Planning & Marketing, Exhibit/Trade Shows, Financial, Food Service, Graphic Design, Health Care Services, Hispanic Market, In-Store Advertising, Industrial, Integrated Marketing, Internet/Web Design, Local Marketing, Logo & Package Design, Magazines, Market Research, Media Buying Services, Media Planning, Merchandising, Mobile Marketing, New Product Development, Newspapers & Magazines, Outdoor, Package Design, Planning & Consultation, Point of Purchase, Print, Production, Production (Ad, Film, Broadcast), Promotions, Public Relations, Publicity/Promotions, Radio, Recruitment, Retail, Sales Promotion, Shopper Marketing, Social Marketing/Nonprofit, Social Media, Sponsorship, Strategic Planning/Research, Sweepstakes, T.V., Trade & Consumer Magazines, Viral/Buzz/Word of Mouth, Web (Banner Ads, Pop-ups, etc.), Women's Market

Approx. Annual Billings: $11,670,000

William J. Donovan, Jr. *(Pres & CEO)*
Jane Flemming *(COO)*
Mike O'Brien *(Dir-Bus Dev)*

Accounts:
BIC Consumer Products
C-P Flexible Packaging
D.F. Stauffer Biscuit Company
Furmano's
Jel Sert
Keystone Food Products
Milton Hershey School
New World Pasta
Perdue Foods
Rutter's Farm Stores; York, PA
Savory Foods
Yuengling

DOODLE DOG ADVERTISING

2919 Commerce St Ste 192, Dallas, TX 75226
Tel.: (940) 453-1636
E-Mail: info@doodledogadvertising.com
Web Site: www.doodledogadvertising.com

Agency Specializes In: Advertising, Brand Development & Integration, Collateral, Internet/Web Design, Logo & Package Design, Promotions, Search Engine Optimization

Nikki Nuckols *(Owner & Creative Dir)*
Sarah Campbell *(Jr Designer)*

Accounts:
Armstrong Diamonds
Catherine Masi
Juniper Flowers
Kim Armstrong
Knot One Day
Life Styled Group
Real Weddings Magazine
Soulbox Productions
Southern Oaks Plantation
VIP DJ

DOOR NUMBER 3

1050 E 11th St Ste 250, Austin, TX 78702
Tel.: (512) 391-1773
Fax: (512) 391-1926
E-Mail: knock@dn3austin.com
Web Site: www.dn3austin.com

E-Mail for Key Personnel:
President: mp@nourzads.com

Employees: 15
Year Founded: 1994

Agency Specializes In: Automotive, Brand Development & Integration, Business-To-Business, Collateral, Consulting, Consumer Marketing, Corporate Identity, E-Commerce, Event Planning & Marketing, Exhibit/Trade Shows, Fashion/Apparel, Financial, Government/Political, Graphic Design, Health Care Services, High Technology, Internet/Web Design, Logo & Package Design, Media Buying Services, Medical Products, Newspapers & Magazines, Outdoor, Pharmaceutical, Planning & Consultation, Print, Publicity/Promotions, Radio, Real Estate, Recruitment, Strategic Planning/Research, T.V., Travel & Tourism

Approx. Annual Billings: $8,655,599

Breakdown of Gross Billings by Media: Fees: 23%; Outdoor: 6%; Print: 19%; Production: 18%; Radio: 18%; T.V.: 14%; Worldwide Web Sites: 2%

M. P. Mueller *(Pres)*
Karen Reiner *(Acct Svcs Dir)*
Zach Cochran *(Dir-Media)*
Ines Morel *(Dir-Art)*
Sally Robb *(Assoc Dir)*

Accounts:
The Alamo
Aramco
Austin Humane Society
Blood Center of Central Texas
Burnet County Tourism
Habitat for Humanity
Premier Research Group
Texas Rangers Baseball Club
Texas.gov
Umlauf Sculpture Garden & Museum; Austin, TX (Pro Bono); 2007

DOREMUS

200 Varick St 11Fl, New York, NY 10014-4810
Tel.: (212) 366-3000
Fax: (212) 366-3060
E-Mail: mbroom@doremus.com
Web Site: www.doremus.com

Employees: 100
Year Founded: 1903

National Agency Associations: 4A's-AAF-ABC-AMA-APA-BMA-BPA

Agency Specializes In: Advertising, Brand Development & Integration, Business-To-Business, Collateral, Communications, Consulting, Consumer Marketing, Corporate Identity, Customer Relationship Management, Direct Response Marketing, Electronic Media, Event Planning & Marketing, Exhibit/Trade Shows, Experience Design, Financial, High Technology, Information Technology, Integrated Marketing, Internet/Web Design, Investor Relations, Leisure, Luxury Products, Magazines, Media Buying Services, Media Planning, Media Relations, Mobile Marketing, New Product Development, New Technologies, Newspaper, Newspapers & Magazines, Out-of-Home Media, Outdoor, Planning & Consultation, Production, Production (Print), Promotions, Public Relations, Sales Promotion, Sponsorship, Strategic Planning/Research, Trade & Consumer Magazines, Yellow Pages Advertising

Breakdown of Gross Billings by Media: Collateral: 5%; D.M.: 5%; Exhibits/Trade Shows: 5%; Internet Adv.: 15%; Mags.: 20%; Newsp.: 15%; Outdoor: 5%; Radio: 3%; Strategic Planning/Research: 10%; T.V.: 17%

Howard Sherman *(Pres & CEO)*
Joe McCormack *(Chief Creative Officer-San Francisco)*
Evelyn Neill *(Chief Creative Officer-New York)*
Matthew Broom *(Pres-Intl & Mng Dir-New York)*
Alasdair Morrison *(Pres-London)*
Allison Womack *(Pres-New York)*
Kevin Jenkins *(VP & Grp Acct Dir)*
David Rowe *(VP & Dir-Media)*
Michael Litchfield *(Exec Dir-Creative)*
Drew Reccius *(Grp Dir-Media)*
Paul Chung *(Sr Dir-Art)*
Lauren Dickinson *(Sr Dir-Art)*
Christine Bailey *(Grp Acct Dir)*
Joanna Berke *(Grp Acct Dir)*
Cate Downes *(Grp Acct Dir)*
Jason Winkler *(Grp Acct Dir)*
Dave Sechko *(Mgmt Supvr)*
Stu Garrett *(Dir-Creative)*
Michael Tucker *(Dir-Creative)*
Arbell Noach *(Assoc Dir-Engagement)*
Elysha Beckerman *(Mgr-Engagement)*
Kelly Higgins *(Mgr-Strategic Partnerships)*
Kali Williams *(Mgr-Digital Campaign)*
Jessica Knight Mendiola *(Acct Supvr)*
Katherine Seipp *(Sr Acct Exec)*

Accounts:
Brocade
CFA Institute; 2007
Hewlett Packard (HP) Campaign: "Get Real. Upgrade and Save.", Printers
Hiscox plc Banner Advertising, Campaign: "Encourage Courage", Cards, Creative, Online, Print
Johnson & Johnson
Marsh & McLennan Companies
Owens-Illinois Campaign: "Glass Is Life", Campaign: "The Living Glass Conversation", Online, Social Media, Social-Content Strategy, TV
QBE Insurance
Quintiles; 2009
Russell Investment Group; 2007
Sun Life Financial; Wellesley Hills, MA Creative, Media
Swift
Truven Health Analytics
UniCredit
Visa
Wall Street Journal Europe

Branch

Doremus (San Francisco)

550 3rd St, San Francisco, CA 94107
Tel.: (415) 273-7800
E-Mail: mgoefft@doremus.com
Web Site: www.doremus.com/

Employees: 50
Year Founded: 1978

National Agency Associations: 4A's-AAF-AMA-ANA-BMA

Agency Specializes In: Advertising, Business-To-Business, Corporate Identity, Direct Response Marketing, Financial, Health Care Services, Information Technology, Internet/Web Design, Media Buying Services, Planning & Consultation, Strategic Planning/Research

Garrett Lawrence *(Pres)*
Joe McCormack *(Exec VP & Dir-Creative)*
Mike Goefft *(Exec Dir-Strategic Partnerships)*
Michael Litchfield *(Creative Dir)*
Lulu Huang *(Mgmt Supvr)*
Artem Peplov *(Mgmt Supvr)*
Bennett Miller *(Dir-Creative)*
Sara Fowler *(Acct Supvr)*
Christina Corrado *(Sr Acct Exec)*
Martin Sargent *(Sr Copywriter)*
Jonathan Handy *(Planner)*
Eric Liu *(Sr Graphic Designer)*

Accounts:
Agility

REDBOOKS
Brands. Marketers. Agencies. Search Less. Find More.
Try out the Online version at www.redbooks.com

Barclays Capital
CFA Institute
Corning Incorporated Campaign: "Brokeface", Campaign: "The Glass Age", Corning Glass, Gorilla Glass, NBT
Hewlett-Packard Company "Power Up", Campaign: "Mac to Z", Content, HP Z workstations, Print, Social Media, online
ING
Knight
Logitech Campaign: "Logitech: The New Office"
Sage North America (Agency of Record) Print & Online Advertising
SonicWall
Uni Credit

International

Doremus (United Kingdom)
10 Regents Wharf All Saints St London, London, N1 9RL United Kingdom
Tel.: (44) 207 778 1500
Fax: (44) 207 778 1515
E-Mail: alasdair.m@doremus.co.uk
Web Site: www.doremus.com

Employees: 12
Year Founded: 1986

National Agency Associations: IAA

Agency Specializes In: Advertising, Business Publications, Business-To-Business, Corporate Communications, Financial, Investor Relations, Magazines, New Technologies, Newspaper, Newspapers & Magazines, Production (Print)

Howard Sherman *(Pres & CEO)*
Richard S. Beccle *(Grp Mng Dir-Asia Pacific)*
Ronnie Brown *(Chief Creative Officer-London)*
Matthew Don *(Chief Innovation Officer)*
Alasdair Morrison *(Pres-London)*
Erica Henninger *(Client Svcs Dir)*

Accounts:
Barclays Capital
Credit Suisse
Danfoss
Deutsche Bank
Quintiles

Doremus (Hong Kong)
Ste 1501 15/F Cityplaza 4, 12 Taikoo Wan Road Taikoo, Hong Kong, China (Hong Kong)
Tel.: (852) 2861 2721
Fax: (852) 2536 9416
E-Mail: richard.beccle@doremus.com.hk
Web Site: www.doremus.com

Employees: 25
Year Founded: 1994

Agency Specializes In: Advertising, Business-To-Business, Financial

Richard Beccle *(Grp Mng Dir-Asia Pacific)*
Calvin Chow *(Grp Acct Dir)*
Macy Au *(Dir-Art)*
Esther Wong *(Dir-Plng)*

Accounts:
ABN AMRO
Barclays
Citigroup
Credit Suisse
JP Morgan
Juniper Networks
Merrill Lynch
Morgan Stanley
SONY Professional Products
Wall Street Journal Asia Campaign: "What in the World Is Going On?"

Advantage Corporate Communications GmbH
Lindle Street 12 3 Stock 3rd fl, 60314 Frankfurt am Main, Germany
Tel.: (49) 69 71005 0
Fax: (49) 69 71005 333
E-Mail: hello@advantage.de
Web Site: www.advantage.de

Employees: 10

Agency Specializes In: Financial

Arman Vardar *(Mng Dir)*
Britta Vardar *(Mng Dir)*
Can Vardar *(Mng Dir)*

Accounts:
Barclay's Capital
Credit Suisse Securities (USA) LLC
Deustche Bank

DORN MARKETING
121 W State St, Geneva, IL 60134-2254
Tel.: (630) 232-2010
Fax: (630) 232-2033
Web Site: www.dornmarketing.com

E-Mail for Key Personnel:
President: james.dorn@dornmarketing.com
Creative Dir.: james.dorn@dornmarketing.com
Media Dir.: kathy.williams@dornmarketing.com

Employees: 10
Year Founded: 1971

National Agency Associations: OAAA

Agency Specializes In: Advertising, Automotive, Brand Development & Integration, Broadcast, Business Publications, Business-To-Business, Cable T.V., Collateral, Commercial Photography, Communications, Consulting, Consumer Marketing, Consumer Publications, Corporate Identity, Digital/Interactive, Direct Response Marketing, E-Commerce, Electronic Media, Engineering, Event Planning & Marketing, Exhibit/Trade Shows, Fashion/Apparel, Financial, Food Service, Graphic Design, Health Care Services, High Technology, Industrial, Infomercials, Information Technology, Internet/Web Design, Investor Relations, Logo & Package Design, Magazines, Media Buying Services, Medical Products, Merchandising, Multimedia, New Product Development, Newspaper, Newspapers & Magazines, Outdoor, Pharmaceutical, Planning & Consultation, Point of Purchase, Point of Sale, Print, Production, Public Relations, Publicity/Promotions, Radio, Real Estate, Recruitment, Restaurant, Retail, Sales Promotion, Seniors' Market, Strategic Planning/Research, T.V., Technical Advertising, Telemarketing, Trade & Consumer Magazines, Travel & Tourism

Approx. Annual Billings: $7,000,000

Dan Roglin *(Sr VP-Strategy & Insights)*
Joseph Caruso *(Dir-Creative)*
John Minorini *(Dir-Tech)*
Neil Ruffolo *(Dir-Digital Mktg)*
Rachel Pankow *(Sr Acct Mgr)*
Kathleen Williams *(Sr Acct Mgr)*
Kerrie Martin *(Mgr-Online Mktg)*
James Sudeikis *(Sr Designer)*
Katherine Frankenthal *(Coord-Mktg)*

Accounts:
Bolingbrook Park District
Bosch Tools
Bowlingbrook Park District
Columbian Tools
Fellows Office Products
Panther Vision
Quality Checked Dairies
Remke Industries
Shanghai Daisy
Wilton Tools

DORNENBURG KALLENBACH ADVERTISING
16 Southwood Dr, Bloomfield, CT 06002
Tel.: (860) 726-9740
Fax: (860) 726-9745
Web Site: www.dornenburggroup.com

Year Founded: 1994

Agency Specializes In: Advertising, Brand Development & Integration, Collateral, Internet/Web Design, Media Buying Services, Promotions, Public Relations, Social Media

Jeff Dornenburg *(Pres)*
Nancy Dornenburg *(Partner-Strategic Bus)*
Tod Kallenbach *(VP)*

Accounts:
University of Connecticut Cooperative Corporation

DORSEY STUDIOS
243 Macdonnell Street, Toronto, ON M6R 2A9 Canada
Tel.: (647) 938-5449
Web Site: www.dorseystudios.ca

Agency Specializes In: Advertising, Brand Development & Integration, Digital/Interactive, Graphic Design, Logo & Package Design, Package Design

Stephen Dorsey *(CEO & Strategist)*
Megan Khan *(Coord-PR & Comm)*

Accounts:
Stephanos Secret Stash
Temporal Power Ltd

DOTBOX
(Acquired by MDC Partners Inc.)

DOUBLE-TEAM BUSINESS PLANS
1725 Ocean Ave, Santa Monica, CA 90401
Tel.: (310) 878-4300
E-Mail: doug@double-team-bp.com
Web Site: www.double-team-bp.com

Employees: 4
Year Founded: 1980

Agency Specializes In: Advertising, Broadcast, Business Publications, Business-To-Business, Cable T.V., Co-op Advertising, Collateral, Consulting, Consumer Goods, Consumer Marketing, Content, Corporate Communications, Corporate Identity, Cosmetics, Direct Response Marketing, Direct-to-Consumer, E-Commerce, Electronic Media, Email, Environmental, Exhibit/Trade Shows, Financial, Government/Political, High Technology, Identity Marketing, Integrated Marketing, Internet/Web Design, Luxury Products, Magazines, Market Research, Media Buying Services, Media Planning, New Product Development, New Technologies, Newspaper, Newspapers & Magazines, Out-of-Home Media, Outdoor, Planning & Consultation, Print, Sales Promotion, Social Media, Sports Market, Strategic Planning/Research, Sweepstakes, T.V., Telemarketing, Trade & Consumer Magazines, Travel & Tourism, Viral/Buzz/Word of Mouth

Approx. Annual Billings: $1,225,000

Doug R. Hedlund *(CEO)*

Accounts:
HedgePort Associates; Los Angeles, CA Outsourced Hedge Fund Services; 2009
La Cantina Italiana; Hollywood, FL Wine & Spirits Importer; 2003
NutriScience Corporation; Hermosa Beach, CA "Energize For Life" Health Program, Protein Shakes; 2004
RAAM Corp.; Los Angeles, CA Financial Real Estate Services; 1993
Rapid Brands Corporation; Flint, MI GreatDay Household-Cleaning Brand, Quick & Healthy Pet-Cleaning Brand; 2004
Resolve Capital LLC; Santa Monica, CA Hedge Fund; 2006
Scoremate Partners, Ltd.; Hawthorne, CA Scorekeeping Wristband for Tennis Players; 1992

DOUBLE XXPOSURE MEDIA RELATIONS INC
2037 Lemoine Ave Ste 205, Fort Lee, NJ 7024
Tel.: (201) 224-6570
E-Mail: theellerbeegroup@aol.com
Web Site: www.dxxnyc.com

Year Founded: 1972

Agency Specializes In: Advertising, Brand Development & Integration, Electronic Media, Event Planning & Marketing, Internet/Web Design, Media Relations, Media Training, Print, Public Relations, Social Media

Angelo Ellerbee *(Founder, Pres & CEO)*

Accounts:
New-Music Mogul

DOUBLEPOSITIVE MARKETING GROUP, INC.
1501 S Clinton St Ste 1520, Baltimore, MD 21224
Tel.: (410) 332-0464
Fax: (410) 332-1059
Toll Free: (888) 376-7484
E-Mail: info@doublepositive.com
Web Site: www.doublepositive.com

Employees: 13
Year Founded: 2004

Revenue: $3,700,000

Joey Liner *(Co-Founder & Exec VP-Sls)*
Sean Fenlon *(CEO)*
Joe Tagliareni *(COO)*
Paul Didonno *(VP-Strategic Client Svcs)*
Jodi Swartz *(VP-Mktg)*
Rich Dent *(Acct Dir-Mgmt)*
Lory Cerato *(Dir-Admin)*

DOUGLAS MARKETING GROUP, LLC
10900 Harper Rd Ste 100, Detroit, MI 48213
Tel.: (313) 571-1858
Fax: (888) 761-5164
E-Mail: info@experiencedmg.com
Web Site: www.experiencedmg.com

Year Founded: 1991

Agency Specializes In: Advertising, Collateral, Event Planning & Marketing, Graphic Design, Internet/Web Design, Public Relations, Social Media

Liz Farano *(VP-Mktg & Dir-Creative)*
Amanda Iera *(VP-Mktg)*
Sebastian Agosta *(Dir-Online Mktg)*
Andrew Siracki *(Dir-Web Dev)*
Jason Trepanier *(Dir-Creative)*

Accounts:
Thomas Utopia Brand

DOUGSERGE+PARTNERS
(Name Changed to dsp+p)

DOVETAIL
12 Maryland Plz, Saint Louis, MO 63108-1502
Tel.: (314) 361-9800
Fax: (314) 361-9801
E-Mail: info@dovetail-stl.com
Web Site: www.dovetail-stl.com

E-Mail for Key Personnel:
Media Dir.: susan@maringweissman.com

Employees: 12
Year Founded: 1979

National Agency Associations: 4A's

Agency Specializes In: Business-To-Business, Consumer Marketing, Education, Environmental, Health Care Services, High Technology, Real Estate, Seniors' Market, Travel & Tourism

Approx. Annual Billings: $10,000,000

Susan Weissman *(Pres)*
Tom Etling *(Partner-Strategy & Innovation)*
Donna MacDonald *(Sr VP-Brand Mgmt)*
Scott Leisler *(Exec Dir-Creative)*
Hunter Lansche *(Assoc Dir-Creative)*
Jennifer Schmid *(Sr Brand Mgr)*
Jenna Green *(Brand Mgr)*
Jennifer Anania *(Mgr-Fin)*

Accounts:
Buckingham Asset Management; Saint Louis, MO Investment Advice
Citizens Equity First Credit Union (CEFCU); Peoria, IL
The Gateway Arch Riverfront; Saint Louis, MO National Monument
Money Center 24

DOWNTOWN PARTNERS CHICAGO
200 E Randolph St 34th Fl, Chicago, IL 60601
Tel.: (312) 552-5800
Fax: (312) 552-2330
Web Site: www.downtownpartners.com

Employees: 22

National Agency Associations: 4A's

Agency Specializes In: Advertising, Production (Ad, Film, Broadcast), Production (Print), Sponsorship

Diane Kerwin *(Sr Dir-Art)*
Dan Consiglio *(Creative Dir)*
Caroline Chen *(Dir-Social & Digital)*
Dimitri Poulios *(Dir-Design)*
Louise Rasmussen *(Dir-Plng)*
Caitlin Klag *(Acct Mgr)*
Christine Vonch *(Acct Supvr)*
Julie Sestan *(Acct Exec)*
Matthew Vaske *(Acct Exec)*

Accounts:
Chicago Children's Advocacy Center Campaign: "Bear"
Chicago Convention & Tourism Bureau
Get Covered Illinois
Green Planet
Illinois State Lottery Campaign: "Anything's Possible", Digital
The Land of Nod
Northern Trust
Walgreen's Campaign: "Twins"
World Business Chicago

THE DOZIER COMPANY
2547 Farrington St, Dallas, TX 75207-6607
Tel.: (214) 744-2800
Fax: (214) 744-1240
E-Mail: doz@thedoziercompany.com
Web Site: www.thedoziercompany.com

E-Mail for Key Personnel:
Creative Dir.: connie@thedoziercompany.com
Public Relations: connie@thedoziercompany.com

Employees: 10
Year Founded: 1987

Agency Specializes In: Brand Development & Integration, Business Publications, Business-To-Business, Co-op Advertising, Collateral, Commercial Photography, Communications, Consulting, Consumer Marketing, Consumer Publications, Corporate Identity, Direct Response Marketing, E-Commerce, Education, Electronic Media, Event Planning & Marketing, Exhibit/Trade Shows, Fashion/Apparel, Financial, Graphic Design, Health Care Services, In-Store Advertising, Industrial, Internet/Web Design, Legal Services, Local Marketing, Logo & Package Design, Magazines, Media Buying Services, Medical Products, Merchandising, Multimedia, New Product Development, Newspaper, Newspapers & Magazines, Outdoor, Pharmaceutical, Planning & Consultation, Point of Purchase, Point of Sale, Print, Production, Public Relations, Publicity/Promotions, Radio, Real Estate, Restaurant, Retail, Sales Promotion, Strategic Planning/Research, Trade & Consumer Magazines, Travel & Tourism, Yellow Pages Advertising

Approx. Annual Billings: $18,000,000

Breakdown of Gross Billings by Media: Bus. Publs.: $1,800,000; Collateral: $2,700,000; Consulting: $1,800,000; Fees: $2,700,000; Newsp.: $2,700,000; Outdoor: $900,000; Plng. & Consultation: $900,000; Promos.: $360,000; Pub. Rels.: $1,800,000; Radio & T.V.: $540,000; Trade & Consumer Mags.: $900,000; Worldwide Web Sites: $900,000

Michael Dozier *(Pres)*
Connie Dozier *(Principal)*
David C. Dozier *(Principal)*

Accounts:
American Land Title Assoc.; Washington, DC
Barclay Commercial; Dallas, TX Real Estate Brokerage
CAPSTAR Commercial Real Estate Services; Dallas, TX
DFW Advisors; Dallas, TX Real Estate Brokerage
Heatley Capital; Dallas, TX
MRK Plumbing Supply; Houston, TX
NorthMarq Capital; Minneapolis, MN Investment Bankers
Silverwing Development; Concord, CA Real Estate Developer
Ticor Title; Dallas, TX
TIG Real Estate Services; Dallas, TX
Westmount Realty Capital; Dallas, TX
Winston Capital; Dallas, TX

DRADDY INFUSION
401 E 80th St Ste 25, New York, NY 10075
Tel.: (212) 600-1375
Fax: (212) 679-0576
Web Site: www.draddyinfusion.com

E-Mail for Key Personnel:
President: sdraddy@draddyinfusion.com

Agency Specializes In: Business-To-Business,

Communications, Consumer Marketing, Event Planning & Marketing, Sales Promotion, Strategic Planning/Research

Sue Draddy *(Pres & Mng Partner)*

Accounts:
DK
Random House
tic tac

DRAKE COOPER INC.
416 S 8th 3rd Fl, Boise, ID 83702-5471
Tel.: (208) 342-0925
Fax: (208) 342-0635
E-Mail: info@drakecooper.com
Web Site: www.drakecooper.com

E-Mail for Key Personnel:
President: bdrake@esdrake.com
Creative Dir.: wlassen@esdrake.com
Production Mgr.: lhawkes@esdrake.com

Employees: 36
Year Founded: 1987

Agency Specializes In: Advertising, Brand Development & Integration, Broadcast, Business Publications, Business-To-Business, Cable T.V., Co-op Advertising, Collateral, Communications, Consulting, Consumer Publications, Digital/Interactive, Direct Response Marketing, Education, Electronic Media, Event Planning & Marketing, Exhibit/Trade Shows, Government/Political, Graphic Design, Health Care Services, High Technology, Infomercials, Internet/Web Design, Logo & Package Design, Magazines, Market Research, Media Buying Services, Newspaper, Newspapers & Magazines, Outdoor, Point of Purchase, Point of Sale, Print, Production, Promotions, Public Relations, Publicity/Promotions, Radio, Sales Promotion, Sponsorship, Strategic Planning/Research, T.V., Trade & Consumer Magazines, Transportation, Travel & Tourism, Web (Banner Ads, Pop-ups, etc.), Yellow Pages Advertising

Breakdown of Gross Billings by Media: Collateral: 28%; Internet Adv.: 6%; Mags.: 9%; Newsp.: 3%; Outdoor: 5%; Radio: 20%; T.V.: 29%

Jamie Cooper *(CEO)*
Katie S. Nichols *(Sr Dir-Art)*
Sara Chase *(Acct Svcs Dir)*
Jennie Myers *(Creative Dir)*
Cale Cathey *(Dir-Art)*
Meghan Rae *(Dir-Media)*
Brad Weigle *(Dir-Digital)*
Annie Takagi *(Media Buyer)*

Accounts:
Big Bear Lake
CBH Homes; Boise, ID Builder; 2007
Home Federal; Boise, ID Financial Institution; 2003
Hubble Homes; Boise, ID; 2004
Idaho Beef Council
Idaho Dairy Products; Boise, ID Dairy; 2008
Idaho Department of Commerce
Idaho Dept of Agriculture; Boise, ID Agriculture; 2002
Idaho Dept. of Health & Welfare; Boise, ID Social & Health Issues; 1994
Idaho Transportation Department; Boise, ID Transportation; 2006
Idaho Wines
Jensen Jewelers; Jensen, ID Jewelry; 2005
Papa Murphy's; Boise, ID Pizza; 2002
Qualis Health; Boise, ID Health Care; 2003
University of Idaho; Moscow, ID Education; 1996
Zoo Boise

DRAW
(Formerly Last Exit)
The Leathermarket, Building1-2, Weston Street, London, SE1 3ER United Kingdom
Tel.: (44) 207 7407 7666
E-Mail: hello@drawgroup.com
Web Site: drawgroup.com

Employees: 18
Year Founded: 2003

Agency Specializes In: Advertising, Brand Development & Integration, Email, Logo & Package Design, Market Research, Print, Search Engine Optimization, Strategic Planning/Research, Web (Banner Ads, Pop-ups, etc.)

Fred Brown *(Mng Dir)*
Nick Elsom *(Mng Dir-Content)*
Steven Blackman *(Head-Media & Entertainment)*
Rob Robinson *(Creative Dir)*
Kent Valentine *(Dir)*
Joe Minett *(Sr Acct Mgr)*
James Bullman *(Acct Mgr)*
Daniel Stolz *(Designer)*
Adam Taylor *(Designer)*
Gary Wadsworth *(Designer)*

Accounts:
Absolut Vodka
BathHouse
Betty Crocker
Canon
McCann Erickson New York
Panasonic
Ray-Ban
Salisbury Cathedral
Serengeti Partners International Inc
Toyota
Unilever Group of Companies Online Healthcare Services

DRB PARTNERS, INC.
2328 Walsh Ave, Santa Clara, CA 95051
Tel.: (408) 943-0515
Fax: (408) 943-1904
Toll Free: (877) 234-2094
E-Mail: info@drbpartners.com
Web Site: www.drbpartners.com

E-Mail for Key Personnel:
President: ray@drbmar.com
Creative Dir.: ken@drbmar.com

Employees: 10
Year Founded: 1985

National Agency Associations: BMA

Agency Specializes In: Advertising, Advertising Specialties, Automotive, Brand Development & Integration, Broadcast, Business Publications, Business-To-Business, Co-op Advertising, Collateral, Communications, Computers & Software, Consulting, Corporate Communications, Corporate Identity, Digital/Interactive, Direct Response Marketing, E-Commerce, Electronic Media, Electronics, Email, Engineering, Exhibit/Trade Shows, Faith Based, Graphic Design, Health Care Services, High Technology, Identity Marketing, Industrial, Information Technology, Integrated Marketing, Internet/Web Design, Local Marketing, Logo & Package Design, Magazines, Media Buying Services, Media Planning, Media Relations, Medical Products, Newspaper, Newspapers & Magazines, Outdoor, Package Design, Planning & Consultation, Point of Purchase, Print, Production, Production (Print), Promotions, Public Relations, Publicity/Promotions, Radio, Social Marketing/Nonprofit, Social Media, Strategic Planning/Research, Technical Advertising, Trade & Consumer Magazines, Transportation, Viral/Buzz/Word of Mouth, Web (Banner Ads, Pop-ups, etc.)

Approx. Annual Billings: $2,000,000

Breakdown of Gross Billings by Media: Graphic Design: $600,000; Logo & Package Design: $400,000; Pub. Rels.: $500,000; Trade & Consumer Mags.: $500,000

Raymond Brown *(Owner)*
Ken Camozzi *(Dir-Creative)*
Dee Brown *(Office Mgr)*

Accounts:
Linear Technology Corp.; Milpitas, CA Analog Semiconductors; 1994
SPX Corporation; Cleveland, OH Automotive Aftermarket; 2003

DREAMBEAR, LLC
111 Jewel St, Brooklyn, NY 11222
Tel.: (917) 391-8962
Web Site: www.dreambear.org

Year Founded: 2011

Agency Specializes In: Production, Production (Ad, Film, Broadcast)

Evan Brown *(Dir-Video Production)*

Accounts:
New-ANTI- Records
New-BANDIER
New-Brand Knew
New-Dartmouth College
New-DJ Dirty South
New-E!
New-Epitaph Records
New-Gabriel Moreno
New-Irving Harvey
New-The Jefferson Awards Foundation
New-The Jewish Federations of North America
New-LifeStation
New-Medical Alert Monitoring Association
New-Palm Beach Show Group
New-RCA Records
New-Riot Act Media
New-Sherwin Williams
New-Talib Kweli

DREAMENTIA INC
453 S Spring St Ste 1101, Los Angeles, CA 90013
Tel.: (213) 347-6000
Fax: (213) 347-6001
E-Mail: dcl@dreamentia.com
Web Site: www.dreamentia.com

Year Founded: 2006

Agency Specializes In: Advertising, Brand Development & Integration, Content, Digital/Interactive, Graphic Design, Outdoor, Package Design, Print, Radio, Social Media

Jim Olen *(Pres & Chief Creative Officer)*
Brandi West *(Dir-Mktg)*
Jameca Lyttle *(Sr Acct Exec)*

Accounts:
Animal Specialty Group
The Bolin Firm
Brigitte Beaute
Coachella Event Parking
Formosa Entertainment
Historic Downtown BID
Joes Auto Parks
L&R Group of Companies
Offerwise
Shinkafa
WallyPark
Zankou Chicken

DREAMSCAPE MULTIMEDIA

120 N Washington Sq Ste 805, Lansing, MI 48933
Tel.: (517) 394-3000
Web Site: www.dreamscapemultimedia.com

Agency Specializes In: Advertising, Brand Development & Integration, Graphic Design, Public Relations, Search Engine Optimization, Social Media

Matt Schoenherr *(Pres)*

Accounts:
New-Governmental Consultant Services Inc.

DREW ADVERTISING
314 El Paso St, San Antonio, TX 78207
Tel.: (210) 807-8798
E-Mail: inquiry@drewadvertising.com
Web Site: www.drewadvertising.com

Year Founded: 2007

Agency Specializes In: Advertising, Graphic Design, Internet/Web Design, Public Relations, Social Media

Andrew M. Anguiano *(CEO)*
Carmina Reyes *(Acct Mgr)*
Shelbi Long *(Acct Exec)*

Accounts:
Rise Recovery

DRIFTWOOD MEDIA
11215 Raw Sienna, Helotes, TX 78023
Tel.: (210) 259-8491
Fax: (512) 551-0140
Web Site: www.driftwoodmediablog.com

Agency Specializes In: Brand Development & Integration, Communications, Media Relations, Public Relations

Eddie Stevenson *(Pres)*

Accounts:
New Breed Archery
Weatherby

DRINKPR
3055 Scott St, San Francisco, CA 94123
Tel.: (415) 567-6988
Web Site: drinkpr.com/

Agency Specializes In: Advertising, Event Planning & Marketing, Public Relations

Debbie Rizzo *(Founder)*
Colin Baugh *(Principal)*
Emily Nordee *(Dir)*
Rena Ramirez *(Specialist-Lifestyle PR)*

Accounts:
Bluecoat
Crescent
Elixir
Martin Millers Gin Beverages
The Perfect Puree
Royal Combier
Vieux Carre
Whiskey Fiest

DRIVE BRAND STUDIO
(Formerly Glen Group, Inc.)
170 Kearsarge St, North Conway, NH 03860
Tel.: (603) 356-3030
Fax: (603) 356-3991
Web Site: www.drivebrandstudio.com

Employees: 10
Year Founded: 1976

Agency Specializes In: Advertising, Advertising Specialties, Brand Development & Integration, Broadcast, Business-To-Business, Collateral, Communications, Consulting, Consumer Marketing, Consumer Publications, Corporate Communications, Corporate Identity, Digital/Interactive, Direct Response Marketing, Electronic Media, Event Planning & Marketing, Exhibit/Trade Shows, Fashion/Apparel, Financial, Food Service, Government/Political, Graphic Design, Health Care Services, High Technology, In-Store Advertising, Industrial, Information Technology, Internet/Web Design, Leisure, Local Marketing, Logo & Package Design, Magazines, Media Buying Services, New Product Development, Newspaper, Newspapers & Magazines, Outdoor, Planning & Consultation, Point of Purchase, Point of Sale, Print, Public Relations, Publicity/Promotions, Real Estate, Restaurant, Retail, Sales Promotion, Sports Market, Strategic Planning/Research, Trade & Consumer Magazines, Travel & Tourism, Yellow Pages Advertising

Nancy Clark *(Owner)*
Kristopher Mariani *(Dir-Art)*

Accounts:
American Airlines; Woburn, MA (Events)
Aquatic
CannonBall Pub
Pearl Izumi; Broomfield, CO Cycling & Running Clothing & Footwear; 2004
Ski NH; North Woodstock, NH

DRIVE COMMUNICATIONS INC.
133 W 19th St Fifth Fl, New York, NY 10011
Tel.: (212) 989-5103
E-Mail: chat@drivecom.com
Web Site: www.drivecom.com

Agency Specializes In: Advertising, Brand Development & Integration, Digital/Interactive, Graphic Design, Internet/Web Design, Logo & Package Design

Michael Graziolo *(Founder & Principal)*

Accounts:
New-Ballyshear

DRIVE CREATIVE
2626 SW Corbett Ave Ste 200, Portland, OR 97201
Tel.: (503) 303-8499
Web Site: www.drivecreative.agency

Year Founded: 2011

Agency Specializes In: Advertising, Brand Development & Integration, Collateral, Digital/Interactive, Internet/Web Design

Eric Weckert *(CEO)*
Chandler Lettin *(Dir-Design)*
Kalina Torino *(Dir-Motion Graphics)*
Kevin Haselwander *(Acct Mgr-DriveMG-Natl)*
Ron Hawk *(Acct Mgr-DriveMG)*

Accounts:
Howl Supply

DRIVE INTERACTIVE
587 Oakmont Ln, Lake Arrowhead, CA 92352
Tel.: (714) 305-3841
E-Mail: info@drive-interactive.com

Employees: 10
Year Founded: 2009

Agency Specializes In: Advertising, Advertising Specialties, Bilingual Market, Brand Development & Integration, Business Publications, Catalogs, Co-op Advertising, Collateral, Consumer Marketing, Consumer Publications, Custom Publishing, Digital/Interactive, Direct Response Marketing, Direct-to-Consumer, E-Commerce, Electronic Media, Email, Graphic Design, Hispanic Market, In-Store Advertising, Integrated Marketing, Internet/Web Design, Local Marketing, Logo & Package Design, Magazines, Media Buying Services, Media Planning, Mobile Marketing, Multicultural, Multimedia, Newspaper, Newspapers & Magazines, Outdoor, Package Design, Paid Searches, Point of Purchase, Point of Sale, Production, Promotions, Publishing, Sales Promotion, Search Engine Optimization, Technical Advertising, Urban Market, Web (Banner Ads, Pop-ups, etc.), Yellow Pages Advertising

Approx. Annual Billings: $5,000,000

Glen Cummins *(Sr VP-Bus Dev)*
Van Flanigan *(VP & Gen Mgr)*
Pam Lefevre *(VP-Mktg)*
Andre Luongo *(VP-Product Dev)*

Accounts:
Pepsi Cola North America; Purchase, NY

DRIVEN SOLUTIONS INC.
320 w 9 Mile Rd Ste b, Ferndale, MI 48220
Tel.: (248) 548-3393
E-Mail: info@drivensolutionsinc.com
Web Site: www.drivensolutionsinc.com

Agency Specializes In: Advertising, Brand Development & Integration, Content, Digital/Interactive, Media Buying Services, Media Planning, Public Relations, Search Engine Optimization, Social Media

Kevin Woods *(Principal & COO)*
Brian Cusac *(Principal & Chief Creative Officer)*
Laura McCann *(Art Dir)*
Lauren Gregory *(Acct Supvr)*

Accounts:
New-Westborn Market

DROGA5
120 Wall St 11th Fl, New York, NY 10005
Tel.: (917) 237-8888
Fax: (917) 237-8889
E-Mail: businessdevelopment@droga5.com
Web Site: www.droga5.com

Employees: 110
Year Founded: 2006

Agency Specializes In: Advertising, Faith Based, Sponsorship

Susie Nam *(COO)*
Chris Wollen *(CMO)*
Jonny Bauer *(Global Chief Strategy Officer)*
Ted Royer *(Chief Creative Officer)*
Andrew Colon *(Head-Production)*
Ben Davies *(Head-Brdcst Production)*
Daniel Gonda *(Head-Acct Mgmt)*
Chet Gulland *(Head-Strategy)*
Erika Kipreos *(Head-HR, Office Svcs & Facilities)*
Niklas Lindstrom *(Head-Interactive Production)*
Rob Lugo *(Head-Print Production)*
Marianne Stefanowicz *(Global Head-Comm)*
Neil Heymann *(Exec Dir-Creative)*
Rob Trostle *(Exec Dir-Design)*
Scott Bell *(Grp Dir-Creative)*
George Bennett *(Grp Dir-Strategy)*
Kevin Brady *(Grp Dir-Creative)*
Tim Gordon *(Grp Dir-Creative)*

Matt Ian *(Grp Dir-Creative)*
Nick Klinkert *(Grp Dir-Creative)*
Colm Murphy *(Grp Dir-Strategy)*
Harry Roman *(Grp Dir-Strategy)*
Don Shelford *(Grp Dir-Creative)*
Adrian Chan *(Sr Dir-Art)*
Andy Grant *(Sr Dir-Art)*
Ben Grube *(Sr Dir-Art)*
Jennifer Hays *(Sr Dir-Art)*
Dan Kenneally *(Sr Dir-Art)*
Jen Lu *(Sr Dir-Art)*
Beth O'Brien *(Sr Dir-Art)*
Evan Schultz *(Sr Dir-Art)*
Matt Ahumada *(Grp Acct Dir)*
Blake Crosbie *(Grp Acct Dir)*
Agnes Fischer *(Grp Acct Dir)*
Tamera Geddes *(Grp Acct Dir)*
Angela Kosniewski *(Grp Acct Dir)*
Ben Myers *(Grp Acct Dir)*
Melissa Nelson *(Grp Acct Dir)*
Bola Adekoya *(Acct Dir)*
Kristoffer Aldorsson *(Acct Dir)*
Bill Berg *(Producer-Brdcst)*
Brian d'Entremont *(Acct Dir)*
Chris Einhauser *(Acct Dir)*
Chris Eyerman *(Creative Dir)*
Michelle Feeley *(Acct Dir)*
Spencer Hansen *(Art Dir)*
Inna Kofman *(Art Dir)*
Samuel Marx *(Assoc Producer-Brdcst)*
Steven Panariello *(Acct Dir)*
Sebastian Piacentini *(Art Dir)*
Miranda Pountney *(Acct Dir)*
Bryan Yasko *(Bus Dir-Global)*
Katy Alonzo *(Dir-Strategy)*
Mary Dauterman *(Dir-Art)*
Rick Dodds *(Dir-Creative)*
Max Friedman *(Jr Dir-Art)*
Matthew Gardner *(Dir-Brand Influence)*
David Gibson *(Dir-Creative)*
Rich Greco *(Dir-Design)*
Tom Haslow *(Dir-Strategy)*
Jerry Hoak *(Dir-Creative)*
Erik Hogfeldt *(Dir-Creative)*
Stephen Howell *(Dir-Creative)*
Sean Lackey *(Dir-New Bus)*
Jocelyn S. Lai *(Dir-Recruitment)*
Nathan Lennon *(Dir-Creative)*
Paul Mcgeiver *(Dir-Photography)*
Daniel Neumann *(Dir-Digital Strategy)*
Alexander Nowak *(Dir-Creative)*
Daniel Perlin *(Dir-User Experience)*
Andrew Prondak *(Dir-Tech)*
Elaine Purcell *(Dir-Strategy)*
Casey Rand *(Dir-Creative)*
Dianne Richter *(Dir-Integrated Production & Bus Affairs)*
Felix Richter *(Dir-Creative)*
Vignesh Seshadri *(Jr Dir-Art)*
Daniel Sumarna *(Dir-Art)*
Conner Tobiason *(Dir-Art)*
Kevin Weir *(Dir-Art)*
Amy Wheeler *(Jr Dir-Art)*
Aaron Wiggan *(Dir-Strategy)*
Dan Wilkos *(Dir-Brand Strategy)*
Katie Willis *(Jr Dir-Art)*
Devon Tsz-Kin Hong *(Assoc Dir-Creative)*
Tara Lawall *(Assoc Dir-Creative)*
Ashton Atlas *(Acct Mgr)*
Belinda Bonar *(Acct Mgr)*
Sara Fletcher *(Acct Mgr)*
Josh Freeland *(Acct Mgr)*
Kirsten Kates *(Office Mgr)*
Lucie Kittel *(Assoc Acct Mgr)*
Cory McCollum *(Acct Mgr)*
Trevor Mundt *(Acct Mgr)*
Lucy Santilli *(Acct Mgr)*
Valeria Sosa *(Acct Mgr)*
Kate Tyler *(Acct Mgr)*
Michelle Villarreal *(Acct Mgr)*
Leo Wong *(Assoc Acct Mgr)*
Joan Wortmann *(Acct Mgr)*
Zack Cohn *(Sr Brand Strategist)*
Kimberly Sanford *(Mgr-HR)*
Hillary Heath *(Sr Strategist-Comm)*
Elsa Stahura *(Sr Strategist-Comm)*
Dakota Green *(Strategist)*
Bryn Little *(Strategist-Comm)*
Kevin Wilkerson *(Strategist-Comm)*
Sam Bauer *(Jr Copywriter)*
Nicholas Bauman *(Copywriter)*
Chris Colliton *(Copywriter)*
Brian Eden *(Copywriter)*
Craig Gerringer *(Copywriter)*
German Rivera Hudders *(Copywriter)*
Kathryn Kvas *(Jr Copywriter)*
Jen Lally *(Designer-Studio)*
Sarah Lloyd *(Copywriter)*
Colin Lord *(Copywriter)*
Matt McCarron *(Copywriter)*
Yahkeema Moffitt *(Copywriter)*
Tori Nygren *(Jr Copywriter)*
Nick Partyka *(Copywriter)*
April Pascua *(Designer)*
Indah Shillingford *(Designer)*
Ryan Snyder *(Jr Copywriter)*
Deanna Solis *(Designer)*
Mark Yoon *(Designer)*
Karlee Thomas *(Coord-Digital Production)*
Donny Jensen *(Grp Brand Dir-Strategy)*
Morgan Mendel *(Assoc Producer-Interactive)*
Emmie Nostitz *(Sr Art Dir)*
Justin Ruben *(Grp Creative Dir)*

Accounts:

Activision Blizzard, Inc
American Express
Bill, Hillary & Chelsea Clinton Foundation Campaign: "Not There"
Chase
New-Coach
The Coca-Cola Company Campaign: "You're on"
Coca-Cola Refreshments USA, Inc. Broadcast, Campaign: "Economy Class", Campaign: "Get A Taste", Campaign: "Kittens", Campaign: "Brackets", Campaign: "Car Wash", Campaign: "Coke Zero Sweater Generator", Campaign: "Enjoy Everything", Campaign: "It's Not Your Fault", Campaign: "Motherpiece", Campaign: "Music That Moves", Campaign: "Stay Extraordinary", Diet Coke, Online, Smartwater, TV
De-De Campaign: "Thunderclap"
Dun & Bradstreet (Creative Agency of Record) Strategy
Georgia-Pacific Campaign: "Birds", Campaign: "Conductor Randy", Campaign: "Daddy Gator", Campaign: "Dark for Dinner", Campaign: "Designed to be Forgotten", Campaign: "Great Grandpa Thaddeus", Campaign: "Little Miss Puffytail", Campaign: "Sir Froggy", Creative, Dixie Tableware, Quilted Northern Bath Tissue, TV
Google Android, Campaign: "Friends Furever"
Harry's Brand Marketing, Print, TV
Heineken USA Inc. "Behind-The-Scenes", Amstel Light, Cabbie Black Ale, Campaign: "Award", Campaign: "Band of Brands", Campaign: "Brewer", Campaign: "CABVERTISING", Campaign: "Chores", Campaign: "Cider at its Bestest", Campaign: "If We Made It", Campaign: "If We Won", Campaign: "Mega Football Ad we didn't actually make.", Campaign: "No Bollocks 2013", Campaign: "Slow Motion Horse", Campaign: "Three Sunsets", Creative, Digital, In-Bar Signage, Newcastle Brown Ale, OOH, Online, Posters, Radio, Social Media, Strongbow Cider, Strongbow Hard Apple Cider, TV
Hennessy Campaign: "Manny", Campaign: "The Man Who Couldn't Slow Down", Campaign: "Wild Rabbit", Creative
New-Hillary Rodham Clinton
Jockey International Inc. (Agency of Record) Campaign: "Planets", Campaign: "Supporting Greatness", Creative, Print, Strategy
Johnsonville Sausage, LLC Bratsgiving, Campaign: "Ballad of Bratsgiving", Campaign: "Bratfest in Bed", Campaign: "Sausage Sunday", Campaign: "We Don't Make Sausage. We Make Family. And Sausage.", Creative, Social Media
MakerBot
Mondelez International, Inc. "#NotBroken", Athenos, BelVita, Campaign: "#MorningWin", Campaign: "4 de Julio", Campaign: "Blind Date", Campaign: "First S'more", Campaign: "How to Make Apple & Cheddar Melts", Campaign: "Morning Win Swag Shop", Campaign: "ShareSmore", Campaign: "This Is Wholesome", Cracker Barrel, Creative, Digital, Honey Maid, Honey Maid Grahamfuls, MadeCo., Media, MilkBite, Radio, Social Media, TV
Mondelez North America
Motorola Mobility LLC (Agency of Record) Campaign: "A Watch for Our Times", Campaign: "Chad", Campaign: "Choose Choice", Campaign: "Designed by you. Assembled in the USA", Campaign: "Lazy Phone", Campaign: "The Longest Search", Campaign: "The Maker", Moto 360, Moto E, Moto G, Moto Hint, Moto X, creative
National Women's Law Center Campaign: "Equal Payback Project"
New-NBTY, Inc. (Agency of Record) Met-Rx, Nature's Bounty, Osteo Bi-Flex, Pure Protein, Sundown Naturals
The New Museum of Contemporary Art Campaign: "Recalling 1993"
New York City Department of Education
New York City Football Club (Agency of Record)
NRG Energy Campaign: "The Power Behind the Plug", Marketing
Prudential Financial, Inc. Campaign: "Challenge Lab", Campaign: "Chapter Two", Campaign: "Race for Retirement", Campaign: "Week of Odds", Creative, Day One: Mujahid, Social
Reckitt Benckiser Inc. Air Wick, Broadcast, Campaign: "Give the Gift of Home", Campaign: "Home is in the Air", Campaign: "Interruption", Campaign: "Let's Be Clear", Campaign: "Teacher Truths", Clearasil, Creative, Digital, Marketing, Online, Point-of-Sale, Print, Public Relations, Social, TV, Video
Scottish & Newcastle
Sony Campaign: "If We Made It", PlayStation
Strongbow Campaign: "All You Need Is Ice"
Toyota Campaign: "Fueled by Bullsh*t", Campaign: "Fueled by Everything", Campaign: "The Turning Point", Campaign: "Weird, Right?", Creative, Digital, Hydrogen Fuel Cell vehicle, Media, Mirai, Online, Scion
Under Armour, Inc. (Creative Agency of Record) Campaign: "Flash", Campaign: "I Will What I Want", Campaign: "Rule Yourself", Campaign: "Slay Your Next Giant", Curry Two, Digital, Outdoor, TV
UNICEF "10 Minutes", Campaign: "Power of a Glass", Campaign: "Water Network", NY Tap, Tap Project
Unilever Suave
New-Viber Creative
West Elm Creative, Social Media
William Morris Entertainment
YMCA of the USA (Agency of Record) Advertising, Creative Strategy

Branches

droga5
12-14 Denman Street, Soho London, W1D 7HJ United Kingdom
Tel.: (44) 207 287 5928
Web Site: droga5.com/

Bill Scott *(CEO)*
Nick Simons *(Mng Dir)*
David Kolbusz *(Chief Creative Officer)*
Amy Garrett *(Head-Client Dev)*
Mico Toledo *(Dir-Art)*
Jo Forel *(Copywriter)*
Iona Ratcliffe *(Jr Planner-Strategic)*

Accounts:
All Market Inc Advertising, Campaign: "Stupidly Simple", TV, Vita Coco
New-Belstaff Creative, Digital, Out-of-Home, Print, Social, TV
Diageo Ciroc Vodka
Farfetch Campaign: "Unfollow", Creative, Digital, Experiential, Global Advertising, Print
G7+1 Russia's out
New-Hepatitis C Trust Creative
New-Hobbs CRM, Creative Advertising, In-Store
KidsCo Online, TV
Mondelez Advertising, Belvita, Digital, Social Activation, TV
New-Unilever Global Creative, Impulse

DROY ADVERTISING

10000 E Yale Ave Ste 13, Denver, CO 80231
Tel.: (303) 368-5480
Web Site: www.droyadvertising.com

Year Founded: 1983

Agency Specializes In: Advertising, Corporate Identity, Direct Response Marketing, Event Planning & Marketing, Package Design, Print

Brad Droy *(Pres & Dir-Creative)*
D. Perkins *(VP)*

Accounts:
Geneva Marsam
Windsor Floor Maintenance

DRS & ASSOCIATES

11684 Ventura Blvd 861, Studio City, CA 91604
Tel.: (818) 981-8210
E-Mail: info@drsandassociates.com
Web Site: www.drsandassociates.com

Agency Specializes In: Advertising, Graphic Design, Internet/Web Design, Public Relations

David R. Schlocker *(Pres & CEO)*
Natalie Schlocker *(Dir-Creative)*
Jon Sklaroff *(Sr Mgr-Online & Social Media Mktg)*
Mariakay Chakos *(Sr Acct Mgr)*
Jocelyn Hutt *(Sr Acct Mgr-East Coast Div)*
Jennifer Cash *(Coord-Mktg & PR)*

Accounts:
Bulthaup Corp
Sonneman - A Way of Light Digital, PR, Social Media Campaigns

THE DRUCKER GROUP

1440 N Dayton St Ste 202, Chicago, IL 60642
Tel.: (312) 867-4960
Fax: (312) 867-4967
E-Mail: info@druckergroup.com
Web Site: www.druckergroup.com

Employees: 7
Year Founded: 2003

Agency Specializes In: Advertising, Brand Development & Integration, Business Publications, Business-To-Business, Communications, Consulting, Consumer Marketing, Corporate Communications, Cosmetics, Exhibit/Trade Shows, Food Service, Health Care Services, High Technology, Industrial, Information Technology, Local Marketing, Market Research, Medical Products, New Product Development, Newspapers & Magazines, Pharmaceutical, Planning & Consultation, Public Relations, Retail, Technical Advertising, Trade & Consumer Magazines, Transportation

Approx. Annual Billings: $4,000,000

Scott Drucker *(Mng Partner)*
Tim Terchek *(Partner & Exec Dir-Creative)*
Nick Andrus *(Partner)*
Jim Samson *(Head-Visual Creative & Dir-Creative)*
Bob Wolff *(Dir-PR)*

Accounts:
Alcoa; Cleveland, OH Transportation Group; 2008
Amcor PET Packaging; Ann Arbor, MI Food & Beverage Packaging; 2008
Baxter Healthcare; Deerfield, IL; 2006
ITW/Miller Electric; Appleton, OH
Master Lock Company; Milwaukee, WI; 2004
Pactiv Corporation; Lake Forest, IL; 2006
Presidio; 2003
Silgan Containers; Woodland Hills, CA; 2003

DRUMROLL

301 Congress Ave Ste 1525, Austin, TX 78701
Tel.: (512) 651-3532
Fax: (512) 501-3660
E-Mail: innovate@drumroll.com
Web Site: www.drumroll.com

Agency Specializes In: Advertising, Digital/Interactive, Email, Environmental, Strategic Planning/Research

Kirk Drummond *(Co-Founder & CEO)*
Andrea Whitenight *(Grp Head & Dir-Production)*
Nicole Sanchez *(Dir)*
Olivia Clark *(Acct Supvr)*
Meredith Darling *(Acct Exec)*
Jonathan Hall *(Acct Exec)*
Clare Campa *(Asst Acct Exec)*
Gage Kelsey *(Asst Acct Exec)*

Accounts:
AT&T Communications Corp.
Golfsmith International Holdings, Inc.
Microsoft Corporation Msn, Bing
Skype
Sony Corporation of America
Toyota Motor North America, Inc.
UGO Entertainment, Inc.

DSA MEDIA GROUP LLC

1271 Ave Americas, New York, NY 10020
Tel.: (646) 417-8198
Fax: (646) 417-8198
E-Mail: info@dsamediagroup.com
Web Site: www.dsamediagroup.com

Agency Specializes In: Advertising, Content, Media Buying Services, Media Relations, Public Relations, Social Media

Dante Simpson *(Pres & CEO)*

Accounts:
New-Associated Press

DSC (DILEONARDO SIANO CASERTA) ADVERTISING

237 Chestnut St, Philadelphia, PA 19106
Tel.: (215) 923-3200
Fax: (215) 923-0972
E-Mail: info@dscadv.com
Web Site: www.dscadv.com

Employees: 25
Year Founded: 2001

National Agency Associations: FVW-MCA

Agency Specializes In: Advertising, Advertising Specialties, Brand Development & Integration, Broadcast, Business Publications, Business-To-Business, Cable T.V., Children's Market, Collateral, Communications, Consulting, Consumer Marketing, Consumer Publications, Corporate Identity, Cosmetics, Digital/Interactive, Direct Response Marketing, E-Commerce, Education, Electronic Media, Engineering, Entertainment, Environmental, Event Planning & Marketing, Exhibit/Trade Shows, Government/Political, Graphic Design, Health Care Services, High Technology, Industrial, Information Technology, Internet/Web Design, Investor Relations, Leisure, Logo & Package Design, Magazines, Media Buying Services, Medical Products, Merchandising, Multimedia, New Product Development, Newspaper, Newspapers & Magazines, Out-of-Home Media, Outdoor, Pharmaceutical, Planning & Consultation, Point of Purchase, Point of Sale, Print, Production, Public Relations, Publicity/Promotions, Radio, Recruitment, Restaurant, Retail, Sales Promotion, Strategic Planning/Research, T.V., Technical Advertising, Telemarketing, Trade & Consumer Magazines, Transportation

Joseph Caserta *(Pres & Chief Creative Officer)*
Joseph Dileonardo *(CEO)*
Ken Suman *(Sr VP-Acct Mgmt)*
Rich Caserta *(Sr Dir-Art)*
Bruno Circolo *(Dir-Art)*
Tony Leone *(Dir-Traffic & Production)*
Matt Mungan *(Dir-Interactive Svcs)*

Accounts:
Amplifier Research & Amplifier/Research/Kalmus; Souderton, PA Test Equipment; 1997
AR Modular RF
Catch, Inc.; Philadelphia, PA Health Care; 1983
Conestoga Bank
Foundations; Moorestown, NJ Educational Enrichment Programs; 2000
FXI-Foamex Innovations
The Philadelphia Coalition; Philadelphia, PA Behavioral Health Management; 1999
Philadelphia Visitors Center
Pinnacle Textiles

DSP+P

(Formerly dougserge+partners)
380 Wellington St W 2nd Fl, Toronto, ON M5V 1E3 Canada
Tel.: (416) 203-3470
Fax: (416) 203-9338
Web Site: dougsergepartners.com/

Employees: 40

Agency Specializes In: Brand Development & Integration, Digital/Interactive, Electronic Media

Doug Robinson *(Founder & Partner)*
Carolyn Rutherford *(CFO)*
Kristin Burnham *(Head-Plng)*
Brian Murray *(Dir-Creative)*
Mike Jones *(Assoc Dir-Creative)*
Tom Stephenson *(Acct Mgr)*
Natasha De Melis *(Designer)*

Accounts:
American Standard
B2B Bank
Branksome Hall
Canon
Clover Leaf Seafoods Creative, Toppers
Dulux (Canadian Agency of Record)
Go RVing
GoodLife Fitness Campaign: "Live Your Good Life", Health Care Services
Miele
Mucho Burrito Campaign: "Authentic Mexican"
NEI Investments
Ontario Honda Dealers Association Campaign: "Toys Can't Make It Without Your Help", Honda Civic EX Sedan
University of New Brunswick
York University

D.TRIO

401 N 3rd St Ste 480, Minneapolis, MN 55401
Tel.: (612) 787-3333
Fax: (612) 436-0324
E-Mail: pwhite@dtrio.com
Web Site: www.dtrio.com

Employees: 12
Year Founded: 2000

Agency Specializes In: Direct Response Marketing, Outdoor, Print, Production (Print), Strategic Planning/Research

Megan Devine *(Owner)*
Fred Driver *(Partner)*
Maureen Dyvig *(Partner)*
Sheryl Doyle *(Client Svcs Dir)*
Melissa Herman *(Dir-Bus Dev)*
Victoria Hoshal *(Dir-Bus Dev)*
Beth Seitzberg *(Dir-Art)*
Catherine Smalley *(Sr Acct Exec)*
Tim Swenson *(Acct Exec)*

Accounts:
University Of Minnesota Educational Services

DUBS & DASH

26 Hasler Cres, Guelph, ON N1L 0A2 Canada
Tel.: (519) 836-4335
Fax: (519) 836-7109
E-Mail: thebetterway@dubsanddash.com
Web Site: www.dubsanddash.com

Year Founded: 1999

Amitav Dash *(Mng Partner)*
Bill Dubs *(Partner-Creative)*

Accounts:
Motos for Moms; 2006

DUDNYK HEALTHCARE GROUP

5 Walnut Grove Dr Ste 280, Horsham, PA 19044
Tel.: (215) 443-9406
Fax: (215) 443-0207
E-Mail: info@dudnyk.com
Web Site: www.dudnyk.com

E-Mail for Key Personnel:
President: lweir@dudnyk.com

Employees: 45
Year Founded: 1993

Agency Specializes In: Advertising, Brand Development & Integration, Health Care Services

Lou Iovino *(Sr VP & Client Svcs Dir)*
John Kemble *(Sr VP & Dir-Creative)*
Jay Geipel *(VP & Acct Dir)*
Daniel Zaksas *(VP & Dir-Scientific)*
Kathie Carnes *(VP-HR)*
Ellen Schneider *(VP-Corp Comm)*
Cindy Gassler *(Sr Dir-Art)*
Heather Wagoner *(Acct Dir)*
Amanda Eutsey *(Dir-Art)*
Allie Focht *(Sr Acct Exec)*
Adewale Adefemi *(Acct Exec)*

Accounts:
Abbott Labs
AMAG
Bausch & Lomb
CSL Behring
ENDO Pharmaceuticals
HMR
MiddleBrook Pharmaceuticals
Nicox, Inc. AdenoPlus, Branding, Marketing Strategy, Messaging, Product Positioning
OmniGuide
OraPharma
Sanofi-Synthelabo
Shire US Inc. Agrylin, Carbatrol, Fareston, ProAmatine; 1999

Branch

Dudnyk

434 Pacific Ave, San Francisco, CA 94133
Tel.: (415) 397-3667
Fax: (415) 397-3668
Web Site: www.dudnyk.com

Employees: 25
Year Founded: 1997

Agency Specializes In: Above-the-Line, Advertising, Advertising Specialties, Below-the-Line, Brand Development & Integration, Broadcast, Business-To-Business, Cable T.V., Co-op Advertising, Collateral, Communications, Consulting, Consumer Marketing, Corporate Communications, Corporate Identity, Digital/Interactive, Direct Response Marketing, Direct-to-Consumer, Education, Electronic Media, Email, Graphic Design, Health Care Services, In-Store Advertising, Infomercials, Integrated Marketing, Internet/Web Design, Logo & Package Design, Media Buying Services, Media Planning, Medical Products, New Technologies, Newspaper, Out-of-Home Media, Outdoor, Package Design, Paid Searches, Pharmaceutical, Planning & Consultation, Podcasting, Point of Purchase, Point of Sale, Print, Production (Print), Radio, Strategic Planning/Research, T.V., Viral/Buzz/Word of Mouth

Heather Aton *(Chief Innovation Officer)*
Scott Harper *(VP-Bus Plng & Ops)*
John Kemble *(Dir-Creative & Art)*
Monica Burnette *(Mgr-Traffic)*

Accounts:
Aardvark Medical; Ross, CA Nasal Irrigator/Aspirator; 2008
e-Neura; Sunnyvale, CA Migraine Treatment; 2010
John Muir Health; Walnut Creek, CA Healthcare Services; 2009
Roche Molecular Systems; Pleasanton, CA Molecular Diagnostics; 2011
Valeant Pharmaceuticals; Bridgewater, NJ Renova; 2007
ZONARE; Mountain View, CA Diagnostic Ultrasound; 2011

DUE NORTH COMMUNICATIONS INC.

(Name Changed to Sandbox)

DUFFEY PETROSKY

38505 Country Club Dr, Farmington Hills, MI 48331
Tel.: (248) 489-8300
Fax: (248) 994-1600
E-Mail: info@duffeypetrosky.com
Web Site: www.duffeypetrosky.com

E-Mail for Key Personnel:
Creative Dir.: bduffey@dp-company.com

Employees: 50
Year Founded: 1997

National Agency Associations: 4A's

Agency Specializes In: Advertising, Automotive, Brand Development & Integration, Broadcast, Business Publications, Business-To-Business, Cable T.V., Co-op Advertising, Collateral, Commercial Photography, Communications, Consulting, Consumer Marketing, Consumer Publications, Corporate Identity, Digital/Interactive, Direct Response Marketing, E-Commerce, Electronic Media, Event Planning & Marketing, Financial, Graphic Design, Health Care Services, High Technology, Internet/Web Design, Logo & Package Design, Magazines, Media Buying Services, Merchandising, New Product Development, Newspaper, Newspapers & Magazines, Out-of-Home Media, Outdoor, Planning & Consultation, Point of Purchase, Point of Sale, Print, Production, Public Relations, Publicity/Promotions, Radio, Recruitment, Restaurant, Retail, Sales Promotion, Sports Market, Strategic Planning/Research, Sweepstakes, T.V., Technical Advertising, Telemarketing, Trade & Consumer Magazines, Transportation

Jeff Scott *(Pres)*
Jimmy Kollin *(Chief Creative Officer)*
Jo Bourjaily *(Mng Dir-Duffey Petrosky)*
Carrie Sweeney *(Acct Dir)*
Paul Murray *(Dir-Media Plng, Negotiation & Res)*
Alison Atwater *(Assoc Dir-Creative)*
Laurie Schutte *(Assoc Dir-Media)*
Yasmin Tekyi-Mensah *(Acct Mgr-PR)*
Joseph Stromski *(Sr Acct Exec)*

Accounts:
Ally Auto (Agency of Record) Digital, Mobile, Social
Ally Financial Inc Digital Channels, Print
Ascension Health Digital Communications, Marketing
Blue Cross Blue Shield of Michigan
Comcast Michigan; 2005
Consumers Energy Company (Advertising & Marketing Services Agency of Record) Creative, Digital Marketing, Media Analytics, Strategic Planning
Falcon Waterfree Technologies Marketing, Strategic Branding
FCA US LLC
Ford Racing Performance Parts
Ford Rotunda
Ford Technical Support Operations
Genuine Ford Accessories

Branch

Embark Digital

38505 Country Club Dr, Farmington Hills, MI 48331
(See Separate Listing)

DUFFY & SHANLEY, INC.

10 Charles St, Providence, RI 02904
Tel.: (401) 274-0001
Fax: (401) 274-3535
E-Mail: info@duffyshanley.com
Web Site: www.duffyshanley.com

E-Mail for Key Personnel:
President: jonduffy@duffyshanley.com

Employees: 25
Year Founded: 1973

Agency Specializes In: Advertising, Brand Development & Integration, Broadcast, Business-To-Business, Cable T.V., Collateral, Communications, Consumer Marketing, Consumer Publications, Corporate Identity, Digital/Interactive, Direct Response Marketing, Entertainment, Fashion/Apparel, Financial, Government/Political, Graphic Design, High Technology, Information Technology, Internet/Web Design, Leisure, Magazines, New Product Development, Newspaper, Newspapers & Magazines, Out-of-Home Media, Outdoor, Print, Production, Public Relations, Publicity/Promotions, Radio, Restaurant, Sports Market, Strategic Planning/Research, T.V., Trade & Consumer Magazines, Travel & Tourism

Approx. Annual Billings: $30,000,000

Jonathan D. Duffy *(Pres)*

Robert Hart *(CFO)*
Peter Marcionetti *(Chief Creative Officer)*
Rae Mancini *(VP)*
Jesse Snyder *(Sr Dir-Art-Creative)*
Karen Maia *(Office Mgr)*
Shawna Hassett *(Acct Supvr-PR)*
Cait Arsenault *(Acct Exec)*
Caitlin Hostetler *(Acct Exec-PR)*

Accounts:
The Barrett Group
Brahmin Leather Works
Cox Communications; West Warwick, RI
CVS Pharmacy; Woonsocket, RI
Deepwater Wind
Delta Dental of Rhode Island
Dorel Juvenile Group; Columhus, IN Quinny
ESPN; Bristol, CT
FGX International Corinne McCormack, Foster Grant Sunglasses
Foster Grant
Gevity HR, Inc.; 2007
Jumpstart
Kasporsey Lab; Woburn, MA; 2007
New-Luca + Danni (Agency of Record) Media Relations, Social Media
Magnivision
National Grid; Providence, RI
Navigant Credit Union; Smithfield, RI Financial Services; 2007
Nike Golf; Portland, OR
Peter Pan Bus Lines; Springfield, MA
Sagus International Education Public Service Campaign
Staples Inc. (Public Relations)
The Stride Rite Corporation; Lexington, MA
Summer Infant, Inc.
Swarovski North America Limited; Cranston, RI
Taste of Nature (Agency Of Record) Digital, Event Sponsorships, Media Relations, PR, Social Media
U.S. Mills, LLC

DUFOUR ADVERTISING

532 S 8th St, Sheboygan, WI 53081
Tel.: (920) 457-9191
Fax: (920) 457-1854
Toll Free: (800) 236-3848
E-Mail: info@dufour.com
Web Site: www.dufour.com

E-Mail for Key Personnel:
Creative Dir.: roman@dufour.com
Production Mgr.: kath@dufour.com

Employees: 7
Year Founded: 1980

National Agency Associations: AAF-Second Wind Limited

Agency Specializes In: Agriculture, Brand Development & Integration, Business Publications, Business-To-Business, Collateral, Communications, Consulting, Consumer Publications, Corporate Identity, Direct Response Marketing, E-Commerce, Education, Engineering, Event Planning & Marketing, Exhibit/Trade Shows, Financial, Food Service, Graphic Design, Health Care Services, High Technology, Industrial, Information Technology, Internet/Web Design, Local Marketing, Logo & Package Design, Marine, Media Buying Services, Merchandising, Newspaper, Newspapers & Magazines, Out-of-Home Media, Outdoor, Planning & Consultation, Point of Purchase, Point of Sale, Print, Production, Public Relations, Radio, Restaurant, Retail, Sales Promotion, Sports Market, Strategic Planning/Research, Trade & Consumer Magazines, Transportation, Travel & Tourism

Kathryn Wade DuFour *(Owner & Project Mgr)*
Timothy F. DuFour *(Owner)*
C. J. Skelton *(Gen Mgr-WebTech)*
Roman Draughon *(Dir-Creative)*

Accounts:
Acuity Insurance; Sheboygan, WI Property & Casualty Insurance; 1999
Aldag-Honold Mechanical, Inc
Curt G. Joa, Inc.; Sheboygan Falls, WI Specialty Machine Builder; 1986
Sheboygan Chamber of Commerce; Sheboygan, WI; 1998

DUKE MARKETING

4040 Civic Center Dr Ste 200, San Rafael, CA 94903
Tel.: (415) 492-4534
E-Mail: info@dukemarketing.com
Web Site: www.dukemarketing.com/

Year Founded: 1989

Linda Duke *(Principal & CEO)*
Michael Fagen *(COO)*

Accounts:
Le Boulanger, Inc. (Marketing Agency of Record) Marketing, Strategy
New-Long John Silver's, Inc. (Agency of Record) Marketing

DULLIGAN DESIGN

PO Box 598, Montville, NJ 07045
Tel.: (973) 387-5612
E-Mail: info@dulligan.com
Web Site: www.dulligan.com

Employees: 3

Agency Specializes In: Advertising, Communications, Consulting, Corporate Identity, Customer Relationship Management, E-Commerce, Email, Graphic Design, Information Technology, Internet/Web Design, Pharmaceutical, Production, Search Engine Optimization, Social Media, Web (Banner Ads, Pop-ups, etc.)

Approx. Annual Billings: $500,000

Mike Dulligan *(Owner & Principal)*

DUNCAN CHANNON

114 Sansome St 14th Fl, San Francisco, CA 94104
Tel.: (415) 306-9200
Fax: (415) 306-9201
E-Mail: andyb@duncanchannon.com
Web Site: www.duncanchannon.com

Employees: 38
Year Founded: 1990

National Agency Associations: 4A's

Agency Specializes In: Advertising, Brand Development & Integration, Broadcast, Business-To-Business, Cable T.V., Direct Response Marketing, E-Commerce, Information Technology, Magazines, New Product Development, Newspaper, Newspapers & Magazines, Outdoor, Planning & Consultation, Print, Production, Radio, Sponsorship, Strategic Planning/Research, Syndication, T.V., Trade & Consumer Magazines

Approx. Annual Billings: $40,000,000

Robert Duncan *(Owner & Exec Dir-Creative)*
Michael Lemme *(Partner & Chief Creative Officer)*
Andy Berkenfield *(Chief Strategy Officer)*
Eric Kozak *(Sr Producer-Digital)*
Christina Chern *(Dir-Art)*
Leslie Diard *(Dir-Comm Plng)*
Allan Johnson *(Dir-Brand Strategy)*
Tiffany Pan *(Dir-Art)*
Nick Gustafson *(Sr Acct Exec)*
Paulo Delacruz *(Sr Planner-Comm)*
Michael Euphrat *(Acct Exec)*
Brandon Sugarman *(Sr Planner-Comm)*
Kelsey Bucsko *(Planner-Comm)*
Jenn Ko *(Planner-Comm)*
Sydney Paine *(Acct Coord)*

Accounts:
Ancestry.com (Agency of Record)
Blurb Campaign: "Haircut"
California Department of Public Health
California Tobacco Control Program Advertising Agency of Record, Creative, Media, Strategy
Diamond Foods, Inc. Advertising Strategy, Branding, Campaign: "Made for Homemade", Creative, Diamond of California (Agency of Record), Media, Pop Secret (Agency of Record), Social Media
DriveTime Automotive Group, Inc. Campaign: "A New Lease on Life", Campaign: "Couples", Campaign: "Hold the Lemon", Campaign: "Matchmaker", Campaign: "Rescued", Campaign: "Taken for a Ride", Radio, TV
Farrier Wines Farrier Wines Packaging
GoToMeeting Campaign: "Water"
Gree
Hard Rock Cafe Foundation, Inc.
John Muir Health
Kona Brewing Company (Agency of Record) Brand Strategy, Branding, Campaign: "Dear Mainland", Campaign: "Sad Hour", Campaign: "Single-Tasking", Creative, Digital, Integrated Marketing, Out-of-Home, TV
The Palms Casino & Resort
Redhook Brewery (Advertising Agency of Record) Creative, Media, Strategy
The Ritz-Carlton Residencies
Sega of America
Sephora Website
Stride Rite Corporation "Built for Childhood", Brand Positioning, Campaign: "Doggie Door", Campaign: "Ice Cream 5 Second Rule", Creative, Digital, Mobile, Online, Print, Social, Strategy, Video
StubHub (Lead Creative Agency) Campaign: "Couples Counseling", Campaign: "I Love You", Campaign: "Latte", Design, Ticket Oak
Tahoe South Campaign: "Team Summer"

DUNCAN/DAY ADVERTISING

6513 Preston Rd Ste 200, Plano, TX 75024
Tel.: (469) 429-1974
Fax: (469) 429-1979
E-Mail: art@duncanday.com
Web Site: www.duncanday.com

Employees: 9
Year Founded: 1986

National Agency Associations: Second Wind Limited

Stacey Day *(Owner & Dir-Creative)*
Leslie Duncan *(Owner)*
Danalyn West *(Dir-Web Dev)*
Laura McCaskill *(Sr Art Dir)*

Accounts:
GE

DUNCAN GRANT ADVERTISING

117 Alpine Cr Ste 500, Columbia, SC 29223
Tel.: (803) 736-2527
Fax: (803) 736-3404
E-Mail: duncan@duncangrant.com

Employees: 2
Year Founded: 1983

Agency Specializes In: Advertising, Print

Duncan Grant *(Owner)*
Kay Jackson *(Dir-Art & Designer)*

Accounts:
ESE Marketing

DUNCAN MCCALL, INC.

4400 Bayou Blvd Ste 11, Pensacola, FL 32503-2691
Tel.: (850) 476-5035
Fax: (850) 476-1556
Toll Free: (800) 897-7775
E-Mail: info@duncanmccall.com
Web Site: www.duncanmccall.com

E-Mail for Key Personnel:
President: michael@duncanmccall.com
Creative Dir.: elaine@duncanmccall.com
Media Dir.: mary@duncanmccall.com

Employees: 6
Year Founded: 1994

Agency Specializes In: Advertising, Business-To-Business, Collateral, Commercial Photography, Financial, Graphic Design, Health Care Services, Industrial, Local Marketing, Logo & Package Design, Medical Products, Restaurant, Retail, Travel & Tourism

Approx. Annual Billings: $4,000,000

Breakdown of Gross Billings by Media: Collateral: $720,000; Newsp. & Mags.: $800,000; Outdoor: $720,000; Pub. Rels.: $80,000; Radio: $560,000; Strategic Planning/Research: $80,000; T.V.: $1,040,000

Bryan McCall *(Partner)*
Mary Nolan *(Dir-Media)*
Shellie McCall *(Office Mgr)*
Nick Johnson *(Graphic Designer & Designer-Web)*

Accounts:
Anestat; Pensacola, FL Medical Staffing Services; 1990
Gulf Coast Plastic Surgery
Gulfwinds Federal Credit Union
National Museum of Naval Aviation/Flight Deck Store; Pensacola, FL Aviation Gifts & Memorabilia; 1998
West Florida Healthcare; Pensacola, FL Hospital & Related Services; 2000

DUNN&CO

202 S 22nd St Ste 202, Tampa, FL 33605
Tel.: (813) 350-7990
Fax: (813) 273-8116
E-Mail: dunn@dunn-co.com
Web Site: www.dunn-co.com

Year Founded: 2003

Agency Specializes In: Advertising, Brand Development & Integration, Media Planning, Promotions, Strategic Planning/Research

Troy Dunn *(Pres & Chief Creative Officer)*
Jamie Miller *(Grp Acct Dir)*
Mike Delach *(Art Dir & Designer)*
Seth Allen *(Dir-Trade Show)*
Glen Hosking *(Dir-Creative)*
Sarah Waldie *(Sr Acct Exec)*
Lexi LaFleur *(Specialist-Social Media)*

Accounts:
ALS Association Scientific Research Services
Baxter Healthcare
GE Healthcare
Hexa Watches
Joffrey's Coffee & Tea Company; Tampa, FL Marketing, Packaging, Website
Majestic Apparel
Monin Gourmet Flavorings Branding, Packaging
Ralph's Mob Armada FC, Indy Eleven, Kicking and screaming, Miracle workers, Scorpions, Strikers, United FC, Win fans
Sabal Trust Company Brand Communications, Digital, Print, Public Relations, TV
Sempermed Gloves Mfr
Tampa Bay Lightning Puck Drop
Tampa Bay Rowdies Campaign: "Tickets"
Valpak Campaign: "Coming Home"
Wok Chi USA Brand Awareness

DUSTLAND

100 Corporate Pointe Ste 120, Culver City, CA 90230
Tel.: (818) 279-2683
Web Site: www.dustland.com

Agency Specializes In: Advertising, Content, Digital/Interactive, Internet/Web Design, Social Media, Strategic Planning/Research

Minh Le *(Mng Partner & VP-Client Svcs)*
Chris Ottinger *(Exec Creative Dir)*
Vanessa West *(Project Mgr-Digital)*

Accounts:
Sitecore

DVA ADVERTISING

109 NW Greenwood Ave Ste 103, Bend, OR 97701
Tel.: (541) 389-2411
Fax: (541) 389-1208
E-Mail: dvaadv@dvaadv.com
Web Site: www.dvaadv.com

E-Mail for Key Personnel:
President: david@dvaadv.com
Media Dir.: desi@dvaadv.com

Employees: 14
Year Founded: 1990

Agency Specializes In: Communications, Public Relations, Sports Market, Travel & Tourism

David R. Day *(Owner)*
Mary Angelo *(Partner & Client Svcs Dir)*
Justin Yax *(Partner & Dir-PR)*
Gary Fulkerson *(Principal & Dir-Creative Svcs)*
Desi Bresler *(Controller & Media Buyer)*
Michelle Roats *(Acct Exec)*

Accounts:
Bandon Dunes Golf Resort; 1998
Carrera Motors
Chambers Bay Golf
Kemper Kaiser Lesnik; 1999
Oxford Hotel Group
The Reserves Vineyard & Golf Club

DVL PUBLIC RELATIONS & ADVERTISING

(Merged with Seigenthaler Public Relations to form DVL Seigenthaler)

DVL SEIGENTHALER

(Acquired by Finn Partners)

DW ADVERTISING

682 Bloomfield Ave, Bloomfield, CT 6002
Tel.: (860) 461-7402
E-Mail: dwteam@dw-advertising.com
Web Site: www.dw-advertising.com

Agency Specializes In: Advertising, Brand Development & Integration, Content, Digital/Interactive, Logo & Package Design, Media Planning, Paid Searches, Print, Social Media, T.V.

Steve Jones *(Art Dir)*
Jeff Durham *(Creative Dir)*
Kim Wilson *(Acct Exec)*

Accounts:
New-My Pillow Inc

DXAGENCY

75 Gorge Rd, Edgewater, NJ 07020
Tel.: (201) 313-1100
Fax: (201) 840-8492
E-Mail: info@dxagency.com
Web Site: www.dxagency.com

Year Founded: 2004

Agency Specializes In: Advertising, Digital/Interactive, Email, Media Buying Services, Media Planning, Search Engine Optimization

Sandy Rubinstein *(CEO)*
Michael Dub *(Partner)*
Benjamin Hordell *(Partner)*
Steve Golub *(VP-Acct Mgmt)*
Adam Reinhardt *(VP-Dev)*
Jill Harrow *(Sr Dir-Accts & SEO)*
Mark Klein *(Mgr)*

Accounts:
Comcast SportsNet Mid-Atlantic (Digital Agency of Record)
DirecTV
Dr. Schar Advertising Agency of Record, Marketing Agency of Record, Social Media Agency of Record
HBO
Kmart
Madison Square Garden
National Geographic Books
Sour Jacks Mobile Ads, Social Ads
Welch's Fruit Snacks Mobile Ads, Social Ads

DYE, VAN MOL & LAWRENCE

209 7th Ave N, Nashville, TN 37219-1802
Tel.: (615) 244-1818
Fax: (615) 780-3301
Web Site: www.dvl.com

E-Mail for Key Personnel:
Creative Dir.: nelson.eddy@dvl.com

Employees: 45
Year Founded: 1980

Agency Specializes In: Automotive, Digital/Interactive, Entertainment, Event Planning & Marketing, Fashion/Apparel, Food Service, Health Care Services, Investor Relations, Media Buying Services, Publicity/Promotions, Sports Market, Strategic Planning/Research

Tom Lawrence *(Founder & Partner)*
Ronald Roberts *(Pres, CEO & Partner-Strategy & Plng)*
Nelson Eddy *(Mng Partner-Creative)*
Jimmy Chaffin *(Partner-Strategy & Plng)*
Jerry Southwood *(CFO)*
Jonathan Carpenter *(VP & Sr Dir-Art-Interactive)*
Robert Hoskins *(VP)*

Accounts:
Bridgestone Americas, Inc.
Bridgestone/Firestone, Inc. Corporate, Off Road Tires
Harpeth Valley Utilities District; 1995
J. Alexander's Corporation
J. Alexander's Restaurants; 1983
Jack Daniels Family of Brands
Tractor Supply Co.; 2000
YWCA of Middle Tennessee; 1999

YWCA of Nashville & Middle Tennessee

DYMUN + COMPANY

200 1st Ave, Pittsburgh, PA 15222-1512
Tel.: (412) 281-2345
Fax: (412) 281-3493
E-Mail: contact@dymun.com
Web Site: www.dymun.com

E-Mail for Key Personnel:
Chairman: jdymun@dymun.com
President: mkurtzrock@dymun.com
Production Mgr.: lbehrhorst@dymun.com
Public Relations: jfaines@dymun.com

Employees: 17
Year Founded: 1987

Agency Specializes In: Advertising, Advertising Specialties, Brand Development & Integration, Broadcast, Business-To-Business, Collateral, College, Communications, Consulting, Consumer Goods, Consumer Marketing, Corporate Communications, Corporate Identity, Digital/Interactive, Direct-to-Consumer, Event Planning & Marketing, Exhibit/Trade Shows, Graphic Design, Health Care Services, High Technology, In-Store Advertising, Integrated Marketing, Logo & Package Design, Market Research, Media Buying Services, Media Planning, Media Relations, Mobile Marketing, New Product Development, Package Design, Point of Purchase, Print, Production, Public Relations, Publicity/Promotions, Radio, Sales Promotion, Social Media, Strategic Planning/Research, T.V., Technical Advertising, Trade & Consumer Magazines, Travel & Tourism

Approx. Annual Billings: $13,527,800 Capitalized

John Dymun *(Chm & Pres)*
Mike Provenzano *(Mng Partner & COO)*
David Tysarczyk *(Partner & CFO)*
Craig Otto *(Partner & Dir-Creative)*
Linda Behrhorst *(Mgr-Production)*
Chris Beregi *(Acct Svcs Mgr & Assoc Mgr-Production)*

Accounts:
California University of Pennsylvania
Carnegie Learning
Oticon, Inc.; Summit, NJ Hearing Devices

DYNAMEDIA OF AMERICA, INC.

(Acquired & Absorbed by Intermark Group, Inc.)

DYNAMIC DIGITAL ADVERTISING, LLC.

1265 Industrial Blvd, Southampton, PA 18966
Tel.: (215) 355-6442
Fax: (215) 396-8779
E-Mail: sales@ddapa.com
Web Site: www.zeroonezero.com

Employees: 15

Agency Specializes In: Advertising

David Katz *(Pres)*
Andrew Jung *(Dir-Bus Dev)*

Accounts:
Allied Dental
Chains-and-Charms.com
Galil Medical
Girsh Development, Inc.
Mobile Diagnostic Services, Inc.
Schlotter Precision Products, Inc.

DYNAMIC INC

1526 S 12th St, Sheboygan, WI 53081
Tel.: (920) 459-8889
Web Site: www.dynamicagency.com

Year Founded: 2006

Agency Specializes In: Advertising, Brand Development & Integration, Digital/Interactive, Logo & Package Design, Print, Public Relations, Social Media

James Grunewald *(Partner & CEO)*
Jason Irish *(COO)*
Julie Hirt *(Acct Svc Dir)*
Jamie Fleming *(Mgr-Production)*
Danielle George *(Acct Exec)*
Casey Irish *(Acct Exec)*

Accounts:
Illinois Tool Works

DZINE ALASKA

3705 Arctic Blvd Ste 2445, Anchorage, AK 99503
Tel.: (907) 240-1380
Web Site: www.dzinealaska.com

Agency Specializes In: Advertising, Brand Development & Integration, Event Planning & Marketing, Graphic Design, Internet/Web Design, Print, Public Relations, Social Media

Don Poynter *(Pres & Creative Dir)*
Kasha Smith-Poynter *(Mgr-Acct & Project)*

Accounts:
StatMedx
ZomBeans Coffee House

E&M ADVERTISING

462 7th Ave 8th Fl, New York, NY 10018-7606
Tel.: (212) 981-5900
Fax: (212) 981-2121
E-Mail: jtarsitano@emadv.com
Web Site: www.emadv.com

E-Mail for Key Personnel:
President: mmedico@emadv.com
Creative Dir.: jwyant@emadv.com
Media Dir.: lcapitelli@emadv.com

Employees: 30
Year Founded: 1981

National Agency Associations: DMA

Agency Specializes In: Affiliate Marketing, Cable T.V., Consulting, Consumer Marketing, Direct Response Marketing, Direct-to-Consumer, Electronic Media, Infomercials, Internet/Web Design, Media Buying Services, Media Planning, Mobile Marketing, New Technologies, Radio, Search Engine Optimization, Syndication, T.V.

Approx. Annual Billings: $42,000,000

Breakdown of Gross Billings by Media: Cable T.V.: 60%; Internet Adv.: 5%; Radio: 5%; Spot T.V.: 20%; Syndication: 10%

Anthony Medico *(Pres)*
Jeffrey R. Wyant *(Exec VP)*
Tom Farrell *(Sr VP-Fin & Admin)*
Jennifer Tarsitano *(VP-Mktg)*

Accounts:
AAA Auto Insurance South
Bargain Network
Life Alert
Lincoln Educational Services
MBI
SMC Corp. (Specialty Merchandising Corp.)
Telebrands; Fairfield, NJ; 1992

Branch

E&M Media Group

1410 Broadway Ste 1002, New York, NY 10018-3704
Tel.: (212) 455-0177
Fax: (212) 455-0176
Web Site: www.emtvsales.com

Employees: 10
Year Founded: 1997

Agency Specializes In: Advertising, Direct Response Marketing, Food Service, Infomercials, Media Buying Services

Bonnie Schalle *(Owner & Pres)*
Sheldon Finkle *(CFO)*
Paola Carlino *(Dir-Media & Mgr-Traffic)*
Maria Miranda *(Dir-Media-Spanish TV & Radio)*
Samina Qureshi *(Dir-Media-Short Form)*
Elise Wexler *(Dir-Media-Long Form)*
Diane Zeit *(Dir-Media & Radio)*

Accounts:
Art Instruction School; Minneapolis, MN Lead Generation; 1998

E-B DISPLAY CO., INC.

1369 Sanders Ave SW, Massillon, OH 44647-7632
Tel.: (330) 833-4101
Fax: (330) 833-9844
Toll Free: (800) 321-9869
E-Mail: display@ebdisplay.com
Web Site: www.ebdisplay.com

Employees: 115
Year Founded: 1952

Agency Specializes In: Advertising Specialties, Cosmetics, Merchandising, Point of Purchase, Point of Sale, Print, Sales Promotion

Approx. Annual Billings: $20,000,000

Michael Rotolo *(Pres & CEO)*
Rick Catazaro *(CFO)*
Richard Philyaw *(VP-Natl Accounts)*
Ken Loy *(Dir-Creative)*
Kathy Ferry *(Mgr-Graphics)*
Steve Metz *(Mgr-Production)*
Denise Leppla *(Acct Exec)*

Accounts:
Ryobi

E-STORM INTERNATIONAL, INC.

(d/b/a E-Storm)
530 Bush St Ste 600, San Francisco, CA 94108
Tel.: (415) 352-1214
Fax: (415) 352-1254
Web Site: www.estorm.com

Employees: 22
Year Founded: 1998

Agency Specializes In: Advertising, Digital/Interactive, Planning & Consultation

William Gaultier *(Co-Founder & CEO)*
Nancy Riveong *(CFO & COO)*
Daniel Riveong *(Gen Mgr-Asia)*
Tracy Clark Green *(Dir-Ops)*
Ivana Petraskova *(Dir-Mktg Svcs)*
Russell Lovegren *(Assoc Dir-Media)*

Accounts:
Affiliated Computer Services
Ebates
Microsoft
National University
Seagate Media Planning & Buying
Verizon

Wells Fargo

E21 CORPORATION

39111 Paseo Padre Pkwy Ste 212, Fremont, CA 94538
Tel.: (510) 818-9600
Fax: (510) 226-0679
E-Mail: maggie.yuan@e21mm.com
Web Site: www.e21mm.com

Employees: 150
Year Founded: 1989

Agency Specializes In: Advertising, Asian Market, Bilingual Market, Brand Development & Integration, Business Publications, Business-To-Business, Co-op Advertising, Collateral, Communications, Consumer Marketing, Corporate Identity, Digital/Interactive, Direct Response Marketing, E-Commerce, Electronic Media, Engineering, Event Planning & Marketing, Exhibit/Trade Shows, Graphic Design, High Technology, Industrial, Information Technology, Internet/Web Design, Logo & Package Design, Magazines, Media Buying Services, New Product Development, Point of Purchase, Point of Sale, Print, Public Relations, Publicity/Promotions, Strategic Planning/Research

Approx. Annual Billings: $15,000,000

Breakdown of Gross Billings by Media: Brdcst.: 10%; D.M.: 5%; Event Mktg.: 20%; Exhibits/Trade Shows: 10%; Graphic Design: 10%; Internet Adv.: 5%; Pub. Rels.: 20%; Worldwide Web Sites: 20%

Joseph Sun *(CEO)*
Maggie Yuan *(Client Svcs Dir)*

Accounts:
7-Eleven
ASI
Intel
Konka Group, Ltd.
Logitech
Nike
Oracle America, Inc.
Polaroid
Samsung
Semiconductor Equipment & Material International (SEMI)
TSMC (Taiwan Semiconductor Manufacturing Co.)
Unigen

E3

419 5th Ave NE, Grand Rapids, MN 55744
Tel.: (218) 326-0728
Fax: (218) 326-8021
E-Mail: info@e3cs.com
Web Site: www.e3cs.com

Year Founded: 1999

Agency Specializes In: Communications, Event Planning & Marketing, Integrated Marketing, Internet/Web Design, Promotions

Eric Eiesland *(Pres)*

Accounts:
Arcadia Lodge
Grand Rapids Dental Care
Kokomo Resort
Minnesota Fishing Connections
Terex ASV, Inc.
Visions North Lodging Association

E3 LOCAL MARKETING

2601 Malsbary Rd, Cincinnati, OH 45242
Toll Free: (888) 878-2768
Web Site: e3local.com

Agency Specializes In: Advertising, Broadcast, Digital/Interactive, Local Marketing, Print

Kevin Slattery *(Owner & CEO)*
Kerry McKiernan *(Pres)*
Suzy Schneider *(Dir)*
Terri Wolke *(Dir-Ops)*

Accounts:
BGR
Champion
Donatos
Pearle Vision
Sears Home Services

EAB MARKETING, CORP.

(d/b/a The Barber Shop Marketing)
(Private-Parent-Single Location)
8140 Walnut Hill Ln, Dallas, TX 75231
Tel.: (214) 217-7177
Web Site: www.thebarbershopmarketing.com

Employees: 16
Year Founded: 2003

Agency Specializes In: Advertising, Collateral, Digital/Interactive, Print, Public Relations, Radio, Social Media, T.V.

Revenue: $3,200,000

Liz Barber *(Pres)*
Lindsay Hart *(Dir-Creative)*
Richard Schiera *(Dir-Creative)*

Accounts:
Dallas County Community College District

EAG GROUP

6790 Coral Way 2nd Fl, Miami, FL 33155
Tel.: (305) 597-5454
Fax: (305) 597-2116
E-Mail: info@eaggroup.com
Web Site: www.eaggroup.com

Agency Specializes In: Advertising, Brand Development & Integration, Media Buying Services, Media Planning, Public Relations

William Riveron *(Founder & Pres)*
Devi San Emeterio *(Mng Dir)*
Vivian Estevez *(Dir-Media)*
Pascal Jacquelin *(Creative Dir)*
Ana Rivera *(Dir-Event Mktg)*
Danny Sibai *(Dir-Online Campaign)*
Zenia Navarro *(Media Buyer)*

Accounts:
Al Hendrickson Toyota

EAST BANK COMMUNICATIONS INC.

215 SE 9th Ave Ste 202, Portland, OR 97214
Tel.: (503) 230-8959
Fax: (503) 230-8960
E-Mail: mail@eastbankcom.net
Web Site: www.eastbankcom.net

Employees: 5
Year Founded: 1977

National Agency Associations: Second Wind Limited

Agency Specializes In: Advertising, Brand Development & Integration, Broadcast, Business-To-Business, Cable T.V., Children's Market, Collateral, Consumer Marketing, Corporate Identity, Digital/Interactive, Direct Response Marketing, E-Commerce, Environmental, Exhibit/Trade Shows, Food Service, Graphic Design, Industrial, Internet/Web Design, Leisure, Logo & Package Design, Media Buying Services, Point of Purchase, Point of Sale, Production, Restaurant, Retail, Strategic Planning/Research, T.V., Travel & Tourism

Approx. Annual Billings: $2,246,000

Breakdown of Gross Billings by Media: Collateral: $786,000; D.M.: $180,000; Exhibits/Trade Shows: $235,000; Graphic Design: $180,000; Mags.: $160,000; Newsp.: $315,000; Point of Sale: $225,000; Radio: $165,000

Richard J. Petralia *(Mng Dir)*
Bryan Murphy *(Dir-Creative)*

Accounts:
Grassland Oregon
Hardwood Industries
Northwest Hardwoods
O'Loughlin Trade Shows; Portland, OR; 1984
Smithco Manufacturing; Portland, OR; 1990

EAST COAST CATALYST

300 Summer St, Boston, MA 02210
Tel.: (617) 314-6400
Web Site: www.eastcoastcatalyst.com

Employees: 5
Year Founded: 2010

Agency Specializes In: Arts, Brand Development & Integration, Business-To-Business, College, Computers & Software, Consulting, Content, Corporate Identity, Customer Relationship Management, Digital/Interactive, E-Commerce, Education, Entertainment, Event Planning & Marketing, Government/Political, Graphic Design, High Technology, Identity Marketing, Information Technology, Integrated Marketing, Internet/Web Design, Logo & Package Design, Market Research, Media Planning, New Technologies, Paid Searches, Planning & Consultation, Restaurant, Search Engine Optimization, Social Media, Strategic Planning/Research, Web (Banner Ads, Pop-ups, etc.)

Approx. Annual Billings: $1,000,000

Tim Bourgeois *(Partner & Strategist-Digital)*
David Polcaro *(Dir-Creative)*

Accounts:
Apperian Digital Design, Digital Marketing; 2012
Fortis College Digital Marketing Audit; 2012
GlideMagazine.com Digital Marketing Optimization; 2013
RAMP Digital Marketing; 2014
Resolution Digital Strategy; 2012
Signiant Digital Design, Digital Marketing; 2014

EAST HOUSE CREATIVE

120 Sylvan Ave Ste 108A, Englewood Cliffs, NJ 07632
Tel.: (201) 408-5775
Fax: (201) 408-5774
E-Mail: info@east-house.com
Web Site: www.east-house.com

Employees: 4

Agency Specializes In: Advertising, Advertising Specialties, Brand Development & Integration, Business Publications, Catalogs, Collateral, Corporate Identity, Custom Publishing, Graphic Design, Health Care Services, Internet/Web Design, Local Marketing, Logo & Package Design, Media Buying Services, Media Planning, New Product Development, Newspapers & Magazines, Package Design, Pharmaceutical, Print, Product Placement, Production (Ad, Film, Broadcast), Publicity/Promotions, Publishing, Real Estate, Search Engine Optimization, Social

Marketing/Nonprofit, T.V., Web (Banner Ads, Pop-ups, etc.)

Approx. Annual Billings: $2,500,000

Silvia Avramov *(Partner & Dir-Design)*
Youlian Avramov *(Partner & Dir-Creative)*
Annmarie Lockhart *(Copywriter)*

Accounts:
Alden Staffing Services; NJ Collateral Design, Web Design
Chestnut Investment Group; NJ Brand ID, Web Site Development
Coldwell Banker; NJ Collateral Design
McGraw Hill
Onboard LLC

EAST MEETS WEST PRODUCTIONS INC.

1024 Leopard St., Corpus Christi, TX 78401
Tel.: (361) 904-0044
Web Site: www.eastmeetswestproductions.com

Employees: 45
Year Founded: 1991

Agency Specializes In: Above-the-Line, Advertising, Advertising Specialties, Affiliate Marketing, Affluent Market, African-American Market, Alternative Advertising, Arts, Asian Market, Automotive, Aviation & Aerospace, Below-the-Line, Bilingual Market, Brand Development & Integration, Branded Entertainment, Broadcast, Business Publications, Business-To-Business, Cable T.V., Children's Market, Co-op Advertising, Collateral, Communications, Computers & Software, Consulting, Consumer Publications, Content, Corporate Communications, Corporate Identity, Crisis Communications, Custom Publishing, Customer Relationship Management, Digital/Interactive, Direct Response Marketing, Direct-to-Consumer, E-Commerce, Education, Electronic Media, Electronics, Email, Engineering, Entertainment, Environmental, Event Planning & Marketing, Exhibit/Trade Shows, Experience Design, Faith Based, Fashion/Apparel, Financial, Food Service, Government/Political, Graphic Design, Health Care Services, High Technology, Hispanic Market, Hospitality, Household Goods, Identity Marketing, Industrial, Information Technology, Integrated Marketing, International, Internet/Web Design, Investor Relations, Legal Services, Leisure, Local Marketing, Logo & Package Design, Magazines, Marine, Market Research, Media Buying Services, Media Planning, Media Relations, Media Training, Medical Products, Men's Market, Merchandising, Mobile Marketing, Multicultural, Multimedia, New Product Development, New Technologies, Newspaper, Newspapers & Magazines, Out-of-Home Media, Outdoor, Over-50 Market, Paid Searches, Planning & Consultation, Podcasting, Point of Purchase, Point of Sale, Print, Product Placement, Production, Production (Ad, Film, Broadcast), Production (Print), Promotions, Public Relations, Publicity/Promotions, Publishing, RSS (Really Simple Syndication), Radio, Real Estate, Recruitment, Regional, Restaurant, Retail, Sales Promotion, Search Engine Optimization, Seniors' Market, Social Marketing/Nonprofit, Social Media, Sponsorship, Sports Market, Stakeholders, Strategic Planning/Research, Syndication, T.V., Technical Advertising, Teen Market, Trade & Consumer Magazines, Transportation, Travel & Tourism, Tween Market, Urban Market, Viral/Buzz/Word of Mouth, Web (Banner Ads, Pop-ups, etc.), Women's Market, Yellow Pages Advertising

Approx. Annual Billings: $3,000,000

Darlene Gregory *(CEO)*
Doug Burrell *(CTO)*

Accounts:
Best Western Hotels
Bradleys Hermetics
Bradleys Motors Inc.
Cessna Aircraft
Comfort Life Pillow Co.
E.I. DuPont de Nemours Inc.
FMC/Moorco
Gainco Environmental
The Growth Coach
Lankford Co. Inc.
Medical Z Corp.
Oxymar/Occidental Petroleum Corp.
Port Authority of New Jersey & New York
Rabalais Electric
Sears, Roebuck & Co.
Sperry Van Ness
Texas Youth Commission
Turning Point
University of S. Florida Coastal Engineering Center
U.S. Army Corps of Engineers
U.S. Geological Survey
U.S. Navy

EASTPOINT GROUP

7601 Paragon Rd Ste 300, Dayton, OH 45459
Tel.: (937) 424-2200
Fax: (937) 424-1777
Toll Free: (800) 305-8331
E-Mail: mark.safran@theeastpointgroup.com
Web Site: www.theeastpointgroup.com

Employees: 15

Revenue: $2,500,000

James Hassler *(VP & Controller)*
Trish Cooper *(Assoc Dir-Production)*
Diane Morris *(Mgr-Production)*

Accounts:
LexisNexis
P&G Pet Care
Vandalia Municipal Court

EASTWEST MARKETING GROUP

575 8th Ave Ste 2114, New York, NY 10018
Tel.: (212) 951-7220
Fax: (212) 951-7201
E-Mail: info@eastwestmg.com
Web Site: www.eastwestmg.com

Employees: 75
Year Founded: 1983

Agency Specializes In: Advertising, Brand Development & Integration, Children's Market, Consumer Marketing, Event Planning & Marketing, In-Store Advertising, Mobile Marketing, Production (Print), Publicity/Promotions, Restaurant, Sales Promotion, Sponsorship, T.V.

Approx. Annual Billings: $20,000,000

Len Zabala *(Owner)*
Lou Ramery *(CEO)*
Keith Manzella *(VP & Grp Dir-Creative)*
Joyce Lu *(VP-Strategic Plng)*
Craig Moser *(VP)*
Todd Drosselmeier *(Sr Dir-Art)*
Traci Basile *(Acct Mgr & Ops Mgr)*

Accounts:
Costco
Mondelez International, Inc. Altoids, Cool Whip, Corn Nuts, Creme Savers, Handi-Snacks, Jell-O, Kids Group, Life Savers, Milk-Bone, Nabisco Fun Fruits, Oreo, Planters, Scale Group Events, Terry's Chocolates, Trolli
Nabisco
Post
Travelodge
Unicef U.S. Fund Tap Project, Trick-or-Treat for Unicef; 2007
Universal Studios
Warner Brothers Studios, Universal Studios, Genius Products

EAT SLEEP WORK

360 N Sepulveda Blvd Ste 1056, El Segundo, CA 90245
Tel.: (310) 450-9102
E-Mail: bff@eatsleepwork.com
Web Site: www.eatsleepwork.com

Year Founded: 2004

Agency Specializes In: Advertising, Collateral, Graphic Design, Internet/Web Design, Print

Jonathan Wang *(CEO & Dir-Creative)*
John Chimmy *(Partner-Accounts)*
Chrissie Canino *(COO)*
Silvana Perolini *(Dir-Art)*

Accounts:
Team Rubicon

E.B. LANE

(Merged with Terralever to Form LaneTerralever)

E.B. WALL + ASSOCIATES

1520 Harper Ave NW, Lenoir, NC 28645
Tel.: (828) 757-0047
Fax: (828) 758-7394
E-Mail: info@ebwall.com
Web Site: www.ebwall.com

Employees: 2
Year Founded: 1989

Agency Specializes In: Advertising, Arts, Communications, Digital/Interactive, Entertainment, Hospitality, Identity Marketing, Local Marketing, Media Planning, Print, Promotions, Public Relations, Real Estate, Strategic Planning/Research, Travel & Tourism

Ewa Powell *(Sr Dir-Art)*
Shawn Bradley *(Mgr-Production)*

Accounts:
Broyhill

EBAY ENTERPRISE DISPLAY & RETARGETING

(Formerly FetchBack Inc.)
100 W University Ste 101, Tempe, AZ 85281
Tel.: (480) 289-5555
Fax: (480) 289-5550
Web Site:
ebayenterprise.com/marketing_solutions/display_retargeting/

Agency Specializes In: Advertising, Direct Response Marketing

Emily Miller *(Partner-Talent Acq)*
Frank Paleno *(CIO)*
Stephen Denton *(VP-Mktg Solutions)*
Michael Lavoie *(Head-Client Svcs, Email & Database Svcs)*
Bill Mills *(Head-Corp Dev & Strategy)*
Kelly Jordan *(Sr Mgr-Talent Acq-Global Omnichannel Ops)*

Accounts:
ABACUS
Awards International Inc. Promotional Product Supplier
Grand Canyon University

True Religion

EBUYMEDIA
332 S Main St, Plymouth, MI 48170
Tel.: (734) 451-6666
Web Site: www.ebuymedia.com

Agency Specializes In: Advertising, Graphic Design, Internet/Web Design, Media Buying Services, Outdoor, T.V.

Andy Winnie *(Pres)*
Franz Vorenkamp *(Head-Creative Team)*

Accounts:
Cauley Automotive
CMC Telecom, Inc
Fraza Forklifts

ECHO FACTORY
9360 Santa Anita Ave Ste 100, Rancho Cucamonga, CA 91730
Tel.: (909) 758-5171
Fax: (909) 912-8273
Web Site: www.echo-factory.com

Employees: 10

Agency Specializes In: Brand Development & Integration, Collateral, Email, Graphic Design, Logo & Package Design, Media Relations, Print, Public Relations, Radio

Michael Schaffer *(Owner)*
Sandra Schaffer *(Controller)*
Carl Custodio *(Dir-Art)*
Sandra Wissa *(Project Mgr & Specialist-Online Mktg)*
Larry Schaffer *(Mgr-IT)*
Hayley Raynes *(Strategist-Brand)*
Nicole Rohrer *(Strategist-Brand)*
Syble Harrison *(Copywriter)*

Accounts:
Allied Anesthesia Medical Group Inc. Medical Services
NALMCO Facilities Management & Training Services

ECHO-FACTORY INC
36 W Colorado Ste 200, Pasadena, CA 91105
Tel.: (626) 993-3770
Fax: (909) 912-8273
E-Mail: info@echo-factory.com
Web Site: www.echo-factory.com

Agency Specializes In: Advertising, Graphic Design, Internet/Web Design, Public Relations, Search Engine Optimization, Social Media

Mike Schaffer *(CEO)*
Dea Goldsmith *(Dir-Creative)*
Mustafa Abou Taleb *(Acct Mgr)*

Accounts:
New-Rockview Family Farms (Agency of Record)
New-ZPower LLC

ECHO MEDIA GROUP
12711 Newport Ave Ste H, Tustin, CA 92780
Tel.: (714) 573-0899
Fax: (714) 573-0898
E-Mail: info@echomediapr.com
Web Site: www.echomediapr.com

Agency Specializes In: Brand Development & Integration, Corporate Identity, Crisis Communications, Internet/Web Design, Media Relations, Media Training, Multimedia, Print, Production, Public Relations, Strategic Planning/Research

Kim Sherman *(Founder & Mng Principal)*
Kim Long *(Owner)*
Nancy Andrews *(Mng Dir & Sr VP)*
Lisa Mendenhall *(Sr VP)*
Sabrina Suarez *(VP)*
Christine Welch *(VP)*
Vivian Slater *(Asst VP)*
Amy Wallace *(Sr Acct Exec)*
Taylor King *(Jr Acct Exec)*

Accounts:
Be There Bedtime Stories
Concordia University Irvine Brand Awareness, Media Outreach, Media Relations
Fisher & Phillips LLP
Irvine Extension
The Joy Factory
REOMAC
RSI Development
Toyota Material Handling USA
U.S.A Inc
University of California
Villeroy & Boch Bath & Wellness Division Public Relations
Wahoo's

ECITY INTERACTIVE INC
1501 Walnut St, Philadelphia, PA 19102
Tel.: (215) 557-0767
E-Mail: info@ecityinteractive.com
Web Site: www.ecityinteractive.com

Year Founded: 1999

Agency Specializes In: Internet/Web Design, Strategic Planning/Research

Louis Miller *(Mng Dir-Strategy)*
Jd Barksdale *(Sr Producer-Interactive)*
Sarah Ruggieri *(Project Mgr & Producer-Interactive)*
Pak Lee *(Dir-Web Svcs)*
Kevin Renton *(Dir-Bus Dev)*

Accounts:
Comcast Ventures Entertainment, Communications & Digital Technology Providers
Smiths Group Benefit Center Healthcare & Welfare Services

ECKEL & VAUGHAN
706 Hillsborough St Ste 102, Raleigh, NC 27603
Tel.: (919) 858-6909
Web Site: www.eandvgroup.com

Agency Specializes In: Advertising, Brand Development & Integration, Digital/Interactive, Public Relations, Social Media

Albert Eckel *(Founder & Partner)*
Harris Vaughan *(Partner)*
Matt Ferraguto *(Partner & Dir-Client Svcs)*
Pres Davenport *(Dir-Bus Dev)*
McGavock Edwards *(Dir-Strategic Comm)*
Amy McLeod *(Acct Mgr)*
Laney Wilke *(Acct Mgr)*
Greyson Kane *(Acct Mgr)*

Accounts:
New-North Hills

ECLIPSE ADVERTISING, INC.
(Private-Parent-Single Location)
2255 N Ontario St Ste 230, Burbank, CA 91504
Tel.: (818) 238-9388
Fax: (818) 238-9193
E-Mail: info@eclipsead.com
Web Site: www.eclipsead.com

Employees: 44
Year Founded: 2000

Agency Specializes In: Advertising, Brand Development & Integration, Digital/Interactive, Internet/Web Design, Print, T.V.

Revenue: $2,300,000

Steve Dubb *(Founder & Pres)*
Rod Ige *(Sr VP)*
Dean Sona *(Sr VP-Theatrical)*
Kevin Williams *(VP & Creative Dir)*
Jeff Rodriguez *(VP-Creative)*
Tony Nuss *(Creative Dir)*
Klarissa Curtis *(Acct Mgr)*

Accounts:
NBC
Walt Disney

ECLIPSE CREATIVE INC.
Ste 200 388 Harbour Rd, Victoria, BC V9A 3S1 Canada
Tel.: (250) 382-1103
Fax: (250) 382-1163
E-Mail: hello@eclipsecreative.ca
Web Site: www.eclipsecreative.ca

Agency Specializes In: Advertising, Brand Development & Integration, Corporate Identity, Digital/Interactive, Package Design, Print, Social Media, Strategic Planning/Research

Jenny Marshall *(Owner)*
Annika Lavigne *(Sr Dir-Art)*
Jason Dauphinee *(Dir-Creative)*
Pip Knott *(Dir-Art)*
Trina M'Lot *(Dir-Art)*
Gina Armstrong *(Mgr-Strategic Svcs)*
Alexandra Cruikshank *(Mgr-Strategic Svcs)*
Lindsay Morgan *(Mgr-Strategic Svcs)*
Kyle Marshall *(Acct Coord)*

Accounts:
Victoria Downtown Public Market Society

ECLIPSE MARKETING
11 Villamoura, Laguna Niguel, CA 92677
Tel.: (949) 363-5340
E-Mail: eclipsemarketing@cox.net
Web Site: www.eclipsemarketing.net

Employees: 5

Agency Specializes In: Advertising, Brand Development & Integration, Market Research, Package Design, Public Relations, Strategic Planning/Research, Trade & Consumer Magazines

Leslie Stevens *(Pres)*
John Nugent *(Sr Dir-Strategic Partnerships)*
Chris Bachler *(Dir-Strategic Partnerships)*
Christine Iglesias *(Dir-Strategic Partnerships)*
Lilia Muniz *(Supvr-Mktg & Client Svcs)*

Accounts:
Benq
Elysium Inc.
Express Contractors Inc.
Ginni Designs
Pioneer
SpeakerCraft Speakers Mfr
VisionArt

ECLIPSE MARKETING SERVICES, INC.
240 Cedar Knolls Rd, Cedar Knolls, NJ 07927
Toll Free: (800) 837-4648
Web Site: www.eclipsemarketingservices.com/

Employees: 40

Year Founded: 1992

Joan Coyne *(Sr VP-Mktg & Client Svcs)*
Sandy Bowden *(VP-Strategic Partnerships)*
John Rapp *(VP-New Bus Dev)*
Ellie Brady *(Sr Dir-Strategic Plng)*
John Nugent *(Sr Dir-Strategic Partnership Svcs)*
Chris Bachler *(Dir-Strategic Partnerships)*
Meredith Hopken *(Dir-Mktg & Client Svcs)*

Accounts:
Cablevision
Charter
Comcast
Cox Communications
Disney
HBO
Mediacom
Showtime Networks
Suddenlink
Time Warner Cable
Universal Studios
U.S. National Guard

ECU COMMUNICATIONS LLC
12775 Randolph Ridge Ln Ste 201, Manassas, VA 20109
Tel.: (703) 754-7728
Fax: (703) 754-7709
Web Site: www.ecucomm.com

Agency Specializes In: Advertising, Brand Development & Integration, Content, Corporate Identity, Digital/Interactive, Graphic Design, Media Buying Services, Media Planning, Social Media

Jacqueline Krick *(Founder & CEO)*
Scott Dickerson *(Dir-Creative)*
Steven Joseph *(Dir-Web Comm)*
Anthony Nesbitt *(Acct Mgr)*

Accounts:
Prince William County Department of Economic Dev

THE EDELMAN GROUP
110 W 40th St Ste 2302, New York, NY 10018
Tel.: (212) 825-9200
Fax: (212) 825-1900
E-Mail: info@edelmangroup.com
Web Site: www.edelmangroup.com

Employees: 8
Year Founded: 1982

National Agency Associations: WOMMA

Agency Specializes In: Bilingual Market, Business-To-Business, Collateral, Communications, Consulting, Corporate Identity, Direct Response Marketing, E-Commerce, Electronic Media, Exhibit/Trade Shows, Financial, Graphic Design, Internet/Web Design, Logo & Package Design, Media Buying Services, Planning & Consultation, Point of Purchase, Point of Sale, Print, Production, Sales Promotion, Sponsorship, Strategic Planning/Research

Paul Leys *(Exec VP-Digital)*
Lauren Dugdale *(VP-Digital)*
Abby Ryan Echenique *(VP-Digital)*
Charles Stefko *(VP)*
Ashley A. Cox *(Assoc Dir-Media)*
Katie Greene *(Sr Acct Supvr)*
Valerie Ferreyra *(Acct Supvr-Digital)*
Kristin Wooten *(Acct Supvr)*
Anne Mitchell *(Sr Acct Exec)*

Accounts:
ADP
American Express
American International Group
Atlantic Trust
Avaya
Blackrock Financial Management
Hitachi
JP Morgan Chase
Kriendler & Kriendler LLP
MetLife
Morgan Stanley
NY Water Authority
Oppenheimer Funds
Pitney Bowes
RR Donnelley
Sector
UBS

EDELSBACHER DESIGN GROUP
7158 Captain Kidd Ave, Sarasota, FL 34231
Tel.: (941) 925-4921
Fax: (941) 925-8648
Web Site: www.edelsbacher.com

Agency Specializes In: Advertising, Brand Development & Integration, Internet/Web Design, Logo & Package Design, Print, Search Engine Optimization, Social Media

Guenther Edelsbacher *(Owner)*
Elke Edelsbacher *(VP)*

Accounts:
Absolute Aluminum Inc
Pizza SRQ

EDGE COLLECTIVE
611 Broadway 5th Fl, New York, NY 10012
Tel.: (917) 512-9591
E-Mail: contact@edge-collective.com
Web Site: www.edge-collective.com

Year Founded: 2012

Agency Specializes In: Advertising, Digital/Interactive, Email, Promotions, Social Media, Strategic Planning/Research

Ryan Aynes *(Mng Dir)*
Kelly Black *(Acct Dir)*
Magnus Erhardt *(Dir-Creative)*
Sarah Malvin *(Strategist-Brand)*
Kim Gynnerstedt *(Coord-Brand Mktg)*

Accounts:
Absolut Vodka Vodka; 2015
Bing Bing & Young Hollywood Awards; 2012
Ciroc Vodka Vodka; 2012
Google Small Business Marketing; 2014
Jabra Wireless Headphones & Speakers; 2013
Pernod Ricard Wine & Champagne; 2013
Sotheby's Diamonds & Jewelry; 2012
Steve Madden Fashion & Music; 2013
TripAdvisor Online Travel Experiences; 2014

EDGE MULTIMEDIA
PO Box 90057, Portland, OR 97290
Tel.: (503) 828-0849
E-Mail: hello@edgemultimedia.com
Web Site: www.edgemm.com

Year Founded: 2001

Agency Specializes In: Advertising, Media Buying Services, Media Planning, Social Media

Dan Herman *(Owner, Mng Partner & Head-Creative)*
Scott Chadwick *(Pres & Mng Partner)*
Stephanie Chadwick *(Partner & Exec VP-Sls & Mktg)*
Zack Stack *(Mgr-Creative Svcs)*

Accounts:
Knowledge Vault
Legend Homes Companies
Mars Hill Church
Top Murphy

EDGE PARTNERSHIPS
117 E Kalamazoo St, Lansing, MI 48933
Tel.: (517) 853-6787
Web Site: www.edgepartnerships.com

Agency Specializes In: Advertising, Brand Development & Integration, Event Planning & Marketing, Media Relations, Public Relations

Angela Witwer *(Owner & Pres)*
Lorri Rishar *(CEO)*
Aaron Pumfery *(Art Dir)*

Accounts:
New-Inforum

EDGECORE
(Formerly .Com Marketing)
400 N Wymore Rd, Winter Park, FL 32789
Tel.: (407) 774-4606
Fax: (407) 774-9959
Toll Free: (866) 266-6584
Web Site: edgecore.com/

E-Mail for Key Personnel:
President: bressler@commarketing.com

Employees: 10
Year Founded: 1997

National Agency Associations: AAF-AMA

Agency Specializes In: Advertising, Business-To-Business, Digital/Interactive, Direct Response Marketing, E-Commerce, Internet/Web Design, Media Buying Services, Travel & Tourism

Scott Stackhouse *(CEO)*
Devin Range *(CMO)*
David Wheeler *(VP-Ops)*
Brandi Church *(Media Dir)*
Alex Cue *(Dir-Creative Svcs)*
Doug Drees *(Dir-Digital Sls)*
Leslie Fordham *(Dir-Acct Svcs)*
Zac Keeney *(Dir-Bus Dev)*
Megan Pralle *(Dir-Creative Svcs)*
Jessica Wienhold *(Dir-Ops & Acct Svcs)*
Heather Lyles *(Mgr-Digital Mktg)*

EDSA
1512 E Broward Blvd Ste 110, Fort Lauderdale, FL 33301-2126
Tel.: (954) 524-3330
Fax: (954) 524-0177
E-Mail: info@edsaplan.com
Web Site: www.edsaplan.com

Employees: 200
Year Founded: 1960

Agency Specializes In: Health Care Services, Leisure, Marine, Real Estate, Travel & Tourism

Joseph J. Lalli *(Chm & Principal)*
Doug Smith *(Pres, Principal)*
Paul D. Kissinger *(COO & Principal)*
Gregg Sutton *(Principal)*
Jill Martinez *(Dir-Mktg)*
Rich Hallick *(Assoc Principal)*

Accounts:
Disney's Old Key West Resort
EDSA
Fairmont Hotel; Acapulco
Fairmont Mayakoba
Los Prados; San Juan, PR
Nova Southeastern University

Porto Bahia
Terra; San Juan, PR
University of Florida Historic Master Plan
Yucatan Country Club

EDWARD J. QUIGLEY ASSOCIATES
114 Bradford Ln Ste 100, Lansdale, PA 19446
Tel.: (215) 699-1127
Fax: (215) 699-1128
E-Mail: ejquig@verizon.net

Employees: 5
Year Founded: 1980

Agency Specializes In: Advertising, Brand Development & Integration, Business-To-Business, Communications, Consumer Marketing, Graphic Design, Logo & Package Design, Multimedia, Newspaper, Pharmaceutical

Ed Quigley *(Pres)*

Accounts:
AICS/LHK Partners; Newtown Square, PA Recruitment
Blizzard Express, Ltd.; Goose-Bay, CA Delivery Services
Minipi Camps; Labrador-Newfoundland, CA Vacation Lodge
Newfoundland-Labrador Tourism & Outfitters Destination Branding & Promotion
Quadra Graphics; Pennsauken, NJ Printing Services
Tax Management Associates; Berwyn, PA Sales Tax Control Services

EFFECTIVE MEDIA SOLUTIONS
554 Pine Links Dr, Tega Cay, SC 29708
Tel.: (803) 396-8283
Web Site: www.myeffectivemedia.com

Agency Specializes In: Advertising, Internet/Web Design, Logo & Package Design, Media Buying Services, Media Planning, Print, Radio, T.V.

Dave Brown *(Mng Partner)*

Accounts:
Patterson Heating & Air

EFFECTIVEUI INC.
(Acquired by WPP plc)

EFG CREATIVE INC.
318 Central Ave SE, Albuquerque, NM 87102
Tel.: (505) 344-1333
Fax: (505) 344-4757
E-Mail: info@efgcreative.com
Web Site: www.efgcreative.com

Agency Specializes In: Advertising, Brand Development & Integration, Graphic Design, Package Design, Public Relations, Social Media

Eric F. Garcia *(Owner & Dir-Creative)*

Accounts:
B&D Industries, Inc Logo, Website
Carolyn Pollack
SilkFeet

EFK GROUP
1027 S Clinton Ave, Trenton, NJ 8611
Tel.: (609) 393-5838
E-Mail: info@efkgroup.com
Web Site: www.efkgroup.com

Agency Specializes In: Advertising, Brand Development & Integration, Collateral, Internet/Web Design, Logo & Package Design, Print, Social Media, T.V.

Eleanor Kubacki *(CEO)*
Peter Hipsz *(Dir-Creative)*
Chris McKay *(Dir-Digital)*
Jackie Pentz *(Office Mgr)*
Bryce Rudolph *(Acct Mgr)*

Accounts:
Kean University
Mercy Health System
Prince Global Sports
St Johns University

EFM AGENCY
624 Bdwy Ste 502, San Diego, CA 92101
Tel.: (619) 232-8800
Fax: (619) 232-8801
E-Mail: hello@efmagency.com
Web Site: www.experiencesformankind.com

Year Founded: 1997

Agency Specializes In: Advertising, Brand Development & Integration, Digital/Interactive, Email, Internet/Web Design, Sponsorship

Charles Tassos *(Founder & Sr Dir-Creative)*
Jessica Martinez *(Acct Dir)*
David Coulson *(Dir-Digital Strategy)*
Summer Jackson *(Dir-Art)*
Dylan Jones *(Assoc Dir-Creative)*
Morgan Graham *(Sr Acct Mgr)*
David Fried *(Sr Copywriter & Strategist)*
Eduardo Garcia *(Designer-Visual)*

Accounts:
GE Lighting, LLC
The Mirage Hotel & Casino; Las Vegas, NV Digital Media
Nik Software
Racor Storage Solutions
Siemens Healthcare Diagnostics
Sony Electronics, Inc.

EG INTEGRATED
11820 Nicholas St Ste 102, Omaha, NE 68154
Tel.: (402) 614-3000
Fax: (402) 614-1586
Web Site: www.egintegrated.com

Year Founded: 2007

Agency Specializes In: Advertising, Brand Development & Integration, Broadcast, Event Planning & Marketing, Media Buying Services, Media Planning, Media Training, Print, Public Relations, Social Media

Tom Ervin *(Principal & Dir-Creative)*
Bill Ervin *(Principal)*
Kathleen Al-Marhoon *(Dir-PR)*
Olivia Poggenpohl *(Dir-Strategic Plng)*
Lynnette Roxburgh *(Sr Acct Exec)*
Bridget Bear *(Acct Exec)*

Accounts:
ACI Worldwide Inc.
Albeck & Associates
Barrier Systems, Inc.
Carl Jarl
Creighton Prep Jesuit School
DeLaguardia Cigars
Greenfield
Hancock & Dana Accountants
Hoegemeyer Hybrids
Kelly Klosure Systems
Lindsay Corporation
LMC Equipment
Lucky Bug
Lutheran Family Services
Marian High School
QuikServe Solutions
Railroad Products
Villotta Homes
Watertronics
Zimmatic

THE EGC GROUP
1175 Walt Whitman Rd Ste 200, Melville, NY 11747-3030
Tel.: (516) 935-4944
Fax: (516) 942-3915
E-Mail: contact@egcgroup.com
Web Site: www.egcgroup.com

Employees: 35
Year Founded: 1985

National Agency Associations: 4A's

Agency Specializes In: Advertising, Automotive, Brand Development & Integration, Co-op Advertising, Direct Response Marketing, Education, Event Planning & Marketing, Food Service, Graphic Design, Internet/Web Design, Media Buying Services, Point of Purchase, Public Relations, Publicity/Promotions, Restaurant, Retail, Sales Promotion

Nicole Larrauri *(Pres)*
Fred Appel *(Sr Dir-Art)*
Graham C. Byer *(Dir-Strategic Plng)*
Steve Castro *(Dir-Digital Dev)*
Rich DeSimone *(Dir-Creative)*
Angela Mertz *(Dir-Media)*
Len Rothberg *(Sr Acct Mgr)*
Jeanne Mitchell *(Acct Mgr)*
Stephanie Steudte *(Acct Exec)*

Accounts:
Brother International; 2005
New-Canon
Dorsey Schools; 2006
Dowling College; Oakdale, NY; 1998
Heart of Bethpage
Hopsteiner Social Media
Island Federal Credit Union Marketing
Jiffy Lube; 2005
Lord & Taylor Event Marketing, Public Relations
New-Nature's Truth LLC (Marketing & Digital Agency of Record) Branding, National Retail Marketing Strategy, Social Media
Pine Lawn Memorial Park; Melville, NY; 1996
Premier Home Health Care Digital, Marketing
Red Mango Creative, Digital, Local Store Marketing, Marketing & Advertising, Social Media, Strategy
Scotto Brothers Restaurants; 1986
Southern Container Manufacturer; 2002
Sterling Optical Uniondale, NY Eyewear; 2004
Storage Deluxe; NY; 2006
New-Thomson Reuters
New-VOXX Electronics Digital, Marketing Strategy, Singtrix, Social Media

EGG
10613 SW 138th St, Vashon, WA 98070
Tel.: (206) 352-1600
Fax: (206) 352-1601
E-Mail: hello@eggbranding.com
Web Site: www.eggbranding.com

Employees: 7
Year Founded: 2003

Agency Specializes In: Advertising, Agriculture, Alternative Advertising, Broadcast, Environmental, Internet/Web Design, Multimedia, Newspapers & Magazines, Planning & Consultation, Production (Print), Social Marketing/Nonprofit, Viral/Buzz/Word of Mouth, Web (Banner Ads, Pop-ups, etc.)

Chris Cobb *(Head-Client Svcs-Accts & Projects)*
Marty McDonald *(Dir-Creative)*

Accounts:
The Alliance for Puget Sound Shorelines
Artscorps
Better World Books
Earthbound Earm
Puget Sound Energy
Slowfood USA
Southwest Wind Power
Wholesome & Hearty Foods Company

EGG STRATEGY

1360 Walnut St Ste 102, Boulder, CO 80302
Tel.: (303) 546-9311
Fax: (303) 546-9237
E-Mail: heather@eggstrategy.com
Web Site: www.eggstrategy.com

Employees: 36
Year Founded: 1996

Agency Specializes In: Affluent Market, Automotive, Brand Development & Integration, Communications, Consulting, Consumer Goods, Consumer Marketing, Cosmetics, Electronics, Entertainment, Experience Design, Food Service, Health Care Services, High Technology, Hospitality, Household Goods, Integrated Marketing, International, Luxury Products, Market Research, Medical Products, Men's Market, Multicultural, New Product Development, Over-50 Market, Package Design, Pets , Pharmaceutical, Planning & Consultation, Restaurant, Seniors' Market, Stakeholders, Strategic Planning/Research, Teen Market, Transportation, Travel & Tourism, Tween Market, Urban Market, Women's Market

Jonathan Rodd *(Partner & Pres-Egg Boulder)*
Matthew Singer *(Partner)*
Christopher Wilshire *(Partner)*
Dave Trifiletti *(Gen Mgr-Boulder, Chicago & Vancouver)*
Sam Evans *(Dir-Strategy & Innovation)*
Kathleen Kennedy *(Mgr-Strategic Plng)*
Jessica Campion *(Strategist)*
Hannah Jones *(Strategist)*
Georgia Patera *(Strategist)*
Kathryn Rhine *(Strategist)*

Accounts:
PetSmart
Shire
WhiteWave Foods

EGGFIRST

B-52/206 Eggfirst Villa, Siddharth Nagar 2, Goregaon (W), Mumbai, Maharashtra 400 104 India
Tel.: (91) 22 4241 7200
E-Mail: unscramble@eggfirst.com
Web Site: www.eggfirst.com

Year Founded: 1999

Agency Specializes In: Advertising, Advertising Specialties, Asian Market, Brand Development & Integration, Business Publications, Business-To-Business, Collateral, Corporate Communications, Email, Internet/Web Design, Logo & Package Design, Multimedia, Print, Strategic Planning/Research

Ravikant Banka *(Founder)*
Ashish Banka *(Sr VP)*
Vasudev Rao *(Head-Bus Dev)*
Vijay Anand *(Grp Acct Dir)*
Manoj Choudhari *(Dir-Creative)*
Kaanchan Shah *(Dir-Client Svcs)*
Rajeevkumar Singh *(Sr Acct Mgr)*
Sunita Menezes *(Mgr-HR)*

Accounts:
3 Global Services; Mumbai, India; 2004
Ashland; Netherlands; 2006
Castrol
CitiGroup Global Services; Mumbai, India; 2005
Honeywell
JP Morgan; Mumbai, India; 2006
JUST Diabetes Creative
QLC
Stratitude; 2007
Talwalkars Hi-Fi, NuForm, Reduce, Transform, Zumba
TATA
Ten Sports
Volkswagen Finance Creative, Social Media

EICHENBAUM/ASSOCIATES, INC.

219 N Milwaukee St, Milwaukee, WI 53202-5818
Tel.: (414) 225-0011
Fax: (414) 225-0022
E-Mail: nealb@eichenbaum.net
Web Site: www.eichenbaum.net

Employees: 13
Year Founded: 1989

Agency Specializes In: Advertising, Brand Development & Integration, Broadcast, Business-To-Business, Cable T.V., Co-op Advertising, Collateral, Communications, Consulting, Consumer Marketing, Consumer Publications, Corporate Identity, Direct Response Marketing, Entertainment, Fashion/Apparel, Financial, Government/Political, Graphic Design, Health Care Services, Internet/Web Design, Leisure, Logo & Package Design, Magazines, Media Buying Services, Medical Products, Newspaper, Newspapers & Magazines, Out-of-Home Media, Outdoor, Pets , Planning & Consultation, Point of Purchase, Point of Sale, Print, Public Relations, Publicity/Promotions, Radio, Real Estate, Restaurant, Retail, Sales Promotion, Sports Market, Strategic Planning/Research, T.V., Trade & Consumer Magazines, Travel & Tourism

Approx. Annual Billings: $18,000,000

Steve Eichenbaum *(Pres & Creative Dir)*
Neal Bardele *(Partner & Client Svcs Dir)*
Jerry Hayes *(Art Dir)*
Kristen Johnson *(Dir-Media)*

Accounts:
Fromm Family Pet Foods Campaign: "Cats", Campaign: "Entree", Campaign: "Imitations", Campaign: "Polynesian", Campaign: "Wait"; 1998
Koss Stereophones; Milwaukee, WI; 1983
Landmark Credit Union; 2011
OnKol Monitoring Device; 2012
Providence Hospital

EIGHT ELEVEN INC.

1315 Walnut St Ste 700, Philadelphia, PA 19107
Tel.: (215) 875-8590
Fax: (609) 482-8395
E-Mail: info@eight-eleven.com

Agency Specializes In: Advertising, Brand Development & Integration, Collateral, Logo & Package Design, Public Relations, Search Engine Optimization, Social Media, Web (Banner Ads, Pop-ups, etc.)

Aaron Haydn McLean *(Co-Founder & COO)*
Glenda Laudisio *(Pres & CEO)*
Andrew Keller *(Dir-Web)*
Paul Ricci *(Dir-Fin)*
Bernadette Mackin *(Sr Graphic Designer)*

Accounts:
Medical Solutions Supplier

EIGHT HORSES

4790 Irvine Blvd, Irvine, CA 92620
Tel.: (888) 580-9975
Web Site: www.eighthorses.com

Year Founded: 2004

Agency Specializes In: Advertising, Collateral, Event Planning & Marketing, Graphic Design, Internet/Web Design, Logo & Package Design, Print, Promotions, Social Media

John H. Park *(CEO)*
Albert Hong *(Exec Dir-Art)*
Kyla Yusay *(Acct Coord-Svcs)*
Dave Grantham *(Coord)*

Accounts:
Dorco Co ltd
Event Planners Association
National Notary Association
NuGenTec
Pace Shave

THE EIGHTH FLOOR LLC

20 W 20th St Ste 905, New York, NY 10011
Tel.: (212) 561-5488
Web Site: www.theeighthfloor.com

Agency Specializes In: Brand Development & Integration, Corporate Communications, Digital/Interactive, Public Relations, Social Media

Matthew Marchak *(Pres & CEO)*
Lindsay Siwiec *(Acct Dir)*

Accounts:
New-Benefit Cosmetics

EISEN MANAGEMENT GROUP

515 Monmouth St Ste 302, Newport, KY 41071
Tel.: (859) 291-4302
Fax: (859) 291-4360
E-Mail: info@theeisenagency.com
Web Site: www.theeisenagency.com

Employees: 8

Agency Specializes In: Advertising, Brand Development & Integration, Collateral, Communications, E-Commerce, Event Planning & Marketing, Exhibit/Trade Shows, Graphic Design, Guerilla Marketing, Internet/Web Design, Media Buying Services, Media Planning, Media Relations, Podcasting, Print, Public Relations, Radio, T.V.

Rodger Roeser *(Owner)*
Elizabeth Schuler *(Acct Mgr)*

Accounts:
The Cincinnati Rotary Club Direct Response Programs, Interactive, Media Relations, Membership Campaigns, Social Media
Roto-Rooter

EISENBERG & ASSOCIATES

511 NE 3rd Ave, Fort Lauderdale, FL 33301-3235
Tel.: (954) 760-9500
Fax: (954) 760-9594
E-Mail: info@eisenberginc.com
Web Site: www.eisenberginc.com

E-Mail for Key Personnel:
President: arthure@eisenberginc.com

Employees: 10
Year Founded: 1980

National Agency Associations: AAF

Agency Specializes In: Advertising, Advertising Specialties, Alternative Advertising, Automotive, Bilingual Market, Brand Development & Integration, Business-To-Business, Cable T.V., Catalogs, Children's Market, Collateral, Consulting, Consumer Marketing, Consumer Publications, Corporate Communications, Corporate Identity, Digital/Interactive, Direct Response Marketing, Direct-to-Consumer, E-Commerce, Electronic Media, Email, Exhibit/Trade Shows, Government/Political, Graphic Design, Health Care Services, Hispanic Market, Hospitality, Integrated Marketing, Internet/Web Design, Investor Relations, Legal Services, Leisure, Local Marketing, Logo & Package Design, Magazines, Marine, Market Research, Media Buying Services, Media Planning, Media Relations, Medical Products, Merchandising, New Product Development, Newspaper, Newspapers & Magazines, Out-of-Home Media, Outdoor, Over-50 Market, Paid Searches, Pharmaceutical, Planning & Consultation, Point of Purchase, Point of Sale, Print, Product Placement, Production, Production (Ad, Film, Broadcast), Production (Print), Promotions, Radio, Recruitment, Regional, Restaurant, Retail, Sales Promotion, Search Engine Optimization, Seniors' Market, Social Marketing/Nonprofit, Sports Market, Strategic Planning/Research, T.V., Trade & Consumer Magazines, Travel & Tourism

Approx. Annual Billings: $18,200,000 Capitalized

Breakdown of Gross Billings by Media: Bus. Publs.: 5%; Collateral: 10%; D.M.: 5%; Graphic Design: 5%; Mags.: 10%; Newsp.: 20%; Out-of-Home Media: 10%; Point of Purchase: 5%; Production: 10%; Radio: 5%; T.V.: 10%; Worldwide Web Sites: 5%

Josie Eisenberg *(Sr Acct Exec)*

Accounts:
AeroTurbine
America National Bank; Ft Lauderdale, FL; 2005
Aqua Wizard; Ft. Lauderdale, Fl Pool Chemical Monitors; 2002
Atlas Metals; Miami, FL; 2005
Blockbuster's Story Garden Films
Cobia Boat Company; Fort Pierce, FL; 2005
Concentra
Denbury Resources Inc
Eisenberg Skatepark
Fastaff Travel Nursing; Denver, CO; 2002
Independence Broadcast Services
Standard Pre-Cast Walls; SC; 2005
University Hospital & Medical Center; Tamarac, FL
Westside Regional Medical Center; Plantation, FL

Branch

Eisenberg & Associates
3102 Oak Lawn LB 104, Dallas, TX 75219
Tel.: (214) 528-5990
Fax: (214) 521-8536
E-Mail: josiee@eisenberginc.com
Web Site: www.eisenberginc.com

Employees: 29

Liz Kline *(Principal & VP-Acct Svcs & New Bus Dev)*
Lindsey Bock *(Sr Dir-Art)*
Sharon Lee *(Sr Dir-Art)*
Arlo Eisenberg *(Mgr-Creative & Traffic)*
Josie Eisenberg *(Sr Acct Exec)*
Brian Kelley *(Acct Exec)*

Accounts:
ADDVantage Technologies
AeroTurbine
Dell Perot Systems Corporation
Denbury Resources Inc.
National Breast Cancer Foundation
Smith & Weber Construction
Stampede Brewing Company, Inc.; Dallas, TX Stampede Light Plus

EISENBERG, VITAL & RYZE ADVERTISING
(Formerly Vital & Ryze)
155 Dow St Ste 101, Manchester, NH 03101
Tel.: (603) 647-8606
Fax: (603) 647-8607
Web Site: www.evradvertising.com

Employees: 16
Year Founded: 1990

Agency Specializes In: Broadcast, Digital/Interactive, Print

Terry Vital *(Founder)*
Jeff Eisenberg *(Pres)*
Deb Choate *(VP-Ops)*
Mike DeBlasi *(Dir-Strategic Mktg)*
Jim Fennell *(Dir-PR & Content Svcs)*
Margo Johnson *(Dir-Creative)*
Christine Blinn *(Acct Mgr)*
Alaina Gonzalez *(Mgr-Social Media)*
Elyse Barry *(Specialist-Res & Strategy)*
Mariah Ehrgott *(Specialist-Digital Analytics)*
Lauren Hettler *(Acct Exec)*
Matt Lawson *(Specialist-Digital Mktg)*
Dan Powers *(Designer-Web)*
Briana Proctor *(Media Buyer)*

Accounts:
Bellwether Community Credit Union (Agency of Record)
The New Hampshire Liquor Commission (Agency of Record)

EISENMAN ASSOCIATES INC.
401 Broadway 22nd Fl, New York, NY 10013
Tel.: (212) 941-0550
Fax: (212) 941-0710
E-Mail: info@eisenman.com
Web Site: www.eisenman.com

Employees: 8
Year Founded: 1962

National Agency Associations: AMA

Agency Specializes In: Fashion/Apparel, Graphic Design, Internet/Web Design, Investor Relations

Approx. Annual Billings: $8,000,000

Breakdown of Gross Billings by Media: Consumer Publs.: $1,000,000; D.M.: $1,000,000; Fees: $2,000,000; Mags.: $2,000,000; Newsp.: $2,000,000

Accounts:
Aetna
Arthur Lipper Corporation
Bower & Gardner
Popeyes Louisiana Kitchen, Inc.
Valiant Hire; Australia Web Site Design

EJW ASSOCIATES, INC.
Crabapple Village Office Park 1602 Abbey Ct, Alpharetta, GA 30004
Tel.: (770) 664-9322
Fax: (770) 664-9324
E-Mail: advertise@ejwassoc.com
Web Site: www.ejwassoc.com

Employees: 3
Year Founded: 1982

Agency Specializes In: Advertising, Aviation & Aerospace, Brand Development & Integration, Business Publications, Business-To-Business, Catalogs, Collateral, Commercial Photography, Communications, Computers & Software, Consulting, Content, Corporate Communications, Corporate Identity, Custom Publishing, Digital/Interactive, Direct Response Marketing, E-Commerce, Electronic Media, Email, Environmental, Graphic Design, Health Care Services, High Technology, Identity Marketing, Industrial, Information Technology, Integrated Marketing, International, Internet/Web Design, Legal Services, Local Marketing, Logo & Package Design, Market Research, Media Buying Services, Media Planning, Media Relations, Multimedia, New Product Development, New Technologies, Paid Searches, Planning & Consultation, Print, Production, Public Relations, Publicity/Promotions, Radio, Real Estate, Regional, Social Marketing/Nonprofit, Strategic Planning/Research, Technical Advertising, Trade & Consumer Magazines

Approx. Annual Billings: $990,000

Breakdown of Gross Billings by Media: Collateral: $10,000; Consulting: $70,000; D.M.: $50,000; E-Commerce: $70,000; Graphic Design: $80,000; Internet Adv.: $80,000; Logo & Package Design: $50,000; Print: $80,000; Pub. Rels.: $100,000; Strategic Planning/Research: $50,000; Trade & Consumer Mags.: $50,000; Worldwide Web Sites: $300,000

Emil Walcek *(Pres)*
Sean Walcek *(Mgr-New Media)*

Accounts:
ACI Vitro; Memphis, TN Glass, Glass Equipment & Supplies; 2006
AFT Aikawa Group Paper Processing Equipment; 2010
Aikawa Fiber Technologies (AFT); Quebec, Canada Pulp & Paper Industry Systems & Equipment; 2011
Altama Footwear; Atlanta, GA Military Footwear
Andritz; Graz, Austria Pulp & Paper Equipment; 2002
Bluefields Capital; Norcross, GA Financial Services; 2002
Cornell University College of Engineering; New York, NY Space Technology Research; 2006
CTI Electronics Corp.; Stratford, CT Computer Interface Equipment & Components; 2006
EB Medicine; Norcross, GA Medical Training & Certification; 2008
Energy Efficient Components; Atlanta, GA Electronic Components; 2010
Foxfire Technologies; Six Mile, SC Supply Chain Software Systems; 2003
Imagetrak; Greenville, SC Document Tracking Software; 1999
IMCorp Inc Data capture, communication systems & equipment; 2013
Kavali Plastic Surgery; Atlanta, GA Medical Services; 2007
Kingway Material Handling Systems; Dallas, TX Material Handling Equipment; 2002
LXE Inc; Norcross, GA Logistics Systems Manufacturing
Matcutter; Lake Hartwell, GA Wholesale Art Mat Manufacturing; 2002
Micasa Industries; Roswell, GA Residential Services; 2005
Nordic Aluminum; Atlanta, GA Lighting Track; 1992
Nordic Components; Hutchinson, MN Precision-Machined Aluminum Parts; 2005
Pak-Lite; Duluth, GA Custom Packaging, Die-Cut Parts, Extrusions, Flooring Underlayment, Foam Components, Insulation, Loose Fill Packaging, Tapes; 2006
PDQ; Ellijay, GA Chemicals Manufacturing; 2005

Plichta Alavi & Associates; Marietta, GA Legal Services; 2006
Quality Gunite Works; Deland, FL Pool Building Services, Trade Services; 2003
Savannah Luggage Works; Vidalia, GA Textile Fabrication Manufacturing; 1996
SDI Supply Chain Solutions; 2012
Seeburger Inc; Atlanta, GA IS Technology; 2001
Senscient Inc.; Houston, TX Fixed Gas Detection Systems; 2005
Sensidyne Gas Monitoring Systems; 2004
Southern Aluminum Finishing; Atlanta, GA Aluminum Extension, Sheets & Finishing Services; 1994
Syskin Medical Employment Agency; 2003
Taylor Chemical Co. Specialty Chemicals; 1999
Tele-Track; Norcross, GA Consumer Information; 1988
Thermal Gas Systems; Roswell, GA Gas Monitoring Instruments; 1986
Tigerflow; Dallas, TX Mechanical Systems Mfg; 1996
Title Credit Loans; Norcross, GA Financial Services; 2012
Triad Health Management of GA; Alpharetta, GA Health Management Services; 2002
Vista Storage Corp.; Atlanta, GA Data Management Systems, Enterprise; 2004
Waldron Dentistry; Marietta, GA Dental Services; 2006
Xcess Casualty; Atlanta, GA Specialty Insurance; 2005
Zellweger Analytics Gas Detection Systems

EL CREATIVE, INC.

3816 San Jacinto, Dallas, TX 75204
Tel.: (214) 742-0700
E-Mail: michael@elcreative.com
Web Site: www.elcreative.com

E-Mail for Key Personnel:
Creative Dir.: brian@elcreative.com

Employees: 8
Year Founded: 2003

Agency Specializes In: Advertising, Advertising Specialties, Affluent Market, African-American Market, Alternative Advertising, Arts, Automotive, Aviation & Aerospace, Bilingual Market, Brand Development & Integration, Broadcast, Business Publications, Business-To-Business, Cable T.V., Catalogs, Children's Market, Co-op Advertising, Collateral, College, Commercial Photography, Communications, Computers & Software, Consulting, Consumer Goods, Consumer Marketing, Consumer Publications, Corporate Communications, Corporate Identity, Cosmetics, Digital/Interactive, Direct Response Marketing, Direct-to-Consumer, E-Commerce, Education, Electronic Media, Electronics, Email, Entertainment, Environmental, Event Planning & Marketing, Exhibit/Trade Shows, Experience Design, Faith Based, Fashion/Apparel, Financial, Food Service, Gay & Lesbian Market, Government/Political, Graphic Design, Guerilla Marketing, Health Care Services, High Technology, Hispanic Market, Hospitality, Household Goods, Identity Marketing, In-Store Advertising, Industrial, Infomercials, Information Technology, Integrated Marketing, International, Internet/Web Design, Leisure, Local Marketing, Logo & Package Design, Luxury Products, Magazines, Marine, Medical Products, Men's Market, Mobile Marketing, Multicultural, Multimedia, New Product Development, New Technologies, Newspaper, Newspapers & Magazines, Outdoor, Over-50 Market, Package Design, Pharmaceutical, Planning & Consultation, Point of Purchase, Point of Sale, Print, Production, Production (Print), Promotions, Public Relations, Publicity/Promotions, Publishing, Radio, Real Estate, Regional, Restaurant, Retail, Sales Promotion, Search Engine Optimization, Seniors' Market, Social Marketing/Nonprofit, Sponsorship, Sports Market, T.V., Technical Advertising, Teen Market, Telemarketing, Trade & Consumer Magazines, Transportation, Travel & Tourism, Tween Market, Urban Market, Viral/Buzz/Word of Mouth, Web (Banner Ads, Pop-ups, etc.), Women's Market

Revenue: $1,000,000

Michael Gonzalez *(Pres & Dir-Creative)*
Robert Zepeda *(Principal & Dir-Creative)*
Victor Gonzalez *(Dir-New Bus)*
Brian Keith *(Dir-Creative)*

Accounts:
CareNow; Coppell, TX Healthcare; 2008
Clamato
Coca-Cola Refreshments USA, Inc.
Stranix; Irving, TX Technology; 2007
Wingstop Restaurants, Inc.; Richardson, TX QSR; 2006

ELA (EVERYTHINGLA)

18101 Von Karman Ave Ste 550, Irvine, CA 92612
Tel.: (310) 849-5100
E-Mail: info@ela1.com
Web Site: www.ela1.com

Employees: 87
Year Founded: 2004

Agency Specializes In: Above-the-Line, Branded Entertainment, Broadcast, Digital/Interactive, Experience Design, Mobile Marketing, Newspapers & Magazines, Out-of-Home Media, Outdoor, Print, Production, Production (Print), Promotions, Radio, Social Media, T.V., Viral/Buzz/Word of Mouth, Web (Banner Ads, Pop-ups, etc.)

Approx. Annual Billings: $127,000,000

Andre Filip *(CEO)*
Pakko De La Torre *(Partner, VP & Dir-Creative)*
Carlos Musquez *(Exec Dir-Creative)*
Michelle Nein *(Acct Dir)*
Jeremiah Jones *(Dir-Creative)*
Joanna Gardner *(Acct Supvr)*

Accounts:
Curacao; 2014
IMAX; 2010
Intel Corporation; 2009
Irvine Company; 2012
Katzkin; 2015
MGM Grand; 2009
NFL; 2010
Slaters 50/50; 2015
Thermador; 2014
Verizon Wireless; 2007
Warner Bros.; 2008
Wix.com; 2015

ELEMENT ADVERTISING LLC

1 Tingle Alley, Asheville, NC 28801
Tel.: (828) 545-8159
Web Site: www.elementadvertising.com

Agency Specializes In: Advertising, Brand Development & Integration, Corporate Identity, Internet/Web Design, Outdoor, Package Design, Print, Public Relations, Social Media

Jack Becker *(Partner, Dir-Creative & Strategist-Brand)*
Rob Young *(Partner & Dir-Media & Res)*
Mackenzie Sedelbauer *(Project Mgr, Acct Exec & Jr Strategist-Brand)*
John Melton *(Designer)*

Accounts:
Asheville Outlets

ELEMENT ELEVEN

588 E Hwy CC Ste 1, Nixa, MO 65714
Tel.: (417) 724-9427
E-Mail: contact@elementeleven.com
Web Site: www.elementeleven.com

Agency Specializes In: Advertising, Brand Development & Integration, Graphic Design, Internet/Web Design, Logo & Package Design, Print, Search Engine Optimization

Dan Bennett *(Partner & Dir-Creative)*
Daniel Mayfield *(Partner)*

Accounts:
Askinosie Chocolate
Nixa Fire Protection District

ELEVATE CREATIVE LLC

(Formerly Hall & Lien Creative Agency)
925 B St Ste 604, San Diego, CA 92101
Fax: (858) 605-4229
Toll Free: (877) 858-2991
Web Site: www.elevatecreativeinc.com

Year Founded: 2011

Agency Specializes In: Advertising, Logo & Package Design

Tori Hall *(Co-Founder & Dir)*

Accounts:
Althea Technologies, Inc.
Blue Beach Resort
CQ Mixer
Davis Ink Interior Design Co.
Guild Mortgage Company
Radiology Oncology Systems
Zinetti Foods

ELEVATE STUDIOS

328 S Jefferson St Ste 540, Chicago, IL 60661
Tel.: (312) 932-1104
Fax: (312) 640-1597
Web Site: www.elevatestudios.com

Year Founded: 2003

Agency Specializes In: Advertising, Content, Digital/Interactive, Internet/Web Design, Social Media, Sponsorship

Lawrence Bak *(Pres & Exec Dir-Creative)*
Kate Vein *(VP)*
Jason Crichton *(Dir-Interactive)*
Sara Novak *(Assoc Dir-Creative)*
Patti Gamble *(Sr Mgr-HR & Ops)*
Sarah Hamilton *(Acct Mgr)*
Nicole Bono *(Mgr-Project Mgmt)*
Samantha Dietz *(Sr Designer-UX)*
Michael Tri *(Designer-Interactive)*
Lauren Clark *(Sr Designer-Interactive)*

Accounts:
HanesBrands (Digital Agency of Record) Champion, Hanes, One Hanes Place
Mario Tricoci Hair Salons
Matrix Content Planning & Strategy, Design, Information Architecture
Redken 5th Avenue Website Design
Restaurant.com

ELEVATED THIRD

535 16th St, Denver, CO 80202
Tel.: (303) 436-9113
E-Mail: info@elevatedthird.com
Web Site: www.elevatedthird.com

Employees: 28
Year Founded: 2005

Agency Specializes In: Advertising, Advertising Specialties, Alternative Advertising, Brand Development & Integration, Business-To-Business, Consulting, Content, Digital/Interactive, E-Commerce, Email, Experience Design, Graphic Design, Integrated Marketing, Internet/Web Design, Local Marketing, Logo & Package Design, Market Research, Mobile Marketing, Paid Searches, Print, Search Engine Optimization, Social Marketing/Nonprofit, Social Media, Strategic Planning/Research, Technical Advertising, Viral/Buzz/Word of Mouth, Web (Banner Ads, Pop-ups, etc.)

Jeff Calderone *(Pres)*
Michael Lander *(Dir-Technical)*
Harrison Liss *(Dir-Bus Dev)*
Judd Mercer *(Dir-Creative)*
Betsy Sherertz *(Dir-Art)*
Nick Switzer *(Dir-Dev)*
Taylor Laitsch *(Acct Mgr)*
Erica Ellingsen *(Mgr-Ops)*
Shannon Flowerday *(Designer-Digital)*

Accounts:
Colorado Public Employees Retirement Association Public Facing Website; 2014
Comcast Business-to-Business Services; 2013
Core Power Yoga; 2013
Hunsucker Law Firm; 2014
Kaiser Permanente Intranet; 2014
Sprint Federal Relay Services; 2012

ELEVATION
1027 33rd St NW Ste 260, Washington, DC 20007
Tel.: (202) 380-3230
Fax: (202) 337-1228
E-Mail: info@elevation-us.com
Web Site: www.elevation-us.com

Employees: 18
Year Founded: 2002

National Agency Associations: ADC-AHAA

Agency Specializes In: Advertising, Affluent Market, Alternative Advertising, Automotive, Bilingual Market, Brand Development & Integration, Branded Entertainment, Broadcast, Business-To-Business, Cable T.V., Children's Market, Collateral, Commercial Photography, Consulting, Consumer Goods, Consumer Marketing, Consumer Publications, Corporate Communications, Corporate Identity, Digital/Interactive, Direct Response Marketing, Entertainment, Environmental, Event Planning & Marketing, Fashion/Apparel, Government/Political, Graphic Design, Guerilla Marketing, Health Care Services, Hispanic Market, Hospitality, Integrated Marketing, International, Internet/Web Design, Leisure, Local Marketing, Logo & Package Design, Luxury Products, Magazines, Media Buying Services, Media Planning, Media Relations, Men's Market, Merchandising, Multicultural, Multimedia, New Product Development, Newspapers & Magazines, Out-of-Home Media, Outdoor, Package Design, Planning & Consultation, Point of Sale, Print, Production, Production (Ad, Film, Broadcast), Production (Print), Promotions, Public Relations, Publicity/Promotions, Radio, Recruitment, Regional, Restaurant, Retail, Search Engine Optimization, Social Marketing/Nonprofit, Sponsorship, Sports Market, Stakeholders, Strategic Planning/Research, Sweepstakes, T.V., Teen Market, Trade & Consumer Magazines, Transportation, Travel & Tourism, Urban Market, Viral/Buzz/Word of Mouth, Web (Banner Ads, Pop-ups, etc.), Women's Market

Approx. Annual Billings: $20,000,000

Breakdown of Gross Billings by Media: Cable T.V.: 15%; Event Mktg.: 2%; Foreign: 5%; Graphic Design: 3%; Internet Adv.: 10%; Network T.V.: 5%; Newsp. & Mags.: 15%; Out-of-Home Media: 5%; Production: 20%; Pub. Rels.: 5%; Spot Radio: 10%; Strategic Planning/Research: 5%

Pablo Izquierdo *(Co-Founder & Exec VP)*
James H. Learned *(Owner)*
Guayi Fernandez *(Sr Dir-Art)*
Rodolfo Hernandez *(Dir-Creative)*
Taylor Cylke *(Sr Acct Exec)*
Jimena Paz *(Sr Acct Exec)*

Accounts:
American Lung Association - DC Chapter; Washington, DC Hispanic & Urban Initiatives, Tobacco Free Families
Black and Orange Burger Collateral Material Development, Consumer Research, Social Media Design, Strategic Communications
Hola Ciudad
Natural Resources Defense Council; Washington, DC La Onda Verde, Hispanic Initiative; 2004
NRDC
Penske; Reading, PA Penske Truck Rental; 2006
Poison Control
US Customs & Border Patrol; Washington, DC Border Safety Initiative; 2008
Virginia Housing Devl Authority

Branch

Elevation
139 Fulton St Ste 211, New York, NY 10007
Tel.: (646) 688-4960
Fax: (202) 337-1228
E-Mail: nyinfo@elevation-us.com
Web Site: www.elevation-us.com

Employees: 13

Roger McNamee *(Co-Founder)*
Avie Tevanian *(Mng Dir)*

Accounts:
American Lung Association
Comcast
Homeland Security
NDN
Northern Virginia Community Hospital
US Department of Health & Human Services
Western Hemisphere Northern Initiative

ELEVATION ADVERTISING LLC
9 W Main St, Richmond, VA 23220
Tel.: (804) 780-2300
Fax: (804) 780-2323
Web Site: www.elevationadvertising.com

Year Founded: 2001

Agency Specializes In: Advertising, Brand Development & Integration, Communications, Corporate Communications, Logo & Package Design, Outdoor, Print, Radio, Sponsorship, Strategic Planning/Research, T.V.

Aaron Dotson *(Co-Founder & Creative Dir)*
Stacie Elliott *(COO)*
Frank Gilliam *(Principal & Dir-Creative)*
Dana Hoeck *(Sr Art Dir)*
Emily Greenwood *(Sr Acct Mgr)*
Dionne Kumpe *(Sr Acct Mgr)*
Kim Moore *(Sr Acct Mgr)*
Stephanie Cardwell *(Acct Mgr)*

Accounts:
Duke's Mayonnaise

ELEVATOR
2965 Roosevelt St Ste C, Carlsbad, CA 92009
Tel.: (760) 494-7590
Fax: (619) 374-2892
E-Mail: hello@elevatoragency.com
Web Site: www.elevatoragency.com

Agency Specializes In: Advertising, Brand Development & Integration, Digital/Interactive, Social Media, Sponsorship

Frank Cowell *(Founder & Pres)*
Joseph Freeman *(VP-Tech & Experience)*
Sarah Szilagyi *(VP-Strategy & Client Svcs)*
Erika Ellis *(Acct Exec)*
Jed Bridges *(Sr Designer-Web & Designer-Identity)*

Accounts:
Asian Real Estate Association of America
The Corky McMillin Companies Brand Audit, Digital Marketing, Language, Liberty Station
Factor Technologies Strategic Brand Language
Logic 9s
LPL Financial Corporation
Pacific Divorce Management
Pilgrim Studios
QUALCOMM Incorporated
Stage 21 Bikes

ELEVATOR STRATEGY, ADVERTISING & DESIGN
300-1505 W 2nd Ave, Granville Island, Vancouver, BC V6H 3Y4 Canada
Tel.: (604) 737-4346
Fax: (604) 737-4348
Web Site: www.elevatorstrategy.com

Employees: 15

Agency Specializes In: Advertising

Bob Stamnes *(Pres)*
Friso Halbertsma *(Sr Dir-Art)*
Dean Butler *(Acct Dir & Dir-Media Svcs)*
Allan Black *(Client Svcs Dir)*
Bruce Fraser *(Dir-Creative)*
Zina Minchenko *(Assoc Dir-Media)*
Aubrey Perez *(Mgr-Media)*
Debbie Hoover *(Acct Exec & Media Buyer)*
Della Shellard *(Sr Accountant)*

Accounts:
Bernardin Ltd. Mason Jars
Coast Hotels & Resorts
Medichair
Rowenta (Public Relations Agency of Record) Floor Care Products, High-End Garment Care
T-Fal (Public Relations Agency of Record) Cookware, Kitchen Appliances, Linen Care
TaskTools
Toyota Dealers of BC

ELEVEN INC.
500 Sansome St., San Francisco, CA 94111
Tel.: (415) 707-1111
Fax: (415) 707-1100
E-Mail: newbusiness@eleveninc.com
Web Site: www.eleveninc.com

E-Mail for Key Personnel:
President: courtney@eleveninc.com

Employees: 120
Year Founded: 1999

National Agency Associations: 4A's

Agency Specializes In: Advertising, Automotive, Below-the-Line, Brand Development & Integration, Broadcast, Business Publications, Business-To-Business, Collateral, Communications, Computers & Software, Consumer Goods, Consumer

Advertising Agencies

Marketing, Corporate Communications, Corporate Identity, Digital/Interactive, Direct Response Marketing, E-Commerce, Education, Electronic Media, Email, Entertainment, Event Planning & Marketing, Fashion/Apparel, Financial, Graphic Design, High Technology, In-Store Advertising, Integrated Marketing, Internet/Web Design, Investor Relations, Leisure, Logo & Package Design, Luxury Products, Merchandising, Multimedia, New Technologies, Newspaper, Newspapers & Magazines, Out-of-Home Media, Outdoor, Package Design, Planning & Consultation, Point of Purchase, Point of Sale, Print, Radio, Restaurant, Retail, Sales Promotion, Social Media, Sponsorship, Strategic Planning/Research, T.V., Trade & Consumer Magazines, Travel & Tourism, Viral/Buzz/Word of Mouth

Approx. Annual Billings: $1,350,000,000

Breakdown of Gross Billings by Media: Collateral: 5%; Consumer Publs.: 5%; D.M.: 10%; Event Mktg.: 5%; Graphic Design: 10%; Internet Adv.: 15%; Logo & Package Design: 5%; Newsp. & Mags.: 5%; Outdoor: 5%; Spot Radio: 5%; Spot T.V.: 10%; Strategic Planning/Research: 10%; Trade & Consumer Mags.: 5%; Worldwide Web Sites: 5%

Michael Borosky *(Founder & Dir-Creative)*
Rob Price *(Founder & Dir-Creative)*
Ken Kula *(Owner & CFO)*
Courtney Buechert *(CEO)*
Alison Fowler *(Partner)*
Clay Eichner *(Grp Dir-Media)*
T. J. Tshionyi *(Exec Producer-Digital)*
Aryan Aminzadeh *(Creative Dir)*
Lily Byrne *(Acct Dir)*
Wood Simmons *(Jr Art Dir)*
Tristan Besse *(Mgmt Supvr)*
Hannah Bell *(Dir-Ad Ops-Activation)*
Ted Bluey *(Assoc Partner & Dir-Design)*
Enrique Camacho *(Dir-Creative)*
Margie Chidley *(Dir-Creative)*
Flavia Gonzalez *(Dir-Art)*
Turner Johnson *(Dir-Art)*
Aaron Richard *(Dir-Innovation)*
Ricard Valero *(Dir-Creative)*
Meghan Bush *(Acct Mgr)*
Marisa Millisic *(Copywriter)*
Rob Thiemann *(Copywriter)*

Accounts:
AAA Northern California, Nevada & Utah Campaign: "Live to Help"
Apple Inc; Cupertino, CA; 2006
Aria Resort & Casino Creative, Design, Digital, On-Site, Out-of-Home, Print, Social, TV
Dignity Health (Agency of Record)
Julep
Lyft Campaign: "Driving You Happy", Digital, Out-of-Home, Social
Oakley, Inc. (Lead Creative Agency) Advertising, Campaign: "LiveYours", Campaign: "One Obsession", Online, Outdoor, Print
San Francisco Jewish Film Festival
San Francisco Travel Assn.; San Francisco, CA Tourism; 2009
Sun Valley; Sun Valley, ID Campaign: "Experience Sun Valley", Ski Resort & Town; 2010
Treasury Wine Estates Campaign: "19 Crimes wine"
Union Bank N.A.; San Francisco, CA Campaign: "Doing Right, It's Just Good Business", Digital, Marketing Campaign, Mobile, Social, TV
Virgin America; Burlingame, CA "Have You Been Flying BLAH Airlines?", Campaign: "Departure Date", Campaign: "Experience Virgin America Site", Creative, Online; 2008
VISA; San Francisco, CA Financial Services; 2005

ELEVEN19 COMMUNICATIONS INC.

900 S 74th Plz Ste 100, Omaha, NE 68114
Tel.: (402) 408-3072
Web Site: www.eleven19.com

Agency Specializes In: Advertising, Graphic Design, Internet/Web Design, Logo & Package Design, Print

Marc Butterfield *(Co-Owner)*
Donovan Beery *(Co-Owner)*

Accounts:
D2 Center
Jons Naturals
Montessori Childrens Room
Neenah Paper
Pug Partners of Nebraska

ELEVENDY

7311 Galilee Rd, Roseville, CA 95678
Tel.: (916) 242-8292
Web Site: www.elevendy.com

Year Founded: 2011

Agency Specializes In: Advertising, Graphic Design, Internet/Web Design, Media Planning, Production, Social Media, Sponsorship

Dave Cox *(CEO & Sr Strategist-Creative)*
Dustin Ljung *(Client Svcs Dir)*

Accounts:
California Family Fitness Campaign: "Discover What's Inside", Campaign: "The Climb", Campaign: "The Ride"
Danger Maiden Productions Geek Girls 'A' Team, Team Unicorn
Electronic Arts Inc.
From Dates To Diapers.com Campaign: "Supermom"
Mikuni Sushi Campaign: "Some call it magic..."
MobileMed
Muerto Spirits, Inc. Tequila Logo
Nerdist.com Campaign: "Games, Gadgets, Girls..."
PepsiCo Inc.
Phase 5 Tactical Ambidextrous Battle Latch
Prism Renova Logo
Qusik App UI Design, Logo
Sacramento Kings Campaign: "Bold. Beautiful. Epic", Campaign: "Defiance", Dancers Calendar, Defiant King
Toyota Motor Corporation
Ubisoft Entertainment S.A. Splinter Cell

ELEVENTY GROUP

453 S High St, Akron, OH 44311
Tel.: (330) 294-1120
Web Site: www.eleventygroup.com

Year Founded: 2011

Agency Specializes In: Advertising, Content, Digital/Interactive, Internet/Web Design, Print, Social Media

Ken Dawson *(Pres)*
Jeff Birkner *(VP-Mktg & Strategy)*
Angie Moore *(VP-Strategy & Dev)*
James Moran *(Dir-Mktg Intelligence & Analytics)*

Accounts:
Holy Apostles Soup Kitchen
Special Olympics International, Inc.

ELF

2332 Galiano St 2nd Fl, Coral Gables, FL 33134
Tel.: (802) 735-1298
Web Site: www.elfproductions.com

Employees: 10
Year Founded: 2007

Agency Specializes In: Branded Entertainment, Business Publications, Collateral, Consumer Publications, Custom Publishing, Digital/Interactive, Electronic Media, Experience Design, Mobile Marketing, Multimedia, Paid Searches, Promotions, Publishing, Search Engine Optimization, Social Media

Approx. Annual Billings: $5,000,000

Jan Manon *(Dir)*

Accounts:
Intercontinental Hotels Group; 2012

ELIAS SAVION ADVERTISING, PUBLIC RELATIONS & INTERACTIVE

Dominion Tower 24th Fl, Pittsburgh, PA 15206
Tel.: (412) 642-7700
Fax: (412) 642-2277
Web Site: www.elias-savion.com

Employees: 30
Year Founded: 1976

Agency Specializes In: Advertising, Sponsorship

Ronnie Savion *(Co-Founder, Chief Creative Officer & Exec VP)*
Joseph Parente *(CTO & VP-Digital Svcs)*
Dan McCarthy *(Exec VP-Strategic & Creative Dev)*
Tina L. Richardson *(VP-Comm)*
Michael Cope *(Dir-Content)*
Genny Lewis *(Mgr-HR)*
Marilyn Schmidt *(Specialist-Media)*

Accounts:
AIRMALL
Alcoa, Inc.
Buffalo Wings & Rings
Center for Organ Recovery & Education; Pittsburgh, PA (Agency of Record) Branding, Creative, Marketing, Media Planning & Buying, Public Relations, Strategic Development, Website Design
Columbia Gas of Maryland (Agency of Record)
Columbia Gas of Pennsylvania (Agency of Record)
Deceuninck North America
Kroff Inc.
Liberty Tire Recycling
Pittsburgh Leadership Foundation
TrueFit Solutions
Wheeling Corrugating

ELISCO ADVERTISING, INC.

3707 Butler St, Pittsburgh, PA 15201
Tel.: (412) 586-5840
E-Mail: ads@elisco.com
Web Site: www.elisco.com

E-Mail for Key Personnel:
President: jelisco@elisco.com
Creative Dir.: belisco@elisco.com
Media Dir.: nnascone@elisco.com

Employees: 8
Year Founded: 1978

National Agency Associations: Second Wind Limited

Agency Specializes In: Brand Development & Integration, Broadcast, Communications, Corporate Identity, Financial, Health Care Services, Internet/Web Design, Logo & Package Design, New Product Development, Newspapers & Magazines, Outdoor, Planning & Consultation, Print, Strategic Planning/Research, Trade & Consumer Magazines

Approx. Annual Billings: $2,500,000

John Elisco *(Mng Partner & Principal)*
Anna Miskella *(VP)*
Anna Radder *(VP)*
Clint Branch *(Dir-Art)*
John Caruso *(Acct Exec)*
Bruce Boul *(Copywriter)*
Nicole Christ *(Media Planner & Buyer-Digital)*

Accounts:
Adelphia Business Solutions
Allegheny Valley Bank
Carnegie Mellon University
Catanese Group
Conemaugh Health System
Easley & Rivers; Monroeville, PA Business-to-Business; 2000
Idlewild Park
Jefferson Regional Medical Center; Pittsburgh, PA Hospital; 2007
Jenny Lee Bakery
Kennywood Park
Lawrenceville Development Corporation
Medsage Technologies
Mid Atlantic Institutional Service
Mosso's Medical Supply
Pittsburgh Wine Festival
Rosen, Louik & Perry
Singer Vacuum Cleaners
Vocelli Pizza
Wendell August

ELL CREATIVE
629 W 22nd St Ste 4, Houston, TX 77008
Tel.: (713) 695-4441
E-Mail: info@ellcreative.com
Web Site: www.ellcreative.com

Agency Specializes In: Advertising, Brand Development & Integration, Digital/Interactive, Email, Outdoor, Print, Social Media

Jose Cordova *(Partner)*
David Saxe *(Partner)*
Thomas Watts *(Partner)*
Jack Wang *(Dir-Art)*
Brad Sebastian *(Acct Exec)*
Ben Berkowitz *(Copywriter)*

Accounts:
Reliant Energy

ELLEN MILLER
75 Capwell Ave, Pawtucket, RI 02860
Tel.: (401) 724-3773
E-Mail: esmiller@cox.net

Agency Specializes In: Advertising

Ellen Miller *(Owner)*

Accounts:
Bluebonnet Nutrition
Guylian Chocolates

ELLEV LLC
807 Main St, Myrtle Beach, SC 29577
Tel.: (843) 902-7107
E-Mail: info@ellev.com
Web Site: www.ellev.com

Agency Specializes In: Advertising, Brand Development & Integration, Event Planning & Marketing, Graphic Design, Internet/Web Design, Print, Public Relations, Social Media

Clifton Parker *(Dir-Creative & Photography Art)*

Accounts:
Surfrider Grand Strand

ELLINGSEN BRADY ADVERTISING (EBA)
207 E Buffalo St Ste 400, Milwaukee, WI 53202
Tel.: (414) 224-9424
Fax: (414) 224-9432
E-Mail: info@ebadvertising.com
Web Site: www.ellingsenbrady.com

Employees: 8
Year Founded: 1994

Agency Specializes In: Collateral, Corporate Identity, Direct Response Marketing, Exhibit/Trade Shows, Internet/Web Design, Media Buying Services, Outdoor, Print, Public Relations, Radio, T.V.

Don Ellingsen *(Owner)*
Tim Brady *(VP & Dir-Creative)*
Rachel Farina *(Acct Exec)*

Accounts:
Gauthier Biomedical

ELLIPSIS SOLUTIONS
30812 Periwinkle Dr, Union City, CA 94587
Tel.: (855) 355-4774
Web Site: www.ellipsissolutions.com

Year Founded: 2010

Agency Specializes In: Direct Response Marketing, Email, Local Marketing, Newspaper, Newspapers & Magazines, Paid Searches, Print, Production (Print), Search Engine Optimization, Social Media, Web (Banner Ads, Pop-ups, etc.), Yellow Pages Advertising

Gautam Tandon *(CEO)*

Accounts:
Bay Jewelers Jewelery; 2014

ELLIS-HARPER ADVERTISING
710 Old Stage Rd, Auburn, AL 36831
Tel.: (334) 887-6536
Fax: (334) 887-6539
E-Mail: ddh@ellisharper.com
Web Site: www.ellisharper.com

E-Mail for Key Personnel:
President: ddh@ellisharper.com
Media Dir.: enewton@ellisharper.com
Production Mgr.: lkrehling@ellisharper.com

Employees: 7
Year Founded: 1981

Agency Specializes In: Advertising, Advertising Specialties, Consulting, Consumer Marketing, Direct Response Marketing, Graphic Design, Internet/Web Design, Logo & Package Design, Media Buying Services, Planning & Consultation, Production, Public Relations, Sales Promotion

Approx. Annual Billings: $150,000

Dee Dee Harper *(Owner & Pres)*
Joyce G. Boggs *(Dir-Admin Svcs)*
Jim Buford *(Dir-Mgmt Div)*
Mike Davenport *(Dir-Bus Dev)*
David McCormick *(Dir-Creative)*
Evelyn M. Newton *(Dir-Ops & Media)*
Leigh Krehling *(Mgr)*
Kristie Martins *(Specialist-Social Media)*

Accounts:
Bonnie Plant Farm
Charter Bank
Opelika Parks
The United Way

ELLISON MEDIA COMPANY
14804 N Cave Creek Rd, Phoenix, AZ 85032-4945
Tel.: (602) 404-4000
Fax: (602) 404-1700
E-Mail: info@ellisonmedia.com
Web Site: www.ellisonmedia.com

E-Mail for Key Personnel:
Media Dir.: barbara.griesman@ellisonmedia.com

Employees: 40
Year Founded: 1972

Agency Specializes In: Direct Response Marketing, E-Commerce, Faith Based, Media Buying Services, Print, Telemarketing

Approx. Annual Billings: $22,000,000

Michael R. Ellison *(Founder & CEO)*
Don Kurtenbach *(CFO & Treas)*
Jay Griffin *(Sr VP-Client Svcs)*
Barbara Griesman *(VP-Media)*
Judd Jackson *(VP-Bus Dev)*

ELSEWHERE ADVERTISING
525 Brannan St Ste 206, San Francisco, CA 94107
Tel.: (415) 722-3068
Web Site: www.elsewhereadvertising.com

Agency Specializes In: Advertising

Cathy Leiden *(Pres)*

Accounts:
American Midstream Partners, LP
Cisco Systems, Inc.
Oracle America, Inc.
Raffa Wealth Management

EM MEDIA INC
2728 Sunset Blvd, Steubenville, OH 43952
Tel.: (740) 264-2186
E-Mail: info@em-media.com
Web Site: www.em-media.com

Agency Specializes In: Advertising, Brand Development & Integration, Corporate Identity, Digital/Interactive, Event Planning & Marketing, Media Buying Services, Media Planning, Media Relations, Public Relations, Social Media

Jim Emmerling *(Owner & Pres)*
Wayne Hardy *(VP)*
Larae Messer *(Dir-Creative)*
Rose Orsatti *(Mgr-Ops)*
Renee Cardelli-Contumelio *(Strategist-Digital Content & PR)*

Accounts:
Guess Motors Inc.

EMAGINATION UNLIMITED INC.
1225 W Gregory St, Pensacola, FL 32502
Tel.: (850) 473-8808
Web Site: www.getemagination.com

Year Founded: 2002

Agency Specializes In: Advertising, Logo & Package Design, Media Buying Services, Outdoor, Public Relations

Chip Henderson *(Pres & CEO)*

Accounts:
Covenant Hospice
Pensacola Young Professionals
Zarzaur Law

Advertising Agencies

EMAILDIRECT.COM
3101 Zinfandel Dr, Rancho Cordova, CA 95670
Tel.: (916) 378-0323
E-Mail: support@emaildirect.com
Web Site: www.emaildirect.com

Year Founded: 2005

Agency Specializes In: Advertising, Digital/Interactive, Email, Integrated Marketing, Social Media

Chris Bryan *(Co-Founder & COO)*
Kevin Linden *(CEO)*
Richard King *(Partner & CTO)*
Kristine Dobson *(VP-Ops)*
Rhonda Merrill *(Mgr-Support)*
Jeanine Derner *(Specialist-Mktg)*
Chelsey Rioux *(Specialist-Email Mktg)*

Accounts:
Books Publisher priceline.com Incorporated
Natural Food Retailers Savannah College of Art & Design
Online Ticket Booking Service Providers New Condos Online Inc
Radio Network Service Providers SUBWAY
Real Estate Agency Services Airfare.com
Restaurant Services SheKnows LLC
Wedding Supplies & Service Providers Earth Fare Inc.

EMBRYO CREATIVE
1085 Commonwealth Ave Ste 371, Boston, MA 02215
Tel.: (617) 543-7444
Web Site: www.embryocreativegroup.com

Year Founded: 2007

Agency Specializes In: Advertising, Brand Development & Integration, Broadcast, Internet/Web Design, Logo & Package Design, Print

Shannon Luttge *(Partner)*
Ryan Ferland *(Principal & Dir-Art)*
Allan Shinohara *(Principal)*
Jaynemarie Hunt *(Sr Acct Mgr)*

Accounts:
Boston University On The move
Commonwealth Financial Monsters
HitTrax
ICE Center
Jewish Family & Children's Service Caring for Generations
Wbur On Point

EMERGE INTERACTIVE
930 NW 14th Ave Ste 280, Portland, OR 97209
Tel.: (503) 922-3483
Fax: (503) 296-5784
E-Mail: info@emergeinteractive.com
Web Site: www.emergeinteractive.com

Employees: 20
Year Founded: 1998

Agency Specializes In: Advertising, Brand Development & Integration, Content, Digital/Interactive, Internet/Web Design, Social Media

Jonathan Hensley *(CEO & Chief Creative Officer)*
Parker Gindele *(Dir-Art & Sr Designer)*
Scott Rich *(Dir-Client Strategy)*
Adam Evans *(Designer-Interaction)*
Linnea Johnson *(Coord-Mktg)*

Accounts:
Stanford Woods Institute for the Environment; 2011

EMERGE PR
300 Congress St Ste 204, Quincy, MA 02169
Tel.: (617) 934-2483
Fax: (617) 689-0454
E-Mail: info@emergepr.com
Web Site: www.emergepr.com

Employees: 10

Agency Specializes In: Exhibit/Trade Shows, Public Relations, Publicity/Promotions, Strategic Planning/Research

Revenue: $2,000,000

Mara Stefan *(Pres)*
Eileen Cahill O'Donoghue *(Controller)*

Accounts:
Caps
Destination Cellars
DYMO
Experian QAS
Mimio
Quaero
Red Bend Software, Inc.; Framingham, MA

EMERGING MARKETING
29 W 3rd Ave, Columbus, OH 43201
Tel.: (614) 923-6000
Fax: (614) 424-6200
Web Site: www.emergingmarketing.com

E-Mail for Key Personnel:
President: cmcgovern@emergingmarketing.com

Employees: 11
Year Founded: 1994

Agency Specializes In: Above-the-Line, Advertising, Affluent Market, African-American Market, Agriculture, Alternative Advertising, Aviation & Aerospace, Below-the-Line, Brand Development & Integration, Business Publications, Business-To-Business, Collateral, College, Communications, Computers & Software, Consulting, Corporate Communications, Corporate Identity, Customer Relationship Management, Digital/Interactive, Direct Response Marketing, E-Commerce, Education, Electronic Media, Electronics, Email, Engineering, Environmental, Exhibit/Trade Shows, Experience Design, Financial, Game Integration, Government/Political, Graphic Design, Health Care Services, High Technology, Hispanic Market, Identity Marketing, Industrial, Information Technology, Integrated Marketing, International, Internet/Web Design, Legal Services, Local Marketing, Logo & Package Design, Magazines, Marine, Medical Products, Mobile Marketing, Multicultural, Multimedia, New Product Development, New Technologies, Newspaper, Newspapers & Magazines, Outdoor, Over-50 Market, Pharmaceutical, Planning & Consultation, Podcasting, Point of Purchase, Point of Sale, Print, Production, Production (Print), Promotions, Public Relations, Publicity/Promotions, Radio, Regional, Search Engine Optimization, Social Marketing/Nonprofit, Social Media, Sponsorship, Stakeholders, Strategic Planning/Research, Technical Advertising, Trade & Consumer Magazines, Transportation, Travel & Tourism, Urban Market, Viral/Buzz/Word of Mouth, Web (Banner Ads, Pop-ups, etc.), Yellow Pages Advertising

Approx. Annual Billings: $1,400,000

Chris McGovern *(Pres)*

Accounts:
Emerson Network Power
IBM
Lincoln Financial Group
Scotts

EMERY ADVERTISING
4213 Bay Laurel Ct, Wake Forest, NC 27587
Tel.: (919) 790-2600
Fax: (919) 790-2601
E-Mail: contact@emeryad.com
Web Site: www.emeryad.com/

E-Mail for Key Personnel:
President: ray@emeryad.com

Employees: 6
Year Founded: 1987

Agency Specializes In: Advertising, Advertising Specialties, Brand Development & Integration, Branded Entertainment, Broadcast, Business Publications, Business-To-Business, Catalogs, Children's Market, Collateral, Commercial Photography, Communications, Computers & Software, Consulting, Consumer Goods, Consumer Marketing, Consumer Publications, Corporate Communications, Corporate Identity, Digital/Interactive, Direct Response Marketing, Education, Electronic Media, Email, Engineering, Entertainment, Exhibit/Trade Shows, Financial, Food Service, Graphic Design, Guerilla Marketing, Health Care Services, High Technology, Hospitality, Identity Marketing, In-Store Advertising, Industrial, Information Technology, Integrated Marketing, International, Internet/Web Design, Legal Services, Local Marketing, Logo & Package Design, Luxury Products, Magazines, Market Research, Media Buying Services, Medical Products, Merchandising, Mobile Marketing, Multimedia, New Product Development, New Technologies, Newspaper, Newspapers & Magazines, Outdoor, Over-50 Market, Package Design, Point of Purchase, Point of Sale, Print, Product Placement, Production, Production (Print), Promotions, Public Relations, Publicity/Promotions, Radio, Real Estate, Restaurant, Retail, Sales Promotion, Seniors' Market, Social Marketing/Nonprofit, Sponsorship, Sports Market, Strategic Planning/Research, Sweepstakes, T.V., Technical Advertising, Teen Market, Telemarketing, Trade & Consumer Magazines, Transportation, Travel & Tourism, Urban Market, Women's Market

Approx. Annual Billings: $2,300,000

Ray E. Emery *(Pres & CEO)*
Pat Emery *(Dir-Creative)*

Accounts:
Diamond Financial; Raleigh, NC Business Franchise Financing; 2006
Eagle Home Medical; Roanoke Rapids, NC Home Medical Supplies; 2004
Gregory Poole; Raleigh, NC Construction Equipment; 2007
Ixia; 2007
Sweet Magnolia Catering; Raleigh, NC Catering Services; 2006

EMFLUENCE
106 W 11th St Ste 2220, Kansas City, MO 64105
Tel.: (877) 813-6245
Fax: (816) 472-8855
Web Site: www.emfluence.com

Employees: 20
Year Founded: 2003

Agency Specializes In: Brand Development & Integration, Email, Internet/Web Design, Search Engine Optimization, Web (Banner Ads, Pop-ups, etc.)

Todd Sandoval *(VP-Digital Strategy)*
Marlana Allaman *(Controller)*
Tyler Barnes *(Dir-Search)*
Michael Tipton *(Dir-Bus Dev)*
Chad Anderson *(Sr Acct Mgr)*
Krissy Head *(Acct Mgr-Mktg)*
Chris Zeller *(Sr Engr-Software)*

Accounts:
Bikers for Babies
Hallmark Greeting Cards Mfr
HEMP
Indigo World
Payless Footwear Producers
ZuPreem

EMG - ETHNIC MARKETING GROUP, INC.
(Name Changed to Shopper Marketing Group Advertising Inc.)

EMLEY DESIGN GROUP
8010 Illinois Rd, Fort Wayne, IN 46804
Tel.: (260) 436-9039
E-Mail: admin@edg-dmc.com
Web Site: www.edg-dmc.com

Year Founded: 1989

Agency Specializes In: Automotive, Aviation & Aerospace, Bilingual Market, Brand Development & Integration, Business-To-Business, Collateral, Communications, Consumer Marketing, Corporate Communications, Corporate Identity, Cosmetics, Direct Response Marketing, E-Commerce, Education, Engineering, Entertainment, Event Planning & Marketing, Exhibit/Trade Shows, Fashion/Apparel, Financial, Food Service, Government/Political, Graphic Design, Health Care Services, High Technology, Internet/Web Design, Investor Relations, Legal Services, Leisure, Logo & Package Design, Magazines, Marine, Newspapers & Magazines, Over-50 Market, Pharmaceutical, Planning & Consultation, Point of Purchase, Point of Sale, Print, Production, Public Relations, Real Estate, Restaurant, Retail, Seniors' Market, Sports Market, Strategic Planning/Research, Teen Market, Trade & Consumer Magazines, Transportation, Travel & Tourism

Dennis Emley *(Owner & Dir-Mktg)*
Donna Emley *(Principal & Dir-Creative)*

Accounts:
American Tissue Services Foundation
Eye Pro, Inc.
Lincoln Museum Lincoln Lore Magazine

EMPIRE MEDIA GROUP
1412 13th St, Monroe, WI 53566
Tel.: (608) 325-2384
E-Mail: info@empiremediagroupusa.com
Web Site: www.empiremediagroupusa.com

Year Founded: 2011

Agency Specializes In: Advertising, Brand Development & Integration, Logo & Package Design, Print, Radio, T.V.

Adam Bansley *(Owner & Dir-Creative)*

Accounts:
Pleasant View

EMRL
1020 10th St, Sacramento, CA 95814
Tel.: (916) 446-2440
E-Mail: office@emrl.com
Web Site: www.emrl.com

Agency Specializes In: Advertising, Brand Development & Integration

Floyd Diebel *(Creative Dir)*

Accounts:
New-Temple Coffee & Tea

ENA HEALTHCARE COMMUNICATIONS
740 River Rd Ste 209, Fair Haven, NJ 07704
Tel.: (732) 576-1519
Fax: (732) 530-2803
E-Mail: info@ena-inc.com
Web Site: www.ena-inc.com

Employees: 6
Year Founded: 1985

Agency Specializes In: Advertising, Brand Development & Integration, Health Care Services, Medical Products, Pharmaceutical, Trade & Consumer Magazines

Breakdown of Gross Billings by Media: Bus. Publs.: 15%; Collateral: 10%; D.M.: 25%; Exhibits/Trade Shows: 10%; Sls. Promo.: 25%; Worldwide Web Sites: 15%

Robert Newland *(Mng Partner)*
Claire Reilly-Taylor *(VP & Dir-Creative)*
Blake McCrossin *(Mgr-Bus Dev)*
Alicia Holmgren *(Acct Grp Supvr)*

Accounts:
CSL Behring; King of Prussia, PA; 1997
Pfizer, Inc.; New York, NY; 1992

ENCITE INTERNATIONAL
9995 E Harvard Ave, Denver, CO 80231
Tel.: (303) 332-3908
Web Site: www.enciteinternational.com

Agency Specializes In: Advertising, Digital/Interactive, Event Planning & Marketing, Internet/Web Design, Media Buying Services, Media Planning, Print, Radio, Social Media, Strategic Planning/Research

Adam Oleary *(Pres)*
Jeff Peterson *(Dir-Creative)*
Jennifer Croft *(Search Engine Optimization)*

Accounts:
Tara Properties

ENCODE
P.O. Box 600534, Jacksonville, FL 32260
Tel.: (316) 708-6264
E-Mail: jelena@encodepr.com
Web Site: www.encodepr.com

Employees: 3
Year Founded: 2013

Agency Specializes In: Advertising, Affluent Market, Agriculture, Alternative Advertising, Arts, Automotive, Aviation & Aerospace, Bilingual Market, Brand Development & Integration, Business Publications, Business-To-Business, Children's Market, Collateral, Commercial Photography, Communications, Computers & Software, Consulting, Consumer Goods, Consumer Marketing, Content, Corporate Communications, Cosmetics, Customer Relationship Management, Digital/Interactive, Direct-to-Consumer, Education, Electronic Media, Email, Engineering, Entertainment, Event Planning & Marketing, Exhibit/Trade Shows, Experience Design, Fashion/Apparel, Financial, Food Service, Government/Political, Graphic Design, Guerilla Marketing, Health Care Services, High Technology, Hospitality, Household Goods, Identity Marketing, Industrial, Information Technology, Integrated Marketing, International, Internet/Web Design, Legal Services, Leisure, Local Marketing, Logo & Package Design, Luxury Products, Magazines, Marine, Market Research, Media Relations, Medical Products, Men's Market, Merchandising, Multicultural, Multimedia, New Technologies, Newspaper, Newspapers & Magazines, Pharmaceutical, Planning & Consultation, Podcasting, Print, Promotions, Publicity/Promotions, Publishing, Real Estate, Recruitment, Restaurant, Retail, Search Engine Optimization, Social Marketing/Nonprofit, Social Media, Sports Market, Stakeholders, Strategic Planning/Research, Trade & Consumer Magazines, Transportation, Travel & Tourism, Viral/Buzz/Word of Mouth, Web (Banner Ads, Pop-ups, etc.), Women's Market

Jelena Brezjanovic *(Owner)*
Uros Brezjanovic *(Project Mgr-IT)*

Accounts:
Best Western Grand Venice Hotel; 2002
Dr. Valerie Drake-Albert Medical Practice, OB-GYN; 2013
ODA Global International Business Consulting; 2011
Singletree Stables Equestrian Sports Facility; 2012
Society of Women Engineers - Central Indiana Non-Profit Trade Association
Vision Consulting Financial Planning/Accounting/CPA; 2012

ENDEAVOUR MARKETING & MEDIA, LLC
151 Heritage Park Dr Ste 102, Murfreesboro, TN 37129
Tel.: (615) 907-5332
Fax: (615) 907-5334
E-Mail: info@endeavour2m.com
Web Site: www.endeavour2m.com

Employees: 10
Year Founded: 2007

Agency Specializes In: Advertising, Broadcast, Business-To-Business, Cable T.V., Collateral, Consumer Marketing, Corporate Identity, Customer Relationship Management, Digital/Interactive, Direct Response Marketing, Direct-to-Consumer, E-Commerce, Electronic Media, Email, Graphic Design, In-Store Advertising, Integrated Marketing, Internet/Web Design, Local Marketing, Media Buying Services, Media Planning, Mobile Marketing, Multimedia, New Technologies, Newspaper, Newspapers & Magazines, Out-of-Home Media, Outdoor, Paid Searches, Planning & Consultation, Podcasting, Print, Production (Print), RSS (Really Simple Syndication), Restaurant, Search Engine Optimization, Social Marketing/Nonprofit, Strategic Planning/Research, Viral/Buzz/Word of Mouth

Harold E. Henn, Jr. *(Partner & CMO)*
Herman Nelson *(COO)*
Jason M. Ehleben *(Dir-Creative)*

Accounts:
Hancock Diabetes

ENDRIZZI ADVERTISING AGENCY LLC
610 McCarthy Dr, King George, VA 22485
Tel.: (540) 775-2458
Web Site: www.endrizziadvertising.com

Agency Specializes In: Advertising, Brand Development & Integration, Exhibit/Trade Shows, Internet/Web Design, Logo & Package Design, Print, Radio, Search Engine Optimization, T.V.

Melissa Endrizzi *(Founder & CEO)*

Accounts:
Affordable Sheds Company
Rejuvalase

ENGEL O'NEILL ADVERTISING & PUBLIC RELATIONS
2124 Sassafras St, Erie, PA 16502
Tel.: (814) 454-3111
Fax: (814) 456-7879
E-Mail: info@engeloneill.com
Web Site: www.engeloneill.com

Employees: 10

Greg Engel *(Partner)*
Nancy O'Neill *(Partner)*
Ahmet Hulusi Hamamcioglu *(Dir-Art)*
Sue Lucas *(Dir-Media)*
Julie Monaghan *(Office Mgr)*
Tim Rogala *(Mgr-Support Svcs)*
Dana Pontillo *(Acct Exec & Writer)*

Accounts:
Bayfront
Erie Business Center
Erie Times News
Medical Associates
Mercyhurst College
MFC Group
National Fuel
Titusville Area Hospital
Valley Tire Co.,Inc.

ENGELBRECHT ADVERTISING, LLC.
(Private-Parent-Single Location)
1000 Esplanade, Chico, CA 95926
Tel.: (530) 891-1988
Fax: (530) 891-1987
E-Mail: info@engelads.com
Web Site: www.engelads.com

Employees: 15
Year Founded: 1994

Agency Specializes In: Advertising, Digital/Interactive, Email, Media Buying Services, Print, Radio, Search Engine Optimization

Revenue: $1,200,000

Greg Engelbrecht *(Pres)*
Michele Dwyer *(Controller)*
Keri Brennan *(Acct Exec)*

Accounts:
Alternative Energy Systems Inc
Chico Back & Neck Pain Center

THE ENGINE ROOM
109 Night Heron Ln, Aliso Viejo, CA 92656
Tel.: (949) 683-3227
Fax: (949) 586-4647
E-Mail: mailroom@the-engine-room.net
Web Site: www.the-engine-room.net

Employees: 2

Agency Specializes In: Advertising, Brand Development & Integration, Catalogs, Consumer Publications, Direct Response Marketing, Direct-to-Consumer, Internet/Web Design, Logo & Package Design, Outdoor, Radio, Sales Promotion

Steve Lauri *(Pres & Dir-Creative)*
Scott Henderson *(Designer & Specialist-Tread)*
Mike Mahoney *(Copywriter)*

ENGLE CREATIVE SOLUTIONS LLC
4807 Walnut Rdg Ct, Columbia, MO 65203
Tel.: (573) 823-4723
Web Site: www.engle-creative.com

Agency Specializes In: Advertising, Digital/Interactive, Event Planning & Marketing, Market Research, Media Buying Services, Media Planning, Promotions, Public Relations, Strategic Planning/Research

Steve Engle *(Pres & Chief Creative Officer)*

Accounts:
Ace Pump
Fine Americas, Inc.
Gowan Company LLC
Kalo, Inc.
Origo (Advertising, PR & Marketing Services Agency of Record)
Z Tags North America L.P
Zetor North America, Inc.

ENLARGE MEDIA GROUP
307 3rd St Ste 101, Huntington Beach, CA 92648
Tel.: (714) 374-5200
Fax: (714) 374-5211
Web Site: www.enlargemedia.com

Rob Kee *(Owner)*
Jay Brown *(Partner & Dir-Creative Team)*
Bert Gragg *(Mgr-Social Media Mktg)*

Accounts:
HB Surround Sound

ENLIGHTEN
3027 Miller Rd, Ann Arbor, MI 48103
Tel.: (734) 668-6678
Fax: (734) 668-1883
E-Mail: info@enlighten.com
Web Site: www.enlighten.com

Employees: 75
Year Founded: 1983

Agency Specializes In: Brand Development & Integration, Consulting, Digital/Interactive, Graphic Design, Internet/Web Design, Sponsorship

Tom Beck *(Pres)*
Adam Wilson *(Partner & Chief Creative Officer)*
Dwayne Raupp *(Chief Creative Officer)*
Rod Smith *(CTO)*
Sathish Kolluri *(VP-Tech & Ops)*
Brad Brief *(Dir-Social Mktg)*
Tessa Wegert *(Dir-Comm)*

Accounts:
Ally Financial Inc.
Amgen
Audi of America; Auburn Hills, MI
Biore
Comerica
Curel
Fine Living
Fruit2O
HBO
Hunter Douglas (Agency of Record)
Jergens
Jimmy John's
John Frieda Collection
Johnson & Johnson
MGA Entertainment
Nickelodeon
Pittsburg Paints
Richmond American Homes
Sony

ENRE@CH INC.
640 N LaSalle St Ste 555, Chicago, IL 60654
Tel.: (312) 951-1900
Fax: (312) 951-1904
Web Site: www.enreachinc.com

Agency Specializes In: Advertising, Brand Development & Integration, Business-To-Business, Email, Exhibit/Trade Shows, Media Buying Services, Media Planning, Promotions, Search Engine Optimization, Technical Advertising

Daniel Townsend *(Co-Founder & Partner)*
Mark Stevens *(Creative Dir-Plum Tree Grp)*

Accounts:
The Black Ensemble Theater

ENSEMBLE CREATIVE & MARKETING
20790 Holyoke Ave 2nd Fl PO Box 899, Lakeville, MN 55044
Tel.: (952) 469-9460
E-Mail: info@ensemblecreative.com
Web Site: www.ensemblecreative.com

Agency Specializes In: Advertising, Brand Development & Integration, Graphic Design, Internet/Web Design

Kristina Murto *(Owner & Creative Dir)*
Steve Volavka *(Owner)*

Accounts:
New-Nemesis Defense

ENSO COLLABORATIVE LLC
1526 Cloverfield Blvd, Santa Monica, CA 90404
Tel.: (310) 526-8273
E-Mail: hello@enso.com
Web Site: http://www.storaenso.com/

Year Founded: 2012

Agency Specializes In: Advertising, Communications, Strategic Planning/Research

Carla Fernandez *(Gen Mgr)*
Lyla Morrison *(Sr Dir-Art)*
Catherine Nieves *(Sr Producer-Digital)*
Amy Cheng-Tran *(Dir-Strategic Partnerships)*
Michelle Moye Da Silva *(Dir-Ops)*
Jason Nichols *(Dir-Creative)*
Seema Thakker *(Dir-Strategic Partnerships)*
Katey Scanlon *(Mgr-Strategic Partnerships)*
Aaron Small *(Sr Writer)*

Accounts:
Google Inc.

ENTERTAINMENT EVENTS AZ LLC
(Formerly Erodz Agency)
1661 E Camelback Rd Ste 380, Phoenix, AZ 85016
Tel.: (602) 753-4770
Web Site: www.eeaz.net

Agency Specializes In: Advertising, Collateral, Graphic Design, Media Training, Print, Public Relations, Search Engine Optimization, Social Media

Ernesto Rodriguez *(CEO)*
Martin Flores *(Mng Partner)*

Accounts:
iVeyo

ENTICE ADVERTISING & DESIGN LLC
6707 Fletcher Creek Cove, Memphis, TN 38133
Tel.: (901) 384-4504
Fax: (901) 384-4504
Web Site: www.enticecreative.com

Agency Specializes In: Advertising, Internet/Web Design, Print, Radio, T.V.

Glynnis Anderson-Smith *(Mng Partner & Designer)*
Maja Price *(Partner)*

Accounts:
Holy Rosary School
Memphis City Schools Volunteer Services
New Direction Christian Church

ENTREPRENEUR ADVERTISING GROUP

2120 Washington Street, Kansas City, MO 64108
Tel.: (816) 842-0100
Fax: (816) 283-0411
E-Mail: info@eagadv.com
Web Site: www.smallbusinessmiracles.com

Year Founded: 2003

Agency Specializes In: Advertising, Brand Development & Integration, Direct Response Marketing, Mobile Marketing, Out-of-Home Media, Web (Banner Ads, Pop-ups, etc.)

Michele Markham *(Pres)*
Paul Weber *(CEO & Chief Strategy Officer)*
Cinda Fisher *(Acct Dir)*
Dawn Kidwell *(Acct Dir)*
Brenda Galloway *(Dir-Content)*
Julianne Gross *(Dir-Art)*
Jason Keeler *(Dir-Digital Mktg)*
Skeet Hanks *(Assoc Dir-Creative)*
Lindsey Weber *(Sr Acct Mgr)*
Kelly Thompson *(Project Mgr-Digital)*

Accounts:
Adams Dairy Bank Banking Services
Boyer & Corporon Wealth Management Financial & Consulting Services
Brookside Personal Shopping
Invision Technology Solutions & Services
Livers Bronze Co. Lighting Services
Sharma-Crawford Attorneys at Law Immigration Litigation Services

ENVIROMEDIA SOCIAL MARKETING

2021 E 5th St, Austin, TX 78702
Tel.: (512) 476-4368
Fax: (512) 476-4392
E-Mail: info@enviromedia.com
Web Site: www.enviromedia.com

Employees: 50
Year Founded: 1997

Agency Specializes In: Advertising, Environmental, Local Marketing, Media Buying Services, Media Planning, Public Relations, Strategic Planning/Research

Valerie Davis *(Co-Founder)*
Ted Burton *(Exec VP)*
Tamala Barksdale *(VP)*
Sara Beechner *(VP-Creative)*
Sharon Henry *(Producer-Digital)*
Susan Rosenzweig *(Creative Dir)*
Millie Salinas *(Dir-Hispanic Mktg)*
Sean Price *(Mgr-Comm & Quality Assurance)*

Accounts:
Car2Go Campaign: "#car2golife"
Department of State Health Services Campaign: "Share Air"
Green Mountain Energy
Litter force
OSU
TEA

ENVISION CREATIVE

(Name Changed to Envision Dennis Romano, LLC)

ENVISION DENNIS ROMANO, LLC

(Formerly enVision Creative)
20 Stonehenge Dr, Ocean, NJ 07712
Tel.: (732) 922-8800
E-Mail: dromano@envisiondr.com
Web Site: www.envisiondr.com

E-Mail for Key Personnel:
President: dromano@envisiondr.com

Employees: 3
Year Founded: 2002

Agency Specializes In: Advertising, Business-To-Business, Communications, Consulting, Email, Graphic Design, Integrated Marketing, Internet/Web Design, Logo & Package Design, Medical Products, Pharmaceutical, Print, Search Engine Optimization

Dennis Romano *(Pres)*

Accounts:
Altaflo High Performance Fluoropolymer and Fluoroplastic Tubing and Pipe
Dotcom Distribution eCommerce and Multi-Channel Logistics; 2014
Porzio Life Sciences Life Sciences Regulatory Compliance Software Solutions, Products, and Services; 2009

ENVISION RESPONSE INC.

2151 N Northlake Way 1st Fl, Seattle, WA 98103
Tel.: (800) 809-8397
Fax: (206) 299-3562
E-Mail: sean@envisiontv.com
Web Site: www.envisiontv.com

Employees: 10
Year Founded: 2003

Agency Specializes In: Broadcast, Consumer Marketing, Direct Response Marketing, Infomercials, Production (Ad, Film, Broadcast), Social Media, Strategic Planning/Research

Sean K. Fay *(CEO & Dir-Creative)*
Mike Johnson *(Exec VP & Dir-Creative)*

ENVISIONIT MEDIA

130 E Randolph St, Chicago, IL 60601
Tel.: (312) 236-2000
Fax: (312) 277-4500
E-Mail: inquiry@eimchicago.com
Web Site: envisionitagency.com

Employees: 51
Year Founded: 2002

Agency Specializes In: Advertising, Brand Development & Integration, Broadcast, Business-To-Business, Consumer Goods, Digital/Interactive, E-Commerce, Email, Food Service, Graphic Design, Identity Marketing, Integrated Marketing, Internet/Web Design, Leisure, Mobile Marketing, Multimedia, New Technologies, Out-of-Home Media, Podcasting, Print, Production (Print), Retail, Search Engine Optimization, Social Marketing/Nonprofit, Social Media, Trade & Consumer Magazines, Travel & Tourism, Viral/Buzz/Word of Mouth, Web (Banner Ads, Pop-ups, etc.)

Approx. Annual Billings: $15,000,000

Todd Brook *(CEO)*
David Silverstein *(COO & Sr Strategist)*
Jason Goldberg *(Exec VP & Dir-Creative)*
Steve Ziemba *(Head-Social Media)*
Amber Davis *(Assoc Dir-Creative)*
Michael Phillips *(Assoc Dir-Creative)*
Stephanie Bakula *(Acct Mgr)*
Sarah Rucinski *(Sr Exec Asst)*

Accounts:
Alva Amco; Niles, IL OTC
Fairmont Hotel, Millenium Park; Chicago, IL Hotels
Performance Trust; Chicago, IL Financial Services

ENYE MEDIA, LLC

301 1/2 E Main St, Norman, OK 73069
Tel.: (405) 579-3693
Fax: (405) 579-6220
E-Mail: info@enye.com
Web Site: matildeballon.com/enye

Employees: 3
Year Founded: 2006

Agency Specializes In: Advertising, Advertising Specialties, Bilingual Market, Branded Entertainment, Broadcast, Business Publications, Cable T.V., Collateral, Commercial Photography, Communications, Computers & Software, Consulting, Consumer Marketing, Content, Corporate Identity, Direct Response Marketing, E-Commerce, Email, Entertainment, Event Planning & Marketing, Exhibit/Trade Shows, Graphic Design, High Technology, Hispanic Market, In-Store Advertising, Infomercials, Information Technology, Internet/Web Design, Legal Services, Local Marketing, Logo & Package Design, Magazines, Market Research, Media Buying Services, Media Planning, Media Relations, Multicultural, Multimedia, New Product Development, Newspaper, Newspapers & Magazines, Outdoor, Planning & Consultation, Print, Production, Promotions, Public Relations, Publicity/Promotions, RSS (Really Simple Syndication), Radio, Recruitment, Regional, Restaurant, Retail, Sales Promotion, Search Engine Optimization, Social Marketing/Nonprofit, Sponsorship, Strategic Planning/Research, T.V.

Breakdown of Gross Billings by Media: Collateral: 4%; Consulting: 5%; E-Commerce: 5%; Graphic Design: 5%; Logo & Package Design: 2%; Mags.: 2%; Newsp.: 20%; Production: 13%; Pub. Rels.: 5%; Radio: 9%; T.V.: 30%

Robert M. Ruiz *(Partner)*
Wilmari Ruiz *(Partner)*
Ricardo Sasaki *(Partner)*
Lance Rivas *(Dir-Photography)*

Accounts:
Buy for Less
El Nacional; Oklahoma City, OK Newspaper, Paginas Amarillas, Super Auto Mercado, Vibraciones; 2006
State Hispanic Chamber of Oklahoma; Oklahoma City, OK; 2006
Viva OKC Latin Music Festival; Oklahoma City, OK; 2007

EO INTEGRATION

419 Park Ave S 2nd Fl, New York, NY 10016
Tel.: (646) 346-9213
E-Mail: mail@eointegration.com
Web Site: www.eointegration.com

Year Founded: 2009

Agency Specializes In: Advertising

Roberto Alcazar *(Founder & Partner)*

EPHRICON WEB MARKETING

(Acquired by Straight North, LLC.)

EPIC CREATIVE

3014 E Progress Dr, West Bend, WI 53095
Tel.: (262) 338-3700
Web Site: www.epiccreative.com

Agency Specializes In: Advertising, Brand Development & Integration, Print, Public Relations, Social Media

Julie Purcell *(Founder & Pres)*
Jim Becker *(CEO)*
Keith Pawlak *(Dir, Mgr-Production & Producer)*
Dan Augustine *(Dir-Creative)*
Fuzz Martin *(Dir-PR & Social Media)*
Timmothy Merath *(Dir-Creative Svcs)*
Will Skaggs *(Dir-Art)*
Geri Weiland *(Dir-Integrated Mktg)*
Sara Johansen *(Sr Acct Mgr)*
Nicole Wagner *(Acct Mgr)*

Accounts:
Floratine Products Group
The Garlock Family of Companies
Precision Laboratories, Inc.

EPIC MARKETING
12356 S 900 E Ste 105, Draper, UT 84020
Tel.: (801) 657-4383
E-Mail: info@marketingepic.com
Web Site: www.marketingepic.com

Agency Specializes In: Advertising, Brand Development & Integration, Graphic Design, Internet/Web Design, Print, Public Relations, Radio, Search Engine Optimization, Social Media, T.V.

Nick White *(Pres)*
Dave Ostler *(VP-Bus Dev)*
Jeff Martin *(Dir-Creative)*
Josh Yamamoto *(Dir-Art)*
Tandy Lee *(Office Mgr)*
David Ludwig *(Mgr-Production)*
Jared Cannon *(Sr Acct Exec)*

Accounts:
Recovery Ways

EPIC MULTIMEDIA
(Name Changed to Epicosity)

EPICOSITY
(Formerly Epic Multimedia)
1741 S Cleveland Ave Ste 302, Sioux Falls, SD 57103-3295
Tel.: (605) 274-0842
Fax: (605) 274-0842
Web Site: www.epicosity.com

Employees: 10
Year Founded: 2006

Agency Specializes In: Advertising, Advertising Specialties, Agriculture, Alternative Advertising, Brand Development & Integration, Branded Entertainment, Broadcast, Business-To-Business, Cable T.V., Catalogs, Collateral, Commercial Photography, Communications, Consulting, Consumer Marketing, Corporate Communications, Corporate Identity, Customer Relationship Management, Direct-to-Consumer, Education, Email, Entertainment, Environmental, Event Planning & Marketing, Exhibit/Trade Shows, Faith Based, Financial, Government/Political, Graphic Design, Health Care Services, High Technology, Identity Marketing, Industrial, Infomercials, Information Technology, Logo & Package Design, Market Research, Media Buying Services, Media Planning, Media Relations, Media Training, Multimedia, New Product Development, New Technologies, Outdoor, Over-50 Market, Package Design, Print, Production (Ad, Film, Broadcast), Production (Print), Public Relations, Publicity/Promotions, Radio, Recruitment, Sales Promotion, Search Engine Optimization, Seniors' Market, Social Marketing/Nonprofit, Social Media, Strategic Planning/Research, T.V., Travel & Tourism, Web (Banner Ads, Pop-ups, etc.)

Justin Smorawske *(Partner & CMO)*
Scott Ostman *(Creative Dir)*
Jeremy Peters *(Art Dir)*
Cheryl Elbers *(Dir-Client Rels)*
Kristi Korver *(Designer)*

Accounts:
CFM; Sioux Falls, SD Graphic Design, Web, Video, Email, Media Placement, Strategy
CorBon; Sturgis, SD Graphic Design, Web, Video, Email, Media Placement, Strategy
Eagle Imports Brand Structuring, Creative, Digital Advertising, Marketing, Marketing Agency of Record, Print Advertising, Website
FAB Defense (Marketing Agency of Record) Creative Development, Media Placement, Public Relations
Rock Island Armory
SD Department of Health; Pierre, SD Web, Social Media, TV, Radio, Print, Design, Strategy
Shur-Co; Yankton, SD Video, Web, Strategy
Sun Optics USA Digital Advertising, Marketing Agency of Record, Marketing Strategies, Print Media, Public Relations, Social Media, Website Development
University of South Dakota; Vermillion, SD Graphic Design, Video, Media Placement

EPIQ SYSTEMS, INC.
10300 SW Allen Blvd, Beaverton, OR 97005-4833
Tel.: (503) 350-5800
Fax: (503) 350-5890
Toll Free: (800) 557-4407
Web Site: www.epiqsystems.com

Employees: 200
Year Founded: 1987

Agency Specializes In: Advertising, Broadcast, Cable T.V., Internet/Web Design, Legal Services, Newspapers & Magazines, Planning & Consultation, Public Relations, T.V.

Approx. Annual Billings: $4,000,000

Tom W. Olofson *(Chm & CEO)*
Brad D. Scott *(Pres & COO)*
Karin-Joyce Tjon *(CFO & Exec VP)*
Terry Gaylord *(Sr VP-HR)*
Paul Liljegren *(Sr VP-Fin)*
Jennifer E. Mercer *(Sr VP-Strategic Comm)*
Jennifer Meyerowitz *(VP & Dir-Bus Dev)*
Sebastian Ko *(Dir-Document Review Svcs-Hong Kong)*
Sara Brown *(Sr Mgr-Strategic Comm)*
Kelly Bailey *(Mgr-IR)*
Kyle Bingham *(Media Planner)*

Accounts:
First Alert
Louisiana Pacific

EPPS ADVERTISING
184 W Main St, Trappe, PA 19426
Tel.: (610) 489-6211
Fax: (610) 489-6758
Web Site: www.eppsadvertising.com

Agency Specializes In: Advertising, Brand Development & Integration, Graphic Design, Internet/Web Design, Logo & Package Design, Print, Public Relations

Shirley Epps *(Pres)*
Richard Moon *(Designer-Web)*
Leann Shultz *(Acct Coord)*

Accounts:
Avalon Yacht Club
Capano Management
Cherrys Natural Foods
The James A. Michener Art Museum

EPSILON DATA MANAGEMENT, LLC
6021 Connection Dr, Irving, TX 75039
Tel.: (469) 262-0600
Toll Free: (800) 309-0505
E-Mail: info@epsilon.com
Web Site: www.epsilon.com

Employees: 600

Agency Specializes In: Direct Response Marketing, Direct-to-Consumer

Approx. Annual Billings: $300,000,000

Keith Morrow *(CIO & Exec VP-Shared Svcs)*
Jeanette Fitzgerald *(Gen Counsel & Sr VP)*
Lissa Napolillo *(Sr VP & Head-Retail Sector)*
Roberto Siewczynski *(Sr VP & Grp Dir)*
Jane Huston *(Sr VP-HR)*
Judy Loschen *(VP-Digital Analytics)*
Mike Lund *(VP-Conversant)*

Accounts:
Kellogg Co. CRM, Database Marketing
KeyCorp Direct Mail Production, Direct Marketing Strategy, Email Marketing Strategy
Nature's Way (Digital Agency of Record) Creative, Digital Marketing, Email, Mobile, Online Advertising, Shopper Marketing, Social Media, Video Content Strategy, Website

Branches

Aspen Marketing Services
224 N Desplaines, Chicago, IL 60661
(See Separate Listing)

Epsilon International, LLC
4401 Regent Blvd, Irving, TX 75063
Tel.: (972) 582-9600
Fax: (972) 582-9700
Web Site: www.epsilon.com

Employees: 20

Bryan Kennedy *(CEO)*
Jane Huston *(Sr VP-HR)*
Laurie Fry *(VP-HR)*
Brittni Lovelace *(Mgr-Digital & Project)*
Greg Berry *(Sr Recruiter)*
Kristina Mehaffey *(Corp Recruiter)*
Bryan Wimpee *(Sr Recruiter)*

Epsilon International
88 Cumberland St Suite 22 Level 1, The Rocks, Sydney, NSW 2000 Australia
Tel.: (61) 292715400
Fax: (61) 2 9271 5499
E-Mail: apac-info@epsilon.com
Web Site: www.epsilon.com

Employees: 16

Dominic Powers *(Sr VP & Mng Dir-Ops-Intl)*
Michael Kustreba *(Mng Dir-Asia Pacific)*

Accounts:
Ad Age

Epsilon International
Rm 1507 15/F Wantong Ctr Block C 6A

Chaoyangmen Wai Ave, Beijing, 100020 China
Tel.: (86) 1059073001
Fax: (86) 10 5907 3002
E-Mail: apac-info@epsilon.com
Web Site: www.epsilon.com

Dominic Powers *(Sr VP & Mng Dir-Ops-Intl)*
Maggie Liu *(Acct Mgr)*

Epsilon International
Rm 2502 25/F Hopewell Ctr 183 Queen's Rd E, Wanchai, China (Hong Kong)
Tel.: (852) 3589 6300
Fax: (852) 3101 2892
E-Mail: apac-info@epsilon.com
Web Site: www.epsilon.com

Employees: 13

Dominic Powers *(Sr VP & Mng Dir-Ops-Intl)*
Yoann Riou *(Sr Dir-Tech-APAC)*
Raul Simon Cantor Lopez *(Client Svcs Dir-Asia)*
Ginny Wong *(Acct Dir-APAC)*
Asa Choi *(Dir-Technical-Digital)*
Robert Freeman *(Dir-Strategy & Insights-APAC)*
Waseem Khan *(Dir-Ops)*
Winnie Wong *(Sr Mgr-Mktg-APAC)*
Tracy Iun *(Sr Generalist-HR-APAC)*

Epsilon International
Ste 103 Block D Red Town, 570 Huai Hai Rd W, Shanghai, 200052 China
Tel.: (86) 21 6132 3890
Fax: (86) 21 6335 2575
E-Mail: apac-info@epsilon.com
Web Site: www.epsilon.com

Dominic Powers *(Sr VP & Mng Dir-Ops-Intl)*
Vivien Deng *(Client Svcs Dir & Office Head)*
Maggie Liu *(Acct Mgr)*
Julian Wang *(Sls Mgr)*

Epsilon International
Room 2019 20/F Tian Qi Yi HongXiang Building, 611 Tian He Bei Road, Guangzhou, China
Tel.: (86) 20 3847 3736
E-Mail: apac-info@epsilon.com
Web Site: www.epsilon.com

Dominic Powers *(Sr VP & Mng Dir-Ops-Intl)*
Janet Seet Ling Low *(VP-Client Svcs-APAC)*

Accounts:
Americas Gardening Resource
Barnes & Noble
Brookstone
Johnston & Murphy
Masune
Netezza
New York & Company
TIAA-CREF
Walter Drake

Epsilon International
8 Eu Tong Sen St #18-98 Office 1, The Central, Singapore, 059818 Singapore
Tel.: (65) 6603 5088
E-Mail: apac-info@epsilon.com
Web Site: www.epsilon.com

Dominic Powers *(Sr VP & Mng Dir-Ops-Intl)*
Patrick Teh *(Acct Dir)*
Lydia Wong *(Acct Mgr)*
Albert Tay *(Product Mgr)*
Calvin Chong *(Acct Exec-Asia)*

Epsilon
2550 Crescent Dr, Lafayette, CO 80026
Tel.: (303) 410-5100
Fax: (303) 410-5595
Web Site: www.epsilon.com

Employees: 400

Tim Prunk *(Exec VP-Global Mktg Grp)*
Jane Huston *(Sr VP-HR)*
Arlene Lacharite *(Mng Dir-Data Delivery)*
Jean-Yves Sabot *(VP-Retail Bus Dev)*
Laura Wojtalik *(Sr Dir-Epsilon Mktg Tech)*
Andy Haversack *(Dir-New Product Dev)*
David Lytle *(Dir-New Bus Dev)*
Jen Bouvat-Johnson *(Acct Exec)*
Jacob Maloney *(Sr Analyst-Bus Sys-Digital Campaign)*

Accounts:
Brookstone, Inc.

Epsilon
(Formerly Ryan Partnership)
233 N Michigan Ave Ste 810, Chicago, IL 60601
Tel.: (312) 454-1000
Web Site: www.epsilon.com

Employees: 60

Cathy Lang *(Pres-Client Svcs)*
John Vierheller *(Exec VP-Client Svcs)*
Jessica Branson *(Sr VP & Grp Dir)*
Nicole Creel *(VP & Gen Mgr-Client Svcs)*
Monte Wehrkamp *(VP & Exec Creative Dir)*
Jamie Christner *(VP-Acct Analytics)*
Fiore Dinovi *(VP & Counsel-Legal)*
Dan Maher *(VP-Client Svcs)*
Jim Wesley *(VP-Tech)*
Barbara Roering *(Sr Dir-Social Media-Epsilon)*
Peter Mcsherry *(Dir-Strategy & Digital Analytics)*
Kelly Logan *(Acct Supvr)*
Calid Bowen *(Sr Strategist-Social Media)*

Accounts:
Ashley Furniture Media planning & Execution, Print, Radio, Social, Strategy, TV, Web, ZZZ
Bel
Cintas
GSK
Office Depot
SC Johnson
Wrigley Orbit Gum

Epsilon
1100 E Woodfield Rd Ste 500, Schaumburg, IL 60173
Tel.: (847) 330-1313
Fax: (847) 330-9155
Web Site: www.epsilon.com

Employees: 85

Bryan Kennedy *(CEO)*
Greg Dowd *(Pres-Local Mktg)*
Michael Lavoie *(Exec VP-Client Svcs)*
Garrin Kapecki *(Sr VP & Head-Portfolio)*
Daniel DeZutter *(Sr VP-Mktg Technologies)*
Kim Finnerty *(Sr VP-Consumer & Shopper Insights)*
Jane Huston *(Sr VP-HR)*
Mark Wollney *(Sr VP)*
Denise Bernat *(Sr Dir-Mktg Tech)*
Jim Montalbano *(Sr Dir-Technical)*

Accounts:
Barnes & Noble
Best Buy
Brookstone
Fabulous-Furs
Johnston & Murphy
KeyBank
New York & Company

Epsilon
601 Edgewater Dr, Wakefield, MA 01880-6235
Tel.: (781) 685-6000
Fax: (781) 685-0830
Web Site: www.epsilon.com

Employees: 500

Bryan Kennedy *(CEO)*
Paul Kramer *(Mng Dir)*
Paul Dundon *(CFO)*
Kevin Elwood *(Pres-Client Svcs)*
Jeanette Fitzgerald *(Gen Counsel & Exec VP)*
Bob Zurek *(Sr VP-Products)*
Wayne Townsend *(Mng Dir-Digital Channel Delivery)*
George Carino *(VP-Sls)*
David Lucey *(Sr Dir-Recruiting)*
Lauren Kent *(Corp Recruiter)*
Stephanie Perkins *(Sr Recruiter-Campus)*

Accounts:
Barnes & Noble
Best Buy
Brookstone
Fender
Firststreet
Johnston & Murphy
KeyBank

Epsilon
1 American Eagle Plz, Earth City, MO 63045
Tel.: (314) 344-3380
Fax: (314) 344-9966
Web Site: www.epsilon.com

Employees: 500

Tom Edwards *(Chief Digital Officer)*
Kerry Morris *(Sr VP & Gen Mgr-Digital Media Solutions Practice)*
John Bartold *(Sr VP-L & CX)*
Jane Huston *(Sr VP-HR)*
Richard McDonald *(Sr VP-Strategy & Bus Dev-CPG & Retail)*
Ed Connor *(VP-Tech)*
Paul Mouer *(Sr Dir-Creative)*
Mirza Baig *(Dir-Digital Solutions Consulting)*

Accounts:
Barnes & Noble
Brookstone
Johnston & Murphy
KeyBank
Masune

Epsilon
16 W 20th St, New York, NY 10011
Tel.: (212) 457-7000
Fax: (212) 457-7040
Web Site: www.epsilon.com

Employees: 15

Agency Specializes In: Sponsorship

Andrew Frawley *(Pres)*
Roberto Siewczynski *(Sr VP & Grp Dir)*
Bruce Grant *(Sr VP-Strategy)*
Mark Hertenstein *(Sr VP-Sls-Epsilon Targeting)*
Quinn Jalli *(Sr VP-Digital Mktg Svcs)*
Robert Powers *(Sr VP-Strategic Growth & Dev)*
Eric Presbrey *(Sr VP)*
John Rohloff *(VP & Gen Mgr-Client Svcs)*
Garrick Gelinas *(VP-Client Svcs)*
Anne Rambow *(Sr Acct Dir-Client Svcs)*
Beth Billingsley *(Sls Dir-Online Solutions)*
Mirza Baig *(Dir-Digital Solutions Consulting)*
Michael Boggs *(Dir-Strategic Consulting & Digital Analysis)*
Sam Gaidemak *(Dir-Sls)*
Steve Smith *(Dir-Tech)*

Stacey Reney *(Sr Mgr-Relationship)*

Epsilon
445 Lake Forest Dr Ste 200, Cincinnati, OH 45242
Tel.: (513) 248-2882
Fax: (513) 248-2672
Web Site: www.epsilon.com

Employees: 100

Bryan Kennedy *(Pres & CEO)*
Mark Smith *(Sr VP & Exec Dir-Creative)*
Bob Moorhead *(VP & Gen Mgr)*
Michael Schneidman *(VP-Brand Strategy)*
Jennifer Browers *(Dir-Retail Strategy-Epsilon)*
Tia Kuchik *(Sr Acct Mgr)*
Alyssa Mollica *(Acct Supvr)*
Andrea Goedde *(Acct Exec)*
Jesse Ouimet *(Copywriter)*

Epsilon
1100 N Glebe Rd Ste 1000, Arlington, VA 22201
Tel.: (703) 312-0509
Fax: (703) 312-9407
E-Mail: info@epsilon.com
Web Site: www.epsilon.com

Employees: 7

Andrew Frawley *(CEO)*
Bryan Kennedy *(CEO)*
Paul Dundon *(CFO)*
Keith Morrow *(CIO & Exec VP-Shared Svcs)*
Catherine Lang *(Pres-Client Svcs)*
Jeanette Fitzgerald *(Gen Counsel & Exec VP)*
Taleen Ghazarian *(Exec VP-Strategy)*
Eric Stein *(Exec VP)*
Janet Barker-Evans *(Sr VP & Exec Dir-Creative)*
Jane Huston *(Sr VP-HR)*
Christopher Harrison *(Mng Dir-Platform Delivery)*

EPSILON MARKETING
(Formerly Aspen Marketing)
7428 Trade St, San Diego, CA 92121
Tel.: (858) 397-1400
Fax: (858) 397-1401
E-Mail: sales@epsilonlocal.com
Web Site: epsilonlocal.com

Employees: 21
Year Founded: 2003

Agency Specializes In: Advertising, Direct Response Marketing, Print, Sponsorship, Web (Banner Ads, Pop-ups, etc.)

Beth Davies *(Acct Supvr)*

EQUALS THREE COMMUNICATIONS
7910 Woodmont Ave Ste 200, Bethesda, MD 20814-3015
Tel.: (301) 656-3100
Fax: (301) 652-5264
E-Mail: info@equals3.com
Web Site: www.equals3.com

Employees: 12
Year Founded: 1984

Agency Specializes In: Brand Development & Integration, Multicultural, Public Relations, Strategic Planning/Research

Eugene M. Faison *(Chm & CEO)*
Robin Meredith *(Corp Sec & VP)*

Accounts:
National Institute of Mental Health

ER MARKETING
512 Delaware St, Kansas City, MO 64105-1100
Tel.: (816) 471-1400
Fax: (816) 471-1419
E-Mail: emayfield@ermarketing.net
Web Site: www.ermarketing.net

Employees: 12
Year Founded: 2001

National Agency Associations: AAF-BMA

Agency Specializes In: Advertising, Advertising Specialties, Alternative Advertising, Automotive, Brand Development & Integration, Business-To-Business, Co-op Advertising, Collateral, College, Communications, Consulting, Consumer Goods, Consumer Marketing, Content, Corporate Communications, Corporate Identity, Crisis Communications, Custom Publishing, Customer Relationship Management, Digital/Interactive, Direct Response Marketing, Direct-to-Consumer, Education, Electronic Media, Email, Engineering, Environmental, Event Planning & Marketing, Exhibit/Trade Shows, Experience Design, Financial, Food Service, Graphic Design, Guerilla Marketing, Health Care Services, Household Goods, Identity Marketing, In-Store Advertising, International, Internet/Web Design, Investor Relations, Local Marketing, Logo & Package Design, Marine, Market Research, Media Planning, Media Relations, Merchandising, Mobile Marketing, Multimedia, New Product Development, Outdoor, Package Design, Paid Searches, Pets , Planning & Consultation, Point of Purchase, Point of Sale, Print, Production, Promotions, Public Relations, Publicity/Promotions, Radio, Real Estate, Recruitment, Restaurant, Retail, Sales Promotion, Search Engine Optimization, Sponsorship, Stakeholders, Strategic Planning/Research, Viral/Buzz/Word of Mouth, Web (Banner Ads, Pop-ups, etc.)

Breakdown of Gross Billings by Media: Collateral: 10%; D.M.: 10%; Event Mktg.: 5%; Exhibits/Trade Shows: 5%; Graphic Design: 20%; Logo & Package Design: 10%; Strategic Planning/Research: 10%; Worldwide Web Sites: 30%

Elton Mayfield *(Co-Founder & Partner)*
Renae Gonner *(Partner)*
Kc Rudolph *(Dir-Art)*
Matthew Bartlett *(Acct Mgr)*
Chris McCutcheon *(Mgr-Interactive)*
Whitney Riker *(Acct Exec)*
Kevin Wright *(Jr Copywriter)*
Lexi Copeland *(Acct Coord)*

Accounts:
ALCO Stores, Inc. Retail Website, email Communications; 2002
Country Club Bank; Kansas City, MO Website Strategy; 2007
Davinci Roofscapes Product Videos; 2011
Fortress Railing Products (Agency of Record) Branding, Channel Communications, Creative Services, Digital, Lead Generation
Goldblatt Tools Events, Product Launch, Rebranding, Website; 2009
Home Building Products.; Saint Louis, MO Huttig Building Products, Masonite Doors, Therma Tru Doors; 2004
IBT, Inc. Branding, Events, Integrated Marketing Communications; 2012
Integrated Healthcare Strategies; Kansas City, MO; Minneapolis, MN Branding, Content, Events, Marketing Collateral, Websites; 2005
ITW Instinct, Trussteel
Ply Gem Industries; Kansas City, MO; Cary, NC Cellwood Vinyl Siding, Durabuilt Vinyl Siding, GP Vinyl Sliding, Leaf Relief Gutter Protection Systems, Ply Gem Windows, Richwood Shutters & Accessories; 2002
SPX; Overland Park, KS; NC Clear Sky Plume Abatement; 2009
ThyssenKrupp Access Home Elevators, stairlifts; 2010
VeriShip (Agency of Record) Creative, Marketing, Public Relations

ERASERFARM
3123 E 4th Ave, Tampa, FL 33605
Tel.: (813) 865-3095
E-Mail: hello@eraserfarm.com
Web Site: www.eraserfarm.com

Agency Specializes In: Above-the-Line, Advertising, Alternative Advertising, Brand Development & Integration, Broadcast, Business Publications, Cable T.V., Co-op Advertising, Consumer Publications, Custom Publishing, Digital/Interactive, Direct Response Marketing, Electronic Media, Email, Exhibit/Trade Shows, Experience Design, Guerilla Marketing, In-Store Advertising, Internet/Web Design, Local Marketing, Magazines, Media Buying Services, Media Planning, Multimedia, Newspaper, Newspapers & Magazines, Out-of-Home Media, Outdoor, Package Design, Print, Production (Print), Promotions, Public Relations, Publishing, Radio, Search Engine Optimization, Social Media, Strategic Planning/Research, Syndication, T.V., Trade & Consumer Magazines, Viral/Buzz/Word of Mouth, Web (Banner Ads, Pop-ups, etc.)

Cindy Haynes *(Partner & Mng Dir)*
James Rosene *(Partner & Dir-Creative)*
Margaret Mariani *(Partner & Strategist-Brand)*

Accounts:
Carmel Kitchen & Wine Bar (Agency of Record) Creative Development, Social Media, Strategic Planning
New-Health First Brand Positioning, Creative Strategy, Strategy
Intrepid Powerboats (Agency of Record) Creative Development, Social Media, Strategic Planning
Kinney, Fernandez & Boire, P.A. (Creative Agency of Record) Social Media, Strategic & Brand Planning
The New York Yankees
North American Soccer League
New-Pacific Life Insurance Creative
Safeguarding a Future for Africa's Elephants (S.A.F.E.); 2013
Strategic Property Partners Real Estate; 2013

ERBACH COMMUNICATIONS GROUP, INC.
1099 Wall St W Ste 175, Lyndhurst, NJ 07071-3623
Tel.: (201) 935-3030
Fax: (201) 935-3555
E-Mail: info@erbachcom.com
Web Site: www.erbachcom.com

E-Mail for Key Personnel:
President: bart@erbachcom.com

Employees: 7
Year Founded: 1988

Agency Specializes In: Advertising, Advertising Specialties, Bilingual Market, Brand Development & Integration, Cable T.V., Collateral, Communications, Consulting, Consumer Publications, Corporate Identity, Direct Response Marketing, Education, Exhibit/Trade Shows, Government/Political, Graphic Design, Health Care Services, Hispanic Market, Internet/Web Design, Logo & Package Design, Media Buying Services, Medical Products, New Product Development, Newspaper, Newspapers & Magazines, Outdoor, Pharmaceutical, Planning & Consultation, Print, Production, Public Relations, Radio, Seniors'

Market, Strategic Planning/Research, T.V.

Approx. Annual Billings: $1,000,000

Bart Erbach *(Pres & Dir-Creative)*
Kristen Kelly Volkland *(VP-Acct Svc)*
Katherine Noyes *(VP-Ops)*
Lynn Martin *(Sr Dir-Art)*
Don Kilcoyne *(Dir-Creative)*
Mary Massaro *(Dir-Art)*
Liz Pagan *(Supvr-Art & Editorial)*
Lauren Ricca *(Acct Exec)*

Accounts:
Cable Vision
Chicago Tribune
Daily News
Friendship Inns
UMDNJ

ERIC MOWER + ASSOCIATES

211 West Jefferson St., Syracuse, NY 13202
Tel.: (315) 466-1000
Fax: (315) 466-2000
E-Mail: lhuggins@mower.com
Web Site: www.mower.com

Employees: 250
Year Founded: 1968

National Agency Associations: 4A's-BMA-DMA-IPREX-MMA-PMA

Agency Specializes In: Above-the-Line, Advertising, Below-the-Line, Brand Development & Integration, Broadcast, Business Publications, Business-To-Business, Cable T.V., Children's Market, Collateral, Communications, Consulting, Consumer Goods, Consumer Marketing, Content, Corporate Communications, Corporate Identity, Crisis Communications, Customer Relationship Management, Digital/Interactive, Direct Response Marketing, Electronic Media, Email, Engineering, Environmental, Exhibit/Trade Shows, Financial, Government/Political, Graphic Design, Health Care Services, Hospitality, Industrial, Integrated Marketing, Internet/Web Design, Local Marketing, Logo & Package Design, Market Research, Media Buying Services, Media Planning, Media Relations, Media Training, Medical Products, Merchandising, Mobile Marketing, Multimedia, Newspaper, Newspapers & Magazines, Out-of-Home Media, Outdoor, Paid Searches, Planning & Consultation, Point of Purchase, Point of Sale, Print, Production, Production (Print), Promotions, Public Relations, Publicity/Promotions, Radio, Regional, Restaurant, Retail, Sales Promotion, Search Engine Optimization, Shopper Marketing, Social Media, Sponsorship, Strategic Planning/Research, Sweepstakes, T.V., Trade & Consumer Magazines, Travel & Tourism, Viral/Buzz/Word of Mouth, Web (Banner Ads, Pop-ups, etc.), Women's Market

Approx. Annual Billings: $250,000,000 Capitalized

Eric Mower *(Chm & CEO)*
Francis T. Nichols *(Vice Chm)*
John Favalo *(Mng Partner-Grp B2B)*
Greg Loh *(Mng Partner-PR & Pub Affairs)*
Stephanie Crockett *(Partner & Acct Dir)*
Robin Farewell *(Partner & Dir-B2B Media)*
John O'Hara *(Partner & Dir-Content Strategy)*
Marty Peterson *(Partner & Dir-Production)*
Hal Goodman *(Partner)*
John Lacey *(Mgmt Supvr-Pub Affairs)*
Nicole LeClair *(Mgmt Supvr)*
Donna Ricciardi *(Mgmt Supvr)*
Chuck Beeler *(Dir & Sr Strategist-PR)*
Diana Comerford *(Dir-Project Mgmt)*
Matthew M. Petrocci *(Dir-Interactive Production)*
Kevin Tripodi *(Sr Partner & Dir-Creative)*
Martin Briggs *(Assoc Dir-Creative)*
Tom Collins *(Assoc Dir-Creative)*
Ryan Garland *(Assoc Dir-Media)*
Danielle Gerhart *(Sr Mgr-Content & PR)*
Patrick Spadafore *(Sr Mgr-Content & PR)*
Meredith Dropkin *(Sr Acct Supvr-PR)*
John Leibrick *(Sr Planner-Strategic)*
A. J. Pellicciotti *(Coord-Media)*
Kristin Gray *(Sr Supvr-Project)*
James Henderson *(Sr Partner)*

Accounts:
Bausch & Lomb
Blue Cross and Blue Shield of Western New York
Carowinds Earned Media, Fury 325, Guerilla Marketing, Public Relations, Social Media
ClosetMaid
Community Bank
Constellation Energy
Dresser-Rand
George Little Management
KI Furniture
Lenox/Newell Rubbermaid
Pass & Seymour/Legrand
Preferred Mutual Insurance Company Branding, Marketing Communications
Rockfon Brand Expression, Brand Position, Digital, Direct Marketing, Marketing Communications, Media Strategy, PR Campaign, Sales
Schick Technologies
Sensus (Marketing Agency of Record) Brand Identity, Creative Services, Digital, Media Buying, Media Planning, Strategic Planning
Sirona Dental Systems, Inc. Brand Management, Digital Development, Integrated Marketing Communications, Media Planning, Public Relations, Social Media, Strategic Planning
Sun Chemical Corporation; Parsippany, NJ (Agency of Record) Agency of Record, Brand Development, Marketing Communications, Public Relations, Strategic Planning
Verizon Wireless

Branches

EMA Public Relations Services

211 W Jefferson St, Syracuse, NY 13202-2561
Tel.: (315) 466-1000
Fax: (315) 466-2000
Web Site: www.mower.com

Agency Specializes In: Advertising, Brand Development & Integration, Broadcast, Business-To-Business, Collateral, Communications, Consumer Goods, Consumer Marketing, Corporate Communications, Corporate Identity, Crisis Communications, Customer Relationship Management, Digital/Interactive, Direct Response Marketing, Electronic Media, Email, Exhibit/Trade Shows, Financial, Government/Political, Graphic Design, Health Care Services, Hospitality, Industrial, Integrated Marketing, Internet/Web Design, Logo & Package Design, Market Research, Media Buying Services, Media Planning, Media Relations, Media Training, Medical Products, Merchandising, Mobile Marketing, Multicultural, Planning & Consultation, Point of Purchase, Point of Sale, Print, Production, Production (Ad, Film, Broadcast), Production (Print), Promotions, Public Relations, Publicity/Promotions, RSS (Really Simple Syndication), Radio, Regional, Restaurant, Retail, Sales Promotion, Search Engine Optimization, Social Media, Strategic Planning/Research, T.V., Trade & Consumer Magazines, Travel & Tourism

Greg Loh *(Mng Partner-PR & Pub Affairs)*
John O'Hara *(Partner & Dir-Content Strategy)*
Patrick Spadafore *(Mgmt Supvr)*
Chuck Beeler *(Dir & Sr Strategist-PR)*
Peter Kapcio *(Dir-Reputation Mgmt Svcs)*
Danielle Gerhart *(Sr Mgr-Content & PR)*
Matt Parry *(Sr Mgr-Content-PR)*
John Lacey *(Supvr-Mgmt)*

Accounts:
Applebee's
BlueCrossBlueShield
Bosch
Constellation Energy Nuclear Group
Corning, Inc.
KeyBank
Kodak Graphic Communications Group
Legrand/Pass & Seymour
Lenox
North American Breweries
Sun Chemical

Eric Mower + Associates

201 17th St NW, Atlanta, GA 30363
(See Separate Listing)

Eric Mower + Associates

(Formerly Eric Mower and Associates)
1001 Morehead Sq Dr 5th Fl, Charlotte, NC 28203
(See Separate Listing)

Eric Mower + Associates

30 S Pearl St Ste 1210, Albany, NY 12207
Tel.: (518) 449-3000
Fax: (518) 449-4000
E-Mail: lhuggins@mower.com
Web Site: www.mower.com

E-Mail for Key Personnel:
President: sawchukp@sawchukbrown.com

Employees: 250
Year Founded: 1968

National Agency Associations: 4A's-AMA-PRSA

Agency Specializes In: Above-the-Line, Advertising, Below-the-Line, Brand Development & Integration, Broadcast, Business Publications, Business-To-Business, Cable T.V., Children's Market, Collateral, Communications, Consulting, Consumer Goods, Consumer Marketing, Content, Corporate Communications, Corporate Identity, Crisis Communications, Customer Relationship Management, Digital/Interactive, Direct Response Marketing, Electronic Media, Email, Engineering, Environmental, Exhibit/Trade Shows, Financial, Government/Political, Graphic Design, Health Care Services, Hospitality, Industrial, Integrated Marketing, Internet/Web Design, Local Marketing, Logo & Package Design, Market Research, Media Buying Services, Media Planning, Media Relations, Media Training, Medical Products, Merchandising, Mobile Marketing, Multimedia, Newspaper, Newspapers & Magazines, Out-of-Home Media, Outdoor, Paid Searches, Planning & Consultation, Point of Purchase, Point of Sale, Print, Production, Production (Ad, Film, Broadcast), Production (Print), Promotions, Public Relations, Publicity/Promotions, Radio, Regional, Restaurant, Retail, Sales Promotion, Search Engine Optimization, Shopper Marketing, Social Media, Strategic Planning/Research, Sweepstakes, T.V., Trade & Consumer Magazines, Travel & Tourism, Viral/Buzz/Word of Mouth, Web (Banner Ads, Pop-ups, etc.), Women's Market

Sean L. Casey *(Partner & Dir-Pub Affairs)*
Saleem Cheeks *(Mgmt Supvr-Pub Affairs)*
Brendan Kennedy *(Sr Mgr-Content-PR)*
Michael Hochanadel *(Acct Supvr-PR & Pub Affairs)*
Matt Maguire *(Sr Counselor)*
Andrew Rush *(Sr Counselor)*

Accounts:
Alcoholism & Substance Abuse Providers
Feld Entertainment
Greenberg Traurig
KeyBank NA
Lafarge NA

National Heritage Academies
New York State Laborers; 1991
The Picotte Companies; Albany, NY; 1979
Susan G. Komen Race for the Cure Northeastern NY
Transmission Developers Inc.

Eric Mower + Associates
50 Fountain Plz Ste 1300, Buffalo, NY 14202
(See Separate Listing)

Eric Mower + Associates
(Formerly Eric Mower and Associates)
1st Federal Plz 28 E Main St Ste 1960, Rochester, NY 14614-1915
(See Separate Listing)

Eric Mower + Associates
830 Main St 10th Fl, Cincinnati, OH 45202
(See Separate Listing)

HB/Eric Mower + Associates
(Formerly Hart-Boillot, LLC)
134 Rumford Ave Ste 307, Newton, MA 02466-1378
Tel.: (781) 893-0053
Fax: (781) 209-1307
Web Site: www.mower.com

Employees: 12

Agency Specializes In: Advertising, Collateral, Corporate Identity, Digital/Interactive, Direct Response Marketing, Exhibit/Trade Shows, Identity Marketing, Public Relations

Kevin Hart *(Pres & Dir-Creative)*
Mark O'Toole *(Mng Dir-PR & Content Mktg)*
Chuck Tanowitz *(VP-PR & Editorial Svcs)*
Alex Jafarzadeh *(Sr Acct Exec-PR)*
Dawn Sullivan *(Strategist-PR)*
Christine Tesseo *(Strategist-Creative)*
Julia Bucchianeri *(Asst Acct Exec)*

Accounts:
ALS Fundraiser Invitation
American University of Antigua Public Relations
Aquanima Direct Marketing Campaign
Attivio; Newton, MA Integrated Communications
Baxa Corporation
Boston GreenFest
Cleantech Open Northeast
ForHealth Technology Pharmacy Automation Systems; 2007
Greentown Labs
Harvard University
Mollie Johnson Interiors Website
NanoHorizons Branding
New England Clean Energy Council
Northeastern University
Ocean Thermal Energy Corporation Brand Identity, Design Development, Public Relations Campaigns, Website
Tail-f Systems
Terraclime Geothermal Branding

M&G/Eric Mower + Associates
(Formerly Middleton & Gendron, Inc.)
845 3rd Ave, New York, NY 10022
(See Separate Listing)

ERIC ROB & ISAAC
509 President Clinton Ave, Little Rock, AR 72201
Tel.: (501) 978-6329
E-Mail: info@ericrobisaac.com
Web Site: www.ericrobisaac.com

Year Founded: 2004

Agency Specializes In: Advertising, Brand Development & Integration, Collateral, Crisis Communications, Digital/Interactive, Event Planning & Marketing, Logo & Package Design, Media Planning, Media Relations, Print

Eric Lancaster *(Owner)*
Isaac Alexander *(Principal)*
Rob Bell *(Principal)*
Brooke Vines *(Dir-Media)*
Meghan Foster *(Mgr-Traffic)*
Ben Johnson *(Designer & Strategist-Brand)*
Michelle Pugh *(Acct Exec)*

Accounts:
Argenta Arts Foundation
Arkansas Capital, Corp.
Mountain Valley Spring Water
New Balance Stores

ERODZ AGENCY
(Name Changed to Entertainment Events AZ LLC)

EROI, INC.
505 NW Couch St Ste 300, Portland, OR 97209
Tel.: (503) 221-6200
Fax: (503) 228-4249
E-Mail: info@eroi.com
Web Site: www.eroi.com

Employees: 40
Year Founded: 2002

Revenue: $4,100,000

Ryan Buchanan *(Founder & CEO)*
Phil Herbert *(Head-Strategy)*
Keely Mckay *(Head-Acct)*
Karen Butler-Kennedy *(Controller & Dir-HR)*
Tyler West *(Acct Exec)*
Robin Clerk *(Designer-Visual)*

Accounts:
CBS Sports
Kettle
Micro Power
Microsoft
Modern Luxury Media
Publicis
Wacom

ERVIN & SMITH
16934 Frances St Ste 200, Omaha, NE 68130
Tel.: (402) 829-8032
Fax: (402) 334-5557
Toll Free: (877) 334-0569
E-Mail: info@ervinandsmith.com
Web Site: www.ervinandsmith.com

E-Mail for Key Personnel:
President: dougs@ervinandsmith.com
Creative Dir.: betsyp@ervinandsmith.com
Production Mgr.: kayh@ervinandsmith.com

Employees: 50
Year Founded: 1983

National Agency Associations: PRSA

Agency Specializes In: Advertising, Advertising Specialties, Agriculture, Alternative Advertising, Arts, Brand Development & Integration, Broadcast, Business Publications, Business-To-Business, Cable T.V., Catalogs, Co-op Advertising, Collateral, College, Commercial Photography, Communications, Consulting, Consumer Marketing, Consumer Publications, Corporate Communications, Corporate Identity, Crisis Communications, Digital/Interactive, Direct Response Marketing, Direct-to-Consumer, E-Commerce, Education, Electronic Media, Email, Event Planning & Marketing, Exhibit/Trade Shows, Financial, Food Service, Graphic Design, Guerilla Marketing, Health Care Services, High Technology, In-Store Advertising, Information Technology, Integrated Marketing, Internet/Web Design, Investor Relations, Local Marketing, Logo & Package Design, Magazines, Market Research, Media Buying Services, Media Planning, Media Relations, Media Training, Medical Products, Merchandising, Mobile Marketing, Multimedia, New Product Development, New Technologies, Newspaper, Newspapers & Magazines, Out-of-Home Media, Outdoor, Paid Searches, Planning & Consultation, Podcasting, Point of Purchase, Point of Sale, Print, Production, Production (Print), Promotions, Public Relations, Publicity/Promotions, RSS (Really Simple Syndication), Radio, Real Estate, Recruitment, Retail, Sales Promotion, Search Engine Optimization, Strategic Planning/Research, T.V., Teen Market, Telemarketing, Trade & Consumer Magazines, Transportation, Travel & Tourism, Viral/Buzz/Word of Mouth, Web (Banner Ads, Pop-ups, etc.), Women's Market, Yellow Pages Advertising

Approx. Annual Billings: $4,850,000

Breakdown of Gross Billings by Media: Collateral: 4%; Consumer Publs.: 3%; Corp. Communications: 10%; D.M.: 4%; Graphic Design: 15%; Internet Adv.: 10%; Logo & Package Design: 8%; Newsp. & Mags.: 3%; Plng. & Consultation: 10%; Production: 7%; Pub. Rels.: 5%; Radio & T.V.: 1%; Radio: 3%; Trade & Consumer Mags.: 5%; Trade Shows: 2%; Worldwide Web Sites: 10%

Betsy Perez *(Chief Creative Officer)*
Katie Herzog *(Dir-Mktg)*
Jennifer Kieffe *(Dir-Fin)*
Aaron Christensen *(Assoc Dir-Creative)*

Accounts:
Allstate
American Academy of Cosmetic Surgery
Ameritas Advisor Services
Barrier Systems, Inc.
Blue Cross Blue Shield Nebraska
Cy Wakeman Inc.
First National Bank Omaha; Omaha, NE Banking Services, Credit Cards; 1983

ERVIN MARKETING CREATIVE COMMUNICATIONS
(Acquired & Absorbed by Geile Leon Marketing Communications)

ERWIN-PENLAND
125 E Broad St, Greenville, SC 29601
Tel.: (864) 271-0500
Fax: (864) 235-5941
E-Mail: shannon.wilbanks@erwinpenland.com
Web Site: www.erwinpenland.com

E-Mail for Key Personnel:
President: joe.erwin@erwinpenland.com

Employees: 300
Year Founded: 1986

National Agency Associations: 4A's

Agency Specializes In: Advertising, African-American Market, Automotive, Bilingual Market, Brand Development & Integration, Broadcast, Business Publications, Business-To-Business, Cable T.V., Co-op Advertising, Collateral, Communications, Consumer Marketing, Corporate Communications, Corporate Identity, Digital/Interactive, Direct Response Marketing, E-Commerce, Electronic Media, Event Planning & Marketing, Exhibit/Trade Shows, Fashion/Apparel, Financial, Food Service, Government/Political, Graphic Design, Health Care Services, High Technology, Hispanic Market, In-Store Advertising,

Industrial, Information Technology, Internet/Web Design, Leisure, Local Marketing, Logo & Package Design, Magazines, Marine, Media Buying Services, Medical Products, Merchandising, Multimedia, New Product Development, Newspaper, Newspapers & Magazines, Out-of-Home Media, Outdoor, Planning & Consultation, Point of Purchase, Point of Sale, Print, Production, Public Relations, Publicity/Promotions, Radio, Real Estate, Restaurant, Retail, Sales Promotion, Seniors' Market, Sponsorship, Sports Market, Strategic Planning/Research, T.V., Technical Advertising, Teen Market, Telemarketing, Trade & Consumer Magazines, Transportation, Travel & Tourism, Yellow Pages Advertising

Joe Saracino *(Pres)*
Roger Beasley *(Chief Strategy Officer)*
Peter Coles *(Exec VP & Exec Dir-Ops)*
Bill Reynolds *(Exec VP & Exec Dir-Media)*
Ty Thornhill *(Sr VP & Grp Acct Dir)*
Stephen Childress *(VP & Grp Dir-Creative)*
Danny Miller *(VP & Sr Producer-Content)*
Peyton Burke Lewis *(VP & Acct Dir)*
Angela Griggs *(Sr Dir-Art)*
Bryan Cherok *(Assoc Dir-Analytics)*
Christie Dwyer *(Assoc Dir-Production)*
Bee Reynolds *(Assoc Dir-Creative)*
Austin Scott *(Assoc Dir-Creative)*
Ryan Brown *(Mgr-Production)*
Lauren Hunt *(Acct Supvr-Content)*
Jessica Puder *(Acct Supvr)*
Rebecca Lynch *(Sr Acct Exec-PR)*
Lauren N. Verdi *(Sr Acct Exec)*
Austin Huff *(Acct Exec)*
Jessy Segal *(Acct Exec)*
Kylie Wall *(Acct Exec)*
Orlando Asson *(Designer-Motion Graphics)*
Scott Wilkins *(Media Buyer)*
Emma Church *(Sr Media Buyer)*

Accounts:
Advance America Cash Advance Centers; Spartanburg, SC Financial Services; 2002
Bi-Lo; Mauldin, SC Regional Grocery Chain; 2007
CIT Bank (Agency of Record) Brand Strategy, Creative, Digital, Retail Marketing
Clemson University
Confluence Watersports Adventure Technology, Confluence Watersports, Dagger, Harmony Gear, Mad River Canoe, Perception, Wave Sports, Web Site Development & Redesign, Wilderness Systems
New-Denny's Brand Awareness
New-Disney XD
General Motors
Greenville Drive Campaign: "Ribbon Cutting"
Greenville Humane Society; SC Pro Bono
Hands on Greenville
Hanesbrands L'eggs
L.L. Bean, Inc. (Agency of Record) Campaign: "Guaranteed Season After Season", Creative, Digital, Marketing Strategy, OOH, Out of Home, Print, Retail, Social, TV
Microsoft
ScanSource, Inc.; Greenville, SC Technology Distribution
Seven & I Holdings Co., Ltd "Greatest Hits Remixed", "The Grand Slams", Local Advertising, Menus, Merchandising, TV
Uniroyal
New-The UPS Store "#3DPWeek"
VAYA Pharma Global Brand Strategy
Verizon Campaign: "Break in the Action", Wireless Communications; 1988
Wells Fargo

Branch

Erwin Penland
622 Third Ave, New York, NY 10017
Tel.: (212) 905-7000
Web Site: www.erwinpenland.com

National Agency Associations: 4A's

Agency Specializes In: Advertising, Brand Development & Integration, Collateral, Digital/Interactive, Event Planning & Marketing, Logo & Package Design, Outdoor, Promotions, Public Relations, Sponsorship, T.V.

Con Williamson *(Chief Creative Officer)*
Jessica Navas *(Chief Plng Officer)*
Peter Kearney *(Sr VP & Exec Creative Dir)*
Jeff Hoffman *(Sr VP & Grp Acct Dir-Social Media & Content)*
Will Lee *(Sr VP & Grp Acct Dir)*
Zac Painter *(Sr VP & Grp Acct Dir)*
Steve Rodriguez *(Sr VP & Dir-Creative Svcs)*
Adrienne Barber *(Sr VP-Sports & Entertainment)*
Jimmy Collins *(VP & Creative Dir)*
Kristofer Delaney *(VP & Creative Dir)*
Vicky Gonzalez *(VP & Dir-Print Production)*
Wesley Westenberg *(VP-Office Svcs & Office Mgr)*
Chris Plating *(VP-Brand Strategy)*
Alex Lea *(Exec Creative Dir)*
Jane Lee *(Sr Dir-Art)*
Kat Shafer *(Grp Acct Dir)*
Beth Moats *(Acct Dir)*
Jennifer Noll *(Producer-Digital)*
Taylor Lucas *(Dir-Art)*
Steven Lund *(Dir-Art)*
Morgan Crego *(Mgr-Community)*
Jennifer Cammarota *(Acct Supvr)*
Jessica Dalati *(Acct Supvr)*
Amanda Dwyer *(Acct Supvr)*
Lauren Hunt *(Acct Supvr-Content)*
Ashley Butturini *(Supvr-Content)*
Morgan Wilkins *(Sr Acct Exec-Digital)*
Brittany Hunley *(Sr Strategist-Social)*
Erin Mehaffey *(Sr Specialist-Digital Asset)*
Erica Cinque *(Acct Exec)*
David Jacks *(Acct Exec)*
Jessy Segal *(Acct Exec)*
Haley Winther *(Acct Exec)*
Jimmy McDonald *(Copywriter)*
Kelsey Spellman *(Community Mgr)*

Accounts:
New-Califia Farms (Agency of Record) Business Strategy, Creative, Digital, Media, Social
CIT Bank
Evolve Campaign: "American Man"
Seven & I Holdings Co., Ltd

ES ADVERTISING
6222 Wilshire Blvd Ste 302, Los Angeles, CA 90048
Tel.: (323) 964-9001
Fax: (323) 964-9801
E-Mail: ester@esadvertising.net
Web Site: www.esadvertising.net

Employees: 25
Year Founded: 1999

Agency Specializes In: Advertising, Asian Market, Automotive, Bilingual Market, Business-To-Business, Co-op Advertising, Collateral, Consumer Marketing, Corporate Communications, Cosmetics, Crisis Communications, Digital/Interactive, Direct Response Marketing, Direct-to-Consumer, Entertainment, Event Planning & Marketing, Exhibit/Trade Shows, Financial, Government/Political, Guerilla Marketing, Integrated Marketing, Local Marketing, Market Research, Media Buying Services, Media Planning, Media Relations, Multicultural, Point of Purchase, Point of Sale, Print, Production, Promotions, Public Relations, Publicity/Promotions, Radio, Sales Promotion, South Asian Market, Strategic Planning/Research, Trade & Consumer Magazines

Approx. Annual Billings: $10,000,000

Billie Jung *(VP-Creative)*
Heidi Hsu *(Mgr-PR & Promos)*

Accounts:
California Bank & Trust; Irvine, CA Banking, Campaign: "The Golden Little Dragon"
Time Warner Cable

ESB ADVERTISING
PO Box 5022, Springfield, VA 22150
Tel.: (703) 988-2307
Web Site: www.esbadvertising.com

Agency Specializes In: Advertising, Internet/Web Design, Media Buying Services, Public Relations, Radio, Search Engine Optimization, T.V.

Jim Folliard *(Dir)*
Sasha Semyonova *(Mgr-Fin)*
Emilie Bair *(Acct Exec)*
Samantha Bass *(Acct Exec)*
Rebecca Miller *(Acct Exec)*
Jackie Toth *(Acct Exec)*
Lynn Martin *(Media Buyer)*

Accounts:
Long Fence Company Inc.

ESCAPE POD
400 N Peoria St, Chicago, IL 60642
Tel.: (312) 274-1180
Fax: (312) 274-0996
E-Mail: normbilow@theescapepodagency.com
Web Site: www.theescapepod.com

Employees: 12

Agency Specializes In: Advertising, Sponsorship

Norm Bilow *(Founder & Mng Dir)*
Vinny Warren *(Owner)*
Bob Sutter *(Pres & Dir-Accts)*
Brad Demarea *(Dir-Art & Designer)*
Matt Wilcox *(Dir-Creative & Copywriter)*
Eric Jurkovic *(Dir-Art)*
Kurt Lenard *(Dir-Creative)*
Lov Carpenter *(Mgr-Bus Affairs & Community Mgr)*
Meg Wohlschlaeger *(Acct Supvr)*
Felicity Pal *(Copywriter)*

Accounts:
Budweiser
Ego Power Lawn Mowers, Power Tools
FECKiN Irish Whiskey
Lunchables
Mondelez International, Inc. Campaign: "Falling Letters", TV, Wheat Thins
Toys "R" Us, Inc. Campaign: "Joys of toys", Campaign: "Make All Their Wishes Come True"
Volkswagen Group of America, Inc.

ESD & ASSOCIATES
1202 W Bitters Bldg 9, San Antonio, TX 78216
Tel.: (210) 348-8008
Fax: (210) 348-9944
E-Mail: info@esdandassociates.com
Web Site: www.esdandassociates.com

Agency Specializes In: Advertising, Brand Development & Integration, Event Planning & Marketing, Graphic Design, Internet/Web Design, Outdoor, Print, Public Relations, Social Media, Strategic Planning/Research

Erik Simpson *(Partner & Dir-Creative)*
Robert Crowe *(Dir-Comm)*
Lindsay Maulden *(Dir-HR)*
Johanna Salazar *(Mgr-Traffic & Acct Exec)*
John Garcia *(Specialist-Digital Mktg)*
Danielle Vanzandt *(Coord-PR)*

Accounts:
Institute for Womens Health

ESP BRANDS
(Formerly GroupM ESP)
825 7th Ave, New York, NY 10019
Tel.: (212) 973-9898
Fax: (212) 973-1999
Web Site: brands.espglobal.com/brands

Employees: 20

Ellen Drury *(Mng Partner & Pres-Local Brdcst)*
Lyle Schwartz *(Mng Partner)*
Jessica Weiss *(Partner & Assoc Dir)*
Ernie Simon *(Pres-Consulting Svcs)*
Jennifer Hageney *(Exec VP)*
Benjamin Dick *(Assoc Dir-Digital Trading)*
Michele Porri *(Mgr-Print)*
Michael Dowd *(Sr Partner)*

Accounts:
Jones Group, Inc.; 2005

ESPARZA ADVERTISING
423 Cooper Ave NW, Albuquerque, NM 87102
Tel.: (505) 765-1505
Fax: (505) 765-1518
E-Mail: info@esparzaadvertising.com
Web Site: letsmakeascene.com

Employees: 16

National Agency Associations: AMA

Agency Specializes In: Advertising, Bilingual Market, Graphic Design, Hispanic Market, Logo & Package Design, Media Buying Services, Merchandising, Outdoor, Pharmaceutical, Print, T.V.

Approx. Annual Billings: $13,000,000

Del Esparza *(Pres)*
Roberta Clark *(CFO & Principal)*
Emily Griebel *(VP)*
Donna Soulsby *(Office Mgr)*
Kiki Lopez *(Mgr-Production & Traffic)*

Accounts:
Blue Cross Blue Shield of New Mexico
MADD New Mexico
Memorial Medical Center; Las Cruces, NM
Mini Cooper
New Mexico Clean & Beautiful Campaign: "Trash Talking"
Oppenheimer Funds
Pardo Salons
Rhythm for a Reason
Sandia BMW
Sandia Mini
Santa Fe BMW
Skydive New Mexico
United Way of Central NM

ESPN CREATIVEWORKS
77 W 66th St, New York, NY 10023
Tel.: (646) 547-5408
Web Site: http://showcase.espncreativeworks.com/

Agency Specializes In: Advertising, Digital/Interactive, Event Planning & Marketing, T.V.

Vikram Somaya *(Sr VP)*
John Skeffington *(Head-Production)*
Steve Mottershead *(Exec Creative Dir)*
Christina Carey-Dunleavy *(Acct Dir)*
Jay Marrotte *(Creative Dir)*
Michael Anastasi *(Designer)*

Accounts:
New-AT&T

ESROCK PARTNERS
14550 S 94th Ave, Orland Park, IL 60462-2652
Tel.: (708) 349-8400
Fax: (708) 349-8471
E-Mail: clay@esrock.com
Web Site: www.esrock.com

E-Mail for Key Personnel:
President: coughlin@esrock.com

Employees: 30
Year Founded: 1978

Agency Specializes In: Brand Development & Integration, Business-To-Business, Collateral, Communications, Corporate Identity, Direct Response Marketing, Electronic Media, Food Service, Graphic Design, Internet/Web Design, Logo & Package Design, Media Buying Services, Planning & Consultation, Point of Sale, Print, Production, Public Relations, Recruitment, Sales Promotion, Sponsorship, Strategic Planning/Research, Trade & Consumer Magazines

Jack Coughlin *(Owner)*
Kevin Wilson *(Pres & Partner)*
Don Peterson *(VP-Mktg)*
Vicki Gawlinski *(Sr Acct Mgr)*
Helen Lipke *(Mgr-Recruitment Adv)*
Tracy Subka *(Mgr-HR, Bus & Fin)*
Melissa Rose *(Acct Coord-Media & Analyst-Res)*
Sharyl Syring *(Media Planner)*

Accounts:
Chiquita
McCain Foods
Nonni's

ESTEY-HOOVER INC. ADVERTISING-PUBLIC RELATIONS
20201 SW Birch St Ste 150, Newport Beach, CA 92660
Tel.: (949) 756-8501
Fax: (949) 756-8506
E-Mail: info@estey-hoover.com
Web Site: www.estey-hoover.com

E-Mail for Key Personnel:
President: hoover@estey-hoover.com
Creative Dir.: jcooper@estey-hoover.com

Employees: 18
Year Founded: 1975

National Agency Associations: 4A's-AAF

Agency Specializes In: Advertising, Automotive, Aviation & Aerospace, Brand Development & Integration, Broadcast, Business Publications, Business-To-Business, Cable T.V., Co-op Advertising, Collateral, Consumer Marketing, Corporate Identity, Cosmetics, Direct Response Marketing, Environmental, Event Planning & Marketing, Exhibit/Trade Shows, Fashion/Apparel, Financial, Food Service, Graphic Design, Health Care Services, High Technology, Hispanic Market, Industrial, Internet/Web Design, Leisure, Logo & Package Design, Magazines, Marine, Media Buying Services, Medical Products, Merchandising, New Product Development, Newspaper, Newspapers & Magazines, Out-of-Home Media, Outdoor, Over-50 Market, Pharmaceutical, Planning & Consultation, Point of Purchase, Point of Sale, Print, Production, Public Relations, Publicity/Promotions, Radio, Real Estate, Retail, Sales Promotion, Seniors' Market, Sports Market, Strategic Planning/Research, T.V., Teen Market, Trade & Consumer Magazines, Transportation, Travel & Tourism

Approx. Annual Billings: $12,750,000

Breakdown of Gross Billings by Media: Bus. Publs.: 12%; Cable T.V.: 5%; Collateral: 12%; Consumer Publs.: 17%; D.M.: 2%; Exhibits/Trade Shows: 1%; Fees: 3%; Graphic Design: 7%; Internet Adv.: 4%; Logo & Package Design: 1%; Newsp.: 3%; Outdoor: 1%; Point of Purchase: 1%; Pub. Rels.: 13%; Spot Radio: 8%; Spot T.V.: 2%; Strategic Planning/Research: 2%; Worldwide Web Sites: 6%

Daniel W. Hoover *(Founder, Pres & CEO)*
John Cooper *(VP-Creative & Co-Dir-Creative)*
Joan Carol *(VP-Ops)*
Shirley Goya *(Mgr-Media)*

Accounts:
California Schools Joint Powers Authority Pooled Funds for School District Employee Benefits & Risk Management; 2012
Camguard Security Systems; 2004
Fast Systems Builders; 2002
Fibercare Baths Fiberglass Bathtubs & Showers; 2004
HRC Auction Marketing; Newport Beach, CA; 2002
La Paz Products Cocktail Mixes & Tequila; 1987
McCormack Roofing Residential & Commercial Roofing; 2012
MK Battery Batteries for Solar Systems, Wheelchairs/Scooters, Marine, and More; 2012
Professional Sport Images, Sports Marketing Co.; 1993
Royal Thai Massage & Day Spa; 2007
Spireon GPS Products & Monitoring Systems; 2014
VCI Event Technology (Formerly Videocam) Audio, Video, Lighting, Staging & Productions; 2001

ESTIPONA GROUP
PO Box 10606, Reno, NV 89511
Tel.: (775) 786-4445
Fax: (775) 313-9914
E-Mail: info@estiponagroup.com
Web Site: www.estiponagroup.com

Year Founded: 2009

Agency Specializes In: Advertising, Brand Development & Integration, Event Planning & Marketing, Internet/Web Design, Logo & Package Design, Media Planning, Media Relations, Public Relations, Social Media

Edward Estipona *(Pres)*
Jackie Shelton *(VP-PR)*
Brian Raszka *(Sr Dir-Art)*
Maren Rush *(Sr Dir-Art)*
Mikalee Byerman *(Dir-Audience Engagement)*
Paige Galeoto *(Dir-Creative)*

Accounts:
New-American Higher Education Development Corp American Higher Education College (Agency of Record), Rockford Career College (Agency of Record)
Career Quest (Agency of Record) Online Advertising, Public Relations, Social Media, Strategic Communications
Charter College Marketing
Discalced Carmelite Friars
Immunize Nevada

E.SULLIVAN ADVERTISING & DESIGN
448 Orleans St, Beaumont, TX 77701
Tel.: (409) 832-2027
Web Site: www.esullivanadvertising.com

Agency Specializes In: Advertising, Collateral, Internet/Web Design, Logo & Package Design, Print

Eric Sullivan *(Owner & Principal)*

Accounts:
Jack Brooks Regional Airport

ESWSTORYLAB

(Formerly Ebel Signorelli Welke LLC)
(d/b/a ESW Partners)
910 W Van Buren St, Chicago, IL 60607
Tel.: (312) 762-7400
Fax: (312) 762-7449
Web Site: www.eswstorylab.com

E-Mail for Key Personnel:
Chairman: jimsl@eswpartners.com
Media Dir.: davidf@eswpartners.com

Employees: 40
Year Founded: 2003

National Agency Associations: AMA

Agency Specializes In: Advertising, Bilingual Market, Brand Development & Integration, Broadcast, Business Publications, Business-To-Business, Cable T.V., Children's Market, Co-op Advertising, Collateral, Communications, Consulting, Consumer Marketing, Consumer Publications, Direct Response Marketing, E-Commerce, Electronic Media, Event Planning & Marketing, Financial, Food Service, Graphic Design, Health Care Services, Internet/Web Design, Investor Relations, Legal Services, Leisure, Logo & Package Design, Magazines, Media Buying Services, Merchandising, New Product Development, Newspaper, Newspapers & Magazines, Outdoor, Pharmaceutical, Point of Sale, Print, Production, Public Relations, Publicity/Promotions, Radio, Restaurant, Retail, Sales Promotion, Sponsorship, Strategic Planning/Research, T.V., Trade & Consumer Magazines, Travel & Tourism

Approx. Annual Billings: $5,000,000

Breakdown of Gross Billings by Media: Newsp. & Mags.: 10%; Out-of-Home Media: 5%; Print: 5%; Spot Radio: 20%; Spot T.V.: 50%; T.V.: 10%

James Signorelli *(Chm & CEO)*
Chris Hayano *(Partner & Grp Dir-Creative)*
Phillip Lanier *(Exec Dir-Creative)*
Carl Haseman *(Dir-Creative)*
Joe Przybylski *(Dir-Interactive Creative)*
Randy Rohn *(Dir-Creative)*

Accounts:
American Marketing Association Mplanet 2009
BAB, Inc.; Deerfield, IL
Bagels
Chicago Archdiocese
Chicago Symphony Orchestra
Chicago Wolves
Church's Chicken Broadcast, Campaign: "Life's too Short to Skimp on Chicken", Creative, In-store & Interactive Media, Print
City Pool Hall
KFC
MotorCity Casino
Republic Tobacco
Shavitz
St. John's Providence
Taco Bell; CA; Michigan, Wisconsin, Kentucky, Missouri, & Iowa; 2000
TradeStation Securities
TZ

ETA ADVERTISING

301 Pine Ave Ste B, Long Beach, CA 90802
Tel.: (562) 499-2305
Fax: (562) 499-2306
Web Site: www.etaadvertising.com

Agency Specializes In: Advertising, Brand Development & Integration, Digital/Interactive, Internet/Web Design, Media Buying Services, Media Planning, Public Relations, Social Media, Strategic Planning/Research

Cindy Allen *(Pres)*
Malinee Saechee *(Sr Art Dir)*
Niko Dahilig *(Art Dir)*
Mike Frey *(Creative Dir)*
Cassandra Popli *(Dir-Acct Svcs)*
Ismael Ford *(Assoc Dir-Creative)*
Ian McGee *(Sr Acct Exec)*
Rachel Shelley *(Acct Exec)*
Andrea Esquivel *(Acct Exec)*

Accounts:
LBS Financial Credit Union

ETARGETMEDIA.COM, INC.

6810 Lyons Technology Circle Ste 160, Coconut Creek, FL 33073
Tel.: (954) 480-8470
Fax: (954) 480-8489
Toll Free: (888) 805-3282
E-Mail: info@etargetmedia.com
Web Site: www.etargetmedia.com

National Agency Associations: DMA-MMA

Agency Specializes In: Advertising, Advertising Specialties, African-American Market, Asian Market, Automotive, Brand Development & Integration, Business-To-Business, Catalogs, College, Computers & Software, Consulting, Consumer Goods, Consumer Marketing, Digital/Interactive, Direct Response Marketing, Direct-to-Consumer, E-Commerce, Education, Electronic Media, Email, Entertainment, Financial, Health Care Services, High Technology, Hispanic Market, Information Technology, Integrated Marketing, International, Internet/Web Design, Market Research, Media Buying Services, Media Planning, Medical Products, Men's Market, Pharmaceutical, Real Estate, Restaurant, Retail, Sports Market, Strategic Planning/Research, Sweepstakes, Travel & Tourism

Breakdown of Gross Billings by Media: D.M.: 35%; Internet Adv.: 65%

Harris Kreichman *(Mng Partner)*
Karen Waddell *(VP-List Svcs)*

Accounts:
Anthem Health Plans of Virginia
BlackBerry
DirecTV
The Hartford
Nissan
Pitney Bowes
Sprint
TGIF (Friday's Restaurants)
United States Army
The Wall Street Journal
Xerox
Yahoo!

ETC ADVERTISING & PROMOTIONS LLC

7930 State Line Rd Ste 208, Prairie Village, KS 66208
Tel.: (913) 341-6248
Fax: (913) 385-2243
Web Site: www.etcadvertising.com

Agency Specializes In: Advertising, Collateral, Digital/Interactive, Media Buying Services, Outdoor, Print, Promotions, Public Relations, Radio, T.V.

Sherry Lieberman *(CEO)*

Accounts:
Mays Asian Cuisine
One Stop Decorating Center, Inc.
Stark Pharmacy
Stuart Woodbury Insurance

ETHICOM

801 Boush St Ste 200, Norfolk, VA 23510-1531
Tel.: (757) 626-3867
Fax: (757) 626-3917
E-Mail: info@ethi.com
Web Site: www.ethi.com

Employees: 10

National Agency Associations: Second Wind Limited

Agency Specializes In: Advertising, Faith Based

Keith Andrus *(Founder & Pres)*
Linda Andrus *(Owner)*

Accounts:
Albemarle Hospital
Baker McNiff
Carpet One
Cenit Bank for Savings
Center for Christian Statesmanship
City of Suffolk
E.T. Gresham Company
Fox 43
Hermes Abrasives
Regent University Undergraduate Education
Virginia Stage Company

ETHNIC PRINT MEDIA GROUP

414 Jutland Drive, San Diego, CA 92117
Tel.: (858) 272-9023
Fax: (858) 272-7275
E-Mail: info@epmg360.com
Web Site: www.epmg360.com

Employees: 25

Agency Specializes In: African-American Market, Hispanic Market, Media Buying Services, Media Planning, Media Relations, Multicultural

Juan Carlos Balarezo *(Dir-Media Rels)*
Nicole Kuklewicz *(Dir-Acct Mgmt & Midwest Bus Dev)*
Kathy Souza *(Dir-Fin)*
Becky We *(Sr Acct Mgr)*
Ashley Anderson *(Acct Mgr)*
Alicia Longo *(Mgr-Media Ops)*
Aura Acosta *(Media Planner & Media Buyer)*
Emmanuel Lemas *(Coord-Media)*

Accounts:
The Oregonian Cancha

ETHNICOM GROUP

45 E City Ave Ste 512, Bala Cynwyd, PA 19107
Tel.: (610) 617-8800
Fax: (610) 616-5630
E-Mail: contact@ethnicom.net
Web Site: www.nmspress.com

Employees: 10
Year Founded: 2002

Dan Tsao *(Pres & Publr)*
Yali Wang *(Dir-Creative)*
Thanh Lam *(Mgr-Metro Viet)*
Vivien Xu *(Mgr-Ops)*
Jane Chen *(Sr Graphic Designer)*
Ling Lin *(Sr Graphic Designer)*

Accounts:
Asian American Times
Asian Bank

Hansen Financial
Hotel Windsor
Old Town Buffet
Splendor of China
Washington Mutual
Wilkie Lexus

ETHOS MARKETING & DESIGN

907 Main St, Westbrook, ME 04092
Tel.: (207) 856-2610
Fax: (207) 856-2610
E-Mail: info@ethos-marketing.com
Web Site: www.ethos-marketing.com

Year Founded: 1999

Agency Specializes In: Advertising, Brand Development & Integration, Internet/Web Design, Media Buying Services, Media Planning, Public Relations

Judy Trepal *(Co-Founder, Dir-Creative & Principal)*
Glenn Rudberg *(Owner)*
Daria Cullen *(Dir-Media)*
Belinda Donovan *(Dir-PR)*
Jessica Laracy *(Dir-Art)*
Kiyo Tabery *(Dir-Art)*
Lori Keenan *(Mgr-Billing)*

Accounts:
OA Centers for Orthopaedics

EUROPRINT, INC.

14271 Jeffrey Rd #305, Irvine, CA 92620
Tel.: (714) 962-3771
Fax: (949) 574-2159
Web Site: www.europrintusa.com

Employees: 3
Year Founded: 2001

Agency Specializes In: Advertising, Graphic Design

Tim Garth *(Pres)*

Accounts:
Custom Window Applications
Green Eco-friendly Materials
Posters

EVANS ALLIANCE ADVERTISING

72 Cobbler Sq, Sparta, NJ 07871
Tel.: (973) 250-4040
Fax: (877) 987-7836
Toll Free: (866) 808-2851
E-Mail: info@evansalliance.com
Web Site: www.evansalliance.com

Employees: 5
Year Founded: 1998

Agency Specializes In: Advertising, Advertising Specialties, Affluent Market, Agriculture, Arts, Asian Market, Automotive, Aviation & Aerospace, Bilingual Market, Brand Development & Integration, Broadcast, Business Publications, Business-To-Business, Cable T.V., Catalogs, Children's Market, Co-op Advertising, Collateral, College, Commercial Photography, Communications, Computers & Software, Consulting, Consumer Goods, Consumer Marketing, Consumer Publications, Content, Corporate Communications, Corporate Identity, Cosmetics, Crisis Communications, Custom Publishing, Customer Relationship Management, Digital/Interactive, Direct Response Marketing, Direct-to-Consumer, E-Commerce, Education, Electronic Media, Electronics, Email, Engineering, Entertainment, Environmental, Event Planning & Marketing, Exhibit/Trade Shows, Faith Based, Fashion/Apparel, Financial, Food Service, Gay & Lesbian Market, Government/Political, Graphic Design, Health Care Services, High Technology, Hispanic Market, Hospitality, Household Goods, Identity Marketing, In-Store Advertising, Industrial, Infomercials, Information Technology, Integrated Marketing, International, Internet/Web Design, Investor Relations, Legal Services, Leisure, Local Marketing, Logo & Package Design, Luxury Products, Magazines, Marine, Market Research, Media Buying Services, Media Planning, Media Relations, Media Training, Medical Products, Men's Market, Merchandising, Mobile Marketing, Multicultural, Multimedia, New Product Development, New Technologies, Newspaper, Newspapers & Magazines, Out-of-Home Media, Outdoor, Over-50 Market, Package Design, Paid Searches, Pets , Pharmaceutical, Planning & Consultation, Point of Purchase, Point of Sale, Print, Product Placement, Production, Production (Ad, Film, Broadcast), Production (Print), Promotions, Public Relations, Publicity/Promotions, Publishing, RSS (Really Simple Syndication), Radio, Real Estate, Recruitment, Regional, Restaurant, Retail, Sales Promotion, Search Engine Optimization, Seniors' Market, Social Marketing/Nonprofit, Social Media, South Asian Market, Sponsorship, Sports Market, Stakeholders, Strategic Planning/Research, T.V., Technical Advertising, Telemarketing, Trade & Consumer Magazines, Transportation, Travel & Tourism, Urban Market, Viral/Buzz/Word of Mouth, Web (Banner Ads, Pop-ups, etc.), Women's Market, Yellow Pages Advertising

Approx. Annual Billings: $2,500,000

Christian Evans *(Pres & CEO)*

Accounts:
A&R Interiors Interior Design & Fine Furnishings; 2012
Bid Global; Scottsdale, AZ Jewelry Auctions - Asia Pacific & US; 2008
Bridgeall, Ltd.; Isle of Man, UK Fine Art & Master Graphics Auctions; 2007
DB Trading, Inc; Tenafly, NJ Fine Art Auctions; 2009
Denville Medical & Sports Rehabilitation; Denville, NJ Chiropractic, Wellness, Sports Rehabilitation; 2007
Diligent Board Member Services, Inc; New York, NY Corporate Governance-SAAS; 2009
Estate Liquidation & Auction Services; Pittsburgh, PA Estate Auctions
Fein Construction Luxury Residential Construction; 2012
Fuda Tile Retail Tile, Marble & Granite; 2011
Gerlach's Jewelers Retail & Fine Estate Jewelry; 2011
Global Life Rejuvenation Health Care; 2011
Hackensack Sleep & Pulmonary Center Health Care; 2011
Hollywood Tans; Daytona Beach, FL Tanning; 2008
Kimsey Auction Team Real Estate Auction; 2012
NJ Rug Warehouse; Carlstadt, NJ Oriental Rugs
Olympic Pool & Spa Pool & Spa; 2013
RJ Foods Gourmet Seafood for Food Services Industry; 2013
Santos Oil; Dover, NJ Heating Oil; 2010
Sponzilli Landscape Group Commercial & Residential Landscaping; 2010
Superior Structures, LLC (Agency of Record) Social Media, Website
US Auction Corporation; Leonia, NJ Fine Art Auction
Vibrance MedSpa; Denville, NJ Medspa & Skin Rejuvination; 2009

EVANS MEDIA GROUP

341 S College Rd #11, Wilmington, NC 28403
Tel.: (203) 512-0250
E-Mail: info@evansmediagroup.com
Web Site: www.evansmediagroup.com

Year Founded: 2002

Agency Specializes In: Media Planning, Media Relations, Search Engine Optimization

Paul Evans *(Pres & CMO)*
Sara Paxton *(Mng Partner)*
Michelle Truax *(Asst VP-Mktg & Media Strategies)*
Tyler Cook *(Dir-Bus Dev)*

Accounts:
Custom Color Imaging Services
KC Sports & Business Alliance (Agency of Record) Business Networking Services
Media Corp Creative Design Agencies

EVANSHARDY & YOUNG, INC.

829 De La Vina St, Santa Barbara, CA 93101-3238
Tel.: (805) 963-5841
Fax: (805) 564-4279
E-Mail: dhardy@ehy.com
Web Site: www.ehy.com

E-Mail for Key Personnel:
President: jevans@ehy.com
Creative Dir.: scott@ehy.com
Production Mgr.: ssonna@ehy.com

Employees: 40
Year Founded: 1986

Agency Specializes In: Advertising, Agriculture, Automotive, Brand Development & Integration, Broadcast, Business Publications, Business-To-Business, Cable T.V., Co-op Advertising, Collateral, Consulting, Consumer Goods, Consumer Marketing, Consumer Publications, Corporate Identity, Crisis Communications, Digital/Interactive, Electronic Media, Financial, Food Service, In-Store Advertising, Infomercials, Internet/Web Design, Leisure, Logo & Package Design, Magazines, Market Research, Media Buying Services, Media Planning, Media Relations, Medical Products, Merchandising, New Technologies, Newspaper, Newspapers & Magazines, Out-of-Home Media, Outdoor, Planning & Consultation, Print, Production, Public Relations, Publicity/Promotions, Radio, Restaurant, Retail, Strategic Planning/Research, T.V., Trade & Consumer Magazines, Transportation, Travel & Tourism

Approx. Annual Billings: $45,000,000

Breakdown of Gross Billings by Media: Brdcst.: 49%; Bus. Publs.: 3%; Consumer Publs.: 10%; Fees: 5%; Newsp.: 15%; Production: 13%; Pub. Rels.: 2%; Worldwide Web Sites: 3%

Dennis Hardy *(Co-Founder & Pres)*
Jim Evans *(Co-Founder & CEO)*
Scott Young *(Exec VP & Dir-Creative)*
Lily Katz-Smolenske *(Sr VP & Dir-Media)*
Kirk Evans *(VP & Dir-Creative)*
Pamela Landis *(VP & Dir-Brdcst Media)*
Suzan Sonna *(Mgr-Production)*

Accounts:
Baja Fresh; Anaheim, CA Fresh Mexican Restaurant; 2007
California Walnut Board; 2010
Chilean Fresh Fruit Association; Sacramento, CO Fresh Fruit from Chile; 2003
The Chumash Casino Resort; Santa Ynez, CA; 2004
Discover Today's Motorcycling Consumer Relations Program
Idaho Potato Commission; Boise, ID Idaho Potatoes; 1998
La Salsa; Anaheim, CA Fresh Mexican Restaurant; 2009

National Honey Board; Firestone, CO Industry Relations, Media Relations, Public Relations, Pure Honey; 2010
Peruvian Avocado Commission Hass Avocados from Peru; 2013
Tony Chachere's Creole Foods; Opelousas, LA; 2003
Viva Bene; Santa Barbara, CA Jenny Craig Franchise; 2007

EVB
(Formerly Evolution Bureau)
1740 Telegraph Ave, Oakland, CA 94612
Tel.: (415) 281-3950
Fax: (415) 281-3957
E-Mail: info@evb.com
Web Site: www.evb.com

Employees: 80
Year Founded: 2000

Agency Specializes In: Sponsorship

Revenue: $1,500,000

Daniel Stein *(Founder & CEO)*
Shane Ginsberg *(Pres)*
Gary Brown *(VP-Fin & Ops)*
Troy Burrows *(Exec Dir-Creative)*
Valerie Carlson *(Exec Dir-Creative-Design Innovation)*
Patrick Maravilla *(Grp Dir-Creative)*
David Byrd *(Dir-Design & Creative)*
Alex Grinton *(Assoc Dir-Creative)*
Jessica Josendale *(Acct Supvr)*
Meg Gallagher *(Copywriter)*

Accounts:
Absolut Campaign: "Absolut Miami", Campaign: "Absolut SF"
Adobe Campaign: "Adobe Remix"
Altoids Campaign: "The Stars on Facebook"
Analon Campaign: "Whisk Takers"
Arizona Jeans Co. Campaign: "Be Ridiculously You"
Big Heart Pet Brands Campaign: "Meowmix Cat Starter", Campaign: 9-Lives "Cat's Eye View"
Chivas Regal Campaign: "The Legend of Cannes"
College Inn Campaign: "Social Kitchen"
Contadina Campaign: "Famous Kitchens with Meg Ryan", Crushed Tomatoes, Tomato Sauce
Ebates
Facebook Campaign: "Facebook Studio Award", Campaign: "Facebook Studio"
Ferrara Candy Company Campaign: "Lemonhead"
General Electric Campaign: "The GE Air Show"
Gevalia Campaign: "Social Fika with Johan"
Glad Campaign: "Trashsmart"
International Delight Campaign: "Fifty Shades of International Delight"
Jameson Irish Whiskey Campaign: "Jameson 1780"
Jimmy John's Campaign: "Sandwich Cannon"
NFL Campaign: "Game Pass Rewind"
Nike Campaign: "Paint the Town Black Mamba"
Office Max Campaign: "Elf Yourself"
Silk Campaign: "Silk Ice Carver"
Skittles Campaign: "Mob the Rainbow"
Sumin Campaign: "Ballet But..."
Sunglass Hut Campaign: "Wow Mom Try on Tool"
Westfield Campaign: "Loliday Cards"
Wrigley's Campaign: "Bleeping Clean", Campaign: "Clean it Up", Campaign: "Serenading Unicorn", Campaign: "Sweet Talk 2.0", Campaign: "Your Life on a Pack"
Zynga Campaign: "I Heart Play"

EVE SECO DISPLAY INC.
209 Waters Edge, Valley Cottage, NY 10989
Tel.: (845) 268-5111
Fax: (845) 268-5115
E-Mail: johna@evesecodisplay.com
Web Site: www.evesecodisplay.com

Employees: 3
Year Founded: 1999

Agency Specializes In: Consulting, Electronics, Entertainment, Fashion/Apparel, Graphic Design, Luxury Products, Point of Purchase, Point of Sale, Production, Production (Print), Promotions, Retail, Sales Promotion

Approx. Annual Billings: $1,000,000

John Amtmann *(Owner & Pres)*

Accounts:
Chanel
Clarins
Korg USA; Melville, NY
LVMH
Tommy Bahama
Victoria's Secret

THE EVENT AGENCY
100 S Ola Vista, San Clemente, CA 92672
Tel.: (949) 542-4830
Fax: (949) 218-9038
E-Mail: information@eventagent.us
Web Site: eventagent.us

Employees: 5
Year Founded: 2003

Agency Specializes In: Advertising, Advertising Specialties, Alternative Advertising, Broadcast, Business-To-Business, Cable T.V., Children's Market, Co-op Advertising, Collateral, Consumer Marketing, Corporate Communications, Direct Response Marketing, Event Planning & Marketing, Exhibit/Trade Shows, Experience Design, Graphic Design, In-Store Advertising, Local Marketing, Magazines, Media Buying Services, Media Relations, Newspaper, Newspapers & Magazines, Outdoor, Planning & Consultation, Print, Promotions, Publicity/Promotions, Radio, Sales Promotion, Sports Market, Strategic Planning/Research, T.V., Teen Market

Brian Bouquet *(Pres)*

Accounts:
The High Kings Traveling Live Entertainment; 2007
Jig-A-Loo Lubricant; Ontario, Canada Silicone Lubricant; 2005
Long Beach Convention & Visitors Bureau; Long Beach, CA Events; 2004
Outdoor Adventure & Winter Sports Expo; Ontario, CA Outdoor Retail Expo; 2007
Silverback Music; Los Angeles, CA Music Artist Management; 2007
Theatre League; Kansas City, MO Theatrical Touring; 2005

EVENTIGE MEDIA GROUP
1501 Broadway 12th Fl, New York, NY 10036
Tel.: (646) 998-5445
Fax: (646) 786-5542
E-Mail: info@eventige.com
Web Site: www.eventige.com

Year Founded: 2008

Agency Specializes In: Advertising, Digital/Interactive, Social Media, Strategic Planning/Research

Alexei Alankin *(Founder & CEO)*
Roman Rabinovich *(VP-Ops)*
Mike Manuel *(Dir-Creative)*
Marissa Puttagio *(Dir-Creative)*
Anthony Choice *(Mgr-Event)*

Accounts:
Boost Promotions

EVENTIV (MARKETING, DESIGN & DISPLAY)
10116 Blue Creek N, Whitehouse, OH 43571
Tel.: (419) 877-5711
E-Mail: jan@eventiv.com
Web Site: www.eventiv.com

E-Mail for Key Personnel:
President: jan@eventiv.com

Employees: 3
Year Founded: 1999

Agency Specializes In: Advertising, Advertising Specialties, Brand Development & Integration, Broadcast, Business Publications, Business-To-Business, Cable T.V., Catalogs, Collateral, Commercial Photography, Communications, Consulting, Consumer Goods, Corporate Communications, Corporate Identity, Digital/Interactive, Direct Response Marketing, Direct-to-Consumer, Electronic Media, Email, Environmental, Event Planning & Marketing, Exhibit/Trade Shows, Graphic Design, Health Care Services, High Technology, Identity Marketing, In-Store Advertising, Industrial, Internet/Web Design, Local Marketing, Logo & Package Design, Magazines, Marine, Media Buying Services, Merchandising, Multimedia, Newspaper, Newspapers & Magazines, Outdoor, Planning & Consultation, Point of Purchase, Point of Sale, Print, Production, Promotions, Publicity/Promotions, Sales Promotion, Strategic Planning/Research, T.V., Technical Advertising, Trade & Consumer Magazines, Transportation

Approx. Annual Billings: $500,000

Breakdown of Gross Billings by Media: Bus. Publs.: $25,000; Collateral: $200,000; Exhibits/Trade Shows: $200,000; Other: $25,000; Plng. & Consultation: $50,000

Janice Robie *(Owner)*

Accounts:
Toledo Refinery
VP Oil

EVERETT STUDIOS
5 N Greenwich Rd, Armonk, NY 10504
Tel.: (914) 997-2200
Fax: (914) 997-2479
E-Mail: robbie@goeverett.com
Web Site: www.goeverett.com

Employees: 30
Year Founded: 1961

Agency Specializes In: Business-To-Business, Sales Promotion

Approx. Annual Billings: $3,500,000

Robbie Everett *(Owner)*
Howard Davies *(Dir-Creative)*
Bill Loscher *(Dir-Creative)*
Kathleen Zazzaro *(Mgr-Graphic Display)*
Paul Kiley *(Acct Exec)*

Accounts:
Dannon
Gerber; Parsippany, NJ; 1998
Heineken; White Plains, NY; 1996
IBM; Armonk, NY; 1961
Kraft
Mastercard

THE EVERSOLE GROUP, LLC
402A Legacy Pk, Ridgeland, MS 39157
Tel.: (601) 366-6814
Fax: (601) 977-5224
E-Mail: info@theeversolegroup.com
Web Site: www.theeversolegroup.com

Employees: 6

Agency Specializes In: Advertising

Craig Eversole *(Pres)*

Accounts:
Albany Bank & Trust
Atlantic BacGroup Inc.
Texas National

EVERY IDEA MARKETING
355 NE Lafayette Ave, Bend, OR 97701
Tel.: (541) 383-2669
Fax: (541) 383-2072
E-Mail: ideas@every-idea.com
Web Site: www.every-idea.com

Agency Specializes In: Advertising, Brand Development & Integration, Broadcast, Print, Public Relations, Strategic Planning/Research

Wendie Every *(Principal)*

Accounts:
Michi Designs

EVOK ADVERTISING
1485 International Pwky, Heathrow, FL 32746
Tel.: (407) 302-4416
Fax: (407) 302-4417
E-Mail: info@evokad.com
Web Site: www.evokad.com

E-Mail for Key Personnel:
President: larry@evokad.com
Creative Dir.: scott@evokad.com

Employees: 30
Year Founded: 2002

National Agency Associations: AAF-PRSA

Agency Specializes In: Advertising, Bilingual Market, Brand Development & Integration, Broadcast, Business Publications, Business-To-Business, Cable T.V., Collateral, Communications, Consumer Marketing, Consumer Publications, Corporate Communications, Corporate Identity, Digital/Interactive, Direct Response Marketing, E-Commerce, Electronic Media, Entertainment, Event Planning & Marketing, Exhibit/Trade Shows, Gay & Lesbian Market, Graphic Design, Health Care Services, High Technology, Internet/Web Design, Legal Services, Leisure, Local Marketing, Logo & Package Design, Magazines, Marine, Media Buying Services, Merchandising, New Product Development, Newspaper, Newspapers & Magazines, Outdoor, Over-50 Market, Planning & Consultation, Point of Purchase, Point of Sale, Print, Public Relations, Publicity/Promotions, Radio, Recruitment, Restaurant, Sales Promotion, Sports Market, Strategic Planning/Research, Sweepstakes, T.V., Trade & Consumer Magazines, Transportation, Travel & Tourism, Yellow Pages Advertising

Approx. Annual Billings: $32,000,000

Larry Meador *(CEO)*
Mark Holt *(Mng Partner)*
Terry Mooney *(COO)*
Chris LeBlanc *(VP & Exec Dir-Creative)*
Jim Roxbury *(VP & Client Svcs Dir)*
Stewart Hill *(VP-Strategic Plng)*
Kathy Fordham *(Acct Dir)*
Kerri Nagy Byrd *(Dir-Media)*
Donna Tinoco *(Dir-PR)*
Carly Laskey *(Sr Acct Mgr)*
Cheryl Parker *(Acct Supvr)*

Accounts:
Hilton Hotels New York Hilton
New-Hoop Culture (Advertising Agency of Record)
Kenwood Car Audio (Agency of Record)
Moe's Southwest Grill
Ocala/Marion County Visitors & Convention Bureau Brand Development, Marketing, PR, Planning, Social Media

EVOKE HEALTH
101 Ave of the Americas 13th Fl, New York, NY 10013
Tel.: (212) 228-7200
E-Mail: info@evokehealth.com
Web Site: www.evokehealth.com

National Agency Associations: 4A's

Agency Specializes In: Advertising

Reid Connolly *(CEO)*
Heather Torak *(COO)*
Elissa Sherman *(SVP)*
Katherine Menges *(VP)*

Accounts:
New-Celgene Otezla

EVOKE IDEA GROUP, INC.
902 S Randall Rd Ste 336C, Saint Charles, IL 60174
Tel.: (630) 879-3846
Fax: (630) 761-9407
Toll Free: (866) 842-7424
E-Mail: jsailer@evokeideagroup.com
Web Site: www.evokeideagroup.com

E-Mail for Key Personnel:
President: jsailer@evokeideagroup.com

Employees: 10
Year Founded: 1996

National Agency Associations: AMA

Agency Specializes In: Advertising, Brand Development & Integration, Business-To-Business, Catalogs, Children's Market, Co-op Advertising, Collateral, Communications, Consumer Goods, Consumer Marketing, Consumer Publications, Corporate Communications, Corporate Identity, Direct Response Marketing, Direct-to-Consumer, Email, Event Planning & Marketing, Exhibit/Trade Shows, Graphic Design, Health Care Services, High Technology, Identity Marketing, In-Store Advertising, Industrial, Internet/Web Design, Leisure, Logo & Package Design, Medical Products, New Product Development, Newspapers & Magazines, Outdoor, Package Design, Point of Purchase, Point of Sale, Print, Production (Print), Retail, Sales Promotion, Trade & Consumer Magazines, Travel & Tourism, Web (Banner Ads, Pop-ups, etc.)

Jennifer Sailer *(Pres)*

Accounts:
Boise Paper Solutions; 1997

EVOL8TION LLC
33 W 37th St, New York, NY 10018
Tel.: (650) 265-0802
E-Mail: info@startupsforbrands.com
Web Site: www.startupsforbrands.com

Year Founded: 2012

Agency Specializes In: Advertising, Brand Development & Integration

Joseph Jaffe *(Co-Founder & CEO)*
Gina Waldhorn *(Co-Founder & COO)*
Lauren Brown *(Dir-Partnership)*

Accounts:
DreamIT Ventures
Kraft
Mondelez
Sumpto

EVOLUTION BUREAU
(Name Changed to EVB)

EVOLVE, INC.
1210 E Arlington Blvd, Greenville, NC 27858
Tel.: (252) 754-2957
Fax: (252) 754-2832
E-Mail: prittani@evolveinc.com
Web Site: www.evolveinc.com

Employees: 18
Year Founded: 2003

Agency Specializes In: Advertising, Advertising Specialties, Affluent Market, Arts, Automotive, Bilingual Market, Brand Development & Integration, Broadcast, Business-To-Business, Cable T.V., Catalogs, Co-op Advertising, Commercial Photography, Communications, Consulting, Consumer Goods, Consumer Marketing, Corporate Communications, Corporate Identity, Crisis Communications, Digital/Interactive, Direct Response Marketing, E-Commerce, Engineering, Exhibit/Trade Shows, Experience Design, Financial, Graphic Design, Health Care Services, High Technology, Infomercials, Integrated Marketing, Internet/Web Design, Local Marketing, Logo & Package Design, Marine, Market Research, Media Buying Services, Media Planning, Media Relations, Medical Products, Mobile Marketing, Multimedia, Newspaper, Out-of-Home Media, Package Design, Planning & Consultation, Point of Purchase, Point of Sale, Print, Production (Ad, Film, Broadcast), Production (Print), Public Relations, Radio, Regional, Sales Promotion, Search Engine Optimization, Strategic Planning/Research, T.V., Web (Banner Ads, Pop-ups, etc.), Yellow Pages Advertising

Approx. Annual Billings: $2,000,000

Tya Young *(Co-Founder & Gen Mgr)*
Will Daugherty *(CEO)*
Matt Fawcett *(Dir-Info Sys)*
Brad Long *(Dir-Digital Strategy)*
Brian Taylor *(Dir-Creative)*
Kevin Trenga *(Dir-Acct Svcs)*
Shannon Lewis *(Mgr-Acctg & HR)*
Lee Parker *(Acct Exec)*

EVOLVE MEDIA LLC
(Formerly Gorilla Nation Media, LLC)
5140 W Goldleaf Cir Fl 3, Los Angeles, CA 90056
Tel.: (310) 449-1890
Fax: (310) 449-1891
Web Site: www.evolvemediallc.com

Employees: 120

Agency Specializes In: Advertising, Advertising Specialties, Affluent Market, Brand Development & Integration, Email, Entertainment, Guerilla Marketing, Internet/Web Design, Logo & Package Design, Luxury Products, New Product Development, New Technologies, Web (Banner Ads, Pop-ups, etc.)

Brian Fitzgerald *(Co-Founder & Pres)*

Travlin McCormack *(CTO)*
John Keefer *(VP & Gen Mgr-CraveOnline)*
Betsy Flounders Novak *(VP-Sls-Crave Online)*
Jessie McIntosh *(Sr Producer-Digital Mktg)*
Jessica Naughton *(Sr Producer-Digital Mktg)*
Adam Landau *(Assoc Dir-Mktg Production)*
Carolyn Johnson *(Mgr-Integrated Mktg & Strategy-TotallyHer)*
Danielle Shinn *(Acct Exec)*

Accounts:
Cookie Jar Entertainment Children's Entertainment; 2007
Deloitte
Gawker Media
Hallmark Cards, Inc
Mattel Properties Online Display Ad Inventory; 2008
Playboy Enterprises Playboy Online; 2007
Reuters Canada
Singingfool.com
Times of India
World Wrestling Entertainment

Branch

DogTime Media Inc.
27 Maiden Ln Ste 700, San Francisco, CA 94508
(See Separate Listing)

E.W. BULLOCK ASSOCIATES
730 Bayfront Pkwy Ste 5, Pensacola, FL 32502-6250
Tel.: (850) 438-4015
Fax: (850) 433-6104
E-Mail: ads@ewbullock.com
Web Site: www.ewbullock.com

E-Mail for Key Personnel:
President: ewb@ewbullock.com
Creative Dir.: saraht@ewbullock.com
Public Relations: ashley@ewbullock.com

Employees: 12
Year Founded: 1982

National Agency Associations: AAF

Agency Specializes In: Advertising, Co-op Advertising, Communications, Digital/Interactive, Event Planning & Marketing, Graphic Design, Internet/Web Design, Market Research, Media Buying Services, Media Planning, Newspapers & Magazines, Outdoor, Production, Production (Ad, Film, Broadcast), Production (Print), Public Relations, Radio, T.V., Travel & Tourism, Web (Banner Ads, Pop-ups, etc.)

Ellis W. Bullock, III *(Founder)*
Pete Gurtowsky *(Dir-Art)*
Trisha Idoni *(Dir-Art)*
Sarah Turner *(Dir-Art & Creative)*
Sandy Bartoszewicz *(Office Mgr)*

Accounts:
Appriver, Inc.
Beck Property Inc.
Bullock Tice Associates
Centennial Imports
Crowne Plaza Grand Hotel
Emerald Coast Utilities Authority
Escambia County Emergency Management/Public Information
Fiesta of Five Flags
Gulf Shores Golf Association
Modica Market
Morris Agency
National Naval Aviation Museum
O'Sullivan Creel LLP
Santa Rosa Island Authority
Sterling Companies
Village of Baytowne Wharf
Virtual Media Integration

EWI WORLDWIDE
834 Inman Village Pkwy NE Ste 150B, Atlanta, GA 30307
Tel.: (734) 525-9010
Fax: (734) 762-3310
E-Mail: contact@ewiworldwide.com
Web Site: www.ewiworldwide.com

Agency Specializes In: Brand Development & Integration, Communications, Exhibit/Trade Shows, Product Placement

Dominic Silvio *(Chm & CEO)*
Tony Barras *(Pres-Labor)*
Alan LaFreniere *(Pres-Retail)*
Arlene Petrush *(Exec VP-Sls)*
Kevin Pritchard *(Sr VP-Intl)*
Sheri Sullivan *(Sr VP-Strategy)*
Angela Heiple *(VP-Mktg & Comm)*

Accounts:
Coca-Cola Refreshments USA, Inc.
Mooney

EXCELER8
301 Clematis St Ste 3000, West Palm Beach, FL 33401
Tel.: (561) 584-9088
E-Mail: info@exceler8.com
Web Site: www.exceler8.com

Year Founded: 2005

Agency Specializes In: Advertising, Brand Development & Integration, Business-To-Business, Communications, Consulting, Consumer Marketing, Digital/Interactive, Direct-to-Consumer, Electronic Media, Graphic Design, Guerilla Marketing, High Technology, Information Technology, Internet/Web Design, Local Marketing, Media Buying Services, Media Training, Multicultural, Newspaper, Newspapers & Magazines, Paid Searches, Podcasting, Print, Publishing, RSS (Really Simple Syndication), Recruitment, Sales Promotion, Search Engine Optimization, Social Marketing/Nonprofit, Viral/Buzz/Word of Mouth, Web (Banner Ads, Pop-ups, etc.), Yellow Pages Advertising

Julian Seery Gude *(Pres & Dir-Creative)*

Accounts:
Allianz Life; Minneapolis, MN; 2005
Knight Ridder Digital; San Jose, CA
R Croot Inc; West Palm Beach, FL; 2006
Russell Investment Group; Tacoma, WA; 2006

EXCLAIM LLC
2125 Western Ave Ste 302, Seattle, WA 98121
Tel.: (206) 368-0121
E-Mail: info@exclaimllc.com
Web Site: www.exclaimllc.com

Year Founded: 1998

Agency Specializes In: Advertising, Brand Development & Integration, Media Buying Services, Public Relations, Strategic Planning/Research

John Schuler *(Owner & Dir-Creative)*
Deanna Waters *(Acct Dir)*

Accounts:
Sport Restaurant & Bar

EXECUTIVE1 MEDIA GROUP
12366 Blazing Star Ln, Victorville, CA 92323
Tel.: (760) 561-5500
Web Site: www.e1mgmedia.com

Employees: 4
Year Founded: 2003

Agency Specializes In: Affluent Market, African-American Market, Cable T.V., Digital/Interactive, Email, Infomercials, Local Marketing, Mobile Marketing, Newspaper, Newspapers & Magazines, Out-of-Home Media, Outdoor, Print, Production, Promotions, Radio, T.V., Web (Banner Ads, Pop-ups, etc.)

Derrick Dzurko *(Owner)*

Accounts:
Curls Hair Products

EXIT
1509 Louisiana St, Little Rock, AR 72202
Tel.: (501) 907-7337
Fax: (501) 907-7339
Web Site: www.exitmarketing.net

Employees: 6
Year Founded: 2004

Shawn Solloway *(Pres)*
Matt Owen *(Creative Dir)*
Alexandria Cantrell *(Mgr-Acct & Social Media)*

Accounts:
Allied Bank; Mulberry, AK
Arkansas Hospital Association
Keeton International
Little Sicilian Sauces
Make A Wish
Qualchoice

EXIT10
323 W Camden St, Baltimore, MD 21201
Tel.: (443) 573-8210
Fax: (443) 573-8220
E-Mail: info@exit10.com
Web Site: www.exit10.com

Year Founded: 2006

Agency Specializes In: Brand Development & Integration, Guerilla Marketing

Jonathan Helfman *(Owner & Dir-Creative)*
David White *(Mng Partner)*
Ali Byro *(Dir-Client Ops)*
Eric Lindstrom *(Dir-Digital)*
Dan Rapp *(Mgr-Production & Acct Supvr)*
Elizabeth Merchant *(Sr Designer)*
Sara Tomko *(Sr Designer)*
Cassie Fick *(Coord)*
Rachel Ventura *(Jr Graphic Designer)*

Accounts:
McGraw Hill

EXPECT ADVERTISING, INC.
1033 Route 46, Clifton, NJ 07013
Tel.: (973) 777-8886
E-Mail: info@expectad.com
Web Site: www.expectad.com

Employees: 20
Year Founded: 2000

Agency Specializes In: Above-the-Line, Advertising, Advertising Specialties, Affiliate Marketing, Affluent Market, African-American Market, Agriculture, Alternative Advertising, Arts, Asian Market, Automotive, Aviation & Aerospace, Below-the-Line, Bilingual Market, Brand Development & Integration, Branded Entertainment, Broadcast, Business Publications,

Business-To-Business, Cable T.V., Catalogs, Children's Market, Co-op Advertising, Collateral, College, Commercial Photography, Communications, Computers & Software, Consulting, Consumer Goods, Consumer Marketing, Consumer Publications, Content, Corporate Communications, Corporate Identity, Cosmetics, Crisis Communications, Custom Publishing, Customer Relationship Management, Digital/Interactive, Direct Response Marketing, Direct-to-Consumer, E-Commerce, Education, Electronic Media, Electronics, Email, Engineering, Entertainment, Environmental, Event Planning & Marketing, Exhibit/Trade Shows, Experience Design, Faith Based, Fashion/Apparel, Financial, Food Service, Game Integration, Gay & Lesbian Market, Government/Political, Graphic Design, Guerilla Marketing, Health Care Services, High Technology, Hispanic Market, Hospitality, Household Goods, Identity Marketing, In-Store Advertising, Industrial, Infomercials, Information Technology, Integrated Marketing, International, Internet/Web Design, Investor Relations, Legal Services, Leisure, Local Marketing, Logo & Package Design, Luxury Products, Magazines, Marine, Market Research, Media Buying Services, Media Planning, Media Relations, Media Training, Medical Products, Men's Market, Merchandising, Mobile Marketing, Multicultural, Multimedia, New Product Development, New Technologies, Newspaper, Newspapers & Magazines, Out-of-Home Media, Outdoor, Over-50 Market, Package Design, Paid Searches, Pets , Pharmaceutical, Planning & Consultation, Podcasting, Point of Purchase, Point of Sale, Print, Product Placement, Production (Ad, Film, Broadcast), Production (Print), Promotions, Public Relations, Publicity/Promotions, Publishing, RSS (Really Simple Syndication), Radio, Real Estate, Recruitment, Regional, Restaurant, Retail, Sales Promotion, Search Engine Optimization, Seniors' Market, Social Marketing/Nonprofit, Social Media, South Asian Market, Sponsorship, Sports Market, Stakeholders, Strategic Planning/Research, Sweepstakes, Syndication, T.V., Technical Advertising, Teen Market, Telemarketing, Trade & Consumer Magazines, Transportation, Travel & Tourism, Tween Market, Urban Market, Viral/Buzz/Word of Mouth, Web (Banner Ads, Pop-ups, etc.), Women's Market, Yellow Pages Advertising

Approx. Annual Billings: $2,200,000

Paul Gilliam *(Sr Dir-Art)*
Daniel Fox *(Dir-Digital Media, Digital Photography & Digital Production)*
Susan Levant *(Dir-Creative)*
Rick Pirman *(Dir-Creative & Art)*

Accounts:
Amylin; San Diego, CA Byetta, Symlin; 2008
Bolton Medical Relay Stent Grafts
Cordis; Somerset, NJ Cordis Products; 2008
DCA; 2011
DPA; 2012
Johnson & Johnson; 2010
Newell; 2011
Orasure; Bethlehem, CA Histofreezer; 2010
Ortho Biotech; Horsham, PA Procrit; 2008
Pepsi Sales Force Training; 2009
RBM; Dallas, TX RBM; 2009
Saiom Technologies; 2011

EXPERIAN MARKETING SERVICES

475 Anton Blvd, Costa Mesa, CA 92626
Tel.: (714) 830-7000
Toll Free: (866) 626-6479
Web Site: www.experian.com/marketing-services

Employees: 17,000

Agency Specializes In: Consumer Marketing

Pasquale Pellegrini *(Chief Res Officer/Gen Mgr-Consumer Insights Bus)*
Matt Seeley *(Pres-North America)*
Michael Meltz *(Exec VP-Strategy-Global)*
Emad Georgy *(Sr VP-Global Product Dev)*
Ashley Johnston *(Sr VP-Mktg-Global)*
Ian Wright *(VP-Global Product Mgmt-Targeting NA)*
Kristine Snyder *(Sr Mgr-PR)*

Accounts:
The Hearst Corporation

Branch

Experian Marketing Services

29 Broadway 6th Fl, New York, NY 10006
Toll Free: (866) 626-6479
Web Site: www.experian.com/marketing-services

Jonathan Hulford-Funnell *(Mng Dir)*
Matt Seeley *(Pres-North America)*
Michael Meltz *(Exec VP-Strategy-Global)*
Michael Kennedy *(VP-Fin-NA Mktg Svcs)*
Jay Stocki *(VP-Digital Svcs)*
Caliopie Walsh *(VP-HR)*
Michael Puffer *(Mgr-Mobile Mktg)*

Accounts:
The Hearst Corporation

EXPERIENCE ADVERTISING INC

10871 NW 52nd St, Sunrise, FL 33351
Tel.: (877) 743-0345
Web Site: www.experienceadvertising.com

Year Founded: 2007

Agency Specializes In: Advertising, Email, Internet/Web Design, Search Engine Optimization, Social Media

Evan Weber *(CEO)*

Accounts:
A. Jaffe Online Marketing, Social Media
Diamondscape
HancockFabrics.com
HookedonPhonics.com
iHomeAudio.com
Phone.com

EXPOSURE

393 Broadway 2nd Fl, New York, NY 10013
Tel.: (212) 226-2530
E-Mail: info-ny@exposure.net
Web Site: america.exposure.net

Year Founded: 2004

Agency Specializes In: Advertising, Digital/Interactive, Event Planning & Marketing, Social Media, Strategic Planning/Research

Tom Phillips *(Mng Partner & Creative Dir)*
John Benson *(Mng Dir)*
Carrie Roberts *(Head-Production)*
D. J. Hardy *(Acct Dir)*
Irwin Tobias Matutina *(Dir-Art)*
Sam Rookwood *(Dir-Client Svcs)*
Virgilio Serrano *(Dir-IT)*
Thomas Liriano *(Mgr-Fin)*
Joanna Hughes *(Coord-Showroom)*

Accounts:
Bill Blass Group Media Relations, Public Relations
Coca-Cola
Dr. Martens

EXSEL ADVERTISING

559 Main St., Sturbridge, MA 01518
Tel.: (774) 241-0041
Fax: (774) 241-0129
Web Site: www.exselad.com

Agency Specializes In: Advertising, Brand Development & Integration, Logo & Package Design, Media Planning, Strategic Planning/Research

Rich Suitum *(Pres)*
Kathy Ruddy *(VP-Ops)*

Accounts:
Higgins Powersports
Hometown Insurance Center
Mylec (Agency of Record)

EXTRA STRENGTH MARKETING COMMUNICATIONS

1804 S Pearl St, Denver, CO 80210
Tel.: (303) 744-8089
Fax: (303) 744-8243
E-Mail: info@extrastrength.net
Web Site: www.extrastrength.net

Employees: 6
Year Founded: 1994

Steve Koloskus *(Principal)*

Accounts:
Affiliated Banks
American Heart Association
Armstrong Vineyards
Big Brothers & Big Sisters of Colorado
Colorado Ballet
Colorado Division of Wildlife
Epoch Estate
Gateway Battered Women's Shelter
Peaberry Coffee
Rainbow Rewards
Rocky Mountain Health Centers
Shea Homes
Shea Properties
Urban Peak

EXTRACTABLE, INC.

612 Howard St Ste 300, San Francisco, CA 94105
Tel.: (415) 426-3600
Fax: (415) 426-3601
Web Site: www.extractable.com

Year Founded: 1999

Agency Specializes In: Advertising, Digital/Interactive, Mobile Marketing, Social Media

Craig McLaughlin *(Co-Founder & CEO)*
Mark Ryan *(Co-Founder)*
Esther Scanlan *(CFO)*
Melanie Lowe *(COO)*
Sean Brown *(CTO)*
Simon Mathews *(Chief Strategy Officer)*
Ernie Chan *(VP-Client Svcs)*
Gordon McNee *(VP-Creative)*
Joel Oxman *(VP-Bus Dev)*
Jon Chiappa *(Dir-Project Mgmt)*

Accounts:
Avago Technologies
BlueCross BlueShield
CareCredit
FedEx
GIA
GoPro
International Association of Business Communicators Digital, Iabc.com, Redesign
Kodak Imaging Network, Inc.
Leapfrog
Lending Tree

Logix Federal Credit Union
Micron
Netgear, Inc.
The Newport Group Design, Strategy, UX
RS Investments
Solta Medical, Inc.
Sunset Magazine
Symantec Corporation
TRUSTe
Visa

EXTREME MEASURES CREATIVE

4737 Sterling Cross, Nashville, TN 37211
Tel.: (615) 331-5649
Fax: (615) 828-7125
E-Mail: info@extrememeasurescreative.com
Web Site: www.extrememeasurescreative.com

Agency Specializes In: Advertising, Graphic Design, Internet/Web Design, Logo & Package Design, Media Buying Services, Radio, Social Media, T.V.

Jason R. Coleman *(Owner & Pres)*

Accounts:
Acumen Realty
Advanced Technical Services

EYE CUE, INC.

3257 Lk Park Cir, Anchorage, AK 99517
Tel.: (907) 248-7663
Fax: (907) 243-1520
Toll Free: (877) 297-7445
E-Mail: info@eye-cue.com
Web Site: www.facebook.com/pages/Eye-Cue-Productions/232001283641141

Employees: 2
Year Founded: 1988

Agency Specializes In: Advertising, Production, Radio

John Wedin *(Owner)*

Accounts:
AutoMax
Capitol Bank
Century Bank
First National Bank
Hawaiian Vacations
Kenai Coastal Tours
Optus Communications
Pacific Telecom, Inc.
Payless Drugstores
Prime Cable
PTI NET
Westmark Hotels

EYEBALL ON THE FLOOR, INC.

(Private-Parent-Single Location)
187 Lafayette St Fl 2, New York, NY 10013
Tel.: (212) 431-5324
Fax: (212) 431-6793
E-Mail: info@eyeballnyc.com
Web Site: www.eyeballnyc.com

Employees: 15
Year Founded: 1991

Agency Specializes In: Brand Development & Integration, Digital/Interactive, Print, Search Engine Optimization

Revenue: $1,000,000

David Edelstein *(Mng Dir)*

Accounts:
New-AOL

Branch

Eyeball Digital

444 Brickell Ave, Miami, FL 33131
Tel.: (786) 615-6720
E-Mail: info@eyeballnyc.com
Web Site: www.eyeballnyc.com

Agency Specializes In: Advertising, Brand Development & Integration, Digital/Interactive, Print, Search Engine Optimization, Social Media

Erica Amalfitano *(Strategist-Content)*
Samantha Henry *(Jr Copywriter)*

Accounts:
New-Polaroid Brand (Global Agency of Record)

EYESEA SOLUTIONS

825 Brickell Bay Dr Ste 246, Miami, FL 33131
Tel.: (786) 602-9114
E-Mail: contact@eyeseasolutions.com
Web Site: www.eyeseasolutions.com

Agency Specializes In: Advertising, Email, Event Planning & Marketing, Internet/Web Design, Logo & Package Design, Media Planning, Radio, Search Engine Optimization, Social Media, T.V.

Gabriel Carvalho *(Pres)*
Juliana Bittencourt *(Dir-Mktg & Comm)*

Accounts:
AcheiUSA
Banco do Brasil S.A.
TAM S.A.

FABCOM

7819 E Greenway Rd Ste 5, Scottsdale, AZ 85260
Tel.: (480) 922-1122
Fax: (480) 922-0606
E-Mail: brian@fabianocom.com
Web Site: www.fabcomlive.com

Employees: 25
Year Founded: 1992

Agency Specializes In: Advertising, Brand Development & Integration, Strategic Planning/Research

Approx. Annual Billings: $30,700,000

Brian Fabiano *(Founder & CEO)*
Mark Weber *(CFO)*
Chris Blaine *(Sr Dir-Interactive Art)*
Latham Floyde *(Sr Dir-Art)*
Sean Appelmann *(Dir-Creative)*
Yoni Novik *(Dir-Tech Integration)*
Ty Sugg *(Dir-Photography)*
Brianna Jennings *(Acct Supvr)*

Accounts:
America West Airlines
American Heart Association
Bank One
Disney
FedEx
HBO
IBM
Mitel; Chandler,AZ Telecommunications; 1999
Motorola Solutions, Inc.
Novartis
University of Advancing Technology
Vestiage Inc Advertising, Marketing, Monterey Bay Nutraceuticals, RegiMEN

FACTION MEDIA

1730 Blake St Ste 200, Denver, CO 80202
Tel.: (303) 339-0206
E-Mail: info@factionmedia.com
Web Site: www.factionmedia.com

Employees: 25

Agency Specializes In: Advertising, Affiliate Marketing, Alternative Advertising, Brand Development & Integration, Content, Digital/Interactive, Direct Response Marketing, Email, Event Planning & Marketing, Logo & Package Design, Market Research, Media Buying Services, Media Planning, Multicultural, Print, Promotions, Radio, Search Engine Optimization, Sponsorship, Strategic Planning/Research, T.V., Web (Banner Ads, Pop-ups, etc.)

Breakdown of Gross Billings by Media: D.M.: 5%; Fees: 5%; Graphic Design: 15%; Internet Adv.: 40%; Other: 5%; Plng. & Consultation: 5%; Print: 10%; Strategic Planning/Research: 5%; Worldwide Web Sites: 10%

Aaron Batte *(Co-Founder & Pres)*
Dave Greves *(Founder & CEO)*
Mike Swainey *(Acct Dir)*
Liz Burgess *(Dir-Ops)*
John Gilbert *(Dir-Integrated Svcs)*
Dan Schrad *(Dir-Creative Svcs)*
Melaina Daniel *(Acct Mgr)*
Todd Nieber *(Graphic Designer & Designer-Web)*
Christina Donegan *(Sr Program Mgr)*

Accounts:
New-Dawn Food Products (Digital Agency of Record)
Johns Manville
TW Telecom

FACTOR1 STUDIOS

2121 S Mill Ave Ste 203, Tempe, AZ 85282
Tel.: (602) 334-4806
E-Mail: sayhello@factor1studios.com
Web Site: www.factor1studios.com

Year Founded: 2004

Agency Specializes In: Advertising, Digital/Interactive, Internet/Web Design

Matt Adams *(Owner)*

Accounts:
Techpinions

FACTOR360 DESIGN + TECHNOLOGY

120 Euclid Ave, Pierre, SD 57501
Tel.: (605) 945-1101
E-Mail: dennis@factor360.com
Web Site: www.factor360.com

Employees: 10
Year Founded: 1993

Agency Specializes In: Advertising, Advertising Specialties, Alternative Advertising, Arts, Automotive, Broadcast, Business-To-Business, Cable T.V., Catalogs, Children's Market, Co-op Advertising, Collateral, College, Commercial Photography, Communications, Computers & Software, Consulting, Consumer Marketing, Consumer Publications, Content, Corporate Communications, Digital/Interactive, Direct Response Marketing, Direct-to-Consumer, E-Commerce, Education, Electronic Media, Email, Engineering, Environmental, Exhibit/Trade Shows, Financial, Food Service, Gay & Lesbian Market, Government/Political, Graphic Design, Guerilla Marketing, Health Care Services, Hospitality, Identity Marketing, In-Store Advertising, Industrial, Information Technology, Integrated Marketing, Internet/Web Design, Legal Services, Leisure,

Local Marketing, Logo & Package Design, Luxury Products, Magazines, Market Research, Media Relations, Medical Products, Men's Market, Multimedia, New Product Development, Newspaper, Newspapers & Magazines, Out-of-Home Media, Outdoor, Over-50 Market, Package Design, Paid Searches, Planning & Consultation, Point of Purchase, Point of Sale, Print, Production, Production (Ad, Film, Broadcast), Production (Print), Promotions, Public Relations, Publicity/Promotions, Radio, Recruitment, Regional, Retail, Sales Promotion, Search Engine Optimization, Seniors' Market, Sponsorship, Stakeholders, T.V., Technical Advertising, Trade & Consumer Magazines, Transportation, Travel & Tourism, Urban Market, Web (Banner Ads, Pop-ups, etc.), Women's Market

Dennis Ryckman *(Founder & CEO)*
Aftin Eich *(Dir-Creative & Mktg)*
Carolyn Ryckman *(Engr-Web & Designer-Database)*
Joanne Pullman *(Designer)*

Accounts:
Chautauqua County Humane Society
Grand Lodge Hunting
Human Society
Lehman Trikes
Millers Sellers Heroux Architect
Sioux Falls Humane Society
South Dakota Realtors Association
South Dakota University Center
Tumbleweed Lodge

FACTORY DESIGN LABS

158 Fillmore St, Denver, CO 80206
Tel.: (888) 663-5282
Fax: (303) 573-5975
Web Site: www.factorylabs.com

Employees: 95
Year Founded: 1997

Agency Specializes In: Advertising, Automotive, Brand Development & Integration, Branded Entertainment, Collateral, Customer Relationship Management, Entertainment, Graphic Design, Internet/Web Design, Luxury Products, Media Buying Services, Media Planning, Point of Sale, Print, Sponsorship, Sports Market, Strategic Planning/Research

Approx. Annual Billings: $27,805,603

Breakdown of Gross Billings by Media: Audio/Visual: $155,738; Brdcst.: $1,555,750; Fees: $15,335,271; Internet Adv.: $1,742,190; Other: $1,567,581; Out-of-Home Media: $542,372; Print: $6,287,262; Production: $619,439

Bob Reimer *(Pres)*
Scott Mellin *(CEO)*
Michael Bennett *(CFO)*
Andrew Price *(Global Chief Creative Officer)*
Andee Conner Foutch *(Exec VP-Media Svcs)*
Yaniv Kanfi *(Exec VP-Digital)*
Derek Effinger *(Brand Dir)*
Steve Hurd *(Assoc Dir-Creative)*

Accounts:
Aspen Skiing Company Campaign: "Before"; 2009
Audi A7 app
Beam Global Spirits & Wines Casa Sauza, El Tesoro
IKEA Campaign: "Kitchen Party"
Nike 360 Football Boot
Oakley, Inc. Campaign: "Pampered", Campaign: "Peace In The Chaos", Oakley Women's; 2005
Odyssey Golf
Powershares Campaign: "Red Carpet"
Revo; 2008
Snowmass Tourism Campaign: "Before"
Sports Authority Campaign: "All Things Sporting Good", On-Air Radio, Online, Print

FACTORY PR

263 11th Ave 6th Fl, New York, NY 10001
Tel.: (212) 941-9394
E-Mail: info@factorypr.com
Web Site: www.factorypr.com

Agency Specializes In: Advertising, Brand Development & Integration, Digital/Interactive, Event Planning & Marketing, Media Planning, Public Relations

Jeff Woodward *(COO)*
Lauren Fisch *(Partner)*
Mark Silver *(Partner)*
Kevin Giss *(Acct Dir)*
Amanda Dawson *(Mgr-Strategic Dev)*
Bridget O'Hara Hale *(Sr Acct Exec)*
Megan Thomas *(Acct Exec)*

Accounts:
New-Betsey Johnson
New-Ruthie Davis

FAHLGREN MORTINE

(Formerly Fahlgren Advertising)
4030 Easton Sta Ste 300, Columbus, OH 43219
Tel.: (614) 383-1500
Fax: (614) 383-1501
E-Mail: info@fahlgren.com
Web Site: www.fahlgrenmortine.com

Employees: 170
Year Founded: 1962

National Agency Associations: AAF-AMA-COPF-PRSA

Agency Specializes In: Above-the-Line, Advertising, Advertising Specialties, Affluent Market, African-American Market, Agriculture, Arts, Automotive, Bilingual Market, Brand Development & Integration, Broadcast, Business Publications, Business-To-Business, Cable T.V., Children's Market, Co-op Advertising, Collateral, College, Communications, Consulting, Consumer Goods, Consumer Marketing, Consumer Publications, Content, Corporate Communications, Corporate Identity, Crisis Communications, Digital/Interactive, Direct Response Marketing, Direct-to-Consumer, E-Commerce, Education, Electronic Media, Electronics, Email, Engineering, Entertainment, Environmental, Event Planning & Marketing, Exhibit/Trade Shows, Experience Design, Fashion/Apparel, Financial, Food Service, Game Integration, Government/Political, Graphic Design, Guerilla Marketing, Health Care Services, High Technology, Hispanic Market, Hospitality, Household Goods, Identity Marketing, In-Store Advertising, Industrial, Information Technology, Integrated Marketing, International, Internet/Web Design, Investor Relations, Leisure, Local Marketing, Logo & Package Design, Market Research, Media Buying Services, Media Planning, Media Relations, Media Training, Medical Products, Men's Market, Mobile Marketing, Multicultural, Multimedia, New Product Development, New Technologies, Newspaper, Newspapers & Magazines, Out-of-Home Media, Outdoor, Over-50 Market, Package Design, Paid Searches, Pharmaceutical, Planning & Consultation, Point of Purchase, Point of Sale, Print, Production, Production (Ad, Film, Broadcast), Production (Print), Promotions, Public Relations, Publicity/Promotions, Radio, Real Estate, Regional, Restaurant, Retail, Sales Promotion, Search Engine Optimization, Seniors' Market, Social Marketing/Nonprofit, Social Media, Sponsorship, Sports Market, Stakeholders, Strategic Planning/Research, Sweepstakes, T.V., Technical Advertising, Teen Market, Trade & Consumer Magazines, Transportation, Travel & Tourism, Tween Market, Urban Market, Viral/Buzz/Word of Mouth, Web (Banner Ads, Pop-ups, etc.), Women's Market

Approx. Annual Billings: $75,000,000

Neil Mortine *(Pres & CEO)*
Brent Holbert *(CFO)*
Mel Windley *(Exec VP)*
Sean Cowan *(Sr VP & Dir-Digital Experience)*
Chrystie Reep *(Sr VP & Dir-Media Connections)*
Aaron Brown *(Sr VP)*
Wendy Cramer *(Sr VP)*
Patrick Gallagher *(Sr VP)*
Edward K. Miller *(Sr VP)*
Paul Vetter *(Sr VP)*
Aaron Reiser *(VP & Dir-Creative & UX)*
Mark Berry *(VP)*
Leslie Holbrook *(Assoc VP)*
Kailyn Longoria *(Assoc VP)*
Gretchen Torres *(Assoc VP)*
Lesley Waldsmith *(Assoc VP)*
Angela Hall *(Acct Dir)*
Michelle Spalding *(Producer-Brdcst)*
Mark Grieves *(Dir-Creative)*
Ed Patterson *(Dir-IT)*
Carrie Morris *(Assoc Dir-Creative)*
Julia Bastaja *(Sr Project Mgr-Digital)*
Heather Hattery *(Project Mgr-Digital)*
Amy Harman *(Acct Supvr)*
Courtenay Hollington *(Acct Supvr)*
Erin Maggied *(Acct Supvr)*
Renee LeGendre *(Sr Acct Exec)*
Caroline Allan *(Acct Exec)*
Giselle Bravo *(Acct Exec)*
Kelsey Short *(Acct Exec)*
Megan Smuckler *(Sr Planner-Media Connections & Buyer)*
Erik Beckett *(Sr Designer)*
Amanda Rearick *(Designer-Production)*
Heather Bartman *(Coord)*

Accounts:
Ansell Healthcare; Red Bank, NJ Industrial Gloves, Safety Products; 1993
Arcelor Mittal; Princeton, WV; 2010
Balloon Time; Columbus, OH Helium Tank & Party Balloon Kits; 2003
Boise CVB
Cardinal Health, Inc.; Dublin, OH; 2004
CareFusion; San Diego, CA
CareSource; Dayton, OH
Chart Industries; Garfield Heights, OH
Chemical Fabrics & Film Association; Cleveland, OH
ClearSaleing; Columbus, OH
Cliff's Natural Resources; Cleveland, OH Mining
Columbus Area Chamber of Commerce; Columbus, OH
Columbus Blue Jackets Foundation; Columbus, OH; 2007
Columbus Image; Columbus, OH; 2010
Cooper Tires
Crown Equipment Corporation; New Bremen, OH Material Handling Equipment Manufacturer; 2008
Dayton/Montgomery County CVB
Delta Air Elite; Cincinnati, OH; 2009
DHL Excel Supply Chain; Westerville, OH; 1991
Diamond HIll Investment Group; Columbus, OH; 2003
Donatos Pizzeria Corporation; Columbus, OH Pizzeria Restaurant Chain; 2006
DPL Energy; Dayton, OH; 2010
Elmer's Products, Inc.; Columbus, OH; 2009
Emerson Climate Technologies; Sidney, OH; 2006
Emerson Network Power; Columbus, OH Business-Critical Continuity Service Provider; 2006
Experience Columbus
FIAMM; Italy; 2010
Franklin Park Conservatory and Botanical Gardens; Columbus, OH; 2006

Gatlinburg Convention & Visitors' Bureau; Gatlinburg, TN Tourism, Travel; 2009
Grange Insurance; Columbus, OH; 2004
Hill-Rom; Batesville, IN Medical Devices; 2010
Holophane Corporation; Newark, OH; 2002
Huntington Federal S&L; Huntington, WV Banking; 1978
Kent State University; Kent, OH Campaign: "Experience for Life", Higher Education; 2009
Kidde
The Kroger Company, Columbus Division
The Kroger Co. of Michigan
Lifeline of Ohio; Columbus, OH
Materion; 2010
McDonald's Cincinnati Co-Op McDonald's; 2009
McDonald's MACOCO Co-op; Columbus, OH McDonald's
McDonald's MACOM Co-op; Toledo, OH McDonald's
McDonald's Southeast Marketing Assocation; FL McDonald's
McDonald's Southwest Marketing Assocation; FL McDonald's
McDonald's West Palm Beach Marketing Association; FL McDonald's
Midmark; Versailles, OH; 2009
The Myrtle Beach Area Chamber of Commerce/CVB National PR
Nationwide Children's Hospital; Columbus, OH Healthcare; 2006
NDI Medical; Cleveland, OH; 2005
Nevada Division of Tourism (Integrated Marketing Agency of Record)
NewPage Corp.; Miamisburg, OH; 2005
North Dakota Department of Commerce
New-North Dakota Tourism (Public Relations Agency of Record)
Nova Southeastern University Campaign: "NSU Rise Up"
Ohio Coalition for Home Care & Hospice; 2010
Ohio Manufacturers' Association; Columbus, OH; 2010
Ohio Tourism Division; Columbus, OH; 2000
Panama City Beach & Convention and Visitor's Bureau; Panama City Beach, FL; 2009
Parma Community General Hospital
Pelotonia
Savannah College of Art and Design Content Marketing, Digital, Media, Social Media
Scentsy; Meridian, ID; 2009
West Virginia Department of Health & Human Resources
School Choice Ohio; Columbus, OH; 2010
Sherwin-Williams; Cleveland, OH; 2010
Standard Register; Dayton, OH; 2006
United Bank; Parkersburg, WV; 1980
West Virginia Department of Health and Human Resources
West Virginia Lottery; WV State Lottery; 2010
West Virginia University Healthcare
Worthington Industries; Worthington, OH Worthington Cylinders; 1998
WOSU Public Media Public Television & Radio; 2010
Wyoming Office of Tourism (Public Relations Agency of Record)
Young Presidents Organization/World Presidents Organization; 2010

Branches

Fahlgren Mortine (Cincinnati)
414 Walnut St Ste 1006, Cincinnati, OH 45202
Tel.: (513) 241-9200
Fax: (513) 241-5982
Web Site: www.fahlgrenmortine.com

Employees: 3
Year Founded: 1962

Agency Specializes In: Advertising

Lisa Morales Cook *(Sr VP-Brand Plng)*

Fahlgren Mortine (Dayton)
4380 Buckeye Ln Ste 210, Beavercreek, OH 45440
Tel.: (937) 560-2840
Fax: (937) 560-2841
E-Mail: info@fahlgren.com
Web Site: www.fahlgrenmortine.com

Employees: 12
Year Founded: 1938

National Agency Associations: COPF

Agency Specializes In: Advertising, Affluent Market

Christy Bykowski *(Sr VP & Mng Dir)*
John Curtis *(Mng Dir & Sr VP)*
Marty McDonald *(Mng Dir & Sr VP)*
Mark Grieves *(Sr VP & Dir-Creative)*
Matt Sutton *(Acct Dir)*
Lisa Kennedy *(Acct Supvr)*
Julie Lechleiter *(Acct Supvr)*
Cari Wildasinn *(Acct Supvr)*
Caroline Allan *(Acct Exec)*
Lauren Church *(Acct Exec)*

Accounts:
Colfax Corporation
Emerson Climate Technologies.; Sidney, OH Compressors
Emerson Network Power
Emerson Network Power
Midmark
The University of Dayton
Win Wholesale

Fahlgren Mortine (Toledo)
One Seagate Ste 901, Toledo, OH 43604
Tel.: (419) 247-5200
Fax: (419) 247-5298
E-Mail: info@fahlgrenmortine.com
Web Site: www.fahlgrenmortine.com

Employees: 1
Year Founded: 1962

National Agency Associations: COPF

Agency Specializes In: Advertising, Cable T.V., Digital/Interactive, Market Research, Media Buying Services, Media Planning, Media Relations, Promotions, Public Relations, Publicity/Promotions, Radio, Social Marketing/Nonprofit, Social Media, T.V., Travel & Tourism, Web (Banner Ads, Pop-ups, etc.)

Katie McGrath *(Sr VP-HR)*

FAHRENHEIT 212
665 Broadway, New York, NY 10012
Tel.: (646) 654-1212
Fax: (646) 225-7172
E-Mail: email@fahrenheit-212.com
Web Site: www.fahrenheit-212.com

Employees: 25

Agency Specializes In: Advertising

Mark Payne *(Pres & Head-Innovation)*
Todd Rovak *(CEO & Mng Partner)*
Bob Dennen *(CFO)*
Chris Cook *(Dir-Design)*
Nithya George *(Dir-Engagement-Comml Strategy)*
Jagatjoti Khalsa *(Dir-Innovation)*
Nicholas Partridge *(Dir-Innovation)*
Sandra Steving Villegas *(Dir-Innovation)*
Mary von Aue *(Mgr-Content)*
Alfia Ilicheva *(Mgr-Engagement & Strategy-Comml)*
Victoria Ozdemir *(Mgr-Fin & HR)*
Jamie Podhaizer *(Mgr-Engagement)*
Alex Stock *(Mgr-Engagement & Strategy-Comml)*

Accounts:
Adidas
Coca-Cola Refreshments USA, Inc.
Diageo
Fonterra
General Mills
The Gucci Group
Hershey
Mashreq
NBC Universal
Nestle
Samsung
Starbucks

FAHRENHEIT CREATIVE
3695 Okemos Rd Ste 100, Okemos, MI 48864
Tel.: (517) 347-9733
Fax: (517) 347-9738
E-Mail: fahrenheit@fahrenheitcreative.com
Web Site: www.fahrenheitcreative.com

Agency Specializes In: Advertising, Brand Development & Integration, Graphic Design, Internet/Web Design, Print, Radio, Social Media, T.V.

Marc Rakas *(Pres)*
Dennis Green *(Creative Dir)*
Jess Foxen *(Asst Acct Exec)*

Accounts:
Capital Prime

FAIRLY PAINLESS ADVERTISING
44 E 8th St Ste 300, Holland, MI 49423
Tel.: (616) 394-5900
Fax: (616) 394-5903
E-Mail: info@fairlypainless.com
Web Site: www.fairlypainless.com

Employees: 18
Year Founded: 1992

Chris Cook *(Owner)*
Cheryl Bell *(Partner & Dir-Design)*
Drake Evans *(Dir-Art)*
Ryan Lockwood *(Dir-Art)*
Jane Smith *(Dir-Interactive)*
Kimberly Dekker *(Office Mgr)*
Lyndsay Mccarthy *(Acct Mgr)*
Beth Taylor *(Strategist)*
David Smith *(Designer-Interactive)*

Accounts:
Fox Motors Campaign: "The Fox Difference"
Grand Rapids Label Website
Greenleaf Trust Campaign: "True Story"
Talco Electronics Campaign: "I Am Here"

FAIRMONT PRESS, INC.
700 Indian Trail Lilburn Rd NW, Lilburn, GA 30047-3724
Tel.: (770) 925-9388
Fax: (770) 381-9865
Web Site: www.fairmontpress.com

E-Mail for Key Personnel:
Creative Dir.: lori@fairmontpress.com

Employees: 15
Year Founded: 1973

Agency Specializes In: Technical Advertising

Linda Hutchings *(VP)*
Valerie Oviatt *(Dir-Seminar & Internet Training)*

Accounts:

Association of Energy Engineers; Atlanta, GA
Professional Society

FAITH CREATIVE MEDIA
1260 York Ave, Howell, MI 48843
Tel.: (248) 921-0919
E-Mail: info@faithcreativemedia.com
Web Site: www.faithcreativemedia.com

Agency Specializes In: Advertising, Broadcast, Graphic Design, Internet/Web Design, Logo & Package Design, Print, Search Engine Optimization

Joe Hochgreve *(CEO & Creative Dir)*
Alex Stawara *(Art Dir)*
Michelle Baber *(Dir-Mktg)*

Accounts:
Smart Diet Scale

FALK HARRISON
1300 Baur Blvd, Saint Louis, MO 63132
Tel.: (314) 531-1410
Fax: (314) 535-8640
E-Mail: info@falkharrison.com
Web Site: www.falkharrison.com

Agency Specializes In: Brand Development & Integration, Business-To-Business, Communications, Digital/Interactive, Financial, Print

Steve Harrison *(Pres & Dir-Creative)*
Matthew Falk *(Exec VP & Dir-Creative)*
Jon Falk *(Exec VP-Sls & Mktg)*
Sadeth Phimphavong *(Acct Dir-Strategic-Monsanto)*
Corey Helling *(Dir-Art)*
Traci Moore *(Dir-Creative)*
Lilly Huxhold *(Asst Dir-Art)*
Jake Walker *(Asst Dir-Art)*
Nermin Zimic *(Asst Dir-Art)*
Ed Mehler *(Assoc Dir-Creative)*
Robert Bierman *(Mgr-Creative Ops)*
Carol Braun *(Mgr-Fin & Benefits)*
Bunny Reiss *(Asst Mgr-Bus Dev)*

Accounts:
Arch Coal Inc Coal Producers

FALL ADVERTISING
10960 Wheatlands Ave Ste 106, Santee, CA 92071-5617
Tel.: (619) 258-6225
Fax: (619) 258-7752
E-Mail: donaldf@fallads.com
Web Site: www.fallads.com

E-Mail for Key Personnel:
President: donaldf@fallads.com
Creative Dir.: russt@fallads.com
Media Dir.: ginac@fallads.com

Employees: 5
Year Founded: 1965

National Agency Associations: AD CLUB

Agency Specializes In: Advertising, Automotive, Business-To-Business, Consumer Marketing, Corporate Identity, E-Commerce, Exhibit/Trade Shows, Industrial, Logo & Package Design, New Product Development, Newspaper, Outdoor, Point of Purchase, Point of Sale, Print, Production, Public Relations, Radio, Retail, Sales Promotion, T.V., Trade & Consumer Magazines, Yellow Pages Advertising

Donald R. Fall *(Owner)*
Russ Turner *(Sr VP, Dir-Creative & Acct Supvr)*
Dan Fall *(Media Buyer)*

Accounts:
KC Hilites, Inc.; Williams, AZ
NHT
Total Seal Inc.

FALLON MEDICA LLC
620 Shrewsbury Ave, Tinton Falls, NJ 07701
Tel.: (732) 345-3550
Fax: (732) 212-1926
E-Mail: timf@fallonmedica.com
Web Site: fallonmedica.com

Employees: 30
Year Founded: 2002

Agency Specializes In: Pharmaceutical

Timothy Fallon *(Pres)*
Bina O'Brien *(Exec VP-Ops)*
Kerry Coffee *(Sr VP & Head-Practice)*
Mitchell Firger *(VP)*
Katie Turpin-Lawlor *(Dir-New Bus Dev)*
Kelsey Guttormsen *(Assoc Acct Mgr)*
Kelly Ludwinski *(Acct Supvr)*
Payal Desai *(Coord-Client Svcs)*
Kristen Holgerson *(Sr Client Svcs Dir)*

Accounts:
Genentech, Inc Rituxan
Pfizer Caduet, Lipitor, NEF, Neurontin
Takeda Febuxostat, Prevacid
Watson Pharma Ferrelcit

FALLON WORLDWIDE
901 Marquette Ave Ste 2400, Minneapolis, MN 55402
Tel.: (612) 758-2345
Fax: (612) 758-2346
E-Mail: info@fallon.com
Web Site: www.fallon.com

Employees: 150
Year Founded: 1981

Agency Specializes In: Advertising, Digital/Interactive, Event Planning & Marketing, Graphic Design, Integrated Marketing, Internet/Web Design, Media Planning, Pets , Print, Production (Print), T.V.

Breakdown of Gross Billings by Media: Cable T.V.: 25%; Internet Adv.: 3%; Mags.: 24%; Network T.V.: 15%; Newsp.: 10%; Out-of-Home Media: 6%; Radio: 3%; Spot T.V.: 14%

Jeff Kling *(Chief Creative Officer)*
Anette Lillegard *(Chief Strategy Officer)*
David Sigel *(Mng Dir-Strategic Growth)*
Beth Freedman *(Head-Acct Mgmt)*
Myles Allpress *(Sr Dir-Art)*
Marc Mason *(Grp Acct Dir)*
Chris Campbell *(Acct Dir)*
Josh Combs *(Creative Dir)*
Chris Lawrence *(Acct Mgmt Dir)*
Charlie Kuhn *(Copywriter)*
Sara Welch *(Media Buyer)*

Accounts:
Arby's "We Have the Meats"
Big Ten Network (Agency of Record) Campaign: "First Robin of Spring", Digital, Experiential Marketing, Offline, Social Media, TV, Web Sites
Brown-Forman (Global Creative Agency of Record)
Cargill Truvia (Social Agency of Record)
Children's Defense Fund BeCarefulWhatYouCut.com; 1986
Comedy Central
The Cosmopolitan Hotel of Las Vegas Campaign: "Let Me Go"
H&R Block Broadcast, Campaign: "Detroit Second Look", Campaign: "Get Your Billion Back America", Campaign: "Nein Nein Nein", Campaign: "Nine Nine Tee Nine", Never Settle for Less
Henkel Creative, Loctite Adhesives
Independent Film Channel
Quicken Loans
Talenti Gelato & Sorbetto Advertising, Campaign: "The Talenti Story", Digital, Videos

Branches

Fallon London
Elsley Court, 20-22 Great Titchfield Street, London, W1W 8BE United Kingdom
Tel.: (44) 20 7494 9120
Fax: (44) 20 7494 9130
Web Site: www.fallon.co.uk

Employees: 120
Year Founded: 1998

National Agency Associations: IPA

Agency Specializes In: Advertising

Gareth Collins *(CEO)*
David Hackworthy *(Chief Strategy Officer)*
Lulu Skinner *(Grp Acct Dir)*
Lucy Kozac *(Acct Dir)*
Aoife O'Dea *(Acct Dir)*
Dan Watts *(Dir-Creative)*
Sigi Egedal *(Copywriter)*
Chloe Grindle *(Copywriter)*
Dan Montgomery *(Designer)*
Susie Morley *(Art Buyer)*

Accounts:
Alzheimer's Society "Gone", Advertising, Brand Creative, Campaign: "Erase", Digital, Media, Out-of-Home, Print, TV
ASDA Group; Leeds Campaign: "Autumn/Winter Collection", George, TV; 2007
Axa Campaign: "Where others ask why? Axa asks why not?", Outdoor, Print
Cadbury Trebor Bassett Campaign: "Unwrap Joy with Cadbury this Christmas"
Cushelle Campaign: "Koala Storybook"
Elephant Family & Action for Children Campaign: "Faberge Big Egg Hunt"
Giffgaff Campaign: "Different Doesn't Have to be Scary", Campaign: "Different Takes Guts", Campaign: "Don't Be Scared", Campaign: "Zombies", Digital, Social Media, TV, Website Design
Grazia
Kerry Foods; Ireland "Brave Bones Club", Cheesestrings, LowLow Cheese
Mondelez International Cadbury Caramel Nibbles, Cadbury Creme Egg, Cadbury Crispello, Cadbury Maynards, Cadbury's Wispa Hot Chocolate, Cadbury: "Cadbury Taste", Campaign: "7 Flavours of Keith", Campaign: "Cadbury Dairy Milk Bubbly", Campaign: "Have a Fling", Campaign: "Joyville Magnificent Musical Chocolate Fountain", Campaign: "Joyville", Campaign: "Opening Ceremony", Campaign: "The Frothybeast", Campaign: "The Search is On", Campaign: "Yes Sir, I WILL Boogie in the Office", Dairy Milk, Digital, Lu, Mikado, OOH, Pan-European, Ritz, Social Media, Terry's Chocolate Orange
More Than; 2005
Nokia Campaign: "Tortoise", Vertu
Orange plc Campaign: "Intermission", Orange Gold Spots Movie Trailers - The A-Team
Orchid
Oxfam International
Peta UK Campaign: "Do It Like They Do"
Raisio PLC Above-the-Line, Benecol, European Advertising
SCA Hygiene TV Advertisement, Velvet
Scottish Power Advertising
Skoda UK Campaign: "More Power", Campaign:

"Skoda Puzzle", Lead Creative Agency, Made of Meaner Stuff, Octavia vRS; 1999
Think Money

Fallon Minneapolis

901 Marquette Ave Ste 2400, Minneapolis, MN 55402
Tel.: (612) 758-2345
Fax: (612) 758-2346
Toll Free: (866) 758-2345
E-Mail: reception@fallon.com
Web Site: www.fallon.com

Employees: 170
Year Founded: 1981

National Agency Associations: 4A's

Agency Specializes In: Advertising, Sponsorship

Rocky Novak *(Mng Dir & Dir-Digital Dev)*
John King *(Chief Mktg Officer)*
Charlie Wolff *(Head-Creative & Copywriter)*
Greg Brinker *(Grp Acct Dir)*
Marc Mason *(Grp Acct Dir)*
Harry Awe *(Producer-Media)*
Jordan Rossman *(Acct Dir)*
Jason Bottenus *(Dir-Creative & Art)*
Anthony DiNicola *(Dir-Art)*
Niki Dobratz *(Dir-Media)*
Patrick Figueroa *(Dir-Design)*
Matt Heath *(Dir-Creative-Arby's)*
Andrew Koningen *(Dir-Production)*
Julie McBride *(Dir-Talent & Comm)*
Jonathan Moehnke *(Dir-Art)*
Julianna Simon *(Dir-Strategic Plng)*
Marty Wetherall *(Dir-Innovation)*
Becky Chaffee *(Assoc Dir-Media-Digital)*
Rachel Quinlan *(Assoc Dir-Media)*
Mona Morris *(Mgr-Integrated Bus Affairs)*
Nick Bondeson *(Acct Supvr)*
Liz O'Reilly *(Acct Supvr)*
Kelly Holley *(Planner-Strategic)*
Emily Skahan *(Coord-Creative)*

Accounts:
Abu Dhabi Commercial Bank
Arby's Restaurant (Agency of Record) Bacon, Beefy Sandwiches, Campaign: "Fear not the Meats", Campaign: "This Is Meatcraft", Campaign: "We Have The Meats", Creative, Digital, Print, Radio, Roast Beef, TV, Television, Turkey
Basilica Of St. Mary Block Party
Big Wood
Camp Heartland; Milwaukee, WI; 1997
Charter Communications Campaign: "Motor Mouth", TV On Demand
Comedy Central
The Cosmopolitan of Las Vegas Campaign: "Just the right amount of wrong", Campaign: "Let Me Go"
Cruzan Rum
Deluxe Corp
General Mills Creative, Old El Paso
H&R Block Campaign: "Second Look Detroit", Financial Services, Tax Services
Henkel Advertising, Campaign: "Breakage", Campaign: "Win At Glue", Digital, Loctite Super Glue, Public Relations
IFC
Loctite Adhesives Campaign: "Positive Feelings", Super Bowl 2015
Nestle Beverages
Nordstrom; Seattle, WA; 1998
The Phoenix Coyotes
Woodford Reserve Bourbon

Saatchi & Saatchi Fallon Tokyo

4-9-3 Jingumae, Shibuya-ku, Tokyo, 150-0001 Japan
Tel.: (81) 3 6438 1255
Fax: (81) 3 6438 1223
Web Site: www.ssftokyo.co.jp

Employees: 40

Naoki Ishikawa *(CFO)*
Luca Grelli *(Exec Dir-Creative)*
Maiko Itami *(Client Svcs Dir)*
Kenji Moriuchi *(Art Dir)*
Takei Yoshishige *(Creative Dir)*
Dominic Byrnes *(Dir-Digital)*
Darren Rogers *(Dir-Integrated Comm)*
Nick Ashley *(Planner)*

Accounts:
Godiva Japan
Reebok Easytone Shoes
Toot
New-Toyota Motor Campaign: "Dream Car of the Day"

THE FALLS AGENCY

900 6th Ave SE Ste 105, Minneapolis, MN 55414-1379
Tel.: (612) 872-6372
Fax: (612) 872-1018
Toll Free: (800) 339-1119
E-Mail: info@fallsagency.com
Web Site: www.fallsagency.com

E-Mail for Key Personnel:
President: s.lund@fallsagency.com
Creative Dir.: k.franson@fallsagency.com

Employees: 25
Year Founded: 1982

Agency Specializes In: Advertising, Business-To-Business, Co-op Advertising, Leisure, Marine, Production, Sponsorship

Sharon Lund *(Pres)*
Robert Falls *(CEO)*
Deanna Davis *(Controller)*
Lisa Rothschild *(Sr Acct Supvr)*
Megan Bren *(Acct Exec)*
Kara Schuette *(Asst Acct Exec)*

Accounts:
Kawasaki Power Products; MI Garden Tools; 1998
Kawasaki Rail Car, Inc.; NY Transportation; 2002
The Saint Paul Hotel
The St Paul Grill

FAME

60 S Sixth St Ste 2600, Minneapolis, MN 55402
Tel.: (612) 746-3263
Fax: (612) 746-3333
Web Site: www.fameretail.com

Employees: 55
Year Founded: 1990

Agency Specializes In: Brand Development & Integration, Communications, Corporate Identity, Event Planning & Marketing, Government/Political, In-Store Advertising, Logo & Package Design, Media Buying Services, New Product Development, Outdoor, Point of Purchase, Point of Sale, Print, Public Relations, Radio, Retail, T.V.

Lynne Robertson *(Pres & CEO)*
Megan Hanson *(VP & Grp Acct Dir)*
Yves Roux *(VP-Creative & Dir)*
Julie Feyerer *(Dir-Creative)*
Jennifer Sheeler *(Dir-Design)*
Emily Barry *(Acct Mgr)*
Terri Dahl *(Office Mgr)*
Iva Devcic *(Asst Acct Mgr)*

Accounts:
Best Buy
SuperValu Creative; 2008

THE FAMILY ROOM

(Formerly Just Kid, Inc.)
27 Ann St, Norwalk, CT 06854
Tel.: (203) 523-7878
Fax: (203) 523-7888
E-Mail: info@familyroomllc.com
Web Site: www.familyroomllc.com/

Employees: 20
Year Founded: 1993

Agency Specializes In: Brand Development & Integration, Children's Market, New Product Development, Strategic Planning/Research

Sales: $10,000,000

George Carey *(Founder & CEO)*
Philip Kurien *(Mng Dir-Strategy & Innovation)*
Laurie Klein *(VP-Bus Dev)*
Eric Wolfeiler *(Dir-Quantitative Res)*

Accounts:
Crayola
Discovery Kids
Dixie
Dymo
Eggo
Heinz
Kellogg's
McDonald's
Mondelez International, Inc.
National Children's Museum
Nestle

FANCY LLC

401 Broadway Ste 1410, New York, NY 10013
Tel.: (212) 343-2629
E-Mail: hello@fancynyc.com
Web Site: www.fancynyc.com

Agency Specializes In: Advertising, Brand Development & Integration, Digital/Interactive, Print

Andrew Tuch *(Gen Counsel & Exec VP-Ops)*
Melissa Schulz *(Exec VP & Acct Dir)*
Nicole Brunwasser *(VP-Comm)*
Brandon Nieuw *(VP-Ops)*
Erica Fite Horvath *(Dir-Creative)*
Katie Keating *(Dir-Creative)*
Paige Williams *(Product Mgr)*
Jake Siegal *(Product VP)*

Accounts:
P&G Clairol Color, Pantene
Ponds

FANCY RHINO

800 Market St Ste 201, Chattanooga, TN 37402
Tel.: (423) 402-0988
Web Site: www.fancyrhino.com

Agency Specializes In: Advertising, Brand Development & Integration, Digital/Interactive, Graphic Design, Social Media

Vann Graves *(Pres & COO)*
Katie Nelson *(Head-Production)*
Joe Scalo *(Art Dir & Copywriter)*
Kate Lamb *(Strategist)*
Sally Lynch *(Acct Exec)*

Accounts:
New-Torch

FANGOHR, LLC

10 Jay St Ste 408, Brooklyn, NY 11201-1162
Tel.: (718) 577-1204

Fax: (718) 577-1204
E-Mail: info@fangohr.com
Web Site: www.fangohr.com

Employees: 4
Year Founded: 2004

National Agency Associations: AD CLUB

Agency Specializes In: Advertising, Advertising Specialties, Affluent Market, Alternative Advertising, Arts, Asian Market, Brand Development & Integration, Branded Entertainment, Business Publications, Business-To-Business, Catalogs, Collateral, Communications, Consulting, Consumer Publications, Content, Corporate Communications, Corporate Identity, Cosmetics, Digital/Interactive, E-Commerce, Electronic Media, Email, Experience Design, Financial, Game Integration, Government/Political, Graphic Design, Information Technology, International, Internet/Web Design, Investor Relations, Logo & Package Design, Luxury Products, Magazines, Men's Market, Multicultural, Multimedia, New Product Development, New Technologies, Package Design, Pharmaceutical, Print, Production (Print), Publishing, Real Estate, Restaurant, Search Engine Optimization, Teen Market, Transportation, Urban Market, Web (Banner Ads, Pop-ups, etc.)

Approx. Annual Billings: $600,000

Breakdown of Gross Billings by Media: Corp. Communications: $75,000; E-Commerce: $75,000; Graphic Design: $75,000; Logo & Package Design: $75,000; Mags.: $75,000; Print: $75,000; Worldwide Web Sites: $150,000

Florian Fangohr *(Dir-Design)*
Roger Xu *(Mgr-Dev)*

Accounts:
Detention Watch Network; Washington, DC Non-profit Organization; 2007
Interesting New York; New York, NY Conference; 2008
Pitchfork Music; Chicago, IL Media Buying; 2008

FANSCAPE INC.
4721 Alla Rd, Marina Del Rey, CA 90292
Tel.: (323) 851-3267
Fax: (323) 785-7101
E-Mail: info@fanscape.com
Web Site: www.fanscape.com

Employees: 23
Year Founded: 1998

Agency Specializes In: Advertising, Sponsorship, Web (Banner Ads, Pop-ups, etc.)

Terry Dry *(Co-Founder, Owner & Pres)*
Larry Weintraub *(CEO)*
Greg Boles *(COO)*
Caroline Conroy *(Acct Mgr)*
Nick Cernoch *(Mgr-Community)*
Courtney Davidson *(Copywriter)*

Accounts:
Electronic Arts
GameStop Corp. Entertainment
Gillette
Hilton Worldwide
Honda
Kodak Graphic Communications Group
Mars, Inc. Snickers, Social Media
Monster.com
MTV
Samsung

THE FANTASTICAL
33 Union St, 4th Fl, Boston, MA 02108
Tel.: (508) 726-2555
Web Site: www.thefantastical.com

Employees: 12
Year Founded: 2012

Agency Specializes In: Advertising, Content, Digital/Interactive

Michael Ancevic *(Mng Partner & Chief Creative Officer)*
Steve Mietelski *(Mng Partner & Chief Creative Officer)*
Jenn Foster *(Acct Dir)*
Will Doherty *(Dir-Bus Dev)*
Kerry Shea Downey *(Dir-Creative)*
Samantha Hodian *(Dir-Art)*
Iona Holloway *(Dir-Art)*
Sarah Hamilton *(Acct Mgr)*

Accounts:
'47 Brand; 2013
Four Seasons Hotel & Resorts
International Olympic Committee
McAlister's Deli
Olympus; 2012
Panera Bread; 2012
Row NYC; 2013
Sam Adams; 2012
New-Society of Grownups Campaign: "You're a Grownup now. Don't Panic"
TripAdvisor, Inc.; 2013

FANTICH MEDIA GROUP
3700 N 10th St, McAllen, TX 78501
Tel.: (956) 928-0500
Fax: (956) 928-0501
E-Mail: marc@fantichmedia.com
Web Site: www.fantichmedia.com

Employees: 8
Year Founded: 1995

Marc Fantich *(Founder)*
Eric Fantich *(Dir-Creative)*
Manny Garza *(Dir-Creative)*
Mary King *(Mgr-Mktg)*
Melyne Martin *(Mgr-Mktg)*

Accounts:
Buy Direct
D-Tronics
Pizza Hut
Rainbow Play Systems

FARAGO+PARTNERS
71 Broadway, New York, NY 10006
Tel.: (212) 344-9472
Fax: (212) 243-1682
E-Mail: peter@farago.com

E-Mail for Key Personnel:
President: peter@farago.com

Employees: 25
Year Founded: 1988

Agency Specializes In: Collateral, Direct Response Marketing

Peter Farago *(Pres)*

Accounts:
Barnes & Noble Bookstores
Brown & Williamson; Louisville, KY Cigarettes; 2000
Dow Jones Newswire
Loehmann's Discount Designer Fashion
Mitsubishi America
Pantone
Prudential
Siskiyou Aerospace Instruments
Sun-Times Media Group Magazines, Newspapers

FARINELLA
1942 Mountain Blvd, Oakland, CA 94611
Tel.: (510) 339-9922
E-Mail: info@farinella.com
Web Site: www.farinella.com

Agency Specializes In: Advertising, Brand Development & Integration, Collateral, Email, Internet/Web Design, Logo & Package Design, Print, Public Relations, Radio, Social Media

David Farinella *(Dir-Creative)*
Will Lettieri *(Sr Designer-Web)*

Accounts:
The Oakland Food Pantry

THE FARM
611 Broadway, New York, NY 10012
Tel.: (212) 982-8500
E-Mail: info@thefarm.com
Web Site: www.thefarm.com

Employees: 10

Agency Specializes In: Advertising, Affluent Market, Automotive, Broadcast, Business-To-Business, Cable T.V., Collateral, College, Communications, Consulting, Content, Corporate Communications, Corporate Identity, Cosmetics, Digital/Interactive, Electronic Media, Experience Design, Fashion/Apparel, Financial, Graphic Design, Health Care Services, Hospitality, Identity Marketing, In-Store Advertising, Leisure, Logo & Package Design, Luxury Products, Market Research, Men's Market, Multimedia, Outdoor, Package Design, Print, Production, Radio, Regional, Restaurant, Retail, Sports Market, T.V., Travel & Tourism, Web (Banner Ads, Pop-ups, etc.), Women's Market

John Anderson *(Owner)*

Accounts:
CBS; New York, NY TV; 1992
Gannett
Lifetime Television; New York, NY TV Network; 1997
NBC
Reebok
SHOWTIME
USA Today

FARMHOUSE
97 S Front St, Memphis, TN 38103
Tel.: (901) 527-0599
E-Mail: info@farmhousemarketing.com
Web Site: www.farmhousemarketing.com

Agency Specializes In: Advertising, Brand Development & Integration, Collateral, Internet/Web Design, Package Design, Print, Social Media

Ben Fant *(Principal & Dir-Creative)*
Jason Prater *(Sr Dir-Art)*

Accounts:
20twelve
Chestnut Hall Interiors
Graham Reese Design Group
The Mighty Olive
Oshi Burger Bar

FASONE & PARTNERS
4003 Pennsylvania Ave, Kansas City, MO 64111
Tel.: (816) 753-7272

Fax: (816) 753-7229
E-Mail: roar@fasonepartners.com
Web Site: www.fasonepartners.com

Employees: 20
Year Founded: 1975

Agency Specializes In: Advertising, Brand Development & Integration, Broadcast, Business-To-Business, Cable T.V., Children's Market, Co-op Advertising, Collateral, Communications, Consumer Marketing, Consumer Publications, Corporate Identity, Direct Response Marketing, E-Commerce, Electronic Media, Event Planning & Marketing, Financial, Food Service, Graphic Design, Health Care Services, High Technology, Hispanic Market, Industrial, Internet/Web Design, Legal Services, Leisure, Logo & Package Design, Magazines, Media Buying Services, Medical Products, Merchandising, Multimedia, New Product Development, Newspaper, Newspapers & Magazines, Out-of-Home Media, Outdoor, Pharmaceutical, Planning & Consultation, Point of Purchase, Point of Sale, Print, Production, Publicity/Promotions, Radio, Real Estate, Recruitment, Retail, Sales Promotion, Seniors' Market, Strategic Planning/Research, T.V., Technical Advertising, Telemarketing, Trade & Consumer Magazines, Transportation

Breakdown of Gross Billings by Media: Outdoor: 4%; Print: 3%; Production: 5%; Radio: 26%; T.V.: 62%

Toni Kerr *(Partner)*
Julie Records *(Partner)*
Karol Albert *(VP & Acct Exec)*
Kathy Davis *(Dir-Media)*
Darren Roubinek *(Dir-Creative)*
Alyson Harper *(Mgr-Production)*
Laura Strecker *(Acct Exec)*

Accounts:
Brotherhood Bank
Builder's Surplus
Wendy's of Missouri
Window World

FAST HORSE
240 N 9th Ave, Minneapolis, MN 55401
Tel.: (612) 746-4610
Fax: (612) 746-4620
E-Mail: info@fasthorseinc.com
Web Site: www.fasthorseinc.com

Employees: 13

National Agency Associations: 4A's

Agency Specializes In: Consumer Goods, Corporate Identity, Digital/Interactive, Email, Environmental, Media Relations, Newspaper, Sponsorship, Sports Market

Jorg Pierach *(Founder & Dir-Creative)*
Allison Checco *(Sr Dir)*
Cydney Strommen *(Acct Dir)*
Jake Anderson *(Mgr-Client Relationship)*
Katherine Krois *(Mgr-Client Relationship)*
Andrew Miller *(Mgr-Client Relationship)*
Alexandra Weaver *(Mgr-Client Relationship)*
Shayla Thiel Stern *(Sr Strategist-Digital)*
Natalie Marquez *(Client Relationship Dir)*
Johnna Vogelbacher *(Client Relationship Dir)*

Accounts:
Allianz
Champs Sports PR
Coca-Cola Refreshments USA, Inc.
Deluxe Corporation (Integrated Marketing Agency of Record)
Great Tile
Heineken USA Campaign: "Mega Football Ad we didn't actually make.", Campaign: "No Bollocks", Newcastle Brown Ale, PR
Insight School
MacPhail Center for Music
Marvin
Newcastle Campaign: "No Bollocks", Public Relations
Radisson
UnitedHealth Group

FASTLANE
261 Madison Ave 9th Fl, New York, NY 10016
Tel.: (855) 677-5263
E-Mail: info@fast-lane.net
Web Site: fastlane.co

Employees: 18
Year Founded: 2006

National Agency Associations: AMA-BMA-IAB-PRSA

Agency Specializes In: Advertising, Brand Development & Integration, Communications, Corporate Communications, E-Commerce, High Technology, Multimedia, Pets , Podcasting, Public Relations, Social Marketing/Nonprofit, Web (Banner Ads, Pop-ups, etc.)

Christopher Faust *(Founder & CEO)*
Eduardo Pires *(Co-Owner & Dir-Creative)*
Alex Pires *(Partner & VP-Client Rels)*
Kevin Levi *(Mng Dir)*
Patty Buchanan *(Mng Dir-PR & Mktg Comm)*
Gaspare J. Marturano *(Mng Dir-Digital Mktg & Social Media)*

Accounts:
Advantedge Healthcare Solutions; Warren, NJ
Astir Analytics
Bluewolf
Brinton Eaton Public Relations
Chief Executive Group (Agency of Record) Editorial Design Services, Event, PR
Collabera
D&G
Education for Employment Foundation; New York, NY
Food Allergy Initiative
Global Ocean Security Technologies Social Media
Golkow
JDC
MaxMara
My-Villages (Agency of Record) Branding, Messaging, Public Relations, Social Media
NJFair
North Star
NorthStar Systems International, Inc.
OceanLED LED Marine Lighting, Social Media
Poliwogg Branding, Marketing, PR, Social Media
Therapeutic Pet Solutions
Venda
Verizon Wireless

FAT CHIMP STUDIOS LLC
2055 Walton Rd, Saint Louis, MO 63114
Tel.: (314) 222-0375
Web Site: www.fatchimpstudios.com

Employees: 18
Year Founded: 2001

Agency Specializes In: Branded Entertainment, Broadcast, Cable T.V., Co-op Advertising, Collateral, Digital/Interactive, Direct Response Marketing, Email, Exhibit/Trade Shows, Game Integration, Guerilla Marketing, In-Store Advertising, Infomercials, Local Marketing, Mobile Marketing, Multimedia, Point of Sale, Product Placement, Production, Promotions, Radio, Social Media, Sponsorship, Sweepstakes, T.V., Telemarketing

Ruth Gerchen *(Sr Acct Exec)*

Accounts:
DynaLabs LLC Corporate Overview Video
Imo's Pizza
MSLA 2015 High School Lacrosse State Championships

FAT FREE COMMUNICATIONS
2 Eaton Ave, Toronto, ON M4J 2Z5 Canada
Tel.: (416) 778-4959
E-Mail: dinnis@fatfreecommunications.ca
Web Site: www.fatfreecommunications.ca

Employees: 5

Agency Specializes In: Advertising, Advertising Specialties, Asian Market, Planning & Consultation

Approx. Annual Billings: $200,000

David Innis *(Dir-Creative)*

Accounts:
Bell Express VU
CFI Financial Services
IKEA
State Bank of India; Toronto, Canada
Sunrocket; VA
Wayne Bourque's Boxercise; Toronto, Canada Boxing Gym

FATHOM COMMUNICATIONS
437 Madison Ave, New York, NY 10022
Tel.: (212) 817-6600
Fax: (212) 415-3514
E-Mail: inquiry@fathomcommunications.com
Web Site: www.fathomcommunications.com

Employees: 36
Year Founded: 2001

Agency Specializes In: Above-the-Line, Advertising, Brand Development & Integration, Business-To-Business, Consulting, Consumer Goods, Consumer Marketing, Corporate Identity, Digital/Interactive, Direct Response Marketing, Direct-to-Consumer, Entertainment, Experience Design, Integrated Marketing, Internet/Web Design, Market Research, Merchandising, New Product Development, New Technologies, Planning & Consultation, Promotions, Sales Promotion, Sponsorship, Sports Market, Strategic Planning/Research, Sweepstakes, Trade & Consumer Magazines, Viral/Buzz/Word of Mouth, Web (Banner Ads, Pop-ups, etc.)

Approx. Annual Billings: $75,000,000

Breakdown of Gross Billings by Media: Consulting: 10%; D.M.: 20%; E-Commerce: 5%; Internet Adv.: 15%; Local Mktg.: 10%; Plng. & Consultation: 15%; Sls. Promo.: 10%; Strategic Planning/Research: 15%

Peter Groome *(CEO)*
Stephanie Shum *(Acct Dir)*
Andy Orge *(Dir-Art)*
Leslie Vanderbrook *(Acct Supvr)*
Courtney Echols *(Acct Exec)*
Elyse Hara *(Acct Exec)*
Victoria Hill *(Acct Exec)*

Accounts:
Arts & Entertainment (A&E) The Glades Crime Mystery Series
Gatorade Creative, Propel
Hasbro; Pawtucket, RI e-Kara Dare to Diva; 2002

Branch

Fathom Communications
200 E Randolf St Ste 3800, Chicago, IL 60601-6436
Tel.: (312) 552-6900
Fax: (312) 552-6990
E-Mail: elni.petridis@fathomcomunications.com
Web Site: fathomcommunications.com/

Employees: 30

National Agency Associations: 4A's

Agency Specializes In: Sponsorship

Linda Poe *(CFO)*
Stephanie Shum *(Acct Dir)*
Tim Evans *(Dir-Production)*
Jo Lyons *(Dir-People & Performance)*
Peter Saint John *(Mgr-Integrated Production)*
Calvin Lai *(Supvr-Creative)*
Elyse Hara *(Acct Exec)*
Victoria Hill *(Acct Exec)*

Accounts:
Hunter Fan Company (Agency of Record) Brand Positioning, Brand Strategy, Broadcast, Creative, Digital, Print
International Trucks
Navistar Inc

FATHOM WORKS
(Formerly Perry Ballard Incorporated)
1101 Broad St Ste 316, Saint Joseph, MI 49085
Tel.: (269) 983-0611
Fax: (269) 983-0747
Toll Free: (800) 800-9547

Employees: 17
Year Founded: 1977

Agency Specializes In: Advertising, Business Publications, Business-To-Business, Collateral, Communications, Consumer Marketing, Consumer Publications, Corporate Identity, E-Commerce, Electronic Media, Email, Engineering, Financial, Graphic Design, Health Care Services, Industrial, Internet/Web Design, Logo & Package Design, Media Buying Services, New Product Development, Newspaper, Outdoor, Planning & Consultation, Print, Production, Public Relations, Sales Promotion, Search Engine Optimization, Strategic Planning/Research, Technical Advertising, Travel & Tourism

Approx. Annual Billings: $11,000,000 Capitalized

Chris Bailey *(Dir-Tech)*

Accounts:
Arnold Transit; Mackinac Island, MI Tourism/Ferry Services; 2005
AUSCO Products, Inc.; Benton Harbor, MI Braking Systems; 2000
Cook Energy Information Center, Indiana Michigan Power; Bridgman, MI Industrial Tourism; 1986
DO IT Corp.; South Haven, MI Hang Tabs
Indiana Michigan Power; Bridgman, MI Industrial Tourism
Rexam; Chicago, IL Beverage Cans; 2001
Select Products Ltd.; Portage, MI Industrial Hinges; 2002
Silver Beach Carousel
The Small Business Association of Michigan; Lansing, MI; 2004
Southwestern Michigan Tourist Council; Benton Harbor, MI
Vail Rubber; Saint Joseph, MI Industrial Rubber
Wolverine Mutual Insurance; Dowagiac, MI Personal Insurance

F.BIZ
(Acquired by WPP plc)

FCB GLOBAL
(Formerly Draftfcb Worldwide)
100 W 33rd St, New York, NY 10001
Tel.: (212) 885-3000
Fax: (212) 885-3300
E-Mail: hello@fcb.com
Web Site: fcb.com

Employees: 8,000
Year Founded: 1873

National Agency Associations: 4A's-AC-AD CLUB-AMA-AWNY-BMA-DMA-IAA-IAB-PMA-PPA-RAMA-WDMI

Agency Specializes In: Above-the-Line, Advertising, Advertising Specialties, Affiliate Marketing, Affluent Market, Alternative Advertising, Arts, Automotive, Aviation & Aerospace, Below-the-Line, Bilingual Market, Brand Development & Integration, Branded Entertainment, Business Publications, Business-To-Business, Cable T.V., Catalogs, Children's Market, Co-op Advertising, Collateral, College, Communications, Computers & Software, Consulting, Consumer Goods, Consumer Marketing, Consumer Publications, Content, Corporate Communications, Corporate Identity, Cosmetics, Crisis Communications, Customer Relationship Management, Digital/Interactive, Direct Response Marketing, Direct-to-Consumer, E-Commerce, Education, Electronic Media, Electronics, Email, Entertainment, Environmental, Event Planning & Marketing, Exhibit/Trade Shows, Experience Design, Fashion/Apparel, Financial, Food Service, Game Integration, Gay & Lesbian Market, Government/Political, Graphic Design, Guerilla Marketing, Health Care Services, High Technology, Hispanic Market, Hospitality, Household Goods, Identity Marketing, In-Store Advertising, Industrial, Infomercials, Information Technology, Integrated Marketing, International, Internet/Web Design, Investor Relations, Leisure, Local Marketing, Logo & Package Design, Luxury Products, Magazines, Market Research, Media Planning, Media Relations, Men's Market, Mobile Marketing, Multicultural, Multimedia, New Product Development, New Technologies, Newspaper, Newspapers & Magazines, Out-of-Home Media, Outdoor, Over-50 Market, Package Design, Paid Searches, Pets , Pharmaceutical, Planning & Consultation, Podcasting, Point of Purchase, Point of Sale, Print, Product Placement, Production, Production (Print), Promotions, Public Relations, Publicity/Promotions, Publishing, Radio, Restaurant, Retail, Sales Promotion, Search Engine Optimization, Seniors' Market, Shopper Marketing, Social Marketing/Nonprofit, Social Media, South Asian Market, Sponsorship, Sports Market, Stakeholders, Strategic Planning/Research, T.V., Technical Advertising, Teen Market, Telemarketing, Trade & Consumer Magazines, Transportation, Travel & Tourism, Tween Market, Urban Market, Viral/Buzz/Word of Mouth, Web (Banner Ads, Pop-ups, etc.), Women's Market

Jonathan Harries *(Chm & Chief Creative Officer-Global)*
Bryan Crawford *(Vice Chm)*
Carter Murray *(CEO)*
Chris Shumaker *(CMO)*
Nigel Jones *(Chief Strategy Officer-Global)*
Stephen Martincic *(Exec VP-Global Branding & Corp Affaires)*
Elyssa Phillips *(Exec VP)*
Tom Theys *(Exec VP-Global Strategy)*
Michael Pruskowski *(Sr VP & Dir-Engagement)*
Holly Brittingham *(Sr VP-Talent & Org Dev-Global)*
Susan Simons *(VP & Project Mgr-Worldwide)*
Akos Papp *(Sr Dir-Art)*
Ian Brown *(Acct Dir)*
Anna Pogosova *(Acct Dir)*
Christopher Arco *(Dir-Client Fin)*
Stephanie Sipe *(Mgr-Corp Comm)*
Katherine Butler *(Acct Exec-Big Heart Pet Brands Acct-Shopper Mktg)*
April Candler *(Acct Exec)*
Quinn Schwellinger *(Asst Acct Exec)*
Howard Draft *(Exec Chm)*

Accounts:
Aramark B2B, Brand Marketing
Beiersdorf 8X4, Eucerin, Hansaplast, Nivea; 1907
Dow Chemical Campaign: "Solutionism. The New Optimism.", Campaign: "Train", Human Element Campaign; 2006
Electronic Arts Mass Effect 3, Video Games
Food & Drug Administration Anti-Smoking
Hewlett Packard; 1997
Jamaica Tourist Board; 1985
Janssen Biotech Campaign: "2nd Thoughts"
Kmart Campaign: "Kmart Smart", Campaign: "Show Your Joe", Creative
Levi Strauss "Live in Levi's", Ads, Cinema, Digital, Dockers, Marketing, Social Marketing, TV
Mondelez International Campaign: "Daily Twist", Nabisco, Nilla, Oreo
Peru's University of Engineering and Technology
Yum! Brands Double Down, KFC, Restaurant, Taco Bell, Taco Bell (Direct Daniella); 1981

Parent Company of:

FCB Health
(Formerly Draftfcb HealthCare NY)
100 W 33rd St, New York, NY 10001
(See Separate Listing)

Hacker Agency
(Formerly Hacker Group)
1215 4th Ave Ste 2100, Seattle, WA 98161-1018
Tel.: (206) 805-1500
Fax: (206) 805-1599
E-Mail: info@hal2l.com
Web Site: hal2l.com

Employees: 300
Year Founded: 1986

National Agency Associations: 4A's

Agency Specializes In: Direct Response Marketing, Electronic Media, Sponsorship

Spyro Kourtis *(Pres & CEO)*
Richard Jacroux *(CFO & VP)*
Stephan Horvath *(CMO-Global)*
Haydn Sweterlitsch *(Global Chief Creative Officer)*
Matt Witter *(Exec VP & Gen Mgr)*
Jason Grollman *(VP-Ops)*
Mark Capps *(Exec Dir)*
Michael Goerz *(Exec Acct Dir)*
Bryan Chaffe *(Dir-Strategic Analytics)*
Scott Fasser *(Dir-Digital Innovation)*
Lauren Collins *(Acct Exec)*
Jessica Deeken *(Strategist-Targeting & Media-Strategic Accts)*
Kyrsten Hendrickson *(Acct Exec)*

Accounts:
AAA
AT&T; 1995
BlueCross BlueShield
Carnival Cruise Line
Coca-Cola

Essence Healthcare, Inc
Global Hyatt
Highmark Blue Cross Blue Shield
Microsoft
One Medical Group Marketing
Skoda
Volkswagen
YMCA

ICC
(Formerly ICC Lowe)
5 Sylvan Way, Parsippany, NJ 07054
(See Separate Listing)

NeON
1400 Broadway, New York, NY 10018
Tel.: (212) 727-5600
Web Site: www.neon-nyc.com

Employees: 95

Agency Specializes In: Health Care Services, Sponsorship

Mark Arnold *(Mng Dir & Exec VP)*
Kevin McHale *(Exec VP & Mng Dir-Creative)*
Kate Knouse *(Sr VP & Acct Grp Supvr)*
Sabrina R. Prince *(Sr VP & Grp Acct Supvr)*
Courtney Lynch *(VP & Assoc Dir-Creative)*
Nicole Habib *(VP & Acct Grp Supvr)*
Manning Krull *(Dir-Tech)*
Meg Holland *(Acct Supvr)*
Pornima Tavkar *(Supvr-Art)*
Jorge Batista *(Assoc Producer)*
Pierce Gaynor *(Grp Supvr-Copy)*

Accounts:
Boehringer Ingelheim GmbH Mycardis, Telmisartan, Twynsta
Gilead Sciences Inc. Atripla
Johnson & Johnson Canagliflozin
Pfizer Inc Cleocin, Coverject, Depo

Segal Licensing
219 Dufferin Street, Toronto, ON M6K 3JI Canada
Tel.: (416) 588-8727
E-Mail: toronto@fcb.com
Web Site: www.fcbtoronto.com

Employees: 25
Year Founded: 1994

Agency Specializes In: Above-the-Line, Advertising, Below-the-Line, Broadcast, Digital/Interactive, Exhibit/Trade Shows, Promotions, Sports Market

Stuart Pollock *(Pres)*
Carol Lovell *(Dir-Licensing & Promotions)*
Natasha Palmieri *(Mgr-Licensing & Mktg)*

DraftFCB North America

FCB Chicago
(Formerly Draftfcb)
875 N Michigan Ave, Chicago, IL 60611
Tel.: (312) 425-5000
Fax: (312) 425-5010
E-Mail: chicago@fcb.com
Web Site: https://fcbchi.com/

Employees: 600
Year Founded: 1873

National Agency Associations: 4A's-AC-AD CLUB-AMA-AWNY-BMA-DMA-IAA-IAB-PMA-PPA-RAMA-WDMI

Agency Specializes In: Above-the-Line, Advertising, Advertising Specialties, Affiliate Marketing, Affluent Market, Alternative Advertising, Arts, Automotive, Aviation & Aerospace, Below-the-Line, Bilingual Market, Brand Development & Integration, Branded Entertainment, Broadcast, Business Publications, Business-To-Business, Cable T.V., Catalogs, Children's Market, Co-op Advertising, Collateral, College, Commercial Photography, Communications, Computers & Software, Consulting, Consumer Goods, Consumer Marketing, Consumer Publications, Content, Corporate Communications, Corporate Identity, Cosmetics, Crisis Communications, Custom Publishing, Customer Relationship Management, Digital/Interactive, Direct Response Marketing, Direct-to-Consumer, E-Commerce, Education, Electronic Media, Electronics, Email, Engineering, Entertainment, Environmental, Event Planning & Marketing, Exhibit/Trade Shows, Experience Design, Fashion/Apparel, Financial, Food Service, Game Integration, Government/Political, Graphic Design, Guerilla Marketing, Health Care Services, High Technology, Hispanic Market, Hospitality, Household Goods, Identity Marketing, In-Store Advertising, Industrial, Infomercials, Information Technology, Integrated Marketing, International, Internet/Web Design, Investor Relations, Legal Services, Leisure, Local Marketing, Logo & Package Design, Luxury Products, Magazines, Marine, Market Research, Media Buying Services, Media Planning, Media Relations, Media Training, Men's Market, Mobile Marketing, Multicultural, Multimedia, New Product Development, New Technologies, Newspaper, Newspapers & Magazines, Out-of-Home Media, Outdoor, Over-50 Market, Package Design, Paid Searches, Pharmaceutical, Planning & Consultation, Podcasting, Point of Purchase, Point of Sale, Print, Product Placement, Production, Production (Print), Promotions, Public Relations, Publicity/Promotions, Publishing, Radio, Retail, Sales Promotion, Search Engine Optimization, Seniors' Market, Social Marketing/Nonprofit, South Asian Market, Sponsorship, Sports Market, Stakeholders, Strategic Planning/Research, Sweepstakes, Syndication, T.V., Technical Advertising, Teen Market, Telemarketing, Trade & Consumer Magazines, Transportation, Travel & Tourism, Urban Market, Viral/Buzz/Word of Mouth, Women's Market, Yellow Pages Advertising

Michael Fassnacht *(Pres & CEO)*
Sue Redington *(Sr VP & Dir-Bus Dev)*
Mark Jungwirth *(CFO)*
Todd Tilford *(Chief Creative Officer)*
Tina Manikas *(Pres-FCB & RED)*
Susan Treacy *(Exec VP & Exec Dir-Creative)*
Teddy Brown *(Exec VP & Grp Dir-Creative)*
Kelly Graves *(Exec VP & Grp Dir-Mgmt)*
Cary Pierce *(Exec VP & Grp Dir-Mgmt)*
Bella Patel *(Exec VP & Dir-HR)*
Max Geraldo *(Sr VP & Exec Dir-Creative)*
Curtis Munk *(Sr VP & Grp Dir-Plng)*
Michael Pruskowski *(Sr VP & Grp Dir-Engagement)*
Christine Lindquist *(Sr VP & Grp Mgmt Dir-Healthcare)*
Jennifer Neumann *(Sr VP & Grp Mgmt Dir)*
Edward Stojakovic *(VP & Dir-Experience Plng)*
Tim Hawkey *(Exec Creative Dir)*
John Claxton *(Grp Dir-Creative)*
Joel Wheat *(Sr Dir-Art)*
Melanie Hellenga *(Grp Acct Dir)*
Josh Hurley *(Creative Dir)*
Andy Kohman *(Creative Dir)*
Lauren Lenart *(Art Dir)*
Paula Searing *(Art Dir)*
Luis Sierra *(Art Dir)*
Lauren Swago *(Art Dir)*
Tyler Hattery *(Dir-Creative)*
Nick Kraska *(Dir-Digital Products)*
Sarah Kruse *(Dir-Strategic Plng)*
Gabriel Schmitt *(Dir-Creative)*
Blair Spector *(Mgr-HR)*
Katie Stapor *(Mgr-HR)*
Alex Marquard *(Acct Exec)*
Ashley Pierre-Louis *(Acct Exec)*
Amanda Strauss *(Acct Exec)*
Matthaus Everts *(Copywriter)*
Lily Hoffman *(Copywriter)*
Lauren Hystead *(Copywriter)*
Laura Potucek *(Assoc Creative Dir)*

Accounts:
Ace Hardware Campaign: "Helpful Is Beautiful", The Paint Studio
Anheuser-Busch InBev Bud Light Lime, Creative Advertising, Michelob Ultra, MixxTail, Ritas
ARAMARK Global Business
Beiersdorf, Inc. Eucerin, Nivea, Nivea Body Care, Nivea for Men
Big Heart Pet Brands
Boeing; 2001
Brown-Forman Below-the-Line, Campaign: "Tonight. Two Words. Jack Fire", Casa Herradura, Jack Daniel's, Tennessee Fire
Choose Chicago Creative
Coca-Cola Refreshments USA, Inc. Shopper Marketing; 2010
Copic Thick + Fine
Cox Communications Social Media Strategy
Diner's Club International; 1991
Discover Financial Services
Dow Chemical Campaign: "Giant Chalkboard", Campaign: "Hopeful"; 2006
Electronic Arts
Fleetmatics
New-GOJO Industries, Inc. Purell
Humane Society Maddie's Fund
Janssen Biotech, Inc.
Kikkoman International, Inc. Kikkoman, Kikkoman International, Inc.
Arediths Miracles Colon Cancer Foundation
MFS Investment Management (Agency of Record) Media Planning & Buying
MilkPEP
Motorola Solutions, Inc. MotoActv
Nestle USA, Inc. Gerber, Nesquik, Outshine, Pure Life
PACCAR
New-Pizza
Raybern Foods
Sears Holdings Corporation "Cavernous", "Dinner Party", "User Name", Creative, Home Appliances and Services, Kmart, Online, TV
Sony
State Farm
Tombstone
Valspar Campaign: "Cityscapes", Campaign: "Color For All", Digital, Print, TV; 2010
Verisign .com & .net Registration, Advertising, Campaign: "Fish on a Bus", Campaign: "Make Your Idea Official"

FCB Garfinkel
(Formerly FCB New York)
100 W 33rd St, New York, NY 10001
Tel.: (212) 885-3000
Fax: (212) 885-3300
E-Mail: hello@fcb.com
Web Site: www.fcb.com

Employees: 100
Year Founded: 1873

National Agency Associations: 4A's

Agency Specializes In: Above-the-Line, Advertising, Alternative Advertising, Below-the-Line, Broadcast, Customer Relationship Management, Digital/Interactive, Direct Response Marketing, Guerilla Marketing, In-Store Advertising, Integrated Marketing, Mobile Marketing, Multimedia, Newspaper, Newspapers & Magazines, Outdoor, Promotions, Shopper Marketing, Social Media, Sponsorship, Viral/Buzz/Word of Mouth

Lee Garfinkel *(CEO)*
Kofi Amoo-Gottfried *(Chief Strategy Officer & Exec*

VP)
Leo Mamorsky *(Exec VP & Grp Dir-Mgmt)*
Jennifer Comiteau *(Sr VP & Dir-Corp Comm-North America)*
Mariela Orochena *(VP & Dir-Talent Acquisition)*
Greg Wikoff *(VP & Assoc Dir-Creative)*
Akos Papp *(Sr Dir-Art)*
Patrick Carella *(Creative Dir)*
Liz King *(Creative Dir)*
Maggie Thomas *(Acct Dir)*
John Riccobono *(Assoc Dir-Talent Acq)*

Accounts:
Beiersdorf Aquaphor, Eucerin, Nivea, Nivea For Men; 1999
FDA
Fisher Price; 2001
Jamaica Tourist Board Campaign: "Bikini", Campaign: "Chicken", Campaign: "Jamaica, Home of All Right", Campaign: "One Team-One Love", Campaign: "Scuba", Campaign: "Waterfall", Campaign: "Wedding"; 1990
New-Lincoln Financial Group (Creative Agency of Record)
National Railroad Passenger Corporation Acela Express, Amtrak, Campaign: "500 Destinations. Infinite Stories", Campaign: "Take Off", Digital, OOH, Print, Social Media, TV; 2012
Nestle Waters North America (Lead Agency) Brand Strategy, Regional Spring Water Portfolio
Partnership Drug Free America
SeaWorld Parks & Entertainment; Orlando, FL Busch Gardens, Sea World, Sesame Place
Tourism Jamaica Campaign: "Jamaica Valentine"
U.S. FDA Campaign: "The Real Cost", FDA Anti-Smoking, Online, Out of Home, Print, Radio; 2013
USDA Child & Adult Care Food Program, New Food Pyramid
Vonage Holdings Corporation (Agency of Record) B2B Marketing, Brand Strategy, Campaign: "The Business of Better", Campaign: "The Didn't Hit", Digital, Online, Print, Radio, TV

FCB/RED
875 N Michigan Ave, Chicago, IL 60611
Tel.: (312) 425-5000
Web Site: www.fcb.com

Agency Specializes In: Shopper Marketing

Tina Manikas *(Pres)*
Suzanna Bierwith *(Sr VP & Dir-Creative)*
Howard Klein, *(Sr VP & Grp Mgmt Dir)*
Jon Morrow *(Sr Dir-Art)*
Lindsay Tomek *(Acct Dir-Global)*
Brendan Fitzpatrick *(Dir-Experience Design-FCB Chicago)*
Jason Methner *(Dir-Analytics)*
Jennifer Asai *(Supvr-Analytics)*

Accounts:
Fleetmatics
Ghiradelli Chocolate Company Web Design

FCB Seattle
(Formerly Draftfcb)
1425 4th Ave Ste 1000, Seattle, WA 98101
Tel.: (206) 223-6464
Fax: (206) 223-2765
E-Mail: hello@fcb.com
Web Site: www.fcb.com

Employees: 20

Agency Specializes In: Advertising, Digital/Interactive, Direct Response Marketing, Integrated Marketing, Promotions, Sponsorship

Jaime Krummel *(Mng Dir & Sr VP)*
Dustin Cook *(Acct Supvr)*

Accounts:
Hewlett Packard; 2002

FCB West
(Formerly Draftfcb)
200 Mildred Ave, Venice, CA 90291
Tel.: (415) 820-8000
Fax: (415) 820-8087
E-Mail: hello@fcb.com
Web Site: www.fcb.com

Employees: 20

Agency Specializes In: Advertising, Brand Development & Integration, Event Planning & Marketing, Media Planning, Strategic Planning/Research

Karin Onsager-Birch *(Chief Creative Officer)*
Dominic Whittles *(CEO-FCB West)*

Accounts:
Taco Bell
US Forest Service Smokes Bear

FCB West
(Formerly Draftfcb West)
1160 Battery St Ste 250, San Francisco, CA 94111
Tel.: (415) 820-8000
Fax: (415) 820-8087
Web Site: www.fcb.com

Employees: 80
Year Founded: 1873

National Agency Associations: 4A's

Agency Specializes In: Advertising, Digital/Interactive, Direct Response Marketing, Electronic Media, Event Planning & Marketing, Integrated Marketing, Promotions, Sponsorship, Sports Market, Strategic Planning/Research

Dominic Whittles *(CEO)*
Ted Manyon *(CFO)*
Vicki McRae *(Sr VP & COO)*
Karin Onsager-Birch *(Chief Creative Officer)*
Colin McRae *(Grp Creative Dir)*
Brooks Day *(Sr VP-Bus Dev-FCB Global)*
Eileen McCarthy *(Sr VP-HR)*
Isaac Clemens *(VP & Acct Dir)*
Rachel Gill *(Acct Dir)*
Amy Matheu *(Art Dir)*
Drew Meiser *(Art Dir)*
Jacob Pepper *(Art Dir)*
Carla Madden *(Dir-Creative & Copywriter)*
Christina De La Cruz *(Assoc Dir-Creative)*
Lauren Geismar *(Acct Supvr)*
Elaine Cox *(Assoc Creative Dir)*
Crystal Thomas *(Acct Exec)*
Frank Fusco *(Copywriter)*
Abby McBeth *(Asst Acct Exec)*

Accounts:
Air New Zealand (Agency of Record)
Big Heart Pet Brands Meow Mix, Milo's Kitchen, Nature's Recipe
Dockers
Electronic Arts Inc. "Quest for the Red Lyrium Reapers", Broadcast, Campaign: "Battlefield Hardline", Campaign: "Fight", Campaign: "Lead Them or Fall", Campaign: "The Breach", Campaign: "Your Mom Hates Dead Space 2", Content, Dragon Age Inquisition, Online
Ghirardelli Chocolate Co. Creative; 2014
Kikkoman International, Inc. Campaign: "Make Haste Slowly:The Kikkoman Creed", Kikkoman, Kikkoman International, Inc.
Levi's 501 CT, Campaign: "Beautiful Morning", Campaign: "For Every Woman. For Every Original", Campaign: "Just Don't Bore Them", Campaign: "Live in Levi's", Creative, Denim Pants, Global Marketing, Social, TV
PG&E
Taco Bell Corp. In-Store, Merchandising, Packaging; 2000
Trulia Campaign: "Look", Campaign: "Moment of Trulia", Campaign: "Shower", Digital, Outdoor, Radio, TV

Canada

FCB Montreal
(Formerly Draftfcb Montreal)
1751 rue Richardson Suite 6.200, Montreal, QC H3K 1G6 Canada
Tel.: (514) 938-4141
Fax: (514) 938-2022
E-Mail: bonjour@fcb.com
Web Site: www.fcbmontreal.com

Employees: 45
Year Founded: 1989

Agency Specializes In: Advertising, Communications, Direct Response Marketing

Rachelle Claveau *(Pres)*
Joe Spilak *(VP & Dir-Production)*
Carole Morin *(VP-Ops)*
Radu Zmeureanu *(Head-Digital & CRM Practice)*
Gaelle Cayrol *(Acct Dir)*
Camille Fortier-Jordan *(Acct Dir)*
Karine Camirand *(Acct Mgr)*
Naomi Ko *(Acct Exec)*
Anne-Marie Lavoie *(Graphic Designer & Designer-Web)*
Joel Letarte *(Copywriter)*
Nicolas Cote-Bruneau *(Acct Coord-FCB Global)*
Hugo Monin *(Acct Coord-FCB Global)*

Accounts:
Air Canada
Beiersdorf
Fido
Loto-Quebec
Royal Canadian Mint
Tetra Pak
Weight Watchers

FCB Toronto
(Formerly Draftfcb Toronto)
219 Dufferin Street, Toronto, ON M6K 3JI Canada
Tel.: (416) 483-3600
Fax: (416) 489-8782
E-Mail: toronto@fcb.com
Web Site: fcbtoronto.com/

Employees: 200
Year Founded: 1951

National Agency Associations: ICA

Agency Specializes In: Advertising, Communications, Digital/Interactive, Direct Response Marketing, Publicity/Promotions

Ricky Jacobs *(Mng Dir, VP & Head-Digital)*
Jon Flannery *(Chief Creative Officer)*
Jeff Hilts *(VP & Grp Head-Creative)*
Nancy Crimi-Lamanna *(VP & Dir-Creative)*
Sunil Sekhar *(VP & Dir-Mgmt)*
Naeem Walji *(Dir-Art)*
Matthaus Frost *(Assoc Dir-Creative)*
Carmen Steger *(Acct Mgr)*
Jason Freeman *(Acct Exec)*
Sabiha Chaudry *(Copywriter-Global)*

Accounts:
Anheuser-Busch InBev Creative Advertising, Michelob Ultra
BMO (Lead Agency) Campaign: "Bank that Knows Ball", Creative
BMW; 2010

Canadian Institute of Chartered Accountants; 2008
Dole; 2010
Fairmont Hotels
Foodland Ontario
Government of Ontario Ministries
Jamaica Tourism
Levi Strauss
Mondelez Chips Ahoy!, Oreo
Mongrel Media Marketing, Media Buying
Nestle Delissio
Ontario Lottery & Gaming (OLG)
Ontario Power Authority
The Ontario Tourism Marketing Partnership Corporation 2015 Pan Am Games, Campaign: "Epic is on", Campaign: "Invade"; 2010
Ontario Tourism; 2010
Paradise Pools Campaign: "Better"
Pflag Canada Campaign: "Jazz"
Sun Life Financial Branding, Marketing
Sunkist Growers
Toronto Jewish Film Festival
Weight Watchers
WSIB

Austria

FCB Neuwien
(Formerly FCB Vienna)
Mariahilfer Strasse 17, 1060 Vienna, Austria
Tel.: (43) 1379110
Fax: (43) 1379111030
E-Mail: vienna@fcb.com
Web Site: www.fcbneuwien.at

Employees: 35

Agency Specializes In: Above-the-Line, Advertising, Below-the-Line, Digital/Interactive, Direct Response Marketing, Retail

Rudi Kobza *(CEO)*
Christoph Schlossnikel *(Dir-Creative)*

Accounts:
Amnesty International
Beiersdorf; 2002
EVN
IONIT; 2011
Laurens Spethman Milford Tee
Lindt & Spruengli
Marionnaud; 2013
OBB
OMV
Unibail-Rodamco Donauzentrum; 2010
Unicredit Bank Austria
Verein Wiener Frauenhauser Campaign: "Offensive Pop-Up for Women's Shelters"
Vienna Insurance Group; 2011
West Africa Children's Aid Donation Appeal
Western Union

Bulgaria

FCB Sofia
(Formerly Business Data Ltd.)
6 Maragidik St, Sofia, 1505 Bulgaria
Tel.: (359) 2 943 4451
Fax: (359) 29434165
E-Mail: hello@fcbsofia.bg
Web Site: www.fcb.com

Employees: 35
Year Founded: 1992

Agency Specializes In: Advertising, Direct Response Marketing, Media Buying Services, Promotions, Public Relations, Sales Promotion

Ivan Sidzhakov *(Mng Dir & Head-Creative)*
Irena Stavreva *(Mng Dir)*
Boryana Pasheva *(Dir-Media)*

Accounts:
Beiersdorf Eucerin, Nivea
Mondelez Oreo
Panasonic
Tchibo
Wizz Air

Czech Republic

FCB Prague
(Formerly Draftfcb s r.o.)
Zerotinova 1133/32, Prague, 130 00 Czech Republic
Tel.: (420) 225 384 666
Fax: (420) 225 384 685
E-Mail: ahoj@fcbprague.cz
Web Site: www.fcb.com

Employees: 25

Agency Specializes In: Advertising, Digital/Interactive, Direct Response Marketing, Exhibit/Trade Shows, Mobile Marketing, Promotions

Petr Bartos *(CEO)*
Liz Gump *(Mng Dir & Sr VP)*
Katerina Pauzarova *(Acct Dir)*
Radek Rytina *(Dir-Creative)*

Accounts:
Beiersdorf; 1996
Berentzen
HDK Music Theater
Kika
Mondelez Oreo, TUC
UNIQA
UPC

France

FCB Paris
(Formerly Draftfcb)
21 rue de Berri, 75008 Paris, France
Tel.: (33) 141067500
Fax: (33) 158749081
E-Mail: info@fcbparis.fr
Web Site: www.fcb.com

Employees: 25
Year Founded: 1964

National Agency Associations: AACC

Agency Specializes In: Advertising, Digital/Interactive, Direct Response Marketing

Nathalie Cogis *(Pres)*
Laure Poquet *(Deputy Dir Gen)*
Virginie Clerget *(Head-New Bus & Strategy)*
Julien Rotterman *(Dir-Creative)*

Accounts:
Beiersdorf Eucerin, Nivea; 1997
Blini Atelier, Blini; 2014
Branded Apparel Playtex; 2013
Mondelez International, Inc. Oreo, Tuc; 2009
SNCF; 2005
Sygma Bank; 2014

Germany

FCB Hamburg
(Formerly Draftfcb)
Bleichenbruecke 10, D-20354 Hamburg, Germany
Tel.: (49) 40 28 810
Fax: (49) 40 28 81 1270
E-Mail: hamburg.info@fcb.com
Web Site: www.fcb.com

Employees: 130

Agency Specializes In: Above-the-Line, Advertising, Below-the-Line, Digital/Interactive, Direct Response Marketing, Promotions

Janina Levy *(Mng Dir)*
Erika Darmstaedter *(Chief Client Officer-Beiersdorf Acct)*
Constantin Kaloff *(Exec Dir-Creative-Global)*
Patricia Nassauer *(Acct Dir-Global)*
Christina Appleton *(Planner-Strategic)*
James Dodd *(Copywriter)*
Valerie Gast *(Planner-Global Brand)*

Accounts:
Aramark; 2014
Beiersdorf Eucerin, Lead Global Creative Agency, Nivea Sun; 1978
Heidelberger Leben
Iberia Airlines
Igepa
JTI Camel
Lieken Brot & Backwaren Lieken Urkorn Golden Toast; 2007
Lindt & Spruengli Lindt
Mondelez Oreo, Tuc; 2001
Peter Koelin Koelin Muesli; 2012
Philharmoniker Hamburg Campaign: "When Music Flows into Pictures"
New-Zoover

Greece

FCB Gnomi
(Formerly Gnomi + Draftfcb)
Iroos Matsi & Archaiou Theatrou Str, Alimos, Athens, 17456 Greece
Tel.: (30) 210 962 6707
Fax: (30) 210 960 1722
E-Mail: fcbgnomi@fcbgnomi.gr
Web Site: www.fcb.com

Employees: 30
Year Founded: 1953

National Agency Associations: IAA

Agency Specializes In: Advertising, Digital/Interactive, Direct Response Marketing, Promotions, Public Relations, Strategic Planning/Research

Christina Hohlakidis *(Mng Dir)*
George Vacondios *(Gen Mgr)*
Yiannis Barboutis *(Dir-Creative)*

Accounts:
Attica Group Blue Star & Superfast Ferries
Beiersdorf Duo, Eucerin, Futuro, Nivea, Tesa; 1999
BSH
Druckfarben Kraft Paints; 2014
EPSA; 2014
Grigoris Mini Lunches
Karamolegos
Mondelez International, Inc. Oreo
Novartis
Revoil; 2005
Toi & Moi

Italy

FCB Milan
(Formerly Draftfcb Milan)
Via Spadolini 7, Milan, 20144 Italy
Tel.: (39) 02 77 411
Fax: (39) 02 78 12 63
E-Mail: milano@fcb.com
Web Site: www.fcb.com

Employees: 65

Agency Specializes In: Advertising, Digital/Interactive, Direct Response Marketing, Promotions

Franco Ricchiuti *(Pres & CEO)*
Luis Silva Dias *(Chief Creative Officer)*
Giorgia Francescato *(Exec VP)*
Susanna Revoltella *(Head-Plng)*
Michele Costante *(Art Dir)*
Gianluca Belmonte *(Assoc Dir-Creative)*
Agnese Salvatore *(Acct Supvr)*

Accounts:
Beiersdorf; 1997
BSH Bosch; 2014
Fila; 2011
Lan Tam; 2014
Lufthansa; 2011
Metro Metro Cash & Carry; 2011
Mondelez Oreo, TUC
Poste Italiene
TAM Airlines
Viacom Nickelodeon; 2010
World Children's Fund

Netherlands

FCB Amsterdam
(Formerly Draftfcb)
Bovenkerkerweg 6-8, Amsterdam, 1185 XE Netherlands
Tel.: (31) 20 573 1111
Fax: (31) 20 573 1310
E-Mail: info.amsterdam@fcb.com
Web Site: www.fcb.com

Employees: 50
Year Founded: 1988

Agency Specializes In: Advertising, Digital/Interactive, Direct Response Marketing, Promotions

Benjamin Messelink *(Chm & Mng Dir)*
Peter Custers *(Creative Dir)*
Lisette Peperkamp *(Client Svcs Dir)*
Joost Van Der Pol *(Jr Producer)*

Accounts:
AON Insurance; 2012
Beiersdorf Eucerin, Nivea
Budget Rent A Car; 2012
Fashioncheque; 2013
Habitat for Humanity; 2013
ING; 2011
KPN; 2011
Mitsubishi Motors Campaign: "Letter"; 2010
Mondelez Oreo, Tuc
MVO Nederland; 2014
PACCAR
Salvation Army Campaign: "Cut for Christmas"
Unilever Blue Band
New-Zoover

Poland

FCB Warsaw
(Formerly Draftfcb)
ul Cybernetyki 19A, 02-677 Warsaw, Poland
Tel.: (48) 224808400
Fax: (48) 224808401
E-Mail: poland.info@fcb.com
Web Site: www.fcb.com

Employees: 20

Agency Specializes In: Above-the-Line, Advertising, Below-the-Line, Digital/Interactive, Direct Response Marketing, Promotions

Marcin Godlewski *(Mng Dir)*
Gosia Drozdowska *(Sr Dir-Art & Dir-Creative)*
Agnieszka Klimczak *(Dir-Creative & Sr Copywriter)*
Ilona Keciek *(Acct Mgr)*
Katarzyna Kociuba *(Acct Mgr)*

Accounts:
Beiersdorf Eucerin, Nivea; 1997
D.E. Master Blenders 1753 Douwe Egberts, Prima; 2008
Lotto Lotto Ekstea Pensja Mini Lotek
Mondelez Oreo, Tuc
Prima Cafe
RWE; 2012

Portugal

FCB Lisbon
(Formerly meredith xcelerated)
Rua Braamcamp No 40 7th Floor, 1250-050 Lisbon, Portugal
Tel.: (351) 2 1381 1200
Fax: (351) 213811279
E-Mail: geral.lisboa@fcb.pt
Web Site: www.fcb.com

Employees: 30
Year Founded: 1981

National Agency Associations: APAP (Portugal)

Agency Specializes In: Advertising, Below-the-Line, Digital/Interactive, Direct Response Marketing, Media Buying Services, Promotions

Edson Athayde *(CEO & Chief Creative Officer)*
Vera Barros *(CFO)*
Luis Silva Dias *(Chief Creative Officer)*
Eduardo Tavares *(Sr Dir-Art)*
Carlos Baptista *(Acct Dir)*
David Rafachinho *(Art Dir)*
Victor Afonso *(Dir-Creative)*
Ian Guimaraes *(Dir-Art)*
Filipa Pinto *(Dir-Art)*
Pedro Santos *(Acct Exec)*
Viton Araujo *(Copywriter)*

Accounts:
New-Alma Lasers, Ltd
New-APAV - Portuguese Association for Victim Support
ATA; 2011
Bayer HealthCare
Beiersdorf Eucerin, Nivea; 2000
New-Botaminuto
CIC Group Cofidis; 2009
Controlinveste Journal de Noticias, Media, O Jogo
Granacer; 2010
Harmony XL Campaign: "For He Who Has More", Campaign: "Looong-Lasting Pleasure", Print
Lidl; 2013
Mondelez Oreo, Tuc
Mundicenter II
Nova University
Prime Drinks Balverie, Glenfiddich, Hendricks; 2010
ReMax; 2010
SATA Azorean Spirit; 2011
SCC Luso; 2014
Secil Secil; 2009
Turismo de Portugal

Romania

FCB Bucharest
(Formerly Draftfcb)
31bis Intrarea Rigas 1st District, Bucharest, 334013 Romania
Tel.: (40) 21 231 4092
Fax: (40) 21 231 4062
E-Mail: office@fcb.ro
Web Site: www.fcb.com

Employees: 75

Agency Specializes In: Above-the-Line, Advertising, Below-the-Line, Digital/Interactive, Direct Response Marketing, Promotions

Bogdan Santea *(Pres & CEO)*
Miruna Macsoda *(Acct Dir & Coord-Digital)*
Ana-Maria Oila *(Acct Dir)*
Claudiu Dobrita *(Dir-Creative)*
Andreea Serbu *(Acct Mgr)*
Ana Velici *(Mgr-Event)*
Diana Focea *(Sr Acct Exec)*
Alexandru Tigoianu *(Copywriter)*

Accounts:
Beiersdorf; 2001
JTI
Lavazza; 2005
New-Lego
Mondelez Milka, Oreo, Tuc; 2007
New-Staropramen
Vodafone; 2008

Serbia

FCB Afirma
(Formerly Draftfcb Afirma)
Cara Dusana 42, 11000 Belgrade, Serbia
Tel.: (381) 11 1328 4620
Fax: (381) 11 1262 2645
E-Mail: office@fcbafirma.rs
Web Site: www.fcb.rs

Employees: 35

Agency Specializes In: Above-the-Line, Advertising, Below-the-Line, Customer Relationship Management, Digital/Interactive, Media Buying Services, Promotions

Dejan Nedic *(CEO)*
Goran Ruskuc *(Head-Creative)*
Borivoje Ljubicic *(Sr Dir-Art)*
Bozidar Cvetkovic *(Dir-Creative)*
Karim Salim *(Dir-Digital Creative)*
Ljiljana Balic *(Sr Acct Mgr)*
Ana Savic *(Acct Mgr)*
Vesna Latas *(Copywriter-Web)*
Marko Milin *(Sr Designer)*
Bojana Rajicic *(Designer)*
Marko Samardzija *(Sr Designer-Web)*

Accounts:
Beiersdorf; 2002
Grand Kafa Grand Gold
Ikea; 2008
Mondelez
Neoplanta
Serbian National Lottery Lotto

Spain

FCB Spain
(Formerly Draftfcb)
Doctor Forquet 29, 28012 Madrid, Spain
Tel.: (34) 913104549
Fax: (34) 913104840
E-Mail: spain@fcb.com
Web Site: www.fcb.com

Employees: 40

Agency Specializes In: Advertising, Digital/Interactive, Direct Response Marketing, Promotions, Strategic Planning/Research

Pablo Munoz *(Pres & CEO)*
Marc Wiederkehr *(CFO)*
Manuel Lopez Pineiro *(Head-Strategy)*
Pedro Soler *(Exec Dir-Creative)*

Juan Ramon Ortega *(Grp Acct Dir)*
Antonio Otero *(Dir-Bus Dev, PR & Comm)*
Courtney Imel *(Sr Analyst-Digital)*

Accounts:
Acciona Transmediterranea; 2013
Beiersdorf Eucerin, Nivea
Canal+ Campaign: "Leave Wilhelm Alone"
Coca-Cola; 2013
Deutsche Bank
Heineken Desperados; 2012
JTI; 2004
McDonald's; 2013
Mondelez; 2009
PACCAR Parts; 2009
Varma Barcelo Rum, Hendrick's Gin, Sailor Jerry; 2008

FCB Spain
(Formerly Draftfcb)
Muntaner 240-242 5 2a, 08021 Barcelona, Spain
Tel.: (34) 932065800
Fax: (34) 932065802
E-Mail: spain@fcb.com
Web Site: www.fcb.com

Employees: 10

Agency Specializes In: Advertising, Digital/Interactive, Direct Response Marketing, Promotions, Strategic Planning/Research

Pablo Munoz *(Pres & CEO)*

Accounts:
Beiersdorf Eucerin, Nivea
Mondelez Oreo, TUC

Sweden

FCB Faltman & Malmen
Valhallavagen 86, Stockholm, 100 41 Sweden
Tel.: (46) 8 406 6500
E-Mail: info@faltman-malmen.se
Web Site: www.faltman-malmen.se

Employees: 35
Year Founded: 1965

Agency Specializes In: Advertising

Ellen Strom *(Partner, Sr Dir-Art & Dir-Digital)*
Johan Eriksson *(Partner & Sr Dir-Art)*
Add Hovqvist *(VP-HR)*
Jessica Hemmingsson *(Acct Dir)*
Magnus Faltman *(Dir-Creative)*
Johanna Linander *(Dir-New Bus)*
Fred Raaum *(Dir-Client Svcs)*
Emmelie Engstrom *(Office Mgr)*
Gunilla Lundqvist *(Strategist-PR)*
Luke Klepke *(Designer-Final Art)*
Viktor Olsson *(Copywriter)*
Add Willborg *(Planner)*

Accounts:
The Absolut Company Campaign: "Absolut Illusion"
Beiersdorf
Giovanni Rana Campaign: "Italification"
Hewlett Packard
HSB Stockholm
JTI Camel, Winston
Mondelez International, Inc.
The National Museum
Siemens
Stockholm Arlanda Airport Campaign: "There's always a good reason to travel"
Swedavia Campaign: "The Office"
Trygga Barnen Foundation

Switzerland

FCB Zurich
(Formerly Draftfcb)
Heinrichstrasse 267, Zurich, 8005 Switzerland
Tel.: (41) 44 877 8787
Fax: (41) 44 877 8750
E-Mail: info@fcbzuerich.com
Web Site: www.fcbzuerich.com

Employees: 30
Year Founded: 1962

National Agency Associations: BSW

Agency Specializes In: Advertising, Digital/Interactive, Direct Response Marketing, Promotions, Strategic Planning/Research

Cornelia Harder *(Pres)*
Johannes Eisenhut *(Head-Strategy)*
Dennis Lueck *(Exec Dir-Creative)*
Flavio Meroni *(Acct Dir)*
Mark Becher *(Dir-Client Svc & Strategic Plng)*
Nina Danner *(Client Svc Dir)*
Marie-Theres Ott *(Client Svc Dir)*

Accounts:
Beiersdorf Nivea, Eucerin, Labello, Hansaplast; 2000
Greenpeace Campaign: "Goliath Chainsaw"
New-Hero Group Global Advertising, Masterbrand
MTV
National MS Society
Nespresso
Neuroth Campaign: "Hearing Test Concert"
SVV-TCS
Swiss Youth Symphony Orchestra
Swisshaus
Unilever Knorr

Turkey

FCB Artgroup
(Formerly FCB Istanbul)
Kilic Ali Pasa Caddesi No:12 K:5, 34425 Tophane, Istanbul, Turkey
Tel.: (90) 2122924242
Fax: (90) 2122924243
E-Mail: info.turkey@fcb.com
Web Site: www.fcb.com

Employees: 40

Agency Specializes In: Advertising

Fehmi Ozkan *(Co-Pres)*
Ozgur Saglam *(Co-Pres)*
Vedat Sertoglu *(Sr VP)*
Ali Doganli *(Exec Creative Dir)*
Yavuzhan Gel *(Dir-Creative)*

Accounts:
Adel Kalemcilik; 2013
Akyurek Pazarlama Cafe Breno; 2013
Beiersdorf 8x4, Nivea
Coca-Cola Refreshments USA, Inc. Cappy, Coca-Cola, Fanta, Sprite; 2003
Dogtas; 2013
Girisim Pazarlama Egos, Hijyenmax; 2013
Mercedes Car Group; 2013
Mondelez International Oreo, Tuc; 2004
Suzuki
Tesco Tesco Kipa; 2013

United Kingdom

FCB Inferno
(Formerly Inferno + Draftfcb)
31 Great Queen Street, Covent Garden, London, WC2B 5AE United Kingdom
Tel.: (44) 20 3048 0000
E-Mail: hello@fcbinferno.com
Web Site: www.fcbinferno.com

Employees: 200

Agency Specializes In: Above-the-Line, Advertising, Below-the-Line, Customer Relationship Management, Digital/Interactive, Direct Response Marketing, Health Care Services, Strategic Planning/Research

Katy Wright *(Mng Partner)*
Sharon Jiggins *(Mng Dir)*
Tim Doust *(CMO-Bus Dev)*
Owen Lee *(Co-Chief Creative Officer)*
Simon White *(Chief Strategy Officer)*
Jonathan Acton *(Head-Interactive Delivery)*
Gilles Bestley *(Head-Interactive Design)*
Elspeth Lynn *(Grp Dir-Creative)*
Raymond Chan *(Art Dir)*
Helena Georghiou *(Acct Dir)*
Chris Spore *(Art Dir)*
Paul Blundell *(Dir-Interactive & Innovation)*
Isabelle Soskice *(Sr Acct Mgr)*

Accounts:
Allergan; 2013
Beiersdorf
Nivea Deodorant, Nivea Cream, Nivea Men Creme, TV
BMW (UK) Ltd BMW 3, Broadcast, Campaign: "Curiosity", Campaign: "xDrive", Creative, Online, hybrid i8
Coca-Cola Refreshments USA, Inc.; 2010
COI TDA
Columbia Threadneedle (Lead Digital & Integrated Marketing Agency)
Flip-Flop Havaianas, Social Media
Grant's Whisky Online
Hyundai; 2011
Jamaica Tourist Board
LVMH Acqua di Parma; 2012
Mondelez Oreo, Print, Tuc
National Savings & Investment; 2014
Nestle Purina PetCare Purina; 2014
New-Pearson plc
Post Office Ltd. Advertising, Campaign: "Get Christmas All Wrapped Up", Digital, Direct Mail, Retail, Social, TV
Royal Mail Group Post Office
Sailor Jerry Rum Global Digital
Sport England Campaign: "This Girl Can", TV
Sported; 2011
Taco Bell; 2010
Valspar (Lead Creative & Strategic Agency) Campaign: "Colour Outside The Lines", Online, Social Media, TV; 2013
William Grant & Sons; 2014

Draftfcb Middle East Network

Horizon FCB Beirut
Badaro Trade Center, El-Fata Street, Beirut, Lebanon
Tel.: (961) 138 7600
Fax: (961) 11387604
E-Mail: beirut@horizonfcb.com
Web Site: www.fcb.com

Employees: 15

Agency Specializes In: Advertising, Direct Response Marketing, Promotions, Sports Market

Johnny Henoud *(Gen Mgr & Dir-Plng)*
David Bekhazi *(Dir-Creative)*
Siham Saad *(Assoc Dir-Creative)*

Accounts:
Arabia Insurance Company; 2014
Berytech; 2011
BSL
Middle East Airlines

Mondelez Oreo
Optimum Invest; 2011
Swatch Group
Tamanna Campaign: "September Christmas"

Horizon FCB Dubai
(Formerly Horizon Draftfcb Dubai)
Capricorn Tower 10th Floor, PO Box 112411, Sheikh Zayed Road, Dubai, United Arab Emirates
Tel.: (971) 4 354 4458
Fax: (971) 4 354 4459
E-Mail: dubai@horizonfcb.com
Web Site: www.fcb.com

Employees: 45
Year Founded: 1976

Agency Specializes In: Advertising, Digital/Interactive, Direct Response Marketing, Exhibit/Trade Shows, Promotions, Strategic Planning/Research

Mazen Jawad *(Grp Mng Dir)*
Christian Khoury *(Exec Dir-Creative)*
Sanjay Bhatia *(Grp Acct Dir)*
Rona Saadeh *(Dir-Plng)*
Yesser Melhem *(Acct Mgr)*

Accounts:
Abu Dhabi University; 2013
Agthia Yoplait
American University of Beirut Medical Center Brave Heart Fund; 2014
Azadea Group Kosebasi; 2014
Beiersdorf 8X4, Hansaplast, NFM, Nivea
Boeing
Citibank Global Consumer Banking CitiCards, CitiGold, Citibank; 2014
Emami Intl; 2014
Emirates; 2012
H.J. Heinz Farley's, Heinz; 2014
Lamb Weston; 2014
Landmark Group Fun Works; 2013
Mondelez Oreo, Tuc
Nestle Klim; 2013
Oasis Mall Creative
Rivoli Group; 2012
Unilever Tresemme; 2014

Horizon FCB Jeddah
(Formerly Horizon Draftfcb Jeddah)
King Abdullah St Intl Economy Tower 3rd Floor, Jeddah, 21433 Saudi Arabia
Mailing Address:
PO Box 10310, Jeddah, 21433 Saudi Arabia
Tel.: (966) 2 650 3100
Fax: (966) 2 650 3090
E-Mail: admin.jeddah@horizonfcb.com
Web Site: www.fcb.com

Employees: 25
Year Founded: 1984

Agency Specializes In: Advertising, Digital/Interactive, Direct Response Marketing, Media Buying Services, Promotions, Strategic Planning/Research

Tony Rouhana *(VP-Saudi Arabia & Levant)*
Charbel Nasser *(Head-Creative & Sr Dir-Creative)*
Ramy Amm *(Dir-Art)*
Moutaz Jad *(Mgr-Client Svcs & Strategic Plng)*

Accounts:
Advanced Petroleum
Al Madinah Press
Al Murjan Design; 2013
Basamh Industrial Perfetto; 2010
Coach; 2014
Foster Clark
Hyundai Motors; 2005
Islamic Development Bank
National Food Industries Luna
Nestle Kit Kat, Nescafe, Nesquik, Nestle Fitness, Nido; 2012
Saudi Radwa Food Radwa Chicken
Sherwin-Williams; 2014
Toyota; 2013

Horizon FCB Kuwait
(Formerly Horizon.Draftfcb Kuwait)
Al Arabiya Tower Ahmed Al Jaber Street, Sharq Kuwait City, Kuwait, 13062 Kuwait
Tel.: (965) 2226 7371
Fax: (965) 2226 7374
E-Mail: kuwait@horizonfcb.com
Web Site: www.fcb.com

Employees: 24
Year Founded: 1976

Agency Specializes In: Advertising, Digital/Interactive, Direct Response Marketing, Media Buying Services, Promotions

Said Zeneddine *(Mng Dir)*
Richard Halabi *(Dir-Creative)*

Accounts:
Ahli Bank; 2012
Automak; 2013
Behbehani Watches; 2004
Caribou Coffee; 2013
Dow Chemical
Elite Brands Sport Direct; 2013
KAPICO Group Auto 1
Kout Food Group Pizza Hut, Taco Bell; 2010
Kuwait & Gulf Link Transport (KGL)
MS Retail Baroue; 2013
Sama Medical Services Royal Hayat
The Scientific Center
Yasra Fashion

Horizon FCB Riyadh
(Formerly Horizon.Draftfcb Riyadh)
Al Mas Plaza Thahlia Street Office # 205, 2nd Floor, Riyadh, 11474 Saudi Arabia
Tel.: (966) 1 461 7557
Fax: (966) 1 463 3848
E-Mail: riyadh@horizonfcb.com
Web Site: www.fcb.com

Employees: 30
Year Founded: 1970

Agency Specializes In: Advertising, Direct Response Marketing, Media Buying Services, Mobile Marketing, Promotions

Walid Soueidi *(Grp Mng Dir)*
Gregory Bauarschi *(Dir-Plng)*
Nayef Mujaes *(Dir-Creative)*

Accounts:
Al Yamamah University; 2013
Banque Saudi Fransi
GSK Vaccine Unit
Mohammed Al Raijhi & Sons; 2011
National Company for Learning & Education Tarbiah Namozajiah Schools; 2013
Riyadh Food Industries; 2011
Saha Co for Healthcare Dietwatchers; 2013
Saudi Arabian Ministry of Health

Horizon FCB
(Formerly Horizon Draftfcb Cairo)
26 Nadi El Jadeed St, Cairo, Egypt
Tel.: (20) 227555700
Fax: (20) 227555701
E-Mail: cairo@horizonfcb.com
Web Site: www.fcb.com

Employees: 58

Agency Specializes In: Advertising, Digital/Interactive, Direct Response Marketing, Media Buying Services, Promotions, Sports Market

Ayham Semaan *(Mng Dir-Egypt & North Africa)*
Mohamed Saber *(Dir-Creative)*
Tamer Gabr *(Mgr-IT)*

Accounts:
Abu Ghaly Motors
Chrysler Group Chrysler, Dodge, Jeep
Citibank Global Consumer Banking Citibank
G6 Hospitality LLC Coralia Club, Ibis, Novotel, Pullman, Sofitel
Grohe
Moevenpick Hotels
Mondelez International, Inc. Borio, Nity, Rasco, Tuc
Pyramids Cosmetics
Trane

Israel

FCB Shimoni Finkelstein Barki
(Formerly Draftfcb Shimoni Finkelstein)
57 Rothschild Blvd, 65785 Tel Aviv, Israel
Tel.: (972) 747177777
Fax: (972) 747177700
Web Site: www.fcb.com

Employees: 40

Agency Specializes In: Advertising, Digital/Interactive, Direct Response Marketing, Mobile Marketing, Promotions, Strategic Planning/Research

Dudi Shimoni *(Pres & Co-CEO)*
Karin Attal *(Co-CEO)*
Mira Finkelstein *(CEO)*
Yosefa Galante *(Grp Acct Dir)*
Shlomi Vashdi *(Art Dir)*
Efi Wolf *(Dir-Fin)*
Assaf Appelboim *(Copywriter)*

Accounts:
Aliya
Arla Foods
Austrian Airlines Business Flights; 2010
Automotive Equipment Group Campaign: "Car Stickers", Daimler Chrysler, Jeep, Porsche, Suzuki
Bahlsen HIT; 2014
Baiit Balev; 2012
Channel 9; 2011
Ferrero Kinder, Nutella, Rocher, Tic Tac
Friends Of The Swifts NPO
Hebrew University of Jerusalem; 2010
Hewlett-Packard HP Printers; 2013
H.Y. Group Ariston, LG, Que; 2005
The Israel Parkinson Association Parkinson's Patients Writing Ads
Michael Nevin; 2014
Tadiran; 2012

Argentina

FCB Buenos Aires
(Formerly Draftfcb)
Luis Maria Campos 46, Capital Federal, C1425GEN Buenos Aires, Argentina
Tel.: (54) 11 3221 9700
Fax: (54) 11 3221 9720
E-Mail: info.ar@fcb.com
Web Site: www.fcb.com

Employees: 63
Year Founded: 1974

Agency Specializes In: Advertising,

Digital/Interactive, Direct Response Marketing, Promotions

Pablo Dagna *(CFO)*
Tony Waissmann *(Exec Dir-Creative)*
Emiliano Cortez *(Art Dir)*
Lulo Calio *(Dir-Creative)*
Daniel Arango *(Copywriter)*
Dardo Perez *(Copywriter)*
Sebastian Regiani *(Copywriter)*

Accounts:
Advanta; 2010
Beiersdorf
Editorial Atlantida Campaign: "Chair", Campaign: "Tsunami", Para Ti Deco Magazine
Electronic Media ATMA; 2013
Fargo Pan Lactal Fargo; 2012
Fiat Chrysler Jeep; 2013
Fundacion Argentina De Trasplante Campaign: "Soul"
Garbarino; 2012
Johnson & Johnson Campaign: "Dot it, Dot it", Campaign: "I Love It", Ky Gel, Softlotion
Mondelez; 1994
Newsan Braun
Pearle Europe MasVision; 2010
Pequeno Editor Tree Book Tree
Pernod Ricard; 2014
Piero; 2012
SABMiller Miller Lite; 2013
San Up; 2013
Sunstar; 2014

Bolivia

Gramma FCB
(Formerly G. Publicidad SRL)
Torre Empresarial Cainco Piso 7 Oficina 4, Santa Cruz, Bolivia
Tel.: (591) 3339 5426
Fax: (591) 33395420
Web Site: www.fcb.com

Employees: 15

Agency Specializes In: Advertising, Production, Production (Print), Promotions, Publicity/Promotions, Strategic Planning/Research

Arlene R. Arce *(Partner & Dir)*
Renzo Mori *(Dir-Creative)*
Sergio Torrelio *(Dir)*

Brazil

FCB Rio de Janeiro
(Formerly Giovanni Draftfcb)
Av Joao Cabral de Melo Neto 400-7 andar Peninsula Corporate, Barra da Tijuca, Rio de Janeiro, CEP 22359-990 Brazil
Tel.: (55) 21 3501 8500
Fax: (55) 21 2553 5807
E-Mail: contato@fcb.com
Web Site: www.fcb.com/location/rio-de-janeiro

Employees: 75
Year Founded: 1973

Agency Specializes In: Advertising, Direct Response Marketing, Integrated Marketing, Mobile Marketing, Strategic Planning/Research

Pedro Cruz *(COO & Chief Culture Officer)*
Aurelio Lopes *(Pres-Brazil)*
Gustavo Oliveira *(VP-Rio)*
Daniel Brito *(Dir-Creative)*
Maria Cacaia *(Dir-PR)*

Accounts:
Aggreko; 2010
Carta Fabril
Golden Cross; 2012
IBMR; 2010
Instituto Metasocial
Limppano Campaign: "Dirty Mind-Lust"
Mondelez International, Inc.
Multiplan Emprendimentos Imobilarios; 2010
Sony Pictures Entertainment Buena Vista Columbia Tristar
TIM; 2001

FCB Sao Paulo
(Formerly Giovanni Draftfcb)
Av das Nacoes Unidas No 12 901-17 fl Cojunto 1702, Torre Norte 17th Floor, Sao Paulo, CEP 04578-000 Brazil
Tel.: (55) 11 2186 0800
Fax: (55) 11 2186 0911
E-Mail: contato@fcb.com
Web Site: www.facebook.com/agenciafcbbrasil

Employees: 300

Agency Specializes In: Advertising, Digital/Interactive, Direct Response Marketing, Media Buying Services, Mobile Marketing, Promotions, Strategic Planning/Research

Joanna Monteiro *(Chief Creative Officer)*
Aurelio Lopes *(Pres-Brazil)*
Mauro Silveira *(VP-Svcs & New Bus)*
Adriano Alarcon *(Dir-Creative)*
Romulo Caballero *(Dir-Art)*
Sandra Denes *(Dir-HR)*
Thiago Di Gregorio *(Dir-Art)*
Tiago Freitas *(Dir-Art)*
Eddy Guimaraes *(Dir-Art)*
Andre Mancini *(Dir-Art)*
Camila Rodrigues *(Dir-Art)*
Carlos Schleder *(Dir-Creative)*
Jose De Oliveira *(Asst Dir-Art)*
Andre Bittar *(Copywriter)*
Sofia Calvit *(Copywriter)*
Cesar Fuster *(Planner)*
Daniel Japa *(Copywriter)*
Leonardo Konjedic *(Copywriter)*
Lui Lima *(Copywriter)*
Juliano Teixeira *(Planner)*
Ricardo Silveira *(Art Dir)*

Accounts:
New-Beiersdorf Nivea Doll
British Sky Broadcasting Group
Campari; 2012
CNA "Speaking Exchange", Campaign: "Hello Pizza", Campaign: "You Like It. You Learn It"; 2012
Cruzeiro do Sul University Campaign: "Learn Hair Aesthetics"
Disque-denuncia
DPA
Gol Linhas Smiles; 2013
Hewlett Packard Campaign: "Print for Help"
Hope Campaign: "Hope Teaches", Campaign: "Super Push Up"
Mondelez Campaign: "Is This Love", Oreo
RioSport
Sanford L.P
Sky Brasil
Trip Book Smiles
Zap Imoveis

Chile

FCB Mayo
(Formerly Mayo Publicidad)
Avda Apoquindo 3846, Las Condes, CP 7550 123 Santiago, Chile
Tel.: (56) 23777910
Web Site: www.fcbmayo.com

Employees: 65

Agency Specializes In: Advertising, Digital/Interactive, Direct Response Marketing, Media Planning, Promotions

Celeste Benavides *(VP & Head-Plng)*
Javier Yranzo *(Gen Mgr)*
Andres Reyes Donoso *(Editor-Creative)*
Carolina Larach *(Acct Dir)*
Diego Cruz *(Dir-Creative-MAYO Digital)*
Ximena Hernandez Pons *(Dir-Art)*
Maria Paz Perez Merlet *(Acct Exec-Digital)*
Mario Riquelme Guerrero *(Planner-Digital)*
Karen Harvey *(Planner-Digital)*
Daniela Troncoso *(Designer-Digital Dev)*

Accounts:
Banco Santander
Behr Paints; 2009
Beiersdorf
Falabella Banco Falabella, Campaign: "Hypnotic"; 2009
Mondelez Oreo
Nextel
Soprole; 2001

Colombia

FCB Mayo
(Formerly Mayo Publicidad)
Ctro Empresarial Torre Platino Av Cra 19, No 95-31/55 Piso 7, Bogota, Colombia
Tel.: (57) 1 487 5353
Fax: (57) 1 487 3747
E-Mail: bogota@fcbmayo.com
Web Site: www.fcbmayo.com

Employees: 33
Year Founded: 1979

Agency Specializes In: Advertising, Digital/Interactive, Direct Response Marketing, Promotions, Strategic Planning/Research

Maria Marchant *(Gen Mgr)*
Enrique Gomez *(Acct Dir)*

Accounts:
Alimentos Polar Harina P.A.N.; 2011
Beiersdorf Eucerin; 2005
Mondelez Club Social, Oreo

Costa Rica

CREA Publicidad
Torre La Sabana Sabana N Piso 1, San Jose, Costa Rica
Tel.: (506) 2291 3162
Fax: (506) 291 3167
E-Mail: info@crea.co.cr
Web Site: www.fcb.com

Employees: 15
Year Founded: 1978

Agency Specializes In: Advertising, Digital/Interactive, Direct Response Marketing, Media Buying Services, Promotions, Strategic Planning/Research

Borja Prado *(Mng Dir)*
Carlos Jimenez *(Creative Dir)*

Accounts:
Banco Promerica; 2011
Beiersdorf
Bimbo; 2002
BLANK Project
Bticino; 2011
Central American Broadcasting News; 2011
Cerveceria Nacional Panama; 2011

Ivermectina
Laboratorios Calox
Mondelez ChocQuQi, Oreo, Ritz, Tubolin
Panasonic Lumix, Viera
Sindolan

Dominican Republic

360 MC FCB
(Formerly 360 Marketing Communications & Contacts)
c/Luis F. Thomen 620A, El Millon, Santo Domingo, Dominican Republic
Tel.: (809) 7326256
Fax: (809) 7326251
Web Site: www.fcb.com

Employees: 21
Year Founded: 1923

Agency Specializes In: Advertising, Digital/Interactive, Media Buying Services, Mobile Marketing, Promotions, Strategic Planning/Research

Jorge Pantano *(Gen Mgr)*
Guillermo Mueses *(Dir-Creative)*

Accounts:
APAP
Banco Promerica
Mondelez Chips Ahoy!, Club Social, Oreo
Nestle Maggi
Pasteurizadora Rica
Pinturas Populares Domastur, Glidden, Popular; 2005

Ecuador

FCB Mayo
(Formerly Mayo Ecuador)
Av Orellana E11-75 y Coruna, Edificio Albra Office 608, Quito, Ecuador
Tel.: (593) 2 382 6147
Fax: (593) 23826192
E-Mail: quito@fcbmayo.com
Web Site: www.fcbmayo.com

Employees: 30

Agency Specializes In: Advertising, Direct Response Marketing, Media Buying Services, Promotions, Strategic Planning/Research

Diana Smoliji *(Dir Gen-Creative)*
Felipe Navascues *(Exec VP-Andean Reg)*
Oscar Correa *(Acct Dir-New Bus)*
Daniel Zarate Ayala *(Dir-Art)*
Carlos Cisneros *(Dir-Creative)*
Pablo Coronel Paredes *(Dir-Art)*
Paula Barrera *(Acct Exec)*

Accounts:
Beiersdorf Campaign: "Hot Action", Duo, Eucerin, Hansaplast, Nivea, Nivea for Men
Dominos Pizza; 2010
DPA Svelty, La Lechera, Natura, Huesitos
Jaboneria Wilson Cierto, Lava, Macho
Lafarge
Mondelez International, Inc. Oreo, Club Social, Ritz
Petro Comercial

El Salvador

FCB CREA
(Formerly CREA Publicidad)
Boulevard Los Proceres 288, San Salvador, El Salvador
Tel.: (503) 2244 5466
Fax: (503) 22071391
Web Site: www.fcb.com

Employees: 20
Year Founded: 1985

Agency Specializes In: Advertising, Digital/Interactive, Direct Response Marketing, Media Buying Services, Promotions, Strategic Planning/Research

Diego Deon *(Gen Dir-Creative)*
Rodrigo Argueta *(Dir)*

Accounts:
Banco Promerica; 2011
Bimbo Bimbo, Milpa Real
Diprisa
Econoparts; 2010
Empresa Turistica Salvadorena Parque Monte Grande
FEDECACES
ITCA/FEPADE

Guatemala

FCB Dos Puntos CREA
(Formerly Dos Puntos CREA)
Km 8.6 antigua Carretera a El Salvador Ctro Corp Muxbal, Torre Este Nivel 9, Guatemala, Guatemala
Tel.: (502) 23263800
Fax: (502) 23263838
E-Mail: info@dpcrea.com.gt

Employees: 45
Year Founded: 1972

Agency Specializes In: Advertising, Media Buying Services, Media Planning, Promotions, Strategic Planning/Research

Estuardo Aguilar *(Pres & CEO)*
Miguel Medina *(Gen Dir-Creative)*
Evelyn De Leon *(Dir-Media)*

Accounts:
Banco Promerica Promerica; 2011
Beiersdorf 8X4, Duo, Eucerin, Nivea
Bimbo; 2001
Casa Medica
Continental Motores Volkswagen; 2012
El Zeppelin; 2011
Productos Lacteos de Centroamerica LALA; 2012

Honduras

FCB CREA
(Formerly CREA Publicidad)
Edif Mall El Dorado Bulevard Morazan, Tegucigalpa, Honduras
Tel.: (504) 22215534
Fax: (504) 422215546
E-Mail: hello@fcb.com
Web Site: www.fcb.com

Employees: 15
Year Founded: 1988

Agency Specializes In: Advertising, Media Buying Services, Media Planning, Promotions, Sports Market, Strategic Planning/Research

Lorna Osorio *(Gen Mgr)*
Victor Bertrand *(Dir-Creative)*

Accounts:
ABC Foods; 2011
Banco Promerica
Bimbo
Detektor
Taca

Jamaica

Lindo/FCB
14 Ruthven Road, Kingston, 10 WI Jamaica
Tel.: (876) 926 1194
Fax: (876) 929 7548
E-Mail: lindofcb@cwjamaica.com
Web Site: www.fcb.com

Employees: 15

Agency Specializes In: Advertising, Direct Response Marketing, Media Buying Services, Media Planning, Promotions, Strategic Planning/Research

Jason Lindo *(Mng Dir)*

Mexico

FCB Mexico City
(Formerly DraftFCB)
Miguel de Cervantes Saavedra #193, Colonia Granada, Mexico, 11520 Mexico
Tel.: (52) 55 5350 7900
Fax: (52) 55 5282 4640
E-Mail: comunicaciones.mx@fcb.com
Web Site: www.fcbmexico.com.mx

Employees: 130

Agency Specializes In: Advertising, Digital/Interactive, Direct Response Marketing, Media Planning, Mobile Marketing

Carole Richaud *(COO)*
Jose Arce *(Exec VP & Dir-Creative)*
Jimena Macias Albanes *(Acct Dir)*
Rocio Fernandez *(Dir-Plng)*
Gabriel Ramos *(Dir-Creative)*
Paulina Fernandez *(Acct Mgr)*
Aldiva Cortes Lezama *(Acct Supvr)*
Yessica Gabriela Mancera Munoz *(Acct Supvr)*
Alan Trejo *(Acct Supvr)*
Mario Orea *(Reg Acct Grp Dir)*

Accounts:
Allied Bakeries; 2011
AutoZone; 2014
Banco Compartamos; 2014
Banorte
Beiersdorf
Bimbo
Campbell Soup Company V8
Diageo
New-Heel Foundation
Interceramic; 2014
MasporMas Campaign: "Paper Towel Dispenser News"
Mondelez Oreo
Penafiel Aguas Minerales Canada Dry, Penafiel; 2011
Reckitt Benckiser Graneodin; Sal de Uvas Picot, Tempra
Reebok; 2013
Samsonite; 2014

Panama

FCB Markez
(Formerly Marquez Worldwide)
Calle 63B Los Angeles #20, Panama, Panama
Mailing Address:
PO Box 083101015, Paitilla, Panama, Panama
Tel.: (507) 236 0755
Fax: (507) 260 0960
E-Mail: info@fcbmarkez.com
Web Site: fcbmarkez.com

Employees: 35
Year Founded: 1991

Agency Specializes In: Advertising

Bolivar Marquez *(Pres)*
Cristhian Martinez *(Sr Dir-Creative)*
Analisa Brostella *(Dir-Client Svcs)*

Accounts:
Agencias Feduro
Bimbo
Caja de Ahorros
Fidanque Hermanos
Momi
Productos de Prestigio
Thrifty Car Rental

Peru

FCB Mayo
Av Salaverry 2423, San Isidro, Lima, 27 Peru
Tel.: (51) 1 617 6500
Fax: (51) 1 617 6501
E-Mail: contacto.peru@fcbmayo.com
Web Site: www.fcbmayo.com

Employees: 120

Agency Specializes In: Advertising, Digital/Interactive, Direct Response Marketing, Media Buying Services, Media Planning, Promotions, Strategic Planning/Research

Humberto Polar *(CEO)*
Ricardo Ortiz *(COO & VP)*
Maria Beatriz Rodo *(VP-Client Svcs)*
Alonso Palomino *(Head-Production)*
Flavio Pantigoso *(Exec Dir-Creative)*
Daniel Sacroisky *(Creative Dir)*
Carmen Aburto *(Dir-Fin)*
Silvia Angulo *(Copywriter)*
Richard Gervacio *(Copywriter)*
Juan Saux *(Exec Chm)*

Accounts:
America Movil CLARO; 2005
Beiersdorf
Cencosud Plaza Lima Sur, Wong Hipermercados, Metro/Eco Almacenes
E. Wong Plaza Norte
Ministerio de Salud
Mondelez International, Inc.
PECSA
Peruvian Cancer Foundation Campaign: "Searching For Hearts"
Quimica Suiza
Radio Filarmonia
Sancela
UNACEM
University of Engineering and Technology Air-Purifying Billboard, Campaign: "Water-harvesting Billboard"
UTEC
Western Union Campaign: "Moving Warmth For Better"

Uruguay

EFPZ
Wilson Ferreira Aldunate 1212, Montevideo, 11100 Uruguay
Tel.: (598) 29 032 803
Fax: (598) 29 032 803
E-Mail: efpz@efpz.com.uy
Web Site: www.efpz.com.uy

Employees: 22

Agency Specializes In: Advertising, Digital/Interactive, Direct Response Marketing, Media Planning, Promotions

Agostina Ponzoni *(Gen Mgr)*
Massimiliano Di Murro *(Exec Dir-Creative)*
Marcelo Vergara Fernandez *(Dir)*
Andrea Fleitas *(Dir)*
Erni Garcia *(Dir-Art)*

Accounts:
Adecco; 2010
Adium Pharma; 2012
ASSE; 2009
Beiersdorf Nivea Deo; 2009
Bimbo
Duty Free Americas
Mondelez International, Inc.
Vendome Revlon; 2010

Venezuela

AJL Park
Torre Multinvest Piso 4 Plaza La Castellana Chacao, Caracas, 1060-A Venezuela
Mailing Address:
PO Box 60.684, Caracas, 1060-A Venezuela
Tel.: (58) 212 263 2355
Fax: (58) 212 263 2785
Web Site: www.fcb.com/location/caracas-ajl-park

Employees: 25

Agency Specializes In: Advertising, Media Buying Services, Media Planning, Strategic Planning/Research

Tony Lutz *(Mng Dir)*

Accounts:
Coposa
Demasa
INLACA Huesitos, Mi Vaca, Yoplait
Laboratorios Calox

FCB Caracas
(Formerly Draftfcb)
Av.Libertador cruce c/Avila, Bello Campo Chacao, Caracas, 1060 Venezuela
Tel.: (58) 212 201 7811
Fax: (58) 212 201 7801
E-Mail: fcb.venezuela@fcb.com
Web Site: www.fcb.com

Employees: 80
Year Founded: 1985

Agency Specializes In: Advertising, Digital/Interactive, Direct Response Marketing, Media Buying Services, Media Planning, Promotions, Strategic Planning/Research

Lucia Acosta *(VP-Accounts)*
Mirna Esposito *(VP-Client Svcs)*
Enrique Pena *(VP-Creative)*
Irene Aguilera *(Gen Mgr)*
Yasna Pradenas *(Acct Dir)*

Accounts:
Alimentos Polar
Bacardi; 2014
Bancaribe; 2014
Beiersdorf 8x4, Duo, Eucerin, Nivea
Bonsai Sushi
Cerveceria Polar
Importadora Occidental Pickens; 2012
Mastercard Intl Maestro
Mondelez Belvita, Oreo
Pernod Ricard
Zurich Insurance

China

FCB Shanghai
(Formerly Draftfcb)
20/F Huai Hai Plaza 1045 Huai Hai Zhong Rd, Shanghai, 200031 China
Tel.: (86) 21 2411 0388
Fax: (86) 21 2411 0399
E-Mail: info.china@fcb.com
Web Site: www.fcb.com

Employees: 75
Year Founded: 1985

Agency Specializes In: Advertising, Digital/Interactive, Direct Response Marketing

Wei Fei *(Chief Creative Officer-Greater China)*
Edward Bell *(CEO-Greater China)*
Willy Wong *(Head-Strategy & Plng-Greater China)*
Josephine Pan *(Gen Mgr)*
Andy Chan *(Exec Dir-Creative)*
Mung Ng *(Sr Acct Dir)*
Tiger Chen *(Creative Dir)*
Ashley Chin *(Art Dir)*
Simon He *(Creative Dir)*

Accounts:
Beiersdorf Nivea
Boeing; 2011
New-Bosch Power Tools Creative
Citic Bank; 2013
New-Hisense Group Brand & Product Communications, Vidaa
Levi Strauss Levi's, Print; 2014
MATTEL, INC. Barbie, Brand Strategy, Content, Creative, Social Media
Mengniu Dairy Group; 2013
Mondelez International, Inc. Oreo
Quangxin Guangxin; 2013
Shanghai Volkswagen Branding, Fabia, Skoda (Agency of Record), Superb
Skoda
Uni-President Foods
Zheijiang Supor; 2012

India

FCB Ulka
(Formerly Draftfcb Ulka)
Vallamattam Estate Mahatma Gandhi Road, Ravipuram, Kochi, 682 015 India
Tel.: (91) 4846066000
Fax: (91) 4842373935
E-Mail: centrepoint@fcbulka.com
Web Site: www.fcbulka.in

Employees: 15

Agency Specializes In: Advertising

Anees Salim *(Head-Creative)*
Rajeev Menon *(Branch Mgr)*

Accounts:
Kalyan Silks
M M Publications
Malabar Cements
Mxc Solutions India Pvt Ltd Cartrade.com

FCB Ulka
(Formerly Draftfcb Ulka Mumbai)
Nirmal 4th Floor Nariman Point, Mumbai, 400 021 India
Tel.: (91) 22 6670 7070
Fax: (91) 22 6670 7172
E-Mail: centrepoint@fcbulka.com
Web Site: www.fcbulka.in

Employees: 255

Agency Specializes In: Above-the-Line, Advertising, Below-the-Line, Digital/Interactive,

Direct Response Marketing, Health Care Services, Media Buying Services, Media Planning, Mobile Marketing, Promotions, Strategic Planning/Research

Kulvinder Ahluwalia *(Sr VP)*
Dennis Koshy *(VP-Bangalore)*
Bambi Diventry *(Head-New Bus Initiatives)*
M.G. Parameswaran *(Exec Dir)*
Anand N. Krishnan *(Dir-Client Servicing)*
Pranay Merchant *(Dir-Client Servicing)*
Aparna Naik *(Dir-HR)*
Nagesh Alai *(Grp Chm-FCB ULKA Group)*

Accounts:
Abbott Nutrition Campaign: "Treadmill"
Agrotech; 1998
Air India
New-Cargill Nature Fish
Cholamandalam Investment & Finance
Elder Pharmaceuticals; 2012
Guarjarat Co-op Milk Marketing Federation "Catch Up", Amul Ice Creams, Amul Mithai Mate, Campaign: "Bhaag Milkha Bhaag", Campaign: "Eats Milk With Every Meal"
Hero MotoCorp. Campaign: "Such a Boy Thing", Creative, Ignitor
Hygiene Research Institute
ICICI Bank; 2004
Indian Oil; 2009
Kensai Nerolac Paints
Life Insurance Corp of India
Mumbai Police Campaign: "A Blank Tweet"
Oerlikon; 2012
Reserve Bank of India RBI; 2012
Salaam Bombay Foundation Campaign: "Project Resume"
Tata Chemicals Ltd
Tata Consultancy
Tata Motors Campaign: "Challenge the Minutes", Campaign: "Designed to Thrill", Campaign: "Don't get your Hands Dirty", Tata Manza, Tata Safari Storme, Tata Vista D90
Trent Landmark, Star Bazaar; 2004
Zee Entertainment Zee Cafe, Zee TV; 2003

FCB Ulka

(Formerly Draftfcb Ulka)
Golden Tower 1st Floor 262 Royapettha High Road, Chennai, 600 004 India
Tel.: (91) 44 6455 5271
Fax: (91) 44 2813 0259
E-Mail: centrepoint@fcbulka.com
Web Site: www.fcbulka.in

Employees: 29

Agency Specializes In: Advertising

Elango Mahalingam *(VP)*
Sharad Mathur *(VP)*

FCB Ulka

Unitech Trade Ctre Sushant Lik hase I Sector 43, Gurgaon, Haryana 122 001 India
Tel.: (91) 124 668 1600
Fax: (91) 124 668 1747
E-Mail: centrepoint@fcbulka.com
Web Site: www.fcbulka.in

Employees: 136

Agency Specializes In: Advertising, Digital/Interactive, Direct Response Marketing, Media Planning, Promotions, South Asian Market, Strategic Planning/Research

Sridhar Iyer *(Sr VP)*
Sharad Mathur *(VP)*
Sachin Das Burma *(Grp Dir-Creative)*
Shiveshwar Raj Singh *(Grp Dir-Creative)*
Sanjay Sharma *(Grp Dir-Creative)*
Vasudha Misra *(Sr Dir-Creative)*

Accounts:
Ambience Mall; 2011
Bausch & Lomb Campaign: "Load"
Cosmic Kitchen Campaign: "Candy Wrapper Business Card", Chokola; 2011
Godfrey Phillips India
HCL Enterprise Campaign: "On Fire Teaser"
Hero Honda Motors Hero Pleasure
Info Edge 99acres.com, jeevansathi.com, naukri.com
ITC John Players
Jasper Infotech Campaign: "Sale-O-Shayari", Digital, OOH, Print, Snapdeal, Social Media, TV; 2011
OBI Mobiles
Rohit Surfactants Red Chief Shoes
Usha Intl.
Whirlpool Of India Limited Air Conditioners, Campaign: "Skin Shirt", Microwaves, Refrigerators, Washing Machines

FCB Ulka

(Formerly Draftfcb Ulka)
1/2 Lord Sinha Road, Kolkata, 700 071 India
Tel.: (91) 33 6499 8200
Fax: (91) 33 2282 4834
E-Mail: centrepoint@fcbulka.com
Web Site: www.fcbulka.in

Employees: 10

Agency Specializes In: Advertising

Nitin Karkare *(COO)*
Sanjoy Mukherjee *(Dir-Creative)*

FCB Ulka

(Formerly Draftfcb Ulka)
1103 11th Floor Barton Centre 84 MG Road, Bengaluru, 560001 India
Tel.: (91) 8065399800
Fax: (91) 8025583955
E-Mail: centrepoint@fcbulka.com
Web Site: www.fcbulka.in

Employees: 60

Agency Specializes In: Advertising, Digital/Interactive, Direct Response Marketing

Dennis Koshy *(VP-Bangalore)*
C. Suresh *(Grp Dir-Fin)*
Mehul Patil *(Dir-Creative)*
Dharmesh Shah *(Dir-Creative)*

Accounts:
Indian Tobacco Company
ITC Campaign: "Magical World", Candyman Creme Lacto, Delishus
Paragon Polymer School World; 2011
Wipro Enterprises Campaign: "Anthem Film", Campaign: "Mistaken Identity", Campaign: "Skating", Chandrika, Santoor Body Lotion, Wipro Baby Soft

Interface Communications Ltd.

A Wing-206 2nd Fl Phoenix House Phoenix Mills Compound, SenapatiBapat Marg Lower Parel, Mumbai, 400 013 India
Tel.: (91) 22 6666 4400
Fax: (91) 22 6666 4411
E-Mail: advantage@interfacecom.com
Web Site: fcbulka.in

Employees: 80

Agency Specializes In: Advertising, Digital/Interactive, Direct Response Marketing, Media Buying Services, Media Planning, Mobile Marketing, Strategic Planning/Research

Joe Thaliath *(COO)*
Roopesh Shah *(Head-Interactive Svcs)*
Arthi Basak *(Gen Mgr)*
Ruchita Purohit *(Gen Mgr)*
Mitushi Verma *(Gen Mgr)*
Binal Kavale *(Acct Dir)*
Abhay Godbole *(Dir-Client Servicing)*
Robby Mathew *(Dir-Creative-Natl)*
Santosh Ramaswamy *(Dir-Client Servicing)*

Accounts:
Beiersdorf Nivea
Blue Star Air Conditioners, Campaign: "Cool the Boss", Campaign: "No Sweat", Campaign: "Office-like Cooling at Home"
Business Line
Cadbury India Oreo
Chola MS Campaign: "Choice Chinnappa"
Henkel Margo
Mahindra & Mahindra Ltd. Campaign: " It's Great To Be Me", Campaign: "A Weekend Feeling", Campaign: "Bond", Campaign: "Drive Less", Campaign: "Everybody Loves A Good Sport", Campaign: "Get more", Campaign: "Indulge the Connoisseur in You", Campaign: "May Your Life be Full of Stories", Campaign: "New Look", Campaign: "Trust Of Mahindra", Campaign: "UnCut Version", Centuro, New Generation Scorpio, Tractors, XUV500
Murugappa Group Campaign: "Bet We've Met", Creative
Nathella Sampath Jewellery; 2014
Prabhat
Sanofi Creative, Seacod
Valvoline; 2013

Indonesia

FCB Jakarta

(Formerly Draftfcb)
12th Floor Menara Mulia Jl.Jend.Gatot Subroto Kav. 9-11, Jakarta, 10340 Indonesia
Tel.: (62) 2152921868
Fax: (62) 2152921867
Web Site: www.fcb.com

Employees: 20
Year Founded: 1991

National Agency Associations: IAA

Agency Specializes In: Advertising, Promotions

Sony Nichani *(Gen Mgr)*
Bhaskar Rao *(Dir)*
Yongky Ismono *(Fin Mgr-HR)*

Accounts:
Beiersdorf
Mondelez Oreo
Moneygram Intl
Perfetti Van Melle Big Babol
PT M-150; 2014
Symantec Norton; 2011
Taisho Pharma Counterpain; 2011
Universal Zwitsal
UNZA

Korea

FCB Seoul

(Formerly Draftfcb)
7/F Hyeongji Bldg 257-4 Sinsa Dong, Gangnam-Gu, Seoul, 135-888 Korea (South)
Tel.: (82) 2 3438 3600
Fax: (82) 2 3438 3686
Web Site: www.fcb.com

Employees: 10

Agency Specializes In: Advertising, Direct Response Marketing, Promotions, Strategic Planning/Research

Sam Kim *(Gen Mgr)*
Gab-Soo Kang *(Exec Dir-Creative)*
Min-Su Kim *(Dir-Fin & Admin)*

Accounts:
Bausch & Lomb
Beiersdorf Eucerin, Nivea; 2001
Cotton Council
Daum My People; 2013
Halla Meister Mando Footloose; 2013
Sunkist Growers; 2001

Malaysia

FCB Kuala Lumpur
(Formerly Draftfcb)
17th Floor Menara IGB No 1 The Boulevard Mid Valley City, Lingkaran Syed Putra, Kuala Lumpur, 59200 Malaysia
Tel.: (60) 3 2296 3600
Fax: (60) 3 2283 2588
E-Mail: fcb.kualalumpur@fcb.com
Web Site: www.fcb.com

Employees: 110

Agency Specializes In: Advertising, Digital/Interactive, Direct Response Marketing, Media Planning, Promotions, Strategic Planning/Research

T. Renganathan *(CEO)*
Shaun Tay *(Mng Dir)*
Shi-Ping Ong *(Chief Creative Officer)*
Nick Gordon *(Head-Creative)*
Alvin Ho *(Grp Head-Creative)*
LiLian Hor *(Head-Digital)*
Alvin Ng *(Creative Dir)*
James Voon *(Art Dir-Digital)*

Accounts:
Ajinomoto
Celcom Celcom Axiata
CIMB Merchant Bank
Commerce Trust; 2005
Edaran Tan Chong Motor Nissan; 2013
Green Spot V-Soy
Mondelez International, Inc.
Telekom Malaysia
UNZA

Philippines

FCB Manila
(Formerly Draftfcb)
4F 6780 Ayala Avenue, Makati, 1220 Philippines
Tel.: (63) 281 20 471
Fax: (63) 281 38 775
E-Mail: mail@fcbmanila.com
Web Site: www.fcbmanila.com

Employees: 85

Agency Specializes In: Above-the-Line, Advertising, Below-the-Line, Digital/Interactive, Direct Response Marketing, In-Store Advertising, Promotions, Social Media

Arnold Liong *(Chm & CEO)*
Tommy Eugenio *(Pres & COO)*
James Bernardo *(Chief Creative Officer)*
Lizette Santos *(Chief Strategic Officer)*
Sydney Samodio *(Exec Dir-Creative)*
Larry Ducut *(Mgr-Fin)*
Laurie Lee *(Client Svc Dir)*

Accounts:
Asia Brewery
Beiersdorf Nivea, Nivea for Men
Coco Fresh
Dole Food Company Creative
Manila Electric Company Meralco; 2014
Mondelez
Philex Mining; 2011
PLDT (Philippines Long Distance Telecommunications)
Smart Communications
Universal Motors

Taiwan

FCB Taipei
(Formerly Draftfcb)
7F No 1 Sec 5 Nanking E Road, Taipei, Taiwan
Tel.: (886) 2 2762 7889
Fax: (886) 2 2762 9009
Web Site: www.fcb.com

Employees: 25
Year Founded: 1962

National Agency Associations: IAA

Agency Specializes In: Advertising, Customer Relationship Management, Digital/Interactive, Promotions

Amy Lee *(Gen Mgr)*
Coco Chen *(Exec Dir-Creative)*
Candice Tsai *(Mgr-Fin)*

Accounts:
1028 Visual Therapy; 2014
3M Campaign: "Making difference", Multi-Purpose Super Glue; 2008
Beiersdorf Nivea; 2011
Heineken; 2013
Hey Song; 2007
Joie; 2012
Jumbo Garment Co Bobson Jeans; 2009
Leotek Electronics; 2013
Merck Sharpe & Dohme; 2014
Mondelez Oreo, Tuc; 1998
Pernod Ricard; 2009
Sanyang Industry
Tokuyo Biotech Campaign: "Stairs"; 2012
Young Energy Source Yes Mineral Water; 2011

Thailand

FCB Bangkok
(Formerly FCB Thailand)
159/25 Serm-Mit Tower Sukhumvit 21 Road, North Klongtoey Wattana, Bangkok, 10110 Thailand
Tel.: (66) 22614240
Fax: (66) 22614246
E-Mail: secretary@fcbbangkok.com
Web Site: www.fcb.com

Employees: 70
Year Founded: 1978

Agency Specializes In: Advertising, Digital/Interactive, Direct Response Marketing, Media Buying Services, Media Planning, Mobile Marketing, Promotions, Strategic Planning/Research

Vasadome Rasmidatta *(Mng Partner)*
Kingrak Ingkawat *(Chief Creative Officer)*
Laddavan Phonboribooncharoen *(Gen Mgr & Exec Dir-Client Svcs)*
Bheemkij Charuchandra *(Dir-Bus Dev)*

Accounts:
Mondelez Oreo; 1999

Australia

AJF Partnership
(Formerly FCB Sydney)
Level 1, 66-72 Reservoir St, Surry Hills, NSW 2010 Australia
Tel.: (61) 2 9213-2000
Web Site: www.fcb.com

Employees: 30
Year Founded: 1992

National Agency Associations: AFA

Agency Specializes In: Advertising, Digital/Interactive, Direct Response Marketing, Mobile Marketing, Promotions, Strategic Planning/Research

Digby Richards *(Founder & Mng Dir)*
Clinton Bell *(Head-Production)*
Jayne Windus *(Head-Acct Mgmt)*
Tom Hart-Brown *(Acct Dir)*
Kristen Sandberg *(Acct Dir)*
Jody Elston *(Dir-Strategy)*
Adam Rose *(Dir-Creative)*
Cait Foxwell *(Acct Mgr)*
Kate Heatley *(Grp Bus Dir)*

Accounts:
Beiersdorf; 2001
Crust Pizza
Donut King
Lindt & Sprungli Excellence, Lindor, Lindt, Lindt Chocolates; 1997
Liquorland
Mondelez Oreo
Officeworks
Perpetual Brand Strategy, Communications, Marketing
Stan
Target Creative
Valspar; 2013
Wattyl; 2012

New Zealand

FCB Auckland
(Formerly Draftfcb)
57 Wellington Street, Freemans Bay, Auckland, New Zealand
Mailing Address:
PO Box 3898, Auckland, New Zealand
Tel.: (64) 93566222
Fax: (64) 93566240
E-Mail: info_nz@fcb.com
Web Site: www.fcb.co.nz

Employees: 210
Year Founded: 1967

Agency Specializes In: Advertising, Digital/Interactive, Direct Response Marketing, Health Care Services, Media Buying Services, Media Planning, Mobile Marketing, Strategic Planning/Research

Bryan Crawford *(Vice Chm)*
Brian van den Hurk *(CEO)*
Niki Pettifer *(CFO)*
Angela Spain *(Head-Media, PR, Activation & Social)*
Kamran Kazalbash *(Gen Mgr-Retail)*
Brent Chambers *(Exec Creative Dir)*
James Mok *(Exec Creative Dir-Regional)*
Dave Nash *(Exec Creative Dir)*
Leisa Wall *(Sr Dir-Art)*
Karla Fisher *(Grp Acct Dir)*
Jane Wardlaw *(Grp Acct Dir)*
Toby Sellers *(Grp Acct Dir)*
Hannah Downes *(Acct Dir)*
Chanelle McDonald *(Acct Mgr)*
Thomas Gledhill *(Art Dir)*

Michelle Koome *(Acct Dir)*
Bruno Regalo *(Creative Dir)*
Greg Wood *(Creative Dir-Digital)*
Matt Barnes *(Dir-Digital Creative)*
Kate Grigg *(Dir-Digital Media)*
Rachel Leyland *(Dir-Media)*
Ele Quigan *(Dir-Brand Experience)*
Alice Eade *(Acct Mgr-PR)*
Emily Jagger *(Acct Mgr)*
Nicole Earnshaw *(Mgr-Media)*
Hywel James *(Sr Copywriter)*
Laura Little *(Acct Exec)*
Mike Braid *(Designer)*
Lennie Galloway *(Copywriter)*
Mike Howie *(Designer)*
Nick McFarlane *(Designer)*
David Thomason *(Planner)*
Peter Vegas *(Copywriter)*
Matt Williams *(Copywriter)*

Accounts:
Air New Zealand
ANZ Bank
APN NZ Herald, NZ Listener
AS Colour Campaign: "Colourmatic"
Bell Tea
Brothers In Arms Youth Mentoring
Cerebos Greggs Campaign: "Eat the impossible - Knife/Fork"
Electric Authority Campaign: "Bear", Campaign: "What's My Number"; 2011
European Motor Distributors Audi, Media, Porsche, Skoda, VW
Flight Center; 2013
Foodstuffs Auckland PAK'nSAVE
Health Promotion Agency Campaign: "Cool Dad", Campaign: "Ease up"
New-HOME magazine
Housing New Zealand; 2009
Hoyts Distribution; 2010
Inland Revenue; 2014
L'Oreal Group
Maritime NZ Campaign: "Death At The Docks"
Mercury Energy; 2014
Ministry of Education Teach NZ
Ministry of Health
Ministry of Social Development It's Not OK
Mitre 10
National Screening Unit (NSU); 2014
Neurological Foundation of New Zealand
New-New Zealand Fire Service
Noel Leeming Bond & Bond; 2007
New-NZ Health Promotion Agency
NZI (New Zealand Insurance) Campaign: "Devil's Chair"
Paper Plus Group Creative, Digital, Media Planning & Buying, PR
New-Parkinsons New Zealand
Peter Buckton
Rabobank; 2006
Shine
Sky Network Prime TV; 2006
Sony Campaign: "Octographer", Cyber Shot TX30
Tourism Queensland; 2014
Unicef Campaign: "Food Photos Save Lives"
New-The Valspar Corporation
Vodafone Campaign: "Instant Astronaut", Campaign: "More Kiwis connect in more places with SuperNet", Campaign: "Piggy Sue", SuperNet

Regional Headquarters

FCB South Africa
(Formerly Draftfcb South Africa)
164 Katherine Street, Pin Mill Farm, Johannesburg, 2146 South Africa
Tel.: (27) 11 566 6000
Fax: (27) 11 566 6664
Web Site: www.fcb.co.za

Employees: 10

Agency Specializes In: Advertising

Brett Morris *(Grp CEO)*
Graham Vivian *(Grp COO)*
Rita Doherty *(Chief Strategy Officer)*
Philip Van Rensburg *(Mng Dir-Africa)*

Accounts:
Cell C
New-South African Tourism (Lead Marketing Agency) Coordination Services, Integrated Marketing, Media Buying, Planning

Ghana

AdMedia
37 Third Crescent Asylum Down, Accra, Ghana
Tel.: (233) 21 250 123
Fax: (233) 21 23 3889
E-Mail: admediafcb@yahoo.com
Web Site: www.fcb.com

Employees: 30

Agency Specializes In: Advertising, Direct Response Marketing, Promotions

Emmanuel A. Addo *(Mng Dir)*

Accounts:
Activa
Aluworks; 2013
Beiersdorf; 2014
C. Woerman; 1997
Engen
Mechanical Lloyd BMW, Ford, Massey Fergusson
Moneygram International; 2007
Shoprite
Trellidor
Unilever
Wingscorp Boom, Soklin; 2013

Mauritius

Cread
Les 5 Palmiers, Route Royale, Beau Bassin, Mauritius
Tel.: (230) 454 6414
Fax: (230) 454 6405
E-Mail: cread@intnet.mu
Web Site: www.fcb.com

Employees: 25

Agency Specializes In: Advertising, Media Buying Services, Media Planning, Promotions, Strategic Planning/Research

Vino Sookloll *(CEO & Exec Dir-Creative)*
Amaresh Ramlugan *(Exec Dir)*

Accounts:
Engen
Momentum
Shoprite
Trellidor
Wingscorp

South Africa

FCB Cape Town
(Formerly Draftfcb Cape Town)
5 Armdale Street, Woodstock, Cape Town, 7700 South Africa
Tel.: (27) 214040300
Fax: (27) 214040302
Web Site: www.fcb.co.za

Employees: 90
Year Founded: 1946

National Agency Associations: ACA

Agency Specializes In: Advertising, Digital/Interactive, Direct Response Marketing, Financial, Internet/Web Design, Mobile Marketing, Public Relations, Retail, Strategic Planning/Research

Elizanne Rauch *(Deputy Mng Dir)*
Mike Barnwell *(Exec Dir-Creative)*
Aaron Harris *(Creative Dir)*
Annie Ibbotson *(Art Dir)*
Hannes Esterhuyse *(Dir-Art)*
Natasha Reddy *(Mgr-HR)*
Chris de Villiers *(Sr Copywriter)*
Andre De Wet *(Copywriter)*
Liora Friedkland *(Copywriter)*

Accounts:
AJ North
BMW Motorcycles; 2014
Cape Union Mart
Carrol Boyes; 2009
Clicks; 2012
Distell Amarula, Gordon's, Klipdrift, Savanna
Savanna Campaign: "Peacock", Hard Cider, Marketing
Engen
Gidani Powerball
Media 24 Campaign: "In or Out?", Die Burger Newspaper
Peninsula School Feeding Association Campaign: "Banana", Campaign: "Cindy", Campaign: "Drumstick", Campaign: "Lunch Is On Me", Campaign: "Pear"
Retsol; 2011
Safarilink.co.za
Tiger Brands; 2013
Vital Health Foods Campaign: "Bedtime", Campaign: "The World's Smallest Idea", Enduramax

FCB Johannesburg
(Formerly Draftfcb Johannesburg)
Pin Mill Farm 164 Katherine Street, Sandown, Johannesburg, 2196 South Africa
Mailing Address:
PO Box 78014, Sandton, Johannesburg, 2146 South Africa
Tel.: (27) 11 566 6000
Fax: (27) 115666656
Web Site: www.fcb.co.za

Employees: 105
Year Founded: 1926

National Agency Associations: ACA

Agency Specializes In: Advertising, Digital/Interactive, Direct Response Marketing, Event Planning & Marketing, Media Planning, Mobile Marketing, Promotions, Strategic Planning/Research

Thabang Skwambane *(Mng Dir)*
Brett Morris *(Chief Creative Officer)*
Jonathan Deeb *(Exec Dir-Creative)*
Stuart Stobbs *(Exec Creative Dir)*
Sergio Penzo *(Creative Dir & Copywriter)*
Alex Christodoulou *(Art Dir)*
Mathew Barnes *(Dir-Creative)*
Toni Hughes *(Dir-Creative)*
Gila Shapiro *(Copywriter)*

Accounts:
Adcock Ingram
Cell C Campaign: "Don't Hang Up"
Coca-Cola Refreshments USA, Inc. Campaign: "Rainbow Nation", Coca-Cola, Coca-Cola Light, Coca-Cola Zero, Tab; 2011
Development Bank of Southern Africa (DBSA)
Eskom Campaign: "Glow in the Dark"; 2007
Famous Brands Mgmt Debonairs, FishAways,

Wimpy; 2012
Lonely Road Foundation Radio
Mondelez Nabisco Grahams, Oreo; 1999
Moneygram; 2013
National Film & Video Foundation; 2014
Old Mutual Properties Campaign: "Dreams"
So. African Revenue Service SARS; 2012
Tiger Brands Campaign: "Koo Bees"; 2005
Toyota Campaign: "Cliches", Campaign: "Pardon the Foley", Hilux, Lexus, RAV4; 1961
University of So. Africa UNISA; 2011

FCB HEALTH

(Formerly Draftfcb HealthCare NY)
100 W 33rd St, New York, NY 10001
Tel.: (212) 672-2300
Fax: (212) 672-2301
E-Mail: hello@fcbhealthcare.com
Web Site: www.fcbhealthcare.com

Employees: 550
Year Founded: 1977

National Agency Associations: 4A's-PMA

Agency Specializes In: Health Care Services, Sponsorship

Dana Maiman *(Pres & CEO)*
Michael Guarino *(Chief Strategy Officer)*
Rich Levy *(Chief Creative Officer)*
Mike Lyman *(Sr VP & Grp Mgmt Dir)*
Rob Esposito *(VP & Dir-Mgmt)*
Jon Evoy *(Dir-Strategic Plng)*
Karin Sweeney *(Acct Supvr)*
Jessica Chiulli *(Sr Acct Exec)*

Accounts:
Abbott Laboratories Flomax, Meridia, Zemplar
Amerifit Brands; 2007
Boehringer Ingelheim
Bristol-Myers Squibb
Cephalon
Crouse Hospital "Beware the Chair", Outdoor, Print, Social Media
GlaxoSmithKline; 1991
Johnson & Johnson Family of Companies Aveeno, Purpose
Lilly; 2011
MedImmune
Merck Arcoxia, Cozaar, Fosamax, Propecia, Zocor; 1981
Osteoporosis
Pfizer
Talecris
Vivus

Branch

Halesway

36 East Street, Andover, Hampshire SP10 1ES United Kingdom
Tel.: (44) 1264 339955
Web Site: www.halesway.com

Agency Specializes In: Digital/Interactive, Health Care Services, Strategic Planning/Research

Liz Rawlingson *(Founder & Pres)*
Neil Padgett *(Mng Dir-Creative)*
Ian Richardson *(Sr Acct Dir)*
Niki Crossley *(Client Svcs Dir)*
Niki Dean *(Client Svcs Dir)*
Damion Hampton *(Acct Dir)*
Zoe Hayton *(Acct Dir)*
Stephen Lewis *(Acct Dir)*
Ekta Jain *(Dir-Digital Strategy)*
Lana Suhova *(Acct Mgr)*
Zoe Lock *(Acct Exec)*

Accounts:
Abbott
Baxter
Boehringer Ingelheim
Hospira
MSD
Novartis
Reckitt Benckiser
Smith & Nephew

FD2S

3601 S Congress Ave, Austin, TX 78704
Tel.: (512) 476-7733
Fax: (512) 473-2202
E-Mail: mdenton@fd2s.com
Web Site: www.fd2s.com

Employees: 11
Year Founded: 1985

Agency Specializes In: Brand Development & Integration, Business-To-Business, Collateral, Communications, Corporate Identity, E-Commerce, Education, Graphic Design, Health Care Services, Leisure, Logo & Package Design, Point of Purchase, Point of Sale, Publicity/Promotions, Retail, Sales Promotion, Strategic Planning/Research

Sales: $3,000,000

Curtis Roberts *(Principal)*
Steven L. Stamper *(Principal)*
Cynthia Hall *(Dir-Engagement)*
Rick Smits *(Assoc Dir-Design)*
Krystal Rose *(Mgr-Ops)*
Jennifer Choi *(Designer)*

Accounts:
Second Street District

FDG CREATIVE

(Name Changed to Prismatic)

FEAR NOT AGENCY

1740 Blake St, Denver, CO 80202
Tel.: (303) 990-2928
E-Mail: info@fearnotagency.com
Web Site: www.fearnotagency.com

Agency Specializes In: Advertising, Internet/Web Design, Strategic Planning/Research

Blake Ebel *(Founder & Chief Creative Officer)*
Jorge Lamora *(Dir-Creative)*
Amy Corwin *(Assoc Dir-Creative)*
Mike King *(Assoc Dir-Creative)*
Meagan Nelson *(Acct Supvr)*
Samantha Clements *(Sr Acct Exec)*

Accounts:
Albert Bartlett (Advertising Agency of Record)
Bellco Credit Union
Corvus Coffee
Lauren Harper Collection
PowerShares SuperSlam

THE FEARLESS GROUP

12 W 21 St Fl 5, New York, NY 10010
Tel.: (646) 789-4789
Fax: (212) 967-1210
E-Mail: info@fearless.agency
Web Site: fearless.agency/

Year Founded: 2010

Agency Specializes In: Advertising, Media Relations, Social Media

Robert Davidman *(Partner)*
Peter Gibb *(Partner)*
Mike Head *(Partner)*
Jerry Judge *(Partner)*
Mark Voysey *(Partner)*

Accounts:
Hard Rock International (Media Buying Agency of Record) Advertising, Digital, Mobile, Strategic Analysis
ICM Registry LLC XXX Financial Times

FEARWORM HAUNTVERTISING

11044 Research Blvd A-525, Austin, TX 78759
Tel.: (512) 554-8867
E-Mail: info@fearworm.com
Web Site: www.fearworm.com

Agency Specializes In: Advertising, Brand Development & Integration, Content, Digital/Interactive, Graphic Design, Internet/Web Design, Media Buying Services, Media Planning, Print, Social Media

Ernest Corder *(Dir-Acct Svcs)*
Patrick Stanger *(Dir-Creative Svcs)*

Accounts:
Fear Town Productions LLC
House Of Horrors & Haunted Catacombs

FECHTOR ADVERTISING LLC

145 N High St Ste 500, Columbus, OH 43215
Tel.: (614) 222-1055
Fax: (614) 222-1057
Web Site: www.fechtor.com

Year Founded: 2003

Agency Specializes In: Advertising, Broadcast, Digital/Interactive, Outdoor, Print

Stephen Fechtor *(Principal)*
Luke Deady *(Dir-Art & Design)*
Luanne Mann *(Assoc Dir-Creative)*

Accounts:
Cota
Dine Originals
Leo Alfred Jewelers
Vorys, Sater, Seymour & Pease

FEDERATED MEDIA

1 Beach St Ste 301, San Francisco, CA 94133
Tel.: (415) 332-6955
Fax: (877) 723-0150
E-Mail: info@federatedmedia.net
Web Site: www.federatedmedia.net

Employees: 60

Agency Specializes In: Advertising

Jordan Hoffner *(CEO)*
Laney Whitcanack *(Exec VP-Employee Experience)*
Alyssa Vitrano *(Exec Producer-Content Strategy)*
Emily Meyer *(Acct Exec)*
Alexandra Wong *(Strategist-Mktg Solutions)*

Accounts:
Apartment Therapy Media
Mixx
Springwise

FEED COMPANY

1015 N Cahuenga Blvd Ste 4322, Los Angeles, CA 90038
Tel.: (323) 469-3052
Fax: (323) 469-9841
E-Mail: hung@feedcompany.com
Web Site: www.feedcompany.com

Agency Specializes In: Planning & Consultation, Strategic Planning/Research

Josh Warner *(Pres)*

Accounts:
Activision Blizzard, Inc
California Milk Processor Board
Capital One
Gillette
Haagen-Dazs
Levi Strauss & Co.
OfficeMax
PepsiCo.
Ray-Ban
Sears
Stealth Advertising Advertising Services
Taco Bell Restaurant Services

FELDER COMMUNICATIONS GROUP
1593 Galbraith Ave Se Ste 201, Grand Rapids, MI 49546-9032
Tel.: (616) 459-1200
Fax: (616) 459-2080
E-Mail: info@felder.com
Web Site: www.felder.com

E-Mail for Key Personnel:
President: stan@felder.com
Creative Dir.: mike@felder.com

Employees: 10
Year Founded: 1994

Agency Specializes In: Advertising, Advertising Specialties, Affluent Market, Agriculture, Automotive, Aviation & Aerospace, Brand Development & Integration, Business Publications, Business-To-Business, Cable T.V., Catalogs, Co-op Advertising, Collateral, Commercial Photography, Communications, Consulting, Consumer Goods, Consumer Marketing, Consumer Publications, Corporate Communications, Corporate Identity, Crisis Communications, Digital/Interactive, Direct Response Marketing, Direct-to-Consumer, E-Commerce, Education, Electronic Media, Engineering, Entertainment, Environmental, Event Planning & Marketing, Exhibit/Trade Shows, Financial, Food Service, Government/Political, Graphic Design, Health Care Services, High Technology, Hospitality, Household Goods, Identity Marketing, In-Store Advertising, Industrial, Infomercials, Information Technology, Integrated Marketing, Internet/Web Design, Legal Services, Leisure, Local Marketing, Logo & Package Design, Luxury Products, Magazines, Marine, Market Research, Media Planning, Media Relations, Medical Products, Merchandising, Multimedia, New Product Development, Newspaper, Newspapers & Magazines, Out-of-Home Media, Outdoor, Over-50 Market, Package Design, Pharmaceutical, Planning & Consultation, Podcasting, Point of Purchase, Point of Sale, Print, Production, Public Relations, Publicity/Promotions, RSS (Really Simple Syndication), Radio, Recruitment, Restaurant, Retail, Sales Promotion, Search Engine Optimization, Seniors' Market, Sports Market, Strategic Planning/Research, Sweepstakes, T.V., Technical Advertising, Telemarketing, Trade & Consumer Magazines, Transportation, Travel & Tourism, Web (Banner Ads, Pop-ups, etc.), Yellow Pages Advertising

Approx. Annual Billings: $8,500,000

Breakdown of Gross Billings by Media: Audio/Visual: 15%; Brdcst.: 20%; Co-op Adv.: 10%; Consulting: 20%; Fees: 20%; Worldwide Web Sites: 15%

Stan Felder *(Pres & CEO)*
Mike Harley *(Sr Dir-Art)*
Erin Alt *(Dir-Art)*
Erin Vandenberg *(Dir-Art)*
Sue McIntire *(Mgr-Fin)*

Accounts:
2/90 Sign Systems; Grand Rapids, MI Signage; 2006
Bates Footwear; Rockford, MI Boots & Shoes; 2006
Gentex; Zeeland, MI Automotive Parts; 1995
Gill Industries; Grand Rapids, MI Automotive Products; 2006
Harbor Hospice; Muskegon, MI Hospice Services; 2006
Haworth Office Furniture; Holland, MI Office Furniture; 1992
IBOA International; Grand Rapids, MI Business Owners Association; 2004
Michigan Turkey Producers; Grand Rapids, MI; 2005
MPI Research; Mattawan, MI Pre-Clinical Testing; 2009
Priority Health; Grand Rapids, MI Health Insurance; 2005
Rowe International; Grand Rapids, MI Jukeboxes; 2002
Wings of Hope Hospice; Allegan, MI Hospice Services; 2008

FELLOW
2609 Aldrich Ave S #103, Minneapolis, MN 55408
Tel.: (612) 605-1712
Web Site: www.fellowinc.com

Year Founded: 2010

Agency Specializes In: Alternative Advertising, Branded Entertainment, Broadcast, Co-op Advertising, Collateral, Consumer Publications, Digital/Interactive, Experience Design, Guerilla Marketing, In-Store Advertising, Local Marketing, Magazines, Newspapers & Magazines, Outdoor, Point of Purchase, Point of Sale, Print, Radio, T.V., Viral/Buzz/Word of Mouth, Web (Banner Ads, Pop-ups, etc.)

Eric Luoma *(Co-Founder & Dir-Creative)*
Karl Wolf *(Co-Founder & Dir-Creative)*
Kari Luoma *(Controller)*
Will Gunderson *(Assoc Dir-Creative)*

Accounts:
JCPenney
Mayo Clinic
ResQwater
Target

FENESTRA MEDIA
PO Box 340662, Sacramento, CA 95834
Tel.: (916) 601-4329
Fax: (888) 411-7015
E-Mail: info@fenestramedia.com
Web Site: www.fenestramedia.com

Agency Specializes In: Advertising, Event Planning & Marketing, Media Buying Services, Media Planning

Lucy Camacho *(Owner)*

Accounts:
Pets To Go

FENTON
630 Ninth Ave Ste 910, New York, NY 10036
Tel.: (212) 584-5000
Fax: (212) 584-5045
E-Mail: info@fenton.com
Web Site: www.fenton.com

Agency Specializes In: Advertising, Brand Development & Integration, Digital/Interactive, Media Relations

Bill Werde *(CEO)*
Ben Branham *(Mng Dir)*
Sandy Skees *(Mng Dir)*
Elke Dochtermann *(Chief Creative Officer)*
William Hamilton *(Exec VP)*
Jennifer Hahn *(Sr VP)*
Alyssa Singer *(Sr Acct Exec)*

Accounts:
New-Bread for the World
New-The Robert Wood Johnson Foundation

THE FENTON GROUP
44 Weybosset St, Providence, RI 02903
Tel.: (401) 490-4888
Fax: (401) 490-4666
E-Mail: info@thefentongroup.net
Web Site: www.thefentongroup.net

Employees: 4

Agency Specializes In: Sponsorship

Joshua Fenton *(CEO)*

Accounts:
Campaign for a Healthy Rhode Island
Fair Insurance Rhode Island
Fit & Fresh
Fresh Brigido's Market
GE Money
Giving Rhode Island
Gore Creative Technologies Worldwide
Guertin
Harrahs
Holliston
Medport
Nordt Company
The Promenade
Qualidigm
Quality Partners of Rhode Island
Supreme

FEREBEE LANE & CO.
734 South Main St B, Greenville, SC 29601
Tel.: (864) 370-9692
Web Site: www.ferebeelane.com

Year Founded: 2005

National Agency Associations: 4A's

Agency Specializes In: Advertising

Matt Ferebee *(Owner & Dir-Creative)*
Josh Lane *(Principal & Dir-Strategic)*
Jivan Dave *(Dir-Art)*
Chris Waldrop *(Dir-Art)*
Jamie Demumbreum *(Sr Mgr-Production)*
Janis Leidlein *(Office Mgr)*
Hannah Lascola *(Strategist-Digital)*

Accounts:
Bayerische Motoren Werke Aktiengesellschaft
BlackBerry Blackberry
Hickory Chair Furniture Co.
Le Creuset

FERGUSON ADVERTISING INC.
803 S Calhoun St 6th Fl, Fort Wayne, IN 46802-2319
Tel.: (260) 426-4401
Fax: (260) 422-6417
E-Mail: rich@fai2.com
Web Site: www.fai2.com

Employees: 17
Year Founded: 1975

Agency Specializes In: Business-To-Business, Collateral, Communications, Customer Relationship Management, Electronic Media, Financial, Graphic Design, Health Care Services, Industrial, Internet/Web Design, Logo & Package Design, New Product Development, Newspaper, Newspapers & Magazines, Out-of-Home Media, Outdoor, Point of Purchase, Point of Sale, Public Relations, Publicity/Promotions, Radio, Sales Promotion, Strategic Planning/Research, T.V., Technical Advertising, Trade & Consumer Magazines

Approx. Annual Billings: $14,000,000

Breakdown of Gross Billings by Media: Outdoor: $1,000,000; Print: $4,000,000; Radio: $3,000,000; T.V.: $5,000,000; Worldwide Web Sites: $1,000,000

John Ferguson *(Owner & Acct Exec)*
Nancy J. Wright *(CEO, Acct Supvr & Exec Dir-Creative)*
Bob Kiel *(VP & Dir-Creative)*
Kyle Martin *(VP-Acct Svcs)*
Jason McFarland *(Sr Dir-Art)*
Brian Art *(Dir-Art)*
Brittany Reed *(Dir-Media)*
Greg Smith *(Dir-Art)*
Carol Havers *(Mgr-Production)*
Gena Taylor *(Strategist & Sr Writer)*

Accounts:
ALFE; Fort Wayne, IN Metal Heat Treater; 1994
Blue Octopus Printing Company
The Community Foundation of Greater Fort Wayne
Dekko Foundation; Kendallville, IN; 2005
Do It Best Corp.; Fort Wayne, IN (Agency of Record) Creative, Marketing, Public Relations, Strategic Planning
Entrex; Washington, DC Private Equity Exchange; 2002
Fort Wayne Metals Research; Fort Wayne, IN Precision Metal Wire; 1999
Indiana Tech; Fort Wayne, IN; 2005
Kroger/Scotts; Fort Wayne, IN Regional Supermarket Chain
Lutheran Foundation; Fort Wayne, IN; 2005
Medical Protective; Fort Wayne, IN Medical Malpractice Insurer; 1998
Northeast Indiana Regional Partnership; Fort Wayne, IN Economic Development; 2006
Purdue Employees Federal Credit Union; Lafayette, IN; 2000
Rea Magnet Wire; Fort Wayne, IN Magnet Wire Producer; 2003
Shindigz; South Whitley, IN Direct Party Goods; 2007
The Strahm Group; Fort Wayne, IN Construction, Furnishings, Interior Design; 1996
Summit Brand; Fort Wayne, IN Consumer Cleaning Products; 1994
Tower Bank; Fort Wayne, IN; 2007
Zimmer Corp; Warsaw, IN Orthopedic Products; 2006

FEROCIOUS COW
315 E 77 St 6th Fl, New York, NY 10075
Tel.: (917) 331-0496
Fax: (212) 396-9295
E-Mail: info@ferociouscow.com
Web Site: www.ferociouscow.com

Agency Specializes In: Advertising, Event Planning & Marketing, Print, Public Relations, Sponsorship

Jason Volper *(Dir-Creative & Exec Producer)*
Rohan Caesar *(Dir-Creative)*

Accounts:
American Express Company
Canadian Club
Century 21 Gold Standard
Verizon Communications Inc.

FERRARA & COMPANY
301C College Rd E, Princeton, NJ 08540
Tel.: (609) 945-8700
Fax: (609) 945-8700
E-Mail: info@ferraracompany.com
Web Site: www.ferraracompany.com

Employees: 40
Year Founded: 1986

Agency Specializes In: Advertising, Event Planning & Marketing, Exhibit/Trade Shows, Hospitality, Internet/Web Design, Local Marketing, New Product Development, Print, Promotions, Radio, Sales Promotion, Sponsorship, Strategic Planning/Research, T.V.

Linda Rosenthal *(Partner & Mng Dir)*
Bob Sullivan *(Chief Creative Officer & Exec VP)*
George Biava *(Exec VP)*
Benjamin J. Weisman *(Exec Dir-Creative)*
Aaron Brown *(Dir-Creative)*
Chris Greenberg *(Dir-Fin)*
Christine Mariani *(Dir-Project Mgmt)*
Elle McComsey *(Dir-Digital Strategy)*
Deborah LaPlante-Rosta *(Mgr-HR)*

Accounts:
ACT
Arm & Hammer
Magni Vision
New Jersey Lottery Advertising, Creative
Orajel
Oxi Clean
Trojan
Unisom

FETCH
650 Mission St 3rd Fl, San Francisco, CA 94105
Tel.: (415) 523-0350
Web Site: www.wearefetch.com

National Agency Associations: 4A's

Agency Specializes In: Advertising, Brand Development & Integration, Media Planning, Social Media

James Connelly *(CEO)*
Greg Grimmer *(COO)*
Guillaume Lelait *(Gen Mgr)*
Paul-Eric Lefebvre *(Creative Dir)*
Frank Lipari *(Creative Dir)*
Christina Higham *(Mgr-Mktg)*
Kristen Pezda *(Acct Coord)*

Accounts:
New-Expedia
New-Hotels.com
New-Uber

FG CREATIVE INC
74020 Alessandro Dr Ste E, Palm Desert, CA 92260
Tel.: (760) 773-1707
Web Site: www.fgcreative.com

Year Founded: 2002

Agency Specializes In: Advertising, Brand Development & Integration, Broadcast, Graphic Design, Internet/Web Design, Logo & Package Design, Media Planning, Public Relations, Social Media, Strategic Planning/Research

Stephanie D. Greene *(CEO)*
Cindy Czarnowski *(Office Mgr & Controller)*
Jeff Day *(Dir-Art & Graphic Designer)*
Emily Diefendorf *(Mgr-Production)*
Judith Salkin *(Mgr-PR)*
Andrea Carter *(Sr Acct Exec)*
Chris Martello *(Sr Strategist-PR)*

Accounts:
El Paseo Shopping
Hi-Desert Med Center
Y Be Fit Palm Desert Challenge

FGM INTERNET MARKETING
1625 Old Plymouth St, Bridgewater, MA 2324
Tel.: (843) 822-3773
Web Site: www.fgminternetmarketing.com

Year Founded: 2011

Agency Specializes In: Advertising, Email, Search Engine Optimization, Social Media

Fiona G. Martin *(Founder)*

FH GROUP
2320 W 8th St, Erie, PA 16505
Tel.: (814) 459-2443
Fax: (814) 459-6862
Web Site: www.fh-group.com

Year Founded: 2001

Agency Specializes In: Advertising, Brand Development & Integration, Digital/Interactive, Email, Internet/Web Design

Gary Fritts *(Founder)*
Andy Fritts *(Pres & CEO)*
Molly Fritts *(Dir-Client Rels)*

Accounts:
EagleBurgmann Industries LP

FIELD DAY INC.
171 E Liberty St Ste 320, Toronto, ON M6K 3P6 Canada
Tel.: (416) 408-4446
Fax: (416) 408-4447
E-Mail: info@fieldday.com
Web Site: www.fieldday.com

Employees: 10
Year Founded: 1989

Agency Specializes In: Advertising, Brand Development & Integration, Business-To-Business, Communications, Entertainment, Pharmaceutical, Sports Market

Andrew Arntfield *(Pres & Planner-Strategic)*
Lynn Kozak *(Partner & Sr Acct Dir)*
Sandy Zita *(Partner & Dir-Art)*
Samantha Elliott *(Mgr-Digital Content & Office Mgr)*
Leah Rose *(Acct Mgr)*

Accounts:
Canadian National Exhibition
Epson Canada
Jays Care Foundation
Living Arts Center
Maple Leaf Sports & Entertainment Ltd.; Toronto, Ontario; 1999
Metro Toronto Convention Centre; 2004
NBA Canada
OLG
Rogers Media
Toronto Blue Jays
Vision TV; Toronto, Ontario; 2004
Warner Home Video Canada
Warner Home Video Canada
XM Canada

FIFTEEN MINUTES
8436 W 3rd St Ste 650, Los Angeles, CA 90048
Tel.: (323) 556-9700
Fax: (323) 556-9710
E-Mail: info@fifteenminutes.com
Web Site: www.fifteenminutes.com

Employees: 21
Year Founded: 2005

Agency Specializes In: Advertising, Media Buying Services, Media Planning, Media Relations, Public Relations, Strategic Planning/Research

Howard Bragman *(Founder & Chm)*
Ryan Croy *(Mng Partner)*
Lisa Perkins *(Partner & Dir-Talent)*
Dawn Stramer *(CFO)*
Victoria Greene *(VP-Comm & Mktg)*
Megan Sekkas *(VP-Lifestyle Brands & Personalities)*
Karen Marines *(Sr Acct Exec-Corp Entertainment)*

Accounts:
Carter Oosterhouse
Dr. Lisa Masterson
eHarmony Inc. Relationship Services Provider
New-FirstLook Media Relations, Thought Leadership
Greg Louganis
New-Headcase VR Media Relations, Thought Leadership

FIFTY EIGHT ADVERTISING LLC
433 Bishop St NW, Atlanta, GA 30318
Tel.: (404) 733-6872
Web Site: www.58advertising.com

Year Founded: 2009

Agency Specializes In: Internet/Web Design, Print, T.V.

Mike Gustafson *(Owner & Dir-Creative)*

Accounts:
Campbell & Brannon Real Estate Attorneys; 2011
Floor & Decor Inc Flooring Retailer; 2012
nFinanSe Inc. Prepaid Card Services; 2009
Stone Mountain Golf Club Marriott Golf; 2010

FIG ADVERTISING
110 16th St Ste 940, Denver, CO 80202
Tel.: (303) 260-7840
Fax: (720) 359-1000
Web Site: www.figadvertising.com

Year Founded: 2009

Agency Specializes In: Advertising, Brand Development & Integration, Collateral, Corporate Identity, E-Commerce, Internet/Web Design, Logo & Package Design, Market Research, Media Buying Services

Zachary Rischitelli *(Mng Dir-Acct Svcs)*
Brian Leugs *(Copywriter)*

Accounts:
Active Rx
ATD Foundation & Football Camp
Barnacle Bookkeeping
Environmental Logistics
Metro Building Services, Inc.

FIGLIULO&PARTNERS
225 Pk Ave S, New York, NY 10003
Tel.: (212) 966-9525
E-Mail: hello@figliuloandpartners.com
Web Site: www.figliuloandpartners.com

National Agency Associations: 4A's

Agency Specializes In: Advertising, Brand Development & Integration, Broadcast, Sponsorship, T.V.

Mark Figliulo *(Founder & CEO)*
Judith Carr-Rodriguez *(Pres)*
Richard Tan *(Partner & CFO)*
Caroline Wellman Krediet *(Partner & Head-Strategy)*
Jay Wee *(Sr Dir-Art)*
Emily Lalime *(Acct Dir)*
Kelly Stevens *(Dir-Client & New Bus Dev)*
Meghan Luck *(Brand Strategist)*

Accounts:
New-Seabourn Cruise Line (Agency of Record) Creative, Marketing
Sprint Corporation Campaign: "Count On It", Campaign: "Frobinsons", Campaign: "Spin Off", Family Plan, Television
Virgin Atlantic Airways Ltd. (North American Creative Agency of Record) Campaign: "Business Is an Adventure", Campaign: "Let it Fly", Digital, Online, Out-of-Home

FIGMENT DESIGN
2977 McFarlane Rd 2nd Fl, Miami, FL 33133
Tel.: (305) 593-7488
Fax: (305) 593-7468
Web Site: www.figmentdesign.com

Agency Specializes In: Advertising, Brand Development & Integration, Collateral, Graphic Design, Internet/Web Design, Logo & Package Design, Media Buying Services, Media Planning, Outdoor, Print

Jeffrey Pankey *(Founder & Pres)*

Accounts:
Diamusica

FILTER CREATIVE GROUP
5908 Barton Ave, Los Angeles, CA 90038
Tel.: (323) 464-4170
Fax: (323) 464-4294
Web Site: www.filtercreativegroup.com

Year Founded: 1999

Agency Specializes In: Advertising, Brand Development & Integration, Event Planning & Marketing, Public Relations, Social Marketing/Nonprofit, T.V., Web (Banner Ads, Pop-ups, etc.)

Accounts:
Guitar Center, Inc
Toyota Motor Corporation
Ty Ku Campaign: "Share on"

FINCH BRANDS
325 Chestnut St Ste 1313, Philadelphia, PA 19106
Tel.: (215) 413-2686
Fax: (215) 413-2687
E-Mail: info@finchbrands.com
Web Site: www.finchbrands.com

E-Mail for Key Personnel:
President: derlbaum@kanterinternational.com
Creative Dir.: jgoldenberg@kanterinternational.com
Public Relations: jkramer@kanterinternational.com

Employees: 17
Year Founded: 1996

Agency Specializes In: Above-the-Line, Advertising, Affluent Market, Automotive, Below-the-Line, Brand Development & Integration, Business-To-Business, Collateral, College, Communications, Consulting, Consumer Goods, Consumer Marketing, Corporate Communications, Corporate Identity, Digital/Interactive, Direct Response Marketing, Education, Electronic Media, Exhibit/Trade Shows, Experience Design, Graphic Design, Guerilla Marketing, High Technology, Hospitality, Identity Marketing, Industrial, Information Technology, Integrated Marketing, Internet/Web Design, Leisure, Local Marketing, Logo & Package Design, Luxury Products, Market Research, Men's Market, Mobile Marketing, New Product Development, New Technologies, Newspapers & Magazines, Outdoor, Point of Sale, Print, Restaurant, Retail, Social Marketing/Nonprofit, Sponsorship, Sports Market, Strategic Planning/Research, Transportation, Travel & Tourism, Women's Market

Daniel Erlbaum *(CEO)*
Scott Richards *(Sr Dir-Art)*
Andrew Moore *(Dir-Integrated Mktg)*
Annette Saggiomo *(Sr Brand Strategist)*
Tracy Grimes *(Mgr-Acctg)*
Valerie Slade *(Mgr-Mktg)*
Kiana Moore *(Strategist-Brand)*
Jennifer Govberg *(Coord-Integrated Mktg)*

Accounts:
Fathead Licensed Retail Line, Customized Wall Art; 2011
Herman Miller; Zeeland, MI Home Furniture Group; 2006
Nutrisystem
World Wrestling Entertainment; Stamford, CT Integrated Media & Entertainment Company; 2005

FINE DOG CREATIVE
103 W Lockwood Ave Ste 201, Saint Louis, MO 63119
Tel.: (314) 968-1200
Fax: (314) 255-3585
Web Site: www.finedogcreative.com

Year Founded: 2003

Agency Specializes In: Advertising, Brand Development & Integration, Environmental, Internet/Web Design, Package Design, Print

Bryan McAllister *(Owner & Creative Dir)*

Accounts:
DataServ, L.L.C.
The Home Depot, Inc.
J.D. Conrad & Associates, Inc.
Nutrahealth Solutions LLC
Ranken Technical College

FINN PARTNERS
301 E 57th St, New York, NY 10022
Tel.: (212) 593-6400
Web Site: www.finnpartners.com

National Agency Associations: COPF

Agency Specializes In: Arts, Corporate Communications, Crisis Communications, Digital/Interactive, Government/Political, Health Care Services, Internet/Web Design, Media Relations, Multicultural, Public Relations, Social Media, Travel & Tourism, Viral/Buzz/Word of Mouth, Web (Banner Ads, Pop-ups, etc.)

Peter Finn *(Founder & Partner)*
Noah Finn *(Mng Partner)*
Morris Silver *(Mng Partner)*
Amy Terpeluk *(Partner & Sr VP)*
Miranda Harper *(Partner)*

Mark Singer *(CFO)*
Sakura Amend *(VP-CSR & Social Issues Practice)*
Aik Wye Ng *(VP)*
Cliff Berman *(Sr Partner & Dir-Consumer Mktg)*
Ashley Aberbach *(Sr Acct Exec)*
Elizabeth Levit *(Sr Acct Exec)*
Haley Schwartz *(Acct Exec)*
Richard Funess *(Sr Mng Partner)*
Helen Shelton *(Sr Partner)*

Accounts:
AVG
Bosch Home Appliances
Carbonite Executive Positioning, Media Relations, Social media
Cinnabon, Inc. (Public Relations Agency of Record) Social Media
Crystal Cruises (North American Public Relations Agency of Record) Brand Management, Image Management, Marketing, Media Relations, Promotions, Special Events, Strategic Partnerships & Alliances
EKOS Campaign: "All you Need is Ecuador", Communication, Creative, Marketing, Media Relations, Public Relations
New-Empire State Development Campaign: "I Love New York", Public Relations
Fujitsu America PR
Green Festivals Inc Corporate Communications, Media Relations
Hyundai Hope on Wheels
Hyundai
IEEE
International Council of Shopping Centers
Invest Atlanta Communication Strategy, Media Relations
The Jamaica Tourist Board
Marvell
MD Anderson
MOMA
Newegg Media
The North Face
Robert Wood Johnson Foundation
Rosetta Stone (Public Relations Agency of Record)
Strength of Nature Global Brands, LLC Corporate Relations, Creative, Media Relations, Sponsorship Activation, Women of Color
StubHub
SUNGARD
Thermador
The Verizon Foundation

Branches

DVL Seigenthaler
(Formerly DVL Public Relations & Advertising)
700 12th Ave S Ste 400, Nashville, TN 37203
(See Separate Listing)

Finn Partners
(Formerly Ruder Finn)
8 Hartum Street, PO Box 45138, Har Hotzvim, Jerusalem, 91450 Israel
Tel.: (972) 2 589 2000
Fax: (972) 2 581 8999
E-Mail: goel@finnpartners.co.il
Web Site: www.finnpartners.com/israel/

Employees: 10
Year Founded: 1997

Agency Specializes In: Public Relations

Glenn Jasper *(Sr Partner & Mng Dir)*
Rafael Fischer *(VP)*
Elie Klein *(Assoc VP)*
Ellie Gorlin Hanson *(Acct Supvr)*
Ayala Young *(Acct Exec)*
Nicole Grubner *(Asst Acct Exec)*

Accounts:
AORA
Amiad Filtrations Systems
AudioCodes Ltd
ECI Telecom
Ectel
Elbit Imaging
Energtek
Global Energy
Lavie TimeTECH
Mazor Surgical Technologies
Metrolight
Nishmat
Oramed
Orthocrat
Radware

Finn Partners
(Formerly Ruder Finn, Inc.)
1875 Century Park East, Ste 200, Los Angeles, CA 90067
Tel.: (310) 552-6922
Web Site: www.finnpartners.com

Employees: 12
Year Founded: 1996

National Agency Associations: COPF

Howard Solomon *(Mng Partner)*
Jeff Seedman *(Partner & Sr VP)*
Joe Foster *(Partner)*
Christine Bock *(Sr Partner, Exec VP & Head-Global Mobile & Telecom Practice)*
Aik Wye Ng *(VP)*
Erica Cohen Coltun *(Assoc VP)*
Whitney Snow *(Acct Supvr)*
Katherine Leibrandt *(Acct Exec)*

Accounts:
BSH Home Appliances (Public Relations Agency of Record)
Crystal Cruises (Public Relations Agency of Record) Strategy
Hyundai Hope on Wheels (Agency of Record)
NetZero 4G Broadband Service
Thermador Brand Awareness

Finn Partners
(Formerly Ruder Finn West)
388 Market St Ste 1400, San Francisco, CA 94111-5316
Tel.: (415) 541-0750
Fax: (415) 541-0720
E-Mail: solomonh@ruderfinn.com
Web Site: www.finnpartners.com

Employees: 13

National Agency Associations: COPF

Agency Specializes In: Public Relations, Sponsorship

Chantal Bowman-Boyles *(Mng Partner)*
Anne Glauber *(Mng Partner)*
Dena Merriam *(Mng Partner)*
Daniel Pooley *(Mng Partner)*
Ron Rogers *(Mng Partner)*
Howard Solomon *(Mng Partner)*
Alicia Young *(Mng Partner)*
Jeff Seedman *(Partner & Sr VP)*
Gabriella Asmus *(VP)*
Brenda Lynch *(Sr Partner)*

Accounts:
All-America Rose Selections, Inc.
Dreamerz Foods; 2007
The Good Earth Company Good Earth Coffee; 2008
Jamba Juice (Agency of Record) Public Relations, Social Media
LIVESTRONG.COM
Moxtra Public Relations
Specific Media
StubHub, Inc.; 2007
TiVo
Voce

Finn Partners
(Formerly Ruder Finn, Inc.)
1667 K St NW Ste 950, Washington, DC 20006
Tel.: (202) 466-7800
Fax: (202) 974-5060
Web Site: www.finnpartners.com

Employees: 9

National Agency Associations: COPF

Jessica Berk Ross *(Mng Partner & Gen Mgr)*
Jason Smith *(Mng Partner)*
Barry Reicherter *(Partner-Digital Insights & Sr VP)*
Robin Crawford *(Partner)*
Mark Martin *(Sr VP-Fin)*
Nebyat Ejigu *(VP & Dir-Digital Production)*
Sharon Keating *(VP-Ops-Ruder Finn)*
Christopher Lawrence *(Dir-Res)*
Erin Robertson *(Acct Supvr-Digital)*
Matt Price *(Deputy Dir-Res)*

Accounts:
American Institute of Cancer Research
Center of Substance Abuse Treatment (CSAT)
Jamaica Tourist Board
Novartis
New-The Recording Academy
Weight Watchers

Finn Partners
(Formerly Ruder Finn, Inc.)
625 N Michigan Ave Ste 2300, Chicago, IL 60611
Tel.: (312) 329-3916
Fax: (312) 932-0367
E-Mail: dan@finnpartners.com
Web Site: www.finnpartners.com

Employees: 32

National Agency Associations: COPF

Agency Specializes In: Public Relations

Dan Pooley *(Mng Partner)*
Alicia Young *(Mng Partner)*
Ann Morris *(Partner)*
Shelly Holmes *(Sr Partner & Exec VP)*
Emily Shirden *(VP)*
Kristen Berry *(Assoc VP-Health Practice)*
Taryn Williams-Clark *(Assoc VP)*
Rosalie M. Hagel *(Sr Partner)*
Bill Nowling *(Sr Partner)*

Accounts:
New-The Recording Academy
Xchanging Technology (Lead Agency) Global Public Relations

Horn Group Inc.
612 Howard St Ste 100, San Francisco, CA 94105
(See Separate Listing)

Johnson King Public Relations
93 Great Suffolk St, London, SE1 0BX United Kingdom
Tel.: (44) 20 7401 7968
Fax: (44) 20 7928 2672
Web Site: www.johnsonking.com

Employees: 20
Year Founded: 1992

Agency Specializes In: Business-To-Business, Public Relations

Mike King *(Founder & Chm)*

Flora Haslam *(Mng Dir)*
Richard Scarlett *(Acct Dir)*
Jonathan Mathias *(Sr Acct Mgr)*
Lindsey Challis *(Acct Mgr)*
Hannah Townsend *(Acct Mgr)*
Mike Marquiss *(Sr Acct Exec)*
Kasia Murphy *(Sr Acct Exec)*
Aidan Murphy *(Acct Exec)*
Gemma White *(Acct Exec)*
Claire Ayles *(Sr Partner)*

Accounts:
Alcatel Intra-Office Communications Systems
Aruba Networks Wireless LAN Systems
Keynote Systems
Sophos (Agency of Record)
TE Connectivity

M. Silver/A Division of Finn Partners
(Formerly M. Silver Associates Inc. - Public Relations)
747 3rd Ave Fl 23, New York, NY 10017-2803
(See Separate Listing)

Widmeyer Communications
1129 NW 20th St Ste 200, Washington, DC 20036
(See Separate Listing)

FIORE ASSOCIATES, INC.
109 Washington St, Morristown, NJ 07960
Tel.: (973) 359-4444
Fax: (973) 359-4449
Toll Free: (800) 835-0641
E-Mail: info@fioreinspires.com
Web Site: www.fioreinspires.com

E-Mail for Key Personnel:
President: pat@fioreassociates.com

Employees: 17
Year Founded: 1983

National Agency Associations: AD CLUB-PRSA

Agency Specializes In: New Product Development, Public Relations, Strategic Planning/Research

Patricia C. Fiore *(Founder & Strategist)*

Accounts:
Aussie Imports, LLC
BENEO Inc.
Bograd's Furniture; 1992
The CIT Group
King of the Sea Tuna
Madison Area YMCA
National Starch Food Innovation
Orafti
Oved Diamond Company
Viva The Chef
Yanina & Co. Jewelry

FIREFLI MEDIA
1327 Grandin Rd Ste A, Roanoke, VA 24015
Tel.: (540) 985-3473
Web Site: www.fireflimedia.com

Year Founded: 2009

Agency Specializes In: Advertising, Brand Development & Integration, Content, Digital/Interactive, Internet/Web Design, Logo & Package Design, Print, Social Media

Greg Brock *(Pres)*
John Cornthwait *(Dir-Digital Media)*
Matthew Sams *(Dir-Digital Strategy)*
Maria Bocanegra *(Specialist-Client Relationship)*
Beth Klinefelter *(Specialist-Social Media & PR)*
Aidan O'Connor *(Copywriter)*

Accounts:
Carilion Clinic
Grand Home Furnishings
Member One
Richfield Retirement Community
Standup Foundation
VirginiaTech

FIREFLY CREATIVE, INC.
2556 Apple Valley Rd Ste 200, Atlanta, GA 30319
Tel.: (404) 262-7424
Fax: (404) 365-9616
E-Mail: barton@fireflyatlanta.com
Web Site: www.fireflyatlanta.com

Employees: 5
Year Founded: 1969

Agency Specializes In: Advertising Specialties, Bilingual Market, Brand Development & Integration, Business-To-Business, Cable T.V., Children's Market, Co-op Advertising, Collateral, Communications, Consumer Marketing, Corporate Identity, Education, Entertainment, Environmental, Exhibit/Trade Shows, Financial, Food Service, Graphic Design, Health Care Services, High Technology, Industrial, Investor Relations, Leisure, Logo & Package Design, Magazines, Medical Products, Merchandising, New Product Development, Newspaper, Newspapers & Magazines, Pharmaceutical, Point of Purchase, Point of Sale, Print, Real Estate, Restaurant, Retail, Sweepstakes, Travel & Tourism

Approx. Annual Billings: $4,878,450

Barton Wood *(Pres)*
Alyssa Felda *(CEO & CMO)*
Brad Lawley *(Dir-Creative)*

Accounts:
Inhibitex; Atlanta, GA; 2002

FIREMAN CREATIVE
33 Terminal Way Ste 527, Pittsburgh, PA 15219
Tel.: (412) 325-3333
Fax: (412) 325-3330
Web Site: www.firemancreative.com

Agency Specializes In: Advertising, Graphic Design, Internet/Web Design, Print

Paul Fireman *(Pres)*
Melissa Cullin *(Dir-Project Mgmt)*

Accounts:
Bob O'Connor Golf Course
The Forbes Funds
Heartland Homes, Inc.

FIRESPRING
(Formerly 42)
1201 Infinity Ct, Lincoln, NE 68512
Tel.: (402) 261-8952
Web Site: creative.firespring.com

Agency Specializes In: Advertising, Digital/Interactive

Dustin Wilbourn *(Dir-Photography)*
Christian Habib *(Acct Exec)*

Accounts:
SL Green Realty Corp

FIREVINE INC.
69950 M-62, Edwardsburg, MI 49112
Tel.: (269) 663-5500
E-Mail: info@firevine.com
Web Site: www.firevine.com

Year Founded: 2008

Agency Specializes In: Advertising, Brand Development & Integration, Collateral, Content, Digital/Interactive, Graphic Design, Internet/Web Design, Public Relations, Search Engine Optimization, Social Media

Matt Harlow *(Partner & VP-Acct Svc)*
Jack Wilkinson *(Acct Dir)*
Tim Eash *(Dir-Tech)*
Mike Pecina *(Dir-Creative)*
Dustin Potts *(Dir-Brand Dev)*
Ryan Williams *(Dir-Art)*

Accounts:
Afdent

FIRMANI & ASSOCIATES
306 Fairview Ave N, Seattle, WA 98109-5313
Tel.: (206) 443-9357
Fax: (206) 443-9365
E-Mail: info@firmani.com
Web Site: www.firmani.com

Employees: 6
Year Founded: 1994

Agency Specializes In: Brand Development & Integration, Market Research, Media Planning, Newspaper, Planning & Consultation, Print, Public Relations

Approx. Annual Billings: $3,000,000

Breakdown of Gross Billings by Media: Brdcst.: $500,000; Print: $500,000; Pub. Rels.: $1,500,000; Radio: $500,000

Mark Firmani *(Pres)*
Kristi Herriott *(Partner)*
Keena Bean *(Acct Exec)*
Christa Van Wieringen *(Coord-Community Events Field)*

Accounts:
HBSS; Seattle, WA

FIRST EXPERIENCE COMMUNICATIONS
381 Hubbard St, Glastonbury, CT 06033
Tel.: (860) 657-3815
Fax: (860) 657-4379
Toll Free: (800) 426-5170
E-Mail: iwyellen@firstexperience.com
Web Site: www.firstexperience.com

Employees: 7
Year Founded: 1983

National Agency Associations: AMA-PRSA

Agency Specializes In: Advertising, Brand Development & Integration, Business-To-Business, Collateral, Commercial Photography, Communications, Consulting, E-Commerce, Education, Event Planning & Marketing, Graphic Design, High Technology, Information Technology, Integrated Marketing, Internet/Web Design, Logo & Package Design, Market Research, Media Planning, Media Relations, Over-50 Market, Paid Searches, Planning & Consultation, Podcasting, Public Relations, Publicity/Promotions, Search Engine Optimization, Social Media, Strategic Planning/Research

Breakdown of Gross Billings by Media: Collateral: 10%; Plng. & Consultation: 10%; Pub. Rels.: 25%; Strategic Planning/Research: 20%; Worldwide Web Sites: 35%

Ira W. Yellen *(Pres & CEO)*
Alison Karam *(Dir-PR, Mktg & Res)*

Lynette Viviani *(Sr Strategist-PR)*
Alaina Tobin *(Specialist-Graphic Design & Production)*
Holly Pelton *(Designer)*

Accounts:
Best of Care; Quincy, MA Home Care; 2011
CT Association for Homecare & Hospice; Wallingford, CT Trade Association; 2011
CT Technology Council; Hartford, CT Professional Trade Association; 2005
Oak Hill; Hartford, CT Social Services for the Disabled; 2004
VNA of South Worcester County; Worcester, MA Home Healthcare Agency; 2011

FIRST GENERATION
410 Allentown Dr, Allentown, PA 18109
Tel.: (610) 437-4300
Fax: (610) 437-3200
E-Mail: contact@firstgencom.com
Web Site: www.firstgencom.com

Year Founded: 1987

Agency Specializes In: Advertising, Brand Development & Integration, Digital/Interactive, Exhibit/Trade Shows, Media Planning, Print

Bill Carmody *(CEO)*
John Costello *(Dir & Sr Producer)*
Jenny Wuerstle *(Sr Producer-Mktg)*
Ashley Dobosh *(Producer-Integrated Mktg)*
Christina Pagano *(Jr Art Dir-Interactive)*
Lisabeth Flynn *(Acct Mgr-Event)*
Alicia Marinelli *(Acct Exec)*

Accounts:
Carpenter Technology Corporation

FIRST MEDIA GROUP INC.
120 E Washington St Ste 721, Syracuse, NY 13202
Tel.: (315) 471-7800
Fax: (315) 471-7811
E-Mail: info@firstmediagroup.com
Web Site: www.firstmediagroup.com

E-Mail for Key Personnel:
President: Mich@firstmediagroup.com

Employees: 8
Year Founded: 1980

Agency Specializes In: Advertising Specialties, Brand Development & Integration, Business Publications, Business-To-Business, Collateral, Communications, Consulting, Corporate Communications, Corporate Identity, Digital/Interactive, Direct Response Marketing, E-Commerce, Electronic Media, Financial, Graphic Design, Health Care Services, High Technology, Industrial, Internet/Web Design, Logo & Package Design, Media Buying Services, Medical Products, Print, Production, Public Relations, Trade & Consumer Magazines

Michael Hamidi *(Pres)*
Iris Wee *(CMO)*
Gail Hamidi *(VP)*

Accounts:
Boys and Girls Club of Syracuse
Cayuga Community College; Auburn, NY
Colgate University; Hamilton, NY
GE Inspection Technologies; Skaneateles, NY
Huber and Breuer; Syracuse, NY
Nottingham Senior Living; Syracuse, NY
Onondaga County Economic of Development

FIRSTBORN
32 Avenue Of the Americas, New York, NY 10013
Tel.: (212) 574-5300
Fax: (212) 765-7605
E-Mail: info@firstborn.com
Web Site: www.firstborn.com/

National Agency Associations: 4A's

Agency Specializes In: Advertising, Arts, Automotive, College, Content, Corporate Identity, Digital/Interactive, E-Commerce, Education, Food Service, Identity Marketing, Internet/Web Design, Magazines, Multimedia, Retail, Sponsorship, T.V., Web (Banner Ads, Pop-ups, etc.)

Dan LaCivita *(Pres)*
Eugene Chung *(Sr VP-Strategy & Analytics)*
Gabriel Garner *(Sr VP-Bus Plng)*
Alex Krawitz *(Sr VP-Content Dev)*
Eric Decker *(VP-Tech)*
Will Russell *(Head-Production)*
Benny Campa *(Dir-Creative)*
Adam Rubin *(Dir-Creative)*
Michele Bavitz *(Assoc Dir-Program)*
David Vale *(Assoc Dir-Creative)*
Daniel Viedma *(Assoc Dir-Tech)*
Bruno Perotto *(Assoc Creative Dir)*

Accounts:
Adobe
Aflac Digital
All Nippon Airways Digital, Print, Social, TV
Apple Campaign: "Try A New Look App", Digital, SoBe
AT&T Communications Corp.
Audible, Inc. Branding, Campaign: "Stories That Surround You", Creative, Digital, Online, Print, Radio, TV, WhisperSync
Dasani
Dentsu Campaign: "DentsuNetwork.com"
Digital Kitchen
Dorel Industries Cannondale, Digital, Mongoose, Strategy, Website
Expedition Titanic
FCUK Fragrances
Fidelity Investments Campaign: "Personal Economy", Saving Stories
Ford Mustang
HP
JCPenney
Lands' End
L'oreal Clarisonic, Concept development, Creative, Digital Marketing, Digital Strategy, Giorgio Armani, Kiehl's, Lancome, Luxe, Redken, Urban Decay, Yves Saint Laurent Beaute
Mars Canada M&M's
Morgans Hotel Group Content, Digital Strategy, Global Website
National Grid Website; 2008
The Patron Spirits Company Patron
PepsiCo Inc. Content, Mountain Dew, Oculus VR
Puma L.I.F.T. Shoe
RMS Titanic
Rolex
Saatchi & Saatchi
Sierra Mist Digital Creative
Skittles ShareSkittles.com
Sony America Digital Marketing, Make.believe, Mobile, OOH, Social
Tommy Bahama Rum
Unilever
UNIQLO Campaign: "Dry Mesh Project"
Wrigley

FISH ADVERTISING
25 Autumn Ln, West Kingston, RI 2892
Tel.: (401) 418-4929
Web Site: www.fishadvertising.com

Agency Specializes In: Advertising, Broadcast, Graphic Design, Media Buying Services, Radio, T.V.

Blair Fish *(Pres)*
Tom Broderick *(Dir-Media)*

Accounts:
Bald Hill Dodge Chrysler Jeep Ram

FISH CONSULTING, INC.
2001 Hollywood Blvd Ste 310, Hollywood, FL 33020
Tel.: (954) 893-9150
Fax: (954) 893-9168
Web Site: www.fish-consulting.com

Year Founded: 2004

Agency Specializes In: Advertising, Brand Development & Integration, Communications, Consulting, Crisis Communications, Graphic Design, Internet/Web Design, Media Relations, Public Relations, Social Media, Sponsorship

Chad Cohen *(Sr VP)*
Kim Ryan *(VP)*
Lauren Simo *(Acct Dir)*
Toby Srebnik *(Dir-Social Media)*
Amanda Bortzfield *(Sr Acct Mgr)*
Elayne Sommers *(Sr Acct Mgr)*
Andie Biederman *(Acct Mgr)*
Claibourne Smith *(Acct Mgr)*
Rachel Tabacnic *(Acct Mgr)*

Accounts:
AAMCO Transmissions Marketing, Public Relations
AlphaGraphics Business-to-Business PR, Marketing
Baskin-Robbins
BIP Capital BIP Franchise, Promotions
Blink Fitness Brand Awareness, Creative
Burger 21 Inc. (PR Agency of Record)
Captain D's, LLC Advertising, Communications, Consumer PR, Content Marketing, Digital Media, Media Relations, Public Relations, Strategic Media Relations
Coverall North America Brand Awareness, Public Relations
Del Taco Marketing
Dunkin' Donuts Event Marketing, Public Relations, Social Media
New-The Dwyer Group, Inc. Aire Serv, Glass Doctor, Mr. Appliance, Mr. Rooter, Public Relations, Rainbow International
Front Burner Brands, Inc Fish, Public Relations, The Melting Pot
Goddard Systems, Inc
New-Great Clips
i9 Sports Consumer, Content Marketing, Strategic Media Relations
International Franchise Association Educational Foundation Campaign: "Franchising Gives Back", Public Relations, Website
New-Kids 'R' Kids Learning Academies
Lo-Lo's Chicken & Waffles Public Relations
Massage Envy
National Restaurant Association Educational Foundation Business-to-Business PR, Marketing
Orangetheory Fitness Public Relations, Social Media
Pearle Vision Marketing Communications
Pinot's Palette
Polaroid Fotobar Public Relations
Smoothie King Marketing Communications
New-Tin Drum Asiacafe
Tropical Smoothie Cafe Content Marketing, Strategic Media Relations
Valpak
New-World of Beer

FISH MARKETING
107 SE Washington St Ste 620, Portland, OR 97214
Tel.: (503) 635-0007
Fax: (503) 635-1995

E-Mail: info@fish-marketing.com
Web Site: www.fish-marketing.com

Employees: 24
Year Founded: 2003

Agency Specializes In: Advertising, Brand Development & Integration, Digital/Interactive, Email, Media Buying Services, Public Relations, Search Engine Optimization, Social Media

Revenue: $5,500,000

Doug Fish *(Pres)*
Laurie Richings *(Controller)*
Alex Brauer *(Acct Dir)*
Michael Griffin *(Dir-Inbound Mktg)*
John Moore *(Dir-Digital)*
Kristen O'Toole *(Dir-Art & Sr Graphic Designer)*
Don Skramovsky *(Dir-Media)*

Accounts:
Ashland Bay
Gamakatsu
HEVI-Shot
Maxima Fishing Line
Mt. Hood Skibowl
Renaissance Marine Group
Snowbasin Resort
Steven's Marine
Subaru Mountain Partnerships
Timberline Lodge
Yakima Bait

FISHERMEARS ASSOCIATES, LLC
1830 Rt 52, Liberty, NY 12754
Tel.: (845) 295-5400
Web Site: www.fishermears.com

Agency Specializes In: Advertising, Brand Development & Integration, Internet/Web Design, Print, Radio

Karen Fisher *(Pres)*
Anne Dubrovsky *(VP)*

Accounts:
Bethel Woods Center for the Arts
Sullivan Renaissance

FISLER COMMUNICATIONS
26 Dartmouth Way, Newbury, MA 01951
Tel.: (978) 499-8448
E-Mail: parke@thefizzbiz.com
Web Site: www.thefizzbiz.com/

Employees: 3
Year Founded: 2000

Agency Specializes In: Advertising, Broadcast, Business-To-Business, Cable T.V., Communications, Computers & Software, Consumer Goods, Direct Response Marketing, Direct-to-Consumer, Entertainment, Event Planning & Marketing, Exhibit/Trade Shows, Government/Political, Health Care Services, High Technology, Industrial, Information Technology, Legal Services, Local Marketing, Newspaper, Pharmaceutical, Point of Purchase, Print, Production, Radio, Restaurant, Social Marketing/Nonprofit, Social Media, Sports Market, T.V., Women's Market

Parke Fisler *(Dir-Creative & Copywriter)*

Accounts:
Hologic; MA Corporate & Other Devices; 2003
Intertek ETL; 2000

FISTER
(Formerly Fister Lauberth, Inc.)
5401 itaska St, Saint Louis, MO 63109
Tel.: (314) 367-5600
Fax: (314) 367-2288
E-Mail: info@fister-inc.com
Web Site: www.fister-inc.com

E-Mail for Key Personnel:
President: aefister@fister-inc.com

Employees: 11
Year Founded: 1988

Agency Specializes In: Advertising, Advertising Specialties, Brand Development & Integration, Business Publications, Business-To-Business, Collateral, Commercial Photography, Communications, Consulting, Consumer Publications, Corporate Identity, Direct Response Marketing, Education, Electronic Media, Environmental, Event Planning & Marketing, Exhibit/Trade Shows, Financial, Graphic Design, Health Care Services, Internet/Web Design, Logo & Package Design, Media Buying Services, Medical Products, Pharmaceutical, Planning & Consultation, Point of Purchase, Point of Sale, Print, Production, Public Relations, Publicity/Promotions, Recruitment, Sales Promotion, Strategic Planning/Research, Trade & Consumer Magazines

Approx. Annual Billings: $4,000,000

Breakdown of Gross Billings by Media: Bus. Publs.: $400,000; Collateral: $2,000,000; Exhibits/Trade Shows: $200,000; Logo & Package Design: $400,000; Strategic Planning/Research: $400,000; Trade & Consumer Mags.: $600,000

Amy Fister *(Co-Founder)*
Kristen Templin *(Mgr-Mktg)*

Accounts:
Ascension Health
Mercer
Mississippi Lime
Sisters of St. Joseph of Carondelet

FITCH
121-141 Westbourne Terrace, London, W2 6JR United Kingdom
Tel.: (44) 207 479 0900
Fax: (44) 207 479 0600
E-Mail: info@fitch.com
Web Site: www.fitch.com

Employees: 80
Year Founded: 1972

Agency Specializes In: Automotive, Aviation & Aerospace, Brand Development & Integration, Broadcast, Children's Market, Corporate Identity, Environmental, Exhibit/Trade Shows, Fashion/Apparel, Financial, Graphic Design, Internet/Web Design, Investor Relations, Logo & Package Design, Merchandising, New Product Development, Planning & Consultation, Point of Purchase, Point of Sale, Restaurant, Retail, Transportation, Travel & Tourism

Tim Greenhalgh *(Chm & Chief Creative Officer)*
David Blair *(CEO-EMEIA)*
Simon Bolton *(CEO-Worldwide)*
Aaron Shields *(Head-Strategy-EMEA)*
Alasdair Lennox *(Exec Dir-Creative-EMEA)*
Kevin Doherty *(Client Svcs Dir)*
Piers Guilar *(Dir-Strategy-EMEA)*
Phil Heys *(Dir-Creative)*
John Regan *(Dir-Creative)*

Accounts:
BAT (British American Tobacco)
Bharti Retail
New-Butlins Brand, Design
Carhartt
HSBC
The Lexi Cinema Campaign: "The Nomad Cinema"
Molton Brown Campaign: "Navigations through Scent"
Morrisons Campaign: "M Local"
Nokia
Sberbank
Tesco Prague
Virgin Racing
White Wind Digital

United States

Fitch
585 S front st Ste 50, Columbus, OH 43215
Tel.: (614) 885-3453
Fax: (614) 885-4289
Web Site: www.fitch.com

Employees: 33
Year Founded: 1998

Agency Specializes In: Sponsorship

Larry Stewart *(Mng Dir)*
Hermann Behrens *(CEO-North America)*
Christian Davies *(Exec Creative Dir-Americas)*
David Hogrefe *(Acct Dir-Global & Dir-Client Svcs & Dev)*
Iain Webster *(Client Svcs Dir)*
Sean McGuinness *(Dir-Bus Dev)*
Alana Thompson *(Dir-Bus Dev)*

Accounts:
Dell
Microsoft
Nickelodeon Campaign: "Spongebob: Absorbent"
Target

Fitch
16435 N Scottsdale Rd Ste 195, Scottsdale, AZ 85254-1649
Tel.: (480) 998-4200
Fax: (480) 905-9423
Web Site: www.fitch.com

Employees: 50
Year Founded: 1998

Tim Greenhalgh *(Chief Creative Officer)*

Europe/Middle East

Fitch:London
121-141 Westbourne Terrace, London, W2 6JR United Kingdom
Tel.: (44) 207 479 0900
Fax: (44) 207 479 0600
E-Mail: ashley.goodall@fitch.com
Web Site: www.fitch.com

Employees: 20
Year Founded: 1978

Agency Specializes In: Brand Development & Integration

Tim Greenhalgh *(Chm & Chief Creative Officer)*
Alasdair Lennox *(Exec Dir-Creative-EMEA)*
Anna Chimes *(Dir-Design)*
Phil Heys *(Dir-Creative)*
John Regan *(Dir-Design)*
Nathan Watts *(Dir-Design-Experiential branding)*
Eleanor Holton *(Assoc Dir-Design)*
Gemma McDonnell *(Assoc Dir-Design)*
Sophia Lengui *(Mgr-HR)*
Christina Miles *(Mgr-Resourcing)*
Lucy Manski *(Designer-Middle Weight 3D)*
Vilma Vaiciule *(Sr Designer)*

Accounts:
Aditya Birla
BAT (British American Tobacco)
Hutchison 3G Cellular Phones
ING Bank
Lego
Microsoft
My for Tesco
Procter & Gamble
Singapore Tourism Board
Virgin Trains
Vodafone
White Wind Digital
Zurich Finance

Asia Pacific

Fitch Design Pvt. Ltd.
78 Amoy St #03-01, Singapore, 069897 Singapore
Tel.: (65) 6538 2988
Fax: (65) 6438 3188
E-Mail: ian.bellhouse@fitch.com
Web Site: www.fitch.com

Employees: 35
Year Founded: 1997

Ian Bellhouse *(CEO-Asia Pacific & Greater China)*
Danny Lye *(Gen Mgr)*
Darren Watson *(Exec Creative Dir)*
Jessalynn Chen *(Dir-Client)*
Christophe Guillot *(Dir-Bus Dev-Asia Pacific)*
Kristian Jones *(Dir-Design)*
Yukiko Kawabata *(Assoc Dir-Design)*
Scott Nelson *(Assoc Dir-Strategy)*
Cher Joven *(Sr Mgr-Client)*
Georgina Fielding *(Mgr-HR)*
Ben Yi Lim *(Client Mgr)*

Accounts:
Asian Paints
Hewlett-Packard
Singapore Tourism
Valore

FITZGERALD & MASTROIANNI, INC.
32 Hampden St, Springfield, MA 01103
Tel.: (413) 737-8757
Fax: (413) 731-1488
E-Mail: suem@fandmadvertising.com

Employees: 2
Year Founded: 2005

Agency Specializes In: Advertising, Advertising Specialties, Media Buying Services, Media Relations, Newspaper, Radio, Retail

Gerry Fitzgerald *(Owner)*
Susan Mastroianni *(Dir-Media Svcs)*

Accounts:
Columbia Gas of Massachusetts; 1996
Divorce Mediation Group; Springfield, MA; 2001
Polish National Credit Union
The Ranch Golf Club; Southwick, MA; 2002

FITZGERALD+CO
3333 Piedmont Rd NE Ste 100, Atlanta, GA 30305
Tel.: (404) 504-6900
Fax: (404) 239-0548
E-Mail: info@fitzco.com
Web Site: www.fitzco.com

Employees: 120
Year Founded: 1983

National Agency Associations: 4A's-AAF

Agency Specializes In: Advertising, Advertising Specialties, Brand Development & Integration, Broadcast, Cable T.V., Collateral, Communications, Consulting, Consumer Marketing, Corporate Communications, Corporate Identity, Direct Response Marketing, Graphic Design, In-Store Advertising, Internet/Web Design, Investor Relations, Local Marketing, Logo & Package Design, Media Buying Services, Newspaper, Newspapers & Magazines, Out-of-Home Media, Outdoor, Planning & Consultation, Point of Purchase, Point of Sale, Print, Production, Public Relations, Publicity/Promotions, Radio, Sponsorship, Strategic Planning/Research, T.V., Trade & Consumer Magazines, Travel & Tourism

Approx. Annual Billings: $200,000,000

David P. Fitzgerald *(Chm)*
Evan Levy *(Mng Dir)*
Keri Palmer *(CFO & Exec VP)*
Liz Daney *(Chief Media Officer & Exec VP)*
David Matathia *(Chief Strategy Officer)*
Pam Piligian *(Sr VP & Grp Acct Dir)*
Joyce Faulkner *(Sr VP & Acct Dir-New Bus)*
Christine Sigety *(Sr VP & Dir-Integrated Production)*
Anna Sherrill *(VP & Grp Dir-Media)*
Pam Hood *(VP & Dir-Media Brdcst Svcs)*
Brad Harvey *(Grp Dir-Creative)*
Jeff Quick *(Acct Dir)*
Maria Beasley *(Dir-HR)*
Mike McGarry *(Dir-Bus-Fitzco//McCann Coca-Cola)*
Katie Mellor *(Dir-Art)*
Stephanie Hue *(Acct Mgr)*
Sydne Cooper *(Mgr-HR)*
Erin Bishop *(Acct Supvr)*
Seth McWhorter *(Designer)*
Melanie Sherman *(Coord-Mktg)*
Betsy Bartlett *(Asst Media Planner)*
Zorah Byrd *(Jr Media Buyer-Brdcst)*
Ryan Henry *(Asst Media Planner)*
Kate Renwick *(Asst Media Planner)*
Lucy Webster *(Sr Media Planner)*

Accounts:
Amway
Atlanta St. Patrick's Day Parade Campaign: "Irish Eyes"
Black & Decker
Bulwark Campaign: "Because People Burn"
Carrabba's Italian Grill (Lead Creative Agency)
Clio Awards 2015 Clio Awards
The Coca-Cola Company Campaign: "Earn It", Coca-Cola Life, Coke Zero
Coca-Cola Refreshments USA, Inc. Campaign: "Roller Coaster"
Cryovac Division of Sealed Air Corp.; 1998
Delta
Durex
Hooters of America, LLC; Atlanta, GA Campaign: "Lifeguard", Creative, Radio, Social Media, TV
Howard's Auto Body
Mellow Mushroom Campaign: "Follow Me and I'll Follow You"
National Kidney Foundation (Agency of Record)
Navy Federal Credit Union
Nutrilite
Ocean Futures Society Campaign: "Beluga"
Porter Cable
The QUIKRETE Companies; 1989
RaceTrac
Synovus
TVA
Wal-Mart Stores, Inc. Campaign: "Earn It"
Wendy's

Branch:

Fitzgerald Media
(Formerly The Media Investment Group)
3333 Piedmont Rd NE Ste 100, Atlanta, GA 30305
(See Separate Listing)

FIXATION MARKETING
4340 E-W Hwy Ste 200, Bethesda, MD 20814
Tel.: (240) 207-2009
Fax: (301) 718-1940
E-Mail: info@fixation.com
Web Site: www.fixation.com

E-Mail for Key Personnel:
President: jean@fixation.com
Creative Dir.: bruce@fixation.com

Employees: 22
Year Founded: 1963

National Agency Associations: AAF

Agency Specializes In: Business-To-Business, Direct Response Marketing, Education, Entertainment, Event Planning & Marketing, Faith Based, Graphic Design, Internet/Web Design, Medical Products, Planning & Consultation, Strategic Planning/Research, Trade & Consumer Magazines

Breakdown of Gross Billings by Media: D.M.: 45%; Logo & Package Design: 5%; Print: 30%; Trade & Consumer Mags.: 10%; Worldwide Web Sites: 10%

Jean Whiddon *(Pres & CEO)*
Sharyn G. Collinson *(Mng Dir & VP)*
Randy Guseman *(Sr Dir-Art)*
Megan Campbell *(Acct Svcs Dir)*
Julie Parsons *(Acct Mgr)*
Amelia Whiddon *(Acct Mgr)*
Lori Kurtyka *(Specialist-Mktg-Intl)*
Elizabeth Ellen *(Sr Designer)*
John Frantz *(Sr Designer)*

Accounts:
Biotechnology Industry Organization
Can Manufacturers Institute
Direct Marketing Association
Recreational Vehicle Industry Association; Reston, VA

FJORD WEST
(Acquired by Cossette Inc. & Name Changed to Cossette Communications)

FKM
(Name Changed to The Company of Others)

FKQ ADVERTISING + MARKETING
15351 Roosevelt Blvd, Clearwater, FL 33760-3534
Tel.: (727) 539-8800
Fax: (866) 707-6648
Web Site: www.fkq.com

Employees: 81
Year Founded: 1961

Agency Specializes In: Advertising, Automotive, Bilingual Market, Brand Development & Integration, Broadcast, Business-To-Business, Cable T.V., Co-op Advertising, Collateral, Consumer Goods, Consumer Marketing, Consumer Publications, Corporate Communications, Corporate Identity, Customer Relationship Management, Digital/Interactive, Direct Response Marketing, Direct-to-Consumer, E-Commerce, Electronic Media, Email, Engineering, Entertainment, Event Planning & Marketing, Exhibit/Trade Shows, Experience Design, Financial, Food Service, Graphic Design, Guerilla Marketing, Health Care Services, High Technology, Hispanic Market, Hospitality, Household Goods, Identity Marketing, In-Store Advertising, Information Technology, Integrated Marketing, International, Internet/Web Design, Investor Relations, Leisure, Local Marketing, Logo & Package Design, Luxury

Products, Magazines, Media Buying Services, Media Planning, Media Relations, Medical Products, Merchandising, Mobile Marketing, New Product Development, Newspaper, Newspapers & Magazines, Out-of-Home Media, Outdoor, Package Design, Paid Searches, Point of Purchase, Point of Sale, Print, Production, Production (Print), Promotions, Public Relations, Publicity/Promotions, Radio, Real Estate, Restaurant, Retail, Sales Promotion, Search Engine Optimization, Social Marketing/Nonprofit, Social Media, Sponsorship, Sports Market, Strategic Planning/Research, T.V., Trade & Consumer Magazines, Transportation, Travel & Tourism, Viral/Buzz/Word of Mouth, Web (Banner Ads, Pop-ups, etc.), Yellow Pages Advertising

Approx. Annual Billings: $77,291,234

Lisa M. Faller *(Pres)*
Stacy Howell *(Sr VP)*
Gina Kline *(Grp Dir-Media)*
John Afflebach *(Acct Dir)*
Ken Barnes *(Dir-Production)*
Kathleen Ferlita *(Dir-Digital Media)*
Christine Karner-Johnson *(Dir-Media)*
Kip Pyle *(Dir-Brdcst Svcs)*
Aaron Barker *(Sr Project Mgr-Interactive)*
Jennifer Barilla *(Mgr-Interactive Project)*
Jessica Fox *(Mgr-PR)*
Richard Levine *(Mgr-Digital Media)*
Fred Caro *(Supvr-Accts Payable)*
David Stob *(Supvr-Media)*
Jessica Ramsey *(Sr Strategist-Email Mktg)*
Ryan Walbridge *(Strategist-Digital Media)*
Shauna Sinclair *(Media Buyer)*
Melissa Pollock *(Asst Acct Exec)*
Jenna Tinney *(Asst Acct Exec)*
Megan Blizard *(Coord-Traffic)*
Yu Chun Lai *(Coord-Social Media)*
Alex Bernardi *(Sr Media Planner & Sr Media Buyer)*

Accounts:
Badcock Furniture & More
Dollar Thrift Automotive Group; Tulsa, OK Dollar Rent-A-Car, Thrifty Car Rental; 1985
McDonald's Corporation
McDonald's Tampa Bay Co-Op; Tampa, FL Quick Service Restaurants; 1996
Melitta USA, Inc. Choc Raspberry, Cinn Rasberry, Colombian Decaf, Colombian Estate, Colombian Supremo, Costa Rican Estate, Decaffeinated French Vanilla, Decaffeinated Hazelnut Creme, Enchanting Evening, French Roast, French Vanilla, Hawaii Estate, Hazelnut, Hazelnut Creme, Italian Espresso, Kona Blend, Melitta Coffeemaker, Melitta Traditional, Melitta USA, Inc., Mini Brick, Morning Bliss, Morning Decadence, Original Estate, South American Estate, Sun and Moon, Van Almond
Nash Finch; Minneapolis, MN Food Wholesaler; 1999
Niemann Foods; Quincy, IL; 2005
Tampa Bay Lightning NHL Franchise; 2001
Tampa General Hospital; Tampa, FL; 2002
W.S. Badcock Furniture Company; Mulberry, FL Home Furnishings; 1998

FLANIGAN COMMUNICATIONS INC.
54 W Hubbard St Concourse Level E, Chicago, IL 60654
Tel.: (312) 464-9668
Web Site: www.flanigancom.com

Agency Specializes In: Advertising, Media Relations, Public Relations

Dyana K. Flanigan *(Principal)*

Accounts:
New-Bob Domenz

FLAPJACK CREATIVE
303 S Paterson Ste 7, Madison, WI 53703
Tel.: (608) 251-8215
Web Site: www.flapjackcreative.com

Year Founded: 2009

Agency Specializes In: Advertising, Corporate Identity, Internet/Web Design, Print, Radio, T.V.

Gerald Mortensen *(Founder & Dir-Creative)*
Dan Shoman *(CFO)*

Accounts:
Roastar
Sconnis Alehouse & Eatery

FLASH POINT COMMUNICATIONS LLC
3070 Bristol St Ste 580, Costa Mesa, CA 92626
Tel.: (657) 212-8505
Fax: (949) 306-0368
Web Site: www.flashpointcommunications.com

Agency Specializes In: Advertising, Digital/Interactive, Email, Internet/Web Design, Promotions, Social Media

Scott Empringham *(Pres & CEO)*
Michael Klarin *(CFO)*
Jennifer Losey *(Mgmt Supvr)*
Eric Davies *(Dir-Bus Dev)*
Masha Gelfer Empringham *(Dir-HR)*
Shannon Romo *(Office Mgr)*
Kyle Nishi *(Mgr-Social Media)*
April Lee *(Acct Exec)*
Jean Liu *(Acct Exec)*

Accounts:
Ford Motor Company

FLASHPOINT MEDICA, LLC
158 W 29th St 5th Fl, New York, NY 10001
Tel.: (212) 894-9750
Fax: (212) 894-9751
E-Mail: info@flashpointmedica.com
Web Site: www.flashpointmedica.com

Employees: 80
Year Founded: 2005

Agency Specializes In: Health Care Services, Pharmaceutical

Helen Appelbaum *(Pres & Partner)*
Charlene Prounis *(CEO & Mng Partner)*
Kerry Baker *(Sr VP & Dir-Creative)*
Nicole Johnson *(Sr VP & Dir-Digital Strategy)*
Shira Lawlor *(Sr VP & Dir-Bus Strategy)*
Steve Witt *(Sr VP & Dir-Creative)*
Donna Filanovsky *(VP & Assoc Dir-Creative)*
Michael Ward *(VP & Assoc Dir-Creative-Copy)*
Heida Jonsson *(Dir-Project Mgmt)*

Accounts:
Acorda Pharmaceuticals, Inc Ampyra
American Reagent Injectafer
Celgene Abraxane
Crescendo Biosciences Vectra DA
Genentech, Inc. Tarceva
Gilead HIV Franchise
Novartis Afinitor, Jakavi
Prostraken Sancuso

THE FLATLAND
(Formerly Seal Ideas)
614 Massachusetts Ave Ste D, Indianapolis, IN 46204
Tel.: (317) 536-6073
E-Mail: info@theflatland.com
Web Site: theflatland.com/

Agency Specializes In: Advertising, Collateral, Logo & Package Design, Outdoor, Print, Radio, T.V.

Brian Gray *(Partner)*
Rebecca Seal *(CFO)*
Ben Seal *(Principal)*

Accounts:
Kingdom Martial Arts
Milto Cleaners

FLEK, INC.
370 Railroad St Ste 4, Saint Johnsbury, VT 05819
Tel.: (802) 748-7113
Web Site: www.flekvt.com

Agency Specializes In: Advertising, Graphic Design, Internet/Web Design, Logo & Package Design

Florence Chamberlin *(Principal & Dir-Creative)*
Amy Hale *(Principal)*

Accounts:
Numia Medical Technologies

FLEMING & COMPANY INC.
31 America's Cup Ave, Newport, RI 02840
Tel.: (401) 848-2300
Web Site: www.flemingandcompany.com

E-Mail for Key Personnel:
President: paulf@flemingandcompany.com

Employees: 10
Year Founded: 1993

National Agency Associations: AAF

Agency Specializes In: Advertising, Advertising Specialties, Agriculture, Aviation & Aerospace, Bilingual Market, Brand Development & Integration, Business-To-Business, Cable T.V., Catalogs, Co-op Advertising, Collateral, Communications, Consulting, Consumer Goods, Consumer Marketing, Consumer Publications, Corporate Communications, Corporate Identity, Cosmetics, Direct Response Marketing, Direct-to-Consumer, E-Commerce, Electronic Media, Electronics, Email, Entertainment, Environmental, Event Planning & Marketing, Exhibit/Trade Shows, Fashion/Apparel, Financial, Government/Political, Graphic Design, Guerilla Marketing, Health Care Services, High Technology, Hospitality, Household Goods, In-Store Advertising, Integrated Marketing, Internet/Web Design, Leisure, Logo & Package Design, Luxury Products, Magazines, Marine, Market Research, Media Buying Services, Media Planning, Media Relations, Medical Products, Merchandising, Multimedia, New Product Development, Newspaper, Newspapers & Magazines, Out-of-Home Media, Outdoor, Over-50 Market, Package Design, Paid Searches, Pharmaceutical, Planning & Consultation, Point of Purchase, Point of Sale, Print, Production, Public Relations, Publicity/Promotions, Radio, Real Estate, Regional, Restaurant, Retail, Sales Promotion, Search Engine Optimization, Seniors' Market, Social Marketing/Nonprofit, Sponsorship, Sports Market, Strategic Planning/Research, Sweepstakes, T.V., Trade & Consumer Magazines, Transportation, Travel & Tourism, Women's Market

Approx. Annual Billings: $5,150,000

Breakdown of Gross Billings by Media: Bus. Publs.: 5%; Collateral: 10%; D.M.: 5%; E-Commerce: 10%; Graphic Design: 10%; Logo & Package Design: 10%; Mags.: 25%; Newsp.: 10%; Outdoor: 5%; T.V.: 5%; Transit: 5%

Paul Fleming *(Pres & CEO)*
Jane Fleming *(Controller)*
Lisa Reilly-Sicilian *(Acct Dir)*
Norma Burnell *(Dir-Web Svcs)*

Accounts:
ETCO Inc.; Warwick, RI Metal Stamped Products
Goetz Custom Technologies LLC; Bristol, RI Yachts; 2008
Newport County Convention & Visitors Bureau Tourism; 1994
Schaeper Marine; New Bedford,MA

FLEMING CREATIVE GROUP
181 Bluffton Rd Ste C-103, Bluffton, SC 29910
Tel.: (843) 757-5620
E-Mail: info@fcgadvertising.com
Web Site: www.fcgadvertising.com

Agency Specializes In: Advertising, Broadcast, Collateral, Corporate Identity, Digital/Interactive, Event Planning & Marketing, Graphic Design, Logo & Package Design, Media Buying Services, Print

Carolyn Fleming *(Pres)*

Accounts:
Centex Homes Atlanta
Centex Homes Charlotte
Centex Homes Coastal Carolina
Centex Homes North Carolina
Centex Homes San Antonio
Centex Homes Texas CityHomes & Fox & Jacobs
The Goldsmith Shop
Great Swamp Sanctuary
Hilton Head Island Chamber of Commerce
Holistic Skincare by Elisabeth Cortes
Macfarlan Capital Partners
Magnolia Village Business Park
Reliant Electrical
Shalimar Interiors
Suburban Mortgage
Terramesa Resorts

FLETCH CREATIVE
585 Waterview Trl, Atlanta, GA 30022
Tel.: (404) 931-3665
Web Site: www.fletchcreative.com

Agency Specializes In: Advertising, Brand Development & Integration, Digital/Interactive, Logo & Package Design, Print

Keith Fletcher *(Pres & Dir-Creative)*

Accounts:
Anatabloc
Kimberly-Clark Healthcare
Wear Your Soul Foundation

FLETCHER & ROWLEY INC
1720 W End Ste 630, Nashville, TN 37203
Tel.: (615) 329-9559
Fax: (615) 329-9633
Web Site: www.fletcherrowley.com

Agency Specializes In: Advertising, Brand Development & Integration, Digital/Interactive, Graphic Design, Logo & Package Design, Media Training, Outdoor, Print, Strategic Planning/Research

Bill Fletcher *(Partner)*
John Rowley *(Partner)*
Katie Bumgardner *(Dir-Media & Res)*
Jill Jeffries *(Dir-Ops)*
Jason Russell *(Dir-Production)*

Accounts:
Marc Veasey

FLETCHER & WILDER COMMUNICATIONS
(Name Changed to Fletcher Media Group)

FLETCHER KNIGHT
1 Dock St 620, Stamford, CT 06902
Tel.: (203) 276-6262, ext. 4606
Fax: (203) 276-6276
E-Mail: info@fletcherknight.com
Web Site: www.fletcherknight.com

Employees: 10
Year Founded: 2001

Agency Specializes In: Brand Development & Integration, Consumer Marketing, Market Research, Web (Banner Ads, Pop-ups, etc.)

Laurence Knight *(Founder & Principal)*
Michael Terranova *(Sr Dir-Creative)*
Lana Buccieri *(Office Mgr)*

Accounts:
Alberto Culver
American Greetings
Avon Cosmetics
Breyers
Dove
Irish Spring
Kraft Foods Chocolate
McCormick
McGraw Hill Publishing,Financial,Information & Media Services
Novartis Health Care Products Mfr
Oregon Scientific
Rogaine
Trident
Unilever Consumer Goods Mfr
Yale University

FLETCHER MEDIA GROUP
(Formerly Fletcher & Wilder Communications)
94 Grove St, Peterborough, NH 03458
Tel.: (603) 924-6383
Fax: (603) 924-6562
Web Site: fletchermedia.com/

Employees: 6
Year Founded: 1996

National Agency Associations: DMA

Agency Specializes In: Advertising, Advertising Specialties, Brand Development & Integration, Business Publications, Business-To-Business, Children's Market, Co-op Advertising, Collateral, Communications, Consumer Marketing, Consumer Publications, Corporate Identity, Direct Response Marketing, E-Commerce, Entertainment, Exhibit/Trade Shows, Financial, Food Service, Graphic Design, Internet/Web Design, Local Marketing, Logo & Package Design, Magazines, New Product Development, Newspaper, Newspapers & Magazines, Outdoor, Point of Purchase, Print, Production, Public Relations, Publicity/Promotions, Radio, Real Estate, Restaurant, Retail, Sales Promotion, Sports Market, Strategic Planning/Research, Sweepstakes, Teen Market, Trade & Consumer Magazines, Travel & Tourism

Approx. Annual Billings: $500,000

Jim Fletcher *(Pres)*

Accounts:
BBC Music
Belletetes
Birding Business Magazine
Boating
Brookwood Capital
Builder Magazine
CFO Magazine
Classic's Today.com
Conde Nast Traveler
Disney Publications
FeltCrafts
Gracewood Groves
Guideposts
Helmers Publications
Norwood Looms
Odyssey Magazine
Peterboro Basket Company
Popular Photography
Trikeenan Tileworks
Webs Yarn Distributor
Woman's Day
Women in Periodical Publishing

FLIGHT PATH CREATIVE
117 S Union St, Traverse City, MI 49684
Tel.: (231) 946-7255
Fax: (231) 946-5746
E-Mail: info@flightpathcreative.com
Web Site: www.flightpathcreative.com

Year Founded: 2004

Agency Specializes In: Advertising, Collateral, Corporate Identity, Graphic Design, Internet/Web Design, Outdoor, Package Design, Print, Promotions

Aaron Swanker *(Co-Founder & Dir-Creative)*
Dan Smith *(Principal)*
Heather Bolton *(Dir-Art)*
Heather Swanker *(Dir-Art)*
Sabrina Maxwell *(Sr Graphic Designer)*

Accounts:
Grand Traverse Endodontics
Northbound Outfitters
Tiger Shark Golf

FLIGHTPATH INC
36 W 25th St 9th Fl, New York, NY 10010
Tel.: (212) 674-5600
Fax: (212) 674-6956
Web Site: www.flightpath.com

Year Founded: 1994

Agency Specializes In: Advertising, Digital/Interactive, Internet/Web Design, Social Media, Sponsorship

Jon Fox *(Pres)*
Denise de Castro *(VP & Client Svcs Dir)*
John Lee *(Sr Dir-Digital Mktg)*
Alex Lindgren *(Dir-Tech)*
Steven Louie *(Dir-Creative)*

Accounts:
Computer Generated Solutions Inc.
Goya Foods Digital, Media
Landice, Inc.
Minwax
Showtime Networks Inc.
TransitChek
Union for Reform Judaism

FLINT COMMUNICATIONS
101 10th St N, Fargo, ND 58102
Tel.: (701) 237-4850
Fax: (701) 234-9680
E-Mail: info@flintcom.com
Web Site: www.flint-group.com/offices

E-Mail for Key Personnel:
President: rogerr@flintcom.com
Creative Dir.: kimk@flintcom.com
Media Dir.: donnad@flintcom.com

Employees: 78
Year Founded: 1946

National Agency Associations: ABC-BPA

Agency Specializes In: Agriculture, Financial, Health Care Services, Industrial, Travel & Tourism

Approx. Annual Billings: $29,816,000 Capitalized

Roger Reierson *(CEO-Flint Group. RR46)*
Jodi Duncan *(VP-Bus Dev & Channel Strategy)*
Kimberly Janke *(VP-Acct Plng & Brand Strategy)*
Andy Reierson *(VP-Digital Ops)*
Chris Hagen *(Dir-PR)*
Kim Kemmer *(Dir-Customer Insight)*
Shanna Flanagan *(Sr Acct Mgr)*
Tara Olson *(Acct Mgr)*
Mariah Madsen *(Media Planner)*
Kim Matter *(Media Buyer)*

Accounts:
American Crystal Sugar
Bobcat
Fargo-Moorhead Convention & Visitors Bureau
Moorhead Healthy Community Initiative
Sales & Marketing Executives of Fargo-Moorhead

Hatling Flint
330 Hwy 10 S, Saint Cloud, MN 56304
Tel.: (320) 259-7976
Fax: (320) 259-0082
Web Site: www.flint-group.com

Employees: 8
Year Founded: 1988

Bill Hatling *(Pres)*

Accounts:
3M Abrasives
CentraCare Healthcare System
Spee-Dee Delivery

SimmonsFlint
33 S Third St Ste D, Grand Forks, ND 58201
Mailing Address:
PO Box 5700, Grand Forks, ND 58206-5700
Tel.: (701) 746-4573
Fax: (701) 746-8067
Web Site: www.flint-group.com

Employees: 5
Year Founded: 1947

Agency Specializes In: Graphic Design, Logo & Package Design, Planning & Consultation, Public Relations, Strategic Planning/Research

Susan Mickelson *(Mng Partner)*
Mary Schieve *(Sr Copywriter & Specialist-PR)*
Linda Muus *(Acct Exec)*

Accounts:
Case IH Farm Machinery
Greater Grand Forks Convention & Visitors Bureau
North Dakota Eye Clinic
UND Athletics

Flint Interactive
11 E Superior St Ste 514, Duluth, MN 55802
Tel.: (218) 740-3516
Fax: (218) 733-0463
Web Site: www.flint-group.com

Employees: 10

Melanie Goldish *(VP-Client Svcs)*
Ken Zakovich *(Dir-Creative)*
Lydia Degrood *(Acct Mgr)*
Brittney Hanson *(Specialist-Digital PR & Social Media)*
Jen Reierson *(Strategist-PR)*
Kelly Harth *(Copywriter)*

Accounts:
AdFarm
Maurices
Media Productions
Praxis Strategy Group
Prime Contact

FLIPELEVEN LLC
710 N Plankinton Ave Ste 300, Milwaukee, WI 53203
Tel.: (414) 272-3547
E-Mail: info@flipeleven.com
Web Site: www.flipeleven.com

Employees: 17
Year Founded: 2005

Agency Specializes In: Advertising, Arts, Automotive, Aviation & Aerospace, Broadcast, Cable T.V., Content, Digital/Interactive, Education, Electronic Media, Entertainment, Experience Design, Graphic Design, Health Care Services, Hospitality, Industrial, Infomercials, Internet/Web Design, Logo & Package Design, Mobile Marketing, Multimedia, New Technologies, Production, Production (Ad, Film, Broadcast), Promotions, Social Marketing/Nonprofit, Social Media, Sports Market, Strategic Planning/Research, T.V., Web (Banner Ads, Pop-ups, etc.)

Kyle Buckley *(Partner & Dir-Media)*
Justin Schnor *(Partner & Dir-Creative Technical)*
Betty Allen *(Editor & Supvr-Post-Production)*
Michael Marten *(Art Dir & Designer)*
Anders Rahm *(Mktg Mgr & Acct Mgr)*
Lora Steinmetz *(Acct Exec)*

Accounts:
2C Media Website; 2014
Bostik Microsites, Web Videos
Manpower Group Web Videos
Milwaukee Ballet Company; 2013
Streamfit.com Websites & Videos
Yell & Tell Non-Profit, PSAs; 2013

FLIPPIES
772 Armonk Rd, Mount Kisco, NY 10549
Tel.: (914) 244-1954
E-Mail: jkay@flippies.com
Web Site: www.flippies.com

Employees: 5

Agency Specializes In: Advertising, Advertising Specialties, Collateral, Custom Publishing, Multimedia, Print, Production (Print), Publicity/Promotions, Publishing, Sales Promotion, Viral/Buzz/Word of Mouth

Approx. Annual Billings: $2,500,000

Breakdown of Gross Billings by Media: Adv. Specialities: $1,000,000; Collateral: $1,500,000

Jeffrey Kay *(Pres)*

Accounts:
Barry Manilow
L'Oreal; New York, NY
MTV; New York, NY
National Geographic Motion
Nickelodeon; New York, NY
Starz Network
Twentieth Century Fox; Los Angeles, CA

FLOURISH INC.
1001 Huron Rd E Ste 102, Cleveland, OH 44115-1755
Tel.: (216) 696-9116
Fax: (216) 696-4771
E-Mail: info@flourishagency.com
Web Site: www.flourishagency.com

Employees: 10
Year Founded: 1998

National Agency Associations: AD CLUB

Christopher Ferranti *(CEO)*
Chris Haas *(Sr Dir-Art)*
Lisa Ferranti *(Dir-Media)*
Steve Shuman *(Dir-Creative)*
Diane Ha *(Acct Exec)*
Morgan Miller *(Acct Exec)*
Patti Harman *(Designer)*

Accounts:
American Woodmark
Aodk,Inc
Jewish Community Federation

FLUID ADVERTISING
1065 S 500 W, Bountiful, UT 84010
Tel.: (801) 295-9820
E-Mail: info@getfluid.com
Web Site: www.getfluid.com

Agency Specializes In: Advertising, Brand Development & Integration, Internet/Web Design, Media Buying Services, Print, Search Engine Optimization, Social Media

Frank Imler *(Dir-Art)*
Ryan Anderson *(Creative Dir)*
Marianne Neff *(Designer)*

Accounts:
New-Creamies
New-Pasture Road LLC

FLUID STUDIO
1065 S 500 W, Bountiful, UT 84010
Tel.: (801) 663-7792
E-Mail: info@getfluid.com
Web Site: www.getfluid.com

Year Founded: 2000

Agency Specializes In: Advertising, Exhibit/Trade Shows, Graphic Design, Internet/Web Design, Logo & Package Design, Market Research, Print, Radio, Search Engine Optimization, Social Media

Phil Case *(Partner & Mng Dir)*
Ryan Anderson *(Partner & Dir-Creative)*
Jessie Roberts *(Acct Mgr & Mgr-Workflow)*
Jonathan Rodriguez *(Mgr-Digital Mktg)*
Frank Imler *(Designer-Interactive)*
Matthew Nieuwland *(Designer)*

Accounts:
Cameron Construction
Creamies
The Gallivan Center
Orbit Irrigation Products, Inc.
Staker Parson Companies

FLY COMMUNICATIONS
40 W 25th St, New York, NY 10010
Tel.: (212) 675-8484
Fax: (212) 675-3677
E-Mail: contactus@flycommunications.com
Web Site: www.flycommunications.com

Employees: 15
Year Founded: 2001

Agency Specializes In: Brand Development & Integration, Broadcast, Digital/Interactive, Direct Response Marketing, Print, Production (Ad, Film, Broadcast), Sponsorship, Strategic Planning/Research, Technical Advertising, Web (Banner Ads, Pop-ups, etc.)

Larry Rowen *(Co-Founder)*
Dave Warren *(Co-Founder)*
Chantel Zapata *(Sr Dir-Art & Dir-Creative)*
Katie Hukill *(Acct Dir & Strategist-Digital)*
Malcolm Kerr *(Acct Mgr)*
Marco Serino *(Acct Mgr)*

Accounts:
American Express
Anchor Blue
Chivas
CIT
ESPN
New-Iconic Brands Inc. (Advertising Agency of Record) BiVi Sicilian Vodka, Outdoor, Print, Radio, Social Media, TV
New York Jets New Stadium Promotion; 2008
Stolichnaya

FLY N HOG MEDIA GROUP
525 S School Ave Ste 110, Fayetteville, AR 72701
Tel.: (866) 983-3322
Fax: (866) 734-1453
E-Mail: contactus@flynhog.com
Web Site: www.flynhog.com

Year Founded: 2009

Agency Specializes In: Advertising, Digital/Interactive, Graphic Design, Outdoor

Brent Robinson *(Co-Owner)*
Susan Robinson *(Co-Owner)*
Esther Oehlke *(Office Mgr)*

Accounts:
Field Agent

FLYING CORK MEDIA
320 Fort Duquesne Blvd Ste 200, Pittsburgh, PA 15222
Tel.: (412) 926-1020
E-Mail: info@flyingcorkmedia.com
Web Site: www.flyingcorkmedia.com

Year Founded: 2009

Agency Specializes In: Advertising, Brand Development & Integration, Digital/Interactive, Media Planning, Social Media

Terri Deasy *(VP-Bus Dev)*
Dan Monarko *(VP)*
Betsy Piasente *(Client Svcs Dir)*
Aart Balk *(Dir-Interactive Creative)*
James Trembulak *(Acct Mgr-Search)*
Krystal Clark *(Mgr-Email)*
Justin Sperandeo *(Strategist-Creative)*
Gina Ciarrocchi *(Coord-Digital Mktg)*

Accounts:
Batch Foundation

FLYING MACHINE
270 Lafayette St, New York, NY 10012
Tel.: (212) 226-7733
Fax: (212) 226-7122
Web Site: www.flyingmachine.tv

Agency Specializes In: Advertising, Brand Development & Integration, Package Design, Print, Web (Banner Ads, Pop-ups, etc.)

Micha Riss *(Mng Partner & Dir-Creative)*
Daniel Acharkan *(VP-Tel Aviv-Israel)*
Daisuke Endo *(Dir-Creative)*
Yuki Muramatsu *(Dir-Art)*
Hsin-Ying Wu *(Sr Designer)*

FLYING POINT DIGITAL
35 W 36th St, New York, NY 10018
Tel.: (212) 629-4960
Fax: (212) 629-4967
E-Mail: info@flyingpt.com
Web Site: www.flyingpointdigital.com

Employees: 20
Year Founded: 2002

Agency Specializes In: Advertising, Advertising Specialties, Business-To-Business, Consulting, Content, Cosmetics, Digital/Interactive, Direct Response Marketing, Direct-to-Consumer, Electronics, Entertainment, Fashion/Apparel, High Technology, Hospitality, Identity Marketing, Integrated Marketing, Internet/Web Design, Legal Services, Luxury Products, Media Buying Services, Men's Market, Paid Searches, Pharmaceutical, Real Estate, Retail, Sales Promotion, Search Engine Optimization, Social Marketing/Nonprofit, Teen Market, Travel & Tourism, Women's Market

Approx. Annual Billings: $19,300,000

Alan Pearlstein *(Founder & CEO)*
Brandon Heagle *(Pres & COO)*
Vlaga Briks *(Acct Dir)*
Jenna Manula *(Dir-Social Media Mktg)*
Matt Strietelmeier *(Dir-Paid Search)*
Lily Faden *(Assoc Dir-Search Engine Optimization)*
Jessica Boyd *(Mgr-Campaign Paid Search)*

Accounts:
Destination XL Group

FLYNN & FRIENDS
437 Franklin St, Buffalo, NY 14202
Tel.: (716) 881-2697
Fax: (716) 881-2711
Toll Free: (877) 883-5966
E-Mail: info@flynnandfriends.com
Web Site: www.flynnandfriends.com

Employees: 8
Year Founded: 1986

National Agency Associations: Second Wind Limited

Marc Adler *(VP-Client Svcs)*
Justine Jopp *(Office Mgr)*
Laura Elia *(Copywriter)*
Kristen Taylor *(Designer)*

Accounts:
Buffalo Urban League; Buffalo, NY
Hilbert College Web Site

FLYNN WRIGHT
1408 Locust St, Des Moines, IA 50309-3014
Tel.: (515) 243-2845
Fax: (515) 243-6351
E-Mail: info@flynnwright.com
Web Site: www.flynnwright.com

Employees: 40
Year Founded: 1984

National Agency Associations: Second Wind Limited

Agency Specializes In: Advertising

Paul Schlueter *(VP-Res & Interactive Media)*
Jon Miller *(Acct Svcs Dir)*
Maggie Baker *(Acct Exec)*
Andy Ireland *(Acct Exec)*
Andrea Tagtow *(Sr Media Planner & Strategist)*
Joey Gale *(Acct Coord)*
Katie Peeper *(Coord-Media)*

Accounts:
MidAmerican Energy Company
OnMedia

FLYWHEEL
536 Broadway 4th Fl, New York, NY 10012
Tel.: (646) 448-9898
E-Mail: miller@flywheelpartners.com
Web Site: flywheelpartners.com

Employees: 18
Year Founded: 2006

Agency Specializes In: Advertising, Brand Development & Integration, Business-To-Business, Consulting, Experience Design, Health Care Services, Integrated Marketing, Medical Products, Pharmaceutical

Approx. Annual Billings: $5,000,000

Breakdown of Gross Billings by Media: Consulting: $5,000,000

Jung Lee *(Mng Partner)*
Dave Miller *(Mng Partner)*
Billy Derby *(Mng Dir)*
Colleen Mcmahon *(Mng Dir)*
Jill Jannsen *(Dir-Content Strategy & Dev)*
Emily Cheesman *(Acct Mgr)*

FMB ADVERTISING
145 S Gay St, Knoxville, TN 37902-1004
Tel.: (865) 525-1554
Fax: (865) 525-0118
Toll Free: (877) 345-4281
E-Mail: info@engagefmb.com
Web Site: www.engagefmb.com

E-Mail for Key Personnel:
President: mfreeman@fmbadvertising.com
Creative Dir.: mfreeman@fmbadvertising.com
Media Dir.: ebryant@fmbadvertising.com
Public Relations: oshults@fmbadvertising.com

Employees: 9
Year Founded: 1986

National Agency Associations: AAF-AMA

Agency Specializes In: Advertising, Advertising Specialties, Affluent Market, Agriculture, Automotive, Aviation & Aerospace, Bilingual Market, Brand Development & Integration, Branded Entertainment, Broadcast, Business Publications, Business-To-Business, Cable T.V., Catalogs, Co-op Advertising, Collateral, College, Consulting, Consumer Marketing, Consumer Publications, Corporate Identity, Crisis Communications, Direct Response Marketing, Direct-to-Consumer, Education, Electronic Media, Exhibit/Trade Shows, Financial, Food Service, Graphic Design, Guerilla Marketing, Health Care Services, High Technology, Hispanic Market, Industrial, Internet/Web Design, Legal Services, Local Marketing, Logo & Package Design, Luxury Products, Magazines, Market Research, Media Buying Services, Media Planning, Medical Products, Newspaper, Newspapers & Magazines, Out-of-Home Media, Outdoor, Package Design, Planning & Consultation, Point of Purchase, Point of Sale, Print, Production, Production (Ad, Film, Broadcast), Production (Print), Publishing, Radio, Restaurant, Seniors' Market, Social Marketing/Nonprofit, Sports Market, Strategic Planning/Research, T.V., Technical Advertising, Trade & Consumer Magazines, Travel & Tourism, Web (Banner Ads, Pop-ups, etc.)

Approx. Annual Billings: $4,080,000

Breakdown of Gross Billings by Media: Bus. Publs.: $75,000; Cable T.V.: $400,000; Collateral: $350,000; Consulting: $75,000; D.M.: $200,000; Graphic Design: $150,000; Mags.: $200,000; Mdsg./POP: $25,000; Newsp.: $150,000; Other: $50,000; Outdoor: $40,000; Point of Purchase: $50,000; Print: $450,000; Radio: $325,000; Radio & T.V.: $350,000; Sports Mktg.: $100,000; Spot Radio: $55,000; Spot T.V.: $450,000; Strategic Planning/Research: $135,000; T.V.: $325,000; Trade Shows: $50,000; Worldwide Web Sites: $75,000

Jody M. Freeman *(Pres)*
Odette Shults *(Sr VP)*
Brett Melancon *(VP & Dir-Art)*
Diette Crockett *(Office Mgr)*
Lori Herron *(Acct Supvr)*

Accounts:
Campbellsville University; Campbellsville, KY Brand Identity Communications; 2001
Eastern Kentucky University; Richmond, KY Alumni Magazine, Brand Identity, Student Admissions; 2003
Knoxville TVA Employees Credit Union; Knoxville, TN Financial Services; 1996
Parkwest Medical Center; Knoxville, TN Healthcare; 2006
Proficiency Testing Service; Brownsville, TX Testing Services for Laboratories; 1998
University of Tennessee Women's & Men's Athletic Department; Knoxville, TN Sporting Advertising & Promotion; 1996
YMCA of East Tennessee Philanthropic; 2001

THE FOCUS GROUP

11545 Old Hwy 49, Gulfport, MS 39505
Tel.: (228) 832-3667
Fax: (228) 314-2387
E-Mail: info@focusgroupms.com
Web Site: www.focusgroupms.com

Agency Specializes In: Advertising, Brand Development & Integration, Graphic Design, Internet/Web Design, Logo & Package Design, Print, Search Engine Optimization, Social Media

John Allen *(Dir-Brdcst & Digital)*
Thomas Broadus *(Dir-Interactive & New Media)*
F. Cliff Kirkland *(Dir-Gaming Div)*
Cecelia Shabazz *(Dir-Creative)*

Accounts:
Charter Bank
Mississippi Gulf Coast Scenic Byways

FOCUSED IMAGE

2941 Fairview Park Dr Ste 650, Falls Church, VA 22042
Tel.: (703) 739-8803
Fax: (703) 739-8809
E-Mail: info@focusedimage.com
Web Site: www.focusedimage.com

Employees: 15

National Agency Associations: PRSA

Toby Eckhardt *(Pres)*
Dave Scanlon *(Exec VP-Strategic Plng)*
Kristina Messner *(Sr VP-PR & Social Media)*
Greg German *(VP)*
Matt Marsden *(VP-Bus Dev)*
Sis Pittman *(Dir-Creative & Print)*
Stacey Salsman *(Sr Acct Exec)*

Accounts:
CSC Holdings, LLC
DeWALT
HealthExtra
SOME (So Others Might Eat)

FOLLOW THE EYES

PO Box 717, Lima, OH 45802
Tel.: (419) 302-8430
E-Mail: info@fteyes.com
Web Site: www.fteyes.com

Year Founded: 2011

Agency Specializes In: Advertising, Brand Development & Integration, Digital/Interactive, Internet/Web Design, Outdoor, Print, Public Relations, Radio, Social Media

David Crnkovich *(Pres)*

Accounts:
Buckeye Mechanical Insulation

THE FOOD GROUP

589 8th Ave 4th Fl, New York, NY 10018
Tel.: (212) 725-5766
Fax: (212) 686-2901
E-Mail: tfg-ny@thefoodgroup.com
Web Site: www.thefoodgroup.com

Employees: 15
Year Founded: 1969

Agency Specializes In: Food Service

Mark Cotter *(CEO)*
John Zebell *(Mng Dir & VP)*
JoAnn Maloney *(Sr VP)*
Kyle Kraus *(VP-Bus Strategy & Dev)*
Carrie Nevaril *(Exec Dir-Creative)*
John McGee *(Sr Dir-Art)*
Deborah Bush *(Acct Exec-Dannon Foodservice)*
Audrey Prior *(Media Planner)*

Accounts:
Kraft Foodservice
Louisiana Seafood Promotion
PepsiCo inc.; Purchase, NY
Polly-O; Mineola, NY Fresh Water-Packed Mozzarella, Italian Cheeses
Tabasco Foodservice

The Food Group (Tampa)

3820 Northdale Blvd Suite 205A, Tampa, FL 33624
Tel.: (813) 933-0683
Fax: (813) 932-1232
E-Mail: mark.cotter@thefoodgroup.com
Web Site: www.thefoodgroup.com

Employees: 9
Year Founded: 1988

Agency Specializes In: Food Service

Joann Maloney *(Sr VP)*
Elissa Ferenbach *(VP & Grp Acct Dir)*
Catherine Dazevedo *(VP & Dir-Media & Content Distr)*
Kyle Kraus *(VP-Bus Strategy & Dev)*
Carrie Holtkamp *(Exec Dir-Creative)*
Megan Hage *(Acct Dir)*
Jan Soran *(Dir-HR)*
Annette Miranda *(Asst Controller)*

Accounts:
McIlhenny Company Tabasco Brand Pepper Sauce
State of Florida Department of Citrus Captain Citrus, Commodity Board Promoting Florida Citrus Products

The Food Group (Chicago)

233 N Michigan Ave 16th Fl, Chicago, IL 60601
Tel.: (312) 596-3333
Fax: (312) 596-3338
Web Site: www.thefoodgroup.com

Employees: 19
Year Founded: 1994

Agency Specializes In: Food Service

John Zabell *(Mng Dir)*

Accounts:
ConAgra
Kraft
National Restaurant Association
Rich-SeaPak Frozen Appetizers, Shrimp

FOODMIX MARKETING COMMUNICATIONS

103 W Arthur St, Elmhurst, IL 60126
Tel.: (630) 366-7500
Fax: (630) 366-7519
E-Mail: doc@foodmix.net
Web Site: www.foodmix.net

Employees: 30
Year Founded: 2000

Agency Specializes In: Advertising, Advertising Specialties, Brand Development & Integration, Business Publications, Business-To-Business, Collateral, Communications, Consulting, Consumer Marketing, Corporate Identity, Digital/Interactive, Direct Response Marketing, Food Service, In-Store Advertising, Industrial, Internet/Web Design, Local Marketing, Logo & Package Design, Magazines, Merchandising, Multimedia, New Product Development, Planning & Consultation, Point of Purchase, Point of Sale, Print, Production, Public Relations, Publicity/Promotions, Radio, Restaurant, Retail, Sales Promotion, Sponsorship, Strategic Planning/Research, T.V., Trade & Consumer Magazines

Approx. Annual Billings: $25,000,000 (Capitalized)

Breakdown of Gross Billings by Media: Collateral: $2,500,000; Consulting: $10,000,000; D.M.: $2,500,000; Promos.: $2,500,000; Strategic Planning/Research: $2,500,000; Trade & Consumer Mags.: $2,500,000; Worldwide Web Sites: $2,500,000

Dan O'Connell *(Founder & CEO)*
Eric Olson *(Sr VP & Exec Dir-Creative)*
Gina Hampe *(Acct Dir)*
Peter Baughman *(Dir-Media)*
Hannah Schober *(Dir-Art)*
Matthew Woo *(Assoc Dir-Creative)*
Jennifer Jaacks *(Acct Mgr-PR & Social Mktg)*
Lisa Ramatowski *(Acct Mgr)*
Mary Ramirez-Murphy *(Mgr-Traffic)*
Sarah Blau *(Asst Acct Exec)*

Accounts:
Coca-Cola Foodservice; Atlanta, GA
Insight Beverages
Lactalis Foodservice; Buffalo, NY
Mizkan Americas, Inc.; Mount Prospect, IL; 2001
Pennant
Taylor Company; Rockton, IL

FOOTSTEPS

220 E 42nd St, New York, NY 10017
Tel.: (212) 336-9743
Fax: (212) 924-5669
E-Mail: vjohnson@footstepsgroup.com
Web Site: www.footstepsgroup.com

Employees: 37
Year Founded: 2000

Agency Specializes In: African-American Market, Asian Market, Hispanic Market, Sponsorship

Verdia Johnson *(Co-Founder & Pres)*
Charles N. Jamison, Jr. *(Pres & Dir-Brand Strategy & Creative Rels)*
David Pilgrim *(Exec Dir-Creative)*
Ingrid Almonte *(Grp Acct Dir)*
Roxanne Fleming *(Acct Dir)*
Marcqui Akins *(Dir-Digital Art)*
Madi Benjamin *(Sr Strategist-Digital)*

Accounts:
Blue Cross & Blue Shield of Florida; Jacksonville, FL
Continuum Health Partners
Gillette
Lowe's Home Improvement Warehouse
Visa

FORCE 5 MEDIA, INC.
1433 Northside Blvd, South Bend, IN 46615
Tel.: (574) 234-2060
Web Site: www.discoverforce5.com

Year Founded: 2000

Agency Specializes In: Advertising, Brand Development & Integration, Event Planning & Marketing, Print

Deb Defreeuw *(Pres & Strategist-Certified Brand)*
David Morgan *(VP & Strategist-Certified Brand)*
Beth North *(Dir-Bus Dev)*
Marty Heirty *(Acct Strategist)*

Accounts:
South Bend ON

FORCE MARKETING LLC
5955 Shiloh Rd E Ste 204, Atlanta, GA 30005
Tel.: (678) 208-0667
Fax: (678) 208-0673
Toll Free: (800) 818-2651
E-Mail: rsieger@forcemktg.com
Web Site: www.forcemktg.com

Employees: 47
Year Founded: 2004

Revenue: $6,500,000

John Fitzpatrick *(Pres & CEO)*
Kate Andra *(Dir-Strategy)*
Jessica Sims *(Dir-Events & Acct Svcs)*
Bladimir Liriano *(Reg Mgr-Sls)*
Jackie Hewett *(Sr Acct Exec)*
Megan Crumpton *(Acct Exec-Sls)*
Amy Farley *(Specialist-Digital Mktg)*
Jillian Garcia *(Acct Exec)*
Alicia Armstrong *(Reg Acct Mgr)*
Ashleigh Smith *(Reg Acct Dir)*

FORESIGHT GROUP, INC.
2822 N Martin Luther King Jr Blvd, Lansing, MI 48906-2927
Tel.: (517) 485-5700
Fax: (517) 485-0202
Toll Free: (800) 766-2355
E-Mail: info@thinkdodeliver.com
Web Site: www.foresightgroup.net

E-Mail for Key Personnel:
President: Bill@foresightgr.com

Employees: 45
Year Founded: 1986

National Agency Associations: AAF

Agency Specializes In: Advertising, Automotive, Broadcast, Business Publications, Business-To-Business, Communications, Consulting, Corporate Identity, Education, Electronic Media, Exhibit/Trade Shows, Government/Political, Graphic Design, Health Care Services, Industrial, Infomercials, Internet/Web Design, Logo & Package Design, Media Buying Services, Medical Products, Multimedia, Out-of-Home Media, Outdoor, Planning & Consultation, Point of Purchase, Print, Production, Public Relations, Publicity/Promotions, Radio, Strategic Planning/Research, T.V.

Approx. Annual Billings: $6,000,000

Bill Christofferson *(Pres)*
Russell Healey *(Partner)*
Linda Getzmeyer *(Mgr-Acctg)*
Scott Mossbarger *(Mgr-Ops)*
Dave Page *(Mgr-Mail Dept)*
Chris Hyland *(Supvr-Pre-Press)*
Jill Dimmitt *(Acct Exec)*
Stacey Trzeciak *(Rep-Sls)*

FOREST HOME MEDIA
1059 Barrel Springs Hollow Rd, Franklin, TN 37069
Tel.: (615) 582-0554
Web Site: www.foresthomemedia.com

Year Founded: 2012

Agency Specializes In: Advertising, Content, Internet/Web Design, Media Relations, Public Relations, Social Media

Nancy McNulty *(Partner)*
Dana Tucker *(Partner)*
Geinger Hill *(Coord-Mktg)*

Accounts:
Carbine & Associates
Nashville Area Home Tours

FORGE MEDIA & DESIGN
135 Liberty Street Ste 300, Toronto, ON M6K 1A7 Canada
Tel.: (416) 533-3674
E-Mail: info@forgemedia.ca
Web Site: forgemedia.ca

Year Founded: 2005

Agency Specializes In: Advertising, Brand Development & Integration, Corporate Communications, Graphic Design, Internet/Web Design

Stussy Tschudin *(CFO, COO, Principal & Dir-Design)*
Gregory Neely *(Principal)*
Laurence Roberts *(Principal)*

Accounts:
Children's Hospital of Philadelphia

FORGE WORLDWIDE
142 Berkeley St, Boston, MA 02116
Tel.: (857) 305-3429
E-Mail: info@forgeworldwide.com
Web Site: www.forgeworldwide.com

Employees: 26
Year Founded: 2005

National Agency Associations: AMA

Agency Specializes In: Advertising, Brand Development & Integration, College, Consumer Marketing, Corporate Identity, Digital/Interactive, Education, Financial, Graphic Design, High Technology, Integrated Marketing, Internet/Web Design, Multimedia, Sponsorship

Approx. Annual Billings: $19,250,000

Harry G. Chapin *(CEO)*
Rob Stewart *(Chief Creative Officer-Brand Strategy)*
Jeffrey Porzio *(Exec Dir-Digital Mktg)*
Mike Gustafson *(Sr Dir-Art)*
Errin Chapin *(Dir-Acctg)*
Melissa Koehler *(Dir-Mktg)*
Jesse Strawbridge *(Dir-Mktg)*
Tara Kearney *(Assoc Dir-Art)*
Andrew Riley *(Assoc Dir-Creative)*
Sarah Bruce *(Acct Mgr)*
Laura Mortenson *(Acct Mgr)*
Nick Vitalie *(Mgr-Studio)*

Accounts:
American International College; Springfield, MA Rebranding
Brigham and Women's Hospital
Cisco C-suite
Dragon
Emerson Hospital Branding, Marketing
Franklin Sports, Inc.; Stoughton, MA
Friendly's Ice Cream Campaign: "Come Get Happy", Out-of-Home Advertising, Print, Radio, Social Media, Television
Harvey Building Products Television, Vinyl Windows
Herb Chambers Companies Branding, Print Advertising
International Yacht Restoration School; Newport, R.I. Brand Reposition
Iron Mountain Digital
Isenberg School of Management
Kaspersky Lab
McLean Hospital Marketing
MIT
Partners Health Care
Privateer American Rum Brand Strategy, Event Communications, Point-of-Purchase, Social Media
Rockland Trust Company; Hanover, MA Brand Strategy
Room to Grow
SBLI
Spaulding Rehabilitation Network
Uno Chicago Grill
Verizon Communications Inc.
Virgin Healthmiles
WPI

FORGELIGHT CREATIVE
1227 New Hampshire St, Lincoln, NE 68508
Tel.: (308) 380-3732
Web Site: www.forgelightcreative.com

Year Founded: 2013

Agency Specializes In: Advertising, Brand Development & Integration, Internet/Web Design, Print, Search Engine Optimization, Social Media

Derek Maze *(Co-Owner & Dir-Creative)*
Tyler Sprunk *(Co-Owner & Acct Exec)*

Accounts:
FleatSocks
Lincoln Beer Week
The Nebraska Cup

FORMATIVE
(Formerly Lavalobe)
1301 5th Ave Ste 2600, Seattle, WA 98101
Tel.: (206) 792-5129
Web Site: www.formativeco.com

Year Founded: 2005

Agency Specializes In: Advertising, Brand

Development & Integration, Digital/Interactive, Internet/Web Design, Media Buying Services, Social Media

Lee Sherman *(Chief Media Officer)*
Joshua Downs *(Dir-Creative)*
Blake Kirstine *(Dir-Creative)*
Shanda Boyett *(Mgr-Social Media Program)*
Sarah Matthews *(Designer-Production)*
Dawn Friedland *(Client Program Dir)*

Accounts:
Inrix, Inc.

FORMIUM
(Name Changed to Kindred)

FORMULA PR
(Acquired by Havas & Name Changed to Havas Formula)

FORREST & BLAKE INC.
1139 Spruce Dr 2nd Fl, Mountainside, NJ 07092
Tel.: (908) 789-6800
Fax: (908) 789-6764
E-Mail: info@forrestandblake.com
Web Site: www.forrestandblake.com

E-Mail for Key Personnel:
President: anns@forrestandblake.com

Employees: 12
Year Founded: 1994

National Agency Associations: Second Wind Limited

Agency Specializes In: Advertising, Automotive, Brand Development & Integration, Broadcast, Cable T.V., Co-op Advertising, Consulting, Digital/Interactive, Direct Response Marketing, Electronic Media, Graphic Design, Infomercials, Internet/Web Design, Market Research, Media Relations, Newspapers & Magazines, Outdoor, Point of Purchase, Print, Production, Production (Print), Public Relations, Publicity/Promotions, Radio, Recruitment, Retail, Search Engine Optimization, T.V., Transportation, Web (Banner Ads, Pop-ups, etc.)

Ann Shallcross *(Pres)*
Wayne A. Freitag *(VP & Dir-Creative)*
Cheryl C. Gaffney *(Dir-Media & Client Svcs Dir)*
Kristen Costello *(Acct Coord)*
Maria Okun *(Acct Coord)*

Accounts:
Douglas Auto Group

FORSYTHE & BUTLER CO., INC.
10777 Westheimer Rd Ste 1100, Houston, TX 77042-3462
Tel.: (713) 783-0775
Fax: (713) 783-0868
E-Mail: contact@forsythebutler.com
Web Site: www.forsythebutler.com

Employees: 5
Year Founded: 1983

Agency Specializes In: Automotive, Consumer Marketing, Retail

Approx. Annual Billings: $5,100,000

Breakdown of Gross Billings by Media: Consulting: $255,000; Newsp.: $1,275,000; Newsp. & Mags.: $510,000; Radio & T.V.: $3,060,000

Brad Forsythe *(Pres & Exec Dir-Creative)*

Accounts:
Amazing Siding Corp.
Maui Good for You Beverage Company; Maui, HI
Turner-Chapman Fine Art Gallery; Houston, TX

FORT GROUP
100 Challenger Rd 8th Fl, Ridgefield Park, NJ 07660
Tel.: (201) 445-0202
Fax: (201) 445-0626
Web Site: www.fortgroupinc.com

Employees: 40
Year Founded: 1970

National Agency Associations: DMA

Agency Specializes In: Advertising, Broadcast, Cable T.V., Consulting, Consumer Marketing, Consumer Publications, Direct Response Marketing, Financial, Newspaper, Newspapers & Magazines, T.V.

Approx. Annual Billings: $30,465,000

Breakdown of Gross Billings by Media: Bus. Publs.: $675,000; Cable T.V.: $10,500,000; Collateral: $270,000; D.M.: $270,000; Internet Adv.: $2,000,000; Mags.: $270,000; Newsp.: $1,080,000; Out-of-Home Media: $250,000; Production: $1,525,000; Radio: $3,530,000; T.V.: $9,845,000; Transit: $250,000

Frank DiGioia *(Pres & CEO)*
Jeff Wolfson *(CMO)*
Joe Moran *(VP & Gen Mgr)*
Pamela Lorusso *(VP & Dir-Creative)*
Anthony Forte *(VP-Digital Strategy)*
Jerry Putruele *(Gen Mgr-HouseSmarts Television Properties)*

Accounts:
All Hallows
Barrons Newspaper
Building Materials Distributors, Inc.
Forward Newspaper
Golf Digest
Golf World
Marvin Windows and Doors
Somerset Tire Service, Inc.

FORT INTEGRATED MARKETING GROUP
100 Challenger Rd 8th Fl, Ridgefield Park, NJ 07660
Tel.: (201) 445-0202
Fax: (201) 445-0626
Toll Free: (800) 633-3678
E-Mail: info@fortgroupinc.com
Web Site: www.fortgroupinc.com

Employees: 35

National Agency Associations: Second Wind Limited

Frank DiGioia *(Pres & CEO)*
Jerry Putruele *(Partner & Gen Mgr)*
Jeff Wolfson *(CMO)*
Steven A. Laux *(Exec VP)*
Joseph Moran *(VP & Gen Mgr-FORT Grp NJ)*
Pamela Lorusso *(VP & Dir-Creative)*
Anthony Forte *(VP-Digital Strategy)*

Accounts:
Best Tile
HouseSmarts
Marvin Windows & Doors
Samsung
Sheplers
St. Maarten

FORTE GROUP INC.
Two Hillcrest Green 12720 Hillcrest Rd Ste 600, Dallas, TX 75230
Tel.: (214) 890-7912
E-Mail: info@fortegroupinc.com
Web Site: www.fortegroupinc.com

Agency Specializes In: Advertising, Brand Development & Integration, Digital/Interactive, Internet/Web Design, Public Relations

Beth Wilbins *(Founder & Pres)*
Jade Falldine *(COO)*

Accounts:
New-Presbyterian Village North

FORTE-THE COLLECTIVE
117 W 9th St Ste 721, Los Angeles, CA 90015
Tel.: (213) 973-9725
Web Site: www.fortethecollective.com

Employees: 6
Year Founded: 2010

Mark Quest *(Co-Founder & Dir-Creative)*
Bryan Alano *(Principal)*

Accounts:
Los Angeles Clippers

FORTY FORTY AGENCY
PO Box 2866, San Francisco, CA 94126
Tel.: (510) 559-1036
E-Mail: contact@4040agency.com
Web Site: www.4040agency.com

Employees: 15
Year Founded: 2002

Approx. Annual Billings: $3,000,000

John Trotter *(Co-Founder)*

Accounts:
Acorn Footwear; Lewiston, ME Brand & Campaign Positioning (Joint Venture with KSV Agency); 2011
America's Cup; San Francisco, CA 2 1/2 Marketing Strategy & Launch Campaign; 2011
Atlanta Braves; Atlanta, GA Brand Experience & Sponsor Integration Design; 2008
Citizens Bank Park; Philadelphia, PA Co-branding, Brand Experience, Naming Rights; 2007
The Climate Corporation; San Francisco, CA Integrated Marketing & Advertising, Rebranding & Renaming; 2011
Jacksonville Jaguars; Jacksonville, FL Naming Rights Branding; 2010
MTV Networks Entertainment Group; New York, NY Brand Strategy & Creative; 2011
Spike TV; New York, NY Brand Strategy & Creative; 2010
UFC; Las Vegas, NV Co-Branding Strategy & Creative; 2010
Washington Nationals; Washington DC (Agency of Record) Brand Development; 2010

FORTYTWOEIGHTYNINE
(Formerly Cummings Group)
5301 E State St Ste 301, Rockford, IL 61108
Tel.: (815) 398-4289
Fax: (815) 394-0291
E-Mail: pingus@42en.com
Web Site: http://www.fortytwoeightynine.com/

Employees: 9
Year Founded: 1906

Agency Specializes In: Advertising, Business Publications, Business-To-Business, Collateral, Communications, Consulting, Corporate Identity,

Cosmetics, Direct Response Marketing, E-Commerce, Electronic Media, Engineering, Exhibit/Trade Shows, Food Service, Graphic Design, Health Care Services, High Technology, Industrial, Information Technology, Internet/Web Design, New Product Development, Pharmaceutical, Planning & Consultation, Point of Purchase, Point of Sale, Print, Production, Public Relations, Publicity/Promotions, Strategic Planning/Research, Technical Advertising, Transportation

Approx. Annual Billings: $6,000,000

Breakdown of Gross Billings by Media: Mags.: $3,000,000; Newsp.: $3,000,000

Rick Belinson *(Owner & Pres)*
Carol Merry *(Sr Dir-Art)*
Amanda Nyen *(Dir-Media)*
Jennifer Hankins *(Mgr-Acctg & Office Mgr)*
Larry Schubert *(Sr Acct Exec)*
Arlene Coll-Dimayo *(Acct Exec-B2B Mktg)*
Christine Chaney *(Designer-Multimedia & Visual)*

Accounts:
DSM
Hutchens Industries Inc.; Springfield, MO
Nalco
Woodward Aircraft Engine Systems

FORZA MARKETING
313 W 4th St, Cincinnati, OH 45202
Tel.: (513) 231-5115
E-Mail: info@forza-marketing.com
Web Site: www.forza-marketing.com

Year Founded: 2013

Agency Specializes In: Advertising, Collateral, Corporate Identity, Internet/Web Design, Logo & Package Design, Media Planning, Media Training, Public Relations, Social Media, Strategic Planning/Research

Jill Z. McBride *(Pres)*
Laura Zazanis *(Mng Dir)*
Kurt Allen *(VP)*
Carol Bross-Mcmahon *(VP)*
Tim Sansbury *(VP)*
Karen Bells *(Assoc Dir)*
Sheryl Waite *(Office Mgr)*

Accounts:
The Urology Group

FORZA MIGLIOZZI, LLC
5419 Hollywood Blvd, Hollywood, CA 90027
Tel.: (213) 973-4001
E-Mail: info@forzamigliozzi.com
Web Site: www.forzamigliozzi.com

Employees: 24
Year Founded: 2007

Agency Specializes In: Advertising, Alternative Advertising, Brand Development & Integration, Branded Entertainment, Broadcast, Business-To-Business, Cable T.V., Co-op Advertising, Communications, Consumer Goods, Consumer Marketing, Corporate Identity, Crisis Communications, Entertainment, Event Planning & Marketing, Experience Design, Fashion/Apparel, Graphic Design, Guerilla Marketing, Household Goods, In-Store Advertising, Integrated Marketing, Internet/Web Design, Leisure, Logo & Package Design, Luxury Products, Market Research, Men's Market, Merchandising, Mobile Marketing, Newspaper, Newspapers & Magazines, Outdoor, Package Design, Podcasting, Point of Purchase, Point of Sale, Print, Product Placement, Production (Print), Promotions, Public Relations, Publicity/Promotions, Radio, Sales Promotion, Sports Market, Strategic Planning/Research, T.V., Teen Market, Transportation, Travel & Tourism, Urban Market, Viral/Buzz/Word of Mouth, Women's Market

Approx. Annual Billings: $24,000,000

Breakdown of Gross Billings by Media: Brdcst.: $8,000,000; Event Mktg.: $2,000,000; Newsp. & Mags.: $3,000,000; Other: $7,000,000; Radio: $2,000,000; Worldwide Web Sites: $2,000,000

Michael Migliozzi *(Mng Partner & Dir-Creative)*

Accounts:
AdvancePierre Fast Fixin', Barber Foods, Steak-EZE, Pierre Drive Thru
After Party Beverage
Armed Music; Los Angeles, CA Entertainment
Chris' & Pitt's
Cost Plus World Market Promotion
The Counter QSR
Diocese of Brooklyn Promotion
Hyperbolic Audio; New York, NY Audio Services
Innove Real Estate
Invitation Homes Real Estate
LA Car Guy Subaru, Audi, Fisker, Porsche, Volkswagen, Toyota
NBCSN Promotion
New Evangelization Television TV Launch
Nisum Technologies IT Services
Poms & Associates Insurance
RelaxZen Beverage
Skyscraper Brewing Company; El Monte, CA Beer
Wedbush Bank Financial
Wedbush Securities Financial
WSH&B Legal Services

FORZA STUDIOS INC
1322A N Robinson, Oklahoma City, OK 73103
Tel.: (405) 367-9239
E-Mail: info@forzastudios.com
Web Site: www.forzastudios.com

Agency Specializes In: Advertising, Broadcast, Digital/Interactive, Social Media, T.V.

Chris Forza *(Dir & Writer)*

Accounts:
True Tech Home Services
Urban Wineworks

FOSTER MARKETING COMMUNICATIONS
3909-F Ambassador Caffrey, Lafayette, LA 70503
Tel.: (337) 235-1848
Fax: (337) 237-7246
Web Site: www.fostermarketing.com

E-Mail for Key Personnel:
President: gfoster@fostermarketing.com
Production Mgr.: vwyatt@fostermarketing.com
Public Relations: vwyatt@fostermarketing.com

Employees: 12
Year Founded: 1980

National Agency Associations: AAF-AMA-BMA-PRSA

Agency Specializes In: Advertising, Advertising Specialties, Aviation & Aerospace, Brand Development & Integration, Broadcast, Business Publications, Business-To-Business, Catalogs, Collateral, Communications, Consulting, Corporate Communications, Corporate Identity, Crisis Communications, Customer Relationship Management, Direct Response Marketing, E-Commerce, Electronic Media, Environmental, Event Planning & Marketing, Exhibit/Trade Shows, Financial, Food Service, Graphic Design, Industrial, Integrated Marketing, International, Internet/Web Design, Investor Relations, Logo & Package Design, Magazines, Marine, Market Research, Media Buying Services, Media Planning, Media Relations, Multimedia, New Product Development, New Technologies, Newspaper, Newspapers & Magazines, Outdoor, Package Design, Print, Production, Production (Print), Public Relations, Publicity/Promotions, Radio, Real Estate, Sales Promotion, Search Engine Optimization, Strategic Planning/Research, Technical Advertising, Telemarketing, Trade & Consumer Magazines

Approx. Annual Billings: $5,740,000 Capitalized

Breakdown of Gross Billings by Media: Adv. Specialities: $74,000; Bus. Publs.: $2,570,000; Collateral: $1,080,000; Comml. Photography: $28,000; D.M.: $41,000; Fees: $753,000; Newsp.: $21,000; Outdoor: $101,000; Pub. Rels.: $72,000; Trade Shows: $1,000,000

Tiffany Harris *(Pres)*
George Foster *(CEO)*
Kristy Bonner *(VP-Digital Svcs)*
Vicki Wyatt *(VP-Creative Svcs)*
Gary Meeks *(Controller)*
Laurel Hess *(Acct Exec)*
Kari Schoeffler *(Acct Exec)*
Tiffany Soileau *(Acct Exec)*

Accounts:
Acteon
Fugro NV
GE Energy
GE Transportation
Superior Energy Services

Branch

Foster Marketing Communications
1160 Dairy Ashford Ste 310, Houston, TX 77079
Tel.: (281) 448-3435
Fax: (281) 445-1362
Web Site: www.fostermarketing.com

Employees: 14
Year Founded: 1980

National Agency Associations: AAF-BMA-Second Wind Limited

Agency Specializes In: Advertising, Aviation & Aerospace, Brand Development & Integration, Business Publications, Business-To-Business, Collateral, Corporate Identity, Direct Response Marketing, Environmental, Event Planning & Marketing, Exhibit/Trade Shows, Graphic Design, Investor Relations, Media Buying Services, New Product Development, Print, Public Relations, Real Estate, Sales Promotion, Strategic Planning/Research

Rachel Bonnette *(Dir-Mktg)*
Bob Lytle *(Acct Supvr)*
Kari Schoeffler *(Acct Exec)*
Lindsay Brown *(Coord-Trade Show)*
Megan Schreckenbach *(Coord-Trade Show)*

Accounts:
GE Transportation

FOUNDRY 9 LLC
44 W 28th St 6th Fl, New York, NY 10001
Tel.: (212) 989-7999
Fax: (212) 989-7190
E-Mail: info@foundry9.com
Web Site: www.foundry9.com

Year Founded: 2004

Agency Specializes In: Advertising, Brand

Development & Integration, Digital/Interactive, Email, Graphic Design, Media Buying Services, Media Planning, Print, Social Media

Matthew Bernardini *(Co-Founder, Pres & CEO)*
Christer Manning *(Co-Founder, VP & Exec Dir-Creative)*
Godfrey Baker *(CTO-Foundry9 Div)*
Steve Kandetzke *(VP-Program Mgmt)*
Maggie Knight *(VP-Mktg Solutions)*
Michael Rimpel *(Dir-Media)*
Kwong Sai *(Dir-Strategy & Analysis)*
Keith Chu *(Div CIO)*

Accounts:
Carbonite, Inc. Digital, Marketing, Media Buying, Media Planning

THE FOUNDRY AGENCY
5855 Sandy Springs Cir NE Ste 200, Atlanta, GA 30328-6275
Tel.: (404) 549-8897
Fax: (770) 874-5807
E-Mail: info@thefoundryagency.com
Web Site: www.thefoundryagency.com

Agency Specializes In: Collateral, Digital/Interactive, Logo & Package Design, Print, Production (Print), Web (Banner Ads, Pop-ups, etc.)

Bryan Beard *(Pres-Foundry Local)*

Accounts:
Allsource
ATDC
Edward Lowe Foundation; 2006
GreenbergFarrow
guardedNet
Leading the Way
Luckie Marietta District; Atlanta, GA Brand Awareness; 2008
The Simpson Company
Sweetie's Gifts
TaxConnex

FOUR BROTHERS MEDIA
2089 Alder Springs Ln, Victor, MT 59875
Tel.: (406) 642-3244
E-Mail: contact@fourbrothersmedia.com
Web Site: www.fourbrothersmedia.com

Year Founded: 2013

Agency Specializes In: Advertising, Brand Development & Integration, Email, Graphic Design, Internet/Web Design, Search Engine Optimization, Social Media

Josh Hallahan *(Founder, CEO & Dir-Sls & Mktg)*
Erin Hallahan *(Mgr-Sls)*
Lisa Hallahan *(Mgr-Social Media Mktg)*

Accounts:
Bob Brandon Runnymede School
Todd Willman Questions About Christianity

FOUR DEEP MULTIMEDIA LLC
501 E Franklin St Ste 619, Richmond, VA 23219
Tel.: (804) 521-4455
Toll Free: (866) 671-8554
Web Site: www.fourdeepmultimedia.com

Agency Specializes In: Advertising, Brand Development & Integration, Crisis Communications, Graphic Design, Internet/Web Design, Media Buying Services, Print, Social Marketing/Nonprofit

J. T. Logan *(Owner & Dir-Creative)*
Ena Ampy *(CEO)*

Accounts:
Mount Olive Baptist Church
Zion Baptist Church

FOURTH IDEA
1109 Delaware Ave, Buffalo, NY 14209
Tel.: (716) 931-9948
E-Mail: hello@fourthidea.com
Web Site: www.fourthidea.com

Agency Specializes In: Advertising, Brand Development & Integration, Digital/Interactive, Package Design, Print

Thomas Mooney *(CEO)*
Sean Daly *(Art Dir)*
Mike Tripi *(Art Dir)*
Arielle Blanchard *(Acct Exec)*
Megan Burget *(Acct Exec)*
Nicole Brown *(Coord-Office)*

Accounts:
Delaware North Companies Inc
KanJam
Kegworks
Moleskine
University at Buffalo

FOXTROT BRAVO ALPHA
638 Tillery St, Austin, TX 78702
Tel.: (512) 637-8999
Web Site: www.foxtrotbravoalpha.com

Year Founded: 2008

Agency Specializes In: Advertising, Brand Development & Integration, Digital/Interactive, Logo & Package Design, Print, Search Engine Optimization, Strategic Planning/Research

Maureen Serrao Cole *(Mng Dir)*
Brad Phillips *(Principal & Dir-Experience & Interaction)*
Jann Baskett *(Principal-Brand & Strategy)*
Ryan Thompson *(Dir-Art)*
Oscar Morris *(Sr Designer)*

Accounts:
Emancipet
Gigaom
SXSW LLC
Starling
Verb

FRANCESCHI ADVERTISING & PUBLIC RELATIONS, INC.
PO Box 1773, Tallahassee, FL 32302
Tel.: (850) 385-2900
Fax: (850) 385-4446
Toll Free: (800) 293-2741
E-Mail: contactus@franadvertising.com
Web Site: www.franadvertising.com

Employees: 7
Year Founded: 1968

National Agency Associations: AAF

Agency Specializes In: Advertising, Automotive, Brand Development & Integration, Business-To-Business, Commercial Photography, E-Commerce, Financial, Government/Political, Graphic Design, Integrated Marketing, Internet/Web Design, Media Buying Services, Media Planning, Over-50 Market, Planning & Consultation, Public Relations, Real Estate, Seniors' Market, Travel & Tourism

Duane Franceschi *(Owner)*
Lee Ann Franceschi *(Pres)*

Accounts:
Adventures In Travel; Tallahassee, FL Resale Travel, Wholesale Tour; 1980
Cook Insurance Agency; Apalachicola, FL; 2004
Cost-Rite Warehouse Club; Nassau, Bahamas Consumer Products
d'Arville Group; Nassau, Bahamas
FLAG Credit Union; Tallahassee, FL; 1998
Gulf County LLC; Port Saint Joe, FL Real Estate Investments; 2006
Higdon Grocery Company; Cairo, GA Wholesale Grocers; 2001
Jim's Piano's; Tallahassee, FL; 2003
Pichard Publishing; Tallahassee, FL Book Publisher; 2007
The Steinway Piano Gallery; Tallahassee, FL; 2003
Taylor's Window & Door; Eastpoint & Tallahassee, FL Andersen Windows; 1999

FRANK ABOUT WOMEN
101 N Cherry St Ste 600, Winston Salem, NC 27101
Tel.: (336) 765-3630
Fax: (336) 774-9550
Web Site: www.frankaboutwomen.com

Year Founded: 2001

National Agency Associations: 4A's

Agency Specializes In: Advertising, Automotive, Brand Development & Integration, Communications, Consumer Goods, Entertainment, Experience Design, Fashion/Apparel, Financial, Food Service, Health Care Services, Internet/Web Design, Local Marketing, Media Buying Services, Media Planning, Media Relations, Package Design, Promotions, Public Relations, Publishing, Restaurant, Retail, Travel & Tourism

Jennifer Ganshirt *(Co-Founder & Mng Partner)*
Shaun Stripling *(Chief Strategy Officer)*
Christy Blain *(Sr VP & Grp Dir-Creative)*
Kate Wilson Masten *(Sr VP & Grp Dir-Media)*
Kate Hanley *(VP & Assoc Dir-Strategic Plng)*
Seton McGowan *(VP & Assoc Dir-Social Strategy)*

Accounts:
Abbott Nutrition; 2012
Food Lion; 2011
Hanes Hosiery; 2011
PBS Sprout Cable TV Network for Children; 2011
Sylvan Learning; 2013
TREsemme; 2010

THE FRANK AGENCY INC
(Formerly BKV Inc.)
10561 Barkley St Ste 200, Overland Park, KS 66212
Tel.: (913) 648-8333
Fax: (913) 648-5024
Web Site: thefrankagency.com/

E-Mail for Key Personnel:
President: haask@weyforth-haas.com

Employees: 52
Year Founded: 1981

National Agency Associations: ICOM

Agency Specializes In: Advertising, Advertising Specialties, Affiliate Marketing, Affluent Market, Agriculture, Alternative Advertising, Arts, Automotive, Below-the-Line, Bilingual Market, Brand Development & Integration, Broadcast, Business Publications, Business-To-Business, Cable T.V., Catalogs, Co-op Advertising, Collateral, College, Communications, Computers & Software, Consulting, Consumer Goods, Consumer Marketing, Consumer Publications, Corporate Communications, Corporate Identity, Custom Publishing, Customer Relationship Management,

Digital/Interactive, Direct Response Marketing, Direct-to-Consumer, E-Commerce, Education, Electronic Media, Electronics, Email, Entertainment, Environmental, Event Planning & Marketing, Exhibit/Trade Shows, Financial, Government/Political, Graphic Design, Guerilla Marketing, Health Care Services, High Technology, Hospitality, Household Goods, Identity Marketing, In-Store Advertising, Industrial, Infomercials, Information Technology, Integrated Marketing, International, Internet/Web Design, Leisure, Local Marketing, Logo & Package Design, Magazines, Marine, Market Research, Media Buying Services, Media Planning, Media Relations, Media Training, Men's Market, Merchandising, Mobile Marketing, Multimedia, New Product Development, New Technologies, Newspapers & Magazines, Out-of-Home Media, Outdoor, Paid Searches, Planning & Consultation, Point of Purchase, Point of Sale, Print, Production, Production (Print), Promotions, Public Relations, Publicity/Promotions, Publishing, RSS (Really Simple Syndication), Radio, Real Estate, Recruitment, Regional, Retail, Sales Promotion, Search Engine Optimization, Social Marketing/Nonprofit, Sponsorship, Strategic Planning/Research, Sweepstakes, T.V., Technical Advertising, Telemarketing, Trade & Consumer Magazines, Transportation, Travel & Tourism, Viral/Buzz/Word of Mouth, Yellow Pages Advertising

Approx. Annual Billings: $100,000,000

Breakdown of Gross Billings by Media: Bus. Publs.: 5%; Collateral: 5%; Consulting: 5%; D.M.: 10%; E-Commerce: 10%; Internet Adv.: 10%; Mdsg./POP: 5%; Plng. & Consultation: 5%; Production: 5%; Pub. Rels.: 5%; Sls. Promo.: 5%; Strategic Planning/Research: 10%; T.V.: 10%; Worldwide Web Sites: 10%

Tony Ali *(Pres & CEO)*
Virginia Doty *(Mng Partner & Exec VP-Mktg)*
Alan Blose *(Chief Creative Officer & Exec VP)*
Stacy Pierce *(Chief Media Officer & Exec VP)*
Maribett Varner *(Pres-Atlanta)*
Angela Hilton *(Sr VP & Grp Acct Dir)*
Bree Roe *(VP & Dir-Media)*
Andrew Booth *(VP-Interactive Mktg)*
Katherine Jianas *(Assoc Dir-Media)*
Samantha Halpin *(Supvr-Media)*
Nurain Alicharan *(Strategist-Social Media)*
Alyson Klugman *(Media Planner)*
Carly Ambrose *(Asst Acct Exec)*
Ashton Ross *(Acct Coord)*
Kelsey Chadwick *(Asst Media Planner)*

Accounts:
American Red Cross National Fundraising
Arby's Restaurant Group
Armed Forces Insurance; Leavenworth, KS; 2004
Dell SecureWorks
Delta TechOps
Equifax
iContact
Kool Smiles
Mercedes-Benz USA
Navy Federal Credit Union
NCM Associates
PetSafe
Six Flags Entertainment Corp.; Atlanta, GA Theme Park & Water Park, Tourism & Hospitality; 2003
Spanx

FRANK COLLECTIVE
20 Jay St Ste 638, Brooklyn, NY 11201
Tel.: (646) 606-2211
Web Site: www.frankcollective.com

Employees: 10
Year Founded: 2011

Agency Specializes In: Above-the-Line, Below-the-Line, Branded Entertainment, Broadcast, Collateral, Digital/Interactive, In-Store Advertising, Multimedia, Point of Purchase, Point of Sale, Print, Production, Web (Banner Ads, Pop-ups, etc.)

Approx. Annual Billings: $1,500,000

Mike Wasilewski *(Founder, Partner & Dir-Creative)*
Jiffy Iuen *(Co-Founder & Partner-Creative)*
Aisling Flynn *(Sr Graphic Designer)*

Accounts:
American Express; 2013
Blue Apron; 2013
Bombas; 2014
Conde Nast Dove, TreSemme, US Trust; 2012
Lo & Sons; 2014
Relay Graduate School; 2014
Tourneau; 2013

FRANK CREATIVE INC
2505 SE 11th Ave Ste 245, Portland, OR 97214
Tel.: (503) 546-3626
Fax: (503) 546-3636
E-Mail: info@frankcreative.com
Web Site: www.frankcreative.com

Agency Specializes In: Advertising, Broadcast, Collateral, Internet/Web Design, Print

Sue Parker *(Founder & CEO)*
Sarah Gensert *(Dir-Art & Sr Graphic Designer)*
David Karstad *(Dir-Creative)*
Aaron Jones *(Sr Acct Mgr)*
Alexander Cherin *(Acct Mgr)*
Ashley Mastrine *(Coord-Mktg)*

Accounts:
The Conservation Alliance
GoLite Footwear

FRANK STRATEGIC MARKETING
8775 Ctr Park Dr ste 253, Columbia, MD 21045
Tel.: (410) 203-1228
Fax: (410) 203-2002
E-Mail: gfrank@frankbiz.com
Web Site: www.frankbiz.com

Employees: 10
Year Founded: 1995

National Agency Associations: Second Wind Limited

Agency Specializes In: Advertising

Gerry Frank *(Chief Creative Officer)*
Lisa P. Howard *(Acct Svcs Dir)*
Pete Burch *(Dir-Creative)*
Sean Sutherland *(Acct Exec)*
Christina Bittinger *(Sr Graphic Designer)*

Accounts:
Attendee Interactive
CEDIA
Consumer Electronics Show
Craig Coyne Jewelers
Food Marketing Institute
Goldwell
I-Fund of Maryland
Kenseal Construction Products
U.S. Foodservice

FRANK UNLIMITED
2819 Elliott Ave Ste 204, Seattle, WA 98121
Tel.: (206) 441-5950
Web Site: www.frankunlimited.com

Year Founded: 2010

Nick Hunt *(Partner, Gen Mgr & Client Svcs Dir)*
Forrest Healy *(Principal & Dir-Creative)*
Zach Hitner *(Principal & Dir-Creative)*
LeeAnna Buis *(Dir-Media)*
Curtis Jackson *(Mgr-Studio)*

Accounts:
Alliance Proton Therapy; Seattle, WA Event Marketing, Online Advertising, Print, Radio
The Everett Clinic; Everett, WA (Agency of Record) Broadcast, Online & Non-traditional Media, Outdoor, Print
Redhook Beer
Sound Credit Union; Tacoma, WA
Zulily

FRANKEL MEDIA GROUP
105 SW 128th St Ste 200, Newberry, FL 32669-3244
Tel.: (352) 331-5558
Fax: (352) 331-5449
Web Site: www.frankelmedia.com

Employees: 8
Year Founded: 2004

Agency Specializes In: Advertising, Brand Development & Integration, Corporate Identity, Direct Response Marketing, Event Planning & Marketing, Graphic Design, Internet/Web Design, Media Buying Services, Media Planning, Strategic Planning/Research

Ryan Frankel *(Pres & Dir-Creative)*
Channing Casey *(VP-Ops)*
Robert Hedges *(Assoc Dir-Creative)*
Jeannette Baer *(Mgr-HR)*
Josh Garland *(Sr Acct Exec)*
Danna Miller *(Acct Exec & Specialist-PR)*
Kelsey Frost *(Acct Exec)*
Mehgan McLendon *(Coord-Digital)*

FRANKLIN ADVERTISING ASSOCIATES, INC.
441 Main St, Yarmouth Port, MA 02675
Tel.: (508) 362-7472
Fax: (508) 362-5975
E-Mail: contact@franklinad.com
Web Site: www.franklinad.com

Employees: 5
Year Founded: 1970

Agency Specializes In: Business-To-Business, Co-op Advertising, Collateral, Consumer Publications, Corporate Communications, E-Commerce, Financial, Graphic Design, In-Store Advertising, Internet/Web Design, Leisure, Newspaper, Newspapers & Magazines, Point of Purchase, Print, Production, Restaurant, Trade & Consumer Magazines, Travel & Tourism

Approx. Annual Billings: $2,500,000

Breakdown of Gross Billings by Media: Bus. Publs.: $60,000; Collateral: $1,140,000; Consumer Publs.: $600,000; Newsp.: $60,000; Print: $640,000

Martin A. Summerfield *(Owner)*

Accounts:
Bound To Stay Bound Books, Inc.; Jacksonville, IL Prebound Books for Schools & Libraries; 1953
Cape Cod Chamber of Commerce; Hyannis, MA Cape-Wide Guidebooks; 1999
Divi Aruba & Divi Tamarijn; Aruba All-Inclusive Resorts; 1994
The Soundings; Dennisport, MA Full Service Resort
Tidewater Inn; West Yarmouth, MA AAA 3 Diamond Lodging Facility
Yarmouth Area Chamber of Commerce; Yarmouth, MA Design & Production of Annual Guidebook,

Other Promotional Materials & Print Advertising; 1992

FRANKLIN STREET MARKETING

9700 Farrar Ct, Richmond, VA 23236
Tel.: (804) 320-3838
Fax: (804) 320-1999
Toll Free: (800) 644-8555
E-Mail: mail@franklinstreet.com
Web Site: www.franklinstreet.com

E-Mail for Key Personnel:
President: flynn@franklinstreet.com

Employees: 19
Year Founded: 1986

Agency Specializes In: Advertising, Brand Development & Integration, Collateral, Corporate Communications, Corporate Identity, Event Planning & Marketing, Health Care Services, Logo & Package Design, Magazines, Media Buying Services, Medical Products, Newspaper, Outdoor, Print, Production, Public Relations, Recruitment

Breakdown of Gross Billings by Media: Collateral: 20%; Logo & Package Design: 10%; Newsp. & Mags.: 15%; Outdoor: 5%; Pub. Rels.: 10%; Radio & T.V.: 30%; Trade & Consumer Mags.: 5%; Worldwide Web Sites: 5%

William B. Flynn *(Pres)*
Tim Roberts *(Partner)*
Dean Ruth *(VP-Production)*
Whitney Pratt *(Assoc Dir-Creative)*
Allison Van Pelt *(Sr Acct Mgr)*
Kelly Jackson *(Mgr-Fin)*

Accounts:
Centra
Martin Memorial Health Systems; Stuart, FL
Methodist Hospitals

FRASER COMMUNICATIONS

1631 Pontius Ave, Los Angeles, CA 90025
Tel.: (310) 319-3737
Fax: (310) 319-1537
E-Mail: rfraser@frasercommunications.com
Web Site: www.frasercommunications.com

E-Mail for Key Personnel:
President: rfraser@frasercommunications.com
Media Dir.: bdundore@frasercommunications.com

Employees: 32
Year Founded: 1992

National Agency Associations: AAF-AD CLUB

Agency Specializes In: Advertising, African-American Market, Alternative Advertising, Asian Market, Automotive, Brand Development & Integration, Broadcast, Business-To-Business, Cable T.V., Children's Market, Collateral, Communications, Consumer Marketing, Corporate Communications, Corporate Identity, Cosmetics, Crisis Communications, Digital/Interactive, Education, Electronic Media, Entertainment, Environmental, Fashion/Apparel, Financial, Gay & Lesbian Market, Government/Political, Guerilla Marketing, Health Care Services, Hispanic Market, Internet/Web Design, Logo & Package Design, Market Research, Media Buying Services, Media Planning, Media Relations, Medical Products, Multicultural, Multimedia, Out-of-Home Media, Outdoor, Package Design, Paid Searches, Print, Production (Ad, Film, Broadcast), Production (Print), Public Relations, Publicity/Promotions, Radio, Search Engine Optimization, Seniors' Market, Social Marketing/Nonprofit, Sponsorship, Strategic Planning/Research, T.V., Viral/Buzz/Word of Mouth, Web (Banner Ads, Pop-ups, etc.), Women's Market

Approx. Annual Billings: $40,000,000

Breakdown of Gross Billings by Media: Cable T.V.: 12%; Collateral: 1%; Internet Adv.: 3%; Newsp. & Mags.: 10%; Outdoor: 7%; Radio: 67%

Renee White Fraser *(Pres & CEO)*
Jennie Crandall *(CFO)*
Neelam Tolani *(CFO)*
Ilene Prince *(Sr VP & Client Svcs Dir)*
Sergio Belletini *(VP & Dir-Creative)*
Lisa Schellenbach *(Dir-Integrated Media)*

Accounts:
East West Bank; San Marino, CA; 2002
Metropolitan Water District
UCLA Extension

FRASER WALLACE ADVERTISING LTD

(Name Changed to Wallace & Company)

FRATERNITY ADVERTISING

2301 W I 44 Service Rd, Oklahoma City, OK 73112
Tel.: (855) 832-6895
Toll Free: (855) 832-6895
Web Site: www.fraternityadv.com

Year Founded: 2011

Agency Specializes In: Advertising, Brand Development & Integration, Internet/Web Design, Production

Drake Scifers *(Co-Founder)*
Christopher Lloyd *(Dir-Media)*

Accounts:
Piper Valve Systems

FRCH DESIGN WORLDWIDE

311 Elm St Ste 600, Cincinnati, OH 45202
Tel.: (513) 241-3000
Fax: (513) 241-5015
E-Mail: info@frch.com
Web Site: www.frch.com

Employees: 150

Agency Specializes In: Brand Development & Integration, Corporate Communications, Entertainment, Graphic Design, Hospitality, Media Relations, Restaurant, Retail, Sponsorship

James R. Tippmann *(CEO & Partner)*
Paul Lechleiter *(Chief Creative Officer)*
Jim Harkin *(Principal & Sr VP)*
James Stapleton *(Principal)*
Michael Chaney *(Mng Dir-Creative-Specialty Design)*
Heesun Kim *(VP & Dir-Creative)*
Rob Depp *(VP-Client Svcs & Specialty Retail Design Studio)*
Robyn Novak *(VP)*
Rob Rink *(VP)*
Scott Rink *(VP)*
Dave Zelman *(VP)*
Phillip Freer *(Dir-Creative)*
Cassie Koch *(Dir-Retail & Mixed-Use)*
Kelli Lear *(Dir-Graphic Design)*
Monica Lowry *(Dir)*
Nicole McDevitt *(Dir-Specialty Architecture)*
Ryan McNally *(Dir-Architect)*
Dave Middendorf *(Dir-Brand Strategy & Insights)*
Mari Miura *(Dir-Interior Design)*
Amy Rink *(Dir-Studio Ops)*
Nicole Roberts *(Dir)*
Jonathan Rolke *(Dir-Specialty Architecture)*
Brian Sullivan *(Dir-Large Format)*
Cristina Ferrari *(Assoc Dir-Brand Strategy)*
Mike Ruehlman *(Assoc Dir-Graphic Design)*
Melissa Chrin *(Mgr-Bus Dev)*
Raejean Downs *(Sr Designer-Interior-Hospitality)*
Erin Hood *(Designer)*
Caitlin Terry *(Designer-Interior)*
Jason Patterson *(Sr Team Head)*

Accounts:
Aveda Corporation
Hilton Worldwide Home2 Suites

FRED AGENCY

826 Juniper St NE, Atlanta, GA 30308
Tel.: (404) 720-0995
Web Site: www.fredagency.com

Agency Specializes In: Advertising, Brand Development & Integration, Corporate Identity, Digital/Interactive, Internet/Web Design, Media Buying Services, Media Planning, Print, Radio, T.V.

Fred Adkins *(Pres & Chief Creative Officer)*
Donny Adkins *(Partner, VP-Production & Dir-Digital Dev)*
Ryan Highfield *(Controller)*
Amanda Burrow *(Dir-Creative)*
Terry Muth *(Dir-Mktg Media)*
Chris Pastir *(Dir-Creative)*
Natalie Ricker *(Designer-Digital)*

Accounts:
Seventh Midtown

FRED H. EBERSOLD, INC.

6040 Main St, Downers Grove, IL 60516
Tel.: (630) 512-9922
Fax: (630) 512-0033
E-Mail: kent@ebersoldinc.com
Web Site: www.ebersoldinc.com

Employees: 3
Year Founded: 1932

Agency Specializes In: Industrial

Approx. Annual Billings: $700,000

Keith Ebersold *(Pres & Treas)*

Accounts:
Kennedy-Webster Electric Co.; Chicago, IL Instrument Lamps
Naylor Pipe Co.; Chicago, IL

FREDERICK SWANSTON

11800 Amberpark Dr Ste 100, Alpharetta, GA 30009
Tel.: (770) 642-7900
Web Site: www.frederickswanston.com

Employees: 38
Year Founded: 1999

Agency Specializes In: Advertising, Brand Development & Integration, Digital/Interactive, Market Research, Sponsorship

Approx. Annual Billings: $10,500,000

Una Hutton Newman *(Sr Dir-Healthcare Div)*
Patty Kinney *(Dir-Creative Svcs)*
Bryan Keith Nixon *(Dir-Creative)*
Dustin Hall *(Assoc Dir-Creative)*
Cassie Twilley *(Sr Acct Supvr)*
Jessica Cochran *(Sr Acct Exec)*
Brittany Fryman *(Sr Acct Exec)*
Caitlin Kinney *(Sr Acct Exec)*
Michael Hersh *(Asst Acct Exec)*
Morgan Metraw *(Asst Acct Exec)*
Heather Moore *(Acct Coord)*

Accounts:

Exide Technologies
Iberostar Hotels & Resorts
JoAnn's Fabrics
Kosair Children's Hospital
Metro Health
Norton Hospital Norton Healthcare
VeriFone Systems, Inc.

FREE AGENTS MARKETING

4800 Cox Rd, Glen Allen, VA 23060
Tel.: (804) 762-9400
Fax: (804) 762-7337
E-Mail: info@freeagentsmarketing.com
Web Site: www.freeagentsmarketing.com

Employees: 13

Agency Specializes In: Broadcast, Collateral, Internet/Web Design, Media Buying Services, Print, Public Relations, Radio, Strategic Planning/Research, T.V.

Ken Wayland *(Pres)*
Todd Williams *(Dir-Art)*
Dawn Young *(Dir-Dev)*
Ha Koehler *(Sr Acct Exec)*
Kristen Greer *(Acct Exec)*
Becky McIntyre *(Strategist-Media)*
Marisa Norona *(Acct Coord)*

Accounts:
Bon Secours Richmond Health System; Richmond, VA
Bon Secours Washington Redskins Training Center Campaign: "Redskins Fandemonium"

FREE ENERGY MEDIA

23 Winged Foot Dr, Larchmont, NY 10538
Tel.: (914) 715-8862
Web Site: www.freeenergymedia.com

Employees: 5
Year Founded: 2012

Agency Specializes In: Digital/Interactive, Direct Response Marketing, Email, Experience Design, Game Integration, Mobile Marketing, Paid Searches, Promotions, Social Media, Sponsorship, Viral/Buzz/Word of Mouth, Web (Banner Ads, Pop-ups, etc.)

Approx. Annual Billings: $800,000

Alex Borsody *(CTO)*

Accounts:
Changecorp SmartWoman; 2014
Internet Society File Library; 2013
Pratt University http://prattcenter.net; 2012
Startalk Radio Startalk Share Widget; 2012
Wanderlust Festival Wanderlustfestival.com; 2012

FREE ENTERPRISE LLC

495 Broadway 4th Fl, New York, NY 10012
Tel.: (212) 625-8740
Fax: (212) 625-8745
E-Mail: info@freeenterprisellc.com
Web Site: www.freeenterprisellc.com

Year Founded: 2002

Agency Specializes In: Advertising, Broadcast, Digital/Interactive, Media Planning, Social Media

Gerry O'Reilly *(Writer, Producer & Strategist)*
Marcus Kemp *(Dir-Creative & Art)*
Laramie Lifton *(Dir-Art)*
Paul Wolfe *(Dir-Creative)*
Steve Soldano *(Sr Strategist-Media & Planner)*

Accounts:
Lovesac

FREE FOR ALL MARKETING INC

33 Bloor Street East Suite 900, Toronto, ON M4W 3H1 Canada
Tel.: (416) 920-5699
Web Site: www.freeforallmarketing.ca

Year Founded: 1999

Agency Specializes In: Retail, Social Media, Sponsorship, Strategic Planning/Research, Trade & Consumer Magazines

Mary Beth Denomy *(Pres)*
Lisa Barrans *(Sr VP)*
Christine Ross *(Sr VP)*
Kelly Power *(VP)*
Marie Bedard *(Acct Dir)*
Madison Denouden *(Sr Acct Mgr)*
Erica Vig *(Sr Acct Mgr)*

Accounts:
Johnson & Johnson Services Inc. Health Care Products Mfr & Distr
Kijiji International Limited Local Classifields Service Providers
MasterCard Financial Transaction Payment Card Providers

FREE RANGE STUDIOS

1605 Connecticut Ave NW 4th Fl, Washington, DC 20009
Tel.: (202) 234-5613
Fax: (202) 318-3037
Web Site: freerange.com/

Employees: 10
Year Founded: 2000

Agency Specializes In: Collateral, Communications, Corporate Identity, Digital/Interactive, Government/Political, Graphic Design, Internet/Web Design, Logo & Package Design, Multimedia, Outdoor, Point of Sale, Print, Radio, Viral/Buzz/Word of Mouth

Approx. Annual Billings: $1,500,000

Jonah Sachs *(Co-Founder & CEO)*
Ben Hester *(Sr Dir-Client Svcs)*
Cymbeline Johnson *(Sr Dir-Sls & Mktg)*
Ruben Deluna *(Dir-Creative)*
Naoto De Silva *(Dir-Fin & Ops)*
Mandy Townsend *(Dir-People Svcs)*
Zoe Maurer *(Sr Acct Mgr)*
Emily Dransfield *(Mgr-Creative Svcs)*
Andrea Falke *(Designer-Visual & UX)*
Darshita Mistry *(Sr Designer-Visual & UX)*

Accounts:
African Wildlife Foundation
Alliance for Climate Education
Discovery Channel
Earth Justice
Green Mountain
Greenpeace
Human Rights Campaign
Planned Parenthood
WRTC
WWF

FREEBAIRN & CO.

3384 Peachtree Rd, Atlanta, GA 30326
Tel.: (404) 487-6106
Fax: (404) 231-2214
E-Mail: jcobb@freebairn.com
Web Site: www.freebairn.com

E-Mail for Key Personnel:
President: jfreebairn@freebairn.com
Creative Dir.: mkirkpatrick@freebairn.com
Media Dir.: schapman@freebairn.com

Employees: 17
Year Founded: 1980

National Agency Associations: PRSA-TAAN

Agency Specializes In: Advertising, Advertising Specialties, Agriculture, Brand Development & Integration, Broadcast, Business Publications, Business-To-Business, Cable T.V., Collateral, College, Consumer Goods, Consumer Marketing, Consumer Publications, Corporate Identity, Digital/Interactive, Direct Response Marketing, E-Commerce, Education, Electronic Media, Event Planning & Marketing, Exhibit/Trade Shows, Financial, Graphic Design, Health Care Services, High Technology, Household Goods, Information Technology, Integrated Marketing, Internet/Web Design, Legal Services, Leisure, Logo & Package Design, Magazines, Media Planning, Media Relations, Multimedia, New Product Development, Newspaper, Newspapers & Magazines, Out-of-Home Media, Outdoor, Package Design, Planning & Consultation, Point of Purchase, Point of Sale, Print, Production, Promotions, Public Relations, Publicity/Promotions, Radio, Retail, Sales Promotion, Sponsorship, Sports Market, Strategic Planning/Research, T.V., Trade & Consumer Magazines, Transportation, Travel & Tourism

Approx. Annual Billings: $17,000,000

John C. Freebairn *(Pres)*
Toni Cooper *(CFO)*
Jean G. Cobb *(Sr VP & Mgmt Supvr)*
Sandy Chapman *(Sr VP & Dir-Media)*
Don Patton *(Sr Dir-Art)*
Jay Hatfield *(Dir-Art)*
Mack Kirkpatrick *(Dir-Creative)*
Kit Becker *(Sr Designer-Interactive)*

Accounts:
Norit Americas; Atlanta, GA Activated Carbon; 1997
Progressive Lighting
University of Georgia Center for Continuing Education
The University of Georgia-Terry College of Business; Atlanta, GA Evening & Executive MBA Programs; 2005
YKK AP; Austell, GA Architectural Products; 1996

Branch

Freebairn & Company Public Relations

3475 Lenox Rd Ste 900, Atlanta, GA 30326
(See Separate Listing)

FREED ADVERTISING

1650 Hwy 6 Ste 400, Sugar Land, TX 77478
Tel.: (281) 240-4949
Fax: (281) 240-4999
Web Site: www.freedad.com

E-Mail for Key Personnel:
President: gfreed@freedad.com

Employees: 20
Year Founded: 1984

National Agency Associations: 4A's-AAF

Agency Specializes In: Advertising, Automotive, Brand Development & Integration, Business-To-Business, Collateral, Communications, Corporate Identity, Direct Response Marketing, Electronic Media, Entertainment, Exhibit/Trade Shows, Faith Based, Financial, Food Service, Health Care Services, High Technology, Industrial, Internet/Web Design, Legal Services, Leisure, Logo & Package Design, Media Buying Services, Medical Products,

Merchandising, New Product Development, Newspaper, Newspapers & Magazines, Out-of-Home Media, Outdoor, Pharmaceutical, Point of Purchase, Point of Sale, Print, Production, Public Relations, Radio, Real Estate, Recruitment, Restaurant, Retail, Sales Promotion, Sports Market, Strategic Planning/Research, T.V., Technical Advertising, Trade & Consumer Magazines, Transportation, Travel & Tourism, Yellow Pages Advertising

Approx. Annual Billings: $21,000,000

Gerald Freed *(Founder & CEO)*
Mandy Deleon *(Sr Acct Dir)*
Nancy Self *(Dir-Creative)*
Rosa Serrano *(Dir-Media Strategy)*
Martha Baxter *(Office Mgr)*
Jordan Lippman *(Media Planner & Media Buyer)*

Accounts:
Baker Nissan
Firethorn; Houston, TX Master-planned Community
Hochheim Prairie Insurance
IKEA IKEA North America Services, LLC
Imperial Sugar
Mercedes-Benz of Sugar Land
MountainKing Potatoes
Redstone Companies; TX Redstone Golf Club, The Houstonian Hotel, The Houstonian, Country Club, Blackhorse Golf Club, Shadow hawk Golf Club

FREESTYLE MARKETING GROUP

211 E Bdwy No 214, Salt Lake City, UT 84111
Tel.: (801) 364-3764
Fax: (801) 322-2168
Web Site: www.freestylemg.com

Year Founded: 2000

Agency Specializes In: Advertising, Collateral, Internet/Web Design, Media Planning

Jason Harrison *(Partner & Dir-Creative)*
Michael Stoll *(COO & VP Sls)*
Naomi Halpern *(Dir-Bus Dev)*
Chase Carpenter *(Assoc Dir-Art)*
Courtney Lissauer *(Sr Acct Mgr)*
Shawna Gunther *(Acct Mgr)*
Philip Johnson *(Mgr-Social Media)*
Nancy Di Modica Swan *(Acct Exec)*
Staci Duke *(Acct Planner)*
Bakir Hamza *(Assoc Acct Exec)*
Elaine Parker *(Corp Acct Exec)*

Accounts:
Arriva E-Commerce
The Colony at White Pine Canyon
Danish Furniture
DogTread
East Zion Development
Mezze Fine Food

FRENCH/BLITZER/SCOTT LLC

275 Madison Ave 4th Fl, New York, NY 10016
Tel.: (212) 255-2650
Fax: (212) 255-0383
E-Mail: rscott@frenchblitzerscott.com
Web Site: www.frenchblitzerscott.com

E-Mail for Key Personnel:
President: RScott@frenchblitzerscott.com

Employees: 5
Year Founded: 1985

Agency Specializes In: Aviation & Aerospace, Business-To-Business, Financial, Print

Robert Scott *(Pres)*
Ray Gaulke *(CMO)*

Accounts:
Alan James Group
Bronxville Historical Conservancy
Country Living
Credit Suisse
Premio Foods; Hawthorne, NJ Sausage Products; 1999
Sheppard Mullin Richter & Hampton

FRENCH CREATIVE GROUP

2007 Roselawn Ave, Monroe, LA 71201
Tel.: (318) 325-5883
Fax: (318) 325-2787
Web Site: www.frenchcreative.com

Agency Specializes In: Advertising, Brand Development & Integration, Internet/Web Design, Print, Public Relations, Social Media

Vici French *(Pres)*
Susan Robley *(Mgr-Production)*
Erin French *(Acct Exec)*

Accounts:
Chennault Aviation & Military Museum
Delta Textiles Manufacturing
Heard McElroy & Vestal
Johnnys Pizza House
P&S Surgical Hospital
Progressive Bank
Scott Powerline & Utility Equipment

FRENCH/WEST/VAUGHAN, INC.

112 E Hargett St, Raleigh, NC 27601
Tel.: (919) 832-6300
Fax: (919) 832-6360
Web Site: www.fwv-us.com

Employees: 50
Year Founded: 2001

National Agency Associations: ABC-COPF

Agency Specializes In: Advertising, Advertising Specialties, Affluent Market, Aviation & Aerospace, Brand Development & Integration, Broadcast, Business Publications, Business-To-Business, Cable T.V., Collateral, College, Communications, Consulting, Consumer Goods, Consumer Marketing, Consumer Publications, Corporate Communications, Corporate Identity, Digital/Interactive, Direct-to-Consumer, Education, Exhibit/Trade Shows, Fashion/Apparel, Financial, Food Service, Graphic Design, Guerilla Marketing, Health Care Services, Identity Marketing, In-Store Advertising, Information Technology, Integrated Marketing, Internet/Web Design, Local Marketing, Logo & Package Design, Luxury Products, Magazines, Market Research, Media Buying Services, Media Planning, Medical Products, Men's Market, Multimedia, New Technologies, Newspaper, Newspapers & Magazines, Out-of-Home Media, Outdoor, Package Design, Pharmaceutical, Point of Purchase, Point of Sale, Print, Promotions, Radio, Real Estate, Recruitment, Regional, Restaurant, Retail, Sales Promotion, Search Engine Optimization, Seniors' Market, Social Marketing/Nonprofit, Sponsorship, Sports Market, Strategic Planning/Research, T.V., Teen Market, Trade & Consumer Magazines, Transportation, Urban Market, Viral/Buzz/Word of Mouth, Web (Banner Ads, Pop-ups, etc.), Women's Market, Yellow Pages Advertising

Approx. Annual Billings: $55,000,000

David Gwyn *(Pres)*
Natalie Best *(Exec VP & Dir-Client Svc)*
Barrie Hancock *(Sr VP)*
Wendy McCarthy *(Sr VP)*
Chris Shigas *(Sr VP)*
Jenny Pilewski *(VP)*
Melissa Timney *(VP)*
Lauren Kinelski *(Assoc VP)*
Leah Knepper *(Assoc VP)*
Shannon Burton *(Grp Acct Dir)*
Katie Johnson *(Grp Acct Dir)*
Amelia Lacker *(Grp Acct Dir)*
Rachel Wing *(Grp Acct Dir)*
Rich Griffis *(Art Dir)*
Mibbie Majors *(Dir-Media)*
Dawn Marie Strzepek *(Assoc Dir-Creative)*
Alexandra Ellis *(Acct Supvr)*
Justin Champion *(Supvr-Digital Mktg)*
Kathryn DeLong *(Acct Exec)*
Lauren Towns *(Acct Exec)*
Caitlin Vargas *(Acct Exec)*
Shina Jackson *(Asst Acct Exec)*
Sally Van Denover *(Acct Coord)*
Charli McKee *(Coord-Studio)*

Accounts:
Absorption Pharmaceuticals Advertising, Brand Positioning, Digital, Point-of-Sale, Promescent (Marketing & Public Relations Agency of Record), Retail, Social Media
A.J. Fletcher Foundation Marketing, PR, Strategic Communications
Arena North America Swimwear
Arian Foster
B2G Sports (Agency Of Record) Marketing, Public Relations
Bassett Furniture Event Planning, Grassroots Marketing, Media Outreach, Media Relations
Brand Napa Valley (Agency of Record) Brand Strategy, Integrated Marketing, Positioning
Cabela's Media, Public Relations
Campbell University PR, School of Osteopathic Medicine
The Central Intercollegiate Athletic Association
Chris Canty Chris Canty Foundation, Marketing, Public Relations
CompareCards.com
Concord Hospitality Enterprises Company (PR & Creative Services Agency of Record)
Dahntay Jones
Dey Pharmaceuticals
Divi Resorts
Dominion Realty Partners, LLC
Downtown Raleigh Alliance
Elevation Burger (Agency of Record) Advertising, Events, Public Relations, Social Media
eWinWin
Fleet Feet Sports (Public Relations Agency of Record)
The Free Enterprise Nation
Gear4 Consumer Marketing, PR
Glen Davis
Glover Quin
Good Look Ink
Greater Raleigh Convention and Visitors Bureau (Creative Services Agency of Record)
HCA Holdings Inc.
Healthy Living Academies; 2008
Hood River Distillers Broker's Gin, Creative Campaigns, Pendleton Whisky, ULLR Nordic Libation, Yazi Ginger Vodka
House-Autry Mills
International Gemological Institute
Island Club Brands
The Jimmy V Foundation
Justin Boot Co.
New-K4Connect Public Relations
Marc John Jefferies (Public Relations Agency of Record) Marketing, Media Relations
Medcryption
Melitta Coffee
Michael Vick
Moe's Southwest Grill Raleigh Co-Op (Agency of Record) Integrated Marketing Campaign; 2010
MoGo Sport Athlete Endorsements, PR, Social Media
NATHAN PR, Social Media Marketing, Strategic Media Relations
New-National Pro Fastpitch (Public Relations, Marketing & Sponsorship Development Agency

of Record) Media Relations
Nestle USA, Inc. Gold Peak, Nestea
Nfinity Shoes (Agency of Record) Women's Athletic Footwear; 2008
NOCQUA Adventure Gear Marketing, PR
New-Nolan Carroll Marketing
Optek Music Systems
Osceola County Advertising, Branding, Creative Services, Marketing, Public Relations, RAM National Circuit Finals Rodeo, Social Media
Paralyzed Veterans of America "Racing to Empower Veterans", Creative, Digital Marketing, Marketing, Media Relations, Public Relations, Social Media, Strategic Brand Development
Pfizer
Pogo Health
Polar Ice House
Professional Rodeo Cowboys Association
Pulse Health & Wellness Initiatives; 2007
Rashad Jennings (Public Relations, Marketing & Endorsement Agency of Record) New York Giants Running Back
RBC Bank
Respirics
Russell Wilson
Ryan Mundy (Agency of Record) Brand Development, Marketing, Public Relations, Social Media
SAS
Skins International PR
New-Southern Season (Public Relations Agency of Record)
Southwestern Athletic Conference Marketing, PR, Social Media
Sports Endeavors Inc. Brand Strategy, Creative
Stacey Lee Agency (Agency of Record)
Strata Solar Public Relations
Structure House
Tasc Performance; New Orleans, LA Digital Advertising, Event Sponsorships, Grassroots Activities, PR Campaign, SEO, Social Media
Teradata Corporation
TigerSwan
New-Trailways Transportation System (Marketing Agency of Record)
Tweetsie Railroad
U.S. Polo Association
USA Futsal Marketing, Public Relations
The Variable Public Relations Campaign
New-Veteran Golfers Association Public Relations, Sponsorship
Wallace Family Racing Endorsement, Marketing, PR, Sponsorship
The Warnaco Group, Inc. Speedo
Wrangler Advanced Comfort Jeans, Social Media, Traditional Public Relations

Branches

French/West/Vaughan, Inc.
185 Madison Ave Ste 401, New York, NY 10016
Tel.: (212) 213-8562
Web Site: www.fwv-us.com

National Agency Associations: COPF

Agency Specializes In: Advertising

Rick French *(Chm & CEO)*
Barrie Hancock *(Sr VP)*
Chris Shigas *(Sr VP)*
Hayes Grooms *(VP-Sports & Entertainment)*
Alexander Aigen *(Acct Coord)*

Accounts:
Cardiac Wellness
Continental Teves
Dunn
Gitano
Natural Pleasures
Swatch
TrustAtlantic Financial
VF Imagewear

French/West/Vaughan, Inc.
2211 E 7th Ave, Tampa, FL 33605
Tel.: (727) 647-0770
E-Mail: jglasure@fwv-us.com
Web Site: www.fwv-us.com

Employees: 70

National Agency Associations: COPF

Agency Specializes In: Advertising

David Gwyn *(Pres)*
Natalie Best *(Exec VP & Dir-Client Svc)*
Barrie Hancock *(Sr VP)*
Chris Shigas *(Sr VP)*
Melissa Rivera *(VP)*

Accounts:
Luol Deng - Miami Heat Forward (Marketing & Endorsement Agency of Record)
Wrangler

FRESH MEDIA GROUP
382 W Chestnut St Ste 109, Washington, PA 15301
Tel.: (724) 503-4826
Web Site: www.freshmediagroup.us

Year Founded: 2012

Agency Specializes In: Advertising, Brand Development & Integration, Graphic Design, Internet/Web Design, Media Buying Services, Print, Social Media

A. J. Brach *(Co-Owner)*
Jennifer Trapuzzano *(Owner)*
Fawn Schooley *(Office Mgr)*

Accounts:
Casa Vite Imagine Design
Dunkin' Brands Group, Inc.
Four Seasons Resort
General Industries
Golf Club of Washington
John Bruner
Krencys Bakery
Sarris Candies
Washington Area Credit Union
Washington Health System Robotics

FRESHBRICK, INC.
761 Koehler Ave, Ronkonkoma, NY 11779
Tel.: (631) 285-7825
Fax: (631) 285-7826
E-Mail: dd@freshbrick.com
Web Site: www.freshbrick.com

Employees: 10
Year Founded: 2000

Don Donaudy *(Partner-Creative & Production)*
Lori Thomas *(Partner-Accounts & Plng)*
Teresa Pelio *(Acct Supvr)*

Accounts:
Cohen's Fashion Optical
Dazzle D Productions
DengTV
Empire National Bank
MSW Group International
New York Commercial Bank
Sterling Optical
United States Rebar
Widex

FRESHBUZZ MEDIA, INC.
263 Harloe Ave Ste 100, Pismo Beach, CA 93449
Tel.: (805) 242-2618
Fax: (805) 244-9292
Toll Free: (877) 285-0857
E-Mail: info@freshbuzzmedia.com
Web Site: www.freshbuzzmedia.com

Employees: 12
Year Founded: 2010

Agency Specializes In: Content, Graphic Design, Social Marketing/Nonprofit, Social Media, Strategic Planning/Research

Judith L. Cohen *(Founder & Pres)*
Jonni Biaggini *(Dir-Mktg Strategy)*
Pacha Hornaday *(Dir-Creative & Interactive)*
Chris Johns *(Dir-Search Mktg)*
Molly Schiff *(Mgr-Content & Community)*

Accounts:
Aveda, Inc. (Agency of Record) Digital/Social & Community Engagement; 2014
Domaine Porto Carras (Greece) (Agency of Record) Digital/Social & Community Engagement; 2015
Educational Employees Credit Union (EECU) Social Promotional Application Design & Campaign; 2014
Graco Baby Products; 2014
Grand Millennium Hotel Group Social Applications & Campaign; 2013
Habitat Home and Garden (Agency of Record) Digital/Social & Community Engagement; 2014
Sotheby's International Realty (Agency of Record) Digital/Social & Community Engagement; 2014
Starwood Hotels and Resorts Agency AOR, Digital/Social & Community Engagement; 2014
Sunset Magazine and SAVOR the Central Coast (Agency of Record) Digital/Social & Community Engagement; 2014
Wines of Naoussa (Greece) (Agency of Record) Digital/Social & Community Engagement; 2015

FREYDELL+TORRES DIVERSITY
436 E 58th St Ste 3D, New York, NY 10022
Tel.: (917) 797-6189
E-Mail: hfreydell@godiversity.com
Web Site: godiversity.com/

Humberto Freydell *(Owner)*

Accounts:
AARP
Catholic Relief Services
The Hartford
Virgin Mobile USA, Inc.

FROEHLICH COMMUNICATIONS, INC.
309 Ct Ave Ste 234, Des Moines, IA 50309
Tel.: (515) 699-8502
Fax: (515) 699-8503
Web Site: www.froehlichcomm.com

Agency Specializes In: Advertising, Collateral, Event Planning & Marketing, Internet/Web Design, Logo & Package Design, Media Planning, Print, Strategic Planning/Research

Scott Froehlich *(Pres)*

Accounts:
American Standard
Maytag

FRONTIER 3 ADVERTISING
15127 Kercheval Ave, Grosse Pointe Park, MI 48230
Tel.: (313) 347-0333
Web Site: www.frontier3.com

Year Founded: 2002

Agency Specializes In: Advertising, Collateral, Logo & Package Design, Market Research, Media Planning, Out-of-Home Media, Outdoor, Print, Radio, T.V.

Bill Mestdagh *(Pres & CEO)*
Eric Turin *(Partner & Exec VP)*
Andrew Roa *(Dir-Social Media & Internet Mktg)*
Jody Yacobucci *(Dir-Media)*

Accounts:
The Old Club

FRONTLINE ADVERTISING, INC.
52 Conmar Dr, Rochester, NY 14609
Tel.: (585) 787-9000
Fax: (585) 787-9001
E-Mail: frank@frontlineadvertising.com
Web Site: www.frontlineadvertising.com

Employees: 10
Year Founded: 1994

Agency Specializes In: Brand Development & Integration, Broadcast, Business-To-Business, Collateral, Consumer Marketing, Corporate Identity, Direct Response Marketing, Electronic Media, Event Planning & Marketing, Graphic Design, Internet/Web Design, Logo & Package Design, Multimedia, Newspapers & Magazines, Out-of-Home Media, Outdoor, Production, Public Relations, Publicity/Promotions, Radio, Retail, Sales Promotion

Approx. Annual Billings: $12,300,000

Breakdown of Gross Billings by Media: Brdcst.: 40%; Collateral: 10%; Event Mktg.: 10%; Graphic Design: 20%; Logo & Package Design: 10%; Newsp.: 10%

Frank Contestabile *(Pres)*
June Provenzano *(Dir-Media)*

Accounts:
Arts & Cultural Council of Greater Rochester
Charlotte Furniture & Appliance; Rochester, NY
Dorschel Automotive
Renaissance Square; Rochester, NY
Rochester Athletic Club; Rochester, NY
Rochester Colonial Manufacturing; Rochester, NY
Rochester Genesee Regional Transit Authority
The Ski Company

FROZEN FIRE
420 S Cesar Chavez Blvd, Dallas, TX 75201
Tel.: (214) 745-3456
Web Site: www.frozenfire.com

Year Founded: 1999

Agency Specializes In: Advertising, Brand Development & Integration, Digital/Interactive, Graphic Design, Internet/Web Design, Social Media

Brad Davis *(Owner & CEO)*
Greg Spindler *(Chief Strategy Officer)*
Nikki Canga *(Acct Dir)*
Pete Warren *(Dir-Ops)*
Mindi Long *(Chief Relationship Officer)*

Accounts:
Ace Cash Express, Inc.
IDEA Public Schools

FRUITT COMMUNICATIONS, INC.
229 Massachusetts Ave Ste 3, Lexington, MA 02420-4040
Tel.: (781) 274-0330
Fax: (781) 674-9192
E-Mail: lisa@fruittcomm.com
Web Site: www.fruittcomm.com

Lisa Fruitt *(Owner)*

Accounts:
Atlantic Western Consulting
Babson Interactive
Chestnut Children's Center
The Druker Company
Maimonides School
McNeil Real Estate

FRY COMMUNICATIONS INC.
800 W Church Rd, Mechanicsburg, PA 17055-3179
Tel.: (717) 766-0211
Fax: (717) 691-0341
Toll Free: (800) 334-1429
E-Mail: info@frycomm.com
Web Site: www.frycomm.com

Employees: 1,850
Year Founded: 1934

Henry Fry *(Chm)*
David Fry *(CTO)*
Mark Stoner *(Gen Mgr-Plng Ops & Customer Svc)*
Melissa Durborow *(Dir-Mktg)*
Glenn Sollenberger *(Dir-Postal Affairs & Distr)*
Mike Weber *(Dir-Mfg)*
Brad Reynolds *(Mgr-Customer Svc)*
Harry Warner *(Mgr-Quality Assurance)*
Terry Yeh *(Mgr-MIS)*

Accounts:
Snyder-Diamond; Santa Monica, CA Marketing Agency

FRY/HAMMOND/BARR INCORPORATED
(Name Changed to &Barr)

FSC MARKETING + DIGITAL
(Formerly FSC Marketing Communications)
1 Oxford Ctr, Pittsburgh, PA 15219
Tel.: (412) 471-3700
Fax: (412) 471-9323
E-Mail: info@fscmarketing.com
Web Site: fscmarketing.com/

Employees: 10
Year Founded: 1956

Agency Specializes In: Advertising, Brand Development & Integration, Business-To-Business, Collateral, Communications, Consulting, Consumer Goods, Consumer Marketing, Corporate Identity, Customer Relationship Management, Digital/Interactive, Direct Response Marketing, Exhibit/Trade Shows, Health Care Services, Hospitality, In-Store Advertising, Integrated Marketing, International, Internet/Web Design, Legal Services, Logo & Package Design, Market Research, Medical Products, New Product Development, Package Design, Planning & Consultation, Point of Purchase, Point of Sale, Promotions, Public Relations, Radio, Sales Promotion, Social Marketing/Nonprofit, Strategic Planning/Research, Transportation

Approx. Annual Billings: $22,646,000

Breakdown of Gross Billings by Media: Collateral: 10%; Consulting: 20%; D.M.: 10%; Exhibits/Trade Shows: 5%; Logo & Package Design: 5%; Point of Purchase: 5%; Production: 5%; Pub. Rels.: 10%; Radio & T.V.: 5%; Sls. Promo.: 25%

Rich Hurey *(CFO & Controller)*
Sadie Nius *(Dir-Ops)*
Brooke Neal *(Mgr-Creative Svcs)*

Accounts:
Conroy Foods; Pittsburgh, PA Consumer Goods; 2003
Gulf Chemical & Metallurgical Corp.
North American Scientific/NOMOS Radiation Oncology
Pittsburgh Downtown Partnership; Pittsburgh, PA
Santinelli International; New York, NY
The W.W. Henry Company; Alliquipa, PA; 2001

FTI CONSULTING
(Formerly FD Americas Public Affairs)
1101 K St NW 9th Fl, Washington, DC 20005
Tel.: (202) 312-9100
Fax: (202) 312-9101
Web Site: www.fticonsulting.com

Year Founded: 1993

National Agency Associations: PAC

Agency Specializes In: Agriculture, Automotive, Aviation & Aerospace, Brand Development & Integration, Broadcast, Cable T.V., Collateral, Communications, Consulting, Consumer Marketing, Corporate Communications, Corporate Identity, Direct Response Marketing, Education, Environmental, Event Planning & Marketing, Financial, Government/Political, Graphic Design, High Technology, Hispanic Market, Information Technology, Internet/Web Design, Logo & Package Design, Pharmaceutical, Public Relations, Strategic Planning/Research, Transportation

Kristina Moore *(Mng Dir)*
David M. Johnson *(CFO)*
Paul Linton *(Chief Strategy Officer)*
Edward Reilly *(CEO-Strategic Comm)*
Curtis Lu *(Gen Counsel)*
Tom Conway *(Sr Mng Dir-Strategic Comm)*
Jackson Dunn *(Sr Mng Dir-Strategic Comm)*
Casey Clark *(Mng Dir-Strategic Comm)*
Matthew Blunt *(VP-Global Talent Acq)*

Accounts:
Fluor Corporation
Pan American Health & Education Organization Foundation Global Violence Prevention; 2008
The Portland Cement Association; 2008
The Salt River Project

FUEGO COMMUNICATIONS & MARKETING INC
6900 Turkey Lake Rd, Orlando, FL 32819
Tel.: (407) 641-4460
Web Site: www.fuegocommunications.com

Year Founded: 2005

Agency Specializes In: Advertising, Brand Development & Integration, Logo & Package Design, Public Relations

Andres Goyanes *(Exec Dir)*

Accounts:
Braven Painting
Classic Real Estate School
Dyches Funeral Home
KuberneoCPA
Red Road LLC

FUEL
1705 N Oak St, Myrtle Beach, SC 29577
Tel.: (843) 839-1456
Fax: (843) 839-1460
E-Mail: info@fueltravel.com
Web Site: www.fueltravel.com

Employees: 20

Agency Specializes In: Consulting, Digital/Interactive, Email, Local Marketing, Media Relations, Search Engine Optimization, Web (Banner Ads, Pop-ups, etc.)

Scott Brandon *(CEO)*
Stuart Butler *(COO)*
David Day *(CTO)*
Nick McNeill *(Chief Creative Officer)*
Pete Dimaio *(VP-Bus Strategy)*
Jay Juan Garcia *(Dir-Sls & Mktg)*
Melissa Kavanagh *(Dir-Analytics)*
Bryce Pate *(Dir-Support-Guestdesk & IQrez)*
Alyssa Fate *(Specialist-Client Success)*

Accounts:
Century 21 Boling & Associates, Inc.
Debordieu Vacation Guide
Endless Fun Resorts
Myrtle Beach Golf Holiday
Myrtle Beach National Brittain Property Management
MyrtleBeachHotels.com
Wilmington & Beaches Convention & Visitors Bureau

FUEL AGENCY, INC.
1300 Clay St 6th Fl, Oakland, CA 94612
Tel.: (510) 834-1400
Fax: (510) 482-5593
E-Mail: kmonte@fuelagency.com
Web Site: www.fuelagency.com

Employees: 12
Year Founded: 1989

Agency Specializes In: Advertising, Brand Development & Integration, Consumer Publications, Corporate Identity, Graphic Design, Internet/Web Design, Logo & Package Design, Media Buying Services, New Product Development, Newspapers & Magazines, Out-of-Home Media, Planning & Consultation, Point of Purchase, Radio, Strategic Planning/Research

Approx. Annual Billings: $12,000,000

Breakdown of Gross Billings by Media: Bus. Publs.: $1,200,000; Collateral: $1,680,000; Comml. Photography: $600,000; Consulting: $1,800,000; Consumer Publs.: $2,400,000; Newsp.: $3,600,000; Strategic Planning/Research: $720,000

Guy Needham *(Partner & Dir-Creative)*
Patrick Meehan *(Head-Creative)*
Pedro Bexiga *(Dir-Creative)*
Marcelo Lourenco *(Dir-Creative)*
Heather Jaboor *(Acct Mgr)*
Adam O'Neill *(Mgr-Creative Svcs & Production)*
Richard Warrell *(Copywriter)*
Sebastian Sarria *(Senior Graphic Designer)*

Accounts:
Alliance Laundry Systems
Avago Technologies; Santa Clara, CA; 2005
Department of Education & Early Childhood Development
Fresh Choice Restaurants, LLC; Morgan Hill, CA; 1998
National Semiconductor; Santa Clara, CA; 2002
Shebeen

FUEL CREATIVE GROUP
2321 P St 2nd Fl, Sacramento, CA 95816
Tel.: (916) 669-1591
Web Site: www.fuelcreativegroup.com

Year Founded: 2004

Agency Specializes In: Advertising, Brand Development & Integration, Graphic Design, Print, Social Media

Brent Rector *(Principal & Art Dir)*
Steve Worth *(Principal & Designer)*
Niki Kangas *(Acct Exec)*
Haley Titus *(Designer)*

Accounts:
New-Mazda Raceway Laguna Seca

FUEL MARKETING
703 E 1700 S, Salt Lake City, UT 84105
Tel.: (801) 484-2888
Fax: (801) 484-2944
Web Site: www.fuelmarketing.com

Agency Specializes In: Advertising, Broadcast, Digital/Interactive, Print, Public Relations

Donna Lifsey-Foster *(Partner)*
Paul Eagleston *(Dir-Creative)*
Christine Grafer *(Specialist-Social Media)*

Accounts:
American Library Association
Challenger School
Control4 Corporation
DirectBuy, Inc.
Gold's Gym International, Inc
Low Book Sales
Physician Group of Utah, Inc

FUEL PARTNERSHIPS
6111 Broken Sound Pkwy NW Ste 265, Boca Raton, FL 33487
Tel.: (561) 961-5436
Web Site: www.fuelpartnerships.com

Year Founded: 2011

Agency Specializes In: Advertising, Brand Development & Integration, Consulting, Consumer Marketing, Digital/Interactive, Email, Event Planning & Marketing, Graphic Design, In-Store Advertising, Internet/Web Design, Local Marketing, Market Research, Media Buying Services, Media Planning, Media Relations, Out-of-Home Media, Outdoor, Planning & Consultation, Point of Purchase, Point of Sale, Production (Ad, Film, Broadcast), Promotions, Publicity/Promotions, Retail, Sales Promotion, Social Marketing/Nonprofit, Social Media, Strategic Planning/Research, Sweepstakes, Web (Banner Ads, Pop-ups, etc.)

Erik Rosenstrauch *(Pres & CEO)*
Matt Custage *(VP-Client Svcs)*
Justin Stephens *(Dir-Retail Mktg & Bus Dev)*
Caitlin Connors *(Acct Coord)*

Accounts:
Sheets Brand Sheets Energy Strips, Sleep Sheets; 2011

FUEL YOUTH ENGAGEMENT
(Formerly Fuel Industries)
7 Hinton Ave N Ste 100, Ottawa, ON K1Y 4P1 Canada
Tel.: (613) 224-6738
Fax: (613) 224-6802
E-Mail: engage@fuelyouth.com
Web Site: www.fuelyouth.com/

Employees: 70
Year Founded: 1999

National Agency Associations: IAB

Agency Specializes In: Advertising, Advertising Specialties, Branded Entertainment, Digital/Interactive, Electronic Media, Entertainment, Internet/Web Design, Publicity/Promotions, Sales Promotion, Strategic Planning/Research, Teen Market, Viral/Buzz/Word of Mouth

Approx. Annual Billings: $20,000,000

Breakdown of Gross Billings by Media: Internet Adv.: 100%

Dave Ozipko *(Founder, Partner, COO, Exec Dir-Creative)*
Chris Greenfield *(Pres)*
Nick Tremmaglia *(Product Dir)*
Jeff Bacon *(Dir-Production)*
Jarret Peterson *(Dir-Quality Assurance, Release Mgmt & Live Ops)*
Colin Tisdall *(Dir-IT & Facilities)*
Russell Mullins *(Mgr-Resource)*

Accounts:
Bestbuy Online Executive Games
BMW Mini www.motormate.com
Coors Coors Golf Games
New-DreamWorks
FedEx Football, Golf
Gap www.watchmechange.com
GE Eco Sites
GM My GM Link
New-Hasbro
HBO
New-Mattel
McDonald's Campaign: "McDonald's Happy Studio"
New-Microsoft
New-NASCAR
New-NFL
Wrigleys

FULL CIRCLE
648 Monroe Ave NW Ste 500, Grand Rapids, MI 49503
Tel.: (616) 301-3400
Fax: (616) 301-8069
E-Mail: info@thinkfullcircle.com
Web Site: www.thinkfullcircle.com

Year Founded: 2001

Agency Specializes In: Advertising, Brand Development & Integration, Logo & Package Design, Social Media

Steve Harney *(Principal & Strategist-Brand)*
Gregg Burns *(Art Dir)*
Adam Mikrut *(Dir-Creative)*
Morgan Moallemian *(Dir-Art)*
Kellie Vandyke *(Dir-Art)*

Accounts:
Belden Brick & Supply Company
Garrison Dental
Health & Wellness company
Kent Power
Magnum Coffee
New-Two Men and a Truck
Universal Forest Products, Inc.
Wegmans Food Markets, Inc.
Wisinski Group

FULL CIRCLE MARKETING
5372 Southern Ave, Dallas, TX 75209
Tel.: (214) 738-6538
Toll Free: (800) 727-7335
Web Site: www.fullcirclemkt.com

E-Mail for Key Personnel:
President: ghomsey@fullcirclemkt.com
Media Dir.: ADunford@fullcirclemkt.com

Employees: 9
Year Founded: 1981

Agency Specializes In: Advertising, Brand

Development & Integration, Business-To-Business, Collateral, Direct Response Marketing, Financial, Health Care Services, High Technology, Internet/Web Design, Investor Relations, Logo & Package Design, Point of Purchase, Public Relations, Real Estate, Sales Promotion

Approx. Annual Billings: $1,000,000 Fees Capitalized

Breakdown of Gross Billings by Media: Bus. Publs.: $300,000; Collateral: $200,000; D.M.: $100,000; Other: $100,000; Pub. Rels.: $300,000

Gary L. Homsey *(Owner)*

FULL CONTACT ADVERTISING

186 Lincoln St, Boston, MA 02111
Tel.: (617) 948-5400
Fax: (617) 249-0144
E-Mail: amy.brownweber@gofullcontact.com
Web Site: www.gofullcontact.com

Employees: 35
Year Founded: 2006

Agency Specializes In: Above-the-Line, Advertising, Advertising Specialties, Affluent Market, Arts, Automotive, Brand Development & Integration, Branded Entertainment, Broadcast, Business-To-Business, Cable T.V., Children's Market, Collateral, Communications, Computers & Software, Consulting, Consumer Goods, Consumer Marketing, Consumer Publications, Content, Corporate Communications, Corporate Identity, Digital/Interactive, Direct Response Marketing, Direct-to-Consumer, E-Commerce, Electronics, Email, Entertainment, Environmental, Event Planning & Marketing, Exhibit/Trade Shows, Experience Design, Fashion/Apparel, Financial, Food Service, Graphic Design, Health Care Services, High Technology, Hospitality, Household Goods, Identity Marketing, In-Store Advertising, Integrated Marketing, International, Internet/Web Design, Leisure, Local Marketing, Logo & Package Design, Luxury Products, Magazines, Market Research, Men's Market, Merchandising, Mobile Marketing, Multicultural, Multimedia, New Product Development, New Technologies, Newspaper, Newspapers & Magazines, Out-of-Home Media, Outdoor, Package Design, Pets , Planning & Consultation, Point of Purchase, Point of Sale, Print, Production, Production (Ad, Film, Broadcast), Promotions, Public Relations, Publicity/Promotions, Radio, Real Estate, Regional, Restaurant, Retail, Sales Promotion, Search Engine Optimization, Social Marketing/Nonprofit, Social Media, Sponsorship, Sports Market, Strategic Planning/Research, Sweepstakes, T.V., Teen Market, Trade & Consumer Magazines, Transportation, Travel & Tourism, Tween Market, Urban Market, Viral/Buzz/Word of Mouth, Web (Banner Ads, Pop-ups, etc.), Women's Market

Approx. Annual Billings: $30,000,000

Tim Foley *(Partner & Creative Dir)*
Marty Donohue *(Partner & Dir-Creative)*
Jennifer Maltby *(Chief Strategy Officer)*
Brian Dedering *(Sr Dir-Art)*
Lauren Kimball *(Dir-Acct Mgmt)*
Rick Butler *(Acct Dir)*
Amy Brown Weber *(Dir-Bus Dev)*
Sara Capaccio *(Acct Mgr)*

Accounts:
Arbella Insurance Personal & Commercial Insurance; 2012
Atlantic Broadband Telecommunications; 2012
Boston Beer Company; 2011
New-Cambridge Savings Bank (Agency of Record) Digital, Media Strategy
Cumberland Farms; Framingham, MA Broadcast, Campaign: "Moving Day", Campaign: "The Cumberland Farms Taste Test", Farmouse Blend, OOH, Radio, Retail; 2008
D'Angelo; 2014
Fisher-Price Creative Strategy, Digital, Global Broadcast, Thomas & Friends (Advertising Agency of Record); 2015
New-Moo; 2015
One Mission; 2013
Papa Gino's Fast Casual Dining & Delivery
Symmons Commercial/Residential Shower Systems & Faucets; 2014

FULL COURT PRESS COMMUNICATIONS

409 13th St 13th Fl, Oakland, CA 94612
Tel.: (510) 271-0640
E-Mail: info@fcpcommunications.com
Web Site: www.fcpcommunications.com

Year Founded: 2001

Agency Specializes In: Brand Development & Integration, Crisis Communications, Event Planning & Marketing, Government/Political, Media Relations, Media Training, Social Marketing/Nonprofit, Strategic Planning/Research

Dan Cohen *(Owner)*
Sarah Hersh *(VP)*

Accounts:
American Civil Liberties Union
Death Penalty Focus
East Bay Asian Youth Center
Organic Power
Pacific Forest
Park Day School
Solano Avenue Association

FULL SPECTRUM BRANDING, LLC

19514 Encino Spur, San Antonio, TX 78259
Tel.: (210) 215-0905
E-Mail: ralph@fullspectrumbranding.com
Web Site: www.fullspectrumbranding.com

Agency Specializes In: Advertising, Brand Development & Integration, Internet/Web Design, Logo & Package Design, Social Media

Ralph D. Klonz *(Gen Mgr-Sls)*
Ernest Castanon *(Designer)*

Accounts:
San Antonio School for the Performing Arts
William J. Cruse DDS

FULL STEAM MARKETING & DESIGN

60 W Market St Ste 150, Salinas, CA 93901
Tel.: (831) 757-4164
Fax: (831) 757-7574
E-Mail: info@fullsteam.com
Web Site: www.fullsteam.com

Employees: 14
Year Founded: 1984

National Agency Associations: Second Wind Limited

Agency Specializes In: Advertising, Agriculture, Bilingual Market, Brand Development & Integration, Business-To-Business, Cable T.V., Collateral, Consulting, Consumer Goods, Consumer Marketing, Consumer Publications, Corporate Communications, Corporate Identity, Direct-to-Consumer, Food Service, Graphic Design, Hispanic Market, Identity Marketing, In-Store Advertising, Integrated Marketing, Internet/Web Design, Logo & Package Design, Media Buying Services, Media Planning, Medical Products, Merchandising, Multicultural, Multimedia, New Product Development, Newspapers & Magazines, Outdoor, Package Design, Podcasting, Point of Purchase, Point of Sale, Print, Production, Production (Print), Radio, Real Estate, Retail, Sales Promotion, Seniors' Market, Social Marketing/Nonprofit, Social Media, T.V., Teen Market, Trade & Consumer Magazines, Travel & Tourism, Web (Banner Ads, Pop-ups, etc.), Women's Market

Approx. Annual Billings: $2,300,000

Breakdown of Gross Billings by Media: Brdcst.: $50,000; Corp. Communications: $300,000; Graphic Design: $400,000; Logo & Package Design: $700,000; Point of Sale: $850,000

Craig Kaufman *(Owner)*
Kathy Matthews *(Controller)*

Accounts:
Big Sur Land Trust; Carmel, CA
The California Department of Forestry & Fire Protection, Monterey-San Benito Unit
Earthbound Farm; San Juan Bautista; CA
Fresh Express; Salinas, CA; 1984
HSBC
Language Line Services Holdings Inc.; Monterey, CA
Monterey Bay Aquarium; Monterey, CA; 2010
Monterey Meeting Connection; Monterey, CA
Ocean Mist Farms; Castroville, CA; 2008
Pacific International Marketing
River Ranch Foods LLC; Salinas, CA; 2008
Robert Mann Packaging
Urban Community Partners; Monterey, CA; 2008

FULL-THROTTLE COMMUNICATIONS INC.

668 Flinn Ave Ste 28, Moorpark, CA 93021
Tel.: (805) 529-3700
Fax: (805) 529-3701
E-Mail: info@full-throttlecom.com
Web Site: www.full-throttlecom.com

Agency Specializes In: Advertising, Brand Development & Integration, Broadcast, Collateral, Corporate Identity, Digital/Interactive, Media Buying Services, Media Planning, Print, Public Relations

Jason Bear *(Pres & CEO)*
Jonina Costello *(Mgr-PR)*

Accounts:
The Bullet Bunker (Agency of Record) Advertising, Marketing, Public Relations
Canyon Coolers Marketing, Public Relations
Midland Radio Corporation (Agency of Record) Public Relations, Strategic Marketing, X-Talker Series
Optisan Marketing

FULL TILT ADVERTISING

2550 Meridian Blvd Ste 200, Franklin, TN 37067
Tel.: (615) 528-2663
Web Site: www.fulltiltadvertising.com

Agency Specializes In: Advertising, Email, Outdoor, Print, Radio, T.V.

Carl Brenner *(Founder & Pres)*

Accounts:
Walker Chevrolet

FULLHOUSE INTERACTIVE

(Acquired & Absorbed by Laughlin/Constable, Inc.)

FULLSIXADVERTISING

(Acquired by Havas)

FUNK/LEVIS & ASSOCIATES
931 Oak St, Eugene, OR 97401
Tel.: (541) 485-1932
Fax: (541) 485-3460
E-Mail: info@funklevis.com
Web Site: www.funklevis.com

Employees: 11
Year Founded: 1980

Agency Specializes In: Advertising, Brand Development & Integration, Communications, Corporate Identity, Graphic Design, Logo & Package Design

Revenue: $13,000,000

Anne Marie Levis *(Pres & Dir-Creative)*
Mindy Deforest *(Acct Mgr)*
Jessica Crossley *(Copywriter & Strategist-Social Media)*
Anna Knutson *(Acct Exec)*
Trevor Steele *(Strategist-Digital Comm)*
Christopher Berner *(Sr Designer)*

Accounts:
University of Oregon

FUNKHAUS
1855 Industrial St Ste 103, Los Angeles, CA 90021
Tel.: (213) 259-3865
E-Mail: info@funkhausdesign.com
Web Site: www.funkhaus.us

Year Founded: 2011

Agency Specializes In: Advertising, Brand Development & Integration, Content, Digital/Interactive, Exhibit/Trade Shows, Logo & Package Design, Print, Production

David Funkhouser *(Owner & Dir-Creative)*
Drew Baker *(Partner & Head-Tech)*
Nicholas Dies *(Partner & Exec Producer)*

Accounts:
Black Dog Film
Cap Gun Collective
Carbon VFX
Community Films
Demand Media, Inc.
Emoto Music
Harvest Films
MJZ
Mutato
O Positive
The Peach Kings
Prettybird
Raconteur
The True East
Whitehouse Post

FUOR DIGITAL
444 N Wells Ste 502, Chicago, IL 60654
Tel.: (312) 257-2240
Fax: (312) 278-0200
E-Mail: media@fuor.net
Web Site: fuor.com

Year Founded: 2006

Agency Specializes In: Advertising, Email, Mobile Marketing, Search Engine Optimization, Web (Banner Ads, Pop-ups, etc.)

Rachel Jarvis *(COO)*

Accounts:
Cargill
FPL
Loyola University Chicago
MSG
NOCC
Republic of Peru Tourism Services
Zimmer

FURBER ADVERTISING, LLC
(Formerly Furber Advertising)
2840 Commercial Center Blvd, Katy, TX 77494
Tel.: (713) 524-0382
E-Mail: info@furberadvertising.com
Web Site: www.furberadvertising.com

Employees: 3
Year Founded: 2002

Agency Specializes In: Advertising, Advertising Specialties, Bilingual Market, Hispanic Market, Local Marketing, Media Buying Services, Media Relations, Outdoor, Production, Radio, Recruitment, Retail, Sports Market, T.V.

Paola Plaza *(Principal)*

Accounts:
Goodman Financial

FURMAN ROTH ADVERTISING
801 2nd Ave 14th Fl, New York, NY 10017-4706
Tel.: (212) 687-2300
Fax: (212) 687-0858
E-Mail: eroth@furmanroth.com
Web Site: www.furmanroth.com

E-Mail for Key Personnel:
Media Dir.: mlefkowitz@furmanroth.com

Employees: 25
Year Founded: 1954

National Agency Associations: 4A's-LAA

Agency Specializes In: Electronic Media, Media Buying Services, Out-of-Home Media, Print, Radio, Retail, T.V.

Ernie Roth *(Pres & CEO)*
Jacki Friedman *(Partner, Sr VP & Dir-Acct Svcs)*
Stephen Friedman *(Partner, Sr VP & Dir-Acct Svcs)*
Barry Glenn *(Sr Dir-Art)*
Sally Mutafopulos *(Office Mgr)*
Jake Rabinowitz *(Supvr-Creative)*

Accounts:
B&H
Cohen's Fashion Optical; 2006
Gold's
New York Methodist Hospital
The New York Times
Sabra
Seton Hall University
Valley Health System

Branch

Furman, Feiner Advertising
560 Sylvan Ave, Englewood Cliffs, NJ 07632
Tel.: (201) 568-1634
Fax: (201) 568-6262
E-Mail: eroth@furmanroth.com
Web Site: www.furmanroth.com

Employees: 15
Year Founded: 1972

Agency Specializes In: Recruitment, Retail

Ernie Roth *(Pres)*
Vilma Sindoni *(Mng Dir & VP)*
Mark Lefkowitz *(Exec VP & Dir-Partner Media)*
Maria LoPiccolo *(Sr VP)*
Rosemary Metz *(VP)*
Barry Glenn *(Dir-Creative)*

Accounts:
Ann Taylor
Avenue
Christmas Tree Shop
Cohens
Loft
MapQuest, Inc.
New York Methodist Hospital
Nutrisystem
Season
Seton Hall University
Sterling National Bank

FURY ADVERTISING
990 Biscayne Blvd Ste 503, Miami, FL 33132
Tel.: (305) 394-5626
E-Mail: info@furyadvertising.com
Web Site: www.furyadvertising.com

Year Founded: 2013

Agency Specializes In: Advertising, Brand Development & Integration, Broadcast, Digital/Interactive, Event Planning & Marketing, Print, Search Engine Optimization, Strategic Planning/Research

Victor Amaro *(Dir-Integrated Media)*
Jeffrey Craig *(Dir-Creative)*
Jennifer Lee *(Dir-Strategy)*
Chris Payne *(Dir-Accts)*

Accounts:
Catalyst Miami
Truck Oci

FUSE/IDEAS
8 Winchester Pl, Winchester, MA 01890
Tel.: (617) 776-5800
Fax: (617) 776-5821
E-Mail: info@fuseideas.com
Web Site: www.fuseideas.com

Employees: 40

Agency Specializes In: Advertising, Brand Development & Integration, Collateral, Exhibit/Trade Shows, Internet/Web Design, Multimedia, Radio, Sponsorship, T.V., Web (Banner Ads, Pop-ups, etc.)

Approx. Annual Billings: $50,000,000

Dennis Franczak *(CEO)*
Craig Goldstein *(VP & Gen Mgr)*
Rich Malak *(VP-Engrg)*
Vanessa Levin *(Exec Creative Dir)*
Kristin Ingeneri *(Acct Dir)*
Yeliza Centeio *(Dir-Analytics)*
Alaine Hansen *(Specialist-Social Media)*

Accounts:
Adidas
Bermuda Department of Tourism
Comcast
Disney
ESPN
FOX Cable Networks
HBO
Johnson & Wales University Marketing & Communication
Maine State Lottery (Advertising Agency of Record)
Massachusetts State Lottery Commission
Mercantile Bank (Agency of Record) Broadcast, Online & Social Media, Print
Nokia
Tourism Santa Fe Advertising, Broadcast, Creative, Digital, Marketing, Print, Social Media

FUSE INTERACTIVE
775 Laguna Canyon Rd, Laguna Beach, CA 92651
Tel.: (949) 376-0438
Fax: (949) 376-0498
E-Mail: info@gofuse.com
Web Site: www.gofuse.com

Employees: 50
Year Founded: 1994

Agency Specializes In: Digital/Interactive, E-Commerce, Electronic Media, Graphic Design, Information Technology, Internet/Web Design, New Product Development, Strategic Planning/Research

Approx. Annual Billings: $6,500,000

Stefan Drust *(CEO & Exec Dir-Creative)*
Brett McMillin *(Sr Dir-Art)*
Matt DeAngelo *(Assoc Dir-Creative)*
April Peron *(Mgr-Project Mgmt Team)*
Jeff Wicken *(Sr Acct Exec)*
Kelly Barrett *(Acct Exec)*
Renee Gaudio *(Acct Exec)*

Accounts:
Kawasaki

FUSEBOXWEST
6101 Del Valle Dr, Los Angeles, CA 90048
Tel.: (310) 993-7073
Web Site: fuseboxwest.com

Agency Specializes In: Advertising, Brand Development & Integration, Broadcast, Commercial Photography, Consumer Goods, Digital/Interactive, Direct Response Marketing, Event Planning & Marketing, Financial, Health Care Services, Local Marketing, Logo & Package Design, Media Planning, Mobile Marketing, Pharmaceutical, Production (Ad, Film, Broadcast), Production (Print), Promotions, Search Engine Optimization, Social Media, Strategic Planning/Research, Urban Market, Web (Banner Ads, Pop-ups, etc.)

Serafin Canchola *(Founder, CEO & Creative Dir)*
Christopher Medina *(Supvr-Mgmt)*

Accounts:
Dakota Financial
John Kelly Chocolates
Jordan Vineyards
L.A. County Department of Public Health

FUSION IDEA LAB
506 N Clark St, Chicago, IL 60654
Tel.: (312) 670-9060
Fax: (312) 670-9061
E-Mail: info@fusionidealab.com
Web Site: www.fusionidealab.com

E-Mail for Key Personnel:
President: oberman@fusionidealab.com

Employees: 10
Year Founded: 1998

Agency Specializes In: Advertising, Brand Development & Integration, Broadcast, Business Publications, Business-To-Business, Cable T.V., Children's Market, Collateral, Consumer Marketing, Consumer Publications, Corporate Identity, Direct Response Marketing, Electronic Media, Entertainment, Event Planning & Marketing, Food Service, Gay & Lesbian Market, Graphic Design, In-Store Advertising, Internet/Web Design, Local Marketing, Logo & Package Design, Magazines, New Product Development, Newspaper, Out-of-Home Media, Outdoor, Point of Sale, Print, Production, Radio, Restaurant, Retail, Sports Market, Strategic Planning/Research, T.V., Trade & Consumer Magazines, Transportation, Travel & Tourism

Mike Oberman *(Founder, Pres & Chief Creative Officer)*

Accounts:
Anheuser Busch
Budweiser
Expedia
Fox Family
Jonhson & Johnson
Lincoln Snacks
Playboy
Reed's Advertising
Remington
Target Corp.
Warner Brothers

FUSION92
440 W Ontario St, Chicago, IL 60654
Tel.: (312) 725-7784
E-Mail: info@fusion92.com
Web Site: www.fusion92.com

Agency Specializes In: Advertising, Digital/Interactive, Search Engine Optimization, Social Media

Matt Murphy *(Founder & CEO)*
Andrea Soper *(Designer)*

Accounts:
New-AT&T

FUSIONFARM
500 3rd Ave SE, Cedar Rapids, IA 52401
Tel.: (319) 368-8959
E-Mail: contact@fusionfarm.com
Web Site: www.fusionfarm.com

Year Founded: 2011

Agency Specializes In: Advertising, Brand Development & Integration, Internet/Web Design, Print, Social Media

Chris Edwards *(VP-Sls & Customer Care)*
Seth Smith *(Sr Dir-Art)*
Neil Brewster *(Dir-Art)*
Kelly Homewood *(Dir-Svcs)*
Kurt Sempf *(Dir-Creative Svcs)*
Jake Vardaman *(Dir-Art-Motion Design)*
Michael Zydzik *(Dir-Creative)*
Joe Matar *(Product Mgr)*
Stacey Stefani *(Product Mgr)*
Andy Sulhoff *(Specialist-Content Mktg)*
Ashleen Baker *(Coord-Sls)*

Accounts:
Collins Community Credit Union

FUSZION COLLABORATIVE
1420 Prince St Ste 100, Alexandria, VA 22314-2868
Tel.: (703) 548-8080
Fax: (703) 548-8382
E-Mail: fuszioninfo@fuszion.com
Web Site: www.fuszion.com

Employees: 7
Year Founded: 1996

Agency Specializes In: Advertising, Internet/Web Design, Pets , T.V.

Rick Heffner *(Owner)*
Sue Smith *(VP-Fin & Admin)*
Greg Spraker *(Sr Dir-Art)*

Accounts:
1Worldspace Satellite Radio Stations
A&E Television Network
Animal Planet Paws Across the Planet
BET Network
CNN Your Choice, Your Voice
Discovery Communications Media Literacy
Discovery Multimedia Skywatching
Discovery Networks
Discovery.com
ESPN Classic Affiliate
Fox Family Channel
FX/Nascar
The History Channel Millennium Memory Game
National Geographic Out There
Pepsi-Cola Co. Star Wars Collector's Cans
Smithsonian Brown v. Board Exhibit, Flag Day Festival, NASM Hazy Center CD-Rom
Speed Channel
Sundance Industries Custom Furniture
Teenbeat Records Sisterhood CD
Time Life Books Total Golf Maglog
Time Life Music Body & Soul, Classic Jazz
Travel Channel Barbeque Sauce
WE Television Network

FUTUREBRAND
233 Park Ave S Fl 2, New York, NY 10003
Tel.: (212) 931-6300
Fax: (212) 931-6310
E-Mail: infona@futurebrand.com
Web Site: www.futurebrand.com

Employees: 75
Year Founded: 1992

National Agency Associations: 4A's

Agency Specializes In: Brand Development & Integration

Christopher Nurko *(Chm)*
Sven Seger *(Chief Creative Officer-Americas)*
Kari Blanchard *(Exec Dir-Strategy)*
Shane Greeves *(Exec Dir-Creative-Global)*
Megan Tafelski *(Acct Exec)*
Ana Gannod *(Assoc Acct Dir)*

Accounts:
ABInBev
American Airlines AA, Logo
Casella Wines
CECP
Disney Corporate Citizenship
The Dow Chemical Company
DuPont Performance Coatings
Elanco
IHOP
John Wiley & Sons
McKesson
McKinsey & Company
Nestle Waters
Pfizer
Pitney Bowes Branding Strategy, Digital
SAE International
Teletech
Unilever
The US Army
USAA
The World Gold Council

Branches

FutureBrand
2 Waterhouse Square 140 Holborn, London, EC1N 2AE United Kingdom
Tel.: (44) 207 067 0010
Fax: (44) 870 990 5467
E-Mail: contact-london@futurebrand.com
Web Site: www.futurebrand.com

Patrick Smith *(Global CEO)*
Nick Sykes *(Pres-EMEA & CEO-London)*
Tom Adams *(Head-Strategy-Global)*
Ian Kirk *(Head-Strategy-UK)*
Simon Hill *(Gen Mgr)*
Shane Greeves *(Exec Dir-Creative-Global)*
Cerys Tusabe James *(Client Svcs Dir)*
Paul Wood *(Acct Dir)*
Stuart Dickinson *(Dir-Creative Environments & Digital)*
Polly Hopkins *(Dir-Client)*
Charles Skinner *(Dir-Strategy)*
Stefanie Mathewson *(Sr Acct Mgr)*
Leonora Peralta *(Sr Acct Mgr)*
Clare Louise Smith *(Sr Acct Mgr)*

Accounts:
Cricket Australia Campaign: "T20"
LOCOG
Morrisons Strategy
Xstrata Campaign: "Xstrata Difference"

FutureBrand
8/F Oxford House Taikoo Place, 979 King's Rd, Quarry Bay, China (Hong Kong)
Tel.: (852) 2501 7979
Fax: (852) 2544 0600
E-Mail: Jochan@futurebrand.com
Web Site: www.futurebrand.com

Lucien Harrington *(Mng Dir-Greater China)*
Josephine Chan *(Exec Dir)*
Klara Chan *(Dir-Strategy)*
Aimee Liu *(Dir-Client)*
Edwina Chan *(Sr Mgr-Comml)*
Venus Lin *(Mgr-Studio)*
Gareth Joe *(Strategist-Creative)*
Celia Leung *(Sr Designer)*
Marlboro Ma *(Sr Designer)*
Debbie Poon *(Designer)*

Accounts:
Cathay Pacific
CLP Power
Commonwealth Bank
eBay China
Joincare
Lenovo
Marco Polo Hotel Group
Shanghai Pudong Development Bank
Swire

FutureBrand
520 Bourke St Level 4, West, Melbourne, VIC 3000 Australia
Tel.: (61) 3 9604 2777
Fax: (61) 3 9604 2799
E-Mail: eputignano@futurebrand.com
Web Site: www.futurebrand.com

Employees: 20

Richard Curtis *(CEO)*
Harley Augustine *(Exec Dir-Strategy)*
Katherine Monk *(Acct Dir)*
Tanya Sulewski *(Acct Dir)*
Tony Charlton *(Dir-Creative)*
Josh Mcgregor *(Dir-Design)*
Douglas Nash *(Dir-Strategy)*
Hannes Zirknitzer *(Strategist-Brand)*

Accounts:
12th FINA World Championships
7 Eleven Munch
Amcal Max
BHP Bilton
ConnectEast Breeze
Crown Entertainment
Diners Club International
Hayman
Mitsubishi; Chadstone, Australia
OPSM
Perfolas
Streets Sunday
Yellow

FutureBrand
69 Blvd du General, Leclerc, 92583 Clichy, France
Tel.: (33) 1 55 63 13 20
Fax: (33) 1 55 63 13 21
E-Mail: contact-paris@futurebrand.com
Web Site: www.futurebrand.com

Employees: 200

Agency Specializes In: Advertising

Suzanne Stahlie *(Mng Dir)*
Magali Tardy-Guyot *(Head-Strategy)*
Jessica Girard *(Controller-Fin)*
Nicolas Gallouin *(Sr Dir-Design)*
Emmanuelle Clermont *(Acct Dir)*
Jerome Lhermenier *(Client Svcs Dir)*
Pierre Abel *(Dir-Creative)*
Maud Mulder *(Dir-Creative)*
Marc Usmati *(Dir-Design-Product & Retail)*
Barbara Viana *(Mgr-Bus Dev & Comm)*
Adeline Joffret *(Acct Exec)*

Accounts:
ACE Aviation Holdings Inc.
Barilla
Beck's Vier
Dolce Gusto
Egis
GMF
Hennessy
Latin America Skies
Martini
Mini
Movenpick
Mulino Bianco
Nespresso
Pullman
St.Lucia

FutureBrand
Avenida El Bosque Norte, Oficina 1003 Las Condes, Santiago, Chile
Tel.: (56) 2 374 2350
Fax: (56) 2 374 2249
E-Mail: contact-santiagodechile@futurebrand.com
Web Site: www.futurebrand.com

Employees: 9

Gabriel Badagnani *(Mng Dir)*
Gustavo Koniszczer *(Mng Dir-Spanish Latin America)*
Cristian Oyharcabal *(Dir-Design)*
Ivan Viquez Solorzano *(Client Dir)*

Accounts:
Arabian Canal
Breeze
Chevron
Concha y Toro
Cooper Tools
Hayman
IGY
LanChile
ME Elecmetal
Oriental Hotel Tokyo Bay
Quatar
Smart City
Smartcom
Veneto

FutureBrand
18/F Huai Hai Plaza, 1045 Huai Hai Zhong Rd, Shanghai, 200031 China
Tel.: (86) 10 8580 4250, ext. 232
Fax: (86) 10 8580 6415
E-Mail: contact-shanghai@futurebrand.com
Web Site: www.futurebrand.com

Johnson Gu *(Dir-Creative-North Asia)*

Accounts:
Corporate Avenue
Dopod
ebay
Nissan

FUZZCO INC.
85 1/2 Spring St, Charleston, SC 29403
Tel.: (843) 723-1665
Web Site: www.fuzzco.com

Year Founded: 2005

Agency Specializes In: Advertising, Brand Development & Integration, Collateral, Communications, Graphic Design, Internet/Web Design, Logo & Package Design, Print

Josh Nissenboim *(Founder & Dir-Creative)*
Cory Etzkorn *(Designer)*
Colin Pinegar *(Designer)*
Melanie Richards *(Sr Designer-Web)*

Accounts:
GIANT
Tokai Polytechnic College

FVM STRATEGIC COMMUNICATIONS
(Formerly Fleming & Van Metre)
630 W Germantown Pke Ste 400, Plymouth Meeting, PA 19462
Tel.: (610) 941-0395
Fax: (610) 941-0580
E-Mail: info@thinkfvm.com
Web Site: www.thinkfvm.com/

Employees: 25
Year Founded: 1987

Agency Specializes In: Business-To-Business, Consumer Marketing, Retail

Paul Fleming *(CEO)*
Jon Cohen *(Exec VP)*
Helen Smith *(VP & Bus Mgr)*
Jordy Pickel *(Dir-Digital Dev)*
Tom O'Brien *(Mgr-Mktg)*
Brian Taylor *(Sr Acct Exec)*
Coleman Rigg *(Jr Acct Exec)*
Emily Walsh *(Jr Acct Exec)*

Accounts:
Archdiocese of Philadelphia
Arraya Solutions Brand Positioning, Content Marketing, Website Design & Development
BASF
Commvault
ESOP Economics Content Marketing, Digital Strategy, Event Strategy, Media Planning, Social Media
Market Street Advisors Content Marketing, Creative Services
Perinatal Research Consortium Design
Philadelphia Gear
Smartsolutions
Strategic Distribution, Inc.; Bensalem, PA
UNIVAR
US Armor

FYI BRAND COMMUNICATIONS
174 5th Ave Ste 404, New York, NY 10010
Tel.: (212) 586-2240
Fax: (212) 586-2234
E-Mail: info@fyipr.com
Web Site: www.fyibrandcomm.com

Year Founded: 2001

Agency Specializes In: Advertising, Public Relations

Tammy Brook *(Pres)*

Accounts:
New-Mike Tyson
New-Russell Westbrook

G&G ADVERTISING, INC.

2804 3rd Ave N, Billings, MT 59101
Tel.: (406) 294-8113
Fax: (406) 294-8120
E-Mail: mgray@gng.net
Web Site: www.gng.net

E-Mail for Key Personnel:
President: mgray@gng.net

Employees: 10
Year Founded: 1997

Agency Specializes In: Advertising, Brand Development & Integration, Business-To-Business, Cable T.V., Collateral, Communications, Consumer Marketing, Corporate Identity, Direct Response Marketing, Entertainment, Event Planning & Marketing, Financial, Government/Political, Graphic Design, Logo & Package Design, Media Buying Services, Media Planning, Medical Products, Newspaper, Newspapers & Magazines, Out-of-Home Media, Outdoor, Print, Production, Production (Ad, Film, Broadcast), Public Relations, Radio, Recruitment, Sports Market, T.V., Teen Market, Travel & Tourism

Michael J. Gray *(Pres & Dir-Creative)*
Gerald Gray, Jr. *(VP)*
Joani Gray *(Dir-Art)*

Accounts:
Montana Tourism
Office of National Drug Control Policy; Washington, DC Anti-Drug Campaign; 1998
Us Census Bureau
W.K. Kellogg Foundation; Lansing, MI Enlace/Nahei Programs; 2003

G&G OUTFITTERS INC.

4901 Forbes Blvd, Lanham, MD 20706
Tel.: (301) 731-2099
Fax: (301) 731-5199
E-Mail: info@ggoutfitters.com
Web Site: www.ggoutfitters.com

Employees: 5

David Johnson *(CFO)*
Robert W. Crowe, Jr. *(Pres-Licensed Sports Grp)*
Christine Kenney *(Pres-Beverage Div)*
Pete Papilion *(Pres-G&G Intl Sourcing Div)*
Rusty Pepper *(Pres-Strategic Accounts Grp)*
Rich Gergar *(Exec VP)*
Wing Pokrywka *(Dir-Mktg)*
Diane Trevanthan *(Dir-Supply Chain & Procurement)*
Denise Wittmeyer *(Dir-Motorsports)*

Accounts:
Adams Automotive
Aerotec
Allegis Group
Best Western
Coca-Cola Refreshments USA, Inc.
Comcast
FannieMae
Frontier Airlines
ING Direct
Lexus
NASCAR

G&M PLUMBING

119 W Torrance Blvd Ste 2, Redondo Beach, CA 90277
Tel.: (310) 727-3555
E-Mail: laurie@gmplumbing.com
Web Site: www.gmplumbing.com

Employees: 20
Year Founded: 1999

Agency Specializes In: Advertising, Affiliate Marketing, Alternative Advertising, Automotive, Brand Development & Integration, Branded Entertainment, Broadcast, Cable T.V., Consumer Marketing, Consumer Publications, Entertainment, Food Service, Integrated Marketing, Leisure, Luxury Products, Multimedia, Newspaper, Newspapers & Magazines, Out-of-Home Media, Outdoor, Planning & Consultation, Print, Production, Production (Ad, Film, Broadcast), Production (Print), Radio, Restaurant, Strategic Planning/Research, T.V., Travel & Tourism

Mickey Taylor *(Owner)*
Glenn Miller *(Partner & Dir-Creative)*

Accounts:
Comcast
Del Taco LLC
HBO
Red Robin
Robbins Bros
THQ

G-COMMUNICATIONS

224 N Broadway Ste 302, Milwaukee, WI 53202
Tel.: (414) 225-9901
Fax: (414) 225-9930
E-Mail: gcom1289@gcom-inc.com
Web Site: www.gcom-marketing.com

Employees: 5
Year Founded: 1996

Agency Specializes In: Communications, Consulting, Recruitment, Strategic Planning/Research

Approx. Annual Billings: $2,000,000

Brandon G. Adams *(Pres)*
Dave Conde *(Dir-Art)*

G L'AGENCE

(Formerly G Branding & Design, Inc.)
465 Saint-Jean St Studio 700, Montreal, QC H2Y 2R6 Canada
Tel.: (514) 985-4181
Fax: (514) 985-4188
E-Mail: info@glagence.ca
Web Site: glagence.ca/

Employees: 10
Year Founded: 1987

Agency Specializes In: Brand Development & Integration, Graphic Design, Logo & Package Design

Luc Goodhue *(Pres)*
Sebastien Provost *(Dir-Artistic)*

Accounts:
Fruits & Passion
La Maison des Futailles

THE G3 GROUP

832 Oregon Ave Ste L, Linthicum, MD 21090
Tel.: (410) 789-7007
Fax: (410) 789-7005
Toll Free: (800) 783-1799
E-Mail: mary@graphics3.com
Web Site: www.g3group.com

Employees: 17
Year Founded: 1984

Agency Specializes In: Advertising, Automotive, Broadcast, Business-To-Business, Cable T.V., Collateral, Commercial Photography, Communications, Consumer Marketing, Digital/Interactive, Direct Response Marketing, E-Commerce, Exhibit/Trade Shows, Food Service, Graphic Design, Health Care Services, In-Store Advertising, Internet/Web Design, Local Marketing, Logo & Package Design, Magazines, Media Buying Services, Medical Products, New Product Development, Newspaper, Outdoor, Pharmaceutical, Planning & Consultation, Print, Public Relations, Radio, T.V., Yellow Pages Advertising

Mary Berman *(Co-Owner)*
Anita Schott *(Owner)*
Dan Appleget *(Dir-Mktg)*
John Pusey *(Dir-Dev & Hosting)*
Andy Goolsby *(Mgr-Admin)*
Theodore Schott *(Specialist-IT)*

Accounts:
Chesapeake Bay Crab Cake Company
Mama Mancini's
Mars Supermarkets; 1988
University of Maryland

G7 ENTERTAINMENT MARKETING

4000 Centre Pointe Dr, La Vergne, TN 37086
Tel.: (615) 768-3200
E-Mail: info@g7marketing.com
Web Site: www.g7marketing.com

Agency Specializes In: Advertising, Brand Development & Integration, Digital/Interactive, Sponsorship

Andre Gaccetta *(VP)*
Wayne Leeloy *(Head-Brand Partnerships & Digital Strategy)*
Brian Thurman *(Dir-New Bus Dev & Strategic Partnerships)*
Niki Tyree *(Acct Mgr)*
Christian Henderson *(Acct Exec)*
Kathleen Chandler Wright *(Acct Exec)*

Accounts:
The Procter & Gamble Company Covergirl

GA COMMUNICATIONS INC.

(Name Changed to PureRED)

GA CREATIVE INC

10900 NE 8th St Ste 1660, Bellevue, WA 98004
Tel.: (425) 454-0101
E-Mail: info@gacreative.com
Web Site: www.gacreative.com

Year Founded: 1984

Agency Specializes In: Advertising, Digital/Interactive, Graphic Design

Karen Axtell *(Principal)*
Julie Burke *(Principal-Brand Strategy)*
Wally Lloyd *(Principal)*
Sara Patillo *(Principal-Creative Svcs)*
Jeff Welsh *(Principal-Creative Svcs)*

Accounts:
Kidney Research Institute
PACCAR Inc.

GA HEALTHCARE COMMUNICATION

(Formerly Goble & Associates, Inc.)
1 E Wacker Dr 32nd Fl, Chicago, IL 60601-2002
Tel.: (312) 803-1900
Fax: (312) 803-1999
E-Mail: info@gacommunication.com
Web Site: www.gacommunication.com

Year Founded: 1982

Agency Specializes In: Health Care Services

Mark Goble *(Pres & COO)*
Joseph E. Kuchta *(CEO)*
Barclay Missen *(Chief Creative Officer & VP)*
Geoff Melick *(Chief Innovation Officer & Exec VP)*
Nancy Finigan *(Exec VP & Acct Grp Dir)*
Ryan Van Pelt *(Sr VP & Mng Dir-Consumer)*
Jody Cahill *(Sr VP & Dir-Ops)*

Accounts:
Baxter
Biomarin
Hospira
iBIO
Merz Pharma
Mylan
Obagi Medical Products
Sakura
Shire HGT
Shire Regenerative Medicine
Upsher-Smith
Valeritas
Vidara

THE GAB GROUP

95 S Federal Hgwy Ste 201, Boca Raton, FL 33432
Tel.: (561) 750-3500
Fax: (561) 982-4649
E-Mail: info@thegabgroup.com
Web Site: www.thegabgroup.com

Year Founded: 2004

Agency Specializes In: Advertising, Event Planning & Marketing, Graphic Design, Public Relations

Michelle Soudry *(Founder & Dir-PR)*
Simon Soudry *(CFO)*
Alison Griffiths *(Office Mgr)*
Allyson Berg *(Asst Brand Mgr)*
Elysia Volpe *(Acct Exec)*
Denise Jocson *(Sr Designer)*

Accounts:
Apura Juicery & Coffeehouse Brand Identity Marketing, Public Relations, Social Media & website design
Berman Plastic Surgery and Spa Marketing, Public Relations, Website Design
Crossroads Financial (Agency of Record) Event Planning, Golf Tournament, Marketing, Public Relations
DiscountMedicalSupplies.com Public Relations
Farmer's Table Restaurant Branding, Marketing, Public Relations, Social Media, Web Design
Fork & Knife Restaurant Design, Marketing, Public Relations, Social Media
Home Angels by NeoForm Design, Marketing, Public Relations, Social Media
Hudson at Waterway East (Agency of Record) Brand Development, Strategic Public Relations
Jim Karol
Laser Pain Care
New-The Little Chalet (Public Relations Agency of Record)
New-Melissa Weinberg Tanning & Beauty (Agency of Record)
Mellow Mushroom Pizza Bakers (Agency Of Record) Marketing, Strategic Public Relations
Oceans 234
New-Perfect Glow Sunless (Agency of Record)
Red, The Steakhouse Marketing, PR, Social Media
RegistryFinder.com
Rhino Doughnuts & Coffee Graphic Design, Marketing, Public Relations
Siemens Group Akoya
The Spirit of Giving Network (Agency of Record) Brand Identity Marketing, Website
STEAM Nightclub Public Relations
VIPwink Corp Public Relations, VIPwink
White Glove Drivers Public Relations, Social Media, Web Design
Wolfgang's Steakhouse Miami Public Relations
Yoko-San (Agency of Record) Marketing, Public Relations, Tech-at-the-Table Offering

GABRIEL DEGROOD BENDT

608 2nd Ave S Ste 129, Minneapolis, MN 55402
Tel.: (612) 547-5000
Fax: (612) 547-5090
E-Mail: info@always-thinking.com
Web Site: gdbagency.com

E-Mail for Key Personnel:
President: jbendt@always-thinking.com
Creative Dir.: tgabriel@always-thinking.com

Employees: 37
Year Founded: 1997

National Agency Associations: 4A's

Agency Specializes In: Advertising, Advertising Specialties, Affluent Market, Agriculture, Alternative Advertising, Arts, Automotive, Brand Development & Integration, Branded Entertainment, Broadcast, Business-To-Business, Cable T.V., Catalogs, Children's Market, Collateral, College, Communications, Computers & Software, Consulting, Consumer Goods, Consumer Marketing, Consumer Publications, Corporate Communications, Corporate Identity, Crisis Communications, Digital/Interactive, Direct Response Marketing, Direct-to-Consumer, E-Commerce, Education, Electronic Media, Electronics, Email, Entertainment, Environmental, Event Planning & Marketing, Exhibit/Trade Shows, Experience Design, Fashion/Apparel, Financial, Game Integration, Gay & Lesbian Market, Government/Political, Graphic Design, Guerilla Marketing, Health Care Services, High Technology, Hospitality, Household Goods, Identity Marketing, In-Store Advertising, Information Technology, Integrated Marketing, Internet/Web Design, Leisure, Local Marketing, Logo & Package Design, Luxury Products, Magazines, Marine, Market Research, Media Buying Services, Media Planning, Media Relations, Media Training, Medical Products, Men's Market, Merchandising, Mobile Marketing, Multicultural, Multimedia, New Product Development, New Technologies, Newspaper, Newspapers & Magazines, Out-of-Home Media, Outdoor, Over-50 Market, Package Design, Pets , Planning & Consultation, Point of Purchase, Point of Sale, Print, Production, Production (Print), Promotions, Public Relations, Publicity/Promotions, Radio, Regional, Restaurant, Retail, Sales Promotion, Search Engine Optimization, Seniors' Market, Social Marketing/Nonprofit, Social Media, Sponsorship, Sports Market, Stakeholders, Strategic Planning/Research, Sweepstakes, T.V., Teen Market, Trade & Consumer Magazines, Transportation, Travel & Tourism, Tween Market, Urban Market, Viral/Buzz/Word of Mouth, Web (Banner Ads, Pop-ups, etc.), Women's Market

Katie Warren *(Pres)*
Tom Gabriel *(CEO)*
Clark Lamm *(Sr Dir-Art)*
Hallee Conkey *(Supvr-Traffic & Producer-Brdcst)*
Lori Shepard *(Dir-Digital Experience)*
Maggie Thoele *(Dir-Media)*
Amy Oeth *(Mgr-Ops)*
Jacey Berg *(Supvr-Media)*
Betsy Defenbaugh *(Media Planner)*

Accounts:
3M Healthcare - Infection Prevention Div
Abbey's Hope
Activision Blizzard, Inc
AmericInn
Anytime Fitness
Bailey Nurseries
Black Forest Inn
Chuck & Don's Online, Outdoor
Crystal Farms
Game-Mill
Genesis Archery Brand Strategy, Digital, Public Relations
Hammer Made
Nuveen Investment, LLC
Park Dental Brand Development, Brand Positioning, Campaign Development, Campaign: "Smile, you've got Park Dental", Media Planning & Buying
Red Wing Shoe Company
Samsung Staron Surfaces
Science Museum of MN; Saint Paul, MN
Summit Brewing Company
Western International University
Zebco; Tulsa, OK

THE GAGE TEAM

601 S Phillips, Sioux Falls, SD 57104
Tel.: (605) 332-1242
Web Site: www.thegageteam.com

Year Founded: 2005

Agency Specializes In: Advertising, Brand Development & Integration, Event Planning & Marketing, Graphic Design, Internet/Web Design, Logo & Package Design, Print, Public Relations, Radio, T.V.

Chris Carlson *(Dir-IT)*
Chris Stanley *(Dir-Web Programming)*
Steve Veenhof *(Dir-Creative)*
Matt Gage *(Sr Mgr-Ops)*

Accounts:
Kory Davis Realty
Midway Drive In
Oahe, Inc.

GAGGI MEDIA COMMUNICATIONS, INC.

2200 Yonge Street, Suite 1711, Toronto, ON M4S 2C6 Canada
Tel.: (416) 222-4364
Fax: (416) 482-9672
Web Site: www.gaggimedia.com

Employees: 11
Year Founded: 1992

Agency Specializes In: Advertising, Event Planning & Marketing, Internet/Web Design, Local Marketing, Magazines, Media Buying Services, Media Planning, Media Relations, Newspaper, Out-of-Home Media, Promotions, Public Relations, Radio, Retail, Sponsorship, Strategic Planning/Research, T.V., Web (Banner Ads, Pop-ups, etc.)

Kelly Dutton *(Pres)*
Laura Gaggi *(CEO)*
Kirsten Carney *(VP & Acct Dir)*
Ken Kirk *(VP & Dir-Strategic Plng & Admin)*
Susan Robb *(Acct Dir)*
Jessica Petty *(Dir-Media Strategy)*
Sue Underwood *(Mgr-Fin)*

Accounts:
The Arthritis Society
Biore
Canadian Cancer Society

Canadian Life and Health Insurance
CHCH
CNE
Curel
Fort Erie Race Track
The Globe & Mail
Holt Renfrew
Humber River Hospital
Jergens
John Frieda
Kao Brands Inc.
Mackenzie Investments
Prevora
Price Waterhouse Cooper
RBC Canadian Open
Rent-a-Center
SCENE
Smoker's Helpline
Weedman

GALEWILL DESIGN

1841 Bdwy Ste 810, New York, NY 10023
Tel.: (212) 664-0606
Web Site: www.galewill.com

Agency Specializes In: Advertising, Collateral, Event Planning & Marketing, Internet/Web Design, Social Media

Bob Mckinnon *(Pres)*
Kathryn Kahler Vose *(Mng Dir)*
Yvonne Carrasco *(Dir-Grantee Rels)*
Joseph Pullen *(Dir-Partnerships)*

Accounts:
National Geographic Channel
The Robert Wood Johnson Foundation
Shape Your World

GALLAGHER ADVERTISING INCORPORATED

PO Box 2085, Linden, NJ 07036
Mailing Address:
PO BOX 2085, Linden, NJ 07036-0010
Tel.: (908) 718-5487
E-Mail: gallwebmaster@galadv.com
Web Site: www.galadv.com

Year Founded: 1976

Agency Specializes In: Advertising, Corporate Identity, Email, Exhibit/Trade Shows, Internet/Web Design, Multimedia, Print

Revenue: $225,000

Brian Gallagher *(Owner)*

Accounts:
Somerset County Park Commission

GALVANEK & WAHL LLC

842 New Charleston Dr, Fuquay Varina, NC 27526
Tel.: (919) 341-2623
E-Mail: contact@gwadagency.com
Web Site: www.gwadagency.com

Employees: 5
Year Founded: 2003

Agency Specializes In: Advertising, Advertising Specialties, Brand Development & Integration, Branded Entertainment, Broadcast, Business Publications, Business-To-Business, Cable T.V., College, Communications, Consulting, Consumer Goods, Corporate Identity, Digital/Interactive, Direct Response Marketing, Electronics, Environmental, Event Planning & Marketing, Exhibit/Trade Shows, Experience Design, Financial, Government/Political, Graphic Design, Health Care Services, Identity Marketing, Infomercials, Information Technology, Integrated Marketing, Internet/Web Design, Local Marketing, Logo & Package Design, Media Buying Services, Media Planning, Multimedia, New Technologies, Newspaper, Outdoor, Over-50 Market, Print, Production, Production (Ad, Film, Broadcast), Production (Print), Promotions, Public Relations, Publishing, Radio, Real Estate, Recruitment, Search Engine Optimization, Seniors' Market, Social Marketing/Nonprofit, Sponsorship, Teen Market, Travel & Tourism, Web (Banner Ads, Pop-ups, etc.)

Revenue: $1,000,000

Jessica Galvanek *(Partner & Dir-Ops)*
Jenna Roderick *(Creative Dir)*
Sean Barkume *(Sr Graphic Designer)*

Accounts:
AR Service Direct
Greenwich Family Dental
Stratotainment
Verizon Wireless

THE GAME AGENCY

18 E 16th St 7th Fl, New York, NY 10003
Tel.: (877) 986-4263
Fax: (347) 695-1270
E-Mail: stephen.baer@thegameagency.com
Web Site: thegameagency.com

Employees: 50

Agency Specializes In: Digital/Interactive, Entertainment, Game Integration, Graphic Design, Local Marketing, Promotions

Stephen Baer *(Mng Partner)*
Richard Lowenthal *(Mng Partner)*
Joseph McDonald *(Mng Partner)*
Rajeev Paliwal *(Partner)*
Corey Redlien *(VP-Tech)*

Accounts:
American Express
Disney
EA
Intel
Lexus
McDonald's
Nintendo
Pfizer

GAME CHANGER COMMUNICATIONS

13064 Elderberry Ct, Apple Valley, MN 55124
Tel.: (612) 327-1886
Web Site: www.gamechangercommunications.com

Year Founded: 2012

Agency Specializes In: Advertising, Brand Development & Integration, Crisis Communications, Digital/Interactive, Event Planning & Marketing, Internet/Web Design, Media Relations, Media Training, Public Relations, Social Media

Jason Sprenger *(Founder & Pres)*

Accounts:
New-Forius

THE GAMS GROUP, INC.

308 W Erie St Ste 400, Chicago, IL 60654-3624
Tel.: (312) 280-2740
Fax: (312) 280-7323
E-Mail: info@gamsgroup.com
Web Site: www.gamscom.com

E-Mail for Key Personnel:
President: dave@gamsgroup.com

Employees: 20
Year Founded: 1974

Agency Specializes In: Advertising, Brand Development & Integration, Broadcast, Business-To-Business, Cable T.V., Co-op Advertising, Collateral, Communications, Consulting, Consumer Marketing, Digital/Interactive, Direct Response Marketing, E-Commerce, Electronic Media, Graphic Design, High Technology, Industrial, Infomercials, Internet/Web Design, Logo & Package Design, Magazines, Media Buying Services, New Product Development, Newspaper, Newspapers & Magazines, Out-of-Home Media, Outdoor, Pharmaceutical, Planning & Consultation, Point of Purchase, Point of Sale, Print, Production, Radio, Real Estate, Restaurant, Retail, Sales Promotion, Sweepstakes, T.V., Trade & Consumer Magazines, Travel & Tourism

Approx. Annual Billings: $38,000,000

Sylvia Garcia *(Office Mgr)*
Voni Giambrone *(Acct Exec)*

GANGWAY ADVERTISING

4313 Purdue Ave, Dallas, TX 75225
Tel.: (214) 265-7976
Web Site: www.gangwayadvertising.com

Year Founded: 2006

Randy Smoot *(Pres)*
Cynthia Smoot *(Strategist-Mktg)*

Accounts:
Waitressville
Me & Re Design

GARAGE BRANDING

410 W 4th St Ste 100, Winston Salem, NC 27101
Tel.: (336) 721-1610
Fax: (336) 721-1984
E-Mail: info@garagebranding.com
Web Site: www.garagebranding.com

Employees: 8
Year Founded: 2003

Agency Specializes In: Brand Development & Integration, Event Planning & Marketing, Guerilla Marketing, Internet/Web Design, Logo & Package Design, Media Relations, Print, Public Relations

Denzil Strickland *(Owner)*
Neil Shoffner *(Acct Svcs Dir)*
Katherine White *(Dir-Acct Svc)*
Ec Vance *(Production Mgr)*
Carloyn Strickland *(Copywriter)*

Accounts:
Audi
Bush's Baked Beans
Dial Soap
GlaxoSmithKline
Hanes
Legg Mason
Olive Garden
Remington Arms
Sealy
Syngenta
Wachovia

THE GARAGE TEAM MAZDA

3200 Bristol St Ste 300, Costa Mesa, CA 92626
Tel.: (714) 913-9900
Web Site: www.garageteammazda.com

Year Founded: 2010

National Agency Associations: 4A's

Agency Specializes In: Advertising, Sponsorship

Michael Buttlar *(CEO)*
Harvey Marco *(Chief Creative Officer)*
Brad Audet *(Exec VP & Gen Mgr)*
Stephanie Kendrick *(Sr VP & Grp Acct Dir)*
Olga Weinraub *(VP & Dir-Media & Digital-Mazda USA)*
Dan Yates *(VP & Reg Acct Dir)*
Jeffrey Dixon *(Assoc Dir-Media)*
Christy Wills *(Sr Acct Exec-Digital)*
Charles Pendleton *(Planner-Digital Media)*
Pita Rodriguez *(Asst Media Planner)*

Accounts:
Mazda Motor Corporation Advertisement, Campaign: "A Driver's Life", Campaign: "Driving Matters", Campaign: "Game Changers"', Campaign: "Superstrada", Campaign: "Zoom-Zoom", Digital, In-Print, Mazda6, Media, TV

GARD COMMUNICATIONS
1140 SW 11th Ave, Portland, OR 97205
Tel.: (503) 221-0100
Fax: (503) 226-4854
Toll Free: (800) 800-7132
E-Mail: bgard@gardcommunications.com
Web Site: www.gardcommunications.com

E-Mail for Key Personnel:
Creative Dir.: jplymale@gardcommunications.com

Employees: 20
Year Founded: 1979

Agency Specializes In: Advertising, Brand Development & Integration, Collateral, Corporate Communications, Corporate Identity, Crisis Communications, Event Planning & Marketing, Government/Political, Graphic Design, Health Care Services, Internet/Web Design, Media Buying Services, Media Planning, Media Relations, Planning & Consultation, Promotions, Public Relations, Strategic Planning/Research

Approx. Annual Billings: $12,000,000

Brian Gard *(Pres)*
Liz Fuller *(Mng Dir)*
Scott Sparling *(Sr VP)*
Valarie Grudier Edwards *(Dir-Fin & Ops)*
Michelle Helm-Carpinelli *(Dir-Media & Promo)*
John Plymale *(Dir-Creative)*
Luciana Trevisan *(Sr Acct Mgr)*
Julia Stoops *(Strategist-Digital Media)*

Accounts:
Ambre Energy North America
Huron Healthcare
O'Loughlin Trade Shows
ODS Companies
Portland General Electric
The Standard

GARDNER KEATON, INC.
3536 East Forest Lk Dr, Sarasota, FL 34232
Tel.: (941) 924-7216
Fax: (941) 924-7194
E-Mail: keaton@gardnerkeaton.com
Web Site: blog.gardnerkeaton.com/

Employees: 5
Year Founded: 1975

Agency Specializes In: Graphic Design, Internet/Web Design

Approx. Annual Billings: $800,000

Breakdown of Gross Billings by Media: Collateral: $360,000; Logo & Package Design: $160,000; Mags.: $200,000; Worldwide Web Sites: $80,000

Jim Keaton *(Designer-Visual)*

Accounts:
American Electronics Association; Washington, DC; 1996
American Shipbuilding
Bloomberg BNA
The Financial Services Roundtable; Washington, D.C.
Howell Construction Inc.
Lancaster Homes
Molloy Marketing Services
Omnifics; Alexandria, VA Office Furniture; 1985
Tagnetics
Viking Healthcare Solutions

GARFIELD GROUP
60 Blacksmith Rd, Newtown, PA 18940
Tel.: (215) 867-8600
Fax: (215) 867-8610
E-Mail: info@garfieldgroup.com
Web Site: www.garfieldgroup.com

Employees: 25
Year Founded: 1990

Agency Specializes In: Advertising, Public Relations

Revenue: $45,000,000

Larry Garfield *(Pres)*
Les Brokaw *(COO & VP)*
Bryon Lomas *(VP & Dir-Creative)*
Matt Pfluger *(VP-Digital Strategy)*
Alexa DiGaetano *(Acct Exec)*
Shannon Kelly *(Assoc Acct Exec)*

Accounts:
Accolade
Almac
ASTM
Bioclinica
DialConnection
Duff & Phelps
FamilyWize
iMedX
InstaMed
NextDocs
Opportunity Finance Network
ThinkShift
Vertex

GARMEZY MEDIA
53 Lindsley Ave, Nashville, TN 37210
Tel.: (615) 242-6878
E-Mail: frontdesk@garmezymedia.com
Web Site: www.garmezymedia.com

Employees: 5

Agency Specializes In: Advertising, Automotive, Infomercials, Local Marketing, Print, Production (Ad, Film, Broadcast), Production (Print), Radio, T.V.

Melissa Thompson *(Partner)*
Andy Garmezy *(Editor-News Assignment & Mgr-TV Station Promos)*
Pat Parker *(Dir-Media)*

GARRAND & COMPANY
Ste 201 75 Washington Ave, Portland, ME 04101-2665
Tel.: (207) 772-3119
Fax: (207) 828-1699
E-Mail: info@garrand.com
Web Site: http://garrandpartners.com/

E-Mail for Key Personnel:
President: bgarrand@garrand.com
Production Mgr.: cmazuzan@garrand.com

Employees: 20
Year Founded: 1989

National Agency Associations: 4A's

Agency Specializes In: Brand Development & Integration, Broadcast, Business-To-Business, Collateral, Consumer Goods, Consumer Marketing, E-Commerce, Electronic Media, Environmental, Event Planning & Marketing, Exhibit/Trade Shows, Government/Political, Graphic Design, High Technology, Internet/Web Design, Media Planning, Media Relations, Media Training, Medical Products, Planning & Consultation, Print, Production, Promotions, Public Relations, Strategic Planning/Research, T.V., Teen Market, Trade & Consumer Magazines, Web (Banner Ads, Pop-ups, etc.)

Approx. Annual Billings: $27,000,000

Breakdown of Gross Billings by Media: Cable T.V.: 10%; Network T.V.: 10%; Point of Sale: 10%; Spot Radio: 10%; Spot T.V.: 15%; Strategic Planning/Research: 15%; Syndication: 20%; Trade & Consumer Mags.: 10%

Mary Baumgartner *(Pres)*
Brenda Garrand *(CEO)*
Larry Vine *(Chief Creative Officer)*
Allison Blackstone *(Dir-Creative)*
Matthew Caffelle *(Dir-Creative)*
Christine Campbell *(Dir-Media)*
Emily Trescot *(Dir-Art)*
Ted O'Meara *(Mng Principal)*

Accounts:
Bedard Pharmacy
Eaton Peabody
FairPoint
H.P. Hood Dairy
ITN America
Lakewood Camps
Lion Brand Yarn
Maine Medical Center; ME
Popcornopolis
University of Maine

THE GARRIGAN LYMAN GROUP, INC
1524 Fifth Ave 4th Fl, Seattle, WA 98101
Tel.: (206) 223-5548
Web Site: www.glg.com

Year Founded: 1993

Agency Specializes In: Advertising, Digital/Interactive, Graphic Design, Sponsorship

Tim Garrigan *(Founder, CEO & Principal)*
Cheronne Wong *(CFO)*
Bryan Cummings *(Chief Creative Officer)*
Chris Geiser *(CTO)*
Rebecca Lyman *(Principal)*
Lisa Illingworth *(Dir-HR)*
Kurt Reifschneider *(Dir-Creative)*
Emily Rice *(Assoc Acct Mgr)*

Accounts:
Herman Miller, Inc.
Microsoft Corporation
The Museum of Flight
Philips Electronics North America
Thompson's Water Seal
Umpqua Bank

GARRISON ADVERTISING
3043 Old Forge Dr, Baton Rouge, LA 70808
Tel.: (225) 761-1000

Fax: (225) 761-9000
Toll Free: (888) CME4ADS
E-Mail: gerald@garrisonadvertising.com
Web Site: www.garrisonadvertising.com

E-Mail for Key Personnel:
President: ggarrison@br-adgroup.com

Employees: 10
Year Founded: 1978

National Agency Associations: AFA-PRSA

Agency Specializes In: Advertising, Advertising Specialties, Business-To-Business, Co-op Advertising, Food Service, Graphic Design, Media Buying Services, New Product Development, Out-of-Home Media, Point of Purchase, Point of Sale, Production, Public Relations, Publicity/Promotions, Restaurant, Retail, Sales Promotion, T.V.

Approx. Annual Billings: $5,000,000

Breakdown of Gross Billings by Media: D.M.: $1,000,000; Radio: $1,200,000; T.V.: $2,800,000

Gerald Garrison *(Pres)*
Chris Garrison *(Acct Supvr)*
Lynn Ross *(Media Buyer)*

Accounts:
McDonald's; Monroe, LA Fast Food Chain; 1986
McDonald's; Shreveport, LA Fast Food Chain; 1991

GARRISON HUGHES
211 Fort Pitt Blvd, Pittsburgh, PA 15222
Tel.: (412) 338-0123
E-Mail: bgarrison@garrisonhughes.com
Web Site: www.garrisonhughes.com

Agency Specializes In: Advertising, Collateral, Graphic Design, Logo & Package Design, Newspapers & Magazines, Radio, Sales Promotion, T.V.

Bob Brown *(Dir-Design-UPMC Mktg)*
Dave Hughes *(Dir-Art)*
Dave Popelka *(Dir-Strategy & Bus Dev)*
Corinne Stenander *(Dir-Art)*
Jenn Reed *(Acct Exec)*
Corinne Kunselman *(Media Planner & Media Buyer)*
Bill Garrison *(Copywriter)*
Mike Giunta *(Copywriter)*

Accounts:
Bruschetta's Bar & Grille; Pittsburgh, PA
Children's Hospital of Pittsburgh of UPMC; Pittsburgh, PA Children's Hospital's Suburban Campaign, Direct Mail, Magazine, Radio, Suburban, Television
Education Management Corporation; Pittsburgh, PA
John Heinz History Center; Pittsburgh, PA
Nemacolin Woodlands Resort; Pittsburgh, PA (Agency of Record) Advertising
Pittsburgh Post-Gazette; Pittsburgh, PA
PNC; Pittsburgh, PA
PPG Industries; Pittsburgh, PA Advertising, Community & Business Leaders, Doing Well, Doing Good, Magazine
ReedSmith LLP
Schneider Downs; Pittsburgh, PA
Western Pennyslvania Sports Museum; Pittsburgh, PA

GARRITANO GROUP
(Formerly Penn Garritano Direct Response Marketing)
305 Minnetonka Ave S Ste 200, Wayzata, MN 55391
Tel.: (612) 333-3775
Fax: (612) 333-3778
Web Site: www.garritano-group.com

Employees: 42
Year Founded: 1999

National Agency Associations: DMA

Agency Specializes In: Direct Response Marketing

Joe Garritano *(Founder & Pres)*
Jerry Mlekoday *(Sr Dir-Art & Web Designer)*
Ryan Campbell *(Acct Svcs Dir)*

Accounts:
Ameriprise Financial
Assurant Affordable Health
Ecolab; Saint Paul, MN; 2004
Minnesota Historical Society
Minnesota Twins
Mutual of Omaha
National Geographic
Nutrisystem
Toro
Truven Health Analytics
TUI University
United Business Mail

THE GARY GROUP
1546 7th St, Santa Monica, CA 90401
Tel.: (310) 449-7626
Fax: (310) 264-9744
E-Mail: info@garygroup.com
Web Site: www.garygroup.com

E-Mail for Key Personnel:
President: egary@garygroup.com

Employees: 30
Year Founded: 1976

Agency Specializes In: Advertising, Advertising Specialties, Broadcast, Cable T.V., Consumer Marketing, Electronic Media, Entertainment, Event Planning & Marketing, Graphic Design, Leisure, Magazines, Media Buying Services, Merchandising, Out-of-Home Media, Point of Purchase, Point of Sale, Print, Production, Publicity/Promotions, Radio, Sales Promotion, Sports Market, Sweepstakes, Syndication

Richard M. Gary *(Owner)*
Rick Rogers *(Pres)*
Elsa H. Gary *(Principal)*
Dana Chung *(Supvr-Media)*
Anna Elema *(Media Planner-Digital & Buyer)*
Marcy Ellenbogen *(Media Buyer)*

Accounts:
Affliction
Amazon
ASCAP
Atlantis
Brand Asset Group
Code Black Entertainment
Country Music Association
Fox Home Entertainment
GMR Marketing
Golden Boy Promotions
NOW
Sony BMG
Universal Music Group
Warner Music Group; Los Angeles, CA

GARZA CREATIVE GROUP
2601 Hibernia St Ste 200, Dallas, TX 75204
Tel.: (214) 720-3888
Fax: (214) 720-3889
E-Mail: vicki@garzacreative.com
Web Site: www.garzacreative.com

Employees: 3
Year Founded: 1991

Agency Specializes In: Advertising, Bilingual Market, Brand Development & Integration, Business-To-Business, Collateral, Communications, Consulting, Corporate Communications, Corporate Identity, Direct Response Marketing, Event Planning & Marketing, Graphic Design, High Technology, Hispanic Market, Local Marketing, Logo & Package Design, Media Buying Services, Planning & Consultation, Print, Public Relations, Publicity/Promotions, Radio, Real Estate, Strategic Planning/Research, T.V.

Breakdown of Gross Billings by Media: Bus. Publs.: 20%; Mags.: 15%; Pub. Rels.: 10%; Radio: 20%; T.V.: 20%; Transit: 15%

Paco Garza *(Pres & Sr Dir-Creative)*
Vicki Garza *(CEO)*
David Schmidt *(Dir-IT Svcs)*

Accounts:
Atmos Energy; Dallas, TX Gas; 2004
ROSS-HR; Dallas, TX Electric Delivery; 1993
Texas Instruments; Dallas, TX High Technology Collateral; 1995

GAS LAMP MEDIA
363 5th Ave Ste 300, San Diego, CA 92101
Tel.: (619) 955-6995
Fax: (619) 955-7607
E-Mail: chris@gaslampmedia.com
Web Site: www.gaslampmedia.com

Employees: 12

Agency Specializes In: Brand Development & Integration, Identity Marketing, Print, Web (Banner Ads, Pop-ups, etc.)

Christopher Shaughnessy *(Partner)*
Thai Yin *(Partner)*

Accounts:
1031 & TIC Investments
Alcon Laboratories
Dorcas House
Focus Asia Partners
Heart to Heart International
ITPathworx
Me Body & Bath
Nine Points Management & Research
Office Furniture Outlet
Olive Services
Pro Sports Healing
Pure Strength
San Diego Boys & Girls Club
San Diego Home Source
Sharp Reese-Stealy
Trabuco Hills High School
Vivoli & Associates

GASLIGHT CREATIVE
501 W Saint Germain St Ste 304, Saint Cloud, MN 56301
Tel.: (320) 257-2242
Fax: (320) 257-2243
Web Site: www.gaslightcreative.com

Year Founded: 2009

Agency Specializes In: Advertising, Event Planning & Marketing, Graphic Design, Internet/Web Design, Logo & Package Design, Print, Public Relations, Radio, Social Media, T.V.

Jodie Pundsack *(Co-Founder & Strategist-Creative)*
Michael Nelsen *(Dir-Interactive Media)*
Sara Judson Brown *(Strategist-Content & Copywriter)*

Sarah Cords *(Strategist-Mktg)*
Amy Imdieke *(Sr Graphic Designer)*

Accounts:
Albany Apothecary
Great River Energy
Vision Woodworking, Inc.

GASQUE ADVERTISING, INC.

3195 Leaphart Rd, West Columbia, SC 29169-3001
Tel.: (803) 791-0952
Fax: (803) 791-0955
Toll Free: (800) 281-5153
E-Mail: ken@gasque.com
Web Site: www.gasque.com

E-Mail for Key Personnel:
President: ken@gasque.com
Media Dir.: jillian@gasque.com
Production Mgr.: mary@gasque.com
Public Relations: hayley@gasque.com

Employees: 6
Year Founded: 1973

National Agency Associations: Second Wind Limited

Agency Specializes In: Advertising, Arts, Brand Development & Integration, Business Publications, Business-To-Business, Consulting, Corporate Identity, Email, Graphic Design, Guerilla Marketing, Identity Marketing, Industrial, Logo & Package Design, Media Planning, Point of Purchase, Print, Publicity/Promotions, Radio, Trade & Consumer Magazines, Viral/Buzz/Word of Mouth

Breakdown of Gross Billings by Media: Bus. Publs.: 10%; Collateral: 5%; Consulting: 15%; D.M.: 10%; Fees: 10%; Graphic Design: 5%; Internet Adv.: 10%; Plng. & Consultation: 15%; Pub. Rels.: 5%; Trade & Consumer Mags.: 5%; Worldwide Web Sites: 10%

Ken Gasque *(Dir-Creative, Planner-Mktg & Designer)*
Mary Gasque *(Office Mgr)*

Accounts:
Reynolds Industries
SC Heart Center Health Care

THE GATE WORLDWIDE NEW YORK

71 5th Ave, New York, NY 10003
Tel.: (212) 508-3400
Fax: (212) 508-3502
E-Mail: contact@thegateworldwide.com
Web Site: www.thegateworldwide.com

E-Mail for Key Personnel:
Creative Dir.: bill.schwab@thegateworldwide.com
Production Mgr.:
charlie.katz@thegateworldwide.com

Employees: 50
Year Founded: 1872

Agency Specializes In: Above-the-Line, Advertising, Affluent Market, Alternative Advertising, Automotive, Aviation & Aerospace, Below-the-Line, Brand Development & Integration, Broadcast, Business Publications, Business-To-Business, Collateral, Communications, Computers & Software, Consulting, Consumer Goods, Consumer Marketing, Corporate Communications, Corporate Identity, Digital/Interactive, E-Commerce, Electronics, Engineering, Entertainment, Event Planning & Marketing, Fashion/Apparel, Financial, Government/Political, Graphic Design, Guerilla Marketing, High Technology, Hospitality, Household Goods, Identity Marketing, Industrial, Integrated Marketing, International, Internet/Web Design, Investor Relations, Leisure, Local Marketing, Logo & Package Design, Luxury Products, Magazines, Media Buying Services, Media Planning, Men's Market, Mobile Marketing, New Product Development, Newspaper, Newspapers & Magazines, Out-of-Home Media, Outdoor, Planning & Consultation, Podcasting, Print, Production, Production (Print), Promotions, Radio, Real Estate, Recruitment, Regional, Restaurant, Retail, Social Marketing/Nonprofit, Sponsorship, Sports Market, Stakeholders, Strategic Planning/Research, Syndication, T.V., Trade & Consumer Magazines, Transportation, Travel & Tourism, Women's Market

Approx. Annual Billings: $85,000,000

Breakdown of Gross Billings by Media: Cable T.V.: 10%; Consumer Publs.: 24%; D.M.: 2%; Internet Adv.: 10%; Network T.V.: 5%; Newsp.: 15%; Out-of-Home Media: 5%; Radio: 5%; Spot T.V.: 8%; Syndication: 2%; Trade & Consumer Mags.: 14%

David Bernstein *(Chief Creative Officer)*
Eric van den Huevel *(Mng Dir-The Gate Media)*
Elaine Hall *(Grp Dir-Media)*
Klaus Heesch *(Sr Dir-Digital Creative)*
Bill Moclair *(Grp Acct Dir)*
Gina Graham *(Producer-Digital)*
Brian Evans *(Mgmt Supvr)*
Kunick Kapadia *(Dir-Performance Mktg)*
Charlie Katz *(Dir-Production)*
Timothy Cozzi *(Sr Mgr-Studio & Agency Ops)*
Rachel Gorman *(Mgr-Media Ops)*
Mary Klindworth *(Asst Acct Exec)*
Charles Chang *(Assoc Creative Dir)*

Accounts:
Consolidated Edison, Inc.
Duxiana
Lawrence Hospital Group
Nasdaq OMX Group Campaign: "Ignite Your Ambition", Online, Social Media
Project Management Institute Analytics, Search
SPDR Gold Shares Campaign: "Precise in a World that isn't", Digital, Print

GATE6, INC.

23460 N 19th Ave Ste 110, Phoenix, AZ 85027
Tel.: (623) 572-7725
Fax: (623) 572-7726
Web Site: www.gate6.com

Employees: 80
Year Founded: 1996

Agency Specializes In: Advertising, Digital/Interactive, Email, Media Buying Services, Media Planning, Mobile Marketing, Paid Searches, Social Media, Strategic Planning/Research, Yellow Pages Advertising

Manish Mamnani *(Founder & CEO)*
Cathy Eckstein *(CMO)*
Atul Shukla *(CTO & Dir-Tech)*
Rebecca Heft *(Dir-Strategy)*
Jenna Hopkins *(Dir-Art)*
Nathan Kinkead *(Dir-Infrastructure & Support)*
Alex Linderman *(Dir-Creative)*
David J. Pond *(Mgr-Bus Dev & Sls)*

Accounts:
Free Arts of Arizona
Gourmet Orchards
PlayersTowel
New-Vantage Mobility International (VMI); 2015
Webgility Inc.

GATEHOUSE MEDIA PARTNERS

32 W Hoster St Ste 250, Columbus, OH 43215
Tel.: (614) 444-1515
Web Site: www.gatehousemedia.com

Agency Specializes In: Advertising, Digital/Interactive, Media Buying Services, Radio, Social Media, Strategic Planning/Research, T.V.

Marsha Young *(Pres)*
Nikki Bragg *(Acct Mgr)*

Accounts:
Oliver Winery

GATESMAN+DAVE

(Formerly GatesmanMarmion+Dave)
2730 Sidney St Bldg 2 Ste 300, Pittsburgh, PA 15203
Tel.: (412) 381-5400
Fax: (412) 381-9770
E-Mail: info@gatesmandave.com
Web Site: www.gatesmandave.com

Employees: 80
Year Founded: 2006

National Agency Associations: 4A's-PRSA-Second Wind Limited

Agency Specializes In: Advertising, Automotive, Brand Development & Integration, Broadcast, Business Publications, Business-To-Business, Cable T.V., Co-op Advertising, Collateral, Communications, Consumer Marketing, Corporate Identity, Digital/Interactive, Email, Fashion/Apparel, Financial, Graphic Design, In-Store Advertising, Industrial, Integrated Marketing, Internet/Web Design, Logo & Package Design, Magazines, Media Planning, Media Relations, Newspaper, Newspapers & Magazines, Out-of-Home Media, Outdoor, Planning & Consultation, Point of Purchase, Point of Sale, Print, Public Relations, Publicity/Promotions, Radio, Restaurant, Retail, Search Engine Optimization, Social Marketing/Nonprofit, Social Media, Sponsorship, Strategic Planning/Research, T.V., Travel & Tourism, Viral/Buzz/Word of Mouth, Web (Banner Ads, Pop-ups, etc.)

Approx. Annual Billings: $91,000,000

John Gatesman *(Pres & CEO)*
Dave Kwasnick *(Partner & Chief Creative Officer)*
Shannon Baker-Meyer *(Partner & Exec VP-PR & Social Media)*
David Nard *(CTO & Sr VP)*
Stuart Glassman *(Sr VP & Acct Mgmt Dir)*
Debbie Zappia *(VP & Controller)*
Beth Vukmir *(VP & Grp Acct Strategy Dir)*
Beth Thompson *(Acct Dir)*
Jamil Buie *(Dir-Bus Dev)*
Tim Friez *(Dir-IT)*
Kathy Morrell *(Dir-Media)*
Mary Kate Joyce *(Acct Supvr-PR)*
Johanna Ortmann *(Supvr-Media)*
Meredith Klein *(Sr Acct Exec-PR & Social Media)*
Blake Lightholder *(Sr Acct Exec)*
Shannon Matula *(Sr Acct Exec)*
Allison Hartman *(Strategist-SEM)*
Elizabeth Horvat *(Sr Media Planner & Strategist-Digital)*
Katie Stout *(Sr Planner-Media)*
Lauren Wenzel *(Acct Exec-PR)*
Alison Kretschman *(Media Planner)*
Paige Blawas *(Asst Acct Exec-PR)*
Jamie Kurke *(Asst Acct Exec)*
Rachael Denny *(Coord-Media)*
Sydney Loveday *(Coord-Media)*
Kendra Reith *(Asst Media Buyer)*

Accounts:
CeaseFirePa
Coen Oil Ruff Creek Markets; 2015
New-CONSOL Energy; 2014
Del Monte; 2004
New-Duquesne Light Company; 2015
Hormel Foods House of Tsang; 2013

New-Mine Safety Appliance Fixed Gas & Fire Detection; 2015
New-Mylan Pharmaceuticals; 2003
New-National Inventors Hall of Fame; 2014
North Shore LIJ Health System; 2012
Pittsburgh Penguins NHL Franchise; 2007
PPG Architectural Coatings Pittsburgh Paints & Stains; 2015
PPG Specialty Coatings & Materials Optical; 2007
Quaker Steak & Lube; Sharon, PA The Lube; 2007
S&T Bank (Agency of Record) Advertising, Brand Positioning, Digital, Media Buying, Media Planning, Public Relations, Social Media
Shop 'n Save; Pittsburgh, PA Supermarket Chain; 2007
StarKist Website, starkist.com; 2004
SUPERVALU Foodland, Shop'n Save
UPMC Children's Hospital Of Pittsburgh Of UPMC, Health Plan, Health System, Media Planning & Buying, UPMC Hamot; 2012

GATEWAY DESIGN, INC.

2425 W Loop S Ste 200, Houston, TX 77027
Tel.: (713) 822-4716
Web Site: www.gatewaydesign.com

Employees: 15
Year Founded: 1989

Agency Specializes In: Above-the-Line, Advertising, Advertising Specialties, Affiliate Marketing, Affluent Market, African-American Market, Agriculture, Alternative Advertising, Arts, Asian Market, Automotive, Aviation & Aerospace, Below-the-Line, Bilingual Market, Brand Development & Integration, Branded Entertainment, Broadcast, Business Publications, Business-To-Business, Cable T.V., Catalogs, Children's Market, Co-op Advertising, Collateral, College, Commercial Photography, Communications, Computers & Software, Consulting, Consumer Goods, Consumer Marketing, Consumer Publications, Content, Corporate Communications, Corporate Identity, Cosmetics, Crisis Communications, Custom Publishing, Customer Relationship Management, Digital/Interactive, Direct Response Marketing, Direct-to-Consumer, E-Commerce, Education, Electronic Media, Electronics, Email, Engineering, Entertainment, Environmental, Event Planning & Marketing, Exhibit/Trade Shows, Experience Design, Faith Based, Fashion/Apparel, Financial, Food Service, Game Integration, Gay & Lesbian Market, Government/Political, Graphic Design, Guerilla Marketing, Health Care Services, High Technology, Hispanic Market, Hospitality, Household Goods, Identity Marketing, In-Store Advertising, Industrial, Infomercials, Information Technology, Integrated Marketing, International, Internet/Web Design, Investor Relations, Legal Services, Leisure, Local Marketing, Logo & Package Design, Luxury Products, Magazines, Marine, Market Research, Media Buying Services, Media Planning, Media Relations, Media Training, Medical Products, Men's Market, Merchandising, Mobile Marketing, Multicultural, Multimedia, New Product Development, New Technologies, Newspaper, Newspapers & Magazines, Out-of-Home Media, Outdoor, Over-50 Market, Package Design, Paid Searches, Pets , Pharmaceutical, Planning & Consultation, Podcasting, Point of Purchase, Point of Sale, Print, Product Placement, Production, Production (Ad, Film, Broadcast), Production (Print), Promotions, Public Relations, Publicity/Promotions, Publishing, RSS (Really Simple Syndication), Radio, Real Estate, Recruitment, Regional, Restaurant, Retail, Sales Promotion, Search Engine Optimization, Seniors' Market, Shopper Marketing, Social Marketing/Nonprofit, Social Media, South Asian Market, Sponsorship, Sports Market, Stakeholders, Strategic Planning/Research, Sweepstakes, Syndication, T.V., Technical Advertising, Teen Market, Telemarketing, Trade & Consumer Magazines, Transportation, Travel & Tourism, Tween Market, Urban Market, Viral/Buzz/Word of Mouth, Web (Banner Ads, Pop-ups, etc.), Women's Market, Yellow Pages Advertising

Approx. Annual Billings: $5,000,000

Chris Norton *(Pres)*
Austin Wright *(Dir-Bus Dev-Mktg & Adv)*
Chase Woods *(Graphic Designer & Designer-Web)*

Accounts:
Amegy Bank of Texas; 2014
The Coca-Cola Company Minute Maid; 2012
MetroMedia Technologies; 2014
New Valves International; 2012
Neway
Phillips 66
Shell Lubricants; 2013

GAUGER + ASSOCIATES

360 Post St, San Francisco, CA 94108
Tel.: (415) 434-0303
Fax: (415) 434-0524
E-Mail: hello@gauger-associates.com
Web Site: www.gauger-associates.com

Employees: 20
Year Founded: 1974

National Agency Associations: IAN

Agency Specializes In: Advertising, Brand Development & Integration, Graphic Design, New Product Development, Public Relations, Strategic Planning/Research

David Gauger *(Pres & Dir-Creative)*
Marcus Young *(Exec VP)*
Sam Matza *(VP & Dir-Media)*
John F. Porter *(Controller)*
Isabelle Laporte *(Sr Dir-Art)*
Lori Murphy *(Sr Dir-Art)*
Carol Muth *(Sr Exec Dir-Creative)*

Accounts:
Artisana Foods; 2014
Baker Ranch Master Planned Community; 2012
Carmel Valley Manor Retirement Community; 2013
DeNova Homes New Homes; 2015
Dividend Homes, Inc.; Santa Clara, CA New Homes; 1974
The Dunes Master Planned Community; 2006
Espetus Food Service; 2013
Galaxy Desserts Bakery; 2000
Geneva Holdings; 2001
Golbon Food Service; 2014
Heritage on the Marina Retirement Community; 2013
Karoun Dairies Food & Beverage; 2013
Kiper Homes; 2003
Lock It Up Self-Storage; 1985
Monogram Residential Trust; 2014
Museum of Craft and Design Non-Profit; 2011
NCPHS Retirement Communities; 2010
The Peninsula Regent Retirement Community; 2010
Ramar Foods Frozen Foods; 2012
Redwood Hill Farm Food & Beverage; 2010
San-J International; San Francisco, CA Natural Foods; 1984
Shea Homes Northern California New Homes; 1992
Supernutrition; San Francisco, CA Supplements, Vitamins; 1996
The Tea Room Confections; 2008
TH Herbals Beverage; 2013
Toll Brothers New Homes; 2005
Truwhip Dessert Topping; 2010
Vitathinq Confections; 2014
Wallaby Yogurt Food & Beverage; 2004

GAUL ADVERTISING, INC.

1553 Ulster Cir, West Chester, PA 19380
Tel.: (215) 817-1834
Fax: (610) 225-0766
E-Mail: gaul6028@aol.com
Web Site: www.gauladvertising.com

Employees: 6
Year Founded: 1988

National Agency Associations: BPA

Agency Specializes In: Advertising, Brand Development & Integration, Business Publications, Business-To-Business, Collateral, Communications, Consulting, Corporate Identity, Direct Response Marketing, Engineering, Environmental, Event Planning & Marketing, Exhibit/Trade Shows, Graphic Design, High Technology, Industrial, Investor Relations, Logo & Package Design, Media Buying Services, New Product Development, Over-50 Market, Planning & Consultation, Point of Sale, Print, Production, Public Relations, Publicity/Promotions, Strategic Planning/Research, Trade & Consumer Magazines

Approx. Annual Billings: $4,000,000

Breakdown of Gross Billings by Media: Bus. Publs.: $800,000; Collateral: $770,000; Fees: $605,000; Newsp.: $202,500; Newsp. & Mags.: $667,500; Other: $500,000; Production: $320,000; Sls. Promo.: $135,000

Richard G. Webster *(Partner)*
Rob Devitis *(Principal)*

GAVIN ADVERTISING

110 N George St 3rd Fl, York, PA 17401
Tel.: (717) 848-8155
Fax: (717) 855-2292
E-Mail: gavin@gavinadv.com
Web Site: www.gavinadvertising.com

Employees: 13
Year Founded: 2011

Agency Specializes In: Advertising, Brand Development & Integration, Crisis Communications, Customer Relationship Management, International, Logo & Package Design, Media Buying Services, Media Relations, Public Relations, Search Engine Optimization

Mandy Arnold *(Pres)*
Tracey Johnston *(Dir-Digital Accts)*
George Migash *(Dir-Art-Multimedia)*
Amanda Mitcheltree *(Project Mgr-Digital)*
Sarah Chain *(Mgr-Mktg & PR)*
Ryan Tarkowski *(Mgr-PR & Mktg)*
Eden Fitzkee *(Coord-Mktg & Comm)*

Accounts:
C.S. Davidson Inc.
MINI of Baltimore

GAVIN & GAVIN ADVERTISING INC.

2900 4th Ave Ste 100, San Diego, CA 92103
Tel.: (619) 686-8500
Fax: (619) 686-8510
E-Mail: adv@gavinandgavin.com
Web Site: www.gavinandgavin.com

Employees: 3
Year Founded: 1991

Agency Specializes In: Advertising, Collateral, Consumer Marketing, Graphic Design, Media Buying Services, Media Planning, Newspaper, Production, Restaurant

Approx. Annual Billings: $7,000,000

Breakdown of Gross Billings by Media: Collateral: 10%; Graphic Design: 30%; Radio: 30%; T.V.: 30%

Sally P. Gavin *(Co-Owner & Dir-Art)*

Accounts:
Bachrach & Associates National Seminar Speaker; 1995
San Diego Regional Economic Development Corporation; 1991

GCG ADVERTISING
(Name Changed to GCG Marketing)

GCG MARKETING
(Formerly GCG Advertising)
2421 W 7th St Ste 400, Fort Worth, TX 76107-2388
Tel.: (817) 332-4600
Fax: (817) 877-4616
E-Mail: turner@gcgadvertising.com
Web Site: www.gcgmarketing.com

Employees: 27
Year Founded: 1973

Agency Specializes In: Advertising, Business Publications, Business-To-Business, Collateral, Communications, Consulting, Corporate Identity, Direct Response Marketing, Engineering, Event Planning & Marketing, Fashion/Apparel, Financial, Graphic Design, Health Care Services, High Technology, Industrial, Information Technology, Internet/Web Design, Investor Relations, Logo & Package Design, Magazines, Medical Products, New Product Development, Newspaper, Newspapers & Magazines, Out-of-Home Media, Outdoor, Pharmaceutical, Planning & Consultation, Point of Purchase, Point of Sale, Print, Production, Radio, Sales Promotion, Strategic Planning/Research, Technical Advertising, Trade & Consumer Magazines

Approx. Annual Billings: $25,790,000

Neil Foster *(Pres)*
Scott Turner *(CEO)*
Brian Wilburn *(Sr Dir-Art)*
Lauren Coleman *(Art Dir)*
Kris Copeland *(Dir-Creative)*
Allyson Cross *(Dir-Mktg)*
Pat Gabriel *(Dir-Creative)*
Becky Johnson *(Dir-Medical Education)*
Dominique Finkbeiner *(Sr Acct Exec)*
Claire Dunn *(Acct Exec)*
Marcie Heffley *(Acct Coord)*

Accounts:
7-Eleven, Inc.
7-Eleven Talent Acquisition
Aqua Pharmaceuticals
BNSF Railways
Cash America International
Colonial Companies
DFB Holdings; Fort Worth, TX
DUSA Pharmaceuticals
EECU
ExxonMobil; Irving, TX
PolyJohn Enterprises
Ranbaxy Laboratories
Rheem
Saladmaster
Steadmed
Taro Pharma
Vertex Energy
XTO Energy; Fort Worth, TX Oil & Gas Corporation

GD SQUARED
4900 N Talman Ave Ste 1, Chicago, IL 60625
Tel.: (773) 293-1896
Fax: (773) 293-6245
E-Mail: gd@gdsquared.com
Web Site: www.gdsquared.com

Year Founded: 2007

Agency Specializes In: Advertising, Brand Development & Integration, Graphic Design, Internet/Web Design, Web (Banner Ads, Pop-ups, etc.)

Garrett Bowhall *(Designer)*

GEARBOX FUNCTIONAL CREATIVE INC.
412 37th Ave N, Saint Cloud, MN 56303
Tel.: (320) 266-4660
E-Mail: info@gearboxfc.com
Web Site: www.gearboxfc.com

Agency Specializes In: Advertising, Brand Development & Integration, Broadcast, Graphic Design, Internet/Web Design, Media Planning, Print, Search Engine Optimization, Social Media

Glenn Richards *(CEO & Partner)*
Sara Mohs *(Partner, VP & Copywriter)*
Zach Arvidson *(Designer)*

Accounts:
Marco Technology

GEARSHIFT ADVERTISING
930 W 16th St Ste E2, Costa Mesa, CA 92627
Tel.: (714) 856-8254
E-Mail: info@gearshiftads.com
Web Site: www.gearshiftads.com

Year Founded: 2013

Agency Specializes In: Advertising, Brand Development & Integration, Digital/Interactive

Thomas Blinn *(Pres & Partner)*
Eric Cwiertny *(Partner & Dir-Creative)*
Roger Feldman *(Partner & Dir-Creative)*
Nevin Safyurtlu *(Partner & Dir-Production)*
Norm Tribe *(Partner & Dir-Creative & Digital)*

Accounts:
Sage Hill School (Agency of Record)
Yamaha Corporation of America

THE GEARY COMPANY
3136 E Russell Rd, Las Vegas, NV 89120-3463
Tel.: (702) 382-9610
Fax: (702) 382-0920
E-Mail: contact@gearycompany.com
Web Site: www.gearycompany.com

Employees: 18
Year Founded: 1969

National Agency Associations: AAF-IAB

Agency Specializes In: Advertising, Advertising Specialties, Automotive, Broadcast, Business Publications, Business-To-Business, Cable T.V., Co-op Advertising, Collateral, Communications, Consumer Marketing, Consumer Publications, Digital/Interactive, Direct Response Marketing, E-Commerce, Electronic Media, Email, Entertainment, Graphic Design, Infomercials, Integrated Marketing, Internet/Web Design, Leisure, Local Marketing, Logo & Package Design, Luxury Products, Magazines, Media Buying Services, Media Planning, Men's Market, Mobile Marketing, Multimedia, Newspaper, Newspapers & Magazines, Out-of-Home Media, Outdoor, Over-50 Market, Paid Searches, Print, Production, Production (Ad, Film, Broadcast), Production (Print), Promotions, Public Relations, Publicity/Promotions, Radio, Real Estate, Restaurant, Retail, Sales Promotion, Search Engine Optimization, Seniors' Market, Sports Market, T.V., Trade & Consumer Magazines, Transportation, Travel & Tourism, Web (Banner Ads, Pop-ups, etc.), Women's Market

Approx. Annual Billings: $12,000,000

Breakdown of Gross Billings by Media: Cable T.V.: 5%; Fees: 2%; Graphic Design: 6%; Logo & Package Design: 2%; Newsp. & Mags.: 35%; Outdoor: 15%; Production: 5%; Radio & T.V.: 30%

James D. McKusick *(CEO & Partner)*
Teri Mckusick *(Comptroller)*
Bob Burch *(Dir-Art)*
Glenn Larsen *(Dir-Creative)*
Kenny Shore *(Dir-Creative)*
Dirk Hanson *(Acct Mgr)*
Jessica Sclafani *(Mgr-Production)*
Jeff Croshaw *(Acct Exec)*
Olivia Kuntz *(Designer)*
Debbie Mclaughlin *(Media Buyer)*
Michael Severin *(Designer)*

Accounts:
Cannery Casino Resorts; LAs Vegas, NV & Washington, PA Gaming/Entertainment/Restaurants/Special Events/Rooms; 2011
Courtesy Auto Group; Las Vegas, NV Automotive Sales for Kia, Mazda, Mitsubishi, Lotus & Pre-Owned; 2005
Fitz Casino and Hotel; Tunica, MS Gaming/Entertainment/Special Events/Restaurants/Rooms; 2011
Friendly Ford; Las Vegas, NV Automotive Sales & Service; 1991
Golden Gaming; Las Vegas, NV Gaming/Taverns/Pubs/Promotions; 2011
The Good Dog Food Company
Heness & Haight Attorneys; Las Vegas, NV Personal Injury; 2008
Lotus Broadcasting; Las Vegas, NV Radio Stations
Pacifica Companies; San Diego, CA New Homes; 2005
Rich Little; Las Vegas, NV Entertainer; 2011
Sam Schwartz Attorney; Las Vegas, NV Bankruptcy & Short Sales; 2010

Branches

Geary Interactive
401 W A St Ste 360, San Diego, CA 92101
Tel.: (619) 756-6700
Fax: (619) 234-8668
E-Mail: info@gearyi.com
Web Site: www.gearylsf.com

Employees: 60
Year Founded: 2000

National Agency Associations: AAF-IAB

Agency Specializes In: Advertising, Advertising Specialties, Business Publications, Business-To-Business, Collateral, Communications, Consumer Publications, Digital/Interactive, E-Commerce, Email, Entertainment, Hospitality, Integrated Marketing, Internet/Web Design, Leisure, Local Marketing, Logo & Package Design, Luxury Products, Magazines, Men's Market, Mobile Marketing, Multimedia, Newspaper, Newspapers & Magazines, Out-of-Home Media, Over-50 Market, Paid Searches, Print, Production, Production (Ad, Film, Broadcast), Production (Print), Promotions, Public Relations, Radio, Real Estate, Restaurant, Retail, Search Engine Optimization, Seniors' Market, Sports Market, T.V., Trade & Consumer Magazines, Transportation, Travel & Tourism, Web (Banner Ads, Pop-ups, etc.), Women's Market

Karen Kovaleski *(Pres & CEO)*
Paul McKnight *(CFO)*
Ramsay Crooks *(Exec VP-Product)*
Ryan Adami *(VP-Strategy)*
Kevin Hird *(Dir-Creative)*
Anna Mikituk *(Dir-HR)*
Said Hamaid *(Sr Acct Mgr-Svcs-SEO & PPC)*
Kathryn Petersen *(Mgr-Media)*
Alex Hitchcock *(Acct Exec)*
Trevor Morrissey *(Planner-Media)*
Nick Altmann *(Acct Coord)*

Accounts:
20th Century Fox
CBM Media
Harrah's
Hyatt
Kyocera
M&T Bank
Marriott
MGA Entertainment
Paramount Parks
PG&E
Trump
Warner Brothers

GEILE LEON MARKETING COMMUNICATIONS

130 S Bemiston Ste 800, Saint Louis, MO 63105
Tel.: (314) 727-5850
Fax: (314) 727-5819
E-Mail: info@geileon.com
Web Site: www.geileon.com

Employees: 15
Year Founded: 1989

National Agency Associations: Second Wind Limited

Agency Specializes In: Broadcast, Business-To-Business, Collateral, Direct Response Marketing, Internet/Web Design, Print, Retail, Sales Promotion, T.V.

Approx. Annual Billings: $14,000,000

Breakdown of Gross Billings by Media: Brdcst.: $270,000; Bus. Publs.: $200,000; Cable T.V.: $65,000; Collateral: $275,000; D.M.: $340,000; Farm Publs.: $320,000; Internet Adv.: $35,000; Logo & Package Design: $75,000; Newsp. & Mags.: $370,000; Outdoor: $320,000; Point of Purchase: $310,000; Point of Sale: $330,000; Pub. Rels.: $90,000; Radio: $600,000; Sls. Promo.: $675,000; Strategic Planning/Research: $100,000; T.V.: $410,000; Trade Shows: $30,000; Transit: $65,000; Worldwide Web Sites: $120,000

Dave Geile *(Mng Partner & Dir-Creative)*
Randy Micheletti *(VP & Dir-Acct Svc)*
Dan Diveley *(VP)*
Mary Roddy Sawyer *(VP)*
Ben Edmonson *(Sr Dir-Art)*
James Coston *(Mgr-Digital Mktg)*
Luke Smith *(Sr Acct Exec)*
Kyle Bryant *(Copywriter)*
Meg Strange *(Asst Acct Exec)*

Accounts:
Metro Imaging

GELIA-MEDIA, INC.

390 S Youngs Rd, Williamsville, NY 14221
Tel.: (716) 629-3200
Fax: (716) 629-3299
E-Mail: info@gelia.com
Web Site: www.gelia.com

E-Mail for Key Personnel:
President: jphipps@gelia.com

Employees: 85
Year Founded: 1961

Agency Specializes In: Advertising, Advertising Specialties, Automotive, Aviation & Aerospace, Bilingual Market, Brand Development & Integration, Broadcast, Business Publications, Cable T.V., Catalogs, Co-op Advertising, Collateral, Commercial Photography, Communications, Consulting, Consumer Goods, Consumer Publications, Corporate Identity, Customer Relationship Management, Direct Response Marketing, Event Planning & Marketing, Health Care Services, Identity Marketing, In-Store Advertising, International, Internet/Web Design, Logo & Package Design, Market Research, Media Planning, Media Relations, Medical Products, New Product Development, Newspapers & Magazines, Package Design, Point of Purchase, Print, Product Placement, Production (Ad, Film, Broadcast), Production (Print), Public Relations, Publicity/Promotions, Radio, Recruitment, Retail, Sales Promotion, Seniors' Market, Strategic Planning/Research, T.V., Telemarketing, Yellow Pages Advertising

Approx. Annual Billings: $52,500,000

James L. Phipps *(Pres & CEO)*
Tom Weber *(VP & Exec Dir-Creative)*
Jon Boal *(VP-Client Svc Ops & Media)*
Lisa Scott *(Acct Svcs Dir & Strategist-Digital)*
Jason Yates *(Art Dir)*
Bob Chase *(Dir-PR)*
Karen Rushford *(Dir-Media)*
Kellie Mazur *(Coord-PR Acct & Copywriter)*
Kerri Linsenbigler *(Acct Coord-PR & Copywirter)*
Brian Orzechowski *(Acct Coord-Svc)*

Accounts:
Queen City Roller Girls

GEM ADVERTISING

2558 Whitney Ave Ste 104, Hamden, CT 06518
Tel.: (203) 506-0040
E-Mail: info@thinkgem.com
Web Site: www.gem-advertising.com

Year Founded: 2008

Agency Specializes In: Advertising, Broadcast, Collateral, Digital/Interactive, Media Buying Services, Print, Promotions, Public Relations, Radio, T.V.

Chris Bartlett *(Co-Founder & CEO)*
Peter Kozodoy *(Partner & Chief Strategy Officer)*
Lauren Downer *(Dir-Social Media)*
Gary Doyens *(Dir-Media Plng)*
Spencer Mahar *(Dir-Art)*
Levon Powell *(Dir-Digital)*
Anna Salatto *(Mgr-Design)*
Adina Munk *(Copywriter)*

Accounts:
Sundae Spa

GEMINI STUDIO

1120 Bloomfield Ave Ste 201, West Caldwell, NJ 07006
Tel.: (973) 276-9576
Fax: (973) 276-9586
E-Mail: mari@geministudio.com
Web Site: www.geministudio.com

E-Mail for Key Personnel:
President: dtirico@geministudio.com

Employees: 7
Year Founded: 1978

Agency Specializes In: Business-To-Business, Health Care Services, Retail, Travel & Tourism

Deborah Gale Tirico *(Principal)*
Mari Ippolito *(Dir-Art)*
Susan Burnham *(Acct Rep)*

Accounts:
Frederic Goodman Fine Jewelers
Little Tots Academy
Pemberley House

GENERAL LEVITATION

1635 Tower Grove Dr, Beverly Hills, CA 90210
Tel.: (310) 454-1188
E-Mail: rcgenlev@gmail.com

Employees: 10
Year Founded: 1995

Agency Specializes In: Automotive, Aviation & Aerospace, Business-To-Business, Consumer Publications, Entertainment, Financial, High Technology, Information Technology, Out-of-Home Media, Outdoor, Transportation

Approx. Annual Billings: $3,500,000

Breakdown of Gross Billings by Media: Collateral: $350,000; Consulting: $175,000; Logo & Package Design: $175,000; Mags.: $175,000; Network T.V.: $875,000; Newsp. & Mags.: $1,750,000

Robert C. Chandler *(CEO, Principal & Dir-Creative)*

Accounts:
Baja Fresh; Thousand Oaks, CA; 2003
Care.com; Boston, MA Online Services; 2009
CISCO Systems; San Jose, CA
Congressman Ed Whitfield; 2002
The Joan English Fund (Non-Profit); Los Angeles, CA; 2003
NXTV; Woodland Hills, CA Digital Entertainment Delivery Technology & Systems; 2000
Saybrook Capital; Santa Monica, CA Financial Services; 2003
Sitrick & Company; Los Angeles, CA
Splashdown Toys (The Skrumps); Los Angeles, CA; 1999
United Online & NetZero; Woodland Hills, CA

GENERATOR MEDIA + ANALYTICS

(Formerly Gotham Direct)
353 Lexington Ave 14th Fl, New York, NY 10016
Tel.: (212) 279-1474
Fax: (212) 279-1475
Web Site: www.generatormedia.com

Employees: 25

Agency Specializes In: Advertising, Digital/Interactive, Direct Response Marketing, Internet/Web Design, Sponsorship, Web (Banner Ads, Pop-ups, etc.)

Chris Gilbertie *(Co-Founder, Mng Partner & Sr VP)*
Shattuck Groome *(CMO)*
Nathan Perez *(Acct Svcs Dir)*
Andrew Antaki *(Assoc Dir-Comm Strategy)*
Jaime Durante *(Assoc Dir-Comm Analytics)*
Nicole Cross *(Mgr-SEM)*
Kelly Epps *(Sr Planner-Comm Strategy)*
Jonathan Gong *(Sr Planner-Comm)*
Regina Sica *(Sr Planner-Comm Strategy)*
Kara Borbely *(Asst Strategist-Comm)*
Katie Bow *(Asst Strategist-Comm)*
Leah Guecia *(Planner-Comm Strategy)*
Mariel Milner *(Planner-Comm Strategy)*

Accounts:
1800 TEQUILA
Atkins
Bayer
Chiquita Brands International Inc. Campaign: "ChiquitaSingOff", Chiquita, Chiquita Sing-Off

Contest, Digital, Media, Mobile Strategy, Social Campaign
New-Cholula Hot Sauce; 2015
Curves
EQUINOX Fitness Centers
Gore-Tex
Hotwire.com
Illy
Jenny Craig
JPMorgan Chase
La Compagnie (Media Agency of Record) Analytics, Media Buying, Media Planning
Lane Bryant
M&M's
My M&Ms
New York University Brennan Center for Justice at NYU School of Law, New York University Medical Center, Stern School of Business
OTC Pharma
PEER 1
ProFoot
Proximo Spirits Jose Cuervo, Media
Sundance
Top Of The Rock
Trane Inc.
New-The University of Virginia Darden School of Business
Woolrich

GENUINE INTERACTIVE

(Acquired by Jack Morton Worldwide)

GENUINE INTERACTIVE

500 Harrison Ave 5R, Boston, MA 02118
Tel.: (617) 451-9700
Fax: (617) 451-9705
E-Mail: hello@genuineinteractive.com
Web Site: www.genuineinteractive.com/

Employees: 100

Agency Specializes In: Advertising, Content, E-Commerce, Internet/Web Design, Market Research, Public Relations, Search Engine Optimization, Viral/Buzz/Word of Mouth

John Grayson *(Pres)*
Stephen Potter *(Sr VP & Dir-Creative)*
Mike Norman *(VP-Tech)*
Chris Pape *(Exec Dir-Creative)*
Mary Ann DiThomas *(Sr Producer-Digital)*
Jahnavi Bhangley *(Producer-Interactive)*
Halbert Evans *(Acct Dir)*
Joanna Field *(Acct Dir)*
Andrea Palumbo *(Producer-Interactive)*
Paul Devlin *(Acct Supvr)*
Lexi Korwin *(Acct Supvr)*
Matt Manganiello *(Acct Supvr)*

Accounts:
Advil Consumer Healthcare Products Mfr
Barbara's Digital
DIRECTV
Fuze Beverages Producer
Gilbane Construction Services
Novartis AG
Qualis Health Healthcare Consulting & Management Services

GEOFFREY CARLSON GAGE, LLC

125 Lake St W Ste 212, Wayzata, MN 55391-1573
Tel.: (952) 923-1081
Fax: (952) 923-1094
E-Mail: info@gcgage.com
Web Site: www.gcgage.com

E-Mail for Key Personnel:
President: geoff@gcgage.com

Employees: 8
Year Founded: 1999

National Agency Associations: ADFED

Agency Specializes In: Advertising, Advertising Specialties, Brand Development & Integration, Business Publications, Business-To-Business, Collateral, Communications, Consulting, Consumer Marketing, Consumer Publications, Corporate Identity, Digital/Interactive, Direct Response Marketing, E-Commerce, Electronic Media, Event Planning & Marketing, Exhibit/Trade Shows, Graphic Design, High Technology, Industrial, Internet/Web Design, Logo & Package Design, Magazines, Media Buying Services, Newspaper, Newspapers & Magazines, Outdoor, Point of Purchase, Point of Sale, Print, Production, Public Relations, Publicity/Promotions, Radio, Sales Promotion, Strategic Planning/Research, Trade & Consumer Magazines, Yellow Pages Advertising

Approx. Annual Billings: $648,001

Breakdown of Gross Billings by Media: Adv. Specialities: $1; D.M.: $70,000; E-Commerce: $10,000; Graphic Design: $60,000; Internet Adv.: $30,000; Logo & Package Design: $60,000; Print: $60,000; Promos.: $18,000; Trade & Consumer Mags.: $30,000; Trade Shows: $40,000; Worldwide Web Sites: $270,000

Geoffrey Carlson Gage *(Owner & Pres)*

Accounts:
Bull Run Roasting; Golden Valley, MN Gourmet Coffee & Tea; 2001
Children's Heartlink Worldwide Children's Health & Heart Services & Education; 2002
Cinequipt; Saint Paul, MN Equipment Rental
Condor Corporation Property Management
Eagle Elevator; Saint Paul, MN; 2004
Gloria Tew; Minnetonka, MN Sculptor
Minnesuing Acres; Lake Minnesuing, WI Lodge & Resort
Prime Group
Radisson Hotel & Conference Center; Plymouth, MN
Window Support Systems; Bloomington, MN Bay Window Support Kits & Systems; 2002

GEOMETRY GLOBAL

636 11th Ave, New York, NY 10036
Tel.: (212) 537-3700
E-Mail: lindsay.fellows@geometry.com
Web Site: www.geometry.com

Employees: 4,000
Year Founded: 2013

National Agency Associations: 4A's

Agency Specializes In: Advertising, Advertising Specialties, Alternative Advertising, Below-the-Line, Digital/Interactive, Guerilla Marketing, In-Store Advertising, Mobile Marketing, Point of Purchase, Point of Sale, Shopper Marketing, Sponsorship

Steve Harding *(CEO)*
Jon Hamm *(Chief Creative Officer-Global)*
Carl Hartman *(CEO-North America)*
Soche Picard *(Exec VP & Grp Acct Dir)*
Angela Burton *(Sr VP & Gen Mgr)*
Julian Roca *(Sr VP & Grp Dir)*
Taylor Nicholls *(Sr VP & Grp Acct Dir)*
Gregory Simon *(Sr VP & Grp Acct Dir-Partnership Mktg)*
Katherine Barks *(Sr VP-Plnng)*
Tim Ferguson *(Sr VP-Relationship Mktg Practice)*
Pam Morrisroe *(Mng Dir-East)*
Michael Kaplan *(VP & Grp Acct Dir)*
Brent Shedd *(Reg Mgr & Exec Dir)*
Paul Velardi *(Exec Dir)*
Chris Cooper *(Grp Dir-Plng & Digital Strategy)*
Lisa Lally *(Grp Acct Dir-Shopper Mktg)*
Sarah Walsh *(Grp Acct Dir)*
Susan Chelte *(Acct Dir-ShopperWorks)*
Monica Nadela *(Creative Dir-Multicultural)*
Andrey Panasyuk *(Dir-Creative-Retail)*
Devin DeFago *(Assoc Dir-Digital Media)*
Lindsay Fellows *(Assoc Dir-New Bus)*
Joanna Kennedy *(Assoc Dir-Project Mgmt-Digital)*
Ron Hudas *(Acct Supvr)*
John McCullagh *(Acct Supvr)*
Blair Martinez *(Sr Acct Exec)*
Elissa Mendez-Renk *(Acct Exec)*
Carl Preller *(Chief Performance Officer)*
Mathew Searcy *(Grp Creative Dir)*

Accounts:
Adobe
New-Aetna
American Express
Blue Cross Blue Shield
Build-A-Bear Workshop, Inc. Shopper
New-Campbell's
The Coca Cola Company
EJ Gallo
New-Emirates Airline
General Mills Advertising, Display, Ecommerce, Multi-Cultural, Shopper Insight, Shopper-Marketing
Heineken USA (Hispanic, Total Market Retail & Shopper Marketing Agency of Record) Heineken, Heineken Light, Strategy, Tecate, Tecate Light
New-Jim Beam
Kimberly-Clark Shopper Marketing
Lego
Lenovo
New-Liberty Mutual
Mondelez International Oreo
New-Pirelli
Sanofi-Aventis
SF SPCA Campaign: "Animal Instincts"
Time Warner Cable
Unilever Shopper Marketing
URC Snack Foods (M) Sdn Bhd
Waste Management

Branches

Geometry Global

215 Rue Saint-Jacques Bureau 333, QC H2Y 1M6 Montreal, QC Canada
Tel.: (514) 861-1811

Nathalie Laplace *(Mng Dir)*
Nuala Byles *(Exec Creative Dir)*
Jennifer Hearn *(Acct Dir)*
Greg Muhlbock *(Art Dir)*
Vincent LeBlanc, *(Copywriter)*
Ian Mackellar *(Copywriter)*
Martin Bujold *(Sr Supvr-Creative)*

Accounts:
Kimberly-Clark Inc. Broadcast, Campaign: "Share The Care", Kleenex, OOH, Online, Print

Geometry Global

350 N Orleans St, Chicago, IL 60654
Tel.: (312) 229-8500

National Agency Associations: 4A's

Scott McCallum *(Exec Acct Dir-Kimberly Clark)*
Kevin Shelhamer, *(Exec Acct Dir)*

Accounts:
New-Kimberly-Clark
New-Mondelez

Geometry Global

388 S Main St, Akron, OH 44311
Tel.: (330) 376-6148
Web Site: www.geometry.com

Employees: 200

National Agency Associations: 4A's

Agency Specializes In: Advertising, Sponsorship

Tony Bell *(VP & Grp Acct Dir)*
Susan Ladd *(VP & Grp Acct Dir)*
Johan Ohlson *(Dir-Creative)*
Michael Sammons *(Assoc Dir-Media)*
Lindsay Moll *(Sr Acct Exec)*

Accounts:
General Mills
New-John Deere
New-Nestle

GEORGE P. JOHNSON

11 E 26th St Fl 12, New York, NY 10010
Tel.: (212) 401-7800
Fax: (212) 401-7801
Web Site: www.gpj.com

Agency Specializes In: Advertising

Jennifer Shifman *(VP & Gen Mgr-Austin)*
Jorge E. Narvaez-Arango *(VP-Creative & Exec Dir-Creative)*
Darrell Coetzee *(Gen Mgr-Boston & New York)*

GEORGE P. JOHNSON COMPANY, INC.

3600 Giddings Rd, Auburn Hills, MI 48326-1515
Tel.: (248) 475-2500
Fax: (248) 475-2325
E-Mail: info@gpj.com
Web Site: www.gpj.com

Employees: 1,300
Year Founded: 1914

Agency Specializes In: Event Planning & Marketing, Strategic Planning/Research

Denise Wong *(Pres)*
Chris Meyer *(CEO)*
Jennifer Shifman *(VP & Gen Mgr-Austin)*
Robert Albitz *(VP-Creative-Worldwide)*
Scott Kellner *(VP-Mktg)*
Eva Miller *(Sr Dir-HR)*

Accounts:
American Ultimate Disc League Agency of Record, Sports Marketing
Chrysler, LLC All Chrysler & Fiat Brands Including Maserati
Cisco Conference/Experiential
Honda Acura, Auto Show/Experiential
IBM Global Experiential Agency of Record
Infiniti Division, Nissan North America Auto Show/Experiential
Lexus Auto Show/Experiential
LG Campaign: "LG at CTIA"
MWV Conference/Experiential
Sage Conference/Experiential
Salesforce.com Annual Dreamforce Event Strategy, Production & Management
Samsung Live Event/Gala Production
Scion Auto Show/Experiential
Tesla Global Experiential Agency of Record
Toyota Auto Show/Experiential
Tridium Conference/Experiential
Under Armour Sports & Experiential Marketing

Branches

George P. Johnson Company, Inc.

711 Atlantic Ave Fl 6, Boston, MA 02111
Tel.: (617) 535-9800
Fax: (617) 535-9797
E-Mail: info@gpj.com
Web Site: www.gpj.com

Employees: 60

John Trinanes *(Sr VP & Exec Dir-Creative)*
Scott Kellner *(VP-Mktg)*
David Rich *(VP-Strategic Mktg-Worldwide)*
Ed Sypek *(VP-Ops-Latin America)*
Darrell Coetzee *(Gen Mgr)*
Tom Maher *(Exec Dir-Client Svcs)*
Carol Krugman *(Client Svcs Dir)*
Gary Lebrun *(Dir-Creative)*
Marc Ruggiero *(Dir-Production Design)*
Keith Capobianco *(Assoc Dir-Creative)*

Accounts:
Alfa Bank Campaign: "Moscow Day"
Dodge
Fiat USA Campaign: "Fiat Gallery at 18 Wooster"
IBM Corp
Toyota Motor Campaign: "Scion Surface Experience"

George P. Johnson Company, Inc.

4000 Centre Pointe Dr, La Vergne, TN 37086
Tel.: (615) 768-3200
Fax: (615) 768-3201
Web Site: www.gpj.com

Employees: 25

Jennifer Shifman *(VP & Gen Mgr-Austin)*
Ryan Burke *(VP-Client Svcs)*
Bernie Clincke *(Exec Dir-Production)*
Michael Greenberg *(Dir-Project Mgmt-Estimating)*
Cherise Nunes *(Acct Mgr)*
Amy Jones *(Sr Acct Exec)*
Ashley Lee *(Sr Acct Exec)*
Eric Peters *(Acct Exec-Client Svcs-Infiniti)*

George P. Johnson Company, Inc.

18500 Crenshaw Blvd, Torrance, CA 90504
Tel.: (310) 965-4300
Fax: (310) 965-4696
Web Site: www.gpj.com

Employees: 130

Agency Specializes In: Advertising

Denise Wong *(Pres)*
Chris Meyer *(CEO)*
Chris Murphy *(Exec VP-Global Automotive)*
John Capano *(Sr VP & Gen Mgr-Los Angeles)*
Jennifer Shifman *(VP & Gen Mgr-Austin)*
Doug Ryan *(VP & Acct Dir)*
James Updike *(VP)*
James Christian *(Exec Dir-Creative)*
Geoffrey Mye *(Dir-Creative)*

Accounts:
New-Infiniti
New-Nissan
New-Toyota Group

George P. Johnson Company, Inc.

999 Skyway Rd Ste 300, San Carlos, CA 94070
Tel.: (650) 226-0600
Fax: (650) 226-0601
E-Mail: richard.toscano@gpj.com
Web Site: www.gpj.com

Employees: 100

Agency Specializes In: Sponsorship

Denise Wong *(Pres)*
Tara Higgins *(Exec VP-Ops)*
Jack Derusha *(Sr VP & Gen Mgr-San Francisco & San Carlos)*
Paolo Zeppa *(Sr VP-Client Success & Co-Gen Mgr)*
Kevin Bartram *(Sr VP-Sports Mktg)*
Jennifer Shifman *(VP & Gen Mgr-Austin)*
Scott Kellner *(VP-Mktg)*
Scott Burns *(Exec Dir-Creative)*
Melissa Powers *(Exec Dir-Client Svcs)*
Richard Toscano *(Sr Dir-Special Events)*
Linda Yu *(Mgr-HR)*

Accounts:
New-Charles Schwab
Cisco

George P. Johnson (UK) Ltd

Picton House 52 High St, Kingston, KT1 1HN United Kingdom
Tel.: (44) 208 879 2200
Fax: (44) 208 879 2201
Web Site: www.gpj.com

Employees: 70

Agency Specializes In: Advertising

Marina Mcmahon *(Grp Acct Dir)*
Pete Davies *(Acct Dir-Global)*
Lizzie. Mildinhall *(Acct Dir)*
Grace Nacchia *(Dir-Event)*
Kirsty Healy *(Sr Mgr-Event)*
Duncan Millar *(Mgr-Bus Dev-North America)*

Accounts:
VMware

George P. Johnson (France) SARL

74 Rue Rouget de Lisle, 92150 Suresnes, France
Tel.: (33) 1 4783 7587
Fax: (33) 1 4279 0583

Employees: 1

Agency Specializes In: Advertising

Victoria Connor *(Sr Acct Dir)*
Laura Sabouret *(Sr Strategist-Mktg-IBM Central Eastern Europe)*

George P. Johnson Event Marketing Co. Ltd.

Unit 1202 Capital Tower 6A Jianguomenwai St, Chaoyang District, Beijing, 100022 China
Tel.: (86) 10 5166 7333
Fax: (86) 10 6563 0103
E-Mail: inbox@gpjco.com

Employees: 40

Agency Specializes In: Advertising

Phyllis Teo *(VP & Gen Mgr-GCG)*
Felix Jun Gonzales *(VP-Client Svcs-Greater China)*
Eric S. Diehl *(Asst Gen Mgr)*
Jessie Li *(Asst Gen Mgr)*
Mimi Ng *(Sr Acct Dir)*
Reggy Lu *(Dir-Event Svcs)*
Katherine Huang *(Assoc Dir-Strategy & Plng Svc-China Reg)*

George P. Johnson (Australia) Pty., Ltd.

Suite 101 Level 1 63-79 Miller St, Pyrmont, Sydney, NSW 2009 Australia
Tel.: (61) 2 8569 7600
Fax: (61) 2 8569 7610
E-Mail: gpjaustralia@gpj.com
Web Site: www.gpj.com

Employees: 60

Agency Specializes In: Advertising

Peter Rix *(Mng Dir & Sr VP)*
Caleb Bush *(VP & Gen Mgr)*
Gareth Davies *(Head-Production)*
Chloe Noel De Kerbrech *(Client Svcs Dir)*

Accounts:
APEC
General Motors
Hyundai
IBM
Kluger
Lexus
Nissan
Smart Light Sydney

GEOVISION
75 N Beacon St, Watertown, MA 02472
Tel.: (617) 926-5454
Fax: (617) 925-5411
E-Mail: info@geovisiononline.com
Web Site: www.geovisiononline.com

Year Founded: 1989

National Agency Associations: AHAA

Agency Specializes In: Hispanic Market, Sponsorship

Juan Mandelbaum *(Pres & Dir-Creative)*
Michelle Jimenez *(Acct Dir)*

Accounts:
Children's Television Workshop Sesame Street
Coca-Cola/McCann-Erickson Worldwide
D.C. Heath
Massachusetts Environmental Trust
McDonald's/Arnold Worldwide
Volkswagen/Arnold Worldwide
WGBH-TV

THE GEPPETTO GROUP
636 11th Ave, New York, NY 10036
Tel.: (212) 462-8140
Fax: (212) 462-8197
E-Mail: info@geppettogroup.com
Web Site: www.geppettogroup.com

E-Mail for Key Personnel:
Creative Dir.: cmckee@geppettogroup.com

Employees: 20
Year Founded: 1997

National Agency Associations: 4A's

Agency Specializes In: Advertising Specialties, Brand Development & Integration, Children's Market, Collateral, Communications, Consulting, Consumer Marketing, Consumer Publications, Digital/Interactive, Graphic Design, In-Store Advertising, Integrated Marketing, New Product Development, Pharmaceutical, Planning & Consultation, Point of Purchase, Point of Sale, Print, Production, Promotions, Publicity/Promotions, Radio, Sales Promotion, Sports Market, Strategic Planning/Research, T.V.

Chris McKee *(Chief Creative Officer)*
Marc Greengrass *(Client Svcs Dir)*

Accounts:
Cadbury Adams
Del Monte Foods; San Francisco, CA
Frito Lay; Plano, TX; 2001
Hershey's; Hershey, PA
Lego; Enfield, CT; 2001
Mondelez International, Inc.
P&G/Gillette; Boston, MA

GERSHONI
785 Market St The Dome, San Francisco, CA 94103
Tel.: (415) 397-6900
E-Mail: info@gershoni.com
Web Site: www.gershoni.com

Agency Specializes In: Advertising

Amy Gershoni *(Co-Founder & Pres)*
Gil Gershoni *(Co-Founder & Dir-Creative)*
Kelly McCloskey *(Sr Acct Mgr)*
Jake Durrett *(Coord-Creative)*
Timothy Bott *(Jr Designer)*

Accounts:
Bank of America
Hewlett-Packard
Kai Vodka
Patron Spirits Co.
Silicon Graphics

GHG
200 5th Ave, New York, NY 10010
Tel.: (212) 886-3000
Fax: (212) 886-3297
E-Mail: ghgnewsroom@ghgroup.com
Web Site: www.ghgroup.com

Employees: 300
Year Founded: 1978

National Agency Associations: PRSA

Agency Specializes In: Advertising, Advertising Specialties, Bilingual Market, Brand Development & Integration, Business-To-Business, Collateral, Communications, Consulting, Consumer Marketing, Corporate Identity, Digital/Interactive, Direct Response Marketing, Education, Electronic Media, Event Planning & Marketing, Exhibit/Trade Shows, Graphic Design, Health Care Services, Hispanic Market, Information Technology, Internet/Web Design, Local Marketing, Logo & Package Design, Medical Products, Pharmaceutical, Print, Public Relations, Publicity/Promotions, Retail, Sales Promotion, Sponsorship, Strategic Planning/Research, Telemarketing, Trade & Consumer Magazines

Lynn O'Connor-Vos *(CEO)*
John Dietz *(Mng Partner & Dir-Brand Strategy)*
Justin Reed *(Sr VP & Dir-Creative)*
Dan Relton *(Sr VP & Dir-HR)*
Megan Fabry *(VP-Interactive Strategy)*

Accounts:
Allergan
AstraZeneca Pharmaceuticals LP
Boehringer Ingelheim Dulcolax, Viramune
Eli Lilly Global Branding
Essilor
Jed Foundation (Pro-Bono)
Pfizer Advil Cold and Sinus, Alavert, Celebrex, Dimetapp, Robitussin
Procter & Gamble
Text4baby

Branches

Grey Healthcare Group
1656 Washington Ste 300, Kansas City, MO 64108
Tel.: (816) 842-8656
Fax: (816) 842-1522
Web Site: www.ghgroup.com

Employees: 48

National Agency Associations: 4A's

Bill Werbaneth *(Sr VP & Dir-Creative-Copy)*
Shelley Hanna *(VP & Exec Dir-Creative)*
Marissa Packer *(Acct Supvr)*
Janet Turley *(Acct Supvr-PR)*
Matthew Brennan *(Sr Acct Exec)*
Kristen Haun *(Sr Acct Exec)*
Emily Stein *(Sr Acct Exec)*
Erin Unterstein *(Sr Acct Exec)*
Amy Westrich *(Sr Acct Exec)*
Joshua Burke *(Acct Exec)*
Ryan Mazar *(Acct Exec)*
Elizabeth Whitcomb *(Acct Exec)*
Alanna Cerino *(Asst Acct Exec)*
Christina Gonsalves *(Asst Acct Exec)*
Bethany Tanno *(Grp Acct Supvr)*

Accounts:
Hills Pet Nutrition

Grey Healthcare Paris
63 bis rue de Sevres, 92100 Boulogne-Billancourt, France
Tel.: (33) 1 46 84 85 72
Fax: (33) 1 46 84 86 17
E-Mail: info@ghgroup.com
Web Site: www.ghgroup.com

Employees: 17

Agency Specializes In: Health Care Services, Pharmaceutical

Thierry Kermorvant *(Mng Dir)*

Accounts:
Galderma
Johnson & Johnson
Pfizer
Sanofi Pasteur

Grey Healthcare
New Bridge Street House 30-34 New Bridge St, London, EC4V 6BJ United Kingdom
Tel.: (44) 203 037 3600
Fax: (44) 203 037 3610
Web Site: www.ghgroup.com

Employees: 30
Year Founded: 1979

Agency Specializes In: Health Care Services

Tamsine Foggin *(Bus Dir)*
Albert Ponnelle *(Acct Dir)*
Jonathan Rands *(Art Dir)*
Darren Wright *(Dir-Creative)*
Matthew Gouma *(Office Mgr)*

Accounts:
AstraZeneca; Sweden
British Heart Foundation Campaign: "Bhf-Vinnie"
GlaxoSmithKline plc Campaign: "The Heat", Lucozade Sport Conditions Zone
News UK
Pfizer
Roche; Switzerland
Scope
The Sunday Times
Vodafone Ireland

Grey Healthcare
Northpoint Building Level 18 100 Miller Street, North, Sydney, NSW 2060 Australia
Tel.: (61) 2 9936 2700
Fax: (61) 2 9936 2701
Web Site: www.ghgroup.com

Employees: 7
Year Founded: 1996

Agency Specializes In: Media Buying Services

Charles Huntington *(Mng Partner)*
Nicholas Brown *(Sr Dir-Art)*

Jessica Woodfield *(Grp Acct Dir)*
Bree McKenzie *(Acct Dir)*
Tim Brierley *(Dir-Creative)*
Elly Price *(Dir)*
Linda Richards *(Dir-Editorial)*
Jessica Bayfield *(Sr Acct Mgr)*
Christina Eltania *(Mgr-Comml)*
Bruce Wright *(Mgr-Studio)*

Accounts:
Abbott
Allergan
AMRRIC
Drontal Allwormer
Eli Lilly
GSK
Pfizer
Roche
Shire

Phase Five Communications
114 5th Ave, New York, NY 10011-5604
Tel.: (212) 886-3047
Fax: (212) 886-3271
E-Mail: wbalter@ghgroup.com
Web Site: www.phase-five.com

Employees: 80

Agency Specializes In: Health Care Services, Pharmaceutical, Planning & Consultation

Wendy Balter *(Pres)*
Carolyn Oddo *(Mng Dir & Exec VP)*
Meredith Wilson *(Sr VP & Acct Dir)*
Pauline Ng *(VP & Grp Acct Supvr)*

GIAMBRONE + PARTNERS
5177 Salem Hills Ln, Cincinnati, OH 45230
Tel.: (513) 231-5146
Fax: (513) 231-5126
E-Mail: markg@giambroneandpartners.com
Web Site: www.giambroneandpartners.com/

Employees: 8
Year Founded: 2002

Agency Specializes In: Advertising, Affluent Market, Alternative Advertising, Broadcast, Business-To-Business, Cable T.V., Catalogs, Children's Market, Co-op Advertising, Collateral, Computers & Software, Consulting, Consumer Goods, Consumer Publications, Corporate Communications, Corporate Identity, Cosmetics, Direct Response Marketing, Direct-to-Consumer, Exhibit/Trade Shows, Fashion/Apparel, Food Service, Graphic Design, Health Care Services, Hospitality, Household Goods, In-Store Advertising, Internet/Web Design, Leisure, Local Marketing, Logo & Package Design, Luxury Products, Magazines, Men's Market, Multimedia, New Product Development, Newspaper, Newspapers & Magazines, Out-of-Home Media, Outdoor, Package Design, Point of Purchase, Point of Sale, Print, Production, Production (Ad, Film, Broadcast), Production (Print), Promotions, Radio, Real Estate, Regional, Sales Promotion, Sponsorship, Sports Market, Sweepstakes, T.V., Trade & Consumer Magazines, Transportation, Travel & Tourism, Web (Banner Ads, Pop-ups, etc.)

Approx. Annual Billings: $500,000

Ken Giambrone *(Chief Creative Officer & Principal)*
Mark Giambrone *(Principal & Exec Dir-Creative)*

Accounts:
Haversham & Baker Golf Expeditions
JeniLee Cosmetics
Newport Aquarium
Procter & Gamble

GIANT CREATIVE/STRATEGY, LLC
1700 Montgomery St, San Francisco, CA 94111
Tel.: (415) 655-5200
Fax: (415) 655-5201
E-Mail: info@giantsf.com
Web Site: www.giantagency.com

Employees: 16
Year Founded: 2002

Agency Specializes In: Digital/Interactive, Exhibit/Trade Shows, Health Care Services, Internet/Web Design, Logo & Package Design, Pharmaceutical, Print, Production, Public Relations, Strategic Planning/Research

Steven Gold *(CEO)*
Jeffrey Nemy *(CFO)*
Adam Gelling *(Principal)*
Michele Adams *(Sr VP & Dir-Creative)*
Jonathan Peischl *(Sr VP & Dir-Innovation & Digital Mktg)*
Alyse Sukalski *(Sr VP & Dir-Ops)*
Rebecca Greenberg *(Sr VP & Mng Grp Dir)*
Angela Busa *(VP & Mgmt Supvr)*
Jan Vennari *(VP & Mgmt Supvr)*
John Stacey *(VP & Dir-Digital Production)*
Josh Yoburn *(VP & Dir-Scientific)*
Gabe Isaacs *(VP-Digital Strategy)*
Angie Matta *(Sr Dir-Digital & Print Art)*
Geoff Lee *(Dir-UX)*

Accounts:
Actelion
APP Pharmaceuticals, Inc.
ArthroCare EMT
BioGen Idec
BioMarin Pharmaceutical
Conor Medsystems
Gilead Sciences, Inc. SpeakFromTheHeart.com
Neutrogena Corp
Otsuka America
PDL BioPharma
Synarc
Verus Corp.

GIANT SPOON
101 S La Brea Ave, Los Angeles, CA 90036
E-Mail: hello@giantspoon.com
Web Site: www.giantspoon.com

Agency Specializes In: Advertising, Content, Digital/Interactive, Strategic Planning/Research

Trevor Guthrie *(Co-Founder)*
Marc Simons *(Co-Founder)*
John Ohara *(Sr VP-Strategy)*
Jon Michael Herrmann *(Dir-Strategy)*
Mikael Greenlief *(Assoc Dir-Strategy)*
Caleb Smith *(Assoc Dir-Strategy)*
Adam Wiese *(Assoc Dir-Strategy)*

Accounts:
Amazon
Cole Haan
Conde Nast
General Electric
HP
Keek Marketing, Media
Lego
Lincoln Motor Co
NBC

GIANTS & GENTLEMEN
145 Berkeley St Ste 200, Toronto, ON M5A 2X1 Canada
Tel.: (416) 568-0811
Web Site: www.giantsandgents.com

Year Founded: 2012

Agency Specializes In: Advertising, Digital/Interactive, Media Planning, Public Relations, Social Media

Gino Cantalini *(Co-Founder & Mng Dir)*
Natalie Armata *(Partner & Dir-Creative)*
Alanna Nathanson *(Partner & Dir-Creative)*
J. P. Spanbauer *(Art Dir)*
Rhianna Padamsey *(Acct Mgr)*
Brandon Tralman-Baker *(Copywriter)*

Accounts:
Dr. Bernstein Diet & Health Clinics (Agency of Record)
New-Fisherman's Friend Campaign: "Suck it Up"
One at Keswick

GIBBONS/PECK MARKETING COMMUNICATION
(Formerly Gibbons/Peck)
7 S Laurens St Ste 200, Greenville, SC 29601
Tel.: (864) 232-0927
Fax: (864) 232-2213
E-Mail: jgibbons@gibbonspeck.com
Web Site: www.gibbonspeck.com

Employees: 9
Year Founded: 1994

Anne Peck Gibbons *(Owner & Dir-Creative)*
James Gibbons *(Owner)*
Sandra Fraser *(Office Mgr)*
Elizabeth Bordeaux *(Mgr-Traffic & Coord-Media)*
Vivian Calzada Loveless *(Acct Exec)*

Accounts:
AMAMCO Tool
AnMed Health
Asheville Christian Academy
Baptist Easley Hospital
Central Pacific Bank (Hawaii)
Converse College
Greenwood Hills Conference Center
Hometrust Bank
Isothermal Community College
Mission Health
Northeast State Technical Community College
The Palmetto Bank
Paragon Bank
The Peace Center for the Performing Arts
Pittsboro Christian Village
Planter's Peanuts
Riverside National Bank
Two Chefs Restaurants

GIBENS CREATIVE GROUP
1014 N Gloster Ste C, Tupelo, MS 38804
Tel.: (662) 844-9007
Fax: (662) 840-3839
Web Site: www.gibenscreativegroup.com

Agency Specializes In: Advertising, Brand Development & Integration, Corporate Identity, Graphic Design, Internet/Web Design, Logo & Package Design, Print

Eric Gibens *(Pres & CEO)*
Cass Phipps *(Dir-Creative)*
Betsy Davis *(Acct Exec)*

Accounts:
B&B Concrete Company Inc.
Dont Be Cruel BBQ Duel
Elvis Presley Birthplace
Kruzzer Kaddy
Lone Cypress
Old Wavery
Shape
Sportsman Camo Covers
Sweet Cheeks Donut
Urology Associates

GIESKEN OUTDOOR ADVERTISING
115 Sophia's Lane, Ottawa, OH 45875
Tel.: (313) 462-0789
Toll Free: (866) 443-7536
E-Mail: tom@gieskenoutdoor.com
Web Site: www.gieskenoutdoor.com/

Tom Geisken *(Pres & CEO)*

Accounts:
Bob Evans
Hype Athletics
Tim Horton's Outdoors

GIGANTE VAZ PARTNERS
BRANDING • ADVERTISING • INTERACTIVE • MEDIA

GIGANTE VAZ PARTNERS ADVERTISING, INC.
915 Broadway, Ste 1408, New York, NY 10010
Tel.: (212) 343-0004
Fax: (212) 343-0776
Web Site: www.gigantevaz.com

Employees: 28
Year Founded: 1989

National Agency Associations: AAF-AWNY

Agency Specializes In: Advertising, Brand Development & Integration, Broadcast, Business Publications, Business-To-Business, Cable T.V., Co-op Advertising, Collateral, Consumer Marketing, Consumer Publications, Corporate Identity, Cosmetics, Digital/Interactive, Direct Response Marketing, Email, Fashion/Apparel, Financial, Graphic Design, Health Care Services, High Technology, In-Store Advertising, Information Technology, Internet/Web Design, Logo & Package Design, Magazines, Media Buying Services, Merchandising, New Product Development, Newspaper, Newspapers & Magazines, Out-of-Home Media, Outdoor, Package Design, Pharmaceutical, Point of Purchase, Point of Sale, Print, Production, Production (Ad, Film, Broadcast), Publicity/Promotions, Publishing, RSS (Really Simple Syndication), Radio, Search Engine Optimization, Sponsorship, Strategic Planning/Research, Sweepstakes, T.V., Technical Advertising, Trade & Consumer Magazines, Transportation, Web (Banner Ads, Pop-ups, etc.)

Approx. Annual Billings: $71,000,000

Breakdown of Gross Billings by Media: Cable T.V.: 8%; D.M.: 3%; Internet Adv.: 11%; Network T.V.: 20%; Newsp. & Mags.: 20%; Out-of-Home Media: 4%; Radio: 10%; Spot T.V.: 10%; Syndication: 4%; Trade & Consumer Mags.: 10%

Jim McHugh *(Pres & Dir-Media)*
Paul Gigante *(CEO & Chief Creative Officer)*
Madeline Vaz *(COO & Head-Client Svcs)*
Kathleen Smith *(Sr Acct Supvr)*

Accounts:
Botkier Designer Handbags & Accessories
Chubb Insurance
The College Board Education
Crillon Importers Spirits
New-EFI
New-iCIMS Business Technology
Mack-Cali Realty Corp. Real Estate
St. Martin's Press Entertainment, Publishing

GIGASAVVY
14988 Sand Canyon Ave Studio 4, Irvine, CA 92618
Tel.: (877) 728-8901
E-Mail: info@gigasavvy.com
Web Site: www.gigasavvy.com

Agency Specializes In: Advertising, Brand Development & Integration, Digital/Interactive, Graphic Design, Media Buying Services, Print, Search Engine Optimization, Social Media

Sven Johnston *(Partner & Sr VP)*
Kyle Johnston *(Partner & VP)*
Trina Parkin *(Designer)*
Olivia Taylor *(Designer)*

Accounts:
New-Johnny Rockets

GIGUNDA GROUP, INC.
150 Dow St Tower 3 5th Fl, Manchester, NH 03101
Tel.: (603) 314-5000
Fax: (603) 314-5001
E-Mail: info@gigundagroup.com
Web Site: www.gigundagroup.com

Employees: 30
Year Founded: 1994

Agency Specializes In: Sponsorship

Paul Owen *(Chief Creative Officer)*
Ross Mosher *(Dir-Production Svcs)*
Ethan Foss *(Sr Mgr-Production)*
Erik Cannon *(Sr Acct Exec)*
Caralyn Cornett *(Acct Exec)*
Devin Hallahan *(Acct Exec)*
Kevin Matte *(Acct Coord)*

Accounts:
Advil
Animal Planet
Assa Abloy
Bounty
Duracell
Eukanuba
Guitar Hero
Kelloggs
Mars Snackfood
Nike
P&G
Pedigree
Shell
Sony
Stanley
Tide
Valvoline
Yahoo

GILBREATH COMMUNICATIONS, INC.
15995 N Barkers Landing Ste 100, Houston, TX 77079
Tel.: (281) 649-9595
Fax: (281) 752-6899
E-Mail: info@gilbcomm.com
Web Site: www.gilbcomm.com

Employees: 12
Year Founded: 1989

National Agency Associations: AAF-AMA-PRSA

Agency Specializes In: Above-the-Line, Advertising, African-American Market, Alternative Advertising, Below-the-Line, Broadcast, Business Publications, Business-To-Business, Cable T.V., Collateral, College, Communications, Consulting, Consumer Marketing, Corporate Communications, Corporate Identity, Digital/Interactive, Direct-to-Consumer, Electronic Media, Environmental, Event Planning & Marketing, Exhibit/Trade Shows, Financial, Graphic Design, Internet/Web Design, Local Marketing, Logo & Package Design, Media Planning, Media Relations, Men's Market, Multicultural, Multimedia, Newspaper, Newspapers & Magazines, Out-of-Home Media, Outdoor, Package Design, Planning & Consultation, Point of Purchase, Point of Sale, Production, Production (Ad, Film, Broadcast), Production (Print), Public Relations, Publicity/Promotions, Radio, Recruitment, Regional, Retail, Sales Promotion, Social Marketing/Nonprofit, Strategic Planning/Research, T.V., Transportation, Urban Market, Web (Banner Ads, Pop-ups, etc.), Women's Market

Approx. Annual Billings: $4,000,000

Wardell Gilbreath *(CFO & VP)*
Bettie DeBruhl *(VP-Mktg Comm)*
Damon Yerian *(Sr Dir-Creative)*
Denise Rohrer *(Acct Mgr)*
Latoya Thomas *(Acct Exec)*
Kelly Musebeck *(Sr Graphic Designer)*
Robert Alfaro *(Jr Graphic Designer)*

Accounts:
Houston-Galveston Area Council Clean Air & Commuting Solutions
Port Authority of Houston Cargo to Economic Dev., Environment
Shell Oil Supplier Diversity, Community Rel.
Workforce Solutions Employment

GILL FISHMAN ASSOCIATES
675 Massachusetts Ave, Cambridge, MA 02139
Tel.: (617) 492-5666
Fax: (617) 492-5408
E-Mail: gfa@gillfishmandesign.com
Web Site: www.gillfishmandesign.com

Agency Specializes In: Advertising, Collateral, Digital/Interactive, Internet/Web Design

Gill Fishman *(Founder & CEO)*
Michael Persons *(Sr Designer)*

Accounts:
Alnylam Pharmaceuticals, Inc
Brown University
The Davis Companies
Gloucester Pharmaceuticals Inc.
Harvard University
Mass Technology Leadership Council
The Rashi School
Sapient Corporation
Spaulding Rehabilitation Hospital

THE GILLESPIE AGENCY
3007 Millwood Ave, Columbia, SC 29205
Tel.: (803) 779-2126
Fax: (803) 254-4833
E-Mail: Elaine@TheGillespieAgency.com
Web Site: www.thegillespieagency.com

E-Mail for Key Personnel:
President: elaine@thegillespieagency.com

Employees: 6
Year Founded: 1985

Agency Specializes In: Business-To-Business, Corporate Identity, Health Care Services, Transportation

Elaine Gillespie *(Founder & Pres)*
Trey Floyd *(Dir-Art)*

Accounts:
Ducane Gas Grills
Hand Picked

GILLESPIE GROUP
101 N Providence Rd, Wallingford, PA 19086
Tel.: (610) 924-0900
Fax: (610) 924-0909
Web Site: www.gillespiegroup.com

Employees: 11
Year Founded: 1992

Agency Specializes In: Advertising, Automotive, Collateral, Education, Entertainment, Health Care Services, Internet/Web Design, Local Marketing, Media Buying Services, Print, Radio, Retail, Social Marketing/Nonprofit, T.V.

Mike Gillespie, Sr. *(Pres & CEO)*
Sean Gillespie *(VP-Creative)*
Debbie Field *(Sr Mgr-Media)*
Holly Rafferty *(Mgr-Media)*

Accounts:
Catholic Health Care Services
Pacifico Marple

GILMORE MARKETING CONCEPTS, INC.
142 Glenbrook Cir, Gilberts, IL 60136
Tel.: (847) 931-1511
E-Mail: info@gmcicreative.com
Web Site: gmcicreative.com

Year Founded: 1991

Agency Specializes In: Advertising, Brand Development & Integration, Event Planning & Marketing, Internet/Web Design, Print, Public Relations, Social Media

Kim Gilmore *(Pres)*
Ben Lampe *(Coord-Web Dev & Designer)*

Accounts:
Algonquin Commons
School District U-46

GIN LANE MEDIA
263 Bowery 3rd Fl, New York, NY 10002
Tel.: (212) 260-9565
E-Mail: hello@ginlanemedia.com
Web Site: ginlane.com

Year Founded: 2008

Agency Specializes In: Advertising, Brand Development & Integration, Content, Digital/Interactive, Internet/Web Design

Emmett Shine *(Pres)*
Suze Dowling *(Dir-Accounts)*
Dan Kenger *(Dir-Digital Creative)*
Dmitri Vassilev *(Dir-Technical)*
Conor O'Hollaren *(Sr Product Strategist)*

Accounts:
Black Seed Bagels

GINESTRA WATSON
907 E State St, Rockford, IL 61104
Tel.: (815) 968-9502
Fax: (815) 968-9503
E-Mail: info@ginestrawatson.com
Web Site: www.ginestrawatson.com

E-Mail for Key Personnel:
President: jay@ginestrawatson.com
Creative Dir.: keith@ginestrawatson.com

Employees: 6
Year Founded: 2000

Agency Specializes In: Advertising, Automotive, Brand Development & Integration, Business-To-Business, Consumer Marketing, E-Commerce, Health Care Services, Internet/Web Design, Logo & Package Design, Public Relations, Recruitment, Trade & Consumer Magazines

Approx. Annual Billings: $1,800,000

Breakdown of Gross Billings by Media: Collateral: $225,000; D.M.: $150,000; Logo & Package Design: $150,000; Newsp. & Mags.: $500,000; Plng. & Consultation: $150,000; Pub. Rels.: $150,000; Radio & T.V.: $100,000; Trade & Consumer Mags.: $225,000; Worldwide Web Sites: $150,000

Keith Watson *(Owner)*
Jay Ginestra *(Partner)*

Accounts:
A. Vision Chicago; Chicago, IL Event Planning; 2004
Arcon Associates; Lombard, IL Architecture; 2001
Chicago Rockford International Airport
Edgebrook
Ginestrawatson
OSF Health Care; Peoria, IL Health Care; 2001
OSF Saint Anthony Medical Center; Rockford, IL Health Care; 2000
Oxford Pest Control
River District
Toyoda Machinery; Chicago, IL; 2000

GINGER GAUTHIER & ASSOCIATES
PO Box 249, Floresville, TX 78114
Tel.: (830) 216-4290
Fax: (830) 216-4295
E-Mail: ginger@ggadesign.com
Web Site: www.ggadesign.com

Employees: 2
Year Founded: 1987

Agency Specializes In: Advertising

Ginger Gauthier *(Pres)*

Accounts:
Chemcel
Lone Star Boutique

GINGER GRIFFIN MARKETING & DESIGN
19109 W Catawba Ave Ste 114, Cornelius, NC 28031
Tel.: (704) 896-2479
Web Site: www.wehaveideas.com

Agency Specializes In: Advertising, Collateral, Internet/Web Design, Logo & Package Design, Package Design, Social Media

Ginger Ervin Griffin *(Principal)*
Gianni Masciopinto *(Dir-Art)*
Becky Rishel *(Designer-Web)*

Accounts:
Charlotte Skyline Terrace
Griffin Brothers Tires, Inc.

GIOVATTO ADVERTISING & CONSULTING INC.
95 Rte 17 S, Paramus, NJ 07652
Tel.: (201) 226-9700
Fax: (201) 226-9694
E-Mail: results@giovatto.com
Web Site: www.giovatto.com

E-Mail for Key Personnel:
President: jgiovatto@giovatto.com
Creative Dir.: jbriggs@giovatto.com

Employees: 45
Year Founded: 1988

Agency Specializes In: Automotive, Fashion/Apparel, Financial, Food Service, Internet/Web Design, Print, Radio, T.V.

Approx. Annual Billings: $55,000,000

Mario Giovatto *(Principal)*
Dave Manno *(VP)*
Brian Tomasella *(Controller)*
Gina Giovatto *(Sr Acct Dir)*
Michael Earle *(Dir-Art)*
Michael Messano *(Dir-Creative Svcs)*
Anthony Oade *(Dir-Art)*
Meredith Palmer *(Acct Mgr)*
Dominic Capone *(Acct Exec)*
Therese Ptak *(Copywriter)*

Accounts:
Blackberry
Crestron
Jack Daniels
Konica Minolta
Nokia
Samsung
Sony Ericsson
T-Mobile US
Wal Mart

GIRARD ADVERTISING LLC
604 DW Hwy Ste 105, Merrimack, NH 03054
Tel.: (603) 429-0100
Fax: (603) 429-0120
E-Mail: advertise@girardadvertising.com
Web Site: www.girardadvertising.com

Year Founded: 2002

Agency Specializes In: Advertising, Graphic Design, Internet/Web Design, Media Buying Services, Public Relations, Social Media

Karen Girard *(Owner)*

Accounts:
Al Terry Plumbing & Heating, Inc.
Artistic Tile Inc.
Black Forest Restaurant
Upton & Hatfield

GIST & ERDMANN, INC.
1978 The Alameda, San Jose, CA 95126
Tel.: (408) 551-0290
Fax: (408) 551-0294
E-Mail: info@gist-erd.com
Web Site: www.gist-erd.com

Employees: 10
Year Founded: 1988
National Agency Associations: AMA-DMA

Agency Specializes In: High Technology, Information Technology

Gerald Gist *(Owner)*

Accounts:
GE Sensing
General Electric
Intel
iPark
Oracle
StatsChipPac

GK COMMUNICATIONS, INC.
149 S Barrington Ave Ste 780, Los Angeles, CA 90049
Tel.: (310) 849-8295
Fax: (310) 440-0645

E-Mail: info@gkcommunications.net
Web Site: www.gkcommunications.net

Agency Specializes In: Brand Development & Integration, Collateral, Communications, Consulting, Crisis Communications, Exhibit/Trade Shows, Local Marketing, Media Relations, Media Training, Public Relations

Amy Goldsmith *(Owner)*
Greg Kalish *(Owner)*

Accounts:
Billy Blues
Cheng Cohen
Goldcentral.com
Inwindow Outdoor
Pulmuone
Radlink
StanBio Laboratory
Staubach
Woodward Laboratory

GKV COMMUNICATIONS
1500 Whetstone Way 4th Fl, Baltimore, MD 21230
Tel.: (410) 539-5400
Fax: (410) 234-2441
E-Mail: newbusiness@gkv.com
Web Site: www.gkv.com

E-Mail for Key Personnel:
President: rogerg@gkv.com
Creative Dir.: jeffm@gkv.com
Production Mgr.: darrenm@gkv.com

Employees: 80
Year Founded: 1981

National Agency Associations: 4A's-ABC-AMIN-APA-BPA

Agency Specializes In: Advertising, Brand Development & Integration, Direct Response Marketing, Financial, Graphic Design, Media Buying Services, Public Relations, Sponsorship

Approx. Annual Billings: $150,000,000

Kevin Kempske *(Partner & Exec VP)*
Garry Raim *(Partner & Exec VP-Direct & Interactive Mktg)*
Dan Collins *(Partner & Sr VP-Strategic Plng & Res)*
Cathy Kowalewski *(CFO & VP)*
David Blum *(Sr VP & Acct Mgmt Dir)*
Dan Robinson *(Sr VP & Dir-Media Svcs)*
Carrie Dudley *(VP & Dir-Experiential Mktg-GKV Reach)*
John Marsh *(VP & Dir-Client Digital Svcs)*
Jessica Loewe *(VP & Assoc Dir-Media)*
Shannon Gardiner *(VP & Acct Supvr)*
Mike Hilton *(Dir-IT)*
Rick Hebert *(Sr Acct Exec-PR)*
Courtney LaSalle *(Acct Exec)*
Amelia Miller *(Acct Exec)*
Karen Kowalewski *(Asst Acct Exec)*
Stacey Wynia *(Dept Head-PR & Social Media)*

Accounts:
About Faces Salons Social Marketing Strategy
Aerotek
Baltimore Ravens
BG&E Home
Blue Shield of California
CareFirst BlueCross BlueShield
CareFirst
Coventry Health Care
DSM Nutritional Products
Elderplan
L-3 Communications
Martek Biosciences
Maryland Lottery
Maryland Physicians Care
Medifast, Inc. (Agency of Record) Branding, Campaign: "Your Whole World Gets Better", Creative Development, Digital, Market Research, Multi-Media, Print, Radio, Strategic Planning, TV
Network Health (Agency of Record) Creative Development, Digital, Media Buying, Media Planning, Medicare Age-In, Medicare Annual Enrollment Period, Strategic Planning, TV
Pandora Jewelry LLC. (Marketing Agency of Record-North America) Brand Development, North American Marketing, Strategic Planning
Shentel Wireless
Thinq
Toms Snack Foods

GLANTZ DESIGN INC
1840 Oak Ave, Evanston, IL 60201
Tel.: (847) 864-8003
E-Mail: info@glantz.net
Web Site: www.glantz.net

Year Founded: 2008

Agency Specializes In: Advertising, Brand Development & Integration, Collateral, Internet/Web Design, Logo & Package Design, Media Buying Services, Print, Promotions, Social Media, Strategic Planning/Research

Keith Glantz *(Pres & Dir-Creative)*
Anne Weber *(Chief Strategy Officer)*
Chelsea Leasure *(Dir-Art)*
Kim Volk *(Assoc Dir-Creative)*

Accounts:
Foov Fitness
NUTennis.com

GLASS AGENCY
(Formerly Glass McClure)
2700 J St 2nd Fl, Sacramento, CA 95816
Tel.: (916) 448-6956
Fax: (916) 448-2049
E-Mail: amber@glassagency.com
Web Site: www.glassagency.com

Employees: 30
Year Founded: 1991

Agency Specializes In: Advertising, Advertising Specialties, Agriculture, Alternative Advertising, Arts, Brand Development & Integration, Broadcast, Cable T.V., Co-op Advertising, Collateral, Consulting, Consumer Goods, Consumer Marketing, Consumer Publications, Corporate Identity, Entertainment, Event Planning & Marketing, Experience Design, Fashion/Apparel, Food Service, Government/Political, Graphic Design, Guerilla Marketing, Health Care Services, Leisure, Logo & Package Design, Luxury Products, Magazines, Market Research, Media Buying Services, Media Planning, Newspaper, Newspapers & Magazines, Out-of-Home Media, Outdoor, Package Design, Print, Production, Production (Ad, Film, Broadcast), Production (Print), Promotions, Radio, Regional, Restaurant, Retail, Social Marketing/Nonprofit, Sponsorship, Sports Market, Strategic Planning/Research, T.V., Teen Market, Trade & Consumer Magazines, Transportation, Travel & Tourism, Viral/Buzz/Word of Mouth, Web (Banner Ads, Pop-ups, etc.), Women's Market

Amber Williams *(Pres)*
Siobhann Mansour *(VP & Dir-Media)*
Brantley Payne *(VP & Dir-Creative)*
Abbey Biehl *(Brand Dir)*
Stephanie Black *(Sr Media Buyer)*
Ashley Karin-Kincey *(Sr Media Planner)*

Accounts:
FoodMaxx Discount Fresh Market; 2004
Hinode Rice Campaign: "How healthy is your rice?", Consumer Packaged Goods; 2009
Lucky & Save Mart Supermarkets Campaign: "Lucky Four to Grow", Campaign: "Save Our Pools", Retail Supermarket; 2004
Sacramento Kings Sports Entertainment; 2012
State of CA, Office of Traffic Safety Anti-Distracted Driving & Anti DUI; 2011
Stratmish.com Sports Online Gaming; 2012
Togo's Sandwiches Dip Diving, Quick Service Restaurant; 2011

GLASS & MARKER
311 Oak St Ste 110, Oakland, CA 94607
Tel.: (510) 922-8907
E-Mail: info@glassandmarker.com
Web Site: www.glassandmarker.com

Agency Specializes In: Advertising, Digital/Interactive

Nick Markham *(Exec Dir-Creative)*
Jesse Tarnoff *(Exec Dir-Creative)*

Accounts:
Estimote Inc
Indochino
Luna Video
Soylent

GLEN GROUP, INC.
(Name Changed to Drive Brand Studio)

THE GLENN GROUP
50 Washington St, Reno, NV 89503-5603
Tel.: (775) 686-7777
Fax: (775) 686-7750
E-Mail: agency@theglenngroup.com
Web Site: www.theglenngroup.com

E-Mail for Key Personnel:
Chairman: jglenn@theglenngroup.com
President: vglenn@theglenngroup.com
Creative Dir.: BLedoux@theglenngroup.com
Media Dir.: jevans@theglenngroup.com
Public Relations: teast@theglenngroup.com

Employees: 70
Year Founded: 1969

Agency Specializes In: Advertising, Brand Development & Integration, Broadcast, Business-To-Business, Collateral, Communications, Consumer Marketing, Corporate Communications, Corporate Identity, Crisis Communications, Digital/Interactive, Direct Response Marketing, Direct-to-Consumer, E-Commerce, Electronic Media, Email, Entertainment, Event Planning & Marketing, Exhibit/Trade Shows, Financial, Government/Political, Graphic Design, Health Care Services, Hospitality, Identity Marketing, Integrated Marketing, Internet/Web Design, Local Marketing, Logo & Package Design, Magazines, Market Research, Media Buying Services, Media Planning, Media Relations, Media Training, Mobile Marketing, Multimedia, New Product Development, Newspaper, Newspapers & Magazines, Out-of-Home Media, Outdoor, Package Design, Paid Searches, Planning & Consultation, Point of Purchase, Point of Sale, Print, Production, Production (Ad, Film, Broadcast), Production (Print), Promotions, Public Relations, Publicity/Promotions, Publishing, RSS (Really Simple Syndication), Radio, Real Estate, Recruitment, Regional, Restaurant, Retail, Search Engine Optimization, Social Marketing/Nonprofit, Sponsorship, Sports Market, Strategic Planning/Research, T.V., Trade & Consumer Magazines, Transportation, Travel & Tourism, Viral/Buzz/Word of Mouth, Web (Banner Ads, Pop-ups, etc.)

Approx. Annual Billings: $65,000,000

Breakdown of Gross Billings by Media: Brdcst.: 30%; Collateral: 11%; D.M.: 12%; Internet Adv.: 10%; Print: 35%; Worldwide Web Sites: 2%

B. C. LeDoux *(Pres & Partner)*
Merl Rose *(CFO)*
Phil Rose *(CFO)*
Gina Brooks *(Exec VP & Acct Svc Dir)*
Jennifer Evans *(Exec VP-Media Strategy)*
Flip Wright *(Exec VP-Strategy & Innovation)*
Tiffany East *(VP-PR)*
Dennis Wanbaugh *(Sr Dir-Art)*
Jan Johnson *(Dir-Print Production)*
Brett Rhyne *(Dir-Creative)*
Allison Dunn *(Media Buyer)*

Accounts:
Bally Technologies, Inc.
Boeing
Capriotti
Employers Insurance; Reno, NV Photography Flag Plastic; 1998
Employers Campaign: "Americans at Work"
Feather Falls Casino; Oroville, CA
FireKeepers Development Authority; Battle Creek, MI
Gold Strike Casino
Grand Sierra Resort & Casino
Grand Victoria Hotel & Casino; Chicago, IL
IGT (International Gaming Technologies); Reno & Las Vegas, NV
Las Vegas Review Journal
Mandalay Bay
The Mob Museum
Nevada Commission on Tourism
Nevada Department of Public Safety; Reno, NV
ReMax
Reno Air Race Association
Reno Real Estate Ventures LLC; Chicago, IL Rebranding
Renown
Shark Reef at Mandalay Bay
Smith Center
Table Mountain Casino; Friant, CA

GLIMMER, INC.
9 S Columbia St, Naperville, IL 60540
Tel.: (630) 330-8747
Fax: (630) 355-4211
E-Mail: info@glimmerco.com
Web Site: glimmerchicago.com

Employees: 11
Year Founded: 2004

Agency Specializes In: Advertising, Advertising Specialties, Brand Development & Integration, Business Publications, Business-To-Business, Co-op Advertising, Collateral, Consulting, Consumer Marketing, Consumer Publications, Corporate Identity, Direct Response Marketing, Electronic Media, Email, Event Planning & Marketing, Exhibit/Trade Shows, Gay & Lesbian Market, Graphic Design, Health Care Services, Hispanic Market, In-Store Advertising, Internet/Web Design, Local Marketing, Logo & Package Design, Magazines, Media Buying Services, Merchandising, New Product Development, Newspaper, Newspapers & Magazines, Outdoor, Planning & Consultation, Point of Purchase, Point of Sale, Print, Promotions, Publicity/Promotions, Radio, Real Estate, Recruitment, Retail, Sales Promotion, Sports Market, Trade & Consumer Magazines, Web (Banner Ads, Pop-ups, etc.)

Breakdown of Gross Billings by Media: Adv. Specialities: 10%; Collateral: 10%; Local Mktg.: 5%; Newsp. & Mags.: 40%; Print: 20%; Promos.: 15%

Brian Eveslage *(Pres)*
Katie Wyzukovicz *(Partner-Bus)*

Accounts:
Advent Product Development
Cassidy Tire & Service
Chicago Tribune
Meisner Electric
Portillo Restaurant Group
Provena Health
San Diego Union Tribune
Thorek Hospital
Two Fish Art Glass
US Energy Savings
Vee Pak, Inc.

GLINT ADVERTISING
235 NE Loop 820 Ste 304, Hurst, TX 76053
Tel.: (817) 616-0320
Fax: (817) 616-0325
Web Site: www.glintadv.com

Year Founded: 2000

Agency Specializes In: Advertising, Brand Development & Integration, Digital/Interactive, Logo & Package Design, Media Buying Services, Media Planning, Media Relations, Public Relations, Social Media, Strategic Planning/Research

Craig Lloyd *(Pres)*
Patty Marshall *(VP)*

Accounts:
Craigs Collision
Fix It Fast Cellular

GLO CREATIVE
1221 Brickell Ave Ste 900, Miami, FL 33131
Tel.: (305) 347-5130
Web Site: www.glocreative.com

Agency Specializes In: Advertising, Broadcast, Digital/Interactive, Internet/Web Design, Print, Public Relations, T.V.

Michael Glovaski *(Co-Founder & Exec Dir-Creative)*
Sebastian Darcyl *(Pres)*
Veronica Miranda *(Designer-Web)*

Accounts:
Gerda Locks
NewsMax Media, Inc.

GLOBAL ADVERTISING STRATEGIES
55 Broad St 8th Fl, New York, NY 10004
Tel.: (212) 964-0030
Fax: (212) 964-2022
E-Mail: info@global-ny.com
Web Site: www.global-ny.com

Employees: 45
Year Founded: 1999

Agency Specializes In: Advertising, Advertising Specialties, African-American Market, Asian Market, Bilingual Market, Business-To-Business, Co-op Advertising, Communications, Consulting, Corporate Identity, Cosmetics, Direct Response Marketing, E-Commerce, Event Planning & Marketing, Financial, Hispanic Market, Internet/Web Design, Investor Relations, Logo & Package Design, Media Buying Services, New Product Development, Outdoor, Pharmaceutical, Planning & Consultation, Public Relations, Strategic Planning/Research

Approx. Annual Billings: $18,600,000

Givi Topchishvili *(Founder & Pres-9 8 Grp)*
Alexander Aksenov *(Chief Creative Officer)*
Leiann S. Kaytmaz *(Dir-HR)*
Jesse Williamson *(Dir-Bus Dev)*

Accounts:
Aeroflot
AeroSvit
EGYPTAIR (Agency of Record) Marketing, North American Rebranding Campaign
Landy
Lufthansa
Lukoil
Medek Wine & Spirits
Nemiroff
Nikoil
Novartis
Novaya Zarya
Primus Telecommunications; McLean, VA Primus Wireless
Red Pocket Mobile
SAP Global Marketing
Stanley Capital Mortgage Company; 2004
The Tourist Office of Spain Digital, Social Media
Transportation Logistics International
Tropicana Casino & Resort; Atlantic City, NJ
Wimm-Bill-Dann
YveGeny

GLOBAL EXPERIENCE SPECIALISTS, INC.
7000 Lindell Rd, Las Vegas, NV 89118
Tel.: (702) 515-5500
Web Site: ges.com

Employees: 3,000

Agency Specializes In: Event Planning & Marketing, Exhibit/Trade Shows, Promotions, Retail

Steve Moster *(Pres)*
Mike Lecour *(Exec VP-Canada)*
David Saef *(Exec VP-Marketworks & Strategy)*
Vin Saia *(Exec VP-Corp Accts)*
Terry Campanaro *(Sr VP-Client Rels-Corp Accts)*
Chris Elam *(Sr VP-Customer Svc)*
John Woo *(VP-Creative & Design)*
Terry Marsh *(Head-Consumer Event Sls)*
Betty Bergeron *(Dir-Corp Svcs)*
Debra Goodlett *(Specialist-Corp Event & Experiential Mktg)*

Accounts:
Los Angeles Auto Show

GLOBAL IMMIGRATION RECRUITING LLC
13575 58th St N, Clearwater, FL 33760
Tel.: (727) 538-4143
Web Site: http://globalimmigrationadvertising.com/

Employees: 6
Year Founded: 2015

Agency Specializes In: Business Publications, Electronic Media, Email, Newspaper, Print, Radio, Trade & Consumer Magazines

Carol Perry *(Co-Founder & Pres)*
Dan Perry *(VP)*

Accounts:
Computer Advertising Solutions Multi-Media; 2013
J.D. Goss Auto House Automobiles; 2013

GLOBAL STUDIO
285 E Parr Blvd, Reno, NV 89512-1003
Tel.: (775) 853-8333
Fax: (775) 853-0200
Toll Free: (800) 932-2787
E-Mail: info@globalstudio.com
Web Site: www.globalstudio.com

Employees: 8

Agency Specializes In: Web (Banner Ads, Pop-ups, etc.)

Michael Reynolds *(Owner-Bus)*

Accounts:
Sani-Hut Company, Inc.

GLOBAL THINKING

3670 Wheeler Ave, Alexandria, VA 22304
Tel.: (571) 527-4160
E-Mail: ideas@globalthinking.com
Web Site: www.globalthinking.com

Agency Specializes In: Advertising, Brand Development & Integration, Internet/Web Design, Social Media

Jason Kowal *(Principal)*
Omar Shiblaq *(Principal)*
Laura Chwirut *(Art Dir)*
Angela Parrotta *(Art Dir)*
Jamin Hoyle *(Creative Dir)*

Accounts:
New-LIFT

GLOBALHUE

Ste 1600 4000 Town Ctr, Southfield, MI 48076
Tel.: (248) 223-8900
Web Site: www.globalhue.com

Employees: 200
Year Founded: 1988

National Agency Associations: AHAA

Agency Specializes In: Above-the-Line, Advertising, Advertising Specialties, African-American Market, Alternative Advertising, Arts, Asian Market, Automotive, Below-the-Line, Bilingual Market, Brand Development & Integration, Branded Entertainment, Broadcast, Business Publications, Cable T.V., Co-op Advertising, Collateral, Commercial Photography, Communications, Consumer Goods, Consumer Marketing, Consumer Publications, Content, Corporate Identity, Digital/Interactive, Education, Electronic Media, Entertainment, Event Planning & Marketing, Exhibit/Trade Shows, Experience Design, Faith Based, Financial, Food Service, Government/Political, Graphic Design, Guerilla Marketing, Hispanic Market, Household Goods, Identity Marketing, In-Store Advertising, Integrated Marketing, Internet/Web Design, Leisure, Marine, Market Research, Media Buying Services, Media Planning, Media Relations, Men's Market, Mobile Marketing, Multicultural, Multimedia, New Product Development, New Technologies, Newspaper, Newspapers & Magazines, Out-of-Home Media, Outdoor, Over-50 Market, Planning & Consultation, Point of Purchase, Point of Sale, Print, Product Placement, Production, Production (Ad, Film, Broadcast), Production (Print), Promotions, Public Relations, Publicity/Promotions, Radio, Recruitment, Regional, Restaurant, Retail, Sales Promotion, Shopper Marketing, Social Marketing/Nonprofit, Social Media, Sponsorship, Sports Market, Strategic Planning/Research, Sweepstakes, T.V., Trade & Consumer Magazines, Transportation, Travel & Tourism, Urban Market, Viral/Buzz/Word of Mouth, Web (Banner Ads, Pop-ups, etc.), Women's Market

Approx. Annual Billings: $834,533,000 Fees Capitalized

Don Coleman *(Chm & CEO)*
Kelli Coleman *(Exec VP-Corp Comm)*
Tracey Jennings *(Exec VP)*
Carlos Munoz *(SVP & Grp Acct Dir)*
Dawn Elledge *(Dir-Art)*
Tony Kause *(Dir-Creative)*
Jonathan Garay *(Assoc Dir-Creative)*
Albert Loera *(Assoc Dir-Creative)*

Accounts:
Autozone (Hispanic Agency of Record) Hispanic Segment; 2014
Coca-Cola (African American Agency of Record); 2014
HBO
Hip Hop Hall of Fame (Agency of Record)
Microsoft
NBA
OneMain Financial; 2010
Orasure Oraquick; 2012
Prudential; 2012
St. Jude Children's Research Hospital African American, Asian American and Hispanic Segments; 2015
United Airlines
U.S Bank (Multicultural Agency of Record) Multicultural Consumer Segments
WalMart; Bentonville, AR; 2007

Branches

GlobalHue

123 William St Ste 1700, New York, NY 10038
Tel.: (646) 871-6200
E-Mail: info@globalhue.com
Web Site: www.globalhue.com

Employees: 200
Year Founded: 1988

Agency Specializes In: Above-the-Line, Advertising, Advertising Specialties, African-American Market, Alternative Advertising, Arts, Asian Market, Automotive, Below-the-Line, Bilingual Market, Brand Development & Integration, Branded Entertainment, Broadcast, Business Publications, Cable T.V., Co-op Advertising, Collateral, Communications, Consumer Marketing, Consumer Publications, Content, Corporate Identity, Education, Electronic Media, Entertainment, Event Planning & Marketing, Exhibit/Trade Shows, Experience Design, Faith Based, Financial, Food Service, Government/Political, Graphic Design, Guerilla Marketing, Hispanic Market, Household Goods, Identity Marketing, In-Store Advertising, Integrated Marketing, Internet/Web Design, Leisure, Marine, Market Research, Media Buying Services, Media Planning, Media Relations, Men's Market, Mobile Marketing, Multicultural, Multimedia, New Product Development, New Technologies, Newspapers & Magazines, Out-of-Home Media, Outdoor, Over-50 Market, Planning & Consultation, Point of Purchase, Point of Sale, Print, Product Placement, Production, Production (Ad, Film, Broadcast), Production (Print), Promotions, Radio, Recruitment, Regional, Retail, Sales Promotion, Shopper Marketing, Social Marketing/Nonprofit, Social Media, Sponsorship, Sports Market, Strategic Planning/Research, Sweepstakes, T.V., Trade & Consumer Magazines, Transportation, Travel & Tourism, Urban Market, Viral/Buzz/Word of Mouth, Web (Banner Ads, Pop-ups, etc.), Women's Market

Don Coleman *(Chm & CEO)*
Kelli Coleman *(Exec VP)*
Chris Surrey *(Exec Dir-Creative)*
Mallie Mickens *(Creative Dir)*
Phillip Shung *(Creative Dir)*
Amany Mroueh *(Dir-Creative & Copywriter)*
Bryann Kellum *(Acct Supvr)*

Accounts:
Chrysler LLC Dodge, Fiat, Jeep; 1996
OneMain Financial; 2010
United States Navy; 2002
Verizon Wireless; 2001
WalMart, Bentonville, AR; 2007

GLOBALWORKS

220 5th Ave, New York, NY 10001
Tel.: (212) 252-8800
Fax: (212) 252-0002
Web Site: www.globalworks.com

Employees: 70

Agency Specializes In: Above-the-Line, Advertising, Advertising Specialties, African-American Market, Asian Market, Below-the-Line, Bilingual Market, Brand Development & Integration, Branded Entertainment, Broadcast, Business-To-Business, Cable T.V., Communications, Computers & Software, Consulting, Consumer Marketing, Corporate Communications, Corporate Identity, Cosmetics, Digital/Interactive, Direct Response Marketing, Direct-to-Consumer, E-Commerce, Email, Entertainment, Fashion/Apparel, Financial, Gay & Lesbian Market, Graphic Design, Health Care Services, Hispanic Market, Household Goods, In-Store Advertising, Information Technology, Integrated Marketing, Internet/Web Design, Local Marketing, Logo & Package Design, Market Research, Media Buying Services, Media Planning, Medical Products, Multicultural, Multimedia, Newspaper, Newspapers & Magazines, Outdoor, Over-50 Market, Package Design, Pharmaceutical, Planning & Consultation, Point of Purchase, Point of Sale, Print, Production, Production (Print), Radio, Retail, Search Engine Optimization, Social Marketing/Nonprofit, South Asian Market, Sponsorship, Strategic Planning/Research, T.V., Technical Advertising, Teen Market, Telemarketing, Tween Market, Urban Market, Viral/Buzz/Word of Mouth, Women's Market

Yuri Radzievsky *(Founder, Chm & CEO)*
Brian Ng *(Partner & Mng Dir-Graphic Production)*
Beatriz Valdes *(Partner-Acctg Plng & Svcs)*
Mans Angantyr *(Sr Partner & Chief Digital Officer)*
Valentin Polyakov *(VP-Media Svcs)*
Roberto Alcazar *(Exec Dir-Creative)*
Alka Chamrolia *(Assoc Dir-Creative)*
Karthik Krishnan *(Project Mgr-Digital)*

Accounts:
Avaya
Cablevision
Harvard Business School
Hughes
Kendall-Jackson App Development, Branding, Creative
Penn World Voice Festival
U.S. Bank

THE GLOVER PARK GROUP

1025 F St NW 9th Fl, Washington, DC 20004-1409
Tel.: (202) 337-0808
Fax: (202) 337-9137
Web Site: gpg.com

Year Founded: 2001

Agency Specializes In: Advertising, Corporate Communications, Crisis Communications, Media Relations, Media Training, Public Relations, Sponsorship

Michael Feldman *(Founder, Partner & Mng Dir)*
Chip A. Smith *(CEO)*
Jonathan Kopp *(Mng Dir & Sr Strategist-Interactive)*
Arik Ben-Zvi *(Mng Dir)*
Susan Brophy *(Mng Dir)*
Jon Gans *(Mng Dir)*
Brian Gaston *(Mng Dir)*

Jenni LeCompte *(Mng Dir)*
Jocelyn Moore *(Mng Dir)*
Oliver Phillips *(Mng Dir)*
Catharine Cyr Ransom *(Mng Dir)*
Lee Jenkins *(Sr VP & Mgr-Creative Studio)*
Jason Boxt *(Sr VP)*
Joseph Caruso *(Sr VP-Pub Affairs)*
Tod Preston *(Sr VP)*
Kim James *(Mng Dir-Health & Wellness Practice)*
Nedra Pickler *(Mng Dir-Strategic Comm Practice)*
Joshua Gross *(VP-Govt Rels & Intl Affairs)*
Robert Harris *(Dir-Govt Affairs)*
Ashley Hickey *(Dir-Strategic Comm)*
Kat Mavengere *(Dir-Pub Affairs)*
Katharine Torgersen *(Dir-Strategic Transformations)*
Ward Cole *(Assoc Dir-Creative-Digital)*

Accounts:
AARP
ADP
Campaign For Women's LIfe
New-FanDuel
New-The J.G. Wentworth Company
Pfizer
Society for Human Resource Management
Verizon Wireless

THE GLOVER PARK GROUP
(Acquired by WPP plc)

GLOW INTERACTIVE, INC.
105 Chambers St Fl 2, New York, NY 10007
Tel.: (212) 206-7370
Fax: (212) 208-0910
E-Mail: info@weareglow.com
Web Site: www.weareglow.com/

Employees: 25
Year Founded: 1999

Agency Specializes In: Game Integration, Mobile Marketing, Sponsorship

Peter Levin *(Co-Founder & CEO)*
Mike Molnar *(Mng Partner)*
Meagan Burns *(Dir-Interactive Art)*
Jesse McLean *(Dir-Creative)*
Clayton Benn *(Sr Acct Exec-Creative Strategy)*
Sean Lynam *(Strategist-Digital)*
Emily Babich *(Coord-Social Media)*

Accounts:
USA Network Campaign: "White Collar HTML 5 In-browser Rich Media"

GLUTTONY NEW YORK
114 W 17th St 2nd Fl, New York, NY 10011
Tel.: (212) 229-0907
Fax: (212) 229-0476
E-Mail: email@gluttony.com
Web Site: www.gluttony.com

Agency Specializes In: Branded Entertainment, Digital/Interactive, Print, Social Media, Strategic Planning/Research

Alex Denholm *(Exec Dir-Creative)*
Carver Low *(Acct Mgr)*

Accounts:
Bulova Watches (Agency of Record) Accu-Swiss, Caravelle New York
New-Stephen Silver (Agency of Record)

GLYNNDEVINS ADVERTISING & MARKETING
11230 College Blvd, Overland Park, KS 66210-2700
Tel.: (913) 491-0600
Fax: (913) 491-1369
E-Mail: csmith@glynndevins.com
Web Site: www.glynndevins.com

E-Mail for Key Personnel:
President: gdevins@glynndevins.com
Creative Dir.: kgrazier@glynndevins.com
Media Dir.: sbogan@glynndevins.com

Employees: 76
Year Founded: 1987

National Agency Associations: 4A's

Agency Specializes In: Above-the-Line, Advertising, Brand Development & Integration, Broadcast, Cable T.V., Collateral, Communications, Consulting, Corporate Identity, Crisis Communications, Digital/Interactive, Direct Response Marketing, Direct-to-Consumer, Electronic Media, Email, Event Planning & Marketing, Faith Based, Graphic Design, Health Care Services, Internet/Web Design, Market Research, Media Buying Services, Newspaper, Newspapers & Magazines, Outdoor, Over-50 Market, Production, Public Relations, Publicity/Promotions, Radio, Search Engine Optimization, Seniors' Market, Social Media, Strategic Planning/Research, T.V., Travel & Tourism, Web (Banner Ads, Pop-ups, etc.), Yellow Pages Advertising

Approx. Annual Billings: $80,000,000 Capitalized

Christopher J. Smith *(CFO)*
James T. Glynn *(Principal)*
Susan Bogan *(Exec VP-Client Rels)*
Randy Eilts *(VP-PR)*
Lea Ann Hodson *(VP-Client Svc)*
Jeremy Johnson *(VP-Creative)*
Mark Johnston *(VP-CRM & Data Analytics)*
Janel Wait *(VP-Digital)*
Candice Yagmin *(VP-Client Svc)*
Scott Finnerty *(Exec Dir-Digital Tech)*
Jen White *(Exec Creative Dir)*
Lindsey Riechers *(Sr Dir-Art)*
Edd Timmons *(Sr Dir-Art)*
AJennifer Anderson *(Acct Grp Dir)*
Lisa Groener *(Acct Dir)*
Gwen Benefield *(Dir-Acctg)*
Hayley Gallagher *(Dir-Art)*
Charles Harris *(Dir-Creative)*
Kendra Leikam *(Dir-Art)*
Kay Moore *(Dir-Talent Dev)*
Lora Siemer *(Dir-Art)*
Matt Whitney *(Dir-Tech)*
Hannah Loftus *(Assoc Dir-Art)*
Lisa Bade *(Sr Mgr-Digital & Search Mktg)*
Brandon Atkins *(Mgr-Digital Dev)*
Jennifer Barr *(Mgr-Production)*
Jonathan Hurst-Sneh *(Mgr-Digital UX)*
Andres Ospino *(Mgr-Search Mktg)*
Shawn Woodward *(Mgr-Print Production)*
Ashley Alpert *(Acct Supvr)*
Travis Bridges *(Acct Supvr)*
Kelsey Dolezal *(Acct Supvr)*
Alyson Langenkamp *(Acct Supvr)*
Jeff Bell *(Sr Acct Exec-PR)*
Megan Higgins *(Sr Acct Exec)*
Madeline Mayer *(Sr Acct Exec)*
Alexis McGraw *(Sr Acct Exec)*
Morgan Schaeffer *(Sr Acct Exec-PR)*
Lauren Schneider *(Sr Acct Exec)*
Yosa Addiss *(Strategist-CRM)*
Greg Blackman *(Strategist-Mktg Automation)*
Joshua Brill *(Specialist-IT)*
Lisa Korte *(Acct Exec)*
Chelsea March *(Acct Exec-PR)*
Brooke Rollison *(Acct Exec)*
Christiana Ryder *(Acct Exec)*
Lisa Wojcehowicz *(Acct Exec)*
Jillian Berger *(Asst Acct Exec)*
Emily Bordner *(Asst Acct Exec)*
Lauren Hamilton *(Asst Acct Exec)*
Kate McEnerney *(Asst Acct Exec)*
Katie Medlar *(Asst Acct Exec)*
Jordan Toomey *(Asst Acct Exec)*
Genesee Jones *(Coord-Media)*

Accounts:
John Knox Village
Life Care Services
Presbyterian Manors of Mid-America

GLYPH INTERFACE
(Formerly Craig Jackson & Partners)
110 Banks Dr Ste 200, Chapel Hill, NC 27514
Tel.: (919) 967-0329
Fax: (919) 967-5918
E-Mail: info@glyphinterface.com
Web Site: www.glyphinterface.com

Employees: 15

Agency Specializes In: Health Care Services

Craig Jackson *(CEO)*
Jennifer Parker *(Acct Mgr)*

Accounts:
All American Pet Resorts
East 54

GLYPHIX ADVERTISING
6964 Shoup Ave, West Hills, CA 91307
Tel.: (818) 704-3994
Fax: (818) 704-8850
E-Mail: cohen@glyphix.com
Web Site: www.glyphix.com

E-Mail for Key Personnel:
President: cohen@glyphix.com

Employees: 7
Year Founded: 1995

Agency Specializes In: Advertising, Brand Development & Integration, Business-To-Business, Collateral, Consumer Marketing, Consumer Publications, Corporate Communications, Corporate Identity, E-Commerce, Graphic Design, Internet/Web Design, Logo & Package Design, Magazines, New Product Development, Newspapers & Magazines, Out-of-Home Media, Outdoor, Print, Production, Radio, Strategic Planning/Research, T.V.

Approx. Annual Billings: $3,000,000

Breakdown of Gross Billings by Media: Bus. Publs.: 15%; Collateral: 20%; Consumer Publs.: 5%; Graphic Design: 15%; Logo & Package Design: 10%; Out-of-Home Media: 10%; Worldwide Web Sites: 25%

Larry Cohen *(Co-Founder, Pres & Partner)*
Brad Brizendine *(Co-Founder & CTO)*
Brad Wilder *(Co-Founder & Dir-Creative)*

Accounts:
Davis Colors
ECJ; Beverly Hills, CA Law Firm
Farmers Insurance; CA Website; 2009
Montage Development
Morpheus Music
Mumy; 1989
Newmedia Invision Awards; 1996
Ohmega Technologies; 1996
The Peloton; Boulder, CO Real Estate Development
Transdimension
Walt Disney Records Music Videos; 2010
Water Music
Western Commercial Bank

GMC+COMPANY
365 Canal St Ste 2260, New Orleans, LA 70130

Tel.: (504) 524-8117
Fax: (504) 523-7068
E-Mail: info@gmcadvertising.com
Web Site: www.gmcadvertising.com

Employees: 5

Agency Specializes In: Advertising

Glenda McKinley English *(Pres & Dir-Creative)*

Accounts:
Audubon Golf Trail
Louisiana Office of Tourism

GMG ADVERTISING

13500 N Kendall Dr Ste 115, Miami, FL 33186
Tel.: (305) 752-2512
Web Site: www.gmgadvertising.com

Year Founded: 2007

Agency Specializes In: Advertising, Broadcast, Crisis Communications, Graphic Design, Internet/Web Design, Logo & Package Design, Outdoor, Print, Public Relations, Social Media

Michael Beovides *(Founder, Pres & CEO)*
Yalennie Vinas *(Owner)*
Victoria Labarta *(Client Svcs Dir)*
Ines Ayra *(Dir-PR & Events)*
Erick Coego *(Dir-Creative & Art)*
Andres Munoz *(Dir-Web Mktg Team)*
Jose Basso *(Acct Exec)*
Lilian Figueroa *(Sr Graphic Designer)*
Ines Diaz *(Coord-Event & Production)*

Accounts:
Ace Hardware Corporation
Amercanex Corp (Agency of Record)

GMLV LLC

53 Edison Pl Level 3, Newark, NJ 7102
Tel.: (973) 848-1100
Fax: (973) 624-3836
Web Site: www.gmlv.co

National Agency Associations: 4A's

Agency Specializes In: Advertising, Brand Development & Integration, Corporate Identity, Event Planning & Marketing, Media Buying Services, Media Planning, Outdoor, Public Relations, Search Engine Optimization, Social Media, Sponsorship

Ray Levy *(Partner)*
Loretta Volpe *(Partner)*
Robert St. Jacques *(Creative Dir)*
Vishal Rupani *(Acct Mgr-Media Plng & Buying)*
Allison Howard *(Strategist-Media)*
Grant Moffitt *(Media Planner & Buyer)*

Accounts:
320 Sports
Barnes & Noble
Chefs Diet Advertising & Marketing Agency of Record, Branding, Public Relations
Chubb Insurance
Jordache
Twist and Smash'd
Unitex

GO APE MARKETING

2101 Cedar Springs Rd Ste 1050, Dallas, TX 75201
Tel.: (214) 310-0336
Web Site: www.goapemarketing.com

Year Founded: 2005

Agency Specializes In: Advertising, Brand Development & Integration, Broadcast, Digital/Interactive, Event Planning & Marketing, Outdoor, Print, Public Relations, Search Engine Optimization, Social Media

Cheryl Rios *(CEO)*

Accounts:
Earthwater PLC (Global Public Relations & Online Marketing Agency of Record)

GO BIG MARKETING

1000 N Magnolia Ave, Orlando, FL 32803
Tel.: (407) 862-1228
Web Site: gobigmarketing.com

Agency Specializes In: Advertising, Content, Graphic Design, Media Buying Services, Public Relations, Radio, Search Engine Optimization, Social Media, T.V.

Sue Hanna *(Pres)*
Hannah Zuk *(Acct Exec)*

Accounts:
Crime Prevention Security Systems

GO EAST

(Name Changed to Thread Connected Content)

GO FETCH MARKETING & DESIGN

7613 Ashleywood Dr, Louisville, KY 40241
Tel.: (502) 415-7405
Fax: (502) 773-5671
E-Mail: info@gofetchmarketing.com
Web Site: www.gofetchmarketing.com

Year Founded: 2004

Agency Specializes In: Advertising, Email, Graphic Design, Internet/Web Design, Logo & Package Design, Media Buying Services, Print, Public Relations, Search Engine Optimization, Social Media

Brad Howard *(Owner)*
Jennifer Griffin *(Pres)*

Accounts:
Venture Connectors
The Waterfront Challenge

GO MEDIA

4507 Lorain Ave, Cleveland, OH 44102
Tel.: (216) 939-0000
Fax: (216) 803-8100
E-Mail: thomas@gomedia.com
Web Site: gomedia.com

Employees: 20
Year Founded: 1998

Agency Specializes In: Advertising, Arts, Brand Development & Integration, Collateral, Corporate Identity, Graphic Design, Guerilla Marketing, High Technology, Identity Marketing, Internet/Web Design, Local Marketing, Logo & Package Design, Mobile Marketing, Multimedia, Point of Purchase, Print, Production, Production (Ad, Film, Broadcast), Production (Print), Publicity/Promotions, Urban Market, Web (Banner Ads, Pop-ups, etc.)

Approx. Annual Billings: $2,000,000

Breakdown of Gross Billings by Media: Graphic Design: $2,000,000

William A. Beachy *(Owner & Pres)*
Jeff Finley *(VP & Designer)*
Wilson Revehl *(VP)*
Jason Chesire *(Dir-Art)*
Kim Finley *(Office Mgr)*
Jana Dvorin *(Mgr-Ops)*
Jamie Esposito *(Strategist-Digital)*
Chris Comella *(Designer)*

GO VERTICAL CREATIVE

3801 McKelvey Rd Ste 201, Bridgeton, MO 63044
Tel.: (636) 244-5550
Fax: (866) 814-4873
E-Mail: info@goverticalcreative.com
Web Site: www.goverticalcreative.com

Year Founded: 2010

Agency Specializes In: Advertising, Graphic Design, Internet/Web Design, Mobile Marketing, Print

Jason Polsgrove *(Strategist-Digital Mktg)*

Accounts:
Durbin Garage Doors

GO WELSH

3055 Yellow Goose Rd, Lancaster, PA 17601
Tel.: (717) 898-9000
Fax: (717) 898-9010
Toll Free: (866) 469-3574
E-Mail: info@gowelsh.com
Web Site: www.gowelsh.com

Employees: 5

National Agency Associations: AAF-ADC

Agency Specializes In: Advertising, Graphic Design, Public Relations

Craig Welsh *(Owner)*

Accounts:
Armstrong World Industries Inc.
Royer's Flowers & Gifts
Society of Design Campaign: "Inviting Hische"

GO2 ADVERTISING

2265 E Enterprise Pkwy, Twinsburg, OH 44087
Tel.: (330) 650-5300
Fax: (330) 650-6416
Web Site: www.go2advertising.com

Year Founded: 2010

Agency Specializes In: Advertising, Brand Development & Integration, Digital/Interactive, Social Media, Strategic Planning/Research

Pete Rubin *(Co-Founder & Partner)*
Marc Okicich *(Sr Dir-Strategic Accts)*
Peter Roth *(Sr Art Dir)*
Chris Bushway *(Sr Art Dir)*
Michelle Gadus *(Dir-Acct Svc)*
Loretta Vaxman *(Dir-Ops)*
Kimberly Kenst *(Acct Mgr)*

Accounts:
American Heart Association

GOALEN GROUP MEDIA

2700 Neilson Way #329, Santa Monica, CA 90405
Tel.: (310) 612-0303
Fax: (310) 396-2361
E-Mail: goalen@goalengroup.com
Web Site: www.goalengroup.com

Employees: 2
Year Founded: 1984

Agency Specializes In: Brand Development & Integration, Collateral, Corporate Identity, Event Planning & Marketing, Exhibit/Trade Shows, Graphic Design, Media Buying Services, Multimedia, Point of Sale

James Goalen *(Dir & Writer)*
Matthew Goalen *(Coord-Production)*

GOBLE & ASSOCIATES, INC.
(Name Changed to GA Healthcare Communication)

GOCONVERGENCE
4545 36th St, Orlando, FL 32811
Tel.: (407) 235-3210
Fax: (407) 299-9907
E-Mail: info@thegoco.com
Web Site: www.goconvergence.com

Employees: 32
Year Founded: 1997

National Agency Associations: AAF

Agency Specializes In: Above-the-Line, Advertising, Advertising Specialties, Affluent Market, African-American Market, Alternative Advertising, Arts, Automotive, Aviation & Aerospace, Below-the-Line, Bilingual Market, Brand Development & Integration, Branded Entertainment, Broadcast, Business Publications, Business-To-Business, Cable T.V., Catalogs, Children's Market, Co-op Advertising, Collateral, College, Commercial Photography, Communications, Computers & Software, Consulting, Consumer Goods, Consumer Marketing, Consumer Publications, Content, Corporate Communications, Corporate Identity, Crisis Communications, Digital/Interactive, Direct Response Marketing, Direct-to-Consumer, E-Commerce, Education, Electronic Media, Electronics, Email, Entertainment, Environmental, Event Planning & Marketing, Exhibit/Trade Shows, Experience Design, Fashion/Apparel, Financial, Food Service, Game Integration, Government/Political, Graphic Design, Guerilla Marketing, Health Care Services, High Technology, Hispanic Market, Hospitality, Household Goods, Identity Marketing, In-Store Advertising, Industrial, Infomercials, Information Technology, Integrated Marketing, International, Internet/Web Design, Leisure, Local Marketing, Logo & Package Design, Luxury Products, Magazines, Marine, Market Research, Media Buying Services, Media Planning, Media Relations, Medical Products, Men's Market, Merchandising, Mobile Marketing, Multicultural, Multimedia, New Product Development, New Technologies, Newspaper, Newspapers & Magazines, Out-of-Home Media, Outdoor, Over-50 Market, Package Design, Paid Searches, Pharmaceutical, Planning & Consultation, Podcasting, Point of Purchase, Point of Sale, Print, Product Placement, Production, Production (Print), Promotions, Public Relations, Publicity/Promotions, Publishing, Radio, Real Estate, Recruitment, Regional, Restaurant, Retail, Sales Promotion, Search Engine Optimization, Seniors' Market, Social Marketing/Nonprofit, Social Media, Sponsorship, Sports Market, Stakeholders, Strategic Planning/Research, T.V., Technical Advertising, Teen Market, Trade & Consumer Magazines, Transportation, Travel & Tourism, Tween Market, Urban Market, Viral/Buzz/Word of Mouth, Web (Banner Ads, Pop-ups, etc.), Women's Market

Approx. Annual Billings: $26,000,000

Breakdown of Gross Billings by Media: Brdcst.: $12,000,000; Cable T.V.: $8,000,000; Print: $6,000,000

Mish Tucker Clark *(VP-Strategy & Accounts)*
Brad Moore *(VP-Creative Svcs)*
Brian Townsend *(Head-New Bus Dev)*
Aaron Reed *(Sr Dir-Art)*
R. Christian Andersen *(Dir-Interactive Media)*
Toby Dalsgaard *(Dir-Creative Svcs)*
Smithy Sipes *(Dir)*
Courtney Karolick *(Acct Mgr)*
Danielle Levine *(Acct Exec)*
Heather Lodispoto *(Acct Exec)*
Ashley Plumley *(Coord-Traffic)*

Accounts:
3M Health Information Systems; MN Agency of Record; 2011
3M; MN; 2005
Atlantis Resort & Casino; Paradise Island, Bahamas Agency of Record, Creative & TV Production, Destination Marketing; 2010
Cirrus Aircraft; MN Agency of Record; 2008
Disney Vacation Club; FL TV Production, Direct Response TV Production, Video on Demand; 2005
Disney Youth Group Marketing; FL Print, Web; 2006
Google; CA Special Venue Experience, Web; 2005
Nassau Paradise Island Promotion Board; Paradise Island, Bahamas Agency of Record, Creative & Broadcast Production, Destination Marketing; 2009
Orlando Magic; FL Brand Marketing Strategy, Print, In-Game Experiences; TV & Radio Commercials; 1997
SIMCOM; FL Professional National Flight Simulator Training Centers; 2011
Wilson Tennis; IL TV Commercial Production & Website Development; 2005

GODA ADVERTISING
1603 Colonial Pkwy, Inverness, IL 60067
Tel.: (847) 776-9900
Fax: (847) 776-9901
E-Mail: info@goda.com
Web Site: www.goda.com

E-Mail for Key Personnel:
President: pgoda@goda.com
Creative Dir.: LKang@goda.com

Employees: 6
Year Founded: 1985

Agency Specializes In: Advertising, Asian Market, Bilingual Market, Business Publications, Business-To-Business, Children's Market, Collateral, Commercial Photography, Corporate Identity, Direct Response Marketing, E-Commerce, Electronic Media, Electronics, Email, Engineering, Event Planning & Marketing, Exhibit/Trade Shows, Health Care Services, High Technology, Industrial, Information Technology, Integrated Marketing, Internet/Web Design, Logo & Package Design, Magazines, Media Buying Services, Media Planning, Medical Products, Newspapers & Magazines, Paid Searches, Print, Production, Public Relations, Publicity/Promotions, Sales Promotion, Search Engine Optimization, Social Media, Technical Advertising, Trade & Consumer Magazines

Approx. Annual Billings: $3,000,000

Elizabeth Kang *(VP & Dir-Creative)*
Kim Maley *(Copywriter)*

Accounts:
Fuji
Lyndex-Nikken, Inc.
Mitsubishi
Pat Mooney - The Saw Company
Sumitomo

GODFREY ADVERTISING
40 N Christian St, Lancaster, PA 17602
Tel.: (717) 393-3831
Fax: (717) 393-1403
E-Mail: info@godfrey.com
Web Site: www.godfrey.com

E-Mail for Key Personnel:
President: val@godfrey.com
Creative Dir.: jcastanzo@godfrey.com
Media Dir.: swhisel@godfrey.com
Production Mgr.: lynn@godfrey.com
Public Relations: chuck@godfrey.com

Employees: 67
Year Founded: 1947

Agency Specializes In: Brand Development & Integration, Business-To-Business, Co-op Advertising, Collateral, Commercial Photography, Communications, Corporate Identity, Digital/Interactive, Direct Response Marketing, E-Commerce, Electronic Media, Event Planning & Marketing, Exhibit/Trade Shows, Graphic Design, High Technology, Industrial, Internet/Web Design, Media Buying Services, New Product Development, Planning & Consultation, Print, Production, Public Relations, Publicity/Promotions, Sales Promotion, Sponsorship, Sports Market, Strategic Planning/Research, Technical Advertising

Approx. Annual Billings: $41,000,000 Capitalized

Russ Green *(Partner & Exec VP)*
Stacy Whisel *(Sr VP-Customer Insight & Strategic Media Programs)*
Melissa Zane *(VP & Dir-Creative Svcs)*
Mark Stoner *(Sr Dir-Art)*
Steven S. Graham *(Dir-PR)*
Bradley Corvelle *(Acct Mgr)*
Debbie Crawford *(Acct Mgr)*
Jim Everhart *(Acct Planner)*
Donna Harris *(Acct Planner)*
Stephanie Brooks *(Coord-Media Traffic)*

Accounts:
Ashland
Bosch Rexroth Corp. Factory Automation & Hydraulics; 2000
Caterpillar
Coleman Heating & Air Conditioning Residential & Light Commercial HVAC Products Marketed by York International Corp.; 1982
Danfoss Mechanical & Electrical Components
Danfoss
Glatfelter Specialty Papers & Engineered Products
Harrington Hoists Industrial Cranes & Hoists; 1990
HSM Solutions; Hickory, NC Strategic Communications
Interface Solutions, Inc. Engineered Composite Materials, Sealing Systems, Unique Specialty Papers
JLG Industries Aerial Work Platforms & Construction Machinery
Kingspan Insulated Panels
Kluber Lubrication North America, LP Specialty Lubricants
Luxaire Heating & Air Conditioning Residential & Light Commercial Products Marketed by York International Corp.; 1982
Murray Insurance Associates, Inc. Commercial Risk Management Services
Nora Rubber Flooring Commercial Rubber Flooring Systems
Rexroth Bosch Group
Timken Company Engineered Bearings & Alloy Steels
Toolinc Dynamics
Veeco Instruments
Wind-Lock Corporation Tools & Accessories for the Commercial Construction Industry
YORK Label Pressure Sensitive Labels

GODFREY Q & PARTNERS

100 California St 9th Fl, San Francisco, CA 94111
Tel.: (415) 217-2800
Fax: (415) 217-2898
Web Site: godfreyq.com/

Employees: 50

National Agency Associations: 4A's

Agency Specializes In: Advertising, Advertising Specialties, Electronic Media, Electronics, Multimedia, New Technologies, T.V., Technical Advertising

Dennis O'Rourke *(Owner)*
Patrick Godfrey *(Pres & Mng Partner)*
Dev Finley *(Partner & Dir-Client Svcs)*
Hugo Lai *(Head-Global Comm & Dir-Bus Dev ASIA)*
Clark Katayama *(Grp Dir-Media)*
Danielle Bird *(Acct Dir)*
Erik Welch *(Dir-Production)*
Andy Mera *(Assoc Dir-Creative & Copywriter)*
Sarah Haar *(Sr Acct Mgr)*
Alex Wilbanks *(Sr Acct Mgr)*
Alexandra O'Rourke *(Acct Mgr)*

Accounts:
Borland
Cisco Systems
Dolby
Riverbed
SAP
Symantec Campaign: "Do It All", Creative, Norton

GODIVERSITY

177 Main St, Huntington, NY 11743
Tel.: (917) 797-6189
E-Mail: hfreydell@godiversity.com
Web Site: www.GoDiversity.com

Employees: 25
Year Founded: 2004

Agency Specializes In: Above-the-Line, Advertising, Alternative Advertising, Asian Market, Automotive, Bilingual Market, Business-To-Business, Cable T.V., Catalogs, Collateral, Communications, Computers & Software, Consumer Goods, Corporate Communications, Corporate Identity, Direct Response Marketing, Direct-to-Consumer, E-Commerce, Email, Financial, Food Service, Government/Political, Guerilla Marketing, Health Care Services, Hispanic Market, Hospitality, Infomercials, International, Internet/Web Design, Legal Services, Logo & Package Design, Mobile Marketing, Multicultural, New Product Development, Newspaper, Newspapers & Magazines, Out-of-Home Media, Outdoor, Over-50 Market, Paid Searches, Pharmaceutical, Planning & Consultation, Podcasting, Point of Purchase, Point of Sale, Production, Production (Ad, Film, Broadcast), Production (Print), Radio, Restaurant, Search Engine Optimization, Seniors' Market, Shopper Marketing, Social Marketing/Nonprofit, Social Media, Sponsorship, Strategic Planning/Research, T.V., Teen Market, Tween Market, Web (Banner Ads, Pop-ups, etc.)

Humberto Freydell *(CEO)*

Accounts:
AARP; 2005
Century Chicken; 2009
Checkers; 2014
IDT; 2007
MLA; 2010
Virgin Mobile; 2008
Viva La Pizza; 2008

GODWIN ADVERTISING AGENCY, INC.

(d/b/a Godwin Group)
1 Jackson Pl 188 E Capitol St Ste 800, Jackson, MS 39201
Tel.: (601) 354-5711
Fax: (601) 960-5869
E-Mail: pshirley@godwin.com
Web Site: www.godwin.com

E-Mail for Key Personnel:
President: pshirley@godwin.com
Creative Dir.: tballard@godwin.com
Media Dir.: kmoss@godwin.com
Public Relations: lragland@godwin.com

Employees: 80
Year Founded: 1937

National Agency Associations: ABC-MAGNET-MCA

Agency Specializes In: Brand Development & Integration, Broadcast, Collateral, Communications, Consulting, Consumer Marketing, Corporate Identity, Direct Response Marketing, E-Commerce, Environmental, Financial, Food Service, Health Care Services, High Technology, Internet/Web Design, Media Buying Services, Over-50 Market, Public Relations, Restaurant, Retail, Seniors' Market, Sponsorship, Transportation, Travel & Tourism

Approx. Annual Billings: $67,000,000

Breakdown of Gross Billings by Media: Brdcst.: 6%; Collateral: 4%; Consumer Publs.: 3%; D.M.: 3%; Fees: 29%; Newsp.: 14%; Other: 1%; Out-of-Home Media: 1%; Print: 1%; Production: 1%; Pub. Rels.: 4%; Radio: 12%; T.V.: 15%; Trade & Consumer Mags.: 3%; Worldwide Web Sites: 3%

Philip Shirley *(Chm, CEO & Sr Partner)*
John McKie *(Mng Partner & Exec VP)*
Susan Graves *(CFO, Partner & Exec VP)*
Donna Ritchey *(Partner & Exec VP)*
Stacye Rinehart *(Sr VP & Grp Dir-Creative)*
Glenn Owens *(Sr VP-Digital Strategy & User Experience)*
Lee Ragland *(VP & Dir-PR)*
Karen Johnson *(VP-Print Production)*
Sue Templeman *(VP)*
Tal McNeill *(Exec Dir-Creative)*
Steve Alderman *(Sr Mgr-PR)*

Accounts:
Brown Bottling Company
Hancock Bank; Gulfport, MS; 1997
Louisville Slugger; Lousville, KY; 1999
MedjetAssist
Mississippi Baptist Health Systems; Jackson, MS Healthcare; 1985
Trustmark National Bank; Jackson, MS Banking; 1937

Branch

GodwinGroup

1617 25th Ave, Gulfport, MS 39501
(See Separate Listing)

GODWINGROUP

1617 25th Ave, Gulfport, MS 39501
Mailing Address:
PO Box 4728, Biloxi, MS 39535-4728
Tel.: (228) 388-8511
Fax: (228) 388-8782
Web Site: www.godwin.com

Employees: 55
Year Founded: 1976

Agency Specializes In: Environmental, Financial, Health Care Services, Travel & Tourism

John Mckie *(Mng Partner)*
Kami Wert *(Partner & Gen Mgr-Godwin Gulf Coast)*
Tal Mcneill *(Sr VP & Grp Dir-Creative)*
Lee Ragland *(VP & Dir-PR)*
Melissa Crosby *(VP-Brand Mgmt)*
Karen Johnson *(VP-Print Production)*
Donna Lindsey *(Sr Dir-Art)*
Steve Alderman *(Sr Mgr-PR)*
Lauren Mozingo *(Sr Brand Mgr)*
Jennie Truhett *(Brand Mgr)*
Melissa Weinberger *(Strategist-Integrated Media)*
Karl Allen *(Sr Media Planner & Buyer)*

Accounts:
Gulf Coast Regional Tourism Partnership
Hancock Bank
Hancock Holding Company; Gulfport, MS
Horne LLP
Louisville Slugger
Medjet Assist
Sandestin Golf & Beach Resort
Traditions

GOING INTERACTIVE

912 Holcomb Bridge Rd, Roswell, GA 30076
Tel.: (770) 643-3014
E-Mail: hello@goinginteractive.com
Web Site: www.goinginteractive.com

Year Founded: 1999

Agency Specializes In: Advertising, Digital/Interactive, Internet/Web Design, Social Media

Jason Davenport *(Co-Founder & Dir-Creative)*
Douglas Davenport *(Principal & Dir-Strategic)*
Phil Brane *(Producer & Designer)*

Accounts:
Future Foundation
Prime Time Toys

GOING TO THE SUN MARKETING ASSOCIATES, LLC

1250 Whitefish Hills Dr, Whitefish, MT 59937
Tel.: (406) 862-2870
E-Mail: buildyourbrand@gttsmarketing.com
Web Site: www.gttsmarketing.com

Year Founded: 2004

Agency Specializes In: Advertising, Brand Development & Integration, Internet/Web Design, Media Planning, Print, Public Relations, Radio, Social Media

Michael Moffitt *(Pres)*

GOLD DOG COMMUNICATIONS

6609 Goldsboro Rd, Falls Church, VA 22042
Tel.: (703) 534-3990
Web Site: www.golddogcommunications.com

Agency Specializes In: Advertising, Brand Development & Integration, Digital/Interactive, Internet/Web Design, Social Media

Jean Komendera *(Pres)*
Christina Ortiz *(Sr Art Dir)*
Pete Fazio *(Art Dir)*
Kristina Billingsley *(Dir-Bus & HR)*
Kate Sonnick *(Creative Dir)*
John Quigley *(Dir-Tech)*
Emily Fazio *(Acct Mgr)*
Jenny Patterson *(Acct Supvr)*
Rachel Fink *(Acct Exec)*

Accounts:

450K
Bethesda Row

GOLD N FISH MARKETING GROUP LLC

53 Old Route 22, Armonk, NY 10504
Tel.: (914) 273-2275
E-Mail: info@gnfmarketing.com
Web Site: www.gnfmarketing.com

Agency Specializes In: Advertising

Caren Berlin *(CEO)*
Ross Cooper *(Mng Dir)*
Steve Gold *(Chief Creative Officer)*
Angela Vecchio *(Exec Dir-Creative)*
Marc Weilheimer *(Dir-Entertainment Mktg)*
Nicole Pasternak *(Office Mgr-Ops)*

Accounts:
Boost Mobile, LLC
Cadbury Adams Stride Gum
Virgin Mobile USA, Inc.

GOLDSTEIN GROUP COMMUNICATIONS

30500 Solon Industrial Pkwy, Solon, OH 44139
Tel.: (440) 914-4700
Fax: (440) 914-4701
E-Mail: info@ggcomm.com
Web Site: www.ggcomm.com

Employees: 12
Year Founded: 1992

Agency Specializes In: Advertising, Brand Development & Integration, Catalogs, Collateral, Direct Response Marketing, Market Research, Product Placement, Public Relations, Trade & Consumer Magazines, Web (Banner Ads, Pop-ups, etc.)

Mark Johnson *(VP)*
Jeff Spencer *(Dir-Creative)*
Angela Arnold *(Acct Mgr)*
James Pugh *(Mgr-Technical Accounts)*
Cyndi Friedel *(Acct Exec-Online)*

Accounts:
Abanaki Pollution Control Equipment Manufacturer
Bud Industries Electronic enclosures
Danaher
Dynamotors
Keithley
LJ Star

GONZALEZ MARKETING LLC

4450 Cordova St Ste 110, Anchorage, AK 99503
Tel.: (907) 562-8640
Web Site: www.gonzalezmarketing.com

Year Founded: 2001

Agency Specializes In: Advertising, Digital/Interactive, Event Planning & Marketing, Graphic Design, Internet/Web Design, Media Buying Services, Media Planning, Promotions, Public Relations, Radio

Stephen L. Gonzalez *(Pres)*
Mary Gonzalez *(CFO)*
Jenny Thomasson *(VP-Client Svcs)*
Tom Anderson *(Mgr-Video Production)*

Accounts:
Chevrolet of South Anchorage
Lithia Chrysler Jeep Dodge of South Anchorage

GOOD ADVERTISING, INC.

5100 Poplar Ave Ste 1700, Memphis, TN 38137
Tel.: (901) 761-0741
Fax: (901) 682-2568
Toll Free: (800) 325-9857
E-Mail: dcox@goodadvertising.com
Web Site: www.goodadvertising.com

E-Mail for Key Personnel:
President: dale.cox@goodadvertising.com
Creative Dir.:
ellen.isaacman@goodadvertising.com

Employees: 25
Year Founded: 1982

Agency Specializes In: Advertising, Brand Development & Integration, Business-To-Business, Consumer Marketing, Direct Response Marketing, E-Commerce, Electronic Media, Graphic Design, Health Care Services, High Technology, Industrial, Internet/Web Design, Logo & Package Design, Medical Products, Point of Sale, Print, Public Relations, Publicity/Promotions, Retail

Approx. Annual Billings: $10,000,000

Dale Cox *(Pres)*
Ellen Isaacman *(Exec VP-Creative)*
Barney Street *(Exec VP)*
Megan Dwan *(Sr Dir-Art)*
Chris Fiveash *(Dir-Art)*
Karen Crutchfield *(Supvr-Acctg)*
Jim Rich *(Copywriter)*

Accounts:
FedEx Alliance Marketing; Memphis, TN
FedEx Corporation; Memphis, TN; 1984
FedEx Freight Marketing; Memphis, TN
FedEx Government & Sales Support; Memphis, TN
FedEx International; Memphis, TN
FedEx Logistics & Electronics Commerce; Memphis, TN
FedEx Retail Marketing; Memphis, TN
The Food Bank; Memphis, TN; 2006
GKM; Indianapolis, IN; 2005
International Paper Co.; Memphis, TN; 2004
The Memphis Zoo; 1996

GOOD GROUP, LLC

580 W Main St Ste 3, Trappe, PA 19426-1940
Tel.: (484) 902-8914
Fax: (610) 935-7074
E-Mail: info@goodgroupllc.com
Web Site: www.goodgroupllc.com

Employees: 7

Shannon Good *(Owner & Pres)*
Brad Good *(Partner-Strategic Mktg Plng & Dev)*
Missie Souders *(Office Mgr & Mgr-Traffic & Production Mgmt)*

Accounts:
Hero To Hero
Sam's Italian Deli

GOOD KARMA CREATIVE

37 W 12th St, New York, NY 10011
Tel.: (212) 691-8879
Fax: (212) 645-0871
Web Site: www.goodkarmacreative.com

Agency Specializes In: Advertising, Internet/Web Design

Luke Lois *(Mng Dir)*

Accounts:
Boulder Creek
Superfocus
Travalo
Youtoo Technologies

GOODBY, SILVERSTEIN & PARTNERS, INC.

720 California St, San Francisco, CA 94108-2404
Tel.: (415) 392-0669
Fax: (415) 788-4303
E-Mail: contact@gspsf.com
Web Site: goodbysilverstein.com

Employees: 300
Year Founded: 1983

Agency Specializes In: Advertising, Sponsorship

Breakdown of Gross Billings by Media: Cable T.V.: 6%; Fees: 8%; Internet Adv.: 2%; Newsp. & Mags.: 8%; Outdoor: 4%; Production: 15%; Radio: 7%; T.V.: 50%

Robert Riccardi *(Mng Partner)*
Derek Robson *(Mng Partner)*
Margaret Johnson *(Partner & Exec Dir-Creative)*
William Elliott *(Assoc Partner)*
Adam Reeves *(Exec Creative Dir)*
Dong Kim *(Grp Dir-Comm Strategy)*
John Thorpe *(Assoc Partner & Grp Dir-Brand Strategy)*
Bonnie Wan *(Assoc Partner & Grp Dir-Brand Strategy)*
Andrew Livingston *(Sr Dir-Art)*
Leslie Barrett *(Grp Acct Dir)*
Todd Porter *(Supvr-Music & Exec Producer-Experiential)*
Sean Farrell *(Dir-Art)*
Theo Abel *(Acct Dir)*
Ed Allt-Graham *(Acct Dir)*
Jason Bedecarre *(Acct Dir)*
Kate Catalinac *(Creative Dir)*
Michael Crain *(Acct Dir)*
Conor Duignan *(Producer-Brdcst)*
Cassi Norman *(Acct Dir)*
Meredith Williams *(Acct Dir)*
Mandi Lin *(Dir-Art & Designer)*
Carlo Barreto *(Dir-Art)*
Heather Barrett *(Dir-Res Strategy)*
Fabio Benedetto *(Dir-Art)*
Maggie Bradshaw *(Dir-Art)*
Bess Cocke *(Dir-Bus Affairs)*
Kelly Evans-Pfeifer *(Dir-Brand Strategy)*
Danny Gonzalez *(Dir-Creative)*
Mike Long *(Dir-Creative)*
Austin O'Connor *(Dir-Art)*
Tod Puckett *(Dir-Content Production)*
Nicole Richards *(Dir-Comm Strategy)*
David Suarez *(Dir-Creative)*
Hanna Wittmark *(Dir-Art)*
Ben Wolan *(Dir-Creative)*
Shane Fleming *(Assoc Dir-Creative)*
Kristin Graham *(Assoc Dir-Creative)*
Kevin Koller *(Assoc Dir-Creative)*
Judy Ybarra *(Assoc Dir-Bus Affairs)*
Edgar Ornelas *(Sr Mgr-Brdcst Traffic)*
Ashley Brittain *(Acct Mgr)*
Melissa Buck *(Acct Mgr)*
Melody Cheung *(Acct Mgr)*
Michelle Farhang *(Acct Mgr)*
Kateri McLucas *(Acct Mgr)*
Rachel Stermer *(Acct Mgr)*
Liza Stokes *(Acct Mgr)*
Heidi Killeen *(Mgr-Bus Affairs)*
Chrissy Shearer *(Mgr-Bus Affairs)*
Etienne Ma *(Strategist-Brand)*
Ursula Meeks-Wagner *(Strategist-Comm)*
Suhail Shaikh *(Strategist-Brand)*
Gabriella Svensk *(Strategist-Brand)*
Kate Baynham *(Copywriter)*
Simon Bruyn *(Copywriter)*
Kevin Steele *(Copywriter)*
Jasper Yu *(Designer)*
Mallory Guraya *(Asst Producer-Brdcst)*
Olivia Mullen *(Asst Acct Mgr-SONIC Drive-In)*

Accounts:
Adobe Systems Incorporated Adobe Creative Suite 2, Adobe Creative Suite 2.3, Adobe Marketing Cloud, Campaign: "Dream On", Campaign: "I

Am the New Creative", Campaign: "Logo Remix", Campaign: "Metrics, not Myths", Campaign: "The Launch", Campaign: "The New Creatives", Campaign: "Woo Woo", Photoshop, Social
American Rivers Campaign: "Get More Green Tool"
New-Apple Inc. Campaign: "I Am A Witness", iOS
Autism Speaks Campaign: "I Want to Say"
Bay Area Council Billboards, Bus-Shelter Ads, Campaign: "Talking Is Teaching: Talk, Read, Sing", Radio, TV, Vocabulary, Website, talkreadsing.org
BevMo! (Agency of Record) Digital & Social Marketing, E-Commerce Support, Media Planning
California Milk Advisory Board
California Milk Processor Board #SongsForMom, Campaign: "Brave", Campaign: "Champion", Campaign: "Defending Dairy", Campaign: "Food Loves Milk", Campaign: "Got milk?", Campaign: "History", Campaign: "Milk Fuels A Better Future", Digital, Get the Glass!, Milk, Social Media; 1993
The Center for Investigative Reporting Poster series, Web Films, Website Design
Cisco Systems Billboard, Branding, Campaign: "Building Tomorrow Today", Campaign: "Circle Story", Campaign: "THE INTERNET OF EVERYTHING", Campaign: "The Last Traffic Jam", Campaign: "Tomorrow Starts Here"
Comcast (Agency of Record) Campaign: "For the Kids", Campaign: "Homecoming", Campaign: "Name Game", Campaign: "Names Are Made Here", Campaign: "Out There", Consumer Advertising, Digital, Dish Head, Internet Service, Nascar Xfinity Series, PowerBoost, Triple Play Service, Xfinity
Dali Museum Campaign: "Staring Contest", iPhone App
Dreyer's Ice Cream; Oakland, CA Haagen-Dazs, Premium; 1999
eBay Inc. Campaign: "Come to Think of it, eBay", Campaign: "Shop a Song", Campaign: "Shop the World", Creative, Media, Social, Strategy, TV
Fancast
Foster Farms Campaign: "Amazing Chicken", Campaign: "Human League", Campaign: "Night Ranger", Campaign: "Toto"
Frito-Lay, Inc.; Plano, TX Campaign: "Chocolate Bunny", Campaign: "Crash The Super Bowl", Campaign: "No Features", Campaign: "Press Conference", Cheetos, Creative, Dips, Doritos, Doritos Collisions, Doritos Late Night Rihanna, Sweetos, Tostitos; 2006
General Motors Campaign: "Chevy Runs Deep", Campaign: "Chevy Sonic Integrated", Campaign: "Night Swimming", Campaign: "Street Art", Campaign: "Then & Now", Chevrolet - Lead Creative Agency, Chevy Volt
Golden Gate National Park Association Campaign: "Golden Gate Bridge 75th Anniversary"
Google Campaign: "Balloons", Campaign: "Hall & Oates", Campaign: "Love Story", Campaign: "May be the best ads are just answers.", Google Docs Demo-Masters Edition, Google+, YouTube
Haagen-Dazs HelptheHoneyBees.com, Television
Hyundai Motor America Genesis, Santa Fe, Tucson, Veracruz; 2007
Logitech Logitech Revue
Marmot (Agency of Record)
Motorola Mobility LLC Motorola
National Audobon Society Birding the Net
Nest Campaign: "Happy Homes"
Nestle USA Campaign: "La Dolce Vita", Digital, Dreyer's/Edy's, Haagen-Dazs, Print, TV
Netflix
Nintendo
Old Spice Campaign: "Jingle Hoops"
PepsiCo Campaign: "Best Summer Job", Campaign: "Crash the Superbowl" Super Bowl 2014, Campaign: "For the Bold", Campaign: "Joy Ride", Campaign: "Now or Never", Campaign: "The Crash Ambassador", Cheetos, Digital, Doritos, Fritos, Project T.P., Rold Gold, TV; 2008
POPSUGAR Creative
Princess Cruises Campaign: "Come Back New", Digital, Marketing, Radio
Seagate Technology Brand Strategy
Sonic Corp. Campaign: "Drive-In", Campaign: "Dunk", Campaign: "Heart's Desire", Campaign: "One on One on One", Campaign: "Sipsters", Campaign: "Sweeter", Campaign: "Train Your 'Buds", Campaign: "Wolfman", Creative, Sonic Drive-In, Wingtoberfest
Sony Ericsson
Specialized Bicycles Campaign: "Life of Speed", Campaign: "Thumbs Of Glory", Pedal-Powered Machine Contest
TD AMERITRADE Holding Corporation
Twitter Brand Marketing, Campaign: "Love Every Second", Campaign: "World Cup of Twitter", World Cup Video
Xfinity 3D
Yahoo! Yahoo Bus Stop Derby

GOODMAN MARKETING PARTNERS

4340 Redwood Hwy Ste B-52, San Rafael, CA 94903
Tel.: (415) 507-9060
E-Mail: info@goodmanmarketing.com
Web Site: www.goodmanmarketing.com

Year Founded: 2002

Agency Specializes In: Advertising, Collateral, Email, Internet/Web Design, Sales Promotion, Social Media

Denise Williams *(Dir-Strategic Mktg & New Bus Dev)*
Anyra Papsys *(Acct Mgr)*

Accounts:
McRoskey Mattress Company

GOODMAN MEDIA INTERNATIONAL, INC.

750 7th Ave 28th Fl, New York, NY 10016
Tel.: (212) 576-2700
Fax: (212) 576-2701
E-Mail: info@goodmanmedia.com
Web Site: www.goodmanmedia.com

Employees: 30

Agency Specializes In: Advertising, Advertising Specialties, Consulting, Environmental, Event Planning & Marketing, Multimedia, Publicity/Promotions, Sponsorship, T.V.

Tom Goodman *(Pres & CEO)*
Henry Miller *(COO)*
Virginia Anagnos *(Exec VP)*
John Michael Kennedy *(VP)*
Bennett Kleinberg *(VP)*
Liane Ramirez Swierk *(VP)*
Sabrina Strauss *(VP)*
Regine Labossiere *(Acct Mgr)*

Accounts:
Abbott Point of Care i-STAT Medical Diagnostic System; 2007
ABC News
American Library Association
The Buoniconti Fund
Charles H. Revson Foundation
Children's Book Council; 2008
Discover Magazine; 2007
Environmental Defense Fund
Free to Chose Media The Power of the Poor Documentary; 2008
GE (General Electric) General Electric Theater Television Series
GQ
Grand Central Terminal; New York, NY Event, Media, Retail
Greater Boston Physicians For Social Responsibility Environmental Threats to Healthy Aging Study
HDNet Dan Rather Reports; 2007
Hospital for Special Surgery Public Relations
Island Press; 2008
The John Merck Fund
Latinum Network Consumer Media Relations
Lifetime
Lincoln Center for the Performing Arts
Macmillan Children's Publishing Cool Creations in 35 Pieces, I'd Know You Anywhere, My Love
MAD Magazine Totally MAD
Mailman School of Public Health
McCormick Distilling Co. 360 Vodka; 2007
MediaPost MEDIA Magazine; 2008
Mental Health Association of New York
MSNBC
Nabbr, Inc.
National Geographic
National NeighborWorks Association
NCC Media Trade & Consumer Business
Next Avenue NextAvenue.org
PBS Michael Feinstein's American Songbook, Pioneers of Television
Penguin Books Madeline & The Cats of Rome; 2008
Private Communications Corporation National Media Relations
Rauch Foundation
Research Corporation; 2007
Scholastic National Media Outreach
SmartPower MyGulfAction.com (Agency of Record), Not-for-Profit Energy Efficiency, Online Campaign, Social Media Campaign
Starmount Life Insurance Company
Student Conservation Association
Time Warner
TLC
TRA, Inc.
TV Guide Magazine National Publicity
Walter Dean Myers; 2006
WNBA
World Science Festival

GOODMEDIA COMMUNICATIONS

(Acquired & Absorbed by Frozen Fire)

THE GOODNESS COMPANY

820 Baker St, Wisconsin Rapids, WI 54494
Tel.: (715) 423-1255
Toll Free: (866) 265-1001
E-Mail: patrick@goodnesscompany.com
Web Site: www.goodnesscompany.com

E-Mail for Key Personnel:
President: patrick@goodnesscompany.com
Creative Dir.: terri@goodnesscompany.com
Media Dir.: patrick@goodnesscompany.com
Public Relations: info@goodnesscompany.com

Employees: 14
Year Founded: 1994

National Agency Associations: AMA

Agency Specializes In: Advertising, Affluent Market, African-American Market, Automotive, Bilingual Market, Brand Development & Integration, Business Publications, Business-To-Business, Children's Market, Co-op Advertising, Collateral, Communications, Consulting, Consumer Goods, Consumer Marketing, Consumer Publications, Corporate Communications, Corporate Identity, Digital/Interactive, Direct Response Marketing, E-Commerce, Education, Electronic Media, Email, Entertainment, Environmental, Fashion/Apparel, Financial, Food Service, Government/Political, Graphic Design, Health Care Services, High Technology, Hispanic Market, Identity Marketing, Industrial, Information Technology, International, Internet/Web Design, Investor Relations, Leisure, Local Marketing, Logo & Package Design, Luxury

Advertising Agencies

Products, Magazines, Marine, Media Buying Services, Medical Products, Multicultural, Multimedia, New Product Development, Newspaper, Newspapers & Magazines, Out-of-Home Media, Outdoor, Over-50 Market, Pharmaceutical, Planning & Consultation, Point of Purchase, Point of Sale, Print, Production, Public Relations, Publicity/Promotions, Real Estate, Recruitment, Restaurant, Retail, Sales Promotion, Seniors' Market, Strategic Planning/Research, Teen Market, Trade & Consumer Magazines, Transportation, Travel & Tourism, Web (Banner Ads, Pop-ups, etc.), Women's Market, Yellow Pages Advertising

Patrick Goodness *(CEO)*
Terri Goodness *(Dir-Creative)*
Ronald Rojas *(Mgr-Video)*
Joctan Rodriguez *(Designer-Print & Web)*

Accounts:
3PEC; MI Automotive; 2004
Administration for Native Americans; Washington, D.C.; 2003
Advanced Audio & Video; WI Home Audio Products; 2003
Adventure 212 Fitness
Allstate Insurance Company; Northbrook, IL; 1994
American Lung Association; Springfield, IL Tobacco QuitLine; 2005
Antioch Rescue Squad
Architectural Designs Inc.; WI; 2002
Bahamas Medical Center
Bancroft State Bank
BFG Tech; Lake Forest, IL Internet Traffic Cop; 2005
Buhrman Design Group; IL Landscaping Services; 1995
Capuchin-Franciscan Vocations Religious Vocation Recruitment; 2007
Cardinal Health
CIB Bank; IL Financial Services; 2002
Colina Dental
Colony Brands Inc.
Costa Rica Dental Team
Custom Gutter Corporation; IL Construction Services; 2001
Day Elevator & Lift; Lynbrook, NY Elevators, Lifts; 2005
DeKind Computer Consultants; 2005
Easter Seals
Energy Composites Corporation
Fabric Source; MN Fabric; 1999
Fey Printing
The Financial Centre Investment Services; 2007
Florida Health Systems
Hasbro Childrens Hospital
Interactive Business Products; IL; 2002
Luna Carpet; IL Retail & Commercial Carpeting; 1998
Made Rite Bedding; IL Mattresses; 1999
Manning Silverman; Lincolnshire, IL Accounting Services; 2006
Master Key Consulting; MD Government Consulting; 2002
Michels Corporation; WI Construction Services; 2004
Microsoft Corp.; Redmond, WA Accessibility - Disabilities Group; 1998
Midnight Velvet; WI Women's Clothing, Accessories & Home Accents; 2004
Monroe & Main; WI Women's Clothing; 2005
North Shore Trust & Savings; Chicago, IL Mid-Size Bank; 2005
Nurtrativa Global Health Foods; 2008
Pediatric Solutions; IL Pediatrics Franchise; 2005
Prime Wine, Inc.; IL Wine; 2004
RainTrade Corporation; IL Construction Services; 2001
Rapid Control Systems
Sundance Photo; Jackson, WI Photo Services; 2007
Village of Antioch; Antioch, IL Village Brand & Collateral Materials; 2005
West Suburban Orthodontics; Elmhurst, IL Dental Services; 2007
Westphal's Printing; WI Printing Services; 2003

GOODNESS MFG.
(Acquired by & Name Changed to Deep Focus)

GOODRUM ADVERTISING INC.
1211 Bakers Work Rd, Burns, TN 37029
Tel.: (615) 797-5959
Fax: (615) 797-5946
E-Mail: hcgads@aol.com

Employees: 4
Year Founded: 1971

Agency Specializes In: Advertising, Brand Development & Integration, Broadcast, Business Publications, Business-To-Business, Cable T.V., Co-op Advertising, Collateral, Communications, Consulting, Consumer Marketing, Consumer Publications, Corporate Identity, Direct Response Marketing, Electronic Media, Environmental, Event Planning & Marketing, Exhibit/Trade Shows, Fashion/Apparel, Financial, Food Service, Graphic Design, High Technology, Industrial, Infomercials, Leisure, Logo & Package Design, Magazines, Media Buying Services, Merchandising, Multimedia, New Product Development, Newspaper, Newspapers & Magazines, Outdoor, Planning & Consultation, Point of Purchase, Point of Sale, Print, Production, Public Relations, Publicity/Promotions, Radio, Recruitment, Restaurant, Retail, Sales Promotion, Seniors' Market, Sports Market, Strategic Planning/Research, T.V., Technical Advertising, Trade & Consumer Magazines, Travel & Tourism, Yellow Pages Advertising

Approx. Annual Billings: $1,900,000

Breakdown of Gross Billings by Media: Brdcst.: $1,425,000; Collateral: $237,500; Newsp. & Mags.: $237,500

Accounts:
Clifty Farms; Paris, TN; 1977
Grace's; Nashville, TN; 1980
Hardaway Group; Nashville, TN; 1982
Tennessee Valley Ham Co.; Paris, TN; 1977

GORA COMMUNICATIONS
3 Front St, Stonington, CT 06378
Tel.: (401) 354-9229
Fax: (401) 223-6444
Web Site: www.goracommunications.com

Year Founded: 1990

Agency Specializes In: Advertising, Brand Development & Integration, Graphic Design, Media Relations, Strategic Planning/Research

Angela Abele-Gora *(Pres & Dir-Creative)*

Accounts:
Greater Providence Chamber of Commerce
The Providence Center Symmetry at Duncan Lodge
RI Catholic
Saint Antoine Community Ultimate

GORDLEY GROUP
(Private-Parent-Single Location)
2540 N Tucson Blvd, Tucson, AZ 85716
Tel.: (520) 327-6077
Fax: (520) 327-4687
E-Mail: info@gordleygroup.com
Web Site: www.gordleydesign.com

Employees: 15
Year Founded: 1991

Agency Specializes In: Advertising, Brand Development & Integration, Event Planning & Marketing, Media Relations, Public Relations, Strategic Planning/Research

Revenue: $1,000,000

Jan Gordley *(Pres)*
Jennifer LaHue-Smith *(Creative Dir)*
Sulochana Konur *(Dir-Acctg)*
Alice Templeton *(Dir-Community Rels)*
Dawn Hosack *(Media Planner & Coord-Public Involvement)*

Accounts:
Pima Community College

GORILLA 76 LLC
408 N Euclid Ave 3rd Fl, Saint Louis, MO 63108
Tel.: (314) 332-1020
Web Site: www.gorilla76.com

Agency Specializes In: Advertising, Brand Development & Integration, Content, Internet/Web Design, Search Engine Optimization, Social Media

Jon Franko *(Partner)*
Joe Sullivan *(Partner)*
Randall Zaitz *(Designer)*

Accounts:
The Korte Company
TruQC LLC

THE GOSS AGENCY INC.
49 Broadway Ste 202, Asheville, NC 28801
Tel.: (828) 259-9910
Fax: (828) 225-6999
E-Mail: info@thegossagency.com
Web Site: www.thegossagency.com

Employees: 12
Year Founded: 1998

Agency Specializes In: Above-the-Line, Advertising, Advertising Specialties, Affiliate Marketing, Affluent Market, African-American Market, Agriculture, Alternative Advertising, Arts, Asian Market, Automotive, Aviation & Aerospace, Below-the-Line, Bilingual Market, Brand Development & Integration, Branded Entertainment, Broadcast, Business Publications, Business-To-Business, Cable T.V., Catalogs, Children's Market, Co-op Advertising, Collateral, College, Commercial Photography, Communications, Computers & Software, Consulting, Consumer Goods, Consumer Marketing, Consumer Publications, Content, Corporate Communications, Corporate Identity, Cosmetics, Crisis Communications, Custom Publishing, Customer Relationship Management, Digital/Interactive, Direct Response Marketing, Direct-to-Consumer, E-Commerce, Education, Electronic Media, Electronics, Email, Engineering, Entertainment, Environmental, Event Planning & Marketing, Exhibit/Trade Shows, Experience Design, Fashion/Apparel, Financial, Food Service, Game Integration, Gay & Lesbian Market, Government/Political, Graphic Design, Guerilla Marketing, Health Care Services, High Technology, Hispanic Market, Hospitality, Household Goods, Identity Marketing, In-Store Advertising, Industrial, Infomercials, Information Technology, Integrated Marketing, International, Internet/Web Design, Investor Relations, Legal Services, Leisure, Local Marketing, Logo & Package Design, Luxury Products, Magazines, Marine, Market Research, Media Buying Services, Media Planning, Media Relations, Media Training, Medical Products, Men's

Market, Merchandising, Mobile Marketing, Multicultural, Multimedia, New Product Development, New Technologies, Newspaper, Newspapers & Magazines, Out-of-Home Media, Outdoor, Over-50 Market, Package Design, Paid Searches, Pharmaceutical, Planning & Consultation, Podcasting, Point of Purchase, Point of Sale, Print, Product Placement, Production, Production (Ad, Film, Broadcast), Production (Print), Promotions, Public Relations, Publicity/Promotions, Publishing, RSS (Really Simple Syndication), Radio, Real Estate, Recruitment, Regional, Restaurant, Retail, Sales Promotion, Search Engine Optimization, Seniors' Market, Social Marketing/Nonprofit, Sponsorship, Sports Market, Stakeholders, Strategic Planning/Research, Sweepstakes, Syndication, T.V., Technical Advertising, Teen Market, Telemarketing, Trade & Consumer Magazines, Transportation, Travel & Tourism, Urban Market, Viral/Buzz/Word of Mouth, Web (Banner Ads, Pop-ups, etc.), Women's Market, Yellow Pages Advertising

Jeffrey E. Goss *(Pres)*
Mark Schofield *(Sr VP-Acct Leadership)*
Gordon Farquhar *(Dir-Political & Client Svcs Dir)*
Neil Romaine *(Dir-Strategic Media Mktg)*
Karen Goss *(Office Mgr)*
Dari Mullins *(Acct Mgr)*
Bob Davies *(Strategist-Brand)*

Accounts:
Haywood County Tourism; 2014
Historic Biltmore Village Branding
Paradise Beach Resort Brand Image, Website
New-Visit Natchez Convention & Visitors Bureau

GOTHAM DIRECT
(Name Changed to Generator Media + Analytics)

GOTHAM INCORPORATED
(Name Changed to beauty@gotham)

GOTHAM PUBLIC RELATIONS
400 W. Broadway, New York, NY 10012
Tel.: (212) 352-2147
E-Mail: courtney@gothampr.com
Web Site: www.gothampr.com

Year Founded: 2002

Agency Specializes In: Advertising, Arts, Brand Development & Integration, Branded Entertainment, Entertainment, Event Planning & Marketing, Hospitality

Courtney Lukitsch *(Founder)*
Peter McGuinness *(Chm & CEO)*
Allison Birmingham *(Acct Exec)*
Hannah Miller *(Acct Exec)*

Accounts:
Adjmi-Andreoli
AFNY
Corinth Films (Agency of Record)
New-Fitzgerald Fine Arts (Agency of Record)
Flavor Paper Business Development, Global Marketing
New-GHWArchitects (Agency of Record)
Hudson Furniture Business Development, Global Marketing
Jennifer Post Design
Luis Pons D-Lab
Messana O'Rorke
Morris Adjmi Architects
Olighting.com (Agency of Record)
Pryor Callaway Design
Relative Space (Agency of Record) Flooring & Textile Showroom
Sebastian+Barquet Business Development, Global Marketing
New-Subject (Agency of Record)
New-Whitehall Interiors (Agency of Record)
Workshop/apd
The World of Interiors Business Development, Global Marketing

THE GOULDING AGENCY, INC.
1367-C S Railrd Ave, Chipley, FL 32428
Tel.: (850) 625-6888
E-Mail: info@thegouldingagency.com
Web Site: www.thegouldingagency.com

Agency Specializes In: Advertising, Internet/Web Design, Media Buying Services, Media Planning, Print, Public Relations, Radio

Debbie Goulding *(VP)*

Accounts:
Hard Labor Creek Shooting Sports
Jackson County The Real Florida
Jeep Sullivan's Outdoor Adventures
Real Florida Magazine
Wausau Possum Festival

GOURMET MARKETING
307 7th Ave Ste 1104, New York, NY 10001
Tel.: (646) 854-4320
E-Mail: info@gourmetmarketing.net
Web Site: www.gourmetmarketing.net

Agency Specializes In: Advertising, Internet/Web Design, Search Engine Optimization, Social Media

Gene Herts *(Pres)*
Emrah Tuzun *(Mgr-Mktg)*

Accounts:
New-Ayza Wine & Chocolate Bar

GRADY BRITTON
107 SE Washington St Ste 300, Portland, OR 97214-2613
Tel.: (503) 228-4118
Fax: (503) 273-8817
E-Mail: info@gradybritton.com
Web Site: www.gradybritton.com

E-Mail for Key Personnel:
Creative Dir.: andya@gradybritton.com
Media Dir.: sarahp@gradybritton.com
Production Mgr.: kellyb@gradybritton.com
Public Relations: ering@gradybritton.com

Employees: 20
Year Founded: 1974

National Agency Associations: 4A's

Agency Specializes In: Advertising, Brand Development & Integration, Broadcast, Business-To-Business, Collateral, Communications, Corporate Communications, Corporate Identity, Financial, High Technology, Media Buying Services, Media Planning, Multimedia, Public Relations, Real Estate, Sponsorship, Strategic Planning/Research, Transportation, Web (Banner Ads, Pop-ups, etc.)

Approx. Annual Billings: $6,200,000

Paige McCarthy *(Pres & Partner)*
Andy Askren *(Partner & Exec Dir-Creative)*
Becky Engel *(Dir-PR & Acct Dir)*
Emma Oliver *(Dir-Fin)*
Sarah Prince *(Dir-Media)*
Kelly Burns *(Sr Acct Mgr)*
Jill Hrycyk *(Acct Mgr)*

Accounts:
Bob's Red Mill
Port of Vancouver (Agency of Record)
Travel Portland

GRAFICAGROUP
67 E Park Pl, Morristown, NJ 07960
Tel.: (973) 309-7500
Fax: (908) 879-2569
E-Mail: info@grafica.com
Web Site: www.grafica.com

E-Mail for Key Personnel:
President: Dtaeschler@grafica.com
Creative Dir.: john_p@grafica.com
Production Mgr.: colleenr@grafica.com

Employees: 37
Year Founded: 1986

National Agency Associations: AWNY-DMA-NJ Ad Club-PRSA-Second Wind Limited

Agency Specializes In: Above-the-Line, Advertising, Advertising Specialties, Affluent Market, Alternative Advertising, Automotive, Below-the-Line, Bilingual Market, Brand Development & Integration, Branded Entertainment, Broadcast, Business Publications, Business-To-Business, Cable T.V., Co-op Advertising, Collateral, College, Commercial Photography, Communications, Computers & Software, Consulting, Consumer Goods, Consumer Marketing, Consumer Publications, Content, Corporate Communications, Corporate Identity, Customer Relationship Management, Digital/Interactive, Direct Response Marketing, Direct-to-Consumer, E-Commerce, Education, Electronic Media, Email, Engineering, Exhibit/Trade Shows, Experience Design, Financial, Food Service, Government/Political, Graphic Design, Guerilla Marketing, Health Care Services, High Technology, Hispanic Market, Hospitality, Identity Marketing, In-Store Advertising, Industrial, Information Technology, Integrated Marketing, International, Internet/Web Design, Leisure, Luxury Products, Magazines, Media Buying Services, Media Planning, Medical Products, Mobile Marketing, Multicultural, Multimedia, New Product Development, New Technologies, Newspaper, Newspapers & Magazines, Out-of-Home Media, Outdoor, Package Design, Paid Searches, Pharmaceutical, Planning & Consultation, Podcasting, Point of Purchase, Point of Sale, Print, Production, Production (Ad, Film, Broadcast), Production (Print), Promotions, Public Relations, Publicity/Promotions, Publishing, RSS (Really Simple Syndication), Radio, Real Estate, Recruitment, Regional, Restaurant, Retail, Sales Promotion, Search Engine Optimization, Seniors' Market, Social Media, Sponsorship, Strategic Planning/Research, Sweepstakes, T.V., Technical Advertising, Teen Market, Trade & Consumer Magazines, Transportation, Travel & Tourism, Viral/Buzz/Word of Mouth, Web (Banner Ads, Pop-ups, etc.), Women's Market, Yellow Pages Advertising

Approx. Annual Billings: $14,168,660

Debra A. Taeschler *(Founder, Pres & CEO)*
John Puglionisi *(Co-Founder & VP-Creative)*
Ed Miller *(CFO)*
Cheryle Barnett *(VP & Dir-Acct Mgmt)*
Jacob Usawicz *(VP-Creative Tech)*

Accounts:
AT&T
Gill Saint Bernards
Horizon Blue Cross Blue Shield of New Jersey
Jackson Hewitt Tax Service
The New Jersey Board of Public Utilities
New Jersey Office of Clean Energy
PSE&G Energy Technologies Inc.
PSE&G Worry Free Service Contracts
Wells Fargo Home Mortgage

GRAFICAINTER.ACTIVE, LTD.
525 E Main St, Chester, NJ 07930-2627
Tel.: (908) 879-2169
Fax: (908) 879-2569
E-Mail: info@grafica.com
Web Site: www.grafica.com

Employees: 27
Year Founded: 1996

National Agency Associations: AD CLUB-ADC-AWNY-DMA-PRSA-Second Wind Limited

Agency Specializes In: Advertising, Bilingual Market, Brand Development & Integration, Broadcast, Business Publications, Business-To-Business, Cable T.V., Collateral, Communications, Consulting, Consumer Marketing, Corporate Identity, Digital/Interactive, Direct Response Marketing, E-Commerce, Education, Electronic Media, Environmental, Event Planning & Marketing, Exhibit/Trade Shows, Financial, Government/Political, Graphic Design, Health Care Services, High Technology, Industrial, Information Technology, Internet/Web Design, Logo & Package Design, Magazines, Media Buying Services, Multimedia, New Product Development, Newspaper, Newspapers & Magazines, Outdoor, Pharmaceutical, Point of Purchase, Point of Sale, Print, Production, Public Relations, Publicity/Promotions, Radio, Real Estate, Retail, Strategic Planning/Research, Sweepstakes, T.V., Technical Advertising, Telemarketing, Yellow Pages Advertising

Approx. Annual Billings: $14,100,000

Debra A. Taeschler *(Founder, Pres & CEO)*
John Puglionisi *(Co-Founder, VP & Dir-Creative)*
Ed Miller *(CFO)*
Cheryle Barnett *(VP-Acct Mgmt)*
Jacob Usawicz *(Dir-Creative-Digital)*

Accounts:
AT&T Network Enterprising
AT&T Teleconference Services
Beneficial Management
Cathedral
First Morris Bank and Trust
Hasbro
Horizon BlueCross BlueShield of New Jersey
Jackson-Hewitt Tax Services
KPMG LLP
New Jersey Lottery
New Jersey Office of the Attorney General
PSE&G
Purchase College
Summit Medical Group
Trane
Trinity Biotech

GRAFIK MARKETING COMMUNICATIONS
625 N Washington St, Alexandria, VA 22314
Tel.: (703) 299-4500
Fax: (703) 299-5999
E-Mail: info@grafik.com
Web Site: www.grafik.com

Employees: 25

Agency Specializes In: Advertising, Broadcast, Collateral, Corporate Identity, Digital/Interactive, Direct Response Marketing, Email, Event Planning & Marketing, Exhibit/Trade Shows, Experience Design, Internet/Web Design, Local Marketing, Mobile Marketing, Outdoor, Paid Searches, Print, Production (Print), Promotions, Radio, Retail, Search Engine Optimization, Social Media, Web (Banner Ads, Pop-ups, etc.)

Lance Wain *(CEO)*
David Collins *(Principal & Dir-Creative)*
Gregg Glaviano *(Principal & Dir-Creative)*
Johnny Vitorovich *(Principal & Dir-Creative)*
Lynn Umemoto *(Principal-Client Strategy)*
Cheryl Haar *(Sr VP-Client Strategy)*
Mikah Sellers *(Sr VP-Strategic Dev)*
Arthur Hsu *(Dir-Art)*
Sun Yun *(Dir-Interactive Creative)*
Jennifer Parker *(Mgr-Mktg)*
Hal Swetnam *(Sr Strategist-Creative)*

Accounts:
AdvicePeriod; 2013
AES Internal Brand; 2013
Akre Capital Management; 2014
Anybill; 2011
The Brady Campaign Campaign Design; 2014
Carsquare; 2014
Convergent Wealth Advisor; 2007
Cystic Fibrosis Foundation; 2006
DC Prep; 2007
EYA Corporate Brand; 2005
Gennum; 2007
Global Automakers; 2010
Honda in America Advocacy; 2003
JK Moving Services; 2010
National Museum of the American Indian; 2000
National Trust for Historic Preservation; 2011
Neustar; 2013
Smithsonian Institution Corporate Advertising; 2001
Software AG Corporate Advertising; 2010
Spree Commerce; 2013
Waldron Private Wealth; 2014
WTOP; 2014

GRAFITZ GROUP NETWORK
1102 3rd Ave Ste 204, Huntington, WV 25701
Tel.: (304) 581-4689
E-Mail: info@grafitz.com
Web Site: www.grafitz.com

Agency Specializes In: Advertising, Email, Graphic Design, Internet/Web Design, Logo & Package Design, Media Planning, Print, Radio

Shawn Fitzpatrick *(Owner)*
Perry Ryan Bentley *(VP, Sr Dir-Creative, Designer-Web & Graphic Designer)*
Tanya Taul *(Sr Dir-Strategic Mktg)*
Terra Ramsey *(Office Mgr)*
Bud Preece *(Specialist-Sls & Mktg)*
Bryan Ousley *(Designer-Web & Graphic Design)*
Josh Robirds *(Designer-Branding)*

Accounts:
Hope's Place

GRAGG ADVERTISING
450 E 4th St Ste 100, Kansas City, MO 64106
Tel.: (816) 931-0050
Fax: (816) 931-0051
Toll Free: (800) 649-4225
E-Mail: info@graggadv.com
Web Site: www.graggadv.com

Employees: 51
Year Founded: 1993

National Agency Associations: AAF-DMA

Agency Specializes In: Advertising, Aviation & Aerospace, Broadcast, Business-To-Business, Cable T.V., Digital/Interactive, Direct Response Marketing, E-Commerce, Electronic Media, Graphic Design, Internet/Web Design, Logo & Package Design, Media Buying Services, Newspaper, Newspapers & Magazines, Outdoor, Planning & Consultation, Point of Purchase, Point of Sale, Print, Production, Radio, Recruitment, Restaurant, Retail, Strategic Planning/Research, T.V.

Breakdown of Gross Billings by Media: Audio/Visual: 2%; Bus. Publs.: 5%; Collateral: 5%; Consulting: 5%; D.M.: 10%; E-Commerce: 5%; Event Mktg.: 1%; Exhibits/Trade Shows: 1%; Fees: 10%; Graphic Design: 7%; Logo & Package Design: 1%; Mags.: 3%; Newsp.: 5%; Outdoor: 3%; Plng. & Consultation: 2%; Radio: 5%; Spot T.V.: 20%; Strategic Planning/Research: 5%; Worldwide Web Sites: 5%

Darryl Mattox *(Pres, Partner & COO)*
Gregory Gragg *(CEO)*
Fred Frantz *(Exec VP)*
Mark Buchele *(Dir-Media)*
Cathryn Vaughn *(Dir-Digital Mktg Grp)*
Lisa Olmedo *(Mgr-EDU Mktg-Western US & Canada)*

Accounts:
American Career Institute Buying, Planning and Placement, Online Marketing Strategies, Search Engine Marketing and Optimization, Traditional Media, Website Redesign
American School of Technology Integrated Marketing Strategy
Brookline College Integrated Marketing Strategy
Central Penn College Integrated Marketing Strategy
Globe University Integrated Marketing Strategy
Michigan Institute of Aviation and Technology Online, Interactive Marketing, Traditional Advertising
Miller-Motte College Online
Ntimus Clinic (Agency of Record) Brand Development, Offline & Online Marketing, Search Engine Marketing, Website Design
Pat Riha Productions
Topsy's Popcorn

GRAHAM & COMPANY ADVERTISING, INC.
510 Broadhollow Rd Ste 301, Melville, NY 11747
Tel.: (631) 393-6492
E-Mail: info@grahamandcompany.com
Web Site: www.grahamandcompany.com

Employees: 7
Year Founded: 1974

Agency Specializes In: Advertising, Brand Development & Integration, Business-To-Business, Children's Market, Consumer Marketing, Electronic Media, Food Service, Graphic Design, Industrial, Internet/Web Design, Logo & Package Design, Print, Real Estate, Strategic Planning/Research

Approx. Annual Billings: $1,200,000

Henry Graham *(VP-Mktg & Bus Dev)*
Mark Bellucci *(Co-Dir-Creative & Copywriter)*

Accounts:
Air Charters
Corteq
Delco Tableware
Gallant & Wein
Garanimals
H.A. Guden Co., Inc.; Ronkonkoma, NY Hardware for Industry
Hastings Manufacturing; Hastings, MI
IDP Consulting
The Law Firm of Jerome A. Wisselman; Great Neck, NY
Marathon Communications Inc.
Paragon Slide Cabinets; Brooklyn, NY Slide Cabinets; 2003
Preload Co., Inc.; Garden City, NY Builders of Prestressed Concrete Tanks
Tesorino

THE GRAHAM GROUP
2014 W Pinhook Rd Ste 210, Lafayette, LA 70508-3297

Tel.: (337) 232-8214
Fax: (337) 235-3787
E-Mail: graham@graham-group.com
Web Site: www.graham-group.com

E-Mail for Key Personnel:
President: graham@graham-group.com
Media Dir.: natalie@graham-group.com

Employees: 30
Year Founded: 1979

Agency Specializes In: Financial, Health Care Services, Travel & Tourism

Approx. Annual Billings: $23,700,000

George Graham *(CEO)*
Michelle Constantin *(COO)*
Kathy Andersen *(Sr VP-Acct Svc)*
Kerry Palmer *(Mng Dir-Art)*
Natalie Lemoine *(VP & Dir-Media)*
Raymond Credeur *(Creative Dir)*
Denise Bishop *(Media Planner & Media Buyer)*
Donna Weber *(Media Buyer)*

Accounts:
Christus Saint Patrick Hospital
Demco; Baton Rouge, LA Utilities
Los Angeles Department of Transportation
Louisiana Health System
Louisiana Lottery Corporation

Branch

The Graham Group
11505 Perkins Rd Bldg 3 Ste 3, Baton Rouge, LA 70810
Tel.: (225) 767-8520
Fax: (225) 761-0870
E-Mail: graham@graham-group.com
Web Site: www.graham-group.com

Employees: 20
Year Founded: 1993

Agency Specializes In: Financial, Health Care Services, Travel & Tourism

Kees Cusveller *(VP-Bus Dev)*

Accounts:
Louisiana Lottery
Terrebonne general Medical Center

GRAHAM GROUP INTERACTIVE
2014 W Pinhook Rd Ste 210, Lafayette, LA 70508-8504
Tel.: (337) 232-8214
Fax: (337) 235-3787
E-Mail: info@graham-group.com
Web Site: www.graham-group.com

E-Mail for Key Personnel:
President: graham@graham-group.com

Employees: 27
Year Founded: 1995

Agency Specializes In: Consulting, Consumer Marketing, Electronic Media, Internet/Web Design, Multimedia, Publicity/Promotions, Web (Banner Ads, Pop-ups, etc.)

Approx. Annual Billings: $3,900,000

Breakdown of Gross Billings by Media: Worldwide Web Sites: 100%

George Graham *(CEO)*
Michelle Constantin *(COO)*
Sylvia Brown *(Mgr-Talent Acq-Natl)*

GRAHAM MEDIA PARTNERS
512 Saint Davids Rd, Wayne, PA 19087
Tel.: (610) 688-2060
Web Site: www.grahammediapartners.com

Year Founded: 2014

Agency Specializes In: Advertising, Brand Development & Integration, Business-To-Business, Internet/Web Design, Logo & Package Design, Print, Public Relations, Social Media

Lisa Graham *(CEO)*
Steve Graham *(COO)*
Corey Pontz *(Creative Dir)*

Accounts:
New-Walz IT LLC

GRAHAM OLESON
(Formerly Graham Advertising)
525 Communication Cir, Colorado Springs, CO 80905-1736
Tel.: (719) 635-7335
Fax: (719) 635-1143
Toll Free: (800) 776-7336
E-Mail: info@grahamadvertising.com
Web Site: www.grahamoleson.com

Employees: 55
Year Founded: 1977

Agency Specializes In: Advertising, Automotive, Brand Development & Integration, Broadcast, Business-To-Business, Cable T.V., Co-op Advertising, Collateral, Corporate Identity, Digital/Interactive, Direct Response Marketing, Direct-to-Consumer, Email, Graphic Design, Guerilla Marketing, Hispanic Market, Identity Marketing, In-Store Advertising, Infomercials, Integrated Marketing, Internet/Web Design, Local Marketing, Logo & Package Design, Magazines, Market Research, Media Buying Services, Media Planning, Merchandising, Newspaper, Newspapers & Magazines, Out-of-Home Media, Outdoor, Planning & Consultation, Point of Purchase, Point of Sale, Print, Sales Promotion, Search Engine Optimization, Sponsorship, Sports Market, Strategic Planning/Research, Web (Banner Ads, Pop-ups, etc.)

Approx. Annual Billings: $40,000,000

Sandy Emmert *(Pres)*
Kirk Oleson *(CEO)*
Rhonda Maehara *(Exec VP)*
Edward Kahn *(Acct Dir)*
Jared Tague *(Dir-IT)*
Georgia Schreiner *(Mgr-Media)*
Sharon Sutter-Holm *(Mgr-Media & Digital Strategy)*
Kristi Davis *(Sr Acct Exec)*
Joni Melendrez *(Sr Acct Exec)*
Jess Horst *(Acct Exec)*
Dawn Wood *(Acct Exec)*
Jennifer Ridler *(Media Buyer)*
Amber Ross *(Acct Coord)*
Cory Webb *(Assoc Strategist-Digital)*

Accounts:
Ford
Honda
Land Rover
Lexus
Lincoln
Toyota

GRAHAM STANLEY ADVERTISING
75 S Broadway 4th Fl, White Plains, NY 10601
Tel.: (212) 710-4329
Fax: (212) 450-1620
E-Mail: database@grahamstan.com
Web Site: www.grahamstan.com

Employees: 21

Agency Specializes In: Advertising, Digital/Interactive, Graphic Design, Internet/Web Design, Media Buying Services, Public Relations, Social Media, Strategic Planning/Research

Revenue: $2,000,000

Breakdown of Gross Billings by Media: Digital/Interactive: $350,000; Newsp. & Mags.: $1,000,000; Pub. Rels.: $150,000; T.V.: $500,000

Larry Woodward *(Principal)*

Accounts:
Cox Communications; Atlanta, GA Cable, Internet, Telephone; 2011
Eurobasket.com (Agency of Record)
Gunter Media Group; New York, NY Syndicated Research; 2011
Sweet Spot Apparel; Atlanta, GA Apparel; 2010

GRANT MARKETING
800 Boylston St 16th Fl, Boston, MA 02199
Tel.: (857) 453-6744
E-Mail: info@grantmarketing.com
Web Site: www.grantmarketing.com

Employees: 8
Year Founded: 1986

National Agency Associations: AMA-BMA-Second Wind Limited

Agency Specializes In: Advertising, Brand Development & Integration, Broadcast, Business-To-Business, Catalogs, Collateral, Commercial Photography, Consulting, Corporate Communications, Corporate Identity, Digital/Interactive, E-Commerce, Email, Exhibit/Trade Shows, Graphic Design, High Technology, Identity Marketing, Industrial, Integrated Marketing, Internet/Web Design, Logo & Package Design, Market Research, Media Buying Services, Media Planning, Media Relations, Paid Searches, Planning & Consultation, Print, Public Relations, RSS (Really Simple Syndication), Search Engine Optimization, Social Marketing/Nonprofit, Strategic Planning/Research

Bob Grant *(Pres)*
Grant Penny *(Dir-Art)*
Cam Mirisola-Bynum *(Mgr-Inbound Mktg)*
Vidushi Bhardwaj *(Specialist-Content Mktg)*

Accounts:
Alliance Scales; Canton, MA Scales, Weighing Systems
Alpha Rho Plastics Corp.; Fitchburg, MA Plastic Boxes
ICL-Imaging; Framingham, MA Large Format Printing
ikaSystems
Interstate Specialty Products; Sutton, MA Die Cutting Services, Gaskets
JI Morris Company; Southbridge, MA Fasteners; 2000
Koch Membrane Systems Filtration Systems
Mass Coalition for Suicide Prevention; Boston, MA; 2007
Standard Rivet; Boston, MA Decorative Rivets

GRANTSTREET CREATIVE
137 E Iron Ave 2nd Fl, Dover, OH 44622
Tel.: (330) 243-0651
Web Site: www.grantstreetcreative.com

Agency Specializes In: Advertising, Brand Development & Integration, Internet/Web Design,

Logo & Package Design, Social Media

Dave Ramsell *(Dir-Creative)*

Accounts:
ACI Services Inc
Tuscarawas County Convention & Visitors Bureau

GRAPEVINE COMMUNICATIONS INC

5201 Paylor Ln, Sarasota, FL 34240
Tel.: (941) 351-0024
Fax: (941) 351-0034
E-Mail: wowme@grapeinc.com
Web Site: www.grapeinc.com

Agency Specializes In: Advertising, Collateral, Internet/Web Design, Logo & Package Design, Outdoor, Print, Public Relations, Radio, Social Media, T.V.

Angela Massaro-Fain *(Founder & Pres)*
John Fain *(Partner & Exec VP)*
Gabriele Vest *(VP-Bus Dev)*
Eric Buchanan *(Dir-Art)*
Michael Hamlin *(Dir-Art)*
John Butzko *(Mgr-PR)*
Shelby Isaacson *(Mgr-Social Media & PR)*
Nick Mayer *(Mgr-Client Rels)*
Sara Englund *(Acct Coord)*

Accounts:
New-ANKO Products
ASO Group
BK Ventures Group
New-Cabot Cove of Largo
New-Dan Dannheisser Personal Injury Attorney
Datum Corporation
Dr. Joshua Colkmire Restorative & Cosmetic Dentistry
Duncan Real Estate
New-Florida Mediator Services
Garage King, Inc
New-GreenZone Heroes
J Dawes Group
New-Karins Engineering Group
New-The Lakeshore Condominiums
New-Manasota Air Conditioning Contractors Association
Ocean Blue Pool Services
Omega Communities
PGT Industries, Inc.
Practice Works MD
Sarasota School of Arts & Sciences
Sky Zone Sarasota
Southport Capital
Synergy Building Corp
Tarpon Shores Dental
New-TreeUmph! Adventure Course
Vold Vision

GRAPHIC ANGELS DESIGN GROUP

370 Turrell Ave, South Orange, NJ 07079
Tel.: (973) 378-3394
E-Mail: scalera@graphicangels.com
Web Site: www.graphicangels.com

Employees: 3
Year Founded: 1997

National Agency Associations: ADC

Agency Specializes In: Advertising, Advertising Specialties, Alternative Advertising, Arts, Automotive, Aviation & Aerospace, Brand Development & Integration, Broadcast, Business-To-Business, Cable T.V., Catalogs, Co-op Advertising, Collateral, Communications, Corporate Identity, Entertainment, Exhibit/Trade Shows, Graphic Design, Guerilla Marketing, In-Store Advertising, Internet/Web Design, Logo & Package Design, Luxury Products, Men's Market, Package Design, Planning & Consultation, Point of Purchase, Print, Production (Ad, Film, Broadcast), Sports Market, T.V., Trade & Consumer Magazines, Transportation, Urban Market, Web (Banner Ads, Pop-ups, etc.)

Revenue: $150,000

Tomm Scalera *(Owner & Dir-Creative)*

Accounts:
American Collectors Insurance; NJ Auto Insurance; 2004
Geraldine R Dodge Foundation; NJ Foundation Grants; 2002
Kanter Auto Products; NJ Auto Products; 2001

GRAPHIC D-SIGNS INC

279 Rte 31 S Ste 4, Washington, NJ 07882
Tel.: (908) 835-9000
Fax: (866) 274-6880
E-Mail: letstalk@graphicd-signs.com
Web Site: www.graphicd-signs.com

Agency Specializes In: Advertising, Collateral, Corporate Identity, Digital/Interactive, Graphic Design, Logo & Package Design, Outdoor, Print, Social Media

Dan Antonelli *(Pres & Dir-Creative)*
Joan Olkowski *(Dir-Art & Graphic Designer)*
Danny Albeck *(Dir-Web Dev)*
Danielle Massad *(Dir-Mktg)*
Jennifer Baker *(Acct Mgr)*

Accounts:
Air Zero
Clear the Air
Trico Poly Systems

GRAPHIC PERSUASION, INC.

169 Tequesta Dr Ste 31E, Tequesta, FL 33469
Tel.: (561) 746-2422
Fax: (561) 746-2204

Employees: 3
Year Founded: 1965

Agency Specializes In: Print

Approx. Annual Billings: $1,000,000

Breakdown of Gross Billings by Media: Mags.: $1,000,000

David T. Robinson, Jr. *(Pres)*
Glenn M. Robinson *(Dir-Art)*

GRAPHICMACHINE INC.

2300 Main St Ste 900, Kansas City, MO 64108
Tel.: (212) 260-2410
E-Mail: hello@graphicmachine.com
Web Site: www.graphicmachine.com

Year Founded: 1999

Agency Specializes In: Advertising, Brand Development & Integration, Digital/Interactive, E-Commerce, Email, Internet/Web Design, Print, Search Engine Optimization, Social Media

Brian Jones *(Founder)*
Patience Jones *(Partner)*
Matthew Staub *(Partner)*

Accounts:
Kpb Architects

GRAVINA ONLINE STRATEGIES

49 Archdale St Ste 2G, Charleston, SC 29401
Tel.: (843) 580-2820
Web Site: www.engagegravina.com

Year Founded: 2013

Agency Specializes In: Advertising, Digital/Interactive, Public Relations, Social Media

Curt Mercadante *(Founder & Principal)*
Chandler Howell *(Dir-Digital Svcs)*

Accounts:
Radiate Technologies

GRAVITY DIGITAL

12603 Hwy 105 W Ste 204, Conroe, TX 77304
Tel.: (936) 588-2882
Fax: (936) 588-2884
Web Site: www.gravitydigital.com

Year Founded: 2000

Agency Specializes In: Advertising, Brand Development & Integration, Collateral, Graphic Design, Internet/Web Design, Logo & Package Design, Media Buying Services, Print, Radio, Social Media

Casey OQuinn *(Owner)*
Matt Brannon *(Creative Dir)*

Accounts:
The Arbor Gate

GRAVITY GROUP

107 E Water St, Harrisonburg, VA 22801
Tel.: (540) 433-3071
Fax: (540) 433-3076
E-Mail: info@gravitygroup.com
Web Site: www.gravitygroup.com

Agency Specializes In: Advertising, Social Media

Steve Gilman *(Pres-Mktg & Strategist-Brand)*
Christian Perritt *(VP & Dir-Creative)*
Mark Fenton *(Specialist-Media)*
Lindsey Laughlin *(Specialist-Mktg Comm)*

Accounts:
DuPont Community Credit Union
The Frazier Quarry Inc.
RMH Healthcare
Universal Postal Union
VMRC Foundation

GRAVITY MEDIA

114 W 26th St 8th Fl, New York, NY 10001
Tel.: (646) 486-0000
Fax: (646) 486-0030
E-Mail: hello@mediagravity.com
Web Site: www.mediagravity.com

Year Founded: 2009

Agency Specializes In: Advertising, Event Planning & Marketing, Internet/Web Design, Media Buying Services, Media Planning, Public Relations, Social Media, Sponsorship, Strategic Planning/Research

Artur Melentin *(Co-Founder & Chief Creative Officer)*
Luba Tolkachyov *(Co-Founder-New Media Dev)*
Rob Douglas *(VP-Client Svcs, Media & Corp Dev)*
Tim Carter *(Dir-AV Production)*
Candy Tse *(Dir-Production)*
Mir Akhgar *(Assoc Dir-Client Svcs)*
Lilian Laskin *(Sr Mgr-Ops & HR)*
Olga Parks *(Sr Acct Mgr)*
Shweta Kapuria *(Acct Mgr)*
Boris Litvinov *(Mgr-Digital)*

Accounts:

Caesars Entertainment "Lunar New Year", Campaign: "Reveal Your Fortune"
CenterLight Healthcare
Dish Campaign: "DISH, the Home of South Asian TV Entertainment", Campaign: "Hum Hain Bollywood"
IDT Corporation
Melia Hotels International Gran Melia, ME, North & South America Digital Marketing, Paradisus
United States Army
Western Union
Xfinity Creative, Home Services, Internet, Media, Phone, Strategy, Television

GRAY LOON MARKETING GROUP, INC.

300 SE Riverside Dr Ste 200, Evansville, IN 47713
Tel.: (812) 422-9999
Fax: (812) 422-3342
Toll Free: (888) GRAYLOON
E-Mail: info@grayloon.com
Web Site: www.grayloon.com

Employees: 28
Year Founded: 1994

Agency Specializes In: Advertising, Brand Development & Integration, Business Publications, Business-To-Business, Collateral, Commercial Photography, Communications, Consumer Goods, Consumer Marketing, Consumer Publications, Content, Corporate Communications, Corporate Identity, Customer Relationship Management, Digital/Interactive, Direct Response Marketing, Direct-to-Consumer, E-Commerce, Education, Electronic Media, Email, Exhibit/Trade Shows, Graphic Design, Industrial, Infomercials, Information Technology, Internet/Web Design, Leisure, Logo & Package Design, Magazines, Media Planning, Media Relations, Merchandising, Mobile Marketing, Multimedia, New Product Development, Newspapers & Magazines, Out-of-Home Media, Outdoor, Package Design, Pets , Pharmaceutical, Podcasting, Point of Purchase, Point of Sale, Print, Production, Public Relations, RSS (Really Simple Syndication), Sales Promotion, Search Engine Optimization, Social Media, Sports Market, Technical Advertising, Trade & Consumer Magazines, Travel & Tourism

Approx. Annual Billings: $4,000,000

Katie Dausmann *(Office Mgr & Controller)*
Kaitlyn Leslie *(Dir-Project Mgmt & Acct Mgr)*
Bryan Horstman *(Dir-Art)*
Jason Ludwig *(Dir-Web Dev)*
Greg Gehlhausen *(Assoc Dir-Design)*
Clint Davis *(Mgr-IT)*
Brita Lewis *(Acct Exec & Strategist)*

Accounts:
Accuride Corporation accuridecorp.com
Ambassador Travel
Benelli benelliusa.com
Burris Optics burrisoptics.com
Duck Commander duckcommander.com
Economic Development Coalition
EVSC
Hoosier Energy hoosiersites.com
Hoyt
Mead Johnson Nutrition
Realtree Camo realtreeoutdoors.com
Steiner Optics steiner-optics.com
Thomson Center

GRAY MATTER AGENCY INC.

94 Station St, Hingham, MA 02043
Tel.: (781) 740-4001
Fax: (781) 740-4002
E-Mail: kthompson@graymatteragency.com
Web Site: www.graymatter.agency/

Employees: 10
Year Founded: 2006

National Agency Associations: AA

Agency Specializes In: Advertising, Brand Development & Integration, Business-To-Business, Communications, Consumer Marketing, Corporate Communications, Direct Response Marketing, Health Care Services, Investor Relations, Market Research, Medical Products, Planning & Consultation, Production, Sales Promotion, Strategic Planning/Research

John Springer *(Owner & Dir-Creative)*
Tom Kennedy *(Acct Dir)*

GREAT AMERICAN FOODS CORP.

(d/b/a David Beard's Catfish King)
3684 FM 161 N, Hughes Springs, TX 75656
Tel.: (903) 639-1482
Fax: (903) 639-1483
Web Site: www.davidbeards.com/index2.php

Employees: 5

Sales: $21,000,000

David Beard *(Pres)*

GREAT COMMUNICATORS, INC.

2625 Ponce de Leon Blvd Ste 101, Coral Gables, FL 33134
Tel.: (305) 448-1456
Fax: (305) 448-1482
E-Mail: info@greatcom.com
Web Site: www.greatcom.com

Employees: 7
Year Founded: 1990

Agency Specializes In: Brand Development & Integration, Collateral, Crisis Communications, Financial, Government/Political, Internet/Web Design, Investor Relations, Media Relations, Multimedia, Newspaper, Product Placement, Promotions, Publicity/Promotions

David Stiefel *(Pres & CEO)*

Accounts:
Berenfeld Spritzer Shechter & Sheer
Greater Miami Jewish Federation (Agency of Record)
Jewish Community Services of South Florida
Meland Russin & Budwick
Miami Jewish Film Festival (Public Relations Agency of Record) Media
Zadok Art Gallery

GREAT DAY ADVERTISING

8335 Sunset Blvd Ste 220, Los Angeles, CA 90069
Tel.: (323) 791-1116
Fax: (323) 337-9034
E-Mail: info@greatdayadvertising.com
Web Site: www.greatdayadvertising.com

E-Mail for Key Personnel:
Creative Dir.: mniles@greatdayradio.com

Employees: 8

Agency Specializes In: Advertising, Alternative Advertising, Bilingual Market, Broadcast, Cable T.V., Communications, Entertainment, Media Buying Services, Production (Ad, Film, Broadcast), Promotions, Radio, Sales Promotion, Web (Banner Ads, Pop-ups, etc.)

Michael Niles *(Owner)*

Accounts:
Coca-Cola Refreshments USA, Inc.
Cox Communications
Disneyland
East West Bank
Levi Strauss
McCracken Brooks
Virgin Megastore

GREAT RIVER CREATIVE

233 S Wacker Dr 84th Fl, Chicago, IL 60606
Tel.: (312) 235-6560
E-Mail: grc@greatrivercreative.com
Web Site: www.greatrivercreative.com

Year Founded: 2009

Agency Specializes In: Advertising, Brand Development & Integration, Event Planning & Marketing, Internet/Web Design, Media Buying Services, Social Media, Strategic Planning/Research

Sarah Dickinson *(Pres)*
Dorian Dickinson *(Partner & Dir-Strategic Dev)*
Jason Antoine *(Dir)*
Matthew Brown *(Dir-Creative)*
Nick Skislak *(Dir-Digital Solutions)*

Accounts:
Great Lakes Region USA Volleyball Brand Awareness, Windy City National Qualifier (Sponsorship Sales Agency of Record)
The H Foundation Events & Media Relation, Inbound Marketing, Public Relations, Strategic & Content Marketing, Strategic Planning
Lakes to Locks Passage
Mainstreet Steak & Chophouse
Vintage Illinois

GREATER THAN ONE

395 Hudson St, New York, NY 10014
Tel.: (212) 252-1999
Fax: (212) 252-7364
Web Site: www.greaterthanone.com

Employees: 70
Year Founded: 2000

Agency Specializes In: Advertising, Affiliate Marketing, Brand Development & Integration, Business-To-Business, Consulting, Consumer Marketing, Consumer Publications, Content, Corporate Communications, Digital/Interactive, Direct-to-Consumer, E-Commerce, Education, Electronic Media, Electronics, Email, Entertainment, Environmental, Gay & Lesbian Market, Hispanic Market, Hospitality, Integrated Marketing, Internet/Web Design, Media Buying Services, Media Planning, Mobile Marketing, Paid Searches, Podcasting, RSS (Really Simple Syndication), Retail, Search Engine Optimization, Social Marketing/Nonprofit, Strategic Planning/Research, Travel & Tourism, Viral/Buzz/Word of Mouth, Web (Banner Ads, Pop-ups, etc.), Women's Market

Approx. Annual Billings: $30,000,000

Breakdown of Gross Billings by Media: Internet Adv.: $15,000,000; Other: $4,000,000; Strategic Planning/Research: $11,000,000

Elizabeth Izard Apelles *(Founder & CEO)*
Pilar Belhumeur *(Partner & Exec Dir-Creative)*
Gregory Gross *(Partner & Exec Dir-Creative)*
John Mahler *(Partner & Dir-Strategy)*
Pamela Pinta *(Partner & Chief Strategic Officer)*
Christa Toole *(Partner-Search Mktg & Web Analytics)*

Accounts:
BET

Genetech
Genzyme
Lunesta
MEDA
Medtronic
MSNBC
New York Presbyterian Hospital
New York University
Novartis
Sunovion Campaign: "Omnaris Integrated"
Transit Center
Vail Resorts

GREATEST COMMON FACTORY

2000 E 6th St, Austin, TX 78702
Tel.: (512) 410-1313
E-Mail: getstarted@gcfactory.com
Web Site: www.gcfactory.com

Year Founded: 2011

Agency Specializes In: Advertising, Content, Strategic Planning/Research

John Trahar *(Founder & Dir-Creative)*
Karen Jacobs *(Mng Partner-Content Production)*
Charlie Pomykal *(Head-Creative Bus Dev)*
Katie Johnson *(Dir-Art)*
Elvira Marin *(Office Mgr)*

Accounts:
Arise Ventures
Nike, Inc.
SafeAuto Insurance Company

GREATEST CREATIVE FACTOR

3000 Chestnut Avenue Suite 400, Baltimore, MD 21211
Tel.: (410) 467-4672
Fax: (410) 467-4672
Web Site: www.gcfonline.com

Agency Specializes In: Advertising, Brand Development & Integration, Digital/Interactive, Internet/Web Design, Logo & Package Design, Print, Social Media

Brenda Foster *(Partner)*
Domenica Genovese *(Partner-Creative)*
Nicole Montecalvo *(Acct Mgr)*
William Shain *(Specialist-Admissions Mktg & Ops)*
Jason Rosenberg *(Designer-Website)*

Accounts:
Johns Hopkins University
Widener University

GREEN ADVERTISING

7301 N Federal Hwy Studio B, Boca Raton, FL 33487
Tel.: (561) 989-9550
Fax: (561) 989-9515
Toll Free: (800) 852-1717
E-Mail: court@greenad.com
Web Site: www.greenad.com

Employees: 19
Year Founded: 1986

Agency Specializes In: Advertising, Advertising Specialties, Aviation & Aerospace, Bilingual Market, Broadcast, Cable T.V., Communications, Direct Response Marketing, Graphic Design, Health Care Services, High Technology, Medical Products, Multimedia, Newspaper, Newspapers & Magazines, Production, Public Relations, Publicity/Promotions, Radio, Real Estate, T.V.

Phyllis M. Green *(Chm)*
Courtland McQuire *(Pres & Exec Dir-Creative)*
Donna Golden-Uliano *(Exec VP)*
Edward Uzzle *(Mgr-Social Media & Producer)*
Julie Bricker *(Dir-Media)*
Jeannie Schnurr *(Sr Acct Mgr)*
Matthew Doyle *(Sr Acct Exec)*
Sheldon Senzon *(Strategist-Media)*
Ryan Mascarenhas *(Acct Coord)*

Accounts:
Boca Raton Regional Hospital
Calder Casino & Race Course (Agency of Record)
Florida Atlantic University
Southern Technical College Digital, Marketing

Branch

Stalder/Green Advertising

1101 N Kentucky Ave Ste 200, Winter Park, FL 32789
Tel.: (407) 645-1113
Fax: (407) 645-1513
Web Site: www.greenad.com

Employees: 10
Year Founded: 2003

Agency Specializes In: Advertising

Lindy Stalder *(Owner)*

GREEN DOOR MEDIAWORKS

263 Soda Creek Ct, Dillon, CO 80435
Tel.: (970) 485-0670
E-Mail: info@greendoormediaworks.com
Web Site: www.greendoormediaworks.com

Year Founded: 2012

Agency Specializes In: Crisis Communications, Media Relations, Media Training, Production, Public Relations, Social Media

Ryan Whaley *(Founder & Owner)*
Thomas Whaley *(Co-Owner)*
Nicole Lloyd *(Mng Partner)*
Chad Whaley *(Specialist-Media)*

Accounts:
Lake View Condominiums
Sandusky Main Street Association

GREEN DOT ADVERTISING & MARKETING

5400 NE 4th Ct, Miami, FL 33137
Tel.: (305) 674-8406
Fax: (305) 674-7898
E-Mail: info@greendotadvertising.com
Web Site: www.greendotadvertising.com

Employees: 5
Year Founded: 1995

Agency Specializes In: Advertising

Revenue: $1,000,000

Mario Behr *(Pres & Dir-Creative)*

Accounts:
Act Mortgage
Brightstar
Chapman Partnership
Fernandez Bay Village
Frontier Golf
Hook & Tackle Apparel
IMACS
Research In Motion/Blackberry
Sea Vee Boats
Sony Electronics
Sony Latin America
U Health
Wish Restaurant

GREEN GRASS MARKETING & ADVERTISING

4539 36th St, Orlando, FL 32811
Tel.: (407) 299-7990
E-Mail: info@greengrass4me.com
Web Site: www.greengrass4me.com

Year Founded: 2008

Agency Specializes In: Advertising, Email, Graphic Design, Internet/Web Design, Media Buying Services, Radio, Social Media, T.V.

Jim Ford *(Dir-Technical)*

Accounts:
Healing Revolutions
Trobo

GREEN ROOM PUBLIC RELATIONS

333 W Main St Ste 1, Boonton, NJ 7005
Tel.: (973) 263-8585
Fax: (201) 526-8351
E-Mail: info@greenroompr.com
Web Site: www.greenroompr.com

Agency Specializes In: Broadcast, Corporate Communications, Crisis Communications, Internet/Web Design, Media Relations, Planning & Consultation, Public Relations

Deborah Sittig *(Co-Founder & Mng Partner)*
Karen Carolonza *(Mng Partner)*

Accounts:
Alpharma Animal Health Animal Drugs Mfr
Becton Dickinson & Company Medical Equipment & Supplies Mfr
Biogen Idec & Elan Pharmaceutical Products Mfr
ExL Pharma Pharmaceutical Training & Educational Support Services
GlaxoSmithKline Pharmaceutical Products Mfr
Merck Pharmaceutical Products Mfr
Novartis Oncology Cancer Medicine Mfr
Publicis Consultants Public Relations

GREEN TEAM ADVERTISING, INC.

261 Madison Ave, New York, NY 10016
Tel.: (212) 966-6365
Fax: (212) 966-6178
E-Mail: info@greenteamusa.com
Web Site: www.greenteamglobal.com

E-Mail for Key Personnel:
President: hugh@greenteamusa.com

Employees: 14
Year Founded: 1993

Agency Specializes In: Corporate Identity, Environmental, Travel & Tourism

Hugh Hough *(Owner)*
Milton Kapelus *(Partner & Client Svcs Dir)*
Nubia Zagami *(CFO)*
Hank Stewart *(Exec VP-Comm Strategy)*
Maria Guilger *(Dir-Art)*

Accounts:
Johnson & Johnson
Rainforest Alliance
Scottish Tourist Board
VisitScotland Tourism Services

GREEN ZEBRA CREATIVE

4660 Main St, Springfield, OR 97477
Tel.: (541) 410-5143
E-Mail: info@greenzebracreative.com

Web Site: www.greenzebracreative.com

Agency Specializes In: Advertising, Brand Development & Integration, Graphic Design, Internet/Web Design, Package Design, Print

Terrance Scott *(Owner)*
Todd Gobeille *(Dir-Art & Designer)*

Accounts:
Buncks Garage
Holy Water Vape Juice

GREENAWAY & ASSOCIATES COMMUNICATIONS LTD.

3381 Ridge Blvd, Westbank, Kelowna, BC V4T 2V6 Canada
Tel.: (250) 768-1240
E-Mail: teresa@greenaway.ca
Web Site: www.greenaway.ca

E-Mail for Key Personnel:
President: steven@greenaway.ca

Employees: 2
Year Founded: 1993

Agency Specializes In: Communications, Electronic Media, Government/Political, Newspaper, Print, Public Relations, Radio, T.V.

Approx. Annual Billings: $1,000,000

Steven Greenaway *(Pres)*
Teresa Greenaway *(VP)*

Accounts:
Okanagan Specialty Fruit

GREENCARD CREATIVE

220 E 42nd St 3rd Fl, New York, NY 10017
Tel.: (212) 459-5359
Web Site: www.greencardcreative.com

Agency Specializes In: Advertising, Brand Development & Integration, Digital/Interactive, Social Media

Tatiana Pages *(CEO, Chief Creative Officer & Chief Strategy Officer)*
Jae Kim *(Dir-Graphic Design & Web Dev)*
David Marte *(Dir-Art)*

Accounts:
The Dannon Company, Inc.
Frito-Lay North America Inc.
Goya Foods, Inc.
Heineken USA Inc.
The Partnership at Drugfree.org
Pepsi-Cola North America
The Procter & Gamble Company Pantene, Gillette

GREENFIELD ADVERTISING GROUP

12551 New Brittany Blvd Bldg 26, Fort Myers, FL 33907-3625
Tel.: (239) 437-0000
Web Site: www.greenfieldadvertising.com

Agency Specializes In: Advertising, Digital/Interactive, Exhibit/Trade Shows, Internet/Web Design, Media Planning, Point of Sale, Production, Radio, Search Engine Optimization, T.V.

Deborah A Greenfield *(Owner)*

Accounts:
Absolute Law

GREENLIGHT MEDIA & MARKETING, LLC

8439 Sunset Blvd W, Hollywood, CA 90069
Tel.: (310) 273-2266
E-Mail: info@greenlightmm.com
Web Site: www.greenlightmm.com

Agency Specializes In: Advertising, Digital/Interactive

Dominic Sandifer *(Pres & Mng Partner)*
Eric Block *(Gen Mgr)*
Nick Davidge *(Exec Dir-Creative)*
Noah Carlstrom *(Sr Dir-Art)*
Rudi Anthony *(Dir-Cultural Mktg)*
Nathan Winston *(Sr Acct Mgr)*

Accounts:
Hyundai Motor America Campaign: "Generation Music Project", Content
Logitech
Lytro Brand Strategy, Creative, Digital, Media, Production
Under Armour "Huddle Up"

GREENMARK PUBLIC RELATIONS

1200 Darnell Dr Ste L, Mundelein, IL 60060-1084
Tel.: (847) 970-9160
Fax: (847) 970-9170
E-Mail: info@greenmarkpr.com
Web Site: www.greenmarkpr.com

Agency Specializes In: Business-To-Business, Commercial Photography, Consulting, Email, Environmental, Exhibit/Trade Shows, Graphic Design, Local Marketing, Media Relations, Print, Public Relations, Web (Banner Ads, Pop-ups, etc.)

Sue Markgraf *(Founder & Pres)*
Gina Tedesco *(VP)*
Sharon Hentsch *(Dir-Bus Dev)*
Lynn Petrak *(Dir-Media Rels)*
Matt Markgraf *(Mgr-Online & Viral Comm)*

Accounts:
Chalet Landscaping, Nursery & Garden Center
Chicago Gateway Green
Chicago Trees Initiative
Global Explorers
Green Exchange
Greenspace
The Lurie Garden
ROC Exhibitions
SpiceStack

GREENRUBINO

1938 Fairview Ave E Ste 200, Seattle, WA 98102
Tel.: (206) 447-4747
Fax: (206) 447-9494
E-Mail: info@greenrubino.com
Web Site: www.greenrubino.com

Employees: 47
Year Founded: 1977

National Agency Associations: AMA

Agency Specializes In: Advertising, Advertising Specialties, Alternative Advertising, Arts, Automotive, Aviation & Aerospace, Brand Development & Integration, Broadcast, Business Publications, Cable T.V., Catalogs, Co-op Advertising, Collateral, Communications, Computers & Software, Consumer Goods, Consumer Marketing, Consumer Publications, Content, Corporate Communications, Corporate Identity, Cosmetics, Crisis Communications, Custom Publishing, Customer Relationship Management, Digital/Interactive, Direct Response Marketing, Direct-to-Consumer, E-Commerce, Education, Electronic Media, Electronics, Email, Engineering, Entertainment, Environmental, Event Planning & Marketing, Exhibit/Trade Shows, Fashion/Apparel, Financial, Food Service, Game Integration, Gay & Lesbian Market, Government/Political, Graphic Design, Guerilla Marketing, Health Care Services, High Technology, Hospitality, Household Goods, Identity Marketing, In-Store Advertising, Information Technology, Integrated Marketing, International, Internet/Web Design, Investor Relations, Legal Services, Leisure, Local Marketing, Logo & Package Design, Luxury Products, Magazines, Marine, Market Research, Media Buying Services, Media Planning, Media Relations, Media Training, Medical Products, Men's Market, Mobile Marketing, Multicultural, Multimedia, New Product Development, New Technologies, Newspaper, Newspapers & Magazines, Out-of-Home Media, Outdoor, Over-50 Market, Package Design, Paid Searches, Pets , Pharmaceutical, Planning & Consultation, Point of Purchase, Point of Sale, Print, Product Placement, Production, Production (Print), Promotions, Public Relations, Publicity/Promotions, RSS (Really Simple Syndication), Radio, Real Estate, Recruitment, Regional, Restaurant, Retail, Sales Promotion, Search Engine Optimization, Seniors' Market, Social Marketing/Nonprofit, Social Media, Sponsorship, Sports Market, Stakeholders, Strategic Planning/Research, Syndication, T.V., Technical Advertising, Teen Market, Trade & Consumer Magazines, Transportation, Travel & Tourism, Tween Market, Urban Market, Viral/Buzz/Word of Mouth, Web (Banner Ads, Pop-ups, etc.), Women's Market, Yellow Pages Advertising

Approx. Annual Billings: $21,500,000

Breakdown of Gross Billings by Media: Brdcst.: $5,000,000; Collateral: $1,500,000; D.M.: $1,000,000; E-Commerce: $3,000,000; Event Mktg.: $750,000; Graphic Design: $2,500,000; Newsp. & Mags.: $1,500,000; Out-of-Home Media: $1,250,000; Pub. Rels.: $1,000,000; Worldwide Web Sites: $4,000,000

John Rubino *(Pres)*
Cameron Green *(CEO & Dir-Creative)*
Lynn Parker *(Principal & Specialist)*
Hamilton McCulloh *(Exec Dir)*
Kimanh Moreau *(Sr Producer-Digital)*
Crystal Inge *(Client Svcs Dir)*
Briana Marrah *(Brand Dir)*
Joe Quatrone *(Dir-Creative)*
Jon Njos *(Sr Mgr-Media)*
Thomas Bobson *(Acct Mgr)*
Chelsea Asplund *(Acct Exec)*

Accounts:
Avanade; Seattle, WA Business Consulting; 2008
The Columbia Bank Financial; 1992
Delta Dental Dental Insurance; 2011
Fred Hutch Cancer Research; 2011
Microsoft; Redmond, WA Software; 2000
PAWS; Seattle, WA Animal Welfare/Non-Profit; 2000
Ryan Law; Seattle, WA Legal Services; 2009
Snoqualmie Casino Gaming; 2012
Sound Transit Transportation; 2008
Washington State Wine Commission Wine; 2008

GREENSTREET MARKETING

245 Michigan Ave W, Battle Creek, MI 49017-3601
Tel.: (269) 963-9922
Fax: (269) 963-7831
E-Mail: info@greenstreetmkg.com
Web Site: www.greenstreetmkg.com

Employees: 7
Year Founded: 1995

National Agency Associations: DMA

Agency Specializes In: Advertising, Advertising Specialties, Automotive, Brand Development &

Integration, Business Publications, Business-To-Business, Cable T.V., Co-op Advertising, Collateral, Commercial Photography, Communications, Consulting, Consumer Marketing, Consumer Publications, Corporate Identity, Direct Response Marketing, Event Planning & Marketing, Financial, Food Service, Graphic Design, Health Care Services, Hispanic Market, Internet/Web Design, Logo & Package Design, Magazines, Newspaper, Newspapers & Magazines, Outdoor, Planning & Consultation, Point of Purchase, Point of Sale, Print, Production, Public Relations, Radio, Restaurant, Retail, Sales Promotion, Strategic Planning/Research, T.V., Trade & Consumer Magazines, Transportation, Travel & Tourism

Kathleen McKay Samson *(Owner)*
Laura Hosler *(Sr Graphic Designer)*

Accounts:
360 Encompassing Cuisine
American Museum of Magic
Battle Creek Area Catholic Schools; Battle Creek, MI; 2000
Battle Creek Community Foundation; Battle Creek, MI; 2009
BC Area Chamber of Commerce; Battle Creek, MI; 2011
Calhoun County Intermediate School District; Marshall, MI; 2010
CTS Telecom; Galesburg, MI; 2009
Kellogg Community Federal Credit Union; 2000
Malia Mediterranean Bistro; Battle Creek, MI; 2010
McFee Medical Technologies; Battle Creek, MI; 2009
Southern Michigan Orthopaedics; Battle Creek & Marshall, MI; 2011

GREENTARGET STRATEGIC COMMUNICATIONS

1 N LaSalle St 27th Fl, Chicago, IL 60602
Tel.: (312) 252-4100
E-Mail: contactus@greentarget.com
Web Site: www.greentarget.com

Employees: 15

National Agency Associations: COPF

Agency Specializes In: Brand Development & Integration, Business-To-Business, Crisis Communications, Public Relations

John E. Corey *(Founder, Pres & Partner)*
Laura Miller *(Exec VP)*
Steven J. DiMattia *(Sr VP)*
Larry Larsen *(Sr VP)*
Chris Gale *(VP)*
Ashley Kyle *(Assoc VP)*
Joseph Cascio *(Dir-Ops)*
Kevin Iredell *(Dir-Res)*

Accounts:
BT
Detroit Mercy School of Law
Foley & Lardner, LLP.
HBOS
Hogan & Hartson
Miller & Chevalier

GREGIS ADVERTISING, INC.

3601 Concord Rd, York, PA 17402
Tel.: (717) 840-9670
Fax: (717) 840-9761
E-Mail: bob@gregis.com
Web Site: www.gregis.com

Employees: 5
Year Founded: 1986

Agency Specializes In: Advertising, Business Publications, Business-To-Business, Collateral, Consulting, Digital/Interactive, Direct Response Marketing, Engineering, Exhibit/Trade Shows, Graphic Design, Industrial, Internet/Web Design, Logo & Package Design, Media Buying Services, New Product Development, Point of Purchase, Point of Sale, Production, Public Relations, Publicity/Promotions, Sales Promotion, Technical Advertising

Approx. Annual Billings: $1,500,000

Breakdown of Gross Billings by Media: Collateral: $1,050,000; Pub. Rels.: $150,000; Worldwide Web Sites: $300,000

Robert J. Gregis *(Pres)*

Accounts:
Aesys Technologies; York, PA Boilers & HVAC Equipment; 2000
Crescent Stonco ExceLine Lighting; Union, NJ Fluorescent Lighting; 1998
Doucette Industries; York, PA Heat Exchangers; 1997
Nautica Dehumidifiers
PoolPak International; York, PA Indoor Pool Dehumidification Equipment; 1991
Security Lighting; Buffalo Grove, IL Interior & Exterior Commercial Lighting Products; 2001
Sieling & Jones; New Freedom, PA Wood Veneer Products; 1995
Thermacore, Inc; Lancaster, PA Specialized Heat Exchanger Components; 1998
United CoolAir Corporation; York, PA Commercial Air Conditioning Equipment; 1990
Wilke Enginuity

GREMILLION & POU

2800 Centenary Blvd, Shreveport, LA 71104
Tel.: (318) 424-2676
Fax: (318) 221-3442
E-Mail: info@gpmarketinginc.com
Web Site: www.gpmarketinginc.com

Employees: 35
Year Founded: 1981

Agency Specializes In: Advertising, Automotive, Brand Development & Integration, Broadcast, Business-To-Business, Communications, Consumer Marketing, Digital/Interactive, Direct Response Marketing, Direct-to-Consumer, E-Commerce, Electronic Media, Email, Graphic Design, Integrated Marketing, Internet/Web Design, Media Buying Services, Media Planning, Media Relations, Newspaper, Out-of-Home Media, Outdoor, Planning & Consultation, Print, Publicity/Promotions, Radio, Strategic Planning/Research, T.V., Travel & Tourism

Approx. Annual Billings: $15,000,000

Breakdown of Gross Billings by Media: Internet Adv.: 5%; Outdoor: 5%; Print: 5%; Radio: 35%; T.V.: 50%

Anne Gremillion *(Principal)*
Robert Pou *(Principal)*
John Gayle *(VP & Grp Acct Dir)*
Jeffrey Romph *(VP-Casino Mktg)*
Robin Hines *(Dir-Creative)*
Cynthia Green *(Media Buyer)*

GRENADIER

1221 Pennsylvania Ave, Boulder, CO 80302
Tel.: (303) 386-3957
E-Mail: info@grenadierco.com
Web Site: www.grenadierco.com

Employees: 18
Year Founded: 2012

National Agency Associations: 4A's

Agency Specializes In: Advertising, Brand Development & Integration, Communications, Content, Corporate Communications, Corporate Identity, Graphic Design, Integrated Marketing, Internet/Web Design, Logo & Package Design, Market Research, Package Design, Sponsorship, Strategic Planning/Research

Approx. Annual Billings: $3,000,000

Mark St. Amant *(Co-Founder & Partner-Creative)*
Wade Paschall *(Partner & Dir-Creative)*
Jeff Graham *(Partner-Acct)*
Rob Hofferman *(Partner-Acct)*
Randall Rogers *(Partner-Creative)*
Eric Forsyth *(Head-Acct)*
Ryan Smith *(Acct Supvr)*

Accounts:
Adidas North America Inc Creative Projects
Coinstar Coinstar, Coinstar Exchange; 2013
Fresh Produce Clothing; 2014
Husky Liners; 2013
Intrawest Intrawest Pass Products; 2015
Original Penguin Creative Projects; 2013
Portalupi Wine Company Vaso di Marina; 2012
Purina Petcare Creative Projects; 2013
Rio Grande Mexican Restaurants; 2014
SolidFire SolidFire Enterprise Storage System; 2013
Suerte Tequila; 2012
Sunny Delight Beverages Co. Campaign: "Grape Drink", Creative, Fruit2o, Marketing, SunnyD; 2012
Water Pik, Inc. Showerhead & Faucet Division; 2012
Winter Park Resort; 2013
Woody Creek Distillers Woody Creek Vodka; 2013

GRETEMAN GROUP

1425 E Douglas 2nd Fl, Wichita, KS 67211
Tel.: (316) 263-1004
Fax: (316) 263-1060
E-Mail: info@gretemangroup.com
Web Site: www.gretemangroup.com

E-Mail for Key Personnel:
President: sgreteman@gretemangroup.com
Creative Dir.: sgreteman@gretemangroup.com
Media Dir.: jgore@gretemangroup.com
Production Mgr.: lheinz@gretemangroup.com
Public Relations: dharms@gretemangroup.com

Employees: 21
Year Founded: 1989

National Agency Associations: ADFED-PRSA

Agency Specializes In: Advertising, Affluent Market, Arts, Aviation & Aerospace, Brand Development & Integration, Broadcast, Business Publications, Business-To-Business, Catalogs, Collateral, Consumer Marketing, Corporate Communications, Corporate Identity, Electronic Media, Event Planning & Marketing, Exhibit/Trade Shows, Experience Design, Financial, Graphic Design, Guerilla Marketing, Health Care Services, High Technology, Hospitality, Identity Marketing, Integrated Marketing, Internet/Web Design, Investor Relations, Leisure, Logo & Package Design, Luxury Products, Magazines, Media Relations, Media Training, Medical Products, Men's Market, Merchandising, Multicultural, Outdoor, Over-50 Market, Package Design, Point of Purchase, Point of Sale, Print, Production (Ad, Film, Broadcast), Production (Print), Public Relations, Publicity/Promotions, Radio, Recruitment, Retail, Social Marketing/Nonprofit, Strategic Planning/Research, Trade & Consumer Magazines, Travel & Tourism, Viral/Buzz/Word of Mouth, Web (Banner Ads, Pop-ups, etc.), Women's

Market

Randy Bradbury *(VP & Sr Writer)*
Chaney Kimball *(Sr Dir-Digital)*
Rachel Groene *(Brand Dir)*
Landon Barton *(Dir-Art)*
Jordan Walker *(Dir-Digital)*
Lori Heinz *(Mgr-Production)*
Jordan Bradbury *(Coord-Brand)*

Accounts:
Adobe Home
BlueBike Architects
Bombardier Bombardier Aerospace, Bombardier Flexjet, Bombardier Learjet
City of Wichita
Dallas Airmotive
Envision
FlightSafety International
Foxwoods Development
Gossen Livingston Architects
HOW Magazine Creative, Gift of Lift
Hutton Construction LogoLounge 8
IdeaTek
Jackson, Wade & Blanck LLC
Kansas Aviation Museum
Kansas Health Foundation
Kansas State Fair
Laham Development
LawKingdon Architecture
Newport Television
OLC Global
PIM Aviation Insurance (Agency of Record)
Preferred Health Systems (Agency of Record)
R. Messner Construction
Riordan Clinic
Rockwell Collins
Royal Caribbean International
Signature Flight Support
Spirit AeroSystems
USAIGNY (Agency of Record) Branding
Versus Bank
Vibe-It
WaterWalk Development
WDM Architects
Wichita Area Technical College
Wichita Mid-Continent Airport
Woodside Health & Tennis

GREY CANADA

46 Spadina Ave Ste 500, Toronto, ON M5V 2H8 Canada
Tel.: (416) 486-0700
Fax: (416) 486-3244
Web Site: grey.com/canada

E-Mail for Key Personnel:
President: Ann_Nurock@grey.net

Employees: 50
Year Founded: 1958

Agency Specializes In: Advertising, Advertising Specialties, Automotive, Business-To-Business, Communications, Consumer Goods, Consumer Marketing, Corporate Communications, Corporate Identity, Digital/Interactive, Direct Response Marketing, Direct-to-Consumer, Education, Email, In-Store Advertising, Infomercials, International, Internet/Web Design, Local Marketing, Mobile Marketing, Multimedia, Newspaper, Newspapers & Magazines, Out-of-Home Media, Outdoor, Over-50 Market, Paid Searches, Pharmaceutical, Podcasting, Point of Purchase, Print, Production, Production (Print), Promotions, RSS (Really Simple Syndication), Radio, Regional, Retail, Search Engine Optimization, Seniors' Market, Social Marketing/Nonprofit, Stakeholders, Sweepstakes, T.V., Teen Market, Telemarketing, Trade & Consumer Magazines, Transportation, Travel & Tourism, Urban Market, Women's Market

Stephanie Nerlich *(Pres & CEO)*
Darlene Remlinger *(Mng Dir & Sr VP)*
Patrick Scissons *(Chief Creative Officer)*
Andrew Carty *(VP-Strategy & Innovation)*
Rob Trickey *(Sr Dir-Art)*
Mike Kirkland *(Art Dir)*
James Ansley *(Dir-Creative)*
Logan Gabel *(Dir-Art)*
Terri Vegso *(Dir-Production Mgmt)*
Francesca Saraco *(Strategist-Social Media)*
James McGuire *(Copywriter)*

Accounts:
Brown-Forman Herradura Tequila (Digital CRM & Below the Line Marketing)
Canadian Cancer Society; 2005
Canadian Special Olympics CSO, Sports Celebrities Festival; 1998
Diageo Canada Campaign: "Window Pints", Captain Morgan, Crown Royal; 2004
Eli Lilly Canada Cialis; 2004
Everytown for Gun Safety Campaign: "Lockdown"
GlaxoSmithKline Abreva, Campaign: "Time in Wings", Contac, Nytol, Polident, Poligrip, Sensodyne (Paste, Brush, Floss); 1983
Glentel
Government of Ontario Ministry of Education, Ministry of Health & Long Term Care, Ministry of Health Promotion
JTI MacDonald
Missing Children Society of Canada Campaign: "Milk Carton 2.0", Campaign: "World's Most Valuable Search Engine"
Moms Demand Action for Gun Sense in America Broadcast Media, Campaign: "Choose One", Campaign: "Lockdown", Campaign: "Not Allowed", Digital, Print, Radio
Mr.Clean
OSEG (Ottawa Sports & Entertainment Group)
Playtex Baby Magic, Banana Boat, Diaper Genie, Infant Feeding, Tampons, Wet Ones; 1968
Post Foods Canada Campaign: "The First15 Project"
Post Foods U.S.
Post Holdings, Inc.
Procter & Gamble Auto Dry, Clean Mop, Magic Eraser, Mr. Clean (North America), Pantene, Pringles Jalapeno; 1974
Sagicor
Salvation Army of Canada & Bermuda Campaign: "Bottle, Drugs, Gun", Campaign: "Frank", Campaign: "No One Chooses to Eat Garbage"
Special Olympics Canada
Special Olympics Campaign: "Kevin"
SUBWAY Restaurants Creative, Marketing, Strategy
Volvo Canada

Branch Offices:

Grey Vancouver

736 Granville St, Vancouver, BC V6Z 1G3 Canada
(See Separate Listing)

GREY GROUP

200 5th Ave, New York, NY 10010
Tel.: (212) 546-2000
Fax: (212) 546-2001
E-Mail: Inquiries@grey.com
Web Site: www.grey.com

Employees: 10,500
Year Founded: 1917

National Agency Associations: 4A's-AAF-ABC-APA-BPA-CBP-DMA-MCA-NYPAA-TAB

Agency Specializes In: Children's Market, Communications, Consulting, Digital/Interactive, Direct Response Marketing, Event Planning & Marketing, Government/Political, Hispanic Market, Internet/Web Design, Logo & Package Design, Public Relations, Sales Promotion, Sponsorship

James R. Heekin, III *(Chm & CEO)*
Jane Reiss *(Mng Dir)*
Christopher Ross *(Mng Dir)*
Robert Walsh *(CIO-Global)*
David Patton *(Pres/CEO-EMEA)*
Amy Tunick *(Pres-GREY Activation & PR)*
Michael Houston *(CEO-North America)*
Joe Lampertius *(CEO-Shopper Mktg-Global)*
John Grudzina *(Gen Counsel & Exec VP)*
Mark Schwatka *(Exec VP & Exec Dir-Creative)*
Debby Reiner *(Exec VP & Grp Dir)*
Emma Armstrong *(Exec VP & Acct Dir-Global)*
Jean Donahue *(Exec VP & Acct Dir-Global)*
Josh Rabinowitz *(Exec VP & Dir-Music)*
Ben Tauber *(Exec VP & Dir-Bus Dev)*
Tania Salter *(Sr VP & Exec Producer)*
Courtney Berry *(Sr VP & Acct Dir)*
Jennifer Chanowitz *(Sr VP & Acct Dir)*
Tara Cosentino *(Sr VP & Acct Dir)*
Beth Culley *(Sr VP & Acct Dir)*
Denise D'Agostino *(Sr VP & Acct Dir)*
Beth Galloway *(Sr VP & Acct Dir)*
Chree Taylor *(Sr VP & Acct Dir)*
Brian Weston *(Sr VP & Acct Dir-Global)*
Ron Castillo *(Sr VP & Dir-Creative)*
David Pitts *(Sr VP)*
Kerry Quinn *(Sr VP-Global Client Fin)*
Mark Suster *(Sr VP-Global Client Fin & Ops)*
Danielle Avedon *(VP & Acct Dir)*
John Baker *(VP & Acct Dir)*
Diana Blau *(VP & Acct Dir)*
Melanie Cortese *(VP & Acct Dir)*
Juliette Dealy *(VP & Acct Dir)*
Emily Giordano Dimakopoulos *(VP & Acct Dir)*
Snigdha Gollamudi *(VP & Acct Dir)*
Josh Mattes *(VP & Acct Dir-Global)*
Erin Metcalf *(VP & Acct Dir)*
Alexis Stember *(VP & Producer)*
Donna Stokes *(VP & Producer)*
Rong Zhang *(VP & Acct Dir)*
Paul Safsel *(VP & Dir-Creative)*
Rita Seredenko *(VP & Dir-HRIS)*
Courtney Engel *(VP-PR & Mktg)*
Peter Loftus *(VP-Bus Dev)*
Caitlin Ewing *(Exec Dir-Creative & Writer)*
Jason Brandt *(Exec Dir-Global Digital-P&G)*
Dave Cohen *(Exec Dir-Creative)*
Rob Lenois *(Exec Dir-Creative)*
Howard Roberts *(Exec Dir-Strategy)*
Nicholas Pringle *(Grp Dir-Creative)*
Leo Savage *(Grp Dir-Creative)*
Jeff Stamp *(Grp Dir-Creative)*
Steve Wakelam *(Grp Dir-Creative)*
Matthew DeCoste *(Sr Dir-Art)*
Matt Rogers *(Sr Dir-Art)*
Marcel Baker *(Sr Producer-Digital)*
Christopher Izzo *(Sr Producer-Digital)*
Joe Mongognia *(Creative Dir)*
Laura Chavoen *(Dir-Social Media Strategy)*
Joao Coutinho *(Dir-Creative)*
Jan Egan *(Dir-Creative)*
Kristen Finch *(Dir-Digital Production)*
Marques Gartrell *(Dir-Art)*
Mike Giannone *(Dir-Plng)*
Jay Hunt *(Dir-Creative)*
Steve Krauss *(Dir-Creative)*
Brad Mancuso *(Dir-Creative)*
Spiro Mifsud *(Dir-Tech)*
Steve Nathans *(Dir-Creative)*
Denise O'Bleness *(Dir-Creative)*
Lance Parrish *(Dir-Creative)*
Damion Sammarco *(Dir-Creative)*
Susan LaScala Wood *(Dir-Creative)*
Andrew Antaki *(Assoc Dir-Media)*
Natsuko Bosaka *(Assoc Dir-Creative)*
Mary Coco *(Assoc Dir-Creative)*
Michelle Moscone *(Assoc Dir-Project Mgmt)*
Rachel West *(Mgr-Creative Reputation)*
Gabrielle Barbuto *(Acct Supvr)*
Yudelka Candelario *(Acct Supvr)*
Danielle Granderson *(Acct Supvr)*
Courtney Griffin *(Acct Supvr)*
Sarah Haman *(Acct Supvr)*

Advertising Agencies

Ashley Hughes *(Acct Supvr)*
Reina Kim *(Acct Supvr)*
Caroline Manning *(Acct Supvr)*
Ethan Nadel *(Acct Supvr)*
Kelly Norris *(Acct Supvr-Downy NA & Global)*
Brenda O'Donovan *(Acct Supvr)*
Sam White *(Acct Supvr)*
Alex Baum *(Sr Strategist-Digital-Global)*
Jessica Rodriguez *(Sr Strategist-Brand-Downy Lenor Global-North America)*
Monisha Tripathi *(Sr Strategist-Digital)*
Lauren Aziz *(Acct Exec-Digital)*
Jessica Chaiparnich *(Acct Exec)*
Alexandra Isabelle *(Acct Exec)*
Melina Jagnandan *(Acct Exec)*
Jillian Kettler *(Acct Exec)*
Hannah Park *(Acct Exec)*
Courtney Ridenhour *(Acct Exec)*
Dan Finer *(Planner)*
Latoya Grant *(Analyst-Client)*
Kim Nguyen *(Copywriter)*
Laura Rose *(Media Planner-Grey Grp)*
Reagan Ward *(Copywriter)*
Jennifer Consaga *(Asst Acct Exec)*
Elizabeth McDonnell *(Asst Acct Exec)*
Emily Darby *(Assoc Producer)*
Zachary Fleming *(Assoc Producer)*
Michele Kay *(Grp Exec VP)*
Per Pedersen *(Deputy Chief Creative Officer-Worldwide)*
Canon Wu *(Chief Digital Creative Officer-Greater China)*

Accounts:
3M
AB Volvo
Allianz Life Insurance Company of North America
Ally Bank
Bausch & Lomb (Global Advertising Duties) Eye Drops, Prescription Medicines & Vitamins
Boehringer Ingelheim
Canon Inc. Campaign: "Long Live Imagination, Project Imagin8ion"
Champions Against Bullying Campaign: "The Bullies"
Darden Restaurants
Diageo
DirecTV Campaign: "Don't just watch TV. DirecTV.", Creative
Eli Lilly
Friends of the National Park Foundation
Gillette Fusion TV
GlaxoSmithKline Panadol Pain Relief
Hasbro, Inc.
J.M. Smucker
Kellogg Company
Marriott Hotels & Resorts
Mike's Hard Beverage Company Mike's Hard Lemonade
National Football League Properties National Football League, Inc.
The NFL
Nokia, Inc.
The Procter & Gamble Company Blades & Razor, Campaign: "One Stroke Shave", Digital Communications, Gillette, Gillette Fusion ProGlide, Global Brand Agency Leader(BAL), Global Creative, Men's Gillette, Personal Care
States United To Prevent Gun Violence
Symantec
T.J. Maxx (Agency of Record)
Turner Broadcasting Inc.
Volvo Trucks North America, Inc.

GHG
200 5th Ave, New York, NY 10010
(See Separate Listing)

Grey New York
200 5th Ave, New York, NY 10010
(See Separate Listing)

Grey Puerto Rico
PO Box 367, San Juan, PR 00918
(See Separate Listing)

Wing
200 5th Ave 3rd Fl, New York, NY 10010
(See Separate Listing)

GREY NEW YORK
200 5th Ave, New York, NY 10010
Tel.: (212) 546-2000
Fax: (212) 546-1495
E-Mail: gwwinfo@grey.com
Web Site: www.grey.com/newyork

Employees: 700
Year Founded: 1925

National Agency Associations: AAF-ABC-APA-BPA-CBP-DMA-MCA-NYPAA-TAB

Agency Specializes In: Advertising, Advertising Specialties, Brand Development & Integration, Business-To-Business, Children's Market, Communications, Consumer Marketing, Cosmetics, Health Care Services, High Technology, Industrial, Leisure, Multimedia, Pharmaceutical, Restaurant, Retail, Sponsorship, Strategic Planning/Research, Teen Market

Rick Cusato *(Partner)*
Jonathan Lee *(Chief Strategy Officer)*
Linda Mummiani *(Exec VP & Grp Dir-Creative)*
Jean Donahue *(Exec VP & Acct Dir-Global)*
Suresh Nair *(Exec VP & Dir-Strategic Plng-Global)*
Alice Ericsson *(Exec VP-Creative Direction)*
Elizabeth Gilchrist *(Sr VP & Acct Dir-Gillette & Gun Violence Prevention)*
Peter Zenobi *(Sr VP & Acct Dir-Integrated)*
Robert Wilson *(VP-Fin-Worldwide)*
Stephen Krauss *(Exec Creative Dir)*
Derek Barnes *(Exec Creative Dir)*
Matt O'Rourke *(Exec Dir-Creative-Volvo)*
Rob Perillo *(Exec Creative Dir)*
David Cuccinello *(Copywriter)*
Leo Savage *(Grp Dir-Creative)*
Jeff Stamp *(Grp Dir-Creative)*
Tony Muller *(Creative Dir & Copywriter)*
Kira Gotbatkin *(Art Dir)*
Oliver Handlos *(Co-Creative Dir-Activation & PR)*
Katy Hill *(Producer-Brdcst)*
Carla Johnson *(Art Dir)*
Stu Mair *(Grp Creative Dir)*
Jerome Marucci *(Art Dir)*
Lance Parrish *(Creative Dir)*
Rob Carducci *(Dir-Creative)*
Doug Fallon *(Dir-Creative)*
Fred Gerantabee *(Dir-Creative Tech)*
Han Lin *(Grp Creative Dir)*
Ian Liu *(Dir-Art)*
Ricky Lu *(Dir-Creative)*
Bennett McCarroll *(Dir-Film Production)*
Marie Ronn *(Dir-Creative)*
Liz Delp *(Assoc Dir-Creative)*
Melissa Saks *(Acct Supvr)*
Abel Gachou *(Acct Exec)*
Genevieve Gray *(Acct Exec)*
Steve Mcelligott *(Copywriter)*
Anthony De Carolis *(Grp Creative Dir)*
Alison Horn *(Assoc Producer)*

Accounts:
3M Company "Tough as Nana", Campaign: "Nana vs. Water", Campaign: "Brand Colors of the World", Campaign: "Nana vs. Dirt", Campaign: "Will It Or Won't It", Digital, Nexcare; 1995
New-9/11 Day
AARP
Ad Desk Instagram
Advil
Aetna; 2001
Ally Bank Campaign: "Facts of Life", Campaign: "Shopping", Campaign: "Suitcase", Creative
American Egg Board Campaign: "Side of Kevin", Online; 1993
B&G Foods Campaign: "Parking Lot"
New-Best Buy CRM, Campaign: "Win the Holidays at Best Buy", Creative Development, Design, Digital, Social Strategy
Bosch Purolator
Bosch Spark Plug Line (Agency of Record) Consumer Advertising, Marketing Communications
Breathe Right Campaign: "The Bedtime Stakes"
Canon U.S.A., Inc. Brand Strategy, Campaign: "Concert", Campaign: "Eulogy", Campaign: "Inspired", Campaign: "Never Again", Campaign: "PIXMA PRO", Campaign: "Project Imagination", Campaign: "Rebel With A Cause", Campaign: "See Impossible", Campaign: "Touchdown", Creative, DSLR Camera, Digital, Event, Promotional, Public Relations
CIBA Vision
Crown Royal Campaign: "Reign Anthem"
Darden Restaurants, Inc. Creative, Longhorn Steakhouse, Olive Garden; 1984
Diageo Campaign: "Reign On", Captain Morgan, Crown Royal Canadian, Don Julio, Godiva Liqueur, Ketel One, Myer's Dark Rum, Parrot Bay, Seagram 7, Tanqueray Gin, Tanqueray Ten; 2009
DirecTV "Football on Your Phone", Campaign: "Arts & Craftsy", Campaign: "Bad Comedian", Campaign: "Cable Effects", Campaign: "Chase", Campaign: "Creepy", Campaign: "Don't Become a Local Fisherman,", Campaign: "Don't Get Body Slammed by a Lowland Gorilla.", Campaign: "Don't Have Your House Explode", Campaign: "Fantasy Football Fantasy", Campaign: "House", Campaign: "Less Attractive", Campaign: "Marionettes", Campaign: "Motorcycle", Campaign: "Painfully Awkward", Campaign: "Road Trip", Campaign: "Scrawny Arms", Campaign: "The World's Most Powerful Fans", Campaign: "Troll", Campaign: "Versus", NFL Sunday Ticket, Robots, Submarine
Dynamics ePlate Campaign: "Aquarium"
Earth 911 Campaign: "Recycle: Wolf"
Eli Lilly; 2000
New-Emirates Airline Brand Communications
Filtration Americas
GlaxoSmithKline Campaign: "Live Loud", Digital Advertising, Polident, Poligrip; 1955
Green Earth Technologies Creative, Public Relations
Hasbro Digital Advertising, Furby, Hulk, Iron Man, Littlest Pet Shop, My Little Pony, Spider-Man, Star Wars, Telepods, Transformers; 1977
JIF
The J.M. Smucker Company Folgers, Millstone; 2002
Kellogg's Pringles
Longhorn Steakhouse (Agency of Record)
Marriott International Branding, Campaign: "#LoveTravels", Campaign: "Let's Go Somewhere Brilliant", Campaign: "Travel Brilliantly", Campaign: "Travel is a Journey", Creative, Digital Advertising, Logo, Marriott Hotels & Resorts, Print, Public Relations, Social Media
National Park Foundation Campaign: "Find Your Park", Digital, Outdoor, Print, Social Media
National Park Service Broadcast, Campaign: "Find Your Park", Campaign: "Parks"
Nestle USA, Inc. Campaign: "Feed Your Phenomenal", Campaign: "The Phenomenal Effect of Elizabeth Ryan", Creative, Digital, Haagen Dazs, Lean Cuisine, Online, Stouffer's, TV
NFL Campaign: "Leon Sandcastle", Campaign: "No more", Campaign: "Speech", Campaign: "Super Bowl Rally", Campaign: "The Ball", Super Bowl 2015, Wind Beneath My Wings
NOMORE.org Campaign: "No More"
NYC Recycles Campaign: "Recycle Eveything"
PANDORA A/S (Advertising Agency of Record)

Campaign: "The Art of You", Communications, Creative, Digital, In-Store, Print, Public Relations, Social Media, TV
Papa John (Agency of Record) Campaign: "Better Ingredients, Better Pizza, Better Football", Campaign: "Get to Know Better", Creative, Digital, Social Media, Television
Penguin Books
Pfizer Advil, Alavert, Dimetapp, Preparation H, Robitussin, ThermaCare
Playtex Products, Inc. Campaign: "Censored"; 1968
The Procter & Gamble Company Art of Shaving, Braun, Campaign: "Piano", Campaign: "Shine Strong", Cover Girl, Creative, Digital Advertising, Duracell, Gillette, Global Shopper-Marketing, Pantene, Venus; 1956
Purolator Campaign: "Burglar", Campaign: "If They Can - Amish", Campaign: "If They Can - Granny", Campaign: "If They Can"
Robert Bosch (Agency of Record)
States United to Prevent Gun Violence Campaign: "Ed-A Petition for Stronger Gun Laws", Campaign: "Holes", Campaign: "The Monster Is Real"
T. J. Maxx
Terlato Wines International; Lake Bluff, IL Rutherford Hill; 2007
TNT "Dallas", Campaign: "Timeline", Marketing
TruTV
Turner Entertainment Network Campaign: "Clear Gaze"
United Van Lines "There's Moving and there's moving United" Campaign
The University of Pittsburgh Medical Center Branding, Marketing
U.S. Department of Health and Social Services Substance & Mental Health Services Administration
Volvo (North America Agency of Record) Campaign: "The Greatest Interception Ever", Creative, Social, Volvo XC60, Volvo XC90
Wet Ones Campaign: "Beautiful mess"
The Whitney Museum of American Art (Agency of Record) Brand Strategy, Creative Advertising, Out-of-Home, Print, Television
World Baseball Classic
World Trade Center "The Rise of See Forever: One World Observatory"

U.S. Agency Information

Grey San Francisco

303 2nd St Ste 800 S Tower, San Francisco, CA 94107
(See Separate Listing)

EMEA Regional Headquarters

Grey London

The Johnson Building 77 Hatton Garden, London, EC1N 8JS United Kingdom
Tel.: (44) 20 3037 3000
Fax: (44) 20 3037 3001
Web Site: www.grey.co.uk

Employees: 260
Year Founded: 1969

Agency Specializes In: Advertising, Digital/Interactive, Event Planning & Marketing, Media Planning, Package Design, Viral/Buzz/Word of Mouth

Nils Leonard *(Chm & Chief Creative Officer)*
Lucy Jameson *(CEO)*
Matt Springate *(Mng Partner-Plng)*
Alistair Green *(Partner-Plng)*
Alice McGinn *(Partner-Plng)*
Sarah Jenkins *(CMO)*
Jacqueline Dobrin *(Head-Production)*
Jessica Ringshall *(Deputy Head-Production)*
Ben Clapp *(Exec Dir-Creative)*
Darren O'Beirne *(Art Dir)*
Darren Wright *(Creative Dir)*
Erika Bataillard *(Acct Dir)*
Clare Campbell *(Bus Dir)*
Lex Down *(Creative Dir)*
Sophie Fredheim *(Acct Dir)*
Eleni Sarla *(Acct Dir)*
Tamsin Allen *(Dir-Creative)*
Miguel Gonzales *(Dir-Art)*
Fiona Keyte *(Dir-Plng)*
Andy Lockley *(Dir-Creative)*
Jay Marlow *(Dir-Creative)*
Gary McNulty *(Dir-Creative)*
Paul Moran *(Dir-Creative)*
Liam Riddler *(Dir-Art)*
Wiktor Skoog *(Dir-Strategic Design)*
Sander Vos *(Dir-Art & Creative)*
Mel Caplan *(Sr Acct Mgr)*
Mike Alhadeff *(Planner)*
Theo Bayani *(Copywriter)*
Ben Buswell *(Copywriter)*
Holly Clancey *(Planner)*
Lex Firth *(Copywriter)*
Rob Greaves *(Copywriter)*
Andy Hyland *(Planner)*
Matt Kemp *(Planner)*
Mike Kennedy *(Copywriter)*
Stuart Leung *(Designer)*
Neil Mcguirk *(Copywriter)*
Tom Reas *(Copywriter-Creative)*
Hazel Reed *(Planner)*
Aisling Ryan *(Planner)*
Natasha Sales *(Planner)*
Matt Tanter *(Planner)*
Chris Whitson *(Planner)*
Amy Witter *(Planner)*

Accounts:
3M Company
Allianz Group Brand Awareness, Campaign: "School Run"
Arcadia
Bold
Boss
BreatheRight
Brother International Europe Campaign: "141% - Brother", Campaign: "141% Blows People Away", Campaign: "Architect", Campaign: "Cafe", Campaign: "Make Great Ideas 141% Greater", Campaign: "Make Your Client 141% More Speechless", Campaign: "Your Ambitions 141% Sooner", Social Media Campaign
Cathedral City Campaign: "Cathedral City, the nation's favourite cheese", Campaign: "Come Home"
Corega
Country Life The Great British Picnic App
Dairy Crest Campaign: "Big Smile Giveaway", Campaign: "Choir", Campaign: "Future Rulers", Campaign: "Get Involved", Campaign: "If you can't play, manage", Clover Clover Lighter & Clover Life Lovers, Country Life butter, Dream Team, Frijj, Jamie Oliver, Online & Offline Marketing, Radio, Sun+
Duracell 2 Boys in a Boat, Campaign: "Christmas Homage", Global Advertising
New-Emirates Airline Brand Communications
Fairy Campaign: "Make a Wish Starring Sean Bean", Campaign: "Make a Wish", Dish Washing Liquid, Rowers, TV
Fairy Liquid Creative
Farm & Countryside Education
Febreze
Fidelity (Lead Marketing Agency)
Findus
New-Fintro
Flash
Flixonase Allergy
Fortis Curve Campaign, Television; 2007
Gartmore
General Mills, Inc. (Lead Creative Agency) Campaign: "Cook Like the Locals", Green Giant, Haagen-Dazs, Jus-Rol, Nature Valley, Old El Paso
Georgia-Pacific
GlaxoSmithKline Advertising, Beechams, Campaign: "Difference", Campaign: "I Believe", Campaign: "Last Man Standing", Campaign: "Mo Farah", Campaign: "Powered by Glucose", Campaign: "Spitting Blood", Campaign: "The Arrival", Campaign: "The Wild Ones", Campaign: "Witness My Revival", Digital, In-Store, Lucozade Energy, Lucozade Lite, Lucozade Revive, McCleans, Outdoor, Panadol, Parodontax, Piriton, Press, Sensodyne, TV, Through-the-Line, YES Positioning
Go Ahead Campaign: "The Most Important Snack of the Day"
Greene King Campaign: "Crafted for the Moment", Campaign: "Dub Hop"
Helly Hansen Digital, Experiential, Global Creative, Point-of-sale, TV
Homeserve plc; Walsall, UK
Honda Honda CR-V, Honda CR-Z
Hong Kong Tourist Board
Horlicks
HSBC Campaign: "It's Never Just Business", Campaign: "Lift", Creative, Retail
Jordans Digital
New-Kiss Awkward Goodbye
New-Koovs.com Campaign: "Step Into KOOVS.COM"
Kuoni Travel Campaign: "Find Your Amazing", Digital, Integrated, Online, Print, Retail, Social, Social Media, TV, Video
Lenor
Lucozade Ribena Suntory Brand Positioning, Broadcast, Campaign: "C'est Shook", Campaign: "Find Your Flow", Campaign: "Last Man Standing", Campaign: "The Wild Ones", Campaign: "Witness My Revival", Energy, Lite, OOH, Orangina, Revive, Sport
McCormick Creative
McVitie's BN Biscuits, Campaign: "Sweeet"
The Ministry of Sound Campaign: "In Pieces"
Mumsnet
NFU Mutual Brand Identity, Brand Positioning, Campaign: "It's About Time", Campaign: "Tea"
Nytol
Piriton
Pringles
Procter & Gamble Campaign: "100 Years of Hair", Campaign: "Fairyconomy", Campaign: "Make a Wish", Clairol, Fairy Dish Washing Liquid, Fairy Rowers, Gillette, Gillette BODY, Pantene
Fairy Campaign: "Make a Wish", Dish Washing Liquid, Rowers
Puma Fragrances Campaign: "Dance Dictionary"
Renegades
Ryvita Above the Line, Digital, Social Media
Samsung JET
Schwartz Campaign: "The Sound of Taste"
Scope End the Awkward, Social Media, TV
Semta Government Apprenticeship
Sensodyne
Sixt Above-the-Line, Brand Awareness, Digital, Press
Sony Bravia, Campaign: "Sony - Di"; 2010
Stop Accidents Happy Faces
The Sun Campaign: "Big Smile Giveaway", Campaign: "Future Rulers", Campaign: "Get Involved", Campaign: "If you can't play, manage", Dream Team, Jamie Oliver, Online & Offline Marketing, Radio, Reality TV's Richest, Sun+, TV
Suntory Holdings Ltd Ribena (Global Advertising)
New-Tate Britain Creative, Press
Times Newspapers Ltd. "Icons", "Making Of", Campaign: "'Fashion Royalty", Campaign: "Incredible Edibles Ultimate Cookbook", Campaign: "Irish Edition Launch", Digital, Media, Outdoor, Press, Print, Style Magazine Best Dressed List, The Sunday Times, The Times
Toshiba Space Chair
Twinings
United Biscuits (Holdings) Limited Campaign:

"Creeepy", Campaign: "Sweeet", Campaign: "The Most Important Snack of the Day", Creative, Digestive, Hob Nobs, Jacob's, Jaffa Cakes, McVitie's Digestives, McVitie's Victoria
Utterly Butterly
New-Vodafone Ireland
Vodafone UK (Agency of Record) Advertising, Below-the-Line, Campaign: "Ass Roasting", Campaign: "Good Things Should Last Forever", Campaign: "If You Don't Get that Call, It's Probably Not Our Network", Campaign: "Make Someone Happy", Campaign: "The Call", Campaign: "The Kiss", Creative, Digital, Mobile Phone Provider, Online, Outdoor, Print, Public Relations, TV
Volvo Campaign: "Be Safe, Be Scary", Campaign: "From Sweden Not Hollywood", Campaign: "Seek Feeling", Campaign: "Swedish Air", Campaign: "The Swell", Global Print, LifePaint, Online, Volvo XC90
Warburtons
Women's Aid Cabinet of Dreams, Domestic Violence Awareness
Yoobot

Austria

Grey Group Austria
Paradistasse 51, 1190 Vienna, Austria
Tel.: (43) 1 328 4060
Fax: (43) 1 328 6931

Employees: 10
Year Founded: 1968

Agency Specializes In: Consumer Marketing, Direct Response Marketing

Michael Himmer *(CEO)*

Accounts:
3M
Allianz
Buena Vista
GSK
Nokia Mobile Phones; 1992
Pfizer
Sara Lee
Vandal Pesticide
Volkswagen Group of America, Inc.
Wuestenrot Financial Services

Belgium

Grey Possible Benelux
(Formerly Grey Group Belgium)
Rue Jules Cockxstraat 8-10, B-1160 Brussels, Belgium
Tel.: (32) 2 773 1711
Fax: (32) 2 771 2690
Web Site: grey.com/benelux

E-Mail for Key Personnel:
President: patrick_stichelmans@grey.be

Employees: 25
Year Founded: 1946

Agency Specializes In: Advertising

Doeke de Steur *(Bus Dir-Benelux)*

Accounts:
Child Focus Campaign: "Stop Child Porno"
Helly Hansen
Info Mazot
Leaseplan
Seat
Skoda Cars; 1994
VivaCite

Bulgaria

Grey Group Bulgaria
23 Mizia Strasse 2nd Floor, 1330 Sofia, Bulgaria
Tel.: (359) 2 401 5073
Fax: (359) 2 401 5073
E-Mail: office@grey.bg
Web Site: bulgaria.grey.com/us

Employees: 28
Year Founded: 1995

Agency Specializes In: Advertising

Albena Zdravkova *(Mng Partner)*
Mariyana Koseva *(Acct Mgr)*

Accounts:
British American Tobacco
Emirates
GM
GSK
Mars
New Yorker
P&G
Pfizer

Croatia

Grey Group Croatia
Trg Bana Jelacica 3, 10 000 Zagreb, Croatia
Tel.: (385) 1 4896 999
Fax: (385) 1 4816 205
E-Mail: office@grey.hr
Web Site: grey.com/croatia/

Employees: 24
Year Founded: 1994

Agency Specializes In: Advertising

Iva Hlavka *(Mng Dir)*
Durbavko Opasic *(COO & Client Svcs Dir)*
Natasa Buljan *(Dir-Creative)*
Ida Pandur *(Dir-Digital)*

Accounts:
Procter & Gamble Company
VIP

Czech Republic

WMC/Grey
Belgicka 115/40, 12000 Prague, 2 Czech Republic
Tel.: (420) 2 667 98 100
Fax: (420) 2 667 98 103
E-Mail: info@wmcgrey.cz
Web Site: www.grey.cz

Employees: 35
Year Founded: 1991

Agency Specializes In: Advertising

Accounts:
Ambiente Restaurants
The Baxter Theatre
Centrum
GlaxoSmithKline
Globus
Heineken
Laufen
Odol
PREkolo
Prevenar
Procter & Gamble
Red Bull
Red Group
Roca
Starobrno

Denmark

Uncle Grey A/S
Studsgade 35, DK 8000 Arhus, Denmark
Tel.: (45) 702 71100
Fax: (45) 702 71101
E-Mail: cb@unclegrey.dk
Web Site: unclegrey.dk/

Employees: 25
Year Founded: 1983

Agency Specializes In: Advertising

Rolf Bach Chrestensen *(CEO-GREY Denmark)*
Jimmy Blom *(Exec Dir-Creative)*
Lukas Lund *(Sr Dir-Art)*
Charlotte Porsager *(Acct Dir)*
Jesper Hansen *(Dir-Creative & Art, Copywriter)*
Rune Dueholm Braemer *(Dir-Art)*
Celina Aagaard *(Acct Mgr)*

Accounts:
Aarhus University
Bolia Campaign: "Home Book"
CPI
Danish Cyclist Association Campaign: "Dead Angle"
Etu Forsikring Insurance
Fakta; 1999
Fleggaard
Jbs Campaign: "Its Hard to Improve Perfect"
Jem & Fix
Kia Motors Dk Campaign: "Seductively Sensible - Picanto"
Lust
Magasin
Morgenavisen Jyllands-Posten
ONLY Campaign: "The Liberation", Website
Opel
Peugeot
Royal Copenhagen Campaign: "Handpainted Outdoors"
Thor
Urban Ears Campaign: "Scratch Posters"
WWF Campaign: "Chimpanse"
Zederkof Campaign: "The Fight"

Estonia

Inorek & Grey
Mafina 20, 10144 Tallinn, Estonia
Tel.: (372) 6 109 370
Fax: (372) 6 109 371
E-Mail: grey@grey.ee

Employees: 10
Year Founded: 1996

Sven Rannavali *(Partner)*

Accounts:
Adobe
Allergan
DanSukker
Frontier
GlaxoSmithKline Coldrex, Corega, Parodontax, Sensodyne
Instrumentarium
Kraft
Mars
Max 123
Nestle
P&G
Santa Maria
Sara Lee
Subaru
Visa

Finland

SEK & Grey

Annankatu 28, 00100 Helsinki, Finland
Tel.: (358) 9 695 71
Fax: (358) 9 695 7200
E-Mail: marco.makinen@sek.fi
Web Site: sek.fi/

Employees: 122
Year Founded: 1987

Agency Specializes In: Advertising

Jaakko Rantala *(COO)*
Jari Ullakko *(Creative Dir)*
Marja Vattulainen *(Acct Dir)*
Joni Furstenborg *(Dir-Art)*
Sami Kelahaara *(Dir-Art)*
Suvi Lahde *(Copywriter)*

Accounts:
Alko Alcoholic Beverages
Amnesty International
Berner XZ Shampoo
Dna Campaign: "C Cassette Teaser", Campaign: "The Kingdom of Entertainment"
Expert
Fazer
Finlayson
Finnair
Fonecta Campaign: "Fonecta 020202 Service"
Gasum
The Mannerheim League For Child Welfare Children's Hopes
Nokia
Paulig Presidentti 3D Coffee Box
PILTTI
Sanoma Magazines Tietokonelehti IT-Magazine
Tapiola Insurance Company
TNT
V&S Finland Festivo Wine
Valio Dairy Products Cream, Oltermanni Cheese
Valio International
Valtra

France

Grey Paris

(Formerly Grey: Callegari Berville Grey)
92 Avenue Des Ternes, 75017 Paris, France
Tel.: (33) 1 44 09 15 15
Fax: (33) 1 44 09 15 00
Web Site: grey.com/france

Employees: 50
Year Founded: 1964

Agency Specializes In: Communications

Thierry Astier *(Exec Dir-Creative)*
Vicken Adjennian *(Art Dir)*
Mehdi Benkaci *(Art Dir)*
Laurence Cormier *(Bus Dir)*
Cedric Auzannet *(Dir-Artistic)*

Accounts:
Albal
Asonor
Banette
BreatheRight
British American Tobacco Barclay, Pall Mall
Brother
Dulux Valentine
Dylon Fabric Dye
Far Cry 4
Findus Findus Fraich'Frites
GlaxoSmithKline Parodontax Toothpaste
Ideal
Kickers
Lego Campaign: "Computer", Campaign: "Creativity forgives everything", Campaign: "Fridge", Campaign: "Haunted House", Campaign: "Parachutes"
McNeil
Nokia Mobile Phones
Oracle Corporation; Redwood Shores, CA High-Tech Software Equipment; 1999
P&G Fabric Care Ace, Campaign: "Eau de Lacoste L.12.12 Blue", Campaign: "Eau de Lacoste L.12.12 Green", Campaign: "Eau de Lacoste L.12.12 White", Campaign: "Eau de Lacoste L.12.12", Dash, Lacoste, Lenore, Nicolas Feuillatte, P&G Fragrances
P&G Home Care Campaign: "La Machine L.12.12 By Lacoste", Febreze, Mr. Propre
Pringles
Sanofi MSD
SEAT (Group Volkswagen) Cars
Ubisoft

Germany

Grey Group Germany

Platz der Ideen 1, PO Box 101051, 40476 Dusseldorf, Germany
Tel.: (49) 211 3807 0
Fax: (49) 211 3807 367
E-Mail: contact@grey.de
Web Site: grey.com/germany

Employees: 300
Year Founded: 1953

Agency Specializes In: Advertising

Andre Schieck *(Mng Dir & Chief Digital Officer)*
Michael Rewald *(Mng Dir)*
Fabian Kirner *(Chief Creative Officer)*
Neil Elliott *(Exec Creative Dir)*
Phillip Benner *(Creative Dir & Copywriter)*
Alexandros Antoniadis *(Creative Dir)*
David Baertz *(Art Dir)*
Alexander Bertschat *(Art Dir)*
Franziska Fischer *(Acct Dir)*
Marc Schade *(Sr Art Dir)*
Martin Venn *(Creative Dir)*
saurabh Kejriwal *(Copywriter)*

Accounts:
Ay Yildiz Online & Offline, TV
British-American Tobacco (Germany) GmbH; Hamburg Captain Black Cigars, Dunhill Cigars & Cigarettes
Bundesverband Alphabetisierung
Bundesverband Volks-und Raiffeisenbanken
Deichmann Schuhe GmbH & Co. Vertriebs KG Campaign: "Occupy Banksy!", Campaign: "Running Shoes", Deichmann, Shoes
Deutsche Verkehrswacht Campaign: "Skeleton"
Deutscher Tierschutzbund
Docmorris International Retail Campaign: "Sauna"
Duracell
Durex Pleasuremax
Erdogan Campaign: "Freedom of tweets"
Febreze Kitchen Campaign: "Holiday"
Geers
New-Germanwings
GlaxoSmithKline Chlorhexamed, Contac, Corega Tabs, Corsodyl, Dr. Best, Lactacyd, Odol, Olod-med 3, Pilca, Sensodyne
Handelsblatt
HanseMerkur Travel Insurance
IFM Europe Coraya
International Children's Fund Campaign: "The Lost Choir-Mad World"
Kellogg Company Pringles
Klosterfrau Campaign: "Sheep"
Langenscheidt Campaign: "Decodicons"
Loyalty Partner Payback
Maredo Restaurants Holding Campaign: "Brandy"
Mars North America Amicelli, Balisto, Bisc, Kit Kat, Mars, Milky Way, Seramis, Twix
Melitta Haushaltsprodukte GmbH & Co. KG Aclimat, Swirl
MTV Networks Campaign: "Sexidents"
NOAH Campaign: "Children's E-Book"
Procter & Gamble Baldessarini, Boss, Campaign: "Lovely Skirt", Fairy, Febreze Campaign: "Breathe Happy", Febreze Campaign: "Febreze Experiment: Communal Bathroom", Febreze Campaign: "Febreze Experiment: Couch" & Febreze Campaign: "Man in a Box", Giorgio Beverly Hills, Helmut Lang, Hugo, Lacoste, Laura, Pantene, Roma, Sensodyne, Vanezia, Yohji Yamamoto
Punica
Scotch Brite
Seat Brake Energy Recovery System, Campaign: "Taxi Fare"
New-SoundCloud
Toshiba
Viacom International Media Networks Northern Europe Campaign: "The Non-Interactive, Interactive Comedy"
Victory Shoes
Vitasprint B12 Campaign: "Running Alarm"
Volkswagen AG

Grey

Schwedter St 6, 60314 Frankfurt, Germany
Tel.: (49) 69 42 72 82 500
Fax: (49) 69 42 72 82 555
Web Site: grey.com/germany

Employees: 20

Agency Specializes In: Advertising

Fabian Kirner *(Chief Creative Officer)*
Isabelle Jubin *(Head-Global Brand & Sr Acct Dir)*
Bodo Schiefer *(Head-Global Client & Client Svcs Dir)*
Mark Hendy *(Dir-Creative)*
Thiago Jacon *(Dir-Art)*
Markus Werner *(Dir-Art)*
Christiano Rocco *(Copywriter)*
Bettina Chamier *(Client Svc Dir)*

Accounts:
HanseMerkur
Langenscheidt GmbH & Co. KG TV
Procter & Gamble Service GmbH (Duracell Germany) Radio

Hungary

Grey Group Hungary

1061 Andrassy ut 9, BP-1061 Budapest, Hungary
Tel.: (36) 1 214 6750
Fax: (36) 1 214 6758
E-Mail: info@grey.hu
Web Site: www.grey.com/hungary/

Employees: 75
Year Founded: 1990

Agency Specializes In: Advertising

David Patton *(Pres/CEO-EMEA)*

Accounts:
Allianz
Amway
Chevrolet
Coca-Cola Refreshments USA, Inc.
Full Tilt Poker
Gefco
GlaxoSmithKline Coldrex, Corega, Lactacyd, Opilca, Panadol, Paradontax, Respir'Activ
Parodontax
Procter & Gamble Bold, Jar, Lenor, Mr Proper, Pantene
Unicef

Israel

Adler, Chomski Grey

154 Menacham Begin Road, 154 Tel Aviv, 64921 Israel
Tel.: (972) 3 608 8888
Fax: (972) 3 608 8881
E-Mail: amir_guy@acw-grey.co.il

Employees: 300
Year Founded: 1980

Agency Specializes In: Advertising

Ariel Berenson *(CEO)*
Karin Gross *(Sr Dir-Art)*
Sharon Suliman *(Sr Dir-Art)*
Daphna Gan *(Sr Acct Dir)*
Ira Gimpelevich *(Art Dir)*
Ziv Meiri *(Creative Dir)*
Idan Regev *(Creative Dir)*
Liron Ezratty *(Acct Mgr)*
Maayan Ben-Shoham *(Acct Supvr)*
Shay Chikotay *(Copywriter)*

Accounts:
Audi
Berlitz
Bezeq International Campaign: "Stork", Next Generation Network
Bezeqint
Cancerhelp.org.il. Campaign: "Spot.A.Dot"
Delta Lingerie Campaign: "A One-Time Sale", Machtonim, Poke Campaign
Delta Underwear
El Halev Self Defense
Electra Chef
Emda Alzheimer Campaign: "The wrong movie"
Fairy
Greenpeace
GSK Sensodyne
Ha'eer Bevarod Gay Magazine
Home Center Clear Out Sale, Furniture
Ken Lazken Senior Rights Awareness
Lighting Networks
L.O. Organization
losec
Lotto Israeli Lottery Campaign: "Selfie"
Marom Musical Instruments
Offer Avnir Piaggio MP3, Vespa
Or Yarok Preventing Road Accidents
Oracle
Pantene
Pelephone Campaign: "Cloud"
Piaggio - Ofer Avnir
Procter & Gamble Washing Up Liquid
Reshet Shoken Campaign: "Get rid of that brief", Goldfish
Schweppes Campaign: "Cannibals"
Seat Ibiza
Shanti House Donation Appel
Shoken Campaign: "Print one"
Skoda Campaign: "Big space conversation", Superb
Spring Tea
Tambour Paint
Tzabar Travel Agency
Volkswagen Group of America, Inc. Campaign: "Elvis", Campaign: "From 0 to 100 km", Golf GTI, Hill Hold Assist, Touareg
WWF Environmental Awareness

Grey Tel Aviv

154 Menachem Begin Road, Tel Aviv, Israel
Tel.: (972) 36088888
Web Site: www.grey.com

Agency Specializes In: Advertising, Brand Development & Integration, Production

Sharon Suliman *(Sr Dir-Art)*
Gabi Kikozashvili *(Art Dir)*
Elad Hermel *(Dir-Creative Plng)*
Ziv Meiri *(Dir-Creative)*

Accounts:
Bezeq
Delta Lingerie Campaign: "A One-Time Sale"
Steimatzky Books Campaign: "The right book will always keep you company."
Volkswagen Fatique Detection System

Italy

Grey Italia S.p.A

Via Alberto Mario 19, 20149 Milan, Italy
Tel.: (39) 02 3616 7500
Fax: (39) 02 349 763 21
E-Mail: info@grey.it
Web Site: www.grey.com/italy/

Employees: 82
Year Founded: 1964

Barbara Cicalini *(Reg Dir-Creative)*
Veronica Ciceri *(Dir-Art)*
Delphine Hawrylko *(Dir-Art)*
Daria Paraboni *(Dir-Art)*
Alice Pozzi *(Dir-Art)*
Luca Beato *(Assoc Dir-Creative)*
Massimo Verrone *(Assoc Dir-Creative)*
Irene Bassani *(Acct Mgr)*
Emanuele Accurli Abenante *(Copywriter)*
Manuela Bandiera *(Client Svc Dir)*

Accounts:
Alcatraz
AMSA
Emirates Airlines
Evonik Chemicals
Ferrero
GCAP
Glaxo SmithKline
Green Peace Campaign: "The Fashion Duel"
Harley Davidson
Ministry of Health
Nokia Cellular Phones
O.N.Da
Oracle
Pfizer
Procter & Gamble Campaign: "Slippery Floors", Fabric and Home Care, Fine Fragrances, Health & Beauty Care, Snacks, Food and Beverage
Sara Lee
Seat Leon Cupra
Shun Restaurant
SISAL
Telecom Italia
UN Millenium Campaign
The Wind of Unchanged

GreyUnited

(Formerly 1861United)
Via Galvano Fiamma 18, Milan, 20149 Italy
Tel.: (39) 02 321 1141
Fax: (39) 02 321 11 44 01
Web Site: grey.com/italy

Agency Specializes In: Advertising, Commercial Photography, Print

Roberto Battaglia *(Chm & Exec Dir-Creative)*
Pino Rozzi *(CEO & Exec Dir-Creative)*
Peppe Cirillo *(Dir-Creative)*
Serena Di Bruno *(Dir-Creative)*

Accounts:
Diners Club International
Disney
IKEA Campaign: "Bathroom", Campaign: "Invasion", Campaign: "Who Said A Bathroom Should Be Just A Loo?"
Il Samaritano
Police Sunglasses Producer
Sky Campaign: "Make Christmas more cinematic.", Entertainment Services
Tonic Gym
Yamaha Lifestyle & Entertainment Services, Marine Motors F300V6

Lebanon

Grey Middle East Network

Beit Mery Roundabout Rouwaisy Grey Compound Beit Mery, PO Box 55-477, Beirut, Lebanon
Tel.: (961) 4 873 607
Fax: (961) 4 873 043
Web Site: www.greyme.com

Employees: 60

Agency Specializes In: Advertising

Eric Hanna *(CEO-Middle East & North Africa)*

Accounts:
Aetna
Canon
Diageo
GSK
Mars
P&G
Pfizer
Sara Lee
Toshiba
Versace
Visa
YASA Lebanon

Netherlands

Grey Amsterdam

Watertorenplein 4b, 1051 PA Amsterdam, Netherlands
Mailing Address:
P.O. Box 7364, 1007 JJ Amsterdam, Netherlands
Tel.: (31) 20 577 5111
Fax: (31) 20 577 5100
E-Mail: Patrick.Joore@GreyPOSSIBLE.nl
Web Site: http://grey.com/benelux

Employees: 60
Year Founded: 1975

Agency Specializes In: Advertising

Patrick Joore *(CEO)*
Ecco Vos *(Sr Dir-Art)*

Accounts:
Abbott Nederland
Becel Butter
Council of Europe The Underwear Rule
Eli Lilly
Energieveilig
Fashioncheque
GlaxoSmithKline Lactacyd, Williams
Manpower
Pink Ribbon Foundation
Pink Ribbon Magazine
Roche
Sanoma Publishers
Stichting Nederland Schoon
Unilever Nederland

Norway

Uncle Grey Oslo

Sorkedalsveien 6, 0365 Oslo, Norway
Tel.: (47) 21 60 34 00
Fax: (47) 21 60 33 02
E-Mail: rune@uncle.dk
Web Site: unclegrey.dk

Employees: 30
Year Founded: 1976

Agency Specializes In: Advertising

Birgitte Kjaer *(Acct Dir)*
Charlotte Porsager *(Acct Dir)*
Terje Jacobsen *(Dir-Art)*
Mia Lykkegaard *(Dir-Art)*
Michael Mandrup *(Dir-Design)*
Christian Kurt Rahn *(Dir-Digital Art)*
Rasmus Veggerby *(Dir-Art)*

Accounts:
Aker
Dagens Naeringsliv
Findus
First Hotels
Honcho Records
Oslo Sporveier
Peugeot
Storebrand Kapitalforvaltning
Visma Software

Poland

Grey Group Poland
Ul Jasna 24, 00-054 Warsaw, Poland
Tel.: (48) 22 332 9300
Fax: (48) 22 332 9303
E-Mail: info@grey.com.pl
Web Site: grey.com/poland/

Employees: 80
Year Founded: 1991

Agency Specializes In: Advertising

Anna Panczyk *(CEO)*
Gosia Skorwider *(Mng Dir)*
Rafal Rys *(Creative Dir)*
Marta Sawicka *(Acct Dir)*
Ireneusz Turski *(Acct Dir)*
Helena Olecka *(Mgr-Digital Comm)*
Krzysztof Bogdalik *(Planner-Strategic)*
Szymon Demirkol *(Sr Art Dir)*
Monika Salamon *(Reg Acct Dir)*

Accounts:
3M
British American Tobacco
Chevrolet
DWS
ESKA
Fresh St Market
Glue-invest
Hochland
Krzysztof Gusta Glueinvest Campaign: "Taboo. Set for Adults"
Nobody's Children Foundation
Pfizer
Prima
Procter & Gamble Campaign: "Extraordinary Experiment 1", Fabric Softener
New-Samsung Samsung Galaxy S6
Viva! Action For Animals Foundation

Romania

Geometry Global
(Formerly Grey Group Romania)
Frumoasa St 39, Sector 1, Bucharest, Romania
Tel.: (40) 2 1 310 6506
Fax: (40) 2 1 310 6509
E-Mail: office@grey.ro
Web Site: www.geometry.com/

Employees: 100
Year Founded: 1992

Agency Specializes In: Advertising

Mircea Pascu *(Mng Dir)*
Florina Voevod *(Dir-Fin-Grey Worldwide Romania-WPP Group)*
Ada Iftodi *(Acct Mgr)*

Accounts:
3M
ActiveWatch
Antena
Bosch
British American Tobacco
Chevrolet
Cosmopolis
New-elefant.ro
Emirates
GSK
Hapi Hap
Lenor
Observator Campaign: "The RGB News"
P&G Ace
Parodontax
Romtelecom
Titan
Weber

Russia

Grey CIS
5th Yamskogo Polya Str 7 Bldg 2, 125040 Moscow, Russia
Tel.: (7) 495 792 31 33
Fax: (7) 495 792 31 35
E-Mail: grey-reception@grey.ru
Web Site: www.grey.com/russia/

Employees: 170
Year Founded: 1993

Agency Specializes In: Advertising

Jon Williams *(Chief Digital Officer & Exec Dir-Creative)*
Alexey Kovylov *(Pres/CEO-Grey Group Russia)*
Andrey Sivkov *(Deputy Dir-Creative)*

Accounts:
Ambi Pur Campaign: "Absorbs Odours"
British American Tobacco
Chevrolet
GlaxoSmithKline
Novartis Consumer Health
Opel Opel Mokka
Procter & Gamble

Saudi Arabia

Grey Group Saudi Arabia
NCCI Building (Abraj Towers), King Fahad Road, Riyadh, Saudi Arabia
Mailing Address:
PO Box 40601, Jeddah, Saudi Arabia
Tel.: (966) 1 218 0290
Fax: (966) 1 218 0299
E-Mail: info@greyjeddah.com
Web Site: www.greyme.com

Employees: 40
Year Founded: 1989

Agency Specializes In: Advertising

Marc Bouharb *(Mng Dir)*
Moustafa Majzoub *(Client Svc Dir)*

Accounts:
Nadec

Serbia & Montenegro

Grey d.o.o. Belgrade
Bade Pivljanina 39, Belgrade, 11000 Serbia
Tel.: (381) 111 367 5765
Fax: (381) 111 367 5768
Web Site: www.grey.com

Employees: 70

Marin Simurina *(Mng Partner)*
Predrag Vrhovski *(Dir-Creative)*

Accounts:
Eurobank
Menosoya
Mercedes-Benz

Slovenia

Grey Ljubljana d.o.o.
(d/b/a Grey Group Slovenia)
Bravnicarjeva ulica 13, 1000 Ljubljana, Slovenia
Tel.: (386) 1 5132 600
Fax: (386) 1 5132 617
Web Site: grey.com/slovenia

Employees: 20
Year Founded: 1993

Spela Zorz *(Mng Dir)*
Nikola Bubanj *(CEO-Adriatic & Balkans)*
Lili Cizelj *(Exec Dir-Media)*
Petra Krulc *(Exec Dir-Creative)*
Matjaz Butara *(Dir-Digital & Acct)*
Ana Zeleznik *(Acct Mgr)*
Mihela Cerne *(Client Svc Dir)*

Accounts:
Raiffeisen Bank Campaign: "World's Smallest Aparatment"
Woodworking Bobic

Spain

Grey Barcelona
Santalo 10, 08021 Barcelona, Spain
Tel.: (34) 93 365 0200
Fax: (34) 93 365 0201
Web Site: www.grey.com/spain

Employees: 100

Javier Suso *(CEO)*
Roberto Sanchez Simon *(Gen Dir)*
Lucia Gomez Hortiguela *(Acct Dir)*
Isabel Tana *(Mgr-Comm)*
Fran Nieves *(Sr Acct Exec)*

Accounts:
Albal
Almirall
ANAR Foundation Campaign: "If Somebody Hurts You, Phone Us & We'll Help You", Campaign: "Only For Chidren"
Asociacion De Editores De Madrid Campaign: "Don Quixote", Campaign: "Moby Dick", Campaign: "The Little"
California Walnut Commission
Domino's Pizza
G+J Publications Campaign: "75 Anniversary of Guernica Bombing"
Loterias Y Apuestas Del Estado Campaign: "The Dreams Factory App"
McNeil
Mitsubishi Electric
Muy Historia
Pilot
Port Aventura
Procter & Gamble
Room Mate Hotels
Sony Campaign: "Exhausted Heros", PlayStation 4
Termoplast

Ubisoft

Grey Madrid
Paseo de la Castellana ,53, 20046 Madrid, Spain
Tel.: (34) 91 597 1750
Fax: (34) 91 556 6530
E-Mail: john.lynn@grey.es
Web Site: www.grey.com/spain

Employees: 100
Year Founded: 1980

Agency Specializes In: Advertising

Enric Nel-lo *(Chief Creative Officer)*
Nana Korke *(Exec Dir-Beauty & Reg Dir-Creative-Pantene Europe)*
Javier Monserrat *(Exec Dir-Creative)*
Tontcho Ponsoda *(Art Dir)*
ALEJANDRO DE ANTONIO *(Dir-Art)*
Jose Carlos Gomez *(Dir-Art)*
Nacho Hernandez *(Dir-Creative)*
Damian Lucas *(Dir-Intl Accounts)*
Jesus Martinez *(Dir-Art)*
Matias Lopez Navajas *(Dir-Creative)*
Juanjo Rogado *(Dir-Art-Online)*
Nuno Martin *(Supvr-Creative & Copy)*
Jorge Manzaneque *(Copywriter)*

Accounts:
3M; 1996
Adidas AG
Aje Group
Albal
Almirall; 2009
Cris Against Cancer
Febe
Fenix Directo
G + J Campaign: "Alois Hitler", MUY HISTORIA
GlaxoSmithKline; 1986
Procter & Gamble Pantene Hair Hang; 1980
UbiSoft

Sweden

INGO
(Formerly Grey Stockholm)
Master Samuelsgatan 56, 114 80 Stockholm, Sweden
Tel.: (46) 8 410 981 00
Fax: (46) 8 458 2801
E-Mail: info@ingostockholm.se
Web Site: ingostockholm.se

Johan Thunmarker *(Head-Activation & Acct Dir)*
Bjorn Stahl *(Exec Dir-Creative)*
Richard Baynham *(Art Dir)*
Timo Orre *(Art Dir)*
Rikard Holst *(Dir-Art)*
Bjorn Persson *(Copywriter)*

Accounts:
AB Electrolux (Lead Agency) Eureka
Lidl Campaign: "Dill", Campaign: "Say it with meat"
Renault
Situation Stockholm Campaign: "CV"

Turkey

Grey Istanbul
Beybi Giz Plaza Dereboyu Caddesi, Meydan Sok No 28 Kat 5 Maslak, 80670 Istanbul, Turkey
Tel.: (90) 212 290 28 10
Fax: (90) 212 290 2811
E-Mail: grey@grey.com.tr
Web Site: www.grey.com.tr

Employees: 100
Year Founded: 1990

Agency Specializes In: Advertising

Meltem Kose *(Head-Production)*
Burcu Gunister *(Sr Dir-Art)*
Engin Kafadar *(Sr Dir-Creative-Geometry Global & Istanbul)*
Tolga Ozbakir *(Art Dir)*
Fatih Yilmaz *(Dir-Art)*
Caglar Kurtaran *(Copywriter)*
Ergin Binyildiz *(Deputy Dir-Creative)*

Accounts:
3M
ACE
AdPrint Festival Campaign: "Nothing Touches Like Print"
Amnesty International Campaign: "Frame of Speech"
Antalya Alkollu Icecekler
Capital Radio Campaign: "The Story of The 80's", Campaign: "The story of 90's"
Corega
Duracell
Fairy
Glaxosmithkline Consumer Health Campaign: "Unhealty Gums"
Google
Koc Allianz
Mon Ami
Nexcare
Nokia
Procter & Gamble
Pronet Security System
Quiksilver
Samet Campaign: "Hinge"
Samsung
Topkapi Raki Campaign: "Just You"
Ulker

Ukraine

Grey Group Ukraine
4A Verhnii Val St, 04071 Kiev, 01004 Ukraine
Tel.: (380) 44 499 0166
Fax: (380) 44 287 7163
E-Mail: info@grey.ua
Web Site: www.grey.ua

Year Founded: 1996

Dan Medria *(CEO-Grey Ukraine & Bulgaria)*
Tatiana Shumilvich *(Deputy Mng Dir-Ukraine)*
Roman Breiman *(Dir-Creative)*

Accounts:
BAT
Chevrolet
Credit West Bank
GSK
Hapkido School
Koktebel
Nar Mobile
P & G
Sab Miller
VIASAT

United Arab Emirates

Grey Group Middle East Network
10th Fl API Tower Sheikh Zayed Rd, Dubai, United Arab Emirates
Mailing Address:
PO Box 60416, Dubai, United Arab Emirates
Tel.: (971) 4 3310 331
Fax: (971) 4 3310 553
E-Mail: tina.mascarenhas@greydubai.com
Web Site: www.greyme.com

Employees: 45
Year Founded: 1989

Agency Specializes In: Advertising

Nadim Khoury *(COO)*
Eric Hanna *(CEO-Middle East & North Africa)*
Dzila Dik *(Acct Dir)*
Vidya Manmohan *(Dir-Creative)*
Alisdair Miller *(Dir-Creative)*

Accounts:
Al Mobidoon
Audi
Barwa Bank Group Integrated Communication
Champion Sprayon Fresh Carpet
Dreamland
Ferrero Ferrero Rocher, Kinder Bueno, Kinder Chocolate, Kinder Country, Kinder Joy, Kinder Schoko-Bons, Raffaello
Volkswagen Group of America, Inc.

Uzbekistan

Grey Group Uzbekistan
Ivlieva St 44, 100070 Tashkent, Uzbekistan
Tel.: (998) 71 361 3041
Fax: (998) 71 361 4165
E-Mail: akovylov@grey.ru
Web Site: www.grey.com

Employees: 20
Year Founded: 1998

Agency Specializes In: Advertising

Alexey Kovylov *(Pres & CEO)*

Mauritius

Orange Communications
6th Floor TN Tower, St Georges Street, Port Louis, Mauritius
Tel.: (230) 211 5782
Fax: (230) 211 4769
E-Mail: orangecomm@intnet.mu

Employees: 12

Agency Specializes In: Advertising

Alix Chung *(Dir)*

Accounts:
GlaxoSmithKline

Nigeria

All Seasons Mediacom
(Formerly Insight Communications)
No 50 Adekunle Fajuyi Way, GRA Ikeja, Lagos, Nigeria
Tel.: (234) 17745021
Fax: (234) 14932697
Web Site: www.mediacom.com

Employees: 41

Agency Specializes In: Media Buying Services

Jimi Awosika *(Mng Dir)*
Kayode Situ *(Exec Dir-Sys & Fin)*
Mowunmi Fatodu *(Dir-Bus Process-Insight Grey)*
Ayo Owoeye *(Office Mgr)*

Accounts:
Amstel
BankPHB
Cobranet
Dublin City Council Sponsorship, Tourism
Dunlop
Emirates
eTranzact

Jagal Pharma
Nestle
Nigeria Breweries
PepsiCo
Samsung
Stallion Motors
Sterling Bank
Suzuki
Yudoo

South Africa

Grey Group South Africa
17 Muswell Road South Block A, Wedgefield Office Park, Bryanston, Gauteng 2021 South Africa
Tel.: (27) 11 706 3060
Fax: (27) 11 463 6043
Web Site: www.grey.com/southafrica

Employees: 65
Year Founded: 1977

Sizakele Marutlulle *(CEO)*

Accounts:
Brandhouse
British American Tobacco
Endangered Wildlife Trust
Findyofayah.org Campaign: "Fighting a virus with a virus"
GSK
Heineken Amstel, Heineken
Mazda
Namepak
Procter & Gamble Pantene
Volvo Cars Campaign: "A New Beginning"

Canada

Grey Canada
46 Spadina Ave Ste 500, Toronto, ON M5V 2H8 Canada
(See Separate Listing)

Argentina

Grey Argentina
Balafco 845, C 1414 AQQ Buenos Aires, Argentina
Tel.: (54) 11 5555 1800
Fax: (54) 11 5555 1801
E-Mail: recepcion@grey.com.ar
Web Site: www.grey.com

Employees: 70
Year Founded: 1972

Agency Specializes In: Advertising

Maximo Lorenzo *(CEO)*
Florencia Pereyra *(VP & Client Svcs Dir)*
Hernan Zamora *(VP-Digital-Latin America)*
Montserrat Villafane Molina *(Gen Mgr)*
Alejandro Devoto *(Dir-Creative)*
Javier Garcia *(Dir-Art)*
Sebastian Graccioli *(Dir-Creative)*
Florencia Loda *(Dir-Art)*
Sol Martin *(Dir-Strategic Plng)*
Jorge Martinez *(Dir-Art)*
Diego Gueler Montero *(Dir-Creative)*
Estefania Prieto *(Acct Exec)*
Gomez Adrover *(Copywriter)*
Facundo Martinelli *(Copywriter)*
Dario Porterie *(Copywriter)*
Juan Manuel Quintero *(Copywriter)*
Jorge Villar *(Reg Acct Dir)*

Accounts:
Artear
Ayudin
Belesana
Boehringer Ingelheim
Coca-Cola Refreshments USA, Inc.
Comedy Central
Covergirl
New-El campo Cine
New-Fundacion Favaloro Campaign: "The Salt You Can See"
Grupo Q Campaign: "Playboy Tweetgrid"
GSK
Hospital Aleman
New-LG Electronics
Magistral
Mr. Clean Wall Eraser
MTV
P&G Campaign: "Magistral Dishwasher: Big Drops"
Playboy Casting
RCI
VH1

Brazil

Grey
(Formerly Matos Grey)
Avenida Major Sylvio de Magalnaes Padiha Edificio Philadelphia 1st Fl, 5200 Condominio America Bus Pk, CEP 05693-000 Sao Paulo, Brazil
Tel.: (55) 11 3755 8200
Fax: (55) 11 3755 8214
Web Site: grey.com/brasil

Employees: 180

Mariangela Silvani *(Dir Gen-Creation)*
Sylvia Panico *(COO)*
Alain Groenendaal *(Pres/CEO-Latin America)*
Sergio Fonseca *(Gen Dir-Creation)*
Daniel Perez *(Exec Dir-Creative)*
Pedro Rocha *(Dir-Art)*
Camila Hoffman *(Acct Exec)*
Janaina Luna *(Acct Exec)*
Marcelle Palermo *(Acct Exec)*
Adriano Matos *(Copywriter)*

Accounts:
3M Nexcare Campaign: "Wash Your Bill", Waterproof bandages
Acao Crianca
New-Aruba
Avon
Boehringer Ingelheim
BR4Dogs
Bracor
Coca-Cola Campaign: "Don't Look Back"
EDP
Foca
New-Green Nation
Hospital Do Cancer De Barretos
Human Rights Foundation Campaign: "War shows the worse side of life"
Mercedes-Benz
Mexican Red Cross
Post-it
Procter & Gamble Campaign: "Everlasting Seconds - Eye", Gillette, Gillette Mach3
Reclame Aqui
Rolling Stone Magazine
Scotch Brite
Sensodyne
WWF Campaign: "Deforested Field"

Chile

Grey Chile
Eleodoro Yanez 2376, Providencia Las Condes, 7510451 Santiago, Chile
Tel.: (56) 2 584 9900
Fax: (56) 2 584 9902
Web Site: www.grey.com/chile/

Employees: 75
Year Founded: 1978

Agency Specializes In: Advertising

Armando Alcazar *(Pres/CEO-Grey, Ogilvy & Geometry Chile)*
Miguel Angel Cerdeira *(Gen Dir-Creative)*
Gonzalo Ferrada *(Creative Dir)*
Pedro Quilaqueo *(Dir-Creative & Copywriter)*
Carles Puig *(Dir-Creative)*

Accounts:
B.A.T. Belmont, Kent
Codeco
Hasbro Twister Bicycle
Hawaiian Tropic
Loto
Polla Chilena De Beneficencia Campaign: "Window"
Pringles Extreme
Procter & Gamble Camay, Moncler, Oil of Olay, Old Spice, Pantene, Pringles
Toto 3 Campaign: "The same problems, with more money"
Vina Maipo Gran Devocion Blended Wines
VTR.com Campaign: "Internet Parental Control: Violence", Campaign: "Some words are hard to reach. Unlimeted minutes plan."

Colombia

Grey: REP
Calle 94 #16-57, Bogota, Colombia
Tel.: (57) 1 530 3131
Fax: (57) 1 236 0252
E-Mail: ggamba@rep.com.co
Web Site: www.grey.com

Employees: 80

Andres Quintero *(Pres)*
Juan Palma *(Chief Creative Officer)*
Beatriz Garzon *(Acct Dir)*
Andres Lancheros *(Art Dir)*
Camilo Monzon *(Dir-Art & Creative)*
Silvana Noguera *(Acct Exec)*
Diego Arenas *(Copywriter)*

Accounts:
Colcafe
New-Compania Nacional de Chocolates
Dolex Gripa
Procter & Gamble

Costa Rica

jotabequ Advertising
(Affiliate of Grey Worldwide)
Avenue 1 & 3, San Jose, Costa Rica
Mailing Address:
PO Box 60-2050, San Jose, Costa Rica
Tel.: (506) 284 9800
Fax: (506) 225 5512
E-Mail: jotabequ@jotabequ.com
Web Site: www.jotabequ.com

Employees: 150

Jaime Jimenez *(Owner)*
Alberto Quiros *(Partner)*
Wagner Cornejo *(Gen Mgr)*

Accounts:
Belmont
Dos Pinos
Gold's Gym
Grupo Nacion Perfil, Revistas
La Florida
Purdy Motor
Roche
World Wildlife Foundation

Guatemala

La Fabrica Jotabequ GREY
Ruta 4 5-33 Zona 4, Guatemala, Guatemala
Tel.: (502) 2416 4900
Web Site: http://grey.com/guatemala

Agency Specializes In: Advertising, Brand Development & Integration, Digital/Interactive, Print

Sergio Estrada *(Creative Dir)*
Natalia Cereser *(Dir-Pro Svcs)*
Jose Fernando Gutierrez *(Dir)*

Accounts:
Aetna
Allianz
American Brasserie Dorada ICE
Campbells
Canon
Coca-Cola Refreshments USA, Inc.
Diageo
Frontier
P & G
Toshiba
Visa

Honduras

Talento Grey Publicidad
Colonia La Modern 22 Avenida, 7a Calle Casa no 720, San Pedro Sula, Honduras
Mailing Address:
Apartado Postal 3353, Tegucigalpa, MDC Honduras
Tel.: (504) 557 6426
Fax: (504) 557 6427
Web Site: grey.com/us

Year Founded: 1993

Augusto Hernandez *(Mgr)*

Mexico

Grey Mexico, S.A. de C.V
Jaime Balmes No 8-104 Col Los Morales Polanco, 11510 Mexico, DF Mexico
Tel.: (52) 55 5350 3700
Fax: (52) 55 5280 1292
E-Mail: greymx@attmail.com
Web Site: www.grey.com/mexico/

Employees: 150
Year Founded: 1984

National Agency Associations: AMAP

Agency Specializes In: Advertising

Pedro Egea *(Pres/CEO-Mexico)*
Alfonso Borreguero *(VP-Strategic Plng-Grey Mexico & Latin America)*
Victor Figueroa *(Grp Head-Creative)*
Cesar Salazar *(Grp Dir-Plng)*
Bernardo Rodirguez Pons *(Reg Dir-Creative)*
Laura Alcala *(Art Dir)*
Laura Abril Chimal *(Art Dir)*
Mariana de Pina *(Acct Dir)*
Pola Sanchez *(Art Dir)*
Raul Rivera *(Dir-Creative)*
Diego Angeles *(Copywriter)*
Miguel Ottati *(Copywriter)*
Tania Rubio *(Jr Planner-Strategic)*

Accounts:
3M Mexico Consumer Products, Corporate; 1996
BAT; 1997
Boehringer Ingelheim
Coca Cola
Diageo
Energizer Mexico
FIAT Campaign: "Digital Cargo"
Gillette Campaign: "Money"
GlaxoSmithKline Breath Right Strips, Campaign: "Asteroids", Campaign: "Tums Drive In", Corega Denture Adhesive, Heartburn Tablet, Nytol
Greenpeace Campaign: "Iceberg"
Hasbro Campaign: "Spiderman", Toys, Upwords
Heineken
Hitcase
Hitcasepro 10
HSBC
Mexico Red Cross
Motor Master
Playtex
Procter & Gamble de Mexico City Campaign: "Gillette For Women Nature", Campaign: "Led Tail", Covergirl, Hair Care, Macleans, Soaps
Rotoplas Water Filters
Sangre Negra Cafe Gourmet Campaign: "The Coffee that Speaks"
New-Secouya Care Center

Peru

Grey GCG Peru S.A.C.
Av Arequipa No 4080, Miraflores, Lima, 18 Peru
Tel.: (51) 1 411 4900
Fax: (51) 1 411 4915

Employees: 60
Year Founded: 1998

National Agency Associations: APAP (Portugal)

Agency Specializes In: Advertising

Emiliano Gonzalez *(Exec Dir-Creative-Circus Grey)*
Carlos Cardenas *(Art Dir)*
Christian Merino *(Copywriter)*

Accounts:
BAT
Deterperu/Procter & Gamble Ariel, Camay, Moncler, Pantene, Pringles, Salvo
GlaxoSmithKline
Good Foods
Lenor Fabric Softener
Magia
Novartis
San Cela
Vencedor
Visa
Volt Energy Drink

Trinidad & Tobago

Valdez & Torry Advertising Limited
46 Murray St, Woodbrook, Port of Spain, Trinidad & Tobago
Tel.: (868) 622 7103
Fax: (868) 622 7136
E-Mail: ideas@vtinternational.net
Web Site: www.vtinternational.net

Employees: 35
Year Founded: 1996

Agency Specializes In: Advertising

Christian Torry *(Pres)*
Lisa Williams *(Exec VP-Creative)*
Nadine Khan-Seemongal *(VP-Media)*
Vikash Rampersad *(VP-Creative)*
Gilla Ferreira *(Mgr-Traffic)*

Accounts:
Francis Fashions/Shoe Locker
Kapok Hotel
Magna
Scotiabank
SportWorld
Tatil
Top Imports
TruValu
TTPost

Uruguay

Grey, Casares, Vernazza & Associados S.A.
Blvd Artigas 1913, 11800 Montevideo, Uruguay
Tel.: (598) 2 400 0066
Fax: (598) 2 408 4924
E-Mail: info@grey.com.uy
Web Site: grey.com/uruguay

Employees: 30

Carlos Martinatto *(Mng Dir)*

Accounts:
Algorta S.A. Old Spice, Pantene; 1993
Banco de Seguros del Estado
Compania Industrial de Tabacos Monte Paz S.A.
EFFEM Mars, Pedigree, Whiskas; 1996
GlaxoSmithKline; 1996
Harrington S.A. Institutional; 1976
Informes 20 Institutional; 1993
Instituto Anglo; 1990
La Cigale Institutional; 1976
Novartis Uruguaya S.A.; 1983
Roche International Ltd. Berocca, Redoxon, Supraydn; 1995

Asia Pacific Regional Headquarters

Grey Group Asia Pacific
No 1 Magazine Road #03-07 Central Mall, Singapore, 059567 Singapore
Tel.: (65) 65117600
Fax: (65) 62238992
Web Site: www.grey.com/asiapacific

Agency Specializes In: Advertising, Advertising Specialties, Asian Market, Automotive, Aviation & Aerospace, Bilingual Market, Brand Development & Integration, Broadcast, Business Publications, Business-To-Business, Cable T.V., Children's Market, Co-op Advertising, Collateral, Commercial Photography, Communications, Consulting, Consumer Marketing, Consumer Publications, Corporate Identity, Cosmetics, Digital/Interactive, Direct Response Marketing, E-Commerce, Education, Electronic Media, Engineering, Entertainment, Environmental, Event Planning & Marketing, Exhibit/Trade Shows, Fashion/Apparel, Financial, Food Service, Gay & Lesbian Market, Government/Political, Graphic Design, Health Care Services, High Technology, Industrial, Infomercials, Information Technology, Internet/Web Design, Investor Relations, Leisure, Logo & Package Design, Magazines, Marine, Media Buying Services, Medical Products, Merchandising, Multimedia, New Product Development, Newspaper, Newspapers & Magazines, Out-of-Home Media, Outdoor, Over-50 Market, Pharmaceutical, Planning & Consultation, Point of Purchase, Point of Sale, Print, Production, Public Relations, Publicity/Promotions, Radio, Real Estate, Recruitment, Restaurant, Retail, Sales Promotion, Seniors' Market, Sports Market, Strategic Planning/Research, Sweepstakes, Syndication, T.V., Technical Advertising, Teen Market, Telemarketing, Trade & Consumer Magazines, Transportation, Travel & Tourism, Yellow Pages Advertising

Subbaraju Alluri *(Grp CEO)*
Ali Shabaz *(Chief Creative Officer)*

Alina Kessel *(Exec VP & Mng Dir-Global Client Svc)*
Konstantin Popovic *(Exec VP & Bus Dir-Global)*
Fernando Beretta *(Exec VP-Asia Pacific)*
Sanjay Chaudhari *(Sr VP & Reg Dir-Client Svc-APAC Gillette)*
Shahvez Afridi *(Head-Strategy-P&G Asia-Pacific)*
Sanjana Chappalli *(Head-Plng-Southeast Asia)*
Suresh Ramaswamy *(Reg Dir-SEA)*
Juhi Manwani *(Acct Dir)*
Antonio Bonifacio *(Dir-Creative-Global)*

Accounts:
3M Lint Roller; 1984
AKIJ Cement
AXA
British Council Campaign: "Know Your English"
Brother International Above-The-Line, Below-The-Line Creative, Laser & Inkjet Printers, Online
China Mobile
CV. Gold Elite Industries
Double A
ESPN ESPN Star Sports
F&N
Ferrero SEA Brand Activation, Digital, Ferrero Rocher, Kinder Bueno, Point-Of-Sale marketing
GE Money
GlaxoSmithKline Eye-Mo Eye Drops, Panadol
Heineken
Invida Singapore
KFC Global Delights Series
Lasalle College of the Arts
Malaysia Dairy Industries
Vitagen Less Sugar
Microsoft
Procter & Gamble Duracell, The Gillette Company
Sennheiser
Sentosa Development Corporation Campaign: "The Fun Movement"
New-SG50
TAC
Wildlife Reserves Singapore
WWF Campaign: "Water"

Grey Pty. Ltd.
470 St Kilda Rd Level 5, Melbourne, VIC 3004 Australia
Tel.: (61) 3 9208 1800
Fax: (61) 3 9820 9703
Web Site: www.grey.com.au

Employees: 50
Year Founded: 1966

Agency Specializes In: Government/Political, Logo & Package Design, Pharmaceutical, Retail

Lauren Doolan *(Art Dir)*
Mel Peters *(Creative Dir-Interactive)*
Danish Chan *(Dir-Plng-Natl)*
David Dumas *(Dir-Bus)*
Aaron Rocca *(Acct Exec)*
Harrison Steinhart *(Strategist)*
Renee Luri *(Designer)*
Sally Richmond *(Copywriter)*
Andrew Trewern *(Designer)*

Accounts:
Bauer Trader Media
Building Better Lives
Bulla Dairy Foods Digital
Cloud 9 Frozen Yoghurt Campaign: "Frozen in the clouds"
Hello Sunday Morning Campaign: "Text"
Holden
Melbourne Storm Campaign Name: "No Ordinary Team"
MS Australia
Open Family
Pental Campaign: "Maids", White King Power Clean
Procter & Gamble
Sara Lee Household & Body Care
Seeing MS Campaign: "Exposing the Invisible Disease"
Sportsbet Sportsbet Collar
Transport Accident Commission Campaign: " Wipe Off 5", Campaign: "A place to remember", Campaign: "BLIND", Campaign: "If you drive on drugs, you're out of your mind.", Campaign: "Mother's Day", Campaign: "Out of Your Mind", Campaign: "Party's Over", Campaign: "Thursday Arvo", Campaign: "Ungiven Gifts", Drink Drive; 1989
Victorian Racing Club
Worksafe Australia Campaign: "The Pain Game"

Bangladesh

Grey Bangladesh Ltd.
House 06 5th Floor Road 137 Block SE(D), Gulshan 1, Dhaka, 1212 Bangladesh
Tel.: (880) 2 882 7862
Fax: (880) 2 881 1541
E-Mail: gousul.shaon@grey.com
Web Site: www.grey.com/bangladesh

Employees: 21
Year Founded: 1996

Agency Specializes In: Advertising, South Asian Market

Salahuddin Shahed *(Asst VP)*
Masud Parvez *(Acct Dir)*
Jaiyyanul Huq *(Dir-Creative)*
Saniar Rahman *(Dir-Art)*
Javed Akter Suman *(Dir-Creative)*
Nurur Rahman *(Assoc Dir-Creative)*
Syed Tariq *(Client Svc Dir)*

Accounts:
Coca Cola Campaign: "Happiness Arcade"
HBMR Bicycle Locks
LG Electronics LG Refrigerator
Ministry of Religious Affairs
Paradote
Ucash Campaign: "City, Sea, Forest"
Xcel Chewing Gum

China

Grey Beijing
607 Tower W3 Oriental Plaza 1 East Chang An Avenue, Dong Cheng District, Beijing, 100 738 China
Tel.: (86) 10 8518 1988
Fax: (86) 10 8518 5500
E-Mail: tammy.sheu@grey.com
Web Site: www.grey.com

Employees: 84
Year Founded: 1992

Oliver Xu *(Chief Integration Officer-Grey China & Mng Dir-Grey Beijing)*
T. H. Peng *(Chm/CEO-Grey Grp China)*
Bernard Wong *(Gen Mgr)*
Chee Guan Yue *(Exec Dir-Creative)*
Yang Jianfeng *(Art Dir)*
Kevin Bi *(Dir-Creative Svcs)*
Afra Hou *(Acct Mgr)*
Li Ning *(Sr Art Dir)*

Accounts:
Beijing Cosmeceutical Dispensary
Beijing Subway
Blue Ocean Paper Recycling Technology Company
Bridge 8 Company
China Mobile
Corelle Campaign: "Vending Machine", Dinnerware
Double A Paper; 2008
Ethan Allen
Friends Of Nature
GlaxoSmithKline Eyemo Eye Drops
Guinness
Harmony Bioscience
Met-Rx Campaign: "Size Up"
Neuro-PS
Panadol
Playtex Infant Campaign: "Yakuza Baby"
Shanghai Essilor Optical Co.
Tencent
Tsingtao Beer
Tui Travel Campaign: "Iceberg", Campaign: "Travel more, see more"
World Kitchen Campaign: "Vending Machine"
Xiaomi Social Media, Traditional Media
Yingda Taihe Life Insurance

Grey Shanghai
3/F Block 3 The Bridge 8 Phase III, 550 Jumen Road, Shanghai, 200023 China
Tel.: (86) 21 2320 2288
Fax: (86) 21 2320 2200
E-Mail: danny.mok@grey.com
Web Site: www.grey.com/china

Employees: 119
Year Founded: 1994

June Lyloc *(Mng Dir)*
Oliver Xu *(Chief Integration Officer-Grey China & Mng Dir-Grey Beijing)*
Canon Wu *(Chief Digital Creative Officer)*
Bernard Wong *(Gen Mgr-Beijing)*
Haidong Guan *(Exec Dir-Plng)*
Alvin Lim *(Exec Creative Dir)*
Cain Huang *(Project Dir & Grp Acct Dir)*
Kate Sun *(Acct Dir)*
Yu Ming Cho *(Dir-Creative)*
Joseph Tsang *(Dir-Digital Bus)*
Greg Sutcliffe *(Copywriter)*

Accounts:
ChangYu Pioneer Wine
CITIC Pacific
Gold Dalo Hygiene Products Co.
OSIM
Ping An Creative
Proya Sunblock
Vanke Shanghai
Volvo Creative, XC60
World Wildlife Fund China Campaign: "Earth Overshoot Day", Campaign: "Save the Vanishing Tree", OOH, Print, social Media

Hong Kong

Grey Hong Kong
31/F 169 Electric Rd, North Point, China (Hong Kong)
Tel.: (852) 2510 6888
Fax: (852) 2510 7541
Web Site: www.grey.com

Year Founded: 1978

Keith Ho *(Mng Partner & Chief Creative Officer)*
Fernando Beretta *(Exec VP-Asia Pacific)*
Desmond Chan *(Gen Mgr)*

Accounts:
3M Nexcare
7-Eleven
A Drop of Life Campaign: "Words From Water"
Abbott Laboratories BoneSure
Asfour Crystal; Egypt
Banana Boat
Brand's Essence of Chicken
New-California Walnut Commission
Car Free Day
Cat Society
Chondroitin Plus
Color Paradise Hong Kong Campaign: "World's

Smallest Art Gallery"
Earthwatch Institute
Epson
Fubon Bank
GlaxoSmithKline Breathe Right, Dequadin, Eno
Great Treasure Group Campaign: "Union Jack"
Green Sense
Handheld Culture Campaign: "Read while you are Waiting"
Haomei Aluminum
Hawaiian Tropic
Hong Kong Cancer Fund
Hong Kong Tourism Board
IceGel Campaign: "The Smallest Art Gallery"
JBL
LCCS (HK) Ltd.
Life Nutrition International Co., Ltd.
Lisa Hoffman
The List Campaign: "Local Speaker"
Lotus Light Charity Society
Mentholatum Campaign: "Bubble Wrap", Campaign: "Lava", Campaign: "Leaf Poems"
Pfizer Campaign: "I am Ugly But I Got the Hotty"
Pringles
Procter & Gamble Creative, Pantene
Respect Magazine
Scott's Emulsion Cod Liver Oil
SHK Finance Branding Campaign, Print
Special Children Parent Club
Sunplay
Sunsense
UA Cinemas
Voulez Vous
WBA Campaign: "Moon Cake Lunar Module"
Wellcome Creative
Yahoo
Zoo Records

India

Grey (India) Ltd. (Bangalore)

Mount Kailash No 33/5 2nd Floor Meanee Avenue Road, Bengaluru, 560 042 India
Tel.: (91) 80 4357 8181
Fax: (91) 80 2228 0339
E-Mail: hari_k@greyindia.com
Web Site: www.grey.com

Agency Specializes In: Advertising

Vishal Ahluwalia *(VP & Branch Head)*
Mark Flory *(Head-Art & Sr Dir-Creative)*
Salil Inamdar *(Head-Digital, Creative & Content-Natl)*
Ram Jayaraman *(Exec Dir-Creative)*
Shihab Karim *(Dir-Art)*
Shezah Salam *(Copywriter)*

Accounts:
3M India Campaign: "Sticky On Both Sides", Scotch Magic Tape, Scotch-brite Sponge Wipe
Britannia Industries Ltd. Britannia Goodday Cakes, Campaign: "Britannia Cakes. Achhaiyon se bhara", Kwality's Glucose, Kwality's Marie, Kwality's Pusti, Kwality's Salt & Sweet, Nutrine Cookies
Britannia New Zealand Foods Pvt. Ltd. Britannia Milkman Butter, Britannia Milkman Cheese, Britannia Milkman Dairy Whitener, Britannia Milkman Ghee, Brittania Milkman Fresh Milk
DHL
Duracell
Fortis Hospital Creative
Fujifilm India Campaign: "360", Campaign: "Ultra-zoom"
Glaxo Smithkline Campaign: "Make Peace with Food"
Intex
Muthoot Group Creative
Pigeon Home Appliances Creative
Reliance Communications 3G Launch, Campaign: "Freezer", Campaign: "Youtube", Wireless Business
Stovekraft Pvt Ltd Pigeon Super Cooker
UB Group

Grey (India) Pvt. Ltd.

Grey House 28 Dr E Borge Road Oppos Dr Shirodkar High School, Parel, Mumbai, 400 012 India
Tel.: (91) 22 4036 6201
Fax: (91) 22 4036 6220
E-Mail: errol_goveas@greyindia.com
Web Site: www.grey.com

Employees: 290
Year Founded: 1987

Agency Specializes In: Communications, Digital/Interactive, Direct Response Marketing, Exhibit/Trade Shows, Financial, Health Care Services, Media Buying Services, Public Relations, South Asian Market

Jishnu Sen *(Pres & CEO)*
Sandipan Bhattacharyya *(Chief Creative Officer)*
Dheeraj Sinha *(Chief Strategy Officer)*
Vineet Singh *(VP & Dir-Client Svcs)*
Louella Rebello *(Sr Exec Creative Dir)*
Ines Etchenique *(Sr Acct Exec)*
Mudassir Ansari *(Assoc Acct Dir)*

Accounts:
3M
Bennett Coleman & Co
Bharti AXA
Cupid Condoms Campaign: "The Slow Cycling Race"
Dell India Campaign: "Laser Lockdown", Dell Inspiron Laptops, Integrated Marketing
Duracell Camera, Campaign: "Positive & Negative", Remote Control
Ferrero Group Campaign: "Theatre", Ferrero Rocher, Kinder, Nutella, Tic Tac; 2010
Fiat Chrysler India Advertising, Campaign: "Life Just Became More Interesting", Punto Evo
Fujifilm India Campaign: "Two-Faced Beauty Pageant"
Government Of India
New-Indian Army
Infosys
Janhit Manch Campaign: "Mumbai's Beauty in Your Hands"
Kewal Kiran Clothing Campaign: "Strip the Summer", Killer Jeans
Ministry of Women & Child Development
Network 18
Oil & Natural Gas Corp. Ltd. (ONCG)
One Life Network
New-Parakh Agro Industries Creative
Parle Agro Pvt. Ltd. Lactobite, Melody, Parle Marie, Smoothies, Tangy
Procter & Gamble Home Products Downy Fabric Softener, Pantene
Reliance Broadcast Network Limited Big CBS Love, Big CBS Prime, Big RTL Thrill
Reliance Communications Creative
Reliance Mobiles Reliance 3G
Sapat International Pvt. Ltd.
Times Centre for Learning Femina Believe Learning Academy
Volkswagen Campaign: "Anything4Jetta"
Wella India Hair Cosmetics Pvt Ltd. Creative
Zee Group

Grey (India) Pvt. Pty. Ltd. (Delhi)

Park Centra 503-505 Sector 30 NH-8, Opp 32nd Milestone, Gurgaon, 122 001 India
Tel.: (91) 124 497 3200
Fax: (91) 124 497 3208
Web Site: www.grey.com

Samir Datar *(VP & Head-Branch)*
Varun Goswami *(Exec Dir-Creative)*
Pranav Harihar Sharma *(Exec Dir-Creative)*
Gautam Bhasin *(Sr Dir-Creative)*
Piyush Jain *(Sr Dir-Creative)*
Ashish Kumar *(Art Dir)*
Karan Raghav *(Dir-Creative)*
Dushyant Chopra *(Assoc Dir-Creative)*

Accounts:
3M India Scotch-brite Sponge Wipe
Actionaid
Alstrong Creative
Collage Group Below the Line, Creative, Print
Crocin Cold & Flu Max
Fenesta Building Systems
Fox International Channels Campaign: "Chatni", Campaign: "Not Enough", Creative, Fox History & Traveller, National Geographic Channel
Fuji Film India Above the Line & Below the Line Media, Creative
Fujifilm
Genpact
GlaxoSmithKline Crocin
Gujarat Ambuja Cements
Indian Oil Corporation Limited
Intex Technologies Mobile Phones, Widescreen TV
John Keells Food; 2009
Living Media India Ltd.
Muthoot Group Creative
Nirmaya Charitable Trust
Novartis
Onida
Parle Agro
Procter & Gamble Ambipur Air Freshener, Campaign: "Guess the Smell", Downy, Duracell, Pantene
Ranbaxy Laboratories Ltd.
Reliance Broadcast Network Limited Big FM, Big Magic, Spark Punjabi
Sricure Herbs India Campaign: "Matchsticks"
Suzuki
New-Usha International Creative, Usha Fans
Wrigley India Pvt. Ltd.

Indonesia

Grey Group Indonesia

5th Fl Tetra Pak Building, Jl Buncit Raya Kav 100, Jakarta, 12510 Indonesia
Tel.: (62) 21 7919 2129
Fax: (62) 21 7919 7755
E-Mail: info@greyindo.com
Web Site: www.grey.com

Employees: 120
Year Founded: 1976

Agus Sudradjat *(Chm & CEO)*
Ali Shabaz *(Chief Creative Officer)*
Ekananta Joesoepadi *(Sr Acct Dir)*
Iqbal Ari *(Art Dir)*
Yohane Chayadi *(Dir-Art)*
Vito Winarko *(Dir-Creative)*
Wawan Ismanto *(Acct Exec)*
Bramuhadi Satria *(Copywriter)*

Accounts:
ABC Heinz Indonesia ABC Syrup
Allianz Indonesia
Astra Honda Motor OOH, POS, Print, Radio, TV, Verza 150
BMW Indonesia
Conservation International
CV. Gold Elite Industries Bubbles Pet Cologne
GlaxoSmithKline Campaign: "The old bar"
Jaringan Advokasi Tambang Campaign: "A Gift of Innocence For Mr. President"
Kumon Campaign: "Daily Fun Math"
Maggi Seasoning
Microsoft
P&G Ambipur, Campaign: "Family's Picnic"
PT Astra Honda Motor Above-the-Line, Below-the-Line, Creative, Digital, Honda CB150R Streetfire,

Ou-of-Home, Print, Radio, TV
PT Bank Central Asia Tbk (Agency of Record) Creative, Integrated Marketing Communications Strategy
PT Krama Yudha Tiga Berlian Motors Mitsubishi Outlander Sport
Pt Massindo International
PT Mitra Alami Sejahtera Sentosa Campaign: "Stewardess"
Softex Indonesia Above the Line, Brand Activation, Creative, Digital
Sterling Products Indonesia Panadol
Telkom Speedy Monitoring Campaign: "Whatch your home everywhere you go"
World Ocean Conference
Yayasan Jantung Indonesia Heart Disease Awareness

Japan

Grey Group Japan

Ebisu Square, 1-23-23 Ebisu, Shibuya-ku, Tokyo, 150-0013 Japan
Tel.: (81) 3 5423 1711
Fax: (81) 3 5423 1741
E-Mail: info@greygroup.jp
Web Site: grey.co.jp/

Employees: 120
Year Founded: 1963

National Agency Associations: IAAA-JAAA

Agency Specializes In: Communications

Yumi Shibuya *(Pres & CEO)*
Jon Hussey *(Pres & Mng Dir-Japan)*
Yohei Irie *(Chief Creative Officer)*
Yukiko Ochiai *(VP & Exec Acct Dir)*
Yasushi Ogata *(Exec Creative Dir)*
Takanori Sakamoto *(Sr Dir-Art)*
Shinmei Yamamoto *(Dir-Art)*
Kei Oki *(Assoc Dir-Creative & Copywriter)*
Sayaka Adachi *(Acct Supvr)*

Accounts:
Cadbury Japan
CEATEC Japan
Ciba Vision
Cisco Systems
Diesel Japan Co., Ltd.
Ginza Aster
GlaxoSmithKline
Hakusetsusha Dry Cleaning
Kagatani Knife
New-KOOWHO
Korean Bbq House Toku-Chan Campaign: "Carnivorous"
Kyoraku
Lindt
Manpower
McAfee
Nike Japan
Ninseikan Karate School Campaign: "Karate for Kids", Campaign: "Trashed Guns"
Novartis Animal Health
Procter & Gamble Campaign: "Febreze for car", Campaign: "Resilient and Shine Hair", Pantene
SORA Fukushima Dogs & Cats Rescue
Sumitomo 3M
Toku-Chan Korean BBQ House
Washin Optical
Wrigley

Korea

Grey Group Korea

2 & 3F ISA Bldg 600-1, Gangnam-Gu, Seoul, 135-815 Korea (South)
Tel.: (82) 2 3015 5800
Fax: (82) 2 3015 5900
Web Site: www.grey.com/korea

E-Mail for Key Personnel:
Media Dir.: joonhoy@greyworldwide.co.kr

Employees: 100
Year Founded: 2000

National Agency Associations: ACA

Scott Rhee *(CEO-Korea)*

Accounts:
3M
7 Luck Casino
Audi
Boehringer Ingelheim
Boram Sangjo
British American Tobacco
Daewon Pharmaceuticals
Dell
GlaxoSmithKline
Google
Heineken
ING
KOTRA
LG
Louis Quartoze
Oral-B
Procter & Gamble
Subway
Volkswagen Group of America, Inc.

Malaysia

Grey Group Malaysia

15th Floor Wisma Genting, Jalan Sultan Ismail, Kuala Lumpur, 50250 Malaysia
Tel.: (60) 3 2178 0000
Fax: (60) 3 2162 6363
E-Mail: nicky.lim@grey.com
Web Site: www.grey.com

Employees: 200
Year Founded: 1986

Agency Specializes In: Advertising, Advertising Specialties

Irene Wong *(CEO)*
Tan Yong Hin *(CFO)*
Nik Lim *(Chief Digital Officer)*
Abhijit Das *(Head-Plng)*
Ramanjit Singh Gulati *(Creative Dir)*
Phoecus Lee *(Dir-Art)*
Alex Wong *(Assoc Dir-Creative)*

Accounts:
Assa Abloy Campaign: "Home"
Auto Bavaria
AXA
Bandaraya Developments
The Body Shop Campaign: "Needless Deaths"
Carex Slovakia
Digi Telecommunications Sdn Bhd
Disposable Soft Goods Campaign: "No Angry Spells When Baby Sleeps Well", Campaign: "Nursery", Motherhood Made Easy
Dyslexia Association of Malaysia
Ep Plus Group Campaign: "Forgetful"
Fitness First Campaign: "Calendar"
Fluff & Stuff Cookies
Fluff & Stuff
Genting Highlands Resorts
GlaxoSmithKline Consumer Healthcare Campaign: "Chapter 22", Horlicks; 1986
Joo Ngan Professional Bike Centre Campaign: "Mountain Bike"
Kedai Ubat Uyee
LG
Malaysian Nature Society Belum Temengor Petition Campaign
Maybank
Mega Lifesciences Vietnam Campaign: "Angry Women"
Procter & Gamble (M) Sdn Bhd Campaign: "Dyslexic Media Invite", Pantene, Pringles
Quick & Easy Convenience Store
Royal Selangor
Sara Lee
Sincere Watches
Special Olympics Malaysia Campaign: "Brain"
Tiger FC
Unilever
URC Snack Foods (M) Sdn Bhd

Pakistan

Prestige Communications Pvt. Ltd.

9 Karachi Chambers Hasrat Mohani Road, Karachi, 74000 Pakistan
Tel.: (92) 21 241 2506
Fax: (92) 21 241 7219

Employees: 55
Year Founded: 1960

Agency Specializes In: Advertising, South Asian Market

A. Jamal Mir *(Mng Dir)*

Accounts:
Emirates Airlines
English Biscuit Manufacturers (Pvt.) Ltd.
NIB Bank
Packages Ltd.
Pakistan Tobacco Co.
Procter & Gamble
Zulfeqar Industries Ltd.

Philippines

Campaigns & Grey

2723 Sabio Street, Chino Roces Avenue, Makati, 1231 Philippines
Tel.: (63) 2 884 7398
Fax: (63) 2 810 3854
E-Mail: campaignsinfo.manila@grey.com
Web Site: www.grey.com/philippines

E-Mail for Key Personnel:
President: yolyo@campaignandgrey.net

Employees: 121
Year Founded: 1986

Agency Specializes In: Advertising

Cherry Gutierrez *(CEO)*
Boboy Consunji *(Mng Dir)*
Noel Orosa *(Exec Dir-Creative)*
Mags Sandoval *(Deputy Exec Dir-Creative)*
Rizzo Tangan *(Exec Dir-Creative)*
Mel Aguinaldo *(Assoc Dir-Creative)*
Lovel Aniag *(Assoc Dir-Creative)*
Jody Castillo *(Assoc Dir-Creative)*
Yolanda Villanueva-Ong *(Grp Chm)*

Accounts:
A. Tung Chingco Ligo Sardines
Academy for Educational Development
Andoks Campaign: "Perfect Breast"
Artha Land
Ayala Land
Bantay Kalikasan Foundation Inc.
Boehringer Ingelheim
Cetaphil
Consolidated Distillers
Davies Paints
Del Monte Philippines
Digital Mobile
Dulcolax Campaign: "Louis"
Felcris Centrale Above-the-Line, Creative, Out of

Home
Ginebra San Miguel Blue
Glaxo SmithKline Astring-O-Sol, Eye Mo, Sensodyne
Harlbon Foundation
HBC
IDS Logistics
JMC
Lacoste Footwear
Lamolyan
Ligo
Mirant Philippines
Novartis
Nutrience
Pediatrica
Penstar Sports
Pfizer
Philippine Match
Procter & Gamble Downy, Global Handwashing Day, Joy, P&G 75th Anniversary, Pantene, Zest
Quezon Province
Rockwell
Sara Lee
Solar Entertainment Corporation Campaign: "Clapper"
UNICEF
Unilab
Universal Robina Corporation Maxx Iceman
Widus Hotel & Casino Creative

Singapore

Grey Digital

(Formerly Yolk)
No. 1 Magazine Road, #03-07 Central Mall, Singapore, 059567 Singapore
Tel.: (65) 6221 2748
Fax: (65) 62212768
E-Mail: yellowfellows@yolk.com.sg
Web Site: www.yolk.com.sg

Employees: 40

Agency Specializes In: Advertising, Communications, Digital/Interactive, Internet/Web Design, South Asian Market

Subbaraju Alluri *(CEO-Grey Grp Singapore, Grey Grp Thailand & Area Dir)*
Sharon Siew *(Head-Digital Client Svcs)*
Gavin Tan *(Head-Social & Content)*
Low Jun Jek *(Exec Creative Dir)*
Nur Azerinna *(Strategist-Social Media & Content)*
Emily Yeunhwa Lee *(Planner-Digital)*

Accounts:
Microsoft

Grey Singapore

No1 Magazine Road, #03-07 Central Mall, Singapore, 059567 Singapore
Tel.: (65) 6511 7600
Fax: (65) 6223 8992
E-Mail: frontdesk.singapore@grey.com
Web Site: www.grey.com

Ali Shabaz *(Chief Creative Officer)*
Tom Evans *(Exec VP & Reg Dir-Client Svcs)*
Rishi Randhawa *(Sr Acct Dir)*
Jorge Thauby *(Creative Dir)*
Tan Ziwei *(Art Dir)*
Madina Kalyayeva *(Sr Acct Mgr)*
Amanda Rendell *(Acct Mgr)*
Michelle Yiu *(Acct Mgr)*
Bobby Koh *(Mgr-Production)*
Sashi Kumar *(Planner)*
Jennifer Sim *(Reg Grp Acct Dir)*

Accounts:
3M Lint Roller
Actal Antacid Campaign: "Feel Stuffed No More"
Alzheimer's Disease Association of Singapore Campaign: "Sort Me Out"
Ambi Pur
The Arcade Stationery
AXA
BAT
British Council
China Mobile
Cry Child Rights & You Campaign: "Resume"
Diageo
ESPN STAR Sports Campaign: "Football Clock"
Eureka Call Centre System Campaign: "Lend An Eye"
GE Money
GlaxoSmithKline Eye Mo
Greenlam Asia Pacific Campaign: "Greenlam Woodpecker"
Harry's Holdings Above-the-Line, Brand Reposition, Creative, Digital, In-House
Invida Campaign: "Indian Food"
Kentucky Fried Chicken Campaign: "Bad Dog", Campaign: "Enjoy the Zinger You Love - in a Spicy New Way!", Campaign: "Fulfill a Hero's Appetite with a Hero-Sized Burger", Campaign: "Hero-Sized", Campaign: "KFC Delivery Life Gets Easier", Campaign: "Transportation", In-Store, Outdoor, Print, TV, Zinger Chicken Rice, Zinger Double Down Max Burger
Lasalle College of the Arts Singapore Campaign: "The Art of Inspiration"
Metro Campaign: "Every Bag has a Story"
MPAN
Neelvasant Medical Foundation and Research Center Campaign: "Life Saving Dot"
Oculus Campaign: "Bubbles"
Pfizer
Procter & Gamble Campaign: "Endless Energy", Campaign: "Some Toys Never Die", Duracell
Qatar Airways Campaign: "A Few Good Men"
Sacoor Brothers Above the Line, Below the Line, Brand Strategy, Creative, Event Management, Media Planning
Salon De Choix
Sara Lee
Sentosa Development Authority
TAC
Wildlife Reserves Singapore
Workplace Safety and Health Council Campaign: "This Could Be You"
WWF Circle of Life
Zoo Education Programmes

Thailand

Grey Thailand

8th Fl Q House Ploenjit Bldg 598 Ploenchite Rd, Lumpini Pathumwan, Bangkok, 10330 Thailand
Tel.: (66) 2 685 2000
Fax: (66) 66 2 685 2097-99
Web Site: www.grey.com/thailand

Employees: 28
Year Founded: 1990

Pattaraporn Wongmesak *(Assoc VP & Country Mgr)*

Accounts:
304 Industrial Park (Agency of Record) Digital Marketing, Event Management, Out of Home Advertising, Print, Public Relations, Television
Ambi Pur
AXA
Bausch & Lomb
Certainty (Agency of Record) Brand Strategy, Corporate Social Responsibility, Event Management, Public Relations
Disposable Soft Goods
Emirates Airlines
Febreze
General Drugs House
GlaxoSmithKline Parodontax, Sensodyne
Hong Kong Tourisim Board
Krung Tai AXA
Mansion 7
Mass Marketing Co. Mosquito Repellent
Polident
Procter & Gamble Pantene
Rottapharm
Siam Park City
Transview Golf
Whizdom Condominium

GREY PUERTO RICO

PO Box 367, San Juan, PR 00918
Tel.: (787) 999-9000
Fax: (787) 999-6711
Web Site: grey.com/puerto_rico

Employees: 75
Year Founded: 1933

National Agency Associations: 4A's

Agency Specializes In: Advertising, Direct Response Marketing, Media Buying Services, Public Relations, Sales Promotion

Carmen Yanes *(CFO)*
Vanessa Torres *(Mgr-Print Production)*
Wilmari Villafane *(Acct Exec)*

Accounts:
Procter & Gamble

GREY SAN FRANCISCO

303 2nd St Ste 800 S Tower, San Francisco, CA 94107
Tel.: (415) 403-8000
Web Site: www.grey.com/us

Employees: 100
Year Founded: 1917

National Agency Associations: 4A's

Agency Specializes In: Above-the-Line, Advertising, Alternative Advertising, Below-the-Line, Business Publications, Cable T.V., Co-op Advertising, Digital/Interactive, Electronic Media, Email, Entertainment, Guerilla Marketing, Health Care Services, Hispanic Market, In-Store Advertising, Integrated Marketing, Magazines, Media Relations, Mobile Marketing, Multimedia, Newspaper, Newspapers & Magazines, Out-of-Home Media, Outdoor, Point of Purchase, Point of Sale, Print, Product Placement, Production, Production (Print), Promotions, Public Relations, Publishing, Radio, Shopper Marketing, Social Media, Sponsorship, Sweepstakes, Syndication, T.V., Viral/Buzz/Word of Mouth, Web (Banner Ads, Pop-ups, etc.)

Milan Martin *(Pres)*
Tricia Clark *(Sr VP, Head-New Bus & Grp Dir)*
Liz Franks *(Sr VP & Dir-Media)*
Ben Warden *(VP & Acct Dir)*
Jocelyn Lee *(VP & Grp Media Dir)*
Mark Butorac *(Sr Dir-Art)*
Mike Huntley *(Dir-Interactive Production)*

Accounts:
LendingTree Creative
NRG Energy, Inc. Campaign: "Smart Dog"
New-Pernod-Ricard Graffigna
The Salt Institute, Alexandria, VA Campaign: "Olde Salty Campaign"; 2011
Sun Edison (Lead Creative Agency) B2B Advertising, Consumer, Digital Marketing; 2015
Symantec Corporation Norton; 2005
Technicolor; 2014

GREY VANCOUVER

736 Granville St, Vancouver, BC V6Z 1G3 Canada
Tel.: (604) 687-1001

Fax: (604) 682-1827
Toll Free: (877) 250-2275
E-Mail: vancouver_reception@greyvancouver.com
Web Site: grey.com/canada

E-Mail for Key Personnel:
President: timjohnson@grey.net

Employees: 20
Year Founded: 1987

Agency Specializes In: Advertising, Brand Development & Integration, Digital/Interactive, Production, Public Relations

Approx. Annual Billings: $5,000,000

Maria Kennedy *(Mng Dir & Dir-Natl Design)*
Neil McPhedran *(Gen Mgr)*
Maureen Atchison *(Grp Acct Dir)*
Maya Lange *(Grp Acct Dir)*
Katie Ainsworth *(Dir-Creative)*
Andrew Mckinley *(Dir-Art)*
Leah Moy *(Dir-Art)*
Lisa Chen-Wing *(Assoc Dir-Creative)*
Geoff Dawson *(Assoc Dir-Creative)*

Accounts:
ADT Security
BC Used Oil Management Association
Better Environmentally Sound Transportation
Bike Month
Canfor Corp.
GGRP Sound
GraphTech Guitar Labs
Liquor Stores of BC
New-OK Tire
The Regional Municipality of Wood Buffalo
Starbucks
Thrifty Foods
TransLink
Walk BC
Warner Bros.
WIRELESEWAVE

GRIFF/SMC
(Name Changed to Griff/SMC, Inc. Medical Marketing Communications)

GRIFF/SMC, INC. MEDICAL MARKETING COMMUNICATIONS
(Formerly Griff/SMC)
954 Pearl St, Boulder, CO 80302
Tel.: (303) 443-7602
E-Mail: griff@griffsmc.com
Web Site: www.griffsmc.com

Employees: 2
Year Founded: 1975

National Agency Associations: BMA

Agency Specializes In: Advertising, Advertising Specialties, Brand Development & Integration, Broadcast, Business Publications, Business-To-Business, Co-op Advertising, Collateral, Communications, Consulting, Consumer Marketing, Consumer Publications, Corporate Identity, Digital/Interactive, Direct Response Marketing, Direct-to-Consumer, E-Commerce, Electronic Media, Exhibit/Trade Shows, Graphic Design, Health Care Services, High Technology, Industrial, Integrated Marketing, Internet/Web Design, Logo & Package Design, Magazines, Media Buying Services, Media Planning, Media Relations, Medical Products, Multimedia, Newspaper, Newspapers & Magazines, Outdoor, Over-50 Market, Package Design, Pharmaceutical, Planning & Consultation, Point of Purchase, Point of Sale, Print, Production, Production (Print), Promotions, Public Relations, Publicity/Promotions, Radio, Sales Promotion, Seniors' Market, Strategic Planning/Research, Technical Advertising, Trade & Consumer Magazines, Web (Banner Ads, Pop-ups, etc.), Women's Market, Yellow Pages Advertising

Bob Griff *(Pres & Dir-Creative)*

Accounts:
Enhance Skin Products Inc Visible Youth

GRIFFIN & ASSOCIATES
119 Dartmouth Dr SE, Albuquerque, NM 87106
Tel.: (505) 764-4444
E-Mail: info@griffinassoc.com
Web Site: www.griffinassoc.com

Agency Specializes In: Advertising, Graphic Design, Media Relations, Media Training, Social Media, Strategic Planning/Research

Joan Griffin *(Pres)*
David Empey *(VP)*
Dezaree Vega-Garcia *(VP-Client Svcs)*
Patricia Garrett *(Controller)*
Barbara Rudolf *(Dir-Creative)*
Alyssa Velasquez *(Acct Mgr)*

Accounts:
Durango Area Tourism Office
Los Alamos County
Town of Taos
Visit Big Sky Media Relations

GRIFFIN ARCHER
126 N 3rd St Ste 204, Minneapolis, MN 55401
Tel.: (612) 309-2050
Web Site: www.griffinarcher.com

Agency Specializes In: Advertising, Communications, Print, Public Relations, T.V.

Kelly Thompson *(Pres & Chief Strategy Officer)*
Ellie Anderson *(CEO)*

Accounts:
Arta Tequila Online, Outdoor, Point-of-Sale, Social Media
Denver Museum of Nature & Science
LearningRx
Luminara Worldwide
Magic Straws Brand Planning, Creative, Media, Public Relations

GRIFFIN COMMUNICATIONS GROUP
3101 NASA Parkway Ste L, Seabrook, TX 77586
Tel.: (281) 335-0200
Fax: (281) 333-1414
Web Site: www.griffincommgroup.com

Employees: 15
Year Founded: 1997

Agency Specializes In: Advertising, Brand Development & Integration, Communications, Consulting, Corporate Communications, Corporate Identity, Custom Publishing, Event Planning & Marketing, Exhibit/Trade Shows, Logo & Package Design, Magazines, Market Research, Media Buying Services, Media Planning, Media Relations, Media Training, Out-of-Home Media, Planning & Consultation, Production (Ad, Film, Broadcast), Production (Print), Public Relations, Sponsorship, Strategic Planning/Research

Gwen Griffin *(Founder & CEO)*
Jeff Carr *(Pres)*
Brooke Baumer Crawford *(Acct Dir)*
Deanna Wilke *(Acct Svcs Dir)*
Jaime Napoli *(Dir-Fin & Admin)*
Julie Arnold *(Sr Acct Mgr)*
Mandy Pierson *(Office Mgr)*
Kristin Kleven *(Sr Acct Coord)*

GRIFFIN COMMUNICATIONS, INC.
1001 Rolandvue Rd, Towson, MD 21204-6816
Tel.: (410) 296-7777
Fax: (410) 339-5292
Web Site: www.griffcom.com

E-Mail for Key Personnel:
President: info@griffcom.com
Creative Dir.: norm@griffcom.com
Media Dir.: kim@griffcom.com

Employees: 4
Year Founded: 1987

Agency Specializes In: Business Publications, Collateral, Exhibit/Trade Shows, Information Technology, Internet/Web Design, Multimedia, New Product Development, Planning & Consultation, Production, Strategic Planning/Research, Technical Advertising

Approx. Annual Billings: $1,700,000

Wade Deaver *(VP-Sls)*
Steve Foerster *(VP-Corp Dev)*
Kathy Haney *(VP-HR)*
Trevor Wiseman *(VP-Tech)*
Jen Bartlett *(Dir-HR)*
Derek Criss *(Dir-Local Sls)*
Jaime Napoli *(Dir-Fin & Admin)*
Elizabeth Taylor Semtner *(Dir-Mktg Svcs)*
Lex Sehl *(Mgr-Local Sls)*
Mark Moore *(Acct Exec)*
Nancy Ruth *(Acct Exec)*

Accounts:
Avista Solutions International
Creative Cow

GRIFFIN WINK ADVERTISING
6306 Iola Ave, Lubbock, TX 79424
Tel.: (806) 791-0045
Fax: (806) 791-0048
Toll Free: (800) 753-1375
E-Mail: rusty@griffinwink.com
Web Site: www.griffinwink.com

Employees: 5
Year Founded: 1975

National Agency Associations: AAF

Agency Specializes In: Advertising, Advertising Specialties, Affluent Market, Agriculture, Automotive, Bilingual Market, Brand Development & Integration, Broadcast, Business Publications, Business-To-Business, Cable T.V., Catalogs, Co-op Advertising, Collateral, College, Commercial Photography, Communications, Consulting, Consumer Goods, Consumer Marketing, Consumer Publications, Corporate Identity, Digital/Interactive, Direct Response Marketing, E-Commerce, Education, Electronic Media, Engineering, Entertainment, Environmental, Event Planning & Marketing, Exhibit/Trade Shows, Financial, Food Service, Government/Political, Graphic Design, Health Care Services, High Technology, Household Goods, Identity Marketing, Industrial, Infomercials, Information Technology, Internet/Web Design, Leisure, Local Marketing, Logo & Package Design, Magazines, Market Research, Media Buying Services, Media Planning, Medical Products, Men's Market, Merchandising, Multimedia, New Product Development, Newspaper, Newspapers & Magazines, Outdoor, Package Design, Pharmaceutical, Planning & Consultation, Point of Purchase, Point of Sale, Print, Production, Production (Print), Promotions, Public Relations, Publicity/Promotions, Radio, Real Estate, Restaurant, Retail, Sales Promotion, Social Marketing/Nonprofit, Sponsorship, Sports Market, Strategic Planning/Research, T.V., Technical Advertising, Trade & Consumer Magazines,

Transportation, Travel & Tourism

Approx. Annual Billings: $960,000

Breakdown of Gross Billings by Media: Collateral: 20%; Network Radio: 50%; T.V.: 30%

Rusty Griffin *(Owner)*
Brian Wink *(Pres)*
Randy Wink *(Partner & COO)*
Carly Deckert *(Media Buyer)*
Carly Sherman *(Media Buyer)*

Accounts:
Dana Palmer Turf Management
Interim Healthcare
Schlotzsky's (Lubbock Area Advertising)
Taco Villa
Watermaster Irrigation

GRIFFITH & COE ADVERTISING, INC.
801 Jerry Ct, Martinsburg, WV 25401
Tel.: (304) 263-1453
E-Mail: jim@jim-coe.com
Web Site: www.jim-coe.com

Employees: 4
Year Founded: 1983

National Agency Associations: MCA

Agency Specializes In: Automotive, Brand Development & Integration, Business-To-Business, Co-op Advertising, Collateral, Commercial Photography, Consulting, Consumer Marketing, Corporate Identity, Electronic Media, Exhibit/Trade Shows, Graphic Design, Industrial, Internet/Web Design, Logo & Package Design, Media Buying Services, Merchandising, New Product Development, Newspapers & Magazines, Out-of-Home Media, Outdoor, Over-50 Market, Planning & Consultation, Point of Purchase, Point of Sale, Print, Production, Public Relations, Publicity/Promotions, Radio, Retail, Sales Promotion, Seniors' Market, Strategic Planning/Research, Technical Advertising, Trade & Consumer Magazines, Transportation

James A. Coe *(Co-Founder & Pres)*

Accounts:
Action Products, Inc.
Floridin Company
Keystone Country Sports; Hagerstown, MD; 1997
Midwest Filter Resources, Inc.
Roach Energy
Rocs Convenience Stores

GRIGG GRAPHIC SERVICES, INC.
20982 Bridge St, Southfield, MI 48033-4033
Tel.: (248) 356-5005
Fax: (248) 356-5636
Web Site: www.grigg.com

Employees: 15
Year Founded: 1967

Agency Specializes In: Advertising, Advertising Specialties, Brand Development & Integration, Corporate Identity, Graphic Design, Logo & Package Design, Outdoor, Planning & Consultation, Print

Stuart Grigg *(Pres)*
Geoff Spencer *(Dir-Art)*
Kate Walsh *(Dir-Art)*
Dawn Bender *(Mgr-Creative Svcs)*

Accounts:
Hutzel Women's Hospital; Detroit, MI Hospital Services

GRINLEY CREATIVE LLC
28 Benjamin Dr, Goffstown, NH 3045
Tel.: (603) 497-2583
Web Site: www.grinleycreative.com

Year Founded: 2013

Agency Specializes In: Advertising, Brand Development & Integration, Internet/Web Design, Logo & Package Design, Outdoor, Print, Radio, Social Media, T.V.

Dan Grinley *(Principal-Creative)*

Accounts:
Pope Memorial SPCA
Russound

GRIP DESIGN, INC.
1128 N Ashland Ave, Chicago, IL 60185
Tel.: (312) 906-8020
Fax: (773) 235-4747
E-Mail: info@gripdesign.com
Web Site: www.gripdesign.com

Agency Specializes In: Advertising, Brand Development & Integration, Collateral, Digital/Interactive, Package Design

Kelly Kaminski *(Principal)*
Kevin McConkey *(Principal)*
Joshua Blaylock *(Dir-Creative)*
Lonnie Tapia *(Dir-Accts)*
Noelle Bullion *(Designer)*

Accounts:
Bengtson Center
Cassiday Schade LLP
Keeley Funds
Kellogg Company
The Nielsen Company B.V.
Romi Chopra Group

GRIP LTD.
179 John St 6th Fl, Toronto, ON M5T 1X4 Canada
Tel.: (416) 340-7111
Fax: (416) 340-7776
Web Site: www.griplimited.com

Employees: 150
Year Founded: 2002

Agency Specializes In: Advertising, Brand Development & Integration, Radio, Social Media, T.V.

Rich Pryce-Jones *(Owner)*
David Chiavegato *(Partner)*
David Crichton *(Partner)*
Randy Stein *(Partner-Creative)*
Ron Dunstan *(CFO)*
Ben Weinberg *(Creative Dir)*
Julia Morra *(Dir-Art)*
Anton Ratinsky *(Dir-Art)*
Ben Steele *(Assoc Dir-Creative)*
Nicholas Hillier *(Acct Mgr)*
Justine Leetham *(Acct Mgr)*
Dane Boaz *(Copywriter)*
Jeff Collins *(Copywriter)*

Accounts:
Acura
Budweiser
Dare
Expedia Broadcast, Campaign: "Escape Winter", Campaign: "Paradise", Campaign: "World Traveler", Online, Print, Social Media
HBO Campaign: "Dragon Bowl", Game Of Thrones
Honda Motor Company, Ltd. Roadside Assistance
Johnson and Johnson
Labatt Canada Campaign: "The Movie out Here", Labatt Blue, Labatt Blue Light
Oshawa Centre B2B, Creative, Social Media
New-RBC
The Sunnybrook Foundation
Taco Bell Canada "The Waiting Game", Campaign: "Eat Your Words"
Testicular Cancer Canada Campaign: "Cop", Campaign: "Mechanic"
Toronto Humane Society
Yum! Restaurants International (Canada) Co. (Agency of Record) KFC, Pizza Hut, Taco Bell

GRISKO
400 W Erie St Ste 400, Chicago, IL 60654
Tel.: (312) 335-0100
Fax: (312) 335-0103
E-Mail: info@grisko.com
Web Site: www.grisko.com

Year Founded: 1995

National Agency Associations: 4A's

Agency Specializes In: Advertising, Brand Development & Integration, Crisis Communications, Public Relations, Social Media

Carolyn Grisko *(Pres & CEO)*
Garlanda Freeze *(VP-Mktg Comm)*
Ambar Mentor-Truppa *(VP)*
Jeff Steinhouse *(Exec Dir-Creative)*
Methon Markadonis *(Sr Dir-Art)*
Greg Martinsen *(Dir-Energy & Environment)*
Eric Nelson *(Mgr-Campaign)*

Accounts:
R.M. Chin & Associates

GRIZZARD COMMUNICATIONS
229 Peachtree St NE Ste 1400, Atlanta, GA 30303-1606
Tel.: (404) 522-8330
Fax: (404) 335-0313
Toll Free: (800) 241-9351
E-Mail: webmaster@grizzard.com
Web Site: www.grizzard.com

Employees: 100
Year Founded: 1919

National Agency Associations: ADMA-AMA-DMA

Agency Specializes In: Direct Response Marketing, Pets , Sponsorship

Approx. Annual Billings: $145,466,000 Capitalized

Breakdown of Gross Billings by Media: D.M.: $145,466,000

Douglas Wilson *(CFO)*
Gary Jones *(Chief HR Officer)*
Chip Grizzard *(CEO-Grizzard Comm Grp)*
Phil Stolberg *(Sr VP & Gen Mgr)*
Tonie Howard *(Sr VP-Animal Care)*
Jody Adkison *(VP-Production & Procurement)*
Sheryl Larson *(VP-Media)*
Clifford Marshall *(VP-Salvation Army Team)*
Andrea Kantargis *(Acct Dir)*
Dustin Riddle *(Specialist-Online Mktg)*
Kristina Soler *(Media Planner & Media Buyer)*

Accounts:
AARP Foundation
ALS Association (Agency of Record)
American Red Cross
Duke Medicine
Food Banks
Fred Hutchinson Cancer Research Center; Seattle, WA Brand Awareness, Direct Response
Habitat for Humanity
Leader Dogs for the Blind Fundraising Campaigns
National Cancer Institute

Parents Television Council Digital Fundraising Programs, Direct Mail, Telemarketing
Prostate Cancer Foundation
The Salvation Army Nashville Area Command Campaign: "Chinese Radio Show", Direct Response Fundraising, Fundraising, Integrated Marketing
State Sheriffs Associations
Union Rescue Mission; Los Angeles, CA (Agency of Record) Campaign: "Pops-The Story of Transformation", Direct Mail, Newsletters, Social Media, eNewsletters
University of Pittsburgh Cancer Institute

Grizzard/Los Angeles

110 N Maryland Ave, Glendale, CA 91206
Tel.: (818) 543-1315
Fax: (818) 543-1308
Toll Free: (800) 325-4892
E-Mail: webmaster@grizzard.com
Web Site: www.grizzard.com

Employees: 50
Year Founded: 1985

Agency Specializes In: Direct Response Marketing, Sponsorship

Phil Stolberg *(Sr VP & Gen Mgr)*
Christina Grigg *(Mgr-Sys Trng)*

GROCERY SHOPPING NETWORK

900 Lumber Exchange Bldg 10 S 5th St, Minneapolis, MN 55402
Tel.: (612) 746-4232
Fax: (612) 746-4237
Toll Free: (888) 673-4663
E-Mail: andy@groceryshopping.net
Web Site: www.groceryshopping.net

Employees: 30
Year Founded: 1996

Agency Specializes In: Communications, Consulting, Consumer Marketing, Digital/Interactive, Direct Response Marketing, E-Commerce, Education, Electronic Media, Health Care Services, High Technology

Approx. Annual Billings: $2,000,000

Breakdown of Gross Billings by Media: D.M.: $2,000,000

John Gaughan *(VP-Digital Media)*
Scott Simerlein *(VP-Tech & Retailer Ops)*
Jennifer Odonnell *(Controller)*
Andrea Darsow *(Dir-Project Mgmt)*
Bill Blaney *(Reg Mgr-Retail Sls)*
Pam Whitaker *(Mgr-Client Performance)*
Andy Parker *(Client Svc Mgr)*

Accounts:
ACH Food Companies, Inc.
C&S
Discover Financial Services
Folgers
General Mills
IGA Inc.; Chicago, IL; 1999
Kraft
Nestle
Ocean Spray
P&G
Ruiz Foods
SuperValu; Minneapolis, MN Store Locations & Online Grocery Shopping; 1997

GROK

20 W 22nd St Ste 502, New York, NY 10010
Tel.: (212) 249-9900
Web Site: www.groknyc.com

Agency Specializes In: Advertising, Internet/Web Design, Public Relations

Julie Bauer *(Founder, CEO & Partner)*
Steve Landsberg *(Founder, Partner & Chief Creative Officer)*
Tod Seisser *(Founder, Partner & Chief Creative Officer)*
Thomas Mori *(Dir-Art)*
Paige Harbert *(Mgr-Bus Dev)*
Shley Platt *(Copywriter)*

Accounts:
AZO Bladder Control Campaign: "Go Less. Worry Less"
D'Agostino's Food & Beverage Mfr & Retailers
Estroven Campaign: "The Menopause Monologues", Digital, Health Care Service Providers, Social Media, TV
i-Health Inc. Brain Health Products Mfr & Distr
Johnson Controls Inc. Electronic Appliances Mfr
The New York Burger Co Restaurant Services
Taleo Corporation Prepackaged Software Publishers
VMware Inc. Virtualization Software Providers

GROOMS ATHLETIC MANAGEMENT & ENTERTAINMENT

(Acquired & Absorbed by French/West/Vaughan, Inc.)

GROPPI ADVERTISING DESIGN

25 Braintree Hill Park Ste 200, Braintree, MA 02184
Tel.: (508) 747-9878
Fax: (508) 747-7646
E-Mail: ken@groppi.com
Web Site: www.groppi.com

E-Mail for Key Personnel:
President: ken@groppi.com

Employees: 7
Year Founded: 1982

Agency Specializes In: Advertising, Brand Development & Integration, Business-To-Business, Collateral, Consulting, Corporate Identity, Direct Response Marketing, Environmental, Food Service, Graphic Design, Internet/Web Design, Investor Relations, Logo & Package Design, Point of Sale, Print, Real Estate, Restaurant, Travel & Tourism

Ken Groppi *(Owner)*

Accounts:
A.D. Makepeace Company
American Automobile Association
CDF Corporation
Massachusetts Association of Insurance Agents
Spang Animation Studios

GROUP 365 (CHICAGO) LLC

1111 E Warrenville Rd, Naperville, IL 60653
Tel.: (630) 671-0365
Fax: (630) 671-0366
E-Mail: bill@group365.com
Web Site: www.group365.com

Employees: 9
Year Founded: 1990

National Agency Associations: Second Wind Limited

Agency Specializes In: Advertising, Advertising Specialties, Automotive, Below-the-Line, Brand Development & Integration, Business Publications, Business-To-Business, Cable T.V., Co-op Advertising, Collateral, Commercial Photography, Communications, Computers & Software, Consulting, Consumer Marketing, Consumer Publications, Corporate Communications, Corporate Identity, Digital/Interactive, Direct Response Marketing, E-Commerce, Education, Electronic Media, Electronics, Email, Engineering, Environmental, Event Planning & Marketing, Exhibit/Trade Shows, Financial, Food Service, Government/Political, Graphic Design, Health Care Services, High Technology, Hospitality, Household Goods, Identity Marketing, In-Store Advertising, Industrial, Infomercials, Information Technology, Integrated Marketing, Internet/Web Design, Legal Services, Leisure, Local Marketing, Logo & Package Design, Magazines, Media Buying Services, Media Planning, Medical Products, Merchandising, New Product Development, Newspaper, Newspapers & Magazines, Out-of-Home Media, Outdoor, Paid Searches, Pharmaceutical, Planning & Consultation, Podcasting, Point of Purchase, Point of Sale, Print, Production, Production (Print), Promotions, Public Relations, Publicity/Promotions, RSS (Really Simple Syndication), Radio, Real Estate, Regional, Restaurant, Retail, Sales Promotion, Seniors' Market, Sports Market, Strategic Planning/Research, Sweepstakes, T.V., Technical Advertising, Telemarketing, Trade & Consumer Magazines, Transportation, Travel & Tourism, Web (Banner Ads, Pop-ups, etc.)

Approx. Annual Billings: $6,000,000

Breakdown of Gross Billings by Media: Co-op Adv.: 15%; Collateral: 10%; Comml. Photography: 2%; Consulting: 15%; D.M.: 8%; Exhibits/Trade Shows: 5%; Fees: 10%; Mags.: 18%; Point of Purchase: 2%; Pub. Rels.: 10%; Sls. Promo.: 5%

Bill Kimball *(Mng Partner)*
David Miller *(Partner & Dir-Creative)*

Accounts:
Conspec Chemicals; Kansas City, KS Construction Chemicals; 2005
Dayton Superior Construction Accessories; Dayton, OH Concrete Construction Accessories; 2004
Dayton Superior Specialty Chemicals; Kansas City, KS Construction Chemicals; 2005
Rand McNally; Skokie, IL Commercial Transportation Software; 2002
Sunbeam Health Division; Aurora, IL Health Products, Scales; 2003
Symons Corp.; Des Plaines, IL Concrete Forming Equipment; 1985

GROUP 4

147 Simsbury Rd, Avon, CT 06001
Tel.: (860) 678-1570
Fax: (860) 678-0783
Web Site: www.groupfour.com

Year Founded: 1972

Agency Specializes In: Brand Development & Integration, Market Research, Package Design, Product Placement, Strategic Planning/Research

Frank von Holzhausen *(Pres)*
Mona L. Kelly *(CFO & COO)*
Matthew Phillips *(Dir-Engrg)*
Michael Solomson *(Mgr-Bus Dev)*

Accounts:
Aiwa
Alsons
Combe
Coty
Dannon
Eli Lilly
First Alert
MSA
Panasonic Electronic Equipment

Snap-On Tools
USG
Wagner USA Consumer Painting Products
X-ACTO Office Tools Manufacturer

GROUP 5 WEST, INC.

810 W Second St, Little Rock, AR 72201-2118
Tel.: (501) 372-7151
Fax: (501) 372-3089
E-Mail: g5w@swbell.net
Web Site: www.groupfivewest.com

Employees: 7
Year Founded: 1963

Agency Specializes In: Business-To-Business, Industrial, Medical Products

Richard Hinkle *(Chm)*
Lisa Hemme *(Pres)*

Branch

Group 5 West, Inc.

197 Walnut Gardens Dr, Memphis, TN 38018-2907
Tel.: (901) 624-3956
Fax: (901) 737-0936
E-Mail: lisa.hemme@comcast.net
Web Site: www.groupfivewest.com

Employees: 6

Agency Specializes In: Public Relations

Lisa Hemme *(VP)*

Accounts:
Chris Woods Construction Company
Jolly Roofing & Contracting
Logical Systems Inc.

GROUP 7EVEN

158 Napoleon St Ste 220, Valparaiso, IN 46383
Tel.: (219) 476-3704
E-Mail: info@group7even.com
Web Site: www.group7even.com

Agency Specializes In: Advertising, Brand Development & Integration, Internet/Web Design, Logo & Package Design, Media Buying Services, Media Planning, Print, Radio, Strategic Planning/Research, T.V.

Michelle Andres *(Pres)*
Grant Andres *(VP-Tech)*
Rebecca Arnett *(Acct Exec)*
Gabrielle Phillips *(Acct Exec)*

Accounts:
Qubit Networks

THE GROUP ADVERTISING

1221 N Mills Ave Ste B, Orlando, FL 32803
Tel.: (407) 898-2409
E-Mail: info@thegroupads.com
Web Site: www.thegroupadvertising.com

Year Founded: 2006

Agency Specializes In: Advertising, Brand Development & Integration, Digital/Interactive, Multicultural, Public Relations

Hernan Tagliani *(Founder & Pres)*
Hector L. Torres *(Dir-New Bus)*

Accounts:
Body Blaster
CFE Federal Credit Union
Don Mealy's Sport Mazda
Foundation For Foster Children
Hooters
The Nature Conservancy
Negocios
Orlando Science Center
Perfume Provider of America
Santa Barbara Beach & Golf Resort

GROUP FIFTY FIVE MARKETING

3011 W Grand Blvd, Detroit, MI 48202
Tel.: (313) 875-1155
Fax: (313) 875-4349
E-Mail: info@group55.com
Web Site: www.group55.com

Employees: 20
Year Founded: 1982

National Agency Associations: Second Wind Limited

Agency Specializes In: Collateral, Communications, Consumer Marketing, Corporate Identity, Public Relations

Approx. Annual Billings: $5,000,000

Catherine Clare Lapico *(Owner & CEO)*
Michael A. Lapico *(Pres & COO)*
Heather Schabel *(Sr Dir-Art)*
Stacey Shires *(Acct Dir & Copywriter)*
John Shoemaker *(Mgr-Ops)*

Accounts:
Agency Services Group
Amcor
Amerisure Insurance
Atlas Oil
Beztak Properties
BrassCraft
Central Global
Comerica Bank
Conway MacKenzie
Covidien
DMC
DTE
First State Bank
Health Plus
Judson Center
Kirk in the Hills
Lear Corporation
Letica
Livonia Public Schools
Michigan Lottery
Pioneer State Mutual Insurance Company
Ronnisch Construction Group
Schostak Brothers
St John Health System
Stryker
Terumo
Wayne-Westland Community Schools
Webasto

GROUP LEAF LLC

PO Box 546, Hudson, WI 54016
Tel.: (715) 381-0123
Fax: (651) 204-2262
E-Mail: info@groupleaf.com
Web Site: www.groupleaf.com

Year Founded: 2003

Agency Specializes In: Advertising, Brand Development & Integration, Collateral, Crisis Communications, Internet/Web Design, Logo & Package Design, Media Buying Services, Public Relations

Greg Leaf *(Principal)*
Jessica Krasin *(Acct Exec)*
Laura Rapp *(Designer)*
Sami Woodford *(Designer)*

Accounts:
Legacy Post & Beam
Nygaard Associates

GROUP M5

42 O'Leary Avenue, Saint John's, NL A1B 4B7 Canada
Tel.: (709) 753-5559
Web Site: www.m5.ca

Agency Specializes In: Communications, Digital/Interactive, Market Research, Public Relations

Craig Tucker *(Mng Partner)*
Chris MacInnes *(Sr VP)*

Accounts:
General Motors
Marine Atlantic
Nalcor
Southwestern Energy

GROUP TWO ADVERTISING, INC.

2002 Ludlow St, Philadelphia, PA 19103
Tel.: (215) 561-2200
Fax: (215) 561-2842
Web Site: www.grouptwo.com

E-Mail for Key Personnel:
President: relkman@grouptwo.com

Employees: 12
Year Founded: 1970

Agency Specializes In: Real Estate

Richard Elkman *(Founder & Strategist)*
Mollie Elkman *(Owner & Pres)*
Daniel Gerson *(COO)*

Accounts:
Kettler Forlines
Wayne Homes

GROUP360 WORLDWIDE

1227 Washington Ave, Saint Louis, MO 63103
Tel.: (314) 260-6360
Web Site: www.group360.com

Agency Specializes In: Advertising, Brand Development & Integration

Tim Rutter *(Pres & CEO)*
Michael Benson *(COO)*
Stephanie Pfund *(Acct Mgr)*

Accounts:
New-Dr Pepper Snapple Group All Natural Snapple

GROUP46

1323 May River Rd Ste 202, Bluffton, SC 22910
Tel.: (843) 540-0567
Web Site: grp46.com

Employees: 6
Year Founded: 2014

Agency Specializes In: Above-the-Line, Advertising, Advertising Specialties, Affiliate Marketing, Affluent Market, African-American Market, Agriculture, Alternative Advertising, Arts, Asian Market, Automotive, Aviation & Aerospace, Below-the-Line, Bilingual Market, Brand Development & Integration, Branded Entertainment, Broadcast, Business Publications, Business-To-Business, Cable T.V., Catalogs,

Children's Market, Co-op Advertising, Collateral, College, Commercial Photography, Communications, Computers & Software, Consulting, Consumer Goods, Consumer Marketing, Consumer Publications, Content, Corporate Communications, Corporate Identity, Cosmetics, Crisis Communications, Custom Publishing, Customer Relationship Management, Digital/Interactive, Direct Response Marketing, Direct-to-Consumer, E-Commerce, Education, Electronic Media, Electronics, Email, Engineering, Entertainment, Environmental, Event Planning & Marketing, Exhibit/Trade Shows, Experience Design, Faith Based, Fashion/Apparel, Financial, Food Service, Game Integration, Gay & Lesbian Market, Government/Political, Graphic Design, Guerilla Marketing, Health Care Services, High Technology, Hispanic Market, Hospitality, Household Goods, Identity Marketing, In-Store Advertising, Industrial, Infomercials, Information Technology, Integrated Marketing, International, Internet/Web Design, Investor Relations, Legal Services, Leisure, Local Marketing, Logo & Package Design, Luxury Products, Magazines, Marine, Market Research, Media Buying Services, Media Planning, Media Relations, Media Training, Medical Products, Men's Market, Merchandising, Mobile Marketing, Multicultural, Multimedia, New Product Development, New Technologies, Newspaper, Newspapers & Magazines, Out-of-Home Media, Outdoor, Over-50 Market, Package Design, Paid Searches, Pets , Pharmaceutical, Planning & Consultation, Podcasting, Point of Purchase, Point of Sale, Print, Product Placement, Production, Production (Ad, Film, Broadcast), Production (Print), Promotions, Public Relations, Publicity/Promotions, Publishing, RSS (Really Simple Syndication), Radio, Real Estate, Recruitment, Regional, Restaurant, Retail, Sales Promotion, Search Engine Optimization, Seniors' Market, Shopper Marketing, Social Marketing/Nonprofit, Social Media, South Asian Market, Sponsorship, Sports Market, Stakeholders, Strategic Planning/Research, Sweepstakes, Syndication, T.V., Technical Advertising, Teen Market, Telemarketing, Trade & Consumer Magazines, Transportation, Travel & Tourism, Tween Market, Urban Market, Viral/Buzz/Word of Mouth, Web (Banner Ads, Pop-ups, etc.), Women's Market, Yellow Pages Advertising

Donna Thomas *(Dir-Art)*
Michael Weaver *(Dir-Creative)*
Rochelle Zuercher *(Dir-Art)*
Jane Fielden *(Acct Exec)*

Accounts:
Belfair Plantation; 2013
K&K Interiors Home Furnishings; 2009
Pierce Kelly Hunt Real Estate; 2014
Vineyard 55; 2014

GROUPE RINALDI COMMUNICATION MARKETING

Ste 400 6750 av de l'Esplanade, Montreal, QC H2V 4M1 Canada
Tel.: (514) 274-1177
Fax: (514) 274-2766
E-Mail: info@agencerinaldi.com
Web Site: www.agencerinaldi.com

Employees: 20
Year Founded: 1994

Maurice Rinaldi *(Pres & CEO)*
Michel Van Houtte *(Creative Dir & Copywriter)*
Andre Bouchard *(Dir-Strategic Plng & Acct Servicing)*
Patrick D'Anjou *(Dir-Art)*
Judith Mathieu *(Dir-Artistic)*
Aurelie Pinceloup *(Dir-Interactive & Social Media)*
Joanne Rinaldi *(Mgr-HR)*
Khaeddy Chanthavongnasaeng *(Acct Exec)*
Sonia Genovesi *(Acct Exec)*
Jean-Charles Bullot *(Copywriter)*

Accounts:
Chop Crazy
Discount
Engel Chevalier
Fraser Furniture
Mont Sutton
Subaru

GROUPM ENTERTAINMENT

2425 Olympic Blvd, Santa Monica, CA 90404-4030
Tel.: (310) 309-8700
Web Site: www.groupm.com

National Agency Associations: 4A's

Agency Specializes In: Advertising

Peter Tortorici *(CEO)*
Adam Pincus *(Exec VP-Programming & Production)*
Raunak Munot *(Dir-Social Strategy)*
Drew Fauser *(Mgr-Print)*
Caitlin Reach *(Mgr-Print)*

Accounts:
American Express Company
Lenovo Group Ltd
Motorola Solutions, Inc.
Nestle US Digital, Media Planning & Buying, Nespresso USA, Nestle Health Sciences, Nestle Nutrition, Nestle Purina PetCare, Nestle USA, Nestle Waters North America
Unilever United States Inc.
Yahoo! How Money Works, Superfoods

GROUPM ESP

(Name Changed to ESP Brands)

GROW

427 Granby St, Norfolk, VA 23510
Tel.: (757) 431-7710
Fax: (757) 431-7709
E-Mail: info@thisisgrow.com
Web Site: www.thisisgrow.com

Employees: 35
Year Founded: 2004

Agency Specializes In: Advertising, Digital/Interactive

Drew Ungvarsky *(CEO & Exec Dir-Creative)*
Matt Paddock *(Gen Mgr)*
Joe Branton *(Dir-Design)*
Sabrina Cassar *(Dir-Ops)*
Eric Green *(Dir-Bus Dev & Mktg)*
Quan Hoang *(Dir-Creative)*
Brian Walker *(Dir-Tech)*
Eamon Wyse *(Dir-Production)*
Josh Newton *(Designer)*

Accounts:
Acura
Adobe
Axe
BFGoodrich
Coca-Cola
EA
Google Campaign: "Burberry Kisses" for Burberry, Campaign: "Hilltop Re-Imagined for Coca-Cola", Campaign: "Madden GIFERATOR" for EA Sports, Campaign: "Phenomenal Shot" for Nike, Campaign: "Uncover Your World"
HP
JC Penney Digital/Interactive, Rock Your Look
Motorola Solutions, Inc.
NASA
NBC
Nike
Rdio
Sprint Campaign: "Sprint - All. Together. Now."
YouTube

GROW MARKETING

570 Pacific Ave 3rd Fl, San Francisco, CA 94133
Tel.: (415) 440-4769
Fax: (415) 440-4779
E-Mail: contact@grow-marketing.com
Web Site: www.grow-marketing.com

Employees: 80

Agency Specializes In: Sponsorship

Gabrey Means *(Co-Founder & Dir-Creative)*
Cassie Hughes *(Co-Founder)*
Tami Anderson *(Mng Dir)*
Kimberly Macke *(Sr Acct Mgr)*
Thao Bui *(Acct Supvr)*
Laura E. Fogelman *(Assoc Acct Dir)*

Accounts:
Pernod Ricard Glenlivet
Tazo Event, Marketing, PR, Social Media Campaigns

GRUPO GALLEGOS

300 Pacific Coast Hwy Ste 200, Huntington Beach, CA 92648
Tel.: (714) 794-6400
Fax: (714) 794-6420
E-Mail: grupogallegos@grupogallegos.com
Web Site: www.grupogallegos.com

Employees: 80
Year Founded: 2001

National Agency Associations: 4A's

Agency Specializes In: Hispanic Market, Pets , Sponsorship

Approx. Annual Billings: $67,500,000

John Gallegos *(Founder, Pres & CEO)*
Jose Pablo Rodriguez *(Grp Acct Dir & Co-Head-Acct Mgmt)*
Sebastian Garin *(Exec Creative Dir)*
Rachel Gilmour *(Grp Acct Dir)*
Caro D'Antuono *(Acct Dir)*
Julie Beall *(Dir-Fin)*
Silvina Cendra *(Dir-Plng)*
Catarina Goncalves *(Dir-Plng)*
Maria Maldini *(Dir-Creative Svcs)*
Carlos Tornell *(Dir-Creative)*
Claudia Canas *(Assoc Dir-Creative)*
Sharon Cleary *(Assoc Dir-Creative)*
Sharon Cooper *(Assoc Dir-Media)*
Franz Rio de la Loza *(Assoc Dir-Creative)*
Nora Ayala *(Acct Supvr)*
Alexandra Bellis *(Acct Supvr)*
Lucia Malam *(Acct Supvr)*
Joanne Martin *(Acct Supvr)*
Sandra Ochoa *(Acct Exec)*

Accounts:
Alzheimer's Association Campaign: "Daughter", Campaign: "Forgetting Little things", Campaign: "Forgot Your Password?"
The California Milk Processors Board "Medusa", Campaign: "Battle", Campaign: "Brave", Campaign: "Champion", Campaign: "Milk Fuels A Better Future"; 2005
Carnival Cruise Lines
Church's Chicken Multi-Cultural Marketing
The Clorox Company
New-Coca-Cola
Comcast Cable Services
Constru-guia
Foster Farms

Fruit of the Loom; 2003
New-General Mills
JC Penney (Hispanic Agency of Record)
La Cocina VA
New-Mitsubishi
Motel 6
Toshiba America Information Systems, Inc. Brand Identity, Latin America Advertising, Media, Portege, Qosimo, Satellite, Strategic Planning, Tecra
Valvoline
Wonderful Pistachios

GRW ADVERTISING

28 W 25th St Second Fl, New York, NY 10010-2705
Tel.: (212) 620-0519
Fax: (212) 620-0549
E-Mail: contact@grwadvertising.com
Web Site: www.grwadvertising.com

E-Mail for Key Personnel:
President: edronk@aol.com

Employees: 8
Year Founded: 1994

Agency Specializes In: Advertising, Brand Development & Integration, Business-To-Business, Entertainment, Graphic Design, Internet/Web Design, Logo & Package Design, Magazines, Newspapers & Magazines, Out-of-Home Media, Print, Radio, Retail, Strategic Planning/Research, Trade & Consumer Magazines, Travel & Tourism

Revenue: $5,000,000

Ed Ronk *(Pres)*
Glen Wielgus *(Dir-Art)*

Accounts:
Empire Theatre Company
Pride Institute
Rioult Dance Theatre

GS&F

209 10th Ave S Ste 222, Nashville, TN 37203
Tel.: (615) 385-1100
Fax: (615) 783-0500
E-Mail: biz@gsandf.com
Web Site: gsandf.com

E-Mail for Key Personnel:
President: jlipscomb@gsandf.com
Creative Dir.: rgibbons@gsandf.com
Media Dir.: llawson@gsandf.com

Employees: 75
Year Founded: 1978

Agency Specializes In: Advertising, Automotive, Brand Development & Integration, Business-To-Business, Cable T.V., Catalogs, Co-op Advertising, Collateral, Consumer Goods, Consumer Marketing, Consumer Publications, Corporate Communications, Corporate Identity, Crisis Communications, Digital/Interactive, Direct Response Marketing, Electronic Media, Entertainment, Event Planning & Marketing, Exhibit/Trade Shows, Financial, Food Service, Gay & Lesbian Market, Graphic Design, Health Care Services, Hospitality, Household Goods, In-Store Advertising, Industrial, Integrated Marketing, Internet/Web Design, Leisure, Local Marketing, Logo & Package Design, Luxury Products, Market Research, Media Buying Services, Media Planning, Media Relations, Multicultural, Multimedia, Newspapers & Magazines, Out-of-Home Media, Package Design, Planning & Consultation, Point of Purchase, Point of Sale, Print, Production (Print), Promotions, Public Relations, Publicity/Promotions, Radio, Restaurant, Retail, Sales Promotion, Social Marketing/Nonprofit, Sponsorship, Sports Market, Strategic Planning/Research, T.V., Trade & Consumer Magazines, Transportation, Travel & Tourism, Yellow Pages Advertising

Approx. Annual Billings: $52,000,000

Breakdown of Gross Billings by Media: Fees: $3,500,000; Graphic Design: $300,000; Internet Adv.: $400,000; Mags.: $12,000,000; Newsp.: $2,000,000; Out-of-Home Media: $1,000,000; Production: $16,900,000; Pub. Rels.: $2,000,000; Radio: $5,000,000; T.V.: $8,000,000; Worldwide Web Sites: $800,000; Yellow Page Adv.: $100,000

Jeff Lipscomb *(Owner & CEO)*
Gregg Boling *(Mng Dir, Exec VP & Exec Dir-Creative)*
Laramey Lawson *(Sr VP & Dir-Media)*
David Camma *(Grp Acct Dir)*
Betsy Curran *(Grp Acct Dir)*
Paige Thompson *(Dir-Art)*
Scott Brooks *(Mgr-Xmedia)*
Derek Hollis *(Mgr-Interactive Ops)*
Abbey Griswold *(Acct Supvr)*
Michael Dean *(Acct Exec)*
Stephen McAllister *(Acct Exec)*
Molly Russell *(Acct Exec)*
Nicole Parker *(Coord-Strategic Plng)*

Accounts:
A.O. Smith; Ashland City, TN Commercial & Residential Water Heaters; 2006
Angela Bacon-Kidwell Photography
Asurion; Nashville, TN Wireless Communications Services; 2003
Bridgestone Americas; Nashville, TN Consumer Tires, Motorcycle Tires, Motorsports; 1994
Hunt Brothers Pizza; Nashville, TN Convenience Store Pizza Shops; 2008
International Comfort Products (ICP); Lewisburg, TN Heating/Cooling Products; 1982
LP; Nashville, TN Building Products; 2008
Minnie Pearl Cancer Foundation; Nashville, TN Services for Cancer Patients & Families; 1996
Monroe Harding; Nashville, TN Counseling & Residential Care for Displaced Youth; 2003
Nashville Convention & Visitors Bureau; Nashville, TN Destination Marketing Organization; 2005
Nashville Predators; Nashville, TN NHL Team; 2008
National College; Roanoke, VA Career College; 2009
Sweet CeCe's Branding, Communications, Creative, Project Management, Public & Media Relations, Social Media, Web Design
Tennessee Titans; Nashville, TN NFL Football Team; 1995
Universal Lighting Technologies; Nashville, TN Lighting Ballasts; 1996
University of Tennessee Medical Center; Knoxville, TN Regional Academic & Medical Center; 2007

GSD&M

828 W 6th St, Austin, TX 78703
Tel.: (512) 242-4736
Fax: (512) 242-4700
Web Site: www.gsdm.com

E-Mail for Key Personnel:
President: roy_spence@gsdm.com
Media Dir.: judy_trabulsi@gsdm.com

Employees: 500
Year Founded: 1971

National Agency Associations: 4A's-AAF-ARF-PRSA-WOMMA

Agency Specializes In: Advertising, Brand Development & Integration, Broadcast, Digital/Interactive, Education, Entertainment, Environmental, Financial, Food Service, Government/Political, Health Care Services, Leisure, Media Buying Services, Newspaper, Over-50 Market, Print, Restaurant, Retail, T.V., Transportation, Travel & Tourism

Judy Trabulsi *(Co-Founder)*
Marianne Malina *(Pres)*
Duff Stewart *(CEO)*
Betty Pat McCoy *(Mng Dir, Sr VP & Dir-Investment)*
J. B. Raftus *(CMO & Exec VP)*
Jay Russell *(Chief Creative Officer & Exec VP)*
Carter Nance *(Chief Client Officer & Sr VP)*
Carmen Graf *(Sr VP & Exec Dir-Media)*
Victor Camozzi *(Sr VP & Grp Dir-Creative)*
Brent Ladd *(Sr VP & Grp Dir-Creative)*
Bo Bradbury *(Sr VP & Grp Acct Dir)*
Carrie Hines *(Sr VP & Acct Dir)*
Jack Epsteen *(Sr VP & Dir-Production)*
Jeanne Crockett *(Sr VP-Ops)*
Andrew Teagle *(Sr VP-Strategy & Insights)*
Jeff Orth *(VP & Acct Dir)*
Coley Platt *(VP & Acct Dir)*
Adrienne Walpole *(VP & Acct Dir)*
Michael Dezso *(VP & Dir-Strategy)*
Kirya Francis *(VP & Dir-Media & Res Tech)*
Madhavi Reese *(VP & Dir-Plng)*
Nancy Ryan *(VP & Dir-Bus Dev)*
Melanie Mahaffey *(VP-Comm)*
David Rockwood *(VP-Community Rels)*
Ryan Carroll *(Grp Dir-Creative)*
Tom Hamling *(Grp Dir-Creative)*
Bill Marceau *(Grp Dir-Creative)*
Chris Carlberg *(Sr Dir-Art)*
Carly Conrad *(Sr Dir-Art)*
Beth Bonargo *(Acct Dir)*
Will Chau *(Creative Dir)*
Michael Griffith *(Art Dir)*
Sean Keith *(Creative Dir)*
Ana Leen *(Acct Dir)*
Judd Oberly *(Dir-Art & Assoc Dir-Creative)*
Joel Williams *(Dir-Art & Assoc Dir-Creative)*
Jeffrey Butterworth *(Dir-Creative & Writer)*
Jeff Maki *(Dir-Creative & Writer)*
Leslie Schaffer *(Dir-Creative & Copywriter)*
Carlotta Stankiewicz *(Dir-Creative & Writer)*
Jennifer Billiot *(Dir-Brand Strategy)*
Lara Bridger *(Dir-Creative)*
Jake Camozzi *(Dir-Creative)*
Christopher Colton *(Dir-Creative)*
Nicole Dumouchel Davis *(Dir-Creative)*
Michelle Dickens *(Dir-Strategy)*
Derek Dollahite *(Dir-Experience)*
Joel Guidry *(Dir-Creative)*
Clay Hudson *(Dir-Creative)*
Sean LaBounty *(Dir-Creative)*
Daniel Leal *(Dir-Digital Strategy & Digital Media)*
Ray Longoria *(Dir-Creative)*
Morgan McDonald *(Dir-Art)*
Mark Snow *(Dir-Creative)*
Arthur Stewart *(Dir-Art)*
Janice Suter *(Dir-Social Media)*
Phil Davies *(Assoc Dir-Creative & Writer)*
Elyse Clark *(Assoc Dir-Media)*
Ryan Kunz *(Assoc Dir-Media)*
Jo Ella Mathis *(Assoc Dir-Bus Affairs)*
Kevin Taylor *(Assoc Dir-Creative)*
Chelsea Davis *(Sr Mgr-Social Media)*
Katherine Colburn *(Acct Mgr)*
Teezal Gaji *(Acct Mgr)*
Samantha Rendon *(Acct Mgr)*
Laurie Pascoe *(Mgr-Bus Affairs)*
Sarah Stuchbery *(Mgr-New Bus)*
Amy Rodgers *(Acct Supvr)*
Claire Tudor *(Acct Supvr)*
Kendra Baumann *(Supvr-Media)*
Kelsey Caulkins *(Supvr-Media)*
Pooja Iyer *(Supvr-Media)*
Sarah Denney *(Sr Planner-Media)*
Meredith Cooper *(Media Planner)*
Matt Garcia *(Copywriter)*
Diana Jimenez *(Media Planner)*
Celina McGraw *(Media Planner)*
David Neilson *(Media Planner)*
Janeanne Yeager *(Media Planner)*
Scott Brewer *(Grp Creative Dir)*
Karla Esquivel *(Asst Media Buyer)*

Cheyenne Gallion *(Assoc Creative Dir)*
Paige Gummere *(Asst Media Planner)*
Dylan Heimbrock *(Assoc Producer)*
Emma Lacouture *(Asst Media Planner)*
Susana Skinner *(Sr Media Buyer)*
Kristi Van Herweg *(Asst Media Planner)*

Accounts:
AARP; Washington, D.C. Campaign: "Car Wash", Creative, Media Buying; 2002
AT&T, Inc. AT&T U-Verse, AT&T, Inc.
Austin City Limits (Creative Agency of Record); 2011
Avocados From Mexico Campaign: 'FirstDraftEver", Creative, Super Bowl 2015
Caesars Palace
Campbell Soup Co. Campbell Skillet Sauces, Dinner Sauce, Slow Cooker Sauces
Charles Schwab
Chipotle Creative, Media Buying, Media Planning, Traditional Advertising
The Goodyear Tire & Rubber Company; Akron, OH Campaign: "Battle Tested, Road Ready", Marketing Campaign, NASCAR
Harrah's Louisiana Downs Casino & Racetrack; 2009
Hilton Worldwide Creative, Digital, Hampton Inn, Hilton Garden Inn, Hilton Hotels & Resorts, Portfolio Marketing
Horseshoe Casinos Campaign: "Slots"
Incista B.V. Stainmaster
Jarritos Campaign: "Double Straw", Campaign: "Flex", Campaign: "Glassblowers", Campaign: "Involuntary Taste Test"
John Deere Campaign: "Bump Track"
Land Rover
LeapFrog Media
Lee Jeans Creative
Lennox International Inc. Creative & Media
Northwestern Mutual (Lead Agency) Creative
Pacifico Campaign: "Yellow Caps"
Perio Inc Campaign: "Shave Like a Man", Campaign: "War Hero", Pure Silk
PGA Tour; Ponte Verde, FL Creative, Media; 1989
Popeye's Chicken & Biscuits; Atlanta, GA Campaign: "#LoveThatChicken", Campaign: "Chicken Waffle Tenders", Creative, Media Buying & Planning, TV; 2008
Seton Healthcare Family
Southwest Airlines Co. "Bags Fly Free", Advertising, Broadcast, Business Select, Campaign: "Garage Band", Campaign: "Love Moment", Campaign: "Smile", Campaign: "Wanna get away", Campaign: "Water-Cannon", Campaign: "Wedding", Campaign: "Weddings 2.0", Campaigns: "Fireworks", Marketing, Rapid Rewards Business; 1981
Sport Clips Media
Stork Media
Sysco Corporation
United States Air Force; Washington, D.C. "Aim High", "Barrier Breakers", Campaign: "America's Future", Campaign: "American Airmen", Campaign: "Make It Fly", Campaign: "New Frontiers", Campaign: "The Collaboratory', Digital Media Buy, It's Not Science Fiction, Online; 2000
University of Texas Campaign: "Leave Your Mark"
Unscrew America (Pro Bono) Energy-Saving Lightbulbs; 2008
Walgreen Co. (Agency of Record) Branding, Broadcast, Campaign: "At the Corner of Happy & Healthy", Campaign: "Faces", Campaign: "Get a Shot Give a Shot", Campaign: "Scraps", Creative, Digital Strategy, Outdoor, Print
Whole Foods Market, Inc. Media Buying, Media Planning
Zale Corp. Campaign: "Friend Your Mom", Campaign: "Let Love Shine", Zales Holiday Series

Branches:

GSD&M Chicago
211 E Chicago Ave 14th Fl, Chicago, IL 60611
Tel.: (312) 725-5750
Fax: (312) 573-5790
Web Site: www.gsdm.com

Employees: 75

National Agency Associations: 4A's

Agency Specializes In: Media Buying Services, Sponsorship

Betty Pat McCoy *(Mng Dir, Sr VP & Dir-Investment)*
Jack Epsteen *(Sr VP & Dir-Production)*
Ulian Valkov *(VP & Assoc Dir-Natl Investment)*
Ryan Carroll *(Grp Dir-Creative)*
Bill Marceau *(Grp Dir-Creative)*
Dale Austin *(Sr Dir-Art)*
Lara Bridger *(Dir-Creative)*
Sean LaBounty *(Dir-Creative)*
Erin Bernethy *(Assoc Dir-Media)*
Jodi Bucciarelli *(Acct Mgr)*
Cat Snyder *(Acct Mgr)*
Amy Lyon *(Acct Supvr)*
Les Stipp *(Supvr-Media & Media Buyer)*
Kendra Baumann *(Supvr-Media)*
Megan Eatherton *(Media Planner)*
David Neilson *(Media Planner)*
Janeanne Yeager *(Media Planner)*
Audsley Dunavant *(Asst Media Planner)*
Karla Esquivel *(Asst Media Buyer)*
Marisol Gonzalez *(Asst Media Planner)*
Paige Gummere *(Asst Media Planner)*
Amy Hatcher *(Asst Media Planner)*
Lucas Indrikovs *(Asst Media Planner)*
Christine Kwak *(Asst Media Planner)*
Emma Lacouture *(Asst Media Planner)*
Jessica Moore *(Asst Media Buyer)*

Accounts:
AARP
American Express
AT&T, Inc.
Hallmark
U.S. Air Force Services
Zale Corporation Gordon's Jewelers, Peoples Jewelry, Piercing Pagoda, Zale Corporation

Sibling
828 W 6th Street, Austin, TX 78703
Tel.: (512) 242-4736

Year Founded: 2015

Rafael Serrano, *(Dir-Creative)*

Accounts:
Popeyes Louisiana Kitchen
Southwest Airlines

GSG PRODUCTION AGENCY
(Formerly GSG Design)
33 E 17th St, New York, NY 10003
Tel.: (212) 242-8787
Fax: (212) 228-8500

Employees: 135
Year Founded: 1980

Agency Specializes In: Broadcast, Business-To-Business, Collateral, Communications, Consumer Goods, Consumer Marketing, Email, Event Planning & Marketing, Exhibit/Trade Shows, Graphic Design, Guerilla Marketing, In-Store Advertising, Information Technology, Integrated Marketing, Internet/Web Design, Local Marketing, Logo & Package Design, Market Research, New Product Development, Out-of-Home Media, Package Design, Point of Purchase, Point of Sale, Production (Ad, Film, Broadcast), Promotions, Retail, Web (Banner Ads, Pop-ups, etc.)

Bill Hufstader *(Partner)*
Anne-Marie Bazzani *(CFO)*
Glen Fix *(COO)*
Richard Paganello *(COO)*
Lidia Latrowski *(Chief Sls Officer)*
Carmine Corinella *(Dir-Creative Imaging)*
Jeffrey Giniger *(Dir-Strategic Accounts)*
Brian O'Neill *(Dir-Innovation)*
Ruben Pimentel *(Mgr-Visual Mdsg)*
Peggy McGuinness *(Sr Acct Exec)*
Rebecca Mummert Swartz *(Sr Acct Coord)*

Accounts:
FAO Schwarz Harry Potter
Major League Baseball
Ralph Lauren

GSS COMMUNICATIONS, INC.
5042 Wilshire Blvd Ste 317, Los Angeles, CA 90036
Tel.: (323) 939-1181
Fax: (888) 387-5717
E-Mail: agraham@gssla.com
Web Site: www.gssla.com

Employees: 9
Year Founded: 1983

Agency Specializes In: Brand Development & Integration, Business Publications, Business-To-Business, Collateral, Communications, Consulting, Corporate Identity, Direct Response Marketing, Financial, Health Care Services, Leisure, Outdoor, Print, Strategic Planning/Research, Travel & Tourism

Approx. Annual Billings: $8,500,000

Andrea Graham *(Pres)*

Accounts:
Esotouric; Los Angeles, CA Entertainment/Tourism; 2007
Health Access Solutions; Foster City, CA; Woodland Hills, CA Medical Software; 2007
Marketing Strategic Group; Westlake Village, CA
Philadelphia County Dental Society; 1998
Physiquality; Calabasas, CA Consumer Healthcare; 2007
Swett & Crawford Group; Atlanta, GA Wholesale Insurance Brokerage; 1978
West Hollywood Convention & Visitors Bureau

GSW WORLDWIDE
(Formerly GSW Worldwide Fueled by Blue Diesel)
500 Olde Worthington Rd, Westerville, OH 43082
Tel.: (614) 848-4848
Fax: (614) 848-3477
E-Mail: columbus@gsw-w.com
Web Site: www.gsw-w.com

Employees: 300
Year Founded: 1977

National Agency Associations: AAF-DMA-PRSA

Agency Specializes In: Advertising, Brand Development & Integration, Broadcast, Business-To-Business, Collateral, Communications, Consulting, Consumer Marketing, Corporate Identity, Direct Response Marketing, Financial, Graphic Design, Health Care Services, Media Buying Services, Medical Products, New Product Development, Pharmaceutical, Planning & Consultation, Print, Production, Public Relations, Publicity/Promotions, Radio, Retail, Sales Promotion, Sponsorship, Strategic Planning/Research, T.V., Technical Advertising

Approx. Annual Billings: $415,900,000

Joe Daley *(Pres)*

Stephen Wheatley *(Mng Dir)*
Scott Page *(Exec VP & Gen Mgr)*
Kevin Fox *(Exec VP & Exec Dir-Creative)*
David Sonderman *(Exec VP & Exec Dir-Creative)*
Jon Parkinson *(Sr VP & Dir-Integrated Production)*
Mark Stinson *(Sr VP-Brand Experience Strategy)*
Ryan Kurty *(Acct Dir)*
Wayne Fassett *(Dir-Creative & Writer)*
Stacy Richard *(Dir-Art)*
Chris Sonderman *(Assoc Dir-Design)*
Kristen Kunk *(Acct Supvr)*
Jess Lawrence *(Sr Strategist-Digital)*
Christine Krapohl *(Acct Exec)*
Abby Scott *(Sr Designer-Brand)*
Eric Davis *(Assoc Creative Dir)*

Accounts:
Allergan, Inc.
Altana
American Medical Systems
Azur Pharma
Baxter BioSurgery
Biogen Avonex
Dyax
Eli Lilly & Company Campaign: "Beyond The Moment", Cymbalta, Duloxetine SUI, Evista, Forteo, Gemzar, Humalog/Humulin, Strattera, Xigris, Zyprexa
Graceway Pharmaceuticals
Haemonetics Corp.
ImClone Systems
Janssen Biotech, Inc.
KV Pharma
Lilly Oncology Campaign: "The Moment"
Nodality, Inc.
Ohio Health
Premier Health Partners
Protopic
Roche Tamiflu; 2006
TAP Pharmaceuticals
Temple University Health Systems
Uloric

Branch

ENE Life
(Formerly ENE Publicidad SA Barcelona)
Calle Villarroell 216, 08036 Barcelona, Spain
Tel.: (34) 93 439 1848
Fax: (34) 93 419 0238
E-Mail: spain@gsw-w.com
Web Site: www.ene.es

Employees: 3
Year Founded: 1990

Alberto Rosa *(Exec Dir-Creative)*
Silvia Montes Garcia *(Dir-Art)*
Aurelio Moreno *(Exec Mgr-Digital)*
Maria Jose Zapata *(Acct Mgr-Barcelona)*
Maria Angeles Torres *(Mgr-Fin)*
Maria De Elio *(Copywriter-Digital Strategy Plng & Creative)*
Guillermo Fernandez *(Exec Gen Mgr)*

Accounts:
Bayer
Bristol-Myers Squibb
Coolmore
GlaxoSmithKline
Menarini
Novartis
Salvat

GTM
239 Walker St, Atlanta, GA 30313
Tel.: (866) 680-0486
E-Mail: info@gtmcentral.com
Web Site: www.gtmcentral.com

Agency Specializes In: Advertising

Samantha Fennell *(VP-Branded Entertainment)*
Alex Morgan *(Sr Dir-Art)*
Toni Davis *(Dir-HR & Ops)*
B. Ray Sams *(Dir-Creative)*

Accounts:
The Coca-Cola Company Sprite
Harley-Davidson Motorcycles
The Humane Society of the United States
Kaiser Family Foundation
L'Oreal USA, Inc.
Nissan Motor Co., Ltd.
Procter & Gamble
Sony Corporation of America
Volkswagen Group of America, Inc.

GUD MARKETING
(Formerly Pace & Partners)
1223 Turner St Ste 101, Lansing, MI 48906
Tel.: (517) 267-9800
Fax: (517) 267-9815
E-Mail: Hello@GudMarketing.com
Web Site: www.gudmarketing.com/

Employees: 22
Year Founded: 1978

Agency Specializes In: Advertising, Agriculture, Automotive, Brand Development & Integration, Broadcast, Business-To-Business, Children's Market, Collateral, Communications, Consulting, Consumer Marketing, Consumer Publications, Corporate Communications, Corporate Identity, Direct Response Marketing, Education, Electronic Media, Environmental, Event Planning & Marketing, Exhibit/Trade Shows, Food Service, Graphic Design, Health Care Services, Internet/Web Design, Leisure, Logo & Package Design, Magazines, Media Buying Services, Medical Products, New Product Development, Newspaper, Newspapers & Magazines, Outdoor, Planning & Consultation, Point of Purchase, Point of Sale, Print, Production, Public Relations, Publicity/Promotions, Radio, Sales Promotion, Strategic Planning/Research, T.V., Trade & Consumer Magazines, Travel & Tourism

Dennis Pace *(Founder)*
Debbie Horak *(Partner & Chief Growth Officer)*
Lisa Crumley *(Principal & Sr Strategist)*
Larry Amburgey *(Dir-Fin)*
Jill Holden *(Dir-Strategic Plng)*
Nancy Metzger *(Dir-Media)*
Emmie Musser *(Dir-Media)*
Kate Stanton *(Coord-Bus & Media)*

GUERILLA SUIT
1208 E 7th St 2nd Fl, Austin, TX 78702
Tel.: (512) 480-5900
E-Mail: hello@guerillasuit.com
Web Site: www.guerillasuit.com

Year Founded: 2010

Agency Specializes In: Advertising, Collateral, Digital/Interactive, Logo & Package Design, Print

Ryan Goeller *(Mgr-Production)*
Luigi Maldonado *(Designer)*
Naema Showery *(Coord-Traffic)*

Accounts:
Circuit of the Americas (Agency of Record)
Pearl Brewery

GUERRILLA TACTICS MEDIA
(d/b/a GTM... It Means A Lot)
239 Walker St, Atlanta, GA 30313
Tel.: (404) 522-0486
Fax: (404) 522-2486
E-Mail: info@gtmcentral.com
Web Site: www.gtmcentral.com

Employees: 10

Agency Specializes In: Advertising, African-American Market, College, Education, Entertainment, Event Planning & Marketing, Experience Design, Guerilla Marketing, Integrated Marketing, Local Marketing, Media Planning, Multicultural, Multimedia, Outdoor, Promotions, Publicity/Promotions, Sponsorship, Strategic Planning/Research, Teen Market, Viral/Buzz/Word of Mouth

Karl Carter *(Co-Founder & CEO)*
Shawn Howard *(Co-Founder & Partner)*
Courtney Counts *(Exec VP-Partnerships & Possibilities)*
Toni Davis *(Dir-HR & Ops)*

GUEST RELATIONS MARKETING
1375 Peachtree St Ste 360, Atlanta, GA 30309
Tel.: (404) 343-4377
Fax: (404) 343-4538
Web Site: www.guestrelationsmarketing.com

Year Founded: 2006

Agency Specializes In: Advertising, Social Media, Strategic Planning/Research

Mike Tyre *(Mng Partner)*
April Voris *(Partner)*
Sarah Scott *(Dir-Online Mktg)*
Virginia Williams *(Mgr-Social Media)*
Alexis Foster *(Coord-Mktg)*

Accounts:
Allan Vigil Dealerships
New-The Kahala Hotel & Resort
New-Maternal Science healthy mama

GUIDE PUBLICATIONS
422 Morris Ave Ste 5, Long Branch, NJ 07740
Tel.: (732) 263-9675
Fax: (732) 263-0494
Web Site: www.njguidepublications.com

Employees: 6
Year Founded: 2000

Agency Specializes In: Advertising, Newspaper, Outdoor, Recruitment, Sales Promotion

Approx. Annual Billings: $250,000

Mike Beson *(Pres)*
Paul Petraccoro *(Dir-Art)*
Cathy Harlow *(Acct Mgr)*
Stacey LaBruno *(Acct Exec-Sls)*

Accounts:
AT Systems
Coca-Cola Refreshments USA, Inc.
Manor by the Sea; Ocean Grove, NJ; 2002
Nordion Inc.
Pepsi Bottling Group Inc.
ProClean
ResCare
Veolia Transportation
WEL Companies

GUMAS ADVERTISING
99 Shotwell St, San Francisco, CA 94103-3625
Tel.: (415) 621-7575
Fax: (415) 255-8804
Web Site: www.gumas.com

E-Mail for Key Personnel:
President: jgumas@gumas.com
Creative Dir.: bjones@gumas.com

Media Dir.: JHearn@gumas.com

Employees: 20
Year Founded: 1984

Agency Specializes In: Advertising, Advertising Specialties, Affluent Market, Agriculture, Alternative Advertising, Arts, Automotive, Aviation & Aerospace, Brand Development & Integration, Broadcast, Business Publications, Business-To-Business, Cable T.V., Catalogs, Children's Market, Co-op Advertising, Collateral, College, Commercial Photography, Communications, Computers & Software, Consulting, Consumer Goods, Consumer Marketing, Consumer Publications, Content, Corporate Communications, Corporate Identity, Cosmetics, Customer Relationship Management, Digital/Interactive, Direct Response Marketing, Direct-to-Consumer, E-Commerce, Education, Electronic Media, Electronics, Email, Engineering, Entertainment, Environmental, Exhibit/Trade Shows, Experience Design, Fashion/Apparel, Financial, Food Service, Gay & Lesbian Market, Government/Political, Graphic Design, Guerilla Marketing, Health Care Services, High Technology, Hospitality, Household Goods, Identity Marketing, In-Store Advertising, Industrial, Infomercials, Information Technology, Integrated Marketing, International, Internet/Web Design, Legal Services, Leisure, Local Marketing, Logo & Package Design, Luxury Products, Magazines, Market Research, Media Buying Services, Media Planning, Medical Products, Men's Market, Mobile Marketing, Multicultural, Multimedia, New Product Development, New Technologies, Newspaper, Newspapers & Magazines, Out-of-Home Media, Outdoor, Over-50 Market, Package Design, Paid Searches, Pets , Pharmaceutical, Planning & Consultation, Podcasting, Point of Purchase, Point of Sale, Print, Product Placement, Production, Production (Print), Promotions, Public Relations, Publicity/Promotions, Radio, Real Estate, Recruitment, Regional, Restaurant, Retail, Sales Promotion, Search Engine Optimization, Seniors' Market, Social Marketing/Nonprofit, Social Media, Sponsorship, Sports Market, Strategic Planning/Research, Sweepstakes, T.V., Teen Market, Telemarketing, Trade & Consumer Magazines, Transportation, Travel & Tourism, Tween Market, Urban Market, Viral/Buzz/Word of Mouth, Women's Market

Approx. Annual Billings: $10,500,000

Breakdown of Gross Billings by Media: Brdcst.: 5%; Bus. Publs.: 10%; Collateral: 20%; D.M.: 10%; Internet Adv.: 20%; Logo & Package Design: 15%; Mags.: 10%; Newsp.: 5%; Outdoor: 5%

John Gumas *(Pres)*
Pat Demiris *(Sr VP & Dir-Ops)*
Craig Alexander *(Sr VP-Client Svcs)*
Jon Polkinghorn *(Sr Acct Mgr)*
Rita Ipsen *(Acct Mgr)*

Accounts:
Aldila
Array Networks; San Jose, CA; 2004
Bell Investment Advisors; Oakland, CA Financial Services; 2010
Burr Pilger & Mayer, LLP; San Francisco, CA Accounting Services, Business Consulting Services, Wealth Management Services; 2005
Criticial Logic; Burlingame, CA Software Testing Services; 2005
HP; Mountainview, CA
Netgear; San Jose, CA Range Extenders, Routers, Wireless Adapters
Petcamp; San Francisco, CA Pet Care For Dogs & Cats; 2011
San Francisco Chamber of Commerce; San Francisco, CA; 2007
San Francisco Giants Community Fund
SanDisk Corp.; Sunnyvale, CA Hi-Tech Products, Memory Cards; 2002
Skins
Trip Insurance; Monte Sereno, CA; 2011
U.S. First Credit Union of San Mateo (Agency of Record)
Yonex; Torrence, CA

THE GUNTER AGENCY

N9191 Cardinal Crest Ln, New Glarus, WI 53574
Tel.: (608) 527-4800
E-Mail: contact@gunteragency.com
Web Site: www.gunteragency.com

Employees: 3
Year Founded: 1996

National Agency Associations: AAF-Second Wind Limited

Agency Specializes In: Advertising, Agriculture, Brand Development & Integration, Broadcast, Business Publications, Business-To-Business, Cable T.V., Children's Market, Co-op Advertising, Collateral, Commercial Photography, Communications, Consulting, Consumer Marketing, Consumer Publications, Corporate Identity, Digital/Interactive, Direct Response Marketing, E-Commerce, Electronic Media, Entertainment, Exhibit/Trade Shows, Financial, Food Service, Graphic Design, Health Care Services, High Technology, Industrial, Internet/Web Design, Logo & Package Design, Magazines, Media Buying Services, Medical Products, Merchandising, Multimedia, New Product Development, Newspaper, Newspapers & Magazines, Out-of-Home Media, Outdoor, Planning & Consultation, Point of Purchase, Point of Sale, Print, Production, Public Relations, Publicity/Promotions, Radio, Retail, Sales Promotion, Sports Market, Strategic Planning/Research, T.V., Technical Advertising, Trade & Consumer Magazines, Travel & Tourism, Yellow Pages Advertising

Approx. Annual Billings: $3,500,000

Breakdown of Gross Billings by Media: E-Commerce: $175,000; Farm Publs.: $175,000; Graphic Design: $350,000; Logo & Package Design: $350,000; Newsp. & Mags.: $175,000; Other: $175,000; Outdoor: $175,000; Point of Sale: $175,000; Print: $700,000; Pub. Rels.: $175,000; Radio & T.V.: $350,000; Strategic Planning/Research: $350,000; Worldwide Web Sites: $175,000

Lucinda E. Gunter *(Pres)*
Randel H. Gunter *(Partner)*

Accounts:
The Employer Group PEO Services; 2010
Furst-McNess Agricultural Products; 2008
General Beverage Beverage Distribution; 2004
The Industrial Athlete Healthcare Services; 2010
Quality Technology International Agricultural Specialty Products; 2004

GUSTIN ADVERTISING

115 Dean Ave Ste 100, Franklin, MA 02038
Tel.: (508) 541-1238
Fax: (508) 541-8006
E-Mail: information@gustinadvertising.com
Web Site: www.gustinadvertising.com

Year Founded: 1998

Agency Specializes In: Advertising, Graphic Design, Internet/Web Design, Print, Social Media

Sally Gustin *(Pres)*
Debra Martin *(Dir-Copy)*
Veronica Maroun *(Acct Mgr)*
Renee Slovick *(Copywriter)*

Accounts:
The Asgard & The Kinsale
Capts Waterfront Grill & Pub

GUTMAN ADVERTISING LLC

6743 National Rd, Triadelphia, WV 26059
Tel.: (304) 214-4700
Fax: (304) 214-4705
E-Mail: greatads@gutmanadvertising.com

Employees: 5
Year Founded: 1926

National Agency Associations: ABC-BPA-MCA

J. Milton Gutman *(Owner)*

Accounts:
Almeyer Funeral Homes; Wheeling, WV
Belmont Savings Bank; Bellaire, OH; 1972
Pree Insurance Centers
United Way of the Upper Ohio Valley; Wheeling, WV; 1996

GWA COMMUNICATIONS, INC.

5200 Upper Metro Pl Ste 110, Dublin, OH 43017-5378
Tel.: (614) 526-7015
Fax: (614) 526-7020
E-Mail: mriggs@hbdeo.com

E-Mail for Key Personnel:
President: mriggs@hbdeo.com

Employees: 20
Year Founded: 1972

National Agency Associations: ABC-ADFED-BPA

Agency Specializes In: Advertising, Advertising Specialties, Affiliate Marketing, Agriculture, Automotive, Aviation & Aerospace, Brand Development & Integration, Broadcast, Business Publications, Business-To-Business, Cable T.V., Catalogs, Co-op Advertising, Collateral, Commercial Photography, Communications, Consulting, Consumer Marketing, Corporate Communications, Corporate Identity, Crisis Communications, Digital/Interactive, Direct Response Marketing, E-Commerce, Education, Electronic Media, Electronics, Engineering, Event Planning & Marketing, Exhibit/Trade Shows, Financial, Graphic Design, High Technology, Identity Marketing, In-Store Advertising, Industrial, Infomercials, Integrated Marketing, International, Internet/Web Design, Logo & Package Design, Magazines, Market Research, Media Buying Services, Media Planning, Media Relations, Media Training, Medical Products, Multimedia, New Product Development, New Technologies, Package Design, Planning & Consultation, Point of Purchase, Point of Sale, Print, Product Placement, Production, Production (Print), Promotions, Public Relations, Publicity/Promotions, Sales Promotion, Search Engine Optimization, Strategic Planning/Research, Technical Advertising, Telemarketing, Transportation, Web (Banner Ads, Pop-ups, etc.), Yellow Pages Advertising

Breakdown of Gross Billings by Media: Adv. Specialties: 2%; Audio/Visual: 3%; Bus. Publs.: 15%; Comml. Photography: 2%; Consulting: 2%; D.M.: 8%; Exhibits/Trade Shows: 15%; Graphic Design: 3%; Internet Adv.: 5%; Logo & Package Design: 2%; Mdsg./POP: 3%; Point of Sale: 5%; Print: 10%; Production: 8%; Pub. Rels.: 4%; Sls. Promo.: 8%; Worldwide Web Sites: 5%

Mark Riggs *(Exec Dir)*

Accounts:

California Drop Forge, Inc.; Los Angeles, CA Closed Die Forgings & Precision Components for the Aerospace & Medical Industries; 2003
Carolina Rubber Rolls; Salisbury, NC Rubber Rolls & Roll Coverings; 1972
HBD Industries, Inc.; Dublin, OH Standard & Custom-Designed Industrial Products; 1971
HBD/Thermoid, Inc.; Oneida, TN Hose Products, PVC Conveyor Belts, Rubber Conveyor Belts; 1972
Ohio Electric Motors Inc.; Barnardsville, NC AC/DC Electric Motors; 1982
Ohio Magnetics, Inc.; Maple Heights, OH Lifting Magnets, Magnetic Separation Equipment; 1979
Peerless Electric; Warren, OH DC Standard & Custom Electric Motors; 1968
Peerless-Winsmith, Inc.; Springville, NY Torque Controls, Variable Speed Drives, Winsmith Gear Reducers; 1989
Perfection Gear Inc.; Asheville, NC Swing & Rotation Drive Products for Aerial Trucks & Lift Equipment; 1990
Powertech Industrial Motors Inc.; Rock Hill, SC Brushless DC Electric Motors & Drive Controls; 2000
Precision Metal Products, Inc.; El Cajon, CA Precision Forged & Complex Machined Metal Forgings for Aerospace, Defense, Industrial & Medical Applications; 2007

GWA/GREGORY WELTEROTH ADVERTISING

356 Laurens Rd, Montoursville, PA 17754
Tel.: (570) 433-3366
Fax: (866) 294-5765
E-Mail: info@gwa-inc.com
Web Site: www.gwa-inc.com

Employees: 15

Agency Specializes In: Sponsorship

Matt Hoff *(VP-Sls)*
Michele Kautz *(VP-Accts)*
Jeff Morrison *(Acct Dir)*
Steve Fagnano *(Dir-Media)*
Robyn Fagnano *(Acct Mgr)*
Aaron Kilcoyne *(Acct Exec)*
Terri Harris *(Media Planner & Media Buyer)*
Angela Abell *(Coord-Media)*

Accounts:
Air Jamaica
Alltel
Ariens/Gravely
Husqvarna
Rock Island Auction Co.
Shop-Vac

GWP BRAND ENGINEERING

365 Bloor St E Ste 1900, Toronto, ON M4W 3L4 Canada
Tel.: (416) 593-4000, ext. 227
Fax: (416) 593-4001
E-Mail: robertm@brandengineering.com
Web Site: www.brandengineering.com

Employees: 15
Year Founded: 1996

National Agency Associations: AMIN

Agency Specializes In: Strategic Planning/Research

Robert Morand *(Exec VP & Dir-Client Svcs)*
Debra Collett *(Gen Mgr)*
Becky Tomlinson *(Acct Dir)*
Sue Belbeck *(Dir-Client Mktg)*
Kiley Woodland *(Dir-Art)*
Philippe Garneau *(Pres & Co-Founder-GWP Brand Engrg)*

Accounts:
Borrowell Consumer Marketplace Lending Platform; 2014
Credit Unions of Ontario Ontario Association for Credit Unions; 2013
D+H Financial Technologies; 2014
Ferrero Rocher Kinder Chocolate, Kinder Surprise; 1997
Teachers Life Life & LTD Insurance; 2013

GWP, INC.

32 Park Ave, Montclair, NJ 07042
Tel.: (973) 746-0500
Fax: (973) 746-5563
E-Mail: elanel@gwpinc.com
Web Site: www.gwpinc.com

E-Mail for Key Personnel:
Creative Dir.: tcryan@gwpinc.com

Employees: 12
Year Founded: 1991

National Agency Associations: APMA WORLDWIDE

Agency Specializes In: Advertising, Advertising Specialties, Affluent Market, Alternative Advertising, Below-the-Line, Brand Development & Integration, Branded Entertainment, Broadcast, Business Publications, Business-To-Business, Cable T.V., Catalogs, Co-op Advertising, Collateral, College, Consulting, Consumer Goods, Consumer Marketing, Consumer Publications, Corporate Communications, Customer Relationship Management, Digital/Interactive, Direct Response Marketing, Direct-to-Consumer, Event Planning & Marketing, Exhibit/Trade Shows, Experience Design, Financial, Game Integration, Graphic Design, Guerilla Marketing, Health Care Services, Identity Marketing, In-Store Advertising, Infomercials, Integrated Marketing, International, Local Marketing, Logo & Package Design, Magazines, Media Buying Services, Media Planning, Media Relations, Medical Products, Mobile Marketing, Multimedia, New Product Development, New Technologies, Newspaper, Newspapers & Magazines, Out-of-Home Media, Outdoor, Over-50 Market, Package Design, Paid Searches, Pharmaceutical, Planning & Consultation, Point of Purchase, Point of Sale, Print, Product Placement, Production, Production (Ad, Film, Broadcast), Production (Print), Promotions, Publicity/Promotions, Radio, Recruitment, Retail, Sales Promotion, Search Engine Optimization, Seniors' Market, Sponsorship, Strategic Planning/Research, Sweepstakes, T.V., Teen Market, Transportation, Urban Market, Viral/Buzz/Word of Mouth, Web (Banner Ads, Pop-ups, etc.), Women's Market

Approx. Annual Billings: $5,535,000

Breakdown of Gross Billings by Media: Event Mktg.: $75,000; Graphic Design: $200,000; Internet Adv.: $600,000; Logo & Package Design: $100,000; Newsp. & Mags.: $50,000; Plng. & Consultation: $1,500,000; Promos.: $1,500,000; Radio & T.V.: $1,500,000; Spot T.V.: $10,000

Eric Lanel *(Pres)*
Michelle Lewis *(Gen Mgr)*

Accounts:
beano
Cold Stone Creamery; Englewood, NJ
GlaxoSmithKline; Parsippany, NJ Beano, Contac, Ecotrin, Gaviscon, Phazyme, Polident, Tagamet, Viverin
HON Corp.
Polident
Wayne Tile; Wayne, NJ Tile

GYKANTLER

(Formerly Griffin York & Krause)
121 River Front Dr, Manchester, NH 03102
Tel.: (603) 625-5713
Fax: (603) 222-2329
Web Site: gykantler.com/

Employees: 50
Year Founded: 1974

Agency Specializes In: Consumer Marketing, Government/Political, High Technology, Public Relations, Strategic Planning/Research

Approx. Annual Billings: $20,000,000 Fees Capitalized

Travis York *(Pres & CEO)*
Brady Sadler *(Exec VP-Growth & Innovation)*
Sophia Cigliano *(Sr VP & Client Svcs Dir)*
Elaine S. Krause *(Sr VP & Dir-Creative)*
Nancy Boyle *(Sr VP-Creative Svcs)*
Evan York *(VP & Dir-Reporting & Analytics)*
Dustin Ruoff *(Dir-IT)*
Samantha J. Mahoney *(Acct Supvr)*
Heather Whitney *(Coord-Media)*

Accounts:
Bear Lake Reserve
Bensonwood Homes
Centex Destination Properties
Citizens Bank
Cruiserworks, L.L.C.
CW Capital
Devine Millimet
ECHN
Globe Manufacturing
Home Hill Inn
Inns & Spa at Mill Falls
Lindner Dental Associates PC
Meredith Harley Davidson
New Hampshire Coalition on Domestic & Sexual Violence
New Hampshire Lottery Public Gaming
South Peak Resort
St. Joseph Hospital
St. Mary's Bank
Stop & Shop
Story Land
Tri-State Lottery Commission Public Gaming
Westbridge Community Services

Branches

GYK Antler

181 South St, Boston, MA 02111
Tel.: (617) 423-0011
Fax: (617) 423-0009
Web Site: gykantler.com

Agency Specializes In: Digital/Interactive, Event Planning & Marketing, Experience Design, Social Media

Michael Wachs *(Chief Creative Officer)*
Brian Costello *(Chief Digital Officer)*
Matthew Doyle *(Exec VP-Brdcst Production)*
Brian Gladstein *(Exec VP-Tech Mktg)*
Brady Sadler *(Exec VP-Growth & Innovation)*
Shana Malik *(VP-Integrated Media)*
Kate Montanile *(Acct Dir)*
Tina Yanuszewski *(Dir-HR)*
Jackie Bourque *(Mgr-User Experience)*
Kelsey Benjamin *(Acct Exec)*
Amber Provenzano *(Sr Media Planner)*

Accounts:
Magners Irish Cider

GYRO

31 W 27th St, New York, NY 10001

Tel.: (212) 915-2490
Fax: (212) 915-2491
Web Site: www.gyro.com

Employees: 550
Year Founded: 1981

National Agency Associations: AAF-ANA-BMA-DMA-IAB-IPA-MCA-PRSA

Agency Specializes In: Above-the-Line, Advertising, Advertising Specialties, Affiliate Marketing, Affluent Market, Agriculture, Arts, Aviation & Aerospace, Below-the-Line, Brand Development & Integration, Broadcast, Co-op Advertising, Collateral, Commercial Photography, Communications, Computers & Software, Consulting, Consumer Goods, Consumer Marketing, Consumer Publications, Content, Corporate Communications, Corporate Identity, Crisis Communications, Custom Publishing, Customer Relationship Management, Digital/Interactive, Direct Response Marketing, Direct-to-Consumer, Education, Electronic Media, Electronics, Email, Engineering, Environmental, Event Planning & Marketing, Exhibit/Trade Shows, Experience Design, Financial, Food Service, Government/Political, Graphic Design, Health Care Services, High Technology, Hispanic Market, Household Goods, Identity Marketing, In-Store Advertising, Industrial, Information Technology, Integrated Marketing, International, Internet/Web Design, Investor Relations, Leisure, Local Marketing, Logo & Package Design, Luxury Products, Magazines, Market Research, Media Buying Services, Media Planning, Media Relations, Media Training, Medical Products, Merchandising, Mobile Marketing, New Product Development, New Technologies, Newspaper, Out-of-Home Media, Outdoor, Package Design, Paid Searches, Pharmaceutical, Planning & Consultation, Podcasting, Point of Purchase, Point of Sale, Print, Product Placement, Production, Production (Ad, Film, Broadcast), Production (Print), Promotions, Public Relations, Publicity/Promotions, Publishing, RSS (Really Simple Syndication), Real Estate, Restaurant, Retail, Sales Promotion, Search Engine Optimization, Social Marketing/Nonprofit, Social Media, Sponsorship, Stakeholders, Strategic Planning/Research, T.V., Technical Advertising, Trade & Consumer Magazines, Transportation, Viral/Buzz/Word of Mouth, Web (Banner Ads, Pop-ups, etc.)

Approx. Annual Billings: $100,000,000

Keith Turco *(Pres & Gen Mgr)*
Christoph Becker *(CEO & Chief Creative Officer)*
Drew Meyers *(Pres-San Francisco)*
Christopher Hill *(Sr VP & Dir-Acct Mgmt)*
Paul Neal *(Sr VP-Global Bus Dev)*
Wendy Lurrie *(Mng Dir-Gyro Human)*
Vito Zarrillo *(Grp Dir-Creative)*
Paul Hackett *(Dir-Creative)*
Kenneth Hein *(Dir-Mktg-Global)*
Howard Herrarte *(Sr Art Dir)*
Richard Lefkowitz *(Dir-Connection Plng)*
Steve Mawhinney *(Dir-Creative)*
Heather Burmester *(Project Mgr-Digital)*
Semira Menghes *(Acct Supvr)*
Nicole Paladino *(Sr Acct Exec)*
Quarn Corley *(Designer)*
Anthony Chelette *(Assoc Creative Dir)*
Patrick O'Hara *(Chief Strategic Officer)*

Accounts:
Adobe
American Express
Audi
BlackBerry (Global Agency of Record) BlackBerry Passport, Campaign: "Work Wide", Enterprise Software & Services
BT
Cannon
DAF
Delta Airlines
Federal Express Pan-European Integrated
Fidelity
First Data
Forbes Campaign: "Change the World"
Fujitsu
GE
Google
ITT
John Deere Campaign: "You're On Trade Show"
Kelloggs
Kennametal
LifeCell Brand Identity
Mobile
Oracle
Panasonic
Polk
Polyphony Campaign: "You Can't Hear Our Differences"
PotashCorp
Shell
Sky
Sony
Tetra Pak Campaign: "Perfectly Squared"
Time Inc. (Agency of Record) Brand Positioning, Campaign: "Open the Experience", Outdoor
Turn Creative
United Stationers
UPS
USG Corporation Campaign: "The Weight Has Been Lifted"
Virgin Atlantic
William Grant & Sons Grant's

Branches

Gyro Amsterdam
(Formerly GyroHSR Amsterdam)
Peperstraat 7, 1011 TJ Amsterdam, Netherlands
Tel.: (31) 203 209 799
E-Mail: michelle.henley@gyro.com
Web Site: www.gyro.com/#/contact-us-now/everywhere/amsterdam/

Michelle Henley *(Mng Dir & Exec Dir-Creative)*

Accounts:
Adobe
First Data
Genencor
Google
Hi-Tec
NXP
Oracle
SKY
Sony
T Mobil
USG

Gyro Cincinnati
(Formerly GyroHSR Cincinnati)
7755 Montgomery Rd Ste 300, Cincinnati, OH 45236
(See Separate Listing)

Branches

Gyro Denver
1625 Broadway Ste 2800, Denver, CO 80202
(See Separate Listing)

GyroHSR Chicago
20 W Kinzie Ste 1400, Chicago, IL 60654
Tel.: (312) 595-0203
Fax: (312) 595-0212
Web Site: www.gyro.com

Employees: 40

Agency Specializes In: Sponsorship

Brian Peters *(Pres & Dir-Creative)*
Mike Hensley *(Exec VP & Gen Mgr)*
Mark Witthoefft *(Head-Plng)*
Dan Fergus *(Grp Dir-Creative)*
Paul Brusatori *(Grp Acct Dir)*
Casey Bright *(Acct Dir)*
Wendy Klein *(Acct Dir)*
Matt Ritondaro *(Assoc Dir-Creative)*
Ken Wagner *(Acct Supvr)*
Lindsay Wagner *(Asst Media Buyer & Planner)*

Accounts:
American Express
Canon
Cars.com Campaign: "Before it's Too Late", Print Ads
John Deere Campaign: "You're On"
Kimberly-Clark
Oracle
Sanofi Pasteur
Sony
USG Corp Brand Awareness, Campaign: "It's Your World. Build It", Online Video, Social Media

Gyro Paris
(Formerly GyroHSR Paris)
38 bis rue du fer a Moulin, 75005 Paris, France
Tel.: (33) 1 55 43 50 00
E-Mail: paris@gyro.com
Web Site: www.gyro.com

Employees: 15

Didier Stora *(Pres & Gen Mgr)*
Sebastien Zanini *(Exec Dir-Creative)*
Evelyne Bourdonne *(Dir-Strategic Plng)*
Berengere Bonfils *(Sr Acct Mgr)*
Marion Lasselin *(Acct Exec)*
Margaux Castanier *(Copywriter)*
Marc Sinegre *(Copywriter)*

Accounts:
Adobe
American Express
Canon
Credit Foncier
Google
New-Oxford The Flying Notebooks
Pitney Bowes
Playstation 3
T-Mobile US
Virgin Atlantic
New-ZEISS Vision Care ZEISS DriveSafe Lenses

Gyro
1025 Sansome St, San Francisco, CA 94111
(See Separate Listing)

maxIIGyroHSR
Munich Lindwurmstr 76, 80337 Munich, Germany
Tel.: (49) 89 76 77 34 0
Fax: (49) 89 76 77 34 70
Web Site: www.gyro.com/#/contact-us-now/everywhere/munich/

Employees: 15

Claudia Leischner *(Pres & Gen Mgr)*
Jurgen Muller-Nedebock *(Exec Dir-Creative)*

Accounts:
Neff

GYRO CINCINNATI
(Formerly GyroHSR Cincinnati)
7755 Montgomery Rd Ste 300, Cincinnati, OH 45236
Tel.: (513) 671-3811

Fax: (513) 671-8163
Toll Free: (800) 243-2648
Web Site: www.gyro.com

Employees: 130
Year Founded: 1981

National Agency Associations: AAF-BMA-DMA-PRSA

Agency Specializes In: Advertising, Aviation & Aerospace, Brand Development & Integration, Business-To-Business, Corporate Identity, Digital/Interactive, Direct Response Marketing, Engineering, Financial, Food Service, Health Care Services, High Technology, Industrial, Information Technology, Internet/Web Design, Legal Services, Marine, Medical Products, Pharmaceutical, Public Relations, Sponsorship, Technical Advertising, Trade & Consumer Magazines, Transportation

Adryanna Sutherland *(Pres-Cincinnati)*
Jon Schneider *(Acct Dir)*
Scott Emond *(Dir-Creative)*
Preeti Thakar *(Dir-Engagement)*
Francis McCoy *(Project Mgr-Digital)*
Maura Pearson *(Acct Exec)*
Margot Richey *(Acct Exec)*
Michael Kochersperger *(Designer)*
Lindsay Wagner *(Media Planner)*
Ashley Frondorf *(Asst Media Buyer)*

Accounts:
AK Steel; 1994
Avaya (Agency of Record) "Avaya Stadium Shootout", Branding, Out-of-Home
Baker Hughers INTEQ; 2006
BCB Holdings Limited
Cincinnati Bell; 1998
Contech; 2003
Convergys; 1999
Deere & Company
Delta Dental
Dymo Labeling Identification Solutions Creative, Media Planning & Buying, Strategic Planning
Fidelity Investments
Flowserve Corporation; 2006
Johns Manville Corporation
Kellogg's; 2006
Kennametal Inc.
Magnode Corporation; 1981
Makino, Inc.; 1992
Nucor Steel
Pall Corporation; 1998
Pitney Bowes; 2007
SAP
Scotsman Ice
SHP Design; 1983
Tate & Lyle Campaign: "Believe It", Creative, Dolcia Prima, Media, Online Advertising, Online Videos, PR, Print
TE Connectivity Ltd.
USG Corporation Sheetrock; 2006

GYRO DENVER

1625 Broadway Ste 2800, Denver, CO 80202
Tel.: (303) 294-9944
Fax: (303) 294-9997
Toll Free: (800) 243-2648
E-Mail: daphne.fink@gyro.com
Web Site: www.gyro.com/

Employees: 20
Year Founded: 1988

National Agency Associations: BMA-INBA

Agency Specializes In: Advertising, Automotive, Brand Development & Integration, Business Publications, Business-To-Business, Cable T.V., Collateral, Communications, Consulting, Corporate Identity, Direct Response Marketing, E-Commerce, Electronic Media, Engineering, Event Planning & Marketing, Exhibit/Trade Shows, Graphic Design, High Technology, Industrial, Internet/Web Design, Logo & Package Design, Magazines, Media Buying Services, New Product Development, Newspaper, Newspapers & Magazines, Outdoor, Planning & Consultation, Point of Purchase, Point of Sale, Print, Production, Public Relations, Publicity/Promotions, Sales Promotion, Sports Market, Strategic Planning/Research, Technical Advertising, Transportation, Travel & Tourism

Approx. Annual Billings: $20,000,000

Breakdown of Gross Billings by Media: Bus. Publs.: 8%; Collateral: 32%; D.M.: 2%; Fees: 20%; Pub. Rels.: 10%; Sls. Promo.: 25%; Trade Shows: 3%

Frank Garamy *(VP-Technical Plng)*
Andy Duttlinger *(Art Dir)*
Andy Mamott *(Creative Dir)*
Robert Tucker *(Mgmt Supvr)*
Nancy Casey *(Dir-Studio)*
Kim Lauersdorf *(Dir-Strategic)*
Heather Burmester *(Project Mgr-Digital)*
Kari Wiens *(Acct Supvr)*
Justin Horrigan *(Sr Copywriter)*

Accounts:
DCP Midstream
Ice-O-Matic
Johns Manville Commercial & Industrial Division; Denver, CO Mechanical Insulations & Air Handling Products; 1988
Johns Manville Corporate Relations; Denver, CO Corporate Brand Management; 1998
Johns Manville Roofing Systems; Denver, CO Commercial & Industrial Products & Systems; 1988
Milliken & Co
Tw Telecom
Vubiquity (Global Agency of Record) Brand Positioning, Design
WOW!

H&K GRAPHICS

8374 Market St Ste 489, Bradenton, FL 34202
Tel.: (941) 758-2200
Fax: (941) 758-0400
Toll Free: (800) 345-2439
E-Mail: bill@hkgraphicsinc.com
Web Site: www.hkgraphicsinc.com

Employees: 2
Year Founded: 1989

Agency Specializes In: Newspapers & Magazines

Breakdown of Gross Billings by Media: Adv. Specialities: 10%; Mags.: 10%; Newsp.: 70%; Print: 10%

William T. Kalter *(Owner)*
Janet Heller *(Exec VP)*

Accounts:
AJ Willner & Co. Auctions; 1994
David Gary; 2003
Destiny Auctions
Perillo Auctions; 1994
TSD Advanced Personnel; 1999

H&L PARTNERS

(Formerly Hoffman/Lewis)
353 Sacramento St 21st Fl, San Francisco, CA 94111
Tel.: (415) 434-8500
Fax: (415) 544-4151
Web Site: www.handlpartners.com

Employees: 85
Year Founded: 1985

National Agency Associations: 4A's-AMIN

Agency Specializes In: Advertising, Direct Response Marketing, Hispanic Market, Media Buying Services, Planning & Consultation

Approx. Annual Billings: $120,000,000

Breakdown of Gross Billings by Media: Bus. Publs.: $1,200,000; Cable T.V.: $10,800,000; Consumer Publs.: $3,600,000; D.M.: $1,200,000; Fees: $3,600,000; Internet Adv.: $4,800,000; Newsp.: $9,600,000; Outdoor: $12,000,000; Production: $14,400,000; Radio: $20,400,000; Spot T.V.: $38,400,000

Josh Nichol *(Pres)*
Andrea Alfano *(Partner & COO)*
Mark Manion *(Partner, Sr VP & Dir-Creative-St Louis)*
Michael Convey *(CFO)*
Mark Schaeffer *(Pres-St Louis)*
Trey Curtola *(Exec VP)*
Sue Ream *(Sr VP & Dir-Media)*
Tyler Martin *(VP & Client Svcs Dir)*
Maribel Orozco *(VP & Dir-Multicultural Mktg)*

Accounts:
McDonald's Co-ops; San Francisco Bay Area, CA, Saint Louis Metro Area, MO Campaign: "Good Morning", Regional Fast Food Advertising Cooperative
Missouri Division of Tourism Campaign: "Enjoy the Show", Campaign: "Show-Me State", Travel/Tourism
Oakland Museum of California
Saint Louis Convention & Visitors Commission; Saint Louis, MO Campaign: "The Meeting Guru", Travel/Tourism
San Francisco Bulls
Touchston Energy; Arlington, VA Energy Cooperative
Toyota; Northern California, CA Auto Dealer Association
University of Southern California (USC)

Branch

H&L Partners

(Formerly Hoffman/Lewis)
30 Maryland Plz, Saint Louis, MO 63108-1526
Tel.: (314) 454-3400
Web Site: www.handlpartners.com

E-Mail for Key Personnel:
President: mschaeffer@handlpartners.com
Creative Dir.: mmanion@handlpartners.com
Media Dir.: tmartin@hoffmanlewis.com

Employees: 30
Year Founded: 2001

National Agency Associations: 4A's-AMIN

Agency Specializes In: Advertising, Direct Response Marketing, Hispanic Market, Media Buying Services, Sponsorship

Mark Schaeffer *(Pres-St Louis)*
Mark Manion *(Sr VP & Dir-Creative)*
Tyler Martin *(VP & Client Svcs Dir)*
Chris Kilcullen *(VP & Dir-Digital)*
Shaun Young *(Sr Dir-Interactive Art)*
John Weller *(Acct Dir)*
Peter Boggeman *(Acct Exec)*
Jennifer Evans *(Specialist-Client Acct Billing)*
Matt Kinsell *(Media Planner)*

Accounts:
CPC Logistics; 2012
McDonald's Advertising Co-op of Saint Louis Campaign: "Unexpected Moments", McDonald's Breakfast, QSR; 2001
McDonald's Corporation
Mercy Health Branding, Service Line Marketing; 2011

Missouri Division of Tourism State Tourism; 2006
Phillips Furniture Home furnishing retail; 2004
Saint Louis Convention & Visitors Commission Destination Tourism; 2006
Tacony Corporation Maytag Vacuums; 2012
Touchstone Energy Cooperatives Electric energy to rural America; 2008

H+A INTERNATIONAL, INC.

70 E Lake St Ste 1220, Chicago, IL 60601
Tel.: (312) 332-4650
Fax: (312) 332-3905
E-Mail: gpedroni@h-a-intl.com
Web Site: www.h-a-intl.com

Employees: 12
Year Founded: 1984

Agency Specializes In: Advertising, Brand Development & Integration, Communications, Direct Response Marketing, Email, International, Internet/Web Design, Local Marketing, Print, Public Relations, Publicity/Promotions

Beate Halligan *(Pres)*
Roger Halligan *(CEO)*
Tim Ward *(Dir-Accounts & Social Media)*

Accounts:
CMM International
Craft Hobby Trade Shows
Emergency Response Conference & Expo
International Home & Housewares Show

H+M COMMUNICATIONS

8648 Holloway Plaza Dr, West Hollywood, CA 90069
Tel.: (310) 289-5066
Fax: (310) 289-5068
Web Site: www.hm-com.com

Year Founded: 2003

Agency Specializes In: Advertising, Crisis Communications, Digital/Interactive, Event Planning & Marketing, Graphic Design, Media Buying Services, Media Planning, Media Relations, Media Training, Social Media

Inma Carbajal-Fogel *(Partner & Exec VP)*
Etienne Hernandez-Medina *(Pres & CEO)*

Accounts:
New-Comcast

H2R AGENCY

5106 Lebsack Ln, Loveland, CO 80537
Tel.: (720) 226-3229
E-Mail: findoutmore@h2ragency.com
Web Site: www.h2ragency.com

Agency Specializes In: Advertising, Brand Development & Integration, Internet/Web Design, Radio, Strategic Planning/Research, T.V.

Ivy Cooper-Rice *(Pres)*
Rick Harshman *(CEO)*
Steve Hammond *(Exec Dir-Creative)*

Accounts:
Treasure Bay Casino & Hotel

H3O COMMUNICATIONS

171 2nd St Ste 500, San Francisco, CA 94105
Tel.: (415) 618-8800
E-Mail: info@h3ocommunication.com
Web Site: www.h3ocommunications.com

Agency Specializes In: Advertising, Digital/Interactive, Graphic Design, Media Planning, Media Relations, Print, Public Relations, Search Engine Optimization, Social Media

Kristen Sharbaugh *(Sr VP)*

Accounts:
New-ChimpChange

HAAN MARKETING & COMMUNICATIONS

(Name Changed to Dearing Group)

HABERMAN & ASSOCIATES, INC.

119 N 4th St Ste 301, Minneapolis, MN 55410
Tel.: (612) 338-3900
Fax: (612) 338-4844
E-Mail: mail@modernstorytellers.com
Web Site: www.modernstorytellers.com/

Employees: 30

Fred Haberman *(Co-Founder & CEO)*
Sarah Haberman *(Co-Founder)*
Brian Wachtler *(Mng Partner)*
Sunny Fenton *(Dir-Bus Dev)*
Katlyn Daoust *(Acct Mgr)*
Megan Mell *(Acct Mgr)*
Adam Benscoter *(Acct Supvr)*
Claudine Galloway *(Acct Supvr)*
Rachel Gray *(Acct Supvr)*
Jessica Snell *(Acct Supvr)*

Accounts:
Amery Regional Medical Center Brand
The August Schell Brewing Company Campaign: "We are German Craft", Digital, Outdoor, Print, Radio
Biogenic Reagents Infographics Development, Marketing Communications
Earthbound Farm Organic Digital, PR, Social, Website
Gearworks
GO Veggie! Public Relations
Late July Organic Snacks Social Marketing
LeafLine Labs (Agency of Record) Communication, Marketing, Public Relations, Website
Parent Aware for School Readiness
Prana Event Planning, Marketing Planning, PR, Social
Traditional Medicinals "Plant Power Journal", Brand Publishing, Campaign: "Plant Power For A Better You", Communications, Content Marketing, Digital, Media Buying, Online, Print Advertising, Public Relations, Social Media
Volvo Cars of North America

HADELER KRUEGER

(Formerly SKSW)
1255 W 15th St Ste 500, Plano, TX 75075
Tel.: (972) 424-3000
Fax: (972) 424-3011
E-Mail: info@hadelerkrueger.com
Web Site: www.hadelerkrueger.com

Employees: 13
Year Founded: 1996

Agency Specializes In: Advertising, Automotive, Brand Development & Integration, Business-To-Business, Cable T.V., Catalogs, Collateral, Corporate Identity, Direct-to-Consumer, E-Commerce, Exhibit/Trade Shows, Graphic Design, Integrated Marketing, Internet/Web Design, Local Marketing, Over-50 Market, Point of Purchase, Point of Sale, Print, Production, Production (Print), Promotions, Radio, Seniors' Market, Trade & Consumer Magazines

Approx. Annual Billings: $5,000,000

Janice Krueger *(Founder & Owner)*
David Hadeler *(Pres)*
Bill Krueger *(Partner & Dir-Interactive Svcs)*
Eric Brule *(Dir-Art)*
Kimberly Smith *(Dir-Creative)*
Tony Stubbs *(Dir-Creative)*

Accounts:
ADW Corporation
Beta Land Services
CorePLUS; Dallas, TX On-demand Hardware & Software; 2011
Daikin AC; Irving, TX HVAC Products; 2011
Distribaire
Eagle Land Services; Dallas, TX Landman Services; 2007
Essilor; Dallas, TX Eyeglass Lens; 2011
M-Pak
Novation; Dallas, TX Group Purchasing; 2007
Smart Sales
Time Warner; Dallas, TX Cable & Internet Services; 2006
Tour & Andersson; Dallas, TX Balancing Valves; 2008
True Brew; Plano, TX Organic Tea & Fruit Juices; 2011
ViewPoint Bank; Plano, TX; 2011

HADFIELD COMMUNICATIONS

8313 Rio Grande Street, Houston, TX 77040
Tel.: (281) 900-8649
Fax: (888) 373-0165
E-Mail: info@hadfield.net
Web Site: www.hadfield.net

Employees: 8
Year Founded: 1993

Agency Specializes In: Advertising, Advertising Specialties, Brand Development & Integration, Business-To-Business, Co-op Advertising, Collateral, Commercial Photography, Consumer Marketing, Consumer Publications, Corporate Identity, Direct Response Marketing, E-Commerce, Event Planning & Marketing, Exhibit/Trade Shows, Graphic Design, In-Store Advertising, Internet/Web Design, Local Marketing, Logo & Package Design, Point of Purchase, Point of Sale, Print, Production, Public Relations, Publicity/Promotions, Radio, Restaurant, Sales Promotion, Strategic Planning/Research, Trade & Consumer Magazines

Approx. Annual Billings: $1,000,000

Breakdown of Gross Billings by Media: Comml. Photography: $100,000; Graphic Design: $750,000; Other: $100,000; Print: $50,000

Linda Hadfield *(Founder, Owner & CEO)*
Kelly Denney *(Mgr-Traffic)*

HADROUT ADVERTISING & TECHNOLOGY

195 W Nine Mile, Ferndale, MI 48220
Tel.: (313) 444-9323
E-Mail: info@hadrout.com
Web Site: www.hadrout.com

Employees: 10
Year Founded: 2004

Agency Specializes In: Advertising, Event Planning & Marketing, Internet/Web Design, Logo & Package Design, Outdoor, Print, Radio, Social Media

Maria Petrenko *(Founder & Dir-Creative)*
Nikita Goldberg *(CTO)*
Eduard Verkhoturov *(Dir-Networks)*
Ivan Petrenko *(Mgr-Ops-Russia)*
Maja Henderson *(Acct Exec-Chicago & Bosnia)*
Xenia Ivanova *(Acct Exec)*
Nedim Kunic *(Acct Exec)*
Terry Gorski *(Rep-Bus Dev)*

Accounts:
Academy of Russian Classical Ballet
Scribe Publishing Company

HAESE & WOOD MARKETING & PUBLIC RELATIONS
1223 Wilshire Blvd Ste 100, Santa Monica, CA 90403
Tel.: (310) 684-3626
Web Site: www.haesewood.com

Agency Specializes In: Advertising, Brand Development & Integration, Content, Crisis Communications, Media Relations, Public Relations, Social Media

Marilyn Haese *(Principal)*
Warren Cereghino *(Principal)*
Cat Nuwer *(Coord-Media)*

Accounts:
Orange County Transportation Authority

HAFENBRACK MARKETING & COMMUNICATIONS
15 W 4th St Ste 410, Dayton, OH 45402
Tel.: (937) 424-8950
Fax: (937) 424-8951
E-Mail: info@hafenbrack.com
Web Site: www.goupward.com/hafenbrack.html

Employees: 15

Agency Specializes In: Advertising

Revenue: $15,000,000

Dave Hafenbrack *(Pres & CEO)*
John Fimiani *(Partner & Dir-Brand & Strategy-Upward Brand Interactions)*
Pat Arrowood *(Mgr-Acctg)*
Margaret Schryver *(Designer)*

Accounts:
Ali Industries
Clark County Red Cross
F&S Harley
Hafenbrack Marketing
JatroDiesel
National Funeral Directors Association

HAGAN ASSOCIATES
(Formerly Kaza Hagan Associates)
1233 Shelburne Rd Ste C3, South Burlington, VT 05403-7753
Tel.: (802) 863-5956
Fax: (802) 864-8232
Web Site: haganmarketing.com/

Employees: 15
Year Founded: 1981

Agency Specializes In: Financial, Health Care Services, Travel & Tourism

Approx. Annual Billings: $8,000,000

Breakdown of Gross Billings by Media: Bus. Publs.: $400,000; D.M.: $400,000; Farm Publs.: $400,000; Mags.: $800,000; Newsp.: $4,000,000; Radio: $500,000; T.V.: $1,500,000

Paul Kaza *(Pres & Dir-Creative)*

Accounts:
Fletcher Allen Health Care
Vermont Symphony Orchestra

HAGGERTY & ASSOCIATES
12 Alfred St Ste 300, Woburn, MA 01801
Tel.: (781) 935-5220
Fax: (781) 935-1666
E-Mail: info@haggertycompanies.com
Web Site: www.haggertycompanies.com

E-Mail for Key Personnel:
President: thaggerty@haggertycompanies.com

Employees: 6
Year Founded: 1991

Agency Specializes In: Advertising, Automotive, Brand Development & Integration, Broadcast, Business Publications, Business-To-Business, Cable T.V., Co-op Advertising, Collateral, Communications, Consumer Marketing, Consumer Publications, Corporate Identity, Digital/Interactive, Direct Response Marketing, E-Commerce, Electronic Media, Entertainment, Environmental, Exhibit/Trade Shows, Financial, Food Service, Graphic Design, Health Care Services, High Technology, Industrial, Information Technology, Internet/Web Design, Logo & Package Design, Magazines, Media Buying Services, Medical Products, New Product Development, Newspaper, Newspapers & Magazines, Outdoor, Over-50 Market, Planning & Consultation, Point of Purchase, Point of Sale, Print, Production, Public Relations, Publicity/Promotions, Radio, Real Estate, Recruitment, Restaurant, Retail, Sales Promotion, Seniors' Market, Strategic Planning/Research, Sweepstakes, T.V., Technical Advertising, Trade & Consumer Magazines, Travel & Tourism, Yellow Pages Advertising

Approx. Annual Billings: $2,900,000

Breakdown of Gross Billings by Media: Bus. Publs.: $290,000; Collateral: $290,000; D.M.: $290,000; Mags.: $290,000; Newsp.: $290,000; Other: $290,000; Outdoor: $290,000; Pub. Rels.: $290,000; Radio: $290,000; T.V.: $290,000

Timothy F. Haggerty *(Pres)*
Rick Hydren *(Dir-Art)*
Michael A. McCullough *(Acct Exec-PR)*

Accounts:
AEA Technology, QSA Radiography Equipment Sales
American Environmental Hazardous Waste Clean Up
The Bank of Canton
Boston Financial Financial Management
Boyle Insurance Agency
Briar Restaurant Group Irish Restaurants & Pubs
Butler Bank
Century Financial Services Investment Services
Country Club Heights Senior Retirement Community
D.L. Maher Companies Environmental Drilling
Drs. Coakley & Trainor Dental Practice
E.B. Horn Company Jeweler
Elia Financial
The First National Bank of Ipswich Full-Service Community Bank
Franklin Park Zoo Metropolitan Zoo
Gables at Winchester Senior Retirement Community
Grandwireless Verizon Cellular Phone Services
Hendersons Wharf Inn & Residential Property
Heritage at Stoneridge
Leominster Credit Union
Longwood Place at Reading
McLaughlin Insurance Insurance Agency
Mulrenan Physical Therapy
Next Generation Network Electronic Media
Northern Bank & Trust Co. Commercial Savings Bank
ProEx Physical Therapy Full Service Wellness Center
River Bay Club Senior Retirement Community
Salem Five Boyle Insurance Services
Saugus Bank Full-Service Community Bank
Senior Retirement Community
Suffolk Downs Thoroughbred Racetrack
Sunrise Senior Living
Superior Friction Auto Disc Brakes
Technical Personnel Services Technical Placement Services
Whitehall Estates Senior Retirement Community
Winchester Hospital
Winchester Savings Bank Full-Service Savings Bank
Winn Management Company Property Management Services

HAGGMAN, INC.
39 Dodge St PMB 331, Beverly, MA 01915
Tel.: (978) 525-3742
Fax: (978) 525-4867
Web Site: www.haggman.com

E-Mail for Key Personnel:
President: eric@haggman.com

Employees: 12
Year Founded: 1991

Agency Specializes In: Advertising, Broadcast, Cable T.V., Co-op Advertising, Collateral, Consumer Marketing, Corporate Identity, Environmental, Financial, Food Service, Graphic Design, Health Care Services, Newspapers & Magazines, Outdoor, Public Relations, Publicity/Promotions, Radio, Restaurant, Strategic Planning/Research, T.V.

Breakdown of Gross Billings by Media: Newsp. & Mags.: 21%; Pub. Rels.: 10%; Radio: 19%; T.V.: 50%

Eric Haggman *(CEO & Dir-Creative)*
Emily F. Haggman *(Exec VP & Dir-Acct Svc)*
Ann Messenger *(VP & Sr Dir-Art)*
Alicia Crichton *(Sr Acct Dir)*
Linda Russo *(Sr Strategist-Mktg)*
Melissa Langdon *(Asst Bus Mgr & Coord-IT)*

Accounts:
Care New England; Providence, RI Hospitals & Services; 2000
CSG/NYSERDA; Westborough, MA Energy Star, Home Performance; 2000
Select Restaurants, Inc.; Cleveland, OH; 1994

HAGON DESIGN
72 St Leger St Ste 321, Kitchener, Ontario N2H 6R4 Canada
Tel.: (519) 954-9263
E-Mail: info@hagondesign.com
Web Site: www.hagondesign.com

Agency Specializes In: Advertising, Brand Development & Integration, Corporate Communications, Digital/Interactive, Exhibit/Trade Shows, Logo & Package Design, Print, Radio, Social Media, T.V.

Crystal Eagles *(Dir-Ops)*
Joshua Emberlin *(Sr Designer)*

Accounts:
Farrow Group

HAHN PUBLIC COMMUNICATIONS
(Formerly Hahn, Texas)
4315 Guadalupe St, Austin, TX 78751
Tel.: (512) 344-2010
E-Mail: info@hahntexas.com
Web Site: www.hahnpublic.com

E-Mail for Key Personnel:
President: jhahn@hahntexas.com

Employees: 16
Year Founded: 1991

Agency Specializes In: Brand Development & Integration, Public Relations, Sponsorship

Approx. Annual Billings: $3,000,000

Jeff Hahn *(Principal)*
Brian Dolezal *(VP)*
Russ Rhea *(VP-Media Svcs)*
Steve Lanier *(Controller)*
Amanda Blease *(Client Svcs Mgr)*
Ariadyn Hansen *(Client Svcs Mgr)*
Lauren Seegers *(Coord-Client Svcs)*
Caitlin Gooch *(Sr Client Svcs Mgr)*

Accounts:
Capital Metropolitan Transportation Authority
Catellus Commercial Group
Circuit of The Americas
Grande Communications
Samsung Semiconductor; Austin, TX
Seton Medical Group
Texas Commission of the Arts

HAKUHODO INCORPORATED

Akasaka Biz Tower 5-3-1 Akasaka, Minato-ku, Tokyo, 107-6322 Japan
Tel.: (81) 3 6441 6161
Fax: (81) 3 6441 6166
E-Mail: koho.mail@hakuhodo.co.jp
Web Site: www.hakuhodo.co.jp

Employees: 3,151
Year Founded: 1895

National Agency Associations: IAA-JAAA

Agency Specializes In: Above-the-Line, Advertising, Advertising Specialties, Affiliate Marketing, Affluent Market, African-American Market, Agriculture, Alternative Advertising, Arts, Asian Market, Automotive, Aviation & Aerospace, Below-the-Line, Bilingual Market, Brand Development & Integration, Branded Entertainment, Broadcast, Business Publications, Business-To-Business, Cable T.V., Catalogs, Children's Market, Co-op Advertising, Collateral, College, Commercial Photography, Communications, Computers & Software, Consulting, Consumer Goods, Consumer Marketing, Consumer Publications, Content, Corporate Communications, Corporate Identity, Cosmetics, Crisis Communications, Custom Publishing, Customer Relationship Management, Digital/Interactive, Direct Response Marketing, Direct-to-Consumer, E-Commerce, Education, Electronic Media, Electronics, Email, Engineering, Entertainment, Environmental, Event Planning & Marketing, Exhibit/Trade Shows, Experience Design, Fashion/Apparel, Financial, Food Service, Game Integration, Gay & Lesbian Market, Government/Political, Graphic Design, Guerilla Marketing, Health Care Services, High Technology, Hispanic Market, Hospitality, Household Goods, Identity Marketing, In-Store Advertising, Industrial, Infomercials, Information Technology, Integrated Marketing, International, Internet/Web Design, Investor Relations, Legal Services, Leisure, Local Marketing, Logo & Package Design, Luxury Products, Magazines, Marine, Market Research, Media Buying Services, Media Planning, Media Relations, Media Training, Medical Products, Men's Market, Merchandising, Mobile Marketing, Multicultural, Multimedia, New Product Development, New Technologies, Newspaper, Newspapers & Magazines, Out-of-Home Media, Outdoor, Over-50 Market, Package Design, Paid Searches, Pharmaceutical, Planning & Consultation, Podcasting, Point of Purchase, Point of Sale, Print, Product Placement, Production, Production (Ad, Film, Broadcast), Production (Print), Promotions, Public Relations, Publicity/Promotions, Publishing, RSS (Really Simple Syndication), Radio, Real Estate, Recruitment, Regional, Restaurant, Retail, Sales Promotion, Search Engine Optimization, Seniors' Market, Social Marketing/Nonprofit, Sponsorship, Sports Market, Stakeholders, Strategic Planning/Research, Sweepstakes, Syndication, T.V., Technical Advertising, Teen Market, Telemarketing, Trade & Consumer Magazines, Transportation, Travel & Tourism, Urban Market, Viral/Buzz/Word of Mouth, Web (Banner Ads, Pop-ups, etc.), Women's Market, Yellow Pages Advertising

Makoto Nakamura *(Sr Dir)*
Yusuke Ono *(Art Dir & Creative Dir)*
Shota Nakajima *(Art Dir)*
Ken Okamuro *(Art Dir)*
Tatsuya Saito *(Art Dir)*
Jorge Takahashi *(Bus Dir-Intl)*
Katsuhiko Suzuki *(Dir-Creative & Art)*
Muro Takeshi *(Dir-Investment & Mgmt Div)*
Koji Tonegashi *(Supvr-Kansai)*
Miwa Goroku *(Copywriter)*
So Kawaguchi *(Gen Producer)*

Accounts:
Acer Calendar
Adidas Campaign: "School Days Shoot"
Adobe Systems Co., Ltd. Campaign: "Font Me", Creative Cloud
Aipo Jspca
Asabiraki
The Asahi Shimbun Company Campaign: "Massaging Circulation"
The Big Issue Japan Campaign: "A Homeless Success Story"
Bureau Kikuchi Campaign: "Kikuchi Naruyoshi-Jazz"
Canon Marketing Japan Campaign: "Hollywood Dad", Campaign: "Ivis Do"
Dai Nippon Printing Campaign: "Reconstructed Kanji 'Ice, Snow'"
Dear Japan Project
Dmg Events Japan Campaign: "White Shadow"
Domino's Pizza Mobile Application
Eishin Foods Campaign: "Porxer - Fight for the King of Meat"
Flash Reproductions
Google Campaign: "Maps 8-Bit", Campaign: "Memories for the future", Campaign: "OK Go - All Is Not Lost"
Gucci Group
Gunze Campaign: "Bored"
Hanasake Nippon Campaign: "Drink for Tohoku", Campaign: "No Sake, No Life"
Hi-Chew Campaign: "Toothbrush Hero"
Hiroshima Peace Memorial Museum
Inakadate Village
Infas Publications, Inc.
Instant Pet House Animal Relief Headquarters
The Iwate Nippo Co Ltd. Campaign: "Nurse"
IWATTE Campaign: "Your Happy News Is Our Top Story"
J-dech
Japan Maritime Self Defense Forces Campaign: "Cheer for Move Project"
Jaxa Campaign: "Space Tanzaku"
JSPCA Campaign: "Relief Pet House"
Kagome
KDDI Corporation Campaign: "Puchi Puchi Earth", Campaign: "Ramen Mobile Championship"
Keihan Dentetsu
Kirin Brewery Company, Ltd.
Kodansha Campaign: "Social Bookmark"
Kose Corporation Campaign: "School Days Shoot", Campaign: "Shootter"
K's Japan Guitars SMASH: BORN TO BE DESTROYED
Laforet Museum Campaign: "All Is Made From Nature' Installation", Campaign: "Be Noisy.", Harajuku
match.com Campaign: "Takumi Match Project"
Meiji Co.
Mercedes Benz Co., Ltd Campaign: "NEXT A-Class"
Mitsubishi Motors Corporation Campaign: "I-Miev Nebuta Project"
Mitsui Real Estate
Molson Coors
Mori Building Tokyo City Symphony
Morinaga Milk Campaign: "Finishing"
NEC Mobiling Campaign: "And Market Brand Design"
Ni Consulting Co. Campaign: "Good-On-Paper Consultant"
Nissan Campaign: "Space Tanzaku"
Onward Holdings
Paby Campaign: "Parent & Baby Cam"
Panasonic Corporation Campaign: "Triathlon", Rechargeable Evolta Batteries, Vacuum Insulation
Recruit Co.
Relations Inc. Campaign: "Turntable Rider"
Samsonite Campaign: "Suitcase Guitar"
Samsung Electronics Japan Campaign: "Space Balloon Project", Campaign: "Word-Of-Mouth Can Be More Powerful"
Shiga Art School
Sony Japan Bravia
BRAVIA
Southern Comfort
Staff Service
S.T.Corporation
Subaru Campaign: "Proposal-Your Story With Subaru"
Sunshine Aquarium Penguin Navi
Suntory Holdings Limited Campaign: "Hibiki Glass"
Suntory Campaign: "Recycloop", Campaign: "Timeline Greening Banner", Mineral Water
Takasu Clinic Campaign: "Crabs"
Tokyo Metro Campaign: "Listen! Wonderground"
Tomita Shuzo Inc.
Toyota Campaign: "BIG SHARE ! Full version", Ractis
Uha Mikakuto
Utsunomiya City Office
Wacoal
WWD Japan
Yahoo!

Domestic Office:

Hakuhodo Inc. Kyushu Office

Hakata Riverain East Site 2-1 Shimokawabata-machi, Fukuoka, 812-0027 Japan
Tel.: (81) 92 263 4560
Fax: (81) 92 263 4555
E-Mail: go.mizushima@hakuhodo.co.jp
Web Site: www.hakuhodo.co.jp

Employees: 100
Year Founded: 1955

Junji Narita *(Chm & CEO)*

Affiliated & Subsidiary Companies

Digital Advertising Consortium, Inc.

Yebisu Garden Place Twr 33F 4-20-3 Ebisu, Shibuya-ku, Tokyo, 150-6033 Japan
Tel.: (81) 3 5449 6360
Fax: (81) 3 5449 6201
E-Mail: int-dac@dac.co.jp
Web Site: www.dac.co.jp

Employees: 400
Year Founded: 1996

Agency Specializes In: Consulting, Electronic Media, Media Buying Services, Strategic Planning/Research

Hirotake Yajima *(Pres & CEO)*

Akihiko Tokuhisa *(CMO)*
Hisaharu Terai *(Head-ASEAN Ops & Exec Dir)*
Yu Murakami *(Gen Mgr-Media Dept 3)*
Noriyuki Nagamatsu *(Gen Mgr-AD-Tech Laboratory)*
Kazuhiro Sunada *(Gen Mgr)*
Mitsuru Saito *(Sr Dir)*
Yoshihisa Nakagawa *(Mgr)*
Shuhei Ueda *(Mgr)*
Keita Mihara *(Supvr-Solutions Dev)*

Accounts:
Eyeblaster, Inc.
Mediba Inc.

Hakuhodo Erg, Inc.

11th Floor Hakata Riverain East Site 2-1 Shimokawabata-machi, Hakata-ku, Fukuoka, 812-0027 Japan
Tel.: (81) 92 263 3811
Fax: (81) 92 263 3819
E-Mail: info@hakuhodo-erg.co.jp
Web Site: www.hakuhodo.jp

Employees: 100
Year Founded: 1993

Agency Specializes In: Publicity/Promotions

Junji Narita *(Chm & CEO)*

Accounts:
Hotto Motto

Hakuhodo i-studio, Inc.

NBF Toyosu Gardenfront 9F 5-6-15 Toyosu, Koto-ku, Tokyo, 135-8621 Japan
Tel.: (81) 3 5144 7700
Fax: (81) 3 5144 7709
E-Mail: webmaster@i-studio.co.jp
Web Site: www.i-studio.co.jp

Employees: 240
Year Founded: 2000

Agency Specializes In: Digital/Interactive, Electronic Media, Internet/Web Design

Seiichi Hirabayashi *(Pres)*

Accounts:
Nissan Motor
Suntory Holdings Campaign: "Kuro Oolong Tea Burns Fat!"

Asia-Pacific

Cheil Worldwide Inc.

222 Itaewon-ro, Youngsan-gu, Seoul, Korea (South)
Tel.: (82) 2 3780 2114
Fax: (82) 2 3780 2483
E-Mail: webmaster@cheil.co.kr
Web Site: www.cheil.com

Employees: 883
Year Founded: 1973

Agency Specializes In: Corporate Identity, Media Buying Services, Sales Promotion

Keesoo Kim *(Pres & Head-Regional HQ)*
Nalla Chui Ping Chan *(Mng Dir)*
Neysa Horsburgh *(Mng Dir)*
Thoai Phan *(Mng Dir)*
Michael Kim *(Global COO)*
Lotta Malm Hallqvist *(Chief Growth Officer-Global)*
Peter Kim *(Chief Digital Officer)*
Volker Selle *(Pres/CEO-Cheil Germany)*
Shiv Sethuraman *(Grp Pres-Southwest Asia)*
Wiwat Taksinwarajan *(Deputy Mng Dir)*
Jeongkeun Yoo *(Exec VP)*
Claus Adams *(Sr VP-Cheil Central Europe-Cheil Germany GmbH)*
Andrew Swinton *(Mng Dir-Australia)*
Dong-Sik Kim *(VP)*
Arun Sharma *(VP-Integrated Strategic Plng)*
Monika Niechajewicz *(Head-Strategy)*
Kate Hyewon Oh *(Exec Dir-Creative)*
Navin Theeng *(Grp Dir-Creative)*
Hadley Newman *(Reg Dir)*
Joo-Mee Song *(Grp Acct Dir)*
Yeongkuk Kwon *(Creative Dir)*
Hyungkyun Oh *(Art Dir)*
Luke Ashton *(Dir-Creative-Global)*
Marc Mangi Baek *(Dir-Creative)*
Jasper Cho *(Dir-Art)*
Abhishek Gupta *(Dir-Digital Creative)*
Suntaeck Kim *(Dir-Art)*
Eunmin Lee *(Dir-Art)*
Joohoon Lee *(Dir-Creative)*
Moonkyo Lee *(Dir-Creative)*
Sunghoon Min *(Dir-Art)*
Narang Park *(Dir-Art)*
Dean Pinnington *(Dir-Creative-Global)*
Junggi Seo *(Dir-Art)*
Randy Woo *(Sr Acct Mgr)*
Seulah Sophia Yoo *(Acct Mgr)*
Yongjun Jung *(Copywriter)*

Accounts:
Amorepacific Dark Circle Brightener, White-e Toothpaste
Binggrae Campaign: "Banana flavored milk", Campaign: "Farm"
BR Korea Campaign: "Flavour Radio"
Burger King Campaign: "Breakfast Like a King", King Americano
Cj Cheiljedang Campaign: "Donating 2-Barcode Water"
CJ Entertainment Campaign: "Wi-Fi poster"
Deutsche Bahn Digital, Mobile Marketing Strategy
Dong-A Pharmaceutical Campaign: "Morning Care Investigation"
Dubai Electricity & Water Authority Strategic Planning & Communication
Dunkin Donuts Campaign: "Flavor Radio", Campaign: "Radio Spray"
Emart Campaign: "Sunny QR code", Campaign: "Sunny Sale", Flying Store
New-Etihad Airways Campaign: "Flying Reimagined", Digital
Hankook Tire Campaign: "Be One with It Winter"
Hi-mo
Home Plus
Hong Kong Disneyland
New-Ijota White
Korean Air
New-Korean Ministry of Unification Piano of Unification
KT Campaign: "Olleh Building With Feet"
L'Oreal Paris Campaign: "The L'Oreal My Girls Go Glam with Sonam", Casting Creme Gloss, Digital, Shopper Marketing, Social Media
Maeil Dairies Kobe Kitchen Range
Morning Care
NHN Campaign: "Me2Day 60Day Project"
Olympic Winter Games 2018; Pyeongchang, South Korea Logo Design
Oriental Brewery Campaign: "Beer Cocktail"
S-OiL Campaign: "Here Balloon"
Samsonite Korea Creative
Samsung Electronics "Look at Me", Billboards, Camera, Campaign: "#RideFor", Campaign: "#WinnerTakesEarth", Campaign: "All Created By Galaxynote", Campaign: "Be a Star", Campaign: "Be the Master of Payments", Campaign: "Bigger Forests", Campaign: "How to Share Smart - Insight", Campaign: "How to live smart - Smart Sticker", Campaign: "Minus One Project", Campaign: "Non Stop Life", Campaign: "The Match Part 1, Campaign: "The Match Part", Campaign: "The Match", Campaign: "WinnerTakesEarth", Galaxy, Galaxy 11, Galaxy Alpha, Galaxy Note, Galaxy S, Galaxy S5, Galaxy Tab S, Gear Circle Bluetooth Headset, Mobile Telephones & Pagers, Printers, S Health app, S6 Edge, Samsung AC, Samsung Galaxy S6, Samsung NX 200, Samsung Pay, Samsung SD
Samsung Life Insurance Campaign: "Bridge of Life", Campaign: "Just Once Again"
Samsung Tesco Homeplus, Retail, Supermarket
Shinhan Financial Group
UNHCR Refugee Exhibition Campaign: "Invisible People"
UNICEF
The Walt Disney Company Disney Fashion Stations/Stores, Disney Marvel, Disney Princess Academy, Planes, Shopper Marketing
Woongjin
Zaps Campaign: "Only Invisible In Your Eyes"

Foresight Research Co., Ltd.

11th Fl Rajapark Bldg 163 Sukhumvit 21, Klong-Toey-Nua Wattana, Bangkok, 10110 Thailand
Tel.: (66) 2 661 7788
Fax: (66) 2 661 6097
Web Site: www.hakuhodo.co.jp

Employees: 35

Agency Specializes In: Planning & Consultation, Strategic Planning/Research

Hakuhodo Hong Kong Ltd.

25th F Prosperity Mellennia Traza 663 Kings Road, North Point, China (Hong Kong)
Tel.: (852) 2865 1861
Fax: (852) 2865 0952
E-Mail: hakuhodo@hakuhodo.co.hk
Web Site: www.hakuhodo.jp

Employees: 40
Year Founded: 1988

Chan Carol *(Gen Mgr)*
Yutaka Shimizu *(Gen Mgr-HAKUHODO Dy Holdings)*
Gigi Ng *(Acct Dir)*
Lai Elsa *(Dir-Media)*
Lina Tun *(Dir-Creative)*
Lorell Pang *(Sr Acct Mgr)*
Yinwa Chan *(Sr Acct Exec)*
Kelly Lau *(Sr Acct Exec)*
Matthew Leung *(Sr Acct Exec)*
Tony Wong *(Sr Acct Exec)*

Accounts:
Kao Creative
Seiko Creative, Media, Media Planning & Buying, Strategic Planning

Hakuhodo & Saigon Advertising Co., Ltd.

10th Floor Room 6 Saigon Centre 65 Le Loi St, District 1, Ho Chi Minh City, Vietnam
Tel.: (84) 8 3825 0140
Fax: (84) 8 3825 0143
E-Mail: van.vu@hakuhodosac.com
Web Site: www.hakuhodo.jp

Employees: 30
Year Founded: 1995

Jiro Kuba *(Mng Dir)*
Phan Quynh *(Acct Dir)*
Ton Thien *(Acct Mgr)*
Do Hoang Linh Chi *(Sr Acct Exec)*
Phan An *(Copywriter)*

Hakuhodo Malaysia Sdn. Bhd.

9Fl Bldg A Peremba Square Saujana Resort Section U2, 40150 Kuala Lumpur, Shah Alam Selangor Malaysia

Tel.: (60) 3 7848 3384
Fax: (60) 3 7848 3385
E-Mail: admin@hakuhodo.com.my
Web Site: www.hakuhodo.com.my

Employees: 50
Year Founded: 1973

Toru Watanabe *(Mng Dir)*

Accounts:
Yaunco

Hakuhodo Percept Pvt. Ltd.
P22, Raghuvanshi Estate, 11/12, Senapati Bapat Marg, Lower Parel, Mumbai, 400 013 India
Tel.: (91) 22 -2491 1281
E-Mail: hakuhododelhi@hakuhodopercept.com
Web Site: www.perceptindia.in/hakuhodo_percept.html

Harindra Singh *(Vice Chm & Mng Dir)*
Elvis Sequeira *(COO)*
Pooja Malhotra *(Sr VP)*
Kosuke Kataoka *(Exec Dir)*
Shobhit Mathur *(Exec Dir-Creative)*
Sabuj Sengupta *(Exec Dir-Creative)*
Saurav Dasgupta *(Creative Dir)*
Jayanto Banerjee *(Dir-Plng-Natl)*
Ajay Chandwani *(Dir)*

Accounts:
Century Plyboards
Costa Coffee
Hindware
Line Campaign: "Katrina Kaif, Neighbour", Campaign: "Shopping", Campaign: "Stickers"
Maruti Suzuki Creative, Integrated Brand
Numero Uno Jeanswear Creative
Panasonic
Phive Rivers
New-Royzez.com
Sharp Mobile
New-Sheela Foam Group Creative, Sleepwell
Sony India Below-the-Line, Bravia Triluminos HD LED TV, Campaign: "Lets the Picture Say Much More", Campaign: "There is More to a Picture", Creative, Cyber-shot, Digital, Exmor R Sensors, Print, Xperia Z
Toshiba
Yakult Danone Creative

Hakuhodo Singapore Pte. Ltd.
111 Somerset Rd 12-01 Singapore Power Building, 238164 Singapore, Singapore
Tel.: (65) 6734 5451
Fax: (65) 6734 4489
Web Site: www.hakuhodo.co.jp

Employees: 35
Year Founded: 1974

Patrick Ng *(Grp Head-Creative & Sr Art Dir)*
Dinesh Sandhu *(Reg Dir-Touchpoints-SEA)*
Woon Hoh *(Reg Exec Dir-Creative)*
Tanner Nagib *(Reg Client Svc Dir)*
Jacky Wong *(Sr Art Dir)*

Accounts:
All Nippon Airlines
Biore UV Watery Essence OOH, Print, TV
Canon Campaign: "Struck a Chord at the Local Level", Canon EOS, Canon EOS M, Creative, Digital, Point-of-Sale, Print, TV
Daiken Toshiba
Seiko

MJW Hakuhodo
Level 5 The Frank Hurley Grandstand Driver Ave Fox Studios, Moore Park, Sydney, NSW 2021 Australia
Tel.: (61) 0285148300
Fax: (61) 2 8353 3444
E-Mail: paulm@mjwadvertising.com.au
Web Site: mjw.com.au

Employees: 14
Year Founded: 1946

National Agency Associations: AFA

Scott Davis *(Head-Strategy)*
Ricardo Larriera *(Gen Mgr)*
Tristan Hay *(Grp Acct Dir)*
Luke Chess *(Creative Dir)*
Jon Foye *(Art Dir)*

Accounts:
Beak & Sons
Kmart Tyre & Auto Campaign: "All Year Low Prices", Campaign: "Everyday Low Prices", Creative
Layby
Manassen Foods Pty. Ltd.; 1996
Mirabella
National Rugby League Campaign: "League Of Mums", Campaign: "Women in League", Online, Print, Radio, Social Media, TV
Nilfisk Campaign: "The Clean Way To Clean"
Stockland Retail
Stuart Alexander Campaign: "Colin", Fisherman's Friend
Valvoline

MJW Hakuhodo
Ste 2 Upper Deck Jones Bay Wharf, 26-32 Pirrama Road, Pyrmont, NSW 2009 Australia
Tel.: (61) 2 8514 8300
Web Site: mjw.com.au

Employees: 8
Year Founded: 1994

Paul Mckay *(CEO)*
Ricardo Larriera *(Gen Mgr)*
Linda Spina *(Acct Dir)*
Stephen Davis *(Dir-Client Svc)*

Accounts:
Biozet
Kao
Konica Minolta
Laughing Cow
Layby
NRL
Sharp
Trident
Vittel
Wokka

Europe

Hakuhodo France S.A.
59 bd Exelmans, 75016 Paris, France
Tel.: (33) 1 40 71 35 00
Fax: (33) 1 46 51 57 96
Web Site: www.hakuhodo.fr

Employees: 20
Year Founded: 1989

Masahiko Ilyama *(Sr Dir-Strategic Plng)*
Marc Desmazieres *(Dir-Creative)*

Southpaw Communications Ltd.
(Formerly Media by Design)
Multimedia House Hill Street, Tunbridge Wells, Kent TN1 2BY United Kingdom
Tel.: (44) 18 9251 7777
Fax: (44) 18 9251 7295
Web Site: www.southpawagency.com

Employees: 60
Year Founded: 1996

National Agency Associations: IPA-PPA

Agency Specializes In: Media Buying Services, Planning & Consultation

Abi Holden *(Grp Dir-Creative)*
Abi Day *(Grp Acct Dir)*
Amy Stewart *(Grp Acct Dir)*
Jo Cornford *(Acct Dir)*
Claire Lambell *(Acct Dir)*
Alex Ponsford *(Dir-Media & Comm)*
Katie Salt *(Sr Acct Mgr)*
Emma Porter *(Acct Mgr)*
Scott Wackett *(Mgr-Studio)*
Emily Simkins *(Sr Acct Exec)*
Kamran Akram *(Sr Designer)*

Accounts:
Callaway
Conde Nast
Cunald
Cunard
Daikin Air Conditioning
Honda
Konica Minolta
Mikimoto
SHARP Electronics
Suzuki Automobiles, Motorcycles

Southpaw
(Formerly Nexus/H Ltd.)
The Warehouse Hill Street, Tunbridge Wells, Kent TN1 2BY United Kingdom
Tel.: (44) 18 9251 7777
Fax: (44) 18 9251 6795
Web Site: www.southpawagency.com

Employees: 65

Tom Poynter *(Mng Dir)*
Abigail Day *(Grp Acct Dir)*
James Osborn *(Client Svcs Dir)*
Dan Harold *(Dir-Creative Svcs)*
Alex Ponsford *(Dir-Strategy & Investment)*
Craig Roderick *(Dir-Creative)*
Glenn Smith *(Dir-Creative)*

Accounts:
Autoglym Media Planning & Buying
Baskin Robbins Digital, Media, Social Media
Callaway Golf
Dunkin' Donuts Creative, Marketing
Hitachi
Honda
Japan Airlines Pan-European
Kobayashi
The Ladies European Tour Creative, The Solheim Cup
Mondial Assistance
SABMiller
Miller Genuine Draft Digital, Media Planning & Buying, Social Media
New-Sanctuary (Lead Strategic & Creative Agency) #LetGo
Sharp
Unipart Automotive Creative, Media, You'll Find Us Better

HALL & LIEN CREATIVE AGENCY
(Name Changed to Elevate Creative LLC)

HALL AND PARTNERS
711 3rd Ave 19th Fl, New York, NY 10017
Tel.: (212) 925-7844
Fax: (212) 343-1270
E-Mail: newyork@hall-and-partners.com
Web Site: www.hallandpartners.com

Employees: 50

Agency Specializes In: Advertising

Approx. Annual Billings: $1,000,000

Josh Shames *(Mng Partner)*
Laurie Slover Visee *(Partner)*
Albert Alcaraz *(Acct Dir)*
Nicole Citron *(Acct Dir)*
D. Erica Pascual *(Acct Dir)*
Jason Beltran *(Dir-Mktg)*
Matt Vicenzi *(Dir-Res)*
Rebecca Brown *(Acct Mgr)*
Kristy Lin *(Acct Mgr)*

HALLARON ADVERTISING

2202 Timberloch Pl Ste 128, The Woodlands, TX 77380
Tel.: (281) 299-0538
E-Mail: info@hallaronadvertising.com
Web Site: www.hallaronadvertising.com

Year Founded: 2003

Agency Specializes In: Advertising, Brand Development & Integration, Graphic Design, Internet/Web Design, Logo & Package Design, Media Planning, Radio, Social Media, T.V.

Megan McDonnell *(Mgr-Social Media)*

Accounts:
Allo French Rotisserie
Cotton Logistics
Ink Jet, Inc.
Red Tiger Security

HALLOCK & BRANCH

(Formerly Hallock Agency)
2445 NW Irving St, Portland, OR 97210
Tel.: (503) 224-1711
Fax: (503) 224-3026
E-Mail: jhallock@hallockagency.com
Web Site: www.hallockandbranch.com/

Employees: 6
Year Founded: 1959

Agency Specializes In: Government/Political, Health Care Services, Internet/Web Design, Real Estate, Restaurant, Retail, Travel & Tourism

Mike Branch *(Dir-Social Media & Website Dev)*

Accounts:
King Retail Solutions
Nodal Exchange
Oregon Zoo
The Portland

THE HALO GROUP

350 7th Ave 21st Fl, New York, NY 10001
Tel.: (212) 643-9700
Fax: (212) 871-0150
Toll Free: (888) 999-3313
E-Mail: info@thehalogroup.net
Web Site: thehalogroup.com

Employees: 30
Year Founded: 1994

National Agency Associations: DMA-PRSA

Agency Specializes In: Advertising, Affluent Market, Agriculture, Alternative Advertising, Aviation & Aerospace, Below-the-Line, Brand Development & Integration, Broadcast, Business Publications, Business-To-Business, Catalogs, Collateral, College, Communications, Computers & Software, Consulting, Consumer Goods, Consumer Marketing, Corporate Communications, Corporate Identity, Cosmetics, Digital/Interactive, Direct-to-Consumer, Education, Electronic Media, Electronics, Entertainment, Exhibit/Trade Shows, Experience Design, Fashion/Apparel, Financial, Food Service, Graphic Design, Guerilla Marketing, Health Care Services, High Technology, Hospitality, Household Goods, Industrial, Integrated Marketing, International, Internet/Web Design, Leisure, Local Marketing, Logo & Package Design, Luxury Products, Magazines, Market Research, Media Buying Services, Media Planning, Media Relations, Men's Market, Mobile Marketing, Multicultural, Multimedia, New Product Development, New Technologies, Newspaper, Newspapers & Magazines, Out-of-Home Media, Outdoor, Over-50 Market, Package Design, Paid Searches, Planning & Consultation, Podcasting, Point of Purchase, Point of Sale, Print, Production, Production (Print), Promotions, Public Relations, Publicity/Promotions, Radio, Recruitment, Restaurant, Sales Promotion, Search Engine Optimization, Social Media, Sports Market, Strategic Planning/Research, T.V., Trade & Consumer Magazines, Travel & Tourism, Viral/Buzz/Word of Mouth, Women's Market

Approx. Annual Billings: $31,000,000

Breakdown of Gross Billings by Media: D.M.: 2%; Internet Adv.: 41%; Newsp. & Mags.: 37%; Outdoor: 10%; Radio & T.V.: 10%

Denise Goodwin Pace *(Co-Founder, Partner & Chief Comm Officer)*
Tom Cunningham *(CMO)*
Michael Gambino *(Sr VP-Connection Plng)*
Michael Pierre *(Sr VP-Connection Plng)*
Toni Racioppo *(Sr VP-Media Svcs)*
Chris Barredo *(VP-Brand Strategy)*
Fran Alaimo *(Sr Media Buyer & Media Planner)*

Accounts:
Advertising and Marketing International Network
Bank of Smithtown; Smithtown, NY Community Bank; 2001
Flossy Shoes Social Media
Guy Carpenter; New York, NY Reinsurance; 2006
International Beverage USA Speyburn
Liebherr Refrigeration Campaign: "Splurge Wisely", Digital, PR, Print, Search Engine Optimization, Trade/Event Promotion, Website Design
Mount Airy Casino Resort
New-The New York Conservatory for Dramatic Arts
Retail Gaming Solutions Lottery Rewards
St. George's University Campaign: "One Small Change"; 1994
New-Toy Industry Association Branding, Paid Media, Public Relations, Social

HAMAZAKI WONG MARKETING GROUP

1155 Pender St W Ste 700, Vancouver, BC V6E 2P4 Canada
Tel.: (604) 669-8282
Fax: (604) 669-2288
E-Mail: aspire@hamazakiwong.com
Web Site: www.hamazakiwong.com

Employees: 10
Year Founded: 1989

Agency Specializes In: Advertising, Asian Market

William Wong *(Gen Mgr)*
Michael Wong *(Dir-Art)*
Lilian Chen *(Acct Mgr)*
Stewart Wong *(Mgr-Production)*
Theresa Chong *(Designer)*

Accounts:
Artspoints
The BMW Store
Coast Capital Savings
Dinosaurs Unearthed
OpenRoad Auto Group
Tropicana

HAMELIN MARTINEAU INC.

505 Maisonneuve Blvd W Ste 300, Montreal, QC H3A 3C2 Canada
Tel.: (514) 842-4416
Fax: (514) 844-9343
E-Mail: info@hamelin-martineau.ca
Web Site: www.hamelin-martineau.ca

Employees: 10
Year Founded: 1988

Agency Specializes In: Advertising, Business-To-Business, Graphic Design, Logo & Package Design, Media Buying Services, Media Planning, Public Relations, Strategic Planning/Research

Robert Martineau *(Owner)*
Diane Hamelin *(VP)*
Marie-Josee Bisaillon *(Dir-Art & Designer)*

Accounts:
Peak of Catering
Pilot Pens
Prescott SM
Reitmans
TD Insurance
TD Meloche Monnex

HAMILTON & BOND ADVERTISING INC.

3003 Foxmoor Dr, Montgomery, IL 60538-4091
Tel.: (630) 293-0071
E-Mail: information@hamiltonbond.com
Web Site: www.hamiltonbond.com

Employees: 5
Year Founded: 1984

National Agency Associations: BPA

Agency Specializes In: Business-To-Business, Communications, Digital/Interactive, E-Commerce, Internet/Web Design, Search Engine Optimization, Web (Banner Ads, Pop-ups, etc.)

Approx. Annual Billings: $4,000,000 Capitalized

Breakdown of Gross Billings by Media: Internet Adv.: 63%; Print: 37%

Marion L. Bond *(Owner)*

Accounts:
Cardwell Westinghouse; Chicago, IL
Chemical Waste Management
Chicago Clock Company
General Services Administration
NIS Group Co., Ltd
Universal Railway Devices, Inc.; Chicago, IL
WDCB
World Dryer Corporation
Worldwide Airline Customer Relations Association

HAMILTON COMMUNICATIONS GROUP, INC.

20 N Wacker Dr Ste 1960, Chicago, IL 60606
Tel.: (312) 321-5000
Fax: (312) 321-5005
E-Mail: badkins@hamiltongrp.com
Web Site: www.hamiltongrp.com

E-Mail for Key Personnel:
Production Mgr.: pboulware@hamiltongrp.com

Employees: 45
Year Founded: 1982

Agency Specializes In: Communications, Health Care Services

Approx. Annual Billings: $140,000,000

Breakdown of Gross Billings by Media: Mags.: $70,000,000; Newsp.: $70,000,000

James D. Lee *(Chief Strategy Officer & Principal)*
Penny Hart *(Sr Dir-Print & Digital Production)*
Rob Merk *(Dir-Creative & Art)*

Accounts:
Jazz Pharmaceuticals
medPointe
TAP
Vysis

HAMLYN SENIOR MARKETING
25 Chestnut St, Haddonfield, NJ 08033
Tel.: (856) 857-0800
Fax: (856) 857-0808
E-Mail: marketing@hamlynmarketing.com
Web Site: www.hamlynmarketing.com

Employees: 9
Year Founded: 2003

Agency Specializes In: Advertising, Collateral, Communications, Consumer Marketing, Direct Response Marketing, Event Planning & Marketing, Market Research, Media Buying Services, Media Relations, New Product Development, Newspaper, Over-50 Market, Print, Promotions, Publicity/Promotions, Radio, Real Estate, Sales Promotion, Seniors' Market, Strategic Planning/Research, Telemarketing, Yellow Pages Advertising

Approx. Annual Billings: $475,000

Breakdown of Gross Billings by Media: Collateral: 5%; D.M.: 60%; Event Mktg.: 10%; Graphic Design: 12%; Newsp. & Mags.: 13%

Catherine S. Martin *(Pres)*
Marybeth Vento *(Dir-Fin)*
Kathy Martin *(Fin Mgr)*

HAMMER CREATIVE
6311 Romaine St Ste 7316, Hollywood, CA 90038
Tel.: (323) 606-4700
Fax: (323) 463-8130
E-Mail: info@hammercreative.com
Web Site: www.hammercreative.com

Employees: 30
Year Founded: 1988

Agency Specializes In: Entertainment, Multimedia, Production (Ad, Film, Broadcast)

Breakdown of Gross Billings by Media: Production: 100%

Mark Pierce *(Founder & Pres)*
Scott Hayman *(Exec Dir-Creative)*
Austin Anderson *(Dir-Art)*
Brett Hocker *(Dir-Creative)*
Mike Berenson *(Sr Editor-Creative)*
Shane Free *(Sr Editor-Creative)*

Accounts:
Big Beach Films
EA Games
Ubisoft
Warner Independent Pictures

HAMMERQUIST STUDIOS
(Formerly Hammerquist Nebeker)
221 Yale Ave N, Seattle, WA 98109
Tel.: (206) 463-3714
Web Site: hammerquiststudios.com

Employees: 12
Year Founded: 2005

Fred Hammerquist *(Founder & Dir-Creative)*
Monica Gussow *(Sr Dir-Art & Designer)*
John Ide *(Dir-Art & Sr Designer)*
Keith Karlick *(Dir-Interactive)*
Brenda Rigor *(Sr Project Mgr & Acct Mgr)*
Alexis Oltman *(Sr Project Mgr-Interactive)*

Accounts:
Canadian Mountain Holidays
Diamondback Bicycles
eVent Fabrics
Heavenly Mountain Resort
Polartec
Sage Fly Fishing
Sea To Summit
SOG Knives
Taos Ski Valley

HAMPTON CREATIVE
3939 S Harvard Ave Ste 204, Tulsa, OK 74135
Tel.: (918) 877-5577
E-Mail: info@hamptoncreative.com
Web Site: www.hamptoncreative.com

Agency Specializes In: Advertising, Brand Development & Integration, Collateral, Digital/Interactive, Logo & Package Design, Media Buying Services, Media Planning, Package Design, Search Engine Optimization, Social Media

Piper Messimore *(CFO)*
Brian Cuff *(Dir-Digital Strategy)*
Christian Ensor *(Dir-Bus Dev)*
Brian Fowler *(Dir-Art)*
David Lichtenwalter *(Dir-Art)*
Stephen Posey *(Mgr-Relationship)*
Nate Olsen *(Designer)*

Accounts:
CherryBerry Enterprises LLC
In Touch Ministries

HANCOCK ADVERTISING AGENCY
PO Box 630010, Nacogdoches, TX 75963-0010
Tel.: (936) 564-9559
Fax: (936) 560-0845
E-Mail: info@hancockadvertising.com
Web Site: www.hancockadvertising.com

E-Mail for Key Personnel:
President: chris@hancockadvertising.com
Creative Dir.: lance@hancockadvertising.com

Employees: 10
Year Founded: 1973

National Agency Associations: AAF

Agency Specializes In: Advertising, Advertising Specialties, Brand Development & Integration, Broadcast, Business Publications, Business-To-Business, Cable T.V., Co-op Advertising, Collateral, Consulting, Corporate Identity, Direct Response Marketing, Electronic Media, Environmental, Financial, Graphic Design, Health Care Services, Internet/Web Design, Legal Services, Logo & Package Design, Magazines, Medical Products, Newspaper, Newspapers & Magazines, Outdoor, Public Relations, Publicity/Promotions, Radio, Restaurant, Sales Promotion, T.V., Trade & Consumer Magazines, Yellow Pages Advertising

Breakdown of Gross Billings by Media: Brdcst.: 10%; Exhibits/Trade Shows: 5%; Internet Adv.: 10%; Other: 20%; Outdoor: 10%; Production: 20%; T.V.: 20%; Trade Shows: 5%

Charles A. Hancock *(Owner)*
Lance Kitchen *(Dir-Art)*
Michele Flippen *(Office Mgr)*
Abigail Christensen *(Acct Exec)*
Claire Nelson *(Acct Exec)*

Accounts:
BBVA Bancorp
Citizens National Bank
First State Bank and Trust; Carthage
First State Bank; Central TX
Klaberg Bank
Legacy Texas National Bank

HANCOCK ADVERTISING GROUP, INC.
3300 N A Bldg 1 Ste 302, Midland, TX 79705-5356
Tel.: (432) 694-2181
Fax: (432) 694-2290
E-Mail: jdh@hancockgroup.net
Web Site: www.hancockgroup.net

Employees: 5
Year Founded: 1986

Agency Specializes In: Industrial, Retail

Valerie Hale *(Acct Mgr)*
Abby Christensen *(Acct Exec)*

Accounts:
First Capital
Manor Park Retirement Community
Rogers Ford; Midland, TX Autos; 1992

HANGAR 30 INC
4500 Cherry Creek Dr S Ste 1150, Denver, CO 80246
Tel.: (303) 990-8330
Fax: (303) 997-2170
E-Mail: info@hangar30.com
Web Site: www.hangar30.com

Year Founded: 2009

Agency Specializes In: Advertising, Brand Development & Integration, Internet/Web Design, Social Media, Strategic Planning/Research

Lucy Hansen *(Creative Dir)*
Jordan White *(Project Mgr-Technical)*

Accounts:
Air National Guard Ready54, The Wingman Project, Wingman Day
Mesa Verde Foundation

HANK - A DIGITAL PRODUCTION AGENCY
10 Pender St E Ste 202, Vancouver, BC V6A 1T1 Canada
Tel.: (604) 259-0330
Web Site: www.hankstudios.com

Employees: 8
Year Founded: 2011

Agency Specializes In: Advertising, Advertising Specialties, African-American Market, Asian Market, Bilingual Market, Brand Development & Integration, Branded Entertainment, Children's Market, Communications, Digital/Interactive, Direct Response Marketing, Electronic Media, Graphic Design, Hispanic Market, Integrated Marketing, Internet/Web Design, Logo & Package Design, Multicultural, Production (Ad, Film, Broadcast), Seniors' Market, South Asian Market, Strategic Planning/Research, Teen Market, Women's Market

Approx. Annual Billings: $1,400,000

Ayda Mehrjou *(Mgr-Fin)*

Accounts:
American Family Insurance Data-Driven Video

Creation; 2013
Caltech Surveys Website Redesign; 2013
EXAN Group Axium Dental Software; 2013
Future Shop futureshop.ca; 2013
Odlum Brown 90th Anniversary Video Presentation; 2012
Partnerships BC; 2013
Red Cross Japanese Tsunami Relief Video; 2011

HANLEY WOOD MARKETING
430 1st Ave N Ste 550, Minneapolis, MN 55401
Tel.: (612) 338-8300
Fax: (612) 338-7044
Web Site: www.hanleywoodmarketing.com

Agency Specializes In: Advertising, Brand Development & Integration, Content, Digital/Interactive, Email, Event Planning & Marketing, Internet/Web Design, Print, Social Media, Sponsorship

Frank Anton *(CEO)*
Matthew Flynn *(CFO)*
Ron Spink *(Pres-Design Grp)*
Paul Tourbaf *(Exec VP)*
Keith Rosenbloom *(VP & Corp Controller)*
Dan Colunio *(VP-Sls-Comml Design Grp)*
Trow Meier *(VP-Corp Sls)*
Jamie Volpe *(Sr Acct Dir-Strategic)*
Clare O'Dower *(Acct Dir-Strategic)*
Jeff Davis *(Dir)*
Melissa Gehrig *(Dir-Design)*
Ed Kraft *(Dir-Sls-Natl)*
Rohn Jay Miller *(Dir-Digital Strategy)*

Accounts:
The Sherwin-Williams Company

HANLON CREATIVE
1744 Sumneytown Pike, Kulpsville, PA 19443
Tel.: (267) 421-5755
Fax: (484) 466-0466
Web Site: www.hanloncreative.com

Year Founded: 2000

Agency Specializes In: Advertising, Broadcast, Digital/Interactive, Market Research, Media Buying Services, Media Planning, Print, Radio, Search Engine Optimization, T.V.

Andrew Hanlon *(Founder & Pres)*
Christopher Hanlon *(Founder & Dir-Creative)*
Toby Eberly *(VP-Mktg)*
Adam Garman *(VP-Interactive)*
Janet Hanlon *(Controller)*
Brian Loper *(Sr Dir-Art)*
Nicole Dimotsis *(Dir-Art)*
Michael Lees *(Dir-Print & Signage Mgmt Solutions)*
Michelle Thomas *(Dir-Art)*

Accounts:
Children's Hospital of Pennsylvania
Good Neighbor Pharmacy
Office of Child & Youth Protection Build

HANNA & ASSOCIATES INC.
1100 E Lakeshore Dr Ste 201, Coeur D'Alene, ID 83814
Mailing Address:
PO Box 2025, Coeur D'Alene, ID 83816
Tel.: (208) 667-2428
Fax: (208) 765-8044
Web Site: www.hanna-advertising.com

E-Mail for Key Personnel:
President: dayneh@hanna-advertising.com
Creative Dir.: JohnB@hanna-advertising.com
Media Dir.: jeffh@hanna-advertising.com
Production Mgr.: ShannonP@hanna-advertising.com

Employees: 25
Year Founded: 1976

National Agency Associations: 4A's-AAF

Agency Specializes In: Brand Development & Integration, Broadcast, Business Publications, Business-To-Business, Cable T.V., Communications, Consulting, Consumer Marketing, Consumer Publications, Corporate Identity, Direct Response Marketing, Education, Electronic Media, Engineering, Entertainment, Event Planning & Marketing, Exhibit/Trade Shows, Financial, Graphic Design, High Technology, Industrial, Information Technology, Internet/Web Design, Investor Relations, Legal Services, Leisure, Logo & Package Design, Magazines, Media Buying Services, Medical Products, Merchandising, Newspaper, Newspapers & Magazines, Outdoor, Planning & Consultation, Point of Purchase, Point of Sale, Print, Publicity/Promotions, Radio, Restaurant, Retail, Sports Market, Strategic Planning/Research, T.V., Trade & Consumer Magazines, Travel & Tourism

Dayne G. Hanna *(Pres)*
John Baechler *(VP & Dir-Creative)*
Jeff Hanna *(VP & Dir-Media)*
Dwain Smart *(Assoc Dir-Creative)*
Mary Ann Sleeth *(Sr Acct Supvr)*
Rebecca Reeves *(Sr Acct Exec)*
Justin Childers *(Media Planner & Media Buyer)*
Cathy Duer *(Media Planner & Media Buyer)*
Shannon Pyle *(Acct Coord)*

Accounts:
Avista
ESPN Throwdown
Inland Northwest Community Foundation
Jacksons Food Store
NW Tile and Floor
Spokesman Review; Spokane, WA Regional Newspaper
Sterling Action
University of Virginia
Washington State University Athletics; Pullman, WA Intercollegiate Athletics
Zak Designs Packaging

HANNA LEE COMMUNICATIONS, INC.
575 Madison Ave 8th Fl, New York, NY 10022
Tel.: (212) 721-2090
Fax: (212) 721-2091
E-Mail: info@hannaleecommunications.com
Web Site: www.hannaleecommunications.com

Employees: 10
Year Founded: 2004

Agency Specializes In: Advertising, Brand Development & Integration, Business Publications, Communications, Corporate Communications, Event Planning & Marketing, Exhibit/Trade Shows, Food Service, Hospitality, Industrial, Internet/Web Design, Local Marketing, Media Training, Newspaper, Product Placement, Public Relations, Sponsorship, Strategic Planning/Research

Hanna Lee *(Founder & Pres)*
Jen Neugeboren *(Dir-Media Rels)*

Accounts:
Atsby New York Vermouth
Bacchanal Restaurant
Bar Celona (Agency of Record)
Bortolomiol Prosecco
Campari Campaign: "Year of the Negroni", PR
Conway Family Wines; Arroyo Grande, CA Public Relations
The Cooper Spirits Co
The Dead Rabbit
Forcella Pizza Restaurant Group
The French Culinary Institute
G7 Portuguese Wine Consortium
Goats do Roam
Gourmet Latino Festival
GRACE Restaurant
Hangar 1 Vodka
Japan Week
Kyochon Restaurant Group
Leblon Cachaca (Agency of Record) Brazil's Handcrafted Spririt
Louis Royer Cognacs Event Management, Media Relations, Public Relations
Lowell International Foods (Agency of Record)
Manhattan Cocktail Classic (Agency of Record)
Marie Brizard Liqueurs
Michael's New York
Mionetto Wines
NYC & Company
PAMA Pomegranate Liqueur Digital, Event Marketing, Media Relations, Public Relations, Social Media Strategy
Pisco Control C "Million Rays of Sunshine", Event Marketing, PR, Social Media Strategy
Rayuela Restaurant
San Domenico
Santa Teresa Rum
Sobieski Vodka
Terra Andina (Agency of Record)
TINCUP American Whiskey
Wines of Croatia

HANON MCKENDRY
(Merged with CSK to form DOMOREGOOD Hannon McKendry)

HANSON ASSOCIATES, INC.
161 Leverington Ave, Philadelphia, PA 19127
Tel.: (215) 487-7051
Fax: (215) 487-7052
E-Mail: info@hansondesign.com
Web Site: www.hansondesign.com

Employees: 15

Agency Specializes In: Brand Development & Integration, Communications, Digital/Interactive, Internet/Web Design, Local Marketing, Package Design, Retail, Strategic Planning/Research

Gil Hanson *(Pres)*
Jeff Lorenz *(Sr Dir-Rich Media)*
Michael McDonald *(Dir-Creative)*
Kent Murray *(Dir-Adv Creative)*

Accounts:
Zero Water

HANSON DODGE INC.
220 E Buffalo St, Milwaukee, WI 53202
Tel.: (414) 347-1266
Fax: (414) 347-0493
E-Mail: info@hansondodge.com
Web Site: www.hansondodge.com

Employees: 65

Agency Specializes In: Advertising, Below-the-Line, Brand Development & Integration, Collateral, College, Consumer Marketing, Corporate Identity, Digital/Interactive, Direct Response Marketing, E-Commerce, Education, Email, Experience Design, Information Technology, Integrated Marketing, Internet/Web Design, Planning & Consultation, Podcasting, Sales Promotion, Search Engine Optimization, Social Media, Sports Market, Teen Market, Travel & Tourism, Web (Banner Ads, Pop-ups, etc.)

Ken Hanson *(Founder & CEO)*
Tim Dodge *(Pres)*
Sally Siegel *(VP-Acct Svcs & Acct Dir)*
Tom Flierl *(VP-Sls & Mktg)*

Rick Miller *(VP-ECommerce & Digital Mktg)*
Angela Rothen *(VP-Tech)*
Chris Buhrman *(Exec Dir-Creative)*
Brandon Powell *(Dir-Digital Mktg)*
Sarah Van Elzen *(Dir-Social Media)*

Accounts:
SOG Specialty Knives and Tools Campaign: "Rise to the Occasion"
Trek Bicycle Corporation TREK Madone
Wilson Sporting Goods

HANSON WATSON ASSOCIATES
1411 15th St, Moline, IL 61265
Tel.: (309) 764-8315
Fax: (309) 764-8336
Web Site: www.hansonwatson.com

E-Mail for Key Personnel:
Creative Dir.: kathy@hansonwatson.com

Employees: 6
Year Founded: 1945

National Agency Associations: AAF-Second Wind Limited

Agency Specializes In: Brand Development & Integration, Broadcast, Business Publications, Business-To-Business, Collateral, Communications, Corporate Communications, Corporate Identity, Direct Response Marketing, Event Planning & Marketing, Exhibit/Trade Shows, Graphic Design, Health Care Services, Hispanic Market, Internet/Web Design, Logo & Package Design, Magazines, Media Buying Services, Medical Products, Newspaper, Newspapers & Magazines, Outdoor, Planning & Consultation, Print, Public Relations, Publicity/Promotions, Radio, Sports Market, Strategic Planning/Research, T.V.

James S. Watson *(Pres)*
Katherine Betcher *(Dir-Art & Creative)*
Tim Wilkinson *(Dir-Bus Dev)*
Josh Wray *(Analyst-Social Media & Res)*

Accounts:
Club Choice
Community Health Care
Davenport Country Club; Davenport, IA; 1995
Johnson Contracting Company, Inc

Division

Latin Connection
1411 15th St, Moline, IL 61265
Tel.: (309) 764-8315
Fax: (309) 764-8336
Web Site: www.qclatinoconnection.com

Employees: 5

Katherine Betcher *(Dir-Art)*

Accounts:
Casa
Las Ranas
Latino Guide
Sonido Camaney
Sonido Estrella
Zaldivar Foundation

HAPPY COG
109 S 13th St Unit 3 S, Philadelphia, PA 19107
Tel.: (215) 701-3936
Web Site: www.happycog.com

Agency Specializes In: Digital/Interactive, Internet/Web Design

Jeffrey Zeldman *(Founder & Chm)*
Greg Hoy *(Principal)*
Dave DeRuchie *(VP-Ops & Gen Mgr)*
Joe Rinaldi *(VP-Bus Dev)*
Mark Huot *(Dir-Tech & Dev)*

Accounts:
The Amanda Project Story Book Providers
Georgetown University Educational Institution
MTV Campaign: "O Music Awards"
W. W. Norton & Company Inc. Academic Books Publisher
Zappos Development Inc. Consutling Services

HAPPY MEDIUM
1717 Ingersoll Ave Ste 117, Des Moines, IA 50309
Tel.: (515) 440-0006
Fax: (515) 440-0964
E-Mail: info@itsahappymedium.com
Web Site: www.itsahappymedium.com

Year Founded: 2011

Agency Specializes In: Advertising, Digital/Interactive, Graphic Design, Internet/Web Design, Media Buying Services, Social Media

Katie Stocking *(Owner)*
Doug Choi *(Dir-Art)*
Nick Renkoski *(Dir-Creative)*
Julie Welch *(Dir-Media & Culture)*
Lauren Reuland *(Office Mgr)*
Tabitha Jamerson *(Strategist-Social Media)*
Kristen Walker *(Acct Exec)*
Sarah Fisch *(Designer-Visual)*
Jill Patterson *(Acct Coord)*
Andrew Rubenbauer *(Acct Coord)*

Accounts:
Kum & Go

THE HARBOUR GROUP LLC
1200 New Hampshire Ave NW Ste 850, Washington, DC 20036
Tel.: (202) 295-8787
E-Mail: contact@harbourgrp.com
Web Site: www.harbourgrp.com

Agency Specializes In: Advertising, Crisis Communications, Digital/Interactive, Public Relations

Gayle Kansagor Hope *(VP)*
Matthew Epperly *(VP)*

Accounts:
New-Conoco
New-Government of Libya
New-Kraft Foods
New-Major League Baseball Player's Association
New-Pfizer Inc.
New-PhHRMA
New-Republic of Georgia
New-US Airways

HARBURGER/SCOTT ADVERTISING
72 Balmville Rd, Newburgh, NY 12550
Tel.: (845) 787-0031
Web Site: www.harburgerscottadvtg.com

Employees: 2
Year Founded: 1982

Agency Specializes In: Brand Development & Integration, Business-To-Business, Collateral, Consumer Marketing, Cosmetics, Fashion/Apparel, Financial, Internet/Web Design, New Product Development, Newspapers & Magazines, Over-50 Market, Planning & Consultation, Print, Restaurant, Retail, Strategic Planning/Research, Travel & Tourism

Revenue: $200,000

Brenda Harburger *(Pres & CEO)*
Ian Campbell *(VP)*

Accounts:
Glenn & Breheney

HARD BEAT COMMUNICATIONS, INC.
1515 Broadway 11th Fl, New York, NY 10036
Tel.: (718) 476-3616
Fax: (718) 710-7478
Toll Free: (800) 789-3062
E-Mail: marketing@caribpr.com
Web Site: www.hardbeatcommunications.com

Employees: 5
Year Founded: 2004

Agency Specializes In: Advertising, Advertising Specialties, African-American Market, Broadcast, Cable T.V., Communications, Corporate Communications, E-Commerce, Event Planning & Marketing, Graphic Design, Internet/Web Design, Media Buying Services, Newspaper, Newspapers & Magazines, Planning & Consultation, Print, Public Relations, Publicity/Promotions, Radio, Recruitment, Strategic Planning/Research, T.V., Yellow Pages Advertising

Approx. Annual Billings: $250,000

Felicia Persuad *(CMO)*
Anthony Phills *(CTO)*
Joe Bernstein *(Coord-Partnership & Investment)*
Kathy Bronson *(Coord-Comm)*

Accounts:
Caribbean Tourism Organization Website & Newsletter; 2010
Invest Caribbean Now Sponsorship & Event Planning; 2010
One Caribbean Television Advertising & Promotion; 2010
PR Newswire Caribbean & Caribbean American Press Releases; 2009

HARDY COMMUNICATIONS DEVELOPMENT
(Name Changed to Brandscapes)

HARFIELD & ASSOCIATES
Ste 320 - 1385 W 8th Ave, Vancouver, BC V6H 3V9 Canada
Tel.: (604) 684-7100
Fax: (604) 684-7307
E-Mail: info@harfield.com
Web Site: www.harfield.com

Employees: 25
Year Founded: 1981

National Agency Associations: Second Wind Limited

Agency Specializes In: Advertising, Advertising Specialties, Digital/Interactive, Direct Response Marketing, E-Commerce, Internet/Web Design, Strategic Planning/Research

Kieth Harfield *(Pres & CEO)*
Britt Dolleren Cornfoot *(Designer)*
Steve Robinson *(Sr Graphic Designer)*

Accounts:
Honda Western Canada

HARGER, HOWE & WALSH
1 Van De Graaff Dr Ste 401, Burlington, MA 01803
Tel.: (781) 425-5005

Fax: (781) 425-5004
Toll Free: (800) 699-6891
E-Mail: mwalsh@hargerhowe.com
Web Site: www.hargerhowe.com

Employees: 20
Year Founded: 1968

Agency Specializes In: Advertising Specialties, Brand Development & Integration, Broadcast, Business Publications, Cable T.V., Collateral, Communications, Consulting, Corporate Identity, Direct Response Marketing, E-Commerce, Electronic Media, Event Planning & Marketing, Exhibit/Trade Shows, Graphic Design, Health Care Services, High Technology, Internet/Web Design, Logo & Package Design, Media Buying Services, Multimedia, Newspaper, Newspapers & Magazines, Out-of-Home Media, Outdoor, Point of Purchase, Point of Sale, Print, Production, Publicity/Promotions, Radio, Recruitment, Sales Promotion, Strategic Planning/Research, T.V., Trade & Consumer Magazines

Approx. Annual Billings: $7,000,000

Jennifer Sopczak *(Mng Partner)*
Michelle Swarts *(Mng Partner-Harger Howe & Associates)*
Mark Wedes *(Mng Partner-Harger Howe & Associates)*
Mike Walsh *(Pres-Harger Howe Adv)*
Catherine Ellett *(Dir-Creative)*

Accounts:
Ixia
Memorial Hermann Healthcare System
Texas Children Hospital

HARLAND CLARKE CORP.

10931 Laureate Dr, San Antonio, TX 78249
Toll Free: (800) 382-0818
E-Mail: info@harlandclarke.com
Web Site: www.harlandclarke.com

Employees: 45
Year Founded: 1994

Agency Specializes In: Financial

Dan Singleton *(Pres & CEO)*
Peter A. Fera, Jr. *(CFO & Exec VP)*
Judy Norris *(Gen Counsel & Sr VP)*
Bob Madrid *(VP-Mktg & eCommerce-Retail Channels Div)*
Karen Salamone *(VP-Mktg-Go to Market)*
Sharon Leighton *(Dir-ECommerce)*

Accounts:
Branch Banking & Trust (BB&T)
Frost Bank
HSBC
Knowledge Learning Centers
Marshall & Ilsley Corporation
Regions
Twin City Federal

HARLO INTERACTIVE INC.

537 SE Ash Ste 107, Portland, OR 97214
Tel.: (503) 517-8074
Web Site: www.harlointeractive.com

Year Founded: 2004

Agency Specializes In: Advertising, Brand Development & Integration, Collateral, Digital/Interactive, E-Commerce, Internet/Web Design, Logo & Package Design, Package Design, Social Media

Danny Decker *(Founder & Partner)*
Cody Galloway *(Partner)*
Paco Allen *(Mng Dir & Dir-Brand Strategy)*
Anna Lott *(Producer-Digital)*
Rae Owen *(Dir-Client Svcs & Strategy)*
Mark Sanders *(Dir-Digital Mktg Strategy & Tech)*
Brad Vornholt *(Dir-Mobile Dev)*
Stephen Leineweber *(Assoc Dir-Creative)*
Michael Manny *(Assoc Dir-Creative)*
Tim Plumb *(Designer-UX)*

Accounts:
MediaSilo
Portland Opportunities Industrialization Center, Inc. Rosemary Anderson High School

THE HARMON GROUP

807 3rd Ave S, Nashville, TN 37210
Tel.: (615) 256-3393
Fax: (615) 256-3464
E-Mail: info@harmongrp.com
Web Site: www.harmongrp.com

Employees: 20

Agency Specializes In: Advertising, Communications, Sponsorship

Revenue: $10,000,000

Rick Arnemann *(CEO)*
Hank Sterner *(VP-Sls)*
Charles Priddy *(Sr Dir-Art)*
Amy Kinard *(Dir-Art)*
Virginia Cradick *(Mgr-Ops & Acctg)*
Chris Gentry *(Designer)*

HAROLD WARNER ADVERTISING, INC.

700 Parkside Ave, Buffalo, NY 14216
Tel.: (716) 852-4410
Fax: (716) 852-4725
E-Mail: mail@haroldwarner.com
Web Site: www.haroldwarner.com

Employees: 5
Year Founded: 1945

Agency Specializes In: Advertising, Business Publications, Business-To-Business, Collateral, Consulting, Corporate Communications, Corporate Identity, Digital/Interactive, Direct Response Marketing, E-Commerce, Electronic Media, Graphic Design, Industrial, Internet/Web Design, Magazines, Media Buying Services, Planning & Consultation, Print, Public Relations, Publicity/Promotions, Technical Advertising, Trade & Consumer Magazines

Paul V. Offermann *(Pres)*
Joanne M. Kij *(Mgr-Traffic)*
Jill Gelzer Walsh *(Mgr-Production)*
Ken Boos *(Acct Exec)*

Accounts:
ACT Associates
Batavia Engineering, Inc.
Buffalo Metal Casting Co., Inc.; Buffalo, NY Nonferrous Castings of Aluminum, Brass Bronze & Conductive Copper
Easyfit
Envirospec Inc.; Buffalo, NY & Toronto, ON, Canada Patented System For Elevating & Uniform Spacing of Paver Stones On Waterproofed Areas
Envoy; Buffalo, NY
Griffco Valve
Infinitex; Clarence, NY Wastewater Treatment Systems
Kee Safety, Inc.
LNA Solutions
Milward Alloys; Lockport, NY Alloying Additives, Aluminum & Copper Master Alloys, Custom Alloys
Neutrex
Niagara Fiberboard Inc.; Lockport, NY Wallboard & Prefabricated Soffets
Niagara Transformer Corp.; Buffalo, NY Power & Distribution Transformers
Pentalift Equipment Corp.; Guelph, ON, Canada Materials Handling & Docking Equipment
Polymer Molding; Erie, PA
Revvo Caster Company, Inc.; Buffalo, NY Industrial Casters & Wheels; 1997
SurveyorTemp
Titan Tool Supply Co., Inc.; Buffalo, NY Optical Metrology for Metalworking, Electronics & Quality Control
Ttarp Industries Inc.; Buffalo, NY Die Cutting, Heat Laminators & Vertical Band Saws; 1997
Unidex, Inc.; Warsaw, NY Ergonomic Manipulators, Material Handling Equipment, Workstations; 1999
Vandemark Chemical
Vent-A-Kiln Corp.; Buffalo, NY Fume & Heat Exhaust System For Kilns
W.T. Height Company, Inc. Casters, Leveling Mounts, Wheels
Wanner Engineering
WSF Industrial, Inc.; Tonawanda, NY Autoclaves, Reactor Retorts, Other Processing Equipment & Systems, Vacuum Impregnation Vessels

HARRIMAN CREATIVE, INC

1310 NW Naito Pkwy Ste 111, Portland, OR 97209
Tel.: (503) 796-1813
Fax: (503) 241-9475
E-Mail: brianh@harrimancreative.com
Web Site: www.harrimancreative.com

Employees: 2
Year Founded: 1996

Agency Specializes In: Advertising, Advertising Specialties, Alternative Advertising, Brand Development & Integration, Business Publications, Business-To-Business, Catalogs, Collateral, Communications, Corporate Communications, Corporate Identity, Direct Response Marketing, Gay & Lesbian Market, Graphic Design, Guerilla Marketing, Health Care Services, Identity Marketing, Integrated Marketing, Internet/Web Design, Logo & Package Design, Media Buying Services, Media Planning, Out-of-Home Media, Package Design, Print, Production (Print), Promotions, Social Marketing/Nonprofit, Trade & Consumer Magazines, Urban Market

Breakdown of Gross Billings by Media: Adv. Specialities: 10%; Collateral: 25%; Exhibits/Trade Shows: 10%; Graphic Design: 25%; Print: 30%

Brian R. Harriman *(Pres)*

Accounts:
HemoBand Corporation; Portland, OR HemoBand
Jordco, Incorporated; Beaverton, OR EndoGel, Endoring, Endoring FileCaddy

HARRIS AGENCY

2250 Kalakaua Ave Ste 313, Honolulu, HI 96815
Tel.: (808) 946-6116
Fax: (808) 946-6556
E-Mail: info@harris-agency.com
Web Site: www.harris-agency.com

Year Founded: 2006

Agency Specializes In: Advertising, Brand Development & Integration, Digital/Interactive, Event Planning & Marketing, Media Buying Services, Media Planning, Print, Public Relations, Social Media, Strategic Planning/Research

Darren Flores *(CFO)*

Accounts:
Burger King Holdings Inc.

HARRIS, BAIO & MCCULLOUGH INC.
520 S Frnt St, Philadelphia, PA 19147-1723
Tel.: (215) 440-9800
Fax: (215) 440-9812
E-Mail: info@hbm.com
Web Site: www.hbmadv.com

Employees: 50
Year Founded: 1983

Agency Specializes In: Business-To-Business, Consumer Marketing, Direct Response Marketing, Event Planning & Marketing, Health Care Services, Public Relations, Publicity/Promotions, Sponsorship, Sports Market

Approx. Annual Billings: $78,831,056

Breakdown of Gross Billings by Media: Bus. Publs.: $15,766,211; Collateral: $7,883,106; Fees: $3,941,553; Internet Adv.: $1,576,621; Network T.V.: $3,941,553; Newsp. & Mags.: $1,576,621; Point of Purchase: $5,518,174; Promos.: $6,306,484; Pub. Rels.: $9,459,727; Sports Mktg.: $1,576,621; Spot T.V.: $1,576,621; T.V.: $3,941,553; Trade & Consumer Mags.: $11,824,658; Yellow Page Adv.: $3,941,553

Camille Dager *(Sr VP)*
Kristin A. Campbell *(VP)*
Brett Harrell *(VP)*
Rob Janssen *(Sr Dir-Art)*
David Burt *(Dir-Interactive Media)*
Alexander Rodriguez *(Dir-IT)*
Ron Kalina *(Assoc Dir-Creative-Design)*
Michele Brown *(Sr Acct Exec)*
Kurt Andersen *(Acct Exec)*

Accounts:
American Biltrite, Inc. Protective Masking Materials
American Cancer Society
Chron's & Colitis Foundation of America
EnerSys Corporation
GlaxoSmithKline plc
NASCAR Network of Automotive Repair & Parts Stores, Roush Racing
Rockwood Specialties Inc. Chemical Additives for Paints, Inks, Grease & Cosmetics
SKF USA Inc. Ball & Rolling Bearings
SKF/VSM Europe Automotive Aftermarket, Bearing Products, Specialized Replacement Kits
Subaru of America Outback, Legacy & Impreza
Yuasa Specialty Batteries

HARRIS D. MCKINNEY
(Merged with Zoomedia to form HDM/Zoomedia)

HARRIS MARKETING GROUP
102 Pierce St, Birmingham, MI 48009-6018
Tel.: (248) 723-6300
Fax: (248) 723-6301
E-Mail: info@harris-hmg.com
Web Site: www.harris-hmg.com

Employees: 30
Year Founded: 1976

Agency Specializes In: Advertising, Women's Market

Janice Rosenhaus *(CEO)*
Denise McQuillan *(VP-Creative & Dir)*
Karen Black Morelli *(Acct Mgr)*
Allison Mullen *(Acct Exec)*
John Clarey *(Sr Designer)*

Accounts:
ARC Pacific (Agency of Record)
First Federal Bank of Wisconsin (Agency of Record)
Lifeway Foods; Chicago, IL
Uniland Construction; Bloomfield Hills; MI
WNBA
YMCA Metro Detroit; Detroit, MI

HARRISON AND STAR LLC
75 Varick St 6th Fl, New York, NY 10013
Tel.: (212) 727-1330
Fax: (212) 822-6590
Web Site: www.harrisonandstar.com

E-Mail for Key Personnel:
President: tcurran@hs-ideas.com
Creative Dir.: kmcshane@hs-ideas.com

Employees: 275
Year Founded: 1987

Agency Specializes In: Advertising, Health Care Services, Pharmaceutical

Ty Curran *(Chm & CEO)*
Mardene Miller *(Pres)*
Mario Muredda *(Pres)*
Charles Doomany *(CFO, COO & Exec VP)*
Rob Perota *(Sr VP & Grp Dir-Creative)*
Michael Norkin *(Sr VP & Sr Dir-Creative)*
Kathy Magnuson *(Sr VP & Client Svcs Dir)*
Lenny Bishop *(Sr VP & Dir-Innovation & User Experience)*
Brad Davidson *(Sr VP & Planner-Strategic)*
Bob Gemignani *(Sr VP-HR)*
Michael Steiner *(Sr VP & Experience Planner)*
Christa M. E. Moeller *(VP & Assoc Dir-Creative & Art)*
Ryan Steward *(VP & Grp Acct Supvr)*
Marjorie Vincent *(Creative Dir)*
Stacey Richter *(Mgr-Learning & Dev Medical Specialists Comm Grp)*
Sarah Stout *(Acct Supvr)*
Darrell Ann Smith *(Sr Acct Exec)*
Elyse Coyle *(Grp Acct Supvr)*

Accounts:
Abbott Humira
Bayer Corp.
Genentech, Inc. Avastin, Herceptin, Rituxan, Tarceva, Xeloda
Lucentis
Novartis Ophthalmics
Novartis Pharmaceuticals Corp.
Roche
Santarus, Inc.
Teva Neurosciences, Inc.
Valeant Pharmaceuticals Campaign: "Tackle It", Jublia, Super Bowl 2015

HARRISON LEIFER DIMARCO, INC.
(Name Changed to HLD Communications)

HARRISON MARKETING & ADVERTISING
333 Palmer Dr Ste 220, Bakersfield, CA 93309
Tel.: (661) 283-1999
Fax: (661) 283-1998
E-Mail: info@teamhma.com
Web Site: www.teamhma.com

Employees: 5
Year Founded: 1992

Agency Specializes In: Advertising, Digital/Interactive, Direct Response Marketing, Event Planning & Marketing, Graphic Design, Internet/Web Design, Logo & Package Design, Media Buying Services, New Product Development, Print, Production, Public Relations, Radio, T.V.

Dan Harrison *(Pres)*
Cris Peterson *(Dir-Art)*
Kristina Kinnett *(Office Mgr & Media Buyer)*
Jeff Opie *(Designer)*
Pam Sill *(Designer-Graphic)*

Accounts:
Agape International
Bakersfield Memorial Hospital
Clifford & Bradford
Clinica Sierra Vista
River Ranch
Salinas Valley Memorial Hospital
Sierra Printers

HARRISON MEDIA
24416 Crocker Blvd, Clinton Township, MI 48036
Tel.: (586) 465-3855
Fax: (586) 465-2726
E-Mail: mark@harrisonmedia.net
Web Site: www.harrisonmedia.net

Agency Specializes In: Advertising, Event Planning & Marketing

Patti Harrison *(Founder)*
Mark Harrison *(Controller)*
Ashley Jackson *(Specialist-Media)*
Samantha Babcock *(Media Buyer)*
Jeff Radzinski *(Media Buyer-Digital)*
Katie Cichowski *(Sr Media Buyer)*

Accounts:
Hap
Henry Ford Health System Media Buying

HARRISONRAND ADVERTISING
6823 Bergenline Ave, Guttenberg, NJ 7093
Tel.: (201) 861-5600
E-Mail: info@harrisonrand.com
Web Site: www.harrisonrand.com

Agency Specializes In: Advertising, Brand Development & Integration, Event Planning & Marketing, Public Relations, Social Media

Daryl Harrison-Rand *(Pres)*
David Rand *(Partner)*
Anya Kougasian *(Dir-Art & Mgr-Production)*
Adam McNicholas *(Asst Acct Exec)*
Nick Santaniello *(Asst Acct Exec)*

Accounts:
Choose New Jersey
LibertyHealth Foundation
New Jersey City University

THE HART AGENCY, INC.
4330 Shawnee Mission Pkwy Ste 105, Fairway, KS 66205-2521
Tel.: (913) 362-7121
Fax: (913) 362-8213
Web Site: www.thebobhartagency.com

E-Mail for Key Personnel:
President: bhart@hartagency.com

Employees: 3
Year Founded: 1985

Agency Specializes In: Business-To-Business, Direct Response Marketing

Approx. Annual Billings: $2,300,000

Robert W. Hart *(Owner)*
Lynn Cobbley *(Acct Mgr)*
Diane Schmidt *(Mgr-Production)*
Suzanne Doss *(Rep-Personal & Comml Customer Svcs)*

HART ASSOCIATES, INC.

1915 Indian Wood Cir, Maumee, OH 43537-4002
Tel.: (419) 893-9600
Fax: (419) 893-9070
Web Site: www.hartinc.com

E-Mail for Key Personnel:
President: mhart@hartinc.com
Creative Dir.: MBell@hartinc.com
Public Relations: mschroder@hartinc.com

Employees: 56
Year Founded: 1965

National Agency Associations: 4A's-PRSA-Second Wind Limited

Agency Specializes In: Advertising, Automotive, Brand Development & Integration, Broadcast, Business-To-Business, Cable T.V., Collateral, Consumer Marketing, Corporate Identity, Direct Response Marketing, Education, Electronic Media, Exhibit/Trade Shows, Financial, Government/Political, Graphic Design, Health Care Services, Industrial, Internet/Web Design, Investor Relations, Logo & Package Design, Media Buying Services, Multimedia, Newspaper, Outdoor, Production, Public Relations, Search Engine Optimization, Social Marketing/Nonprofit, Social Media, Trade & Consumer Magazines, Transportation, Travel & Tourism

Approx. Annual Billings: $55,000,000 Capitalized

Michael K. Hart *(Pres & CEO)*
Susan Degens *(VP-Media)*
Ryan DeShazer *(VP-Digital Experience)*
Rich Kretz *(VP-Video Svcs)*
Leslie Verral *(Acct Svcs Dir)*
Sharon Stemen *(Mgr-New Bus Dev)*
Logan Hecklinger *(Jr Graphic Designer)*
Jeff Payden *(Sr Art Dir)*

Accounts:
Cabell Huntington Hospital; 2013
Caterpillar; 2015
Certified Angus Beef; Wooster, OH; 2001
Croghan Colonial Bank; 2014
HCR Manor Care; Toledo, OH; 2005
La-Z-Boy; Monroe, MI; 2000
Lima Memorial Health System; 2012
Lourdes University; 2014
Mercy Health; 2013
Ohio Department of Transportation; 2014
Ohio Lottery; 2009
Paramount Health Care; Toledo, OH; 2004
ProMedica Health System; 2004
New-Seafood Nutrition Partnership
Therma-Tru Doors; 2007
Toledo Area Regional Transit Authority; Toledo, OH
Tween Brands; 2014
URS Corporation
Wacker Chemical Corp

HART-BOILLOT, LLC
(Acquired by Eric Mower & Name Changed to HB/Eric Mower + Associates)

HARTE-HANKS, INC.
9601 McAllister Freeway Ste 610, San Antonio, TX 78216
Tel.: (210) 829-9000
Fax: (210) 829-9403
Toll Free: (800) 456-9748
E-Mail: contactus@harte-hanks.com
Web Site: www.hartehanks.com

Employees: 5,389
Year Founded: 1920

Agency Specializes In: Business Publications, Direct Response Marketing, Direct-to-Consumer

Revenue: $553,676,000

Karen Puckett *(Pres & CEO)*
Robert Neill *(CIO)*
Frank Grillo *(CMO)*
Robert L. R. Munden *(Gen Counsel, Sec & Sr VP)*
Andrew Harrison *(Sr VP)*
George Shafer *(Sr Dir-Demand Generation Center)*
Shannon Bryant *(Mgr-Bus Dev)*
Nicole Bump *(Mgr-Content Mktg)*
Desiree Smith *(Asst Controller)*

Accounts:
AstraZeneca
Comcast
Flumist
JCPenney
Sony Electronics
Symantec

Branches

Harte-Hanks, Inc.
1525 NW Third St Ste 21, Deerfield Beach, FL 33442-1667
Tel.: (954) 429-3771
Fax: (954) 570-1100
Web Site: hhl1.harte-hanks.com/hitsweb/

Employees: 130
Year Founded: 1990

Christen Regan *(Partner-HR Bus & VP)*
Robert Colucci *(VP)*
Steve Garizio *(Acct Dir)*

Harte-Hanks, Inc.
165 New Commerce Blvd, Wilkes Barre, PA 18706-1439
Tel.: (570) 826-0414
Fax: (570) 826-0488
Web Site: www.hartehanks.com

Employees: 150

Robert Kuhl *(Mng Dir)*
Gavin Pommernelle *(Chief HR Officer & Exec VP)*
Philip Galati *(CEO-Trillium)*
Rick J. Carbone *(Sr VP-Customer Delivery)*
Joseph Voica *(Sr VP-Sls)*
Darlene Phillips *(Mgr-HR)*

Subsidiaries

Harte-Hanks Direct Marketing/Baltimore, Inc.
4545 Annapolis Rd, Baltimore, MD 21227-4817
Tel.: (410) 636-6660
Fax: (410) 636-2638
E-Mail: contactus@harte-hanks.com

Employees: 350

Kyle Kennedy *(Grp Mng Dir)*
Bob Kuhl *(Mng Dir)*
Joseph Voica *(Chief Revenue Officer & Sr VP-Sls)*
Robert Munden *(Gen Counsel, Sec & Sr VP)*
Andrew Harrison *(Sr VP)*
Lauri Kearnes *(Grp VP-Fin)*
Roberto Lopez *(VP-Fin & Head-Project Costing)*
Carlos Alvarado *(VP & Corp Controller)*
Amy Laird *(VP-Client Svcs)*
Michelle Mogielnicki *(VP-Fin)*
Michele Maltby *(Mgr-Acctg)*
John Henigan *(Asst Controller)*

Harte-Hanks Direct Marketing/Dallas, L.P.
2750 114th St Ste 100, Grand Prairie, TX 75050-8737
Tel.: (972) 660-4242
Fax: (972) 660-3137
E-Mail: info@harte-hanks.com
Web Site: www.hartehanks.com

Employees: 100

Kyle Kennedy *(Grp Mng Dir)*
Gavin Pommernelle *(Chief HR Officer & Exec VP)*
Robert Munden *(Gen Counsel, Sec & Sr VP)*
Craig H. Murray *(Sr VP-Retail Solutions Grp)*
Lauri Kearnes *(Grp VP-Fin)*
Michael Dwyer *(VP & Head-Sls Ops & Sls Engrg-Global)*
Roberto Lopez *(VP-Fin & Head-Project Costing)*
Carlos Alvarado *(VP & Corp Controller)*
Michele Fitzpatrick *(VP-CRM Strategy & Sls Engrg)*
Michele Maltby *(Mgr-Acctg)*
John Henigan *(Asst Controller)*

Harte-Hanks Direct Marketing/Fullerton, Inc.
680 Langsdorf Dr, Fullerton, CA 92831-3702
Tel.: (714) 996-8900
Fax: (714) 441-1577
E-Mail: media@hartehanks.com
Web Site: www.hartehanks.com

Employees: 20

Doug Shepard *(CFO & Exec VP)*
Robert Neill *(CIO)*
Gavin Pommernelle *(Chief HR Officer & Exec VP)*
Joseph Voica *(Chief Revenue Officer & Sr VP-Sls)*
Robert Munden *(Gen Counsel, Sec & Sr VP)*
Rick J. Carbone *(Sr VP-Ops)*
Seth Romanow *(Sr VP-Mktg Strategy & Analytics)*
Johnny Castaneda *(VP-IT)*
Michele Fitzpatrick *(VP-CRM Strategy & Sls Engrg)*

Aberdeen Group
(Formerly Harte-Hanks Market Intelligence, Inc.)
9980 Huennekens St, San Diego, CA 92121
Tel.: (800) 854-8409
Fax: (858) 452-6857
E-Mail: hello@aberdeen.com
Web Site: www.aberdeenservices.com

Employees: 250

Agency Specializes In: Strategic Planning/Research

Gary Skidmore *(CEO)*
Marissa Parillo *(Partner-Talent Acq)*
Charlie Allieri *(Mng Dir & Chief Data Officer)*
John Dusett *(Mng Dir)*
Gavin Pommernelle *(Chief HR Officer & Exec VP)*
Andrew Harrison *(Sr VP)*
Nina Hall *(Dir-HR)*
Carolyn Oatman *(Dir-Employee Benefits)*
Gary Ronan *(Mgr-HR)*
Danielle Nesbitt *(Sr Partner-Talent Acq)*

Harte-Hanks Response Management/Boston, Inc.
600 N Bedford St, East Bridgewater, MA 02333
Tel.: (508) 894-1500
Fax: (508) 378-8448
E-Mail: contactus@harte-hanks.com

Employees: 400

Kyle Kennedy *(Grp Mng Dir)*
Bob Kuhl *(Mng Dir)*
Joseph Voica *(Chief Revenue Officer & Sr VP-Sls)*
Robert Munden *(Gen Counsel, Sec & Sr VP)*
Andrew Harrison *(Sr VP)*
Lauri Kearnes *(Grp VP-Fin)*
Michael Dwyer *(VP & Head-Sls Ops & Sls Engrg-*

Global)
Roberto Lopez *(VP-Fin & Head-Project Costing)*
Carlos Alvarado *(VP & Corp Controller)*
Michele Fitzpatrick *(VP-CRM Strategy & Sls Engrg)*
Michelle Mogielnicki *(VP-Fin)*
Michele Maltby *(Mgr-Acctg)*
John Henigan *(Asst Controller)*

Harte-Hanks Data Services LLC
6701 Baymeadow Dr Ste D, Glen Burnie, MD 21060-6405
Tel.: (410) 412-1662
Fax: (410) 412-1659
E-Mail: contactus@harte-hanks.com
Web Site: www.hartehanks.com

Employees: 100

Kyle Kennedy *(Grp Mng Dir)*
Doug Shepard *(CFO & Exec VP)*
Robert Neill *(CIO)*
Gavin Pommernelle *(Chief HR Officer & Exec VP)*
Robert Munden *(Gen Counsel & Sec & Sr VP)*
Andrew Harrison *(Sr VP)*

Accounts:
PennysaverUSA.com
TheFlyer.com

Harte-Hanks Direct, Inc.
777 Township Line Rd Ste 300, Yardley, PA 19067
Tel.: (215) 750-6600
Fax: (215) 944-9710
Web Site: www.hartehanks.com

E-Mail for Key Personnel:
President: frank_harvey@harte-hanks.com

Employees: 180
Year Founded: 1983

Agency Specializes In: Sponsorship

Doug C. Shepard *(CFO & Exec VP)*
Brian J. Dames *(CMO)*
Robert L.R. Munden *(Gen Counsel, Sec & Sr VP)*
Michele Fitzpatrick *(VP-CRM Strategy & Sls Engrg)*
Federico Ortiz *(VP-Tax)*

Aberdeen Group, Inc.
451D St 7th Fl Ste 710, Boston, MA 02210
Tel.: (617) 723-7890
Fax: (617) 723-7897
Toll Free: (800) 577-7891
E-Mail: member.services@aberdeen.com
Web Site: www.aberdeen.com

Employees: 100
Year Founded: 1998

Jay Adams *(CFO)*
James Cabral *(Chief Sls Officer)*
Peter Ostrow *(VP & Grp Dir-Res)*
Derek Brink *(VP)*
Tamara Graves *(Sr Dir-Mktg)*
Jim Rapoza *(Dir-Editorial & Sr Analyst-Res)*
Matt Grant *(Dir-Content Strategy)*
Michael M. Moon *(Dir-Res & Human Capital Mgmt)*
Jonathan Ryan *(Dir-Mktg Tech)*
Matthew Lewis *(Mgr-Mktg Ops)*

Accounts:
Acxiom
Gardner Denver
Industry Canada

Harte-Hanks Direct Marketing/Jacksonville, LLC
7498 Fullerton St, Jacksonville, FL 32256-3508
Tel.: (904) 363-6313
Fax: (904) 363-6867
E-Mail: contactus@harte-hanks.com
Web Site: www.hartehanks.com

Employees: 125
Year Founded: 1972

Agency Specializes In: Direct Response Marketing

Robert Neill *(CIO)*
Steve Lester *(Dir-Bus Sys)*

Non-U.S. Subsidiaries

Harte-Hanks CRM Services Belgium N.V.
Ekkelgaarden 6, 3500 Hasselt, Belgium
Tel.: (32) 11 300 300
Fax: (32) 11 300 310
E-Mail: info@harte-hanks.be
Web Site: www.hartehanks.com

Employees: 50

Agency Specializes In: Communications, Consulting, Direct-to-Consumer, Media Planning, New Technologies, Strategic Planning/Research

Ger Schuivens *(Mng Dir)*
Jeff Slough *(Mng Dir)*
Pascal Schroyen *(Dir-Fin & Admin)*

Harte-Hanks do Brazil Consultoria e Servicos Ltda.
Av marcoes Unidas 13797 Abandar 94 CJ3, SP 04794-000 Sao Paulo, Brazil
Tel.: (55) 11 2161 6199
Fax: (55) 11 2161 6198
Web Site: www.hartehanks.com

Employees: 70

Agency Specializes In: Direct Response Marketing

Toni Munoz *(Sr Mgr-Ops)*

HARVEST CREATIVE
348 N Main, Memphis, TN 38103
Tel.: (901) 526-6244
Web Site: www.harvestcreative.com

Agency Specializes In: Advertising, Brand Development & Integration, Graphic Design, Logo & Package Design

Ursula Gutowski *(Sr Dir-Art)*
Daniel Brown *(Dir-Creative)*
Mike Force *(Assoc Dir-Creative)*
Jenna Kaufman *(Acct Mgr)*
Hunter Mitchell *(Copywriter)*

Accounts:
Tractor Supply Co. Inc.

HARVEST CREATIVE SERVICES
1011 North Washington, Lansing, MI 48906
Tel.: (517) 887-6555
Web Site: harvestcreativeservices.com/

Agency Specializes In: Advertising, Brand Development & Integration, Strategic Planning/Research

Pam Jodway *(Sr VP-Market Dev)*
Mark Miller *(VP-Music Svcs)*
Matthew Reinbold *(Editor-Media & Motion Graphics)*
Jenny Berggren *(Mgr-Production)*

Accounts:
Biggby Coffee

HARVEY & DAUGHTERS, INC./ H&D BRANDING
952 Ridgebrook Rd Ste 1000, Sparks, MD 21152
Tel.: (410) 771-5566
Fax: (410) 771-5559
E-Mail: jperkins@hd-branding.com
Web Site: www.harveyagency.com

Employees: 32
Year Founded: 1986

National Agency Associations: AAF-IN-Second Wind Limited

Agency Specializes In: Advertising, Brand Development & Integration, Communications, Consumer Marketing, Guerilla Marketing, Integrated Marketing, Internet/Web Design, Package Design, Point of Purchase, Promotions, Publicity/Promotions, Retail, Strategic Planning/Research

Approx. Annual Billings: $28,000,000 Capitalized

Sue Baile *(Dir-Production & Studio)*
John Makowski *(Dir-Creative)*
Brian Knowles *(Mgr-Print Production)*
Claire Joyce *(Designer)*
Alexandra Geisler *(Acct Coord)*
Lexi Geisler *(Acct Coord)*
Shannon Taylor *(Coord-Traffic)*

Accounts:
Black & Decker
Blanx
CoverGirl
Delta Carbona
DeWalt
Dr. Scholl's
H&S Bakery/Schmidt's
Hershey's
McCormick Foodservice, Retail
Olay
Phillips Seafood
Procter & Gamble Cosmetics Oil of Olay, Max Factor & Cover Girl; 1986
Schmidt Baking
Scotts
Season Brand
Turkey Hill
U.S. Foodservice

HARVEY ASSOCIATES-DIRECT MARKETING SOLUTIONS
2 Knollwoods, Oakland, NJ 07436
Tel.: (201) 962-8463
E-Mail: harveyfnj@optonline.net
Web Site: www.harveyfeldman.com

Employees: 5
Year Founded: 1986

National Agency Associations: DMA

Agency Specializes In: Advertising, Brand Development & Integration, Business Publications, Business-To-Business, Children's Market, Co-op Advertising, Collateral, Communications, Consulting, Consumer Marketing, Consumer Publications, Corporate Identity, Cosmetics, Digital/Interactive, Direct Response Marketing, E-Commerce, Education, Electronic Media, Engineering, Event Planning & Marketing, Exhibit/Trade Shows, Fashion/Apparel, Financial, Food Service, Government/Political, Graphic Design, Health Care Services, High Technology, In-Store Advertising, Industrial, Information Technology, Legal Services, Leisure, Local Marketing, Logo & Package Design, Magazines, Medical Products, Merchandising, New Product

Development, Newspapers & Magazines, Over-50 Market, Package Design, Pharmaceutical, Planning & Consultation, Point of Purchase, Point of Sale, Print, Production, Public Relations, Publicity/Promotions, Real Estate, Restaurant, Retail, Sales Promotion, Seniors' Market, Sports Market, Strategic Planning/Research, Syndication, Technical Advertising, Trade & Consumer Magazines, Transportation, Travel & Tourism

Approx. Annual Billings: $1,000,000

Breakdown of Gross Billings by Media: Bus. Publs.: $100,000; Consulting: $250,000; D.M.: $400,000; Point of Purchase: $50,000; Strategic Planning/Research: $200,000

Harvey A. Feldman *(Pres)*

Accounts:
General Foods; White Plains, NY Gevalia Kaffe
Hanover Direct; Weehawken, NJ Catalogs
Liberty Richter; Saddle Brook, NJ Food, Gifts
Management Concepts; Vienna, VA Business-to-Business Publishing
McGraw Hill; Heightstown, NJ Publisher
Mosby-Year Book; Chicago, IL Professional Publications
Myron Manufacturing; Maywood, NJ Personalized Gifts
Pain Relief Technology; Boca Raton, FL Health Products
Prentice Hall Direct; Paramus, NJ Publisher
TX Technology; Randolph, NJ Communications Technology

HASTINGS DESIGN CO

PO Box 8813, Roanoke, VA 24014
Tel.: (540) 808-2233
E-Mail: mary@hastingsdesign.com
Web Site: www.hastingsdesign.com

Employees: 1

Mary Hastings *(Pres)*

Accounts:
Bontex, Inc.

HATCH MARKETING

(Formerly Dibona, Bornstein & Random, Inc.)
46 Waltham St, Boston, MA 02118
Tel.: (617) 267-6262
Fax: (617) 267-3870
Web Site: www.engagehatch.com/

E-Mail for Key Personnel:
Media Dir.: tgauvreau@dbrnet.com

Employees: 12
Year Founded: 1989

National Agency Associations: ICOM

Agency Specializes In: Advertising

Approx. Annual Billings: $3,000,000

Breakdown of Gross Billings by Media: Bus. Publs.: $60,000; Collateral: $870,000; D.M.: $150,000; Mags.: $90,000; Newsp.: $450,000; Other: $90,000; Outdoor: $510,000; Pub. Rels.: $30,000; Radio: $150,000; T.V.: $600,000

Stanley Bornstein *(Pres & CEO)*
Jacqueline Holland *(Sr Dir-Art)*
Vic Meredith *(Sr Acct Mgr)*

Accounts:
Sodexho; Gaithersburg, MD

HAUSER ADVERTISING

309 Bellino Dr, Pacific Palisades, CA 90272
Tel.: (310) 459-5911
E-Mail: moreinfo@hauser-advertising.com
Web Site: www.hauser-advertising.com

E-Mail for Key Personnel:
President: chauser@hauser-advertising.com

Employees: 1
Year Founded: 1987

Agency Specializes In: Advertising, Brand Development & Integration, Branded Entertainment, Broadcast, Business-To-Business, Catalogs, Collateral, College, Computers & Software, Consulting, Consumer Marketing, Corporate Identity, E-Commerce, Education, Email, Entertainment, Financial, Graphic Design, High Technology, Hospitality, Identity Marketing, Internet/Web Design, Logo & Package Design, Marine, Outdoor, Planning & Consultation, Print, Production, Production (Print), Radio, Real Estate, Regional, Sales Promotion, Strategic Planning/Research, Syndication, T.V., Technical Advertising, Travel & Tourism

Breakdown of Gross Billings by Media: Collateral: 10%; Consulting: 10%; Foreign: 10%; Graphic Design: 30%; Logo & Package Design: 10%; Outdoor: 5%; Print: 10%; Worldwide Web Sites: 15%

Cliff Hauser *(Pres)*
David Miller *(Sr VP-Mktg)*

Accounts:
Alfred A. Knopf
Bank of America
Cousteau Resorts
Disney; Burbank, CA
Hughes JVC Technical Corp.; Carlsbad, CA
Johnson & Johnson; New Brunswick, NJ
Random House
Twentieth Century Fox; Los Angeles, CA
Universal Pictures; Universal City, CA
Vela Resorts
The Venetian Hotel
Vintage/Anchor Books
Warner Brothers; Burbank, CA

THE HAUSER GROUP INC.

13354 Manchester Rd Ste 200, Saint Louis, MO 63131
Tel.: (314) 436-9090
Fax: (314) 436-9212
Web Site: www.hausergrouppr.com

Agency Specializes In: Advertising, Crisis Communications, Media Relations, Media Training, Public Relations, Social Media, Strategic Planning/Research

Julie Hauser *(Pres)*
Kelly Harris *(Dir-PR)*
Pamela Powell *(Sr Acct Exec)*
Jeni Ross *(Acct Exec)*

Accounts:
New-Gateway Greening
New-Great Rivers Greenway

HAVAS

29/30 quai de Dion Bouton, 92817 Puteaux, Cedex France
Tel.: (33) 1 58 47 81 00
Fax: (33) 1 58 47 90 38
E-Mail: havas.communications@havas.com
Web Site: www.havas.com

Employees: 15,419
Year Founded: 1835

National Agency Associations: AACC-ADC

Agency Specializes In: Above-the-Line, Advertising, Advertising Specialties, Below-the-Line, Brand Development & Integration, Branded Entertainment, Communications, Consulting, Content, Corporate Communications, Corporate Identity, Crisis Communications, Customer Relationship Management, Digital/Interactive, Direct Response Marketing, Direct-to-Consumer, Entertainment, Environmental, Event Planning & Marketing, Experience Design, Financial, In-Store Advertising, Internet/Web Design, Investor Relations, Logo & Package Design, Market Research, Media Buying Services, Media Planning, Media Relations, Media Training, Mobile Marketing, Outdoor, Package Design, Pharmaceutical, Planning & Consultation, Point of Purchase, Point of Sale, Production (Print), Promotions, Public Relations, Publicity/Promotions, Publishing, Sales Promotion, Shopper Marketing, Social Media, Sponsorship, Sports Market, Viral/Buzz/Word of Mouth, Web (Banner Ads, Pop-ups, etc.)

Approx. Annual Billings: $2,285,419,000

Mercedes Erra *(Exec Pres & Founder-BETC)*
Yannick Bollore *(Chm & CEO)*
Stephane Fouks *(Exec Co-Chm-Havas Worldwide, CEO-France & VP-Havas Grp)*
Remi Babinet *(Chm-BETC & Dir-Global Creative-BETC)*
Alfonso Rodes Vila *(CEO-Havas Media)*
Thomas Derouault *(Exec Dir-Creative)*
Gael Caron *(Dir-Art)*
Aurelie Jolion *(Dir-IR)*
Alban Penicaut *(Dir-Creative)*
Marielle Postec *(Dir-Art)*
Michel Dobkine *(Gen Sec)*

Accounts:
The Architecture Museum
B&B Hotels
Carrefour
Cite de l'architecture & du patrimoine
Citroen
Danone
EDF
France Telecom
GlaxoSmithKline
Grupo Carso
Hershey Foods
Hyundai
Joey Starr / Lickshot
Les Restaurants du Coeur
LVMH
McDonald's
Merck
Mondelez International, Inc.
Moutardes du Vexin
Novartis Nicotinell
Peugeot
Pfizer
Reckitt Benckiser
Sanofi

Havas Creative Group

Arnold Furnace

(Formerly The Furnace)
Level 11 60 Miller St, Sydney, NSW 2060 Australia
Tel.: (61) 2 8248 5000
Fax: (61) 2 8248 5050
Web Site: www.arnoldfurnace.com/

Employees: 30

Agency Specializes In: Sports Market

Danielle Davies *(Sr Acct Mgr)*
Natalia Kowalczyk *(Acct Mgr)*
Helen Macdougall *(Copywriter)*
Anthony Gregorio *(Group CEO)*
Michael Stevenson *(Client Svc Dir)*

Accounts:
Atkins Nutritionals
Brown-Forman Australia Campaign: "Christmas Hub", Campaign: "Jack's Holiday Holograms", Campaign: "The Bar That Jack Built", Campaign: "The Spirit of Music"
Cenovis
Disney Channel
Jack Daniel's Tennessee Honey "Holiday Holograms", Campaign: "Birthdays, Loved, Legend, Unchanged", Campaign: "Holiday Select", Campaign: "Postcards From Lynchburg", Campaign: "The Spirit of Music"
Olympus
Peugeot
Skins
Surfrider Foundation Plastic Pollution Awareness, Print
Tour East

Arnold Worldwide
10 Summer St, Boston, MA 02110
(See Separate Listing)

fullsixadvertising
(Formerly 6:AM)
157 Rue Anatole, 92300 Levallois-Perret, France
Tel.: (33) 149687300
E-Mail: communication@fullsix.com
Web Site: fullsixadvertising.fr

Employees: 600

Agency Specializes In: Advertising

Marco Tinelli *(Pres)*
Stephanie Boisson *(Assoc Dir)*

Accounts:
New-Dodo SAS
French Red Cross Campaign: "The light of donation"

Havas Formula
(Formerly Formula PR)
810 Parkview Dr N, El Segundo, CA 90245
(See Separate Listing)

Havas Sports & Entertainment
(Formerly uncommon)
Avenida General Peron, 38 Planta 10,, 28020 Madrid, Spain
Tel.: (34) 914569090
Fax: (34) 91 319 8238
Web Site: www.aisspain.es

Employees: 100

Agency Specializes In: Direct Response Marketing

Frodoric Sounillac *(Dir-Creative)*
Cristina Lera Garcia *(Mgr-Analytics)*
Teresa Veron Sanchez *(Analyst-Digital)*

Accounts:
International Association of Athletics Federations Public Relations

Havas Worldwide Chicago
36 E Grand Ave, Chicago, IL 60611
(See Separate Listing)

Havas Worldwide
(Formerly Euro RSCG Worldwide HQ)
200 Hudson St, New York, NY 10013
(See Separate Listing)

Helia
(Formerly Havas EHS London)
6 Briset Street, London, EC1M 5NR United Kingdom
Tel.: (44) 207 017 1000
Fax: (44) 207 017 1001
Web Site: www.havashelia.com

Employees: 100
Year Founded: 1967

Agency Specializes In: Direct Response Marketing

Tash Whitmey *(CEO)*
Dan Gibson *(Mng Partner)*
Tony Miller *(Mng Partner)*
Matt Fanshawe *(Grp COO)*
Ben Silcox *(Chief Data & Digital Officer)*
Mark Taylor *(Mng Dir-FULCRM)*
Andy Buist *(Assoc Global Brand Dir)*
Aaron Howard *(Dir-Creative)*
Liz Tang *(Dir-Client Svcs)*
Sarah Wood *(Assoc Dir-Creative)*
Lauren McIlroy *(Planner)*
Steven Bennett-Day *(Grp Exec Dir-Creative)*

Accounts:
Barclays
Barkley Cars International
BBC CRM
The Co-operative Bank
D.E Master Blenders Global Media
Diageo
EasyJet
Heathrow
Nestle
Pets at Home
Peugeot UK Campaign: "Carkour", Campaign: "Envy Whodunnit", Campaign: "See the city in a different light", Campaign: "Show Your Character"
New-Royal Mail Customer Engagement
Sky Card Credit Card; 2008
Southwestern Distillery Campaign: "FaceTime", Tarquin's Gin
Tesco CRM, Clubcard
TSB Direct Marketing
Unilever Digital Display Communications, Dove (Global Digital Agency of Record), Dove Men+Care (Global Digital Agency of Record), Surf (Global Digital Agency of Record)
Viking Cruises
Volvo Cars, Digital, V40 R-Design
New-Westfield CRM
Whitbread Beefeater Grill, Brewers Fayre, CRM, Premier Inn, Table Table, Taybarns

Helia
(Formerly Havas EHS Cirencester)
Phoenix Way, Cirencester, Glos GL7 1RY United Kingdom
Tel.: (44) 1285 644744
Fax: (44) 1285 654952
Web Site: www.havashelia.com

Employees: 110

Agency Specializes In: Direct Response Marketing

David Williams *(Mng Dir)*
Simon Cromey *(Head-Plng)*
Jon McWee *(Head-Digital Design)*
Aaron McCarthy *(Sr Dir-Art)*
Ewan Gee *(Dir-Global Creative-Volvo Cars)*
Sue Vizor *(Dir-Ops)*

Accounts:
Comparethemarket.com
Heinz Baby Food
Pets at Home CRM

Victors & Spoils
1904 Pearl St, Boulder, CO 80302
(See Separate Listing)

W & Cie
19 rue Klock, Clichy, 92586 France
Tel.: (33) 1 72 27 00 00
Fax: (33) 1 72 27 00 07
E-Mail: d.gancel@wcie.fr
Web Site: www.wcie.fr

Employees: 95

Agency Specializes In: Advertising, Production (Print)

Francols Lamotte *(Dir Gen)*
Martin Pion *(Dir Gen)*
Gregoire Weil *(Deputy Mng Dir)*
Thomas Stern *(VP & Dir-Creative)*
Aurelie Leaute *(Acct Dir)*
Paul Groves *(Dir-Creative)*
Catherine Parmentier *(Dir-Admin & Fin)*
Catherine Alquier *(Assoc Dir-Digital)*

Accounts:
AFG
Airports of Paris
Canard
E.Leclerc
Federation Nationale Femmes Campaign: "The monsters - Freddy Krueger"
Federation Nationale Solidarite Femmes Campaign: "Breath"
G6 Hospitality LLC
IClaro
Jardi
Ligue contre le cancer Campaign: "Donate and life goes one"
Loiret
Mercure Hotels
Ministry of National Education Campaign: "Take Action Against Bullying at School"
Peugeot
Reseau Ferre de France Campaign: "Tomorrow on Track Today"
SITA

Havas Media Group

Affiperf
8 rue Godefroy, 92800 Puteaux, France
Tel.: (33) 1 58 47 80 00
Fax: (33) 1 58 47 90 38
E-Mail: contact@affiperf.com
Web Site: www.affiperf.com

Deborah Wits *(Acct Dir)*
Laure De Longvilliers Prest *(Dir-France)*
Fabien Josiere *(Dir-Programmatic Media)*
Xavier-denis Picard *(Mgr-Intl Programmatic)*

Arena BLM
247 Tottenham Court Rd, London, W1T 7QX United Kingdom
Tel.: (44) 20 7182 6400
Fax: (44) 20 7287 8769
E-Mail: info@arenablm.co.uk
Web Site: www.arenamedia.co.uk

Employees: 90
Year Founded: 1990

Agency Specializes In: Media Buying Services

Pedro Avery *(CEO)*
Beatrice Boue *(Mng Partner)*
Henry Daglish *(Mng Dir)*
Peter Hall *(Art Dir)*
Janine Green *(Dir-Plng)*
Jenna Walker *(Copywriter)*

Accounts:
All Leisure Group Just You, Media, Media Planning & Buying, Swan Hellenic, Travelsphere, Voyages of Discovery
Betfair Media Planning & Buying, SEO, Social
Blinkbox Planning & Buying
Bourne Leisure
Brittany Ferries
Canti Media
Character Options
Dominos Pizza Campaign: "#Lookdown", Campaign: "A dough in the life"
New-Electronic Arts International Media Planning & Buying
ESPN
Eurostar
Flight Centre Buying, Media
GX Networks Ltd. Media Planning & Buying
Indeed Laboratories In-House, Media, Nanoblur, Outdoor, Press
Innovation Norway
Jaeger
King of Shaves
LG Global Media
Merck Consumer Health Hailborange, Seven Seas
Monsanto
Pizza Group Domino's, Online Sitcom, The Support Group
QVC
Ricola Media Planning & Buying, TV
Roundup
Royal Botanical Gardens Kew
New-Royal Mail Media
Scotts Miracle-Gro Media Planning & Buying
Scotts
Suzuki
Three Mobile
Vapestick
VSO
Warner Vision
Westfield

Havas Digital
11 Square Leon Blum, 92806 Puteaux, Cedex France
Tel.: (33) 1 46 93 33 33
Fax: (33) 1 46 93 35 37

Agency Specializes In: Media Buying Services

Stephanie Marie *(COO)*
Pascal Dasseux *(Sr VP & Acct Mgmt Dir)*
Thomas Derouault *(Exec Dir-Creative)*
Gael Caron *(Dir-Art)*
Lucas Polato *(Dir-Media)*
Michel Tonieti *(Dir-Art)*
Otavio Mastrogiuseppe *(Copywriter)*

Accounts:
AACD - Association for Assistance to Handicapped Children Campaign: "Forgotten Bill"
Accor-Hotels.com
Adidas
Air France-KLM Group
Alampco
Areva Energy
Audi
AXA
B&B Hotels
Barclays
Bayer
BBC
BNP Paribas
Center Parcs
Coca-Cola Refreshments USA, Inc.
Danone
DG Digital, MediaMind, Online, TV Campaign Optimization, VideoFusion
EDF
Francaise des Jeux
France Telecom
Orange ABC Annual Report, Cellular Phones
Santander
SEB/Tefal/Calor

Havas Media
(Formerly MPG)
200 Hudson St, New York, NY 10013
(See Separate Listing)

Havas Sports & Entertainment Cake
(Formerly Cake Group Ltd.)
15 Bedford St, Covent Garden, London, WC2E 9HE United Kingdom
Tel.: (44) 207 307 3100
Fax: (44) 207 307 3101
E-Mail: info@cakegroup.com
Web Site: www.cakegroup.com

Employees: 50
Year Founded: 1998

Agency Specializes In: Brand Development & Integration, Public Relations

Adrian Pettett *(CEO)*
Jim Dowling *(Mng Dir)*
Lizzy Pollott *(CMO)*
Martin Smith *(Chief Strategy Officer)*
Andrew Casher *(Head-Experiential & Dir)*
Ria Elizabeth Thomas *(Acct Dir-PR & Experiential)*
Justin Kiszegi *(Dir-Digital Creative)*
Neil Mortimer *(Dir-Production)*
Kathryn Renshaw *(Dir-Bus Dev)*
Hannah Jackson *(Acct Mgr)*
Daniel Lipman *(Acct Mgr-PR & Social Media)*

Accounts:
Alton Towers Resort Consumer PR, Creative, The Smiler, Theme Park & Resort, Viral Campaign
Ben & Jerry's
The Big Lottery Fund
The Big Lunch
British Airways
Burger King
Carling
Chivas
Coca-Cola Refreshments USA, Inc.
COI
New-Electronic Arts Public Relations
HMV
Honda Social Media
Hyundai Motor Company Campaign: "Car Parts for the World"
Microsoft
Morrisons Consumer PR, Nutmeg
Motorola Solutions, Inc.
One Direction Campaign: "Our Moment"
Orange
PG Tips
Sainsburys Mobile
Shop Direct Consumer Public Relations, SEO, Social Media
Sony UK Experiential, Online, Public Relations, SmartBand, Social Media, Wristband
Tourism Ireland Adventure Sports-Tourism
Unilever
United Biscuits
V Festival 20th Anniversary, Consumer Public Relations, Media, Press
Virgin Atlantic #FlightDecks, 787 Aircraft, Birthday Girl, Concept Creation, Consumer Public Relations, Event Production, Microsite, Talent Handling
Visit London
Vodafone
Weetabix Alpen, Online Social Strategy, Social Media
Yahoo

Just Health Communications
37 Point Pleasant, River House, London, SW18 1NN United Kingdom
Tel.: (44) 20 8877 8400
Fax: (44) 20 8874 2453
E-Mail: ask@justhealthcomms.com
Web Site: www.justhealthcomms.com

Employees: 33

Agency Specializes In: Brand Development & Integration, Communications, Consulting, Consumer Publications, Health Care Services, Media Relations, Public Relations, Strategic Planning/Research

Emma Crozier *(Mng Dir)*
Kirsty Mearns *(Mng Dir)*
Jennie Talman *(Mng Dir)*
Catherine Barnett *(Dir)*
Glen Halliwell *(Dir-Client)*

Accounts:
Caris Life Sciences Integrated PR, Public Affairs
MiniCol

HAVAS HEALTH
200 Madison Ave, New York, NY 10016
Tel.: (212) 532-1000
Fax: (212) 251-2766
E-Mail: hhww.managingpartners@havashealth.com
Web Site: www.havashealth.com

Employees: 2,500

National Agency Associations: 4A's

Agency Specializes In: Communications, Health Care Services, Sponsorship

Donna Murphy *(Co-CEO & Partner)*
Edward Stapor *(Partner & Brand Dir-Global)*
William Kemp *(Exec VP & Client Svcs Dir)*
Meredith Levy *(Sr VP & Dir-Bus Dev)*
James Akhbari *(VP & Dir-Digital Media)*
Michele Coppa *(VP-HR)*
Michelle Wang *(Mgr-Creative Svcs)*
April Boykin *(Generalist-HR)*
Adriana Erin Rivera *(Asst Media Planner)*

United States

Havas Life Metro
(Formerly Euro RSCG Life LM&P)
200 Madison Ave, New York, NY 10016
Tel.: (212) 532-1000
Fax: (212) 251-2766
Web Site: www.havaslife.com/

Year Founded: 1980

Agency Specializes In: Health Care Services, Pharmaceutical

Allison Ceraso *(Mng Dir & Chief Creative Officer)*
Donna Murphy *(CEO-Havas Health-Global)*
Matt Silver *(Sr VP & Mgmt Supvr)*
Joseph Speiser *(Sr VP & Dir-Tech)*
Claire Kane *(Sr VP & Planner)*
Ellen Funk *(VP & Acct Grp Supvr)*
Scott Kelson *(VP & Acct Grp Supvr)*
Ryan Phippen *(VP & Acct Grp Supvr)*
Kim Rostovskis *(VP & Acct Grp Supvr)*
Cailean O'Connor *(Acct Supvr)*
Amanda Vitta *(Acct Supvr)*

Accounts:
Bausch & Lomb
Biogen Idec
Bristol-Myers Squibb
ENDO Pharmaceuticals
Genentech
Lansinoh Laboratories
Medicis

Havas Life and Wellness
200 Madison Ave, New York, NY 10016
Tel.: (212) 884-1400
E-Mail: hello@havaslifeandwellness.com
Web Site: www.havaslifeandwellness.com

Employees: 50
Year Founded: 2014

Laurel Rossi *(Pres)*

Havas Lynx
200 Madison Ave, New York, NY 10016
Tel.: (212) 251-8800
Web Site: www.havaslynx.com

Employees: 100
Year Founded: 1986

Larry Mickelberg *(Pres)*

Havas Life New York
200 Madison Ave, New York, NY 10016
Tel.: (212) 726-5050
Web Site: www.havaslife.com

Employees: 125
Year Founded: 2003

National Agency Associations: 4A's

Allison Ceraso *(Co-Mng Dir & Chief Creative Officer)*
Michael McNamara *(Co-Mng Dir)*

H4B Chelsea
75 9th Ave, New York, NY 10011
Tel.: (212) 299-5000
E-Mail: mpeto@Health4Brands.com
Web Site: www.health4brands.com

Employees: 325
Year Founded: 2004

National Agency Associations: 4A's

Agency Specializes In: Advertising, Health Care Services

Christian Bauman *(Mng Dir & Chief Creative Officer)*
Steven Nothel *(Mng Dir)*
Mike Peto *(Mng Dir)*
George Lepore *(Exec VP & Exec Dir-Creative)*
Tracey O'Brien *(Exec VP & Client Svcs Dir)*
Jan Chau *(Sr Dir-Art)*
Charles Ross *(Acct Exec)*

Managed Edge
(Formerly Havas Life Managed Edge)
200 Madison Ave, New York, NY 10016
Tel.: (212) 532-1000
E-Mail: khawar.khokhar@havashealth.com
Web Site: www.havashealth.com

Employees: 45
Year Founded: 1997

Agency Specializes In: Health Care Services

Gaynor Hayburn *(Grp Mng Dir)*
Doug Burcin *(CEO-Havas Health-Global)*
Donna Murphy *(CEO-Havas Health-Global)*
Janine Serio *(Sr VP & Assoc Dir-Creative)*
Alison Czarnecki *(Coord)*

Havas Life Metro
(Formerly Euro RSCG Life LM&P)
36 E Grand Ave, Chicago, IL 60611
Tel.: (312) 640-6800
Fax: (312) 640-3219
Web Site: www.havaslife.com

Employees: 45
Year Founded: 2000

Agency Specializes In: Health Care Services

Jill Mennenga *(Exec VP & Grp Acct Dir)*
Stephen Bell *(VP & Acct Supvr)*
Doug Fox *(VP & Acct Supvr)*

Adrenaline- A Havas Company
(Formerly Euro RSCG Life Adrenaline)
350 Hudson St, New York, NY 10014
Tel.: (212) 519-3700
Web Site: www.adrenaline-havas.com/

National Agency Associations: 4A's

Agency Specializes In: Consumer Marketing, Health Care Services

Rich Russo *(Mng Dir & Chief Creative Officer)*
Larry Pollare *(Co-Mng Dir)*
Pablo Hernandez *(Grp Acct Dir)*
Lauren Berlamino *(Acct Dir-Global Brands)*
Alicia De Armas *(Acct Dir-Global)*
Irina Shlafman *(Acct Supvr)*

Accounts:
Benefiber
Coalitionforthehomeless.org
Excedrin
Gas-X
PetArmor Plus

Havas PR
(Formerly Euro RSCG Life PR)
200 Madison Ave, New York, NY 10016
Tel.: (646) 361-1837
Fax: (212) 367-6839
Web Site: www.us.havaspr.com

Employees: 80

Agency Specializes In: Health Care Services, Investor Relations, Public Relations

Matt Weiss *(Mng Partner & CMO)*
Tim Maleeny *(Mng Partner & Chief Strategy Officer)*
Israel Garber *(Grp Exec Dir-Creative & Mng Dir)*
Jason Musante *(Grp Exec Dir-Creative & Mng Dir)*
Andrew Benett *(CEO-Havas Worldwide & Havas Creative Grp)*
Dustin Duke *(Exec Dir-Creative)*
Jim Hord *(Exec Dir-Creative)*
Kurt Nossan *(Exec Dir-Creative)*
Matt Hock *(Assoc Dir-Creative)*
Jon Vall *(Assoc Dir-Creative)*
Susanne Collin *(Sr Acct Mgr)*
James Mann *(Coord-PR-North America)*

Canada

Havas Life
(Formerly Euro RSCG Life)
20 Richmond St E 6th Fl, Toronto, ON M5C 2R9 Canada
Tel.: (416) 925-9005
Fax: (416) 925-6568
Web Site: www.havaslife.com

Employees: 25

Agency Specializes In: Health Care Services

Pam Park *(Pres)*
Kristina Sauter *(VP & Client Svcs Dir)*
Chantal Innes *(VP & Dir-Creative)*
Cecile Hustin *(VP-Strategic Plng)*
Danielle Nicholas *(Sr Acct Dir)*
Patrick Hammill *(Acct Dir)*
Marie-Claude Turgeon *(Acct Dir)*
Anoush Thorose *(Dir-Art)*
Kelsey Macdonald *(Assoc Dir-Creative & Copy)*
Marjorie Davies *(Copywriter)*

Accounts:
Abbott
Bayer BP Canada
Bayer BP Global
Boehringer Ingelheim
Janssen Ortho

Italy

Havas Life Rome
(Formerly Euro RSCG Life)
Via del Poggio Laurentino 118, 00144 Rome, Italy
Tel.: (39) 0654550498
E-Mail: Cristina.Dalo@havasww.com
Web Site: www.havaslife.com

Employees: 4
Year Founded: 2004

Agency Specializes In: Health Care Services

Carola Salvato *(Mng Dir)*
Fabrizio Vettori *(Client Svcs Dir)*
Alessandra Bordigato *(Dir-Bus Developer)*
Elisabetta Grioni *(Dir & Strategic Planner)*
Olgamaria Pacchioni *(Dir-Bus Unit)*
Michela Carella *(Sr Acct Mgr)*
Michela Ferron *(Sr Acct Mgr)*

Germany

Havas Life Bird & Schulte
Urachstrasse 19, 79102 Freiburg, Germany
Tel.: (49) 07618885480
Web Site: www.bird-schulte.de

Employees: 30
Year Founded: 2008

Jeremy Bird *(Mng Dir)*
Monika Schulte *(Mng Dir)*

Havas Lynx
168-173, Berkshire House, London, WC1V7AA United Kingdom
Tel.: (44) (0)20 3763 5780
Web Site: www.havaslynx.com

Employees: 35
Year Founded: 2012

Tim Woodcock *(Co-Mng Dir)*
Jon Linscott *(Co-Mng Dir)*
Tom Richards *(Chief Creative Officer)*
Jon Chapman *(Creative Dir)*
Helen Godley *(Creative Dir)*
Stuart Hornby *(Client Svcs Dir)*

Accounts:
New-Teva #Laugh4Lungs

Havas Life Medicom UK
Ferry Works, Summer Road, Thames Ditton, KT7 0QJ United Kingdom
Tel.: (44) (0) 208 481 8100

Employees: 100
Year Founded: 2003

Gaynor Hayburn *(Group Mng Dir)*
Chris Bartley *(Deputy Mng Dir)*

Sarah Dyson *(Deputy Mng Dir)*

HAVAS WORLDWIDE

(Formerly Euro RSCG Worldwide HQ)
200 Hudson St, New York, NY 10013
Tel.: (212) 886-2000
Fax: (212) 886-5013
Web Site: www.havasworldwide.com/

Employees: 11,000
Year Founded: 1991

National Agency Associations: 4A's

Agency Specializes In: Above-the-Line, Advertising, Advertising Specialties, Automotive, Aviation & Aerospace, Below-the-Line, Brand Development & Integration, Branded Entertainment, Business-To-Business, Communications, Content, Corporate Communications, Cosmetics, Digital/Interactive, Event Planning & Marketing, Fashion/Apparel, Financial, Food Service, Health Care Services, High Technology, International, Leisure, Luxury Products, Medical Products, Men's Market, Multicultural, Pharmaceutical, Planning & Consultation, Public Relations, Retail, Social Marketing/Nonprofit, Social Media, Sponsorship, Strategic Planning/Research, Teen Market, Travel & Tourism, Urban Market, Women's Market

Matt Weiss *(Mng Partner-New York & CMO-Global)*
Tim Maleeny *(Mng Partner & Chief Strategy Officer)*
Rachel Conlan *(Mng Dir & Sr VP)*
Julie Hall *(Mng Dir)*
Jason Musante *(Grp Exec Dir-Creative & Mng Dir)*
Beth Pasciucco *(Mng Dir)*
Frank Mangano *(CFO & COO-NA & NY)*
Jessica Ellison *(Editor-Digital Content)*
Dustin Duke *(Exec Dir-Creative)*
Jim Hord *(Exec Dir-Creative)*
John Nussbaum *(Grp Dir-Creative)*
Joe Koecher *(Sr Dir-Art)*
Ryan Wi *(Sr Dir-Art)*
Gene Fischer *(Sr Acct Dir-Digital Strategy & Integration)*
Julie Lister *(Grp Acct Dir)*
Suzanne Winkelman *(Grp Acct Dir)*
Daniel Cioni *(Sr Producer-Digital)*
Anna Santiago *(Sr Producer-Digital)*
Ashley Heltne *(Acct Dir-Digital)*
Cheryl Ryan *(Bus Dir)*
Rolando Cordova *(Dir-Creative)*
Josh Greenspan *(Dir-Creative)*
Maggie Gross *(Dir-Brand & Digital Strategy)*
Luke Hughett *(Dir-Creative)*
Daniel Korn *(Dir-Bus Dev)*
Sherrod Melvin *(Dir-Creative)*
Rita Senders *(Dir-Creative)*
Mark Tallis *(Dir-Art)*
David Fredette *(Assoc Dir-Creative)*
Matthew Hock *(Assoc Dir-Creative)*
Jon Vall *(Assoc Dir-Creative)*
Susan Schaefer *(Sr Mgr-Brdcst Bus)*
Deborah Steeg *(Sr Mgr-Brdcst Bus)*
Rhona Press *(Mgr-Editorial Proofreading)*
Frank Rega *(Mgr-Production Billing-Havas Media)*
Jason Desmarais *(Acct Grp Supvr)*
Rebecca Padrick *(Acct Supvr)*
Lindsay Stanislau *(Acct Supvr)*
Andy Chang *(Acct Exec)*
Stephanie Pollitt *(Acct Exec-New Bus)*
Kara Brown *(Media Planner & Media Buyer)*
Marty Bonacorso *(Copywriter)*
Madeline Toro *(Analyst-Fin)*
Lauren Wojciechowski *(Asst Acct Exec)*
Katharine Barker *(Jr Producer-Digital)*
Seth Rothberg *(Sr Developer-Interactive)*

Accounts:
The Ad Council Campaign: "Awkward Times"
Air France-KLM Group
Chivas
Citroen
Coca Cola
Cracker Barrel Old Country Store, Inc. Campaign: "Match", Campaign: "Pictures", Campfire Meals, Cracker Barrel, Digital, Radio, Search, Social
Credit Suisse
D-CON Campaign: "Mouse Missing"
Dish Network
Dos Equis "Bobsled", Campaign: "Dog Sledder", Campaign: "Dogsled", Campaign: "Legend" Winter Olympics 2014, Campaign: "Life Saver", Campaign: "Memory Foam Mattresses", Campaign: "Surgery Fixer", Campaign: "The Most Interesting Man's Dos Nog Recipe"
Durex (Agency of Record) Campaign: "Don't Fake It"
Evian
GlaxoSmithKline
Heineken USA
Hershey Co Digital
IBM
Ikea
New-Italian Institute of Frozen Food Freeze the Waste
Jacob's Creek
Jenny Craig
Keurig Green Mountain Inc. (Creative Agency of Record) Campaign: "Make Your Favorite Cold Drinks", Keurig Kold
KLM Group - Air France
Lacoste
LG Electronics
Liberty Mutual Campaign: "Rise" Winter Olympics 2014, Creative
L'Oreal
LVMH
MakeMyTrip.com; India
Malaria No More
Merck
The National Campaign to Prevent Teen & Unplanned Pregnancy Campaign: "Don't Give Up"
NetJets Digital Marketing
Optimus
P&G
PayPal Campaign: "People Rule", Global Creative
Pernod Ricard
Peugeot
Pfizer
PSA Peugeot Citroen
Reckitt Benckiser Dettol
Sanofi SA
Sauza Campaign: "Make it with a Fireman"
Schering-Plough Claritin, Coppertone, Dr. Scholl's, Levitra
Shire Pharmaceuticals
TD Ameritrade (Lead Creative Agency) Campaign: "Lamb", Campaign: "Type E", Campaign: "You Got This", Digital, In-Store, Print, Social, TV
Unilever Digital
New-Weight Watchers International, Inc. Creative

United States

Abernathy MacGregor Group-Los Angeles

(Formerly Abernathy MacGregor Group, Inc.)
707 Wilshire Blvd Ste 3950, Los Angeles, CA 90017-3110
Tel.: (213) 630-6550
Fax: (213) 489-3443
E-Mail: idc@abmac.com
Web Site: www.abmac.com

Employees: 15
Year Founded: 1998

Agency Specializes In: Financial, Public Relations

Ian D. Campbell *(Vice Chm)*
David Schneiderman *(Mng Dir & Head-San Francisco Office)*
Chuck Dohrenwend *(Mng Dir)*
James B. Lucas *(Mng Dir)*
Shawn H. Pattison *(Mng Dir)*
Sydney Isaacs *(Exec VP)*
Glen L. Orr *(Exec VP)*
Alan Oshiki *(Exec VP)*
Allyson Vento *(Exec VP)*
Heather Wilson *(Exec VP)*
Amy Feng *(Sr VP)*

Abernathy MacGregor Group-New York

(Formerly Abernathy MacGregor Group, Inc.)
501 Madison Ave 13th Fl, New York, NY 10022-5617
(See Separate Listing)

Havas Edge Boston

(Formerly Euro RSCG Edge)
10 Summer St, Boston, MA 02110
Tel.: (617) 585-3000
Fax: (617) 585-3001
E-Mail: info@havasedge.com
Web Site: www.havasedge.com

Employees: 22

Agency Specializes In: Advertising, Sponsorship

Greg D. Johnson *(Pres & COO)*
Eric Bush *(CFO)*
Bill Marks *(Exec VP & Grp Dir)*
George Sylva *(Sr VP-DRTV Agency Ops)*
Mike Lodge *(VP-Digital Strategy)*
Karla Tateosian *(Acct Dir-Strategic)*
Jeff Donnelley *(Dir-Bus Dev)*
Adam Lynch *(Planner-Digital Media)*

Accounts:
Vistaprint Media Buying

Havas Edge Portland

(Formerly Euro RSCG EDGE)
920 Sw 6th Ave, Portland, OR 97204
Tel.: (503) 228-5555
Fax: (503) 228-0560
Web Site: www.havasedge.com

Employees: 60
Year Founded: 1988

Agency Specializes In: Advertising Specialties, Direct Response Marketing, Infomercials, Sponsorship, T.V.

Greg Johnson *(Pres & COO)*
David Antos *(CTO)*
Mary Webb *(Exec VP & Exec Dir-Creative)*
Abed Abusaleh *(Exec VP-Long-Form Brdcst Media)*
George Sylva *(Sr VP-DRTV Agency Ops)*
Andy Kling *(VP & Grp Acct Dir)*
Dalton Mangin *(VP-Bus Dev)*
Dan Schlafman *(VP-Analytics & Modeling)*

Accounts:
Body by Jake
Brita Water
Cadillac
Callaway Golf Hex Ball; 2000
Char-Broil; 2000
Clorox
Countrywide Financial
Direct TV
Harrah's Casino
Louisiana Pacific
Merck Propecia
Select Comfort

Havas Edge

(Formerly Euro RSCG Edge)
2173 Salk Ave Ste 300, Carlsbad, CA 92008

Tel.: (760) 929-0041
Fax: (760) 929-0104
E-Mail: info@havasedge.com
Web Site: www.havasedge.com

Employees: 100
Year Founded: 2001

National Agency Associations: 4A's

Agency Specializes In: Advertising, Advertising Specialties, Direct Response Marketing, Electronic Media, Infomercials, Media Buying Services, Media Planning, Production, Sponsorship, Strategic Planning/Research, T.V., Telemarketing

Greg D. Johnson *(Pres & COO)*
Steve Netzley *(CEO)*
Shannon Ellis *(Exec VP-Bus Dev)*
Jennifer Peabody *(Exec VP-Short Form Media)*
Taft Zitoun *(VP-Long Form Media)*
Michael Thomas *(Producer-Digital)*
Nicky DeLaSalle *(Dir-Bus Dev)*

Accounts:
CarMD.com Media
Debt Free
Euro-Pro
Sanyo-Fisher

Havas Health
200 Madison Ave, New York, NY 10016
(See Separate Listing)

Havas Impact Chicago
(Formerly Euro RSCG 4D)
36 E Grand Ave Stes 3 & 4, Chicago, IL 60611
Tel.: (312) 799-7000
Fax: (312) 799-7100
Web Site: www.havasimpact.com

Employees: 50

Agency Specializes In: Direct Response Marketing

Bill Meyer *(CEO)*
Marc Broccoli *(Sr VP-Life stage Mktg)*
Julie Obrien *(VP & Acct Dir)*
Cathy Babiez *(VP-Ops & Acct Svcs)*
Linda Burns *(VP)*
Ralph Hollingsworth *(Exec Dir-Creative & Copywriter-Recovering)*
Lisa Zelenko Krutiak *(Dir-Mktg Res)*
Gina Giordano *(Sr Acct Exec)*
Katy Shoemaker *(Sr Acct Exec)*

Accounts:
Barilla
Groupon Customer Relationship Marketing
PureCircle (Agency of Record)
Sprint Digital Marketing (Agency of Record)
Valspar Paints & Stains

Havas Impact
(Formerly Euro RSCG 4D Impact)
2885 Pacific Dr Ste A, Norcross, GA 30071-1807
Tel.: (888) 788-5918
Fax: (770) 248-9014
Toll Free: (888) 788-5918
Web Site: www.havasimpact.com

Employees: 50

National Agency Associations: 4A's

Agency Specializes In: Brand Development & Integration, Consumer Marketing, Event Planning & Marketing, Exhibit/Trade Shows, Merchandising, Out-of-Home Media, Sales Promotion, Sports Market, Strategic Planning/Research

Bill Meyer *(CEO)*
Marc Broccoli *(Sr VP-Life Stage Mktg)*
John Frantz *(VP-Ops)*
John Cavaliero *(Dir-Ops & Experiential Mktg)*
Todd Hoffnagle *(Sr Mgr-Production)*

Accounts:
Boots Healthcare
Bristol Myers Squibb
Clorox
General Motors
Johnson & Johnson
Kellogg USA
Kraft
Merck
Mertz Pharmaceutical
Nestle USA
PepsiCo
Procter & Gamble
Sanofi Aventis
Unilever

Havas Impact
(Formerly Euro RSCG 4D Impact)
36 E Grand Ave, Chicago, IL 60611-3506
Tel.: (312) 799-7000
Fax: (312) 799-7100
Web Site: www.havasimpact.com

Agency Specializes In: Advertising Specialties, Exhibit/Trade Shows, Out-of-Home Media, Sales Promotion

Bill Meyer *(CEO)*
Julie Obrien *(VP & Acct Dir)*
Cathy Babiez *(VP-Ops & Acct Svcs)*
Linda Burns *(VP)*
Ralph Hollingsworth *(Exec Dir-Creative & Copywriter-Recovering)*
John Cavaliero *(Dir-Ops & Experiential Mktg)*
Joe Wangler *(Dir-Art)*
Gina Giordano *(Sr Acct Exec)*

Accounts:
Beiersdorf
Bristol Myers Squibb
Chevrolet
Church & Dwight
Clorox
Corona Brands
Discovery Networks
Friendship Dairies
Johnson & Johnson
Kraft
Mars North America
Merck
Novartis
Procter & Gamble
Reckitt Benckiser
Unilever

Havas PR
(Formerly Euro RSCG Worldwide PR)
200 Madison Ave, New York, NY 10016
(See Separate Listing)

Havas Worldwide New York
(Formerly Euro RSCG Worldwide)
200 Hudson St, New York, NY 10013
Tel.: (212) 886-2000
Fax: (212) 886-2016
Web Site: www.havas.com

Employees: 1,500
Year Founded: 1986

National Agency Associations: 4A's-DMA-PRSA

Agency Specializes In: Advertising, Advertising Specialties, Automotive, Brand Development & Integration, Broadcast, Business-To-Business, Communications, Consulting, Consumer Marketing, Corporate Identity, Digital/Interactive, Direct Response Marketing, Event Planning & Marketing, Fashion/Apparel, Financial, Food Service, Health Care Services, High Technology, Hispanic Market, Internet/Web Design, Investor Relations, Medical Products, New Product Development, Outdoor, Pharmaceutical, Planning & Consultation, Point of Purchase, Point of Sale, Print, Production, Public Relations, Publicity/Promotions, Restaurant, Sales Promotion, Strategic Planning/Research, Sweepstakes, T.V., Teen Market

Jason Musante *(Mng Dir & Grp Exec Dir-Creative)*
Vanessa Romann *(Exec Dir-Strategy-Performance North America)*
Bernardo Gomez *(Grp Dir-Creative)*
Paul Johnson *(Grp Dir-Creative)*
Keith Scott *(Grp Dir-Creative)*
Rosemary Calderone *(Acct Dir)*
Jenni Finch *(Acct Dir)*
Casey Ritts *(Acct Dir)*
Betsy Simons *(Brand Dir-Global)*
Anders Da Silva *(Dir-Creative)*
Andrea Gustafson *(Dir-Design)*
Andrew Jeske *(Dir-Creative)*
Jeremy Pippenger *(Dir-Creative)*
Laure Ayel *(Acct Mgr)*
Olivia Kaufman *(Acct Supvr)*
Mary Klauser *(Acct Supvr)*
Stephanie Pollitt *(Acct Exec-New Bus)*

Accounts:
Air France-KLM Group
Amgen Neulasta, Vera; 2002
Bedsider.org Campaign: "Dog", Campaign: "Grandma", Campaign: "The Talk"
Cash4Gold
Children's Health Fund (Pro-Bono)
Chivas
Citigroup
Edible Arrangements (Lead Creative Agency)
GlaxoSmithKline, Inc. Advair, Boniva, Valtrex, Vesicare; 1999
Heineken Campaign: "Luna Rising", Campaign: "Most Interesting Man in the World", Campaign: "The Most Interesting Man in the World Wins on Land, Sea, Air and Beyond", Campaign: "The Most Interesting Man in the World on Cinco de Mayo", Dos Equis, Heineken, Heineken Light; 2004
IBM
Keurig Green Mountain Campaign: "The Cup Half Full"
Kraft
Liberty Mutual Insurance (Advertising Agency of Record) Campaign: "See Car Insurance In A Whole New Light", Creative
Merck
Nestle
Novartis BeneFiber, Keri Lotion, Nicotinell, Vagistat; 2004
Partnership for a Drug-Free America (Pro-Bono)
Pfizer, Inc. Chantix, Oporia
Reckitt Benckiser Inc.; Wayne, NJ AirWick, Cattlemen's Barbeque, Clearasil, D-Con, Easy Off Bam, Electrasol, Frank's Original Red Hot, French's Gourmayo, French's Mustard, French's Potato Sticks, French's Taste Toppers, French's Worcestershire Sauce, Hippo, Jet Dry, Lime-Away, Lysol, Old English, Resolve, Rid-X, Spray n Wash, Veet, Woolite; 2001
Sanofi-Aventis Pharmaceutical Apidra, Lantus, Lovenox
Schering-Plough HealthCare Products Corp; Kenilworth, NJ A&D Ointment, Afrin Nasal Spray, Bain de Soleil, Chlor-Trimeton, Claritin, Coppertone, Coricidin, Correctol, Dr. Scholl's, Drixoral, Lotrimin AF, Tinactin; 1984
The Skin Cancer Foundation (Pro-Bono)
Verizon Business
Volvo Car Corp.; Goteborg, Sweden Global Lead Agency; 1991
Volvo Cars of Europe; 2000
Volvo Local Market Tactical Organization;

Rockleigh, NJ Handled by Fuel North America
WeddingWire
Yahoo

Havas Worldwide - San Francisco
1725 Montgomery St, San Francisco, CA 94111
Tel.: (415) 345-7700
Fax: (415) 345-7705
Web Site: www.sf.havasworldwide.com/

Employees: 34
Year Founded: 1999

National Agency Associations: 4A's

Agency Specializes In: Advertising, Bilingual Market, Brand Development & Integration, Broadcast, Corporate Identity, Digital/Interactive, Direct Response Marketing, Electronic Media, Event Planning & Marketing, Information Technology, Internet/Web Design, Investor Relations, Radio, Retail, Sponsorship, Strategic Planning/Research

Alan Burgis *(CEO)*
Jim Lightner *(CFO)*
Taylor Wynne *(VP & Dir-Media)*
Ernie Lageson *(Exec Dir-Creative)*
Lyndsey Sferro Konrad *(Dir-HR)*
Peter Lenn *(Dir-Project Mgmt)*
Diana Manning *(Dir-Tech)*
Greg Hawkins *(Assoc Dir-Creative)*

Accounts:
Adobe
Barclays Global Investors
Genetech
Google
Grotto Cellars; 2008
Hainan Airlines; 2008
Method Products; San Francisco, CA
SanDisk Corp; Sunnyvale, CA Flash Memory Cards; 2004
Seagate B2B, B2C, Campaign: "Cello", Campaign: "Popcorn", Creative, Strategy
Silver Oak Cellars Website
Sony Campaign: "Twisted Metal"
Visa
Wells Fargo; San Francisco, CA
wine.com, Inc.

Havas Worldwide-Strat Farm
(Formerly Euro RSCG Worldwide Strat Farm)
200 Madison Ave 2nd Fl, New York, NY 10016
Tel.: (212) 367-6800
Web Site: www.stratfarm.com/

Employees: 10

Agency Specializes In: Brand Development & Integration, Digital/Interactive, Social Media

Laurel Rossi *(Chm & Pres)*
Pamela Vahdat *(Exec VP & Exec Dir-Creative)*
Chris Jarrin *(Sr VP & Dir-Creative & Art)*
Laura Dartnall *(Grp Acct Dir)*
Pablo Hernandez *(Grp Acct Dir)*
Lauren Berlamino *(Acct Dir-Global Brands)*
Vanessa Difebo *(Client Svcs Dir)*
Lauri Liebenstein *(Acct Dir)*
Sam Higgins *(Dir-Creative & Writer)*
Peter Coutroulis *(Dir-Creative)*
Yvonne Desanti *(Dir-Creative)*
Mark Durney *(Dir-Social Media)*
Kristen Gold *(Dir-Benefits)*
Bari Greenstein *(Project Mgr-Global New Bus)*
Rob Conger *(Mgr-Presentation)*
Nancy Frycz *(Mgr-Admin)*

Accounts:
Capgemini North America
EmblemHealth Broadcast, Campaign: "Our Legacy of Care", Campaign: "What Care Feels Like for the Dawson Family", Campaign: "What Care Feels Like for the Martinez Family", Campaign: "What Care Feels Like", Creative, Digital, Media, Social, Strategic, Subway Advertising
Johns Hopkins Medicine
Mastercard
Weight Watchers

Havas Worldwide Tonic
(Formerly Euro RSCG Tonic)
200 Hudson St, New York, NY 10013
Tel.: (212) 886-4100
Fax: (212) 886-2016
Web Site: ny.havasworldwide.com

Employees: 400
Year Founded: 2005

National Agency Associations: 4A's

Agency Specializes In: Advertising, Health Care Services, Pharmaceutical

Matt Weiss *(CMO-Global & Mng Partner-HWW NY)*
Paul Klein *(Mng Partner)*
Phil Silvestri *(Mng Dir & Chief Creative Officer)*
Jason Musante *(Mng Dir & Grp Exec Dir-Creative)*
Frank Mangano *(CFO & COO-NA & NY)*
Rachel Conlan *(Dir-Global Growth)*
Abby Grozenski *(Dir-Talent Acq)*
Larry Lac *(Dir-Social Media Mktg)*
Tiffany Tutson *(Sr Mgr-Talent Acq)*

Accounts:
GlaxoSmithKline

Helia
(Formerly Havas Discovery)
372 Danbury Rd Ste 100, Wilton, CT 06897
Tel.: (203) 563-3300
Fax: (203) 563-3435
Web Site: http://www.HavasHeliaNA.com/

Year Founded: 1978

Agency Specializes In: Direct Response Marketing

Jason Peterson *(Chief Creative Officer)*
Killian Schaffer *(Mng Dir-CRM)*
Cara Cameron *(VP-Client Svcs)*

Accounts:
Canadian Tire
SONIC Corporation Menus, Packaging, Point of Sale; 2010

Helia
(Formerly Havas Discovery Baltimore)
400 E Pratt St 10th Fl, Baltimore, MD 21202-6174
Tel.: (410) 230-3700
Fax: (410) 752-6689
Web Site: http://www.HavasHeliaNA.com/

Employees: 45
Year Founded: 1988

Agency Specializes In: Advertising, Direct Response Marketing, Sponsorship

Cara Cameron *(Mng Dir)*
Jason Peterson *(Chief Creative Officer)*
Paul Marobella *(CEO-Havas Chicago Group)*
Jamie Gray *(Sr Dir-Interactive Art)*
Kate Fulks *(Client Svcs Dir)*
Heather Lyons *(Producer-Digital)*
Mia Carosi *(Sr Acct Exec)*
Kyle Britt *(Sr Strategist-Digital)*

Accounts:
JP Morgan Chase
Perceptive Software; 2008

Helia
(Formerly Havas Discovery Richmond)
4490 Cox Rd, Glen Allen, VA 23060
Tel.: (804) 968-7400
Fax: (804) 968-7450
Web Site: http://www.HavasHeliaNA.com/

Paul Marobella *(CEO-Havas Chicago Group)*
Ward Thomas *(Gen Mgr & Dir-Analytics)*
Mia Carosi *(Acct Supvr)*
Kelli Gibbs *(Acct Supvr)*
Judith Calvert *(Sr Acct Exec)*
Kyle Britt *(Strategist-Digital)*
Stephanie DuVal *(Acct Exec)*

Accounts:
AARP
Chase
Diageo
Humana
Hyatt
Liberty Mutual
Sprint

Canada

Havas Worldwide Canada
(Formerly PALM + HAVAS)
1253 McGill College Ave 3rd Fl, Montreal, QC H3B 2Y5 Canada
Tel.: (514) 845-7256
Fax: (514) 845-0975
E-Mail: info.montreal@havasww.com
Web Site: www.havasworldwide.ca

Employees: 74
Year Founded: 1986

Agency Specializes In: Advertising

Helen Pak *(CEO)*
Tom Olesinski *(CFO)*
Christian Ayotte *(VP-Digital)*
Patrick Hotte *(VP-Strategy & Brand Integration)*
John C. Parlea *(VP-CRM)*
Marie Helene Rivard *(VP-Strategy & Integration Brands)*
Rachel Letellier *(Acct Dir)*
Natee Likitsuwankool *(Dir-Art)*
Alexandra Damiani *(Strategist-Content & Sr Planner-Digital)*
Deric Moore *(Copywriter)*
Chloe Gascon *(Acct Coord-Digital-Brand Strategy & Brand Integration)*

Accounts:
Cadillac Fairview
Couche-Tard Circle K Banner, Creative, Strategy
Hershey Canada
New-Kruger Products OOH, Scotties
Loblawas Loblaws, Maxi, President's Choice, Provigo
New-New Balance Canada
VIA Rail
Volkswagen Canada 24 Tremblant

Havas Worldwide Digital Canada
(Formerly Euro RSCG 4D)
473 Adelaide St W Ste 300, Toronto, ON M4S 3E4 Canada
Tel.: (416) 920-6864
Fax: (416) 920-5043
Web Site: www.havasworldwide.com/contact-us/north-america/canada/havas-worldwide-digital-canada

Employees: 150

Agency Specializes In: Direct Response Marketing

Elda Bylykbashi *(Dir-Fin)*

Paul McClimond *(Dir-Creative)*
Michael Pallister *(Mgr-Studio)*
Daffodil Stewart-Morris *(Mgr-Fin Acctg)*
Dawn Kim *(Coord-Media)*
Samantha Miller *(Coord-Media)*

Accounts:
Agilent Technologies
CDW
Evian
Kraft
Reckitt Benckiser

Havas Worldwide Toronto
(Formerly Euro RSCG Toronto)
473 Adelaide St W Ste 300, Toronto, ON M5V 1T1 Canada
Tel.: (416) 920-6864
Fax: (416) 920-5043
E-Mail: info.toronto@havasww.com
Web Site: www.havasworldwide.ca/

Employees: 150

Agency Specializes In: Advertising, Co-op Advertising, Digital/Interactive, Direct Response Marketing, Event Planning & Marketing, Internet/Web Design

Helen Pak *(COO)*
Tom Olesinski *(CEO-Havas Media Canada & CFO-Havas Canada Grp)*
Richard Hill *(Sr VP & Grp Acct Dir)*
Ian Bryce-Buchanan *(VP & Grp Acct Dir)*
Sarah Jue *(VP & Grp Acct Dir)*
Christian Ayotte *(VP-Digital)*
Marie Helene Rivard *(VP-Strategy & Integration Brands)*
Rachel Letellier *(Acct Dir)*
Avi Soudack *(Dir-User Experience)*
Amanda Chen *(Strategist-Digital)*
Bill Shaefer *(Copywriter)*

Accounts:
Agilent Technologies
Argus Insurance Bermuda
CDW
Fairmont Hotels
Fidelity
GlaxoSmithKline (GSK)
Groupe Media TFO Digital, Social Media
Hershey's
Home Hardware
Jacob's Creek
Jean Coutu Group Digital Initiatives, Media Buying, Social
John Hancock
Kraft Canada
Mondelez
Monster Factory
New Balance
Novartis
Reckitt Benckiser Air Wick, Airwick, Durex Condoms, Finish, Lysol, Woolite, Zero
Schering-Plough
Sears Canada
Terago

Plastic Mobile
171 E Liberty St Ste 204, Toronto, ON M6K 3P6 Canada
(See Separate Listing)

Regional Headquarters

Havas Worldwide-Europe
29/30 quai de Dion Bouton, Puteaux, Cedex 92817 France
Tel.: (33) 1 58 47 80 00
Fax: (33) 1 58 47 85 12
Web Site: www.havasworldwide.com/

Employees: 1,200

Agency Specializes In: Advertising

Gilles Berouard *(Reg CEO-Eastern Europe & Mng Dir-Europe)*
Remi Arnaud *(Dir-Artistic)*
Nicolas Favier *(Assoc Dir)*

Austria

Havas Worldwide Vienna
(Formerly Euro RSCG Vienna)
Hasnerstrasse 123, 1160 Vienna, Austria
Tel.: (43) 1 5011 80
Fax: (43) 1 5011 8150
E-Mail: wien@havasww.com
Web Site: www.havasworldwide.at/

Employees: 50
Year Founded: 1992

Frank Bodin *(Chm & CEO)*

Accounts:
Begas
Citroen C-Zero
Ekazent
Olympus Campaign: "Abstract Art Klee"
Peugeot
Sanofi Aventis

Belgium

Havas Worldwide Brussels
(Formerly Euro RSCG Brussels)
Dekenijstraat 58 rue du Doyenne, Brussels, 1180 Belgium
Tel.: (32) 2 348 38 00
Fax: (32) 2 347 59 11
Web Site: www.havasworldwide.be/

Employees: 43

Agency Specializes In: Brand Development & Integration, Consumer Marketing, Corporate Communications, Direct Response Marketing, Health Care Services, Internet/Web Design, Public Relations

Christian de La Villehuchet *(CEO-Europe)*
Tom Loockx *(Exec Dir-Creative)*
Ruben Goots *(Exec Producer)*
Kato Maes *(Exec Producer)*
Stephane Daniel *(Dir-Creative & Copywriter)*
Hugo Battistel *(Dir-Creative)*

Accounts:
Brasschaat Travel Cruise Travel
Candico
Cruise Plus Brasschaat
Disneyland Resort Paris; 2005
EDF; 2007
Foorire FM
Friesland Foods Appelsientje; 2002
ING Campaign: "Ing Bache Bag"; 2004
Mondelez International, Inc.; 1997
Mutualite Chretienne Campaign: "Solidarity. It begins by putting oneself in the shoes of the others."
Opera & Ballet Flanders
Raffinerie Tiriemontoise
The Reading Foundation
Sara Lee Douwe Egberts Jacqmotte
SNCB (Societe des Chemins de Fer Belges); 2006
Tele Moustique; 1999
Tiense Suiker Campaign: "T-man"
Tirlemont Candico Sugar, Morceaux Durs Sugar

Havas Worldwide Digital Brussels
(Formerly Euro RSCG 4D Brussels)
58 rue du Doyenne, 1180 Brussels, Belgium
Tel.: (32) 2 348 38 00
Fax: (32) 2 348 38 12
Web Site: www.havasworldwide.be

Employees: 80

Thierry Debievre *(Mng Partner)*
Ann Voorspoels *(Mng Dir)*
Christian de la Villehuchet *(CEO-Europe)*
Kacper Wozniak *(Head-Strategy)*
Tom Loockx *(Exec Dir-Creative)*
Chantal Claes *(Grp Acct Dir)*
Murielle Segers *(Acct Dir)*
Stephane Daniel *(Dir-Creative & Copywriter)*
Hugo Battistel *(Dir-Creative)*
Philippe Haine *(Strategist-Digital)*

Accounts:
3 Suisses
Actimel
Balade
Be Tv
Belvita
Bongrain Benelux
Chaumes
Chavroux
Citroen
Cracotte
Danone
Danone Waters Evian
Galeria Inno
ING Go to 18; 2004
L'Oreal; 2006
Mondelez International, Inc.
Peugeot Belgique-Luxembourg; 2006
Sara Lee Douwe Egberts Non-Alcoholic Beverage
SNCB
Yamaha

The Retail Company
Chausee de Ruisbroek 368, Drogenbos, 1620 Belgium
Tel.: (32) 2 245 60 60
Fax: (32) 2 245 70 11
Web Site: www.havasworldwide.com/contact-us/europe/belgium/the-new-retail-company

Employees: 50

Bulgaria

Havas Worldwide Sofia
(Formerly Euro RSCG Sofia)
16, Tundja Str. Sofia, Sofia, 1164 Bulgaria
Tel.: (359) 2 963 17 51
Fax: (359) 2 400 9401
Web Site: www.havasworldwide.bg/

Employees: 7
Year Founded: 1995

Agency Specializes In: Advertising, Consumer Marketing

Gilles Berouard *(CEO-New Europe & Mng Dir-Europe)*
Velichka Slavcheva *(Acct Dir)*
Ivena Hlebarova *(Acct Exec)*
Plamen Hristov *(Designer)*

Croatia

Havas Worldwide Zagreb
(Formerly Euro RSCG Zagreb)
Ilica 26, 10000 Zagreb, Croatia
Tel.: (385) 1 4831253
Fax: (385) 1 4831254

Advertising Agencies

E-Mail: marina.bolancaradunovic@unex.hr
Web Site: www.unex.hr/unex-group/home/c239/

E-Mail for Key Personnel:
Creative Dir.: kruno@unex.hr

Employees: 80
Year Founded: 1991

Agency Specializes In: Advertising, Corporate Communications, Digital/Interactive, Direct Response Marketing, Event Planning & Marketing, Internet/Web Design, Media Buying Services, Public Relations, Publicity/Promotions, Sales Promotion

Krunoslav Serdar *(Chief Creative Officer & Dir-Creative)*

Accounts:
CEMEX
Generali
Kozmo
PBZ
Perutnina Pruj
Pik
Sanofi-Aventis Research & Development

Czech Republic

Havas Worldwide Digital Prague
(Formerly Euro RSCG 4D)
Expo 58 Letenske sady 1500, 170 00 Prague, 7 Czech Republic
Tel.: (420) 220397600
Fax: (420) 220397601
Web Site: www.havasworldwide.cz

Employees: 200

Agency Specializes In: Business-To-Business, Consumer Marketing, Digital/Interactive, Direct Response Marketing, Event Planning & Marketing, Internet/Web Design

Eda Kauba *(Chief Creative Officer)*
Gilles Berouard *(CEO-New Europe & Mng Dir-Europe)*
Ondrej Fiala *(Sr Brand Dir)*
Sarka Doehring *(Dir-HR)*
Jakub Kolarik *(Dir-Art)*
Martina Kozlerova *(Sr Brand Mgr & Mgr-PR)*
Klara Kajanus *(Production Mgr-Sound-ENA)*
Tomas Machata *(Specialist-IT)*
Agnieszka Kargul *(Project Exec)*
Michal Vlasak *(Deputy Dir)*

Accounts:
Assoufid
Bernard
Citroen
Czech Philharmonic Orchestra
Danfoss
EKO-KOM Campaign: "Ekokom Samosebou", Campaign: "Recycling"
Jack Daniels
Komercni Banka Campaign: "Moneymaker"
Novartis
Opavia
Peugeot
Tetra Pak
Triola Campaign: "Brassiere"

Havas Worldwide Prague
(Formerly Euro RSCG Prague)
Expo 58 Letenske Sady 1500, 170 00 Prague, 7 Czech Republic
Tel.: (420) 220 397 600
Fax: (420) 220 397 601
Web Site: www.havasworldwide.cz/

Employees: 120
Year Founded: 1994

Agency Specializes In: Advertising, Brand Development & Integration, Business-To-Business, Consulting, Consumer Marketing, Corporate Communications, Digital/Interactive, Direct Response Marketing, Event Planning & Marketing, Health Care Services, Internet/Web Design, Publicity/Promotions, Sales Promotion

Gilles Berouard *(CEO & Mng Dir-Havas Worldwide Europe)*
Eda Kauba *(Chief Creative Officer)*
Pavel Fris *(Creative Dir & Copywriter)*
Pavel Slovacek *(Art Dir)*
Jakub Kolarik *(Dir-Art)*

Accounts:
Amnesty International Campaign: "Stones for Sakineh", Campaign: "The Wall"
Citroen
EKO-KOM
KB
Opavia
P&G
Styx
Unicef

Denmark

Havas Worldwide Copenhagen
(Formerly Euro RSCG Copenhagen)
Jagtvej 169B, 2100 Copenhagen, Denmark
Tel.: (45) 77 33 44 00
Fax: (45) 77 33 44 33
Web Site: www.havasworldwide.dk/

Employees: 20
Year Founded: 1989

Agency Specializes In: Advertising, Corporate Communications, Digital/Interactive, Direct Response Marketing, Event Planning & Marketing, Health Care Services, Publicity/Promotions, Sales Promotion

Anker Brandt Nielsen *(CFO)*
Steffan Kjaer Madsen *(Dir-Art & Graphic Designer)*
Rasmus Nybo Andersen *(Dir-Art)*
Kim Madsen *(Dir-Art)*
Benny Steen Moller *(Dir-Comm)*
Lars Moller *(Dir-Comm)*
Mette Karlog *(Mgr-Production)*
Helena Aagreen *(Graphic Designer & Designer-Web)*

Accounts:
Citroen
Reckitt Benckiser Calgon

Finland

Havas Worldwide Helsinki
(Formerly Euro RSCG Helsinki)
Peramiehenkatu 12 E, Helsinki, 00150 Finland
Tel.: (358) 9 425 00200
Fax: (358) 9 42500 201
E-Mail: info@havasww.fi
Web Site: www.havasww.fi/en/

Employees: 35

Agency Specializes In: Advertising

Paul Earl *(Mng Dir)*
Johanna Vuorensola *(Acct Dir & Planner)*
Jon Gustavson *(Dir-Art)*
Marco Voransola *(Dir-Art)*
Marko Vuorensola *(Dir-Creative)*
Liisa Vilkkumaa *(Copywriter)*
Muusa Salminen *(Project Planner)*

Accounts:
Cancer Society of Finland Campaign: "Baby Love", Campaign: "The Breath Holder"
Coca-Cola Refreshments USA, Inc.
Finland Campaign: "The Breath Holder"
Fragile Childhood Organization "Orphanage", Campaign: "Monsters", PSA
Lasinen Lapsuus Parental Alcohol Misuse Awareness
McDonald's
Nokia
Outokumpu

France

BETC Life
(Formerly BETC Euro RSCG)
85/87 rue du Faubourg Saint Martin, Passage du Desir CEDEX, 75010 Paris, France
Tel.: (33) 1 56 41 35 00
Fax: (33) 1 56 41 35 01
Web Site: www.betc-life.com

Employees: 500

Agency Specializes In: Magazines, Newspaper, Newspapers & Magazines

Mercedes Erra *(Founder & Mng Dir)*
Shawn Lacy *(Mng Dir)*
Ivan Beczkowski *(Pres-BETC DIGITAL)*
Alasdhair Macgregor Hastie *(VP & Exec Dir-Creative-Intl Clients)*
Nathalie Dupont *(Editor & Designer)*
Alban Gallee *(Editor & Designer)*
Richard Desrousseaux *(Exec Dir-Creative)*
Etienne Turquet *(Exec Dir-Creative)*
Arnaud Assouline *(Creative Dir & Copywriter)*
Jean-Michel Alirol *(Art Dir)*
Marie Baillot *(Art Dir)*
Pierre Cauret *(Art Dir)*
Christophe Clapier *(Creative Dir)*
Francis De-Ligt *(Art Dir)*
Fabien Hujeux *(Art Dir)*
Sylvain Paradis *(Art Dir)*
Steven Poindron *(Art Dir)*
Nicolas Prado *(Art Dir)*
Thomas Renaudin *(Art Dir)*
Jean-Christophe Royer *(Dir-Creative & Sr Copywriter)*
Eric Astorgue *(Dir-Art)*
Vincent Behaeghel *(Dir-Creative-Intl)*
Damien Binello *(Dir-Art)*
Sophian Bouadjera *(Dir-Art)*
Mathilde Fallot *(Dir-Art)*
Jane Girard *(Dir-Artistic)*
Jacques Jolly *(Dir-Creative)*
Jasmine Loignon *(Dir-Creative)*
Flavie Macaigne *(Dir-Artistic)*
Emmanuelle Maliakas *(Dir-Art)*
Emilie Roy *(Dir-Customer)*
Marie-Eve Schoettl *(Dir-Art)*
Landry Stark *(Dir-Artistic)*
Annick Teboul *(Dir-Creative)*
Stephanie Thomasson *(Dir-Artistic)*
Romain Van Den Plas *(Assoc Dir)*
Guillaume Espinet *(Acct Supvr)*
David Aronson *(Copywriter)*
Gabrielle Attia *(Copywriter)*
Gullit Baku *(Copywriter)*
Paul Delmas *(Copywriter)*
Patrice Dumas *(Copywriter)*
Fabien Le Roux *(Planner-Strategic)*
Dominique Marchand *(Copywriter)*
Fanny Molins *(Copywriter)*
Samuel Moore *(Copywriter)*
Guillaume Rebbot *(Copywriter-BETC Paris)*
Adrian Skenderovic *(Copywriter-Integrated)*
Morgan Sommet *(Copywriter)*
Victoria Vingtdeux *(Art Buyer)*
Daniele Manasseh *(Client Dir-Integrated)*
Guillaume Martin *(Assoc Head-Plng)*

Accounts:
13th Street Campaign: "Bathroom Suspect", Campaign: "I kill a friend 2", Campaign: "The Target"
Aides
Aids Africa Solidarity Fund
Aigle
Air France-KLM Group Campaign: "France is in the Air", Campaign: "L'envol", Campaign: "The A380 Inspiration project"
ATD Fourth World
Black Opium
Braderie Aides Campaign: "Fashion fights HIV", Fashion Sale For Aids
New-Breast Cancer Awareness Month
Calorilight
Canal + Campaign: "Borgia App", Campaign: "Cameramen", Campaign: "Fuel For Fans", Campaign: "Making Sport Bigger is Our Sport", Campaign: "More Cinema", Campaign: "Subtitles", Campaign: "The Bear", Campaign: "The Clowns", Campaign: "The Wise Man", Carlos, TV, Tick
Cerruti, Paris Cerruti, Cerruti 1881, Cerruti RR 1881
Cidil
Club Med
Cockburn's Port Campaign: "12 Incher"
Collectif De Lutte Contre Les Violences Faites Aux Femmes
Collectif Don du Rein Campaign: "More of the same"
Comex
Concorde Hotels & Resorts Campaign: "Lutatia Le Discret"
D&AD
Danone Campaign: "Baby & Me", Campaign: "Baby Inside", Campaign: "Badoit New Identity", Campaign: "Little Big Baby", Campaign: "Live Young", Campaign: "The Amazing Baby & Me", Evian, Outdoor, Print
Decathlon Campaign: "Team Mates", Campaign: "Tired footballer", Campaign: "We Make Sport Easier", Print
Disney Parks & Resorts Campaign: "Giants", Campaign: "Santa"
Disneyland Resorts
Dulux Paint
FDJ (French Lottery)
Gant Lead Creative Agency
GMO/CartCom
Graffiti General
I Tele Morning News
Ibis Campaign: "Sleep Art", Campaign: "The Ultimate Sleep"
IBM
Kwixo
La Poste
La Roche-Posay
Lacoste Campaign: "Life is a Beautiful Sport", Campaign: "The Big Leap"
Le Parisien
Leroy Merlin
Les Enfants Du Noma
Les Revenants Campaign: "Ghosts"
Loto Campaign: "Knock On Wood"
Louis Vuitton Campaign: "Venice - Director's Cut"
LVMH
McDonald's
MCM Campaign: "MCM Pizzas", Campaign: "Speed Rabbit Pizza"
Medecins du Monde Campaign: "Names not Numbers"
PagesJaunes Campaign: "Optical Illusion", Campaign: "Pursuit", Campaign: "Yellow Pages", Campaign: "You are here"
Petit Bateau Campaign: "The Mini Factory"
Peugeot 206 HDi, 208, 307 SW, 407 Hdi, 407 SW, Bb1, Campaign: "Bodyway", Campaign: "Like a Candle in the Wind", Campaign: "PINOCCHIO 2.08", Let Your Body Drive, Peugeot GTI
Philharmonie de Paris
Renaloo Campaign: "60th Anniversary", Kidney Transplantations
Reporters Without Borders 'Kim Jong Un'
Schneider Electric
Sephora Campaign: "Where Beauty Beats"
Shots
Sixt Advertising
Sky Team Alliance
Sodiaal Riches Monts; 2007
Stop Harcelement de Rue
Super Loto Campaign: "Lucky Gloves"
SXSW
Ubisoft Campaign: "Amazing Street Hack", Campaign: "Hide By Watch Dogs", Watch Dogs
Victimes & Citoyens Campaign: "Don't let alcohol drive you to the wrong place"
Volvo
Yellow Pages Directory
Young Director Award Campaign: "The light is your friend"

Havas 360-Annecy

(Formerly Compagnie 360 Euro RSCG-Annecy Le Vieux)
7 ave du Pre Felin, Parc des Glaisins, Annecy-le-Vieux, 74940 France
Tel.: (33) 4 50 10 20 50
Fax: (33) 4 50 10 20 74
Web Site: www.havas360.com/fr

Employees: 20

Christophe De Jandin *(Partner & Dir)*
Thomas Derouault *(Dir-Creative)*
Alban Penicaut *(Dir-Creative)*
Marielle Postec *(Dir-Art)*
Anne-Flore Seringe *(Dir-Customer)*
Marie-Claude Morat *(Sr Mgr-Adv)*
Ophelie Dumay *(Acct Mgr)*
Antoine Palle *(Copywriter)*
Florent Roux *(Copywriter)*
Vanessa Bernard-Granger *(Key Acct Mgr)*

Accounts:
APREC Campaign: "Vote Life"
Atd Quart Monde Campaign: "Give for Good"
Athana Campaign: "Partnership"
Credit Agricole Banking
Eminence
Joupi Toy Shop Campaign: "Don't fear finding the perfect present", Joupi Bag
King Jouet Toys Retailer
leboncoin.fr
Megeve Alps Ski Resort
Mobilier de France Home Equipment
Point P Building Materials Retailer
SPIT Campaign: "SPIT, Extra Strong Fixings"
Tefal Cooking Equipment
Villa Plancha Restaurants

Havas 360 Rennes

(Formerly Compagnie 360 Euro RSCG-Rennes)
17 rue de la Quintaine, Rennes, 35000 France
Tel.: (33) 2 99 65 55 55
Fax: (33) 2 99 30 72 27
Web Site: www.havas360.com/fr

Employees: 65
Year Founded: 2001

Agency Specializes In: Communications, Consumer Marketing, Internet/Web Design

Matthieu Habra *(Co-CEO)*
Florent Roux *(Editor & Designer)*
Alban Penicaut *(Exec Dir-Creative)*
Thomas Derouault *(Dir-Creative)*
Ophelie Dumay *(Dir-Comml)*
Alexandre Jozefowicz *(Dir-Comml)*
Marielle Postec *(Dir-Art)*
Corinne Schorpp *(Dir-Customer)*
Edouard Dorbais *(Copywriter)*
Jeremy Prevost *(Copywriter)*

Accounts:
CNCT National Committee Campaign: "Tobacco weighs annually 47 billion Euro on French society"
Michelin
Slate.fr

Germany

Havas Worldwide Central Europe

(Formerly Euro RSCG Worldwide)
Kaiserwerther Strasse 135, Dusseldorf, D-40474 Germany
Tel.: (49) 21 199 16488
Fax: (49) 21 199 16 496
Web Site: www.havasworldwide.com

Employees: 180

Andreas Geyr *(CEO-Havas Worldwide Europe & Germany)*

Accounts:
Granini
LG
Mondelez International, Inc.
Rinti
Riopan
Sagrotan
Tebonin
Vanish
Veet
Vichy
Woolite

Havas Worldwide Digital Dusseldorf

(Formerly Euro RSCG 4D)
Kaiserwerther Strasse 135, Dusseldorf, 40474 Germany
Tel.: (49) 211 9916 0
Fax: (49) 211 991 64 96
Web Site: www.havasww.de

Employees: 150

Agency Specializes In: Advertising, Broadcast, Cable T.V., Digital/Interactive, Direct Response Marketing, Internet/Web Design, Publicity/Promotions, Sales Promotion, Strategic Planning/Research

Andreas Geyr *(CEO)*
Vincent Behaeghel *(Creative Dir)*
Guido Korfer *(Client Svcs Dir)*
Caroline Saurbier *(Jr Acct Mgr)*

Accounts:
Airwick
Bundesministerium der Verteidigung
Calgon
CALIDA Caritas
Citroen
LG
Peugeot Deutschland GmbH The Legend Returns
Regus
Riopan
Toshiba
Vanish
Weight Watchers

Havas Worldwide Dusseldorf

(Formerly Euro RSCG ABC GmbH)
Kaiserwerther Strasse 135, 40474 Dusseldorf, Germany
Tel.: (49) 21191496
Fax: (49) 2119149757
E-Mail: jan.steinbach@havasww.com
Web Site: www.havasww.de

Employees: 180

Year Founded: 1965

Agency Specializes In: Brand Development & Integration, Communications, Consulting, Corporate Communications, Corporate Identity, Food Service, Public Relations, Transportation

Felix Glauner *(Chief Creative Officer)*
Andreas Geyr *(CEO-Europe)*
Marjorieth Sanmartin *(Creative Dir)*
Beverly Jones *(Dir-Bus Unit)*
Annika Weber *(Dir-Art)*
Deepti Gera *(Assoc Dir-Creative)*
Jan Billmann *(Copywriter)*

Accounts:
Brandt Zwieback-Scholkladen GmbH
The European Central Bank Direct Marketing, Online Advertising, Outdoor, PR, Print, Radio, TV
Fiftyfifty Campaign: "Frozen Cinema", Homeless
Lloyds Pharmacy
N-TV Campaign: "Showing the idea closer to the news literally"
Peugeot 208 GTi, Campaign: "The Legend Returns", Online
United Parcel Service Europe, Brussels
United Technologies Corporation

Havas Worldwide Hamburg
(Formerly Euro RSCG ABC Hamburg Agentur fur Kommunikation GmbH)
Brahms Kontor Johannes-Brahms-Platz 1, 20355 Hamburg, Germany
Tel.: (49) 40 43175 0
Fax: (49) 40 43175 110
E-Mail: ulrike.hanky-mehner@havaspr.com
Web Site: www.havasww.de

Employees: 20

Agency Specializes In: Consulting, Corporate Communications, Public Relations

Joachim Klopsch *(CEO)*
Patrik Buchtien *(Mng Partner)*
Ulrike Hanky-Mehner *(Mng Partner)*
Guido Korfer *(Mng Dir)*
Andreas Geyr *(CEO-Europe)*
Christian Claus *(Mng Dir-Europe & COO-Germany)*
Martina Kafka *(Dir)*
Caroline Saurbier *(Jr Acct Mgr)*

Accounts:
Abfallwirtschaftsgesellschaft Stormarn mbH
Aoste
Audioline
Bundesministerium der Verteidigung
Bundeswehr
Burgerschaft der Freien und Hansestadt Hamburg
Jacobs
Kofax
LMV
MHG Heiztechnik
Mondelez International, Inc. Jakobs, Milka, Tassimo
Sanofi Aventis
United Technologies
Zentralverband Naturdarm e.V.

Greece

Havas Worldwide Athens
(Formerly Euro RSCG Athens)
226 Snygrou Avenue, 176 72 Athens, Greece
Tel.: (30) 210 952 0109
Fax: (30) 210 952 0209
E-Mail: infoathens@havas.com
Web Site: www.havasworldwide.gr/en/

Employees: 60
Year Founded: 1979

Manos Palavidis *(CEO)*
Takis Theophilopoulos *(Mgr-Bus Dev)*
Diana Barbatsarou *(Sr Acct Supvr)*

Accounts:
Air France-KLM Group
Exalco
Quanto
Reckitt Benckiser Airwick, Calgon, Calgonit, Dosia, Karpex, Quanto, Woolite
Sanofi-Aventis
Somfy
Veet
Vichy

Hungary

Havas Worldwide Budapest
(Formerly Euro RSCG Budapest)
Nagyszombat u 1, 1036 Budapest, Hungary
Tel.: (36) 1436 7270
Fax: (36) 1436 7810
Web Site: www.havasworldwide.hu/

Employees: 30
Year Founded: 1990

Agency Specializes In: Advertising

Sandor Piller *(CEO)*
Balazs Csurgo *(Mng Dir)*
Mercedes Erra *(Exec Pres & Mng Dir)*
Viktor Manuel Imre *(Chief Creative Officer)*

Accounts:
Air France-KLM Group
Mondelez International, Inc.

Ireland

Havas Worldwide Dublin
(Formerly Euro RSCG Young)
64 Lower Leeson St, Dublin, 2 Ireland
Tel.: (353) 1 614 5300
Fax: (353) 1 661 1992
Web Site: www.havasworldwide.com

Employees: 50
Year Founded: 1943

Agency Specializes In: Consumer Marketing

Tony Caravousanos *(Head-Adv)*
Peter O'Dwyer *(Exec Creative Dir)*
Gary Boylan *(Art Dir)*
Judy O'Broin *(Creative Dir)*
Glen O'Rourke *(Art Dir)*
Aoife Surgeon *(Acct Dir)*

Accounts:
AIL Group
Aurivo Consumer Foods Campaign: "Connacht Gold Low Fat Butter"
Birds Eye Ireland
BMI
Brainwave
Bulmers
Cuisine de France
The Doyle Collection
EMI
New-Heineken
Hyundai Cars Ireland
Irish League of Credit Unions
Mondelez International, Inc.
Pavilions
Premier Foods Ireland
Premier Foods PLC
Reckitt Benckiser
Valeo Foods
Findlander Grants
Institute of Education
The Irish Council Society
JustEat.ie
Mercedes
Mitsubishi
MyHome.ie Campaign: "My Home My World"
Pfizer Healthcare

Italy

Havas Worldwide Digital Milan
(Formerly Euro RSCG 4D)
Via San Vito, 7, 20123 Milan, Italy
Tel.: (39) 02 8020 2275
Fax: (39) 02 7200 0027
Web Site: www.havasworldwide.com

Employees: 21
Year Founded: 1998

Agency Specializes In: Above-the-Line, Advertising, Automotive, Below-the-Line, Digital/Interactive, Health Care Services

Selmi Barissever *(Creative Dir)*
Lorenzo Crespi *(Creative Dir)*
Enzo Di Sciullo *(Dir-Art)*
Erick Loi *(Dir-Creative)*
Dario Villa *(Dir-Creative)*
Vincenzo Garzillo *(Copywriter)*
Giustina Gnasso *(Copywriter)*

Accounts:
Campari Campaign: "Celebrating Friendship", Comparisoda
Durex Campaign: "Loveville"
Ferrarelle Water
Legambiente

Havas Worldwide Milan
(Formerly Euro RSCG Milan)
Via San Vito 7, 20123 Milan, Italy
Tel.: (39) 02 802021
Fax: (39) 02 72000027
Web Site: www.havasworldwide.it

Employees: 120
Year Founded: 1982

Agency Specializes In: Advertising

Simone Cresciani *(Gen Mgr)*
Jeanne Wu *(Grp Acct Dir)*
Diego Campana *(Art Dir)*
Elisa Rizzuto *(Acct Dir)*
Michele Romani *(Art Dir)*
Erick Loi *(Dir-Creative)*
Dario Villa *(Dir-Creative)*
Riccardo Walchhutter *(Copywriter)*
Salvatore Zanfrisco *(Sr Art Dir)*

Accounts:
Air France-KLM Group
ANIA Foundation
Camparisoda Campaign: "Orange Passion"
Cesvi
Citroen Campaign: "Deejay Range", Campaign: "Yes Man", Citroen C1
Darty Italia
Davide Campari Campaign: "It's the End of the World, Baby"
Disney
Ferrarelle Spa Mineral Water
Fiere Milano Tech
General Group
IGAM
Kraft Foods Italia Campaign: "Gnome"
Legambiente Campaign: "No Nuke Project - A Yes to Say No", Campaign: "Vote Yes to say No spot"
Mediaset Campaign: "Street"
MSC Cruises

Peugeot Italia Spa
Provincia di Torino
Reckitt Benckiser Campaign: "Happy New Year"
RTI
Saiwa Kraft
TUC Krek
Vitasnella
Zucchetti Spa Fittings

Lebanon

Havas Worldwide Beirut
(Formerly Euro RSCG Beirut)
Voice of Lebanon Bldg, Achrafieh,, PO Box 116-5106, Beirut, Lebanon
Tel.: (961) 1 217 137
Fax: (961) 1 217 156
Web Site: www.havasworldwide.com/contact-us/middle-east/lebanon/havas-worldwide-beirut

Employees: 20

Agency Specializes In: Advertising

Nabil Maalouf *(Gen Mgr-Middle East Dubai)*

Accounts:
Air France-KLM Group
Danone
General Mills Mena Haagen-dazs

The Netherlands

Havas Worldwide Amsterdam
(Formerly Euro RSCG Amsterdam)
Sarphatistraat 370, Amsterdam, 1018 GW Netherlands
Tel.: (31) 20 456 5000
Fax: (31) 20 664 39 49
Web Site: www.havasworldwide.nl/

Employees: 70
Year Founded: 1987

Agency Specializes In: Advertising

Remko Herremans *(Head-Strategy)*
Edgar Kuipers *(Client Svcs Dir)*
Shaun Voogd *(Dir-Art)*
Bieneke Glijn *(Sr Mgr-Traffic)*
Sheila Da Silva *(Acct Mgr)*
Milo Duyff *(Acct Mgr)*
Regina Kroon *(Acct Mgr)*
Nicolet Sloothaak *(Acct Mgr)*
Lisette Timmer *(Acct Mgr)*
Bart Van De Winkel *(Copywriter)*

Accounts:
Air France-KLM Group
Citroen Campaign: "Nordic sweater", DS5, Twitter Race
Dokters van de Wereld
Evian
Het Rijk
Kentucky Fried Chicken
LU General Biscuits
Metropole Orchestra Campaign: "Metropole Tweetphony", Campaign: "Save an Orchestra"
Novartis
Peugeot
Reckitt Benckiser
Top Gear Magazine

Poland

Digital One
Dowborczykow 25 st, 90-019 Lodz, Lodz, 90-019 Poland
Tel.: (48) 42 677 1477
Fax: (48) 42 677 1478
E-Mail: info@digitalone.pl
Web Site: www.digitalone.pl

Employees: 45

Agency Specializes In: Advertising

Olgierd Cygan *(CEO & Mng Partner)*
Iza Zajfert *(Acct Dir)*
Ewa Przyborowska *(Sr Acct Mgr)*
Malgorzata Tomczyk *(Acct Mgr)*
Anna Stepkowska *(Mgr-HR)*
Monika Wojcik *(Sr Acct Exec)*
Michal Hejduk *(Planner-Strategy)*
Katarzyna Kolasinska *(Jr Copywriter)*

Accounts:
Cephalon
Clinique
Estee Lauder
Onet.pl
PZU
Pepsi
Polpharma
Roche
Storck

Havas Worldwide Poland
(Formerly Euro RSCG Warsaw)
Ul Marynarska 11, 02-674 Warsaw, Poland
Tel.: (48) 22 444 0999
Fax: (48) 22 444 0998
Web Site: www.havasworldwide.pl/

Employees: 80
Year Founded: 1992

Agency Specializes In: Advertising

Katarzyna Kaminska *(COO)*
Malgorzata Begier *(Exec Dir-Activation)*
Michal Imbierowicz *(Exec Dir-Creative)*
Sylwia Rekawek Michon *(Sr Dir-Art)*
Agata Stanczyk-Dabrowska *(Grp Acct Dir)*
Anna Roman *(Assoc Dir-Strategy)*

Accounts:
5aSec
Anida
Boots Healthcare
Cadbury-Wedel
Canal + Creative, Digital, Online, e-Marketing
Citroen
H&M Campaign: "Mammogram scanning"
Hortex
IKEA
NC+ Creative, Digital, Online, e-Marketing
Peugeot Campaign: "Foreign Parts"
The Polish Federation Of Cancer Survivors
Polish Union of Transplantation Medicine
Rak'n'roll Foundation Cancer Research
Reckitt Benckiser Air Wick, Campaign: "Woolite Blouse"
Rip Curl Pro Store Braille Clothing Tags
Sanofi-Aventis
Vichy
Wienerberger
Woolite
World Wildlife Federation

Marketing House
(Formerly Euro RSCG 4D Marketing House)
Ul Marynarska 11, Warsaw, 02-674 Poland
Tel.: (48) 22 444 0888
Fax: (48) 22 444 0887
Web Site: www.marketing-house.pl

Employees: 80
Year Founded: 1998

Agency Specializes In: Direct Response Marketing

Sylwester Nowalski *(Dir-Integrated Data Solutions Dept)*
Aleksandra Siejka *(Coord-Loyalty Program)*
Ewa Goralska *(Sr Project Coord)*
Sylwia Kobus *(Sr Project Coord)*
Anna Wilczynska *(Sr Project Coord)*

Accounts:
Canal+
Danone
Hewlett Packard
Kraft Foods Polska
Okocim
PTK Centertel
Peugeot
Unilever
Volvo

Portugal

Havas Experience Lisbon
Alameda dos Oceanos Torre Euro RSCG, Parque das Nacoes, 1990-223 Lisbon, Portugal
Tel.: (351) 21 891 0600
Fax: (351) 21 892 2600
Web Site: www.havasww.pt/

Employees: 175
Year Founded: 1990

Augusto Rebelo De Andrade *(CFO)*
Rui Lourenco *(Chief Creative Officer-Havas Worldwide Digital Portugal)*
Joao P. Ferreira *(CEO-Havas Worldwide Digital)*

Accounts:
Amnesty International
Banco Best
Cabo
Citroen
ICEP
LG
Modelo Continente Hipermercados Campaign: "Chef Online App"
Optimus Campaign: "Unlikely Duets"
Portugal Tourism
Reckitt Benckiser
Sonae
Tranquilidade

Havas Worldwide Digital Portugal
(Formerly Euro RSCG 4D)
Zona Intervencao Expo 98 Alameda dos Oceanos, Pav Exposicoes, Lisbon, 1990-223 Portugal
Tel.: (351) 21 891 06 00
Fax: (351) 21 892 26 97
Web Site: www.havas.com

Employees: 14

Joao Ferreira *(CEO & VP)*
Rui Lourenco *(Chief Creative Officer)*
Paulo Pinto *(Exec Dir-Creative)*
Ines Lopes *(Acct Dir)*
Paulo Perdigaao *(Art Dir)*
Jose Vieira *(Dir-Creative)*
Ricardo Silva *(Supvr-Creative)*
Leo Gomez *(Copywriter)*
Tiago Vital *(Copywriter)*
Luis Silva *(Mgr Dir)*

Accounts:
Amnesty International Campaign: "Mugshots"
C-Optima
Coca-Cola Company
Control
F.Lima
New-NOS
Optimus
Peugeot 308 Campaign: "Shadows in Motion"
Portuguese Association For Victim Support
SOS Racismo

Unicer
Zas Odorless Firelighters

Romania

Havas Worldwide Bucharest

(Formerly Euro RSCG Bucharest)
Calea Victoriei 141 Sector 1, Bucharest, 010071 Romania
Tel.: (40) 21 318 1447
Fax: (40) 21 31 29 159

Employees: 25
Year Founded: 1999

Agency Specializes In: Advertising

Adrian Dura *(CEO)*
Iulia Paraschiv *(Sr Acct Mgr)*

Accounts:
Pims
Tymbrk

Spain

Havas Design Plus Madrid

(Formerly Euro RSCG 4D Madrid)
Plaza de Castellana 259 C, Planta 28 & 29, Madrid, 28046 Spain
Tel.: (34) 91 330 23 23
Fax: (34) 91 330 23 45
E-Mail: M.Gardie@havasdesignplus.com
Web Site: www.havasworldwide.com/contact-us/europe/spain/havas-design-plus---spain

Employees: 40
Year Founded: 1993

Ricardo Montero *(Pres)*

Accounts:
Bibliotecas
Electrolux
Ford
Zurich

Havas Worldwide Digital Spain

(Formerly Euro RSCG Worldwide)
Plaza de Canalejas 3, Madrid, 28014 Spain
Tel.: (34) 349 133 02323
Fax: (34) 349 133 02345
Web Site: http://www.havasworldwide.com/

Employees: 75
Year Founded: 1998

Juan Rocamora *(CEO-Southern Europe)*
Trinidad Cortes *(Acct Dir)*
Berta Pascual *(Dir-Art)*

Accounts:
Henkel
IBM

Havas Worldwide Southern Spain

(Formerly Euro RSCG Madrid)
Plaza de Canalejas No 3, 28014 Madrid, Spain
Tel.: (34) 91 330 2323
Fax: (34) 91 330 2345
Web Site: www.havasworldwide.com

Employees: 75

Juan Rocamora *(CEO-Southern Europe)*
Trinidad Cortes *(Dir-Accts)*
Berta Pascual *(Dir-Art)*

Accounts:
Air France-KLM Group
Alcampo Auchan, Hypermarket
Citroen
Greenpeace Campaign: "Stampede"
LG Electronics
Peugeot Automobiles Campaign: "Toys - Finger Print"
Piaget Watches
Reckitt & Benckiser Campaign: "Soccer"
Sara Lee Playtex, Wonderbra
Strepsils
Toshiba Campaign: "Eyes - Fat Man", Toshiba 3D Glasses Free TV

Sweden

Havas Worldwide Granath

(Formerly Granath RSCG Stockholm)
Peter Myndes Backe 8, Box 17089, 10462 Stockholm, Sweden
Tel.: (46) 852246000
Fax: (46) 852246099
Web Site: www.granathreklam.se/

Employees: 35
Year Founded: 1992

Agency Specializes In: Above-the-Line, Advertising, Affluent Market, Automotive, Aviation & Aerospace, Internet/Web Design, Pharmaceutical

David Granath *(Owner & Mng Dir)*
Goran Berggard *(Acct Dir)*
Fredrik Espmark *(Dir-Creative)*
Maria Lamke *(Dir-Art)*

Accounts:
Actavis
Air France-KLM Group
Bayer
Fidelity Funds
Gardasil
Medical Protection Agency
Novartis
Sanofi-Aventis
Statoil
Swedish Environmental Protection Agency
The Swedish Police
Ticnet

Switzerland

Havas Worldwide Geneva

(Formerly Euro RSCG Geneva)
42 rue du XXXI Decembre, 1211 Geneva, 6 Switzerland
Tel.: (41) 22 718 9494
Fax: (41) 22 718 9495
Web Site: www.havasworldwide.ch/

Employees: 20
Year Founded: 1992

Agency Specializes In: Communications, Corporate Identity, Direct Response Marketing, Logo & Package Design, Pharmaceutical, Sales Promotion

Henri Balladur *(Co-Mng Dir-Geneva)*
Roger Giger *(Co-Mng Dir-Geneva)*
Delphine Saulnier *(Acct Dir)*
Gabriel Mauron *(Dir-Creative)*
Pauline Richard Charuel *(Acct Mgr)*
Laurine Bersier *(Acct Exec)*
Mathias Bart *(Copywriter)*

Accounts:
New-Action Innocence
Air France-KLM Group
Credit Agricole
EIM
Riposa
SIG Electricity
Vichy

Havas Worldwide Zurich

(Formerly Euro RSCG Zurich)
Gutstrasse 73, PO Box 428, 8047 Zurich, Switzerland
Tel.: (41) 444666777
Fax: (41) 466 67 22
E-Mail: info-zurich@havasww.com
Web Site: www.havasworldwide.ch/zurich

Employees: 50
Year Founded: 1959

National Agency Associations: BSW

Agency Specializes In: Public Relations

Frank Bodin *(Chm & CEO)*
Peter Schaefer *(Dir-Plng)*
Maria Ebnother *(Acct Mgr)*
Samuel Reichmuth *(Designer)*
Walter Tagliaferri *(Client Svc Dir)*

Accounts:
3M Health Care, Red Dot
Arena 225
BAB
Credit Suisse Charity Event
Danone
DU Kulturmagazin
Econoniesuisse
En Vogue
Evian
Federal Office of Public Health Campaign: "Itching-Pizza"
Greenpeace
Haecky Fine Food AG
IG Motorrad
IP Multimedia
IPL
Kult Productions
Laserpraxis Campaign: "Mermaid"
M-Electronic
Nigros
Novartis
One Young World Campaign: "Time Change, Mind Change"
Peugeot Campaign: "Original Parts", Campaign: "Reaction Time", Lugano, RCZ
Riposa Campaign: "Swiss Sleep: A colorful dream"
Ristorante Cantina
SAM Campaign: "Filling Station"
SMH Verlag AG
Swiss Cancer Foundation
Swiss Health Department Campaign: "Pizza"
Swiss Post International Campaign: "Scratchcard Mailing"
Swiss Railroad Company (SBB)
Swiss Tibetan Friendship
Switzerland Cheese
Walter Moretto
WeightWatchers
Zurich Chamber Orchestra Campaign: "Sound", Classical Music

Turkey

Havas Life Istanbul

(Formerly Euro RSCG 4D - Istanbul)
Istiklal Cad No 284-286 Odakule Is Merkezi Kat 16, Beyoglu, Istanbul, 34430 Turkey
Tel.: (90) 212 245 83 00
Fax: (90) 212 245 83 21
Web Site: www.havaslife.com

Employees: 14

Agency Specializes In: Consumer Marketing, Direct Response Marketing, Event Planning & Marketing,

Internet/Web Design, Publicity/Promotions, Sales Promotion

Gulru Berk *(Mng Partner)*
Erol Batislam *(CEO-Havas Worldwide Istanbul)*

Accounts:
Benetton
Efes Pilsen Beer
Fujitsu Siemens
IS Bankasi
Millenicom
Oracle
Sutas
Yurtici Kargo

Havas Worldwide Istanbul
(Formerly Euro RSCG Istanbul)
Istiklal Caddesi No 284-286 Odakule Is Merkezi Kat 16, Beyoglu, Istanbul, 34430 Turkey
Tel.: (90) 212 245 8300
Fax: (90) 212 245 8310
Web Site: www.havasworldwide.com.tr/

Employees: 40

Agency Specializes In: Broadcast, Communications, Consumer Marketing, Direct Response Marketing, Internet/Web Design, Strategic Planning/Research

Mali Erdogan *(COO)*
Arzu Emre Ozbek *(Grp Head-Creative)*
Ergin Binyildiz *(Exec Dir-Creative)*
Ediz Kurtbarlas *(Exec Dir-Creative)*
Hasan Yildirim *(Art Dir)*
Cabbar Ozdemir *(Dir-Creative)*
Seyma Keklik *(Copywriter)*
Merve Selamet *(Copywriter)*
Ahmet Sefer *(Sr Art Dir)*

Accounts:
Acik Radyo/Open Radio Campaign: "Music of the People"
Dettol
Durex Easy Roll On
Faber-Castell
Next Navigation Systems
Peugeot
Reckitt Benckiser Campaign: "Dirty Stranger", Campaign: "Make wools happy", Durex, Woolite
Total
Turk Telekom Campaign: "BaskADball", Campaign: "BaskeTweet", Campaign: "BasketPad"
Vanish

Ukraine

Havas Worldwide Kiev
(Formerly Euro RSCG Kiev)
79 Vladimirskaya St 2nd Fl, Kiev, 01033 Ukraine
Tel.: (380) 44 230 3561
Fax: (380) 44 201 3562
E-Mail: becoolwith@havaswwkiev.com.ua
Web Site: www.havasworldwidekiev.com.ua/

Employees: 70
Year Founded: 2004

Agency Specializes In: Advertising

Kseniya Morozova *(Mng Dir)*
Ivan Akinin *(Sr Dir-Art)*
Olga Kazkova *(Acct Dir)*
Masha Polishchuk *(Acct Dir)*
Alexander Zelenko *(Dir-Digital Creative)*
Ruslan Dobzhynsky *(Sr Acct Mgr)*
Alena Gulak *(Acct Mgr)*
Julia Shvedun *(Acct Mgr)*
Iryna Ivanenko *(Mgr-SMM)*
Kateryna Burlyay *(Client Svc Dir)*

Accounts:
Anti-AIDS
Askold
Batik
Foxtrot
Kyivstar
Overline Myagkov, Shturman
Productinvest Shake
Revo Energy
Rosava
Skvortsova
Swedbank
TNK-BP

United Kingdom

Havas People Birmingham
(Formerly Euro RSCG Riley)
Ground Fl 39 Dominion Ct Sta Rd Solihull, Birmingham, B91 3RT United Kingdom
Tel.: (44) 121 711 3433
Fax: (44) 121 711 7769
Web Site: www.havaspeople.com

Employees: 25
Year Founded: 2003

Wendy Peoples *(CFO)*
Danni Brace *(Head-Global Client Dev)*
Jessica Carrington *(Acct Dir)*
Dawn Cronin *(Acct Dir)*
April Bryce *(Dir-Creative)*
Susie Roe *(Dir-Resourcing)*
Graeme Wright *(Dir-Strategy)*
Charlotte Fenney *(Client Partner)*
Sian Dutton *(Acct Exec)*
Helen Jenkins *(Media Planner & Media Buyer)*
Jack Morgan *(Media Planner-Digital & Buyer)*

Havas People Glasgow
(Formerly Euro RSCG Riley)
Standard Building 3rd Floor 94 Hope Street, Glasgow, G2 6PH United Kingdom
Tel.: (44) 141 332 2020
Fax: (44) 141 332 7665
Web Site: www.havaspeople.com

Employees: 8
Year Founded: 1982

Agency Specializes In: Communications, Recruitment

Fiona Morris *(Head-Sls & Mktg)*
Gaynor Burksfield *(Reg Dir)*
Rebecca Baynes *(Grp Acct Dir)*
Alasdair Devenney *(Acct Dir)*
Susie Roe *(Dir-Resourcing)*
Charlotte Fenney *(Client Partner)*

Accounts:
Lothian

Havas People London
(Formerly Euro RSCG Riley)
6 Briset Street, London, EC1M 5NR United Kingdom
Tel.: (44) 207 022 4000
Fax: (44) 207 022 4005
Web Site: www.havaspeople.com

Employees: 60
Year Founded: 1947

National Agency Associations: IPA-PPA

Agency Specializes In: Advertising, Business-To-Business, Consulting, Graphic Design, Internet/Web Design, Print, Recruitment

Rupert Grose *(CEO)*
Charlotte Fenney *(Partner-Client)*
Chris Le'cand-Harwood *(Head-Social Media)*
Gaynor Burksfield *(Reg Dir)*
Alasdair Devenney *(Acct Dir)*
Emma Hawker *(Dir-Ops)*
Susie Roe *(Dir-Resourcing)*
Graeme Wright *(Dir-Strategy)*
Sara Brooks *(Acct Exec)*

Accounts:
Allen & Overy
Central School of Speech & Drama
Direct Line Group
The Ministry of Defence Campaign: "MOD Police Constables"
Staffordshire University Media Planning & Buying

Havas People Manchester
(Formerly Euro RSCG Riley)
Trafford House Chester Rd, Stretford, Manchester, M32 0RS United Kingdom
Tel.: (44) 161 610 2200
Fax: (44) 161 872 3351
Web Site: www.havaspeople.com

Employees: 7

Agency Specializes In: Recruitment

Brian Beech *(Mng Dir-Havas PR UK)*
Simon Bracewell *(Dir-Education & Pub Sector)*

Accounts:
McCurrach
Thomas Cook Press

Havas PR London
(Formerly Euro RSCG Biss Lancaster)
Cupola House 15 Alfred Pl, London, WC1E 7EB United Kingdom
Tel.: (44) 207 467 9200
Fax: (44) 207 467 9201
E-Mail: enquiries@havasww.com
Web Site: www.havaspr.co.uk/

Employees: 50
Year Founded: 1978

National Agency Associations: IAA

Agency Specializes In: Business-To-Business, Communications, Corporate Communications, Investor Relations, Pharmaceutical, Public Relations

Gerry Moira *(Chm-Creative)*
Alethea Sibois *(Head-Bus Dev)*
Philip Beaumont *(Sr Dir-Art)*
Anthony Edwards *(Dir-Strategy)*
Paola Nicolaides *(Dir-Consumer Brands)*
Russell Schaller *(Dir-Creative)*
Lauren Stewart *(Assoc Dir-PR & Social Media)*

Accounts:
Arla Foods Castello, Digital, Lactofree, PR, Social Media
Bae Systems
Diageo
Hogg Robinson Corporation
Ideal Standard International Consumer & Trade PR
Kimberly Clark
Vileda PR

Havas Work Club
(Formerly Work Club)
Axe & Bottle Court, 70 Newcomen St, London, SE1 1YT United Kingdom
Tel.: (44) 20 7407 7800
Fax: (44) 20 7681 1573
E-Mail: hello@work-club.com
Web Site: www.work-club.com

Employees: 100

Agency Specializes In: Advertising, Digital/Interactive

Jon Claydon *(Chm)*
Martin Brooks *(Co-CEO)*
Patrick Griffith *(CEO)*
Lisa De Bonis *(Partner-Strategy)*
Ben Mooge *(Partner-Creative)*
Jane McNeill *(COO)*
Tom Sneddon *(Sr Acct Dir)*
Eduardo de Felipe *(Dir-Creative-Work Club)*

Accounts:
Adidas Social Media
Alfa Romeo Global
ASDA Asda.com, Campaign: "#savesummer", Creative, Digital, Strategic
BBC
BT Business Insights
Coca-Cola
General Mills Digital, Haagen-Dazs, Old El Paso
Google
Heineken Desperados, Global Digital, Strongbow Gold
Iglo
Jack Wills Creative, Digital, Strategic
McLaren F1
Mondelez International, Inc. Campaign: "Seductively Silky", Carte Noire, Mellow Bird, Seductive Servers
Nationwide Building Society Campaign: "People Powered Digital Services", Media, Online
New-Nature's Bounty International Communications, Digital, Nature's Bounty, Solgar, Strategy
Nokia Nokia N85; 2009
Paddy Power
Pernod Ricard Ballantine's, Campaign: "T-Shirt OS"
Plum Baby
Rentokil Digital
Sanctuary Spa YouTube Channel
Sharp Brand & Digital Advertising, Experiential, Print, TV
Sony BMG
Sony Computer Entertainment America LLC Advertising, PlayStation Plus
Walmart / ASDA
Work Club Ginger Pig

Havas Worldwide London
(Formerly Euro RSCG London)
Cupola House 15 Alfred Place, London, WC1E 7EB United Kingdom
Tel.: (44) 207 240 4111
Fax: (44) 207 467 9210
E-Mail: enquiries@havasww.com
Web Site: www.havasworldwide.co.uk

Employees: 200
Year Founded: 1990

National Agency Associations: IAA

Agency Specializes In: Communications, Public Relations

Martin Brooks *(Co-CEO-Havas Work Club)*
Tracey Barber *(CMO-UK)*
Gerry Moira *(Chm-Creative)*
Chris Hirst *(CEO-Europe)*
Andre Moreira *(Head-Art & Dir-Creative-Global)*
Michael Olaye *(Head-Tech & Innovation)*
Paul Ward *(Grp Head-Ops & Innovation)*
Andy Sandoz *(Exec Dir-Creative)*
Phil Beaumont *(Sr Dir-Art)*
Jess Tarpey *(Grp Acct Dir)*
Alasdair Graham *(Creative Dir)*
Mihiri Kanjirath *(Acct Dir)*
Andy Preston *(Art Dir)*
Russell Schaller *(Creative Dir)*
Minnie Vaughan *(Acct Dir)*
Samantha Alonso *(Dir-Plng)*
David Burn *(Dir-Creative & Art)*
Yann-Gael Cobigo *(Dir-Art)*
Rory Cunningham *(Dir-Strategy-Global)*
Ed Edwards *(Dir-Strategy)*
Susan Poole *(Dir-Plng)*
Sam Shepherd *(Dir-Art)*
Mathieu Grichois *(Copywriter)*
Tim Langford *(Copywriter)*
Joe Williams *(Copywriter)*
Caroline Saunders *(Grp Bus Dir)*

Accounts:
Akzo Nobel Dulux
Alberto Culver Pageant 90', VO5 Extreme Style
Arla Foods Advertising, Baby & Me Organic, Creative
Aunt Bessie's
Birds Eye Campaign: "Comedy Dad", Captain Birds Eye
BMI
New-Carl F Bucherer (Global Advertising Agency) Creative, Digital
Central Office of Information
Chivas Regal Campaign: "Here's To Big Bear"
Citroen UK Campaign: "Anti Retro", Campaign: "Footballet", Campaign: "Refined Redefined", Geisha Diesel Engine, Idiot Abroad
CLIC Sargent The Joke Appeal
Comet Branding
Cote d'Or
Credit Suisse Campaign: "Leonardo Di Vinci App", Campaign: "Metamorphosis"
Danone
Evian Campaign: "Live Young"
De Witt
Ella's Kitchen Campaign: "Give A Sprout", Creative, Digital
Harrod's Brand Campaign, Creative
Hobbycraft Consumer PR
Ideal Standard
J. R. Simplot Company
Joe's Advertising National Campaign for the Homeless
La Senza Underwear
LG Electronics
London & Partners Public Relations
Loveflutter Campaign: "Quirky Me"
Maggie's Digital
Mothercare Creative Advertising, Design, Retail
Myhomemove Search Ranking
Pernod Ricard Above-the-Line, Below-the-Line, Campaign: "Art of Hosting", Chivas, Chivas Big Bear, Chivas Brothers, Chivas MASHTUN, Chivas Regal, Digital, Global Advertising, Social Media, Vinyl 50, Vodka Brands
Peugeot Motor Company PLC Citroen
Peugeot Campaign: "Just Add FuelTM", Creative, Peugeot 1007, Peugeot 207, Verve 207/308
Platinum Guild International Media Relations Campaign
Reckitt Benckiser Campaign: "Explore", Campaign: "Get In Sync", Campaign: "When It's On It's On", Creative, Durex Condoms, E-Commerce Website, Mobile App, Strepsils, TV, Vinyl 40', Vinyl 50"
RNID
Santander Campaign: "123 Current Account", Campaign: "Dog Grooming", Cinema, Outdoor, Staples, TV
Thomas Cook Brand-Building TV, Campaign: "Water Slide", Customer Awareness
Travelodge
Unilever Campaign: "Pageant 90", VO5
VO5 Campaign: "Pageant"
Yakult; 2007

Helia
(Formerly Havas EHS London)
6 Briset Street, London, EC1M 5NR United Kingdom
Tel.: (44) 207 017 1000
Fax: (44) 207 017 1001
Web Site: www.havashelia.com

Employees: 100
Year Founded: 1967

Agency Specializes In: Direct Response Marketing

Tash Whitmey *(CEO)*
Dan Gibson *(Mng Partner)*
Tony Miller *(Mng Partner)*
Matt Fanshawe *(Grp COO)*
Ben Silcox *(Chief Data & Digital Officer)*
Mark Taylor *(Mng Dir-FULCRM)*
Andy Buist *(Assoc Global Brand Dir)*
Aaron Howard *(Dir-Creative)*
Liz Tang *(Dir-Client Svcs)*
Sarah Wood *(Assoc Dir-Creative)*
Lauren McIlroy *(Planner)*
Steven Bennett-Day *(Grp Exec Dir-Creative)*

Accounts:
Barclays
Barkley Cars International
BBC CRM
The Co-operative Bank
D.E Master Blenders Global Media
Diageo
EasyJet
Heathrow
Nestle
Pets at Home
Peugeot UK Campaign: "Carkour", Campaign: "Envy Whodunnit", Campaign: "See the city in a different light", Campaign: "Show Your Character"
New-Royal Mail Customer Engagement
Sky Card Credit Card; 2008
Southwestern Distillery Campaign: "FaceTime", Tarquin's Gin
Tesco CRM, Clubcard
TSB Direct Marketing
Unilever Digital Display Communications, Dove (Global Digital Agency of Record), Dove Men+Care (Global Digital Agency of Record), Surf (Global Digital Agency of Record)
Viking Cruises
Volvo Cars, Digital, V40 R-Design
New-Westfield CRM
Whitbread Beefeater Grill, Brewers Fayre, CRM, Premier Inn, Table Table, Taybarns

Helia
(Formerly Havas EHS Cirencester)
Phoenix Way, Cirencester, Glos GL7 1RY United Kingdom
Tel.: (44) 1285 644744
Fax: (44) 1285 654952
Web Site: www.havashelia.com

Employees: 110

Agency Specializes In: Direct Response Marketing

David Williams *(Mng Dir)*
Simon Cromey *(Head-Plng)*
Jon McWee *(Head-Digital Design)*
Aaron McCarthy *(Sr Dir-Art)*
Ewan Gee *(Dir-Global Creative-Volvo Cars)*
Sue Vizor *(Dir-Ops)*

Accounts:
Comparethemarket.com
Heinz Baby Food
Pets at Home CRM

The Maitland Consultancy
Orion House 5 Upper St Martins Ln, London, WC2H 9EA United Kingdom
Tel.: (44) 20 7379 5151
Fax: (44) 20 7379 6161
E-Mail: info@maitland.co.uk
Web Site: www.maitland.co.uk

Employees: 50
Year Founded: 1994

Agency Specializes In: Brand Development & Integration, Corporate Communications, Financial, Investor Relations, Pharmaceutical, Planning & Consultation

Angus Maitland *(Chm)*
William Clutterbuck *(Vice Chm & Head-Fin Svcs & Litigation PR)*
Neil Bennett *(CEO)*
Steve Marinker *(Partner & Head-Maitland Corp)*
Emma Burdett *(Partner)*
Greg Lawless *(Partner)*
Martin Leeburn *(Partner)*
Ella Mason *(Partner)*
Kate O'Neill *(Partner-Capital Markets Advisory)*
Jeremy Dorling *(CFO)*

Accounts:
Aberdeen Asset Management
Ashtead
B&M Retail
Balfour Beatty Corporate & Financial Communications, Financial PR
Cath Kidston
Catlin Group
Debiopharm SA
New-Domino's Pizza Group Financial & Corporate Public Relations
EIM
Epwin Group Communications
Essar
GlaxoSmithKline
Halfords
The Harley Medical Group Communications, Reputation Management
Howdens
Kleinwort Benson Corporate Communications, PR
The Laird Group Plc
Moneysupermarket.com Group Plc Corporate PR, Financial Communications
Monsoon Accessorize
Mysale Group Communications
OCH-ZIFF
Oriel Securities Communications Strategy
Permal
Pets at Home
Premier Foods
SAB Miller
Schroders
TDR Capital
Tesco
Weir Group plc
Zoopla IPO communications

Regional Headquarters

Havas Worldwide Latin America
(Formerly Euro RSCG Worldwide Latin America)
Av. Sao Gabriel 301, Itaim Bibi, C1414BKK Sao Paulo, 01435-001 Brazil
Tel.: (55) 11-2126 1000
Fax: (55) 11-2126 1100
Web Site: www.havasworldwide.com

Employees: 538
Year Founded: 2002

Agency Specializes In: Advertising, Business-To-Business, Consumer Marketing, Digital/Interactive, Direct Response Marketing

Marcelo Bresciani *(Dir-Creative)*
Victor Britto *(Dir-Art)*
Rodrigo Corbari *(Dir-Creative)*
Cristian Firmino *(Dir-Art)*
Felipe Perles *(Dir-Art)*
Akira Tateyama *(Dir-Creative)*
Raul Torres *(Dir-Art)*
Anabela Borges *(Sr Acct Mgr-Digital)*

Accounts:
Arcor Campaign: "Good hand, Bad hand", Saladix
BBVA Bank Campaign: "Ping Pong"
Citroen Campaign: "Always Use Original Parts", Campaign: "Telephone", Citroen C4, Citroen DS3
New-Mortein Pro
Pao de Acucar
Peugeot C4 Hatch
Pirelli
Reckitt Benckiser

Dominican Republic

AS Publicidad
Jose Contreras no 62, Zona Universitaria, Santo Domingo, Dominican Republic
Tel.: (809) 535 3264
Fax: (809) 535 2303

Employees: 15

Agency Specializes In: Advertising

Raul Bartolome *(Owner)*

Guatemala

ICU Publicidad
13 Calle 2-60 Edificio Topacio Azul 10 Fl, Oficina, 1001 Guatemala, Guatemala
Tel.: (502) 2332 8938
Fax: (502) 2332 8941
E-Mail: gerencia@icupublicidad.com
Web Site: www.icupublicidad.com

Employees: 21

Agency Specializes In: Advertising

Silvia Carazo *(Gen Mgr)*
David Quiroa *(Assoc Dir-Creative)*

Accounts:
Ciruelax
Fox Channel International
Grupo Tecun
Hyundai
Mazda De Didea
National Geographic Channel
Pastas La Moderna
Peugeot
Sanofi Aventis
Sky Television
Utilisima TV

Mexico

Havas Worldwide Mexico
(Formerly Euro RSCG Beker)
Av Insurgentes Sur 694-9, Mexico, CP 031000 Mexico
Tel.: (52) 55 5626 61 00
Fax: (52) 55 5687 7406
Web Site: www.havasworldwide.com

Employees: 40

Agency Specializes In: Advertising, T.V.

Carolina Torres *(Head-Plng)*
Aida Arvide *(Sr Acct Dir)*
Sergio Galindo *(Art Dir)*
Martin Gandarillas *(Acct Dir)*
Paola Gonzalez *(Acct Dir)*
Ray Lopez *(Creative Dir)*
Beatriz Torres *(Acct Dir)*
Laurence Rossignol *(Dir-HR)*
Lorena Johansen *(Sr Acct Supvr)*
Paulina Campos *(Planner)*
Jaime Canales *(Copywriter)*
David Gaona *(Planner-Digital)*
Juan Marindia *(Copywriter)*

Accounts:
Anheuser-Busch InBev Media
AXA Insurance
Bafar
Cinemex
Clamato
Continental
Henkel
Liverpool
Nacional Monte De Piedad Comic Sensus
Play City
Sanofi Aventis
Sky
Squirt
Television Foundation
Walmart Supercenter

Regional Headquarters

The Face - Melbourne
(Formerly The Face Euro RSCG - Melbourne)
Level 1 132 B Gwynne St, Richmond, VIC 3121 Australia
Tel.: (61) 3 9426 5399
Fax: (61) 3 9427 7537
E-Mail: katie.fowles@thefaceaustralia.com.au
Web Site: www.havaspeople.com.au

Employees: 10
Year Founded: 1992

Agency Specializes In: Recruitment

Havas Worldwide Australia
(Formerly Euro RSCG Group Australia)
Level 12 60 Miller Street, North Sydney, NSW 2060 Australia
Tel.: (61) 2 9963 7711
Fax: (61) 2 9957 5766
Web Site: www.havasworldwide.com.au

Employees: 100
Year Founded: 1990

Agency Specializes In: Digital/Interactive

Imogen Hewitt *(Head-Strategy)*
Tim Green *(Exec Dir-Creative)*
Alex Ball *(Sr Acct Dir)*
Alice Mason *(Sr Acct Dir)*
Steve Osaer *(Sr Acct Dir)*
Mick Healy *(Dir-Art)*
Seamus Higgins *(Dir-Creative)*
Christopher Johnson *(Dir-Creative)*
Eryl Thomas *(Dir-Plng)*
Stuart Turner *(Dir-Creative)*
Scott Balalas *(Sr Acct Mgr)*
Julie Bouissin *(Sr Acct Mgr)*
Ray Ali *(Copywriter)*
James Wright *(Grp COO)*

Accounts:
Australian Defence Force
Australian Wool Innovation
Boehringer Ingelheim
Defence Force Recruiting Campaign: "Do what you love", Creative, Digital
New-eBay
Goodman Fielder Creative, Meadow Lea, Media Strategy, Olive Grove, Praise, White Wings
Jacob's Creek Campaign: "Made By"
Novartis
Save Our Sons & Duchenne Foundation Campaign: "The Most Powerful Arm Ever Invented"
Sony Australia Campaign: "DSLR GEAR NO IDEA"

Havas Worldwide Southeast Asia
(Formerly Euro RSCG APAC)
150 Cantonment Road, Block B, Cantonment Centre #03-06/07/08, Singapore, 089762 Singapore
Tel.: (65) 6317 6600
Fax: (65) 6317 6700
Web Site: www.havasworldwide.com

Employees: 95

Agency Specializes In: Advertising, Consumer Marketing, Digital/Interactive, Direct Response Marketing, Internet/Web Design, Public Relations, Social Media

Juan Rocamora *(Chm-Asia Pacific & CEO)*
Andrea Conyard *(Grp Mng Dir)*
Stefano Augello *(Chief Strategy Officer-South-East Asia)*
Levent Guenes *(CEO-Southeast Asia)*
Karen Flynn *(Mng Dir-Siren)*
Vj Yamat *(Mng Dir-Healthcare Ops-Southeast Asia)*
Andrew Hook *(Exec Dir-Creative)*
Jacob Joseph Puthenparambil *(Dir-Comm Strategy)*

Accounts:
Anna Sui Beauty
Carlsberg Beer, Campaign: "Cars In Control"
China Telecom
DBS Financial Services
IBM Technology
Lee Hwa Jewellery Jewelry
Microsoft Technology
Novartis Pharmaceuticals
NTUC Fair Price Telecommunications; 2008
Orange Telecommunications
Pernod Ricard Spirits
Peugeot Auto
Reckitt Benckiser FMCG
Sanofi Aventis FMCG, Pharmaceuticals
Singapore Association of the Visually Handicapped Campaign: "Blind Faith"
Sony Consumer Electronics

Havas Worldwide Sydney
(Formerly Euro RSCG Sydney)
60 Miller Street Level 12, North, Sydney, NSW 2060 Australia
Tel.: (61) 2 9963 7711
Fax: (61) 2 9957 5766
E-Mail: andrewknox@eurorscg.com.au
Web Site: www.havasworldwide.com.au

Employees: 120

Agency Specializes In: Consumer Marketing

Darren Cole *(Designer)*
Steve Coll *(Exec Dir-Creative)*
Kat Thomas *(Exec Creative Dir)*
Jason Carnew *(Sr Acct Dir)*
Steve Osaer *(Sr Acct Dir)*
Scott Portelli *(Project Dir-Digital)*
Dan Smith *(Client Svcs Dir)*
Stuart Turner *(Creative Dir)*
Nicole Hetherington *(Dir-Art)*
Micah Howard *(Dir-Client Ops)*
Adam Shutler *(Dir-Digital Design)*
Julie Bouissin *(Acct Mgr)*

Accounts:
Citroen Brochures, Community Management, Creative, Strategic Planning
Durex Brand Positioning, Campaign: "Fundawear", Campaign: "Touch Over The Internet", Durex Fetherlite Intense, Durexperiment
eBay Campaign: "Know What They Like, What They Love", Creative
New-Expedia Lastminute.com.au, Out-of-Home, Radio, Video
Fairfax Media Creative, MyCareer
Greenpeace Campaign: "Turtle", Outdoor & Print Campaign
Intel
Novartis
Nurofen
PayPal Inc.
Pernod Ricard Brancott Estate, Jacob's Creek
Personal Broadband Australia iBurst
Peugeot
Pine O'Cleen Campaign: "The wipe with a flipside"
Reckitt Benckiser Campaign: "Durexperiment Fundawear", Campaign: "Sponsor the White House", Campaign: "The Harpic Toilet Confessions", Harpic, Mortein, Pea Beu, Vanish
Sony Campaign: "DSLR Gear No Idea", Campaign: "Like Nothing You've Ever Experienced", Campaign: "Multimillion Dollar", Campaign: "No More Bad Photos", Online, Social Media, Sony NEX, Ultra HD TV
Sydney IVF
Virgin Mobile Campaign: "Fair Go Bro", Campaign: "Game of Phones", Campaign: "Meal For A Meal"
YSL Beaute

China

Havas Worldwide Beijing
(Formerly Euro RSCG Beijing)
19/F Tower B Global Trade Center No 36 Bei San Huan East Road, Dongcheng District, Beijing, 100013 China
Tel.: (86) 10 5923 2700
Fax: (86) 10 5825 6172
Web Site: www.havasworldwide.com

Employees: 150
Year Founded: 1993

Ben Wong *(Mng Dir)*
Rosita Chang *(VP)*
Ami Qian *(Head-Acct Mgmt & Sr Bus Dir)*
Lewis Rosa *(Head-Social Strategy)*
Monica Wang *(Sr Dir-Art)*
Kaka Ling Kaka *(Dir-Creative)*
Jonathan Chan *(Assoc Dir-Creative)*
Vencent Chen *(Assoc Dir-Creative)*
Circle Lee *(Assoc Acct Dir)*

Havas Worldwide Hong Kong
(Formerly Euro RSCG Hong Kong)
9/F Northeast Warwick House Taikoo Place, 979 King's Road, Island East, Hong Kong, China (Hong Kong)
Tel.: (852) 2590 1800
Fax: (852) 2516 5411
Web Site: www.havasworldwide.com

Employees: 65

Agency Specializes In: Advertising

C. C. Tang *(Chm & Chief Creative Officer-Greater China)*
Mitchell Tan *(Mng Dir)*
Ivan Tang *(Acct Mgr)*
Ivy Chow *(Reg Acct Mgr)*
Ng Kaima *(Assoc Acct Dir)*

Accounts:
Air France-KLM Group
Anna Sui Super Black Mascara
Hong Kong International Airport Brand Management, Communication, Creative, Strategic Planning, Through the Line
Peugeot
Pizza Hut Digital Communications
Shangri-La Hotel (Global Media Planning & Buying) The Shard Hotel
Sony Bravia, Handycam, Vaio, Walkman

Havas Worldwide Shanghai
(Formerly Euro RSCG Shanghai)
11/F, Novel Building, 887 Huaihai Zhong Road, Shanghai, 200020 China
Tel.: (86) 21 6467 5868
Fax: (86) 21 6467 5869
Web Site: www.havasworldwide.com.cn/

Employees: 55

Brendan Tansey *(CEO)*
Simone Zhang *(Chief Strategy Officer)*
Mason Lin *(CEO-China)*
Ami Qian *(Head-Acct Mgmt & Sr Bus Dir)*
Lewis Rosa *(Head-Strategy)*
Kaka Ling Kaka *(Dir-Creative)*
Jonathan Chan *(Assoc Dir-Creative)*
Circle Lee *(Assoc Acct Dir)*

Accounts:
New-Ariston
Balabala
China Bank of Communications
Chivas
New-Citroen
Dulux
Hangzhou Nabel Group
Hershey Company Hershey Kisses; 2008
Johnson & Johnson Viactiv
LoLo Group Mei Yan Fang; 2008
New-OSM
New-Reckitt Benckiser
Sanofi-Aventis
Shandong Bohi Industry Co. Bohi
Suning Appliance Co.
Vichy
Yili Chang Qing; Pureday Yogurt, QQ Star Children's Milk, QQ Star Yogurt, Satine, Yili Adult Milk
Zhengzhou Sanquan Foods Co. Sanquan Champion

Socialistic China
11/F Novel Building No 887 Huaihai Zhong Road, Shanghai, 200020 China
Tel.: (86) 21 6467 5868
Fax: (86) 21 6467 5869
Web Site: www.havasworldwide.com

Employees: 20

Agency Specializes In: Digital/Interactive

Brendan Tansey *(Founder)*

Accounts:
Danone Infant Nutrition
Freescale
Hersheys
Ivory Baby
Jala
Peugeot
Seagate

Korea

Havas Worldwide Seoul
(Formerly Euro RSCG NEXT)
10th Fl Dongwon Bldg 128 27 Dangju-dong, Jongro-gu, Seoul, 110-759 Korea (South)
Tel.: (82) 2 757 33 23
Fax: (82) 2 794 66 86
Web Site: www.havasworldwide.co.kr/

Employees: 60
Year Founded: 1997

Agency Specializes In: Advertising, Digital/Interactive, Direct Response Marketing, Internet/Web Design

JuneKyu Park *(Pres)*
Jinnie Kim *(Acct Exec)*

Accounts:
Air France-KLM Group
Cartier
Emirates Airlines
JTI Lucia, Premier One
Korea Telecom
L'Oreal Vichy
Omega
Reckitt Benckiser Oxy
Sanofi-Aventis
Sky Team
Trane Inc.

Malaysia

Havas Worldwide Kuala Lumpur
(Formerly Euro RSCG Kuala Lumpur)
11F, The Crest, 3 Two Square 2 Jalan 19/1, Petaling Jaya, 46300 Malaysia
Tel.: (60) 3 2718 6600
Fax: (60) 3 2718 6704
Web Site: www.havasworldwide.com/

Employees: 50
Year Founded: 1980

Andrew Lee *(Mng Dir)*
Ezra Foo *(Head-Creative)*
Tjon Tsin Kim Marcus *(Mgr-Digital)*
Renee Ong *(Mgr-Digital)*
Marry Tai *(Mgr-Digital Media)*

Accounts:
Aivoria Group Bonita, Brand Management, Elianto, Tiamo
AmBank
Amnesty International Malaysia
Carlsberg
DiGi Creative Agency of Record
Old Town White Coffee Brand Management
Peugeot Catalogue, Creative, Print, TVC
Reckitt Benckiser Dettol For Men, Digital, Fibre Drink, Shower Gel, Social Media

Philippines

Havas Worldwide Manila
16F Robinsons Equitable Bank Tower 4 ADB, Pasig, 1605 Philippines
Tel.: (63) 2 638 6063
Fax: (63) 2 634 6854
E-Mail: info.ph@havasww.com
Web Site: www.havasworldwide.ph/

Employees: 74
Year Founded: 1998

Agency Specializes In: Advertising, Communications, Consumer Marketing, Digital/Interactive, Direct Response Marketing, Health Care Services, Internet/Web Design

Singapore

Havas Worldwide Bangkok
(Formerly Euro RSCG 4D-Bangkok)
29 Bangkok Business Center Building 28th Floor Room 2802 Soi Ekamai, Sukhumvit 63 Klongton Nua Watt, Bangkok, 10110 Thailand
Tel.: (66) 2 382 1722
Fax: (66) 2 382 1727
Web Site: www.havasworldwide.com/contact-us/asia-pacific/thailand/havas-worldwide-bangkok

Employees: 20

Agency Specializes In: Business-To-Business, Consumer Marketing, Digital/Interactive, Direct Response Marketing, Event Planning & Marketing, Internet/Web Design, Publicity/Promotions

Ricardo Turcios *(Exec Dir-Creative)*
Sarah Ko *(Reg Dir-Creative)*
Sunny Hermano *(Dir-Bus Dev & Integration-Southeast Asia)*
Sahaphon Phanpakdee *(Sr Graphic Designer)*

Accounts:
Trane Inc.
Jotun
Osram
Shieldtox Naturgard
Unilever

Havas Worldwide Singapore
(Formerly Euro RSCG Singapore)
80 Robinson Road #20-02, Singapore, 068898 Singapore
Tel.: (65) 6317 6714
Fax: (65) 6317 6700
Web Site: www.havasworldwide.com/

Employees: 130
Year Founded: 1974

Anna Chew *(Gen Mgr)*
Andrew Hook *(Exec Dir-Creative)*
Sharon Koh-Mitchell *(Client Svcs Dir)*

Accounts:
Agilent Technologies
Air France-KLM Group Content Creation, Corporate Communications, Media Strategies, Public Relations, Strategic Counselling
Allied World B2B, Brand Campaign, Creative, Digital, OOH, Print, Public Relations
New-Aspial Corporation Digital, Media
Bose
Carlsberg
Dell
Diageo
EPINS Branding
Fox Fashion Apparel
Lion Capital Management
Microsoft APAC
Nikon
Novartis
Reckitt Benckiser Durex
Seagate
Tiger Airways
Tokio Marine Asia Communication
Trane
Universitas Global
Volvo
Yahoo!

India

Havas Worldwide Bangalore
(Formerly Euro RSCG Bangalore)
4016 First Cross 17th Main, HAL II Stage - Domlur, Indiran, Bengaluru, 560 008 India
Tel.: (91) 80 49195333
Fax: (91) 80 49195399
Web Site: www.havasworldwide.co.in/

Agency Specializes In: Internet/Web Design

Anita Nayyar *(CEO-India & South Asia)*
Tiraz Balaporia *(Sr VP)*
Chandy Mohapatra *(Sr VP-Digital & Adv)*
Gaurav Soi *(Sr VP-Mumbai)*
Mohit Joshi *(Mng Dir-Havas Media India)*
Ashish Chandra *(Assoc VP)*

Accounts:
Air Wick Campaign: "Family", Campaign: "Freshness", Campaign: "Life is Bright"
Airtel
Bharat Petroleum
New-BlueStone.com Digital, Mobile Media
Durex
Gaana.com
Google
New-HolidayIQ.com Integrated Media
HSBC
IBM
Indiatimes.com
Luxpresso.com
Makemytrip.com
Pajero
New-Quikr Media
Reckitt Benckiser Dettol, Veet
Times Internet Limited
Unilever
Webex
Zigwheels.com

Havas Worldwide Delhi
(Formerly Euro RSCG New Delhi)
5th Floor Tower A Building No 9, DLF Cyber City Phase III, Gurgaon, 122002 India
Tel.: (91) 124 468 4500
Fax: (91) 124 468 4599
E-Mail: info@havasworldwide.co.in
Web Site: www.havasworldwide.co.in/

Mohit Joshi *(Mng Dir)*
Anita Nayyar *(CEO-India & South Asia)*
Chandy Mohapatra *(Sr VP-Digital & Adv)*
Vikas Parihar *(Sr VP-Digital)*
Lokesh Sah *(VP-Reckitt Benckiser Bus)*
Ankit Rastogi *(Joint Mng Dir & Head-Media Buying-Natl)*
Punita Lakhani *(Assoc VP-Digital Strategy)*
Uday Mohan *(Exec Dir)*
Nakul Sharma *(Exec Dir-Creative)*

Accounts:
Amway India Artistry, Attitude, Beauty Vertical, Media Planning & Buying
BSNL Data One, One India
CareerBuilder India Digital
Caterpillar India Digital Media
Child Survival India Campaign: "No Child Brides"
New-Clovia Digital, Mobile
New-Doctor 24x7 Digital, Media, Mobile
New-FoodCloud.in Digital, Media, Outdoor, Print, Radio, TV
Indiatimes.com
iOrderFresh Digital, Mobile, Social, Traditional Media Buying, Traditional Media Planning
Mann Public School
Max New York Life
Mortien
Neo Milk Products Media
OCM India Digital Media, Traditional
Ranbaxy (Digital Agency of Record) Consumer Healthcare
Reckitt Benckiser Campaign: "Happy Mornings", Campaign: "Kids Dreams", Dettol Antiseptic Soap, Disprin, Harpic Toilet Cleaner, Lizol Floor Cleaner, Strepsils, Veet Hair Removal Cream
Volvo
Wonder Cement Media
Yepme.com Media
Zee Business Creative, Marketing Communication

Havas Worldwide Digital Delhi
(Formerly Euro RSCG 4D-New Delhi)
Map 5th Floor - Tower A, Building No.9 - DLF Cyber City, Phase III, 122 002 Gurgaon, India
Tel.: (91) 124 468 4500
Fax: (91) 124 468 4599
Web Site: www.havasworldwide.com/contact-us/asia-pacific/india/havas-worldwide-digital-delhi

Agency Specializes In: Consumer Marketing, Digital/Interactive, Direct Response Marketing, Event Planning & Marketing, Internet/Web Design,

Publicity/Promotions, Sales Promotion

Gaurav Soi *(Sr VP-Mumbai)*
Mohit Joshi *(Mng Dir-Havas Media India)*
Roopali Sharma *(VP)*
Ranjoy Dey *(Head-Digital)*
Ankit Rastogi *(Joint Mng Dir & Head-Media Buying-Natl)*
Ashish Chandra *(Assoc VP)*
Gaurav Pandey *(Grp Dir-Tech)*
Saurabh Bhatnagar *(Grp Acct Dir-Digital)*
Adil Sanwari *(Sr Acct Mgr)*
Salome Singhal *(Acct Mgr)*

Accounts:
Airtel
Beam Global Spirits & Wine Below the Line Activities, Creative, Developing Insights, Surrogate Ads
Dalmia Continental Join the Change. Go Indiano, Leonardo Olive Oil
HDFC Bank
HSBC
IBM
Inditimes.com
Nokia Digital
Reckitt Benckiser Campaign: "Family", Campaign: "Happy Mornings", Campaign: "The Energy", Mortein NaturGard
Unilever
Uninor Creative, Strategy

Havas Worldwide Mumbai
(Formerly Euro RSCG Mumbai)
Valencia Building - 4th floor, Raj Kamal Marg, Off Dr SS Rao Road, Parel, Mumbai, India
Tel.: (91) 22 6177 6177
Fax: (91) 22 6177 6178
Web Site: www.havasworldwide.co.in/

Employees: 190

Agency Specializes In: Advertising, Brand Development & Integration, Consumer Marketing, Corporate Communications, Digital/Interactive, Direct Response Marketing, Health Care Services, Public Relations, South Asian Market

Nirmalya Sen *(CEO-India)*
Gaurav Soi *(VP-Mumbai)*
Rayomand J. Patell *(Exec Dir-Creative)*
Ajeet Shukla *(Sr Dir-Creative)*

Accounts:
Borosil Media
BPCL
Cobra Beer
Dell
DS Group Communications, Tansen
Finish
Grand Hyatt
HDFC Bank HDFC Credit Cards
New-Jaslok Hospital & Research Centre Creative, Integrated Communications
Mitsubishi Motors Cedia, Creative, Lancer, Montero, Outlander, Pajero
Multi Screen Media Pvt Ltd
Nimbus Sport Creative, World Hockey Series
Paras Pharmaceutical Creative, D'Cold, Dermicool, Itchguard, Krack, Moov
Rohit Surfactants Creative, Personal Care & Home Care Products
Yepme.com Media

South Africa

Havas Worldwide Johannesburg
(Formerly Euro RSCG South Africa)
Cedarwood House Ballywoods Office Park Bally Clare Dr, 2194 Bryanston, South Africa
Tel.: (27) 11 549 3600
Fax: (27) 11 706 5377
Web Site: www.havas.co.za

Employees: 62

Agency Specializes In: Advertising

Eoin Welsh *(Chief Creative Officer)*
Lynn Madeley *(CEO-Southern Africa)*
Annie Lazarevski *(Grp Acct Dir)*
Ryan Jones *(Dir-Art)*
Fiona O' Connor *(Dir-Creative)*
Greg Dennis *(Acct Mgr)*
Jeff Harvey *(Copywriter)*

Accounts:
Air France-KLM Group
Autopax
Bonjela
Calmdog
Citroen
Durex Play Campaign: "Durex Play Woman"
Mortein Campaign: "Jeremy"
Mr. Min
Peermont Hotels, Casinos & Resorts
PNet Behind the Scenes
PSN Campaign: "Intruder"
Reckitt Benckiser Campaign: "Entomology", Strepsils
Revlon 24 Seven, Aquamarine, ColorSilk, Cutex, Flex, Mitchum
Target Mortein Campaign: "Easy Reach: Tap"

United Arab Emirates

Havas Worldwide Middle East
(Formerly Euro RSCG Worldwide Middle East Headquarters)
Choueiri Building, 1st Floor Al Sufouh 2 St., Knowledge Village P.O. Box 21448, Dubai, 21448 United Arab Emirates
Tel.: (971) 4-455-6000
Fax: (971) 4 455 6299
Web Site: www.havasworldwide.com/contact-us/middle-east/united-arab-emirates/havas-worldwide-middle-east

Employees: 60
Year Founded: 2001

Agency Specializes In: Consumer Marketing, Public Relations

Kavita Dhyani *(Head-Media)*
Mayang Gore *(Head-Performance Media)*
Bushair Muhammadunni *(Dir-Digital Buying)*
Rana Zeidan *(Dir-Media)*
Dany El Zein *(Dir-Bus Unit)*
Liliane Alghadban *(Mgr-Media)*
Myriam Calvo *(Sr Media Planner)*
Dany Naaman *(Reg Mng Dir)*
Thais Perosa *(Sr Media Planner)*

Accounts:
Air France-KLM Group
And So To Bed
Haagen-Dazs
Peugeot
Pif Paf
Reckitt Benckiser Campaign: "Dettol Re-Energize", Campaign: "Germ Stamps", Dettol, Pifpaf Insect Repellent
Saks Fifth Avenue
Sanofi-Aventis
Strepsils
Vanish

HAVAS WORLDWIDE CHICAGO
36 E Grand Ave, Chicago, IL 60611
Tel.: (312) 640-6800
Fax: (312) 640-6801
E-Mail: chicago@havasww.com
Web Site: www.chi.havasworldwide.com

National Agency Associations: 4A's

Agency Specializes In: Advertising, Brand Development & Integration, Sponsorship

Paul Marobella *(Grp CEO)*
Angelo Kritikos *(CFO & Dir-Ops)*
Tatia Torrey *(Chief Client Officer)*
Drew Donatelle *(Exec Creative Dir)*
Jon Eckman *(Grp Dir-Creative)*
Chris Gyorgy *(Grp Dir-Creative)*
Michelle Tucker *(Grp Dir-Creative-Ragu)*
Meagan Huskisson *(Sr Acct Dir)*
Lisa Evia *(Grp Acct Dir)*
Shelby Georgis *(Creative Dir)*
Marisa Scime *(Acct Dir)*
Carolyn Tubekis *(Art Dir)*
Bethany Whipple *(Acct Dir)*
Chuck Anderson *(Dir-Creative-Design)*
Ian Beacraft *(Dir-Digital Strategy)*
Rachel Bottlinger *(Dir-Art)*
Eric Kripas *(Assoc Dir-Creative)*
Elizabeth Pearce *(Sr Project Mgr-Interactive)*
Adam Crouch *(Supvr-Social Media)*
John Courtland *(Sr Acct Exec)*
Marcella Astini *(Acct Exec)*
Taylor DuFour *(Acct Exec)*
Caitlin Kennedy *(Acct Exec)*
Ellie Brzezenski *(Media Planner)*
Zack Carlstrom *(Copywriter)*
Alex Hoogland *(Asst Media Planner & Media Buyer)*
Jason LaFlore *(Designer-Digital)*
Justin Miller *(Copywriter)*
Will Ryan *(Designer-Digital Production)*
Megan Roman *(Asst Media Planner & Buyer-Traditional & Digital)*

Accounts:
Autolite Campaign: "Mysterion"
AutoZone Advertising
Beam, Inc. Campaign: "Make It Easy with a Lifeguard", Sauza Tequila
Citigroup Inc.
Dish Network Campaign: "Mobile Basketball", Campaign: "Streaker", Campaign: "The Beautiful Game", DISH Anywhere App, Digital, DishLATINO, Online
New-Hefty Campaign: "#SaidNoSchoolEver", Online
Pearle Vision Digital
R&B Foods, Inc. Bertolli (Creative & Digital Agency of Record), Digital, In-Store, Packaging, Print, Radio, Ragu (Creative & Digital Agency of Record), TV
Reynolds Consumer Products Aluminum Foil, Campaign: "Party Hard Moms", Campaign: "Ultimate Cubs Game", Campaign: "Ultimate Garbage Men", Hefty Cups, Online, Televisions
Sauza Tequila
Sears Holdings Corp. Craftsman (Agency of Record), Creative, Die Hard (Agency of Record), Digital Media, Kenmore (Agency of Record), Kmart, Sears, Social Media
Sony Corporation PlayStation
Terminix Attractive Targeted Sugar Bait, Branding, Campaign: "Death to Mosquitoes", Print, TV

HAVIT ADVERTISING, LLC
1010 Wisconsin Ave NW Ste 205, Washington, DC 20007
Tel.: (202) 695-8055
Fax: (301) 604-2843
E-Mail: hello@havitad.com
Web Site: www.havitad.com

Employees: 10
Year Founded: 2003

Agency Specializes In: Advertising, Consumer Marketing, Direct Response Marketing, High Technology, Retail

Approx. Annual Billings: $7,000,000

Breakdown of Gross Billings by Media: Collateral: 10%; D.M.: 40%; Outdoor: 10%; Print: 40%

Scott Mikolajczyk *(CEO)*
Shannon Foy Leaf *(Mng Dir & Grp Acct Dir)*
Carolina Skelly *(Exec VP)*
Amy Looney *(Acct Dir)*
Adam Unger *(Acct Dir)*
Eric Sackett *(Mgr-Studio)*
Jocelyn L. Zobitz *(Acct Supvr)*

Accounts:
Comcast; Baltimore, MD Cable Television, High-Speed Internet; 2003
Mount Vernon Campaign: "One Man Stands Out"

HAVRILLAGROUP
22E E Roseville Rd, Lancaster, PA 17601
Tel.: (717) 569-6902
Fax: (717) 569-6930
E-Mail: jhavrilla@havrillagroup.com
Web Site: www.havrillagroup.com

Employees: 10
Year Founded: 1980

National Agency Associations: AMA-BMA

Agency Specializes In: Advertising, Advertising Specialties, Brand Development & Integration, Broadcast, Business Publications, Business-To-Business, Cable T.V., Co-op Advertising, Collateral, Communications, Consulting, Consumer Marketing, Consumer Publications, Corporate Identity, Direct Response Marketing, E-Commerce, Education, Electronic Media, Event Planning & Marketing, Exhibit/Trade Shows, Financial, Government/Political, Graphic Design, Health Care Services, High Technology, Information Technology, Internet/Web Design, Investor Relations, Leisure, Logo & Package Design, Magazines, Media Buying Services, Medical Products, Merchandising, New Product Development, Newspaper, Newspapers & Magazines, Out-of-Home Media, Outdoor, Over-50 Market, Planning & Consultation, Point of Purchase, Point of Sale, Print, Production, Public Relations, Publicity/Promotions, Radio, Real Estate, Retail, Sales Promotion, Seniors' Market, Strategic Planning/Research, Sweepstakes, Syndication, T.V., Technical Advertising, Telemarketing, Trade & Consumer Magazines, Transportation, Travel & Tourism

Approx. Annual Billings: $4,000,000

Linda Duncan *(Dir-Media)*

Accounts:
Dermatology Associates

HAWK ASSOCIATES, INC.
227 Atlantic Blvd, Key Largo, FL 33037
Tel.: (305) 451-1888
E-Mail: info@hawkassociates.com
Web Site: www.hawkassociates.com

Employees: 5
Year Founded: 1995

Agency Specializes In: Brand Development & Integration, Crisis Communications, Email, Internet/Web Design, Investor Relations, Media Relations

Julie W. Marshall *(Pres)*
Frank N. Hawkins *(CEO)*
Peter D'Agostino *(Mng Dir)*

Accounts:
Manhattan Scientifics, Inc.
NeoGenomics, Inc.

HAWK MARKETING SERVICES
77 Vaughan Harvey Blvd 4th Fl Unit 28, Moncton, NB E1C 0K2 Canada
Tel.: (506) 877-1400
Fax: (506) 877-1503
Web Site: www.hawk.ca

Employees: 28
Year Founded: 1978

Bill Whalen *(CEO)*
Susan Jones *(COO & VP-Strategy)*
Francois Giroux *(VP & Dir-Creative)*
Andre Levesque *(VP-Client Svcs)*
Steve Thompson *(Dir-Sls)*
Chris Farella *(Assoc Dir-Creative & Sr Writer-Creative)*
Ruth Macdonnell *(Mgr-HR)*
Kara Arsenault *(Acct Exec)*
Katelyn Hebert *(Acct Exec)*

HAWTHORNE DIRECT INC.
300 N 16th St, Fairfield, IA 52556-2604
Tel.: (641) 472-3800
Fax: (641) 472-4553
E-Mail: solutions@hawthornedirect.com
Web Site: www.hawthornedirect.com

E-Mail for Key Personnel:
Creative Dir.: thawthorne@hawthornedirect.com
Public Relations: kcrawfordkerr@hawthornedirect.com

Employees: 75
Year Founded: 1986

National Agency Associations: DMA

Agency Specializes In: Advertising, Automotive, Branded Entertainment, Broadcast, Business-To-Business, Computers & Software, Consumer Goods, Cosmetics, Direct Response Marketing, Education, Electronics, Entertainment, Fashion/Apparel, Financial, Health Care Services, Household Goods, Infomercials, Integrated Marketing, Internet/Web Design, Media Buying Services, Media Planning, Medical Products, Mobile Marketing, Multimedia, New Technologies, Pharmaceutical, Production, Production (Ad, Film, Broadcast), Retail, Sponsorship, Sports Market, Strategic Planning/Research, T.V., Telemarketing

Approx. Annual Billings: $103,000,000

Jessica Hawthorne-Castro *(CEO)*
Stephen Kelley *(CTO)*
John Pucci *(Chief Creative Officer)*
George Leon *(Sr VP-Media & Acct Mgmt)*
Lauren Bronchtein *(VP & Acct Dir-DentalPlans.com-Equifax)*
Bob Dashtizad *(Sr Dir-Digital Media)*
Jared Lake *(Dir-Digital Media)*
Ray Widjaja *(Dir-Art)*
Kurt Werderman *(Strategist-Media & Analyst)*

Accounts:
3M
Bose Corp.
Braun
Church & Dwight Co., Inc.
Discover Card
Eons
Evinrude
Hamilton Beach
High Plains Bison
Holloway House
Humminbird
J.G. Wentworth
Lawn Boy
Rowenta
Time-Life Inc.; Alexandria, VA Music Collections
Transamerica
The United States Navy
United States Navy
Urban Rebounding System
Wagner Power Paint

HAYNES MARKETING NETWORK, INC.
4149 Arkwright Rd, Macon, GA 31210
Tel.: (478) 742-5266
Fax: (478) 742-5334
Web Site: www.haynesmarketing.com

E-Mail for Key Personnel:
President: phil@haynesmarketing.com
Creative Dir.: amelia@haynemarketing.com

Employees: 2
Year Founded: 1976

Agency Specializes In: Advertising, Automotive, Broadcast, Business-To-Business, Cable T.V., Collateral, Consulting, Consumer Marketing, Consumer Publications, Corporate Communications, Corporate Identity, Direct Response Marketing, Electronic Media, Financial, Government/Political, Graphic Design, Industrial, Integrated Marketing, Magazines, Market Research, Media Buying Services, Media Planning, Mobile Marketing, Newspaper, Newspapers & Magazines, Out-of-Home Media, Outdoor, Planning & Consultation, Print, Production (Ad, Film, Broadcast), Publicity/Promotions, Radio, Retail, Strategic Planning/Research, T.V., Transportation, Yellow Pages Advertising

Phil Haynes *(Pres)*
Amelia Haynes *(VP & Graphic Designer)*

Accounts:
Bashinski Fine Gems & Jewelry; Macon, GA Jewelry; 2002
GBIS Disability, Inc
L.E. Schwartz & Sons; Macon, GA Roofing Services; 1988
Schwartz Precision Manufacturing; Macon, GA Laser Cutting; 1996
Youmans Chevrolet; Macon, GA Chevrolet; 1978

HAYWORTH PUBLIC RELATIONS
(Formerly Hayworth Creative Public Relations)
700 W Granada Blvd Ste 100, Ormond Beach, FL 32174
Tel.: (386) 677-7000
Fax: (386) 677-7393
E-Mail: info@hayworthpr.com
Web Site: hayworthpr.com/

Year Founded: 1999

Agency Specializes In: Public Relations, Retail, Strategic Planning/Research, Travel & Tourism

Kevin Hayworth *(Owner)*
Lauren Swoboda *(Mng Dir)*
Kelly Prieto *(VP)*
Hope Sarzier *(Reg Dir-Southeast)*
Brittany Najmy *(Acct Exec)*

Accounts:
Payless Car Rental Automobile Rental Services
The Shores Resort & Spa Tourism Services
Wyndham Sugar Bay Resort & Spa Tourism Services

HC&B HEALTHCARE COMMUNICATIONS
701 Brazos St Ste 1100, Austin, TX 78701-3232
Tel.: (512) 320-8511
Fax: (512) 320-8990
E-Mail: kerryh@hcandb.com
Web Site: www.hcbhealth.com/

E-Mail for Key Personnel:
President: kerryh@brsg.com
Media Dir.: georgec@brsg.com

Employees: 20
Year Founded: 2001

Agency Specializes In: Advertising, Business-To-Business, Collateral, Health Care Services, High Technology, Medical Products, Pharmaceutical, Real Estate, Retail, Strategic Planning/Research, Travel & Tourism

Approx. Annual Billings: $15,000,000

Breakdown of Gross Billings by Media: Brdcst.: 5%; Collateral: 20%; E-Commerce: 5%; Exhibits/Trade Shows: 5%; Logo & Package Design: 5%; Newsp.: 5%; Outdoor: 5%; Print: 30%; Production: 5%; Radio: 5%; Strategic Planning/Research: 10%

Nancy Beesley *(Partner & CMO)*
Kim Carpenter *(VP-Acct Svcs)*
Joe Doyle *(VP-Digital Strategy)*
Lori Lipscomb *(Controller)*
Michele Evans *(Sr Dir-Art)*
David Walker *(Dir-Creative)*
Marcus Rice *(Assoc Dir-Creative)*
Susan Dore *(Mgr-Production)*

Accounts:
Agennex
Alcon
ANS
Association for the Advancement of Wound Care; Atlanta, GA; 2004
Boral
Menninger
Optima Health
Scott & White Hospital Network
Solis
University of Texas System

HCB HEALTH
701 Brazos Ste 1100, Austin, TX 78701
Tel.: (512) 320-8511
Fax: (512) 320-8990
Web Site: www.hcbhealth.com

Year Founded: 2001

Agency Specializes In: Advertising, Brand Development & Integration, Broadcast, Business-To-Business, Cable T.V., Communications, Consumer Publications, Content, Corporate Communications, Corporate Identity, Crisis Communications, Digital/Interactive, Direct Response Marketing, Direct-to-Consumer, Electronic Media, Email, Exhibit/Trade Shows, Graphic Design, Health Care Services, High Technology, Identity Marketing, Integrated Marketing, International, Internet/Web Design, Local Marketing, Logo & Package Design, Magazines, Market Research, Media Buying Services, Media Planning, Media Relations, Medical Products, Mobile Marketing, Multicultural, Multimedia, New Product Development, New Technologies, Newspaper, Newspapers & Magazines, Out-of-Home Media, Outdoor, Package Design, Paid Searches, Pharmaceutical, Planning & Consultation, Print, Production (Ad, Film, Broadcast), Public Relations, Publicity/Promotions, Radio, Regional, Sales Promotion, Search Engine Optimization, Social Marketing/Nonprofit, Social Media, Sponsorship, Strategic Planning/Research, Syndication, T.V., Technical Advertising, Trade & Consumer Magazines, Web (Banner Ads, Pop-ups, etc.)

Kerry Hilton *(CEO & Exec Dir-Creative)*
Nancy Beesley *(Partner & CMO)*
Amy Dowell *(Exec VP)*
Abby Mansfield *(Sr VP & Dir-Creative)*
Joe Doyle *(VP-Digital Strategy)*
Meg Nohe *(Dir-Strategic Dev)*
Erin Schwarz *(Assoc Dir-Creative)*
Alexia Ybarra *(Sr Project Mgr-Interactive)*

Accounts:
Alcon Laboratories
Alcon Surgical (Global & US Agency of Record)
AposTherapy
California Pacific Medical Center-Sutter Health
CareFusion
Cochlear
Edgemont Pharmaceuticals
Harden Healthcare
Hollister
invisalign
KCI
Lanx
LDR
LIVESTRONG
Luminex
McKesson Specialty Health
Medtronic
The Menninger Clinic
On-X Life Technologies
Schumachergroup
Scott & White Health Plan
Smith & Nephew
Texas Oncology
THANC Foundation
The US Oncology Network
Vaser
Zeus Scientific

Subsidiary

HCB Health Chicago
(Formerly Topin & Associates, Inc.)
205 N Michigan Ave Ste 2315, Chicago, IL 60601-5923
(See Separate Listing)

HCB HEALTH CHICAGO
(Formerly Topin & Associates, Inc.)
205 N Michigan Ave Ste 2315, Chicago, IL 60601-5923
Tel.: (312) 645-0100
Fax: (312) 645-0120
Web Site: www.hcbhealth.com

Employees: 30
Year Founded: 1982

National Agency Associations: 4A's

Agency Specializes In: Advertising, Brand Development & Integration, Consulting, Health Care Services, Internet/Web Design, Medical Products, Pharmaceutical

Alan Topin *(Pres)*
Katie Keblusek *(VP-Fin & Ops)*
Betsy Kramer *(VP-Acct Svcs)*
Yuliya Chepurnaya *(Sr Dir-Art)*
Lori Kewin *(Acct Dir)*
Alexander Leavitt *(Acct Dir)*
Tommy Schenck *(Acct Dir)*
Erin Schwarz *(Assoc Dir-Creative)*

Accounts:
Mission Pharmacal
Myriad Genetics
Terumo Cardiovascular Systems
Teva Neuroscience, Inc./Eisai Inc.
Vetter Pharma

HCC MARKETING, INC.
(Formerly Hurley Chandler & Chaffer)
57 Maple Ave, Barrington, RI 02806
Tel.: (401) 273-5530
Fax: (401) 331-2061
Web Site: www.hccmarketing.com

Employees: 14
Year Founded: 1982

Kerry Chaffer *(Partner & Sr Acct Mgr)*
Bill De Witt *(Partner & Sr Acct Mgr)*
Scott Clark *(Exec Dir-Art)*
Julia Brough *(Acct Mgr)*
Mary Dewitt *(Mgr-Ops)*
Susan Lincoln *(Acct Exec)*

Accounts:
Harbor One Credit Union
Milford National Bank
PeoplesBank

HCK2 PARTNERS
16775 Addison Rd Ste 550, Addison, TX 75001
Tel.: (972) 716-0500
Fax: (972) 716-0599
E-Mail: hcapps@hck2.com
Web Site: www.hck2.com

E-Mail for Key Personnel:
President: hcapps@michaelpartners.com

Employees: 30
Year Founded: 1998

Agency Specializes In: Advertising, Advertising Specialties, Brand Development & Integration, Business Publications, Business-To-Business, Collateral, Consulting, Consumer Goods, Consumer Marketing, Consumer Publications, Corporate Communications, Corporate Identity, Cosmetics, Crisis Communications, Digital/Interactive, Direct Response Marketing, E-Commerce, Electronic Media, Email, Event Planning & Marketing, Exhibit/Trade Shows, Fashion/Apparel, Financial, Food Service, Graphic Design, Health Care Services, High Technology, In-Store Advertising, Information Technology, Integrated Marketing, Internet/Web Design, Investor Relations, Local Marketing, Logo & Package Design, Media Buying Services, Media Planning, Media Relations, Medical Products, Multimedia, New Product Development, Newspaper, Newspapers & Magazines, Outdoor, Package Design, Pharmaceutical, Planning & Consultation, Point of Purchase, Point of Sale, Print, Production, Production (Print), Promotions, Public Relations, Publicity/Promotions, Radio, Real Estate, Restaurant, Retail, Social Marketing/Nonprofit, Strategic Planning/Research, T.V., Trade & Consumer Magazines, Travel & Tourism, Women's Market

Kenneth Kracmer *(Owner & Mng Partner)*
Heather Capps *(Pres & CEO)*
Elizabeth Browne Cornelius *(VP-Acct Svc)*
Kerri Fulks *(Mgr-PR Ops & Acct Dir)*
Thomas Moore *(Acct Dir)*
Martin Eggert *(Dir-Interactive Svcs)*
Jordan LaMons *(Dir-Tech)*
Emi FitzGerald *(Supvr-Interactive Svcs)*
Erin Groover *(Sr Acct Exec)*

Accounts:
A & A Optical
Advanced Data Spectrum
AdvoCare
AfriCeuticals, Inc
Ambit Energy
Applebee's
Autobuses Americanos
Celanese
City of Cedar Hill
Dependable Auto Shippers
FCS Equipment
FITCO
Garfield Traub Development
GMR

Grand Prairie AirHogs
Heritage Health Solutions
HG Trial Resource
Holiday Card Campaign: "Naughty or Nice Game"
Ignis Petroleum, Inc
Kimberly-Clark
LenderServ Partners
Lockton Dunning
Marazzi Tile
MASERGY Communications
MedSynergies
Minerva Real Estate
OneSource Virtual
Pinnacle Family of Companies
Plexon
Redmoon Broadband
Texas Power (Agency of Record) Marketing Communications, Media Outreach
Town of Addison
Victory Bank
Virallock
Wischmeyer Benefit Partners
Yo! Bus
Zix Corporation

HDE, LLC.

22 E Victory St, Phoenix, AZ 85040
Tel.: (602) 276-2499
Fax: (815) 642-4836
Web Site: www.hdeagency.com

Agency Specializes In: Advertising, Brand Development & Integration, Graphic Design, Internet/Web Design, Logo & Package Design, Print, Public Relations, Radio, Social Media, Strategic Planning/Research

Landon Evans *(Owner & Dir-Creative)*
Elena Evans *(Controller)*
Shane Gadberry *(Dir-Print & Graphic Designer)*
Jennifer Pruett *(Mgr-PR)*
Kellie Threadgill *(Coord-Sponsor & Vendor)*

Accounts:
Accelerated Beverages
Arctic Fox Heating & Air Conditioning
Arizona Restaurant Systems, Inc.
Brat Haus (Agency of Record) Creative Development, Design, Marketing, Public Relations
Crowne Plaza San Marcos Hotel
Crust Restaurants (Agency of Record) Brand Marketing, Public Relations
El Palacio Brand Development, Marketing, Public Relations
Hunter Contracting Company
Pincus & Associates
Pizza Me! Design, Marketing, Public Relations
SanTan Brewing Company
New-Scottsdale League for the Arts (Marketing & Public Relations Agency of Record) Scottsdale Culinary Festival
World of Beer Franchise Marketing, Promotional Development, Public Relations

HDM/ZOOMEDIA

(Formerly Harris D. McKinney)
55 W Wacker Dr, Chicago, IL 60601
Tel.: (312) 506-5200
Fax: (312) 506-5201
Web Site: hdmz.com/

Employees: 20
Year Founded: 1936

National Agency Associations: 4A's

Agency Specializes In: Business-To-Business, Internet/Web Design, Public Relations, Sponsorship

Daniel E. Hoexter *(Pres & CEO)*
Sam Recenello *(CFO)*
Dave Marcou *(Sr VP-Bus Dev)*
Dillon Allie *(VP-Client Svcs)*
Hooshna Amaria *(VP-Client Svcs)*
Ryan Ferrell *(Dir-Scientific Comm)*
Seth Schwartz *(Dir-Digital Solutions)*
Alan Zachary *(Dir-Media Rels)*
Laura Mayronne *(Acct Exec-Natl)*
Meagan Metkowski *(Acct Exec)*

Accounts:
Abimba Manufacturing
Agilent Technologies
Applied Biosystems
Bimba
BioSante Pharmaceuticals
Gilead
InterMune
Life Technologies
Medtronic
The Nugene Product
Regeneron
Remel
Rosetta Genomics
Sigma-Aldrich
Sirna Therapeutics
Thermo Fisher Scientific
Trustwave
XTRA Lease

Branch

HDM/Zoomedia

(Formerly Zoomedia, Inc.)
1620 Montgomery St, San Francisco, CA 94111
Tel.: (415) 474-1192
Fax: (415) 474-8146
Web Site: hdmz.com/

Year Founded: 1994

National Agency Associations: 4A's

Agency Specializes In: Health Care Services, Medical Products, Pharmaceutical

Justin Bane *(Dir-Tech)*
Seth Schwartz *(Dir-Digital Solutions)*
Christine Bennett *(Specialist-Client Svcs)*

Accounts:
Celera Corp; Alameda, CA
Genencor International
Gilead Sciences
Rigel Pharmaceuticals

HDSF

450 Geary St Unit 301, San Francisco, CA 94102
Tel.: (415) 685-2800
E-Mail: info@hdsf.com
Web Site: www.hdsf.com

Year Founded: 2003

Agency Specializes In: Advertising, Digital/Interactive, Graphic Design, Internet/Web Design, Media Planning, Print

Sue Hutner *(CEO & Principal)*
Justine Descollonges *(Principal & Dir-Creative)*
Timothy Preut *(Designer-Visual)*

Accounts:
Hathaway Dinwiddie Construction Company

HEADFIRST CREATIVE

30150 Walser, Chapel Hill, NC 27517
Tel.: (919) 338-1098
Fax: (919) 338-1446
Web Site: www.headfirstcreative.com

Agency Specializes In: Advertising, Brand Development & Integration, Email, Internet/Web Design, Logo & Package Design, Print, Radio, Social Media, T.V.

Scott Whitney *(Principal & Creative Dir)*
Jake Garver *(Art Dir)*
Jason Quintiliano *(Art Dir)*
Tim McCracken *(Creative Dir-Interactive)*

Accounts:
GoFileRoom
MXenergy
Maurice Villency
Thomson Reuters Tax & Accounting

HEADSPACE MARKETING

2323 Yonge St Ste 204, Toronto, ON M4P 2C9 Canada
Tel.: (416) 221-3770
Fax: (416) 221-9436
E-Mail: eblais@headspacemarketing.com
Web Site: www.headspacemarketing.com

Agency Specializes In: Advertising, Brand Development & Integration, Communications

Eric Blais *(Pres)*
Manon Varin *(Dir-Project Mgmt)*

Accounts:
Bio-Oil
D'Italiano
Dormex-Vous
Durex
Tim Hortons
Virgin Mobile USA, Inc.

HEALTH SCIENCE COMMUNICATIONS

711 3rd Ave Ste 17, New York, NY 10017
Tel.: (212) 849-7900
Fax: (212) 627-4764
E-Mail: dbottiglieri@hsci.com
Web Site: www.hsci.com

E-Mail for Key Personnel:
President: dbottiglieri@hsci.com

Employees: 120
Year Founded: 1987

Agency Specializes In: Education, Health Care Services, Medical Products, Pharmaceutical

Fariba Ghodrati *(Sr VP-Client Svcs)*
Tara Regan *(Sr VP-Health Science Comm)*
Kathleen Young *(Sr VP-Client Svcs, Health Science Comm)*
David Ferguson *(VP & Dir-Creative-Scientific Visual Strategy)*
Nina Leeds *(VP-Medical & Scientific Svcs)*
Charity Miller *(VP-Client Svcs)*
Stephen Towers *(Sr Dir-Medical)*
Alison Pantelic *(Acct Dir)*
Josh Rodman *(Dir-Medical)*
Nicole Sabaliauskas *(Assoc Dir-Medical)*

Accounts:
Bristol-Myers Squibb Company
Bristol-Myers Squibb Medical Imaging
Genentech
Merck & Company
Merck/Schering-Plough
Novartis
Pfizer Inc.
Schering-Plough International
Schering-Plough Pharmaceuticals

THE HEALTHCARE CONSULTANCY GROUP

711 3rd Ave 17th Fl, New York, NY 10017
Tel.: (212) 849-7900

Fax: (212) 627-4764
Web Site: www.hcgrp.com

Year Founded: 1987

Agency Specializes In: Advertising

Denise Bottiglieri *(CEO)*
Brian Kielty *(CFO, COO & Exec VP)*
Delphine Dubois *(Pres-Health Science Comm)*
Jan-willem Van Doorn *(Mng Dir-Medical & Scientific Svcs & Exec VP)*
Tejinder Kaur *(Exec VP-Learning & Dev)*
Natasha Moningka *(Exec VP-Learning & Dev)*
Elizabeth Robinson *(Exec VP-Learning & Dev)*
Jenny Song *(Exec VP-Learning & Dev)*
Joe Walsh *(Dir-Ops-Health Science Comm)*
Karen Colbert *(Assoc Dir-Medical)*
Sarah Guttenplan *(Assoc Dir-Medical)*
Diala Habib *(Assoc Dir-Medical)*
Cheryl Williams *(Mgr-HR-Talent Acq)*
Catherine Hauer *(Sr Analyst-Fin)*

Accounts:
Clovis Oncology

HEALTHCARE SUCCESS STRATEGIES
8961 Research DrSte 200, Irvine, CA 92618
Toll Free: (800) 656-0907
E-Mail: info@healthcaresuccess.com
Web Site: www.healthcaresuccess.com

Agency Specializes In: Advertising, Brand Development & Integration, Email, Health Care Services, Internet/Web Design, Local Marketing, Logo & Package Design, Media Buying Services, Newspapers & Magazines, Public Relations, Publicity/Promotions, Radio, Search Engine Optimization, T.V., Web (Banner Ads, Pop-ups, etc.)

Stewart Gandolf *(Co-Founder & CEO)*
Jamie Roney *(Client Svcs Dir)*
Simona Ramos *(Assoc Dir-Creative)*
Steven Jacobs *(Mgr & Analyst-SEO)*
Stephen Gregg *(Mgr-Mktg Comm)*
Kathy Roy Gaughran *(Sr Strategist-Mktg)*
Lori Waltz *(Specialist-Trng)*

HEALTHED
100 Walnut Ave Ste 407, Clark, NJ 07066
Tel.: (908) 654-4440
Fax: (732) 388-5203
E-Mail: info@healthed.com
Web Site: www.healthed.com

Employees: 140
Year Founded: 1989

Agency Specializes In: Graphic Design, Print, Telemarketing

Joe Poggi *(Mng Dir)*
Lauren Musto *(Controller)*
Courtney L. Johnson *(Acct Supvr)*
Debra Podolsky *(Acct Supvr)*

Accounts:
Bristol-Myers Squibb Company
Genentech
The Leukemia & Lymphoma Society
Merck & Co Pharmaceutical Product Mfr

HEALTHSTAR COMMUNICATIONS, INC.
1000 Wyckoff Ave, Mahwah, NJ 07430
Tel.: (201) 560-5370
Fax: (201) 891-2380
E-Mail: marketing@healthstarcom.com
Web Site: www.healthstarcom.com

Year Founded: 2001

Agency Specializes In: Health Care Services, Medical Products

Approx. Annual Billings: $213,000,000

Al Mahafzah *(CTO & Sr VP)*
Patty Brock *(Sr VP-HR & Admin)*
Bryan Fuerst *(Sr VP-Fin)*
Lew Campanaro *(VP-Acct Svcs)*
James King *(VP)*
Alanna Kirschbaum *(VP-HR)*
Karen Smith *(VP-Acct)*
Simone Virgilio *(Acct Dir)*
Angela Browne *(Dir-Virtual & Creative Ops)*
Scott Salvatore *(Dir-IT)*

Accounts:
AstraZeneca Pharmaceuticals
Bayer Pharmaceuticals Corp.
Biogen, Inc.
Boehringer Ingelheim Corp.
Eli Lilly & Co.
Merck & Co., Inc.
Nabi Biopharmaceuticals
Novartis Pharmaceuticals Corp. Lamisil DermGel
Obagi Medical Products, Inc
Pfizer Inc.
Reliant Pharmaceuticals
Sankyo Pharma
Sanofi-Synthelabo Inc.
University of Texas

Branches

Centron
90 5th Ave, New York, NY 10011
Tel.: (646) 722-8900
Fax: (646) 722-8988
Web Site: www.centroncom.com

Employees: 80

Agency Specializes In: Health Care Services, Medical Products, Pharmaceutical

Marcia McLaughlin *(Pres & CEO)*
Madeleine Gold *(Mng Dir & Exec VP)*
Shannyn Smith *(Mng Dir & Exec VP)*
Michael Metelenis *(Chief Creative Officer)*
Letty Albarran *(Exec VP & Dir-Creative)*
Frederick Rescott *(Exec VP & Dir-Creative)*
Glynis Samuel *(Assoc Dir-Project Mgmt)*
Anne Giaquinto *(Acct Grp Supvr)*
Christine Pezza *(Acct Exec)*
Jenny Krieger *(Grp Acct Supvr)*

Accounts:
Eisai Inc. Ontak, Targretin
Genta Ganite, Genasense
Lundbeck/Solvey
Lundbeck/Takeda
Merz

HEALTHSTAR PUBLIC RELATIONS
112 Madison Ave, New York, NY 10016
Tel.: (212) 532-0909
Fax: (212) 532-6907
E-Mail: info@healthstarpr.com
Web Site: www.healthstarpr.com

Employees: 20

Agency Specializes In: Advertising, Broadcast, Communications, Corporate Communications, Direct Response Marketing, Guerilla Marketing, Health Care Services, Internet/Web Design, Medical Products, Pharmaceutical, Print, Public Relations, Publicity/Promotions

Erinn White *(Founder & Pres)*
David Bashaw *(Exec VP)*
Abhi Basu *(VP)*
Stacey Cooper *(Acct Supvr)*

Accounts:
Almirall
Bayer Consumer Care
European Alliance for Access to Safe Medicines
Forest Laboratories
Genentech
Henry Ford Hospital
Mead Johnson Nutritional

HEART
500 Harrison Ave Ste 3R, Boston, MA 02118
Tel.: (508) 981-7315
Web Site: wemakeheart.com

Year Founded: 2013

Agency Specializes In: Above-the-Line, Advertising, Advertising Specialties, Alternative Advertising, Below-the-Line, Brand Development & Integration, Branded Entertainment, Broadcast, Cable T.V., Communications, Consulting, Content, Corporate Identity, Custom Publishing, Digital/Interactive, Experience Design, Graphic Design, Identity Marketing, In-Store Advertising, Integrated Marketing, Logo & Package Design, Magazines, Mobile Marketing, New Product Development, Newspaper, Out-of-Home Media, Outdoor, Package Design, Planning & Consultation, Point of Purchase, Point of Sale, Print, Social Media, Sponsorship, Strategic Planning/Research, T.V., Viral/Buzz/Word of Mouth, Web (Banner Ads, Pop-ups, etc.)

Thomas O'Connell *(Founder)*
Brandon Bird *(Partner)*

Accounts:
Gemvara Retail/Online; 2013

HEARTBEAT DIGITAL
200 Hudson St 9th Fl, New York, NY 10013
Tel.: (212) 812-2233
Fax: (212) 812-6380
Toll Free: (888) 941-9590
E-Mail: info@heartbeatideas.com
Web Site: www.heartbeatideas.com

Employees: 100

Agency Specializes In: Advertising, Media Buying Services, Media Planning, Search Engine Optimization, Viral/Buzz/Word of Mouth

Bill Drummy *(Founder & CEO)*
Janelle Starr *(Sr VP & Gen Mgr)*
James Talerico *(Sr VP & Exec Dir-Creative)*
Lee Slovitt *(Sr VP-Media)*
Jennifer Campanaro *(Sr Dir-Interactive Mktg)*
Chris Whaites *(Dir-Creative)*
Dan Haller *(Assoc Dir-Media)*
Andrew Simon *(Sr Media Planner)*

Accounts:
Abbott Laboratories
Amgen
Baxter Bioscience
BD
Biogen
Genentech
GSK
Memorial Sloan-Kettering
Merck
Millennium
MSD Pharmaceuticals Private Limited
Roche Diagnostics
Sanofi Aventis
Sephora
UCB

XYZAL

HEAT

1100 Sansome St, San Francisco, CA 94111
Tel.: (415) 477-1999
Fax: (415) 477-1990
E-Mail: elder@sfheat.com
Web Site: www.sfheat.com

Employees: 55
Year Founded: 2005

Agency Specializes In: Digital/Interactive, Internet/Web Design, Print, Production, Sponsorship

Approx. Annual Billings: $12,000,000

Steve Stone *(Chm & Exec Dir-Creative)*
John Elder *(Pres)*
Mike Barrett *(Mng Dir-Media & Comm Plng)*
Emily Palmer *(Acct Dir)*
Warren Cockrel *(Dir-Creative & Copywriter)*
Liza Bobrow *(Dir-Ops)*
Molly Cabe *(Dir-Strategy)*
Aaron Clinger *(Dir-Digital)*
Brian Coate *(Dir-Production)*
Teri Miller *(Dir-Mktg)*
Julie Petruzzo *(Dir-Bus Affairs)*
Shawn Raissi *(Dir-Art)*
Katie Ramp *(Dir-Talent)*
Nick Reggars *(Dir-Content Strategy)*
Anna Rowland *(Dir-Creative & Art)*
Kim Shores *(Dir-Comm Plng)*
Kirby Todd *(Dir-Social Media)*
Ryan Hartsfield *(Assoc Dir-Creative)*
Matt Stafford *(Assoc Dir-Creative)*
MacKenzie Huff *(Acct Mgr)*
Kevin John *(Acct Mgr)*
Rachel Majors *(Acct Mgr)*
Ian Anderson *(Mgr-Fin Plng & Analysis)*
Libby Dunn *(Acct Supvr)*
Julia Wu *(Acct Supvr)*
Ashley Wurzel *(Acct Supvr)*
Jon Korn *(Sr Writer)*
Zach Moranville *(Designer-Production)*
Ben Pfutzenreuter *(Copywriter)*
Erica Lizarraga *(Asst Media Planner)*

Accounts:
AOL
New-Arlo (Agency of Record)
Bank of the West; San Francisco, CA (Agency of Record) Campaign: "A to Z"
EA Sports (Agency of Record) Campaign: "Become More Powerful", Campaign: "Born to Madden", Campaign: "Get Ready", Campaign: "Madden 25: Running Back Sons", Campaign: "Madden NFL 12 Smack Shack", Campaign: "Madden Season", Campaign: "Madden: The Movie", Campaign: "NCAA True Friend", Campaign: "Shadow", Campaign: "The Rumble", Campaign: "Titanfall", Digital, Madden NFL 15, NHL 16, Star Wars Battlefront, Tiger Woods PGA Tour 14., UFC
Hotwire (Agency of Record) Account Planning, Creative, Discount Travel Site, Strategy
Kendall-Jackson Digital, Point-of-Purchase, Print
La Crema Winery Digital, Experiential, POS, Print, Trade Development
Levi's Stadium Digital, Outdoor, Print, Radio, Social Media Marketing
MINI Dealership Complementary Campaign, Digital, Print, Radio, Social Media, TV
NFL Campaign: "Madden NFL 15 Madden Season", Campaign: "Madden: The Movie"
Nike
Nikon
Riverbed
Sunrun
SW
Weebly Campaign: "We Believe", Online, TV
Yelp
YouSendIt Campaign: "Consumer-Facing", Digital, Experiential

HEATHCOTT ASSOCIATES

(Acquired & Absorbed by Cranford Johnson Robinson Woods)

HEAVENSPOT

1800 S Brand Blvd Ste 205, Glendale, CA 91204
Tel.: (323) 463-1092
Fax: (323) 463-1605
E-Mail: information@heavenspot.com
Web Site: www.heavenspot.com

Year Founded: 1997

Agency Specializes In: Advertising, Brand Development & Integration, Digital/Interactive, Internet/Web Design, Print

Kathryn Schotthoefer *(Sr VP-Social Media)*
Julia Bartine *(VP-Strategy)*
Eric Lamb *(Dir-Creative)*
Geoff Oki *(Assoc Dir-Creative)*
Nicole Breanne *(Sr Mgr-Social Media)*
Katie Hutchings *(Sr Mgr-Social Media)*
Lindsey Shaw *(Sr Mgr-Social Media)*
Laura Caccavo *(Mgr-Social Media)*
Mathilde Medeiros *(Specialist-Social Media)*

Accounts:
Goldenvoice, Llc.
Mattel, Inc.
Universal Pictures

HECKLER ASSOCIATES

(Private-Parent-Single Location)
2701 1st Ave Ste 530, Seattle, WA 98121
Tel.: (206) 352-1010
Fax: (206) 352-1011
E-Mail: inquiries@hecklerassociates.com

Employees: 23
Year Founded: 1970

Agency Specializes In: Advertising, Digital/Interactive, Internet/Web Design, Logo & Package Design, Outdoor, Package Design, Print, Radio, Sponsorship, T.V.

Revenue: $1,500,000

Terry Heckler *(Pres)*
Doug Brody *(Dir-Creative & Writer)*
Kristin Fortino *(Acct Mgr)*
Erik Bell *(Designer)*
Rob Humphrey *(Designer-2D & 3D)*
Kristien Ziska *(Designer)*

Accounts:
Sage

HEILBRICE

9840 Irvine Center Dr, Irvine, CA 92618
Tel.: (949) 336-8800
Fax: (949) 336-8819
E-Mail: ideas@heilbrice.com
Web Site: www.heilbrice.com

E-Mail for Key Personnel:
President: hal.brice@heilbrice.com

Employees: 40
Year Founded: 1987

Agency Specializes In: Advertising, Advertising Specialties, Affluent Market, Bilingual Market, Brand Development & Integration, Broadcast, Business-To-Business, Cable T.V., Co-op Advertising, Collateral, Communications, Consumer Goods, Consumer Marketing, Corporate Communications, Corporate Identity, Digital/Interactive, Direct Response Marketing, Food Service, Government/Political, Hispanic Market, In-Store Advertising, Integrated Marketing, Internet/Web Design, Local Marketing, Logo & Package Design, Magazines, Market Research, Media Buying Services, Media Planning, Media Relations, Merchandising, Multicultural, Multimedia, Newspaper, Newspapers & Magazines, Out-of-Home Media, Outdoor, Package Design, Point of Purchase, Point of Sale, Print, Production, Production (Ad, Film, Broadcast), Production (Print), Promotions, Public Relations, Publicity/Promotions, Radio, Restaurant, Retail, Search Engine Optimization, Social Marketing/Nonprofit, Sponsorship, T.V., Trade & Consumer Magazines, Travel & Tourism, Web (Banner Ads, Pop-ups, etc.), Women's Market

Revenue: $80,000,000

Hal Brice *(Co-Founder & Co-CEO)*
Jeff Morris *(Pres)*
Robert Guevarra *(VP-Ops)*
Brian Cruse *(Acct Dir)*
Tim Ruiz *(Dir-Tech & Project Mgr-Interactive)*
Joni Parenti *(Dir-Creative)*
Doris Heil *(Mgr-HR)*
Matt Furman *(Acct Exec)*

Accounts:
Cirque du Soleil
The Great Atlantic & Pacific Tea Company A&P, A&P Liquor, AC Healthy Kids, America's Choice, Best Cellars, Food Basics, Gold Quality, Green Way, Hartford Reserve, LiveBetter, Master Choice, Pathmark, Smart Price, Superfresh, The Food Emporium, The Great Atlantic & Pacific Tea Company, Inc., Via Roma, Waldbaum's
Jana Water North America Consumer Engagement, Social Media
Los Angeles Clippers; Los Angeles, CA Basketball Team; 1999
Los Angeles Tourism & Convention Board Creative & Strategy Agency of Record, Integrated Consumer Marketing
Manhattan Beach Chamber of Commerce
Marie Callender's Restaurant & Bakery Creative
Ralph's Grocery Company Food 4 Less Supermarkets, Ralph's Grocery Company
Roth Capital Partners
Smart & Final

HEINRICH MARKETING

2228 Blake St Ste 200, Denver, CO 80205-2120
Tel.: (303) 233-8660
Fax: (303) 239-5373
Toll Free: (800) 356-5036
E-Mail: info@heinrich.com
Web Site: www.heinrich.com

E-Mail for Key Personnel:
President: georgeeddy@heinrich.com
Media Dir.: laurasonderup@heinrich.com
Public Relations: laurasonderup@heinrich.com

Employees: 55
Year Founded: 1977

National Agency Associations: DMA

Agency Specializes In: Direct Response Marketing, Sponsorship

Approx. Annual Billings: $18,000,000

Laura Sonderup *(Mng Dir & Sr Strategist-Multicultural)*
Erin Iwata *(VP-Digital Mktg)*
Steven Greenwald *(Dir-Media)*
Robert L. McPhee *(Dir-Creative)*
Linds Johnson *(Assoc Dir-Media)*
Erika Lidster *(Sr Mgr-Print Production)*
Cathy Peeper *(Acct Exec)*

Pamela Talley *(Acct Exec)*

Accounts:
COUNTRY Financial
First Data Corporation; 1996
Macy's West; San Francisco, CA
Merrick Bank
Wells Fargo

Heinrich Hawaii

900 Fort St Mall Ste 860, Honolulu, HI 96813
Tel.: (808) 275-1021
Fax: (808) 275-1152
E-Mail: mwitter@heinrich.com
Web Site: www.heinrichhawaii.com

Employees: 20

Patrick Bullard *(Principal)*
Erin Iwata *(VP-Digital Mktg)*
Jay Rael *(Acct Dir)*
Rafael Rodriguez *(Acct Dir)*
Steven Greenwald *(Dir-Media)*
Robert Mason *(Dir-Creative)*
Rob McPhee *(Dir-Creative)*
Erika Lidster *(Mgr-Production)*
Angee Jackson *(Acct Exec)*
Pat Nohara Ho *(Media Buyer)*
Amber Vega *(Asst Acct Exec)*

Accounts:
The Cookie Corner
Hawaii Coffee Company
Humana
HWB
Paradise
Saint Louis Alumni
Saint Louis School
Sizzler

HEINZEROTH MARKETING GROUP

415 Y Blvd, Rockford, IL 61107-3059
Tel.: (815) 967-0929
Fax: (815) 967-0983
E-Mail: ideas@heinzeroth.com
Web Site: www.heinzeroth.com

Employees: 11
Year Founded: 1993

National Agency Associations: Second Wind Limited

Agency Specializes In: Advertising, Aviation & Aerospace, Bilingual Market, Brand Development & Integration, Business Publications, Business-To-Business, Cable T.V., Catalogs, Co-op Advertising, Collateral, Commercial Photography, Communications, Consumer Goods, Consumer Marketing, Consumer Publications, Corporate Communications, Corporate Identity, Digital/Interactive, Direct Response Marketing, E-Commerce, Electronic Media, Email, Event Planning & Marketing, Exhibit/Trade Shows, Graphic Design, High Technology, Household Goods, In-Store Advertising, Industrial, Integrated Marketing, Internet/Web Design, Legal Services, Leisure, Local Marketing, Logo & Package Design, Luxury Products, Magazines, Marine, Market Research, Media Planning, Media Relations, Merchandising, Multimedia, New Product Development, Newspapers & Magazines, Out-of-Home Media, Outdoor, Package Design, Paid Searches, Pharmaceutical, Planning & Consultation, Point of Purchase, Point of Sale, Print, Production, Promotions, Public Relations, Publicity/Promotions, Radio, Sales Promotion, Search Engine Optimization, Social Marketing/Nonprofit, Social Media, Strategic Planning/Research, T.V., Technical Advertising, Trade & Consumer Magazines

Loren Heinzeroth *(Pres)*
Greg Surufka *(VP-Creative & Dir)*
Roger Peterson *(Sr Acct Mgr)*
Scott Heinzeroth *(Acct Exec)*
Lisa Nielsen *(Acct Exec-PR & Media Buy)*

Accounts:
Altra Industrial Motion; South Beloit, IL
Concentric
Culligan
Horton Automatics
Northern Illinois Hospice & Grief Center; Rockford, IL
Rain Bird Corporation; Azusa, CA

HEISE MEDIA GROUP

1400 Easton Dr Ste 148, Bakersfield, CA 93309
Tel.: (661) 323-8594
Fax: (661) 323-1120
E-Mail: info@heisemedia.com
Web Site: www.heisemedia.com

Agency Specializes In: Advertising, Graphic Design, Internet/Web Design, Media Buying Services, Media Planning, Public Relations

Marlene B. Heise *(Owner & Chief Strategic Officer)*

Accounts:
The Aviator Casino
Finnery's Coffee Brewing Company
HealthSouth Bakersfield Rehabilitation Hospital

HELIUS CREATIVE ADVERTISING LLC

1935 E Vine St Ste 290, Murray, UT 84121
Tel.: (801) 424-5005
Fax: (801) 424-5006
E-Mail: q@heliuscreative.com
Web Site: www.heliuscreative.com

Agency Specializes In: Advertising, Brand Development & Integration, Corporate Identity, Graphic Design, Internet/Web Design, Logo & Package Design, Outdoor, Print

Rod Burkholz *(Owner, Dir-Art & Designer)*

Accounts:
Solstice Spices

HELIX EDUCATION

(Formerly Datamark Inc.)
175 SW Temple Ste 700, Salt Lake City, UT 84101
Tel.: (801) 886-2002
Fax: (801) 886-0102
Toll Free: (800) 279-9335
E-Mail: info@helixeducation.com
Web Site: www.helixeducation.com/

Employees: 140
Year Founded: 1987

Agency Specializes In: Broadcast, Commercial Photography, Communications, Direct Response Marketing, E-Commerce, Education, Electronic Media, Infomercials, Internet/Web Design, Magazines, Media Buying Services, New Product Development, Newspaper, Newspapers & Magazines, Outdoor, Planning & Consultation, Print, Production, Radio, Recruitment, Strategic Planning/Research, Telemarketing, Yellow Pages Advertising

Seth Odell *(Sr VP-Creative & Mktg Strategy)*
Brett Tippetts *(VP-Client Svcs)*
Michelle Shurtz *(Acct Dir)*
Sara Bohmholdt *(Dir-Traditional Media)*
Rachel Lemieux *(Dir-CPL Media)*
Kara Snyder *(Dir-Corp Mktg)*
Craig Larson *(Media Planner-Interactive)*
Matt Maddox *(Media Planner)*

HELKEN & HORN

107 N Cortez St Ste 300, Prescott, AZ 86301
Tel.: (928) 776-0234
E-Mail: info@azadagency.com
Web Site: www.azadagency.com

Agency Specializes In: Advertising, Internet/Web Design, Radio, Social Media, T.V.

Tracey Horn *(Pres & Founder)*
Donna Werking *(Client Svcs Dir)*
Sue Marceau *(Copywriter)*
Dina Ponder *(Sr Graphic Designer)*

Accounts:
Alarm Connection
Barrett Propane
The Dells
Enchanted Canyon
Executive Transportation Services
Freedom Station Family Fun
The Palace Restaurant & Saloon
Pinnacle Capital Mortgage
Realty Executives Northern Arizona
Yavapai County Contractors Association

HELLERMAN BARETZ COMMUNICATIONS

5335 Wisconsin Ave NW Ste 640, Washington, DC 20015
Tel.: (202) 274-4751
Web Site: www.hellermanbaretz.com

Agency Specializes In: Content, Crisis Communications, Media Relations, Public Relations, Social Media, Strategic Planning/Research

John Hellerman *(Partner)*
Spencer Baretz *(Partner)*
Kelsey Nason *(VP)*
Poonam Jain *(Mgr-Ops)*
Sarah Andries *(Sr Acct Exec)*
Jessica Klein *(Acct Exec)*
Madeline OConnor *(Acct Exec)*

Accounts:
New-Corinthian

HELLMAN

1225 W 4th St, Waterloo, IA 50702
Tel.: (319) 234-7055
Fax: (319) 234-2089
Toll Free: (800) 747-7055
Web Site: www.hellman.com

Employees: 36
Year Founded: 1967

Agency Specializes In: Broadcast, Business Publications, Cable T.V., Catalogs, Collateral, Consumer Publications, Digital/Interactive, Direct Response Marketing, Electronic Media, Email, Exhibit/Trade Shows, Local Marketing, Magazines, Mobile Marketing, Multimedia, Newspaper, Newspapers & Magazines, Outdoor, Print, Production (Print), Promotions, Publishing, Radio, Social Media, T.V., Trade & Consumer Magazines, Web (Banner Ads, Pop-ups, etc.)

Approx. Annual Billings: $48,000,000

Breakdown of Gross Billings by Media: Cable T.V.: 5%; Collateral: 10%; D.M.: 5%; E-Commerce: 10%; Exhibits/Trade Shows: 5%; Graphic Design: 5%; Logo & Package Design: 5%; Outdoor: 5%; Point of Purchase: 10%; Pub. Rels.: 10%; Radio & T.V.: 15%; Worldwide Web Sites: 15%

David McNurlen *(Co-Pres)*
Mike Ruane *(CFO)*
Tony Luetkehans *(COO)*
Ila Scott-Ford *(CMO)*
Dwight Fritts *(Exec VP)*
Ross Bruno *(VP-Bus Dev)*
Jolan Cockrell *(Dir-Art)*
Aaron Smock *(Dir-Creative)*
Kim Rogers *(Acct Mgr)*

Accounts:
3M
Ecolab
General Electric
John Deere

Branch

Hellman
Ste 250 The Gilbert Bldg 413 Wacouta Street, Saint Paul, MN 55101
Tel.: (612) 375-9598
Fax: (612) 375-0215

Employees: 45

Agency Specializes In: Advertising, Agriculture, Aviation & Aerospace, Brand Development & Integration, Business-To-Business, Collateral, Consumer Marketing, Corporate Identity, E-Commerce, Email, Exhibit/Trade Shows, Health Care Services, In-Store Advertising, Industrial, Integrated Marketing, Internet/Web Design, Logo & Package Design, Market Research, Media Buying Services, Media Planning, Media Relations, Media Training, Medical Products, Merchandising, New Product Development, Outdoor, Package Design, Pharmaceutical, Point of Purchase, Point of Sale, Print, Production (Ad, Film, Broadcast), Production (Print), Promotions, Public Relations, Publicity/Promotions, Radio, Retail, Sales Promotion, Search Engine Optimization, Strategic Planning/Research, Technical Advertising, Trade & Consumer Magazines, Travel & Tourism, Web (Banner Ads, Pop-ups, etc.)

Kathy Forslund *(Exec VP & Acct Exec)*
Ross Bruno *(VP-Bus Dev)*

HELLO DESIGN
10305 Jefferson Blvd, Culver City, CA 90232
Tel.: (310) 839-4885
Fax: (310) 839-4886
E-Mail: hello@hellodesign.com
Web Site: www.hellodesign.com

Agency Specializes In: Advertising, Brand Development & Integration, E-Commerce, Graphic Design, Internet/Web Design, Mobile Marketing, Search Engine Optimization

David Lai *(CEO & Dir-Creative)*
Scott Arenstein *(Partner & Acct Dir)*
Hiro Niwa *(Dir-Creative)*
Elizabeth Aldana *(Sr Head-Project)*

Accounts:
Callaway Golf
Dermalogica
General Mills
Intel
Mattel
Nike
Sesame Workshop
Speedo Campaign: "Fueled by Water"
TaylorMade Golf

HELLOWORLD
(Formerly ePrize, Inc.)
1 ePrize Dr, Pleasant Ridge, MI 48069
Tel.: (877) 837-7493
Fax: (248) 543-3777
Web Site: www.helloworld.com/

Agency Specializes In: Brand Development & Integration, Local Marketing, Mobile Marketing, Sponsorship, Sports Market

Peter DeNunzio *(CEO)*
Ira Schlussel *(Gen Counsel & Sr VP)*
Chris Wayman *(Sr VP & Acct Mgmt Dir)*
Lisa Feldberg *(Sr VP-Client Mgmt)*
Kim Smith *(Sr VP-Product)*
Meredith Hillman *(Reg VP)*
Nora McGillicuddy *(VP & Acct Dir)*
Tia Sollecito *(VP-Client Leadership & Bus Dev)*
Meaghan Cleary *(Acct Dir)*
Tia Einarsen *(Dir-Bus Dev)*
Tony Bartish *(Acct Mgr-Mobile)*
Kyla Berden *(Acct Mgr)*

Accounts:
Belk, Inc. "Santa Baby Sweepstakes"
Billy Graham Evangelistic Association
CMO Club
New-Coca-Cola
Ford Fusion
GAC TV
Justin Bieber
Kenny Chesney
Rascal Flatts
Rock the Vote
Sony BMG Music Entertainment
Trulia Brand Awareness, Content, Mobile, Online Videos
Virgin Mobile USA, Inc.

HELPSGOOD
6627 Valjean Ave, Van Nuys, CA 91406
Tel.: (818) 787-4444
Web Site: www.helpsgood.com

Year Founded: 2011

Agency Specializes In: Advertising, Brand Development & Integration, Content, Graphic Design, Internet/Web Design, Promotions, Public Relations, Social Media

Michael Bellavia *(CEO)*
Ferry Permadi *(Dir-Tech)*
Amanda Lehner *(Sr Strategist)*
Tara Fisher *(Acct Exec)*

Accounts:
Brave Trails
Fountain House
Tias Hope

HELVETICA CREATIVE
1752 Hyde St, San Francisco, CA 94109
Tel.: (310) 361-6809
Fax: (360) 368-0039
E-Mail: infosf@helveticacreative.com
Web Site: www.helveticacreative.com

Employees: 10
Year Founded: 2008

Agency Specializes In: Above-the-Line, Advertising, Advertising Specialties, Affiliate Marketing, Affluent Market, African-American Market, Agriculture, Alternative Advertising, Arts, Asian Market, Automotive, Aviation & Aerospace, Below-the-Line, Bilingual Market, Brand Development & Integration, Branded Entertainment, Broadcast, Business Publications, Business-To-Business, Cable T.V., Catalogs, Children's Market, Co-op Advertising, Collateral, College, Commercial Photography, Communications, Computers & Software, Consulting, Consumer Goods, Consumer Marketing, Consumer Publications, Content, Corporate Communications, Corporate Identity, Cosmetics, Crisis Communications, Custom Publishing, Customer Relationship Management, Digital/Interactive, Direct Response Marketing, Direct-to-Consumer, E-Commerce, Education, Electronic Media, Electronics, Email, Engineering, Entertainment, Environmental, Event Planning & Marketing, Exhibit/Trade Shows, Experience Design, Fashion/Apparel, Financial, Food Service, Game Integration, Gay & Lesbian Market, Government/Political, Graphic Design, Guerilla Marketing, Health Care Services, High Technology, Hispanic Market, Hospitality, Household Goods, Identity Marketing, In-Store Advertising, Industrial, Infomercials, Information Technology, Integrated Marketing, International, Internet/Web Design, Investor Relations, Legal Services, Leisure, Local Marketing, Logo & Package Design, Luxury Products, Magazines, Marine, Market Research, Media Buying Services, Media Planning, Media Relations, Media Training, Medical Products, Men's Market, Merchandising, Mobile Marketing, Multicultural, Multimedia, New Product Development, New Technologies, Newspaper, Newspapers & Magazines, Out-of-Home Media, Outdoor, Over-50 Market, Package Design, Paid Searches, Pharmaceutical, Planning & Consultation, Podcasting, Point of Purchase, Point of Sale, Print, Product Placement, Production, Production (Ad, Film, Broadcast), Production (Print), Promotions, Public Relations, Publicity/Promotions, Publishing, RSS (Really Simple Syndication), Radio, Real Estate, Recruitment, Regional, Restaurant, Retail, Sales Promotion, Search Engine Optimization, Seniors' Market, Social Marketing/Nonprofit, South Asian Market, Sponsorship, Sports Market, Stakeholders, Strategic Planning/Research, Sweepstakes, Syndication, T.V., Technical Advertising, Teen Market, Telemarketing, Trade & Consumer Magazines, Transportation, Travel & Tourism, Urban Market, Viral/Buzz/Word of Mouth, Web (Banner Ads, Pop-ups, etc.), Women's Market, Yellow Pages Advertising

Sultan Mirza *(Principal & Sr Dir-Creative)*
Jeff Kerrin *(Dir-Creative)*
Jack Rose *(Dir-Digital Media)*
Bill Wade *(Dir-Design)*

Accounts:
CBS
Geebo.com
NATAS
Resch Productions

HEMLINE CREATIVE MARKETING
506 S Main Ste 201, Memphis, TN 38103
Tel.: (901) 529-9092
E-Mail: info@hemlinetheory.com
Web Site: www.hemlinetheory.com

Agency Specializes In: Advertising, Brand Development & Integration, Logo & Package Design, Public Relations, Social Media

Cynthia Saatkamp *(Owner)*
Kelley Morice *(Partner)*
Megan Glenn *(Brand Mgr)*
Aimee McMillin *(Specialist-Comm)*

Accounts:
Apple Grove
The Assisi Foundation of Memphis
Ballet Memphis
Bella Vita & Itty Bitty Bella
Clark/Dixon Architects
Destination King
GTx, Inc.
Memphis Crisis Center
Memphis Medical Center
Onyx Medical Corporation

THE HENDERSON ROBB GROUP

401 Bay St Ste 1600, Toronto, ON M5H 2Y4 Canada
Tel.: (416) 646-6604
Fax: (416) 363-0460
E-Mail: info@hendersonrobb.com
Web Site: www.hendersonrobbmarketing.com/

National Agency Associations: Second Wind Limited

Agency Specializes In: Advertising, Brand Development & Integration, Business-To-Business, Internet/Web Design, Market Research

Peter Henderson *(Pres & Dir-Creative)*
Bill Robb *(Mng Dir & VP)*

Accounts:
Alias
Compugen
MCI, LLC

HENDRICK & ASSOCIATES MARKETING SERVICES INC.

1015 Fourth St SW Ste 750, Calgary, AB T2R 1J4 Canada
Tel.: (403) 571-0760
Fax: (403) 571-0769
E-Mail: gary@hendrick.ca
Web Site: www.hendrick.ca

Employees: 6
Year Founded: 1995

National Agency Associations: ICA

Gary Hendrick *(Pres)*
Gaylene Hendrick *(Sec)*

Accounts:
Canadian North
Cetelex Systems
Sunpine Forest Products
Surrey Eye Care Centre
Tim Hortons

Subsidiary

BlessAd Christian Communications

1015 4th St SW, Ste 750, Calgary, AB T2R 1J4 Canada
Tel.: (403) 571-0760
Fax: (403) 571-0769
Web Site: www.blessad.ca

Employees: 4

Gary W. Hendrick *(Pres)*

Accounts:
Bible Research Institute, Peterborough
Christian Life Assembly - Langley, BC
Church of the Nazarene Canada, Toronto
Edmonton Christian Schools, Edmonton
First Assembly Church, Calgary
Harvest Worship Centre; Brampton, ON
Lifeline Malawi; 2006
Mission Fest,Edmonton
PAOC - Eastern Ontario Womens Ministries

HENKE & ASSOCIATES, INC.

236 Hamilton Rd, Cedarburg, WI 53012
Tel.: (262) 375-9090
Fax: (262) 375-2262
E-Mail: bhenke@henkeinc.com
Web Site: www.henkeinc.com

Employees: 9
Year Founded: 1986

National Agency Associations: Second Wind Limited

Agency Specializes In: Advertising, Advertising Specialties, Automotive, Brand Development & Integration, Broadcast, Business Publications, Business-To-Business, Cable T.V., Catalogs, Co-op Advertising, Collateral, Commercial Photography, Communications, Consulting, Consumer Goods, Consumer Marketing, Consumer Publications, Corporate Communications, Corporate Identity, Cosmetics, Crisis Communications, Customer Relationship Management, Digital/Interactive, Direct Response Marketing, Direct-to-Consumer, E-Commerce, Electronic Media, Email, Engineering, Entertainment, Environmental, Event Planning & Marketing, Exhibit/Trade Shows, Financial, Food Service, Government/Political, Graphic Design, Health Care Services, High Technology, In-Store Advertising, Industrial, Infomercials, Information Technology, Integrated Marketing, Internet/Web Design, Investor Relations, Legal Services, Leisure, Local Marketing, Logo & Package Design, Magazines, Marine, Market Research, Media Buying Services, Media Planning, Media Relations, Medical Products, Men's Market, Merchandising, Mobile Marketing, Multimedia, New Product Development, Newspaper, Newspapers & Magazines, Out-of-Home Media, Outdoor, Over-50 Market, Package Design, Planning & Consultation, Point of Purchase, Point of Sale, Print, Production, Production (Print), Promotions, Public Relations, Publicity/Promotions, Radio, Real Estate, Recruitment, Regional, Restaurant, Retail, Sales Promotion, Search Engine Optimization, Seniors' Market, Social Marketing/Nonprofit, Social Media, Sponsorship, Sports Market, Strategic Planning/Research, Sweepstakes, Syndication, T.V., Teen Market, Telemarketing, Trade & Consumer Magazines, Transportation, Travel & Tourism, Viral/Buzz/Word of Mouth, Web (Banner Ads, Pop-ups, etc.), Yellow Pages Advertising

Approx. Annual Billings: $5,000,000

Breakdown of Gross Billings by Media: Consumer Publs.: $400,000; D.M.: $100,000; Mags.: $100,000; Newsp.: $550,000; Other: $100,000; Point of Purchase: $500,000; Production: $200,000; Radio: $1,000,000; Sls. Promo.: $50,000; T.V.: $2,000,000

William J. Henke *(Owner)*
Mark Boyce *(Dir-Art & Designer)*
Annette Murtos *(Dir-Media)*
Carolyn Kassander *(Media Buyer)*

HENKINSCHULTZ

6201 S Pinnacle Pl, Sioux Falls, SD 57108
Tel.: (605) 331-2155
Fax: (605) 331-2556
E-Mail: hello@henkinschultz.com
Web Site: www.henkinschultz.com

Agency Specializes In: Advertising, Brand Development & Integration, Digital/Interactive, Event Planning & Marketing, Logo & Package Design

Joe Henkin *(Partner)*
Teresa Jackson *(Partner-New Bus)*
Kirby Schultz *(Partner)*
Emily Schilling *(Office Mgr)*
Chris Huls *(Media Buyer)*
Jason Jellis *(Designer)*
Melissa Rohwedder *(Copywriter)*
Paul Thompson *(Media Buyer)*

Accounts:
South Dakota State University

HEPCATSMARKETING.COM

1861 Banks Rd, Margate, FL 33063
Tel.: (954) 532-0645
Web Site: www.hepcatsmarketing.com

Year Founded: 2012

Agency Specializes In: Affiliate Marketing, Alternative Advertising, Catalogs, Digital/Interactive, Direct Response Marketing, Electronic Media, Email, Guerilla Marketing, Local Marketing, Magazines, Multimedia, Newspaper, Paid Searches, Print, Search Engine Optimization, Shopper Marketing, Social Media, Viral/Buzz/Word of Mouth, Web (Banner Ads, Pop-ups, etc.)

Luis Quinones *(CEO)*
Thomas Hurley *(Partner)*

HERB GILLEN AGENCY

1953 S Mallway Ave, Columbus, OH 43221
Tel.: (614) 488-2828
Fax: (614) 488-3945
Web Site: www.herbgillen.com

Agency Specializes In: Advertising, Collateral, Digital/Interactive, Event Planning & Marketing, Logo & Package Design, Print, Public Relations, Radio, Strategic Planning/Research, T.V.

Herb Gillen *(Pres)*
Vanessa Ward *(Sr Graphic Designer)*

Accounts:
Rdp Foodservice, Ltd.
Thunder Over Michigan
Vectren Dayton Air Show

HERB GROSS & COMPANY, INC.

10000 Gatehouse Ct, Charlotte, NC 28277-8730
Tel.: (704) 846-0199
Fax: (704) 841-9014
Toll Free: (800) 257-0772
E-Mail: herb@herbgross.com
Web Site: www.herbgross.com

Employees: 4
Year Founded: 1970

Agency Specializes In: Broadcast, Print, Retail

Herb Gross *(Pres)*

Accounts:
Felluca Garage Doors; Rochester, NY; 1997
Quality Overhead Doors; Toledo, OH
Thompson Garage Doors; Reno, NV; 1998
Wayne Dalton; Mount Hope, OH; 2001

HERCKY PASQUA HERMAN, INC.

324 Chestnut St, Roselle Park, NJ 07204
Tel.: (908) 241-9474
Fax: (908) 241-8961
E-Mail: hercky@hph-comm.com
Web Site: www.hph-comm.com

Employees: 10
Year Founded: 1985

Agency Specializes In: Business-To-Business, Retail

Approx. Annual Billings: $4,200,000

Peter Hercky *(Owner)*
Michael A. Pasqua *(Partner)*

HERESY, LLC

10304 Nolina Cove, Austin, TX 78759-6413
Tel.: (512) 415-1698

Web Site: www.heresy.co

Year Founded: 2010

Agency Specializes In: Advertising, Digital/Interactive, Graphic Design, Internet/Web Design

Josh Sklar *(Pres & Dir-Creative)*

Accounts:
The Coca-Cola Company
Colgate-Palmolive Company
Dell Inc.

HERMAN ASSOCIATES, INC.

275 Madison Ave Ste 800, New York, NY 10016
Tel.: (212) 616-1190
Fax: (212) 725-0172
E-Mail: hainfo@hermanassociatesnewyork.com
Web Site: www.hermanassociatesnewyork.com

E-Mail for Key Personnel:
President:
sherman@hermanassociatesnewyork.com
Production Mgr.:
dlarrabure@hermanassociatesnewyork.com
Public Relations:
malmonte@hermanassociatesnewyork.com

Employees: 9
Year Founded: 1973

Agency Specializes In: Advertising, Brand Development & Integration, Broadcast, Business-To-Business, Collateral, Consulting, Consumer Marketing, Corporate Communications, Corporate Identity, Digital/Interactive, Direct Response Marketing, Email, Financial, Graphic Design, Health Care Services, High Technology, Industrial, Integrated Marketing, Internet/Web Design, Leisure, Magazines, Marine, Media Buying Services, Media Relations, Newspaper, Newspapers & Magazines, Out-of-Home Media, Outdoor, Over-50 Market, Planning & Consultation, Print, Production (Ad, Film, Broadcast), Public Relations, Publicity/Promotions, Radio, Sales Promotion, Strategic Planning/Research, Trade & Consumer Magazines, Transportation, Travel & Tourism, Web (Banner Ads, Pop-ups, etc.)

Approx. Annual Billings: $2,500,000

Breakdown of Gross Billings by Media: Audio/Visual: $10,000; Brdcst.: $150,000; Bus. Publs.: $750,000; Collateral: $350,000; Corp. Communications: $75,000; Exhibits/Trade Shows: $10,000; Fees: $30,000; Graphic Design: $125,000; Internet Adv.: $100,000; Mags.: $750,000; Newsp.: $150,000

Stuart Herman *(Pres)*
Paula Herman *(CEO)*
Mario Almonte *(Mng Partner)*

Accounts:
Air-India; New York, NY
Big Brothers Big Sisters of New York City
Carpet Export Promotion Council; India Hand-Woven Rugs; 2008
Christie, Inc.; Cypress, CA Digital Cinema Projection Equipment, Film Equipment
Clearwater Festival; Poughkeepsie, NY; 2004
Masterlooms, Inc.; Secaucus, NJ Imported Area Rugs
Senior Health Partners; New York, NY
Wallenius Wilhelmsen Logistics; Woodcliff Lake, NJ Global Logistics, Ocean Cargo, Transport

Branch

Herman & Almonte Public Relations, LLC
(Formerly Herman Associates Public Relations)
275 Madison Ave Ste 800, New York, NY 10016
(See Separate Listing)

HERO FARM

3525 Hessmer Ave, Metairie, LA 70002
Tel.: (504) 451-4282
E-Mail: signal@hero-farm.com
Web Site: www.hero-farm.com

Year Founded: 2009

Agency Specializes In: Advertising, Event Planning & Marketing, Internet/Web Design, Logo & Package Design, Print, Public Relations

Shaun Walker *(Co-Founder, Partner & Creative Dir)*
Reid Stone *(Co-Founder, Partner & Strategist)*
Jason Taix *(Art Dir)*

Accounts:
WRBH 88.3 FM

HERON AGENCY

1528 W Fullerton, Chicago, IL 60614
Tel.: (773) 969-5200
Fax: (773) 477-7388
E-Mail: info@heronagency.com
Web Site: www.heronagency.com

Agency Specializes In: Advertising, Brand Development & Integration, Crisis Communications, Event Planning & Marketing, Public Relations, Search Engine Optimization, Social Media

Noreen Heron *(Pres)*
Lianne Wiker Hedditch *(VP)*
Jennifer Vander Sanden *(VP)*

Accounts:
New-Le Meridien Chicago
New-Renaissance Chicago Downtown

HERRMANN ADVERTISING DESIGN/COMMUNICATIONS

30 W St, Annapolis, MD 21401
Tel.: (410) 267-6522
Fax: (410) 295-0266
E-Mail: info@herrmann.com
Web Site: www.herrmann.com

Employees: 25
Year Founded: 1979

National Agency Associations: Second Wind Limited

Judi Hermann Dunn *(Pres & Dir-Creative)*
John Albert *(Chief Bus Dev Officer & Sr Acct Exec)*
Alexis Gatto *(Dir-Media & Sr Acct Exec)*
Mary Regan *(Dir-Bus Dev)*
Jane Farrell *(Sr Acct Exec)*
Stephanie Blank *(Acct Exec)*
Samantha Smith *(Acct Coord)*

Accounts:
CAIS Internet
Cellular One
Center for the Advancement of Food Service Education
Central Supply Company
Cooperative Development Foundation
Disclosure, Inc.
Dissen & Juhn Corporation
e.spire
Earthlan (Metropolitan Area Networks)
Indian Creek School
InterCAD
KMC Telecom
Maryland Saltwater Sport Fishing Association
Maryland Scenic Byways
Maryland State Teachers Association
Mustique
National Association for Senior Living Industry
National Electrical Manufacturers Association
Navy League of the United States
SkyTel
United Cerebral Palsy Associations
United Service Organization
University of Maryland
USi
Yacht Magazine

THE HESTER GROUP LLC

100 N Laura St Ste 802, Jacksonville, FL 32202
Tel.: (904) 739-2338
Fax: (904) 739-2339
E-Mail: info@hester-group.com
Web Site: www.hester-group.com

Employees: 30
Year Founded: 1998

National Agency Associations: Second Wind Limited

Agency Specializes In: Advertising, Education, Food Service, Regional, Restaurant

Hester Clark *(Pres & CEO)*
Ricki Fairley *(Strategist-Mktg)*

Accounts:
National Urban League
PBS&J
Ritzi
RS&H

HEY ADVERTISING

911 Western Ave Ste 408, Seattle, WA 98104
Tel.: (206) 829-9782
Web Site: www.heyadvertising.com

Year Founded: 2009

Agency Specializes In: Advertising, Brand Development & Integration, Digital/Interactive, Social Media

Eric Gutierrez *(Partner & Dir-Creative)*
Chris Lloyd *(Partner)*
Leslee Stockton *(Acct Dir)*
Sitha Ngy *(Assoc Dir-Creative)*
Matthew Betz *(Planner-Strategic)*

HEYWOOD FORMATICS & SYNDICATION

1103 Colonial Blvd NE, Canton, OH 44714-1837
Tel.: (330) 456-2592
Fax: (330) 456-2592
E-Mail: max@heywoodformatics.com
Web Site: www.heywoodformatics.com

E-Mail for Key Personnel:
President: max@heywoodformatics.com

Employees: 3
Year Founded: 1978

Agency Specializes In: Advertising, Broadcast, Communications, Consulting, Consumer Marketing, Engineering, Event Planning & Marketing, Financial, Food Service, Industrial, Information Technology, Legal Services, Media Buying Services, Medical Products, Multimedia, New Product Development, Point of Sale, Production, Public Relations, Publicity/Promotions, Radio, Restaurant, Retail, Sales Promotion, Technical Advertising, Teen Market

Breakdown of Gross Billings by Media: Newsp.: 10%; Other: 5%; Out-of-Home Media: 5%; Outdoor: 5%; Production: 5%; Radio: 65%; T.V.:

5%

Max Heywood *(Owner)*

Accounts:
Alltronics; Mishawaka, IN Electronics, Stereos, TVs; 1989
Blackhawk Powersports Suzuki; 2005
Brubakers Pub; Green, OH; 2008
Buchanan Oil/Bucky Mart; New Philadelphia, OH Convenience Stores; 2005
Classic Q Billiards; Fort Walton Beach, FL; 2007
Cousins Motor Cars; Canton, OH Used Car Dealership
CYBMedia; Canton, OH Web Site Design; 1999
Ganley Lincoln-Mercury; Canton, OH New & Used Vehicles; 1999
Greg's Eagle Tire; Canton, OH; 2006
Hi Fi Buys; Akron, OH; Canton, OH Home & Car Stereos; 1989
Itolo's Pizza; Canton, OH; 2002
J Honda; Cleveland, OH; 2005
Jeff's Motor Cars; North Canton, OH Porsche, Lexus & BMW; 1999
Leonard's; Dover, OH Restaurant & Lounge; 1978
LT & Associates; Canton, OH; 2007
Mardi Gras; Cleveland, OH Restaurant & Lounge; 1985
Midwest Homes
Morris Loan; Canton, OH; 2007
Needful Things Jewelry; Akron, OH; 2007
Nicole's Connection; Akron, OH; 2002
The Pub Nightclub; 1988
Red Dog Saloon; Canton, OH Night Club, Restaurant
Schwartz Homes; Saint Clairsville, OH Mobile Homes; 1995
Scorchers
Utterback Dental Group; Canton/Alliance, OH Dental Services
Walther's Cafe Sports Bar
West Harbor Landings; Marblehead, OH Real Estate & Condominiums; 1997

HFB ADVERTISING, INC.

1406 Washington Ave, West Islip, NY 11795
Tel.: (631) 383-1693
Toll Free: (877) 432-2231
E-Mail: hfbadvertising@hfbadvertising.com
Web Site: www.hfbadvertising.com

Employees: 10

Agency Specializes In: Advertising, Advertising Specialties, Alternative Advertising, Automotive, Broadcast, Business Publications, Business-To-Business, Cable T.V., Co-op Advertising, Collateral, Commercial Photography, Computers & Software, Consulting, Consumer Publications, Corporate Communications, Corporate Identity, Direct Response Marketing, Direct-to-Consumer, Email, Exhibit/Trade Shows, Financial, Food Service, Government/Political, Graphic Design, In-Store Advertising, Internet/Web Design, Local Marketing, Logo & Package Design, Magazines, Media Buying Services, Media Planning, Medical Products, Newspaper, Newspapers & Magazines, Outdoor, Paid Searches, Planning & Consultation, Point of Sale, Print, Production, Production (Ad, Film, Broadcast), Production (Print), Promotions, Publicity/Promotions, Real Estate, Recruitment, Restaurant, Retail, Seniors' Market, Sweepstakes, T.V., Trade & Consumer Magazines, Transportation, Travel & Tourism, Urban Market, Web (Banner Ads, Pop-ups, etc.), Women's Market

Approx. Annual Billings: $1,000,000

Breakdown of Gross Billings by Media: Graphic Design: $1,000,000

Lance Rocha *(VP)*
Harris Brown *(Dir-Art & Sr Graphic Designer)*

HG MEDIA, INC.

31 Airpark Rd Ste 6, Princeton, NJ 08540-1524
Tel.: (609) 921-6200
E-Mail: info@hg-media.com
Web Site: www.hg-media.com

Employees: 4

Agency Specializes In: Graphic Design, Internet/Web Design

Kenneth Greenberg *(Founder & CEO)*

Accounts:
Community Options
Digimax
Foxtons
Hi Tops of Princeton
Kevmar
Laurie Altman
Neutrogena
Niece Lumber Company
Nutrafruit
Princeton Business News
Revlon
TORC Financial
TradeSpeed
Visionary Vehicles

HGA INC

300 Marconi Blvd 3rd Fl, Columbus, OH 43215
Tel.: (614) 827-9712
E-Mail: info@hga.com
Web Site: hga.com

Employees: 23
Year Founded: 1997

Agency Specializes In: Advertising, Advertising Specialties, Alternative Advertising, Brand Development & Integration, Broadcast, Business Publications, Cable T.V., Catalogs, Co-op Advertising, Collateral, Communications, Consulting, Consumer Goods, Consumer Marketing, Consumer Publications, Corporate Identity, Customer Relationship Management, Digital/Interactive, Direct Response Marketing, Direct-to-Consumer, E-Commerce, Electronic Media, Email, Event Planning & Marketing, Exhibit/Trade Shows, Graphic Design, Household Goods, Identity Marketing, In-Store Advertising, Infomercials, Information Technology, Integrated Marketing, Internet/Web Design, Local Marketing, Logo & Package Design, Magazines, Market Research, Media Buying Services, Media Planning, Merchandising, Mobile Marketing, Multimedia, New Product Development, New Technologies, Newspaper, Newspapers & Magazines, Out-of-Home Media, Outdoor, Planning & Consultation, Podcasting, Point of Purchase, Point of Sale, Production, Production (Print), Promotions, Radio, Sales Promotion, Search Engine Optimization, Social Marketing/Nonprofit, Social Media, Strategic Planning/Research, Sweepstakes, T.V., Trade & Consumer Magazines, Viral/Buzz/Word of Mouth, Yellow Pages Advertising

Approx. Annual Billings: $25,000,000

Breakdown of Gross Billings by Media: Brdcst.: $1,250,000; Bus. Publs.: $1,250,000; Collateral: $2,500,000; Consulting: $3,750,000; Consumer Publs.: $1,250,000; Internet Adv.: $3,750,000; Radio & T.V.: $6,250,000; Worldwide Web Sites: $5,000,000

Bill Gallagher *(Owner)*
Rick Adams *(Principal)*
Cindy Carvour *(Mgmt Supvr)*

Accounts:
Abbott Nutrition Ensure, Glucerna, Juven, Pediasure; 2003
Eagle Manufacturing Crusher Plants; 2002
Grief Corporation Load Securement, Packaging; 2001
NiSource; PA, VA, MD, IN Columbia Gas; 2007
Stanley Steemer Carpet Cleaning, Water Damage Restoration; 1998

HI-GLOSS

1666 Kennedy Causeway, Miami Beach, FL 33141
Tel.: (305) 759-7288
Web Site: www.hi-gloss.com/

Year Founded: 2004

Agency Specializes In: Above-the-Line, Advertising, Advertising Specialties, Affiliate Marketing, Affluent Market, Arts, Aviation & Aerospace, Below-the-Line, Bilingual Market, Brand Development & Integration, Branded Entertainment, Broadcast, Business-To-Business, Catalogs, Co-op Advertising, Collateral, Consumer Marketing, Consumer Publications, Content, Corporate Identity, Cosmetics, Digital/Interactive, Direct-to-Consumer, E-Commerce, Email, Fashion/Apparel, Food Service, Gay & Lesbian Market, Government/Political, Graphic Design, Health Care Services, High Technology, Hispanic Market, Hospitality, Identity Marketing, Integrated Marketing, International, Internet/Web Design, Leisure, Logo & Package Design, Luxury Products, Magazines, Marine, Media Buying Services, Media Planning, Medical Products, Men's Market, Mobile Marketing, Multimedia, New Product Development, Newspaper, Newspapers & Magazines, Out-of-Home Media, Outdoor, Package Design, Paid Searches, Pharmaceutical, Planning & Consultation, Print, Production, Production (Ad, Film, Broadcast), Production (Print), Promotions, Radio, Real Estate, Recruitment, Regional, Restaurant, Retail, Search Engine Optimization, Social Marketing/Nonprofit, Social Media, Sponsorship, Sports Market, Strategic Planning/Research, Sweepstakes, T.V., Technical Advertising, Travel & Tourism, Viral/Buzz/Word of Mouth, Web (Banner Ads, Pop-ups, etc.), Women's Market

Robert Villazon *(CEO)*
Carrie Copeland *(VP)*

Accounts:
New-Adrienne Arsht Center Entertainment; 2010
New-Fontainebleau Miami Beach Hospitality; 2008
New-W South Beach Hospitality; 2012

HIDALGO & DE VRIES, INC.

560 5th St Ste 401, Grand Rapids, MI 49504
Tel.: (616) 493-5000
Fax: (616) 493-5001
E-Mail: info@hidalgodevries.com
Web Site: www.hidalgodevries.com

Year Founded: 1989

Agency Specializes In: Customer Relationship Management, Integrated Marketing, New Product Development, Strategic Planning/Research

Carlos Hidalgo *(Pres)*

Accounts:
Advantage Health
ALTL
CitiVision
Manatron, Inc.; Portage, MI
Medtronics
Vichem
Zondervan

HIEBING

315 Wisconsin Ave, Madison, WI 53703-2107
Tel.: (608) 256-6357
Fax: (608) 256-0693
E-Mail: letstalk@hiebing.com
Web Site: www.hiebing.com

E-Mail for Key Personnel:
President: dflorin@hiebing.com
Creative Dir.: smullen@hiebing.com
Media Dir.: BEdison@hiebing.com
Production Mgr.: crichards@hiebing.com
Public Relations: bhernandez@hiebing.com

Employees: 54
Year Founded: 1981

Agency Specializes In: Advertising, Broadcast, Business-To-Business, Collateral, Communications, Consulting, Consumer Marketing, Corporate Identity, Direct Response Marketing, Event Planning & Marketing, Financial, Graphic Design, Health Care Services, Internet/Web Design, Logo & Package Design, Magazines, Marine, Media Buying Services, Newspaper, Newspapers & Magazines, Outdoor, Planning & Consultation, Point of Purchase, Point of Sale, Print, Public Relations, Radio, Retail, Sales Promotion, Sponsorship, Strategic Planning/Research, T.V., Trade & Consumer Magazines, Yellow Pages Advertising

Dave Florin *(Pres)*
Barry Edison *(Partner & Dir-Touchpoint Plng)*
Jeane Kropp *(Partner & Dir-Brand Strategy)*
Mike Pratzel *(Partner)*
Sean Mullen *(VP & Dir-Creative)*
Dana Arnold *(Dir-PR & Social Media)*
Ann Dencker *(Dir-Insight & Strategic Res)*
Lynn Borkenhagen *(Assoc Dir-Media)*
Amanda Broderick *(Acct Mgr-PR & Social Media)*
Grant Gunderson *(Acct Exec-PR & Social Media)*
Sara Tetzloff *(Acct Exec-PR & Social Media)*
Leanne Havertape *(Media Planner & Media Buyer)*
Erin Nelson *(Jr Copywriter)*
Emily Connors *(Acct Coord)*

Accounts:
American Family Insurance; Madison, WI
American Girl
Anchor Bank; Madison, WI Financial Services
BioAg Gateway
Brown Shoe Company, Inc
The Coca-Cola Company
Culver's (Agency of Record) Campaign: "Welcome to Delicious"
Dean HMO & Medical Group; Madison, WI Healthcare Services
Design Concepts, Inc
General Casualty; Sun Prairie, WI Insurance
New-Kerry Group
Kinetico
Kwik Trip; La Crosse, WI
Madison Museum of Contemporary Art
Nestle
New-Quaker Oats Company
Saint Mary's Hospital & Medical Center; Madison, WI
Schneider National
ThedaCare/Touchpoint Health Plan; Appleton, WI Health Care

HIGH TIDE CREATIVE

245 Craven St, New Bern, NC 28560
Tel.: (252) 671-7087
E-Mail: info@hightidecreative.com
Web Site: www.hightidecreative.com

Year Founded: 2005

Agency Specializes In: Advertising, Collateral, Corporate Identity, Outdoor, Package Design, Print, Radio, T.V.

Todd Willis *(Pres)*
Kim Kruger *(Partner & Dir-Media)*
Tom Lewis *(VP & Dir-Creative)*
Alicia Hawkins *(Dir-Art)*
Shawna Black *(Project Mgr & Mgr-Traffic)*
Dawn Osterlund-martin *(Mgr-Traffic)*

Accounts:
New-Carolina Orthopedics Sports Medicine & Physical Therapy (Advertising Agency of Record) Marketing
TyraTech Inc

HIGH-TOUCH COMMUNICATIONS INC.

372 Ste-Catherine St W Ste 320, Montreal, QC H3B 1A2 Canada
Tel.: (514) 739-2461
Fax: (514) 739-6121
Web Site: www.htc.ca

Employees: 20
Year Founded: 1982

Agency Specializes In: Brand Development & Integration, Communications, Internet/Web Design, Planning & Consultation, Strategic Planning/Research

Tom Kouri *(Pres)*
Pat Yoshida *(Acct Dir)*

Accounts:
The Cedar Cancer Institute
Inro
Unisource Canada
Velan
YES

HIGH WIDE & HANDSOME

9430 West Washington Blvd, Culver City, CA 90232
Tel.: (310) 751-6931
E-Mail: info@wearehwh.com
Web Site: www.highwidehandsome.com

Employees: 15
Year Founded: 2009

Agency Specializes In: Above-the-Line, Advertising, Below-the-Line, Brand Development & Integration, Broadcast, Collateral, Corporate Identity, Digital/Interactive, Email, Exhibit/Trade Shows, Experience Design, Graphic Design, In-Store Advertising, Internet/Web Design, Logo & Package Design, Magazines, Market Research, Newspaper, Newspapers & Magazines, Outdoor, Package Design, Planning & Consultation, Point of Purchase, Point of Sale, Print, Production (Print), Radio, Search Engine Optimization, Social Media, Strategic Planning/Research, T.V., Trade & Consumer Magazines, Viral/Buzz/Word of Mouth, Web (Banner Ads, Pop-ups, etc.)

Approx. Annual Billings: $20,000,000

Dani Churchill *(Partner & Acct Dir)*
Sheena Ruffin *(Partner & Dir-Social Media)*
Nina Tooley *(CMO)*
Ashley Katona *(Sr Dir-Art)*
Damian Fraticelli *(Dir-Creative)*
Emma Cardenas *(Mgr-Social Media)*
Ginny Turner *(Mgr-Production)*

Accounts:
CCP Games DUST 514, EVE Online; 2012
Constellation Brands Arbor Mist, Black Box Wine, Clos du Bois, NPD, Paul Masson, Rex Goliath; 2010
The Habit Burger Grill; 2013
Motiga Gigantic; 2015
Toshiba; 2012
Trion Worlds Archeage, Defiance, RIFT; 2010
Ventura Foods Dean's Dip, LouAna Cooking Oils, Marie's Salad Dressings; 2013

HIGHER GROUND CREATIVE AGENCY

11650 Elcadore St, Las Vegas, NV 89193
Tel.: (775) 600-7885
Web Site: www.highergroundadvertising.com/

Employees: 15
Year Founded: 2015

Agency Specializes In: Above-the-Line, Affluent Market, African-American Market, Alternative Advertising, Below-the-Line, Branded Entertainment, Business Publications, Business-To-Business, Cable T.V., Catalogs, Children's Market, Co-op Advertising, Collateral, College, Consumer Marketing, Consumer Publications, Digital/Interactive, Direct Response Marketing, Direct-to-Consumer, Electronic Media, Email, Exhibit/Trade Shows, Gay & Lesbian Market, Guerilla Marketing, High Technology, Hispanic Market, In-Store Advertising, International, Local Marketing, Luxury Products, Magazines, Men's Market, Mobile Marketing, Multicultural, Multimedia, Newspaper, Newspapers & Magazines, Out-of-Home Media, Outdoor, Over-50 Market, Paid Searches, Pets , Podcasting, Point of Purchase, Print, Product Placement, Production, Production (Print), Promotions, Publishing, Radio, Search Engine Optimization, Seniors' Market, Shopper Marketing, Social Media, T.V., Teen Market, Trade & Consumer Magazines, Tween Market, Urban Market, Viral/Buzz/Word of Mouth, Web (Banner Ads, Pop-ups, etc.), Women's Market

Julia Lopez *(Pres)*
Jacob Gallegos *(Exec Creative Dir)*
Shahab Zargari *(Exec Dir-Mktg)*
Kevin Sanders *(Acct Mgr)*

Accounts:
New-AZ PRoductions Commercial, Music Video & Movie Production Company; 2015

HIGHER IMAGES INC.

300 Bursca Dr 301, Bridgeville, PA 15017
Tel.: (412) 203-1996
Fax: (412) 220-7771
Toll Free: (888) 207-4414
E-Mail: admin@higherimages.net
Web Site: www.higherimages.com

Agency Specializes In: Advertising, Brand Development & Integration, Digital/Interactive, Graphic Design, Internet/Web Design, Paid Searches, Print, Public Relations, Search Engine Optimization

Bryan Thornberg *(Pres & CEO)*
Daniel Harmon *(VP)*
Robin Dugas *(COO)*
Alexandra Hepler *(Creative Dir)*

Accounts:
New-Fitness Werqs

HIGHTOWER AGENCY

970 Ebenezer Blvd, Madison, MS 39110
Tel.: (601) 853-1822
Fax: (601) 853-1069
E-Mail: eoh@hightowerservices.com
Web Site: www.hightoweragency.com

Employees: 30
Year Founded: 1990

Agency Specializes In: Recruitment, Transportation

Eddie Hightower *(Pres)*

James Hickman *(Exec VP)*
Christina Wright *(VP-Ops)*
Chuck Bradford *(Dir-Creative)*
Vickie Burkes *(Dir-Traffic)*
Randy Scheel *(Dir-Sls)*
Sissy Musgrove *(Coord-Media)*
Ashley Purvis *(Coord-Media)*
Jessica Troth *(Coord-Media)*

Accounts:
Hill Brothers
USA Truck

HIGLEY DESIGN
389 Taylor St, Ashland, OR 97520
Tel.: (541) 482-8805
E-Mail: info@higleydesign.com
Web Site: www.higleydesign.com

Agency Specializes In: Advertising, Brand Development & Integration, Exhibit/Trade Shows, Graphic Design, Logo & Package Design

John Higley *(Dir-Creative & Designer)*

Accounts:
eSuperStock
Hill Station
Sapling Bicycle Company

HILE DESIGN LLC
4844 Jackson Rd Ste 125, Ann Arbor, MI 48103
Tel.: (734) 995-1245
Fax: (734) 995-5173
Web Site: hilecreative.com

Year Founded: 1984

Dave HILE *(Founder & Pres)*
Mike Bell *(Dir-Creative)*
Matthew Restorff *(Dir-Web Dev)*
Laura Abramson *(Mgr-Web)*
Julie Tibus *(Strategist-Brand)*
Charlie Szczygiel *(Designer)*

Accounts:
Beaumont Health System myBeaumontChart
Scio Economic Development

HILL AEVIUM
34215 Hwy 6 Ste 204, Edwards, CO 81632
Tel.: (970) 926-6700
Fax: (970) 926-6705
E-Mail: info@hillaevium.com
Web Site: www.hillaevium.com

Year Founded: 2004

Agency Specializes In: Advertising, Brand Development & Integration, Digital/Interactive, Market Research, Multimedia

Linda Hill *(Pres)*
Mark Beresniewicz *(Sr Dir-Art)*
Steve Litt *(Dir-Fin & HR)*
Michelle Parenti *(Dir-Digital Mktg)*

Accounts:
Advanced Systems Group
Black Tie Ski Rentals
Crazy Mountain Brewery
Glenwood Hot Springs

HILL & PARTNERS INCORPORATED
25 Mathewson Dr Ste 200, East Weymouth, MA 02189-2345
Tel.: (857) 403-0312
Fax: (617) 471-7914
E-Mail: info@hillpartners.com
Web Site: www.hillpartners.com

Employees: 15
Year Founded: 1995

Michael McMahon *(Pres)*
Jonathan Raimond *(VP-Sls)*
Mark Holme *(Dir-Creative)*
Joseph Brosnan *(Sr Acct Mgr)*
Amy Connery *(Office Mgr & Mgr-Facilities)*
Rachelle Kulak *(Acct Mgr)*

Accounts:
Dunkin' Brands Group, Inc.
GTECH
National Grid; Waltham, MA
Polartec LLC
Samsonite

HILL HOLLIDAY
53 State St, Boston, MA 02109
Tel.: (617) 366-4000
E-Mail: info@hhcc.com
Web Site: www.hhcc.com

Employees: 373
Year Founded: 1968

National Agency Associations: 4A's-AD CLUB

Agency Specializes In: Advertising, Brand Development & Integration, Broadcast, Business-To-Business, Collateral, Communications, Consulting, Consumer Marketing, Corporate Identity, Digital/Interactive, Direct Response Marketing, E-Commerce, Fashion/Apparel, Financial, Food Service, Health Care Services, High Technology, Hispanic Market, Internet/Web Design, Logo & Package Design, Media Buying Services, Newspaper, Newspapers & Magazines, Out-of-Home Media, Outdoor, Pharmaceutical, Publicity/Promotions, Radio, Retail, Sponsorship, Strategic Planning/Research, Telemarketing

Approx. Annual Billings: $850,000,000

Breakdown of Gross Billings by Media: D.M.: 1%; Internet Adv.: 1%; Network T.V.: 34%; Newsp. & Mags.: 20%; Other: 2%; Outdoor: 3%; Radio: 13%; Spot T.V.: 26%

Karen Kaplan *(CEO)*
Steve Andrews *(CFO & Exec VP)*
Lance Jensen *(Chief Creative Officer & Exec VP)*
Lesley Bielby *(Chief Strategy Officer)*
Brent Feldman *(Exec VP & Grp Acct Dir)*
Karen Agresti *(Exec VP & Dir-Local Investments)*
Seb Maitra *(Exec VP & Dir-Analytics)*
Bryan Sweeney *(Exec VP & Dir-Creative Production)*
Chris Wallrapp *(Exec VP & Dir-Mktg)*
Leslee Lenoff Kiley *(Exec VP)*
Phil Chadwick *(Sr VP & Controller)*
Will Uronis *(Sr VP, Grp Dir-Creative & Dir-Art)*
Scott Simpson *(Sr VP & Grp Dir-Plng)*
Scott Hainline *(Sr VP & Exec Producer-Brdcst)*
Steve Briggs *(Sr VP & Acct Dir)*
Joan Golden *(Sr VP & Acct Dir)*
Scott Noble *(Sr VP & Dir-Creative)*
Rowena Alston *(Sr VP-Strategy & Plng)*
Brian Gosnar *(VP & Exec Producer-Brdcst)*
Clifford Stevens *(VP & Acct Dir)*
Andrew Still *(VP & Acct Dir)*
Lawson Clarke *(VP-Creative & Dir)*
Jamie Scheu *(VP & Dir-Experience Design)*
Liz Brown *(VP & Assoc Dir-Media)*
Alicia Petersen *(VP & Assoc Dir-Media)*
Kelly McSheffrey *(VP & Program Mgr)*
Noah King *(VP-Digital Strategy)*
Danielle Stern *(Mgmt Supvr)*
Kevin Daley *(Dir-Creative)*
Brett Brown *(Assoc Dir-Creative)*
Kelly Butterworth *(Assoc Dir-Media)*
Marianne Gaudelli *(Assoc Dir-Media)*
Michelle Cohen Sherman *(Assoc Dir-Media)*
Jessica Schnur *(Sr Brand Strategist)*
Liane Nadeau *(Mgr-Platform Media-Trilia Media)*
Anna Plotnikova *(Mgr-Platform Media)*
Anna Albani *(Acct Supvr)*
Laurel Janssen *(Acct Supvr)*
Malia Estes *(Supvr-Media)*
Brittany French *(Supvr-Mgmt)*
Jacqueline Klein *(Supvr-Media)*
Steph Dilorio *(Sr Planner-Integrated Media)*
Jason Gary *(Sr Planner-Integrated & Digital Media)*
Kristina Hedberg *(Acct Exec)*
Heather Ward *(Acct Exec)*
Allie Alesi *(Media Planner)*
Kelsey Gillen *(Media Buyer)*
Elizabeth Hawkins *(Media Buyer)*
Rebecca Lehman *(Media Planner)*
Emily Nichols *(Media Buyer)*
Kar-Kate Parenteau *(Designer)*
Dhruva Patel *(Media Buyer)*
Jerry Roach *(Copywriter)*
Ryan Sheppard *(Media Buyer)*
Bryn Colum *(Asst Media Buyer)*
Amanda Cuoco *(Assoc Strategist-Social Media)*

Accounts:
Anheuser-Busch Budweiser; 2001
Bank of America Corporation "Invisible-U2" Super Bowl 2014, Brand Positioning, Campaign: "Gladly Tuesday", Campaign: "Life's Better When We're Connected", Campaign: "Portraits", Campaign: "Power of the Right Advisor", Lead Creative, Merrill Lynch, NCAA Championship
Boston Children's Museum
Boston Healthcare for the Homeless Program
Boston Police Department
Capella University Creative, Digital, Media
Chili's Grill & Bar Broadcast, Creative, Media Planning & Buying
Clark Bar Campaign: "Are you Clark enough?"
Dell
Dunkin' Brands Group, Inc. Campaign: "#DunkinReplay", Campaign: "#MyDunkin", Campaign: "Donuts & the Sims Social", Campaign: "Dunkin' Iced Coffee Creator", Digital Media Planning/Buying, Flatbread Sandwiches, Personal Pizzas, Wake-up Wrap; 1998
General Motors Campaign: "Strong", Chevrolet, Strategy
Great Wolf Resorts, Inc.; Madison, WI (Agency of Record) Account Management, Brand Management, Creative Development, Data Analytics, Great Wolf Lodge, Marketing Communications, Media Planning & Purchasing, Strategic Planning & Research
Harvard Pilgrim Health Care Campaign: "Dog Loves Guitar", Campaign: "Nine Golfers ", Campaign: "Talking Twins "; 1990
The J.M. Smucker Company Dunkin' Brands
John Hancock Financial Services, Inc. Campaign: "Life Comes Next", Campaign: "Real Life, Real Answers"; 1985
The LG Home Appliance Campaign: "#MomConfessions", Dish Washer, Oven, Refrigerator, TV, Washing Machine
Liberty Mutual Group Inc. Campaign: "Human", Campaign: "Passion For What We Do", Digital Media, Print, Radio, Video
Marshalls Media
Massachusetts State Lottery; 2003
Museum of Fine Arts (Media); Boston, MA; 2003
The New England Confectionery Company Inc. "Color Your Own", Campaign: "#Tweethearts", Necco Candy Buttons
Newsweek Daily Beast Co. Mad Men
Novartis Pharmaceuticals Corp. Diovan
Oxfam America (Agency of Record) Brand Campaign, Campaign: "Food Fight"
Partners Healthcare; 1996
Partnership for Drug Free Kids Campaign: "WeGotYou", Campaign: "Who Controls You?", Campaign: "Your Brain on Drugs", Emoji, Mobile, Outdoor, Print, wegotyou.life
Procter & Gamble

Putnam Investments; 2003
RED
Safeco Insurance
Spike TV
St. Jude Children's Research Hospitals
Supercuts, Inc. Media, Media Strategy, Planning & Buying
T.J. Maxx (Media); 2001
VH1
WHOLE WORLD Water (Agency of Record) #WholeWorldWater, Creative, Digital, Media
Wolverine Worldwide Creative, Merrell (Agency of Record)

Branches

Hill Holliday/New York
622 3rd Ave 14th Fl, New York, NY 10017
(See Separate Listing)

Gray Matter Agency Inc.
94 Station St, Hingham, MA 02043
(See Separate Listing)

Erwin-Penland
125 E Broad St, Greenville, SC 29601
(See Separate Listing)

HILL HOLLIDAY/NEW YORK
622 3rd Ave 14th Fl, New York, NY 10017
Tel.: (212) 905-7000
Fax: (212) 905-7100
E-Mail: lrossi@hhny.com
Web Site: www.hhcc.com

Employees: 140
Year Founded: 1976

National Agency Associations: 4A's

Agency Specializes In: Advertising, Brand Development & Integration, Broadcast, Business-To-Business, Cable T.V., Collateral, Communications, Consulting, Consumer Marketing, Consumer Publications, Corporate Communications, Corporate Identity, Digital/Interactive, Direct Response Marketing, E-Commerce, Electronic Media, Entertainment, Financial, Graphic Design, High Technology, In-Store Advertising, Internet/Web Design, Local Marketing, Logo & Package Design, Magazines, Merchandising, Newspaper, Newspapers & Magazines, Out-of-Home Media, Outdoor, Pharmaceutical, Planning & Consultation, Point of Purchase, Point of Sale, Print, Production, Publicity/Promotions, Radio, Retail, Sales Promotion, Strategic Planning/Research, T.V., Trade & Consumer Magazines

Approx. Annual Billings: $180,000,000

Lauren Herman *(Sr VP & Dir-Creative)*
Jennifer Prince *(Sr VP & Dir-Brdcst-Natl)*
Brian Gonsar *(VP & Exec Producer)*
Kristen Anderson *(VP & Acct Dir)*
Christian Castellano *(VP & Mgmt Supvr)*
Erin Cockren *(VP & Mgmt Supvr)*
Danielle Gorsha *(VP & Mgmt Supvr)*
Lisa Kleinman *(VP & Assoc Dir-Media)*
Solange Collins *(VP & Mgr-HR)*
Riomar Welch *(Sr Dir-Art)*
Rachel Rawlinson *(Producer-Brdcst)*
Jarard Isler *(Dir-Art & Graphic Designer)*
Jessica McNulty *(Assoc Dir-Media-Natl Television Investment)*
Janice McOwen *(Assoc Dir-Media)*
Justine Moncrief *(Assoc Dir-Creative)*
Joe Scopazzi *(Mgr-Production)*
Christopher Soares *(Mgr-Production)*
Jordan Calia *(Acct Supvr)*
Phoebe Juggan *(Acct Supvr)*
Alyson DaPrile *(Asst Acct Exec)*
Jana Frankel *(Asst Media Buyer)*

Accounts:
Dunkin' Donuts Media Buying
Merrill Lynch & Co., Inc. Campaign: "TrailScape"
The TJX Companies, Inc. Media
Verizon Wireless; 2000

HILTON & MYERS ADVERTISING, INC.
3350 N Country Club Rd, Tucson, AZ 85716
Tel.: (520) 881-4550
Fax: (520) 881-4696
E-Mail: info@hiltonmyersadv.com
Web Site: www.hiltonmyersadv.com

Employees: 5
Year Founded: 1986

Agency Specializes In: Advertising, Media Buying Services, Print, Production, Production (Print)

Lisa Hilton *(Founder)*

Accounts:
Lexus of Tucson
Magpies Gourmet Pizza Logo
Royal Automotive Group
TMC Foundation Invitation
Tucson Medical Center Report to Our Community

HIMMELRICH PR
3600 Clipper Mill Rd Ste 425, Baltimore, MD 21211
Tel.: (410) 528-5400
Fax: (410) 528-1515
E-Mail: info@himmelrich.com
Web Site: www.himmelrich.com

Employees: 7

Agency Specializes In: Arts, Media Relations, Promotions, Public Relations

Steven Himmelrich *(Pres)*
Garrett Berberich *(Acct Exec)*
Dan Wiznitzer *(Acct Exec)*
Dennis Mizzoni *(Acct Coord)*
Catherine Rinaldo *(Acct Coord)*

Accounts:
Allfirst Bank
Anderson Coe & King
Bebe Paluzza Baby & Toddler Expo
JPB Enterprises
Merrill Corporation
Mobil Oil
Sugarloaf Moutain Works

HINDSIGHT MANAGEMENT INC.
2213 Morris Ave Ste 2020, Birmingham, AL 35203-4214
Tel.: (205) 324-9960
E-Mail: jriley@hindsightmanagement.com
Web Site: www.hindsightmanagement.com

E-Mail for Key Personnel:
President: jriley@hindsightsystems.com

Employees: 2
Year Founded: 1987

Agency Specializes In: Advertising, Brand Development & Integration, Business-To-Business, Consulting, Consumer Marketing, Consumer Publications, Corporate Communications, Health Care Services, Investor Relations, Medical Products, Over-50 Market, Planning & Consultation, Seniors' Market, Strategic Planning/Research

Approx. Annual Billings: $6,000,000

Breakdown of Gross Billings by Media: Bus. Publs.: $120,000; D.M.: $300,000; Fees: $1,080,000; Logo & Package Design: $600,000; Mdsg./POP: $300,000; Newsp.: $600,000; Plng. & Consultation: $600,000; Production: $300,000; Sls. Promo.: $600,000; Strategic Planning/Research: $600,000; Trade & Consumer Mags.: $600,000; Worldwide Web Sites: $300,000

James E. Riley *(Owner)*

Accounts:
PointClear Solutions; Birmingham, AL

HINTON COMMUNICATIONS
1215 19th St NW, Washington, DC 20036
Tel.: (703) 798-3109
Fax: (480) 275-3554
E-Mail: karen@hintoncommunications.com
Web Site: www.hintoncommunications.com

Agency Specializes In: Event Planning & Marketing, Media Relations, Media Training, Print, Radio, Strategic Planning/Research, T.V.

Karen Hinton *(Owner)*

Accounts:
Amazon Defense Coalition
Gradient Analytics

HIP ADVERTISING
2809 Mansion Rd Ste A, Springfield, IL 62711
Tel.: (217) 789-4447
Web Site: www.hipadvertising.com

Agency Specializes In: Advertising, Digital/Interactive, Event Planning & Marketing, Internet/Web Design, Logo & Package Design, Outdoor, Public Relations, Radio, Social Media, Strategic Planning/Research

Myra Hoffman *(Owner & Pres)*
Angela Parks *(Dir-Creative & Graphic Designer)*
Molly Ballinger *(Acct Exec)*
Julie Craig *(Media Planner & Media Buyer)*
Betsey Heidrick *(Planner-Social Media)*
Sanya Kushak *(Designer-Web)*

Accounts:
University of Spa & Cosmetology Arts
Zaras Collision Center Inc.

THE HIP EVENT
356 Bloomfield Ave Ste 5, Montclair, NJ 7042
Tel.: (973) 707-7125
Web Site: www.thehipevent.com

Year Founded: 2007

Agency Specializes In: Advertising, Event Planning & Marketing, Public Relations, Social Media

Jessica Evans *(Mgr-PR)*

Accounts:
New-The Connie Dwyer Breast Center

HIPCRICKET
4400 Carillon Pt # 4, Kirkland, WA 98033-7353
Tel.: (425) 452-1111
Fax: (425) 827-1561
E-Mail: info@hipcricket.com
Web Site: www.hipcricket.com

Employees: 40

Agency Specializes In: Brand Development & Integration, Mobile Marketing, Radio, Sponsorship, T.V.

Doug Stovall *(Pres & COO)*
David W. Hostetter *(CTO)*
Kate Farley *(Sr VP-Bus Ops)*
Sandy Glickman *(Dir-Brand Solutions)*

Accounts:
California Milk Processor Board
The City of Baltimore
Clear Channel Radio
Coca-Cola Refreshments USA, Inc.
Ford
Hershey
Jameson
Kiss FM
Macy's
Nestle Waters
Premiere Radio Networks
Sandusky Broadcasting
Staples
Wiley Publishing

HIPERVINCULO
7774 NW 46th ST, Doral, FL 33166
Tel.: (786) 529-0679
E-Mail: info@hipervinculo.net
Web Site: www.hipervinculo.net/en/

Year Founded: 2004

Agency Specializes In: Computers & Software, Digital/Interactive, E-Commerce, Electronics, Engineering, Fashion/Apparel, Hispanic Market, Internet/Web Design, Market Research, Media Buying Services, Media Planning, Paid Searches, Real Estate, Strategic Planning/Research

Maria Luisa Sarquis *(Acct Mgr)*
Rowland Saer *(Mgr-Analog Resources)*
Fabiola Santana *(Mgr-Admin)*
Miguel Camacho *(Strategist-Digital Media Mktg Campaigns)*
Orianna Amoni *(Jr Designer)*
Haydana Perez *(Marketing Specialist)*
Ida Tovar *(Jr Designer)*

Accounts:
Chrissie24 Hair Products; 2011
Flexoven Packages Plastics; 2012
TWC Latin American Computer Wholesaler; 2012
Zerma Americas Recycling Industrial Machinery; 2013

HIRECLIX LLC
3 Heritage Way, Gloucester, MA 01930
Tel.: (617) 299-8889
E-Mail: contact@hireclix.com
Web Site: www.hireclix.com

Employees: 10
Year Founded: 2010

Agency Specializes In: Advertising, Recruitment, Search Engine Optimization, Social Media

Neil Costa *(Founder & CEO)*
Scott Ryan *(VP-Client Svcs)*
Tracy Scollo *(Mgr-Bus Dev)*
Corinne Hopkins *(Analyst-Digital Mktg)*
Michael Campbell *(Coord-Digital Mktg)*
Olivia Wilson *(Coord-Digital Mktg)*

HIRONS & COMPANY
422 E New York St, Indianapolis, IN 46202
Tel.: (317) 977-2206
Fax: (317) 977-2208
E-Mail: info@hirons.com
Web Site: www.hirons.com

E-Mail for Key Personnel:
President: thirons@hirons.com
Public Relations: jparham@hirons.com

Employees: 50
Year Founded: 1978

Agency Specializes In: Advertising, Advertising Specialties, Bilingual Market, Brand Development & Integration, Broadcast, Business-To-Business, Collateral, Consumer Publications, Corporate Identity, Direct Response Marketing, Education, Electronic Media, Event Planning & Marketing, Food Service, Government/Political, Graphic Design, Health Care Services, Internet/Web Design, Logo & Package Design, Magazines, Media Buying Services, Multimedia, Newspaper, Newspapers & Magazines, Outdoor, Print, Public Relations, Radio, Real Estate, Restaurant, Sports Market, Strategic Planning/Research, Trade & Consumer Magazines, Travel & Tourism

Approx. Annual Billings: $30,000,000

Tom Hirons *(Pres & CEO)*
Jim Parham *(COO)*
Kelsey Brewer *(Acct Mgr & Producer)*
Erin Ladyman *(Acct Coord)*
Blair Tilson *(Acct Coord)*
Liz Robinson *(Sr Media Planner & Buyer)*

Accounts:
Department of the Navy - NAVSEA Crane
Eiteljorg Museum of American Indians & Western Art
Indiana University
Indianapolis Indians
Indianapolis Symphony Orchestra
Indianapolis Zoo
Verizon Wireless

HIRSHORN ZUCKERMAN DESIGN GROUP
(d/b/a HZDG)
10101 Molecular Dr, Rockville, MD 20850
Tel.: (301) 294-6302
Fax: (301) 294-6305
E-Mail: info@hzdg.com
Web Site: www.hzdg.com

Employees: 100

Agency Specializes In: Brand Development & Integration, Broadcast, Digital/Interactive, Direct Response Marketing, E-Commerce, Electronic Media, Graphic Design, Internet/Web Design, Multimedia, Print

Karen Zuckerman *(Founder, Pres & Chief Creative Officer)*
Jerry Zuckerman *(CEO)*
Ed Illig *(VP & Dir-Creative)*
Stacey Deorzio *(VP-Client Rels)*
Sean Conrad *(Sr Dir-Interactive Art)*
Jason Drumheller *(Sr Dir-Art)*
Jon Leon *(Sr Dir-Art)*
Justine Song *(Acct Dir)*
Chad Stockton *(Dir-Creative)*
Gillian Goodman *(Assoc Dir-Creative)*
Ashley Gharib *(Acct Exec)*

Accounts:
Affinia Hotels
Again Restaurants
Alexan Solero
New-Conair Campaign: "Your Confidence is Showing", Conair for Men
The Georgian
Half Street
National Jean Co

HISPANIC GROUP
8181 NW 14th St Ste 250, Miami, FL 33126
Tel.: (305) 477-5483
Fax: (305) 436-1953
E-Mail: nbcontact@hispanicgroup.net
Web Site: www.hispanicgroup.net

Employees: 40
Year Founded: 2002

Agency Specializes In: Sponsorship

Jose Luis Valderrama *(CEO)*
Marily Maguina *(CFO)*
Ivan Dibos *(VP & Dir-Bus Dev)*
Ximena Pazos *(VP & Dir-Media)*
Kurt Pflucker *(VP)*
Franciso Morilo *(Media Planner-Digital & Buyer)*

Accounts:
Dish Network- Dish Latino; 2005

HISPANIDAD
2228 Blake St Ste 200, Denver, CO 80205
Tel.: (303) 233-8660
Toll Free: (800) 356-5036
Web Site: www.heinrichhispanidad.com

Agency Specializes In: Advertising, Event Planning & Marketing, Media Planning, Print, Strategic Planning/Research

Laura Sonderup *(Mng Dir)*

Accounts:
Wyoming Department of Transportation

HITCHCOCK FLEMING & ASSOCIATES, INC.
500 Wolf Ledges Pkwy, Akron, OH 44311-1022
Tel.: (888) 376-7601
Fax: (330) 966-7060
E-Mail: info@teamhfa.com
Web Site: www.teamhfa.com

E-Mail for Key Personnel:
Creative Dir.: mcollins@teamhfa.com

Employees: 102
Year Founded: 1940

National Agency Associations: 4A's-AAF-AMA-BPA-DMA-PRSA

Agency Specializes In: Advertising, Advertising Specialties, Alternative Advertising, Arts, Automotive, Aviation & Aerospace, Bilingual Market, Brand Development & Integration, Branded Entertainment, Business Publications, Business-To-Business, Cable T.V., Co-op Advertising, Collateral, Communications, Consulting, Consumer Goods, Consumer Marketing, Consumer Publications, Corporate Communications, Corporate Identity, Customer Relationship Management, Digital/Interactive, Direct Response Marketing, Direct-to-Consumer, E-Commerce, Education, Electronic Media, Email, Engineering, Entertainment, Environmental, Event Planning & Marketing, Exhibit/Trade Shows, Food Service, Government/Political, Graphic Design, Health Care Services, High Technology, Hispanic Market, Hospitality, Household Goods, Identity Marketing, In-Store Advertising, Industrial, Information Technology, Integrated Marketing, International, Internet/Web Design, Investor Relations, Leisure, Local Marketing, Logo & Package Design, Magazines, Market Research, Media Buying Services, Media Planning, Media Relations, Medical Products, Merchandising, Mobile Marketing, New Product Development, Newspaper, Newspapers & Magazines, Out-of-Home Media, Outdoor, Over-50 Market, Package Design, Paid Searches, Pharmaceutical, Planning & Consultation, Podcasting, Point of Purchase, Point of Sale, Print, Product Placement, Production, Production (Print), Promotions, Public Relations, Publicity/Promotions, Radio, Recruitment, Regional, Restaurant, Retail, Sales Promotion, Search Engine Optimization, Seniors' Market, Social Marketing/Nonprofit, Sponsorship, Strategic Planning/Research, Sweepstakes, T.V., Technical Advertising, Teen Market, Telemarketing, Trade & Consumer Magazines, Transportation, Travel & Tourism, Viral/Buzz/Word of Mouth

Approx. Annual Billings: $90,000,000

Charles Abraham *(Mng Partner)*
Kevin Kinsley *(Partner-Client Dev)*
Shirley Shriver *(Partner-Strategy & Insights)*
Dale Elwell *(VP-Acct Svcs)*
Rene McCann *(Sr Dir-Art-Interactive)*
Sandi Fellmeth-Nelson *(Dir-Production)*
Kelly Wanstrath *(Sr Mgr-Res)*
Patrick Kunklier *(Sr Acct Mgr-PR)*
Jason Nicolacakis *(Sr Acct Mgr)*
Angela Dublikar *(Acct Mgr)*
Katie Greenwald *(Acct Mgr-PR)*
Doug Snider *(Acct Mgr)*
Keith Busch *(Client Partner-Dev)*
Ellen Murray *(Mgr-Brdcst Traffic)*
Ted Paynter *(Acct Supvr)*
Shelly Morton *(Supvr-Project Mgmt)*
Karen Lahovich *(Sr Specialist-Integrated Media)*
Lauren Reed *(Sr Acct Planner)*
Alyssa Trowbridge *(Asst Project Mgr)*

Accounts:
Akron Beacon Journal
Akron Marathon Charitable Corporation 10 Year Commemorative Book
Akron Road Runner Marathon
Akron Summit County Convention & Visitors Bureau; Akron, OH
BlueLinx
Buffalo Wild Wings Marketing Group Media
City of Akron
Clopay Buying, Creative Design, Paid Media, Strategic Planning, Strategy
Dunlop Tires
Gemini Automotive Care
The Goodyear Tire & Rubber Company; Akron, OH Aviation, Commercial Truck, Just Tires Stores, North American Tires, Off-the-Road Tires
Greater Akron Chamber of Commerce
JRayl Transport Inc. Brand Positioning, Media Planning & Buying, Public Relations, Website Design
Just Tires
Keep Akron Beautiful
Liquid Nails
LP Building Products Media Planning & Buying, Research & Creative Development.
LP SmartSide Trim and Siding
Nexa Autocolor; Westlake, OH
PPG Industries Creative, Media, PPG PAINTS, PPG PITTSBURGH PAINTS, Public Relations
Saint-Gobain Creative, Process Systems Business, Public Relations
Schneller Inc.; Kent, OH Decorative Laminates for the Transportation & Architectural Interiors Industries
SPA.GIENE LLC; Kirtland, OH
Summa Health System
Tremco Roofing & Building Maintenance; Beachwood, OH Renovation, Maintenance & Repair Solutions; 2005
University of Akron
Zellmed

THE HIVE
544 King St W, Toronto, Ontario M5V 1M3 Canada
Tel.: (416) 923-3800
Fax: (416) 923-4123
E-Mail: info@thehiveinc.com
Web Site: www.thehiveinc.com

Agency Specializes In: Advertising, Brand Development & Integration, Broadcast, Corporate Identity, Digital/Interactive, Outdoor, Print, Promotions, Social Media, Strategic Planning/Research

Andy Krupski *(Pres & CEO)*
Simon Creet *(Chief Creative Officer & VP)*
Trent Fulton *(VP-Client Svcs)*
Christian Buer *(Dir-Art)*
Meagan Eveleigh *(Dir-Art)*
Paul Parolin *(Assoc Dir-Creative)*

Accounts:
The Bicycle Factory
Jack Daniel's
Mondelez

THE HIVE ADVERTISING
724 Pine St, San Francisco, CA 94108
Tel.: (415) 255-3000
Fax: (415) 255-3005
E-Mail: info@thehivesf.com
Web Site: thehivesf.com/

Employees: 18
Year Founded: 2003

National Agency Associations: 4A's

Agency Specializes In: Advertising, Brand Development & Integration, Consumer Goods, Out-of-Home Media, Outdoor, Print, T.V., Web (Banner Ads, Pop-ups, etc.)

Approx. Annual Billings: $12,000,000

DeeAnn Budney *(Founder, CEO & Dir-Creative)*
Sushil Pandit *(Owner)*
Harold Sogard *(Pres)*
Genevieve Wiersema *(VP-Palisades Media)*
Mary King *(Dir-Ops)*
Barbara Wingate *(Dir-Brand Strategy)*

Accounts:
Big Brothers Big Sisters of the Bay Area
Boudin Bakery
Torani Consumer-Oriented Campaign
University of California at San Francisco Medical Center

HJMT COMMUNICATIONS, LLC
145 Pinelawn Rd, Melville, NY 11747
Tel.: (631) 393-0220
Fax: (516) 997-1740
E-Mail: info@hjmt.com
Web Site: www.hjmt.com

Employees: 15

Agency Specializes In: Event Planning & Marketing, Graphic Design, Local Marketing, Media Relations, Publicity/Promotions

Hilary Topper *(Pres & CEO)*
Lisa Gordon *(Sr VP-PR)*
Lori Alexy *(VP-Client Svcs)*
Elizabeth Montoya *(Sr Acct Exec)*

Accounts:
B Well NY Corporate Wellness Consultants
Esquire Bank

HK ADVERTISING, INC.
41 Bisbee Ct Ste A-1, Santa Fe, NM 87508
Tel.: (505) 988-9299
Fax: (505) 983-5804
Toll Free: (800) 766-2092
E-Mail: hkadv@hkadv.com
Web Site: www.hkadv.com

E-Mail for Key Personnel:
President: david@hkadv.com

Employees: 8
Year Founded: 1982

National Agency Associations: AAF

Agency Specializes In: Government/Political, Retail, Travel & Tourism

Approx. Annual Billings: $3,750,000 (Capitalized)

Breakdown of Gross Billings by Media: Collateral: 27%; Mags.: 1%; Newsp.: 17%; Outdoor: 8%; Point of Purchase: 2%; Radio: 23%; T.V.: 22%

David C. Hayduk *(Pres & CEO)*
Ben Matthews *(Mgr-Accts)*

Accounts:
Bishops Lodge Resort & Spa
Buffalo Thunder Resort & Spa
Camel Rock Casino
Dancing Eagle Casino
Los Alamos Medical Center
Molecular Informatics
New Mexico Finance Authority
New Mexico National Guard
New Mexico North Central Region
Regional Development Corporation
Route 66 Casino Hotel

HL GROUP
853 Broadway 18th Fl, New York, NY 10003
Tel.: (212) 529-5533
Fax: (212) 673-3131
Web Site: www.hlgrp.com

Year Founded: 2001

Agency Specializes In: Brand Development & Integration, Communications, Crisis Communications, Event Planning & Marketing, Market Research, Media Relations

Hamilton South *(Founder & Partner)*
Robert Harwood-Matthews *(CEO)*
Sharna Ettenberg *(Mng Dir)*
Matthew Levison *(Mng Dir)*
Dave McNamee *(VP)*
Devon Nagle *(VP)*
Anne Reingold *(VP)*
Tara Kurobe *(Acct Dir)*
Kelsey London *(Acct Mgr)*
Maureen Thon *(Acct Mgr)*
Julianna Da Silva *(Acct Coord)*
Evan Rome *(Coord-PR)*

Accounts:
Bolthouse Farms Public Relations
Expedia.Com Online Travel Agency
Hilton Worldwide Conrad Hotels & Resorts, Waldorf Astoria
Mattel Barbie, Public Relations

HLD COMMUNICATIONS
(Formerly Harrison Leifer DiMarco, Inc.)
330 Old Country Rd Ste 206, Mineola, NY 11501
Tel.: (516) 536-2020
Fax: (516) 536-2641
Toll Free: (888) 571-2500
E-Mail: info@hldnow.com
Web Site: hldcommunications.com

Employees: 75
Year Founded: 1986

Agency Specializes In: Advertising, Alternative Advertising, Brand Development & Integration, Business-To-Business, Cable T.V., Collateral, Consumer Marketing, Consumer Publications, Corporate Communications, Corporate Identity,

Crisis Communications, Digital/Interactive, Direct Response Marketing, E-Commerce, Electronic Media, Electronics, Environmental, Event Planning & Marketing, Exhibit/Trade Shows, Health Care Services, High Technology, Household Goods, Integrated Marketing, Internet/Web Design, Legal Services, Logo & Package Design, Media Buying Services, Media Planning, Medical Products, New Product Development, New Technologies, Package Design, Pharmaceutical, Planning & Consultation, Point of Purchase, Point of Sale, Production, Public Relations, Real Estate, Search Engine Optimization, Social Marketing/Nonprofit, Strategic Planning/Research, Trade & Consumer Magazines, Web (Banner Ads, Pop-ups, etc.)

Approx. Annual Billings: $29,300,000

Breakdown of Gross Billings by Media: Bus. Publs.: $10,000,000; Collateral: $1,000,000; Consumer Publs.: $1,500,000; D.M.: $1,500,000; Internet Adv.: $1,000,000; Newsp.: $3,000,000; Production: $3,500,000; Pub. Rels.: $2,000,000; Radio: $2,000,000; T.V.: $3,000,000; Worldwide Web Sites: $800,000

Don Miller *(Exec VP)*
Renee Marquardt *(Sr VP-Client Svcs)*
Elizabeth Burke *(VP-PR)*
Josephine Acampora *(Client Svcs Dir)*
John Decker *(Dir-Creative)*
Jill Ferrone *(Dir-Media)*
Dale Moskowitz *(Dir-Fin)*
Leah Bush *(Acct Mgr)*

Accounts:
Aladdin Remodelers
Albanese & Albanese Attorneys at Law; Garden City, NY
Albanese Development Corp.; Garden City, NY Genesis Networks, The Vanguard Chelsea, Verdesian
Albrecht, Viggiano, Zureck & Company, P.C.
Certilman Balin Adler & Hyman, LLP
Decof, Decof & Barry, P.C Content Marketing, Social Media
Developmental Disabilities Institute; Smithtown, NY (Agency of Record)
Elias Property Management; Jericho, NY
Empower
Flushing Savings Bank iGOBanking.com
Fougera
Graf Repetti & Company; New York, NY
Hansgrohe
Island Harvest
Long Island Junior Soccer League
M&R Management
Margolin/Winer/Evans; Garden City, NY
Medical Action Industries (MAI); Hauppauge , NY
New Island Hospital of Bethpage
Sheffield Tools
Westbury Schools
Westfield Group LLC Public Relations, Westfield South Shore, Westfield Sunrise

HLG HEALTH COMMUNICATIONS

(Formerly The Hal Lewis Group Inc.)
1700 Market St Sixth Fl, Philadelphia, PA 19103-3913
Tel.: (215) 563-4461
Fax: (215) 563-1148
E-Mail: info@hlg.com
Web Site: www.hlg.com

E-Mail for Key Personnel:
President: dwinigrad@hlg.com

Employees: 40
Year Founded: 1967

Agency Specializes In: Communications, Medical Products, Planning & Consultation

Approx. Annual Billings: $70,000,000

Breakdown of Gross Billings by Media: Audio/Visual: 2%; Bus. Publs.: 15%; Collateral: 35%; Consumer Publs.: 2%; D.M.: 15%; Fees: 10%; Internet Adv.: 5%; Newsp.: 2%; Other: 5%; Production: 1%; Pub. Rels.: 2%; Radio & T.V.: 3%; Trade Shows: 3%

David Winigrad *(Pres & Exec Dir-Creative)*
Jami Stover *(VP & Grp Acct Dir)*
Dawn Hastings *(Dir-Creative-Copy)*
Halley Yankanich *(Sr Acct Exec)*

Accounts:
Abbott Laboratories
Ariad Pharmaceuticals
Aspect Medical Systems Bis
Azur Pharma
Baxter Healthcare Corp.
BMS Imaging Cardiolite, Definity
Bristol-Myers Squibb Atazanavir, Corporate, Coumadin, Sustiva
GE Healthcare
Healthpoint Accuzyme, Panafil
MDS Pharma Services
MEDA Pharmaceuticals
Merck & Co., Inc. Merck Managed Care, Merck Ophthalmics
Neuronetics
Organogenesis

HMC ADVERTISING

453 D St Ste C, Chula Vista, CA 91910
Tel.: (619) 420-4586
Toll Free: (888) 330-7637
E-Mail: info@hmcadvertising.com
Web Site: www.hmcadvertising.com

E-Mail for Key Personnel:
President: lroberts@hmcadvertising.com
Media Dir.: rnava@hmcadvertising.com

Employees: 7
Year Founded: 1990

National Agency Associations: AHAA

Agency Specializes In: Advertising, Advertising Specialties, Bilingual Market, Brand Development & Integration, Broadcast, Consulting, Corporate Identity, Entertainment, Event Planning & Marketing, Exhibit/Trade Shows, Government/Political, Graphic Design, Hispanic Market, Internet/Web Design, Local Marketing, Logo & Package Design, Media Buying Services, Multimedia, Newspaper, Newspapers & Magazines, Outdoor, Planning & Consultation, Public Relations, Publicity/Promotions, Radio, Retail, Strategic Planning/Research, T.V., Travel & Tourism

Lucy Roberts *(Owner)*
Jennifer Garcia-Hinkle *(Pres)*
Rosa Nava *(Dir-Media)*
Olivia Ramos *(Mgr-Production)*

Accounts:
Baja Duty Free Retail Duty-Free Products
Feld Entertainment Disney on Ice, Ringling Brothers & Barnum & Bailey; 1990

HMC ADVERTISING LLC

(d/b/a HMC2)
65 Millet St Ste 301, Richmond, VT 05477
Tel.: (802) 434-7141
Fax: (802) 434-7140
E-Mail: info@wearehmc.com
Web Site: www.wearehmc.com/

Employees: 15
Year Founded: 1980

National Agency Associations: 4A's

Agency Specializes In: Advertising, Brand Development & Integration, Branded Entertainment, Collateral, College, Consumer Goods, Consumer Marketing, Corporate Communications, Direct Response Marketing, Education, Email, Entertainment, Event Planning & Marketing, Financial, Graphic Design, Health Care Services, Integrated Marketing, Internet/Web Design, Local Marketing, Logo & Package Design, Magazines, Market Research, Media Buying Services, Media Planning, Media Training, Medical Products, Newspaper, Newspapers & Magazines, Package Design, Print, Production, Production (Ad, Film, Broadcast), Production (Print), Public Relations, Radio, Regional, Strategic Planning/Research, Travel & Tourism, Viral/Buzz/Word of Mouth, Web (Banner Ads, Pop-ups, etc.), Women's Market, Yellow Pages Advertising

Breakdown of Gross Billings by Media: Newsp. & Mags.: 50%; Print: 35%; Radio & T.V.: 10%; Worldwide Web Sites: 5%

Tom Holmes *(Pres)*
Paula Bazluke *(VP & Dir-Media)*
Bill Patton *(VP-Creative Tech)*
Jessie Angus *(Dir-Plng & Strategy)*
Susan Weeks *(Dir-Mktg)*
Katie Rutherford *(Assoc Dir-Creative)*
Kate Connolly *(Media Planner & Media Buyer)*

Accounts:
Smugglers' Notch Resort; Smugglers' Notch, VT; 1988
State of Vermont; Montpelier, VT
Vermont Information Technology
Vermont Student Assistance Corp.; Winooski, VT Student Loans; 2004

HMH

1800 SW 1st Ave Ste 250, Portland, OR 97201
Tel.: (503) 295-1922
Fax: (503) 295-1938
E-Mail: portland@hmhagency.com
Web Site: www.hmhagency.com

E-Mail for Key Personnel:
President: edh@thinkhmh.com
Creative Dir.: daveb@thinkhmh.com
Media Dir.: jille@thinkhmh.com
Production Mgr.: paulap@thinkhmh.com
Public Relations: marianm@thinkhmh.com

Employees: 30
Year Founded: 1978

National Agency Associations: 4A's

Agency Specializes In: Advertising, Advertising Specialties, African-American Market, Agriculture, Asian Market, Automotive, Aviation & Aerospace, Bilingual Market, Brand Development & Integration, Broadcast, Business Publications, Business-To-Business, Cable T.V., Children's Market, Co-op Advertising, Collateral, Commercial Photography, Communications, Consulting, Consumer Marketing, Consumer Publications, Corporate Communications, Corporate Identity, Cosmetics, Digital/Interactive, Direct Response Marketing, E-Commerce, Education, Electronic Media, Engineering, Entertainment, Environmental, Event Planning & Marketing, Exhibit/Trade Shows, Fashion/Apparel, Financial, Food Service, Gay & Lesbian Market, Government/Political, Graphic Design, Health Care Services, High Technology, Hispanic Market, In-Store Advertising, Industrial, Infomercials, Information Technology, Internet/Web Design, Investor Relations, Legal Services, Leisure, Local Marketing, Logo & Package Design, Magazines, Marine, Media Buying Services, Medical Products, Merchandising, Multimedia, New Product Development, Newspaper, Newspapers & Magazines, Outdoor, Over-50 Market,

Pharmaceutical, Planning & Consultation, Point of Purchase, Point of Sale, Print, Production, Public Relations, Publicity/Promotions, Radio, Real Estate, Recruitment, Restaurant, Retail, Sales Promotion, Seniors' Market, Sports Market, Strategic Planning/Research, Sweepstakes, Syndication, T.V., Technical Advertising, Teen Market, Telemarketing, Trade & Consumer Magazines, Transportation, Travel & Tourism, Yellow Pages Advertising

Approx. Annual Billings: $5,200,000

Ed Herinckx *(Pres-Portland)*
Megan Miller *(VP & Client Svcs Dir)*
Paula Phillis *(VP-Portland)*
Melissa Anderson *(Dir-Media)*
Kevin Archer *(Dir-Creative)*
Denise Hollingsworth *(Dir-Brand Strategy)*
Teddy Shipley *(Assoc Dir-Creative)*
Robb Beck *(Mgr-Analytics & Digital Campaign)*
Cindi Elsom *(Acct Supvr)*

Accounts:
Alliance Truck Parts
New-Central Oregon Visitors Authority
Crescent Communities Residential Division
Epiq Systems
Fluke Networks
Freightliner Trucks
New-Harrison Dental
Idaho Power
LP Building Products
New-Mecklenburg Livable Communities
Mercedes-Benz Financial Services
New-North Carolina State Ports Authority
Oregon Community Credit Uniion
PacificSource
The Partners Group
New-Superior Tape & Label
New-Teleflex
Thomas Built Buses; High Point, NC
Tolko Industries
New-Transportation Fairness Alliance
TriMet
TruWood
Watchguard Technologies

Satellite Offices

HMH
(Formerly Citrus)
19797 Village Office Ct, Bend, OR 97702
Tel.: (541) 388-2003
Fax: (541) 388-4381
Web Site: www.hmhagency.com

Employees: 10
Year Founded: 1986

National Agency Associations: 4A's-Second Wind Limited

Agency Specializes In: Broadcast, Business-To-Business, Cable T.V., Consulting, Corporate Identity, Digital/Interactive, Direct Response Marketing, Financial, Graphic Design, Health Care Services, High Technology, Internet/Web Design, Leisure, Logo & Package Design, Magazines, Medical Products, Newspaper, Newspapers & Magazines, Planning & Consultation, Podcasting, Point of Sale, Print, Production, Production (Print), Radio, Seniors' Market, Sponsorship, Strategic Planning/Research, T.V., Trade & Consumer Magazines, Travel & Tourism

Ed Herinckx *(Pres)*
Paula Phillis *(VP)*
Kevin Archer *(Dir-Creative)*

Accounts:
Montana Lottery
Nike
The Oregon State Fair

HMH-Charlotte N.C.
1435 W Morehead St Ste 140, Charlotte, NC 28208
Tel.: (704) 323-4444
Fax: (704) 323-4440
Toll Free: (888) 527-62327
Web Site: www.hmhagency.com

Employees: 10
Year Founded: 1999

National Agency Associations: 4A's

Sally Auguston *(VP)*
Donna Forbes *(Gen Mgr)*
Shawn Kelley *(Exec Dir-Creative)*
Kevin Prenoveau *(Acct Dir)*
Jennifer Hausman *(Assoc Dir-Media & Supvr-Media)*
Betsy Grant *(Sr Acct Exec)*
Lauren Dixon *(Asst Acct Exec)*

Accounts:
Freightliner

HN MEDIA & MARKETING
275 Madison Ave Ste 2200, New York, NY 10016
Tel.: (212) 490-1300
Fax: (212) 490-0777
E-Mail: info@hnmediamarketing.com
Web Site: www.hnmedia.com

Employees: 9

Robin Golden *(COO)*
Marla Arum *(VP & Dir-Media Buying)*
Chelsea Lerch *(Sr Acct Dir & Strategist-Media)*
Dessy O'Keefe *(Sr Acct Dir & Strategist-Cross-Media)*
Sheldon Kawer *(Acct Mgmt Dir)*
Justin Young *(Strategist-Media)*
Christina Riccitelli *(Assoc Strategist-Media)*

HODGES ADVERTISING INC
3727 Rose Lake Dr Ste 101, Charlotte, NC 28217
Tel.: (704) 357-3560
Web Site: www.hodgesadvertising.com

Agency Specializes In: Advertising, Media Buying Services, Promotions, Radio, T.V.

Chris Hodges *(Founder & Pres)*
David Hodges *(VP-Sls)*
Terri Hodges *(Office Mgr)*

Accounts:
Elite 5 Chevy Dealers

HODGES & ASSOCIATES
The Dr Pepper Bldg Ste 300 2829 2nd Ave S, Birmingham, AL 35233
Tel.: (205) 328-4357
Fax: (205) 328-4366
E-Mail: hodges@thehighroad.com
Web Site: www.thehighroad.com

Employees: 7

Marynell Ford *(Strategist-Mktg)*

Accounts:
The Community Foundation of Greater Birmingham
Daniel Corp.
Davis Architects
Medical Properties Trust, LLP

HODGES ASSOCIATES, INC.
912 Hay St, Fayetteville, NC 28305-5314
Tel.: (910) 483-8489
Fax: (910) 483-7197
E-Mail: info@hodgesassoc.com
Web Site: www.hodgesassoc.com

E-Mail for Key Personnel:
President: anna@hodgesassoc.com
Creative Dir.: jerri@hodgesassoc.com
Production Mgr.: chuck@hodgesassoc.com

Employees: 7
Year Founded: 1974

National Agency Associations: AAF

Agency Specializes In: Agriculture, Automotive, Brand Development & Integration, Broadcast, Business Publications, Business-To-Business, Cable T.V., Catalogs, Co-op Advertising, Collateral, Commercial Photography, Communications, Consulting, Consumer Marketing, Consumer Publications, Corporate Identity, Digital/Interactive, Direct Response Marketing, E-Commerce, Education, Electronic Media, Engineering, Entertainment, Environmental, Event Planning & Marketing, Exhibit/Trade Shows, Faith Based, Fashion/Apparel, Financial, Food Service, Government/Political, Graphic Design, Health Care Services, High Technology, Hispanic Market, Industrial, Internet/Web Design, Legal Services, Leisure, Logo & Package Design, Magazines, Marine, Media Buying Services, Media Planning, Media Relations, Medical Products, Merchandising, Multimedia, New Product Development, Newspaper, Newspapers & Magazines, Out-of-Home Media, Outdoor, Over-50 Market, Package Design, Pharmaceutical, Planning & Consultation, Point of Purchase, Point of Sale, Print, Production, Production (Print), Public Relations, Publicity/Promotions, Radio, Real Estate, Recruitment, Restaurant, Retail, Sales Promotion, Seniors' Market, Sports Market, Strategic Planning/Research, T.V., Technical Advertising, Teen Market, Trade & Consumer Magazines, Transportation, Travel & Tourism, Yellow Pages Advertising

Approx. Annual Billings: $3,000,000

Breakdown of Gross Billings by Media: Bus. Publs.: $733,000; Collateral: $295,000; D.M.: $29,000; Mags.: $130,000; Newsp.: $480,500; Outdoor: $115,000; Point of Purchase: $10,000; Production: $477,000; Radio: $280,000; Sls. Promo.: $135,500; T.V.: $315,000

Anna Hodges Smith *(Pres & Acct Exec)*
Chuck Smith *(VP)*
Jerri L. Allison *(Sr Dir-Art)*
Pat Mingle *(Sr Acct Exec)*
Colette Moore *(Copywriter)*

Accounts:
A La Cart; Charlotte, NC Food Service Equipment; 2000
Aberdeen & Rockfish Railroad; Aberdeen, NC; 1995
All America Mortgage; Fayetteville, NC; 2005
Blood & Cancer Clinic; Fayetteville, NC Medical
Cape Fear Botanical Garden; Fayetteville, NC
Cape Fear Cardiology; Fayetteville, NC Medical; 2009
Carolina Regional Radiology; Fayetteville, NC Medical; 2007
Carolina Turf Farm; Raeford, NC Commercial Sod
Cavin's Business Solutions; Fayetteville, NC Business Products; 2009
City of Fayetteville Leaf Pick-Up Program; Fayetteville, NC
Cottages at North Ramsey; Fayetteville, NC Real Estate Development; 2008
ESAB Welding Products; Florence, SC Welding & Cutting Equipment Manufacturer
Fayetteville Area Convention & Tourism; 1998

G & G HealthCare
Guaranty Savings & Loan
Highland Presbyterian Church; Fayetteville, NC; 2005
House Autry Farms
Hutchens, Senter & Britton; Fayetteville, NC Legal Services
Jerry Gregory & Associates; Fayetteville, NC Legal Services; 2005
John Boyle & Co.; Statesville, NC Industrial Manufacturers
The Logistics Company; Fayetteville, NC Computers/Internet
Natvar Company
North Carolina's Southeast; Elizabethtown, NC Economic Development; 2006
Olde Fayetteville Insurance; Fayetteville, NC Insurance Services
Pilch, Inc
Public Works Commission; Fayetteville, NC Utilities
Reed-Lallier (Agency of Record) Advertising, Chevrolet, Marketing, Public Relations
Rego-Cryo Flow; Burlington, NC Regulators, Valves; 1997
Resinal Corp; Severn, NC Inks
Riverside Sports Center; Fayetteville, NC
Saint Patrick Church; Fayetteville, NC; 2004
Snyder Memorial Baptist Church; Fayetteville, NC; 2002
Stedman Housing Mart
Valley Regional Imaging; Fayetteville, NC Radiology/Imaging; 2009
Woodbridge Alternative Inc.; Fayetteville, NC Residential Treatment for At-Risk Youth; 2003

HOEGGER COMMUNICATIONS

2304 Midwestern Pkwy Ste 104A, Wichita Falls, TX 76308
Tel.: (940) 692-7999
Web Site: www.hoeggercommunications.com

Agency Specializes In: Advertising, Event Planning & Marketing, Internet/Web Design, Logo & Package Design, Print, Radio, Social Media, T.V.

Jackie Hoegger *(Owner & Pres)*

Accounts:
Berend Bros
Four Stars Auto Ranch
Neighborhood Autos
Next Concept LLC

HOFF COMMUNICATIONS

23 S Lansdowne Ave, Lansdowne, PA 19050
Tel.: (610) 623-2091
Fax: (610) 623-2041
E-Mail: service@hoffcomm.com
Web Site: hoffcomm.com

Employees: 8
Year Founded: 1988

Agency Specializes In: Business-To-Business

Approx. Annual Billings: $1,000,000

Jennifer Hoff *(Founder & Pres)*

Accounts:
Celebration Theater
Landsdowne Professional Association

HOFFMAN AND PARTNERS

44 Adams St, Braintree, MA 02184
Tel.: (617) 354-8600
Fax: (781) 843-9799
Web Site: www.hoffmanandpartners.net

E-Mail for Key Personnel:
President: bob@hoffmanandpartners.net

Employees: 35
Year Founded: 2012

Agency Specializes In: Advertising, Brand Development & Integration, Broadcast, Business-To-Business, Cable T.V., Collateral, Consumer Goods, Consumer Marketing, Consumer Publications, Corporate Identity, Digital/Interactive, Direct Response Marketing, Direct-to-Consumer, E-Commerce, Email, Financial, Guerilla Marketing, Health Care Services, In-Store Advertising, Internet/Web Design, Local Marketing, Logo & Package Design, Luxury Products, Magazines, Market Research, Media Buying Services, Media Planning, Mobile Marketing, Newspaper, Newspapers & Magazines, Out-of-Home Media, Outdoor, Paid Searches, Planning & Consultation, Point of Purchase, Point of Sale, Print, Production, Production (Ad, Film, Broadcast), Production (Print), Promotions, Radio, Regional, Restaurant, Retail, Search Engine Optimization, Seniors' Market, Social Marketing/Nonprofit, Social Media, Strategic Planning/Research, T.V., Trade & Consumer Magazines, Travel & Tourism, Web (Banner Ads, Pop-ups, etc.), Women's Market

Approx. Annual Billings: $15,000,000

Breakdown of Gross Billings by Media: Collateral: 5%; Consulting: 10%; D.M.: 5%; E-Commerce: 10%; Internet Adv.: 10%; Newsp. & Mags.: 15%; Out-of-Home Media: 5%; Radio: 10%; T.V.: 30%

Bob Hoffman *(Pres, Creative Dir & Copywriter)*
Bill Drake *(Sr VP & Dir-Creative)*
Jennifer Reuss *(Sr VP & Dir-Media)*
Darcy Doyle *(VP & Dir-Creative)*
Scott Hodgdon *(Dir-Digital Design)*
Katie Alabiso *(Acct Supvr)*

Accounts:
Boston Interiors Furniture Retailer
Capital Growth Management CGM Mutual Funds
Fusion Worldwide International Electronics
MB Trading Online Trading Services
Scottrade; Saint Louis, MO Financial Services

HOFFMAN/LEWIS

(Name Changed to H&L Partners)

HOFFMANN PUBLISHING GROUP

(Formerly Niemczyk Hoffmann Group)
2921 Windmill Rd Ste 4, Reading, PA 19608
Tel.: (610) 685-0914
Fax: (610) 685-0916
Web Site: www.hoffmannpublishing.com

Employees: 15
Year Founded: 1990

Revenue: $2,000,000

Tracy Hoffmann *(Pres)*
Linda Hoffmann *(COO)*
Brad Hess *(Exec VP-Sls & Mktg)*
Karen Zach *(Sr VP-Reg Media Sls)*
Kay Shuey *(Dir-Reg Media Sls)*
Alicia Lee *(Acct Exec-Media)*
Mark Schelling *(Reg Acct Exec-Media)*

Accounts:
Benson Settlement Company
Eagleville Hospital; 2004

HOGARTH WORLDWIDE

230 Park Ave S 11th Fl, New York, NY 10003
Tel.: (646) 480-6444
Web Site: www.us.hogarthww.com

Employees: 300

National Agency Associations: 4A's

Agency Specializes In: Bilingual Market, Broadcast, Co-op Advertising, Integrated Marketing, International, Local Marketing, Magazines, Merchandising, Multimedia, Newspaper, Newspapers & Magazines, Outdoor, Point of Sale, Print, Production, Production (Print), T.V., Web (Banner Ads, Pop-ups, etc.)

Approx. Annual Billings: $90,000,000

Breakdown of Gross Billings by Media: Brdcst.: $30,000,000; Print: $30,000,000; Production: $30,000,000

Meritxell Guitart *(Pres-Hogarth Americas)*
Kristen Martini *(Client Svcs Dir)*
David Chant *(Dir-Ops-Canada)*
Kate Dohaney *(Dir-The Box)*

Accounts:
New-Emirates Airline

HOLBERG DESIGN, INC.

391 Greendale Rd, York, PA 17403
Tel.: (717) 843-4048
Fax: (717) 848-2163
E-Mail: info@holbergdesign.com
Web Site: www.holbergdesign.com

Agency Specializes In: Advertising, Brand Development & Integration, Internet/Web Design, Media Planning, Print, Strategic Planning/Research

Richard Holberg *(Pres)*
Vincent Reedy *(Dir-Creative)*
Michael Waltemeyer *(Dir-New Bus Dev)*

Accounts:
Reinsel Kuntz Lesher LLP

HOLLAND ADVERTISING:INTERACTIVE

8040 Hosbrook Rd, Cincinnati, OH 45236
Tel.: (877) 865-0977
Fax: (513) 721-1269
Web Site: www.HollandAdvertising.com

E-Mail for Key Personnel:
President: bholland@hollandroi.com

Employees: 10
Year Founded: 1937

National Agency Associations: AAF-AMA-DMA

Agency Specializes In: Advertising, Advertising Specialties, African-American Market, Brand Development & Integration, Broadcast, Business Publications, Business-To-Business, Cable T.V., Co-op Advertising, Collateral, Communications, Consulting, Consumer Goods, Consumer Marketing, Consumer Publications, Corporate Communications, Corporate Identity, Cosmetics, Customer Relationship Management, Digital/Interactive, Direct Response Marketing, Direct-to-Consumer, Electronic Media, Entertainment, Event Planning & Marketing, Financial, Government/Political, Graphic Design, Guerilla Marketing, Health Care Services, Hospitality, Identity Marketing, In-Store Advertising, Information Technology, Integrated Marketing, Internet/Web Design, Leisure, Luxury Products, Magazines, Market Research, Media Buying Services, Media Planning, Media Relations, Medical Products, Men's Market, Mobile Marketing, New Product Development, Newspaper, Newspapers & Magazines, Out-of-Home Media, Outdoor, Over-50 Market, Package Design, Pets , Pharmaceutical, Planning & Consultation, Podcasting, Point of Purchase, Print, Production (Print), Public Relations, RSS (Really Simple Syndication), Radio, Recruitment, Regional,

Restaurant, Retail, Sales Promotion, Search Engine Optimization, Seniors' Market, Social Marketing/Nonprofit, Social Media, Strategic Planning/Research, T.V., Trade & Consumer Magazines, Travel & Tourism, Urban Market, Viral/Buzz/Word of Mouth, Women's Market, Yellow Pages Advertising

Approx. Annual Billings: $10,000,000

Breakdown of Gross Billings by Media: Brdcst.: 35%; Consulting: 10%; D.M.: 10%; Internet Adv.: 30%; Print: 15%

Mark S. Holland *(Partner & Sr Strategist-Acct)*
Bryan Holland *(Partner)*
Lisa Nicholas *(VP & Dir-Media)*
Andy Hemmer *(Dir-PR)*
Lauren Bausano *(Mgr-Acctg)*
Justin Ellison *(Designer-Digital)*

Accounts:
ABS Business Products; Cincinnati, Columbus & Dayton, OH B2B; 1994
Advance Dentistry; Cincinnati, OH Dental Practice; 2010
Aquatic & Garden Decor; Cincinnati, OH; 1991
The Cincinnatian Hotel; Cincinnati, Ohio Hospitality; 2010
Esther Price Candy; Dayton, OH; 2010
Floturn; 1983
Mason Company Kennel Mfr; 1983
Mike-Sells Snack Foods; 2009
Mullaney's Home Health Care Medical, Pharmacy, Compounding; 1996
Procter & Gamble; 1963
The Rug Gallery; Cincinnati, OH; 1990
Towne Condominiums
Troyke Manufacturing; 1972
Widmer's Cleaners; 2003

HOLLAND MARK
727 Atlantic Ave, Boston, MA 02111
Tel.: (617) 247-1111
Web Site: www.holland-mark.com

Employees: 20

Agency Specializes In: Advertising, Brand Development & Integration, Broadcast, Digital/Interactive, Direct-to-Consumer

Approx. Annual Billings: $5,000,000

Rob Waldeck *(Pres)*
Chris Haff *(CTO)*
Renee Bolz *(VP & Dir-Client Svcs)*
Matt Gorlaski *(Assoc Dir-Art)*
Holly Monacelli *(Assoc Dir-Creative)*
Jim Magary *(Strategist-Media)*

Accounts:
Stonyfield Farms
Virgin Money USA
Zipcar

HOLLYWOOD BRANDED INC.
110 Lomita St, El Segundo, CA 90245
Tel.: (310) 606-2030
Fax: (310) 606-2063
E-Mail: info@hollywoodbranded.com
Web Site: www.hollywoodbranded.com

Employees: 12
Year Founded: 2007

Agency Specializes In: Above-the-Line, Advertising, Advertising Specialties, African-American Market, Asian Market, Below-the-Line, Bilingual Market, Brand Development & Integration, Branded Entertainment, Communications, Consulting, Consumer Goods, Consumer Marketing, Content, Corporate Communications, Corporate Identity, Cosmetics, Entertainment, Environmental, Fashion/Apparel, Game Integration, Gay & Lesbian Market, Hispanic Market, Identity Marketing, In-Store Advertising, Integrated Marketing, International, Leisure, Luxury Products, Magazines, Marine, Media Buying Services, Medical Products, Men's Market, Mobile Marketing, Multicultural, New Technologies, Over-50 Market, Pharmaceutical, Point of Purchase, Product Placement, Promotions, Public Relations, Publicity/Promotions, Publishing, Restaurant, Seniors' Market, Social Marketing/Nonprofit, Sponsorship, Strategic Planning/Research, Sweepstakes, Syndication, T.V., Teen Market, Transportation, Travel & Tourism, Urban Market, Viral/Buzz/Word of Mouth, Women's Market

Approx. Annual Billings: $3,000,000

Breakdown of Gross Billings by Media: Cable T.V.: 10%; Consulting: 15%; Corp. Communications: 15%; Game Shows: 5%; Network T.V.: 10%; Promos.: 10%; Strategic Planning/Research: 15%; Syndication: 10%; T.V.: 10%

Stacy Jones *(Founder & CEO)*
Michelle Hughes *(Mgr-Mktg Media)*

Accounts:
BlackBerry Blackberry; 2007
Coffee Beanery; 2011
FLIR Extech, FLIR, Lorex Technology, Raymarine; 2014
Mezzetta; 2014
PassionRoses PassionRoses, Passion Growers; 2010

HOLLYWOOD BRANDING INTERNATIONAL
2616 Indiana Avenue Rear, Saint Louis, MO 63118
Tel.: (917) 596-9040
Fax: (206) 350-4375
E-Mail: hollywoodbranding@gmail.com
Web Site: www.hollywoodbranding.com

Employees: 12
Year Founded: 2001

Agency Specializes In: Advertising, Alternative Advertising, Automotive, Brand Development & Integration, Branded Entertainment, Digital/Interactive, Direct-to-Consumer, Electronic Media, Entertainment, Event Planning & Marketing, Experience Design, Game Integration, Government/Political, International, Market Research, Media Buying Services, Media Planning, Mobile Marketing, New Technologies, Out-of-Home Media, Outdoor, Point of Purchase, Point of Sale, Publicity/Promotions, Sales Promotion, Social Marketing/Nonprofit, Social Media, Sponsorship, Teen Market, Tween Market, Viral/Buzz/Word of Mouth

Approx. Annual Billings: $2,000,000

Breakdown of Gross Billings by Media: Out-of-Home Media: $2,000,000

Beverly Nation *(Pres)*

HOLMES MILLET ADVERTISING
4161 McKinney Ave Ste 200, Dallas, TX 75204
Tel.: (214) 526-4885
Fax: (214) 526-4887
E-Mail: info@holmesmillet.com
Web Site: www.holmesmillet.com

Agency Specializes In: Advertising, Brand Development & Integration, Collateral, Digital/Interactive, Graphic Design, Internet/Web Design, Package Design, Print, Radio, T.V.

Jeffrey W. Millet *(Partner)*
David G. Holmes *(Mng Dir-Bus Dev & Acct Svcs)*
Tom Miller *(Mng Dir-Concept, Design & Production Svcs)*
Brittany Johnson *(Dir-Art)*

Accounts:
Curry Printing Inc.
Guida, Slavich & Flores, P.C.
Hermes Sargent Bates, L.L.P.
Inter-American Corporation Helium
Markland Hanley
The Melrose Hotel
Vidar Systems Corporation
Winstead Sechrest & Minick Pc

HOLSTED MARKETING, INC.
135 Madison Ave, New York, NY 10016
Tel.: (212) 686-8537
Fax: (212) 481-0415
E-Mail: preulbach@holstedmarketing.com
Web Site: www.holstedmarketing.com

Employees: 46
Year Founded: 1971

Agency Specializes In: Direct Response Marketing, Merchandising, Sales Promotion

Carolyn Kraft *(Sr VP-Mktg & Adv)*
Roy Rathbun *(Sr VP-Fin)*
Paul Reulbach *(Sr VP-Partnership Mktg Dev)*
Coleen Boyle *(VP-Product Dev)*
Jim Malloy *(VP-Mktg)*
John Cesaro *(Controller)*
John Zhang *(Dir-Ops)*

Accounts:
Exxon
Fingerhut
Otto
Redcats
Sears
Texaco

HOLT CREATIVE GROUP
5307 E Mockingbird Ln 5th Fl, Dallas, TX 75206
Tel.: (214) 826-9802
Toll Free: (888) 707-0447
Web Site: www.holtcreativegroup.com

Agency Specializes In: Advertising, Brand Development & Integration, Digital/Interactive, Internet/Web Design, Logo & Package Design, Social Media

Edwin Holt *(CEO)*
John O'Dell *(VP & Sr Strategist-Mktg)*
Cyndi Behrend *(Sr Dir-Art)*
Erin Porterfield *(Sr Dir-Creative)*
Jennifer Burk *(Dir-Media)*
Lacy Judd *(Strategist-SEO & Social Media)*
Reagan Judd *(Acct Strategist-Digital)*

Accounts:
Dallas Symphony Orchestra

HOLTON SENTIVAN AND GURY
7 E Skippack Pike, Ambler, PA 19002
Tel.: (215) 619-7600
Fax: (215) 619-7621
E-Mail: jholton@hsgadv.com
Web Site: www.hsgadv.com

Employees: 22
Year Founded: 1983

National Agency Associations: ADC

Agency Specializes In: Advertising, Alternative Advertising, Automotive, Below-the-Line, Broadcast, Business-To-Business, Cable T.V., Co-op Advertising, Consulting, Consumer Marketing, Consumer Publications, Corporate Identity, Direct Response Marketing, E-Commerce, Education, Electronics, Email, Exhibit/Trade Shows, Fashion/Apparel, Graphic Design, Health Care Services, High Technology, Hospitality, Household Goods, Identity Marketing, In-Store Advertising, Industrial, Integrated Marketing, Internet/Web Design, Leisure, Logo & Package Design, Luxury Products, Men's Market, Mobile Marketing, Multimedia, Newspaper, Out-of-Home Media, Outdoor, Over-50 Market, Planning & Consultation, Point of Purchase, Point of Sale, Print, Production, Production (Ad, Film, Broadcast), Production (Print), Promotions, RSS (Really Simple Syndication), Radio, Real Estate, Retail, Sales Promotion, Seniors' Market, Social Marketing/Nonprofit, Social Media, Strategic Planning/Research, Sweepstakes, T.V., Teen Market, Trade & Consumer Magazines, Transportation, Travel & Tourism, Web (Banner Ads, Pop-ups, etc.)

Approx. Annual Billings: $24,500,000

Breakdown of Gross Billings by Media: D.M.: $6,500,000; E-Commerce: $3,000,000; Mags.: $3,400,000; Newsp.: $3,600,000; Radio: $1,400,000; T.V.: $3,600,000; Worldwide Web Sites: $3,000,000

Jack Holton *(CEO)*
Glenn Gury *(Dir-Creative)*
Drew Sentivan *(Dir-Art & Interactive)*
Bob Peischel *(Assoc Dir-Creative-Copy)*

Accounts:
Adams County National Bank
Clean Earth
Cutting Crew
Deloitte Interactive
Kreischer Miller
Main Line Health; Radnor, PA Interactive, Multi-Media
The National Constitution Center; Philadelphia, PA Interactive
Right Management; Philadelphia, PA
Rosenberg & Parker; King of Prussia, Pa Surety Bond Brokers

HOLYSTONE STUDIOS
12417 Ocean Gateway Bldg B11 Ste 116, Ocean City, MD 21842
Tel.: (443) 924-6350
E-Mail: inquiry@holystonestudios.com
Web Site: www.holystonestudios.com

Year Founded: 2009

Agency Specializes In: Advertising, Email, Graphic Design, Internet/Web Design, Logo & Package Design, Print, Search Engine Optimization, Social Media

Colin Campbell *(Partner & Principal)*

Accounts:
Jeffrey L Premo PA
Videre Consulting
Wags to Riches Pet Grooming

THE HONEY AGENCY
1050 20th St Ste 220, Sacramento, CA 95811
Tel.: (916) 444-0203
E-Mail: buzz@honeyagency.com
Web Site: www.honeyagency.com

Year Founded: 2008

Agency Specializes In: Advertising, Brand Development & Integration, Internet/Web Design, Search Engine Optimization, Social Media

Rachael Lankford *(Acct Dir)*

Accounts:
New-Farm to Fork Capital of America

HOOAH LLC.
807 S Orlando Ave Ste P, Winter Park, FL 32789
Tel.: (407) 362-7715
Web Site: www.hooah.cc

Year Founded: 2003

Agency Specializes In: Advertising, Digital/Interactive, Media Buying Services, Public Relations, Social Media

Jorge Suria *(Pres & Dir-Creative)*
Tanya Zeiher *(VP)*
Ricardo Ortiz *(Dir-Production)*

Accounts:
Department of Defense
Orlando Utilities Commission

HOOK
522 King St, Charleston, SC 29403
Tel.: (843) 853-5532
E-Mail: info@hookusa.com
Web Site: hookworldwide.com

Year Founded: 2005

Agency Specializes In: Advertising, Broadcast, Collateral, Logo & Package Design, Outdoor, Print

Brady Waggoner *(Owner)*
Tom Jeffrey *(Partner & Dir-Creative)*
Phil Waggoner *(Partner)*
Suzie Barrow *(Acct Dir)*
Trish Ward *(Dir-Art)*
Jennifer Waggoner *(Media Buyer)*

Accounts:
Charleston Mix
PeopleMatterHR
Studio Strut
Titin Tech

HOOKLEAD
(Formerly Diadem Agency)
2120 Noisette Blvd Ste 120, Charleston, SC 29405
Tel.: (740) 500-4665
E-Mail: contact@hooklead.com
Web Site: www.hooklead.com/

Year Founded: 2009

Agency Specializes In: Advertising, Brand Development & Integration, Internet/Web Design, Media Planning, Print, Social Media

Allen Bayless *(Principal)*

Accounts:
East Bay Deli

HOOPLA MARKETING & PUBLIC RELATIONS
2011 Walnut St, Philadelphia, PA 19103
Tel.: (215) 964-9943
E-Mail: info@hooplaphilly.com
Web Site: www.hooplaphilly.com

Year Founded: 2010

Melissa Kennedy *(Partner)*
Amanda Wozniak *(Partner)*

Accounts:
New Balance of Philadelphia

HOPE-BECKHAM, INC.
17 Executive Park Dr Ste 600, Atlanta, GA 30329
Tel.: (404) 636-8200
Fax: (404) 636-0530
Web Site: www.hopebeckham.com

Employees: 20
Year Founded: 1994

Agency Specializes In: Business-To-Business, Communications, Entertainment, Exhibit/Trade Shows, Government/Political, Hospitality, Investor Relations, Local Marketing, Mobile Marketing, Public Relations, Sponsorship, Sports Market

Paul D. Beckham *(Co-Founder & Chm)*
Bob Hope *(Co-Owner & Pres)*
Jennifer Jones-Mitchell *(Mng Dir & Exec VP)*
Ann Nelson *(VP-Fin & Admin)*
Allison Ritter *(VP)*
Jaime Griffon *(Dir-Bus Dev)*
Andrew Thompson *(Acct Exec)*

Accounts:
Arris, Inc.
Atlanta Sports Council
Atlanta Track Club
Belk Department Stores
Collegiate Licensing Company
Georgia Education Articulation Committee
The TOUR Championship

THE HORAH GROUP
351 Manville Rd #105, Pleasantville, NY 10570
Tel.: (914) 495-3200
Fax: (914) 769-8802
E-Mail: dgoldsmith@horah.com
Web Site: www.horah.com

E-Mail for Key Personnel:
Chairman: dick@horah.com

Employees: 2
Year Founded: 1982

National Agency Associations: DMA

Agency Specializes In: Business Publications, Business-To-Business, Cable T.V., Catalogs, Co-op Advertising, Collateral, Communications, Consumer Marketing, Consumer Publications, Customer Relationship Management, Direct Response Marketing, Direct-to-Consumer, Education, Entertainment, Financial, Graphic Design, Health Care Services, Internet/Web Design, Mobile Marketing, Newspapers & Magazines, Out-of-Home Media, Point of Sale, Print, Production, Radio, Strategic Planning/Research, T.V., Telemarketing

Approx. Annual Billings: $1,000,000

Breakdown of Gross Billings by Media: D.M.: $1,000,000

Dick Goldsmith *(Chm)*

Accounts:
American Diabetes Foundation
Consumers Union
Kids Discover Magazine
Quadrant HealthCom

HORICH HECTOR LEBOW
101 Schilling Rd Ste 30, Hunt Valley, MD 21031
Tel.: (410) 823-5020
Fax: (410) 329-1210

Toll Free: (800) 878-8989
E-Mail: jparks@hpladv.com
Web Site: www.hpladv.com

Employees: 35
Year Founded: 1989

Agency Specializes In: Advertising, Cable T.V., Consumer Marketing, Household Goods, Newspaper, Planning & Consultation, Radio, Retail, T.V.

Approx. Annual Billings: $25,000,000

Chip Hector *(Partner & COO)*
David Weinstein *(Partner & Sr VP)*
Miles Anderson *(Creative Dir)*
Kristin Hollis *(Mgr-Production)*
Liz Healey *(Supvr-Media)*
Ashley Downes *(Planner-Digital Media)*
Ana Dietz *(Coord-Traffic)*
Kris Fauntleroy *(Coord-Production)*

Accounts:
Becker Furniture
Benchcraft Furniture
Darvin Furniture
Flexsteel Industries
Goldsteins Furniture
John V. Schultz Furniture
Morris Home Furnishings
Pilgrim Furniture City
Powell's Furniture
Superstore Furniture
Vermont Furniture Galleries
Walker Furniture
Wolf Furniture

HORIZON MARKETING GROUP, INC.
1197 Neipsic Rd, Glastonbury, CT 06033
Mailing Address:
PO Box 1468, Glastonbury, CT 06033
Tel.: (727) 525-0034
Web Site: www.hmgcompany.com

Employees: 55
Year Founded: 1998

Agency Specializes In: Advertising, Brand Development & Integration, Corporate Communications, Corporate Identity, Email, Internet/Web Design, Media Buying Services, Multicultural, Planning & Consultation, Public Relations, Social Media, Web (Banner Ads, Pop-ups, etc.)

Bob Watson *(Owner & CEO)*
Bill Harper *(Owner)*
Michele Grimes *(Pres)*
Brian Grimes *(CFO)*
Monica Kozak *(Chief Strategy Officer)*
Jordan Falcone *(VP-Ops)*

Accounts:
Boeing
Carter's
Chico's
Imagination at Work
Joe Boxer
Liberty
Logitech
Rimmel
The Scooter Store
Wrigley

HORN GROUP INC.
612 Howard St Ste 100, San Francisco, CA 94105
Tel.: (415) 905-4000
Fax: (415) 905-4001
E-Mail: info@horngroup.com
Web Site: www.horngroup.com

Employees: 52
Year Founded: 1991

National Agency Associations: COPF

Agency Specializes In: Business-To-Business, Digital/Interactive, Graphic Design, High Technology, Integrated Marketing, Media Relations, Media Training, Public Relations

Approx. Annual Billings: $9,000,000

Sabrina Horn *(Founder, Pres & CEO)*
Debra Raine *(Partner)*
Brian Sinderson *(Sr Mng Dir & Gen Mgr)*
Bryan Adams *(VP-Ops)*
Vicky Paar *(Controller)*
Gustavo Llamas *(Dir-HR)*
Samantha Kops *(Acct Supvr)*
Toni Leigh *(Sr Acct Exec)*
Jack Ortner *(Acct Exec)*
Jonelle Taylor *(Acct Exec)*

Accounts:
Absolute Software Interactive Marketing, PR, Social Media
Bay Alarm Medical Consumer Communications
BitDefender
NorseCorp
StrongMail PR
TigerLogic Corporation Media Relations, Messaging, Postano (Digital Communications Agency of Record)
Validity
Whiptail Analyst Relations, Media, PR
WhiteFence (Agency of Record)
WhiteHat Security

Branch

Horn Group
55 Broad St Fl 29, New York, NY 10004
Tel.: (646) 202-9750
Fax: (646) 826-0022
E-Mail: info@horngroup.com
Web Site: www.horngroup.com

Employees: 17

Sabrina Horn *(Pres & CEO)*
Brian Sinderson *(Sr Mng Dir & Gen Mgr)*
Seth Rosenstein *(VP-Fin & Controller)*
Erica Mcdonald *(VP)*
Allyne Mills *(VP)*
Eric Kim *(Dir-Creative)*
Elliot Schimel *(Dir)*

Accounts:
AppSense
CT Corporation Content Creation, Public Relations
DataCore Brand Awareness, Media Relations, Strategic Counsel
Forbes Media PR
ORC International Brand Identity, Brand Positioning, Digital Communications, Website

HORN GROUP INC.
(Acquired by Finn Partners)

HORNALL ANDERSON
710 2nd Ave Ste 1300, Seattle, WA 98104-1712
Tel.: (206) 467-5800
Fax: (206) 467-6411
E-Mail: us@hornallanderson.com
Web Site: www.hornallanderson.com/

Employees: 125
Year Founded: 1982

Agency Specializes In: Affluent Market, Automotive, Aviation & Aerospace, Brand Development & Integration, Branded Entertainment, Business Publications, Business-To-Business, Catalogs, Collateral, Communications, Computers & Software, Consulting, Consumer Goods, Consumer Marketing, Content, Corporate Identity, Cosmetics, Customer Relationship Management, Digital/Interactive, Direct-to-Consumer, E-Commerce, Education, Electronic Media, Electronics, Engineering, Environmental, Exhibit/Trade Shows, Experience Design, Fashion/Apparel, Financial, Food Service, Game Integration, Graphic Design, Health Care Services, High Technology, Hospitality, Household Goods, Identity Marketing, In-Store Advertising, Information Technology, Integrated Marketing, International, Internet/Web Design, Leisure, Logo & Package Design, Luxury Products, Marine, Market Research, Medical Products, Men's Market, Mobile Marketing, New Technologies, Package Design, Pets , Pharmaceutical, Point of Purchase, Point of Sale, Print, Production (Print), Real Estate, Regional, Retail, Shopper Marketing, Sponsorship, Sports Market, Transportation, Travel & Tourism, Web (Banner Ads, Pop-ups, etc.), Women's Market

Jack Anderson *(Founder & Chm)*
John Anicker *(Pres & CEO)*
Michael Connors *(VP-Design)*
Erin Crosier *(VP-Client Dev)*
Maureen Estep *(VP-Client Svcs)*
Ricki Pasinelli *(Grp Acct Dir)*
Laura Masters *(Acct Dir)*
April Melchiode *(Acct Dir)*
Annette Wilder *(Acct Dir)*
Nory Emori *(Dir & Strategist)*
Michael Ausich *(Dir-Design)*
Mark Buchalter *(Dir-Innovation & Design Strategy)*
Heidi Durham *(Dir-Strategy)*
Jay Hilburn *(Dir-Design)*
Jennifer Jacobson *(Dir-HR)*
Marcy Kelley *(Dir-Resource Mgmt)*
Jen Orth *(Dir-Creative)*
Carly Schlenker *(Acct Mgr)*
Laura Running *(Mgr-Client Dev)*
Mandy Robertson *(Acct Supvr)*
Christina Arbini *(Supvr-PR)*
Euan Fraser *(Strategist-Innovation)*
Maxwell Churchill *(Designer)*
Jon Graeff *(Sr Designer)*

Accounts:
Airbus
Amazon
ASDA
Ciena
CitationShares
Clearwire
Empire State Building
Eos
Garlic Jim's
Hewlett-Packard
Holland America Line
L'Oreal
Lovin' Scoopful
Madison Square Garden
Marmite Campaign: "Ma'amite"
Microsoft
OMD
PepsiCo
Redhook Brewery Campaign: "Packaging"
Riverplace
Space Needle
Starbucks Campaign: "Evolution Fresh Brand Experience", Campaign: "Starbucks Via Extension"
T-Mobile US Sidekick
Tommy Bahama
Unilever
University of Washington National Branding
Virgin Atlantic
Weyerhaeuser
Widmer Brothers; Portland, OR SnowPlow Winter Beer

HORNERCOM
(Formerly Jack Horner Communications)
474 Main St, Harleysville, PA 19438
Tel.: (267) 932-8760
Fax: (267) 932-8759
E-Mail: info@hornercom.com
Web Site: www.hornercom.com

Employees: 22
Year Founded: 1992

Agency Specializes In: Collateral, Communications, Corporate Identity, Direct Response Marketing, Event Planning & Marketing, Exhibit/Trade Shows, Graphic Design, Internet/Web Design, Magazines, Media Buying Services, Planning & Consultation, Public Relations, Publicity/Promotions, Retail, T.V.

Jack Horner *(Pres)*
Meg Horner *(CEO)*
Alana Suko *(Exec Dir)*
Kari Gill *(Mgr-Promotional Products Sls)*
Jeff Shurilla *(Acct Supvr)*
Emily Watts *(Acct Supvr)*
Bria Annie *(Acct Coord)*
Rachel Jakubowitcz *(Acct Coord)*
Richard Page *(Graphic Artist)*

Accounts:
American Liver Foundation
Applebee's
Blumling & Glusky Legal Services
Burn Foundation
Corrado & Sons, Inc
Courier Times
Dollar Bank
Ductmate Industries, Inc.
ESPN
Feld Entertainment
GlaxoSmithKline
Hard Rock Pittsburgh
Hunter Truck Sales & Service, Inc.; Butler, PA
Iolta
Jefferson School of Pharmacy
The Mario Lemieux Foundation
The Pace School; Churchill, PA
PNC

HORNSBY BRAND DESIGN
PO Box 51204, Knoxville, TN 37950
Tel.: (865) 660-7261
Fax: (865) 690-7265
E-Mail: info@hornsbybrandesign.com
Web Site: www.hornsbybrandesign.com

Year Founded: 2003

Agency Specializes In: Advertising, Brand Development & Integration, Internet/Web Design, Logo & Package Design

Chris Hornsby *(Pres)*
Bridget Hornsby *(CEO & Principal)*

Accounts:
Finish Point
Knoxville Area Transit
Memphis Urban Area MPO

HOSPITALITY-MARKETING LLC
200 S Andrews Ave Ste 503, Fort Lauderdale, FL 33301
Tel.: (954) 213-6666
Fax: (954) 213-6677
E-Mail: info@h-mllc.com
Web Site: www.h-mllc.com

Agency Specializes In: Advertising, Public Relations, Social Media

David Rojas *(Creative Dir)*

Accounts:
New-Boca Raton Resort & Club
New-Casa Marina
New-El Conquistador Resort
New-The London NYC

HOT DISH ADVERTISING
800 Washington Ave N Ste 200, Minneapolis, MN 55401
Tel.: (612) 341-3100
Fax: (612) 341-0555
E-Mail: glindberg@hotdishad.com
Web Site: www.hotdishad.com

Employees: 15
Year Founded: 1999

Agency Specializes In: Advertising, Automotive, Brand Development & Integration, Broadcast, Business Publications, Business-To-Business, Cable T.V., Co-op Advertising, Collateral, Consulting, Consumer Goods, Consumer Marketing, Consumer Publications, Direct-to-Consumer, Identity Marketing, In-Store Advertising, Integrated Marketing, Internet/Web Design, Local Marketing, Logo & Package Design, Magazines, Media Buying Services, Media Planning, Merchandising, Newspaper, Newspapers & Magazines, Out-of-Home Media, Outdoor, Package Design, Planning & Consultation, Point of Purchase, Point of Sale, Print, Production (Print), Promotions, Radio, Regional, Retail, Sales Promotion, Strategic Planning/Research, T.V., Trade & Consumer Magazines

Approx. Annual Billings: $6,300,000 Capitalized

Breakdown of Gross Billings by Media: Adv. Specialities: $76,000; Cable T.V.: $155,000; Co-op Adv.: $885,000; Comml. Photography: $171,000; D.M.: $165,000; Fees: $510,000; Graphic Design: $223,000; In-Store Adv.: $32,000; Internet Adv.: $263,000; Logo & Package Design: $60,000; Mags.: $1,750,000; Network T.V.: $205,000; Newsp.: $315,000; Outdoor: $175,000; Plng. & Consultation: $210,000; Print: $215,000; Production: $485,000; Radio: $135,000; Strategic Planning/Research: $155,000; Worldwide Web Sites: $115,000

Greg Lindberg *(Owner & CFO)*
Dawn Kane *(Pres)*
Jennifer Campbell *(VP & Acct Dir)*
Ruth Harvey *(VP & Dir-Creative)*
Pete Bakanowski *(Sr Dir-Art)*
Brian George *(Dir-Art)*
Jen Barton *(Acct Supvr)*
Hilary Chang *(Acct Exec)*
Megan Reed *(Acct Exec)*
Emilee Sirek *(Acct Exec)*
Kaylee Brist *(Acct Coord)*

Accounts:
Budget Blinds; Orange County, CA Window Treatments
Edible Arrangements; CT Fresh Fruit Bouquets
Fruitation; CT Fresh Fruit Smoothies
Lawn Doctor; NJ Lawn Services
Menchie's; California Frozen Yogurt
Novus; Minnesota Automotive Glass Repair
Primrose Schools; Georgia Schools

HOT TOMALI COMMUNICATIONS INC
1441 E Pender St, Vancouver, BC V5L 1V7 Canada
Tel.: (604) 893-8347
Fax: (604) 893-8346
E-Mail: info@hottomali.com
Web Site: www.hottomali.com

Year Founded: 1998

Agency Specializes In: Brand Development & Integration, Broadcast, Corporate Identity, Digital/Interactive, Graphic Design, Internet/Web Design, Media Buying Services, Mobile Marketing, Search Engine Optimization

Thomas Stringham *(Pres & Dir-Creative)*
Davinder Deo *(Dir-Art & Designer)*
Kate Alvarenga *(Acct Mgr)*
Alice Openysheva *(Office Mgr)*

Accounts:
7-Eleven Canada Slurpee Frozen Drinks
New-AmericanEHR
CanadianEMR Healthcare Services Provider
Chop Shop Hair Designing Services
City of Vancouver Campaign: "Pedestrian"
Fairmont Hot Springs Resort
PacBlue Printing Printing Services
Silver Star Mountain Resort

HOUSER & HENNESSEE
6000 Dixie Hwy, Bridgeport, MI 48722
Tel.: (989) 921-1172
Fax: (989) 921-1175
Toll Free: (800) 878-1172
Web Site: www.houserhennessee.com

Cliff Houser *(Owner)*
Larry Hennessee *(CEO)*
Kim Gouin *(VP)*
Mike Grocholski *(Dir-Art)*
Kyle Arnett *(Mgr-Signage)*
Mel Justice *(Media Buyer)*

Accounts:
Koegel Meats
Little Caesar's

HOWARD M. SCHWARTZ & ASSOCIATES, INC.
One Marketing Ctr 19020 Emerald Dr, Brookfield, WI 53045
Tel.: (262) 879-0165
Fax: (262) 879-1132
E-Mail: hms@execpc.com

Employees: 25
Year Founded: 1964

Agency Specializes In: Advertising, Advertising Specialties, Broadcast, Business-To-Business, Cable T.V., Co-op Advertising, Collateral, Communications, Consulting, Consumer Marketing, Exhibit/Trade Shows, Faith Based, Graphic Design, Local Marketing, Newspapers & Magazines, Over-50 Market, Point of Purchase, Point of Sale, Print, Production, Public Relations, Publicity/Promotions, Sales Promotion

Approx. Annual Billings: $26,530,000

Breakdown of Gross Billings by Media: Bus. Publs.: $6,000,000; D.M.: $11,000,000; Mags.: $680,000; Newsp.: $3,000,000; Pub. Rels.: $1,500,000; Radio: $350,000; T.V.: $4,000,000

Howard M. Schwartz *(CEO)*

Accounts:
Abington Friends School; Abington, PA; 1980
Center for the Blind; New York, NY
Council for Advancement & Support of Education; Washington, DC; 1985
Engle Associates, Inc.; Jenkintown, PA Marketing Managers; 1980
Institute for Communications Research & Planning; Philadelphia, PA
Kraft Publishing Co.; Philadelphia, PA; 1980

Philadelphia College of Art; Philadelphia, PA
Philadelphia Geriatric Center; Philadelphia, PA
Philadelphia Hearing Society; Philadelphia, PA
Shulman Air Freight; Philadelphia, PA

HOWARD, MERRELL & PARTNERS, INC.

4800 Falls of Neuse Rd, Raleigh, NC 27609
Tel.: (919) 848-2400
Fax: (919) 845-9845
E-Mail: sstyons@merrellgroup.com
Web Site: www.howardmerrell.com/

E-Mail for Key Personnel:
Media Dir.: dmercer@merrellgroup.com
Production Mgr.: SDunford@merrellgroup.com
Public Relations: mganey@merrellgroup.com

Employees: 45
Year Founded: 1976

National Agency Associations: ARF-DMA

Agency Specializes In: Above-the-Line, Advertising, Advertising Specialties, Affiliate Marketing, Affluent Market, Agriculture, Alternative Advertising, Arts, Asian Market, Automotive, Aviation & Aerospace, Below-the-Line, Bilingual Market, Brand Development & Integration, Branded Entertainment, Broadcast, Business Publications, Business-To-Business, Cable T.V., Catalogs, Children's Market, Co-op Advertising, Collateral, College, Commercial Photography, Communications, Computers & Software, Consulting, Consumer Goods, Consumer Marketing, Consumer Publications, Content, Corporate Communications, Corporate Identity, Cosmetics, Crisis Communications, Custom Publishing, Customer Relationship Management, Digital/Interactive, Direct Response Marketing, Direct-to-Consumer, E-Commerce, Education, Electronic Media, Electronics, Email, Engineering, Entertainment, Environmental, Event Planning & Marketing, Exhibit/Trade Shows, Experience Design, Fashion/Apparel, Financial, Food Service, Health Care Services, High Technology, Hispanic Market, Hospitality, Household Goods, Identity Marketing, In-Store Advertising, Industrial, Infomercials, Information Technology, Integrated Marketing, International, Internet/Web Design, Investor Relations, Legal Services, Leisure, Local Marketing, Logo & Package Design, Luxury Products, Magazines, Marine, Market Research, Media Buying Services, Media Planning, Media Relations, Media Training, Medical Products, Men's Market, Merchandising, Mobile Marketing, Multicultural, Multimedia, New Product Development, New Technologies, Newspaper, Newspapers & Magazines, Out-of-Home Media, Outdoor, Over-50 Market, Package Design, Paid Searches, Pharmaceutical, Planning & Consultation, Podcasting, Point of Purchase, Point of Sale, Print, Product Placement, Production, Production (Ad, Film, Broadcast), Production (Print), Promotions, Public Relations, Publicity/Promotions, Publishing, RSS (Really Simple Syndication), Radio, Real Estate, Recruitment, Regional, Restaurant, Retail, Sales Promotion, Search Engine Optimization, Seniors' Market, Social Marketing/Nonprofit, South Asian Market, Sponsorship, Sports Market, Stakeholders, Strategic Planning/Research, Sweepstakes, Syndication, T.V., Technical Advertising, Teen Market, Telemarketing, Trade & Consumer Magazines, Transportation, Travel & Tourism, Web (Banner Ads, Pop-ups, etc.)

Breakdown of Gross Billings by Media: Bus. Publs.: 15%; Collateral: 2%; Consulting: 10%; D.M.: 3%; Mags.: 22%; Newsp.: 5%; Other: 1%; Outdoor: 2%; Radio: 5%; T.V.: 35%

Jim Cobb *(Pres & CEO)*
Billy Barnes *(Dir-Creative)*
Ellen Wayland *(Dir-Media)*
Laura Gross *(Mgr-Event Svcs-PR)*
Denise Lingenfelser *(Mgr-Studio)*
Cindy Honickman *(Sr Acct Exec)*
Anastasia Ellis *(Acct Exec)*
Andria Rosell *(Mng Supvr & Strategist-Social)*
Julie Orsini *(Assoc Acct Exec)*
Joseph Williams *(Acct Coord)*

Accounts:
Aquatic Life
Atlantic South Power
BASF NutriDense
BioResource International
Cisco
Cordura Durability Experience Module
Dixie
El Pueblo
enMotion
Eschelon Experiences (Agency of Record) Event Planning, Marketing, Press, Social Media
Georgia-Pacific Professional Food Services Solutions (Agency of Record)
Happy Jack Inc (Agency of Record) Integrated Brand Communications, Market Research, Media Planning, Website Design
Invacare
INVISTA Cordura; 2007
KIOTI Tractor Integrated Communications, Interactive, Media Planning & Buying, PR
O2 Fitness; Raleigh, NC; 2008
Oliver Twist; Raleigh, NC; 2008
Precise Pet Products (Agency of Record)
New-Premiere Communications & Consulting (Agency of Record)
The Produce Box (Agency of Record) Content Marketing, Public Relations, Social Media, Strategic Marketing
Sappi
Step2 Holdings Company, LLC Brand Management, Creative, Event Planning, Marketing, Public Relations, Social Media

HOWARD MILLER ASSOCIATES, INC.

20A E Roseville Rd, Lancaster, PA 17601
Tel.: (717) 581-1919
Fax: (717) 581-1972
E-Mail: drew@hmab2b.com
Web Site: www.globalhma.com

Employees: 10
Year Founded: 1979

National Agency Associations: 4A's

Agency Specializes In: Advertising, Brand Development & Integration, Broadcast, Business Publications, Business-To-Business, Catalogs, Collateral, Communications, Consulting, Content, Corporate Identity, Digital/Interactive, Email, Environmental, Event Planning & Marketing, Health Care Services, Industrial, Information Technology, Integrated Marketing, Internet/Web Design, Magazines, Media Relations, Multimedia, Planning & Consultation, Print, Production (Ad, Film, Broadcast), Production (Print), Public Relations, Search Engine Optimization, Social Media, Strategic Planning/Research, Technical Advertising, Trade & Consumer Magazines

Approx. Annual Billings: $3,000,000

Drew Dorgan *(Owner)*
Erin Lebo *(Strategist-Creative)*
Mandy Thudium *(Acct Exec)*
Jamie Wilson *(Acct Exec)*
Jason Getz *(Designer-Interactive)*
Sean Heisey *(Designer-Video & Interactive)*

Accounts:
Trent, Inc.; Philadelphia, PA

HOWELL, LIBERATORE & ASSOCIATES, INC.

(Formerly Howell, Liberatore & Wickham, Inc.)
50 Pennsylvania Ave, Elmira, NY 14902
Tel.: (607) 733-5666
Fax: (607) 734-5233
E-Mail: service@HLAmarketing.com
Web Site: www.hlamarketing.com

E-Mail for Key Personnel:
President: esmith@hlamarketing.com

Employees: 7
Year Founded: 1942

National Agency Associations: ABC-Second Wind Limited

Agency Specializes In: Brand Development & Integration, Business-To-Business, Collateral, Communications, Consulting, Corporate Identity, Direct Response Marketing, Education, Electronic Media, Entertainment, Event Planning & Marketing, Exhibit/Trade Shows, Financial, Graphic Design, Health Care Services, Industrial, Internet/Web Design, Logo & Package Design, Magazines, Media Buying Services, Medical Products, Multimedia, Newspaper, Newspapers & Magazines, Outdoor, Planning & Consultation, Point of Purchase, Print, Public Relations, Publicity/Promotions, Radio, Strategic Planning/Research, T.V., Travel & Tourism

Approx. Annual Billings: $1,500,000

Eiron Smith *(Pres)*
Brett Powell *(Dir-Client Svcs & Bus Dev)*
Donna Wujastyk *(Office Mgr)*
Shelby Button *(Acct Strategist)*

Accounts:
Edger Enterprises Website
Elmira Savings Bank
Fagan Engineers & Land Surveyors, P.C Website
Great-Circle Technologies
Watkins Glen International
Welliver

HOWERTON+WHITE

520 E Douglas, Wichita, KS 67202
Tel.: (316) 262-6644
E-Mail: info@howertonwhite.com
Web Site: www.howertonwhite.com

Year Founded: 2002

Agency Specializes In: Advertising, Market Research, Media Relations, Public Relations, Strategic Planning/Research

Nicole Howerton *(Principal & Creative Dir)*
Ken White *(Principal & Dir-Interactive)*
Craig Tomson *(Sr Dir-Art)*
Bryan Malone *(Creative Dir & Dir-Brdcst)*
Josh Becker *(Dir-Art)*
Dustin Commer *(Dir-Art)*
Doug Minson *(Acct Exec & Brand Mgr)*
Melody Mynatt *(Acct Exec)*
Sharon Bullard *(Acct Coord)*

Accounts:
Ambassador Hotel Collection Advertising Agency of Record
First National Bank of Hutchinson
Wichita Collegiate School

HOWLANDMOSER

3220 W Cavedale Dr, Phoenix, AZ 85083
Tel.: (602) 282-8081
Toll Free: (888) 382-4807
E-Mail: info@howlandmoser.com
Web Site: www.howlandmoser.com

Year Founded: 2010

Agency Specializes In: Advertising, Brand Development & Integration, Collateral, Content, Digital/Interactive, Media Planning, Print, Public Relations, Social Media, Strategic Planning/Research

Brandon Moser *(Co-Pres & CEO)*
Chris Howland *(Co-Pres & Chief Creative Officer)*
Shay Moser *(Exec VP-Comm & Digital Strategy)*
Georgette McNally *(Sr VP-Ops)*

Accounts:
Continuance Health Solutions

HR ADWORKS LTD.
(Formerly Corporate Human Resource Communications Ltd.)
280 Smith Street Main Floor, Winnipeg, MB R3C 1K2 Canada
Tel.: (204) 943-3312
Fax: (204) 943-6192
Toll Free: (877) 943-3312
E-Mail: llicharson@hradworks.ca
Web Site: www.hradworks.ca

Employees: 14
Year Founded: 1984

Agency Specializes In: Recruitment

Approx. Annual Billings: $5,150,000

Larry Licharson *(Owner & Mgr)*
Gabrielle Beckmann *(Controller)*
Jeff Aquino *(Mgr-Customer Svc)*
Paul Bennett *(Acct Exec)*
Susan Velie *(Media Buyer & Planner)*
Carly Anderson *(Designer)*
July Minsky *(Designer)*
Glen Zelinsky *(Media Buyer)*

HUB MEDIA
827 State St Ste 24, Santa Barbara, CA 93101
Tel.: (805) 963-4200
Fax: (805) 963-4225
E-Mail: dawn@hub-media.com
Web Site: www.hub-media.com

Agency Specializes In: Brand Development & Integration, Broadcast, Cable T.V., Communications, Corporate Communications, Corporate Identity, Entertainment, Integrated Marketing, Media Relations, Multimedia, Product Placement, Production, Production (Ad, Film, Broadcast), Production (Print), Social Marketing/Nonprofit, Syndication, T.V.

Approx. Annual Billings: $900,000

Breakdown of Gross Billings by Media: Production: 100%

Gary Sugarman *(CEO)*
Scott Wick *(Chief Sls Officer & Exec VP)*

Accounts:
Audi; U.K., USA
CMP; U.K. Tradeshows & Publications

HUB STRATEGY AND COMMUNICATION
39 Mesa St Ste 212, San Francisco, CA 94129
Tel.: (415) 561-4345
Fax: (415) 771-5965
E-Mail: info@hubstrategy.com
Web Site: hubsanfrancisco.com

Employees: 20
Year Founded: 2002

Agency Specializes In: Advertising, Sponsorship

D. J. O'Neil *(CEO & Dir-Creative)*
Peter Judd *(Partner & Dir-Creative)*
Chris Ferko *(Grp Acct Dir)*
Angelina Dilg *(Acct Dir & Producer)*
Elaine Harris Smith *(Acct Dir)*
Jason Rothman *(Dir-Design)*
Valerie Nerio *(Acct Mgr)*
Emily Grigone *(Designer)*
Zoe Drazen *(Acct Coord)*
Spencer Terris *(Asst Acct Mgr)*

Accounts:
Accidentally Extraordinary
Blue Shield of California
Eat24
Google
Levi's Levi's Stadium Museum
Lyve Minds (Agency of Record)
Microsoft
Nimble Storage Inc. Campaign: "Adaptive Flash Challenge", Online Advertising, Social Media
Oakland Athletics Branding, Campaign: "Curveball", Campaign: "Peripheral Vision", Creative, Integrated Marketing
Personal Capital (Agency of Record) Brand Awareness, Creative, Outdoor Media, Radio
Sling Media; San Mateo, CA Slingbox
Smart
New-Texture (Agency of Record)

HUDSON MIND
833 Broadway, New York, NY 10003
Tel.: (201) 993-7014
Web Site: hudsonmind.com

Employees: 25

Agency Specializes In: Arts, Commercial Photography, Communications, Computers & Software, Consulting, Consumer Goods, Cosmetics, Digital/Interactive, E-Commerce, Email, Entertainment, Fashion/Apparel, Health Care Services, Information Technology, Internet/Web Design, Production (Ad, Film, Broadcast), Retail, Search Engine Optimization, Social Marketing/Nonprofit, Social Media, Travel & Tourism, Viral/Buzz/Word of Mouth

Lucie Andre *(CEO)*

Accounts:
New-Hexagon Consulting Network Online Marketing (SEO & SMM); 2015

HUDSON ROUGE
257 Park Ave S 20th Fl, New York, NY 10010
Tel.: (212) 845-0500
E-Mail: hello@hudsonrouge.com
Web Site: www.hudsonrouge.com

Employees: 130
Year Founded: 2011

National Agency Associations: 4A's

Agency Specializes In: Advertising, Brand Development & Integration, Digital/Interactive, Media Planning, Social Media

Jon Pearce *(COO)*
Jess Harper Heckerling *(Sr VP & Dir-Brand Plng)*
Monique Frumberg *(Sr VP-Brand Content & Alliances)*
Ross Maupin *(VP-Integrated Creative Dir)*
Austin Muncy *(Sr Dir-Art)*
Paul Miser *(Grp Acct Dir-Digital)*
Patricia Brinkmann *(Dir-Art)*
Ashley Davidson *(Dir-Brand Content & Social Spaces)*
Adam Flanagan *(Assoc Dir-Creative)*
Tavia Moore *(Project Mgr-Social)*
Emily Richie *(Acct Exec)*
Mark Abellera *(Copywriter)*

Accounts:
Lincoln Motor Company Campaign: "The Winning Hand", Lincoln MKX

HUDSONYARDS
80 Broad St 26th Fl, New York, NY 10004
Tel.: (212) 716-6600
Fax: (212) 716-6700
E-Mail: info@hyards.com
Web Site: www.hudson-yards.com

Employees: 200

Agency Specializes In: Advertising, Advertising Specialties, Affluent Market, Automotive, Bilingual Market, Branded Entertainment, Business Publications, Business-To-Business, Catalogs, Co-op Advertising, Collateral, Communications, Consulting, Consumer Goods, Consumer Publications, Corporate Identity, Cosmetics, Custom Publishing, E-Commerce, Entertainment, Exhibit/Trade Shows, Food Service, Graphic Design, High Technology, In-Store Advertising, Internet/Web Design, Leisure, Logo & Package Design, Luxury Products, Media Buying Services, Multimedia, Newspaper, Out-of-Home Media, Outdoor, Package Design, Pharmaceutical, Point of Purchase, Point of Sale, Print, Product Placement, Production, Production (Ad, Film, Broadcast), Production (Print), Promotions, Publishing, Restaurant, Search Engine Optimization, Technical Advertising, Trade & Consumer Magazines, Transportation, Travel & Tourism, Urban Market, Web (Banner Ads, Pop-ups, etc.), Yellow Pages Advertising

Approx. Annual Billings: $90,000,000

Diane Romano *(Pres & CEO)*
Neil O'Callaghan *(Exec VP & Gen Mgr)*
Steve Finnerty *(Exec VP-Sls)*
Mark Potter *(Exec VP-Sls & Mktg)*
John A. Regina *(Sr VP-Sls)*
Ed Saturn *(VP-Sls)*

Accounts:
Aleve
Kraft
L'Oreal
Miller Lite
Nestle
Quaker
Ritz
Windex

HUE STUDIOS
222 Water St Ste 228, Binghamton, NY 13901
Tel.: (607) 722-5156
Fax: (800) 513-9084
E-Mail: contact@huestudios.com
Web Site: www.huestudios.com

Agency Specializes In: Advertising, Content, Digital/Interactive, Graphic Design, Internet/Web Design, Logo & Package Design, Media Planning, Print, Public Relations, Social Media

Camilla Hoffman *(Art Dir)*
Peter Hoffman *(Dir-Web)*

Accounts:
Greater Binghamton Chamber of Commerce
MaineSource Food & Party Warehouse
Opportunities for Broome, Inc.
Warehouse Carpet Outlet

HUGE
45 Main St Ste 220, Brooklyn, NY 11201
Tel.: (718) 625-4843

Fax: (718) 625-5157
E-Mail: makesomething@hugeinc.com
Web Site: www.hugeinc.com

Employees: 1,000
Year Founded: 1999

National Agency Associations: 4A's

Agency Specializes In: Above-the-Line, Advertising, Advertising Specialties, Affiliate Marketing, Affluent Market, African-American Market, Agriculture, Alternative Advertising, Arts, Asian Market, Automotive, Aviation & Aerospace, Below-the-Line, Bilingual Market, Brand Development & Integration, Branded Entertainment, Broadcast, Business Publications, Business-To-Business, Cable T.V., Catalogs, Children's Market, Co-op Advertising, Collateral, College, Commercial Photography, Communications, Computers & Software, Consulting, Consumer Goods, Consumer Marketing, Consumer Publications, Content, Corporate Communications, Corporate Identity, Cosmetics, Crisis Communications, Custom Publishing, Customer Relationship Management, Digital/Interactive, Direct Response Marketing, Direct-to-Consumer, E-Commerce, Education, Electronic Media, Electronics, Email, Engineering, Entertainment, Environmental, Event Planning & Marketing, Exhibit/Trade Shows, Experience Design, Faith Based, Fashion/Apparel, Financial, Food Service, Game Integration, Gay & Lesbian Market, Government/Political, Graphic Design, Guerilla Marketing, Health Care Services, High Technology, Hispanic Market, Hospitality, Household Goods, Identity Marketing, In-Store Advertising, Industrial, Infomercials, Information Technology, Integrated Marketing, International, Internet/Web Design, Investor Relations, Legal Services, Leisure, Local Marketing, Logo & Package Design, Luxury Products, Magazines, Marine, Market Research, Media Buying Services, Media Planning, Media Relations, Media Training, Medical Products, Men's Market, Merchandising, Mobile Marketing, Multicultural, Multimedia, New Product Development, New Technologies, Newspaper, Newspapers & Magazines, Out-of-Home Media, Outdoor, Over-50 Market, Package Design, Paid Searches, Pets , Pharmaceutical, Planning & Consultation, Podcasting, Point of Purchase, Point of Sale, Print, Product Placement, Production, Production (Ad, Film, Broadcast), Production (Print), Promotions, Public Relations, Publicity/Promotions, Publishing, RSS (Really Simple Syndication), Radio, Real Estate, Recruitment, Regional, Restaurant, Retail, Sales Promotion, Search Engine Optimization, Seniors' Market, Shopper Marketing, Social Marketing/Nonprofit, Social Media, South Asian Market, Sponsorship, Sports Market, Stakeholders, Strategic Planning/Research, Sweepstakes, Syndication, T.V., Technical Advertising, Teen Market, Telemarketing, Trade & Consumer Magazines, Transportation, Travel & Tourism, Tween Market, Urban Market, Viral/Buzz/Word of Mouth, Web (Banner Ads, Pop-ups, etc.), Women's Market, Yellow Pages Advertising

Paul Burns *(Mng Dir)*
Kate Watts *(Mng Dir)*
Jason Whiting *(Mng Dir)*
Raj Singhal *(CFO)*
Jeff Brooks *(Pres-New York)*
Eric Moore *(Pres-Client Svcs-Global)*
Kevin Sweeney *(Dir-Fin & Grp VP)*
Eduardo Torres *(Mng Dir-Brazil & VP)*
Michael Claypool *(Mng Dir-Portland)*
Randy Rubino *(Mng Dir-Fin)*
Brock Boddie *(VP-Project Mgmt)*
Michelle Burnham *(VP-Media Activation)*
Carrie Clarke *(VP-Bus Dev)*
Todd Coen *(VP)*
Beth Fetzer *(VP-Plng & Strategy)*
Jon Gibs *(VP-Data Science & Analytics)*
Beth Lind *(VP-Bus Dev)*
Adam Slagowski *(VP-Govt Solutions)*
Peter Sommers *(VP-Media)*
Mark Stojack *(VP-Client Svcs)*
Lawson Waring *(VP)*
Brittany Nugent *(Head-Plng)*
Allison Sims *(Head-Media Plng)*
Trey Trenchard *(Head-Analytics-Strategy Grp)*
Derek Fridman *(Grp Dir-Creative)*
Charles Fulford *(Grp Dir-Creative)*
Tim Nolan *(Grp Dir-Creative)*
Becky Kitlan *(Sr Dir-Art)*
Andrew Delamarter *(Dir-Search & Inbound Mktg)*
Ryan Kellogg *(Dir-Creative)*
Marcela Lay *(Dir-Engagement)*
Michelle Pulman *(Dir-Comm)*
Yashoda Sampath *(Dir-Res)*
Courtney Scott *(Dir-Plng)*
Jeff Small *(Dir-Tech)*
Irene Tien *(Dir-Bus Strategy)*
Dave Tupper *(Dir-Creative)*
Tom Westerlin *(Dir-Creative)*
Jayme Bednarski *(Mgr-Client Engagement)*
Blake Bensman *(Mgr-Engagement)*
Allison Chait *(Mgr-Engagement)*
Evan Kosowski *(Sr Designer-Visual)*
Thomas Nicholas *(Sr Designer-Visual)*

Accounts:
American Express
Audi
Cap'n Crunch
Comcast Web
Dick's Sporting Goods, Inc. (Social Agency of Record) Content Creation, Social Media Strategy
New-Fiat Chrysler Chrysler, Dodge, FIAT North America, Jeep, Online Advertising, Ram
FX
Google
Gucci
Lowe's
Mass Mutual
Morgan Stanley Campaign: "Capital Creates Change", Digital, Print, Social, Website
Nike
Samsung
TED
Unilever
Vans
New-The White House Campaign: "Heads Up America"

Branches

Huge
60 Sloane Avenue, London, SW3 3XB United Kingdom
Tel.: (44) 2078945030
E-Mail: london@hugeinc.com
Web Site: www.hugeinc.com

Year Founded: 2011

Agency Specializes In: Advertising, Digital/Interactive, Social Media

Shirley Au *(Pres & COO)*
Nathan Weyer *(Mng Dir-Europe)*
Ben Callis *(Grp Dir-Creative)*
Mark Tipper *(Grp Dir-Creative)*
Brian Brady *(Dir-Creative)*
Andy Thomas *(Dir-Creative-Europe)*

Accounts:
Diageo plc Alexander & James
Samsung Campaign: "Looking For Myself", Smart TV
Volkswagen Marketing, Seat

Huge
6100 Wilshire Blvd 2nd Fl, Los Angeles, CA 90048
Tel.: (310) 499-7700
E-Mail: losangeles@hugeinc.com
Web Site: www.hugeinc.com

Year Founded: 2006

National Agency Associations: 4A's

Agency Specializes In: Advertising, Digital/Interactive, Integrated Marketing, Internet/Web Design, Sponsorship, Strategic Planning/Research

Patricia Korth-McDonnell *(CMO-Global)*
Daryan Dehghanpisheh *(VP-Strategy-Huge)*
Clark Morgan *(Grp Dir-Creative)*
Kristen Purdy Benel *(Project Mgr-CSM & Sr Producer-Digital)*
Tiffany Bacon *(Dir-Engagement)*
Evan Dody *(Dir-Creative-Huge)*
Gillian Gutierrez *(Dir-Engagement)*
Matt Murray *(Dir-Creative)*
Sean Rosenberg *(Dir-Engagement)*
Laura Yetter *(Dir-Engagement)*
Tyler Starrine *(Assoc Dir-Strategy)*
Virginia A. Vickery *(Assoc Dir-Creative)*
Nikolas Alexoff *(Mgr-Bus)*
Blake Bensman *(Mgr-Engagement)*
Jen Kuenzig *(Mgr-Bus Dev)*
Josie Capuano *(Coord-Bus Dev)*

Accounts:
Tempur Sealy International, Inc.

HUGHES AGENCY LLC
104 S Main St Ste 110, Greenville, SC 29601
Tel.: (864) 271-0718
Fax: (864) 271-7522
E-Mail: info@hughes-agency.com
Web Site: www.hughes-agency.com

Agency Specializes In: Advertising, Brand Development & Integration, Event Planning & Marketing, Media Relations, Public Relations, Strategic Planning/Research

Velda Hughes *(Owner & Pres)*
Amanda Long *(Acct Dir)*
Elise Nichols *(Acct Dir)*
Anna Mcninch *(Acct Mgr)*
Deborah Pressley *(Mgr-Fin)*
Jennifer Spellman *(Supvr-Media)*
Eliza Bostian *(Sr Acct Exec)*
Sheldon Johnson *(Sr Acct Exec)*
Lauren Neely *(Sr Acct Exec)*

Accounts:
Clements Kindness Fund

HUGHES & STUART, INC.
6050 Greenwood Pl Blvd Ste 130, Greenwood Village, CO 80111
Tel.: (303) 798-0601
E-Mail: mgoetz@hughesstuart.com
Web Site: www.hughesstuart.com

Year Founded: 1979

Agency Specializes In: Advertising, Graphic Design, Media Relations, Media Training, Social Media

Melanie Hughes Goetz *(Pres)*
Denise Keller *(Dir-Creative & Designer)*
Elizabeth Gee *(Dir-Comm)*
Tony Walt *(Dir-3D & Motion Design)*
Bryan Bisel *(Program Mgr-IT)*

Accounts:
DC Clear
Purgatoire Watershed

Wheatlands Metropolitan District

HUGHES LEAHY KARLOVIC

1415 Park Ave W, Denver, CO 80205
Tel.: (844) 455-3377
E-Mail: hello@hlkagency.com
Web Site: www.hlkagency.com

Agency Specializes In: Advertising, Brand Development & Integration, Digital/Interactive, Media Buying Services, Media Planning

Joe Leahy *(Partner & Chief Creative Officer)*
Ellen Crouch *(Acct Mgr)*
Erin Smith *(Acct Mgr)*

Accounts:
New-SCL Health
New-St. Louis Browns

HUGHESLEAHYKARLOVIC

1141 S 7th St, Saint Louis, MO 63104
Tel.: (314) 571-6300
E-Mail: jobs@hlkagency.com
Web Site: www.hlkagency.com

E-Mail for Key Personnel:
President: jschnurbusch@hughes-stl.com

Employees: 50
Year Founded: 1977

National Agency Associations: MAGNET

Agency Specializes In: Automotive, Aviation & Aerospace, Brand Development & Integration, Broadcast, Business Publications, Business-To-Business, Cable T.V., Children's Market, Co-op Advertising, Collateral, College, Communications, Consulting, Consumer Marketing, Consumer Publications, Corporate Communications, Corporate Identity, Crisis Communications, Customer Relationship Management, Digital/Interactive, Direct Response Marketing, E-Commerce, Education, Electronic Media, Email, Engineering, Entertainment, Event Planning & Marketing, Exhibit/Trade Shows, Experience Design, Fashion/Apparel, Financial, Food Service, Game Integration, Graphic Design, Guerilla Marketing, Health Care Services, High Technology, Hospitality, Household Goods, In-Store Advertising, Industrial, Integrated Marketing, International, Internet/Web Design, Leisure, Local Marketing, Logo & Package Design, Magazines, Marine, Market Research, Media Buying Services, Media Planning, Media Relations, Medical Products, Merchandising, Mobile Marketing, Multimedia, New Product Development, New Technologies, Newspaper, Newspapers & Magazines, Out-of-Home Media, Outdoor, Package Design, Paid Searches, Pharmaceutical, Planning & Consultation, Podcasting, Point of Purchase, Point of Sale, Print, Production, Production (Ad, Film, Broadcast), Production (Print), Promotions, Public Relations, Publicity/Promotions, RSS (Really Simple Syndication), Radio, Recruitment, Regional, Restaurant, Retail, Sales Promotion, Search Engine Optimization, Social Marketing/Nonprofit, Sponsorship, Sports Market, Strategic Planning/Research, Sweepstakes, T.V., Teen Market, Trade & Consumer Magazines, Transportation, Travel & Tourism, Web (Banner Ads, Pop-ups, etc.), Yellow Pages Advertising

Approx. Annual Billings: $37,500,000

Breakdown of Gross Billings by Media: Brdcst.: 20%; Bus. Publs.: 20%; Consumer Publs.: 25%; Fees: 10%; Production: 10%; Pub. Rels.: 10%; Strategic Planning/Research: 5%

William F. Hughes *(Mng Partner)*
Eric Karlovic *(Partner)*
Monica Giardina *(Sr Dir-Art)*
Mike Roberts *(Sr Producer-Digital)*
Bob Sherron *(Dir-Tech)*
Ryan Doggendorf *(Assoc Dir-Creative)*
Heath Harris *(Assoc Dir-Creative)*
Patty Alt *(Sr Acct Mgr)*
Patrick Keefe *(Strategist-Brand)*
Luke Yamnitz *(Jr Strategist)*

Accounts:
AAA
Enterprise
Missouri Municipal League
MiTek
Race For The Cure
RubinBrown; Saint Louis, MO
Saint Louis Public Library
Steel Joist Institute
Webster University

HULT MARKETING

(Formerly Hult Fritz Matuszak)
401 SW Water St Ste 601, Peoria, IL 61602-1586
Tel.: (309) 673-8191
Fax: (309) 674-5530
Web Site: www.hultmarketing.com/

Employees: 20
Year Founded: 1956

National Agency Associations: MCA-NAAN-Second Wind Limited

Agency Specializes In: Advertising, Automotive, Bilingual Market, Brand Development & Integration, Broadcast, Business Publications, Business-To-Business, Cable T.V., Co-op Advertising, Collateral, Commercial Photography, Communications, Consulting, Consumer Marketing, Consumer Publications, Corporate Identity, Digital/Interactive, Direct Response Marketing, Education, Electronic Media, Event Planning & Marketing, Fashion/Apparel, Financial, Government/Political, Graphic Design, Health Care Services, High Technology, Industrial, Infomercials, Information Technology, Internet/Web Design, Logo & Package Design, Media Buying Services, Medical Products, Multimedia, New Product Development, Newspaper, Newspapers & Magazines, Out-of-Home Media, Outdoor, Over-50 Market, Pharmaceutical, Planning & Consultation, Point of Purchase, Point of Sale, Print, Production, Public Relations, Publicity/Promotions, Radio, Sales Promotion, Seniors' Market, Strategic Planning/Research, T.V., Technical Advertising, Trade & Consumer Magazines, Travel & Tourism, Yellow Pages Advertising

Approx. Annual Billings: $10,000,000

Breakdown of Gross Billings by Media: Adv. Specialities: 5%; Brdcst.: 10%; Bus. Publs.: 10%; Collateral: 20%; D.M.: 15%; Logo & Package Design: 5%; Newsp. & Mags.: 5%; Newsp.: 5%; Outdoor: 5%; Point of Purchase: 5%; Pub. Rels.: 5%; Worldwide Web Sites: 10%

James Flynn *(Pres & CEO)*

HUMANAUT

1428 Williams St Ste C-1, Chattanooga, TN 37408
Tel.: (423) 771-9646
E-Mail: hello@humanaut.is
Web Site: humanaut.is

Agency Specializes In: Brand Development & Integration, Digital/Interactive, Mobile Marketing, Public Relations

Andrew Clark *(Co-Founder & Chief Strategist)*
David Littlejohn *(Chief Creative Officer)*
Matt Denyer *(Dir-Art)*
Daniel Edelman *(Dir-Art)*
Stephanie Gelabert *(Dir-Art)*
Mike Cessario *(Assoc Dir-Creative & Copywriter)*
Andrew Ure *(Copywriter)*

Accounts:
A Mother's Pledge
Lyft
Organic Valley Campaign: "Save the Bros", Organic Fuel
Soda Stream Direct, LLC Campaign: "Sorry, Coke & Pepsi" Super Bowl 2014

HUMMINGBIRD CREATIVE GROUP

160 NE Maynard Rd Ste 205, Cary, NC 27513
Tel.: (919) 854-9100
Fax: (919) 854-9101
E-Mail: info@hummingbird-creative.com
Web Site: www.hummingbird-creative.com

Employees: 4
Year Founded: 1995

Agency Specializes In: Advertising, Brand Development & Integration, Direct Response Marketing, Direct-to-Consumer, Email, Internet/Web Design, Logo & Package Design, Production, Production (Print), Promotions, Public Relations, Sales Promotion

Wendy Coulter *(CEO)*
Dan Gregory *(VP & Gen Mgr)*
Sherry Mitchell *(Dir-Brand Strategies)*
Mike Neel *(Dir-Creative)*

Accounts:
Exhibit Resources Collateral, Marketing Strategy, Public Relations, Social Media
Integrated Audio Video Branding Strategy, Collateral, Marketing Strategy, PPC Campaigns, Public Relations, Social Media, Web Marketing, Website Design
REUL Brand Branding Strategy, Collateral, Marketing Strategy, PPC Campaigns, Public Relations, Social Media, Web Marketing, Website Design
Technology Savants Branding Strategy, Collateral, Marketing Strategy, PPC Campaigns, Public Relations, Social Media, Web Marketing, Website Design

HUMPHREY ASSOCIATES INC

233 S Detroit Ste 201, Tulsa, OK 74120
Tel.: (918) 584-4774
Fax: (918) 584-4773
Web Site: www.humphreyad.com

Agency Specializes In: Advertising, Brand Development & Integration, Internet/Web Design, Media Planning, Print, Public Relations, Radio, T.V.

Jim Humphrey *(Pres)*

Accounts:
Enacomm

HUNT ADKINS

15 S 5th St, Minneapolis, MN 55402
Tel.: (612) 339-8003
Fax: (612) 339-8104
Web Site: www.huntadkins.com

E-Mail for Key Personnel:
President: phunt@huntadkins.com
Creative Dir.: dadkins@huntadkins.com
Media Dir.: lsteig@huntadkins.com

Employees: 20
Year Founded: 1991

Agency Specializes In: Advertising, Alternative Advertising, Brand Development & Integration,

Broadcast, Business-To-Business, Cable T.V., Collateral, College, Computers & Software, Consumer Goods, Consumer Marketing, Corporate Identity, Digital/Interactive, E-Commerce, Email, Entertainment, Financial, Graphic Design, Guerilla Marketing, Health Care Services, High Technology, In-Store Advertising, Internet/Web Design, Leisure, Logo & Package Design, Magazines, Media Buying Services, Media Planning, Medical Products, Men's Market, Mobile Marketing, New Product Development, Newspaper, Newspapers & Magazines, Out-of-Home Media, Outdoor, Package Design, Point of Purchase, Point of Sale, Print, Production, Production (Print), Radio, Restaurant, Retail, Social Marketing/Nonprofit, Sponsorship, Sports Market, Strategic Planning/Research, T.V., Teen Market, Trade & Consumer Magazines, Travel & Tourism, Viral/Buzz/Word of Mouth

Approx. Annual Billings: $25,000,000

Breakdown of Gross Billings by Media: Brdcst.: 20%; Collateral: 10%; Digital/Interactive: 25%; Graphic Design: 15%; Internet Adv.: 10%; Logo & Package Design: 10%; Trade & Consumer Mags.: 10%

Patrick Hunt *(Pres & CEO)*
Doug Adkins *(Chief Creative Officer & Copywriter)*
Betsey Ruesink *(Acct Dir)*
Shanna Apitz *(Dir-Digital Strategy)*
Michelle Gilstead *(Dir-Art)*
Shelley Wicinske *(Dir-Studio)*
Jennifer Broman *(Sr Acct Mgr)*
Mariah Becchetti *(Office Mgr)*
Joe Mielzarek *(Acct Mgr)*
Theresa Connelly *(Acct Supvr)*

Accounts:
Calabrio; Plymouth, MN Software; 2010
Canterbury Park
Concord USA; Minneapolis, MN Technology Consulting; 2011
Gettington.com
iWireless
Lola's Lakehouse; Waconia, MN Restaurant; 2007
UnitedHealthcare; Minneapolis, MN Insurance; 2011
University of Minnesota Athletics

HUNTER
204 Julie Dr, Parkesburg, PA 19365
Tel.: (610) 909-4884
Toll Free: (877) 363-0606
E-Mail: info@rjhunter.com
Web Site: www.rjhunter.com

E-Mail for Key Personnel:
President: john@rjhunter.com

Employees: 3
Year Founded: 1986

Agency Specializes In: Advertising, Brand Development & Integration, Public Relations

Andrew Nazari *(VP-Corp & Sr Dir-New Bus Dev)*
Norm Malone *(VP-Sls & Mktg-Fabrication Div)*
Christine Mikler *(VP-Fin-Fabrication Div)*
Bruce D. Milley *(VP)*
Amy Gagliano *(Product Dir & Brand Dir)*
Earl Franz *(Dir-Brand Dev)*
David Parrett *(Dir-Dealer Mktg Programs)*
Paula Cerna *(Brand Mgr & Product Mgr)*
Kelly Foster *(Brand Mgr & Product Mgr)*
Debi Borowski *(Mgr-Mktg)*
Kirsten Clark *(Mgr-Mktg)*

Accounts:
Conestoga Wood
Eastern Instruments; Wilmington, NC
Furmano Foods
Hill & Associates; Wilmington, NC
Philadelphia Gear

HUNTSINGER & JEFFER
809 Brook Hill Cir, Richmond, VA 23227-2503
Tel.: (804) 266-2499
Fax: (804) 266-8563
Toll Free: (800) 969-3342
E-Mail: info@huntsingerjeffer.com
Web Site: www.huntsinger-jeffer.com

E-Mail for Key Personnel:
President: vickil@huntsinger-jeffer.com
Public Relations: willis@huntsinger-jeffer.com

Employees: 14
Year Founded: 1964

National Agency Associations: DMA

Agency Specializes In: Direct Response Marketing

Approx. Annual Billings: $3,348,000

Victoria S. Lester *(Pres)*
Cheryl Martin *(VP)*
Chris Pitzer *(Sr Dir-Art)*
Shannon Holleman *(Dir-List Svcs)*
Mary Richardson *(Dir-Strategic Plng)*
Kelly Woodward *(Mgr-Ops)*
Willis Turner *(Sr Writer)*

Accounts:
American Red Cross; 1996
Englewood Hospital & Medical Center Foundation; 2013
Military Officers Association of America; 2011
National Association of Police Organizations; Washington, DC; 1985
VFW National Home for Children; 2010
Volunteers of America; Washington, DC; 2004

HURLEY CHANDLER & CHAFFER
(Name Changed to HCC Marketing, Inc.)

HUSEBO ADVERTISING & PUBLIC RELATIONS
1319 Shelfer St, Leesburg, FL 34748
Tel.: (352) 787-5777
Fax: (352) 787-5510
E-Mail: info@husebo.com
Web Site: www.husebo.com

Agency Specializes In: Advertising, Internet/Web Design, Print, Public Relations, Radio, T.V.

Lanny Husebo *(Pres & CEO)*
Brooke Robles *(Dir-Interactive Mktg & Strategy)*

Accounts:
Vac-Tron Equipment

HUXLEY QUAYLE VON BISMARK, INC.
2 Berkeley St Ste 301, Toronto, ON M5A 4J5 Canada
Tel.: (416) 864-1700
Fax: (416) 864-1701
E-Mail: chris@huxleyquayle.com
Web Site: hqvb.ca

Employees: 10

Agency Specializes In: Advertising, Brand Development & Integration

Approx. Annual Billings: $750,000

Chris Hall *(Pres)*
Joaquin Gravel *(Head-Creative & Dir-Art)*

Accounts:
Appleton Estate Jamaica Rum

HY CONNECT
(Formerly Hoffman York)
142 E Ontario St Ste 13, Chicago, IL 60611-2818
Tel.: (312) 787-2330
Fax: (312) 787-2320
E-Mail: dsheehan@hyc.com
Web Site: www.hyc.com

E-Mail for Key Personnel:
President: dsheehan@hyc.com
Creative Dir.: tbonilla@hyc.com
Media Dir.: pbacke@hyc.com
Production Mgr.: KHayes@hyc.com

Employees: 27
Year Founded: 1994

National Agency Associations: AMA-AMIN-DMA

Agency Specializes In: Advertising, Brand Development & Integration, Broadcast, Business-To-Business, Cable T.V., Children's Market, Collateral, Consumer Marketing, Corporate Identity, Digital/Interactive, Direct Response Marketing, E-Commerce, Education, Event Planning & Marketing, Exhibit/Trade Shows, Graphic Design, Internet/Web Design, Logo & Package Design, Magazines, Media Buying Services, Medical Products, Newspaper, Newspapers & Magazines, Out-of-Home Media, Outdoor, Pharmaceutical, Print, Production, Radio, Restaurant, Sponsorship, Strategic Planning/Research, T.V., Trade & Consumer Magazines, Travel & Tourism

Approx. Annual Billings: $70,000,000

Breakdown of Gross Billings by Media: Mags.: $6,800,000; Newsp.: $13,600,000; Outdoor: $13,600,000; Radio: $17,000,000; T.V.: $19,000,000

Rich Levy *(CEO)*
Jim Roots *(Partner & Exec VP-Strategy & Analytics)*
Sharon Boeldt *(Partner & Dir-Earned Media)*
Elissa Polston *(Chief Strategy Officer & Exec VP)*
Susan Flinn Cobian *(Sr VP & Acct Dir)*
Michael A. Smith *(Sr VP-Client Svcs)*
Kevin Houlihan *(Exec Creative Dir)*
Kelly Hampton *(Sr Dir-Art)*
Kip Russell *(Sr Mgr-Community)*
Jacob Robinson *(Sr Acct Exec)*

Accounts:
Academy of Dermatology
Advocate Healthcare; Chicago, IL Hospitals; 2002
Arlington Park; Arlington Heights, IL; 2000
Bakers Square (Agency of Record)
Blue Cross Blue Shield Campaign: "Birthday"
Cherdon
Chicago's First Lady Cruises (Agency of Record) Creative, Digital, Marketing, Media Buying, Media Planning, Strategy
Design Center
Emerson Network Power
First Tennessee Bank Media Buying, Media Planning
Health Care Service Corporation
Indiana University Health
Land O'Frost (Advertising Agency of Record) Consumer
Merillat
Museum of Science and Industry
The Museum of Science and Industry (Agency of Record)
Napoleon Products Advertising & Marketing Agency of Record, Pro 665 Grill
NetCredit
Peapod Campaign: "Get Fresh", Creative, Radio
ProMedica
Roche Diagnostics Advertising, Digital Communications, Marketing, Strategic Planning
Turtle Wax, Inc. Turtle Wax Ice, Turtle Wax, Inc.

University of Notre Dame-Mendoza College of Business
Wahl Products
Weber Grill Restaurants
Wisconsin Lottery
Yamaha

Branches:

HY Connect
(Formerly Hoffman York)
1000 N Water St Ste 1600, Milwaukee, WI 53202-6667
Tel.: (414) 289-9700
Fax: (414) 289-0417
Toll Free: (800) 842-3020
E-Mail: tpeterson@hyc.com
Web Site: www.hyc.com/

E-Mail for Key Personnel:
Public Relations: sboeldt@hyc.com

Employees: 80
Year Founded: 1933

National Agency Associations: AMIN-DMA

Agency Specializes In: Advertising, Brand Development & Integration, Broadcast, Business-To-Business, Cable T.V., Co-op Advertising, Collateral, Consulting, Consumer Marketing, Corporate Identity, Digital/Interactive, Event Planning & Marketing, Exhibit/Trade Shows, Food Service, Graphic Design, Health Care Services, Internet/Web Design, Logo & Package Design, Magazines, Marine, Newspapers & Magazines, Outdoor, Planning & Consultation, Point of Purchase, Point of Sale, Public Relations, Publicity/Promotions, Radio, Retail, Strategic Planning/Research, T.V., Telemarketing, Trade & Consumer Magazines, Travel & Tourism

Dave Brown *(Partner)*
Vivian Moller *(CFO)*
Emily Dold *(VP & Media Dir)*
Kyle Krueger *(VP & Media Dir)*
Megan Finkelman *(VP & Mgmt Supvr)*
Robin Finco *(VP & Dir-Production)*
Angie Dorrington *(VP & Acct Supvr)*
Patrick Kopisckie *(VP-Acct Mgmt)*
Eric Oken *(Creative Dir)*
Cathy Brendel *(Mgr-HR)*
Brooke Renzelmann *(Supvr-Media)*
Luke Bell *(Sr Media Planner)*
Kendell Lee *(Sr Media Planner)*

Accounts:
Advocate Health Care
Chicago Museum of Science & Industry
Egg Innovations; Port Washington, WI Food Products; 2002
Focus on energy
Grainger; Lake Forest, IL Industrial Supplies; 2001
Merillat Industries, Inc., Div. of MASCO; Adrian, MI (Agency of Record) Cabinetmakers; 1994
Turtle Wax, Inc. Turtle Wax Ice, Turtle Wax, Inc.
University of Notre Dame
WAHL
Yamaha; Kennesaw, GA Water Vehicles; 1995

HYDROGEN ADVERTISING
1520 4th Ave Ste 600, Seattle, WA 98101
Tel.: (206) 389-9500
Fax: (206) 389-4849
E-Mail: info@hydrogenadvertising.com
Web Site: http://hydrogenadvertising.com/

Employees: 10

Agency Specializes In: Advertising, Brand Development & Integration, Business-To-Business, Collateral, Graphic Design, Print, Radio, Sponsorship, T.V.

Rick Peterson *(Pres)*
Mary Knight *(Principal & Exec Dir-Creative)*
Tom Scherer *(VP & Exec Dir-Creative)*
Kim Yale *(VP & Dir-Accounts)*
Hillary Miller *(VP-Acct Strategy)*
Mike McGrath *(Dir-Creative & Art)*
Lauren Meadows-Rose *(Mgr-Media)*
Noel Fountain *(Copywriter)*
Brian McCartney *(Designer-Digital)*

Accounts:
AegisLiving
Agilent
American Advertising Federation Creative
BDA
The Center for Colorectal Health
CRH Medical Corporation
DaVinci Gourmet
Eating Disorder Prevention
EBay
Family Services
Heritage Bank Advertising, Digital, Print, Radio, Television
Insight Schools, Inc.
Kenworth Truck Company
Keysight Technologies Advertising, Global Advertising, Online, Print
Microsoft B2B Campaign for Online Services
MultiCare Health System
National Multiple Sclerosis Society
The Polyclinic Campaign: "Physician Owned, Physician Run"
Precor
Quadrant Homes (Agency of Record); 2008
Rolling Stone Ringtones
Schnitzer West
Trammell Crow
Whole Foods
Windermere Real Estate Campaign: "Your Story is Our Story"

HYPE GROUP LLC
433 Central Ave Ste 205, Saint Petersburg, FL 33701
Tel.: (727) 623-9085
Fax: (727) 803-6836
E-Mail: info@hypegroup.net
Web Site: www.hypegroup.net

Year Founded: 2009

Agency Specializes In: Advertising, Brand Development & Integration, Graphic Design, Internet/Web Design, Print, Public Relations, Social Media

Brooke Boyd *(Pres)*
Kenny Coil *(Dir-Creative)*
Lisa Williams *(Dir-Mktg & Comm)*
Maureen Horan *(Sr Graphic Designer)*

Accounts:
the AVENUE eat/drink
Flippers Pizzeria Campaign Planning, Creative Design, Market Research, Marketing Strategy, PR, Social Media
The Grape @ Coconut Point
Nova HRC

HYPERAKT
401 Smith St, Brooklyn, NY 11231
Tel.: (718) 855-4250
Fax: (718) 855-2754
E-Mail: whatsup@hyperakt.com
Web Site: www.hyperakt.com

Year Founded: 2001

Agency Specializes In: Advertising, Brand Development & Integration, Internet/Web Design, Print

Julia Vakser Zeltser *(Co-Founder & Dir-Creative)*
Deroy Peraza *(Principal & Dir-Creative)*
Jason Lynch *(Dir-Art)*
Eric Fensterheim *(Sr Designer-UI & UX)*
Wen Ping Huang *(Designer)*
Radhika Unnikrishnan *(Designer)*

Accounts:
Bill & Melinda Gates Foundation
Collaborative Fund
Girl Scouts of the United States of America
Good Magazine
Hunchworks
Ted Conferences, LLC
Thomson Reuters Foundation

THE HYPERFACTORY (USA) INC.
(Acquired by Meredith Corporation & Name Changed to MXM Mobile)

HYPERQUAKE
205 W Fourth St Ste 1010, Cincinnati, OH 45202
Tel.: (513) 563-6555
Fax: (513) 563-6080
E-Mail: chris.heile@hyperquake.com
Web Site: www.hyperquake.com

Employees: 35

Agency Specializes In: Advertising, Brand Development & Integration, Branded Entertainment, Digital/Interactive

Colin Crotty *(Pres & Partner)*
Steve Bruce *(CEO)*
Dan Barczak *(Partner & Dir-Creative)*
Jeanne Bruce *(CFO & Principal)*
Shari Ernst *(Dir-Client Leadership)*
Molly Danks *(Mgr-HR)*

Accounts:
Bounce
Cover Girl
DIY Network
Ethicon
Food Network
GE Healthcare
HGTV
New Balance
Pampers
Procter & Gamble
Scripps Networks
Sea Pak
Takeda
Vicks
Warner Bros. Pictures
Welch's Interactive

HYPERRELEVANCE
(Formerly The Coakley Heagerty Advertising & Public Relations Co.)
1165 Lincoln Ave Ste 208, San Jose, CA 95125
Tel.: (408) 275-9400
Fax: (408) 995-0600
E-Mail: contact@hyperrelevance.com
Web Site: www.hyperrelevance.com/

Employees: 12
Year Founded: 1961

National Agency Associations: MAGNET

Agency Specializes In: Advertising, Asian Market, Bilingual Market, Brand Development & Integration, Broadcast, Business-To-Business, Collateral, Consulting, Consumer Marketing, Corporate Communications, Corporate Identity, Education, Electronic Media, Event Planning & Marketing, Exhibit/Trade Shows, Fashion/Apparel, Financial, Food Service, Government/Political, Graphic Design, Health Care Services, High Technology,

Hispanic Market, Internet/Web Design, Local Marketing, Logo & Package Design, Magazines, Media Buying Services, Medical Products, Newspaper, Out-of-Home Media, Over-50 Market, Planning & Consultation, Print, Production, Public Relations, Publicity/Promotions, Radio, Real Estate, Restaurant, Retail, Seniors' Market, Strategic Planning/Research, T.V., Trade & Consumer Magazines, Travel & Tourism, Yellow Pages Advertising

Approx. Annual Billings: $3,800,000

Breakdown of Gross Billings by Media: Brdcst.: 15%; Print: 65%; Pub. Rels.: 20%

Tom Tso *(CFO)*

Accounts:
Cisco Systems Inc. Campaign: "Hackers of Troy"
KACE International Raceway
Palo Alto Medical
Ricoh Innovations iCandy
Santana Row; San Jose, CA Fashion Apparel; 2005
Standard Pacific Homes Home Builder, Real Estate; 1976

HYPHEN COMMUNICATIONS
110-375 Water St, Vancouver, BC V6B 5C6 Canada
Tel.: (604) 694-0844
Fax: (604) 694-0845
Web Site: www.hyphenweb.com

Employees: 5

Agency Specializes In: Advertising

David Martin *(Pres & Dir-Creative)*

Accounts:
City of Richmond
Goldcorp
Northshore Auto Mall

HYPHEN DIGITAL
711 3rd Ave 17th Fl, New York, NY 10017
Tel.: (212) 856-8700
Fax: (212) 856-8602
E-Mail: info@hyphenhealth.com
Web Site: www.hyphenhealth.com

Employees: 15
Year Founded: 2001

Agency Specializes In: Advertising, Communications, Digital/Interactive, E-Commerce, Electronic Media, Health Care Services, New Product Development, Pharmaceutical

Greg Imber *(Mng Dir-Hyphen Digital)*
Deborah Pagano *(VP & Dir-Production)*

Accounts:
Bristol-Myers Squibb
ConjuChem
Genentech
Merck
Myogen/Gilead
Novartis
Sanofi-Aventis
Schering-Plough

THE I AM GROUP, INC.
2875 East Timberwood, Hernando, FL 34442
Fax: (305) 646-0144
Toll Free: (800) 421-2358
E-Mail: rachael@iamgroupinc.com
Web Site: www.iamgroupinc.com

Employees: 5

Agency Specializes In: Advertising, Affluent Market, Alternative Advertising, Arts, Brand Development & Integration, Branded Entertainment, Broadcast, Business Publications, Business-To-Business, Cable T.V., Children's Market, Communications, Consulting, Consumer Goods, Corporate Communications, Corporate Identity, Cosmetics, Engineering, Entertainment, Event Planning & Marketing, Financial, Graphic Design, Identity Marketing, Information Technology, Integrated Marketing, Internet/Web Design, Legal Services, Leisure, Logo & Package Design, Luxury Products, Magazines, Market Research, Medical Products, New Product Development, Newspapers & Magazines, Package Design, Point of Purchase, Print, Production, Production (Print), Promotions, Public Relations, Publicity/Promotions, Publishing, Radio, Real Estate, Restaurant, Sales Promotion, Social Marketing/Nonprofit, Strategic Planning/Research, T.V., Viral/Buzz/Word of Mouth

Approx. Annual Billings: $1,000,000

Breakdown of Gross Billings by Media: Corp. Communications: $1,000,000

Lee Elliot *(Pres & Dir-Mktg)*
Rachael Miller *(Exec VP-Design)*
Victor Valla *(Sr VP-Fine Art)*

I IMAGINE STUDIO
1603 Orrington Ave Ste 1090, Evanston, IL 60201
Tel.: (855) 792-7263
Fax: (866) 372-4390
E-Mail: info@iimaginestudio.com
Web Site: www.iimaginestudio.com

Year Founded: 2000

Alena Tsimis *(Mng Dir)*
Larry Minsky *(VP-Adv)*
Vladimir Moskvin *(VP-IT)*
Kurt Zoller *(VP-Acct Svcs)*
Olga Weiss *(Exec Dir-Creative)*
Jesse Jacobs *(Dir-Creative)*
Dmitriy Naymark *(Dir-Search Engine Mktg)*
Kristi Huber *(Mgr-Mktg)*

Accounts:
Lamin-Art, Inc.

I-SITE, INC.
15 S Third St Ste 200, Philadelphia, PA 19106-2801
Tel.: (215) 413-3135
Fax: (215) 413-3128
E-Mail: info@i-site.com
Web Site: www.i-site.com

E-Mail for Key Personnel:
President: ian@i-site.com

Employees: 13
Year Founded: 1996

Agency Specializes In: Children's Market, Consumer Marketing, E-Commerce, Education, Electronic Media, Food Service, Health Care Services, Internet/Web Design, Multimedia, Pharmaceutical

Steven Mangione *(Dir-Dev)*

Accounts:
Anacostia Watershed
Deloitte
National Dairy Council
Nxtup
Redbud Native Plant
Virunga National Park
Welcoming Center for New Pennsylvanians

I2 MARKETING INC
120 Coxe Ave Ste 2C, Asheville, NC 28801
Tel.: (828) 575-2268
Web Site: www.i2mktg.com

Year Founded: 2010

Agency Specializes In: Advertising, Brand Development & Integration, Email, Internet/Web Design, Public Relations, Social Media

Megan Gurney *(Partner, Dir-Accts & Strategist-Brand)*
Betsy Watson *(Dir-PR & Copywriter-Mktg)*
Jaki Brendle *(Dir-Media)*
Caitlin Trew *(Project Mgr & Acct Exec)*

Accounts:
Herrmann International
Mission Foundation

IBARRA STRATEGY GROUP INC.
1140 Connecticut Ave NW Ste 1100, Washington, DC 20036-4001
Tel.: (202) 969-8777
Fax: (202) 969-8778
E-Mail: mickey@IbarraStrategy.com
Web Site: www.ibarrastrategy.com

Agency Specializes In: Corporate Identity, Customer Relationship Management, Education, Email, Entertainment, Event Planning & Marketing, Hispanic Market, Media Relations, Pharmaceutical, Public Relations, Recruitment, Strategic Planning/Research

Mickey Ibarra *(Founder & Pres)*
Roxana Cazares Olivas *(VP)*
Laly Rivera Perez *(Mgr-Bus Ops)*

IBEL AGENCY
1055 N High St, Columbus, OH 43201
Tel.: (614) 294-0662
Fax: (614) 294-0663
E-Mail: contact@ibelagency.com
Web Site: www.ibelagency.com

Agency Specializes In: Advertising, Brand Development & Integration, Digital/Interactive, Internet/Web Design, Print, Social Media

Sebastian Ibel *(Founder & Pres)*
Jessica Jordan *(Art Dir)*
Alyssa Degeorge *(Dir-Art)*

Accounts:
The Benchmark
The Cleaning Fleet
CMH Fashion Week
Corporate One Federal Credit Union
Dress for Success
Hostd
Ohio Capital Corporation for Housing

ICC
(Formerly ICC Lowe)
5 Sylvan Way, Parsippany, NJ 07054
Tel.: (973) 984-2755
Fax: (973) 984-2759
E-Mail: dana.maiman@fcb.com
Web Site: www.icc-hc.com

Employees: 250

National Agency Associations: 4A's

Agency Specializes In: Health Care Services

Frank Galella *(CFO & COO)*
Chet Moss *(Exec VP & Dir-Creative)*
David Renner *(Exec VP & Dir-Creative)*
Dawn Contillo *(VP & Acct Grp Supvr)*
Anna Humphreys *(Dir-Media Strategy)*
Paul Kaiser *(Dir-Engagement Strategy)*

Accounts:
Bausch & Lomb
Glaxo Smith Kline
ICC Redshift
Novartis AG
Sepracor
Shire Pharmaceuticals

ICEBREAKER CONSULTING

475 5th Ave, New York, NY 10016
Tel.: (917) 477-7957
Web Site: icebreakerconsulting.com

Employees: 15
Year Founded: 2003

Agency Specializes In: Advertising, Affluent Market, Arts, Automotive, Brand Development & Integration, Business-To-Business, Communications, Computers & Software, Consulting, Consumer Goods, Consumer Marketing, Content, Corporate Communications, Corporate Identity, Custom Publishing, E-Commerce, Education, Electronic Media, Electronics, Email, Entertainment, Environmental, Fashion/Apparel, Graphic Design, Health Care Services, High Technology, Hispanic Market, Household Goods, Industrial, Information Technology, Internet/Web Design, Logo & Package Design, Luxury Products, Market Research, Media Buying Services, Media Planning, Media Relations, Media Training, Multimedia, New Product Development, Over-50 Market, Package Design, Planning & Consultation, Promotions, Public Relations, Publicity/Promotions, RSS (Really Simple Syndication), Radio, Restaurant, Retail, Sales Promotion, Search Engine Optimization, Social Marketing/Nonprofit, Social Media, Strategic Planning/Research, Sweepstakes, Travel & Tourism, Tween Market, Urban Market, Viral/Buzz/Word of Mouth, Women's Market

Approx. Annual Billings: $1,000,000

Aaron Mandelbaum *(CEO)*
Lea Mansour *(Sr Dir-Art)*

Accounts:
NBC The Biggest Loser; 2001

ICIDIGITAL

(Formerly Billups Design)
650 W Lake St Ste 330, Chicago, IL 60661
Tel.: (312) 930-1145
Web Site: www.icidigital.com

Year Founded: 2003

Agency Specializes In: Advertising, Digital/Interactive, Internet/Web Design

Ted Billups *(Principal-Creative)*
Charles Stevenson *(Principal-Ops)*

Accounts:
Indigo
United Airlines, Inc.

ICM PARTNERS

10250 Constellation Blvd., Los Angeles, CA 90067
Tel.: (310) 550-4278
Web Site: www.icmtalent.com

Agency Specializes In: Branded Entertainment, Consulting, Entertainment, Event Planning & Marketing, Planning & Consultation, Product Placement, Promotions, Sponsorship

Carol Goll *(Partner & Head-Global Branded Entertainment)*
Keyvan Peymani *(Mng Dir-Digital Strategy Div)*

Accounts:
Jaguar; 2013
Land Rover; 2013

ICON ADVERTISING & DESIGN INC

67 Sharp St, Hingham, MA 2043
Tel.: (781) 413-0001
E-Mail: info@iconadvertising.com
Web Site: www.iconadvertising.com

Agency Specializes In: Advertising, Brand Development & Integration, Graphic Design, Logo & Package Design, Package Design, Print, Public Relations, Search Engine Optimization, Social Media

Denis Concannon *(Pres)*

Accounts:
Convenient Auto Repair Specialists
Gibson Allen Design Build
TC Training

ICONOLOGIC

40 Inwood Cir, Atlanta, GA 30309
Tel.: (404) 260-4500
Fax: (404) 260-4581
E-Mail: info@iconologic.com
Web Site: www.iconologic.com

Employees: 20

Agency Specializes In: Advertising, Aviation & Aerospace, Brand Development & Integration, Communications, Consulting, Food Service, Government/Political, Internet/Web Design, Logo & Package Design, Men's Market, New Technologies, Restaurant, Sports Market

Ben Friedman *(Owner)*
Brad Copeland *(Pres)*
Ward Copeland *(Partner & COO)*
Juliet D'Ambrosio *(Partner & Dir-Editorial)*
Matt Rollins *(Partner & Dir-Creative)*

Accounts:
Andre Benjamin
Auburn University
The Coca-Cola Company

ICR

761 Main Ave, Norwalk, CT 06851
Tel.: (203) 682-8268
E-Mail: info@icrinc.com
Web Site: www.icrinc.com

Employees: 4

Agency Specializes In: Crisis Communications, Digital/Interactive, Entertainment, Financial, Health Care Services, Information Technology, Investor Relations, Market Research, Media Relations, Public Relations, Real Estate, Retail

Timothy Dolan *(Mng Partner)*
Michael R. Fox *(Mng Partner)*
Brad Cohen *(Mng Dir)*
Michael Robinson *(Mng Dir)*
Don Duffy *(Pres-Leisure, Gaming, Fin Svcs & Restaurants)*
John C. Sorensen *(COO-Consumer Goods, Private Equity & Fin Svcs)*
Anthony Depasquale *(Sr VP-Creative Content Production-Television/Video)*
Jessica Liddell *(Sr VP)*
Brian Ruby *(Sr VP)*
William Zima *(Mng Dir-Consumer Goods, Retail & Industrials-Asia)*
Kate Ottavio *(Acct Supvr)*

Accounts:
American Eagle Outfitters
Blackbaud
Chipotle
Circuit City
Inuvo, Inc.
Kenexa
LookSmart, Ltd.; San Francisco, CA
Metabolix
Multiband Corporation
New-Noodles & Co Publicity
Sentient Jet
New-SoulCycle Financial Communications
Swisher Hygiene
Titan Machinery
New-Wingstop Inc.
New-Zoe's Kitchen

ID29

425 River St, Troy, NY 12180
Tel.: (518) 687-0268
Fax: (518) 687-0607
Web Site: www.id29.com

Employees: 8

Agency Specializes In: Above-the-Line, Advertising, Advertising Specialties, Affiliate Marketing, Affluent Market, Alternative Advertising, Below-the-Line, Brand Development & Integration, Branded Entertainment, Co-op Advertising, College, Communications, Computers & Software, Consumer Goods, Consumer Marketing, Consumer Publications, Corporate Identity, Cosmetics, Direct Response Marketing, Direct-to-Consumer, Education, Electronic Media, Electronics, Entertainment, Event Planning & Marketing, Exhibit/Trade Shows, Experience Design, Fashion/Apparel, Financial, Food Service, Game Integration, Graphic Design, Guerilla Marketing, Identity Marketing, In-Store Advertising, Infomercials, Integrated Marketing, Internet/Web Design, Investor Relations, Leisure, Local Marketing, Luxury Products, Marine, Merchandising, Mobile Marketing, Multimedia, New Product Development, Newspapers & Magazines, Out-of-Home Media, Outdoor, Package Design, Point of Purchase, Point of Sale, Print, Production, Production (Print), Promotions, Recruitment, Sales Promotion, Search Engine Optimization, Sponsorship, Sports Market, Stakeholders, Sweepstakes, T.V., Technical Advertising, Teen Market, Trade & Consumer Magazines, Transportation, Travel & Tourism, Urban Market, Viral/Buzz/Word of Mouth, Web (Banner Ads, Pop-ups, etc.), Women's Market, Yellow Pages Advertising

Approx. Annual Billings: $1,000,000

Doug Bartow *(Principal & Dir-Design)*
Michael Fallone *(Principal & Dir-Creative)*
James Morrison *(Acct Dir)*
Andrew Neufeld *(Acct Dir)*
Jake Wright *(Sr Designer)*

Accounts:
The Case Foundation
Davidson Brothers Brand & Marketing Communication, Creative Strategy
EMPAC
Litespeed
Novell
Realtime Worlds
The Travel Channel
Troy Night Out

Union College

I.D.E.A.
(Formerly Fishtank)
444 W Beech St 4th Fl, San Diego, CA 92101
Tel.: (619) 295-8232
Fax: (619) 295-8234
Web Site: www.theideabrand.com/

Employees: 12

Agency Specializes In: Advertising, Brand Development & Integration, Collateral, Digital/Interactive, Direct Response Marketing, Electronic Media, Electronics, Event Planning & Marketing, Logo & Package Design, Media Buying Services, Media Planning, Multimedia, New Technologies, Outdoor, Production (Ad, Film, Broadcast), Production (Print), Radio, Sponsorship, T.V.

Jonathan Bailey *(Founder)*
Ryan Berman *(Founder & Chief Idea Officer)*
Indra Gardiner Bowers *(Founder)*
Daniel Andreani *(Sr VP & Exec Dir-Creative)*
Amy Martin Winhoven *(Sr VP-Strategy & Plng)*
Amon Rappaport *(VP-Brand Purpose)*
Melina Ramos *(Specialist-Ops)*
Clarissa Slagle *(Specialist-Social Media)*
Lisa Prentis *(Jr Strategist-Digital Media)*

Accounts:
New-Eddie Bauer
National University Broadcast, Campaign: "Spiders", Campaign: "Sports", Digital, Outdoor, Print
Olevia
New-Qualcomm
Scheib
New-UFC Gym
Unicef
New-Visit Newport Beach
Vivitar
Von Dutch

IDEA AGENCY
(Formerly Smith & Jones)
76 Main St, Sturbridge, MA 01566-1260
Tel.: (508) 347-7793
Fax: (508) 347-7796
Web Site: www.ideaagency.biz/

Employees: 15
Year Founded: 1995

Agency Specializes In: Advertising, Brand Development & Integration, Broadcast, Business-To-Business, Collateral, Communications, Consulting, Consumer Marketing, Corporate Identity, Graphic Design, Internet/Web Design, Logo & Package Design, New Product Development, Newspaper, Newspapers & Magazines, Outdoor, Pets , Point of Sale, Print, Production, Publicity/Promotions, Sales Promotion, Strategic Planning/Research, Trade & Consumer Magazines

Christine Tieri *(Pres & Strategist-Certified Brand)*
Jennifer Day *(Acct Mgr)*
Jessica Adams *(Mgr-Content)*
Alex Quinn *(Mgr-Ops)*
Susan Stebbins *(Mgr-Traffic)*
Vivian Brooks *(Strategist-Comm)*
Caitlin Ryan *(Strategist-Media)*

Accounts:
Hudson Valley Community College Campaign: "Be bold. Be a Viking."
Venus Wafers Nejaimes Lavasch

IDEA ASSOCIATES, INC.
2245 Perimeter Park Dr Ste 1, Atlanta, GA 30341
Tel.: (770) 234-9407
Fax: (770) 234-9410
E-Mail: sales@ideaassociates.com
Web Site: www.ideaassociates.com

Employees: 7
Year Founded: 1988

Agency Specializes In: Real Estate

Approx. Annual Billings: $4,500,000

Breakdown of Gross Billings by Media: Other: 40%; Print: 60%

Bruce Freides *(Principal)*
Sibet Burch Freides *(Principal)*
Jeff Stevens *(Dir-Creative)*

Accounts:
Achasta; Dahlonega, GA
Sobu Flats; Atlanta, GA

IDEA BANK MARKETING
701 W Second St, Hastings, NE 68901
Tel.: (402) 463-0588
Fax: (402) 463-2187
E-Mail: mail@ideadbankmarketing.com
Web Site: www.ideabankmarketing.com

E-Mail for Key Personnel:
President: ann@ideabankmarketing.com
Creative Dir.: sherma@ideabankmarketing.com

Employees: 12
Year Founded: 1982

National Agency Associations: Second Wind Limited

Agency Specializes In: Agriculture, Brand Development & Integration, Broadcast, Business Publications, Cable T.V., Co-op Advertising, Collateral, Communications, Consulting, Consumer Marketing, Corporate Identity, Direct Response Marketing, Electronic Media, Exhibit/Trade Shows, Graphic Design, Industrial, Internet/Web Design, Logo & Package Design, Magazines, Media Buying Services, Multimedia, New Product Development, Newspaper, Newspapers & Magazines, Point of Purchase, Point of Sale, Print, Production, Public Relations, Radio, Sales Promotion, T.V., Telemarketing, Yellow Pages Advertising

Approx. Annual Billings: $2,000,000

Ann Martin *(Founder & Pres)*
Sherma Jones *(Owner)*
Karen Stroebel *(Office Mgr)*
Tamera Schlueter *(Acct Planner & Copywriter)*

Accounts:
Bruckman Rubber Co.
Centennial Plastics, Inc
Central Community College
Chief Agri/Industrial Products; Kearney, ME Agriculture; 2002
Chief Custom Products
Chief Fabrication Division; Grand Island, NE Agri Building
Community Hospital - McCook; McCook, NE; 1996
The Equitable Federal Savings Bank; Grand Island, NE; 2002
Family Medical Center; Hastings, NE; 2002
Family Resources of Greater Nebraska; Grand Island, NE; 2000
First Bank & Trust Company
First National Bank; Minden, NE Financial; 2000
Five Points Bank; Grand Island, NE Banking; 1999
General Collection, Inc.
Hal Maggiore Photography
Hornady Manufacturing Company; Grand Island, NE Bullets, Handguns, Rifles; 2001
Industrial Irrigation & Engine Services; Hastings, NE; 1984
Peterson Industries; Smith Center, KS RV Trailers; 1994

THE I.D.E.A. BRAND
444 W Beech St 4th Fl, San Diego, CA 92101
Tel.: (619) 295-8232
Fax: (619) 295-8234
Web Site: www.theideabrand.com

Year Founded: 2012

Agency Specializes In: Advertising, Brand Development & Integration, Digital/Interactive, Public Relations, Social Media

Ryan Berman *(Founder & Chief Creative Officer)*
Jonathan Bailey *(Co-Founder)*
Indra Gardiner Bowers *(Co-Founder)*
Michaela Krams *(VP-Media)*
Julie Messing-Paea *(VP-Reputation)*
James White *(VP-Brand Mgmt)*
Bryan Hansen *(Mgr-Reputation)*
Torie Wohlwend *(Mgr-Reputation)*
Amanda Duncan *(Supvr-Brand)*
Venice Fahey *(Coord-Reputation)*

Accounts:
ecoATM Brand Identity, Brand Positioning, Crisis Communication, Media Relations, Messaging, PR, Planning, Social Media Strategy, Website Development
Harrah's Rincon Casino & Resort
Hot Spring Spas Creative Branding Development, Print

THE IDEA CENTER
3991 Glenside Dr Ste H, Richmond, VA 23228
Tel.: (804) 264-3067
Web Site: www.theideacenter.com

Agency Specializes In: Advertising, Internet/Web Design, Print, Radio, Search Engine Optimization, Social Media, T.V.

Barry Martin *(Pres)*
Peyton Gregory *(Dir-Art)*
Kyle Milwit *(Acct Mgr)*
Taylor Quinn *(Specialist-Media)*

Accounts:
HCA Virginia

IDEA ENGINEERING, INC.
21 E Carrillo St, Santa Barbara, CA 93101
Tel.: (805) 963-5399
Fax: (805) 963-5339
E-Mail: info@ideaengineering.com
Web Site: www.ideaengineering.com

Employees: 10
Year Founded: 2000

Agency Specializes In: Advertising, Brand Development & Integration, Media Buying Services

Simon Dixon *(CEO)*
Joyce Valentino *(CFO)*
Richard Gregoire *(Principal & Mgr-Process Engrg)*
Wallace Reinecke *(VP)*
Alicia Chasse *(Controller)*
Ron Lucas *(Sr Dir-Art)*
Jeanne Spencer *(Dir-Creative)*

Accounts:
Bryant & Sons, Ltd.
CenCal Health
The Home Depot Foundation; 2003
Sansum Clinic; Santa Barbara, CA Medical Services; 2005

University of Santa Barbara; Santa Barbara, CA

THE IDEA FACTORY

122 E 42nd St Ste 2900, New York, NY 10168
Tel.: (917) 371-7754
E-Mail: vc@theideafactory.biz
Web Site: www.theideafactory.biz

Employees: 5
Year Founded: 1992

Agency Specializes In: Advertising, Affluent Market, Alternative Advertising, Automotive, Below-the-Line, Brand Development & Integration, Broadcast, Business-To-Business, Cable T.V., Catalogs, Collateral, College, Communications, Computers & Software, Consulting, Consumer Goods, Consumer Marketing, Consumer Publications, Corporate Communications, Corporate Identity, Cosmetics, Digital/Interactive, Direct Response Marketing, Direct-to-Consumer, E-Commerce, Electronic Media, Fashion/Apparel, Financial, Food Service, Graphic Design, Guerilla Marketing, Health Care Services, High Technology, Hospitality, Household Goods, In-Store Advertising, Industrial, Infomercials, Internet/Web Design, Legal Services, Local Marketing, Logo & Package Design, Magazines, Market Research, Media Planning, Media Relations, Medical Products, Men's Market, New Product Development, Over-50 Market, Package Design, Paid Searches, Pharmaceutical, Point of Purchase, Point of Sale, Print, Production (Ad, Film, Broadcast), Production (Print), Promotions, Public Relations, Publicity/Promotions, Publishing, Radio, Regional, Restaurant, Retail, Sales Promotion, Search Engine Optimization, Seniors' Market, Sponsorship, Sports Market, Strategic Planning/Research, T.V., Teen Market, Trade & Consumer Magazines, Travel & Tourism, Urban Market, Women's Market

Approx. Annual Billings: $2,000,000

Breakdown of Gross Billings by Media: Brdcst.: 30%; Cable T.V.: 20%; Consulting: 10%; Fees: 15%; Print: 10%; Radio: 15%

Vincent Conti *(Exec Dir-Creative & Sr Strategist)*

IDEA GROVE

14800 Quorum Dr Ste 320, Dallas, TX 75254
Tel.: (972) 235-3439
E-Mail: inquiries@ideagrove.com
Web Site: www.ideagrove.com

Agency Specializes In: Advertising, Internet/Web Design, Public Relations, Search Engine Optimization, Social Media, Sponsorship

Margaret Pacheco *(COO & Sr VP)*
Michelle Doss *(VP-Acct Svcs)*
Jamie Rudolph *(Acct Dir)*
Elizabeth Bari *(Acct Dir)*
Brant Schroeder *(Creative Dir)*
Brigid OConnor *(Dir-Fin & Ops)*
Kristy Blackmon *(Sr Mgr-Content)*
Jarrett Rush *(Sr Mgr-Content)*
Michelle Malina *(Mgr-Social Media)*
Taylon Chandler *(Mgr-Paid Search)*

Accounts:
Pivot3 (Integrated Marketing & Public Relations AOR)

IDEA HALL

Metro Pointe 950 S Coast Dr Ste 280, Costa Mesa, CA 92626
Tel.: (714) 436-0855
E-Mail: info@ideahall.com
Web Site: www.ideahall.com

Employees: 18
Year Founded: 2003

Agency Specializes In: Advertising, Brand Development & Integration, Direct Response Marketing, Mobile Marketing, Multicultural, Product Placement, Public Relations

Randy Hall *(Principal)*
Tempel Watson *(Controller)*
Daniel Rhodes *(Gen Mgr)*
Mike Kornoff *(Sr Dir-Art & Dir-Creative)*
Jeff Cole *(Sr Producer-Creative & Digital Media)*
Meghan Curtiss *(Acct Mgr)*
Lisa Harris *(Mgr-Mktg)*
Martina Uhlirova *(Mgr-Mktg)*
Megan Barry *(Acct Exec)*
Nicole Inal *(Acct Exec)*
Tiffany Trias *(Asst Acct Exec)*

Accounts:
Birtcher Land Company Corporate and asset branding, PR, advertising, websites; 2006
Kaiser Permanente Orange County (Agency of Record)
Pumpkin Glow (Agency of Record)
Roll Real Estate Development (Agency of Record)
Sabal Financial Corporate and business line branding, Direct Response, PR; 2010

THE IDEA MILL

6101 Penn Ave Ste 400, Pittsburgh, PA 15206
Tel.: (412) 924-0027
Fax: (412) 924-0034
E-Mail: grzym@ideamill.com
Web Site: www.ideamill.com

Employees: 4
Year Founded: 1998

Agency Specializes In: Advertising

Anthony Musmanno *(Chief Creative Officer)*
Doug Kochmanski *(Dir-Art)*

Accounts:
Arterati
Cochran Automotive
Dockers
Flynn Construction
Georgia Museum of Art
Irish and Classical Theatre
Jeffrey's Salon
King's Family Restaurants
TravelCenters of America, LLC Services for Professional Truck Drivers; 2005

IDEABASE

138 E Main St Ste 203, Kent, OH 44240
Tel.: (330) 672-7300
Fax: (330) 672-7373
Web Site: www.ideabasekent.com

Agency Specializes In: Advertising, Brand Development & Integration, Broadcast, Digital/Interactive, Media Planning, Media Relations, Print, Public Relations, Radio, T.V.

Kristin Dowling *(Mgr-Bus Dev)*

Accounts:
College of Communication & Information

IDEAHAUS

1014 Stratford Ct, Del Mar, CA 92014
Tel.: (844) 433-2428
E-Mail: sandiego@ideahaus.com
Web Site: www.ideahaus.com

Year Founded: 1990

Agency Specializes In: Advertising, Graphic Design, Internet/Web Design

Kevin Popovic *(Founder & CEO)*

Accounts:
Alliance Healthcare Foundation
Blue Sky Broadcast
GotUWired
PT Services Group
Take Shape For Life

IDEAOLOGY ADVERTISING INC.

4223 Glencoe Ave Ste A 127, Marina Del Rey, CA 90292
Tel.: (310) 306-6501
Fax: (310) 306-6508
E-Mail: csacks@ideaology.biz
Web Site: www.ideaology.biz

Employees: 6

Cary Sacks *(Pres)*
Louis Plotkin *(Partner)*
John Crosson *(Exec VP & Gen Mgr)*
Kim Ashton *(Acct Dir)*
Dino Santili *(Dir-Creative)*

Accounts:
Bank of America
Bank of Hawaii
Cerritos Auto Square
Mattress Firm
Sit'nSleep Mattresses

IDEAS COLLIDE INC.

6125 E Indian School Rd Studio Ste 1005, Scottsdale, AZ 85251
Tel.: (480) 659-4520
E-Mail: info@ideascollide.com
Web Site: www.ideascollide.com

Agency Specializes In: Advertising, Digital/Interactive, Email, Market Research, Strategic Planning/Research

Rebecca Clyde *(Co-Founder)*
Matthew Clyde *(Pres & Sr Strategist)*
Mike Mason *(VP-Creative Svcs & Brand Dev)*
Bridget Daly *(Acct Dir)*
Colin Bennett *(Mgr-Traffic)*
Joel Eberhart *(Mgr-Mktg)*

Accounts:
Best Western International, Inc.

IDEASCAPE, INC.

57 Newcomb Rd, Stoneham, MA 02180
Tel.: (781) 665-3700
E-Mail: rl@ideascape.com
Web Site: www.ideascape.com

E-Mail for Key Personnel:
President: rl@ideascape.com

Employees: 5
Year Founded: 1990

Agency Specializes In: Brand Development & Integration, Business-To-Business, Catalogs, Collateral, Corporate Identity, Direct Response Marketing, E-Commerce, Fashion/Apparel, Graphic Design, Health Care Services, High Technology, Internet/Web Design, Leisure, Logo & Package Design, Medical Products, Print, Production, Sports Market, Travel & Tourism

Approx. Annual Billings: $1,000,000

Ralph Lucier *(Pres)*

IDEAWORK STUDIOS
735 State St Ste 100, Santa Barbara, CA 93101
Tel.: (805) 962-2468
Web Site: www.ideawork.com

Jay Schwartz *(Chief Creative Officer)*
David Rayner *(VP-Strategy & Dev)*

Accounts:
Australia's Thunder from Down Under
Bally Technologies
Barona Resort and Casino
Crunch Fitness 21st Birthday Campaign, Contest, E-Mail, Out of Home Marketing, Social Media
Hard Rock Hotel & Casino
Harrah's
MGM Grand's Crazy Horse Paris

IDEAWORKS, INC.
1110 N Palafox St, Pensacola, FL 32501-2608
Tel.: (850) 434-9095
Fax: (850) 434-5753
E-Mail: info@ideaworksusa.com
Web Site: www.ideaworksusa.com

E-Mail for Key Personnel:
President: carons@ideaworksusa.com
Creative Dir.: michelleo@ideaworksusa.com

Employees: 10
Year Founded: 1995

Agency Specializes In: Advertising, Brand Development & Integration, Business Publications, Co-op Advertising, Collateral, Communications, Consulting, Corporate Identity, Direct Response Marketing, E-Commerce, Event Planning & Marketing, Exhibit/Trade Shows, Financial, Graphic Design, Health Care Services, Internet/Web Design, Investor Relations, Media Buying Services, Medical Products, New Product Development, Newspaper, Newspapers & Magazines, Out-of-Home Media, Outdoor, Over-50 Market, Planning & Consultation, Point of Purchase, Point of Sale, Print, Production, Public Relations, Publicity/Promotions, Radio, Real Estate, Restaurant, Retail, Seniors' Market, Sports Market, Strategic Planning/Research, T.V., Trade & Consumer Magazines, Travel & Tourism, Yellow Pages Advertising

Breakdown of Gross Billings by Media: Co-op Adv.: 2%; Consulting: 5%; Fees: 3%; Graphic Design: 10%; Mags.: 21%; Outdoor: 4%; Point of Purchase: 2%; Point of Sale: 2%; Promos.: 10%; Radio: 14%; Sls. Promo.: 10%; Strategic Planning/Research: 5%; T.V.: 12%

Caron Sjoberg *(Pres & CEO)*
Michelle Ortiz-Miguez *(VP & Dir-Creative)*
Jade Lantz *(Coord-Mktg)*

Accounts:
Baptist Health Care
Northwest Florida Regional Planning Council

IDENTITY
400 W 14th St 3rd Fl, New York, NY 10014
Tel.: (212) 683-2500
Fax: (212) 683-2502
Web Site: www.identityid.com

National Agency Associations: 4A's

Agency Specializes In: Advertising

Joe Masi *(Owner & Exec Producer)*
Deidre Smalls-Landau *(Mng Dir & Exec VP)*

Accounts:
Covered California Media Planning & Buying
Dr Pepper Snapple Group, Inc. 7up
Gucci America Inc.
Honda North America, Inc.
Nissan North America, Inc. Infiniti
Tommy Hilfiger USA

THE IDENTITY GROUP
440 W First St Ste 204, Tustin, CA 92780-3047
Tel.: (714) 573-0010
Fax: (714) 573-2084
E-Mail: jmerkow@theidgroup.com
Web Site: www.theidgroup.com

Employees: 11
Year Founded: 1991

Agency Specializes In: Automotive, Business Publications, Business-To-Business, Communications, Consumer Marketing, Consumer Publications, Corporate Identity, Direct Response Marketing, Financial, Graphic Design, Health Care Services, Logo & Package Design, Magazines, Point of Purchase, Print, Production, Publicity/Promotions, Sales Promotion

Approx. Annual Billings: $2,000,000

Paul Parkinson *(Owner & Partner)*

Accounts:
Bank Of America
Cal Optima
Doheny Eye Institute
Employee Benefits America
Financial Network Investment Corporation
First Interstate Bank
Gibraltar Savings & Loan
Glendale Memorial Hospital
Houlihan, Lakey, Howard & Zukin, Inc.
Institute for Healthcare Advancement
Integrated Medical Management
Kaiser Permanente Orange County
Keenan & Associates
Methodist Hospital of Southern California
Saint John's Hospitals (CHW)
USC School of Journalism

IDEOPIA
4270 Ivy Pointe Blvd Ste 120, Cincinnati, OH 45245
Tel.: (513) 947-1444, ext. 10
E-Mail: info@ideopia.com
Web Site: www.ideopia.com

Employees: 16
Year Founded: 1990

Agency Specializes In: Advertising, Affluent Market, Arts, Collateral, Computers & Software, Consulting, Consumer Goods, Consumer Marketing, Consumer Publications, Content, Corporate Communications, Corporate Identity, Crisis Communications, E-Commerce, Education, Environmental, Event Planning & Marketing, Exhibit/Trade Shows, Experience Design, Financial, Graphic Design, Health Care Services, High Technology, Household Goods, In-Store Advertising, Information Technology, Integrated Marketing, Internet/Web Design, Luxury Products, Market Research, Media Relations, Media Training, Medical Products, Mobile Marketing, New Product Development, Newspaper, Newspapers & Magazines, Outdoor, Over-50 Market, Print, Production (Print), Promotions, Public Relations, Real Estate, Restaurant, Retail, Social Marketing/Nonprofit, Strategic Planning/Research, Technical Advertising, Travel & Tourism

Approx. Annual Billings: $3,500,000

Bill Abramovitz *(CEO)*
Susan Abramovitz *(Pres-Ideopia, B2B & B2C Integrated Mktg)*
Mike Bober *(Dir-Online Strategy)*
Ben Singleton *(Dir-PR)*
Curt Staubach *(Dir-Web Dev & Interactive)*
Tori Tarvin *(Dir-Social Media)*
Toni Parker *(Mgr-Brand Grp Support)*
Emily Babel *(Designer-Interactive)*
Eric House *(Copywriter)*
Joel Steczynski *(Sr Designer)*

Accounts:
Avure Technologies HPP Food Processing Machines; 2014
Hamilton Caster Heavy Duty Casters, Wheels & Carts; 2008
Mercy Health System; 2010
Reichert Technologies; Buffalo, NY Medical Diagnostic Devices & Equipment; 2012

Division

Ideopia Medical Marketing
4270 Ivy Pointe Blvd Ste 120, Cincinnati, OH 45245
Tel.: (513) 947-1444
Web Site: www.ideopiamedical.com

Employees: 15
Year Founded: 1990

Agency Specializes In: Advertising, Affluent Market, Alternative Advertising, Brand Development & Integration, Broadcast, Business-To-Business, Cable T.V., Collateral, Consumer Marketing, Content, Corporate Identity, Cosmetics, Direct Response Marketing, E-Commerce, Email, Event Planning & Marketing, Fashion/Apparel, Graphic Design, Guerilla Marketing, Health Care Services, High Technology, Identity Marketing, Information Technology, International, Internet/Web Design, Logo & Package Design, Luxury Products, Market Research, Media Training, Medical Products, Mobile Marketing, New Product Development, New Technologies, Newspaper, Newspapers & Magazines, Out-of-Home Media, Outdoor, Over-50 Market, Paid Searches, Podcasting, Point of Purchase, Point of Sale, Print, Production (Ad, Film, Broadcast), Public Relations, RSS (Really Simple Syndication), Radio, Regional, Sales Promotion, Seniors' Market, Social Marketing/Nonprofit, Social Media, Strategic Planning/Research, Sweepstakes, T.V., Trade & Consumer Magazines, Web (Banner Ads, Pop-ups, etc.)

Susan Abramovitz *(Pres & Dir-Brand Planning)*
Bill Abramovitz *(CEO & Creative Dir)*
Mike Bober *(Dir-Integrated Mktg)*
Ben Singleton *(Dir-PR)*
Curt Staubach *(Dir-Web Dev)*
Tori Tarvin *(Dir-Social Media)*

Accounts:
Bell Ophthalmic Technologies National Ophthalmic Distributor; 2005
Haag-Streit All Diagnostic Brands, ENT, ER, Neuro, Ophthalmic, Surgical; 1990
Invision Eye Fitness and Health Multi-location Ophthalmic Practice; 2006
Mercy Health System Bariatric, Branding, General Hospital, Orthopaedic, Pediatrics; 2012
Reichert Medical Technologies Ophthalmic Diagnostic Devices; 2012
Volk Optical Surgical & Diagnostic Lenses; 2008

IDEX CREATIVE MARKETING
1655 Wynne Rd Ste 101, Cordova, TN 38016-4905
Tel.: (901) 373-7500
Fax: (901) 373-7171
E-Mail: jtumbrink@idexcreative.com
Web Site: www.idexcreative.com

E-Mail for Key Personnel:
President: lpardue@idexcreative.com
Creative Dir.: rmunoz@idexcreative.com

Employees: 10
Year Founded: 1992

Agency Specializes In: Advertising, Brand Development & Integration, Business-To-Business, Collateral, Consumer Marketing, Consumer Publications, Corporate Identity, Direct Response Marketing, Food Service, Graphic Design, Logo & Package Design, Newspapers & Magazines, Point of Purchase, Point of Sale, Print, Restaurant, Retail, Sales Promotion, Trade & Consumer Magazines, Travel & Tourism

Larry Pardue *(CEO)*
Jim Tumbrink *(Principal)*

Accounts:
Morgan Keegan
Pyramex
Raymond James
Semco
Smith & Nephew

IDFIVE
3600 Clipper Mill Rd, Baltimore, MD 21211
Tel.: (410) 837-5555
Fax: (410) 783-0999
E-Mail: hi@idfive.com
Web Site: www.idfive.com

Employees: 30
Year Founded: 2005

Agency Specializes In: Advertising, Business-To-Business, College, Digital/Interactive, Graphic Design, Integrated Marketing, Internet/Web Design, Media Planning, Paid Searches, Search Engine Optimization, Strategic Planning/Research, Technical Advertising, Web (Banner Ads, Pop-ups, etc.)

Approx. Annual Billings: $6,000,000

Andres Zapata *(Co-Founder & Exec VP-Strategy)*
Chris Smith *(Dir-Strategy)*
Sam Borowy *(Assoc Dir-Creative)*
Maddie Forrester *(Acct Supvr)*
Ira Gewanter *(Acct Supvr)*
Jessica Hinton *(Acct Supvr)*
Max Kellner *(Acct Supvr)*
Jodi Hey *(Sr Acct Exec)*
Caitlin Currey-Ortiz *(Acct Exec)*
Kelly Driver *(Sr Designer)*

Accounts:
Academbot.com
Ally Financial Inc.
Johns Hopkins Carey School of Business
Jophns Hopkins School of Public Health
University of Baltimore; 2008
University of Dallas
Vaccinogen
Whitman, Requardt & Associates

IDIRECT MARKETING, INC.
6789 Quail Hill Pkwy Ste 550, Irvine, CA 92603
Tel.: (949) 753-7300
Fax: (949) 269-0198
E-Mail: dhastings@idirectmarketing.com
Web Site: www.idirectmarketing.com

Employees: 9

Agency Specializes In: Customer Relationship Management, Direct Response Marketing, Direct-to-Consumer, Integrated Marketing, Internet/Web Design, Local Marketing, Market Research, Media Buying Services, Media Planning, Multimedia, Planning & Consultation, Promotions, Publicity/Promotions, Real Estate, Sales Promotion, Strategic Planning/Research, Viral/Buzz/Word of Mouth, Web (Banner Ads, Pop-ups, etc.)

Approx. Annual Billings: $9,079,524

Dennis J. Hastings *(Owner)*

IDYLLWILD ADVERTISING
8184 S Highland Dr Ste C7, Salt Lake City, UT 84093
Tel.: (801) 733-8400
Web Site: http://www.idydigital.com/

Year Founded: 2007

Agency Specializes In: Advertising, Email, Internet/Web Design, Search Engine Optimization, Social Media

Michelle Smith *(Founder & CEO)*
Greg Bay *(VP-Mktg & Dev)*
Laura Barlow *(Dir-Social Media & Mgr-Mktg)*
Scott Collett *(Dir-Art)*
Hannah Halstrom *(Project Mgr & Copywriter)*

Accounts:
Connor Sports Flooring
Nashville Mosquito Squad
Showtime Custom Floors
Solitude Mountain Resort
Sport Court International Inc.

IGNITE COMMUNICATIONS
11445 JohnsCreek Pkwy, Duluth, GA 30097
Tel.: (770) 232-1711
Fax: (770) 232-1722
E-Mail: pball@ignitecommunications.com
Web Site: www.ignitecommunications.com

Agency Specializes In: Advertising, Business-To-Business, Communications, Corporate Communications, Direct Response Marketing, Direct-to-Consumer, Food Service, Industrial, Integrated Marketing, Local Marketing, Logo & Package Design, Point of Sale, Promotions, Telemarketing

Doug Pickert *(Pres)*
Pam Ball *(CFO)*
Pam Waken *(VP-Acct Svc)*

Accounts:
Agility
Arby's Restaurant Group, Inc.
Giles Industries
Moe's Southwest Grill
Pactiv Packaging North America Protective Packaging
Paradise Tomato Kitchens
ProMarketing; Atlanta, GA; 2008
Rich Products; Buffalo, NY
Surge; Atlanta, GA; 2008
Ted's Montana Grill

IGNITE DESIGN AND ADVERTISING, INC.
8480 Utica Ave, Rancho Cucamonga, CA 91730
Tel.: (909) 948-6704
Web Site: www.clickandcombust.com

Agency Specializes In: Automotive, Education, Entertainment, Fashion/Apparel, Government/Political, Health Care Services, Legal Services, Pets , Real Estate, Sports Market

Chris Wheeler *(Pres & CEO)*
Audrey Pentz Kikos *(Dir-Client Solutions)*
Philip Mastroianni *(Dir-Digital Solutions)*
Gregory Poutre *(Dir-Art)*
Carolyn Hayes Uber *(Dir-Brand Strategies)*
Kimberli Wheeler *(Dir-Bus Ops)*
Jami Sams *(Assoc Acct Mgr)*
Joaquin Barranco *(Designer-Digital Media)*
Mannie Gonzales, III *(Designer-Web & Creative)*

Accounts:
Kumho Tire

IGNITED
2150 Park Pl, El Segundo, CA 90245
Tel.: (310) 773-3100
Fax: (310) 773-3101
E-Mail: brosenthal@ignitedusa.com
Web Site: www.ignitedusa.com

Employees: 80
Year Founded: 1999

National Agency Associations: 4A's-THINKLA

Agency Specializes In: Above-the-Line, Advertising, Automotive, Below-the-Line, Brand Development & Integration, Business-To-Business, Collateral, Communications, Computers & Software, Consulting, Consumer Goods, Consumer Marketing, Content, Cosmetics, Customer Relationship Management, Digital/Interactive, Direct-to-Consumer, E-Commerce, Electronic Media, Electronics, Entertainment, Event Planning & Marketing, Exhibit/Trade Shows, Experience Design, Food Service, Game Integration, Government/Political, Graphic Design, High Technology, Hospitality, In-Store Advertising, Industrial, Information Technology, Internet/Web Design, Leisure, Logo & Package Design, Luxury Products, Market Research, Media Buying Services, Media Planning, Men's Market, Merchandising, Mobile Marketing, Multimedia, New Technologies, Newspaper, Newspapers & Magazines, Out-of-Home Media, Outdoor, Package Design, Paid Searches, Planning & Consultation, Point of Purchase, Print, Production, Production (Print), Real Estate, Sales Promotion, Search Engine Optimization, Social Marketing/Nonprofit, Social Media, Sponsorship, Sports Market, Strategic Planning/Research, T.V., Technical Advertising, Teen Market, Trade & Consumer Magazines, Transportation, Travel & Tourism, Viral/Buzz/Word of Mouth, Web (Banner Ads, Pop-ups, etc.)

Approx. Annual Billings: $178,000,000

Bill Rosenthal *(COO)*
Eric Springer *(Chief Creative Officer)*
Stacy Sanchez *(Grp Dir-Media)*
Amy Matheu *(Dir-Art)*
Alexandria Oliver *(Dir-Plng)*
Whitney Stephenson *(Dir-Fin)*
Tiffany Fudge *(Supvr-Media)*
Nicole Meadows *(Supvr-Media)*
Maria Aintablian *(Media Planner)*
Brian Hallisey *(Copywriter)*
Torin Ladewig *(Planner-Digital Media)*
Emily O'Donnell *(Planner-Digital Media)*
Tate Adams *(Jr Analyst)*
Christopher Yeh *(Asst Media Planner)*

Accounts:
Activision Blizzard, Inc; Santa Monica, CA "Call of Duty", "Destiny", "Guitar Hero", "Skylanders", Campaign: "Deadpool Does Comic-Con", Experiential Marketing, Video Games; 1999
Bravo Social
Contiki Vacations
Deckers Outdoor Corporation Brand Awareness, Campaign: "#1 Fan", Campaign: "Always Sanuk", Campaign: "Drummer Boy", Campaign: "Never Uncomfortable", Creative, Digital, Media Planning & Buying, Radio, Sanuk Footwear (Agency of Record), Social
DTS, Inc. Campaign: "Dts Anthem", Campaign:

"We're All Ears", Headphone X
Fisker Automotive Digital
Fresh & Easy Neighborhood Market Inc Campaign: "It's About Time", Campaign: "Smarter Market", Digital Media, Experiential, Out-of-Home, Radio, Social, TV, Video
gumi "Brave Frontier", "Chain Chronicle", Experiential Marketing; 2014
New-Johnnie-O
Konami Digital Entertainment Campaign: "Metal Gear Rising: Revengeance"
LA Derby Dolls Campaign: "Gori Spelling"
MGA Entertainment
MTV "Rebel Music"; 2014
NBC Universal Motion Pictures; Los Angeles, CA Movie & DVD Media Planning & Buying; 2007
NBC Universal Television Networks Group
NFL Campaign: "NFL Rivalry Fashion"
Pinkberry Inc.
Scopely
Sony Electronics; San Diego, CA VAIO Laptops; 2005
Syfy; New York, NY SyFy Channel Shows
Trion Media Planning & Buying
Turtle Beach Experiential Marketing, Video Production; 2012
United States Army; Washington, DC Education & Outreach, Marketing, Recruiting; 2001
New-U.S. Securities & Exchange Commission (SEC) Integrated Marketing, Public Service Campaign; 2015
VEEV Media Planning & Buying
Zico; El Segundo, CA Campaign: "Naturally Powered", Coconut Water; 2010

Branch

Ignited
915 Bdwy Ste 605, New York, NY 10010
(See Separate Listing)

IGNITION BRANDING
2211 E 7th Ave, Tampa, FL 33605
Tel.: (813) 356-0556
E-Mail: jglasure@ignitionbranding.com
Web Site: www.ignitionbranding.com

Agency Specializes In: Advertising, Crisis Communications, Digital/Interactive, Exhibit/Trade Shows, Graphic Design, Media Training, Print, Public Relations, Search Engine Optimization, Strategic Planning/Research

Goktug Sarioz *(Partner & Exec Dir-Creative)*
Martin Kistler *(Partner & Dir-Creative)*
Jon Simon *(Sr VP-Brand Mktg & Strategy)*
Matt Silverman *(Mng Dir-Motion Design & Producer)*
Emmett James *(VP & Dir-Creative)*
Louie Lorenzo *(Dir-Digital Production)*
Tomasz Opasinski *(Dir-Creative)*

Accounts:
Ambassador Limousine
BlackBerry Blackberry

IGNITION INTERACTIVE
12959 Coral Tree Pl, Los Angeles, CA 90066
Tel.: (310) 586-1670
Web Site: www.ignitioncreative.net

Agency Specializes In: Advertising, Broadcast, Game Integration, Print

Martin Kistler *(Founder & Chief Creative Officer)*
Dale Lanier *(Exec VP-Brdcst Adv)*
Andrew Reed *(Exec Dir-Creative)*
Jason Herron *(Sr Dir-Art)*
Dang Nguyen *(Sr Dir-Art)*
Michael Brittain *(Creative Dir-Print)*
Matt Clack *(Dir-Creative)*
David Ikeda *(Dir-Creative)*
Patrick Sayre *(Dir-Art)*
Gary Sertyan *(Sr Supvr-Media)*

Accounts:
20th Century Fox Campaign: "X-Men: Days of Future Past"
Arrested Development Campaign: "ManGo", www.insertmeanywhere.biz
Lions Gate Entertainment Corp. The Hunger Games
Netflix Campaign: "Superfan", House of Cards, Lilyhammer, Orange is the New Black
Resident Evil Campaign: "Eat Like A Tyrant"
Trask Industries

IGRAFIX CREATIVE LLC
50 Depot St, Collinsville, CT 6019
Tel.: (860) 521-6567
Web Site: www.igrafix.com

Agency Specializes In: Advertising, Internet/Web Design, Logo & Package Design, Print, Social Media

Brigitte DiBenedetto *(Principal)*

Accounts:
New-Harmony Home Care Services LLC

IKON3
(Name Changed to Noble People)

ILAN GEVA & FRIENDS
850 W Erie Ste 1E, Chicago, IL 60642
Tel.: (312) 497-2233
Fax: (312) 666-5823
E-Mail: ilan@ilanandfriends.com
Web Site: www.ilanandfriends.com

Employees: 2
Year Founded: 1993

Agency Specializes In: Advertising, Automotive, Bilingual Market, Brand Development & Integration, Business-To-Business, Collateral, Consulting, Consumer Marketing, Corporate Identity, Direct Response Marketing, Education, Exhibit/Trade Shows, Financial, Food Service, Graphic Design, Health Care Services, Hispanic Market, Internet/Web Design, Leisure, Logo & Package Design, Medical Products, Merchandising, Outdoor, Over-50 Market, Point of Purchase, Point of Sale, Print, Production, Public Relations, Publicity/Promotions, Radio, Real Estate, Restaurant, Retail, Sales Promotion, Sports Market, Strategic Planning/Research, T.V., Trade & Consumer Magazines, Transportation, Travel & Tourism

Approx. Annual Billings: $2,500,000

Breakdown of Gross Billings by Media: Collateral: $375,000; D.M.: $750,000; Graphic Design: $125,000; Logo & Package Design: $250,000; Newsp. & Mags.: $250,000; Point of Sale: $125,000; Strategic Planning/Research: $625,000

Ilan Geva *(Owner)*
Jeff Weinman *(Dir-Travel & Hospitality)*

Accounts:
Chicago Arts Orchestra; Chicago, IL; 2009
Lisbon Convention Bureau; 2007
Medical Travel Insight; 2012
MediTour Expo: NY; 2011
Meeting Incentive Experts; Chicago, IL; 2003
Murphy/Jahn; 2012

ILFUSION INC
209 S Main St, Fort Worth, TX 76104
Tel.: (888) 420-5115
Web Site: www.ilfusion.com

Year Founded: 2010

Agency Specializes In: Advertising, Brand Development & Integration, Digital/Interactive, Internet/Web Design, Print, Social Media

Blake Hooser *(CEO)*
Jeff Langhammer *(Partner)*
Clif Mattix *(CMO)*
Elsa Newsome *(VP)*
Lee Littlefield *(Dir-Creative)*
Hillary Dupriest *(Strategist-Social Media)*

Accounts:
Hope Center For Autism
Walls Outdoors Clothing

ILLUME COMMUNICATIONS
805 E Baltimore St, Baltimore, MD 21202
Tel.: (410) 783-2627
Fax: (410) 783-2650
E-Mail: noboundaries@illumecommunications.com
Web Site: illumecomm.com

Agency Specializes In: Brand Development & Integration, Consumer Marketing, Guerilla Marketing, Internet/Web Design, Media Buying Services, Print, Promotions, Public Relations, T.V.

James Evans *(CEO & Dir-Creative)*
Seth McMillan *(Dir-Digital)*
Alan Reisberg *(Dir-Media)*

ILLUMINATION ADVERTISING INC.
650 Cleveland St Ste 1236, Clearwater, FL 33757
Tel.: (813) 507-9392
E-Mail: hello@illuminationadvertising.com
Web Site: www.illuminationadvertising.com

Agency Specializes In: Advertising, Graphic Design, Print, Public Relations, Search Engine Optimization, Social Media

Sarah L. Stone *(Owner & Pres)*
Robyn Clarke *(Art Dir)*

Accounts:
Baking by the Sea

ILM MARKETING
225 S Water St Ste M, Wilmington, NC 28401
Tel.: (910) 547-6910
E-Mail: info@marketingilm.com
Web Site: www.ilmmarketing.com

Agency Specializes In: Advertising, Brand Development & Integration, Media Buying Services, Public Relations

Nat Criss *(Pres)*

Accounts:
New-Rolesville Pet Resort & Spa

IM IMAGE MARKETING
2979 Whispering Pines Dr, Canfield, OH 44406
Tel.: (330) 272-1493
Web Site: www.imimagemarketing.com

Year Founded: 2005

Agency Specializes In: Advertising, Brand Development & Integration, Graphic Design, Internet/Web Design, Print, Social Media

Mike Tarantino *(CEO & Designer)*

Sam Morris *(Project Mgr-Sls)*

Accounts:
Aamco transmissions of Boardman
Eric Allshouse LLC
Lisa Herold
Matt Gambrel Attorney at Law

IMAGE ASSOCIATES LLC

700 Virginia St E Ste 220, Charleston, WV 25301
Tel.: (304) 345-4429
Fax: (304) 345-4445
Web Site: www.imageassociatesllc.com

Agency Specializes In: Advertising, Brand Development & Integration, Internet/Web Design, Logo & Package Design, T.V.

Sharon A. Harms *(Partner & Dir-Art)*
William F. Hogan *(Creative Dir)*

Accounts:
Frontier Communications Corporation
The West Virginia Housing Development Fund

THE IMAGE GROUP

31 E 8th St Ste 200, Holland, MI 49423
Tel.: (616) 393-9588
Fax: (616) 393-2137
E-Mail: image@imagegroup.com
Web Site: www.imagegroup.com

Employees: 20

Agency Specializes In: Advertising, Brand Development & Integration, Broadcast, Corporate Identity, Digital/Interactive, Internet/Web Design, Logo & Package Design, Multimedia, Planning & Consultation, Print, Public Relations

Mark Tanis *(Founder & CEO)*
Rich Evenhouse *(Pres & Dir-Digital Design)*
Scott Kramer *(Sr Dir-Art)*
Andrea Beckman *(Dir-Art & Design)*
Tim Hackney *(Dir-Creative)*
Ed Van Poolen *(Dir-Creative)*
Julie Berghoef *(Sr Acct Exec)*
Katy Johnson *(Copywriter)*

Accounts:
Macatawa Pointe Development
Metro Health
Point West 1 LLC Campaign: "Everything Old is New"

IMAGE MAKERS ADVERTISING INC

139 E North St, Waukesha, WI 53188
Tel.: (262) 650-8300
Fax: (262) 650-1595
E-Mail: im@imagemakersadv.com
Web Site: www.imagemakersadv.com

Agency Specializes In: Advertising, Internet/Web Design, Media Buying Services, Outdoor, Print, Public Relations, Radio, Social Media, Strategic Planning/Research, T.V.

Tom Sheffield *(VP-Fin & Admin)*
Ginny Ripley *(Dir-Creative)*
Tim Vogel *(Dir-Fin & Admin)*
John Leutermann *(Mgr-Emerging Media)*
Sara Gooding *(Graphic Designer & Designer-Web)*
Margaret Odya *(Media Buyer-Print & Project Coord)*
Susie Austin *(Coord-Agency Svcs)*
Sarah Zubarik *(Coord-Social Media, PR, Direct Mail & Radio Promos)*

Accounts:
Arts Cameras Plus

IMAGE MEDIA SERVICES, INC.

1521 W Branch Dr Ste 650, McLean, VA 22102-3328
Tel.: (703) 893-8080
Fax: (703) 893-9480
E-Mail: info@imsja.com
Web Site: www.imagemediaservices.com

E-Mail for Key Personnel:
President: jahn@imsja.com

Employees: 18
Year Founded: 1989

Agency Specializes In: Advertising, Advertising Specialties, Asian Market, Bilingual Market, Brand Development & Integration, Broadcast, Business Publications, Business-To-Business, Cable T.V., Co-op Advertising, Collateral, Consumer Marketing, Consumer Publications, Corporate Identity, Direct Response Marketing, E-Commerce, Electronic Media, Event Planning & Marketing, Exhibit/Trade Shows, Government/Political, Graphic Design, Hispanic Market, Internet/Web Design, Logo & Package Design, Magazines, Media Buying Services, Newspaper, Newspapers & Magazines, Out-of-Home Media, Outdoor, Print, Production, Public Relations, Publicity/Promotions, Radio, Recruitment, Sales Promotion, Strategic Planning/Research, T.V., Technical Advertising, Trade & Consumer Magazines

Approx. Annual Billings: $3,000,000

Breakdown of Gross Billings by Media: D.M.: 5%; Internet Adv.: 5%; Mags.: 10%; Newsp.: 60%; Radio & T.V.: 15%; Transit: 5%

Jennifer Ahn *(Founder & Pres)*
Jeffry Davis *(VP)*
Jeehoon Park *(VP-Ops-Intl)*
Kathryn Clark *(Dir-Art)*
Bryan Johnson *(Dir-Media)*
Hanna Yun *(Project Mgr-Mktg)*

Accounts:
Centers for Medicare and Medicaid Services
Customs and Border Protection
United States Coast Guard

IMAGEHAUS

718 Washington Ave N #214, Minneapolis, MN 55401
Tel.: (612) 377-8700
Fax: (612) 374-2956
E-Mail: info@imagehaus.net
Web Site: www.imagehaus.net

Employees: 6

National Agency Associations: AAF

Agency Specializes In: Brand Development & Integration, Collateral, Consulting, Consumer Goods, Consumer Marketing, Corporate Communications, Cosmetics, Fashion/Apparel, Gay & Lesbian Market, Graphic Design, Health Care Services, Household Goods, In-Store Advertising, Logo & Package Design, Marine, Medical Products, Package Design, Point of Purchase, Point of Sale, Print, Retail, Social Marketing/Nonprofit

Breakdown of Gross Billings by Media: Collateral: 20%; Digital/Interactive: 10%; Graphic Design: 30%; Logo & Package Design: 20%; Mdsg./POP: 20%

Jay Miller *(Owner & Dir-Creative)*

Accounts:
All Seasons Wild Bird Store
CVS Pharmacy; 2008
Kangaroo Korner
Minute Clinic Health Care; 2009
Napa Jack's
OfficeMax; 2006
Otto Bock; Minneapolis, MN Medical Products; 2001
Schimidty's
Target
UBS
Urban Retreat
Wilson's Leather

IMAGEMAKERS INC.

514 Lincoln Ave, Wamego, KS 66547
Tel.: (888) 865-8511
Fax: (785) 380-2556
E-Mail: info@imagemakers-inc.com
Web Site: www.imagemakers-inc.com

Year Founded: 2001

Agency Specializes In: Advertising, Email, Event Planning & Marketing, Internet/Web Design, Logo & Package Design, Print, Public Relations, Search Engine Optimization, Social Media

Dan Holmgren *(Pres & Creative Dir)*
Ben York *(Art Dir)*
Jaclyn Collins *(Acct Dir)*
Dusty Thomas *(Dir-Bus Dev)*
Carrie Rich *(Acct Exec)*
John Holcomb *(Designer)*

Accounts:
Back Nine Development

IMAGEMARK, INC.

12 Godfrey Pl 3rd Fl, Wilton, CT 06897
Tel.: (203) 761-0025
Fax: (203) 761-8624
E-Mail: info@imagemark.net
Web Site: www.imagemark.net

Employees: 7
Year Founded: 1996

Agency Specializes In: Brand Development & Integration, Digital/Interactive

Peter Baker *(Partner & Dir-Creative)*
Greg Mursko *(Acct Dir & Dir-Creative)*
Jenny Pemberton *(Mgr-Fin)*

Accounts:
Bellagio
Citibank
Cold Stone
Drug Free America
Elm Bank
Fairfield Magazine
Global Design
Health Prize
Hot Dog On A Stick
Manpower
Mozart.com
Nabors
The National Geographic Channel
Northwest Mutual
Qualified Bookkeepers
Shaklee
Street Smart Technology
The Weather Channel
Yale Cancer Center

IMAGEN

800 Douglas Rd La Puerta del Sol Ste 101, Coral Gables, FL 33134
Tel.: (305) 774-9443
Fax: (305) 774-9043
Web Site: www.imagentma.com

Agency Specializes In: Advertising, Crisis Communications, Event Planning & Marketing, Media Buying Services, Media Planning, Outdoor, Print, Public Relations, Radio, Social Media

Roxana Fernandez *(Pres)*
Mari J. Garcia *(Exec VP)*
Alexis Regalado *(Acct Exec)*

Accounts:
Ocean Bank
VaporFi

IMAGERY CREATIVE

7400 SW 50th Terrace, Miami, FL 33155
Tel.: (305) 667-4468
Fax: (786) 953-7168
E-Mail: info@imagerycreative.com
Web Site: www.imagerycreative.com

Employees: 10
Year Founded: 2002

Agency Specializes In: Advertising, Advertising Specialties, Alternative Advertising, Aviation & Aerospace, Bilingual Market, Brand Development & Integration, Broadcast, Business-To-Business, Cable T.V., Collateral, Commercial Photography, Communications, Computers & Software, Consulting, Consumer Goods, Consumer Marketing, Content, Corporate Communications, Corporate Identity, Digital/Interactive, Direct-to-Consumer, E-Commerce, Electronic Media, Electronics, Email, Environmental, Event Planning & Marketing, Exhibit/Trade Shows, Financial, Food Service, Graphic Design, Guerilla Marketing, Health Care Services, High Technology, Hospitality, Identity Marketing, In-Store Advertising, Integrated Marketing, Internet/Web Design, Investor Relations, Leisure, Local Marketing, Logo & Package Design, Luxury Products, Magazines, Market Research, Media Buying Services, Medical Products, Multicultural, Multimedia, New Product Development, Newspapers & Magazines, Out-of-Home Media, Outdoor, Package Design, Paid Searches, Planning & Consultation, Point of Purchase, Point of Sale, Print, Production, Production (Ad, Film, Broadcast), Production (Print), Promotions, Public Relations, Publicity/Promotions, Radio, Real Estate, Regional, Restaurant, Retail, Sales Promotion, Search Engine Optimization, Social Marketing/Nonprofit, Social Media, Sponsorship, Strategic Planning/Research, T.V., Technical Advertising, Teen Market, Transportation, Travel & Tourism, Viral/Buzz/Word of Mouth, Web (Banner Ads, Pop-ups, etc.)

Julio Sanchez *(Pres & Chief Creative Officer)*

Accounts:
ACGG Development
Advance Roofing
Bacardi USA
Bahri Development
Baja Fresh
Bayview Financial
Cointreau
DonQ
Dreamquest Foundation
Express Equity
Franklin Credit
Grove Developer
International Finance Bank
Lighthouse CMHC
MedCare International
Mercy Hospital
National Asset Direct
Noble House Hotels & Resorts
Ocean Key
Pangaea Hard Rock
Premiere Beverage
Republic Nation
Santa's LLC
Sony Electronics
South Florida Golf Foundation
Southern Wine & Spirits
Taha Properties
Tiva Healthcare
TM Real Estate Group
TotalBank

IMAGES USA

1320 Ellsworth Industrial Blvd, Atlanta, GA 30318
Tel.: (404) 892-2931
Fax: (404) 892-8651
E-Mail: p.hammond@imagesusa.net
Web Site: www.imagesusa.net

E-Mail for Key Personnel:
President: b.mcneil@imagesusa.net

Employees: 47
Year Founded: 1989

National Agency Associations: AAF-AMA

Agency Specializes In: Advertising, Advertising Specialties, African-American Market, Asian Market, Automotive, Bilingual Market, Brand Development & Integration, Broadcast, Business-To-Business, Cable T.V., Children's Market, Co-op Advertising, Collateral, Communications, Consulting, Consumer Marketing, Corporate Communications, Corporate Identity, Cosmetics, Digital/Interactive, Direct Response Marketing, Education, Electronic Media, Engineering, Entertainment, Environmental, Event Planning & Marketing, Fashion/Apparel, Financial, Food Service, Gay & Lesbian Market, Government/Political, Graphic Design, Health Care Services, High Technology, Hispanic Market, In-Store Advertising, Industrial, Internet/Web Design, Leisure, Local Marketing, Logo & Package Design, Magazines, Media Buying Services, Medical Products, Merchandising, New Product Development, Newspaper, Newspapers & Magazines, Out-of-Home Media, Outdoor, Over-50 Market, Pharmaceutical, Planning & Consultation, Point of Purchase, Point of Sale, Print, Production, Public Relations, Publicity/Promotions, Radio, Real Estate, Recruitment, Restaurant, Retail, Sales Promotion, Seniors' Market, Sponsorship, Sports Market, Strategic Planning/Research, Sweepstakes, T.V., Technical Advertising, Teen Market, Telemarketing, Trade & Consumer Magazines, Transportation, Travel & Tourism

Approx. Annual Billings: $62,000,000

Robert L. McNeil, Jr. *(Pres & CEO)*
John Lockyer *(Partner & COO)*
Juan Quevedo *(Dir-Market Res)*
Ahmad Abdul-Ali *(Acct Exec)*

Accounts:
AARP
Amtrak
Astrazeneca
International Speedway Corporation
Wachovia

IMAGINASIUM INC.

110 S Washington St, Green Bay, WI 54301
Tel.: (920) 431-7872
Fax: (920) 431-7875
Toll Free: (800) 820-4624
E-Mail: dkreft@imaginasium.com
Web Site: www.imaginasium.com

E-Mail for Key Personnel:
President: pat@imaginasium.com
Creative Dir.: joe@imaginasium.com
Media Dir.: annette@imaginasium.com
Production Mgr.: shelly@imaginasium.com
Public Relations: pat@imaginasium.com

Employees: 23
Year Founded: 1996

National Agency Associations: AAF-Second Wind Limited

Agency Specializes In: Advertising, Brand Development & Integration, Broadcast, Business-To-Business, Consulting, Consumer Marketing, Corporate Communications, Corporate Identity, Digital/Interactive, Direct Response Marketing, Education, Environmental, Event Planning & Marketing, Exhibit/Trade Shows, Financial, Graphic Design, Health Care Services, Integrated Marketing, Internet/Web Design, Leisure, Logo & Package Design, Market Research, Media Planning, Medical Products, Planning & Consultation, Print, Production (Print), Recruitment, Retail, Sponsorship, Sports Market, Strategic Planning/Research, Travel & Tourism, Web (Banner Ads, Pop-ups, etc.)

Approx. Annual Billings: $5,000,000

Patrick J. Hopkins *(Pres)*
Kris Neveau *(Gen Mgr)*
Laura Myers *(Client Svcs Dir)*
Joseph Bergner *(Dir-Experience Design)*
Matthew George *(Dir-Ops)*
Denis Kreft *(Dir-Bus Dev)*
Kory Lax *(Dir-Creative)*
Shelly DeBouche *(Mgr-Production)*
Jennifer Ducat *(Mgr-Support Svcs)*
Melinda Morella *(Specialist-Bus Dev)*

Accounts:
Boldt

IMAGINATION (CANADA) LTD.

22 Wellesley St E Ste 2202, Toronto, ON MAY 1G3 Canada
Tel.: (416) 929-1260
Fax: (416) 572-2212
E-Mail: andrew.horberry@imagination.com
Web Site: www.imagination.com

Agency Specializes In: Advertising

Douglas Broadley *(Grp CEO & Dir-Creative-Global)*
Andrew Horberry *(Gen Mgr)*

Accounts:
BBC
British Airways
Ford of Canada
Jaguar
Mazda
One World
Samsung
Shell
Sony
V&A
Vodafone

THE IMAGINATION COMPANY

920 Campbell Rd, Bethel, VT 5032
Tel.: (802) 234-5809
E-Mail: info@theimaginationcompany.com
Web Site: www.theimaginationcompany.com

Agency Specializes In: Advertising, Brand Development & Integration, Graphic Design, Internet/Web Design, Print, Public Relations

Jim Giberti *(Pres & Creative Dir)*
Kristen Smith *(VP & Art Dir)*

Accounts:
New-Killington Resort
New-Northstar Fireworks
New-Packard Fuels

THE IMAGINATION FACTORY
15 Ionia Ave SW Ste 220, Grand Rapids, MI 49503
Tel.: (616) 356-2545
Fax: (616) 356-2546
E-Mail: imagine@what-if.com
Web Site: www.what-if.com

Employees: 6
Year Founded: 1985

Agency Specializes In: Consulting, Consumer Marketing, Digital/Interactive, Electronic Media, Internet/Web Design, Publicity/Promotions

Mike McCrindle *(Graphic Designer & Designer-Media)*

Accounts:
Amway
Apple
Bosch
Church Organizations
Dow Chemical
Michigan Dept
Sacramento Kings

THE IMAGINATION GROUP
25 Store St, South Crescent, London, WC1E 7BL United Kingdom
Tel.: (44) 207 323 3300
Fax: (44) 207 323 5801
E-Mail: jake.moore@imagination.com
Web Site: www.imagination.com

Employees: 300
Year Founded: 1978

Agency Specializes In: Advertising, Automotive, Brand Development & Integration, Corporate Identity, Event Planning & Marketing, Exhibit/Trade Shows, Financial, Planning & Consultation

Anton Christodoulou *(CTO-EMEA)*
Patrick Reid *(CEO-EMEA)*
Christopher Wade *(Head-IT-Global)*
Rob Day *(Acct Dir-Global)*
Michael Flood *(Acct Dir)*
Cassandra Green *(Acct Dir-Jaguar & Land Rover)*
Tony Currie *(Dir-Creative Tech-Automotive)*
Chris Shepherd-Barron *(Dir-Ops & Automotive)*
Rebecca Taylor *(Mgr-HR)*

Accounts:
BBC
Commonwealth Bank Campaign: "Community Seeds"
Disney
Disneyland Paris
Jaguar Land Rover Campaign: "Range Rover: The All-New Experience"
Land Rover
Orange
Shell Campaign: "An Expression of Innovation"
Swire Properties Campaign: "Pacific Place"
Tate Modern Launch

Branches

Imagination the Americas
(Formerly Imagination (USA) Inc.)
155 Franklin St, New York, NY 10013
Tel.: (212) 813-6400
Fax: (212) 813-6401
E-Mail: info@imagination.com
Web Site: www.imagination.com

Employees: 30

Douglas Broadley *(Grp CEO & Dir-Creative-Global)*
Rob Bullen *(CFO)*
Gabrielle Chamberlain *(Acct Dir-The Americas)*
Geoffrey Hayes *(Acct Dir)*
Ronald Pawlicki *(Dir-Creative Imagination)*
John Leen *(Sr Mgr-Production)*
Anthony Lacey *(Sr Acct Mgr-Jaguar Land Rover North America)*
William Gorncy *(Project Mgr-Digital)*
Katelyn Patterson Wheeler *(Project Mgr-Digital)*

Accounts:
Akzo Noble
British Airways
Christies
Disney Land
Ford
Jaguar
Mazda
One World
Samsung
Sony
Virgin Mobile USA, Inc.
Vodafone

Imagination (USA) Inc.
290 Town Center Dr 7th Fl, Dearborn, MI 48126-2765
Tel.: (313) 996-7000
Fax: (313) 563-8606
E-Mail: christopher.gerlach@imagination.com
Web Site: www.imagination.com

Employees: 28

Rob Bullen *(CFO)*
Gabrielle Chamberlain *(Acct Dir)*
Candice Dias *(Dir-Bus & Strategy)*
Chris Israelski *(Dir-Investor Comm-The Americas)*
Paul Skomra *(Sr Mgr-Comml)*
Joshua Chu *(Mgr-IT)*
Brittany Frattini-Cox *(Mgr-Comml)*
Amy Myers-Delaney *(Mgr-Production)*
Mark Rennoldson *(Sr Bus Mgr)*

Imagination (Canada) Ltd.
22 Wellesley St E Ste 2202, Toronto, ON MAY 1G3 Canada
(See Separate Listing)

Imagination (Scandinavia) AB
Gotgatan 48 1st Fl, SE-118 26 Stockholm, Sweden
Tel.: (46) 8 442 1848
Fax: (46) 8 442 1831

Employees: 1

Guy Stevenson *(Client Svcs Dir)*

Imagination Australia
Ste 121 Jones Bay Wharf, 26-32 Pirrama Rd, Pyrmont, 2009 Australia
Tel.: (61) 2 8572 8700
Fax: (61) 2 9660 2800
Web Site: www.imagination.com

Employees: 135
Year Founded: 2006

Antony Gowthorp *(Mng Dir)*
Mark Davies *(Exec Producer-Digital)*
Katrina Rae *(Bus Dir-Telstra)*
Mae Ann Tan *(Producer-Digital)*
Gerry Breislin *(Dir-Comm)*
Kate Daly *(Dir-Bus)*
Adrian Goldthorp *(Dir-Creative)*
Lisa Taylor *(Dir-Creative)*
Brodie Melrose *(Acct Mgr)*
Sarah Vierod *(Mgr-Resource)*

Accounts:
BMW
City of Sydney
Commonwealth Bank of Australia
Ford
Interface
Land Rover
Nike
Samsung
Shell
Telstra

IMAGINE GLOBAL COMMUNICATIONS
262 W 38th St Ste 502, New York, NY 10018-9192
Tel.: (212) 922-1961
Fax: (212) 922-1962
Web Site: www.imagine-team.com

Agency Specializes In: Travel & Tourism

Gabriele Klink *(Owner)*
Cassie Lovett *(Sr Acct Exec)*
Anna Patrick *(Acct Exec)*
Rachel Peace *(Acct Exec)*

Accounts:
Aurelio Lech
Jacada Travel Public Relations
Pezula Resort Hotel and Spa
The Safari Collection
Singapore Airlines
Singita
South Pacific Tourism Organisation
Uncharted Africa Safari Co
Zambezi Queen

IMAGINE IT MEDIA
318 N Palm Canyon Dr, Palm Springs, CA 92262
Tel.: (760) 325-6998
Fax: (866) 902-0435
E-Mail: info@imagineitmedia.com
Web Site: www.imagineitmedia.com

Year Founded: 2002

Agency Specializes In: Advertising, Collateral, Graphic Design, Internet/Web Design, Logo & Package Design, Print, Public Relations, Search Engine Optimization

Jeff Shotwell *(Pres & Dir-Creative)*
Scott Jones *(VP)*

Accounts:
Desert Business Association
LGBT Legal Forms
Modern Misting Systems

IMAGINE THIS, INC.
43 Corporate Park, Irvine, CA 92606
Tel.: (949) 486-4598
Fax: (714) 384-0444
E-Mail: patrick@imaginethispromo.com
Web Site: www.imaginethispromo.com

Employees: 32
Year Founded: 1999

Agency Specializes In: Advertising

Revenue: $22,000,000

Patrick Papaccio *(Pres)*
Danny Saenz *(Dir-Bus Dev)*
Barry Waldron *(Dir-Sls)*
Amy French *(Mgr-Acctg & Bus Mgr)*
Nancy McCarthy *(Mgr-Vendor Rels)*
Joseph Guiste *(Sr Strategist-Mktg)*
Gretchen Krebs *(Acct Exec-Sls)*
Joanne Nguyen *(Acct Coord)*
Adam Bullock *(Exec Strategist-Mktg)*
Russ Scarce *(Sr Exec-Mktg)*

Accounts:
Ameristar
Auto Club
Heinz
Hyundai
MGM Grand
Nissan
Smuckers

IMAGO COMMUNICATIONS
200-168 rue Notre-Dame Nord, Sainte-Marie, QC G6E 3Z9 Canada
Tel.: (418) 387-4781
Fax: (418) 387-1826
Web Site: www.goimago.com/

Employees: 20

Agency Specializes In: Communications, Internet/Web Design, Production, Public Relations, Strategic Planning/Research

Jean Savoie *(Pres)*

Accounts:
MBI Plastic (Mouleurs de Beauce Inc.)

IMAJ ASSOCIATES
11 William Reynolds Farm Rd, West Kingston, RI 02892
Tel.: (401) 491-9665
Fax: (401) 654-6667
Web Site: www.imajassociates.com

Employees: 10

Jami Oullette *(Founder, Pres & Creative Dir & Dir-Branding)*
Kristine Allard *(Sr Strategist-Media Rels)*
Jennifer Allison *(Planner)*
Shawn Buckless *(Planner-Strategic)*
Katie Schibler *(Sr Client Svcs Mgr & Project Head)*

Accounts:
Atlantic Hearing
Bishop Hendricken High School
Care New England
CityFinds
Meckley & Associates
Rhode Island Housing HelpCenter
The Virta Insurance Agency

IMARKETING LTD, INC.
(Acquired by Mercury Media, Inc.)

IMBUE CREATIVE
31 N Sugan Rd Ste 3A, New Hope, PA 18938
Tel.: (215) 862-2248
E-Mail: info@imbuecreative.com
Web Site: www.imbuecreative.com

Agency Specializes In: Advertising, Digital/Interactive, Graphic Design, Internet/Web Design

Joe Kubiak *(Mng Dir)*
Michael Piperno *(Principal & Dir-Creative)*
Laura Dickerman *(Sr Acct Mgr)*
Wendy Stasolla *(Project Mgr & Designer)*
Michael Olson *(Designer)*
Mark Yearick *(Copywriter)*

Accounts:
Bucks County Playhouse
Mistral
Westminster Conservatory of Music

IMG COLLEGE
540 North Trade St, Winston Salem, NC 27101
Tel.: (336) 831-0700
Fax: (859) 226-4242
Web Site: www.imgcollege.com

Employees: 300
Year Founded: 1972

Agency Specializes In: Sports Market

Revenue: $81,800,000

Roger Vandersnick *(CMO, Chief Sls Officer & Sr VP)*
Cory Moss *(Sr VP & Mng Dir-The Collegiate Licensing Company)*
Jim Connelly *(Sr VP-Special Projects)*
Steve Cornwell *(Sr VP-Ops)*
Kelli Hilliard *(Sr VP-Bus Dev & Partnership Mgmt)*
Andrew Judelson *(Sr VP-Natl Sls-IMG College & US Bus Dev-IMG)*
Cameron Scholvin *(Reg VP-Midwest Reg-IMG College)*
John Harden *(VP & Dir-Print Svcs)*
John Hite *(VP-Stadium Seating)*
Scott MacKenzie *(VP-Conference-Big 12 & CUSA West)*
Jason Wilmoth *(Dir-Partnership Mktg)*

Accounts:
Alltel
Chobani Content, Digital, Greek Yogurt, Print Ads, Product Sampling, Radio Ads
Dodge
Foot Locker
IBM
Kraft Foods Content, Jell-O, Social-Media, Video Boards

IMMERSION ACTIVE
16 E Patrick St, Frederick, MD 21701
Tel.: (301) 631-9277
Fax: (301) 631-9276
E-Mail: info@immersionactive.com
Web Site: www.immersionactive.com

Employees: 12
Year Founded: 1998

National Agency Associations: AAF

Agency Specializes In: Advertising, Affiliate Marketing, Affluent Market, Aviation & Aerospace, Consulting, Consumer Marketing, Content, Corporate Identity, Digital/Interactive, Direct Response Marketing, E-Commerce, Email, Game Integration, Graphic Design, Internet/Web Design, Leisure, Luxury Products, Media Buying Services, Media Planning, Mobile Marketing, Multimedia, Over-50 Market, Paid Searches, Podcasting, RSS (Really Simple Syndication), Search Engine Optimization, Seniors' Market, Strategic Planning/Research, Viral/Buzz/Word of Mouth

Approx. Annual Billings: $1,500,000

Breakdown of Gross Billings by Media: Internet Adv.: $1,500,000

David Weigelt *(Co-Founder & Pres)*
Jonathan Boehman *(Partner)*
Joe Ford *(VP-Digital Mktg Practices)*
Alix Locke *(VP-Acct Strategy)*
Kathi Scharf *(VP-Ops)*
Alayna Allen *(Dir-Bus Dev)*
John Sears *(Dir-Interactive)*
Gina Pagliaro *(Mgr-Email Mktg)*
Lisa Young *(Strategist-Acct)*
Kelsey Waddingham *(Acct Strategist)*

IMMOTION STUDIOS
4717 Fletcher Ave, Fort Worth, TX 76107
Tel.: (817) 731-4176
Web Site: www.immotionstudios.com

Agency Specializes In: Advertising, Brand Development & Integration, Graphic Design, Internet/Web Design, Public Relations, Social Media

Lindsey Hurr *(VP)*
Coleman Anderson *(Acct Exec & Producer-Video)*
Patti Nelson Bandy *(Dir-Art-Styling)*
Colin Coolidge *(Dir-Web)*
Jonathan Graf *(Dir-Art)*
Kristin Peaks *(Dir-PR & Social Media)*
Tom Schuller *(Dir-Creative)*
Shelly Raifsnider *(Acct Mgr)*
Marie Simon *(Acct Mgr)*

Accounts:
Insight Complete Eye Care Public Relations, Social Media
Junior Achievement of the Chisholm Trail, Inc Design, Event Planning, Public Relations, Social Media, Strategy
Shoot Smart Indoor Range & Training Center

IMPACT MARKETING & PUBLIC RELATIONS, INC.
6177 Silver Arrows Way, Columbia, MD 21045
Tel.: (410) 312-0081
Fax: (410) 872-0890
Web Site: www.impactmarketing.net/

Employees: 2
Year Founded: 1990

Agency Specializes In: Communications

Duane Carey *(Owner)*
Kevin Hansen *(CMO)*
Kimberly Hopkins *(Dir-Art)*
Chrissy Hoffmaster *(Project Mgr & Copywriter)*
Emily Crider *(Project Mgr-Social Media & Mktg)*
Terri Hesse *(Client Coord & Project Coord)*

Accounts:
Howard County Chamber of Commerce
The Melting Pot

IMPACT XM - NEW JERSEY
250 Ridge Rd, Dayton, NJ 08810
Tel.: (732) 274-2000
Fax: (732) 274-2417
E-Mail: experience@impact-xm.com
Web Site: www.impact-xm.com

Employees: 150
Year Founded: 1973

Agency Specializes In: Brand Development & Integration, Corporate Communications, Entertainment, Exhibit/Trade Shows, Market Research, Strategic Planning/Research

Richard Nelson *(Chm)*
Ken Payne *(Pres)*
Donna Bernero *(Exec Acct Dir)*
Kevin Padden *(Exec Dir-Meeting & Comm Strategies)*
Ed Salge *(Exec Dir-Ops & IT)*
Krupali Desai *(Dir-Mktg & Comm)*
Kristi Ruskuski *(Sr Acct Mgr)*

Accounts:
Canton of St. Gallen City Details

IMPRESS PUBLIC RELATIONS, INC.
777 W Roosevelt St Bldg 5, Phoenix, AZ 85007
Tel.: (602) 443-0030
Fax: (602) 443-0027
E-Mail: info@impresslabs.com
Web Site: impresslabs.com

Employees: 10

Agency Specializes In: Business-To-Business, Communications, Environmental, Integrated Marketing, Strategic Planning/Research, Technical Advertising

Martijn Pierik *(Mng Partner)*
Amy Smith *(Sr Acct Dir-Semiconductor Lab)*
Tom Cheyney *(Dir-Solar Practice)*
German Wegbrait *(Dir-Creative)*

Accounts:
ASM International
Entrepix
Flexible Display Center
OmniVision
Rohm & Haas Electronic Materials
SAFC Global
SAFC Hitech
Sigma Life Science (Agency of Record)

Branches

IMPRESS Public Relations, Inc.

632 Commercial St Ste 200, San Francisco, CA 94111
Tel.: (415) 992-7255
Fax: (866) 738-7190
E-Mail: info@impress-pr.com
Web Site: www.impresslabs.com

Agency Specializes In: Public Relations

Martijn Pierik *(Mng Partner)*
Amy Smith *(Sr Acct Dir-Semiconductor Lab)*
Ina Chu *(Dir-Ops-Asia Pacific)*
German Wegbrait *(Dir-Creative)*

IMPRESSIONS-A.B.A. INDUSTRIES, INC.

393 Jericho Tpk, Mineola, NY 11501
Tel.: (516) 739-3210
Fax: (516) 739-9246
E-Mail: info@impressionsaba.com
Web Site: www.impressionsaba.com

E-Mail for Key Personnel:
President: aschettino@impressionsaba.com

Employees: 30
Year Founded: 1971

Agency Specializes In: Advertising, Brand Development & Integration, Broadcast, Business Publications, Business-To-Business, Collateral, Communications, Computers & Software, Consulting, Consumer Publications, Corporate Identity, Customer Relationship Management, Direct Response Marketing, Electronics, Engineering, Event Planning & Marketing, Exhibit/Trade Shows, Financial, Graphic Design, Health Care Services, High Technology, Identity Marketing, Industrial, Information Technology, Integrated Marketing, Internet/Web Design, Investor Relations, Luxury Products, Magazines, Marine, Market Research, Media Buying Services, Media Planning, Media Relations, Medical Products, Multimedia, New Product Development, New Technologies, Paid Searches, Pharmaceutical, Planning & Consultation, Print, Production, Production (Ad, Film, Broadcast), Production (Print), Promotions, Publicity/Promotions, Publishing, Sales Promotion, Search Engine Optimization, Strategic Planning/Research, Technical Advertising, Telemarketing, Trade & Consumer Magazines

Approx. Annual Billings: $25,000,000 Capitalized

Breakdown of Gross Billings by Media: Collateral: 10%; D.M.: 40%; Exhibits/Trade Shows: 10%; Plng. & Consultation: 20%; Sls. Promo.: 10%; Trade & Consumer Mags.: 10%

Anthony M. Schettino *(Founder & Pres)*
Jeff Thurau *(Sr Dir-Art & Dir-IT)*
LouAnn Pugliese *(Acct Supvr)*

Accounts:
Ameriprise
Broadridge
International Paper
Mastercard International
Mercer
National Grid
Schneider Electric
SNL Financial
Tyco/ADT
Unica/IBM
Wesco

IMPRESTIGE MEDIA MARKETING

4402 W 95th St, Prairie Village, KS 66207
Tel.: (913) 232-9098
Fax: (913) 904-0858
E-Mail: randy@imprestige.com
Web Site: www.imprestige.com

Employees: 9

Agency Specializes In: Advertising, Advertising Specialties, Alternative Advertising, Automotive, Brand Development & Integration, Broadcast, Business Publications, Cable T.V., Catalogs, Co-op Advertising, Collateral, College, Commercial Photography, Consulting, Consumer Publications, Corporate Identity, Customer Relationship Management, Direct Response Marketing, Education, Electronic Media, Email, Event Planning & Marketing, Experience Design, Graphic Design, Guerilla Marketing, Health Care Services, In-Store Advertising, Infomercials, Internet/Web Design, Local Marketing, Logo & Package Design, Magazines, Media Buying Services, Media Planning, Media Relations, Media Training, Multicultural, Multimedia, New Product Development, Newspaper, Newspapers & Magazines, Outdoor, Planning & Consultation, Point of Purchase, Print, Production, Production (Ad, Film, Broadcast), Production (Print), Promotions, Public Relations, Publicity/Promotions, Publishing, Radio, Retail, Sales Promotion, Search Engine Optimization, Strategic Planning/Research, T.V., Teen Market, Travel & Tourism, Urban Market, Viral/Buzz/Word of Mouth, Web (Banner Ads, Pop-ups, etc.), Yellow Pages Advertising

Approx. Annual Billings: $3,000,000

Breakdown of Gross Billings by Media: Brdcst.: $2,000,000; Cable T.V.: $250,000; Collateral: $50,000; Comml. Photography: $20,000; Event Mktg.: $100,000; Graphic Design: $10,000; Internet Adv.: $3,000; Newsp.: $50,000; T.V.: $500,000; Worldwide Web Sites: $17,000

Dan Neustadter *(COO & Dir-Youth Mktg)*

Accounts:
A1 Mortgage; Lee's Summit, MO Mortgage Services; 2007
BigDataSummitKC (Agency of Record)
Comfort Tours; Kansas City, MO Travel & Leisure; 2007
Marvin's Midtown Chiropractic; Kansas City, MO Chiropractic Services; 2007
Meridian Mortgage Solutions; Carmel, IN Mortgage Services
Smart Wholesale Lending; Saint Louis, MO Mortgage Services; 2007
Sunshine Home Improvement; Drexel, MO Windows, Siding & Patio; 2007

IMPRINT PROJECTS

215 Centre St 2nd Fl, New York, NY 10013
Tel.: (212) 925-2968
E-Mail: info@imprintprojects.com
Web Site: www.imprintprojects.com

Agency Specializes In: Advertising, Brand Development & Integration, Digital/Interactive, Print, Strategic Planning/Research

Dina Pugh *(Co-Founder & Exec Producer)*
Adam Katz *(Pres)*
Anna Simonse *(Mng Dir)*
Nina Sers *(Gen Mgr)*
David Jacob Kramer *(Dir-Creative)*
Kristen Leung *(Acct Mgr)*
Carson Salter *(Strategist)*

Accounts:
Moogfest
RVCA

IMPULSE CONCEPT GROUP

18 Leonard St, Norwalk, CT 6850
Tel.: (203) 945-9262
Web Site: www.impulseconceptgroup.com

Year Founded: 2013

Agency Specializes In: Advertising, Brand Development & Integration, Digital/Interactive, Graphic Design, Internet/Web Design, Print, Promotions, T.V.

Matthew Conciatore *(Mng Partner & Dir-Creative)*

Accounts:
University of Saint Joseph

IMRE

909 Ridgebrook Rd Ste 300, Baltimore, MD 21152
Tel.: (410) 821-8220
Fax: (410) 821-5619
E-Mail: info@imre.com
Web Site: www.imre.com/

Employees: 50

National Agency Associations: COPF

Agency Specializes In: Sponsorship

Mark Eber *(Owner)*
Dave Imre *(Partner & CEO)*
Jeff Williams *(Sr VP-Home & Building)*
Kevin Windorf *(Sr VP-Fin Svcs)*
Ryan Jordan *(VP & Creative Dir)*
Lindsay Hughes *(Acct Dir)*
Matt Saler *(Dir-Sports & Mktg)*
Jason Burelle *(Assoc Dir-Creative)*
Erin Hampton *(Sr Mgr-Production)*
Katy Funk Long *(Acct Mgr)*
Nichole Addison Hart *(Sr Acct Exec)*
Caitlin Haskins *(Sr Acct Exec)*
Courtney Nelson *(Copywriter)*

Accounts:
ABC Merit Choice
AkzoNobel Glidden Professional, Marketing, PR
The American Institute of Architects
Ames True Temper Ames, Dynamic Design, Hound Dog, Jackson, Razor-Back, True Temper, UnionTools
AmWINS Group Benefits
Beazer Homes Single-Family Homes; 2008
Benjamin Obdyke
Boral Bricks; 2008
CoreNet Global
Corporate Coverage
Dal-Tile Corporation (Agency of Record) American Olean, Creative, Daltile, Public Relations, Social Marketing

Deere & Company; Moline, IL Public Relations
EFI Global
EngagePoint Marketing
Fiber Composites, LLC (Agency of Record) Fiberon
Gravie Campaign: "Gravie Makes Everything Better"
The Home Depot, Inc.
Irrigation Association Education Foundation
John Deere
Kwikset Campaign: "Made for the World You Live In", Consumer, Digital Advertising, Social Content, Videos, Web
Liberty Hardware Manufacturing Corporation
Mannington Mills Flooring; 2008
MetLife
PowerBar (Public Relations, Social Media & Creative Agency of Record)
Travelers Championship
Travelers
United Industries Consumer Products; 2008

Branches

IMRE
6100 Wilshire Blvd Ste 1110, Los Angeles, CA 90048
Tel.: (213) 289-9190
E-Mail: info@imre.com
Web Site: www.imre.com

Agency Specializes In: Advertising, Digital/Interactive, Public Relations, Social Media

John Bentz *(Sr VP)*

Accounts:
New-Kwikset

IMRE
50 Broadway Fl 31, New York, NY 10004
Tel.: (917) 477-4800
Fax: (410) 821-5619
E-Mail: info@imre.com
Web Site: www.imre.com

Agency Specializes In: Advertising, Digital/Interactive, Public Relations, Social Media

John Bentz *(Sr VP)*
Bob Cavosi *(Sr VP-Fin Svcs)*
Christine Pierpoint *(Sr VP-Digital Strategy)*
Ryan Jordan *(VP-Creative & Dir)*
Anne Denford *(VP-HR)*
Brian Simmons *(Dir-Client Rels)*
Benjamin Myers *(Assoc Dir-Creative)*
Sarah Findle *(Sr Acct Exec)*
Amy M. Jones *(Acct Exec)*
Stephanie Sones *(Acct Exec)*

Accounts:
Travelers & Target

IMS ADVERTISING LLC
769 Newfield St Ste 6, Middletown, CT 6457
Tel.: (860) 316-2541
Fax: (860) 316-2551
E-Mail: info@imsadvertising.com
Web Site: www.imsadvertising.com

Agency Specializes In: Advertising, Brand Development & Integration, Internet/Web Design, Logo & Package Design, Search Engine Optimization, Social Media

Bob Russo *(Pres)*

Accounts:
All Services Electric
Bruce Solomon Plumbing Heating & Air
Service Roundtable

IN HOUSE ADVERTISING
8946 S Erie Ave, Tulsa, OK 74137
Tel.: (918) 481-6499
Fax: (918) 481-1677
E-Mail: rprofitt@hotmail.com

Year Founded: 2003

Agency Specializes In: Advertising, Aviation & Aerospace, Broadcast, Cable T.V., College, Consulting, Education, Entertainment, Event Planning & Marketing, Exhibit/Trade Shows, Financial, Food Service, Graphic Design, Health Care Services, Internet/Web Design, Local Marketing, Logo & Package Design, Market Research, Media Buying Services, Media Relations, Print, Production, Promotions, Public Relations, Publicity/Promotions, Radio, Restaurant, Retail, Seniors' Market, T.V.

Approx. Annual Billings: $1,000,000

Renee Profitt *(Owner)*

Accounts:
Gleam Guard; Tulsa, OK Wood Re-Finishing; 2004
The Hamlet; Tulsa, OK HoneyBaked Hams; 2002
Just Between Friends; Tulsa, OK; 2004
Ludger's Restaurant & Catering; Tulsa, OK Cakes & Catering; 2003
Trip Crosby Campaign: "A Conference Call In Real Life"
Tulsa Wedding Show; Tulsa, OK Event; 2002
Tulsa Welding School; Tulsa, OK Trade School; 2002
Zippo Campaign: "Share the Pain"

THE IN-HOUSE AGENCY, INC.
55 Madison Ave Ste 400, Morristown, NJ 07960
Tel.: (973) 285-3259
Fax: (908) 996-3593
E-Mail: dougm@in-houseagency.com
Web Site: www.theinhouseagency.com

Employees: 5
Year Founded: 1996

Agency Specializes In: Above-the-Line, Advertising, Affluent Market, Alternative Advertising, Arts, Automotive, Below-the-Line, Brand Development & Integration, Broadcast, Business Publications, Business-To-Business, Cable T.V., Co-op Advertising, Collateral, College, Commercial Photography, Communications, Computers & Software, Consulting, Consumer Goods, Consumer Marketing, Consumer Publications, Corporate Communications, Corporate Identity, Cosmetics, Digital/Interactive, Direct Response Marketing, Direct-to-Consumer, E-Commerce, Education, Electronic Media, Electronics, Email, Entertainment, Event Planning & Marketing, Exhibit/Trade Shows, Fashion/Apparel, Financial, Government/Political, Graphic Design, Guerilla Marketing, Health Care Services, High Technology, Hospitality, Household Goods, Identity Marketing, In-Store Advertising, Industrial, Information Technology, Integrated Marketing, Internet/Web Design, Investor Relations, Leisure, Local Marketing, Logo & Package Design, Luxury Products, Magazines, Market Research, Media Planning, Media Relations, Medical Products, Men's Market, Merchandising, Mobile Marketing, Multicultural, Multimedia, New Product Development, New Technologies, Newspaper, Newspapers & Magazines, Out-of-Home Media, Outdoor, Package Design, Paid Searches, Planning & Consultation, Podcasting, Point of Purchase, Point of Sale, Print, Production, Production (Print), Promotions, Publicity/Promotions, Publishing, Radio, Real Estate, Recruitment, Regional, Restaurant, Retail, Sales Promotion, Search Engine Optimization, Social Media, Sports Market, Strategic Planning/Research, Sweepstakes, T.V., Technical Advertising, Teen Market, Trade & Consumer Magazines, Transportation, Travel & Tourism, Urban Market, Viral/Buzz/Word of Mouth, Women's Market, Yellow Pages Advertising

Approx. Annual Billings: $5,000,000

Doug MacGibbon *(Owner)*
Sarah Cavicchi *(Exec Dir)*
Emily Foster *(Program Mgr & Mgr-Traffic)*

Accounts:
Chobani
JOHNNIE WALKER BLUE LABEL
Mattel
Microsoft

IN PLACE MARKETING
410 S Cedar Ave, Tampa, FL 33606
Tel.: (813) 933-1810
Fax: (813) 932-8512
E-Mail: info@inplacemarketing.com
Web Site: www.inplacemarketing.com

Employees: 8
Year Founded: 1971

Agency Specializes In: Real Estate

Approx. Annual Billings: $1,500,000

Breakdown of Gross Billings by Media: Mags.: $600,000; Newsp.: $450,000; Outdoor: $450,000

Barbara Commesso *(Pres)*
Joseph Commesso *(VP)*
Kristi Shaw *(VP-Client Svcs)*
Peter Masem *(Dir-Creative)*
Annie Goodwin *(Acct Mgr)*
Sarah Watson *(Strategist-Brand Engagement)*
Kayla Bradley *(Designer)*
Donnie White *(Designer)*

Accounts:
Arlington Ridge
Blair Communities
Blair Homecrafters
Bridgewater Place
Crosland
Hannah Bartoletta
Lennar Homes
Metro Development
Ryland Homes
Tradition Communities
William Ryan Homes

INDEPENDENT FLOORCOVERINGS DEALERS OF AMERICA, INC.
110 Mirramont Lake Dr, Woodstock, GA 30189
Tel.: (770) 592-5858
Fax: (770) 592-5508
Toll Free: (888) 261-4332
E-Mail: contact@ifda.net
Web Site: www.ifda.net

Employees: 6

Agency Specializes In: Direct-to-Consumer, Promotions, Radio, T.V.

John Harris *(Mng Dir)*
Anne Brown *(VP)*

Accounts:
Bob's Carpets
Durfee's Floor Center
The Flooring Network
Palmetto Carpet
Stainmaster

Townsend Floors
Vallejo Floor Company

INDEPENDENT GRAPHICS INC.

1679 River Rd, Pittston, PA 18640
Tel.: (570) 654-4040
Web Site: www.independentgraphics.com

Agency Specializes In: Graphic Design

Lou Ciampi, Jr. *(Owner & Pres)*
Stan Brozena *(Mgr-Production)*
Jim Ciampi *(Mgr-Customer Svc)*
Jeff Fusco *(Mgr-PrePress)*
Rich Mattei *(Mgr-Customer Satisfaction)*
Jim Murphy *(Mgr-Mailroom)*

Accounts:
Bridon American Corp.

INDUSTRIAL IMAGE

111 S 2nd Ave, Alpena, MI 49707
Tel.: (989) 358-7100
Web Site: www.ind-image.com

Andy Osthoff *(Mgr-Bus Dev)*

Accounts:
Besser Company

INDUSTRIAL STRENGTH MARKETING

8115 Isabella Ln Ste 4, Brentwood, TN 37027
Tel.: (615) 577-2015
Web Site: www.marketstrong.com

Employees: 22
Year Founded: 2003

Agency Specializes In: Affiliate Marketing, Alternative Advertising, Business Publications, Catalogs, Collateral, Consumer Publications, Custom Publishing, Digital/Interactive, Direct Response Marketing, Electronic Media, Email, Exhibit/Trade Shows, Experience Design, Guerilla Marketing, Local Marketing, Magazines, Mobile Marketing, Multimedia, Newspapers & Magazines, Paid Searches, Point of Sale, Print, Product Placement, Production, Production (Print), Promotions, Publishing, RSS (Really Simple Syndication), Search Engine Optimization, Social Media, Trade & Consumer Magazines, Web (Banner Ads, Pop-ups, etc.)

James Soto *(Founder & CEO)*
Kevin Brown *(Mng Dir)*
Sheri Wofford *(Controller)*
Rafael Encarnacion *(Dir-Content)*
Jake Gerli *(Dir-Comm)*
Brent Lathrop *(Dir-Web Dev)*
Joey Strawn *(Dir-Integrated Mktg)*

Accounts:
Bailey Parks Urethane National Brand, Urethane Molding; 2008
E-Com Seating Chair Manufacturing & Distribution, Laboratory Seating, National Brand; 2010
Mills Products Hydroforming, Metal Forming, National Brand, Roll Forming
National Boiler Service Boiler Repair, Boiler Service, National Brand; 2010
Nth-Works Metal Stamping; 2012
Power Technology Laser Diode Manufacturing, National Brand; 2011
Process Baron Air Handling, Ash Handling, Fuel Handling, Industrial Fans, Material Handling, National Brand; 2008
Southern Metal Fabricators Metal Fabrication, National Brand; 2010
Tennessee Children's Home Child Care Services, Christian Ministry, National Brand; 2012

INDUSTRIUM

(Formerly Kemp Goldberg Partners)
280 Fore St Ste 301, Portland, ME 04101-7101
Tel.: (207) 773-0700
Fax: (207) 773-0900
Web Site: www.industrium.com

Employees: 42
Year Founded: 2005

Agency Specializes In: Advertising, Brand Development & Integration, Business-To-Business, Collateral, Communications, Corporate Communications, Digital/Interactive, Direct Response Marketing, Game Integration, Graphic Design, Integrated Marketing, Internet/Web Design, Logo & Package Design, Media Buying Services, Media Planning, Media Relations, Multimedia, Podcasting, Print, Production (Print), Public Relations, Publicity/Promotions, Recruitment, Search Engine Optimization, Strategic Planning/Research, Transportation, Viral/Buzz/Word of Mouth, Web (Banner Ads, Pop-ups, etc.)

Approx. Annual Billings: $6,000,000

Don Fibich *(Partner & Dir-Creative)*
Dan Ventura *(Partner & Dir-Interactive)*
David Goldberg *(Partner)*
Tim Mathis *(Dir-Retail Innovation-The Retail Innovation Grp)*
Chris Philbrook *(Dir-Pub Affairs)*
Mark Kunert *(Assoc Dir-Creative)*
Leah Sommer *(Supvr-Media-Industrium)*

Accounts:
Blue Tarp
Camden National Bank
Concord Coach
Conway Inc.
Globe
Intermed
Menlo
The Nature Conservancy Campaign: "Future of Nature"
Putney Vet
Verrill Dana
Ways to Work
Wreaths Across America
Yale Cordage

INFERNO

505 Tennessee St Ste 108, Memphis, TN 38103
Tel.: (901) 278-3773
Fax: (901) 278-3774
E-Mail: tim@creativeinferno.com
Web Site: www.creativeinferno.com

Employees: 30
Year Founded: 1999
National Agency Associations: AAF-PRSA

Agency Specializes In: Advertising, Affluent Market, Brand Development & Integration, Broadcast, Business Publications, Business-To-Business, Cable T.V., Collateral, Communications, Computers & Software, Consulting, Consumer Goods, Consumer Marketing, Consumer Publications, Corporate Communications, Corporate Identity, Digital/Interactive, Direct Response Marketing, Direct-to-Consumer, Electronic Media, Email, Entertainment, Event Planning & Marketing, Fashion/Apparel, Financial, Government/Political, Graphic Design, Guerilla Marketing, Health Care Services, Hospitality, In-Store Advertising, Information Technology, Integrated Marketing, International, Internet/Web Design, Local Marketing, Magazines, Market Research, Media Buying Services, Media Planning, Media Relations, Media Training, Medical Products, Merchandising, New Product Development, Newspaper, Newspapers & Magazines, Out-of-Home Media, Outdoor, Over-50 Market, Package Design, Pharmaceutical, Planning & Consultation, Podcasting, Point of Purchase, Point of Sale, Print, Production, Production (Ad, Film, Broadcast), Production (Print), Promotions, Public Relations, RSS (Really Simple Syndication), Radio, Recruitment, Regional, Retail, Sales Promotion, Search Engine Optimization, Social Marketing/Nonprofit, Strategic Planning/Research, T.V., Technical Advertising, Trade & Consumer Magazines, Transportation, Travel & Tourism, Viral/Buzz/Word of Mouth, Web (Banner Ads, Pop-ups, etc.), Women's Market, Yellow Pages Advertising

Approx. Annual Billings: $14,600,000

Breakdown of Gross Billings by Media: Corp. Communications: $730,000; Exhibits/Trade Shows: $1,460,000; Graphic Design: $1,460,000; Logo & Package Design: $2,190,000; Production: $1,460,000; Pub. Rels.: $2,190,000; Strategic Planning/Research: $2,190,000; Worldwide Web Sites: $2,920,000

Michael Overton *(Partner & Dir-Creative)*
Dan O'Brien *(Partner)*
Tim Sellers *(Partner)*
Amy Lind *(Sr Art Dir)*
Lindsey Woodard *(Acct Mgr)*
Isabelle Blais *(Acct Exec-PR)*
Nicole Hinson *(Acct Exec)*
Tarryn Sanchez *(Acct Exec)*
Brandon Davis *(Copywriter)*
Kyle Monteverde *(Acct Coord-PR)*
Jackson Knight *(Team Head)*

Accounts:
Eclectic Eye; Memphis, TN Eyewear, Optical Services; 2003
Fullen Dock & Warehouse; Memphis, TN Transportation Management Systems; 2003
Memphis Public Links; Memphis, TN Golf Courses; 2001
The Motorcycle Industry Association
NuVasive; San Diego, CA Orthopedic Devices; 2002
Prudential
Smith & Nephew; Memphis, TN Orthopedic Devices; 2003

THE INFINITE AGENCY

220 E Las Colinas Blvd, Irving, TX 75039
Tel.: (469) 310-5870
E-Mail: hello@theinfiniteagency.com
Web Site: www.theinfiniteagency.com

Year Founded: 2010

Agency Specializes In: Advertising, Brand Development & Integration, Collateral, Digital/Interactive, Graphic Design, Internet/Web Design, Logo & Package Design, Print, Social Media, T.V.

Flip Croft Caderao *(Principal & Dir-Interactive)*
Jonathan Ogle *(Principal & Dir-Creative)*
Don Pelham *(Dir-Bus Dev)*
Steve Swaim *(Dir-Ops)*
Steve Wade *(Dir-Digital Mktg)*
Alex Pelham *(Acct Mgr)*

Accounts:
Spree

INFINITE PUBLIC RELATIONS, LLC

275 Madison Ave 6th Fl, New York, NY 10016
Tel.: (212) 687-0935
Fax: (212) 208-2945
Web Site: www.infinitepr.com

Employees: 10

Agency Specializes In: Communications, Crisis Communications, Media Relations

Jamie Diaferia *(Owner)*
Nick Gaffney *(Partner)*
Steven Andersen *(VP-Content & Client Strategy)*

Accounts:
Avvo, Inc.
eGain

INFINITEE COMMUNICATIONS, INC.
3400 Peachtree Rd NE Ste 921, Atlanta, GA 30326
Tel.: (404) 231-3481
Fax: (404) 231-4576
Toll Free: (800) 886-3481
Web Site: www.infinitee.com

Agency Specializes In: Advertising, Brand Development & Integration, Business-To-Business, Digital/Interactive, Integrated Marketing, Promotions

Barbara McGraw *(Founder & CMO)*
Jocelyn Smith *(CEO & Mng Partner)*
Janet Smith *(VP-Brand Mgmt)*
Amy Norton *(Sr Acct Dir)*
Shannon Petty *(Dir-Creative)*
Marcia Schlehuber *(Sr Brand Mgr)*
Taylor Cochran *(Acct Exec)*

Accounts:
Athens First Bank & Trust Company
Atlanta Center for Self Sufficiency
New-Avison Young Branding, Digital Media, Public Relations
Banyan Street Properties Media, PR
Buckhead Atlanta
Citadel Outlets
Cousins Properties Incorporated
Craig Realty Group
DiversiTech Corporation
The Eric R. Beverly Family Foundation
Fuqua Development
Gables Residential Strategic Branding
Hill Partners, Inc. (Agency of Record) Branding, Marketing, Messaging, Specialty Shops
King's Ridge Christian School
Lennar Commercial Investments
Meals By Grace
Monolith
OliverMcmillan
Parkway Properties, Inc.
PM Realty Group LP
RaCo Real Estate Advisors
Royal Oak
Safe Havens International
Sandestination
Tanger Outlet Centers
United Bankshares, Inc.

INFINITY CONCEPTS
5331 Triangle Ln, Export, PA 15632
Tel.: (724) 733-1200
Fax: (724) 733-1201
E-Mail: info@infinityconcepts.net
Web Site: www.infinityconcepts.net

Agency Specializes In: Advertising, Direct Response Marketing, Graphic Design, Internet/Web Design, Media Relations, Strategic Planning/Research

Mark Dreistadt *(Founder, Pres & CEO)*
Susie Dreistadt *(CFO)*
Darrell Law *(Client Svcs Dir)*
Jason Dreistadt *(Dir-Creative & Ops)*
George Konetes *(Dir-Digital Media)*
Paul McDonald *(Dir-Media)*
Kirstie Ansell *(Acct Exec)*
Christina Mason *(Acct Coord)*

Accounts:
Boston Catholics Holy Place
First Baptist Church of Oakeola Holy Place
University of Notre Dame Educational Services

INFINITY MARKETING
874 S Pleasantburg Dr, Greenville, SC 29607
Tel.: (864) 235-1700
Fax: (864) 235-3100
E-Mail: info@infinitymkt.com
Web Site: www.infinitymkt.com

Employees: 31
Year Founded: 1993

Agency Specializes In: Advertising, Alternative Advertising, Broadcast, Cable T.V., Collateral, Corporate Communications, Digital/Interactive, Direct-to-Consumer, Electronic Media, Email, Event Planning & Marketing, Graphic Design, Hispanic Market, Identity Marketing, In-Store Advertising, Integrated Marketing, Internet/Web Design, Local Marketing, Logo & Package Design, Media Buying Services, Media Planning, Media Relations, Multimedia, Newspaper, Newspapers & Magazines, Outdoor, Print, Production, Production (Ad, Film, Broadcast), Production (Print), Promotions, Radio, Regional, T.V., Web (Banner Ads, Pop-ups, etc.), Yellow Pages Advertising

Tim Morrison *(Exec VP-Ops)*
Bill Shatten *(Client Svcs Dir)*
Amanda Stewart *(Mgr-Digital Media)*
Tim Collins *(Supvr-Production)*
Chelsea Lawdahl *(Specialist-Media)*
Lindsey Mainhart *(Sr Graphic Designer)*
Erin Ehrhardt *(Sr Designer-Multimedia)*
Christy Gordon *(Copywriter)*
Caroline Hallman *(Coord-Integrated Mktg)*
Mark Havens *(Coord-Digital Media)*
Ryan King *(Coord-Production)*
Ross McIlwain *(Coord-Client Svcs)*
Brittney Piescik *(Coord-Media)*
Chris Sweeney *(Coord-Analytics)*
Jeanne Morrison *(Asst-Social Media)*

Accounts:
New-ARCpoint Labs Multimedia Creative, Production Services
Chesnee Communications, Inc.
Comcast Cable; 2005
Limestone College (Agency of Record) Branding, Extended Campus, Marketing, Media Buying, Media Planning
Live More
MSO
Nano Cleaning Solutions Communication Strategies, Marketing Services, Media Buying, Media Planning, Search Engine Optimization, Website Design
Newwave
Suddenlink Communications; 2004
Sylvan Learning Direct Mail, Radio, Social Media

INFLIGHT CREATIONS
15030 N Hayden Rd Ste 120, Scottsdale, AZ 85260
Tel.: (480) 331-4621
E-Mail: takeoff@inflightcreations.com
Web Site: www.inflightcreations.com

Agency Specializes In: Advertising, Brand Development & Integration, Digital/Interactive, Graphic Design, Internet/Web Design, Logo & Package Design, Print, Social Media

Carson Poe *(Co-Founder & Pres)*
Trevor Shaffer *(Co-Founder & Dir-Creative)*
Issac Packnett *(Acct Supvr)*

Accounts:
Dre Mack
Ford Motor Company
Innovative Products Operations
The Phoenician Scottsdale
Skaas & Co

INFLUENT50
650 F Street NW, Washington, DC 20004
Tel.: (202) 434-7600
E-Mail: hello@influent50.com
Web Site: www.influent50.com

Agency Specializes In: Advertising, Media Planning

Katharine Vlcek Lazarus *(Acct Dir)*
Paige Greenberg *(Acct Exec)*

Accounts:
New-Avis Budget
New-UnitedHealthcare

INFORM, INC.
415 1st Ave NW, Hickory, NC 28601
Tel.: (828) 322-7766
Fax: (828) 322-4868
Web Site: www.informinc.net

Employees: 5
Year Founded: 1967

Agency Specializes In: Business-To-Business, Pets , Public Relations

Approx. Annual Billings: $624,000

Breakdown of Gross Billings by Media: Collateral: $187,200; Mags.: $31,200; Outdoor: $312,000; Radio: $31,200; T.V.: $62,400

Paul Fogleman, Jr. *(Pres)*

Accounts:
Accordis Yarn; Charlotte, NC
Carolina Hosiery Association; Hickory, NC
Century Furniture; Hickory, NC; 1967
City of Hickory; Hickory, NC
Conover Plastics; Hickory, NC
Faith In America; Hudson, NC
Greenville Colorants
Henerson Machinery
Legware Trends & Fashion; Hickory, NC; 1967
Pets Plus Homecare
Twin City

INFORM VENTURES
606 N Larchmont Blvd Ste 306, Los Angeles, CA 90004
Tel.: (323) 906-0724
Fax: (323) 906-0725
E-Mail: patrick@inform-ventures.com
Web Site: www.inform-ventures.com

Employees: 10

Agency Specializes In: Entertainment

Adryana Cortez *(Co-Owner)*
Patrick Courrielche *(Co-Owner)*

Accounts:
Toyota Lexus, Scion

INFORMATION ANALYTICS, INC.
301 S 70th St Ste 300, Lincoln, NE 68510
Mailing Address:
7205 S Hampton Rd, Lincoln, NE 68506
Tel.: (402) 477-8300
Fax: (402) 695-7375

Toll Free: (866) 477-8300
Web Site: www.4w.com

E-Mail for Key Personnel:
President: KLivingston@4w.com
Creative Dir.: rcurtis@4w.com
Media Dir.: rcurtis@4w.com
Production Mgr.: rcurtis@4w.com
Public Relations: rcurtis@4w.com

Employees: 15
Year Founded: 1995

Agency Specializes In: Automotive, Aviation & Aerospace, Business-To-Business, Consulting, Consumer Marketing, Digital/Interactive, Direct Response Marketing, E-Commerce, Electronic Media, Engineering, Graphic Design, High Technology, Information Technology, Internet/Web Design, Legal Services, Merchandising, Publicity/Promotions, Real Estate, Seniors' Market, Technical Advertising, Trade & Consumer Magazines

Approx. Annual Billings: $800,000

Breakdown of Gross Billings by Media: D.M.: 73%; Mags.: 9%; Radio: 9%; T.V.: 9%

Mark Dahmke *(Co-Owner & VP)*
Kenneth Livingston *(Pres)*

Accounts:
City of Lincoln; Lincoln, NE; 1998
Duncan Aviation; Lincoln, NE; 1997
Exmark Manufacturing; Beatrice, NE; 1997
State of Nebraska Division of Tourism; Lincoln, NE; 1998

INFUSION DIRECT MARKETING & ADVERTISING INC
350 Motor Pky Ste 410, Hauppauge, NY 11788
Tel.: (631) 846-1558
E-Mail: info@infusiondirect.com
Web Site: www.infusiondirect.com

Agency Specializes In: Advertising, Graphic Design, Internet/Web Design, Logo & Package Design, Print, Public Relations

Monique Merhige *(Pres)*

Accounts:
Commtech Design (Agency of Record) Public Relations
Idesco, Corp.
OffSite Vision Holdings, Inc. (Public Relations Agency of Record)

INFUZE MARKETING
455 Capitol Mall Ste 317, Sacramento, CA 95814
Tel.: (916) 662-0008
E-Mail: info@infuzemarketing.com
Web Site: www.infuzemarketing.com

Agency Specializes In: Advertising, Brand Development & Integration, Event Planning & Marketing, Graphic Design, Internet/Web Design, Public Relations, Social Media

Stacey Heater Divine *(CEO & Creative Dir)*

Accounts:
New-El Dorado Winery Association

INITIO, INC.
212 3rd Ave N Ste 510, Minneapolis, MN 55401-1440
Tel.: (612) 339-7195
Fax: (612) 333-0632
E-Mail: info@initioadvertising.com
Web Site: www.initioadvertising.com

E-Mail for Key Personnel:
President: geoffg@initioadvertising.com
Creative Dir.: paul@initioadvertising.com
Media Dir.: mary@initioadvertising.com

Employees: 15
Year Founded: 1991

Agency Specializes In: Advertising, Brand Development & Integration, Broadcast, Business-To-Business, Cable T.V., Co-op Advertising, Collateral, Communications, Consulting, Consumer Marketing, Corporate Communications, Corporate Identity, Digital/Interactive, E-Commerce, Electronic Media, Event Planning & Marketing, Exhibit/Trade Shows, Financial, Government/Political, Graphic Design, Health Care Services, High Technology, In-Store Advertising, Information Technology, Integrated Marketing, Internet/Web Design, Investor Relations, Logo & Package Design, Magazines, Market Research, Media Buying Services, Media Planning, Medical Products, New Product Development, Newspaper, Newspapers & Magazines, Out-of-Home Media, Outdoor, Over-50 Market, Planning & Consultation, Point of Purchase, Point of Sale, Print, Production, Promotions, Radio, Sales Promotion, Search Engine Optimization, Seniors' Market, Social Media, Sports Market, Strategic Planning/Research, T.V., Teen Market, Trade & Consumer Magazines

Approx. Annual Billings: $15,000,000

Scott Sample *(Founder, Partner & Exec Dir-Creative)*
Paul Chapin *(Owner)*
Lee Ericksen *(Controller-Admin)*
Tom Chapman *(Client Svcs Dir)*
Mary Murphy *(Dir-Media)*
Wade Weidner *(Dir-Media)*

Accounts:
Calcium Products Inc Soil Products; 2011
enVision Ideas Consumer Products; 2012
LTS Partners; 2012
UCare (Agency of Record) Health Insurance; 2000
UltraGreen Packaging Biodegradable Food & Personal Products; 2008

INK
38 Discovery Ste 100, Irvine, CA 92618
Tel.: (949) 596-4500
Fax: (949) 502-3773
E-Mail: info@inkagency.com
Web Site: www.inkagency.com

Year Founded: 2007

Agency Specializes In: Advertising, Brand Development & Integration

Todd Henderson *(Founder & Pres)*
Dennis Pettigrew *(Exec Dir-Creative)*
Justin Hannis *(Sr Dir-Art)*
Carlo Tresser *(Brand Dir)*
Kelly Ward *(Brand Dir)*
Shannon Schofield *(Dir-Digital Ops)*
Stephanie Burns *(Sr Brand Mgr)*
Lindsay Reilly *(Brand Mgr)*

Accounts:
Agile360
Baja Fresh
DocuTech
Edwards Lifesciences
Hoag Health
Orange County Department of Education
Raleigh Enterprises
RF Surgical Systems
Santa Monica Convention and Visitors Bureau
SchoolsFirst Federal Credit Union
SmartRoom
Time Warner Cable Business Class
Yokohama Tire Corporation

THE INK TANK
2461 Queen St E, Toronto, ON M4E 1H8 Canada
Tel.: (416) 690-7557
Fax: (416) 690-9236
E-Mail: js@theinktank.com
Web Site: www.theinktank.com

Employees: 6
Year Founded: 1984

Agency Specializes In: Agriculture, Financial, Food Service, Pets , Real Estate, Restaurant, Travel & Tourism

Jim Murray *(Strategist, Writer & Producer-Brdcst)*
Bill Tibbles *(Dir-Creative, Strategist & Designer)*
Jacqueline Spicer *(Dir-Creative & Designer-Mktg)*

Accounts:
Ensemble Travel
JJ Barnicke
Miniature Transportation

INLANDLIGHT LLC
20343 N Hayden Rd Ste 105-116, Scottsdale, AZ 85255
Tel.: (480) 788-5219
E-Mail: info@inlandlight.com
Web Site: www.inlandlight.com

Agency Specializes In: Advertising, Brand Development & Integration, Content, Digital/Interactive, Internet/Web Design, Media Buying Services, Search Engine Optimization, Social Media

Brendan O'Malley Jr. *(Exec VP-Mktg & Product Dev)*
Sarah B. Lovell *(Dir-Production & Social Media)*

Accounts:
The Interior Design

INNER CIRCLE LABS
333 1St St Ste A, San Francisco, CA 94105
Tel.: (415) 684-9400
E-Mail: tellmemore@innercirclelabs.com
Web Site: www.innercirclelabs.com

Agency Specializes In: Public Relations

Julie Crabill *(Founder & CEO)*
Jonathan Neri *(Founder & COO)*
Audrey Jacobson *(VP)*
Brittany Votto *(Sr Mgr)*
Julie Zappelli *(Sr Mgr)*
Meredith Klee *(Sr Acct Mgr)*
Mallory Cloutier *(Mgr)*
Melissa Roxas *(Mgr)*

Accounts:
BlogHer
Time

INNER SPARK CREATIVE
1735 E University Dr Ste 104, Auburn, AL 36830
Tel.: (334) 826-7502
E-Mail: info@innersparkcreative.com
Web Site: www.innersparkcreative.com

Year Founded: 2014

Agency Specializes In: Advertising, Brand Development & Integration, Collateral, Corporate Identity, Electronic Media, Graphic Design,

Internet/Web Design, Local Marketing, Logo & Package Design, Mobile Marketing, Outdoor, Print, RSS (Really Simple Syndication), Radio, Search Engine Optimization, Social Media, Web (Banner Ads, Pop-ups, etc.)

Dayton Cook *(Dir-Art)*
Jarrett Moore *(Dir-Creative)*
Joel Moore *(Dir-Ops)*

Accounts:
New-Holland Homes Custom Home Builder; 2015
New-Initial Outfitters Direct Sales; 2015
New-University Ace Hardware; 2015

INNERACTION MEDIA LLC

1440 Ctr Hill Ave Ste 4, Morgantown, WV 26505
Tel.: (304) 288-1503
Web Site: www.inneractionmedia.com

Year Founded: 2011

Agency Specializes In: Advertising, Brand Development & Integration, Internet/Web Design, Logo & Package Design, Public Relations, Radio, Social Media, Strategic Planning/Research, T.V.

Jim Matuga *(Founder & CEO)*
Hayley Boso *(Assoc Graphic Designer)*

Accounts:
Allegheny Design Services
Mon General Hospital
Mountainstate Orthopedic Associates Inc

INNERSPIN MARKETING

3250 Wilshire Blvd Ste 2150, Los Angeles, CA 90010
Tel.: (213) 251-1500
Web Site: www.innerspin.com

Employees: 22

Agency Specializes In: Above-the-Line, Advertising, Advertising Specialties, Affluent Market, Arts, Asian Market, Below-the-Line, Bilingual Market, Brand Development & Integration, Broadcast, Business-To-Business, Collateral, College, Communications, Consulting, Consumer Goods, Consumer Marketing, Content, Corporate Communications, Corporate Identity, Customer Relationship Management, Digital/Interactive, Direct-to-Consumer, E-Commerce, Education, Electronics, Entertainment, Environmental, Event Planning & Marketing, Fashion/Apparel, Financial, Food Service, Graphic Design, Identity Marketing, In-Store Advertising, Integrated Marketing, Internet/Web Design, Logo & Package Design, Luxury Products, Magazines, Market Research, Media Buying Services, Media Planning, Media Relations, Mobile Marketing, Multicultural, Newspapers & Magazines, Out-of-Home Media, Over-50 Market, Package Design, Point of Purchase, Point of Sale, Print, Production, Production (Ad, Film, Broadcast), Production (Print), Promotions, Restaurant, Retail, Search Engine Optimization, Shopper Marketing, Social Marketing/Nonprofit, Social Media, South Asian Market, Sponsorship, Strategic Planning/Research, Sweepstakes, T.V., Technical Advertising, Teen Market, Urban Market, Web (Banner Ads, Pop-ups, etc.), Women's Market

Approx. Annual Billings: $5,000,000

Elcid Choi *(Pres)*
John Meyer *(Partner & Chief Creative Officer)*
Anthony Shin *(Dir-Interactive & Social Media)*
Jeanette Low *(Sr Acct Exec)*
Michael Chingoo Lee *(Asst Acct Exec)*

Accounts:
Bliss Fuzz Off, Print
Escena Golf & Grill, Real Estate; 2011
Mrs. Cubbinsons Salad Toppings, Stuffing; 2011
Paula Deen Paula Deen Foods; 2012
Sugar Foods Food Service; 2011
Walgreens Balance Rewards; 2011

INNERWEST ADVERTISING

170 S Virginia St Ste 202, Reno, NV 89501
Tel.: (775) 323-4500
Fax: (775) 323-5572
E-Mail: moreinfo@innerwestadv.com
Web Site: www.innerwestadv.com

Agency Specializes In: Advertising, Brand Development & Integration, Internet/Web Design, Media Buying Services, Media Planning, Public Relations, Strategic Planning/Research

Dan Morgan *(Pres & CEO)*
Rachael Ferrari *(COO)*
Angela Comphel *(Dir-Media)*

Accounts:
Hot August Nights

INNIS MAGGIORE GROUP, INC.

4715 Whipple Ave NW, Canton, OH 44718-2651
Tel.: (800) 460-4111
Fax: (330) 492-5568
E-Mail: dick@innismaggiore.com
Web Site: www.innismaggiore.com

E-Mail for Key Personnel:
President: dick@innismaggiore.com

Employees: 32
Year Founded: 1974

National Agency Associations: 4A's-AMA-PRSA

Agency Specializes In: Above-the-Line, Advertising, Advertising Specialties, Affiliate Marketing, Affluent Market, Agriculture, Alternative Advertising, Arts, Automotive, Aviation & Aerospace, Below-the-Line, Brand Development & Integration, Branded Entertainment, Broadcast, Business Publications, Business-To-Business, Cable T.V., Catalogs, Children's Market, Co-op Advertising, Collateral, College, Commercial Photography, Communications, Computers & Software, Consulting, Consumer Goods, Consumer Marketing, Consumer Publications, Content, Corporate Communications, Corporate Identity, Cosmetics, Crisis Communications, Custom Publishing, Customer Relationship Management, Digital/Interactive, Direct Response Marketing, Direct-to-Consumer, E-Commerce, Education, Electronic Media, Electronics, Email, Engineering, Entertainment, Environmental, Event Planning & Marketing, Exhibit/Trade Shows, Experience Design, Faith Based, Fashion/Apparel, Financial, Food Service, Game Integration, Government/Political, Graphic Design, Guerilla Marketing, Health Care Services, High Technology, Hispanic Market, Hospitality, Household Goods, Identity Marketing, In-Store Advertising, Industrial, Infomercials, Information Technology, Integrated Marketing, International, Internet/Web Design, Investor Relations, Legal Services, Leisure, Local Marketing, Logo & Package Design, Luxury Products, Magazines, Marine, Market Research, Media Buying Services, Media Planning, Media Relations, Media Training, Medical Products, Men's Market, Merchandising, Mobile Marketing, Multicultural, Multimedia, New Product Development, New Technologies, Newspaper, Newspapers & Magazines, Out-of-Home Media, Outdoor, Over-50 Market, Package Design, Paid Searches, Pets , Pharmaceutical, Planning & Consultation, Podcasting, Point of Purchase, Point of Sale, Print, Product Placement, Production, Production (Ad, Film, Broadcast), Production (Print), Promotions, Public Relations, Publicity/Promotions, Publishing, RSS (Really Simple Syndication), Radio, Real Estate, Recruitment, Regional, Restaurant, Retail, Sales Promotion, Search Engine Optimization, Seniors' Market, Social Marketing/Nonprofit, Social Media, Sponsorship, Sports Market, Stakeholders, Strategic Planning/Research, Sweepstakes, Syndication, T.V., Technical Advertising, Teen Market, Telemarketing, Trade & Consumer Magazines, Transportation, Travel & Tourism, Tween Market, Urban Market, Viral/Buzz/Word of Mouth, Web (Banner Ads, Pop-ups, etc.), Women's Market, Yellow Pages Advertising

Approx. Annual Billings: $26,000,000

Dick Maggiore *(Pres & CEO)*
Lorraine Kessler *(Principal-Strategy & Client Svcs)*
Mark Vandegrift *(Principal-Web & Digital Svcs)*
Scott Edwards *(Exec Dir-Creative)*
Emily Mays *(Dir-Art)*
Marty Richmond *(Dir-PR)*
Jack Wollitz *(Dir-PR)*

Accounts:
Advanced Power
Aero Communications Inc
Alside; Cuyahoga Falls, OH Building Products; 2002
Apple Growth Partners; Akron, OH Financial Services; 2006
AultCare; Canton, OH Health Insurance; 1996
Aultman Health Foundation; Canton, OH Healthcare; 1996
Aultman Hospital; Canton, OH Healthcare; 1996
Aultman Orrville
Baird Brothers; Canfield, OH Building Products; 2006
Bank of America; Charlotte, NC Financial Services; 2004
FSBO
Gebauer Company
GOJO Industries, Inc Creative, Sustainability Report; 2008
Goodyear - Aviation Division; Akron, OH Tires; 2007
Goodyear - Off Road Division; Akron, OH Tires; 2007
Guidestone Financial Services; Dallas, TX Financial Services; 2006
JOMAC Ltd
Kendall House, Inc
Nickles Bakery Inc.; Navarre, OH Baked Goods Manufacturer; 1998
Ohio Civil Service Employee Association
Old Carolina ICHOR
Republic Steel; Canton, OH Steel; 1988
RTI International Metals; Warren, OH Titanium; 1999
Stark Community Foundation
Stark County District Library
The Village Network

INNOCEAN USA

(Formerly Innocean Americas Worldwide)
180 5th St Ste 200, Huntington Beach, CA 92648
Tel.: (714) 861-5200
Fax: (714) 861-5337
Web Site: www.innoceanusa.com

Employees: 100

National Agency Associations: 4A's

Agency Specializes In: Advertising, Brand Development & Integration, Digital/Interactive, Event Planning & Marketing, Sponsorship

Timothy Blett *(Mng Dir & Exec VP)*
Brad Fogel *(COO)*
Chad Saul *(Chief Growth Officer)*
William Lee *(CEO-Americas)*
Cynthia Jensen *(Sr VP-Media Ops)*

Frank Striefler *(Sr VP-Strategic Plng)*
Barney Goldberg *(VP & Grp Dir-Creative)*
Juli Swingle *(VP & Acct Dir-Social CRM)*
Kathleen Kindle *(VP & Dir-Plng)*
Carol Lombard *(VP & Dir-Integrated Production)*
Fabrizia Cannalonga *(VP-Hyundai Promos & Exhibitions)*
Marisstella Marinkovic *(VP-Acct Svcs)*
Sanjay Rana *(VP-Digital Strategy)*
Jose Eslinger *(Sr Dir-Art)*
Mike Lind *(Sr Dir-Art)*
Miranda Jacobucci *(Art Dir)*
Max Godsil *(Dir-Creative & Writer)*
Jill Pool *(Dir-Creative Resources & Recruiter)*
Kerri Bailey *(Dir-Media Plng & Buying)*
Shane Diver *(Dir-Art & Creative)*
Nguyen Duong *(Dir-Digital Strategy)*
Joanne Fulford *(Dir-Media)*
Scott Muckenthaler *(Dir-Creative)*
Doug Palmer *(Dir-Creative Tech & Digital Innovation)*
Arnie Presiado *(Dir-Art)*
Bob Rayburn *(Dir-Creative)*
Kiran Koshy *(Assoc Dir-Creative)*
David Mesfin *(Assoc Dir-Creative)*
Christie Borowski *(Mgr-Media-Kia Media Plng)*
Parker Collins *(Supvr-Bus Dev)*
Edgar Gamez *(Sr Acct Exec-Digital)*
Lawrence Chow *(Specialist-Product Info)*
Giansimone Graziosi *(Specialist-Dealer Mktg)*
Katie Nevin *(Acct Exec-Digital)*
Gina Pautazzo *(Analyst-Social Media)*
Mehta Mehta *(Grp Creative Dir)*

Accounts:
Alpina Foods (Agency Of Record) Yogurt
Atomic Candy Campaign: "Explore Your Sweet Side"
New-CarePossible Campaign: "Checkout and Alarm Clock"
FootJoy Broadcast, Campaign: "FJ. The Mark of a Player", Digital, Mobile, Social Marketing
New-Hankook Tire America Campaign: "Never Halfway", Digital, Print, Social Media, TV
Hyundai Motor America (Agency of Record) 2015 Sonata, Campaign: "#Because Futbol", Campaign: "Bell Tower", Campaign: "Blind Test Drive", Campaign: "Boom", Campaign: "Cheetah", Campaign: "Co-Pilot", Campaign: "Cooler", Campaign: "Dad's Sixth Sense" Super Bowl 2014, Campaign: "Difference", Campaign: "Don't Tell", Campaign: "Driveway Decision Maker", Campaign: "Epic Play Date", Campaign: "Excited", Campaign: "Mobile Site", Campaign: "New Sonata", Campaign: "Nice" Super Bowl 2014", Campaign: "Sonata Spotted", Campaign: "Speech", Campaign: "Stuck", Campaign: "The Walking Dead Chop Shop App 2.0", Campaign: "The Walking Dead Chop Shop", Campaign: "Welcome to Hyundai Test Town", Campaign: "What kind of car is that?", Campaign: "Youtube Redesign", Creative, Hyundai Equus, Hyundai Tucson, Media Planning, NCAA, Sonata Turbo, The Elantra, Veloster Turbo
Kia Motors "Fight for your Picanto", PicantoLeaks
NRG Energy Inc
New-Thousand Dollar Shave Society Campaign: "Baby On Purpose"

INNOVA DESIGN & ADVERTISING
9211 W Rd Ste 143-109, Houston, TX 77064
Tel.: (713) 623-4432
Fax: (713) 623-2714
E-Mail: info@innovadesign.com
Web Site: www.innovadesign.com

Year Founded: 1990

Agency Specializes In: Advertising, Brand Development & Integration, Collateral, Corporate Identity, Internet/Web Design, Media Buying Services, Outdoor, Package Design, Print, Promotions

J. B. Jarman Jr. *(Pres & Dir-Creative)*

Accounts:
Azulino Tequila labels

INNOVATIVE ADVERTISING
4250 Hwy 22, Mandeville, LA 70471
Tel.: (985) 809-1975
E-Mail: info@peoplewhothink.com
Web Site: peoplewhothink.com

Emily Carlson *(Head-Acct)*
Casey Colomb *(Head-Acct)*
Lena Liller *(Dir-Acct Leadership)*
Gordon Reese *(Dir-Political & Govt Affairs)*
Jordan Von Tress *(Strategist-Digital)*
Laurie Mayeux *(Media Buyer-Digital)*
Meredith Nolan *(Acct Coord)*

Accounts:
Abita Beer
Painting with a Twist (Advertising Agency of Record)

INNOVISION ADVERTISING, LLC
5140 30th Ave, New York, NY 11377
Tel.: (212) 380-6744
E-Mail: chelsey@innovisionadvertising.com
Web Site: www.innovisionadvertising.com

Employees: 5
Year Founded: 2009

Agency Specializes In: Advertising, Broadcast, Business Publications, Cable T.V., Co-op Advertising, Consulting, Direct Response Marketing, Email, Infomercials, Magazines, Media Buying Services, Media Planning, Newspaper, Newspapers & Magazines, Out-of-Home Media, Outdoor, Print, Radio, Social Media, Strategic Planning/Research, Syndication, T.V., Yellow Pages Advertising

Approx. Annual Billings: $975,000

Charles Pendock *(Partner & Dir-Fin & Tech)*

INNOVISION MARKETING GROUP
10620 Treena St Ste 120, San Diego, CA 92131
Tel.: (619) 356-3020
E-Mail: info@innovisionnow.com
Web Site: www.innovisionnow.com

Agency Specializes In: Advertising, Brand Development & Integration, Print

Ric Militi *(CEO & Creative Dir)*
Giselle Campos *(Sr Art Dir)*
Alanna Markey *(Acct Supvr)*
Carolina Oaks *(Acct Supvr)*
Lynnea Schnelle *(Acct Exec)*
Bianca Kasawdish *(Jr Copywriter)*

Accounts:
New-San Diego Gulls (Agency of Record)

INQUEST MARKETING
(Formerly Wilson Chapman)
9249 Ward Pkwy, Kansas City, MO 64114
Tel.: (816) 994-0994
Fax: (816) 994-0999
E-Mail: info@inquestmarketing.com
Web Site: www.inquestmarketing.com

E-Mail for Key Personnel:
Production Mgr.: dennis@inquestmarketing.com

Employees: 22
Year Founded: 1986

Agency Specializes In: Advertising, Advertising Specialties, Brand Development & Integration, Broadcast, Business Publications, Business-To-Business, Cable T.V., Collateral, Commercial Photography, Communications, Consulting, Consumer Goods, Consumer Marketing, Consumer Publications, Corporate Communications, Corporate Identity, Crisis Communications, Customer Relationship Management, Digital/Interactive, Direct Response Marketing, Direct-to-Consumer, E-Commerce, Education, Electronic Media, Email, Entertainment, Event Planning & Marketing, Exhibit/Trade Shows, Faith Based, Financial, Food Service, Graphic Design, Health Care Services, High Technology, Hispanic Market, In-Store Advertising, Industrial, Information Technology, Integrated Marketing, Internet/Web Design, Local Marketing, Logo & Package Design, Magazines, Market Research, Media Buying Services, Media Planning, Media Relations, Medical Products, Merchandising, Multimedia, New Product Development, New Technologies, Newspaper, Newspapers & Magazines, Outdoor, Paid Searches, Pets , Pharmaceutical, Planning & Consultation, Point of Purchase, Point of Sale, Print, Production, Production (Print), Public Relations, Publicity/Promotions, Radio, Restaurant, Retail, Sales Promotion, Search Engine Optimization, Social Marketing/Nonprofit, Social Media, Sports Market, Strategic Planning/Research, Sweepstakes, T.V., Trade & Consumer Magazines, Viral/Buzz/Word of Mouth

Approx. Annual Billings: $8,000,000

Breakdown of Gross Billings by Media: Brdcst.: $2,000,000; Collateral: $2,500,000; Consulting: $2,500,000; E-Commerce: $500,000; Graphic Design: $500,000

Brian Olson *(Owner)*
Joe Myers *(Acct Dir-Mgmt Dept)*
Drew Eldridge *(Dir-Video Production)*
Kristi Sherer *(Dir-Database)*
Stacie Tindle *(Dir-Bus Dev)*
Dennis Michael *(Mgr-Production)*
Anna Lynch *(Acct Coord)*

Accounts:
A.B. May Heating & Cooling Contractor
Ace Imagewear Uniform Services
Belfonte Dairy Products Ice Cream; 1996
Faultless Bon Ami Garden Tools
Fujifilm Sericol Graphic Ink
Postal Uniform Direct Post Office Uniforms
Price Chopper Grocery Retail
Starlight Theatre Outdoor Theatre
WellPet Pet Food

INSIDE OUT COMMUNICATIONS
24 Water St, Holliston, MA 01746
Tel.: (508) 429-8184
Fax: (508) 429-3970
E-Mail: mstearns@iocomm.com
Web Site: www.iocomm.com

Employees: 12
Year Founded: 1987

Agency Specializes In: Advertising

Alicia Frick Laguarda *(Pres)*
Maria Stearns *(VP-Client Svcs)*
Matt Lynch *(Dir-Creative)*
Rebecca Palmer *(Dir-Ops)*

Accounts:
Caterpillar
Genesis Consolidated Services Employee Benefits Packages, Human Resources Management, Payroll Administration, Risk Management Services, Tax Administration

Iwaki America
Lenze/Americas
Milton CAT
Nurse Power

INSIGHT CREATIVE GROUP
19 NE 9th St, Oklahoma City, OK 73104
Tel.: (405) 728-3062
E-Mail: ideas@icgadv.com
Web Site: www.icgadv.com

Year Founded: 2006

Agency Specializes In: Advertising, Brand Development & Integration, Internet/Web Design, Media Buying Services, Print, Social Media

Eric Joiner *(CEO)*
Doug Farthing *(Partner & Chief Creative Officer)*
Rusty Duncan *(Partner)*
Bobbie Earles *(Dir-Bus Dev)*
Jason Reynolds *(Dir-Gaming)*
Steve Loftis *(Strategist-Brand)*
Sharee Farmer *(Sr Acct Planner)*
Alexa Macmillan *(Media Buyer)*

Accounts:
Big Brothers Big Sisters of Oklahoma
Novo Ministries
St. Anthony Hospital

INSIGHT CREATIVE INC.
1816 Sal St, Green Bay, WI 54302
Tel.: (920) 468-7459
Fax: (920) 468-0830
Web Site: www.insightcreative.com

Agency Specializes In: Advertising, Digital/Interactive, Public Relations, Social Media

Jim von Hoff *(Pres)*
Stacy J. Allen *(Dir-Brand Strategy)*
Jay Bauer *(Dir-Creative)*
Niki Petit *(Dir-Bus Dev)*
Cindy Struensee *(Dir-Bus)*
Emily Morehart *(Specialist-PR & Copywriter)*
Jenny Brandenburg *(Media Buyer)*
Bart Raboin *(Designer-Interactive & Web)*
Andrea Parins *(Sr Coord-Social Media)*
Molly Setzer *(Sr Media Buyer)*

Accounts:
Domino Printing Sciences plc

INSIGHT MARKETING DESIGN
401 E 8th St Ste 304, Sioux Falls, SD 57103
Tel.: (605) 275-0011
Fax: (605) 275-0056
E-Mail: info@insightmarketingdesign.com
Web Site: www.insightmarketingdesign.com

Year Founded: 2003

Agency Specializes In: Advertising, Brand Development & Integration, Digital/Interactive, Internet/Web Design, Media Planning, Radio, Search Engine Optimization, Strategic Planning/Research, T.V.

Candy Van Dam *(Partner & Chief Strategy Officer)*
Doug Moss *(Partner & Exec Creative Dir)*
Ben Hodgins *(Art Dir)*
Gaye Grider *(Dir-Media)*
Jon Carroll *(Creative Dir)*
Lori Intveld *(Dir-Bus Dev)*
Kari Geraets *(Mgr-Production & Traffic)*
Joan Meyers *(Office Mgr)*
Ashleigh Walton *(Strategist-Mktg)*
Jill Smith *(Designer)*

Accounts:
Quality BioResources

INSIVIA
5000 Euclid Ave, Cleveland, OH 44103
Tel.: (216) 373-1080
Web Site: www.insivia.com/

Employees: 14
Year Founded: 2002

Agency Specializes In: Advertising, Brand Development & Integration, Content, Digital/Interactive, Event Planning & Marketing, Graphic Design, Integrated Marketing, Internet/Web Design, Mobile Marketing, Production, Production (Print), Search Engine Optimization, Social Marketing/Nonprofit, Social Media, Strategic Planning/Research, Web (Banner Ads, Pop-ups, etc.)

Andy Halko *(CEO)*
Justine Timoteo *(Strategist-Inbound Marketing)*

Accounts:
Collect Next Logo Design
Fan Mosaics Nascar Mobile App
Midtown Cleveland Video
Solupay Collateral System
Yonanas Microsite

INSPIRE!
3625 N Hall St Ste 1100, Dallas, TX 75219
Tel.: (214) 521-7373
Fax: (214) 252-1722
Web Site: inspireagency.com/

Employees: 20
Year Founded: 1998

National Agency Associations: 4A's

Agency Specializes In: Advertising, Bilingual Market, Brand Development & Integration, Hispanic Market, Integrated Marketing, Media Buying Services, Media Planning, Multicultural, Retail, Sponsorship, Teen Market, Urban Market

Breakdown of Gross Billings by Media: Cable T.V.: 7%; D.M.: 1%; Internet Adv.: 2%; Network Radio: 1%; Network T.V.: 28%; Newsp. & Mags.: 5%; Other: 3%; Out-of-Home Media: 4%; Spot Radio: 29%; Spot T.V.: 19%; Trade & Consumer Mags.: 1%

Tommy Thompson *(Chm & CEO)*
Elba Intriago *(Mng Partner)*
Rafael Ramirez *(Chief Creative Officer)*
Maria Cardenas *(Assoc Media Buyer)*
Ricardo Marti *(Jr Copywriter)*

Accounts:
Boost Mobile Hispanic Marketing, Mobile Phone Service, Sin Abusos Campaign
Coca-Cola Refreshments USA, Inc. Soft Drinks & Beverage Products
Heineken USA Campaign: "Con caracter", Digital, Indio, Media Buying, OOH, Outdoor, Radio
Mattress Giant Mattresses
McDonald's Fast Food Restaurants
Sprint
Western Union Caribbean/Latin American Remittances

INSPIRE CREATIVE STUDIOS
St George Technology Bldg, Wilmington, NC 28405
Tel.: (910) 395-0200
Toll Free: (866) 814-4427
E-Mail: info@inspirenc.com
Web Site: www.inspirecreativestudios.com

Employees: 5
Year Founded: 2005

Agency Specializes In: Advertising, Advertising Specialties, Alternative Advertising, Brand Development & Integration, Broadcast, Business-To-Business, Cable T.V., Catalogs, Co-op Advertising, Collateral, College, Commercial Photography, Communications, Consulting, Consumer Goods, Consumer Marketing, Consumer Publications, Content, Corporate Communications, Corporate Identity, Crisis Communications, Custom Publishing, Digital/Interactive, Direct Response Marketing, Direct-to-Consumer, E-Commerce, Electronic Media, Email, Event Planning & Marketing, Exhibit/Trade Shows, Food Service, Government/Political, Graphic Design, Health Care Services, Hospitality, Identity Marketing, In-Store Advertising, Industrial, Infomercials, Integrated Marketing, Internet/Web Design, Leisure, Logo & Package Design, Luxury Products, Market Research, Media Buying Services, Media Planning, Media Relations, Media Training, Multimedia, Newspaper, Newspapers & Magazines, Outdoor, Package Design, Paid Searches, Pharmaceutical, Planning & Consultation, Podcasting, Point of Purchase, Point of Sale, Print, Product Placement, Production, Production (Ad, Film, Broadcast), Production (Print), Promotions, Public Relations, Publicity/Promotions, Publishing, RSS (Really Simple Syndication), Radio, Real Estate, Restaurant, Retail, Search Engine Optimization, Seniors' Market, Social Marketing/Nonprofit, Sponsorship, Sports Market, Strategic Planning/Research, Syndication, T.V., Technical Advertising, Trade & Consumer Magazines, Travel & Tourism, Viral/Buzz/Word of Mouth, Web (Banner Ads, Pop-ups, etc.), Yellow Pages Advertising

Curtis Thieman *(Co-Founder & Dir-Creative)*
Robin Devido *(Dir-Content Mktg)*
Jake Pierce *(Mgr-Creative Ops)*
Ira Bass *(Media Buyer)*

Accounts:
Cape Fear Restaurants; Wilmington, NC; 2006

INSPIRIAMEDIA
10 Mitchell Pl Ste 201, White Plains, NY 10601
Tel.: (914) 239-3421
Fax: (914) 729-0989
E-Mail: adinfo@inspiriamedia.com
Web Site: www.InspiriaMedia.com

Employees: 5
Year Founded: 2007

Agency Specializes In: Advertising, Advertising Specialties, Business-To-Business, Co-op Advertising, Integrated Marketing, Media Buying Services, Media Planning, Mobile Marketing, Out-of-Home Media, Outdoor, Search Engine Optimization, Social Media, Web (Banner Ads, Pop-ups, etc.)

Approx. Annual Billings: $1,000,000

Ronnie Ram *(Co-Founder & Pres)*
Nick Simard *(Co-Founder & VP)*
Micky Huizinga *(Dir-Creative)*
Andy Seraita *(Dir-Outdoor Adv)*
Amanda L. Gomez *(Coord-Inbound Mktg)*
Theresa Mailhot *(Coord-Client Svcs)*

INSTINCT MARKETING
5700 Granite Pkwy Ste 410, Plano, TX 75024
Tel.: (214) 269-1700
Web Site: www.instinctmarketing.com

Employees: 24

Advertising Agencies

Agency Specializes In: Customer Relationship Management, Direct Response Marketing, Market Research, Search Engine Optimization, Web (Banner Ads, Pop-ups, etc.)

Revenue: $7,500,000

William F. Broadbent, Sr. *(CEO)*
Brian Broadbent *(CFO-Instinct Mktg)*
Yung-Yao Shen *(VP-Tech)*
Monica Serrano *(Controller-Fin)*

Accounts:
Conversion Graphics
Search Wisdom

INSTRUMENT
419 NE 10th Ave, Portland, OR 97232
Tel.: (503) 928-3188
Fax: (503) 231-9902
E-Mail: hello@instrument.com
Web Site: www.instrument.com/

Year Founded: 2002

Agency Specializes In: Advertising, Brand Development & Integration, Digital/Interactive, E-Commerce, Graphic Design

Vince LaVecchia *(CO-Founder & COO)*
Steven Denekas *(Exec Dir-Creative)*
Toby Grubb *(Dir-Creative)*
Robin Cornuelle *(Planner-Strategic)*
Jordan A. Smith *(Designer-Interactive)*

INSYNTRIX
3457 Ringsby Ct Ste 323, Denver, CO 80216
Tel.: (303) 280-0014
E-Mail: info@insyntrix.com
Web Site: www.insyntrix.com

Agency Specializes In: Advertising, Brand Development & Integration, Graphic Design, Internet/Web Design, Social Media, Strategic Planning/Research

Ian Atchison *(Pres)*
Robert Young *(Dir-Art)*

Accounts:
HP

INTANDEM INC.
1302 E Firetower Rd, Greenville, NC 27858
Tel.: (252) 321-1111
Fax: (252) 321-1169
Web Site: www.intandeminc.com

Agency Specializes In: Advertising, Communications, Corporate Identity, Graphic Design, Internet/Web Design, Logo & Package Design, Print, Public Relations

Georgina Quinn *(Creative Dir)*

Accounts:
Earp Dentistry
Rooks Dentistry
Spine In Motion

THE INTEGER GROUP, LLC
7245 W Alaska Dr, Lakewood, CO 80226
Tel.: (303) 393-3000
Fax: (303) 393-3730
E-Mail: nicolesouza@integer.com
Web Site: www.integer.com

Employees: 902
Year Founded: 1993

Agency Specializes In: Advertising, Advertising Specialties, Asian Market, Bilingual Market, Brand Development & Integration, Broadcast, Business-To-Business, Catalogs, Collateral, Communications, Consumer Goods, Consumer Marketing, Customer Relationship Management, Digital/Interactive, Direct Response Marketing, Direct-to-Consumer, E-Commerce, Entertainment, Event Planning & Marketing, Exhibit/Trade Shows, Experience Design, Financial, Graphic Design, Hispanic Market, Household Goods, In-Store Advertising, Integrated Marketing, International, Internet/Web Design, Local Marketing, Logo & Package Design, Market Research, Media Buying Services, Media Planning, Men's Market, Merchandising, Mobile Marketing, Multicultural, Multimedia, Newspapers & Magazines, Out-of-Home Media, Outdoor, Package Design, Pharmaceutical, Planning & Consultation, Point of Purchase, Point of Sale, Print, Production, Promotions, Publicity/Promotions, Radio, Regional, Retail, Sales Promotion, Shopper Marketing, Sponsorship, Sports Market, Strategic Planning/Research, Sweepstakes, T.V., Telemarketing, Trade & Consumer Magazines, Urban Market, Viral/Buzz/Word of Mouth, Women's Market

Jeremy Pagden *(Chm)*
Mike Sweeney *(CEO)*
Frank Maher *(COO & Grp Pres-Midwest)*
Christine Stoeber *(Grp CFO & Exec VP)*
Craig Elston *(Sr VP-Insight & Strategy)*
Nicole Souza *(Sr VP-Bus Dev)*
Sam An *(VP-Ops & Bus Solutions)*
Katie Dickens *(Acct Dir)*
Jennine Friess *(Dir-Network Comm)*
Michael Salamon *(Dir-Digital Production)*
Sydney Stoehr *(Acct Exec)*
Jeanette Brown-Green *(Reg Acct Supvr-MillerCoors)*
Erin Kelly *(Reg Sr Acct Exec-MillerCoors)*

Accounts:
7-Eleven
Allsteel Office Furniture; 2008
AT&T Communications Corp.
BancVue; 2005
Benjamin Moore Paints; 2005
Bimbo Bakeries, USA
Carpet One Flooring Retailers; 2011
Dr. Oetker
Electrolux Frigidaire; 2007
FedEX Office
Georgia Lottery
Gillette Razor
GlaxoSmithKline
Grocery Manufacturers Association
Homes Murphy & Associates Insurance Brokerage; 1986
Illinois Lottery
Iowa Department of Economic Development; 1987
Iowa Governor's Traffic Safety Bureau; 1989
Iowa Lottery; 2002
Johnson & Johnson Acuvue, LifeScan
Kellogg's Cheez-It, Frosted Flakes, Mini Wheats, Rice Krispies adult brands; 2010
Kohler
Mars
Mercy Medical Center Healthcare; 2010
Michelin BFGoodrich, Michelin; 2006
MillerCoors Blue Moon, Campaign: "Brewmaster's Inspiration"; 1993
Mohawk Industries Columbia Flooring, Daltile, Quick-Step; 2006
OnMedia/Mediacom Internet Services; 2010
Pella Corporation Doors, Windows; 1997
Procter & Gamble
Red Robin Gourmet Burgers Merchandising
Regency Energy Partners
Shell Pennzoil, Quaker State, Rotella Lubricants; 2010
Slurpee
Starbucks At Home Coffee, Channel Brand Management (Lead Agency), Marketing
Transamerica (Lead Brand Agency) Marketing
Veridian Credit Union Financial Services; 2010

Branches

The Integer Group-Dallas
1999 Bryan St Ste 1700, Dallas, TX 75201
(See Separate Listing)

The Integer Group - Denver
7245 W Alaska Dr, Lakewood, CO 80226
(See Separate Listing)

The Integer Group-Midwest
2633 Fleur Dr, Des Moines, IA 50321-1753
(See Separate Listing)

INTEGRAPHIX, INC.
305 N Eric Dr Ste E, Palatine, IL 60067
Tel.: (847) 537-0067
E-Mail: info@integraphix.com
Web Site: www.integraphix.com

Agency Specializes In: Advertising, Brand Development & Integration, Graphic Design, Internet/Web Design, Logo & Package Design, Print

Scott Ventura *(Dir-Creative)*
Geoff Fuller *(Specialist-Mktg)*

Accounts:
Elemental Media
Number 4 Designs
The Traveling Pot

INTEGRATED MARKETING GROUP
(Name Changed to brandhive)

INTEGRATED MARKETING SERVICES
279 Wall St Research Park, Princeton, NJ 08540-1519
Tel.: (609) 683-9055
Fax: (609) 683-8398
E-Mail: lkaufman@imsworld.com
Web Site: www.imsworld.com

E-Mail for Key Personnel:
President: lkaufman@imsworld.com

Employees: 50
Year Founded: 1981

Agency Specializes In: Advertising, Brand Development & Integration, Business Publications, Business-To-Business, Collateral, Communications, Consumer Marketing, Consumer Publications, Corporate Communications, Corporate Identity, Digital/Interactive, Direct Response Marketing, E-Commerce, Education, Electronic Media, Engineering, Environmental, Exhibit/Trade Shows, Financial, Graphic Design, Health Care Services, High Technology, Hispanic Market, Industrial, Information Technology, Internet/Web Design, Investor Relations, Legal Services, Logo & Package Design, Magazines, Media Buying Services, Medical Products, New Product Development, Newspaper, Newspapers & Magazines, Over-50 Market, Pharmaceutical, Point of Purchase, Print, Production, Public Relations, Publicity/Promotions, Seniors' Market, Strategic Planning/Research, Trade & Consumer Magazines, Travel & Tourism

Approx. Annual Billings: $11,000,000

Breakdown of Gross Billings by Media: Bus. Publs.: $3,000,000; Newsp.: $8,000,000

Lois Kaufman *(Pres)*
Anthony Casale *(CEO)*
Allison Welker *(VP-Client Svc)*
Roseann Rosetta *(Dir-Acct Mgmt)*

Accounts:
Siemens
SoupMan, Inc. Marketing, Merchandising, Traditional & Digital Media
Tribune Co.; Chicago, IL

INTELLIGENT COMMUNITIES GROUP
(Formerly Alan/Anthony, Inc.)
250 Park Ave 7th Fl, New York, NY 10177
Tel.: (212) 825-1582
Fax: (212) 825-0075
E-Mail: info@creating-communities.com
Web Site: www.creating-communities.com

Employees: 4
Year Founded: 1983

Agency Specializes In: Infomercials, New Product Development, Public Relations, Real Estate

Approx. Annual Billings: $750,000

Louis A. Zacharilla *(Mng Dir)*
Robert A. Bell *(VP)*
Tamera Bond *(Dir-Ops)*
Orly Konig-Lopez *(Mgr-Comm)*

Accounts:
Allied Signal
Dex One Corporation
JSAT
Louis Dreyfus
The REIS Reports
Society of Satellite Professionals International
Stuart Dean
Vestcom International

INTERACTIVE AVENUES PVT. LTD.
(Acquired by The Interpublic Group of Companies, Inc.)

INTERACTIVE STRATEGIES
1140 Connecticut Ave NW Ste 1008, Washington, DC 20036
Tel.: (202) 223-8656
Web Site: www.interactivestrategies.com

Year Founded: 2001

Agency Specializes In: Advertising, Brand Development & Integration, Content, Digital/Interactive, Internet/Web Design, Logo & Package Design, Social Media

Bruce Namerow *(Founder & Sr Strategist)*
Dean Burney *(Mng Partner & Dir-Design & UX)*
Kye Tiernan *(Mng Partner & Dir-Client Svcs)*
Mark Davenport *(Acct Dir)*
Levi Wardell *(Dir-Digital Mktg)*
Brian Bieniowski *(Sr Project Mgr-Digital)*
Lori Evans *(Mgr-Ops)*
Ryan McBurney *(Mgr-Digital Mktg)*

Accounts:
Apartment Search
Edelman Financial Services
Envision

INTERACTIVITY MARKETING
408 Main St, Conway, SC 29526
Tel.: (843) 438-8262
Web Site: www.interactivitydigital.com

Year Founded: 2009

Agency Specializes In: Advertising, Brand Development & Integration, Content, Email, Internet/Web Design, Logo & Package Design, Mobile Marketing, Search Engine Optimization, Social Marketing/Nonprofit

Gary Henderson *(Founder & CEO)*
Melanie McMurrain *(Sr Analyst-Strategy & Digital Mktg)*
Dustin T. Marcum *(Jr Analyst)*
Ian Ostrowski *(Jr Analyst-Digital)*

Accounts:
Distinctive Eyewear
Myrtle Beach Zipline Adventures

INTERBRAND
4000 Smith Rd, Cincinnati, OH 45209
Tel.: (513) 421-2210
Fax: (513) 421-2386
E-Mail: info@interbrand.com
Web Site: www.interbrand.com

Employees: 75

Agency Specializes In: Advertising, Brand Development & Integration, Digital/Interactive

Jez Frampton *(Pres)*
Stuart Green *(Pres-Asia Pacific)*
Victoria Leavitt *(CEO-Consumer & Retail Brand Experience-North America)*
Daniel Binns *(Exec Dir-Global Brand Engr)*
Jonathan Redman *(Sr Dir-Client Svcs)*
Krista Danias *(Assoc Dir-Bus Dev & Client Svc)*
Shane Jallick *(Assoc Dir-Creative)*

Accounts:
3M 3M Post-it
BALS
CSC Holdings, LLC
Wm. Wrigley Jr. Company Orbit Gum, Packaging Design; 2008
YP

INTERBRAND CORPORATION
130 5th Ave, New York, NY 10011-4306
Tel.: (212) 798-7500
Fax: (212) 798-7501
E-Mail: usinfo@interbrand.com
Web Site: www.interbrand.com

Employees: 110

Agency Specializes In: Brand Development & Integration, Environmental, Logo & Package Design, Sponsorship

Tom Zara *(Pres)*
Andrea Sullivan *(CMO-North America)*
Antoine Veliz *(Chief Experience Officer)*
Josh Feldmeth *(CEO-North America)*
Jez Frampton *(CEO-Global)*
Vicky Leavitt *(CEO-Consumer & Retail Brand Experience-North America)*
Zach Newcomb *(Head-NA Practice & Exec Dir-Client Engagement)*
Chris Campbell *(Exec Dir-Creative)*
Jonathan Redman *(Sr Dir-Client Svcs)*
Ross Clugston *(Dir-Design)*
Kristin Reagan *(Dir-Mktg-Global)*
Natalie Silverstein *(Coord-Mktg)*

Accounts:
3M Post-It
Applebee's
AT&T Communications Corp.
Aviage Systems
AWARD
Banco Popular
Barclays
Best Buy
BMW Mini
Boots
Canon
City of Johannesburg
Ebay
Humana
Kellogg's Branding
Mandela Poster Project
Montecasino
National Geographic
Nissan West Europe SAS Brand Strategy
Oxfam
PricewaterhouseCoopers
Procter & Gamble Aussie, Noxzema, Tag
Repsol YPF Oil Company
Samsung
Schering-Plough Bridion
SFR Mobile Phones
Singapore Mozaic
Synchrony Financial Branding, Campaign: "Engage With Us", Logo
Terranova
Thai Airways
Unilever Foodsolutions Knorr
Unionpay Bank Card Processing
Wrigley Campaign: "Wrigley Brand Identity"
Xerox

Branches

Interbrand
85 Strand, London, WC2R 0DW United Kingdom
Tel.: (44) 20 7554 1000
Fax: (44) 20 7554 1001
E-Mail: reception@interbrand.com
Web Site: www.interbrand.com

Employees: 130

Christian Purser *(CEO)*
Vincent Baroin *(Chief Creative Officer & CFO-EMEA & Latham)*
Jez Frampton *(CEO-Global)*
Fred Burt *(Mng Dir-Clients-Global)*
Dan Howarth *(Dir-Creative)*
Kristin Reagan *(Dir-Global Mktg & Comm)*
Rebecca Robins *(Dir-EMEA & LatAm)*
Michael Rocha *(Dir-Brand Valuation-Global)*

Accounts:
Image of the Studio
Npower Strategy
Telefonica

InterbrandHealth
130 5th Ave, New York, NY 10011
Tel.: (212) 798-7600
Fax: (212) 798-7501
Web Site: www.interbrand.com

Employees: 200

Jane Parker *(CEO)*
John Breen *(Exec Dir-Analytics)*
Nichole Davies *(Exec Dir-Global Engagement & Ops)*
R. John Fidelino *(Exec Dir-Creative)*
Barry Silverstein *(Exec Dir-Client Svc)*
Wes Wilkes *(Exec Dir-Global Strategy)*
Ramya Kartikeyan *(Dir-Res & Analytics)*
Aurelie Castel *(Sr Mgr-Res)*
Trisha Carr *(Mgr-Res)*
Nicole Diamant *(Mgr-Mktg)*

INTERBRAND DESIGN FORUM
7575 Paragon Rd, Dayton, OH 45459-5316
Tel.: (937) 439-4400

Fax: (937) 439-4340
E-Mail: scott.smith@interbrand.com
Web Site: www.interbranddesignforum.com/

Employees: 150
Year Founded: 1978

Agency Specializes In: Sponsorship

Scott Smith *(Sr VP)*
Thomas Kowalski *(VP-Design)*
Tim Raberding *(VP-Engrg)*
Ginger Scherbarth *(Exec Dir-HR)*
Amanda Kohnen *(Sr Dir-Design)*
Glen Middleton *(Sr Dir)*
Missy Donahoe *(Dir-Plng)*
Beth Ling *(Dir-PR)*
Tracy Heppes *(Program Mgr-Automotive-Client Svc)*
Ashlie Wilmetti *(Designer-Interior & Planner)*
Amanda Handermann *(Designer-Environmental)*
Haley Kunka *(Designer-Graphic Comm)*

Accounts:
Applebee's
Burger King
Dunkin' Donuts
FedEx
Gold's Gym
KFC
Land Rover
Mazda
McDonald's
Microsoft
Porsche
Subway
Yankee Candle

Branches

Interbrand Design Forum
(Formerly Design Forum Los Angeles)
15375 Barranca Pkwy Ste E106, Irvine, CA 92618
Tel.: (949) 450-1101
Fax: (949) 450-9967
E-Mail: JWilliamson@designforum.com
Web Site: www.interbranddesignforum.com/

Employees: 10

Agency Specializes In: Advertising

Scott Smith *(CMO)*
Jim Williamson *(Sr VP-Ops-Los Angeles)*
Beth Ling *(Dir-PR)*

Interbrand San Francisco
555 Market St Ste 500, San Francisco, CA 94105
Tel.: (415) 848-5000
Fax: (415) 848-5020
E-Mail: sarah.lent@interbrand.com
Web Site: www.interbrand.com

Employees: 20

Agency Specializes In: Advertising

Tom Zara *(Pres)*
Beth Viner *(CEO-New York & San Francisco)*
Dominik Prinz *(Exec Dir-Strategy)*
Craig Stout *(Exec Dir-Creative)*
Jonathan Redman *(Sr Dir-Client Svcs)*
Kurt Munger *(Dir-Creative)*
Alan Roll *(Dir-Creative)*
Caren Williams *(Dir-Brand Strategy)*

Accounts:
3M 3M Post-it
Ambre
Applebee's
BALS

INTERCEPT GROUP - CAMPUS INTERCEPT / CONSUMER INTERCEPT
(Formerly Campus Intercept)
251 Consumers Rd 3rd Fl, Toronto, ON M2J 4R3 Canada
Tel.: (416) 479-4200, ext. 321
E-Mail: info@interceptgroup.com
Web Site: www.interceptgroup.com

Employees: 50
Year Founded: 2006

Agency Specializes In: Advertising, Advertising Specialties, Below-the-Line, Branded Entertainment, College, Consumer Marketing, Direct-to-Consumer, Electronics, Entertainment, Event Planning & Marketing, Integrated Marketing, Mobile Marketing, Planning & Consultation, Point of Sale, Sales Promotion, Social Media, Sponsorship, Strategic Planning/Research, Urban Market

Approx. Annual Billings: $10,000,000

Andrew Au *(Pres)*
Shaheen Yazdani *(VP-Client Svc)*
Daisy Magboo *(Sr Mgr-Staffing & Acct Mgr)*
Jessica Gorassi *(Sr Acct Mgr)*
Julian Ibe *(Acct Mgr)*
Jennifer Jesson *(Acct Mgr)*
Richard Pay *(Mgr-Production)*
Vyvy Truong *(Coord-Staffing)*

Accounts:
3M Canada
7-Eleven
HP
Pepsico
Unilever

INTERCOMMUNICATIONS INC.
1375 Dove St Ste 200, Newport Beach, CA 92660
Tel.: (949) 644-7520
Fax: (949) 640-5739
E-Mail: intercom@intercommunications.com
Web Site: www.intercommunications.com

E-Mail for Key Personnel:
President: ta@intercommunications.com

Employees: 15
Year Founded: 1984

National Agency Associations: 4A's

Agency Specializes In: Strategic Planning/Research

Breakdown of Gross Billings by Media: Collateral: 40%; Consulting: 30%; Newsp. & Mags.: 30%

Toni Alexander *(Pres & Dir-Creative)*
Pat Cherpeski *(Sr VP-Admin Ops)*
Bob Weil *(VP-Digital Engagement)*
Richard Darner *(Sr Dir-Art)*
Carolyn Marek *(Dir-Media & Acct Mgr)*
Barbara Landa *(Supvr-Production)*

Accounts:
Four Seasons Residences LA
Hasko Development
Lincoln Property Co - Villages at Playa Vista
Luxury Estates - Utopia
McCaffrey Group
Tero Viejo Inc.

INTERKOM CREATIVE MARKETING
720 Guelph Line Ste 304, Burlington, ON L7R 4E2 Canada
Tel.: (905) 332-8315
Fax: (905) 332-8316
Toll Free: (800) 565-0571
E-Mail: solutions@interkom.ca
Web Site: www.interkom.ca

Employees: 20
Year Founded: 1981

Martin van Zon *(Pres)*
Lee Zhang *(Client Svcs Dir)*
Kayla Van Zon *(Acct Mgr)*
Willem Van Zon *(Strategist)*

Accounts:
Amgen
Burlington Art Centre
Halton Women's Place & ErinOak Kids
Injection Molding Systems
PictorVision
Young Drivers of Canada

INTERLEX COMMUNICATIONS INC.
4005 Broadway Ste B, San Antonio, TX 78209-6311
Tel.: (210) 930-3339
Fax: (210) 930-3383
Toll Free: (866) 430-3339
E-Mail: info@interlexusa.com
Web Site: www.interlexusa.com

Employees: 33
Year Founded: 1995

Agency Specializes In: Above-the-Line, Advertising, Advertising Specialties, Affluent Market, African-American Market, Agriculture, Alternative Advertising, Arts, Asian Market, Automotive, Below-the-Line, Bilingual Market, Brand Development & Integration, Branded Entertainment, Broadcast, Business Publications, Business-To-Business, Cable T.V., Children's Market, Co-op Advertising, Collateral, College, Commercial Photography, Communications, Consulting, Consumer Goods, Consumer Marketing, Consumer Publications, Content, Corporate Communications, Corporate Identity, Cosmetics, Customer Relationship Management, Digital/Interactive, Direct Response Marketing, Direct-to-Consumer, E-Commerce, Education, Electronic Media, Electronics, Environmental, Event Planning & Marketing, Exhibit/Trade Shows, Experience Design, Faith Based, Fashion/Apparel, Financial, Food Service, Game Integration, Gay & Lesbian Market, Government/Political, Graphic Design, Guerilla Marketing, Health Care Services, Hispanic Market, Hospitality, Household Goods, Identity Marketing, In-Store Advertising, Infomercials, Integrated Marketing, International, Internet/Web Design, Local Marketing, Logo & Package Design, Luxury Products, Magazines, Market Research, Media Buying Services, Media Planning, Media Relations, Medical Products, Men's Market, Merchandising, Mobile Marketing, Multicultural, Multimedia, New Product Development, Newspaper, Newspapers & Magazines, Out-of-Home Media, Outdoor, Over-50 Market, Package Design, Paid Searches, Pharmaceutical, Planning & Consultation, Podcasting, Point of Purchase, Point of Sale, Print, Product Placement, Production (Ad, Film, Broadcast), Production (Print), Promotions, Public Relations, Publicity/Promotions, Radio, Real Estate, Recruitment, Regional, Restaurant, Retail, Sales Promotion, Search Engine Optimization, Seniors' Market, Social Marketing/Nonprofit, Social Media, South Asian Market, Sponsorship, Sports Market, Stakeholders, Strategic Planning/Research, T.V., Teen Market, Transportation, Travel & Tourism, Tween Market, Urban Market, Web (Banner Ads, Pop-ups, etc.), Women's Market

Approx. Annual Billings: $31,000,000

Breakdown of Gross Billings by Media: Brdcst.: $28,000,000; Radio: $3,000,000

Heather Kristina Ruiz *(Co-Founder & Dir-Creative)*
Rudy Ruiz *(Pres & CEO)*
Joseph Garcia *(COO)*
Leah Delagarza *(VP-Ops & Integration)*
Thomas Schlenker *(Dir-Medical)*
Irasema Ortiz *(Acct Exec)*
Ana Ramos *(Media Planner & Buyer)*
Krystal Ortega *(Sr Media Planner & Buyer)*

Accounts:
American Airlines
American Express
Amigo Energy
Amoco
AT&T West
Balise
Department of Homeland Security
Texas Department of State Health Services

INTERMARK GROUP, INC.

101 25th St N, Birmingham, AL 35203
Tel.: (205) 803-0000
Fax: (205) 870-3843
Toll Free: (800) 554-0218
Web Site: www.intermarkgroup.com

E-Mail for Key Personnel:
President: jake.mckerzie@intermarkgroup.com

Employees: 185
Year Founded: 1977

National Agency Associations: PRSA

Agency Specializes In: Advertising, Alternative Advertising, Automotive, Brand Development & Integration, Broadcast, Business Publications, Business-To-Business, Cable T.V., Co-op Advertising, Collateral, Communications, Consulting, Consumer Goods, Consumer Marketing, Consumer Publications, Corporate Communications, Corporate Identity, Crisis Communications, Digital/Interactive, Direct Response Marketing, E-Commerce, Electronic Media, Email, Entertainment, Environmental, Event Planning & Marketing, Exhibit/Trade Shows, Financial, Food Service, Graphic Design, Health Care Services, Hispanic Market, In-Store Advertising, Industrial, Infomercials, Information Technology, Integrated Marketing, Internet/Web Design, Legal Services, Leisure, Logo & Package Design, Media Buying Services, Media Planning, Media Relations, Media Training, Medical Products, Merchandising, Mobile Marketing, Multimedia, New Product Development, Newspaper, Newspapers & Magazines, Outdoor, Over-50 Market, Package Design, Pharmaceutical, Planning & Consultation, Point of Purchase, Point of Sale, Print, Production, Production (Print), Promotions, Public Relations, Publicity/Promotions, Radio, Real Estate, Regional, Restaurant, Retail, Sales Promotion, Search Engine Optimization, Seniors' Market, Social Media, Sponsorship, Sports Market, Strategic Planning/Research, T.V., Technical Advertising, Trade & Consumer Magazines, Transportation, Travel & Tourism, Viral/Buzz/Word of Mouth, Yellow Pages Advertising

Approx. Annual Billings: $100,000,000

Breakdown of Gross Billings by Media: Cable T.V.: $12,467,984; Internet Adv.: $5,818,392; Mags.: $831,199; Newsp.: $831,199; Out-of-Home Media: $831,199; Production: $16,348,774; Pub. Rels.: $531,335; Radio: $8,311,989; T.V.: $54,027,929

Jake McKenzie *(CEO)*
Billy Sanford *(CFO)*
Josh Simpson *(Chief Strategy Officer)*
Becci Hart *(Pres-PR)*
Neal Fondren *(Sr VP-Interactive Strategy)*
Paul Brusatori *(VP & Grp Acct Dir)*
Keith Otter *(Exec Dir-Creative)*
Michel Le *(Dir-Art)*
Jim Poh *(Dir-Media)*
Blake Young *(Dir-Art)*
Elizabeth Bishop *(Acct Supvr)*
Kelly Darden *(Acct Supvr)*
Tracie Ray *(Acct Supvr)*
Madison Elkin *(Sr Acct Exec)*
Ale Bowman *(Acct Exec-Automotive)*
Jade Chesser *(Copywriter)*
David Dulock *(Copywriter)*
Drew Granthum *(Asst Acct Exec)*
Alex Hawkins *(Asst Acct Exec)*
Ashlyn McClellan *(Asst Acct Exec)*
Amber Parket *(Asst Acct Exec)*
Julie LaForce *(Acct Coord)*
Brian Gordon *(Sr Media Buyer)*
Sheena Robinson *(Sr Media Planner)*

Accounts:
Alabama Tourism Department (Agency of Record) Advertising, Campaign: "Year of", Marketing
American Buildings Company; Eufaula, AL
Cadence Bank Brand Strategy, Creative, Marketing Campaign, Media Planning & Buying, Online, PR, Research
Chevrolet Local Marketing Association; Bettendorf, IA/Davenport, IA/East Moline, IL/Rock Island, IL
Chevrolet Local Marketing Association; Birmingham, AL
Chevrolet Local Marketing Association; Cedar Rapids, IA
Chevrolet Local Marketing Association; Charlotte, NC
Chevrolet Local Marketing Association; Denver, CO
Chevrolet Local Marketing Association; Dothan, AL/Montgomery, AL
Chevrolet Local Marketing Association; Grand Junction, CO
Chevrolet Local Marketing Association; Huntsville, AL
Chevrolet Local Marketing Association; Mobile, AL/Pensacola, FL
Chevrolet Local Marketing Association; Nashville, TN
Chevrolet Local Marketing Association; South Bend, IN
Chevrolet Local Marketing Association; Tallahassee, FL/Panama City, FL
Chevrolet Local Marketing Association; Washington, DC
EGS Commercial Real Estate; Birmingham, AL
Mohawk Industries; Dalton, GA
Office Furniture USA; Birmingham, AL
Parrish Medical Center (Advertising Agency of Record)
Red Diamond Coffee; Birmingham, AL
Southeast Toyota Distributors; Deerfield Beach, FL
St. Vincent's Health System; Birmingham, AL
Talladega Superspeedway Creative, Marketing Strategy, Media
University of Alabama; Tuscaloosa, AL

INTERMUNDO MEDIA

1433 Pearl St 2nd Fl, Boulder, CO 80302
Tel.: (303) 633-4993
Fax: (303) 633-4998
E-Mail: info@intermundomedia.com
Web Site: extramundomedia.com

Agency Specializes In: Advertising, Digital/Interactive, Email, Media Buying Services, Search Engine Optimization, Social Media

Ian Woods *(Chief Engagement Officer)*
Stacey Paznokas *(Exec VP-Client Svcs)*
Kyle Taylor *(Sr VP & Exec Dir-Creative)*
Zach Baze *(Sr VP-Strategy & Insights)*
Gina Lee *(Sr VP-Solutions)*
Keith Pieper *(VP-Tech)*
Kelly Roe *(Dir-Customer Value Mgmt)*

Accounts:
Brinker International Interactive Media, Strategy
Chili's Grill & Bar "Baby Back Ribs" Jingle, Social, Videos
Roku Digital Marketing

INTERNECTION

1577 Riverview Cir W, Ripon, CA 95366-9330
Tel.: (800) 893-8458
Fax: (209) 599-6600
Web Site: www.internec.com

E-Mail for Key Personnel:
Production Mgr.: ktucker@internec.com

Employees: 9
Year Founded: 1995

Agency Specializes In: Advertising, Business Publications, Collateral, Graphic Design, Internet/Web Design, Logo & Package Design, Magazines, Newspaper, Newspapers & Magazines, Print, Recruitment, Restaurant, Trade & Consumer Magazines

Approx. Annual Billings: $6,100,000

Jane Kraft *(Owner)*
Martin J. Kraft *(Owner)*
Shana Adams *(Acct Mgr-Natl)*

Accounts:
Airoom Architects & Builders
Antech Diagnostics
Associated Health Professionals
Barton Protective Services
Bristol Industries
College Hospital
Crystal Springs Water Co.; Mableton, GA
El Pollo Loco
Eurest Services
Granite Construction
Jet Delivery
Kelly Services; San Jose, CA Recruitment
LTD Commodities, LLC
Manpower Technical
Medfinders, Inc.
Monroe Truck Equipment
Pacific Rim Mechanical
Placement Pros
PrideStaff
RCR Companies
Red Lion Hotels
Restaurant Management Careers
Smart & Final
Sony Entertainment America; Foster City, CA Recruitment; 1998
Southern Wine & Spirits
Sparkletts
Surf & Sand Resort
Tripp Lite; Chicago, IL Recruitment Advertising
Unimark
Winbond Microelectronics; San Jose, CA; 1996

INTERNET DISTRIBUTION SERVICES, INC.

665 Wellsbury Way, Palo Alto, CA 94306
Tel.: (650) 327-3385
Fax: (650) 327-3302
E-Mail: marc@service.com

Employees: 3
Year Founded: 1994

Agency Specializes In: Internet/Web Design

Marc Fleischmann *(Pres)*

Accounts:
Alliance Cost Containment
Ashley Lighting
DVDPlay

Exfreight Zeta
PRN
SAMS Customer Catalog Service

INTERNET EXPOSURE, INC.
1101 Washington Ave S, Minneapolis, MN 55415
Tel.: (612) 676-1946
E-Mail: info@ieexposure.com
Web Site: www.iexposure.com

Employees: 15
Year Founded: 1995

Agency Specializes In: Digital/Interactive, Game Integration, Local Marketing, Mobile Marketing, Paid Searches, Search Engine Optimization, Social Media, Web (Banner Ads, Pop-ups, etc.)

Jeff Hahn *(Owner)*
Kristy Collins *(Office Mgr)*

Accounts:
Summit Brewing; 2013

INTERNET MARKETING, INC.
10620 Treena St Ste 250, San Diego, CA 92131
Tel.: (866) 563-0620
Fax: (866) 780-5126
E-Mail: info@internetmarketinginc.com
Web Site: www.internetmarketinginc.com

Year Founded: 2005

Agency Specializes In: Advertising, Email, Internet/Web Design, Search Engine Optimization, Social Media

Brent Gleeson *(Co-Founder & CMO)*
Brandon Fishman *(CEO)*
Dan Romeo *(CFO)*
Benj Arriola *(VP-SEO)*
Michael Montgomery *(VP-Bus Dev)*
Justin Mayerick *(Dir-SEM)*
Ann Smarty *(Community Mgr & Brand Mgr)*
Jeff King *(Acct Exec-Digital)*

INTERPLANETARY
175 Varick St, New York, NY 10014
Tel.: (212) 488-4769
Web Site: www.interplanetaryhq.com

Agency Specializes In: Advertising, Brand Development & Integration, Broadcast, Digital/Interactive, Multimedia, Newspapers & Magazines, Out-of-Home Media, Outdoor, Print, Radio, T.V.

Chris Parker *(Partner-Creative)*
Joseph A Dessi *(Mng Dir)*
Bruce Lee *(Dir-Creative)*
Jill McClabb *(Dir-Creative & Art)*
Andy Semons *(Dir-Strategic Plng)*

Accounts:
New-Astoria Bank
New-City of Hope Hospital
Leukemia & Lymphoma Society

THE INTERPUBLIC GROUP OF COMPANIES, INC.
1114 Ave of the Americas 19th Fl, New York, NY 10036
Tel.: (212) 704-1200
Fax: (212) 704-1201
E-Mail: info@interpublic.com
Web Site: www.interpublic.com

Employees: 47,400
Year Founded: 1902

National Agency Associations: 4A's-AAF-AC-ARF-IAA-PMA

Agency Specializes In: Advertising, African-American Market, Asian Market, Brand Development & Integration, Corporate Identity, Digital/Interactive, Direct Response Marketing, Event Planning & Marketing, Health Care Services, Hispanic Market, Internet/Web Design, Investor Relations, Logo & Package Design, Media Buying Services, Newspaper, Out-of-Home Media, Outdoor, Print, Public Relations, Sales Promotion, Sponsorship, Sports Market, Strategic Planning/Research, T.V., Teen Market

Revenue: $7,537,100,000

Michael Roth *(Chm & CEO)*
Terry Peigh *(Mng Dir & Sr VP)*
Frank Mergenthaler *(CFO & Exec VP)*
Joseph W. Farrelly *(CIO & Sr VP)*
Eliseo Rojas *(Chief Procurement Officer & VP)*
Julie Connors *(Chief Risk Officer & Sr VP)*
Heide Gardner *(Chief Diversity Officer & Sr VP)*
Simon Bond *(Chief Growth Officer)*
Nicholas J. Camera *(Gen Counsel)*
Ellen T. Johnson *(Treas & Sr VP)*
Peter Leinroth *(Sr VP & Mng Dir-Client Svcs)*
Marjorie Hoey *(Sr VP & Dir-Talent-Global)*
Anthony G. Alexandrou *(Sr VP-Taxation-Global)*
Matt Carrasco *(Sr VP-Digital Media & Mktg)*
Richard J. Haray *(Sr VP-Corp Svcs)*
Jerry Leshne *(Sr VP-IR)*
Jemma Gould *(Dir-Content Creation)*
Leslie LaPlante *(Dir-Mktg & Online Svcs)*
Tim Jensen *(Mgr-Global Engrg-Unified Comm)*
Miriam Sampson *(Mgr-IT Program & Comm)*
Joseph G. Clemente *(Engr-Unified Comm)*
Anca Cornis-Pop *(Sr Counsel)*
Ilyssa London *(Counsel-Adv-Digital Media & Production)*

Accounts:
General Motors
Home Depot
Johnson & Johnson Family of Companies
Markwins Beauty Products Communications, Integrated PR, Marketing, Social Media, Wet n Wild
Merck & Co., Inc.; Whitehouse Station, NJ
Microsoft Corporation Advertising, Creative, Deployment
MillerCoors
Walmart
Zurich Insurance Group Global Marketing

McCann-Erickson WorldGroup (Part of the Interpublic Group)

AFG&
(Formerly Avrett Free Ginsberg)
1 Dag Hammarskjold Plz 885 2nd Ave, New York, NY 10017-2205
(See Separate Listing)

beauty@gotham
(Formerly Gotham Incorporated)
150 E 42nd St 12th Fl, New York, NY 10017
(See Separate Listing)

Fitzgerald+CO
3333 Piedmont Rd NE Ste 100, Atlanta, GA 30305
(See Separate Listing)

The Martin Agency
One Shockoe Plz, Richmond, VA 23219
(See Separate Listing)

McCann Erickson Worldwide
622 3rd Ave, New York, NY 10017-6707
(See Separate Listing)

McCann Worldgroup
622 3rd Ave, New York, NY 10017
(See Separate Listing)

Mithun
(Formerly Campbell Mithun, Inc.)
Campbell Mithun Tower 222 S 9th St, Minneapolis, MN 55402-3389
(See Separate Listing)

NAS Recruitment Innovation
9700 Rockside Rd Ste 170, Cleveland, OH 44125
(See Separate Listing)

TM Advertising
3030 Olive St, Dallas, TX 75219-7690
(See Separate Listing)

Draftfcb Group: (Part of the Interpublic Group)

FCB Global
(Formerly Draftfcb Worldwide)
100 W 33rd St, New York, NY 10001
(See Separate Listing)

FCB Health
(Formerly Draftfcb HealthCare NY)
100 W 33rd St, New York, NY 10001
(See Separate Listing)

Hacker Agency
(Formerly Hacker Group)
1215 4th Ave Ste 2100, Seattle, WA 98161-1018
Tel.: (206) 805-1500
Fax: (206) 805-1599
E-Mail: info@hal2l.com
Web Site: hal2l.com

Employees: 300
Year Founded: 1986
National Agency Associations: 4A's

Agency Specializes In: Direct Response Marketing, Electronic Media, Sponsorship

Spyro Kourtis *(Pres & CEO)*
Richard Jacroux *(CFO & VP)*
Stephan Horvath *(CMO-Global)*
Haydn Sweterlitsch *(Global Chief Creative Officer)*
Matt Witter *(Exec VP & Gen Mgr)*
Jason Grollman *(VP-Ops)*
Mark Capps *(Exec Dir)*
Michael Goerz *(Exec Acct Dir)*
Bryan Chaffe *(Dir-Strategic Analytics)*
Scott Fasser *(Dir-Digital Innovation)*
Lauren Collins *(Acct Exec)*
Jessica Deeken *(Strategist-Targeting & Media-Strategic Accts)*
Kyrsten Hendrickson *(Acct Exec)*

Accounts:
AAA
AT&T; 1995
BlueCross BlueShield
Carnival Cruise Line
Coca-Cola
Essence Healthcare, Inc
Global Hyatt
Highmark Blue Cross Blue Shield
Microsoft
One Medical Group Marketing
Skoda
Volkswagen
YMCA

Mullen Lowe Group
(Formerly Mullen)
40 Broad St, Boston, MA 02109
(See Separate Listing)

R/GA
350 W 39th St, New York, NY 10018-1402
(See Separate Listing)

Interpublic Aligned Companies: (Part of the Interpublic Group)

Adcomm
House 7A Road 41 Gulshan 2, Dhaka, 1212 Bangladesh
Tel.: (880) 2 885 3222
Fax: (880) 2 885 3255
E-Mail: champa@adcommad.com
Web Site: www.adcommad.com/

The Axis Agency
8687 Melrose Ave 9th Fl, Los Angeles, CA 90069
(See Separate Listing)

BB&M Lowe & Partners
Ave Ricardo Arango y Calle 54 Urbanizacion Obarrio 4, Panama, Panama
Tel.: (507) 263 9300
Fax: (507) 263 9692
E-Mail: info@bbm-panama.com
Web Site: www.bbm-panama.com

Employees: 62
Year Founded: 1971

Rafael E. Barcenas *(Pres-BBM Publicidad)*
Jaimie Sosa *(VP-Plng)*

Accounts:
Movil
Novartis
Unilever

Campbell Ewald
(Formerly Lowe Campbell Ewald)
2000 Brush St Ste 601, Detroit, MI 48226
(See Separate Listing)

Branches

Campbell Ewald Los Angeles
(Formerly Lowe Campbell Ewald Los Angeles)
8687 Melrose Ave Ste G510, West Hollywood, CA 90069
Tel.: (310) 358-4800
Web Site: www.c-e.com

Employees: 40
Year Founded: 1962

National Agency Associations: 4A's-THINKLA

Agency Specializes In: Advertising, Sponsorship

Jim Palmer *(CEO)*
Mark Simon *(Chief Creative Officer)*
Craig Kleber *(Exec Dir-Strategy)*
Jo Shoesmith *(Exec Creative Dir)*
Zenaida Torres Marvin *(Grp Acct Dir)*
Paula Pletcher *(Mgmt Supvr)*
Cheryl Liu *(Dir-Media Plng-Life Lock, WGU, Energy Upgrade & PIMCO)*
Debbie Osborne *(Dir-HR)*
Vanessa Witter *(Assoc Dir-Creative)*
Derek Padilla Ravega *(Sr Media Planner)*

Accounts:
Chicken of the Sea International; San Diego, CA (Agency of Record)
Covered California (Agency of Record) Creative Implementation, Digital, Media Buying, Media Planning, Social Communications, Strategy
Energy Upgrade California Education, Energy, Marketing, Outreach, Water
Kaiser Permanente Insurance
Keep Oakland Beautiful Campaign: "Litter is Bad"
Los Angeles Tourism & Convention Board
McKesson

Campbell Ewald New York
(Formerly Lowe Campbell Ewald New York)
386 Park Ave S, New York, NY 10016
Tel.: (646) 762-6700
Web Site: www.c-e.com

Employees: 30

National Agency Associations: 4A's

Agency Specializes In: Advertising, Collateral, Content, Digital/Interactive, Event Planning & Marketing, Logo & Package Design, Print, Sponsorship

Sal Taibi *(Pres)*
Jonathan Lange *(Exec VP & Grp Acct Dir)*
Rebecca Ginsberg *(Sr VP & Grp Acct Dir)*
Kelley Samanka *(Sr Dir-Art & Graphic Designer)*
Erica Turner *(Sr Dir-Art)*
Emily Goodwin *(Sr Acct Supvr)*
Alyssa Tigue *(Acct Supvr)*
Nathalie Rocklin *(Media Buyer & Media Planner)*
Devin Golestani *(Asst Media Planner)*

Accounts:
CFA Institute Brand Planning, Content Strategy, Creative
New-Empire State Development Advertising, Digital Marketing, Media Buying, Media Planning
Energy Upgrade California
General Motors Below-the-Line, Cadillac, Customer
MilkPEP
The Sun Products Corporation Campaign: "Crescendo", Snuggle Fresh Spring Flowers, TV
United Nations Children's Fund Advocacy, Digital, Education, Fundraising, Mobile, Social, Traditional

Campbell Ewald San Antonio
(Formerly Lowe Campbell Ewald San Antonio)
816 Camaron Ste 102, San Antonio, TX 78212
Tel.: (210) 242-3760
Web Site: www.c-e.com

Employees: 30

National Agency Associations: 4A's

Kevin Wertz *(Pres)*
Keith Clark *(Mng Dir)*
Barb Rozman-Stokes *(Chief People Officer)*
David Bierman *(Grp Dir-Creative)*
Tom Talbert *(Grp Dir-Media Svcs)*
Matthew Zelley *(Grp Dir-Creative)*
Anthony Giordano *(Creative Dir)*
Jim Millis *(Dir-Creative)*
Brian Phelps *(Dir-Bus Dev)*
Wojtek Szumowski *(Dir-Invention Strategy)*
Walter Harris *(Grp Mgmt Supvr)*

Accounts:
USAA Creative

Carmichael Lynch
110 N 5th St, Minneapolis, MN 55403
(See Separate Listing)

Change Communications GmbH
Solmstrasse 4, 60486 Frankfurt am Main, Germany
Mailing Address:
Postfach 90 06 65, 60446 Frankfurt am Main, Germany
Tel.: (49) 69 97 5010
Fax: (49) 69 97 501 141
E-Mail: klaus.flettner@change.de
Web Site: www.change.de

Employees: 60
Year Founded: 1978

Klaus Flettner *(CEO)*
Gabriela Rado *(Mng Dir)*

Accounts:
Carefree
Guiuant
National Savings Bank
Novartis
Penaten
Toyota Germany
Unilever
United Continental Holdings

Current Lifestyle Marketing
875 N Michigan Ave Ste 2700, Chicago, IL 60611
(See Separate Listing)

Dailey & Associates
(Sub. of The Interpublic Group of Cos., Inc.)
8687 Melrose Ave Ste G300, West Hollywood, CA 90069-5701
(See Separate Listing)

Deutsch, Inc.
330 W 34th St, New York, NY 10001
(See Separate Listing)

DeVries Global
(Formerly DeVries Public Relations)
909 Third Ave, New York, NY 10022
(See Separate Listing)

Frank About Women
101 N Cherry St Ste 600, Winston Salem, NC 27101
(See Separate Listing)

Frukt Communications
No 2 Warehouse Sq, 140 Holborn, London, EC1N 2AE United Kingdom
Tel.: (44) 207 751 2900
E-Mail: london@wearefrukt.com
Web Site: wearefrukt.com

Agency Specializes In: Entertainment

Jack Horner *(Founder & Exec Dir-Creative)*
Dominic Hodge *(Mng Partner & Head-Plng)*
Jim Robinson *(Mng Partner)*
Julie Petard *(Head-Strategic Acct)*
Jon Kell *(Acct Dir)*
Lynne Maltman *(Acct Dir)*
Rees Hitchcock *(Planner-Creative)*
Erin Schlissel *(Acct Planner)*

Accounts:
Coca Cola
Mast-Jagermeister UK Consumer Activation, Jagermeister

Grape Communications
Duckyang Building 31-5 Jangchoong-Dong, Jung-Ku, Seoul, 100 391 Korea (South)
Tel.: (82) 2 2260 5400

Fax: (82) 2 2268 5470
E-Mail: hj.jeong@grapecomm.co.kr
Web Site: www.grapecomm.co.kr

Employees: 30
Year Founded: 1983

Agency Specializes In: Advertising, Advertising Specialties, Asian Market, Bilingual Market, Broadcast, Co-op Advertising, Collateral, Communications, Consumer Marketing, Direct Response Marketing, Event Planning & Marketing, Exhibit/Trade Shows, Fashion/Apparel, Financial, Graphic Design, Internet/Web Design, Magazines, Media Buying Services, Merchandising, Multimedia, New Product Development, Newspaper, Newspapers & Magazines, Outdoor, Pharmaceutical, Point of Purchase, Print, Production, Publicity/Promotions, Radio, Sales Promotion, Strategic Planning/Research, T.V., Trade & Consumer Magazines

John Pak *(Grp CEO)*
Ian Choi *(Exec Dir-Global Bus & Network Rels)*

Hill Holliday

53 State St, Boston, MA 02109
(See Separate Listing)

Huge

45 Main St Ste 220, Brooklyn, NY 11201
(See Separate Listing)

Interactive Avenues Pvt. Ltd.

First Floor Kagalwala House C Block - East Wing, Metro Estate 175 CST Road, Mumbai, 400098 India
Tel.: (91) 66753000
Fax: (91) 66753005
Web Site: www.interactiveavenues.com

Employees: 200
Year Founded: 2006

Agency Specializes In: Advertising, Internet/Web Design, Search Engine Optimization, Social Media

Amar Deep Singh *(CEO)*
Shantanu Sirohi *(COO)*
Suraj Nambiar *(VP)*
Mangala Bhattacharjee *(Grp Head-Creative)*
Nikhil Sarna *(Dir-Creative)*
Abbhishek Chadha *(Assoc Dir-Media)*
Sindhu Janardhan *(Assoc Dir-Creative & Digital)*
Sathya Narayanan *(Assoc Dir-Creative)*
Gaurav Phanasgaonkar *(Assoc Dir-Creative)*
Aswathy Nambiar *(Sr Acct Exec)*
Mushahid Abbas *(Assoc Grp Head-Media Plng & Buying)*

IPG Mediabrands

100 W 33rd St 9th Fl, New York, NY 10001
(See Separate Listing)

Lola Madrid

C. Marques de Cubas, 4, Madrid, 28014 Spain
Tel.: (34) 696 499 580
E-Mail: cristina.abril@lola-madrid.com
Web Site: hello-lola.com

Chacho Puebla *(Partner & Chief Creative Officer)*
Francisco Cassis *(Exec Dir-Creative)*
Daniele Cicini *(Client Svcs Dir)*
Saulo Rocha *(Art Dir)*
Carlos Solchaga *(Acct Dir-Global)*
Paulo Areas *(Dir-Creative)*
Nacho Onate *(Dir-Creative)*
Tomas Ostiglia *(Dir-Creative-Global)*
Ausias Perez *(Dir-Art)*
Aida Pozuelo *(Dir-Art)*
Juan Sevilla *(Dir-Creative)*
Nicolas Gomez Cal *(Assoc Dir-Creative)*
Beatriz Moreno *(Acct Mgr-Global)*
Lucas Reis *(Designer)*

Accounts:
Buccaneer
Click Seguros Campaign: "Very Very Amicable Report"
Fight Club Gym Campaign: "Mountain"
Fyne Formacion Campaign: "Speak Fluent Chinese"
Kiss TV Campaign: "I Know You Want Me"
Lesac Campaign: "Soho"
Libero Magazine
Magnum 5 Kisses
Mattel Barbie, Digital, Hot Wheels, Max Steel, Monster High, Scrabble
Miami Ad School Campaign: "The Worstfolio"
Monkey Week Campaign: "Music Beer"
Monsieur Gordo Brewery
Nomad Skateboards Campaign: "The board that should have arrived 100 years ago, is here.", Campaign: "Very Old School", Campaign: "We Are The Same"
Revista Libero
Scrabble
Unilever Campaign: "Flag"
Upload Cinema Campaign: "Hikikimori", Campaign: "Internet On A Zip"
Visionlab Campaign: "Gratu-Gratu-Ito-Ito"
Volkswagen Seat
Wall's Ice Cream Cornetto, Magnum Ice Cream, Magnum Mini
Wide Campaign: "Men & Women"

MAS Communications

Sir Ugo Mifsud Street, Ta' Xbiex, MSD11 Malta
Tel.: (356) 21 332 036
Fax: (356) 21 338 605
Web Site: www.mas.com.mt

Marc Spiteri *(Owner)*
Yana Carabott *(Head-Plng & Office Mgr)*
Chris Psaila *(Dir-Art)*
Claire Kennington *(Mgr-Bus Dev)*

Middle East Communication Networks - MCN

Emarat Atrium Bldg 4th Fl, PO Box 6834, Sheikh Zayed Rd, Dubai, United Arab Emirates
Tel.: (971) 4 321 0007
Fax: (971) 4 321 1540
E-Mail: info@promoseven.com
Web Site: www.mcnholding.com

Employees: 375

Akram Miknas *(Chm)*
Rami Omran *(CEO & Partner-MCN Syria)*
Mohamad Haidar *(COO)*
Tom Roychoudhury *(Chief Innovation Officer)*
Faraz Raja *(Dir-HR-Asia, Middle East & Africa-Sector HQ)*

Accounts:
Carrefour
Coca-Cola Refreshments USA, Inc.
HP
Johnson & Johnson
L'Oreal
MasterCard
Nestle
Nivea
Nokia
Sony
Unilever

Momentum Worldwide

250 Hudson St, New York, NY 10013
(See Separate Listing)

Mullen Lowe Brasil - Sao Paulo

(Formerly Borghi Lowe)
Rua Gomes De Carvalho 1195, 5 e 6 Andares, Vila Olimpia, Sao Paulo, SP CEP 04547-004 Brazil
Tel.: (55) 11 3299 2999
Fax: (55) 11 3845 7708
Web Site: mullenlowegroup.com

Year Founded: 1957

Jose Henrique Borghi *(Co-CEO)*
Andre Gomes *(Co-CEO)*
Agustin Acosta *(Art Dir)*
Piu Afonseca *(Dir-Art)*
Robert Filshill *(Reg Bus Dir & Dir-Svc)*
Fernando Nobre *(Dir-Creative)*
Roberto Ulhoa *(Dir-Art)*
Patricia Venturini *(Dir-New Bus)*
Thais Frazao *(Planner)*
Ricardo Scarpa *(Copywriter)*
Gabriela Soares *(Planner)*
Murilo Torezan *(Copywriter)*
Raphael Zem *(Planner)*

Accounts:
9 de Julho Campaign: "Small Change. All Change."
Anador Campaign: "Every headache has the same solution.", Campaign: "Head"
Antistax Campaign: "Synchronized Swimming"
Asics Campaign: "Let it Go", Campaign: "Perfect Pace", Campaign: "Pizza, Cake"
Bic Campaign: "Falling - Cup", Campaign: "Love Declaration", Cristal
Boehringer Ingelheim Campaign: "Synchronized Swimming"
CCSP Campaign: "Geese", Yearbook Festival
Cream Studio Campaign: "Double Life"
Ducoco
Fashion Floor
FEI College of Engineering Campaign: "For those things you were too busy at school to learn.", Campaign: "Foundation Project", Campaign: "Join the Dots", Campaign: "Medium-Voltage Project"
FINI
FSP Campaign: "Brain", Top Of Mind
Johnson & Johnson Campaign: "The Sound Replacer"
K-Y Campaign: "Sandwich"
Magazine Store Campaign: "Travellin Hands"
Pepsodent Campaign: "Reaches Impossible Places"
Pobre Juan
Revistaria D'Amauri Campaign: "Lolita/Mother Teresa"
Rubbermaid Campaign: "Pick-Up Lines"
Runner's Magazine
Sao Paulo Creative Club Campaign: "Blank Sheet of Paper"
SASP Furniture Donation Appeal, Social Assistance
Skip
Unica (Brazilian Sugarcane Industry Association)
Unilever Campaign: "Kissdemic", Campaign: "Knorr Quick: Ping Pong", Close Up, Knorr Quick Campaign: "Kitchen", Personal Care Products, Rexona & Axe Deodorants, Signal, Gessy, & Cristal
University of Industrial Engineering
Uol Portal
Uol Campaign: "Condom", Gravedigger

Octagon

800 Connecticut Ave 2nd Fl, Norwalk, CT 06854
(See Separate Listing)

Orion Trading

622 3rd Ave, New York, NY 10017
(See Separate Listing)

PACE Advertising
230 Park Ave S 12th Fl, New York, NY 10003
(See Separate Listing)

PMK*BNC
8687 Melrose Ave 8th Fl, Los Angeles, CA 90069
Tel.: (310) 854-4800
Fax: (310) 289-6677
E-Mail: info@pmkbnc.com
Web Site: www.pmkbnc.com

Employees: 30

National Agency Associations: 4A's

Agency Specializes In: Entertainment, Public Relations, Publicity/Promotions, Sponsorship

Brad Cafarelli *(Vice Chm)*
Kevin Gessay *(Mng Dir)*
Joseph Assad *(COO & Exec VP)*
Monica Chun *(COO-Brand Mktg & Comm & Exec VP)*
Rebecca Waits *(Exec VP-People Svcs)*
Steve Janisse *(Sr VP)*
Joanne Melzer *(Sr VP-Insights & Analytics)*
Taj Sullivan *(Sr VP-Brand Mktg)*
Joanna Cichocki *(VP-Special Events)*
Krista Guilfoyle *(VP)*
Monica Jaramillo *(VP-Entertainment Mktg)*
Brian Tsao *(Acct Dir)*
Michelle Ravelo-Santos *(Dir)*
Mark Y Van Lommel *(Dir-Brand Mktg & Comm)*
Nicholas Pietryga *(Mgr-Strategic Insights & Analytics)*
Erica Urquiza *(Sr Acct Exec)*
Steve Willis *(Sr Acct Exec)*
Kristin Busk *(Sr Strategist-Digital)*

Accounts:
Lucky Strike Lanes Event Planning, Media Relations, Social Media

PMK*BNC
622 3rd Ave 8th Fl, New York, NY 10017
Tel.: (212) 582-1111
Fax: (212) 582-6666
Web Site: www.pmkbnc.com

Employees: 34

National Agency Associations: 4A's

Agency Specializes In: Entertainment, Public Relations, Publicity/Promotions, Sponsorship

Cindi Berger *(Co-Chm & CEO)*
Genesa Garbarino *(Sr VP)*
Rick McCabe *(Sr VP-Brand Comm)*
Cliff Carson *(VP)*
Omar Gonzales *(VP-Natl Publicity)*
Michelle Nelson *(Sr Dir)*
Paul Downs *(Copywriter)*

Accounts:
American Express Sponsorship
Audi of America Campaign: "Spock vs. Spock", Campaign: "The Challenge", Digital, Social Content, Strategic Planning, US Public Relations
Beats by Dr. Dre Digital, Marketing, Public Relations
Diageo Haig Club, Public Relations, Social
IMDb Digital, Marketing, PR
JCPenney Co. (Agency of Record)
PepsiCo Aquafina FlavorSplash, PR, Pepsi, Pepsi Limon
The Player's Tribune Public Relations
New-Samsung
Verizon Events & Promotion

Ponce Buenos Aires
Avenida del Libertador 14950, Acassuso, 1641 Buenos Aires, Argentina
Tel.: (54) 11 4733 5100
Fax: (54) 11 4733 5101
E-Mail: hernan.ponce@poncebuenosaires.com
Web Site: www.poncebuenosaires.com

Employees: 70
Year Founded: 1997

Agency Specializes In: Advertising, Consumer Goods, Consumer Marketing, Household Goods

Ricardo Armentano *(Gen Dir-Creative)*
Matias Ballada *(Exec Dir-Creative)*
Luigi Ghidotti *(Exec Dir-Creative)*
Kevin Cabuli *(Art Dir)*
Lucas Cambiano *(Creative Dir)*
Matias Eusebi *(Dir-Creative)*
Dante Zamboni *(Dir-Art)*
Carolina Brancos *(Sr Acct Exec)*
Francisco Odriozola *(Acct Exec)*

Accounts:
Fundacion Temaiken Campaign: "Birds Vs Wallabies"
Stella Artois
Temaiken Biopark
Unilever Axe, Axe Bowling, Axe Distance, Campaign: "Evidence 1", Campaign: "La Donna e Mobile", Campaign: "THE LOOK", Campaign: "The Cleaner", Deodorant, Detergents, Foods, Gold Temptation, Mother, Rexona, Television, Toiletries

Publicidad Comercial
Edificio Comercial, Avenida el Espino No.77, Urbanizacion Madre Selva Antig, La Libertad, El Salvador
Tel.: (503) 22 44 22 22
Fax: (503) 244 3363
E-Mail: Juan.Salaverria@corp.ipgnetwork.com
Web Site: www.pcomercial.com

Herbert Alvarado *(Chief Creative Officer)*
Emerson Huezo *(Chief Creative Officer)*
Juan Federico Salaverria *(Exec Dir)*
Orlando Alvarez *(Dir-Creative)*
Rodrigo Canjura *(Dir-Creative)*
Gerardo Muyshondt *(Dir)*
Camila Trigueros *(Acct Exec)*

Accounts:
El Faro Campaign: "The Citizen's Comic Book"

Quadrant Communications Ltd.
Raut Sadan, Ground Floor, Kadeshwari Road, Bandra West, Mumbai, 400 050 India
Tel.: (91) 22 2645 1836
Fax: (91) 22 2645 1837
E-Mail: mumbai-info@quadrantcom.com

Year Founded: 1970

Pradnesh Vaidya *(Asst Dir-Media)*
Preeti Wankhede *(Sr Acct Exec)*

Accounts:
Balaji Telefilms ATL, Communication, Institute of Creative Excellence, Print, Radio
EMGEE Group Creative, Media
New-Kirloskar Proprietary Ltd
Paranjape Schemes (Construction) Ltd. Creative
Pravin Masalewale Campaign: "Chatkar Khusakhusheet Khamang"
Quick Heal Technologies Creative
Samrat Atta
Tiger Balm Campaign: "Class Room"

Tierney Communications
The Bellevue 200 S Broad St, Philadelphia, PA 19102-3803
(See Separate Listing)

Translation LLC
(Formerly Translation Consulting & Brand Imaging)
145 W 45th St 12th Fl, New York, NY 10036
(See Separate Listing)

Constituency Management: (Part of the Interpublic Group)

Casanova Pendrill
275-A McCormick Ave Ste 100, Costa Mesa, CA 92626-3369
(See Separate Listing)

FutureBrand
233 Park Ave S Fl 2, New York, NY 10003
(See Separate Listing)

Golin
(Formerly GolinHarris)
875 N. Michigan Ave 26th Fl, Chicago, IL 60611
(See Separate Listing)

IW Group, Inc.
8687 Melrose Ave Ste G540, West Hollywood, CA 90069
(See Separate Listing)

Jack Morton Worldwide
142 Berkeley St, Boston, MA 02116
(See Separate Listing)

Weber Shandwick
909 3rd Ave, New York, NY 10022
(See Separate Listing)

INTERTREND COMMUNICATIONS, INC.
213 E Broadway, Long Beach, CA 90802-5003
Tel.: (562) 733-1888
Fax: (562) 733-1889
E-Mail: info@intertrend.com
Web Site: www.intertrend.com

E-Mail for Key Personnel:
President: julia@intertrend.com
Creative Dir.: stephanine@intertrend.com
Media Dir.: michael@intertrend.com

Employees: 50
Year Founded: 1991

National Agency Associations: AAF-DMA

Agency Specializes In: Advertising, Advertising Specialties, Affluent Market, Alternative Advertising, Arts, Asian Market, Automotive, Bilingual Market, Brand Development & Integration, Branded Entertainment, Broadcast, Business Publications, Business-To-Business, Cable T.V., Catalogs, Children's Market, Co-op Advertising, Collateral, College, Commercial Photography, Communications, Computers & Software, Consulting, Consumer Goods, Consumer Marketing, Consumer Publications, Content, Corporate Communications, Corporate Identity, Digital/Interactive, Direct Response Marketing, Direct-to-Consumer, E-Commerce, Education, Electronic Media, Electronics, Email, Entertainment, Event Planning & Marketing, Exhibit/Trade Shows, Experience Design, Fashion/Apparel, Financial, Food Service, Game Integration, Government/Political, Graphic Design, Guerilla Marketing, Health Care Services, High Technology, Hospitality, Household Goods, Identity Marketing, In-Store Advertising, Integrated Marketing, Internet/Web Design, Leisure, Local

Marketing, Logo & Package Design, Luxury Products, Magazines, Market Research, Media Buying Services, Media Planning, Media Relations, Media Training, Merchandising, Mobile Marketing, Multicultural, Multimedia, New Product Development, New Technologies, Newspaper, Newspapers & Magazines, Out-of-Home Media, Outdoor, Over-50 Market, Package Design, Paid Searches, Pharmaceutical, Planning & Consultation, Podcasting, Point of Purchase, Point of Sale, Print, Product Placement, Production, Production (Print), Public Relations, Publicity/Promotions, Publishing, Radio, Real Estate, Regional, Restaurant, Retail, Sales Promotion, Seniors' Market, Social Marketing/Nonprofit, Sponsorship, Sports Market, Strategic Planning/Research, Sweepstakes, T.V., Technical Advertising, Teen Market, Trade & Consumer Magazines, Transportation, Travel & Tourism, Urban Market, Viral/Buzz/Word of Mouth, Women's Market, Yellow Pages Advertising

Approx. Annual Billings: $70,000,000

Breakdown of Gross Billings by Media: Collateral: 5%; D.M.: 5%; Internet Adv.: 5%; Newsp.: 30%; Outdoor: 5%; Production: 20%; Pub. Rels.: 5%; Radio: 10%; T.V.: 15%

Julia Y. Huang *(Pres)*
Wade Guang *(VP-Ops)*
Joe Min *(Grp Acct Dir)*
Joyce Lu *(Dir-Platform & Application)*
Anna Xie *(Dir-Strategic Plng)*
Joys Wong *(Mgr-Media Ops)*
Neil Sadhu *(Copywriter)*

Accounts:
American Cancer Society
Asia American Symphony
AT&T Communications Corp.
J.C. Penney; Dallas, TX; 1996
JPMorgan Chase
State Farm Insurance; Bloomington, IL (Asia Agency of Record); 1999
Toyota Motor Company Matrix
Western Union

INTREPID MARKETING GROUP

6500 Creedmoor Rd Ste 216, Raleigh, NC 27613
Tel.: (919) 845-2467
Web Site: www.intrepidmg.com

Agency Specializes In: Advertising, Promotions, Public Relations, Social Media

Mike Dixon *(Partner)*
Ann Marie Sales *(Partner)*

Accounts:
New-Teamworks

INTRINZIC MARKETING + DESIGN INC.

1 Levee Way Ste 3121, Newport, KY 41071
Tel.: (859) 261-2200
Fax: (859) 261-2102
E-Mail: justin@intrinzicinc.com
Web Site: www.intrinzicinc.com

Employees: 20

Agency Specializes In: Corporate Identity, Market Research

Wendy Vonderhaar *(Owner)*
Chris Heile *(Chief Strategy Officer)*
Katie Peters *(Acct Dir)*
Jenn Riegert *(Acct Dir)*
David Kaufmann *(Sr Mgr-Realization)*
Tami Beattie *(Office Mgr)*
Kelli Haller *(Acct Mgr)*
Sarah Petracco *(Acct Mgr)*
Rob Pasquinucci *(Strategist-Content)*
Elaine Zeinner *(Strategist-Content)*
Sarah Eisenman *(Sr Graphic Designer)*

Accounts:
Anthem
Baker Concrete Construction
Boys & Girls Club of Cincinnati
Cincinnati Live
Johnson & Johnson Vision Care - Vistakon
Johnson Investment Council
Kumon cosmic Club
Miami University MBA Program
ProSource
The Redmoor
Senco
Spectrum
St. Elizabeth Healthcare
Transportation Authority of Northern Kentucky (TANK)
U.S Bank
U.S Bank Flexparks
Western Southern

INTROWORKS, INC.

(d/b/a Freytag Mcmillen)
13911 Ridgedale Dr Ste 280, Minnetonka, MN 55305
Tel.: (952) 593-1800
Fax: (952) 593-1900
E-Mail: inquiry@introworks.net
Web Site: www.introworks.net

Employees: 12
Year Founded: 1992

Agency Specializes In: Advertising, Brand Development & Integration, Communications, Financial, Identity Marketing, Information Technology, Medical Products

Approx. Annual Billings: $2,000,000

Bob Freytag *(Pres)*
Mike McMillan *(Partner & Chief Creative Officer)*
Nancy Chesser *(Partner & Acct Dir)*
Matt Fahrner *(Partner & Mgr-Studio)*
Alison Lapoint *(VP-Acct Svcs)*
Jamaal Gilbert *(Copywriter)*

INTUIT MEDIA GROUP

1239 NE 8th Ave, Fort Lauderdale, FL 33304
Tel.: (954) 716-6341
E-Mail: info@intuitmediagroup.com
Web Site: www.intuitmediagroup.com

Agency Specializes In: Advertising, Brand Development & Integration, Graphic Design, Internet/Web Design, Logo & Package Design, Print, Search Engine Optimization, Social Media

John Paul *(Pres & Dir-Mktg)*
Lawrence Smith *(VP & Creative Dir)*

Accounts:
Blue & Green Films
Nitro Displays

INVENTIV HEALTH INC.

(Formerly inVentiv Communications Inc.)
1 Van de Graaff Dr, Burlington, MA 01803
Tel.: (781) 425-4600
Toll Free: (800) 416-0555
E-Mail: info@inventivhealth.com
Web Site: www.inventivhealth.com

Employees: 600
Year Founded: 1977

Agency Specializes In: Advertising, Brand Development & Integration, Broadcast, Business-To-Business, Collateral, Communications, Consulting, Consumer Marketing, Corporate Identity, Digital/Interactive, Direct Response Marketing, E-Commerce, Education, Electronic Media, Event Planning & Marketing, Exhibit/Trade Shows, Financial, Graphic Design, Health Care Services, High Technology, Information Technology, Internet/Web Design, Logo & Package Design, Media Buying Services, Medical Products, New Product Development, Pharmaceutical, Planning & Consultation, Print, Production, Public Relations, Publicity/Promotions, Radio, Retail, Sales Promotion, Strategic Planning/Research, T.V., Technical Advertising

Approx. Annual Billings: $734,000,000

Michael Bell *(Chm & CEO)*
Jeffrey McMullen *(Vice Chm)*
Joseph Solfaro *(CIO-Global)*
Michael A. Griffith *(Pres-Comml Div & Exec VP)*
Jeffrey Wilks *(Pres-Adv)*
Michael McKelvey *(Exec VP)*
Jennifer O'Neill *(VP-Bus Dev)*
Leslie Taylor *(Head-Digital & Innovation-Global)*

Branches

Cadent Medical Communications

1707 Market Pl Blvd Ste 350, Irving, TX 75063
(See Separate Listing)

Chandler Chicco Agency

450 W 15th St 7th Fl, New York, NY 10011
(See Separate Listing)

Palio+Ignite

(Formerly Palio)
260 Broadway, Saratoga Springs, NY 12866
(See Separate Listing)

inVentiv Health Clinical

(Formerly PharmaNet Development Group, Inc.)
504 Carnegie Ctr, Princeton, NJ 08540
Tel.: (609) 951-6800
Fax: (609) 514-0390
Web Site: www.inventivhealthclinical.com

Employees: 2,400
Year Founded: 1999

Jeffrey P. McMullen *(Chm)*
Michael McKelvey *(Pres)*
Rick Shimota *(CFO)*
Paul A. Taylor *(Pres-Taylor Technology Inc)*
Lynn Okamoto *(Exec VP-Late Stage)*
George Scott *(VP-Bioanalytical Svcs)*
Jose Chavarro *(Mgr-Corp Comm)*
Monica Freeman-Greene *(Mgr-HR)*

INVENTIVA

19179 Blanco Rd, San Antonio, TX 78258-4009
Tel.: (830) 438-4679
Web Site: www.inventiva.com

E-Mail for Key Personnel:
Chairman: heberto@inventiva.com
President: glia@inventiva.com
Media Dir.: mpolovina@inventiva.com

Employees: 11
Year Founded: 1989

National Agency Associations: AAF-AMA

Agency Specializes In: Advertising, Bilingual Market, Communications, Consulting, Food Service, Government/Political, Hispanic Market, Leisure, Media Buying Services, Media Planning, Multicultural, Outdoor, Over-50 Market,

Pharmaceutical, Planning & Consultation, Retail, Sponsorship, Strategic Planning/Research

Approx. Annual Billings: $8,000,000

G. Lia Gutierrez *(Principal)*
Heberto Gutierrez *(Principal)*

Accounts:
American Electric Power Utilities; 1997
American Quarter Horse Association; 2003
Central Power & Light Utilities
Laredo National Bank
Pioneer Flour Mills
Southwest Electric & Power
Texas Department of Health; 1994
Tony Lama Boots
Valero Energy Corporation

INVERSE MARKETING

180 N Stetson Ave Ste 1401, Chicago, IL 60601-6710
Tel.: (312) 944-7833
Fax: (312) 944-5756
E-Mail: rick@inversem.com
Web Site: www.inversem.com

Employees: 4
Year Founded: 1990

Agency Specializes In: Advertising, Brand Development & Integration, Business-To-Business, Communications, Consulting, Consumer Marketing, Internet/Web Design, Planning & Consultation, Radio, Strategic Planning/Research

Approx. Annual Billings: $500,000

Rick Marzec *(Founder & Partner)*
Patrick Navin *(Partner)*

Accounts:
Liberty Bank
Mercedes Benz
National Collegiate Scouting Association
Pinkerton
Prudential Capital

INVERVE MARKETING

(Formerly Spoke8 Marketing)
1035 N Washington Ave, Lansing, MI 48906
Tel.: (517) 485-7237
E-Mail: info@invervemarketing.com
Web Site: https://invervemarketing.com/

Agency Specializes In: Advertising, Brand Development & Integration, Graphic Design, Internet/Web Design, Media Buying Services, Search Engine Optimization, Social Media

Lisa Smith *(Pres)*
Fran Russell *(Creative Dir)*

Accounts:
New-Asahi Kasei Plastics

INVNT

295 Lafayette St Fl 7, New York, NY 10012
Tel.: (212) 334-3415
E-Mail: newyork@invnt.com
Web Site: www.invnt.com

Year Founded: 2008

Agency Specializes In: Advertising, Brand Development & Integration, Broadcast, Digital/Interactive, Graphic Design, Internet/Web Design, Social Media

Scott Cullather *(Founder & Mng Partner-Global)*
Shannon Washington *(Sr Dir-Creative)*
Audrey Fowler *(Dir-HR & Ops)*
Allie Mercurio *(Coord-Production)*
Alexandra Serowoky *(Coord-Graphics)*
Jonathan Serluco *(Sr Coord-Production)*

Accounts:
ESPN, Inc.
General Motors
Intel
New-Juniper Networks
New-Merck
Miele Inc.
New-Outdoor Advertising Association of America
PepsiCo Inc.
Subway

INVOKE MEDIA

37 Dunlevy Ave, Vancouver, BC V6A 3A3 Canada
Tel.: (604) 484-8902
Fax: (604) 909-5178
E-Mail: info@invokemedia.com
Web Site: www.invokemedia.com

Agency Specializes In: Digital/Interactive, Social Media

Chris Miller *(Partner & Mng Dir)*
Vincent Cauwet *(Head-Production)*
Jordan Eshpeter *(Head-Client Engagement)*
Carmen Chau *(Project Mgr-Digital)*
Ben Adams *(Strategist-Digital Media)*
Dustin Borek *(Designer-UX & UI)*
Natalie Zawadzki *(Designer-Interaction)*

Accounts:
Electronic Arts
MSN
The Onion Onion Magic Answer Ball App
State Farm Insurance
Viacom
Wells Fargo

INXPO

770 N Halsted St Ste 6S Ste 207, Chicago, IL 60642
Tel.: (312) 962-3724
Web Site: www.inxpo.com

Year Founded: 2003

Agency Specializes In: Brand Development & Integration, Event Planning & Marketing, Production

Drew VanVooren *(Co-Founder & Pres)*
Malcolm L. Lotzof *(CEO)*
David Aniol *(CFO, Treas & Sec)*
Scott Cotter *(Chief Mktg Officer)*
Jeff Pryhuber *(CTO)*
Rich Hawkinson *(Exec VP-Product Svcs)*
Daniel Lotzof *(Exec VP-Sls)*
Nick Gates *(VP-Pro Svcs)*

Accounts:
Forbes Publishing & Media Company
HIMSS Healthcare Services
IDG
Ingram Micro
Monster
Neilson
P&G
SAP Software Solutions Provider
Sears
The Wall Street Journal
Ziff Davis Media

IOMEDIA

640 W 28th St, New York, NY 10001
Tel.: (212) 352-1115
Fax: (212) 352-1117
Web Site: www.io-media.com

Employees: 35
Year Founded: 1997

Agency Specializes In: Content, Graphic Design, Production, Strategic Planning/Research

Peter Korian *(Founder & Pres)*
Ashwan Wadhwa *(Sr VP-R&D)*
Brady Walcott *(Sr VP-Mktg & Dev)*
Ray Battaglia *(VP & Dir-Ops)*
Mark Calveric *(VP-Tech)*
Megan Doran *(Dir-Ops)*
Melanie Gargano *(Assoc Dir-Creative)*
Karen Patel *(Mgr-HR)*

Accounts:
Abbott Health Care Services
Baxter Healthcare Products Mfr
Bristol Myers Squibb
Genetech Medical Products Producers
Janssen Biotech, Inc.
King Phamaceuticals Pharmaceutical Product Producers

ION BRAND DESIGN

(Formerly Ion Branding + Design)
948 West 7th Ave, Vancouver, BC V5Z 1C3 Canada
Tel.: (604) 682-6787
Fax: (604) 682-6769
Toll Free: (888) 336-2466
E-Mail: info@iondesign.ca
Web Site: www.iondesign.ca

Employees: 6
Year Founded: 1988

Agency Specializes In: Brand Development & Integration, Media Planning, Strategic Planning/Research

Rod Roodenburg *(Partner & Dir-Creative)*
David Coates *(Partner)*
Casey Hrynkow *(Sr Brand Strategist)*

Accounts:
Sustainable Solutions International

IONIC MEDIA

21300 Victory Blvd, Woodland Hills, CA 91367
Tel.: (818) 849-3737
Fax: (818) 905-7800
Toll Free: (877) 905-7800
E-Mail: inquiry@ionicmedia.com
Web Site: www.ionicmedia.com

Employees: 40
Year Founded: 2002

Agency Specializes In: Above-the-Line, Advertising, Advertising Specialties, Affluent Market, Alternative Advertising, Automotive, Bilingual Market, Branded Entertainment, Broadcast, Business-To-Business, Cable T.V., Catalogs, College, Communications, Consulting, Consumer Goods, Consumer Marketing, Consumer Publications, Content, Customer Relationship Management, Digital/Interactive, Direct Response Marketing, Direct-to-Consumer, E-Commerce, Electronics, Email, Entertainment, Experience Design, Financial, Gay & Lesbian Market, Guerilla Marketing, Hispanic Market, Household Goods, In-Store Advertising, Infomercials, Integrated Marketing, International, Internet/Web Design, Legal Services, Local Marketing, Magazines, Market Research, Media Buying Services, Media Relations, Men's Market, Mobile Marketing, Multicultural, New Technologies, Newspaper, Out-of-Home Media, Over-50 Market, Paid Searches, Pharmaceutical, Planning & Consultation, Print, Product Placement, Radio,

Regional, Retail, Search Engine Optimization, Seniors' Market, Sponsorship, Sports Market, Strategic Planning/Research, Sweepstakes, Syndication, T.V., Telemarketing, Transportation, Urban Market, Web (Banner Ads, Pop-ups, etc.)

Approx. Annual Billings: $100,000,000

Breakdown of Gross Billings by Media: Brdcst.: 40%; Internet Adv.: 50%; Strategic Planning/Research: 10%

Michael Kubin *(CEO & Mng Dir)*
Catherine Hahn *(VP-Plng & Acct Mgmt)*
Nancy Martinez *(Mgr-SEO & Social Media)*
Sharon Bender *(Media Planner & Buyer-Digital)*

Accounts:
Bausch & Lomb
Children's Hospital of Philadelphia
Cooking.com
Disney
Marriott
Relax the Back
Smith & Hawken
Therative
Verizon Wireless
Virgin

IOSTUDIO
565 Marriott Dr Ste 100, Nashville, TN 37214
Tel.: (615) 256-6282
E-Mail: info@iostudio.com
Web Site: www.iostudio.com

Year Founded: 2001

Agency Specializes In: Advertising, Brand Development & Integration, Digital/Interactive, Production

Andy Blenkle *(Pres)*
Mitch Powers *(Partner & CEO)*
Ed Brown *(Partner & CFO)*
Chris West *(Partner)*
Bryan Detwiler *(Acct Supvr)*
Jen Mears *(Acct Supvr)*
Steve Wright *(Copywriter-Digital)*

Accounts:
Goodall Homes
SPEAKeasy Spirits Strategic Marketing Campaign, Whisper Creek Tennessee Sipping Cream
United States Army National Guard

IPG MEDIABRANDS
100 W 33rd St 9th Fl, New York, NY 10001
Tel.: (212) 883-4751
E-Mail: contact@mbww.com
Web Site: www.mbww.com

Employees: 7,500
Year Founded: 2007

National Agency Associations: 4A's

Agency Specializes In: Advertising, Media Buying Services, Media Planning, Media Relations, Media Training

Mitchell Weinstein *(Mng Partner, Sr VP & Dir-Ad Ops-US)*
Carrie Herron *(Partner-Talent Acq Bus)*
Samuel Chesterman *(CIO)*
Mat Baxter *(Chief Strategy & Creative Officer-Global)*
Russell Marsh *(Chief Data Officer)*
Dervilla Kelly *(Chief Client Officer-Global)*
Alastair Procter *(Chief HR Officer)*
John Sintras *(Pres-Global Bus Dev & Product Innovation)*
Cary Huang *(CEO-China)*
Cesar Angulo *(Sr VP-Bus Dev & Svcs)*
Fernando Monedero *(Mng Dir-Miami)*
Holly Myles *(Acct Dir)*
Nnenna Orji *(Dir-Art)*
Josh Shabtai *(Dir-Creative)*
Chris Siciliano *(Sr Mgr-Community)*
Noor Yousif *(Acct Exec)*
Courtney Carr *(Asst Acct Exec)*

Branches

Cadreon
100 W 33rd St 9th Fl, New York, NY 10001
(See Separate Listing)

ID Media
100 W 33rd St, New York, NY 10001
(See Separate Listing)

Identity
400 W 14th St 3rd Fl, New York, NY 10014
(See Separate Listing)

Initiative Worldwide
100 W 33rd St, New York, NY 10001
(See Separate Listing)

Initiative
42 St John Square, London, EC1M 4EA United Kingdom
Tel.: (44) 20 7663 7000
Fax: (44) 20 7663 7001
E-Mail: tony.manwaring@uk.initiative.com
Web Site: www.initiative.com

Employees: 80
Year Founded: 1970

Agency Specializes In: Consulting, Media Buying Services

Gary Birtles *(Mng Dir)*
Sally Weavers *(Mng Dir-United Kingdom)*
James Temperley *(Head-Brdcst)*
Deborah Mackay *(Sr Acct Dir)*
Jack Winter *(Sr Acct Exec)*

Accounts:
Ancestry.co.uk
Bernard Matthews
Dorchester Collection Media, Micro App
Flight Centre Corporate Traveller, FCM, First & Business Class, Media Planning & Buying, Round the World Experts
Hays
Hertz Media Buying & Planning
London Zoo
Quorn Foods Media Planning & Buying
TGI Fridays
Travelodge Media Buying, Media Planning

MAGNA GLOBAL
100 W 33rd St 9th Fl, New York, NY 10001
(See Separate Listing)

Reprise Media Asia
Rm. 1302-04, Oxford House, Taikoo Pl., 979 King's Rd., Quarry Bay, China (Hong Kong)
Tel.: (852) 2901 8400
Web Site: www.reprisemedia.com

Employees: 5

Accounts:
Langham Hotels

Reprise Media Australia
Level 1, 166 William St, Sydney, NSW 2011 Australia
Tel.: (61) 2 9994.4200
Web Site: www.reprisemedia.com.au/

Craig Ellis *(CEO)*
James Luty *(Acct Dir-Reprise)*
David Coats *(Dir-SEO)*
Chris Brennan *(Sr Acct Mgr)*
Thomas Delafosse *(Mgr-Performance-Paid Search)*

Accounts:
Bunnings
Dreamworld
Hyundai
News Queensland
RACQ
Target
Unilever Australia
ZUJI

Reprise Media
100 W 33rd St Ste 921, New York, NY 10001
Tel.: (212) 444-7474
Toll Free: (800) 218-9476
Web Site: www.reprisemedia.com

National Agency Associations: 4A's

Agency Specializes In: Search Engine Optimization

Adam Edwards *(VP-SEO)*
Craig Lister *(Head-Reprise Media-UK & EMEA)*
Susila Pokar *(Head-Ops-UK)*
Michael Higgins *(Dir-Search & Innovation)*

Accounts:
Cathay Pacific
Honda
KIA
L'Oreal
Maidenform Brands, Inc.
Mastercard
Microsoft, Inc; Redmond, WA
Raymour & Flanigan
Verizon

UM NY
(Formerly Universal McCann)
100 W 33rd St, New York, NY 10001
(See Separate Listing)

IPROSPECT
1 S Station, Boston, MA 02110
Tel.: (617) 449-4300
Fax: (617) 923-7004
E-Mail: interest@iprospect.com
Web Site: www.iprospect.com

Employees: 150

National Agency Associations: 4A's

Agency Specializes In: Search Engine Optimization

Revenue: $10,000,000

Matt Kropp *(Mng Dir & Sr VP-Client Svc)*
Sara Si *(CEO-China)*
Thad Ward *(Mng Dir-Boston & VP)*
Erica Barth *(VP & Grp Acct Dir)*
Diana Naguib *(VP & Grp Acct Dir)*
Max Cheprasov *(VP-Project Mgmt & Ops-Digital Mktg)*
Adnan Avdic *(Reg Dir-Paid Search-East)*
Herndon Hasty *(Reg Dir-SEO)*
Krysten Muldoon *(Acct Supvr)*

Accounts:
American Eagle Outfitters

Anheuser-Busch InBev N.V./S.A.
AT&T Communications Corp.
Circuit City
Panasonic
Xerox

IQ 360
800 W El Camino Real Ste 180, Mountain View, CA 94040
Tel.: (408) 348-3651
E-Mail: info@iq360inc.com
Web Site: www.iq360inc.com

Agency Specializes In: Advertising, Crisis Communications, Digital/Interactive, Media Relations, Public Relations, Social Media

Lori Teranishi *(Principal)*
John Williamson *(Sr VP)*
Elisabeth Hershman *(VP)*

Accounts:
New-Kaiser Permanente

IQ SOLUTIONS
11300 Rockville Pk Ste 901, Rockville, MD 20852
Tel.: (301) 984-1471
Fax: (301) 984-1471
E-Mail: info@iqsolutions.com
Web Site: www.iqsolutions.com

Employees: 275

Agency Specializes In: E-Commerce, Health Care Services, Information Technology, Strategic Planning/Research, Web (Banner Ads, Pop-ups, etc.)

Ileana Quintas *(CEO)*
Tom Brackett *(CFO)*
David Tondreau *(CTO)*
Stephanie Adams *(VP-Health Intelligence)*
Kim Barnes *(VP-Program Dev)*

Accounts:
National Institute for Health
National Institute of Arthritis & Musculoskeletal & Skin Diseases Messaging

IRON CREATIVE COMMUNICATION
120 2nd St Fl 3, San Francisco, CA 94105
Tel.: (415) 227-9975
Web Site: www.ironcreative.com

Year Founded: 2003

Agency Specializes In: Advertising, Brand Development & Integration, Digital/Interactive, E-Commerce, Graphic Design, Radio, Social Media

David Jamison *(CFO)*
Rick Byrne *(Dir-Creative)*
Dave Caraker *(Dir-Creative)*
Zach Morvant *(Dir-Creative-Copy)*
Drashti Patel *(Acct Mgr & Strategist-Brand)*
Kate Torres *(Sr Project Mgr-Digital)*
Marcela Carrillo *(Sr Designer)*

Accounts:
Bticino S.p.A.
Levi Strauss & Co.
NewSchools Venture Fund
The North Face, Inc.
Patelco Credit Union
Purcell Murray Company Inc.
TRX Marketing

IRONCLAD MARKETING
PO Box 733, West Fargo, ND 58078
Tel.: (701) 373-0062
Web Site: www.ironcladmktg.com

Year Founded: 2009

Agency Specializes In: Advertising, Internet/Web Design, Logo & Package Design, Public Relations

Denise Stoppleworth *(Owner & Pres)*
Amy Wieser Willson *(VP-Client Svcs)*
Mitchell Wagner *(Dir-Art)*
Darren Ebensteiner *(Acct Mgr)*
Kari Kleingartner *(Acct Mgr)*
Meredith Wathne *(Strategist-Online Mktg & Writer)*

Accounts:
Atlas Copco Construction Equipment Brand Awareness, Construction, Marketing, Public Relations
Blastcrete Equipment Company, Inc.

ISA ADVERTISING
845 3rd Ave, New York, NY 10022
Tel.: (646) 290-5227
Fax: (212) 293-3779
E-Mail: ishokoff@isaadvertising.com
Web Site: www.isaadvertising.com

E-Mail for Key Personnel:
President: ishokoff@irisshokoff.com

Employees: 15
Year Founded: 1989

National Agency Associations: DMA

Agency Specializes In: Advertising, Advertising Specialties, African-American Market, Asian Market, Automotive, Aviation & Aerospace, Brand Development & Integration, Broadcast, Business-To-Business, Cable T.V., Children's Market, Co-op Advertising, Collateral, Communications, Consulting, Consumer Marketing, Cosmetics, Direct Response Marketing, Education, Fashion/Apparel, Financial, Food Service, Gay & Lesbian Market, Government/Political, Health Care Services, High Technology, Hispanic Market, Infomercials, Information Technology, Leisure, Logo & Package Design, Magazines, Media Buying Services, Medical Products, Newspaper, Newspapers & Magazines, Outdoor, Over-50 Market, Pharmaceutical, Planning & Consultation, Print, Production, Radio, Seniors' Market, Strategic Planning/Research, T.V., Teen Market, Trade & Consumer Magazines, Transportation, Travel & Tourism

Approx. Annual Billings: $34,000,000

Breakdown of Gross Billings by Media: Cable T.V.: 25%; Consumer Publs.: 20%; Internet Adv.: 10%; Newsp.: 15%; Out-of-Home Media: 5%; Radio: 15%; Spot T.V.: 10%

Iris Shokoff *(Founder & CEO)*
Suzanne Ghosh *(Grp Acct Dir)*
Shannon Entin *(Strategist-Social Media)*
Beth Wrubleski *(Acct Exec)*

Accounts:
Bookspan; Garden City, NY All Clubs; 1995
Omaha Steaks; Omaha, NE; 1999
Pace University; New York, NY; 1989
Rider University; Princeton, NJ

ISM
(Acquired by Connelly Partners & Name Changed to ISM/CP Travel & Lifestyle Group)

ISOBAR
(Formerly Roundarch Isobar)
140 Bdwy Ste 4520, New York, NY 10005
Tel.: (212) 909-2300
E-Mail: info@us-isobar.com
Web Site: www.isobar.com/us/home

Year Founded: 2000

National Agency Associations: 4A's

Agency Specializes In: Advertising, Brand Development & Integration, Communications, Search Engine Optimization, Social Media

Jim Butler *(Pres)*
Geoff Cubitt *(Co-CEO)*
Jeff Maling *(Co-CEO)*
Bruce Posner *(CFO)*
Paul Buranosky *(Mktg Dir)*
Tim Dunn *(Dir-Strategy)*
Dana Demas *(Assoc Dir-Creative)*
Shawna Cermak *(Acct Mgr)*
Megan Madaris *(Mgr-PR)*
Steven Moy *(Chief Commerce Officer)*

Accounts:
The Coca-Cola Company The Bubbler
Enterprise Holdings, Inc. (Digital Agency of Record) Mobile, Strategy, Web
Harmon Kardon
KCRW Music Mine iPad
Lonza

ISOBAR US
One S Station, Boston, MA 02110
Tel.: (617) 936-1600
Fax: (617) 449-4200
Web Site: www.isobar.com

E-Mail for Key Personnel:
President: sarah.fay@isobar.net

Employees: 700
Year Founded: 2004

National Agency Associations: 4A's

Agency Specializes In: Digital/Interactive, Direct Response Marketing, Direct-to-Consumer, High Technology, Integrated Marketing, Internet/Web Design, New Technologies

Geoff Cubitt *(Co-CEO)*
Jeff Maling *(Co-CEO)*
Dave Meeker *(VP & Head-Isobar Nowlab-Global)*
Javier Frank *(Dir-Tech & Commerce)*
Dana Demas *(Assoc Dir-Creative)*
Paul Buranosky *(Mgr-Mktg)*

Accounts:
Coca-Cola Refreshments USA, Inc. Sprite (Digital Agency of Record)
Dolby Laboratories Campaign: "Dolby Update Theater"
Electronic Arts
Lowe's
Motorola Solutions, Inc.
Papa Johns
Sprite Global Digital Agency of Record
Yahoo! Sports Campaign: "Yahoo! Sports Grudge Judge"

Branches

Isobar Brazil
Rua Wisard 298 - 5 andar, vila Madalena, Sao Paulo, 05434-000 Brazil
Tel.: (55) 11 3759 3600
E-Mail: comunicacao@isobar.com.br
Web Site: www.isobar.com/br/home

Agency Specializes In: Advertising

Frederico Saldanha *(Chief Creative Officer)*
Eliel Allebrandt *(VP-Bus & Ops)*
Rose Campiani *(VP-Media)*

Claudio Souza *(VP-Bus & Ops)*
Eduardo Battiston *(Exec Dir-Creative)*
Rafael Campos *(Copywriter)*

Accounts:
Adidas Campaign: "Shoelace Business Card"
Aviotur Campaign: "Alley"
Brazilian Red Cross Campaign: "Rain"
Camp Nectar Campaign: "Real Fruit Invitation"
Fiat Group Automobiles S.p.A Campaign: "Big Little Car", Campaign: "Live Store", Campaign: "Social Drive"
Gang Campaign: "Chewable Pencil"
Limited Edition Campaign: "Real Toy Soldier"
Nivea Campaign: "Sun Art"
Sadia Campaign: "Hot Combat Battle"
Salao Duas Rodas Campaign: "Invitation Tatoo"
Save Brasil Campaign: "Savetones"
Sky Company #SKYREC, Campaign: "Wind", Digital, Hashtag
Sony Ericsson Campaign: "Soccer"
Voicez Campaign: "Stories"

Isobar Hong Kong
16/F 633 King's Rd, North Point, China (Hong Kong)
Tel.: (852) 39624500
Fax: (852) 39624567
E-Mail: dwanye.serjeantx@isobar.com
Web Site: www.isobar.com/hk/home

Agency Specializes In: Digital/Interactive, Internet/Web Design

David Jessop *(Mng Dir)*
Cally Cheng *(Grp Acct Dir)*
Jonathan Evans *(Dir-Creative)*
Astrar Lam *(Dir-Technical)*
Andrew Ryder *(Dir-Strategic Plng)*
Edward Williams *(Dir-Bus)*
Katheryn Lui *(Mgr-Strategy Plng)*

Accounts:
AIA
New-Audi Hong Kong Digital
The Coca-Cola Company
Hong Kong Broadband Network Website Redevelopment
Kellogg's (Digital Agency of Record) Digital
Rosewood Hotels & Resorts Digital, Website Redesign

Isobar India
7th Floor B Wing Poonam Chambers II Dr Annie, Besant Road, Mumbai, 400018 India
Tel.: (91) 2230248103
Web Site: www.isobar.com

Agency Specializes In: Advertising, Digital/Interactive, Media Relations, Social Media

Shamsuddin Jasani *(Mng Dir)*
Gopa Kumar *(VP)*
Gopa Menon *(VP)*
Sonali Banerji *(Grp Head-Creative)*
Anish Behera *(Head-Strategy-North)*
Prachi Karan *(Grp Head-Media)*
Anish Varghese *(Grp Dir-Creative)*
Praveen Raj *(Dir-Creative-West & South)*
Anish Daniel *(Assoc Dir-Media)*
Sanjeev Patel *(Sr Mgr-Media Plng)*
Vartika Anand *(Media Planner)*

Accounts:
Barbeque Nation Digital
New-Hachette Book Publishing India Digital
IndiaFirst Life Insurance Digital, Website
JK Tyres (Digital Agency of Record)
Sterling Holiday Resorts Social Media
New-TimesofMoney Digital

Isobar North America
343 Arsenal St, Watertown, MA 02472
Tel.: (617) 218-6500
Fax: (617) 218-6700
Web Site: www.isobar.com

Employees: 120

National Agency Associations: 4A's

Geoff Cubitt *(Co-CEO)*
Jeff Maling *(CEO-Isobar US)*
Dave Meeker *(VP & Head-Isobar Nowlab-Global)*
Saurab Bhargava *(VP)*
Riccardo La Rosa *(VP-Engrg)*
James Lazar *(VP)*
Mark Ferry *(Dir-Tech)*

Accounts:
Adidas
Nikon

Isobar UK
(Formerly glue London Ltd.)
10 Triton Street Regents Place, London, NW1 3BF United Kingdom
Tel.: (44) 20 3535 9700
Fax: (44) 20 7920 7381
Web Site: www.isobar.com

Employees: 125

Steven Moy *(CEO)*
Simon Clancy *(Grp Dir-Creative)*
James Leigh *(Assoc Dir & Creative Dir-Kellogg's & Pringles)*
Darren Giles *(Dir-Creative)*
Mona Hakky *(Dir-Experience Design)*
Jeani Rodgers *(Dir-Mktg Comm-Global)*

Accounts:
3 Mobile
Adidas Campaign: "The Adizero D Rose 2"
AkzoNobel Creative, Cuprinol, Digital Creative, Digital Strategy, Dulux, Hammerite, Polycell, Social Media
Auto Trader Digital, Digital Display, Public Relations, Strategy
Aviva RAC
Bacardi Global Digital Advertising
Brown-Forman Chambord, Digital, Social
New-Burger King (Digital Agency of Record) Digital Communications, Digital Strategy
Coca-Cola Refreshments USA, Inc.
Eurostar
Google Digital, Google Music All Access, Print
Guardian News & Media Campaign: "The Whole picture", Digital
New-Huawei Global Digital Marketing
Kellogg Company Campaign: "Cash Calls", Campaign: "It's All Lies, They're Not Even Square", Campaign: "Squeeze in the best bits of BRKFSt", Digital Campaign, Krave, Nutri-Grain, Rice Krispies, Squares
Pringles Campaign: "Bursting with Flavour", Campaign: "Fan Versus Flavour", Creative Development, Digital Strategy, Roast Chicken Flavour, Social Media
Magners Digital
McCain Potatoes
NatWest Campaign: "The Natwest Secret Cricketer"
News Group Newspapers The Sun; 2007
News of the World
Nokia
Philips
ScottishPower Creative, Digital Advertising, Social Media
Sony Corporation Campaign: "One Stadium", Digital, Fifa World Cup 2014, One Stadium Live
Toyota UK Aygo, Campaign: "All New Yaris - Social Snap Shot", Campaign: "YNOT", Digital, Prius, Social Media, Yaris; 2008
Visit Sweden
Woolworths

Isobar
875 Howard St 6th Fl, San Francisco, CA 94103
Tel.: (415) 541-2710
Web Site: www.isobar.com

Jeff Maling *(Co-CEO-Isobar US)*
Jean Lin *(CEO-Global)*
Saurab Bhargava *(VP)*
Robert Goerke *(Dir-Art)*
Mike Mulligan *(Dir-Global Comml & Ops)*
Jeani Rodgers *(Dir-Mktg & Comm-Global)*
Heather Schonmeier *(Acct Exec)*
Claire Savage *(Project Head)*

Pjure Isobar
Ignaz Kock Strasse 17, 1210 Vienna, Austria
Tel.: (43) 1 503 98 82
Web Site: www.isobar.com

Agency Specializes In: Digital/Interactive

Helmut Kosa, *(CEO)*
Christian Kdolsky *(Dir-Technical)*
Wolfgang Kindermann *(Dir-Creative)*
Sascha Mahdavi *(Acct Mgr)*

Accounts:
Allianz
Bahlsen
Maestro
MasterCard
Stiefelkonig

TUS Isobar
(Formerly The Upper Storey)
One Raffles Place Tower 2, #28-61, Singapore, 048616 Singapore
Tel.: (65) 6501 3571
Fax: (65) 67322757

Employees: 30
Year Founded: 2001

Agency Specializes In: Advertising, Email, Multimedia, Public Relations, Strategic Planning/Research

Jean Lin *(CEO-Isobar)*
Sven Huberts *(Mng Dir-Asia Pacific)*
Lynn Hoi *(Sr Acct Mgr)*
Kriti Mishra *(Sr Acct Mgr)*
Rachel Tan *(Sr Acct Exec)*
Royston Teoh *(Sr Acct Exec)*
Saachi Aurora *(Reg Sr Acct Exec)*

Accounts:
New-Coca-Cola Campaign: "Share a Coke", Campaign: "Share a Feeling", Digital Engagement, Outdoor, Social Media, TV ad, Video Content
eBay
Huawei Digital Marketing
Intel Corporation Computer Processor Developers
LG Consumer Electronics Distr
Microsoft
OCBC Bank Consumer Financial Services, Digital, Frank, Operations
Thuraya Telecommunications Mobile Satellite Operating Services

wwwins Isobar
Suite 103 1st Floor, Block G Huai Hai Xi Road, Shanghai, 200052 China
Tel.: (86) 21 5238 1333
Fax: (86) 21 5238 6873
Web Site: www.isobar.com

Employees: 300

Year Founded: 1999

Agency Specializes In: Advertising, Digital/Interactive, Local Marketing, Media Buying Services, Media Planning, Strategic Planning/Research

Jane Lin-Baden *(CEO)*
Alvin Huang *(Mng Partner-Integrated Media-China)*
Rohan Lightfoot *(Mng Dir)*
Tim Doherty *(Chief Creative Officer-China)*
Wen Louie *(Grp Dir-Creative)*
Francis Lam *(Dir-Creative Tech)*
Christina Lu *(Client Partner)*
Devin Zhao *(Sr Creative Dir)*

Accounts:
7-Eleven Campaign: "Facebook Management"
Adidas
New-Bacardi
Coca-Cola Refreshments USA, Inc. Campaign: "Release Your Summer in 100 Ways", Campaign: "Share a Coke", Digital, Minute Maid, Sprite, Video
Delta
Emirates Hotels & Resorts
HSBC
Huawei Digital Marketing
New-KFC
Mondelez International Campaign: "Share a bonding moment", Creative, Digital, Oreo
Nissan
Northwest Airlines, Inc.
The Peninsula Hotel
Procter & Gamble
New-Volkswagen
Yahoo

ISOM GLOBAL STRATEGIES
701 8th St NW Ste 350, Washington, DC 20001
Tel.: (202) 347-3374
E-Mail: info@isomglobal.com
Web Site: http://isomglobal.com/

Agency Specializes In: Advertising, Public Relations

Towan Isom *(Pres & CEO)*
Erika Singletary *(COO)*
Ashley Siegle *(Sr Acct Exec)*

Accounts:
New-U.S. Department of Health & Human Services

ISTRATEGYLABS
1630 Connecticut Ave NW 7th Fl, Washington, DC 20009
Tel.: (202) 683-9980
Web Site: https://isl.co/

Year Founded: 2007

Agency Specializes In: Advertising, Digital/Interactive, Internet/Web Design, Media Planning

Peter Corbett *(CEO)*
D. J. Saul *(CMO & Mng Dir)*
Zach Goodwin *(Dir-Creative)*
Zach Saale *(Dir-Ops)*
Audrey Matthias *(Sr Strategist-Creative)*
Eric Shutt *(Sr Strategist-Creative)*
Erica Goodwin *(Strategist-Creative)*
Will Dove *(Jr Designer)*

Accounts:
New-Dramamine
The Kroger Co. (Social Media Agency of Record)
William Grant & Sons (Digital & Social Media Agency of Record) Flor De Cana Rum, Glenfiddich, Hendrick's Gin, Milagro Tequila, Sailor Jerry Rum, The Balvenie, Tullamore D.E.W.

ITALIA PARTNERS
3500 W Olive Ave Ste 300, Burbank, CA 91505
Tel.: (818) 973-2701
Fax: (818) 973-2702
Web Site: www.italiapartners.com

Employees: 32
Year Founded: 1983

Agency Specializes In: Event Planning & Marketing, Exhibit/Trade Shows, Graphic Design, Logo & Package Design, Media Buying Services, Newspapers & Magazines, Point of Purchase, Point of Sale, Print, Production, Radio, Real Estate, Restaurant

Approx. Annual Billings: $95,000,000

Breakdown of Gross Billings by Media: D.M.: 3%; Mags.: 15%; Newsp.: 10%; Outdoor: 2%; Radio: 45%; T.V.: 25%

Carmen Italia *(Pres)*
Monica Hecht *(Controller)*

Accounts:
3M
AT&T Communications Corp.
Bravo Restaurants
CompUSA
Del Taco LLC
Denver Post
EAS, Inc.; Golden, CO Dietary Supplements; 1999
Gart Sports
Panasonic
Primestar
Wells Fargo
Wintrust Financial

ITC
6404 Wilshire Blvd Ste 850 8th Fl, Los Angeles, CA 90048
Tel.: (800) 590-6953
Fax: (323) 544-6206
E-Mail: info@itcfirm.com
Web Site: www.itcfirm.com

Year Founded: 1995

Agency Specializes In: Advertising, Brand Development & Integration, Digital/Interactive, Paid Searches, Public Relations, Search Engine Optimization, Social Media

Ash Sobhe *(Founder & CEO)*
Desiree Duffy *(VP)*

Accounts:
New-The Fashion Bookstore

ITEAM CREATIVE
405 W Washington St, Brainerd, MN 56401
Tel.: (651) 278-4429
E-Mail: info@iteamcreative.com
Web Site: www.iteamcreative.com

Agency Specializes In: Advertising, Brand Development & Integration, Graphic Design, Internet/Web Design, Logo & Package Design, Print, Radio, Search Engine Optimization, Social Media

Robert Foster *(Mng Partner)*

Accounts:
Jennifer Arnhold MD

ITI DIRECT MAIL
115 W California Blvd Ste 286, Pasadena, CA 91105
Toll Free: (866) 558-6365
Web Site: www.letterprinting.net

Employees: 28
Year Founded: 1999

Agency Specializes In: Print, Publishing

Alan Barseghian *(Dir-Mktg)*

Accounts:
MediVet America
Practice Promotions

IVIE & ASSOCIATES INC. MARKETING COMMUNICATIONS
601 Silveron Blvd Ste 200, Flower Mound, TX 75028
Tel.: (972) 899-5000
Fax: (972) 899-5050
E-Mail: ivieinc@ivieinc.com
Web Site: www.ivieinc.com

Employees: 550

Agency Specializes In: Advertising, Broadcast, Commercial Photography, Digital/Interactive, Internet/Web Design, Media Buying Services, Media Planning, Media Relations, Point of Sale, Production (Ad, Film, Broadcast), Production (Print), Sponsorship

Warren Ivie *(Founder & CEO)*
Buddy Martensen *(CMO & Sr VP)*
Renee Rawlings *(Pres-Emerging Markets)*
Kay Ivie *(Exec VP)*
David Needham *(Exec VP-Client Svcs)*
Jodi Marsh *(Sr VP-Comm & Digital Mktg)*
Pat Quinn *(VP)*
Joe Worley *(VP-Client Svcs)*
Darrell Basgall *(Dir-Creative)*
Evelyn Camp *(Dir-Media)*
Lauren Hayman *(Project Mgr-Digital)*
Stacey Diamond *(Mgr-Media Svcs)*
Barry Johnson *(Mgr-Direct Mktg)*
Rick Meekes *(Coord-On-Site Mktg)*

Branch

CLM Marketing & Advertising
588 W Idaho St, Boise, ID 83702-5928
(See Separate Listing)

IVUE DIGITAL ADVERTISING, INC.
3527 Grafton Ave N, Oakdale, MN 55128
Tel.: (651) 307-0120
Web Site: www.ivueda.com

Agency Specializes In: Advertising, Digital/Interactive, Social Media

John Ruiz *(Owner)*
Dan Olson *(Mgr-Mktg & Ops)*

Accounts:
Abra Auto Body & Glass
Eastview Family Chiropractic
Valley Services Inc.
The Work Connection of Hudson

IVY CREATIVE
214 N Main St Ste 102, Natick, MA 1760
Tel.: (774) 290-0013
Fax: (774) 290-0015
E-Mail: info@ivycreative.com
Web Site: www.ivycreative.com

Year Founded: 2007

Agency Specializes In: Advertising, Brand Development & Integration, Internet/Web Design, T.V.

Rick Felty *(Principal & Sr Dir-Creative)*
Steve Ratner *(Principal & Dir-Creative)*
Tom Segale *(Principal & Dir-Production)*
Robert Hebert *(Dir-Design)*

Accounts:
Arbella Insurance
Begley Law Group
Boston University
The Cavan Group
Comcast SportsNet
Dunkin Brands Group, Inc.
GateHouse Media, Inc.
The Goodyear Tire & Rubber Company
Harvard Athletics
Ivy League Sports

THE IVY GROUP, LTD.

1001 E Market St Ste 202, Charlottesville, VA 22902
Tel.: (434) 979-2678
Fax: (434) 979-8433
Toll Free: (800) IVY-1250
E-Mail: contact@ivygroup.com
Web Site: www.ivygroup.com

E-Mail for Key Personnel:
President: fitzgerald@ivygroup.com

Employees: 11
Year Founded: 1989

Agency Specializes In: Advertising, Advertising Specialties, Brand Development & Integration, Broadcast, Business-To-Business, Collateral, Communications, Consulting, Consumer Marketing, Consumer Publications, Corporate Identity, Digital/Interactive, Direct Response Marketing, E-Commerce, Education, Environmental, Event Planning & Marketing, Exhibit/Trade Shows, Graphic Design, Health Care Services, High Technology, Information Technology, Internet/Web Design, Leisure, Logo & Package Design, Magazines, Media Buying Services, New Product Development, Newspaper, Newspapers & Magazines, Outdoor, Planning & Consultation, Point of Purchase, Print, Production, Public Relations, Publicity/Promotions, Radio, Recruitment, Restaurant, Retail, Seniors' Market, Strategic Planning/Research, Telemarketing, Travel & Tourism, Yellow Pages Advertising

Pamela Fitzgerald *(Mng Partner)*
Chris Fitzgerald *(CFO & Mgr-Video, Design & Audio Production)*
Mark B. Goodson *(Dir-Bus Dev)*
Stephen Burden *(Sr Graphic Designer)*
Julia Prince *(Project Specialist)*

Accounts:
Tiger Fuel
Vietnam Children's Fund

Branch

The Ivy Group, Ltd.

1489 Baltimore Pike Suite 215, Springfield, PA 19064
Tel.: (610) 544-4040
Fax: (610) 544-4055
E-Mail: info@ivygroup.com
Web Site: www.ivylibrary.com

Year Founded: 1989

Agency Specializes In: Advertising

Nancy Davis *(Owner)*
Chris Fitzgerald *(Specialist-Production)*
Stephen J. Burden *(Sr Graphic Designer)*

Accounts:
National Trust for Historic Preservation
Pennsylvania Library Association/Commonwealth Library

IW GROUP, INC.

8687 Melrose Ave Ste G540, West Hollywood, CA 90069
Tel.: (310) 289-5500
Fax: (310) 289-5501
E-Mail: info@iwgroupinc.com
Web Site: www.iwgroupinc.com

E-Mail for Key Personnel:
Chairman: bimada@iwgroupinc.com
President: nsung@iwgroupinc.com
Media Dir.: jchen@iwgroupinc.com

Employees: 64
Year Founded: 1990

National Agency Associations: 4A's

Agency Specializes In: Advertising, Asian Market, Aviation & Aerospace, Consumer Goods, Consumer Marketing, Financial, Government/Political, Public Relations, Sponsorship

Breakdown of Gross Billings by Media: Brdcst.: 35%; Collateral: 15%; Consumer Publs.: 50%

Bill Imada *(Chm)*
Nita Song *(Pres & COO)*
Wendy Liao *(Grp Acct Dir)*
Sally Choi *(Acct Dir)*
Shagorika Ghosh *(Acct Dir)*
Mia Hu *(Dir-Interactive Experience)*
Martin Yang *(Dir-Fin)*
Ting Lin *(Assoc Dir-Creative)*
Benjamin Hyun *(Sr Acct Exec)*
Henry Ngo *(Sr Acct Exec)*

Accounts:
American Airlines
American Cancer Society
American Legacy Foundation; 1999
Blue Cross of California
California Children & Families Commission (F5 CA)
California Department of Food & Agriculture
California Department of Highways
California Public Utilities Commission; CA Electric Deregulation Outreach; 1997
Chrysler
The Coca-Cola Company
Covered California Asian Americans
Dish Network
GODIVA Chocolatier Campaign: "Victory"
McDonald's Corporation Sirloin Burger
Met Life
Nissan North America
United States Army
Wal-Mart Stores, Bentonville, AR; 2007

Branches

IW Group

33 New Montgomery St Ste 990, San Francisco, CA 94105
Tel.: (415) 268-1828
Fax: (415) 905-0376
E-Mail: info@iwgroupinc.com
Web Site: www.iwgroupinc.com

Employees: 10
Year Founded: 1991

National Agency Associations: 4A's

Agency Specializes In: Asian Market

Charmaine David *(Mng Dir & VP)*
Stan Toyama *(Exec Dir-Creative)*
Eloisa Hubilla *(Grp Dir-Plng)*
Stone Mays *(Sr Dir-Art)*
Sisi Zhang *(Sr Dir-Art)*
Flora Zhao *(Grp Acct Dir)*
John Author *(Exec Producer)*
Mia Hu *(Dir-Interactive Experience)*
Tim Thom *(Dir-Media)*
Wonee Paek *(Assoc Dir-Creative)*
Henry Ngo *(Sr Acct Exec)*
Benjamin Hyun *(Acct Exec)*
Hesham Mohsem *(Media Planner)*

Accounts:
Bank of America
The Coca-Cola Company
FDIC
KTSF
L'Oreal USA, Inc.
McDonald's
Merrill Lynch
MetLife, Inc.
Nissan North America
US Army
U.S. Census Bureau
Wal-Mart Stores, Inc.
WaMu

IW Group

100 W 33rd St 5th Fl, New York, NY 10001
Tel.: (212) 494-8676
Fax: (212) 885-3944
E-Mail: hhatanaka@iwgroupinc.com
Web Site: www.iwgroupinc.com

Employees: 3

National Agency Associations: 4A's

Bill Imada *(Chm)*
Martin Yang *(Dir-Fin)*

Accounts:
American Airlines
Christopher & Dana Reeve Foundation
Glaxo Smith Kline
McDonald's

J&M MARKETING COMMUNICATIONS, LLC

177 Parkside Dr, Princeton, NJ 08540-4814
Tel.: (609) 924-1083
E-Mail: jandmads@aol.com
Web Site: www.jandmads.com

Employees: 5
Year Founded: 1981

Agency Specializes In: Automotive, Brand Development & Integration, Consumer Marketing, Financial, Internet/Web Design, Outdoor, Print, Promotions, Real Estate, Restaurant, Retail, Strategic Planning/Research, Web (Banner Ads, Pop-ups, etc.)

Approx. Annual Billings: $5,000,000

Margaret L. Van Dagens *(Owner)*
Gordon Bennett *(Partner)*

Accounts:
Holman Studios; Dorset, VT Furniture; 2009

J DANIEL AGENCY

583 Donofrio Dr Ste 218, Madison, WI 53719
Tel.: (608) 535-9428
E-Mail: info@jdanielagency.com

Web Site: www.jdanielagency.com

Year Founded: 2007

Agency Specializes In: Advertising, Brand Development & Integration, Digital/Interactive, Email, Graphic Design, Internet/Web Design, Print, Social Media

Jeremy Tyler *(Founder & CEO)*

Accounts:
Hello Referrals
Neverfar
ReviewUs

J. FITZGERALD GROUP

12 W Main St, Lockport, NY 14094
Tel.: (716) 433-7688
Fax: (716) 433-6772
E-Mail: contact@jfitzgeraldgroup.com
Web Site: www.jfitzgeraldgroup.com

Agency Specializes In: Advertising, Brand Development & Integration, Crisis Communications, Internet/Web Design, Logo & Package Design, Media Planning, Public Relations, Search Engine Optimization, Social Media, Strategic Planning/Research

Carmel Cerullo Beiter *(Partner)*
Jack Martin *(Partner)*
Ken Dobmeier *(Dir-Media)*
Ron Koscinski *(Creative Dir)*

Accounts:
Cornerstone Community Federal Credit Union
Mullane Motors (Advertising Agency of Record)

J. GREG SMITH, INC.

Seville Square 1 14707 California St Ste 6, Omaha, NE 68154
Tel.: (402) 444-1600
Fax: (402) 444-1610
E-Mail: jgreg@jgregsmith.com
Web Site: www.jgregsmith.com

E-Mail for Key Personnel:
President: jgreg@radiks.net
Media Dir.: jsmith@radiks.net

Employees: 10
Year Founded: 1970

Agency Specializes In: Advertising, Affluent Market, Brand Development & Integration, Broadcast, Business Publications, Business-To-Business, Cable T.V., Children's Market, Co-op Advertising, Collateral, Commercial Photography, Communications, Consulting, Consumer Goods, Consumer Marketing, Corporate Communications, Corporate Identity, Crisis Communications, Direct Response Marketing, Education, Environmental, Event Planning & Marketing, Exhibit/Trade Shows, Experience Design, Faith Based, Financial, Food Service, Government/Political, Graphic Design, Hospitality, Household Goods, Identity Marketing, In-Store Advertising, Industrial, Integrated Marketing, Internet/Web Design, Investor Relations, Leisure, Local Marketing, Logo & Package Design, Luxury Products, Magazines, Media Planning, Media Relations, Medical Products, Merchandising, Multimedia, New Product Development, Newspaper, Newspapers & Magazines, Out-of-Home Media, Outdoor, Over-50 Market, Package Design, Planning & Consultation, Point of Purchase, Point of Sale, Print, Production, Production (Print), Promotions, Public Relations, Publicity/Promotions, Radio, Real Estate, Regional, Restaurant, Retail, Sales Promotion, Seniors' Market, Social Marketing/Nonprofit, Sponsorship, Stakeholders, Strategic Planning/Research, Sweepstakes, T.V., Trade & Consumer Magazines, Transportation, Travel & Tourism

Approx. Annual Billings: $3,000,000

Breakdown of Gross Billings by Media: Brdcst.: 25%; Logo & Package Design: 5%; Newsp.: 20%; Plng. & Consultation: 20%; Radio: 5%; Spot T.V.: 15%; Strategic Planning/Research: 10%

Jeff S. Smith *(VP)*

Accounts:
General Douglas MacArthur Foundation; Norfolk, VA; 2007
Great Plains Black History Museum
Lewis and Clark Trail
National Arbor Day Foundation; Lincoln, NE Trees for America, Tree City USA, Conservation Trees & Rain Forest, Replanting Our National Forests; 1972

J. LINCOLN GROUP

9595 Six Pines Dr Ste 8210, The Woodlands, TX 77380
Tel.: (832) 631-6050
Fax: (832) 631-6001
E-Mail: info@jlincolngroup.com
Web Site: www.jlincolngroup.com

Agency Specializes In: Advertising, Brand Development & Integration, Internet/Web Design, Logo & Package Design, Media Buying Services, Print, Radio, T.V.

Jason Breshears *(Creative Dir)*
Dan Arnold *(Media Buyer)*
Crystal Griffith *(Media Buyer)*
Ronald Lowrey *(Media Buyer)*

Accounts:
Honda Of Lake Jackson
Honda of Brazosport
Jaguar Cars Limited
Land Rover
Lone Star Cowboy Church
Motorcycle Gear Extravaganza
The Progressive Corporation
Re-Bath
Safeco Insurance Company of America
Sports Culture

J-U CARTER, INC.

555 N El Camino Rel St A 462, San Clemente, CA 92672
Tel.: (949) 852-5960
Fax: (949) 852-5960
Web Site: www.j-u.com

E-Mail for Key Personnel:
President: donnac@j-u.com
Creative Dir.: sandral@j-u.com
Media Dir.: marianneb@j-u.com

Employees: 12
Year Founded: 1991

National Agency Associations: AAF

Agency Specializes In: Advertising, Brand Development & Integration, Broadcast, Business Publications, Business-To-Business, Cable T.V., Children's Market, Co-op Advertising, Collateral, College, Consumer Marketing, Corporate Communications, Corporate Identity, Customer Relationship Management, Digital/Interactive, Direct Response Marketing, Direct-to-Consumer, Electronic Media, Email, Environmental, Event Planning & Marketing, Government/Political, Graphic Design, Guerilla Marketing, Health Care Services, Hispanic Market, Household Goods, Identity Marketing, In-Store Advertising, Integrated Marketing, Internet/Web Design, Local Marketing, Logo & Package Design, Media Buying Services, Media Planning, Mobile Marketing, Multimedia, Newspaper, Newspapers & Magazines, Out-of-Home Media, Outdoor, Over-50 Market, Paid Searches, Podcasting, Point of Purchase, Point of Sale, Print, Production (Ad, Film, Broadcast), Production (Print), Promotions, RSS (Really Simple Syndication), Radio, Real Estate, Recruitment, Regional, Restaurant, Retail, Sales Promotion, Search Engine Optimization, Seniors' Market, Social Marketing/Nonprofit, Sports Market, Strategic Planning/Research, T.V., Technical Advertising, Transportation, Viral/Buzz/Word of Mouth, Web (Banner Ads, Pop-ups, etc.), Women's Market

Breakdown of Gross Billings by Media: Internet Adv.: 15%; Newsp. & Mags.: 20%; Out-of-Home Media: 5%; Radio & T.V.: 45%; Trade & Consumer Mags.: 15%

Donna Carter *(Pres & Sr Strategist-Acct)*

Accounts:
Anthem Inc.; 1996
Black & Decker HHI: Lake Forest, CA Branding Initiatives; 2007
Black Angus Steakhouse Restaurant; Los Altos, CA Branding, Local Initiatives; 2007
Healthnet; Woodland Hills, CA; 2007
Mattel; El Segundo, CA Creative Services; 2007
McClellan Nichols Sports Syndicate
Metropolitan Water District of Southern California; Los Angeles, CA Water Conservation; 2005
Overnite Express
Plus Orthopedics
Real Mex Restaurants; Cypress, CA Local Store Branding & Marketing; 2007
The Toll Roads - Transportation Corridor Agencies
Warner Pacific Insurance Services
Wells Fargo Century

J. WALTER THOMPSON

(Formerly JWT)
466 Lexington Ave, New York, NY 10017-3140
Tel.: (212) 210-7000
Fax: (212) 210-7299
E-Mail: maggie.connors@jwt.com
Web Site: www.jwt.com

E-Mail for Key Personnel:
Chairman: bob.jeffrey@jwt.com

Employees: 650
Year Founded: 1864

National Agency Associations: 4A's-AAF-AD CLUB-AWNY-MCA-NEW YORK/AMA-OAAA-THINKLA

Agency Specializes In: Advertising, Sponsorship

Lynn Power *(Pres)*
Laura Selfridge *(Partner & Dir-Ops-Global)*
Lida Burpee *(Mng Dir & Exec VP)*
Erin Johnson *(Chief Comm Officer)*
Brian Yessian *(Chief Creative Officer)*
Lyle Tick *(Global Chief Growth Officer)*
Alison Burns *(CEO-London)*
Howard Courtemanche *(CEO-Health)*
Todd Ruthven *(Sr VP & Dir-Creative)*
Kai Yen *(Mng Dir-New York)*
Lisa Setten *(Head-Integrated Production)*
Charly Wehbe *(Head-Digital, Channel & Tech Plng)*

Sarah Barclay *(Exec Dir-Creative)*
Cathy Clift *(Exec Dir-Plng)*
Robert Frost *(Exec Dir-Creative)*
Marta La Rock *(Exec Dir-Plng-NY)*
Emmanuel Lalleve *(Exec Dir-Creative)*
Ian Thomas *(Exec Dir-Creative)*
Paul Turzio *(Exec Dir-Analytics)*
Eric Weisberg *(Exec Dir-Creative-Global)*
Jon Zast *(Exec Dir-Creative-New York)*
Joseph Mueller *(Sr Dir-Art)*
Nadine Andros *(Acct Dir)*
Will Bright *(Creative Dir)*
Alex Ciociola *(Acct Dir)*
John Codling *(Creative Dir)*
Alex Mailman *(Bus Dir)*
Michelle Mancero *(Acct Dir-Estee Lauder)*
Charlie Martyn *(Acct Dir)*
Dan Morales *(Creative Dir)*
Mike Potter *(Art Dir)*
Glenn Sciachitano *(Acct Dir-Global)*
Stephanie Tanguay *(Acct Dir)*
Lindsey Tatgenhorst *(Acct Dir)*
Erik Wagner *(Acct Dir)*
Dave Wasserman *(Creative Dir)*
Kate Wheeler *(Acct Dir-Johnson & Johnson)*
Derrick Goss *(Dir-Plng-Global & Strategist-Brand)*
Chad Baker *(Dir-Creative)*
Betsy Decker *(Dir-Creative)*
Billy Faraut *(Dir-Creative)*
Bill Finnegan *(Dir-Brand Production)*
Chad Gilchrist *(Dir-Fin Analysis)*
Lucie Greene *(Dir-Innovation Grp-Worldwide)*
Anaka Kobzev *(Dir-Comm)*
Howard Lenn *(Dir-Creative)*
Ludovic Marrocco *(Dir-Creative)*
Ben Morejon *(Dir-Art)*
Zach Roif *(Dir-Art)*
Robert Rosswaag *(Dir-Creative)*
Mark Truss *(Dir-Brand Intelligence-Global)*
Jordan Young *(Sr Art Dir)*
Samantha Cho *(Acct Mgr)*
Erin Cross *(Acct Mgr)*
Stephanie Reedy *(Acct Mgr)*
Gemma Swinglehurst *(Acct Mgr)*
Daniela Obando *(Sr Designer)*
Steve Panawek *(Planner-Strategic)*
Nicolas Piris *(Acct Planner)*
Linda Acheampong *(Coord-Fin)*
Robin Bardolia *(Chief Strategic Officer-North America)*
Tom O`Connell *(Sr Partner)*

Accounts:
AB Electrolux Eureka
ADC Portfolio Night
Bayer Coppertone, Creative, Miralax, Phillips
Bristol-Myers Squibb
New-Cobra Puma Golf (Lead Creative Agency)
Edgewell Personal Care Advertising, Banana Boat, Campaign: "Beachball", Campaign: "Schick & Pitch Perfect 2 Present "Ready, Shave, Shine"", Campaign: "Swordplay Meets Foreplay", Creative, Fresh + Sexy Wipes, Hawaiian Tropic, Playtex Tampons, Schick, Schick Hydro, Schick Hydro Silk, Schick Intuition, Skintimate, Video, Wilkinson Sword
The Estee Lauder Companies Inc. Clinique
Ford Motor Co. Ford Everest, Ranger
Google Creative, Energizer Personal Care, Enterprise Assignment
HSBC Little Investor, Museum of Procrastination
Jansen
Johnson & Johnson Benadryl, Bengay, Campaign: "For Everything We Do", Campaign: "For What Matters Most", Campaign: "Glambulance", Campaign: "Like Crazy", Listerine, Reach, Tylenol
Kellogg Company Creative, Special K
Kimberly-Clark Advertising, Campaign: "Achoo", Campaign: "Do My Thing", Kleenex, TV
KPMG Campaign: "Glass Ceiling", Global Creative
Macy's Inc.; Cincinnati, OH Believe Campaign (Benefits Make-A-Wish Foundation), Campaign: "Macy's Backstage Pass", Campaign: "Screamers", Campaign: "Week of Wonderful", Campaign: "What's in store?", Creative, Macy's, Yes, Virginia
McNEIL-PPC, Inc. Campaign: "How We Family", Online, Tylenol
Nestle Campaign: "Snack Brighter", Carnation, Drumstick, Libby's, Mac Cups, Outshine Frozen Fruit Bars, Skinny Cow, Stouffers, Tollhouse
Nokia Global Creative; 2007
North Shore-LIJ Health System Advertising, Creative, Marketing, Strategy
Pfizer Inc.
Puma Campaign: "Calling All Troublemakers", Campaign: "Forever Faster", Campaign: "Rihanna trains for platinum", Creative
Rolex Campaign: "Deepest Dive"
Shell
T. Rowe Price
Treasury Wine Estates Global Marketing, Marketing Communications, Marketing Strategy, Public Relations, Shopper Marketing
Unilever Sunsilk
United Health Group
United States Marine Corps

Subsidiaries

J. Walter Thompson INSIDE
(Formerly JWT Inside)
6300 Wishire Blvd, Los Angeles, CA 90048
(See Separate Listing)

J. Walter Thompson U.S.A., Inc.
466 Lexington Ave, New York, NY 10017-3140
(See Separate Listing)

J. Walter Thompson
591 Camino De La Reina Ste 314, San Diego, CA 92108-3105
Tel.: (619) 297-9334
Fax: (619) 297-9208
Web Site: www.jwt.com

Agency Specializes In: Advertising

Brian Daly *(Sr VP)*
Tibor van Ginkel *(Sr Dir-Creative & Art-JWT Amsterdam)*
James Cooper *(Dir-Mgmt)*
Michael Antoine *(Supvr-Post Production)*

Accounts:
Microsoft
Nature's Recipe Pet Food Campaign: "Nature's Recipe for Moments"

J. Walter Thompson
222 Merchandise Mart Plz Ste 250, Chicago, IL 60654
(See Separate Listing)

Canada

J. Walter Thompson Canada
630 Sherbrooke W Suite 710, Montreal, QC H3A 1E4 Canada
Tel.: (514) 287-3597
Fax: (514) 287-9007
Web Site: www.jwtcanada.ca

Employees: 20
Year Founded: 2004

Agency Specializes In: Advertising

David Gibb *(Mng Dir & Exec VP)*
Andre LaChance *(VP & Gen Mgr)*
Christian Desrosiers *(VP & Dir-Creative)*
Chris Edmeades *(Acct Dir)*
Julie Guimond *(Mgr-Print Production)*
Brigitte Ledermann *(Copywriter)*

Accounts:
Bayer
Energizer
HSBC
Johnson & Johnson
Kraft
Kraft Foods
Nokia
Shell
Tim Hortons

J. Walter Thompson Canada
160 Bloor St E Ste 800, Toronto, ON M4W 3P7 Canada
(See Separate Listing)

Ghana

Adam Advertising
(Formerly JWT Ghana)
Hse No F874/2 Eleventh Close, Osu Former Citirock Building, 233 Accra, Ghana
Tel.: (233) 0302 784 685
E-Mail: info@jwtghana.com
Web Site: www.adamsghana.com

Year Founded: 2001

Don Obilor *(Mng Dir)*
Bithia Awuku-Asante *(Head-Strategic Plng & Media)*
Elsie Amorin *(Sr Client Svc Mgr)*
Dinah Freeman *(Client Svc Dir)*

Nigeria

LTC Advertising Lagos
2nd Fl Motorway Centre 1 Motorway Ave, PMB 21772 Ikeja, Lagos, Nigeria
Tel.: (234) 1 471 2056
Fax: (234) 1 554 7897
E-Mail: info@ltc-jwtlagos.net
Web Site: www.ltc-jwtlagos.net

Year Founded: 1986

Billy K. Lawson *(Chm)*
Charles O. Abraham *(CEO-LTC-JWT Lagos)*
Aderonke Ladi-Awotinde *(Grp Head-New Bus)*
Tunji Oladejo *(Grp Head-Bus Dev)*
Bisi Afolabi *(Dir-Bus Dev)*
Bola Thomas *(Dir)*
Adebayo Toib Adelabu *(Asst Dir-Copy)*
Abiola Olawumi *(Sr Acct Mgr)*
Modupe Awe *(Acct Mgr-Microsoft Mobile Devices & Svcs)*
Martina Feese *(Copywriter-Creative)*

Accounts:
AVIS Nigeria
Cadbury Nigeria Plc
Coca-Cola Nigeria limited
Crusader Sterling Pension
Federal Inland Revenue Service
FedEx Courier
Muritala Mohammed Airport (MMA2)
Reckitt Benckiser Nig
Society for Family Health
Unilever Nigeria Plc

South Africa

J. Walter Thompson Cape Town
30 Keerom Street 3rd Floor, 8001 Cape Town, 8001 South Africa

Mailing Address:
PO Box 7234, Roggebaai, 8012 Cape Town, South Africa
Tel.: (27) 21 426 2880
Fax: (27) 21 426 2890
Web Site: www.jwt.com

Employees: 45
Year Founded: 1928

Jim Faulds *(CEO)*
Jonathan Commerford *(Grp Head-Creative & Copywriter)*
Jonathan Lang *(Exec Dir-Creative)*
Claire Markwell *(Grp Acct Dir)*
Paul Lawrence *(Art Dir)*
Mkhuseli Mancotywa *(Dir-Bus Unit-Digital & Social)*
Nikki Miller *(Dir-Bus Unit)*
Martine Levy *(Mgr-Production)*

Accounts:
A Nation's Pride
Barloworld Digital
Bokomo Foods Campaign: "Big Flavour Big Taste"
Everlast Boxing Campaign: "Born Fighters"
Ford Road Safety
Gautrain Campaign: "Boy, Dog, Baby", Campaign: "By Car By Train", Campaign: "For People On The Move"
Green Cross
Johnson & Johnson Campaign: "Benylin Cough Cough"
Kalahari.com Campaign: "Bloodsport", Campaign: "Taken Aweigh", Campaign: "Textbook Beer Burger Shoe"
Kellogg Company
Lewis
Lucky Star Analytics, Lead Creative Agency, Public Relations, Social Media
Mardi Gras
Panarottis Campaign: "Family Board Game Boxes"
Shell SA
Smirnoff
True Blue Surf Travel

J. Walter Thompson
34 Homestead Rd cnr 12th Ave & Rivonia Rd, Rivonia, 2128 South Africa
Mailing Address:
PO Box 3939, Rivonia, 2128 South Africa
Tel.: (27) 11 806 8000
Fax: (27) 11 806 8010
Web Site: www.jwt.com

Employees: 110
Year Founded: 1928

National Agency Associations: ACA

Modise Makhene *(CEO)*
Jonathan Lang *(Exec Dir-Creative)*
Claire Markwell *(Grp Acct Dir)*
Natalie Pierpoint *(Grp Acct Dir)*
Hannes De Beer *(Dir-Art)*
Ronnie Malden *(Dir-Creative)*
Ilka Mourao *(Dir-Art)*
Stephen Roth *(Dir-Art)*
Paul Strappini *(Dir-Creative)*
Collin Makhubela *(Copywriter)*

Accounts:
Bayer Healthcare
Bombela Gautrain
Kelloggs
Kraft
Nestle
Nokia
Shell
Unilever

Tunisia

J. Walter Thompson
91 Avenue Louis Braille, Cite El-Khadrah, Tunis, 1003 Tunisia
Tel.: (216) 71 806 250
Fax: (216) 71 860 082
Web Site: www.jwt.com

Ahmed Mahjoub *(Mng Dir)*
Ghassan Nejmeh *(CEO-North Africa)*
El Zoghlami Ahmed *(Exec Dir-Creative-North Africa)*
Lori Beal *(Bus Dir)*
Ben Abdelghaffar Ahmed *(Dir-Art)*
Kaddour Hazem *(Dir-Plng)*
Kaouther Boumaiza *(Mgr-Talent)*

Accounts:
ADDA Campaign: "Illegal Downloading Kills Games"
ARFT Campaign: "Pulp Fiction"
B Cosmic
Confiserie Triki Florida Chewing Gum
Lilas
Samsung
SIVO Lenses Campaign: "Kidnapping", Campaign: "What you see isn't always true."
Tounsia TV Campaign: "Defies time on Tounsia TV", Campaign: "Goldorak"
Tunisiana Campaign: "Story of Life"

Australia

J. Walter Thompson Australia
Bldg 18A 64 Ballmain St, Richmond, VIC 3121 Australia
Mailing Address:
P.O. Box 6182, Melbourne, VIC 3004 Australia
Tel.: (61) 3 9868 9111
Fax: (61) 3 9867 7568
E-Mail: melb.info@jwt.com
Web Site: www.jwt.com.au

Employees: 65
Year Founded: 1929

National Agency Associations: AFA

John Gutteridge *(CEO-Australasia)*
Angela Morris *(Exec Dir-Plng-Melbourne)*
Richard Muntz *(Exec Dir-Creative-JWT Melbourne)*
Tim Yates *(Sr Dir-Art)*
Jessica Johnson *(Sr Acct Dir)*
Tim Holmes *(Creative Dir)*
Jem Prehar *(Acct Dir)*
Josie Brown *(Dir-Digital-APAC)*

Accounts:
Australian Department of Health & Ageing Campaign: "Swap it where is"
Cancer Center
Ford Motor Company Campaign: "Face to Facebook", Ford Territory, G Series (Television)
IFAW Australia
Kraft Campaign: "It pays to sell Peanut Butter like Ice Cream"
Melbourne Writers Festival Campaign: "Wi-Fiction"
Mondelez Australia Campaign: "Right Kinda Nuts"
Mylanta Campaign: "Chilli Con Carnage", Campaign: "Sushiti", Print Campaign
Quit Victoria Campaign: "Last Dance", Campaign: "The Wait"
New-RAC Electric Highway
Royal Dutch Shell plc
Unilever
VicRoads

J. Walter Thompson
Level 14 338 Pitt Street, Sydney, NSW 2000 Australia
Tel.: (61) 2 9947 2222
Fax: (61) 2 9947 2299
E-Mail: syd.info@jwt.com
Web Site: www.jwt.com

Year Founded: 1929

Agency Specializes In: Direct Response Marketing, Sales Promotion

Laurie Geddes *(Grp Head-Creative)*
Jenny Willits *(Gen Mgr)*
Simon Langley *(Exec Dir-Creative-Sydney)*
Peta Parker *(Sr Acct Dir)*
Milly Hall *(Grp Acct Dir)*
Fiona Wilson *(Grp Acct Dir)*
Alex Antoniou *(Art Dir)*
Simon Hayes *(Art Dir)*
Tim Holmes *(Creative Dir)*
Jarrod Lowe *(Creative Dir)*
Jay Morgan *(Creative Dir-Digital Grp)*
Rachel Wintle *(Acct Dir)*
Patrick Allenby *(Dir-Art)*
Delphine Perret *(Dir-Art)*
Amanda Slayter *(Dir-Brdcst)*
Dav Tabeshfar *(Dir-Creative)*
Chris Badger *(Assoc Dir-Creative)*
Will Edwards *(Assoc Dir-Creative)*
John Lam *(Assoc Dir-Creative)*
Amanda Porritt *(Acct Mgr)*
Ali Clemesha *(Acct Exec)*
Sinead Roarty *(Copywriter)*
Elliott White *(Copywriter)*

Accounts:
AMP
Banlice
Cancer Council NSW Campaign: "I Touch Myself"
Challenger Creative
FaHCSIA
Federal Government Department of Health & Aging National Sexually Transmissible Infections Prevention Program
Foodbank
Ford Campaign: "You're The Voice"
Hero Condoms
Japan Earthquake Appeal Campaign: "Sushi Train"
Johnson & Johnson Campaign: "Crawl", Campaign: "Flirtilator", Combantrin, Imodium, Nicorette, Regaine, Sudafed Day & Night
Kellogg's Coco Pops, Crunchy Nut Cornflakes, In-Store, Special K
Kimberly-Clark Brand Strategy, Campaign: "Share the Softness", Campaign: "The 'Wash Test", Creative, Digital, In-Store, Kleenex Cottonelle, Social Media, TV
Kraft Campaign: "Darwin", Vegemite
LWP Property Group
McMillan Shakespeare
McNeil-PPC, Inc K-Y, Yours + Mine
Melbourne Writers Festival Campaign: "Stories Unbound"
Merck & Co., Inc.
Mylanta
Nestle Confectionery Campaign: "Noooo", Campaign: "The Final Fifty", Cookies & Cream Kit Kat, Kit Kat, Limited Edition KIT KAT
Nokia Corporation Beautifully Simple
New-NSW Government Campaign: "Stop Before it Gets Ugly", Print, Rural Fire Service
Patak Social Media
Piaggio Vespa Australia
RAC Campaign: "Attention Powered Car", Creative, Roadside Assistance
Schick Quattro
Sega Sonic Vision
Shell
Smirnoff
Unilever Australia Ltd.
Unilever Campaign: "Blogged & Bound", Campaign: "Daydream Lilly", Creative, Digital, Sunsilk, Toni & Guy
Vegemite
Youth Off The Streets Campaign: "Graham & Linda", Homeless Charity

Bangladesh

Asiatic Marketing Communications, Ltd.

Asiatic Ctr House 63 Rd 7B Block H Banal Model Town, Dhaka, 1213 Bangladesh
Tel.: (880) 2 989 3303
Fax: (880) 2 987 0222
Web Site: www.jwt.com

Year Founded: 1995

Aly Zaker *(Chm CEO & Mng Dir)*

China

J. Walter Thompson

25/F No 989 Chang Le Road The Center, Shanghai, 200031 China
Tel.: (86) 21 2405 0000
Fax: (86) 21 2405 0001
Web Site: www.jwtchina.com

Employees: 250
Year Founded: 1986

Tom Doctoroff *(CEO-JWT APAC-JWT Shanghai)*
Dan Ingall *(Mng Dir-JWT Shanghai)*
George Shi *(Gen Mgr)*
Fei Wei *(Sr Dir-Creative-Interactive)*
Rojana Chuasakul *(Dir-Art & Creative)*
Bill Chan *(Creative Dir)*
Mike Nash *(Bus Dir-Changan Ford)*
Ratan Malli *(Dir-Strategic Plng-Asia Pacific-JWT Shanghai)*
Marchille Yan *(Dir-Fin-North East Asia-JWT Shanghai)*
Jun Qian *(Copywriter)*

Accounts:
Air New Zealand
New-AliCloud Campaign: "For Values Beyond Computing", Print, TV
New-Alipay (Agency of Record)
Anta Sports Products Campaign: "Anta Fitness Delivery"
CEPF Campaign: "CEO Bus Pool"
China Merchants Bank Campaign: "Listen", Wealth Management
DTC
Ford
GNC Campaign: "Tangled ColonDuck"
Guangzhou Liby Enterprise Campaign: "Skiing"
GZL International Travel Service Campaign: "Tiger"
Haier Campaign: "Cleaning Fish", Corporate Branding Business
Henkel Campaign: "Chinese Wedding"
HSBC Group
INESA Brand Strategy
Johnson & Johnson Tylenol
KFC Fast Food
Levi's Campaign: "Kung Fu", Campaign: "We Are Explorers", Denizen
Lily Brand Campaign
Listerine Campaign: " Smelly Flipbook"
Maxam Campaign: "Civilization-Egypt"
Metersbonwe Brand Image, Campaign: "The Skate Wash Denim", Fashion & Accessories, Mjeans
Pizza Hut
New-SAKURA SAKURA (water Exercise) Of the share a shower
Samsonite Campaign: "Kid Proof", Cosmolite Suitcase, Heaven & Hell
New-Skullcandy
Sofy
Starbucks China Digital, Social Media
Tourism New Zealand
Treasury Wine Estates Global Marketing, Marketing Communications, Marketing Strategy, Public Relations, Shopper Marketing
Uni-President Enterprises Aha Coffee, Creative, Iced Tea, President Milk Tea, Verlet Milk Tea
Unicharm
Unilever Lux
Walt Disney CRM, Digital, TV

J. Walter Thompson Beijing

RM 501, 5/F Jin Bao Tower, 89 Jin Bao St., Beijing, 100000 China
Tel.: (86) 10 851 59599
Fax: (86) 1085159590
Web Site: www.jwt.com

Year Founded: 1986

Jeffrey Yu *(Mng Dir)*
Polly Chu *(Chief Creative Officer)*
Sean Chuah *(Sr Acct Dir)*

Accounts:
Baby Back Home Missing Children App
Baixiang Food
China National Cereals, Oils & Foodstuffs (COFCO) Creative, Lohas Fruit Juice, Wu Gu Dao Chang
Cofco Limited Campaign: "Ferrari"
Dacheng; 2007
Gome Brand Strategy, Creative Business, Digital Marketing, New Media Marketing, Promotion
Halls
Huiyuan Group; 2007
Intel Campaign: "Look Inside,"
Lenovo Group Limited; 2007
Microsoft Creative, Online Advertising, Online App, Out-of-Home Billboards, Print, Viral Videos, Windows 8
Nestle
Nokia Campaign: "Unfollow"
Red Bull; 2008
Renren.com Brand Strategy, Nuomi.com
Shell
Yili Jian Dian; 2007

Hong Kong

J. Walter Thompson

36/F PCCW Tower Taikoo Place 979 King's Road, Quarry Bay, China (Hong Kong)
Tel.: (852) 2280 3333
Fax: (852) 2280 3533
Web Site: www.jwt.com

Year Founded: 1973

Agency Specializes In: Advertising Specialties

Barbara Fu *(Co-Exec Dir-Creative-Hong Kong)*
Jam Wu *(Dir-Creative)*
Kate Desmarais *(Copywriter)*
Frankie Fung *(Grp Creative Dir)*
Samuel Yu *(Assoc Acct Dir)*

Accounts:
Banana Boat Solar Protection
Cooper Wheelock Loft-Style Real Estate; 2007
DIAGEO plc
Friends of the Earth Campaign: "Drown The World"
International Fund for Animal Welfare Campaign: "Free the Moon Bear"
Jiayuan.com International Campaign: "Finding Your Other Half"
Johnson & Johnson Campaign: "Flipbook With Bad Breath", Listerine
Nissin Foods Below-the-Line, Cup Noodles, Digital, Print, TV
Nokia Corporation
Pink Beauty Campaign: "Armpit Tsunami"
Samsonite Asia Limited Campaign: "Step Out", Campaign: "Take on the World"
SmarTone-Vodafone

India

Contract Advertising (India) Limited

Vaswani Chambers 264 Dr Annie Bessant Road, Mumbai, 400 030 India
Tel.: (91) 22 40569696
Fax: (91) 22 2430 3808
Web Site: www.contractindia.co.in

Year Founded: 1947

National Agency Associations: AAAI (INDIA)

Rana Barua *(CEO)*
Rohit Srivastava *(Exec VP)*
Kunal Chakravarty *(Sr VP)*
Rahul Ghosh *(Sr VP & Sr Creative Dir)*
Pooja Malhotra *(Sr VP)*
Geet Nazir *(Sr VP)*
Kapil Mishra *(Head-Creative)*
Prateek Suri *(Grp Head-Creative)*
Ayesha Ghosh *(Gen Mgr)*
Mayur Hola *(Exec Dir-Creative)*
Ashish Chakravarty *(Creative Dir-Natl)*
Nikhil Mehrotra *(Dir-Creative)*

Accounts:
Acer Creative, Digital, Out-Of-Home, Print, Radio, TV
Aditya Birla Group Louis Philippe
New-Air Pegasus
New-Amarprakash Developers
Amira Nature Foods Ltd Digital Media, Media, Print, Radio, Television
Asian Paints Campaign: "The Wall Takes it All", Creative, Royale, Tractor
Bajaj Electricals
Cadbury India Campaign: "Cadbury Celebrations Lonely Maa", Campaign: "Choose your Face", Campaign: "Made with Love", Celebrations Candy, Eclairs, Halls
CaratLane
CNBC TV18 Campaign: "Hello Dreamers"
Corelle Campaign: "Relax"
Crompton Greaves Creative
Dabur India Ltd Campaign: "Rose Glow", Vatika-Anti-Dandruff Shampoo; 2005
Del Monte
Dominos Pizza India Ltd Campaign: "Football", Campaign: "Theatre", Oven-Baked Subwich
New-Droom Creative, Digital, Print, TV
Edelweiss Tokio Life Insurance
New-Electrolux Creative, Kelvinator
Firstpost.com Campaign: "Got An Opinion?", Campaign: "Journalist"
New-Fortune India Communication, Creative, Creative Strategy, Digital Strategy
GNIIT
New-Godrej
New-GPI
New-Hotstar
HSBC
HSIL Ltd
Hypercity
Infomedia Yellow Pages
New-ITC
New-Jaypee Associates
JK Tyre Campaign: "Soles with Souls", Digital, OOH, Print, Radio
Jockey International Campaign: "Sweep Him Off His Feet or Stay Single"
Jubilant Foodworks Campaign: "Kidney or Heart", Campaign: "Lost", Campaign: "Rishton Ka Time"
New-Kenstar
New-KOEL- Gensets
New-Life OK
New-LINE
Mankind Pharma Manforce
New-Mantri Developers
Marico
Mondelez India Kraft-Cadbury
Network18 Campaign: "Got An Opinion?", Creative, Marketing, Moneycontrol.com
NIIT

Piramal Realty Creative
New-Portea Medical
Provogue india Ltd Campaign: "Make Your Mark"
Religare Star Child Plans
New-Revlon
Samsonite Corporation American Tourister, Campaign: "Survivor", Samsonite; 2009
New-Sansui Creative
New-Shell
Shoppers Stop Ltd Campaign: "Every Wife Doesn't Know", Campaign: "Get Knotty", Campaign: "Go Gaga Over You", Campaign: "Loud Entrance", Campaign: "Tidy Up In Style", Campaign: "Unlock Extra", Start Something New
Sound Art Campaign: "Sound Drives"
Star Plus Campaign: "Knife", Creative
Sugar Free Gold Campaign: "Meetha on, Calories Gone"
New-Tango Media Creative
Tara Jewellers Campaign: "For Life's Unbreakable Relationships", Campaign: "Promise", Campaign: "Sorry Papa"
Tata Docomo Campaign: "Bhalai Ki Supply", Campaign: "Duckface Selfie", Campaign: "Falooda", Campaign: "More Data, More Bhalai", Campaign: "Open Up", Campaign: "Poser", Campaign: "Selfiesh", Campaign: "Snowball"
New-Tata Motors
New-Tata Tele Services
New-Truecaller Brand Campaign, Brand Marketing, Creative
New-Truly Madly
United Breweries Campaign: "Vladivar Scream"
New-United Spirits Limited
UTI Mutual Fund Creative, Digital, OOH, Print, Radio, TV
New-Vectus Industries
New-VIP
Whirlpool India Campaign: "New for longer", Campaign: "Permanent Stain", Campaign: "Stain Terminator"
New-Wills lifestyle
Zydus Wellness

J. Walter Thompson

301 Peninsula Chambers Ganpatrao Kadam Marg, Lower Parel West, Mumbai, 400 013 India
Tel.: (91) 22 40985555
Fax: (91) 22 40985656
E-Mail: colvyn.harris@jwt.com
Web Site: www.jwt.com

Year Founded: 1929

Rajesh Gangwani *(Mng Partner & Sr VP)*
Bindu Sethi *(Chief Strategy Officer-India)*
Anupama Ahluwalia *(VP & Head-Films-Natl-India)*
Rajeev Sharma *(VP & Head-Digital)*
Priya Pardiwalla *(VP & Exec Dir-Creative)*
Sayam Bhadra *(VP)*
Anupama Ramaswamy *(Assoc VP & Sr Dir-Creative)*
Mark Samuel *(Assoc VP & Sr Dir-Creative-JWT Mindset Hyderabad)*
Sonia Bhatnagar *(Exec Dir-Creative)*
Colvyn Harris *(Exec Dir-Global Growth & Client Dev)*
Hanoz Mogrelia *(Exec Dir-Creative-Radiant-Global)*
Partha Chowdhury *(Sr Dir-Creative)*
Kashyap Joshi *(Sr Dir-Creative)*
Anagha Nigwekar *(Sr Dir-Creative)*
Somitra Chaturvedi *(Acct Dir)*
Siddhant Lahiri *(Acct Plng Dir)*
Preethi Maroli *(Bus Dir-Global)*
Shourabh Verma *(Acct Dir)*
Vinayak Gaikwad *(Dir-Art & Copywriter)*
Shweta Iyer *(Dir-Creative)*
Shubhrojyoti Roy *(Dir-Plng)*
Tina Sachdev *(Dir-Creative)*
Simran Sahni *(Dir-Creative)*
Subhash Sudhakaran *(Dir-Art)*
Deep Singh *(Acct Mgr-Plng)*
Suyash Barve *(Supvr-Creative)*
Uttaran Chowdhury *(Copywriter)*
Babita Baruah *(Exec Bus Dir-Delhi)*

Accounts:
ADF Foods Creative, Soul Pickle
Aditya Birla Insurance Brockers
All India Congress Committee
Amit Enterprises
The Apollo Hospitals Group
Bay Beat Collective The Genomusic Project
Beans and Beyond
Bennett Coleman & Co. Ltd. Campaign: "A Day in the Life of Kerala", Campaign: "Traffic Jam", Times Kerala Launch Campaign
Bharti Airtel Airtel Digital TV Campaign: "Life Badlo - Quick Service", Campaign: "Hip Hop", Campaign: "Movie Crashers"
Bombay Elektrik Projekt
CADD India Campaign: "Car"
Cargill Sweekar Sunflower Oil
CommonFloor.com Campaign: "No Darr. Find Ghar", Cinema, Digital, Outdoor, Print, Radio
Denizen
Diageo Campaign: "Smirnoff Spin The Bottle Board Game Packaging", Smirnoff Green Apple
Disney UTV Campaign: "Indiagames.com: Mom"
Ford Motor Company Campaign: "Don't Text While Driving", Endeavour 4x4, Fiesta, Ford Figo
Friends for Education Campaign: "Dracula"
Fuji Film Campaign: "Orgasm", Campaign: "Real Smile", Finepix F 70
Gitanjali Jewels
Glaxosmithkline Consumer Healthcare Ltd Boost, Campaign: "Child Experiments", Campaign: "Office", Horlicks, Nutribic Biscuits
GM Pens International
Godrej & Boyce Mfg Company Ltd Campaign: "Ab Musibat se Darna Kaisa", Campaign: "Birthday Party", Campaign: "Thoughts will remain thoughts", Godrej Safes, Godrej Security Solutions
New-Godrej Consumer Products Campaign: "Subah Bolo Good Knight", Good Knight
Gripone
Hamstech Institute Campaign: "Your Name Here - Blazer"
Hero Motocorp Campaign: "50 Million", Glamour, Hero HF Deluxe, Hero Splendor
Ihaveanidea Inc Campaign: "Women"
ILLBAN Remedies
The Indian Express
Is-Travel & Tourism
Kellogg Company Campaign: "Big Meeting", Campaign: "Game", Campaign: "Perfect Figure", Campaign: "Uff Yeh Honey Loops", Honey Loops, Kellogg's All Bran, Kellogg's Chocos, Kellogg's Special K
KidZania Creative, OOH, Print
Kotak Life Insurance
Landmark Group Campaign: "Lifestyle Baddie Bags"
Life Insurance Corporation
Listerine Campaign: "No one follows bad breath"
Maharashtra Janvikas Kendra
Microsoft Corporation India Pvt Ltd
Mid Day Infomedia
Mountain Dew
Multi Commodities Exchange of India Business to Consumer, Creative
Multi Screen Media Campaign: "Old Couple", Campaign: "Police", Campaign: "Role Reversal", Campaign: "Seats"
National Geographic
National Payments Corporation of India Above the Line, Advertising, Below-the-Line, Creative, Digital, RuPay, RuPay Card Scheme, Strategy
Naturals Creative, Marketing, Online, Print, Social Media, TV
Nestle India Campaign: "Dancing Babies", Campaign: "Shor", Campaign: "To Love is To Share", Campaign: "Virat as Mr. Vaali", Chocolate Business, Kit Kat, Munch, Nestle Alpino
Nike Campaign: "Make Every Yard Count"
Nokia Campaign: "Congratulates Croma", Campaign: "Directions (Mandarin - French)", Campaign: "Nokia Translator", Campaign: "Pinning", Lumia 920, N8, Nokia C2 -00, Nokia Lumia, Ovi Maps, Social Media
PepsiCo India Andhra Bangkok Curry, Campaign: "Ab Ras Barsega", Campaign: "Football vs Cricket", Campaign: "Free recharge, Priyanka Chopra", Campaign: "Hit Hai", Campaign: "It's Good to be Alive", Campaign: "Oh Yes Abhi!", Campaign: "Party Invitation", Campaign: "T20 Film", Campaign: "Try Tedha Yaar", Creative, Kurkure, Lay's, Punjabi Pizza, Rajasthani Manchurian, Slice, Tropicana
Frito-Lay Campaign: "Lay's Best Buddies", Campaign: "The Secret is Out", Lay's
Peta India
Petroleum Conservation Research Association
Pizza Hut Campaign: "Thought Bubble", Campaign: "iPan"
Regency Tiles
Rotary International National Polio Plus Committee
SET Max Movie/Special Events Channel
Shaadi.com Matrimonials
Starbucks Creative
Sunrisers Group Campaign: "Rise Up to Every Challenge, IPL"
Tata AIA Life Insurance
Thomas Cook Campaign: "Surprisingly Swift Money Transfers"
Timex Group India Ltd. Campaign: "Floating Bed"
Unilever Campaign: "Rin Eraser"
Univercell Campaign: "Goodbye in Homam"

J. Walter Thompson

26 Ethiraj Salai, Egmore, Chennai, 600 008 India
Mailing Address:
Bag No. 1401, Chennai, 600 008 India
Tel.: (91) 44 4292 9600
Fax: (91) 44 4292 9701
E-Mail: anita.gupta@jwt.com
Web Site: www.jwt.com

Employees: 60
Year Founded: 1955

Bindu Sethi *(Chief Strategy Officer-India)*
Mythili Chandrasekar *(Sr VP & Exec Dir-Plng-JWT Delhi)*
M. L. Raghavan *(VP & Gen Mgr-JWT Chennai)*
Shujoy Dutta *(VP & Exec Dir-Plng)*
Ayan Chakraborty *(VP & Dir-Client Svcs)*
Rinku Roy Choudhury *(VP & Dir-Strategic Plng)*
Divya Sharma *(Asst VP & Dir-Strategic Plng)*
Bhaskar Thakur *(Asst VP & Dir-Strategic Plng)*
Sonia Bhatnagar *(Exec Dir-Creative)*
Nilakshi Medhi *(Acct Plng Dir)*
Kamakshi Thareja *(Acct Plng Dir)*
Varun Kalkal *(Dir-Brand Strategy)*

Accounts:
Bennett, Coleman & Co. Campaign: "God's Own Delivery Boys"
CavinKare Creative
Chettinad Hospital
Ethical Nutrients Ironmax
G R Thanga Maligai Jewellery
Gallop Campaign: "Spirit Of Sport"
GlaxoSmithKline Consumer Healthcare Ltd Horlicks Chocolate
GRT Radisson Hotels
New-Info Edge India
K7 Computing 360-Degree Communications, Brand Positioning, Creative
MRF
Nippon Paint
Orient Electricals Orient AC
Peta
Rexine House
RmKV Silks Creative
Sun Group 360-Degree Multimedia Campaign, Indian Premier League
The Times of India Campaign: "Naaka Mukka-A

Day In The Life Of Chennai"
Univercell
Yalla Yall Burqa

J. Walter Thompson
30 Bondel Road, Kolkata, 700 019 India
Tel.: (91) 33 2282 8361
Fax: (91) 33 2287 7545
E-Mail: raji.ramaswamy@jwt.com
Web Site: www.jwt.com

Year Founded: 1934

Raji Ramaswamy *(Sr VP & Mng Partner-JWT Kolkata)*
Pinaki Bhattacharya *(VP & Exec Dir-Plng)*
Rinku Roy Choudhury *(VP & Dir-Strategic Plng)*
Rohit Sharma *(VP & Exec Bus Dir)*
Hanoz Mogrelia *(Exec Dir-Creative-Radiant-Global)*
Sumonto Ghosh *(Sr Dir-Creative)*
Jatishankar Bhowmik *(Art Dir)*
Megha Manchanda *(Acct Plng Dir)*
Urmi Roy *(Acct Exec)*
Anurag Acharya *(Copywriter)*
Arjun Mukherjee *(Sr Creative Dir)*

Accounts:
Aditya Birla Group
New-Atletico de Kolkata Creative, Digital, Merchandising, Outdoor, Print
Berger Paints (India) Limited
Bharti Telemedia
Birla Motor Insurance
Exide Industries Exide, Standard Furukawa
New-Getit Infoservices
Godrej & Boyce
Godrej Security Solutions Break in, Campaign: "Guest on Lunch", Godrej Sizzle, Metal Bank, Museum, Pension, Will
Hamdard Laboratories Pvt Ltd Creative, RoohAfza, Safi, Suvalin
Hero Cycles Campaign: "Baisakhi", Campaign: "Boyfriend"
Hero Honda Motors Ltd
ITC Ltd
Ivy League
Khaitan Fans
Khaitan India Ltd Campaign: "Fruits"
Konark Cement Campaign: "Seesaw"
Mayur Ply Campaign: "Office"
Nestle Kit Kat
Nokia Asha 311, Nokia X
Nutribic
P.C.Chandra Jewellers Pvt. Ltd.
The Peerless Inn
Pepsico India Holdings Ltd Campaign: "Tattooo Quiz", Campaign: "Tongue Twister", Kurkure, Mirinda Orange, Orange Mango, Orange Masala, Slice
Rotary Club International
Sony Max
South City Projects Ltd
Tata Chemicals Ltd
Tea Board of India Creative
New-Turtle
Wonder Cement Campaign: "Ek Perfect Shuruat"
Zovi.com

J. Walter Thompson
9th Floor Embassy Heights 13 Magrath Road, Bengaluru, 560 025 India
Tel.: (91) 80 42612100
Fax: (91) 80 42612249
E-Mail: dhunji.wadia@jwt.com
Web Site: www.jwt.com

Employees: 85
Year Founded: 1929

Himanshu Saxena *(Pres-JWT Group)*
Vigyan Verma *(VP & Client Svcs Dir)*
Divya Khanna *(VP & Dir-Strategic Plng)*
Priya Shivakumar *(Exec Dir-Creative)*
Sumonto Ghosh *(Sr Dir-Creative)*
Senthil Kumar *(Dir-Natl Creative-JWT India)*
Akshay Shetty *(Supvr-Creative)*

Accounts:
Airtel
Black Dog
BSA Foldman
Ford Endeavour
ING Vysya Bank
Kingfisher
Levi's
Lifestyle Campaign: "Lifestyle Baddie Bags", Campaign: "StylePlay"
Nike Campaign: "Make Every Yard Count", Campaign: "Parallel Journeys"
Times of India
Titan Industries Creative
Univercell Campaign: "Keep Your Number.Change Your Network."
VDot
Whyte & Mackay Dalmore, Isle of Jura, Whyte & Mackay Scotch

Indonesia

J. Walter Thompson
Jalan Proklamasi No 46, Jakarta, 10320 Indonesia
Tel.: (62) 21 310 0367
Fax: (62) 21 314 4292
Web Site: www.jwt.com

Year Founded: 1972

National Agency Associations: PPPI

Lulut Asmoro *(Pres)*
Ivan Hady Wibowo *(Exec Dir-Creative)*
Jonathan Nata *(Art Dir)*
Leonard Wiguna *(Dir-Art)*
Adam Pamungkas *(Assoc Dir-Creative)*
Rasus Subarkah *(Acct Mgr)*
Astrid Anggawirya *(Copywriter)*

Accounts:
ACE Hardware Indonesia Campaign: "Playing Ipad"
American Standard Above-the-Line, Digital
Bahtera Cipta Raga Prima
Bayer Indonesia Osteoporosis Awareness
Box Inovasi Indonesia Campaign: "Commitment"
Ford Indonesia Campaign: "Wedding", Ford Fiesta
Iabri Campaign: "Life Changing Donation Box"
Indosat IM3, Matrix, Mentari
KPAI
Krisbow
Krisview Campaign: "No More Blind Pots"
Kruha Water That Kills
Leuch'Tech
Nokia Campaign: "Morning, Day, Night", GPS, Nseries
Perwatusi Campaign: "Osteocessories By Perwatusi"
Phapros
Pt Ace Hardware Indonesia Campaign: "Playing Ipad"
Pt Box Inovasi Indonesia Campaign: "Commitment"
Sara Lee Indonesia Dranex Drain Cleaner
Seitenbacher Musli Cereal
Wwf Campaign: "Cycle For Life"
Yamaha Motorcycles Outdoor Media, Print, Radio, TV

Japan

J. Walter Thompson Japan
Yebisu Garden Place Tower 30th Floor 4-20-3 Ebisu, Shibuya-ku, Tokyo, 150 6030 Japan
Tel.: (81) 3 3280 9500
Fax: (81) 3 3280 7104
Web Site: www.jwt.com/japan

Employees: 140
Year Founded: 1956

Hironobu Kitajima *(Mng Dir)*
Takumi Ichihara *(Gen Mgr)*
Keizo Mugita *(Sr Dir-Creative)*
Kumiko Ohashi *(Sr Dir-Plng)*
Hironaga Yai *(Sr Dir-Plng)*
Marco Koeder *(Bus Dir-Digital)*
Tomohiko Nakano *(Producer-Creative)*
Shizuka Aizawa *(Dir-Creative)*
Akira Sato *(Dir-Creative)*
Shinsuke Sawasaki *(Dir-Creative)*
Hiroaki Shinkai *(Dir-Creative)*
Keita Fukumoto *(Supvr-HR Grp)*
Kohei Kawasaki *(Sr Creative Dir)*

Accounts:
Aero
Aflac Creative
Diageo Kirin Company Limited
Disney Entertainment
DTC
HSBC
Jack Daniels
Jaguar
Johnson & Johnson
Kellogg Company
Mondelez International, Inc. Parmesan Cheese
Nestle Japan
Rolex
Schick Japan Campaign: "Schick Unplugged"
Suntory
Taylormade
Unilever Lux

Korea

J. Walter Thompson Korea
8F JS Tower 144 20 Samsung-dong, Kangnam-gu, Seoul, 135-090 Korea (South)
Tel.: (82) 2 3148 3600
Fax: (82) 2 3148 3601
E-Mail: eunkung.an@jwt.com
Web Site: www.jwt.com

Employees: 31
Year Founded: 1989

Junghwan Kim *(Mng Dir)*
Unju Terry Rah *(Acct Dir)*
Saerom Hong *(Acct Mgr)*

Accounts:
EBay
Google
Kellogg Campaign: "Jeans Donation Box"
Nike
The North Face Campaign: "Exploring Seoul"
PAYCO (Agency of Record)
Vidal Sassoon

Malaysia

J. Walter Thompson
Level 6 Wismean Anta Jalan Changtat Senantan, Damansara Heights, Kuala Lumpur, 50490 Malaysia
Tel.: (60) 3 271 06688
Fax: (60) 3 271 06616

Employees: 60
Year Founded: 1975

Nicole Tan *(Mng Dir)*
Andrea Ma *(Grp Acct Dir)*
Alvin Edison *(Dir-Art)*
Nixon Lee *(Dir-Digital Integration-JWT Digital Malaysia)*

Hasnah Mohammed Samidin *(Dir-Creative)*
Eugene Nyam *(Assoc Acct Dir)*

Accounts:
Dutch Lady Milk Industries Berhad Campaign: "Womb Scan"
FindIt Malaysia (Agency of Record) Digital, Social Media
Ford Campaign: "Fiesta Wheel Of Fortune", Ford Mondeo
Scott Kitchen Towels
YTL Communications 4G Mobile Internet Network

Myanmar

Mango Marketing Services Company Ltd.
No 51 C Golden Valley Street Golden Valley Ward 2 Bahan Tsp, Yangon, Myanmar
Tel.: (95) 1523338
Fax: (95) 1512884
E-Mail: info@mango.com.mm
Web Site: www.jwt.com/mangomarketing

Agency Specializes In: Advertising, Event Planning & Marketing, Media Buying Services, Media Planning, Radio, T.V.

Lynn Lynn Tin Htun *(Mng Dir)*
Khin Thet Khaing *(Gen Mgr)*
Alyssa Rogier *(Acct Dir)*
Soe Moe Kyaw *(Asst Dir-Art)*
May Mon Thu *(Acct Mgr-PR)*
Swan Htet *(Mgr-Media)*
Htoo Htoo *(Acct Exec)*
Thaw Tar *(Acct Exec)*
Rani Robelus *(Copywriter)*

Accounts:
Dagon Brewery Co., Ltd. Meat Mfr

New Zealand

J. Walter Thompson International
The Axis Bldg CNR 91 St Georges Bay & Cleveland Roads, Parnell, Auckland, New Zealand
Mailing Address:
PO Box 2566, Auckland, New Zealand
Tel.: (64) 9 379 9625
Fax: (64) 9 357 0825
E-Mail: nz.info@jwt.com
Web Site: www.jwt.co.nz

Employees: 35
Year Founded: 1976

Agency Specializes In: Direct Response Marketing, Public Relations

Simon Lendrum *(Mng Dir-New Zealand)*
Jacqueline Smart *(Head-Plng)*
Rod Prosser *(Sr Dir-Art)*
Lisa Aalton *(Sr Acct Dir)*
Jo Simpson *(Sr Acct Dir)*
Mariona Wesselo-Comas *(Dir-Art)*
Jordan Young *(Dir-Art)*
Natalie Allen *(Sr Acct Mgr)*
Sam Dickson *(Copywriter)*
Mike Ramsay *(Copywriter-New Zealand)*

Accounts:
Contact Energy Creative, Retail, Strategic Counsel
Ford Campaign: "Ford Fiesta Cross Stitch", Campaign: "Paseengers"
HSBC
Kellogg's
Trade Me Jobs Campaign: "Family Names"

Pakistan

J. Walter Thompson
4th Floor Executive Tower Dolmen City, Marine Drive, Karachi, Sindh 75600 Pakistan
Tel.: (92) 21 569 3401
Fax: (92) 21 568 8444
Web Site: www.jwt.com

Year Founded: 1963

Imran Afzal *(CEO)*
Omer Yousuf Murad *(CFO & Dir-WPP Mktg Comm)*
Adil Muhammad *(Grp Head-Creative)*
Syed Shakeel Hasan *(Exec Dir-Creative)*
Tahir Yousuf *(Grp Acct Dir)*
Fakhar Abdullah *(Acct Dir)*
Mariam Keeriyo *(Acct Dir)*
Zulqarnain Afzal *(Dir-Creative)*
Fawad Parvez Fazli *(Dir-Plng & Digital)*
Sarah Moquim *(Dir-Creative)*
Kiran Yazdani *(Assoc Dir-Creative)*
Shams Mansur *(Copywriter)*

Accounts:
EPOS E-Commerce, easestore.com
Geo TV
Ideas By Gul Ahmed Creative
Vaseline Creative

Philippines

J. Walter Thompson
7th F Equitable Bank Tower 8751 Paseo de Roxas, Salcedo Village, Makati, 1227 Philippines
Tel.: (63) 2 864 8560
Fax: (63) 2 884 8563
E-Mail: maggie.madayag@jwt.com
Web Site: www.jwt.com

Employees: 55
Year Founded: 1947

Carol Pe Benito *(Head-Print & Mgr-Studio-Manila)*
Dave Ferrer *(Exec Dir-Creative)*
Drea Dizon *(Art Dir)*
Golda Roldan *(Dir-Client Svc)*
Boyet Custodio *(Assoc Dir-Creative-JWT Manila)*
Brian Lontok *(Acct Mgr)*
Maan Bautista *(Sr Copywriter-Manila)*
Kaye Matriano *(Copywriter)*
Bob Cruz *(Assoc Creative Dir)*

Accounts:
Bayer Philippines Campaign: "Concert"
Berlitz
Del Monte Foods, Inc.
Edgewell Personal Care Schick
Ford
GNC Live Well Campaign: "Swamp", Campaign: "Wine Bottle"
McNEIL-PPC, Inc.
Mondelez International Campaign: "Unsilent Night"
Sunsilk
Unilever Cream Silk
Zain

Singapore

J. Walter Thompson Singapore
50 Scotts Rd Unit 01-01, Singapore, 228242 Singapore
Tel.: (65) 6880 5088
Fax: (65) 6227 8183
Web Site: www.jwt.com

Employees: 90
Year Founded: 1978

Peter Womersley *(CEO)*
Sapna Srivastava *(Chief Talent Officer-JWT Asia Pacific)*
Michael Maedel *(Pres-JWT Asia Pacific)*
Jordan Price *(Exec Dir-Strategic Plng & Head-Plng Dept)*
Selwyn Low *(Grp Head-Creative)*
Gayle Lim *(Creative Dir)*
Leon Traazil *(Acct Dir)*
Alan Leong *(Dir-Creative)*
Chiao Woon Lim *(Dir-Creative)*
Thomas Ong *(Dir-Bus Dev)*
Lynette Chua *(Sr Acct Mgr)*
Khoo Kai Qi *(Acct Mgr)*
Tay Guan Hin *(Reg Exec Dir-Creative)*

Accounts:
Association of Women for Action & Research Campaign: "The Guardian Angel "
Bayer Berocca
Changi Airport Group Brand & Tactical Communications, Creative, Social Media, Websites
Fourtrimesters Campaign: "Tissue Card"
Friso Digital Out-of-Home Campaign, Social Media
Hewlett Packard Asia Pacific Campaign: "This Isn't a Banner"
The Hongkong & Shanghai Banking Corporation HSBC
Icm Pharma Campaign: "Victory At The Commode"
Johnson & Johnson Listerine
Mizmor Campaign: "Table Of Cloth"
Nestle Kit Kat
Nikon Singapore Creative
Pizza Hut Creative
Screening Room Campaign: "King Kong", Campaign: "Where Food Meets Film"
Singapore Economic Development Board
Singapore Tourism Board Creative
TEDx Campaign: "Bright Ideas", Campaign: "Bulb"
Unilever Campaign: "Fragrance Sticks", Campaign: "Magic Shower Rooms", Cream Silk, Lux, Radiant, Sunsilk
Vue Privee Campaign: "Window Paintings"

Taiwan

J. Walter Thompson
11F No. 35, Lane 11 GuangFu N. Rd, Taipei, 105 Taiwan
Tel.: (886) 2 3766 1000
Fax: (886) 2 2766 3298
Web Site: www.jwt.com/taipei

Employees: 100
Year Founded: 1988

Agency Specializes In: Above-the-Line, Advertising, Advertising Specialties, Automotive, Consumer Goods, Digital/Interactive, Event Planning & Marketing, Shopper Marketing

Evan Teng *(Mng Dir-Taipei)*
I-Fei Chang *(Exec Dir-Creative-Taipei)*
Ian Chen *(Grp Dir-Creative-Taipei)*
Maurice Huang *(Dir-Digital-Taipei)*
K. S. Yeh *(Dir-Creative-Taipei)*

Accounts:
AIA Group Creative
ASO Creative
FamilyMart Coffee; 2010
Ford Motor Ford
HB Realty
Kengyih Campaign: "The Tallest FB X'mas Tree", Flowers
Kespri New Zealand Kiwi Fruit
Kimberly-Clark Kleenex
Kuai-Kuai
Sakura
Simple Beauty Plastic Surgery Clinic Campaign: "Family Portrait - Suits"
Win Sing Development Campaign: "Bamboo"

Thailand

J. Walter Thompson Thailand
591 19/F UBC 2 Bldg Sukhumvit 33 Road, Klongton Nua Wattana, Bangkok, 10110 Thailand
Tel.: (66) 2 204 8000
E-Mail: chanintorn.sinwat@jwt.com
Web Site: www.jwt.com

E-Mail for Key Personnel:
Creative Dir.: pinit.chantaprateep@jwt.com

Year Founded: 1983

Ratchanida Nakpresha *(CFO)*
Bob Hekkelman *(CEO-Southeast Asia-Bangkok)*
Satit Jantawiwat *(Exec Dir-Creative)*
Chaowalek Julaketpotichai *(Sr Dir-Art)*
Mark Webster *(Reg Dir-Bus Dev)*
Torsak Cheunprapar *(Creative Dir)*
Charnpanu Suchaxaya *(Art Dir)*
Supachai Toemtechatpong *(Creative Dir)*
Sittichai Okkararojkij *(Assoc Dir-Creative)*
Parinyaporn Srangsomwong *(Acct Mgr)*
Nopharit Dusadeedumkoeng *(Copywriter)*

Accounts:
3M Cushion Wrap Ceramic, Crystal, Marble
AIS 3G 2100
Bayer Healthcare Alka Seltzer, Birth Control
Bumrungrad International Hospital; 2008
Cadbury Adams Thailand Halls Mentholyptus
Carrefour; Thailand
European Food Public Company Campaign: "Pregnant "
Ford Sales & Service Thailand
Hair Max Shampoo
Inbisco Thailand Campaign: "Engineer"
Kit Kat
Kraft Food Thailand Campaign: "Earth God"
New-Mattel East Asia Hot Wheels
MK Suki; Thailand Restaurant Chain
O.P. Natural Product Co. Campaign: "Woman Society"
Pace; Thailand Property Development
Panasonic Lumix
Ruam Charoen Pattana Co. Campaign: "The Eyes"
The Siam Commercial Bank Campaign: "I Missed Already"
Siam Ocean World
SNP Trading Co.
Thai Airways International Creative, Thai Smile
Thai Asia Pacific Brewery Campaign: "Shoot the Music by Heineken", Campaign: "Tiger Bloody Ring"
TMB Bank Public Company Limited Campaign: "Last Day"
Top Charoen Optical
WeChat

Austria

J. Walter Thompson Werbeagentur GmbH
Muthgasse 109, A-1190 Vienna, Austria
Tel.: (43) 1 93 9990
Fax: (43) 1 93 999 99
E-Mail: vienna@jwt.com
Web Site: www.jwt.com

Employees: 40
Year Founded: 1930

Andreas Schwarz *(Controller)*
Sabrina Saeuerl *(Dir-Fin)*

Accounts:
Allianz Campaign: "Live Banner"
Knorr
Nestle
Nokia
Osterreichische Sportwetten
Viva

Belgium

J. Walter Thompson Dialogue
86 Avenue Franklin Roosevelt, 1050 Brussels, Belgium
Tel.: (32) 2 890 90 00
Fax: (32) 2 890 90 99
Web Site: https://www.jwt.com/brussels

Employees: 25

Agency Specializes In: Corporate Communications, Web (Banner Ads, Pop-ups, etc.)

Johnny Baka *(CFO)*
Sabrina Munoz *(Acct Dir-Digital)*
Delphine Remy *(Acct Dir)*
Chris Rustin *(Acct Dir)*
Jean-Luc Walraff *(Dir-Creative)*
Muriel Degreef *(Office Mgr)*
Olivia Gathy *(Acct Mgr)*
Michel Scouflaire *(Mgr-IT & Sr Accountant)*

J. Walter Thompson
Avenue Franklin Roosevelt 86, B-1050 Brussels, Belgium
Tel.: (32) 2 775 0020
Fax: (32) 2 771 6005
E-Mail: jean-jacques.luycx@jwt.com
Web Site: www.jwt.com

Employees: 45
Year Founded: 1930

Jean-Jacques Luycx *(CEO)*
Xavier Caytan *(Mng Dir)*
Sabrina Munoz *(Acct Dir-Digital)*
Renaud Lavency *(Dir-Art)*
Jean-Luc Walraff *(Dir-Creative)*
Olivia Gathy *(Acct Mgr)*
Natalia Konovaloff *(Designer-Web)*

Accounts:
Nestle KitKat
UNHCR
Wilkinson

Bosnia & Herzegovina

Studio Marketing J. Walter Thompson
Cobanija 20, 71000 Sarajevo, Bosnia & Herzegovina
Tel.: (387) 33 265 600
Fax: (387) 33 200 739
E-Mail: info@smjwt.ba
Web Site: www.sm-studiomarketing.com

Employees: 10

Minka Gazibara *(Gen Mgr)*
Haris Radzo *(Gen Mgr)*

Accounts:
Nestle
Samsung

Bulgaria

Huts J. Walter Thompson Sofia
Iztok District 14 B Charles Darwin Street, 1113 Sofia, Bulgaria
Tel.: (359) 2 971 7182
Fax: (359) 2 971 7178
E-Mail: info@hutsjwt.com
Web Site: www.hutsjwt.com

Employees: 40
Year Founded: 1994

Alexander Petrov *(Client Svc Dir & Gen Mgr)*
Galina Troeva *(Gen Mgr)*
Maria Bikova *(Dir-Creative)*
Tatyana Kuchinova *(Dir-Plng & New Bus)*
Sashka Sashova *(Dir-Strategic Plng & Bus Acceleration)*

Accounts:
Bayer OTC
Clinique
Everbel
Grazia
Jacobs 3in1
Jacobs Monarch
Maxim
Nestle Confectionery Brands
Nestle Ice Cream Brands
Nova Brasilia Coffee
Oriflame
Peshterska Rakia
Playboy
Savex
Semana
Shell
Teo Bebe
Vodafone

Croatia

Studio Marketing J. Walter Thompson
Draskoviceva 5, HR-10000 Zagreb, Croatia
Tel.: (385) 1 4628 333
Fax: (385) 1 4628 340
E-Mail: smjwt@smjwt.hr
Web Site: www.sm-studiomarketing.com/en

Employees: 15
Year Founded: 1998

Ivana Palatinus *(Gen Mgr)*

Accounts:
Fructal

Denmark

J. Walter Thompson Copenhagen
(Formerly Halbye Kaag J. Walter Thompson)
Toldbodgade 55, 1253 Copenhagen, Denmark
Tel.: (45) 3332 6031
Fax: (45) 3332 6041
E-Mail: thomas.thorstholm@jwt.com
Web Site: jwt.dk

Employees: 40
Year Founded: 1967

Kasper Heumann Kristensen *(CFO)*
Rasmus Petersen *(Sr Dir)*
Lasse Hinke *(Art Dir)*
Jesper Lykke *(Client Svcs Dir)*
Annette Pryce *(Client Svcs Dir)*
David Asmussen *(Dir-Creative)*
Rasmus Sanko *(Dir-Digital)*

Accounts:
Adventuredk
Danish Cancer Society & Trygfonden Campaign: "Elephant Bikini"
DFDS
Hamley's
Mazda Denmark Campaign: "Open House"
Quiksilver

Finland

J. Walter Thompson

Itanerenkatu 1, 00180 Helsinki, Finland
Tel.: (358) 9 8562 6200
Fax: (358) 9 8562 6214
E-Mail: jean.gallen@jwt.com
Web Site: www.jwt.com

E-Mail for Key Personnel:
President: jean.gallen@jwt.fi

Year Founded: 1964

National Agency Associations: MTL

Jarno Varis *(Dir-Creative)*
Sara Varjoranta *(Copywriter)*

Accounts:
Aino
Bepanthol
Berocca
Blue1
Canesten
Classic
Dumle
Muru
Nokia
Pingviini
Rolex
Shell
Stora Enso
SunSilk
Superpops
Unilever Foodsolutions
WWF

France

J. Walter Thompson France
88 Avenue Charles de Gaulle, 92200 Neuilly-sur-Seine, Cedex France
Tel.: (33) 1 41 05 80 00
Fax: (33) 1 41 05 80 01
E-Mail: jwt.france@jwt.com
Web Site: www.jwt.com

Employees: 150
Year Founded: 1928

National Agency Associations: AACC

Agency Specializes In: Advertising

Claude Chaffiotte *(CEO)*
Anne-Cecile Tauleigne *(Exec Dir-Creative)*
Cindy Manautou *(Sr Dir-Art)*
Julien Chesne *(Dir-Art)*
Julien Foulatier *(Dir-Creative)*
Thierry Brioul *(Sr Copywriter-Adv & Digital)*
Thomas Blanc *(Copywriter)*

Accounts:
13e Rue TV
AIDES Campaign: "Sexy Fingers"
Bepanthen
BMW Series 1
Calzaturificio Buttero
Daily Tattoo
Galileo GPS
Hawaiian Tropic Campaign: "More Protection"
Lipton
Nestle Campaign: "Crunch Pulls Norman Out Of His Room", Extreme Chocolate Crisp Ice Cream, Kit Kat
Reporters Without Borders Campaign: "Cyber-Tag"
Rolex
Timotei
Wilkinson Quattro Love Needs A Bit of Upkeep

Germany

J. Walter Thompson GmbH
Schwedlerstrasse 6, 60314 Frankfurt am Main, Germany
Mailing Address:
PO Box 111911, 60054 Frankfurt, Germany
Tel.: (49) 69 405 76 0
Fax: (49) 69 405 764 14
E-Mail: jwtffm@jwt.com
Web Site: www.jwt.com

Employees: 100
Year Founded: 1952

Bernd Adams *(Mng Dir)*
Ingo Sanchez *(Mng Dir)*
Wolfgang Zimmerer *(Mng Dir)*
Eddy Greenwood *(Exec Dir-Creative)*
Mark Karatas *(Exec Dir-Creative)*
Pedro Americo *(Sr Dir-Art)*
Annette Endrass *(Dir-HR-JWT Germany)*
Danyel Kassner *(Dir-Art)*
Laura Cuenca Fernandez *(Copywriter)*

Accounts:
Economic Development Board Singapore Campaign: "Wrong Side of the Road Driving School"
Hinz & Kunzt Campaign: "Cardboards against Homelessness", Streetmagazine
Isabel Schwartau Campaign: "Cardboard Ambient Posters"
Kraft Foods Deutschland Campaign: "Really Stimulating Coffee"
Love Rocks Campaign: "Neck"
Mazda Campaign: "Heightened Senses"
Nestle Campaign: "Advent Calendar", Campaign: "Kit Kat Traffic Break Experiment", Kit Kat

Hungary

J. Walter Thompson Budapest
(Formerly Partners/JWT Budapest)
Revesz 27-29, 1123 Budapest, Hungary
Tel.: (36) 1488 0500
Fax: (36) 1488 0501
E-Mail: cskiss@partnersjwt.hu
Web Site: www.jwt.com

E-Mail for Key Personnel:
Creative Dir.: TaFarago@partnersjwt.hu

Year Founded: 1992

Agency Specializes In: Advertising, Digital/Interactive, Guerilla Marketing

Ildiko Tollasi *(Mng Dir)*
Vince Pataky *(Head-Digital)*
Tamas Farago *(Dir-Creative)*
Tunde Csapo *(Acct Mgr)*

Accounts:
New-Hungary Government

Ireland

DDFH&B Advertising Ltd.
3 Christ Church Square, Dublin, 8 Ireland
Tel.: (353) 141 066 66
Fax: (353) 141 066 99
E-Mail: ddfhbinfo@ddfhb.ie
Web Site: www.ddfhb.ie

Employees: 90
Year Founded: 1983

Jim Donnelly *(Chm)*
Miriam Hughes *(Grp CEO)*
Gavin O'Sullivan *(Partner-Creative)*
Vanessa Carswell *(Grp Acct Dir)*
Fiona Byrne *(Acct Dir)*
Roisin Keown *(Dir-Creative & Copywriter)*
Ronnie Trouton *(Dir-Creative)*
Sarah Wood *(Dir)*
Emma Kavanagh *(Sr Acct Exec)*
Mick Loftus *(Copywriter)*

Accounts:
Aero
Dublin City Council Campaign: "Dublin Icons", Campaign: "Inner City Illegal Dumping", Campaign: "Rubbish Dumping", DCC P.O.T.I
eircom Limited Campaign: "Horizon"
Google Campaign: "10 years in Ireland"
IAPI ADFX
New-Littlewoods Ireland Autumn & Winter Campaign
Lucozade
Mazda
Millionaire Raffle
Mondelez International, Inc.
National Lottery Campaign: "Missing"
Nestle
Nokia
SuperValu Advertising, Campaign: "Good Food Karma", Digital, Press, Social Media, TV
Unilever
Vichy
Wilkinson Sword

Italy

J. Walter Thompson Milan
Via Lomazzo 19, 20154 Milan, Italy
Tel.: (39) 02 33634 1
Fax: (39) 02 33634 400
E-Mail: milan.reception@jwt.com
Web Site: www.jwt.com/italy

Employees: 100
Year Founded: 1951

Agency Specializes In: Advertising

Enrico Dorizza *(Chief Creative Officer & Exec VP)*
Sergio Rodriguez *(Chief Creative Officer & Exec VP)*
Flavio Mainoli *(Exec Dir-Creative)*
Daniela Radice *(Exec Dir-Creative)*
Paolo Cesano *(Dir-Creative)*
Massimiliano Traschitti *(Dir-Art)*
Luca Zamboni *(Dir-Creative)*
Antonio Codina *(Copywriter-Italy)*
Giovanna Curti *(Client Svc Dir)*
Valentina Salice *(Client Head)*

Accounts:
Barilla G. e R. F.lli Campaign: "The Man of the Mill"
Bayer Campaign: "Pin Up", Citrosodina Digestive Soda
Fitosonno
Heineken
New-Hotpoint
Huggies Newborn
Indesit Creative
Kraft Italia Campaign: "Live Exhibit Banner"
Lamborghini Campaign: "Hexagon Huracan"
Mazda Campaign: "The Purple Card"
Museo Nazionale del Fumetto
Nestle Campaign: "Break Time Friday", Campaign: "Design Break", Kit Kat
Onda Onlus Campaign: "Tags For Life"
Pam - Panorama Campaign: "Traps - Ocean"
UNA ONLUS Campaign: "HATE"
Wilkinson Sword Campaign: "Play Now"

J. Walter Thompson
Via del Commercio 36, 00154 Rome, Italy
Tel.: (39) 065 710 81
Fax: (39) 065 783 233
E-Mail: rome.reception@jwt.com
Web Site: www.jwt.com/italy

Employees: 50

Year Founded: 1951

Agency Specializes In: Advertising

Francesco Basile *(Sr Dir-Art)*
Nicoletta Cernuto *(Creative Dir)*
Enrico Giraudi *(Dir-Bus Dev-JWT Milan & Sr Planner-Strategic)*
Francesca Costanzo *(Acct Mgr)*
Francesco Muzzopappa *(Sr Copywriter)*
Antonio Codina *(Copywriter-Italy)*
cristiano nardo *(Copywriter)*

Accounts:
The English FunBus
New-Forevermark Limited
Johnson & Johnson Campaign: "Bungalow", Campaign: "Holidays"
Mazda Motor Italia Campaign: "Purple Card"
Seneca

Latvia

San Baltic J. Walter Thompson
(Formerly SAN Riga)
Tirgonu Str 8, LV-1050 Riga, Latvia
Tel.: (371) 721 5221
Fax: (371) 721 5224
E-Mail: welcome@san.lv

Year Founded: 1998

Mudite Krumina *(Mng Dir)*

Lithuania

J. Walter Thompson Lithuania San Vilnius
Pylimo Street 30/2, Lt-01135 Vilnius, Lithuania
Tel.: (370) 5 2333 520
Fax: (370) 5 2330 927
E-Mail: agencies@san.lt
Web Site: www.san.lt/lithuania

Employees: 10
Year Founded: 1998

Kristofers Sics *(Mng Dir)*
Sabina Daukantaite *(Grp Dir-Creative)*
Violeta Kalinauskiene *(Acct Dir)*
Tomas Jankauskas *(Dir-Creative)*
Sarune Susniene *(Acct Mgr)*
Danylo Torbovskyi *(Copywriter)*

Accounts:
New-Lithuanian State Symphony Orchestra
Nestle

Netherlands

Ubachswisbrun J. Walter Thompson
Rietlandpark 301, 1019 DW Amsterdam, Netherlands
Mailing Address:
PO Box 904, 1000 AX Amsterdam, Netherlands
Tel.: (31) 20 301 9696
Fax: (31) 20 301 9600
Web Site: jwt.amsterdam/en/home

Employees: 50
Year Founded: 1957

Agency Specializes In: Advertising

Rolf Wisbrun *(Mng Partner)*
Robert Harrison *(Publr-Creative Desktop)*
Jeena van der Heul *(Art Dir)*
Andreas Moller *(Acct Dir)*
Chris Sant *(Art Dir)*
Friso Ludenhoff *(Dir-Art & Copywriter)*
Agustin Soriano *(Dir-Strategy)*
Joep Drummen *(Copywriter)*
Guney Soykan *(Designer)*

Accounts:
Agis Health Insurance
Apollo Vredestein Tyres Global Creative
Assent
Bayer
Belangenbehartiging Amsterdamse Dak- en Thuislozen (BADT) Campaign: "A piggy bank for the homeless"
BMW BMWi3, Broadcast, Campaign: "Driving Pleasure Reinvented", Campaign: "Glance Back", Campaign: "Matchbox"
Bridgestone
Dutch Tax and Customs Administration Campaign: "Sea Lion"
New-Elan Languages
Gall & Gall
Gamma
ING Financial Services Campaign: "A Penny For Your Thoughts", Campaign: "What's It Going To Be?", Personal Property Insurance
MINI Campaign: "Dakar"
Ministerie Van Justitie Campaign: "Spreekwapens/Wordweapons"
Nationale Nederlanden Campaign: "Do Re Mi", Campaign: "In Love"
Nestle Campaign: "Guy In A Waiting Line", Campaign: "New Ipad Launch", Kit Kat
Nukuhiva "The Traceable Coat Hanger"
Opel Nederland Campaign: "500 Km"
PEFC Campaign: "Save The Green"
Shell
Top Gear Magazine
Unilever Campaign: "Baltimor Gold Race Champions"
Upc Nederland Campaign: "Glossy Newspaper Insert"

Poland

J. Walter Thompson Poland
Ul Zurawia 45, 00-680 Warsaw, Poland
Tel.: (48) 22 440 1200
Fax: (48) 22 440 1201
E-Mail: office@jwt.com.pl
Web Site: www.jwt.com/lemonskyjwalterthompsonpoland

Employees: 40
Year Founded: 1992

Daniel Swiatkowski *(Chief Innovation Officer)*
Agata Aniol *(Dir-Internal Quality)*
Pawel Jakubowski *(Dir-Strategy)*
Mariusz Pitura *(Dir-Creative)*
Gawel Podwysocki *(Mgr-Print Production & Studio DTP)*
Monika Lapczynska-Zygan *(Client Svc Dir)*

Accounts:
Bayer
Ben - Gay
Bepanthen
Biovital
Chipita
Halls
IKEA
Nestle Kit Kat
Nokia Campaign: "Around the World in 80 days", Campaign: "Around the world on one battery"
Polish Humanitarian Action Campaign: "1 Like, 1 Drop"
Rennie
Saga
Velvet

Portugal

J. Walter Thompson
Centro Cultural de Belem, Rua Bartolomeu Dias, 1449-003 Lisbon, Portugal
Tel.: (351) 21 413 8200
Fax: (351) 21 410 4574
Web Site: www.jwt.com

E-Mail for Key Personnel:
President: susana.decarvalho@jwt.com

Employees: 18
Year Founded: 1981

National Agency Associations: APAP (Portugal)

Agency Specializes In: Advertising

Susana de Carvalho *(CEO)*
Jorge Barrote *(Dir-Creative)*
Joao Oliveira *(Dir-Creative)*
Nuno Melo Da Silva *(Dir-Client Svc & Strategic Plng)*
Assuncao Albuquerque *(Client Svc Dir)*

Accounts:
CIN Woodtec
Exercito de Salvacao
Santa Casa Da Misericordia
Sumol
Vodafone Campaign: "Motocross", Campaign: "Supper"

Romania

Scala/J. Walter Thompson
Str Trotusului Nr 39 Sector 1, 012141 Bucharest, Romania
Tel.: (40) 121 224 1460
Fax: (40) 21 224 1461
E-Mail: plilana.slavascu@jwt.com

Year Founded: 1994

Mihaela Vacarus *(CFO)*

Serbia & Montenegro

Studio Marketing
Bul Arsenija Carnojevica 52/34, 11000 Belgrade, Serbia
Tel.: (381) 11 361 8383
Fax: (381) 11 2685 558
E-Mail: marko@smjwt.rs
Web Site: www.sm-studiomarketing.com

Year Founded: 1998

Nikola Jovanetic *(Dir-Art)*

Accounts:
Point cafe

Slovenia

Studio Marketing
Vojkova 50, SI-1000 Ljubljana, Slovenia
Tel.: (386) 1 589 6810
Fax: (386) 1 589 6862
E-Mail: info@smjwt.com
Web Site: www.sm-studiomarketing.com

E-Mail for Key Personnel:
President: jernej.repovs@smjwt.com

Employees: 30
Year Founded: 1973

Jernej Repovs *(Pres & Reg Dir-Creative)*
Tina Bolcar *(CEO-Studio Marketing JWT)*
Petra Ravnik *(Dir-Client Svc)*

Accounts:
Mazda

Spain

J. Walter Thompson
(Formerly Delvico)
La Palma # 10, 28004 Madrid, Spain
Tel.: (34) 91 592 3300
Fax: (34) 91 310 42 16
E-Mail: comunicacion@jwt.com
Web Site: www.jwt.com/#!/jwtspain

Employees: 150
Year Founded: 1971

National Agency Associations: AEAP

Agency Specializes In: Advertising

Jordi Palomar *(CEO-JWT Group Spain & JWT Madrid)*
Ugo Ceria *(Head-Strategy-JWT Spain, Nestle Ice Cream GBU & JWT Madrid)*
Jaime Chavarri *(Exec Dir-Creative)*
Alejandro Lobo *(Sr Dir-Art & Creative)*
Ivan de Dios *(Dir-Creative-Madrid)*
Paco Garcia *(Dir-Creative)*
Francesco Minopoli *(Dir-Art-Madrid)*
Alvaro Gonzalez *(Copywriter)*
Carolina Pineiro *(Copywriter)*

Accounts:
Amnesty International
Bodybell
Corona Campaign: "Drink Responsibly", Campaign: "It's On Me. No It's On Me.", Campaign: "Turtle", Django
La Ciudad de La Raqueta Campaign: "Ballrocking"
Nestle

J. Walter Thompson
Via Augusta 281 4a Planta, 08017 Barcelona, Spain
Tel.: (34) 93 413 1414
Fax: (34) 93 413 1415
E-Mail: contacto.barcelona@jwt.com
Web Site: www.jwt.com

E-Mail for Key Personnel:
Creative Dir.: alex.martinez@jwt.com

Employees: 25
Year Founded: 1966

Agency Specializes In: Communications

Jordi Palomar *(Chm & CEO)*
Alex Martinez *(Gen Dir-Creative)*
Jordi Iglesias *(Dir-Customer Svc)*
Javier Lores *(Dir-Art)*
Helena Marzo *(Dir-Creative)*
Oscar Galan *(Copywriter)*

Accounts:
Amnesty International Campaign: "Democracy", Chilean
Bayer Consumer Care Campaign: "Make a better choice", Priorin
Corona Extra
Diagonal Mar Shopping Centre Campaign: "The First Bag That Raises Your Self-Esteem"
Diagonal Mar Campaign: "Forest", Campaign: "The Sales Season is on"
Dunkin Campaign: "Coffee & DoNut Always together"
Freixenet Campaign: "Among the Bubbles", Global Positioning
Fundacion Ideas Campaign: "Customs"
Gmodelo Campaign: "Garbage Beach"
Unilever
Viajes Century Travel Agency Campaign: "Van Gogh"
World March for Peace

Switzerland

J. Walter Thompson Fabrikant
(Formerly JWT & Hostettler & Fabrikant)
Binzmuhlestrasse 170, CH-8050 Zurich, Switzerland
Mailing Address:
Postfach 8037, 8005 Zurich, Switzerland
Tel.: (41) 44 277 7111
Fax: (41) 44 277 7112
E-Mail: info@jwtf.ch
Web Site: www.jwtfabrikant.ch

Employees: 18
Year Founded: 1965

National Agency Associations: BSW

Agency Specializes In: Advertising

Remy Fabrikant *(CEO)*

Accounts:
Bayer
Deutsche Bank
Heineken
Kimberly Clark Campaign: "100% Recycling", Campaign: "See you later", Hakle
Kraft
Mazda Campaign: "Sumo"
Pink Cloud
Swiss People

Turkey

Manajans Thompson Istanbul
Buyukdere Cad Harman Sokak No 4 Kat 7 Levent, 80498 Istanbul, Turkey
Tel.: (90) 212 317 2000
Fax: (90) 212 282 6477
Web Site: www.manajans-jwt.com/

Employees: 75
Year Founded: 1964

Baran Gunes *(Grp Head-Creative)*
Firat Yildiz *(Grp Head-Creative)*
Ozlem Ozdemir *(Dir-Art)*
Pelin Karagoz *(Acct Supvr)*
Fulya Ozari *(Acct Supvr)*
Kaan Ertuz *(Deputy Dir-Creative-JWT ISTANBUL)*

Accounts:
Association of Shelter Volunteers & Animal Rights
Bayer
Bosch Campaign: "Obsession", Campaign: "Ride", IXO
Dockers
Levis
Mazda
Miller Brewery Campaign: "Miller Boombox"
Nokia
Rebul Perfume
Sarelle
Shell
TELE2
Turkcell
Ulker Musli Bar
Ulker
UNICEF Campaign: "3 Secs"
Wusthof Campaign: "Sliced Posters"

United Kingdom

Cheetham Bell
(Formerly Cheetham Bell/JWT)
Astley House Quay St, Manchester, M3 4AS United Kingdom
Tel.: (44) 161 832 8884
Fax: (44) 161 835 1436
Web Site: www.cheethambelljwt.com

E-Mail for Key Personnel:
Creative Dir.: andy.cheetham@jwt.com

Employees: 80
Year Founded: 1919

Agency Specializes In: Brand Development & Integration, Communications, Graphic Design, Retail

David Bell *(CEO)*
Steve McCarron *(Mng Dir)*
Liz Jacobs *(Grp Acct Dir)*
Martin Smith *(Creative Dir)*
Andy Huntingdon *(Dir-Creative)*
Jennie McBeath *(Dir-Bus Dev)*
Liz Hughes *(Acct Mgr)*

Accounts:
British Car Auctions
Dreams Creative
Jersey Telecom Campaign: "Mycool Bolt-On", Consumer Brands, Corporate Identity, Through the Line
John West Campaign: "Discover The Story Behind Every Can - Combover", Campaign: "Lucky Pete", Campaign: "The Clue Is The Name", Creative
La Redoute Advertising
Magnet Kitchens Campaign: "Find the beauty within", Social Media
Magnet
On the Beach Campaign: "Totally Beaching Holidays"
Siemens Home Appliances (Lead Creative Agency)
Taste Inc Campaign: "Wrestler"
Victoria Plumb

J. Walter Thompson
1 Knightsbridge Green, London, SW1X 7NW United Kingdom
Tel.: (44) 20 7656 7000
Fax: (44) 20 7656 7010
E-Mail: hello@jwt.com
Web Site: www.jwt.co.uk

Employees: 464
Year Founded: 1926

National Agency Associations: IAA

Agency Specializes In: Advertising

Toby Hoare *(CEO)*
Barry Christie *(Partner-Creative)*
Dave Dye *(Head-Art & Creative Dir)*
Christiano Neves *(Head-Integrated-Art & Dir-Creative)*
Ricardo Figueira *(Exec Dir-Creative-Digital-London)*
Pipo Virgos *(Sr Dir-Creative)*
Patrick Netherton *(Sr Acct Dir)*
Tom Ring *(Sr Acct Dir-JWT London)*
Jean-Louis Roche *(Reg Dir-Europe)*
Denise Connell *(Sr Producer-Brdcst)*
Anne Deane *(Acct Dir)*
Angus Flockhart *(Acct Dir-JWT London)*
Rebeca Hernandez *(Acct Dir)*
Matthew Hounsell *(Bus Dir-CRM)*
Phil Ridsdale *(Acct Dir)*
Ronnie Vlcek *(Art Dir)*
Doug Wade *(Producer-Brdcst)*
Alex Walker *(Acct Dir)*
Yoni Alter *(Dir-Art)*
Chris Bailey *(Dir-Plng-UK & EMEA-JWT London)*
Toby Clifton *(Dir-Integrated Production)*
Giles Hepworth *(Dir-Art)*
Alex Huzzey *(Dir-Plng)*
Anne McCreary *(Dir-Plng-Global)*
Gillian Milner *(Dir-Bus)*

Guy Murphy *(Dir-Plng-Worldwide)*
Adam Scholes *(Dir-Creative-London)*
Jaspar Shelbourne *(Dir-Global Creative)*
Simon Sworn *(Dir-Creative)*
Anna Hall *(Sr Acct Mgr-Global)*
Sophia Redgrave *(Sr Acct Mgr)*
Jessica Deakin *(Acct Mgr)*
Charlotte Humphries *(Acct Mgr)*
Alex Peacock *(Acct Mgr)*
Alex Ball *(Copywriter)*
Jonathan Budds *(Copywriter)*
Kat Thomas *(Copywriter)*

Accounts:
AB World Foods Campaign: "Put some Music in your Food", Campaign: "Young Spice", Patak's, Blue Dragon, Reggae Reggae Sauce
Age UK Campaign: "No Friends"
Alzheimer's Society
Anti-Slavery International Campaign: "Victorian Newspaper"
Apollo Tyres Global Creative
Army Reserve
Army Army Recruitment, Campaign: "Step Up", Creative
ASPIRE Campaign: "Andy's Story"
Bayer AG
Blue Dragon Campaign: "'Legendary Stir Fry", Campaign: "Make Your Stir Fry Legendary With Blue Dragon", Experiential, Shopper Marketing
Bridgestone Tyres Campaign: "Everywhere"
British Army Campaign: "Step Up", Digital Outdoor, Radio, Social Media, TV, Video-on-Demand
CADD Anti-Drunk Driving
Canon EMEA Campaign: "Come and See", Campaign: "Urban Deer", Creative, Digital, Online, Outdoor, Press
Care For The Wild Campaign: "Cat Aid", Campaign: "The Tooth Fairy", Donation Appeal
Carlsberg
COI IEA
Crowne Plaza Campaign: "You First", Print
De Beers Consolidated Mines Limited Campaign: "As One", Creative, Forevermark, TV
Debenhams Campaign: "Butterfly", Campaign: "Found it", Campaign: "Wishes Made Fabulous", Online, Radio, Social Media, TV
Diageo Smirnoff
Diesel Diesel Black Gold
Ed's Easy Diner Campaign: "Eat the 50s", Outdoor, Press
Energizer Uk Wilkinson Sword
First Direct Campaign: "Relaunch", Campaign: "Unexpected", Content, Creative, Digital, Outdoor, Press, Social Media, TV, campaign: "Little Frill"
New-GlaxoSmithKline plc
Google Inc.
HSBC Campaign: "150th Anniversary", Campaign: "British & Irish Lions Tour", Campaign: "Date", Campaign: "In The Future", Campaign: "Microdot", Campaign: "Serious Play - The Mint", Campaign: "The Pink Ladies", Campaign: "Wedding Present", Global Brand Marketing, HSBC Advance Bank, Lemon Grove, Retail, TV
InterContinental Hotels Group Campaign: "Secrets in the City", Creative, Insider Experiences, Marketing, Online, Print, Social Media
Johnson & Johnson Anusol, Benadryl, Benylin, Calpol, Campaign: "Feel Every Smile", Campaign: "Mouth Vs Life", Campaign: "Power To Your Mouth", Imodium, Listerine, Sudafed Olynth
Kenwood Campaign: "Leeks", Campaign: "What Do You See?", Chef, kMix
Kimberly-Clark Andrex, Kleenex
KPMG Global Creative
Kraft Foods Inc
Lastminute.com CRM
Legal & General Creative, Media
Lego Duplo
Live Life Then Give Life Campaign: "Falling in Love Again", Campaign: "Let Love Live On"
Microsoft Bing
Mondelez International Campaign: "Coffee vs Gangs", Campaign: "Dude, Where'S My Chicken?", Creative, Digital, Halls, Kenco, Philadelphia Cream Cheese, Public Relations, Strategic, TV
National Centre for Domestic Violence Campaign: "Drag Him Away", Campaign: "House Hunt", Hands
Nestle Aero, Rowntree's, Rolo, Yorkie, Milky Bar, Quality Street, Campaign: "Chunky Champion", Campaign: "Chunky Mail", Campaign: "Have A Break Have A Kit Kat", Campaign: "The First Sign of Christmas", Digital, Digital Marketing, Kit Kat, Outdoor, Quality Street, Radio, TV
Nokia Campaign: "Uv Box"
Premier Foods PLC Ambrosia, Best of Both, Billboard, Campaign: "Exceedingly Good Cakes", Campaign: "Life is Better With Cake", Campaign: "Now Tastes Even Better", Campaign: "Salvation Army", Campaign: "Snowball Fight", Campaign: "The Magic Cube", Campaign: "The Magic Touch", Creative, Halloween campaign, Mr. Kipling, Online, Oxo, Print, TV
RHM plc
Rimmel Digital
Rolex
Rolls Royce Engines
Seraphine Campaign: "Congratulations M'um", Campaign: "Is it a girl? Is it a boy?", Outdoor Campaign
Shell Campaign: "Supercars"; 2007
Suntory Holdings Ltd Campaign: "You can't get any more Ribenary", Marketing, Outdoor, Ribena, Social Media, Strategic, TV, Video-on-Demand
Territorial Army Campaign: "Caption at Work", Campaign: "Night Time Sangar Handover", Campaign: "The Apache", Campaign: "The Briefing"
Tilda Creative
Treasury Wine Estates Global Marketing, Marketing Communications, Marketing Strategy, Public Relations, Shopper Marketing
Unilever Campaign: "Hair Meet Wardrobe", LUX, Sunsilk, Timotei, Toni & Guy
Watkins Books Campaign: "Fenopalm"
WWF

Afghanistan

Altai Communications
House 733-124 St 4 Qala-e-Fatullah, Kabul, Afghanistan
Tel.: (93) 79 888 000
Web Site: www.altaiconsulting.com

Year Founded: 2004

Emmanuel De Dinechin *(Partner)*

Bahrain

J. Walter Thompson
502 Almoayyad Tower, Seef District, Manama, 18490 Bahrain
Tel.: (973) 17563700
Web Site: www.jwt.com

Year Founded: 2003

Vatche Keverian *(CEO-JWT MENA & JWT MEA)*
Adnan Al-Arrayed *(Dir)*
Susano Saguil *(Dir-Art)*
Samar Ameer *(Acct Mgr)*
Catherine Hughes *(Mgr-Strategic Plng-Bahrain)*

Accounts:
Kleenex

Egypt

J. Walter Thompson Cairo
306 Cornish El Nile, Maadi, 124 Cairo, Egypt
Mailing Address:
El Giza PO-Imbaba, PO Box 435, Imbaba, 12411 Cairo, Egypt
Tel.: (20) 225254740
Fax: (20) 225254740
Web Site: www.jwt.com/jwtcairo

Year Founded: 1987

Agency Specializes In: Advertising

Mohammed Sabry *(Mng Dir)*
Amal El Masri *(Chief Strategy Officer-JWT MEA)*
Ramsey Naja *(Chief Creative Officer-JWT MEA)*
Islam Serag *(Head-BTL & Sr Dir-Art)*
Sally Ghally *(Sr Dir-Art)*
Khaled Zaki *(Mgr-Content & Producer-TV)*
Shaimaa El Hout *(Acct Dir)*
Sherif Atef Gergis *(Dir-Fin)*
Nihal Nashed *(Acct Mgr-Kraft, Jawwal & Red Bull)*

Accounts:
Dolceca Ice Cream Campaign: "Aqua Mangos"
Egyptian Tourism Authority
Kraft Foods
Nestle Kimo Cono, Dolceca, Maxibon
OSN Terrible Accident
Red Bull
Vodafone Campaign: "Fakka", Campaign: "How to make small seem big"

Israel

J. Walter Thompson
6 Kremenetski Street, Tel Aviv, 67899 Israel
Tel.: (972) 3 623 1111
Fax: (972) 3 623 1100
E-Mail: liata@jwt.co.il
Web Site:
www.jwt.com/#!/en/network/israel/tel+aviv/jwtisrael

Employees: 100
Year Founded: 1995

Yoram Dembinsky *(CEO & Partner-Israel)*
Liav Gutstein *(Dir-Art)*
Shirly Engel *(Acct Exec)*
Noam Krauza *(Copywriter)*

Accounts:
Bissell Electra Campaign: "The Cheating Dog"
Materna
Orange
Subaru Forester

Kuwait

J. Walter Thompson
Wataniya Tower 10th Floor Fahed Al Salem Street, Daiya, 35454 Kuwait
Mailing Address:
PO Box 15363, Daiya, 35454 Kuwait
Tel.: (965) 2460234
Fax: (965) 2460231
E-Mail: karim.bitar@jwt.com
Web Site: www.jwt.com

Year Founded: 1987

Karim Bitar *(Mng Dir)*
Mazen Fayad *(Exec Dir-Creative)*

Accounts:
International Vegetarian Union
MTC Atheer
Nestle Campaign: "Car"
PETA

Taiba Hospital
World Food Programme Campaign: "Listen.Help"
Zain

Lebanon

J. Walter Thompson

47 Patriarch Howeiyek Street Sabbagh Bld 3rd Floor, Bab Idriss, 11-3093 Beirut, Lebanon
Tel.: (961) 1 973 030
Fax: (961) 1 972 929
E-Mail: pascale.khoury@jwt.com
Web Site: www.jwt.com

Employees: 80
Year Founded: 1987

Dikran Kalaydjian *(CFO)*
Mazen Khater *(CMO)*
Charly Wehbe *(Head-Digital, Channel & Tech Plng)*
Nicolas Geahchan *(Exec Dir-Creative)*
Maria Akmakji *(Sr Acct Dir)*
Marc Anthony Haddad *(Acct Dir-Levant)*
Randa Chehab *(Dir-Talent)*
Mohamed Kabbani *(Assoc Dir-Creative)*
Paola Mounla *(Assoc Dir-Creative)*
Christine Mardirian *(Coord-Talent)*

Accounts:
A&H Property Development
Amnesty International Chile Campaign: "Every Signature Makes It Harder"
Cadbury Adams Middle East
Depechemode Campaign: "605 Corporate Id"
Diageo Lebanon Campaign: "Double Trouble", Smirnoff Red
Fransabank
Heineken Brasserie Almaza, Campaign: "What's Christmas without Red and Green"
Le Mall
Mercedes
T.Gargour & Fils Campaign: "Unlock Beirut"
Touch Campaign: "My Plan", Creative

Syria

J. Walter Thompson

Shoshara Building Hilal Al Bizim Street, Malki, Damascus, Syria
Mailing Address:
PO Box 5566, Damascus, Syria
Tel.: (963) 11 373 5528
Fax: (963) 11 373 7924
Web Site: www.jwt.com

Employees: 20
Year Founded: 1995

Iyad Krayem *(Exec Dir)*
Susan Bazzi *(Dir-Media)*
Udai Al Jundi *(Mgr-Traffic)*
Oula Alayoubi *(Sr Accountant)*

Accounts:
Syria Duty Free

United Arab Emirates

J. Walter Thompson

Business Central Tower Block B 36 Rd, PO Box 202032, Media City, Dubai, United Arab Emirates
Mailing Address:
PO Box 4327, Dubai, United Arab Emirates
Tel.: (971) 4 369 8400
Fax: (971) 4 369 8401
Web Site: www.jwt.com

Employees: 150
Year Founded: 1987

Vatche Keverian *(CEO-Gulf)*
Chafic Haddad *(Exec Dir-Creative)*
Mahesh Powar *(Sr Dir-Art)*
Richard Hol *(Reg Dir-Creative)*
Rayyan Aoun *(Dir-Creative)*
Yulia Kurdina *(Sr Acct Mgr)*

Accounts:
Atlantis Atlantis The Palm
New-Coca-Cola
HSBC Campaign: "E-Greeting"
Johnson & Johnson
Kinokuniya Campaign: "Bookends"
Nestle Arabia Campaign: "Have a break. Have a KitKat.", Campaign: "Kit Kat-Boss", Campaign: "Silence Your Hunger"
Nike Sports Campaign: "Nike Sticker Wall"
Nokia Campaign: "Student Code Developer"
Pink Caravan
Polo Mints
Saudi Telecom Mobile
Suraya Foundation
The Times
Tunisiana Campaign: "Desert"

Argentina

J. Walter Thompson

Alsina 465, C1087 AAE Buenos Aires, Argentina
Tel.: (54) 1 1 4339 6100
Fax: (54) 1 1 4339 3675
Web Site: www.jwt.com

Employees: 100
Year Founded: 1929

Agency Specializes In: Advertising

Vanina Rudaeff *(CEO)*
James Evans *(CEO-BlueHive Europe)*
Gonzalo Vecino *(Exec Dir-Creative)*
Joaquin Ares *(Dir-Creative & Art, Copywriter)*
Fernando Bozzoletti *(Dir-Strategic Plng)*
Victoria Carrano *(Dir-Trademark)*
Juan Lodola *(Dir-Art)*
Luciano Griessi *(Copywriter)*
Sebastian Lombroni *(Copywriter)*

Accounts:
Abbott Campaign: "Speed up your mind.", Ensure Active M2
Air Brahma Brahma Beer
Alzas Bajas Magazine Campaign: "More Information, Less Risk"
Berocca Campaign: "#BeroccaMechanicalDesk"
The Coca-Cola Company Campaign: "Superheroes"
Conduciendo a Conciencia Campaign: "Drive Safely"
Editorial Conyuntura Campaign: "Hope"
Ejercito De Salvacion
Ford Campaign: "Ecosport Runner X", Campaign: "Strong Men", Ford Fiesta, Ford KA
HSBC Campaign: "Laptop"
L.A.L.C.E.C
Mercado Business Magazine Campaign: "Flags - China-India", Campaign: "The world is a hard place to understand."
Mondelez International, Inc. Campaign: "Birds", Gum, Halls Creamy, Halls XS
Nestle Campaign: "Site Mixer", Campaign: "The Rackelitas"
Salvation Army Mr. Love

Brazil

J. Walter Thompson

Rua Mario Amaral 50, Paraiso, 04002-20 Sao Paulo, SP Brazil
Tel.: (55) 11 3888 8000
Fax: (55) 11 3887 0173
Web Site: www.jwt.com/brasil

Year Founded: 1929

Agency Specializes In: Advertising

Fernand Alphen *(Chief Strategy Officer)*
Ezra Geld *(CEO-Brazil)*
Marcia Lacaze *(Head-Brdcst-Brazil)*
Vico Benevides *(Exec Creative Dir)*
Enoch Lan *(Exec Dir-Creative)*
Vitor Veras *(Sr Dir-Interactive Art)*
Waldemar Cardozo *(Art Dir)*
Filipe Cuvero *(Art Dir)*
Felipe Giacon *(Acct Dir)*
Marcelo Mariano *(Creative Dir)*
Pedro Ricci *(Art Dir)*
Santiago Dulce *(Dir-Creative-Brazil)*
Rodolfo Garcia *(Dir-Art)*
Ricardo Marques *(Dir-Creative)*
Daniel Massih *(Dir-Creative & Art)*
Marcelo Monzillo *(Dir-Art)*
Hernan Rebalderia *(Dir-Creative)*
Erick Rosa *(Dir-Creative)*
Diego Vieira *(Dir-Art)*
Rafael Hessel *(Copywriter)*
Caio Lekecinskas *(Copywriter)*
Gabriel Morais *(Copywriter)*
Lucas Tristao *(Copywriter)*
Julia Velo *(Copywriter)*
Yves Rodrigues *(Reg Acct Supvr)*
Hiroito Takahashi *(Jr Editor)*

Accounts:
91 Rock 91 Rock Clock, Campaign: "Deaths", Campaign: "Vocals"
AC Camargo Hospital Campaign: "Anti Cancer Paste Up", Campaign: "The Running Finger", Campaign: "The Unexpected Choir", Super-Powerful Campaign, Superformula
AfroReggae Campaign: "Electric Pee", Campaign: "Putting Favelas On The Map"
Alcoholics Anonymous Campaign: "The Crash Cooler"
Alpino
Bayer Argentina S.A. Bepantol, Campaign: "Ballet Dancer X Dog", Supradyn Vitamins
Bon Vivant Grater Card
Buzina Gourmet Food Truck
Cadbury Adams
Cadence
Coca-Cola Refreshments USA, Inc. Campaign: "A Bridge for Santa", Campaign: "Goals", Campaign: "Magazine Amplifier", Campaign: "Women Cry For Everything"
Costume House Campaign: "Mask Up"
Diageo Smirnoff
Editora Brasileira Pele 70
Florecer Ngo Campaign: "Tomorrow in a Box"
Ford Campaign: "Fairy Tale", Campaign: "Ford Ecosport Wearble Calendar", Campaign: "Ford-Reading Your Mind", Campaign: "Ogres"
Gapa
Gazeta Mercantil
Gomes Da Costa Campaign: "Fresh Fish Packing"
Gustavo Borges Swimming School
Hospital A.C.Camargo Cancer Center Campaign: "Superformula"
Hotel Emiliano Campaign: "The Menu that Became a Book"
HSBC Campaign: "Hsbc in the Future - Money Parking Ticket", Insurance
Johnson & Johnson Band Aid, Campaign: "Deep Blue Sea", Campaign: "The Little Woundies", Creative, FIFA World Cup 2014
Kiss Radio FM Campaign: "The Turnstile of Rock"
Kleenex
Lavanderia Wash
Liga Do Rosa
Listerine
Livraria da Vila Bookstore Campaign: "Check-In at Imaginary Places"

Losango
Master Blenders Pilao Decaf
Meta Real Campaign: "Virtual Fridge Lock"
Microsoft Internet Explorer 9
Mobilize Brasil
Nestle Kit Kat Pillow
Nokia Ovi Maps GPS Service
Ong Florescer Campaign: "Tomorrow in a Box"
Other Images Campaign: "Cold War"
Raizen Campaign: "Used Oil Poster"
Rolex
Santa Casa de Misericordia de Porto Alegre
Shell
Tramontina The Bible of Barbecue
Troller T4, T4 4x4
Unilever Campaign: "Shampoo Paper Invitation"
Warner Bros

J. Walter Thompson
Av Atlantica 1130 10th Fl, Copacabana, 22021-000 Rio de Janeiro, RJ Brazil
Tel.: (55) 21 3873 8200
Fax: (55) 21 3873 8279
Web Site: www.jwt.com/brasil

Year Founded: 1931

Aurora Magalhaes Ellingsen *(Acct Supvr)*
Tbssia Massumi *(Acct Supvr)*

Accounts:
Alcoholics Anonymous
Grupo de Apoio a Prevencao a AIDS da Baixada Santista
Hospital A.C. Camargo
Pernambucanas
SHELL

Chile

J. Walter Thompson
Avenida Ricardo Lyon 1262 Providencia, Santiago, Chile
Tel.: (56) 2 230 9000
Fax: (56) 2 225 4593
Web Site: www.jwt.com

Employees: 50
Year Founded: 1944

National Agency Associations: ACHAP-IAA

Agency Specializes In: Consumer Marketing

Vicente Valjalo *(CEO)*
Pablo Herrera *(Creative Dir & Copywriter)*
Felipe Porte *(Creative Dir & Copywriter)*
Karl Neumann *(Dir-Art)*
Pablo Orozco *(Dir-Art)*

Accounts:
Bayer Berocca Plus
CCU
Chilean Red Cross
Copesa Campaign: "Diversity"
Empresa Periodistica La Tercera Campaign: "Earthquake"
Ford Chile
Fundacion Maria Ayuda Campaign: "One Minute"
Johnson & Johnson
Kraft Foods Campaign: "Catapult"
Las Condes City Hall Campaign: "Walls"
Maria Ayuda Campaign: "Hiding Nightmares"
Mattel Scrabble
Mirax
Mondelez
Nestle
Puma
Unicef
Unilever Sedal (Placard Campaign)
United Nations

Colombia

J. Walter Thompson
Calle 98 No 22 64 Floor 12, Bogota, Colombia
Mailing Address:
Apartado Aereo 89173, Bogota, Colombia
Tel.: (57) 1 621 6060
Fax: (57) 1 621 6060
E-Mail: jwt.colombia@jwt.com
Web Site: www.jwt.com

Employees: 120
Year Founded: 1939

Agency Specializes In: Consumer Marketing

Armando De Leon Arcos *(Fin Dir)*
Juan Pablo Rocha *(Pres-Colombia)*
Rodolfo Borrell *(VP-Creative)*
Adriana Pineda *(VP-Integrated Comm Plng)*
Lisseth Trejos *(Acct Dir)*
Nicolas Acosta *(Sr Art Dir)*
Diego Contreras *(Dir-Creative)*
Jaime Perea *(Dir-Creative)*
Andres Norato *(Assoc Dir-Creative)*
Claudia Murillo *(Assoc Creative Dir)*

Accounts:
Bavaria-Sab Miller Campaign: "50Th Anniversary"
The Clorox Company Campaign: "Clorox Drops of Life"
Comcel Campaign: "Acho"
Ford Campaign: "The Guy with More Traffic Tickets in Colombia"
Fundacion Clinica Shaio
Juan Valdez Campaign: "Big Bang"
Nestle Kit-Kat
Telmex Colombia Campaign: "High Speeds"
Telmex
Unilever
Vision Mundial Campaign: "Where is the Child?"

Ecuador

Norlop J. Walter Thompson
Tulcan 1017 y Luque, PO Box 0901, 5063 Guayaquil, Ecuador
Tel.: (593) 4 245 1811
Fax: (593) 4 245 1652
E-Mail: fsola@norlopjwt.com.ec

Employees: 100
Year Founded: 1963

National Agency Associations: AEAP

Agency Specializes In: Advertising, Brand Development & Integration, Commercial Photography, Consumer Marketing, Corporate Identity, Direct Response Marketing, Event Planning & Marketing, Financial, Graphic Design, Hispanic Market, Logo & Package Design, Magazines, Merchandising, Multimedia, Newspaper, Production, Public Relations, Publicity/Promotions, Radio, Sales Promotion, Seniors' Market, Strategic Planning/Research, T.V., Telemarketing, Trade & Consumer Magazines

Fausto Acosta *(Dir-Art)*
Ivan Coello *(Dir-Creative)*
Milton Cordova *(Dir-Art)*
Wilson Franco *(Dir-Creative)*
Josue Granda *(Dir-Art)*
Leon Perez *(Dir-Creative)*
Emilio Silva *(Dir-Art)*
Gabriela Valenzuela *(Dir-Art)*
Javier Maldonado *(Copywriter)*
Susan Valverde *(Copywriter)*
Francisco Sola Medina *(Exec Chm)*

Accounts:
Ecuatoriano Suiza
Hospital Sotomayor Campaign: "Windows of Hope"
New-Instituto de Neurociencias
Solca Charity
Teatro Sanchez Aguilar
Telconet
Wildaid

El Salvador

J. Walter Thompson
Calle Circunvalacion No 332, Colonia San Benito, San Salvador, El Salvador
Tel.: (503) 2264 3505
Fax: (503) 2264 3512
Web Site: www.jwt.com

Employees: 29
Year Founded: 1978

Agency Specializes In: Advertising

Reynaldo Pino *(Gen Dir-Creative-JWT El Salvador)*
Elizabeth De Guardado *(Dir-Media)*
Argentina De Merlos *(Acct Mgr)*

Accounts:
Secretary of Education of El Salvador Campaign: "Silence"

Mexico

J. Walter Thompson
Avenue Ejercito Nacional No 519, Col Granada, CP 11520 Mexico, DF Mexico
Tel.: (52) 55 5729 4000
Fax: (52) 55 5279 4093
Web Site: www.jwt.com

Year Founded: 1943

Agency Specializes In: Advertising

Andres Martinez *(VP-Creative-JWT Mexico City)*
Enrique Codesido *(Exec Dir-Creative)*
Martin Giudicessi *(Dir-Art & Creative)*
Edgar Elorza *(Creative Dir & Copywriter)*
Cesar Pavel Mendez *(Art Dir)*
Raul Pineda *(Creative Dir)*
Veronica Pugliese *(Acct Dir)*
Silvia Gomez *(Dir-Photography Production)*
Rafael Hidalgo *(Copywriter)*
Luis Gaitan *(Gen Creative Dir)*
Gabriel Vazquez *(VP Creative)*

Accounts:
Alukim Foil
Canon Campaign: "'Don't Let A Call Interrupt Your Photo", Canon EOS
New-Crown Imports LLC Victoria
Dramamine
Electrolux Campaign: "Stadium"
Ford Campaign: "Gps", Edge, Explorer, Ford Vehicles, Lobo, Transit
Henkel AG Fester
Johnson & Johnson Campaign: "Flying Fish"
Kraft
Mexican Red Cross Campaign: "Phonebooth > Moneybox", Charity, Charity Fundraising
Nestle Campaign: "Smartphone"
Nike Campaign: "Bid Your Sweat"
Schering-Plough Dramamine Sickness Remedy
Unilever

Panama

J. Walter Thompson
Entre Calle 64 y 65 Edificio Star Communications & Holding, Piso 1 Mezzanine, Panama, Panama

Tel.: (507) 322 0050
Fax: (507) 322 0053
Web Site: www.jwt.com

Year Founded: 1980

Agency Specializes In: Advertising

Saul Zayat *(Gen Mgr)*
Francisco Gonzalez *(Creative Dir)*

Accounts:
Ford
Freixenet
HSBC
Nelka
Nestle
Nike
Nokia
Shell
Thrifty
Unilever

Peru

J. Walter Thompson
Paseo de la Republica 5883, Lima, 18 Peru
Tel.: (51) 1 610 6767
Fax: (51) 1 610 6768
E-Mail: milagros.plaza@jwt.com
Web Site: www.jwt.com

Employees: 60
Year Founded: 1957

Agency Specializes In: Advertising

Ivan Malqui *(Art Dir)*
Eduardo Meza *(Dir-Art)*
Alberto Portugal *(Dir-Art)*
Monica Torres *(Dir-Production)*
Alvaro Montufar *(Acct Supvr)*
Alejandro Gutierrez *(Copywriter)*
Diego Millagui *(Copywriter)*
Juan Pablo Peschiera *(Copywriter)*

Accounts:
Ambev Peru
Belcorp
Billboard Dogs
Casa Andina
Enersur GDF Suez Campaign: "Leaving The Light Off"
Flora Tristan
Hogar Clinica San Juan De Dios
Interbank
Kraft Campaign: "Boobs"
La Canasta Basketball School
Nestle
Peruvian Association of Alzheimer's Disease
Teleton
Wwf Campaign: "The Plantmen"

Puerto Rico

J. Walter Thompson
Calle C 60 Urb Industrial Mario Julia, San Juan, PR 00920
Mailing Address:
PO Box 2125, San Juan, PR 00922-2125
Tel.: (787) 474-2501
Fax: (787) 474-2506
E-Mail: srasances.pagan@jwt.com
Web Site: www.jwt.com

E-Mail for Key Personnel:
President: jorge.rodriguez@jwt.com

Employees: 100
Year Founded: 1955

Jorge Rodriguez *(Pres)*
Jaime Rosado *(VP & Reg Dir-Creative)*
Richard Pascual *(VP & Grp Acct Dir)*
Diana Hernandez *(Dir-Art)*
Nicole Perez *(Dir-Art)*
Johanna Santiago *(Assoc Dir-Creative)*
Andrea Vega *(Copywriter)*
Rafael Sepulveda *(Gen Creative Dir)*

Accounts:
Banco Popular Campaign: "The Most Popular Song"
Dc Shoes Campaign: "Spray The Word"
Department of Economic Development & Commerce of Puerto Rico
Heineken
Mendez & Co
Muscular Dystrophy Association
Pepsico Campaign: "Fueling Buzz", Gatorade, Pepsi
Susan G. Komen Breast Cancer Foundation Campaign: "5 Women, 5 Races"

Uruguay

Corporacion / J. Walter Thompson
Convencion 1343 Piso 8, Montevideo, Uruguay
Tel.: (598) 2 902 3434
Fax: (598) 2 902 0719
E-Mail: secretaria@jwt.com.uy
Web Site: www.jwt.com.uy

Employees: 50
Year Founded: 1976

National Agency Associations: AUDAP

Agency Specializes In: Advertising, Food Service, Production (Ad, Film, Broadcast), Travel & Tourism

Cecilia Drever *(Acct Dir)*
Martin Cedes *(Dir-Art)*
Andres Techera *(Dir-Creative)*
Lucia De Soto *(Acct Exec)*
Carolina Barreiro *(Writer-Creative)*

Accounts:
Abitab
ABN AMRO Bank
Bayer Berocca, Redoxon, Supradyn
Kraft Foods Bubbaloo, Chiclets, Halls, Vita-C
Life Cinemas Life Cinemas Mobile App
Paso Los Torris
Pepsi 7up, Mirinda, Paso Toros, Pepsi Light
Sedal
Ta-Ta
UNICEF
Unilever UK Foods Bull-Dog, Knorr, Lipton, Lux, Nevex

Venezuela

J. Walter Thompson
Centro Banaven Torre C Piso 3 Ave La Estancia Chuao, Caracas, 1061 Venezuela
Tel.: (58) 212 991 3544
Fax: (58) 212 902 3227
Web Site: www.jwt.com

Employees: 200
Year Founded: 1964

Agency Specializes In: Advertising, Hispanic Market

Roberto Pol *(Pres)*
Eugenio Reyes *(Gen Dir-Creative)*
Sylvia Navas Faria *(Acct Dir)*
Bernardo Tortolero *(Dir-Creative)*
Ana Teresa Vasquez Arroyo *(Dir-Audiovisual & BTL Production)*
Tatiana Ferro *(Gen Acct Dir)*

Accounts:
Amnesty International Campaign: "If Your Friends Were"
Dramamine
Ford Motor Company Campaign: "Hydrant", Campaign: "Tree"
Johnson & Johnson Dramamine Motion Sickness Tablets

J. WALTER THOMPSON ATLANTA
3630 Peachtree Road NE Ste 1200, Atlanta, GA 30326
Tel.: (404) 365-7300
Fax: (770) 668-5707
Web Site: www.jwt.com/atlanta

E-Mail for Key Personnel:
President: Ridge.White@jwttech.com
Creative Dir.: roy.trimble@jwttech.com
Media Dir.: cindy.giller@jwttech.com
Production Mgr.: kim.bohlayer@jwttech.com

Employees: 80
Year Founded: 1947

National Agency Associations: 4A's

Agency Specializes In: Advertising, Brand Development & Integration, Broadcast, Business Publications, Business-To-Business, Cable T.V., Co-op Advertising, Consulting, Consumer Marketing, Consumer Publications, Corporate Communications, Corporate Identity, Digital/Interactive, Direct Response Marketing, Electronic Media, High Technology, Information Technology, Internet/Web Design, Magazines, Media Buying Services, Newspaper, Newspapers & Magazines, Outdoor, Planning & Consultation, Print, Production, Radio, Retail, Sponsorship, Strategic Planning/Research, T.V., Technical Advertising, Trade & Consumer Magazines

Marshall Lauck *(COO)*
Deana Strauss *(Sr VP-Strategic Plng)*
Jeremy Jones *(Exec Creative Dir)*
Ann McClintock *(Sr Dir-HR)*
Chris Hooper *(Grp Acct Dir)*
Sean McNeeley *(Grp Acct Dir)*
Erin Fillingam *(Art Dir)*
Chris Wilson *(Acct Mgmt Dir)*
Rod Armbruster *(Sr Partner & Dir-Fin)*
Peter Blitzer *(Dir-Integrated Production Atlanta, Dallas & Houston)*
Paul Schoknecht *(Sr Partner & Dir-Digital Experience)*
Sunni Thompson *(Dir-Content)*
Matt Genne *(Assoc Dir-Creative)*
Lucas Heck *(Assoc Dir-Creative)*
Melissa Schulte *(Acct Supvr)*
Nathalie Espinol *(Sr Strategist-Social Media)*
Adriana Meneses *(Jr Acct Planner)*

Accounts:
Blue Coat Systems
BMC Software
Bridgestone Golf Bridgestone Golf
Brother
Build-A-Bear Workshop, Inc. (Lead Creative Agency) Communications, Marketing, Retail
FEMA
Foundation Rwanda
Jiffy Lube International, Inc. Broadcast, Campaign: "Every Corner", Campaign: "Leave Worry Behind(SM)", Digital, OOH, Radio, Social
Randstad
Royal Dutch Shell plc Brand Strategy, Campaign: "Airlift Drift", Campaign: "Complete Protection", Campaign: "Pennzoil", Creative Development, Pennzoil, Quaker State, TV
Scana
SimDesk
New-SOPUS Products Pennzoil AirLift Drift

Texas Instruments
United States Marine Corps Campaign: "Toward the Sounds of Chaos", USMC/UFC Integrated Campaign
US Marine Corps Campaign: "Home of the Brave", Campaign: "The Few, the Proud", Campaign: "The Land We Love", Campaign: "Toward the Sounds of Chaos", Campaign: "Wall", Communications, Digital, Media, Social
U.S. Virgin Islands Department of Tourism Media Relations
Zultys Technologies

J. WALTER THOMPSON CANADA

160 Bloor St E Ste 800, Toronto, ON M4W 3P7 Canada
Tel.: (416) 926-7300
Fax: (416) 967-2859
E-Mail: torjwtresumes@jwt.com
Web Site: www.jwtcanada.ca

E-Mail for Key Personnel:
President: paul.wales@enterprisecs.com

Employees: 175
Year Founded: 1975

Agency Specializes In: Advertising Specialties

Susan Kim-Kirkland *(Pres & CEO)*
Rob Elliott *(CFO & VP)*
Scott Miskie *(Sr VP & Bus Dir)*
Carolyn Bingham *(Sr VP-Creative Ops)*
Ari Elkouby *(VP & Creative Dir)*
Matt Syberg-Olsen *(VP & Dir-Creative)*
Don Saynor *(VP & Assoc Dir-Creative)*
Rebecca Brown *(Exec Dir-Content Mktg)*
Chris Page *(Grp Dir-Creative)*
Patrick Schroen *(Grp Dir-Digital Tech & Innovation)*
Dan Bache *(Sr Dir-Art-JWT Toronto)*
Yen Chu *(Creative Dir-Design)*
Troy Geoghegan *(Art Dir)*
Alex Newman *(Art Dir)*
Gary Westgate *(Creative Dir)*
Jed Churcher *(Dir-Creative)*
Craig Hum *(Dir-Bus Insights & Analytics)*
Ian Westworth *(Dir-Strategic Plng)*
Nicole Ellerton *(Assoc Dir-Creative)*
Megan Brescacin *(Acct Mgr)*
Susan Goodfellow *(Mgr-Production)*
Tanya Grenville *(Acct Supvr)*
Mike DeCandido *(Copywriter)*
Kyla Galloway *(Copywriter)*
Kareem Halfawi *(Copywriter)*
William Ruzvidzo *(Community Mgr)*

Accounts:
Air Canada Creative
Bayer Cadbury
Brandaid
Canadian Film Fest Broadcast, Campaign: "Canadian Zombie", Campaign: "Its Hard Being A Canadian Actor", Campaign: "The Academy of Cliche"
Canon
Diageo
HSBC Campaign: "Bamboo City"
Johnson & Johnson Band Aid, Campaign: "Hopscotch", Tylenol
Mazda Canada "Long Drive Home", Campaign: "Cineplex TimePlay", Campaign: "Game Changer", Social Media
McCormick Canada; 1997
Nestle Kit Kat
ReStore Habitat for Humanity, Social Media, Videos
Tim Horton Children's Foundation
Tim Hortons, Inc. Campaign: "Dark Experiment", Campaign: "Good Ol Hockey Game", Dark Roast Coffee Blend, Tim Horton Donuts; 1991
Tourism Ireland
TVB Bessies
University of Toronto
Wal-Mart Campaign: "Lives For Halloween Mom", Wal-Mart Flyer

J. WALTER THOMPSON INSIDE

(Formerly JWT Inside)
6300 Wishire Blvd, Los Angeles, CA 90048
Tel.: (310) 309-8282
Fax: (310) 309-8283
E-Mail: conversations@jwtinside.com
Web Site: www.jwtinside.com

Year Founded: 1949

National Agency Associations: 4A's-AMA

Agency Specializes In: Advertising, Advertising Specialties, Business-To-Business, Consulting, Corporate Identity, Over-50 Market, Recruitment

Leslie Salmon *(Sr Partner & Mng Dir)*
Jeff Press *(CFO)*
Erin Seedman *(Sr Dir-Client)*
Bruce Carey *(Dir-Creative-INSIDE-Los Angeles)*
Elaine Ng *(Dir-Art)*
Mark Overbaugh *(Dir-Natl Creative Svcs)*
Janice Chung *(Client Dir)*
Kathy Dowd *(Sr Client Dir)*

Accounts:
Atos Consulting
B&Q
Boeing
Merrill Lynch
Metropolitan Police
Microsoft
Nordstrom Career Site
United States Department of State Career Site

Branches

J. Walter Thompson Inside

3630 Peachtree Rd, Ste 1200, Atlanta, GA 30326
Tel.: (404) 365-7300
Web Site: www.jwt.com

Employees: 14

National Agency Associations: 4A's

Agency Specializes In: Communications, Recruitment

John Windolph *(Pres-Washington)*
Ron D. Payton *(Acct Dir)*
Julia Toth *(Dir-Creative)*
Sheila Meyer *(Acct Supvr)*
Jenn Patterson *(Acct Supvr)*
Peter Price *(Planner & Sr Strategist)*
Julie Roth *(Acct Exec)*
Ben Litoff *(Asst Acct Exec)*
Cami Nezam *(Acct Coord)*
Victoria Skinner *(Acct Coord)*

Accounts:
Capital One
Catholic Health Care West
Children's Healthcare of Atlanta
Dreyers
Expedia inc
The Home Depot
Jet Blue Airways
Merrill Lynch
Microsoft
Shell
U.S Border Patrol

J. Walter Thompson Inside

1001 Fannin St 500, Houston, TX 77002
Tel.: (713) 952-4290
Fax: (713) 977-9127
Web Site: www.jwt.com/jwtinside

Employees: 1
Year Founded: 1984

National Agency Associations: 4A's

Agency Specializes In: Communications, Public Relations, Recruitment

Janice Chung *(Dir-Client)*
Karen Joyce *(Dir-HR)*
Kay Rangel *(Mgr-Creative Svcs)*
Megan Keleshian *(Acct Supvr)*

Accounts:
Dreyers
Ferguson

J. Walter Thompson Inside

466 Lexington Ave 4th Fl, New York, NY 10017-3166
Tel.: (212) 856-0045
Fax: (212) 210-1097
Web Site: www.jwt.com/jwtinside

Employees: 35

National Agency Associations: 4A's

Agency Specializes In: Communications, Recruitment, Sponsorship

Kai Yen *(CTO)*
Ian Kaplan *(Head-Bus Dev & Dir-Natl Sls)*
Peggy Brogan Woods *(Sr Dir-Client)*
Dave Levin *(Sr Producer-Interactive)*
Doug Shonrock *(Dir-Tech Products)*
Stephen Nemeth *(Planner)*
Trish Golden *(Client Dir)*

Accounts:
American Express Company

J. Walter Thompson Inside

11973 Westline Industrial Ste 100, Saint Louis, MO 63146
Tel.: (314) 275-8600
Fax: (314) 205-1398
E-Mail: jonathan.redman@jwt.com
Web Site: www.jwt.com/jwtinside

Employees: 30

National Agency Associations: 4A's

Agency Specializes In: Communications, Recruitment

Jenn Strathmann *(Dir-Studio)*

Accounts:
B&Q
Capital One
Catholic Healthcare West
Childrens Hospital Los Angeles
Comcast
Dreyers
Ferguson
jet Blue Airways
Microsoft
UCLA Health Systems
University of Michigan

International

J. Walter Thompson Inside

160 Bloor St E 8th Floor, Toronto, ON M4W 3P7 Canada
Tel.: (416) 926-7304
Fax: (416) 926-7316
E-Mail: lauri.richardson@jwt.com
Web Site: www.jwt.com/jwtinside

Agency Specializes In: Communications, Recruitment

David Gibb *(Mng Dir & Exec VP)*
Ryan Spelliscy *(Sr VP & Exec Dir-Creative)*
Dean Foerter *(VP & Head-Integrated Mktg Strategy)*
Craig Hum *(Dir-Bus Insights & Analytics)*

J. Walter Thompson Inside
Level 12 99 Walker St I, Sydney, NSW 2060 Australia
Tel.: (61) 2 9947 2285
Fax: (61) 2 9770 7810
E-Mail: allison.doorbar@jwt.com
Web Site: www.jwt.com/jwtinside

Employees: 8

Agency Specializes In: Communications, Recruitment

John Gutteridge *(CEO-Australasia)*
Angela Morris *(Exec Dir-Plng)*
Richard Muntz *(Exec Dir-Creative)*
Alexandra Antoniou *(Sr Dir-Art)*
Vanessa O'Brien *(Sr Acct Dir)*
Milly Hall *(Grp Acct Dir)*
Fiona Wilson *(Grp Acct Dir)*
Daniella Adam *(Dir-Art & Sr Designer)*
Andrew Mccowan *(Dir-Plng-Sydney)*

Accounts:
HSBC Holdings plc
Kimberly-Clark Corporation
Nokia Corporation
Unilever Australia Ltd.

Global Partners

ORC Image & Strategies d'Employeur
6 boulevard des Capucines, 75441 Paris, Cedex 9 France
Tel.: (33) 1 47 61 58 00
Fax: (33) 1 49 10 95 72
E-Mail: info@orc.fr
Web Site: www.orc.fr

Employees: 80
Year Founded: 1988

Agency Specializes In: Communications, Planning & Consultation, Recruitment

Fabrice Fournier *(Owner)*
Thierry Delorme *(Partner)*
Corinne Leveque *(Acct Dir)*
Elodie Biagiotti Walk *(Acct Dir)*
Emmanuelle Laurent *(Dir-Brands)*
Fanny Caumont *(Assoc Dir)*
Christina Pastoret *(Sr Acct Mgr)*
Sylvie Shamsoudine *(Sr Acct Mgr)*
Laure Schlissinger *(Acct Mgr)*
Jean-Christophe Tixier *(Mgr-Media)*

Accounts:
Auchan
Aylin Conseil
Cadbury France
Cetlem
Robert Hall
Total
Toyota
Xerox

AIMS Polska sp. z o.o.
ul Flory 9/10, 00-586 Warsaw, Poland
Tel.: (48) 22 331 66 67
Fax: (48) 22 331 66 94
E-Mail: info@aims.pl
Web Site: www.aims.pl

Employees: 2
Year Founded: 1996

Agency Specializes In: Communications, Planning & Consultation, Recruitment

Jerzy Potocki *(Pres-AIMS Intl Poland)*

J. WALTER THOMPSON U.S.A., INC.
466 Lexington Ave, New York, NY 10017-3140
Tel.: (212) 210-7000
Fax: (212) 210-7299
E-Mail: request@jwt.com
Web Site: www.jwt.com

Year Founded: 1864

Agency Specializes In: Advertising

Gustavo Martinez *(Chm & CEO)*
Jamie McLellan *(CTO-J. Walter Thompson Company)*
Rishap Malhotra *(VP-Corp Dev)*
Anaka Kobzev *(Dir-Comm-JWT North America)*
Michael Powell *(Dir-Creative)*
Jinal Shah *(Dir-Digital Strategy-Global)*

Accounts:
Baobeihuijia.com Campaign: "Missing Children"
Bloomberg
Energizer Personal Care
GoodNites Underwear
Intel
Kimberly-Clark Corporation
Macy's
Nestle
Schick-Wilkinson Sword Schick Quattro

Principal Offices

J. Walter Thompson U.S.A., Inc.
1001 Fannin Ste 500, Houston, TX 77002
Tel.: (713) 659-6688
Fax: (713) 759-0034
E-Mail: request@jwt.com
Web Site: www.jwt.com

Employees: 25
Year Founded: 2000

Ray Redding *(Mng Dir & Sr VP)*
Jaime Rosado *(VP & Reg Dir-Creative)*
Lorna Muniz-Paz *(Acct Dir)*

Accounts:
Houston Ford Dealers Assoc.
Shell Lubricants
Shell Oil Company; Houston, TX Shell Chemical Company, Shell Oil Products, Shell Trading
Shell Oil Products U.S. Shell Oil Products U.S., Shell Rimula, Shell Stations

J. Walter Thompson Atlanta
3630 Peachtree Road NE Ste 1200, Atlanta, GA 30326
(See Separate Listing)

Service Offices:

J. Walter Thompson U.S.A., Inc.
175 W Ostend St Ste #A-2, Baltimore, MD 21230
Tel.: (410) 567-8910
Fax: (410) 567-9001
Web Site: www.jwt.com

Employees: 4

Steve Diebold *(Sr VP & Grp Acct Dir)*
Jaime Rosado *(VP & Reg Dir-Creative)*

J. Walter Thompson U.S.A., Inc.
2600 Douglas Ave Ste 610, Coral Gables, FL 33134
Tel.: (305) 476-7702
Fax: (305) 476-7710
E-Mail: request@jwt.com
Web Site: www.jwt.com

Employees: 11
Year Founded: 2000

Chris Hooper *(Grp Acct Dir)*
Sean McNeeley *(Grp Acct Dir)*
Andrea Villa *(Acct Dir-Brand Messaging)*
Chris Wilson *(Acct Mgmt Dir)*
Emmakate Young *(Acct Dir)*
Sunni Thompson *(Dir-Content)*
Marjanee Shook *(Acct Supvr)*
Nathalie Espinol *(Sr Strategist-Social Media)*
Sydney Busby *(Strategist-Content)*
Christopher Perkowski *(Coord-Social Media)*

J. Walter Thompson U.S.A., Inc.
1 Dallas Ctr 350 N Saint Paul St Ste 2410, Dallas, TX 75201
Tel.: (214) 468-3460
Fax: (214) 754-7199
E-Mail: request@jwt.com
Web Site: www.jwt.com

Employees: 11

Chris Von Selle *(COO)*
Lo Sheung Yan *(Chm-Asia Pacific & Worldwide Creative Councils)*
Toby Hoare *(CEO-Europe)*
Jaime Rosado *(VP & Reg Dir-Creative)*
Mike Apple *(Acct Dir)*

J. Walter Thompson U.S.A., Inc.
455 Pennsylvania Ave Ste 136, Fort Washington, PA 19034
Tel.: (215) 643-9700
Fax: (215) 643-9730
E-Mail: request@jwt.com
Web Site: www.jwt.com

Employees: 5

Phil Alandt *(Sr VP & Acct Dir)*
Andrea Villa *(Acct Dir-Brand Messaging)*
Chris Wilson *(Dir-Acct Mgmt)*
Breanna Rotell Caldwell *(Acct Supvr)*
Marjanee Shook *(Acct Supvr)*
Christine Smith *(Acct Supvr)*
Chelsea Gattung *(Supvr-Social Media)*
Nathalie Espinol *(Sr Strategist-Social Media)*
Alex Lieppe *(Acct Exec)*
Christopher Perkowski *(Coord-Social Media)*

J. Walter Thompson U.S.A., Inc.
10401 N Meridian St Ste 216, Indianapolis, IN 46290-1090
Tel.: (317) 844-5181
Fax: (317) 844-5240
E-Mail: request@jwt.com
Web Site: www.jwt.com

Employees: 4

Jaime Rosado *(VP & Reg Dir-Creative)*
Eric Kwiatkowski *(VP & Acct Mgr)*

J. Walter Thompson U.S.A., Inc.
7666 E 61st St Ste 130, Tulsa, OK 74145
Tel.: (918) 250-1884

Fax: (918) 250-0875
E-Mail: request@jwt.com
Web Site: www.jwt.com

Employees: 10

Kyle McQuaid *(Sr VP)*
Jaime Rosado *(VP & Reg Dir-Creative)*

Accounts:
Ford
HSBC
Nestle
Nike
Shell
Unilever

J. WINSPER & CO.
(See Under Winsper)

J3 NEW YORK
1400 Broadway, New York, NY 10018
Tel.: (917) 265-2700
Web Site: www.umww.com

National Agency Associations: 4A's

Agency Specializes In: Advertising, Media Planning, Sponsorship

Eileen Kiernan *(Pres)*
Matthew Baker *(VP & Grp Partner-Integrated Plng)*
Jamie Kozma *(VP & Grp Partner-Integrated Plng)*
Alison Menius *(Partner-Integrated Plng)*
Erin Akselrod-Quintana *(Client Mng Partner & Exec VP)*
Corinne Shaffer *(Sr VP & Client Bus Partner-Integrated Plng-UM)*
Nicole Bouquet *(VP & Grp Partner-Integrated Plng)*
Sarah Kadish *(Grp Partner-Integrated Plng)*

Accounts:
Johnson & Johnson Global Media, Listerine

JAB ADVERTISING
203 Market Ave S Ste 212, Canton, OH 44702
Tel.: (330) 936-4083
Web Site: www.jabvertising.com

Agency Specializes In: Advertising, Brand Development & Integration, Collateral, Internet/Web Design, Package Design, Promotions

Doug Bennett *(Owner)*

Accounts:
Historic Onesto Lofts

JACK MORTON WORLDWIDE
142 Berkeley St, Boston, MA 02116
Tel.: (617) 585-7000
Fax: (617) 585-7171
E-Mail: experience@jackmorton.com
Web Site: www.jackmorton.com

Employees: 850
Year Founded: 1939

National Agency Associations: 4A's-AMA-ANA-ARF-DMA-PMA-PRSA-WOMMA

Agency Specializes In: Advertising Specialties, Below-the-Line, Business-To-Business, College, Consulting, Consumer Marketing, Corporate Communications, Corporate Identity, Digital/Interactive, Direct-to-Consumer, Entertainment, Environmental, Event Planning & Marketing, Exhibit/Trade Shows, Experience Design, Financial, Graphic Design, Guerilla Marketing, Health Care Services, Hispanic Market, Integrated Marketing, Internet/Web Design, Investor Relations, Local Marketing, Market Research, Medical Products, Mobile Marketing, Multicultural, Pharmaceutical, Planning & Consultation, Podcasting, Print, Production, Production (Print), Promotions, Recruitment, Social Marketing/Nonprofit, Social Media, Sponsorship, Sports Market, Stakeholders, Strategic Planning/Research, Viral/Buzz/Word of Mouth

Steve Mooney *(Mng Dir)*
Bill Davies *(CFO)*
Bruce Henderson *(Chief Creative Officer)*
Charlotte Merrell *(Exec VP-HR-Worldwide)*
Phil Collyer *(Sr VP & Head-Creative)*
Jeb Blatt *(Sr VP)*
Ben Grossman *(VP & Dir-Strategy)*
Rachel Vingsness *(VP & Dir-HR)*
Tammy Falvey *(Mgr-Recruiting)*
Joeli Gewirtz *(Mgr-Strategic Sourcing & Risk Mgmt)*

Accounts:
Bank of America Event Marketing
Cotton Inc.
Lego Star Wars
Liberty Mutual Insurance (Brand Experience Agency of Record)
Procter & Gamble Event Marketing, Wella
Samsung Event Marketing, Experiential
Scott & White Healthcare; Temple, TX Employee Engagement
Subway Experiential
Truven Health Analytics Event Marketing, Experiential
Verizon Employee Engagement
VMware Event Marketing, Experiential

Branches

Genuine Interactive
500 Harrison Ave 5R, Boston, MA 02118
(See Separate Listing)

Jack Morton Worldwide (Sao Paulo)
Av Antonio Joaquim de Moura Andrade, 425, Vila Nova Conceicao, 04507-0001 Sao Paulo, Brazil
Tel.: (55) 16175857135
Web Site: www.jackmorton.com/offices/sao-paulo/

Employees: 850
Year Founded: 1939

Agency Specializes In: Above-the-Line, Affiliate Marketing, Alternative Advertising, Below-the-Line, Branded Entertainment, Broadcast, Digital/Interactive, Exhibit/Trade Shows, Experience Design, Guerilla Marketing, In-Store Advertising, Mobile Marketing, Out-of-Home Media, Shopper Marketing, Social Media, Sponsorship

Bill Davies *(CFO)*

Jack Morton Worldwide (Dubai)
Office 2201-2202, PO Box 212148, Bayswater Tower, Dubai, United Arab Emirates
Tel.: (971) 971044312389
Web Site: www.jackmorton.com/offices/dubai/

Employees: 850
Year Founded: 1939

Agency Specializes In: Above-the-Line, Alternative Advertising, Branded Entertainment, Broadcast, Digital/Interactive, Exhibit/Trade Shows, Experience Design, In-Store Advertising, Local Marketing, Mobile Marketing, Out-of-Home Media, Promotions, Shopper Marketing, Social Media, Sponsorship, Trade & Consumer Magazines

Alex Apthorpe *(Mng Dir & Sr VP)*
Yvonne Hoffzimmer *(Mng Dir & Sr VP)*

Accounts:
Abraaji Capital
Emirates

Jack Morton Worldwide (Dusseldorf)
Rochusstrasse 47, 40479 Dusseldorf, Germany
Tel.: (49) 49021149554504
Web Site: www.jackmorton.com/offices/dusseldorf

Employees: 850
Year Founded: 1939

Agency Specializes In: Above-the-Line, Branded Entertainment, Broadcast, Digital/Interactive, Exhibit/Trade Shows, Experience Design, Guerilla Marketing, In-Store Advertising, Local Marketing, Mobile Marketing, Multimedia, Out-of-Home Media, Outdoor, Promotions, Shopper Marketing, Social Media, Sponsorship, Trade & Consumer Magazines

Jens Mayer *(Mng Dir & Vp)*

Accounts:
Vodafone

Jack Morton Worldwide (Singapore)
40A Orchard Road, #07-01 MacDonald House, 238838 Singapore, Singapore
Tel.: (65) 6564998800
Web Site: www.jackmorton.com/offices/singapore/

Employees: 850
Year Founded: 1939

Agency Specializes In: Branded Entertainment, Broadcast, Digital/Interactive, Exhibit/Trade Shows, Experience Design, Guerilla Marketing, In-Store Advertising, Local Marketing, Outdoor, Promotions, Shopper Marketing, Social Media, Sponsorship

Charles Robinson *(Mng Dir)*

Accounts:
Google
Nike

Jack Morton Worldwide (Seoul)
Dae-gong Building, 4/F, Gangnam-gu, Seoul, Korea (South)
Tel.: (82) 4402087352000
Web Site: www.jackmorton.com/offices/seoul/

Employees: 850
Year Founded: 1939

Agency Specializes In: Broadcast, Digital/Interactive, Exhibit/Trade Shows, Experience Design, Guerilla Marketing, In-Store Advertising, Local Marketing, Promotions, Shopper Marketing, Social Media, Sponsorship, Trade & Consumer Magazines

Mike Kunheim *(Mng Dir & Sr VP)*

Accounts:
Samsung Electronics

Jack Morton Worldwide (Hong Kong)
10/F Oxford House TaiKoo Place, Quarry Bay, Hong Kong, China (Hong Kong)
Tel.: (852) 8522805176
Web Site: www.jackmorton.com/offices/hong-kong/

Employees: 850
Year Founded: 1939

Agency Specializes In: Digital/Interactive,

Exhibit/Trade Shows, Experience Design, Guerilla Marketing, Local Marketing, Promotions, Shopper Marketing, Sponsorship

Natalie Ackerman *(Mng Dir)*
Justin Bonnett *(VP & Dir-Bus)*

Accounts:
K-Mart
Marriott

Jack Morton Worldwide (Shanghai)
1045 Huaihai Zhong Road, 16/F Huai Hai Plaza, 200031 Shanghai, China
Tel.: (86) 862124110157
Web Site: www.jackmorton.com/offices/shanghai/

Employees: 850
Year Founded: 1939

Adam Charles *(Sr Vp & Mng Dir)*

Accounts:
HSBC
TMall

Jack Morton Exhibits
10 Applegate Dr, Robbinsville, NJ 08691
Tel.: (609) 259-0500
Fax: (609) 259-4055
E-Mail: experience@jackmorton.com
Web Site: www.jackmorton.com

Employees: 850
Year Founded: 1939

Agency Specializes In: Advertising

Cyndi Davis *(Sr VP & Mng Dir-Jack Morton Exhibits)*
Jim Cavanaugh *(Sr VP-New Bus & Grp Acct Dir)*
Sheila Bermel *(Dir-Environments & Logistics)*

Accounts:
2(X)IST
Bank of America
Dow

Jack Morton Worldwide
16-18 Acton Pk Estate Stanley Gardens, The Vale, London, W3 7QE United Kingdom
Tel.: (44) 208 735 2000
Fax: (44) 208 735 2020
E-Mail: experience@jackmorton.com
Web Site: www.jackmorton.com/

Employees: 850
Year Founded: 1939

Richard Vincent *(Sr VP & Head-Consumer & Digital)*
Henry Simonds *(Sr VP & Grp Acct Dir)*
Suzi Thrift *(VP & Dir-Production & Consumer Mktg)*
Keith Chamarette *(Head-Digital)*
Jim Donald *(Head-Production)*
Michael Kent *(Deputy Head-Technical Svcs)*
Joanne Sackett *(Acct Dir)*
Paul Visser *(Sr Mgr-Production)*
Laurence Keep *(Mgr-Production)*
Regno Saminather *(Mgr-IT)*
Craig Wilson *(Mgr-Production)*
Illango Nelson *(Specialist-IT)*

Accounts:
Freeview Campaign: "Entertainment. It's Even Better When it's Free"
King Digital Entertainment PLC Candy Crush Soda Saga
Nivea Dare to Dip
P&G Wella

Jack Morton Worldwide
Royal Navy House 32 Grosvenor St, The Rocks, Sydney, NSW 2000 Australia
Tel.: (61) 2 8231 4500
Fax: (61) 2 8231 4555
E-Mail: experience@jackmorton.com
Web Site: www.jackmorton.com

Employees: 850
Year Founded: 1939

Katie Chatfield *(VP & Head-Strategy & Digital)*
Dan Pearce *(VP & Dir-Ops Australia)*
Kate Russell *(Head-Production)*
Richard Bradley *(Exec Dir-Creative)*
Kate Carulli *(Acct Dir)*
Jasmine Russell *(Assoc Producer)*
Kate Williams *(Assoc Producer)*

Accounts:
Google

Jack Morton Worldwide
Level 4, 520 Bourke Street, Melbourne, VIC 3000 Australia
Tel.: (61) 386442100
E-Mail: experience@jackmorton.com
Web Site: www.jackmorton.com

Employees: 850
Year Founded: 1939

Thomas Manion *(Dir-Creative)*

Accounts:
Casella Yellow Tail
Google
Nespresso

Jack Morton Worldwide
600 Battery St 2nd Fl, San Francisco, CA 94111
Tel.: (415) 318-4300
E-Mail: experience@jackmorton.com
Web Site: www.jackmorton.com

Employees: 850
Year Founded: 1939

National Agency Associations: 4A's

Agency Specializes In: Advertising

Edward Scott *(Sr VP & Mng Dir-West Coast)*
Lindsay Grinstead *(Sr VP & Sr Acct Dir)*
Mo Husseini *(VP, Sr Dir-Creative & & Dir-Design)*
Vince Belizario *(VP & Sr Acct Dir)*
Armando Orubeondo *(Dir-Environments & Acct Mgr)*
Tom Manion *(Dir-Creative)*
Tom Michael *(Dir-Strategy)*
Pete Scanlon *(Assoc Strategist)*

Accounts:
T-Mobile Telecommunications

Jack Morton Worldwide
8687 Melrose Ave Ste G700, West Hollywood, CA 90069
Tel.: (310) 967-2400
Fax: (310) 967-2450
E-Mail: experience@jackmorton.com
Web Site: www.jackmorton.com

Employees: 850
Year Founded: 1939

National Agency Associations: 4A's

Agency Specializes In: Advertising, Sponsorship

Edward Scott *(Sr VP & Mng Dir-West Coast)*

Jack Morton Worldwide
800 Connecticut Ave, Norwalk, CT 06854
Tel.: (203) 851-7800
E-Mail: experience@jackmorton.com
Web Site: www.jackmorton.com

Employees: 850
Year Founded: 1939

National Agency Associations: 4A's

Paula DeFeo *(Sr VP & Mng Dir)*

Accounts:
eBay
HP
Intel

Jack Morton Worldwide
875 N Michigan Ave 27th Fl, Chicago, IL 60611
Tel.: (312) 274-6060
Fax: (312) 274-6061
E-Mail: experience@jackmorton.com
Web Site: www.jackmorton.com

Employees: 850
Year Founded: 1939

National Agency Associations: 4A's

Agency Specializes In: Advertising

Josh McCall *(Chm & CEO)*
Bill Davies *(COO)*
Stacie Sefcik *(Sr VP-Dir-Client Svc)*
Craig Chaplin *(VP & Sr Dir-Creative-Chicago)*
Sharon Wilson *(VP & Exec Producer)*
Jennifer Funches *(VP & Dir-Production)*
Michelle Gallagher *(VP & Dir-Bus Dev)*
Rebecca Sanders *(Assoc Dir)*
Jordan Hensley *(Sr Assoc Producer)*

Accounts:
Abbott
Abbvie
P&G
Target

Jack Morton Worldwide
1 Woodward Ave, Detroit, MI 48226-3430
Tel.: (313) 596-9100
E-Mail: experience@jackmorton.com
Web Site: www.jackmorton.com

Employees: 40
Year Founded: 1939

National Agency Associations: 4A's

Agency Specializes In: Advertising, Sponsorship

Josh McCall *(Chm & CEO)*
Brian Patterson *(Exec VP & Mng Dir-Detroit)*
Charlotte Merrell *(Exec VP-HR-Worldwide)*
Janet Greenberg *(VP & Head-Creative Svcs-NYC)*
Dave Silcox *(Sr Dir-Creative)*
Erika Eraqi *(Sr Acct Dir-Cadillac)*
Mary Trybus *(Dir-Creative)*
Erin Abbott *(Sr Acct Mgr)*

Accounts:
Bayer Schering Plough
CME Group
Dell
Ebay
ESPN
General Motors Event Marketing, Experiential Marketing, Promotions, Sponsorships
HP
Hyundai
IBM

Microsoft

Jack Morton Worldwide
909 3rd Ave 11th Floor, New York, NY 10022
Tel.: (212) 401-7000
Fax: (212) 401-7010
E-Mail: experience@jackmorton.com
Web Site: www.jackmorton.com

Employees: 850
Year Founded: 1939

National Agency Associations: 4A's

Agency Specializes In: Advertising, Affluent Market, Arts, Automotive, Brand Development & Integration, Broadcast, Communications, Computers & Software, Consumer Goods, Consumer Marketing, Cosmetics, Digital/Interactive, Direct-to-Consumer, Entertainment, Event Planning & Marketing, Fashion/Apparel, Financial, Food Service, Graphic Design, Health Care Services, High Technology, Hospitality, Integrated Marketing, International, Luxury Products, Market Research, Multimedia, Package Design, Pharmaceutical, Print, Production, Production (Ad, Film, Broadcast), Promotions, Public Relations, Publicity/Promotions, Retail, Sales Promotion, Social Media, Sponsorship, Strategic Planning/Research, T.V., Travel & Tourism, Web (Banner Ads, Pop-ups, etc.)

Bill Davies *(CFO & COO)*
Charlotte Merrell *(Exec VP-HR-Worldwide)*
Craig Millon *(Exec VP-Consumer Mktg)*
Abbie Walker *(Sr VP & Head-Strategy)*
Carley Faircloth *(Sr VP & Acct Dir)*
Sharon Foo *(Sr VP & Acct Dir)*
Leesa Wytock *(VP & Head-Creative Tech)*
Carol Katz *(VP & Sr Producer)*
Traci Kleinman *(VP & Acct Dir)*
Dan Carter *(VP & Dir-Creative)*
Jonathan Singer *(VP-HR)*
Peter Sun *(VP-Brand Mktg)*
Andy Herman *(Dir-Event Sls)*
Mandi Zansky *(Assoc Dir-Creative)*
Brendan Steiner *(Acct Mgr)*
Christina Houghton *(Strategist)*

Accounts:
British Petroleum Energy
Cotton Manufacturing
Emblem Health Insurance
Google Fiber Optics
IBM Technology
Samsung Technology
Verizon Communications Telecommunications

JACK MYERS MEDIA BUSINESS REPORT
PO Box 27740, Las Vegas, NV 89126
Tel.: (201) 572-8675
Fax: (973) 267-1514
Web Site: www.jackmyers.com

E-Mail for Key Personnel:
President: jack@jackmyers.com

Employees: 2
Year Founded: 1981

Agency Specializes In: Business-To-Business, Cable T.V., Consulting, Entertainment, Planning & Consultation, Strategic Planning/Research, T.V.

Jack Myers *(Chm)*
Maryann Teller *(VP-Ops-Res)*
Ed Martin *(Dir-Editorial)*

Accounts:
ABC Cable Networks
AOL, LLC
CBS Television
Disney On Line
Hallmark
McCann Erickson
MTV Networks Comedy Central
Rainbow Media
Scripps Networks
Turner Broadcasting
The Weather Channel
Zenith

JACKSON MARKETING GROUP
2 Task Ct, Greenville, SC 29607
Tel.: (864) 272-3000
Fax: (864) 272-3040
Web Site: www.jacksonmg.com

Employees: 85
Year Founded: 1988

National Agency Associations: BMA-PRSA-Second Wind Limited

Agency Specializes In: Advertising, Automotive, Aviation & Aerospace, Brand Development & Integration, Collateral, College, Communications, Consumer Marketing, Corporate Communications, Corporate Identity, Crisis Communications, Digital/Interactive, Event Planning & Marketing, Exhibit/Trade Shows, Experience Design, Financial, Graphic Design, Guerilla Marketing, Health Care Services, Identity Marketing, Integrated Marketing, Internet/Web Design, Logo & Package Design, Market Research, Media Buying Services, Media Planning, Media Relations, Mobile Marketing, Pharmaceutical, Production (Print), Public Relations, Publicity/Promotions, Search Engine Optimization, Sponsorship, Strategic Planning/Research, Transportation

Darrell Jackson *(CEO)*
Kevin Johnson *(COO & Exec VP)*
David Jones *(CMO & VP)*
Joe Clark *(Exec Dir-Video & Bus Theater)*
JoAnne Laffey Abed *(Dir-PR)*
Benjamin Adams *(Dir-Art)*
Josh Lyall *(Dir-Strategic Plng)*
Mike Weston *(Dir-Creative)*
Alyssa Guerrero *(Assoc Dir-Art)*
Monique Bearden *(Acct Supvr)*

Accounts:
American Red Cross of the Upstate
Artisphere
BF Goodrich Tires
BMW Charity ProAm
BMW Manufacturing Corp.
BMW Motorrad
BNSF Railway
Capsugel
Hyster Lift Trucks; Greenville, NC; 2009
Metropolitan Arts Council
Michelin Aircraft Tires
Michelin Earthmover Tires
Michelin North America
Michelin Truck Tires
Milliken & Co.
The Palmetto Bank Smart phone
Peace Center; Greenville, SC Performing Arts; 2009
Wiley X Eyewear
Yale Lift Trucks; Greenville, NC; 2009

JACOB TYLER BRAND COMMUNICATIONS
625 Broadway Ste 1025, San Diego, CA 92101
Tel.: (619) 573-1061
Fax: (619) 696-8633
Toll Free: (866) 735-3438
E-Mail: info@jacobtyler.com
Web Site: www.jacobtyler.com

Agency Specializes In: Advertising, Brand Development & Integration, Corporate Identity, Graphic Design, Internet/Web Design, Logo & Package Design, Outdoor, Print, Search Engine Optimization, Social Media

Les Kollegian *(Founder & CEO)*
Charlie Van Vechten *(Pres & Chief Creative Officer)*
Timothy Mutrie *(Chief Strategy Officer)*
Victoria Hodgkins *(Client Svcs Dir)*
Michelle Peck *(Assoc Dir-Creative)*

Accounts:
JBS International
Soundcast Company

JACOBS AGENCY
308 W Erie 2nd Fl, Chicago, IL 60654
Tel.: (312) 664-5000
Fax: (312) 664-5080
E-Mail: newbusiness@jacobsagency.com
Web Site: www.jacobsagency.com

Employees: 13
Year Founded: 1997

National Agency Associations: BMA

Agency Specializes In: Above-the-Line, Advertising, Alternative Advertising, Below-the-Line, Brand Development & Integration, Business-To-Business, Cable T.V., Co-op Advertising, Collateral, Communications, Computers & Software, Consumer Marketing, Corporate Communications, Corporate Identity, Digital/Interactive, E-Commerce, Electronics, Email, Financial, Graphic Design, High Technology, Identity Marketing, Industrial, Internet/Web Design, Local Marketing, Logo & Package Design, Media Planning, Merchandising, Multimedia, New Technologies, Out-of-Home Media, Package Design, Planning & Consultation, Podcasting, Point of Purchase, Point of Sale, Print, Promotions, Radio, Regional, Retail, Sales Promotion, Search Engine Optimization, Sports Market, Strategic Planning/Research, Sweepstakes, Transportation, Urban Market, Viral/Buzz/Word of Mouth, Web (Banner Ads, Pop-ups, etc.), Women's Market

Tom Jacobs *(Principal)*
Flora Caputo *(VP & Exec Dir-Creative)*
Bill Tourlas *(VP & Client Svcs Dir)*
Bernie Pitzel *(Grp Dir-Creative)*
Joanna Mirowska *(Dir-Art)*
Rachel Ryan *(Assoc Dir-Creative)*
Monica Arcaro *(Acct Mgr)*

Accounts:
Accenture
ACCO
Amtrak Regional Advertising
Comcast
Fair Oaks Farms
HomeDirectUSA
John Morrell Food Group Advertising
Kellogg
Microsoft
Mondelez International, Inc.
Nicor
OTTO
Turano Baking Company
WE Energies
Weston Food Brands

JACOBS & CLEVENGER, INC.
303 E Wacker Dr, Chicago, IL 60601
Tel.: (312) 894-3000
Fax: (312) 894-3005
E-Mail: mail3250@jacobsclevenger.com
Web Site: www.jacobsclevenger.com

Employees: 30
Year Founded: 1982

National Agency Associations: 4A's-AMA-DMA

Agency Specializes In: Advertising, Automotive, Bilingual Market, Business Publications, Business-To-Business, Cable T.V., Collateral, Communications, Consulting, Consumer Marketing, Cosmetics, Direct Response Marketing, E-Commerce, Education, Electronic Media, Financial, Food Service, Graphic Design, Health Care Services, High Technology, Hispanic Market, Information Technology, Internet/Web Design, Leisure, Logo & Package Design, Magazines, New Product Development, Newspapers & Magazines, Over-50 Market, Planning & Consultation, Point of Sale, Print, Public Relations, Radio, Retail, Strategic Planning/Research, T.V., Telemarketing, Trade & Consumer Magazines, Travel & Tourism

Approx. Annual Billings: $30,000,000

Breakdown of Gross Billings by Media: D.M.: $28,000,000; Other: $2,000,000

Ron Jacobs *(Pres)*
Sheera Eby *(Exec VP-Strategy & Client Svcs)*
Kim Redlin *(VP & Dir-Creative)*
Penny Clevenger *(VP-Fin & Admin)*
John Kissane *(Dir-Creative Svcs)*
Jessica Kumor *(Assoc Dir-Content Mktg & Editing)*
Randy Mitchell *(Assoc Dir-Creative)*

Accounts:
American Marketing Association; Chicago, IL
Cintas Uniforms
Consumers Energy; Jackson, MI
The Direct Marketing Association
National Restaurant Association Educational Foundation

JACOBSON ROST

233 N Water St 6th Fl, Milwaukee, WI 53202
Tel.: (414) 220-4888
Fax: (414) 220-4889
Web Site: www.jacobsonrost.com

E-Mail for Key Personnel:
President: jflemma@jacobsonrost.com
Creative Dir.: srussell@jacobsonrost.com
Media Dir.: JEmery@jacobsonrost.com
Public Relations: mbrophy@jacobsonrost.com

Employees: 50
Year Founded: 1956

National Agency Associations: MCA

Agency Specializes In: Advertising, Brand Development & Integration, Broadcast, Business-To-Business, Cable T.V., Collateral, Consumer Marketing, Consumer Publications, Digital/Interactive, Event Planning & Marketing, Exhibit/Trade Shows, Food Service, In-Store Advertising, Internet/Web Design, Leisure, Logo & Package Design, Magazines, Marine, Newspaper, Out-of-Home Media, Outdoor, Planning & Consultation, Point of Sale, Print, Production, Public Relations, Radio, Restaurant, Retail, Sales Promotion, Sponsorship, Sports Market, Strategic Planning/Research, T.V., Travel & Tourism

Approx. Annual Billings: $64,000,000

Jerry Flemma *(Pres & COO)*
Pat Goggin *(Partner & Chief Strategy Officer)*
Steve Simoncic *(Chief Creative Officer)*
Mary Brophy *(Dir-PR)*
C. K. Lim *(Dir-Art)*
Laura Hinrichsen *(Assoc Dir-Media)*
Aimee Westerbeke *(Sr Acct Exec)*
Ashleigh Christopherson *(Acct Exec)*
Kurt Schultz *(Acct Exec)*

Accounts:
Boss Snowplows; Iron Mountain, MI Snow Removal Equipment; 1998
Carl Buddig & Company Carl Buddig & Company, Deli Cuts, Extra Thin, Fix Quix
Cellcom Israel Ltd.
Jacob Leinenkugel Brewing Co.
Kohler Company; Kohler, WI Plumbing Products
MillerCoors LLC Campaign: "Great Beer Great Responsibility", Miller Lite Brewers Collection
Nemschoff, Inc.
Old Wisconsin Sausage; Sheboygan, WI; 2001
Society Insurance; Fond du Lac, WI; 1998
Stein Gardens & Gifts

JADI COMMUNICATIONS

1110 Glenneyre St, Laguna Beach, CA 92651
Tel.: (949) 494-8900
Fax: (949) 494-4153
E-Mail: studio@jadicom.com
Web Site: www.jadicom.com

Agency Specializes In: Advertising, Brand Development & Integration, Broadcast, Corporate Identity, Digital/Interactive, Internet/Web Design, Outdoor, Print, Public Relations, Radio

Tim Morra *(Exec Dir-Creative)*
Lauren Ivy *(Sr Dir-Art)*
Ashley Pringle *(Sr Dir-Art)*
Alec Boehm *(Dir-Visual)*
Gary Brewer *(Dir-Social Media)*
Lisa Roberson-Beery *(Dir-Dev)*
Chris Walker *(Dir-Digital)*

Accounts:
AMA Skincare Marketing, Strategic Branding
Epson America Inc.

JAEGER, INC.

8981 Timberedge Dr, North Ridgeville, OH 44039
Tel.: (440) 243-8700
Toll Free: (800) 237-7585
Web Site: www.jaegerinc.com

E-Mail for Key Personnel:
President: auble@jaegerinc.com

Employees: 1
Year Founded: 1972

Agency Specializes In: Advertising, Aviation & Aerospace, Business-To-Business, Collateral, Communications, Corporate Identity, E-Commerce, Education, Electronic Media, Engineering, Exhibit/Trade Shows, Financial, Graphic Design, Health Care Services, High Technology, Industrial, Internet/Web Design, Logo & Package Design, Magazines, Marine, Multimedia, Newspaper, Newspapers & Magazines, Outdoor, Print, Production, Public Relations, Publicity/Promotions, Radio, Recruitment, Strategic Planning/Research, Technical Advertising, Trade & Consumer Magazines

Donald C. Auble *(Founder)*

Accounts:
The Sherwin-Williams Co.
TA-Petro
Truckstops of America
Yokohama Tire Corp.

JAFFE & PARTNERS

148 Madison Ave 12th Fl, New York, NY 10016-5109
Tel.: (212) 696-5555
Fax: (212) 696-4998
E-Mail: stevej@jaffeandpartners.com
Web Site: www.jaffeandpartners.com

Employees: 13
Year Founded: 1991

Agency Specializes In: Brand Development & Integration, Direct Response Marketing, Event Planning & Marketing, Exhibit/Trade Shows, Graphic Design, Internet/Web Design, Logo & Package Design, New Product Development, Point of Purchase, Publicity/Promotions, Sales Promotion

Approx. Annual Billings: $5,000,000

Breakdown of Gross Billings by Media: Brdcst.: $1,000,000; Collateral: $1,000,000; Fees: $2,500,000; Point of Purchase: $250,000; Trade Shows: $250,000

Steven R. Jaffe *(Partner)*
Betty Wall *(Partner)*
Chris Clary *(Dir-Creative)*
Dan Weiss *(Dir-Creative)*

Accounts:
American Express; New York, NY; 1991
Cheeses of France, Inc.
Pentagon Federal Credit Union
Software Business Consulting

JAJO, INC.

200 N Broadway Ste 110, Wichita, KS 67202
Tel.: (316) 267-6700
Fax: (316) 267-3531
E-Mail: info@jajo.net
Web Site: www.jajo.net

Employees: 6
Year Founded: 2003

Agency Specializes In: Advertising, Aviation & Aerospace, Brand Development & Integration, Broadcast, Business-To-Business, Cable T.V., College, Consumer Marketing, Corporate Identity, Digital/Interactive, Direct Response Marketing, E-Commerce, Event Planning & Marketing, Exhibit/Trade Shows, Financial, Graphic Design, Health Care Services, High Technology, Hospitality, Identity Marketing, Industrial, Integrated Marketing, Internet/Web Design, Leisure, Logo & Package Design, Luxury Products, Marine, Market Research, Media Buying Services, Multimedia, Outdoor, Planning & Consultation, Print, Promotions, Public Relations, Radio, Retail, Seniors' Market, Strategic Planning/Research, T.V., Trade & Consumer Magazines, Transportation, Travel & Tourism

Steve Randa *(Mng Partner)*
Shawn Stuckey *(Mng Partner)*
Mike Gangwere *(Dir-Art)*
Cole Winblad *(Assoc Dir-Creative)*
Jessica Fagherazzi *(Coord-Brand)*

Accounts:
Cox Business; Wichita, KS Business Voice, Data & Video Services; 2009
Great Lakes Polymer Technologies
ICM, Inc.; Colwich, KS; 2008

JAM3

171 E Liberty St Ste 252, Toronto, ON M6K 3P6 Canada
Tel.: (416) 531-5263
Fax: (416) 532-5263
Web Site: www.jam3.com

Agency Specializes In: Advertising, Digital/Interactive, Internet/Web Design

Mark McQuillan *(Mng Dir)*
Mikko Haapoja *(Dir-Creative Tech)*
Aaron Morris *(Dir-Technical)*

Pablo Vio *(Dir-Creative)*
Kuba Bogaczynski *(Assoc Dir-Creative)*
Amanda Westerhout *(Mgr-Talent)*

Accounts:
Dean West
Fathom Film Group Campaign: "Inside North Korea", Campaign: "The Defector: Escape from North Korea"
New-MTV
National Film Board of Canada Bear 71
Orange SA Campaign: "Future Self", Digital
Royal Canadian Mint Campaign: "Heart of the Arctic"
Skittles Campaign: "Create The Rainbow", Online

THE JAMES AGENCY
8100 E Indian School Rd Ste 201, Scottsdale, AZ 85251
Tel.: (480) 248-6710
Fax: (480) 323-2208
E-Mail: info@thejamesagency.com
Web Site: www.thejamesagency.com

Year Founded: 2005

Agency Specializes In: Advertising, Collateral, Corporate Identity, Event Planning & Marketing, Graphic Design, Internet/Web Design, Media Buying Services, Media Planning, Public Relations, Strategic Planning/Research

Cristin Andrews *(Controller)*
Jennifer Adler *(Dir-PR)*
Jillian Green *(Dir-Production)*
Angie Miller *(Dir-PR)*
Natalie Niekro *(Dir-Media)*
Darren Tang Simoes *(Dir-Art)*
Shane Tang *(Dir-Creative)*
Jamie Britton *(Sr Graphic Designer)*
Wesley Chaderton *(Jr Copywriter)*
Bryan Zavala *(Coord-Traffic)*

Accounts:
City of Scottsdale
Norbu Designs
Octane Raceway
Potty Pals Club
Spinatos Pizzeria

JAMES & THOMAS, INC.
6N397 Corron Rd Ste 100, Saint Charles, IL 60175-8420
Tel.: (630) 587-9901
Fax: (630) 587-9911
Web Site: www.jamesthomasinc.com

E-Mail for Key Personnel:
President: bbloch@aol.com

Employees: 4
Year Founded: 1965

Agency Specializes In: Advertising, Business-To-Business, Consulting, Direct Response Marketing, Engineering, Environmental, Financial, Graphic Design, Health Care Services, Logo & Package Design, Medical Products, Newspaper, Newspapers & Magazines, Point of Purchase, Print, Production, Public Relations, Publicity/Promotions, Radio, Recruitment, T.V., Trade & Consumer Magazines, Transportation, Yellow Pages Advertising

Breakdown of Gross Billings by Media: Bus. Publs.: 3%; Collateral: 3%; Comml. Photography: 2%; D.M.: 3%; Fees: 6%; Game Shows: 4%; Mags.: 1%; Network Radio: 6%; Newsp. & Mags.: 2%; Newsp.: 26%; Outdoor: 1%; Point of Purchase: 2%; Print: 3%; Production: 4%; Pub. Rels.: 2%; Radio & T.V.: 32%

William Bloch *(Owner)*

Accounts:
Business Learning Inc.; 1987
CAE Service, Inc.; 2000
Conroy Physical Therapy; 2000
CTE AECOM; 1967
Family Pac
IL Chip Services
Illinois Masonic Childrens Home; 1999
Illinois Masonic Homes Endowment Fund
Topel Forman Accounting Services

THE JAMES GROUP
38 Greene St 5th Fl, New York, NY 10013
Tel.: (212) 243-2022
Fax: (212) 243-6797
E-Mail: contact@thejamesgroup.com
Web Site: www.thejamesgroup.com

E-Mail for Key Personnel:
Creative Dir.: paul@thejamesgroup.com

Employees: 7
Year Founded: 1996

Agency Specializes In: Advertising, Advertising Specialties, Brand Development & Integration, Broadcast, Business Publications, Business-To-Business, Cable T.V., Children's Market, Collateral, Communications, Consulting, Consumer Marketing, Consumer Publications, Corporate Communications, Corporate Identity, Cosmetics, Digital/Interactive, Direct Response Marketing, E-Commerce, Education, Electronic Media, Engineering, Entertainment, Event Planning & Marketing, Exhibit/Trade Shows, Fashion/Apparel, Financial, Food Service, Graphic Design, Health Care Services, High Technology, In-Store Advertising, Information Technology, Internet/Web Design, Leisure, Local Marketing, Logo & Package Design, Magazines, Marine, Media Buying Services, Medical Products, Merchandising, Multimedia, New Product Development, Newspaper, Newspapers & Magazines, Out-of-Home Media, Outdoor, Pharmaceutical, Planning & Consultation, Point of Purchase, Point of Sale, Print, Production, Public Relations, Publicity/Promotions, Radio, Real Estate, Restaurant, Retail, Sales Promotion, Strategic Planning/Research, Sweepstakes, T.V., Trade & Consumer Magazines, Travel & Tourism, Yellow Pages Advertising

Approx. Annual Billings: $5,000,000

Breakdown of Gross Billings by Media: Cable T.V.: $2,500,000; Consulting: $1,225,000; D.M.: $575,000; Internet Adv.: $200,000; Newsp. & Mags.: $500,000

Enda Mcshane *(Principal)*

Accounts:
Apex Mills; Long Island, NY Industrial Fabrics; 2004

JAMES PLESSAS INC.
207 Miller Ave, Mill Valley, CA 94941-2817
Tel.: (415) 388-2996

Employees: 3
Year Founded: 1961

National Agency Associations: 4A's

Agency Specializes In: Advertising

Approx. Annual Billings: $1,000,000

Jim Plessas *(Pres)*
Mary Plessas *(VP)*

JAMES ROSS ADVERTISING
1180 SW 36th Ave Ste 101, Pompano Beach, FL 33069
Tel.: (954) 974-6640
Fax: (954) 974-6621
E-Mail: neil@jamesrossadvertising.com
Web Site: www.jamesrossadvertising.com

Employees: 12
Year Founded: 2003

Agency Specializes In: Advertising, Affiliate Marketing, Affluent Market, African-American Market, Alternative Advertising, Automotive, Aviation & Aerospace, Bilingual Market, Brand Development & Integration, Branded Entertainment, Business Publications, Business-To-Business, Cable T.V., Catalogs, Children's Market, Collateral, Commercial Photography, Communications, Consumer Goods, Consumer Marketing, Consumer Publications, Corporate Communications, Corporate Identity, Cosmetics, Custom Publishing, Digital/Interactive, Direct Response Marketing, Direct-to-Consumer, E-Commerce, Electronic Media, Electronics, Email, Entertainment, Environmental, Event Planning & Marketing, Exhibit/Trade Shows, Fashion/Apparel, Financial, Food Service, Gay & Lesbian Market, Graphic Design, Guerilla Marketing, Health Care Services, High Technology, Hispanic Market, Hospitality, Household Goods, Identity Marketing, In-Store Advertising, Internet/Web Design, Leisure, Local Marketing, Logo & Package Design, Luxury Products, Magazines, Marine, Media Buying Services, Media Planning, Medical Products, Merchandising, Mobile Marketing, Multicultural, Multimedia, New Product Development, New Technologies, Newspaper, Newspapers & Magazines, Out-of-Home Media, Outdoor, Over-50 Market, Package Design, Paid Searches, Pharmaceutical, Planning & Consultation, Point of Purchase, Point of Sale, Print, Production, Production (Print), Promotions, Publishing, Radio, Real Estate, Restaurant, Retail, Sales Promotion, Search Engine Optimization, Seniors' Market, Social Marketing/Nonprofit, Sports Market, Technical Advertising, Trade & Consumer Magazines, Transportation, Travel & Tourism, Viral/Buzz/Word of Mouth, Web (Banner Ads, Pop-ups, etc.)

Approx. Annual Billings: $18,000,000

Breakdown of Gross Billings by Media: Collateral: 5%; D.M.: 2%; Graphic Design: 10%; Outdoor: 2%; Point of Sale: 5%; Print: 32%; Production: 3%; Sls. Promo.: 3%; Trade & Consumer Mags.: 10%; Trade Shows: 3%; Worldwide Web Sites: 25%

Jim Potts *(Pres)*
Neil Ross *(CEO)*
Julian Narvaez *(Dir-Art)*
Paige Ross *(Dir-HR & Benefits)*
Lara Hershbein *(Mgr-Traffic Production)*

Accounts:
AshBritt
Dolphin Encounters
Gardens Memorial Park
Heico
Javalution Coffee Company
MD Science Lab
Techno Derm

JAMES STREET ASSOCIATES, LTD.
2441 W Vermont St Ste 298, Blue Island, IL 60406
Tel.: (708) 371-0110
Fax: (708) 371-1979
E-Mail: media@jamesstreetassoc.com
Web Site: jamesstreetassoc.com

Employees: 10

Agency Specializes In: Advertising, Brand Development & Integration, Collateral, Consulting, Email, Integrated Marketing, Internet/Web Design, Logo & Package Design, Production, Publicity/Promotions, Strategic Planning/Research, Web (Banner Ads, Pop-ups, etc.)

Martha Anderson *(Partner)*
Bill Fahrenwald *(Exec Dir)*

Accounts:
Kenco Media Relations
Pacer International

JAMPOLE COMMUNICATIONS, INC.
428 Forbes Ave, Pittsburgh, PA 15219-1620
Tel.: (412) 471-2463
Fax: (412) 471-5861
E-Mail: office@jampole.com
Web Site: www.jampole.com

Employees: 4

Marc Jampole *(Pres)*
Elizabeth Almes *(VP)*

JAN KELLEY MARKETING
1005 Skyview Dr Ste 322, Burlington, ON L7P 5B1 Canada
Tel.: (905) 631-7934
Fax: (905) 632-6924
E-Mail: jletwin@jankelley.com
Web Site: www.jankelley.com

E-Mail for Key Personnel:
President: jletwin@jankelleymarketing.com
Media Dir.: cpreston@jankelleymarketing.com
Production Mgr.: splace@jankelleymarketing.com

Employees: 48
Year Founded: 2001

National Agency Associations: CMA

Agency Specializes In: Advertising, Advertising Specialties, Automotive, Brand Development & Integration, Broadcast, Business Publications, Business-To-Business, Co-op Advertising, Communications, Consulting, Consumer Marketing, Consumer Publications, Corporate Identity, Direct Response Marketing, Education, Event Planning & Marketing, Food Service, Graphic Design, Health Care Services, Internet/Web Design, Logo & Package Design, Marine, Media Buying Services, Medical Products, Merchandising, New Product Development, Outdoor, Planning & Consultation, Point of Purchase, Point of Sale, Print, Production, Public Relations, Publicity/Promotions, Radio, Strategic Planning/Research

Approx. Annual Billings: $10,000,000

Breakdown of Gross Billings by Media: Consulting: 18%; D.M.: 9%; Exhibits/Trade Shows: 1%; Fees: 5%; Graphic Design: 15%; Logo & Package Design: 5%; Newsp.: 5%; Point of Sale: 5%; Radio: 10%; Strategic Planning/Research: 10%; T.V.: 10%; Trade & Consumer Mags.: 5%; Worldwide Web Sites: 2%

Ken Nicholson *(CFO & VP)*
Chantel Broten *(Chief Strategy Officer & VP)*
Geoff Redwood *(Sr Dir-Art)*
Mike Bzowski *(Dir-Video & Graphic Designer-Motion)*
Dave Barnes *(Dir-Art)*
Anita Kitchen *(Assoc Dir-Creative)*
Peter Petch *(Specialist-Dealer Mktg)*
Chris Sanislo *(Copywriter)*

Accounts:
ArcelorMittal Dofasco Inc.
Armstrong Milling
AweStruck Wildlife Removal
Big Brothers Big Sisters
Bulk Burn
Canadian Tire Dealers' Association
Cosella Dorken
Deeley Harley-Davidson
Hamilton Health Sciences
Imperial Oil Ltd.
Jiffy Lube
Knowledge First Financial
Melitta Coffee
Ministry of Finance
Municipal Property Assessment Corporation
Ontario Medical Association
Ontario Pharmaceutical
Ontario Telemedicine Network
Peller Estates
Ranpro Inc.
RiteRate
Rust-Oleum
Sevita (PRO Seeds)
SIR Corp.
Suncor Lubricants
Toronto Transit Commission
VicWest
The Works Burger

JANIS BROWN & ASSOCIATES
19434 4th Pl, Escondido, CA 92029-8111
Tel.: (760) 743-1795
Fax: (760) 746-1691
E-Mail: info@janisbrown.com
Web Site: www.janisbrown.com

Employees: 15
Year Founded: 1977

Agency Specializes In: Advertising, Bilingual Market, Brand Development & Integration, Broadcast, Cable T.V., Co-op Advertising, Collateral, Consulting, Consumer Marketing, Corporate Identity, Direct Response Marketing, E-Commerce, Electronic Media, Entertainment, Event Planning & Marketing, Fashion/Apparel, Food Service, Graphic Design, High Technology, Hispanic Market, Infomercials, Internet/Web Design, Leisure, Logo & Package Design, Magazines, Media Buying Services, Newspaper, Newspapers & Magazines, Out-of-Home Media, Outdoor, Over-50 Market, Planning & Consultation, Point of Purchase, Point of Sale, Print, Production, Publicity/Promotions, Radio, Real Estate, Restaurant, Retail, Sales Promotion, Strategic Planning/Research, Sweepstakes, T.V., Teen Market, Trade & Consumer Magazines, Travel & Tourism

Approx. Annual Billings: $6,000,000

Breakdown of Gross Billings by Media: Collateral: 10%; Internet Adv.: 2%; Out-of-Home Media: 20%; Print: 30%; Radio: 13%; T.V.: 25%

Janis Brown *(Principal)*
Kim Keeline *(Coord-Events & Copywriter)*

Accounts:
City North
Jones Lang LaSalle
Pine Street Development; Seattle, WA
Serramonte Center; Daly City, CA
Urban Retail Properties; Chicago, IL

JANKOWSKICO.
570 Kirts Blvd Ste 202, Troy, MI 48084
Tel.: (248) 404-9900
Fax: (248) 404-9905
E-Mail: possiblities@jankowskico.com
Web Site: www.jankowskico.com

E-Mail for Key Personnel:
President: rjankowski@jankowskico.com

Employees: 8
Year Founded: 1998

National Agency Associations: AAF

Agency Specializes In: Advertising, Brand Development & Integration, Corporate Identity, Education, Financial, Sponsorship

Roger Jankowski *(Pres & Chief Creative Officer)*
Cheryl Collins *(Dir-Media)*

Accounts:
Wayne State University Physicians Group
West Michigan Academy of Environmental Science

JARRARD PHILLIPS CATE & HANCOCK, INC.
219 Ward Cir Ste 3, Brentwood, TN 37027
Tel.: (615) 254-0575
Fax: (615) 843-8431
E-Mail: info@jarrardinc.com
Web Site: www.jarrardinc.com

Employees: 8

Agency Specializes In: Communications, Government/Political, Health Care Services

David Jarrard *(Pres & CEO)*
Molly Cate *(Partner)*
Kim Fox *(Sr VP)*
Debbie Landers *(Sr VP)*
Lauren Fulton *(VP)*
Kendra Rodgers *(Dir-Mktg)*

JASE GROUP, LLC
614 Georgia Ave, Norfolk, VA 23508
Tel.: (757) 962-0134
Web Site: www.jasegroup.com

Year Founded: 1997

Agency Specializes In: Advertising, Brand Development & Integration, Internet/Web Design, Social Media

Keith Parnell *(CEO)*
Walt Taylor *(Dir-Creative)*
Cameron Muro *(Mgr-Comm)*

Accounts:
New-Advance Short Sale Service (Creative Agency of Record) Search Engine Optimization, Social Media
Arvon Staffing Virginia, LLC (Creative Agency of Record)
Dragas Mortgage Company
Iggles Cheesesteaks & Burgers (Advertising Agency of Record) Creative
La Bella in Ghent (Advertising Agency of Record)
New-NuMerchant Pro (Advertising & Creative Agency of Record) Search Engine Optimization, Social Media
Philly Style Steaks & Subs (Advertising Agency of Record) Website
New-Royal Oak Eye Care (Advertising & Creative Agency of Record) Search Engine Optimization, Social Media Integration
New-Vancostas Mediterranean Restaurant (Advertising & Creative Agency of Record) Search Engine Optimization, Social Media

JASON SCHULTE DESIGN, INC.
1060 Capp St, San Francisco, CA 94110
Tel.: (415) 447-9850
E-Mail: hello@visitoffice.com
Web Site: www.visitoffice.com

Year Founded: 2003

Agency Specializes In: Advertising, Brand Development & Integration, Digital/Interactive, Package Design, Strategic Planning/Research

Jason Schulte *(Founder & Dir-Creative)*
Jill Robertson *(Pres)*
Cindy Wu *(Acct Dir)*
Rob Alexander *(Dir-Creative)*
Will Ecke *(Dir-Design)*
Nate Luetkehans *(Designer)*
Gilbert Van Citters *(Designer)*

Accounts:
Bigfoot Art Show
Wee Society

JAVELIN MARKETING GROUP

(Formerly Javelin)
7850 N Belt Line Rd, Irving, TX 75063-6098
Tel.: (972) 443-7000
Fax: (972) 443-7194
E-Mail: info@javelinmarketinggroup.com
Web Site: javelin.mg

Employees: 190
Year Founded: 2004

National Agency Associations: 4A's-AAF-AMA-DMA

Agency Specializes In: Advertising, Automotive, Business-To-Business, Collateral, Communications, Consulting, Consumer Marketing, Corporate Communications, Digital/Interactive, Direct Response Marketing, Direct-to-Consumer, Electronic Media, Financial, Graphic Design, Health Care Services, High Technology, Information Technology, Internet/Web Design, Local Marketing, Pharmaceutical, Planning & Consultation, Print, Production, Sponsorship, Strategic Planning/Research, Sweepstakes

Mike McCartin *(Pres)*
Pam Larrick *(CEO)*
Leigh Ober *(Chief People Officer)*
Michael Radigan *(Sr VP-Digital)*
Derek Harding *(Mng Dir-Javelin Labs)*
David Selwood *(Mng Dir-Enterprise Spectrum)*
Amy Stratton *(Acct Dir)*
Ashley Spooner *(Acct Supvr)*
Hannah Clayton *(Acct Exec)*
Jully Joseph *(Acct Coord)*

Accounts:
Allstate
AT&T, Inc. AT&T U-Verse
Citi
Gerber Life Insurance Company
Heritage Union
The Humane Society of the United States Call Center Management, Creative, DRTV, Media Planning & Buying
Hyatt
New Zealand Telecom
PEPBOYS Auto
The Scooter Store
TruGreen; Memphis, TN Lawn Care

JAY ADVERTISING, INC.

170 Linden Oaks, Rochester, NY 14625-2836
Tel.: (585) 264-3600
Fax: (585) 264-3650
Toll Free: (800) 836-6800
E-Mail: gregory.smith@jayww.com
Web Site: www.jayww.com

E-Mail for Key Personnel:
President: gregory.w.smith@jayww.com

Employees: 50
Year Founded: 1973

National Agency Associations: 4A's

Agency Specializes In: Advertising, Automotive, Brand Development & Integration, Broadcast, Cable T.V., Co-op Advertising, Communications, Consumer Marketing, Consumer Publications, Direct-to-Consumer, Entertainment, Health Care Services, Magazines, Media Buying Services, Media Planning, Newspaper, Newspapers & Magazines, Out-of-Home Media, Outdoor, Over-50 Market, Pharmaceutical, Point of Purchase, Point of Sale, Print, Production, Publicity/Promotions, Radio, Restaurant, Retail, Sales Promotion, Social Media, Sponsorship, Sports Market, Sweepstakes, T.V., Trade & Consumer Magazines

Approx. Annual Billings: $24,000,000

Gregory W. Smith *(Pres & COO)*
Ferdinand Jay Smith, III *(CEO & Exec Dir-Creative)*
Roxie Barrett *(CFO & VP)*
Bob Nisson *(Chief Creative Officer)*
Guy S. Smith *(VP)*
David Ianucci *(Acct Dir)*
Lisa Brown *(Mgr-Media)*
Elizabeth Gallea *(Acct Exec)*
Jennifer Barone *(Media Planner)*
Marisa Quinn *(Sr Media Planner & Sr Media Buyer)*

Accounts:
First Niagara Financial Group; Lockport, NY Bank & Consumer Commercial Services; 2007
General Motors Pontiac Retail, Buick & GMC Truck Retail Advertising, Chevrolet Retail
HBO
Nikon Inc (Agency of Record)
Raymour & Flanigan Furniture; Liverpool, NY Furniture; 2005
Rochester Red Wings Baseball Team
Sealy Corporation; Trinity, NC Mattresses
St. John Fisher College; Rochester, NY Liberal Arts College; 2006
Wegmans Food & Pharmacy

JAYNE AGENCY

400 N. State St, Chicago, IL 60654
Tel.: (312) 464-8100
Web Site: www.jayneagency.com

Employees: 15
Year Founded: 2009

Brooke Foley *(CEO)*

Accounts:
Big Lots!; 2014
College Illinois! Prepaid Tuition Program; 2012
Free Market Ventures; 2012

JAYRAY, A COMMUNICATIONS CONSULTANCY

535 E Dock St Ste 205, Tacoma, WA 98402-4630
Tel.: (253) 627-9128
Fax: (253) 627-6548
E-Mail: scampbell@jayray.com
Web Site: www.jayray.com

Employees: 12
Year Founded: 1970

Agency Specializes In: Advertising, Brand Development & Integration, Consulting, Corporate Identity, Event Planning & Marketing, Financial, Graphic Design, Health Care Services, Internet/Web Design, Legal Services, Media Relations, Media Training, Public Relations, Real Estate, Strategic Planning/Research

Approx. Annual Billings: $9,000,000 (Capitalized)

Breakdown of Gross Billings by Media: Bus. Publs.: 21%; Collateral: 14%; D.M.: 5%; Mags.: 17%; Newsp.: 26%; Outdoor: 6%; Point of Sale: 1%; T.V.: 5%; Transit: 5%

Kathleen Deakins *(Pres)*
Bridget Baeth *(Designer)*
Bethany Doane *(Coord-Admin)*

Accounts:
Broadway Center for the Performing Arts
Catholic Health Initiatives; Denver, CO Health Care
Green Diamond Resource Co.
Harborstone Credit Union
KPS Health Plans
Lacey Fire District Three
LeRoy Jewelers; Tacoma, WA
Lucks Food Decorating Co.; Tacoma, WA Cake Decorations; 1992
Mercy Medical Center
Metro Parks Tacoma
Northwest Cascade, Inc.
Palmer Scholars
Pierce County Library System
Pierce County Public Works & Utilities
Port of Tacoma
Simpson Lumber Company, LLC; Tacoma, WA; 1985
Simpson Tacoma Kraft Co.; Tacoma, WA Paper, Pulp
Sound Credit Union
St. Anthony Hospital
Threshold Group
Thurston County Department of Water & Waste
The Union Credit Union

JB CHICAGO

435 N LaSalle Ste 201, Chicago, IL 60654
Tel.: (312) 442-7223
Fax: (312) 264-0138
E-Mail: info@jbchicago.com
Web Site: www.jbchicago.com

Employees: 10

Agency Specializes In: Integrated Marketing

Steve Gaither *(CEO)*
Christina Calderon *(COO & Dir-Creative)*
Ann Hlavach *(Mgr-Billing)*
Kimberly Laughlin *(Sr Copywriter & Strategist-Brand)*
Lindsey Lullo *(Acct Exec)*
Katelyn Diveley *(Asst Acct Exec)*

Accounts:
Albert's Diamond Jewelers
American Auto Insurance
ASHA Salon & Spa
Koncept Promotions
Nate Berkus & Associates
Virtual Care Provider, Inc

J.C. THOMAS MARKETING COMMUNICATIONS

1230 W Morehead St Ste 208, Charlotte, NC 28208
Tel.: (704) 377-9660
Fax: (704) 377-9662
E-Mail: info@jcthomas.com

Joel B. Thomas *(Owner)*

Accounts:
Johnson & Johnson
The McGill & Hill Group Financial Advisory Firm; 2010

JCDECAUX NORTH AMERICA

3 Park Ave 33rd Fl, New York, NY 10016
Tel.: (646) 834-1200

Fax: (646) 834-1201
Web Site: www.jcdecauxna.com

Employees: 180
Year Founded: 1994

Agency Specializes In: Out-of-Home Media, Outdoor

Jean-Luc Decaux *(Co-CEO)*
Nicolas Clochard-Bossuet *(COO)*
Paul J. Meyer *(Pres-Digital Sign Svcs)*
Gabrielle Brussel *(Gen Counsel)*
Bob Cilia *(Exec VP)*
Faith Garbolino *(Exec VP-Sls & Mktg)*
Andrew Korniczky *(VP-Intl Client Svcs-USA)*
Thomas Mason *(VP-HR)*
Jennifer Gilhooley *(Mgr-Sls)*
Jessica Krol *(Acct Exec-Natl)*

Accounts:
American InterContinental University
Starbucks
Toyota

JD GORDON CREATIVE LABS
312 Court St, Sioux City, IA 51101
Tel.: (712) 255-5882
Web Site: www.jdgcreativelabs.com

Year Founded: 2002

Agency Specializes In: Advertising, Brand Development & Integration, Graphic Design, Media Buying Services, Package Design, Print, Public Relations, Radio, Social Media, T.V.

Kim Gordon *(Principal & Acct Dir)*
Jeff Gordon *(Principal & Dir-Creative)*
Jan Swanson *(Dir-Media)*
William Brandt *(Strategist-Brand)*
Jim Braunschweig *(Strategist-New Bus Dev & Social Media)*
Jess Anderson *(Designer-Web)*

Accounts:
Downtown Partners Sioux City

JDA FRONTLINE
1667 K St NW Ste 520, Washington, DC 20006
Tel.: (202) 559-0290
E-Mail: info@jdafrontline.com
Web Site: www.jdafrontline.com/

Year Founded: 1976

Agency Specializes In: Advertising

Jim Dyke *(Pres)*
Trevor Francis *(Exec VP & Mng Partner)*
Kelly Cushman *(Exec VP)*
Chris Billeter *(VP-Digital Media)*
Laurie Rossbach *(VP-Pub Affairs)*
Adam Temple *(VP-Pub Affairs)*

Branch

JDA Frontline
(Formerly Jim Dyke & Associates)
438 King St Ste B, Charleston, SC 29403
Tel.: (843) 722-9670
Fax: (843) 722-9672
E-Mail: info@jdafrontline.com
Web Site: www.jdafrontline.com

Year Founded: 2005

Agency Specializes In: Advertising, Communications, Crisis Communications, Media Training, Public Relations, Strategic Planning/Research, Web (Banner Ads, Pop-ups, etc.)

Jim Dyke *(Pres)*
Thomas Otis *(Exec VP-Fin)*
Adam Temple *(VP-Pub Affairs)*

Accounts:
Edo Interactive Digital Marketing

JDCOMMUNICATIONS INC
742 Washington St, Canton, MA 02021
Tel.: (781) 828-0323
Fax: (810) 885-2048
E-Mail: info@jdcomm.biz
Web Site: www.jdcomm.biz

Agency Specializes In: Advertising, Collateral, Graphic Design, Media Buying Services, Print, Public Relations

Joanne DiFrancesco *(Owner & Pres)*
Yvonne Lauziere *(Dir-Art)*
Sarah Gale *(Acct Coord)*
Ashley Francis *(Coord-Mktg & Social Media)*

Accounts:
Eleven Interiors
GerrityStone Granite Stone Fabrications

JEFFREY ALEC COMMUNICATIONS
149 S Barrington Ave Ste 331, Los Angeles, CA 90049
Tel.: (310) 265-1700
Fax: (310) 476-6770
E-Mail: info@jeffreyalec.com
Web Site: www.jeffreyalec.com

E-Mail for Key Personnel:
President: jlevine@jeffreyalec.com
Creative Dir.: jlevine@jeffreyalec.com
Production Mgr.: tgleason@jeffreyalec.com
Public Relations: lmori@jeffreyalec.com

Employees: 4
Year Founded: 1985

National Agency Associations: Second Wind Limited

Agency Specializes In: Advertising, African-American Market, Automotive, Aviation & Aerospace, Brand Development & Integration, Broadcast, Business Publications, Business-To-Business, Cable T.V., Catalogs, Collateral, Communications, Consulting, Corporate Communications, Corporate Identity, Digital/Interactive, Direct Response Marketing, E-Commerce, Electronic Media, Event Planning & Marketing, Exhibit/Trade Shows, Fashion/Apparel, Financial, Food Service, Graphic Design, Health Care Services, High Technology, Identity Marketing, Industrial, Internet/Web Design, Investor Relations, Leisure, Logo & Package Design, Luxury Products, Marine, Market Research, Media Buying Services, Media Planning, Media Relations, Medical Products, Multimedia, Newspaper, Outdoor, Package Design, Planning & Consultation, Point of Purchase, Print, Production, Production (Print), Public Relations, Publicity/Promotions, Radio, Real Estate, Restaurant, Retail, Sales Promotion, Social Marketing/Nonprofit, Strategic Planning/Research, Trade & Consumer Magazines, Transportation, Travel & Tourism

Approx. Annual Billings: $1,000,000

Breakdown of Gross Billings by Media: Collateral: 25%; Consulting: 25%; Graphic Design: 15%; Logo & Package Design: 10%; Worldwide Web Sites: 25%

Jeff Levine *(Pres & Dir-Creative)*

Accounts:
ATI Tools; Escondido, CA Aircraft Tools; 2007
CDI Torque Products; City of Industry, CA Calibration Equipment, Torque Products; 1988
Pipeline Apparel; Gardena, CA Men's & Young Men's Surf Apparel; 2002
Progressive Management Systems; Los Angeles, CA Consulting; 2004
Remy Leather Fashions Fashion; 1995
Signature Estate & Investment Advisors, LLC; Los Angeles, CA Financial; 2006
Weyco Group Inc. Fashion; 1999
Zimmer Museum (Non-Profit); Los Angeles, CA; 2003

JEFFREY SCOTT AGENCY
670 P St, Fresno, CA 93721
Tel.: (559) 268-9741
Fax: (559) 268-9759
Web Site: www.jsaweb.com

Agency Specializes In: Advertising, Brand Development & Integration, Event Planning & Marketing, Media Planning, Media Relations, Outdoor, Print, Public Relations, Social Media, Strategic Planning/Research

Bruce Batti *(Pres)*
Wendy Batti *(CFO)*
Suzanne Davis *(Dir-Art)*
Cathleen Figura *(Dir-Ops)*
Kerry Sabbatini *(Dir-Traffic & Production)*
Jennifer Seita *(Dir-Client Strategies)*

Accounts:
Barrels Unlimited, Inc.
Tioga-Sequoia Brewing

JEKYLL AND HYDE
(Formerly Western Creative, Inc.)
26135 Plymouth Rd, Redford, MI 48239
Tel.: (800) 500-4210
Toll Free: (800) 500-4210
Web Site: jekyllhydeagency.com/

Employees: 16
Year Founded: 1996

Agency Specializes In: Advertising, Brand Development & Integration, Consumer Goods, Direct Response Marketing, Logo & Package Design, Media Planning, Multimedia, Package Design, Print, Production, Radio, Strategic Planning/Research, T.V., Web (Banner Ads, Pop-ups, etc.)

Revenue: $7,000,000

Sally Young *(Pres)*
Robb Taylor *(Chief Creative Officer, Dir-Creative & Strategist-Brand)*
Millie Elston *(Exec Dir-Accts)*
David Alan Olender *(Dir-Ops)*
Angelica Pietrasik *(Dir-Print Art-Western Creative)*
Rob Cozad *(Designer)*
May Lopez *(Media Planner & Buyer)*

Accounts:
Andover (Agency of Record)
Australian Dream Media Purchasing, Strategy
Cremo Company Shave Cream
Delicious Brands L.L.C.; Dallas, TX (Agency of Record)
DenTek Dental Guards
H2Ocean Extreme Tattoo Care Kit, Television
Holmquist Healthcare LLC (Agency of Record)
Innovative Body Solutions (Agency of Record) Resistance Stretching DVD
Jackson Precious Metals Inc.; Redford, MI (Agency of Record)
P&M Products L.L.C; Kirkland, WA (Agency of

Record)
Remedent Inc (Agency of Record)
Solos Footwear (Agency of Record)
Sunset Malibu; Malibu, CA (Agency of Record)
Triumph Pharmaceuticals (Agency of Record)

JENNINGS & COMPANY

104-A N Elliott Rd, Chapel Hill, NC 27514
Tel.: (919) 929-0225
Fax: (919) 968-8278
E-Mail: pzinn@jenningsco.com
Web Site: jenningshealthcaremarketing.com

Employees: 25
Year Founded: 1985

Dan Dunlop *(Principal)*
Dewey Mooring *(VP & Acct Svcs Dir)*
Barri Burch *(Dir-Production)*
Suzanne Williams *(Dir-Art)*
Kathleen Anzenberger *(Assoc Dir-Art)*
Cheryl Witherspoon *(Mgr-Acctg)*
Tim Brennan *(Acct Supvr)*
Kate Rudy *(Specialist-Digital Engagement)*

Accounts:
The Nasher Museum of Art at Duke University; 2007
Truliant
Volvo Fleet
Volvo Owner-Ops
Volvo Trucks North America, Inc. Autocar, Volvo VHD, Volvo VHD 430, Volvo VN, Volvo VN 430, Volvo VN 630, Volvo VN 670, Volvo VN 730, Volvo VN 780, Volvo VNL 300, Volvo VNM 200, X Peditor

JENNINGS PUBLIC RELATIONS & ADVERTISING

(Name Changed to Jennings Social Media Marketing)

JENNINGS SOCIAL MEDIA MARKETING

(Formerly Jennings Public Relations & Advertising)
1656 Washington Ste 150, Kansas City, KS 64108
Tel.: (816) 221-1040
E-Mail: info@jenningssocialmedia.com
Web Site: www.jenningssocialmedia.com

Employees: 6
Year Founded: 2003

Agency Specializes In: Advertising, Collateral, Consulting, Corporate Communications, Corporate Identity, Direct Response Marketing, Graphic Design, Internet/Web Design, Media Buying Services, Media Planning, Media Relations, Print, Public Relations, Publicity/Promotions, Radio, Sponsorship, Sports Market, T.V., Web (Banner Ads, Pop-ups, etc.)

Valerie Jennings *(Founder & CEO)*
Heather Waugh *(Client Svcs Mgr)*
Christina Howard *(Specialist-Social Media Mktg)*

Accounts:
Emfluence
Kansas City Sports Commission

JESS3

1707 L St NW Ste 1000, Washington, DC 20036
Tel.: (571) 213-4308
E-Mail: hi@jess3.com
Web Site: www.jess3.com

Year Founded: 1982

Agency Specializes In: Advertising, Brand Development & Integration, Internet/Web Design, Social Media, Sponsorship, Travel & Tourism

Jesse Thomas *(Founder & CEO)*
Xiyao Yang *(Dir-Project Mgmt & Strategy)*

Accounts:
American Express Company
ESPN, Inc. TV Ratings 101
The Estee Lauder Companies Inc.
Forbes Magazine The Zen of Steve Jobs
Google Inc. Google Politics & Elections 2012
Samsung America, Inc. SXSWi 2012 Smart Wall
United Nations Foundation

JET MARKETING

1929 W County Rd 56, Fort Collins, CO 80524
Tel.: (970) 218-4797
Web Site: www.jetmarketing.net

Agency Specializes In: Advertising, Brand Development & Integration, Internet/Web Design, Logo & Package Design, Media Planning

Jackie Ohara *(Owner & Acct Mgr)*
Erin Rogers *(Creative Dir)*
Lynn Nichols *(Mgr-Publications & Copywriter)*

Accounts:
University of Colorado Hospital

JETSET STUDIOS

2211 Corinth Ave Ste 103, Los Angeles, CA 90064
Tel.: (310) 235-1014
Fax: (310) 914-0469
E-Mail: info@jetsetstudios.com
Web Site: www.jetsetstudios.com

Employees: 15
Year Founded: 1999

Agency Specializes In: Advertising, Entertainment, Game Integration, Internet/Web Design, Viral/Buzz/Word of Mouth

Patrick Young *(Co-Founder & Pres)*
Russell Scott *(CEO & Dir-Creative)*
Krissi Grant *(Producer-Digital)*
Jeremy McDonald *(Dir-Creative)*
Peter Soldinger *(Dir-Creative-Content & Strategy)*
Scott Leeds *(Mgr-Creative)*

Accounts:
Fox Broadcasting Services
Sony Entertainment Services
Universal Studios Entertainment Services
Warner Bros

JETSTREAM PUBLIC RELATIONS

6210 Campbell Rd Ste 203, Dallas, TX 75248
Tel.: (972) 788-9456
Fax: (972) 788-9189
E-Mail: humphrey@jetstreampr.com
Web Site: www.jetstreampr.com

Employees: 6
Year Founded: 2002

Agency Specializes In: Business-To-Business, Communications, Consulting, Corporate Communications, Corporate Identity, Digital/Interactive, Entertainment, Financial, Government/Political, High Technology, Internet/Web Design, Retail

Revenue: $1,000,000

Tony Katsulos *(Pres)*
Tracee Larson *(Sr Acct Supvr)*
Katie Hartfield *(Acct Exec)*
Allison Klingsick *(Acct Coord)*

Accounts:
Cistera Networks; 2007
Dell Computer Corporation
The Southland Corporation
Tesoro Petroleum Corporation

JFD ADVERTISING & PUBLIC RELATIONS

(Name Changed to Jones Foster Deal Advertising & Public Relations, Inc.)

JFLAROUCHE ADVERTISING AGENCY

799 Rue Jacques-Berthiaume, Quebec, QC G1V 3T3 Canada
Tel.: (418) 651-8777
Fax: (418) 651-9229
E-Mail: jflarouche@jflarouchepublicite.com
Web Site: www.jflarouchepublicite.com

Employees: 7
Year Founded: 2006

Agency Specializes In: Advertising

Jean-Francois Larouche *(CEO & Dir-Creative)*
Celine Kirouac *(Dir-Studio & Acct Mgr)*
Bernard Dagenais *(Dir-Content & Strategist-Web)*
Raynald Laflamme *(Dir-Art)*
Myriam Larouche *(Acct Mgr)*

Accounts:
APN
Apocalypse Zero
CEOBois
Julien
Lepine Cloutier Funeral Home; 2005
Prolam
Q-Web
Urgel Bourgie Funeral Home; 2005
Verity Audio Loudspeakers; 2005

J.G. SULLIVAN INTERACTIVE, INC.

6101 Nimtz Pkwy, South Bend, IN 46628-6111
Tel.: (312) 943-1600
Fax: (574) 234-1490
Toll Free: (800) 363-9196
E-Mail: pr@jgsullivan.com
Web Site: www.jgsullivan.com

Employees: 30
Year Founded: 1955

National Agency Associations: BPA

Agency Specializes In: Digital/Interactive

Brett Knobloch *(Pres-Content on Demand)*

Accounts:
Adelphia
Armstrong Flooring
Bendix
Fisher & Paykel
John Deere
Lowe's Home Improvement
Michelin
Nibco; IN
Norelco
Philips
Sears
Stanley
Waterpik
Whirlpool Corp.; Benton Harbor, MI Home Appliances (Special Projects)
York Coleman & Luxaire

Branch

J.G. Sullivan Interactive Inc.
343 W Erie St Ste 440, Chicago, IL 60654
Tel.: (312) 943-1600

Fax: (773) 439-2130
Toll Free: (800) 363-9196
E-Mail: intel@jgsullivan.com
Web Site: www.jgsullivan.com

Employees: 20

Agency Specializes In: Internet/Web Design

Al Croke *(Pres & CEO)*

Accounts:
DAL-Tile
John Deere
Johnson Controls
Omni Hotels

JH&A ADVERTISING INC.
2312 Western Trl Ste 303C, Austin, TX 78745
Tel.: (512) 444-0716
Fax: (512) 444-0865
E-Mail: info@jhaadvertising.com
Web Site: www.jhaadvertising.com

Employees: 15

Agency Specializes In: Advertising, Collateral, Commercial Photography, Consulting, Corporate Identity, Digital/Interactive, Direct Response Marketing, Event Planning & Marketing, Exhibit/Trade Shows, Financial, Graphic Design, High Technology, Internet/Web Design, Print

John Hamm *(Pres)*
Patrick Cline *(Mng Partner & VP)*
Crystal Bristow *(Acct Dir)*
Paula Logan *(Office Mgr)*
Lori Owens *(Project Mgr & Designer)*

Accounts:
3M
Adams Globalization
Alereons
Avaire
Dell
NetQos
QuickArrow
Semicon Groups
Silicon Labs
Spinal Concepts
TMG Consulting
Unwired Buyer
VIEO
Visionedge
Wifi alliance
Wilsonart International

JH COMMUNICATIONS LLC
111 Wayland Ave, Providence, RI 02906
Tel.: (401) 831-6123
E-Mail: info@jhcom.net
Web Site: www.jhcom.net

Year Founded: 2002

Agency Specializes In: Advertising, Communications, Digital/Interactive, Print, Public Relations, Radio, T.V.

John Houle *(Pres)*
Pete Lucas *(VP-Bus Dev)*
Anna Romano *(Office Mgr)*
Sydney Weymouth *(Acct Exec)*

Accounts:
RI Medical Imaging

JIBE MEDIA
774 S 300 W Unit B, Salt Lake City, UT 84101
Tel.: (801) 433-5423
Fax: (801) 364-5423
E-Mail: info@jibemedia.com
Web Site: www.jibemedia.com

Year Founded: 2001

Agency Specializes In: Advertising, Brand Development & Integration, Social Media

Joel Farr *(Owner & Partner)*
Gregory Lowe *(COO)*
Sam Demastrie *(Dir-Art)*
Elise Bowen *(Designer)*
Paula Dalby *(Coord-Acctg & Admin Svcs)*

Accounts:
Davis Education Foundation
Ivory Homes
Mule Deer Foundation
Reaction Polymers, Inc.
Uptown Cheapskate
Xinsurance

JIGSAW LLC
710 N Plankinton Ave Empire Bldg 9th Fl, Milwaukee, WI 53203
Tel.: (414) 271-0200
Fax: (414) 271-0201
E-Mail: info@jigsawllc.com
Web Site: www.jigsawllc.com

Agency Specializes In: Advertising, Collateral, Digital/Interactive, Print, Promotions, Public Relations, Social Media, Strategic Planning/Research

Steven Marsho *(Pres & Partner)*
Steven Wold *(Partner & Chief Creative Officer)*
Dave Hanneken *(Exec Dir-Creative)*
Erin Reising *(Acct Dir)*
Johnny Abbate *(Dir-Digital Svcs)*
Beki Gonzalez *(Dir-Art)*
Amanda Janssen-Egan *(Dir-Media)*
Anne Linginfelter *(Dir-Art)*

Accounts:
88Nine Radio Milwaukee
BloodCenter of Wisconsin
Dohmen Foundation
Lake Consumer Products
Legacy Private Trust Company
Midwest Orthopedic Specialty Hospital
Sage Technologies
Visit Milwaukee
Wheaton Franciscan Healthcare-Iowa, Inc.
Wisconsin Energy Corporation
Zywave, Inc.

JINGLE NETWORKS
(Acquired & Absorbed by Marchex, Inc.)

JIVALDI
6200 Stoneridge Mall Rd 3rd Fl, Pleasanton, CA 94588
Tel.: (800) 277-5734
E-Mail: info@jivaldi.com
Web Site: www.jivaldi.com

Agency Specializes In: Advertising, Brand Development & Integration, Internet/Web Design

James Ivaldi *(Founder & CEO)*

Accounts:
Forged Clothing
Sunol Valley Golf Club

JIWIN
(Acquired by & Name Changed to Apco Worldwide)

JK DESIGN
465 Amwell Rd, Hillsborough, NJ 08844
Tel.: (908) 428-4700
Web Site: www.jkdesign.com

Employees: 65
Year Founded: 1985

Agency Specializes In: Broadcast, Business Publications, Cable T.V., Catalogs, Co-op Advertising, Collateral, Consumer Publications, Digital/Interactive, Electronic Media, Email, Exhibit/Trade Shows, In-Store Advertising, Local Marketing, Magazines, Mobile Marketing, Multimedia, Newspaper, Newspapers & Magazines, Outdoor, Point of Purchase, Point of Sale, Print, Production, Production (Print), Radio, Social Media, T.V., Trade & Consumer Magazines, Viral/Buzz/Word of Mouth, Web (Banner Ads, Pop-ups, etc.), Yellow Pages Advertising

Jerry Kaulius *(Founder & Chief Creative Officer)*
Brett Fielo *(COO & CTO)*
Martha Marchesi *(COO & Chief Strategy Officer)*
Andrea Wolkofsky *(VP-Strategic Alliances)*

JKR ADVERTISING & MARKETING
1 South Orange Ave Ste 202, Orlando, FL 32801
Tel.: (321) 397-0777
Web Site: www.jkradvertising.com

Employees: 50
Year Founded: 2006

Agency Specializes In: Broadcast, Cable T.V., Co-op Advertising, Electronic Media, Local Marketing, Mobile Marketing, Paid Searches, Production, Radio, Search Engine Optimization, T.V.

Approx. Annual Billings: $47,000,000

Jeff Johnson *(Mng Partner)*
Jon Albert *(Partner)*
Daniel Albert *(CFO)*
Donna Fuller *(Acct Exec)*
Doug Johnson *(Acct Exec)*
Jennifer Lawrence *(Acct Exec)*
James Smith *(Acct Exec)*
Yolanda Pagan *(Media Buyer)*
Jacqui Allain *(Coord-Media)*
Phillip Blevins *(Coord-Media)*
Richard Brauns *(Sr Partner)*

Accounts:
Acura of Augusta
Autoworld KIA
Big M Chevy - Radcliff
Big Red KIA
Bill Doraty KIA
Bloomington Ford
Brewbaker Dodge Chrysler Jeep
Brewbaker Infiniti
Brewbaker KIA
Briggs Chrysler Dodge Jeep Lawrence
Briggs Dodge RAM Topeka
Briggs KIA
Briggs Nissan
Briggs Subaru
Butler Fiat of Indianapolis
Car Town Hyundai
Car Town Kia of Florence
Car Town KIA
Car Town RIchmond
Century KIA
Charlie Obaugh Chevrolet Buick Waynesboro
Crown KIA of Longview
Crown Kia of Tyler
Dothan Chrysler Dodge Jeep
Dothan Kia
Enterprise Chevrolet
New-Father & Sons VW & KIA
Felton Holly KIA
Galeana Chrysler Jeep

Galeana KIA
Good Motor Company
Grand KIA
Hampton Automotive Group
Hatfield KIA
Hawkinson KIA
Hughes Honda
Jack Miller KIA
Jeremy Franklin Suzuki
Kia Autosport Columbus
Kia Autosport Pensacola
The Kia Big 3
KIA of Augusta
KIA of Bradley
KIA Of Chattanooga
KIA Of Duluth
KIA of Muncie
Kia of St. Cloud
KIA of Wilmington
The KIA Stores
Kingdom KIA
Laredo Dodge Chrysler Jeep
Matt Blatt KIA
Metro KIA of Madison
Mike Finnin KIA
Mike Murphy KIA
Nazareth Ford
Orlando KIA
Palm Springs KIA
Pete Franklin's Best Cars
Prestige KIA
Repo Joe-The Kia Big 3
Riverchase KIA
Selbyville Holly KIA
Southeast KIA
Spitzer KIA Mansfield
Sterling Auto Group
Stokes Honda
Stokes KIA
Stokes Volkswagen
Sunset Chevrolet GMC Buick
Suntrup Hyundai
Suntrup KIA
Suntrup Nissan
Taylor Hyundai
Taylor KIA Findlay Lima
Taylor KIA of Boardman
Taylor KIA-Toledo
TKS, Anniston Gadsden
Toyota Direct
Tropical Cadillac
University Chrysler Jeep Dodge Ram
University Chrysler Jeep Dodge
University CJDR - Florence
University Hyundai of Florence
University Hyundai
University KIA, IN
University KIA of Muscle Shoals
University KIA
Ward Chrysler
Ward KIA
Ward Used
Warner KIA
West Brothers Chevrolet Buick GMC
Young Automotive

JLM PARTNERS

1001 4th Ave Ste 2100, Seattle, WA 98154
Tel.: (206) 381-3600
Fax: (206) 381-3607
E-Mail: lrm@jlmpartners.com
Web Site: www.jlm-partners.com

Agency Specializes In: Business-To-Business, Corporate Communications, Crisis Communications

Louise R. Mooney *(CEO)*
Jeremy H. Pemble *(Exec VP)*
Stacy Oaksmith *(Sr VP)*
Renee Burch *(Acct Dir)*

Accounts:
Amazon.com
Cisco
Clearwire Broadband Services
Hillcrest Laboratories
Motorola Solutions, Inc.
RealNetworks

JM FOX ASSOCIATES INC

616 Dekalb St, Norristown, PA 19401
Tel.: (610) 275-5957
Fax: (610) 275-7448
Web Site: www.jmfox.com

Agency Specializes In: Advertising, Brand Development & Integration, Email, Internet/Web Design, Logo & Package Design, Outdoor, Print, Public Relations, Radio, T.V.

Jeff Fox *(Pres)*
Robert Goldwein *(Specialist-Mktg & Acct Exec)*

Accounts:
4 Less Furniture
Blue Bell Physical Therapy
Carrolls Jewelers
Chantilly Floral
D&K Appliances
Da Vinci's Pub
Solemate
Spice Salon

JMC MARKETING COMMUNICATIONS & PR

10 Pearl St, Kingston, NY 12401
Tel.: (845) 331-1200
Fax: (845) 331-1431
Toll Free: (800) 459-3003
E-Mail: info@jmcpr.com
Web Site: www.jmcpr.com

Employees: 12
Year Founded: 1987

National Agency Associations: ABC-PRSA

Agency Specializes In: Commercial Photography, Communications, Direct Response Marketing, Event Planning & Marketing, Exhibit/Trade Shows, Internet/Web Design, Multimedia, Point of Sale, Print, Publicity/Promotions, Sales Promotion

Approx. Annual Billings: $1,000,000

John Mallen *(Owner & Pres)*

Accounts:
Honeywell International
International Association of Outsourcing Professional (IAOP)
Invensys Controls
Messe Frankfurt
Ore Pharmaceuticals Inc.
Performance Fibers
Polymer Group, Inc.
Robertshaw Controls Company

JMD COMMUNICATIONS

760 Calle Bolivar, San Juan, PR 00909
Tel.: (787) 728-3030
Fax: (787) 728-7050
E-Mail: jmd@jmdcom.com
Web Site: www.jmdcom.com

E-Mail for Key Personnel:
President: jjimenez@jmdcom.com

Employees: 35
Year Founded: 1996

Approx. Annual Billings: $25,000,000

Joey Jimenez *(Pres)*
Carlos Davila Rinaldi *(Dir-Creative)*

Accounts:
Cooperativa Zeno Gandia
First Bank
Healthy Lifestyles Fitness Club
Nissan Infinity
Pfizer Caribbean
RJ Reynolds

JNA ADVERTISING

7101 College Blvd Ste 120, Overland Park, KS 66210
Tel.: (913) 327-0055
E-Mail: marketing@jnaadv.com
Web Site: http://www.jna-advertising.com/

Agency Specializes In: Advertising, Brand Development & Integration, Corporate Identity, Digital/Interactive, Internet/Web Design, Print, Social Media, T.V.

John Nohe *(Pres & CEO)*
Lance McCormick *(Chief Creative Officer & VP)*
Jordan Garcia *(VP, Dir-Brand Activation & Gen Mgr)*
Tom Wirt *(Exec Dir-Creative)*
Scott Richards *(Sr Dir-Art)*
Angle Williams *(Acct Dir)*
Allie Palmer *(Mgr-Social Media)*
Kevin Mckernan *(Acct Supvr)*

Accounts:
Ceva Animal Health
Kansas Lottery Commission Campaign: "Big Catch", Campaign: "Big TV", Campaign: "Curtains", Campaign: "Dream Sergeant", Campaign: "Hammock", Campaign: "Meterologist", Campaign: "Monkey", Campaign: "Yard Balloon", TV
Mooney International Corp
Overland Park Convention & Visitors Bureau

JOBELEPHANT.COM INC.

5443 Fremontia Ln, San Diego, CA 92115
Tel.: (619) 795-0837
Fax: (619) 243-1484
Toll Free: (800) 311-0563
E-Mail: info@jobelephant.com
Web Site: www.jobelephant.com

E-Mail for Key Personnel:
President: michael@jobelephant.com

Employees: 8
Year Founded: 2000

Agency Specializes In: African-American Market, Asian Market, Bilingual Market, Business Publications, Cosmetics, Engineering, Financial, Government/Political, Graphic Design, High Technology, Information Technology, Internet/Web Design, Media Buying Services, Newspaper, Newspapers & Magazines, Pharmaceutical, Print, Recruitment, Retail, Trade & Consumer Magazines, Transportation, Travel & Tourism

Adam Connelly *(Creative Dir)*
Ryan Vandergriff *(Sr Acct Exec-Adv)*
Belinda Lopez *(Acct Exec-Adv)*
Edward Ramos *(Designer-Web & Visual)*

Accounts:
City of South Lake Tahoe
Kellogg's
Lassen Group
Norcal Mutual Insurance Company
Planned Parenthood of San Diego
San Jose State University
Stratagene
Time Warner Cable
University of Idaho

University of San Diego

JOCOTO ADVERTISING

331 Jefferson St, Oakland, CA 94607
Tel.: (925) 855-7412
Fax: (925) 855-7413
E-Mail: advertising@jocoto.com
Web Site: www.jocoto.com

Employees: 20

Agency Specializes In: Health Care Services, Medical Products, Pharmaceutical

Revenue: $2,000,000

Tom Collins *(Owner)*

Accounts:
Astra Tech
Bausch & Lomb
Heidelberg Engineering
Medical Marketing Association
SkinMedica
SurgRx

JODYANDIANE CREATIVE COMMUNICATIONS, LLC

111 Wood Hollow Ln, New Rochelle, NY 10804
Tel.: (914) 632-2576
Web Site: www.jodyandiane.com

Agency Specializes In: Advertising, Brand Development & Integration, Collateral, Digital/Interactive, Event Planning & Marketing, Internet/Web Design, Media Buying Services, Media Planning, Promotions, Public Relations

Diane Wade *(Co-Pres)*
Marilyn Knapp *(Sr VP & Dir-Acct Mgmt)*
Jody Rawdin *(VP & Dir-Creative)*

Accounts:
New Rochelle Humane Society From Our Home to Yours

JOE ZEFF DESIGN, INC.

8 Hillside Ave Ste 208, Montclair, NJ 07042
Tel.: (973) 655-0501
Fax: (973) 655-0502
E-Mail: studio@joezeffdesign.com
Web Site: www.joezeffdesign.com

Agency Specializes In: Advertising, Multimedia, Print

Joe Zeff *(Pres)*
Ed Gabel *(VP)*

Accounts:
PepsiCo Inc.
Unisys Corporation

THE JOEY COMPANY

45 Main St Ste 632, Brooklyn, NY 11201
Tel.: (718) 852-7730
Fax: (718) 412-3498
E-Mail: see@thejoeycompany.com
Web Site: www.thejoeycompany.com

Employees: 15
Year Founded: 1993

Agency Specializes In: Above-the-Line, Advertising, Affluent Market, Alternative Advertising, Arts, Automotive, Brand Development & Integration, Broadcast, Business-To-Business, Cable T.V., Co-op Advertising, Consumer Goods, Consumer Marketing, Consumer Publications, Corporate Identity, Cosmetics, Digital/Interactive, Direct Response Marketing, Direct-to-Consumer, Education, Electronics, Entertainment, Fashion/Apparel, Financial, Food Service, Gay & Lesbian Market, Government/Political, Graphic Design, Health Care Services, Hispanic Market, Hospitality, Household Goods, Integrated Marketing, Internet/Web Design, Leisure, Local Marketing, Logo & Package Design, Luxury Products, Marine, Medical Products, Men's Market, New Product Development, New Technologies, Newspapers & Magazines, Out-of-Home Media, Outdoor, Over-50 Market, Pets , Pharmaceutical, Point of Sale, Print, Radio, Real Estate, Restaurant, Retail, Seniors' Market, Social Marketing/Nonprofit, Sponsorship, Sports Market, Strategic Planning/Research, T.V., Teen Market, Trade & Consumer Magazines, Transportation, Travel & Tourism, Tween Market, Urban Market, Women's Market

Approx. Annual Billings: $225,000,000

Breakdown of Gross Billings by Media: Radio & T.V.: $225,000,000

Joey Cummings *(Founder, CEO, Chief Creative Officer & Chief Strategic Officer)*
Steve Brodwolf *(Mng Dir & Dir-Creative)*
David Rosenfeld *(Mng Dir-Strategic & Acct Svcs)*
Matt Flandorfer *(Dir-Art)*
Zivy Johnson *(Dir-Production)*
Mesh Maktal *(Dir-Creative)*
Andrea Steuer *(Dir-Art)*
Jim Trowell *(Dir-Creative)*

Accounts:
CDC; 2009
Church & Dwight Arm & Hammer Baking Soda, Arrid Extra Dry, Close Up Toothpaste, First Response Diagnostic Tests, Nair, Simply Saline, Trojan Condoms, Trojan Lubricants
DCG Autogroup Teen Safety Driving Campaign; 2008
Jarden Myself Pelvic Muscle Trainer; 2009
PURE Insurance; 2008
Sanofi-Aventis/Chattem ACT Mouthwash, Allegra, Bullfrog Sunblock, Capzasin, Dexatrim, Garlique, Gold Bond Body Wash, Gold Bond First Aid, Gold Bond Foot Care, Gold Bond Lotion, Gold Bond Powder, Gold Bond Sanitizing Lotion, Herpecin, Icy Hot, Kaopectate, Pamprin, Phisoderm, Selsun Blue Shampoo, Sun In
Title IX; 2004

JOHN APPLEYARD AGENCY, INC.

(d/b/a Appleyard Agency)
(Private-Parent-Single Location)
4400 Bayou Blvd Ste 34, Pensacola, FL 32503-2668
Tel.: (850) 494-2194
Fax: (850) 494-0289
Web Site: www.appleyardagency.com

Employees: 20
Year Founded: 1959

Agency Specializes In: Advertising, Brand Development & Integration, Graphic Design, Internet/Web Design, Media Planning, Public Relations, Social Media

Revenue: $1,600,000

Dick Appleyard *(Pres)*
Diane Appleyard *(VP)*
Chitra Carroll *(Dir-Art)*
Jeanie Hufford *(Dir-Media)*
Liz Pelt *(Sr Acct Mgr & Media Buyer-Digital)*
Eva Chastain *(Office Mgr)*
Carolyn Appleyard *(Mgr-Fin)*
Riannon Boven *(Mgr-Art Dept)*

Accounts:
Armored Frog

JOHN DOE USA

43 W 24th St, New York, NY 10010
Tel.: (212) 377-7189
E-Mail: info@johndoehub.com
Web Site: www.johndoehub.com

Agency Specializes In: Advertising

Rana Reeve *(Founder)*
Rosie Holden *(Mng Dir)*

Accounts:
Adidas
Beats by Dre (North America Agency of Record) Marketing, Public Relations
Dream Hotels Lifestyle Media Relations
Festival Republic Benicassim, Berlin Festival, Lollapalooza, Media Strategies, Press Strategy, UK Public Relations
Ibiza Rocks
illycaffe North America Inc.
New-Kodak Global Buzz & Influencer Relations
o2
Pernod Ricard UK Malibu, Public Relations
Red Bull Blueberry, Cranberry, Lime Flavors
Siggi's Dairy PR, Skyr
Zaggora Brand Awareness, PR

JOHN LAMBERT ASSOCIATES

4370 Starkey Rd Ste 4D, Roanoke, VA 24018
Tel.: (540) 989-4830
Fax: (540) 772-4405
E-Mail: jlambert@jlapr.com
Web Site: www.jlapr.com

Year Founded: 1977

National Agency Associations: Second Wind Limited

Agency Specializes In: Public Relations

John W. Lambert, Jr. *(Owner)*

Accounts:
Halifax Regional Medical Center
Kroger
North Carolina Hospital Association
Wake Forest University Baptist Medical Center

JOHN MANLOVE ADVERTISING

5125 Preston Ave, Houston, TX 77505
Tel.: (281) 487-6767
Fax: (281) 487-5566
Toll Free: (800) 848-4088
E-Mail: info@johnmanlove.com
Web Site: www.johnmanlove.com

Employees: 12
Year Founded: 1962

National Agency Associations: AAF

Eddy Henry *(Chief Creative Officer)*
Gina Manlove *(VP)*
Melody Manlove *(Mgr-Production & Acct Exec)*
Madison Henry *(Acct Planner)*

Accounts:
Allied Waste
Cameron
HCA Holdings Inc.

JOHN ST.

172 John Street, Toronto, ON M5T 1X5 Canada
Tel.: (416) 348-0048
Fax: (416) 348-0050
E-Mail: afleischmann@johnst.com
Web Site: www.johnst.com

Employees: 100
Year Founded: 2001

Agency Specializes In: Advertising, Brand Development & Integration

Breakdown of Gross Billings by Media: Print: 30%; Radio: 20%; T.V.: 50%

Stephen Jurisic *(Partner & Co-Exec Creative Dir)*
Angus Tucker *(Partner & Co-Exec Creative Dir)*
David Glen *(Art Dir)*
Mark Graham *(Acct Dir)*
Marketa Krivy *(Creative Dir)*
Anna Neilson *(Producer-Brdcst)*
Amy Sawyer *(Acct Dir-Acct Svcs)*
Tina Tieu *(Acct Dir)*
Denver Eastman *(Dir-Art)*
Niall Kelly *(Dir-Creative)*
George Lin *(Dir-Art)*
Jenny Luong *(Dir-Art)*
Hannah Smit *(Dir-Art)*
Kara Wark *(Dir-Art)*
Sebastien Lafaye *(Assoc Dir-Creative)*
Matty Bendavid *(Acct Supvr)*
Pawel Rokicki *(Designer)*
Jessica Schnurr *(Copywriter)*

Accounts:
New-1 Second Everyday
Ad Bands
AstraZeneca
Canadian Safe School Network Campaign: "Kids Read Mean Tweets"
The Cassies Teeneger, Ex, Cop
Coggins Campaign: "ExFEARiential"
Corby Distilleries Wiser's, Wiserhood Purse
Family Channel
Future Shop Campaign: "Future Shopping", Campaign: "Gifts You'll Want Too", Campaign: "Nice List", Digital, Online, Signage, Transit Shelters
ING Direct Brand Strategy, Campaign: "Coffee Cup Car", Campaign: "Old Ways", Campaign: "you get what you save for", Creative, Strategic Counsel
Kobo Campaign: "Reader's Passion", Online, Print, TV
Kruger Products
Lake Huron Campaign: "Stop The Drop"
Little Monster Catvertising
Loblaw Companies Limited (Agency of Record) Advertising, Campaign: "Crave More"
Maple Leaf Foods Campaign: "Always-on", Campaign: "Change Your Life with Bacon", Campaign: "Feed their Potential", Natural Selections, Online, TV, Video
Mitsubishi Motor Sales of Canada Campaign: "Built Better. Backed Better", Campaign: "Commute", Campaign: "Electriphobia", Mitsubishi Mirage
President's Choice Broadcast, Campaign: "Crave More", Marketing, Social Media
Shoppers Drug Mart Corporation (Agency of Record) Creative, Media, Print
Sirius Campaign: "We Love Comedy, 1"
Tata Global Beverages Campaign: "Routine"
Tetley Routine Experiment #1, Routine Experiment #2, Tetley Infusions
Trader Corp Campaign: "Free Parking Day"
Trader Media Autotrader.ca
War Child Canada Surrogaid
Winners Creative
Wiser's Canadian Whisky Campaign: "He-Coy bags"
WWF Canada Campaign: "Crowdsourced Earth Hour Anthem", Campaign: "Granny Call Centre", Campaign: "Lazy Environmentalism - Feed Your Cat", Campaign: "Lazy Environmentalism - Making a Sandwich", Campaign: "Lazy Environmentalist", Campaign: "National Sweater Day", Campaign: "Scratch and Save Adoptions card", Campaign: "We Are All Wildlife", Campaign: "We Don't Farm Like This", Earth Hour, MSC Seafood, Online
Young Guns International Campaign: "Forest"
Zellers Campaign: "Festive Finale"

JOHNNY LIGHTNING STRIKES AGAIN LLC

1818 Wyandotte St Ste 100, Kansas City, MO 64108
Tel.: (877) 664-5572
Fax: (877) 664-5572
E-Mail: omg@jlsa.com
Web Site: www.jlsa.com

Year Founded: 2009

Agency Specializes In: Advertising, Brand Development & Integration, Content, Internet/Web Design, Logo & Package Design, Print

Joshua Davis *(Co-Owner & Creative Dir)*
James Penman *(Co-Owner & Dir-Interactive)*
David Cecil *(Co-Owner & Dir-Strategy)*
Caroline Young *(Strategist & Copywriter)*
Sara Duncan *(Designer)*

Accounts:
KVC Health Systems

JOHNSON & MURPHY

16122 Sherman Way, Van Nuys, CA 91406
Tel.: (818) 787-2170
Fax: (818) 787-2094
Web Site: www.jmadv.com

Employees: 300

Agency Specializes In: Brand Development & Integration, Broadcast, Collateral, Consumer Marketing, Entertainment, Event Planning & Marketing, Exhibit/Trade Shows, Graphic Design, Logo & Package Design, Media Buying Services, Production, Publicity/Promotions, Strategic Planning/Research

Kevin Murphy *(Co-Founder & Owner)*
John Potter *(Dir-Creative)*
Brian Hoffmann *(Designer)*

Accounts:
20th Television
Buena Vista Television
Lions Gate Films
Regal CineMedia Corporation
Revolution Studios
That 70's Show

JOHNSON & SEKIN

800 Jackson St Ste 300, Dallas, TX 75202
Tel.: (214) 244-0690
Web Site: www.johnsonandsekin.com

Agency Specializes In: Advertising, Brand Development & Integration, Internet/Web Design, Print, Social Media, T.V.

Chris Sekin *(Partner & Creative Dir)*
Kent Johnson *(Partner & Creative Dir)*
Janet Mistretta *(Art Dir)*
Krista McCrimmon *(Assoc Dir-Creative)*

Accounts:
New-Meat Fight

JOHNSON DESIGN GROUP

550 River St SE, Ada, MI 49301-9524
Tel.: (616) 676-5557
E-Mail: karen@johnsondesign.com
Web Site: www.johnsondesign.com

Employees: 3
Year Founded: 1985

Agency Specializes In: Advertising, Advertising Specialties, Automotive, Brand Development & Integration, Broadcast, Business Publications, Business-To-Business, Cable T.V., Children's Market, Co-op Advertising, Collateral, Commercial Photography, Communications, Consulting, Consumer Marketing, Consumer Publications, Corporate Communications, Corporate Identity, Cosmetics, Digital/Interactive, Direct Response Marketing, E-Commerce, Education, Electronic Media, Engineering, Entertainment, Environmental, Event Planning & Marketing, Exhibit/Trade Shows, Fashion/Apparel, Financial, Food Service, Government/Political, Graphic Design, Health Care Services, High Technology, Hispanic Market, In-Store Advertising, Industrial, Information Technology, Internet/Web Design, Investor Relations, Legal Services, Leisure, Local Marketing, Logo & Package Design, Magazines, Marine, Media Buying Services, Medical Products, Merchandising, Multimedia, New Product Development, Newspaper, Newspapers & Magazines, Out-of-Home Media, Outdoor, Over-50 Market, Pharmaceutical, Planning & Consultation, Point of Purchase, Point of Sale, Print, Production, Public Relations, Publicity/Promotions, Radio, Real Estate, Recruitment, Restaurant, Retail, Sales Promotion, Seniors' Market, Sports Market, Strategic Planning/Research, Sweepstakes, T.V., Technical Advertising, Teen Market, Trade & Consumer Magazines, Transportation, Travel & Tourism, Yellow Pages Advertising

Karen Johnson *(Principal)*

Accounts:
Garlock Equipments
Hines Corporation
K & H Concrete
Proscan

JOHNSON DIRECT

(Name Changed to Responsory)

JOHNSON GRAY ADVERTISING

15375 Barranca Pkwy Ste F-101, Irvine, CA 92618
Tel.: (949) 955-3781
Web Site: www.johnsongray.com

Agency Specializes In: Advertising, Collateral, Digital/Interactive, Event Planning & Marketing, Internet/Web Design, Media Relations, Print, Radio, Social Media, Strategic Planning/Research

William Johnson *(Pres & Creative Dir)*
Gerry Gomez *(Dir-Creative)*
Kathy McLaughlin *(Dir-Media)*
Priscilla Barbanell *(Acct Exec)*
Hunter Johnson *(Acct Exec)*

THE JOHNSON GROUP

436 Market St, Chattanooga, TN 37402-1203
Tel.: (423) 756-2608
Fax: (423) 267-0475
E-Mail: jjohnson@johngroup.com
Web Site: www.johngroup.com

E-Mail for Key Personnel:
President: jjohnson@johngroup.com
Creative Dir.: pbuckley@johngroup.com
Media Dir.: RDaigh@johngroup.com

Employees: 65
Year Founded: 1996

National Agency Associations: 4A's

Agency Specializes In: Sponsorship

Joe Johnson *(Owner)*

Pat Buckley *(Partner & Mng Dir-Creative)*
Mike Polcari *(Partner & Dir-Creative)*
Roger Vaughn *(Partner & Dir-Creative)*
Sandy Buquo *(Partner)*
Joyce Debter *(Controller)*
Alice Ailey *(Acct Svcs Dir)*
Chris Jones *(Dir-Creative)*
Donna Barton *(Mgr-Process-Customer Svcs)*
Jenny Downs *(Acct Exec)*

Accounts:
Fivestar Ranges; Cleveland, TN Stainless Steel Consumer Ranges
The Krystal Company (Co-op & Media Buying Agency of Record) Marketing, Strategies
Krystal Restaurants; 2003
Pet Dairy; Charlotte, NC; 2006

JOHNSON GROUP
15 S 16th Ave, Saint Cloud, MN 56301
Tel.: (320) 654-0500
E-Mail: info@jgroupmarketing.com
Web Site: www.jgroupmarketing.com

Agency Specializes In: Advertising, Brand Development & Integration, Digital/Interactive, Event Planning & Marketing, Graphic Design, Internet/Web Design, Public Relations, Search Engine Optimization, Social Media

Scott Hondl *(Owner & Acct Exec)*
Pam Raden *(Owner & Acct Exec)*
Crystal Simon *(Art Dir)*

Accounts:
New-Thomsen's Greenhouse & Garden Center
New-UV Vodka

JOHNSON INC.
201 W Broad St Ste 600, Richmond, VA 23220-4216
Tel.: (804) 644-8515
Fax: (804) 644-0835
E-Mail: Lwilliams@johnsonmarketing.com
Web Site: www.johnsonmarketing.com

Employees: 10
Year Founded: 1992

Agency Specializes In: Event Planning & Marketing, Public Relations

Approx. Annual Billings: $2,700,000

Paula Bowens *(Dir-Bus Dev)*
Nicole Reed *(Office Mgr)*
Alyse Rooks *(Mgr-Event)*
Jasmine Roberts *(Sr Client Svcs Dir)*

Accounts:
AES
CIAA
City of Richmond
Friends
Optima Family Health Care
Optima
Philip Morris
Richmond Coliseum
Richmond Redevelopment & Housing Agency
Verizon
Virginia Tourism

JOHNSON KING PUBLIC RELATIONS
(Acquired by Finn Partners)

JOHNSON MARKETING GROUP INC.
15255 S 94th Ave Ste 600, Orland Park, IL 60462
Tel.: (708) 403-4004
Fax: (708) 403-4111
E-Mail: info@jmg-inc.com
Web Site: www.jmg-inc.com

Employees: 10
Year Founded: 1985

Agency Specializes In: Brand Development & Integration, Business-To-Business, Collateral, Corporate Identity, Direct Response Marketing, E-Commerce, Exhibit/Trade Shows, Food Service, High Technology, Industrial, Information Technology, Internet/Web Design, Logo & Package Design, Media Buying Services, New Product Development, Planning & Consultation, Point of Purchase, Point of Sale, Print, Production, Public Relations, Strategic Planning/Research, Technical Advertising

Approx. Annual Billings: $4,000,000

Breakdown of Gross Billings by Media: Bus. Publs.: 20%; Collateral: 55%; D.M.: 15%; Worldwide Web Sites: 10%

Allison Johnson *(Founder & Pres)*
Paul G. Johnson *(CEO)*
James Galligan *(Principal)*

JOHNSONRAUHOFF
2525 Lake Pines Dr, Saint Joseph, MI 49085
Tel.: (269) 428-9212
Fax: (269) 428-3312
Toll Free: (800) 572-3996
Web Site: johnsonrauhoff.com

Employees: 60
Year Founded: 1969

National Agency Associations: AMA-Second Wind Limited

Agency Specializes In: Advertising, Alternative Advertising, Automotive, Brand Development & Integration, Broadcast, Business-To-Business, Catalogs, Children's Market, Collateral, Commercial Photography, Communications, Consumer Goods, Consumer Marketing, Consumer Publications, Content, Corporate Communications, Corporate Identity, Cosmetics, Digital/Interactive, Direct Response Marketing, E-Commerce, Education, Electronic Media, Electronics, Engineering, Event Planning & Marketing, Exhibit/Trade Shows, Faith Based, Fashion/Apparel, Financial, Food Service, Gay & Lesbian Market, Graphic Design, Guerilla Marketing, Health Care Services, High Technology, Household Goods, In-Store Advertising, Industrial, Integrated Marketing, Internet/Web Design, Local Marketing, Logo & Package Design, Magazines, Media Buying Services, Media Planning, Media Relations, Medical Products, Merchandising, Multimedia, New Product Development, New Technologies, Newspaper, Newspapers & Magazines, Outdoor, Over-50 Market, Package Design, Pharmaceutical, Planning & Consultation, Point of Purchase, Point of Sale, Print, Production, Production (Ad, Film, Broadcast), Production (Print), Promotions, Public Relations, Publicity/Promotions, Radio, Real Estate, Regional, Retail, Sales Promotion, Seniors' Market, Social Media, Sports Market, Strategic Planning/Research, Sweepstakes, T.V., Technical Advertising, Teen Market, Trade & Consumer Magazines, Travel & Tourism, Tween Market, Viral/Buzz/Word of Mouth, Web (Banner Ads, Pop-ups, etc.), Women's Market

Approx. Annual Billings: $10,000,000

Breakdown of Gross Billings by Media: Brdcst.: 5%; Collateral: 10%; Comml. Photography: 25%; Production: 25%; Strategic Planning/Research: 10%; Worldwide Web Sites: 25%

Jackie Huie *(Owner)*
Don Johnson *(CEO)*
Elizabeth Kohler *(VP)*
Ralph Lucius *(VP-Acct Svcs)*
Marilyn Simmons Wilson *(Acct Dir)*
Amy Hemphill *(Dir-HR)*
Dawn Williams *(Dir-Creative)*
David Buckland *(Sr Acct Mgr)*
Rob Regovich *(Mgr-Studio)*

Accounts:
Amway; Ada, MI General Merchandise
Hamilton Beach; Glen Allen, VA Portable Appliances; 1997
International Order of the Rainbow for Girls Global Membership; 2007
Johnson Controls; Holland, MI Automotive Products; 1994
KitchenAid; Benton Harbor, MI Small Appliance
Meijer; Grand Rapids, MI General Merchandise (Photography); 1979
Michigan Masons; Alma, MI Regional Membership
Newell Rubbermaid; Atlanta, GA Levolor
Rheem; Montgomery, AL Water Heaters
Sur La Table; Seattle, WA Gourmet Cooking Products; 2005
Walmart; Bentonville, AR General Merchandise; 1980
Whirlpool; Benton Harbor, MI Appliances; 1969

Branches

JohnsonRauhoff Marketing Communications
300 W Britain Ave, Benton Harbor, MI 49022
Tel.: (269) 428-3377
Fax: (269) 925-4549
Web Site: www.johnsonrauhoff.com

Employees: 20

Dawn Williams *(Exec VP)*
Elizabeth Kohler *(VP-Creative)*
Ralph Lucius *(VP-Acct Svcs)*
Marilyn Simmons Wilson *(Acct Dir)*
Amy Hemphill *(Dir-HR)*
David Buckland *(Sr Acct Mgr)*
Jacqueline Forestieri *(Acct Mgr)*
Rob Regovich *(Mgr-Studio)*
Paige Zars *(Acct Exec)*

Accounts:
Amway
Bosch
GE
Johnson Controls
Meijer
Samsung
Sears
Skil
Walmart
Whirlpool

JOHNSTON DUFFY
2424 E York Rd No 215, Philadelphia, PA 19125
Tel.: (215) 389-2888
Fax: (215) 389-2988
E-Mail: info@johnstonduffy.com
Web Site: www.johnstonduffy.com

Employees: 8
Year Founded: 2003

Martin Duffy *(Owner & Dir-Design)*

Accounts:
Aramark
Wawa
Wonderboy Clothing

JONES ADVERTISING

603 Stewart St Ste 600, Seattle, WA 98101
Tel.: (206) 691-3124
Fax: (206) 691-3495
E-Mail: info@jonesadvertising.com
Web Site: www.jonesadvertising.com

Year Founded: 2001

Agency Specializes In: Advertising, Branded Entertainment, Media Planning, Production, Public Relations, Radio, Social Media, T.V.

Mark Jones *(Pres & Dir-Creative)*
Kristin Mackay *(Mgmt Supvr)*
Amber Morton *(Dir-Mktg & Bus Dev)*
David Edgerton *(Assoc Dir-Creative & Acct Mgr)*
Kimberly Lukens *(Acct Svc Dir)*

Accounts:
Rover.com

THE JONES AGENCY

303 N Indian Canyon Dr, Palm Springs, CA 92262-6015
Tel.: (760) 325-1437
Fax: (760) 778-0320
E-Mail: kradke@jonesagency.com
Web Site: www.jonesagency.com

Employees: 9
Year Founded: 1958

Agency Specializes In: Advertising, Advertising Specialties, Automotive, Aviation & Aerospace, Brand Development & Integration, Broadcast, Business Publications, Business-To-Business, Cable T.V., Children's Market, Co-op Advertising, Collateral, Commercial Photography, Communications, Consulting, Consumer Marketing, Consumer Publications, Corporate Identity, Cosmetics, Digital/Interactive, Direct Response Marketing, E-Commerce, Education, Electronic Media, Entertainment, Environmental, Event Planning & Marketing, Exhibit/Trade Shows, Fashion/Apparel, Financial, Food Service, Gay & Lesbian Market, Government/Political, Graphic Design, Health Care Services, High Technology, Infomercials, Information Technology, Internet/Web Design, Investor Relations, Legal Services, Leisure, Logo & Package Design, Magazines, Media Buying Services, Medical Products, Multimedia, New Product Development, Newspaper, Newspapers & Magazines, Out-of-Home Media, Outdoor, Over-50 Market, Pharmaceutical, Point of Purchase, Point of Sale, Production, Public Relations, Publicity/Promotions, Radio, Real Estate, Restaurant, Retail, Sales Promotion, Seniors' Market, Sports Market, Strategic Planning/Research, Sweepstakes, Syndication, T.V., Teen Market, Telemarketing, Trade & Consumer Magazines, Transportation, Travel & Tourism, Yellow Pages Advertising

Approx. Annual Billings: $2,000,000

Kyle Radke *(Sr VP & Gen Mgr)*
Maryanne Coury *(Dir-Media)*
Jessica Surrett *(Mgr-Creative Svcs)*

Accounts:
Buddy Greco's Restaurant; Cathedral City, CA
Canyon National Bank; Palm Springs & Palm Desert, CA
City & Regional Magazine Association; Los Angeles, CA
Desert Partners; Palm Desert, CA
Desert Regional Medical Centre
Hotel Twin Dolphin; Cabo San Lucas, Mexico
Las Casualas Terraza; Palm Springs, CA Restaurant
Palm Hills Land Company
Palm Springs Bureau of Tourism
Palm Springs Desert Resorts Convention & Visitors Authority; Rancho Mirage, CA
The Quarry; La Quinta, CA
US Filter/Veolia; Palm Desert, CA
Villa Porto Fino; Palm Desert, CA
Walter Clark; Palm Desert, CA

JONES & THOMAS, INC.

788 N Sunnyside Rd, Decatur, IL 62522-1156
Tel.: (217) 423-1889
Fax: (217) 425-0680
E-Mail: corp@jonesthomas.com
Web Site: www.jonesthomas.com

E-Mail for Key Personnel:
President: bill@jonesthomas.com

Employees: 15
Year Founded: 1980

Agency Specializes In: Advertising, Agriculture, Brand Development & Integration, Broadcast, Business Publications, Business-To-Business, Co-op Advertising, Collateral, Communications, Consulting, Consumer Marketing, Consumer Publications, Corporate Identity, Direct Response Marketing, Event Planning & Marketing, Exhibit/Trade Shows, Financial, Food Service, Graphic Design, Health Care Services, Industrial, Internet/Web Design, Investor Relations, Logo & Package Design, Magazines, Media Buying Services, Medical Products, Multimedia, New Product Development, Newspaper, Newspapers & Magazines, Outdoor, Over-50 Market, Pharmaceutical, Planning & Consultation, Point of Purchase, Point of Sale, Print, Production, Public Relations, Publicity/Promotions, Radio, Sales Promotion, Seniors' Market, Sports Market, Strategic Planning/Research, T.V., Trade & Consumer Magazines

Bill Lehmann *(Pres)*
Russ Proch *(VP)*
Laura Hunt *(Acct Exec)*

Accounts:
Seno Formal Wear; Decatur, IL; 2005

JONES FOSTER DEAL ADVERTISING & PUBLIC RELATIONS, INC.

(Formerly JFD Advertising & Public Relations)
412 E Madison St, Tampa, FL 33602
Tel.: (813) 223-4545
Fax: (813) 254-7899
E-Mail: jfoster@jfdadvertising.com
Web Site: www.jfdadvertising.com

Employees: 2
Year Founded: 2003

National Agency Associations: AMA

Agency Specializes In: Advertising, Advertising Specialties, Affluent Market, Brand Development & Integration, Broadcast, Business Publications, Business-To-Business, Cable T.V., Catalogs, Co-op Advertising, Collateral, Communications, Computers & Software, Consulting, Consumer Marketing, Consumer Publications, Corporate Communications, Corporate Identity, Crisis Communications, Direct Response Marketing, Direct-to-Consumer, E-Commerce, Electronic Media, Electronics, Event Planning & Marketing, Exhibit/Trade Shows, Financial, Food Service, Graphic Design, Health Care Services, High Technology, Hispanic Market, Hospitality, In-Store Advertising, Industrial, Information Technology, Integrated Marketing, Internet/Web Design, Leisure, Local Marketing, Logo & Package Design, Magazines, Marine, Media Buying Services, Media Planning, Media Relations, Media Training, Medical Products, Merchandising, Mobile Marketing, Multimedia, New Product Development, Newspaper, Newspapers & Magazines, Out-of-Home Media, Outdoor, Package Design, Pharmaceutical, Planning & Consultation, Point of Purchase, Point of Sale, Print, Product Placement, Production, Production (Ad, Film, Broadcast), Production (Print), Promotions, Public Relations, Publicity/Promotions, Publishing, Radio, Real Estate, Recruitment, Regional, Restaurant, Retail, Sales Promotion, Search Engine Optimization, Social Marketing/Nonprofit, Sponsorship, Sports Market, Strategic Planning/Research, T.V., Technical Advertising, Telemarketing, Trade & Consumer Magazines, Transportation, Travel & Tourism, Urban Market, Web (Banner Ads, Pop-ups, etc.), Women's Market, Yellow Pages Advertising

Approx. Annual Billings: $7,600,000

Breakdown of Gross Billings by Media: Bus. Publs.: 20%; Production: 40%; Pub. Rels.: 20%; Radio & T.V.: 20%

Karin Arden *(Partner)*
Jay Foster *(Partner)*

Accounts:
Custom Scripts Rx; Tampa, FL; 2005
Doctor's Walk-In Clinics; Tampa, FL; 2002
Electric Supply Electrical Distributor; 2007
Hollister, Inc. Wound Care Products; 2008
KHS&S Contractors; Tampa, FL Specialty Contractor; 2003
Laser Scalp & Hair Center; Clearwater, FL Hair Transplants; 2011
Markou Medical Center; Clearwater, FL Hair Replacement; 2011
Richie's Cleaners Dry Cleaning Chain; 2013
Superior Communications Communications Systems; 2011
Tye Maner Group; Tampa, FL Sales Training & Motivational Speaker; 2004
Villa Rosa Specialty Housewares; 2014

JONES HUYETT PARTNERS

3200 SW Huntoon St, Topeka, KS 66604-1606
Tel.: (785) 228-0900
Fax: (785) 228-9990
Web Site: www.jhpadv.com

E-Mail for Key Personnel:
President: gjones@jshadv.com
Media Dir.: LPalace@jshadv.com

National Agency Associations: AAF

Agency Specializes In: Advertising, Brand Development & Integration, Broadcast, Business-To-Business, Collateral, Commercial Photography, Communications, Consulting, Consumer Marketing, Corporate Identity, Digital/Interactive, Direct Response Marketing, E-Commerce, Financial, Graphic Design, Health Care Services, Internet/Web Design, Logo & Package Design, Newspaper, Newspapers & Magazines, Out-of-Home Media, Outdoor, Planning & Consultation, Point of Purchase, Point of Sale, Print, Production, Public Relations, Publicity/Promotions, Radio, Sales Promotion, Seniors' Market, Strategic Planning/Research, T.V., Trade & Consumer Magazines

Gary Jones *(Pres & Chief Creative Officer)*
Kurt Eskilson *(CFO & Sr VP)*
Linda Bull *(Sec & Sr VP-HR)*
Jake Huyett *(Exec VP)*
Linda Eisenhut *(Sr VP-Digital Comm)*
Michelle Stubblefield *(VP-Bus Dev)*
Tracey Stratton *(Dir-PR)*
Leslie Palace *(Sr Acct Mgr)*
Alissa Menke *(Sr Strategist-Digital)*
Sherri Wilson *(Media Buyer)*

Accounts:

Aldersgate Village/United Methodist Homes; Topeka, KS; 1992
Bartlett & West Engineers, Inc.; Topeka, KS; 1994
Blue Cross & Blue Shield of Kansas; Topeka, KS; 1999
Newcomer Funeral Service Group; Topeka, KS; 2003
Prairie Band Potawatomi Nation; Mayetta, KS; 1996
Security Benefit; Topeka, KS; 2004
Stormont-Vail Regional HealthCare; Topeka, KS; 1982

JORDAN ASSOCIATES

3111 Quail Springs Pkwy Ste 200, Oklahoma City, OK 73134-2625
Tel.: (405) 840-3201
Fax: (405) 840-4149
E-Mail: info@jordanet.com
Web Site: www.jordanet.com

Employees: 25
Year Founded: 1961

National Agency Associations: 4A's

Agency Specializes In: Advertising, Agriculture, Automotive, Brand Development & Integration, Broadcast, Business-To-Business, Co-op Advertising, Collateral, Communications, Consulting, Consumer Marketing, Consumer Publications, Corporate Communications, Corporate Identity, Direct Response Marketing, E-Commerce, Event Planning & Marketing, Exhibit/Trade Shows, Financial, Food Service, Government/Political, Graphic Design, Health Care Services, High Technology, In-Store Advertising, Local Marketing, Logo & Package Design, Media Buying Services, Medical Products, Merchandising, Multimedia, Over-50 Market, Planning & Consultation, Point of Purchase, Point of Sale, Public Relations, Publicity/Promotions, Restaurant, Retail, Sales Promotion, Seniors' Market, Sponsorship, Sports Market, Strategic Planning/Research, Teen Market

Rhonda Hooper *(Pres & CEO)*
Amy Hindman *(SR VP & Dir-Acct Svc)*
Mike Wilkinson *(Sr VP-Strategic Plng)*
Randy Bradley *(VP & Creative Dir)*
Steve Green *(VP)*
Helen Reinheimer-Mercer *(VP-Media)*
Candace Guy *(Media Buyer)*

Accounts:
AAA Oklahoma (Agency of Record)
Allied Custom Gypsum
American Automobile Association
GHS Insurance
OKC Memorial Foundation
Oklahoma Lottery
Oklahoma Office of Homeland Security (Agency of Record) Red Dirt Ready
Oklahoma Tourism and Recreation Department (Agency of Record)
ONEOK

JOSEPH BROWN & ASSOCIATES INC.

1040 Stanton Rd Ste C, Daphne, AL 36526
Tel.: (251) 445-5370
Fax: (251) 621-3271
E-Mail: info@josephbrownassociates.com
Web Site: www.josephbrownassociates.com

Year Founded: 2006

Agency Specializes In: Advertising, Graphic Design, Internet/Web Design, Print, Social Media

Bryan Smith *(Dir-Image Mgmt)*
Joe Brown *(Strategist-Innovation)*

Accounts:
Advanced Dermatology & Skin Care Centre

JP&R ADVERTISING AGENCY INC.

305 Broadway Ste 200, New York, NY 10007
Tel.: (212) 267-6698
Fax: (212) 608-2147
Toll Free: (800) 660-7050
E-Mail: info@jpandr.com
Web Site: www.jpandr.com

E-Mail for Key Personnel:
President: wmannion@jpandr.com
Public Relations: RDeBoer@jpandr.com

Employees: 4
Year Founded: 1964

Agency Specializes In: Advertising Specialties, Legal Services, Newspaper, Real Estate

Approx. Annual Billings: $2,500,000

Breakdown of Gross Billings by Media: Newsp.: $2,500,000

Tricia Samaroo *(Acct Mgr)*
Twanda Stafford *(Acct Mgr)*

Accounts:
Bekerman & Reddy; New York, NY Legal Notices; 1979
Cadwalader Wickersham & Taft; New York, NY Legal Notices; 1980
Kosterich & Assoc.; Yonkers, NY Legal Notices; 2002
Phillips Lytle; Rochester, NY Legal Notices; 1999
Sweeney Gallo & Reich; Rego Park, NY Legal Notices; 1995

JP MEDIA INC.

149-151 Westchester Ave Ste 22, Port Chester, NY 10573
Tel.: (914) 935-0600
Fax: (914) 935-0606
Toll Free: (866) ADS-0601
E-Mail: info@jpmedia.com
Web Site: www.jpmedia.com

E-Mail for Key Personnel:
President: jpeter@aboutjpmedia.com
Creative Dir.: jpeter@aboutjpmedia.com
Media Dir.: mpeter@aboutjpmedia.com

Employees: 5
Year Founded: 2001

Agency Specializes In: Education, Financial, Graphic Design, Health Care Services, Internet/Web Design, Logo & Package Design, Newspaper, Newspapers & Magazines, Print, Production, Real Estate, Recruitment, Retail

Approx. Annual Billings: $4,000,000

Breakdown of Gross Billings by Media: D.M.: 10%; Graphic Design: 10%; Internet Adv.: 10%; Mags.: 10%; Newsp.: 60%

Jaime Peter *(Pres)*
Matt Peter *(VP)*

Accounts:
Cabrini College
Delaware Hospice
Horizon House, Inc
Kentucky Health Partners
Leslie J. Garfield & Co., Inc.

JPA HEALTH COMMUNICATIONS

(Formerly Jones Public Affairs, Inc.)
1420 K St NW Ste 1050, Washington, DC 20005
Tel.: (202) 591-4000
Fax: (202) 591-4020
Web Site: www.jpa.com/

Employees: 7

Agency Specializes In: Communications, Crisis Communications, Event Planning & Marketing, Government/Political, Health Care Services, Media Relations, Strategic Planning/Research

Carrie Jones *(Mng Dir & Principal)*
Ken Deutsch *(Exec VP)*
Patrick Brady *(Sr VP)*
Valerie Carter *(Sr VP-Policy Support & Govt Rels)*
Berna Diehl *(Sr VP)*
Catherine Brady *(VP)*
Sarah Dick *(Acct Dir)*
Andrea Still Gray *(Acct Dir)*
Deborah Danuser *(Acct Supvr & Coord-Dev)*
Joel Lopez *(Sr Acct Exec)*
Rhonda Slater *(Acct Coord)*

Accounts:
Advancing Excellence in Americas Nursing Homes
Bristol-Myers Squibb Oncology Advocacy Business
Entertainment Industries Council, Inc.
GenSpera, Inc. (Public Relations Agency of Record) Communications
Global Bridges Digital Presence, Network Communications
National Center for Complementary & Alternative Medicine
The Partnership for Safe Medicines

J.R. NAVARRO & ASSOCIATES INC.

212 26th St Ste 315, Santa Monica, CA 90402
Tel.: (310) 472-0589
E-Mail: mnavarro@jrnavarro.com
Web Site: www.jrnavarro.com

E-Mail for Key Personnel:
President: jnavarro@jrnavarro.com

Employees: 17
Year Founded: 1977

Agency Specializes In: Advertising

Approx. Annual Billings: $12,000,000

Mike Navarro *(CEO)*
Paul McCarty *(Dir-Art & Graphic Designer)*

Accounts:
Al Brooks Ticket Agency; Los Angeles, CA Ticket & Tour Service
International Visitors Council of Los Angeles; Los Angeles, CA International Services
Mitsubishi Motors North America; Cypress, CA Automotive
Petersen Automotive Museum; Los Angeles, CA Museum
Rose Bowl Tours; Los Angeles, CA Tour Operator
So. Cal Sports/Entertainment Guide; Los Angeles, CA Entertainment
Watson Land Co.; Carson, CA Commercial Office Development
Wells Fargo Bank; Los Angeles, CA Financial Services

J.R. THOMPSON CO.

26970 Haggerty Rd Ste 100, Farmington Hills, MI 48331
Tel.: (248) 553-4566
Fax: (248) 553-2138
E-Mail: jrt@jrthompson.com
Web Site: www.jrthompson.com

Employees: 65
Year Founded: 1974

National Agency Associations: AMA-BMA-PRSA-

Second Wind Limited

Agency Specializes In: Advertising, Automotive, Brand Development & Integration, Business Publications, Business-To-Business, Communications, Consulting, Corporate Identity, Digital/Interactive, Direct Response Marketing, Event Planning & Marketing, Graphic Design, Internet/Web Design, Logo & Package Design, Magazines, Marine, Merchandising, Planning & Consultation, Point of Purchase, Point of Sale, Print, Production, Public Relations, Publicity/Promotions, Sales Promotion, Strategic Planning/Research, Trade & Consumer Magazines

Jim Yetter *(CMO)*
John McGee *(VP)*
Paul Ranalli *(Sr Dir-Art)*
Terry Ayrault *(Creative Dir)*
Karen Willis *(Mgr-Acctg)*
Cody Yachasz *(Designer-Web & UX)*
Kim McIntyre *(Sr Art Dir)*
James Roach *(Client Svc Mgr)*

Accounts:
Chrysler Corporation Dodge Division; Auburn Hills, MI, Mopar Parts Division; Center Line, MI; 1974
Tecumseh Products Company; Ann Arbor, MI North American Marketing, PR Communications

JS2 COMMUNICATIONS

661 N Harper Ave Ste 208, Los Angeles, CA 90048
Tel.: (323) 866-0880
Fax: (323) 866-0882
Web Site: www.js2comm.com

Employees: 10

Agency Specializes In: Public Relations

Jeff Smith *(Co-Founder, CEO & CFO)*
Jill Sandin *(Owner)*
Lauren Newhouse *(Acct Supvr)*
Kristin Hansel *(Sr Acct Exec)*
Diana Hossfeld *(Sr Acct Exec)*
Amy Mccullaugh *(Sr Acct Exec)*
Katie Rubino *(Asst Acct Exec)*
Kim Brounstein *(Acct Coord)*

Accounts:
ArcLight Cinemas & Pacific Theatres
Boombang
CASA
Chef Danhi
City Tavern Public Relations
The Coffee Bean & Tea Leaf
FARMSHOP Public Relations
Golden Road Brewing
iZO Cleanze
Karlin+Pimsler
MCC Hospitality Group
Nana, What's Cancer?
New School of Cooking; Culver City, LA
Out & About Tours
Payard
Pennyful.com Media Relations, Social Media
Rao's
Rare Concepts Group
RockSugar Pan Asian Kitchen
Rush Street
Shaw Festival
Soho House North America Brand Positioning
Tender Greens
TheSuitest Marketing, Media Outreach, Social Media
Wet International Personal Wellness Products; 2008

Branch

JS2 Communications

41 E 11th St 11th Fl, New York, NY 10003
Tel.: (646) 430-5645
Web Site: www.js2comm.com

Employees: 14

Agency Specializes In: Advertising, Brand Development & Integration, Strategic Planning/Research

Jill Sandin *(Co-Founder & Pres)*
Jeff Smith *(Co-Founder, CEO & CFO)*
Diana Hossfeld *(Sr Acct Exec)*

Accounts:
ArcLight Cinemas
Boombang (Agency of Record) Media Relations; 2008
DAP World Social Media
Kraiko Diamonds
Lawry's The Prime Rib
Moonview Sanctuary
Omni Hotels Corporation
Segway
Susta
Zeke's Smokehouse

JSTOKES AGENCY

1444 N Main St, Walnut Creek, CA 94596-4605
Tel.: (925) 933-1624
Fax: (925) 933-0546
Toll Free: (888) 9STOKES
E-Mail: info@jstokes.com
Web Site: www.jstokes.com

E-Mail for Key Personnel:
President: jim@jstokes.com
Media Dir.: betty@jstokes.com

Employees: 25
Year Founded: 1974

National Agency Associations: 4A's-AAF-AMA

Agency Specializes In: Advertising, Aviation & Aerospace, Brand Development & Integration, Broadcast, Business-To-Business, Cable T.V., Co-op Advertising, Collateral, Communications, Consumer Goods, Consumer Marketing, Consumer Publications, Content, Corporate Identity, Digital/Interactive, Direct Response Marketing, Direct-to-Consumer, Electronic Media, Email, Event Planning & Marketing, Financial, Food Service, Graphic Design, Guerilla Marketing, Health Care Services, Hispanic Market, Hospitality, In-Store Advertising, Integrated Marketing, Internet/Web Design, Local Marketing, Logo & Package Design, Magazines, Media Buying Services, Media Relations, Mobile Marketing, Multimedia, Newspaper, Newspapers & Magazines, Outdoor, Paid Searches, Point of Purchase, Point of Sale, Print, Product Placement, Promotions, Public Relations, Publicity/Promotions, Radio, Real Estate, Regional, Restaurant, Retail, Sales Promotion, Search Engine Optimization, Seniors' Market, Social Marketing/Nonprofit, Social Media, Sponsorship, Strategic Planning/Research, T.V., Teen Market, Trade & Consumer Magazines

Approx. Annual Billings: $25,000,000

James A. Stokes *(Pres)*
Daniel Stokes *(Exec VP)*
Lynn Jackson *(VP-Creative)*
Andrea Hegarty *(Acct Dir)*
Angela Claire Corpus *(Mgmt Supvr-Project)*
Betty Tafoya *(Dir-Media)*
Raffi Apelian *(Mgr-Content & Copywriter)*
Jocelyn Coolbaugh *(Acct Supvr)*
Lindsey Fischesser *(Acct Supvr)*

Accounts:
Bay Alarm; Walnut Creek, CA; 1993
Bishop Ranch
Black Bear Diner Brand Strategy, Social Media
Sedgwick
SpeeDee Oil Change & Tune-Up of the West; 1989
Sunset Development; San Ramon, CA Bishop Ranch Business Park
Zip Realty; US Residential Real Estate Brokerage

J.T. MEGA FOOD MARKETING COMMUNICATIONS

(Formerly J.T. Mega Marketing Communications)
4020 Minnetonka Blvd, Minneapolis, MN 55416-4100
Tel.: (952) 929-1370
Fax: (952) 929-5417
Toll Free: (800) 923-6342
E-Mail: info@jtmega.com
Web Site: www.jtmega.com

E-Mail for Key Personnel:
Media Dir.: mpulver@jtmega.com
Production Mgr.: sdekker@jtmega.com

Employees: 50
Year Founded: 1976

Agency Specializes In: Brand Development & Integration, Business-To-Business, Exhibit/Trade Shows, Food Service, Industrial, Point of Purchase

Approx. Annual Billings: $17,000,000

Breakdown of Gross Billings by Media:
Audio/Visual: 5%; Bus. Publs.: 20%; Collateral: 40%; D.M.: 15%; Fees: 10%; Point of Purchase: 5%; Pub. Rels.: 5%

Philip Lee *(Owner & Pres)*
Tim Glovatsky *(Partner & Exec VP)*
Sandri Dekker *(Partner, VP-Production & Dir-Digital Dev)*
Clarice Hallberg *(VP & Mgmt Supvr)*
Bob Beach *(VP-Creative Svcs)*
Patrick DuPont *(Sr Dir-Art)*
Don Mullen *(Dir-Media)*

Accounts:
Brakebrush Chicken; Westfield, WI; 1988
Di Lusso Deli Company
Hormel Foodservice; Austin, MN Ham, Pork, Bacon, Chili & Stew; 1996
Jennie-O Turkey Store; Willmar, MN
Michael Foods; Wayzata, MN
Precept Foods
Sartori Foods
United Sugars Corporation

JTP FIFTH COLUMN

(Name Changed to The Chapter Media)

JUGULAR LLC

1 Little W 12th St, New York, NY 10014
Tel.: (212) 931-9009, ext. 100
E-Mail: info@jugularnyc.com
Web Site: www.jugularnyc.com

Year Founded: 2006

Agency Specializes In: Advertising, Brand Development & Integration, Internet/Web Design, Outdoor, Print, Promotions, Radio, Search Engine Optimization, Social Media, T.V.

Scott Lackey *(Founder & Pres)*
Erin Lackey *(Dir-Creative)*

Accounts:
ProDirect Sports

JUICE COMMUNICATIONS

(Acquired & Absorbed by Pure Brand

Communications, LLC)

JUICE GROUP
Ste 212-1650 Duranleau St, Vancouver, BC V6H 4B6 Canada
Tel.: (604) 266-4266
Web Site: www.juicegroup.ca

Agency Specializes In: Brand Development & Integration, Internet/Web Design, Social Media

Jonathan Greenstein *(Owner)*
Lara Greenstein *(Owner)*

Accounts:
Camp Hatikvah
Global Shoe Connection
Gloria Latham
Keir Surgical
The Kidz Lounge
Miz Mooz

JUICE PHARMA WORLDWIDE
(Formerly Juice Pharma Advertising, Llc.)
322 8th Ave 10th Fl, New York, NY 10001
Tel.: (212) 647-1595
Fax: (212) 647-1594
Web Site: www.juicepharma.com

Employees: 200
Year Founded: 2002

Revenue: $4,500,000

Lynn Macrone *(Owner)*
Lois Moran *(Pres & CEO)*
Adam Kline *(Exec VP, Mng Dir & Grp Creative Dir)*
Laurence Richards *(Mng Dir & Exec VP)*
Joan Wildermuth *(Exec VP & Grp Creative Dir)*
Anne Davison *(Sr VP-Strategic Planning)*
Alec Pollak *(VP & Dir-User Experience)*

Accounts:
Bristol Myers Squibb
Elan
Merck
Pfizer

JUICEBOX INTERACTIVE
516 3rd St Ste 202, Des Moines, IA 50309
Tel.: (515) 244-6633
E-Mail: hi@juiceboxint.com
Web Site: www.juiceboxinteractive.com

Agency Specializes In: Advertising, Content, Digital/Interactive, Internet/Web Design, Social Media

Dale Bentlage *(Principal & Chief Strategist)*
Aimee Oakley-Runyan *(Strategist-Mktg, Copywriter & Editor)*
Jorunn Musil *(Dir-Art)*
Kevin Vandekrol *(Dir-Tech)*
Jaclyn Zwiefel *(Sr Designer-Web)*

Accounts:
Beza Threads
Encore Properties
Wiedenfeld & McLaughlin LLP

JULIE A. LAITIN ENTERPRISES, INC.
1350 Ave of the Americas 2nd Fl, New York, NY 10019
Tel.: (646) 568-1877
E-Mail: jlaitin@julielaitin.com
Web Site: www.julielaitin.com

Employees: 5
Year Founded: 1982

Agency Specializes In: Collateral, Communications, Direct Response Marketing, E-Commerce, Health Care Services, High Technology, Print, Public Relations, Publicity/Promotions, Sales Promotion

Julie A. Laitin *(Pres)*
Cynthia Amorese *(Sr VP)*
Martha Hall Houck *(Acct Mgr)*
Ravelle Brickman *(Sr Writer)*

Accounts:
HCB Health; 2008
MicroMass Communication; 2008
Publicis Touchpoint Solutions; 2007
StrikeForce Communication; 2010
Triple Threat Communications; 2013

JULIET ZULU
6025 SE Belmont St, Portland, OR 97215
Tel.: (503) 841-5152
E-Mail: info@julietzulu.us
Web Site: www.julietzulu.us

Year Founded: 2009

Agency Specializes In: Advertising, Broadcast, Digital/Interactive, Graphic Design, Internet/Web Design, Print

Jayson Bosteder *(Partner)*
Zak Davis *(Exec Dir-Creative)*
Meg Weber *(Dir-Ops & Sr Producer)*
Everett Yockey *(Producer-Creative)*
Jihad Qutub *(Dir-Art)*

Accounts:
Puma North America, Inc.

JUMBOSHRIMP ADVERTISING, INC.
431 Bryant St, San Francisco, CA 94107
Tel.: (415) 369-0500
Fax: (415) 369-0501
Web Site: www.jumboshrimp.com

Agency Specializes In: Advertising, Brand Development & Integration

Robert Ahearn *(Founder & Owner)*
Michelle Verloop *(Sr Acct Dir)*
Scott Leeper *(Dir-Creative & Writer)*
Shane Diiullo *(Dir-Creative)*

Accounts:
AJA Video Systems
Calypso Technology, Inc.
CBS Interactive Inc.
Cisco Systems, Inc.
Comventures
Continental Airlines Inc.

JUMP!
1417 Mayson St, Atlanta, GA 30324
Tel.: (404) 574-2910
Fax: (404) 574-2915
E-Mail: matt@jumphi.com
Web Site: www.jumphi.com

Employees: 10

Agency Specializes In: Advertising, Brand Development & Integration, Branded Entertainment, Broadcast, Communications, Corporate Communications, Corporate Identity, Graphic Design, Identity Marketing, Local Marketing, Publishing

Rob Jameson *(Pres)*
Hilary Hobbs *(Mgr-Production & Editor)*
Matt Thomason *(Dir-Sls & Mktg)*
Jessie Compton *(Designer-Motion Media)*
Charlie Skinner *(Designer-Motion Media)*

Accounts:
DIY Network
Fine Living
HGTV House Hunters
PGA Tour Superstore
The Sunshine House
TBS
TNTLA

JUMP BRANDING & DESIGN INC.
235 Carlaw Ave Ste 403, Toronto, ON M4M 2S1 Canada
Tel.: (416) 463-5867
Fax: (416) 463-0059
Toll Free: (866) 716-6668
E-Mail: info@howhigh.ca
Web Site: www.howhigh.ca

Year Founded: 2004

Agency Specializes In: Advertising, Brand Development & Integration, Corporate Identity, Email, Internet/Web Design, Package Design, Search Engine Optimization, Social Media, Technical Advertising

Eric M.W. Boulden *(Pres)*
Brigitte Headley *(Mng Dir)*
Jerry Alfieri *(Principal & Dir-Creative)*
Jason Hemsworth *(Principal & Dir-Strategic)*
Kim Machado *(Dir-Digital Media & Strategy)*
Richard Patmore *(Dir-Creative)*
Michelle Mok *(Designer-Intermediate Environmental)*
Paul Volk *(Sr Designer-Interior)*
Andrew Vysick *(Designer-Intermediate)*

Accounts:
Carson, Dunlop & Associates Ltd
Curated Properties
New-DDrops Logo Design, Packaging
Hanson + Jung Architects Inc.
KFC Corporation
South St. Burger Co.
YUM! Brands, Inc. Pizza Hut

JUMP START AGENCY LLC
3530 Central Pke Ste 106, Nashville, TN 37076
Tel.: (615) 656-5277
Web Site: www.jsanow.com

Year Founded: 2011

Agency Specializes In: Advertising, Corporate Identity, Graphic Design, Internet/Web Design, Print, Search Engine Optimization, Social Media

Roger Miller *(CEO)*
Kimberley Britton *(Dir-Creative & Promotional Svcs)*

Accounts:
Mahan & Associates LLC
Westgate Inn & Suites

JUMPSTART AUTOMOTIVE MEDIA
550 Kearny St Ste 500, San Francisco, CA 94108
Tel.: (415) 844-6300
Fax: (415) 399-0868
Web Site: www.jumpstartautomotivegroup.com

Year Founded: 2000

Agency Specializes In: Advertising, Automotive, Financial, Internet/Web Design

Nick Matarazzo *(CEO)*
Laura Schooling *(CMO)*
Choon Choi *(Sr VP-Strategy, Bus Dev & Tech)*

Rob Bollinger *(VP-Channel Dev)*
Jason Koenigsknecht *(VP-Sls-Natl)*
Libby Murad-Patel *(VP-Strategic Insights & Analytics)*
Mat Harris *(Sr Dir-Products)*
Shawn Poe *(Dir-Creative)*
Jillian Gibala *(Sr Mgr-Mktg)*

Accounts:
Consumer Guide Automotive
NADAguides
Shopping.com Dealtime, Epinions, Shopping.com
Vehix

JUMPTAP INC.
(Acquired & Absorbed by Millennial Media Inc.)

JUNE ADVERTISING
420 S 14th St, Omaha, NE 68102
Tel.: (402) 502-6575
E-Mail: info@juneadv.com
Web Site: www.juneadv.com

Year Founded: 2005

Agency Specializes In: Advertising, Digital/Interactive, Email, Internet/Web Design, Logo & Package Design, Outdoor, Print, Radio, T.V.

Sarah Whipkey *(Creative Dir & Copywriter)*
Rob Mucciaccio *(Creative Dir)*

Accounts:
Heritage Communities

JUNGLE DIGITAL ENTERPRISES
530 Emerson St, Palo Alto, CA 94301
Tel.: (650) 326-7622
E-Mail: jungle@jungledigital.com
Web Site: www.jungledigital.com

Employees: 13
Year Founded: 1987

Agency Specializes In: Graphic Design, Newspaper, Newspapers & Magazines, Recruitment

Approx. Annual Billings: $100,000,000

Dang Le *(Partner-Jungle Digital Imaging)*
Kim Bower *(Controller)*

JUST HEALTH COMMUNICATIONS
(Acquired by Havas)

JV MEDIA DESIGN
177 Kestrel Ln, Roseburg, OR 97471
Tel.: (541) 677-7440
E-Mail: info@jvmediadesign.com
Web Site: www.jvmediadesign.com

Year Founded: 1995

Agency Specializes In: Advertising, E-Commerce, Graphic Design, Internet/Web Design, Logo & Package Design, Print, Social Media

Sherry Holub *(Dir-Creative)*

Accounts:
South of the James Productions

JVST
25 Stillman St Ste 200, San Francisco, CA 94107
Tel.: (415) 358-1900
Fax: (415) 358-1901
E-Mail: hello@jvst.us
Web Site: www.jvst.us

Employees: 12
Year Founded: 2008

Agency Specializes In: Above-the-Line, Advertising, Advertising Specialties, Affiliate Marketing, Affluent Market, Agriculture, Alternative Advertising, Arts, Automotive, Aviation & Aerospace, Below-the-Line, Bilingual Market, Brand Development & Integration, Branded Entertainment, Broadcast, Business Publications, Business-To-Business, Cable T.V., Catalogs, Children's Market, Co-op Advertising, Collateral, College, Commercial Photography, Communications, Computers & Software, Consulting, Consumer Goods, Consumer Marketing, Consumer Publications, Content, Corporate Communications, Corporate Identity, Cosmetics, Crisis Communications, Custom Publishing, Customer Relationship Management, Digital/Interactive, Direct Response Marketing, Direct-to-Consumer, E-Commerce, Education, Electronic Media, Electronics, Email, Engineering, Entertainment, Environmental, Event Planning & Marketing, Exhibit/Trade Shows, Experience Design, Fashion/Apparel, Financial, Food Service, Game Integration, Government/Political, Graphic Design, Guerilla Marketing, Health Care Services, High Technology, Hispanic Market, Hospitality, Household Goods, Identity Marketing, In-Store Advertising, Industrial, Infomercials, Information Technology, Integrated Marketing, International, Internet/Web Design, Investor Relations, Legal Services, Leisure, Local Marketing, Logo & Package Design, Luxury Products, Magazines, Marine, Market Research, Media Buying Services, Media Planning, Media Relations, Media Training, Medical Products, Men's Market, Merchandising, Mobile Marketing, Multicultural, Multimedia, New Product Development, New Technologies, Newspaper, Newspapers & Magazines, Out-of-Home Media, Outdoor, Package Design, Paid Searches, Pharmaceutical, Planning & Consultation, Podcasting, Point of Purchase, Point of Sale, Print, Product Placement, Production, Production (Ad, Film, Broadcast), Production (Print), Promotions, Public Relations, Publicity/Promotions, Publishing, RSS (Really Simple Syndication), Radio, Real Estate, Recruitment, Regional, Restaurant, Retail, Sales Promotion, Search Engine Optimization, Seniors' Market, Social Marketing/Nonprofit, South Asian Market, Sponsorship, Sports Market, Stakeholders, Strategic Planning/Research, Sweepstakes, Syndication, T.V., Technical Advertising, Teen Market, Telemarketing, Trade & Consumer Magazines, Transportation, Travel & Tourism, Urban Market, Viral/Buzz/Word of Mouth, Web (Banner Ads, Pop-ups, etc.), Women's Market, Yellow Pages Advertising

Approx. Annual Billings: $5,000,000

Breakdown of Gross Billings by Media: Collateral: $25,000; Graphic Design: $225,000; Internet Adv.: $1,500,000; Logo & Package Design: $10,000; Network T.V.: $400,000; Out-of-Home Media: $40,000; Print: $500,000; Strategic Planning/Research: $100,000; T.V.: $2,000,000; Worldwide Web Sites: $200,000

James Song *(Owner & Exec Dir-Creative)*
Roderick Van Gelder *(Mng Dir & Exec Producer)*

Accounts:
Capcom USA, Inc.
Dash Navigation; San Francisco, CA Dash Express
Eidos Interactive; Redwood City, CA Death Jr. 2, Gauntlet, Shellshock 2, Tomb Raider Underworld
Monterey Bay Aquarium; Monterey, CA Splash Zone
Namco Bandai; Santa Clara, CA Warhammer: Battle March

J.W. MORTON & ASSOCIATES
1924 Saint Andrews Ct NE, Cedar Rapids, IA 52402-5889
Tel.: (319) 378-1081
Fax: (319) 378-1827
E-Mail: spot@jwmorton.com
Web Site: www.jwmorton.com

E-Mail for Key Personnel:
President: dmorton@jwmorton.com

Employees: 14
Year Founded: 1984

Agency Specializes In: Brand Development & Integration, Broadcast, Business-To-Business, Consumer Marketing, Exhibit/Trade Shows, Financial, Health Care Services, High Technology, Industrial, Merchandising, Newspaper, Outdoor, Radio, Strategic Planning/Research, T.V., Trade & Consumer Magazines

Breakdown of Gross Billings by Media: Adv. Specialities: 1%; Audio/Visual: 3%; D.M.: 1%; Exhibits/Trade Shows: 1%; Fees: 15%; Mags.: 12%; Newsp.: 9%; Out-of-Home Media: 3%; Plng. & Consultation: 14%; Print: 9%; Production: 2%; Pub. Rels.: 4%; Radio & T.V.: 12%; Strategic Planning/Research: 14%

Jeff Westrom *(Co-Founder, Pres-Creative Svc & Sr Dir-Creative)*
David Morton *(Pres-Mktg Svcs)*
Connie Collins *(Sr Dir-Art)*
Kevin Northway *(Sr Dir-Art)*
Kristopher Sullens *(Dir-Art)*
Scott Appleget *(Sr Acct Mgr)*
Sandi Lafferty *(Acct Mgr)*
Kim McGuire *(Office Mgr)*
Chris Schulte *(Acct Mgr)*
Nancy Crist *(Specialist-PR & Writer)*
Jessica Joyce *(Specialist-Media)*

Accounts:
Bankers Trust; Cedar Rapids, IA
Iowa City Hospice; Iowa City, IA
Iowa Falls State Bank; Iowa Falls, IA
Lil' Drug Store Products
Panchero's Mexican Grill
St. Luke's Hospital
TaxACT.com
Vi-COR

JWALCHER COMMUNICATIONS
2986 Ivy St, San Diego, CA 92104
Tel.: (619) 295-7140
Fax: (619) 295-7135
E-Mail: pr@jwalcher.com
Web Site: www.jwalcher.com

Employees: 5

Agency Specializes In: Collateral, Email, Internet/Web Design, Local Marketing, Magazines, Media Planning, Media Relations, Newspaper, Publicity/Promotions, Radio, T.V.

Jean Walcher *(Pres)*
Doug Moore *(Dir-Creative & Designer)*
Sandy Young *(Acct Supvr)*
Jenna Brossman *(Sr Acct Exec)*

Accounts:
Bali Hai Restaurant
California Athletic Trainers' Assoc.
The International Council of Systems Engineering
New-Jewish Family Service of San Diego Strategic Public Relations
United States Parachute Assoc

United Way of San Diego
Zephyr Partners

JWALK
419 Pk Ave S, New York, NY 10016
Tel.: (646) 649-2339
E-Mail: info@jwalkny.com
Web Site: www.jwalkny.com

Year Founded: 2008

Agency Specializes In: Advertising, Brand Development & Integration, Digital/Interactive, Social Media

Doug Jacob *(CEO)*
Brooks Cook *(Partner-Ecommerce & Loyalty)*
Katie Naylon *(Dir-Creative)*
Erin Fitzpatrick *(Acct Supvr)*
Andrew McDonald *(Strategist)*

Accounts:
Bare Escentuals
Bebe
DeLeon
Organic Gemini
Proximo Spirits
Pure Leaf tea
RealBeanz Brand Planning, Brand Strategy, Creative, Digital, Experiential, Social
Rubbermaid
Stuart Weitzman

JWT
(Name Changed to J. Walter Thompson)

JWT INSIDE
(Name Changed to J. Walter Thompson INSIDE)

K. FERNANDEZ AND ASSOCIATES, LLC
2935 Thousand Oaks #6, San Antonio, TX 78247
Tel.: (210) 614-1052
E-Mail: info@kfernandez.com
Web Site: www.kfernandez.com

Employees: 10
Year Founded: 1996

National Agency Associations: AAF-AHAA

Agency Specializes In: Advertising, Advertising Specialties, Bilingual Market, Brand Development & Integration, Broadcast, Business-To-Business, Co-op Advertising, Collateral, Commercial Photography, Communications, Consulting, Consumer Marketing, Consumer Publications, Corporate Identity, Cosmetics, Direct Response Marketing, Education, Event Planning & Marketing, Financial, Graphic Design, Health Care Services, Hispanic Market, In-Store Advertising, Local Marketing, Logo & Package Design, Magazines, Media Buying Services, Medical Products, Merchandising, Multicultural, Multimedia, Newspaper, Newspapers & Magazines, Outdoor, Planning & Consultation, Point of Purchase, Point of Sale, Print, Production, Public Relations, Publicity/Promotions, Radio, Sponsorship, Sports Market, Strategic Planning/Research, T.V., Telemarketing

Approx. Annual Billings: $6,300,000

Reni Moczygemba *(Office Mgr)*

Accounts:
The Scooter Store

K. FERNANDEZ AND ASSOCIATES, LLC
(Acquired by Sensis)

K2 COMMUNICATIONS
PO Box 1641, Doylestown, PA 18901-9838
Tel.: (215) 230-7671
Fax: (215) 230-8385
E-Mail: kurt@k2-com.com
Web Site: www.k2-com.com

Employees: 10
Year Founded: 2002

National Agency Associations: BMA

Agency Specializes In: Advertising, Brand Development & Integration, Business-To-Business, Collateral, Communications, Consumer Goods, Corporate Identity, Digital/Interactive, Direct Response Marketing, Direct-to-Consumer, Education, Electronic Media, Exhibit/Trade Shows, Financial, Graphic Design, Health Care Services, High Technology, Industrial, Information Technology, Integrated Marketing, Internet/Web Design, Market Research, Medical Products, New Technologies, Pharmaceutical, Planning & Consultation, Point of Purchase, Point of Sale, Public Relations, Publicity/Promotions, Strategic Planning/Research, T.V., Technical Advertising, Trade & Consumer Magazines, Travel & Tourism

Approx. Annual Billings: $3,000,000

Kurt Krumpholz *(Pres & Exec Dir-Mktg)*
Doug Hill *(Dir-Art & Assoc Dir-Creative)*
Karen Crane *(Dir-Media)*
Robert Lusk, Jr *(Dir-Crowd funding & Social Media)*
Nina Zucker *(Dir-PR)*

Accounts:
Bankers' Information Network
Coppertone Sport Sunglasses
FMC
Hank's Rootbeer
Kodak Graphic Communications Group
Merck
NMS Labs
Opera Company of Philadelphia
Yuengling Brewery

KABOOKABOO MARKETING
396 Alhambra Cir S Twr Ste 210, Coral Gables, FL 33134
Tel.: (305) 569-9154
E-Mail: info@kabookaboo.com
Web Site: www.kabookaboo.com

Year Founded: 2001

Agency Specializes In: Advertising, Brand Development & Integration, Graphic Design, Social Media

Alan Brown *(Principal)*
Ari Rollnick *(Principal)*
Camila Correa *(VP-Ops)*
Sam Rodriguez *(Dir-Creative)*
Arlene Linares *(Community Mgr-Social Media)*

Accounts:
Goldman Properties Website
Miami International Auto Show
Zoo Miami Website

KALA AGENCY
2545 Bookcliff Ave, Grand Junction, CO 81501
Tel.: (970) 640-2655
E-Mail: info@kalaagency.com
Web Site: www.kalaagency.com

Year Founded: 2013

Agency Specializes In: Advertising, Brand Development & Integration, Digital/Interactive, Graphic Design, Internet/Web Design, Media Buying Services, Media Planning, Search Engine Optimization, Social Media

Travis Freeman *(Strategist)*

Accounts:
Essentials in Learning
International Concept Management
R&R Events & Design
Stars

KALEIDOSCOPE
30 Irving Pl 8th Fl, New York, NY 10003
Tel.: (212) 358-7750
Fax: (212) 358-8620
E-Mail: frontdesk@kscopenyc.com
Web Site: www.kscopenyc.com

Employees: 11

National Agency Associations: 4A's

Agency Specializes In: Production

Karen Jorgensen *(Pres & Chief Creative Officer)*
Tara Cacciola *(VP-Creative Svcs & Dir)*
Cheryl Riggins *(VP-Stage Production)*
Jessica Giblin *(Dir-Bus Dev)*
Jen McLaughlin *(Acct Mgr)*

Accounts:
Hewlett-Packard
Intel
Pepsi
Toyota
Wrigley "Seattle Mix", Packaging, Skittles

KALEIDOSCOPE MARKETING AND COMMUNICATIONS INCORPORATED
346 Fairlawn Avenue, Toronto, ON M5M 1T6 Canada
Tel.: (416) 785-8558
E-Mail: ygauthier@KaleidoscopeResults.com
Web Site: www.kaleidoscopemarketing.ca

Agency Specializes In: Advertising, Brand Development & Integration, Digital/Interactive, Event Planning & Marketing, Experience Design, Graphic Design, Print, Public Relations, Social Marketing/Nonprofit, Strategic Planning/Research

Yvette Gauthier *(Founder & Co-CEO)*
Kate Taylor *(Co-CEO)*

KAMP GRIZZLY
1020 NW 18th St, Portland, OR 97209
Tel.: (503) 228-9440
E-Mail: info@kampgrizzly.com
Web Site: www.kampgrizzly.com

Agency Specializes In: Advertising, Brand Development & Integration

Dan Portrait *(Owner)*
Jared Evans *(Dir & Editor)*
Jeff Harding *(Creative Dir)*

Accounts:
Portland Timbers

THE KANTAR GROUP
11 Madison Ave, New York, NY 10010
Tel.: (212) 548-7200
Fax: (212) 548-7201
E-Mail: info@kantar.com
Web Site: www.kantar.com

Employees: 28,500
Year Founded: 1995

Agency Specializes In: Consulting, Market Research

Amanda Hampton *(Partner-HR Bus)*
Robert Bowtell *(CFO)*
Efrain Ribeiro *(Chief Res Officer)*
Terry Kent *(CEO-Kantar Media Adv Intelligence)*
Joel Pacheco *(Sr VP-HR-Kantar Media North America)*
Kevin O'Shea *(VP-Client Consulting Svcs)*
Kelly Ward *(VP-HR)*

Accounts:
AARP Services, Inc

UK Headquarters

The Kantar Group
6 More London Pl, Tooley St, London, SE1 2QY United Kingdom
Tel.: (44) 207 656 5700
Fax: (44) 207 656 5701
E-Mail: Info@Kantar.com
Web Site: www.kantar.com

Employees: 12

Agency Specializes In: Strategic Planning/Research

Robin Dargue *(CIO-Global)*
Tim Kelsall *(Chief Client Officer-Asia)*
Richard Asquith *(CEO-Kantar Media Audiences)*
Jeff Krentz *(Exec VP)*
Aziz Cami *(Dir)*
David Soanes *(Dir-Comml-Client Software)*

Divisions

The Futures Company
11-33 Saint John Street, London, EC1M 4PJ United Kingdom
Tel.: (44) 20 7955 1800
Fax: (44) 20 7955 1900
Web Site: www.thefuturescompany.com

Employees: 50

Agency Specializes In: Planning & Consultation, Strategic Planning/Research

Mark Inskip *(CEO)*
Andre Furstenberg *(CFO)*
Valeria Piaggio *(VP & Head-Multicultural Insights)*
Rob Callender *(Dir-Youth Insights)*
Andrew Curry *(Dir)*
Michelle Trayne *(Dir-Web Applications)*
Karen Kidson *(Mgr-Mktg & Events)*
Kate Turkcan *(Assoc Head-TRU Youth MONITOR)*

Accounts:
Aviva

Millward Brown Inc.
3333 Warrenville Rd, Lisle, IL 60532
(See Separate Listing)

Subsidiaries

Adgooroo
730 W Randolph, Chicago, IL 60661
Toll Free: (866) 263-9900
Web Site: www.adgooroo.com

Employees: 20

Agency Specializes In: Search Engine Optimization

Courtney Christianson *(VP-Customer Success)*
Andy Kras *(VP-Fin)*
Michael Schiro *(VP-Engrg)*
Daniel Navarro *(Acct Mgmt Dir)*
Nicole Clementi *(Dir-HR Bus Partner)*
Whitney Fershee *(Dir-Customer Success & Analytics)*
Jim Leichenko *(Dir-Mktg)*
Kathleen Kenney Winter *(Sr Acct Mgr)*

Accounts:
Discount Party Supplies
Sam Ash

Compete, Inc.
501 Boylston St, Boston, MA 02116
Tel.: (617) 933-5600
Fax: (617) 933-5700
E-Mail: press@compete.com
Web Site: www.compete.com

Employees: 75

Scott Centurino *(COO)*
Gregory Curran *(Mgr-Data)*
Brian Ingalls *(Sr Engr-Software)*

Accounts:
Chrysler
Hyundai Motor America
MSN
Subaru of America, Inc.
Teva Neuroscience
Verizon Wireless

KAPLAN THALER
(Merged with Publicis New York to form Publicis Kaplan Thaler)

KAREN MORSTAD & ASSOCIATES LLC.
79 E Putnam Ave, Greenwich, CT 06830
Tel.: (203) 661-1090
Fax: (203) 661-1091
E-Mail: drabin@karenmorstad.com
Web Site: www.karenmorstad.com

Employees: 52
Year Founded: 2004

Agency Specializes In: Advertising, Collateral, Commercial Photography, Corporate Identity, Digital/Interactive, Direct Response Marketing, Email, Internet/Web Design, Market Research, New Product Development, Newspapers & Magazines, Point of Sale, Public Relations, T.V., Web (Banner Ads, Pop-ups, etc.)

Karen Morstad *(Pres)*

Accounts:
Alger
Atlas Energy Resources LLC. New Marketing Campaign
Byram Archibald Neighborhood Center Children's Sports & Recreation, Pro Bono, Website; 2008
Children
Craig D. Tilford Foundation Pro Bono, Testicular Cancer Research & Education, Website; 2008
Foxhall
Horizon
InvestmentNews
Kenmar
LPL Financial
Paramount
RBS Greenwich Capital
UBS

KARI FEINSTEIN PUBLIC RELATIONS
1638 Abbot Kinney blvd, Venice, CA 90291
Tel.: (323) 957-2700
E-Mail: hello@kfpr.tv
Web Site: www.kfpr.tv

Agency Specializes In: Advertising, Digital/Interactive, Event Planning & Marketing, Public Relations, Social Media

Kari Feinstein *(Owner)*
Megan Eustis *(Acct Exec)*

Accounts:
New-Desigual

KARLEN WILLIAMS GRAYBILL ADVERTISING
512 7th Ave 41st Fl, New York, NY 10018
Tel.: (212) 414-9000
Fax: (212) 414-9561
E-Mail: info@kwgadv.com
Web Site: www.kwgadv.com

Employees: 20
Year Founded: 1967

National Agency Associations: 4A's

Agency Specializes In: Collateral, Consumer Marketing, Direct Response Marketing, Logo & Package Design, New Product Development, Package Design, Public Relations, Sponsorship, Strategic Planning/Research

Approx. Annual Billings: $44,000,000

Jeff Graybill *(Mng Partner)*
Valerie Cipriati *(Sr VP & Dir-Strategic Media)*
Jesse Chen *(Dir-Analytics & Results)*
Christina Chin *(Assoc Dir-Media)*
Dave Duran *(Assoc Dir-Media)*
Kelly Killelea *(Assoc Dir-Digital Media)*
Christopher Manning *(Assoc Dir-Media)*
Maya Milbert *(Assoc Dir-Media)*
Nicole Kingston *(Supvr-Media Buying-Natl Television)*
Henry Johnson *(Sr Acct Exec)*
Matt Murphy *(Media Buyer)*
Matthew Rohrs *(Media Buyer)*
Lisa Vaccarella *(Media Buyer)*
Rebecca Moriarty *(Jr Media Buyer)*

Accounts:
Bull Frog
Capzasin
Ester-C
Ester-E
FLEXALL
Garlique
NewPhase
Pamprin

KARLIN+PIMSLER
115 E 30th St Fl 1, New York, NY 10016-7532
Tel.: (212) 779-3375
Fax: (212) 779-4154
E-Mail: mkarlin@karlinpimsler.com
Web Site: www.karlinpimsler.com

E-Mail for Key Personnel:
President: mkarlin@karlinpimsler.com
Creative Dir.: spimsler@karlinpimsler.com

Employees: 10
Year Founded: 1995

National Agency Associations: DMA

Agency Specializes In: Business-To-Business, Collateral, Consulting, Consumer Marketing, Corporate Identity, Direct Response Marketing, Internet/Web Design, Logo & Package Design, Sales Promotion, Strategic Planning/Research, T.V.

Approx. Annual Billings: $17,000,000

Breakdown of Gross Billings by Media: Collateral: $1,650,000; D.M.: $2,600,000; Internet Adv.: $1,150,000; Radio: $600,000; T.V.: $11,000,000

Malcolm T. Karlin *(Pres & Chief Creative Officer)*
Stephen Pimsler *(Dir-Creative)*

Accounts:
Brava; Coconut Grove, FL
British Airways
Cablevision
Cigna
Citizens Bank
EDiets.com Direct Response TV Creative
Hair Club For Men & Women
Indigene Pharma
J. G. Wentworth
Lippincott OutofYourLife.com
NationsHealth

KARMORY
529 Main St Ste 127, Charlestown, MA 02129
Tel.: (617) 337-2720
Web Site: www.karmory.com

Employees: 20
Year Founded: 2014

Agency Specializes In: Branded Entertainment, Broadcast, Business Publications, Cable T.V., Catalogs, Consumer Publications, Custom Publishing, Digital/Interactive, Direct Response Marketing, Electronic Media, Email, Exhibit/Trade Shows, Experience Design, Game Integration, Guerilla Marketing, In-Store Advertising, Local Marketing, Magazines, Mobile Marketing, Multimedia, Newspaper, Newspapers & Magazines, Out-of-Home Media, Outdoor, Paid Searches, Podcasting, Point of Purchase, Point of Sale, Print, Product Placement, Production, Production (Print), Promotions, Publishing, Radio, Search Engine Optimization, Shopper Marketing, Social Media, Sponsorship, T.V., Trade & Consumer Magazines, Viral/Buzz/Word of Mouth, Web (Banner Ads, Pop-ups, etc.)

Eric Vaden *(Partner)*
Jessica Levine *(Dir-Acct Svcs)*
Madeline Murphy *(Dir-Social Media)*

Accounts:
Bruce Rossmeyer's Harley Davidson
Sweeney Merrigan Law
Virus Zero

KARO GROUP, INC.
1817 10th Ave SW, Calgary, AB T3C 0K2 Canada
Tel.: (403) 266-4094
Fax: (403) 269-1140
E-Mail: info@karo.com
Web Site: www.karo.com

Year Founded: 1971

Agency Specializes In: Advertising, Brand Development & Integration, Communications, Digital/Interactive, Environmental

Joe Strasser *(CFO)*
Gaylene Macdonald *(Mng Dir-Vancouver & VP-Digital Strategy)*
Michael Dangelmaier *(Grp Dir-Creative)*
Lyndsay Wasko *(Dir-Art)*
Caitlin Kangles *(Sr Acct Mgr)*
Jane Farries *(Copywriter)*

Accounts:
FlapJack Finder
HomeFront Calgary
Port Metro Vancouver
TELUS Spark (Agency of Record)
Travel Alberta Campaign: "Families Grow With Water"
The Young Canadians

KARSH & HAGAN COMMUNICATIONS, INC.
685 S Broadway, Denver, CO 80209
Tel.: (303) 296-8400
Fax: (303) 296-2015
E-Mail: kroberts@karsh.com
Web Site: karshhagan.com

E-Mail for Key Personnel:
President: pmarranzino@karsh.com

Employees: 40
Year Founded: 1977

National Agency Associations: 4A's

Agency Specializes In: Advertising, Brand Development & Integration, Broadcast, Co-op Advertising, College, Consumer Marketing, Financial, Graphic Design, Health Care Services, Hospitality, Local Marketing, Logo & Package Design, Magazines, Media Buying Services, Media Planning, Medical Products, Newspaper, Newspapers & Magazines, Out-of-Home Media, Outdoor, Point of Purchase, Point of Sale, Print, Production, Radio, Real Estate, Recruitment, Regional, Restaurant, Retail, Sponsorship, T.V., Travel & Tourism, Women's Market

Pocky Marranzino *(Co-Pres)*
Tracy Broderick *(VP & Dir-Media)*
Becky Ferguson *(VP & Dir-Brdcst Production)*
Lauren Curler *(Head-Acct)*
Camille King *(Sr Dir-Art)*
Lindsey Mills *(Dir-Art)*
David Finkelstein *(Acct Mgr)*
Nikki Burmaster *(Strategist-Digital Media & Media Planner)*
Megan Cohen *(Copywriter)*
Ivy Vaughn *(Coord-Media)*
Darren Brickel *(Assoc Creative Dir)*

Accounts:
American Crew, Inc.
Arrow Electronics Campaign: "Five Year Olds on Five Years Out"
Colorado Tourism Office Campaign: "The Come to Life"
Pinnacle Bancorp.; Central City, NE Financial Services; 2005
Pinnacol Assurance; Denver, CO Workers' Compensation Insurance; 2002
Regis University Private Four Year University; 2000
The State of Colorado Campaign: "Making Colorado"
TD Ameritrade Holding Corporation
Visit Denver

KARSTAN COMMUNICATIONS
700 Doorbell Dr Ste 301, Oakville, ON L6K 3V3 Canada
Tel.: (905) 844-1900
Fax: (905) 844-5200
Web Site: www.karstan.com

Employees: 7

National Agency Associations: Second Wind Limited

Agency Specializes In: Advertising, Brand Development & Integration, Digital/Interactive, Direct Response Marketing, Logo & Package Design, Public Relations

Jeanine Miessner *(Pres)*
Brian Miessner *(VP)*

Accounts:
McCain Foods Ltd.

KASTNER & PARTNERS
5340 Alla Rd Ste 110, Los Angeles, CA 90066
Tel.: (310) 458-2000
Fax: (310) 458-6300
E-Mail: opportunities@kastnernetwork.us
Web Site: www.kastnerandpartners.us

Employees: 60

Agency Specializes In: Advertising, Media Buying Services, Media Planning, Sponsorship

Approx. Annual Billings: $100,000,000

Christian Daul *(Mng Dir)*
Brandon Rochon *(Chief Creative Officer)*
Evelyn Borgatta *(Grp Acct Dir)*
Tim Braybrooks *(Dir-Creative)*
Chad Ford *(Dir-Art)*
Astrid Francis *(Dir-HR)*
McKay Hathaway *(Assoc Dir-Creative)*
Erica Goitia *(Acct Mgr-Red Bull)*
Jill Lundin *(Mgr-Print Production)*
Sara Murray *(Mgr-Mktg)*
Kurt Schellenbach *(Mgr-Studio)*
Samantha Williams *(Acct Supvr)*
Krissy Kobata *(Supvr-Media)*

Accounts:
adidas North America
Carpe Diem
OtterBox
Red Bull Campaign: "Choose Your Wings", Campaign: "The World", Campaign: "Wings for Every Taste", Digital Video, Media, Out-of-Home; 1987
SmartKids

Branches

Kastner & Partners
612 N 2nd St Ste 401, Saint Louis, MO 63102-2553
Tel.: (314) 735-7900
Web Site: www.kastnernetwork.us

Employees: 10

Agency Specializes In: Advertising

Tim Braybrooks *(Dir-Creative)*

KATHODERAY MEDIA INC.
20 Country Estates Rd PO Box 545, Greenville, NY 12083
Tel.: (518) 966-5600
Fax: (518) 966-5629
E-Mail: info@kathoderay.com
Web Site: www.kathoderay.com

Employees: 10
Year Founded: 1997

Agency Specializes In: Advertising, Affluent Market, African-American Market, Alternative Advertising, Catalogs, Children's Market, Collateral, Communications, Content, Corporate Communications, Corporate Identity, Direct Response Marketing, Direct-to-Consumer, E-Commerce, Graphic Design, Information Technology, Integrated Marketing, Internet/Web Design, Multicultural, Multimedia, Production (Print), RSS (Really Simple Syndication), Real Estate, Social Marketing/Nonprofit, Urban Market, Web (Banner Ads, Pop-ups, etc.), Women's Market

Approx. Annual Billings: $350,000

Breakdown of Gross Billings by Media: Corp. Communications: 25%; Graphic Design: 25%; Worldwide Web Sites: 50%

Kathleen Packard *(Founder, Pres & Dir-Creative)*
Tom Clark *(Art Dir)*
Lisa Myron *(Dir-IT)*
Judy Xanthopoulos *(Office Mgr)*

Accounts:
Beyond Wealth Management; Poughkeepsie, NY Financial Services; 2006
InterHealth; Benicia, CA Neutraceuticals; 2005
Jack Schwartz Shoes; New York, NY Lugz Shoes; 1999
The Lincoln Institute; Greenwich, CT; 1998

KAZOO BRANDING

316 E Hennepin Ave Ste 202-203, Minneapolis, MN 55414
Tel.: (612) 378-7050
E-Mail: info@kazoobranding.com
Web Site: www.kazoobranding.com

Year Founded: 1999

Agency Specializes In: Brand Development & Integration, Communications, Strategic Planning/Research

Tom Dupont *(Principal)*
Kelsey Duncan *(Designer)*
Mila Samson *(Designer)*

Accounts:
Hormel Foods
Minneapolis Police Department Police Department
Minnesota Eye Consultants
Northeast Business Association
Pay It Forward Fund
Red Seat
Talent Poole

KBS+

(Formerly kirshenbaum bond senecal + partners)
160 Varick St 4th Fl, New York, NY 10013
Tel.: (212) 633-0080
Fax: (212) 463-8643
E-Mail: khunt@kbsp.com
Web Site: www.kbsp.com

Employees: 300
Year Founded: 1987

National Agency Associations: 4A's

Agency Specializes In: Above-the-Line, Advertising, Advertising Specialties, Affiliate Marketing, Affluent Market, African-American Market, Alternative Advertising, Automotive, Below-the-Line, Brand Development & Integration, Branded Entertainment, Broadcast, Business-To-Business, Cable T.V., Co-op Advertising, Collateral, Consulting, Consumer Goods, Consumer Marketing, Consumer Publications, Corporate Communications, Corporate Identity, Customer Relationship Management, Digital/Interactive, Direct Response Marketing, Direct-to-Consumer, Electronics, Email, Entertainment, Event Planning & Marketing, Experience Design, Fashion/Apparel, Financial, Graphic Design, Guerilla Marketing, In-Store Advertising, Integrated Marketing, Internet/Web Design, Leisure, Logo & Package Design, Luxury Products, Magazines, Market Research, Media Buying Services, Media Planning, Media Relations, Mobile Marketing, Multicultural, Multimedia, Newspaper, Newspapers & Magazines, Out-of-Home Media, Outdoor, Package Design, Pharmaceutical, Planning & Consultation, Point of Purchase, Point of Sale, Print, Production (Print), Promotions, Public Relations, Publicity/Promotions, Radio, Restaurant, Retail, Sales Promotion, Search Engine Optimization, Social Media, Sponsorship, Strategic Planning/Research, Syndication, T.V., Trade & Consumer Magazines, Travel & Tourism, Urban Market, Viral/Buzz/Word of Mouth, Women's Market

Approx. Annual Billings: $700,000,000

Matt Powell *(Co-Pres & CIO)*
Caterina Bartoli *(Partner & Grp Dir)*
Chris Mozolewski *(CFO)*
Jennifer Hohman *(CMO-Global)*
Dan Kelleher *(Co-Chief Creative Officer)*
Jonathan Mackler *(Co-Chief Creative Officer)*
Guy Hayward *(CEO-Global)*
Jenny Read *(Head-Production)*
Jon Goldberg *(Exec Dir-Creative)*
Marc Hartzman *(Grp Dir-Creative)*
Michele Kunken *(Grp Dir-Creative)*
Phillip Schaffer *(Grp Acct Dir)*
Gabriela Benitez *(Acct Dir)*
Douglas Christian *(Acct Dir)*
Angela Denise *(Creative Dir)*
Laurence Gega *(Creative Dir)*
Jason Slack *(Creative Dir)*
Samantha Smeach *(Acct Dir)*
Aileen Calderon *(Dir-Creative)*
Sam Chotiner *(Dir-Strategy)*
Rob Collignon *(Dir-Creative)*
Julie Liu *(Dir-Creative)*
Robin Oksenhendler *(Dir-Content Bus Affairs)*
Angela Renfroe *(Dir-Talent)*
Liz King *(Assoc Dir-Creative & Copywriter)*
Stephen Faulkner *(Assoc Dir-Data & Analytics)*
Bill Graham *(Assoc Dir-Creative)*
Mary O'Keefe *(Assoc Dir-Creative)*
Alex Marinescu *(Mgr-Fin)*
Erin Finestone Kligman *(Acct Supvr)*
Jennifer Kluzek *(Acct Supvr)*
Joshua Safran *(Acct Supvr)*
Benjamin Cascella *(Copywriter)*
Lauren Finn *(Copywriter)*
Amy Lieberthal *(Copywriter)*
Nick Marchese *(Copywriter)*
Jonathan Serrano *(Sr Designer)*
Chris Wernikowski *(Copywriter)*
Carlie Naftolin *(Assoc Producer)*

Accounts:
New-ALS NFL: Game-Changing Moments, 60s
American Express
AOL Inc.
Applebee's International, Inc.
Armani Jeans Interactive, The Room
BMW of North America (North America's Agency of Record) 3-Series Sedan, BMW EVolve App, BMW X1 SUV, BMW i3, BMW i8, Campaign: "A Window Into the Near Future", Campaign: "BMW Innovations", Campaign: "Chapter 1: The New City", Campaign: "Cute Cottage", Campaign: "Hello Future" Winter Olympics 2014, Campaign: "How We'll Learn To Stop Worrying and Love the Future", Campaign: "Looking Forward", Campaign: "Newfangled Idea", Campaign: "Road Home", Campaign: "SHHH" Winter Olympics 2014, Campaign: "Sightings " Winter Olympics 2014, Campaign: "The Future Just Isn't What it Used to Be", Creative, Snowchat, Social Media, Strategy, Super Bowl 2015, TV, Website, X3 Crossover, X4 SUV, X5
Boar's Head
Capital One Financial Corporation
Church's Chicken
Coca-Cola Refreshments USA, Inc.
FTI
GAP, Inc. / Banana Republic / Old Navy
Google Campaign: "If I Had Google Glass", Google Glass
Hero/Whitewave Fruit2Day; 2008
Jay-Z Gold
Keds LLC Creative, Digital, Retail, Strategy
Kwittken + Company
NetJets, Inc. NetJets
Nike SB
Prestige Brands
Prostate Cancer Foundation Prostate Czech
Puma
Rolls-Royce North America, Inc.
Simmons Bedding Co. Beautyrest, Campaign: "Look Out World", ComforPedic, Creative, Digital, Global Marketing, Social, TV
The Steak 'n Shake Company
TE Connectivity (Global Agency of Record)
TJX Home Goods
Vanguard Group; Malvern, PA
VDA: Verband der Automobilindustrie Diesel
Victoria's Secret PINK
Windstream Corporation (Agency of Record); 2006
Ad Council Campaign: "Adopt US Kids", Ice Cream, The Bird

Branches

KBS+

(Formerly kirshenbaum bond senecal + partners Toronto)
340 King St East 5th Fl, Toronto, ON M5A 1K8 Canada
(See Separate Listing)

KBS+

(Formerly kirshenbaum bond senecal + partners montreal)
555 Rene Levesque Blvd W 17th Fl, Montreal, QC H2Z 1B1 Canada
Tel.: (514) 875-7400
Fax: (514) 875-7736
Web Site: www.kbsp.ca

Employees: 60
Year Founded: 1984

Agency Specializes In: Business-To-Business, Direct Response Marketing, Health Care Services, Media Buying Services

Annie Aubert *(Pres)*
Mark McElwain *(Sr VP-Client Svcs)*
Maria Spensieri *(VP & Dir-Media)*
Sacha Ouimet *(Exec Dir-Creative)*

Accounts:
Sun Life
Target Lead Brand Strategy

The Media Kitchen

160 Varick St, New York, NY 10013
(See Separate Listing)

Branch

Kenna

(Formerly henderson bas)
90 Burnhamthorpe Road West 5th Floor, Mississauga, ON L5B 3C3 Canada
(See Separate Listing)

KD&E

(Name Changed to MODCo Group)

KDG ADVERTISING

5404 White Mane, Columbia, MD 21045
Tel.: (443) 539-7802
Web Site: www.kdga.net

Employees: 4
Year Founded: 2006

Agency Specializes In: Above-the-Line, Advertising, Advertising Specialties, Affiliate Marketing, Affluent Market, African-American

Market, Agriculture, Alternative Advertising, Arts, Asian Market, Automotive, Aviation & Aerospace, Below-the-Line, Bilingual Market, Brand Development & Integration, Branded Entertainment, Broadcast, Business Publications, Business-To-Business, Cable T.V., Catalogs, Children's Market, Co-op Advertising, Collateral, College, Commercial Photography, Communications, Computers & Software, Consulting, Consumer Goods, Consumer Marketing, Consumer Publications, Content, Corporate Communications, Corporate Identity, Cosmetics, Crisis Communications, Custom Publishing, Customer Relationship Management, Digital/Interactive, Direct Response Marketing, Direct-to-Consumer, E-Commerce, Education, Electronic Media, Electronics, Email, Engineering, Entertainment, Environmental, Event Planning & Marketing, Exhibit/Trade Shows, Experience Design, Faith Based, Fashion/Apparel, Financial, Food Service, Game Integration, Gay & Lesbian Market, Government/Political, Graphic Design, Guerilla Marketing, Health Care Services, High Technology, Hispanic Market, Hospitality, Household Goods, Identity Marketing, In-Store Advertising, Industrial, Infomercials, Information Technology, Integrated Marketing, International, Internet/Web Design, Investor Relations, Legal Services, Leisure, Local Marketing, Logo & Package Design, Luxury Products, Magazines, Marine, Market Research, Media Buying Services, Media Planning, Media Relations, Media Training, Medical Products, Men's Market, Merchandising, Mobile Marketing, Multicultural, Multimedia, New Product Development, New Technologies, Newspaper, Newspapers & Magazines, Out-of-Home Media, Outdoor, Over-50 Market, Package Design, Paid Searches, Pets , Pharmaceutical, Planning & Consultation, Podcasting, Point of Purchase, Point of Sale, Print, Product Placement, Production, Production (Ad, Film, Broadcast), Production (Print), Promotions, Public Relations, Publicity/Promotions, Publishing, RSS (Really Simple Syndication), Radio, Real Estate, Recruitment, Regional, Restaurant, Retail, Sales Promotion, Search Engine Optimization, Seniors' Market, Shopper Marketing, Social Marketing/Nonprofit, Social Media, South Asian Market, Sponsorship, Sports Market, Stakeholders, Strategic Planning/Research, Sweepstakes, Syndication, T.V., Technical Advertising, Teen Market, Telemarketing, Trade & Consumer Magazines, Transportation, Travel & Tourism, Tween Market, Urban Market, Viral/Buzz/Word of Mouth, Web (Banner Ads, Pop-ups, etc.), Women's Market, Yellow Pages Advertising

Margot Jones *(Dir-Ops)*
Charles Panagopoulos *(Acct Exec)*
Nick Patterson *(Sr Designer-UX)*

Accounts:
Alzheimers Disease International, Inc; 2011
Coca-Cola; 2007
DC Govt - Department of Disability Services; 2011
DC Govt-Officer of Personnel Management; 2011
DC Scores, Inc; 2012
Printing & Graphics Association Mid Atlantic; 2013
Tucker-Diggs Foundation; 2008
Wesley College; 2007

KDR PRODUCTIONS/DOLLARWISE PUBLICATIONS

2500 W Higgins Rd, Hoffman Estates, IL 60169
Tel.: (630) 894-0934
Fax: (630) 894-0953
E-Mail: dino@kdrmarketing.com
Web Site: KDRmarketing.com

Employees: 20
Year Founded: 1992

Agency Specializes In: Direct Response Marketing

Approx. Annual Billings: $2,500,000

Breakdown of Gross Billings by Media: Consumer Publs.: $2,500,000

Dino A. Thanos *(Owner & Mgr-Direct Mktg)*
Kenneth W. Goldman *(Pres)*
Greta Goldman *(Dir-Sls)*

Accounts:
Firestone
Goodyear

KEA ADVERTISING

217 Rte 303 Ste 1, Valley Cottage, NY 10989-2534
Tel.: (845) 268-8686
Fax: (845) 268-8699
E-Mail: keaadvertising@keaadvertising.com
Web Site: www.keaadvertising.com

Employees: 16
Year Founded: 1995

Agency Specializes In: Advertising, Automotive, Collateral, Digital/Interactive, Newspaper, Retail, Web (Banner Ads, Pop-ups, etc.)

Approx. Annual Billings: $15,000,000

Henry Kwartler *(Pres)*
Dean Miller *(VP)*
Brandon Hoffman *(Dir-Internet Mktg)*
Andrea Tully *(Dir-Mktg)*
Linda Augustoni *(Mgr-Direct Mail & Sr Coord-Media)*
Mark Levine *(Mgr-Direct Mail)*

Accounts:
Liberty
Majestic
Quattroporte
Quit Smoking
Skin Centre

KEATING MAGEE MARKETING COMMUNICATIONS

708 Phosphor Ave, Metairie, LA 70005
Tel.: (504) 299-8000
Fax: (504) 525-6647
E-Mail: khiatt@keatingmagee.com
Web Site: www.keatingmagee.com

Employees: 10
Year Founded: 1981

National Agency Associations: AMA

Agency Specializes In: Advertising, Arts, Brand Development & Integration, Broadcast, Business-To-Business, Cable T.V., Co-op Advertising, Collateral, Communications, Consulting, Consumer Publications, Corporate Communications, Corporate Identity, Crisis Communications, Digital/Interactive, Education, Email, Entertainment, Event Planning & Marketing, Exhibit/Trade Shows, Financial, Government/Political, Graphic Design, Guerilla Marketing, Health Care Services, Hospitality, Identity Marketing, Integrated Marketing, Internet/Web Design, Leisure, Luxury Products, Market Research, Media Buying Services, Media Planning, Media Relations, Medical Products, Mobile Marketing, Multimedia, Newspaper, Newspapers & Magazines, Out-of-Home Media, Outdoor, Over-50 Market, Paid Searches, Planning & Consultation, Point of Sale, Print, Production, Production (Ad, Film, Broadcast), Public Relations, Publicity/Promotions, Radio, Real Estate, Retail, Search Engine Optimization, Seniors' Market, Social Marketing/Nonprofit, Sponsorship, Sports Market, Strategic Planning/Research, Sweepstakes, T.V., Trade & Consumer Magazines, Travel & Tourism, Viral/Buzz/Word of Mouth, Web (Banner Ads, Pop-ups, etc.), Women's Market

Approx. Annual Billings: $20,000,000

Jennifer Keating Magee *(CEO)*
Karen Craig *(CFO)*

Accounts:
Louisiana Campaign for Tobacco-Free Living
UnitedHealthcare

KEEGAN ASSOCIATES

50 Clinton Ave, Cortland, NY 13045
Tel.: (607) 753-9696
Web Site: www.keeganinc.com

Agency Specializes In: Advertising, Brand Development & Integration, Business-To-Business, Internet/Web Design, Media Planning, Print, Public Relations, Social Media

Hugh J. Keegan *(Founder & Pres)*
Jennifer King MacKenzie *(Exec VP)*
Betsy Wiggers *(Art Dir)*

Accounts:
New-Madison County Tourism

KEEN BRANDING

30616 Overbrook Ctr Way, Milton, DE 19969
Tel.: (302) 644-6885
E-Mail: info@keenbranding.com
Web Site: www.keenbranding.com

Employees: 15
Year Founded: 2000

Agency Specializes In: Advertising, African-American Market, Asian Market, Automotive, Aviation & Aerospace, Bilingual Market, Brand Development & Integration, Business Publications, Business-To-Business, Cable T.V., Children's Market, Collateral, Communications, Consulting, Consumer Marketing, Corporate Identity, Cosmetics, Digital/Interactive, E-Commerce, Education, Electronic Media, Engineering, Entertainment, Environmental, Fashion/Apparel, Financial, Food Service, Graphic Design, Health Care Services, High Technology, Hispanic Market, Industrial, Infomercials, Information Technology, Internet/Web Design, Legal Services, Leisure, Logo & Package Design, Magazines, Marine, Medical Products, Multimedia, New Product Development, Over-50 Market, Pharmaceutical, Planning & Consultation, Real Estate, Restaurant, Retail, Seniors' Market, Strategic Planning/Research, Transportation, Travel & Tourism

Approx. Annual Billings: $5,000,000

Breakdown of Gross Billings by Media: Logo & Package Design: $1,250,000; Plng. & Consultation: $3,750,000

Alicia Stack *(Partner)*

Branches

Keen Branding

PO Box 416, Nassau, DE 19969
Mailing Address:
PO Box 12372, Charlotte, NC 28220-2372
Tel.: (302) 644-6885
Fax: (704) 295-1101
E-Mail: info@keenbranding.com
Web Site: www.keenbranding.com

E-Mail for Key Personnel:
President: astack@keenbranding.com
Creative Dir.: sownbey@keenbranding.com

Year Founded: 2000

Agency Specializes In: Advertising, African-American Market, Agriculture, Asian Market, Automotive, Aviation & Aerospace, Bilingual Market, Brand Development & Integration, Business Publications, Business-To-Business, Cable T.V., Children's Market, Collateral, Communications, Consulting, Consumer Marketing, Corporate Identity, Cosmetics, Digital/Interactive, E-Commerce, Education, Electronic Media, Engineering, Entertainment, Environmental, Fashion/Apparel, Financial, Food Service, Graphic Design, Health Care Services, High Technology, Hispanic Market, Industrial, Infomercials, Information Technology, Internet/Web Design, Legal Services, Leisure, Logo & Package Design, Magazines, Marine, Medical Products, Multimedia, New Product Development, Over-50 Market, Pharmaceutical, Planning & Consultation, Real Estate, Restaurant, Retail, Seniors' Market, Sports Market, Strategic Planning/Research, Transportation, Travel & Tourism

Alicia Stack *(Partner)*

Accounts:
Block Drug
GlaxoSmithKline
Hewlett-Packard
Kellogg's
KFC
Merck
Procter & Gamble Pharmaceuticals
Sara Lee
Wilson Sporting Goods

KEENAN-NAGLE ADVERTISING
1301 S 12th St, Allentown, PA 18103-3814
Tel.: (610) 797-7100
Fax: (610) 797-8212
Web Site: www.keenannagle.com

E-Mail for Key Personnel:
President: mkeenan@keenannagle.com

Employees: 20
Year Founded: 1985

Agency Specializes In: Financial, Health Care Services, Industrial

James Nicnick *(Dir-Web Dev)*
Alissa Nieli *(Dir-Art)*
Megan Rotondo *(Assoc Dir-Art)*
Gena Cavallo *(Mgr-Print & Production)*
Carol Sarubin *(Mgr-Fin & Ops)*
Rob Burns *(Designer)*

Accounts:
Fuller Bulk Handling Compressor Div
Horsehead Resource Development Co., Inc.; Palmerton, PA
Ingersoll-Dresser Pumps
Lehigh Electric
Michael Dunn Corporation
Premier Bank; Doylestown, PA
Silberline Manufacturing Co., Inc.
Vastex International
Walters Oil, Inc.; Easton, PA & Phillipsburg, NJ
Weidenhammer Systems Corporation

KEITH BATES & ASSOCIATES, INC.
4319 N Lowell Ave, Chicago, IL 60641
Tel.: (773) 205-7992
Fax: (773) 205-7988
E-Mail: keithbates@kbates.com
Web Site: www.kbates.com

Employees: 2
Year Founded: 1970

Agency Specializes In: Business-To-Business, Consulting, Corporate Identity, Direct Response Marketing, High Technology, Information Technology, Internet/Web Design, Planning & Consultation, Strategic Planning/Research, Travel & Tourism, Viral/Buzz/Word of Mouth

Approx. Annual Billings: $500,000

Keith Bates *(Owner)*

Accounts:
ABC Technologies
Antares Alliance Grp.
IBM
Napersoft
Silvon Software
SKK, Inc.
SPSS

KEITH LANE CREATIVE GROUP
301 Lafayette St Ste 2, Salem, MA 01970
Tel.: (781) 258-7364
Web Site: www.keithlanecreativegroup.com

Employees: 3
Year Founded: 2013

Agency Specializes In: Advertising, Advertising Specialties, Affluent Market, Alternative Advertising, Brand Development & Integration, Broadcast, Business-To-Business, Cable T.V., Catalogs, Collateral, Communications, Consulting, Consumer Marketing, Content, Corporate Communications, Corporate Identity, Digital/Interactive, Direct Response Marketing, Direct-to-Consumer, Electronic Media, Graphic Design, Guerilla Marketing, High Technology, Identity Marketing, In-Store Advertising, Integrated Marketing, International, Internet/Web Design, Local Marketing, Logo & Package Design, Luxury Products, Magazines, Media Buying Services, Media Planning, Mobile Marketing, Multimedia, Newspaper, Newspapers & Magazines, Package Design, Paid Searches, Planning & Consultation, Point of Purchase, Point of Sale, Print, Production (Ad, Film, Broadcast), Promotions, Public Relations, Publicity/Promotions, Radio, Regional, Search Engine Optimization, Social Media, T.V., Trade & Consumer Magazines, Viral/Buzz/Word of Mouth, Web (Banner Ads, Pop-ups, etc.)

Approx. Annual Billings: $500,000

Keith Lane *(Chief Creative Officer)*

Accounts:
North Solar Screen Solar Shade; 2013

KEKST & CO.
437 Madison Ave, New York, NY 10022
Tel.: (212) 593-2655
Fax: (212) 521-4900
E-Mail: jeffrey-taufield@kekst.com
Web Site: www.kekst.com

Employees: 75

Agency Specializes In: Sponsorship

Jeffrey Taufield *(Vice Chm)*
Lissa Perlman *(Partner)*
Robert Siegfried *(Partner)*
Molly Morse *(Mng Dir & Co-Head-Retail & Consumer Practice)*
Ruth Pachman *(Mng Dir)*
Frederic Spar *(Mng Dir)*
Thomas Davies *(Sr VP)*
Larry Rand *(Exec Chm)*

Accounts:
CBOCS, Inc.
KKR Financial Holdings LLC
LVMH Moet Hennessy Louis Vuitton
North Castle Partners
Spectrum Brands, Inc.
Tecumseh Products Co.

KELLEN COMMUNICATIONS
355 Lexington Ave Ste 1515, New York, NY 10017
Tel.: (212) 297-2100
Fax: (212) 370-9047
E-Mail: infony@kellenpr.com
Web Site: www.kellenpr.com

Employees: 45
Year Founded: 1945

Agency Specializes In: Consumer Marketing, Corporate Identity, Food Service, High Technology, Industrial, Public Relations, Travel & Tourism

Approx. Annual Billings: $10,000,000

Peter Rush *(Chm & CEO)*
Mike Brooks *(CFO & Exec VP)*
Debra Berliner *(Sr VP)*
Pam Chumley *(Grp VP)*
Russell Lemieux *(Grp VP)*
Bonnie Sonnenschein *(VP)*
Pam Meadows *(Controller)*
Chris Barry *(Dir-Comm)*
Jason Carlbom *(Dir-Creative Svcs)*
Stan Samples *(Sr Acct Supvr)*
Harry Schmitz *(Sr Acct Supvr)*
Kathleen Fletcher *(Acct Exec-PR)*

Accounts:
Association for Dressings & Sauces
Builders Hardware Manufacturers Association
Calorie Control Council
Copper Development Association
Infant Formula Council
National Association of Margarine Manufacturers
National Candle Association
National Pasta Association
New York Women in Communications
Research Chefs Association

Branches

Kellen Communications
1156 15th St NW Ste 900, Washington, DC 20005
Tel.: (202) 207-0915
Fax: (202) 223-9741
E-Mail: infodc@kellenpr.com
Web Site: www.kellenpr.com

Employees: 25

Agency Specializes In: Public Relations

Debra Berliner *(Sr VP)*
Joan Cear *(Sr VP)*
Chris Barry *(Dir-Comm)*
Martin Bay *(Dir-Meetings & Expositions)*
Jason Carlbom *(Dir-Creative Svcs)*
Greg Cashman *(Dir-Fin Plng & Analysis)*
Linda Arcangeli-Story *(Mgr-Meetings)*
Sean Hewitt *(Mgr-Meetings & Expositions)*
Barbara Miller *(Mgr-Comm)*
Jennifer Stone-Rogers *(Mgr-Trade Show & Ops)*
Robert Rankin *(Acct Exec)*

Accounts:
Calorie Control Council
Copper Development Association
International Formula Council
National Association of Margarine Manufacturers

National Candle Association
National Park Association
Pfizer Inc

Kellen Europe

Avenue Jules Bordet 142, 1140 Brussels, Belgium
Tel.: (32) 2 761 16 00
Fax: (32) 2 761 16 99
E-Mail: info@kelleneurope.com
Web Site: www.kelleneurope.com

Year Founded: 2004

Agency Specializes In: Public Relations

Alfons Westgeest *(Mng Partner & Grp VP)*
Maria Teresa Scardigli *(VP)*
Hans Craen *(Mgr)*
Dani Kolb *(Mgr)*
Pascale Lammineur *(Sr Accountant)*

Accounts:
EUROBAT The Association of European Automotive & Industrial Battery Manufacturers
GAMA Global Acetate Manufacturers Association
Global FM - Global Facility Management Association
PDA Europe Polyurea Development Association
PEFRC Phosphate Ester Flame Retardant Consortium
PRISM Professional Records & Information Services Management
STM International Association of Scientific, Technical & Medical Publishers

KELLENFOL ADVERTISING

Gran Via Corts Catalanes, 08020 Barcelona, Spain
Tel.: (34) 933056233
E-Mail: info@kellenfol.com
Web Site: www.kellenfol.com

Employees: 6
Year Founded: 2011

Agency Specializes In: Above-the-Line, Alternative Advertising, Below-the-Line, Branded Entertainment, Catalogs, Digital/Interactive, Electronic Media, Experience Design, Guerilla Marketing, In-Store Advertising, Infomercials, Magazines, Mobile Marketing, Multimedia, Newspapers & Magazines, Outdoor, Social Media, Viral/Buzz/Word of Mouth

Approx. Annual Billings: $1,000,000

Jesus Gordillo *(Gen Mgr)*

Accounts:
Chopard Digital Strategy
Daikin Design Branding
Danone Advertising
Dom Perignon Branding Design
Fujitsu Advertising
ITW / Panreac Advertising
Sanofi Advertising Strategy

KELLETT COMMUNICATIONS

5012 50th Ave, PO Box 1027, Yellowknife, NT X1A 2N7 Canada
Tel.: (867) 669-9344
Fax: (867) 669-9354
Web Site: www.kellett.nt.ca

Employees: 15
Year Founded: 1998

Agency Specializes In: Advertising

Michael Ericsson *(Dir-Art)*
Lee O'Mara *(Dir-Web)*
Amanda Shaw *(Acct Mgr)*
Melissa Bannister *(Mgr-Media & Production)*
Bianca Ericsson *(Mgr-Media & Production)*
Christina Rae Carrigan *(Sr Graphic Designer)*
Joe Fitzgerald *(Copywriter)*

Accounts:
Folk on the Rocks
Kellett
Latitude Wireless
NorthwestTel

KELLEY & ASSOCIATES ADVERTISING

8410 Wolf Lake Dr Ste 104, Bartlett, TN 38133
Tel.: (901) 754-8998
Fax: (901) 754-8060
Web Site: www.kelleyadv.com

Agency Specializes In: Advertising, Brand Development & Integration, Graphic Design, Internet/Web Design, Logo & Package Design, Media Planning, Public Relations

Christi Kelley *(Pres & CEO)*
Kim Strickland *(Sr Dir-Art)*
Elise Herron *(Acct Mgr)*
Ellen Larson *(Coord-Mktg & Media)*

Accounts:
Catholic Charities of West Tennessee
The City of Bartlett
Frost Bake Shop

KELLEY & COMPANY

70 Walnut St, Wellesley, MA 02481
Tel.: (781) 239-8092
Fax: (781) 239-8093
E-Mail: gckelleyco@aol.com
Web Site: www.kelleyandwhoever.com/

Employees: 9
Year Founded: 1993

National Agency Associations: 4A's

Agency Specializes In: Automotive, Brand Development & Integration, Consumer Marketing, Education, Financial, High Technology, Leisure, Retail, Sports Market, Travel & Tourism

Approx. Annual Billings: $11,300,000

Glenn C. Kelley *(Pres/CEO-Kelley & Cohorts)*

Accounts:
Connected Corporation High Technology
Cotuit Development Inc. Real Estate
EMC Corporation
Gosling's Liquor, Spirits
Windemere Development Corp. Real Estate, Resort

KELLEY HABIB JOHN

155 Seaport Blvd, Boston, MA 02210
Tel.: (617) 241-8000
Fax: (617) 241-8110
Web Site: www.khj.com

Employees: 20
Year Founded: 1986

Agency Specializes In: Advertising, Advertising Specialties, Bilingual Market, Brand Development & Integration, Broadcast, Business Publications, Business-To-Business, Collateral, Communications, Consulting, Consumer Marketing, Consumer Publications, Corporate Identity, Digital/Interactive, Direct Response Marketing, Education, Electronic Media, Event Planning & Marketing, Exhibit/Trade Shows, Financial, Government/Political, Graphic Design, Health Care Services, High Technology, Hispanic Market, Industrial, Information Technology, Internet/Web Design, Legal Services, Logo & Package Design, Magazines, Media Buying Services, Medical Products, Merchandising, Multimedia, Newspaper, Newspapers & Magazines, Out-of-Home Media, Outdoor, Over-50 Market, Planning & Consultation, Point of Purchase, Point of Sale, Print, Production, Publicity/Promotions, Radio, Real Estate, Sales Promotion, Seniors' Market, Strategic Planning/Research, T.V., Technical Advertising, Trade & Consumer Magazines, Travel & Tourism

Approx. Annual Billings: $34,700,000

Gregory P. John *(Chm & Principal)*
Judy A. Habib *(Pres & CEO)*
Sylvie Askins *(Principal & Exec VP-Strategy & Plng)*
Adam Cramer *(Principal, Sr VP & Dir-Creative)*
Patricia Marraffa *(VP-Fin & Admin)*
Michelle Karalekas *(Acct Dir)*
Tod Brubaker *(Dir-Creative & Copywriter)*

Accounts:
Delta Dental
Webster Five Cents Savings Bank Commercial & Retail Mutual Bank; 1995

KELLEY SWOFFORD ROY, INC.

(Merged with Navigant Marketing to form Navigant Marketing / KSR)

KELLIHER SAMETS VOLK

212 Battery St, Burlington, VT 05401-5281
Tel.: (802) 862-8261
Fax: (802) 863-4724
E-Mail: tvolk@ksvc.com
Web Site: www.ksvc.com

E-Mail for Key Personnel:
Creative Dir.: bill@ksvc.com
Media Dir.: bob@ksvc.con
Public Relations: claudia@ksvc.con

Employees: 65
Year Founded: 1977

National Agency Associations: MAGNET

Agency Specializes In: Advertising, Brand Development & Integration, Business Publications, Cable T.V., Collateral, Communications, Consumer Marketing, Consumer Publications, Corporate Identity, Crisis Communications, Digital/Interactive, E-Commerce, Event Planning & Marketing, Financial, Government/Political, Graphic Design, Guerilla Marketing, In-Store Advertising, Integrated Marketing, Internet/Web Design, Leisure, Media Buying Services, Media Planning, Media Relations, Newspaper, Newspapers & Magazines, Out-of-Home Media, Outdoor, Over-50 Market, Planning & Consultation, Point of Purchase, Point of Sale, Print, Production, Public Relations, Publicity/Promotions, Radio, Retail, Sponsorship, Sports Market, Strategic Planning/Research, T.V., Teen Market, Trade & Consumer Magazines, Travel & Tourism, Women's Market

Approx. Annual Billings: $40,000,000

Rob Niccolai *(Client Grp Dir & Principal)*
Bob Smith *(VP & Grp Dir-Connections)*
Cavan Chasan *(Exec Dir-Connections)*
Linda Kelliher *(Dir-Creative)*
Brian Mullins *(Dir-Creative)*
Mark Ray *(Dir-PR)*
Bill Stowe *(Dir-Creative)*
Rachel Gage *(Brand Mgr)*
Brent Sitterly *(Mgr-Analytics)*
Tim White *(Mgr-IT)*
Dave Treston *(Sr Acct Planner)*
Derek Bratek *(Sr Designer)*

Accounts:
Arbella Insurance Group
Mass Save; Boston, MA
National Grid
Nellie's Cage Free Eggs
Okemo Mountain Resort
Rural Cellular Corp./Unicel; Alexandria, MN
State Street Corporation
State Street Global Advisors
Totes Isotoner ACORN
Vermont Business Roundtable; South Burlington, VT
Vermont Department of Health; Burlington, VT Smoke Baby
Vermont Energy Investment Corp.; Burlington, VT
Vermont Student Assistance Corp.; Winooski, VT

Branch

Kelliher Samets Volk NY
337 Broome St 3rd Fl, New York, NY 10002
(See Separate Listing)

KELLIHER SAMETS VOLK NY
337 Broome St 3rd Fl, New York, NY 10002
Tel.: (212) 366-4000
Fax: (212) 366-4046
E-Mail: info@ksvc.com
Web Site: www.ksvc.com

Employees: 4
Year Founded: 1977

Agency Specializes In: Advertising, Brand Development & Integration, Communications, Consulting, Consumer Publications, Digital/Interactive, Exhibit/Trade Shows, Graphic Design, In-Store Advertising, Internet/Web Design, Leisure, Local Marketing, Logo & Package Design, Magazines, Media Buying Services, New Product Development, Newspaper, Out-of-Home Media, Outdoor, Pharmaceutical, Planning & Consultation, Print, Real Estate, Restaurant, Retail, Sales Promotion, Travel & Tourism

Ashley Nicholls *(Principal & Dir-Energy Strategy)*
Cavan Chasan *(Exec Dir-Connections)*
Aimee Frost *(Dir-Connections)*
Brian Mullins *(Dir-Creative)*
Mark Ray *(Dir-PR)*
Erin Fagnant *(Brand Mgr)*
Rachel Gage *(Brand Mgr)*
Tucker Wright *(Brand Mgr)*
Tim White *(Mgr-IT)*
Ashley Oakley *(Strategist-Brand)*

Accounts:
Chittenden Bank
Seventh Generation
Stowe
VT Dept of Health

KELLY & COMPANY
3100 N Knoxville Ave Ste 213, Peoria, IL 61603
Tel.: (309) 550-5786
Web Site: www.kellyadvco.com

Agency Specializes In: Advertising, Brand Development & Integration, Internet/Web Design, Logo & Package Design, Print, Radio, T.V.

Kelly Alexander *(Pres)*
Alex Alexander *(VP-Ops)*

Accounts:
Advantage Auto
Bikers for Ta-Tas
Blunier Builders Inc
German-Bliss Equipment
Klasinski Orthopedic Clinic
McMahon's Pints & Plates
Menold Construction & Restoration
Millworks
Woodworkers Shop

KELLY MARCOM
(Name Changed to Mottis)

KELLY MEDIA GROUP
2022 W 11th St, Los Angeles, CA 91786
Tel.: (909) 621-4737
Toll Free: (877) 788-8463

Employees: 72
Year Founded: 2002

National Agency Associations: DMA

Agency Specializes In: Advertising, Advertising Specialties, Broadcast, Direct Response Marketing, Direct-to-Consumer, Internet/Web Design, Media Planning, Media Relations, Media Training, Print, Production (Ad, Film, Broadcast), Sales Promotion, Search Engine Optimization, Social Marketing/Nonprofit, Telemarketing

Approx. Annual Billings: $27,000,000

Breakdown of Gross Billings by Media: Corp. Communications: $27,000,000

jason cardiff *(Pres)*

Accounts:
Kelly Media; Los Angeles, CA

KELSEY ADVERTISING & DESIGN
133 Main St, Lagrange, GA 30240
Tel.: (706) 298-2738
Web Site: www.kelseyads.com

Agency Specializes In: Advertising, Brand Development & Integration, Digital/Interactive, Graphic Design, Integrated Marketing, Logo & Package Design, Outdoor, Print, Public Relations, Strategic Planning/Research

Dawn Harris *(Office Mgr)*
Jessica Brannen *(Acct Exec)*
Stacey Malone *(Acct Exec)*
Niki Studdard *(Sr Designer)*

Accounts:
Thinc Academy

KEMP ADVERTISING & MARKETING
3001 N Main St, High Point, NC 27265
Tel.: (336) 869-2155
Web Site: www.edkemp.com

Agency Specializes In: Advertising, Internet/Web Design, Public Relations, Social Media, Strategic Planning/Research

Ed Kemp *(Co-Founder)*
Jon Kemp *(Owner & Pres)*
Tony Faucette *(Partner & VP)*
Brent Taylor *(Dir-Creative)*

Accounts:
Eanes Heating and Air Direct Mail, Marketing, Online Banner Ads, Print Ads, Television, Web Video
Taylorsville Savings Bank Ssb

KEMP GOLDBERG PARTNERS
(Name Changed to Industrium)

KEN FONG ASSOCIATES, INC.
178 W Adams St, Stockton, CA 95204
Tel.: (209) 466-0366
E-Mail: greatads@kenfongassociates.com
Web Site: www.kenfongassociates.com

Employees: 2
Year Founded: 1952

Approx. Annual Billings: $2,000,000

Breakdown of Gross Billings by Media: Collateral: $300,000; Newsp.: $200,000; T.V.: $1,500,000

Les J. Fong *(Owner & Pres)*

Accounts:
Barbosa Cabinets
Duncan Press
O'Conner Woods
Proco Products
Stanislaus Behavioral Health & Recovery Services

KEN SLAUF & ASSOCIATES, INC.
1 N Main St, Lombard, IL 60148
Tel.: (630) 629-7531
Fax: (630) 629-7534
E-Mail: info@ksa-inc.com
Web Site: www.ksa-inc.com

Employees: 7
Year Founded: 1949

National Agency Associations: BMA

Agency Specializes In: Business-To-Business, Industrial

Approx. Annual Billings: $1,500,000

Kenneth E. Slauf *(Pres)*

Accounts:
Autoblok; Wheeling, IL; 1997
Reishauer; Elgin, IL Machine Tools
ROW, Inc.
Transor Filter; Elk Grove, IL EDM Filtration Systems

KENNA
(Formerly henderson bas)
90 Burnhamthorpe Road West 5th Floor, Mississauga, ON L5B 3C3 Canada
Tel.: (905) 277-2900
Web Site: www.kenna.ca

Employees: 130
Year Founded: 1999

Agency Specializes In: Advertising, Advertising Specialties, Brand Development & Integration, Digital/Interactive, Fashion/Apparel, Financial, Internet/Web Design, Publicity/Promotions, Sports Market, Teen Market

Jeffrey Bowles *(Mng Dir & Exec VP)*
Paul Quigley *(COO)*
Steve Turner *(Grp Acct Dir)*
Jason Griffiths *(Acct Dir)*
Kristine Lang *(Acct Dir)*
Aimee Richard *(Acct Dir-Agriculture)*
Lisa Pratt *(Dir-Social Strategy)*
Mary Mastrangelo *(Acct Supvr)*

Accounts:
New-BASF
New-Capital One
Coca-Cola Refreshments USA, Inc.; 2004
Dockers; Toronto, ON; 2001
New-Dr. Oetker
Dreyfus; 1998
FedEx
Kids Help Phone
Levi's Canada

Mercedes-Benz Canada
Molson Canada; Toronto, ON; 1994
Nintendo of Canada; 2005
Ontario Lottery & Gaming Corporation; 2004
Rogers
New-Sonos
Tim Hortons
Yamaha Motor Canada Ltd.; 2004

KENNEDY COMMUNICATIONS
1701 Broadway St Ste 266, Vancouver, WA 98663
Tel.: (360) 213-5001
Fax: (360) 213-0246
Toll Free: (800) 877-0485
E-Mail: info@kennedyglobal.com
Web Site: www.kennedyglobal.com

Employees: 5

Agency Specializes In: Advertising

Kurt Kennedy *(CEO, Exec Dir-Creative & Sr Strategist)*
Alice Thornton Wright *(Client Svcs Dir)*
Curtis Franklin *(Dir-Creative)*
Kara Brack *(Acct Exec-Digital)*

Accounts:
Adobe
Albertsons
Big Brothers Big Sisters Invitation
Culligan Campaign: "It Pays To See The Difference"
Dell
Nike
Sunglass Hut
Target Optical

KENNETH JAFFE INC.
71 Vly St Ste 201, South Orange, NJ 07079-2835
Tel.: (973) 378-3200
Fax: (973) 378-2010
Web Site: www.kennethjaffeadvertising.com/

Employees: 12
Year Founded: 1969

Agency Specializes In: Advertising, Food Service, Real Estate

Approx. Annual Billings: $5,000,000

Breakdown of Gross Billings by Media: Bus. Publs.: $350,000; Cable T.V.: $50,000; Mags.: $425,000; Newsp.: $2,800,000; Outdoor: $200,000; Radio: $625,000; T.V.: $550,000

Kenneth Jaffe *(Owner)*
Sheldon Greenholtz *(Pres)*

Accounts:
Burger King Franchises; Elmwood Park, NJ
Chas Smith Realtors; Edison, NJ
Main Street Realty; Woodbridge, NJ
Worden & Green Real Estate; Hillsborough, NJ

KENT COMMUNICATIONS
6402 Westchester Cir, Richmond, VA 23225
Tel.: (804) 323-1500
Web Site: www.kentcommunications.net

Agency Specializes In: Advertising, Brand Development & Integration, Broadcast, Collateral, Internet/Web Design, Media Buying Services, Outdoor, Print, Radio

Tom Kent *(Pres)*

Accounts:
JoPa Co

KERIGAN MARKETING ASSOCIATES, INC.
260 Marina Dr, Port Saint Joe, FL 32456
Tel.: (850) 229-4562
Fax: (866) 518-5855
E-Mail: info@kerigan.com
Web Site: keriganmarketing.com

Year Founded: 2000

Agency Specializes In: Advertising, Internet/Web Design, Logo & Package Design, Print, Social Media, T.V.

Jack Kerigan *(Owner)*
Sara Backus *(Dir-Creative)*
Renee Orand *(Office Mgr)*

Accounts:
Florida State University Panama City
Tyndall Federal Credit Union Inc.

KERN
(Formerly The Kern Organization)
20955 Warner Center Ln, Woodland Hills, CA 91367-6511
Tel.: (818) 703-8775
Fax: (818) 703-8458
Toll Free: (800) 335-4244
E-Mail: info@kernagency.com
Web Site: kernagency.com/

Employees: 50
Year Founded: 1991

Agency Specializes In: Direct Response Marketing, Strategic Planning/Research

Russell Kern *(Founder & Pres)*
Camilla Grozian-Lorentzen *(VP)*
Jay Jablonski *(VP-Applied Mktg)*
Scott Levine *(VP-Strategy)*
Tom MacKendrick *(VP-Digital & Data)*
Robert Susnar *(VP-Bus Dev)*
Nilesh Sojitra *(Dir-Dev)*
Jessica Purdy *(Acct Supvr)*
Karina Mohacsy *(Sr Acct Exec-DIRECTV Team)*

Accounts:
DIRECTV

KERVIN MARKETING
14121 NE Airport Way Ste 207572, Portland, OR 97230
Tel.: (250) 204-2108
Web Site: www.kervinmarketing.com

Agency Specializes In: Advertising, Brand Development & Integration, Email, Graphic Design, Internet/Web Design, Logo & Package Design, Print, Search Engine Optimization, Social Media

Jonathan Kervin *(Owner)*

Accounts:
Peniuks Sportfishing
TAP Bookkeeping

KEVIN J. ASH CREATIVE DESIGN, LLC
58 Sax Alley, Northwood, NH 03261
Tel.: (603) 942-8989
E-Mail: kjacd@kjadesign.com
Web Site: www.kjadesign.com

Employees: 6
Year Founded: 1992

Agency Specializes In: Advertising, Brand Development & Integration, Business Publications, Collateral, Consumer Marketing, Corporate Communications, Corporate Identity, Direct Response Marketing, Electronic Media, Exhibit/Trade Shows, Financial, Graphic Design, Health Care Services, High Technology, Internet/Web Design, Logo & Package Design, Magazines, Media Buying Services, Newspaper, Newspapers & Magazines, Outdoor, Print, Production, Radio, Recruitment, Trade & Consumer Magazines

Approx. Annual Billings: $5,000,000

Breakdown of Gross Billings by Media: Corp. Communications: $500,000; Exhibits/Trade Shows: $500,000; Graphic Design: $1,000,000; Newsp. & Mags.: $1,000,000; Radio: $500,000; Trade & Consumer Mags.: $1,000,000; Worldwide Web Sites: $500,000

Kevin J. Ash *(Principal & Dir-Creative)*

Accounts:
Mr. Shower Door Custom Shower/Bath Enclosures; 1993

KEY GORDON COMMUNICATIONS
70 The Esplanade Ste 300, Toronto, ON M5E 1R2 Canada
Tel.: (416) 644-0844
Fax: (416) 362-2387
E-Mail: info@keygordon.com
Web Site: www.keygordon.com

Employees: 7

Grant Gordon *(Pres & Dir-Creative)*
Bruce Roberts *(Mng Dir)*
Rachel Bruner *(Acct Dir)*
Joe Gorecki *(Dir-Art)*
Lena Rubisova *(Dir-Art)*

Accounts:
Feed The Children
Fleishman Hillard
Hydro One
Independent Grocers
Organic Meadow
SierraClub
Starbucks
Toronto Hydro
Triton
WWF

KEYAD, LLC
1723 N Loop 1604 E Ste 211, San Antonio, TX 78232
Tel.: (210) 363-2861
Fax: (210) 568-6630
E-Mail: cmp@keyad.com
Web Site: www.keyad.com

Employees: 25
Year Founded: 1998

Agency Specializes In: Advertising, Advertising Specialties, Alternative Advertising, Automotive, Brand Development & Integration, Branded Entertainment, Business Publications, Business-To-Business, Catalogs, Co-op Advertising, Collateral, Content, Corporate Identity, Cosmetics, Custom Publishing, Direct Response Marketing, Direct-to-Consumer, Education, Electronic Media, Entertainment, Event Planning & Marketing, Exhibit/Trade Shows, Graphic Design, Hospitality, Identity Marketing, Internet/Web Design, Local Marketing, Logo & Package Design, Magazines, Media Buying Services, Media Planning, New Product Development, Out-of-Home Media, Outdoor, Over-50 Market, Package Design, Podcasting, Point of Purchase, Point of Sale, Print, Production (Ad, Film, Broadcast), Production (Print), Public Relations, Publicity/Promotions, RSS

(Really Simple Syndication), Regional, Retail, Sales Promotion, Sports Market, Technical Advertising, Telemarketing, Trade & Consumer Magazines, Transportation, Travel & Tourism, Web (Banner Ads, Pop-ups, etc.)

Revenue: $1,500,000

Mike Pilkilton *(Owner)*

Accounts:
Alpha Jones
Domino's Pizza
Nike
Nikon
Pizza Hut

KEYPATH EDUCATION

(Formerly PlattForm Advertising)
15500 W 113 Ste #200, Lenexa, KS 66219
Tel.: (913) 254-6000
Fax: (913) 538-5078
Web Site: keypathedu.com/

Employees: 300

Agency Specializes In: Advertising, Direct Response Marketing, Education, Internet/Web Design, Newspaper, Print, Radio, T.V., Yellow Pages Advertising

Approx. Annual Billings: $39,000,000

Mike McHugh *(Grp Pres)*
Steve Fireng *(CEO)*
Stephen Rentschler *(Mng Dir)*
Patrick Donoghue *(CFO)*
Jai B. Shankar *(CIO)*
Kris Little *(Sr VP-Mktg Svcs)*
Mallory Curry *(Acct Mgr)*
Valerie McBee *(Mgr-Digital Media)*
Megan Quillin *(Mgr-Digital Media)*
Korab Eland *(Media Buyer-Digital)*
Caitlin Stephens *(Analyst-Media)*
Dave Admire *(Chief Integrity Officer)*
Erik Edmonds *(Sr Media Buyer-Digital)*
Lindsay Parker *(Sr Media Buyer)*

Accounts:
Azusa Pacific University
The Career Centers
The Center for Professional Development at The Art Institute of Colorado
Davison
Dawn
Delta Tech Recruitment
Duluth Business University
EDMC
Hallmark College
The Illinois Institute of Art Recruitment
International Institute of the Americas Recruitment
Liberty University
Lincoln Educational Services Recruitment
Maybe Logic Academy
Modern Gun School
Olympia College Recruitment
Pinnacle Career Institute Recruitment
The Praxis Center
SBB College
Student Loan Solutions, LLC
Students Paths
Thompson Education
Utah Career College

KEYSTONE MARKETING

709 N Main St, Winston Salem, NC 27101
Tel.: (336) 724-9899
Fax: (336) 724-9855
Web Site: www.keystonemarketing.net

Agency Specializes In: Advertising, Communications, Promotions, Strategic Planning/Research

Brad Bennett *(CEO & Principal)*
Denise Appleyard *(CFO)*
Mike Grice *(Principal & Chief Creative Officer)*
Chip Crutchfield *(Dir-Interactive)*
Jonathan Reed *(Assoc Dir-Creative)*
Jacki Petree *(Jr Graphic Designer)*

Accounts:
The Hershey Co.
Mondelez International, Inc. Oreo, Oscar Mayer, A1 Steak Sauce

KG CREATIVE

395 Del Monte Ctr Ste 243, Monterey, CA 93940
Tel.: (831) 333-6294
E-Mail: advertising@kgcreative.com
Web Site: www.kgcreative.com

Employees: 2
Year Founded: 2008

Agency Specializes In: Advertising, Brand Development & Integration, Corporate Identity, Graphic Design, Production (Print), Web (Banner Ads, Pop-ups, etc.)

Kevin Garcia *(Founder & Dir-Art)*

KGBTEXAS

200 E Grayson St, San Antonio, TX 78215
Tel.: (210) 826-8899
Fax: (210) 826-8872
E-Mail: info@kgbtexas.com
Web Site: www.kgbtexas.com

Agency Specializes In: Advertising

Mary McNelis *(VP)*
Melody Patrick *(VP)*
Jeff Coyle *(Dir-Pub Affairs & Govt Rels)*
Matthew Danelo *(Dir-PR & Adv)*
Keoni Viriyapunt *(Assoc Dir-Creative)*
Elaine Matthews *(Sr Acct Exec)*
Laura Elizabeth Morales-Welch *(Sr Acct Exec-Pub Affairs)*
Amy Cantu *(Acct Coord-Pub Affairs)*
Tiffany Heikkila *(Acct Head-AT&T-Grp 42)*

Accounts:
Claro

KGLOBAL

2001 L St NW 6th Fl, Washington, DC 20036
Tel.: (202) 349-7075
E-Mail: hello@kglobal.com
Web Site: www.kglobal.com

Agency Specializes In: Advertising, Brand Development & Integration, Content, Crisis Communications, Digital/Interactive, Media Relations, Public Relations

Randy DeCleene *(Partner)*
Gene Grabowski *(Partner)*
Charles Dolan *(Sr VP)*
Kathryn Harrington *(Sr VP)*
Diana Devaney Moon *(Acct Dir)*
Ming Freer *(Acct Dir)*
Molly Mark *(Acct Dir)*
Joe Malunda *(Sr Acct Exec)*
Brianna Broad *(Acct Exec)*
Collin Lever *(Acct Exec)*

KH COMPLETE ADVERTISING

6280 N Shadeland Ave, Indianapolis, IN 46220
Tel.: (317) 813-0180
Web Site: www.khcompleteadvertising.com

Agency Specializes In: Advertising, Digital/Interactive, Graphic Design, Media Buying Services, Media Relations, Public Relations, Search Engine Optimization, Social Media

Kerrie Henderson *(Owner)*

Accounts:
Indiana Fever

KHEMISTRY

14-16 Brewer Street, London, W1F OSG United Kingdom
Tel.: (44) 20 7437 4084
Fax: (44) 20 7437 4085
E-Mail: kenny@khemistry.ltd.uk
Web Site: www.khemistry.ltd.uk

Employees: 7
Year Founded: 2001

Agency Specializes In: Above-the-Line, Advertising, Advertising Specialties, Arts, Automotive, Aviation & Aerospace, Below-the-Line, Brand Development & Integration, Business Publications, Business-To-Business, Commercial Photography, Communications, Computers & Software, Consumer Goods, Consumer Marketing, Consumer Publications, Corporate Communications, Corporate Identity, Digital/Interactive, Direct Response Marketing, Direct-to-Consumer, E-Commerce, Education, Email, Entertainment, Financial, Food Service, Graphic Design, Household Goods, Information Technology, Integrated Marketing, International, Internet/Web Design, Logo & Package Design, Luxury Products, Magazines, Market Research, Mobile Marketing, New Product Development, New Technologies, Newspaper, Newspapers & Magazines, Outdoor, Package Design, Pharmaceutical, Point of Purchase, Point of Sale, Print, Production, Production (Print), Promotions, Public Relations, Publicity/Promotions, Radio, Retail, Sales Promotion, Search Engine Optimization, Social Media, Strategic Planning/Research, T.V., Trade & Consumer Magazines, Travel & Tourism, Yellow Pages Advertising

Approx. Annual Billings: $500,000

Breakdown of Gross Billings by Media: Adv. Specialities: $100,000; Brdcst.: $150,000; Consumer Publs.: $100,000; Corp. Communications: $50,000; E-Commerce: $100,000

Kenny Nicholas *(Partner & Dir-Creative)*
Anthony Bates *(Partner)*
Jessica Bradley *(Dir-Art & Designer)*

Accounts:
Belazu; UK Food Products
CAI Games; UK Online Gaming
Devonshire Partnership; UK Surveyors
IET Venues; UK Venue Hire
Jasper Littman; UK Savile Row Tailor
KBR Government & Infrastructure
Profile Interiors; UK Interior Fitters
St Patrick's International College; UK & Asia Education
Superman Energy Drink; UK Energy Drink
Vital Europe; UK Dentistry

KICKSTART CONSULTING INC

217 State St, San Mateo, CA 94401
Tel.: (650) 346-8990
E-Mail: pr@kickstartconsulting.com
Web Site: www.kickstartconsulting.com

Agency Specializes In: Media Planning, Media Relations, Public Relations, Strategic Planning/Research, Trade & Consumer Magazines

Annette Shimada *(Principal)*

Accounts:
Accelrys
Accruent
Bristlecone
Clearapp
Conard House Medical Services
Infobright Data Warehousing Services
ITM Software
SeeSaw Networks Media Planning & Buying Services

KIDD GROUP
2074 Centre Point Blvd Ste 200, Tallahassee, FL 32308
Tel.: (850) 878-5433
Fax: (850) 878-6745
Toll Free: (800) 323-4869
E-Mail: info@kidd.com
Web Site: www.kidd.com

E-Mail for Key Personnel:
President: WKidd@kiddtucker.com

Employees: 10
Year Founded: 1980

National Agency Associations: Second Wind Limited

Agency Specializes In: Advertising, Communications, E-Commerce, Education, Financial, Government/Political, Graphic Design, Health Care Services, Internet/Web Design, Market Research, Media Buying Services, Media Planning, Public Relations, Retail, Social Media, Transportation, Web (Banner Ads, Pop-ups, etc.)

Jerry Kidd *(Pres & Dir-Creative)*
Mary Liz Moody *(Dir-Studio & Print)*
Cindy Martin *(Office Mgr)*

Accounts:
Bay Medical Center; Panama City , FL Healthcare Services; 1998
City of Jacksonville Beach Utilities
Florida Department of Health; Tallahassee, FL; 1999

KIDS AT PLAY
959 Cole Ave, Hollywood, CA 90038
Tel.: (323) 462-8100
E-Mail: play@kidsatplaymedia.com
Web Site: www.kidsatplaymedia.com

Year Founded: 2006

Agency Specializes In: Advertising, Brand Development & Integration, Production

Jason Berger *(Founder & CEO)*
Amy Laslett *(Pres & Producer)*
Jim Dolan *(Partner & CFO)*
Emma Berger *(COO)*
Topher Osborn *(Dir-Photography)*

KIDVERTISERS
1133 Broadway Ste 1000, New York, NY 10010
Tel.: (212) 966-2345
Fax: (212) 966-2770
E-Mail: mail@kidvertisers.com
Web Site: www.kidvertisers.com

E-Mail for Key Personnel:
Creative Dir.: vesey@kidvertisers.com

Employees: 10
Year Founded: 1989

Agency Specializes In: Broadcast, Cable T.V., Children's Market, Collateral, Consumer Publications, Education, Entertainment, Graphic Design, Leisure, Magazines, Teen Market

Approx. Annual Billings: $8,000,000

Breakdown of Gross Billings by Media: Bus. Publs.: $250,000; Graphic Design: $250,000; Mags.: $1,000,000; Promos.: $250,000; T.V.: $6,250,000

Larry Nunno *(Owner)*
Mitch Koffler *(Assoc Dir-Creative)*
Nona Bleetstein *(Office Mgr)*

Accounts:
Comedy Central
Disney
National Geographic Little Kids
Networks
Nickelodeon
Paramount
Playskool

KILGANNON
(Acquired by Dalton Agency & Name Changed to Dalton Agency Atlanta)

KILLEEN FURTNEY GROUP, INC.
149 S Barrington Ave Ste 800, Los Angeles, CA 90049-3310
Tel.: (310) 476-6941
Fax: (310) 476-6256
E-Mail: info@killeenfurtneygroup.com
Web Site: www.killeenfurtneygroup.com

Employees: 10

Agency Specializes In: Crisis Communications, Government/Political, Local Marketing, Media Relations, Media Training, Public Relations, Social Marketing/Nonprofit, Strategic Planning/Research, Web (Banner Ads, Pop-ups, etc.)

Joann E. Killeen *(Pres)*

Accounts:
California State Parks
Comeback Institute
DAKA International
David Lustig & Associates
Lifetime Corporation
Litton Industries
Microsoft Corporation
OATH
Wal-Mart

KILLERSPOTS
463 Ohio Pke Ste 102, Cincinnati, OH 45255
Tel.: (800) 639-9728
Fax: (513) 672-0161
E-Mail: sales@killerspots.com
Web Site: www.killerspots.com

Employees: 10
Year Founded: 1997

Storm Bennett *(Pres & CEO)*
Ray Brown *(Sr Dir-Creative)*
Ashley Phillips *(Dir-Social Media)*
Mark Roberts *(Dir-Social Media)*

Accounts:
Beechmont Racquet & Fitness
Cincinnati Tan Company

KILLIAN BRANDING
1113 W Armitage, Chicago, IL 60624
Tel.: (312) 836-0050
Fax: (312) 836-0233
E-Mail: info@killianbranding.com
Web Site: www.killianbranding.com

E-Mail for Key Personnel:
Creative Dir.: bob@killianadvertising.com

Employees: 13
Year Founded: 1987

National Agency Associations: 4A's

Agency Specializes In: Advertising, Affluent Market, Brand Development & Integration, Broadcast, Business Publications, Business-To-Business, Cable T.V., Collateral, College, Communications, Computers & Software, Consulting, Consumer Goods, Consumer Marketing, Consumer Publications, Corporate Communications, Corporate Identity, Digital/Interactive, E-Commerce, Education, Electronic Media, Email, Exhibit/Trade Shows, Financial, Food Service, Graphic Design, Health Care Services, High Technology, Identity Marketing, Industrial, Information Technology, Integrated Marketing, Internet/Web Design, Legal Services, Logo & Package Design, Medical Products, New Product Development, New Technologies, Newspapers & Magazines, Out-of-Home Media, Outdoor, Over-50 Market, Package Design, Paid Searches, Planning & Consultation, Print, Production, Radio, Retail, Sales Promotion, Search Engine Optimization, Seniors' Market, Social Marketing/Nonprofit, Strategic Planning/Research, T.V., Trade & Consumer Magazines

Approx. Annual Billings: $15,200,000

Cat Novak *(VP-Creative Svcs)*
Zack Dessent *(Dir-Art)*
Stephanie Granowicz *(Acct Coord)*

Accounts:
Bounce Logistics; South Bend, IN; 2007
The Diemasters; Elk Grove Village, IL; 2009
Family Credit Management; Rockford, IL; 2006
Grippo & Elden; Chicago, IL Attorneys; 2001
Hermitage Art; Chicago, IL E-Commerce Publishing; 1999
North Shore Pediatric Therapy; Chicago, IL Pediatric Therapy; 2011
Travis Pedersen; Chicago, IL; 2009

KINDLING MEDIA, LLC
2040 N Highland Ave, Los Angeles, CA 90068
Tel.: (310) 954-1379
Web Site: kindlingdigital.com/

Employees: 10
Year Founded: 2010

Agency Specializes In: Above-the-Line, Advertising, Advertising Specialties, Affluent Market, African-American Market, Agriculture, Alternative Advertising, Arts, Asian Market, Automotive, Aviation & Aerospace, Below-the-Line, Bilingual Market, Brand Development & Integration, Branded Entertainment, Business-To-Business, Children's Market, College, Commercial Photography, Computers & Software, Consulting, Consumer Goods, Consumer Marketing, Content, Cosmetics, Digital/Interactive, Direct-to-Consumer, Education, Electronic Media, Electronics, Entertainment, Environmental, Fashion/Apparel, Financial, Food Service, Gay & Lesbian Market, Government/Political, High Technology, Hispanic Market, Hospitality, Household Goods, Industrial, Information Technology, Integrated Marketing, International, Leisure, Luxury Products, Marine, Media Planning, Media Relations, Media Training, Men's Market, Mobile Marketing, Multicultural, New Technologies, Over-50 Market, Pets , Product Placement, Production (Ad, Film, Broadcast), Real Estate, Restaurant, Retail, Seniors' Market, Social Media, South Asian Market, Sports Market, Teen

Market, Transportation, Travel & Tourism, Tween Market, Urban Market, Viral/Buzz/Word of Mouth, Women's Market

Approx. Annual Billings: $2,500,000

Jeremy Katz *(Pres)*
Alex Beguin *(VP-Bus Dev)*
Paul Slagle *(Exec Dir-Media)*
Lauren Kaplow *(Acct Mgr)*

Accounts:
New-E! Online "The Royals", Influencer Marketing, Viral Strategy
New-Zodiac Vodka Advertising Platform, Influencer Activations

KINDRED
(Formerly Formium)
10 Liberty Ship Way Ste 300, Sausalito, CA 94965
Tel.: (415) 944-3310
Fax: (415) 944-3327
Web Site: www.kindredsf.com

Year Founded: 2009

Agency Specializes In: Advertising, Brand Development & Integration, Package Design

Monika Rose *(Founder & Pres)*
Kerry Rose *(Mng Dir-SF)*
Cori Constantine *(Dir-Strategy)*
Lindsey Crawford *(Dir-Art)*
Marian Kwon *(Dir-Strategy)*
Rene Sanchez *(Mgr-Digital Ops)*
Danielle Von Mayrhauser *(Copywriter)*

Accounts:
Ahnu Footwear
Crimson & Quartz Wine

KINER COMMUNICATIONS
43100 Cook St Ste 100, Palm Desert, CA 92211
Tel.: (760) 773-0290
Fax: (760) 773-1750
E-Mail: info@kinercom.com
Web Site: www.kinercom.com

Employees: 16
Year Founded: 1994

Agency Specializes In: Advertising, Collateral, Corporate Identity, Crisis Communications, Digital/Interactive, Media Relations, Print, Promotions, Public Relations, Radio, T.V.

Revenue: $2,500,000

Chris Hunter *(Pres)*
Scott Kiner *(CEO)*
Steve Johnsen *(VP & Dir-Creative)*
Linda Furbee *(VP-Client Svcs)*
Sheila Kiner *(VP)*
Sandy Piedra *(Dir-Media)*

Accounts:
3rd Corner Wine Shop & Bistros
American Jazz Institute
American Red Cross
New-Back Nine Greens (Agency of Record) Advertising, Marketing, Public Relations
Cabazon Band of Mission Indians
Claremont McKenna College
Coachella Valley Economic Partnership
Community Valley Bank
Copper Mountain College
Cuistot Restaurant
Desert Sands Unified School District
Eagle Falls Golf Course
Fantasy Springs Resort Casino
Heckmann Corporation
Links Nursery
Martha's Village & Kitchen
MyPalmSprings.com
Off the Grid Survival Supply Store
Out of the Box Gold Store
Palm Desert Area Chamber of Commerce
The Penta Building Group
Pete Carlson's Golf & Tennis
Prime Time International
Score
SilverRock Resort
Southwest Arts Festival
Tradition Golf Club

KINETIC KNOWLEDGE
620 Harris Ave, Brielle, NJ 08730
Tel.: (732) 722-5915
E-Mail: contact@kineticknowledge.com
Web Site: kineticknowledge.com

Year Founded: 2003

Agency Specializes In: Advertising, Content, Digital/Interactive, Graphic Design, Internet/Web Design, Logo & Package Design, Print, Search Engine Optimization, Social Media

Chris Frerecks *(Owner & Pres)*
Andrew J. Talcott *(CTO)*

Accounts:
Balsamic Nectar
C Rice Global
Greenauer Design Group
Schmidt Realty Group

KINETIX CREATIVE
934 3rd St Ste 401, Alexandria, LA 71301
Tel.: (318) 487-8200
E-Mail: info@brandwithred.com
Web Site: www.brandwithred.com

Year Founded: 2002

Agency Specializes In: Advertising, Brand Development & Integration, Graphic Design, Internet/Web Design, Logo & Package Design, Social Media

Amanda Bolton Chenevert *(Sr Dir-Art)*
Todd Fingleton *(Dir-Creative & Bus Dev)*
Angel Wilkerson *(Designer)*

Accounts:
Alexandria Pineville CVB
Honey Brake Lodge
Louisiana Community Development Authority
Spirits Foods & Friends

THE KING AGENCY
3 N Lombardy St, Richmond, VA 23220
Tel.: (804) 249-7500
E-Mail: info@kingagency.com
Web Site: www.thekingagency.com

Agency Specializes In: Advertising, Graphic Design, Social Media

Dave King *(Pres & Dir-Creative)*
Gus Pistolis *(VP & Sr Strategist-Mktg)*
Bryan Farkas *(Sr Dir-Art)*
Jeff Erickson *(Acct Dir)*
Tena Lustig *(Sr Strategist-Media)*
MaryJo Steinmetz *(Sr Strategist-Media)*
Eric Zirkle *(Sr Graphic Designer)*

Accounts:
Altadis USA, Inc.
Arby's Restaurant Group, Inc.
Bottoms Up Pizza Campaign: "Huge Slices to Huge Decks"
Citizen Community Bank
Dr. Baxter Perkinson & Associates Campaign: "Dentist Crossing"
First Capital Bank
Global Healthcare Alliance, Inc.
Harman Eye Centre
Healthcare Solutions, Inc.
McGeorge Toyota (Agency of Record) Creative Advertising
VCS

KING & PARTNERS, LLC
35 Great Jones St 6th Fl, New York, NY 10012
Tel.: (212) 371-8500
E-Mail: info@kingandpartners.com
Web Site: www.kingandpartners.com

Agency Specializes In: Advertising, Brand Development & Integration, Digital/Interactive, E-Commerce, Graphic Design, Internet/Web Design, Social Media

Justin Grubbs *(Head-Tech)*
Ashley Cecere *(Acct Dir)*
Inii Kim *(Dir-Creative)*
Dan Liu *(Dir-Art)*
Tamara Belopopsky *(Office Mgr)*
Soyeo Jung *(Designer)*
Gillean Yuen *(Designer)*
Barbara Bertisch *(Jr Acct Mgr)*

Accounts:
Victoria Beckham

KING FISH MEDIA
27 Congress St Ste 508, Salem, MA 01970
Tel.: (978) 745-4140
Fax: (978) 745-4725
E-Mail: info@kingfishmedia.com
Web Site: www.kingfishmedia.com

Employees: 7
Year Founded: 2001

Agency Specializes In: Advertising, Content, Digital/Interactive, Email, Event Planning & Marketing, Internet/Web Design, Market Research, Mobile Marketing, Print, Social Media

Revenue: $2,282,000

Cameron K. Brown *(Founder & CEO)*
Missy Kustka *(Controller)*
Sue Twombly *(Sr Acct Dir)*
Kristen Villalongo *(Dir-Art)*
Meredith Yoder *(Dir-Mktg Analytics)*
Tanya O'Hara *(Sr Acct Mgr)*

Accounts:
Avnet
Boston Market
HIMMS
Kretschmer Wheat Germ
Market Forge Industries
Restaurant.com

THE KING GROUP
25550 Chagrin Blvd, Beachwood, OH 44122
Tel.: (216) 831-9330
Fax: (216) 831-8879
Web Site: www.thekinggroup.com

Employees: 8
Year Founded: 1987

Agency Specializes In: Advertising, African-American Market, Hispanic Market

Approx. Annual Billings: $12,000,000

Delva King *(Owner)*
Richard Sippola *(CFO & Analyst)*

Richard G. Bialosky *(Sr VP)*
Julie White *(VP-Leasing & Tenant Relations)*
William J. Nelson, III *(Dir-Ops)*
Amy Licari *(Mgr-Acctg)*

Accounts:
7-Eleven
Sally Beauty Supply; Denton, TX All Markets & African American

KING MEDIA
1555 Watertower Place Ste 200, East Lansing, MI 48823
Tel.: (517) 333-2048
E-Mail: kingmedia@kingmedianow.com
Web Site: www.kingmedianow.com

Year Founded: 1999

Agency Specializes In: Advertising, Brand Development & Integration, Event Planning & Marketing, Graphic Design, Media Relations, Public Relations

Coleen King *(Founder & Pres)*
Laurie DeYoung *(Acct Dir)*

Accounts:
New-Tabor Hill Winery & Restaurant

KINGS ENGLISH LLC
335 S Davie St, Greensboro, NC 27401
Tel.: (336) 574-0304
Web Site: www.thekingsenglish.com

Agency Specializes In: Advertising, Broadcast, Internet/Web Design, Print, Public Relations, Social Media

Marc Barnes *(Dir-PR)*
David McLean *(Dir-PR)*
Greg Monroy *(Dir-Creative)*
Tyler Jeffreys *(Acct Exec)*

Accounts:
Otey Construction
South of France

KINNEY GROUP CREATIVE
424 W 33rd St Ste 570, New York, NY 10001
Tel.: (323) 570-2076
E-Mail: hello@kinneygroupcreative.com
Web Site: www.kinneygroupcreative.com

Year Founded: 2010

Agency Specializes In: Advertising, Brand Development & Integration, Digital/Interactive, Radio

James Kinney *(Founder & CEO)*
Alex Leal *(Client Svcs Dir)*
Brendon Wade *(Brand Mgr)*
Claudia Guzman *(Mgr-Social Media)*
Karim Alston *(Acct Exec)*
Mason Myles *(Acct Exec)*

Accounts:
Aquadopa
Author Phyllis Peters

KINZIEGREEN MARKETING GROUP
915 5th St, Wausau, WI 54403
Tel.: (715) 845-4251
Fax: (715) 842-3399
E-Mail: info@kinziegreen.com
Web Site: www.kinziegreen.com

E-Mail for Key Personnel:
President: kirk@kinziegreen.com
Creative Dir.: tom@kinziegreen.com
Media Dir.: jody@kinziegreen.com

Employees: 11
Year Founded: 1966

Agency Specializes In: Advertising, Brand Development & Integration, Business Publications, Business-To-Business, Collateral, Consulting, Consumer Marketing, Corporate Identity, Digital/Interactive, Direct Response Marketing, Exhibit/Trade Shows, Financial, Health Care Services, Internet/Web Design, Magazines, Media Buying Services, Newspapers & Magazines, Planning & Consultation, Production, Public Relations, Radio, Strategic Planning/Research, T.V., Yellow Pages Advertising

Approx. Annual Billings: $6,986,218 Capitalized

Breakdown of Gross Billings by Media: Fees: $5,030,077; Mags.: $978,071; Newsp.: $69,862; Production: $558,897; Spot Radio: $69,862; Spot T.V.: $69,862; Yellow Page Adv.: $209,587

Kirk E. Howard *(Owner, Pres & Dir-Creative)*
Bridget Leonhard *(VP-Ops)*
Jody McCormick *(Dir-Media & Acct Exec)*
Tom Neal *(Dir-Brand Dev)*
Patti Howard *(Acct Mgr-Svcs)*
Don Celing *(Mgr-Creative Svcs)*
Chris Martin *(Mgr-Interactive Svcs)*

Accounts:
Action Floor
American Society of Laser Medicine & Surgery; 1999
EO Johnson Office Technologies
Greenheck Fan Air Moving Equipment, Kitchen Ventilation Systems; 1966
Ministry HealthCare; Marshfield, WI; 2000
Never Forgotten Honor Flight
WRM America

Branch

Kinziegreen Marketing Group
744 Ryan Dr Ste 101, Hudson, WI 54016
Tel.: (715) 386-8707
Fax: (715) 386-8727
E-Mail: info@kinziegreen.com
Web Site: www.kinziegreen.com

Employees: 8
Year Founded: 2007

Kirk Howard *(Owner, Pres & Dir-Creative)*

KIP HUNTER MARKETING
888 E Las Olas Blvd Ste 500, Fort Lauderdale, FL 33301
Tel.: (954) 765-1329
Fax: (954) 524-3047
E-Mail: contact@kiphuntermarketing.com
Web Site: www.kiphuntermarketing.com

Agency Specializes In: Advertising, Brand Development & Integration, Corporate Identity, Event Planning & Marketing, Media Planning, Media Training, Public Relations, Social Media

Kip Hunter *(Founder & CEO)*
Patricia Kneski *(VP-Mktg)*
Aimee Adler *(VP-PR)*
Adam Jalali *(Dir-Mktg & Graphic Design)*
Michelle Rodrigues Hawthorn *(Dir-PR)*
Melissa Sweredoski *(Mgr-PR)*

Accounts:
New-Hoffmans Chocolates
New-The Village at Gulfstream Park

KIRK COMMUNICATIONS
1 New Hampshire Ave Ste 125, Portsmouth, NH 03801
Tel.: (603) 766-4945
Fax: (603) 766-1901
E-Mail: info@kirkcommunications.com
Web Site: www.kirkcommunications.com

Employees: 2

Nate Tennant *(Founder)*
Michael Havey *(Sr Dir-Art)*

Accounts:
Adder
Animetrics
Annik Technology Services Ltd. Branding, Digital, Marketing, Website Creation
Auger Systems
CBE Technologies (Agency of Record) Web Site; 2008
Cipher Optics
Imprivata
IMT Partners; North Chelmsford, MA
Ipswitch Analyst Relations, New Product Announcements, New Product Introductions, Press Relations, Product Placements, Public Relations, Social Networking, Trade Show Press
ITelagen
Sagamore Systems
SeaNet Technologies
Staff Hunters
Theikos
Thermonexus, LLC
Treeno Software
XyEnterprise

KITCH & SCHREIBER, INC.
(Single Location)
402 Court St, Evansville, IN 47708-1130
Tel.: (812) 424-7710
E-Mail: contact@kitchandschreiber.com
Web Site: www.kitchandschreiber.com

Employees: 7

Agency Specializes In: Advertising, Event Planning & Marketing, Internet/Web Design, Logo & Package Design, Media Planning, Outdoor, Print, Radio, T.V.

Revenue: $1,800,000

Ken Schreiber *(Founder & Pres)*
Scott Schreiber *(VP-Media Svcs)*
Brian Scroggins *(Dir-Creative)*
Pam Myrick *(Office Mgr)*

Accounts:
Carson's Brewery

KITCHEN PUBLIC RELATIONS, LLC
5 Penn Plz, New York, NY 10001
Tel.: (212) 687-8999
Fax: (212) 687-6272
E-Mail: dnorman@kitchenpr.com
Web Site: www.kitchenpr.com

Employees: 10
Year Founded: 1992

Agency Specializes In: Brand Development & Integration, Corporate Communications, Crisis Communications, Exhibit/Trade Shows, Government/Political, Strategic Planning/Research

Revenue: $1,100,000

David Norman *(Mng Dir)*

Accounts:

Conning
Denver Global Products
Employment Resource Group
Preferred Concepts
S'well
Y-cam Solutions

KIWI CREATIVE
611 W Bagley Rd, Berea, OH 44017
Tel.: (440) 973-4250
Fax: (440) 973-4433
Web Site: www.kiwicreative.net

Year Founded: 2007

Agency Specializes In: Advertising, Graphic Design, Internet/Web Design, Media Planning, Print, Social Media

Danni Bennett *(Strategist-Website)*

Accounts:
John Carroll University

KK BOLD
505 E Main Ave Ste 250 PO Box 693, Bismarck, ND 58502-4412
Tel.: (701) 255-3067
Fax: (701) 255-1022
E-Mail: contact@kkbold.com
Web Site: www.kkbold.com

E-Mail for Key Personnel:
President: laroyk@kkcltd.com
Creative Dir.: clayc@kkcltd.com
Media Dir.: marcig@kkcltd.com

Employees: 29
Year Founded: 1969

Agency Specializes In: Agriculture, Broadcast, Collateral, Corporate Identity, Digital/Interactive, Electronic Media, Graphic Design, Health Care Services, Internet/Web Design, Media Buying Services, Newspapers & Magazines, Outdoor, Planning & Consultation, Print, Public Relations, Radio, T.V., Travel & Tourism

LaRoy Kingsley *(Owner & Pres)*
Wayne Kranzler *(CEO)*
Stephanie Schoenrock *(VP)*
Marci Goldade *(Dir-Media)*
Ted Hanson *(Dir-Bus Rels)*
Clay Hove *(Dir-Creative)*
Kalvin Kingsley *(Dir-Ops)*
Jackie Hawkinson *(Office Mgr)*
Nikki Sims *(Mgr-Production)*
Candace Christopherson *(Acct Exec)*
Penny Blotsky *(Media Buyer)*

Accounts:
Bismarck Funeral Home
Bismarck Mandan Development Association
Bismarck-Mandan Chamber of Commerce
Bowman County Development
Cloverdale Meats
Dan's Pantry
Fireside Office Products; Bismarck, ND Office Equipment; 1984
Grand River Casino And Resort
Hatton Prairie Village
Kirkwood Mall; Bismarck, ND Regional Shopping Mall; 1990
Minot State University
Nisqually Red Wind Casino Marketing Agency of Record
Norsk Hostfest
North Dakota Democratic Party; Bismarck, ND; 1982
North Dakota Education Association; Bismarck, ND; 1990
North Dakota John Deere Dealers Co-op; Minneapolis, MN Farm Equipment; 1984
North Dakota State Fair
North Dakota State Lottery
North Dakota University Systems
Prairie Knights Casino; Fort Yates, ND Casino Gambling; 1993
Red River Commodities
Russell's Reserve
Theodore Roosevelt Medora Foundation Marketing, Radio, Television
Unison Bank

KKPR MARKETING & PUBLIC RELATIONS
PO Box 511, Milford, PA 18337
Tel.: (570) 296-2333
E-Mail: info@kkmpr.com
Web Site: kkprnyc.com

Agency Specializes In: Advertising, Brand Development & Integration, Event Planning & Marketing, Internet/Web Design, Media Planning, Public Relations

Katrina Foster *(Founder & Pres)*
Graham Campbell *(Coord-Bus Dev)*
Katie Knapp *(Coord-Mktg)*

KLEBER & ASSOCIATES MARKETING & COMMUNICATIONS
1215 Hightower Trl Bldg C, Atlanta, GA 30350
Tel.: (770) 518-1000
Fax: (770) 518-2700
E-Mail: info@kleberadvertising.com
Web Site: www.kleberandassociates.com

Employees: 20
Year Founded: 1987

National Agency Associations: Second Wind Limited

Agency Specializes In: Advertising, Brand Development & Integration, Business-To-Business, Co-op Advertising, Communications, Consumer Marketing, Corporate Identity, Crisis Communications, Customer Relationship Management, Direct Response Marketing, Direct-to-Consumer, Electronic Media, Email, Exhibit/Trade Shows, Integrated Marketing, Internet/Web Design, Logo & Package Design, Market Research, Media Buying Services, Media Planning, Media Relations, Media Training, Planning & Consultation, Podcasting, Print, Product Placement, Public Relations, Publicity/Promotions, RSS (Really Simple Syndication), Search Engine Optimization, Sponsorship, Strategic Planning/Research, Web (Banner Ads, Pop-ups, etc.)

Steven Kleber *(Owner)*

Accounts:
Altmans Integrated Marketing, Media Relations, Social Media, Strategic
Century Architectural Specialties
DANVER (Agency of Record)
Emira
Feeney, Inc Integrated Marketing, Media Relations, Social Media, Strategic
Georgia-Pacific Gypsum LLC (Advertising Agency of Record) Account Strategy, Creative Advertising, Dens, Digital, Marketing, Media Planning, ToughRock
Gerber Plumbing Fixtures Corporation Plumbing Fixtures; 2008
Hy-lite Integrated Marketing, Media Relations, Social Media, Strategic
KWC America; Norcross, GA High End Kitchen & Bath Plumbing Fixtures
Masonite (Agency of Record) PR, Social Media, Traditional & Digital Channels
Nichiha; Atlanta, GA Fiber Cement Siding Products
Viance's Wood Treatment solutions
Walpole Outdoors Integrated Marketing, Media Relations, Social Media, Strategic
Woodtrack Ceiling System

KLEIDON & ASSOCIATES
320 Springside Dr, Akron, OH 44333
Tel.: (330) 666-5984
Fax: (330) 666-6833
E-Mail: info@kleidon.com
Web Site: www.kleidon.com

Employees: 8
Year Founded: 1975

National Agency Associations: AAF

Agency Specializes In: Advertising, Brand Development & Integration, Business-To-Business, Consumer Marketing, Graphic Design, Logo & Package Design, Public Relations, Strategic Planning/Research, Trade & Consumer Magazines

Revenue: $1,000,000

Rose A.O. Kleidon *(Owner)*
Dennis A. Kleidon *(Pres & CEO)*
Kurt Kleidon *(VP & Gen Mgr)*
Tim Klinger *(Dir-Creative)*
Diana Lueptow *(Dir-Strategic Comm)*
Peggy Schobert *(Dir-Ops & Media Rels)*

Accounts:
Conservancy for CVNP Annual Report, Campaign: "Trails Forever"
Fresco Mexican Grill & Salsa Bar
JDM Structures
Jentner Financial Group
Omega Cabinetry

KLICKPICKS
136 E 57th St, New York, NY 10022
Tel.: (646) 330-4613
E-Mail: info@klickpicks.com
Web Site: www.klickpicks.com

Agency Specializes In: Advertising, Cosmetics, Digital/Interactive, Electronic Media, Production (Ad, Film, Broadcast)

Katherine O'Sullivan *(Co-founder & CEO)*
Jose Pinto *(Co-founder & COO)*
Kevin O'Sullivan *(CTO)*
Niki Sawyer *(VP-Production)*
Alyssa Timoteo *(Lead Digital Media Specialist)*

Accounts:
First in Service Travel Travel Agency
Lysse Fashion
Priv

KLUGE INTERACTIVE
4133 Redwood Ave Unit 4032, Marina Del Rey, CA 90066
Tel.: (310) 382-0267
E-Mail: hello@klugeinteractive.com
Web Site: www.klugeinteractive.com

Year Founded: 2008

Agency Specializes In: Advertising, Brand Development & Integration, Corporate Identity, Digital/Interactive, Internet/Web Design, Strategic Planning/Research

Arturo Perez *(CEO)*
Cameron Wood *(Partner & COO)*
Atina Hartunian *(Strategist-Content)*
Daniel Sabal *(Sr Designer)*
Daniel Garcia *(Sr Engr-Software)*

Accounts:
Runrunes

THE KLUGER AGENCY
1200 Brickell Ave 14th Fl, Miami, FL 33131
Tel.: (305) 639-8750
Fax: (305) 639-8751
E-Mail: info@klugeragency.com
Web Site: www.klugeragency.com

Agency Specializes In: Entertainment, Product Placement

Adam Kluger *(CEO & Head-Global Artist Partnerships)*

KLUNDT HOSMER
216 W Pacific Ste 201, Spokane, WA 99201
Tel.: (509) 456-5576
Fax: (509) 456-5848
Toll Free: (866) 456-5577
E-Mail: info@klundthosmer.com
Web Site: www.klundthosmer.com

Year Founded: 1987

Agency Specializes In: Advertising, Brand Development & Integration, Broadcast, Digital/Interactive, E-Commerce, Email, Internet/Web Design, Search Engine Optimization, Social Media

Rick Hosmer *(Principal & Dir-Creative)*
Darin Klundt *(Principal & Dir-Creative)*
Jean Klundt *(Principal & Dir-Creative)*
Ashley Martin *(Acct Dir)*
Diane Mahan *(Dir-Digital Mktg)*
Mastery Sheets *(Coord-Web)*

Accounts:
Lawton Printing Inc. Commercial Printing Services
Northwest Spokane Pediatrics Offices of Physicians Except Mental Health
Susan Mahan Kohls DDS Dental Care Service Providers

KLUNK & MILLAN ADVERTISING INC.
9999 Hamilton Blvd, Allentown, PA 18031
Tel.: (610) 973-2400
Fax: (610) 973-2407
Web Site: www.klunkmillan.com

Year Founded: 1989

Agency Specializes In: Advertising, Brand Development & Integration, E-Commerce, Logo & Package Design, Media Planning, Mobile Marketing, Print, Public Relations, Search Engine Optimization, Strategic Planning/Research

James Klunk *(Pres)*
Andrew Hall *(Sr VP & Dir-Creative)*
Michelle Gaynor *(VP-Client Svcs)*
Gwenn Lundy *(Dir-Art)*
Jason Ziemba *(Dir-Art)*
Jerry Brahm *(Mgr-Ops)*

Accounts:
Fluortek
Kutztown University
Orbel Corporation

KMGI.COM
228 Park Ave S Ste 16065, New York, NY 10003
Tel.: (212) 873-2211
Fax: (212) 202-4982
Toll Free: (866) 437-3816
Web Site: www.kmgi.com

E-Mail for Key Personnel:
President: ak@kmgi.com
Production Mgr.: eg@kmgi.com

Employees: 19
Year Founded: 1987

Agency Specializes In: Digital/Interactive, E-Commerce, Education, Electronic Media, High Technology, Infomercials, Information Technology, Internet/Web Design, Media Buying Services, Production

Approx. Annual Billings: $4,200,000

Breakdown of Gross Billings by Media: Fees: 10%; Internet Adv.: 25%; Other: 2%; Production: 60%; Pub. Rels.: 3%

Elena Gratcheva *(Owner)*
Alexandre P. Konanykhine *(CEO)*
Nat Kurok *(VP)*

Accounts:
9 Net Avenue, Inc.; NJ Internet-Related Services; 1998
American Airlines; Dallas, TX
Boeing
Brown & Williamson; KY Tobacco; 1999
Canon
CBS
DuPont; New York, NY Corian; 1999
Energizer
Intel
Macromedia, Inc.; San Francisco, CA Software; 1999
MTV
Net 2 Phone, Inc.; Hackensack, NJ IP Telephony; 1999
Siemens
Transatlantic Communications; New York, NY Telecommunications Services; 1998
Verizon
Vivendi Group
Volkswagen Group of America, Inc.
Volvo

KMK MEDIA GROUP
716 N Church St, Rockford, IL 61103
Tel.: (815) 399-2805
Fax: (815) 399-1726
E-Mail: info@kmkmedia.com
Web Site: www.kmkmedia.com

Agency Specializes In: Advertising, Brand Development & Integration, Event Planning & Marketing, Internet/Web Design, Logo & Package Design, Print, Public Relations, Social Media, T.V.

Jeff Klarman *(Pres)*
Pam Maher *(CEO)*
Doug Burton *(Mgr-Mktg)*
Stephanie Lammi *(Mgr-Comm)*
Mitch Brechon *(Sr Acct Exec)*

Accounts:
Caldwell Group
MD Skin Center
Nitrorthopaedics

KMR COMMUNICATIONS
419 Park Ave S, New York, NY 10016
Tel.: (212) 213-6444
Fax: (212) 213-4699
Web Site: www.kmrpr.com

Year Founded: 1998

Katherine M. Rothman *(Pres)*
Lauren Arrington *(Acct Exec)*

KNACK4 DESIGN, INC.
15 Harmon Dr, Huntington, NY 11743
Tel.: (631) 486-2750
Fax: (631) 486-2750
E-Mail: info@knack4design.com
Web Site: www.knack4design.com

Agency Specializes In: Advertising, Brand Development & Integration, Package Design, Strategic Planning/Research

Carol Andersen *(Pres & Dir-Creative)*

Accounts:
A&M Rotondi
Bethpage Federal Credit Union
Ecological Laboratories Inc.
Karon Check Cashing Inc.
Love of Learning Montessori School
Mailmen Inc.
Matthew James Salon
Maxus Media Marketing Solutions
Neilson Associates
Old Westbury College
Palm Bay Imports
Presidio Beverage Company
Quick Tax Inc.
RCG&H Law Firm
Sanna Mattson & Macleod
Terryco Lawn Maintenance
Wine Wave Inc.

KNB COMMUNICATIONS
230 Park Ave 10th Fl Ste 1000, New York, NY 10169
Tel.: (212) 505-2441
Fax: (917) 591-3117
E-Mail: info@knbpr.com
Web Site: http://www.knbcomm.com/

Employees: 12

Agency Specializes In: Communications, Public Relations

Shirin Bhan *(Founder & Pres)*
Marianne Fulgenzi *(VP)*
Courtney Kraemer *(VP)*
Emma Ludwin *(VP)*
Logan Miller *(Mgr-Digital Mktg)*
Katie Newman Vukas *(Sr Acct Exec & Specialist-Media Rels)*

Accounts:
Aprima
Carefx Corporation Medical Services
iMedica Corporation Software Solution Provider
Impelsys Electronic Content Solutions Provider
TeleHealth Services Media Services

THE KNIGHT AGENCY
6895 E Camelback Rd Ste 118, Scottsdale, AZ 85251
Tel.: (480) 447-9996
Web Site: www.knight.agency

Agency Specializes In: Advertising, Event Planning & Marketing, Public Relations

Erica Knight *(Pres)*
Stephanie Ferrer *(Sr Acct Exec-PR)*
Skyler Scott *(Acct Exec)*

Accounts:
New-The Mitchell Group

KNOODLE ADVERTISING
4450 N 12th St Ste 120, Phoenix, AZ 85014
Tel.: (602) 530-9900
Web Site: www.useyourknoodle.com

Agency Specializes In: Advertising, Internet/Web

Design, Logo & Package Design, Media Buying Services, Media Planning, Media Training, Multimedia, Print, Public Relations, Search Engine Optimization

Rosaria Cain *(CEO)*
Scott Cain *(Partner & CFO)*
Matthew Wilson *(Partner & VP-Creative)*
Rob Snyder *(Exec VP & Exec Dir-Creative)*
Larry Winward *(VP)*
Sandra Guadarrama-Baumunk *(Client Svcs Dir)*
Dabi Adeyemi *(Dir-Digital)*
Lad Makinde *(Dir-Digital)*
Maria Ortiz *(Office Mgr)*
Bryan Glasco *(Media Buyer)*

Accounts:
National Kidney Foundation, Inc.
Shamrock Foods Company

KNOW ADVERTISING
422 W 11 Mile Rd, Royal Oak, MI 48067
Tel.: (248) 632-1171
Fax: (248) 542-7316
Web Site: www.knowad.com

Year Founded: 2005

Agency Specializes In: Advertising, Brand Development & Integration, Digital/Interactive, Email, Internet/Web Design, Radio

Rick Van House *(Pres)*
Dylan Shippey *(Sr Dir-Art)*
Joe McGuckin *(Dir-Digital Svcs)*
Earl Barclay *(Mgr-Social Media)*

Accounts:
Niagara LaSalle Corporation
Roberts Restaurant Group

KNUDSEN, GARDNER & HOWE, INC.
2103 Saint Clair Ave NE, Cleveland, OH 44114-4018
Tel.: (216) 781-5000
Fax: (216) 781-5004
E-Mail: info@kghinc.com
Web Site: www.kghinc.com

E-Mail for Key Personnel:
President: tim@kghinc.com

Employees: 4
Year Founded: 1967

Agency Specializes In: Advertising, Automotive, Consumer Goods, Consumer Marketing, Consumer Publications, Financial, Planning & Consultation, Production (Print)

Tim Knudsen *(Pres)*
Allison Knudsen *(Office Mgr)*

Accounts:
Anderson & Vreeland, Inc.; Bryan, OH
Axiom Automotive Technologies; Pittsburgh, PA
Corteco
Custom Flex
Floraline Display Products Corp.; Cleveland, OH
Freudenberg-NOK Distribution Div.; Milan, OH
Light Craft Manufacturing, Inc.; Fremont, OH
Mill-Rose Laboratories; Mentor, OH
Nautica Charity Poker Festival
Nova Polymers
TransTec
Warwick Products, Inc.; Cleveland, OH
Westport Axle Corporation; Cleveland, OH

KNUPP & WATSON & WALLMAN
5201 Old Middleton Rd, Madison, WI 53705-2715
Tel.: (608) 232-2300
Fax: (608) 232-2301
Web Site: www.kw2ideas.com

E-Mail for Key Personnel:
President: tknupp@knupp-watson.com

Employees: 24
Year Founded: 1986

Agency Specializes In: Advertising, Advertising Specialties, African-American Market, Agriculture, Asian Market, Bilingual Market, Brand Development & Integration, Broadcast, Business Publications, Business-To-Business, Cable T.V., Children's Market, Co-op Advertising, Collateral, Commercial Photography, Communications, Consulting, Consumer Marketing, Consumer Publications, Corporate Identity, Digital/Interactive, Direct Response Marketing, E-Commerce, Education, Electronic Media, Entertainment, Environmental, Event Planning & Marketing, Exhibit/Trade Shows, Financial, Food Service, Government/Political, Graphic Design, Health Care Services, High Technology, Hispanic Market, Industrial, Infomercials, Information Technology, Internet/Web Design, Logo & Package Design, Magazines, Media Buying Services, Medical Products, Merchandising, Multimedia, New Product Development, Newspaper, Newspapers & Magazines, Out-of-Home Media, Outdoor, Pharmaceutical, Planning & Consultation, Point of Purchase, Point of Sale, Print, Production, Public Relations, Publicity/Promotions, Radio, Recruitment, Restaurant, Retail, Sales Promotion, Seniors' Market, Sports Market, Strategic Planning/Research, T.V., Technical Advertising, Telemarketing, Trade & Consumer Magazines, Transportation, Travel & Tourism, Yellow Pages Advertising

Theodore H. Knupp *(Owner)*
Andy Wallman *(Pres & Exec Dir-Creative)*
Jennifer Savino *(VP)*
Shelley Beere *(Client Svcs Dir)*
Ellen Paulson *(Media Planner & Buyer)*

Accounts:
Brothers Main
Corona Clipper
Goodstock
Hasumann Johnson
Madison Symphony Orchestra
Mid-State Technical College
Physicians Plus Insurance
Rocky Rococo
Steve Brown Apartments
Western Technical College
Wisconsin Anti-Tobacco
Wisconsin Department of Health Services; 1998
Wisconsin Department of Transportation; 1986
Wisconsin Department of Workforce Development; 1989

KOCHAN & COMPANY MARKETING COMMUNICATIONS
800 Geyer Ave, Saint Louis, MO 63104-4048
Tel.: (314) 621-4455
Fax: (314) 621-1777
E-Mail: bob@kochanandcompany.com
Web Site: www.kochanandcompany.com

E-Mail for Key Personnel:
President: bob@kochanandcompany.com
Media Dir.: kathy@kochanandcompany.com

Employees: 6
Year Founded: 1987

National Agency Associations: AAF

Agency Specializes In: Advertising, Brand Development & Integration, Broadcast, Business-To-Business, Cable T.V., Collateral, Communications, Consumer Marketing, Corporate Identity, Digital/Interactive, Direct Response Marketing, Email, Entertainment, Financial, Graphic Design, Health Care Services, Integrated Marketing, Internet/Web Design, Leisure, Logo & Package Design, Media Buying Services, Media Planning, Newspaper, Newspapers & Magazines, Out-of-Home Media, Outdoor, Point of Purchase, Point of Sale, Print, Production, Promotions, Radio, Restaurant, Retail, Sales Promotion, Social Media, Sports Market, Strategic Planning/Research, T.V., Trade & Consumer Magazines, Travel & Tourism

Approx. Annual Billings: $2,000,000

Breakdown of Gross Billings by Media: Brdcst.: 26%; Collateral: 10%; Consulting: 8%; Internet Adv.: 3%; Outdoor: 5%; Print: 20%; Promos.: 10%; Strategic Planning/Research: 18%

Robert J. Kochan *(Pres & Sr Strategist-Mktg)*
Karen Robben *(Acct Exec)*

Accounts:
Consort Homes; St. Louis, MO Home Builder; 2009
Delta Dental of Missouri; Saint Louis, MO & Kansas City, MO Dental Health Plan; 1998
Hotel Blackhawk; Davenport, IA (Agency of Record)
Laclede's Landing; St. Louis, MO Entertainment District; 2008
The Missouri Valley Conference; Saint Louis, MO College Sports Conference; 2004
National Railroad Hall of Fame; Galesburg, IL Museum; 2007
The Pasta House Co.; Saint Louis, MO Italian Restaurants; 1995
Pool King Recreation; Saint Louis, MO Pool & Spa Dealer; 2005
Pulaski Banks; St Louis, MO Banking/Financial; 2010

KOHNSTAMM COMMUNICATIONS
400 N Robert St Ste 1450 Securian Tower, Saint Paul, MN 55101
Tel.: (651) 228-9141
Fax: (651) 298-0628
E-Mail: media@kohnstamm.com
Web Site: www.kohnstamm.com

Employees: 20
Year Founded: 1991

National Agency Associations: COPF

Agency Specializes In: Brand Development & Integration, Communications, Consumer Marketing, Corporate Communications, Crisis Communications, Digital/Interactive, Event Planning & Marketing, Financial, Guerilla Marketing, Industrial, Local Marketing, Media Relations, Product Placement, Strategic Planning/Research, Trade & Consumer Magazines, Viral/Buzz/Word of Mouth, Web (Banner Ads, Pop-ups, etc.)

Joshua Kohnstamm *(Founder & CEO)*
Alan Newbold *(VP-Consumer Grp)*
Aaron Berstler *(Grp Acct Dir-Bus PR)*
Jessica Olstad *(Acct Dir)*
Jeff Trauring *(Acct Dir)*
Rachel Jones-Pittier *(Acct Supvr)*
Angela Deeney *(Asst Acct Exec)*

Accounts:
3M
Elliott Wave International
Happy Baby Foods
Malt-O-Meal
Pro Uro Care
Thai Kitchen

KOIKO DESIGN LLC

322 Stoughton Ave, Cranford, NJ 07016
Tel.: (908) 272-1113
Web Site: www.koikodesign.com

Agency Specializes In: Arts, Bilingual Market, Brand Development & Integration, Catalogs, Cosmetics, Graphic Design, Local Marketing, Logo & Package Design, Magazines, Newspapers & Magazines, Package Design, Real Estate

Approx. Annual Billings: $140,000

Breakdown of Gross Billings by Media: Graphic Design: $70,000; Newsp. & Mags.: $30,000; Print: $40,000

Irena Pejovic *(Owner & Graphic Designer)*

KOLBECO MARKETING RESOURCES
1676 Bryan Rd Ste 113, Prairie City, MO 63368
Tel.: (636) 379-3895
Fax: (636) 272-3252
E-Mail: info@kolbeco.net
Web Site: www.kolbeco.net

Year Founded: 2000

Agency Specializes In: Advertising, Broadcast, Crisis Communications, Internet/Web Design, Logo & Package Design, Media Training, Print, Public Relations, Social Media, Strategic Planning/Research

Scott Kolbe *(Co-Owner & Dir-Corp Dev)*
Lauren Kolbe *(Co-Owner & Sr Mgr)*
Danieal Broz *(Dir-Accounts & Info)*
Erin Celuch *(Dir-Art)*
Jeremy Nulik *(Acct Exec)*
Erica Skrivan *(Acct Coord)*

Accounts:
ActOn Dentistry
Antennas Direct
Krilogy Financial
True North Management Services

KONCORDIA GROUP
2417 Lancaster Ave, Wilmington, DE 19805
Tel.: (302) 427-8606
Fax: (302) 427-8545
E-Mail: lscott@koncordiagroup.com
Web Site: www.koncordiagroup.com

Employees: 8
Year Founded: 1997

Agency Specializes In: Advertising, Sponsorship

Lisa Scott *(Mng Dir)*
Jon Owen *(COO)*
Rowan Sidd *(Acct Dir)*
Paul DiCampli *(Dir-Creative)*
Gary Watson *(Dir-Strategic Plng)*
Mark Bartman *(Assoc Dir-Creative)*
Sean Chase *(Acct Supvr)*

Accounts:
Accent Energy
AT&T Communications Corp.
Chrysler
Comcast
Con Edison
Ford
GE Healthcare
JPMorgan Chase
Miller Coors

KOOPMAN OSTBO
412 NW 8th Ave, Portland, OR 97209
Tel.: (503) 223-2168
Fax: (503) 223-1819
E-Mail: info@koopmanostbo.com
Web Site: www.koopmanostbo.com

Employees: 15

Agency Specializes In: Advertising, Public Relations, Sponsorship

Revenue: $30,000,000

Ken Koopman *(Owner)*
Craig Ostbo *(Mng Partner)*
Joe Parker *(Partner & Dir-Bus Dev)*
Ted Morgan *(Acct Svcs Dir)*
Tracy Pokarney *(Dir-Media)*
Robert Shepard *(Dir-Creative)*
Ashley Heinonen *(Acct Coord)*

Accounts:
Crater Lake Soda
Gosee Portland
Kroger
Lochmead Farms
Luna & Larry's Coconut Bliss
Recharge
Santa Cruz Organic
Spritzer
Wild Oats

KOSSMAN/KLEIN & CO.
PO Box 38624, Germantown, TN 38183-0624
Tel.: (901) 754-0025
Fax: (901) 754-3980
E-Mail: jerry@kossmankleinco.com
Web Site: www.kossmankleinco.com

Employees: 2
Year Founded: 1981

National Agency Associations: LAA

Agency Specializes In: Automotive, Aviation & Aerospace, Collateral, Corporate Identity, Event Planning & Marketing, Graphic Design, Health Care Services, High Technology, Logo & Package Design, Media Buying Services, Medical Products, Public Relations, Publicity/Promotions, Trade & Consumer Magazines

Jerold L. Klein *(Owner)*
Juliet K. Klein *(Principal)*

Accounts:
Air Repair, Inc.; Cleveland, MS Stearman Airplane Restorer; 1993
Patterson Warehouses, Inc.; Memphis, TN Public Warehouses; 1992

KOSTIAL COMPANY, LLC
(Name Changed to Audience Innovation)

KOVEL/FULLER
9925 Jefferson Blvd, Culver City, CA 90232-3505
Tel.: (310) 841-4444
Fax: (310) 841-4599
E-Mail: info@kovelfuller.com
Web Site: www.kovelfuller.com

E-Mail for Key Personnel:
President: jfuller@kovelfuller.com
Creative Dir.: lkovel@kovelfuller.com

Employees: 50
Year Founded: 1999

Agency Specializes In: Advertising, Automotive, Brand Development & Integration, Broadcast, Business-To-Business, Cable T.V., Co-op Advertising, Collateral, Communications, Consulting, Consumer Goods, Consumer Marketing, Corporate Identity, Digital/Interactive, Direct Response Marketing, E-Commerce, Electronics, Email, Entertainment, Event Planning & Marketing, Fashion/Apparel, Financial, Food Service, Graphic Design, High Technology, Hispanic Market, Internet/Web Design, Leisure, Logo & Package Design, Market Research, Media Buying Services, Media Planning, Newspaper, Newspapers & Magazines, Out-of-Home Media, Outdoor, Paid Searches, Planning & Consultation, Point of Purchase, Point of Sale, Print, Production, Production (Ad, Film, Broadcast), Production (Print), Radio, Restaurant, Retail, Sales Promotion, Sponsorship, Sports Market, Strategic Planning/Research, T.V., Travel & Tourism, Viral/Buzz/Word of Mouth, Web (Banner Ads, Pop-ups, etc.)

John Fuller *(Owner)*
Lee Kovel *(Partner & Chief Creative Officer)*
Maura Gonzalez *(Acct Dir)*
Richard Salinas *(Producer-Digital)*
Ilya Berstenev *(Strategist-Media)*
Adrena Altoonian *(Sr Media Buyer)*

Accounts:
Anna's Linens Inc.; Costa Mesa, CA; 2009
Cash Call Mortgages/Personal Loans; 2003
Ellsworth Bicycles High-End Bicycles; 2000
Mercury Insurance
Pacific Life Insurance Company
Sizzler
Western Sky Financial Personal Unsecured Loans; 2009
Yokohama Tire Company; 2006

KPS3 MARKETING
50 W Liberty St Ste 640, Reno, NV 89501
Tel.: (775) 686-7439
Fax: (775) 334-4313
E-Mail: info@kps3.com
Web Site: www.kps3.com

Year Founded: 1991

Agency Specializes In: Advertising, Brand Development & Integration, Digital/Interactive, Internet/Web Design, Social Media

Stephanie Kruse *(Pres)*
Katie Coleman *(VP-Accts)*
Rob Gaedtke *(VP-Creative Svcs)*
Scott Walquist *(VP-Acct Svcs)*
Chrisie Yabu *(Sr Acct Dir)*
Mike McDowell *(Dir-Web & Digital Mktg & Acct Exec)*
Kevin Jones *(Dir-Art)*
Tammy Abe *(Office Mgr & Bus Mgr)*
Julia Kruper *(Acct Mgr)*

Accounts:
Arch Business System
Nevada Network of Domestic Violence
New-Roundabout Catering & Party Rentals Advertising, Content Development, Design, Digital, Engine Optimization, Marketing Communications, Marketing Strategy, Public Relations, Social Media
United Way of Northern Nevada & The Sierra

KRACOE SZYKULA & TOWNSEND INC.
2950 W Square Lake Rd Ste 112, Troy, MI 48098-5725
Tel.: (248) 641-7500
Fax: (248) 641-4779
E-Mail: rkracoe@ksthip.com
Web Site: www.ksthip.com

E-Mail for Key Personnel:
President: rkracoe@ksthip.com
Creative Dir.: townsend@ksthip.com
Media Dir.: szykula@ksthip.com

Employees: 6

Year Founded: 1991

National Agency Associations: AAF-BMA-BPA

Agency Specializes In: Advertising, Automotive, Brand Development & Integration, Business Publications, Business-To-Business, Catalogs, Collateral, Corporate Communications, Corporate Identity, Engineering, Industrial, Internet/Web Design, Magazines, Media Buying Services, Media Planning, Multimedia, New Product Development, Outdoor, Planning & Consultation, Promotions, Public Relations, Publicity/Promotions, Sales Promotion, Search Engine Optimization, Technical Advertising

Approx. Annual Billings: $4,900,000

Breakdown of Gross Billings by Media: Audio/Visual: 2%; Bus. Publs.: 35%; Print: 12%; Pub. Rels.: 40%; Sls. Promo.: 9%; Worldwide Web Sites: 2%

Edward R. Szykula *(Owner)*
Andrew J. Townsend *(Principal & Dir-Creative)*
Roland R. Kracoe *(Principal)*
Peggy Harrington *(Mgr-Print Production)*

Accounts:
BLM Group; Wixom, MI Tube Processing & Fabricating Machinery
Buck Chuck Co.; Traverse City, MI Chucks; 2007
CIGNYS; Saginaw, MI General Manufacturing; 2002
Creform Corp.; Wixom, MI; Greer, SC Material Handling System; 1996
Doerken Corporation USA; Ann Arbor, MI Engineered Coatings; 2003
FixtureWorks; Fraser, MI Workholding & Fixturing; 2004
HOSCO; Livonia, MI Paint Finishing Systems; 2000
Hougen Manufacturing, Inc.; Flint, MI Holemaking Cutting Tools; 1991
ThermoFlex; Morrison, TN Thermo & Vacuum Forming; 2007
Urgent Plastic Services; Rochester Hills, MI Plastic Prototypes; 1997
VGAGE; Madison Heights, MI Gaging Products & Systems; 2006

KRAFTWORKS LTD.
525 Broadway, New York, NY 10012
Tel.: (212) 431-7501
Fax: (212) 431-7527
E-Mail: info@kraftworksltd.com
Web Site: kraftworksnyc.com

Employees: 20
Year Founded: 2000

Agency Specializes In: Fashion/Apparel, Leisure, Sponsorship, Strategic Planning/Research

Neil Kraft *(Owner)*
Trente Miller *(VP-Ops & Mgmt)*
Karen Lee *(Art Dir)*
Ashley Wenk *(Acct Dir)*
Janessa Gomez *(Dir-Art)*
L. C. Staten *(Acct Exec)*
Elisabeth Smith *(Client Svc Dir)*

Accounts:
HanesBrands Bali
Playtex Apparel Campaign: "Be Uniquely You."
iacc
La Prairie
Swimsuits For All

KRATIVE LLC
350 Center St Ste 208, Wallingford, CT 6492
Tel.: (855) 572-8483
E-Mail: studio@krative.com
Web Site: www.krative.com

Agency Specializes In: Advertising, Brand Development & Integration, Internet/Web Design, Logo & Package Design, Print, Search Engine Optimization

Rick Callahan *(Owner)*

Accounts:
New-The Healing Corner

KRAUS MARKETING
4 Spring St, Morristown, NJ 7960
Tel.: (973) 998-5742
Web Site: www.krausgroupmarketing.com

Agency Specializes In: Advertising, Brand Development & Integration, Internet/Web Design, Search Engine Optimization, Social Media

Nick Kraus *(Founder & CEO)*
Joel Kraus *(Acct Mgr)*

Accounts:
New-Kim's Barkery

KRAUSE ADVERTISING
5307 E Mockingbird Ln Ste 250, Dallas, TX 75206
Tel.: (214) 823-5100
Fax: (214) 823-5108
E-Mail: jim_krause@krauseadvertising.com
Web Site: www.krauseadvertising.com

Employees: 16
Year Founded: 1979

Agency Specializes In: Advertising, Affluent Market, Brand Development & Integration, Branded Entertainment, Broadcast, Collateral, Education, Entertainment, Fashion/Apparel, Financial, Food Service, Graphic Design, Guerilla Marketing, Health Care Services, Hospitality, Leisure, Local Marketing, Logo & Package Design, Luxury Products, Media Buying Services, Production (Ad, Film, Broadcast), Real Estate, Restaurant, Retail, Social Marketing/Nonprofit, Sports Market, Strategic Planning/Research, Syndication, T.V., Travel & Tourism, Viral/Buzz/Word of Mouth

Approx. Annual Billings: $31,500,000

Breakdown of Gross Billings by Media: Bus. Publs.: $787,500; Collateral: $2,835,000; Fees: $1,197,000; Mags.: $3,465,000; Newsp.: $6,520,500; Other: $2,205,000; Outdoor: $1,260,000; Point of Sale: $63,000; Production: $3,402,000; Radio: $6,300,000; T.V.: $3,465,000

Jim Krause *(CEO)*
David Coats *(Principal & Exec Dir-Creative)*
Jim Hradecky *(Principal & Exec Dir-Creative)*
Candace Krause *(VP)*
Gary Perrone *(Sr Dir-Art)*
Emily Black *(Client Svcs Dir)*
Kelly Galloway *(Acct Dir)*
Elisabeth Bardo *(Acct Exec)*

Accounts:
C.J. Charles; La Jolla, CA Fine Jeweler; 2005
Lee Michaels; LA Fine Jewelers; 2002
Louis Glick; New York, NY Wholesale Diamond Jewelry; 2004
Lux Bond & Green; CT & Boston Fine Jewelers; 2002
Park Cities Bank; Dallas, TX; 2004
William Goldberg; NY Diamond Jewelry Wholesaler; 2005

KRE8 MEDIA INC
200 E New England Ave Ste 200, Winter Park, FL 32789
Tel.: (407) 629-5454
E-Mail: info@kre8media.com
Web Site: www.kre8media.com

Agency Specializes In: Brand Development & Integration, Direct Response Marketing, Media Planning, Media Relations, Production (Print), Radio, Strategic Planning/Research

T. Lee Cutler *(Founder, Pres & CEO)*
Eureka Vanterpool *(Sr VP-Ops)*
Eureka Davis *(VP & Acct Grp Dir)*
Stephen Pickens *(VP-Partnership Dev)*
Jay Glanzman *(Dir-Media)*
Eric Hill *(Dir-Media Sys & Traffic)*
Laura Nichols *(Dir-Acct Ops)*
Lauren Atherton *(Supvr-Media)*
Kim Cole *(Media Buyer)*
Kim Serulneck *(Media Buyer)*

Accounts:
BodyBuilding.com
Connect Hearing
DraftStreet
Julep
Medical Alert
nomorerack
OnDeck
PokerStars.net
Premier Care in Bathing DRTV
QuiBids
Rover
TradeKing
Woodbury Health Products
Zulily Campaign: "zulily.com. A Big Selection of Styles for a Small Window of Time."

KREATIVE
9840 Willows Rd NE Ste 100, Redmond, WA 98052
Tel.: (866) 849-0922
E-Mail: hello@kreative.com
Web Site: www.kreative.com

Employees: 50
Year Founded: 2010

Agency Specializes In: Advertising, Arts, Brand Development & Integration, Collateral, Consumer Goods, Content, Digital/Interactive, E-Commerce, Graphic Design, Internet/Web Design, Logo & Package Design, Outdoor, Package Design, Print, Retail, Search Engine Optimization, Social Media, T.V., Web (Banner Ads, Pop-ups, etc.)

Luke Phillips *(Dir-Client Svcs)*
Tylar Espinosa *(Acct Mgr)*
Michael Miner *(Acct Mgr)*
Blake Thiessen *(Acct Mgr)*
Chelsea Eliott *(Acct Mgr)*
Nick Quiro *(Acct Mgr)*
Travis Walsh *(Sr Acct Exec)*
Michael Caporale *(Strategist-Digital Mktg)*
Tifani Johnson *(Copywriter)*

Accounts:
Evolution By Thompson
J Thompson Consulting

KRISTOF CREATIVE, INC.
707 Bob White Ct, Mount Juliet, TN 37122
Tel.: (615) 656-5516
Fax: (480) 275-3659
E-Mail: kristofcreative@gmail.com
Web Site: www.kristofcreative.com

Employees: 10
Year Founded: 1995

Agency Specializes In: Advertising, Brand Development & Integration, Broadcast, Consulting,

Corporate Identity, Cosmetics, Fashion/Apparel, Financial, Food Service, Graphic Design, Health Care Services, Internet/Web Design, Logo & Package Design, Outdoor, Package Design, Print, Restaurant, Travel & Tourism

Approx. Annual Billings: $250,000

Breakdown of Gross Billings by Media: Collateral: 40%; Logo & Package Design: 20%; Trade Shows: 10%; Worldwide Web Sites: 30%

Michael Kristof *(Dir-Creative)*

Accounts:
cMedia Corporation
Fairfax County Federal Credit Union
Ferrin IronWorks
Solatese

KRONER COMMUNICATION
4966 Valhalla Dr, Boulder, CO 80301
Tel.: (303) 478-3044
Fax: (303) 785-7483
Web Site: www.kronercommunications.com

Agency Specializes In: Advertising, Collateral, Exhibit/Trade Shows, Public Relations

Marilyn R. Kroner *(Principal)*

Accounts:
Body Bar Systems Inc.
The Chasen Group
Exhibit Surveys, Inc.
Exhibitor Media Group "EXHIBITOR2014", Public Relations
The Hughes Group Brand Awareness, Public Relations Strategies

KRT MARKETING
3685 Mt Diablo Blvd Ste 255, Lafayette, CA 94549-3776
Tel.: (925) 284-0444
Fax: (925) 284-0448
E-Mail: keith@krtmarketing.com
Web Site: www.krtmarketing.com

E-Mail for Key Personnel:
President: keith@krtmarketing.com
Creative Dir.: henry@krtmarketing.com
Media Dir.: ryan@krtmarketing.com

Employees: 20
Year Founded: 1972

Agency Specializes In: Advertising, Brand Development & Integration, Business Publications, Business-To-Business, Collateral, College, Communications, Computers & Software, Corporate Communications, Corporate Identity, Crisis Communications, Digital/Interactive, Direct Response Marketing, E-Commerce, Email, Event Planning & Marketing, Exhibit/Trade Shows, Financial, Graphic Design, Health Care Services, High Technology, Hospitality, Identity Marketing, Integrated Marketing, Internet/Web Design, Local Marketing, Logo & Package Design, Luxury Products, Marine, Media Buying Services, Media Planning, Media Relations, Medical Products, Newspaper, Print, Production (Print), Public Relations, Publicity/Promotions, Real Estate, Recruitment, Restaurant, Sales Promotion, Social Marketing/Nonprofit, Social Media, Strategic Planning/Research, Sweepstakes, Technical Advertising, Transportation, Travel & Tourism

Approx. Annual Billings: $25,245,000

Keith R. Thomas *(Pres)*
Ryan Christoi *(Partner)*
Eric Holwell *(VP-Ops)*
Marcia Thomas *(VP-Fin)*
Adriana Kevill *(Dir-Online & Social Media Strategy)*
Henry Simpson *(Dir-Creative)*
Jenny Skundrich *(Dir-Client Strategy)*
Mona Tawakali *(Dir-Client Strategy)*
Kara Somsen Diem *(Acct Mgr & Media Buyer)*
Olivia Haro *(Media Planner)*
Nicole Morris *(Media Planner)*

Accounts:
Deere & Company
Fannie Mae; Washington, DC Recruitment; 2005
Hitachi Data Systems; Santa Clara, CA Storage Systems; 2010
PayPal; San Jose, CA Partner Programs; 2009
Philips-Van Heusen; New York, NY Recruitment; 2004
Procter & Gamble; Cincinnati, OH Recruitment; 2005
Saint Mary's College of California; Moraga, CA Graduate Programs; 2009
TIAA-CREF Recruitment; 2007
UnitedHealth Group; New York, NY Recruitment; 2006

KRUEGER COMMUNICATIONS
1222 Preston Way, Venice, CA 90291
Tel.: (310) 995-1971
Fax: (310) 857-1355
E-Mail: john_krueger@kruegerads.com
Web Site: www.kruegerads.com

Employees: 10
Year Founded: 2005

Agency Specializes In: Advertising

John Krueger *(Owner)*
Allen Krueger, Jr. *(Exec VP, Sr Engr-Sys & Sr Engr-Sls & Design)*
Matt Torgerson *(Mgr-Voice & Network Svcs)*
Steve Dykstra *(Acct Exec)*

Accounts:
Auto Insurance Specialists
Garden Fresh Restaurant Corp. (Advertising Agency of Record) Discover Fresh, Print, Radio, Souplantation/Sweet Tomatoes, TV
Nikon

KRUSH DIGITAL ADVERTISING AGENCY
5408 NW 135th StSte B, Oklahoma City, OK 73012
Tel.: (405) 603-5355
Web Site: www.gokrush.com

Year Founded: 2013

Agency Specializes In: Broadcast, Custom Publishing, Digital/Interactive, Electronic Media, Email, Infomercials, Local Marketing, Mobile Marketing, Outdoor, Paid Searches, Print, Promotions, Radio, Search Engine Optimization, Social Media, T.V., Viral/Buzz/Word of Mouth, Web (Banner Ads, Pop-ups, etc.)

Rusty Holzer *(Pres)*

Accounts:
Comfort Masters Insulation; 2013

KRUSKOPF & COMPANY, INC.
(Formerly kruskopf Coontz)
310 4th Ave S 2nd Fl, Minneapolis, MN 55415
Tel.: (612) 338-3870
Fax: (612) 630-5158
E-Mail: info@kctruth.com
Web Site: www.kctruth.com

E-Mail for Key Personnel:
Creative Dir.: skruskopf@kctruth.com

Employees: 20
Year Founded: 1988

National Agency Associations: AMIN

Agency Specializes In: Advertising, Brand Development & Integration, Broadcast, Collateral, Communications, Consumer Marketing, Corporate Identity, Entertainment, Food Service, Graphic Design, Health Care Services, Logo & Package Design, New Product Development, Out-of-Home Media, Outdoor, Point of Sale, Public Relations, Radio, Restaurant, Retail, Sales Promotion, Sponsorship, Strategic Planning/Research, T.V.

Approx. Annual Billings: $25,000,000

Breakdown of Gross Billings by Media: Brdcst.: 35%; Bus. Publs.: 10%; Collateral: 15%; Newsp.: 10%; Out-of-Home Media: 20%; Radio & T.V.: 10%

Robb Burnham *(VP & Dir-Creative)*
Mike Cronin *(VP & Assoc Dir-Creative)*
Aron Shand *(Sr Dir-Art)*
Jeannette Tschida *(Dir-Media)*
Andie Nelson *(Acct Mgr)*
Brandon Tyrell *(Acct Supvr)*
Lauren Akin *(Supvr-Media)*
Randy Grubba *(Copywriter)*

Accounts:
3M Co. 3M ESPE
3M; Maplewood, MN Optical Services Division; 2004
Cost Cutters Communications
Evercare
Fieldnation.com
Fuji Ya; Minneapolis, MN
Herzing University
MyWonderfulLife.com
Nautic Global Group
No Name Steaks
SC Railing Co.
United Healthcare Sonus Hearing Clinics; 2004

KRUTICK ADVERTISING
7 Hollow Ln, Poughkeepsie, NY 12603-5018
Tel.: (845) 462-4188
Fax: (845) 462-8586
E-Mail: ken.krutick@verizon.net

Employees: 3
Year Founded: 1990

Agency Specializes In: Cable T.V., Consumer Marketing, Graphic Design, In-Store Advertising, Local Marketing, Magazines, Media Buying Services, Newspaper, Newspapers & Magazines, Planning & Consultation, Point of Purchase, Print, Production, Radio, Retail, T.V., Trade & Consumer Magazines

Approx. Annual Billings: $1,500,000

Kenneth J. Krutick *(Pres)*

Accounts:
Dutchess Community College; Poughkeepsie, NY Office of Student Activities
LJ Edwards Home Furnishings; Brookfield, CT; 2010

KRYL & COMPANY, INC.
39 S LaSalle St Ste 910, Chicago, IL 60603
Tel.: (312) 961-0928
Fax: (312) 641-0314
E-Mail: info@krylandco.com
Web Site: www.krylandco.com

Employees: 4
Year Founded: 1989

Agency Specializes In: Direct Response Marketing

Approx. Annual Billings: $1,000,000

Susan Kryl *(Pres)*

Accounts:
Alter Ego Networks
British American Drama Academy; Bethel, CT Midsummer in Oxford (Acting Program); 1998
Children's Memorial Medical Center; Chicago, IL; 1998
Compaq
Experian
GE Financial
Informatica; Chicago, IL; 1996
Jockey International

KTK DESIGN

53 W Jackson Blvd Ste 630, Chicago, IL 60604-4277
Tel.: (312) 212-1500
Fax: (312) 212-1796
E-Mail: joe@ktkdesign.com
Web Site: www.ktkdesign.com

E-Mail for Key Personnel:
President: joe@ktkdesign.com

Employees: 2
Year Founded: 1991

Agency Specializes In: Advertising, Brand Development & Integration, Business-To-Business, Collateral, Commercial Photography, Communications, Consulting, Consumer Marketing, Corporate Identity, Direct Response Marketing, E-Commerce, Electronic Media, Event Planning & Marketing, Exhibit/Trade Shows, Gay & Lesbian Market, Graphic Design, Health Care Services, High Technology, Internet/Web Design, Logo & Package Design, Media Buying Services, New Product Development, Newspapers & Magazines, Outdoor, Point of Purchase, Point of Sale, Print, Production, Restaurant, Retail, Sales Promotion, Technical Advertising, Yellow Pages Advertising

Approx. Annual Billings: $750,000

Joseph J. Kozak *(Co-Owner)*
Kristina E. Krumdick *(Co-Owner)*

Accounts:
Desert Willow Golf Resort; Palm Desert, CA
National Association of Realtors; Chicago, IL; 1996
The Segal Company; Chicago, IL Business Publications; 1993

KUHN & ASSOCIATES

10901 W 84th Terr Ste 240, Lenexa, KS 66214
Tel.: (913) 663-5999
E-Mail: contact@kuhnkc.com
Web Site: www.kuhnkc.com

Agency Specializes In: Advertising, Brand Development & Integration, Collateral, Digital/Interactive, Email, Graphic Design, Internet/Web Design, Print, Social Media

Ray Kuhn *(Pres)*
Aaron Kuhn *(Dir-Digital Mktg)*

Accounts:
Aviation Solutions

KUHN & WITTENBORN, INC.

2405 Grand Blvd Ste 600, Kansas City, MO 64108-2519
Tel.: (816) 471-7888
Fax: (816) 471-7530
E-Mail: workwithus@kuhnwitt.com
Web Site: www.kuhnwitt.com

Employees: 50
Year Founded: 1978

National Agency Associations: 4A's-AAF-DMA

Agency Specializes In: Advertising, Brand Development & Integration, Business-To-Business, Collateral, Communications, Consumer Marketing, Corporate Identity, Direct Response Marketing, E-Commerce, Entertainment, Exhibit/Trade Shows, Financial, Graphic Design, Health Care Services, High Technology, Internet/Web Design, Investor Relations, Leisure, Logo & Package Design, Media Buying Services, New Product Development, Out-of-Home Media, Outdoor, Planning & Consultation, Point of Purchase, Point of Sale, Print, Public Relations, Publicity/Promotions, Radio, Sales Promotion, Strategic Planning/Research, T.V., Trade & Consumer Magazines, Travel & Tourism

Breakdown of Gross Billings by Media: Bus. Publs.: 2%; D.M.: 2%; Internet Adv.: 2%; Newsp.: 12%; Outdoor: 6%; Spot Radio: 30%; Spot T.V.: 36%; Trade & Consumer Mags.: 10%

Whitey Kuhn *(Pres & CEO)*
Julie Robinson *(COO & Sr VP)*
Alan Doan *(Chief Creative Officer & Sr VP)*
Lisa Anderson *(Controller)*
Bill Ost *(Exec Dir-Creative)*
Randy Robinson *(Dir-Creative)*
Shelley Porter *(Assoc Dir-Media)*
Amy McNeall *(Sr Media Buyer & Media Planner)*

Accounts:
Assurant Employee Benefits
Federated Rural Electric Insurance Exchange
GEHA Government Employee's Health Association
Kansas City Aviation Department FlyKCI.com
Kansas City Power & Light; Kansas City, MO; 2002
Kansas City Southern
Kansas Speedway; Kansas City, KS; 1999
Liberty Hospital
Stowers Institute for Medical Research; Kansas City, MO; 1999

KWGC WORLDWIDE LLC

(Formerly KWGC, Inc. Advertising & Design)
10206 Conser St, Overland Park, KS 66212
Tel.: (214) 693-7932
Web Site: www.kwgc.com

E-Mail for Key Personnel:
President: kay@kwgc.com

Employees: 7
Year Founded: 1985

Agency Specializes In: Advertising Specialties, Automotive, Aviation & Aerospace, Brand Development & Integration, Broadcast, Business-To-Business, Collateral, Communications, Consulting, Consumer Marketing, Corporate Communications, Corporate Identity, Direct Response Marketing, Event Planning & Marketing, Exhibit/Trade Shows, Graphic Design, Health Care Services, High Technology, Logo & Package Design, New Product Development, Out-of-Home Media, Outdoor, Pharmaceutical, Point of Purchase, Point of Sale, Print, Production, Publicity/Promotions, Radio, Real Estate, Restaurant, Retail, Sales Promotion, Strategic Planning/Research, T.V., Travel & Tourism

Approx. Annual Billings: $5,000,000

Kay Williams *(Mng Partner)*

Accounts:
American Airlines; Dallas, TX; 2000
Galveston Island
Motorola Solutions, Inc.; Chicago, IL Pagers; 1987
Professional Insurance Elite

KWITTKEN & COMPANY

360 Lexington Ave 15th Fl, New York, NY 10017
Tel.: (646) 277-7111
Fax: (646) 658-0880
E-Mail: info@kwitco.com
Web Site: www.kwittken.com

Employees: 22

National Agency Associations: COPF

Agency Specializes In: Automotive, Business-To-Business, Cable T.V., Consulting, Corporate Communications, Crisis Communications, Education, Entertainment, Fashion/Apparel, Financial, Food Service, Hospitality, Household Goods, Internet/Web Design, Investor Relations, Luxury Products, Media Relations, Medical Products, Publishing, Retail, Social Marketing/Nonprofit, Sponsorship, Trade & Consumer Magazines, Travel & Tourism

Aaron R. Kwittken *(Global Chm & CEO)*
Gabrielle Zucker Acevedo *(Partner & Mng Dir)*
Shanee Goss *(Mng Dir)*
Ellie Jones Rossi *(Mng Dir)*
Jason Schlossberg *(Chief Creative Officer)*
Adam Snyder *(Chief Digital Officer)*
William Nikosey *(Sr Acct Dir)*
Jason Morley *(Sr Acct Supvr)*
Glori Perez *(Sr Acct Supvr)*
Katie Bonneau *(Acct Supvr)*

Accounts:
Amadeus
American Eagle Outfitters
New-American Express
Better Homes & Gardens Real Estate
Butterfield Fulcrum (Agency of Record)
Capco
Cengage Learning
Coleman Research Group
CourseSmart
CPower
DSM Biomedical (Agency of Record)
First Advantage
New-HomeAway
Matrixx Initiatives, Inc. Content, Media Relations, Public Relations, Zicam (Communications Agency of Record)
New-Pantone, Inc. (Public Relations Agency of Record)
New-Procter & Gamble Co
Sharp Electronics Consumer, Public Relations
New-TE Connectivity
Trusted Advisor
U.S. News & World Report Public Relations; 2008
New-Virtus Asset Management
New-Windstream

KYK ADVERTISING MARKETING PROMOTIONS

2600 Constant Comment Pl, Louisville, KY 40299
Tel.: (502) 636-0288
Fax: (502) 636-0635
Toll Free: (800) 531-6999
Web Site: www.kykmarketing.com

E-Mail for Key Personnel:
President: jhagerty@kykmarketing.com

Employees: 22
Year Founded: 1980

Agency Specializes In: Collateral, Commercial Photography, Consumer Marketing, Consumer Publications, Corporate Identity, Direct Response Marketing, Food Service, Internet/Web Design, Logo & Package Design, New Product Development, Newspaper, Outdoor, Point of

Purchase, Point of Sale, Radio, Sales Promotion, Strategic Planning/Research

Approx. Annual Billings: $25,000,000

Breakdown of Gross Billings by Media: Collateral: 50%; D.M.: 2%; Point of Purchase: 5%; Sls. Promo.: 43%

Jack Hagerty *(Owner)*
Mark Stivers *(Sr Dir-Creative)*
Paul Plaschke *(Dir-Bus Dev)*
Steve Coburn *(Mgr-Production)*

Accounts:
Brown-Forman Corporation; Louisville, KY
Coca-Cola Bottling; Atlanta, GA

KZSW ADVERTISING
19 Bennetts Rd, Setauket, NY 11733
Tel.: (631) 348-1440
Fax: (631) 348-1449
E-Mail: contact@kzswadvertising.com
Web Site: kzswadvertising.com

Employees: 18
Year Founded: 1980

National Agency Associations: 4A's

Agency Specializes In: Advertising, Brand Development & Integration, Business Publications, Business-To-Business, Collateral, Corporate Identity, Direct Response Marketing, E-Commerce, Education, Exhibit/Trade Shows, Graphic Design, Health Care Services, High Technology, Internet/Web Design, Leisure, Logo & Package Design, Print, Production, Radio, Restaurant, Technical Advertising, Telemarketing, Trade & Consumer Magazines, Travel & Tourism

Approx. Annual Billings: $20,034,000

Breakdown of Gross Billings by Media: Adv. Specialities: $50,000; Bus. Publs.: $2,600,000; Cable T.V.: $160,000; Collateral: $5,100,000; Consumer Publs.: $4,150,000; D.M.: $430,000; E-Commerce: $60,000; Event Mktg.: $30,000; Exhibits/Trade Shows: $40,000; Fees: $230,000; Internet Adv.: $120,000; Logo & Package Design: $30,000; Network Radio: $300,000; Newsp.: $3,100,000; Newsp. & Mags.: $250,000; Outdoor: $50,000; Print: $100,000; Production: $1,640,000; Radio: $50,000; Radio & T.V.: $190,000; Sls. Promo.: $50,000; Spot Radio: $190,000; Spot T.V.: $280,000; Strategic Planning/Research: $100,000; T.V.: $664,000; Trade Shows: $20,000; Video Brochures: $25,000; Worldwide Web Sites: $25,000

Jack Schultheis *(Owner)*
Michael Welch *(Mng Partner)*
Chris Basile *(Dir-Art)*
Richard Shepard *(Supvr-Production)*

Accounts:
Holy Child Academy Independent School; 2007
Long Island Convention & Visitors Bureau Tourism, Meetings & Conventions; 2001
NYCyberKnife RadioSurgery Center; 2014
Winthrop-University Hospital; Mineola, NY Healthcare Services; 1999

L-A ADVERTISING
1541 Alta Dr Ste 202, Whitehall, PA 18052
Tel.: (610) 799-3382
Fax: (610) 365-8027
Web Site: www.l-aadvertising.com

Agency Specializes In: Advertising

Larry Kacyon *(Owner & Specialist-Integrated Mktg)*

Accounts:
Abec Inc.
Aesculap
Amroc Entry Systems
Bethlehem Skateplaza
DORMA Group North America
Hertz Supply Company
HT Lyons
Kutztown University of Pennsylvania
Lear Educational Center
Lehigh Center for Clinical Research
Moravian College Comenius Center for Continuing, Professional & Graduate Studies
Premair Cleaning & Maintenance
TND
Tuscan Dairy Farms

L-AVENUE
11467 Huebner Rd Ste 368, San Antonio, TX 78230
Tel.: (210) 348-1900
E-Mail: l-avenue@l-avenue-ad.com
Web Site: www.l-avenue-ad.com

Employees: 7

Jimmy Clavijo *(Dir-Creative)*
Carlos Jaramillo *(Dir)*

Accounts:
Be Natural
UltraVision

L2 MARKETING
114 W Sixth St, Tyler, TX 75701
Tel.: (903) 526-6864
Fax: (903) 526-6884
E-Mail: info@l2-marketing.com
Web Site: www.l2-marketing.com

Year Founded: 2004

Agency Specializes In: Advertising, Brand Development & Integration, Event Planning & Marketing, Internet/Web Design, Logo & Package Design, Outdoor, Print, T.V.

Linda Warren *(Owner & Pres)*
Doug Warren *(CFO)*

Accounts:
Murphey the Jeweler

L3 ADVERTISING INC.
115 Bowery 3rd Fl, New York, NY 10002-4933
Tel.: (212) 966-7050
Fax: (212) 431-1282
E-Mail: info@l3advertising.com
Web Site: www.l3advertising.com

Employees: 20
Year Founded: 1984

Agency Specializes In: Advertising, Asian Market, Event Planning & Marketing, Financial, Health Care Services, Hospitality, Strategic Planning/Research, Travel & Tourism

Approx. Annual Billings: $4,000,000

Joseph Lam *(Co-Founder & Pres)*
Ellen Lee *(VP-Acct Svcs)*
Jojo Chan *(Dir-Creative)*
Raymond Tam *(Dir-Art)*
Brian Lai *(Acct Exec)*

Accounts:
CAIA-Chinese American Insurance Association
Diageo
Fantasy Springs Hotel & Casino
Johnnie Walker Scotch
Red Egg
Vonage

L7 CREATIVE
(Formerly L7 Creative Communications)
5927 Balfour Ct Ste 104, Carlsbad, CA 92008
Tel.: (760) 931-0777
Toll Free: (877) 572-7888
E-Mail: info@L7creative.com
Web Site: www.L7creative.com

Employees: 20
Year Founded: 2001

Agency Specializes In: Advertising, Alternative Advertising, Brand Development & Integration, Branded Entertainment, Business-To-Business, Collateral, Consumer Marketing, Corporate Communications, Corporate Identity, Digital/Interactive, Direct Response Marketing, Direct-to-Consumer, E-Commerce, Electronic Media, Email, Entertainment, Experience Design, Identity Marketing, In-Store Advertising, Information Technology, Internet/Web Design, Logo & Package Design, Media Planning, Media Relations, Mobile Marketing, Multimedia, New Product Development, New Technologies, Outdoor, Package Design, Podcasting, Point of Purchase, Point of Sale, Product Placement, Promotions, Radio, Recruitment, Social Marketing/Nonprofit, Viral/Buzz/Word of Mouth, Web (Banner Ads, Pop-ups, etc.)

Breakdown of Gross Billings by Media: Brdcst.: 20%; D.M.: 15%; Outdoor: 5%; Print: 25%; Worldwide Web Sites: 35%

Tom Gallego *(Chief Creative Officer)*
Harley Orion *(Exec Producer & Principal)*
Lance Pine *(Principal & Dir-Client Svcs)*
Christine Tarantino-Gallego *(Dir-Fin)*
Christina Gagnon *(Mgr-Production)*
Cody Gutierrez *(Acct Exec)*
Heather Masters *(Acct Planner-Digital)*
Theresa Gallego *(Acct Coord-Digital)*
Nikki Hess *(Acct Coord-Digital)*

Accounts:
Chimei Consumer Electronics; 2007
La Cantina Doors Bi-Fold Door Systems; 2008
National City Mortgage Financial; 2004
Pac West Builders Construction; 2005
VIZIO TV's Consumer Electronics; 2003

L7 CREATIVE COMMUNICATIONS
(Name Changed to L7 Creative)

LA ADS
9018 Balboa Blvd 536, Northridge, CA 91325
Tel.: (800) 991-0625
E-Mail: frontdesk@laadsmarketing.com
Web Site: www.laadsmarketing.com

Year Founded: 2009

Agency Specializes In: Advertising, Public Relations, Social Media

Dan Katz *(Pres)*

Accounts:
New-The Archdiocese Los Angeles

LA AGENCIA DE ORCI & ASOCIADOS
2800 28th St Ste 222, Santa Monica, CA 90405-6202
Tel.: (310) 444-7300
Fax: (310) 478-3587
E-Mail: info@orci.com

Web Site: www.orci.com

E-Mail for Key Personnel:
Creative Dir.: RCardena@laagencia.com

Employees: 35
Year Founded: 1982

National Agency Associations: AAF-AEF-AHAA

Agency Specializes In: Advertising, Advertising Specialties, Automotive, Bilingual Market, Brand Development & Integration, Broadcast, Business-To-Business, Cable T.V., Co-op Advertising, Collateral, Communications, Consumer Marketing, Cosmetics, Digital/Interactive, Direct Response Marketing, Event Planning & Marketing, Financial, Health Care Services, Hispanic Market, Internet/Web Design, Media Buying Services, Newspaper, Newspapers & Magazines, Out-of-Home Media, Outdoor, Planning & Consultation, Point of Purchase, Point of Sale, Print, Production, Public Relations, Publicity/Promotions, Radio, Restaurant, Retail, Sales Promotion, Sponsorship, Strategic Planning/Research, T.V.

Breakdown of Gross Billings by Media: Cable T.V.: 2%; Internet Adv.: 3%; Network Radio: 3%; Network T.V.: 33%; Newsp. & Mags.: 3%; Out-of-Home Media: 5%; Outdoor: 1%; Spot Radio: 14%; Spot T.V.: 36%

Hector Orci *(Chm)*
Andrew Orci *(CEO)*
Marina Filippelli *(Sr VP & Dir-Client Svcs)*
Marielena Tidwell *(Sr VP-HR)*
Juan Jose Quintana *(Exec Dir-Creative)*

Accounts:
American Honda Motor Co., Inc.; Torrance, CA
Angel Soft
Bacardi USA, Inc. Cazadores
Big Brothers Big Sisters of America
CASA; Seattle, WA (Public Relations)
Court Appointed Special Advocates
Georgia Pacific
Jack in the Box
Lactaid
Sempra Energy
Splenda

LA COMUNIDAD
(Acquired by SapientNitro USA, Inc.)

LABOV ADVERTISING, MARKETING AND TRAINING
(Formerly LaBov & Beyond, Inc.)
609 E Cook Rd, Fort Wayne, IN 46825
Tel.: (260) 497-0111
Fax: (260) 497-0007
E-Mail: blabov@labov.com
Web Site: www.labov.com

Employees: 45
Year Founded: 1981

Agency Specializes In: Above-the-Line, Advertising, Affiliate Marketing, Affluent Market, Alternative Advertising, Automotive, Aviation & Aerospace, Below-the-Line, Brand Development & Integration, Business Publications, Business-To-Business, Catalogs, Co-op Advertising, Collateral, Communications, Consulting, Consumer Goods, Consumer Marketing, Consumer Publications, Corporate Communications, Corporate Identity, Custom Publishing, Customer Relationship Management, Digital/Interactive, Direct Response Marketing, Direct-to-Consumer, Electronic Media, Environmental, Event Planning & Marketing, Exhibit/Trade Shows, Experience Design, Financial, Government/Political, Graphic Design, Guerilla Marketing, Health Care Services, Identity Marketing, In-Store Advertising, Industrial, Integrated Marketing, Internet/Web Design, Leisure, Local Marketing, Logo & Package Design, Luxury Products, Magazines, Marine, Market Research, Medical Products, Merchandising, Mobile Marketing, Multimedia, New Product Development, Newspaper, Newspapers & Magazines, Out-of-Home Media, Outdoor, Package Design, Planning & Consultation, Point of Purchase, Point of Sale, Print, Production (Print), Promotions, Public Relations, Publicity/Promotions, Retail, Sales Promotion, Sponsorship, Strategic Planning/Research, Transportation, Viral/Buzz/Word of Mouth

Barry Labov *(Pres & CEO)*
Marc McMillen *(Head-Creative & Dir-Art)*
Pete Piekarski *(Head-Creative & Sr Art Dir)*
Sal Farias *(Acct Mgr)*
Leslie Heller *(Acct Mgr)*
Ginger Hollister *(Acct Mgr)*
Michael Krouse *(Acct Mgr)*
Lucas Smith *(Acct Mgr)*
Jim Baum *(Mgr-Production)*
Mary Gabbard *(Mgr-Traffic)*
Jim Buck *(Designer-Instructional)*

Accounts:
Audi of America; Auburn Hills, MI; 1998
Ferrari; Englewood Cliffs, NJ; 2004
Fleetwood RV Marketing; 2009
FlexJet; 2014
Freightliner; 2000
Harley-Davidson; 2008
Heil Trailer; 2013
Volkswagen Group of America, Inc.; Auburn Hills, MI; 1995
Zimmer Orthopaedics; Warsaw, IN; 2003

LABOV & BEYOND, INC.
(Name Changed to LABOV Advertising, Marketing and Training)

THE LACEK GROUP
900 2nd Ave S Ste 1800, Minneapolis, MN 55402
Tel.: (612) 359-3700
Fax: (612) 359-9395
E-Mail: info@lacek.com
Web Site: www.lacek.com

Employees: 100
Year Founded: 1993

National Agency Associations: 4A's

Agency Specializes In: Direct Response Marketing

William Baker *(Pres)*
Brad Fiery *(Sr Partner & VP-Mktg Analytics & Campaign Ops)*
Chris Hoffman *(VP-HR & Comm)*
Tim Manoles *(VP-Loyalty Consulting)*
Jeff Jones *(Grp Dir-Creative)*
Steve Pederson *(Sr Dir-Art)*
Jennifer Russo *(Sr Dir-Art)*
Myrna Krueger *(Acct Supvr)*
Kevin Deshler *(Acct Exec)*
Jay Walsh *(Copywriter)*
Kristina Fenner *(Project Supvr-Mgmt Office)*

Accounts:
AOL
Carnival Cruise Lines Campaign: "WAVE", Digital Media, Marketing, Print
DuPont Pioneer Campaign: "With You", Marketing, Media Relations, Trade Show Support
National Car Rental
Starwood Hotels & Resorts
United Continental Holdings OnePass Loyalty Program

LAER PEARCE & ASSOCIATES
22892 Mill Creek Dr, Laguna Hills, CA 92653
Tel.: (949) 599-1212
Fax: (949) 599-1213
E-Mail: info@laer.com
Web Site: www.laer.com

Employees: 6

Agency Specializes In: Brand Development & Integration, Communications, Crisis Communications, Email, Environmental, Government/Political, Media Relations, Media Training, Newspaper, Real Estate, Strategic Planning/Research, Web (Banner Ads, Pop-ups, etc.)

Laer Pearce *(Pres)*
Beth Pearce *(CFO & VP)*

Accounts:
Anaheim
BIA
Boeing Realty Corporation
California Geotechnical Engineers Association
CalOptima
Centra Realty
Coalition for Habitat Conservation
Cucamonga Valley Water District
DMB Associates
Grub & Ellis
John Laing Homes
Mesa Consolidated Water District
Mission Landscaping
Newhall Land & Farming
Newhall Ranch
Shea Homes
South Orange County Wastewater Authority
Tejon Ranch Company
Yorba Linda Water District

LAGRANT COMMUNICATIONS
600 Wilshire Blvd Ste 1520, Los Angeles, CA 90017-2920
Tel.: (323) 469-8680
Fax: (323) 469-8683
Web Site: www.lagrantcommunications.com

Employees: 20
Year Founded: 1990

Agency Specializes In: Sponsorship

Kim Hunter *(Pres & CEO)*
Keisha Brown *(Chief Creative Officer, Chief Innovative Officer & Sr VP)*
Paulo Pereira Lima *(VP & Mng Dir-Hispanic Practice)*
Jocelyn Robinson *(VP-Community Engagement)*

Accounts:
American Airlines
American Cancer Society
Bahamas Ministry of Tourism
California Wellness Foundation
City of Los Angeles
CMS
Deloitte
Harley Davidson; 2007
Islands of the Bahamas
Lagrant Foundation
Macy's East
National Marrow Donor Program Multicultural Media Relations Campaign; 2007
Office of National Drug Control Policy
Southern California Edison
United Bank of California
US Army
USC
YWCA

THE LAIDLAW GROUP, LLC
337 Summer St, Boston, MA 02210
Tel.: (617) 423-2801

Fax: (617) 423-2802
E-Mail: info@laidlawgroup.com
Web Site: www.laidlawgroup.com

Employees: 5

Cindy Laidlaw *(Principal)*

Accounts:
Boyce Highlands; Concord, NH Wood Moldings; 2004
Draper Knitting Equipile Performance Wear; 2004
Duckham Architecture & Interiors Web Site
Dujardin Design
Dunkin Donuts
Precast Specialties
Rakks Rangine Corporation
Reebok
Sage Laboratories
Staples

LAIRD+PARTNERS

475 10th Ave 7th Fl, New York, NY 10018
Tel.: (212) 478-8181
Fax: (212) 478-8210
E-Mail: info@lairdandpartners.com
Web Site: www.lairdandpartners.com

Employees: 70

Agency Specializes In: Advertising, Affluent Market, Brand Development & Integration, Cosmetics, Fashion/Apparel, Luxury Products, Newspapers & Magazines, Package Design, Planning & Consultation, Print, Sponsorship, T.V.

Approx. Annual Billings: $200,000,000

LAJEUNESSE COMMUNICATION MARKETING

807 rue Roy Est, Montreal, QC H2L 1E4 Canada
Tel.: (514) 528-8888
Fax: (514) 528-1291
E-Mail: 123go@lacm.ca
Web Site: www.lacm.ca

Employees: 7

Agency Specializes In: Advertising

Mario Larose *(Exec Dir)*
Gilles Guerard *(Mgr-Production)*
Nathalie Daigle *(Coord-Production)*

Accounts:
BP
Gaz Metro

LAKE GROUP MEDIA, INC.

1 Byram Group Pl, Armonk, NY 10504
Tel.: (914) 925-2400
Web Site: www.lakegroupmedia.com

Employees: 68
Year Founded: 1961

Agency Specializes In: Advertising, Affluent Market, African-American Market, Alternative Advertising, Arts, Automotive, Business-To-Business, Children's Market, Co-op Advertising, Consulting, Consumer Goods, Consumer Marketing, Cosmetics, Customer Relationship Management, Digital/Interactive, Direct Response Marketing, Direct-to-Consumer, Education, Electronic Media, Electronics, Email, Engineering, Entertainment, Environmental, Faith Based, Fashion/Apparel, Financial, Gay & Lesbian Market, Government/Political, Health Care Services, High Technology, Hospitality, Household Goods, Information Technology, Integrated Marketing, Investor Relations, Leisure, Local Marketing, Luxury Products, Marine, Media Buying Services, Media Planning, Medical Products, Men's Market, Mobile Marketing, Multimedia, New Technologies, Newspaper, Over-50 Market, Paid Searches, Pets , Pharmaceutical, Planning & Consultation, Print, Production (Print), Real Estate, Retail, Seniors' Market, Shopper Marketing, Social Marketing/Nonprofit, Sports Market, Stakeholders, Sweepstakes, Teen Market, Telemarketing, Transportation, Travel & Tourism, Tween Market, Web (Banner Ads, Pop-ups, etc.), Women's Market

Approx. Annual Billings: $67,000,000

Ryan Lake *(CEO)*
Heather Maylander *(Mng Dir)*
Carolyn Woodruff *(Mng Dir-Brokerage)*
Mike Connolly *(VP-Sls)*
Joanne Elias *(Assoc VP-List Brokerage)*
Carrie French *(Assoc VP)*
Kathy Stivaletti *(Assoc VP-List Brokerage)*
Lenore DeBellis *(Dir-Sls)*
Danny Grubert *(Dir-Sls)*
Elisa Klatt *(Sr Acct Exec)*

Accounts:
American City Business Journals American City Business Journals Subscriptions; 2003
BabyTalk Baby Talk Magazine; 2007
Boardroom Boardroom Reports; 2011
Buena Vista Home Entertainment Disney Movie Club; 2011
Consumers Union Consumer Reports; 2011
Crestline Company Crestline B2B Catalog; 2011
Democratic Congressional Campaign Committee Direct Mail Fundraising; 2008
Experian Z24 Catalog Cooperative; 2013
Fingerhut Fingerhut Credit; 2011
Fisher Investments; 2009
Gerber Life Insurance Grow-Up Plan; 2011
Gerber Products Company Carnation Baby Formula; 2008
Hartford Insurance; 2011
Heifer International Heifer International Fundraising Catalog; 2008
Highlights for Children Continuity Program; 2012
Investor's Business Daily; 2008
Loeb Enterprises Script Relief; 2011
Lorman Education Continuing Education; 2011
Mattel Fisher Price DM; 2013
Mead Johnson Enfamil; 2012
National Geographic Society National Geographic Magazine; 2011
National Magazine Exchange; 2011
The Nature Conservancy Direct Mail Fundraising; 2010
Picture People Retail; 2010
SC Direct Especially Yours Catalog, Paula Young Catalog; 2011
Source Interlink Media Automobile Magazine; 2012
Sprint Assurance Wireless; 2011
Suarez Corporation Biotech Research, International Home Shopping, US Commemorative Gallery
Uline Shipping Supply Specialists Uline B2B Shipping Catalog; 2009

LAKE STRATEGIC MARKETING

2341 Ellis Ave St, Saint Paul, MN 55114
Tel.: (651) 276-8927
Web Site: lakestrategic.com/

Agency Specializes In: Advertising, Brand Development & Integration, Collateral, Content, Digital/Interactive, Package Design, Social Media

James Kolstad *(Pres)*
John Kohl *(VP)*

Accounts:
United States Conceal Carry Association

LAM-ANDREWS INC.

1201 8th Ave S, Nashville, TN 37203
Tel.: (615) 297-7717
Fax: (615) 297-4033
E-Mail: info@lam-andrews.com
Web Site: www.lam-andrews.com

Employees: 10
Year Founded: 1991

Agency Specializes In: Advertising, Advertising Specialties, Brand Development & Integration, Business Publications, Co-op Advertising, Commercial Photography, Communications, Consulting, Consumer Marketing, Consumer Publications, Corporate Identity, Digital/Interactive, Direct Response Marketing, E-Commerce, Electronic Media, Entertainment, Event Planning & Marketing, Exhibit/Trade Shows, Fashion/Apparel, Financial, Graphic Design, Health Care Services, Internet/Web Design, Legal Services, Logo & Package Design, Media Buying Services, Medical Products, New Product Development, Outdoor, Pharmaceutical, Planning & Consultation, Print, Production, Public Relations, Publicity/Promotions, Radio, Real Estate, Retail, Sports Market, T.V., Technical Advertising

Approx. Annual Billings: $4,000,000

Breakdown of Gross Billings by Media: Collateral: 5%; D.M.: 5%; Fees: 30%; Newsp.: 30%; Outdoor: 5%; T.V.: 20%; Trade Shows: 5%

Douglas Andrews *(Pres)*
David Barlar *(Dir-Creative Svcs)*
Jon Kincaid *(Dir-Art)*
John Lam *(Sr Strategist)*
Holly Newsome *(Acct Exec)*

Accounts:
Bradfords; Nashville, TN Furniture; 1991
Cambio Solutions; Brentwood, TN
New Light Imaging; Nashville, TN
Quorum Health Resources; Brentwood, TN
Timberline Properties; Knoxville, TN
Worth Properties

LAMAR ADVERTISING COMPANY

5321 Corporate Blvd, Baton Rouge, LA 70808
Tel.: (225) 926-1000
Fax: (225) 926-1005
Toll Free: (800) 235-2627
E-Mail: infotdoran@lamarhq.com
Web Site: www.lamar.com

E-Mail for Key Personnel:
President: kreilly@lamarhq.com

Employees: 3,200
Year Founded: 1902

Revenue: $1,287,060,000

Kevin P. Reilly, Jr. *(Chm & Pres)*
Keith A. Istre *(CFO & Treas)*
Tommy Teepell *(CMO)*
James R. McIlwain *(Gen Counsel & Sec)*
Brent McCoy *(Exec VP)*
John Miller *(VP & Dir-Natl Sls)*
Tammy Duncan *(VP-HR)*
Hal Kilshaw *(VP-Governmental Rels)*
Mike Mons *(VP)*
Robert B. Switzer *(VP-Ops)*
Brian Henry *(Dir-Creative)*
Chris Landry *(Mgr-Digital Mktg)*
Deborah A. Ruiz *(Mgr-Sls & Mktg)*
Shelby Stilwell *(Mgr-Market-SF Bay Reg)*
Melissa York *(Mgr-SW Washington Market)*
Maritza Norton *(Acct Exec-Natl)*

Accounts:
Barstoolsexpress.com

National Center for Disaster Fraud Pro-Bono

Subsidiaries

Lamar Corporation
5551 Corporate Blvd Ste2-A, Baton Rouge, LA 70808-2567
Tel.: (225) 926-1000
Fax: (225) 923-0658
Toll Free: (800) 235-2627
E-Mail: tdoran@lamar.com
Web Site: www.lamar.com

Employees: 130
Year Founded: 1902

Kevin P. Reilly *(Chm & Pres)*
Sean Reilly *(CEO)*
Keith A. Istre *(CFO & Treas)*

Lamar Advertising Company
700 Southlake Blvd, Richmond, VA 23236
Tel.: (804) 794-7000
Fax: (804) 794-1816
Web Site: www.lamar.com

Employees: 27

Agency Specializes In: Outdoor

Steve Southern *(VP & Gen Mgr-Richmond Virginia)*
Mark Sherwood *(VP & Reg Mgr)*
Robert Switzer *(VP-Ops)*
Paul Gartland *(Reg Mgr)*
Byron Montgomery *(Reg Mgr)*
Don Riley *(Reg Mgr)*
Bill Condon *(Territory Mgr)*

LAMBESIS, INC.
1020 Prospect St., La Jolla, CA 92037
Tel.: (858) 255-4800
Fax: (760) 547-2331
E-Mail: info@lambesis.com
Web Site: www.lambesis.com

E-Mail for Key Personnel:
President: cfarmer@lambesis.com
Production Mgr.: mhayes@lambesis.com

Employees: 35
Year Founded: 1987

National Agency Associations: 4A's

Agency Specializes In: Above-the-Line, Advertising, Affluent Market, Alternative Advertising, Automotive, Brand Development & Integration, Branded Entertainment, Broadcast, Cable T.V., Communications, Consulting, Consumer Goods, Consumer Marketing, Consumer Publications, Content, Corporate Identity, Cosmetics, Direct Response Marketing, E-Commerce, Electronic Media, Electronics, Entertainment, Environmental, Fashion/Apparel, Game Integration, Graphic Design, Hospitality, In-Store Advertising, Information Technology, Integrated Marketing, International, Internet/Web Design, Logo & Package Design, Luxury Products, Magazines, Market Research, Media Buying Services, Media Planning, Multimedia, New Product Development, Out-of-Home Media, Outdoor, Package Design, Planning & Consultation, Point of Purchase, Point of Sale, Print, Product Placement, Production, Production (Print), Search Engine Optimization, Sponsorship, Strategic Planning/Research, T.V., Teen Market, Trade & Consumer Magazines

Approx. Annual Billings: $92,000,000

Breakdown of Gross Billings by Media: Cable T.V.: 22%; Consumer Publs.: 50%; Internet Adv.: 12%; Newsp.: 1%; Outdoor: 15%

Nicholas Lambesis *(Founder & Chm)*
Chad Farmer *(Pres & Exec Dir-Creative)*
Vicki Hoekstra *(COO)*
Brian Munce *(Exec Dir-Brand Mgmt)*
Michael Hayes *(Dir-Print Production)*
Oscar Lutteroth *(Dir-Interactive)*
Colin McGuire *(Dir-IT Infrastructure)*
Hicham Badri *(Assoc Creative Dir)*

Accounts:
Anchor Brewing; 2010
The Coca-Cola Company Campaign: "Flavor-Charged Iced Tea", Dasani, Experiential, Fuze, Gold Peak Coffee, Gold Peak Tea, Honest Tea, Out-of-Home, Sprite Green; 2007
Dasani Essence Flavored Bottled Water; 2008
Fisker Automotive, Inc.
Gruppo Campari; 2004
sbe Entertainment Group & SLS Hotels; 2011
Tacori

LANDAU PUBLIC RELATIONS
(Acquired by The Adcom Group)

LANDERS & PARTNERS, INC.
13555 Automobile Blvd Ste 610, Clearwater, FL 33762
Tel.: (727) 572-5228
Fax: (727) 572-5910
E-Mail: info@landersandpartners.com
Web Site: www.landersandpartners.com

Employees: 22
Year Founded: 1977

Agency Specializes In: Advertising, Broadcast, Consumer Marketing, Electronic Media, Media Buying Services, Merchandising, Point of Purchase, Sponsorship

Approx. Annual Billings: $14,994,001

Breakdown of Gross Billings by Media: Brdcst.: $11,613,000; D.M.: $271,500; Graphic Design: $193,875; Newsp.: $1,401,000; Outdoor: $933,000; Point of Sale: $290,813; Print: $290,813

Michelle Darr *(Pres)*
Jenna Pullaro *(Dir-Media Svcs)*
Will Starks *(Dir-Mid-West)*
Joann Chang *(Acct Exec)*
Virginia Ruppert *(Media Planner & Media Buyer)*

Accounts:
KFC; NC; AL; FL; NY; IN
Long John Silver's; NC; FL
Taco Bell; AL; FL; GA; IN; LA; NC; SC; KY; NY; VA; IL; MI; OH

LANDOR ASSOCIATES
1001 Front St, San Francisco, CA 94111
Tel.: (415) 365-1700
Fax: (415) 365-3190
E-Mail: more_info@landor.com
Web Site: www.landor.com

Year Founded: 1941

National Agency Associations: 4A's

Agency Specializes In: Brand Development & Integration, Sponsorship

Suzie Ivelich *(Mng Dir)*
Allen Adamson *(Mng Dir-Brand Dev & Brand Mgmt)*
Deborah Chae Crudo *(Exec Dir)*
Carolyn Ashburn *(Dir-Design)*
Joe Napier *(Dir-Creative)*
Paisley Schade *(Dir-Creative-Verbal Branding)*
Marc Hershon *(Sr Mgr-Naming & Verbal Identity)*

Accounts:
Advanced Ice Cream Technologies Campaign: "Bardot"
Arts Centre Melbourne Campaign: "Box of Curiosities"
Barclays
BP
Broadview Security
The Children's Creativity Museum
Danone China Robust Dairy Products
DC Comics DC Entertainment, DC Reveal
ECOtality Campaign: "Blink Identity & Visual System", Campaign: "Blink"
FedEx
Frito-Lay
Giant Bicycles Campaign: "Everyday Rider Sponsorships"
ITG Campaign: "Decoding Signal from Noise"
Marriott Hotels & Resorts
MillerCoors Brewing Company Campaign: "Miller High Life Red, White & Blue Summer", MGD (Branding Agency of Record), Miller High Life (Branding Agency of Record), Miller Lite (Branding Agency of Record)
PepsiCo
Procter & Gamble Eukanuba, Global Handwashing Day, Old Spice Classic
SKYY Spirits
Texas Instruments

Branches

Landor Associates
Via Tortona 37, Milan, I-20144 Italy
Tel.: (39) 02 7645 171
Fax: (39) 02 7601 2596
E-Mail: landor.italy@landor.com
Web Site: www.landor.com

Agency Specializes In: Brand Development & Integration

Antonio Marazza *(Gen Mgr)*
Michele Genghi *(Dir-Design)*
Francesca Pannuti *(Dir-Client)*
Vittorio Gagliardi *(Designer)*
Jacopo Tripodi *(Sr Designer)*
Elena Lambertucci *(Client Mgr)*

Accounts:
Alfa Romeo
Atkinsons
Azimut Benetti
Banca Primavera
Fiorucci Food
Flair
Kraft Foods Italia
Marazzi Group
Nostromo
Procter & Gamble

Landor Associates
44 rue des Petites Ecuries, Paris, 75010 France
Tel.: (33) 1 53 34 31 00
Fax: (33) 1 53 34 31 01
Web Site: www.landor.com

Agency Specializes In: Brand Development & Integration

Luc Speisser *(Pres & Mng Dir)*
Stephane Dubard *(Exec Dir-Brand Strategy)*
Oriane Tristani *(Exec Dir-Client Svc)*
Anita Lim *(Dir-Client)*
Melissa Weiss *(Assoc Dir-Client)*
Benedicte Avrillon *(Sr Mgr-Client)*
Anne-Sophie Tomas-Gautier *(Sr Mgr-Client)*
Alexandre Vacante *(Coord-Mktg & Comm)*

Accounts:
BE Health Association Campaign: "Health is Contagious"
Danone
Dim
Evian
France Telecom
HomeAway, Inc. Brand Positioning
Iggesund Campaign: "Iggesund Christmas Card"
Pathe
Sociata D'Amanagement De Zenata Campaign: "City of Zenata"
Totem Theory Campaign: "Papermind"
Uniross Hybiro Batteries

Landor Associates
Rue Lugardon 1, CH-1227 Geneva, Switzerland
Tel.: (41) 22 908 40 66
Fax: (41) 22 908 40 67
Web Site: www.landor.com

Agency Specializes In: Brand Development & Integration

Tessa Westermeyer *(Gen Mgr & Exec Dir-Creative)*
Florence Chevallier *(Dir-Client)*
Ella Elliott *(Assoc Dir-Design)*

Landor Associates
Klamath House, 18 Clerkenwell Green, London, EC1R 0QE United Kingdom
Tel.: (44) 207 880 8000
Fax: (44) 207 880 8001
Web Site: www.landor.com

Employees: 120

Agency Specializes In: Brand Development & Integration

James Bruce *(CFO)*
Jane Geraghty *(Pres-Europe, Middle East & Africa)*
Kirsten Foster *(Exec Dir-Corp Brand Strategy)*
Charlotte Morrison *(Exec Dir)*
Michelle Fero *(Dir-Client)*
Naomi Davie *(Sr Mgr-Client)*
Adnan Habis *(Strategist)*
Ross Ducat *(Assoc Strategist)*
Jonathan Millar *(Client Mgr)*
James Nixon *(Sr Client Mgr)*
Emily Ward *(Client Mgr)*

Accounts:
Austrian Airlines
BDO International
BP
British Airways
De Beers
Diageo
Invensys Campaign: "Invensys Typography"
Jet Airways
Kraft
Land Rover
Medi-Clinic Corporation
Molson Coors Campaign: "Re-Launching A National Treasure"
MoneyGram Brand Identity
Paddy Power Brand Visual Identity, Online, Retail & Marketing
UKTV Business-to-Business, Logo, Rebranding, The Nebula

Landor Associates
An der Alster 47, Hamburg, 20099 Germany
Tel.: (49) 40 378 5670
Fax: (49) 378 567 71
E-Mail: ldhp.reception@landor.com
Web Site: www.landor.com

Year Founded: 1997

Agency Specializes In: Brand Development & Integration

Henning Danckwart *(Dir-Fin)*
Tony Lyons *(Dir-Design)*
Philipp Mokrohs *(Dir-Bus & Client Dev)*
Christopher Wynes *(Dir-Creative)*
Luisa Hallmann *(Strategist)*
Alessandro Ielitro *(Strategist-Brand)*
Anouk Sylvestre *(Designer)*
Andreas Gruss *(Sr Client Mgr)*
Michael Kleinert *(Client Dir)*
Ricarda Schoenbeck *(Sr Client Mgr)*

Accounts:
Bonduelle
Bosch
Der Deutsches Reiseburo
Dm Drogeriemarkt Campaign: "Girls Just Wanna Have Fun"
Merck
Mondelez International, Inc.
MTU
Siemens
UNIQA

Landor Associates
233 N Michigan Ave Ste 1400, Chicago, IL 60601
Tel.: (312) 596-1444
Fax: (312) 596-1464
Web Site: www.landor.com

Year Founded: 1991

Agency Specializes In: Brand Development & Integration

Mary Zalla *(Global Pres-Consumer Brands & Mng Dir-Cincinnati & Chicago)*
John Gass *(Gen Mgr)*
Anne Gibble Vaschetto *(Dir-Design)*
Marco Vaschetto *(Sr Mgr-Bus Dev)*
Jenny Johnston *(Mgr-Client)*
Greg Althoff *(Sr Designer)*

Landor Associates
230 Park Ave S 6th Fl, New York, NY 10003
Tel.: (212) 614-5050
Fax: (212) 614-3966
E-Mail: patricia.wootton@atlanda.com
Web Site: www.landor.com

Employees: 100

National Agency Associations: 4A's

Agency Specializes In: Sponsorship

Stuart Sproule *(Pres-North America)*
Allen P. Adamson *(Mng Dir-Brand Dev & Brand Mgmt)*
Marie Minyo *(Exec Dir-Client Svcs)*
Katie Ryan *(Exec Dir)*
Louis Sciullo *(Exec Dir-Fin Svcs)*
Laura Shuler *(Exec Dir-Brand Engagement)*
Mimi Chakravorti *(Sr Dir-Strategy)*
Ashley Rosenbluth *(Sr Dir-Client)*
Lee Arters *(Dir-Creative)*
Jane Boynton *(Dir-Creative)*
Elyse Kazarinoff *(Dir-Creative-Verbal Branding)*
Danielle Prevete *(Dir-Strategy & Employee Engagement)*
Jasmine Tanasy *(Dir-Verbal Branding)*
Mike Boylan *(Assoc Dir-Design)*
Jennaro Villa *(Sr Mgr-Mktg & Bus Dev)*
Allison Bikshorn *(Project Mgr-Bus Dev)*
Margherita Devine *(Mgr-Naming & Verbal Identity)*
Justin Molina *(Mgr-Client)*
Julia Race *(Mgr-Brand Engagement)*

Accounts:
Central Park Conservancy Communication
Delta Airlines
FedEx Office
HomeAway, Inc. Brand Positioning

Landor Associates
110 Shillito Pl, Cincinnati, OH 45202-2361
Tel.: (513) 419-2300
Fax: (513) 221-3532
Web Site: www.landor.com

Employees: 180

National Agency Associations: 4A's

Agency Specializes In: Brand Development & Integration, Sponsorship

Lois Jacobs *(CEO)*
Dale Doyle *(Exec Dir-Creative)*
Noelle Flood *(Exec Dir-Client Svcs)*
Richard Westendorf *(Exec Dir-Creative)*
Karen Floyd *(Dir-Talent Acq & Rewards-Global)*
Rick Shelton *(Dir-Client)*
Katie Cousino *(Sr Mgr-Client)*
Lani Wilson *(Sr Mgr-Tech)*
Tabitha Schadler *(Client Mgr)*

Accounts:
AIGA Campaign: "The World's Smallest Poster"
Mondelez International, Inc. Campaign: "Gevalia"
Procter & Gamble Campaign: "Old Spice Classic"

LANETERRALEVER
(Formerly E.B. Lane)
725 W McDowell Rd, Phoenix, AZ 85007-1727
Tel.: (602) 258-5263
Fax: (602) 257-8128
E-Mail: info@laneterralever.com
Web Site: www.laneterralever.com

Employees: 100
Year Founded: 1962

National Agency Associations: 4A's-MAGNET

Agency Specializes In: Advertising, Affiliate Marketing, Affluent Market, Alternative Advertising, Arts, Automotive, Brand Development & Integration, Broadcast, Business Publications, Business-To-Business, Cable T.V., Co-op Advertising, Collateral, Communications, Consulting, Consumer Goods, Consumer Marketing, Consumer Publications, Content, Corporate Identity, Customer Relationship Management, Digital/Interactive, Direct Response Marketing, Direct-to-Consumer, E-Commerce, Electronic Media, Email, Entertainment, Environmental, Event Planning & Marketing, Exhibit/Trade Shows, Experience Design, Fashion/Apparel, Financial, Food Service, Game Integration, Graphic Design, Guerilla Marketing, Health Care Services, High Technology, Hispanic Market, Hospitality, Household Goods, Identity Marketing, Infomercials, Integrated Marketing, Internet/Web Design, Investor Relations, Leisure, Local Marketing, Logo & Package Design, Luxury Products, Magazines, Media Buying Services, Media Planning, Media Relations, Media Training, Men's Market, Mobile Marketing, Multimedia, New Product Development, New Technologies, Newspaper, Newspapers & Magazines, Out-of-Home Media, Outdoor, Paid Searches, Planning & Consultation, Podcasting, Point of Purchase, Point of Sale, Print, Product Placement, Production, Production (Ad, Film, Broadcast), Production (Print), Promotions, Public Relations, Publicity/Promotions, RSS (Really Simple Syndication), Radio, Real Estate, Recruitment, Regional, Restaurant, Retail, Sales Promotion, Search Engine Optimization, Seniors' Market, Social Marketing/Nonprofit, Sponsorship, Sports

Market, Stakeholders, Strategic Planning/Research, Sweepstakes, T.V., Trade & Consumer Magazines, Travel & Tourism, Viral/Buzz/Word of Mouth, Web (Banner Ads, Pop-ups, etc.)

Approx. Annual Billings: $100,000,000

Richard Skufza *(CFO & Exec VP)*
Todd Bresnahan *(COO)*
Mark Itkowitz *(Sr VP & Exec Dir-Creative)*
Isabelle Jazo *(Sr VP-Brand Strategy)*
Leigh Dow *(VP-PR)*
Jon Lewis *(VP-Content)*
Gil Rodriguez *(VP-Bus Solutions)*
Niki Blaker *(Dir-Art)*
Alison Rose *(Sr Mgr-PR)*
Jessica Wright *(Mgr-PR)*
Megan Breinig *(Coord-PR)*
Brandon Smith *(Coord-PR)*

Accounts:
Arizona Cardinals
Arizona Lottery
Boots USA
Cable ONE; Phoenix, AZ; 2003
CVS Caremark
First Solar
Greater Phoenix Convention & Visitors Bureau
Honeywell Aerospace
Inspirato with American Express
Massage Envy
Muscular Dystrophy Association
National Bank of Arizona
National Multiple Sclerosis Society, Arizona Chapter (Public Relations Agency of Record) Media Relations, Strategic
Pat Tillman Foundation
PayScan
Phoenix Convention Center
Sports & Orthopedic Specialist
SunCor Development
Time Warner Cable
Wal-Mart
Xanterra Parks & Resorts

Branches

LaneTerralever
(Formerly E.B. Lane Denver)
999 18th St, Denver, CO 80202
Tel.: (303) 296-4100
E-Mail: info@laneterralever.com
Web Site: www.laneterralever.com/

E-Mail for Key Personnel:
Production Mgr.: CRhodes@laneterralever.com

Employees: 5
Year Founded: 2011

National Agency Associations: 4A's-AAF-MAGNET

Agency Specializes In: Business-To-Business, Consumer Marketing

Chris Rhodes *(Mgr-Denver Ops)*

Accounts:
Colorado Succeeds; 2011
Inspirato LLC; 2013

LANGDON FLYNN COMMUNICATIONS
(Acquired by Allied Integrated Marketing)

LANMARK360
(Formerly The Lanmark Group Inc.)
804 Broadway, West Long Branch, NJ 07764
Tel.: (732) 389-4500
Fax: (732) 389-4998
Web Site: www.lanmark360.com/

Employees: 40
Year Founded: 1977

National Agency Associations: ADC-NJ Ad Club

Agency Specializes In: Advertising, Advertising Specialties, Brand Development & Integration, Business Publications, Business-To-Business, Catalogs, Communications, Consulting, Corporate Communications, Corporate Identity, Crisis Communications, Digital/Interactive, Direct Response Marketing, E-Commerce, Education, Electronic Media, Event Planning & Marketing, Exhibit/Trade Shows, Graphic Design, Health Care Services, Integrated Marketing, Internet/Web Design, Local Marketing, Logo & Package Design, Market Research, Media Buying Services, Media Planning, Media Relations, Media Training, Medical Products, Multimedia, New Product Development, New Technologies, Package Design, Pharmaceutical, Planning & Consultation, Podcasting, Point of Purchase, Print, Promotions, Public Relations, Publicity/Promotions, Sales Promotion, Search Engine Optimization, Strategic Planning/Research, Technical Advertising, Telemarketing, Trade & Consumer Magazines, Viral/Buzz/Word of Mouth, Web (Banner Ads, Pop-ups, etc.)

Breakdown of Gross Billings by Media: Adv. Specialities: 3%; Collateral: 8%; Consulting: 10%; Corp. Communications: 5%; Graphic Design: 10%; In-Store Adv.: 5%; Logo & Package Design: 3%; Print: 20%; Production: 3%; Strategic Planning/Research: 13%; Trade & Consumer Mags.: 15%; Trade Shows: 5%

Howard Klein *(Owner & Pres)*
Michael McCarthy *(Chief Strategy Officer & Mng Partner)*
Kurt Algayer *(VP-Production Svcs)*
Danielle Avalone *(VP-Acct Svcs)*
Ed Yasser *(VP-Digital)*
Andrew Saklas *(Dir-Creative)*
Judy Adelman *(Mgr-Media)*

Accounts:
Conair Corporation; Stamford, CT Interplak; 1994
Darby Corporate Solutions; Boston, MA
Darby Dental
Darby Group Companies; Westbury, NY
Dental Trade Alliance
Johnson & Johnson
Novartis Pharmaceuticals; East Hanover, NJ
OraPharma; Warminster, PA Arrestin; 2002
Sirona; Charlotte, NC Erec, Inlab; 1992
Windmill Restaurant
Wrigley
Young Dental; Chicago, IL
Zenith Dental; Englewood, NJ

LANZA GROUP LLC
1710 DeFoor Ave Ph 2, Atlanta, GA 30318
Tel.: (404) 350-0200
Fax: (404) 350-0231
E-Mail: info@lanzagroup.com
Web Site: www.lanzagroup.com

E-Mail for Key Personnel:
Creative Dir.: asamayoa@lanzagroup.com

Employees: 10
Year Founded: 2002

Agency Specializes In: Advertising, Bilingual Market, Broadcast, Event Planning & Marketing, Government/Political, Hispanic Market, Media Planning, Print, Public Relations, Publicity/Promotions, Radio, Social Media, Sponsorship, T.V.

Breakdown of Gross Billings by Media: Consulting: 25%; Event Mktg.: 15%; Pub. Rels.: 35%; Radio & T.V.: 25%

Vanessa Segura *(Coord-Comm)*

Accounts:
AGL
Atlanta Beat
Banco Agricola Bank Remittance Service; 2005
Chick-fil-A; Atlanta, GA Public Relations; 2008
Coca-Cola Refreshments USA, Inc.; Atlanta, GA Activations & Events; 2009
CowParade Atlanta
Girl Scout Council of NW Georgia; Atlanta, GA
Latin American Association; Atlanta, GA
Pilgrims Pride Corporation of Georgia, Inc.
Sharon McSwain Homes
Underground Atlanta
Verizon Wireless
Wade Ford
World of Coca-Cola; Atlanta, GA

LAPIERRES ADVERTISING INC.
1500 Mohawk Trl, Shelburne Falls, MA 01370
Tel.: (413) 625-9279
Web Site: www.lapierre.com

Agency Specializes In: Advertising, Graphic Design, Internet/Web Design, Logo & Package Design, Magazines, Radio, Social Media, T.V.

Rick LaPierre *(Founder & Partner)*
Joan LaPierre *(Co-Owner & Graphic Designer)*

Accounts:
Lessig Oil & Propane
Santarelli & Sons Oil

LAPLACA COHEN
43 W 24th St Tenth Fl, New York, NY 10010-3205
Tel.: (212) 675-4106
Fax: (212) 675-4763
E-Mail: info@laplacacohen.com
Web Site: www.laplacacohen.com

Employees: 25
Year Founded: 1993

Agency Specializes In: Faith Based, Leisure

Approx. Annual Billings: $15,000,000

Breakdown of Gross Billings by Media: Brdcst.: 10%; Newsp. & Mags.: 85%; Outdoor: 3%; Transit: 2%

Aggie Williams *(Dir-Fin & Ops & Controller)*
Maggie Hartnick *(Sr Dir-Strategy & Branding)*
Hannah Speirits *(Acct Mgr)*
Natasha Hernandez *(Mgr-Acctg)*
Allison Jones *(Strategist)*
Hil Moss *(Strategist)*
Taulant Bushi *(Designer)*
Joel P. Johnson *(Sr Designer)*

Accounts:
Copia
Hillwood Museum & Garden
Philadelphia Museum of Art; Philadelphia, PA; 1995

LARA & COMPANY
1317 Montana Ave, El Paso, TX 79902-5530
Tel.: (915) 544-9800
Fax: (915) 544-9200
E-Mail: ric.lara@lrcreative.com
Web Site: www.lrcreative.com

Employees: 7
Year Founded: 1989

Agency Specializes In: Advertising, Automotive, Aviation & Aerospace, Bilingual Market, Brand

Development & Integration, Broadcast, Business Publications, Business-To-Business, Co-op Advertising, Collateral, Commercial Photography, Communications, Consumer Marketing, Corporate Identity, Event Planning & Marketing, Exhibit/Trade Shows, Fashion/Apparel, Graphic Design, Health Care Services, Hispanic Market, Logo & Package Design, Newspapers & Magazines, Outdoor, Point of Purchase, Point of Sale, Public Relations, Publicity/Promotions, Radio, Real Estate, Seniors' Market, Sponsorship, Strategic Planning/Research, Transportation

Approx. Annual Billings: $800,000

Breakdown of Gross Billings by Media: Collateral: 25%; Print: 25%; Radio: 25%; T.V.: 25%

Richard Lara *(Owner)*

LARS & ASSOCIATES, INC.

322 Greenpond Rd, Hibernia, NJ 07842
Tel.: (973) 625-2225
Fax: (973) 625-5025
E-Mail: lou@larsnj.com
Web Site: www.larsnj.com

Employees: 5
Year Founded: 1964

Agency Specializes In: Collateral, Graphic Design, Logo & Package Design, Newspaper, Pharmaceutical, Point of Purchase, Point of Sale, Sales Promotion

Louis S. Sceusi *(Owner)*

Accounts:
B&G Foods, Inc.; Parsippany, NJ
LaFe Foods, Inc. Ethnic Food Products
Mobile Vision; Boonton, NJ
Valio International Finlandia Swiss Cheese & McCadam Cheddar Cheese

LARSEN

7101 York Ave S Ste 120, Minneapolis, MN 55435
Tel.: (952) 835-2271
Fax: (952) 921-3368
E-Mail: info@larsen.com
Web Site: www.larsen.com

Employees: 50

Agency Specializes In: Brand Development & Integration, Collateral, Digital/Interactive, Identity Marketing, Internet/Web Design, Print

Approx. Annual Billings: $8,400,000

Tim Larsen *(Founder & Pres)*
John Barta *(CFO & VP-Fin)*
Jo Davison *(Sr VP-Creative)*
Reid Durbin *(VP-Digital)*
Paul Wharton *(VP-Creative)*
Laura Bates *(Acct Svcs Dir)*
Vicki Homuth *(Acct Dir)*
Peter De Sibour *(Dir-Design)*
Todd Nesser *(Dir-Design)*

Accounts:
Adobe Systems
Alebra Technologies
Ampers
Andersen Corporation
ATMI
Audibel
Banner Engineering
Best Buy
Guthrie Theater
MTS Systems
Target Corporation
US Bancorp
Wells Fargo Foothill

Branch

Larsen

95 El Camino Real, Menlo Park, CA 94025
Tel.: (650) 233-7777
Fax: (650) 233-7770
Web Site: www.larsen.com

Employees: 15
Year Founded: 1998

Tim Larsen *(Founder & Pres)*
Jim Madson *(Dir-Bus Dev)*

Accounts:
Charles Web Schwab

LARSON O'BRIEN MARKETING GROUP

3591 Ridgeway Dr Ste 200, Bethel Park, PA 15102
Tel.: (412) 831-1959
Fax: (412) 833-2838
E-Mail: info@larsonobrien.com
Web Site: www.larsonobrien.com

E-Mail for Key Personnel:
President: jack@larsonobrien.com
Production Mgr.: jeff@larsonobrien.com

Employees: 20
Year Founded: 2001

National Agency Associations: Second Wind Limited

Agency Specializes In: Business-To-Business, Corporate Identity, Digital/Interactive, Print, Public Relations, Publicity/Promotions, Sales Promotion

Approx. Annual Billings: $8,500,000 Fees Capitalized

Jack O'Brien *(Chm & Pres)*
Ronald Larson *(CEO & Dir-Art)*
Garrett Andrae *(Principal & Dir-Creative)*
Jeff Miskis *(Dir-Interactive Svcs)*
Nick Murosky *(Dir-PR)*
Julie Pintar *(Dir-Res & Media)*
Jeff Gray *(Mgr-Production & Media)*
Melinda Maloney *(Acct Exec-PR & Adv)*
Dan Tambellini *(Acct Exec-PR)*

Accounts:
American Hydrotech, Inc. Marketing Communications
Banker Wire PR
Birdair, Inc.; 2007
Butler County Community College; Butler, PA; 1998
Cambridge Architectural
Fabric Structures Association
Follansbee Steel; Follansbee, VA
Greenscan; Los Angeles, CA; 2009
H.B. Fuller Construction Products Inc; Aurora, IL PR, TEC Brand
Hope's PR, Planning & Execution, Strategic Marketing
Hufcor, Inc. PR
LITECONTROL
Nichiha USA
PVSEC
Ronstan
Viracon Marketing Communications
Zurn Industries PR

LASER ADVERTISING

1500 Cordova Rd Ste 205, Fort Lauderdale, FL 33316
Tel.: (954) 760-4667
Fax: (954) 760-7049
Web Site: www.laseradvertising.com

Agency Specializes In: Advertising, Content, Internet/Web Design, Print, Search Engine Optimization

Charles Datlen *(Owner)*

Accounts:
Dona Lola
Luke Brown Yachts
Outer Reef Yachts

LASPATA DECARO

450 W 15th St Ste 600, New York, NY 10011
Tel.: (212) 929-1998
Fax: (212) 243-5305
E-Mail: info@laspatadecaro.com
Web Site: www.laspatadecaro.com

Employees: 15

Agency Specializes In: Advertising

Charles DeCaro *(Co-Owner)*
Rocco Laspata *(Co-Owner)*
Anne Erickson *(Dir-Media & Creative Svcs)*
Yasmeen Jacobs *(Office Mgr)*
Linda Crawford *(Mgr-Media & Creative Svcs)*
William Crompton *(Mgr-Media & Creative Svcs)*

Accounts:
Americana Legend
Americana Manhasset
Perry Ellis; 2007
Ulta

LATCHA+ASSOCIATES

24600 Hallwood Ct, Farmington Hills, MI 48335-1603
Tel.: (248) 482-4500
Fax: (248) 482-4624
E-Mail: dave@latcha.com
Web Site: www.latcha.com

Employees: 105
Year Founded: 1998

Agency Specializes In: Advertising, Automotive, Aviation & Aerospace, Broadcast, Collateral, Communications, Consumer Marketing, Digital/Interactive, Direct Response Marketing, Fashion/Apparel, Graphic Design, Internet/Web Design, Marine, Multimedia, Pharmaceutical, Point of Purchase, Print, Retail, Technical Advertising, Transportation

Approx. Annual Billings: $18,000,000

Breakdown of Gross Billings by Media: E-Commerce: 20%; Print: 70%; Video Brochures: 10%

David Latcha *(Founder & Owner)*
Lisa Chapman *(Pres)*
Jill Davis *(Head-Production)*
Steve Janik *(Dir-Art)*
Annemarie Mccallum *(Acct Mgr)*
Vanessa Tirb *(Acct Mgr)*
Corey Smith *(Project Mgr-Digital)*
Kyle Lindenboom *(Grp Acct Supvr-Audi Acct Strategy)*

Accounts:
Cars.com
Ford Division; Dearborn, MI Ford Cars, Trucks, & SUVs; 2000
Ford Fleet USA; Dearborn, MI; 2003
Ford International; Allen Park, MI Ford, Lincoln, Mercury Cars, Trucks, & SUVs Worldwide; 2002
Lincoln Mercury; Dearborn, MI Lincoln Cars, SUVs,

Mercury Cars, SUVs; 2003
Riverfront Condominiums & Apartments
Swartzmiller Associates

LATIN FUSION GROUP

16520 Harbor Blvd, Fountain Valley, CA 92708
Tel.: (714) 540-8886
Fax: (714) 540-4726
E-Mail: rog@latinfusiongroup.com

Employees: 15
Year Founded: 1990

National Agency Associations: AHAA

Agency Specializes In: Advertising, Advertising Specialties, Bilingual Market, Business-To-Business, Cable T.V., Children's Market, Consumer Marketing, Event Planning & Marketing, Guerilla Marketing, Hispanic Market, Identity Marketing, In-Store Advertising, Infomercials, Integrated Marketing, Logo & Package Design, Media Buying Services, Media Planning, Media Relations, Merchandising, Mobile Marketing, Multicultural, Outdoor, Package Design, Planning & Consultation, Point of Sale, Print, Production, Promotions, Public Relations, Publicity/Promotions, Publishing, Radio, Retail, Sales Promotion, Sponsorship, Sports Market, Strategic Planning/Research, T.V., Teen Market, Urban Market, Women's Market

Approx. Annual Billings: $1,000,000

Rafael Oscal *(VP & Dir-Sls & Mktg)*
Carol Oscal *(VP)*

Accounts:
Crush Soda; Los Angeles, CA; 2008
Gerber Branding; 2000
Pepsi; CA; 2005
S&W Beans; Minneapolis, MN; 2000
Sports Authority Soccer; 2010
Toys for Soccer Foundation

LATIN WORLD ENTERTAINMENT AGENCY

3470 NW 82nd Ave Ste 670, Doral, FL 33122
Tel.: (305) 572-1515
Fax: (305) 572-1510
E-Mail: moreinfo@latinwe.com
Web Site: www.latinwe.com

Employees: 10

Luis Balaguer *(Founder & CEO)*
Sacha Suarez *(Exec VP-Mktg & Endorsements)*
Rebecca Villaescusa *(Exec VP)*
Melissa Gelineau *(VP-Television & Dev)*
Kenchy Ragsdale *(VP-Dev)*
Camila Suarez *(VP-Branded Entertainment-Celebrity Endorsements)*
Melissa Escobar *(Head-Film, TV & Digital Dev-US, US Hispanic & Latin America)*
Valerie Boldrin *(Dir-PR & Client Publicity)*
Keegan Killian *(Brand Mgr & Strategist-Social Media-Sofia Vergara)*

Accounts:
CNET Website Creation
Colgate
General Mills
Pepsi

LATIN3 INC.

6400 N Andrews Ave Ste 490, Fort Lauderdale, FL 33309
Tel.: (954) 893-7305
Fax: (954) 893-7307
E-Mail: info@latin3.com
Web Site: www.latin3.com

Agency Specializes In: Sponsorship

Matias Perel *(Founder & CEO)*
Diego Rubio *(Gen Dir-Creative)*
Adrian Garcia *(Client Svcs Dir)*
Natalia Saibene *(Mgr-Ops)*

Accounts:
General Mills, Inc.
Panasonic System Communications Company (Latin America Agency of Record) B2B, Content Development, Creative, Digital Marketing, Media Buying, Media Planning, Social Media, Strategy, Toughbook, Toughpad, Website
Pepsi
Reebok
Sony
Wachovia

LATINA CREATIVE AGENCY

720 Market St Ste H, Kirkland, WA 98033
Tel.: (425) 968-8013
E-Mail: info@latinacreativeagency.com
Web Site: www.latinacreativeagency.com

Agency Specializes In: Advertising, Brand Development & Integration, Digital/Interactive, Event Planning & Marketing, Media Planning, Media Relations, Media Training, Social Media

Cynarah Ellawala *(Co-Founder & Principal)*

Accounts:
Dustin Tavella
Latino Community Fund

LATINOLANDIA USA

17595 Harvard Ave Ste C5000, Irvine, CA 92614
Fax: (949) 502-8855
Toll Free: (800) 250-7780
E-Mail: info@latinolandia.com
Web Site: www.latinolandia.com

Employees: 10
Year Founded: 2009

Agency Specializes In: Advertising, Affluent Market, African-American Market, Automotive, Aviation & Aerospace, Bilingual Market, Brand Development & Integration, Branded Entertainment, Broadcast, Business-To-Business, Cable T.V., Children's Market, Co-op Advertising, Collateral, College, Communications, Computers & Software, Consulting, Consumer Goods, Consumer Marketing, Consumer Publications, Corporate Identity, Customer Relationship Management, Digital/Interactive, Direct Response Marketing, Direct-to-Consumer, E-Commerce, Education, Electronic Media, Electronics, Email, Entertainment, Environmental, Event Planning & Marketing, Exhibit/Trade Shows, Experience Design, Financial, Food Service, Government/Political, Graphic Design, Guerilla Marketing, Health Care Services, High Technology, Hispanic Market, Hospitality, Household Goods, Identity Marketing, In-Store Advertising, Infomercials, Information Technology, Integrated Marketing, International, Internet/Web Design, Leisure, Local Marketing, Logo & Package Design, Luxury Products, Magazines, Market Research, Media Buying Services, Media Planning, Media Relations, Medical Products, Multicultural, Multimedia, New Product Development, New Technologies, Newspaper, Newspapers & Magazines, Out-of-Home Media, Outdoor, Package Design, Pharmaceutical, Planning & Consultation, Podcasting, Point of Purchase, Point of Sale, Print, Production, Production (Print), Promotions, Public Relations, Publicity/Promotions, Radio, Real Estate, Regional, Restaurant, Retail, Sales Promotion, Search Engine Optimization, Seniors' Market, Social Marketing/Nonprofit, Social Media, Sponsorship, Sports Market, Strategic Planning/Research, T.V., Teen Market, Telemarketing, Trade & Consumer Magazines, Transportation, Travel & Tourism, Urban Market, Viral/Buzz/Word of Mouth

Approx. Annual Billings: $5,000,000

Breakdown of Gross Billings by Media: Brdcst.: 15%; Comml. Photography: 3%; Consulting: 10%; Consumer Publs.: 3%; D.M.: 10%; Event Mktg.: 5%; Exhibits/Trade Shows: 2%; Fees: 5%; Internet Adv.: 10%; Logo & Package Design: 5%; Out-of-Home Media: 10%; Trade & Consumer Mags.: 2%; Worldwide Web Sites: 20%

Alan Torreano *(Exec VP & Dir-Creative)*

Accounts:
Angels Baseball, LP; Anaheim, CA Major League Baseball; 2003
Artimex Bakery; Santa Fe Springs, CA Gourmet & Mexican Baked Goods; 2009
Damafro, Inc.; Montreal; 2009
Del Taco LLC; Lake Forest, CA Mexican Fast Service Restaurants; 2005
Downey Nissan; Downey, CA; 2009
El Gallo Giro; Downey, CA Traditional Mexican Food; 2009
Essential Healthcare Management; Los Angeles, CA & Dallas, TX Healthcare Industry Consulting; 2009
Interdeli SAPI de CV; Mexico Cheese, Hummus; 2009
Maria Elena's Authentic Latino Inc.; Santa Clarita, CA Maria Elena's Certified Organic Drink Mixes
Markzware, Inc.; Santa Ana, CA Graphics, Publishing Software
Nong Shim America, Inc; Seoul, Korea; Rancho Cucamonga, CA Bowl Noodle Instant Soup, Shin Ramyun Noodles
Oncars.com; Aliso Viejo, CA Automotive Information, Product Reviews
Optamis; Lake Forest, CA Financial Services, Insurance
Triomphe Design; Costa Mesa, CA Commercial Interior Design; 2007

LATINWORKS MARKETING, INC.

2500 Bee Caves Rd, Austin, TX 78746
Tel.: (512) 479-6200
Fax: (512) 479-6024
Web Site: www.latinworks.com

Employees: 150
Year Founded: 1998

Agency Specializes In: Above-the-Line, Advertising, Advertising Specialties, Affluent Market, African-American Market, Alternative Advertising, Automotive, Below-the-Line, Bilingual Market, Brand Development & Integration, Branded Entertainment, Broadcast, Cable T.V., Children's Market, Collateral, College, Communications, Consulting, Consumer Goods, Consumer Marketing, Consumer Publications, Content, Digital/Interactive, Direct-to-Consumer, Electronic Media, Email, Entertainment, Experience Design, Financial, Food Service, Gay & Lesbian Market, Government/Political, Graphic Design, Guerilla Marketing, Hispanic Market, Household Goods, Identity Marketing, In-Store Advertising, Integrated Marketing, International, Internet/Web Design, Local Marketing, Logo & Package Design, Magazines, Market Research, Media Buying Services, Media Planning, Men's Market, Mobile Marketing, Multicultural, Multimedia, Newspaper, Out-of-Home Media, Outdoor, Over-50 Market, Paid Searches, Pets , Pharmaceutical, Planning & Consultation, Point of Purchase, Point of Sale, Print, Production, Production (Ad, Film, Broadcast), Production (Print), Promotions, Radio, Regional,

Retail, Sales Promotion, Search Engine Optimization, Seniors' Market, Shopper Marketing, Social Marketing/Nonprofit, Social Media, Sponsorship, Sports Market, Strategic Planning/Research, Sweepstakes, Syndication, T.V., Teen Market, Trade & Consumer Magazines, Travel & Tourism, Tween Market, Urban Market, Viral/Buzz/Word of Mouth, Web (Banner Ads, Pop-ups, etc.), Women's Market

Approx. Annual Billings: $116,000,000

Alejandro Ruelas *(Co-Founder, Mng Partner & CMO)*
Manny Flores *(CEO)*
Scott Radigk *(Sr VP-Fin Ops)*
Marcelo Perrone *(VP-Strategic Plng)*
Melissa Trepinski *(Exec Dir-Bus Dev)*
Chloe King *(Grp Dir-Media Buying)*
del Mar Clark *(Grp Acct Dir)*
Jaime Gonzales-Mir *(Grp Acct Dir)*
Jaime Clausen *(Dir-Media)*
Justin Smith *(Supvr-Bus Dev)*

Accounts:
Anheuser-Busch Inbev Bud Light, Montejo Mexican Beer, Vuvuchela; 2004
New-Capital One; 2013
Domino's; 2005
New-Jack Daniel's; 2013
Kimberly-Clark Corp. Advertising, Digital, Huggies, Kleenex, Pull-Ups; 2007
Lowe's; 2003
New-Major League Baseball; 2014
New-Marriott; 2014
Mars Inc Cesar, Dove, M&M's, Pedigree, Snickers, Starburst, Twix; 2007
Pepsico Aquafina, Frappucino, Manzanita, Mountain Dew, Pepsi, Sierra Mist, Sol, Starbucks; 2011
New-Stripes Laredo Taco Company, Stripes; 2012
Target Broadcast, Campaign: "Arrullo", Campaign: "Sin Traduccion", Campaign: "Sobremesa", Digital Advertising, Experiential, Hispanic Marketing, Print, Radio, TV, Up & Up; 2013
Texas Lottery Instant Scratch-Off, Mega Millions, Powerball; 2008
Wrigley Jr. Company Skittles, Starbursts; 2010

LATORRA, PAUL & MCCANN

120 E Washington St, Syracuse, NY 13202-4000
Tel.: (315) 476-1646
Fax: (315) 476-1611
E-Mail: lpm@lpm-adv.com
Web Site: www.lpm-adv.com

Employees: 40
Year Founded: 1993

National Agency Associations: NAMA-PRSA

Agency Specializes In: Advertising, Advertising Specialties, Agriculture, Brand Development & Integration, Broadcast, Business Publications, Business-To-Business, Cable T.V., Co-op Advertising, Collateral, Communications, Consumer Marketing, Corporate Identity, Direct Response Marketing, Electronic Media, Event Planning & Marketing, Exhibit/Trade Shows, Financial, Graphic Design, Hispanic Market, Industrial, Internet/Web Design, Leisure, Logo & Package Design, Magazines, Media Buying Services, Medical Products, New Product Development, Newspaper, Newspapers & Magazines, Out-of-Home Media, Pets , Pharmaceutical, Planning & Consultation, Point of Purchase, Point of Sale, Print, Production, Public Relations, Publicity/Promotions, Radio, Sales Promotion, Strategic Planning/Research, T.V., Technical Advertising, Trade & Consumer Magazines, Travel & Tourism

Michael Ancillotti *(Pres & CEO)*
Bill Patrick *(VP-Ops & Fin)*
Mark Anderson *(Dir-Media)*
Andy Collins *(Dir-Creative)*
Kimberly Parr *(Dir-PR)*
Barbara Straight *(Sr Mgr-Production)*

Accounts:
American Dairy Association-New York State
Carrier Corporation; Syracuse, NY Room Air Conditioners
Carrier Duct Free Systems; Syracuse, NY; 1998
Dairy One; Ithaca, NY; 2002
Hoard's Dairyman; Fort Atkinson, WI Dairy Industry Magazine; 1999
Nationwide Insurance (N.Y.); Columbus, OH Personal & Commercial Insurance; 1999
Nationwide Insurance (New York State); Syracuse, NY; 1999
St. Bonaventure University

LATREILLE ADVERTISING & TALENT INC

1421 N Leroy St, Fenton, MI 48430
Tel.: (810) 714-4224
Web Site: www.latreilles.com

Agency Specializes In: Advertising, Media Buying Services, Print, Radio, T.V.

Bill Latreille *(Pres)*
Jeremy Chaney *(Dir-Creative & Mgr-Production)*
William Latreille III *(Acct Mgr & Coord-Traffic)*

Accounts:
Dave Lamb Heating & Cooling
Fenton Hotel
Grand Blanc Mercedes-Benz
Grand Blanc Motorcars
Hodges Subaru
Lane Car Company
Panda Water Ice
River Rock Grill
Shane Adams
Sterling Heights Dodge, Inc.

LATTIMER COMMUNICATIONS

934 Glenwood Ave Ste 260, Atlanta, GA 30316
Tel.: (404) 526-9321
Fax: (404) 526-9324
Web Site: www.lattimercommunications.com

Employees: 10
Year Founded: 1998

National Agency Associations: 4A's

Agency Specializes In: African-American Market, Hispanic Market

Revenue: $5,000,000

Sarah Sanders Lattimer *(Pres)*
Gail Warren *(Dir-Media)*
Maya Fizer *(Acct Coord)*

Accounts:
American Cancer Society
Atlanta History Center
Centene Corporation
Dallas Austin Foundation
Dekalb Hospital Hillandale
The Georgia Department of Labor
Georgia Power
Hoop City
John Wieland Homes & Neighborhoods
Marta
Morehouse College
Robert W. Woodruff Library
Southern Co.
SunTrust Bank

LAUGHING SAMURAI

1221-C N Orange Ave, Orlando, FL 32804
Tel.: (407) 982-4350
E-Mail: calvin@laughingsamurai.com
Web Site: www.laughingsamurai.com

Employees: 25

Agency Specializes In: Advertising, Advertising Specialties, Alternative Advertising, Bilingual Market, Brand Development & Integration, Co-op Advertising, Collateral, Consumer Marketing, Direct Response Marketing, Graphic Design, Guerilla Marketing, Identity Marketing, Internet/Web Design, Local Marketing, Logo & Package Design, Market Research, Package Design, Public Relations, Publicity/Promotions, Search Engine Optimization, Social Marketing/Nonprofit, Social Media, Strategic Planning/Research, Web (Banner Ads, Pop-ups, etc.)

Ben Collins *(Co-Founder & Pres)*

Accounts:
Microsoft; New York, NY Marketing, Package Design

LAUGHLIN/CONSTABLE, INC.

207 E Michigan St, Milwaukee, WI 53202-4998
Tel.: (414) 272-2400
Fax: (414) 270-7140
Web Site: www.laughlin.com

Employees: 155
Year Founded: 1976

National Agency Associations: 4A's-AMA-BMA-PRSA

Agency Specializes In: Advertising, Affluent Market, Alternative Advertising, Brand Development & Integration, Branded Entertainment, Broadcast, Business Publications, Business-To-Business, Cable T.V., Catalogs, Children's Market, Co-op Advertising, Collateral, Communications, Consumer Goods, Consumer Marketing, Content, Corporate Communications, Corporate Identity, Cosmetics, Crisis Communications, Customer Relationship Management, Digital/Interactive, Direct Response Marketing, Direct-to-Consumer, E-Commerce, Electronic Media, Email, Entertainment, Experience Design, Fashion/Apparel, Financial, Food Service, Game Integration, Graphic Design, Guerilla Marketing, Health Care Services, Hispanic Market, Hospitality, Household Goods, In-Store Advertising, Information Technology, Integrated Marketing, Internet/Web Design, Leisure, Local Marketing, Logo & Package Design, Luxury Products, Magazines, Market Research, Media Buying Services, Media Planning, Media Relations, Medical Products, Men's Market, Merchandising, Mobile Marketing, Multicultural, Multimedia, New Product Development, Newspaper, Newspapers & Magazines, Out-of-Home Media, Outdoor, Over-50 Market, Package Design, Planning & Consultation, Point of Purchase, Point of Sale, Print, Production, Production (Ad, Film, Broadcast), Promotions, Public Relations, Publicity/Promotions, Publishing, Radio, Regional, Restaurant, Retail, Sales Promotion, Search Engine Optimization, Seniors' Market, Social Marketing/Nonprofit, Sponsorship, Strategic Planning/Research, T.V., Teen Market, Trade & Consumer Magazines, Transportation, Travel & Tourism, Viral/Buzz/Word of Mouth, Web (Banner Ads, Pop-ups, etc.), Yellow Pages Advertising

Approx. Annual Billings: $220,000,000

Michael Jeary *(Pres)*
Mat Lignel *(CEO)*
Michael Baer *(CMO)*
Rich Kohnke *(Chief Creative Officer)*

Paul Brienza *(Exec VP-Digital)*
Renee Haber *(Exec VP-Acct Svcs)*
Brenna Kriviskey Sadler *(Exec VP-PR)*
Mark Carlson *(Sr VP & Dir-Brand Strategies)*
Patrick McSweeney *(VP-PR)*
Ryan Spiering *(Sr Dir-Digital Art)*
Leah Olinyk *(Acct Supvr)*
Julie Huenemann *(Grp Supvr)*

Accounts:
Associated Bank; Milwaukee, WI; 2002
Aurora Healthcare; Milwaukee, WI Saint Luke's Hospital; 2005
Beaufort Memorial Hospital; Beaufort, SC 197 Bed Hospital; 2005
Bon-Ton Department Stores; York, PA Bergner's, Bon-Ton, Boston Store, Carson Pirie Scott, Elder-Beerman, Herberger, Younker's; 1992
Bridgestone/Firestone MasterCare Car Service Auto Service, Tire Retailing; 1997
New-Bright Start/Oppenheimer Funds
Connecture, Inc. IT Service for Processing Health Plans; 2004
CUNA
Delnor Hospital; Geneva, IL 128 Bed Hospital; 2001
Empire Today
Etire
Firestone
New-Food Network
HPCtv; Milwaukee, WI Digital Cable, Real Estate Listings, TV Network Broadcasting; 2005
International Engine Group; Chicago, IL
Master Lock Padlocks; 2004
McDonald's Corporation
Medela (Creative Agency of Record); Chicago, IL Nursing Mothers' Products; 2007
New-MillerCoors
Navistar International Truck Engine; 2005
New-Northwestern Medicine
New-Palermo Villa
Paris Presents Incorporated (Advertising & Digital Marketing Agency of Record) Social Media
New-PDC Brands
Promega; 2006
Salon Selectives; Chicago, IL
New-Sears Holdings
Topper's Pizza; Whitewater, WI Pizza Stores; 2007
UIMCC
ULTA
New-USA Network
Wisconsin Department of Tourism (Agency of Record) Campaign: "Airplane!", Marketing

Branches

Laughlin/Constable, Inc.

200 S Michigan Ave, Chicago, IL 60604
Tel.: (312) 422-5900
Fax: (312) 422-5901
Web Site: www.laughlin.com

Employees: 120
Year Founded: 1997

National Agency Associations: 4A's

Agency Specializes In: Above-the-Line, Advertising, Advertising Specialties, Affiliate Marketing, Affluent Market, Alternative Advertising, Arts, Brand Development & Integration, Branded Entertainment, Broadcast, Business Publications, Business-To-Business, Cable T.V., Catalogs, Children's Market, Co-op Advertising, Collateral, College, Commercial Photography, Communications, Computers & Software, Consulting, Consumer Goods, Consumer Marketing, Consumer Publications, Content, Corporate Communications, Corporate Identity, Cosmetics, Crisis Communications, Custom Publishing, Customer Relationship Management, Digital/Interactive, Direct Response Marketing, Direct-to-Consumer, E-Commerce, Education, Electronic Media, Electronics, Email, Engineering, Entertainment, Environmental, Event Planning & Marketing, Exhibit/Trade Shows, Experience Design, Fashion/Apparel, Financial, Food Service, Game Integration, Government/Political, Graphic Design, Guerilla Marketing, Health Care Services, High Technology, Hispanic Market, Hospitality, Household Goods, Identity Marketing, In-Store Advertising, Industrial, Infomercials, Information Technology, Integrated Marketing, International, Internet/Web Design, Investor Relations, Legal Services, Leisure, Local Marketing, Logo & Package Design, Luxury Products, Magazines, Marine, Market Research, Media Buying Services, Media Planning, Media Relations, Media Training, Medical Products, Men's Market, Merchandising, Mobile Marketing, Multicultural, Multimedia, New Product Development, New Technologies, Newspaper, Newspapers & Magazines, Out-of-Home Media, Outdoor, Over-50 Market, Package Design, Paid Searches, Pharmaceutical, Planning & Consultation, Podcasting, Point of Purchase, Point of Sale, Print, Product Placement, Production, Production (Ad, Film, Broadcast), Production (Print), Promotions, Public Relations, Publicity/Promotions, Publishing, RSS (Really Simple Syndication), Radio, Real Estate, Recruitment, Regional, Restaurant, Retail, Sales Promotion, Search Engine Optimization, Seniors' Market, Social Marketing/Nonprofit, Sponsorship, Sports Market, Stakeholders, Strategic Planning/Research, Sweepstakes, Syndication, T.V., Technical Advertising, Teen Market, Telemarketing, Trade & Consumer Magazines, Transportation, Travel & Tourism, Urban Market, Viral/Buzz/Word of Mouth, Web (Banner Ads, Pop-ups, etc.), Women's Market, Yellow Pages Advertising

Mat Lignel *(CEO)*
Paul Brienza *(Exec VP-Digital)*
Renee Haber *(Exec VP-Acct Svcs)*
Denise Kohnke *(Exec VP-Strategy & Bus Dev)*
Joyce O'Brien *(Exec VP-HR)*
Emily Harley *(VP-Media)*
Kirk Ruhnke *(Exec Dir-Creative)*
Maggie Avram *(Mgr-Social & Content Integration)*
Katie Gurney *(Sr Planner-Online Media)*
Chelsey Wahlstrom *(Acct Exec)*
Hillary Benson *(Sr Media Buyer)*

Accounts:
Associated Bank
Bon-Ton Department Stores; York, PA; 1992
Bridgestone/Firestone; Chicago, IL; 1997
Harley Davidson Museum; Milwaukee, WI; 2007
Medela, Inc. Medela Breastfeeding U.S.
Paris Presents Incorporated (Advertising & Digital Marketing Agency of Record) Social Media
Stacy Adams Collection
Toppers
University of Illinois Hospital & Health Sciences System
Wisconsin Department of Tourism

Laughlin/Constable New York

27 Whitehall St 7th Fl, New York, NY 10004
Tel.: (212) 422-4022
Fax: (212) 422-4078
E-Mail: info@laughlin.com
Web Site: www.laughlin.com

Employees: 8

National Agency Associations: 4A's

Agency Specializes In: Custom Publishing

Michael Jeary *(Pres)*
Denise Kohnke *(Exec VP-Strategy & Bus Dev)*
Lauren Garstecki *(VP-Digital)*
Emily Wong Harley *(VP-Media)*
Jim Rhines *(VP-Web Dev)*
Laura Stmarie *(VP-Digital Strategy)*
Ben Wohlers *(VP-Digital)*
Rosemarie Waraksa *(Acct Supvr)*
Jeff Louis *(Supvr-Digital Media)*
Steven A. Kaufman *(Sr Engr-Front-End)*

Accounts:
Firestone
Jewish Home Life Care
Kleenex
Lung Cancer Alliance (Agency of Record)
Master Look

LAUNCH

351 E Kennedy St, Spartanburg, SC 29302
Tel.: (864) 580-2350
Fax: (864) 583-5276
E-Mail: sims@launchsomething.com
Web Site: www.launchsomething.com

Employees: 6

Agency Specializes In: Advertising, Brand Development & Integration, Broadcast, Business Publications, Collateral, Communications, Consulting, Corporate Communications, Corporate Identity, Event Planning & Marketing, Graphic Design, Internet/Web Design, Logo & Package Design, Media Buying Services, Merchandising, Newspapers & Magazines, Outdoor, Planning & Consultation, Print, Publicity/Promotions, Radio, Strategic Planning/Research

Sims Hammond *(Owner)*
Lesley Mottla *(Sr VP-Customer Experience)*
Mark Miller *(Dir-Art)*
Jaime Wells Nash *(Acct Mgr)*

Accounts:
First National Bank of Spartanburg
Spartanburg Area Chamber of Commerce
Wofford College

LAUNCH AGENCY

4100 Midway Rd Ste 2110, Carrollton, TX 75007
Tel.: (972) 818-4100
Fax: (972) 818-4101
Toll Free: (866) 427-5013
E-Mail: info@launchagency.com
Web Site: www.launchagency.com

E-Mail for Key Personnel:
Creative Dir.: dwilguse@launchagency.com

Employees: 25
Year Founded: 2003

National Agency Associations: 4A's

Agency Specializes In: Advertising

Approx. Annual Billings: $14,000,000

Breakdown of Gross Billings by Media: Brdcst.: 20%; Collateral: 5%; D.M.: 5%; Fees: 25%; In-Store Adv.: 2%; Internet Adv.: 7%; Local Mktg.: 3%; Logo & Package Design: 3%; Mdsg./POP: 3%; Out-of-Home Media: 5%; Print: 5%; Strategic Planning/Research: 10%; Worldwide Web Sites: 7%

Michael Boone *(Principal & Acct Dir)*
Diane Seimetz *(Principal)*
Seth Perisho *(Creative Dir)*
Ellen Marquart Giles *(Dir-Art)*
Carolyn Sexton *(Dir-Art)*
Alexandra Watson *(Dir-Digital Media)*
Jason Giles *(Sr Acct Supvr)*
Ashley Mejia *(Acct Supvr)*
Rebecca Lauten *(Sr Acct Exec)*
Amanda Lewis *(Acct Exec)*

Accounts:

Bed Bath and Beyond
Children's Advocacy Center of Collin County
Children's Medical Center Campaign: "Trust"
Cooper Consulting Partners
The Dallas Wind Symphony
ParkPlace Dealerships; Dallas, TX; 2003
Promised Land Dairy
ViewPoint Bank

LAUNCH DYNAMIC MEDIA, LLC

828 Penn Ave, Wyomissing, PA 19610
Tel.: (610) 898-1330
Fax: (610) 898-8262
E-Mail: info@launchdm.com
Web Site: www.launchdm.com

Employees: 10
Year Founded: 1997

Agency Specializes In: Digital/Interactive, Print, Web (Banner Ads, Pop-ups, etc.)

Rob Wolf *(Founder)*
Noelle Wolf *(Treas)*
Brian Leupold *(Dir-Bus Ops)*
Jason Yeakle *(Dir-Creative)*
Amy Duggan *(Mgr-Acct & Project)*
Cory Embody *(Acct Coord)*
Meghan Miller *(Coord-Salesbuddy Pro Brand & Sls)*
Chris McConney *(Project Relationship Mgr)*

Accounts:
Fujitsu
GiggleWorks
Greth Homes
Hess
Reading Chamber
Reading Truck Body
Smithsonian Institution

LAUNCHFIRE INTERACTIVE INC.

200 Isabella St 5th Fl, Ottawa, ON K1S 1V7 Canada
Tel.: (613) 728-5865
Fax: (613) 728-1527
Toll Free: (800) 896-4115
E-Mail: info@launchfire.com
Web Site: www.launchfire.com

Employees: 20

Agency Specializes In: Advertising, Digital/Interactive, Internet/Web Design, Mobile Marketing, Strategic Planning/Research, Viral/Buzz/Word of Mouth, Web (Banner Ads, Pop-ups, etc.)

John Findlay *(Founder)*
S. Alexandre Lemaire *(CTO)*
A. J. Pratt *(VP-Sls & Mktg)*
Alicia Gutierrez *(Acct Mgr)*
Joshua Mintha *(Acct Mgr)*
Steve Wilson *(Acct Mgr)*
Justin Mcnally *(Designer-Web)*
Ingrid Tam *(Designer-Multimedia)*

Accounts:
AMD
ATI
Canadian Blood Services
Castrol
Dell
DIAGIO
Gillette
Intel
Jewel-Osco
JF Sports Canada
MBNA
Microsoft
Napster
NBC
Nestle
Nintendo
Palm
Procter & Gamble
RSA
Splenda
Tylenol
Yahoo! Music Canada

LAUNCHPAD

100 Galen St 2nd Fl, Watertown, MA 02472
Tel.: (617) 926-8700
Fax: (617) 924-8744
E-Mail: info@launchpad.tv
Web Site: www.launchpad.tv

Employees: 8
Year Founded: 2002

Agency Specializes In: Brand Development & Integration, Communications, Corporate Communications, Corporate Identity, E-Commerce, Internet/Web Design, Production, T.V.

Jacob Eidsmoe *(VP & Dir-Creative)*
John Basile *(Mgr)*

Accounts:
Abbott Diagnostics
Armour
Goal Marketing
Log Cabin
Lycos

LAUNCHPAD ADVERTISING

114 5th Ave 11th Fl, New York, NY 10011
Tel.: (212) 303-7650
E-Mail: info@launchpadadvertising.com
Web Site: www.lpnyc.com

Agency Specializes In: Advertising, Brand Development & Integration, Consumer Marketing, Direct Response Marketing, Strategic Planning/Research, Web (Banner Ads, Pop-ups, etc.)

Scott Elser *(Pres)*
David Low *(Co-Pres)*
Noah Ross *(Partner & Exec Dir-Creative)*
Tom Lamb *(COO & CMO)*
Nukte Tuncok *(Sr VP & Dir-Strategy)*
Mariam Guessous *(Sr Dir-Art)*
Abby Salgado *(Acct Supvr)*
Delia Pavlichko *(Supvr-Bus Dev)*
Ryan Shields *(Acct Exec)*
Julie Anzulewicz *(Asst Acct Exec)*
Emily Hamilton *(Asst Acct Exec)*

Accounts:
CenturyLink Marketing
CONTEXTWEB; New York, NY (Agency of Record) Digital, Media
Jambu (Agency of Record) Creative Advertising, Digital, In-Store, Print, Strategic Advertising
The Pat Tillman Foundation Brand Strategy, Marketing, Print
The Power of Fruit (Agency of Record)
Wall Street Journal

LAUNCHSQUAD

116 New Montgomery St Ste 620, San Francisco, CA 94105
Tel.: (415) 625-8555
Fax: (415) 625-8559
E-Mail: squad@launchsquad.com
Web Site: www.launchsquad.com

Employees: 50
Year Founded: 2000

National Agency Associations: COPF

Agency Specializes In: Brand Development & Integration, Communications, Consumer Marketing, Consumer Publications, Event Planning & Marketing, Exhibit/Trade Shows, Print, Production, Public Relations, Strategic Planning/Research

Jason Mandell *(Co-Founder & Partner)*
Jesse Odell *(Co-Founder & Partner)*
Jason Throckmorton *(Co-Founder & Partner)*
Mike Farber *(Founder-Boston & Gen Mgr)*
Brett Weiner *(Partner)*
Gavin Skillman *(Sr VP-New York)*
Daniel Paul *(VP-Fin & Ops)*
Stephanie Fryer *(Office Mgr & Mgr-HR)*
Molly Galler *(Acct Mgr)*

Accounts:
Aereo Media Relations, Strategy
AnchorFree
BrightRoll
Clair Mail Mobile Technology
Clairmail
ClearStory Data
Evernote
Opower
TIBCO PR, Tibbr
Wine.com (Agency of Record) Media Relations

LAUNDRY SERVICE

(Formerly 247 Laundry Service)
40 W 25th St, New York, NY 10010
Tel.: (212) 812-5671
E-Mail: hi@247laundryservice.com
Web Site: 247laundryservice.com

Employees: 70
Year Founded: 2011

Agency Specializes In: Advertising, Social Media

Jason Stein *(Founder & Pres)*
Don Middleberg *(CEO)*
Matt Cohen *(COO)*
Ross Sheingold *(Chief Strategy Officer)*
Alyson Warshaw *(Chief Creative Officer)*
Liz Eswein *(Exec Dir)*
Shayna Pilnick *(Client Svcs Dir)*
Jeremy Leon *(Dir-Strategy)*
Andrew Lerner *(Mgr-Community)*
Chris Lewis *(Coord-Studio)*

Accounts:
Amazon
Beats by Dre
Jordan Brand
Nike
New-Viber Social Media

LAUNDRY SERVICE

(Acquired by Wasserman Media Group)

LAURA DAVIDSON PUBLIC RELATIONS, INC.

72 Madison Ave, New York, NY 10016
Tel.: (212) 696-0660
Fax: (212) 696-9804
E-Mail: info@ldpr.com
Web Site: www.ldpr.com

Employees: 17
Year Founded: 1991

Agency Specializes In: Consulting, Crisis Communications, Internet/Web Design, Local Marketing, Publicity/Promotions

Revenue: $1,800,000

Laura Davidson *(Founder & Pres)*
Leslie Cohen *(Exec VP)*

Meghna Patel *(Sr VP)*
Sara Geen Hill *(VP)*
Carla Tracy *(VP)*
Dana Curatolo *(Acct Supvr)*

Accounts:
Abercrombie & Kent USA, LLC
Amanresorts
Bal Harbour, Florida
Curtain Bluff Resort, Antigua
Eden Rock; Saint Barts
The Gleneagles Hotel (Public Relations Agency of Record)
Grand Hotel Excelsior Vittoria PR
Grande Lakes Orlando
The Inn at Windmill Lane (Public Relations Agency of Record)
Kittitian Hill Public Relations
Mayflower Renaissance Hotel; Washington, DC
New-Morgans Hotel Group Co. (Public Relations Agency of Record)
Naples Grande Beach Resort
New York Marriott, Brooklyn Bridge (Public Relations Agency of Record)
Newport Marriott (Public Relations Agency of Record)
Ocean Edge Resort & Golf Club; Brewster, MA
Ocean House; Watch Hill, RI OH! Spa, PR, The Weekapaug Inn
The Press Hotel (Public Relations Agency of Record)
Rocco Forte Hotels PR
Sanctuary Retreats
The Thinking Traveller Think Puglia, Think Sicily
TownePlace Suites (Public Relations Agency of Record)
New-Travel Portland (Public Relations Agency of Record)
The Tryall Club
VisitScotland
The Waterfall Group Public Relations

LAVERDAD MARKETING & MEDIA

7817 Cooper Rd, Cincinnati, OH 45242
Tel.: (513) 891-1430
Fax: (815) 301-9664
E-Mail: mike.robinson@laverdadmarketing.com
Web Site: www.laverdadmarketing.com

Employees: 30

National Agency Associations: AMA-MRA-PRSA

Agency Specializes In: African-American Market, Asian Market, Automotive, Bilingual Market, Brand Development & Integration, Consumer Goods, Event Planning & Marketing, Guerilla Marketing, Hispanic Market, Household Goods, International, Market Research, Merchandising, Multicultural, Public Relations, Publicity/Promotions, Social Marketing/Nonprofit, Travel & Tourism

Approx. Annual Billings: $5,000,000

Breakdown of Gross Billings by Media: Adv. Specialities: 20%; Collateral: 30%; Event Mktg.: 20%; Radio: 30%

Mary Robinson *(Mgr-Corp Svcs)*
Lorin Rose Molloy *(Acct Exec-Mktg & Graphic Designer)*

Accounts:
bigg's; Cincinnati, OH Hispanic Category
Ohio Hispanic Chambers of Commerce Branding, Cultural Training, Marketing, PR, Stakeholder Management

LAVIDGE & ASSOCIATES INC.

6700 Baum Dr Ste 25, Knoxville, TN 37919
Tel.: (865) 584-6121
Fax: (865) 584-6756
E-Mail: info@lavidgeinc.com
Web Site: www.lavidgeinc.com

E-Mail for Key Personnel:
Public Relations: towneso@lavidgeinc.com

Employees: 10
Year Founded: 1950

National Agency Associations: APA-MCA

Agency Specializes In: Brand Development & Integration, Broadcast, Cable T.V., Commercial Photography, Event Planning & Marketing, Financial, Internet/Web Design, Logo & Package Design, Magazines, Media Buying Services, Multimedia, New Product Development, Newspaper, Newspapers & Magazines, Out-of-Home Media, Outdoor, Point of Sale, Print, Production, Public Relations, Real Estate, Sales Promotion, Sports Market, Sweepstakes, Travel & Tourism

Approx. Annual Billings: $10,750,000

Breakdown of Gross Billings by Media: Bus. Publs.: $500,000; Collateral: $4,600,000; D.M.: $200,000; Mags.: $500,000; Newsp.: $1,000,000; Other: $500,000; Outdoor: $400,000; Point of Purchase: $50,000; Radio: $1,500,000; T.V.: $1,500,000

Townes Lavidge Osborn *(Pres)*
Hal Bouni Ernest *(Exec VP & Acct Exec)*

Accounts:
Capital
High Hampton Inn & Country Club; Cashiers, NC
Jackson County Travel & Tourism Authority; Sylva, NC
The L.A.M.P. Foundation; Knoxville, TN
Schaad

THE LAVIDGE COMPANY

2777 E Camelback Rd Ste 300, Phoenix, AZ 85016
Tel.: (480) 998-2600
Fax: (480) 998-5525
E-Mail: info@lavidge.com
Web Site: www.lavidge.com

E-Mail for Key Personnel:
Creative Dir.: bcase@lavidge.com

Employees: 75
Year Founded: 1982

National Agency Associations: AAF-PRSA

Agency Specializes In: Advertising, Broadcast, Collateral, Corporate Identity, Event Planning & Marketing, Graphic Design, Integrated Marketing, Internet/Web Design, Logo & Package Design, Media Buying Services, Point of Sale, Print, Production (Ad, Film, Broadcast), Public Relations, Sports Market, Strategic Planning/Research

Approx. Annual Billings: $70,000,000

Alicia Wadas *(COO)*
Bob Case *(Chief Creative Officer)*
Betsey Griffin *(Mng Dir-Media)*
Stephen Heitz *(Mng Dir-Interactive Svcs)*
Ronda Parker *(Dir-Production)*
Juliana Gonzales Scott *(Dir-Interactive Art)*
Kyra Harmanos *(Assoc Dir-Strategy)*
Greg Sexton *(Assoc Dir-PR)*
Kathy Knudson *(Office Mgr)*
Jennifer Whittle *(Acct Supvr)*
Caroline Montgomery *(Acct Exec)*
Brittany Williams *(Acct Exec)*
Melanee Arnett *(Sr Media Planner-Interactive & Media Buyer)*
Abbey Barry *(Jr Acct Exec)*
Beth Logan *(Acct Coord-PR)*
Keller Perry *(Acct Coord-PR)*
Caitlin Wendt *(Acct Coord-PR)*

Accounts:
Banner Health; Phoenix, AZ; 2007
Celebrity Fight Night
College of St. Scholastica
Discount Tire; 2005
Enterprise Bank & Trust
Greenberg Traurig
I/O Data Centers
McDonald's Phoenix Co-op; 2002
Phoenix Area McDonald's
Phoenix International Raceway; Phoenix, AZ; 2006
RSC Rental Equipment
UPN 45 KUTP; 2001
VirTra
WGM

LAWLER BALLARD VAN DURAND

31 Inverness Center Pkwy Ste 110, Birmingham, AL 35242-4822
Tel.: (205) 995-1775
Fax: (205) 991-5141
E-Mail: inquire@lbvd.com
Web Site: www.lbvd.com

E-Mail for Key Personnel:
President: tvandurand@lbvd.com

Employees: 25
Year Founded: 1991

Agency Specializes In: Advertising, Brand Development & Integration, Consumer Goods, Consumer Marketing, Corporate Identity, Financial, Food Service, Graphic Design, Logo & Package Design, Media Buying Services, Media Planning, Multimedia, Newspaper, Newspapers & Magazines, Outdoor, Package Design, Production (Print), Public Relations, Publicity/Promotions, Radio, Regional, Social Media, Strategic Planning/Research, T.V., Women's Market

Approx. Annual Billings: $26,000,000

Tinsley Van Durand *(Owner)*
Gene Taylor *(Exec VP)*
Larry Washington *(Exec Dir-Creative)*
Lrichard Albright *(Assoc Dir-Creative)*
Julia Crigler *(Mgr-Strategic Mktg)*

Accounts:
Alabama Power
National Peanut Board

Branch

Lawler Ballard Van Durand

280 Elizabeth St Ste B201, Atlanta, GA 30307
Tel.: (404) 658-0232
Fax: (404) 658-0237
E-Mail: inquire@lbvd.com
Web Site: www.lbvd.com

Employees: 5

Agency Specializes In: Advertising

Bob Coyle *(Mng Dir-Atlanta)*
Steve Saari *(Dir-Creative)*
Hilary Stiefelmeyer *(Sr Mgr-Mktg)*

Accounts:
Peanut Butter & Co Campaign: "Taste Amazing"

LAWRENCE & SCHILLER, INC.

3932 S Willow Ave, Sioux Falls, SD 57105-6234
Tel.: (605) 338-8000
Fax: (605) 338-8892
Toll Free: (888) 836-6224
E-Mail: contact@l-s.com

Web Site: www.l-s.com

E-Mail for Key Personnel:
President: scott.lawrence@l-s.com
Creative Dir.: john.pohlman@l-s.com

Employees: 55
Year Founded: 1976

National Agency Associations: Second Wind Limited

Agency Specializes In: Agriculture, Automotive, Brand Development & Integration, Broadcast, Business Publications, Business-To-Business, Cable T.V., Children's Market, Co-op Advertising, Collateral, Commercial Photography, Communications, Consulting, Consumer Marketing, Consumer Publications, Corporate Identity, Digital/Interactive, Direct Response Marketing, E-Commerce, Education, Electronic Media, Engineering, Entertainment, Environmental, Event Planning & Marketing, Exhibit/Trade Shows, Financial, Food Service, Government/Political, Graphic Design, Health Care Services, High Technology, Industrial, Infomercials, Information Technology, Internet/Web Design, Investor Relations, Legal Services, Leisure, Logo & Package Design, Magazines, Media Buying Services, Medical Products, Merchandising, Multimedia, New Product Development, Newspaper, Newspapers & Magazines, Out-of-Home Media, Outdoor, Over-50 Market, Pharmaceutical, Planning & Consultation, Point of Purchase, Point of Sale, Print, Production, Public Relations, Publicity/Promotions, Radio, Recruitment, Restaurant, Retail, Sales Promotion, Seniors' Market, Sports Market, Strategic Planning/Research, T.V., Technical Advertising, Teen Market, Telemarketing, Trade & Consumer Magazines, Transportation, Travel & Tourism, Yellow Pages Advertising

Approx. Annual Billings: $13,500,000

Breakdown of Gross Billings by Media: Adv. Specialities: $135,000; Collateral: $1,080,000; Consulting: $270,000; D.M.: $270,000; E-Commerce: $3,510,000; Graphic Design: $135,000; Internet Adv.: $270,000; Mags.: $540,000; Newsp.: $2,160,000; Out-of-Home Media: $405,000; Outdoor: $135,000; Plng. & Consultation: $405,000; Point of Purchase: $1,485,000; Print: $810,000; Radio: $135,000; T.V.: $945,000; Video Brochures: $135,000; Worldwide Web Sites: $675,000

Scott Lawrence *(Pres & CEO)*
Dan Edmonds *(Sr VP & Dir-Design)*
Tom Helland *(Sr VP-Client Rels)*
Dave Haan *(VP-Deployment-Digital, Disruptive & PR)*
Scott Wiechmann *(Sr Dir-Creative)*
Laura Mitchell *(Dir-Digital Mktg)*
Angela Chapman *(Mgr-Customer Svc)*
Joann GoBell *(Supvr-Customer Svc)*
Jamie Bulian *(Acct Exec)*
Lizzy Cranny *(Specialist-Media)*
Mike Edgette *(Specialist-Media)*
Amy Griese *(Strategist-Digital)*
Chelsea Heeren *(Specialist-Media)*
Aubrey Kvasnicka *(Specialist-Media)*
Aubrey Stromberg *(Specialist-Media)*
Sam Gotham *(Assoc Acct Exec)*
Cortney Slaight *(Assoc Acct Exec)*
Jodi Stahl *(Acct Coord)*
Jenna Jares *(Coord-Digital Mktg)*

Accounts:
Augie Mascot
DAKOTACARE
Ed the Energy Guy
Forward Sioux Falls
Great Western Bank
KELO
Koch Hazard Architects
Midcontinent Business Solutions
Midcontinent Communications
Rosenbauer America
Sanford Health
Sanford Kid Zone
Sanford The Gift
South Dakota Department of Tourism Broadcast, Creative, Media, PR, Print
South Dakota State University
South Dakota Symphony
Taco John's International, Inc. (Advertising Agency of Record)
Visit Rapid City
Visit Spearfish

LAZBRO, INC.

13323 Washington Blvd Ste 100, Los Angeles, CA 90066
Tel.: (310) 279-5080
Fax: (866) 273-2652
E-Mail: info@lazbro.com
Web Site: www.lazbro.com

Agency Specializes In: Advertising, Advertising Specialties, Affiliate Marketing, Affluent Market, African-American Market, Alternative Advertising, Arts, Brand Development & Integration, Branded Entertainment, Broadcast, Children's Market, Co-op Advertising, Collateral, College, Consumer Marketing, Cosmetics, Digital/Interactive, Direct Response Marketing, Direct-to-Consumer, E-Commerce, Electronic Media, Email, Entertainment, Event Planning & Marketing, Experience Design, Food Service, Game Integration, Gay & Lesbian Market, Graphic Design, Guerilla Marketing, Health Care Services, High Technology, Hispanic Market, Hospitality, Identity Marketing, Infomercials, Information Technology, Integrated Marketing, Internet/Web Design, Leisure, Local Marketing, Logo & Package Design, Luxury Products, Market Research, Media Buying Services, Men's Market, Mobile Marketing, Multicultural, Multimedia, New Technologies, Package Design, Pets , Pharmaceutical, Planning & Consultation, Podcasting, Production, Production (Ad, Film, Broadcast), Promotions, Public Relations, Publicity/Promotions, Search Engine Optimization, Social Marketing/Nonprofit, Social Media, Strategic Planning/Research, Sweepstakes, Teen Market, Transportation, Travel & Tourism, Tween Market, Urban Market, Viral/Buzz/Word of Mouth, Web (Banner Ads, Pop-ups, etc.), Women's Market

Breakdown of Gross Billings by Media: Audio/Visual: 10%; Collateral: 5%; Digital/Interactive: 70%; Graphic Design: 15%

Jen Lazarus *(Pres)*
Evan Lazarus *(CEO)*
Zachariah Lazarus *(VP-Cuteness)*
Jeff Bernstein *(Dir-Tech)*
Chris Glover *(Dir-Creative)*
Jake Hamilton *(Dir-Content)*
Christopher Houston *(Dir-Mobile Dev)*
Brittany Everett *(Sr Strategist-Digital)*

Accounts:
American Film Institute
Child Care Resource Center
North East Valley Health Corporation
Physicians Formula Cosmetics
Sunless, Inc. Mystic Tan, VersaSpa
Whish Body Products

LBI U.S.

(Merged with MRY and Name Changed to MRY)

LEAD ME MEDIA

1200 NW 17th Ave Ste 17, Delray Beach, FL 33445-2513
Tel.: (888) 445-3282
Fax: (561) 423-7890
Toll Free: (888) 445-3282
E-Mail: info@leadmemedia.com
Web Site: www.leadmemedia.com

Year Founded: 2007

Agency Specializes In: Advertising, Advertising Specialties, Affiliate Marketing, Affluent Market, African-American Market, Arts, Aviation & Aerospace, Bilingual Market, Branded Entertainment, Business-To-Business, Children's Market, Co-op Advertising, College, Communications, Computers & Software, Consulting, Consumer Goods, Consumer Marketing, Content, Corporate Communications, Cosmetics, Crisis Communications, Customer Relationship Management, Digital/Interactive, Direct Response Marketing, Direct-to-Consumer, E-Commerce, Education, Electronic Media, Electronics, Email, Engineering, Entertainment, Environmental, Event Planning & Marketing, Exhibit/Trade Shows, Faith Based, Fashion/Apparel, Financial, Food Service, Government/Political, Graphic Design, Guerilla Marketing, Health Care Services, High Technology, Hispanic Market, Hospitality, Household Goods, Industrial, Information Technology, Integrated Marketing, Internet/Web Design, Investor Relations, Leisure, Local Marketing, Market Research, Media Buying Services, Media Planning, Media Relations, Men's Market, Mobile Marketing, Multicultural, Multimedia, New Product Development, Newspaper, Out-of-Home Media, Outdoor, Over-50 Market, Pets , Pharmaceutical, Planning & Consultation, Point of Sale, Print, Production, Production (Print), Promotions, Publicity/Promotions, Publishing, Radio, Real Estate, Recruitment, Regional, Restaurant, Retail, Sales Promotion, Search Engine Optimization, Seniors' Market, Social Marketing/Nonprofit, Social Media, Sports Market, Strategic Planning/Research, Sweepstakes, T.V., Technical Advertising, Teen Market, Telemarketing, Transportation, Travel & Tourism, Tween Market, Urban Market, Viral/Buzz/Word of Mouth, Web (Banner Ads, Pop-ups, etc.), Women's Market

Breakdown of Gross Billings by Media: Internet Adv.: 100%

Rob Clouse *(Founder)*
Robert Brown *(Exec VP-Major Accounts)*
Debra Robbins *(Dir-Media)*
Jeff Grady *(Sr Mgr-Bus Dev & Mktg)*
Nathali Delgado *(Mgr-Social Media)*
Christian Santamaria *(Acct Exec)*

LEADDOG MARKETING GROUP

159 W 25th St 2nd Fl, New York, NY 10001
Tel.: (212) 488-6500
Web Site: www.leaddogmarketing.com

Year Founded: 1999

Agency Specializes In: Brand Development & Integration, Consumer Marketing, Entertainment, Integrated Marketing, Promotions, Social Marketing/Nonprofit, Sponsorship, Sports Market

Revenue: $14,700,000

Dan Mannix *(Pres & CEO)*
Federico Gomez *(Partner & Sr VP-Creative)*
Dan Jahn *(Partner & Sr VP-Brand Promos & Digital Solutions)*
Donna Providenti *(COO)*
Danit Aronson *(VP-Client Partnerships)*
Nicole Boyar *(VP-Brand Strategy)*
Jayne Bussman-Wise *(Sr Dir-Mktg)*
Ken Blake *(Acct Dir)*

Gaspar Guerra *(Dir-Creative)*
Paola Ortega *(Dir)*
Jason Polan *(Sr Acct Mgr)*

Accounts:
Boston Apparel Group Apparels & Accessories Mfr
Department of Transportation Branding
HBO Television Channel
Jabra (North American Marketing Agency of Record) Digital Strategy
NASCAR Auto Racing
The Orphan Magazine Magazine Publishers
Recreational Equipment, Inc.
TNT Television Channel
Vitamin Water Vitamin Water Mfr

LEADING EDGE COMMUNICATIONS LLC
206 Bridge St, Franklin, TN 37064
Tel.: (615) 790-3718
Fax: (615) 794-4524
E-Mail: info@leadingedgecommunications.com
Web Site: www.leadingedgecommunications.com

Agency Specializes In: Advertising, Corporate Identity, Digital/Interactive, Internet/Web Design, Package Design

Eddie Coutras *(Owner & Pres)*
Darlene Bailey *(Sr Dir-Art)*

Accounts:
Mississippi Turfgrass Association

LEADING EDGES
2100 8th St, Meridian, MS 39301
Tel.: (601) 483-9810
Fax: (601) 485-6976
Web Site: www.leadingedges.net

Agency Specializes In: Advertising, Digital/Interactive, Graphic Design, Internet/Web Design, Logo & Package Design, Media Relations, Print, Promotions, Public Relations, Social Media

Tony Pompelia *(Partner)*
Lynn Combest *(VP-Sls)*
Mark Brentnall *(Dir-Creative)*
Jackie Smith *(Office Mgr)*
Lindsay Taylor *(Mgr-Social Media & Graphic Designer)*
Mary Katherine DeBardeleben *(Acct Exec)*
Leslie Hiatt *(Acct Exec)*
Kristen McCaskill *(Acct Rep)*

Accounts:
New-Citizens National Bank
Lauderdale County Tourism
LPK Architects
MSU Riley Center (Agency of Record)
New-Rush Health Systems
New-Structural Steel Services

LEAN MEAN FIGHTING MACHINE LTD.
(Acquired & Absorbed by M&C Saatchi plc)

LEAP COMMUNICATIONS
1301 Shiloh Rd Ste 1140, Kennesaw, GA 30144
Tel.: (678) 354-4240
Fax: (678) 354-4241
E-Mail: contact@leapcommunication.com
Web Site: www.leapcommunication.com

Year Founded: 2003

Agency Specializes In: Advertising, Brand Development & Integration, Digital/Interactive, Print

Robyn Bilbrey *(Project Mgr & Media Buyer)*

Accounts:
The Mohawk Group

LEAP LLC
(Merged with HudsonWide to form ProperVillains)

LEAP STRATEGIC MARKETING, LLC
N16 W23250 Stone Rdg Dr Ste 4, Waukesha, WI 53188
Tel.: (262) 436-4080
Web Site: www.leapstrategicmarketing.com

Year Founded: 2007

Agency Specializes In: Advertising, Digital/Interactive, Graphic Design, Public Relations, Strategic Planning/Research

John Verre *(Pres & CEO)*
Bruce Geiger *(Acct Dir)*
Laura Komar *(Acct Dir)*
Nancy VonderHeydt Verre *(Dir-Ops)*

Accounts:
Bank of New Glarus
BioLyte Laboratories

LEAPFROG ONLINE
807 Greenwood St, Evanston, IL 60201
Tel.: (847) 492-1968
Fax: (847) 492-1990
E-Mail: info@leapfrogonline.com
Web Site: www.leapfrogonline.com

Year Founded: 1995

Agency Specializes In: Advertising, Automotive, Communications, Consumer Goods, Consumer Marketing, Digital/Interactive, Direct Response Marketing, Direct-to-Consumer, Financial, High Technology, Sponsorship

Scott Epskamp *(Co-Founder & Pres)*
Joel Grossman *(Sr VP)*
Matt Kelley *(Sr VP-Consumer Journey)*
Robyn Simburger *(VP & Gen Mgr)*
Randy Wait *(VP-Corp Dev)*
Scot Wheeler *(VP-Consumer Intelligence & Business Analytics)*
Ruxandra Vidican *(Acct Mgr)*
Claire Cotter *(Mgr-SEM)*

Accounts:
Adelphia
AT&T Broadband
Comcast
Discover Card
Hallmark
Leapfrog
Morningstar
Motorola Solutions, Inc.

LEAPFROG SOLUTIONS, INC.
3201 Jermantown Rd, Fairfax, VA 22030
Tel.: (703) 273-7900
Fax: (703) 273-7902
E-Mail: lfs_info@leapfrogit.com
Web Site: www.leapfrogit.com

Employees: 23

Agency Specializes In: Brand Development & Integration, Event Planning & Marketing, Internet/Web Design, Print, Public Relations, Sponsorship

Revenue: $2,000,000

Lisa Martin *(Founder & CEO)*
Rene Ramos *(Dir-Creative)*
Abbi Boose *(Acct Mgr)*
Kelly Eisenberg *(Brand Mgr-Content)*
Erin Bridges *(Mgr-PR)*
Kati Brown *(Mgr-Client Dev)*
Donna Davidovich *(Mgr-Production)*
Michael Choi *(Sr Graphic Designer)*

Accounts:
American Red Cross
Athena Technologies, Inc.
Cochran & Owen
Deloitte
Eagle Ray, Inc.
Employment Enterprises; 2008
Fairfax Choral Society

LEAVITT COMMUNICATIONS INC
5221 Olive Hill Rd, Fallbrook, CA 92028
Tel.: (760) 639-2900
E-Mail: info@leavcom.com
Web Site: www.leavcom.com

Year Founded: 1991

Agency Specializes In: Advertising, Public Relations, Social Media

Neal Leavitt *(Pres)*
Richard Stehr *(VP)*

Accounts:
New-Cambrios Technologies Corporation

LEE ADVERTISING
4381 Arrowwood Cir, Concord, CA 94521
Tel.: (925) 680-0139
E-Mail: ivan@leeadvertising.com
Web Site: www.leeadvertising.com

Employees: 5

Agency Specializes In: Corporate Identity, Direct Response Marketing, E-Commerce, Internet/Web Design, Magazines, Newspapers & Magazines, Outdoor, Print, T.V.

Ivan Lee *(Dir-Art & Creative & Designer-Web)*

Accounts:
Diamond Systems
Digital Doc
Family Fertility Center
IGN Entertainment
Institutional Real Estate Inc
Rigitoni
Strizzi's Restaurant

LEE BRANDING
945 Broadway St NE Ste 280, Minneapolis, MN 55413
Tel.: (612) 843-8477
Fax: (612) 843-8479
Web Site: www.leebranding.com

Employees: 18
Year Founded: 2011

Agency Specializes In: Advertising, Brand Development & Integration, Collateral, Digital/Interactive, Media Buying Services, Media Planning, Print, Public Relations, Social Media

Revenue: $5,000,000

Tina White *(Mng Dir)*
Terri Lee *(Principal)*
Kari Helling *(Acct Dir)*
Mary Tabery Smith *(Acct Dir)*
Nicole Travis *(Acct Svcs Dir)*
Jack Wilcox *(Dir-Creative)*
Ania Kowalewicz-Hallen *(Acct Supvr)*

Accounts:
612 Brew
Amplifon
Baxter Healthcare
Cardiovascular Systems, Inc. (CSI)
ENKI Brewing
Medtronic
Minnesota Lynx
Orthopaedic and Fracture Clinic

LEE MARKETING & ADVERTISING GROUP, INC.
2322 J St, Sacramento, CA 95816
Tel.: (916) 448-1104
E-Mail: kdog@leeadgroup.net
Web Site: www.leemag.net

Agency Specializes In: Advertising, Brand Development & Integration, Graphic Design, Internet/Web Design, Media Planning, Public Relations, Search Engine Optimization, Social Media

Kenton Lee *(Pres & CEO)*
Jason L. Lee *(CFO)*

Accounts:
New-Rubicon Brewing Company

LEE TILFORD AGENCY
5725 W Hwy 290 Ste 201, Austin, TX 78735
Tel.: (512) 899-1100
E-Mail: info@leetilford.com
Web Site: www.leetilford.com

Agency Specializes In: Advertising, Customer Relationship Management, Digital/Interactive, Direct Response Marketing, Promotions, Radio, Retail, Search Engine Optimization, Social Media, Strategic Planning/Research

Tony Tilford *(Pres)*
John Dillon *(Controller)*
Greg Poszywak *(Dir-Art)*
Jamie Dillon *(Acct Exec)*
Brandon Tilford *(Acct Exec)*
Canaan Henderson *(Copywriter)*
Stephanie Freed *(Sr Media Planner & Buyer)*
Adam Keeton *(Sr Media Planner & Buyer)*

Accounts:
Spec's Family Partners Ltd.

LEFFLER AGENCY
2607 N Charles St, Baltimore, MD 21218
Tel.: (410) 235-5661
Fax: (410) 235-5697
E-Mail: info@leffleragency.com
Web Site: www.leffleragency.com

Employees: 19

Agency Specializes In: Advertising, Brand Development & Integration, Event Planning & Marketing, Public Relations, Social Media

Bob Leffler *(Owner)*
Heather Connellee *(CEO)*
Rachel Lawrence *(Dir-Media Svcs)*
Jeff Sewell *(Dir-Art)*
Jim Hesch *(Acct Mgr & Media Buyer)*

Accounts:
Colonial Athletic Association

LEFT FIELD CREATIVE
2423 S 13th St, Saint Louis, MO 63104
Tel.: (314) 773-1300
Fax: (314) 773-1311
E-Mail: info@leftfieldcreative.com
Web Site: www.leftfieldcreative.com

Agency Specializes In: Advertising

Eric Lee *(Partner)*
Christine Yu *(Sr Dir-Art)*
Isabel Barreto *(Sr Producer-Digital)*
Armando Ceron *(Dir-Creative & Art & Designer)*
Ann French *(Office Mgr)*
Lauren Bernard *(Mgr-Digital Production)*
Heejin Kim *(Designer-Interactive)*

LEGACY MARKETING PARTNERS
640 N LaSalle Dr 5th Fl, Chicago, IL 60654
Tel.: (312) 799-5400
Web Site: www.legacymp.com

Agency Specializes In: Advertising, Brand Development & Integration, Content, Digital/Interactive, Event Planning & Marketing, Social Media, Sponsorship

Chris Kapsalis *(Exec VP & Gen Mgr)*
Mark Driggs *(Exec VP-Bus Ops)*
Justin Kawa *(Acct Dir)*
Shari Moehlenkamp *(Dir-Fin)*
April Quealy *(Dir-Creative)*
Bruce Turner *(Dir-IT)*

Accounts:
Pernod Ricard USA, Inc.

LEGAN ADVERTISING AGENCY
5281 Hayes Rd, Ravenna, OH 44266
Tel.: (330) 221-7947
E-Mail: info@leganadvertising.com
Web Site: www.leganadvertising.com

Agency Specializes In: Advertising, Brand Development & Integration, Corporate Identity, Internet/Web Design, Logo & Package Design, Public Relations, Social Media

Michael Legan *(Owner & Dir-Creative)*

Accounts:
BioTech Medical Inc
Davis Printing Company
SpectraSan
West Branch Bait & Tackle

LEGEND INC.
PO Box 50, Marblehead, MA 01945-0050
Tel.: (781) 990-8707
Fax: (781) 639-2511
Toll Free: (800) 976-0008
E-Mail: bp@legendinc.com
Web Site: www.legendinc.com

E-Mail for Key Personnel:
President: bp@legendinc.com

Employees: 8
Year Founded: 1979

Agency Specializes In: Advertising, Broadcast, Business-To-Business, Cable T.V., Commercial Photography, Communications, Consulting, Digital/Interactive, Direct Response Marketing, E-Commerce, Education, Electronic Media, Entertainment, Event Planning & Marketing, Gay & Lesbian Market, Graphic Design, Health Care Services, High Technology, Information Technology, Internet/Web Design, Leisure, Logo & Package Design, Magazines, Marine, Media Buying Services, Medical Products, New Product Development, Newspaper, Newspapers & Magazines, Outdoor, Planning & Consultation, Point of Purchase, Point of Sale, Print, Production, Public Relations, Publicity/Promotions, Radio, Real Estate, Recruitment, Restaurant, Retail, Sales Promotion, Seniors' Market, Sports Market, Strategic Planning/Research, T.V., Technical Advertising, Trade & Consumer Magazines, Transportation, Travel & Tourism

Approx. Annual Billings: $2,500,000 Capitalized

Breakdown of Gross Billings by Media: Brdcst.: 10%; Bus. Publs.: 18%; Cable T.V.: 3%; Collateral: 5%; D.M.: 3%; Internet Adv.: 7%; Newsp. & Mags.: 20%; Production: 25%; Pub. Rels.: 5%; Radio: 4%

Claudia Rodenstein *(CO-Pres & Sr VP)*
Bill Purdin *(Pres-Adv Agency & Dir-Creative)*
Joy Purdin *(VP)*

Accounts:
Design & Co.
The Duratherm Corporation
Genevieve deManio Photography
Insurers' Recovery Group; Natick, MA Insurance Recovery & Risk Management; 1997
Mazow McCullough
Proofreadnow.com
Union Specialties; Newburyport, MA Specialty Products for Leather Industry

LEGION ADVERTISING
1425 Greenway Dr Ste 100, Irving, TX 75038
Tel.: (817) 784-8544
Fax: (817) 385-0378
E-Mail: eric@legionadvertising.com
Web Site: www.legionadvertising.com

Employees: 22
Year Founded: 2000

Agency Specializes In: Bilingual Market, Digital/Interactive, Hispanic Market, Media Buying Services, Planning & Consultation, Sponsorship, Strategic Planning/Research

Revenue: $15,000,000

Antonio Meraz *(Acct Dir)*
Guille Saucedo *(Dir-Creative & Art)*
Harold Midence *(Client Svc Dir)*

Accounts:
Bimbo Bakeries USA

LEGRAND & ASSOCIATES
3925 Benton Rd, Bossier City, LA 71111
Tel.: (318) 226-4555
Fax: (318) 226-4558
Web Site: www.legrandandassociates.com

Agency Specializes In: Advertising, Graphic Design, Internet/Web Design, Radio

Al LeGrand *(Owner)*
Germaine Benoit *(Mgr-Bus)*
Mary Craigo *(Acct Exec)*

Accounts:
Mclarty Ford

LEHIGH MINING & NAVIGATION
(Formerly Spark)
1 W Broad St, Bethlehem, PA 18018
Tel.: (484) 821-0920
Fax: (484) 821-0921
Web Site: lehighminingandnavigation.com

Employees: 17
Year Founded: 2004

Agency Specializes In: Advertising, Local Marketing, Media Relations, Public Relations

Approx. Annual Billings: $8,600,000

Denis Aumiller *(Mng Partner & Dir-Creative)*
Scott Byers *(Mng Partner-Creative)*
Michael Drabenstott *(Mng Partner)*
Donna Reynolds *(Dir-Bus Dev)*
Michael Merring *(Sr Planner-Media)*

Accounts:
Air Products Specialty Chemicals; 2013
AltusGroup CarbonCast Precast Concrete Technology; 2004
B. Braun OEM Division Medical Devices; 2005
C.F. Martin & Co Martin Guitar, Martin Strings
Discover Lehigh Valley Regional Tourism; 2009
ESSA Bank & Trust Financial Services; 2014
Olympus Consumer Imaging Products; 2005
Paxos Restaurants Blue, Melt, Torre; 2004
PPL EnergyPlus/Talen Energy Retail & Commercial Energy Supply; 2009

LEHMANMILLET
2 Atlantic Ave, Boston, MA 02110
Tel.: (800) 634-5315
Fax: (617) 722-6099
E-Mail: bruce_lehman@millet.com
Web Site: www.lehmanmillet.com

E-Mail for Key Personnel:
President: bruce_lehman@millet.com

Employees: 84
Year Founded: 1978

Agency Specializes In: Advertising, Communications, Consumer Marketing, Corporate Identity, Direct Response Marketing, Education, Event Planning & Marketing, Exhibit/Trade Shows, Graphic Design, Health Care Services, Internet/Web Design, Logo & Package Design, Newspapers & Magazines, Point of Purchase, Point of Sale, Print, Production, Public Relations, Publicity/Promotions, Radio, Sales Promotion, Strategic Planning/Research, Trade & Consumer Magazines

Approx. Annual Billings: $66,396,000

Breakdown of Gross Billings by Media: Bus. Publs.: 70%; Consumer Publs.: 10%; D.M.: 20%

Carolyn Morgan *(Pres)*
Deborah Lotterman *(Chief Creative Officer)*
Kristi Hansen *(Sr VP & Dir-Interactive)*
Bill Green *(VP & Mgmt Supvr)*
Kathleen Carino *(Grp Acct Dir)*
Bob Shiffrar *(Assoc Dir-Creative & Copywriter)*
Heather O'Handley *(Sr Mgr-Bus Dev)*
Shannon Moore *(Acct Mgr)*

Accounts:
Abbott Diagnostics
Amedica Innovative Spine Surgery Products
Ariad Pharmaceuticals Novel Cancer Therapeutics
Auxilium Pharmaceuticals Novel Biologic for Dupytren's Contracture
Bausch & Lomb
Biotronic Cardiac Rhythm Management
CardioDx Novel Cardiovascular Molecular Diagnostics
Conceptus Non-Surgical Permanent Birth Control
Edwards Life Sciences Critical Care
EMD Serono Oncology Franchise
Exact Sciences Novel Cancer Diagnostics
Focus Diagnostics Novel Infectious Disease Diagnostics
Genomic Health Novel Cancer Diagnostics
Genzyme BioSurgery
Glaukos Novel Glaucoma Products
Infinity Pharmaceuticals Novel Cancer Therapeutics
Intuitive Surgical Robotic Surgical Products
Life Technologies Novel Cancer Diagnostics
Medtronic Sofamor Danek
Multiple Myeloma Research Foundation
OvaScience Novel Treatment Products for Infertility
Zimmer Dental

LehmanMillet
3 MacArthur Pl Ste 700, Santa Ana, CA 92707
(See Separate Listing)

THE LEIGH AGENCY
3050 Chain Bridge Rd Ste 201, Fairfax, VA 22030
Tel.: (703) 850-5190
E-Mail: info@leighenergy.com
Web Site: www.leighenergy.com

Employees: 20
Year Founded: 2009

Agency Specializes In: Advertising, Brand Development & Integration, Direct Response Marketing, Identity Marketing, Internet/Web Design, Media Planning, Public Relations, Search Engine Optimization, Strategic Planning/Research

Jodi Leigh *(Pres)*
Frank Bilotto *(Sr Dir-Art)*
Anastasia Zueva *(Designer-Web)*

Accounts:
2 Young Foundation Health Care Services

LEINICKE GROUP
213 Old Meramec Station Rd, Saint Louis, MO 63021
Tel.: (636) 227-4424
Fax: (636) 227-8049
Web Site: www.leinickegroup.com

Year Founded: 1979

Agency Specializes In: Advertising, Brand Development & Integration, Digital/Interactive, Internet/Web Design, Print, Social Media

Connie Leinicke *(Exec VP)*
Bob Gauen *(Dir-Creative)*

Accounts:
12 Days of Giving
Gordon USA

LENNON & ASSOCIATES
734 N Highland Ave, Los Angeles, CA 90038
Tel.: (323) 465-5104
Fax: (323) 463-6463
E-Mail: maria@lennon.com
Web Site: www.lennonla.com

Employees: 5
Year Founded: 1978

Agency Specializes In: Advertising, Advertising Specialties, Broadcast, Cable T.V., Catalogs, Co-op Advertising, Collateral, Commercial Photography, Communications, Consulting, Consumer Marketing, Corporate Communications, Corporate Identity, Environmental, Event Planning & Marketing, Exhibit/Trade Shows, Graphic Design, Hospitality, Household Goods, In-Store Advertising, Infomercials, Information Technology, Integrated Marketing, Internet/Web Design, Logo & Package Design, Magazines, Media Planning, Multimedia, Newspapers & Magazines, Outdoor, Package Design, Planning & Consultation, Point of Sale, Production, Production (Print), Promotions, Public Relations, Publicity/Promotions, Sales Promotion, Search Engine Optimization, Sponsorship, Strategic Planning/Research, T.V., Trade & Consumer Magazines, Web (Banner Ads, Pop-ups, etc.), Yellow Pages Advertising

Approx. Annual Billings: $1,000,000

Dan Lennon *(Dir-Creative)*
James Park *(Dir-Art)*
Sean Funkhouser *(Copywriter)*

Accounts:
Hancock & Moore
Royal Pedic
Westwood Interiors
Wildwood

LENZ MARKETING
119 E Ct Sq Ste 201, Decatur, GA 30030
Tel.: (404) 373-2021
Fax: (404) 371-0293
Web Site: www.lenzmarketing.com

Agency Specializes In: Advertising, Brand Development & Integration, Digital/Interactive, Public Relations, Social Media

Richard J. Lenz *(Founder, Pres & CEO)*
John R. Lenz *(Partner & VP)*
Ben Barnes *(Dir-Art)*
Mike Killeen *(Dir-Mktg)*
Cameron Spivey *(Dir-Creative)*
Rachel Cushing *(Mgr-PR)*

Accounts:
100 Miles
Core Performance Company
Newnan Dermatology
SouthCoast Medical Group

THE LEO AGENCY
17226 Hillcrest Terr SW, Burien, WA 98166
Tel.: (206) 877-3135
E-Mail: info@the-leo-agency.com
Web Site: www.the-leo-agency.com

Agency Specializes In: Advertising, Brand Development & Integration, Digital/Interactive, Graphic Design, Internet/Web Design, Radio, Search Engine Optimization, Social Media

Tony Freeman *(Owner)*

Accounts:
Tacoma Opera

LEO BURNETT BUSINESS
300 Park Ave S, New York, NY 10010
Tel.: (646) 840-8350
Fax: (646) 840-8360
Web Site: www.leoburnettbusiness.com/

Employees: 50
Year Founded: 2000

National Agency Associations: 4A's

Agency Specializes In: Advertising, Brand Development & Integration, Broadcast, Business Publications, Business-To-Business, Collateral, Corporate Communications, Corporate Identity, Digital/Interactive, Education, Financial, Graphic Design, Health Care Services, Industrial, Out-of-Home Media, Print, Production, Radio, Recruitment, Sales Promotion, Travel & Tourism

Breakdown of Gross Billings by Media: Collateral: 20%; Mags.: 10%; Newsp.: 16%; Other: 26%; Out-of-Home Media: 2%; Radio: 2%; T.V.: 24%

Lisa Abbatiello *(CEO)*
Jenny Clark *(VP & Head-Acct Mgmt)*
Rob Allen *(VP & Exec Producer)*
Ken Gilberg *(VP & Exec Producer)*
Tony Wallace *(VP & Exec Producer)*
Lee Goldberg *(Sr Producer-Brdcst)*
Gene Campanelli *(Dir-Creative)*
Peter Powell *(Dir-Creative)*

Noel Nickol *(Copywriter)*

Accounts:
ACE Group Ltd.
New-Ann & Robert H. Lurie Children's Hospital of Chicago (Creative Advertising Agency of Record) Out-of-Home, Social, TV
Avis Budget Group, Inc. Avis, Budget, Payless
Options Industry Council
Stanley
United Nations Office for the Coordination of Humanitarian Affairs Campaign: "#theworldneedsmore"

LEO BURNETT COMPANY LTD.

175 Bloor St E North Twr, Toronto, ON M4W 3R9 Canada
Tel.: (416) 925-5997
Fax: (416) 92-5 3443
Web Site: www.leoburnett.ca

E-Mail for Key Personnel:
Creative Dir.: judy.john@leoburnett.ca
Public Relations: margaret.arnold@leoburnett.ca

Employees: 100
Year Founded: 1935

National Agency Associations: ABC-CBP-NYPAA

Agency Specializes In: Advertising, Bilingual Market, Brand Development & Integration, Broadcast, Business-To-Business, Cable T.V., Children's Market, Co-op Advertising, Collateral, Communications, Consumer Marketing, Corporate Identity, Cosmetics, Digital/Interactive, Direct Response Marketing, E-Commerce, Education, Electronic Media, Entertainment, Event Planning & Marketing, Fashion/Apparel, Financial, Food Service, Health Care Services, High Technology, Infomercials, Internet/Web Design, Media Buying Services, New Product Development, Newspaper, Newspapers & Magazines, Out-of-Home Media, Outdoor, Over-50 Market, Planning & Consultation, Point of Purchase, Point of Sale, Print, Production, Public Relations, Radio, Retail, Seniors' Market, Sports Market, Strategic Planning/Research, Sweepstakes, T.V., Teen Market, Transportation, Travel & Tourism

Judy John *(CEO & Chief Creative Officer)*
Brent Nelsen *(Mng Partner, Sr VP & Dir-Strategic Plng)*
David Kennedy *(COO & Exec VP)*
Lisa Greenberg *(Sr VP, Dir-Creative & Head-Art)*
Richard Bernstein *(Sr VP & Grp Acct Dir)*
David Federico *(Sr VP & Dir-Creative)*
Matt Foulk *(VP & Grp Dir-Plng)*
Lisa Morch *(VP & Dir-Knowledge Mgmt)*
Morgan Kurchak *(Grp Head-Creative)*
Marcus Sagar *(Grp Head-Creative)*
Anthony Chelvanathan *(Grp Dir-Creative)*
David Buckspan *(Grp Acct Dir)*
Natasha Dagenais *(Grp Acct Dir)*
Chris Perron *(Grp Acct Dir)*
Melanie Palmer *(Mgr-Brdcst & Exec Producer)*
Sam Cerullo *(Art Dir & Grp Creative Dir)*
Diana Kelly *(Acct Dir)*
Kelly Zettel *(Grp Creative Dir & Copywriter)*
Lucyed Hernandez *(Dir-Art)*
Sean Ohlenkamp *(Dir-Digital Creative)*
Jeremy Farncomb *(Acct Mgr)*
Kayla Osmond *(Acct Supvr)*
Elizabeth Rivers *(Acct Exec)*
Dejan Djuric *(Designer)*
Matt Doran *(Copywriter)*
Lisa Hart *(Planner)*
Marty Hoefkes *(Copywriter)*
Noreel Asuro *(Grp Creative Dir)*
Dave Thornhill *(Sr Writer)*

Accounts:
AMC Networks Campaign: "The Walking Dead Rotting Finger Countdown"
Bell Media Campaign: "Brought To Life"
Bounce
New-city Ontario Campaign: "Ontario: Who Will You Help"
Derek Royer
Diageo; Canada Smirnoff Ice; 2005
Earls Kitchen + Bar Campaign: "Lobster Party"
Elections Ontario Campaign: "We Make Voting Easy"
Flight Network Campaign: "Gas Station Takeover"
Forbes
IKEA Campaign: "Human Coupons", Campaign: "Ikea Icons", Campaign: "Inspiration Boxes", Campaign: "Learn Ikea", Campaign: "Moving Day Wild Postings", Campaign: "Multiple Choice", Campaign: "Ottawa Interior Beautification Plan", Campaign: "The Ikea Moving Box", Campaign: "The Most Helpful Measuring Tape in the World"
New-The Intern of Bloor Street
Invesco Investment Fund
James Ready Beer Alcohol, Campaign: "50% Awesomer Coasters", Campaign: "How Many Beers for That?", Cover Photo Swap, James Ready Cap Recall
J.M. Smucker Adam's Peanut Butter, Jams; 1996
Kellogg Company Frosted Flakes, Funktown, Special K; 1952
Kraft Canada Inc. Breakstone's, Campaign: "Faces", Campaign: "Made with JELL-O-V-E", Cool Whip, Cracker Barrel, Crystal Light, Jell-O, Philadelphia Cream Cheese, Planters, TV
MillerCoors Campaign: "Say Yes to Yes", Coors Light
Moosehead Breweries; Canada Moosehead Lager; 2005
Nintendo; 1991
Peter Schafrick Campaign: "Flip Books"
Procter & Gamble Always, Bounce, Bounty, Campaign: "Bounce It Off Millions", Campaign: "Bounty Picks It Up", Campaign: "Dig It! Get It!", Campaign: "Like A Girl", Gain, Pet Hair Repellent "Bunnies"; 1958
Raising the Roof Campaign: "Nothing But Potential - Look Down", Campaign: "Repackaging Help", Campaign: "Thank You For Helping the Homeless", Campaign: "The Homeless Read Mean Tweets", Campaign: "The Street House", Campaign: "Toques That Make You Look Good - "Dentist", Homeless Charity
Restore Integrative Health Campaign: "Restore Logo"
Rooster Post Production Campaign: "Calendar of Large Cocks"
The Score; Toronto, Ontario, Canada Television Programming; 2004
Smith Restaurant + Bar Campaign: "Smith.Food For The Everyman."
TDCanada "Automated Thanking Machines"
The Toronto-Dominion Bank Campaign: "MakeTodayMatter"
TSN
TVO "Group Photos - Chefs"
Type Books Campaign: "The Joy of Books"
Yellow Pages Campaign: "Local Lights"

LEO BURNETT DETROIT, INC.

3310 W Big Beaver Rd Ste 107, Troy, MI 48084-2809
Tel.: (248) 458-8300
Fax: (248) 458-8300
Web Site: www.leoburnett.com

Year Founded: 1906

National Agency Associations: 4A's

Agency Specializes In: Communications, Sponsorship

Ian Jones *(Exec VP & Grp Acct Dir)*
Keith Ulrich *(Exec VP & Grp Acct Dir)*
Tony Booth *(Exec VP & Dir-Creative Ops)*
Michael Muscat *(Exec VP & Dir-Brand Plng)*
Kelle Durocher *(Sr VP & Exec Acct Dir)*
Brian McCallum *(Sr VP & Exec Acct Dir-Buick)*
Erik Zaar *(VP & Exec Producer)*
Andrew Bacheller *(VP & Acct Dir)*
Delayne Turner *(VP & Dir-Talent)*
Jeff Wolfe *(Art Dir)*
Jack Crifasi *(Dir-Creative)*
Tim Thomas *(Dir-Creative)*
Bob Veasey *(Dir-Integrated Creative)*
Jessica Smith *(Sr Acct Exec)*
Devann Madden *(Acct Exec-Digital)*

Accounts:
Buick; 2007
Detroit Institute of Arts "Diego Rivera and Frida Kahlo in Detroit", Communications, Creative, Creative Agency of Record, Exhibition, Marketing
Envo Water
GMC (Agency of Record) Campaign: "Fastball", Campaign: "Swish", Digital, Out of Home, Print, Social, TV; 2007
National Collegiate Athletic Association (NCAA) Campaign: "Talking Bench", Creative; 2012

LEO BURNETT WORLDWIDE, INC.

35 W Wacker Dr, Chicago, IL 60601-1723
Tel.: (312) 220-5959
Fax: (312) 220-3299
E-Mail: belief@leoburnett.com
Web Site: www.leoburnett.us/chicago/contact-us/

Employees: 6,844
Year Founded: 1935

National Agency Associations: 4A's-AAF-ABC

Agency Specializes In: Advertising, Advertising Specialties, Brand Development & Integration

Tom Bernardin *(Chm & CEO)*
David Zander *(Pres)*
Susan Credle *(Chief Creative Officer)*
Giles Hedger *(Chief Strategy Officer)*
Mick Mccabe *(Chief Strategy Officer-USA)*
Mark Tutssel *(Chief Creative Officer-Global)*
Bill Hickman *(Chief Growth Officer)*
Mark Renshaw *(Chief Innovation Officer)*
Catherine Guthrie *(Pres-Multi-Natl Accts)*
Jeanie Caggiano *(Exec VP & Exec Dir-Creative)*
Mylene Pollock *(Exec VP & Exec Dir-Creative)*
Charley Wickman *(Exec VP & Exec Dir-Creative)*
Skip Drayton *(Exec VP & Grp Dir-Integrated Mktg)*
Nina Abnee *(Exec VP & Acct Dir)*
David Brot *(Exec VP & Acct Dir)*
Catherine Davis *(Exec VP & Acct Dir)*
Karla Flannery *(Exec VP & Acct Dir)*
Richard Roche *(Exec VP & Acct Dir)*
Louis Slotkin *(Exec VP & Acct Dir)*
John Hansa *(Exec VP & Dir-Creative)*
Lance Koenig *(Exec VP & Dir-Plng)*
Brian Shembeda *(Exec VP & Dir-Creative)*
Angela Whitby *(Exec VP & Dir-Strategy)*
Richard Bennington *(Exec VP-Fin & Ops)*
Ron Nelken *(Exec VP)*
Cliff Schwandner *(Exec VP)*
Josh Crick *(Sr VP & Mng Dir-Digital Integration)*
Brian Ma *(Sr VP & Exec Creative Dir)*
Mike Shanahan *(Sr VP & Exec Dir-Production Ops)*
Denis Giroux *(Sr VP & Exec Producer)*
Varsha Kaura *(Sr VP & Acct Dir)*
Jean-Marc Kuentzmann *(Sr VP & Acct Dir)*
Susan Lulich *(Sr VP & Acct Dir)*
Sarah Paulsen *(Sr VP & Acct Dir)*
Josh Raper *(Sr VP & Acct Dir)*
Gordy Sang *(Sr VP & Creative Dir)*
Susan Stefaniak *(Sr VP & Acct Dir)*
Peter Albrycht *(Sr VP & Dir-Digital Dev & Integration)*
Sarah Block *(Sr VP & Dir-Creative)*
Lilia Arroyo Flores *(Sr VP & Dir-Plng)*

Advertising Agencies

Tony Katalinic *(Sr VP & Dir-Creative)*
Heather Paris *(Sr VP & Dir-Strategy)*
Mikal Pittman *(Sr VP & Dir-Creative)*
Eric Routenberg *(Sr VP & Dir-Creative)*
Mike Siska *(Sr VP & Dir-Strategic Plng)*
Delayne Turner *(Sr VP & Dir-Talent)*
Steve Yuan *(Sr VP & Dir-Global Plng-Samsung Global Brand Mgmt)*
Kevin Zier *(VP, Head-Creative Integration, Dir-Creative & Copywriter)*
Matt Blitz *(VP & Exec Producer)*
A.J. Hassan *(VP & Creative Dir)*
Mike Ward *(VP, Dir-Creative & Writer)*
Sue Broverman *(VP & Dir-Strategy)*
Doug Buffo *(VP & Dir-Info Svcs)*
Amanda Butts *(VP & Dir-Creative)*
Tony Cregler *(VP & Dir-Brand Strategy)*
Tina Janczura *(VP & Dir-External Comm)*
Howard Laubscher *(VP & Dir-Participation Strategy)*
Molly Stewart *(VP & Dir-Talent Mgmt)*
Ray Swift *(VP & Dir-Production Consulting)*
Chris von Ende *(VP & Dir-Art & Creative)*
Peggy Walter *(VP & Dir-Celebrity Svcs)*
Drew Wehrle *(VP & Dir-Publ & Content)*
Jill Fix *(VP & Assoc Dir-Creative)*
Paul Earle *(Exec Dir)*
Dominick Maiolo *(Exec Dir-Creative)*
Jon Wyville *(Exec Dir-Creative)*
Bob Veasey *(Dir-Art & Grp Dir-Creative)*
Glen Hilzinger *(Grp Dir-Creative & Copywriter)*
Doug Burnett *(Sr Dir-Art)*
Niki Condon *(Sr Dir-Art)*
Stephanie Summers *(Sr Dir-Art)*
Waleska Diaz *(Grp Acct Dir)*
Jennifer Cacioppo *(Acct Dir)*
Chris Cole *(Creative Dir)*
Vincent Cook *(Creative Dir)*
Katie George *(Acct Dir-Adv)*
Megan Lally *(Acct Dir)*
Brian McCauley *(Creative Dir)*
C J Nielsen *(Acct Dir)*
Katie Nikolaus *(Acct Dir)*
Ang Puglise *(Art Dir)*
Jason Reno *(Acct Dir)*
Amber Stanze *(Acct Dir)*
Michael Sutton *(Art Dir)*
Mark Wegwerth *(Creative Dir)*
Keith Wisniewski *(Creative Dir)*
Rene Delgado *(Dir-Art)*
Omar Elamin *(Dir-Fin)*
Lisa Hill *(Dir-Content Strategy)*
Natalia Kowaleczko *(Dir-Design)*
AJ Livsey *(Dir-Strategy)*
Britt Nolan *(Dir-Creative)*
Alice O'Hara *(Dir-Legal Ops & Corp Affairs)*
Jill Solarcyk *(Dir-Art)*
Sheila Stanicek *(Dir-Digital Comm)*
Graham Woodall *(Dir-Global Creative)*
Dave Derrick *(Assoc Dir-Creative)*
Pablo Jimenez *(Assoc Dir-Creative)*
Omari Miller *(Assoc Dir-Creative)*
Greg Nobles *(Assoc Dir-Creative)*
Angela Paris *(Assoc Dir-Creative)*
Jennifer Skidgel *(Assoc Dir-Global Awards)*
Kate Sullivan *(Assoc Dir-Creative)*
Ryan Wolin *(Assoc Dir-Creative)*
Sara Anderson *(Mgr-Talent)*
Mao Moua *(Mgr-Creative Resource)*
Julie Dykstra *(Acct Supvr)*
Kelly Mesi *(Acct Supvr)*
Deepti Ramakrishnan *(Acct Supvr)*
Kristen Vandenberg *(Acct Supvr)*
Laura Zimmer *(Acct Supvr)*
Nickay Penado *(Supvr-Mktg-Global)*
Julie Baker *(Sr Acct Exec)*
Lauren Davidson *(Acct Exec)*
Michele Hillman *(Acct Exec)*
Bridget Kuehn *(Strategist)*
Abu Ngauja *(Acct Exec)*
Claudia Steer *(Strategist)*
Becca Wilson *(Acct Exec)*
Leigh Kunkel *(Copywriter)*
Jono Paull *(Copywriter)*
Alan Shen *(Copywriter)*
Shirley Costa *(Sr Bus Mgr)*

Accounts:

Allstate Insurance "Project Aware Share", Campaign: "Blind Spot", Campaign: "Labor", Campaign: "Mayhem Wine Bottle", Campaign: "Mayhem: Apple Video", Campaign: "Out Holding Hands", Campaign: "Raccoon", Campaign: "Streaker", GPS, Holiday Decorator, Interactive, Motorcycle Insurance, Speech, Website; 1957
Altoids Altoids Sours, Campaign: "Mastering the Mother Tongue"
Altria Group, Inc.
Art Institute of Chicago Campaign: "ChicaGO Picasso"
Bridgestone Americas Tire Operations, LLC Campaign: "Drive a Firestone", Firestone, Firestone Complete Auto Care, Strategic & Creative Solutions
Bridgestone/Firestone North American Tire, LLC
Brooks Running (Global Agency of Record)
Cheez-It
Chicago Ideas Week Campaign: "WhatIfChicago"
Coca-Cola Refreshments USA, Inc. Campaign: "Arctic Home", Campaign: "Shine", Campaign: "Snowball Effect", Campaign: "Stare Bear", Campaign: "There's Nothing Soft About It", Campaign: "Thumbprints", Creative
ComEd The Ice Box Derby
DIRECTV "BOXING"
Esurance Campaign: "#EsuranceSave30" Super Bowl 2014, Campaign: "Beatrice", Lead Creative
FEMA Campaign: "Day Before Irene", Campaign: "Day Before Joplin"
Fiat
Fifth Third Bancorp; Cincinnati, OH Campaign: "Challenge", Campaign: "New Shoes", Campaign: "Quiet", Campaign: "The Idea", Campaign: "The curious bank", Digital, Marketing Communications
General Motors Advertising, Buick, GMC, Marketing
Girl Scouts Of America
Greater Chicago Food Depository Campaign: "Pass The Plate"
Hallmark Cards, Inc. Campaign: "Motherbird", Campaign: "Put Your Heart to Paper", Campaign: "Tell Me Family", Campaign: "The Team"
Intel
Jeep
Kellogg Company All-Bran, Campaign: "Defined by a Number", Campaign: "Fight Fat Talk", Campaign: "From Great Starts Come Great Things", Campaign: "L'Eggo My Eggo", Cereal, Corn Flakes, Crunchy Nut, Eggo (Creative Agency), FiberPlus, Frosted Flakes, Gone Nutty, Hispanic, Keebler, Online, Peanut Butter, Pop Tarts, Social Media, TV, Wake Up To Breakfast
The Kraft Heinz Company Campaign: "Faces", JELL-O, TV
Labatt USA LLC Beck's, Leffe; 2002
Marshall's Digital Creative, Traditional Creative
McDonald's Advertising, Ant Can't, Campaign: "APPLE", Campaign: "All-Day Breakfast", Campaign: "Arch Enemies", Campaign: "Dave", Campaign: "Fishin", Campaign: "Go Blackhawks", Campaign: "I'm lovin' it", Campaign: "NFL Rush Zone", Campaign: "Pay with Lovin", Campaign: "Signs", Chicken Burger, Coffee, Creative, Deana's Big Dreams, Digital, Doddi the Dodo Goes to Orlando, Fast Food, Fresh Salads, Happy Meal Choices, Lead Agency, Marketing, Proud Papa, Sirloin Burger, Snack Size Menu, Super Bowl 2015, TV, The Goat Who Ate Everything
Nestle Purina PetCare Company Campaign: "I Make Dog Chow", Creative, Digital, Public Relations, TV
Nintendo of America Campaign: "Legend of You", Campaign: "School's Out", Campaign: "Sleeping Problems", Creative, Digital, Nintendo DS, Nintendogs, Wii; 1991
Norton Campaign: "Enjoy Your Privacy"
Pantone Campaign: "Pantone Queen"
Peace One Day Campaign: "Recipeace", Olive Oil Can
Pfizer Campaign: "Stay on Top of Your Game", Centrum
Philip Morris
Procter & Gamble Always, Campaign: "#LikeAGirl", Campaign: "Gang Up For Good", Campaign: "Mean Stinks", Campaign: "Meanamorphosis", Campaign: "Stronger Together", Campaign: "Unstoppable", Mr. Clean, Super Bowl 2015
Proton
Samsung Electronics Campaign: "Design Your Life", Galaxy Gear, Galaxy Note 3
Seek Campaign: "Volunteer to promote volunteering", Seek Volunteer
Sprint Below-The-Line, Campaign: "Everything's Important", Campaign: "I Am Unlimited", Campaign: "Lost", Campaign: "Pajamas", Campaign: "Probably Not, But Maybe", Campaign: "Thinking About You", Campaign: "Totes McGotes", Campaign: "Unlimited Love Billboard", Creative, Retail
Symantec Campaign: "Stuff Theatre", Norton Internet Security
New-Ty Inc. Campaign: "Peek A Boos"
United Nations Campaign: "The World Needs More", Campaign: "Under Five"
Visa
Western Digital Campaign: "External Hard Drives"
WhiteWave Foods Silk Soymilk
Wikipedia Knowledge is power

Arc Worldwide

35 W Wacker Dr 15th Fl, Chicago, IL 60601
(See Separate Listing)

Lapiz

35 W Wacker Dr 12th Fl, Chicago, IL 60601
Tel.: (312) 220-5000
Fax: (312) 220-6212
E-Mail: info@lapizusa.com
Web Site: www.lapizusa.com

Employees: 40
Year Founded: 1999

National Agency Associations: 4A's

Agency Specializes In: Bilingual Market, Consumer Marketing, Hispanic Market, Public Relations, Sales Promotion, Sponsorship

Diego Figueroa *(Sr VP & Dir-Strategy & Participation)*
Ernesto Adduci *(VP & Acct Dir)*
Marco Azucena *(Acct Dir)*
Maru Bernal *(Creative Dir)*
Carlos Murad *(Dir-Creative)*
Edgardo Olaizola *(Dir-Strategy)*
Bruno Pieroni *(Assoc Dir-Creative)*
Daniela Barcelo *(Acct Supvr)*
Lucille Gratacos *(Acct Supvr)*
Spencer Colvin *(Acct Exec)*
Jonny Arcila *(Jr Art Dir)*

Accounts:

ACH Foods Creative, Mazola; 2008
Allstate Corporation; 2007
Allstate Insurance Hispanic
Brown Forman
The Cara Program Choose
Chase
Chicago Latino Film Festival Campaign: "All About Great Stories", Campaign: "Paternity"
Coca-Cola Refreshments USA, Inc.
General Motors Buick
H&R Block, Inc.; 2007
Hanes
Kellogg Company Keebler
Labatt USA LLC

Lumini Photography Campaign: "Get A Better"
Mars Bounty
Marshalls Hispanic
McDonald's Chicago, North West Indiana
Mexico Tourism Board Campaign: "Los Cabos #Unstoppable", Campaign: "Snow Graffiti", Outdoor, TV
Mujeres Latinas En Accion Campaign: "Flower", Campaign: "Husband", Campaign: "Ring"
Nestle Purina PetCare Company Purina Latin America
Nintendo
Procter & Gamble Always, Bounty Paper Towels, Campaign: "BATHROOM-MADE", Campaign: "Bed", Campaign: "Clear Words", Campaign: "Movie", Campaign: "Quinceanera", Campaign: "Radio Case", Campaign: "Stains Happen", Charmin, Clear Blue, Dawn, Gain with Oxi, Herbal Essences, Outdoor, Prilosec OTC, Print, Puffs
Re/Max Holdings Campaign: "Dream With Your Eyes Open", Digital, Print, Radio, Social Media, Tv
Rofs Pharmaceuticals
The Spirit Initiative
New-UnitedHealthcare Campaign: "Ways In"
U.S. Cellular Hispanic; 2010
Walt Disney Company
Wickes Furniture

Leo Burnett Business

300 Park Ave S, New York, NY 10010
(See Separate Listing)

Leo Burnett Detroit, Inc.

3310 W Big Beaver Rd Ste 107, Troy, MI 48084-2809
(See Separate Listing)

Leo Burnett - Los Angeles

6500 Wilshire Blvd Ste 1950, Los Angeles, CA 90048
Tel.: (323) 866-6020
Fax: (323) 866-6033
E-Mail: info@leoburnett.com
Web Site: www.leoburnett.com

Employees: 5
Year Founded: 1947

National Agency Associations: 4A's

Richard Roche *(Exec VP & Acct Dir)*
Radim Svoboda *(Sr VP-Global Bus Mgmt)*
Sean Pinney *(VP & Producer-Content)*
Tim Howman *(Assoc Dir-Art & Creative)*
Marsha Kabb *(Office Mgr)*
Ian Beacraft *(Mgr-New & Emerging Technologies)*

Accounts:
Nintendo Co., Ltd.
Samsung Campaign: "Sweet Dreams", Galaxy Gear, Note 3

Leo Burnett Tailor Made

300 Park Ave S 7th Fl, New York, NY 10013
Tel.: (646) 840-8300
Fax: (646) 840-8334
E-Mail: lisa.abbatiello@leoburnett.com
Web Site: www.leoburnett.com

Employees: 40

Agency Specializes In: Sponsorship

Mark Tutssel *(Chief Creative Officer-Worldwide)*
Lisa Abbatiello *(CEO-Leo Burnett Bus)*
Dave Skinner *(Exec Dir-Creative)*
Stian Bugten *(Dir-Digital Creative)*

Accounts:
Filip Technologies Campaign: "Best Day Ever"
Hemoba/Esporte Clube Vitoria Campaign: "My Blood is Red and Black"
Village Voice Campaign: "New York Writes Itself", Campaign: "The Chairman"

Leo Burnett USA

35 W Wacker Dr, Chicago, IL 60601-1723
Tel.: (312) 220-5959
Fax: (312) 220-3299
Web Site: www.leoburnett.us

Employees: 1,000
Year Founded: 1935

Agency Specializes In: Advertising, Advertising Specialties, Brand Development & Integration, Sponsorship

Rich Stoddart *(Pres-North America)*
Suellen Ravanas *(CFO-NA & Exec VP)*
Michele Gilbert *(Exec VP & Head-Global P&G)*
Jeanie Caggiano *(Exec VP & Exec Dir-Creative)*
Nancy Hannon *(Exec VP & Exec Dir-Creative)*
Dave Loew *(Exec VP & Exec Dir-Creative)*
John Montgomery *(Exec VP & Exec Dir-Creative)*
Charley Wickman *(Exec VP & Exec Dir-Creative)*
Debbie Bougdanos *(Exec VP & Dir-Talent Acq)*
Lance Koenig *(Exec VP & Dir-Strategy)*
Jenny Cacioppo *(Exec VP)*
Brian Ma *(Sr VP & Exec Dir-Creative-Leo Burnett Interactive)*
Denis Giroux *(Sr VP & Exec Producer)*
Eric King *(Sr VP & Creative Dir)*
Colin Padden *(Sr VP & Acct Dir)*
Antoniette Wico *(Sr VP & Acct Dir)*
Rob Allen *(Sr VP & Dir-Tech)*
Christopher Cole *(Sr VP & Dir-Creative)*
Vince Cook *(Sr VP & Dir-Creative)*
Omar Elamin *(Sr VP & Dir-Fin-Multi Natl Accts)*
Tony Katalinic *(Sr VP & Dir-Creative)*
Enrique Marquez *(Sr VP & Dir-Strategy)*
Gavin McGrath *(Sr VP & Dir-Creative)*
Heather Paris *(Sr VP & Dir-Strategy)*
Sarah Patterson *(Sr VP & Dir-Plng)*
Veronica Puc *(Sr VP & Grp Exec Producer)*
Isabela Ferreira *(VP-Creative & Dir)*
Jill Reformado *(VP & Dir-Recruiting)*
Gina Santana *(VP & Dir-Strategic Plng)*
Chris von Ende *(VP & Dir-Creative & Art)*
Joel Arzu *(Sr Dir-Art)*
Ashley Beam *(Acct Dir)*
Jeff Candido *(Creative Dir)*
Brian Marcus *(Art Dir)*
Andrea Newsom *(Acct Dir-Fifth Third Bank)*
Colleen Raleigh *(Acct Dir-Global)*
Jason Reno *(Acct Dir)*
Brian Shembeda *(Creative Dir)*
Susan Stefaniak *(Acct Dir)*
Laura Wood *(Art Dir)*
Peter Albrycht *(Dir-Digital Dev & Integration)*
Joel Boysen *(Dir-Strategic Vendor Mgmt)*
Scott Fleming *(Dir-Art)*
AJ Hassan *(Dir-Creative)*
Brandan Jenkins *(Dir-Creative)*
Kate Lorenz *(Dir-Content Strategy)*
Andrew Malloy *(Dir-Strategy)*
Melissa Matthews *(Dir-Art)*
Britt Nolan *(Dir-Creative)*
Anca Risca *(Dir-Creative)*
Jon Wyville *(Dir-Creative)*
Brooke Anderson *(Assoc Dir-Creative)*
Julio D'Alfonso *(Assoc Dir-Creative)*
Rene Delgado *(Assoc Dir-Creative)*
Lynsey Elve *(Assoc Dir-Global Reputation & Comm)*
Kevin Goff *(Assoc Dir-Creative)*
Matt Mortimer *(Assoc Dir-Creative)*
Alan Shen *(Assoc Dir-Creative)*
Ryan Stotts *(Assoc Dir-Creative)*
Michael Cowen *(Mgr-External Comm)*
Thy Barnes *(Acct Supvr)*
Lindsey Woerther *(Acct Supvr)*
Nickay Penado *(Supvr-Mktg-Global)*
Hannah Qualley *(Sr Acct Exec-Kellogg's-Morning Foods)*
Diana Saenz *(Sr Acct Exec)*
Samantha Hickey *(Acct Exec)*
Meredith Kelly *(Acct Exec)*
Adriana Zavala *(Acct Exec)*
Jack Dess *(Jr Copywriter)*
Alberto Portas *(Copywriter)*
Jordan Bustin *(Asst Acct Exec)*
Sean Hannaway *(Assoc Creative Dir)*
Jo Shoesmith *(Sr Creative Dir)*

Accounts:
The Allstate Corporation Allstate Homeowner Insurance, The Allstate Corporation
Always Campaign: "Like a Girl"
American Bar Association
The Art Institute of Chicago Campaign: "19th Century Paris Has Come To Chicago"
Avis
Centrum Campaign: "Stay On Top Of Your Game"
The Coca-Cola Company Campaign: "Small World Machines"
Delta Faucet Co. Campaign: "HappiMess Anthem", Campaign: "HappiMess", Campaign: "Here's to the Mess Makers", Digital, Print, Shower Head, Touch-Free Faucet, Touch2O
DeVry University
Esurance, Inc. Campaign: "Sorta Pharmacist", Campaign: "Sorta You Isn't You", Super Bowl 2015
Exelon
FEMA
Fifth Third Bank Campaign: "Checkbook", Campaign: "Curiosity Stands Up to Cancer", Campaign: "Pay to the Order of", Campaign: "Replacements", In-branch, Mobile Banking App, Online, Out-of-home, Radio, Social Media, TV
Firestone Campaign: "Do Truck Stuff", Campaign: "Drive A Firestone", Campaign: "Jump", Campaign: "Pick Up"
General Motors Company Campaign: "Her Horse", Chevy Silverado, Pontiac
Hallmark Cards, Inc. Hallmark Cards, Inc., Hallmark Greeting Cards
New-The Innovation Foundation Chicago Ideas
Invesco Ltd. Campaign: "Intentional Investing", Campaign: "Roger on a Monday"
Kellogg Company Campaign: "Eat Special. Feel Special.", Campaign: "Froot Detector", Campaign: "Shut Down Fat Talk", Campaign: "Tomorrow", Campaign: "What Will You Gain When You Lose?", Digital, Froot Loops Treasures, In-Store Marketing, Print, Public Relations, Raisin Bran Crunch, TV
McDonald's Campaign: "Lucky Penny"
MillerCoors; Chicago, IL Campaign: "How To Speak Australian", Creative, Miller High Life; 2009
NCAA (Agency of Record)
Nintendo Creative, Digital, Donkey Kong Country Returns 3D
Pfizer
Philip Morris U.S.A. Parliament, Philip Morris U.S.A.
The Procter & Gamble Company Biggest Assembly Ever, Campaign: "Mean Stinks", Noxzema
Purina
Samsung "Changes", Campaign: "Design Your Life", Campaign: "Dress Your Device Up, No Matter What The Occasion", Campaign: "Sweet Dreams", Campaign: "The Developer", Campaign: "We AllShare movie trailer", Galaxy Gear, Galaxy Note 3, Galaxy Note 4, Swarovski
Sprint Campaign: "Unlimited Love Billboard"
Tampax
UnitedHealthcare Campaign: "Our Song", Campaign: "Ways In", Digital, Out-of-Home, Radio, Social, TV
U.S. Smokeless Tobacco Company Copenhagen, Skoal; 2009
Walgreens; Chicago, IL; 2009
Walt Disney Company

Advertising Agencies

Canada

Leo Burnett Company Ltd.

175 Bloor St E North Twr, Toronto, ON M4W 3R9 Canada
(See Separate Listing)

Argentina

Leo Burnett Inc., Sucursal Argentina

Olga Cossenttini 1545 Piso 2, C1107 BVA Buenos Aires, Argentina
Tel.: (54) 11 4819 5959
Fax: (54) 11 4819 5900
E-Mail: fernando.bellotti@leoburnett.com.ar
Web Site: www.leoburnettargentina.com

Employees: 87
Year Founded: 1981

Agency Specializes In: Advertising

Carmelo Maselli *(Gen Dir-Creative)*
Agustin Remaggi *(Acct Dir)*
Luis Sanchez Zinny *(Dir-Creative)*
Hernan Cunado *(Gen Acct Dir)*

Accounts:
Arcor Arcor Father-Son, Campaign: "The Juice Mystery"; 1997
Bodegas Callia
Car One "Love Story / Party", Campaign: "Damn License Plates", Campaign: "Previous Owner"
Chrysler Campaign: "GPS to Get Lost"
Fiat Campaign: "Boob Job", Campaign: "First Day", Highway, Love Point, Parking; 1992
Garbarino Campaign: "Back to Garbarino"
Marlboro
McDonald's Corporation
Philip Morris; 1984
Procter & Gamble; 1981
New-Samsung
Walmart

Brazil

Leo Burnett Tailor Made

(Formerly Leo Burnett Publicidade, Ltda.)
Rua Brejo Alegre 93/99, CEP-04557-050 Sao Paulo, SP Brazil
Tel.: (55) 11 5504 1337
Fax: (55) 11 5504 1444
Web Site: www.leoburnett.com.br

Employees: 160
Year Founded: 1969

Marcelo Reis *(Co-Pres)*
Marcio Toscani *(Co-Pres)*
Paulo Giovanni *(CEO)*
Marcello Magalhaes *(Partner & VP-Strategic Plng)*
Andre Nassar *(Exec Dir-Creative)*
Pedro Rosa *(Sr Dir-Art)*
Ricardo Alonso *(Art Dir)*
Eduardo Battiston *(Creative Dir)*
Junior Bottura *(Acct Dir-Fiat Retail & Chrysler Grp)*
Marcelo Bruzzesi *(Creative Dir)*
Cintia Mourao *(Acct Dir)*
Maicon Pinheiro *(Art Dir)*
Alessandro Bernardo *(Dir-Creative)*
Vinny Couto *(Dir-Art & Creative)*
Henri Honda *(Dir-Art)*
Martin Insua *(Dir-Art)*
Marcio Juniot *(Dir-Creative)*
Robison Mattei *(Dir-Creative & Art)*
Antonio Nogueira *(Dir-Creative)*
Alexandre Pagano *(Dir-Art)*
Marcelo Rizerio *(Dir-Art)*
Vitor Menezes *(Asst Dir-Art)*
Giovanna Rodrigues *(Acct Supvr)*
Mirelly Rosa *(Acct Supvr)*
Anelene Putini *(Acct Exec)*
Marco Farah *(Planner)*
Christian Fontana *(Copywriter)*
Alexandre Freire *(Copywriter)*
Roberto Salomao *(Designer-Final Art)*
Ezequiel Soules *(Copywriter)*
Andre Marques *(Exec Client Svcs Dir)*

Accounts:
ABTO- Brazilian Association of Organ Transplant Campaign: "Bentley Burial", Campaign: "Dating", Charity, Donation Badges
The Against Malaria Foundation
Atitude Brasil Campaign: "Laundry"
Brazilian Association of Organ Transplant Campaign: "Bentley Burial"
Camil
Centro de Valorizacao da Vida Campaign: "Inside Every Suicide"
The Chrysler Group Campaign: "Eagle", Campaign: "Risks", Car, Jeep Grand Cherokee
Club SangueBom Campaign: "The Donor Cable"
Coral
CVV; 1999
Daimler AG
Dreft
Emirates
New-FCA US LLC Jeep Deserts
Fiat Campaign "Come to the street", Campaign: "Design", Campaign: "Dont Make-Up & Drive", Campaign: "Hero Hug", Campaign: "Just one non-original part changes the whole story.", Campaign: "Letters: N, F, R", Campaign: "Protect Your Music. Freemont with Soundproof Interior", Fiat 500, Fiat Ambulance, Fiat Bravo, Fiat Ducato, Fiat Original Parts, Fiat Safety Wi-Fi, Linea, New Fiat Uno, Palio, Wolverine; 1995
Gillette
Guitar Player Magazine Campaign: "1985, 2012", Campaign: "Fashion Trends", Campaign: "The Beatles", Campaign: "World Economy", Jimi Hendrix
Hemoba Foundation Campaign: "My Blood Is Red And Black"
Instituto Akatu Campaign: "Fake Shower"
Jacare Grill
Koleston Wella
L&M
Lance Final Shopping Virtual Ltda. Lancefinal.com, Television
Lemonade Films
Livraria Da Vila Campaign: "15 Minutes", Campaign: "Malcolm X"
Morumbi Shopping Mall
Next
Pao & Companhia Campaign: "Bread Wine"
Pea Campaign: "Gallagher Brothers"
Philip Morris; 1975
Procter & Gamble ACE Detergent, Campaign: "Grubby Bra"; 1987
Rimowa Campaign: "Protected Clothing"
Rossi Residencial Fiateci, Real Estate
Samsung Campaign: "Where Is Pancho?", Home Theater, Phone, SH100
Saxsofunny Campaign: "Johann"
Serta Colcha.Es Campaign: "Plane"
Sharpie
Skinmax Depilacao Campaign: "The Waxe Pencil"
Studio Anaca Campaign: "Public Domain"
Topline Gums campaign: "Made For Kissing"
Truth
Vitoria Campaign: "My Blood is Red & Black"

Colombia

Leo Burnett Colombia, S.A.

Carrera 13 N 89-59, Bogota, DC Colombia
Tel.: (57) 1 628 5959
Fax: (57) 1 218 9073
E-Mail: olga.villegas@col-leoburnett.com
Web Site: www.col-leoburnett.com

Employees: 150
Year Founded: 1964

Olga Lucia Villegas *(Pres)*
Mauricio Sarmiento *(VP-Creative)*
Fernando Hernandez *(Grp Dir-Creative)*
Adriana Arjona *(Acct Dir)*
Ana Sanchez *(Dir & Acct Mgr)*
Diego Almanza *(Dir-Art)*
Janet Consuegra *(Dir-Customer Svc)*
Rafael Reina *(Dir-Creative HUB Digital)*
Diego Rodroguez *(Dir-Creative & Digital)*
Jorge Valencia Montenegro *(Team Head-Digital)*

Accounts:
Against Cancer League Cancer Awareness
Aldor Campaign: "Bumba Giants"
Alpina Vibe Yogurt
Art with Wine
New-Asiri Group of Hospitals Ltd. Soap Bus TIcket
Carrefour "LETTUCES"
Cerveza Club Colombia
Coca-Cola Refreshments USA, Inc. Campaign: "The Happiness Passenger"
Colombian Red Cross Campaign: "The Blood Scroll"
Corona
Cruz Roja Colombiana Campaign: "Names of Blood", Campaign: "The Blood Scroll"
Cusezar
Davivienda Banking, Credit For Brazil 2014, Financial Services; 1979
Diageo Campaign: "Art with Wine", Johnny Walker
Diana
DIRECTV Campaign: "King Kong"
ETB
Falabella
Farmatodo
Fundacion Bolivar-Davivienda
ICASA; 2001
Juan Valdez Coffee
Kellogg Company Zucaritas; 1980
Mawbima
Me Encanta
Navarro Correas
Procter & Gamble Campaign: "Chicken"; 1989
Productos Alimenticios Alpina Campaign: "Bon Yurt Neon"
Pronaca
Samsung
Seguros Bolivar Billboard Lighting Rod, Campaign: "Rockstar"; 1997
United Nations Organization "Burning Forest", Shared Responsibility Program
Visa
WWF Campaign: "A Double Gift", Campaign: "One Daily Drop", Wildlife Charity

Mexico

Leo Burnett Mexico S.A. de C.V.

Bosque de Duraznos 65-8P Bosques de las Lomas, 11700 Mexico, DF Mexico
Tel.: (52) 55 5246 5959
Fax: (52) 55 5251 7207
E-Mail: jaguilar@leoburnett.com.mx
Web Site: www.leoburnett.com

Employees: 150
Year Founded: 1969

National Agency Associations: AMAP-IAA

Agency Specializes In: Advertising

Daniel Perez Pallares *(Chief Creative Officer)*
Juan Pablo Camargo *(VP-Strategic Plng)*
Daniel Jimenez-Castro *(Gen Mgr & Acct Dir)*
Fernando Moraga *(Sr Dir-Strategy-Reg & Global)*
Fernando Bellotti *(Creative Dir)*
Emilio Solis *(Creative Dir)*

Marco Vigano *(Dir-Creative)*
Federico Augusto Pellejero Acosta *(Assoc Dir-Creative)*
Ulises Navarro *(Mgr-Customer Svc)*
Ana Luna *(Copywriter)*

Accounts:
ACT2
Allstate Insurance
Always
AXA Insurance
Cannon
Cerveceria Modelo; 2000
Jeep Campaign: "Wash Stencil"
Kellogg's Company All-Bran; 1984
Philip Morris Mexico; 1969
Procter & Gamble; 1982
Unidal Mexico, S.A. de C.V.; 2001
Wrigley Campaign: "Native", Skwinkles

Paraguay

Mass Publicidad S.R.L.

Estados Unidos 961 3rd Floor, Asuncion, Paraguay
Tel.: (595) 21 451 031
Fax: (595) 21 210 772
E-Mail: prubiani@mass.com.py
Web Site: www.mass.com.py

Employees: 34
Year Founded: 1996

Agency Specializes In: Advertising, Public Relations

Pascual Rubiani *(Owner)*
Francis Galeano *(Graphic Designer & Designer-Creative)*

Peru

Circus Communicacion Integrada

(Formerly Leo Burnett Del Peru S.A.)
Av Angamos Oeste #1270, Miraflores, Lima, 18 Peru
Tel.: (51) 1617 9292
Fax: (51) 1617 9274
Web Site: www.leoburnett.com

Employees: 75
Year Founded: 1998

Agency Specializes In: Advertising, Government/Political, Social Marketing/Nonprofit

Juan Carlos Gomez de la Torre *(Pres & Gen Dir-Creative)*
Marco Milesi *(CEO)*
Gisella Ocampo *(Gen Mgr)*
Emiliano Gonzalez *(Exec Dir-Creative)*
Yasu Arakaki *(Sr Dir-Art)*
Viviana Bedoya *(Acct Dir-Spectacular Holistic Circus)*
Ivana Chavez *(Dir-Trademark-Grey Circus Peru)*
Giuliana Garcia *(Dir-Audiovisual Production)*
Ricardo Toyohama *(Dir-Art)*

Accounts:
Asa Alimentos; 1999
Banco de Credito Del Peru; 2001
BCP Bank Campaign: "Very Easy"
BCP Deals App
Claro Peru
Credicorp Capital
DERCO (Suzuki Dealer)
Diageo; 2002
Empresa Editoria El Comercio; 1999
Ideasmusik App
Ponle Corazon (Foundation Against Cancer)
Prima AFP
Procter & Gamble; 1994
Saga Falabella; 2000
San Fernando Poultry Campaign: "Brochette", Chicken Preserved Food
Sodimac
Supermercados Tottus
Techo Campaign: "Pandora Project", Campaign: "Trolling Against Poverty"
Todinno
UPC; 2000
Fundacion Peruana de Lucha contra el Cancer / Ponle Corazon
Samsung
Sony
Visa

EMEA Regional Headquarters

Leo Burnett, Ltd.

Warwick Building Kensington Village, Avonmore Road, London, W14 8HQ United Kingdom
Tel.: (44) 207 751 1800
Fax: (44) 207 348 3855
Web Site: www.leoburnett.co.uk

Employees: 482
Year Founded: 1969

National Agency Associations: IPA

Agency Specializes In: Advertising

Andrew Edwards *(Grp Chm & Grp CEO)*
Paul Lawson *(CEO)*
Josh Bullmore *(Grp Head-Plng)*
Justin Tindall *(Exec Dir-Creative)*
Sarah Baumann *(Grp Dir-Talent Strategy)*
Tara Howell *(Grp Dir-Client Svcs)*
Lewis Beaton *(Art Dir)*
Beri Cheetham *(Creative Dir)*
Charlie Martin *(Creative Dir)*
Phill Meyler *(Creative Dir)*
Steve Robertson *(Art Dir)*
Hugh Todd *(Creative Dir)*
Matt Collier *(Dir-Art & Copywriter)*
Wayne Robinson *(Dir-Art & Copywriter)*
Don Bowen *(Dir-Creative)*
Rik Brown *(Dir-Creative)*
Zoe Crowther *(Dir-Mktg & New Bus)*
Pete Heyes *(Dir-Creative)*
Darren Keff *(Dir-Creative)*
Matt Lee *(Dir-Creative)*
Guy Moore *(Dir-European Creative)*
Richard Robinson *(Dir-Creative)*
Angus Campbell Golding *(Sr Acct Mgr)*
Lorna Burt *(Planner)*
Kit Altin *(Planner)*
Allison Ball *(Designer)*
Caroline Baron *(Planner)*
Anna Bron *(Designer)*
Phil Deacon *(Copywriter)*
Marc Donaldson *(Sr Designer)*
Alexandra Gill *(Planner)*
Richard Ince *(Copywriter)*
Alex Moore *(Copywriter)*
Allison Steven *(Copywriter)*

Accounts:
Amnesty International Campaign: "The Departure Board"
BITC Campaign: "Ban The Box"
Brake
Business In The Community Campaign: "BAN THE BOX"
Channel 4
Chrysler Group UK Creative, Dodge, Jeep
The Co-operative Bank Creative, Smile Internet Bank
Co-operative Electrical Snapchat
Co-operative Funeralcare Campaign: "Here For You, For Life", Campaign: "Smile", Campaign: "Voice of Law", Digital, Outdoor, Press, TV
Co-operative Group Limited Campaign: "Easter Errands", Campaign: "Marzipan!", Campaign: "Wonderful", Creative, TV, The Cooperative Food
The Co-operative Legal Services Campaign: "Ready Meals", Campaign: "Voice of Law"
Coca Cola Campaign: "Share a Bottle", Coke Classic, Coke Zero, Diet Coke; 2007
Energy Brands #shinebright, Vitamin Water
Comfy
Dartmouth Films Campaign: "The Machine"
Department for Transport Campaign: "#publooshocker", Campaign: "THINK"
Design Museum 2015 Exhibition, Design
Dewars
Freeview Brand Campaign, Campaign: "#catandbudgie", Campaign: "Entertainment. It's Even Better When it's Free", Campaign: "Left Behinds", Campaign: "Set Yourself Free", Campaign: "Summer of Sport", Campaign: "Tadpoles", Digital, Freeview Play, Helium balloons, In-Store, Outdoor, Print, Social, Strategy, TV
Homebase Campaign Name: "Containers", Campaign: "Make Your House Your Home"; 2008
IndieLisboa 10th International Independent Film Festival, Campaign: "Noooo!"
Karma Nirvana "National Day of Memory for Honour Killing", Campaign: "RememberShafilea", Campaign: "Suffocation", Print, Social Media Campaign
Kellogg "Henry", Campaign: "72,000 Flavours", Campaign: "Actual Size", Campaign: "Blue Plaque of Lies", Campaign: "Buy Two, Get a Free Boat", Campaign: "Day's Out", Campaign: "Give a Child a Breakfast", Campaign: "Imagine That", Campaign: "It's All Lies", Campaign: "Revolutionary Chocolatier", Campaign: "The Box", Campaign: "The Trouble is They Taste Too Good", Crunchy Nut, Frosties, Marketing, Rice Krispies, Special K, Television; 1977
Leica Store
Lindt & Sprungli
Luerzers International Archive Campaign: "Account Man Monthly", Campaign: "Spreadsheet Enthusiast", Campaign: "Untouchable Covers"
McDonald's "Little Farmers", "McD", A-Z, Cajun Crispy Chicken, Campaign: "Break the Habit of a Lunchtime", Campaign: "Check In", Campaign: "Coffee?", Campaign: "Cow", Campaign: "Dad's Voice", Campaign: "Discover Australia", Campaign: "Good Times", Campaign: "Good to Know", Campaign: "Great Tastes of America", Campaign: "Here's to What Matters", Campaign: "Hunter Gatherer", Campaign: "Just Moved In", Campaign: "Loading Piccadilly Circus", Campaign: "Lonely Hearts", Campaign: "Mascotathon Anthem", Campaign: "Next Stop, McDonald's", Campaign: "Paralympics", Campaign: "Perfume", Campaign: "See One. Want One.", Campaign: "Somewhere Near You", Campaign: "Sun Party", Campaign: "That's what makes McDonald's", Campaign: "The Rest Of The Day Has A Lot To Live Up To", Campaign: "Trust The Tree", Campaign: "We All Make The Games", Chicken Legend, Chicken McBites, Creative, Dave, Digital, Egg McMuffin, Fanta Fruitizz, Favourites, Happy Meals, He's Happy, Online, Outdoor, Print, Public Relations, Sausage, Saver Menu, Social Media, TV, The Journey to Christmas; 1986
MillerCoors
National Careers Service
NHS LifeCheck
NSPCC
Pantone Campaign: "Pantone Queen"
Plan International Campaign: "Mass Construction"
Procter & Gamble #GentleManHunt, Always, Campaign: "#LikeAGirl", Cleaning Product, Daz Confetti, Flash, Old Spice; 1983
Renaissance Photography Prize Campaign: "Renaissance", Campaign: "Saturday, Sunday & Monday", Campaign: "Winter"
Rice Krispies Squares

RNLI
Ronald McDonald House Charities Campaign: "Dad's Voice"
New-Samsung Campaign: "The Time Is Now"
Shelter Homeless Charity
THINK! Campaign: "PubLooShocker", Drunk-Driving PSA, Teenage Road Safety
Tommys
Which?

Belgium

Leo Burnett Belgium

18 Place Eugene Flageyplien, Box 17, 1050 Brussels, Belgium
Tel.: (32) 2 775 65 40
Fax: (32) 2 779 90 36
E-Mail: info@leoburnett.be
Web Site: www.leoburnett.be

Employees: 32
Year Founded: 1975

National Agency Associations: EAAA

Agency Specializes In: Electronics, Food Service, Pharmaceutical

Henet Denis *(Mng Partner)*
Kaat Danneels *(Mng Dir)*
Tom Garcia *(Dir-Creative)*
Jeroen Vernelen *(Acct Mgr)*
Elodie Pagaud *(Acct Exec)*
Wout Geysen *(Copywriter)*

Accounts:
Closedgap
DIAGEO; 1995
Fiat Group Automobiles Campaign: "Jeep Compass Most Remote Postbox"; 1992
H.J. Heinz Company Heinz; 1998
Inbec; 1990
IP TV and Radio
Ixina
Philip Morris; 1975
Procter & Gamble Campaign: "Mannequin"; 1983
The Reading Foundation Out of Office Poetry
Samsung Electronics Campaign: "Speed Deals"
Stichting Lezen Campaign: "Out of Office Poetry"

Cyprus

Innovation Leo Burnett

90 Ifigenias St 2nd Fl, 2003 Strovolos, Nicosia, Cyprus
Mailing Address:
PO Box 16058, 2085 Strovolos Nicosia, Cyprus
Tel.: (357) 22 378 828
Fax: (357) 22 378 577
E-Mail: leoburnett@leoburnett.com.cy
Web Site: www.leoburnett.com

Employees: 20

Agency Specializes In: Advertising

Stavroula Eracleous *(Dir-Fin)*

Accounts:
Christies
G. Charalambous Lavazza Coffee
Lifeline
Marks & Spencer
Natuzzi
Procter & Gamble Always, Ariel, Pantene Shampoo & Conditioner; 1998
Wella

Estonia

Kontuur-Leo Burnett

Parnu Road 142A, 11317 Tallinn, Estonia
Tel.: (372) 683 2000
Fax: (372) 683 2001
E-Mail: info@kontuur.ee
Web Site: www.kontuur.ee

Employees: 65
Year Founded: 1997

Agency Specializes In: Outdoor

Madis Laas *(CEO)*
Jaanus Meri *(Dir-Art)*
Andrus Niit *(Copywriter)*

Accounts:
1188 Infoabi
ADCE Estonia Campaign: "Dying Designer"
Baltika Group; 1996
Etv
Extreme Sport
Hot
Kalev
Kontakt!
Kroonika
Nycomed Sefa; 1997
Rakvere
Statoil

Egypt

AMA Leo Burnett

2005C Corniche El Nil St Ramlet Beaulec, Nile City Towers N Tower, 11221 Cairo, Egypt
Tel.: (20) 2 2461 8000
Fax: (20) 2 2461 9080

Christin Ghobrial *(Deputy Mng Dir)*
Tamer El-Sherbini *(Acct Dir)*
Mohamed Aboul Enein *(Acct Dir)*
Mohammed Yousri *(Dir-Plng)*
Osama Arnaouty *(Assoc Dir-Creative)*
Akram Negm *(Assoc Dir-Creative)*
Magda Ghaly *(Mgr-Admin)*

Accounts:
Birell
Boehringer Ingelheim
Brazil Telecom
Du Life
Egypt Foods Campaign: "Cono is Different", Campaign: "Dog", Cono
Hallmark
Heinz Campaign: "You Can't Eat Without It"
Melody Entertainment
Mobinil Campaign: "Mobinil Hands", Campaign: "We Only Have Each Other"
Phillip Morris
Prisma
SCIB
Telecom-Tim
Tesco
VTB Bank

France

Leo Burnett

12 rue James Watt, Saint Denis, 93200 Paris, France
Tel.: (33) 1 55 84 65 00
Fax: (33) 1 79 62 11 20
E-Mail: jean-paul.brunier@leoburnett.fr
Web Site: www.leoburnett.fr

Employees: 151
Year Founded: 1969

Michel Perret *(Mng Dir)*
Marianne Wagner *(Mng Dir)*
Thierry Miliotis *(CFO)*
Adeline Messiaen *(Editor & Designer)*
Mohamed Bareche *(Art Dir)*
Remi Lascault *(Art Dir)*
Jerome Gonfond *(Art Di)*
Veronique Khayat *(Acct Mgr)*
Luc Lepelletier *(Acct Mgr)*
Elise Baudour *(Copywriter)*
Jean-Francois Le Marec *(Copywriter)*

Accounts:
Aprilia
Atlantic
Charal Campaign: "The Ostrich"; 1993
Chrysler Group Campaign: "Now, man is expected anywhere", Campaign: "Upside Down Doe", Campaign: "Upside Down Elephant", Campaign: "Upside Down Giraffe", Jeep Wrangler
Daimler AG Campaign: "See whatever you want to see"
Delipapier Le Trefle Toilet Paper Campaign: "Sopalin Orange Juice", Emma
Fiat 500
Jeep Campaign: "Beaver", Campaign: "Bike", Campaign: "Boat", Campaign: "Float", Campaign: "Horse", Campaign: "Speedboat", Quiksilver Pro
Kellogg Company; 1986
Krispolis
Lamy Lutti
LDC: Le Gaulois
Le Trefle Campaign: "EMMA", Campaign: "Paper is Necessary"
Mimi Foundation Campaign: "If Only For A Second", Puzzle 1, Puzzle 2, Puzzle 3
Noemi Association
Pfizer Inc.
Prisma Presse
Procter & Gamble Campaign: "Planet"; 1985
Rana
Riches Monts
Samsung Samsung Galaxy
Sidaction
Sopalin
Swiffer
Theatre de la Bastille Campaign: "Edgar & Kelly"
Volvo Trucks Campaign: "If Only for a Second"

Ireland

Leo Burnett Associates

46 Wellington Rd Ballsbridge, Dublin, 4 Ireland
Tel.: (353) 1 668 9627
Fax: (353) 1 668 1341
E-Mail: info@leoburnett.ie
Web Site: www.leoburnett.com

Employees: 25
Year Founded: 1962

Agency Specializes In: Consumer Marketing

Martin Larkin *(Chm)*

Accounts:
Bavaria Beer
Beiersdorf Ireland
Channel 6
Elverys Sports
FIAT
Goodfella's
Home Value Hardware; 1998
Kellogg's
Nawras Campaign: "Piggybacking"
RPII

Italy

Leo Burnett Co., S.r.l.

Via Fatebenefratelli 14, 20121 Milan, Italy
Tel.: (39) 02 63541
Fax: (39) 02 2900 5229

E-Mail: giorgio.brenna@leoburnett.it
Web Site: www.leoburnett.it

Employees: 192
Year Founded: 1969

Daniele Tranchini *(Mng Dir & Bus Dir-Global)*
Niccolo Arletti *(Mng Dir)*
Giorgio Brenna *(Chm/CEO-CWE)*
Enrico Dorizza *(Sr Dir-Creative)*
Luca Ghilino *(Sr Dir-Art)*
Gianluca Ignazzi *(Sr Dir-Art)*
Alessandro Antonini *(Dir-Creative-Global)*
Alessandra Buchignani *(Dir-Art)*
David Campos *(Dir-Art)*
Christopher Jones *(Dir-Creative)*
Anna Meneguzzo *(Dir-Creative)*
Marco Vigano *(Dir-Creative)*
Lisa Marussi *(Assoc Dir-Creative)*
Andrea Marzagalli *(Assoc Dir-Creative)*
Giovanni Salvaggio *(Assoc Dir-Creative)*
Alice Jasmine Crippa *(Copywriter)*
Giovanni Pesce *(Coord-Creative)*

Accounts:
ABN Nephrotic Children's Association; 1995
Anno Sabbatico
Diageo; 1988
Fiat Fiat 500 Cult Yacht, Safety At Work Awareness; 1991
Fontegrafica Campaign: "Sabbatical Year"
Heineken; 1997
Heinz-Plasmon
Hemaviton Stamina Plus
IDI Pharmaceuticals Cinzia Your Skin Friend
Imetec; 1997
ING Direct Financial Services
Jeep Campaign: "Jeep Never Adapt"
Kellogg Company; 1987
Montblanc Campaign: "The Beauty of a Second", Nicolas Rieussec Chronograph
Poste Italiane; 1999
Procter & Gamble Clearblue Easy, Pringles Multigrain; 1986
Samsung Campaign: "Samsung Smart Bikes", Washing Machine
SDA Bocconi; 1992
Theatre de la Bastille
Vivienne Westwood
Walt Disney Co.; 2001
WWF

Leo Burnett Co. S.r.l.

Via San Quintino 28, 10121 Turin, Italy
Tel.: (39) 011 560 1911
Fax: (39) 011 5175 300
Web Site: www.leoburnett.it

Employees: 15
Year Founded: 1969

Agency Specializes In: Advertising

Giorgio Brenna *(Chm/CEO-Continental Western Europe)*
Paolo Griotto *(Acct Dir)*
Alessandro Antonini *(Dir-Creative-Global)*
Luca Boncompagni *(Dir-Art)*
Julie Carpinelli *(Copywriter)*
Diego Tardani *(Copywriter)*
Davide Boscacci *(Grp Creative Dir)*

Accounts:
Domina Hotels
Ferretti Yachts
Fiat Auto Campaign: "Panda"; 1993
Kellogg
McDonald's

Leo Burnett Rome

Via Crescenzio 38, 00193 Rome, Italy
Tel.: (39) 06 684 321
Fax: (39) 06 684 32 513
E-Mail: leoinfo@leoburnett.it
Web Site: www.leoburnett.it

Employees: 50

Agency Specializes In: Advertising

Daniele Tranchini *(Mng Dir & Bus Dir-Global)*
Niccolo Arletti *(Mng Dir)*
Giorgio Brenna *(Chm/CEO-CWE)*
Cristina Leone *(Gen Mgr-Rome Office)*
Joelle Rizk *(Client Svcs Dir)*
Ilaria Fruscio *(Dir & Planner)*
Luca Boncompagni *(Dir-Art)*
Daniele Marrone *(Dir-Creative)*
Martina Barbi *(Acct Exec)*

Accounts:
ABN Nephrotic Children's Association; 1994
Fiat; 1993
Heineken; 1989
Imetc; 1997
Kellogg Company; 1989
McDonald's; 2000
Procter & Gamble; 1999
SDA Bocconi; 1995
Walt Disney Company; 2000

Jordan

Leo Burnett Jordan

18 Al Mutanabi Street 3rd Cicle, 2013, Amman, 11181 Jordan
Tel.: (962) 646 44142
Fax: (962) 646 44142
E-Mail: info@amman-leoburnett.com
Web Site: www.leoburnett.com

Employees: 8

Agency Specializes In: Advertising

Joelle Jammal *(Mng Dir)*
Kamil Kuran *(Mng Dir-Levant Reg)*
Rami Afifi *(Sr Dir-Art)*
Sary Najjar *(Dir-Creative)*

Accounts:
Brasil Telecom
Diageo
Fiat
Kelloggs
McDonald's
Phillip Morris
Samsung
Sipes Paint We Cover Everything
Tesco
Visa

Kenya

Access Leo Burnett

Bishops Garden Towers 4th Floor, PO Box 42379, Nairobi, 00100 Kenya
Tel.: (254) 2 719 501
Fax: (254) 20 2719 533
E-Mail: access@accessleoburnett.com.ke
Web Site: www.leoburnett.com

Employees: 30
Year Founded: 1979

Alison Mcconnell *(Exec VP & Chief Growth Officer-Leo Burnett Worldwide)*

Kuwait

Leo Burnett

Al Khaleeja Building 12th Floor, PO Box 4455, Safat, 13045 Kuwait, Kuwait
Tel.: (965) 240 4967
Fax: (965) 240 7855
E-Mail: kamal.dimachkie@dubai.leoburnett.com
Web Site: www.leoburnett.com

Employees: 8
Year Founded: 1986

Agency Specializes In: Advertising

Kamal Dimachkie *(Exec Reg Mng Dir)*

Accounts:
Kuwait Telecom Company VIVA
Nandos; 2007
The National Bank of Kuwait

Lebanon

H&C, Leo Burnett

Sofil Center 5th Floor Achrafieh, PO Box 55369, Beirut, Lebanon
Tel.: (961) 1 201090
Fax: (961) 1 334219
Web Site: www.leoburnett.com

Employees: 85
Year Founded: 1974

National Agency Associations: IAA-LAA

Agency Specializes In: Consumer Marketing

Bechara Mouzannar *(Chief Creative Officer-MENA)*
Christine Bouyea *(VP & Acct Dir)*
Nayla Baaklini *(Sr Dir-Art)*
Caroline Farra *(Creative Dir)*
Christina Salibi *(Art Dir)*
Alexandre Choucair *(Dir-Creative)*
Youssef Naaman *(Dir-Global Comm & Reg Ops-CEEMEA)*
Daniel Salles *(Dir-Art)*
Said Stephan *(Dir-Fin)*
Kato Tsang *(Assoc Dir-Creative)*
Zaid Alwan *(Assoc Creative Dir & Copywriter)*
Jordan Gabriel *(Copywriter)*
Lama Najjar *(Copywriter-English)*
Malek Ghorayeb *(Reg Exec Dir-Creative)*

Accounts:
Alfa Campaign: "Tariff"
Always
Bank Audi Campaign: "Go Out there Wheel of Life", Campaign: "Make It Big Out Of Little", Credit Card
Bel Group CSR Campaign
Bonux
Brand Protection Group Anti-Counterfeit Awareness, Campaign: "Fake it all"
Cadbury Adams Trident Chewing Gum
Cafa Super Brasil Campaign: "Read the Country's Fortune"
Chateau Ksara
Children Cancer Center Creative
Diageo Campaign: "Keep Walking Lebanon", Johnnie Walker
Exotica
General Motors Corp.; 1999
HARIRI Foundation
Himaya Campaign: "Break the Silence"
Kellogg Company; 1994
Khalil Warde SAL
Koleston Naturals
Ksara; 2000
Lebanese Army
Les Affichages Pikasso
LibanPost
Loubnani Card
Mashrou' Leila
Mondelez International, Inc.; 1991

No Rights No Women
Offre Joie Campaign: "Volunteers Don't Seek Recognition"
Olay 7
Outbox International Short Film Festival Campaign: "The Forest"
Philip Morris; 1981
Pikasso
Procter & Gamble Campaign: "Smoky Eye Effect"; 1983
Virgin Radio Campaign: "Nothing Comes Easy", Campaign: "Say No To Piracy"
Warde Campaign: "Home Is A Quest"

Lithuania

Leo Burnett Vilnius
Birutes 1D, Vilnius, 08117 Lithuania
Tel.: (370) 5 264 7505
Fax: (370) 5 260 9000
E-Mail: office@leoburnett.lt
Web Site: www.leoburnett.com

Employees: 6

Rapolas Vedrickas *(COO)*
German Lapin *(Controller-Fin)*
Pavel Cesnokov *(Dir-Art)*
Nida Zekaite Pakutinskiene *(Dir-Art)*

Accounts:
Phillip Morris

Morocco

Leo Burnett Casablanca
26 Rue Frederic Le Maitre, Quartier Riviera, Casablanca, Morocco
Tel.: (212) 22 22 43 73
Fax: (212) 22 22 24 79
E-Mail: asmaa.dyani@leoburnett.ma
Web Site: www.leoburnett.com

Employees: 20
Year Founded: 1999

Agency Specializes In: Advertising

Abla Ammor *(Mng Dir-Morocco)*
Asmaa Dyani *(Dir-Comm)*
Kamal Elallam *(Dir-Comm)*
Scott Huebscher *(Dir-Creative)*

Accounts:
China Telecom
Dubai Holding
Fiat; 1999
GM
Hallmark
Hiear
Marlboro
Multon
Orange
Phillip Morris
Procter & Gamble; 1999
Red Bull GmbH; 2001
Samsung
Sanofi Aventis
VISA

Nigeria

Rosabel Advertising Ltd.
Rosabel Court 31 Aromire Av, Ikeja, Lagos, Nigeria
Mailing Address:
P.O.Box 12067, Ikega, Lagos, Nigeria
Tel.: (234) 1 497 6210
Fax: (234) 1 497 6214
E-Mail: info@rosabelleoburnett.com
Web Site: www.rosabelleoburnett.com

Employees: 61
Year Founded: 1978

Tunji Abioye *(Exec Dir)*
Kayode Adeboye *(Dir-Bus Dev & Strategic Plng)*

Accounts:
Kraft Foods; 2001

Norway

Kitchen Leo Burnett
Drammensveien 127, 114, BYGG 86,2 ETG, 0212 Oslo, Norway
Tel.: (47) 24 10 3629
Fax: (47) 24 10 39 99
E-Mail: haakon@kitchen.no
Web Site: www.kitchen.no

Employees: 49
Year Founded: 1981

Agency Specializes In: Advertising, Automotive, Consumer Goods, Consumer Marketing

Bjorn Polmar *(Chm & Acct Dir)*
Christian Hygen *(Creative Dir)*
Melissa Kristiansen *(Art Dir)*
Kjetill Nybo *(Art Dir)*
Anne Gravingen *(Dir-Art)*
Anders Holm *(Copywriter)*

Accounts:
1888 Telephone Directory Campaign: "Hair"
BMW; 2002
Brilleland
Canon; 2002
Djuice/Telenor; 2001
Flytoget Campaign: "Slower than fast"
Fretex Campaign: "Coming Soon Maybe", Campaign: "Digital Recycling Bin", Salavation Army Second Hand Shop, Secondhand Clothes
Hansa
JC Decaux
McDonald's; 1989
New-Meny
Norwegian Airlines Campaign: "From Cold To Hot"
Norwegian Handcraft Association 100 Year Anniversary, Campaign: "Taxi"
Rimi; 2001
Salvation Army/Fretex; 2001
Skeive Dager
SpareBank 1 Campaign: "App-Bank", Campaign: "Woman in Black"
Unibet Campaign: "Dee Sings what He Sees"
Uteseksjonen Campaign: "The Complaint"

Poland

Leo Burnett Warsaw SP.Z.O.O.
UL Woloska 9, 02-583 Warsaw, Poland
Tel.: (48) 22 448 9800
Fax: (48) 22 860 9801
Web Site: www.leoburnett.com

Employees: 120
Year Founded: 1991

Agency Specializes In: Advertising

Monika Perek *(Mng Dir)*
Bechara Mouzannar *(Chief Creative Officer)*
Pawel Heinze *(Dir-Creative)*

Accounts:
Amnesty International Campaign: "Empathy Calendars"
Beta
Dreft
Exotica
Fiat Campaign: "The Earthliner,2", Jeep
Grupa Zywiec Campaign: "Faces"
Heineken Poland U-Code
Max Factor
National Museum In Krakow
Procter & Gamble Bonux, Campaign: "Date", Campaign: "Rainbow", Discreet Tanga, Maps, Tide
Ptk Centertel Campaign: "Scales"
Sukiennice Museum

Portugal

Leo Burnett Publicidade, Ltda.
Rua das Flores 7, 1200-193 Lisbon, Portugal
Tel.: (351) 21 326 0800
Fax: (351) 21 326 0895
E-Mail: sofia.barros@leoburnett.pt
Web Site: www.leoburnett.pt

Employees: 57
Year Founded: 1982

Nuno Salvaterra *(Head-Art & Dir-Design Creative)*
Hugo Lage *(Editor-Video, Dir & Producer-Creative)*
Douglas Cardoso *(Dir-Art)*
Paula Lopes *(Dir-Customer Svc)*
Guilherme Nunes *(Dir-Art)*
Leonardo Pinheiro *(Dir-Creative & Art)*
Tiago Reis *(Dir-Bus Dev)*
Lina Ventura *(Dir-Local Fin)*
Jorge Pais *(Acct Exec)*
Emanuel Serodio *(Sr Graphic Designer)*
Antonio Silva *(Sr Designer)*

Accounts:
Amnesty International Campaign: "Stop Torture", Campaign: "Voices for Freedom", Tyrannybook
APCD Campaign: "Andra"
Caos Sustainability Campaign: "Now we are 7 billion. For better. Or for worse."
Carma Campaign: "The Bicycle Made From The Scrap Of A Car"
Coca-Cola Refreshments USA, Inc. Fanta; 1998
Control Arms Campaign: "The exhibition that shouldn't exist"
Corbis Campaign: "Requests Yellow Car"
Dyrup Bondex Wood Protection, Paint, Varnish
EDP Foundation
Fiat Campaign: "Titanic", Environmental Campaign; 1992
Freeport Department Store, Shopping Outlet, Witchcraft Exhibition
Fundacion Altius
Galp Energia; 2000
Gas de Portugal; 1996
IndieLisboa Campaign: "Nooooooooooooooooo", Campaign: "Shower"
Leya
Lidl Supermarkets
Lisbon City Council Campaign: "LX Type"
Louie Louie Campaign: "Gelatery", Campaign: "Kurt"
McDonald's; 2002
Mondelez International, Inc.; 1998
MTV
ORBIS
Pampero Rum
Pfizer
Philip Morris Detroit, L&M, Marlboro; 1994
Portuguese Red Cross Campaign: "Drop of Hope"
Red Cross Portugal
Samsung
Sic Noticias
Sogrape Vinhos; 1991

Romania

Leo Burnett & Target SA

13 Nicolae Iorga Str, Bucharest, 010432 Romania
Tel.: (40) 21 201 6100
Fax: (40) 21 201 6101
E-Mail: office@leoburnett.ro
Web Site: www.facebook.com/LeoBurnettRomania

Employees: 100
Year Founded: 1995

Agency Specializes In: Advertising

Andreea Boaca *(Mng Dir)*
Razvan Capanescu *(Chief Creative Officer & Copywriter)*
Ioana Avram *(Art Dir)*
Ciubotaru Codrina *(Brand Dir-Comm)*
Irina Becher *(Dir-Creative)*
Anca Catarambol *(Dir-HR)*
Andrei Radulescu *(Dir-Fin)*
Victor Stroe *(Dir-Plng)*
Ioana Carp *(Brand Mgr-Comm)*
Cristina Corbu *(Brand Mgr-Comm)*
Madalina Marica *(Brand Mgr-Comm)*
Alexandra Patarlageanu *(Brand Mgr-Comm)*

Accounts:
Altex
Asociatia Pro Democratia
Autoitalia
Bergenbier
BRD Groupe Societe Generale
Groupama
PETROM
Philip Morris; 1996
Procter & Gamble; 1995
Quadrant Amrog Beverage; 1999
Stop Violence Against Women
Strauss

Russia

Leo Burnett Moscow
11 Bldg 2-5 Timur Frunze Str 2nd Fl, Business Centre Red Rose, 119021 Moscow, Russia
Tel.: (7) 495 969 2030
Fax: (7) 495 969 2025
E-Mail: reception.leoburnett@leoburnett.ru
Web Site: www.leoburnett.ru

Employees: 200
Year Founded: 1995

Agency Specializes In: Advertising

Vladimir Tkachev *(Chm/CEO-Russia & Eastern Europe)*
Mikhail Kudashkin *(Exec Dir-Creative)*
Max Kitaev *(Sr Dir-Art)*
Mikhail Yarovikov *(Sr Dir-Art)*
Ivan Dergachev *(Assoc Dir-Creative)*
Irina Aldushina *(Acct Mgr)*

Accounts:
BSGV; 2004
Chilled Chicken Meat
Diageo; 1999
Dirol; 2003
Goodyear Russia
Google Campaign: "Free a Tree"
Jeep Campaign: "Carabiner"
Kraft Foods; 2003
LEGO
MegaFon
MTS Jeans; 2003
Myth
National Cable Networks Campaign: "Scan Your Brain"
Panasonic; 2003
Philip Morris; 1995
Procter & Gamble Dreft; 1995
Russian Ministry of Press
S7 Airlines Campaign: "Catch a Plane", Campaign: "Where Cold is Cool"
Sinteros; 1999
Staropramen Beer
Sun Interbrew; 2003
Surf Leroy Merlin Campaign: "Banknotes"
The Village Campaign: "Death Revealer", Magazine
Vimm-Bill-Dann Campaign: "The softest cheese ever"; 2002
Wimm-Bill-Dann Campaign: "Butcher"
WWF Charity, Sibirian Tiger Protection

Saudi Arabia

Targets/Leo Burnett
Al Faisaliah Tower 7th Fl, PO Box 295797, King Fahd Rd, Riyadh, 11351 Saudi Arabia
Tel.: (966) 1 273 7070
Fax: (966) 1 273 7071
Web Site: www.leoburnett.com

Employees: 45
Year Founded: 2001

Bechara Mouzannar *(Chief Creative Officer)*
Mohammed Albatran *(Dir-Art)*
Roy Ghattas *(Dir-Art)*
Habeeb Najjar *(Dir-Art)*
Feras Shoujah *(Dir-Creative)*
Nader Naamani *(Mgr-PR Comm)*
Khalid Al Khatib *(Sr Graphic Designer)*
Dominic Felix *(Sr Graphic Designer)*
Anthony Azzi *(Sr Art Dir)*

Accounts:
General Motors Corp.; 1999
Invision
Kellogg Company; 1991
Kudu
Mondelez International, Inc.; 1987
Nasair Air Travel
Philip Morris; 1987
Procter & Gamble; 1982

Slovakia

Wiktor/Leo Burnett, s.r.o.
Leskova 5, 811 04 Bratislava, Slovakia
Tel.: (421) 2 5249 7250
Fax: (421) 2 5249 7078
E-Mail: wlb@wlb.sk
Web Site: blog.wlb.sk/

Employees: 50
Year Founded: 1992

Agency Specializes In: Advertising

Peter Kontra *(Mng Dir)*
Peter Kacenka *(Exec Dir-Creative)*
Katarina Kvackajova *(Grp Acct Dir)*
Stefan Andrejco *(Dir-Creative)*
Martin Motacek *(Dir-Creative)*
Raffo Tatarko *(Dir-Creative)*
Jana Machackova *(Sr Acct Mgr)*
Igor Fekiac *(Acct Mgr)*
Marcela Liptajova *(Mgr-Talents & Culture)*
Marek Surovec *(Copywriter)*

Accounts:
Alfa Romeo
Coop Jednota
Dobry Anjel
Edison
Fiat; 1994
Orange Slovakia Campaign: "Lucky Puck"
Orava
Philip Morris; 1996
Quatro Campaign: "Retro In Store", Installment Sale
Saint Nicolaus Vodka
Slovenske Pramene a Zriedia Budis, Fatra; 1996
Sony Ericsson
Tatry Mountain Resorts
New-Transparency International Campaign: "Not every bribe is just a box of chocolates"
Triangel
Unebanke
Union Insurance Campaign: "Announcement", Campaign: "Italy", Campaign: "Truth Well Told", Mandatory Car Insurance

Slovenia

Votan Leo Burnett
Ob Ljubljanici 12, 1000 Ljubljana, Slovenia
Tel.: (386) 1 236 40 50
Fax: (386) 1 236 4051
E-Mail: vlb@votanleoburnett.si
Web Site: www.votan.co

Employees: 14
Year Founded: 1995

Agency Specializes In: Advertising

Natasa Krese *(Acct Dir)*
Mojca Digger *(Dir-PR Dept)*

Accounts:
Jub; 1991
Procter & Gamble; 1996
Radio Hit; 1995
Red Bull GmbH; 1994
Sava Tires; 1999
Skoda

Sweden

Leo Burnett Annonsbyra
Sveavagen 24-26, PO Box 476, 10129 Stockholm, Sweden
Tel.: (46) 8 412 5000
Fax: (46) 8 412 5050
E-Mail: info@leoburnett.se
Web Site: leoburnett.com/

Employees: 20
Year Founded: 1991

Agency Specializes In: Advertising, Food Service

Thomas Gibson *(CEO)*

Switzerland

Spillmann/Felser/Leo Burnett
Armtlerstrasse 201, PO Box 8040, CH-8003 Zurich, Switzerland
Tel.: (41) 43 311 2525
Fax: (41) 43 311 2524
E-Mail: welcome@sflb.ch
Web Site: www.sflb.ch

Employees: 70
Year Founded: 2002

Agency Specializes In: Advertising, Travel & Tourism

Rolf Zimmermann *(Mng Dir)*
Michael Waeber *(CFO)*
Axel Eckstein *(Exec Dir-Creative)*
Johannes Raggio *(Exec Dir-Creative)*
Christian Bircher *(Creative Dir & Copywriter)*
Ilija Gautschi *(Art Dir)*
Barbara Hartmann *(Art Dir)*
David Hugentobler *(Copywriter)*
Bastian Otter *(Copywriter)*
Fabian Windhager *(Copywriter)*

Accounts:
Anna Belle; Zurich
New-Bio Suisse
Die Post Campaign: "Coffeestamp"
Emmentaler Campaign: "Emmentaler Cheese Gotthelf", Campaign: "National Day Emmentaler"
Federal Office of Public Health Switzerland Campaign: "Organ Donation", Campaign: "The Decision"
Fleurop Campaign: "Broken Vase"
Floralp Campaign: "Butter Atop Jelly"
German Stuttering Association
Goldbach Media
GSOA
HG Commerciale; Zurich
HWZ School of Business; Zurich
Interflora Fleurop
Mario Haller
Micasa; Zurich Campaign: "Names-Promotion"
Migros Magazine; Zurich
Neuco; Zurich
Ovomaltine Campaign: "Flakes Banner"
Pet Recycling
Samsung NX Mini
Slow Food
Sunrise; Zurich
Swiss Life; Zurich Campaign: "Life's Turns In A Sentence"
Swiss Post Campaign: "Coffeestamp"
Swissbanking Campaign: "100 Thank You"
Switzerland Tourism Ant Hill, Campaign: "Clocks", Campaign: "Holidays Without Internet", Campaign: "The Visit"
Tages-Anzeiger; Zurich
Verein Zurcher Hausarzte
Victorinox
WOZ Die Wochenzeitung Campaign: "Ads Suck When You'Re Reading", Campaign: "Notebook, Smartphone, Tablet"

Turkey

Markom/Leo Burnett

Buyukdere Cad 26/6 Beytem Plaza, Sisli, 34360 Istanbul, Turkey
Tel.: (90) 212 234 2728
Fax: (90) 212 246 0842
E-Mail: sibel.buyuktezcan@leoburnett.com.tr
Web Site: www.leoburnett.com.tr

Employees: 65
Year Founded: 1983

Ekin Arsiray *(Grp Head-Creative)*
Evren Dinler *(Grp Head-Creative)*
Koray Sahan *(Grp Dir & Dir-Art)*
Emrah Akay *(Creative Dir)*
Tuba Azak *(Acct Dir)*
Umit Senturk *(Art Dir)*
Mert Ozkaner *(Dir-Art)*
Deniz Cavdar *(Copywriter)*
Onur Kamis *(Copywriter)*
Ari Koen *(Copywriter)*
Sezgin Rizaoglu *(Copywriter)*

Accounts:
Be Better Campaign: "Dog"
BEDD Campaign: "Bus"
BGD Stray Animals Foundation
Blendax
Borusan Holding Borusan Technology; 2002
Chrysler Jeep
Estetica
Fiat Campaign: "The Ball", Hillholder, Panic Brake Assistance
Istanbul Toy Museum Campaign: "Soldier"
Jeep
McDonald's Campaign: "Office", Premium Roast Coffee; 2000
Private Pension System Insurance
Procter & Gamble Alldays, Alo Alo Ultra & Alo Campaign: "Spaghetti Napolitan", Campaign: "Auburn Haired Woman", Discreet, Herbal Essence, Max Factor, Orkid, Rejoice, Shamtu, Wella Koleston, Wella New Wave, Wella Wellaflex; 1990
Samsung Campaign: "Hearing Hands"
Solen Menthol Chewing Gum Campaign: "I Love You"
Stray Animals Foundation Pasha
Tema
Tofas
Toy Museum
Turkish Catastrophe Insurance Pool Compulsory Earthquake Insurance
Turkish Natural Habitat Preservation Foundation Environmental Awareness
WWF Campaign: "What Goes Around Comes Around"

Ukraine

Leo Burnett Kiev

24 Vorovskogo Str building 2 2nd floor, 01054 Kiev, Ukraine
Tel.: (380) 44 490 9060
Fax: (380) 44 490 9070
E-Mail: info@leoburnett.ua
Web Site: www.leoburnett.ua

Employees: 50
Year Founded: 1995

Ulrich Tacke *(Mng Dir)*
Tatiana Shumilovich *(Gen Dir)*
Natalia Dundina *(Creative Dir)*
Tatiana Fedorenko *(Creative Dir)*
Dmitry Gunkovsky *(Dir-Client Svc)*
Pavel Mandryk *(Copywriter)*
Volodymyr Navrotskyi *(Copywriter)*
Denys Savchenko *(Sr Art Dir)*

Accounts:
Art Directors Club Ukraine
Delo.ua Campaign: "News briefly", Campaign: "One Glance Is Enough"
Kyivstar Business
MTV Ukraine
Philip Morris; 1995
PocketBook Campaign: "One Page"
Procter & Gamble; 1995

United Arab Emirates

Flip Media FZ-LLC

Dubai Media City Arjaan Al Sufouh Office 108, PO Box 502372, Dubai, United Arab Emirates
Tel.: (971) 44247500
Fax: (971) 43912384
Web Site: www.flipcorp.com

Employees: 100
Year Founded: 2003

Agency Specializes In: Advertising, Branded Entertainment, Digital/Interactive, Graphic Design, Information Technology, Internet/Web Design, Market Research, Search Engine Optimization, Social Media

Kareem Monem *(Mng Dir)*
Wisam Akily *(Dir-Bus)*
Walid Chelala *(Dir-Creative)*
Hani Najjad *(Dir-Ops)*
Murad Daniyel *(Mgr-Bus Growth)*

Accounts:
Aabar Properties LLC
Bourjois Make-up
OSN Creative, Digital Specialist Services

Radius Leo Burnett

Dubai Media City Bldg No 11, PO Box 7534, Dubai, United Arab Emirates
Tel.: (971) 4 3672 600
Fax: (971) 4 3672 611
E-Mail: raja.trad@dubai.leoburnett.com
Web Site: www.leoburnettmena.com

Employees: 225
Year Founded: 1986

National Agency Associations: IAA

Agency Specializes In: New Product Development, Outdoor, Public Relations, Sales Promotion

Bechara Mouzannar *(Chief Creative Officer)*
Munah Zahr *(Exec Dir-Creative)*
Jad Mouhawej *(Reg Dir-Comm)*
Ramzi Sleiman *(Reg Dir-Comm)*
Rondon Fernandes *(Creative Dir)*
Bassel Kakish *(Dir-Fin)*
Nabil Mufarrij *(Dir-Comm Servicing)*
Abraham Varughese *(Dir-Creative)*
Rafael Augusto *(Assoc Dir-Creative)*
Wayne Fernandes *(Copywriter)*
Clevin Antao *(Copywriter-English)*
Sunny Deo *(Copywriter)*
Tariq Ayass *(Assoc Creative Dir-Middle East & North Africa)*

Accounts:
The Box Campaign: "The Moving Commercial", Moving Services
Chevrolet
Diageo; 1991
Dubai Cares Charity, Education Funds
Fox International Channels Middle East Campaign: "The Break-Free Print"
Fox Movies
General Motors Campaign: "The Perfect Storm"
Kellogg Company Special K; 1991
McDonald's Campaign: "Family Time Forever"
Mont Blanc
National Geographic Campaign: "Wild Cards"
Nawras
Philip Morris; 1987
Procter & Gamble Campaign: "Tide Smart Bag", Laundry Detergent, Reusable Shopping Bag, Tide, Washing Powder; 1987
Samsung After-Sales Service, Air Conditioning
Sugar Daddy's

United Kingdom

Leo Burnett London

(Formerly Holler Digital Ltd.)
Kensington Village, Avonmore Road, London, W14 8HQ United Kingdom
Tel.: (44) 207 751 1800
Fax: (44) 2077130822
E-Mail: info@leoburnett.co.uk
Web Site: www.leoburnett.co.uk

Employees: 39
Year Founded: 2001

Agency Specializes In: Brand Development & Integration, Digital/Interactive, Email, Entertainment, Game Integration, Internet/Web Design, Social Media, Technical Advertising, Viral/Buzz/Word of Mouth

Andrew Edwards *(Chm)*
Paul Lawson *(CEO)*
Sarah Baumann *(Deputy CEO)*
Giles Hedger *(Chief Strategy Officer)*
Justin Tindall *(Chief Creative Officer)*

Accounts:
Alfred Dunhill
Avios Content, Digital, Social Media
Co-operative Group Banking, Blogger Outreach,

Campaign: "Snaptop", Community Management, Engagement Production, Food, Seeding, Snapchat, Social Media, Tactical Work
Co-operative Electrical Campaign: "Fight The Price"
The Collective Brand Awareness, Digital
Contiki
Covent Garden
Food Network American Street Feasts, Digital Campaign
Innocent Big Knit, Campaign: "Orange Lovers"
Jergens Naturals
John Frieda Jergens
Logica
Lurpak Digital, Social
Mercedes-Benz UK #YOUDRIVE, Campaign: "Challenge the Van", Campaign: "Van Experience", Digital Strategy, Social Strategy, Twitter Campaign
Now TV
Pretty Green Below the Line, Digital Communications, Sunglasses Launch
Procter & Gamble Always, Campaign: "Like A Girl", Consumer Goods Mfr
Red Bull
Royal Caribbean Social Media
Samsung
Sky Social Media
TravelSupermarket
United Breweries Group Jura Whisky
Whyte & Mackay Campaign: "X Marks the Spot", Jura Whisky

Australia

Leo Burnett Melbourne

Level 7 28 Fresh Water Supply South Bank, Melbourne, VIC 3006 Australia
Tel.: (61) 3 9251 1300
Fax: (61) 3 9251 1350
E-Mail: melinda.geertz@leoburnett.com.au
Web Site: www.leoburnett.com.au

Employees: 42
Year Founded: 1935

Agency Specializes In: Advertising

Christopher Steele *(Head-Social)*
Jason Williams *(Exec Creative Dir)*
Chris Ivanov *(Grp Acct Dir)*
Ari Sztal *(Grp Acct Dir)*
Adam Jaffrey *(Acct Exec-Digital & Producer-Digital)*
Lauralee Cuzner *(Acct Dir)*
Blair Kimber *(Sr Art Dir)*
Michelle Walsh *(Dir-Creative)*
Chloe Erftemeyer *(Sr Acct Mgr)*
Suzi Williamson *(Acct Exec)*
Matt Portch *(Sr Designer)*
Kota Matsuda *(Sr Designer-Digital)*

Accounts:
7-Eleven Stores Campaign: "Slurpee: Reinventing an Icon", Slurpee, Slurpee BYO Cup Day
Arts Centre Melbourne Campaign: "Box of Curiosities"
Berger Paints Campaign: "Man Space"
New-Bonds
The Communications Council Circus Festival
Crikey
Dulux Group
British Paints Paint & Prime
The Famous Spiegeltent
Freehills
General Mills
Giant Everyday Rider Sponsorships
Honda CR-V Series, CR-V Series II, Campaign: "'Power of Dreams", Campaign: "A-Team", Campaign: "Go With It", Campaign: "Human Truth", Cinema, Communications, Creative, Digital, H2O, HR-V, Interactive, Outdoor, Social, TV
New-iSelect (Creative Agency of Record)
Mercer Wealth Solutions
Nestle Maxibon
Nintendo
Peters Ice Cream Campaign: "The Thrill of the Taste", Cinema, Creative, Digital, In-store, Magazine, Outdoor, TV
Philip Morris; 1979
Scenic Tours Digital Strategy
Scope Campaign: "See The Person", Campaign: "What Do I Look Like?", Disability Awareness, See The Person; 2000
SEEK Learning Campaign: "The Learnings from Seek Learning", Campaign: "Volunteer to Promote Volunteering"
SPC Ardmona (Creative Agency of Record) #MyFamilyCan, Baked Beans, Campaign: "Ain't Nobody Got Time For That", Creative, Fruit Cups, SPC, Spaghetti, TV
Sportsbet.com.au
Suzuki
Victoria University

Leo Burnett Sydney

20 Windmill St, McMahons Point, Sydney, NSW 2060 Australia
Tel.: (61) 2 9925 3555
Fax: (61) 2 9925 3617
Web Site: www.leoburnett.com.au

Employees: 160
Year Founded: 1935

Grant McAloon *(Head-Copy & Exec Dir-Creative)*
Justin Carew *(Grp Head-Creative)*
Iggy Rodriguez *(Grp Head-Creative)*
Patrick Rowe *(Gen Mgr)*
Grant MacAloon *(Exec Dir-Creative)*
Laura Dowling *(Sr Dir-Bus)*
Amanda Nicoll *(Grp Acct Dir)*
Jay Gray *(Art Dir-Digital)*
Joe Hill *(Creative Dir)*
Courtney Robertson *(Bus Dir)*
Claus Stangl *(Art Dir)*
Brendan Donnelly *(Dir-Creative)*
Neil Duncan *(Dir-Bus)*
Nils Eberhardt *(Dir-Art)*
Guy Futcher *(Dir-Creative)*
Caroline Ghatt *(Dir-Plng-Brand & Retail)*
Scott Huebscher *(Dir-Creative)*
Misha McDonald *(Dir-Art)*
Kieran Ots *(Dir-Digital Creative)*
Amanda Quested *(Dir-Client Svcs)*
Stuart Tobin *(Dir-Art)*
Joe Van Trump *(Dir-Creative)*
Joanna Steuart *(Sr Acct Mgr)*
Laura Cervin *(Mgr-Bus)*
Jess Ferguson *(Acct Exec)*
Curt McDonald *(Copywriter)*
Bruno Nakano *(Designer-Creative Adv)*
Jason Young *(Sr Designer)*
Dave Varney *(Sr Art Dir)*

Accounts:
7-Eleven BYO Cup Day
Australian Bureau of Statistics & Census Campaign: "Run That Town", Campaign: "Spotlight"
Barbeques Galore
Ben Lee
BIG W (Agency of Record)
Bundaberg Original Rum Campaign: "Road To Recovery"
Bundy Five
Caltex Australia Campaign: "With you all the way"
Canon Campaign: "Darren Jew", Campaign: "Decoy - A Portrait Session With a Twist", Campaign: "PIXMA Endless Creative Possibilitie", Campaign: "Seconds With", Canon Digic Image Processor, Compact Cameras, Gorilla, Large Format Printers, Media Planning
Coca Cola 3D Touchscreens Technology, Campaign: "Small Faces", Campaign: "Small World Machines", Small World Posters
Colonial First State
Diageo Bundaberg Rum, Campaign: "Ain't No Nancy Drink", Campaign: "Bundy 8-Ball", Campaign: "Bundy Bottle", Campaign: "Butterfly", Campaign: "Collective Genius", Campaign: "Lucy Maria", Campaign: "Road to Recovery", Campaign: "Smirnoff Pure", Campaign: "Watermark", Favourable Lie, Johnnie Walker Serious & Important, Master Distiller's Collective, Media Planning, Media Strategy, Pampero, Post Disaster Aid Program, Rum, Television
J&B Campaign: "Mash-Up"
Ebay Campaign: "When Inspiration Strikes", Online Shopping, Website
Energy Australia Above-the-line, Advertising, Brand Strategy, Campaign: "Perfect Plans", Campaign: "Power To Move", Digital, Outdoor, TV
EOS Photochains
Freedom Furniture
Giant Everyday Rider Sponsorships
GIO Trust
Kellogg's Be Natural
Ketel One Vodka Campaign: "'This One's Mine", Creative
Landcom
Marilyn Grace
Maytag; 1999
McDonald's Campaign: "Smurfs 2", Campaign: "Tree of Life", Creative, Frappes, Happy Meals, McCafe, Smoothies
New-NSW Fire & Safety
New-Pacific Brands Limited
Parrot Carrot
Procter & Gamble Herbal Essences, SK-II, Tide; 1985
Rabobank
Ronald McDonald House Charities Campaign: "Tree Of Life"
Samsung Campaign: "Made for Australia", Galaxy S5, Galaxy Tab S2, Gear VR, S-Drive
TRUenergy Creative
Unibet Australia Campaign: "Back Yourself"
Unilever Campaign: "The Priceline & Dove 7 Day Test"
Woolworths Limited (Agency of Record) "Odd Bunch", 85c Bread, Campaign: "Always at Woolworths", Campaign: "Choose Taste Over Waste", Campaign: "Fresh Food People", Campaign: "That is Easy", Digital, Online Shopping, Outdoor, TV
WWF Australia Campaign: "Rhino", Campaign: "Sharks", Campaign: "Stop one.Stop them all", Campaign: "Tigers"

Leo Burnett-Beijing

Room 1308 China World Tower 2 No 1 Jian Guo Meri Wai Avenue, Beijing, 100004 China
Tel.: (86) 10 6505 8838
Fax: (86) 10 6505 6983
E-Mail: benjamin.tsang@bj.leoburnett.com
Web Site: www.leoburnett.com

Year Founded: 1992

Frank Liu *(Mng Dir)*
Eddie Booth *(Reg Chm & CEO-Greater China)*
Danny Mok *(CEO-China)*
Qifei Xu *(Sr Dir-Creative)*
Jennifer Wei *(Sr Mgr-People & Culture)*

Accounts:
New-Baidu, Inc. Baidu Duer, Digital
COFCO Creative, Fortune Oil, Strategy
Huiyuan Group Creative

Leo Burnett-Guangzhou

5/F North Tower Poly International Plaza, Yue Jiang Zhong Road, Guangzhou, 510308 China
Tel.: (86) 20 2836 0333

Fax: (86) 20 2836 0391
E-Mail: chasie.zeng@gz.leoburnett.com
Web Site: www.leoburnett.com

Employees: 60
Year Founded: 1992

Agency Specializes In: Advertising

Alvin Yim *(Gen Mgr)*
Kin Chong *(Exec Dir-Creative)*
Takho Lau *(Exec Dir-Creative)*

Accounts:
Bucalus Campaign: "Sound Wave"
Evergreen Travel
Haomei Aluminum Bucalus Soundproof Windows
Heineken; 2007
Hongguo International Creative, Footwear; 2008
Huawei B2B Communications, Creative
Inse (Agency of Record) Below the Line Creative, Digital, Marketing Strategy, Shopper Marketing
McDonald's; 2000
Procter & Gamble; 2000

Leo Burnett Shanghai Advertising Co., Ltd.
2F Block F Red Town 570 Huai Hai Road (W), Shanghai, 200052 China
Tel.: (86) 21 6281 6611
Fax: (86) 21 5230 5773
Web Site: www.leoburnett.com

Year Founded: 1992

Donald Chen *(Grp CEO-China)*
Sharon Chen *(Chief Strategy Officer)*
Victor Manggunio *(Chief Creative Officer-China)*
Rocky Hao *(Head-Creative)*
Angie Wong *(Gen Mgr)*
Alvin Yim *(Gen Mgr)*
Takho Lau *(Exec Dir-Creative)*
Christopher Annen *(Grp Dir-Creative)*
Eddie Booth *(Reg Chm)*

Accounts:
A.O. Smith Campaign: "Sun Bathing"
Caltrate Open Cap For Strong Bones
Coca-Cola Refreshments USA, Inc. Campaign: "Shine", Coke/Red Lounge, Minute Maid; 2000
Jack & Jones Creative, Rebranding Campaign
Li-Ning Campaign: "Don'T Drive Run"
McDonald's Chicken Nuggets, Creative, McCafe, McDonald's Delivery Service; 2000
Shanghai Qingcongquan training Center Campaign: "The Distance Between Mother and Child"
Shanghai Zendai Himalayas Center Campaign: "Floating Lotus "
Skoda China Digital
Supor Campaign: "Revolving Door", Kitchen Utensils, Knives, Pans, Smokeless Pans, Supor Non-Strick Pans
Uni-President Above the Line, Below-the-Line Merchandising, Branding, Communication Strategy, Content Planning, Digital, Print, Social, Soup Daren (Creative Agency of Record), TV, Uni-Sport, Xiao Ming Tong Xue
Volkswagen Group of America, Inc. Creative
Wyeth Pharmaceuticals Campaign: "Open Cap For Strong Bones"

Hong Kong

Leo Burnett-Hong Kong
6th Fl City Plaza 3 14 Taikoo Wan Road, Quarry Bay, China (Hong Kong)
Tel.: (852) 2567 4333
Fax: (852) 2885 3209
Web Site: www.leoburnett.com

Employees: 180
Year Founded: 1970

Agency Specializes In: Advertising

Eddie Booth *(Reg Chm & CEO-Greater China)*
Alfred Wong *(Exec Dir-Creative)*
May Chan *(Art Dir)*
Ivy Wong *(Dir-Art)*
Alvin Yim *(Dir-Ops)*
Edward Ha *(Grp Brand Dir)*
Margaret Chan *(Acct Supvr)*

Accounts:
Asian Tigers Mobility
Calbee Creative
Casablanca Campaign: "Deep Sleep", Campaign: "Dominos", Campaign: "Dreambot", I-Pillow
Cat Society Cats on Facebook
Che San Stationery 2 Ply Paper Towels
Christina Noble Children's Foundation Fear No Joy, Limit No Love, Worry No Home
Csl 1010 Campaign: "Rearview Mirror"
Dulux B2B, Shopper Marketing
General Mills
Greenpeace Car Free Day
Harmony House Campaign: "Fists"
Hong Kong Animal Adoption Centre Campaign: "Adopt a pet. The stories will follow", Campaign: "Story With My Pet"
IKEA Curtains, Trailer; 2000
Just Diamond Jewellery, Wedding Ring Series
Li Ning Campaign: "Don't Drive...Run"
Lisa Hoffman Mousepad, Perfume
Master Lau Cooking School
McDonald's Fast Food
Orbis Campaign: "Break the Wall"
Organic Baby Food
Pattex Campaign: "C-Hair"
Procter & Gamble Advertising, Campaign: "Smooth Heart Touching Moments", Pert, Rejoice; 1983
The Salvation Army Campaign: "Gift Box"
Shanghai Dai Zhi Men Food & Beverage Management Co. Diamond Coffee
Shanghai Diamond Trade International Campaign: "Sleepy"
Staedtler Campaign: "Architecture", Campaign: "Memoji", Campaign: "The Pencil", Campaign: "Where it all begins."
Sunsense Skin Care, Sunblock Oil
Supor Kitchen Utensils, Non-Stick Pans, Smokeless Pans
Swire Properties Creative, Here I am, Pacific Place, TaiKoo Hui
UA Cinema Campaign: "U-Late Hotline", Limitless Movie
Vigconic Campaign: "Chair"
Zoo Records Alternative Music Shop, Campaign: "Hidden Live", Hidden Sound Campaign

India

Leo Burnett India
Big Apple A, 36 Dr L Shirodkar Rd Parel, Mumbai, 400 012 India
Tel.: (91) 22 6663 4444
Fax: (91) 22 2417 3328
E-Mail: arvind.sharma@leoburnett.co.in
Web Site: www.leoburnett.co.in/

Employees: 250
Year Founded: 1972

Agency Specializes In: Consumer Marketing, Financial, Industrial, South Asian Market

Nitish Mukherjee *(Mng Dir)*
Rakesh Hinduja *(Exec VP)*
Suvadip Ghosh Mazumdar *(VP-Acct Mgmt)*
Hitesh Mehta *(VP)*
Sanju Menon *(VP)*
Sharmine Panthaky *(VP)*
Surbhi Gupta *(Head-People & Culture)*
Aman Mannan *(Grp Exec Dir-Creative)*
Sainath Saraban *(Dir-Creative-Natl)*
Puran Choudhary *(Assoc Dir-Creative)*
Sharan Sabhachandani *(Acct Supvr)*
Hassan Danish *(Copywriter)*
Neeraj Singh *(Copywriter)*
Prajato Guha Thakurta *(Assoc Exec Dir-Creative)*

Accounts:
Adlabs Imagica Creative
Alembic
Amazon Kindle India
Anchor Health & Beauty care
Apple Inc
Asia Motor Works
Bacardi Martini India; 2007
Bajaj Auto Limited ATL, Activation, Bajaj CT100, Bajaj Discover (Agency of Record), Campaign: "Khushiyon Ka Jackpot", Digital, Print, Retail; 1973
Bajaj Electricals Ltd. Bajaj Disney Fans, Bajaj Majesty Irons, Bajaj Pressure Cooker, Campaign: "Cigarette", Campaign: "Reclaim Your Space", Donald Duck, Exhaust Fans, Fans, Hand Blenders; 2001
Birla Sunlife Insurance Co Ltd
Broken Compass Tours & Travels Campaign: "Travelogue"
Campaign Brief Asia
CavinKare Creative, Henna
Coca-Cola Campaign: "Aaj kuch toofani karte hain", Campaign: "Bhaag Bittoo Bhaag", Campaign: "Limca Wali Pyaas", Campaign: "Pyaas Badhao", Campaign: "Reflection of Music - Table Mat", Campaign: "Sounds of Happiness", Campaign: "Toofan to Sab Keanderhai, Bas Dhakkan hi to Hatanahai", Campaign: "WhirlWind", Coke Studio, Creative, Digital Media, Limca, Maaza, Minute Maid Nimbu Fresh, OOH, Radio, Social Media, TV, Thums Up; 1995
New-Craftsvilla
Dinodia Photo Library
Door Step School Campaign: "Ink Pad"
Fiat; 1995
Finit Campaign: "Call them Out"
Fortis Healthcare
Furniture Village
Gandhijifont Campaign: "Different Views, One Vision"
New-General Mills Integrated Communications, Pillsbury
GlaxoSmithKline Consumer Healthcare Campaign: "Aadatein Badal Rahi Hain", Iodex, Ostocalcium
HDFC Bank Campaign: "Har Zaroorat Poori Ho Chutki Mein, Bank Aapki Muthi Mein", Creative
HDFC Standard Life Insurance Company Limited Campaign: "IPL Team", Campaign: "Life of Dignity", Campaign: "YoungStar Plans, Family"
Hero MotoCorp Creative
Hindustan Petroleum Corporation Limited Creative, Finit Insect Repellent
H.J. Heinz Company Campaign: "Classroom", Complan Memory, Heinz Ketchup; 1989
HomeShop18 Campaign: "Diwali Dhamaal"
I am Laadli
Jet Movers & Packers Shift the Station
Kohler Campaign: "Advanced Toilet"
The Little Yellow Box Campaign: "Love Letter"
Loksatta Awaaz - 1
Mahindra Wheels
Maneland Jungle Lodge
McDonald's Campaign: "Absolutely Indian", Campaign: "Bargain", Campaign: "Chinese Whisper", Campaign: "Dare to Choose", Campaign: "Don't Stop, Just Have Pop", Campaign: "Happy Sparrows", Crispy Veggie Pops, Digital, Masala Grill Burger, McSpicy, OOH, Print, Radio, Social Media
Mrs Kapru's Guest House
ParentCircle Branding, Communication Strategy
Perfetti Van Melle India Pvt Ltd Campaign: "Boss, Yeh Mera Dil"

Tata Capital Limited Tata Capital Housing Finance
Tata Chemicals Limited Campaign: "Cucumber Salad", Campaign: "Happy Mother's Day"
Prerana
Procter & Gamble Campaign: "100% Shiksha", Campaign: "South Indian", Tide Detergents, Tide Fragrance - Fisherman, Washing Detergent; 1984
Reliance Communications Creative
Reliance Digital Excuses
Reliance Retail Ltd (Agency of Record) Creative
Saathi Campaign: "Street Kid 1"
Samsung India Electronics Pvt. Ltd. Mobile, Samsung Refrigerator
Sony Entertainment Television Campaign: "A Million Dollar Question (Kaun Banega Crorepati)", Campaign: "Indian Idol Junior"
New-Sterlite Technologies
Strand Book Stall Punishment
Tide Detergent
Tide
Wella Kolestint
Yellow Box Cupcake

Leo Burnett India

24 & 30 Okhla Industrial Real Estate Phase III 3rd Floor, New Delhi, 110 020 India
Tel.: (91) 11 4150 0000
Fax: (91) 11 4161 2152
E-Mail: samir.gangahar@leoburnett.co.in
Web Site: www.leoburnett.com

Employees: 50
Year Founded: 1972

Agency Specializes In: Advertising

Rajdeepak Das *(Chief Creative Officer)*
Amritraj Thakur *(VP-Plng)*
Samir Gangahar *(Exec Dir)*
Shiva Kumar *(Exec Creative Dir)*
Amit Nandwani *(Exec Creative Dir)*
Sainath Saraban *(Exec Dir-Creative)*
Rajesh Minocha *(Creative Dir)*
Ashish Poddar *(Art Dir)*
Venkataraghavan Srinivasan *(Dir-Plng)*

Accounts:
Bacardi Martini India Bacardi Dark Rum, Bacardi White Rum, Bombay Sapphire Gin, Creative, Dewar's Scotch, Eristoff, Grey Goose Vodka
New-Bajaj Auto. Ltd. Bajaj CT100
Coca-Cola Refreshments USA, Inc. Campaign: "Har Mausam Love, Har Mausam Aam", Digital, Maaza, OOH, Point-of-Sales
New-Craftsvilla.com
McDonald's Happy Meal
PayUMoney Creative
Samsung India Campaign: "Bring Out", Galaxy Grand
Snapdeal.com Campaign: "Dil Ki Deal", Electronic, Marketing Campaign, Media, Print
Yatra.com

Orchard Advertising

HAL 3rd Stage No 37 80 Foot Road, Bengaluru, 560 075 India
Tel.: (91) 80 2527 5801
Fax: (91) 80 2527 2506
Web Site: www.orchardindia.com

Employees: 50
Year Founded: 1977

Agency Specializes In: Advertising, South Asian Market

Kaizad Pardiwala *(COO)*
Raj Deepak Das *(Chief Creative Officer)*
Neha Contractor *(VP-Leo Burnett & Head-Branch)*
Neel Roy Cruz *(Exec Creative Dir)*
Vinod Eshwer *(Exec Dir-Creative)*
Hemant Kumar *(Exec Dir-Creative)*
Gunjan Poddar *(Creative Dir-Leo Burnett)*
Sameera Dowerah *(Dir-Creative)*
Sagar Prajapati *(Dir-Art-Creative)*
M. G. Harti *(Supvr-Creative)*

Accounts:
Amazon Kindle
Bigg Boss 7 Below-The-Line, Digital, Mobile, Print, Radio
Blackberry
Deccan Aviation; 1998
Emami Group
Fiat India
i-canhelp
Jyothi Laboratories Campaign: "Insects Dancing", Campaign: "Quiz", Maxo
Lux Cozi ONN
Lux Industries
MAS Holdings Amante, Creative
Peter England
Pico Peta
Piramal Healthcare Campaign: "Chamchi"
South African Breweries
Standard Chartered Bank
New-Vistaprint India Advertising, Campaign: "Chalta Hai ko Chalta Karo"
WaterHealth India BTL, Creative, Media, Print
Wipro Consumer Care Campaign: "Class room", Glucovita

Indonesia

Leo Burnett Kreasindo Indonesia

Menara Thamrin 26th Fl, Jl MH Thamrin Kav3, Jakarta, 10250 Indonesia
Tel.: (62) 21 3983 0118
Fax: (62) 21 3983 0119
E-Mail: steve_bonnell@leoburnettkreasindo.com
Web Site: www.leoburnett.com

Employees: 113
Year Founded: 1990

Agency Specializes In: Advertising

Anne Ridwan *(Grp Mng Dir-Leo Burnett Group)*
Alison McConnell *(Chief Growth Officer-Worldwide)*
Tom Bernardin *(Chm/CEO-Worldwide)*
Berry Dawanas *(Sr Dir-Art)*
Jules Tan *(Creative Dir)*
Brian Charles Capel *(Grp Exec Dir-Creative-Jakarta)*

Accounts:
Bank Danamon Indonesia Tbk; 1999
Darya Varia Laboratoria; 2000
Faber-Castell International Indonesia Pens
Honda; 2001
McDonald's Restaurant, Wrapped; 2004
Metro Department Store; 2006
Nintendo
Philip Morris; 1994
Procter & Gamble; 1994
PT Indofood Chitao (Creative Agency of Record), Popmie (Creative Agency of Record)
Pt Rekso National Food Campaign: "Small Currency"
Samsung Electronics Campaign: "Me Gliding"; 2005
Telekomunikasi Selular; 2000
Telkomsel
Tempo Scan Pacific Campaign: "Mom", Contrexyn, Corporate Communications Campaigns, Hemaviton, Oskadon, Over the Counter, Through the Line, Zevit
TVS Motor Company Motorcycles; 2007

Japan

Beacon Communications K.K.

JR Tokyo Maguro Building 3-1-1 Kami-Osaki, Shinagawa-ku, Tokyo, 141-0021 Japan
Tel.: (81) 3 5437 7200
Fax: (81) 3 5437 7211
E-Mail: tokyo.prbeacon@beaconcom.co.jp
Web Site: www.beaconcom.co.jp

Employees: 350
Year Founded: 2001

National Agency Associations: ABC-IAA-JAAA-JMAA

Nicolas Menat *(Pres)*
Sayori Kato *(Exec Dir-HR)*
Yuhei Takeyama *(Sr Dir-Art)*
Taketo Igarashi *(Creative Dir)*
Ai Yamaguchi *(Art Dir)*
Kazz Ishihara *(Dir-Creative)*
Marie Kobayashi *(Acct Supvr)*
Daisuke Kimura *(Designer)*
Kuniaki Yamamoto *(Copywriter)*
Yasuo Matsubara *(Assoc Creative Dir)*

Accounts:
AIFUL Corp.; 2002
AR Drone Campaign: "Flying Banner"
BMW Japan
Ebara Foods Industry, Inc. Campaign: "Funfair in Your Mouth"
Electronic Arts K.K.
GlaxoSmithKline K.K.
Herman Miller Japan
Human Lab
Lenovo Campaign: "DO.NEXT"
Max Factor K.K. Illume, Muse, SK-II
Merial Japan Frontline Plus, Pet Medications
Mondelez
Nike Japan Campaign: "Play the Real Thing", Football, Nike Five, Sportswear
Nikon Corporation Campaign: "Tears"
Norton Campaign: "Stuff that Matters"
One Eight Promotion Campaign: "Pinch Pinup"
Parrot Campaign: "Flying Banner"
Procter & Gamble Far East Ltd. Ariel, Attento, Braun Oral-B, Campaign: "International Flight Mouth", Campaign: "Life & Dirt", Campaign: "Mom's First Birthday", Campaign: "Transform Audition", Crest Spin Brush, Eukanuba, Herbal Essences, Iams, Joy, Pampers, Rejoy, Vidal Sassoon, WELLA, Whisper; 1983
Puma
Second Harvest Japan
Skymark Airlines Co., Ltd.
Sumitomo 3M Ltd.
Symantec Anti-virus Software, Campaign: "Boy in Love", Campaign: "She Said Daddy", Campaign: "Stuff that Matters", Campaign: "Writer's Story"
Tumi Japan
Wada Elementary School Campaign: "Ribbond Birds"
Whirlpool Campaign: "Corporate Identity"
Wide Corporation

Korea

Leo Burnett Korea

East Wing 15th Fl Signature Towers 100 Cheonggyecheon-ro, Jongno-gu, Seoul, 100-230 Korea (South)
Tel.: (82) 220003600
Fax: (82) 27320082
Web Site: leoburnett.com/

Employees: 120
Year Founded: 1991

Agency Specializes In: Advertising

Youmi Cho *(Mng Dir)*
Sarah Jane Chang *(CFO-HR)*
Hyunjung Song *(VP & Acct Mgmt Dir)*
Shang Woo Bae *(Acct Mgr)*

Miseon Kang *(Acct Mgr)*
Sung Min Kim *(Acct Mgr)*
Ji-hyun Kwon *(Acct Exec)*
Hyo Eun Jeon *(Planner-Strategic)*

Accounts:
ASML
Bayer
Coca Cola
Ferrero; 2000
Gilead
GSK
Kellogg Company; 1992
Korea Ginseng
McDonald's Campaign: "Big Mac Song"; 1991
Pfizer
Philip Morris; 1990
Procter & Gamble Female Hygiene; 1990
Samsung Mobile
Sanofi Aventis
Takeda

Malaysia

Leo Burnett Malaysia
(Formerly Publicis Dialog Malaysia)
Level 5 Menara Olympia, 8 Jalan Raja Chulan, 50200 Kuala Lumpur, Malaysia
Tel.: (60) 3 2031 0998
Fax: (60) 3 2031 0972
E-Mail: tan.kieneng@leoburnett.com.my
Web Site: www.leoburnett.com.my

Employees: 143
Year Founded: 1964

Agency Specializes In: Advertising

Tan Kien Eng *(CEO)*
Iska Hashim *(Grp Head-Creative)*
Yiksee Heng *(Grp Head-Creative)*
Tam Jian Zhong *(Grp Head-Creative)*
Andrew Low *(Exec Dir-Creative)*
Muntip Liew *(Acct Dir)*
Andy Ng *(Acct Dir)*
ZunZheng Liu *(Dir-Art)*
David HK Tan *(Dir-Art)*
Ryan Leong *(Acct Exec)*
Simon Dall *(Copywriter)*
Jodie Hew *(Designer)*
Callum Ng *(Designer)*
Pei Sien *(Copywriter)*
Clara Wijaya *(Designer)*
Jovian Lee *(Grp Creative Head)*

Accounts:
New-AIA PUBLIC Takaful Bhd.
BCWA
BMW Campaign: "7 Signs"
Carlsberg
Dignity for Children's Foundation Campaign: "Jamilah"
Dutch Lady
Golden Arches Campaign: "Save the Sundae Cone"
ING Creative
Kellogg Company; 1995
Kinokuniya Bookstore; 2001
Malaysian Philharmonic Orchestra Cuckoo & Nightingale
Maxis
McDonald's; 1986
Naza TTDI
Petronas
Philip Morris; 1994
Procter & Gamble; 1983
Reckitt Benckiser Durex RealFeel
Samsung Malaysia Campaign: "Samsung Believes in Malaysia", Galaxy S4
Sime Darby
Sunway Group; 2005
Taylor's College
YTL Corporation; 1994

Philippines

Leo Burnett Manila
Enterprise Center Tower 2 24th Fl 6766 Ayala Avenue Corner, Paseo de Roxas, Makati, 1226 Philippines
Tel.: (63) 8848001
Fax: (63) 28848036
E-Mail: gela.pena@ph.leoburnett.com
Web Site: www.leoburnett.ph

Employees: 86
Year Founded: 1935

Agency Specializes In: Advertising

Raymond Arrastia *(Mng Dir)*
Boyet Alvero *(COO)*
Sue Ann Malig-Nolido *(VP & Acct Mgmt Dir)*
Kat Limchoc *(Exec Creative Dir)*
Donny Dingcong *(Grp Acct Dir)*
Alvin Tecson *(Creative Dir & Copywriter)*
Carlo Cruz *(Art Dir)*
Dante Dizon *(Creative Dir)*
Nico Zapanta *(Art Dir)*
Carl Urgino *(Dir-Creative)*
AM Valdez *(Dir-Art)*
Cey Enriquez *(Assoc Dir-Plng)*
Toby Amigo *(Copywriter)*
Joe Dy *(Copywriter)*

Accounts:
Ad Board of the Philippines Campaign: "Horsemen"
Bank of the Philippine Islands Social Media
Camella Homes Property Development
Coca-Cola Refreshments USA, Inc. Campaign: "Xerox Man", Coke Light, Coke Zero, Samurai Energy Drink; 2002
New-Cultural Center of the Philippines
General Motors
Hank & Frank
McDonald's Breakfast McSavers, Campaign: "Flash Cards", Campaign: "Kuya", Campaign: "Restraint", Rainbow; 1996
Philip Morris; 1995
Philippine Airlines
Procter & Gamble Camay, Campaign: "Aid Couture 2", Campaign: "Aid Couture", Tide; 1978
Samurai Campaign: "Xerox Man"
Shell Philippines
WWF Dangers Beneath Exhibit, Earth Hour

Singapore

Leo Burnett
8 Murray Street 02-01, 079522 Singapore, Singapore
Tel.: (65) 6595 9700
Web Site: www.leoburnett.com

Employees: 93
Year Founded: 1946

National Agency Associations: SAA

Agency Specializes In: Advertising Specialties

Chris Chiu *(CEO & Chief Creative Officer)*
Pawan Bahuguna *(COO)*
Jarek Ziebinski *(Chm/CEO-Asia Pacific)*
Saurabh Varma *(CEO-India)*
Simon Holt *(Reg Dir-Retail Activation-Asia Pacific)*
Karen Ellis *(Global Creative Dir)*
Bibiana Lee *(Client Svcs Dir)*
Linus Chen *(Dir-Art)*

Accounts:
Allergan (Regional Creative Agency of Record) Asia-Pacific Integrated Communications, Health Care, Medical Aesthetics
APEX Clubs of Singapore. Somebody RC60s
GEMS World Academy (Creative Agency of Record) Communications, Digital, Outdoor, Print
Great Eastern Campaign: "There Will Never Be Another You"
Ikea Campaign: "Catalogue Launch", Creative
The Patissier Cake-Mouflage
Procter & Gamble SK-II; 1977
Samsung
Singapore Cancer Society Campaign: "No Excuse Not To Screen"
Telco Indonesia
New-Tigerair (Social Media Agency of Record)
United Overseas Bank

Sri Lanka

Leo Burnett Solutions Inc.
No 379 R A de Mel Mawatha, Colombo, 3 Sri Lanka
Tel.: (94) 11 237 2080
Fax: (94) 11 237 2088
E-Mail: ranil_de_silva@leoburnett.lk
Web Site: www.leoburnett.lk

Employees: 80
Year Founded: 1999

Agency Specializes In: Advertising, South Asian Market

Ranil de Silva *(Mng Dir)*
Chrishani Kotalawela *(COO)*
Trevor Kennedy *(Chief Creative Officer)*
Dileep Kulathunga *(Grp Head-Creative)*
Prasad Kulkarni *(Art Dir)*
Nedra Dewapura *(Dir-HR)*
Thushara Malalanayake *(Dir-Art)*
Chandika Samaraweera *(Dir-Art)*
Hasan Samdin *(Dir-Art)*
Sithum Walter *(Dir-Art)*
Athula Kathriarachchi *(Assoc Dir-Creative)*
Firzan Mulafer *(Acct Mgr)*
Juneston Mathana *(Copywriter)*
Farzard Mohideen *(Copywriter)*
Malaka Samith *(Copywriter)*

Accounts:
Akzo Nobel Paints Lanka Campaign: "Washable Cricket Score Wall", Dulux Paints
New-Asiri Group of Hospitals
Cargills Quality Foods; 2001
Ceylon Newspapers Campaign: "Paper Flag"
CIC Paints
Coca-Cola Refreshments USA, Inc.
Columbo Jewelry Stores
DFCC Bank; 2000
Findmyfare.com
Godrej Sara Lee Lanka (Pvt) Ltd
The Hilton Hotel Colombo; 1999
Information Communication Technology Agency of Sri Lanka
Janet Deodorant Campaign: "Nurse, Police Woman"
Jetwing Group Jetwing Hotels & Resorts; 1999
Juliet Coombe Publishing
KV International Campaign: "Durty Scean 01"
Mobitel
Noir
Odel; 2000
Pacific Inter - Link SDN BHD
Procter & Gamble; 1999
Serendipity Publications Around The Fort in 80 Lives, Campaign: "Ride A Book"
Sir Lanka Eye Donation Society Campaign: "Pass it on when you're done with it"
Spa Ceylon
Sri Lanka Insurance Corporation
Sri Lanka Telecom
UNICEF; 2001
Wijeya Newspapers

Taiwan

Leo Burnett
10th F 16 Nanjing E Road Sec 4, Taipei, 10553 Taiwan
Tel.: (886) 2 2577 1211
Fax: (886) 2 2577 3800
E-Mail: margaret_huang@leoburnett.com.tw
Web Site: www.leoburnett.com

Employees: 150
Year Founded: 1984

Agency Specializes In: Advertising

Margaret Huang *(Grp CEO)*
Murphy Chou *(Chief Creative Officer & Copywriter)*
Mikhail Kudashkin *(Exec Dir-Creative-Moscow)*
Kyle Chiu *(Creative Dir)*
Elven Liu *(Sr Art Dir)*
Angela Lai *(Dir-Fin)*

Accounts:
Carrefour Taiwan; 2007
China Airlines Creative
Coca-Cola Refreshments USA, Inc. Coke Zero, Digital Creative, Media Planning & Buying
FEMA
Ferrero; 1999
Heineken; 1997
Hwa-Young Hotel
Johnnie Walker
Line Marketing Campaign
McDonald's; 2001
Mitsubishi Motor; Taiwan Passenger/Commercial Vehicles, Promotional
P&G
Pfizer (Agency of Record) Centrum, Creative, Robitussin
Shin Kong Mitsukoshi Department Stores; 2008
Vedan

Thailand

Leo Burnett
Sindhorn Bldg Tower 1 3rd Fl 130-132 Wireless Rd, Lumpini Pathumwan, Bangkok, 10330 Thailand
Tel.: (66) 2 684 5555
Fax: (66) 2 684 5500
E-Mail: on-usa_l@leoburnett.co.th
Web Site: www.leoburnett.com

Employees: 120
Year Founded: 1965

National Agency Associations:

Agency Specializes In: Direct Response Marketing, Graphic Design, Public Relations, Sales Promotion

Keeratie Chaimoungkalo *(Exec Creative Dir)*
Sompat Trisadikun *(Exec Dir-Creative)*
Ukrit Karnsomwan *(Art Dir)*
Santi Tubtimtong *(Creative Dir)*
Jutarat Kongton *(Dir-Art)*
Putthikon Saeamad *(Dir-Art)*
Sorasak Songnapawuttikul *(Dir-Art)*
Wantaya Thitipaisal *(Dir-Art)*
Park Wannasiri *(Dir-Art)*
Thanachpath Ratanaborvornsethi *(Copywriter)*

Accounts:
Canon Powershot Underwater Campaign: "Photo Fighters"
Center For The Protection Of Children's Rights Foundation Campaign: "A Girl", Campaign: "Child Abuse", Campaign: "It Never Goes Away"
Central Trading
Chemical Tech Co. Grison Ogliss Stain Guard
Chulabhorn Hospital Campaign: "Hope For Hair"
Clima Co. Clima Bicycle Lock
The Department Of Disease Control Campaign: "X-Ray Film Project", Sexual Health Awareness
Don't Drive Drunk Foundation Campaign: "Suicide"
Friesland Campina Campaign: "Nutrition Squad"
Heineken
Italasia
Mahaphant Group Shera; 2008
Mira Electric Campaign: "Angry"
Olan-Kemed Optal Eye Lotion
Osotspa
Procter & Gamble Campaign: "The Giant Bacteria"; 1988
PTG Energy Brand Communications
PTT Plc
Quality Houses Real Estate; 2008
Rasayana Retreat Campaign: "Pig"
Riche Monde; 1983
Samsung Campaign: "Kitchen", Galaxy S4
New-Shutterstock, Inc
Singha Corporation Campaign: "Thailand Be Strong"
Star Reachers Group Campaign: "A Happy Gift"
Taitan International Campaign: "Lover'S Lane"
Tesco Lotus
Thai Asia Pacific Brewery; 1997
TMB Bank Campaign: "Panyee FC"
Tourism Authority of Thailand Campaign: "I Hate Thailand", Campaign: "It Begins with the People", Campaign: "The Way We See The World", TV; 2007
True Corporation Campaign: "Let Them See Love", Organ Donation Awareness
T.S. Patex Co Ltd
Tv Direct Company Twister Sweeper XI

LEO J. BRENNAN, INC.
2359 Livernois Rd, Troy, MI 48083-1692
Tel.: (248) 362-3131
Fax: (248) 362-2355
E-Mail: request@ljbrennan.com
Web Site: www.ljbrennan.com

E-Mail for Key Personnel:
President: lbrennan@ljbrennan.com

Employees: 3
Year Founded: 1969

Agency Specializes In: Advertising Specialties, Automotive, Business Publications, Business-To-Business, Collateral, Consulting, E-Commerce, Engineering, Financial, Graphic Design, Health Care Services, High Technology, Industrial, Information Technology, Internet/Web Design, Logo & Package Design, Marine, Media Buying Services, Medical Products, New Product Development, Newspapers & Magazines, Planning & Consultation, Point of Purchase, Print, Production, Public Relations, Publicity/Promotions, Sales Promotion, Strategic Planning/Research, Technical Advertising

Leo J. Brennan *(Pres)*

Accounts:
Ace Controls
Al Salter Photography, Inc.
E&E Engineering
J.F. Hubert Enterprises
ND Industries
Search Group, Inc.

LEOPARD
555 17th St Ste 300, Denver, CO 80202-3908
Tel.: (303) 527-2900
Fax: (303) 530-3480
E-Mail: req_info@leopard.com
Web Site: www.leopard.com

Employees: 60
Year Founded: 1984

National Agency Associations: 4A's

Agency Specializes In: Business-To-Business, Education, Financial, High Technology, Sponsorship

Bonnie Demoss *(VP & Dir-Mktg Strategy)*
Steve Mudd *(VP & Dir-Mktg Strategy)*
Kelly Hanratty *(Exec Dir-Acct Svc)*
Chad Palm *(Dir-Art)*
Jill Mabary *(Acct Mgr)*
Bryn Lowe *(Acct Exec)*
Felipe Aguilar *(Designer)*
Rich Lopez *(Sr Graphic Designer)*
Jeff Pontes *(Exec Grp Dir)*

Accounts:
Attensity
CDW
Cisco
Intrado
Mentor Graphics
SAP
Siemens

LEOPOLD KETEL & PARTNERS
112 SW 1st Ave, Portland, OR 97204
Tel.: (503) 295-1918
Fax: (503) 295-3601
E-Mail: krissy@leoketel.com
Web Site: www.leoketel.com

E-Mail for Key Personnel:
Creative Dir.: jerryk@leoketel.com

Employees: 22
Year Founded: 1995

National Agency Associations: PRSA

Agency Specializes In: Advertising, Brand Development & Integration, Broadcast, Collateral, Communications, Consumer Marketing, Corporate Identity, Electronic Media, Fashion/Apparel, Financial, Food Service, Graphic Design, Internet/Web Design, Logo & Package Design, Media Buying Services, Newspapers & Magazines, Out-of-Home Media, Outdoor, Planning & Consultation, Point of Purchase, Point of Sale, Print, Public Relations, Publicity/Promotions, Radio, Retail, Strategic Planning/Research, T.V., Trade & Consumer Magazines, Travel & Tourism

Approx. Annual Billings: $22,300,000

Breakdown of Gross Billings by Media: Fees: 26%; Internet Adv.: 1%; Mags.: 27%; Network T.V.: 9%; Newsp.: 13%; Outdoor: 2%; Production: 16%; Radio: 6%

Terra Spencer *(Founder, Partner & Mng Dir)*
Olga Haley *(Mng Dir-PR)*
Holly Zander *(Mgr-PR & Media)*
Jeremy Bolesky *(Designer)*
Sheena McCray *(Coord-Acct & Media)*

Accounts:
Benchmade Knives
Cannon Beach Business Associates
Castelli
Friedrich Air Conditioning
ODS Health Insurance
Oregon Humane Society; 2002
Oregon Public Broadcasting
Pendleton Whisky
Pendleton Woolen Mills
Planned Parenthood
Tillamook County Creamery Association Cheese, Ice Cream - Television Spots

LEPOIDEVIN MARKETING
245 S Executive Dr, Brookfield, WI 53005
Tel.: (262) 754-9505
Web Site: www.LePoidevinMarketing.com

Employees: 12
Year Founded: 1997

Agency Specializes In: Business Publications, Catalogs, Co-op Advertising, Collateral, Custom Publishing, Digital/Interactive, Direct Response Marketing, Electronic Media, Email, Exhibit/Trade Shows, Guerilla Marketing, In-Store Advertising, Infomercials, Local Marketing, Magazines, Mobile Marketing, Multimedia, Newspapers & Magazines, Out-of-Home Media, Outdoor, Paid Searches, Point of Purchase, Point of Sale, Print, Product Placement, Production, Production (Print), Search Engine Optimization, Social Media, Sponsorship, Sweepstakes, Telemarketing, Trade & Consumer Magazines, Viral/Buzz/Word of Mouth, Web (Banner Ads, Pop-ups, etc.)

Approx. Annual Billings: $2,000,000

Dean LePoidevin *(Pres)*
Gregg Kerttula *(Creative Dir)*
Angela Mork *(Dir-Content & Acct Supvr)*
Steve Staedler *(Sr Acct Exec-PR)*
Kelsey Meyer *(Strategist-Digital & Acct Exec)*

Accounts:
Abbott Diagnostics; 2013
Colordyne; 2012
Dorner Manufacturing; 2009
FMC Professional Products; 2013
Jaguar Animal Health Jaguar, Neonorm; 2014
LEM USA; 2011
Liphatech Professional Pest Control Products; 2007
MinXray; 2011
Snap-On Industrial Professional Tool Use & Management Programs, Snap-on Tools; 2008
Spee-Dee Manufacturing; 2012

L.E.R. PR
580 Broadway Ste 309, New York, NY 10012
Tel.: (646) 692-3244
E-Mail: info@lerpr.com
Web Site: www.lerpr.com

Agency Specializes In: Advertising, Brand Development & Integration, Digital/Interactive, Event Planning & Marketing, Internet/Web Design, Media Relations, Public Relations, Social Media

Jane Lerman *(Founder & CEO)*

Accounts:
New-Thaddeus O'Neil

LEROY + CLARKSON
151 Lafayette St 3rd Fl, New York, NY 10013
Tel.: (212) 431-9291
Web Site: www.leroyandclarkson.com

Year Founded: 2001

Agency Specializes In: Advertising, Brand Development & Integration, Content, Digital/Interactive, Graphic Design, Production, Promotions

Kate Hillis *(Mng Dir)*
Daniel Fries *(Principal & Dir-Creative-Live-Action)*
Ethan Christy *(Mgr-Studio)*

Accounts:
A&E Stores, Inc.
American Broadcasting Company Dancing with the Stars Season Three
Cooking Channel
The Discovery Channel
E! Entertainment Television, Inc.
Fuse Knowledge is Power
The History Channel
Home & Garden Television
Lifetime Entertainment Services LLC Network Rebrand
Syfy
USA Suits & Mr Porter Fashion Show
Zipcar, Inc.

LESNIEWICZ ASSOCIATES LLC
500 E Front St, Perrysburg, OH 43551-2134
Tel.: (419) 873-0500
Fax: (419) 873-0600
Toll Free: (800) 809-3093
E-Mail: contactus@designtoinfluence.com
Web Site: http://www.design2influence.com/

Employees: 12

Agency Specializes In: Advertising, Brand Development & Integration, Collateral, Communications, Consulting, Corporate Identity, Digital/Interactive, Graphic Design, Internet/Web Design, Logo & Package Design, Sales Promotion, Strategic Planning/Research

Revenue: $2,000,000

Terrence Lesniewicz *(Chief Creative Officer)*
Jack Bollinger *(Dir-Creative)*
Jeanne Lesniewicz *(Mgr-Resources)*

Accounts:
BASF
Bowling Green State University
Crain Communications
Dana Holding Corporation
TI Automotive
Toledo Mud Hens; Toledo, OH
Toledo Public Schools
TRANE

LESSING-FLYNN ADVERTISING CO.
3106 Ingersoll Ave, Des Moines, IA 50312
Tel.: (515) 274-9271
Fax: (515) 274-9283
E-Mail: jimspoerl@lessingflynn.com
Web Site: www.lessingflynn.com

Employees: 19
Year Founded: 1907

National Agency Associations: APA-MCA-NAMA

Agency Specializes In: Agriculture, Business-To-Business

Approx. Annual Billings: $7,500,000

Joe Rosenberg *(Vice Chm)*
Tom Flynn, III *(Pres)*
Jessica Held *(VP-Acct Svcs)*
Jim Spoerl *(Dir-Electronic Media & Acct Mgr)*
Joel Clifton *(Dir-Art)*
Chris Hanson *(Dir-Art)*
Chris Abrahamson *(Office Mgr)*
Jamie Thomassen *(Acct Mgr)*

Accounts:
Vermeer

LETIZIA MASS MEDIA
5460 Desert Point Dr, Las Vegas, NV 89118
Tel.: (702) 777-2121
Fax: (702) 878-0983
Web Site: http://www.letiziaagency.com/

Agency Specializes In: Brand Development & Integration, Broadcast, Digital/Interactive, Graphic Design, Media Buying Services

Brittany Madsen *(Gen Mgr-Agency Svcs)*
Kevin Bailey *(Dir-Ops)*
Russell Letizia *(Acct Exec)*

Accounts:
El Cortez Hotel & Casino
Fashion Show Mall Shopping Centers
Hyundai Car Dealers
McDonald Fast Food Restaurant

THE LETTER M MARKETING
(Formerly MacMillan Marketing Group)
285 Woolwich St, Guelph, ON N1H 3V8 Canada
Tel.: (519) 836-6183
Fax: (519) 836-3155
Web Site: www.thelettermmarketing.com/

Employees: 15
Year Founded: 1979

Stenna Berry *(Sr Dir-Art)*
Julie Brown-Hallman *(Dir-Art & Graphic Designer)*
Stacey McCarthy *(Acct Mgr)*
Natasha Paterson *(Mgr-Ops)*

Accounts:
The City of Guelph; 2004

LEVATAS
11701 Lk Victoria Gardens Ave, Palm Beach Gardens, FL 33410
Tel.: (561) 622-4511
E-Mail: hello@levatas.com
Web Site: www.levatas.com

Employees: 77
Year Founded: 2006

Agency Specializes In: Communications, Digital/Interactive, Strategic Planning/Research

Chris Nielsen *(Founder, CEO & Partner)*
Ryan Gay *(Mng Partner)*
Daniel Burce *(Exec Dir-Platforms, R&D)*
Ray Popp *(Exec Dir-Mktg)*
Jason Reynolds *(Exec Dir-Strategy)*
Lorin Munchick *(Dir-Bus Dev)*
Annaliese Szymaszek *(Sr Mgr-Relationship)*
Kristen Saumell *(Specialist-Bus Dev)*

Accounts:
BurgerFi
Duffy's Sports Bar
Palm Beach County Tourism Department

LEVEL BRAND
724 N 1st St, Minneapolis, MN 55401-1143
Tel.: (612) 338-8000
Fax: (612) 338-9824
E-Mail: info@levelbrand.com
Web Site: www.levelbrand.com

E-Mail for Key Personnel:
President: johnf@levelbrand.com
Media Dir.: lauras@levelbrand.com

Employees: 40
Year Founded: 1986

Agency Specializes In: Advertising, Agriculture, Brand Development & Integration, Collateral, Communications, Direct Response Marketing, Financial, Graphic Design, Health Care Services, Logo & Package Design, Media Buying Services, Newspaper, Newspapers & Magazines, Outdoor, Point of Purchase, Point of Sale, Print, Production, Public Relations, Radio, Restaurant, Retail, Strategic Planning/Research, T.V., Trade & Consumer Magazines

Approx. Annual Billings: $8,093,181

Breakdown of Gross Billings by Media: Mags.: $201,923; Newsp.: $675,081; Outdoor: $846,431;

Radio: $3,587,044; T.V.: $2,782,702

Lois Dirksen *(Pres & Strategist-Brand)*
John Foley *(CEO & Principal Brand Strategist)*
Laura Shiue *(VP-Strategic Mktg & Media)*
Kim Thelen *(VP-Strategic Plng & Client Svc)*
John Jensen *(Controller)*
Gregg Byers *(Dir-Creative)*
Ruth Edstrum *(Dir-Production)*
Matt Lunneborg *(Assoc Dir-Creative)*
Marisa Gurrola *(Asst Media Planner & Buyer)*

Accounts:
Boldt
Healthsense Branding, Communications Support, Creative Development, Market Insights
Medica; Minnetonka, MN; 2000
Pearson Assessments
Unipower
Western Bank; 2002

LEVELTWO ADVERTISING
302 N Market St Ste 300, Dallas, TX 75202
Tel.: (214) 506-2915
Fax: (214) 824-9784
Toll Free: (888) 894-9782
E-Mail: schoppin@ltwo.com
Web Site: www.ltwo.com

Employees: 26
Year Founded: 1999

Agency Specializes In: Above-the-Line, Advertising, Advertising Specialties, Affiliate Marketing, Affluent Market, Agriculture, Alternative Advertising, Arts, Automotive, Aviation & Aerospace, Below-the-Line, Bilingual Market, Brand Development & Integration, Branded Entertainment, Broadcast, Business Publications, Business-To-Business, Cable T.V., Catalogs, Children's Market, Co-op Advertising, Collateral, College, Commercial Photography, Communications, Computers & Software, Consulting, Consumer Goods, Consumer Marketing, Consumer Publications, Content, Corporate Communications, Corporate Identity, Cosmetics, Customer Relationship Management, Digital/Interactive, Direct Response Marketing, Direct-to-Consumer, E-Commerce, Education, Electronic Media, Electronics, Email, Entertainment, Environmental, Event Planning & Marketing, Exhibit/Trade Shows, Experience Design, Fashion/Apparel, Financial, Food Service, Game Integration, Gay & Lesbian Market, Graphic Design, Guerilla Marketing, Health Care Services, High Technology, Hispanic Market, Hospitality, Household Goods, Identity Marketing, In-Store Advertising, Industrial, Information Technology, Integrated Marketing, Internet/Web Design, Investor Relations, Legal Services, Leisure, Local Marketing, Logo & Package Design, Luxury Products, Magazines, Market Research, Media Buying Services, Media Planning, Medical Products, Men's Market, Merchandising, Mobile Marketing, Multicultural, Multimedia, New Product Development, New Technologies, Newspaper, Newspapers & Magazines, Out-of-Home Media, Outdoor, Over-50 Market, Package Design, Paid Searches, Pharmaceutical, Planning & Consultation, Point of Purchase, Point of Sale, Print, Product Placement, Production, Production (Print), Promotions, Public Relations, Publicity/Promotions, Radio, Real Estate, Regional, Restaurant, Retail, Sales Promotion, Search Engine Optimization, Seniors' Market, Social Marketing/Nonprofit, Social Media, Sponsorship, Sports Market, Stakeholders, Strategic Planning/Research, Sweepstakes, Syndication, T.V., Teen Market, Trade & Consumer Magazines, Transportation, Travel & Tourism, Tween Market, Viral/Buzz/Word of Mouth, Web (Banner Ads, Pop-ups, etc.), Women's Market, Yellow Pages Advertising

Approx. Annual Billings: $24,500,000

Gina Roach *(Dir-Media)*

Accounts:
Adams Golf; Plano, TX Adams Golf, YES! Putters; 2009
Capellon Pharmaceutical; Fort Worth, TX REQ49+; 2009
Compass Professional Healthcare Services; 2013
Dr Pepper Snapple Group; Plano, TX; 2001
Galt Medical; Atlanta, GA; 2006
LegalShield; 2011
Litex Industries Craftmade, Ellington Fans, Jeremiah Lighting; 2011
Puget Sound Surgical Center Bariatric; 2010
Service First Mortgage; Richardson, TX; 2011
T-Mobile US; 2005

LEVENSON GROUP
(Formerly Levenson & Hill, Inc.)
717 N Harwood Ste 2000, Dallas, TX 75201
Tel.: (214) 932-6000
Fax: (214) 880-0630
E-Mail: hello@levensongroup.com
Web Site: www.levensongroup.com

Employees: 70
Year Founded: 1984

Agency Specializes In: Communications, Consumer Marketing, Entertainment, Public Relations, Retail, Sales Promotion, Sponsorship

Barbara L. Levenson *(Pres & CEO)*
Saira Habash *(Mng Partner-Client & Media Svcs)*
Saira Habash *(Mng Partner-Client & Media Svcs)*
Andy Harmon *(Mng Partner)*
Faithe Nicholson *(Chief Acctg Officer & Sr VP)*
Esther Lafuente *(VP & Controller)*
Alison Wenzel *(VP & Assoc Dir-Media)*
Jeff Mallace *(Dir-Branding & Activation)*
Susan Noah *(Assoc Dir-Media & Plng)*
Shareen Hafiz *(Acct Exec)*
Jessica Israel *(Sr Media Buyer)*
Monica Rosa *(Sr Media Planner)*

Accounts:
Church's Chicken Casual Dining, Media Buying for Western U.S.
Dallas Center for the Performing Arts
Gordon's Jewelers; Irving, TX
Marble Slab Creamery; Houston, TX Ice Cream; 2005
Paramount Pictures
Warner Brothers

THE LEVERAGE AGENCY
888 7th Ave, New York, NY 10106
Tel.: (212) 752-2500
Fax: (212) 223-6982
Web Site: www.leverageagency.com

Agency Specializes In: Branded Entertainment, Media Planning, Public Relations, Sales Promotion, Strategic Planning/Research, T.V.

Benjamin Sturner *(Pres & CEO)*
David Rosenfeld *(Mng Partner-Leverage Latino)*
Brad Brown *(Pres-Sports & Entertainment Consulting)*
Ryan Garton *(Exec VP-Bus Dev & Brand Strategy)*
Mandy O'Donnell *(Sr VP-Integrated Mktg)*
Chris Farrell *(VP-Partnership Mktg)*
Marcy Braasch *(Dir-Brdcst & Direct Response Media Buying)*
Kimberly Kasarda *(Dir-Ops)*
Jake Brackman *(Mgr-Mktg-Sports & Entertainment)*

Accounts:
Amway Global Multilevel Marketing Services
AVP Pro Beach Volleyball Sports
FremantleMedia
Jimmy Kimmel
KFC
Mark Burnett
New York Post
The New York Times
NFL Alumni Association (Sponsorship Agency of Record) Super Bowl Weekend
Radical Media
Six Flags Entertainment Corp.
Tic Tac

LEVERAGE MARKETING GROUP
117-119 S Main St, Newtown, CT 06470-2380
Tel.: (203) 270-6699
Fax: (203) 270-3491
E-Mail: info@leverage-marketing.com
Web Site: www.leverage-marketing.com

E-Mail for Key Personnel:
Creative Dir.: david@leverage-marketing.com
Production Mgr.: tomm@leverage-marketing.com

Employees: 8
Year Founded: 1984

National Agency Associations: BMA-Second Wind Limited

Agency Specializes In: Advertising, Business-To-Business, Consumer Marketing, Graphic Design, High Technology, Public Relations, Sales Promotion, Sponsorship

Approx. Annual Billings: $3,000,000

Breakdown of Gross Billings by Media: Bus. Publs.: $720,000; Cable T.V.: $36,000; Collateral: $432,000; Consumer Publs.: $600,000; D.M.: $504,000; E-Commerce: $180,000; Newsp.: $180,000; Outdoor: $36,000; Radio: $180,000; Sls. Promo.: $450,000; T.V.: $72,000

Tom Marks *(CEO & Gen Mgr)*
Sue Kaufman *(Office Mgr)*
Lauren Adiletti *(Acct Exec)*

Accounts:
ATS/MRI VOIP Telephone Services
Bubble Wrap
Cartuf; Danbury, CT; 2001
GE-International Fiber Systems (IFS); Newtown, CT Audio Video & Fiber Optic Data Communication Products; 1998
Photronics; Brookfield, CT PhotoMasks; 1990
Sealed Air Corporation, Corporate Offices; Saddle Brook, NJ Packaging Systems; 1993
Sealed Air Corporation, Engineered Products Div.; Danbury, CT Foam-in-Place Packaging Systems; 1989
Sealed Air Corporation, Korrvu Division; Danbury, CT Suspension & Retention Packaging Systems; 1992
Sealed Air Corporation, Packaging Products Division; Saddle Brook, NJ Bubble Wrap; 1995
Sun Rocket
Newtown School System; Newtown, CT

LEVINE & ASSOCIATES, INC.
1777 Church St NW, Washington, DC 20036
Tel.: (202) 842-3660
Fax: (202) 842-3663
E-Mail: peggy@levinedc.com
Web Site: www.levinedc.com

E-Mail for Key Personnel:
President: barbaral@levinedc.com

Employees: 12
Year Founded: 1988

Agency Specializes In: Advertising, Brand

Development & Integration, Collateral, Corporate Identity, Direct Response Marketing, Entertainment, Exhibit/Trade Shows, Government/Political, Graphic Design, Health Care Services, High Technology, Internet/Web Design, Logo & Package Design, Magazines, Medical Products, Print, Production, Radio, Travel & Tourism

Approx. Annual Billings: $6,000,000

Breakdown of Gross Billings by Media: Collateral: $3,275,000; Mags.: $850,000; Newsp.: $1,625,000; Radio: $250,000

Barbara Levine *(Founder)*

Accounts:
AARP; 2000
American Chemical Society
Children's Defense Fund
Edison National Historic Site
International Youth Foundation
Meat & Livestock Australia; 2004
National Institute on Aging; 1998
The Ocean Conservancy
U.S. Holocaust Memorial Museum; 1985
United States Department of Agriculture
United States Department of Health & Human Services
Urban Institute
Verizon Center
Washington National Opera
Widerthan
WiderThan Americas, Inc.
Wintergreen Resort Advertising Campaign
Wolf Trap Foundation; 1996
Woolly Mammoth

LEVINE COMMUNICATIONS OFFICE
9100 Wilshire Blvd Ste 540E Tower, Beverly Hills, CA 90212-3470
Tel.: (310) 300-0950
Fax: (310) 300-0951
E-Mail: info@lcoonline.com
Web Site: lcopublicity.com

Employees: 15
Year Founded: 1983

Agency Specializes In: Brand Development & Integration, Communications, Event Planning & Marketing, Internet/Web Design, Investor Relations, Media Relations, Media Training, Newspaper, Print, Product Placement, Public Relations, Strategic Planning/Research

Michael Levine *(Founder)*
Shannon Donnelly *(Partner & Sr Acct Mgr)*

Accounts:
geneME Media Outreach, Public Relations
York Shackleton

THE LEVINSON TRACTENBERG GROUP
154 Grand St, New York, NY 10013
Tel.: (646) 568-3166
E-Mail: contact@ltgny.com
Web Site: www.ltgny.com

Agency Specializes In: Advertising

Joel Levinson *(Partner)*
Joel Tractenberg *(Partner)*

Accounts:
NY Spine Institute (Agency of Record) Creative Advertising, Media Buying, Media Planning, Social Media

LEVLANE ADVERTISING/PR/INTERACTIVE
100 Penn Sq E, Philadelphia, PA 19107
Tel.: (215) 825-9600
Fax: (215) 809-1900
E-Mail: info@levlane.com
Web Site: www.levlane.com

E-Mail for Key Personnel:
President: dlane@levlane.com

Employees: 35
Year Founded: 1984

National Agency Associations: 4A's-MAGNET-PRSA

Agency Specializes In: Advertising, Brand Development & Integration, Broadcast, Business-To-Business, Co-op Advertising, Communications, Education, Entertainment, Financial, Food Service, Graphic Design, Health Care Services, High Technology, Internet/Web Design, Logo & Package Design, Media Buying Services, New Product Development, Outdoor, Print, Production, Public Relations, Publicity/Promotions, Restaurant, Retail, Sales Promotion, Seniors' Market, Sponsorship, Strategic Planning/Research, Sweepstakes

Approx. Annual Billings: $40,000,000

Bruce Lev *(Partner & Chief Creative Officer)*
Karen Ruiter *(CFO)*
Debbey Racano *(Sr VP & Dir-Creative)*
Tony Sweeney *(Sr VP & Dir-Media)*
Michael Wood *(Sr VP & Dir-PR)*
Jason Rossano *(VP)*
Bess Denney *(Acct Dir)*
R. J. Cassi *(Dir-Art & Graphic Designer)*
Rich Wood *(Specialist-Digital Media)*
Deborah Artaza *(Designer)*
Jerry Selber *(Copywriter)*

Accounts:
AcquireWeb
American Law Institute-American Bar Association (Agency of Record); Philadelphia, PA
The Atlanta KFC Advertising Co-op (Agency of Record)
The Chester County Economic Council
CorCell Companies, Inc.
De Souza Brown
Fairmount Park Conservancy (Agency of Record) Brand Positioning, Collateral Material, Event-Based Public Relations, Social Media, Traditional Media, Web Site Development
Greater Philadelphia Innovation Cluster for Energy-Efficient Buildings (Agency of Record) Brand Identity
Jomar, Inc. (Agency of Record) Brand Redesign, Social Media
Kennedy Health System
KFC Restaurants; Boston, MA; Miami, FL; Philadelphia, PA; Portland & Bangor, ME; West Palm Beach, FL
Lancaster General Hospital
Massage Envy; Cleveland, OH
Massage Envy Connecticut Broadcast, Digital, Event Marketing, PR, Print, SEM, SEO, Social Media, Website Development
Massage Envy Maryland & Southern Delaware Event Marketing, PR, Social Media
Massage Envy New York Broadcast, Digital, Event Marketing, PR, Print, SEM, SEO, Social Media, Website Development
Massage Envy Northern and Central New Jersey (Agency Of Record) Broadcast, Digital, Event Marketing, PR, Print, SEM, SEO, Social Media, Website Development
Massage Envy Northern Virginia & DC Event Marketing, PR, Social Media
Massage Envy Philadelphia (Agency of Record) Event Marketing, Online, Radio, Search Engine Marketing, Sponsorships, TV
Massage Envy Event Marketing, Online Advertising, Radio, Search Engine Marketing, Sponsorships, TV
Mayor's Office of Transportation and Utilities; Philadelphia, PA Campaign: "Sorta Stop", Traffic Safety
Mayor's Office of Transportation
The Penn Mutual Life
PennFuture
Pennsylvania Horticultural Society; Philadelphia, PA Brand Agency
The Philadelphia Center City District
Philadelphia Corporation for Aging
Philadelphia Financial (Agency of Record) Public Relations
Philadelphia Industrial Development Corporation Strategic Marketing
Philadelphia Mayors Office of Transportation & Utilities
Rothman Institute
Saul Ewing (Agency of Record) Print, Online,Outdoor & Media Buying
Senior Care Development
Seniors Management Services
Taco Bell; Philadelphia, PA Frutista Freeze
Tenet HealthSystems
United Way
West Chester University of Pennsylvania Public Relations

Branch

LevLane Advertising/PR/Interactive-Florida
1326 E Fairfax Cir, Boynton Beach, FL 33436-8612
Tel.: (561) 963-0490
Fax: (561) 963-0860
E-Mail: dlane@levlane.com
Web Site: www.levlane.com

Employees: 1

National Agency Associations: MAGNET-PRSA

Bruce Lev *(Partner & Chief Creative Officer)*
Drake Newkirk *(Sr VP & Dir-Creative-Digital)*
David Koromaus *(VP & Acct Dir)*
Dan Hall *(VP & Dir-Digital Media)*
Josh Lev *(Sr Acct Mgr)*
Chloe Walsh *(Mgr-Traffic)*
Brian Hall *(Supvr-Media)*

LEVO HEALTH
15310 Amberly Dr Ste 207, Tampa, FL 33647
Toll Free: (855) 234-0232
E-Mail: info@levohealth.com
Web Site: www.levohealth.com

Year Founded: 2014

Agency Specializes In: Above-the-Line, Advertising, Advertising Specialties, Affiliate Marketing, Affluent Market, African-American Market, Agriculture, Alternative Advertising, Arts, Asian Market, Automotive, Aviation & Aerospace, Below-the-Line, Bilingual Market, Brand Development & Integration, Branded Entertainment, Broadcast, Business Publications, Business-To-Business, Cable T.V., Catalogs, Children's Market, Co-op Advertising, Collateral, College, Commercial Photography, Communications, Computers & Software, Consulting, Consumer Goods, Consumer Marketing, Consumer Publications, Content, Corporate Communications, Corporate Identity, Cosmetics, Crisis Communications, Custom Publishing, Customer Relationship Management, Digital/Interactive, Direct Response Marketing, Direct-to-Consumer, E-Commerce, Education, Electronic Media, Electronics, Email, Engineering, Entertainment, Environmental, Event Planning & Marketing, Exhibit/Trade Shows, Experience Design, Faith Based, Fashion/Apparel, Financial,

Food Service, Game Integration, Gay & Lesbian Market, Government/Political, Graphic Design, Guerilla Marketing, Health Care Services, High Technology, Hispanic Market, Hospitality, Household Goods, Identity Marketing, In-Store Advertising, Industrial, Infomercials, Information Technology, Integrated Marketing, International, Internet/Web Design, Investor Relations, Legal Services, Leisure, Local Marketing, Logo & Package Design, Luxury Products, Magazines, Marine, Market Research, Media Buying Services, Media Planning, Media Relations, Media Training, Medical Products, Men's Market, Merchandising, Mobile Marketing, Multicultural, Multimedia, New Product Development, New Technologies, Newspaper, Newspapers & Magazines, Out-of-Home Media, Outdoor, Over-50 Market, Package Design, Paid Searches, Pets , Pharmaceutical, Planning & Consultation, Podcasting, Point of Purchase, Point of Sale, Print, Product Placement, Production, Production (Ad, Film, Broadcast), Production (Print), Promotions, Public Relations, Publicity/Promotions, Publishing, RSS (Really Simple Syndication), Radio, Real Estate, Recruitment, Regional, Restaurant, Retail, Sales Promotion, Search Engine Optimization, Seniors' Market, Shopper Marketing, Social Marketing/Nonprofit, Social Media, South Asian Market, Sponsorship, Sports Market, Stakeholders, Strategic Planning/Research, Sweepstakes, Syndication, T.V., Technical Advertising, Teen Market, Telemarketing, Trade & Consumer Magazines, Transportation, Travel & Tourism, Tween Market, Urban Market, Viral/Buzz/Word of Mouth, Web (Banner Ads, Pop-ups, etc.), Women's Market, Yellow Pages Advertising

David M. Williams *(Chief Strategy Officer)*

Accounts:
Darryl Strawberry Recovery Centers

LEVY MG

Four Smithfield St, Pittsburgh, PA 15222-2222
Tel.: (412) 201-1900
Fax: (412) 201-1410
E-Mail: info@levymgi.com
Web Site: www.levymgi.com

E-Mail for Key Personnel:
President: davelevy@levymgi.com
Creative Dir.: lisawittig@levymgi.com
Media Dir.: pennysummers@levymgi.com

Employees: 12
Year Founded: 1987

Agency Specializes In: Advertising, Brand Development & Integration, Business Publications, Business-To-Business, Collateral, Communications, Corporate Identity, Digital/Interactive, Direct Response Marketing, E-Commerce, Electronic Media, Engineering, Event Planning & Marketing, Financial, Graphic Design, Health Care Services, High Technology, Industrial, Information Technology, Internet/Web Design, Legal Services, Medical Products, New Product Development, Newspaper, Newspapers & Magazines, Outdoor, Pharmaceutical, Planning & Consultation, Point of Purchase, Point of Sale, Print, Production, Public Relations, Publicity/Promotions, Radio, Sales Promotion, Strategic Planning/Research, Technical Advertising, Telemarketing

David Levy *(Pres & CEO)*
Lisa Wittig *(VP-Creative)*
Daniel Kerekes *(Sr Dir-Art & Creative)*
Todd Miller *(Dir-PR)*
Penny Summers *(Dir-Media & Ops)*
Charles Sylak *(Dir-Bus Dev)*
Trisha Hineman *(Mgr-Interactive Production)*

Accounts:
Ametek Specialty Metals; Eighty Four, PA Metal Powders & Polymers; 1991
Irwin Car & Equipment; Irwin, PA Industrial Wheel Assemblies; 1992
ITW Sexton Marketing

LEWIS ADVERTISING COMPANY INC.

(d/b/a Lewis Direct)
325 E Oliver St, Baltimore, MD 21202-2999
Tel.: (410) 539-5100
Fax: (410) 685-5144
Toll Free: (800) 533-5394
E-Mail: info@lewisdirect.com
Web Site: www.lewisdirect.com

Employees: 36
Year Founded: 1930

Agency Specializes In: Direct Response Marketing

Approx. Annual Billings: $7,000,000

Marianne Leonard *(Mgr)*

Accounts:
AllFirst Bank
American Printing House for the Blind
Armstrong

LEWIS ADVERTISING, INC.

1050 Country Club Rd, Rocky Mount, NC 27804
Tel.: (252) 443-5131
Fax: (252) 443-9340
Web Site: www.lewisadvertising.com

E-Mail for Key Personnel:
President: dwilliams@lainc.com

Employees: 47
Year Founded: 1969

National Agency Associations: 4A's

Agency Specializes In: Advertising, Agriculture, Brand Development & Integration, Business Publications, Business-To-Business, Cable T.V., Co-op Advertising, Collateral, Commercial Photography, Communications, Digital/Interactive, E-Commerce, Electronic Media, Financial, Food Service, Graphic Design, Guerilla Marketing, Health Care Services, High Technology, Hospitality, In-Store Advertising, Integrated Marketing, International, Internet/Web Design, Local Marketing, Logo & Package Design, Magazines, Market Research, Media Buying Services, Media Planning, Multimedia, New Product Development, Newspaper, Newspapers & Magazines, Out-of-Home Media, Outdoor, Paid Searches, Point of Purchase, Point of Sale, Print, Production, Production (Print), Promotions, Public Relations, Publicity/Promotions, Radio, Real Estate, Regional, Restaurant, Retail, Sales Promotion, Search Engine Optimization, Social Marketing/Nonprofit, Sponsorship, Strategic Planning/Research, T.V., Technical Advertising, Telemarketing, Trade & Consumer Magazines, Transportation, Travel & Tourism, Yellow Pages Advertising

Approx. Annual Billings: $35,000,000

Gene L. Lewis *(Chm)*
Kim Council *(CFO & Sr VP)*
Reese Adams *(Sr VP-Acct Mgmt)*
Ronnie Grillo *(Sr VP)*
Lee Lewis *(Sr VP-Out-Of-Home Media)*
Becky Beaty *(VP & Dir-Media)*
Susan Harper *(VP-Production)*
Jim Lowdermilk *(VP-Acct Mgmt)*
Sandra Everette *(Mgr-Traffic)*
Mark Jackson *(Mgr-IT)*
Ursula Forrester *(Sr Acct Exec)*

Accounts:
A Cleaner World
Builder's Discount Center
CenturyLink
Embarq Business
Fred's Beds
Friendly Check
Hardee's Interview Radio
Hardees Food Systems, Inc.
Kerr Drug
LeafGuard
Nash Health Care
Nash Surgical Weight Loss - Tape Measure
NCPC
North Carolina Pork Council
PenCell Plastics
Perdue, Inc. - Housing Division
Providence Bank
Riverside Brochure

LEWIS COMMUNICATIONS

600 Corporate Pkwy Ste 200, Birmingham, AL 35242
Tel.: (205) 980-0774
Fax: (205) 437-0250
E-Mail: newbiz@lewiscommunications.com
Web Site: www.lewiscommunications.com

E-Mail for Key Personnel:
President: larry@lewiscommunications.com
Creative Dir.: paulc@lewiscommunications.com

Employees: 80
Year Founded: 1951

National Agency Associations: 4A's-ICOM-PRSA

Agency Specializes In: Advertising, Advertising Specialties, Affluent Market, Brand Development & Integration, Broadcast, Cable T.V., Co-op Advertising, Collateral, College, Commercial Photography, Communications, Consumer Goods, Consumer Marketing, Corporate Identity, Customer Relationship Management, Digital/Interactive, Direct-to-Consumer, Electronic Media, Environmental, Event Planning & Marketing, Exhibit/Trade Shows, Financial, Government/Political, Health Care Services, Hospitality, Identity Marketing, Integrated Marketing, Internet/Web Design, Leisure, Logo & Package Design, Luxury Products, Marine, Media Buying Services, Media Planning, Medical Products, Mobile Marketing, Newspaper, Out-of-Home Media, Outdoor, Paid Searches, Print, Production (Ad, Film, Broadcast), Production (Print), Public Relations, Radio, Real Estate, Restaurant, Sports Market, Strategic Planning/Research, T.V., Travel & Tourism, Women's Market

Approx. Annual Billings: $80,000,000

Larry Norris *(Pres & CEO)*
Kenneth Wilson *(Mng Dir & VP)*
Spencer Till *(Sr VP & Exec Dir-Creative)*
Gary Brandon *(VP & Brand Strategist)*
Jim Sealy *(Controller-Bus Svcs)*
Deanna Chisholm *(Sr Dir-Art)*
Stephen Curry *(Dir-Creative)*
Tripp Lewis *(Dir-New Bus Dev)*
Jared Lyvers *(Dir-Interactive Grp)*
Lisa Mahaffey *(Dir-Traffic)*
Leigh Ann Motley *(Dir-Production)*
Scott Piggott *(Dir-Digital & Tech)*
Puffer Thompson *(Dir-Creative)*
Laura Powers *(Assoc Dir-Creative & Copywriter)*
Chrystal Forshee *(Sr Acct Mgr)*
Michelle Kendrick *(Sr Acct Mgr)*
Miriam Strickland *(Sr Acct Mgr)*
Sarah Cooper *(Office Mgr)*
Stefani Raushenberger *(Acct Mgr)*
Catie Bell *(Mgr-Social Media)*
Ben Fine *(Mgr-Traffic & Production)*

Courtney Haupt *(Mgr-Internal Controls)*
Carlton Wood *(Acct Supvr)*
Anne Varner *(Supvr-Client Svcs)*
Mary-Margaret Brown *(Media Planner & Media Buyer)*
Jeff Porter *(Designer)*
Rebecca Roberts *(Media Planner & Buyer)*
Jake Fagan *(Acct Coord)*
John Michael Morris *(Sr Media Planner & Buyer)*

Accounts:
Abeka Books
Alagasco; Birmingham, AL Natural Gas (utility); 2010
Alfa Insurance
Austal, USA; Mobile, AL Commercial & Defense Vessels; 2009
Energy Logic
Good People Brewing
Habitat for Humanity; Birmingham, AL Habitat for Humanity of Greater Birmingham; 2007
The Joseph School; Nashville, TN & Port-au-Prince, Haiti Leadership School in Haiti; 2010
Mobile Area Water & Sewer Service
Mobile Gas; Mobile, AL Natural Gas (Utility); 2011
Shoe Station Advertising, Marketing
Stony Brook Long Island Children's Hospital
Tiffin Motorhomes; Red Bay, AL Motorhomes & RV; 2003
University of Virginia; Charlottesville, VA University of Virginia Health System; University of Virginia; 2006
US Postal Service; Washington D.C. Postal Inspection Service; 2008
Vanderbilt University Medical Center; Nashville, TN Health Care; Academic Medical Center; NCI Designated Cancer Center; Children's Hospital; 1996

Branch

Lewis Communications
30 Burton Hills Blvd Ste 207, Nashville, TN 37215-6184
Tel.: (615) 661-4995
Fax: (615) 661-4772
E-Mail: ken@lewiscommunications.com
Web Site: www.lewiscommunications.com

Employees: 8
Year Founded: 1997

National Agency Associations: 4A's

Agency Specializes In: Advertising, Communications, Public Relations

Ken Wilson *(Mng Dir & VP)*
Jason Headrick *(Art Dir)*
Jason BicKell *(Dir-Art)*
Robert Froedge *(Dir-Creative)*
Laura Powers *(Assoc Dir-Creative & Copywriter)*
Katie Peninger *(Acct Supvr)*

Accounts:
University Hospital

LEWIS MEDIA PARTNERS
500 Libbie Ave Ste 2C, Richmond, VA 23226
Tel.: (804) 741-7115
Fax: (804) 741-7118
E-Mail: info@lewismediapartners.com
Web Site: www.lewismediapartners.com

Beth Saunders *(VP)*
Carrie Watko *(Producer-Digital)*
Jackie Niblock *(Dir-Digital)*
Bg Brinkley *(Mgr-HR)*
Gwendolyn Ford *(Mgr-Fin)*
Christi Barbour *(Sr Buyer-Brdcst)*
Tori Stowers *(Planner-Digital & Buyer)*
Jennifer Ward *(Analyst-Digital)*

LG2
3575 Saint-Laurent Boulevard Suite 900, Montreal, QC H2X 2T7 Canada
Tel.: (514) 281-8901
Fax: (514) 281-0957
E-Mail: infomtl@lg2.com
Web Site: www.lg2.com

Employees: 100

Agency Specializes In: Advertising

Sylvain Labarre *(Partner & Pres)*
Mireille Cote *(Partner, Mng Dir & VP)*
Mathieu Roy *(Partner, Mng Dir & VP)*
Paul Gauthier *(Partner & Chief Brand Officer)*
Jeremy Gayton *(Partner, VP & Gen Mgr)*
Jacques de Varennes *(Partner, VP & Dir-Creative & Design)*
Gilles Chouinard *(Partner & Exec Dir-Creative)*
Nellie Kim *(Partner & Dir-Creative)*
Nicolas Boisvert *(Partner & Copywriter)*
Krista Cressman *(Acct Dir)*
Mathieu Dufour *(Art Dir)*
Vincent Bernard *(Dir-Art)*
Julie Pichette *(Dir-Production)*
Philippe Comeau *(Copywriter)*

Accounts:
1one Production
Arctic Gardens
Automotive Insurance of Quebec
Bell
Bonduelle
Canac Hardware
The Capital Transit Network
Country Time Campaign: "Breakfast time is whenever you're reading this", Campaign: "It's never too late for Bacon""
F. Menard
New-Farnham Ale & Lager
Krispy Kernels Campaign: "Dinosaur, Robot", Campaign: "Meditation", Campaign: "President", Km 43
La Cage Aux Sports
Les Rotisseries Au Coq Ltee
Life Saving Society Campaign: "Hand", Campaign: "Inattention"
Loto-Quebec Campaign: "Billet Noir"
Maison Orphee
Natrel
Nestle
New-Nike
Partenariat du Quartier des Spectacles Campaign: "Luminotherapy"
Quebec Automobile Insurance Corporation
Quebec City Magic Festival "Magic Mop", Campaign: "Magic Hat", Campaign: "Magic Powers"
New-Quebec Hog Farmers
New-Quebec Milk Producers Creative
Rockland
Sanofi-Aventis Campaign: "Dandruff Flakes Typically Occur in Winter", Selsun Blue
Savoura
Sears Optical Campaign: "Makeup, Tail, Boat", Campaign: "The Fabulous Flea Circus"
Societe de l'assurance Automobile Quebec
Ultramar
Valin Custom Tailoring Campaign: "Whatever Your Shape"
Via Capitale Campaign: "Garage"
Village Vacances Valcartier

LGD COMMUNICATIONS, INC.
3819 N Miami Ave, Miami, FL 33137
Tel.: (305) 576-9400
Fax: (305) 576-9200
Web Site: lgdcom.com/

Employees: 20
Year Founded: 2001

Agency Specializes In: Advertising, Affluent Market, Brand Development & Integration, Collateral, Commercial Photography, Corporate Identity, Digital/Interactive, Electronic Media, Internet/Web Design, Logo & Package Design, Luxury Products, Media Buying Services, Media Planning, Print, Radio, Social Media, T.V.

Approx. Annual Billings: $1,600,000

Len Dugow *(Pres & Chief Creative Officer)*
Nancy Cooper *(COO)*
Andrew Smith *(Acct Svcs Dir)*
Vanessa Conde *(Dir-Mktg & New Bus Dev)*
Matthew Dugow *(Dir-New Business & Digital Mktg)*
Kaile Choi *(Office Mgr)*

Accounts:
Gale Boutique Hotel & Residences (Branding, Advertising & Digital Marketing Agency of Record)
Marina Palms Yacht Clubs & Residences Advertising, Branding, Digital Marketing, Web Development
Melia Hotel International Advertising, Branding, Digital Marketing, Web Development
Prive Residences Advertising, Branding, Digital Marketing, Web Development
Sabbia Beach (Branding, Advertising & Digital Marketing Agency of Record) Media Buying, Media Planning, Point of Sale, Print, Website

LH ADVERTISING AGENCY INC.
200 N Central Ave Ste 220, Hartsdale, NY 10530
Tel.: (914) 285-3456
Fax: (914) 285-3450
E-Mail: lh@leonhenryinc.com
Web Site: www.leonhenryinc.com

E-Mail for Key Personnel:
President: lynnh@leonhenryinc.com

Employees: 4
Year Founded: 1968

National Agency Associations: DMA

Agency Specializes In: Business Publications, Business-To-Business, Co-op Advertising, Consumer Marketing, Consumer Publications, Direct Response Marketing, E-Commerce, Out-of-Home Media, Print, Seniors' Market, Sports Market

Approx. Annual Billings: $125,000

Breakdown of Gross Billings by Media: D.M.: $125,000

Lynn Henry *(Pres)*
Gail Henry *(Exec VP & Gen Mgr)*
Barbara Henry *(Exec VP-Branch Office)*
Jackie Gizzo *(VP)*
Jeff Angelini *(Dir-IT)*
Margaret Ginns *(Mgr-Sls)*
Millie Mcfarlane *(Mgr-Acctg Dept)*
Lois Attisani *(Sr Acct Exec)*
Mike Natoli *(Sr Acct Exec)*
Rebecca A. Santaniello *(Sr Acct Exec)*
Sharon Kenyon *(Coord-Promos)*

Accounts:
The American Stationery Company
Bally Total Fitness
Mantis
QCI Direct
Wizard Entertainment

LHWH ADVERTISING & PUBLIC RELATIONS
(Formerly lesnik himmelsbach wilson hearl advertising & public relations)

(d/b/a LHWH)
3005 Hwy 17 Bypass N, Myrtle Beach, SC 29577-6742
Tel.: (843) 448-1123
Fax: (843) 626-2390
E-Mail: alesnik@lhwh.com
Web Site: www.lhwhadvertising.com

E-Mail for Key Personnel:
President: alesnik@lhwh.com
Creative Dir.: swilson@lhwh.com
Public Relations: lgainer@lhwh.com

Employees: 40
Year Founded: 1987

Agency Specializes In: Advertising, Entertainment, Financial, Health Care Services, Real Estate, Travel & Tourism

Approx. Annual Billings: $10,000,000

Andrew Lesnik *(Pres)*
Vern Hearl *(Partner)*
Steve Ellwood *(Sr Dir-Art)*
Leslie Fried *(Sr Dir-Art)*
Lei Gainer *(Dir-PR)*
Dick Gibson *(Mgr-Production)*
Dana Mcdonald *(Mgr-Network)*
Laura Tyler *(Acct Exec)*
Jamie Wilburn *(Coord-PR)*

Accounts:
Burroughs & Chapin
HTC Communications
Marina Inn
McLeod Health
Newland Communities
Silver Companies

LIGHTHOUSE LIST COMPANY
27 SE 24th Ave Ste 6, Pompano Beach, FL 33062
Tel.: (954) 489-3008
Fax: (954) 489-3040
E-Mail: lighthouselist@lighthouselist.com
Web Site: www.lighthouselist.com

Agency Specializes In: Advertising Specialties

Lighthouse List is a premier interactive and mixed channel broker in the United States. Our integrated marketing consists of a promotional mix of direct mail, telemarketing, digital, lead generation, SMS and more. The Lighthouse List Team is knowledgable, experienced, and dedicated to ensuring our clients receive the best possible results. We offer impeccable service at the absolute most competitve pricing. With sixteen years of experience, we continue to evolve and innovate for you, our client.

Robert Orr *(Pres)*
Mark Traverso *(VP-New Bus & Sls)*
Jordan Cothran *(Dir-Digital Mktg)*
Scott Warren *(Dir-Data Mgmt)*
Matt Kowalski *(Mgr-New Bus Dev & Data Acquisition)*
Aleen Newman *(Mgr-Data Acq)*

LIGHTHOUSE MARKETING
5821 Acton St, East Syracuse, NY 13057
Tel.: (315) 656-9922
Fax: (315) 656-9955
Web Site: www.lighthousemkt.com

Year Founded: 2001

Susan M. Beebe *(Founder & Pres)*
Kim McNeill *(CFO)*
Ann Martin *(VP-Agency Svcs)*
Jessy Hugus *(Sr Dir-Art)*
Kevin Powell *(Sr Dir-Art)*
Ashley Jernigan *(Acct Svcs Dir)*
Christine Fallucco *(Dir-Strategic Plng)*
Tracie Cantrell *(Sr Acct Mgr)*
Marina White *(Acct Mgr)*
Vanessa Berry *(Acct Coord)*
Kimberly Klamon *(Acct Coord)*

Accounts:
Brophy Services Inc
Brown & Brown
Eldan Homes
Greek Peak Mountain Resort
John Arquette Properties

LIGHTMAKER
6881 Kingspointe Pkwy Ste 12, Orlando, FL 32819
Tel.: (321) 293-0500
Fax: (321) 293-0501
E-Mail: usa@lightmaker.com
Web Site: www.lightmaker.com

Agency Specializes In: Digital/Interactive

Bill Quinn *(CEO)*
Ben Philyaw *(Chief Client Officer)*
Patrick McNerney *(Exec VP)*
Suzi Albrecht *(Project Mgr & Sr Producer-Digital)*
Kelly Lammers *(Sr Producer-Digital)*
Keith Frechette *(Dir-Bus Dev)*
Kashif Hasan *(Dir-Strategy-UK EMEA)*

Accounts:
Bacardi
BMW
JK Rowling

LIGHTQUEST MEDIA INC
7666 E 61st St Ste 120, Tulsa, OK 74133
Tel.: (918) 794-6464
E-Mail: news@lightquestmedia.com
Web Site: www.lightquestmedia.com

Employees: 8

Agency Specializes In: Graphic Design, Internet/Web Design, Media Buying Services, Media Planning, Media Relations, Product Placement, Production

Chris Busch *(CEO)*
Walter Warren *(Exec VP)*
Cynthia Johnston *(Dir-Ops & Fin)*

Accounts:
Elevate Life Church
Faith Life Now Strategies Sharing Services
Love A Child, Inc.

LIGON MEDIA
PO Box 161776, Sacramento, CA 95816
Tel.: (916) 642-8710
Web Site: www.ligonmedia.com

Agency Specializes In: Advertising, Internet/Web Design, Media Training, Public Relations, Radio, T.V.

David Ligon *(Owner)*

Accounts:
Sacramento Area Commerce & Trade Organization

LILLETHORUP PRODUCTIONS, INC.
5011 Seward St, Omaha, NE 68104
Tel.: (402) 341-5423
Fax: (402) 342-8392
E-Mail: tim@lpvideo.com
Web Site: www.lpvideo.com

Employees: 3
Year Founded: 1990

Approx. Annual Billings: $500,000

Tim Lillethorup *(Owner & Pres)*

LIME VALLEY ADVERTISING, INC.
1620 S Riverfront Dr, Mankato, MN 56001
Tel.: (507) 345-8500
Fax: (507) 387-6901
Toll Free: (800) 896-5419
E-Mail: info@limevalley.com
Web Site: www.limevalley.com

Agency Specializes In: Advertising, Corporate Identity, Digital/Interactive, Graphic Design, Internet/Web Design, Logo & Package Design, Media Buying Services, Print, Public Relations, Social Media

Brian Maciej *(Owner)*
Jim Schill *(VP & Copywriter)*
Marissa Geerdes *(Dir-Admin Svcs)*
Casey Christenson *(Assoc Dir-Art)*

Accounts:
Mankato Marathon

LIME VIZIO
8135 Varna Ave, Van Nuys, CA 91402
Tel.: (818) 284-4683
Fax: (818) 988-5043
Toll Free: (866) 446-1774
E-Mail: tim@limevizio.com
Web Site: www.limevizio.com

Employees: 5

Agency Specializes In: Advertising, Advertising Specialties, Bilingual Market, Business-To-Business, Consumer Marketing, Custom Publishing, Entertainment, Guerilla Marketing, Local Marketing, Logo & Package Design, Luxury Products, Mobile Marketing, Out-of-Home Media, Outdoor, Promotions, Sports Market, Viral/Buzz/Word of Mouth

Timur Kremenetskiy *(Owner)*

Accounts:
Don Ramon Tequila
Nemiroff Vodka
Nissan Dealership

LIMEGREEN
344 N Ogden Ave 5th Fl, Chicago, IL 60607
Tel.: (312) 432-1600
Fax: (312) 602-3836
E-Mail: info@limegreen.net
Web Site: http://lgmoroch.com/

National Agency Associations: 4A's

Agency Specializes In: Advertising, Brand Development & Integration, Digital/Interactive, Media Relations, Media Training, Public Relations, Social Media, Strategic Planning/Research

Allison Lamb *(Co-Founder & Dir-Creative)*
Michon Ellis *(CEO & Mng Partner)*
Ella Britton Gibson *(Mng Dir)*
Michelle Mosley *(Project Mgr & Mgr-Fin)*

Accounts:
AmazingCosmetics
Beam Global Spirits & Wine
BlackDoctor.org
Courvoisier
Cystic Fibrosis Foundation
Kia Motors America Communication Strategy, Creative, Media Relationships

Laphroaig Scotch
Luster Products Inc.
Magic Johnson Bridgescape
McDonald's Corporation
Miami University
University of Chicago

LIMELIGHT ADVERTISING & DESIGN

26 Ontario St Ste 200, Port Hope, ON L1A 2T6 Canada
Tel.: (905) 885-9895
Fax: (905) 885-5699
E-Mail: change@limelight.org
Web Site: www.limelight.org

Employees: 5
Year Founded: 1986

Agency Specializes In: Advertising, Agriculture, Aviation & Aerospace, Brand Development & Integration, Broadcast, Business Publications, Business-To-Business, Catalogs, Co-op Advertising, Collateral, Commercial Photography, Communications, Consulting, Consumer Goods, Content, Corporate Communications, Corporate Identity, Digital/Interactive, E-Commerce, Engineering, Environmental, Event Planning & Marketing, Exhibit/Trade Shows, Financial, Food Service, Government/Political, Graphic Design, Health Care Services, Identity Marketing, In-Store Advertising, Industrial, Integrated Marketing, Internet/Web Design, Logo & Package Design, Magazines, Marine, Market Research, Media Buying Services, Media Planning, Medical Products, New Technologies, Newspaper, Package Design, Planning & Consultation, Point of Purchase, Point of Sale, Print, Production, Production (Print), Public Relations, Publicity/Promotions, Radio, Real Estate, Restaurant, Retail, Social Marketing/Nonprofit, Sponsorship, Strategic Planning/Research, Trade & Consumer Magazines, Transportation, Travel & Tourism, Viral/Buzz/Word of Mouth

Approx. Annual Billings: $750,000

Peter Gabany *(Pres & Dir-Creative)*

LIMELIGHT NETWORKS

222 South Mill Ave Ste 800, Tempe, AZ 85281
Tel.: (602) 850-5000
Fax: (602) 850-5001
E-Mail: media@llnw.com
Web Site: www.limelight.com

Year Founded: 2005

Agency Specializes In: Investor Relations, Media Buying Services, Multimedia

Kurt Silverman *(Sr VP-Dev & Delivery)*
Venu Aravamudan *(VP-R&D)*
Nigel Burmeister *(VP-Product & Solutions Mktg)*
Dan Carney *(VP-Ops)*
Harry Chiu *(VP-Product Mgmt)*
Kevin Odden *(VP-S/s)*
Jason Hofmann *(Sr Dir-Product Mgmt)*
Nivedita Mehra *(Sr Dir-Product Mgmt)*
Michael Shulman *(Sr Dir-Platform Engrg)*
Jason Thibeault *(Sr Dir-Mktg Strategy)*

Accounts:
DoubleClick

LINDSAY, STONE & BRIGGS, INC.

100 State St, Madison, WI 53703-2573
Tel.: (608) 251-7070
Fax: (608) 251-8989
E-Mail: info@lsb.com
Web Site: www.lsb.com

Employees: 35
Year Founded: 1978

National Agency Associations: 4A's

Agency Specializes In: Advertising, Brand Development & Integration, Broadcast, Collateral, Communications, Consulting, Consumer Marketing, Graphic Design, Health Care Services, Internet/Web Design, Logo & Package Design, Media Buying Services, New Product Development, Out-of-Home Media, Planning & Consultation, Print, Production, Public Relations, Publicity/Promotions, Radio, Strategic Planning/Research, T.V., Trade & Consumer Magazines, Travel & Tourism, Viral/Buzz/Word of Mouth

Phil Ouellette *(Pres & COO)*
Marsha Lindsay *(CEO)*
Julie Herfel *(Partner & Dir-Production)*
Bill Winchester *(Chief Creative Officer)*
Rick Stone *(Exec VP & Sr Strategist-Brand)*
Amy Rohn *(Sr VP & Dir-PR)*
Lindsay Ferris *(Sr VP & Sr Strategist-Mktg)*
Shelley DauSchmidt *(Acct Supvr)*

Accounts:
Emergency Physicians Insurance Company (EPIC)
First Weber Group Realtors
Jazz at Five Concert Series
Marshfield Clinic; 2001
Michael Best & Friedrich
Midwest Airlines
Milio's
PremierGarage (Agency of Record)
Stonyfield Farm

LINEAR CREATIVE LLC

4681 Hinckley Pkwy, Cleveland, OH 44019
Tel.: (216) 741-1533
Web Site: www.linearcreative.com

Year Founded: 2003

Agency Specializes In: Advertising, Event Planning & Marketing, Graphic Design, Internet/Web Design, Public Relations, Strategic Planning/Research

Raymond W. Jasinski *(Owner & Dir-Creative)*
Mike Counselman *(Dir-Video Art & Designer)*
Barbara A. Ragon *(Dir-Mktg)*
Elizabeth Ziehm *(Coord-Mktg)*

Accounts:
J&M Machine, Inc.
Northern Ohio Printing, Inc. SculptedUV

LINETT & HARRISON

2500 Morris Ave, Union, NJ 07083
Tel.: (908) 686-0606
Fax: (908) 686-0623
E-Mail: sharrison@linettandharrison.com
Web Site: www.linettandharrison.com

E-Mail for Key Personnel:
President: sharrison@linettandharrison.com

Employees: 20
Year Founded: 1989

Agency Specializes In: Advertising, Brand Development & Integration, Broadcast, Business Publications, Business-To-Business, Cable T.V., Children's Market, Co-op Advertising, Collateral, Commercial Photography, Consumer Marketing, Corporate Identity, Cosmetics, Digital/Interactive, Direct Response Marketing, Education, Exhibit/Trade Shows, Financial, Graphic Design, Health Care Services, High Technology, Hispanic Market, Industrial, Internet/Web Design, Leisure, Logo & Package Design, Magazines, Marine, Media Buying Services, Newspapers & Magazines, Out-of-Home Media, Outdoor, Planning & Consultation, Point of Purchase, Print, Production, Public Relations, Publicity/Promotions, Radio, Real Estate, Recruitment, Retail, Sales Promotion, Strategic Planning/Research, Sweepstakes, Trade & Consumer Magazines, Travel & Tourism

Caryl Linett *(Chm & CEO)*
Sam Harrison *(Pres & Dir-Acct Svcs)*
Diane Ahle *(Dir-Recruitment Adv)*
Jodi Elias *(Acct Mgr)*
Sabine Dorisme *(Mgr-Production & Traffic)*

Accounts:
Chilton Memorial Hospital
College of Saint Elizabeth
Cornerstone Accounting Group
Hospital for Joint Diseases
The Provident Bank of New Jersey Marketing, Media Relations
SI Bank & Trust
The Szikley Borresen Group
University Health Plans
Westminster Hotel

THE LINICK GROUP, INC.

Linick Bldg 7 Putter Ln Dept RB08, Middle Island, NY 11953-0102
Mailing Address:
PO Box 102, Middle Island, NY 11953-0102
Tel.: (631) 924-3888
Fax: (631) 924-8555
E-Mail: linickgrp@att.net
Web Site: www.andrewlinickdirectmarketing.com

Employees: 70
Year Founded: 1972

National Agency Associations: DMA

Agency Specializes In: Advertising, Agriculture, Asian Market, Automotive, Aviation & Aerospace, Brand Development & Integration, Broadcast, Business Publications, Business-To-Business, Cable T.V., Children's Market, Co-op Advertising, Collateral, Commercial Photography, Communications, Consulting, Consumer Marketing, Consumer Publications, Corporate Identity, Cosmetics, Digital/Interactive, Direct Response Marketing, E-Commerce, Education, Electronic Media, Engineering, Entertainment, Environmental, Event Planning & Marketing, Exhibit/Trade Shows, Fashion/Apparel, Financial, Food Service, Graphic Design, Health Care Services, High Technology, Hispanic Market, Industrial, Infomercials, Information Technology, Internet/Web Design, Investor Relations, Legal Services, Leisure, Logo & Package Design, Magazines, Marine, Media Buying Services, Medical Products, Merchandising, Multimedia, New Product Development, Newspaper, Newspapers & Magazines, Out-of-Home Media, Outdoor, Over-50 Market, Pets , Pharmaceutical, Planning & Consultation, Point of Purchase, Point of Sale, Print, Production, Public Relations, Publicity/Promotions, Radio, Real Estate, Recruitment, Restaurant, Retail, Sales Promotion, Seniors' Market, Sports Market, Strategic Planning/Research, Sweepstakes, Syndication, T.V., Technical Advertising, Teen Market, Telemarketing, Trade & Consumer Magazines, Transportation, Travel & Tourism, Yellow Pages Advertising

Approx. Annual Billings: $50,000,000

Breakdown of Gross Billings by Media: Adv. Specialities: 1%; Audio/Visual: 1%; Brdcst.: 2%; Bus. Publs.: 3%; Cable T.V.: 2%; Co-op Adv.: 2%; Collateral: 2%; Comml. Photography: 2%; Consulting: 5%; Consumer Publs.: 2%; Corp. Communications: 2%; D.M.: 8%; E-Commerce: 15%; Event Mktg.: 2%; Exhibits/Trade Shows: 2%;

Fees: 5%; Foreign: 2%; Graphic Design: 2%; In-Store Adv.: 10%; Internet Adv.: 5%; Mags.: 3%; Newsp. & Mags.: 3%; Newsp.: 2%; Plng. & Consultation: 2%; Print: 2%; Production: 3%; Pub. Rels.: 5%; Radio & T.V.: 5%; Trade Shows: 1%; Video Brochures: 1%; Worldwide Web Sites: 1%

Andrew S. Linick *(Chm & CEO)*
Roger Dextor *(VP & Dir-Creative)*
Bruce Linick *(VP)*

Accounts:
ABCNews.com; New York, NY Competitive Intelligence, TV Commercial; 2007
Act Technology Corporation
Arizona Highways Magazine
Checkpoint Systems, Inc.
Duna-Bull Dog Bedz, LLC; 2006
Fortune Magazine
Grow Group, Inc.
IBM
Innovative Speech Therapy Online Training DVD; 2006
McGraw-Hill Publications
Microsoft Corporation

The Linick Group, Inc.
(Formerly L.K. Advertising Agency)
The Linick Building, Middle Island, NY 11953-0102
(See Separate Listing)

LINK ADVERTISING INC.
554 Waterloo St, London, ON N6B 2P9 Canada
Tel.: (519) 432-1634
Fax: (519) 432-4626
Toll Free: (800) 472-5731
E-Mail: info@linkad.com
Web Site: www.linkad.com

Employees: 9
Year Founded: 1987

Anne Hallf *(Pres)*
Michelle Davey-Wright *(Assoc Dir-Creative)*
Danielle Vanhie *(Specialist-Mktg)*

Accounts:
Accucaps Industries
Discovery Air

THE LINK AGENCY
38 Talcott St, Barrington, RI 02806
Tel.: (401) 289-2600
E-Mail: info@thelinkagency.com
Web Site: www.thelinkagency.com

Employees: 14
Year Founded: 2000

Agency Specializes In: Advertising, Advertising Specialties, Direct Response Marketing, Hispanic Market, Logo & Package Design, Public Relations, Sales Promotion, Strategic Planning/Research

Tracy LeRoux *(Founder)*

Accounts:
Bancorp Rhode Island, Inc. (BankRI)
Fidelity Charitable Gift Fund
Goya Foods
International Academy of Low Vision Specialists
RageWorks
Rhode Island Convention Center
Saint Luke's School
TJX Companies
Turning Point
Woman & Infants Hospital

LINKMEDIA 360
Summit 1 4700 Rockside Rd Ste 310, Independence, OH 44131-2148
Tel.: (216) 447-9400
Fax: (216) 447-9412
Toll Free: (877) 843-1091
Web Site: www.linkmedia360.com/

Employees: 16
Year Founded: 1968

National Agency Associations: ADM-YPA

Agency Specializes In: Co-op Advertising, Financial, Health Care Services, Internet/Web Design, Search Engine Optimization, Strategic Planning/Research, T.V., Yellow Pages Advertising

Approx. Annual Billings: $12,000,000

Breakdown of Gross Billings by Media: Yellow Page Adv.: $12,000,000

Betty Brown *(Co-Owner & Pres)*
Chad Luckie *(Mng Partner)*
David Wolf *(Mng Partner)*
Renae Dabney *(Sr VP)*
Cindy Adamek *(VP)*
Patti Spirko *(Dir-Billing & Admin)*
Barra Terrigno *(Sr Acct Exec)*
Paul Bauer *(Acct Exec)*
Fritz Davis *(Specialist-Digital Mktg)*
Christopher Enis *(Acct Exec)*
Candace Graves *(Specialist-Digital Mktg)*
Barbara Le *(Strategist-Digital Mktg)*
Kyle Luckie *(Specialist-Digital Solutions)*

LINKSTORM
1 Penn Plz #6244, New York, NY 10119
Tel.: (646) 649-8799
Fax: (646) 649-8795
Toll Free: (855) 836-6743
E-Mail: info@linkstorm.net
Web Site: www.linkstorms.com

Employees: 14
Year Founded: 2000

Agency Specializes In: Advertising, Digital/Interactive, E-Commerce, Publishing, Web (Banner Ads, Pop-ups, etc.)

Revenue: $1,000,000

Michael B. Healy *(Dir-Client & Ad Ops)*

Accounts:
Audi
Blackberry
Chevrolet; Detroit, MI
Cisco; San Jose, CA
Coca-Cola Refreshments USA, Inc.; Atlanta, GA CokeTag
Hachette Filipacchi; New York, NY
Hewlett-Packard Company; Palo Alto, CA
Microsoft
Ogilvy; New York, NY
Sharebuilder
Verizon
Volvo
Wal-Mart

LINN PRODUCTIONS
1222 Oregon St, Rapid City, SD 57701
Tel.: (605) 348-8675
Fax: (605) 355-0664
Toll Free: (877) 248-8675
E-Mail: studio@linnproductions.com
Web Site: www.linnproductions.com

Employees: 7

Agency Specializes In: Advertising, Advertising Specialties, Digital/Interactive, Internet/Web Design, Production (Ad, Film, Broadcast), Web (Banner Ads, Pop-ups, etc.)

Marc Linn *(Co-Owner)*
Tanya Aby *(Office Mgr & Mgr-Production)*

Accounts:
Fischers Furniture
Riddles Jewelry Christmas

LINNIHAN FOY ADVERTISING
615 1st Ave NE Ste 320, Minneapolis, MN 55413
Tel.: (612) 331-3586
Fax: (612) 238-3000
E-Mail: info@linnihanfoy.com
Web Site: www.linnihanfoy.com

Agency Specializes In: Advertising, Internet/Web Design, Media Buying Services, Media Planning, Public Relations

Neal Linnihan *(Co-Owner & Acct Exec)*
Sean Foy *(Co-Owner)*
Dan Rasmussen *(VP & Acct Dir)*
Brian Ellstrom *(Creative Dir)*
Brian Flis *(Dir-Creative)*
Erin Gibson *(Dir-Media)*
Rhonda Martin *(Dir-Creative)*
Jenna Schuldt *(Office Mgr)*
Christine Wittman *(Office Mgr)*
Liv Tollefson *(Acct Supvr & Sr Strategist-Media)*
Erik Lillejord *(Acct Exec)*
Mark Potter *(Strategist-Digital Mktg)*

Accounts:
Cargill, Inc.
Restonic Mattress Corporation Versalok
Schneiderman's Furniture

LINX COMMUNICATIONS CORP.
155 E Main St 2nd Fl, Smithtown, NY 11787-2808
Tel.: (631) 361-4400
Fax: (631) 361-6400
E-Mail: info@linx.com
Web Site: www.linx.com

E-Mail for Key Personnel:
President: michael@linx.com

Employees: 17
Year Founded: 1996

National Agency Associations: AACC-Second Wind Limited

Agency Specializes In: Advertising, Advertising Specialties, Affluent Market, Alternative Advertising, Brand Development & Integration, Broadcast, Business Publications, Business-To-Business, Cable T.V., Catalogs, Children's Market, Co-op Advertising, Collateral, College, Communications, Computers & Software, Consulting, Consumer Goods, Consumer Marketing, Corporate Communications, Corporate Identity, Custom Publishing, Customer Relationship Management, Digital/Interactive, Direct Response Marketing, Direct-to-Consumer, E-Commerce, Education, Electronic Media, Electronics, Email, Engineering, Entertainment, Environmental, Event Planning & Marketing, Exhibit/Trade Shows, Faith Based, Fashion/Apparel, Financial, Food Service, Government/Political, Graphic Design, Guerilla Marketing, Health Care Services, High Technology, Hospitality, Identity Marketing, In-Store Advertising, Industrial, Infomercials, Information Technology, Integrated Marketing, Internet/Web Design, Investor Relations, Legal Services, Leisure, Local Marketing, Logo & Package Design, Luxury Products, Magazines, Market Research, Media Buying Services, Media Planning, Media Relations, Medical Products, Mobile Marketing, Multimedia, New Product Development, New Technologies, Newspaper, Newspapers & Magazines, Out-of-

Home Media, Outdoor, Over-50 Market, Package Design, Paid Searches, Pharmaceutical, Planning & Consultation, Podcasting, Point of Purchase, Point of Sale, Print, Product Placement, Production (Ad, Film, Broadcast), Production (Print), Promotions, Public Relations, Publicity/Promotions, RSS (Really Simple Syndication), Radio, Real Estate, Recruitment, Regional, Restaurant, Retail, Sales Promotion, Search Engine Optimization, Seniors' Market, Social Marketing/Nonprofit, Social Media, Sponsorship, Sports Market, Strategic Planning/Research, Sweepstakes, T.V., Technical Advertising, Telemarketing, Trade & Consumer Magazines, Transportation, Travel & Tourism, Viral/Buzz/Word of Mouth, Web (Banner Ads, Pop-ups, etc.)

Approx. Annual Billings: $13,000,000

Michael Smith *(Pres & CEO)*
Randee Smith *(VP-Admin)*
Debbie Cosentino *(Dir-Art)*
Jerian Dimattei *(Acct Exec)*
Alex Lougovtsov *(Acct Exec)*
Christina Francesco *(Jr Designer)*

Accounts:
Canon USA; Lake Succes, NY

LIONFISH ADVERTISING

4847 E Virginia St Ste D, Evansville, IN 47715
Tel.: (812) 457-8902
E-Mail: searesults@lionfishadvertising.com
Web Site: www.lionfishadvertising.com

Agency Specializes In: Advertising, Digital/Interactive, Graphic Design, Internet/Web Design, Media Relations, Public Relations, Search Engine Optimization, Social Media, T.V.

Sarah Fortune *(Owner)*

Accounts:
All-Star Lawn Care
Attorney Kevin Bryant
Crane Concrete
Green Tree Plastics

LIPMAN HEARNE, INC.

200 S Michigan Ave Ste 1600, Chicago, IL 60604-2423
Tel.: (312) 356-8000
Fax: (312) 356-4005
E-Mail: lhi@lipmanhearne.com
Web Site: www.lipmanhearne.com

Employees: 50
Year Founded: 1988

National Agency Associations: 4A's

Agency Specializes In: Advertising, Brand Development & Integration, Collateral, College, Communications, Consulting, Crisis Communications, Digital/Interactive, Direct Response Marketing, Education, Government/Political, Graphic Design, Health Care Services, Integrated Marketing, Internet/Web Design, Logo & Package Design, Market Research, Media Buying Services, Media Planning, Media Relations, Media Training, Planning & Consultation, Print, Public Relations, Social Marketing/Nonprofit, Social Media, Strategic Planning/Research

Robert M. Moore *(Pres & CEO)*
Jeremy Ryan *(VP-Digital Svcs)*
Nancy Levner *(Dir-Creative)*
Ryan Wolfe *(Dir-Art)*
Arnie Fishman *(Assoc Dir-Creative)*
Katie Greer *(Sr Acct Exec)*
Donna Bandyk *(Designer-Production)*
Craig Turner *(Coord-IT Support & Office)*

LIPOF ADVERTISING

830 Peters Rd Ste D100, Plantation, FL 33324
Tel.: (954) 472-9999
Fax: (954) 472-1222
E-Mail: media@lipof.com
Web Site: www.lipof.com

Employees: 15

Agency Specializes In: Advertising, Automotive

Mark Lipof *(Pres)*
Matthew Grodzitsky *(Dir-Art)*
Michele Jacobs *(Dir-Media)*
Nathan Lowery *(Dir-Creative)*

Accounts:
Collier Jaguar
Complete Power Solutions
Flanigan's Enterprises, Inc.; Fort Lauderdale, FL
Florida Plumbing-Kitchen & Appliances
Floridian Community Bank
Jaguar
Land Rover
Le Cordon Bleu Culinary School
Miami Subs and Grille
Napleton Hyundai
Ocala Volva
Pet Supermarket
Prestige Infinity
Prestige Nissan
Sea Escape
Shula's Steak Houses, LLP. (Agency of Record) Media, Shula's 2, Shula's 347 Grill, Shula's Bar & Grill, Shula's Grill & Wine Bar, Shula's on the Beach
Tulsa Welding School
University of Florida MBA Program
USA Tile & Marble
Vita Leisure
Warren Henry Automotive Group

LIPPI & CO. ADVERTISING

2820 Selwyn Ave, Charlotte, NC 28209
Tel.: (704) 376-2001
Fax: (704) 374-1535
E-Mail: larry@lippi.com
Web Site: lippi.bfoundbchosen.com/

E-Mail for Key Personnel:
President: larry@lippi.com

Employees: 4
Year Founded: 1987

Agency Specializes In: Broadcast, Collateral, Direct Response Marketing, Print

Larry Lippi *(Owner & Pres)*

Accounts:
Ajax Rolling Ring & Machine Inc.
Diamond Springs
IIDA Carolina
Sycamore Cabinetry
Tri Mountain Gear
Whispering Pines Sportswear

LIPPINCOTT

499 Park Ave, New York, NY 10022-1240
Tel.: (212) 521-0000
Fax: (212) 308-8952
E-Mail: info@lippincott.com
Web Site: www.lippincott.com

Employees: 90
Year Founded: 1943

Agency Specializes In: Advertising, Brand Development & Integration, Communications, Digital/Interactive, Exhibit/Trade Shows, Logo & Package Design

Rick Wise *(CEO)*
Cory Cruser *(Partner-Experience Innovation)*
Fabian Diaz *(Sr Partner)*
Hilary Folger *(Partner-Strategy New York)*
Marc Hohmann *(Partner-Design)*
John Kennedy *(Partner-Bus Dev)*
Heather Stern *(Partner-Marketing & Comm-New York)*
Michael D'Esopo *(Sr Partner & Dir-Brand Strategy)*
John Marshall *(Sr Partner & Dir-Global Strategy-Boston)*
Allen Gove *(Sr Partner-Strategy)*

Accounts:
3M
A&P
Abbott Labs
ABC Television
Actavis
AIGA
Ajilon
Al Ghurair
Allegion
Allstate
American Express
American Greetings
American Heart Association
American Management Association
Amtrak
Andaz
Aptuit
Archstone Communities
Avaya
Avianca
Baker Tilly
Bancroft NeuroHealth
Barclays
Baskin-Robbins
Bausch & Lomb
Bayer
Bayn
BD
Betty Crocker
BMW
BP America Inc. Ampm
Brightheart
British Gas
Buick
Burberrys
C Spire
CA Technologies
Campbell's
Catapult Learning
Centria
Champion Spark Plugs
Chick-fil-A
Childreach
Citgo
Citizens Bank
Clayton, Dubilier & Rice
Coca-Cola
Cognistar
Comcast
Comerica Incorporated
Con Edison, Inc.
Conectiv
Coty, Inc.
Country Road
Daewoo Motor Company
Dell Inc.
Delta Air Lines
Design Management Institute
Doosan Group
Dyneon
Earth Pledge
Ebay Logo
ECornell
Eddie Bauer
Egon Zehnder
Elsevier

Enbridge Inc.
EPEAT EcoSense
ExxonMobil
EyeMed
Farmers Insurance
FiberMark, Inc.
First Citizens Bank
Fluor Corporation
ForeSee
Forethought
Fragomen
The Gillette Company
Giti
GLAAD
Goodwin Procter
Group Health
Grupo Aeroportuario del Pacifico
Guangzhou Honda
Handok Pharmaceuticals
Hayneedle
The Hershey Company Balanced Choices
Holland & Knight
Houghton Mifflin Harcourt
Humana Inc.
Hyatt Corporation
IBM
Inova Health System
Intuit
ITT Corporation
Jamba Juice
JDA Software Brand-Strategy, Campaign: "Plan to Deliver", Communications, Online, Out-of-Home Advertising, Print, Social Media
Johnson Controls
JohnsonDiversey
Kelly Services
Kemper Corporation
Knowles
La Francaise des Jeux La Francaise des Jeux
Lighthouse International
Lincoln Financial Group
Loeb Inc.
Lonely Planet
Manitowoc
Mashreq
MasterCard Advisors
McDonald's
The McGraw-Hill Companies
Meredith
Metafore
Metro-Goldwyn-Mayer
MFS Investment Management
Mobily
Monotype
Neuberger Berman
Nissan Infiniti
Nokia Siemens Networks
Nuveen Investments
OFS
OneMain Financial
Orange
PacifiCare Health Systems
Pathmark
Peter Piper Pizza
Pizza Hut
Power.org
Praxair
Prep for Prep
The Prince's Charities
Princeton National Rowing Association
Principal Financial Group
The Procter & Gamble Company Duracell
Qtel
Quick Chek
The Radio Corporation of America
RCA
Red Lobster
SABIC
Sainsbury's
Sam's Club
Samsung
Sara Lee Corporation
Scana Corporation
Scripps Health
The Shabab Club
Shutterstock
Signature Flight Support
SK
Sonic Drive-In
Southern Company
Southwest Airlines Logo
Sprint
Standard & Poor's
Stanley Black & Decker
Starbucks
Stouffer's
Sutter Health
Sysmex
TAG Aviation
Televisa
Telmex
Telus Corporation
Tenneco
TGV
Time Warner Cable
Truliant
Trustmark National Bank
Turkiye Is Bankasi
United Airlines
United Technologies
UnitedHealth
Vale
Viking
Visa
The Vitamin Shoppe
Walmart
Wana
Western Union
Windstream
Xylem Inc
Yves Rocher

LIQUID ADVERTISING

499 Santa Clara, Venice, CA 90291
Tel.: (310) 450-2653
Fax: (310) 450-2658
E-Mail: info@liquidadvertising.com
Web Site: www.liquidadvertising.com

Employees: 35
Year Founded: 2000

National Agency Associations: 4A's

Agency Specializes In: Advertising, Affluent Market, African-American Market, Alternative Advertising, Asian Market, Automotive, Aviation & Aerospace, Brand Development & Integration, Branded Entertainment, Business-To-Business, Cable T.V., Children's Market, Collateral, College, Communications, Computers & Software, Consulting, Consumer Goods, Consumer Marketing, Corporate Identity, Digital/Interactive, Direct Response Marketing, Direct-to-Consumer, E-Commerce, Education, Electronic Media, Electronics, Email, Entertainment, Event Planning & Marketing, Exhibit/Trade Shows, Experience Design, Fashion/Apparel, Financial, Food Service, Game Integration, Gay & Lesbian Market, Graphic Design, Guerilla Marketing, Health Care Services, High Technology, Hispanic Market, Hospitality, Household Goods, Identity Marketing, In-Store Advertising, Infomercials, Information Technology, International, Internet/Web Design, Legal Services, Leisure, Luxury Products, Market Research, Media Buying Services, Media Planning, Media Relations, Media Training, Medical Products, Men's Market, Mobile Marketing, Multicultural, Multimedia, New Technologies, Newspaper, Newspapers & Magazines, Out-of-Home Media, Outdoor, Package Design, Paid Searches, Pets , Pharmaceutical, Planning & Consultation, Podcasting, Print, Production, Production (Ad, Film, Broadcast), Production (Print), Promotions, Publicity/Promotions, Publishing, RSS (Really Simple Syndication), Radio, Recruitment, Regional, Restaurant, Retail, Sales Promotion, Social Marketing/Nonprofit, Social Media, Sponsorship, Sports Market, Strategic Planning/Research, Sweepstakes, Syndication, T.V., Technical Advertising, Teen Market, Telemarketing, Trade & Consumer Magazines, Transportation, Travel & Tourism, Tween Market, Urban Market, Viral/Buzz/Word of Mouth, Web (Banner Ads, Pop-ups, etc.), Women's Market

Approx. Annual Billings: $4,800,000

Will Akerlof *(Pres & CEO)*
Patrick Runco *(VP & Dir-Creative)*
Marlo Huang *(VP-Strategy)*
Kevin Joyce *(VP-Media)*

Accounts:
Blizzard Entertainment
High Rez
Microsoft
Recovery Channel
Sonos
Turbine

LIQUID AGENCY, INC.

(Private-Parent-Single Location)
448 S Market St, San Jose, CA 95113
Tel.: (408) 850-8800
Fax: (408) 850-8825
Web Site: www.liquidagency.com

Employees: 30
Year Founded: 2000

Agency Specializes In: Advertising, Brand Development & Integration, Digital/Interactive, Internet/Web Design, Logo & Package Design

Scott Gardner *(Pres & CEO)*
Alfredo Muccino *(Chief Creative Officer)*
Hamish Macphail *(VP-Fin)*
Marie McNeely *(Dir-Bus Dev-Global)*

Accounts:
Jive Software Campaign: "Work Better Together", Content Marketing, Marketing, Online, Signage, Social Media
PayPal Brand Strategy, Digital

LIQUIDFISH

401 E California Ave Ste 201, Oklahoma City, OK 73104
Tel.: (405) 606-4445
Fax: (405) 606-4447
E-Mail: info@liquidfish.com
Web Site: liquid.fish

Agency Specializes In: Advertising, Brand Development & Integration, Digital/Interactive, Internet/Web Design, Logo & Package Design, Print, Promotions, Social Media

Cody Blake *(Pres)*
Jennifer Armstrong *(Dir-Creative)*
Wendy Johnson *(Dir-Social Media)*
Melissa Cowan *(Copywriter)*

Accounts:
Colcord Hotel
Cover Oklahoma
Custom Reef Creations
Westpoint Homes

LISAIUS MARKETING

337 College St, Burlington, VT 05401
Tel.: (802) 658-1369
Web Site: www.lisaius.com

Agency Specializes In: Advertising, Brand Development & Integration, Graphic Design, Logo & Package Design, Media Planning, Print, Public

Relations, Social Media, Strategic Planning/Research

Joe Lisaius *(Pres & Dir-Creative)*
Mark Crow *(Partner)*
Bret Murray *(Dir-Art)*
Sarah Morrell *(Brand Mgr)*
Kevin Deutermann *(Jr Graphic Designer)*

Accounts:
Northwestern Medical Center

LITOS STRATEGIC COMMUNICATION

36 N. Water St Ste 1, New Bedford, MA 02740
Tel.: (508) 996-8989
Web Site: www.Litossc.com

Employees: 8
Year Founded: 1984

Agency Specializes In: Advertising, Advertising Specialties, Brand Development & Integration, Broadcast, Business Publications, Business-To-Business, Catalogs, Collateral, Communications, Consulting, Consumer Goods, Corporate Communications, Corporate Identity, Crisis Communications, Digital/Interactive, Direct Response Marketing, Email, Environmental, Event Planning & Marketing, Government/Political, Graphic Design, High Technology, Integrated Marketing, Internet/Web Design, Logo & Package Design, Market Research, New Technologies, Newspaper, Newspapers & Magazines, Outdoor, Package Design, Point of Sale, Print, Production (Print), Promotions, Public Relations, Publicity/Promotions, RSS (Really Simple Syndication), Radio, Search Engine Optimization, Strategic Planning/Research, Trade & Consumer Magazines, Web (Banner Ads, Pop-ups, etc.)

Approx. Annual Billings: $1,500,000

Mark Litos *(Pres)*
Sandra Guglielmo *(Controller)*
Peter Vercellone *(Mgr-Traffic & Production)*

Accounts:
Bridgewater State University; Bridgewater, MA
Department of Energy Smart Grid Initiative
GDF SUEZ Energy North America, Inc.; Houston, TX Energy/Power Generation

LITTLE & COMPANY

920 2nd Ave S Ste 1400, Minneapolis, MN 55402
Tel.: (612) 375-0077
Fax: (612) 375-0423
E-Mail: sunny.fenton@littleco.com
Web Site: littleco.com

Employees: 37
Year Founded: 1979

Agency Specializes In: Advertising, Advertising Specialties, Alternative Advertising, Arts, Brand Development & Integration, Broadcast, Business-To-Business, Catalogs, Collateral, Communications, Consumer Goods, Consumer Marketing, Corporate Communications, Corporate Identity, Digital/Interactive, Environmental, Experience Design, Financial, Graphic Design, Health Care Services, Identity Marketing, In-Store Advertising, Integrated Marketing, Internet/Web Design, Investor Relations, Leisure, Local Marketing, Logo & Package Design, Magazines, Newspaper, Outdoor, Package Design, Point of Purchase, Print, Production, Production (Print), Radio, Recruitment, Retail, Sponsorship, Stakeholders, Trade & Consumer Magazines

Approx. Annual Billings: $13,000,000

Joanne Kuebler *(Owner & Principal)*
Joe Cecere *(Pres & Chief Creative Officer)*
Nancy Everhart *(Principal-Studio)*
Andrea Zimmerman *(Acct Dir)*
Kelly Cusack *(Dir)*
Mike Schacherer *(Dir-Creative)*
Curt Baker *(Acct Supvr)*
Danielle Johnson *(Designer)*

Accounts:
American Public Media
Clinic Sofia; Minneapolis, MN Healthcare/Health Services; 2009
DC Comics, Inc.
Habitat for Humanity International Rebrand
Landscape Structures; Minneapolis, MN Manufacturer/B2B; 2005
Lowe's Companies, Inc.
Medtronic; Minneapolis, MN Medical Device; 2010
Microsoft; Seattle, WA Consumer Products/Technology; 2007
Polaris; Minneapolis, MN Consumer Products/Corporate Communications; 1994
RedBrick Health; Minneapolis, MN Healthcare/Health Services; 2008
New-Ryan Companies U.S., Inc (Brand Agency of Record) Brand Strategy
Saint Paul Great River Park Project; Saint Paul, MN Government/Environmental; 2010
Sealy Corporation Sealy Posturepedic
Target Corporation Retail; 1989
U.S. Bancorp (US Brand Agency of Record)
Way to Grow; Minneapolis, MN Non-Profit; 2009
Wells Fargo; San Francisco, CA Finance/Corporate Communications; 1987

LITTLE BIG BRANDS

Two William St Ste 303, White Plains, NY 10601
Tel.: (914) 437-8686
E-Mail: contactus@littlebigbrands.com
Web Site: www.littlebigbrands.com

Agency Specializes In: Advertising, Brand Development & Integration, Identity Marketing, Logo & Package Design, Product Placement

Pamela Long *(Partner & Client Svcs Dir)*
Crystal Bennett *(Partner)*
John Nunziato *(Chief Creative Officer)*
Karla Finlan *(Acct Dir)*
Richard Palmer *(Dir-Creative)*
Frank Tantao *(Dir-Production)*
Emma Jackson *(Acct Mgr)*
Racine Lovergie *(Mgr-Benefits)*
Colleen Peck *(Mgr-Bus Dev)*

Accounts:
Finesse
Genny Light
Give
The Lion Brewery Beverages
Lionshead
Lypsyl
M5 Magnum
Wisk Eco Energy
Yardley

LITTLE BIRD MARKETING

1037 S Main St, Joplin, MO 64801
Tel.: (417) 782-1780
E-Mail: info@littlebirdmarketing.com
Web Site: www.littlebirdmarketing.com

Agency Specializes In: Advertising, Brand Development & Integration, Content, Internet/Web Design, Logo & Package Design, Print

Priscilla McKinney *(Principal)*
Steve McKinney *(VP)*

Accounts:
Candy House Gourmet Chocolates
Ozark Christian College

LITTLE DOG AGENCY INC.

3850 Bessemer Rd Ste 220, Mount Pleasant, SC 29466
Tel.: (843) 856-9201
Fax: (843) 856-9207
E-Mail: webmaster@littledogagency.com
Web Site: www.littledogagency.com

Employees: 4
Year Founded: 2005

Agency Specializes In: Advertising, Advertising Specialties, African-American Market, Agriculture, Asian Market, Automotive, Aviation & Aerospace, Bilingual Market, Brand Development & Integration, Broadcast, Business Publications, Business-To-Business, Cable T.V., Children's Market, Co-op Advertising, Collateral, Commercial Photography, Communications, Consulting, Consumer Marketing, Consumer Publications, Corporate Communications, Corporate Identity, Cosmetics, Digital/Interactive, Direct Response Marketing, E-Commerce, Education, Electronic Media, Engineering, Entertainment, Environmental, Event Planning & Marketing, Exhibit/Trade Shows, Fashion/Apparel, Financial, Food Service, Gay & Lesbian Market, Government/Political, Graphic Design, Health Care Services, High Technology, Hispanic Market, In-Store Advertising, Industrial, Infomercials, Information Technology, Internet/Web Design, Investor Relations, Legal Services, Leisure, Local Marketing, Logo & Package Design, Magazines, Marine, Media Buying Services, Medical Products, Merchandising, Multimedia, New Product Development, Newspaper, Newspapers & Magazines, Out-of-Home Media, Outdoor, Over-50 Market, Pharmaceutical, Planning & Consultation, Point of Purchase, Point of Sale, Print, Production, Public Relations, Publicity/Promotions, Radio, Real Estate, Recruitment, Restaurant, Retail, Sales Promotion, Seniors' Market, Sports Market, Strategic Planning/Research, Sweepstakes, Syndication, T.V., Technical Advertising, Teen Market, Telemarketing, Trade & Consumer Magazines, Transportation, Travel & Tourism, Yellow Pages Advertising

Brent McKay *(Pres)*
Soraya McKay *(VP)*
Bonnie Schwartz *(Office Mgr)*
Kaili Howard *(Specialist-Mktg & Media Buyer)*
Katey Warren *(Specialist-PR & Social Media)*

Accounts:
82 - Clean
Blackbeard's Cove Family Fun Park
Charleston Restaurant Association
Daniel Island Business Association
Red's 1947 Ice House
Rita's

LITTLE HIGHRISE LLC

237 King St, Charleston, SC 29401
Tel.: (843) 793-1490
Web Site: www.littlehighrise.com

Agency Specializes In: Advertising, Brand Development & Integration, Graphic Design, Internet/Web Design

Stacey Elicker *(Owner & Partner-Strategic)*
Bob Elicker *(Dir-Creative)*

Accounts:
Carolina Food Design
Margaret Donaldson Interiors

LITTLE L COMMUNICATIONS

(Formerly McKinney-Cerne Advertising & Public Relations)

PO Box 63, Geneva, OH 44041
Tel.: (440) 799-7884
Web Site: littlelcomm.biz

Employees: 12
Year Founded: 1936

National Agency Associations: AAF-PRSA

Agency Specializes In: Advertising, Advertising Specialties, Asian Market, Automotive, Brand Development & Integration, Business Publications, Business-To-Business, Children's Market, Co-op Advertising, Collateral, College, Communications, Consulting, Consumer Goods, Consumer Marketing, Consumer Publications, Corporate Communications, Corporate Identity, Crisis Communications, Direct-to-Consumer, E-Commerce, Education, Electronic Media, Engineering, Event Planning & Marketing, Exhibit/Trade Shows, Financial, Food Service, Government/Political, Graphic Design, Health Care Services, High Technology, Industrial, Information Technology, Integrated Marketing, International, Legal Services, Local Marketing, Logo & Package Design, Magazines, Marine, Media Buying Services, Media Planning, Medical Products, Merchandising, Multimedia, New Product Development, Newspaper, Newspapers & Magazines, Out-of-Home Media, Outdoor, Over-50 Market, Package Design, Pharmaceutical, Planning & Consultation, Point of Purchase, Point of Sale, Print, Production, Production (Ad, Film, Broadcast), Public Relations, Publicity/Promotions, RSS (Really Simple Syndication), Radio, Real Estate, Restaurant, Retail, Sales Promotion, Search Engine Optimization, Seniors' Market, Social Marketing/Nonprofit, Strategic Planning/Research, T.V., Technical Advertising, Trade & Consumer Magazines, Travel & Tourism, Urban Market, Web (Banner Ads, Pop-ups, etc.), Women's Market, Yellow Pages Advertising

Breakdown of Gross Billings by Media: Bus. Publs.: 30%; Collateral: 15%; D.M.: 10%; Production: 15%; Pub. Rels.: 30%

Laura Lytle *(Pres & CEO)*

Accounts:
Eye Lighting
The Lake County YMCA

LITTLEFIELD BRAND DEVELOPMENT

(Formerly Littlefield, Inc.)
1350 S Boulder Ave Ste 500, Tulsa, OK 74119-3214
Tel.: (918) 295-1000
Fax: (918) 295-1001
Web Site: www.littlefield.us

E-Mail for Key Personnel:
President: david@littlefieldinc.com
Creative Dir.: lbender@littlefield.us

Employees: 30
Year Founded: 1980

National Agency Associations: AMA-MAGNET-PRSA

Agency Specializes In: Above-the-Line, Advertising, Advertising Specialties, Affiliate Marketing, Affluent Market, African-American Market, Agriculture, Alternative Advertising, Arts, Asian Market, Automotive, Aviation & Aerospace, Below-the-Line, Bilingual Market, Brand Development & Integration, Branded Entertainment, Broadcast, Business Publications, Business-To-Business, Cable T.V., Catalogs, Children's Market, Co-op Advertising, Collateral, College, Commercial Photography, Communications, Computers & Software, Consulting, Consumer Goods, Consumer Marketing, Consumer Publications, Content, Corporate Communications, Corporate Identity, Cosmetics, Crisis Communications, Custom Publishing, Customer Relationship Management, Digital/Interactive, Direct Response Marketing, Direct-to-Consumer, E-Commerce, Education, Electronic Media, Electronics, Email, Engineering, Entertainment, Environmental, Event Planning & Marketing, Exhibit/Trade Shows, Experience Design, Fashion/Apparel, Financial, Food Service, Game Integration, Gay & Lesbian Market, Government/Political, Graphic Design, Guerilla Marketing, Health Care Services, High Technology, Hispanic Market, Hospitality, Household Goods, Identity Marketing, In-Store Advertising, Industrial, Infomercials, Information Technology, Integrated Marketing, International, Internet/Web Design, Investor Relations, Legal Services, Leisure, Local Marketing, Logo & Package Design, Luxury Products, Magazines, Marine, Market Research, Media Buying Services, Media Planning, Media Relations, Media Training, Medical Products, Men's Market, Merchandising, Mobile Marketing, Multicultural, Multimedia, New Product Development, New Technologies, Newspaper, Newspapers & Magazines, Out-of-Home Media, Outdoor, Over-50 Market, Package Design, Paid Searches, Pharmaceutical, Planning & Consultation, Podcasting, Point of Purchase, Point of Sale, Print, Product Placement, Production, Production (Ad, Film, Broadcast), Production (Print), Promotions, Public Relations, Publicity/Promotions, Publishing, RSS (Really Simple Syndication), Radio, Real Estate, Recruitment, Regional, Restaurant, Retail, Sales Promotion, Search Engine Optimization, Seniors' Market, Social Marketing/Nonprofit, Social Media, Sponsorship, Sports Market, Stakeholders, Strategic Planning/Research, Sweepstakes, Syndication, T.V., Technical Advertising, Teen Market, Telemarketing, Trade & Consumer Magazines, Transportation, Travel & Tourism, Urban Market, Viral/Buzz/Word of Mouth, Women's Market, Yellow Pages Advertising

Approx. Annual Billings: $29,145,000

David G. Littlefield *(Pres & CEO)*
Laurie Tilley *(Exec VP-Strategy)*
Mike Rocco *(VP & Dir-Creative)*
Marellie Littlefield *(VP-Fin & HR)*
Steve Roop *(Dir-Interactive Strategy)*
Lauren Esposito *(Acct Mgr)*

Accounts:
Apache Casino
BOK Financial Bank of Albuquerque, Bank of Arizona, Bank of Arkansas, Bank of Kansas City, Bank of Oklahoma, Bank of Texas, Colorado State Bank and Trust; 2002
The Charles Machine Works
Cherokee Nation Entertainment Hard Rock Hotel & Casino Tulsa
Ditch Witch; Perry, OK Underground Construction Equipment; 2002
Fort Sill Apache Casino; Lawton, OK
Groendyke Transport
Head Country Barbecue Analytics, Brand Strategy, Marketing, Media
Quik Print; Tulsa, OK Printing Services; 2003
Tulsa Area United Way
Tulsa Chamber Economic Development
Tulsa Convention & Visitors Bureau
Tulsa CVB; Tulsa, OK Convention & Visitors; 2006
Tulsa Health Department
Tulsa World; Tulsa, OK Regional Newspaper; 2007
Video Gaming Technologies
YMCA of Greater Tulsa; Tulsa, OK

LIVE & BREATHE

Crown House, 143-147 Regent Street, London, W1B 4JB United Kingdom
Tel.: (44) 20 7478 0000
Fax: (44) 20 7478 0001
E-Mail: info@liveandbreathe.co.uk
Web Site: www.liveandbreathe.com

Employees: 70

Agency Specializes In: Advertising, Below-the-Line, Brand Development & Integration, Digital/Interactive, Direct Response Marketing, Experience Design, Retail, Sales Promotion

Adrian Watts *(Chm)*
Stuart Mitchell *(CEO)*
Nick Gray *(Mng Dir)*
Viv Craske *(Head-Digital)*
James Hoxley *(Exec Creative Dir)*
Jamie King *(Exec Dir-Plng)*
Kenny Cox *(Acct Dir)*
Gary Jacobs *(Creative Dir)*

Accounts:
Birds Eye Bake to Perfection, Below the Line Marketing, Experiential, Fish Fusions, Make More Of Midweek Tour, Promotional, Rice Fusions, Sampling Campaign, Shopper Marketing
Blockbuster UK Marketing Strategy
Danone Waters UK & Ireland Ltd Evian & Volvic, In-Store Campaign, Point Of Sale, Tropical Tour, Volvic Touch of Tropical Fruits
Evian Campaign: "Baby and Me", Campaign: "Live young", Campaign: "Wimbledon Whites"
Kwik Fit Below-the-Line, Direct Mail
Morrisons In-Store Communications
Peacocks
Reckitt Benckiser

LIVEAREALABS

3131 Western Ave Ste515, Seattle, WA 98121
Tel.: (206) 521-1105
E-Mail: info@livearealabs.com
Web Site: www.livearealabs.com

Year Founded: 2009

Agency Specializes In: Advertising, Brand Development & Integration, Digital/Interactive, E-Commerce, Internet/Web Design, Mobile Marketing, Strategic Planning/Research

Neil Nylander *(Co-Founder & Pres)*
Mark Moskal *(Co-Founder & Exec Dir-Creative)*
Ben Tudor *(Head-Interactive)*
Aden Ryan *(Acct Dir)*
Naomi Dent *(Dir-Engagement Svcs)*
Michael Francis *(Dir-Creative)*
Jen Dougherty *(Assoc Dir-Creative)*
Peter Kowalczyk *(Sr Engr-Software)*

Accounts:
Brooks Sports, Inc.
London Drugs Limited
Meredith Wendell
World Vision

LJF ASSOCIATES, INC.

26419 Oak Rdg Dr, The Woodlands, TX 77380-1964
Tel.: (281) 367-3922
Fax: (281) 292-7780
E-Mail: forinfo@ljfassoc.com
Web Site: www.ljfmarketing.com

E-Mail for Key Personnel:
President: lfreede@ljfassoc.com

Employees: 7
Year Founded: 1989

National Agency Associations: Second Wind Limited

Agency Specializes In: Advertising, Advertising Specialties, Broadcast, Business Publications,

Business-To-Business, Cable T.V., Collateral, Communications, Consulting, Consumer Publications, Corporate Identity, Direct Response Marketing, Electronic Media, Engineering, Event Planning & Marketing, Exhibit/Trade Shows, Financial, Graphic Design, Health Care Services, High Technology, Industrial, Information Technology, Internet/Web Design, Investor Relations, Legal Services, Local Marketing, Logo & Package Design, Magazines, Media Buying Services, Medical Products, Multimedia, Newspaper, Newspapers & Magazines, Out-of-Home Media, Outdoor, Planning & Consultation, Print, Public Relations, Publicity/Promotions, Radio, Seniors' Market, Strategic Planning/Research, T.V., Technical Advertising, Trade & Consumer Magazines

Linda Freede *(Pres)*

Accounts:
Burditt Consultants; Conroe, TX Urban Forestry; 2005
Fullenweider Wilhite
Huntsville Convention & Visitors Center; Huntsville, TX Tourism
Multi-Seal Inc.; Houston, TX Tire Sealants; 2004

L.K. ADVERTISING AGENCY

(Name Changed to The Linick Group, Inc.)

LKF MARKETING

303 N Rose St Ste 444, Kalamazoo, MI 49007
Tel.: (269) 349-4440
Fax: (269) 349-6128
E-Mail: lkf_info@lkfmarketing.com
Web Site: www.lkfmarketing.com

Agency Specializes In: Advertising, Internet/Web Design, Media Buying Services, Public Relations, Social Media

Carol Fricke *(Pres & CEO)*
Heather Isch *(VP)*
Linda Lewis *(Office Mgr)*
Lisa Moore *(Acct Exec & Specialist-SEO)*
Martha Nicholson *(Acct Exec, Media Planner & Buyer)*
Sara Ramaker *(Acct Coord)*

Accounts:
Envirologic
Premier Vein Center

LKH&S

54 W Hubbard Ste 100, Chicago, IL 60610
Tel.: (312) 595-0200
Fax: (312) 595-0300
E-Mail: lkhs@lkhs.com
Web Site: www.lkhs.com

E-Mail for Key Personnel:
Creative Dir.: kirshenbaum@lkhs.com
Public Relations: lewin@lkhs.com

Employees: 20
Year Founded: 1991

National Agency Associations: BMA

Agency Specializes In: Advertising, Affiliate Marketing, Affluent Market, Agriculture, Alternative Advertising, Arts, Automotive, Brand Development & Integration, Branded Entertainment, Broadcast, Business-To-Business, Collateral, College, Communications, Computers & Software, Consulting, Consumer Goods, Consumer Marketing, Corporate Communications, Corporate Identity, Customer Relationship Management, Digital/Interactive, Direct Response Marketing, Direct-to-Consumer, E-Commerce, Education, Electronic Media, Electronics, Email, Entertainment, Environmental, Exhibit/Trade Shows, Financial, Graphic Design, Guerilla Marketing, Health Care Services, High Technology, Hospitality, Household Goods, Identity Marketing, In-Store Advertising, Industrial, Information Technology, Integrated Marketing, Internet/Web Design, Leisure, Local Marketing, Logo & Package Design, Luxury Products, Magazines, Marine, Market Research, Medical Products, Multimedia, New Product Development, New Technologies, Newspaper, Newspapers & Magazines, Out-of-Home Media, Outdoor, Over-50 Market, Package Design, Point of Purchase, Point of Sale, Print, Production, Production (Ad, Film, Broadcast), Production (Print), Promotions, Public Relations, Publishing, RSS (Really Simple Syndication), Radio, Restaurant, Retail, Sales Promotion, Search Engine Optimization, Social Marketing/Nonprofit, Strategic Planning/Research, Sweepstakes, T.V., Technical Advertising, Telemarketing, Trade & Consumer Magazines, Transportation, Web (Banner Ads, Pop-ups, etc.)

Breakdown of Gross Billings by Media: Bus. Publs.: 20%; D.M.: 35%; Internet Adv.: 15%; Newsp. & Mags.: 5%; Point of Purchase: 5%; Production: 5%; Strategic Planning/Research: 15%

Stanton Lewin *(Chm & CEO)*
Samuel Kirshenbaum *(Principal & Exec Dir-Creative)*
Jim Goldman *(Sr Acct Dir)*
Bill Heuglin *(Assoc Dir-Creative)*
Jennyfer Butzen Dougherty *(Media Planner & Sr Acct Exec)*
Christina Seiwert *(Sr Acct Exec)*

Accounts:
ComEd
DampRid
Leggett & Platt; IL; 2002
Peco; PA; 2002
Walter Payton Liver Center

Branch

LKH&S Louisville

4907 Dunbarvalley Rd, Fisherville, KY 40023
Tel.: (502) 261-9826
Web Site: www.lkhs.com

Year Founded: 2005

Agency Specializes In: Advertising, Affiliate Marketing, Affluent Market, Agriculture, Alternative Advertising, Arts, Automotive, Brand Development & Integration, Branded Entertainment, Broadcast, Business-To-Business, Collateral, College, Communications, Computers & Software, Consulting, Consumer Goods, Consumer Marketing, Corporate Communications, Corporate Identity, Customer Relationship Management, Digital/Interactive, Direct Response Marketing, Direct-to-Consumer, E-Commerce, Education, Electronic Media, Electronics, Email, Entertainment, Environmental, Exhibit/Trade Shows, Financial, Graphic Design, Guerilla Marketing, Health Care Services, High Technology, Hospitality, Household Goods, Identity Marketing, In-Store Advertising, Industrial, Information Technology, Integrated Marketing, Internet/Web Design, Leisure, Local Marketing, Logo & Package Design, Luxury Products, Magazines, Marine, Market Research, Multimedia

Stanton Lewin *(Chm & CEO)*
Samuel Kirshenbaum *(Principal & Exec Dir-Creative)*
Bill Heuglin *(Assoc Dir-Creative)*

LLNS

220 E 42nd St, New York, NY 10017-5806
Tel.: (212) 771-3000
Fax: (212) 771-3010
Web Site: www.llns.com

Employees: 336
Year Founded: 1994

Agency Specializes In: Advertising, Business-To-Business, Consumer Marketing, Direct Response Marketing, Graphic Design, Health Care Services, Logo & Package Design, Media Buying Services, New Product Development, Pharmaceutical, Production, Strategic Planning/Research

Sharon Callahan *(Pres & CEO)*
Ellen Fields *(Pres-Consumer Healthcare)*
Brian Schwartz *(Exec VP-Ops)*
James J. Stringer *(Sr VP & Controller)*
Jordan Lichay *(Sr Acct Exec)*
Kathy Bardong *(Generalist-HR)*

Accounts:
Braintree Laboratories Axid Oral Solution, GoLytely, HalfLytely, NuLytely
Merck Serono International SA Oral Cladribine
Pfizer Inc. Aromasin, Camptosar, Cerenia, Detrol, Ellence, Fesoterodine, Geodon; 1988
UCB Keppra, Rikelta; 1988

LLOBE DESIGN

28 2nd St Ste 300, San Francisco, CA 94105
Tel.: (415) 688-2024
Web Site: llobe.com

Employees: 12
Year Founded: 2009

Agency Specializes In: Digital/Interactive, Experience Design, Mobile Marketing, Search Engine Optimization, Social Media, Viral/Buzz/Word of Mouth, Web (Banner Ads, Pop-ups, etc.)

Melissa Meagher *(Head-Social)*

Accounts:
Caliber Magazine
Consult Your Community
Help Me Get In
Machean Consulting
Side/Project/SF
Sierra Point Group
The Terma Foundation
Travis Shirley Live Design
Video Purveyor

LLOYD & CO.

180 Varick St Ste 1018, New York, NY 10014
Tel.: (212) 414-3100
Fax: (212) 414-3113
E-Mail: info@lloydandco.com
Web Site: www.lloydandco.com

Employees: 25
Year Founded: 1994

Agency Specializes In: Leisure, Luxury Products, Sponsorship, Travel & Tourism

Approx. Annual Billings: $20,000,000

Jodi Sweetbaum *(Pres & Mng Dir)*
Shari Kaufman-Lewis *(Acct Dir)*
Douglas Lloyd *(Creative Dir)*
Rachel Levine *(Dir-Production & Creative Svcs)*

Accounts:
Adidas
Badgley Mischka
Big Magazine
Calvin Klein

Club Monaco
Cole Haan
Concord
Ebel
Estee Lauder Broadcast, Campaign: "Be Daring, Be an Inspiration", Campaign: "Dual Impressions", Modern Muse, Modern Muse Le Rouge, Print, Social Media, TV
Express
Fragile
G Series
Garrard
Glaceau/Vitamin Water
Gucci
John Varvatos
Marie Claire
Max Mara
Movado
Nave
PepsiCo Inc. Advertising, Campaign: "Live for Now", Pepsi
Perry Ellis
Sergio Ross
The Standard Hotel
Tod's
Tommy Hilfiger
Yves Saint Laurent

LMA

2300 Yonge St Ste 1000, PO Box 2302, Toronto, ON M4P 1E4 Canada
Tel.: (416) 440-2500
Fax: (416) 440-2504
Web Site: lma.ca

Employees: 12
Year Founded: 1991

Agency Specializes In: Advertising

Larry Mogelonsky *(Founder & Pres)*
Jerry Grymek *(Acct Dir)*
Juan Hernandez *(Dir-Interactive Art)*
Elizabeth Zemnickis *(Office Mgr)*
Maureen Wright *(Mgr-PR)*
Michelle Robertson *(Acct Exec)*
Ante Miletic *(Acct Coord-PR)*

Accounts:
Artic Combustion
Botox At Home
Brightlights
CLHIO
COMO Hotels
Dine Magazine
Firestone
Israel Tour Guide
Medevaq
New York Hotel PA
Ojai Valley Inn & Spa
Palm Holdings
Performance World
Rics Americas
Steelmen Systems
Surveyors General Insurance
Tridel
Visit Florida
Zarienu

LMD AGENCY

14409 Greenview Dr Ste 200, Laurel, MD 20708
Tel.: (301) 498-6656
Fax: (301) 953-0321
Web Site: www.lmdagency.com

Agency Specializes In: Advertising, Brand Development & Integration, Corporate Identity, Digital/Interactive, Internet/Web Design, Outdoor, Point of Purchase, Print, Public Relations, Strategic Planning/Research

Sarah Pugh *(Pres)*
Karen Killian *(Partner & VP-Strategy & Bus Dev)*
Scott Van Der Meid *(Partner & VP-Creative Svcs)*
Holly Huntley *(Client Svcs Dir)*
Carl Bice *(Dir-Web Svcs & Ops)*
Dan Croft *(Dir-Creative-Web Svcs)*
Kristen Newton *(Dir-Res & Content Strategy)*
Mary Ellen McCormack *(Acct Mgr)*
Katie Slagle *(Acct Mgr)*
Cathy Barrett *(Mgr-Fin & Admin)*

Accounts:
Capitol College
The National Information Exchange Model
SESYNC
U.S. Environmental Protection Agency WaterSense
University of Maryland

LMGPR

(Formerly Loughlin/Michaels Group)
111 W Evelyn Ave Ste 308, Sunnyvale, CA 94086
Tel.: (408) 738-9150
Fax: (408) 738-9100
E-Mail: info@lmgpr.com
Web Site: www.lmgpr.com

Employees: 12
Year Founded: 2002

Agency Specializes In: Event Planning & Marketing, Exhibit/Trade Shows, Local Marketing, Media Relations, Media Training, New Technologies, Public Relations, Publishing, Strategic Planning/Research

Donna Loughlin Michaels *(Founder & Pres)*
Michael Erwin *(Dir-Editorial)*
Paul Fernandez *(Sr Mgr-PR)*

Accounts:
Avocent
Blue Coat
Citrix Systems
Concentric
Crescendo Networks
enKoo
FireEye
frevvo
Infineta Systems (Agency of Record)
Netoptics
Werkadoo (Agency of Record) Online Workplace for Businesses and Contracting Professionals
Wildfire
Zyrion Public Relations

LMI ADVERTISING

24E E Roseville Rd, Lancaster, PA 17601
Tel.: (717) 569-8826
Fax: (717) 569-9463
E-Mail: info@lmiadvertising.com
Web Site: www.lmiadvertising.com

Agency Specializes In: Advertising, Brand Development & Integration, Broadcast, Collateral, Digital/Interactive, Internet/Web Design, Media Planning, Outdoor, Public Relations, Radio

Tina Bellanca *(Pres)*
Gregg R. Rineer *(VP-Creative Svcs)*
Shawna Martin *(Controller)*
Joshua Jones *(Dir-Art)*

Accounts:
Alliance Cancer Specialists

LMO ADVERTISING

1776 Wilson Blvd 5th Fl, Arlington, VA 22209
Tel.: (703) 875-2193
Fax: (703) 875-2199
E-Mail: sherrigreen@lmo.com
Web Site: www.lmo.com

E-Mail for Key Personnel:
President: douglaughlin@lmo.com

Employees: 60
Year Founded: 1995

National Agency Associations: 4A's

Agency Specializes In: Advertising, Brand Development & Integration, Broadcast, Co-op Advertising, Collateral, Consumer Marketing, Corporate Identity, Direct Response Marketing, Government/Political, Internet/Web Design, Media Buying Services, Media Planning, Newspapers & Magazines, Out-of-Home Media, Outdoor, Print, Production, Radio, Recruitment, Sponsorship, Strategic Planning/Research, Teen Market

Chris Laughlin *(Pres)*
Kendria Perry *(Mgmt Supvr)*
Christi Burnum *(Dir-Media)*
Mike Caplanis *(Dir-Creative)*
Panayiotis Karabetis *(Dir-User Experience)*
Jennifer Lennon *(Dir-Traffic)*
Chris Rothrock *(Dir-Media)*
Debbie Simon *(Assoc Dir-Media)*
Ashley Banek *(Sr Mgr-Direct Mktg)*
Christine Chrabot *(Sr Mgr-Content Mktg)*
Robyn Loube *(Sr Mgr-Outreach)*
Kristen Butts *(Mgr-Production)*
Claire Robertson *(Mgr-Mktg)*
Kelly Walter *(Mgr-Proposal)*
Chris Beauchemin *(Acct Supvr)*
Karen Laughlin *(Supvr-Interactive Mktg)*
Alix Montes *(Acct Exec)*
Joacir Soto *(Designer-Interactive)*
J. P. Welch *(Copywriter)*
Takia Robinson *(Acct Coord)*
Max Walker *(Acct Coord)*
Janet Beckley *(Coord-Traffic)*
Ileza Dantzig *(Sr Media Planner & Buyer)*
Ray Tehrani Vargas *(Asst Mgr-HR)*

Accounts:
Avis Budget Group, Inc. Avis Canada, Avis Europe, Avis Rent a Car, Budget Japan, Budget Rent a Car; 2004
Bionic Turtle Advertising, Marketing Strategy, Website Maintenance
Booz Allen Hamilton
Bull Frog
Capital Area Food Bank; 2007
Department of Defense Health.mil, Tricare
Department of Veterans Affairs VetBiz.gov; 2004
New-George Washington University (Digital Media Agency of Record) Digital Strategy, Media Buying
Hargrove Inc. Advertising Strategy
Jordan
Lurn, Inc Visual Design, Web & Mobile
Metro
The National Guard Air National Guard, Army National Guard, Guard Bureau, Recruitment Advertising; 1995
Sears Portrait Studio
Sigma Phi Epsilon
Thanks USA
United States Army National Guard; Crystal City, VA Recruitment, Retention & Public Affairs; 1995
United States Coast Guard Media, Production
Urban Arias
US French Embassy; 2006
Voice for America's Troops
Washington West

Branch

VIM Interactive

2100 Aliceanna St Fl 2, Baltimore, MD 21231
Fax: (443) 969-4191
Toll Free: (800) 704-4846
E-Mail: info@viminteractive.com
Web Site: viminteractive.com

National Agency Associations: 4A's

Agency Specializes In: Digital/Interactive

Stevan Fickus *(Dir-Dev)*
Cory Magin *(Assoc Dir-Engrg & User Experience)*

Accounts:
Marriott

LOADED CREATIVE LLC
141 W High St, Bellefonte, PA 16823
Tel.: (814) 353-0144
Web Site: www.weareloaded.com

Agency Specializes In: Advertising, Brand Development & Integration, Corporate Identity, Digital/Interactive, Internet/Web Design, Package Design, Print, Radio, T.V.

Mark D. Dello Stritto *(Founder & Dir-Creative)*
Daniel J. Evans *(Assoc Dir-Creative, Writer, Producer & Strategist)*
Sean McCauley *(Dir-Art & Designer)*
Darryl Cozza *(Designer-Website)*
William Offutt *(Designer-Website)*

Accounts:
Alpha Fire Company
ORX

LOBO & PETROCINE, INC.
95 Broadhollow Rd Ste D, Melville, NY 11747
Tel.: (631) 421-3142
Fax: (631) 421-3783
E-Mail: info@loboads.com
Web Site: Loboads.com

Employees: 18
Year Founded: 2003

Agency Specializes In: Broadcast, Business Publications, Co-op Advertising, Collateral, Consumer Publications, Direct Response Marketing, Education, Newspapers & Magazines, Out-of-Home Media, Recruitment

Approx. Annual Billings: $6,000,000

Breakdown of Gross Billings by Media: Collateral: 15%; D.M.: 10%; Out-of-Home Media: 5%; Print: 15%; Radio: 15%; T.V.: 40%

Russ Petrocine *(Owner)*
Rick Bodamer *(Partner & Dir-Creative)*
Lou Lopriore *(Partner & Co-Dir-Creative-Art)*
Beth Beyer *(Controller)*
Chad Barnattan *(Acct Dir)*
Sal Annarumma *(Dir-Art)*
Charles DeNatale *(Dir-Media)*
Virginia Suhr *(Dir-Media & Digital)*
Janet Winckler *(Mgr-Production & Traffic)*
Tara Refano *(Supvr-Production)*
Patty Pike *(Media Planner & Media Buyer)*

Accounts:
Alpha Windows; Bay Shore, NY; 2003
Monroe College; Bronx, NY; 2003
Precision International; Bohemia, NY Transmission Kits; 2003
Stevens 112; Patchogue, NY Ford & Kia Dealer; 2003

LOCAL CORPORATION
7555 Irvine Center Dr, Irvine, CA 92618
Tel.: (949) 825-5664
Web Site: www.localcorporation.com

Year Founded: 1999

Agency Specializes In: Advertising, Communications, Consumer Marketing, Digital/Interactive, Media Planning, Over-50 Market, Regional, Web (Banner Ads, Pop-ups, etc.)

Fred Thiel *(Chm & CEO)*
Joe Lindsay *(VP-Tech)*
Eric Orrantia *(VP-Network)*
Brian Singleton *(VP-Innovation)*
Jeff Dillon *(Mgr-Bus Dev-nQuery)*

LOCALITE LA
116 S Catalina Ave Ste 107 & 109, Redondo Beach, CA 90277
Tel.: (424) 254-8391
E-Mail: info@localitela.com
Web Site: www.localitela.com

Agency Specializes In: Advertising, Brand Development & Integration, Digital/Interactive, Event Planning & Marketing, Internet/Web Design, Social Media

Matthew McIvor *(Founder & Pres)*
Jennalee Infanto *(Dir-Publicity)*

Accounts:
New-DOMA Kitchen
New-Richstone Family Center

LOCATION3 MEDIA, INC.
1515 Arapahoe St Tower 2 Ste 400, Denver, CO 80202
Tel.: (303) 291-6984
Fax: (303) 298-1986
Toll Free: (877) 462-9764
E-Mail: info@location3.com
Web Site: www.location3.com

E-Mail for Key Personnel:
President: abeckman@location3.net

Employees: 65
Year Founded: 1999

National Agency Associations: AMA-DMA-SEMPO-WAA

Agency Specializes In: Advertising, Business-To-Business, Consulting, Consumer Marketing, Content, Digital/Interactive, Direct Response Marketing, Direct-to-Consumer, E-Commerce, Email, Graphic Design, High Technology, Hispanic Market, Internet/Web Design, Local Marketing, Media Buying Services, Media Planning, Mobile Marketing, Search Engine Optimization, Social Marketing/Nonprofit, Sponsorship, Web (Banner Ads, Pop-ups, etc.)

Approx. Annual Billings: $3,000,000

Andrew Beckman *(Chm)*
Alex Porter *(Pres)*
Erik Whaley *(Mng Dir & Sr VP)*
Ryan Guilford *(VP-Fin & Acctg)*
Kate Julian *(VP-Client Svcs)*
Jared Schroder *(VP-Data Intelligence & Mktg Tech)*
Gloria Dutton *(Grp Acct Dir)*
Carol Lee *(Dir-Local Bus Dev)*
Robin Arlen *(Acct Mgr)*
Chris Jones *(Assoc Acct Dir)*

LOCKARD & WECHSLER
2 Bridge St Ste 200, Irvington, NY 10533
Tel.: (914) 591-6600
Fax: (914) 591-6652
E-Mail: info@lwdirect.com
Web Site: www.lwdirect.com

Employees: 25
Year Founded: 1967

National Agency Associations: MCA

Agency Specializes In: Direct Response Marketing, Financial

Approx. Annual Billings: $80,000,000

Richard Wechsler *(Founder & CEO)*
Asieya Pine *(Pres)*
Carolyn Sura *(Exec VP & Dir-Brdcst)*
Joan Alev *(Sr VP & Grp Acct Dir)*
Stacey Kaufman *(Sr VP & Dir-Paid Programming)*
Kurt Pisani *(VP-Client Svcs)*
Eddie Wilders *(VP-Res & Analytics)*

Accounts:
American Home Business Association
Idea Village; NJ; 2000
Square One Entertainment, Inc
Studio SB, LLC
Thane International
TriStar Products; Parsippany, NJ; 1998

LOCOMOTION CREATIVE
2535 Franklin Rd Ste 201, Nashville, TN 37204
Tel.: (615) 327-4647
Fax: (615) 327-7670
E-Mail: ajohnsen@locomotioncreative.com
Web Site: www.locomotioncreative.com

Employees: 14
Year Founded: 1998

Agency Specializes In: Advertising

Carol Davis *(Editor & Copywriter)*
Brian Donnenwirth *(Dir-Art & Designer)*
Caitlyn Gibbons *(Dir-Art)*
Amy Ware *(Dir-Art)*
Richard Scaglione *(Strategist-Creative)*
Michelle Myers *(Designer)*
Wes Webb *(Designer)*

Accounts:
American Hometown Publishing
Bass Berry & Sims

LODESTONE ADVERTISING
318 Central Ave, Great Falls, MT 59401
Tel.: (406) 761-0288
Fax: (406) 761-6576
E-Mail: info@lodestoneadvertising.com
Web Site: www.lodestoneadvertising.com

Employees: 4
Year Founded: 1996

National Agency Associations: AAF-AFA

Agency Specializes In: Advertising, Print

Sales: $750,000

Chuck Fulcher *(Owner & Dir-Creative)*

Accounts:
Montana State Fair
Motifs
Ozog Eve Care Laser Center

LODICO & COMPANY
60 McAllister Dr, Carlisle, MA 01741
Tel.: (978) 369-6556
Fax: (978) 369-6284
E-Mail: isabran@lodicoandco.com
Web Site: www.lodicoandco.com

E-Mail for Key Personnel:
President: bsabran@lodicoandco.com

Employees: 5
Year Founded: 1989

National Agency Associations: PRSA

Agency Specializes In: Advertising, Asian Market, Brand Development & Integration, Business Publications, Business-To-Business, Collateral, Commercial Photography, Communications, Consulting, Corporate Communications, Electronic Media, Engineering, Event Planning & Marketing, Graphic Design, High Technology, Logo & Package Design, Media Buying Services, Medical Products, Pharmaceutical, Print, Public Relations, Radio, Strategic Planning/Research, Technical Advertising

Approx. Annual Billings: $9,000,000

Breakdown of Gross Billings by Media: Bus. Publs.: $4,000,000; Collateral: $1,000,000; Pub. Rels.: $4,000,000

Ira Sabran *(Exec VP)*
Barbara L. Sabran *(Dir-Channel Mktg)*

Accounts:
Delta
Melexis
NexTek

LOGAN
4221 Redwood Ave Ste 2A, Los Angeles, CA 90066
Tel.: (310) 822-1500
Fax: (310) 822-2277
Web Site: www.logan.tv

Agency Specializes In: Advertising, Graphic Design

Alexei Tylevich *(Owner & Mng Dir)*
Scott Siegal *(Head-Production)*
Ben Conrad *(Dir)*
Max Hattler *(Dir)*
Hauke Hilberg *(Dir)*
Paul Minor *(Dir)*
Korner Union *(Dir)*

Accounts:
DC Shoes

LOGOWORKS
825 E 1180 S Ste 300, American Fork, UT 84003
Tel.: (801) 805-3700
Toll Free: (888) 710-5646 (LogoMaker)
E-Mail: info@logoworks.com
Web Site: www.logoworks.com

Employees: 100
Year Founded: 2001

Agency Specializes In: Custom Publishing, Internet/Web Design, Logo & Package Design, Multimedia, Production (Print), Promotions

Approx. Annual Billings: $5,700,000

Daniel Wolfson *(Pres)*
Toufan Rahimpour *(COO)*
Aaron Bernabi *(Dir-Client Dev)*
Jenni Wheeler *(Dir-Art)*
Allison Humeniuk *(Mgr-Print)*
Aaron Shapiro *(Mgr-Affiliate Mktg)*

Accounts:
360 Investments
Adventure Camps
Agile
The CraftArt Studio
Global360
Hewlett Packard
HomeWorks
Krewe Outfitters
Morning Moon Cafe
WonderWorks

LOHRE & ASSOCIATES, INCORPORATED
126A W 14th St, Cincinnati, OH 45202
Tel.: (513) 961-1174
E-Mail: sales@lohre.com
Web Site: www.lohre.com

E-Mail for Key Personnel:
President: chuck@lohre.com

Employees: 4
Year Founded: 1935

Agency Specializes In: Advertising, Alternative Advertising, Aviation & Aerospace, Brand Development & Integration, Business-To-Business, Catalogs, Collateral, Commercial Photography, Consulting, Corporate Communications, Corporate Identity, Digital/Interactive, E-Commerce, Email, Engineering, Environmental, Event Planning & Marketing, Exhibit/Trade Shows, Graphic Design, High Technology, Industrial, Integrated Marketing, Internet/Web Design, Logo & Package Design, Magazines, Market Research, Media Planning, Multimedia, Paid Searches, Planning & Consultation, Print, Production, Production (Print), Public Relations, Publicity/Promotions, RSS (Really Simple Syndication), Search Engine Optimization, Social Marketing/Nonprofit, Strategic Planning/Research, Technical Advertising, Viral/Buzz/Word of Mouth

Approx. Annual Billings: $700,000

Breakdown of Gross Billings by Media: Collateral: 50%; Mags.: 50%

Charles Lohre *(Owner)*
Gerald Seeger *(Controller)*
Frank Kaulen *(Acct Dir-European)*
Robert Jeffries *(Dir-Art)*

Accounts:
Beck Paint Hardware; 2004
CAST-FAB; Cincinnati, OH Castings & Fabrications; 1996
CF3 (Cincinnati Form Follows Function) Mid-Century Modern Forum; 2004
Cincinnati Industrial Machinery; Cincinnati, OH Industrial Washers; 1977
Dynamic Industries; Cincinnati, OH Contract Machining; 1977
Hamilton Kettles, Inc.; Cincinnati, OH Food & Drug Processing Equipment; 1977
Hamilton Tool Co.; Cincinnati, OH Web Presses & Collators
Hill and Griffith Co.; Cincinnati, OH Materials Processing; 1977
ILSCO; Cincinnati, OH Electrical Connectors; 1992
Insul-Deck Concrete; Florence, KY Concrete Forms; 1995
International Processing Corporation; Winchester, KY Chemical Processing; 2000
McGraw/Kokosing, Inc.; Middletown, OH Engineers & Constructors; 1978
MED+ Urgent Medical Care Services Urgent Care; 2005
New England Industrial Machine Tool Representative; 2000
ROHR America, Inc.; Lexington, KY Dredging & Aggregate Processing Equipment; 1995
Roto-Disc Process Valves; 1998
SKF Machine Tool Group; Grafton, WI Machine Tool Components; 1992
SKF Precision Technologies Precision Machine Tool Components; 1999
VERTIFLO; Cincinnati, OH Pumps; 1987

LOIS GELLER MARKETING GROUP
1915 Hollywood Blvd Ste 201, Hollywood, FL 33020
Tel.: (646) 723-3231
Fax: (954) 456-2877
E-Mail: info@loisgellermarketinggroup.com
Web Site: www.loisgellermarketinggroup.com

E-Mail for Key Personnel:
President: lois@loisgellermarketinggroup.com

Employees: 5
Year Founded: 1995

National Agency Associations: DMA

Agency Specializes In: Above-the-Line, Advertising, Affluent Market, Automotive, Below-the-Line, Brand Development & Integration, Business Publications, Cable T.V., Catalogs, Collateral, Communications, Consulting, Consumer Marketing, Consumer Publications, Corporate Communications, Custom Publishing, Customer Relationship Management, Digital/Interactive, Direct Response Marketing, Direct-to-Consumer, E-Commerce, Education, Electronic Media, Electronics, Email, Fashion/Apparel, In-Store Advertising, Integrated Marketing, Internet/Web Design, Local Marketing, Luxury Products, Magazines, Multicultural, Newspaper, Planning & Consultation, Point of Sale, Print, Promotions, Publishing, Real Estate, Social Marketing/Nonprofit, Strategic Planning/Research, T.V., Trade & Consumer Magazines, Travel & Tourism, Web (Banner Ads, Pop-ups, etc.), Women's Market

Approx. Annual Billings: $500,000

Lois K. Geller *(Owner & Pres)*
Michael McCormick *(VP)*

LOKKEADVERTISING
7721 El Padre Lane, Dallas, TX 75248
Tel.: (214) 600-2683

Year Founded: 1978

Don Lokke, Jr. *(CEO)*

Accounts:
Atcoa Air Tools, Dallas, TX
Decorative Concrete Supply, Houston, TX

Branch

netPRpro, Inc.
6106 Long Prairie Rd #744-114, Flower Mound, TX 75028
(See Separate Listing)

LONGREN & PARKS
14101 Brandbury Walk, Minnetonka, MN 55345
Tel.: (952) 945-0572
Fax: (952) 945-9970
E-Mail: sales@longrenparks.com
Web Site: www.longrenparks.com

E-Mail for Key Personnel:
President: steve@longrenparks.com

Employees: 6
Year Founded: 1987

Agency Specializes In: Communications, Engineering, Industrial, Print, Public Relations

Steve Longren *(Owner)*
Steve Parks *(VP)*
Carrie Decker *(Dir-Creative & Designer)*
Julie Eleftheriou *(Dir-Editorial)*

Accounts:
APG Sensors
BMG Seltec
Clean Air Products
Empire Magnetics

OMRON Scientific Technologies, Inc.
Pepperl + Fuchs
Portescap
Procorp
SAIA Burgess Ledex & Dormeyer
Sick Stegmann, Inc.
Stegmann, Inc.
Wanner Engineering
Wanner Engineering

LOOKTHINKMAKE, LLC

3701 Airport Blvd, Austin, TX 78722
Tel.: (512) 402-6861
Fax: (512) 672-6112
Web Site: www.lookthinkmake.com

Year Founded: 2008

Agency Specializes In: Brand Development & Integration, Internet/Web Design, Logo & Package Design, Market Research, Mobile Marketing, Print, Public Relations, Search Engine Optimization, Strategic Planning/Research, T.V.

Patricia Buchholtz *(Co-Founder & Partner)*
Sean Thompson *(Partner & Dir-Creative)*
Laura Duncan *(Dir-Art)*
Casey Miller *(Dir-PR)*
Jeff Noel *(Dir-Interactive Art)*
Jordan Jeffus *(Acct Exec)*
Nate Stine *(Copywriter)*
Sean Swanson *(Sr Designer)*
Elle Tse *(Sr Designer)*

Accounts:
Frio Canon
Plum Creek Golf Club
Risher Martin
Sanctuary Lofts
Sims Foundation

THE LOOMIS AGENCY

17120 Dallas Pkwy Ste 200, Dallas, TX 75248-1189
Tel.: (972) 331-7000
Fax: (972) 331-7001
E-Mail: info@theloomisagency.com
Web Site: www.theloomisagency.com

Employees: 40
Year Founded: 1984

Agency Specializes In: Automotive, Brand Development & Integration, Broadcast, Co-op Advertising, Consumer Marketing, Consumer Publications, Corporate Identity, Direct Response Marketing, Entertainment, Food Service, Graphic Design, Logo & Package Design, Magazines, Media Buying Services, New Product Development, Newspapers & Magazines, Out-of-Home Media, Outdoor, Point of Purchase, Point of Sale, Radio, Restaurant, Retail, Sales Promotion, Sponsorship, Strategic Planning/Research, Trade & Consumer Magazines, Travel & Tourism

Approx. Annual Billings: $52,000,000

Breakdown of Gross Billings by Media: D.M.: 10%; Other: 15%; Print: 15%; Radio: 20%; T.V.: 40%

Paul Loomis *(Founder & CEO)*
Mike Sullivan *(Pres & Partner)*
Tina Tackett *(Exec Dir-Creative)*
Chelsea Ratliff *(Brand Dir)*
Aimee Herron *(Dir-Media)*
Melanie Selah *(Dir-Media)*
Katie Ackels *(Brand Mgr)*
Matthew Anderson *(Mgr-Social Media)*
Rachel Brittenham *(Sr Media Buyer)*

Accounts:
Cash America
First United Bank
New-Golden Chick
La Madeleine
Medieval Times
Papa John's International, Inc.
Rug Doctor TV
Sun Tan City

LOONEY ADVERTISING AND DESIGN

7 N Mountain Ave, Montclair, NJ 07042
Tel.: (973) 783-0017
Fax: (973) 783-0613
E-Mail: looneys@looney-advertising.com
Web Site: www.looney-advertising.com

Agency Specializes In: Above-the-Line, Advertising, Advertising Specialties, Affluent Market, Alternative Advertising, Arts, Automotive, Aviation & Aerospace, Below-the-Line, Brand Development & Integration, Branded Entertainment, Broadcast, Business Publications, Business-To-Business, Cable T.V., Children's Market, Co-op Advertising, Collateral, College, Communications, Computers & Software, Consulting, Consumer Goods, Consumer Marketing, Consumer Publications, Content, Corporate Communications, Corporate Identity, Cosmetics, Customer Relationship Management, Digital/Interactive, Direct Response Marketing, Direct-to-Consumer, E-Commerce, Education, Electronic Media, Electronics, Email, Entertainment, Environmental, Event Planning & Marketing, Exhibit/Trade Shows, Experience Design, Fashion/Apparel, Financial, Food Service, Graphic Design, Guerilla Marketing, Health Care Services, High Technology, Hospitality, Household Goods, Identity Marketing, In-Store Advertising, Industrial, Integrated Marketing, International, Internet/Web Design, Leisure, Local Marketing, Logo & Package Design, Luxury Products, Magazines, Marine, Market Research, Media Buying Services, Media Planning, Media Relations, Media Training, Medical Products, Men's Market, Merchandising, Mobile Marketing, Multicultural, Multimedia, New Product Development, New Technologies, Newspaper, Newspapers & Magazines, Out-of-Home Media, Outdoor, Over-50 Market, Package Design, Paid Searches, Pharmaceutical, Planning & Consultation, Podcasting, Point of Purchase, Point of Sale, Print, Product Placement, Production, Production (Ad, Film, Broadcast), Production (Print), Promotions, Public Relations, Publicity/Promotions, RSS (Really Simple Syndication), Radio, Real Estate, Recruitment, Regional, Restaurant, Retail, Sales Promotion, Search Engine Optimization, Seniors' Market, Social Marketing/Nonprofit, Sponsorship, Sports Market, Stakeholders, Strategic Planning/Research, Sweepstakes, Syndication, T.V., Technical Advertising, Teen Market, Telemarketing, Trade & Consumer Magazines, Transportation, Travel & Tourism, Urban Market, Viral/Buzz/Word of Mouth, Web (Banner Ads, Pop-ups, etc.), Women's Market

Approx. Annual Billings: $35,000,000

Debbie Looney *(Partner)*
Michael-Paul Raspanti *(Dir-Art & Graphic Designer)*
Jennifer Seaman *(Dir-Media)*

Accounts:
Applegate Farms Branding, Corporate Communications, Creative Development, Digital Development, Media Planning, Strategic Planning
BuyYourFriendaDrink.com Creative, Media Buying
Charlie Brown's Direct Mail, POP, PR, Print, Social Media, Web
New-ConnectPointz
Gelazzi Italiano Cafes
IronShore Insurance
Izod Creative Development, Media Planning, Strategic Planning
March Associates
Maxim Creative Development, Media Planning, Strategic Planning
Omni Watch & Clock, Inc.
Panera Bread Company
Pierre Fabre Group Eau Thermale Avene
Reeves International Toy Company
Tivo Creative Development, Media Planning, Strategic Planning
Van Heusen Creative Development, Media Planning, Strategic Planning

LOPEZ NEGRETE COMMUNICATIONS, INC.

3336 Richmond Ave Ste 200, Houston, TX 77098
Tel.: (713) 877-8777
Fax: (713) 877-8796
E-Mail: Inc@lopeznegrete.com
Web Site: www.lopeznegrete.com

E-Mail for Key Personnel:
President: alex@lopeznegrete.com

Employees: 250
Year Founded: 1985

National Agency Associations: AAF-AHAA-AMA

Agency Specializes In: Above-the-Line, Advertising, Advertising Specialties, Arts, Automotive, Below-the-Line, Bilingual Market, Brand Development & Integration, Branded Entertainment, Broadcast, Business-To-Business, Cable T.V., Children's Market, Collateral, Communications, Consulting, Consumer Goods, Consumer Marketing, Consumer Publications, Content, Corporate Communications, Corporate Identity, Cosmetics, Crisis Communications, Customer Relationship Management, Digital/Interactive, Direct Response Marketing, Direct-to-Consumer, Electronic Media, Electronics, Entertainment, Event Planning & Marketing, Exhibit/Trade Shows, Experience Design, Fashion/Apparel, Financial, Food Service, Graphic Design, Guerilla Marketing, Health Care Services, Hispanic Market, Household Goods, In-Store Advertising, Internet/Web Design, Local Marketing, Logo & Package Design, Media Buying Services, Media Planning, Media Relations, Media Training, Medical Products, Mobile Marketing, Multicultural, Multimedia, New Product Development, Newspaper, Newspapers & Magazines, Out-of-Home Media, Outdoor, Package Design, Pets , Pharmaceutical, Planning & Consultation, Print, Production, Production (Print), Promotions, Public Relations, Publicity/Promotions, Radio, Real Estate, Regional, Restaurant, Retail, Sales Promotion, Social Marketing/Nonprofit, Sponsorship, Sports Market, Strategic Planning/Research, T.V., Teen Market, Trade & Consumer Magazines, Travel & Tourism, Tween Market, Women's Market

Alex Lopez Negrete *(Co-Founder, Pres & CEO)*
Marisol Cruz *(Exec Dir-Strategic Mktg)*
Luis Gonzalez *(Exec Dir-Creative)*
Marco Walls *(Exec Dir-Creative)*
Mauricio Garcia *(Sr Dir-Art)*
Julie Grayum *(Acct Dir-PR & Social Media)*
Eugenia Archetti *(Dir-Res)*
Gerry Loredo *(Dir-Bus Analytics)*
Tony Parker Marban *(Dir-HR)*
Remo Mazzini *(Mgr-Promos Field)*
Jason Valdez *(Sr Specialist-Channel Strategy)*
Michelle Lopez Negrete *(Acct Exec)*
Yenis Rubio *(Acct Exec)*
Mauricio Cadena *(Assoc Acct Plng Dir)*
Natasha Marquez *(Community Mgr)*
Pablo Miro *(Exec Grp Acct Dir)*

Accounts:
Bank of America Corporation; 1993

Chrysler; 2013
Feld Entertainment; 2014
Fiat Chrysler Automobiles Chrysler 200, Digital, Hispanic, Social, TV
NBC Universal Motion Pictures Group; 2007
Recreational Boating & Fishing Foundation; 2013
Samsung Telecommunications; 2013
Southern California Edison; 2013
Verizon Communications (Hispanic Agency of Record); 2011
Verizon Wireless (Hispanic Agency of Record); 2013
Wal-Mart Stores, Inc (Hispanic Agency of Record); 1995

Branch

Lopez Negrete Communications West, Inc.
2222 W Olive Ave, Burbank, CA 91506
Tel.: (713) 877-8777
Fax: (818) 524-2016
Toll Free: (888) 398-0657
E-Mail: incmailbox@lopeznegrete.com
Web Site: www.lopeznegrete.com

Employees: 200
Year Founded: 2007

Cathy Lopez Negrete *(CFO)*
Howard Brown *(VP & Gen Mgr)*
Julie Jameson Grayum *(Acct Dir-PR & Social Media)*
Rudy Lopez Negrete *(Mgr-Music & Content Dev)*
Nancy Cauich *(Specialist-Channel Investment & Media Buyer)*

Accounts:
Bank of America
LNC
Microsoft
NBC Universal, Inc.
NRG Energy, Inc.
Sonic
Visa
Wal Mart Campaign: "Iceberg"

LOPITO, ILEANA & HOWIE, INC.
Metro Office Park #13 First St, Guaynabo, PR 00968
Tel.: (787) 783-1160
Fax: (787) 783-2273
E-Mail: info@lih.com
Web Site: www.lih.com

Employees: 75
Year Founded: 1972

Approx. Annual Billings: $25,225,415

Jose Luis Alvarez *(Owner)*
Carlos Pepe Rodriguez *(Pres & Chm-LIH Grp)*
Noemi Diaz *(Partner & CFO)*
Tere Davila *(VP-Creative & Dir)*
Alexandra Caraballo *(Gen Mgr & Head-Integrated Media Svc)*
Idy Candanedo *(Acct Dir)*
Maruchi Lopez *(Acct Dir)*
Javier Torres Bonilla *(Dir-Digital)*
Milka Seda *(Dir-Media)*
Jose Alicea *(Mgr-IT)*

Accounts:
Baccardi Caribbean
Caribbean Project Management
Evertec
Festival Casals
GlaxoSmithKline
Horizon Lines
Imdulac
JCPenney
Merck, Sharp & Dohme
Metal Lube
Nestle
Puerto Rico Safe Kids
SPCA
UBS
Worldnet

LORD & LASKER
555 W Grandad Blvd Ste F5, Ormond Beach, FL 32174
Tel.: (386) 615-8170
Fax: (386) 615-8758
E-Mail: mjiloty@lordandlasker.com
Web Site: www.lordandlasker.com

Employees: 2
Year Founded: 1989

National Agency Associations: AAF

Agency Specializes In: Advertising, Brand Development & Integration, Broadcast, Business-To-Business, Cable T.V., Co-op Advertising, Collateral, Communications, Consumer Marketing, Corporate Communications, Corporate Identity, Crisis Communications, Direct Response Marketing, Direct-to-Consumer, Electronic Media, Financial, Graphic Design, Health Care Services, High Technology, Hispanic Market, In-Store Advertising, Infomercials, Integrated Marketing, Internet/Web Design, Local Marketing, Logo & Package Design, Magazines, Market Research, Media Planning, Media Relations, Multimedia, New Technologies, Newspaper, Newspapers & Magazines, Out-of-Home Media, Outdoor, Package Design, Planning & Consultation, Point of Purchase, Point of Sale, Print, Production, Production (Print), Public Relations, Publicity/Promotions, Radio, Retail, Sales Promotion, Strategic Planning/Research, T.V., Technical Advertising, Trade & Consumer Magazines, Travel & Tourism, Web (Banner Ads, Pop-ups, etc.)

Michael Jiloty *(Pres)*

Accounts:
Christopher Bean Coffee; Daytona Beach, FL; 2005
Daytona Beach International Airport; Daytona Beach, FL; 2005
Rice & Rose Law Firm; Daytona, FL; 2005
Volusia County Government; Daytona, FL; 2002

LOREL MARKETING GROUP LLC
590 N Gulth Rd, King of Prussia, PA 19406
Tel.: (610) 337-2343
Fax: (610) 768-9511
E-Mail: info@lorel.com
Web Site: www.lorel.com

Employees: 50
Year Founded: 1987

Agency Specializes In: Brand Development & Integration, Business-To-Business, Collateral, Commercial Photography, Consumer Marketing, Food Service, Health Care Services, Internet/Web Design, Planning & Consultation, Retail

Approx. Annual Billings: $9,400,000

Lorna Rudnick *(Chm)*
Sebastian Pistritto *(Pres)*
Leah Simpson *(VP-Acct Svcs)*
Dawn Flook *(Dir-Ops)*
Nicholas Purifico *(Dir-Art)*
Jackey McConnell *(Office Mgr & Mgr-HR)*
Lorraine Herman *(Mgr-Production)*
Nicole Poulin *(Sr Acct Exec)*
Susan Rushing *(Assoc Acct Exec)*
Sara Brennan *(Sr Acct Coord)*

Accounts:
Amway
Broder
HasbroToyShop.com
Holy Redeemer Health System
Jordan
King of Prussia Mall
Maaco
Magee Rehabilitation
Quest Diagnostics
Rita's Water Ice
Sanofi-Aventis

LORRAINE GREGORY COMMUNICATIONS
110 Schmitt Boulevard, Farmingdale, NY 11735
Tel.: (888) 624-5888
Fax: (631) 694-1501
E-Mail: info@lgcli.com
Web Site: www.lorrainegregory.com

Agency Specializes In: Advertising, Brand Development & Integration, Media Planning, Public Relations

Greg Demetriou *(Pres & CEO)*
Jay Demetriou *(COO)*
Lorraine Demetriou *(Exec VP)*
Carie Falco *(Creative Dir)*
Julie Roventini *(Acct Mgr)*

Accounts:
New-Dominican Sisters of Amityville
New-Hia-li

LOUIS COSTANZA & ASSOCIATES, INC.
17 Point Of Woods Dr, North Brunswick, NJ 08902
Tel.: (732) 297-3800
Fax: (732) 246-4299
E-Mail: lcassociat@aol.com

Employees: 6
Year Founded: 1977

Agency Specializes In: Advertising, Newspaper, Newspapers & Magazines, Public Relations

Approx. Annual Billings: $3,500,000

Breakdown of Gross Billings by Media: Collateral: 5%; Graphic Design: 10%; Newsp.: 80%; Outdoor: 5%

Louis F. Costanza *(Pres)*

LOUNGE LIZARD WORLDWIDE
31 W Main St, Patchogue, NY 11772
Tel.: (888) 444-0110
Fax: (631) 563-6278
Toll Free: (888) 444-0110
Web Site: www.loungelizard.com

Employees: 20
Year Founded: 1996

Agency Specializes In: Advertising

Ken Braun *(Founder & Chief Creative Officer)*
Matthew Carman *(Dir-Creative)*
Rob Schiffman *(Dir-Tech)*
Trevor Magnani *(Asst Project Mgr)*

Accounts:
American Express
FalconStor
Tuesday's Children

LOVE ADVERTISING INC.

770 S Post Oak Ln Ste 101, Houston, TX 77056-1913
Tel.: (713) 552-1055
Fax: (713) 552-9155
Toll Free: (800) 544-5683
E-Mail: billie@loveadv.com
Web Site: www.loveadv.com

E-Mail for Key Personnel:
President: brenda@loveadv.com

Employees: 30
Year Founded: 1979

Agency Specializes In: Advertising, Advertising Specialties, Automotive, Broadcast, Cable T.V., Co-op Advertising, Commercial Photography, Consulting, Direct Response Marketing, Environmental, Event Planning & Marketing, Exhibit/Trade Shows, Food Service, Gay & Lesbian Market, Government/Political, Graphic Design, Hispanic Market, Internet/Web Design, Logo & Package Design, Magazines, Media Buying Services, Multimedia, New Product Development, Newspaper, Newspapers & Magazines, Outdoor, Planning & Consultation, Print, Production, Public Relations, Publicity/Promotions, Radio, Restaurant, Retail, Sales Promotion, Sponsorship, Sports Market, Strategic Planning/Research, T.V., Yellow Pages Advertising

Approx. Annual Billings: $33,000,000

Breakdown of Gross Billings by Media: Other: 10%; Radio: 30%; T.V.: 60%

Mike Albrecht *(Chief Dev Officer & Sr VP-Acct Svcs)*
Billie Van Slyke *(Exec VP & Dir-Creative)*
Shannon Moss *(Sr VP)*
Jessica Manning *(VP-PR)*
Mark Miller *(VP-Media Svcs)*
Thomas Guerrero *(Dir-Creative)*
Lisa Martin *(Acct Supvr-PR)*
Sarah Stubbs *(Acct Supvr)*
Kaelie Marcozzi *(Media Planner & Media Buyer)*
Hank Bell *(Media Planner & Buyer)*
Jennifer Chandler *(Sr Media Planner & Buyer)*

Accounts:
Buffalo Wild Wings, Inc.
C&D Scrap
Centerpoint Energy
Gallery Furniture; Houston, TX; 1989
Genghis Grill
Houston Auto Dealer Association; 1994
Houston Auto Show
HSP
Northwest Honda; Houston, TX Motorcycles; 1999
Papa John's
Tomball Bunch
Westside Tennis Club

LOVE & COMPANY, INC.
1209 N East St, Frederick, MD 21701
Tel.: (301) 663-1239
Fax: (301) 663-1553
E-Mail: info@loveandcompany.com
Web Site: www.loveandcompany.com

E-Mail for Key Personnel:
President: rlove@loveandcompany.com
Creative Dir.: tsprecher@loveandcompany.com
Production Mgr.: pbarto@loveandcompany.com

Employees: 13
Year Founded: 1980

National Agency Associations: AAF-Second Wind Limited

Agency Specializes In: Advertising, Advertising Specialties, Brand Development & Integration, Business Publications, Communications, Consulting, Corporate Identity, Direct Response Marketing, Education, Financial, Graphic Design, Local Marketing, Logo & Package Design, Market Research, Media Buying Services, Media Planning, Media Relations, Multimedia, Over-50 Market, Public Relations, Seniors' Market, Social Marketing/Nonprofit, Strategic Planning/Research, Travel & Tourism

Approx. Annual Billings: $1,000,000

Ann Burnside Love *(Founder & Chm)*
Rob Love *(Pres)*
Tim Bracken *(VP-Bus Dev & Sr Specialist-Mktg)*
Susan Moore *(VP-Sls Svcs)*
Sarah Camp *(Dir-Interactive Comm & Digital Strategy)*
Pat Barto *(Mgr-Traffic & Production)*
Scott Markle *(Specialist-Design & Production)*
Jennifer Adelman *(Coord-Bus Dev)*

LOVE AND WAR ASSOCIATES LLC
414 Broadway 5th Fl, New York, NY 10013
Tel.: (212) 343-3141
E-Mail: info@loveandwar.com
Web Site: www.loveandwar.com

Year Founded: 2006

Agency Specializes In: Advertising, Digital/Interactive, Internet/Web Design, Print, Social Media

Eng San Kho *(Partner)*
Peter Tashjian *(Partner)*
Steve Fine *(Dir-Art)*
James Renouf *(Designer)*
Jennifer Yung *(Designer)*

Accounts:
Denihan Hospitality Group, LLC

LOVE COMMUNICATIONS
546 S 200 W, Salt Lake City, UT 84101
Tel.: (801) 519-8880
Fax: (801) 519-8884
E-Mail: tlove@lovecomm.net
Web Site: www.lovecomm.net

Employees: 30

Richard B. Love *(Partner & Dir-Creative)*
Preston E. Wood *(Partner & Dir-Creative)*
Alan Reighard *(Partner-Brand Plng)*
Joe Evans *(VP & Grp Acct Dir)*
Peggy Conway *(VP & Dir-Media)*
Sarah Nielson *(Dir-Digital Mktg)*
Chip Haskell *(Assoc Dir-Creative)*
Jonathan Smithgall *(Mgr-Digital Media)*
Amanda Chew *(Media Buyer)*

Accounts:
All Seasons Resort Lodging
Cooper Roberts Simonsen Associates
DownEast Home & Clothing
Papa Murphy's International, LLC
Pioneer Theatre Company
Spring Mobile
Standard Optical
Swaner EcoCenter
University Health Care
New-Utah Office of Tourism Media Buying
Wingers Grill & Bar Restaurants

LOVELL COMMUNICATIONS, INC.
2021 Richard Jones Rd Ste 310, Nashville, TN 37215
Tel.: (615) 297-7766
Fax: (615) 297-4697
E-Mail: lovcom@lovell.com
Web Site: www.lovell.com

Employees: 11
Year Founded: 1988

Agency Specializes In: Collateral, Communications, Corporate Communications, Crisis Communications, Email, Entertainment, Event Planning & Marketing, Financial, Government/Political, Health Care Services, Hospitality, Internet/Web Design, Local Marketing, Media Relations, Media Training, Pharmaceutical, Retail, Search Engine Optimization, Social Marketing/Nonprofit

Paula Lovell *(Founder, Chm & CEO)*
Rosemary Plorin *(Pres)*
Rebecca Kirkham *(Sr VP)*
Robin Embry *(VP & Sr Acct Supvr)*
Dana Coleman *(VP)*
Susanne Powelson *(VP)*
Janice Sensing *(Office Mgr)*
Amanda Anderson *(Sr Acct Supvr)*
Katelyn Fish *(Acct Exec)*
Alli Finkelston *(Asst Acct Exec)*

Accounts:
Alive Hospices
AlliedBarton Security Services LLC; Conshohocken, PA
Cadence Bank; Starkville, MS
College Living Experience; Columbia, MD
General Council on Finance & Administration of The United Methodist Church; Nashville, TN
MedQuest Associates; Alpharetta, GA
MedSolutions; Franklin, TN
Superior Energy Services Inc.; New Orleans, LA
Whitney National Bank; New Orleans, LA

LOVELL PUBLIC RELATIONS, INC.
8080 N Central Expwy Ste 1410, Dallas, TX 75026-1817
Tel.: (972) 788-4511
Fax: (972) 788-4322
E-Mail: info@lovellpr.com
Web Site: www.lovellpr.com

Employees: 4

Betty Lovell *(Pres)*

Accounts:
The Macerich Company

LOVGREN MARKETING GROUP
809 N 96th St Ste 2, Omaha, NE 68114
Tel.: (402) 397-7158
Fax: (402) 397-0354
Toll Free: (800) 366-8488
E-Mail: lovgren@lovgren.com
Web Site: www.lovgren.com

Employees: 5

National Agency Associations: AANI

Agency Specializes In: College, Consulting, Consumer Marketing, Education, Financial, Government/Political, Travel & Tourism

Linda Lovgren *(Pres & CEO)*
Tom Nemitz *(Mgr-Creative & Web Production)*

Accounts:
American National Bank
Bridges Investment Management Inc.
Campbell's of London
City of Omaha
Consolidated Telephone
Creighton University (project)
Curt Hofer Construction
Grace University
Lexus of Omaha

Omaha Royals
Reload LLC (Agency of Record) Smashburger Restaurants in Omaha & Lincoln, NE

LOVING + COMPANY
276 5th Ave Ste 801, New York, NY 10001
Tel.: (212) 213-3504
E-Mail: info@lovingandcompany.com
Web Site: www.lovingandcompany.com

Employees: 10

Agency Specializes In: Brand Development & Integration, Crisis Communications, Event Planning & Marketing, Fashion/Apparel, Food Service, Health Care Services, Hospitality, Media Relations, Retail, Social Marketing/Nonprofit, Travel & Tourism

Marry Loving *(Owner)*

Accounts:
J.C. Penney Company, Inc.
Sue Wong (Agency of Record)

LOWRY CREATIVE
2525 Drane Field Rd Ste 12, Lakeland, FL 33811
Tel.: (863) 797-4845
Web Site: www.lowrycreative.com

Agency Specializes In: Advertising, Brand Development & Integration, Digital/Interactive, Internet/Web Design, Print

Warren Davis *(Dir-Live Production & Audio-Visual Design)*
Kyle Dunaway *(Dir-Sound)*
Andrew Pritchett *(Dir-Digital Media)*

Accounts:
New-Bionic Gloves
OMS Group

LOYALKASPAR
13 Crosby St Ste 402, New York, NY 10013
Tel.: (212) 343-1037
Fax: (212) 343-1038
E-Mail: info@loyalkaspar.com
Web Site: www.loyalkaspar.com

Year Founded: 2003

Agency Specializes In: Advertising, Brand Development & Integration, Broadcast, Production

David Herbruck *(Owner)*
Beat Baudenbacher *(Principal & Chief Creative Officer)*
Robert Blatchford *(Chief Dev Officer)*
Geoff Bailey *(Dir-Creative)*
Anna Minkkinen *(Dir-Creative)*
Mika Saulitis *(Strategist & Writer)*
Steven Manuel *(Coord-Mktg)*

Accounts:
AMC Networks Inc. The Walking Dead
Fuse Rebranding
Pop Creative
Screenvision Cinema Network LLC

LP&G MARKETING
(Formerly LP&G, Inc.)
2329 N Tucson Blvd, Tucson, AZ 85716
Tel.: (520) 624-1116
Fax: (520) 624-0272
E-Mail: lperls@lpginc.com
Web Site: www.lpginc.com

E-Mail for Key Personnel:
Creative Dir.: lperls@lpginc.com
Media Dir.: cpalmer@lpginc.com
Production Mgr.: abowles@lpginc.com

Employees: 10
Year Founded: 1993

National Agency Associations: AAF-AMA-PRSA

Agency Specializes In: Advertising, Alternative Advertising, Arts, Brand Development & Integration, Broadcast, Business-To-Business, Cable T.V., Co-op Advertising, Collateral, Communications, Computers & Software, Consumer Marketing, Corporate Identity, Crisis Communications, Digital/Interactive, Direct Response Marketing, Direct-to-Consumer, E-Commerce, Email, Entertainment, Event Planning & Marketing, Exhibit/Trade Shows, Gay & Lesbian Market, Graphic Design, Guerilla Marketing, Health Care Services, High Technology, Hospitality, Integrated Marketing, Internet/Web Design, Leisure, Local Marketing, Logo & Package Design, Luxury Products, Magazines, Market Research, Media Buying Services, Media Relations, Medical Products, Merchandising, New Product Development, Out-of-Home Media, Outdoor, Package Design, Planning & Consultation, Podcasting, Point of Purchase, Point of Sale, Print, Production, Production (Ad, Film, Broadcast), Promotions, Public Relations, Publicity/Promotions, Radio, Real Estate, Restaurant, Sales Promotion, Search Engine Optimization, Seniors' Market, Social Marketing/Nonprofit, Strategic Planning/Research, T.V., Trade & Consumer Magazines, Transportation, Travel & Tourism, Viral/Buzz/Word of Mouth, Web (Banner Ads, Pop-ups, etc.)

Approx. Annual Billings: $1,211,430

Leslie Perls *(Owner, Principal & Dir-Creative)*
Colleen Tierney-Cutshaw *(Principal & Dir-Brand Strategy)*
Alison Gillanders-Daubert *(Assoc Dir-Creative)*
Cindy Jordan-Nowe *(Acct Mgr)*
Krysta Jordan *(Project Mgr-Interactive)*
Jenny Hanke *(Accountant-HR)*
David Wahl *(Sr Writer)*

Accounts:
Blue + White Auto; Tucson, AZ
Bombhair Website
Cascades of Tucson; Tucson, AZ
Environmental Services Dept., City of Tucson; Tucson, AZ
Medical Referral Source; Tucson, AZ
Nextrio; Tucson, AZ
Pima Federal Credit Union; Tucson, AZ
Regier Carr & Monroe; Tucson, AZ
Remodelers' Advantage; Laurel, MD
Save the Cord Foundation; Tucson, AZ
Town of Queen Creek; Queen Creek, AZ
University of Arizona Health Network; Tucson, AZ

LPI COMMUNICATIONS GROUP INC.
101 253 62nd Ave SE, Calgary, AB T2H 0R5 Canada
Tel.: (403) 735-0655
Fax: (403) 735-0530
Toll Free: (888) 835-0655
E-Mail: info@lpi-group.com
Web Site: www.lpi-group.com

Employees: 40

Agency Specializes In: Advertising, Corporate Communications, Digital/Interactive, Direct Response Marketing, Logo & Package Design, Print, Sales Promotion, Sports Market, Strategic Planning/Research, Web (Banner Ads, Pop-ups, etc.)

Melody Macpherson *(VP & Mng Dir-Toronto Office)*
Ken Youngberg *(Mng Dir-Growth & Innovation)*
Erin Henry *(Dir-Client Svcs)*
Rochelle Gracia *(Acct Mgr-Monster Energy & Coca-Cola)*
Suzanne Lacoste *(Acct Mgr)*
Dawn Lapeare *(Acct Mgr)*
Jennifer Simbulan *(Acct Mgr)*
Luke Yates *(Mgr-Rewards & Logistics)*
Chelsea Zaparyniuk *(Acct Exec)*

Accounts:
Calgary Stampede
Easyhome
Kraft
Levi Strauss

Branch

LPi Communications
4220 98th St NW Ste 104, Edmonton, AB T6E 6A1 Canada
Tel.: (780) 452-4160
Fax: (780) 452-2066
E-Mail: edmonton@lpi-group.com
Web Site: www.lpi-group.com

Employees: 12

Agency Specializes In: Advertising

Melody MacPherson *(Mng Dir & VP)*
Erin Henry *(Acct Dir)*
Liz Hulley *(Dir-Client Svcs-Edmonton)*
Becky Foster *(Sr Mgr-Production)*
Rochelle Gracia *(Acct Mgr-Monster Energy & Coca-Cola)*
Jennifer Simbulan *(Acct Mgr)*
Luke Yates *(Mgr-Rewards & Logistics)*

Accounts:
All Weather Windows
Calgary Stampede
The CORE
Full Throttle
Hockey Calgary
Johnson & Johnson
Kraft Canada
Odwalla
Value Drug Mart

LPK
19 Garfield Pl, Cincinnati, OH 45202
Tel.: (513) 241-6401
Fax: (513) 241-1423
Web Site: www.lpk.com

Employees: 400

Agency Specializes In: Brand Development & Integration, Corporate Identity, Identity Marketing

Amy Steinmetz *(Mng Dir & VP-Europe)*
Stacey Rudolf *(Mng Dir)*
Nathan Hendricks *(Chief Creative Officer)*
John Recker *(Pres-Intl)*
Howard McIlvain *(Exec VP & Dir-Creative)*
Liz Grubow *(VP & Grp Dir)*
Andrew Tesnar *(Sr Dir-Creative)*
Randall Houser *(Brand Dir-Adaptation)*
Amy Kletz *(Dir-Design)*
David Volker *(Dir-Creative)*

Accounts:
Excedrin
Gillette
Glad
Hallmark
Hershey
Pampers
Pringles
Tampax
US Bank

Branches

LPK Sarl Geneva
Avenue des Morgines 12, Petit-Lancy, CH-1213 Geneva, Switzerland
Tel.: (41) 22 300 3300
Fax: (41) 22 300 3322
E-Mail: info@lpk.com

Employees: 20

Amy Steinmetz *(Mng Dir)*
Julien Desgarceaux *(Brand Dir)*
Cathy Lowe *(Dir-Bus Dev)*

Accounts:
Hallmark
Hershey
Kellogg's
Olay
Pampers
Pantene
Pringles
Samsung
Sirius
U.S. Bank

LPNY LTD.
135 E 65th St, New York, NY 10021
Tel.: (212) 288-5676
Fax: (212) 288-5679
E-Mail: jlotas@lpny.com
Web Site: www.lpny.com

Employees: 5
Year Founded: 1986

Agency Specializes In: Advertising, Advertising Specialties, Brand Development & Integration, Broadcast, Business-To-Business, Children's Market, Consulting, Consumer Marketing, Consumer Publications, Corporate Identity, Cosmetics, Gay & Lesbian Market, Government/Political, Graphic Design, Health Care Services, Logo & Package Design, Magazines, New Product Development, Outdoor, Over-50 Market, Point of Purchase, Retail, Teen Market

Joanna Patton *(Partner)*
Edward Lehman *(Dir-Creative & Acct Svcs)*
Nina Schuermaier-Lewerenz *(Dir-Creative)*

Accounts:
Ahava Skincare
American Red Cross; Greater New York
Beth Israel
Brooklyn Brewery; Brooklyn, NY Brooklyn Lager, Brooklyn Brown; 1986
Cosmo GIRL
Max Factor
New York Cornell
NYC Children's Services

LSHD ADVERTISING INC.
1974 Westover Rd, Chicopee, MA 1022
Tel.: (413) 593-1114
Fax: (413) 593-1115
E-Mail: info@lshd.com
Web Site: www.lshd.com

Agency Specializes In: Advertising, Brand Development & Integration, Broadcast, Communications, Digital/Interactive, Event Planning & Marketing, Internet/Web Design, Logo & Package Design, Outdoor, Print

Tom Leveille *(Pres)*
Bob Demetrius *(Partner & Sr Dir-Creative)*
Meghan Dewar *(Sr Dir-Art)*
Fred Crisp *(Dir-Art)*
Karl Hammond *(Mgr-Fin & Admin)*
Joanna Surowiec *(Acct Exec)*

Accounts:
Chemex Corporation

LUBICOM MARKETING CONSULTING
1428 36th St, Brooklyn, NY 11218
Tel.: (718) 854-4450
Fax: (718) 854-4474
E-Mail: info@lubicom.com
Web Site: www.lubicom.com

E-Mail for Key Personnel:
President: mlubinsky@lubicom.com

Employees: 12
Year Founded: 1984

Agency Specializes In: Advertising, Business-To-Business, Collateral, Communications, Consulting, Consumer Marketing, Direct Response Marketing, Event Planning & Marketing, Exhibit/Trade Shows, Food Service, Graphic Design, Health Care Services, New Product Development, Newspaper, Over-50 Market, Production, Public Relations

Menachem Lubinsky *(Pres)*
Eda Kram *(Office Mgr)*

Accounts:
Kosher Today
Kosherfest

LUBOW ADVERTISING, INC.
5 Revere Dr Ste 200, Northbrook, IL 60062
Tel.: (847) 509-5880
Fax: (847) 205-5330
E-Mail: info@iubow.com
Web Site: www.lubowadvertising.com

Employees: 10
Year Founded: 1977

Agency Specializes In: Brand Development & Integration, Broadcast, Collateral, Corporate Identity, Direct Response Marketing, Fashion/Apparel, Financial, Logo & Package Design, Media Buying Services, Print, Radio, Real Estate, Retail, Seniors' Market

Approx. Annual Billings: $7,500,000

Mike Lubow *(Pres)*

Accounts:
AIU Online
Amy James Clothing
CA Development
Chestnut Homes
Discovery Clothing
Frankel & Giles
Kensington Homes
Lakewood Homes
MCL Corporation Homebuilder
Residential Homes of America Homebuilder
River East Center

LUCID AGENCY
117 E 5th St 2nd Fl, Tempe, AZ 85281
Tel.: (480) 219-7257
Web Site: www.lucidagency.com

Agency Specializes In: Advertising, Internet/Web Design, Mobile Marketing, Public Relations, Search Engine Optimization, Social Media

Chris Alfano *(VP-Mktg Svcs)*
Ken Bonham *(VP-Bus Dev)*
Carley Coursin *(Sr Acct Mgr)*
Emily Knight *(Copywriter)*
Lilly Babakitis *(Acct Coord-Digital Mktg)*
Danielle Rodriguez *(Asst-Mktg)*

Accounts:
New-Arizona Mexico commission
New-City of Tempe

LUCKIE & COMPANY
600 Luckie Dr Ste 150, Birmingham, AL 35223-2429
Tel.: (205) 879-2121
Fax: (205) 877-9855
E-Mail: info@luckie.com
Web Site: www.luckie.com

E-Mail for Key Personnel:
President: tom.luckie@luckie.com
Creative Dir.: brad.white@luckie.com
Media Dir.: linda.rountree@luckie.com
Public Relations: brian.pia@luckie.com

Employees: 130
Year Founded: 1953

Agency Specializes In: Advertising, Brand Development & Integration, Broadcast, Business Publications, Business-To-Business, Cable T.V., Co-op Advertising, Collateral, Communications, Consulting, Consumer Publications, Corporate Communications, Corporate Identity, Digital/Interactive, Direct Response Marketing, E-Commerce, Education, Electronic Media, Event Planning & Marketing, Exhibit/Trade Shows, Financial, Food Service, Government/Political, Graphic Design, Health Care Services, High Technology, Hispanic Market, In-Store Advertising, Information Technology, Internet/Web Design, Investor Relations, Legal Services, Leisure, Local Marketing, Logo & Package Design, Magazines, Media Buying Services, Medical Products, Merchandising, New Product Development, Newspaper, Newspapers & Magazines, Outdoor, Planning & Consultation, Point of Purchase, Point of Sale, Print, Production, Public Relations, Publicity/Promotions, Radio, Real Estate, Recruitment, Retail, Sales Promotion, Sponsorship, Strategic Planning/Research, T.V., Telemarketing, Trade & Consumer Magazines, Travel & Tourism, Yellow Pages Advertising

Revenue: $15,000,000

Tom Luckie *(Chm & CEO)*
John Gardner *(Pres)*
Ed Mizzell *(Mng Dir & COO)*
Brad White *(Mng Dir & Chief Creative Officer)*
Chris Statt *(COO)*
Jay Waters *(Chief Strategy Officer & Sr VP)*
Laura Long *(Sr VP-Strategic Engagement)*
Keelie Segars *(VP & Grp Acct Dir)*
Tripp Durant *(VP & Acct Dir)*
Eunice Carter *(VP & Dir-Media)*
Stephanie Naman *(VP & Dir-Creative)*
Bill Abel *(VP-User Experience Strategy & Interaction Design)*
Mark Unrein *(VP-Delivery)*
Jane Mantooth *(Controller)*
Brian Conley *(Acct Dir)*
Jenny Griffin *(Acct Dir)*
Andy Odum *(Creative Dir)*
Bo Rumbley *(Dir-Digital Art & Designer)*
Markus Beige *(Dir-Design)*
Jason Martin *(Assoc Dir-Creative)*
Sylvia Adamson *(Sr Mgr-Field Mktg)*
John Cobbs *(Mgr-Dev)*
Erin McGuire *(Mgr-Production)*
Andrea Carver *(Acct Supvr)*
Bill Dinan *(Acct Supvr)*
Megan Dillon *(Supvr-Media)*
Melonie Sturm *(Supvr-Media)*
Mary Bradley Anderson *(Sr Acct Exec)*
Jessica Austin *(Sr Acct Exec)*
Adrienne Gates *(Acct Exec)*

Maree Jones *(Specialist-PR & Social Media)*
Amanda Powell *(Jr Acct Exec)*
Caley Goins *(Acct Coord)*
Lindsay Sexton *(Acct Coord)*
Dannielle Boozer *(Coord-HR)*

Accounts:
Alabama Department of Conservation
Alabama Power Company; Birmingham, AL Media Buying & Planning; 1997
American Cast Iron Pipe Co.; Birmingham, AL; 1956
Asheville Tourism Campaign: "30 Days of Asheville"
AT&T Communications Corp.; Birmingham, AL Direct Mail; 1997
Balch & Bingham LLP
Bayer Advanced
Blue Cross-Blue Shield of Alabama; Birmingham, AL; 1957
Brown-Forman
Char-Broil (Agency of Record) Brand Strategy, Creative, Digital Media, Marketing, Mobile
Gulf Power Company
Kirkland's
Little Debbie Facebook Engagement Ad - Smart Car
McKee Foods Corporation; Collegedale, TN Granola Bars, Little Debbie Snacks, Sunbelt Cereals; 1979
Mercedes-Benz U.S. International
Regions Bank Campaign: "Wheels Of Progress"
Regions Financial
United Way of Central Alabama
Virginia Samford Theatre

Branches

Luckie & Company
3100 Breckinridge Blvd Ste 135, Duluth, GA 30096
Tel.: (404) 397-6144
Web Site: www.luckie.com

Agency Specializes In: Advertising, Brand Development & Integration, Public Relations, Search Engine Optimization, Social Media

Tom Luckie *(Chm & CEO)*
Robert E. Luckie *(Chm)*
John Gardner *(Pres)*
Ed Mizzell *(Mng Dir)*
Chris Statt *(COO)*
John Heenan *(CMO)*
Brad White *(Chief Creative Officer)*
Mary Winslow *(VP-Grp Accts)*
Ginger Williford *(Acct Dir)*
Anne Marie Whatley *(Acct Exec)*

Accounts:
New-Regions Bank

Luckie & Co.
700 St Mary's St Ste 420, San Antonio, TX 78205
Tel.: (210) 223-0516
E-Mail: sanantonio@luckie.com
Web Site: www.luckie.com

Agency Specializes In: Brand Development & Integration, Direct Response Marketing, Planning & Consultation, Public Relations, Social Media

Tom Luckie *(Chm & CEO)*
Robert E. Luckie, III *(Chm)*
Ed Mizzell *(Mng Dir & COO)*
Brad White *(Mng Dir & Chief Creative Officer)*
Jay Waters *(Chief Strategy Officer & Sr VP)*
Melissa Wheeler *(Sr VP-HR)*
Eunice Hong Carter *(VP & Dir-Media)*
Giannina Stephens *(VP & Dir-Print Production)*
Bill Abel *(VP-User Experience Strategy & Interaction Design)*
Jessica Austin *(Acct Exec)*

Accounts:
AT&T Advanced Solutions, Inc.
Balch & Bingham LLP
Bayer Properties, LLC
Giant Impact, LLC.
GlaxoSmithKline
Mercedes-Benz USA Inc.
Pur Minerals

LUCKY BRANDED ENTERTAINMENT
68 Jay St Ste 503, Brooklyn, NY 11201
Tel.: (917) 658-9234
E-Mail: studio@luckyny.com
Web Site: www.luckyny.com

Agency Specializes In: Advertising, Brand Development & Integration, Digital/Interactive, Print, Social Media

Jonathan Rosen *(Founder & Creative Dir)*

Accounts:
New-Ally Bank

LUCKY DOG CREATIVE
(Name Changed to Creative Brand Consulting)

LUCKYFISH
161 Mangum St SW Ste 101, Atlanta, GA 30313
Tel.: (404) 659-1001
E-Mail: greetings@luckyfish.tv
Web Site: www.luckyfish.tv

Agency Specializes In: Brand Development & Integration, Digital/Interactive, Graphic Design, Identity Marketing, Internet/Web Design

Jason Bratton *(Partner & Dir-Art)*

Accounts:
The Coca-Cola Company Beverages Producer
Purple Inc. Counselling & Recovery Services

LUDOMADE
(Formerly Soap)
2001 N Lamar St 4th Fl, Dallas, TX 75202
Tel.: (214) 890-4100
Fax: (214) 890-4155
Web Site: www.ludomade.com

Employees: 40
Year Founded: 2001

Agency Specializes In: Advertising, Branded Entertainment, Communications, Digital/Interactive, E-Commerce, Game Integration, Mobile Marketing

Revenue: $10,000,000

Tony George *(Mng Dir)*
Sean-Michael Daley *(Mng Dir-Dallas)*
Kaitlyn Greer *(Producer-Digital)*
Brett Bimson *(Dir-Creative)*
Mike Chang *(Dir-Technical)*

Accounts:
American Airlines
LEGO Toys Mfr
Microsoft Brand Identity Forum

LUDVIK + PARTNERS
245 E 50th St Ste 4A, New York, NY 10022
Tel.: (347) 586-9862
Fax: (212) 371-3279
Web Site: www.ludvikplus.com

Employees: 5
Year Founded: 2008

Agency Specializes In: Advertising, Advertising Specialties, Brand Development & Integration, Branded Entertainment, Collateral, Commercial Photography, Corporate Identity, Digital/Interactive, Direct Response Marketing, Direct-to-Consumer, Entertainment, Event Planning & Marketing, Exhibit/Trade Shows, Fashion/Apparel, In-Store Advertising, Integrated Marketing, Internet/Web Design, Magazines, Multimedia, Newspaper, Newspapers & Magazines, Out-of-Home Media, Outdoor, Package Design, Podcasting, Point of Purchase, Point of Sale, Print, Product Placement, Production (Print), Publicity/Promotions, Real Estate, Search Engine Optimization, Social Marketing/Nonprofit, Travel & Tourism, Viral/Buzz/Word of Mouth

Approx. Annual Billings: $400,000

Breakdown of Gross Billings by Media: Collateral: 15%; Comml. Photography: 5%; Newsp. & Mags.: 40%; Worldwide Web Sites: 40%

Leskovik Ludvik Nekaj *(Dir-Ops & Billing)*

Accounts:
Bona Tierra Realty; New York, NY Pre-Construction Apartments for Sale & Rental; 2008

LUMINATE ADVERTISING
12303 Airport Way Ste 200, Broomfield, CO 80021
Tel.: (303) 460-8703
Fax: (303) 460-8704
E-Mail: mary@luminateadvertising.com
Web Site: www.luminateadvertising.com

Employees: 5
Year Founded: 1996

Agency Specializes In: Graphic Design, Medical Products, Newspaper, Recruitment

Approx. Annual Billings: $1,000,000

Breakdown of Gross Billings by Media: Newsp.: $900,000; Pub. Rels.: $100,000

Mary H. Tilger *(Dir & Specialist-Employer Brand)*
Terry Weissman *(Sr Engr-Software)*

Accounts:
Alexanders Data Service; Denver, CO Recruitment Advertising; 1996
Laradon; Denver, CO Recruitment Advertising; 1997
Metropolitan State College of Denver
Regis University
Six Flags Elitch Gardens; Denver, CO Recruitment Advertising; 1998
Six Flags Worlds of Adventure; Aurora, OH Recruitment Advertising; 2001
Vail Valley Medical Center; Vail, CO Recruitment Advertising; 1996
Water World

LUMINOR
360 E. 1st Street, Tustin, CA 92780
Tel.: (949) 648-7460
E-Mail: info@luminor.com
Web Site: www.luminor.com

Employees: 20
Year Founded: 1983

Agency Specializes In: Brand Development & Integration

Ron Wilbur *(Owner)*

Accounts:

Alcoa
EDO Corp.
HP
Microsoft Corporation
Sony

LUNA AD

116 Princess St, Wilmington, NC 28401
Tel.: (910) 763-7030
Web Site: www.lunaad.com

Agency Specializes In: Advertising, Brand Development & Integration, Event Planning & Marketing, Graphic Design, Internet/Web Design, Logo & Package Design, Print, Public Relations, Social Media, T.V.

Cathey Luna *(Owner & Dir-Acct Svcs)*

Accounts:
New-Bob King Automall

LUNA CREATIVE DESIGN

15829 N 51st Pl, Scottsdale, AZ 85254
Tel.: (602) 494-4048
Fax: (602) 765-7955
E-Mail: design@mikeluna.com
Web Site: http://www.mlpscottsdale.com/LCD/

Employees: 4
Year Founded: 1989

Agency Specializes In: Collateral, Commercial Photography, Communications, Consulting, Consumer Marketing, E-Commerce, Electronic Media, Graphic Design, Internet/Web Design, Logo & Package Design, Multimedia, New Product Development, Newspapers & Magazines, Package Design, Print, Production, Promotions, Publicity/Promotions, Web (Banner Ads, Pop-ups, etc.), Women's Market

Approx. Annual Billings: $250,000

Michael Luna *(Owner)*

Accounts:
AIGA Knoxville
James Craig Furnishings
Newport Furnishings
Odyssey Homes

LUNCHBUCKET CREATIVE

2153 Chuckwagon Rd Ste 20, Colorado Springs, CO 80919
Tel.: (719) 466-3010
E-Mail: info@lunchbucketcreative.com
Web Site: www.lunchbucketcreative.com

Agency Specializes In: Advertising, Brand Development & Integration, Corporate Identity, Digital/Interactive, Internet/Web Design

Larry Hinkle *(Partner & Copywriter)*
Craig Rae *(Dir-Art)*
Ryan Carsten *(Designer-Interactive)*

Accounts:
Citizens Project

LUNDMARK ADVERTISING + DESIGN INC.

2345 Grand Blvd Ste 200, Kansas City, MO 64108
Tel.: (816) 842-5236
Fax: (816) 221-7175
E-Mail: brandon@lundmarkadv.com
Web Site: www.lundmarkadvertising.com

Employees: 6
Year Founded: 1947

Agency Specializes In: Bilingual Market, Brand Development & Integration, Business-To-Business, Catalogs, Collateral, Consumer Goods, Consumer Marketing, Direct Response Marketing, Graphic Design, In-Store Advertising, Logo & Package Design, Package Design, Point of Purchase, Point of Sale, Print, Production, Production (Print), Promotions, Sales Promotion

Brandon Myers *(Mng Partner)*
Kia Hunt *(Dir-Creative)*
Nick Ogden *(Dir-Design, Print & Interactive)*

Accounts:
Borden Dairy
Faultless Starch/Bon Ami Co.
Hostess Brands
Payless Shoe Source

LUQUIRE GEORGE ANDREWS, INC.

(d/b/a LGA)
4201 Congress St Ste 400, Charlotte, NC 28209
Tel.: (704) 552-6565
Fax: (704) 552-1972
E-Mail: senger@lgaadv.com
Web Site: www.lgaadv.com

Employees: 45
Year Founded: 1984

National Agency Associations: 4A's

Agency Specializes In: Advertising, African-American Market, Automotive, Aviation & Aerospace, Bilingual Market, Brand Development & Integration, Broadcast, Business Publications, Business-To-Business, Cable T.V., Children's Market, Co-op Advertising, Collateral, Communications, Consulting, Consumer Marketing, Consumer Publications, Corporate Communications, Corporate Identity, Digital/Interactive, Direct Response Marketing, E-Commerce, Education, Electronic Media, Engineering, Entertainment, Event Planning & Marketing, Exhibit/Trade Shows, Fashion/Apparel, Financial, Food Service, Gay & Lesbian Market, Government/Political, Graphic Design, Health Care Services, Hispanic Market, Industrial, Internet/Web Design, Investor Relations, Legal Services, Leisure, Logo & Package Design, Magazines, Marine, Medical Products, Merchandising, New Product Development, Newspaper, Newspapers & Magazines, Out-of-Home Media, Outdoor, Over-50 Market, Planning & Consultation, Point of Purchase, Point of Sale, Print, Production, Public Relations, Publicity/Promotions, Radio, Real Estate, Recruitment, Restaurant, Retail, Sales Promotion, Seniors' Market, Sponsorship, Sports Market, Strategic Planning/Research, T.V., Technical Advertising, Teen Market, Trade & Consumer Magazines, Transportation, Travel & Tourism, Yellow Pages Advertising

Approx. Annual Billings: $50,000,000

Steve Luquire *(Founder & CEO)*
Peggy Brookhouse *(Pres & Partner)*
Steve Dunkley *(Partner & Chief Creative Officer)*
Judi Wax *(Exec VP & Dir-PR)*
Todd Aldridge *(Sr VP & Grp Dir-Creative)*
Christine Eubanks *(Sr VP & Co-Dir-Client Svc)*
Brooks Luquire *(Sr VP & Co-Dir-Client Svc)*
David Coburn *(Sr VP)*
Philip Tate *(Sr VP)*
Chuck Griffiths *(VP & Controller)*
Jennifer Jones *(VP & Grp Dir-Creative)*
Stephanie Spicer *(VP & Dir-Brand Strategy)*
Jon Cain *(Sr Dir-Art)*
Kelly Bayett *(Creative Dir)*
Jean-Francois Campeau *(Art Dir)*
Joe Tolley *(Dir-Art & Assoc Dir-Creative)*
Maggie Cote *(Dir-Art)*
Gretchen Voth *(Dir-Content Strategy)*
Mateo Wellman *(Dir-Digital)*
Margaret Bond *(Assoc Dir-Creative & Copywriter)*
Ryan Coleman *(Assoc Dir-Creative)*
Bobbi Adderton *(Sr Mgr-Production)*
Courtney Ottelin *(Project Mgr-Digital)*
Dana Boone *(Mgr-Social Media)*
Stacey McCray *(Sr Acct Supvr-PR)*
Jane Duncan *(Acct Supvr)*
Stephen Hass *(Sr Acct Exec-PR)*
Crandall Turner *(Acct Exec)*
Taryn Dietrich *(Asst Acct Exec)*
Anna Mullen *(Asst Acct Exec-Client Svcs)*
Chelsea Caplan *(Acct Coord)*

Accounts:
AAF Charlotte
ACC Football
American Tire Distributors Aftermarket Tires, Campaign: "Drag Chute"; 2005
Antilles Seaplanes
Babson Capital
Balfour Beatty Construction
BB&T Corp. (Marketing Agency of Record) Broadcast, Print
Blum
Carolina Panthers Sam Mills
Curtiss-Wright Controls, Inc.
ING DIRECT
Lincoln Financial
New-McGladrey Campaign: "The Gauntlet"
Methodist Sports Medicine Campaign: "Comeback Athlete Award"
Molnlycke Health Care
North Carolina State Tourism Campaign: "Wild Horses", Marketing Program, North Carolina Wines, Website Design
Novant Health
Orthocarolina
Piedmont Natural Gas
Premier
PURPLE Campaign: "Peel Back The Paint"
New-RSM US LLP
RT&E Integrated Communications
SHEA Homes
Snyder's-Lance, Inc. Public Relations
Syska Hennessy Group
Thomasville Medical Center
Wix Filtration Products Division

LURE AGENCY

4752 Palm Ave Ste 103, La Mesa, CA 91942
Tel.: (619) 889-8156
Web Site: www.lureagency.com

Year Founded: 2012

Agency Specializes In: Advertising, Brand Development & Integration, Digital/Interactive, Internet/Web Design, Logo & Package Design, Media Buying Services, Media Planning, Public Relations, Social Media, Strategic Planning/Research

Cory Falter *(Chief Creative Officer)*
Melissa Rautenberg *(Dir-Digital Strategy)*
Heather Falter *(Mgr-Fin)*
Zoe Freedman *(Strategist-Content)*

Accounts:
Juice Nation

LURE DESIGN, INC.

1009 Virginia Dr, Orlando, FL 32803
Tel.: (407) 895-5360
Web Site: www.luredesigninc.com

Agency Specializes In: Advertising, Brand Development & Integration, Graphic Design

Jeff Matz *(Owner)*
Sarah Blacksher Collins *(Principal & Designer)*
Paul Mastriani *(Principal & Designer)*

Accounts:
Enzian Theater City of God Cult Classic Poster
YMCA

LUXURIOUS ANIMALS LLC
435 W 19th St, New York, NY 10011
Tel.: (212) 518-1920
E-Mail: info@luxanimals.com
Web Site: www.luxanimals.com

Year Founded: 2008

Agency Specializes In: Advertising, Digital/Interactive, Social Media

Robert Bengraff *(Co-Founder, Owner & CEO)*
Garrett Nantz *(Principal & Dir-Creative)*

Accounts:
Home Box Office, Inc.
Kimberly-Clark Corporation Huggies

L.W. RAMSEY ADVERTISING AGENCY
PO Box 2561, Davenport, IA 52809
Tel.: (563) 326-3333
Fax: (563) 326-0159
Toll Free: (800) 473-0157
Web Site: www.ramseyadagency.com

Employees: 1
Year Founded: 1923

National Agency Associations: APA-BPA

Agency Specializes In: Agriculture, Graphic Design, Public Relations, Social Marketing/Nonprofit

Rick Bopp *(Designer-Adv)*

Accounts:
Ramsey How-To Booklets

LYERLY AGENCY INC.
126 N Main St, Belmont, NC 28012
Tel.: (704) 525-3937
Fax: (704) 525-3938
E-Mail: info@lyerly.com
Web Site: www.lyerly.com

Employees: 9
Year Founded: 1977

National Agency Associations: AD CLUB-AMA-Second Wind Limited

Agency Specializes In: Advertising, Aviation & Aerospace, Brand Development & Integration, Business-To-Business, Co-op Advertising, Collateral, Communications, Consulting, Consumer Marketing, Corporate Identity, Direct Response Marketing, E-Commerce, Event Planning & Marketing, Exhibit/Trade Shows, Financial, Food Service, Graphic Design, Health Care Services, High Technology, Industrial, Internet/Web Design, Leisure, Logo & Package Design, Media Buying Services, Medical Products, Newspaper, Newspapers & Magazines, Out-of-Home Media, Outdoor, Over-50 Market, Pharmaceutical, Planning & Consultation, Point of Purchase, Point of Sale, Print, Production, Public Relations, Publicity/Promotions, Real Estate, Recruitment, Restaurant, Retail, Strategic Planning/Research, Travel & Tourism

Approx. Annual Billings: $15,000,000

Melia L. Lyerly *(Owner)*
Elaine Lyerly *(Pres & CEO)*
Kelly Peace *(VP-Client Svcs)*
Melinda Skutnick *(Dir-PR)*

Accounts:
Bank of Kansas
Cannon School
Central Piedmont Community College
Charlotte Eye Ear Nose Throat Associates (Agency of Record)
Charlotte Mecklenburg School
Charlotte Preparatory School
Evergreen Packaging
First Bank
First Trust Bank
First Union National Bank
Gaston Day School
The PENROD Company; Virginia Beach, VA; 2003
Physicians for Peace
Rowan Jobs Initiative
UNCC Belk College of Business

LYQUIX
620 Chestnut St Ste 1200, Philadelphia, PA 19106
Tel.: (215) 930-0187
Fax: (215) 501-7087
Web Site: www.lyquix.com

Year Founded: 2008

Agency Specializes In: Advertising, Brand Development & Integration, Email, Graphic Design, Market Research, Mobile Marketing, Print, Production, Search Engine Optimization, Social Media

Matt Hyde *(Partner)*
Ruben Reyes *(Principal-Tech & Usability)*
Christian Shea *(Principal-Client Mktg Strategy)*

Accounts:
Intelligent Infrastructure Systems Web

LYTHOS STUDIOS
212-A E Franklin St, Richmond, VA 23219
Tel.: (804) 225-7780
Web Site: www.lythos.com

Employees: 8

Agency Specializes In: Advertising, Brand Development & Integration, Broadcast, Digital/Interactive, Logo & Package Design, Print, Radio, T.V.

Revenue: $1,280,000

Clay Hamner *(Pres)*
Darrell Cahoon *(Dir-Ops)*
Trevor Sandy *(Dir-Art)*

Accounts:
Fiamour

M&C SAATCHI PLC
36 Golden Sq, Soho, London, W1F 9EE United Kingdom
Tel.: (44) 20 7543 4500
Fax: (44) 20 7543 4501
E-Mail: info@mcsaatchi.com
Web Site: www.mcsaatchi.com

Employees: 1,251
Year Founded: 1995

Agency Specializes In: Advertising

Approx. Annual Billings: $756,814,706

Jeremy Sinclair *(Chm)*
Richard Alford *(Mng Dir)*
Michelle Whelan *(Mng Dir)*
Camilla Kemp *(COO)*
Richard Storey *(Chief Strategy Officer-Global)*
Dip Mistry *(Art Dir & Copywriter)*
Laura Evans *(Acct Dir)*
Katie Gilbert *(Bus Dir)*
Ben Middleton *(Creative Dir)*
Neil Ritchie *(Art Dir)*
Yury Vorobev *(Art Dir)*
Will Bate *(Dir-Art & Copywriter-creative)*
Rowland Barran *(Dir-Corp & B2B)*
Luke Boggins *(Dir-Creative)*
Mark Goodwin *(Dir-Creative)*
Dan Harris *(Dir-Art)*
Antonia Harrison *(Dir-Bus Dev-Intl)*
Jeremy Hemmings *(Dir-Client-Global)*
Jamie Hewitt *(Dir-Fin-Worldwide)*
Jason Lawes *(Dir-Creative)*
David Lawrie *(Dir-Art & Creative)*
Gary Monaghan *(Dir-Art)*
Kelly Grindle *(Assoc Dir-Consumer)*
Kat McGettigan *(Assoc Dir)*
Jamie Watson *(Strategist)*
Curtis Brittles *(Copywriter)*
Will Grave *(Copywriter)*
Jonathan Muddell *(Designer)*
Matt Roach *(Copywriter)*
Christopher Ross-Kellam *(Copywriter)*

Accounts:
Adidas
Africa United Campaign: "We've Got Your Back", Online, Radio, TV
Air New Zealand
Ballantine's Campaign: "Stay True", Whisky
Be Clear On Cancer
Beatbullying Campaign: "MindFull", Campaign: "The Big March"
Blue Cross CRM, Consumer PR, Media Planning & Buying, Social Media
Boots Digital, Implementation, Media Strategy
British Airways
New-Byron Consumer & Corporate Communications
Celcom
Change4Life Campaign: "Be Food Smart"
CommBank
DE Master Blenders Global Creative
New-Dinosaur Designs Brand Awareness
Ginsters
GlaxoSmithKline Ladbrokes Bingo, Lucozade Hydroactive, Lucozade Sport, Macleans
Ladbrokes Bingo
Lucozade Sports
Macleans
Google GooglePlay
Havana Club
Investec Private Banking Communications
Jameson
Ladbrokes
Monika's Doggie Rescue
NatWest Campaign: "Goodbye, Hello", Campaign: "Her Big Day", Campaign: "House that Built Jack", Campaign: "Mustang", Get Cash, Outdoor & Digital Channels, Press, TV
Network Rail
New-Nude by Nature Global Public Relations
New-One25 Campaign: "The Green Light District"
Optus
Paddy Power
Penny For London
Public Health England Campaign: "Be Clear On Cancer", Campaign: "Change4Life - 10 Minute Shake Up"
New-Royal Mail Advertising
Samsonite
Fosters
The Silver Line Charity Campaign: "Christmas at Home"
Surfers Against Sewage
Tata Motors Limited Land Rover
Tourism Malaysia
Virgin Holidays Above The Line, Campaign: "Flaunt It", Campaign: "Hair Flick", Campaign: "Mojo the Musical", Campaign: "Unleash Your Mojo", Digital, Hip Hotels, Online, Outdoor, Press, Social, TV, Travel City Direct

VirtualPride.org

Branches

Clear Ideas Ltd.
The Poppy Factory Petersham Rd, Richmond, London TW10 6UW United Kingdom
Tel.: (44) 2084398280
Fax: (44) 2084398281
E-Mail: info@clear-ideas.com
Web Site: www.clear-ideas.com

Employees: 70
Year Founded: 2002

Damian Symons *(Mng Dir-Europe)*
Mark Killey *(Dir & Head-Innovation Skills)*
Jessica Lawson *(Head-HR)*
Adam Rowles *(Head-Bus Dev)*
Anne Imbach *(Grp Dir-Strategy)*
Jim Whelan *(Acct Dir)*
Simon Clarkson *(Dir-Strategy)*
Toby Rogers *(Dir-Res)*

Clear
270 Lafayette St Ste 1107, New York, NY 10012
Tel.: (212) 361-0014
E-Mail: simong@clear-ideas.com
Web Site: www.clear-ideas.com

Employees: 100
Year Founded: 2002

Agency Specializes In: Affluent Market, Brand Development & Integration, Consulting, Consumer Goods, Consumer Marketing, Cosmetics, Electronics, Entertainment, Environmental, Fashion/Apparel, Financial, Food Service, Graphic Design, Health Care Services, Hispanic Market, Household Goods, International, Logo & Package Design, Luxury Products, Market Research, Medical Products, Men's Market, Multicultural, New Product Development, Package Design, Pets , Pharmaceutical, Planning & Consultation, Restaurant, Retail, Seniors' Market, South Asian Market, Strategic Planning/Research, Teen Market, Tween Market, Urban Market, Women's Market

Mike Weber *(Mng Dir)*
Stephanie Herold *(Head-Practice Cultural Insight & Assoc Dir)*
Rhonda Hiatt *(Exec Dir-Strategy)*
Amy Fredrickson *(Dir-Comml Ops)*
Alicia Timpanaro *(Jr Designer)*

Human Digital
Portland House, 4 Great Portland Street, London, W1W 8QL United Kingdom
Tel.: (44) 207 404 6434
Fax: (44) 207 242 2348
Web Site: www.human-digital.com

Agency Specializes In: Social Media

Sarah Ward *(CEO)*
Sophie Wilkinson *(Office Mgr)*

Accounts:
Gatorade
Microsoft
Palmolive

LIDA
36 Golden Square, London, W1F 9EE United Kingdom
Tel.: (44) 20 7544 3700
Fax: (44) 20 7544 3701
E-Mail: lisat@lida.com
Web Site: www.lida.com

Employees: 450
Year Founded: 2000

Agency Specializes In: Brand Development & Integration, Digital/Interactive, Direct Response Marketing

Matthew Heath *(Chm & Chief Strategy Officer)*
Jonathan Goodman *(Mng Dir)*
Louise Whitcombe *(COO)*
Spencer White *(Grp Head-Creative)*
Nicky Bullard *(Exec Creative Dir)*
Camilla Patel *(Client Svcs Dir)*
Joanne Olsen *(Dir-Talent Dev)*

Accounts:
Acas
Alzheimer's Society Digital, OOH, Radio, Television
BA Holidays
Bmi Bmi American Express Credit Card, Direct Marketing
Boots Advantage Card
New-Carnival UK CRM, Creative, Cunard, P&O Cruises, Strategic
COI Inland Revenue
Comparethemarket.com Below-the-Line, CRM, Direct-to-Consumer
Dept of Health
East Midlands Trains Campaign: "Reasons to Take the Train", Direct Marketing, Email, Leaflets, Online, Outdoor
Foyles
Greater London Authority Campaign: "Capital Bee - Saving London's Bees"
The Home Office
HSE
Ikea Campaign: "Make Small Spaces Big", Digital Campaign, Garden Marketing, Online Invite System
John Lewis Financial Services Direct Marketing
KPMG
Land Rover Customer Engagement, Retail Marketing
Leslie Davis
MINI
Miscarriage Association Guerrilla Marketing, Natural Poster
National Trust "50 Things to do Before You're 11", Outdoors
NatWest
O2 Campaign: "Be more dog", Direct Marketing
Oxfam Direct & Digital Fundraising
Royal Airforce
South West Trains; 2008
Tourettes Action
Travelex
Virgin Holidays Below-the-Line, Direct Marketing

M&C Saatchi Hong Kong
29/F Cambridge House 979 King''s Road, Taikoo Place Quarry Bay, Hong Kong, China (Hong Kong)
Tel.: (852) 225252843
Fax: (852) 225814122
Web Site: www.mcsaatchi.com

Employees: 50
Year Founded: 1995

Agency Specializes In: Advertising, Brand Development & Integration

Accounts:
The British Council

M&C Saatchi Milan
Viale Monte Nero 76, 20135 Milan, Italy
Tel.: (39) 236748250
Fax: (39) 236748294
Web Site: www.mcsaatchi.com

Year Founded: 2010

Agency Specializes In: Advertising

Vincenzo Gasbarro *(Co-Founder & Partner-Creative)*
Richard Thompson *(Chm)*
Massimo Capucci *(Head-Plng)*
Lorenzo De Manes *(Sr Dir-Art)*
Anna De Gaetano *(Acct Dir)*
Margherita Zanvit *(Acct Dir-Digital)*
Roberto Ardigo *(Dir-Art)*
Alberto Pinto *(Sr Acct Mgr & Project Mgr)*
Emanuela Goretti *(Acct Mgr)*
Chiara Magnaghi *(Acct Mgr)*
Marzia Puma *(Office Mgr)*
Cristiano Nardo *(Copywriter)*
Daniele Dionisi *(Deputy Dir-Creative)*
Paolo Perrone *(Deputy Dir-Creative)*

Accounts:
Europe Assistance Milan Stunt Campaign: "L1F3"
Fastweb Campaign: "Fastline", Speed
Leroy Merlin
Sky Italia S.r.l. Santa's Team
Unicredit

M&C Saatchi PR
250 Park Ave S 10th Fl, New York, NY 10003
(See Separate Listing)

M&C Saatchi
2032 Broadway, Santa Monica, CA 90404
Tel.: (310) 401-6070
Fax: (310) 264-1910
E-Mail: huw.griffith@mcsaatchi-la.com
Web Site: www.mcsaatchi.com

Employees: 30

National Agency Associations: 4A's-THINKLA

Agency Specializes In: Advertising, Pets

Huw Griffith *(CEO, Partner-LA & Co-CEO-North America)*
Kate Bristow *(Chief Strategy Officer)*
Erickson Ilog *(Exec VP & Dir-Fin & Ops)*
Cole Hartman *(Exec VP-Mktg)*
James Bray *(Exec Creative Dir)*
Jessica Francis *(Acct Dir)*
Daniel Sundin *(Acct Mgr)*
Jackie Ayrault *(Mgr-Market Insights)*
Ana Slavin *(Sr Media Planner & Buyer)*

Accounts:
Beverly Hills Conference & Visitors Bureau; Beverly Hills, CA
City National Bank
Crystal Cruises
Epson America, Inc; Long Beach, CA Campaign: "Finish Strong"
Getty Museum Oudry's Painted Menagerie; 2006
J. Paul Getty Museum Oudry's Painted Menagerie; 2007
J. Paul Getty Trust
Ketel One Vodka
Network Omni Multilingual
Related Collateral, Ocean Avenue South, Online Videos, Print, Rich Media, Standard Digital Banners, Website
San Diego Zoo Safari Park Campaign: "Tiger Power", Campaign: "Welcome To Koalafornia", Digital, Outdoor, Print, TV, Tiger Trail
Sylvester Comprehensive Cancer Center
UGG Australia Brand Positioning, Broadcast, Campaign: "Down Time", Campaign: "For Gamechangers", Campaign: "Passing Out Presents", Campaign: "This Is UGG", Campaign: "This is magic. This is UGG", Campaign: "Twinkling Lights", Creative, Digital, In-Store, Men's Footwear, Outerwear & Accessories, Mobile, OOH, Online, Out-of-Home, Paid-Pre

Roll Media, Social Media, Twinkle Toes, Video
New-UHealth
United States Olympic Committee PR
Zoological Society of San Diego; San Diego, CA

M&C Saatchi Sport & Entertainment
36 Golden Square, London, W1F 9EE United Kingdom
Tel.: (44) 20 7543 4531
Fax: (44) 20 7543 4712
E-Mail: information@mcsaatchi.com
Web Site: www.mcsaatchi.com

Employees: 45

Agency Specializes In: Brand Development & Integration, Entertainment, Event Planning & Marketing, Sports Market

Steve Martin *(CEO)*
Jamie Wynne-Morgan *(Mng Partner)*
Moray MacLennan *(CEO-Worldwide)*
David Roberts *(Deputy Mng Dir)*
Stuart Donovan *(Dir-Plng)*
Emma Watson *(Acct Exec)*

Accounts:
1966 Entertainment Commercial & Charitable Interests, England Football Team
Amir Khan
Asics Digital, Out-Of-Home, POS, Print, TV
Association of Volleyball Professionals Brand Outreach, Strategy
Ballantines "Benjamin Von Wong's Underwater River", Brand Positioning, Campaign: "INSA's Space GIF-ITI", Global PR, Scotch Whisky
Beyond Sport United
Bomber Ski (Public Relations Agency of Record) Media
Carlsberg
Coca-Cola Refreshments USA, Inc. Powerade
New-Contego Sports Brand Development, International Marketing, Public Relations, Social Media
Currys Campaign: "Vader's Visit"
EE
Harlem RBI Events & Talent Relations, Golf Charity Event, Public Relations
Heineken UK Consumer PR, Heineken's Rugby World Cup
Jameson Irish Whiskey
MindFull Campaign: "Let it all out"
O2 Innovation, Technology
Orange
Pernod Ricard Ballantine, Digital, Global Marketing, Public Relations, Social Media
Reebok Public Relations
Sainsbury Active Kids Campaign
Street Soccer USA
Taylormade
Technogym (US Public Relations Agency of Record)
Travelex
Trilogy
United States Olympic Committee

M&C Saatchi
32 rue du Notre Dame des Victoires, 75002 Paris, France
Tel.: (33) 1 55 80 1000
Fax: (33) 1 55 80 10 10
E-Mail: gillesm@mcsgad.com
Web Site: www.mcsaatchi.com

Employees: 60

Agency Specializes In: Advertising, Digital/Interactive, Direct Response Marketing

Gilles Masson *(Founder & Pres)*
Antoine Barthuel *(Co-Founder & Dir-Creative)*
Daniel Fohr *(Owner)*
Madjid Bouzar *(Partner & Dir-Digital)*
Philippe Horeau *(Mng Dir)*
Jean Luc Roux *(VP)*
Jean-Didier Loizeau *(Head-Print Production)*
Jorge Carreno *(Creative Dir)*
Robin de Lestrade *(Creative Dir)*
Thierry Taglioni *(Dir-Comml)*

Accounts:
Coca Cola TV
Comte
Conservation Party
Earthquake Commission
Enfants Maltraites
Freedom Furniture
GIE TNT
Pages Jaunes
Save the Children
Sharp
Sorenza Clothing and Footwear
Yves Rocher

M&C Saatchi
1-26-1 Ebisunishi Shibuya-Ku, Tokyo, 150 0021 Japan
Tel.: (81) 3 5456 6355
Fax: (81) 3 5456 6377
Web Site: www.mcsaatchi.co.jp

Employees: 13

Agency Specializes In: Advertising, Brand Development & Integration, Consulting, Corporate Identity, Digital/Interactive, Luxury Products, Public Relations, Sponsorship

Tamio Koshino *(CEO)*
Nobuhiko Yamamoto *(Dir-Creative & Plng & Copywriter)*
Tetsuya Fumihira *(Sr Acct Planner)*
Chen-Ying Wang *(Designer)*

Accounts:
Sony (China) Limited Creative

M&C Saatchi
Oranienburgerstr 5a, D-10178 Berlin, Germany
Tel.: (49) 30 616 5790
Fax: (49) 30 616 57920
Web Site: www.mcsaatchi.com

Employees: 35

Agency Specializes In: Advertising, Advertising Specialties, Multimedia, New Technologies, Production (Ad, Film, Broadcast), Production (Print), Sponsorship

Dominik Tiemann *(Partner & Mng Dir)*
Darius Gross *(Acct Dir & Dir-New Bus)*
Martin Hoeft *(Dir-Art)*
Jan Lucas *(Dir-Creative)*
Sebastian Graef *(Copywriter)*
Bjoern Koebe *(Copywriter)*
Hannah Scherber *(Copywriter)*

Accounts:
Askania
Bayer Leverkusen Campaign: "We Are Someone Too"
Bundnis 90/Die Grunen
European Maccabi Games
Ferrero
Havana Club
New-HelmMut
HypoVereinsbank
Intro-Verlag
Maya Mate
MTV/VIVA
Oxfam Deutschland
Tourism Australia

M&C Saatchi
99 MacQuarie St, Sydney, NSW 2000 Australia
Tel.: (61) 2 9270 2700
Fax: (61) 2 9270 2775
E-Mail: mariej@mcsaatchi.co.nz
Web Site: www.mcsaatchi.com

Employees: 200

Agency Specializes In: Advertising

Jaimes Leggett *(CEO)*
Mim Haysom *(Mng Partner)*
Andy DiLallo *(Chief Creative Officer)*
Justin Graham *(Chief Strategy Officer)*
Ben Welsh *(Chm-Creative-Asia)*
Brian Jefferson *(Grp Head-Creative)*
Phil Leece *(Grp Head-Creative)*
Nathalie Brady *(Gen Mgr)*
Michael Canning *(Exec Dir-Creative)*
Ross Berthinussen *(Grp Dir-Strategy)*
Chris Cheeseman *(Sr Dir-Art)*
Glenn Christensen *(Sr Dir-Art)*
Ronojoy Ghosh *(Sr Dir-Art)*
Steve Hanzic *(Sr Dir-Art)*
David Jackson *(Sr Dir-Art)*
Lauren Trace *(Sr Acct Dir)*
Chelsey Peace *(Sr Acct Dir)*
Karlee Weatherstone *(Sr Acct Dir)*
Tom McFarlane *(Reg Dir-Creative)*
Manuella Perche *(Grp Acct Dir & Strategist-Brand)*
Yash Gandhi *(Grp Acct Dir)*
Hayley Mathews *(Grp Acct Dir)*
Will Reynolds *(Grp Acct Dir)*
Anthony Harca *(Team Head & Sr Producer-Digital)*
Gary Dawson *(Creative Dir)*
Chris Little *(Dir-Art & Creative)*
Sarah Cunningham *(Acct Dir)*
Simon Dobbin *(Art Dir)*
Jacinta Karras *(Producer-Digital)*
Stephen Reidmiller *(Art Dir)*
Steve Anderson *(Dir-Creative)*
Michael Andrews *(Dir-Creative)*
Matt Ennis *(Dir-Art)*
Andy Flemming *(Dir-Creative)*
Paul Gregson *(Dir-Art)*
Rachael Kimber *(Dir-Strategy)*
Alex Roper *(Dir-Strategy)*
Paula Keamy *(Assoc Dir-Creative)*
Lizzie O'Hara-Boyce *(Assoc Dir-Creative)*
Peter Lewis *(Sr Acct Mgr)*
Ella Speakman *(Acct Exec)*
Blake Arthur *(Copywriter)*
Josh Bryer *(Copywriter)*
Jonathan Flannery *(Copywriter)*
George Organ *(Copywriter)*
Ben Patterson *(Designer)*
Geoff Reid *(Copywriter)*
Claire Stapleton *(Copywriter)*
Chi Yusuf *(Designer)*

Accounts:
Acreis
ANZ
Asics Campaign: "Face A Nation"
Australian Cancer Research Foundation (ACRF)
Big Richard Creative, Marketing Campaigns, Planning, Strategic
Blue Ball Foundation
CommBank Campaign: "Can", Campaign: "Change Your Everyday"
Commonwealth Bank of Australia Campaign: "Leather Hitting Willow", Campaign: "The CommBank Cricket Club", Campaign: "Three Little Letters"
Eftpos Campaign: "A Little Button Can Do A Lot Of Good", Campaign: "Heartland"
Etihad Airways (Lead Creative Agency) Campaign: "Flying Reimagined", Digital, Print, TV
Google Campaign: "Build With Chrome", Campaign: "Google Voice Search", Campaign: "The Perfect Shot", Nexus 7
Greater Western Sydney Giants

Herringbone
Lend Lease Creative
Lexus Campaign: "This is the New Lexus"
Medicins Sans Frontieres Campaign: "Carburetor"
Miroslav Underwear Campaign: "Quality Best Appreciated Up Close"
Monikas Doggie Rescue
Noise International Campaign: "Ping-Pong By Noise", Campaign: "The Art Of Noise"
NRMA Insurance (Agency of Record)
OnePiece Digital, PR, Social
Optus Mobile Pty. Ltd. Campaign: "Clever Buoy", Campaign: "Declaration of Yes", Campaign: "It's Possible", Campaign: "Make Cyberspace A Better Place", Campaign: "On Safari", Creative, In-Store, My Plan, Online, Outdoor, TV
Pepsi Max
Pizza Hut Doritos Crunchy Crust Pizza
Quit
Samsung
Sara Lee Indulge in the Moment
DE Master Blenders Campaign: "Wake Up To Something Special"
Moccona Campaign: "Hint of Chocolate"
Skins
St Vincent de Paul Society Creative, Strategic
Stepping Stone Creations
Sydney Dogs & Cats Home Campaign: "Getting To Zero", Campaign: "Limited Edition"
Tennis Australia Ready Play
Testicular Cancer Awareness
Travelex
Ugg Campaign: "Here Comes Spring", Campaign: "Keep Stepping", Campaign: "Pop Of Summer"
Visualaz
Wotif
Xero (Global Creative Agency) Strategic

M&C Saatchi

141B Shahpur Jat, New Delhi, 110049 India
Tel.: (91) 9818544924
Web Site: mcsaatchi.co.in

Employees: 33

Nirmal Pulickal *(Mng Dir)*
Sanyja Santiago *(Sr Acct Dir & Head-Bus Dev)*
Samya Ghosh *(Dir-Art)*
Jyoti Thukral *(Acct Exec)*
Sanchita Dasgupta *(Acct Planner)*
Vankoor Raina *(Copywriter)*

Accounts:
Aditya Birla Group Campaign: "Trek & Crow"
Cyber Media
Dabbawala Foundation
DC Design
Easy Bill
Franklin Templeton Investments Mutual Fund; 2008
Stargaze
T24 Mobile Campaign: "Mauritius"
TCNS Clothing Company Creative, W
VLCC

M&C Saatchi

No 486 Fuxing Middle Road, Shanghai, 200020 China
Tel.: (86) 21 6267 3183
Fax: (86) 21 6386 3990
E-Mail: angelah@mcsaatchi.com.cn
Web Site: www.mcsaatchi.com

Michael Liu *(Partner-Greater China)*
Tony Liu *(Partner-Greater China)*
Albert Yeo *(Dir-Creative)*
Stephanie Wang *(Acct Exec)*
Henry Fung *(Assoc Acct Dir)*
Jessica Jarl *(Assoc Acct Dir)*

Accounts:
Abbott (Agency of Record) Creative, Infant Milk Formula
Airmate
American International Assurance
Bank of China Olympic-Themed Visa Card; 2007
Cerebos Bird's Nest, Brand's Essence of Chicken, InnerShine Berry Essence, Ying Kao
Christian Dior
Coolpad
Deerway Brand Strategy, Creative
Hong Ya
Uni-President Instant Noodles; 2008
Watsons
Yakult

M&C Saatchi

Level 27 140 William Street, Melbourne, VIC 3000 Australia
Tel.: (61) 3 9670 2225
Fax: (61) 3 9670 2229
E-Mail: davidb@mcsaatchi.com.au
Web Site: www.mcsaatchi.com

Employees: 40

Agency Specializes In: Direct Response Marketing

Paul Taylor *(Exec Dir-Creative)*
Tristan Cornelius *(Sr Dir-Art)*
Jay Lazaro *(Sr Dir-Art)*
Jo Matthews *(Grp Acct Dir)*
Nick Bollard *(Acct Dir)*

Accounts:
CPA Australia Brand, Digital, Marketing, Strategy
CPA
New-Cricket Australia Campaign: "Don't be a Daryl"
Hennessy Australia
KFC
Melbourne Recital Center
Opel Campaign: "Guten Tag Australien", Creative
Slater & Gordon Campaign: "Not A Problem", Marketing Communications, Strategy
Tennis Australia Campaign: "Djokovic"

M&C Saatchi

115 Amoy Street, Singapore, 069935 Singapore
Tel.: (65) 6372 4212
Fax: (65) 6227 3382
E-Mail: whittled@mcsaatchi.com.au
Web Site: www.mcsaatchi.com

Tanuj Philip *(Founder, CEO & Partner)*
Marc Leong *(Sr Dir-Art)*
David Lin *(Sr Dir-Art)*
Neo Shiyi *(Sr Dir-Art)*
Karen Wong *(Sr Dir-Art)*
Dawn Goh *(Dir-Strategy Plng)*

Accounts:
Aviva
Danone
FED; China Women's Footwear; 2007
ITV
Mediacorp Radio
Mount Faber Leisure Group (Marketing Agency of Record) Communications
Network for Electronic Transfers (Agency of Record) B2B, Communications
O2
Regent
SAP
Tourism Australia
Web.com
Yakult

M&C Saatchi

Banguan Malaysia Re 17 Lorong Dungun, 50490 Kuala Lumpur, Malaysia
Tel.: (60) 3 2094 6355
Fax: (60) 3 2093 9355
E-Mail: lara.hussein@mcsaatchi.com
Web Site: www.mcsaatchi.com

Employees: 80

Michael Quay *(Mng Partner & Head-Plng)*
Henry Yap *(Exec Dir-Creative)*
Pauline Ang *(Sr Dir-Art)*
Zen Ngan *(Art Dir)*
Farrah Harith *(Dir-Client Servicing)*
Kin Leong *(Dir-Art)*
Marzuki Maani *(Dir-Creative)*
Ahmad Fariz *(Assoc Dir-Creative)*

Accounts:
Alliance Banking Group
Association Of Accredited Advertising Agents
Boh Camomile Tea Campaign: "Calm Tea Bag"
Bursa
Cancer Research Initiative Foundation Campaign: "Stuntman"
Celcom Axiata Campaign: "Public Places, Hidden Stories"
Kuala Lumpur Sentral Development Marketing Communications, Rebranding
Malaysia Airlines Creative, Digital
Malaysia Airports Holdings Berhad KLIA2
Nike Campaign: "Trouble-Free Man"
Oxford
Petronas Lubricants International
Sime Darby Property Creative
SOTA Consumer Campaign
SPCA Campaign: "There's more play in a pet"
TM International Brand Identity, Celcom
Tourism Malaysia
Volkswagen Group Cross Touran, Jetta, Lead Agency, Passat B7, The People's Car
Wild Asia Environmental Awareness, Green Office Initiative
Yeo Hiap Seng Campaign: "Spicy Curry", Cintan Instant Cup Noodles

M&C Saatchi Abel

Media Quarter, Somerset Road, De Waterkant, Cape Town, 8001 South Africa
Tel.: (27) 21 421 1024
Web Site: mcsaatchiabel.co.za/

Mike Abel, *(Founder & Sr Exec Partner)*
Nick Liatos *(Partner-Creative)*
Jerry Mpufane *(Grp Mng Dir)*
Mick Shepard *(Exec Dir-Creative)*
Carla Bekker *(Art Dir)*
Jurgen Freese *(Art Dir)*
Sharika Jaga *(Acct Dir)*
Ntobeko Ximba *(Dir-Art)*
Faheem Chaudhry *(Strategist)*
Amanda Crawley *(Acct Exec)*
Nyarai Gomiwa *(Acct Exec)*
Kayli Vee Levitan *(Copywriter)*

Accounts:
Boxman
Flight Centre
The Haven Night Shelter
Heineken
Hollard Insurance Campaign: "Mystic Marie"
IZIKO Natural History Museum
Mr Delivery
Q20
Virgin Active South Africa

Lida

(Formerly Mark.)
Level 3 99 Macquarie St, Sydney, NSW 2000 Australia
Tel.: (61) 2 9016 1600
Fax: (61) 2 9019 5747
E-Mail: christine.gardner@lidaaustralia.com.au
Web Site: lidaaustralia.com.au/

Employees: 30

Agency Specializes In: Digital/Interactive, Direct Response Marketing

Victoria Curro *(Partner-Strategy)*
Christine Gardner *(Mng Dir)*
Kerri Chesler *(Acct Mgr)*

Accounts:
ANZ
Audi
Blackberry
Electronic Frontiers Australia
EMI
Google Campaign: "Build With Chrome", Campaign: "Google Voice Search"
NRMA
Optus
Qantas Frequent Flyer
Westfield

Smith & Milton
Elizabeth House 2nd Floor Block 2, 39 York Road, London, SE1 7NJ United Kingdom
Tel.: (44) 20 7803 4711
Fax: (44) 20 7262 6987
E-Mail: info@smith-milton.co.uk
Web Site: www.smithandmilton.com

Employees: 15
Year Founded: 1980

Agency Specializes In: Brand Development & Integration, Corporate Identity

Howard Milton *(Founder & Chm)*
Ben Mott *(Grp Mng Dir)*
Ben Hostler *(Grp Dir-Digital Creative)*
Rob Wade *(Grp Dir-Creative)*
Jay Milton *(Dir)*
Tony Stiles *(Dir-Creative)*
Georgia Buchanan *(Office Mgr)*
Ellen Fearnley *(Acct Mgr)*
Alexandra Hobbs *(Acct Mgr)*
Kevin O'Brien *(Mgr-Production)*
Tom Crawshaw *(Sr Designer)*
Lloyd Parker *(Designer)*
Ruth Pearson *(Designer)*
Tom Walker *(Designer)*

Accounts:
Black Swan
Channel 4 Embarrassing Bodies 1, Embarrassing Bodies 2
Christie + Co Creative
Coca-Cola Refreshments USA, Inc.
COI

Talk PR
3-5 Rathbone Pl, London, W1T 1HJ United Kingdom
Tel.: (44) 207 544 3777
E-Mail: janeb@talkpr.com
Web Site: www.talkpr.com

Employees: 30
Year Founded: 2001

Jane Boardman *(CEO)*
Helena Fisher *(Mng Dir)*
Tanya Hughes *(Pres-SERMO Comm)*
Toby Schuster *(Head-Tech, Social Media & Digital)*
Claudia Crow *(Dir-Creative)*
Sophie Lam *(Assoc Dir-FTC)*
Niravta Mathur *(Assoc Dir)*
Lucy Yates *(Sr Acct Mgr)*
Jessica Shanks *(Acct Mgr)*
Sophie Lee *(Acct Exec)*

Accounts:
American Express
Buena Vista Home Entertainment
Christina Aguilera
Dixons
Dolce & Gabbana
EB Brands Candy Store
ELLE Style Awards
Farfetch.com PR, Press
Fujifilm Social Media
G.H.Mumm Global Public Relations
Hugo Boss
James Bond 007 Fragrances
Lacoste
Mother of Pearl Public Relations
Nailease
Navabi Public Relations
Pencourage
Perfect Moment Media, Public Relations, Ski, Surf
Pernod Ricard Travel Retail Communications, Communications Strategy, Consumer Engagement, Consumer PR, Digital PR, Pernod Ricard, Retail
POPSUGAR Inc. Brand Awareness, Brand Identity, Communications, Media, ShopStyle
Procter & Gamble
The Sanctuary Spa
Scottish & Newcastle Carlsberg, Fosters
ShopStyle UK
SK-II
Stella McCartney
Swarovski Crystallized
Tesco
Twinings
New-Vita Coco Beauty Communications
Vodafone
Wella Professional

M&R MARKETING GROUP
3985 Arkwright Rd Ste 104, Macon, GA 31210
Tel.: (478) 621-4491
E-Mail: hey@mandr-group.com
Web Site: www.mandr-group.com

Year Founded: 2008

Agency Specializes In: Advertising, Brand Development & Integration, Graphic Design, Internet/Web Design, Logo & Package Design, Search Engine Optimization, Social Media

Matthew Michael *(Co-Founder & Dir-Accts)*
Nick Rios *(Co-Founder & Creative Dir)*
Tracie Hill *(Acct Mgr)*
Hannah Jones *(Copywriter)*

Accounts:
Cherry Blossom Festival
Macon Water Authority

M. BOOTH & ASSOCIATES
300 Park Ave S 12th Fl, New York, NY 10010
Tel.: (212) 481-7000
Fax: (212) 481-9440
E-Mail: info@mbooth.com
Web Site: www.mbooth.com

Year Founded: 1985

National Agency Associations: COPF

Agency Specializes In: Sponsorship

Margaret Booth *(Chm)*
Dale S. Bornstein *(CEO)*
Bradford D. Rodney *(Mng Partner)*
Joe Hamrahi *(CFO & COO)*
Adrianna Bevilaqua *(Chief Creative Officer)*
Jeff Bodzewski *(Chief Analytics Officer & Dir-Midwest)*
Richard Goldblatt *(Sr VP & Dir-Consumer Brands & Better4You)*
Mark Schroeder *(Sr VP & Dir-Corp Practice)*
Lauren Swartz *(Sr VP & Dir-Lifestyle, Wine & Spirits)*
Jennifer Teitler *(Sr VP & Dir-Consumer)*
Jon Paul Buchmeyer *(Sr VP-Brand Mktg)*
Frani Lieberman *(VP)*
Amber Roussel *(VP-Digital)*
Shira Zackai *(VP)*
Martha Cid *(Grp Dir-Media)*
Jacqueline Warren *(Sr Acct Supvr-Consumer)*
Maggie Walsh *(Sr Strategist-Digital & Acct Supvr)*
Ali LaFleur *(Acct Supvr)*
Rachel Pancoe *(Acct Supvr)*
Stephanie Bleiberg *(Sr Acct Exec)*
Taylor Foxman *(Specialist-Media Rels-Wine & Spirits Div)*
Vincent Grippi *(Strategist-Digital)*
Abha Gunjal *(Acct Exec)*
Alison Hoachlander *(Acct Exec)*
Megan Hunsicker *(Acct Exec)*
Julia Prey *(Strategist-Digital)*
Caitlin Teahan *(Acct Exec)*
Sofi Biviano *(Asst Acct Exec)*
Jessie Kramer *(Asst Acct Exec)*
Jennifer McTigue *(Assoc Strategist-Digital)*
Bonnie Ulman *(Chief Insights Officer & Chief Plng Officer)*

Accounts:
American Express
The British Virgin Islands Tourist Board Media Relations, PR, Strategic Consulting & Planning
Brooks Sports (Agency of Record) Consumer PR
Brugal
Burlington Coat Factory PR
Campari
Canada Goose Public Relations
Carnival Cruise Line (North American Agency of Record)
coupons.com
Dyson
Evenflo Company, Inc. Bath Tubs, Booster Car Seats, Bottle Feeding, Breast Pumps, Changing Tables, Convertible Car Seats, Cribs, Cups, Doorway Jumpers, Evenflo Company, Inc., Evenflo infant furnishings, ExerSaucer Products, Frame Carriers, Gates, Gerry Pet Gates, High Chairs, Humidifiers, Infant Car Seats, Monitors, Nursing Pads, Pacifiers, Playards, Potties, Snugli Products, Soft Carriers, Strollers, Swings, Travel Systems
The Famous Grouse
Firstbuild
GE
Godiva Chocolatier (Public Relations Agency of Record) Digital, Media Relations, Social Media, Special Events
Goed
Google
Highland Park
Kelley Blue Book (Public Relations Agency of Record) Marketing, Social Media, Strategy
Land's End
Lutron
The Macallan
Mercedes-Benz
Nolet's
Noosa
Patron Spirits Company Public Relations
Rent.com
St. Ives
Steelcase
Sur La Table
Turnstone
Unilever I Can't Believe It's Not Butter!, Vaseline, Wish Bone
University of Pennsylvania Wharton School
Weight Watchers Public Relations

M/C/C
8131 Lyndon B Johnson Fwy Ste 275, Dallas, TX 75251-1352
Tel.: (972) 480-8383
Fax: (972) 669-8447
E-Mail: pam_watkins@mccom.com

Web Site: www.mccom.com

E-Mail for Key Personnel:
President: mike_crawford@mccom.com
Creative Dir.: greg_hansen@mccom.com
Media Dir.: karen_hansen@mccom.com

Employees: 25
Year Founded: 1986

Agency Specializes In: Advertising, Brand Development & Integration, Broadcast, Business Publications, Business-To-Business, Collateral, Communications, Consulting, Consumer Publications, Corporate Identity, Digital/Interactive, Direct Response Marketing, E-Commerce, Electronic Media, Electronics, Entertainment, Financial, Graphic Design, High Technology, Information Technology, Internet/Web Design, Magazines, Media Buying Services, Multimedia, Newspaper, Newspapers & Magazines, Out-of-Home Media, Point of Purchase, Point of Sale, Print, Production, Public Relations, Publicity/Promotions, Radio, Sales Promotion, Social Media, Strategic Planning/Research, T.V., Technical Advertising, Trade & Consumer Magazines

Approx. Annual Billings: $40,000,000

Breakdown of Gross Billings by Media: Brdcst.: 10%; Digital/Interactive: 75%; Print: 15%

Mike Crawford *(Pres)*
Jim Terry *(Sr VP-Acct Svcs)*
Pam Watkins *(Sr VP-Bus & Media Strategy)*
Shannon Sullivan *(VP & Acct Dir)*
Todd Brashear *(VP-Creative)*
Kathy Andrews *(Dir-Ops)*
Sherie Wigder *(Assoc Dir-Media)*

Accounts:
Altium Limited Media Planning & Buying
Animalz by ReTrak Content Marketing, Kid-Friendly Headphones, Public Relations
CommScope
CPS HR Consulting
New-CyrusOne Planning
Harris CapRock Communications; Houston, TX Remote Communications Systems; 1998
Hudson & Marshall
Property Damage Appraisers Brand Development, Marketing Communications
New-Razberi Technologies (Agency of Record)
Texas Instruments Incorporated

M J KRETSINGER

(Private-Parent-Single Location)
3601 W 76th St Ste 50, Minneapolis, MN 55435
Tel.: (612) 327-8067
E-Mail: info@mjkretsinger.com
Web Site: www.mjkretsinger.com

Employees: 10
Year Founded: 2003

Agency Specializes In: Advertising, Brand Development & Integration, Collateral, Digital/Interactive, Internet/Web Design, Social Media

Revenue: $1,000,000

Michael Kretsinger *(CEO & Exec Creative Dir)*
Joe Kocik *(Dir-Art)*

Accounts:
Comstar
KleinBank

M/K ADVERTISING PARTNERS, LTD.

(d/b/a MK)
16 W 22Nd St, New York, NY 10010
Tel.: (212) 367-9225
Fax: (212) 242-7008
E-Mail: info@mkanyc.com
Web Site: mkanyc.com

Employees: 12
Year Founded: 1997

Agency Specializes In: Advertising, Brand Development & Integration, Broadcast, Business-To-Business, Cable T.V., Children's Market, Collateral, Consumer Marketing, Consumer Publications, Direct Response Marketing, Entertainment, Graphic Design, Leisure, Logo & Package Design, Media Buying Services, Print, T.V., Trade & Consumer Magazines

Approx. Annual Billings: $15,000,000

Michael Yuen *(Owner & Principal)*
Ingrid Laub *(Partner & Exec Acct Dir)*
Michele Bavitz *(VP & Acct Dir)*
Jeff Bechtloff *(VP & Dir-Media)*
Larry Freemantle *(Sr Dir-Art)*
Garth Wingfield *(Sr Dir-Copy)*
Brett Rachlin *(Acct Dir)*
Colin Riley *(Mgr-Digital Adv Ops)*
Sara Prober *(Coord-Media)*

Accounts:
ABC Daytime
ABC Family
Cable & Telecommunications Association for Marketing
Cablevision of New York
CBS Daytime
City Center New York
CSTV
Disney Publishing Worldwide; New York, NY
Fox News Channel
Fox News Radio
Kingfisher
Lifetime Networks
MYOB Software US, Inc.; Rockaway, NJ; 2000
National Geographic Channel; Washington, DC; 2000
NBC Cable Networks
NCTA
NFL Network
Penguin Young Readers Group
Showtime Networks
Soapnet
Style
Time Warner Cable
TV One
YES Network

M/PAKT

(Formerly Bergman Associates)
511 W 25th St Ste 804, New York, NY 10001
Tel.: (212) 645-1911
Fax: (212) 645-6226
E-Mail: contact@m-pakt.com
Web Site: www.m-pakt.com/

Employees: 15
Year Founded: 1991

Agency Specializes In: Cosmetics, Fashion/Apparel, Graphic Design

Revenue: $10,000,000

Robert Bergman *(Exec Dir-Creative)*

Accounts:
Alberta Ferretti
Council of Fashion Designers of America; New York, NY; 1997
Forum Jeans
L'Oreal; New York, NY Redken; 1998
Moda Inc.
Redken; New York, NY
Ryuichi Sakamoto
Shu Uemura
Unilever
Warner Bros. Records

M. SILVER ASSOCIATES INC. - PUBLIC RELATIONS

(Acquired by Finn Partners & Name Changed to M. Silver/A Division of Finn Partners)

M SS NG P ECES

68 Greenpoint Ave Ste 4, Brooklyn, NY 11222
Tel.: (646) 290-7931
E-Mail: contactus@mssngpeces.com
Web Site: www.mssngpeces.com

Year Founded: 2005

Agency Specializes In: Advertising

Ari Kuschnir *(Co-Founder, CEO & Exec Producer)*
Brian Latt *(Partner & Exec Producer)*
Kate Oppenheim *(Partner-Strategy & Exec Producer)*
Josh Nussbaum *(Partner & Dir)*
Dave Saltzman *(Head-Production)*
Jonathan Figueroa *(Mgr-Production)*

Accounts:
The Climate Reality Project
Intel
PepsiCo 7UP FREE, Campaign: "Feels Good to be You", Digital, Social Media, TV

M STUDIO

513C Bangs Ave, Asbury Park, NY 7712
Tel.: (732) 721-0890
E-Mail: info@mdidit.com
Web Site: www.mdidit.com

Year Founded: 2004

Agency Specializes In: Advertising, Brand Development & Integration, Event Planning & Marketing, Graphic Design, Internet/Web Design, Media Relations, Media Training, Public Relations, Search Engine Optimization, Social Media

Jenna Zilincar *(Owner & Creative Dir)*

Accounts:
New-Simple Shoes

M3 GROUP

614 Seymour Ave, Lansing, MI 48933
Tel.: (517) 203-3333
Fax: (517) 203-3334
Web Site: www.m3group.biz

Agency Specializes In: Advertising, Brand Development & Integration, Event Planning & Marketing, Graphic Design, Guerilla Marketing, Internet/Web Design, Media Buying Services, Public Relations, Social Media

Tiffany Dowling *(Pres & CEO)*
Jennifer Hodges *(VP-Bus Dev)*
Kelly Mazurkiewicz *(Dir-Mktg)*
Jeffrey Henry *(Acct Exec)*

Accounts:
New-Lansing Economic Area Partnership

M5 NEW HAMPSHIRE

(Formerly The Bedford Granite Group, Inc.)
707 Chestnut St, Manchester, NH 03104
Tel.: (603) 627-9600
Fax: (603) 627-9603
E-Mail: susan@m5nh.com

Web Site: www.m5.ca/

E-Mail for Key Personnel:
Media Dir.: susan@m5nh.com

Employees: 10
Year Founded: 1989

National Agency Associations: Second Wind Limited

Agency Specializes In: Advertising, Automotive, Brand Development & Integration, Broadcast, Business-To-Business, Co-op Advertising, Corporate Identity, Direct Response Marketing, E-Commerce, Electronic Media, Email, Event Planning & Marketing, Exhibit/Trade Shows, Financial, Health Care Services, Integrated Marketing, Market Research, Media Buying Services, Production (Ad, Film, Broadcast), Public Relations, Radio, T.V., Web (Banner Ads, Pop-ups, etc.)

Approx. Annual Billings: $9,100,000 Capitalized

Breakdown of Gross Billings by Media: Brdcst.: 29%; Bus. Publs.: 2%; D.M.: 9%; Fees: 14%; Internet Adv.: 2%; Mags.: 2%; Newsp.: 13%; Outdoor: 3%; Point of Purchase: 2%; Print: 7%; Production: 5%; Radio & T.V.: 9%; Transit: 3%

Karen Sears *(VP-Client Svcs)*
Maria Dauer *(Controller)*
Kristian Sumners *(Sr Dir-Creative)*
Vicki Murphy *(Dir-Creative)*
Andy Ploughman *(Dir-Creative)*
Jordan Walton *(Acct Exec)*

Accounts:
Centrix Bank; Bedford, NH; 1999
Courville Communities
Courville Community; Manchester, NH Assisted Living, Nursing Home; 1995
New Hampshire Association of Broadcasters; Bedford, NH Trade Association; 1974
Secondwind Water Systems

M8 AGENCY
(Formerly Media 8, Inc)
3301 NE 1st Ave Ste Ph6, Miami, FL 33137
Tel.: (786) 623-5500
Fax: (305) 675-8253
Web Site: m8agency.com/

Employees: 87
Year Founded: 2001

Agency Specializes In: Advertising, Below-the-Line, Brand Development & Integration, Digital/Interactive, Hispanic Market, Internet/Web Design, Market Research, Media Planning, Print, Search Engine Optimization

Revenue: $13,600,000

Sergio Barrientos *(Chief Strategy Officer)*
Joaquin Lira *(Chief Creative Officer)*
Daniel Almada *(VP & Grp Acct Dir)*
Tisha Costales *(VP-Client Svcs)*
Flavia Hakkers *(VP-Fin & Ops)*
Audel Alvarez *(Sr Dir-Art)*
Herman Grabosky *(Acct Dir)*
Marcelo Boasso *(Dir-Production)*
Mathew Kunkel *(Supvr-Media)*

Accounts:
Sony Corporation Campaign: "Beach Grenade", PlayStation

M80 SERVICES, INC.
3400 Cahuenga Blvd, Los Angeles, CA 90068
Tel.: (323) 436-6750
Fax: (323) 644-7801
E-Mail: info@m80im.com
Web Site: www.m80.com

Employees: 35

Agency Specializes In: Advertising, Guerilla Marketing, Internet/Web Design, Sponsorship, Viral/Buzz/Word of Mouth, Web (Banner Ads, Pop-ups, etc.)

Jeff Semones *(Pres)*
Todd Steinman *(CEO)*
Kieley Taylor *(Partner & Head-Paid Social)*
Amanda Grant *(Partner & Dir-Social Practice)*
Joe Muran *(Mng Dir)*

Accounts:
20th Century Fox
Ford
Microsoft
Warren & Bros

MA3 AGENCY
540 Broadway 5th Fl, New York, NY 10012
Tel.: (646) 291-6400
E-Mail: hello@ma3agency.com
Web Site: www.ma3agency.com

Agency Specializes In: Advertising, Brand Development & Integration, Event Planning & Marketing, Print, Public Relations, Social Media

Jason Lannert *(Co-Founder, Co-CEO, Chief Strategy Officer & Chief Brand Officer)*
Danielle Ferrazzano *(Dir-Activation-Energyfruits)*
Cyril Stanajic *(Dir-Brand Image & Creative)*
Elise Dicop *(Coord-Production)*

THE MAAC GROUP
333 Waltham St, Lexington, MA 2421
Tel.: (781) 862-1666
Fax: (781) 862-1666
Web Site: www.maacg.com

Agency Specializes In: Brand Development & Integration, Digital/Interactive, Email, Hospitality, Internet/Web Design, Media Relations, Public Relations, Search Engine Optimization, Sponsorship, Travel & Tourism

Melanie Alexander *(Founder)*
Robert Mansfield *(Dir-Creative)*
Marc Hoelscher *(Specialist-Internet Mktg)*

MAC STRATEGIES GROUP
53 W Jackson Blvd, Chicago, IL 60604
Tel.: (312) 588-4102
Fax: (312) 275-7501
E-Mail: info@macstrategiesgroup.com
Web Site: www.macstrategiesgroup.com

Agency Specializes In: Crisis Communications, Media Relations, Public Relations, Strategic Planning/Research

Ryan P. McLaughlin *(Pres)*
Cally C. Eckles *(COO)*
Matt Butterfield *(VP-Pub & Media Rels)*
Catie Sheehan *(Dir-Statehouse Media)*

Accounts:
The Chase Group Professional Recruiting Services
The Chicago Slaughter (Agency of Record)
Illinois Association of Regional Superintendents of Schools; Springfield, IL Campaign: "Restoring Pay to Illinois Regional Superintendents"
Trac Web Based Project Management Services
Woodfield Chicago Northwest Convention Bureau

MACDONALD MEDIA
1306 NW Hoyt St 204, Portland, OR 97209
Tel.: (971) 255-1150
Web Site: www.macdonaldmedia.com

Employees: 25
Year Founded: 1997

National Agency Associations: 4A's

Agency Specializes In: Above-the-Line

Andrea MacDonald *(Pres & CEO)*
David Koppelman *(Mng Dir)*
Stephen Faso *(Dir-Media)*
Peter Macdonald *(Dir-Ops)*
Kathie Wright Montague *(Dir-Media)*
Simone Davis *(Acct Supvr)*
Tamsen Brown *(Supvr-Media)*
Kevin McCabe *(Supvr-Media)*
Kristy Nichols *(Media Planner)*
Makenzi McSmith *(Acct Coord-Media)*
Donovan Zink *(Coord-Media)*

Accounts:
Alaska Airlines
Coffee Bean & Tea Leaf
Delivery.com
ESPN
Facebook
fitflop
Guess
KIND Snacks
Madison Square Garden
Meijer
Nike, Inc.
NY Knicks
NY Rangers
Old Spice
Oris Watches
Premier Exhibitions
Revlon Professional Brands
Roc Nation
Starbucks Coffee
Torrid
UCLA
Union Bank
Viacom
Vita Coco

MACDOUGALL BIOMEDICAL COMMUNICATIONS, INC.
888 Worcester St, Wellesley, MA 02482
Tel.: (781) 235-3060
Fax: (781) 235-3061
Web Site: www.macbiocom.com

Employees: 12

Agency Specializes In: Brand Development & Integration, Business-To-Business, Communications, Corporate Communications, Corporate Identity, Crisis Communications, Education, Email, Internet/Web Design, Investor Relations, Logo & Package Design, Media Relations, Medical Products, Print, Public Relations, Strategic Planning/Research

Douglas MacDougall *(Pres)*
Chris Erdman *(Sr VP)*
Kari M.L. Watson *(Sr VP)*
Heather Savelle *(VP)*
Michelle Avery *(Sr Acct Exec)*
Lynnea Olivarez *(Sr Acct Exec)*
Michelle Vaira *(Designer-Interactive)*

Accounts:
Acetylon Pharmaceuticals, Inc.
Epizyme, Inc.
Rheonix, Inc. Media

MACHINERY
10 N 3rd St 2nd Fl, Philadelphia, PA 19106

Tel.: (609) 410-6614
Web Site: www.machineryphilly.com

Agency Specializes In: Advertising

Ken Cills *(Founder)*
Kristian Summerer *(Principal & Dir-Creative)*
Paul Miller *(Dir-Accounts)*
Brynlee Griffin *(Acct Supvr)*

Accounts:
Auto Lenders Transit Center
Just Born, Inc. Goldenberg Peanut Chews
Newsday Media Group
Philadelphia Craft Show Branding, Collateral, Outdoor, TV, Web
University Medical Center of Princeton

MACK ADVERTISING INCORPORATED

617 1st Ave, Salt Lake City, UT 84103-3403
Tel.: (801) 328-3336
Fax: (801) 328-9898
E-Mail: mackadv@xmission.com

Employees: 2
Year Founded: 1983

Agency Specializes In: Recruitment

Approx. Annual Billings: $220,000

Breakdown of Gross Billings by Media: Newsp.: $220,000

Susan Mack *(Owner)*

MACLAREN MCCANN CANADA INC.

10 Bay St, Toronto, ON M5J 2S3 Canada
Tel.: (416) 594-6000
Fax: (416) 643-7027
E-Mail: newbiz@maclaren.com
Web Site: www.maclaren.com

Employees: 650
Year Founded: 1922

National Agency Associations: ABC-CBP-NYPAA

Agency Specializes In: Advertising

David Leonard *(CEO)*
Mary Chambers *(Chief Strategy Officer)*
Robyn Gorman *(Sr VP & Gen Mgr)*
Chris Munnik *(VP & Grp Dir-Creative)*
Josh Haupert *(VP & Dir-Creative)*
Ryan Timms *(VP & Dir-Client Svc)*
Sarah Michener *(VP & Mgr-Brdcst Production)*
Scott McKay *(VP & Planner-Strategic)*
Jonathan Careless *(Grp Dir-Creative)*
Joe Piccolo *(Grp Dir-Creative)*
Travis Sellar *(Grp Dir-Creative)*
Arron Isaac *(Sr Dir-Art)*
Rizwan Devji *(Grp Acct Dir)*
Sarah Lostracco *(Acct Dir)*
Emily MacLaurin-King *(Acct Dir)*
John Stevenson *(Acct Dir)*
Chad Burnie *(Dir-Art)*
Scott Johnson *(Dir-Creative)*
Rishi Gupta *(Acct Supvr)*
Adam Bercovici *(Acct Exec)*
Nadia Nauth *(Acct Exec)*
Erik Dela Cruz *(Copywriter)*
Gary Lennox *(Grp Creative Dir & Copywriter)*
Ann Solecki *(Designer)*
Natalie Greenspan *(Sr Writer)*

Accounts:
Andrew Murray Roofing
Angel Painting Co
Bayer CropScience
Canadian Film Centre
Carlson Wagonlit Travel (Media Only)
Coca-Cola Canada Ltd.
Dave Thomas Foundation Campaign: "The Story of I"
Developing World Connections Campaign: "Be More"
Earthbound Gardens
El Furniture Warehouse
Fading Fast Campaign: "Peel-off Tattoo Installation"
Freedom to Thrive Campaign: "Rorschach"
General Motors GMAC LLC, General Motors Acceptance Corp., General Motors Credit Card, General Motors Goodwrench Dealer Associations, General Motors Optimum Used Vehicles, General Motors Regional Marketing Advisory Board, General Motors of Canada
Johnson & Johnson Inc.
Labatt Breweries Media
Lotto Max Campaign: "Helicopter", Campaign: "House", Campaign: "Yacht"
Mastercard Canada Campaign: "#internswanted", Campaign: "Accepted", Campaign: "MasterCard's Stylicity", Campaign: "Priceless Surprises", Online
Microsoft Xbox Alan Wake Computer Game, Alan Wake Video Game, Campaign: "Gears of War 3 Butcher Shop"
New Brunswick Power
Novartis Pharmaceuticals Canada Inc.
PowerStream
RBC
Tourism Partnership of Niagara (Marketing Agency of Record) Advertising, Brand Strategy, Media Buying, Media Planning, Planning, Website
New-Trillium Gift of Life Network (Creative Agency of Record) Communications, Creative, Integrated Strategic
Vistakon
Wendy's Restaurants of Canada
Western Canada Lottery
Wind Mobile

Divisions

MacLaren McCann Direct (M2D)

10 Bay St, Toronto, ON M5J 2S3 Canada
Tel.: (416) 594-6000
Fax: (416) 64-3 7030
E-Mail: doug.turney@maclaren.com
Web Site: www.maclaren.com

Employees: 450

Agency Specializes In: Digital/Interactive

Doug Turney *(Pres & CEO)*
Andy Langs *(CTO & Sr VP)*
Mark Thompson *(Pres-MacLaren Momentum)*
Jenn Powell *(VP & Grp Acct Dir)*
Gerard Dolan *(VP & Dir-User Experience)*
Leena Patel *(VP & Dir-Innovation Tech & Performance)*
Ryan Timms *(VP & Dir-Client Svc)*
Mario Gelleny *(Dir-Art)*
Kevin Bryan *(Mgr-Desktop & Technical Support)*
Dee Robinson *(Mgr-Resource-Tech & Project Mgmt Office)*
Pamela De Petrillo *(Acct Supvr)*
Heather Fletcher *(Acct Supvr)*
Brendon Sargent *(Acct Supvr-Digital)*

Accounts:
General Motors
New-Royal Bank of Canada Retirement Designers

Branches

MacLaren McCann/Calgary

238 11 Ave SE Ste 100, Calgary, AB D2G 0X8 Canada
Tel.: (403) 269-6120
Fax: (403) 263-4634
E-Mail: ric.fedyna@maclaren.com
Web Site: www.maclaren.com

Employees: 30

Agency Specializes In: Advertising

Mark Thompson *(Pres-Momentum)*
Raelee Fedyna *(Sr VP & Gen Mgr-Calgary)*
Robyn Gorman *(Sr VP & Gen Mgr)*
Lindsey Feasby *(Sr VP & Dir-HR)*
Gerard Dolan *(VP & Dir-User Experience)*
Mike Meadus *(VP & Dir-Creative)*
Leena Patel *(VP & Dir-Innovation Tech & Performance)*
Ryan Timms *(VP & Dir-Client Svc)*
Peter Vaz *(VP & Dir-Channel Engagement)*
Kristen Landolfi *(Mgr-Trade Mktg)*
Brendan Marley *(Acct Supvr-Digital Ops)*

Accounts:
Buick
Fotolia #1 in Europe
GMC
MasterCard

MacLaren McCann Vancouver

100 W Pender St, Vancouver, BC V6B 1R8 Canada
(See Separate Listing)

Marketel

1100 Rene-Levesque Boulevard West 19th Floor, Montreal, QC H3B 4N4 Canada
(See Separate Listing)

MACLAREN MCCANN VANCOUVER

100 W Pender St, Vancouver, BC V6B 1R8 Canada
Tel.: (604) 689-1131
Fax: (604) 687-6955
Toll Free: (888) 330-1200
E-Mail: hagan.ainsworth@maclaren.com
Web Site: www.maclaren.com

Employees: 27
Year Founded: 1925

Agency Specializes In: Advertising, Advertising Specialties, Asian Market, Automotive, Brand Development & Integration, Broadcast, Business-To-Business, Co-op Advertising, Collateral, Communications, Consulting, Consumer Marketing, Consumer Publications, Corporate Identity, Direct Response Marketing, Event Planning & Marketing, In-Store Advertising, Internet/Web Design, Local Marketing, Logo & Package Design, Magazines, Media Buying Services, Merchandising, Newspaper, Newspapers & Magazines, Out-of-Home Media, Outdoor, Planning & Consultation, Point of Purchase, Point of Sale, Print, Production, Radio, Retail, Sales Promotion, Sports Market, Strategic Planning/Research, T.V., Trade & Consumer Magazines

Breakdown of Gross Billings by Media: Brdcst.: 20%; Mags.: 10%; Newsp.: 50%; Other: 5%; Out-of-Home Media: 5%; Radio: 10%

Ric Fedyna *(Sr VP & Gen Mgr)*
Rick Sanderson *(Sr VP & Gen Mgr)*
Stefanie Kraupa *(Dir-Media)*
Heather Thrash *(Dir-Creative)*

Accounts:
BC Transplant Society
Calona Vineyards Artist Series, Heritage, Sandhill
Canuck Place
Cathay Pacific

CDI College Campaign: "Set Change"
General Motors of Canada Ltd.; B.C. Zone
General Motors Regional Marketing Advertising Boards Buick, Cadillac, Chevrolet, GMC, Goodwrench, Oldsmobile, Pontiac
GM Telus Snowboard
H.R. MacMillan Space Centre
Hell Pizza Ouija
Sevenoaks

MACLYN GROUP

1985 Ohio St, Lisle, IL 60532
Tel.: (630) 852-2057
E-Mail: whoareyou@maclyngroup.com
Web Site: www.maclyngroup.com

Agency Specializes In: Advertising, Brand Development & Integration, Digital/Interactive, Event Planning & Marketing, Internet/Web Design, Logo & Package Design, Outdoor, Public Relations, Search Engine Optimization, Social Media

Bill Murphy *(Owner & Partner)*
Marc Hausmann *(Partner)*
Michael Naples *(Dir-Art)*
Jay Paonessa *(Dir-Creative)*
Jodi Bernicky *(Mgr-Social Media)*
Courtney Brown *(Acct Exec)*

Accounts:
Argus Brewery
Casey's Foods Inc.
Choose DuPage
Dunkin' Donuts

MACQUARIUM INTELLIGENT COMMUNICATIONS

1800 Peachtree St NW Ste 250, Atlanta, GA 30309
Tel.: (404) 554-4000
Fax: (404) 554-4001
E-Mail: info@macquarium.com
Web Site: www.macquarium.com

Employees: 120
Year Founded: 1992

Agency Specializes In: Consulting, Digital/Interactive, Internet/Web Design, Sponsorship, Technical Advertising

Marc F. Adler *(Chm)*
Peter Forsstrom *(COO)*
Jay Cann *(CTO)*
Don Brazil *(VP-Client Engagement)*
Robert Criscione *(VP-Client Engagement)*
Julie Hadden *(VP-Experience Strategy)*
Sharon Carter *(Dir-Experience Design)*
Anja Huebler *(Dir-Creative)*
Stephen Perry *(Dir-Experience Strategy & Design)*
Justin Reilly *(Dir-Experience Strategy)*
Amanda Flashner *(Mgr-Studio)*

Accounts:
AGL Resources
AT&T Communications Corp.
Atlanta Gas Light Company
Atlanta Sports Council
ATS
Bayor Health Care System
The Center for Puppetry Arts
Coca-Cola Refreshments USA, Inc.
Delta Air Lines
Earthlink
Emory University
Executive Wealth Management (EWM)
Georgia Institute of Technology
The Home Depot
HSBC
IBM
Lufthansa
Mastercard
Media Play
Randstad North America
The State of Florida
Suncoast Motion Picture Co.
Turner
United Way
UPS
Yahoo!

MACRO COMMUNICATIONS

9851 Irvine Center Dr, Irvine, CA 92618
Tel.: (949) 940-6037
Fax: (949) 261-8866
E-Mail: info@macrocommunications.com
Web Site: www.macrocommunications.com

Employees: 7
Year Founded: 1987

Agency Specializes In: Advertising, Brand Development & Integration, Collateral, Consulting, Content, Corporate Identity, Digital/Interactive, Direct Response Marketing, Direct-to-Consumer, E-Commerce, Electronic Media, Email, Graphic Design, Internet/Web Design, Local Marketing, Logo & Package Design, Mobile Marketing, Multimedia, New Technologies, Package Design, Paid Searches, Point of Purchase, Point of Sale, Print, Production, Search Engine Optimization, Social Media, Sports Market, Strategic Planning/Research, Viral/Buzz/Word of Mouth, Web (Banner Ads, Pop-ups, etc.)

Patty Carran *(Owner & Dir-Art)*
Kristi Grant *(Sr Graphic Designer)*

Accounts:
Lexus
Mazda
Serface; Rancho Santa Margarita, CA; 2005
Toyota

MACROHYPE

32 Broadway, New York, NY 10004
Tel.: (415) 645-3572
Web Site: www.MacroHype.com

Employees: 6
Year Founded: 2009

Agency Specializes In: Digital/Interactive, Search Engine Optimization, Shopper Marketing

Rehman Siddiq *(CEO)*

Accounts:
Himont Pharmaceutical Ferplex; 2010

MACY + ASSOCIATES INC.

411 Culver Blvd, Los Angeles, CA 90293-7705
Tel.: (310) 821-5300
Fax: (310) 821-8178
E-Mail: kmacy@macyinc.com
Web Site: www.macyinc.com

E-Mail for Key Personnel:
Creative Dir.: kmacy@macyinc.com
Media Dir.: jhalloran@macyinc.com

Employees: 11
Year Founded: 1989

National Agency Associations: 4A's

Agency Specializes In: Brand Development & Integration, Communications, Corporate Communications, Exhibit/Trade Shows, Financial, Government/Political, Industrial, Investor Relations, Logo & Package Design, Newspaper, Newspapers & Magazines, Public Relations, Real Estate, Sponsorship, Strategic Planning/Research

Approx. Annual Billings: $1,000,000

John Halloran *(Dir-Creative Svcs)*
Natalie Weiner *(Acct Coord-PR)*

Accounts:
1100 Wilshire
Amstar
Goodwin Procter LLP; Century City, CA; 2007
Granite Park, Pasadena
Shea Properties

Branch

Macy + Associates Inc.

1750 Montgomery St, San Francisco, CA 94111
Tel.: (415) 954-8550
Fax: (415) 954-8598
E-Mail: kmacy@macyinc.com
Web Site: www.macyinc.com

Employees: 15
Year Founded: 1991

Agency Specializes In: Advertising, Brand Development & Integration, Communications, Electronic Media, Graphic Design, Public Relations

Kimberly Macy *(Pres)*
John Halloran *(Dir-Creative Svcs)*

Accounts:
Buchanan Street Partners
Jefferies & Company

MAD 4 MARKETING

5203 NW 33rd Ave, Fort Lauderdale, FL 33309-6302
Tel.: (954) 485-5448
Fax: (954) 485-5410
E-Mail: info@mad4marketing.com
Web Site: www.mad4marketing.com

E-Mail for Key Personnel:
President: chris@mad4marketing.com

Employees: 14
Year Founded: 1992

National Agency Associations: AAF-AMA-DMA

Agency Specializes In: Advertising, Advertising Specialties, Brand Development & Integration, Broadcast, Business-To-Business, Cable T.V., Children's Market, Collateral, College, Communications, Consumer Marketing, Corporate Identity, Digital/Interactive, Direct Response Marketing, E-Commerce, Event Planning & Marketing, Exhibit/Trade Shows, Gay & Lesbian Market, Graphic Design, Guerilla Marketing, Health Care Services, Internet/Web Design, Leisure, Local Marketing, Logo & Package Design, Magazines, Marine, Media Buying Services, Media Planning, Medical Products, New Product Development, Newspaper, Newspapers & Magazines, Out-of-Home Media, Outdoor, Package Design, Planning & Consultation, Point of Purchase, Point of Sale, Print, Production, Production (Print), Public Relations, Publicity/Promotions, Radio, Real Estate, Recruitment, Restaurant, Retail, Sales Promotion, Search Engine Optimization, Strategic Planning/Research, T.V., Transportation, Travel & Tourism, Viral/Buzz/Word of Mouth

Approx. Annual Billings: $5,000,000

Christine Madsen *(Pres & CEO)*
Elyse Taylor *(VP)*
Brianna O'Connor *(Acct Mgr)*
Laura Pierson *(Sr Strategist-Acct)*

Accounts:
Altman Management Company; Boca Raton, FL Real Estate; 2008
Baptist Outpatient Services; Miami, FL Healthcare; 1997
Broward College; Fort Lauderdale, FL; 2002
East Coast Jewelry
Fishing Hall of Frame & Museum
Phoenix Physicians, LLC
Purigen; Sunrise, FL Nitrogen; 2006
Regent Bank; Fort Lauderdale, FL; 2005
Ulysse Nardin; Boca Raton, FL Watches; 1999
Westrec Marinas; Encino, CA; 2004

MAD DOGS & ENGLISHMEN
363 17th St, Oakland, CA 94612
Tel.: (510) 251-0402
E-Mail: info@maddogsandenglishmen.com
Web Site: www.maddogsandenglishmen.com

Year Founded: 1991

Agency Specializes In: Advertising, Digital/Interactive

Nick Cohen *(Exec Creative Dir)*
Jon Soto *(Exec Creative Dir)*

Accounts:
Brickstr
City Center at Bishop Ranch
Rock Creek Vineyard

MAD GENIUS
279 S Perkins St, Ridgeland, MS 39157
Tel.: (601) 605-6234
Fax: (601) 605-2121
Web Site: www.madg.com

Year Founded: 2005

Agency Specializes In: Advertising, Brand Development & Integration, Digital/Interactive, Print, Social Media, T.V.

Chip Sarver *(Pres)*
Rob Bridges *(Sr VP-Branding & Strategy)*
Eric Hughes *(VP & Dir-Creative)*
Monte Kraus *(Mgr-Production & Sr Producer)*
Ash Taylor *(Sr Producer)*
Frank Owen *(Dir-Social Media & Strategist-Brand)*
Ryan Farmer *(Dir-Interactive Creative)*
Pshone Grace *(Dir-Media)*
Paul Povolni *(Assoc Dir-Creative)*
Kim Sykes *(Mgr-Production)*
Brent Hearn *(Copywriter)*

Accounts:
Roman Catholic Diocese of Jackson
Ronald McDonald House Charities of Mississippi
Seafood Revolution

MAD MEN MARKETING INC.
111 E Bay St Ste 201, Jacksonville, FL 32202
Tel.: (904) 355-1766
E-Mail: support@madmenmarketinginc.com
Web Site: www.madmenmarketinginc.com

Year Founded: 2008

Agency Specializes In: Advertising, Brand Development & Integration, Media Buying Services, Media Planning, Search Engine Optimization

Ryan Blair *(COO)*
Justin DeStefano *(VP & Dir-Production)*
Shannon Mayhugh *(VP-Reg Accounts)*
J. D. Blair *(Dir-Mktg)*
Andy Leyva *(Mgr-Accts)*

Accounts:
Garber Automall

MADDASH E-MEDIA
800 W Cummings Pk Ste 2800, Woburn, MA 01801
Tel.: (781) 935-0015
Fax: (800) 919-0017
Toll Free: (866) MADDASH
E-Mail: shannon.price@maddash.net
Web Site: www.maddash.net

Employees: 22
Year Founded: 2000

National Agency Associations: AMA

Agency Specializes In: Brand Development & Integration, Broadcast, Consulting, Corporate Identity, E-Commerce, Electronic Media, Exhibit/Trade Shows, Internet/Web Design, Multimedia, Production, Recruitment, T.V.

Approx. Annual Billings: $2,500,000

David Grainger, Jr. *(Co-Founder & Mng Partner)*
Shannon Price *(Mng Partner)*

MADDEN BRAND AGENCY
116 S Tennessee Ave Ste 201, Lakeland, FL 33801
Tel.: (863) 248-0822
Web Site: www.brandmadden.com

Agency Specializes In: Advertising, Brand Development & Integration, Collateral, Digital/Interactive, Logo & Package Design, Outdoor, Print, Social Media

Michelle Ledford *(Pres)*
Greg Madden *(Principal)*
Steve Madden *(Principal)*
Jim Battista *(Art Dir)*
Allen Reed *(Creative Dir)*
Mike McLaughlin *(Dir-Digital Strategy)*
Cindy Joyce *(Mgr-Production Design)*

Accounts:
Bank of Central Florida
Florida United Methodist Foundation

MADDOCK DOUGLAS, INC.
111 Adell Pl, Elmhurst, IL 60126
Tel.: (630) 279-3939
Fax: (630) 279-0553
Toll Free: (800) 988-6780
E-Mail: info@maddockdouglas.com
Web Site: www.maddockdouglas.com

Employees: 65
Year Founded: 1991

Agency Specializes In: Advertising, Advertising Specialties, Brand Development & Integration, Business-To-Business, Collateral, Communications, Consulting, Consumer Marketing, Corporate Identity, Digital/Interactive, Direct Response Marketing, E-Commerce, Event Planning & Marketing, Exhibit/Trade Shows, Graphic Design, In-Store Advertising, Internet/Web Design, Local Marketing, Logo & Package Design, Media Buying Services, New Product Development, Out-of-Home Media, Outdoor, Point of Purchase, Point of Sale, Print, Production, Public Relations, Publicity/Promotions, Radio, Real Estate, Recruitment, Retail, Sales Promotion, Strategic Planning/Research

Wes Douglas *(Partner & Exec VP-Innovation)*
Luisa Uriarte *(Partner & Exec VP-Innovation)*
Raphael Louis Viton *(Partner)*
Jerry Leiby *(VP & Principal-Engagement)*
Gino Chirio *(Sr VP-Engagements)*
John Coyle *(Sr VP-Innovation)*
Doug Stone *(Sr VP-Innovation)*
Cindy Kellogg Malone *(VP-Innovation)*
Randy Simms *(VP-Innovation Experience Design)*
Maria Ferrante-Schepis *(Mng Principal-Insurance & Fin Svcs)*

Accounts:
Culligan
DuPont
LG/Zenith Consumer Electronics
Purina
S.C. Johnson
Shure, Inc.
Talaris, Inc.
Verizon
Wise Foods Snack Foods

MADDOCKS
2011 Pontius Ave, Los Angeles, CA 90025
Tel.: (310) 477-4227
Fax: (310) 479-5767
E-Mail: frank@maddocks.com
Web Site: http://maddocksvenice.com/

Employees: 10

Agency Specializes In: Advertising, Identity Marketing, Logo & Package Design, Merchandising, Package Design

Revenue: $5,000,000

Frank Maddocks *(Pres)*
Robert DeSantis *(Pres-Transactional Mktg)*

Accounts:
Coca-Cola Refreshments USA, Inc.
Estee Lauder
Ketel One
Procter & Gamble
Red Bull
The Venetian Hotel

MADE MOVEMENT LLC
2206 Pearl St, Boulder, CO 80302
Tel.: (720) 420-9840
E-Mail: hello@mademovement.com
Web Site: www.mademovement.com

Year Founded: 2012

Agency Specializes In: Advertising, Brand Development & Integration, Sponsorship

Dave Schiff *(Partner & Chief Creative Officer)*
John Kieselhorst *(Partner)*
Dave Moore *(VP-Mobile Architecture)*
Steve Dolan *(Creative Dir)*
Becky Herman *(Acct Dir)*
Marybeth Ledesma *(Art Dir)*
Mariela Rueda *(Dir-Creative & Art)*
Myles Rigg *(Acct Mgr)*
Malory Toscano *(Acct Mgr)*
Heather Barranco *(Strategist)*
David Castellanos *(Sr Writer)*

Accounts:
Church's Chicken (Agency of Record) Digital, Packaging, Point-of-Sale, Radio, TV
Clayton Homes, Inc. (Marketing Agency of Record) Advertising, Clayton Built, Digital, Strategy
Copper Mountain
Evol Foods
New-Lyft Creative
Mozilla
New Belgium Brewing Company, Inc.
Pangea
Repair.com
Seventh Generation, Inc.

T.G.I. Friday's Inc. (Digital, Creative & Technology Agency of Record) Campaign: "Unionize", Digital Content, Online, Social, Social Media, TV
Vegas.com
Walmart

MADISON + MAIN

101 E Cary St, Richmond, VA 23219
Tel.: (804) 521-4141
Fax: (804) 521-4140
Toll Free: (877) 623-6246
E-Mail: shout@madisonmain.com
Web Site: www.madisonmain.com

Employees: 10
Year Founded: 2005

Agency Specializes In: Advertising, Advertising Specialties, Affiliate Marketing, Brand Development & Integration, Broadcast, Cable T.V., Collateral, College, Communications, Consulting, Consumer Goods, Consumer Marketing, Corporate Communications, Corporate Identity, Crisis Communications, Digital/Interactive, Direct Response Marketing, Direct-to-Consumer, E-Commerce, Electronics, Email, Event Planning & Marketing, Graphic Design, Guerilla Marketing, Health Care Services, Hospitality, Identity Marketing, In-Store Advertising, Local Marketing, Logo & Package Design, Market Research, Media Buying Services, Media Planning, Media Relations, Medical Products, Merchandising, Multimedia, New Technologies, Newspaper, Newspapers & Magazines, Outdoor, Paid Searches, Point of Purchase, Point of Sale, Print, Production, Production (Ad, Film, Broadcast), Production (Print), Promotions, Public Relations, Publicity/Promotions, Radio, Retail, Sales Promotion, Search Engine Optimization, Social Marketing/Nonprofit, Strategic Planning/Research

David Saunders *(Pres & Chief Idea Officer)*
Kara Forbis *(VP-Brand Strategy)*
Molly Quarles *(VP-Ops)*
Scott Harris *(Dir-Art & Producer)*
Renita Wade *(Dir-Art)*
Lindsey Durfee *(Acct Mgr)*

Accounts:
Advanced Wellness Centre
Commonwealth Autism
CowanGates
Davis & Green Electrical
The Dragas Group
First Bank
The Lightning Protection Institute
Lucy Corr Village & Springdale at Lucy Corr
The National MS Society
R.A.M.P.S.
Shenandoah Valley Music Festival
Silverback Distillery
Vera's Fine Jewelers
Village Bank
The Virginia Aeronautical Historical Society
Virginia Women's Center
World's Best Cheesecake
Yard Works

MADISON & FIFTH

5 E Long St 8th Fl, Columbus, OH 43215
Tel.: (614) 246-7777
Web Site: www.madisonandfifth.com

Year Founded: 2000

Agency Specializes In: Advertising, Digital/Interactive, Social Media

Chris Shirer *(Pres & CEO)*
Kathy Hart *(Dir-Art)*

Accounts:
Black Falls Natural Angus
Dublin Arts Council
Grandview Yard
Hilton Marco Island
Latitude 41
Mall Properties, Inc.
New Albany Community Foundation
Piada Italian Street Food
Riverboxes
The Wine Bistro

THE MADISON GROUP

1775 Broadway, New York, NY 10019
Tel.: (212) 915-9900
Fax: (212) 210-4340

National Agency Associations: 4A's

Agency Specializes In: Advertising, Graphic Design, Technical Advertising

Michael Romanski *(COO)*

Accounts:
Abbott Laboratories
Citibank N.A.
The Coca-Cola Company
Colgate-Palmolive Company
The Dannon Company, Inc.
Dell Inc.
Diageo North America, Inc.
Microsoft Corporation
Xerox Corporation

MADWELL

243 Boerum St, Brooklyn, NY 11206
Tel.: (347) 713-7486
E-Mail: info@madwellnyc.com
Web Site: www.madwell.com

Agency Specializes In: Advertising, Multimedia

Chris Sojka *(Co-Founder & Dir-Creative)*
David Eisenman *(Co-Founder & Sr Strategist)*
Berto Aguayo *(Producer-Creative)*
Ricky Schweitzer *(Acct Mgr)*
Kate Hannum *(Sr Strategist-Social)*
Lee Benedict *(Designer)*
Matt Fry *(Sr Designer)*
Ana Meza *(Designer)*
Jacob Smiley *(Designer)*
Olena Subchuk *(Designer)*
Allison Supron *(Designer)*
Laura Wasson *(Copywriter)*

Accounts:
All Market, Inc. Vita Coco
New-Babyganics
New-Happy Family
Kind Healthy Snacks
Mamatini
New-New York Botanical Garden Digital
New-Union Square Hospitality Group

MAGIC DOG CREATIVE

477 Madison Ave 2nd Fl Ste 1, New York, NY 10022
Tel.: (347) 508-1080
E-Mail: contact@magicdogcreative.com
Web Site: www.magicdogcreative.com

Year Founded: 2012

Agency Specializes In: Advertising, Collateral, Content, Digital/Interactive, Graphic Design, Media Buying Services, Print, Search Engine Optimization, Social Media, Strategic Planning/Research

Grace Didato *(CFO)*

Accounts:
Ausanil

MAGIC JOHNSON ENTERPRISES

9100 Wilshire Blvd Ste 700 E Tower, Beverly Hills, CA 90212
Tel.: (310) 246-4400
Fax: (310) 786-8796
E-Mail: info@magicjent.com
Web Site: www.magicjohnson.com

Employees: 25

Agency Specializes In: Advertising, African-American Market, Asian Market, Hispanic Market, Multicultural

Earvin 'Magic' Johnson *(Chm & CEO)*
Kawanna Brown *(COO)*
Gerald E. Johnson, II *(CMO)*
Christina Francis *(Sr VP-Mktg)*
Sheila Ewing *(VP-Fin & Ops)*
Shane Jenkins *(VP)*
Chris Morrow *(Dir-Strategic Alliances)*
Ryan L. Smith *(Dir-Investments)*

Accounts:
Aetna
Best Buy
TNT

MAGNA GLOBAL

100 W 33rd St 9th Fl, New York, NY 10001
Tel.: (212) 883-4751
E-Mail: press@magnaglobal.com
Web Site: www.magnaglobal.com

National Agency Associations: 4A's

Agency Specializes In: Strategic Planning/Research

David Cohen *(Pres)*
Ethan Chamberlin *(Sr VP-Programmatic)*
Brian Hughes *(Sr VP-Audience Analysis)*
Saqib Mausoof *(Sr VP-Programmatic Insights & Plng)*
Vin Paolozzi *(Sr VP-Marketplace Dev & Investment)*
Steven Kaufman *(VP-Programmatic)*
Stewart Roberts *(VP-Advanced TV)*
Dani Benowitz *(Dir-Investment)*
Lisa Markou *(Assoc Dir & Specialist-Programmatic)*
Peter Liao *(Assoc Dir-Advanced TV)*

MAGNANI CARUSO DUTTON

138 W 25th St, New York, NY 10001
Tel.: (212) 500-4500
E-Mail: info@mcdpartners.com
Web Site: www.mcdpartners.com

Employees: 65

Agency Specializes In: Advertising, Alternative Advertising, Below-the-Line, Brand Development & Integration, Business-To-Business, Children's Market, Communications, Consumer Goods, Consumer Marketing, Content, Cosmetics, Customer Relationship Management, Digital/Interactive, Direct Response Marketing, Direct-to-Consumer, E-Commerce, Electronic Media, Electronics, Email, Entertainment, Experience Design, Fashion/Apparel, Financial, Graphic Design, Household Goods, Information Technology, Internet/Web Design, Leisure, Logo & Package Design, Luxury Products, Magazines, Mobile Marketing, Multimedia, New Technologies, Paid Searches, Podcasting, Production (Print), Publishing, RSS (Really Simple Syndication), Search Engine Optimization, Social Marketing/Nonprofit, Strategic Planning/Research,

Trade & Consumer Magazines, Travel & Tourism, Viral/Buzz/Word of Mouth, Web (Banner Ads, Pop-ups, etc.)

Approx. Annual Billings: $38,500,000

Breakdown of Gross Billings by Media: E-Commerce: $4,000,000; Graphic Design: $2,000,000; Internet Adv.: $13,500,000; Worldwide Web Sites: $19,000,000

David Eastman *(Mng Partner)*
John Caruso *(Partner & Dir-Creative)*
Wasim Choudhury *(Partner)*
John Dutton *(Partner)*
Bruce Ginsberg *(Sr VP-Bus Dev Digital)*
Scott Immerman *(Grp Acct Dir-Digital)*
Beth Irvin *(Acct Dir)*
James Warren *(Dir-Digital Intelligence & QA)*
Hannah Wurzel *(Strategist-Digital)*

Accounts:
A&E Television A&E.com
Advance Me AdvanceMe.com
AT&T Communications Corp. AT&T.com
Capitol One CapitalOne.com
CIT Group CIT.com
Discover Financial Services Discover.com
Sesame Workshop SesameStreet.com, Sesameworkshop.com
Tiffany & Co. Tiffany.com

MAGNANI CONTINUUM MARKETING
200 South Michigan Ave Ste 500, Chicago, IL 60604
Tel.: (312) 957-0770
Fax: (312) 957-0457
E-Mail: contact_us@magnani.com
Web Site: www.magnani.com

E-Mail for Key Personnel:
President: rudy@magnani.com

Employees: 43
Year Founded: 1985

National Agency Associations: AMA-PRSA

Agency Specializes In: Advertising, Advertising Specialties, Brand Development & Integration, Broadcast, Business-To-Business, Collateral, Communications, Consulting, Consumer Marketing, Corporate Communications, Corporate Identity, Digital/Interactive, Direct Response Marketing, E-Commerce, Education, Entertainment, Event Planning & Marketing, Exhibit/Trade Shows, Fashion/Apparel, Financial, Graphic Design, Health Care Services, High Technology, Hospitality, Internet/Web Design, Leisure, Logo & Package Design, Magazines, Market Research, Medical Products, Merchandising, Multimedia, New Product Development, Newspaper, Newspapers & Magazines, Outdoor, Planning & Consultation, Point of Purchase, Print, Production, Public Relations, Publicity/Promotions, Radio, Restaurant, Retail, Sales Promotion, Sports Market, Strategic Planning/Research, T.V., Trade & Consumer Magazines, Travel & Tourism

Justin Daab *(Pres)*
Felicia Stanczak *(Mng Partner & COO)*
Brian Riley *(Mng Partner & Exec Dir-Creative)*
Ted Hoagland *(CFO)*
Corey Gutwillig *(Dir-Bus Dev)*
Gail Straus *(Dir-Res)*

Accounts:
CME Group; Chicago, IL Derivatives Exchange; 2005
CNA Insurance; Chicago, IL; 2002
Marriott International, Inc. ; Bethesda, MD Hotel/Lodging; 2005
New-Oil-Dri Corporation of America Cat's Pride (Advertising & Marketing Agency of Record)

MAGNER SANBORN
111 N Post Ste 400, Spokane, WA 99201
Tel.: (509) 688-2200
Fax: (509) 688-2299
E-Mail: dmagner@magnersanborn.com
Web Site: www.magnersanborn.com

Employees: 14
Year Founded: 2003

Agency Specializes In: Advertising, Brand Development & Integration, Collateral, Consumer Marketing, Corporate Identity, Exhibit/Trade Shows, Graphic Design, Logo & Package Design, Merchandising, Newspaper, Newspapers & Magazines, Out-of-Home Media, Outdoor, Point of Purchase, Point of Sale, Print

Dennis Magner *(Owner)*
Jeff Sanborn *(Partner & Exec Dir-Creative)*
Brandt Heinemann *(Partner)*
Deanna Hildenbrand *(Acct Dir)*
Scott Anderson *(Dir-Creative)*
Roxy Boone *(Dir-Ops)*
Delaney Nye *(Assoc Dir-Creative)*
Teresa Leighton *(Acct Exec)*

Accounts:
Amtrak
Boost Mobile
Cascades
City of Spokane Parks & Recreation
Eastern Washington University
Gonzaga University
Mario & Son
Sony Pictures Television
Tomlinson
Vaagen

MAGNETIC IMAGE INC.
401 E Indiana, Evansville, IN 47711
Tel.: (812) 423-6088
Fax: (812) 423-7488
Web Site: www.videomi.com

Agency Specializes In: Advertising, Brand Development & Integration, Graphic Design, Internet/Web Design, Media Buying Services, Print, Radio, Social Media

David Jones *(Pres & Dir-Mktg)*
Chris Blair *(VP & Creative Dir)*

Accounts:
HealthSouth Corporation

MAGNETO BRAND ADVERTISING
71 SW Oak St Ste 3N, Portland, OR 97204
Tel.: (503) 222-7477
Fax: (503) 222-7737
E-Mail: info@magnetoworks.com
Web Site: www.magnetoworks.com

Year Founded: 2001

Agency Specializes In: Advertising, Brand Development & Integration, Digital/Interactive, Logo & Package Design, Media Buying Services, Print, Radio, Strategic Planning/Research, T.V.

Craig Opfer *(Owner & Dir-Creative)*
Paul Landaker *(Acct Dir)*
Adom Balcom *(Designer)*
Justina Quagliata *(Acct Coord)*

Accounts:
Northwest Natural Gas Company
Portland International Raceway

MAGNIFICENT MARKETING LLC
511 w 41st St, Austin, TX 78751
Tel.: (512) 777-9539
Web Site: www.magnificent.com

Agency Specializes In: Advertising, Brand Development & Integration, Paid Searches, Print, Search Engine Optimization, Social Media

Steve Viner *(Dir-Mktg)*

Accounts:
New-Sealy Eye Center

MAGNIFY360
5757 W Century Blvd, Los Angeles, CA 90045
Tel.: (866) 861-8878
Fax: (310) 861-8878
Toll Free: (855) 462-4360
E-Mail: info@magnify360.com
Web Site: my.magnify360.com

Employees: 15

Agency Specializes In: Advertising, Internet/Web Design

Olivier Chaine *(Sr VP-Landing Page Optimization-Magnify360 Div)*
Karl Kleinschrodt *(Sr Acct Mgr)*
Treacy Seeley *(Sr Acct Mgr)*
Jay Hayward *(Mgr-Client Success & Engr-Sls)*

Accounts:
Citrix Systems
Continental Warranty
Rhino Marketing, Inc.

MAGNOLIA COMMUNICATIONS
(Formerly Magnolia Marketing Communications)
988 Sauve Ct, North Vancouver, BC V7K 3C8 Canada
Tel.: (604) 760-3085
E-Mail: info@magnoliamc.com
Web Site: www.magnoliamc.com

Employees: 20
Year Founded: 2005

Agency Specializes In: Advertising, Collateral, Digital/Interactive, Event Planning & Marketing, Internet/Web Design, Local Marketing, Media Relations, Public Relations, Publishing

Phoebe Yong *(Principal)*
Kristina Lee *(Head-Client Svcs)*
Jina You *(Sr Dir-Comm)*
Kelly Choi *(Coord-Mktg Comm)*

Accounts:
Fincad
Verrus Mobile Technologies

MAGNUM CREATIVE INC.
807 Powell Street, Vancouver, BC V6A 1H7 Canada
Tel.: (604) 628-7637
Web Site: www.magnumcreative.ca

Year Founded: 2007

Agency Specializes In: Advertising, Brand Development & Integration, Digital/Interactive, Mobile Marketing, Search Engine Optimization, Social Media

Malcolm Ellis *(Founder & Partner)*
Brett Duzita *(Strategist-Digital)*

Accounts:

Diveidc

MAGNUSON DESIGN
1890 E Mortimer Dr, Boise, ID 83712
Tel.: (208) 869-6279
E-Mail: creative@magnusondesign.com
Web Site: www.magnusondesign.com

Agency Specializes In: Advertising, Brand Development & Integration, Corporate Identity, Internet/Web Design, Logo & Package Design, Print

Brett Magnuson *(Owner & Dir-Creative)*

Accounts:
Curt Faus Corp
Givens Pursley
McCall Landscapes & Design
National Vehicle Leasing Association
Tucker & Associates

MAIDEN MEDIA GROUP LLC
130 N 2nd St, Philadelphia, PA 19106
Tel.: (212) 586-3603
Toll Free: (877) 962-4336
Web Site: www.maidenmediagroup.com

Agency Specializes In: Advertising, Digital/Interactive, Game Integration, Mobile Marketing, Social Media

Zain Haseeb *(Co-Founder & Dir-Bus Dev)*

Accounts:
Acqueon Technologies Inc Management Services
America's Mortgage University Educational Services
Energy & Utility Services Website
ForeSite Commercial Realty (Agency of Record) Logo, Website
Healthcare Synergies LLC Healthcare Insurance Services
Johanna Foods, Inc. Campaign: "The Bottomless Cup: A Year of La Yogurt Probiotic Giveaways", Digital, La Yogurt Probiotic, Online Marketing, Social Media Strategy

MAIER ADVERTISING, INC.
1789 New Britain Ave, Farmington, CT 06032-3317
Tel.: (860) 677-4581
Fax: (860) 677-4898
E-Mail: agency@maier.com
Web Site: www.maier.com

E-Mail for Key Personnel:
President: bill@maier.com
Production Mgr.: kim@maier.com
Public Relations: harry@maier.com

Employees: 17
Year Founded: 1971

National Agency Associations: PRSA

Agency Specializes In: Advertising, Brand Development & Integration, Business Publications, Business-To-Business, Collateral, Communications, Consulting, Corporate Communications, Corporate Identity, Direct Response Marketing, Electronic Media, Event Planning & Marketing, Exhibit/Trade Shows, Graphic Design, High Technology, Industrial, Information Technology, Integrated Marketing, Internet/Web Design, Logo & Package Design, Media Buying Services, Media Planning, Media Relations, Multimedia, Pharmaceutical, Planning & Consultation, Point of Purchase, Point of Sale, Print, Production, Production (Print), Public Relations, Publicity/Promotions, Sales Promotion, Sponsorship, Strategic Planning/Research, Technical Advertising, Trade & Consumer Magazines, Web (Banner Ads, Pop-ups, etc.)

Breakdown of Gross Billings by Media: Bus. Publs.: 12%; Collateral: 15%; Corp. Communications: 8%; Graphic Design: 20%; Internet Adv.: 15%; Logo & Package Design: 5%; Print: 10%; Pub. Rels.: 5%; Strategic Planning/Research: 10%

Laura Kennedy *(VP-Fin)*
Rick Mellon *(VP-Creative)*
Brian Connolly *(Client Svcs Dir)*
Bob Dully *(Dir-Art & Designer)*
Bryan Johnson *(Dir-Art)*
Kim Turgeon *(Mgr-Production & Acct Coord)*
Jeff Doemland *(Strategist-Mktg)*

Accounts:
Agilent Technologies
Bridgeport Fittings; Bridgeport, CT Electrical Products; 2004
CIGNA HealthCare
GE Energy; Atlanta, GA Distribution of Power, Smart Grid Technology Products, Solutions for Transmission; 2008
Gexpro; Shelton, CT Electrical & Electronic Products; 1993
Hubbell Inc.; Orange, CT Electrical Products; 2003
Innovative Medical Products
The Lee Company
Mott Corporation; Farmington, CT Filter Media; 1994
Regan Technologies; Wallingford, CT IT Systems Integrator; 2008
TRUMPF

MAIN IDEAS
26485 482nd Ave, Brandon, SD 57005
Tel.: (605) 582-7800
Fax: (605) 582-8922
E-Mail: info@mainideas.com
Web Site: www.mainideas.com

Employees: 3
Year Founded: 1992

National Agency Associations: Second Wind Limited

Agency Specializes In: Advertising, Brand Development & Integration, Business-To-Business, Consumer Marketing

Approx. Annual Billings: $900,000

Lisa Peterson *(Owner)*
Steve Peterson *(Co-Owner)*

Accounts:
Girl Scouts Dakota Horizons
Hurco Industries
Raven Industries, Inc.
Spader Companies
Statistical Surveys Inc.
Vision Care Associates
Western Industries, Inc.

MAIZE MARKETING INC.
17003 Ventura Blvd Ste 202, Encino, CA 91316
Tel.: (818) 849-5114
E-Mail: info@maizemarketing.com
Web Site: www.maizemarketing.com

Year Founded: 2004

Agency Specializes In: Advertising, Content, Internet/Web Design, Logo & Package Design, Print, Public Relations, Social Media

Kevin Friedman *(Pres)*
Tory Hinton *(Mgr-Mktg & PR)*

Accounts:
Association for Science in Autism Treatment
Louroe Electronics
Pacifica First National Bank
Restricted Shoes
Schwartz & Shapiro LLP

MAKAI
211 Nevada St, El Segundo, CA 90245
Tel.: (310) 546-9585
Fax: (310) 321-7933
E-Mail: info@makaievents.com
Web Site: makaiinc.com

Employees: 10
Year Founded: 1995

Agency Specializes In: Brand Development & Integration, College, Corporate Communications, Entertainment, Event Planning & Marketing, Guerilla Marketing, Integrated Marketing, Internet/Web Design, Local Marketing, Merchandising, Mobile Marketing, Multicultural, Package Design, Production (Print), Regional, Retail, Sales Promotion, Sponsorship, Sports Market, Strategic Planning/Research, Technical Advertising, Viral/Buzz/Word of Mouth

Robbie Thain *(CEO)*
Brianna Castillo *(VP-Bus Dev)*
Heath Sorrells *(VP)*
Robert Patin *(Controller)*
Kay Payne *(Sr Acct Mgr)*
Mickey Gordon *(Mgr-Field)*
Alex Guati-Rojo *(Mgr-Field)*
Ruben Garcia *(Asst Acct Coord)*

Accounts:
Adobe
Intel
Nestle
Soyjoy
Suzuki
Wet Planet Beverage, Co. Jolt Soda

MAKE IT POP ADVERTISING
1026 Atlantic Ave, Atlantic City, NJ 08401
Tel.: (609) 428-6446
E-Mail: studio@mipnj.com
Web Site: www.makeitpopadvertising.com

Year Founded: 2004

Agency Specializes In: Advertising, Digital/Interactive, Logo & Package Design, Media Buying Services, Media Planning, Outdoor, Radio, T.V.

Dave Holak *(Partner & Dir-Creative)*
Rina Mackler *(Principal)*

Accounts:
GMS Law

MAKE ME SOCIAL
(Acquired by R2Integrated)

MAKE ME SOCIAL
310 Commerce Lake Dr, Saint Augustine, FL 32095
Tel.: (904) 824-8830
E-Mail: info@makemesocial.net
Web Site: www.makemesocial.net

Agency Specializes In: Advertising, Brand Development & Integration, Content, Internet/Web Design, Social Media, Strategic Planning/Research

Mike Riley *(Chief Revenue Officer)*
Tom Kaczmarek *(Dir-Omni Channel Mktg)*

Mia Horberg *(Mgr-Mktg)*
Krista Savage *(Mgr-Community)*
Samantha Press *(Acct Exec)*

Accounts:
New-Envestnet
New-Summit Golf Brands
New-Thomas & Betts
New-Triboro Quilt Manufacturing

MAKE SEARCH WORK
320 NE Failing St, Portland, OR 97212
Tel.: (503) 850-8187
Web Site: makesearchwork.com

Employees: 5
Year Founded: 2010

Agency Specializes In: Affiliate Marketing, Digital/Interactive, Email, Local Marketing, Mobile Marketing, Publishing, Search Engine Optimization, Social Media, Syndication, Web (Banner Ads, Pop-ups, etc.)

Approx. Annual Billings: $250,000

Jacob Martus *(Partner)*
Troy Steele *(Partner)*
Mark Adams *(Lead Technical Writer)*
Jared Harrington *(Lead Programmer)*

Accounts:
Bridge City Bulk Supplements; 2013
Excel High School Online High School Diploma; 2013
Rockwell Automation Safety Equipment; 2014

MALETZKY MEDIA
450 Fashion Ave, New York, NY 10123
Tel.: (212) 829-0150
Web Site: www.maletzkymedia.com

Agency Specializes In: Advertising, Brand Development & Integration, Media Relations

Karyn Maletzky Ravin *(Founder & Pres)*
Robyn Ungar *(Sr VP-Brand Strategy)*
Noelle Schultz *(Dir-Fin & HR)*
Erica Finkelstein *(Acct Exec)*
Stephanie Rosenblum *(Acct Exec)*

Accounts:
Children's Cardiomyopathy Foundation Public Relations, US Agency of Record
Dalys 1895 Media Relations, US Agency of Record Product of the Year

MALKUS COMMUNICATIONS GROUP
888 Las Olas Blvd Ste 508, Fort Lauderdale, FL 33301
Tel.: (954) 523-4200
Fax: (954) 523-5902
E-Mail: cmalkus@malkus.com
Web Site: www.malkus.com

Year Founded: 1974

Agency Specializes In: Brand Development & Integration, Broadcast, Collateral, Graphic Design, Internet/Web Design, Media Relations, Print, Production (Print), Public Relations

Hillary Reynolds *(VP)*
Mark Budwig *(Dir-Creative)*
Nicholas Scalzo *(Assoc Dir-Creative)*

Accounts:
Advanced Green Technologies
Arthur R. Marshall Foundation Social Services
Atlantic Hotel
Beach Place
Boca Ballet Theatre Entertainment Services
Broward County Fair
Comcast
Cooper City
Digestive CARE Medical Services
Everglades Foundation Inc Environmental Services
Med Time Technology, Inc.
Phil Smith Automotive Group

MALLOF, ABRUZINO & NASH MARKETING
765 Kimberly Dr, Carol Stream, IL 60188-9407
Tel.: (630) 929-5200
Fax: (630) 752-9288
Web Site: www.manmarketing.com

Employees: 20
Year Founded: 1980

Agency Specializes In: Advertising, Advertising Specialties, Automotive, Bilingual Market, Broadcast, Cable T.V., Co-op Advertising, Commercial Photography, Direct Response Marketing, Electronic Media, Email, Graphic Design, Infomercials, Internet/Web Design, Magazines, Media Buying Services, Media Planning, Media Relations, Newspaper, Newspapers & Magazines, Out-of-Home Media, Outdoor, Print, Production, Production (Ad, Film, Broadcast), Publicity/Promotions, Radio, Retail, Sales Promotion, T.V.

Approx. Annual Billings: $18,000,000

Edward G. Mallof *(Pres)*
Lee Zuika *(Controller)*
Antoinette Raddi Mallof *(Dir-Brdcst Media & Producer)*
Lucy Ferrari *(Acct Exec)*
Kelley Stiles *(Acct Exec)*
Michelle Garbarz *(Media Buyer)*
Jamie Golden *(Acct Coord)*

Accounts:
B2B Computer Products
Barrington Volvo
BMW of Peoria
Castle BPG
Currie Motors
Devil's Head Resort
Eaglewood Resort
Ewald's Auto Group
Hotel Arista
Jack Phelan Chevrolet
Libertyville Buick GMC; Libertyville, IL
McCarthy Ford
McGrath Lexus
McGrath Lexus Chicago
McGrath Lexus Westmont
Riverfront Chrysler Plymouth Jeep
Rogers Pontiac/GMC/Buick/Hyundai
Ron Tirapelli Ford
Sam Leman Auto Group
Schaumburg Mitsubishi
Shred Shop
Westfield Ford
Wicksrom Ford & Chevy

MALONEY STRATEGIC COMMUNICATIONS
9441 Lyndon B Johnson Fwy Ste 506, Dallas, TX 75243-4541
Tel.: (214) 342-8385
Fax: (214) 342-8386
Web Site: www.maloneystrategic.com

Employees: 15
Year Founded: 1993

Agency Specializes In: Restaurant, Travel & Tourism

John Maloney *(Owner)*
Brian Thompson *(VP-Mktg)*
Budi Sutomo *(Dir-Creative)*
Donna Payne *(Acct Exec)*

Accounts:
City of Irving, Texas
Cozymels Mexican Grill Restaurants
Destination ImagiNation
The EDS Byron Nelson Classic
Grand Cayman Marriott Beach Resort
The Hilton Baton Rouge Capitol Center
Holiday Inn Express
InterContinental Hotels Group
Irving Convention & Visitors Bureau
Kessler Collins
La Quinta Inn and Suites
The Marriott Grand Cayman Beach Resort
Prism Hotels and Resorts
Reddy Ice Corporation
Royal Bank of Canada
Sabre
Schmidt & Stacy
Sealed Air Corporation

MAMI MEDIA, LLC
261 Old York Rd Ste 930, Jenkintown, PA 19046
Tel.: (609) 334-4418
Web Site: www.mamimedia.com

Employees: 5
Year Founded: 2001

Agency Specializes In: Branded Entertainment, Broadcast, Business Publications, Cable T.V., Co-op Advertising, Consumer Publications, Custom Publishing, Digital/Interactive, Electronic Media, Email, Experience Design, Guerilla Marketing, In-Store Advertising, Infomercials, Magazines, Mobile Marketing, Multimedia, Newspaper, Newspapers & Magazines, Podcasting, Point of Purchase, Print, Product Placement, Production, Production (Print), Promotions, Publishing, RSS (Really Simple Syndication), Radio, Search Engine Optimization, Shopper Marketing, Social Media, Sweepstakes, T.V., Trade & Consumer Magazines, Viral/Buzz/Word of Mouth, Web (Banner Ads, Pop-ups, etc.)

Approx. Annual Billings: $100,000

Algie deWitt *(Founder & Principal)*

MAMMOTH ADVERTISING LLC
45 Main St Ste 1006, Brooklyn, NY 11201
Tel.: (718) 422-7760
Fax: (718) 522-2961
E-Mail: info@mammothnyc.com
Web Site: www.mammothnyc.com

Year Founded: 2005

Agency Specializes In: Advertising, Media Planning, Print, Promotions, Public Relations, Social Media

Robert Nuell *(Co-Founder & Partner)*
Melanie Klein *(VP-Comm)*
Charles Lam *(Dir-Production & Tech)*
Ryan O'Connor *(Dir-Bus Dev)*
Chad Evenson *(Acct Mgr-Digital Strategy & Creative Production)*
Lauren Shugrue *(Acct Mgr-Digital Mktg & Creative Production)*
Brianne Fortuna *(Mgr-PR & Promos)*
Patrick Sammon *(Mgr-Social Media)*
Bonnie Calkins *(Coord-PR)*
Timothy Greene *(Coord-Social Media)*
Alyssa Hackmann *(Sr Coord-PR)*

Accounts:
A&E

Fox Entertainment Group, Inc.
Lions Gate Entertainment Corp.
Paramount Pictures Corporation
Showtime Networks Inc.
Sony Pictures
Universal Studios, Inc.

MAMUS, INC.

81 Scudder Ave 3, Northport, NY 11768
Tel.: (631) 261-2610
E-Mail: more@mamusinc.com
Web Site: www.mamusinc.com

Agency Specializes In: Advertising, Brand Development & Integration, Graphic Design, Internet/Web Design, Print

John Mamus *(Owner)*

Accounts:
AVA Velocity Works
Fila USA, Inc.
Imblim
Noble Biomaterials

MAN MARKETING

765 Kimberly Dr, Carol Stream, IL 60188
Tel.: (630) 929-5200
Fax: (630) 752-9288
Web Site: www.manmarketing.com

Employees: 26
Year Founded: 1980

Agency Specializes In: Advertising, Broadcast, Digital/Interactive, Internet/Web Design, Media Buying Services, Outdoor, Print, Search Engine Optimization, Social Media

Ed Mallof *(Pres)*
Matt Nash *(Exec VP & Creative Dir)*
Lee Zuika *(Controller)*
Guy Lieberman *(Dir-Digital Mktg)*
Lisa Bircher *(Mgr-Acctg)*
Jane Wiedmeyer *(Coord-Adv)*
Michelle Garbarz *(Sr Media Buyer)*

Accounts:
Fox Valley Auto Group
Jerry Biggers Chevrolet

THE MANAHAN GROUP

222 Capitol St, Charleston, WV 25301
Tel.: (304) 343-2800
E-Mail: info@manahangroup.com
Web Site: www.manahangroup.com

Agency Specializes In: Advertising, Broadcast, Digital/Interactive, Event Planning & Marketing, Graphic Design, Logo & Package Design, Media Planning, Print, Public Relations, Strategic Planning/Research

Jennifer Clark *(Pres)*
George Manahan *(CEO)*
Kelly Stadelman *(Principal & VP-Res)*
Ron Jarrett *(Controller & Comptroller)*
Abbey Fiorelli *(Dir-Creative)*
Tammy Harper *(Sr Acct Mgr)*
Matt Minch *(Sr Graphic Designer)*

Accounts:
Pierpont Community & Technical College

MANDALA

2855 NW Crossing Dr Ste 201, Bend, OR 97701-2744
Tel.: (541) 389-6344
Fax: (541) 389-3531
E-Mail: info@mandala.agency
Web Site: mandala.agency/

E-Mail for Key Personnel:
Creative Dir.: paul@mandala-agency.com
Media Dir.: laura@mandala-agency.com

Employees: 7
Year Founded: 1980

National Agency Associations: 4A's-PORTLAND AD FED

Agency Specializes In: Advertising, Aviation & Aerospace, Broadcast, Collateral, College, Consumer Marketing, Corporate Identity, Financial, Graphic Design, Health Care Services, Identity Marketing, Internet/Web Design, Media Buying Services, Media Planning, Newspapers & Magazines, Production (Print), Public Relations, Real Estate, Search Engine Optimization, Social Media

Approx. Annual Billings: $7,000,000 Capitalized

Matthew Bowler *(Partner)*
Laury Benson *(CFO)*
Ryan Crotty *(Sr Dir-Art)*
Laura Bryant *(Dir-Media)*
Paul Grignon *(Dir-Creative)*
Lori Hell *(Dir)*
Ted Olson *(Dir-Digital Engagement)*

Accounts:
Mountain Khakis; 2013
Pronghorn; 2014
Sky Lakes Medical Center Hospital; Klamath Falls, OR; 2005

MANGAN HOLCOMB PARTNERS

2300 Cottondale Ln Ste 300, Little Rock, AR 72202
Tel.: (501) 376-0321
Fax: (501) 376-6127
Web Site: www.manganholcomb.com

Employees: 30
Year Founded: 1972

National Agency Associations: 4A's

Agency Specializes In: Advertising, Advertising Specialties, Agriculture, Brand Development & Integration, Broadcast, Business-To-Business, Co-op Advertising, Communications, Corporate Identity, Financial, Health Care Services, Investor Relations, Media Buying Services, Medical Products, Public Relations, Publicity/Promotions, Strategic Planning/Research, Transportation

Approx. Annual Billings: $10,000,000

Chip Culpepper *(Owner & Chief Creative Officer)*
Sharon Tallach Vogelpohl *(Pres)*
David Rainwater *(CEO & Principal)*
Barbara King Dozier *(Dir-Media)*

Accounts:
Arkansas Pharmacists Association Marketing Communications
Arkansas Repertory Theater
Arkansas Urology
Baxter Regional Medical Center
Bean Hamilton Corporate Benefits
The Buzz 103.7 FM
Centenary College of Louisiana
Children's Hospital of Wisconsin
Chuy
Delta Plastics
Department of Arkansas Heritage
Farmers & Merchants Bank
Greenway Equipment Inc.
Harding University
International Greek Food Festival
J.B. Hunt Transport; Lowell, AR
Keep Arkansas Beautiful
Le Bonheur Children's Hospital; 2005
Metropolitan National Bank
Oleen Pinnacle Healthcare Consulting
Our Lady of the Lake Regional Medical Center
RiceTec Inc.
Sparks Health System; Fort Smith, AR
St. Vincent Health System
University of Arkansas; Little Rock, AR
Verizon Wireless
Winthrop Rockefeller Institute

MANGOS

10 Great Valley Pkwy, Malvern, PA 19355-1316
Tel.: (610) 296-2555
Fax: (610) 640-9291
E-Mail: bradleygast@mangosinc.com
Web Site: www.mangosinc.com

Employees: 20
Year Founded: 1977

Agency Specializes In: Advertising, Brand Development & Integration, Collateral, Health Care Services, Identity Marketing, Media Buying Services, Media Planning, Public Relations, Web (Banner Ads, Pop-ups, etc.)

William Gast *(Partner & CEO)*
Bradley Gast *(Partner)*
Joanne deMenna *(Sr VP & Dir-Strategy)*
Patti Monaco *(Sr VP-Acct Mgmt)*
Joanne Moore *(Sr VP-Admin)*
Mary Ann Sesso *(VP-Acct Mgmt)*
Heidi Habel *(Sr Dir-Art)*
Brooke DeLuise *(Dir-New Media)*
Justin Moll *(Dir-Creative)*
Ingrid Tripple *(Sr Acct Mgr)*
Casey Zweigle *(Acct Coord)*

Accounts:
BlackRock
Bucks County Workforce Investment Board Youth Program
Curtiss-Wright Flow Control Company
Firstrust Bank (Agency of Record)
Lehigh Valley Health Network Campaign: "Through a Child's Eyes"
Liberty Sport
Main Line Health (Agency of Record)
National Museum of American Jewish History; Philadelphia, PA
Olympus
Siemens
Siemens Healthcare; Malvern, PA
University of the Arts
Vibe Hearing Aids
Zix Corp
Zurich

MANHATTAN MARKETING ENSEMBLE

443 Park Ave S 4th Fl, New York, NY 10016-7322
Tel.: (212) 779-2233
Fax: (212) 779-0825
E-Mail: jrowe@mme.net
Web Site: www.mme.net

Employees: 32
Year Founded: 1989

Agency Specializes In: Advertising, Collateral, Food Service, Point of Sale, Retail, Sponsorship

Approx. Annual Billings: $65,000,000

Phil McCann *(Exec Acct Dir)*
Mabel Tong *(Sr Dir-Art)*
Sook H. Kang-Fuentecilla *(Sr Acct Dir)*
Amy Hanna *(Acct Dir)*
Brad Eisenstein *(Dir-Creative)*
Robert Merino *(Dir-Print Production)*
Jimmy Ng *(Assoc Dir-Creative)*

Keisey Fraser *(Acct Exec)*
Maury R. Maniff *(Sr Partner)*
Don Raskin *(Sr Partner)*
Jim Rowe *(Sr Partner)*

Accounts:
Affinia Hospitality; Manhattan, NY; 1999
Belvedere Vodka
The Benjamin
E.T. Browne Drug Company, Inc.
Estates & Wines
Maxell Corp. of America; Fairlawn, NJ Audio & Video Tapes; 1990
Nathan's Famous; Westbury, NY (Agency of Record) Hot Dogs; 1990
Palmers; 1998

MANJON STUDIOS
7650 W Us Hwy 90 Lot 410, San Antonio, TX 78227
Tel.: (210) 764-9321
Web Site: www.manjonstudios.com

Agency Specializes In: Advertising, Digital/Interactive, Graphic Design, Internet/Web Design, Media Buying Services, Radio, T.V.

Capone De Leon *(Owner)*

Accounts:
Ultimate Services Group

MANN ADVERTISING INC
913 Elm St 4th Fl, Manchester, NH 3101
Tel.: (603) 625-5403
Fax: (603) 622-6266
Web Site: www.mannad.com

Agency Specializes In: Advertising, Digital/Interactive, Graphic Design, Logo & Package Design, Radio, Social Media, T.V.

Paul Hanson *(Pres)*
Jessica Rodier *(VP-Ops)*
Hank Simpson *(VP-Client Svcs)*
Peter St. James *(Dir-Creative & Sr Copywriter)*

Accounts:
Motorcycles of Manchester

MANSFIELD + ASSOCIATES, INC.
629 12th St, Manhattan Beach, CA 90266
Tel.: (310) 245-9600
E-Mail: info@mans.com
Web Site: www.mans.com

E-Mail for Key Personnel:
President: peter@mans.com
Creative Dir.: craig@mans.com

Employees: 5
Year Founded: 1992

Agency Specializes In: Digital/Interactive, Internet/Web Design

Approx. Annual Billings: $1,000,000

Peter Mansfield *(Pres)*
Craig Miranda *(Dir-Creative)*
Christopher Adams *(Mgr-Production)*
Kevin Truong *(Mgr-IT Network)*

Accounts:
California Wellness Foundation
The Challenged Athletes Foundation
McGuire Properties
Q Inc. Software

MANSFIELD INC.
(Formerly Mansfield Communications, Inc.)
225 Richmond Street West Suite 302, Toronto, ON M5V 1W2 Canada
Tel.: (416) 599-0024
Fax: (416) 599-7484
Web Site: www.mansfieldinc.com

Agency Specializes In: Advertising, Advertising Specialties, Market Research, Media Buying Services, Media Planning, Media Relations, Media Training, Public Relations, Publicity/Promotions

Hugh W Mansfield *(Founder & Partner)*
Beth Mansfield *(Owner & Principal)*
Andrea Ellison *(Sr VP)*
Ajinkya Kulkarni *(Dir-Analytics & Insights)*
Jeff Payne *(Dir-Strategy & Engagement)*
Sarah Laister *(Sr Acct Exec)*
Jonah Cait *(Strategist-Digital)*
Nicholas Prospero *(Acct Exec)*

Accounts:
Lorus Therapeutics
Speedy Corporation
Yamana Gold; Toronto, Canada

MANTERA ADVERTISING
1902 Three Bridges Way, Bakersfield, CA 93311
Tel.: (661) 201-8790
E-Mail: info@manteramedia.com
Web Site: www.manteramedia.com

Employees: 5
Year Founded: 2008

Agency Specializes In: Above-the-Line, Advertising, Advertising Specialties, Affiliate Marketing, Affluent Market, African-American Market, Agriculture, Alternative Advertising, Arts, Asian Market, Automotive, Aviation & Aerospace, Below-the-Line, Bilingual Market, Brand Development & Integration, Branded Entertainment, Broadcast, Business Publications, Business-To-Business, Cable T.V., Catalogs, Children's Market, Co-op Advertising, Collateral, College, Commercial Photography, Communications, Computers & Software, Consulting, Consumer Goods, Consumer Marketing, Consumer Publications, Content, Corporate Communications, Corporate Identity, Cosmetics, Crisis Communications, Custom Publishing, Customer Relationship Management, Digital/Interactive, Direct Response Marketing, Direct-to-Consumer, E-Commerce, Education, Electronic Media, Electronics, Email, Engineering, Entertainment, Environmental, Event Planning & Marketing, Exhibit/Trade Shows, Experience Design, Faith Based, Fashion/Apparel, Financial, Food Service, Game Integration, Gay & Lesbian Market, Government/Political, Graphic Design, Guerilla Marketing, Health Care Services, High Technology, Hispanic Market, Hospitality, Household Goods, Identity Marketing, In-Store Advertising, Industrial, Infomercials, Information Technology, Integrated Marketing, International, Internet/Web Design, Investor Relations, Legal Services, Leisure, Local Marketing, Logo & Package Design, Luxury Products, Magazines, Marine, Market Research, Media Buying Services, Media Planning, Media Relations, Media Training, Medical Products, Men's Market, Merchandising, Mobile Marketing, Multicultural, Multimedia, New Product Development, New Technologies, Newspaper, Newspapers & Magazines, Out-of-Home Media, Outdoor, Over-50 Market, Package Design, Paid Searches, Pets , Pharmaceutical, Planning & Consultation, Podcasting, Point of Purchase, Point of Sale, Print, Product Placement, Production, Production (Ad, Film, Broadcast), Production (Print), Promotions, Public Relations, Publicity/Promotions, Publishing, RSS (Really Simple Syndication), Radio, Real Estate, Recruitment, Regional, Restaurant, Retail, Sales Promotion, Search Engine Optimization, Seniors' Market, Shopper Marketing, Social Marketing/Nonprofit, Social Media, South Asian Market, Sponsorship, Sports Market, Stakeholders, Strategic Planning/Research, Sweepstakes, Syndication, T.V., Technical Advertising, Teen Market, Telemarketing, Trade & Consumer Magazines, Transportation, Travel & Tourism, Tween Market, Urban Market, Viral/Buzz/Word of Mouth, Web (Banner Ads, Pop-ups, etc.), Women's Market, Yellow Pages Advertising

Matt Molina *(CEO)*
David Reichelt *(Mgr-Mobile Dev)*

Accounts:
Brundage Lane Florist
East Pointe Dance
Karpe Real Estate Billboard, SEO, Website; 2012
Kern River Alliance
The Mission at Kern County Digital, Marketing, Website; 2013
Que Pasa Mexican Restaurants Billboard, Radio, Website; 2011
Stockdale Tile Website; 2014

MANTOOTH MARKETING COMPANY
8334 Coeur DAlene Dr, Fort Collins, CO 80525
Tel.: (970) 663-1888
Fax: (970) 682-1327
Web Site: www.mantoothcompany.com

Agency Specializes In: Advertising, Digital/Interactive, Event Planning & Marketing, Graphic Design, Logo & Package Design, Media Relations, Media Training, Outdoor, Print, Public Relations

Connie Hanrahan *(Owner)*
Isis Rose Diloreti *(Dir-Event & Acct Mgr-Mktg)*
Sarah Lukemire *(Mgr-Digital & Social Media)*
Lindsey Keller *(Mgr-Event)*

Accounts:
Community Foundation of Northern Colorado
Team Fort Collins

MARANON & ASSOCIATES ADVERTISING
2103 Coral Way Ste 604, Miami, FL 33145
Tel.: (305) 854-2002
Fax: (305) 476-5010
E-Mail: info@maranonad.com
Web Site: www.maranonad.com/

Employees: 15
Year Founded: 1985

Agency Specializes In: Bilingual Market, Hispanic Market, Media Buying Services, Publicity/Promotions

Legia Maranon *(Pres)*
Richard Maranon *(CEO)*

Accounts:
Al Flex Exterminators
Amco Insurance
Toyota of South Florida

MARBURY GROUP
16 Terminal Way, Pittsburgh, PA 15219
Tel.: (412) 904-1969
Web Site: www.marburygrp.com

Year Founded: 2012

Agency Specializes In: Advertising, Brand Development & Integration, Internet/Web Design, Media Buying Services, Media Planning, Social Media

Douglas Shriber *(Principal)*
Kathryn Sullivan *(Dir-Acct Svcs)*
Brittany Fradkin *(Acct Mgr)*
John Neenan *(Acct Mgr)*

Accounts:
Andora Restaurant

MARC ATLAN DESIGN, INC.

434 Carroll Canal, Los Angeles, CA 90291
Tel.: (310) 306-8148
Fax: (310) 306-8348
E-Mail: info@marcatlan.com
Web Site: www.marcatlan.com

Agency Specializes In: Advertising, Brand Development & Integration, Event Planning & Marketing, Exhibit/Trade Shows, Logo & Package Design, Print, T.V.

Marc Atlan *(Principal & Dir-Creative)*

Accounts:
Coty Prestige
Fondation Cartier
Helmut Lang
L'Oreal USA, Inc.
Unilever United States, Inc.
Wallpaper Magazine

M/A/R/C RESEARCH

1660 N Westridge Cir, Irving, TX 75038
Fax: (972) 983-0444
Toll Free: (800) 884-6272
Web Site: www.marcresearch.com

Year Founded: 1968

Approx. Annual Billings: $1,000,000

Merrill Dubrow *(Pres & CEO)*
Rob Arnett *(Exec VP)*
Amy Barrentine *(Exec VP)*
Susan Hanks *(Sr VP)*
Susan Hurry *(Sr VP)*
Patricia Wakim *(Sr VP-Fin)*
Nancy Miller *(VP)*
Erika Smith *(VP)*
Shannon Goyda *(Dir-Res)*
Suann Griffin *(Dir-Strategy & Dev)*

MARC USA

225 W Station Square Dr Ste 500, Pittsburgh, PA 15219
Tel.: (412) 562-2000
Fax: (412) 562-2022
E-Mail: bstefanis@marcusa.com
Web Site: www.marcusa.com

Employees: 270
Year Founded: 1955

National Agency Associations: 4A's

Agency Specializes In: Advertising, Advertising Specialties, Affluent Market, Arts, Automotive, Bilingual Market, Brand Development & Integration, Branded Entertainment, Broadcast, Business Publications, Business-To-Business, Cable T.V., Children's Market, Co-op Advertising, Collateral, College, Communications, Consulting, Consumer Goods, Consumer Marketing, Consumer Publications, Content, Corporate Communications, Corporate Identity, Cosmetics, Crisis Communications, Digital/Interactive, Direct Response Marketing, E-Commerce, Education, Electronic Media, Electronics, Email, Entertainment, Event Planning & Marketing, Fashion/Apparel, Financial, Food Service, Game Integration, Graphic Design, Guerilla Marketing, Health Care Services, Hispanic Market, Hospitality, Household Goods, Identity Marketing, In-Store Advertising, Information Technology, Integrated Marketing, Internet/Web Design, Leisure, Local Marketing, Logo & Package Design, Luxury Products, Magazines, Market Research, Media Buying Services, Media Planning, Media Relations, Medical Products, Mobile Marketing, Multicultural, Multimedia, New Product Development, New Technologies, Newspaper, Newspapers & Magazines, Out-of-Home Media, Outdoor, Package Design, Paid Searches, Planning & Consultation, Podcasting, Point of Purchase, Point of Sale, Print, Production, Production (Ad, Film, Broadcast), Promotions, Public Relations, Publicity/Promotions, RSS (Really Simple Syndication), Radio, Real Estate, Regional, Restaurant, Retail, Sales Promotion, Search Engine Optimization, Seniors' Market, Shopper Marketing, Social Marketing/Nonprofit, Social Media, Sponsorship, Sports Market, Strategic Planning/Research, Sweepstakes, Syndication, T.V., Teen Market, Trade & Consumer Magazines, Travel & Tourism, Viral/Buzz/Word of Mouth, Web (Banner Ads, Pop-ups, etc.), Women's Market

Approx. Annual Billings: $30,000,000

Tony Bucci *(Chm)*
Jean McLaren *(CMO & Pres-Chicago)*
Bryan Hadlock *(Chief Creative Officer)*
Chris Heitmann *(Chief Innovation Officer)*
Cari Bucci *(Exec VP & Gen Mgr)*
Karen Leitze *(Exec VP & Dir-Res & Strategic Plng)*
Fran Gargotta *(Exec VP)*
David Shaw *(Sr VP & Client Svcs Dir)*
Nancy Roth *(Sr VP & Dir-Media)*
Cheryl Sills *(Sr VP & Dir-Corp Comm)*
Scott Pool *(VP & Dir-Brdcst-Natl)*
Dave Slinchak *(Sr Dir-Art)*
Alison Hammer *(Creative Dir)*
Dan O'Donnell *(Creative Dir)*
Michelle Fuscaldo *(Mgmt Supvr)*
Greg Edwards *(Dir-Creative & Copywriter)*
Tyler Bergholz *(Dir-Art)*
Marcello Figallo *(Dir-UX)*
Jon Kagan *(Dir-Search & Biddable Media)*
Zachary Cole *(Mgr-Affiliate & Analyst-SEM)*
Kym Recco *(Acct Supvr)*
Jenny Merriman *(Supvr-Media)*
Michael Oravitz *(Sr Acct Exec)*
Nicole Incardone *(Copywriter)*

Accounts:
American Heart Association; 2012
The Andy Warhol Museum Campaign: "Summer's Different Here", Digital, Outdoor, Postcards, Print; 2012
Bryant Heating & Cooling; 1990
Carle Foundation Hospital; 2011
Carrier Corporation; 1987
Cooper Tire and Rubber Company; 2009
DePaul University; 2011
Dish Network DishLatino; 2011
Florida Coalition Against Human Trafficking; 2007
Gold Eagle Company 303 Protectant, STA-BIL 360; 2014
H&R Block; 2014
Health Alliance Insurance; 2011
Huntington Bank; 2014
Independent Insurance Agents & Brokers of America, Inc. Campaign: "Free To Do What's Right For You", Campaign: "Gym", Campaign: "Skydive", Direct Mail, Online, Out-of-Home, Print, Radio, Trusted Choice
Make-A-Wish Foundation; 1998
MAV TV; 2011
Navistar; 2014
Net 10 Wireless; 2013
Oster; 2009
Payless Shoe Source; 2012
The Pennsylvania Lottery; 2002
PharmaVite NatureMade Vitamins; 2011
Rite Aid Corporation Campaign: "Wellness 65+", Digital, Direct Mail, Online, Radio, Videos; 1995
Sunbeam; 2009
TracFone; 2012
True Value Company; 1983

Branches

MARC USA Chicago

325 N La Salle Blvd Ste 750, Chicago, IL 60654
(See Separate Listing)

MARCA Miami

(Formerly MARCA Hispanic)
3390 Mary St Ste 254, Coconut Grove, FL 33133
(See Separate Listing)

MARC USA CHICAGO

325 N La Salle Blvd Ste 750, Chicago, IL 60654
Tel.: (312) 321-9000
Fax: (312) 321-1736
E-Mail: jmclaren@marcusa.com
Web Site: www.marcusa.com

Employees: 270
Year Founded: 1955

National Agency Associations: 4A's

Agency Specializes In: Advertising, Advertising Specialties, Brand Development & Integration, Broadcast, Business Publications, Business-To-Business, Cable T.V., Co-op Advertising, Collateral, Communications, Consulting, Consumer Marketing, Consumer Publications, Corporate Identity, Cosmetics, Digital/Interactive, Direct Response Marketing, Education, Electronic Media, Entertainment, Event Planning & Marketing, Fashion/Apparel, Financial, Food Service, Graphic Design, Health Care Services, Hispanic Market, Internet/Web Design, Investor Relations, Leisure, Logo & Package Design, Magazines, Media Buying Services, New Product Development, Newspaper, Newspapers & Magazines, Out-of-Home Media, Outdoor, Planning & Consultation, Point of Purchase, Point of Sale, Print, Production, Public Relations, Publicity/Promotions, Radio, Real Estate, Recruitment, Restaurant, Retail, Sales Promotion, Sponsorship, Sports Market, Strategic Planning/Research, Sweepstakes, Syndication, T.V., Teen Market, Trade & Consumer Magazines, Travel & Tourism

Approx. Annual Billings: $30,000,000

Breakdown of Gross Billings by Media: Bus. Publs.: 3%; Collateral: 11%; D.M.: 6%; Mags.: 5%; Newsp. & Mags.: 18%; Outdoor: 10%; Radio: 22%; T.V.: 23%; Transit: 2%

Bryan Hadlock *(Chief Creative Officer)*
Cari Bucci *(Exec VP & Gen Mgr)*
Fran Gargotta *(Exec VP)*
Nancy Roth *(Sr VP & Dir-Media)*
Barbara Stefanis-Israel *(Sr VP & Dir-Mktg)*
Bill McCarthy *(VP & Acct Dir)*
Scott Pool *(VP & Dir-Brdcst-Natl)*
Matt Sullivan *(Creative Dir)*
Jeff Norman *(Assoc Dir-Creative & Copywriter)*
Nok Sangdee *(Assoc Dir-Creative)*
Cindy Tomek *(Assoc Dir-Creative)*

Accounts:
American Heart Association; 2012
The Andy Warhol Museum; 2012
Bryant Heating & Cooling; 1990
Carle Foundation Hospital Marketing
Carrier Corporation; 1987
Cooper Tires and Rubber Company; 2009
DePaul University; 2011
Dish Network DishLatino; 2011
Florida Coalition Against Human Trafficking; 2007
Gold Eagle Company 303 Protectant, STA-BIL

360; 2014
H&R Block; 2010
Health Alliance Insurance Marketing
Huntington Bank; 2014
Make-A-Wish Foundation; 1998
MAVTV; 2011
Navistar Inc. (Advertising Agency of Record) Brand Strategy; IC Bus, Campaign: "Uptime", International Truck, Marketing, Online, Print; 2014
Net 10 Wireless; 2013
Oster; 2009
Payless ShoeSource Creative; 2012
The Pennsylvania Lottery; 2002
PharmaVite Nature Made Vitamins; 2011
Rite Aid Corporation Digital, Print, Radio, Social Media; 1995
Sta-Bil Storage
Sunbeam; 2009
TracFone; 2012
True Value Company Easy Care, EasyCare Platinum, Home & Garden Showplace, Taylor Rental, TrueValue; 1983
Trusted Choice Independent Insurance Agents B2B, B2C, Digital, Direct, Marketing, Print, Television, Trusted Choice; 2013

MARCA MIAMI
(Formerly MARCA Hispanic)
3390 Mary St Ste 254, Coconut Grove, FL 33133
Tel.: (305) 423-8300
Fax: (305) 665-3533
E-Mail: tnieves@marcamiami.com
Web Site: www.marcamiami.com

Employees: 32
Year Founded: 2003

National Agency Associations: 4A's

Agency Specializes In: Advertising, Advertising Specialties, Brand Development & Integration, Broadcast, Business Publications, Business-To-Business, Cable T.V., Co-op Advertising, Collateral, Communications, Consulting, Consumer Marketing, Consumer Publications, Corporate Identity, Cosmetics, Direct Response Marketing, Electronic Media, Engineering, Entertainment, Event Planning & Marketing, Fashion/Apparel, Financial, Food Service, Graphic Design, Health Care Services, Hispanic Market, Internet/Web Design, Investor Relations, Leisure, Logo & Package Design, Magazines, Media Buying Services, Merchandising, New Product Development, Newspaper, Newspapers & Magazines, Out-of-Home Media, Outdoor, Planning & Consultation, Point of Purchase, Point of Sale, Print, Production, Public Relations, Publicity/Promotions, Radio, Real Estate, Restaurant, Retail, Sales Promotion, Sponsorship, Sports Market, Strategic Planning/Research, Sweepstakes, Syndication, T.V., Teen Market, Trade & Consumer Magazines, Travel & Tourism

Approx. Annual Billings: $30,000,000

Tony Nieves *(Pres & Partner)*
Armando Hernandez *(Partner & Chief Creative Officer)*
Alejandro Berbari *(Sr VP & Dir-Creative)*
Henry Gomez *(Sr Dir-Strategic Plng)*
Sebastian Moltedo *(Assoc Dir-Creative)*
Amanda Taylor *(Mgr-Social Media)*
Lorena Robles *(Jr Strategist-Digital)*

Accounts:
DishLatino Customer Acquisition, Hispanic, Multimedia Branding, Puerto Rican Market
Florida Coalition Against Human Trafficking Campaign: "Security Camera"
H&R Block
Kyocera Hispanic & Latin American Marketing
Norwegian Cruise Line
Oster

MARCEL DIGITAL
(Formerly Marcel Media)
445 W Erie Ste 211, Chicago, IL 60654
Tel.: (312) 255-8044
Fax: (866) 643-7506
Web Site: www.marceldigital.com

Employees: 20
Year Founded: 2003

Ben Swartz *(Pres)*
Tommy Confar *(Head-Acct)*
Anjali Gumbhir *(Head-Admin)*
Mike Schmidt *(Head-Ops)*
Marjorie Vardo *(Dir-Art)*
Drew Brinckerhoff *(Acct Mgr)*
Marty McKenna *(Mgr-SEO)*
Patrick Delehanty *(Strategist-Digital Mktg)*
Kourtney Elam *(Specialist-Digital Graphic Design)*
Catherine Merton *(Acct Coord)*

Accounts:
Broadway In Chicago
Cole Wire
Hub International
Modern Process Equipment Corporation
Personal Zation
Your Labels Now

MARCHESE COMMUNICATIONS INC.
425 Manitoba St, Playa Del Rey, CA 90293
Tel.: (213) 399-5999
Fax: (310) 821-2819
E-Mail: david@marchesecommunications.com
Web Site: www.marchesecommunications.com

E-Mail for Key Personnel:
Media Dir.:
andrew@marchesecommunications.com

Employees: 5
Year Founded: 1988

Agency Specializes In: Advertising, Below-the-Line, Brand Development & Integration, Co-op Advertising, Consulting, Digital/Interactive, Direct Response Marketing, E-Commerce, Email, Entertainment, Hospitality, Integrated Marketing, Internet/Web Design, Planning & Consultation, Promotions, Retail, Sales Promotion, Strategic Planning/Research, Sweepstakes, T.V., Travel & Tourism, Web (Banner Ads, Pop-ups, etc.)

Breakdown of Gross Billings by Media: Consulting: 5%; D.M.: 5%; Internet Adv.: 40%; Sls. Promo.: 10%; Strategic Planning/Research: 10%; T.V.: 20%; Trade & Consumer Mags.: 5%; Worldwide Web Sites: 5%

Christopher Barnes *(Dir-Email Solutions)*

Accounts:
E-Travel Concepts Inc.; Los Angeles, CA Top10Travelworld.com, www.WineWorldTours.com; 2008
Newton Business Programs; New York, NY Entrepreneurial Employee Performance Enhancement Programs; 2005
Pelletier, Koll & Weill; Los Angeles, CA Liquor, Multilevel, Weight Loss; 2004
Tourism Fiji; Los Angeles, CA Fiji Island Tourism; 2009

MARCHEX, INC.
520 Pike St Ste 2000, Seattle, WA 98101
Tel.: (206) 331-3300
Fax: (206) 331-3695
E-Mail: info@marchex.com
Web Site: www.marchex.com

Employees: 367
Year Founded: 2003

Agency Specializes In: Internet/Web Design, Mobile Marketing

Revenue: $182,644,000

Michael A. Arends *(CFO)*
Gary Nafus *(Chief Revenue Officer)*
Matt Greff *(Product Mgr & Principal)*
Brooks McMahon *(Sr VP & Gen Mgr)*
John Busby *(Sr VP-Mktg & Consumer Insights)*
Travis Fairchild *(Sr VP-Strategy & Dev)*
Matt Muilenburg *(Sr VP-Customer Evangelist)*
Peter Greb *(VP-Natl Client Engagement)*
Simon Sorrell *(VP-Strategic Partnerships)*
Todd Wilson *(VP-Ops)*
Matthew Harris *(Acct Dir)*
Jason Flaks *(Dir-Product & Engrg-Call Svcs)*
Steve Russell *(Dir-Bus Dev-Natl)*
Ken Seligman *(Dir-Bus Dev)*
Kimberly Paul *(Sr Acct Mgr)*
Jamie Dieterich *(Client Svcs Mgr)*
Jennifer McNamee *(Acct Mgr)*
Alina Ottemiller *(Acct Mgr)*
Lori Ward *(Acct Exec)*
Brian Brock *(Sr Partner Mgr)*

Accounts:
AT&T Communications Corp.
Barrington Broadcasting; 2008
Diversified Systems Group, Inc.
Geary LSF
HealthMarkets
IBM
IQ Chart

MARCOM GROUP INC.
1180 Courtneypark Dr E, Mississauga, ON L5T 1P2 Canada
Tel.: (905) 565-0331
Fax: (905) 565-0339
E-Mail: marcom@mgrp.com
Web Site: www.mgrp.com

Employees: 50
Year Founded: 1982

Agency Specializes In: Advertising

Dave Heslop *(Pres)*
Scott Dennison *(Acct Svcs Dir)*
Kevin Kirkwood *(Dir-Art & Designer-Web)*
Dack Heslop *(Acct Mgr)*
David Lambden *(Acct Mgr)*
Ana Fonseca *(Supvr-Data Entry Dept)*
Tabitha Marshall *(Acct Coord)*

Accounts:
Brampton Brick
Chevron/Texaco
Gay Lea
HOYA Vision Care
KitchenAid
OSRAM SYLVANIA
Purolator
Simmons
Whirlpool

MARCOSOLO DESIGN
335 Ridgepoint Dr, Carmel, IN 46032
Tel.: (317) 946-4897
Fax: (317) 575-9943
Web Site: www.marcosolodesign.com

Agency Specializes In: Advertising, Corporate Identity, Email, Event Planning & Marketing, Internet/Web Design, Logo & Package Design, Print

Craig Clayton *(Pres)*

Accounts:
BBG Construction
Cellular Necessities
Fit Livin

THE MARCUS GROUP, INC.
150 Clove Rd 11th Fl, Little Falls, NJ 07424
Tel.: (973) 890-9590
Fax: (973) 890-9130
E-Mail: info@marcusgroup.com
Web Site: www.marcusgroup.com

Employees: 17
Year Founded: 1970

National Agency Associations: PRSA

Agency Specializes In: Advertising, Business-To-Business, Collateral, Communications, Consulting, Corporate Identity, Government/Political, Graphic Design, Health Care Services, Internet/Web Design, Investor Relations, Magazines, Media Relations, Newspaper, Newspapers & Magazines, Out-of-Home Media, Planning & Consultation, Print, Production, Promotions, Public Relations, Publicity/Promotions, Strategic Planning/Research, Web (Banner Ads, Pop-ups, etc.)

Approx. Annual Billings: $4,000,000

Breakdown of Gross Billings by Media: Adv. Specialities: 10%; Bus. Publs.: 5%; Collateral: 10%; Consulting: 20%; Graphic Design: 10%; Newsp. & Mags.: 10%; Print: 10%; Pub. Rels.: 25%

Alan C. Marcus *(Owner)*
Denise Gassner Kuhn *(COO & Exec VP)*
Janel Patti *(Exec VP & Dir-Creative)*
Penny Goldstein *(VP-Ops)*
Angela Middleton *(Dir-Creative)*
Scott Wasserman *(Acct Exec)*
Jeannette Tarquino *(Media Planner & Media Buyer)*

Accounts:
Michael Graves
Nadasky Kopelson
New Jersey Society of Architects

MARCUS THOMAS LLC
4781 Richmond Rd, Cleveland, OH 44128
Tel.: (216) 292-4700
Fax: (216) 378-0396
Toll Free: (888) 482-4455
E-Mail: mbachmann@marcusthomasllc.com
Web Site: www.marcusthomasllc.com

E-Mail for Key Personnel:
Creative Dir.: jkim@marcusthomasllc.com

Employees: 95
Year Founded: 1937

National Agency Associations: 4A's-AAF-AMA-ARF-MAGNET-PRSA

Agency Specializes In: Advertising, Brand Development & Integration, Broadcast, Business Publications, Business-To-Business, Cable T.V., Collateral, Communications, Consumer Goods, Consumer Marketing, Corporate Communications, Direct Response Marketing, Electronic Media, Exhibit/Trade Shows, Financial, Health Care Services, Household Goods, Industrial, Integrated Marketing, Internet/Web Design, Market Research, Media Buying Services, Media Relations, Newspaper, Outdoor, Planning & Consultation, Point of Sale, Print, Public Relations, Publicity/Promotions, Retail, Social Media, Sponsorship, Sports Market, Strategic Planning/Research, T.V., Trade & Consumer Magazines, Transportation, Web (Banner Ads, Pop-ups, etc.)

Approx. Annual Billings: $86,000,000

Breakdown of Gross Billings by Media: E-Commerce: 7%; Mags.: 12%; Newsp.: 3%; Outdoor: 5%; Promos.: 14%; Radio: 12%; T.V.: 47%

Joseph J. Blaha *(Owner)*
Jim Nash *(Mng Partner)*
Lori Hedrick *(Partner & VP-HR)*
Mark E. Bachmann *(Partner)*
Scott Chapin *(Partner-Analytics & Digital Strategy)*
Jennifer Hirt-Marchand *(Partner-Res)*
Ian Verschuren *(CTO & Sr VP-Digital Strategy)*
Amber Zent *(VP & Strategist-Social Media)*
Pat Carlson *(VP-Acct Svc)*
Carrie Ann Kandes *(VP)*
Raphael Rivilla *(VP-Media & Connections Plng)*
Joanne Teets *(VP-Studio Svcs)*
Glenda Terrell *(Mgmt Supvr)*
Doug Herberich *(Dir-Art)*
Laura Seidel *(Dir-Art)*
Jim Sollisch *(Dir-Creative)*
Brian Gillen *(Assoc Dir-Creative)*
Eric Holman *(Assoc Dir-Creative)*
Carolyn Fertig *(Project Mgr-Digital)*
Cathy Rivera *(Mgr-Fin Projects)*
Debbie Pirone *(Acct Supvr)*
Dave Evans *(Sr Acct Exec)*
Sandi Hensel *(Acct Exec)*
Stephanie Burris *(Copywriter)*
Patricia DiFranco *(Copywriter)*
T. J. Prochaska *(Copywriter)*
Max Sollisch *(Copywriter)*
Mary White *(Media Buyer)*

Accounts:
Akron Children's Hospital; 2003
Alcoa Wheel & Forged Products; 2000
Bendix Commercial Vehicle Systems; 1999
The Better Sleep Council Marketing, Public Relations, Social & Digital Media, Strategic Development
Boys & Girls Clubs of Cleveland Campaign: "Save Our Kids"
Diebold Financial Self-Service Division
Diebold; 2008
First Energy
Goo Gone Campaign: "Dice"
Innovative Developments; Cleveland, OH Creative, Digital Marketing Communications, Media, Mycestro, Planning, Public Relations
Lifebanc Campaign: "Bugs"
Metrie
MTD Bolens, Campaign: "How We're Built", Troy-Built, White Outdoor Equipment, Yard-Machine, Yard-Man; 2006
Nestle Buitoni, Creative, Digital, Nescafe, Ovaltine, Refrigerated Pastas, Sauces
Ohio Department of Administrative Services; Columbus, OH Creative, Media
Ohio Lottery Commission Broadcast, Buckeye 5, Campaign: "It's Time for a New Tradition", Campaign: "Mosquitos", Campaign: "Poison Ivy", Cash Explosion, Classic Lotto, Cool Cat, Digital Advertising, Kicker, Marketing, Mega Millions, Mobile, Money Island, Ohio State Lottery, Out-of-Home, Pick 3, Pick 4, Radio, Rolling Cash 5, Ten-OH!; 2003
Okamoto Campaign: "Bareback. Almost.", Campaign: "Fatherhood' Crown Condoms"
Quanex
Sherwin-Williams Paint & Sundries Brands Campaign: "Krylon ColorMaster Challenge", Digital, Dutch Boy, Krylon, Pratt & Lambert, Purdy
New-Shoes and Clothes for Kids
Sirva
The Step2 Company; 2008
Sundries Brands
Swagelok Company; 1999
Tarkett; 1998
TourismOhio Buying, Media, Planning, Strategy
Troy-Bilt Campaign: "Built for Life", Digital, Mobile, POS, Radio, Social Media, TV
U.S. Cotton Swisspers (Agency of Record)

THE MAREK GROUP
(Formerly Brandspring Solutions LLC)
6625 W 78th St Ste 260, Bloomington, MN 55439
Tel.: (952) 345-7273
Fax: (952) 345-7261
E-Mail: dave.maiser@brandspringsolutions.com
Web Site: http://www.marekgroup.com/

E-Mail for Key Personnel:
President:
dave.maiser@brandspringsolutions.com
Production Mgr.:
tara.beyer@brandspringsolutions.com

Employees: 12
Year Founded: 1975

Agency Specializes In: Advertising, Brand Development & Integration, Business Publications, Business-To-Business, Catalogs, Co-op Advertising, Collateral, Consulting, Corporate Communications, Corporate Identity, Digital/Interactive, Direct Response Marketing, E-Commerce, Electronic Media, Engineering, Exhibit/Trade Shows, Financial, Food Service, Graphic Design, Health Care Services, High Technology, Industrial, Information Technology, Integrated Marketing, Internet/Web Design, Local Marketing, Logo & Package Design, Magazines, Marine, Market Research, Media Buying Services, Media Planning, Media Relations, Medical Products, Multimedia, New Technologies, Newspapers & Magazines, Paid Searches, Planning & Consultation, Point of Purchase, Point of Sale, Print, Production, Production (Print), Promotions, Public Relations, Publicity/Promotions, Sales Promotion, Search Engine Optimization, Social Marketing/Nonprofit, Strategic Planning/Research, Technical Advertising, Trade & Consumer Magazines, Web (Banner Ads, Pop-ups, etc.)

Approx. Annual Billings: $2,400,000

Breakdown of Gross Billings by Media: Collateral: 5%; Internet Adv.: 20%; Print: 10%; Trade & Consumer Mags.: 5%; Worldwide Web Sites: 60%

Mark Sprester *(Dir-Art)*
Tara Beyer *(Sr Acct Mgr)*
Charles Stannard *(Acct Exec)*

Accounts:
ASI DataMyte
Continental Hydraulics; Minneapolis, MN Hydraulic Components; 2005
General Mills; Minneapolis, MN Foodservice Flour & Bakery Mixes; 1993
Mirror Disk; Minneapolis, MN Online Backup Services; 2008
OnPoint On Demand; Portsmouth, NH Printing; 2007
Soluxe; Darien, CT Imprinted Products; 2008
Thomas Engineering Co.; Minneapolis, MN Custom Precision Metal Stampings; 1975
Thrivent Financial; Minneapolis, MN Financial Products; 2004
United Health Group; Minneapolis, MN Health Insurance; 2007
University of Minnesota; Minneapolis, MN Landscape Arboretum; 2003

MARICICH BRAND COMMUNICATIONS
18201 McDurmott W Ste A, Irvine, CA 92614
Tel.: (949) 223-6455
Fax: (949) 223-6451
E-Mail: mark@maricich.com
Web Site: www.maricich.com

National Agency Associations: TAAN

Agency Specializes In: Advertising, Brand Development & Integration, Business-To-Business, Cable T.V., Co-op Advertising, Consumer Marketing, Corporate Communications, Corporate Identity, Direct Response Marketing, Direct-to-Consumer, Event Planning & Marketing, Government/Political, Health Care Services, Local Marketing, Media Buying Services, Media Relations, Medical Products, Over-50 Market, Public Relations, Seniors' Market, Viral/Buzz/Word of Mouth

Suzanne Maricich *(Founder-Maricich Healthcare Comm)*
David Maricich *(Pres)*
Mark Maricich *(CEO)*
Debbie Karnowsky *(Exec Dir-Creative)*
Tina Badat *(Dir-Mktg & Bus Dev)*
Kate Jennings *(Dir-PR)*
Cindy Ramirez *(Mgr-Studio)*

Accounts:
Abbott Laboratories
Golden State Water Company
Memorial Care
PCI

MARINA MAHER COMMUNICATIONS
(Acquired by Omnicom Group Inc.)

MARINELLI & COMPANY
25 E 21st St 9th Fl, New York, NY 10010-6207
Tel.: (212) 254-3366
Fax: (212) 477-2282
E-Mail: kmarinelli@marinellic.com
Web Site: www.marinellic.com

E-Mail for Key Personnel:
President: kmarinelli@marinellic.com

Employees: 23
Year Founded: 1974

Agency Specializes In: Advertising, Automotive, Bilingual Market, Brand Development & Integration, Broadcast, Business-To-Business, Children's Market, Collateral, Communications, Consumer Marketing, Corporate Communications, Corporate Identity, Cosmetics, Digital/Interactive, Direct Response Marketing, Direct-to-Consumer, Education, Entertainment, Event Planning & Marketing, Exhibit/Trade Shows, Experience Design, Financial, Food Service, Government/Political, Graphic Design, Guerilla Marketing, Health Care Services, High Technology, Integrated Marketing, Internet/Web Design, Local Marketing, Logo & Package Design, Merchandising, Mobile Marketing, New Product Development, Newspapers & Magazines, Package Design, Pharmaceutical, Point of Purchase, Point of Sale, Print, Production, Production (Print), Promotions, Radio, Restaurant, Retail, Sales Promotion, Sports Market, Strategic Planning/Research, Sweepstakes, Teen Market, Travel & Tourism, Viral/Buzz/Word of Mouth

Approx. Annual Billings: $3,000,000

Breakdown of Gross Billings by Media: Collateral: 10%; D.M.: 10%; Event Mktg.: 10%; Graphic Design: 15%; Logo & Package Design: 10%; Point of Sale: 10%; Print: 10%; Radio & T.V.: 5%; Sls. Promo.: 10%; Strategic Planning/Research: 10%

Ric Sella *(Sr VP)*

Accounts:
Altria
Benzel-Busch Motor Car Corp.; 2000
Celtic Crossing
Colgate Palmolive
Delta Storage
Ecosmart
Elizabeth Arden; New York, NY; 2000
GlaxoSmithKline
Kobrand Corporation St. Francis Wines
Loews Cineplex Entertainment; New York, NY; 2001
Natural Health Science; Geneva, Switzerland
Prelox, Pycnogenol; 2002
Oracle Beauty Brands; NJ
XO Holdings, Inc.; Reston, VA; 2005

THE MARINO ORGANIZATION, INC.
171 Madison Ave 12th Fl, New York, NY 10016
Tel.: (212) 889-0808
Fax: (212) 889-2457
E-Mail: info@themarino.org
Web Site: www.themarino.org

Employees: 20
Year Founded: 1993

Agency Specializes In: Collateral, Communications, Corporate Communications, Crisis Communications, Email, Event Planning & Marketing, Financial, Government/Political, Internet/Web Design, Media Relations, Media Training, Multimedia, Outdoor, Public Relations, Publishing, Real Estate, Retail, Social Marketing/Nonprofit, Strategic Planning/Research, Trade & Consumer Magazines, Travel & Tourism

Revenue: $2,100,000

Lee A. Silberstein *(Exec VP)*
John F. Marino *(Sr VP)*
Russ Colchamiro *(VP-Comml Real Estate)*
Tom Corsillo *(Assoc VP)*
Elizabeth Ferrara-Latino *(Acct Dir)*
Michelle Friedman *(Acct Dir)*
Megan Romano *(Acct Mgr)*
Ross M. Wallenstein *(Sr Acct Supvr)*

Accounts:
Servcorp NYC Public Relations

MARION INTEGRATED MARKETING
2900 Weslayan Ste 610, Houston, TX 77027
Tel.: (713) 623-6444
E-Mail: info2@marion.com
Web Site: www.marion.com

Agency Specializes In: Advertising, Brand Development & Integration, Corporate Identity, Event Planning & Marketing, Graphic Design, Public Relations, Search Engine Optimization, Social Media

John Anger *(Dir-Mktg)*
Arnaldo Larios *(Acct Exec)*

Accounts:
New-The Moody Foundation

MARIS, WEST & BAKER, INC.
18 Northtown Dr, Jackson, MS 39211-3016
Tel.: (601) 977-9200
Fax: (601) 977-9257
E-Mail: peter.marks@mwb.com
Web Site: www.mwb.com

Employees: 21
Year Founded: 1970

Agency Specializes In: Automotive, Financial, Government/Political, Health Care Services, Restaurant

Peter Marks *(Co-Owner & Pres)*
Mike Booth *(CFO)*
Marc Leffler *(VP & Dir-Creative)*
Randy Lynn *(VP & Dir-Creative)*
Angie Smith *(VP & Dir-Media)*
Austin Cannon *(VP-Interactive Svcs)*
Tim Mask *(VP-Brand Plng & Dev)*
Jonathan Pettus *(Sr Acct Exec)*

Accounts:
AMVAC
Cadence Bank
Crossroads Film Festival
Energy Nuclear
Genuine Scooter Company
Jackson Convention/Visitors Bureau
Soulshine Pizza Factory
Sweet Peppers Deli
Thermo-Kool

MARK ADVERTISING AGENCY, INC.
1600 5th St, Sandusky, OH 44870
Tel.: (419) 626-9000
Fax: (419) 626-9934
Web Site: www.markadvertising.com

Employees: 15

Agency Specializes In: Advertising, Brand Development & Integration, Digital/Interactive, Graphic Design, Internet/Web Design, Print, Social Media

Revenue: $1,500,000

Shelly Chesbro *(Pres)*
Katherine Dragon *(Office Mgr)*
Chip Chesbro *(Mgr-Production)*
Jennifer Yochem *(Rep-Sls)*

Accounts:
Bay Manufacturing
Gaymont Nursing Center
Sandusky State Theatre
Stein Hospice

MARKE COMMUNICATIONS
381 5th Ave, New York, NY 10016
Tel.: (212) 201-0600
Fax: (212) 213-0785
E-Mail: sales@marke.com
Web Site: www.marke.com

Year Founded: 2003

Agency Specializes In: Catalogs, Collateral, Corporate Communications, Direct Response Marketing, Fashion/Apparel, Package Design, Point of Sale, Retail

Sandra Cooper *(VP-Creative & Acct Svcs)*
Yolanda Rivera *(Dir-Acctg & Admin)*

Accounts:
CPA2Biz; New York, NY

MARKEN COMMUNICATIONS INC.
3375 Scott Blvd Ste 236, Santa Clara, CA 95054-3113
Tel.: (408) 986-0100
Fax: (408) 986-0162
E-Mail: andy@markencom.com
Web Site: www.markencom.com

E-Mail for Key Personnel:
President: andy@markencom.com

Employees: 9
Year Founded: 1977

National Agency Associations: BPA-PMA-PRSA

Agency Specializes In: Business-To-Business, Consumer Marketing, Consumer Publications, E-Commerce, Electronic Media, Event Planning &

Marketing, Exhibit/Trade Shows, High Technology, Industrial, Information Technology, Internet/Web Design, Investor Relations, Planning & Consultation, Public Relations, Publicity/Promotions, Strategic Planning/Research, Technical Advertising

Approx. Annual Billings: $5,100,000

Breakdown of Gross Billings by Media: Fees: $2,040,000; Mags.: $3,060,000

Andy Marken *(Pres)*
Dan Bell *(VP-Regulatory Compliance & Technical Affairs)*
Kathy Gerson *(VP-US East Coast Ops & Global Customer Svc)*
Ralph Venturini *(VP-Sls)*
Michael Macneir *(Dir-Comml Ops)*
Christine Noble *(Dir-Mktg-Global)*
Ricardo Batarce *(Mgr-Ops)*
Colleen Tabala *(Mgr-HR-Global)*

Accounts:
ADS Tech; Cerritos, CA Audio/Video Hardware & Software; 2002
BrightSign; Los Gatos, CA
Corel
Cyberlink; Fremont, CA Video Production Software; 2007
Dazzle; Fremont, CA
InterVideo; Fremont, CA Software; 2001
Migo Software; Foster City, CA Software; 2005
Mitsubishi Chemical Co; Sunnyvale, CA Storage; 1994
NewTech Infosystems; Orange, CA Software; 2000
Other World Computing; Woodstock, IL
Panasonic; Osaka, Japan
Pinnacle Systems; Mountain View, CA Video Production; 2007
Ulead Software; Fremont, CA Video Software; 2003
Verbatim Inc.; Charlotte, NC Storage Systems & Media; 1996

MARKER SEVEN, INC.

300 Beale St Ste A, San Francisco, CA 94105-2091
Tel.: (415) 447-2841
Fax: (415) 447-2860
Web Site: www.markerseven.com

Employees: 17
Year Founded: 2001

Agency Specializes In: Advertising, Internet/Web Design, Web (Banner Ads, Pop-ups, etc.)

Revenue: $1,600,000

John Clauss *(Founder & CEO)*
Patrick Ford *(Partner)*
Scott Abbott *(Dir-Creative)*
Jeremy Amos *(Dir-Tech)*

Accounts:
Abarca Group
College Media Solutions
Gallagher Sharp West
Green Coast Foundation
Greener World Media
Marriott Residential Suite
US Telecom Association

MARKET CONNECTIONS

82 Patton Ave Ste 710, Asheville, NC 28801
Tel.: (828) 398-5250
Web Site: www.mktconnections.com

Agency Specializes In: Advertising, Brand Development & Integration, Event Planning & Marketing, Graphic Design, Internet/Web Design, Print, Public Relations, Radio, Strategic Planning/Research, T.V.

Karen Tessier *(Pres)*
Brad Campbell *(Dir-Creative)*
Nathan Jordan *(Dir-Creative)*
Katie Rotanz *(Dir-Art)*

Accounts:
Diamond Brand Outdoors
Keystone Camp

MARKET DEVELOPMENT GROUP, INC.

5151 Wisconsin Ave NW 4th Fl, Washington, DC 20016
Tel.: (202) 298-8030
Fax: (202) 244-4999
E-Mail: mdginc@mdginc.org
Web Site: www.mdginc.org

Employees: 33
Year Founded: 1978

Agency Specializes In: Advertising, Advertising Specialties, Direct Response Marketing, Faith Based, Health Care Services, Infomercials, Magazines, New Product Development, Pets , Strategic Planning/Research, Sweepstakes

Approx. Annual Billings: $50,000,000

Breakdown of Gross Billings by Media: Adv. Specialities: $5,000,000; D.M.: $32,500,000; Event Mktg.: $1,000,000; Exhibits/Trade Shows: $1,000,000; Foreign: $5,000,000; Graphic Design: $5,000,000; Spot T.V.: $500,000

John Alahouzos *(Founder, Partner & Exec VP)*
W. Michael Gretschel *(Pres & CEO)*
Ann Papp *(Sr VP)*
Bill Walley *(VP-Real Estate, Construction & Maintenance)*

Accounts:
American Action Fund for Blind Children & Adults
The Humane Society of the United States
International Fund for Animal Welfare
National Federation of the Blind
Southwest Indian Children's Fund

MARKET FORCE, INC.

109 N Boylan Ave, Raleigh, NC 27603
Tel.: (919) 828-7887
Fax: (919) 832-1807
E-Mail: njohnson@theforce.com
Web Site: www.theforce.com

Employees: 5
Year Founded: 1993

National Agency Associations: Second Wind Limited

Agency Specializes In: Advertising, Business-To-Business, Collateral, Consulting, Consumer Marketing, Corporate Identity, Direct Response Marketing, Graphic Design, Logo & Package Design, Media Buying Services, Outdoor, Planning & Consultation, Point of Purchase, Point of Sale, Print, Radio, Real Estate, Strategic Planning/Research, Travel & Tourism

Revenue: $1,000,000

Nancy P. Johnson *(Pres)*

Accounts:
ElectriCities of NC; Raleigh, NC Association of Municipal Utilities; 1991

MARKETEL

1100 Rene-Levesque Boulevard West 19th Floor, Montreal, QC H3B 4N4 Canada
Tel.: (514) 935-9445
Fax: (514) 935-5623
E-Mail: jduval@marketel.com
Web Site: www.marketel.com

Employees: 131
Year Founded: 1977

National Agency Associations: ICA

Agency Specializes In: Advertising

Approx. Annual Billings: $89,000,000

Jacques L. Duval *(Chm & CEO)*
Martin Le Sauteur *(Pres & COO)*
Diane Ridgway-Cross *(Exec VP)*
Jill Edmonds *(Acct Dir)*
Alain Bourgeois *(Dir-Creative & Sr Copywriter)*
Marie Pierre Blanchette *(Dir-Digital Experiences)*
Jo-Ann Munro *(Dir-Creative)*
Genevieve O'Keefe *(Dir-Digital Strategic Resources)*
Sebastien Pelletier *(Dir-Creative)*
Lina Moussaoui *(Acct Exec-Client Svcs)*

Accounts:
AB INBEV Alexander Keith's, Beck's, Brava, Budweiser, Labatt Blue, Michelobe, Rolling Rock, Stella Artois, Ultra
ACE Aviation Holdings Inc.
Air Canada
Canada Savings Bonds
Domaine Pinnacle
FCA Canada Inc.
Fonds de Solidarite FTQ
L'Oreal Paris
Maybelline New York
New-Reitmans Hyba, Marketing
Rogers Wireless
Rougier Pharma

MARKETGARDEN LLC

1504 Argonne Dr, Dallas, TX 75208-3507
Tel.: (214) 232-1674
Fax: (214) 750-6542
E-Mail: info@marketgardenllc.com
Web Site: www.marketgardenllc.com

Employees: 3
Year Founded: 2005

Agency Specializes In: Advertising, Brand Development & Integration, Business-To-Business, Catalogs, Collateral, Communications, Computers & Software, Consulting, Content, Corporate Communications, Corporate Identity

Approx. Annual Billings: $750,000

Bill Reed *(Principal)*

Accounts:
Baylor All Saints Hospital
CANTEX
Cognizant Technology IT; 2005

MARKETING ALTERNATIVES, INC.

21925 Field Pkwy Ste 200, Deer Park, IL 60010-7208
Tel.: (847) 719-2299
Fax: (847) 719-2288
E-Mail: info@mktalt.com
Web Site: www.mktalt.com/index.html

E-Mail for Key Personnel:
President: gjstanko@mktalt.com

Employees: 30
Year Founded: 1983

National Agency Associations: BMA

Agency Specializes In: Business-To-Business, Consumer Marketing, Information Technology, Integrated Marketing, Telemarketing

Approx. Annual Billings: $10,000,000 Fees Capitalized

Gary Jon Stanko *(Pres)*
Joe Lamonica *(CFO)*
Ram Patibandla *(CIO & Exec VP)*
Darcy Tudor *(Exec VP-Call Center Div)*
Scott Roof *(Exec Dir-Strategic Bus Partnerships)*
Darla Maclean *(Dir-HR)*
Jason Carlile *(Mgr-Ops)*

Accounts:
Abbott Laboratories
AllSteel
Allstate
BR-111
Bridgestone/Firestone
Cole Taylor Bank
Crossville Ceramics
Florida Tile
Lowes
Mannington Mills
Mohawk Industries
Pactiv Corp. Hefty
Seaquist Closures
Wilsonart Flooring

MARKETING & ADVERTISING BUSINESS UNLIMITED, INC.

(d/b/a MABU)
1003 Gateway Ave, Bismarck, ND 58503
Tel.: (701) 250-0728
Fax: (701) 250-1788
Toll Free: (800) 568-9346
E-Mail: mmabin@agencymabu.com
Web Site: www.agencymabu.com

Employees: 20
Year Founded: 2001

Agency Specializes In: Advertising, Advertising Specialties, Alternative Advertising, Brand Development & Integration, Broadcast, Business Publications, Business-To-Business, Cable T.V., Collateral, Commercial Photography, Communications, Consulting, Consumer Publications, Content, Corporate Communications, Corporate Identity, Digital/Interactive, E-Commerce, Education, Electronic Media, Email, Event Planning & Marketing, Exhibit/Trade Shows, Government/Political, Graphic Design, Guerilla Marketing, Health Care Services, Hospitality, Identity Marketing, Integrated Marketing, International, Internet/Web Design, Logo & Package Design, Market Research, Media Buying Services, Media Planning, Media Relations, Mobile Marketing, Multicultural, Multimedia, New Technologies, Newspaper, Newspapers & Magazines, Out-of-Home Media, Outdoor, Over-50 Market, Planning & Consultation, Podcasting, Print, Production, Production (Ad, Film, Broadcast), Production (Print), Promotions, Public Relations, Publicity/Promotions, RSS (Really Simple Syndication), Radio, Real Estate, Recruitment, Regional, Sales Promotion, Search Engine Optimization, Seniors' Market, Social Marketing/Nonprofit, Social Media, Stakeholders, Strategic Planning/Research, T.V., Trade & Consumer Magazines, Transportation, Travel & Tourism, Web (Banner Ads, Pop-ups, etc.), Women's Market, Yellow Pages Advertising

Approx. Annual Billings: $2,500,000

Breakdown of Gross Billings by Media: Internet Adv.: 20%; Out-of-Home Media: 10%; Print: 25%; Production: 10%; Radio & T.V.: 25%; Worldwide Web Sites: 10%

Mike Mabin *(Founder)*
Sean Fennington *(Client Svcs Dir)*

Accounts:
U.S. Army Civilian Corps; San Antonio, TX Recruitment for Medical/Dental Personnel; 2009
U.S. Dept. of Justice; Washington, DC Government Meetings & Events; 2009

MARKETING & MEDIA SOLUTIONS, INC.

304 E Gibson St, Haubstadt, IN 47639
Mailing Address:
11497 S 450 E, Haubstadt, IN 47639
Tel.: (812) 768-5555
Fax: (812) 768-5550
Web Site: www.marketingmediasolutions.com

Agency Specializes In: Advertising, Internet/Web Design, Print, Radio, T.V.

Kye Hofman *(Owner)*
Kristie Goedde *(Office Mgr)*

Accounts:
Fehrenbacher Cabinets Inc
Kings Great Buys Plus

MARKETING ARCHITECTS, INC.

(Private-Parent-Single Location)
110 Cheshire Ln Ste 200, Minnetonka, MN 55305
Tel.: (952) 449-2500
E-Mail: info@markarch.com
Web Site: http://www.marketingarchitects.com/

Employees: 92
Year Founded: 1996

Agency Specializes In: Advertising, Media Planning, Search Engine Optimization, Social Media

Revenue: $5,400,000

Charles Hengel *(Founder & CEO)*
Brent Longval *(Pres & CFO)*
Christopher Crowhurst *(CTO)*
Rob DeMars *(Chief Creative Officer)*
Katie Scheetz *(Exec VP-Bus Dev)*
Angela Voss *(Exec VP-Acct Svcs)*
Ryan Kinkaid *(VP-Creative)*
Josh Madigan *(VP-Digital Strategy)*
Eric Pilhofer *(VP-Creative)*

Accounts:
New-Bare Escentuals, Inc.
New-HurryCane LLC
New-Rosetta Stone Inc.

THE MARKETING ARM

1999 Bryan St 18th Fl, Dallas, TX 75201-3125
Tel.: (214) 259-3200
Fax: (214) 259-3201
E-Mail: info@themarketingarm.com
Web Site: www.themarketingarm.com

Employees: 550
Year Founded: 1993

Agency Specializes In: Digital/Interactive, Entertainment, Shopper Marketing, Social Media, Sponsorship

Matt Delzell *(Mng Dir)*
Chris Smith *(Chief Strategy Officer)*
Gregg Hamburger *(Chief Integration Officer)*
Daniel Belmont *(Pres-Sports)*
Jeff Chown *(Pres-Davie Brown Entertainment)*
Jordis Rosenquest *(Exec VP-Plng, Insights & Performance Science)*
Nowell Upham *(Exec VP-Consumer Engagement)*
Doug Dunkin *(Sr VP-Bus Dev)*
Amy Erschen *(Sr VP-Acct Svcs)*
Michelle Palmer *(Sr VP)*
Ben Day *(Grp VP-Creative)*
Trina Roffino *(Grp VP-Acct Svc)*
Dina Light-McNeely *(VP & Head-Strategic Acct)*
Melvin Strobbe *(VP & Dir-Creative)*
Tony Amador *(VP-Bus Dev)*
Jeff Erickson *(VP-Digital Engagement)*
Mary O'Connor *(VP-Global Olympic)*
Lori Sutherland-Thelen *(VP-Acct Svc)*
Andrew Thompson *(VP-TMA Experiential)*
Leo Santos *(Sr Dir-Creative)*
Chris Anderson *(Dir-Comm & Education)*
Genevieve Polito Nguyen *(Assoc Dir-Concept)*
Nikki Cloer *(Acct Mgr)*
Corey Lark *(Acct Supvr-Digital)*
Katherine Araujo *(Sr Acct Exec)*
Sarah Bunner *(Acct Exec)*
Colleen O'Connor *(Acct Exec)*
Chris Morales *(Assoc Acct Dir)*

Accounts:
American Airlines
AT&T, Inc. Campaign: "Be The Fan"
Chili's Grill & Bar
The Dannon Company, Inc.
Dewar's
Frito-Lay Campaign: "Do Us A Flavor", Cheetos, Crash the Super Bowl, Doritos, In-Store Marketing, Lay's, Multipack, Tostitos
GameStop Corp. Promotions
Hilton Worldwide Hospitality, Sports
JC Penney "Oscars Play to Give" Game, Mobile
Mars Entertainment, Talent
Monster.com Digital, Promotions, Talent
Novartis AG
Pepsi Campaign: "Test Drive", Celebrity Talent, Entertainment, PepsiMAX, Uncle Drew
Quaker Chewy Superstar, Shopper Marketing
State Farm Digital, Events, Sports
Unilever Campaign: "Care Makes a Man Stronger", Campaign: "Journey to Comfort", Campaign: "Real Strength", Dove, Dove Men + Care, Super Bowl 2015
Victoria's Secret Entertainment, Mobile

Branches

The Marketing Arm

4721 Alla Rd, Marina Del Rey, CA 90292
Tel.: (310) 754-3000
Fax: (310) 754-3001
Web Site: www.themarketingarm.com

Agency Specializes In: Advertising, Digital/Interactive, Social Media

Chris Smith *(Chief Strategy Officer)*
Brad Alesi *(Chief Digital Officer)*
Tom Meyer *(Pres-Entertainment)*
Andrew Robinson *(Pres-Consumer Engagement)*
Larry Weintraub *(CEO-Social Media)*
Melissa Taylor *(Sr VP & Acct Dir-Digital)*
Melissa Fallon-Miller *(Sr VP-Television, Film & Digital)*
Todd Ervin *(VP-Multicultural)*

Accounts:
PepsiCo Inc. Pepsi Max

The Marketing Arm

711 3rd Ave 11th Fl, New York, NY 10017
Tel.: (212) 284-7686
Web Site: www.themarketingarm.com

Larry Weintraub *(Chief Innovation Officer & Pres-Music Strategy)*
Brad Groves *(Exec VP)*
Robert Familetti *(Exec Dir)*

Charles Black *(Dir-Digital)*

THE MARKETING CENTER OF THE UNIVERSE

1539 Jackson Ave 5th Fl, New Orleans, LA 70130
Tel.: (504) 525-0932
Fax: (504) 525-7011
E-Mail: info@themarketingcenter.com
Web Site: www.themarketingcenter.com

E-Mail for Key Personnel:
President: nchapman@themarketingcenter.com

Employees: 13
Year Founded: 1991

National Agency Associations: AAF-AMA

Agency Specializes In: Advertising, Broadcast, Cable T.V., Digital/Interactive, Direct Response Marketing, Internet/Web Design, Legal Services, Media Buying Services, Media Planning, Media Relations, Outdoor, Print, Production, Production (Print), Publicity/Promotions, Radio, Search Engine Optimization, Syndication, T.V., Yellow Pages Advertising

Approx. Annual Billings: $15,000,000

Breakdown of Gross Billings by Media: Local Mktg.: 100%

Nathan Chapman *(Owner, Founder & Pres)*
Clark Castle *(Assoc Dir-Creative)*
Cindy Bower *(Mgr-Production)*
Alex Ludwig *(Sr Acct Exec)*
Mandy Lee *(Media Buyer)*

Accounts:
Social Security Disability Attorneys
Vieux Carre Property Owners; New Orleans, LA
Workers Compensations Attorneys

MARKETING CONCEPTS GROUP

6 Old Field Rd, Weston, CT 06883
Tel.: (203) 454-0800
Fax: (203) 454-0507
Toll Free: (866) DIJIT01
E-Mail: weaverpd@mcgtec.com
Web Site: www.mcgtec.com

Employees: 5
Year Founded: 1981

Agency Specializes In: Advertising, Automotive, Brand Development & Integration, Co-op Advertising, Collateral, Consulting, Consumer Marketing, Graphic Design, High Technology, Internet/Web Design, Logo & Package Design, New Product Development, Package Design, Point of Purchase, Point of Sale, Print, Sales Promotion, Social Marketing/Nonprofit

Breakdown of Gross Billings by Media: Collateral: 20%; Consulting: 80%

Paul D. Weaver *(Pres)*
Rick Crouch *(Partner)*
Tomas Jablonski *(CTO)*
Lawrence Kilfoy *(Mgr-Bus Dev)*

Accounts:
Boy Scouts of America; Irving, TX Membership, Publications; 1981
Hershey Chocolate USA
NHL; New York, NY E-Commerce; 2001
Salty Snack Food Company
SONY Digital; Amsterdam, Netherlands; Tokyo, Japan Digital Photography, OS; 2001

THE MARKETING DEPARTMENT

457 King St, London, ON N6B 1S8 Canada
Tel.: (519) 439-8080
Fax: (519) 439-8081
Toll Free: (866) 439-8080
Web Site: www.tmd.ca

Employees: 15
Year Founded: 1995

Joseph Farina *(Owner)*
Randy Timmins *(Pres)*
Nancy Gee *(Dir-Strategy & Client Svcs)*
Link Malott *(Dir-Ops)*
Margo Visser *(Dir-Admin, Fin & HR)*
Craig Forsey *(Assoc Dir-Creative)*
Ryan Byrne *(Mgr-Mktg & Client Svcs Mgr)*
Diane Allen *(Mgr-Admin)*
Kari Rennie *(Mgr-Social Media Mktg)*
Nicholas Callender *(Designer-Production)*

Accounts:
Alcon Canada
Arctic
Black Berry
Domus
Huron
Iciniti
Kanter Yachts
Keith Brown Magician
Lawon
LCS
Mountain HardWear
North Star
SISKINDS
Sorel
Summit

MARKETING DIRECTIONS, INC.

28005 Clemens Rd, Cleveland, OH 44145
Tel.: (440) 835-5550
Fax: (440) 892-9195
Web Site: marketingdirectionsinc.com/

E-Mail for Key Personnel:
President: nick@ideaswithapoint.com
Creative Dir.: scott@ideaswithapoint.com
Production Mgr.: marie@ideaswithapoint.com

Employees: 14
Year Founded: 1980

National Agency Associations: ADFED-BMA

Agency Specializes In: Advertising, Automotive, Brand Development & Integration, Business-To-Business, Communications, Consumer Goods, Consumer Marketing, Consumer Publications, Corporate Communications, Corporate Identity, Customer Relationship Management, Direct-to-Consumer, E-Commerce, Electronic Media, Event Planning & Marketing, Food Service, Graphic Design, Health Care Services, In-Store Advertising, Internet/Web Design, Logo & Package Design, Magazines, Media Buying Services, Media Planning, Media Relations, Medical Products, New Product Development, Newspapers & Magazines, Outdoor, Package Design, Point of Sale, Print, Production, Public Relations, Retail, Sales Promotion, Trade & Consumer Magazines

Nicholas J. Lowe *(Pres)*
Marie Bozek *(CFO)*
John Brubaker *(VP & Mgr-Special Projects)*
Scott Camarati *(Dir-Creative)*
Cathy Schwark *(Acct Exec)*
Kelly Sullivan *(Acct Exec)*

Accounts:
Arnold
City of Middleburg Heights
Federal-Mogul Automotive Aftermarket Products; 1998
Napa Gaskets
Rivals Sports Grille; 2007
Saint Luke's Foundation

MARKETING EDGE GROUP

1555 Ruth Rd Units 1 & 2, North Brunswick, NJ 08902
Tel.: (732) 658-1540
Fax: (732) 745-1990
E-Mail: info@medge.com
Web Site: www.megdigital.com/

Employees: 8
Year Founded: 1995

Agency Specializes In: Automotive, Communications, Financial, Logo & Package Design, Medical Products, Pharmaceutical, Real Estate, Retail

Approx. Annual Billings: $5,000,000

Rama Marupilla *(Partner & VP-Software Dev)*
Christine Conant *(Dir-Art)*
Jason Vosu *(Dir-Digital Strategy & Implementation)*
Nancy Cerza *(Acct Mgr)*
Liz Gau *(Acct Mgr)*
Stephanie Stefanelli *(Acct Mgr)*

Accounts:
AT&T Communications Corp.; Bridgewater, NJ Business Services; 1996
Capital Asset Exchange
Digital Source 360
Douglas Laboratories; Pittsburgh, PA; 1999
Granutec, Inc.
Image Stream Productions
JS Group
Marketing Zone
MD On-line
Pfizer
Phillips
Quest Diagnostics; Teterboro, NJ; 1999
Roche Diagnotics
Sea Tel
Tris Pharma
Trius Therapeutics
US HealthConnect
Venodyne; Columbus, MS; 2000

THE MARKETING GARAGE

(Formerly Larter Advertising)
15243 Yonge St, Aurora, ON L4G 1L8 Canada
Tel.: (905) 727-6978
Fax: (905) 727-0103
Toll Free: (855) 223-8313
E-Mail: bob@themarketinggarage.ca
Web Site: www.themarketinggarage.ca

National Agency Associations: Second Wind Limited

Bob Nunn *(Owner & Pres)*

Accounts:
Career Builder Canada
Dawson Dental Centres
Niagara Parks Commission
Pathways to Perennials
Timberland Footwear

MARKETING GROUP

880 Louis Dr, Warminster, PA 18974
Tel.: (215) 259-1500
Fax: (215) 259-0290
E-Mail: rdean@mgadvertising.com
Web Site: www.mgadvertising.com

E-Mail for Key Personnel:
President: jnotte@mgadvertising.com
Media Dir.: rsherwood@mgadvertising.com

Employees: 37
Year Founded: 1975

National Agency Associations: IAAA

Agency Specializes In: Advertising Specialties, Brand Development & Integration, Business Publications, Business-To-Business, Cable T.V., Collateral, Communications, Consulting, Consumer Marketing, Consumer Publications, Corporate Identity, Direct Response Marketing, E-Commerce, Event Planning & Marketing, Exhibit/Trade Shows, Graphic Design, In-Store Advertising, Industrial, Infomercials, Internet/Web Design, Leisure, Logo & Package Design, Magazines, Multimedia, Newspaper, Newspapers & Magazines, Outdoor, Planning & Consultation, Point of Purchase, Point of Sale, Print, Public Relations, Publicity/Promotions, Real Estate, Sales Promotion, Strategic Planning/Research, T.V., Trade & Consumer Magazines, Yellow Pages Advertising

Approx. Annual Billings: $17,450,000

Breakdown of Gross Billings by Media: Adv. Specialities: $565,000; Cable T.V.: $510,000; Collateral: $265,000; Comml. Photography: $375,000; Consulting: $880,000; Consumer Publs.: $400,000; D.M.: $530,000; Fees: $725,000; Graphic Design: $870,000; Logo & Package Design: $85,500; Mags.: $1,440,000; Newsp.: $5,709,000; Outdoor: $125,000; Print: $2,483,500; Production: $625,000; Pub. Rels.: $335,000; Sls. Promo.: $895,000; Spot T.V.: $185,000; Yellow Page Adv.: $447,000

James Notte *(Pres-West)*
Randi Sherwood *(Sr VP)*
Kirk Zucal *(Sr VP)*
Charlie Guardino *(Dir-Media & Sr Acct Mgr)*
Bill Beck *(Sr Acct Supvr)*
Tom Gilmore *(Sr Acct Exec)*

Accounts:
The American Red Cross, Lower Bucks Chapter; Newtown, PA
Anthony & Sylvan Pools; Doylestown, PA Swimming Pools & Spas; 1980
Avalon Real Estate
Baulk Chemical Inc.
Bradford-White Corporation; Philadelphia, PA Water Heaters; 1978
Durasol Awnings
Gemini Bakery Equipment; Philadelphia, PA Bakery Equipment; 1996
Goldsteins Rosenberg Raphael Sacks Funeral Homes
Lux Products Corp.; Mount Laurel, NJ Retail Thermostats, Timers
Luxury Pools Magazine; Warminster, PA
Manor House Publishing
Pool & Spa Living Magazine; Feasterville, PA; 1996
Precision Transmission
St. Mary Medical Center; Langhorne, PA
Waterford Crystal

MARKETING IN COLOR
1515 N Marion St, Tampa, FL 33602
Tel.: (877) 258-3771
E-Mail: info@marketingincolor.com
Web Site: www.marketingincolor.com

Year Founded: 1996

Agency Specializes In: Advertising, Brand Development & Integration, Graphic Design, Internet/Web Design, Media Buying Services, Media Planning, Search Engine Optimization, Social Media

Cheryl Parrish *(Pres & CEO)*
John Parrish *(VP)*
Angela Mitchell *(Assoc Dir-Creative)*
MaryKay Scott *(Acct Exec)*

Accounts:
New-HD Law Partners

MARKETING INITIATIVES
481 Prince Arthur W Ste 301, Montreal, QC H2X 1T4 Canada
Tel.: (514) 271-0800
Fax: (514) 526-6678
E-Mail: markinit@bell.net

Employees: 5
Year Founded: 1989

Agency Specializes In: Advertising, Brand Development & Integration, Co-op Advertising, Collateral, Communications, Consulting, Consumer Goods, Consumer Marketing, Corporate Communications, E-Commerce, Fashion/Apparel, Food Service, Local Marketing, Logo & Package Design, Market Research, Media Buying Services, Media Planning, Media Relations, Men's Market, New Product Development, Out-of-Home Media, Outdoor, Package Design, Planning & Consultation, Production, Production (Print), Public Relations, Social Marketing/Nonprofit, Strategic Planning/Research, Women's Market

Howard Barrett *(Pres)*

Accounts:
United States Department of Commerce
Utex Corporation
Vitalicious Foods; New York, NY

MARKETING INNOVATIONS
6447 E Thunderbird Rd, Scottsdale, AZ 85254
Tel.: (480) 332-1963
E-Mail: info@mktginnovations.com
Web Site: www.mktginnovations.com

Employees: 3
Year Founded: 1975

Agency Specializes In: Advertising Specialties, Collateral, Consulting, Consumer Marketing, Direct Response Marketing, Exhibit/Trade Shows, Graphic Design, Health Care Services, Industrial, Legal Services, Logo & Package Design, Medical Products, New Product Development, Print, Production, Public Relations, Sales Promotion, Strategic Planning/Research

Approx. Annual Billings: $600,000

Breakdown of Gross Billings by Media: Audio/Visual: $150,000; Collateral: $200,000; D.M.: $125,000; Fees: $25,000; Print: $100,000

Kevin Arnold *(Owner)*
Clayton Arnold *(Pres & Dir-Creative)*

MARKETING INSPIRATIONS
(Acquired by Allied Integrated Marketing)

MARKETING MATTERS
2700 N 29th Ave, Hollywood, FL 33020
Tel.: (954) 925-1511
Fax: (954) 925-1549
E-Mail: info@marketingmatters.net
Web Site: www.marketingmatters.net

Employees: 5
Year Founded: 1997

Agency Specializes In: Advertising, Collateral, Entertainment, Event Planning & Marketing, Luxury Products, Newspaper, Product Placement, Public Relations, Publishing, Strategic Planning/Research

Coleen Sterns *(Pres)*
Matt Fleming *(Dir)*
Kyle Glass *(Dir-Mktg)*
Marie Holloway *(Dir-Creative)*
James Farquharson *(Assoc Dir)*

Accounts:
Avad
Cobb
New-KanexPro (Agency of Record) Advertising, Marketing Communications, Public Relations, Social Media
KEF America (Agency of Record)
Niles Audio Corporation
RGB Spectrum Public Relations

MARKETING MEDIA COMMUNICATION
10 W 100 S Ste 710, Salt Lake City, UT 84101
Tel.: (801) 359-8900
Fax: (801) 359-8933
Toll Free: (800) 587-5588
E-Mail: mmc@marketingmediacom.com
Web Site: www.marketingmediacom.com

Employees: 10
Year Founded: 1985

Agency Specializes In: Brand Development & Integration, Health Care Services, Internet/Web Design, Logo & Package Design, Medical Products, Pharmaceutical, Public Relations, Strategic Planning/Research

Stephen Holbrook *(Owner)*

Accounts:
Bard Access Systems
Bard Peripheral Vascular
Beehive Glass
Compass Capital
EMPI
Jeremy Ranch
Specialty Furniture
Weber State University

MARKETING OPTIONS, LLC
7965 Washington Woods Dr, Dayton, OH 45459
Tel.: (937) 436-2648
Fax: (937) 436-6156
E-Mail: info@moptions.com
Web Site: www.moptions.com

E-Mail for Key Personnel:
President: bcast@moptions.com
Media Dir.: mike@moptions.com

Employees: 3
Year Founded: 1987

Agency Specializes In: Advertising, Business Publications, Business-To-Business, Collateral, Communications, Consulting, E-Commerce, Electronic Media, Exhibit/Trade Shows, Graphic Design, Integrated Marketing, Internet/Web Design, Market Research, New Product Development, Print, Production (Print), Public Relations, Search Engine Optimization, Strategic Planning/Research, Trade & Consumer Magazines

Barbara Weber Castilano *(Owner)*
Bryan Strunk *(Dir-Art)*

Accounts:
International Mold Steel
Palmer Manufacturing

THE MARKETING PROS
10825 Caribou Ln, Orland Park, IL 60467
Tel.: (708) 205-2983
Web Site: www.themarketingpros.net

Year Founded: 2009

Agency Specializes In: Broadcast, Cable T.V., Co-op Advertising, Digital/Interactive, Email, Local Marketing, Newspapers & Magazines, Outdoor, Paid Searches, Print, Radio, Social Media, Sponsorship, T.V.

Todd Probasco *(Pres)*

Accounts:
New-Sherlock's Carpet & Tile Carpeting; 2009

MARKETING RESOURCE GROUP

225 S Washington Sq, Lansing, MI 48933
Tel.: (517) 372-4400
Web Site: www.mrgmi.com

Year Founded: 1979

Agency Specializes In: Advertising, Crisis Communications, Media Relations, Public Relations

Tom Shields *(Founder & Pres)*
Dave Doyle *(Exec VP)*
Donna Halinski *(Acct Dir)*
Eric Dimoff *(Acct Exec)*

Accounts:
New-Sparrow Foundation

MARKETING RESULTS INC.

2900 W Horizon Rdg Pkwy Ste 200, Henderson, NV 89052
Tel.: (702) 361-3850
Fax: (702) 361-2905
Web Site: www.marketingresults.net

Year Founded: 1988

Agency Specializes In: Direct Response Marketing, Email, Event Planning & Marketing, Graphic Design, Print

Gary Border *(Pres & COO)*
Patrice Gianni *(CEO)*
Craig Border *(VP-Database Mktg)*
Kevin McElroy *(VP-Creative Svcs)*
Meg Schroeder *(Exec Dir-Ops)*
Amy Morais *(Dir-Multimedia)*
Rebecca Perger *(Sr Acct Exec)*

THE MARKETING SHOP

605 East Baltimore Pike 2nd Fl E, Media, PA 19063
Tel.: (610) 967-1466
Web Site: mshop360.com/

Agency Specializes In: Advertising, Email, Internet/Web Design

Pat DiCola *(Founder & CMO)*
Ryan Fitzpatrick *(CIO & Dir-Tech)*

Accounts:
Difilippos Service Company
Wimpys Original

MARKETING SPECIFICS INC.

3050 Matlock Dr, Kennesaw, GA 30144
Tel.: (770) 426-1107
Fax: (770) 426-1305
Toll Free: (800) 717-8999
E-Mail: info@marketingspecifics.com
Web Site: www.marketingspecifics.com

Year Founded: 1987

National Agency Associations: Second Wind Limited

Agency Specializes In: Advertising, Advertising Specialties, Affluent Market, Brand Development & Integration, Catalogs, Collateral, Communications, Consulting, Consumer Marketing, Corporate Communications, Corporate Identity, Digital/Interactive, Direct Response Marketing, E-Commerce, Email, Event Planning & Marketing, Exhibit/Trade Shows, Graphic Design, Hospitality, Identity Marketing, Integrated Marketing, International, Internet/Web Design, Leisure, Logo & Package Design, Luxury Products, Market Research, Media Planning, Media Relations, Merchandising, Mobile Marketing, Over-50 Market, Point of Purchase, Production (Ad, Film, Broadcast), Production (Print), Public Relations, Publicity/Promotions, RSS (Really Simple Syndication), Radio, Real Estate, Retail, Sales Promotion, Search Engine Optimization, Seniors' Market, Social Marketing/Nonprofit, Social Media, Telemarketing, Web (Banner Ads, Pop-ups, etc.), Women's Market

Joan Barnes *(Founder & Pres)*

Accounts:
The Belknap Company Ltd.; Canaan, NY
Big Canoe; Big Canoe, GA
The Breakstone Group; Miami, FL
BridgeMill Development
B.T. Ventures; Charlotte, NC
Camden Summit, Inc.; Charlotte, NC
Chapel Hills Development; Douglasville, GA
Charter Bank; Marietta, GA
Childress Klein; Atlanta, GA
The Cliffs at Glassy; Landrum, SC
Cobb Rides; Marietta, GA
Cornwallis Development
Corporate Property Investors; New York, NY
Cousins Properties; Atlanta, GA
Crescent Communities
Dan Cowart Development
Dewey Homes; Paole, PA
The DiCanio Organization; Smithtown, NY
Eagle Real Estate Advisors; Duluth, GA
East West Partners; Raleigh, NC; Suffolk, VA
Engineered Structures Inc.; Atlanta, GA
The Equitable, Atlanta, GA
Ernst & Young; Atlanta, GA
Frank Betz & Associates; Atlanta, GA
Goldmark Realty; Atlanta, GA
Governors Club; Brentwood, TN
GTE Wireless; Atlanta, GA
Habersham; Beaufort, SC
Harbor Investments; Atlanta, GA
Havens Properties; Roswell, GA
Hawks Ridge; Alpharetta, GA
Homeland Communities; Norcross, GA
IDI; Atlanta, GA
JHA Enterprises, Inc.; Marietta, GA
John Wieland Homes & Neighborhoods; Atlanta, GA
Kaiser Communities; Atlanta, GA
Kingfort Homes; Greensboro, CA
Landrex Corp.; Toronto, Canada
Laurel Springs Realty; Cumming, GA
Legacy Property Group; Atlanta, GA
Liberty Properties; Greenville, SC
Macauley Homes & Neighborhoods; Marietta, GA
Marketing Results; Atlanta, GA
Miller Clapperton Partnership; Smyrna, GA
Minerva Communities LLP
Neumann Homes; Chicago, IL
New Homes America; Norcross, GA
Newland Communities
Northside Realty; Atlanta, GA
Park Signature Properties
Pathway Communities; Peachtree City, GA
Peachtree Development; Peachtree City, GA
Pulte Home Corp.; Baltimore, MD; Charlotte, NC; Columbus, OH
Reynolds Plantation; Greensboro, GA
Santa Maria Golf & Country Club; Baton Rouge, LA
Sharon McSwain Homes; Atlanta, GA
Shea Homes; Charlotte, NC
Simply Cinco; Katy, TX
SMG Development; Atlanta, GA
Southeast Capital Partnership, Inc.; Atlanta, GA
Southland Development; Norcross, GA
Sugarloaf Golf & Country Club; Duluth, GA
T.D. Page Development Co.; Atlanta, GA
Terrabrook; Orlando, FL; Charlotte, NC
Traton Corp.; Marietta, GA
TriStar Management; Memphis, TN
Wakefield Plantation; Raleigh, NC
West Cobb Developer Associates; Marietta, GA

MARKETING STRATEGIES INC.

4603 Oleander Dr Ste 4, Myrtle Beach, SC 29577
Tel.: (843) 692-9662
Fax: (843) 692-0558
E-Mail: production@marketingstrategiesinc.com
Web Site: www.marketingstrategiesinc.com

Agency Specializes In: Advertising, Brand Development & Integration, Collateral, Digital/Interactive, Graphic Design, Logo & Package Design, Media Relations, Media Training, Public Relations, Social Media

Denise Blackburn-Gay *(Pres & CEO)*
Erica Boardman Thomas *(Dir-Media & Mgr-Client Svcs)*

Accounts:
Lowes Foods

THE MARKETING WORKS

55 Murray St Ste 108, Ottawa, ON K1N 5M3 Canada
Tel.: (613) 241-4167
Fax: (613) 241-7321
E-Mail: info@the-marketing-works.com
Web Site: www.the-marketing-works.com

Employees: 2
Year Founded: 1993

Agency Specializes In: Brand Development & Integration, Business-To-Business, Communications, Consulting, High Technology, Planning & Consultation, Strategic Planning/Research

Rob Woyzbun *(Pres & Mng Partner)*

Accounts:
Bridgewater Systems
Canada Museum of Science and Technology
Canadian Medical Association Practice Solutions
Canadian Museum of Civilization
CMHC
The Electronic Courthouse
Export Development Corporation
The Heart & Stroke Foundation of Canada
Natural Resources Canada
Teknor Corporation
Transport Canada
United Way of Ottawa-Carleton

MARKETING WORKS, INC.

740 Lakeview Plz Blvd Ste 100, Worthington, OH 43085
Tel.: (614) 540-5520
Fax: (614) 540-5524
E-Mail: info@marketing-works.net
Web Site: marketing-works.net

Employees: 10

Agency Specializes In: Advertising, Brand Development & Integration, Communications, Government/Political, Internet/Web Design, Local Marketing, Media Relations, Public Relations, Strategic Planning/Research, Viral/Buzz/Word of Mouth, Web (Banner Ads, Pop-ups, etc.)

Brenda Stier-Anstine *(CEO)*
Bill Kiefaber *(Partner)*
Stacy Wood *(VP & Grp Head-Practice)*
Tom Vranich *(VP-Client Svcs)*
Sandy Wynegar *(Client Svcs Dir)*
Lauren Hartman *(Dir-Acct Mgmt)*
Alexandra Can *(Acct Mgr)*
Mary Trimarche *(Office Mgr)*
Amanda Pierce *(Acct Coord)*

Accounts:
Bob Webb Group
e-Play
Finance Fund
Mid Ohio Oncology/Hematology
Progressive Medical, Inc.; Westerville, OH

MARKETPLAN
1020 Pacific Ave, Manhattan Beach, CA 90266-5854
Tel.: (310) 372-8453
Fax: (310) 372-6024
E-Mail: mrktplnwjr@aol.com
Web Site: mrktpln.com

E-Mail for Key Personnel:
President: mrktplnwjr@aol.com

Employees: 4
Year Founded: 1976

Agency Specializes In: Advertising, Business Publications, Business-To-Business, Collateral, Communications, Event Planning & Marketing, Exhibit/Trade Shows, Financial, Local Marketing, Planning & Consultation, Public Relations, Publicity/Promotions, Real Estate, Retail, Sales Promotion

Breakdown of Gross Billings by Media: Collateral: 10%; D.M.: 65%; Mags.: 5%; Newsp.: 5%; Pub. Rels.: 15%

Theresa Mars *(Mgr-Print Production)*
Anni Pesce *(Acct Exec)*

Accounts:
LACBOR
Wilson

MARKETSHARE
11150 Santa Monica Blvd 5th Fl, Los Angeles, CA 90025
Tel.: (310) 914-5677
Fax: (310) 914-5155
E-Mail: contact@marketshare.com
Web Site: www.marketshare.com

Employees: 4
Year Founded: 1976

Agency Specializes In: Brand Development & Integration, Corporate Identity, Electronic Media, Graphic Design, Internet/Web Design, Logo & Package Design, New Product Development, Strategic Planning/Research

Approx. Annual Billings: $500,000

Jon Vein *(Co-Founder & CEO)*
Wes Nichols *(Co-Founder & CEO-Growth)*
Ted Polmar *(Co-Owner, CMO & Sr Strategist)*
Dirk Beyer *(Chief Innovation Officer & Exec VP)*
Rick Larkin *(Sr VP)*
Marc Rossen *(Exec Dir-Digital Insights Solutions)*
Miriam Ravkin *(Sr Dir-Digital Mktg & Demand Generation)*
Lynn Schlesinger *(Sr Dir-Strategic Mktg & Events)*

Accounts:
Bioject

MARKETSHARE PLUS, INC.
Woodland Plz 1220 Ruston Pass, Fort Wayne, IN 46825
Tel.: (260) 497-9988
Fax: (260) 497-0064
E-Mail: mkst@marketshareplus.com
Web Site: www.marketshareplus.com

Employees: 4
Year Founded: 1992

Agency Specializes In: Children's Market, Food Service

Thomas D. Mattern *(Owner)*
Clark Trexler *(Dir-Creative)*

Accounts:
Access America
Andrew Davis
Challenger Door
Mike Thomas Association, Wayne, IN Sofas, Loveseats, Chairs & Ottomans
Trans Am Series

MARKETSMITHS CONTENT STRATEGISTS LLC
401 Park Ave S, New York, NY 10016
Tel.: (415) 787-5058
E-Mail: info@marketsmiths.com
Web Site: www.marketsmiths.com

Agency Specializes In: Content, Copywriting, Email, Print, Search Engine Optimization, Social Media

Jean Tang *(CEO)*
Sofia Simeonidis *(Office Mgr)*
Gregory M. Lewis *(Copywriter)*
Alison Weissbrot *(Copywriter-Creative)*
Daniel DiGriz *(Chief Strategist)*

Accounts:
Choices in Childbirth
Entrepreneur Online
Ethos Wellness Collective
Forbes.com
Gastronomie491
Greenhouse Eco-Cleaning
IOBY
Jose Rolon Events
Kuncio Orthodontics
LMA Group
NYFU
Rock Paper Team
Rubicon Project
Varghese & Associates

MARKETSTAR CORPORATION
2475 Washington Blvd, Ogden, UT 84401
Tel.: (801) 393-1155
Fax: (801) 393-4115
Toll Free: (800))877-8259
E-Mail: info@marketstar.com
Web Site: www.marketstar.com

Employees: 250
Year Founded: 1988

Agency Specializes In: Business-To-Business, Consumer Marketing, Consumer Publications, Health Care Services, High Technology, Sponsorship

David Treadway *(Pres & CEO)*
E.J. Harris *(CFO & Exec VP)*
Keith Titus *(Exec VP-Strategy & Ops)*
Adam Gunn *(Dir-Mktg & Creative Svcs)*
Regan Howell *(Dir-Cloud & Channel Svcs)*
Adam Price *(Dir-Sls & Mktg Ops)*
Mat Peterson *(Mgr-Bus Dev)*
Jace Garside *(Specialist-Mktg Automation)*
Marshall Snedaker *(Sr Gen Mgr-Demand Mktg)*

Accounts:
Agilsys
Canon
Cisco
Hewlett Packard Compaq
InFocus
KitchenAid
Logitech
Microsoft
Motorola Solutions, Inc.
Office Depot
Sony
Verizon
Whirlpool

THE MARLIN NETWORK, INC.
1200 E Woodhurst Dr, Springfield, MO 65804-4240
Tel.: (417) 885-4500
Fax: (417) 887-3643
E-Mail: marlin@marlinco.com
Web Site: www.marlinco.com

E-Mail for Key Personnel:
President: dkm@marlinco.com

Employees: 70
Year Founded: 1985

Agency Specializes In: Brand Development & Integration, Business-To-Business, Consumer Marketing, Digital/Interactive, Food Service, Graphic Design, Internet/Web Design, New Product Development, Publicity/Promotions, Strategic Planning/Research

Michael M. Stelzer *(Owner)*
Todd Carroll *(CFO)*
Doug Austin *(Sr VP-Growth & Innovation)*
Rob Nelson *(Grp Acct Dir)*
Matt Rose *(Dir-Creative)*
Dionne Reese *(Acct Supvr)*

Accounts:
Akzo Nobel Chemicals
Blue Bunny
Camp Barnabas (Pro Bono)
Mission Food Service
Pinnacle Foods
Splenda
Starbucks Foodservice
Sweet Street Desserts Inc. Foodservice Desserts; 2000

Branches

The Alchemedia Project
(Formerly iMarlin)
1200 E Woodhurst Bldg V, Springfield, MO 65804
Tel.: (417) 885-4500
Fax: (417) 887-3643
E-Mail: hi@thealchemediaproject.com
Web Site: thealchemediaproject.com

Employees: 9

Agency Specializes In: Brand Development & Integration, Business-To-Business, Communications, Consulting, Customer Relationship Management, Digital/Interactive, E-Commerce, Food Service, Graphic Design, High Technology, Information Technology, Integrated Marketing, Internet/Web Design, Paid Searches, Point of Sale, Web (Banner Ads, Pop-ups, etc.)

Jackie Haldiman *(Dir-Media)*
Tom Rankin *(Dir-Tech)*
Meghan Sponenberg *(Dir-Insights)*

Josh Sullivan *(Dir-Art)*
Michael Dockery *(Assoc Dir-Creative)*
Claire McMillin *(Acct Supvr)*
Sarah Reid *(Acct Exec)*
Sarah Jenkins *(Copywriter)*
Jasmine Barnes *(Asst Acct Exec)*

Accounts:
Atlantic Mills
Cavendish Farms
Everpure
H. Walker Foods
Heinz
John Morrell Foodservice
Johnsonville Sausage
Land O'Lakes
MasterFoodServices
McCain
Minors
Mission Foods
Nestle Waters North America
Procter & Gamble

Deep

4350 S National B 110, Springfield, MO 65810
Tel.: (417) 887-7446
Fax: (417) 823-8415
E-Mail: pdaniels@deepgroup.com
Web Site: www.deepgroup.com

Employees: 35

Agency Specializes In: Advertising

Valeri Lea *(Partner)*
Cabot Brothers *(Controller)*
Daniel Green *(Sr Dir-Interactive Art)*
Amy Rosendahl *(Mgr-PR & Social Media)*
Chris Heil *(Acct Exec)*
Desirae Struthers *(Designer)*

Accounts:
DaVinci Gourmet Advertising, Marketing, Smoothies
Lean Cuisine
Minor's
Mission Foods
Nesquik
Stouffer's
Trio

Marlin

1200 E Woodhurst Dr Bldg V, Springfield, MO 65804
Tel.: (417) 887-7446
Fax: (417) 887-3643
E-Mail: info@marlinco.com
Web Site: www.marlinco.com

Employees: 40

Agency Specializes In: Advertising

Doug Austin *(Sr VP-Growth & Innovation)*
Quentin Brown *(Sr Dir-Art)*
Emily Johnson *(Sr Dir-Art)*
Chad Harris *(Grp Acct Dir)*
Scott Bratcher *(Dir-Digital)*
Chris Rock *(Dir-Creative)*
Matt Rose *(Dir-Creative)*
April Speed *(Assoc Dir-Creative)*
Claire Shaffer *(Acct Exec)*
Ashley Sims *(Acct Exec)*
John Manhart *(Designer)*
Sam Pyle *(Copywriter)*
Cecily Robertson *(Copywriter)*

Accounts:
Splenda
Star Bucks Coffee
Sweet Street

MARQUETTE GROUP

222 NE Monroe St Fl 8, Peoria, IL 61602
Mailing Address:
PO Box 1410, Peoria, IL 61602
Tel.: (309) 677-0400
Fax: (309) 677-0407
Toll Free: (800) 548-6214
E-Mail: info@mqgroup.com
Web Site: www.marquettegroup.com

Employees: 155
Year Founded: 1963

National Agency Associations: ADM-YPA

Agency Specializes In: Advertising, Co-op Advertising, Digital/Interactive, Direct Response Marketing, Internet/Web Design, Mobile Marketing, Paid Searches, Search Engine Optimization, Social Media, Sponsorship, Web (Banner Ads, Pop-ups, etc.), Yellow Pages Advertising

Approx. Annual Billings: $150,000,000

Breakdown of Gross Billings by Media: D.M.: $1,000,000; Internet Adv.: $19,000,000; Yellow Page Adv.: $130,000,000

Eric Webb *(Pres)*
Christopher Cummings *(CEO)*
Troy Dowell *(VP-Mktg & Bus Dev)*
Andrea Brandon *(Dir-Mktg Comm)*
Stephanie Casajuana *(Mgr-Paid Search)*
Kevin Samp *(Specialist-Interactive Product)*
Amanda deFreese *(Acct Coord-Interactive)*
Alicia Ruemelin *(Coord-Mktg Comm)*
Dawn Tiller *(Rep-State Farm Corp Hispanic & Asian Display)*

Accounts:
Enterprise Holdings, Inc; St. Louis, MO Auto Rental; 2010
Pizza Hut; Dallas, TX Pizza Restaurants; 2009
Sherwin-Williams; Cleveland, OH Paint; 2009
U-Haul; Phoenix, AZ Vehicle/Storage Rental; 2003

MARRINER MARKETING COMMUNICATIONS, INC.

6731 Columbia Gateway Dr Ste 250, Columbia, MD 21046
Tel.: (410) 715-1500
Fax: (410) 995-3609
Toll Free: (800) 268-6475
Web Site: www.marriner.com

E-Mail for Key Personnel:
Media Dir.: wendy@marriner.com
Production Mgr.: vicki@marriner.com

Employees: 48
Year Founded: 1989

Agency Specializes In: Advertising, Brand Development & Integration, Broadcast, Business Publications, Business-To-Business, Collateral, Consumer Goods, Consumer Marketing, Consumer Publications, Content, Corporate Communications, Corporate Identity, Custom Publishing, Digital/Interactive, Direct Response Marketing, Direct-to-Consumer, Electronic Media, Email, Event Planning & Marketing, Exhibit/Trade Shows, Food Service, Graphic Design, Hospitality, Identity Marketing, In-Store Advertising, Integrated Marketing, Internet/Web Design, Local Marketing, Logo & Package Design, Market Research, Media Buying Services, Media Planning, Mobile Marketing, Multimedia, New Product Development, Out-of-Home Media, Outdoor, Paid Searches, Planning & Consultation, Point of Purchase, Point of Sale, Print, Production, Production (Ad, Film, Broadcast), Promotions, Public Relations, Restaurant, Retail, Sales Promotion, Search Engine Optimization, Social Media, Sponsorship, Strategic Planning/Research, Trade & Consumer Magazines, Travel & Tourism, Web (Banner Ads, Pop-ups, etc.)

Approx. Annual Billings: $60,000,000

Tighe Merkert *(Pres)*
Susan Gunther *(Partner & Client Svcs Dir)*
Rob Levine *(Partner & Dir-Acct Strategy)*
Walt Rampata *(VP-Digital)*
Josie Griffin *(Controller)*
Linda Henley *(Dir-Package Dev)*
Vicki Rummel *(Dir-Production)*
Wendy Simms *(Dir-Media)*
Carrie Gardner *(Mng Supvr)*
Lacey Stryker *(Mng Supvr)*

Accounts:
Butterball
Butterball (Foodservice Agency of Record) Marketing Communications
Hospitality Mints Digital Strategy, E-commerce, Marketing
Knouse Foods
Marriott International
McCormick & Company (Agency of Record)
Meat & Livestock Australia
MICROS Systems
Perdue Farms
Phillips Foods
Reinhart Foodservice
Rich Products
The Sugar Association
USA Rice Federation; 2006
Vulcan, Wolf & Berkel
Zatarain's

THE MARS AGENCY

(Formerly Mars Advertising Group)
25200 Telegraph Rd, Southfield, MI 48033-7496
Tel.: (248) 936-2200
Fax: (248) 936-2760
Toll Free: (800) 521-9317
E-Mail: cookb@themarsagency.com
Web Site: www.themarsagency.com/

Employees: 470
Year Founded: 1973

Agency Specializes In: Advertising, Advertising Specialties, Brand Development & Integration, Broadcast, Business Publications, Cable T.V., Co-op Advertising, Collateral, Consumer Marketing, Direct Response Marketing, Event Planning & Marketing, Food Service, Health Care Services, Hispanic Market, In-Store Advertising, Internet/Web Design, Local Marketing, Magazines, Merchandising, New Product Development, Newspaper, Newspapers & Magazines, Out-of-Home Media, Outdoor, Pharmaceutical, Point of Purchase, Point of Sale, Print, Production, Production (Print), Promotions, Radio, Retail, Sales Promotion, Shopper Marketing, Sponsorship, Strategic Planning/Research, Sweepstakes, T.V.

Approx. Annual Billings: $252,245,461

Breakdown of Gross Billings by Media: Bus. Publs.: $3,940,750; Cable T.V.: $5,946,150; Collateral: $13,632,050; Consumer Publs.: $9,265,450; Fees: $174,068,111; Newsp. & Mags.: $3,462,749; Outdoor: $7,249,757; Point of Sale: $12,900,200; Radio & T.V.: $21,780,244

Marilyn Barnett *(Chm & Pres)*
Jeff Stocker *(Chief Creative Officer)*
Ken Barnett *(CEO-Global)*
Steve Nottingham *(Sr VP & Gen Mgr)*
Carol Butash *(Sr VP-Ops)*
Maribeth Fasseel *(Sr VP-Fin)*
Janine Flaccavento *(Sr VP-Ops & Comml Innovation)*
Gail Hendrickson *(Sr VP-Print Production)*

Geralyn George *(VP & Acct Dir)*
Theresa Lyons *(VP & Dir-Strategic Plng)*
Kris Abrahamson *(VP-Retail Consultancy)*
Chris Baranowski *(VP-Fin)*
Diane Beffa *(VP)*
Lorrie Boone *(VP-Strategic Plng)*
Kathleen Curran *(VP-Comm)*
Mary Evans *(VP-Strategic Plng)*
Ethan Goodman *(VP-Digital & Innovation)*
Barbara Hagen *(VP-Client Leadership)*
Kim Pawlak *(VP-Creative Ops)*
Christie Schiller *(VP-Client Svc)*
Eric Haddad *(Client Svcs Dir)*
Rachel Bateast *(Dir-Strategic Plng)*
Kristen Sabol *(Dir-Client Leadership)*
Clay Crymes *(Assoc Dir-Creative)*
Ryan Hughes *(Assoc Dir-Creative)*
Christina Kane *(Assoc Dir-Creative)*
James Scarsella *(Assoc Dir-Creative)*
Vincent Straszewski *(Assoc Dir-Creative)*
Sherry Galligan *(Supvr-Brdcst-Mars Adv)*
Jacob Barnett *(Sr Acct Exec-Client Leadership)*
Leah Key *(Sr Planner & Buyer-Digital & Planner-Engagement)*
Adam McKay *(Acct Exec)*
Margie Fujarski *(Client Svc Dir)*

Accounts:
Big Y Foods Inc.
Campbell Soup Co.
Cargill Inc; 2010
Chobani Greek Yogurt, Marketing, Strategic Insight
Clorox
Pepperidge Farms
Pfizer Consumer Healthcare; 2010
United Health Group; 2010
UnitedHealthcare

MARSHAD TECHNOLOGY GROUP
12 Desbrosses St, New York, NY 10013
Tel.: (212) 925-8656
E-Mail: info@marshad.com
Web Site: www.marshad.com

Agency Specializes In: Advertising, Broadcast, Digital/Interactive, Education, Entertainment, Financial, Health Care Services, Information Technology, Multimedia, New Technologies, Pharmaceutical, Public Relations, Retail, Travel & Tourism, Web (Banner Ads, Pop-ups, etc.)

Neal Marshad *(Pres)*

Accounts:
Caswell-Massey Creative Development, Online Advertising Strategy & Management, Search Engine Optimization, Social Media Strategy
Colgate Palmolive
Coty, Inc
General Mills
Idamenities Europe SL
NBC Entertainment
Olga Corporation
Pyramid Media Inc
Rita Hazan Salon
Speedo Authentic Fitness
Telerep
Viacom

MARSHFIELD GROUP
9025 Osborne Dr, Mentor, OH 44060
Tel.: (440) 974-8448
Fax: (440) 357-8577
E-Mail: info@marshfield.com
Web Site: www.marshfield.com

Employees: 4
Year Founded: 1979

Agency Specializes In: Communications, Consumer Marketing, Electronic Media, Graphic Design, Internet/Web Design, Multimedia, Planning & Consultation

Tom Mitchell *(Owner)*

Accounts:
Bescast; Painesville, OH
GE; Cleveland, OH Lighting; 1993
Holz Rubber; Lodi, CA
John Palmer's Bistro 44; Concord, OH
Lake Hospital Systems; Concord, OH
NCD Medical Group; Eastlake, OH

MARSTON WEBB INTERNATIONAL
270 Madison Ave, New York, NY 10016
Tel.: (212) 684-6601
Fax: (212) 725-4709
Toll Free: (800) 580-6816
E-Mail: marwebint@cs.com
Web Site: www.marstonwebb.com

E-Mail for Key Personnel:
President: victor@marstonwebb.com
Creative Dir.: george@inetgraphics.com
Media Dir.: madlene@marstonwebb.com

Employees: 11
Year Founded: 1982

Agency Specializes In: Advertising, Advertising Specialties, Business Publications, Business-To-Business, Collateral, Consulting, Consumer Publications, Education, Entertainment, Financial, Government/Political, Health Care Services, High Technology, Internet/Web Design, Investor Relations, Media Buying Services, Newspaper, Newspapers & Magazines, Planning & Consultation, Public Relations, Radio, Real Estate, Recruitment, Sales Promotion

Breakdown of Gross Billings by Media: Collateral: 25%; Fees: 25%; Newsp. & Mags.: 50%

Victor G. Webb *(Pres)*
Robert Schantz *(Treas)*
Madlene Olson *(VP)*
George Haddad *(Dir-Creative Svcs)*

Accounts:
Austrian Trade Commission; New York, NY
Internet Plus; CA Ecommerce Direct
Linden Educational Services; Washington, DC
MBA Tours; Boston, MA Education; 2000
McEn Mining
Metropolitan Area Network; Washington, DC Broadband Wireless Service
World Gold Council; New York, NY & London, UK
Yomiuri Shimbun; Tokyo, Japan Newspaper

MARTIN ADVERTISING
1650-C E Greenville St, Anderson, SC 29621
Tel.: (864) 226-0282
Fax: (864) 226-8215
Web Site: www.ineedmartin.com

Year Founded: 1989

Agency Specializes In: Advertising, Brand Development & Integration, Graphic Design, Internet/Web Design, Logo & Package Design, Media Planning, Print, Promotions, Radio, T.V.

Judy E. Forrest *(Mgr-Fin, Media Planner-Print & Buyer)*
Chloe R. Munch *(Asst Acct Exec & Strategist-Digital)*
Emily B. Holland *(Media Planner-Acct Svcs & Brdcst & Buyer)*

Accounts:
Hill Electric, Inc.
Timms Harley-Davidson

THE MARTIN AGENCY
One Shockoe Plz, Richmond, VA 23219
Tel.: (804) 698-8000
Fax: (804) 698-8001
E-Mail: info@martinagency.com
Web Site: www.martinagency.com

Employees: 483
Year Founded: 1965

National Agency Associations: 4A's-AAF-APA-ARF-BPA-DMA

Agency Specializes In: Advertising, Agriculture, Automotive, Brand Development & Integration, Branded Entertainment, Broadcast, Business Publications, Business-To-Business, Cable T.V., Children's Market, Communications, Consulting, Consumer Marketing, Consumer Publications, Content, Corporate Communications, Digital/Interactive, Direct Response Marketing, E-Commerce, Electronic Media, Electronics, Entertainment, Environmental, Event Planning & Marketing, Fashion/Apparel, Financial, Game Integration, Graphic Design, Health Care Services, High Technology, Information Technology, Integrated Marketing, Internet/Web Design, Investor Relations, Leisure, Logo & Package Design, Magazines, Market Research, Media Buying Services, Media Planning, Merchandising, Mobile Marketing, New Product Development, Newspaper, Newspapers & Magazines, Out-of-Home Media, Outdoor, Over-50 Market, Package Design, Paid Searches, Podcasting, Point of Purchase, Point of Sale, Print, Product Placement, Production, Promotions, Public Relations, Publicity/Promotions, RSS (Really Simple Syndication), Radio, Restaurant, Retail, Sales Promotion, Search Engine Optimization, Sponsorship, Sports Market, Strategic Planning/Research, T.V., Teen Market, Telemarketing, Trade & Consumer Magazines, Travel & Tourism, Viral/Buzz/Word of Mouth, Web (Banner Ads, Pop-ups, etc.), Yellow Pages Advertising

Breakdown of Gross Billings by Media: D.M.: 2%; Internet Adv.: 13%; Newsp.: 18%; Outdoor: 2%; Radio: 9%; T.V.: 46%; Trade & Consumer Mags.: 10%

Bruce Kelley *(Vice Chm)*
Warren Foster *(Pres)*
Matt Williams *(CEO)*
Brad Armstrong *(Partner)*
Beth Rilee-Kelley *(COO & Exec VP)*
Earl C. Cox *(Chief Strategy Officer & Exec VP)*
Joe Alexander *(Chief Creative Officer)*
Dean Jarrett *(Chief Comm Officer)*
Colleen Stein *(Exec VP & Mng Dir-Martin Local)*
Lorri Riddle *(Sr VP & Controller)*
Andy Azula *(Sr VP & Exec Creative Dir)*
Wade Alger *(Sr VP & Grp Dir-Creative)*
Jason Komulainen *(Sr VP & Grp Dir-Creative)*
Fritz Kuhn *(Sr VP & Grp Dir-Plng)*
Danny Robinson *(Sr VP & Grp Dir-Creative)*
Sydney Norton *(Sr VP & Grp Acct Dir)*
Tedd Aurelius *(Sr VP, Acct Dir & Dir-One-to-One Engagement)*
Trent Patterson *(Sr VP, Dir-Creative & Writer)*
Bob Meagher *(Sr VP, Assoc Dir-Creative & Writer)*
Raymond McKinney *(Sr VP & Sr Copywriter)*
Darren Foot *(Sr VP)*
Ian Davidson *(Mng Dir-Intl)*
Matt Mattox *(VP & Grp Dir-Plng)*
Pat Wittich *(VP & Sr Dir-Art)*
Rebecca Smith *(VP & Acct Dir)*
Hugh Callahan *(VP & Dir-Creative)*
Matt Davis *(VP & Dir-Art & Creative)*
Magnus Hierta *(VP & Dir-Creative)*
Mike Kelley *(VP & Dir-Plng)*
Andrew Watson *(VP & Dir-Creative)*
Sissy Estes *(VP & Assoc Dir-Creative)*
Karen Baber *(VP & Supvr-Grp Project Mgmt)*

Shannon Webb *(VP-Brand First Entertainment)*
Jorge Calleja *(Exec Dir-Creative)*
Steve Bassett *(Grp Dir-Creative)*
Tara Gorman *(Sr Dir-Art)*
Justin Harris *(Sr Dir-Art)*
Michael Henry *(Acct Dir)*
Colleen Hopkins *(Producer-Brdcst)*
Liza Miller *(Producer-Brdcst)*
Allison Oxenreiter *(Acct Dir)*
Ben Roberts *(Acct Dir)*
Taj Tedrow *(Creative Dir)*
Ellen Donoghue Carlton *(Dir-Strategy & Content)*
Ty Harper *(Dir-Art)*
Jordi Martinez *(Dir-Creative)*
Sean Riley *(Dir-Creative)*
Dave Padgett *(Assoc Dir-Creative & Art)*
Julie Basham Smith *(Mgr-Production)*
Samantha Tucker *(Mgr-ITS Project Mgmt)*
Carrie Bird *(Acct Supvr)*
Laurel Busony *(Acct Supvr)*
Elizabeth Eldred *(Acct Supvr)*
Gabriella Eljaiek *(Acct Supvr)*
Patti Fox *(Acct Supvr-Fin)*
Jacki Juenger *(Acct Supvr)*
Josh Lybarger *(Acct Supvr)*
Steph Shaw *(Acct Supvr)*
Michelle Daidone *(Supvr-Media-Engagement Team)*
Debbie Douglas *(Supvr-Brdcst Traffic)*
Robin Kaspar *(Supvr-Print Buying)*
Celeste Root *(Supvr-Engagement Team)*
Suzanne Wieringo *(Supvr-Brdcst Bus Affairs)*
Stephanie Brummell *(Acct Exec)*
Allison Hensley *(Acct Exec)*
Lisa Loving *(Acct Exec)*
Andrew Beckman *(Copywriter)*
Sarah Berkheimer *(Sr Designer)*
Kristen Dutton *(Copywriter)*
Mark Habke *(Copywriter)*
Gigi Jordan *(Planner-Strategic)*
Miranda Morgan *(Copywriter)*
Lauren Prociv *(Planner-Strategic-UX)*
Allison Slocum *(Planner-Engagement)*
Lassiter Stone *(Copywriter)*
Erica Archer *(Asst Media Planner)*
Giao Roever *(Grp Supvr-Project Mgmt)*
Maggie Shifflett *(Assoc Producer)*
Emily Taylor *(Assoc Producer)*

Accounts:
Benjamin Moore & Co. (Creative & US Media Agency of Record) Campaign: "Bring the Green Monster to Local Fields", Campaign: "Feats of Can", Campaign: "Main Street Matters"; Campaign: "Scary Good Job"; Creative; Media Planning & Buying; Ultra Spec 500, Campaign: "Meet the Hopsons", Campaign: "Paint Like No Other", Campaign: "Shades of Life", Campaign: "Who Are You Talking To?", Digital, Fenway Collection, Green Monster, Natura "Zero-VOC and Zero Emissions", Online, Print, Radio, Regal Select, Revive Paint, TV
Berkshire Hathaway Inc.
Colonial Williamsburg Brand Campaign, Campaign: "Cannon"
Discover Financial Services, Inc. Campaign: "Surprise", Super Bowl 2015
Earth University
Experian Campaign: "Get Your Credit Swagger On", Campaign: "Hamburger Hot Dog", Campaign: "Home Loan"
ExxonMobile Campaign: "Touchdown"
Ferrero U.S.A., Inc. Strategic, Tic Tac (US Creative Agency of Record)
Fortune Brands Dishes, Dodge Balls, Laundry, Shopping Carts, Sippy Cup, Tools, Toys
Geico "The Genie and Me", Campaign: "Abduction", Campaign: "Ancient Pyramids", Campaign: "Assistant", Campaign: "Boat", Campaign: "Brostache", Campaign: "Camel Cinema", Campaign: "Dating", Campaign: "Did You Know?", Campaign: "Divers", Campaign: "Doughboy", Campaign: "Family", Campaign: "Free Range Chicken", Campaign: "Giant", Campaign: "Happier Than", Campaign: "High Five", Campaign: "Hump Day", Campaign: "Insurance for the Modern World", Campaign: "It's What You Do", Campaign: "Lobby", Campaign: "Old MacDonald", Campaign: "Owl", Campaign: "Pinocchio Yours Truly", Campaign: "Push It", Campaign: "Roommate", Campaign: "Salt-N-Peppa", Campaign: "Unskippable", Car Insurance, GEICO Auctioneer, Online; 1994
Georgia-Pacific Sparkle Paper Towels
Hanesbrands Branded Apparel "Can Michael Jordan Palm It?", Campaign: "Color Wheel", Champion, L'eggs
John F. Kennedy Presidential Library & Museum Campaign: "An Idea Lives on", Campaign: "Clouds Over Cuba", Campaign: "Peace Corps"; 1994
New-Land O'Lakes Inc. Creative Development, Kozy Shack Puddings (Agency of Record), Land O'Lakes Butter (Agency of Record), Media Buying, Media Planning
LG
Manpower Inc. (Agency of Record); 2009
Moen Campaign: "Buy it for looks, buy it for life", Campaign: "Statement Piece"; 2009
Mondelez International "Dare to Wonder", "Thinner", Advertising, Camapaign: "Life's Rich", Campaign: "Colorfilled", Campaign: "Play With Oreo", Campaign: "Wonderfilled", Chips Ahoy!, Cookie Balls, Creative, Marketing, Oreo, Oreo Thins, Print, Ritz Crackers, TV, Transformers, Video
Morgan Stanley Brand Creative Development, Campaign: "The Pursuit/Anthem", Campaign: "What if", Creative, Print & Digital, Strategic Planning, TV
Nespresso
Nexus
The One Club
Penske Truck Leasing (Agency of Record) "Horn", Online, Print, Social Media
Perfetti van Melle Campaign: "Coals", Campaign: "Dragee", Campaign: "Gum Gallery", Campaign: "Punch", Campaign: "Spider", Mentos, UP2U
PING Golf Equipment; 1995
Sabra Dipping Co. (Advertising Agency of Record) Creative, Digital Media, Social Media Strategy, Strategic
Stoli Group USA Campaign: "THE Vodka", Creative, Stolichnaya
Tie the Knot
The Timberland Company The Timberland Company, Timberland
New-Total Wireless
Tracfone Wireless Lovestruck, Net 10
New-UCI Road World Championships
Virginia Museum Of Fine Arts
Wal-Mart Stores, Inc. (Lead Agency) "Straight Talk" Phone Service, Big Sister, Campaign: "Frank the Fruitcake", Campaign: "Yodel Cat", Digital Marketing; 2007

Branches

The Martin Agency Media

(Formerly Ingenuity Media Group at The Martin Agency)
1 Shockoe Plz, Richmond, VA 23219-4132
Tel.: (804) 698-8600
Fax: (804) 698-8401
Web Site: www.martinagency.com

Employees: 85
Year Founded: 1965

Agency Specializes In: Advertising, Affluent Market, Alternative Advertising, Automotive, Brand Development & Integration, Branded Entertainment, Broadcast, Business Publications, Business-To-Business, Cable T.V., Communications, Consumer Goods, Consumer Marketing, Consumer Publications, Content, Digital/Interactive, Direct Response Marketing, Direct-to-Consumer, Electronic Media, Email, Entertainment, Financial, Game Integration, Guerilla Marketing, In-Store Advertising, Integrated Marketing, Local Marketing, Magazines, Market Research, Media Buying Services, Media Planning, Mobile Marketing, Newspaper, Newspapers & Magazines, Out-of-Home Media, Outdoor, Paid Searches, Planning & Consultation, Podcasting, Print, Product Placement, Radio, Regional, Retail, Search Engine Optimization, Social Marketing/Nonprofit, Social Media, Sponsorship, Strategic Planning/Research, Syndication, T.V., Trade & Consumer Magazines, Transportation, Travel & Tourism, Viral/Buzz/Word of Mouth, Web (Banner Ads, Pop-ups, etc.), Women's Market, Yellow Pages Advertising

Randy Freisner *(Sr VP & Dir-Media Ops)*
Julie Findlay *(VP & Assoc Dir-Media)*
Katherine Dorey *(Mgr-Media Rels)*
Gina Whelehan *(Media Buyer-Local Brdcst & Specialist-Market)*
Allison Hensley *(Acct Exec)*
Kendree Thieringer *(Media Buyer-Local Brdcst)*
Tamara Middleton *(Asst Media Buyer)*

Accounts:
901 Tequila; 2010
Bermuda Tourism; 2011
Geico; 1994
Healthmart; 1993
JFK Library & Museum; 1994
Manpower; 2010
Mentos; 2010
MOEN; 2010
Monsanto; 2009
Motrin; 2010
Progress Energy Carolinas; 2009
SAAB; 2010
TV Land; 1998

The Martin Agency-NY

71 5th Ave 4th Fl, New York, NY 10003
Tel.: (212) 405-4800
Fax: (212) 405-4801
E-Mail: info@martinagency.com
Web Site: www.martinagency.com

Employees: 31
Year Founded: 1994

National Agency Associations: 4A's

Agency Specializes In: Advertising, Sponsorship

Joe Alexander *(Chief Creative Officer)*
Elissa Goldman *(Exec VP & Acct Dir)*
Leslie North *(Sr VP & Grp Dir-Plng-UX Strategy)*
Trent Patterson *(Sr VP, Dir-Creative & Writer)*
Demian Brink *(VP & Grp Dir-Engagement)*
Chris Peel *(VP & Assoc Dir-Creative)*
Linda Salzberg *(VP & Mgr-Local Brdcst)*
James Robinson *(Exec Creative Dir)*
Pete Watson *(Grp Acct Dir)*
Jonathan Richman *(Assoc Dir-Creative)*
David Shusterman *(Mgr-Brdcst-Natl)*
Sherri Skellett *(Mgr-Media Svcs)*
Sarah Berkheimer *(Sr Designer)*
Julia Maimone-Medwick *(Planner-Engagement Team)*
Erica Fisher *(Asst Planner-Digital-Engagement Team)*
Diana Cirullo *(Asst Media Planner-Digital)*
Zaneta Reid *(Assoc Dir Media-Digital Engagement-TIAA Cref & Penske)*

Accounts:
Benjamin Moore
Colonial Williamsburg
Expedia.com Creative
Oreo Campaign: "Cookie Balls", Creative
UPS

The Martin Agency
3 Grosvenor Gardens, London, SW1W 0BD United Kingdom
Tel.: (44) 207 979 5600
Web Site: www.martinagency.com

Year Founded: 2014

Agency Specializes In: Advertising, Brand Development & Integration, Digital/Interactive, Event Planning & Marketing, Graphic Design, Internet/Web Design, Print

Ian Davidson *(Exec VP)*
Daniel Fisher *(Exec Creative Dir)*
Brian Williams *(Deputy Exec Dir-Creative)*

Accounts:
Education First
Manpower Group

Martin Local Lead Generation
(Formerly Telmark)
1 Shockoe Plz, Richmond, VA 23219-4132
Mailing Address:
PO Box 2481, Richmond, VA 23218
Tel.: (804) 698-8700
Fax: (804) 698-8701
Toll Free: (800) 476-8124
Web Site: www.martinagency.com

Employees: 15
Year Founded: 1972

National Agency Associations: 4A's-ADM-YPA

Agency Specializes In: Yellow Pages Advertising

Colleen Stein *(Exec VP & Mng Dir-Martin Local)*

Accounts:
Advance Auto Parts
AMF Bowling Worldwide
Barely There
BFGoodrich
Dominion Resources Group
Geico Insurance

MARTIN & CO ADVERTISING
3504 Knight Rd, Whites Creek, TN 37189
Tel.: (615) 876-1822
Fax: (615) 876-9018
Web Site: www.martincoadvertising.com

Agency Specializes In: Advertising, Brand Development & Integration, Content, Digital/Interactive, Event Planning & Marketing, Package Design, Public Relations, Social Media

Zan Martin *(Pres & CEO)*
Randy Martin *(CFO & Dir-Creative)*
Holly Krozel *(VP)*
Jeff Lee *(Dir-Digital Mktg)*

Accounts:
Alignment Simple Solutions
Fontanel Hotel & Resort

MARTIN E. JANIS & COMPANY, INC.
401 N Michigan Ave Ste 2920, Chicago, IL 60611
Tel.: (312) 943-1100
Fax: (312) 943-3583
Web Site: www.janispr.com

Year Founded: 1950

Agency Specializes In: Investor Relations, Media Relations

Beverly Jedynak *(Pres)*

Accounts:
Spare Backup, Inc. Communications Program, Investor Relations, Marketing
Xplore Technologies Corp.

THE MARTIN GROUP, LLC.
487 Main St Ste 200, Buffalo, NY 14203
Tel.: (716) 853-2757
Fax: (716) 853-7366
Web Site: tmgbrandfuel.com/

National Agency Associations: 4A's

Agency Specializes In: Advertising, Brand Development & Integration, Broadcast, Collateral, Digital/Interactive, Environmental, Outdoor, Package Design, Point of Sale, Print

Dion Pender *(Sr VP & Exec Dir-Creative)*
Michael Prezioso *(VP-Ops)*
Lianne Coogan *(Sr Dir-Art)*
Rob Hopkins *(Sr Dir-Art)*
Jim Lynch *(Dir-Media)*
Dave Riley *(Dir-Digital Art & Creative)*
Oliver Hays *(Sr Mgr-PR)*
Kristen Perri *(Sr Brand Mgr)*
Emily Brodhead *(Brand Mgr)*
John Jiloty *(Mgr-Social Media)*
Rosemary Witschard *(Mgr-Traffic)*
Rick Calzi *(Supvr-Creative)*
Sarah DiPofi *(Coord-Brand)*

Accounts:
ECMC
Great Skate
Seneca Gaming Corp Creative Development, Marketing, Media

MARTIN RETAIL GROUP/MARTIN ADVERTISING
2801 University Blvd Ste 200, Birmingham, AL 35233
Tel.: (205) 930-9200
Fax: (205) 933-6949
Web Site: www.martinretail.com

Year Founded: 1977

National Agency Associations: 4A's

Agency Specializes In: Broadcast, Direct Response Marketing, Email, Magazines, Newspaper, Print, Radio, Sponsorship, T.V.

David Martin *(Chm)*
Paul Knapp *(VP & Gen Mgr)*
Scott Metzger *(VP & Gen Mgr)*
Tim Kaiser *(VP & Grp Dir-Premium)*
Ken McCallum *(VP & Acct Dir-Cadillac)*
Brad Maxon *(Gen Mgr)*
Derek Littlefield *(Dir-Art & Writer)*
Pam Satterfield Hayes *(Dir-Media Processes & Compliance)*
Crystal Garcia *(Media Planner & Media Buyer)*
Brooks Gant *(Sr Graphic Designer)*

Accounts:
Allstate
Buick
Cadillac Campaign: "Standard"
GMC

MARTIN THOMAS INTERNATIONAL
42 Riverside Dr, Barrington, RI 02806
Tel.: (401) 245-8500
Fax: (401) 245-0694
E-Mail: contact@martinthomas.com
Web Site: www.martinthomas.com

E-Mail for Key Personnel:
President: mpottle@martinthomas.com

Employees: 5
Year Founded: 1987

National Agency Associations: PRSA

Agency Specializes In: Advertising, Bilingual Market, Business-To-Business, Consulting, Corporate Communications, Corporate Identity, Direct Response Marketing, Exhibit/Trade Shows, Graphic Design, Industrial, Internet/Web Design, Logo & Package Design, Public Relations, Publicity/Promotions, Strategic Planning/Research, Technical Advertising, Trade & Consumer Magazines

Approx. Annual Billings: $1,000,000

Martin K. Pottle *(Founder)*

Accounts:
Alliance Polymers & Services, LLC; Romulus, MI Plastics Resins Distributor, Tech Service Provider
Deerfield Urethane, Inc.; Whately, MA Plastics Films; 1999
Elastocom TPE Technologies, Inc.; Rochester, IL Thermoplastic Elastomers; 2007
G.R. Technical Services, Inc.; Mountainside, NJ Industrial Designers; 1992
National Plastics Center & Museum; Leominster, MA Industry Services, Museum; 1999
Plastics Institute of America, Inc.; Lowell, MA Trade Association; 2002
Polyzen, Inc.; Cary, NC Medical Products; 1998
SEI Chemical; Los Angeles, CA Chemicals

Branch

Martin Thomas International, Public Relations Division
42 Riverside Dr, Barrington, RI 02806
(See Separate Listing)

MARTIN WAYMIRE
426 W Ottawa, Lansing, MI 48933
Tel.: (517) 485-6600
E-Mail: info@mwadvocacy.com
Web Site: www.martinwaymire.com

Agency Specializes In: Advertising, Digital/Interactive, Graphic Design, Internet/Web Design, Media Buying Services, Media Relations, Media Training, Print, Public Relations, Social Media

Jessica Tramontana *(Acct Exec)*

Accounts:
New-Michigan Retailers Association

MARTIN/WILLIAMS ADVERTISING INC.
150 S 5th St, Minneapolis, MN 55402-4428
Tel.: (612) 340-0800
Fax: (612) 342-9700
E-Mail: mgray@martinwilliams.com
Web Site: www.martinwilliams.com

Employees: 200
Year Founded: 1948

National Agency Associations: 4A's

Agency Specializes In: Advertising, Business-To-Business, Consumer Goods, Consumer Marketing, Pets , Pharmaceutical, Retail, Sponsorship, Sports Market

Tom Moudry *(CEO & Chief Creative Officer)*
Glenn Karworski *(Sr VP & Mng Dir)*
Laura Terry *(CMO & Sr VP)*
Tony Lintner *(VP & Grp Dir-Creative)*
Marija Hoehn *(VP & Dir-Activation)*

Stan Prinsen *(VP & Dir-Production)*
Kurtis Benson *(Editor-Creative)*
Emily Almich *(Grp Dir-Media)*
Swapna Desai *(Acct Dir)*
Tara Henderson *(Acct Dir)*
Stephanie Shaw *(Acct Dir)*
Cameron High *(Dir-Art & Assoc Dir-Creative)*
Ryan Libby *(Dir-Studio Svcs)*
Jane Petersen *(Dir-Project Mgmt)*
Bethany Schwichtenberg *(Acct Mgr)*
Laura Wiering *(Acct Mgr)*
Megan Kell *(Acct Supvr)*
Natalie Zamansky *(Acct Supvr)*
Carmen Nesenson *(Strategist-Digital & Planner-Interaction)*
Emily Culp *(Media Planner)*
Lauren Flynn *(Analyst-Media)*

Accounts:
3M; Saint Paul, MN; 1978
Airwalk
Basilica of St. Mary
Boy Scouts of America Campaign: "Bigger than Badges", Letter to the Editor
Cargill; Minneapolis, MN; 1998
CHS
New-Crave Restaurants
Ergotron Advertising, Digital, Website Creation
Finnegans Blonde Ale, Campaign: "Now Floating in a Cooler Near You", Campaign: "Part Blondie/Part Gandhi", Irish Amber, Packaging, Posters
Handsome Cycles
Integrity Windows & Doors Digital
Kill Kancer
Kinze Manufacturing Brand Strategy, Engagement Strategy, Event Marketing, Public Relations, Social Media
Kubota Construction Equipment (Agency of Record) Brand Awareness
Mall of America Broadcast, Campaign: "Level Up", Campaign: "Redefine Your Holiday", Campaign: "Sparkle", Digital Buyers Guide, OOH, Print, Radio
Marvin Windows & Doors; Warroad, MN Campaign: "Milton Glaser"; 1980
Minnesota Chamber of Commerce Brand
Minnesota Timberwolves; Minneapolis, MN
Minnesota Twins Campaign: "Countdown to Cooperstown"
Pastime Foods French Toast, Major League Baseball, Pancakes, Waffles
Pavay Organics Corporation Digital Marketing, Packaging, Strategic & Creative Agency of Record
Pei Wei
Pfizer Animal Health
Raymond James Financial Inc.
Sheex
Steelcase
Syngenta AG Syngenta Crop protection, Syngenta Seeds; 2001
New-Turfco Manufacturing Co.
New-Union Protein
West Central
Wolverine Creative Planning, Strategic Planning

Divisions

TripleInk
60 S 6th St Ste 2800, Minneapolis, MN 55402
(See Separate Listing)

Karwoski & Courage
60 S 6th St Ste 2800, Minneapolis, MN 55402
Tel.: (612) 342-9898
Fax: (612) 342-4340
E-Mail: gkarwosk@creativepr.com
Web Site: www.creativepr.com

Employees: 17
Year Founded: 1992

Agency Specializes In: Public Relations, Sponsorship

Maija Freivalds *(VP & Dir-Interaction Plng & Analytics)*
Tena Murphy *(VP & Dir-HR)*
Stan Prinsen *(VP & Dir-Production)*
Emily Finley *(Acct Dir)*
Steve Renier *(Assoc Dir-HR)*
Coral Graszer *(Acct Mgr)*
Jennifer Hahs *(Mgr-Info Svcs)*
Vanessa de Bruijn *(Acct Supvr)*
Kristin Merchant *(Acct Supvr)*
Jordan Freitag *(Asst Acct Mgr)*
Halli Kubes *(Asst Acct Mgr)*

Accounts:
3M Commercial Graphics
3M Company
3M Healthcare
A-dec, Inc. Media Relations
Boys & Girls Clubs
Felhaber, Larson, Fenlon & Vogt
First American Funds
GlaxoSmithKline
KickedUp Media Group Satellite Media Tour
Kinze Manufacturing
Pavay Organics Corporation Public Relations
P.F. Chang's PR
Pillsbury Food Services

MARTINO & BINZER
(Acquired & Absorbed by Bluespire Marketing)

MARTINO BLUM
2101 Bel Air Rd Ste D, Fallston, MD 21047
Tel.: (410) 893-1700
Fax: (410) 893-2598
Web Site: www.martinoblum.com

Employees: 5
Year Founded: 1987

Agency Specializes In: Consumer Marketing

Approx. Annual Billings: $3,200,000

Michael Blum *(Pres & Dir-Creative)*

Accounts:
Family Recreation Products
Klein's Family Markets
Little House Music
Physicians Pain Care
Regional Pest management

MARTINO FLYNN LLC
175 Sully's Trl Ste 100, Pittsford, NY 14534
Tel.: (585) 421-0100
Fax: (585) 421-0121
E-Mail: info@martinoflynn.com
Web Site: www.martinoflynn.com

Employees: 52
Year Founded: 1967

National Agency Associations: MAGNET

Agency Specializes In: Advertising, Brand Development & Integration, Broadcast, Business-To-Business, Collateral, Consulting, Consumer Marketing, Direct Response Marketing, E-Commerce, Electronic Media, Financial, Graphic Design, Health Care Services, High Technology, Industrial, Internet/Web Design, Logo & Package Design, Media Buying Services, Newspapers & Magazines, Out-of-Home Media, Pharmaceutical, Public Relations, Publicity/Promotions, Radio, Retail, Sponsorship, Sports Market

Approx. Annual Billings: $33,000,000

Kevin Flynn *(Partner)*
Ray Martino *(Partner)*
Greg Monrad *(Controller)*
Tim Downs *(Exec Creative Dir)*
Whit Thompson *(Grp Dir-Creative)*
Charles Bennett *(Sr Dir-Art)*
John Dobles *(Sr Dir-Art)*
Anthony Benedetti *(Acct Dir)*
Megan Connor-Murphy *(Dir-PR & Social Media)*
Julie Wegman *(Dir-Client Dev, Health Care Practice & Mktg Strategy)*
Lisa Hube *(Assoc Dir-Art)*
Charlotte McCabe *(Assoc Dir-Creative)*
Lisa Parenti *(Assoc Dir-Creative)*
Julie Andrews *(Mgr-Sys & Network)*
Jake Pierson *(Acct Supvr)*
Michael Tracy *(Acct Supvr)*
Brianna Bennett *(Supvr-Media)*
Lisa Hare *(Supvr-Creative)*
Ashley Saltzman *(Acct Exec)*
Skylar Jameson *(Asst Acct Exec)*
Janet Wolf *(Assoc Acct Dir)*

Accounts:
The Bonadio Group
Bristol Mountain
Buffalo Bills
Canandaigua National Bank & Trust
Clover Capital Management
CooperVision
Dick's Sporting Goods Campaign: "The Balls to go for it", Top Flite
Dundee Ales & Lagers
Eastman Kodak Company
Financial Freedom
Genesse Cream
Getinge USA; Rochester, NY (Agency of Record) Brand Management, Digital Media Services, Lead Generation, Public Relations, Research, Strategic & Marketing Communications
The Harley School
High Falls Brewery
Mentholatum Co. Rohto Eye Drops
MetLife Bank
Monroe Community
MVP Health New
One Communications
PAETEC Holding Corp.; Perinton, NY (Agency of Record) Corporate Public Relations, Marketing
Rochester Institute of Technology
Seneca Park Zoo Society
Xerox Corporation

MARTOPIA, INC.
3805 E Main St, Saint Charles, IL 60174
Tel.: (630) 587-9944
Fax: (630) 587-5316
Toll Free: (866) 587-9944
E-Mail: info@martopia.com
Web Site: www.martopia.com

Agency Specializes In: Advertising, Brand Development & Integration, Crisis Communications, Digital/Interactive, Email, Exhibit/Trade Shows, Financial, Health Care Services, Industrial, Internet/Web Design, Local Marketing, Media Relations, Newspaper, Podcasting, Promotions, Public Relations, Search Engine Optimization, Strategic Planning/Research

Tami Starck Hernandez *(Owner & Pres)*
Scott Nielsen *(Dir-Creative)*

Accounts:
The Honorable Cause Foundation

MARTY WEISS & FRIENDS
(Formerly Meter Industries)
41 E 11th Street 11th Floor, New York, NY 10003
Tel.: (212) 699-6490
E-Mail: info@martyweissandfriends.com

Web Site: martyweissandfriends.com

Marty Weiss *(Founder & Dir-Creative)*

Accounts:
City & Country School
Dering Hall
Ike Kligerman Barkley
Imperial Brands; Palm Beach Gardens, FL 4 Orange Premium Vodka (Agency of Record), Sobieski; 2007
Rose Tarlow Melrose House
Sobieski Vodka

THE MARTZ AGENCY
(Merged with MP Agency LLC to form Martz Parsons)

THE MARX GROUP
2175 E Francisco Blvd East Ste F, San Rafael, CA 94901
Tel.: (415) 453-0844
Fax: (415) 451-0166
E-Mail: info@themarxgrp.com
Web Site: www.themarxgrp.com

E-Mail for Key Personnel:
President: tmarx@themarxgrp.com
Creative Dir.: kpetersen@themarxgrp.com
Media Dir.: gmedina@themarxgrp.com

Employees: 10
Year Founded: 1984

National Agency Associations: APRA-Second Wind Limited

Agency Specializes In: Advertising, Automotive, Brand Development & Integration, Business-To-Business, Co-op Advertising, Collateral, Communications, Consulting, Consumer Marketing, Consumer Publications, Corporate Communications, Corporate Identity, Direct Response Marketing, E-Commerce, Email, Event Planning & Marketing, Exhibit/Trade Shows, Graphic Design, High Technology, Household Goods, Identity Marketing, Industrial, Information Technology, Integrated Marketing, Internet/Web Design, Leisure, Logo & Package Design, Market Research, Media Buying Services, Media Planning, Media Relations, Package Design, Planning & Consultation, Point of Purchase, Point of Sale, Print, Promotions, Public Relations, Publicity/Promotions, Radio, Real Estate, Sales Promotion, Search Engine Optimization, Social Marketing/Nonprofit, Social Media, Sponsorship, Strategic Planning/Research, Telemarketing, Trade & Consumer Magazines, Transportation, Travel & Tourism

Approx. Annual Billings: $4,300,000

Breakdown of Gross Billings by Media: Collateral: 5%; D.M.: 10%; Exhibits/Trade Shows: 5%; Fees: 15%; Graphic Design: 10%; Logo & Package Design: 5%; Point of Purchase: 5%; Sls. Promo.: 5%; Strategic Planning/Research: 20%; Trade & Consumer Mags.: 5%; Trade Shows: 5%; Worldwide Web Sites: 10%

Tom Marx *(Chm & Co-CEO)*
Devin Hart *(Pres & Co-CEO)*
Kerri Petersen *(VP-Mktg & Creative Svcs)*
Steffanie Savine *(Dir-Mktg & Acct Exec)*
Gloria Medina *(Dir-Mktg)*
Christine Campbell-LeMay *(Mgr-Bus Dev)*
Tim Sayers *(Acct Exec & Specialist-Product & Market)*

Accounts:
Betts Springs; Fresno, CA Heavy Duty Truck Parts & Service; 2012
CADNA Automotive; Memphis, TN Prestone Farm & ArmorMark Brand Automotive Belts, Hoses, Thermostats & Radiator Caps; 2007
CTEK Power USA Marketing, PR
DENSO Sales/US; Long Beach, CA Original Equipment & Aftermarket Parts; 2005
Enerpulse Marketing, PR
FRAS-LE North America; Farmington Hills, MI Friction Products for Light, Medium and Heavy Duty Vehicles; 2010
H3R Performance; Larkspur, CA Portable Premium Fire Extinguishers for Autos, Marine, Off-Road, Garage & Small Business; 2005
King Engine Bearings; Cedar Grove NJ Engine bearings for aviation, automotive, industrial and agriculture; 2009
MAHLE Clevite Inc Marketing, Public Relations
VIPAR Equipment Network; Crystal Lake, IL Program Distribution Group; 2008
VIPAR Heavy Duty; Crystal Lake, IL Program Distribution Group; 2007

MARX LAYNE & COMPANY
31420 Northwestern Hwy Ste 100, Farmington Hills, MI 48334
Tel.: (248) 855-6777
Fax: (248) 855-6719
E-Mail: mlayne@marxlayne.com
Web Site: www.marxlayne.com

Employees: 19
Year Founded: 1987

Agency Specializes In: Public Relations

Frederick Marx *(Owner)*
Michael Layne *(Pres)*
Leslie Pardo *(Sr VP)*
Alan Upchurch *(Sr VP)*
Robyn Gorell *(VP)*
David Stoyka *(Sr Acct Exec)*
Lana Mini *(Acct Exec)*

Accounts:
McDonald's Premium Roast Coffee
Moosejaw Mountaineering
NextDiesel
Toasted Oak Grill & Market (Agency of Record)
TransLogic Auto Carriers (Agency of Record)
Twelve Oaks Mall
Wal-Mart

MARY FISHER DESIGN
1731 Emerson St, Jacksonville, FL 32207
Tel.: (904) 398-3699
Fax: (904) 398-3799
Web Site: www.maryfisherdesign.com

Agency Specializes In: Advertising, Corporate Identity, Internet/Web Design, Media Buying Services, Outdoor, Public Relations, Radio, Search Engine Optimization, Social Media, T.V.

Mary Fisher *(Pres)*
Bruce Floyd *(Sr Dir-Art)*
Kelly Young *(Dir-Art)*
Vicki Floyd *(Copywriter)*

Accounts:
Watson Realty Corp

MASCOLA ADVERTISING
434 Forbes Ave, New Haven, CT 06512-1932
Tel.: (203) 469-6900
Fax: (203) 467-8558
E-Mail: contact@mascola.com
Web Site: www.mascola.com

E-Mail for Key Personnel:
President: chuck@mascola.com
Public Relations: matt@mascola.com

Employees: 10
Year Founded: 1987

Agency Specializes In: Advertising, Advertising Specialties, Affluent Market, African-American Market, Alternative Advertising, Arts, Automotive, Bilingual Market, Brand Development & Integration, Branded Entertainment, Broadcast, Business Publications, Business-To-Business, Cable T.V., Catalogs, Co-op Advertising, Collateral, College, Communications, Consulting, Consumer Goods, Consumer Marketing, Consumer Publications, Content, Corporate Communications, Corporate Identity, Crisis Communications, Customer Relationship Management, Digital/Interactive, Direct Response Marketing, Direct-to-Consumer, E-Commerce, Education, Electronic Media, Electronics, Email, Entertainment, Event Planning & Marketing, Exhibit/Trade Shows, Financial, Food Service, Gay & Lesbian Market, Government/Political, Graphic Design, Guerilla Marketing, High Technology, Hispanic Market, Hospitality, Identity Marketing, In-Store Advertising, Information Technology, Integrated Marketing, International, Internet/Web Design, Investor Relations, Legal Services, Leisure, Local Marketing, Logo & Package Design, Luxury Products, Magazines, Marine, Market Research, Media Buying Services, Media Planning, Media Relations, Media Training, Men's Market, Mobile Marketing, Multicultural, Multimedia, New Product Development, New Technologies, Newspaper, Newspapers & Magazines, Out-of-Home Media, Outdoor, Package Design, Paid Searches, Planning & Consultation, Podcasting, Point of Purchase, Point of Sale, Print, Production, Production (Print), Promotions, Public Relations, Publicity/Promotions, RSS (Really Simple Syndication), Radio, Real Estate, Regional, Restaurant, Sales Promotion, Search Engine Optimization, Social Marketing/Nonprofit, Sponsorship, Sports Market, Strategic Planning/Research, Sweepstakes, Syndication, T.V., Teen Market, Trade & Consumer Magazines, Transportation, Travel & Tourism, Urban Market, Viral/Buzz/Word of Mouth, Web (Banner Ads, Pop-ups, etc.), Women's Market

Approx. Annual Billings: $30,000,000

Breakdown of Gross Billings by Media: Bus. Publs.: 10%; Collateral: 20%; D.M.: 20%; Mags.: 20%; Newsp.: 20%; Radio & T.V.: 10%

Chuck Mascola *(Pres & Strategist-Bus Growth)*
Nick Healy *(Sr Dir-Art)*
Vin DiGioia *(Specialist-Interactive)*
Lauren Leitch *(Specialist-Media)*

Accounts:
Aetna
Big E; West Springfield, MA
Eastern States Exposition; West Springfield, MA
Hancock Shaker Village
ResidenSea (Agency of Record)

MASLANSKY + PARTNERS
200 Varick St, New York, NY 10014
Tel.: (917) 677-9100
Fax: (703) 358-0089
Web Site: www.maslansky.com

Employees: 23

Agency Specializes In: Market Research

Lee Carter *(Partner)*
Keith Yazmir *(Partner-EMEA)*
Patrick Buckley *(VP)*
Chris Manley *(VP)*
Mike Phifer *(VP)*
Clint Sievers *(VP)*
Katie Cronen *(Dir-Language Strategy)*

David Baynham *(Mgr-Social Media & Sr Strategist-Language)*
Margaret Files *(Strategist-Language)*
Sara Snedeker *(Strategist-Language)*

Accounts:
AARP
Alcatel-Lucent
American Medical Association
Amgen
Anheuser-Busch
AT&T Communications Corp.
Bank of America
Bill & Melinda Gates Foundation
Blue Cross Blue Shield
Chase
Citibank
Comcast
Conservation International
Consumer Healthcare Products Association
Continental Airlines
Disney
Dropbox
eBay
eLanco
Emblem Health
Entergy
Estee Lauder
FedEx
Florida Power & Light
General Electric
Hilton Hotels
Insured Retirement Institute
Kindsight
Kroger
McDonald's
Microsoft
Monster
Motion Picture Association of America
National Mining Association
NBC Universal
P&G
Penn Mutual
PepsiCo
Personal Care Products Council
Peter G. Peterson Foundation
Pfizer
PriceWaterhouseCoopers
Property Casualty Insurers Association of America
PSE&G
Shell Oil
Southern California Edison
Starbucks
Tyco International
UBS
Van Kampen Investments
Wachovia
Westfield

MASLOW LUMIA BARTORILLO ADVERTISING

182 N Franklin St, Wilkes Barre, PA 18701-1404
Tel.: (570) 824-1500
Fax: (570) 825-9757
E-Mail: agency3@mlbadvertising.com
Web Site: www.mlbadvertising.com

Employees: 10
Year Founded: 1979

National Agency Associations: 4A's-AAF

Agency Specializes In: Brand Development & Integration, Broadcast, Business Publications, Business-To-Business, Direct Response Marketing, Entertainment, Exhibit/Trade Shows, Food Service, Internet/Web Design, Logo & Package Design, New Product Development, Newspaper, Newspapers & Magazines, Outdoor, Public Relations, Radio, Travel & Tourism

John Nackley, Jr. *(Dir-Mktg & Bus Dev)*
Michael Scholl *(Dir-Art)*
A. J. Zambetti *(Dir-Creative)*

Accounts:
Dincher & Dincher
Greater Wilkes-Barre Chamber of Business & Industry; Wilkes-Barre, PA; 1995
Huntsville Golf Club; Lehman, PA; 1991
Intermountain Health Group
Quad 3
Riverfront Parks of Wilkes-Barre; Wilkes-Barre, PA; 1994
Sagacious Consulting
Tom Hesser (Agency of Record) Online Marketing, Print, Social Media, TV/Radio

MASON, INC.

23 Amity Rd, Bethany, CT 06524-3417
Tel.: (203) 393-1101
Fax: (203) 393-2813
E-Mail: info@mason23.com
Web Site: www.mason23.com

E-Mail for Key Personnel:
President: cmason@masonmadison.com
Creative Dir.: RGamer@masonmadison.com
Media Dir.: pobrien@masonmadison.com
Production Mgr.: aporretta@masonmadison.com
Public Relations: fonofrio@masonmadison.com

Employees: 25
Year Founded: 1951

National Agency Associations: 4A's-MAAN

Agency Specializes In: Advertising, Brand Development & Integration, Business Publications, Business-To-Business, Co-op Advertising, Collateral, Consulting, Consumer Marketing, Consumer Publications, Corporate Identity, Digital/Interactive, Direct Response Marketing, E-Commerce, Electronic Media, Engineering, Environmental, Event Planning & Marketing, Exhibit/Trade Shows, Health Care Services, High Technology, Industrial, Information Technology, Internet/Web Design, Magazines, Medical Products, Merchandising, Out-of-Home Media, Outdoor, Planning & Consultation, Point of Purchase, Point of Sale, Print, Production, Public Relations, Publicity/Promotions, Real Estate, Recruitment, Sales Promotion, Strategic Planning/Research, Sweepstakes, Technical Advertising, Trade & Consumer Magazines, Transportation

Approx. Annual Billings: $20,000,000

Charles T. Mason *(CEO)*
Elmer Grubbs *(VP & Assoc Dir-Creative)*
Angelo Porretta *(VP-Production Svcs)*
Derek Beere *(Dir-Brand Engagement)*
Richard Gamer *(Dir-Creative)*
Neil Johnson *(Dir-Interactive Creative)*
Ryan Winiarski *(Dir-Digital Strategies & Analytics)*
Nick Koutsopoulos *(Sr Mgr-Media)*
Jordana Carideo *(Brand Mgr-PR)*
Danielle Geer *(Brand Mgr & Sr Media Planner)*
Olivia Canada *(Assoc Media Buyer)*

Accounts:
Acadia Insurance
Cohen & Wolf
Connecticut Open Tennis Tournament (Agency of Record) Advertising, Digital Media, Press, Public Relations, Social Media
Connex Credit Union
Cookson Electronics
DYMAX Corporation
Energize CT
Enthone
Gateway Community College
Hospital for Special Care
Odyssey Logistics & Technology
Precision X-Ray
Speedline Technologies
The United Illuminating Company
Yale Center for Clinical Investigation
Yale New Haven Health

MASON INTERACTIVE INC

130 W 29th St 6th Fl, New York, NY 10001
Tel.: (212) 967-7862
E-Mail: hello@masoninteractive.com
Web Site: www.masoninteractive.com

Year Founded: 2008

Agency Specializes In: Advertising, Brand Development & Integration, Content, Corporate Identity, Digital/Interactive, Logo & Package Design, Media Buying Services, Search Engine Optimization, Social Media

Brook Llewellyn Shepard *(CEO & Mng Partner)*
Greg Byrnes *(Mng Partner)*
Craig Handleman *(Mng Partner)*
Julie Eydman *(Dir-Accts)*
Jenna Vaccaro *(Sr Acct Mgr-SEO)*
Nathan Kugel *(Acct Mgr-SEO)*
Brian Poole *(Acct Mgr-eMail & Social Remarketing)*
Claudia Santana *(Acct Mgr-SEO)*

Accounts:
Carini Lang Carpets
The Whisky Explorers Club

MASON SELKOWITZ MARKETING, INC

400 Whitney Rd, Penfield, NY 14526
Tel.: (585) 249-1100
Fax: (585) 249-1060
E-Mail: info@msmmarcom.com
Web Site: www.masonmarketing.com

Employees: 33
Year Founded: 1986

Agency Specializes In: Advertising, Brand Development & Integration, Broadcast, Business-To-Business, Collateral, Communications, Consumer Marketing, Direct Response Marketing, Education, Financial, Graphic Design, Health Care Services, Industrial, Medical Products, Pharmaceutical, Planning & Consultation, Point of Purchase, Point of Sale, Public Relations, Publicity/Promotions, Sales Promotion, Strategic Planning/Research

Approx. Annual Billings: $21,656,750 Capitalized

Breakdown of Gross Billings by Media: Audio/Visual: 5%; Bus. Publs.: 15%; Collateral: 25%; D.M.: 15%; Pub. Rels.: 5%; Sls. Promo.: 20%; Strategic Planning/Research: 10%; Trade & Consumer Mags.: 5%

Timothy J. Mason *(Pres & CEO)*
Brad Schultz *(Chief Creative Officer)*
Terri Cubiotti *(COO-Mason Mktg)*
Mike Cassidy *(Exec VP)*
Greg Danylak *(Sr Dir-Art & Grp Supvr-Creative)*
Jack Pilarski *(Acct Mgr)*
Kaleigh Witzel *(Acct Coord)*

Accounts:
Genesee Regional Bank
Klein Steel
New York Apple Association; Fishers, NY; 2000
Nipro Diagnostics, Inc.; 2001
Tyco Fire & Building Products; Landsdale, PA; 2006

MASONBARONET

1801 N Lamar St Ste 250, Dallas, TX 75202
Tel.: (214) 954-0316
Fax: (214) 855-0460
E-Mail: info@masonbaronet.com

Web Site: www.masonbaronet.com

E-Mail for Key Personnel:
Creative Dir.: Paul@masonbaronet.com

Employees: 6
Year Founded: 1992

Agency Specializes In: Advertising, Brand Development & Integration, Broadcast, Business Publications, Business-To-Business, Collateral, Communications, Consulting, Consumer Marketing, Corporate Communications, Corporate Identity, Digital/Interactive, Direct Response Marketing, Education, Electronic Media, Entertainment, Fashion/Apparel, Financial, Food Service, Gay & Lesbian Market, Graphic Design, Health Care Services, High Technology, Internet/Web Design, Legal Services, Leisure, Logo & Package Design, Magazines, Newspaper, Outdoor, Point of Purchase, Point of Sale, Print, Radio, Real Estate, Restaurant, Retail, Strategic Planning/Research, T.V., Trade & Consumer Magazines

Approx. Annual Billings: $2,000,000

Breakdown of Gross Billings by Media: Collateral: $100,000; Graphic Design: $200,000; Logo & Package Design: $200,000; Print: $800,000; T.V.: $200,000; Worldwide Web Sites: $500,000

Holly Mason *(Owner & Pres)*
Tabitha Bogard *(Creative Dir)*
Sook Lee *(Art Dir-Creative)*
Austin Beavers *(Dir-Art)*
Mary Jane Heard *(Acct Mgr)*
Connor Huff *(Acct Mgr)*

Accounts:
Hanson Brick & Tile
Payne Mitchell Law Group

MASS MEDIA MARKETING
229 Fury's Ferry Rd Ste 123, Augusta, GA 30907
Tel.: (706) 651-0053
Fax: (706) 651-0535
E-Mail: info@m3agency.com
Web Site: www.m3agency.com

E-Mail for Key Personnel:
President: rick@massmediamktg.com
Creative Dir.: lynn@massmediamktg.com
Production Mgr.: mark@massmediamktg.com

Employees: 15
Year Founded: 2000

National Agency Associations: AAF

Agency Specializes In: Broadcast, Co-op Advertising, Food Service, Graphic Design

Approx. Annual Billings: $10,000,000

Rick Donaldson *(Owner)*
Fredna Lynn Forbes *(Dir-Creative)*
Ashley Drummond *(Acct Exec)*
Kim Barrs Jenkins *(Acct Exec)*
Courtney Prouty *(Acct Exec)*
Amy Padgett *(Media Planner)*

Accounts:
First Bank

MASS TRANSMIT
453 W17th St, New York, NY 10011
Tel.: (704) 706-2670
Fax: (704) 447-7262
E-Mail: info@masstransmit.com
Web Site: www.masstransmit.com

E-Mail for Key Personnel:
President: Anthony.Schneider@masstransmit.com
Creative Dir.: rich.barrett@masstransmit.com

Employees: 18
Year Founded: 1996

National Agency Associations: DMA-EEC-WOMMA

Agency Specializes In: Business-To-Business, Consulting, Consumer Marketing, Digital/Interactive, Electronic Media, Email, Information Technology, Internet/Web Design, Mobile Marketing, New Technologies, Paid Searches, Publicity/Promotions, RSS (Really Simple Syndication), Search Engine Optimization, Sweepstakes, Viral/Buzz/Word of Mouth, Web (Banner Ads, Pop-ups, etc.)

Mark Lewis *(Co-Founder & Dir-Tech)*
Anthony Schneider *(Pres)*
Adam Holden-Bache *(CEO)*
Marla Chupack *(VP & Dir-Client Rels)*

Accounts:
American Marketing Association; Chicago, IL; 2007
AOL
Boxwood Technology; Hunt Valley, MD; 2008
CNA Insurance; New York, NY, Chicago, IL; 2000
Comverge; New York, NY; 2005
Equinox
Food Network
Heineken USA; White Plains, NY; 1999
Henry Schein; Melville, NY; 2007
Kimberly-Clark; New York, NY; 2007
Maytag
NBC Universal; New York, NY; 2009
Pearson Assessments
SEGA; Las Vegas, NV Gameworks, World Sports Grille; 2008
Shell Oil; Houston, TX; 2007
SunCom Wireless; Charlotte, NC; 2002
The Wharton School; Philadelphia, PA; 2009

MASSEY COMMUNICATIONS
1736 33rd St, Orlando, FL 32839
Tel.: (407) 581-4222
Fax: (407) 581-4226
E-Mail: info@masseycommunications.com
Web Site: www.masseycommunications.com

Year Founded: 1985

Agency Specializes In: Advertising, Graphic Design, Logo & Package Design, Public Relations, Social Media

Sam Stark *(Pres & CEO)*
Kim Sachse *(VP-Creative Svcs)*
Susan Vernon-Devlin *(VP-PR)*
Katherine Coulthart *(Sr Dir-PR & Mktg)*
Matt Masterson *(Dir-Brand Dev)*
Alison Presley *(Office Mgr)*
Rachel Murphy *(Specialist-PR)*

Accounts:
FAMU College of Law; 2015
Jewish Family Services of Greater Orlando; 2013
Massey Services; 1985

MASSIVEMEDIA
34 W 27th St 6 Fl, New York, NY 10001
Tel.: (212) 730-7222
Fax: (212) 730-7444
E-Mail: info@massivemediainc.com
Web Site: www.massivemediainc.com

Employees: 15
Year Founded: 1995

Agency Specializes In: Advertising, Advertising Specialties, Affluent Market, African-American Market, Alternative Advertising, Arts, Asian Market, Automotive, Bilingual Market, Children's Market, Collateral, College, Consumer Marketing, Direct-to-Consumer, Electronic Media, Entertainment, Event Planning & Marketing, Exhibit/Trade Shows, Experience Design, Gay & Lesbian Market, Guerilla Marketing, Health Care Services, Hispanic Market, Identity Marketing, In-Store Advertising, Integrated Marketing, Leisure, Local Marketing, Luxury Products, Marine, Men's Market, Mobile Marketing, Multicultural, Multimedia, Out-of-Home Media, Outdoor, Over-50 Market, Pets , Point of Purchase, Production, Promotions, Publicity/Promotions, Real Estate, Regional, Restaurant, Sales Promotion, Seniors' Market, Social Marketing/Nonprofit, Sports Market, Sweepstakes, Teen Market, Tween Market, Urban Market, Viral/Buzz/Word of Mouth, Women's Market

Approx. Annual Billings: $6,000,000

Robert Rukstalis *(Pres)*
Carolyn Mcneilly *(Dir-Ops)*
Shakira Smith *(Dir)*

Accounts:
Assurance Wireless
Boost Mobile
Chase
Dunkin Donuts
Hyundai
Nissan
Samsung
Sprint
Verizon
Virgin Mobile USA, Inc.

MASSMEDIA CORPORATE COMMUNICATIONS
2863 St Rose Pkwy, Henderson, NV 89052
Tel.: (702) 433-4331
Fax: (702) 433-4566
E-Mail: carmesha@massmediacc.com
Web Site: www.massmediacc.com

Employees: 18
Year Founded: 1997

Agency Specializes In: Public Relations

Breakdown of Gross Billings by Media: Pub. Rels.: 100%

Kassi Belz *(Pres)*
Paula Yakubik *(Mng Partner)*
Sean Corbett *(VP-Digital Strategy & Plng)*
Georgeann Pizzi *(VP)*
Amanda Arentsen *(Acct Exec)*

Accounts:
ABQ Health Partners
The City of Henderson
Colliers International
HealthCare Partners
Kafoury
LS Power
McDonald Carano Wilson
NAIOP
Nevada Department Of Employment Training & Rehabilitation Campaign: "Opportunity at Work", Creative Development, Media Planning & Placement, Public Relations, Social Media
Nevada Partnership For Homeless Youth
Penta
Pets Best Insurance; Boise, ID Media Inquiries, Public Relations
Pisanelli Bice
Southwest Gas
Women's Health Associates of Southern Nevada

MASSMEDIA, INC.
67 Walnut Hill Rd, Newton, MA 02459-2666

Tel.: (617) 964-1098
Toll Free: (877) MASSMEDIA
E-Mail: info@massmedia.net
Web Site: www.massmedia.net

Employees: 3
Year Founded: 1991

Agency Specializes In: Advertising, Broadcast, Cable T.V., Collateral, Consulting, E-Commerce, Education, Fashion/Apparel, Financial, High Technology, Infomercials, Internet/Web Design, Leisure, Media Buying Services, Multimedia, Outdoor, Planning & Consultation, Production, Radio, Retail, Strategic Planning/Research, T.V., Travel & Tourism

Approx. Annual Billings: $3,000,000

Breakdown of Gross Billings by Media: Newsp.: 5%; Outdoor: 5%; Production: 15%; Radio & T.V.: 50%; Strategic Planning/Research: 10%; Worldwide Web Sites: 15%

Charles N. Shapiro *(Founder & Pres)*
Dana Mattson *(Partner & Dir-New Bus Dev)*
Debra A. Shapiro *(VP & Dir-Creative)*

Accounts:
Chippewa Boots; Fort Worth, TX Footwear; 1999
Congregation Kehillath Israel Branding, Events, Membership; 2008
Connecticut School of Broadcasting Education; 1991
Legends Radio Radio Station; 2014
Massasoit Community College Education; 2014
Mount Wachusett Community College Education; 2012
Santa's Village Entertainment; 2013
State Universities/Commonwealth of Massachusetts Awareness, Branding; 2014
Worcester State University Education; 2014

MASTERMINDS
6727 Delilah Rd, Egg Harbor Township, NJ 08234
Tel.: (609) 484-0009
Fax: (609) 484-1909
Web Site: mastermindsagency.com

Employees: 42
Year Founded: 1985

Agency Specializes In: Above-the-Line, Advertising, Advertising Specialties, Below-the-Line, Brand Development & Integration, Broadcast, Cable T.V., Collateral, Communications, Consulting, Consumer Goods, Consumer Marketing, Corporate Identity, Customer Relationship Management, Direct Response Marketing, Direct-to-Consumer, Entertainment, Graphic Design, Hospitality, Internet/Web Design, Leisure, Logo & Package Design, Magazines, Media Buying Services, Newspaper, Newspapers & Magazines, Out-of-Home Media, Outdoor, Over-50 Market, Planning & Consultation, Point of Purchase, Print, Production, Production (Print), Promotions, Publicity/Promotions, Radio, Regional, Restaurant, Retail, Sales Promotion, Seniors' Market, Sports Market, Strategic Planning/Research, Sweepstakes, T.V., Trade & Consumer Magazines, Travel & Tourism, Web (Banner Ads, Pop-ups, etc.)

Approx. Annual Billings: $35,000,000

Joseph McIntire *(Pres)*
Nancy Smith *(CEO)*
Ryan Leeds *(Partner & Exec VP)*
Jennifer Fink *(VP & Acct Dir)*
George Cortesini *(VP & Dir-Accts)*
Tina Bendl *(VP-Fin & Admin)*
Bill Porter *(VP-Media Svcs)*
James Garrison *(Sr Dir-Art)*
Lani Bouchacourt *(Acct Dir)*
Shawna Hurley *(Acct Supvr)*
Rebecca Veloso *(Acct Coord)*

Accounts:
Cannery Row Casinos; Las Vegas, NV Racetrack & Casino; 2007
Greater Philadelphia Tourism Marketing Corp. Philly Guest of the Day, Philly Overnight Hotel Package
IGT; Reno, NV Branded Slot Machines; 1989
The Mississippi Gulf Coast Regional Convention & Visitors Bureau
Pinnacle Entertainment
The Westfield Group; 2004

MASTERPIECE ADVERTISING
3101 Boardwalk Ste 13, Atlantic City, NJ 8401
Tel.: (609) 344-2400
Fax: (609) 347-3556
E-Mail: getcreative@masterpieceadvertising.com
Web Site: www.masterpieceadvertising.com

Agency Specializes In: Advertising, Brand Development & Integration, Digital/Interactive, Event Planning & Marketing, Internet/Web Design, Print, Promotions, Search Engine Optimization, Social Media, Strategic Planning/Research

Phyllis Lacca *(Owner)*
Hiro Kizuka *(Dir-Interactive Comm)*
Mark Patten *(Dir-Creative)*
Megan Vanett *(Acct Exec)*

Accounts:
New-The Pascale Sykes Foundation (Agency of Record) Marketing
Reliance Medical Group

MATCH MARKETING GROUP
5225 Satellite Drive, Mississauga, ON L4W5P9 Canada
Tel.: (905) 566-2824
E-Mail: info@matchmg.com
Web Site: www.matchmg.com

Agency Specializes In: Shopper Marketing

Brett Farren *(Pres & CEO)*
Christopher Difonzo *(Mng Partner-Match Mktg Grp)*
Mike Duncan *(Mng Partner)*
Antoine Adams *(Partner)*
Andrea Nickel *(CFO)*
Roger Chan *(Acct Dir)*
Kathryn Hill *(Client Svcs Dir)*
Brandon Ram *(Mgr-Talent Acq-Natl)*
Nadia Novello *(Acct Supvr)*
Robert Fleming *(Client Mgr)*
Shelli Kotkovski *(Client Mgr-Match Transact)*

Accounts:
L'Oreal
Mars Canada Advertising, Ben's Beginners, Digital Banners, Public Relations, Social Media, Uncle Ben's
Pepsi
Redbox

MATCHA DESIGN LLC
3513 S Richmond Ave, Tulsa, OK 74135
Tel.: (918) 749-2456
E-Mail: info@matchadesign.com
Web Site: www.matchadesign.com

Year Founded: 2004

Agency Specializes In: Advertising, Brand Development & Integration, Corporate Identity, Digital/Interactive, Email, Internet/Web Design, Logo & Package Design, Print, Social Media

Chris Lo *(Pres & CEO)*

Accounts:
Up With Trees

MATCHBOOK CREATIVE
2507 N Delaware St, Indianapolis, IN 46205
Tel.: (317) 920-1200
Web Site: www.matchbookcreative.com

Year Founded: 2007

Agency Specializes In: Advertising, Brand Development & Integration, Collateral, Corporate Identity, Internet/Web Design, Package Design, Print, Social Media

Christy Gormal *(VP)*
Maris Schiess *(VP)*
Madeline Cole *(Sr Dir-Art)*
Michael Stark *(Designer)*

Accounts:
Humane Society of Indianapolis

MATLOCK ADVERTISING & PUBLIC RELATIONS
107 Luckie St, Atlanta, GA 30303
Tel.: (404) 872-3200
Fax: (404) 876-4929
E-Mail: edward.rutland@matlock-adpr.com
Web Site: www.matlock-adpr.com

Employees: 15
Year Founded: 1986

Agency Specializes In: Advertising, Consumer Marketing, Direct Response Marketing, Public Relations, Sponsorship

Approx. Annual Billings: $25,000,000

Breakdown of Gross Billings by Media: Print: 60%; Spot Radio: 30%; Spot T.V.: 10%

Kent Matlock *(Chm & CEO)*
Lilla Jean Matlock *(Vice Chm & Treas)*
S. Edward Rutland *(Pres)*
Donald Webster *(CFO)*
Kirstin Popper *(Sr VP & Gen Mgr)*
Pamela Bishop *(Sr VP-Client Svcs)*

Accounts:
Atlanta Medical Center Brand Positioning, Creative Strategy, Media, Public Relations
BMW Marketing
Georgia-Pacific
Mini USA
Publix Super Markets; 1993

Branch:

Matlock Advertising & Public Relations-NY
160 Varick St, New York, NY 10013
Tel.: (212) 532-3800
Fax: (212) 532-4010
E-Mail: edward.rutland@matlock-adpr.com
Web Site: www.matlock-adpr.com

Employees: 5
Year Founded: 1993

Agency Specializes In: Advertising, Public Relations

Kent Matlock *(Chm & CEO)*
S. Edward Rutland *(Pres)*
Donald Webster *(CFO)*
Ashley Ihesiaba *(Asst Acct Exec & Chm-Social*

Media)
Kirstin Popper *(Sr VP & Gen Mgr)*
Pamela Foster Bishop *(Sr VP-Client Svcs)*
Chandra Diggs Small *(Acct Dir)*
Pat Burson George *(Specialist-Media Rels)*
Jonathan Dossman *(Coord-Graphics & Social Media)*

Accounts:
BMW
Georgia Pacific
Luster Products
Major League Baseball
Mini
Publix Supermarkets

MATRIX MARKETING GROUP LLC
47 Maple St, Burlington, VT 5401
Tel.: (802) 435-1414
E-Mail: info@matrixmarketinggroup.com
Web Site: www.matrixmarketinggroup.com

Year Founded: 2002

Agency Specializes In: Advertising, Graphic Design, Paid Searches, Public Relations, Search Engine Optimization, Social Media

Robin Emiliani *(VP)*

Accounts:
New-SCApath

MATRIX PARTNERS LTD.
566 W Adams St Ste 720, Chicago, IL 60661
Tel.: (312) 648-9972
Fax: (312) 648-9978
E-Mail: info@matrix1.com
Web Site: www.matrix1.com

Employees: 12
Year Founded: 1996

Agency Specializes In: Brand Development & Integration, Communications, Pets , Strategic Planning/Research

Breakdown of Gross Billings by Media: Bus. Publs.: 10%; Collateral: 10%; D.M.: 10%; Fees: 25%; Internet Adv.: 15%; Mags.: 15%; Point of Purchase: 5%; Pub. Rels.: 5%; Trade Shows: 5%

Don Tomala *(Mng Partner)*
Dennis Abelson *(Partner & Dir-Creative)*
Kristy Boulos *(VP & Acct Supvr)*
Rebecca Tomala *(VP-Client Svcs)*
John Zappia *(VP-Bus Dev)*
George Wielgus *(Sr Dir-Art)*
Stephanie Krol *(Dir-PR)*

Accounts:
Arctic Paws
Custom Foods
Griffith
Hyper Products
McNeil
Pet Care Systems; Detroit Lakes, MN Pet Products; 2001
Quaker
REI
StickySheets
SwheatScoop
Tops
TropiClean

MATRIX2 ADVERTISING
(Private-Parent-Single Location)
1903 NW 97th Ave, Miami, FL 33172
Tel.: (305) 591-7672
Fax: (305) 591-8575
Web Site: www.matrix2advertising.com

Employees: 18
Year Founded: 1977

Agency Specializes In: Advertising, Collateral, Content, Graphic Design, Internet/Web Design, Media Buying Services, Media Planning, Outdoor, Print, Social Media, Strategic Planning/Research

Revenue: $1,200,000

Kathy Maiuri *(Owner)*
Cristina Ruizcalderon *(Dir-Media)*
Bill Thomas *(Dir-Creative)*
KiM Haber *(Sr Acct Exec)*
CleMen Hernandez *(Acct Coord)*

Accounts:
Miramar Cultural Center Artspark

MATTER COMMUNICATIONS
50 Water St, Mill #3, The Tannery, Newburyport, MA 01950
Tel.: (978) 499-9250
Fax: (978) 499-9253
E-Mail: scott@matternow.com
Web Site: www.matternow.com

Agency Specializes In: Communications, Corporate Communications, Crisis Communications, High Technology, Integrated Marketing, Investor Relations, Media Training, Publicity/Promotions, Social Media

Scott Signore *(CEO & Principal)*
Jesse Ciccone *(Mng Dir & VP)*
Patty Barry *(Principal)*
Parry Headrick *(VP-Mktg & Comm)*
Matt Landry *(VP)*
Anne Lines *(VP)*
Jim Baptiste *(Acct Dir)*
Emma Walter *(Acct Exec)*

Accounts:
CVS Pharmacy
ExaGrid
Experience
Harris Corp.
New-JDA Software Group (Public Relations Agency of Record) Social Media, Thought Leadership, Trade Media Relations
Kubota Image Tools
Lexar Media
LoJack Media Relations, PR, Social Strategy
Lowepro
Progress Software Corporation (North American Agency of Record) Creative, Media Outreach, Public Relations, Social Media, Strategic Counsel, Thought Leadership
Spider Holster
Verizon Wireless New England

MATTER CREATIVE GROUP
308 E 8th St 3rd Fl, Cincinnati, OH 45202
Tel.: (513) 398-1700
E-Mail: inquiry@mattercreativegroup.com
Web Site: www.mattercreativegroup.com

Agency Specializes In: Advertising, Brand Development & Integration, Internet/Web Design, Logo & Package Design

Chuck Tabir *(VP-Sls & Mktg)*
Greg Fehrenbach *(VP-Client Engagement)*
Joel Warneke *(Exec Creative Dir)*
Suzette Percival *(Dir-Mktg)*

Accounts:
New-Blue Ash Oral

MATTER UNLIMITED LLC
175 Varick St, New York, NY 10014
Tel.: (646) 664-4472
E-Mail: ican@makethingsmatter.com
Web Site: www.makethingsmatter.com

Year Founded: 2010

Agency Specializes In: Advertising, Brand Development & Integration, Digital/Interactive, Social Media, Strategic Planning/Research

Rob Holzer *(Founder & CEO)*
Alexandra Gordon *(Mng Dir-Acct)*
Sean Donovan *(Dir-Strategy)*
Jake Kahana *(Dir-Creative & Design)*

Accounts:
Enterprise Community Partners Affordable Housing
Hewlett-Packard Company

MATTHEW JAMES CREATIVE, INC.
596 Squaw Run Rd E, Pittsburgh, PA 15238
Tel.: (412) 508-8085
Fax: (412) 906-9580
E-Mail: solutions@matthewjamescreative.com
Web Site: www.matthewjamescreative.com

Year Founded: 2006

Agency Specializes In: Advertising, Business-To-Business, Internet/Web Design, Search Engine Optimization

Jim Balog *(Co-Owner & Partner)*
Matthew Loht *(Co-Owner & Partner)*

Accounts:
Cronimet USA
Universal Manufacturing Corp.

THE MATTHEWS GROUP, INC.
400 Lake St, Bryan, TX 77801
Tel.: (979) 823-3600
Fax: (979) 823-0036
E-Mail: info@thematthewsgroup.com
Web Site: www.thematthewsgroup.com

E-Mail for Key Personnel:
President: drew@thematthewsgroup.com

Employees: 7
Year Founded: 1987

Drew Matthews *(Pres & Dir-Creative)*
Josh Daybery *(Gen Counsel)*
Debbie Brow *(Office Mgr)*
Kim Smith *(Office Mgr)*

Accounts:
First Community Holdings; Houston, TX
St. Joseph Regional Health Center; Bryan, TX

MATTS & DAVIDSON INC.
3 Rye Rdg Plz, Rye Brook, NY 10573
Tel.: (914) 220-6576
Fax: (914) 831-3203
Toll Free: (800) 353-8867
E-Mail: tdavidson@mattsdavidson.com
Web Site: www.mattsdavidson.com

Employees: 20
Year Founded: 2005

Agency Specializes In: Advertising, Advertising Specialties, Affluent Market, Alternative Advertising, Brand Development & Integration, Business Publications, Business-To-Business, Cable T.V., Collateral, Commercial Photography, Consulting, Consumer Marketing, Corporate Identity, Digital/Interactive, Direct Response Marketing, E-Commerce, Email, Entertainment,

Event Planning & Marketing, Graphic Design, In-Store Advertising, Infomercials, Information Technology, Internet/Web Design, Local Marketing, Logo & Package Design, Media Buying Services, Multimedia, New Product Development, Newspaper, Paid Searches, Podcasting, Print, Public Relations, Publicity/Promotions, Sales Promotion, Strategic Planning/Research, Technical Advertising, Women's Market, Yellow Pages Advertising

Approx. Annual Billings: $700,000

Breakdown of Gross Billings by Media: Internet Adv.: 100%

Theresa Davidson *(Owner)*

MATTSON CREATIVE INC

14988 Sand Canyon Ave Studio 8, Irvine, CA 92618
Tel.: (949) 651-8740
E-Mail: info@mattsoncreative.com
Web Site: www.mattsoncreative.com

Agency Specializes In: Advertising, Brand Development & Integration, Digital/Interactive, Graphic Design

Ty Mattson *(Owner)*
Russ Gray *(Dir-Art & Designer-Production)*

Accounts:
Audi of America, Inc.
The Jim Henson Company
SND CYN

MAUDE, LLC

160 Varick St, New York, NY 10013
Tel.: (917) 237-7191
E-Mail: info@maudeny.com
Web Site: www.maudeny.com

Agency Specializes In: Advertising, Media Planning, Public Relations, Social Media

Marc Klatzko *(Chief Creative Officer)*
Margaret Selsam Muhlfelder *(Mng Dir-Acct Mgmt & Client Svc)*
Aaron Goodman *(Sr Dir-Art)*
David Muldoon *(Dir-Creative)*

Accounts:
Comedy Central
MTV Campaign: "MTV Movie Awards Twitter Tracker"
Sony Corporation
Terlato Wines International
Viggle TV Commercial

MAVEN COMMUNICATIONS LLC

123 S Broad St Ste 1645, Philadelphia, PA 19109
Tel.: (215) 434-7190
E-Mail: info@mavenagency.com
Web Site: www.mavenagency.com

Agency Specializes In: Advertising, Event Planning & Marketing, Internet/Web Design, Public Relations, Social Media, Strategic Planning/Research

Rebecca Devine *(Co-Founder & Principal)*
Jessica Sharp *(Co-Founder & Principal)*
Lisa Gimelli *(Exec VP & Client Svcs Dir)*
Sarah Rohlfing *(VP & Sr Acct Dir)*
Sabeen Malik *(Mgmt Supvr-Project)*
Kiersten Tomson *(Dir-New Bus Dev & Media Strategies)*
Veronica Mikitka *(Acct Supvr)*
Meghan McGarrigle *(Sr Acct Exec)*
Amy C. Woolley *(Sr Acct Exec)*

Accounts:
ARCWheeler LLC Real Estate Investment & Development Services
The Arthritis Foundation Inc Health Care & Social Service Provider
Excel Physical Therapy Health Care & Gymnasium Providers
Fisher & Phillips LLP
Futura Mobility
InfoMC Inc Health Care Service Providers
Javers Group Human Resources & Benefit Outsourcing Service Providers
ProPoint Graphics
Prudential Real Estate Affiliates Inc Real Estate Agency Services
Rothman Institute; Philadelphia, PA PR
Vesper Property Group Ltd Real Estate Investment & Development Services

MAVEN CREATIVE

62 W Colonial Dr Ste 302, Orlando, FL 32801
Fax: (888) 606-2836
Toll Free: (888) 606-2836
E-Mail: hello@mavencreative.com
Web Site: mavencreative.com

Year Founded: 2008

Agency Specializes In: Advertising, Brand Development & Integration, Corporate Identity, Digital/Interactive, Print

Chris Stephens *(Principal)*
Corey Curyto *(Principal)*

Accounts:
The Pop Parlour

MAXIMUM BALANCE FOUNDATION

1770 Post Ste 108, San Francisco, CA 94115
Tel.: (415) 691-4264
Fax: (415) 738-7670
E-Mail: johnny@maximumbalancefoundation.com
Web Site: www.maximumbalancefoundation.com

Employees: 5
Year Founded: 2003

Agency Specializes In: Above-the-Line, Advertising, Advertising Specialties, Affiliate Marketing, Affluent Market, African-American Market, Agriculture, Alternative Advertising, Arts, Asian Market, Automotive, Aviation & Aerospace, Below-the-Line, Bilingual Market, Brand Development & Integration, Branded Entertainment, Broadcast, Business Publications, Business-To-Business, Cable T.V., Catalogs, Children's Market, Co-op Advertising, Collateral, College, Commercial Photography, Communications, Computers & Software, Consulting, Consumer Goods, Consumer Marketing, Consumer Publications, Content, Corporate Communications, Corporate Identity, Cosmetics, Crisis Communications, Custom Publishing, Customer Relationship Management, Digital/Interactive, Direct Response Marketing, Direct-to-Consumer, E-Commerce, Education, Electronic Media, Electronics, Email, Engineering, Entertainment, Environmental, Event Planning & Marketing, Exhibit/Trade Shows, Experience Design, Fashion/Apparel, Financial, Food Service, Game Integration, Gay & Lesbian Market, Government/Political, Graphic Design, Guerilla Marketing, Health Care Services, High Technology, Hispanic Market, Hospitality, Household Goods, Identity Marketing, In-Store Advertising, Industrial, Infomercials, Information Technology, Integrated Marketing, International, Internet/Web Design, Investor Relations, Legal Services, Leisure, Local Marketing, Logo & Package Design, Luxury Products, Magazines, Marine, Market Research, Media Buying Services, Media Planning, Media Relations, Media Training, Medical Products, Men's Market, Merchandising, Mobile Marketing, Multicultural, Multimedia, New Product Development, New Technologies, Newspaper, Newspapers & Magazines, Out-of-Home Media, Outdoor, Over-50 Market, Package Design, Paid Searches, Pharmaceutical, Planning & Consultation, Podcasting, Point of Purchase, Point of Sale, Print, Product Placement, Production, Production (Ad, Film, Broadcast), Production (Print), Promotions, Public Relations, Publicity/Promotions, Publishing, RSS (Really Simple Syndication), Radio, Real Estate, Recruitment, Regional, Restaurant, Retail, Sales Promotion, Search Engine Optimization, Seniors' Market, Social Marketing/Nonprofit, South Asian Market, Sponsorship, Sports Market, Stakeholders, Strategic Planning/Research, Sweepstakes, Syndication, T.V., Technical Advertising, Teen Market, Telemarketing, Trade & Consumer Magazines, Transportation, Travel & Tourism, Urban Market, Viral/Buzz/Word of Mouth, Web (Banner Ads, Pop-ups, etc.), Women's Market, Yellow Pages Advertising

Approx. Annual Billings: $7,000,000

Breakdown of Gross Billings by Media: Co-op Adv.: 20%; Event Mktg.: 30%; Local Mktg.: 20%; Plng. & Consultation: 25%; Strategic Planning/Research: 5%

J. Lee Clarke *(Mng Partner)*

MAXIMUM DESIGN & ADVERTISING

7032 Wrightsville Ave Ste 201, Wilmington, NC 28403
Tel.: (910) 256-2320
Fax: (910) 256-5171
E-Mail: kelly@maximumdesign.com
Web Site: maximumrocks.com

Employees: 8
Year Founded: 1998

Agency Specializes In: Brand Development & Integration, Exhibit/Trade Shows, Internet/Web Design, Media Buying Services, Media Planning, Outdoor, Real Estate, Strategic Planning/Research

Kelly Burnette *(Co-Founder & Principal)*
Katie McCormick *(VP-Digital & New Bus Dev)*
Benson Wills *(Mgr-Internet Dev)*

Accounts:
The Ginn Company
The Grove

MAXIMUM MEDIA ENTERPRISES, INC.

100 Corporate Pl Ste 102, Peabody, MA 01960
Tel.: (978) 536-9600
Fax: (978) 536-9604
E-Mail: info@maximummediaagency.com
Web Site: www.maximummediaagency.com

Employees: 7
Year Founded: 2003

National Agency Associations: 4A's

Agency Specializes In: Advertising, Email, Event Planning & Marketing, Graphic Design, Internet/Web Design, Local Marketing, Media Buying Services, Print, Production, Radio, T.V.

Nick DeAngelo *(Owner)*
Cheryl DeAngelo *(Pres)*
Lisa Morello *(Office Mgr-HR & Fin)*

Accounts:
Redwood

MAXWELL & MILLER MARKETING COMMUNICATIONS

141 E Michigan Ste 500, Kalamazoo, MI 49007-3943
Tel.: (269) 382-4060
Fax: (269) 382-0504
E-Mail: millerg@maxwellandmiller.com
Web Site: www.maxwellandmiller.com

E-Mail for Key Personnel:
President: millerg@maxwellandmiller.com
Media Dir.: rnurrie@maxwellandmiller.com

Employees: 10
Year Founded: 1981

Agency Specializes In: Advertising, Brand Development & Integration, Business-To-Business, Communications, Consulting, Consumer Marketing, Consumer Publications, Corporate Identity, Direct Response Marketing, Graphic Design, Logo & Package Design, Newspapers & Magazines, Out-of-Home Media, Outdoor, Travel & Tourism

Breakdown of Gross Billings by Media: Bus. Publs.: 10%; Collateral: 30%; D.M.: 5%; Logo & Package Design: 5%; Mags.: 15%; Newsp.: 15%; Outdoor: 10%; Radio & T.V.: 10%

Gregory A. Miller *(Pres & Dir-Creative)*
Dave Eick *(Partner-Strategic)*
Tom Repp *(Partner-Strategic)*
Ruth Nurrie *(Dir-Media)*
Dan Willoughby *(Assoc Dir-Creative)*

Accounts:
Branns Steakhouses; Grand Rapids, MI; 1997
Jack Brown Produce
Kellogg's
Petoskey Area Visitors Bureau; Petoskey, MI Resort Region; 1988
Whirlpool

MAY SKY, INC.

153 Hunns Lake Rd, Stanfordville, NY 12581
Tel.: (845) 868-3155
Fax: (845) 868-3156
E-Mail: dpress@mayskyinc.com
Web Site: www.mayskyinc.com

Employees: 6
Year Founded: 2003

Agency Specializes In: Advertising, African-American Market, Brand Development & Integration, Business Publications, Business-To-Business, Collateral, Communications, Consumer Publications, Corporate Communications, Corporate Identity, Direct Response Marketing, Education, Electronic Media, Entertainment, Exhibit/Trade Shows, Food Service, Graphic Design, Guerilla Marketing, Hispanic Market, In-Store Advertising, Internet/Web Design, Legal Services, Leisure, Local Marketing, Logo & Package Design, Media Buying Services, New Product Development, Newspaper, Out-of-Home Media, Outdoor, Planning & Consultation, Point of Purchase, Print, Production, Public Relations, Publicity/Promotions, Radio, Restaurant, Retail, Sales Promotion, Strategic Planning/Research, Technical Advertising, Teen Market, Trade & Consumer Magazines, Urban Market, Women's Market

Revenue: $200,000

Darren Press *(Dir-Creative & Mktg & Copywriter)*

Accounts:
107.5 WBLS; New York, NY; 2005
Antique & Vintage Woods
Art Institute of NY
Gallaghers Steakhouse
Interboro University
Mandl School; New York, NY; 2006
Palisade Jewellers
Pawling Corporation
Ronnybrook Farm Dairy; Ancramdale, NY; 2004
SSMP
Technical Career Institute
Williams Lumber; Rhinebeck, NY; 2006
WLIB 1190 AM; New York, NY; 2006

MAYA ADVERTISING & COMMUNICATIONS

1819 L St NW Ste 100, Washington, DC 20036
Tel.: (202) 337-0566
Fax: (202) 337-0548
E-Mail: maya@mayaadvertising.com
Web Site: www.mayaadvertising.com

Employees: 12
Year Founded: 1990

National Agency Associations: AHAA

Agency Specializes In: Bilingual Market, Collateral, Digital/Interactive, Education, Entertainment, Financial, Government/Political, Health Care Services, Hispanic Market, Internet/Web Design, Leisure, Production, Public Relations, Real Estate, Sponsorship, Sports Market, Travel & Tourism

Luis Vasquez-Ajmac *(Pres)*
Rikki Marie George *(VP)*
Giovanny Guzman *(Dir-Creative)*
Bonnie Lee La Madeleine *(Dir-Digital)*

Accounts:
20th Century Fox
Alpha Media Group
Best Buy
BIC USA
Big Apple Circus
Comcast
Conectiv
DC Office of the State Superintendent of Education
Department of Education's Federal Student Aid
The Department of Navy
Dynastar
Friendship Public Charter School
GlaxoSmithKline
Hearst Corporation
Jones Group, Inc.
Kraft Foods
Movies on Demand
The Office of Minority Health
Osse
Payless Shoe Stores
Pepco
Time Inc
Time Warner Cable
U.S. Small Business Administration
United States Department of Health & Human Services
United States Department of Homeland Security
United States Department of Navy
Virginia Housing Development Authority
WASA

THE MAYOROS AGENCY

454 S Anderson Rd Ste 154, Rock Hill, SC 29730
Tel.: (803) 324-9940
E-Mail: info@mayorosagency.com
Web Site: www.mayorosagency.com

Year Founded: 2003

Agency Specializes In: Advertising, Graphic Design, Internet/Web Design, Logo & Package Design, Media Buying Services, Media Planning, Print, Social Media, Strategic Planning/Research

Tim Knol *(Dir-Internet Adv)*

Accounts:
Carolina Lift Stations

MAYR COMMUNICATIONS INC

15 Farview Terr Ste 2, Paramus, NJ 07652
Tel.: (201) 291-9800
Fax: (201) 291-9874
Toll Free: (866) 688-6297
E-Mail: info@mayr.com
Web Site: www.mayr.com

Employees: 3
Year Founded: 1998

Agency Specializes In: Faith Based, Graphic Design, Public Relations

Revenue: $1,500,000

Accounts:
Advanced Viral Research Corporation
Aegis Management
Alita Pharmaceuticals
Barr Pharmaceuticals
Caugherty & Hahn
K2R
LuSheann Caterers and Event Planning
RetailClick

THE MAZEROV GROUP

3600 S Yosemite St, Denver, CO 80237
Tel.: (303) 741-2369
Fax: (303) 741-3126
E-Mail: info@themazerovgroup.com
Web Site: themazerovgroup.com/

Employees: 15

Agency Specializes In: Advertising, Digital/Interactive, Public Relations

Bob Mazerov *(Pres)*

MB PILAND ADVERTISING & MARKETING LLC

3127 Southwest Huntoon, Topeka, KS 66604
Tel.: (785) 232-4156
Web Site: www.mbpiland.com

Agency Specializes In: Advertising, Collateral, Digital/Interactive, Media Planning, Social Media, Strategic Planning/Research

Martha Bartlett Piland *(Pres & CEO)*
Alex Reilly *(Principal & VP)*

Accounts:
Midland Care Connection Inc.

MBLM

7 W 22nd St 10th Fl, New York, NY 10010
Tel.: (212) 979-8200
E-Mail: info.ny@mblm.com
Web Site: www.mblm.com

Year Founded: 2005

Agency Specializes In: Advertising, Brand Development & Integration, Corporate Identity, Digital/Interactive, Internet/Web Design, Package Design, Sponsorship

John Diefenbach *(Chm)*
Mario Natarelli *(Mng Partner)*
Maria Pulido *(Mng Partner)*
Luis Herrera *(Partner & Dir-Creative-Emblem Mexico)*
Jae-Yong Hwang *(Partner)*

Diego Kolsky *(Partner)*
Olaf Kreitz *(Partner)*
Kate Conrad *(Dir-Bus Dev)*

Accounts:
AllianceBernstein Campaign: "Ahead of Tomorrow", Marketing, Online, Print, Website
Madrilena Tequila Xicote Bottle

MBS VALUE PARTNERS, INC.
(Formerly Breakstone Group)
501 Madison Ave Fl 12A, New York, NY 10022
Tel.: (212) 750-5800
Fax: (212) 661-2268
E-Mail: contact@mbsvalue.com
Web Site: mbsvalue.com

Agency Specializes In: Brand Development & Integration, Corporate Communications, Crisis Communications, Financial, Identity Marketing, Investor Relations, Local Marketing, Media Relations, Strategic Planning/Research

Monique Skruzny *(Founder & Partner)*
Betsy Brod *(Partner)*
Fabiane Goldstein *(Partner-Brazil)*
Susan Borinelli *(Mng Dir)*
Barbara J. Cano *(Mng Dir)*
Margaret Mager *(Mng Dir)*

Accounts:
Uruguay Mineral Exploration, Inc.

MBT MARKETING
5331 SW Macadam Ave Ste 370, Portland, OR 97239-3848
Tel.: (503) 232-7202
Fax: (503) 232-7213
E-Mail: info@mbtmarketing.com
Web Site: www.mbtmarketing.com

Employees: 15

Agency Specializes In: Advertising

Approx. Annual Billings: $10,000,000

Scott Thompson *(Mng Partner)*
Elwood Beukelman *(Partner & Dir-Creative)*
Norm Myhr *(Partner & Dir-Creative)*
Katie Gailey *(Dir-Media)*
Lisa Bleser *(Acct Exec)*
Mia Carney *(Acct Exec)*

Accounts:
Allison Smith
BASCO
Dairy Queen
Hecht Group
Home & Garden
Home Builders University
Kroger
Tire Factory
Toy & Joy Drive
Vista

MC COMMUNICATIONS
(d/b/a M/C/C)
8131 LBJ Fwy Ste 275, Dallas, TX 75251
Tel.: (972) 480-8383
Fax: (972) 669-8447
Web Site: www.mccom.com

Employees: 20
Year Founded: 1986

National Agency Associations: PRSA

Agency Specializes In: Advertising, High Technology, Public Relations

Approx. Annual Billings: $6,578,000

Breakdown of Gross Billings by Media: Collateral: 7%; D.M.: 7%; Fees: 25%; Print: 35%; Promos.: 21%; Radio & T.V.: 5%

Jim Terry *(Sr VP-Acct Svc)*
Pam Watkins *(Sr VP-Bus & Media Strategy)*
Shannon Sullivan *(VP & Acct Dir)*
Jennifer Reeves *(Mgr-PR Engagement)*

Accounts:
CapRock Communications
CommScope Enterprise Solutions
Geoworks

MC/K HEALTHCARE
(Acquired by Connelly Partners & Name Changed to Mc/K-CP)

MC SQUARED ADVERTISING AGENCY
325 W Eighth St Ste 405, Los Angeles, CA 90014
Tel.: (213) 612-4488
E-Mail: info@e-mc2.com
Web Site: www.e-mc2.com

Agency Specializes In: Advertising, Brand Development & Integration, Event Planning & Marketing, Internet/Web Design, Public Relations, Social Media

Joe Distefano *(VP)*
Scott Nyzio *(Dir-Digital)*

Accounts:
New-MAD Architects

MCBEE GIBRALTAR
455 Massachusetts Avenue, NW, Washington, DC 20004
Tel.: (202) 234-1224
Web Site: www.mcbeestrategic.com

Employees: 15
Year Founded: 2007

Agency Specializes In: Brand Development & Integration, Communications, Crisis Communications, Financial, Government/Political, Strategic Planning/Research

Kimberly Olson Dorgan *(Mng Dir)*
Ted Anderson *(Exec VP)*
Charles Cooper *(Exec VP)*
Kathleen Frangione *(Exec VP)*
Noe Garcia *(Exec VP)*
Chelsea Koski *(Exec VP)*
Elizabeth Northrup *(Exec VP)*
Julie Bertoson *(VP)*
Bruce Holmes *(VP)*
Ryan Hubbard *(VP-Ops)*
Iman Ghanizada *(Mgr-Info Sys)*
Caroline Andrews *(Coord-Client Rels & Bus Dev)*

MCCABE DUVAL + ASSOCIATES
10 Moulton St, Portland, ME 04101
Tel.: (207) 773-4538
Fax: (207) 773-7245
Toll Free: (800) 603-6069
E-Mail: cduval@mccabe-duval.com
Web Site: www.mccabe-duval.com

E-Mail for Key Personnel:
Creative Dir.: cmccabe@mccabe-duval.com

Employees: 15
Year Founded: 1988

Agency Specializes In: Brand Development & Integration, Business-To-Business, Collateral, Corporate Identity, Direct Response Marketing, E-Commerce, Electronic Media, Financial, Logo & Package Design, Medical Products, Print, Strategic Planning/Research

Approx. Annual Billings: $5,000,000

Breakdown of Gross Billings by Media: Collateral: 15%; D.M.: 15%; E-Commerce: 10%; Fees: 15%; Graphic Design: 10%; Print: 15%; Strategic Planning/Research: 10%; Worldwide Web Sites: 10%

Chris Duval *(Founder & Pres)*
Constance McCabe *(Principal & Dir-Creative)*
Paula Bourassa *(Acct Exec)*

MCCAFFERTY & CO. ADVERTISING
1014 S Floyd St, Louisville, KY 40203
Tel.: (502) 581-9227
Fax: (502) 582-2865
Web Site: www.mccaffertyandcompany.com

Employees: 1

Agency Specializes In: Advertising, Direct Response Marketing, Identity Marketing, Outdoor, Package Design, Print

John McCafferty *(Pres & Dir-Creative)*

Accounts:
Better Business Bureau
Southern Warehouse & Distribution

MCCANN ERICKSON WORLDWIDE
622 3rd Ave, New York, NY 10017-6707
Tel.: (646) 865-2000
Fax: (646) 487-9610
E-Mail: contact@mccann.com
Web Site: www.mccannworldgroup.com

Employees: 10,300
Year Founded: 1902

National Agency Associations: AAF-ABC-APA-BPA-DMA-MCA-TAB-THINKLA

Agency Specializes In: Sponsorship

Approx. Annual Billings: $107,000,000

Daniel DiGiuseppe *(Partner-Integrated Plng)*
Dan Fried *(Partner-UM Studios)*
Jeremy Miller *(Chief Comm Officer & Exec VP)*
Tom Murphy *(Chief Creative Officer)*
Eric Silver *(Chief Creative Officer-North America)*
Dan Hanson *(Mgr-Publr)*
Christine Villanueva *(Exec VP & Exec Dir-Strategy & Analytics)*
Susan Irwin *(Sr VP & Dir-Corp Comm)*
Angie Ahn *(Sr VP & Grp Partner-Strategy)*
Dan Donovan *(Exec Dir-Creative)*
Fabiano Feijo *(Exec Creative Dir)*
Jillian Goger *(Grp Dir-Creative & Writer)*
Mike Potter *(Art Dir)*
Kate Siembieda *(Acct Dir)*
Marley Stellmann *(Art Dir)*
Jeremy Adirim *(Dir-Interactive Production)*
Matt Swinburne *(Dir-Creative)*
Kenny Gold *(Assoc Dir-Social)*
Geordie Larratt-Smith *(Acct Supvr)*
Caitlin Bishop *(Strategist-Digital)*
Kelsey Weidman *(Sr Planner-Digital Media)*
Brittany Anhouse *(Media Buyer)*
Josh Bareno *(Planner-Digital Media)*
Mariah Kelley *(Sr Assoc-Integrated Investment)*
Molly Whybrew *(Asst Media Buyer)*

Accounts:
American Airlines
Biscuits & Bath
Black & Decker
The Brady Campaign to Prevent Gun Violence

Campaign: "Voices Against Violence"
Brady Center to Prevent Gun Violence Campaign: "Voices Against Violence"
Cathay Pacific
Chicco
Cisco Systems, Inc.
Coca-Cola Refreshments USA, Inc.
General Mills Campaign: "Trail View", Creative Advertising, Lucky Charms, Nature Valley, Pillsbury
General Motors Campaign: "Joy"
GlaxoSmithKline
IKEA Campaign: "A World Without Textiles", Creative, IKEA Catalogue (Global Agency of Record), Website
Johnson & Johnson
L'Oreal
MasterCard
New-MGM Resorts International (Creative Agency of Record)
Mondelez International, Inc.
Nestle Campaign: "Fountain of Electrolytenment", Campaign: "Raid", Nestle Waters
New-New York Lottery Campaign: "Holiday Wishes", Online, Out-of-Home, Radio, TV
Novartis
The Parks & Crump Law Firm Campaign: "Millionhoodies for Trayvon Martin"
Pfizer
Purity Organic Inc.
Reckitt Benckiser Airborne, Campaign: "Let's End This", Creative, Delsym, Digestive Advantage, Digital, Marketing, MegaRed, Mucinex (Advertising Agency of Record), Print, Social, TV
San Francisco Arts Commission Campaign: "Graffiti"
Siemens
Sony Ericsson Campaign: "Juggling", Campaign: "Made Of Imagination", Xperia Play
SSL International/Durex
State Street Global Advisors (Lead Creative Agency); 2014
Tiffany
Unilever
US Postal Service Campaign: "Priority:You"
VeriSign, Inc.; Reston, VA
Verizon Fios
Xbox

Branches

Commonwealth

211 Woodside Ave, Detroit, MI 48201
Tel.: (313) 202-3700
Web Site: www.cw-mccann.com

Year Founded: 2012

Agency Specializes In: Sponsorship

Andy Queen *(CFO & Exec VP)*
Linus Karlsson *(Global Chm-Creative)*
Kate MacNevin *(Exec VP & Exec Dir-Global Ops)*
Jonathan Disegi *(Exec VP & Dir-Strategy & Res-Global)*
Samantha Ankeny *(VP & Acct Dir-Ops)*
Dave Paxton *(Acct Dir)*
Chris Balicki *(Gen Mgr)*
Giacomo Bertaina *(Grp Acct Dir)*
Dennis McMillan *(Grp Acct Dir-Chevrolet Retail)*
Noah Schusterbauer *(Exec Producer-Interactive)*
Craig Feigen *(Dir-Creative)*
Tida Ball *(Acct Dir)*
Katherine Brandon *(Acct Dir-Mktg-Global)*
Jacqueline Redmond *(Acct Dir)*
Tim Mahoney *(Dir-Art & Assoc Dir-Creative)*
James Adame *(Dir-Design)*
Iris Coldibelli *(Dir-Strategy-Global)*
Adam Glickman *(Dir-Creative)*
Robert Guisgand *(Dir-Creative)*
Erika Kayuk *(Dir-Creative)*
Charlie Quirk *(Dir-Strategy-Global)*
Scott Lenfestey *(Assoc Dir-Creative)*
Jordan Miller *(Assoc Dir-Creative)*
Victor Quattrin *(Assoc Dir-Creative)*
Richard Weinert *(Assoc Dir-Creative)*
Amy Brede *(Acct Supvr)*
Kathy Carollo *(Acct Supvr)*
Derek Chappo *(Acct Supvr)*
Andrea Goulette *(Acct Supvr)*
Chris Skalsky *(Sr Acct Exec)*
Jackie Carline *(Specialist-Comm Content)*
Nicole Chambers *(Acct Exec)*

Accounts:
General Motors "What Do You #PlayFor", Advertising, Bowtie, Campaign" "#TheNew", Campaign: "#TheNew US" Winter Olympics 2014, Campaign: "All American", Campaign: "Chevrolet Home Derby", Campaign: "Dog & Doe Anthem", Campaign: "Eyes on the Road", Campaign: "Find New Roads", Campaign: "Focus Groups", Campaign: "Lessons", Campaign: "Silent Anthem", Campaign: "Strong", Campaign: "TMI", Campaign: "The Classic is Back", Campaign: "The car for the richest guys on earth", Campaign: "Theme Song", Campaign: "Truck Guy Deodorant", Campaign: "Trucked-Up", Campaign: "Whisper", Campaign: "World's First Reverse Test Drive", Campaign: "You Know You Want a Truck", Chevrolet, Chevrolet Silverado, Chevy Colorado, Corvette Stingray, Creative, Impala, Manchester United Kit, Precision Challenge, Reposition, Social Media, Traverse, Video

McCann Erickson/New York

622 3rd Ave, New York, NY 10017
Tel.: (646) 865-2000
Fax: (646) 487-9610
Web Site: www.mccannny.com/

Employees: 850
Year Founded: 1902

National Agency Associations: 4A's

Agency Specializes In: Above-the-Line, Advertising, Advertising Specialties, Affiliate Marketing, Affluent Market, African-American Market, Agriculture, Alternative Advertising, Arts, Asian Market, Automotive, Aviation & Aerospace, Below-the-Line, Bilingual Market, Brand Development & Integration, Branded Entertainment, Broadcast, Business Publications, Business-To-Business, Cable T.V., Catalogs, Children's Market, Co-op Advertising, Collateral, College, Commercial Photography, Communications, Computers & Software, Consulting, Consumer Goods, Consumer Marketing, Consumer Publications, Content, Corporate Communications, Corporate Identity, Cosmetics, Crisis Communications, Custom Publishing, Customer Relationship Management, Digital/Interactive, Direct Response Marketing, Direct-to-Consumer, E-Commerce, Education, Electronic Media, Electronics, Email, Engineering, Entertainment, Environmental, Event Planning & Marketing, Exhibit/Trade Shows, Experience Design, Faith Based, Fashion/Apparel, Financial, Food Service, Game Integration, Gay & Lesbian Market, Government/Political, Graphic Design, Guerilla Marketing, Health Care Services, High Technology, Hispanic Market, Hospitality, Household Goods, Identity Marketing, In-Store Advertising, Industrial, Infomercials, Information Technology, Integrated Marketing, International, Internet/Web Design, Investor Relations, Legal Services, Leisure, Local Marketing, Logo & Package Design, Luxury Products, Magazines, Marine, Market Research, Media Buying Services, Media Planning, Media Relations, Media Training, Medical Products, Men's Market, Merchandising, Mobile Marketing, Multicultural, Multimedia, New Product Development, New Technologies, Newspaper, Newspapers & Magazines, Out-of-Home Media, Outdoor, Over-50 Market, Package Design, Paid Searches, Pets , Pharmaceutical, Planning & Consultation, Podcasting, Point of Purchase, Point of Sale, Print, Product Placement, Production, Production (Ad, Film, Broadcast), Production (Print), Promotions, Public Relations, Publicity/Promotions, Publishing, RSS (Really Simple Syndication), Radio, Real Estate, Recruitment, Regional, Restaurant, Retail, Sales Promotion, Search Engine Optimization, Seniors' Market, Social Marketing/Nonprofit, Social Media, South Asian Market, Sponsorship, Sports Market, Stakeholders, Strategic Planning/Research, Sweepstakes, Syndication, T.V., Technical Advertising, Teen Market, Telemarketing, Trade & Consumer Magazines, Transportation, Travel & Tourism, Tween Market, Urban Market, Viral/Buzz/Word of Mouth, Web (Banner Ads, Pop-ups, etc.), Women's Market, Yellow Pages Advertising

Steve Zaroff *(Mng Dir & Chief Strategy Officer)*
Kevin Scher *(Grp Mng Dir & Exec VP)*
ToniAnn Bonade *(Grp Mng Dir & Sr VP)*
Andrew Chamlin *(CMO)*
Sean Bryan *(Co-Chief Creative Officer-New York)*
Thomas Murphy *(Co-Chief Creative Officer-New York)*
Eric Silver *(Chief Creative Officer-North America)*
Daniel Bennett *(Chief Digital Officer)*
Leo Tarkovsky *(Pres-North America-McCann HumanCare)*
Tina Galley *(Exec VP & Grp Acct Dir)*
Matthew O'Rourke *(Sr VP & Grp Dir-Creative)*
Tom Sullivan *(Sr VP & Grp Dir-Creative)*
Benjamin Vendramin *(Sr VP & Grp Dir-Creative)*
Lauren LaValle *(Sr VP & Grp Acct Dir)*
Eric David Johnson *(Sr VP & Exec Producer-Music)*
Chioma Aduba *(Sr VP & Dir-New Bus)*
Brad Mintz *(Sr VP & Mgr-Production Svcs)*
Nicole Witover *(VP & Acct Dir)*
Avinash Bajaj *(Head-Creative Team)*
Mat Bisher *(Executive Creative Dir)*
Larry Platt *(Exec Dir-Creative)*
Caprice Yu *(Exec Creative Dir)*
Sherman Winfield *(Sr Dir-Art)*
Olivier Gillaizeau *(Art Dir)*
David Hulin *(Creative Dir)*
Sean Labounty *(Creative Dir)*
Jesse Lunenfeld *(Acct Dir)*
Daniella Rey *(Acct Dir)*
Adam Kanzer *(Dir-Creative & Copywriter)*
Jason Ashlock *(Dir-Creative)*
Scott Higgins *(Dir-Creative)*
Zoe Kessler *(Dir-Art)*
Bruce Stockler *(Dir-Brand Community-Global)*
Chuck Tso *(Dir-Creative & Art)*
Tom Weingard *(Assoc Dir-Creative & Sr Copywriter)*
Cameron Flemming *(Assoc Dir-Creative)*
Ryan Quigley *(Assoc Dir-Creative)*
Eric Monnet *(Mgr-Creative Network)*
Kara DeBuona *(Acct Supvr)*
Preston Wallis *(Acct Supvr)*
Rebecca Ganswindt *(Supvr-New Bus)*
Ian Hartsough *(Sr Strategist-Digital)*
Christopher Alexander *(Acct Exec)*
Brittany Benourida *(Acct Exec)*
Whitnie Hawkins *(Acct Exec)*
Rachel Heiss *(Acct Exec)*
Alexandra Telyan *(Acct Exec)*
Tali Gumbiner *(Copywriter)*
Lex Singer *(Copywriter)*
Denis Mahon *(Asst Acct Exec)*
Colin Parajon *(Assoc Strategist)*

Accounts:
Ad Council
American Airlines Creative
Ashley Furniture Industries, Inc.
Bisquick
Brady Center to Prevent Gun Violence Campaign:

"Conversations", PSA
Bristol Myers Squibb
Choice Hotels International (Lead Creative Agency) Brand Identity, Brand Positioning, Broadcast, Campaign: "Introducing the new Choice Hotels", Campaign: "Stay or Go", Digital, Mobile, Online, Public Relations, Radio, Social Media, Website
Cigna (Lead Creative Agency) Campaign: "Together, All the Way", Digital, TV, Website
Clio Awards
The Coca-Cola Company
Evolve Balloons, Campaign: "Playthings", Claws, Swords
Frozen Food Council
Galderma
General Mills (Agency of Record) Campaign: "Cinnamon Toast Crunch Selfie", Campaign: "Parent Promises"
GlaxoSmithKline Lovaza, Cervarix
Healthy America
Ignite Restaurant Group; Houston, TX Brand Advertising
Brick House Tavern + Tap Strategy
Joe's Crab Shack Campaign: "100% Shore!"
Romano's Macaroni Grill
IKEA IKEA Catalog, Ikea.com
Johnson & Johnson Vistakon Vision Products
Lockheed Martin Creative
L'Oreal USA; New York, NY Hair care, Skin care, Cosmetics
MasterCard Inc. Campaign: "Lost Dog"
Mondelez International Dentyne
Nature Valley Nature Valley Trail View 2.0
New-Nespresso Campaign: "Training Day"
Nestle Waters North America Campaign: "Fountain of Electrolytenment", Campaign: "Nature's Fix"
New York State Lottery Creative, Digital
Novartis AG; East Hanover, NJ Aclasta, RAD, Reclast; 2003
Office Depot (Advertising Agency of Record) Broadcast, Campaign: "Co-Worker Collection", Campaign: "Gear Up For Great", Campaign: "Gearcentric", Color-Coded Filing Systems, Creative, Digital Video, Email, OfficeMax, Portable Printers, Print, Social Media, TV, Tablets
Pfizer Toviaz
Proximo Spirits, Inc. Campaign: "Jose Cuervo Have A Story", Campaign: "The Blacksmith", Campaign: "Write Your Cinco", Creative, Digital Video, Especial Gold, Especial Silver, Social, Website
Sony Ericsson
Sony Xperia Campaign: "Made of Imagination", Campaign: "Mind of a Child", Campaign: "The Most Immersive Xperia"
State Street Global Advisors (Creative Lead Agency)
Unilever UK Foods
United States Army
United States Postal Service Agency of Record, Creative
United Way of America
Verizon Campaign: "Get Out of the Past", Campaign: "Reality Check", Campaign: "Why", Fios (Agency of Record), Live Broadcast Application, Verizon Wireless (Lead Agency), Vision

McCann Erickson North America

622 3rd Ave, New York, NY 10017
Tel.: (646) 865-2000
Fax: (646) 487-9610
Web Site: www.mccann.com

National Agency Associations: 4A's

Agency Specializes In: Advertising

Dana Mansfield *(Chief Talent Officer-North America & Exec VP)*
Megan Rogers *(Head-Client Fin & Dir)*
Dane Yankowich *(Art Dir)*
Laura C. Wilson *(Dir-Learning Strategy)*
Kelley Cox *(Acct Supvr)*
DeNeatra Love *(Acct Supvr-Commonwealth & McCann)*
Sarah Louie *(Sr Acct Exec)*
Brittany Benourida *(Acct Exec-McCann HumanCare)*
Melanie Greenblatt *(Acct Exec)*
Stacie Maurer *(Acct Exec)*

McCann Erickson/Salt Lake City

32 Exchange Pl Ste 200, Salt Lake City, UT 84111-5151
Tel.: (801) 257-7700
Fax: (801) 257-7799

National Agency Associations: 4A's

Lori Feld *(Pres)*
Ted Tsandes *(Exec VP & Exec Dir-Creative-West Reg)*
Kelly Hindley *(Sr VP)*
Scott Kempema *(Sr VP)*
Lori Steele *(Sr VP)*
Barbara Hirsch *(VP & Grp Dir-Strategy)*
John Kiechle *(Dir-Art)*
Mary McBride *(Mgr-Media)*

Accounts:
Intel
MasterCard
Verisign
Verizon

McCann Erickson

360 W Maple Rd, Birmingham, MI 48009
Tel.: (248) 203-8000
Fax: (248) 203-8010
Web Site: www.mccannerickson.com

Agency Specializes In: Advertising

Jon Marchant *(Mng Partner)*
Mike Stocker *(Exec Dir-Creative)*
Robin Chrumka *(Exec VP & Co-Creative Dir)*
Mark Canavan *(Sr VP & Grp Dir-Creative)*
Julianna Katrancha *(Sr VP & Grp Dir-Strategy)*
Michael Crone *(Sr VP & Grp Acct Dir)*
Gary Holme *(Sr VP & Creative Dir-ALDI)*
Mark Reichard *(Sr VP & Dir-Creative)*
Todd Paglia *(VP & Dir-Product Info)*
Desmond Burrows *(VP & Assoc Dir-Creative)*
Vince McSweeney *(Exec Creative Dir)*
Edward Parks *(Sr Art Dir & Copywriter)*
Charlotte Manns *(Acct Dir)*
Ken Sara *(Art Dir)*
George Aytoun *(Dir-Art)*
Jamie Buckingham *(Dir-Art)*
Martin Parkes *(Dir-Creative)*
Nikki Neale *(Assoc Dir)*
Julian Putti *(Assoc Dir-Creative)*
Joe Ivory *(Copywriter)*
Jon Leigh *(Copywriter)*

Accounts:
New-Admiral
Aldi Inc; Batavia, IL (Agency of Record)
Altro
Always A Chance
American Airlines
Ameriprise Financial, Inc. (Lead Creative Agency)
Ashley Furniture
Bentley
Chevrolet
Delphi
E-Lites Digital Outdoor, PR, Press Marketing Communications, TV
Flowers by Gabrielle
General Mills Campaign: "Nature Valley Trail View"
General Motors
Hitachi Business-to-Business, Social Innovation Business
Honeywell Consumer Products Autolite, Fram
James Villa Holidays Creative, TV
Keira Watering Cans Campaign: "Carnivorous Plants", Campaign: "Mobile App", Campaign: "Thumb"
Master Card
Matrix
MFI Retail Creative, Media Buying; 2008
MGM Grand Detroit (Integrated Agency of Record)
Michigan Economic Development Corporation Campaign: "Pure Michigan", Creative, Travel Michigan
Microsoft
New-Miele
Motors Corp
Nestle
Northrop Grumman
Old Jamaica Ginger Beer Man vs. Food Nation Sponsorship
Pfizer
Saab Change Perspective Campaign
Sirius XM Radio
Sunseeker CRM, Creative, Digital, Global Communications, International PR, Media Buying, Strategic Planning
Triumph Motorcycles Global Digital Marketing
Unilever
Vauxhall Astra GTC
World Vision
Xbox

McCann Regan Campbell Ward

622 Third Ave 22nd Fl, New York, NY 10017
(See Separate Listing)

McCann Worldgroup

600 Battery St, San Francisco, CA 94111
Tel.: (415) 262-5600
Fax: (415) 262-5400
E-Mail: info@mccannsf.com
Web Site: www.mccann.com

Employees: 550
Year Founded: 1902

National Agency Associations: 4A's-IPA

Agency Specializes In: Advertising, Brand Development & Integration, Broadcast, Business-To-Business, Cable T.V., Children's Market, Consumer Marketing, High Technology, Information Technology, Magazines, Media Buying Services, Newspaper, Newspapers & Magazines, Out-of-Home Media, Outdoor, Print, Strategic Planning/Research, T.V., Trade & Consumer Magazines

Melanie Smart *(Exec VP & Dir-Integrated Client Svcs)*
Mark Canavan *(Sr VP & Grp Dir-Creative)*
Michael Crone *(Sr VP & Grp Acct Dir)*
Jan O'Malley *(Sr VP & Dir-Brdcst)*
Dylan Lee *(Sr VP & Client Analytics Partner)*
Scott Combs *(VP & Dir-Creative)*
Jon Curcio *(VP & Dir-Field Acct Svcs & Ops)*
Michael Etzel *(Mgmt Supvr)*
Jeremy Oviatt *(Dir-Creative)*
Racquel Ankney *(Mgr-Consumer Insights)*
Leslie Toltzman *(Mgr-Portfolio Mgmt)*
Kimberly Sanders *(Sr Acct Exec)*

Accounts:
General Mills, Inc.
Microsoft; Redmond, WA Xbox

Canada

M2 Universal Communications Management

10 Bay Street, Toronto, ON M5J 2S3 Canada
Tel.: (416) 594-6000

Fax: (416) 643-7030
Web Site: www.maclaren.com

Agency Specializes In: Advertising, Media Buying Services, Media Planning

Doug Turney *(Pres & CEO)*
Andy Langs *(CTO & Sr VP)*
Jack Neary *(Chief Creative Officer)*
Mark Thompson *(Pres-Momentum)*
Robyn Gorman *(Sr VP & Gen Mgr)*
Lindsey Feasby *(Sr VP & Dir-HR)*
Lynn Fletcher *(Sr VP-Integrated Client Strategy)*

Accounts:
Wind Mobile Media

MacLaren McCann Canada Inc.
10 Bay St, Toronto, ON M5J 2S3 Canada
(See Separate Listing)

Marketel
1100 Rene-Levesque Boulevard West 19th Floor, Montreal, QC H3B 4N4 Canada
(See Separate Listing)

Algeria

FP7 McCann Algeria
31 Mohammad khoudi, El Biar, Algiers, Algeria
Tel.: (213) 21 79 22 42
Fax: (213) 21 79 22 39
E-Mail: amourad@mccannalger.com
Web Site: www.fp7.com

Employees: 39

Faycal Kherbachi *(Dir-Art-FP7 & ALG)*
Selima Medjaoui *(Dir-Client Servicing-FP7 & ALG)*
Reda Rouibi *(Dir-Art-FP7 & ALG)*
Amine Zaidi *(Dir-Art-FP7 & ALG)*
Neila Amrane *(Acct Mgr)*
Lamia Bouzid *(Acct Mgr)*
Yacine Bounekraf *(Mgr-IT-FP7 & ALG)*
Souhila Mohammed Azizi *(Acct Exec-FP7/ALG)*
Imene Boussouara *(Acct Exec-FP7/ALG)*

Accounts:
Cevital
Coca Cola
Faderco
FAF
Huawei
La Vache Qui Rit
Nestle
ooredoo

Argentina

McCann Erickson
Esmeralda 1080, 1007 Buenos Aires, Argentina
Tel.: (54) 11 5552 2100
Fax: (54) 11 4315 1254
Web Site: www.mccann.com

Employees: 92
Year Founded: 1935

National Agency Associations: AAAP (Argentina)-IAA

Agency Specializes In: Consumer Marketing

Diego Livachoff *(Gen Dir-Creative)*
Susan Irwin *(Sr VP & Dir-Corp Comm)*
Chavo Demilio *(Exec Dir-Creative)*
Paula Montes *(Acct Dir)*
Victoria Ortelli *(Acct Dir)*
Marian Jethro Legname *(Dir-Creative)*
Rodrigo Polignano *(Dir-Creative)*
Agustina Giffi *(Acct Exec)*

Accounts:
American Airlines
Argentina Diabetes Foundation Pinprick
Bimbo
Black & Decker
Cathay Pacific
Chevrolet
Coca-Cola Refreshments USA, Inc.
Consejo Publicitario Argentino Campaign: "Bilardo"
E.S.S.O.
ExxonMobil
Fundacion Par
Garrahan Foundation
General Mills
General Motors Pick-Up Trucks, Road Safety
Harley Davidson
L'Oreal/Prodesca S.A. Hair Care
Madison Campaign: "Washbowl car"
Mastercard
Microsoft
Nestle Cream, Desserts, Instant Coffees, Spaghetti, Spreadable Cheeses, Yogurts
Novartis
Pfizer
Raaw
Siemens
Sony Ericsson
Tiffany
Unilever Hand & Nail, NesQuick, Vaseline, Vasenol
V.F. Corporation Reef
Xbox
ZonaJobs

Australia

McCann Erickson Advertising Pty. Ltd.
Level 7 574 Saint Kilda, South, Melbourne, VIC 3000 Australia
Tel.: (61) 3 9993 9333
Fax: (61) 3 9993 9300
E-Mail: melbourneteam@mccann.com.au
Web Site: www.mccann.com.au/

Employees: 45
Year Founded: 1960

National Agency Associations: AFA-MCA

Adrian Mills *(Mng Dir)*
Victoria Conners-Bell *(Head-Brdcst)*
David Phillips *(Head-Strategy & Media)*
Patrick Baron *(Exec Creative Dir)*
Anita Deutsch-Burley *(Exec Dir)*
Serrin Dewar *(Exec Dir)*
Alec Hussain *(Grp Acct Dir)*
Matthew Lawson *(Creative Dir)*
Danielle Pollock *(Acct Dir)*
Ryan Clayton *(Dir-Art)*
Corey Thorn *(Dir-Art)*
Alex Wadelton *(Dir-Creative)*
Alex Haigh *(Sr Acct Mgr)*
Alex Stott *(Sr Acct Mgr)*
Dave Budd *(Sr Designer)*
Andrew North *(Sr Writer)*

Accounts:
AGL Energy Limited (Creative Agency of Record) Advertising, Brand, Media
Australian Federal Government
Bendigo Bank
New-Bic
Coca-Cola
Google
Holden Barina Beats
Lion
L'Oreal Paris
Macmillan Publishing
Macquarie Dictionary Phubbing
MasterCard
Melbourne Central
Metro Trains Campaign: "Be Safe Around Valentine's Day ... and Trains", Campaign: "Deck the Halls", Campaign: "Dumb Ways To Die", Campaign: "Dumb Ways to Die 2: The Games", Campaign: "Take Your Time On Game Day", Press
Nimble
Pacific Brands
Specsavers Campaign: "Vespa"
Tiger Airlines Campaign: "Good to Go"
University of Melbourne Campaign: "Where Great Minds Collide", Creative
V/Line Creative
Velvet Jayne Campaign: "Bras & Knickers"
Vic Gambling
Victorian Responsible Gambling Foundation Campaign: "100 Day Challenge", Campaign: "100 Days - Anna", Campaign: "KidBet", Digital Banners, Print, Radio, TV
Victorian WorkCover Authority
WorkSafe

McCann Erickson Advertising Pty. Ltd.
166 William St, Woolloomooloo, NSW 2011 Australia
Tel.: (61) 2 9994 4000
Fax: (61) 2 9994 4010
E-Mail: contact@mccann.com.au
Web Site: www.mccann.com.au/

Employees: 150
Year Founded: 1959

National Agency Associations: AFA-MCA

Agency Specializes In: Health Care Services

Ben Lilley *(Chm)*
Adrian Mills *(Mng Dir-Melbourne)*
Chris Baker *(Head-Social)*
Bradley Moore *(Head-Digital-Natl)*
Nicole Gardner *(Gen Mgr-Sydney)*
Alexandra Baker *(Exec Dir)*
Dejan Rasic *(Exec Dir-Creative-Sydney)*
Roxanne Tyler *(Grp Acct Dir)*
David Ponce De Leon *(Dir-Creative-Melbourne)*
David Phillips *(Dir-Strategy-McCann Melbourne)*
Vince McSweeney *(Grp Exec Dir-Creative)*

Accounts:
Cathay Pacific
Holden Ute
L'Oreal
MasterCard Australia Ltd.
Pfizer
Uncle Toby's

McCann Healthcare Melbourne
Level 7 574 St Kilda Rd, 3001 Melbourne, Australia
Tel.: (61) 03 9993 9344
Fax: (61) 03 9993 9300
Web Site: www.mccann.com.au

Employees: 15

Agency Specializes In: Advertising, Health Care Services, Pharmaceutical

John Cahill *(CEO)*
Adrian Mills *(Mng Dir)*
Jamie Toh *(Art Dir)*

Accounts:
Melbourne Central
Pfizer
New-Public Transport Victoria

McCann Healthcare Sydney
Royal Naval House 32-34 Grosvenor Street, The Rocks, Sydney, 2000 Australia
Tel.: (61) 02 9994 4390
Fax: (61) 02 9994 4010

Web Site: www.mccannhealthcare.com.au

Agency Specializes In: Advertising, Health Care Services, Print

June Laffey *(Exec Dir-Creative)*
Kate Chisnall *(Sr Dir-Art)*
Bob Johnson *(Dir-Art)*

Accounts:
A2 Milk/Freedom Nutritional Products
AAPT
Bristol-Meyers Squibb Pravachol, Taxol
Bushells
George Western Foods
New-Guide Dogs Victoria Campaign: "Opening Doors"
Holden Ute
International Diabetes Institute
Jack Daniels
JR/Duty Free
L'Oreal
Melbourne Central
Merck Serono
Microsoft
Nestle Nutrition Campaign: "Talking Toddlers", NAN Toddler Milks
Novartis
Pfizer Australia
Sanofi-Aventis
SCA Hygiene Australia
V-Line
Xbox

Mccann
32 Grosvenor St The Rocks, Sydney, NSW 2000 Australia
Tel.: (61) 299944000
Fax: (61) 299944010
Web Site: www.mccann.com.au

Year Founded: 1959

Agency Specializes In: Advertising, Brand Development & Integration, Digital/Interactive, Market Research

Ben Lilley *(Chm/CEO-McCann Worldgroup)*
Duncan Shields *(Grp Head-Creative)*
Nicole Gardener *(Gen Mgr-Sydney)*
Lisa FitzGerald *(Acct Dir)*
Sara Shields *(Acct Dir)*
Corey Thorn *(Dir-Art)*
Andy Jones *(Assoc Dir-Creative)*
Daniel Larcombe *(Acct Mgr)*
Chesney Payet *(Copywriter)*

Accounts:
Bushells Tea Tea Drinks Mfr
New-Charles Sturt University Campaign: "Think Again", Media Buying, Online, Social Media, Television
Coca-Cola Amatil Hot Beverages Sprite
Department of Families, Housing, Community Services and Indigenous Affairs Campaign: "Impossible Orchestra"
Freeview More for Free Telecommunication services
Lego Campaign: "Santa's Little Helper", Media, Toys Mfr
Lion Dairy & Drinks Brand Awareness
MasterCard Campaign: "Florence & the Machine", Campaign: "New Zealand", Financial Transaction Payment Cards Provider
Metro Trains Campaign: "Dumb Ways To Die"
Microsoft Xbox
Midas Network Management services
Milo Nutritious Energy Drinks
MTV Exit Foundation
NBN Media
Solaris Paper Emporia, TV
Suzanne Grae
Taubmans Painting Products Mfr
Twinings
Velvet Jayne
World Kitchen Campaign: "Corelle Post-A-Plate", Campaign: "Tipsy Hostess", Corelle, Online

Bahrain

FP7
(Formerly Fortune Promoseven)
609 City Centre Building 6th Floor Government Avenue, PO Box 5989, Manama, Bahrain
Mailing Address:
PO Box 5989, Manama, Bahrain
Tel.: (973) 17 500 777
Fax: (973) 17 224 375
E-Mail: info@fp7.com
Web Site: www.fp7.com

Employees: 200
Year Founded: 1968

Agency Specializes In: Consumer Marketing, Direct Response Marketing, Public Relations

Ehab Lori *(Mng Dir-FP7 & BAH)*
Mohamed Sabra *(Sr Acct Dir)*
Husen Baba *(Dir-Creative)*
Jaison Ben *(Assoc Dir-Creative)*

Accounts:
Al Zamil Air Conditioners
Batelco Audio Signature, Environmental Awareness, INFINITY, Ramadan Promo, Sim Sim O-Net Device, Talk For Free On Friday, Voice SMS, World Cup Promo
Berlitz Language School
BIC Formula One
BigWig
Cathay Pacific Airways Limited
Dubai Duty Free
GulfAir
Joby Gorillapod
L'Oreal
Lux
MasterCard
Nestle
Nido
Orbit
QNB
Rotana
Samsung
Sony
UPS
Vileda
Volvo
Xbox 360 Wireless Controller
Yaquby Stores Joby Gorilapod

Bangladesh

Unitrend Ltd.
House #49 Rd #27, Dhanmondi R/A, Dhaka, 1213 Bangladesh
Tel.: (880) 2 912 4380
Fax: (880) 2 811 0436
E-Mail: info@unitrendbd.com
Web Site: www.unitrendbd.com

Zulfiquar Ahmed Khan *(Owner)*
Muneer Ahmed Khan *(Chm)*
Sushanta Saha *(Head-Ops)*
Tarik Shomi *(Exec Dir-Unisocial)*
Asifur Rahman Khan *(Assoc Dir-Creative)*

Universal Communication
1 Vandammestraat 5-70 B, Hoeilaart, 1560 Brussels, Belgium
Tel.: (32) 26764211
Fax: (32) 26606257
E-Mail: ucb@uc.be
Web Site: www.uc.be

Employees: 22
Year Founded: 1983

Agency Specializes In: Media Buying Services, Media Planning, Multimedia, Production

Mick Daman *(Mng Dir)*
Werner Neirinckx *(Dir-Creative)*

Accounts:
K.U. Leuven
La Poste
Volvo

Bosnia

McCann Erickson Sarajevo
GM Lokateli 21, 71000 Sarajevo, Bosnia & Herzegovina
Tel.: (387) 33 267 111
Fax: (387) 33 267 121
E-Mail: mail@mccann.ba
Web Site: www.mccann.ba

Employees: 30

Zoran Ivancic *(Mng Dir)*
Muamera Kadric *(Dir-Media)*

Accounts:
Coca-Cola Refreshments USA, Inc. Coke, Fanta, Sprite
Gavrilovic
L'Oreal Revitalift
Mercator
Nestle
Raffeisen Bank
Sony
UNIQA
UPS
Violetta

Brazil

McCann Erickson Publicidade Ltda.
Rua Visconde de Ouro Preto 5 12-13 Floors, 22250-180 Rio de Janeiro, Brazil
Tel.: (55) 212 559 2500
Fax: (55) 212 106 7998
E-Mail: mccann@mccann.com.br
Web Site: www.mccann.com.br

Year Founded: 1935

Agency Specializes In: Advertising, Automotive, Consumer Goods, Consumer Marketing, Electronic Media, Electronics, Food Service

Paulo Gregorachi *(Vice-Chm & Chief Creative Officer)*
Viviana Maurman *(Gen Dir-Media)*
Marcio Borges *(Exec VP-Ops, Innovation & Strategic Alliances)*
Maximiliano Lacerda *(Exec VP-Global Clients)*
Rafael Carmineti *(Sr VP)*
Guime Davidson *(VP-Creation)*
Marcelo Hack *(VP-Production)*
Jaqueline Travaglin *(VP-Projects)*
Monica Charoux *(Dir-Corp Comm-Latin America)*

Accounts:
AACD
American Airlines
CARE
CPW
Cadbury Adams
Chicco
Coca-Cola Brasil
Dorina Nowill

IBTA
Intel
Intelig
L'Oreal
MSN
MasterCard
Microsoft
Safekids

McCann Erickson / SP

Rua Loefgreen 2527, CEP 04040- 33 Sao Paulo, Vila Clementino Brazil
Tel.: (55) 11 3775 3000
E-Mail: mccann@mccann.com.br
Web Site: www.mccann.com.br

Employees: 245
Year Founded: 1935

Agency Specializes In: Advertising, Social Marketing/Nonprofit

Washington Olivetto *(Chm-WMcCann Brazil & Chief Creative Officer-Latin America)*
Milton Mastrocessario *(VP-Creative & Dir)*
Angelo Franzao *(Dir-Media)*
Bruno Guimaraes *(Dir-Art)*
Francisco Oliveira *(Dir-Art)*
Fernando Penteado *(Dir-Creative)*
Eric Sulzer *(Dir-Creative)*
Mauro Villas-Boas *(Dir-Art)*
Joao Pires *(Copywriter)*

Accounts:
American Airlines
Bimbo
Casa Mae
Chicco
Coca-Cola Refreshments USA, Inc.
Colgate Sorriso Herbal
Dorina Nowill Foundation
General Motors Corp.; Sao Paulo Chevrolet Vectra Elite 2.0, Omega Upmarket Sedan
Hewlett-Packard (HP)
Hospital de Cancer de Barretos
Kraft Foods Chicklets
L'Oreal
Mastercard International MasterCard
Microsoft Campaign: "Hard Times"
Nestle Purina Alpo, Friskies
Ninho
Nutrella Vitta Natural Bread
Salvation Army Campaign: "Labyrinth"
Tiffany

Paim Comunicacao

Rua Padre Chagas 79 5 Andar, Moinhos de Vento, CEP 90570-080 Porto Alegre, Brazil
Tel.: (55) 51 2102 2577
E-Mail: contato@paim.com.br
Web Site: www.paim.com.br

Employees: 95
Year Founded: 1991

Agency Specializes In: Advertising

Cesar Paim *(Pres)*
Rodrigo Pinto *(Partner & Dir-Creative)*
Willian Zanette *(Head-Digital)*
Aline Lima *(Acct Dir)*
Vanessa Locks *(Art Dir)*
Matheus Mendes *(Art Dir)*
Julia Poloni *(Art Dir)*
Luciano Burger *(Dir-Art)*
Joao Batista Cabral De Melo *(Dir-New Bus & Mktg)*
Marcio Blank *(Copywriter)*
Paula Campani *(Planner)*
Mariana Ferreira *(Copywriter)*
Eduardo Pandolfo *(Copywriter)*
Laura Valmorbida *(Jr Media Planner)*

Accounts:
Ambev
Empresas
New-Instituto de Estudos Empresariais
Kaizen RS
Marisol
Maxxi Atacado
Ministerio Publico do Trabalho
Moinhos
One Store
Polar Beer Campaign: "Cell Phone Nullifier"
Randon
New-SPRS
Via Uno e Zensul
Walmart

Bulgaria

McCann Erickson Sofia

63 Shipchenski Prohod Boulavard, 1574 Sofia, Bulgaria
Tel.: (359) 2 971 9641
Fax: (359) 2 971 9504
E-Mail: office@mccann.bg

Agency Specializes In: Advertising

Alexander Toromanov *(Mng Dir)*
Julia Ratieva *(Dir-Art)*
Reneta Traykova *(Acct Exec)*

Accounts:
American Airlines
Coca-Cola Refreshments USA, Inc.
Credit Suisse
General Motors
Hewlett-Packard
InterContinental Hotels Group
Johnson & Johnson
MasterCard
Microsoft
Pfizer

Cameroon

McCann Erickson Cameroon

39 rue Kitchener Place de la Chamber de Commerce, Douala, Cameroon
Mailing Address:
PO Box 12516, Douala, Cameroon
Tel.: (237) 3343 9188
Fax: (237) 3342 29 02
Web Site: www.mccann.com

Employees: 20
Year Founded: 1986

Agency Specializes In: Advertising

Annie Barla *(Gen Mgr)*
Armel Assohou *(Acct Dir)*
Andre Engoue Tcheukam *(Dir-Artistic)*
Sinclair Teffo *(Dir-Artistic)*
Venant G. Pouemi *(Acct Planner)*

Chile

McCann Erickson S.A. de Publicidad

Ave Andres Bello 2711, 7th Fl, Comuna las Condes, Santiago, Chile
Tel.: (56) 2337 6777
Fax: (56) 2337 6800
Web Site: www.mccann.com

Employees: 150
Year Founded: 1945

National Agency Associations: ACHAP

Agency Specializes In: Advertising, Automotive, Aviation & Aerospace, Consumer Goods, Consumer Marketing, Financial, Food Service, Multimedia, T.V., Teen Market

Francisco Guzman *(Dir-Art & Designer)*
Cesar Aburto *(Dir-Creative)*
Nicolas Briceno *(Dir-Arts & Creative)*
Ricardo Corsaro *(Dir-Creative)*
Patricio Navarrete *(Dir-Creative-Coca-Cola)*
Felipe Abufhele *(Sr Editor-Creative)*

Accounts:
ACT
American Airlines
BCI Campaign: "Bass Drum"
Capel
Coca-Cola de Chile
Entel BCS
Fundacion Las Rosas Campaign: "Reality Show", Campaign: "We Need Volunteers"
General Motors Campaign: "Seatbelt", Chevrolet
Gillette Mach 3
Kraft Foods Dentyne Extra
L'Oreal
Mastercard
Nestle Chile S.A
UPS

China

McCann Erickson Guangming Ltd.

33/F Telecom Plaza, 18 Zhong Shan Er Road, Guangzhou, 510115 China
Tel.: (86) 20 8888 8438
Fax: (86) 20 8888 8439
Web Site: www.mccann.com

Steve Xue *(Chief Strategy Officer)*
Kit Yuchun *(Exec Creative Dir)*
Ginny Wu *(Sr Dir-Art)*
Szeman Cheng *(Bus Dir)*
Xie Martin *(Dir-Bus)*
Henry Shen *(Dir-Plng)*
Christine Sung *(Dir-Bus)*

Accounts:
New-Cadillac
China Telecom OOH, Wifi

UM

(Formerly Universal McCann)
21/F Huaihai Plz, 1045 Huaihai Rd, Shanghai, 200031 China
Tel.: (86) 21 2411 1488
Fax: (86) 21 2411 1468
E-Mail: stella.lee@umww.com
Web Site: www.umww.com/global

Employees: 60
Year Founded: 2000

Agency Specializes In: Media Buying Services

Ying Li *(Grp Acct Dir-Digital Team)*
Sunil Jaryal *(Dir)*
Emma Liu *(Dir-Plng)*
Erika Lin *(Assoc Portfolio Mgr)*
Steve Shi *(Assoc Portfolio Dir-Social)*

Accounts:
CCTV
Coca-Cola Campaign: "Share a Coke"
Conba Pharmaceutical
Heinz Longfeng
MetersBonwe Digital, Media Planning & Buying
Shanghai OnStar Media
Supor

Colombia

McCann Erickson Corp. S.A.
Calle 96 #13A-21/33, Santafe de Bogota, Bogota, Colombia
Tel.: (57) 1487 1010
E-Mail: latam@mccann.com
Web Site: www.mccann.com

Employees: 185
Year Founded: 1945

National Agency Associations: ACA

Samuel Estrada *(VP-Creative)*
Fabiola Andrea Garcia Amaya *(Acct Dir-Digital)*
Daniel Gonzalez *(Creative Dir)*
Lorena Nunez Montero *(Acct Dir)*
Melisa Restrepo *(Acct Dir)*
Cesar Meza *(Dir-Art)*
Lina Maria Serrato *(Sr Acct Mgr-Digital)*

Accounts:
Biblioteca EPM
Editorial Televisa Campaign: "Kick"
Ejercito Nacional De Colombia
EPM Campaign: "Water Museum"
General Motors Campaign: "Reverse"
Insurance ETB
Microsoft Campaign: "Body"
NATIONAL POLICE FORCE
National Symphony Orchestra Of Colombia
Nestle de Colombia Biovita with Cereal, Buitoni, Cerelac Cereal, Chambourcy, Flamby, Lechera Cream Cheese, Nestum, Nido
NOEL Campaign: "Just One"
Pfizer
Portal 80 Shopping Mall
Sabmiller Beer
Spring Mattress
Today Condoms

McCann Erickson Corp. (S.A.)
Edificio Banco Andino Carrera 43A #16A Sur 38, Ofc 1205, Medellin, Colombia
Tel.: (57) 4 313 6622
Fax: (57) 4 313 6822
Web Site: www.mccann.com

Employees: 30
Year Founded: 1997

Agency Specializes In: Advertising

Alvaro Jose Fuentes *(CEO-McCann Worldgroup)*
Alejandro Bermudez *(Dir-Creative)*

Accounts:
NOEL Campaign: "Air"

Croatia

McCann Erickson
Heinzelova 33A, 10 000 Zagreb, Croatia
Tel.: (385) 1 555 51 00
E-Mail: info@mccann.hr
Web Site: www.mccann.hr

Employees: 80

Sandra Cindric *(Acct Dir)*
Goranka Mijic *(Acct Dir)*
Zeljka Ivosevic Valentic *(Acct Dir)*
Ivana Balog Zadkovic *(Acct Dir)*
Goran Bozic *(Dir-Creative)*
Irina Dukic *(Acct Mgr)*
Zarko Kuvalja *(Designer)*

Accounts:
CDS
Cereal Partners
Coca-Cola Adria
GM Opel
Grand Auto
Hobby Cat
MasterCard
Nestle
Tommy
Unilever

Cyprus

De Le Ma/ McCann Erickson
36 Grivas Dighenis Ave, 1066 Nicosia, Cyprus
Mailing Address:
PO Box 21674, 1512 Nicosia, Cyprus
Tel.: (357) 2 2660 300
Fax: (357) 2 2660 303
E-Mail: despo@delema.com
Web Site: www.delema.com

Employees: 52
Year Founded: 1985

Agency Specializes In: Advertising, Advertising Specialties, African-American Market, Agriculture, Asian Market, Automotive, Aviation & Aerospace, Bilingual Market, Brand Development & Integration, Broadcast, Business Publications, Business-To-Business, Cable T.V., Children's Market, Co-op Advertising, Collateral, Commercial Photography, Communications, Consulting, Consumer Marketing, Consumer Publications, Corporate Communications, Corporate Identity, Cosmetics, Digital/Interactive, Direct Response Marketing, E-Commerce, Education, Electronic Media, Engineering, Entertainment, Environmental, Event Planning & Marketing, Exhibit/Trade Shows, Fashion/Apparel, Financial, Food Service, Gay & Lesbian Market, Government/Political, Graphic Design, Health Care Services, High Technology, Hispanic Market, In-Store Advertising, Industrial, Infomercials, Information Technology, Internet/Web Design, Investor Relations, Legal Services, Leisure, Local Marketing, Logo & Package Design, Magazines, Marine, Media Buying Services, Medical Products, Merchandising, Multimedia, New Product Development, Newspaper, Newspapers & Magazines, Out-of-Home Media, Outdoor, Over-50 Market, Pharmaceutical, Planning & Consultation, Point of Purchase, Point of Sale, Print, Production, Public Relations, Publicity/Promotions, Radio, Real Estate, Recruitment, Restaurant, Retail, Sales Promotion, Seniors' Market, Sports Market, Strategic Planning/Research, Sweepstakes, Syndication, T.V., Technical Advertising, Teen Market, Telemarketing, Trade & Consumer Magazines, Transportation, Travel & Tourism, Yellow Pages Advertising

Despo Lefkariti *(CEO)*
Irene Kalogirou-Karaoli *(VP & Exec Dir-Media)*
Costas Constantinou *(Controller-Fin)*
Christiana Chrysostomou *(Acct Dir)*
Efi Christou *(Mgr-Media)*
Joanna Kasoulidou *(Mgr-PR)*
Christos Skordis *(Acct Exec)*
Lina Hamali *(Copywriter-Creative)*
Lily Solomou *(Jr Acct Exec)*

Czech Republic

McCann Erickson Prague
Riegrovy Sady 28, 12000 Prague, 2 Czech Republic
Tel.: (420) 2 2200 9188
Fax: (420) 2 22 723 996
E-Mail: reception.prague@mccann.cz
Web Site: www.mccann.cz

Employees: 60

Jan Binar *(CEO)*
Oldrich Dostal *(Chief Digital Officer)*
Jaroslav Malina *(Head-Tech & Ops)*
Richard Axell *(Art Dir)*
Gerrit John Gerischer *(Art Dir)*
David Cermak *(Dir-Momentum)*
Klara Palmer *(Copywriter)*
Ales Vyhlidal *(Planner-Strategic)*

Accounts:
Ceskomoravska Stavebni Sporitelna
New-Nas Grunt

Denmark

McCann Copenhagen
Gothersgade 14 4, DK-1123 Copenhagen, Denmark
Tel.: (45) 33134243
E-Mail: info@mccann.dk
Web Site: www.mccann.dk

Agency Specializes In: Advertising

Morten Ingemann *(CEO)*
Kim Jong Andersen *(Exec VP)*
Silas Jansson *(Sr Dir-Art)*
Bo Sorensen *(Producer-Creative Digital)*

Accounts:
Coca-Cola Campaign: "The Happy Flag", Logo, Poster
Ikea
Ladbrokes.dk
L'Oreal S.A.
Universal Music Black Sabbath

Egypt

FP7 Cairo
(Formerly Fortune Promoseven Egypt)
12 Al Esraa Street Lebanon Street, PO Box 12411, Mohandessin, Cairo, Egypt
Tel.: (20) 2 3 3446545
E-Mail: info@fp7.com
Web Site: www.fp7.com

Ayman Anwar *(Sr Dir-Art)*
Marize Sami *(Acct Dir)*
Reem Ezzeldin *(Sr Acct Mgr)*
Nahla Hendy *(Sr Acct Mgr)*
Dahlia Mehrez *(Sr Acct Mgr)*
Nihal Alaaq *(Mgr-Internal Corp Comm & Dev)*
Moheb Ayad *(Mgr-Studio)*
Farah Mansour *(Mgr-Plng)*
Hussein Diaa *(Acct Supvr)*
Yara Ali *(Acct Exec)*
Mariam Ghabrial *(Acct Exec)*
Malak Nour *(Acct Exec)*
Khadiga Rehab *(Copywriter)*

Accounts:
Coca-Cola Refreshments USA, Inc.
Frequency
Molto Molto Cheese
Sprite

Finland

Hasan & Partners Oy
Pursimiehenkatu 29-31B, 00150 Helsinki, Finland
Tel.: (358) 424 6711
Fax: (358) 9 177 055
Web Site: www.hasanpartners.fi

Eka Ruola *(CEO & Chief Creative Officer)*
Panu Nordlund *(Deputy CEO)*
Jussi Lindholm *(COO)*
Bruno Ribeiro *(Sr Dir-Art)*
Barbara Sorsa *(Acct Dir)*
Reino Tikkanen *(Acct Dir)*
Sebastian Ramn *(Dir-Art & Designer)*
Sami Anttila *(Dir-Art)*

Alfonso Arbos *(Dir-Art)*
Markku Maenpaa *(Dir-Strategy, Retail & Design)*
Mikael Nemeschansky *(Dir-Art)*
Ossi Piipponen *(Dir-Art)*
Rickard Skogtoft *(Dir-Art)*
Tobias Wacker *(Dir-Creative)*
Ossi Honkanen *(Sr Mgr-Creative & Innovation)*
Jutta Casen *(Acct Mgr)*
Kati Eerola *(Acct Mgr)*
Heidi Eriksson *(Acct Mgr)*
Liisa Frick *(Acct Mgr)*
Johanna Leppanen *(Acct Mgr)*
Johanna Tarvainen *(Mgr-Production)*
Mark Maher *(Copywriter)*
Anu Niemonen *(Copywriter)*
Anni Paltemaa *(Copywriter)*
Mick Scheinin *(Copywriter)*

Accounts:
Abandoned Circuits
Angry Birds Campaign: "Bringing Brands into the Content"
Cancer Society Of Finland Campaign: "Quitter the Game"
DNA Campaign: "Christmas Wish", Campaign: "Follow The Gift"
Fazer Campaign: "Tutti Frutopia"
Felix
Helsingin Sanomat Campaign: "One Story, all the Angles", Daily Newspaper
Karkimedia
Kiosked Campaign: "Web Wide Shop"
Leiras Oy Campaign: "Children's Pain Diagnostics Tool"
Ilta-Sanomat
New-Metsa Wood
Novart Oy
Oy Orthex
Plan Finland Campaign: "Girls Can"
Saarioinen
Sanoma News Campaign: "Print&Pint"
Silja Line
Sinebrychoff Karhu
Stockman
New-Takeda Oy
TDF Entertainment Finland Campaign: "HD Granny"
Urheilusanomat Sports Magazine Campaign: "Dry Season"
Veikkaaja
Vepsalainen Campaign: "Chain of Friends", Campaign: "Egg Chair"
Vilpuri
World Design Capital Campaign: "Kauko Remotely Controlled Design Cafa"
World Kitchen
Yuju Milk

McCann Helsinki

Lautatarhankatu 8 B, 00580 Helsinki, Finland
Tel.: (358) 424 6311
Fax: (358) 424 631 311
E-Mail: hello@mccann.fi
Web Site: www.mccann.fi

Employees: 30
Year Founded: 1924

Kaisa Saarinen *(Acct Dir)*
Timo Silvennoinen *(Dir-Creative)*
Jutta Sutinen *(Dir-Art)*
Janne Uotila *(Dir-Creative Production)*
Yrjo Haavisto *(Project Mgr-Creative Svcs)*
Tuomas Perala *(Copywriter)*

Accounts:
Alcoholics Anonymous Campaign: "If you see this double"
Area Business Travel Agent Campaign: "Spreadsheet the Love"
Cancer Society of Finland Campaign: "The Men Who Swam for Love"
Delta Car Dealership Campaign: "Let's Change The Headlines"
Hammaspeikko Dental Clinic Campaign: "Before & After", Dental Whitening Services
HIV Foundation Campaign: "Man"
HKL
Leiras
L'Oreal Finland Oy Feria
Nestle
New-Nokian Tyres Plc
Nurminen
Omron
Opel
Top-Sport
Trendi & Lily Campaign: "United State of Women"
Viking Line

France

McCann Erickson Paris

69 Blvd du General Leclerc, 92583 Clichy, France
Tel.: (33) 14 759 3456
Fax: (33) 14 748 0757
E-Mail: info@mccann.fr
Web Site: www.mccann.fr

Employees: 188
Year Founded: 1927

Agency Specializes In: Consumer Marketing, Health Care Services

Nannette Dufour *(Pres)*
Ron Ryder *(CEO)*
Jacques Challes *(CIO)*
Michele Ferrebeuf *(CEO-McCann Central Limited Co)*
Bruno Tallent *(CEO-McCann Worldgroup)*
Caroline Montrichard Salle de Chou *(VP)*
Alexandra Dupy *(Gen Mgr)*
Julien Chiapolini *(Exec Dir-Creative)*
Riccardo Fregoso *(Exec Dir-Creative)*
Benjamin Foucaud *(Creative Dir)*
Sylvain Merigeau *(Creative Dir)*
Agathe Dupasquier *(Copywriter)*
Claire Besancon *(Sr Art Dir)*

Accounts:
Capitaine Plouf Music& Sound Design Campaign: "For The Love Of Sound"
Durex
Dymo
European Council on Refugees & Exiles Campaign: "Bloody Stairs"
Fisherman's Friend
Fitness
General Motors France
Inpes Anti-AIDS Campaign
L'Oreal Paris
Martini & Rossi
MasterCard; 1999
Microsoft
Nestle FITNESS PSA
Nestle/Gloria Animal Products, Campaign: "One second of emotions", Nespresso
Opel Campaign: "Strauss"
Tiffany
Unilever/Cogesal Batonnets Max

Georgia

McCann Erickson Georgia

71 Vazha-Pshavela Ave BCV 4th Fl, Tbilisi, 0186 Georgia
Tel.: (995) 32 220 73 55
Fax: (995) 32 220 75 87
E-Mail: office@mccann.com.ge
Web Site: www.mccann.com.ge

Irakli Skhirtladze *(Dir-Creative)*
Lika Chanturia *(Acct Mgr)*
Tamuna Chikvaidze *(Acct Mgr)*
Nata Tskhvediani *(Mgr-BTL)*

Accounts:
Coca-Cola Refreshments USA, Inc.
Nestle
Pfizer

Germany

McCann Erickson Brand Communications Agency

Grosser Hasenpad 44, 60598 Frankfurt am Main, Germany
Tel.: (49) 69 60 50 70
Fax: (49) 69 60 50 76 66
E-Mail: frankfurt@mccann.de
Web Site: www.mccann.de

Andreas Bruckner *(CEO & Mng Dir)*
Laurent Jaulin *(CFO)*
Anja Viemann *(Grp Head-Creative)*
Joerg Scheuerpflug *(Grp Dir-Creative-Experience Design)*
Daniel Gonsior *(Bus Dir-Mktg Solutions)*
Martin M. Rosskopf *(Dir-Art & Designer-Motion)*
Anna Chechetka *(Dir-Art)*
Gabriel Franke *(Dir-Art)*
Barbara Kuehne *(Dir-Client Bus Solutions)*
Johannes Veith *(Dir-Creative)*
Suzana Mitrasinovic *(Acct Mgr)*
Ulrich Weiss *(Mgr-Process)*
Christian Endecott *(Copywriter)*

Accounts:
Bankhaus Ellwanger & Geiger KG; 2004
CDU Frankfurt; 2005
General Motors Astra; 2009
GranataPet #SnackBall
Mammut Sports Group Store ecosystem
New-Master Card
Opel

McCann Erickson Deutschland

Grosser Hasenpfad 44, D-60598 Frankfurt am Main, Germany
Tel.: (49) 6960 5070
Fax: (49) 69 605 07 666
E-Mail: mccann-erickson@mccann.de
Web Site: www.mccann.de

Employees: 1,000
Year Founded: 1928

National Agency Associations: GWA

Bill Biancoli *(Chief Creative Officer-Germany)*
Elke Klinkhammer *(Chief Creative Officer)*
Martin Biela *(Exec Dir-Creative)*
Thomas Keil *(Dir-Creative)*
Benjamin Gebien *(Sr Acct Mgr)*
Juliane Back *(Acct Mgr)*
Tobias von Aesch *(Sr Art Dir)*

Accounts:
Amecke Fruchtsaft Campaign: "Vitamin A"
Coca-Cola Campaign: "Open Happiness"
GranataPet
Mammut Store Ecosystem
Nestle
Stiftung Artenschutz Campaign: "#animachine"

McCann Erickson Hamburg GmbH

Neuer Wall 43, 20354 Hamburg, Germany
Tel.: (49) 4036 0090
Fax: (49) 4036 0092 10
E-Mail: hamburg@mccann.de
Web Site: www.mccann.de

Employees: 20

National Agency Associations: GWA

Ruber Iglesias *(CEO)*
Elke Klinkhammer *(Chief Creative Officer-McCann WorldGroup Germany)*
John Kriwet *(Chief Growth Officer)*
Ralf Menikheim *(Gen Mgr-Artwork)*

Accounts:
New-Aldi Nord (Germany Marketing Agency of Record) Integrated Marketing Communications
Arte Deutschland TV GmbH
Diebels
Durex
Esso A.G.
Haake Beck
Labatt USA LLC
Scholl
Zentis

M.E.C.H.
Schonhauser Allee 37, Kultur Brauerei, D-10435 Berlin, Germany
Tel.: (49) 30 44 03 00
Fax: (49) 30 44 03 01 51
Web Site: www.mccann.de

Employees: 25

Elke Klinkhammer *(Chief Creative Officer-McCann WorldGroup Germany)*
John Kriwet *(Chief Growth Officer)*
Erik Gonan *(Dir-Creative)*

Accounts:
Deutsche Akademie fur Akupunktur
Stiftung Artenschutz

Greece

McCann Erickson Athens
2 Hydras st & 280 Kifissias ave, Halandri, 15232 Athens, Greece
Tel.: (30) 21 0817 1100
Fax: (30) 21 0817 1180
E-Mail: mce.athens@europe.mccann.com
Web Site: www.mccann.gr

Employees: 92
Year Founded: 1972

National Agency Associations: EDEE

Agency Specializes In: Advertising, Advertising Specialties, Communications, Consumer Marketing, Corporate Communications, Corporate Identity, In-Store Advertising, Local Marketing, Logo & Package Design, Sales Promotion

Parianos Harry *(Co-CEO)*
Yannis Goulios *(Mng Dir)*

Accounts:
ActionAid
General Motors Opel
Lufthansa
Mastercard
OTE (Hellenic Telecommunications Organization)
Rea Maternity Hospital Campaign: "Red Line"
SSL Hellas Durex
Unilever Algida, Elais

Guatemala

D4 Mccann
5a Ave 5-55 zona 14 Europlaza Torre I Nivel 7, Guatemala, Guatemala
Tel.: (502) 50223839699
Fax: (502) 50223839698
E-Mail: info@d4mccann.com
Web Site: www.d4mccann.com

Agency Specializes In: Advertising, Brand Development & Integration, Outdoor, Print, Strategic Planning/Research

Herbert Castillo *(Pres)*
Gabriel Castillo *(Gen Mgr)*
Sylvia Batres *(Dir-Strategic Plng)*
Jonathan Bell *(Dir-Creative)*
Erwin Farfan *(Dir-Art)*

Accounts:
Credito Hipotecario Nacional

Hong Kong

McCann Erickson Hong Kong Ltd.
23F Sunning Plz 10 Hysan Ave, Causeway Bay, China (Hong Kong)
Tel.: (852) 2808 7888
Fax: (852) 2576 9136
E-Mail: apac@mccann.com

Employees: 136
Year Founded: 1963

Agency Specializes In: Communications

Spencer Wong *(Chief Creative Officer)*
Alex Huang *(Sr Dir-Creative)*
Rick Kwan *(Creative Dir)*
Agnes Lee *(Sr Art Dir)*
Chester Tang *(Dir-Art)*
Sarah Watson *(Planner-Global)*

Accounts:
Asia Miles
Cathay Pacific Airways Business-Class Cabins, Newspapers, Television
Cathay Pacific Rugby Sevens Tournament
City Chain Solvil Et Titus, Time is Love
Corbis Images Campaign: "Visual Alphabet"
Cyma Creative
HMVideal
Intel; Taiwan; 2008
Jet Li Foundation
Metro Publishing Hong Kong
MTR Elements
Nike Hong Kong; 2008
Wellcome Supermarket

UM
(Formerly Universal McCann)
23rd Floor Sunning Plaza, Hysan Ave, Causeway Bay, China (Hong Kong)
Tel.: (852) 2808 7228
Fax: (852) 2576 7308
Web Site: www.umww.com

Alice Lam *(Mng Dir-Hong Kong)*
Ying Li *(Grp Acct Dir-Digital Team)*
Seven Li *(Assoc Dir)*
Stanley Zhao *(Portfolio Dir)*

Accounts:
Brand Hong Kong Media Buying, Media Planning
Burberry
Financial Times Media
Yeung Gwong

India

End to End Marketing Solutions Pvt. Ltd
#173 9th Cross, Indiranagar 1st Stage, Bengaluru, 560038 India
Tel.: (91) 80 43461200
Fax: (91) 80 25281471
E-Mail: info@endtoend.in
Web Site: endtoend.in

PN Shanavas, *(CEO)*
Manish Raj *(Mgr-Client Servicing)*

Accounts:
Hewlett Packard
Intel
Microsoft

McCann Erickson India
McCann House Dr SS Rao Road, Parel East, Mumbai, 40012 India
Tel.: (91) 22 241 76601
Fax: (91) 22 241 6871
Web Site: www.mccann.com

Prasoon Joshi *(CEO, Chief Creative Officer & Chm-Asia Pacific)*
Dip Sengupta *(Chief Growth Officer & Gen Mgr)*
Vijay Jacob *(Sr VP & Gen Mgr)*
Kishore Chakraborti *(VP-Consumer Insight & Human Futures Dev)*
Puneet Kapoor *(Exec Dir-Creative)*
Vivek Bhambhani *(Creative Dir)*
Abhijeet Bhattacharya *(Acct Dir)*
Subhashish Datta *(Creative Dir)*
Navajyoti Pegu *(Creative Dir)*
Pradyuman Chauhan *(Dir-Creative-Natl)*
Pramod Chavan *(Dir-Art)*
Rohit Devgun *(Dir-Creative)*
O. R. Radhakrishnan *(Dir-Creative)*
Siddhi Yadav *(Dir-Art & Creative)*
Simran Sardana *(Acct Mgr)*
Anushree Chaitanya *(Copywriter)*
Jyotirmoi Deb *(Copywriter)*
Seby John *(Copywriter)*
Mangesh Kavale *(Designer)*
Ashish Nath *(Copywriter)*
Nikhil Waradkar *(Team Head-Creative-Art)*

Accounts:
ACC Cement
Active Total Security Systems Campaign: "Bank", Campaign: "God", Campaign: "High Rise", Campaign: "Keys Are Hard To Find"
AETN-18 Communication Strategy, Creative
Aircel Campaign: "Little Extra"
AkzoNobel Campaign: "Pop Corn", Campaign: "Shade Card", Dulux Paints
Big CBS Campaign: "Cross Connection"
Bombay City Red Cross
Bombay Dyeing
Canterbury
Chevrolet Beat, Campaign: "Reverse Motion Sensor", Captiva, Cruze
CNBC Awaaz
Coca-Cola Refreshments USA, Inc. Campaign: "Crazy for Happiness", Campaign: "Mobile Campaign Shot", Campaign: "Spread happiness Without Reason, Share a Coca-Cola", Khushiyan Baatne Se Hi Badhti Hain
Dabur India Limited Campaign: "Kids", Campaign: "Mosquito", Chyawanprash, Odomos, Pharmaceuticals
Dharampal Satyapal Group Creative, Meetha Maza, Rajnigandha
Dish TV Campaign: "Child Lock", Campaign: "Cock and Pussy", Campaign: "Intermission Interrupted", Campaign: "Intermission Uninterrupted", Dish Sawaar Hai
Durex Performa Condoms
Follihair Campaign: "Anchor"
General Motors India Campaign: "Fuel Efficient", Creative
Good Health Hospital Campaign: "Pee Reflector"
Greenpeace
Happy Dent Gum Happydent Complete
Happy Life Welfare Society & Dabbawala Foundation Campaign: "Share My Dabba"
Harman Kardon
Heal Foundation of India Campaign: "Eunuch"
Help Delhi Breathe Campaign: "Price Tag"
Hindustan Unilever Ltd Pears
Hockey India League
HUL (Hindustan Unilever Ltd) Campaign:

"Masoom", Pears
IDFC Bank Creative, Outdoor, Print, TV
New-Incredible India Creative
Indian Broadcasting Foundation Consumer Awareness Campaign, Creative
Intel
Jagran Prakashan Campaign: "Soulmate"
Jagriti Sewa Sansthan Campaign: "A Journey of Awakening"
Johnson & Johnson Campaign: "Women for Change", Stayfree
Lasky Herbal Campaign: "Delay"
New-LifeCell
L'Oreal
Mahanagar Walefare Society Campaign: "Ban Blue Line"
Maitri Foundation Campaign: "Befriend Life"
Mankind Pharma Campaign: "Tummyville, Gasofast
Marico Limited Campaign: "Aaj ka Special", Campaign: "Add a Shade", Campaign: "Growing Is Beautiful", Campaign: "Love Dobara", Campaign: "Man Offers", Mediker, Parachute Advanced Body Lotion, Parachute Advanced Jasmine Hair Oil, Parachute Advanced Tender Coconut, Saffola, Shanti Amla
MetLife India Insurance Co. Ltd Campaign: "Mobile Store", Campaign: "Pocket Money"
Monte Carlo Creative
Mumbai Indians
Neo Sports Broadcast Campaign: "Religion"
Nerolac
Nestle Campaign: "Switch On Your Morning", Magii, Nescafe Classic, Nutrition & Healthcare Business
Network 18 Campaign: "Cnbc Awaaz"
Nirlep Campaign: "Chicken"
Omron
Onida Onida i21
Park Avenue Campaign: "Less Travelled", Creative, Parx
Paytm
Penguin Group Campaign: "Author Headphones"
Perfetti Van Melle India Pvt. Ltd. Big Babol, Campaign: "Happy Indians", Campaign: "Kid", Campaign: "Red Light"
Piramal Enterprises Ltd Campaign: "Chaale Tujhe Dekh Loonga", Lacto Calamine, QuikKool
Premier Tissues Kitchen Towel
Radio Mirchi Campaign: "IRS Callers"
Raymond Creative
Reebok Campaign: "Live with Fire"
Reliance Life Insurance Co Ltd
Republic of Chicken
Sa Re Ga Ma Campaign: "Keeping The Legend Live"
Saavn Advertising, Creative
Sajah
Samsonite Campaign: "Car Crash", Cosmolite
Sanitol
New-Schimitten and Hoppits
Star Sports & Star Cricket
Ttk Lig Ltd
TVS Motor Company Campaign: "For Front Benchers", Tvs Star City
UNICEF Campaign: "Sakshi & Girl"
Usha International Ltd. Campaign: "Air Basketball Match", Campaign: "AirPlay Challenge - Mom & Son", Fans
Vacha Trust Campaign: "Baby Sitter"
Vanarai Foundation
Viacom18 Media Pvt ltd Campaign: "The Caps On Project", MTV
VIP Industries Creative, Skybags, VIP
Western Union Money Transfer Campaign: "Western Union Demo Billboards"
Xolo Mobiles Campaign: "Built in Translator", Campaign: "English to Swahili", X900
Yatra.com Creative
Young Presidents' Organisation Campaign: "The lighter side of heavy weights"
Zee Network Campaign: "Child Lock"

McCann Erickson India

Landmark Plaza 299 Langford Road, Richmond Town, Bengaluru, 560 025 India
Tel.: (91) 80 2222 9539
Fax: (91) 80 2299 0470
Web Site: www.mccann.com

Accounts:
ACT TV
Britannia Industries Bourbon Biscuits, Campaign: "Dad", Campaign: "For a Coffee", Campaign: "Happy Good Day", Campaign: "Super Market", Campaign: "Zindagi mein life", Cheese Slices, Cookies, Treat-O
Chennai Traffic Police Campaign: "Drink & Get Driven"
DishTV
History Channel
Metrozone
TVS Motor Company Campaign: "A Ride with Boss", Campaign: "Scarily Fast", TVS Apache, TVS Phoenix, TVS Scooty Streak, TVS Star City

McCann Erickson India

8 Balaji Estate Guru Ravi Dass Marg Kalkaji, Near Kailash Colony, New Delhi, 110019 India
Tel.: (91) 11 2600 2600
Fax: (91) 11 2600 2655
E-Mail: sanjay.nayak@ap.mccann.com
Web Site: www.mccann.com

Employees: 260

Neha Chopra *(Sr Dir-Strategic Plng)*
Rohit Devgun *(Dir-Creative)*
Richa Mishra *(Dir-Art)*
Gunjan Gaba *(Copywriter)*
Archit Gadiyar *(Copywriter)*

Accounts:
The 3C Company
ABH Packers & Movers
Aircel (Agency of Record) Campaign: "Joy of a Little Extra", Campaign: "Pappu", Campaign: "Pocket Buddies", Creative, IPL
Badminton Association of India Campaign: "Players"
Chlormint
Coca-Cola
Dermotriad+
DS Group Campaign: "Stadium"
ESPN
General Motors Campaign: "Conference Room"
Greenply Industries Ltd Greenlam Laminates
HP
New-HSIL Hindware, TV
IKFI
Indian Badminton League Creative, Strategic
Indian Oil Corporation Limited Creative, Servo
Insurance ETB
Intel Digital, PC Business
Jagran Campaign: "Largest Print Network of India"
JustDial
Lava International Campaign: "Blink"
Livguard
Lufthansa Campaign: "More Indian Than You Think"
Mankind Pharmaceutical Addiction, Campaign: "Gases", Creative, Gas-o-fast
Mastercard
MetLife India Insurance Co. Ltd. Campaign: "Pocket Money"
Nestle Campaign: "Start Healthy, Stay Healthy"
Odomos
Paytm Creative, Outdoor, Print, TV
Piramal Healthcare Quikkool
Reebok
Sanitol Campaign: "Cleaning Lady"
Skore Condom Campaign: "Lasts Longer Than You Think", Campaign: "Naughty World"
Sporty Solutionz Campaign: "Players"
Subway India Campaign: "Let's Go Rafting", Campaign: "Throw Your Treats at Subway", Creative, Egg & Mayo Sandwich
UNICEF
Usha Fans
Videocon Air Conditioners, Campaign: "The Cascade of Books", Orange Peel
Vodka Smoke
Western Union
Yatra.com Campaign: "Ehsaan Mat Lo, Discount Lo"

Ireland

McCannBlue

(Formerly McCann Dublin)
Malting Tower Grand Canal Quay, Dublin, 2 Ireland
Tel.: (353) 1 234 3900
E-Mail: info@mccannblue.ie
Web Site: mccannblue.ie

Employees: 40
Year Founded: 1991

Jessica Mitton *(Head-Client Svcs)*
Jenny Paetzold *(Dir-Ops)*
Eamonn Rohan *(Dir-Technical)*
Shannon Rushe *(Acct Mgr)*
Amy Satelle *(Acct Exec)*
Jason Fitzgerald *(Designer-Motion)*
Melissa Garlington *(Designer-Interactive)*

Accounts:
Bacardi
Boots Nurofen; 1993
Bord Bia
Boring Vs. Normal
Cheerios
Coca-Cola Ireland Coke (Media), Diet Coke, Fanta, Five Alive, Fruitopia, Lilt; 1993
Dairygold Campaign : "Butter it with Dairygold"
Deep RiverRock Water Cafe, Strategy
Dublin Business School Creative, Digital, Media Buying, Media Planning
Entel PCS
Fuji
Garnier Ambre Solaire, Belle Color, Expression, Neutralia, Synergie
Health and Safety Authority Campaign: "Tractor"
Heineken Sports Sponsorship
Irish Mist
Largo Foods
L'Oreal Skin, Body & Hair Care; 1991
MasterCard
Maybelline
McDonald's
Microsoft
Mobile Network 3
Molloys
Movistar
Nestle Ireland Cereals, Clusters, Coffee, Lucky Charms, Nesquik, Shreddies; 1991
Opel
Powerade
Rape Crisis Centre Campaign: "Fade"
Safefood Campaign: "Childhood Obesity", Campaign: "Folic Acid", Digital Display, Print, Public Relations, Social Media, TV
Siemens
Solero
SuperValu
Tayto
Tullamore Dew Creative
UNICEF

Israel

McCann Erickson

2A Raul Valenberg St, Tel Aviv, 69719 Israel
Tel.: (972) 3 768 6868
Fax: (972) 3 768 6876
E-Mail: lobby@mccann.co.il

Web Site: www.mccann.co.il

Employees: 400

Ami Alush *(Chief Creative Officer)*
Yossi Erez *(CEO-McCann Digital)*
Elav Horwitz *(VP-Clients)*
Sigal Abudi *(Creative Dir)*
Netanel Hagag *(Art Dir)*
Naor Itzhak *(Creative Dir)*
Dan Kashani *(Creative Dir)*
Yelena Ravitz Levi *(Acct Dir)*
Adi Oren *(Acct Dir)*
Dikla Pinhasi *(Acct Dir)*
Yael Slabezki *(Art Dir)*
Udi Avital *(Dir-Creative-McCann Tel Aviv)*
liran Elias *(Dir-Art)*
Nir Hersztadt *(Dir-Art)*
Elias Liran *(Dir-Art)*
Kfir Peretz *(Dir-Art)*
Tal Raviv *(Dir-Creative)*
Amit Margalit *(Acct Mgr)*
Guy Barak *(Acct Supvr)*
Or Zer-Aviv *(Acct Supvr)*
Tomer Abramovitz *(Copywriter)*
Dave Cohen *(Copywriter)*
Rona Cohen *(Copywriter)*
Eddie Gartsman *(Copywriter)*
Ira Klainer *(Copywriter)*
Idan Kravitz *(Copywriter)*
Tal Manor *(Copywriter)*
Ido Mymon *(Copywriter)*
Royi Rokah *(Copywriter)*

Accounts:
Abarbanel Mental Health Center
AEG Campaign: "Noah's Ark"
AIG Campaign: "Vod Takeover"
Association For The Blind
The Association Of Rape Crisis Centers In Israel Campaign: "The Finger"
Axe
Badin Laundry Products
Bank Leumi Campaign: "Are You Young Enough?"
Beitech
BMW Motorrad
Burgeranch ltd Fast Food
Caesarstone
Cathay Pacific
Cellcom Campaign: "Show Urlove"
Clal
Coca-Cola Refreshments USA, Inc.
Credit Suisse
Deus
Domino's Pizza Campaign: "Don't Let Hunger Ruin The Game", Campaign: "The Big Idea"
Dove Heat
El Al Campaign: "South America", Campaign: "The London Present", Switzerland Present
Eran Campaign: "When Facing Distress - Dial 1201"
Eurocom Panasonic
Garage Fitness Club Campaign: "Be prepared to sweat"
General Mills
General Motors
GlaxoSmithKline
HaBezefer School of Art Campaign: "Hack 1"
Hamashbir Latzarchan Campaign: "Present Simple"
Honda Campaign: "Betrayal", Campaign: "Sword", Campaign: "The Treat", Honda CRF250R, Honda CS500F
Huggies Campaign: "Superstar Athletes"
Israel Anti-Drugs Authority Campaign: "Both Sided of Weed", Campaign: "Drugs Set Your Timeline", Facebook Timeline
The Israels Women's Network
JDate Campaign: "Sleeping Beauty"
JNF Campaign: "Filter"
Lake Kinneret
Leiman-Schlussel Campaign: "Kiss - Tuna"
Matar Productions
Mentos Campaign: "Salami"
New-Nestle Nescafe
New-Pharm
Novartis
One in Nine
Opticana Eyewear Campaign: "The Pinch Banner"
Otcot Campaign: "A Door to a New Life"
PAM Oil Spray Campaign: "Egg"
Panasonic
Perfetti Van Melle Mentos Kiss
Pfizer
Purina ProPlan Campaign: "Reverse World"
Ritter Sport
Sapir College
Shorashim Group Campaign: "Donate with Style", Campaign: "The Siren", Fast over
Siemens
New-Tempo Goldstar Beer
Unilever Campaign: "Hiding Body", Dove
Volvo Campaign: "Finger Safety", Campaign: "The Seesaw"
Xbox
Yes Multiroom Campaign: "Game Of Thrones", Campaign: "Move Your Content", Campaign: "Yes Streamer", Campaign: "Yes"
YesGo

Italy

McCann Erickson Italiana S.p.A.
Via Libano 68/74, 00144 Rome, Italy
Tel.: (39) 06 500 991
Fax: (39) 06 5728 9350
E-Mail: eleonora.cinelli@mccan.com
Web Site: www.mccann.com

Employees: 15
Year Founded: 1959

Agency Specializes In: Public Relations

Joyce King Thomas *(Chm & Chief Creative Officer-McCannXBC)*
Alessandro Sabini *(Chief Creative Officer)*
Gaetano Del Pizzo *(Creative Dir)*
Stefano Tunno *(Art Dir)*
Alessandro Polia *(Dir-Art)*
Alessandro M. Sciortino *(Dir-Creative)*
Maria Vittoria Maccon *(Acct Exec)*
Milton Siclari *(Copywriter)*

Accounts:
Althea
FAO Global Petition Against Hunger, The 1 Billion Hungry Project
Gruppo Poste Italiane
Honda Europe SH 125 Mode DCT
L'Oreal
Menarini Youderm
New-Poste Italiane
Telethon
Unipol Banca

McCann Worldgroup S.r.l
Via Valtellena 15/17, 20159 Milan, Italy
(See Separate Listing)

Japan

McCann Erickson Inc.
Aqua Dojima West 19th Floor 1-4-16, Dojimahama Kita-ku, Osaka, 530-0004 Japan
Tel.: (81) 6 6342 6800
Fax: (81) 6 6342 6893
Web Site: www.mccann.co.jp

Employees: 40
Year Founded: 1980

Agency Specializes In: Advertising, Advertising Specialties, Brand Development & Integration, Communications, Consumer Marketing, Corporate Identity, Direct Response Marketing, Event Planning & Marketing, Graphic Design, Outdoor, Planning & Consultation, Sales Promotion, Strategic Planning/Research

John Woodward *(Chief Strategy Officer)*
Jeremy Perrott *(Dir-Global Creative-McCann Health)*
Satoko Takada *(Assoc Creative Dir)*

McCann Erickson Japan Inc.
Shin Aoyama Bldg., E 1-1-1 Minami-Aoyama, Minato-ku, Tokyo, 107-8679 Japan
Mailing Address:
Minato-ku, P.O. Box 90, Tokyo, 107-91 Japan
Tel.: (81) 3 37468111
Fax: (81) 3 37468247
E-Mail: info.pm.me@japan.mccann.com
Web Site: www.mccann.co.jp

Employees: 425
Year Founded: 1960

Agency Specializes In: Advertising, Advertising Specialties, Below-the-Line, Communications, Direct Response Marketing, Event Planning & Marketing, Media Buying Services, Public Relations, Publicity/Promotions, Sales Promotion, Strategic Planning/Research

Masashi Nakai *(Chief Growth Officer & Exec Bus Dir)*
Masaya Abe *(Art Dir)*
Takashi Enomoto *(Bus Dir-Media)*
Kanta Kumazawa *(Art Dir)*
Michiko Nukui *(Acct Dir)*
Shoji Yokota *(Acct Dir)*
Fumihiko Yamanaka *(Dir-Bus)*
Noriko Sekine *(Acct Supvr)*
Yoshihito Tanaka *(Acct Supvr)*

Accounts:
Johnson & Johnson Vision Care Co. Campaign: Hitomi Rhythm 1:2:1
Mars Japan Ltd Media Buying & Planning
MasterCard Campaign: PricelessMaker
MSD K.K. Campaign: "Barber"
Nihon Kraft Foods Inc. Campaign: "Find the Buried One Million Yen", Campaign: "New CM Actor Audition"
Rakuten Campaign: "Rakuten Helping Hand of Love"
New-Toyo Tire & Rubber Co., Ltd.
The Yokohama Rubber Company Campaign: "White Warrior Go With Pride"

Jordan

Afkar Promoseven-Jordan
Um Uthayna Hamza Al Labadi Street Villa No 6, PO Box 851348, Amman, 11185 Jordan
Tel.: (962) 6 551 1144
Fax: (962) 6 551 1140
Web Site: www.fp7.com

Employees: 25
Year Founded: 1994

Agency Specializes In: Public Relations

Issa Marto *(CEO)*

Lebanon

Fortune Promoseven-Lebanon
Ashrafieh 784 Bldg Sodeco, PO Box 116-5288, Beirut, Lebanon
Tel.: (961) 1 428 428
Fax: (961) 1 398 646

E-Mail: george.jabbour@promoseven.com.lb
Web Site: www.fp7.com

Employees: 70
Year Founded: 1969

Agency Specializes In: Consumer Marketing, Public Relations

George Jabbour *(Mng Dir)*

Accounts:
Close Up

Malawi

Cottman McCann Advertising

Hisco House Chipembere Highway, P.O. Box 835, Blantyre, Malawi
Mailing Address:
PO Box 2473, Blantyre, Malawi
Tel.: (265) 1 67 17 20
Fax: (265) 1 671 487
E-Mail: clientservice@hiscohouse.com
Web Site: www.mccann.com

Employees: 12

Banda Mapopa *(Mgr-Ops)*
Atupele Ellah Stambuli *(Mgr-Mktg & Ops)*

Malaysia

McCann Erickson (Malaysia) Sdn. Bhd.

5-01 & 5-02 Wisma LYL No 12 Jalan 51A/223 Petaling Jaya, Selangor Darul Ehsan, 46100 Kuala Lumpur, Malaysia
Tel.: (60) 3 7841 2898
Fax: (60) 3 2712 6668
Web Site: www.mccann.com

Employees: 140
Year Founded: 1965

Agency Specializes In: Communications, Faith Based

Michael Constantine *(Pres & CEO)*
Daniel Loo *(Art Dir & Copywriter)*
Gavin E. Hoh *(Dir-Creative)*
Mag Lim *(Assoc Dir-Creative)*
Adrian Ng *(Exec Brand Dir)*
Richard Chong *(Assoc Creative Dir)*

Accounts:
BFM Media Sdn Bhd Campaign: "Anytime: Audrey, Freda, Yameen"
BookXcess The Receipt That Changed A Nation
Borders Cookbooks Campaign: "Dog", Campaign: "Husbands"
Carrefour Media
Friends 4 Organ Donation Campaign: "DontFeedTheBugs"
Grafa Sdn Bhd Campaign: "Lessons In Riding: Crotch", Campaign: "Lessons In Riding: Penny", Campaign: "Lessons In Riding: Wig"
KFC Malaysia
Lotus Cars Campaign: "Do More With Less", Campaign: "Lghtwght"
Mitsubishi Motors Above the Line, Creative, Pajero Sport VGT
National Cancer Society Malaysia Hello
Nestle Malaysia Sdn. Bhd. Making A Country Fall In Love With Foam
New Straits Times Press Campaign: "Kitchen", Creative
Oh & Ah Campaign: "Reboot - The Robot Project"
Petronas Motorsports

Mexico

McCann Erickson Mexico

Palo Santo No 22, Lomas Altas, 11950 Mexico, DF Mexico
Tel.: (52) 55 5258 5900
Fax: (52) 55 5258 5917
E-Mail: nicolas.guzman@mccann.com.mx
Web Site: www.mccann.com

Employees: 230
Year Founded: 1947

Agency Specializes In: Above-the-Line, Advertising, Brand Development & Integration, Communications, Experience Design, Health Care Services, Integrated Marketing, Promotions, Publicity/Promotions, Strategic Planning/Research

Nicolas Guzman *(CEO)*
Javi Carro *(Exec VP-Creative)*
Jorge Aguilar *(VP-Creative)*
Breno Cotta *(VP-Creative)*
Myriam Barrios *(Art Dir)*
Marcela Berlanga *(Client Svcs Dir)*
Ricardo Montes de Oca *(Dir-Creative & Art)*
Pablo Motta *(Assoc Dir-Creative)*
Christian del Rio *(Acct Supvr)*

Accounts:
Andersen Windows; 1996
Bancomer Education, Insurance; 1997
Barcel Chicharrones, Chicharrones de Cerdo, Chip's con Sal, Adobadas y con Jalapeno, Chipotles, Chirriones, Churritos, Fritos Ricos, Golden Nuts, Hut Nuts, Maxipapas con Maggie, con Sal y con Chamoy, Palis, Palomitas, Palomitas con Chile, Quechitos, Takis, Tostachos con Chipotle, Tostachos con Jalapena
BestDay.com
BIC Twin Lady Razors
Bimbo; 1983
General Motors Campaign: "Don't Text a Driver", Campaign: "Pedestrial Pass", Chevrolet, Chevrolet Tahoe, Print
Janssen Invokana
Johnson & Johnson Band Aids, Reach; 1996
Lara Albitas, Animalitos, Antillanas, Canapinas, Cremositas, Deliciosas, Marias, Nutriavenas, Rosetas, Saladas, Surtido Rico, Suspiros, Trigobran
L'Oreal Elvive Casting, Cosmetics, Elvide, Feria, Imedia, Maybelline, Studio Line; 1979
Marinela-Pasteles y Galletas Barritas, Blingos, Cajas, Canelitas, Choco Wow, Chocorroles, Crujirocks, Gansito, Hit Triki-Trakes, Kg, Lors, Mr. Brown, Napolitano, Pay de Nuez y Pina, Pinguinos, Plativolos, Polvoroes, Principe, Rocko, Rollo, Sponch, Suavicremas, Submarinos, Tubos, X
Microsoft; 1999
Motorola Solutions, Inc. Cellular Phones, Club Beep, Pagers, Radios; 1997
Nestle Buitoni, Capuccino, Decaf, Diplomat, Dolca, Nestea, Nido Clasica, Nido Extracalcio, Nido Kinder, Open Up, Quik, Ristreto; 1947
The Non-Violence Project Mexico
Non Violence
Ricolino Bubulubu, Chocoretas, Dulcigomas, Kirs Bar, Kranky, Micky, Moritas, Paleta Payaso, Panditas, Sorpresa

Morocco

Promoseven-Morocco

237 Bd Zerktouni Residence El Kheir, Casablanca, Morocco
Tel.: (212) 22 364040
Fax: (212) 22 364732
E-Mail: gouza@fp7mccann.co.ma
Web Site: www.fp7.com

Year Founded: 1992

Laszlo Koza *(Gen Mgr)*

Accounts:
Cathay Pacific
Coca-Cola Refreshments USA, Inc. Sprite
L'Oreal
LUX
MasterCard
Nescafe
Nivea
QNB
Rotana
Sony
Vichy
Vileda

Netherlands

McCann Amsterdam

(Formerly McCann Erickson (Nederland) B.V.)
Bovenkerkerweg 6-8, 1185 XE Amstelveen, Netherlands
Tel.: (31) 205030800
Fax: (31) 205030888
E-Mail: info@ifbmccann.com
Web Site: http://www.mccann.nl/

Employees: 36
Year Founded: 1959

Miranda Honselaar *(Mng Dir-Craft Amsterdam)*
Albert Vegers *(Sr Dir-Art)*
Micky Geesink *(Dir-Strategy)*
John Spijkers *(Mgr-Creative)*
Tim Voors *(Interim Dir-Creative)*

Accounts:
Arag
Bataviastad
Cathay Pacific
Het Spoorwegmuseum
Intratuin
L'Oreal Nederland B.V.
MasterCard/Maestro
Maybelline NY
Mediq
Pfizer
Plan-it Brico
Praxis
RedBrand
Remia
Roosvicee
Stegeman
TVM
Van Gils
Venco
Welzorg

Norway

McCann Erickson

Sandakervn 24C Building C1, Box 4228, N-0401 Oslo, Norway
Tel.: (47) 2254 3600
Fax: (47) 2254 3601
E-Mail: info@mccann.no
Web Site: www.mccann.no

Employees: 85

Paal Tarjei Aasheim *(Chief Integration Officer)*
Marius Zachariasen *(Dir-Innovation)*
Jorgen Laure *(Copywriter)*

Accounts:
Coca-Cola Refreshments USA, Inc.
GET
Go Morgen Yogurt
Grilstad Campaign: "The Lucky Pig"

Gule Sider Yellow Pages
Klart Svar Wireless Business
KSL Matmerk Ecological Organic Food
Maarud Campaign: "Hip Pop", Campaign: "Micropop", Estrella Nuts
Munkholm Campaign: "Good things come to those who wait"
Netcom Campaign: "A Phonestory", Campaign: "Nightmare", Campaign: "The Swap"
Norwegian Peoples Aid
Ostecompagniet Campaign: "Drive", Snofrisk Cream Cheese
Rimi Campaign: "Rimi Pluss"
Ringnes Campaign: "Good things Come to those Who Wait", Campaign: "Prais Munkholm!"
Statoil ASA Campaign: "Deep Dive Statoil", Campaign: "The Treasure Hunt", Goodnight, Natural Gas
Stine Sofies Stiftelse Child Welfare
New-Storebrand Campaign: "#Justgonna"
Sunniva Campaign: "The Better Morning App"
TDC
Tine Campaign: "Motherwitch", Campaign: "Refill and refresh in two minutes", Iced Coffee
Toro
TV2 Campaign: "Ham", Sumo
Ulleval Business Class
Universitetet i Oslo
UTE
Wideroe Airline Campaign: "A Summer Without Rain", Campaign: "Grandpa's Magic Trick", Campaign: "The Shortest Url"

Oman

FP7

(Formerly Muscat Promoseven)
1st Fl Homuz Bldg Next Near Ruwi Roundabout, PO Box 2317, 112 Muscat, Oman
Mailing Address:
PO Box 2413, 112 Muscat, Oman
Tel.: (968) 2 4705270
E-Mail: info@fp7.com
Web Site: www.fp7.com/#!/en/dxb/contact/12

Employees: 25
Year Founded: 1988

Agency Specializes In: Consumer Marketing, Direct Response Marketing, Point of Sale, Public Relations

Noufal Ali *(Exec Dir-Creative)*
Wissam Matar *(Dir-Creative)*
Jaison Ben *(Assoc Dir-Creative)*

Accounts:
Al Hilal Islamic Banking Services
Al Mar'a
Al Nahda Resort & Spa
Apollo Medical Centre
Coca-Cola Refreshments USA, Inc.
Delicio
Ford
Mastercard
Micromax Mobile
Muscat Film Festival
Nescafe
Oman Oasis
Sony Micro Vault Tiny 8 GB
Sweets of Oman
Vileda

Paraguay

Biedermann Publicidad S.A.

Alejo Garcia 2589 c/ Rio de la Plata, Asuncion, Paraguay
Tel.: (595) 21 424 735
Fax: (595) 21 571 07
E-Mail: info@biedermann.com.py
Web Site: www.biedermann.com.py

Employees: 65
Year Founded: 1954

National Agency Associations: APAP (Portugal)-IAA

Agency Specializes In: Advertising, Consumer Goods, Consumer Marketing

Enrique Biedermann *(Owner)*
Alejandro Rebull *(Gen Dir-Creative)*
Gaston Cortesi *(Dir-Art)*
Federico Perie *(Dir-Plng)*
Oscar Vera *(Dir-Creative)*
Mariel Jorgge *(Acct Exec)*
Marcos Valdez *(Copywriter)*

Accounts:
British American Tobacco
Chevrolet Trucks
Coca-Cola Refreshments USA, Inc. Diet Coke, Diet Sprite, Fanta, Simba, Sprite, Tab
Diageo
Esso Standard del Paraguay
Johnson & Johnson
Lasca Lab Campaign: "Jinx"
MasterCard
Millicom Campaign: "Rewrite", Campaign: "Slide", Tigo
TAM Airlines
Unilever Axe, Celebrity Endorsement
Vision Banco Campaign: "The Great Jump"

Peru

McCann Erickson (Peru) Publicidad S.A.

Calle Tripoli 102 Miraflores Apartado 180668, L18-0368 Lima, 18 Peru
Tel.: (51) 1 610 8100
Fax: (51) 1 447 8110
E-Mail: latam@mccann.com
Web Site: www.mccannworldgroup.com

Employees: 80
Year Founded: 1946

Mauricio Fernandez-Maldonado *(Chief Creative Officer)*
Rodrigo Revoredo *(VP & Strategist-Creative)*
Luigi Rissi *(Art Dir)*
Andrea Rossello *(Acct Dir)*
Fabrizio Tapia *(Creative Dir)*
Fernando Valladares *(Art Dir)*
Ricardo Aranibar *(Dir-Art)*
Roberto Delgado *(Dir-Creative)*
Giovanni Macco *(Dir-Art)*
Tyto Delgado *(Copywriter)*
Roberto Lopez *(Copywriter)*
Alvaro Soto *(Copywriter)*

Accounts:
American Airlines
Aniquem Campaign: "The Firecracker Project", Robot
Bimbo Wraps
Coca-Cola Refreshments USA, Inc. Campaign: "Happy ID", OOH, Press, Radio, Sprite, TV, Website
Domund Campaign: "Cold"
Ducati
Entel Chile S.A
Flying Dog Hostels
Johnson & Johnson
Kraft Foods
La Tarumba Circus Campaign: "Make it real"
National Blind Unit of Peru The first post in Braille
Papa Con Camote
Peru21 Newspaper
Representaciones Durand
Save the Children #SPEAKFORTHEM, Campaign: "Boy", Campaign: "Girl"
Sodimac
New-UNCP

Philippines

McCann Erickson (Philippines), Inc.

34th Floor GT Tower 6813 Ayala Avenue Corner HV Dela Costa Street, Makati City, Manila, 1229 Philippines
Tel.: (63) 2 757 2333
Web Site: www.mccann.com

Employees: 270
Year Founded: 1963

Raul Castro *(Chief Creative Officer & Exec VP)*
Kathy Hilado *(Acct Dir)*
Randy Tiempo *(Creative Dir)*
Mel Balmaceda *(Acct Mgr)*
Noel Bermejo *(Deputy Exec Dir-Creative)*
Mervin Ignacio *(Assoc Exec Dir-Creative)*

Accounts:
ACS Manufacturing Pride Laundry Detergent, Star Floor Wax, Unique Toothpaste; 1986
Bank of the Philippine Islands
Boehringer Ingelheim; Philippines Media
Boots Company Strepsils
The Coca-Cola Export Corporation Campaign: "Living Billboard", Campaign: "Where Will Happiness Strike Next", Coke, Fanta, Hi-C, Lift, Powerade, Royal, Sprite; 1988
Coca-Cola Refreshments USA, Inc. Campaign: "Living billboard"; 1963
Globe Telecommunications Globelines, Handyphone; 1995
Hummer Campaign: "Pass It Along"
Johnson & Johnson J's Alcohol, J's Diapers, J's Non-Greasy Skin Lotion, Modess, Reach, VAL Pure Essentials; 1982
JS Unitrade Merchandise Campaign : "Walang tatalo sa alagang totoo", EQ Plus Diapers
L'Oreal Casting, Elseve, Imedia-Excellence, Makeup; 1990
Nestle Cappuccino, Carnation, Chocolait, Coffeemate, Decaf, Maggi, Magnolia UHT, Master Roast, Neslac, Nesvita; 1985
Operation Smile Campaign: "Beggar"
Philippine Cancer Society Inc
San Miguel Corporation
UNILAB Biogesic, Ceelin, Creative, Decolgen, Ritemed, Skelan, Tuseran, Unilab Corporate, Westmont Appebon

Poland

Polska McCann Erickson

Cybernetyki 19, 02-677 Warsaw, Poland
Tel.: (48) 22 548 8100
Fax: (48) 22 21 01 101
E-Mail: office_warsaw@mccann.com.pl
Web Site: mccann.com

Employees: 150
Year Founded: 1991

Arek Baranski *(Head-Tech)*
Agnieszka Wichracka-Kuzma *(Head-Acct Mgmt)*
Magdalena Kieferling *(Dir-Comm)*
Michal Krejza *(Dir-Growth)*
Lukasz Krol *(Acct Mgr)*
Katarzyna Grochowska *(Sr Acct Exec)*
Malgorzata Nieciecka *(Sr Acct Exec)*
Monika Sosnowska *(Client Svc Dir)*
Agnieszka Wichracka *(Client Svc Dir)*

Accounts:
Alpika Baby Cream
Apap
Calypso Fitness Club Campaign: "Before & After"
CEDO Campaign: "Hand"

CI Games
Customform Campaign: "Couple"
General Motors (Opel)
Greenpeace Campaign: "Banker"
L'Oreal
Mastercard
Mola Tissues Campaign: "Boy"
MPT
Nestle Maggi, Nesquik
Nobody's Children Foundation
Polmedica Alpica Cream
Saab
US Pharmacia Apap Pain Relief
Verco Campaign: "Boat"
Wik Optik Campaign: "Shark"

Portugal

McCann Worldgroup Portugal
(Formerly McCann Erickson/Hora)
Rua Carlos Alberto da Mota Pinto n 17A, Piso 8, 1070-313 Lisbon, Portugal
Tel.: (351) 217 517 500
Fax: (351) 217 517 504
E-Mail: geral@mccann.pt
Web Site: www.mccann.pt

Employees: 70
Year Founded: 1980

Angelo Costa *(CFO & COO)*
Filipe Moreira *(Chief Strategy Officer)*
Filipe Domingues *(Sr Dir-Art)*
Sofia Belo *(Acct Dir)*
Fred Fannon *(Dir-Creative)*
Cesar Nunes *(Dir-Art)*
Marta D'Orey *(Acct Mgr)*
Mario Nascimento *(Sr Writer)*
Filipa Vasconcelos *(Grp Acct Supvr)*

Accounts:
ACP Portuguese Auto Club Campaign: "Txt & Drive"
Amnesty International Portugal Campaign: "Letter from a Prisoner"
Chiado Publishers
Coca-Cola Refreshments USA, Inc.
Expresso Newspaper
Martini
Nesquik
Nestle
Opel
Oxigenio Radio Station Campaign: "Groove", Campaign: "Hipster", Campaign: "MC"
Portuguese Association for Victim Support
Portuguese League Against Aids Campaign: "Vaccine"
Roche
Tap
Zurich Home Insurance

Qatar

Fortune Promoseven-Qatar
Pearl Towers 4th Fl Al Saad St, PO Box 13645, Doha, Qatar
Tel.: (974) 44 364 385
Fax: (974) 4 364 387
E-Mail: cmezher@promoseven.com
Web Site: www.fp7.com

E-Mail for Key Personnel:
President: cmezher@promoseven.com

Employees: 30
Year Founded: 1994

Simon Bowthorpe *(Mng Dir)*

Accounts:
Nestle Purina PetCare Company Dog Chow
QNB Al Islami

Romania

McCann Erickson Romania
Jules Michelet 18 1st Sector, Bucharest, 010463 Romania
Tel.: (40) 2 1 232 3727
Fax: (40) 2 1 232 3190
E-Mail: reception@mccann.ro
Web Site: www.mccann.ro

Employees: 200
Year Founded: 1996

Nir Refuah *(Chief Innovation Officer)*
Catalin Dobre *(Exec Dir-Creative)*
Alexandru Dumitrescu *(Exec Dir-Creative)*
Bogdan Teodorescu *(Sr Dir-Art)*
Bogdan Dinu *(Dir-Art)*
Vlad Macarie *(Dir-Art)*
Alina Nechita *(Dir-Art)*
Arpad Rezi *(Dir-Art)*
Tiberiu Muneanu *(Mgr-Audio & Video)*
Sandra Bold *(Copywriter)*
Tal Scweiger *(Copywriter)*
Catalin Stanciu *(Copywriter)*

Accounts:
21 Radio
Beko Campaign: "Snooze for Coffee", Global Communications
Caroli
Caroti Foods
Cif
Coca-Cola Refreshments USA, Inc. Campaign: "Let's Eat Together"
Connex-GSM
Dedeman
GlaxoSmithKline
GM-Opel
Heineken
Interbrew
Kandia Dulce Campaign: "American Rom", Campaign: "Bucharest Not Budapest", Campaign: "Romanians are Smart", Chocolate Bar, ROM Campaign: "Romanians are smart" & ROM Chocolates, Snack
KFC
Kraft Foods
L'Oreal
Loteria Romana
MTV
National Movie Archive
Nestle
Renaestara Romania
ROM Candy Campaign: "Bucharest Not Budapest"
Rompetrol
Tnuva
Transilvania
Travel Studio
UniCredit Tiriac Bank
Unilever
Vodafone Group plc Arpad, Sebastian, Salvamont App

Saudi Arabia

Albert Promoseven-Jeddah
Badriyah Towers 1st Floor Al-Rowda Street, PO Box 17775, Jeddah, 21494 Saudi Arabia
Tel.: (966) 2 606 1160
Fax: (966) 2 606 0150
E-Mail: aboulos@promoseven.com
Web Site: www.fp7.com

Year Founded: 1986

Agency Specializes In: Consumer Marketing, Public Relations

Marc Lawandos *(Mng Dir)*

Albert Promoseven-Riyadh
2nd FloorMawhid Center Olaya St N, PO Box 53034, Riyadh, 11583 Saudi Arabia
Mailing Address:
P0 Box 53038, Riyadh, Saudi Arabia
Tel.: (966) 1 215 2211
E-Mail: aboulos@promoseven.com
Web Site: www.fp7.com

Employees: 70
Year Founded: 1982

Agency Specializes In: Consumer Marketing, Event Planning & Marketing, Media Buying Services, Public Relations

Sasan Saeidi *(Mng Dir)*
Claude Abboud *(Gen Mgr-FP7/RUH)*

Accounts:
NAQA
Red Logistics
Tiger

Serbia & Montenegro

McCann Erickson Group
Terazje 7-0, 11000 Belgrade, Serbia
Tel.: (381) 11 202 2200
Web Site: www.mccann.co.rs/

Lidija Milovanovic *(Sr Dir-Art)*
Vladimir Cosic *(Dir-Creative)*
Nenad Dodic *(Dir-Art)*
Marija Milankovic *(Dir-Art)*
Jana Savic Rastovac *(Dir-Creative)*
Milena Kvapil *(Assoc Dir-Creative)*
Milos Stankovic *(Mgr-New Bus)*
Bojan Babic *(Copywriter)*
Zdravko Kevresan *(Sr Designer)*

Accounts:
Alterna Travel Store Campaign: "Life is short. Travel"
City Magazine
FitCurves Gym
Kontext
Maskot
MK Mountain Resort Campaign: "Cotton lungs"
MTV Serbia
Museum of Science & Technology
Nestle
ORCA
Suicide Prevention Center Sos Info Line
White Cane NGO Campaign: "Web Blackout"
Yugoslav Drama Theatre

Singapore

McCann Erickson (Singapore) Private Limited
40A Orchard Road #06-00 the MacDonald House, Singapore, 238838 Singapore
Tel.: (65) 6737 9911
Fax: (65) 6737 1455
E-Mail: sorab.mistry@ap.mccann.com
Web Site: www.mccann.com

Year Founded: 1965

Charles Cadell *(Pres-Asia Pacific)*
Robert Doswell *(CEO-McCann Singapore & Reg Mng Dir-Craft Worldwide)*
Ben Israel *(Head-Digital)*

Accounts:
FHM Calendar
GPS Bay
JA Henckels

KFC Singapore; 2007
Line Digital, Outdoor, Print, Social Media, TV
Nestle Confectionary Products, Milo
Oversea-Chinese Banking Corporation Limited (Creative Agency of Record)
Panasonic Singapore
Prudential Assurance The Face You Can Trust Campaign
REPELLA Insect Repellant
Selleys

McCann Healthcare Singapore
The MacDonald House, 40A Orchard Rd 05-01, Singapore, 238838 Singapore
Tel.: (65) 6739 3485
Fax: (65) 67393349
Web Site: www.mccannhealth.com

Employees: 15

Agency Specializes In: Advertising, Health Care Services, Pharmaceutical

Sean Riley *(Exec Dir-Creative-Singapore & South East Asia)*
Alfred Wee *(Dir-Creative-McCann Worldgroup Singapore)*

Accounts:
AstraZeneca
Bayer Schering
DEY
Eisai/PriCara
ICM Pharma Hexo-Dane Antiseptic Handrub
Impact Campaign: "Accelerated wound healing"
USV Sebamed
Vusion

McCann Worldgroup (Singapore) Pte Ltd
40A Orchard Road, #06-01 The MacDonald House, Singapore, 238838 Singapore
Tel.: (65) 6737 9911
Fax: (65) 6737 1455
Web Site: www.mccannworldgroup.com

Employees: 128
Year Founded: 1965

Agency Specializes In: Communications

Jessica Davey *(CMO-Asia Pacific)*
Patrick Rona *(Chief Digital Officer-Asia Pacific)*
Charles Cadell *(Pres-Asia Pacific)*
Matt Mckay *(Exec VP & Exec Dir-Creative)*
Nick Handel *(Mng Dir-MRM//McCann & Head-m:united-APAC)*
Richard McCabe *(Reg Dir-Strategic Plng-APAC)*
Marina Tolsa *(Assoc Dir-Creative)*
Daniel Foo *(Copywriter)*
Adrian Loo *(Sr Designer)*

Accounts:
L'Oreal Campaign: "Upside Down", Revitalift Laser X3
Panasonic Singapore 3D TV, Viera 3D TV
Singapore Environment Council Environmental Awareness

Slovakia

Mayer/McCann-Erickson s.r.o.
Viedenska Cesta 5, 851 01 Bratislava, Slovakia
Tel.: (421) 2 6726 7101
Fax: (421) 2 62 24 04 18
E-Mail: mayer@mccann.sk
Web Site: www.mayer.sk

Employees: 43

Radovan Grohol *(Co-Owner & Mng Dir)*
Zuzana Kusova *(Co-Owner & Exec Dir)*
Martin Hala *(Acct Dir)*
Viera Sindelarova *(Art Dir)*
Michal Hornicky *(Dir-Art)*
Boris Prexta *(Dir-Creative)*

Accounts:
Bayer
Coca-Cola Refreshments USA, Inc.
Corgon
Heineken Slovensko A.S. Corgon Beer
Intersnack Solvakia
Mastercard Campaign: "Festival shoes"
Miele Vacuum Cleaner
Opel
Rigips
Slovanet
TIPOS Campaign: "LOTO book"
Toyota
UniCredit Bank

Slovenia

Mayer-McCann
Dunajska cesta 163, 1000 Ljubljana, Slovenia
Tel.: (386) 1 563 65 50
Fax: (386) 1 563 6568
E-Mail: agency@mayermccann.com
Web Site: www.mayermccann.com/slo

Employees: 20

Marko Majer *(Founder, CEO & Partner)*
Nenad Cizl *(Art Dir)*
Robert Bohinec *(Dir-Creative)*
Suzana Milenkovic *(Dir-Media)*
Tatjana Seneker *(Acct Mgr)*
Ales Petejan *(Client Svc Dir)*

Accounts:
Hov-Hov Dog Bakery
MasterCard
Post of Slovenia
Snaga

South Africa

McCann Erickson Africa
4 Kikuya Road South Sunninghill, PO Box 10663, 2000 Sandton, 2157 South Africa
Tel.: (27) 11 235 4600
Fax: (27) 11 803 4222
Web Site: www.mccann.co.za/

Employees: 125

Karabo Denalane *(Mng Dir)*
Pierre Odendaal *(Chief Creative Officer-Johannesburg)*
Krishnan Srinivasan *(Mng Dir-Healthcare)*
Dallas Glover *(Dir-Strategic Plng-McCann Johannesburg)*
Fraser Lamb *(Exec Chm)*

Accounts:
Kyocera Mita South Africa
Merck Consumer Healthcare
Telkom 8.ta

McCann Worldgroup Johannesburg
4 Kikuyu Road, Sunninghill, Johannesburg, 2157 South Africa
Mailing Address:
PO Box 10663, Johannesburg, 2000 South Africa
Tel.: (27) 11 235 4600
Fax: (27) 11 803 7566
E-Mail: infosa@mccann.com
Web Site: www.mccann.co.za/

Employees: 125
Year Founded: 1934

Agency Specializes In: Communications

Clyde Mallon *(Gen Mgr-Digital)*
Lee Tan *(Exec Dir-Creative)*
Miguel Bemfica *(Dir-Creative-Global)*
Fraser Lamb *(Exec Chm)*
Jerome Styer *(Reg Head-Bus)*

Accounts:
Coca-Cola Campaign: "Coca-Cola Happy Flag"
General Motors
KAUAI Campaign: "Live The KAUAI Life", Digital
MasterCard
Telkom 8.ta Mobile Network, Emoticon Boy
Zurich Insurance Company "Gator Golf", Campaign: "Bicycle", Campaign: "Warmth"

Spain

McCann Erickson S.A.
Paseo de la Castellana 165, 28046 Madrid, Spain
Tel.: (34) 91 5679 000
Fax: (34) 91 571 2098
Web Site: www.mccann.com

Employees: 262
Year Founded: 1963

Agency Specializes In: Advertising

Monica Moro *(Chief Creative Officer)*
Felix Vicente *(Pres-Spain)*
Gonzalo Sanchez-Taiz *(Gen Dir)*
Jon Lavin *(Exec Creative Dir)*
Raquel Martinez *(Exec Dir-Creative)*
Marta Carreras *(Acct Dir)*
Eduard Cubel *(Art Dir)*
David Fernandez *(Creative Dir)*
Rafael Quilez *(Dir-Art)*
Pedro Rego *(Dir-Creative)*
Marta Grassa *(Acct Supvr)*
Laia Gilibets *(Acct Exec)*
Jaume Rufach *(Copywriter)*

Accounts:
AECC Campaign: "Fix You", Campaign: "Singer", Cancer Association; 2001
Afal
Asefa Estudiantes Basketball Club Campaign: "Sheikh"
Banco Santander Financial Products & Services; 1996
Barcelo Rum
Boots Pharmaceuticals, S.A. Nurofen 400; 1992
Brunete Town Council Campaign: "Poops"
Buitrago Town Council
Caja Duero; 2004
Campofrio food Groups Ashes, Comedians, Finissimas, Naturissimos Ham, Sausages, Toads
Compania Coca-Cola Espana, S.A. Aquabona, Burn Energy Drink, Campaign: "125th anniversary", Campaign: "Instant", Campaign: "Kiss Happiness", Campaign: "Reasons to Believe", Coca Cola, Coca Cola Caffeine Free, Coca Cola Zero, Coca-Cola Light, Fanta, Nestea, Powerade, Soft Drinks, The Swap; 1977
Consejeria de Agricultura y Pesca
Consorcio Regional de Transportes Metro de Madrid
Costa Cruceros Cruise Lines; 1999
Council of Brunete Campaign: "Poo Express"
De Ley; 2005
Emplea
Endesa; 2008
Factoria De Canales
Fundacion Lealtad; 2007
General Motors Agila, Antara, Astra, Astra GTC, Astra SW, Astra Sedan, Astra Twin Top, Combo, Combo Tour, Corsa, Corsavan, Insignia, Meriva,

Movano, Opel GT, Signum, Tigra Twin Top, Vectra, Vectra GTS, Vectra SW, Vivaro, Zafira
Ikea International A/S "The Other Letter", Cookies
Gran Pantalla
Greenpeace Campaign: "Videodegradable", Environmentalism, Institution
Inakadate Village
Johnson & Johnson Acuvue; 1993
Kia Motors Campaign: "Rafa Sells Car"
L'Oreal Productos Publico, S.A. Campaign: "Mirrors", Dermo, Maybelline New York, Sun Expertise; 1976
Movistar Imagenio
NH Hotels
Nisa Hospitals
Opel Campaign: "The Seedling Car"
Pavofrio
Renault Clio Gueropa
Sala Montjuic Campaign: "Truly Independent 1"
Sony Ericsson Xperia Play
New-Teatreneu
Telefonica, S.A. Campaign: "Energy", Campaign: "The Biggest Stadium in the World", IMAGENIO; 1997
Telefonica
Trapote Group Campaign: "The Bathroom Network"

McCann Erickson S.A.

Plaza de America 2 piso 6, 46004 Valencia, Spain
Tel.: (34) 96 316 2990
Fax: (34) 96 395 0765
Web Site: www.mccann.com

Employees: 10

Agency Specializes In: Advertising, Hispanic Market

Luis Pardo *(Dir-Corp Strategy)*

McCann Erickson S.A.

Josep Irla y Bosch 1 3, 08034 Barcelona, Spain
Tel.: (34) 93 252 0400
Fax: (34) 93 2520434
E-Mail: e.jove@mccann.es
Web Site: www.mccann.com

Employees: 55
Year Founded: 1963

National Agency Associations: IAA

Enric Jove Bosch *(Mng Dir)*
Alex Bartumeus *(Chief Digital Officer)*
Ana Brossa *(Exec Dir-Creative)*
Joaquin Espagnol *(Creative Dir-Europe)*
Marta Torrecillas *(Acct Dir)*
Xavi Gimeno *(Dir-Creative)*
Carrillo Maite *(Dir-Creative)*
Carla Tortosa *(Dir-Strategic Plng & Deputy Dir)*
Cristina Sanchez de toro *(Acct Exec)*

Accounts:
New-Alzheimer Foundation Spain
Bacardi; 1972
New-Beko Global Communications
Cereal Partners Espana, S.A. Chocopics, Fibre 1, Fitness, Golden Grahams; 1990
Nestle Espana S.A. Bonka, Maggi, Nesquik, Nestle Selection; 1964
Pokerstars
Spanish National Lottery Campaign: "Vineyards"

Sweden

Storakers McCann

Grev Turegaton 11A, Box 5809, 102 48 Stockholm, Sweden
Tel.: (46) 8 506 50000
Fax: (46) 8 506 50010
E-Mail: info@storakers.se

Employees: 50

Agency Specializes In: Advertising

Adam Kerj *(Chief Creative Officer-Nordic)*
Max Hansson *(Dir-Art)*

Accounts:
3 Sweden Campaign: "Ski Hunt"
Adlibris E-book Store
Dagens Industri
Lantmannen Campaign: "Leftover Dating"
Max Burgers Campaign: "Nobody Puts Burger"
Mer Campaign: "Mer Trailer 46"
Riksgalden
seb Campaign: "55+"
Sony Ericsson
Swedish National Debt Office

Switzerland

McCann Erickson Switzerland

15 Passage Malbuisson, 1211 Geneva, 11 Switzerland
Tel.: (41) 22 317 77 77
Fax: (41) 22 317 77 78
E-Mail: geneva.office@mccann.ch
Web Site: www.mccann.ch

Employees: 50
Year Founded: 1967

National Agency Associations: BSW

Carole Massanes *(Mng Dir)*
Sandy Criquelion *(Controller-Fin)*
Olivier Renaud *(Dir-Art)*
Laura Beetschen *(Office Mgr & Coord-HR)*
Neil Maccormack *(Mgr-IT)*

Accounts:
Bacardi Martini
General Motors
L'Oreal
Mastercard
WattWorld Electric Bikes

Taiwan

McCann Erickson Communications Group

11th Fl No 2 Lane 150 Section 5 Hsin Yi Rd, Taipei, 110 Taiwan
Tel.: (886) 2 2758 5000
Fax: (886) 2 2758 5690
E-Mail: shilyn@mccannerickson.com
Web Site: www.mccann.com

Employees: 100
Year Founded: 1981

Agency Specializes In: Advertising, Direct Response Marketing, Event Planning & Marketing, Sales Promotion

Gary Chi *(Mng Dir)*

Accounts:
Coca Cola
KAO (Japanese Cosmetics)
MasterCard
Nestea

Thailand

McCann Worldgroup Thailand

555 Narathiwas Rd, Bangkok, 10120 Thailand
Tel.: (66) 2 343 6000
Fax: (66) 2 343 6001

Employees: 125
Year Founded: 1965

Agency Specializes In: Communications

Yupin Muntzing *(CEO)*
Varidda Voraakom *(Head-Digital Strategy & Social)*
Suvit Jaturiyasajagul *(Exec Creative Dir)*
Julien Robin *(Reg Dir-Digital Content Production)*
Ekasit Angkarangkool *(Art Dir)*
Anusorn Boorana *(Art Dir)*
Boonasak Bunnahirun *(Dir-Creative)*
Perawich Charoenphan *(Dir-Art)*
Wuthinan Jandafai *(Dir-Art)*
Sypabhas Tiraratanakul *(Dir-Art)*
Jenkanit Rujiramora *(Assoc Dir-Plng)*
Sorn Manawanitcharoen *(Copywriter)*
Nathapat Pianboonwat *(Copywriter)*

Accounts:
ADECCO Consulting Campaign: "Coin of Luck"
Alpha Unitrade Co Campaign: "Ceramic"
Amarin Book Center Campaign: "See from Sound", Pocket Books
Autopoint
Bangkok Distributor Co. Big-Bloom Bubble Gum
Be Bebe Campaign: "Bean Bag"
Big Bloom
BSH Home Appliances Campaign: "Clean Power"
Cadbury Adams Thailand Campaign: "Downward", Car Freshener
Channel V Campaign: "Man in the Mirror"
Clean Plus Campaign: "Let Dirt Speak"
Clorets BTS Skytrain
Dentyne Campaign: "Complete Every Meal"
Fong Hom
Fowin
Hygiene Color Bleach Blue Stain
Italasia Electro Campaign: "The Incredible Sharpness"
IUCN
Jermrid Sanitiser Gel
Kasikornbank Marketing
Kiwi Kleen
LG Electronics Thailand Campaign: "The Real 3D Experience", Infinia TV, LG Lollipop, Washing Machine
Line Campaign: "Code"
Meiji
Naiin.com Campaign: "See from Sound"
Nicomild
Pravit Group
Prompong Ruangjui (Photographer) Campaign: "YEAH! It's You On My Business Card"
PZ Cussons Carex Hand Shower
S.C. Stationery Co. Horse Pen
Siampoolsup Inter-Chemical
Siribuncha Company Limited Campaign: "Keep Your Moment Clean"
Smith & John
Viking Fertiliser
Wematch.co.th
WMF Knife Campaign: "Incredibly Sharp"
Acer Computers; 2008
Ansell
Asia Pacific Breweries Heineken; 2008
Chevrolet Campaign: "Passion On"
Chivas Regal 100 Pipers Malt Premium Whiskey, Master Blend; 2007
International Products Group Consumer Goods; 2007
Sony Thailand
Thai Health Promotion Foundation Campaign: "Hotline"
Tourism Authority of Thailand Campaign: "Thailand At 5Cm", Campaign: "The World's memories of Thailand"; 2007
Boots Body Cream
Carex
Johnson & Johnson (Thailand) Ltd. Acuvue Contact Lenses

L'Oreal
MasterCard
Reckitt Benckiser Durex Performa Condoms
New-SAND-M
Siemen's Energy

Turkey

McCann Erickson WorldGroup Turkey
Buyukdere Caddesi Ecza Sokak No 6, Levent, 34330 Istanbul, Turkey
Tel.: (90) 212 317 5777
Fax: (90) 212 278 9769
Web Site: www.mccann.com

Employees: 150
Year Founded: 1976

Kaan Ayce *(Creative Dir)*
Serdar Bilginer *(Art Dir)*
Elvan Deniz *(Art Dir)*
Ozlem Milor Islam *(Client Svcs Dir)*
Cihan Kavaklpnar *(Creative Dir)*
Funda Hergul *(Acct Mgr)*
Elif Kir *(Acct Mgr)*
Duygu Teser *(Acct Exec)*
Kerem Ceteci *(Copywriter)*
Mesut Kocarslan *(Copywriter)*
Duygu Yazici *(Jr Copywriter)*

Accounts:
3M Scotch Brite Roller
A La Farina
Akbank Short Film Festival
Alzheimer Foundation Campaign: "Knitting"
Aytac
Beko Global Communications
Bocek Avcisi
Chicco
Coca-Cola Refreshments USA, Inc. Campaign: "125th Year Anniversary"; 1978
Dogan Courier
Dogus Otomotiv
Duru Gourmet
Engelleri Kaldir
General Motors
Lezita Chicken Nugget
L'Oreal S.A.
Magic Form
Nestle; 1985
Tetra Pak; 1999
Turkish Airlines Campaign: "Monna Lisa", Campaign: "QR flags"
Volkswagen Group of America, Inc. Amarok, Campaign: "Facebook Flipbook", Igloo

UM
(Formerly Universal McCann)
Buyukdere Caddesi Ecza Sokak No 6, Levent, 34330 Istanbul, Turkey
Tel.: (90) 212 317 5656
Fax: (90) 212 321 1215
Web Site: www.umww.com

Employees: 65

Tolga Uner *(Mng Dir)*
Sinemis Candemir *(Head-Digital Media)*
Erin Iversen *(Head-Digital)*
Nazli Kursunoglu *(Mgr-Digital)*
Tugce Yamanel *(Mgr)*

Accounts:
Beko
C Johnson
Coca-Cola Refreshments USA, Inc.
MasterCard
Turkies Telecom

United Arab Emirates

FP7
(Formerly Fortune Promoseven-HQ)
7th Floor MCN Hive Tecom Section C, PO Box 6834, Dubai, United Arab Emirates
Tel.: (971) 4 4454777
E-Mail: info@fp7.com
Web Site: www.fp7.com

Employees: 300
Year Founded: 1975

Agency Specializes In: Public Relations

Sasan Saeidi *(Mng Dir)*
Tarek Miknas *(CEO-FP7 & MENA)*
Ali Mokdad *(Grp Head-Creative)*
Spiro Malak *(Gen Mgr-Bus Unit)*
Karl Uhlemann *(Gen Mgr-Bus Unit, FP7 & DXB)*
Josephine Younes *(Dir-Art & Assoc Dir-Creative)*
Mo Aram *(Dir-Art)*
Nayaab Rais *(Assoc Dir-Creative & Copywriter)*
Khaled Hamza *(Mgr-Creative Svcs)*
Chris Booth *(Copywriter)*

Accounts:
Al Tayer Maintenance
Berlitz Language Center
Carrefour
Cathay Pacific Airways; Dubai
The Coca-Cola Company Campaign: "Today I Will", Design
Emirates NBD Campaign: "ATM: Awesome Traveling Machine", Campaign: "The Beautiful After", Campaign: "The Culture Dispensing Machine", Creative
Harvey Nichols Campaign: "Influenced by None"
HP
Leatherman
L'Oreal
McDonald's; Sharjah
Microsoft
NCB (National Commerical Bank)
Purina Dog Chow
RAKBank
SmartLife Foundation Campaign: "Dream"
Sony Guld; Dubai Audio Products
Sony Campaign: "Big Day", Campaign: "Mean", Ericsson Xperia Arc, Handycam

United Kingdom

AllofUs
112-116 Old Street, London, EC1V 9BG United Kingdom
Tel.: (44) 20 7553 9250
Fax: (44) 20 7253 9648
E-Mail: studio@allofus.com
Web Site: www.allofus.com

Agency Specializes In: Digital/Interactive

Nick Cristea *(Co-Founder & Dir-Strategy)*
Phil Gerrard *(Mng Dir)*
Ricardo Amorim *(Dir-Creative)*
Michael Chase *(Dir-Creative Tech)*
Hana Sutch *(Dir-Ops)*
Jon Caplin *(Sr Designer)*
Sarah Hodges *(Sr Designer)*
Gemma Lane *(Sr Designer)*

McCann Erickson Advertising Ltd.
7-11 Herbrand Street, London, WC1N 1EX United Kingdom
Tel.: (44) 20 7837 3737
Fax: (44) 20 7837 3773
Web Site: mccannlondon.co.uk

Employees: 265
Year Founded: 1927

Agency Specializes In: Advertising

Rob Doubal *(Co-Pres & Co-Chief Creative Officer)*
Laurence Thomson *(Co-Pres & Co-Chief Creative Officer)*
Jamie Mietz *(Grp Head-Creative)*
Sanjiv Mistry *(Grp Head-Creative)*
Alba Berdala *(Acct Dir)*
Rob Brown *(Creative Dir)*
Melissa Cain *(Creative Dir)*
AJ Coyne *(Acct Dir)*
Kate Douglas *(Acct Dir)*
Adrian Finzelberg *(Creative Dir-Interactive)*
Anna Henderson *(Producer-Creative)*
Jean-Laurent Py *(Creative Dir)*
Andy Tannock *(Art Dir)*
Sarah Clift *(Dir-Creative-Intl)*
Lianne Galazka *(Dir-Art)*
Simon Hepton *(Dir-Creative)*
John Hurst *(Dir-Creative)*
Neil Lancaster *(Dir-Creative)*
Jay Phillips *(Dir-Art)*
Carl Rapp *(Dir-Art)*
James Rooke *(Dir-Art)*
Will Shepherd *(Dir-Creative)*
Duncan Slater *(Dir-Bus Dev)*
Charlotte Habin *(Acct Mgr)*
Andy Williams *(Acct Mgr)*
Dustin de Souza *(Designer)*
Thomas Keane *(Planner)*
Colin Lee *(Sr Designer)*
Jess Mallett *(Copywriter)*
Jim Nilsson *(Copywriter)*

Accounts:
The AA "Stop Jack Frost"
Aldi Stores Campaign: "Like Brands", Campaign: "Like Christmas With Aldi", Campaign: "Tomato Sauce", TV
American Airlines The Individual
Automobile Association
Bayer Alka Seltzer
Birmingham Tourism
Bistro
Black & Decker Ltd. Consumer Power Tools, Household, Outdoor Products
BMW Bikes
British Airways
Cannes Lions (Lead Creative Agency) 2015 Festival, Lions Festival, Press
Cereal Partners UK Clusters, Coco Shreddies, Digital, Frosted Shreddies, Golden Grahams, Honey Nut Cheerios, Lucky Charms, Multi-Cheerios, PR, Print, Shredded Wheat, Shreddies, TV
Coca-Cola Refreshments USA, Inc. Campaign: "Happiness Is Movement"
ComputerTan
Crackdown 2
Department of Health Creative
Evening Standard London Live TV
Fisher Price
Harrods
Homepride
Honey Shreddies
Kaspersky Lab Digital, Outdoor, Print, Social Media
Kraft Foods
LOCOG Campaign: "Oscar", Campaign: "Sport Like Never Before"
L'Oreal Campaign: "Go Louder", Campaign: "The Gold One", Casting, Catwalk to the Sidewalk, Cinema, Elnett Satin, Elseve, Freestyle, Glam Shine Reflexion., Maybelline, Perfection, Print, Studio Line, TV
Maestro
MasterCard UK BRITs My Priceless Gig, Campaign: "'Priceless Remakes", Campaign: "Mastercard Mother's Day Tactical", Campaign: "mother", Digital, Outdoor, Print, Social Media, Somethingforthefans.co.uk, TV
Microsoft Campaign: "Destiny", Campaign: "Kinect Star Wars App", MSN, Online, Press, XBox 360
Momondo
Nestle Nesquik, Shreddies
Nespresso Campaign: "Nespresso. What Else?"

New-Picturehouse Cinemas Creative
Premier Foods PLC Batchelors, Bisto, Campaign: "3 Little Pigs", Campaign: "The Together Project", Creative, Loyd Grossman, Sharwood
Sported Campaign: "Sport Can Change Everything"
Subway BBQ Chicken Temptation, Campaign: "Bruce", Campaign: "Janet", Campaign: "Keith", Campaign: "My Sub, My Way", Campaign: "Stay Picky", Digital, Outdoor, PR, Print, Radio, Subcard Loyalty Communications, TV
Toshiba Encore Campaign: "Look Closer. See More"
Unilever I Can't Believe It's Not Butter
New-Vauxhall

McCann Erickson Bristol

125 Redcliff St, Bristol, BS1 6HU United Kingdom
Tel.: (44) 117 921 1764
Fax: (44) 117 929 0603
E-Mail: fraser.bradshaw@europe.mccann.com
Web Site: www.mccannbristol.co.uk

Employees: 34
Year Founded: 1978

National Agency Associations: IPA

Dean Lovett *(CEO)*
Andy Reid *(Mng Dir)*
Patrick Fraser *(Head-PR)*
Claire Banks *(Dir-Digital Plng)*
Mike Vines *(Copywriter)*

Accounts:
Archery GB Media, National Series Finals, Performance Academies
Brut
Cathay Pacific Airways Above the Line, Branding, Creative, Media Relations, Public Relations, Social Media Strategy
David Salisbury Brand Strategy, Integrated Marketing, Media Relations
Goodyear
HiQ
Pink Lady Apples
SeaLife
Wadworth
Woburn Estates Abbey, Golf Club, PR, Safari Park

McCann Erickson Central

McCann Erickson House Highlands Road, Shirley, Solihull, West Midlands B90 4WE United Kingdom
Tel.: (44) 121 713 3500
Fax: (44) 1217133509
E-Mail: dean.lovett@europe.mccann.com
Web Site: www.mccannbirmingham.co.uk

Employees: 250
Year Founded: 1986

Agency Specializes In: Advertising

Dean Lovett *(CEO)*
Jonathan Jesson *(Chief Growth Officer)*
Iamie Buckingham *(Art Dir)*
Barrie Robinson *(Dir-Art)*
Harry Waine *(Designer)*

Accounts:
Avis Europe
Casio
Chiltern Railway
Daikin
E-Lites Campaign: "Dancing Baby"
Experian
Fuji
General Motors UK Vauxhall, Saab & Chevrolet; 2009
Hardys Wine Campaign: "Boots"
Hitachi
Ideal
ING
Mercedes Benz
Mitchells & Butlers
NHBC
Npower
OKI
Old Jamaica Ginger Beer
RWE Group
Siemens
Sunseeker Yachts
Volvo
Wavin
Westley Richards
Whitbread
Wiltshire Farm Foods Media
Yorkshire Building Society

McCann-Erickson Communications House Ltd , Macclesfield

Bonis Hall, Bonis Hall Lane, Prestbury, Cheshire SK10 4EF United Kingdom
Tel.: (44) 1625 8222 00
Fax: (44) 1625 8295 67
E-Mail: jim.rothnie@europe.mccann.com
Web Site: www.mccannmanchester.com

Employees: 260
Year Founded: 1927

Agency Specializes In: Advertising, Brand Development & Integration, Digital/Interactive, Direct Response Marketing, Media Planning, New Product Development, Public Relations, Telemarketing

Sue Little *(CEO)*
David Donaghue *(Mng Partner)*
Dave Price *(Exec Creative Dir)*
Graham Todd *(Grp Acct Dir)*
Neil Lancaster *(Creative Dir)*
Jennie Madden *(Acct Dir-PR & Social Media)*
Hana Sadat *(Acct Dir)*
Jamie Axford *(Dir-Art)*
Laura McKinlay *(Sr Acct Mgr)*
Tracey Harman *(Mgr-Talent & Dev)*
Rob Gorton *(Copywriter)*
Mick Craven *(Deputy Dir-Creative)*

Accounts:
Aldi "Chocolate Bunnies", Campaign: "Champagne", Campaign: "Endless Table", Campaign: "Gin", Campaign: "Like Brands", Low Fat Cereals, TV
American Airlines
Bargain Booze Campaign: "Doreen"
Britannia Sainsburys Bank
Farnell Element14, Pan-European Communications
Harveys Advertising, Creative, Offline, Online, Strategy
Intercontinental Hotels Group
New-JD Williams Jacamo
Jura
Npower Creative
Peugeot Media Planning/Buying, Public Relations
Pizza Hut Campaign: "Love It", Campaign: "Try It", Hot Dog Pizza
Portland Holidays Direct
Rugby League World Cup Sports Marketing
Sainsbury's Bank

McCann Erickson Worldwide

7-11 Herbrand Street, London, WC1N 1EX United Kingdom
Tel.: (44) 207 837 3737
Fax: (44) 207 837 3773
Web Site: mccannlondon.co.uk

Employees: 400

Agency Specializes In: Advertising

Alex Lubar *(CEO)*
Michael Darragh *(Mng Partner)*
Stephen Guy *(Mng Partner)*
Jon Marchant *(Mng Partner)*
Tom Wong *(Mng Partner-Bus Dev)*
Mike Longhurst *(Sr VP-Bus Dev)*
James Cross *(Grp Head-Creative)*
Nikki Crumpton *(Exec Dir-Plng)*
A. J. Coyne *(Acct Dir)*
David Frymann *(Dir-Plng)*
Irina Kondrashova *(Dir-Strategy)*
Lee Sanderson *(Dir-CRM & Affinity)*
Harjot Singh *(Dir-Strategy-Europe)*

Accounts:
Carlsberg Group Creative
Cheerios
Godolphin Media
Heart Research UK
MasterCard
Microsoft
Paxo Online, The Turkey Whisperer
Premier Foods PLC Batchelors, Bisto, Campaign: "Fred About The House", Homepride, Loyd Grossman, Sharwood's, TV
New-Statoil Marketing
Subway
Tempur
Unilever

Venezuela

McCann Erickson Publicidad

Av Francisco Solano Lopez entre Calles Negrin y Apamates Pisos 18, 1062-A, Sabana Grande Apartado, 68152 Caracas, Venezuela
Tel.: (58) 212 7612464
Fax: (58) 212 7611843
Web Site: www.mccann.com

Employees: 55
Year Founded: 1946

Agency Specializes In: Communications

Norberto Esposito *(Pres)*

Accounts:
Coselca/L'Oreal Cacharel, Dedicace, Elseve, Free Style, Guy Laroche, Imedia Performance, Studio Line
Goodyear Tires
Johnson & Johnson New Products, Reach Oral Care, Sanitary Napkins
Nestle Cereals Nestum, Rica-Chicha & Buitoni, Coffee Mate, Decaf
Unilever Tio Rico Ice Cream, Vasenol, Vasenol Hand & Nail Formula

Vietnam

McCann Erickson Vietnam

27 Le Thanh Ton Street, District 1, Ho Chi Minh City, SR Vietnam
Tel.: (84) 8 824 3296
Fax: (84) 8 824 1904
Web Site: www.mccann.com

Zimbabwe

Upton Fulton McCann Pvt. Ltd.

Building 6 Arundel Office Park Norfolk Road, Box 789, Mount Pleasant, Harare, Zimbabwe
Mailing Address:
PO Box 789 Mount Pleasant, Harare, Zimbabwe
Tel.: (263) 4 33 8418
Fax: (263) 4 33 8426
Web Site: www.mccann.com

Rick Fulton *(Mng Dir)*
Rumbidzayi Chiro *(Client Svcs Dir)*
Tsitsi Nyati *(Dir-Special Projects)*

MCCANN REGAN CAMPBELL WARD
622 Third Ave 22nd Fl, New York, NY 10017
Tel.: (646) 742-2100
Fax: (646) 742-2206
E-Mail: contact@rcw.com
Web Site: www.mccannrcw.com

Employees: 200
Year Founded: 1997

National Agency Associations: 4A's

Agency Specializes In: Advertising, Brand Development & Integration, Education, Health Care Services, Internet/Web Design, Medical Products, Newspapers & Magazines, Pharmaceutical, Trade & Consumer Magazines

Dan Hassan *(Exec Dir-Creative)*

Accounts:
Alexion
Allergan Inc.
American Academy of Family Physicians
Amgen
Daiichi Sankyo
Kowa/Lilly
Novartis Pharmaceuticals Inc.
Sigma-Tau Pharmaceuticals
Stroke Awareness Campaign: "Chokehold"

Branches

Regan Campbell Ward West
4747 Executive Dr Ste 1080, San Diego, CA 92121
Tel.: (858) 526-2400
Fax: (619) 209-4205
E-Mail: jeffrey.sweeney@rcw.com
Web Site: www.mccannrcw.com

Employees: 15
Year Founded: 2002

Agency Specializes In: Advertising, Education, Health Care Services, Internet/Web Design, Pharmaceutical

Jeff Sweeney *(Pres)*
Colleen Hindsley *(Exec VP & Dir-Client Svcs)*
Joni Honig *(VP & Acct Dir)*
Margaret Borchers *(VP & Sr Strategist)*
Kc Dickerson *(VP & Strategist-Digital)*
Vanessa Brown *(Mgr-HR)*
Meredith Krauter *(Acct Supvr)*
Fumiko Funatsubo *(Supvr-Art)*
Linda Enns *(Copywriter)*

Accounts:
Allergan/Inspire Pharmaceuticals

Medrageous
150 E 42nd St 16th Fl, New York, NY 10017
Tel.: (646) 742-2194
Fax: (646) 742-2206
Web Site: www.mccannrcw.com

Employees: 15

Agency Specializes In: Communications, Digital/Interactive, Medical Products

Dan Hassan *(Chief Creative Officer & Exec VP)*
Colleen Hindsley *(Exec VP & Dir-Client Svcs)*
Kent Chang *(Sr Dir-Interactive Art)*

Accounts:
Bayer Pharmaceuticals/Onyx Pharmaceuticals Nexavar
Bayer Schering Pharma AG PTK/ZK
Bayer Schering Pharma AG
Elan Pharmaceuticals Tysabri
Intel
Ligand Pharmaceuticals/Organon Pharmaceuticals USA Avinza
Novartis Reclast, Vildagliptin
Sigma-Tau Pharmaceuticals, Inc.
Valeant Pharmaceuticals International, Inc. Zovirax Cream, Zovirax Ointment

MCCANN TORRE LAZUR
Waterview Corporate Ctr 20 Waterview Blvd, Parsippany, NJ 07054-1295
Tel.: (973) 263-9100
Fax: (973) 263-4113
Web Site: www.mccanntorrelazur.com

Employees: 200

Agency Specializes In: Advertising, Health Care Services, Pharmaceutical, Sponsorship

Marcia Goddard *(Chief Creative Officer)*
Bill McEllen *(Pres-McCann Torre Lazur)*
Hilary Gentile *(Sr VP-Strategic Plng)*

Accounts:
Boehringer Ingelheim Diabetes Franchise
GlaxoSmithKline Advair, Arzerra, Avodart, Bexxar, Entereg, Hycamtin, Pazopanib, Rezonic, Tykerb, Veramyst
Novartis RAD, SBR759
Novartis Vaccines Aflunov, Agrippal, Begrivac, Fluad, Fluvirin, Optaflu
UCB Vimpat

Branches

Echo Torre Lazur
49 Bloomfield Ave, Mountain Lakes, NJ 07046
Tel.: (973) 257-3900
Web Site: http://www.mccannecho.com/

Agency Specializes In: Advertising

Beth Beck *(Mng Dir & Exec VP)*
Tracy Blackwell *(Mng Dir & Exec VP)*
Charlene Leitner *(Mng Dir & Exec VP)*
Juan Ramos *(Exec VP & Exec Dir-Creative)*
Kristy Huszar Caraballo *(Sr VP & Acct Dir)*
Jesse Johanson *(Sr VP & Dir-Strategic Plng)*
Francesco Lucarelli *(Sr VP & Dir-Strategic Plng)*
Hilary Gentile *(Sr VP-Strategic Plng)*
Lauren Lewis *(VP & Acct Dir)*
Scott Sisti *(VP-Customer Experience Architecture)*
Christopher Hefferon *(Head-Tech)*
Leonard Tafro *(Head-Tech)*
Deb Feath *(Assoc Dir-Art & Creative)*

Accounts:
Eisai/PriCara Aciphex
Galderma Differin, Epiduo, Metrogel, Oracea
GlaxoSmithKline Cervarix, Combivir, Epzicom, FluLaval, Fluarix, Lexiva, Relenza, Solzira, Trizivir; 2007
GlaxoSmithKline/Human Genome Science Belimumab
Oscient Antara, Factive

MCCANN WORLDGROUP
622 3rd Ave, New York, NY 10017
Tel.: (646) 865-2000
Fax: (646) 487-9610
E-Mail: contact@mccann.com
Web Site: www.mccannworldgroup.com

Employees: 23,000
Year Founded: 1997

National Agency Associations: 4A's

Agency Specializes In: Above-the-Line

Approx. Annual Billings: $18,700,000,000

Luca Lindner *(Pres)*
Nannette LaFond-Dufour *(Chief Client Officer)*
Rob Reilly *(Chm-Global Creative)*
Fernando Fascioli *(Pres-Latin America & Caribbean)*
Pablo Walker *(Pres-Europe)*
Mark Lund *(CEO-UK)*
Andrew Schirmer *(Exec VP & Mng Dir-McCann HumanCare)*
Matt McKay *(Exec VP & Exec Dir-Creative)*
Craig Bagno *(Sr VP & Grp Dir-Strategic Plng)*
Tracy Kurczaba *(Sr VP & Grp Acct Dir)*
Ji Watson *(Sr VP-Global Client Fin & Dir-Comml-APAC)*
India Woolridge *(Sr VP & Dir-McCann Truth Central)*
Shaheen Salimi *(VP & Acct Dir)*
Mat Bisher *(Exec Creative Dir)*
James Dawson-Hollis *(Exec Dir-Creative-Global)*
Martin Lever *(Exec Dir-Creative)*
John Mescall *(Global Creative Dir)*
Bill Wright *(Exec Dir-Creative-Global)*
Matt Swinburne *(Creative Dir)*
Stewart Alter *(Dir-Editorial)*
Sarah Watson *(Dir-Strategy-Global)*
Eric Monnet *(Mgr-Creative Network)*
Greg Masiakos *(Acct Supvr-Global)*
Steven Parsons *(Acct Supvr)*

Accounts:
Coca-Cola Refreshments USA, Inc.
General Mills, Inc. Campaign: "Amnesia", Campaign: "Inheritance", Campaign: "Murder", Campaign: "The Tiny & The Tasty", French Toast Crunch, Hello, Cereal Lovers, Pillsbury
General Motors Chevrolet
L'Oreal
MasterCard
Microsoft
Nestle
New-Tommee Tippee

Divisions

FutureBrand
233 Park Ave S Fl 2, New York, NY 10003
(See Separate Listing)

McCann Erickson Worldwide
622 3rd Ave, New York, NY 10017-6707
(See Separate Listing)

Momentum Worldwide
250 Hudson St, New York, NY 10013
(See Separate Listing)

MRM McCann
622 3rd Ave, New York, NY 10017-6707
(See Separate Listing)

McCann Torre Lazur
Waterview Corporate Ctr 20 Waterview Blvd, Parsippany, NJ 07054-1295
(See Separate Listing)

Weber Shandwick
909 3rd Ave, New York, NY 10022
(See Separate Listing)

MCCANN WORLDGROUP S.R.L

Via Valtellena 15/17, 20159 Milan, Italy
Tel.: (39) 02 85 291
E-Mail: milan@mccann.com
Web Site: www.mccann.com

Year Founded: 1959

Agency Specializes In: Brand Development & Integration, Customer Relationship Management, Digital/Interactive, Event Planning & Marketing, Public Relations

Paolo Boccardi *(Creative Dir-Digital)*
Marco Zilioli *(Art Dir)*

Accounts:
New-Fondo Ambiente Italiano

Branch

McCann Erickson Italiana S.p.A.

Via Libano 68/74, 00144 Rome, Italy
Tel.: (39) 06 500 991
Fax: (39) 06 5728 9350
E-Mail: eleonora.cinelli@mccan.com
Web Site: www.mccann.com

Employees: 15
Year Founded: 1959

Agency Specializes In: Public Relations

Joyce King Thomas *(Chm & Chief Creative Officer-McCannXBC)*
Alessandro Sabini *(Chief Creative Officer)*
Gaetano Del Pizzo *(Creative Dir)*
Stefano Tunno *(Art Dir)*
Alessandro Polia *(Dir-Art)*
Alessandro M. Sciortino *(Dir-Creative)*
Maria Vittoria Maccon *(Acct Exec)*
Milton Siclari *(Copywriter)*

Accounts:
Althea
FAO Global Petition Against Hunger, The 1 Billion Hungry Project
Gruppo Poste Italiane
Honda Europe SH 125 Mode DCT
L'Oreal
Menarini Youderm
New-Poste Italiane
Telethon
Unipol Banca

Affiliate

UM Italy

(Formerly McCann Erickson Italiana S.p.A.)
Via Valtellina 15/17, 20159 Milan, Italy
Tel.: (39) 02 0066041
Fax: (39) 02 801 207
Web Site: www.universalmccann.it

Employees: 50

Agency Specializes In: Media Buying Services

MCCLAIN MARKETING GROUP

70 Center St, Portland, ME 04101
Tel.: (207) 761-8372
Fax: (207) 780-0155
E-Mail: info@mcclainmarketing.com
Web Site: www.mcclainmarketing.com

Employees: 15

Agency Specializes In: Advertising

Approx. Annual Billings: $3,800,000

Sue-Ellen McClain *(Pres)*
Bob Perkins *(Dir-Creative)*
Paul Engel *(Acct Mgr)*

Accounts:
Dead River Company
Flotation Technologies

MCCORMICK COMPANY

701 S Taylor Ste 400, Amarillo, TX 79101
Tel.: (806) 374-5333
Fax: (806) 372-7040
E-Mail: info@mccormickcompany.com
Web Site: www.mccormickcompany.com

E-Mail for Key Personnel:
President: perrin@mccormickcompany.com

Employees: 100
Year Founded: 1926

National Agency Associations: 4A's-AAF-AMA-APA-BPA-MCA-NAMA-PAC-PRSA

Agency Specializes In: Advertising, Advertising Specialties, Agriculture, Brand Development & Integration, Business-To-Business, Communications, E-Commerce, Financial, Food Service, Graphic Design, Health Care Services, Magazines, Media Buying Services, Newspaper, Outdoor, Planning & Consultation, Print, Public Relations, Publicity/Promotions, Sales Promotion, Strategic Planning/Research

Approx. Annual Billings: $82,000,000

Breakdown of Gross Billings by Media: Adv. Specialities: $820,000; Audio/Visual: $820,000; Bus. Publs.: $3,280,000; Farm Publs.: $5,740,000; Fees: $19,680,000; Graphic Design: $8,200,000; Mags.: $820,000; Newsp.: $1,640,000; Outdoor: $820,000; Point of Purchase: $2,460,000; Print: $8,200,000; Pub. Rels.: $10,660,000; Radio: $2,460,000; Strategic Planning/Research: $10,660,000; T.V.: $4,100,000; Trade & Consumer Mags.: $820,000; Worldwide Web Sites: $820,000

Mark Perrin *(Owner)*
Fran Sheff-Mauer *(Partner)*
Penny Massey *(Sr Dir-Art & Designer)*
Sarah Bankert *(Sr Mgr-Mdsg Innovations)*
Sara Sajadi *(Product Mgr)*

Accounts:
AgriLaboratories Ltd.; Saint Joseph, MO Animal Health Products; 2001
Allflex USA, Inc.; Dallas, TX Livestock Data Tracking Systems; 1990
ASARCO Incorporated
Becker Underwood
Bell Helicopter Textron; Amarillo, TX; 2000
Cal Farley's Boys Ranch
Cook Composites and Polymers
E.I. du Pont de Nemours and Company
Elanco Animal Health
Elanco Companion Animal
Eli Lilly-Elanco; Greensfield, IN Cattle Health
Growth Enhancement Technology Information Team
IVY Natural Solutions
LendTrade, Inc.
Liberty Bank
National Pork Producers Council
PM Beef
Principal Bank; Des Moines, IA Online Bank Services; 2002
Sterling Technologies
United Sorghum Checkoff Program
Unverferth Manufacturing Co., Inc.
West Texas A&M University

Branches

McCormick Company

920 Main St Ste 1850, Kansas City, MO 64105
Tel.: (816) 584-8444
Fax: (816) 584-8310
E-Mail: lmayfield@mccormickcompany.com
Web Site: www.mccormickcompany.com

Employees: 52
Year Founded: 1989

National Agency Associations: 4A's

Agency Specializes In: Advertising, Sponsorship

Laura Mayfield *(Exec VP & Grp Dir)*
Sharon Polk *(Grp VP)*
Zach Tassell *(VP & Media Dir)*
Suzanne Levy *(VP-Acct Svcs)*
Patrick Sheridan *(Sr Dir-Art)*
Patricia Reese *(Media Dir-Ag)*
Lisa Feustle *(Dir-Package Dev)*
Lori Hollis *(Acct Mgr)*
Jeff Salyers *(Mgr-Mktg-Zatarain's Brand)*
Stephen Nottingham *(Grp Creative Dir)*
Lisa Siebert *(Sr Counselor-PR)*

Accounts:
AgriLabs
ASARCO Incorporated
Elanco Animal Health
Elanco Companion Animal
Ivy Natural Solutions
LendTrade Inc
Texas Cattle Feeders Association

McCormick Company

9245 Northpark Dr, Johnston, IA 50131
Tel.: (515) 251-8805
Fax: (515) 251-8909
E-Mail: info@mccormickcompany.com
Web Site: www.mccormickcompany.com

Employees: 28
Year Founded: 1993

National Agency Associations: 4A's

Justin Lobaito *(Head-Digital Creative)*
Dana Scheidegger *(Sr Dir-Art & Mgr-Creative)*
Mike Peterson *(Sr Dir-Art)*
Greta Lang *(Acct Svcs Dir)*
Jennifer Ruggle *(Dir-Digital)*
Janice Keene *(Mgr-Sls)*
Melissa Sudman *(Mgr-Traffic)*
Tiffany Obrecht *(Acct Supvr-Bus Dev)*
Evan Stadlman *(Acct Exec)*
Megan Arnold *(Acct Coord)*
Courtney Rude *(Acct Coord)*

Accounts:
AgriLabs
ASARCO Incorporated
Cal Farley's Boys Ranch
Cattlemen's Beef Board
Cook Composites and Polymers
E.I. du Pont de Nemours and Company
Elanco Animal Health
Elanco Companion Animal
National Cattlemen's Beef Association
PM Beef
West Texas A&M University

MCDANIELS MARKETING COMMUNICATIONS

11 Olt Ave, Pekin, IL 61554-6216
Mailing Address:
PO Box 729, Pekin, IL 61555-0729
Tel.: (309) 346-4230
Fax: (309) 346-2258
Toll Free: (866) 431-4230
E-Mail: info@mcdmarketing.com
Web Site: www.mcdanielsmarketing.com

E-Mail for Key Personnel:
Public Relations: bcalvin@mcdmarketing.com

Employees: 20
Year Founded: 1966

National Agency Associations: APA-MCA

Agency Specializes In: Advertising, Agriculture, Alternative Advertising, Brand Development & Integration, Business-To-Business, Corporate Communications, Corporate Identity, Education, Email, Event Planning & Marketing, Exhibit/Trade Shows, Financial, Health Care Services, Identity Marketing, Industrial, Internet/Web Design, Market Research, Media Relations, New Product Development, Public Relations, Publicity/Promotions, Retail, Strategic Planning/Research

Approx. Annual Billings: $7,000,000

Randy R. McDaniels *(Pres)*
Claudia McDaniels *(VP-Fin)*
Rod Standley *(Sr Dir-Art)*
Brenda Tomlinson *(Dir-PR)*

Accounts:
AgVenture; Kentland, IN; 2010
Illinois Soybean Association; Bloomington, IL; 1993
Innoquest; Woodstock, IL; 2009
Pekin Hospital; Pekin, IL; 1998
Rochelle Community Hospital; Rochelle, IL; 1998
Women's Center for Health; Pekin, IL; 1997
Lincoln Office
First Mid-Illinois Bank & Trust; Mattown, IL
Heritage Bank of Central Illinois
Preston-Hanley Funeral Homes; Pekin, IL
Ray Dennison Chevrolet; Pekin, IL; 1997

MCDONALD MARKETING
2700 Thomas Ave, Dallas, TX 75204-2641
Tel.: (214) 880-1717
Fax: (214) 880-7596
E-Mail: info@mcdonaldmarketing.com
Web Site: www.mcdonaldmarketing.com

Employees: 20

Kelly McDonald *(Owner)*
Sharon Griesing *(Dir-Media)*
Liliana Ramirez *(Dir-Strategic Plng)*

Accounts:
A-Affordable Insurance
InsureOne
Mattress Firm
Subaru

MCDOUGALL & DUVAL
24 Millyard #8, Amesbury, MA 01913
Tel.: (978) 388-3100
Fax: (978) 388-6700
E-Mail: dduval@mcdougallduval.com
Web Site: www.mcdougallduval.com

Employees: 13
Year Founded: 1995

Agency Specializes In: Trade & Consumer Magazines, Travel & Tourism, Yellow Pages Advertising

Dan Duval *(Owner)*
Peter Hale *(VP-Client Rels)*
Dianne Konon *(VP-Production Svcs)*
Julie Rotar *(Co-Dir-Creative)*
Mia Thurlow *(Co-Dir-Creative)*
Paige Moulton *(Acct Exec)*
Lori Martone *(Media Planner & Buyer)*
Deb Valenti *(Designer)*

Accounts:
Clinton Savings Bank
Extreme Adhesives

MCFRANK & WILLIAMS ADVERTISING AGENCY, INC.
266 W 37th St, New York, NY 10018
Tel.: (212) 531-5700
E-Mail: info@mcfrank.com
Web Site: www.mcfrank.com

E-Mail for Key Personnel:
President: mbruce@mcfrank.com

Employees: 35
Year Founded: 1968

Agency Specializes In: Advertising, Advertising Specialties, African-American Market, Bilingual Market, Brand Development & Integration, Broadcast, Business Publications, Business-To-Business, Cable T.V., Collateral, College, Commercial Photography, Communications, Consulting, Consumer Publications, Corporate Identity, Digital/Interactive, Direct Response Marketing, E-Commerce, Education, Electronic Media, Email, Engineering, Exhibit/Trade Shows, Graphic Design, Health Care Services, In-Store Advertising, Infomercials, Information Technology, International, Legal Services, Magazines, Market Research, Media Buying Services, Media Planning, Medical Products, Mobile Marketing, Newspaper, Newspapers & Magazines, Outdoor, Pharmaceutical, Planning & Consultation, Print, Production, Production (Print), Public Relations, Publicity/Promotions, RSS (Really Simple Syndication), Radio, Real Estate, Recruitment, Strategic Planning/Research, T.V., Technical Advertising, Telemarketing, Trade & Consumer Magazines, Transportation, Web (Banner Ads, Pop-ups, etc.)

Approx. Annual Billings: $15,000,000

Michael Bruce *(Founder & Pres)*
Mike Persaud *(Dir-Fin & Ops)*
Edward Lanigan *(Acct Mgr)*
Kevin Abdool *(Client Acct Mgr)*

Accounts:
Beth Abraham Health Services
Coca-Cola Refreshments USA, Inc.
GAF Manufacturing; USA Recruitment; 2000
Leap
McGraw-Hill
Schindler
UNM Hospital
Wackenhut
WorleyParsons Engineering

MCGAFFIC ADVERTISING & MARKETING
433 State Ave, Beaver, PA 15009
Tel.: (724) 774-6341
Web Site: www.mcgafficadvertising.com

Agency Specializes In: Advertising, Graphic Design, Internet/Web Design, Logo & Package Design, Print, Radio, Search Engine Optimization, Social Media, T.V.

David Stuber *(Acct Exec)*

Accounts:
Brighton Hot Dog Shoppe

MCGANN + ZHANG
1441 Bel Air Rd, Los Angeles, CA 90077
Tel.: (424) 256-2584
Fax: (424) 832-8579
E-Mail: info@mcgannzhang.com
Web Site: www.mcgannzhang.com

Year Founded: 2015

Agency Specializes In: Advertising, Digital/Interactive, Social Media

Geoff McGann *(Founder, COO & Dir-Creative)*
Yichi Zhang *(CEO)*
Nomin Boutchard *(Dir-Art)*
Armando Ceron *(Dir-Art)*

Accounts:
New-Air China
New-Los Angeles Coalition for Water Conservation

MCGARRAH JESSEE
121 W 6th St, Austin, TX 78701-2913
Tel.: (512) 225-2000
Fax: (512) 225-2020
Web Site: www.mc-j.com

Employees: 70
Year Founded: 1996

National Agency Associations: 4A's-AAF

Agency Specializes In: Advertising, Catalogs, Food Service, Internet/Web Design, Market Research, Package Design, Point of Purchase, Public Relations, Restaurant, Sponsorship

Approx. Annual Billings: $72,000,000

Breakdown of Gross Billings by Media: Cable T.V.: $592,553; Collateral: $9,237,429; Internet Adv.: $4,830,417; Newsp. & Mags.: $19,467,527; Other: $77,410; Out-of-Home Media: $11,968,809; Production: $884,895; Pub. Rels.: $904,585; Radio: $13,247,228; Spot T.V.: $6,792,139; Strategic Planning/Research: $2,535,438; Worldwide Web Sites: $663,008; Yellow Page Adv.: $798,562

Britton Upham *(Gen Mgr-Mktg & Integration)*
James Mikus *(Exec Dir-Creative)*
Brett Eaton *(Grp Acct Dir)*
Michael Anderson *(Dir-Creative)*
Tim Cole *(Dir-Creative)*
Melissa Fodo *(Dir-Content)*
David Kampa *(Dir-Design)*
Michel Lozen *(Dir-Media)*
Brian Wheelis *(Dir-Media Engagement)*
Andrea Cruz *(Acct Supvr)*
Nick Schulte *(Acct Supvr)*
Derek Bishop *(Copywriter)*
Colin Lapin *(Copywriter)*

Accounts:
Costa Del Mar Sunglasses; 2008
Costa Sunglasses 580P Sunglasses, Website
Cullen / Frost Bankers, Inc.
Frost National Bank Campaign: "Campaign: "Frost Bank - Switch Flowchart Transit Board"
Guitar Center Inc. Brand Development, Campaign: "Drums"
Haggar Clothing Co.
Shiner Beers Advertising, Messaging, Product Development
Spoetzl Brewery Campaign: "Episode 1 Characteristics", Shiner Beer, Shiner Beers 101 Packaging
Sun Mountain Golf
Sweet Leaf Tea Company Branding
Whataburger, Inc. Creative, Media Planning & Buying
Yeti Coolers Bass, Bear, Boulder, Bow hunter, Campaign: "Sword for a Nose", Catfish, Duck, Luchadores, Musky, Offshore, Quail

MCGARRYBOWEN
601 W 26th St, New York, NY 10001
Tel.: (212) 598-2900
Fax: (212) 598-2996

E-Mail: info@mcgarrybowen.com
Web Site: www.mcgarrybowen.com

Employees: 800
Year Founded: 2002

National Agency Associations: 4A's

Agency Specializes In: Advertising, Sponsorship

Approx. Annual Billings: $250,000,000

Gordon Bowen *(Founder, Chm, Chief Creative Officer & CEO-Intl)*
Maureen Falvey *(Grp Mng Dir)*
Peter Geary *(Mng Dir)*
Brian Horwitz *(Grp Mng Dir)*
Ida Rezvani *(Mng Dir)*
Brandon Cooke *(CMO-Global)*
Matthew Bull *(Chief Creative Officer)*
Phil Gaughran *(Chief Strategy Officer)*
Tom Sewell *(Chief Innovation Officer)*
Dante Piacenza *(Mng Dir-Content Production)*
Russell Lambrecht *(Exec Dir-Creative)*
Haydn Morris *(Exec Dir-Creative)*
Craig Cimmino *(Grp Dir-Creative)*
Oliver Dudley *(Grp Dir-Creative)*
Tuesday Poliak *(Grp Dir-Creative)*
Kevin Thoem *(Grp Dir-Creative)*
Frauke Tiemann *(Grp Dir-Creative)*
Kevin Gladwin *(Sr Dir-Art)*
Isaac Lindberg *(Sr Dir-Strategy-Digital & Emerging Platforms)*
Lindsey Schmidt *(Acct Mng Dir)*
Joey Ziarko *(Acct Dir & Acct Supvr)*
Malaika Danovitz *(Creative Dir-Copy)*
Adrienne DeGemmis *(Producer-Digital)*
Trent Dunlop *(Acct Dir)*
Jessica Murray *(Producer-Brdcst)*
Brian Mekjian *(Assoc Dir-Creative)*
Charlotte Housel *(Sr Strategist-Digital)*
Albert Gentry *(Acct Exec)*
Andrew Magrini *(Strategist-Digital)*
Megan Nickerson *(Acct Exec)*
Christa Santa-Donato *(Acct Exec)*
Matas Vilgalys *(Strategist)*
Katie Coe *(Asst Acct Exec)*
Amy Laughlin *(Asst Acct Exec-United Airlines)*
Judy Ocampo *(Asst Acct Exec)*
Janine Perry *(Jr Strategist-Digital-Verizon)*
Stephen Stallings *(Asst Producer-Music)*
Jessica Terlizzi *(Assoc Creative Dir-Art)*
Jessica Zalaznick *(Assoc Creative Dir-Copy)*

Accounts:
BAM
BlueCross Blue Shield Association; 2012
Brooklyn Academy of Music Campaign: "BAM and Then it Hits You", Campaign: "Crank Balls"; 2011
Cars.com Campaign: "ALFIE", Creative
Central Park Conservancy; 2009
Chevron Corporate Image Campaign; 2007
Crayola LLC Campaign: "A Hero Draws Near", Campaign: "Create 2 Destroy", Campaign: "Doodle Magic", Campaign: "Family Portrait", Campaign: "Marker Marker", Campaign: "Melt N Mold", Campaign: "See The Light", Campaign: "This Holiday, Get Creative", Crayola, Girlfitti; 2004
Disney Campaign: "Ursula", Disney Cruise Lines, Disney Parks & Resorts, Disney Vacation Club; 2005
Dr. Pepper/Snapple Group A&W, Campaign: "Cee Lo", Campaign: "Couple", Canada Dry, Creative Assignment, Hawaiian Punch, Sunkist, Welches
E-LAND
Fusion-io (Agency of Record)
Honda; 2012
Intel Corporation (Agency of Record) Campaign: "PC Does What", Creative, Online, Social Media, TV, Videos
New-J.C. Penney Company, Inc. (Creative Agency of Record)
KAO
Kraft Foods Group, Inc. Athenos, Boca, Campaign: "Sophisticated Snacking with Malcolm McDowell", Cheeses, Country Time, Crystal Light, Lunchables, Maxwell House, Oscar Mayer, Singles; 2006
Marriott International Broadcast, Campaign: "Cattle Drive", Campaign: "It's Not A Room, It's A Residence", Campaign: "Make Room for a Little Fun", Campaign: "Take Residence", Campaign: "Vikings", Campaign: "Yukon", Courtyard, Digital, Fairfield Inn, Marriott Rewards, Marriott Vacation Clubs, Residence Inn, Social Content, SpringHill Suites, TownePlace Suites, Website; 2003
Maserati Creative
Mondelez International, Inc. Chips Ahoy, Fig Newtons, Snackwells, Tassimo, Toblerone; 2006
Motorola Solutions, Inc. Campaign: "A Lot Can Happen in 48 Hours", Droid RAZR; 2009
NEC
Nestle Purina Alpo, Mighty Dog; 2013
Northrop Grumman; 2010
Procter & Gamble Aussie, Creative, Digital, Duracell, Social; 2012
Roundabout Theatre Company; 2011
Rust-Oleum Brands; 2010
Staples Advertising, Campaign: "Make More Happen", Campaign: "Staples Price Match Guarantee -- Tom Foolery", Creative, Online, Radio, TV; 2013
United Airlines (Agency of Record) Campaign: "Athletes Aboard" Winter Olympics 2014, Campaign: "Built Around You", Campaign: "Fly the friendly skies", Campaign: "Getting Ready", Campaign: "Orchestra", Campaign: "Satellite", Campaign: "Taxi", Creative, Digital, Out-of-Home, Print, Radio; 2011
United States Tennis Association US Open; 2013
Verizon Wireless Apophis 2029, Campaign: "48 Hours", Campaign: "A Lot Can Happen in 48 Hours", Campaign: "Catch Me If You Can", Campaign: "Football", Campaign: "Supercollider", Campaign: "The Fall with James Franco", Campaign: "Trick or Treat", Creative, Droid Razr, Droid Turbo, Innovation, NFL Mobile, Slice, Tablet, iPhone Trade-in Offer; 2009

Branches

mcgarrybowen
No 44 Ln 1285 Middle Huaihai Rd, Xuhui District, Shanghai, China
Tel.: (86) 21 6433 5099
E-Mail: info@mcgarrybowen.com
Web Site: www.mcgarrybowen.com

Simone Tam *(CEO)*
Jeffry Gamble *(Chief Creative Officer)*
Roland Zhu *(Mng Dir-Bus Dev)*
Andrew Poon *(Dir-Strategic Comm Plng)*

Accounts:
Mondelez International, Inc.
Weight Watchers International, Inc.

mcgarrybowen
515 N State St 29th Fl, Chicago, IL 60654
Tel.: (312) 840-8300
Fax: (312) 840-8396
E-Mail: info@mcgarrybowen.com
Web Site: www.mcgarrybowen.com

Employees: 50

National Agency Associations: 4A's

Agency Specializes In: Advertising, Sponsorship

Laurel Flatt *(Grp Mng Dir)*
Lisa Groot *(Grp Mng Dir)*
Ellen Oberman *(Grp Mng Dir)*
Ned Crowley *(Chief Creative Officer)*
Jeff Mccreesh *(Mng Dir-Ops)*
Kurt Fries *(Exec Dir-Creative)*
Michael Straznickas *(Exec Creative Dir)*
Shoshana Winter *(Exec Dir-Plng-Digital Integration)*
Ludwig Ortiz *(Grp Dir-Plng)*
Lee Remias *(Grp Dir-Creative)*
Kevin Thoem *(Grp Dir-Creative)*
Arturo Marconell *(Acct Mng Dir)*
Betsy Ross *(Acct Mng Dir)*
Sadie Schabdach *(Acct Mng Dir)*
Todd Brusnighan *(Creative Dir)*
Elizabeth Sandoval *(Acct Dir)*
Mike Wegener *(Dir-Art & Assoc Dir-Creative)*
Pat Burke *(Dir-Creative)*
William Cannon *(Dir-Creative)*
Anna Conroy *(Dir-Experience Plng)*
Marianne Newton *(Dir-Content Production)*
Carolyn Reilley *(Dir-Art)*
Steve Ross *(Dir-Content Production)*
Ryan Carter *(Assoc Dir-Creative)*
Brian Culp *(Assoc Dir-Creative)*
Rob Neveau *(Assoc Dir-Creative)*
Amy Henning *(Acct Supvr)*
Orchid Liu *(Acct Supvr)*
Jennifer Rake *(Acct Exec)*
Dani Wachter *(Acct Exec)*
Catherine Morrison *(Asst Acct Exec)*

Accounts:
Blue Cross & Blue Shield Association Consumer Brand Campaign, Creative
Cars.com Campaign: "All Drive. No Drama", Campaign: "Why drama?", Lead Creative, Super Bowl
Century 21
Chase
Chevron
Disney Campaign: "Together as One"
Emirates Airline U.S. Open Series of Tournaments
New-Fairfield Inn & Suites (Creative Agency of Record)
New-J.C. Penney Company, Inc. (Creative Agency of Record)
Kraft Foods Group, Inc. Boca, Campaign: "Dairy", Campaign: "Made", Campaign: "Miracle Whip and proud of it", Campaign: "Why", Crystal Light, Deli Deluxe, Kraft Mayo, Kraft Natural Cheese, Kraft Singles, Lunchables, Oscar Mayer, P3
Mondelez International, Inc. "#Tweet2Lease.", Campaign: "Makers of More", Campaign: "Twisted Minds", Campaign: "Village", Chips Ahoy, Fig Newtons, Kraft Barbecue Sauce, Kraft Mayonnaise, Kraft Salad Dressings, Kraft Singles, Lunchables, Maxwell House, Miracle Whip, Miracle Whip Dipping Sauces, Nabisco 100-Calorie Packs, Online, Oscar Mayer, Print, R, Smokin' Bacon Ranch, Social Media, TV, Triscuit, Wienermobile
New-Olive Garden (Creative Agency of Record)
Pfizer
Reaction
Rust-Oleum Campaign: "Never Seen This"
Sharp
U.S. Tennis Association Marketing
Wall Street Journal

mcgarrybowen
10 Hills Place, London, W1F 7SD United Kingdom
Tel.: (44) 02036405592
Fax: (44) 2075299099
E-Mail: info@mcgarrybowen.com
Web Site: www.mcgarrybowen.com

Year Founded: 2002

Agency Specializes In: Advertising, Brand Development & Integration, Customer Relationship Management, Digital/Interactive, Direct Response Marketing, Media Buying Services, Multicultural

Rick Hirst *(CEO)*
Robbie Black *(Head-Acct Mgmt)*
Paul Jordan *(Exec Creative Dir)*
Angus Macadam *(Exec Dir-Creative-London)*
Alice Tendler *(Bus Dir)*
Yury Vorobev *(Art Dir)*
Richard Dorey *(Dir-Creative)*
Mark McCall *(Dir-Creative)*
William Grave *(Copywriter)*
Michael McCourt *(Planner)*

Accounts:
Branston
New-Bridgestone
Canon Campaign: "Power to Your Next Step", PR, Social Media, Through-the-Line
Fujitsu Brand Marketing, Campaign: "Together We Can Make It Happen"
Honda Europe 2015 CR-V, CR-V 1.6 i-DTEC, Campaign: "An impossible, made possible", Campaign: "Endless Road", Campaign: "Illusions", Campaign: "Stepping", NSX Supercar
HouseTrip Creative
New-Intel
Mizkan "Chutney Mountain", Branston Chutney, Branston Pickle, Campaign: "Make it Special", Campaign: "The Apologist", Campaign: "The Fish and Chip Campaign", Creative, Haywards, Print, Sarson's, TV
Mondelez Tassimo
New-Pernod-Ricard
Scotts Miracle-Gro Campaign: "Say it with Flower Magic", Campaign: "Weeding Right Now", Flower Magic, Online, Pathclear Weedkiller, Social Media, TV, Weedol
Sky Bet Creative, Strategic
New-Western Union #ChainOfBetters

MCGILL BUCKLEY
2206 Anthony Avenue, Ottawa, ON K2B 6V2 Canada
Tel.: (613) 728-4199
Fax: (613) 728-6450
E-Mail: ideasmatter@mcgillbuckley.com
Web Site: www.mcgillbuckley.com

E-Mail for Key Personnel:
President: smcgill@mcgillbuckley.com
Creative Dir.: nbuckley@mcgillbuckley.com

Employees: 4
Year Founded: 1996

National Agency Associations: AMA-CMA

Agency Specializes In: Advertising, Bilingual Market, Brand Development & Integration, Business Publications, Business-To-Business, Collateral, Communications, Consulting, Consumer Marketing, Consumer Publications, Corporate Communications, Digital/Interactive, Direct Response Marketing, Education, Event Planning & Marketing, Financial, Food Service, Gay & Lesbian Market, Government/Political, Graphic Design, Health Care Services, High Technology, Industrial, Legal Services, Leisure, Logo & Package Design, Magazines, Media Buying Services, New Product Development, Out-of-Home Media, Planning & Consultation, Public Relations, Recruitment, Retail, Sports Market, Travel & Tourism

Approx. Annual Billings: $3,000,000

Breakdown of Gross Billings by Media: Collateral: $900,000; Mags.: $900,000; Newsp.: $1,200,000

Stephen McGill *(Pres & Dir-Creative)*
Nadine Buckley *(Dir-Creative Svcs)*

Accounts:
Atlific Hotels & Resorts; Montreal, Canada; 2001
Bruyere Continuing Care Healthcare; 2005
Canadian Centre on Substance Abuse; 2012
Holiday Inn Vancouver Downtown; Vancouver, British Columbia; 2003
Magnolia Hotel & Spa; Victoria, British Columbia; 2005
Marriott Chateau Champlain; Montreal, Quebec; 2003
Queensway Carleton Hospital; 2009
Saint John Ambulance Canada; 2004

MCGOLDRICK MARKETING
10 Burget Ave, Medford, MA 2155
Tel.: (781) 874-9553
E-Mail: newbusiness@mcgoldrickmarketing.com
Web Site: www.mcgoldrickmarketing.com

Year Founded: 2011

Agency Specializes In: Advertising, Digital/Interactive, Graphic Design, Internet/Web Design, Print, Radio, Social Media, T.V.

Jack McGoldrick *(Pres & Chief Creative Officer)*

Accounts:
NAACP

MCGOWAN CRAIN
5257 Shaw Ave Ste 201, Saint Louis, MO 63110
Tel.: (314) 446-6300
Fax: (314) 443-6301
Web Site: www.mcgowancrain.com

Agency Specializes In: Advertising, Brand Development & Integration, Digital/Interactive, Event Planning & Marketing, Logo & Package Design, Print, Social Media, T.V.

Todd Mcgowan *(Partner)*
Rommel Medrano *(VP & Dir-Client Rels)*
Jeff Braun *(Sr Dir-Art)*
Perry Tovrea *(Dir-Digital Strategy)*
Mini Johri *(Sr Acct Mgr)*
Maria Tovrea *(Sr Acct Mgr)*
Madeleine Flucke *(Acct Mgr)*
Jennifer Beidle *(Specialist-PR)*

Accounts:
Margaritaville Spirits
Michaels Bar & Grill
Sazerac Company, Inc.

MC/K-CP
(Formerly Mc/K Healthcare)
200 State St, Boston, MA 02109
Tel.: (617) 482-8228
Fax: (617) 482-4994
Web Site: www.mckcp.com

Employees: 23

Agency Specializes In: Advertising, Brand Development & Integration, Health Care Services, Strategic Planning/Research

Kathryn Wilson *(Acct Dir-CP Health & Wellness)*
Michael McLinden *(Dir-Practice)*

Accounts:
Frova
GLIADEL Wafer
Neupro Medical Services
Niravam
Orapred
TriLyte
Zyflo CR

MCKEE WALLWORK & COMPANY
1030 18th St NW, Albuquerque, NM 87104
Tel.: (505) 821-2999
Toll Free: (888) 821-2999
E-Mail: info@mwcmail.com
Web Site: www.mckeewallwork.com

E-Mail for Key Personnel:
President: smckee@mwcmail.com
Creative Dir.: bcleveland@mwcmail.com
Media Dir.: pwallwork@mwcmail.com
Public Relations: dfriedman@mwcmail.com

Employees: 25
Year Founded: 1997

Agency Specializes In: Advertising, Brand Development & Integration, Business-To-Business, Consumer Marketing, Health Care Services, Media Buying Services, Planning & Consultation, Restaurant, Retail, Strategic Planning/Research, Travel & Tourism

Approx. Annual Billings: $19,000,000

Steve McKee *(Pres)*
Pat Wallwork *(Partner & Dir-Media)*
Jonathan Lewis *(VP & Dir-Strategy)*
Dayna Melvin *(Dir-Fin)*
Dave Ortega *(Dir-Creative)*
Cara Garretson *(Assoc Dir-Media)*
Jasmyn Madison *(Mgr-Content Mktg)*
Katie Delorenzo *(Acct Exec)*
Kimberly Montoya *(Sr Media Buyer)*

Accounts:
Albuquerque Convention & Visitors Bureau
Cliff's Amusement Park
Dion's Campaign: "Street Team Car", Facebook App, Illustrations, Integrated Campaign, Posters, T-shirts, Website
Dwyer Group, Inc. Glass Doctor, Mr. Rooter
Food Packaging Institute
Fred Meyer Jewelers
International Paper Campaign: "Senseless Robot"
Kirtland Federal Credit Union
New Mexico Jiujitsu Academy Milton Poster, Poster Series
Porsche of Albuquerque Doll Poster, Porsche Bear Poster, Porsche Poster Series, Soldier Poster
St Louis Children's Hospital Campaign: "Heart Song Shoestring"
Tobacco Use Prevention Control
University of New Mexico
Wilderness Athlete Campaign: "Alien Yeti", Campaign: "Poster Series", Campaign: "Survival Kit", Campaign: "Wilderness Athlete Bear"

MCKENZIE WAGNER INC.
1702 Interstate Dr, Champaign, IL 61822
Tel.: (217) 355-9533
E-Mail: talk@mckenziewagner.com
Web Site: www.mckenziewagner.com

Agency Specializes In: Advertising, Brand Development & Integration, Collateral, Digital/Interactive, Internet/Web Design, Media Planning, Public Relations

Jill Wagner *(Pres & Dir-Media)*
Chad McKenzie *(Exec VP & Creative Dir)*
Todd Jones *(Producer & Copywriter)*
Matt Farrell *(Designer)*

Accounts:
First Federal Savings Bank

MCKIM
(Formerly McKim Cringan George)
5th Floor 211 Bannatyne Ave, Winnipeg, MB R3B 3P2 Canada
Tel.: (204) 284-2221
Fax: (204) 475-2469
E-Mail: info@mckimcg.ca
Web Site: www.mckimcg.ca

E-Mail for Key Personnel:
President: Peter.George@mckim.ca

Creative Dir.: Ron.Sawchuk@mckimcg.ca

Employees: 40
Year Founded: 1911

National Agency Associations:

Agency Specializes In: Advertising, Advertising Specialties, Agriculture, Automotive, Bilingual Market, Brand Development & Integration, Broadcast, Business Publications, Business-To-Business, Co-op Advertising, Collateral, Communications, Consulting, Consumer Marketing, Consumer Publications, Corporate Communications, Corporate Identity, Direct Response Marketing, E-Commerce, Electronic Media, Entertainment, Event Planning & Marketing, Exhibit/Trade Shows, Fashion/Apparel, Financial, Government/Political, Graphic Design, In-Store Advertising, Information Technology, Internet/Web Design, Local Marketing, Logo & Package Design, Magazines, Media Buying Services, New Product Development, Newspaper, Newspapers & Magazines, Out-of-Home Media, Outdoor, Pharmaceutical, Planning & Consultation, Point of Purchase, Point of Sale, Print, Production, Public Relations, Publicity/Promotions, Radio, Recruitment, Retail, Sales Promotion, Seniors' Market, Sports Market, Strategic Planning/Research, T.V., Teen Market, Trade & Consumer Magazines, Travel & Tourism, Yellow Pages Advertising

Approx. Annual Billings: $12,000,000

Breakdown of Gross Billings by Media: Collateral: 15%; D.M.: 5%; Event Mktg.: 5%; Internet Adv.: 5%; Logo & Package Design: 5%; Mags.: 5%; Newsp. & Mags.: 25%; Radio: 10%; Strategic Planning/Research: 10%; T.V.: 15%

Peter George *(Owner, Pres & CEO)*
Audra Lesosky *(VP-Accounts & Strategic Svcs)*
Ron Sawchuk *(VP-Creative Svcs)*
Glen Sapach *(Art Dir)*
Tamara Bodi *(Dir-PR & Social Media)*
Carey Pradinuk *(Assoc Dir-Creative)*
Tracy Fiett *(Sr Acct Mgr-Bus Dev)*

Accounts:
Federated Co-operatives Limited Media Only; 1991
Hudson Bay Mining & Smelting Co. Ltd.; 1994
Manitoba Club; 2003
Manitoba Floodway Authority; 2005
Manitoba Lotteries Corporation; 2005
Sport Manitoba; 2001
Travel Manitoba Tourism Marketing Campaign
University of Manitoba Asper School of Business, Department of Family Medicine, Faculty of Law; 2003
University of Winnipeg; 2004
Winnipeg Football Club; 2004

MCKINNEY

318 Blackwell St, Durham, NC 27701
Tel.: (919) 313-0802
Fax: (919) 313-0805
E-Mail: hello@mckinney.com
Web Site: mckinney.com/

Employees: 200
Year Founded: 1969

National Agency Associations: 4A's

Agency Specializes In: Automotive, Brand Development & Integration, Broadcast, Business-To-Business, Collateral, Communications, Consumer Marketing, Corporate Identity, E-Commerce, Financial, Graphic Design, Internet/Web Design, Local Marketing, Magazines, Newspaper, Newspapers & Magazines, Out-of-Home Media, Outdoor, Point of Purchase, Print, Production, Radio, Restaurant, Sponsorship, T.V.

Brad Brinegar *(Chm & CEO)*
Jim Russell *(Partner & Chief Digital Officer)*
Janet Northen *(Partner, Exec VP & Dir-Comm)*
Walt Barron *(Chief Strategy Officer)*
Laura Sudar *(Sr VP & Dir-Creative Ops)*
Josh Eggleston *(VP & Exec Producer)*
Stephanie Sumner *(VP & Dir-Bus Dev)*
Liz Paradise *(Exec Dir-Creative)*
C. J. Franzitta *(Grp Dir-Plng)*
Megan Wade *(Sr Producer-Interactive)*
Alex Nassour *(Art Dir)*
Elias Kakomanolis *(Dir-Creative Ops-NY)*
Cody Pate *(Dir-Art)*
Tom Holtz *(Acct Supvr)*
Alissa Sheely *(Acct Supvr)*
Melanie Wallace *(Acct Supvr)*
Kevin Murray *(Sr Acct Planner)*
Robyn Gunn *(Copywriter)*
David McClay *(Copywriter)*
Will Chambliss *(Grp Creative Dir)*
Will Dean *(Grp Creative Dir)*
Jordan Eakin *(Assoc Creative Dir)*
Mike Manganillo *(Grp Media Dir)*
Jenny Nicholson *(Grp Creative Dir)*
Meg Sewell *(Grp Creative Dir)*
Owen Tingle *(Grp Creative Dir)*

Accounts:
Abbott Laboratories Campaign: "Unstoppable Tour 'Boxing"
Above the Influence; 2007
Aprica, Osaka, Japan
Audi
Battle of the Bands
Big Boss Brewing Company Beercade, The Last Barfighter; 2007
Blue Ridge Orthopaedic Campaign: "We've Got Your Back!"
Bonterra Vinyard
Brown Forman Corp. Southern Comfort; 2006
Canines Inc. Dognition.com
CarMax, Inc. (Lead Creative Agency)
CenturyLink
Chambord; 2008
EAS AdvantEdge, Betagen, Campaign: "The Unstoppable Tour", Myoplex, Phospagen
ESPN Campaign: "Animals", Campaign: "Reveille", Golden Girls, SEC Network
Full Frame Film Festival
Gold's Gym
Lenovo Campaign: "Boot Or Bust", Campaign: "RapidBoot", Wild Reality Challenge
Meijer
Mentos Campaign: "Never Surrender"
The NASDAQ OMX Group, Inc.; New York, NY; 2001
Nationwide Insurance (Lead Creative Agency) Campaign: "Baby", Campaign: "Invisible", Campaign: "Join the Nation", Media Planning, Super Bowl 2015
Newell Rubbermaid
Nike; 2008
Old Town Athletic Club Campaign: "Unleash Your Inner Warrior!"
Partnership for a Drug-Free America
Piedmont Press & Graphics Campaign: "Think With Ink!"
Pro Shares; 2007
Qwest Communications; Denver, CO Campaign: "Ultimate Problem Solver", Campaign: "Wired Shaky iPad ad"; 2004
Radio Flyer (Agency of Record) Branding Campaign, Online Advertising, Print, Social Media
Ruby Tuesday, Inc.
Samsung Samsung Galaxy S6
The Sherwin-Williams Company Campaign: "Ask Sherwin-Williams", Campaign: "Color Chips", Chip It!, Color travels, HGTV HOME (Creative Agency of Record)
Southern Comfort; 2006
SUBWAY Restaurant Campaign: "Eggsical"
Tuaca
Twerrible Towel
Urban Ministries Of Durham Campaign: "Names For Change", Homeless Services, Spent
Virgin Mobile USA, Inc. Creative, Mobile Phone Service; 2007

Branch

McKinney New York

15 Watts St, New York, NY 10013
Tel.: (646) 380-5800
E-Mail: hello@mckinney.com
Web Site: mckinney.com

Employees: 40
Year Founded: 2013

National Agency Associations: 4A's

Agency Specializes In: Sponsorship

Kerry Fitzmaurice *(Mng Dir)*
Chris Kim *(Art Dir)*
Mary Liao *(Acct Dir)*
Alex Nassour *(Art Dir)*
Ryan Gardiner *(Acct Supvr)*
Dylan Meagher *(Copywriter)*
Zach Kohn *(Coord-Agency Comm)*
Will Dean *(Assoc Creative Dir)*

Accounts:
Crocs, Inc. (Global Advertising Agency of Record) Brand Positioning, Campaign: "Find Your Fun", Creative, Media Buying, Media Planning, Strategy
Hankook Tires
Perfetti Van Melle Campaign: "Never Surrender", Chewy Mint Rolls, Creative, Mentos
Samsung Activewash Top Load Washer, Campaign: "Crock", Campaign: "Crushing Dinner Parties with Samsung Home Appliances", Campaign: "Home for the Holidays", Campaign: "It Can Do That", Campaign: "The Next Big Thing Is Here", Galaxy Pro, Galaxy Tab S
Sennheiser Campaign: "Let Your Ears Be Loved", Urbanite Headphones
Sherwin-Williams Coastal Cool
ShredYourEx

MCKINNEY-CERNE ADVERTISING & PUBLIC RELATIONS

(Name Changed to Little L Communications)

MCLAREN MARKETING INC.

53 Mountain St, Saint Catharines, ON L2T 2S6 Canada
Tel.: (905) 680-8115
E-Mail: duncan@mclarenmarketing.com
Web Site: www.mclarenmarketing.com

Agency Specializes In: Internet/Web Design, Media Planning, Sales Promotion

Duncan McLaren *(Pres)*

MCLELLAN MARKETING GROUP

2330 Rocklyn Dr, Urbandale, IA 50322
Tel.: (515) 251-8400
Fax: (515) 251-3174
E-Mail: heyyou@mclellanmarketing.com
Web Site: www.mclellanmarketing.com

Year Founded: 1995

Agency Specializes In: Advertising, Brand Development & Integration, Graphic Design, Identity Marketing, Media Planning, Print, Public Relations, Social Media

Robin Blake *(Dir-Art)*

Karen Loehr *(Dir-Fin)*

Accounts:
Woodard Hearing Centers

MCMAHON MARKETING
413 N Flood Ave, Norman, OK 73069
Tel.: (760) 709-1214
Web Site: www.mcmkt.com

Year Founded: 2011

Agency Specializes In: Advertising, Crisis Communications, Event Planning & Marketing, Internet/Web Design, Logo & Package Design, Social Media

Korey McMahon *(Principal)*
Dane Heins *(Dir-Creative)*
Kalie Fry *(Mgr-Social Media)*
Amanda Krueger *(Designer-Visual Comm)*

Accounts:
First Oklahoma Construction Inc.

MCMILLAN GROUP
25 Otter Trail, Westport, CT 6880
Tel.: (203) 227-8696
Fax: (203) 227-2898
Web Site: www.mcmillangroup.com

Agency Specializes In: Advertising, Communications, Exhibit/Trade Shows, Graphic Design, Media Relations

Charles McMillan *(Pres)*

Accounts:
GE Healthcare
Sikorsky Aerospace Services

MCQUEEN MARKETING
3616 Harden Blvd Ste 340, Lakeland, FL 33803
Tel.: (863) 660-0782
Web Site: www.mcqueenmarketingllc.com

Agency Specializes In: Advertising, Media Planning, Media Relations, Print, Public Relations, Social Media

Mary Mcqueen *(CEO)*

Accounts:
Heacock Insurance Group, Inc.
Sessums Law

MDB COMMUNICATIONS, INC.
1150 18th St NW Ste 425, Washington, DC 20036
Tel.: (202) 835-0774
Fax: (202) 835-0656
E-Mail: info@mdbcomm.com
Web Site: www.mdbcomm.com

E-Mail for Key Personnel:
President: chatch@mdbcomm.com
Creative Dir.: rcoad@mdbcomm.com
Media Dir.: sniman@mdbcomm.com

Employees: 27
Year Founded: 1981

National Agency Associations: 4A's-AAF-PRSA

Agency Specializes In: Advertising, Brand Development & Integration, Broadcast, Business-To-Business, Cable T.V., Collateral, Communications, Consumer Goods, Corporate Communications, Digital/Interactive, Direct Response Marketing, Direct-to-Consumer, Education, Financial, Food Service, Graphic Design, High Technology, Hospitality, Information Technology, International, Internet/Web Design, Media Buying Services, New Product Development, Print, Production (Ad, Film, Broadcast), Production (Print), Public Relations, Publicity/Promotions, Radio, Real Estate, Restaurant, Sales Promotion, Strategic Planning/Research, T.V., Trade & Consumer Magazines, Travel & Tourism, Web (Banner Ads, Pop-ups, etc.)

Richard M. Coad *(Chief Creative Officer-Engagement)*
Seth Niman *(Dir-Media Strategy)*
Jodie Warren *(Dir-Campaign Mgmt)*
Joanne Williams *(Dir-Ops)*
O'Keyla Smith *(Sr Acct Exec)*
Bryson Welch *(Sr Media Buyer & Planner)*
Maria George *(Acct Coord)*

Accounts:
Boston Market
DC Lottery DC Daily 6; 2003
Destination DC Creative, Media Planning
Fannie Mae (New Product Launches, Research & Branding); 1998
Hunter Douglas; 2006
Loral Skynet; 2003
National Geographic; 1998
Politico
Prudential
Rapid Advance
ZebraTechnologies

MDC PARTNERS
45 Hazelton Avenue, Toronto, ON M5R 2E3 Canada
Tel.: (416) 960-9000
Web Site: www.mdc-partners.com

Employees: 12

National Agency Associations: 4A's

Agency Specializes In: Health Care Services, Pharmaceutical, Retail

Steve Pustil *(Vice Chm)*
Terence Donnelly *(CMO-Canada)*

Accounts:
Microsoft Xbox

MDC PARTNERS INC.
745 5th Avenue, New York, NY 10151
Tel.: (646) 429-1800
Web Site: www.mdc-partners.com

E-Mail for Key Personnel:
President: mnadal@mdccorp.com
Public Relations: wcampbell@mdccorp.com

Employees: 5,250
Year Founded: 1980

National Agency Associations: 4A's

Agency Specializes In: Advertising

Revenue: $1,223,512,000

Scott L. Kauffman *(Chm & CEO)*
Raffi Grigorian *(Mng Dir)*
Laura Cruz *(CIO)*
Lori Senecal *(Pres/CEO-MDC Partner Network)*
Mitchell S. Gendel *(Gen Counsel)*
Ryan Linder *(Sr VP-Strategic Growth)*
Khartoon Ohan *(Sr VP-Bus Dev)*
Matt Chesler *(VP-IR)*
Rachel Catalani *(Dir-Corp Brand Mgmt)*

Accounts:
Bud Lite
Mini

Branches

Allison & Partners
7135 E Camelback Rd, Scottsdale, AZ 85251
Tel.: (623) 201-5555
Fax: (480) 966-0111
E-Mail: sappel@allisonpr.com
Web Site: www.allisonpr.com

Employees: 12

Cathy Planchard *(Partner & Pres)*
Karyn Barr Amin *(Sr VP-Client Svc)*
Alan Weatherbee *(Sr VP-Talent Search)*
David Wolf *(Mng Dir-Global China Practice-Los Angeles)*
Cortney Read *(Acct Mgr)*
Laura Zilververg *(Acct Mgr)*
Amy Ohara *(Sr Acct Exec)*

Accounts:
Best Western International; Phoenix, AZ
Boost
GE Healthcare
Hasbro
International Game Technology; Las Vegas, NV Campaign: "Ghostbusters Slots Launch"
L'Oreal USA
Progressive
Samsung
Sony
YouTube

Allison & Partners
8880 Rio San Diego Dr Ste 1090, San Diego, CA 92108
Tel.: (619) 533-7978
Fax: (619) 543-0030
E-Mail: timw@allisonpr.com
Web Site: www.allisonpr.com

Brian Brokowski *(Gen Mgr)*
Jeannie Horner *(Acct Mgr)*
Jessica Fix *(Sr Acct Exec)*
Julia Yuryev *(Sr Acct Exec)*
Rebecca Buddingh *(Acct Exec)*
Erin Flemming *(Acct Coord)*

Accounts:
ARAMARK Parks & Destinations
Envision Solar International, Inc. (Agency of Record)
Healthcare Leadership Council
KPMG Corporate Finance
SONY
The Vitamin Shoppe

Allison & Partners
11611 San Vicente Blvd Ste 910, Los Angeles, CA 90049-6510
Tel.: (310) 452-7540
Fax: (310) 452-9005
E-Mail: dawn@allisonpr.com
Web Site: www.allisonpr.com

Employees: 15

Agency Specializes In: Public Relations, Sponsorship

Paul Breton *(Sr VP-Corp Comm Practice)*
David Wolf *(Mng Dir-Global China Practice)*
Emily Wilson *(VP-Consumer)*
Carline Jorgensen *(Gen Mgr)*
Dana Block *(Grp Acct Dir-Technology & Consumer Tech)*
Ashley Wallace *(Dir-Consumer)*
Marilyn Finegold *(Office Mgr)*
Elizabeth Villafan *(Asst Acct Exec)*
Nicole Walker *(Asst Acct Exec)*

Accounts:
ASICS America Corporation ASICS America Corporation

Allison & Partners
505 Sansome St 7th Fl, San Francisco, CA 94111-3310
(See Separate Listing)

Allison & Partners
71 5th Ave, New York, NY 10003
Tel.: (646) 428-0612
Fax: (212) 302-5464
E-Mail: info@allisonpr.com
Web Site: www.allisonpr.com

Employees: 15

Agency Specializes In: Advertising, Sponsorship

Thomas Smith *(Mng Dir)*
Lisa Rosenberg *(Chief Creative Officer)*
Matthew Della Croce *(Pres-Global Corp & Europe)*
Jonathan Heit *(Sr Partner & Pres-Americas)*
Linda Burns *(Sr VP-Media Rels)*
Kevin Nabipour *(Sr VP-Content Strategies)*
Alan Weatherbee *(Sr VP-Talent Search)*
Jenny Braga *(VP)*
Carolina Guana *(VP-Multicultural & Hispanic Practice)*
Jeremy Rosenberg *(Head-Digital)*
Anne Colaiacovo *(Sr Partner & Gen Mgr-New York)*
Cynthia Patnode *(Acct Mgr)*
Amanda Roark *(Sr Acct Exec)*
Cat Forgione *(Asst Acct Exec)*

Accounts:
Affinity
Airbnb Media
Apple
Aramark
Asics
B&G Foods, Inc. Consumer Public Relations, Marketing, Publicity Initiatives, Social Media
Best Western
Boost
Bulova Corporation Digital, Marketing Strategy
Dignity Health
Equity Residential
ForSaleByOwner.com Brand Awareness, Digital, Media, Social, Thought Leadership
GE Health Care
Gowalla
Hasbro
Intermedia Brand Awareness
Johnny Rockets
Joico; New York, NY (Agency of Record) Consumer Activations, Consumer PR, Digital Campaigns, Events, Media Relations, Partnerships, Product Launches, Social Media, Sponsorships
Kimpton Hotel Group
Loreal USA
PhRMA
PKWARE
Progressive
RetailMeNot (Public Relations Agency of Record)
Seventh Generation Public Relations, Social Media
TiVo, Inc.

Anomaly
536 Broadway 11th Fl, New York, NY 10012
(See Separate Listing)

Anomaly
The Old Ink Factory, 22 St James's Walk, London, EC1R 0AP United Kingdom
Tel.: (44) 207 843 0600
E-Mail: camilla@anomaly.com
Web Site: www.anomaly.com/en/call

Camilla Harrisson *(CEO & Partner)*
Oli Beale *(Partner)*
Alex Holder *(Partner-London)*
Stuart Smith *(Partner)*
Richard Lawson *(Mng Dir)*
Simon Robertson *(Head-Comm Strategy)*
Craig Ainsley *(Creative Dir)*
Renee Hyde *(Acct Dir)*
Ewoudt Boonstra *(Dir-Creative)*
Jenny Hudak *(Recruiter-Creative)*

Accounts:
Anti Tobacco League
Budweiser Campaign: "ToTheDream", Creative
Cancer Research UK (Lead Creative Agency)
Captain Morgan Creative
Converse Desire, Made By Facebook App
New-Diageo plc Campaign: "Joy Will Take You Further", Gordon's Gin (Global Creative), Johnnie Walker
Diesel
Gaydar Brand Identity
New-Lyst (Global Agency of Record) Communications Strategy, Creative, Media Planning; 2015
Sky Campaign: "Billy Bass", Fantasy Football
Thetrainline.com (Lead Creative Agency) Campaign: "I am train", Creative
Umbro
The Vaccines
New-Virgin Trains Campaign: "Be Bound For Glory"

Anomaly
46 Spadina, Toronto, ON M5V 2H8 Canada
Tel.: (647) 547-3440
E-Mail: catalent@anomaly.com
Web Site: www.anomaly.com

Year Founded: 2004

Agency Specializes In: Advertising, Brand Development & Integration, Digital/Interactive, Graphic Design, Media Planning, Social Media

Justin Barocas *(Founder & Partner)*
Jason DeLand *(Founder & Partner)*
Richard Mulder *(Founder & Partner)*
Johnny Vulkan *(Founder & Partner)*
Franke Rodriguez *(CEO & Partner)*
Mike Byrne *(Partner & Chief Creative Officer)*
Stuart Smith *(Partner)*
Ihxel Perez *(Head-Production)*
Kevin Filliter *(Sr Dir-Art)*

Accounts:
Anheuser-Busch InBev Bud Light, Corona: Discover your music
Belgian White
BMW Campaign: "MINI Roller Coaster", Campaign: "NOT NORMAL", Mini
Mexx Canada Inc

Antidote 360
160 Varick St, New York, NY 10013
(See Separate Listing)

Bryan Mills Iradesso Corp.
1129 Leslie St, Toronto, ON M3C 2K5 Canada
(See Separate Listing)

Civilian
(Formerly TargetCom, LLC)
444 N Michigan Ave 33rd Fl, Chicago, IL 60611-3905
(See Separate Listing)

Colle+McVoy
400 1st Ave N Ste 700, Minneapolis, MN 55401-1954
(See Separate Listing)

Concentric Pharma Advertising
175 Varick St 9th Fl, New York, NY 10014
(See Separate Listing)

CP+B
3390 Mary St Ste 300, Coconut Grove, FL 33133
(See Separate Listing)

Doner, London
(Formerly Doner Cardwell Hawkins)
60 Charlotte St, London, W1T 2NU United Kingdom
Tel.: (44) 20 7632 7600
E-Mail: talk@doner.co.uk
Web Site: www.doner.co.uk/

Employees: 45
Year Founded: 1995

Agency Specializes In: Advertising, Consumer Goods, Electronics, New Technologies

Nik Margolis *(Mng Partner)*
Nick Constantinou *(Mng Dir)*
Wayne Deakin *(Exec Creative Dir)*
Jenna Stafford *(Acct Dir)*
Nigel Carlos *(Dir-Social Media)*
Nick Gill *(Dir-Plng)*
Matt McMinn *(Dir-Bus Dev)*
Nick Scott *(Dir-Creative)*
Becky Griffiths *(Sr Acct Mgr)*
Ian Cawley *(Copywriter-Creative)*

Accounts:
Align Technology, Inc.
Discovery
Fiat Group Alfa Romeo, Campaign: "Made of Red", Chrysler, Digital, Giulietta, Jeep, MiTo, Online, Press, TV
Fuller's
Nikon Corporation
QVC
Wiltshire Farm Foods Taking Care of Mealtimes

Hello Design
10305 Jefferson Blvd, Culver City, CA 90232
(See Separate Listing)

HL Group
853 Broadway 18th Fl, New York, NY 10003
(See Separate Listing)

KBS+
(Formerly kirshenbaum bond senecal + partners Toronto)
340 King St East 5th Fl, Toronto, ON M5A 1K8 Canada
(See Separate Listing)

KBS+
(Formerly kirshenbaum bond senecal + partners)
160 Varick St 4th Fl, New York, NY 10013
(See Separate Listing)

MDC Partners
45 Hazelton Avenue, Toronto, ON M5R 2E3 Canada
(See Separate Listing)

Customer Relationship Management

mono
1350 Lagoon Ave, Minneapolis, MN 55408
(See Separate Listing)

Redscout LLC
28 W 25th St 10th Fl, New York, NY 10010
(See Separate Listing)

Source Marketing LLC
761 Main Ave, Norwalk, CT 06851
(See Separate Listing)

Team Enterprises, Inc.
110 E Broward Blvd Ste 2450, Fort Lauderdale, FL 33301
Tel.: (954) 252-1338
Fax: (954) 449-0275
E-Mail: info@teament.com
Web Site: www.teamenterprises.com

Employees: 105
Year Founded: 1993

Agency Specializes In: Sponsorship

Michael Shea *(Partner & VP)*
James Vicente *(VP & Mng Field Dir)*
Craig Ducker *(Sr Acct Dir)*
Letty Vargas *(Grp Acct Dir)*
john s. Cicero *(Dir-Trade Advocacy-Natl)*
Kate Page *(Dir-Comm)*
Jason Reece *(Dir-Info Tech)*
Pete Rodriguez *(Dir-Field & Production)*
Ron Williams *(Dir-Creative)*
Amanda Keller *(Mgr-Market-MillerCoors)*

Accounts:
Mondelez International, Inc.
U.S. Cellular Guerilla & Experiential AOR

Trapeze Media
174 Bloor St East, South Tower Ste 900, Toronto, ON M4W 3R8 Canada
(See Separate Listing)

Veritas Communications, Inc.
370 King St W Ste 800, PO Box 46, Toronto, ON M5V 1J9 Canada
Tel.: (416) 482-2248
Fax: (416) 482-2483
E-Mail: info@veritascanada.com
Web Site: www.veritasinc.com

Employees: 30

Krista Webster *(Pres & Partner)*
Martha McKimm *(Exec VP)*
Joe Chidley *(Sr VP)*
Martin McInally *(Sr VP)*
Kim Roman *(Grp VP)*

Accounts:
Art Gallery of Ontario Public Relations, Social Media
New-Best Buy Canada Public Relations
Bristol-Myers Squibb
Canada Dry Mott's
CBC Creative Counsel, PR, Publicity & Promotions, Strategy
Coty Canada PR
Expedia.ca
iShares
Microsoft Canada Cloud Technology, Media Relations, Office, Surface, Windows 8, Windows Azure, Windows Phone, Xbox
Ministry of Health
Pfizer
Subway Campaign: "Subway Commit to Fit"
Target
UNICEF Canada PR
Wind Mobile

Veritas Inc.
(Formerly Integrated Healthcare Communications, Inc.)
370 King St W Ste 800, Box 46, Toronto, ON M5V 1J9 Canada
Tel.: (416) 504-8733
Fax: (416) 504-8737
E-Mail: info@veritascanada.com
Web Site: www.veritasinc.com

Employees: 10

Krista Webster *(Pres & Partner)*
Ray Siu *(Sr VP-Fin & IT)*
Sue Kuruvilla *(VP-Consumer Brands)*
Lisa Pasquin *(VP)*
Libby Stunt *(Acct Dir)*
Sarah Micak *(Sr Acct Mgr)*
Laura Ballantyne *(Acct Mgr)*
Debbie Boyce *(Acct Mgr)*
Nicole Debartolo *(Office Mgr)*

VITRO
2305 Historic Decatur Rd Ste 205, San Diego, CA 92106
(See Separate Listing)

Yamamoto
(Formerly Yamamoto Moss Mackenzie)
252 First Ave N, Minneapolis, MN 55401
Tel.: (612) 375-0180
Fax: (612) 342-2424
E-Mail: sregan@go-yamamoto.com
Web Site: www.go-yamamoto.com

Employees: 30
Year Founded: 2000

National Agency Associations: 4A's

Shelly Regan *(Pres)*
Kathy McCuskey *(CEO)*
Stacey Davies *(CFO)*
Andy Thieman *(Exec Creative Dir)*
Jodi Beaupre *(Dir-Ops)*
Lori Sharbono *(Dir-Bus Dev)*
Attila Szabo *(Dir-Plng & Digital Solutions)*
Rachel Wood *(Mgr-Dev)*
Valerie Inglis *(Acct Supvr)*

U.S. Subsidiaries

72andSunny
12101 W Buffalo Creek Dr, Playa Vista, CA 90094
(See Separate Listing)

Assembly
(Formerly TargetCast tcm)
909 3rd Ave 31st Fl, New York, NY 10022
Tel.: (212) 500-6900
Fax: (212) 500-6880
Web Site: www.media-assembly.com

Employees: 80
Year Founded: 2002

National Agency Associations: 4A's-AD CLUB

Agency Specializes In: Advertising, Automotive, Broadcast, Business Publications, Business-To-Business, Cable T.V., Co-op Advertising, Communications, Consumer Marketing, Consumer Publications, Corporate Communications, Corporate Identity, Cosmetics, Education, Entertainment, Fashion/Apparel, Financial, Government/Political, Health Care Services, High Technology, Internet/Web Design, Leisure, Local Marketing, Magazines, Media Buying Services, Medical Products, Newspaper, Newspapers & Magazines, Out-of-Home Media, Outdoor, Pharmaceutical, Planning & Consultation, Print, Radio, Real Estate, Restaurant, Retail, Seniors' Market, Sponsorship, Strategic Planning/Research, Syndication, T.V., Teen Market, Telemarketing, Transportation, Travel & Tourism

Martin Cass *(CEO)*
Catherine Warburton *(Chief Investment Officer)*
Steve Minichini *(Chief Innovation Officer & Chief Growth Officer)*
Alan Smith *(Chief Digital Officer)*
Emil Panzarino *(Sr VP & Head-Biddable & Search)*
Sara Heydt *(Sr VP)*
Samantha Druss *(Head-Digital Mktg & Supvr-Interactive Comm)*
Casey Boyer *(Supvr-Integrated Comm)*
Sarah Davis *(Supvr-Integrated Comm-AMC)*
Jacqueline Smith *(Planner-DR)*

Accounts:
1-800-Flowers.com
AMC Entertainment Inc.
AMC Networks, Inc.
American Legacy Foundation Digital Media Planning & Buying, Traditional Media Planning & Buying
New-Audible, Inc. Analytics, Media Buying, Media Planning, Strategy
Edmunds Inc.
Elevate (Media Agency of Record) Digital Media Planning & Buying, Traditional Media Planning & Buying
Expedia, Inc. Media Buying, Media Planning
Fonterra Anchor, Tip Top
Gorton's
Hotels.com Media Buying; 2007
Hotwire, Inc. Broadcast, TV Buying
Illva
Janus Group
New World Pasta Company
NZI
Pfizer Consumer Healthcare
Pfizer, Inc. Advil, Advil Cold & Sinus, Advil PM, Alavert, Caltrate, Centrum, Centrum Cardio, Centrum Kids, Centrum Performance, Centrum Silver, Centrum Ultra, Chap Stick, Children's Advil, Pfizer, Inc., Preparation H, Robitussin, Robitussin.com, Thermacare
Rydex SGI (Agency of Record) Digital, Media, Print, Search
Sidney Frank Importing Co. Jacques Cardin Cognac, Jagermeister, Tommy Bahama; 2008
Sun-Maid Growers of California Sun-Maid Raisins; 2008
TIAA-CREF; New York, NY Financial Services, Media Planning & Buying; 2004
New-Timberland (Media Agency of Record); 2014
New-Travelocity US Media
UniGroup Inc.

The Bull-White House
220 E 23rd St No 1005, New York, NY 10010
(See Separate Listing)

Doner
909 N. Sepulveda Blvd, El Segundo, CA 90245-2724
Tel.: (424) 220-7200
Web Site: www.doner.com

Employees: 25

National Agency Associations: 4A's-AAF-DMA-PRSA

Agency Specializes In: Advertising, Digital/Interactive

Zihla Salinas *(Mng Dir & Exec VP)*
Jane Huetter *(Sr VP & Head-Strategic)*

Anita Anderson *(Sr VP & Acct Dir)*
Marlene Calderon *(Sr VP-Strategy & Plng)*
Maria Carr *(Sr VP)*
Brad Emmett *(Exec Dir-Creative)*
Matt Swanson *(Grp Dir-Creative)*
Michelle Musallam *(Sr Dir-Art)*
Kristie Bergmann *(Supvr-Local Brdcst)*
Tina Williams *(Sr Acct Exec)*
Jessye Hand *(Copywriter)*
Alexander Harvilla *(Planner-Strategic)*
Alicia Liken *(Copywriter)*

Accounts:
Arby's West
Avery Dennison Office Products Office & Consumer Products
Detroit Zoo
Fuhu, Inc. Advertising, Nabi Big Tab
Jafra International
Menchies
Minute Maid
Neato Robotics
Neato Campaign: "Card", Campaign: "Hippie Pinata", Campaign: "House Sitter", Campaign: "Neato Knows Your Grandma Misses You", Campaign: "One Night Stand"
Pac Sun
Secure Horizons
UPS Store

Doner
25900 Northwestern Hwy, Southfield, MI 48075
(See Separate Listing)

Doner
The Diamond Bldg 1100 Superior Ave 10th Fl, Cleveland, OH 44114
Tel.: (216) 771-5700
Fax: (216) 771-1308
Web Site: doner.com/

Year Founded: 1988

National Agency Associations: 4A's-AAF-DMA-PRSA

Agency Specializes In: Sponsorship

Liz Boone *(CMO & Exec VP)*
Jennifer Deutsch *(Exec VP & Gen Mgr-Cleveland)*
Sandy Croucher *(Sr VP & Head-Brand)*
Larry Deangelis *(Sr VP & Head-Brand)*
Brian Keir *(VP & Acct Dir)*
Paul Forsyth *(VP & Dir-Creative)*
Laura Owen *(VP & Dir-Creative)*
Pete Heid *(Exec Dir-Creative)*
Jason Tisser *(Assoc Dir-Creative)*

Accounts:
Geisinger Health System & Health Plan
OhioHealth

SEE Insight
55 Ivan Allen Jr Blvd Ste 350, Atlanta, GA 30308
(See Separate Listing)

Sloane & Company LLC
(d/b/a Sloane & Company)
7 Times Sq Tower 17th Fl, New York, NY 10036
(See Separate Listing)

Varick Media Management
160 Varick St, New York, NY 10013
(See Separate Listing)

MDG
13 Water St, Holliston, MA 01746
Tel.: (508) 429-0755
Fax: (508) 429-0766
E-Mail: info@thinkmdg.com
Web Site: www.thinkmdg.com

Employees: 14

Agency Specializes In: Advertising

Tim Merry *(Owner)*
Ann Merry *(Acct Svcs Dir)*
Ben Poulin *(Designer)*

Accounts:
Round Hill Hotel and Villas (Agency of Record)
Vita New York (Agency of Record)

MDVC CREATIVE INC.
121 Payne St, Dallas, TX 75207
Tel.: (214) 742-6382
Fax: (214) 742-6388
E-Mail: info@mdvccreative.com
Web Site: www.mdvccreative.com

Agency Specializes In: Advertising, Internet/Web Design, Media Buying Services, Media Planning, Public Relations

Molly Devoss *(Pres)*

Accounts:
New-Saint Rocco

MDW ADVERTISING SOLUTIONS INC
22454 Glass Ln, Punta Gorda, FL 33980
Tel.: (941) 875-9268
Web Site: www.mdwadvertising.com

Agency Specializes In: Advertising, Brand Development & Integration, Broadcast, Graphic Design, Internet/Web Design, Media Planning, Outdoor, Radio, Social Media

Maria Diaz-Williamson *(Owner)*
Joanne Donaldson *(Designer-Creative)*

Accounts:
Titanz Plumbing

ME CREATIVE AGENCY
287 Roosevelt Ave, Stratford, CT 6615
Tel.: (203) 572-1728
Fax: (256) 213-1975
E-Mail: info@mecreativeagency.com
Web Site: www.mecreativeagency.com

Year Founded: 2013

Agency Specializes In: Advertising, Brand Development & Integration, Graphic Design, Internet/Web Design, Logo & Package Design, Media Buying Services, Social Media

Marck E. Estemil *(Founder & Chief Creative Officer)*

Accounts:
Via New Media Inc

MEADSDURKET
502 10th Ave, San Diego, CA 92101
Tel.: (619) 688-5204
Fax: (619) 574-1644
E-Mail: mail@meadsdurket.com
Web Site: www.meadsdurket.com

Employees: 14
Year Founded: 2004

National Agency Associations: 4A's

Agency Specializes In: Advertising

Gary Meads *(Pres & CEO)*
Erin Bailey *(VP-Client Svcs)*
Carrie Jones *(VP-PR & Social Media)*
Tony Durket *(Dir-Art)*
Kevin Stout *(Assoc Dir-Creative)*
Michelle Wall *(Assoc Dir-Media)*
Kristen Tobiason *(Supvr-Production)*
Corrinne Bollendorf *(Acct Exec)*
Kimberly Cunningham *(Acct Exec)*
Mimi Kotter *(Project Supvr-Digital)*

Accounts:
Del Mar Racetrack
Hoehn Motors; 1984
ISE
MacroAir
Overland Storage; San Diego, CA Data Storage; 2005

MEANS ADVERTISING
4320 Eagle Pt Pkwy, Birmingham, AL 35242
Tel.: (205) 271-9980
Fax: (205) 271-5396
E-Mail: info@meansadv.com
Web Site: www.meansadv.com

Year Founded: 1993

Agency Specializes In: Advertising, Brand Development & Integration, Collateral, Digital/Interactive, Internet/Web Design, Logo & Package Design, Media Planning, Radio, Social Media, Strategic Planning/Research

Kevin Gustin *(VP & Dir-Creative)*
Andrea Catalano *(Dir-Media)*
Christina Helton *(Acct Mgr)*
Whitney Seitz *(Acct Mgr)*

Accounts:
Colonial Brookwood Village See you at the Village Campaign

MEC INTERACTION
1 Paris Garden, London, SE1 8NU United Kingdom
Tel.: (44) 20 7803 2000
Fax: (44) 20 7803 2018
Web Site: www.mecglobal.com

Employees: 40
Year Founded: 1994

Agency Specializes In: Digital/Interactive, Media Buying Services

Matt Bell *(Head-Digital Strategy)*
Nick Dobson *(Head-Digital Engagement)*
Richard Stanton *(Head-Digital Plng)*
Bedir Aydemir *(Grp Dir-Digital Ops)*
Nisha Patel *(Grp Dir-Digital Ops)*
Lafortune Mambu *(Acct Dir-Digital)*
Doyin Akindude *(Dir-Digital Plng)*
Lyndsay Broughton *(Dir-Digital Plng)*
Amanda Fahndrich *(Acct Mgr)*
Carly Quigley *(Acct Mgr-Digital)*
Cameron Vafaey *(Acct Exec-Digital)*

Accounts:
Canon
MBNA Campaign: "Making Life Easier", Media Buying, Media Planning
Nestle Digital Strategy, Volvic
ReactFast PPC

Branches

MEC Interaction
Via Carducci 14, 20123 Milan, Italy
Tel.: (39) 02 467 671

Fax: (39) 02 467 67344
E-Mail: info.mecmilan@mecglobal.com
Web Site: www.mecglobal.com

Employees: 150

Agency Specializes In: Electronic Media

Luca Vergani *(CEO)*
Alessandro Bartolini *(CFO)*
Giuseppe Romeo *(Mgr-Comm)*
Chiara Anselmo *(Supvr-Digital Media)*
Alessandro Ardemagni *(Supvr-Comm)*
Irene Carta *(Supvr-Digital)*
Walter Ferrari *(Supvr-Digital Media)*
Antonio Pianese *(Supvr-Digital-MEC Interaction Rome)*
Francesca Ugo *(Specialist-Digital Media)*
Andrea Buscemi *(Planner-Digital Media)*
Francesca D'Adda *(Planner-Digital Media)*
Maria Serena Lorenzoni *(Planner-Digital Media)*
Daniela Mangano *(Media Planner-Digital)*
Chloe Ripoche *(Planner-Digital)*

MECHANICA

75 Water St Level 2, Newburyport, MA 01950
Tel.: (978) 499-7871
Fax: (978) 499-7876
E-Mail: hello@mechanicausa.com
Web Site: www.mechanicausa.com

Employees: 15

Agency Specializes In: Brand Development & Integration

Jim Garaventi *(Founder, Partner & Dir-Creative)*
Libby Delana *(Founder & Partner)*
Arabella Plum *(Principal & Client Svcs Dir)*
Michelle Arsenault *(Brand Dir)*
Emily Grimes *(Brand Dir)*
Ted Jendrysik *(Dir-Creative)*

Accounts:
New-Akamai
American Heritage Dictionary You Are Your Words
Boingo Wireless
Brahmin Leatherworks
New-Bullhorn
Cheer Networks
Communispace
Fallon Community Health Plan
Healthy Child Healthy World
High Liner Foods Digital Marketing, In-Store, Online Advertising, Print Advertising, Sea Cuisine (Branding Agency of Record)
Houghton Mifflin
Kronos Inc.
LuckyVitamin
New-Neighborhood Health Plan Campaign: "Fear Out of Affordable", Marketing
New-Northeastern University
New-NPR
Nuance Communication Branding, Document Imaging Division
PATS Aircraft Systems
New-PBS
REM Technologies
Saucony (Agency of Record) Campaign: "Find Your Strong"
New-Schnucks
Student/Defend
Symantec
T-2 Biosystems
Time Inc.

MEDAGI DIGITAL AGENCY (US)

4493 3rd Ave, San Francisco, CA 94103
Tel.: (415) 890-6237

Employees: 12

Agency Specializes In: Advertising, Alternative Advertising, Branded Entertainment, Broadcast, Catalogs, Communications, Consumer Marketing, Digital/Interactive, Electronic Media, Electronics, Environmental, Exhibit/Trade Shows, Experience Design, Graphic Design, High Technology, International, Leisure, Local Marketing, Logo & Package Design, Luxury Products, Magazines, Media Buying Services, Media Planning, Media Relations, Media Training, Mobile Marketing, Multicultural, Multimedia, New Technologies, Newspaper, Newspapers & Magazines, Outdoor, Package Design, Print, Production, Production (Ad, Film, Broadcast), Production (Print), Social Media, Sports Market, T.V., Technical Advertising, Travel & Tourism, Web (Banner Ads, Pop-ups, etc.)

Approx. Annual Billings: $6,000,000

Marcus Silverdale *(VP-Mktg)*
David Zhou *(VP-Mgmt & Fin)*
Stephen Kaeppeler *(Gen Mgr)*
John Jacobson *(Dir-Art)*

Accounts:
Double Diamond Backcountry Gear; 2010

MEDDAUGH ADVERTISING INC.

12 Circuit St, Norwell, MA 02061
Tel.: (781) 659-9440
Fax: (877) 270-8856
Web Site: www.meddaugh.net

Year Founded: 1989

Agency Specializes In: Advertising, Broadcast, Exhibit/Trade Shows, Internet/Web Design, Print, Public Relations

John S. Meddaugh *(Founder & Pres)*
Deborah Meddaugh *(CFO & Dir-Creative)*

Accounts:
Microcut Inc.
Tech-Etch Inc.

MEDERGY HEALTHGROUP INC.

790 Township Line Rd Ste 200, Yardley, PA 19067
Tel.: (215) 504-5082
Fax: (215) 504-2916
E-Mail: lwright@medergygroup.com
Web Site: www.medergygroup.com

Employees: 30

Agency Specializes In: Health Care Services, Medical Products, Pharmaceutical

Suzann Schiller *(Exec VP-Strategic Collaborations)*
Debbie Feger *(VP & Dir-Creative Art)*
Bo Choi *(VP & Grp Supvr-Scientific)*
Kim Dittmar *(Assoc Dir-Scientific)*
Jennifer Hardy *(Acct Mgr)*
Tarah Nagel *(Acct Mgr)*
Erin Brant *(Assoc Acct Dir)*

THE MEDIA ADVANTAGE

414 E Michigan Ave Ste 1A, Lansing, MI 48933
Tel.: (517) 913-0100
E-Mail: info@themediaadvantage.com
Web Site: www.themediaadvantage.com

Agency Specializes In: Advertising, Brand Development & Integration, Graphic Design, Internet/Web Design, Print, Search Engine Optimization, Social Media

Scott VanGilder *(Partner & Creative Dir)*
Lauren Godlesky *(Copywriter)*

Accounts:
New-Giggling Grizzly
New-Lansing Parks & Recreation

THE MEDIA & MARKETING GROUP

Vorhees Town Center 220 Laurel Rd, Voorhees, NJ 08043
Tel.: (856) 782-6000
Fax: (856) 385-7155
Web Site: www.2mg.com

Employees: 300
Year Founded: 1994

Agency Specializes In: Production

Approx. Annual Billings: $5,000,000

Frank Palmieri *(Owner)*

Accounts:
Tropicana Casino & Resort

MEDIA & MORE, INC.

100 Trade Ctr, Burlington, MA 01803
Tel.: (781) 569-5410
E-Mail: glangham@mediaandmoreinc.com
Web Site: www.mediaandmoreinc.com

Employees: 5
Year Founded: 1999

Agency Specializes In: Direct Response Marketing, Media Buying Services, Planning & Consultation

Gloria Langham *(Dir-Media)*
Deborah Ring *(Mgr-Fin)*

Accounts:
Analog Devices
Fairchild Semiconductor

MEDIA ARCHITECTS ADVERTISING & DESIGN

11811 N Tatum Blvd Ste 3031, Phoenix, AZ 85028
Tel.: (602) 569-3435
Web Site: www.media-architects.com

Year Founded: 2001

Agency Specializes In: Advertising, Brand Development & Integration, Content, Digital/Interactive, Graphic Design, Internet/Web Design, Media Buying Services, Media Planning, Public Relations, Social Media

John Bevens *(Dir-Creative & Brand Mktg)*

Accounts:
Alcor Life Extension Foundation

MEDIA BRIDGE ADVERTISING

211 N 1st St Ste 325, Minneapolis, MN 55401
Tel.: (612) 210-9438
Web Site: www.mediabridgeadvertising.com

Agency Specializes In: Advertising, Media Buying Services, Media Planning, Print, Radio, T.V.

Jenny Veldkamp *(Controller)*
Maria Hileman *(Dir-Comm)*
Brandon Lanham *(Dir-Sponsorship & Sls)*
Michael Libman *(Dir-Bus Dev)*
Toni Villella *(Dir-Mktg)*

Accounts:
Renters Warehouse
Woodys Furniture

THE MEDIA CENTER

735 McArdle Dr Ste F, Crystal Lake, IL 60014
Tel.: (815) 455-3882
Fax: (815) 455-3904
E-Mail: bpintsak@themediactr.com
Web Site: www.themediactr.com

Employees: 20
Year Founded: 1981

Agency Specializes In: Internet/Web Design, Market Research, Planning & Consultation, Technical Advertising

Bill Pintsak *(VP-Mktg)*
Nancy Prioletti *(Sr Acct Exec)*

Accounts:
Air Products and Chemicals, Inc.
CCCR/CROWN
CENTA Corporation
Chicago Tag & Label
Coastal Hotel Group
Home State Bank
Lexington Healthcare, Inc.
The Lubrizol Corporation
Medtronic Corporation, Inc.
Motorola Solutions, Inc.
North Shore Trust and Savings
Viant, Inc.
Xpelair UK

MEDIA DESIGN

5569 Bowden Rd Ste 5, Jacksonville, FL 32216-8034
Tel.: (904) 636-5131
Fax: (904) 636-5322
Web Site: www.mediadesignjax.com

Employees: 6
Year Founded: 1999

Agency Specializes In: Advertising, Automotive, Cable T.V., Co-op Advertising, Consulting, Consumer Marketing, Direct Response Marketing, Event Planning & Marketing, Graphic Design, Internet/Web Design, Logo & Package Design, Media Buying Services, Newspaper, Outdoor, Planning & Consultation, Print, Publicity/Promotions, Radio, Sports Market, Strategic Planning/Research, T.V.

Keith Ferguson *(Pres)*

Accounts:
Florida Department of Transportation
Jiffy Lube

MEDIA ETC.

2222 Kalakaua Ave Ste 701, Honolulu, HI 96815-2516
Tel.: (808) 922-8974
Fax: (808) 922-8975
Web Site: www.mediaetc.net

Employees: 5
Year Founded: 1992

Agency Specializes In: Asian Market, Collateral, Commercial Photography, Communications, Direct Response Marketing, Media Buying Services, Planning & Consultation, Print, Production, Publicity/Promotions, Sales Promotion, Strategic Planning/Research

Chihiro Lykes *(Pres)*
Kayo Watari *(Treas)*
Mutsumi Matsunobu *(Mgr-Coordination & Writer)*
Yuko Porter *(Mgr-Production)*
Toshie Taniguchi *(Coord-Admin)*

Accounts:
Big Island Abalone Corp.
Canon USA
Hans Hedemann Surf School
Herb Ohta Jr.
Kaimana Kea
Koaloho Ukulele
Le Sportsac
Tanaka of Tokyo Restaurant

MEDIA HORIZONS, INC.

40 Richards Ave, Norwalk, CT 06854
Tel.: (203) 857-0770
Fax: (203) 857-0296
E-Mail: wchistoni@mediahorizons.com
Web Site: www.mediahorizons.com

Employees: 40

Agency Specializes In: Below-the-Line, Consumer Marketing, Consumer Publications, Customer Relationship Management, Direct Response Marketing, Direct-to-Consumer, Integrated Marketing, Magazines, Media Buying Services, Media Planning, Newspapers & Magazines, Over-50 Market, Print, Production (Print), Social Media, Strategic Planning/Research

Approx. Annual Billings: $6,490,000

Tom Reynolds *(Partner & Sr VP)*
Chris Varian *(VP & Creative Dir)*
Jill Arvanitis *(VP-Acct Mgmt)*
Claire Carpenter *(VP-Acct Svcs)*
Erica DePalma *(VP-Digital Mktg)*
LuAnn Romanillo *(Sr Dir-Production)*
Kathy Pond *(Art Dir-Digital)*
Heather Fogarty *(Dir-Digital Mktg)*
Cyrus Karimi *(Dir-Search Mktg & Audience Generation)*
Cheri Adami *(Mgr-HR)*
Katie Brown *(Mgr-Mktg Comm)*
Joanna Soulios *(Mgr-Corp Comm)*
Amy Lorenzen *(Sr Acct Exec)*
Jeremy Kraft *(Acct Exec)*

Accounts:
Bose
GreatCall
Lifestyle Lift

MEDIA II, INC.

2778 SOM Center Rd Ste 200, Willoughby, OH 44094
Tel.: (440) 943-3600
Fax: (440) 943-3660
E-Mail: mediaii@mediaii.com
Web Site: www.mediaii.com

Employees: 7
Year Founded: 1974

National Agency Associations: BPA

Agency Specializes In: Advertising, Advertising Specialties, Automotive, Brand Development & Integration, Business Publications, Business-To-Business, Co-op Advertising, Collateral, Communications, Consulting, Corporate Communications, Corporate Identity, Digital/Interactive, Direct Response Marketing, E-Commerce, Education, Electronic Media, Engineering, Event Planning & Marketing, Exhibit/Trade Shows, Graphic Design, Health Care Services, High Technology, Industrial, Infomercials, Information Technology, Internet/Web Design, Local Marketing, Logo & Package Design, Magazines, Marine, Media Buying Services, Medical Products, Merchandising, Multimedia, New Product Development, Newspapers & Magazines, Planning & Consultation, Point of Purchase, Point of Sale, Print, Production, Public Relations, Publicity/Promotions, Sales Promotion, Strategic Planning/Research, T.V., Technical Advertising

Approx. Annual Billings: $1,000,000

Breakdown of Gross Billings by Media: Collateral: $500,000; Consulting: $500,000

Roy W. Harry *(CEO & Dir-Creative)*

Accounts:
Automated Packaging Systems
Online Development; Knoxville, TN Automation Products; 2003
Ridge Tool
Rockwell Automation/Reliance Electric; Cleveland, OH Industrial Products; 1972
Siemens

MEDIA LOGIC

1 Park Pl, Albany, NY 12205
Tel.: (518) 456-3015
Fax: (518) 456-4279
E-Mail: mail@mlinc.com
Web Site: www.medialogic.com

Employees: 45
Year Founded: 1984

National Agency Associations: AAF-AMA-DMA-PRSA

Agency Specializes In: Advertising, Brand Development & Integration, Business Publications, Business-To-Business, Collateral, College, Communications, Consulting, Consumer Marketing, Corporate Communications, Corporate Identity, Digital/Interactive, Direct Response Marketing, Direct-to-Consumer, E-Commerce, Education, Electronic Media, Email, Event Planning & Marketing, Exhibit/Trade Shows, Financial, Graphic Design, Health Care Services, In-Store Advertising, Industrial, Integrated Marketing, Internet/Web Design, Logo & Package Design, Media Buying Services, Media Planning, Mobile Marketing, New Product Development, Out-of-Home Media, Outdoor, Over-50 Market, Planning & Consultation, Podcasting, Print, Public Relations, Publicity/Promotions, Radio, Recruitment, Sales Promotion, Search Engine Optimization, Sponsorship, Strategic Planning/Research, Sweepstakes, T.V., Technical Advertising

David M. Schultz *(Founder & Pres)*
Jim Sciancalepore *(VP & Sr Dir-Creative)*
Greg Johnson *(Sr Dir-Art & Dir-Design)*
Nicole Johnson *(Mgmt Supvr)*
Carol Ainsburg *(Dir-Studio Svcs)*
Patrick Boegel *(Dir-Media Integration)*
Jim McDonald *(Dir-Bus Dev)*
Christian Salmonsen *(Dir-Art)*
Silvy Lang *(Assoc Dir-Media)*
Carolee Bennett *(Sr Mgr-Social Content)*
Fred Ulrich *(Sr Acct Supvr)*
Vicki Venditti *(Sr Acct Exec)*
Cara Zambri *(Sr Acct Exec)*

Accounts:
Alloy Polymers
Barclay's
Bassett Healthcare; Cooperstown, NY
Cornell University-Johnson School
Excelsior College
Harvard Drug Group
Hofstra
JPMorgan Chase
Landmark College
Microbia (Agency of Record)
Moraine Valley
MVP Health Care; Schenectady, NY Campaign: "Project Go"
Orange Regional Medical Center
Penn Mutual
Senior Services of Albany (Pro Bono)

SI Group
Visa; San Francisco, CA Credit Cards
Webster

MEDIA MATCHED INC

9798 Coors Blvd NW C-305, Albuquerque, NM 87114
Tel.: (505) 431-4524
Fax: (505) 890-0743
Web Site: www.mediamatched.com

Agency Specializes In: Advertising, Graphic Design, Internet/Web Design, Media Buying Services, Public Relations, Social Media

Shelley Gregory *(Pres)*
John Gregory *(CFO & VP)*
Anthony Jio *(Acct Dir)*
Angelique Carrisal *(Dir-Art)*

Accounts:
Christus St. Vincent

THE MEDIA MATTERS INC

PO Box 1442, Lexington, NC 27293
Tel.: (336) 956-2488
Fax: (336) 956-3639
Web Site: www.themediamatters.com

Year Founded: 2000

Agency Specializes In: Advertising, Media Relations, Print, Promotions, Public Relations, T.V.

Kathy D. Wall *(Pres)*
Dawn Brinson *(VP-Strategic Mktg)*
Melissa Walter *(Office Mgr)*
Cathy Lloyd *(Specialist-PR)*

Accounts:
Hospice of Davidson County (Agency of Record) Advertising Strategy, Media, Public Relations, Social Media
Woodard Furniture Communications Strategy, Public Relations

MEDIA MIX

13901 Sutton Pk Dr S Bldg B Ste 400 4th Fl, Jacksonville, FL 32224
Tel.: (904) 294-6962
Fax: (904) 212-1227
Web Site: www.mediamixmarketingsolutions.com

Agency Specializes In: Advertising, Brand Development & Integration, Media Planning, Social Media

Natalie Dunlap *(Pres & CEO)*
Kyle Brumbley *(Creative Dir)*
Lia Galli *(Acct Exec)*
Justin Alley *(Acct Exec)*

Accounts:
New-Key Auto Group
New-McCall Service

MEDIA ON THE GO LTD.

1088 Bedford Ave, Brooklyn, NY 11216
Tel.: (718) 875-1808
Fax: (718) 689-1375
E-Mail: info@mediaotg.com
Web Site: www.mediaotg.com

Year Founded: 2006

Agency Specializes In: Advertising, Brand Development & Integration, Media Buying Services, Media Planning, Public Relations

Isaac Eidlisz *(CEO)*
Rivky Schwartz *(Acct Exec)*
Miri Friedman *(Designer)*

Accounts:
New-RCCS Rofeh Cholim Cancer Society
New-Tuscanini Foods

MEDIA ONE ADVERTISING/MARKETING

3918 S Western Ave, Sioux Falls, SD 57105
Tel.: (605) 339-0000
Fax: (605) 332-8211
E-Mail: info@m-1.com
Web Site: www.mediaone.com

E-Mail for Key Personnel:
President: john@m-1.com
Creative Dir.: greg@m-1.com

Employees: 9
Year Founded: 1974

National Agency Associations: AAF

Agency Specializes In: Crisis Communications, Financial, Food Service, Industrial, Medical Products, Social Media, Travel & Tourism

Greg Blomberg *(Partner)*
Rebecca Goeden *(Controller)*
Steve Brummond *(Sr Dir-Art)*
Eva Hofer *(Sr Dir-Art)*
Anne Allen *(Dir-Media Svcs)*
Anne Eidem *(Dir-Media Svcs)*
Shannon Mccoy *(Dir-PR)*
Bryon Middleton *(Dir-Audio & Video Svcs)*
Jason Shea *(Dir-Interactive Svcs)*
Brad Blomberg *(Acct Exec)*

Accounts:
Brown Clinic; Watertown, SD
Desco Industries; DeSmet, SD Building Components
Sioux Falls Area Chamber of Commerce
Sioux Falls Regional Airport

MEDIA PARTNERS, INC.

8150 E Douglas Ste 40, Wichita, KS 67206
Tel.: (316) 652-2210
Fax: (316) 652-2274
Web Site: www.mpiwichita.com

Agency Specializes In: Advertising, Brand Development & Integration, Collateral, Graphic Design, Media Buying Services, Media Planning, Outdoor, Print

Susan Bowers *(Owner)*
Becky Zeiner *(Media Buyer)*

Accounts:
Kansas Masonic Home (Agency of Record)
Mid America Exteriors
WKDE Radio (Agency of Record)

MEDIA RESPONSE, INC.

3201 Griffin Rd 3rd Fl, Fort Lauderdale, FL 33312
Tel.: (954) 967-9899
Fax: (954) 967-9321
Toll Free: (888) 801-9899
E-Mail: info@media-response.com
Web Site: www.media-response.com

Employees: 6
Year Founded: 1989

Agency Specializes In: Business-To-Business, Financial

Ellis Kahn *(Founder & CEO)*
Bruce Halkin *(Dir-Media)*

MEDIA RESULTS

10 Upton Dr, Wilmington, MA 01887
Tel.: (978) 658-4449
Web Site: www.mediaresults.com

Employees: 20
Year Founded: 1986

Agency Specializes In: Branded Entertainment, Broadcast, Cable T.V., Co-op Advertising, Collateral, Digital/Interactive, Direct Response Marketing, Email, Guerilla Marketing, Infomercials, Local Marketing, Mobile Marketing, Multimedia, Newspaper, Newspapers & Magazines, Outdoor, Paid Searches, Point of Purchase, Print, Production, Production (Print), Promotions, Radio, Search Engine Optimization, Social Media, Sponsorship, T.V., Web (Banner Ads, Pop-ups, etc.)

Andy Vallario *(Pres)*
Ron Le Blanc *(VP-Sls)*
Tricia Devine-freeman *(Dir-Sls-Natl)*
Daniel Milone *(Mgr-Digital Media & Media Buyer)*

Accounts:
Boch Automotive; 2006
Subaru of New England; 2006
Victory Automotive Group; 2009

MEDIA STRATEGIES & RESEARCH

8999 E Vassar Ave, Denver, CO 80231
Tel.: (303) 989-4700
Fax: (303) 989-1910
Web Site: www.mediastrategies.com

Employees: 10

Agency Specializes In: Media Buying Services

Jon Hutchens *(Pres)*
Karen Mallet *(Specialist-Comm)*

MEDIA TWO INTERACTIVE

111 E Hargett St Ste 200, Raleigh, NC 27601
Mailing Address:
PO Box 1119, Clayton, NC 27528-1119
Tel.: (919) 553-1246
Fax: (919) 882-9162
E-Mail: info@mediatwo.net
Web Site: www.mediatwo.net

E-Mail for Key Personnel:
President: mhubbard@mediatwo.net
Creative Dir.: rachel@mediatwo.net

Employees: 10
Year Founded: 1998

National Agency Associations: SEMPO

Agency Specializes In: Advertising, Affiliate Marketing, Brand Development & Integration, Broadcast, Business-To-Business, Cable T.V., Co-op Advertising, College, Consulting, Consumer Marketing, Corporate Identity, Customer Relationship Management, Digital/Interactive, Direct Response Marketing, Direct-to-Consumer, Education, Electronic Media, Email, Exhibit/Trade Shows, Financial, Graphic Design, Health Care Services, Integrated Marketing, Internet/Web Design, Investor Relations, Local Marketing, Logo & Package Design, Magazines, Media Buying Services, Media Planning, Medical Products, Mobile Marketing, Multimedia, Newspaper, Newspapers & Magazines, Paid Searches, Planning & Consultation, Print, Regional, Retail, Search Engine Optimization, Social Marketing/Nonprofit, Social Media, Strategic Planning/Research, T.V., Trade & Consumer Magazines, Web (Banner Ads, Pop-ups, etc.)

Breakdown of Gross Billings by Media: Consulting:

2%; Graphic Design: 8%; Internet Adv.: 90%

Michael Hubbard *(Founder & CEO)*
Seth Hargrave *(VP-Strategy & Ops)*
Heather Morrison *(Dir-Fin)*
Charlotte Rollins *(Assoc Dir-Strategy)*
Kelli Hashimoto *(Strategist-Media)*
Carly Wisse *(Strategist-Programmatic Media)*

Accounts:
3M DDS, Filtrete; 2009
D-Link Cloud Cameras & Routers; 2011
Glock Firearms; 2011
University of North Carolina Kenan-Flagler Business School; 2010
VectorVest Trading Software; 2010

MEDIA VISION ADVERTISING
10 Lagrange Rd, Campbell Hall, NY 10916
Tel.: (845) 294-3228
Fax: (845) 294-3493
E-Mail: info@mediavisionadvertising.com
Web Site: www.mediavisionadvertising.com

Year Founded: 2003

Agency Specializes In: Advertising, Brand Development & Integration, Event Planning & Marketing, Print, Radio, Strategic Planning/Research

James Danella *(Owner)*
Laura Danella *(Copywriter)*

Accounts:
Flannery Animal Hospital
Hudson Valley Kitchen Design & Remodeling
New-The Orange County Chamber of Commerce (Advertising & Public Relations Agency of Record)
Royal Pools & Spas

MEDIABOOM
96 Broad St, Guilford, CT 06437
Tel.: (203) 453-3537
E-Mail: info@mediaboom.com
Web Site: www.mediaboom.com

Year Founded: 2002

Agency Specializes In: Advertising, Brand Development & Integration, Content, Digital/Interactive, Internet/Web Design, Logo & Package Design, Print, Social Media, Strategic Planning/Research

Frank DePino *(Pres)*
Matt Mizerek *(Dir-Interactive)*

Accounts:
Bunk1
The Guilford Savings Bank

MEDIACROSS, INC.
2001 S Hanley Rd, Saint Louis, MO 63144
Tel.: (314) 646-1101
Fax: (314) 646-8795
E-Mail: mailbox@mediacross.com
Web Site: www.mediacross.com

E-Mail for Key Personnel:
President: markt@mediacross.com

Employees: 30
Year Founded: 1987

National Agency Associations: TAAN

Agency Specializes In: Advertising, Brand Development & Integration, Recruitment

Approx. Annual Billings: $6,000,000

Breakdown of Gross Billings by Media: Collateral: 25%; Consulting: 15%; D.M.: 15%; Event Mktg.: 15%; Fees: 10%; Print: 20%

Jennifer Umali *(CEO)*
Gretchen Borzillo *(Dir-Ops)*
Kevin Bennett *(Strategist-Acct & Media Buyer)*

Accounts:
The Army Reserve
Military Sealift Command; Virginia Beach, VA; 2002
Sprint

MEDIAFUEL
12574 Promise Creek Ln Ste 138, Fishers, IN 46038
Tel.: (317) 578-3399
Web Site: www.mediafuel.net

Year Founded: 2002

Agency Specializes In: Advertising, Brand Development & Integration, Digital/Interactive, Graphic Design, Internet/Web Design

Jeff Kivett *(Principal)*

Accounts:
James Dant

MEDIALINKS ADVERTISING
101 E Sandusky St Ste 322, Findlay, OH 45840
Tel.: (419) 422-7150
Fax: (419) 422-7520
Web Site: www.medialinksadv.com

Year Founded: 2005

Agency Specializes In: Advertising, Brand Development & Integration, Graphic Design, Internet/Web Design, Media Buying Services, Media Planning, Package Design, Print, Radio, Social Media

Jim Barger *(Partner & Acct Exec)*
Justin Franks *(Partner)*
Jeff Zellner *(Dir-Creative)*

Accounts:
Dicks Auto Supply

MEDIAMATH
415 Madison Ave 3rd Fl, New York, NY 10017
Tel.: (646) 840-4200
Web Site: www.mediamath.com

Agency Specializes In: Integrated Marketing

Erich Wasserman *(Co-Founder & Chief Revenue Officer-Global)*
Ari Buchalter *(Co-Pres)*
Michael Lamb *(Co-Pres)*
Joe Zawadzki *(CEO)*
Joanna O'Connell *(CMO)*
Roland Cozzolino *(CTO)*
Jeffrey W. Davis *(Sr VP-Corp Acctg & Reporting)*
Wilfried Schobeiri *(Sr VP-Tech)*
Fernando Juarez *(Mng Dir-LATAM)*
Dave Reed *(Mng Dir-EMEA)*
Jesse Parker *(Reg VP-Sls-East)*
Sam Cox *(VP-Open Global Media Partnerships)*
Saurabh Dangwal *(VP-Sls-APAC)*
Jake Engwerda *(VP-Sls-North America)*
Neil Fried *(VP-Corp Dev)*
Joey Hyche *(VP-Platform Solutions)*
Michael Cahan *(Dir-Sls)*
Robyn M. Diamond *(Dir-Bus Ops)*
Francisco Garcia *(Mgr-Platform Solutions- Latin America)*
Orlando Uribe *(Mgr-Platform Solutions-Latin America)*

Accounts:
American Express
General Mills
Prudential

MEDIAMIND TECHNOLOGIES INC.
(Name Changed to Sizmek)

MEDIAPLUS ADVERTISING
200-203 Catherine St, Ottawa, ON K2P 1C3 Canada
Tel.: (613) 230-3875
Fax: (613) 230-1458
E-Mail: info@mediaplusadvertising.com
Web Site: www.mediaplusadvertising.com

Employees: 23
Year Founded: 1984

Don Masters *(Pres & Dir-Creative)*
Jennifer Irwin *(VP)*
Christine Kincaid *(VP)*
Mark Skinner *(Sr Dir-Art)*
Grazyna Szawlowski *(Dir-Interactive Art)*
Aaron Vardon *(Sr Strategist-Media)*

Accounts:
Bluefest
Canada Post
CPAC
Glenn Briggs
Mermaid Pools
OCRI
Odutola
Rogers Television
Tartan
Tartan Homes
TIAC

MEDIATIVE
(Formerly Enquiro Search Solutions, Inc.)
1620 Dickson Ave Ste 410, Kelowna, BC V1Y 9Y2 Canada
Tel.: (250) 861-5252
Fax: (250) 861-5235
Web Site: mediative.com/

Employees: 35
Year Founded: 1999

Agency Specializes In: Search Engine Optimization

Darby Sieben *(Pres)*
Jon de la Mothe *(VP-Platforms & Tech)*
Frederick Ranger *(VP-Mktg)*
Pino Gatto *(Dir-Tech Ops)*
Karen Haughton *(Dir-Customer Experience)*
Brad Krieger *(Dir-Data Insights)*

Accounts:
1-800-Dentist
Academy 123
Business.com
New-CarCostCanada.com
Carson Dunlop
New-Dine.to
DS Waters
ID SuperShop
Kinaxis
Marketo
Siemens
SilkRoad Technology
New-ToutesAutosQuebec.com
VanillaSoft
YouSendIt

MEDIATREE ADVERTISING
PO Box 150069, Nashville, TN 37215

Tel.: (615) 496-7113
E-Mail: info@mediatreeadvertising.com
Web Site: www.mediatreeadvertising.com

Agency Specializes In: Advertising, Internet/Web Design, Media Buying Services, Print

Ryan Vinett *(Pres)*
Rachel Brannon *(Dir-Revenue Mgmt)*
Joe Stevens *(Dir-Web Dev)*

Accounts:
Lindemann Chimney Service

MEDIAURA INC
455 S 4th St Ste 808, Louisville, KY 40202
Tel.: (502) 554-9649
Web Site: www.mediaura.com

Year Founded: 2003

Agency Specializes In: Advertising, Content, Digital/Interactive, Graphic Design, Internet/Web Design, Logo & Package Design, Print, Social Media

Andrew Aebersold *(Founder & CEO)*
Rachel Burgess *(CFO & Acct Dir)*
Amy Aebersold *(COO)*
Ashley Blakemore *(Dir-Sls & Mktg)*
Dawn Geary *(Dir-Digital Mktg)*
Melissa McCarty *(Acct Exec)*
Mary Ragsdale *(Acct Exec)*
Lindsay Ramser *(Acct Exec)*

Accounts:
The Meadows

MEDIAVATION
1260 Mackay St Ste 200, Montreal, QC H3G 2H4 Canada
Tel.: (514) 935-8855
Fax: (514) 935-6894
E-Mail: info@mediavation.ca
Web Site: www.mediavation.ca

Employees: 15

MEDICUS LIFE BRANDS
1675 Broadway 5th Fl, New York, NY 10019-5820
Tel.: (212) 468-3100
Fax: (212) 468-3187
Web Site: www.plbmedicus.com

Employees: 598
Year Founded: 1972

Agency Specializes In: Communications, Health Care Services

Julie Spoleti *(Sr VP & Dir-Relationship Mktg)*
Cheryl Abbott *(Dir-Mktg)*
Wendy Bykowicz *(Supvr-Art)*
Marc Feil *(Grp Art Supvr)*

Accounts:
Bristol-Myers Squibb
Uroxatral

MEDIO SYSTEM, INC.
701 Pike St 15th Fl 1 Convention Pl, Seattle, WA 98101
Tel.: (206) 262-3700
Fax: (206) 262-3799
E-Mail: bd@medio.com
Web Site: www.medio.com

Employees: 40

Agency Specializes In: Advertising, Merchandising, Mobile Marketing

Revenue: $3,000,000

Robert P. Lilleness *(Pres & CEO)*
Jennifer Deonigi *(Dir-HR & Acctg)*

Accounts:
ABC News
Amazon.com
Berggi
CBS Sports
Novauris
Radar
T-Mobile US
Travel Zoo
Verizon Wireless

MEDTHINK COMMUNICATIONS
3301 Benson Dr Ste 400, Raleigh, NC 27609
Tel.: (919) 786-4918
Fax: (919) 786-4926
E-Mail: info@medthink.com
Web Site: www.medthink.com

Employees: 12
Year Founded: 2004

Agency Specializes In: Brand Development & Integration, Business-To-Business, Communications, Health Care Services, Logo & Package Design, Media Buying Services, Medical Products, Pharmaceutical, Print, Public Relations, Sales Promotion, Strategic Planning/Research

Scott Goudy *(Pres)*
Steven Palmisano *(Mng Dir & VP)*
Laura Perry *(Mng Dir & VP)*
Todd A. Parker *(Mng Dir-Scientific Svcs)*
Greg O'Donnell *(Grp Acct Dir)*
Edward Leon *(Acct Svcs Dir)*

Accounts:
Glenveigh
Inspire
Rosetta Genovics
Wilmington

MEDVEC-EPPERS ADVERTISING LTD.
4707 Hwy 61 N, Saint Paul, MN 55110
Tel.: (612) 436-1001
Fax: (612) 436-2846
E-Mail: info@medvec-eppers.com

E-Mail for Key Personnel:
President: jason.m@medvec-eppers.com

Employees: 6
Year Founded: 1994

National Agency Associations: ACA

Agency Specializes In: Brand Development & Integration, Business-To-Business, Consumer Marketing, Corporate Identity, Direct Response Marketing, Entertainment, Financial, Food Service, Graphic Design, Health Care Services, Hospitality, In-Store Advertising, Internet/Web Design, Logo & Package Design, Newspapers & Magazines, Outdoor, Point of Purchase, Point of Sale, Print, Radio, Restaurant, Retail, T.V.

Approx. Annual Billings: $1,500,000

Shawn Eppers *(Dir-Creative)*

Accounts:
Alerus Financial; Grand Forks, ND Financial Services; 2003
Cal Spas; Minneapolis, MN Hot Tubs, Spas; 2008
Jimmy's Salad Dressings & Dips; Stewartville, MN Consumer Packaged Foods; 2005
Marcum Technologies; Anoka, MN Outdoor Products; 1999

MEERS ADVERTISING
1811 Walnut St, Kansas City, MO 64108
Tel.: (816) 474-2920
Fax: (816) 474-2925
Toll Free: (800) 259-7346
E-Mail: info@meers.com
Web Site: www.meers.com

E-Mail for Key Personnel:
President: samm@meers.com

Employees: 16
Year Founded: 1993

National Agency Associations: 4A's-AMA-BMA-DMA

Agency Specializes In: Agriculture, Brand Development & Integration, Broadcast, Business Publications, Business-To-Business, Co-op Advertising, Collateral, Communications, Consulting, Direct Response Marketing, Health Care Services, Information Technology, Internet/Web Design, Medical Products, New Product Development, Planning & Consultation, Print, Production, Radio, Strategic Planning/Research, T.V., Trade & Consumer Magazines

Approx. Annual Billings: $12,000,000

Sam Meers *(Pres & CEO)*
Kathy Luetkenhoelter *(VP & Controller)*
Allisyn Wheeler *(VP-Channel Strategy)*
Dave Altis *(Exec Dir-Creative)*
Krisha Newham *(Client Svcs Dir)*
Lindsay Rankin *(Supvr-Channel Buying)*

Accounts:
Academy Bank Channel Planning & Buying, Creative, Digital, Marketing Communications Planning, Social Media Strategy
Armed Forces Bank Channel Planning & Buying, Creative, Digital, Marketing Communications Planning, Social Media Strategy
Children's Mercy Hospital; Kansas City, MO; 2004
Cobalt Ventures; Kansas City, MO; 2010
Great Plains SPCA
Husch Blackwell; Kansas City, MO; 2011
Kansas City Filmfest; Kansas City, MO; 2012
Kaufman Center for the Performing Arts; Kansas City, MO; 2011
Starlight Theatre; Kansas City, MO; 2011
Virtuous Living, LLC Brand & Identity Development, Digital Marketing, Marketing Communications Planning, Package Design, Social Media Strategy, Website Development
Wellmark Blue Cross Blue Shield; Des Moines, IA; 2011
Whole Person; Kansas City, MO; 2010

MEGA MEDIA ASSOCIATES, INC.
PO Box 4259, Newport Beach, CA 92661-4259
Tel.: (949) 673-2290
Fax: (949) 673-8382
E-Mail: info@megamediaassociates.com
Web Site: www.megamediaassociates.com

Employees: 4
Year Founded: 1978

Agency Specializes In: Consumer Marketing, Consumer Publications, Direct Response Marketing, Magazines, Media Buying Services, Newspaper, Newspapers & Magazines, Over-50 Market, Seniors' Market

Approx. Annual Billings: $3,000,000

Breakdown of Gross Billings by Media: Mags.: $2,500,000; Newsp.: $500,000

Stuart A. Cogan *(Pres & Treas)*
Sharon A. Cogan *(Sec & Exec VP)*
Sally Martindale *(Sr Acct Mgr & Media Buyer)*

Accounts:
Ace Home Employment Program
American Best Marketing Opportunities
CMS Video Opportunity
Computers Made Easy
David Bendah Opportunity
Demor-Rion Opportunity
Fast Track to Wealth Buyers
Information Brokerage Systems
Jenco Opportunity Seekers
Multi Money Makers
Opportunity Today
Profit Now Opportunity Seekers
Steamroller Publications
Target Opportunity Seekers

MEIER
907 Broadway 4th Fl, New York, NY 10010
Tel.: (212) 460-5655
Fax: (212) 460-5957
E-Mail: info@meierbrand.com
Web Site: www.meierbrand.com

Employees: 6
Year Founded: 1979

Agency Specializes In: Advertising, Consumer Goods, Retail

Approx. Annual Billings: $1,500,000

Diane Meier *(Pres)*

Accounts:
Chopard Watches and Fragrance
DeBeers
Elizabeth Arden
Georg Jensen
Kalkin & Co.
Neiman Marcus
Pierre Balmain
Willi Smith/WilliWear

THE MEIERHANS COMPANY
43 W 734 Old Midlothian Rd, Elburn, IL 60119-9662
Tel.: (630) 557-2575
Fax: (630) 557-2626
E-Mail: bob@themeierhans.com

Employees: 3
Year Founded: 1977

Agency Specializes In: Agriculture, Industrial, Local Marketing

Approx. Annual Billings: $1,000,000

Robert E. Meierhans *(Principal)*
Joy A. Meierhans *(VP)*

Accounts:
Colonial Cafe & Ice Cream; Saint Charles, IL Chain of 7 Family Restaurants
Energy Kinetics Inc.; Naperville, IL Natural Gas Vehicle Controls, Shock Absorbers
Farm Credit Services of Western Arkansas; AR Agricultural Financing

MEKANISM
(Formerly Mekanism, Inc.)
640 Second St 3rd Fl, San Francisco, CA 94107
Tel.: (415) 908-4000
Fax: (415) 908-3993
E-Mail: info@mekanism.com
Web Site: www.mekanism.com

Employees: 71
Year Founded: 2000

Agency Specializes In: Advertising, Alternative Advertising, Branded Entertainment, Broadcast, College, Computers & Software, Consumer Goods, Consumer Marketing, Content, Corporate Identity, Cosmetics, Digital/Interactive, Electronic Media, Electronics, Entertainment, Experience Design, Fashion/Apparel, Financial, Game Integration, Graphic Design, High Technology, Hispanic Market, Household Goods, Identity Marketing, In-Store Advertising, Industrial, Integrated Marketing, Internet/Web Design, Leisure, Local Marketing, Logo & Package Design, Magazines, Market Research, Media Buying Services, Media Planning, Men's Market, Mobile Marketing, Multicultural, Multimedia, New Product Development, New Technologies, Newspaper, Newspapers & Magazines, Out-of-Home Media, Outdoor, Package Design, Paid Searches, Podcasting, Point of Purchase, Point of Sale, Print, Production, Production (Ad, Film, Broadcast), Production (Print), Promotions, Public Relations, Publicity/Promotions, RSS (Really Simple Syndication), Radio, Regional, Restaurant, Retail, Sales Promotion, Search Engine Optimization, Sponsorship, Strategic Planning/Research, Sweepstakes, Syndication, T.V., Teen Market, Tween Market, Urban Market, Viral/Buzz/Word of Mouth, Web (Banner Ads, Pop-ups, etc.), Women's Market

Approx. Annual Billings: $26,000,000

Jason Harris *(Pres & CEO)*
Pete Caban *(Partner)*
Michael Zlatoper *(Mng Dir)*
Tommy Means *(Exec Dir-Creative)*
Anna Boyarsky *(Dir-Brand Mgmt)*
Melissa Hill *(Dir-Brand Mgmt)*
Daivd Horowitz *(Dir-Creative)*
Meagan Cotruvo *(Sr Brand Mgr)*
Claire Fallon *(Sr Brand Mgr)*
Emily Brody *(Brand Mgr)*

Accounts:
AB & Bev; 2013
Art.Com; San Francisco, CA; 2011
Ben & Jerry's Brrr-ito, Creative, Video
Charles Schwab; San Francisco, CA; 2010
Fortune Brands
GE; 2011
Google; 2012
Jim Beam (US Digital Agency of Record) Campaign: "#FiredUp", Campaign: "The Kentucky Standard", Campaign: "The Kentucky Tycoon", Campaign: "The Slow Burn", Kentucky Fire, Online, Social
LSI Inc. Broadcast, Campaign: "Wedding", Jack Link's
Method Campaign: "They Meet"; 2011
New-MillerCoors Henry's Hard Soda (Agency of Record), Redd's (Agency of Record), Smith & Forge (Agency of Record)
Muscle Milk; 2012
Nordstrom Rack (Agency of Record) Campaign: "Youphoria"; 2013
The North Face, Inc. Advertising, Campaign: "I Train For", Campaign: "Never Stop ______", Campaign: "Your Land", Digital, Experiential Marketing, Mountain Athletics, OOH, Online, Social, TV
PepsiCo Inc. Aquafina, Campaign: "For Happy Bodies", Campaign: "Halftime Touches Down", Campaign: "Little Can. Epic Satisfaction", Campaign: "Matt Forte gets Hyped for Halftime", Campaign: "Mini Hollywood", Campaign: "Nick Mangold gets Hyped for Halftime", Campaign: "Soundcheck NYC" Super Bowl 2014, Lil' Pepsi, Pepsi (Agency of Record), Super Bowl 2015, TV; 2010
Quirky; 2013
Skinnygirl (Agency of Record)
TaylorMade; 2013
New-Trulia Campaign: "A Different Kind of Housewarming", Campaign: "Gingerbread House Day", Creative, Digital
United States Government Campaign: "It's On Us", Creative, Design, PSA
Virgin Mobile USA, Inc.; 2011
White House Campaign: "It's on Us", Outdoor, Print

Branch

Mekanism
80 Broad St Fl 35, New York, NY 10004
Tel.: (212) 226-2772
Web Site: www.mekanism.com

Agency Specializes In: Advertising, Brand Development & Integration, Social Media, Sponsorship

Ian Kovalik *(Owner)*
Jason Harris *(CEO)*
Jason Lonsdale *(Chief Strategy Officer)*
Anna Boyarsky *(Dir-Brand Mgmt)*
Rick Thornhill *(Dir-Brand Mgmt)*
Cassie Jackson *(Sr Brand Mgr)*

Accounts:
New-It's On Us
New-Jim Beam
New-Nordstrom Rack
New-Skinnygirl

MELT
(Formerly Creative Presence Partners, Inc.)
3630 Peachtree Rd Ste 960, Atlanta, GA 30326
Tel.: (404) 812-1957
Fax: (404) 812-7072
E-Mail: info@meltatl.com
Web Site: www.meltatl.com

Employees: 25

Agency Specializes In: Advertising, Brand Development & Integration, Mobile Marketing, Retail, Sponsorship, Sports Market

Vince Thompson *(Pres & CEO)*
Michelle Grech *(COO)*
David Culbertson *(Chief Creative Officer & Sr VP)*
Travis Rice *(Acct Dir)*
Matt Capobianco *(Dir-Retail Svcs & Shopper Mktg)*
Doug Kroll *(Dir-Digital & Social Mktg)*
Jason Pressman *(Dir-Lifestyle Mktg)*
Sara Beth Davis *(Mgr-Community & PR)*
Lyndon McClusky *(Mgr-Event)*
Darbi Lou Todd *(Acct Exec)*
Daisy Venners *(Acct Exec)*

Accounts:
Coca-Cola Refreshments USA, Inc. Campaign: "It's Possible to Enjoy Everything", Coke Zero
Gold Peak
Maxim Magazine
Nissan
Roswell Food Group
Southern Creations Creative, Event Execution, Grit Chips, Packaging, Retail Promotions, Sampling, Social Media, Sponsorships
New-Thompson Tractor Company (Sports Marketing Agency of Record)

MENTUS
6755 Mira Mesa Blvd Ste 123, San Diego, CA 92121-4311
Tel.: (858) 455-5500
Fax: (858) 455-6872
Web Site: www.mentus.com

Employees: 15
Year Founded: 1981

Agency Specializes In: Corporate Identity, Direct Response Marketing, Financial, Health Care Services, High Technology, Information Technology, Internet/Web Design, Logo & Package Design, Medical Products

Approx. Annual Billings: $5,000,000

Guy Iannuzzi *(Pres & CEO)*
Audrey Miranda *(CFO, Exec VP & Gen Mgr)*
Tracy K. Mitsunaga *(Sr VP & Dir-Creative)*
Tom Okerlund *(Creative Dir)*
Gary Branch *(Dir-Production)*
Leasa Fisher *(Sr Acct Supvr)*
Janine Giambrone *(Acct Supvr)*
Dena Bahar *(Sr Graphic Designer)*

Accounts:
BioMed Realty Trust Inc.
Extra Space Storage Inc.

MEPLUSYOU
(Acquired by Moroch Partners)

MEPLUSYOU
12404 Park Central Dr Ste 400, Dallas, TX 75251
Tel.: (214) 224-1000
Web Site: www.meplusyou.com

Employees: 175
Year Founded: 1995

Agency Specializes In: Advertising, Brand Development & Integration, Branded Entertainment, Broadcast, Business Publications, Business-To-Business, Cable T.V., Catalogs, Children's Market, Collateral, College, Communications, Consumer Goods, Consumer Marketing, Consumer Publications, Content, Corporate Identity, Customer Relationship Management, Digital/Interactive, Direct Response Marketing, Direct-to-Consumer, E-Commerce, Education, Electronic Media, Email, Exhibit/Trade Shows, Experience Design, Fashion/Apparel, Financial, Graphic Design, Guerilla Marketing, Health Care Services, Household Goods, Identity Marketing, In-Store Advertising, Magazines, Market Research, Media Planning, Medical Products, Men's Market, Mobile Marketing, Multicultural, Multimedia, Newspapers & Magazines, Out-of-Home Media, Pets , Pharmaceutical, Planning & Consultation, Point of Purchase, Print, Production, Production (Ad, Film, Broadcast), Promotions, Publicity/Promotions, Radio, Restaurant, Retail, Search Engine Optimization, Seniors' Market, Shopper Marketing, Social Marketing/Nonprofit, Sponsorship, Sports Market, Strategic Planning/Research, Sweepstakes, T.V., Teen Market, Trade & Consumer Magazines, Transportation, Travel & Tourism, Tween Market, Viral/Buzz/Word of Mouth, Web (Banner Ads, Pop-ups, etc.), Women's Market

Approx. Annual Billings: $40,000,000

Colin Turney *(Pres & Chief Client Officer)*
Doug Levy *(CEO)*
Evelyn Henry-Miller *(CFO)*
Jason Shipp *(Grp Dir-Creative)*
Shawn Staley *(Assoc Dir-Creative)*
Chantal Sethi *(Acct Coord)*

Accounts:
The American Diabetes Association; 2000
Boehringer Ingelheim Oncology, Flomax, Dulcolax, Zantac; 2010
The Clorox Company Burt's Bees; 2009
The Coca-Cola Company Diet Coke, Coca-Cola, Corporate; 2007
Dendreon; 2012
GlaxoSmithKline; 2002
New-Haggar
Hillerich & Bradsby Louisville Slugger, Bionic; 2010
Houghton Mifflin Harcourt; 2012
New-Mary Kay
MoneyGram International; 2012
Novartis Pharmaceuticals; 2004
Omni Hotels & Resorts; 2003
Procter & Gamble Secret; 1997
Shire US; 2003
Verizon; 2012
Wells Fargo Small Business; 2012
World Vision International; 2009

MERCURY MAMBO
1107 S 8th St, Austin, TX 78704
Tel.: (512) 447-4440
Fax: (512) 447-5787
E-Mail: info@mercurymambo.com
Web Site: www.mercurymambo.com

Employees: 40

Agency Specializes In: Advertising, Co-op Advertising, Event Planning & Marketing, Hispanic Market, Market Research, Outdoor, Promotions, Retail, Sales Promotion, Sponsorship, Strategic Planning/Research

Becky Arreaga *(Partner)*
Liz Arreaga *(Partner)*
Carmen Murcia *(Dir-Event Mktg)*
Stephanie Beard *(Sr Mgr-Event)*

Accounts:
7-Eleven Inc. Grassroots Marketing, Hispanic, Promotion Efforts
7up
Anheuser-Busch
AOL
Budweiser
Crisco
Crown Royal
Crown Royale
Dr Pepper
Gibsuniel
Grande
Hungry Jake
Mondelez
Nike
Smuckers

MERCURY MEDIA, INC.
520 Broadway Ste 400, Santa Monica, CA 90401
Tel.: (310) 451-2900
Web Site: www.mercurymedia.com

Year Founded: 1989

Agency Specializes In: Direct Response Marketing, Sponsorship

Approx. Annual Billings: $275,000,000

Breakdown of Gross Billings by Media: Brdcst.: $100,000,000; Cable T.V.: $175,000,000

John L. Cabrinha *(Co-Chm)*
Dan Danielson *(Co-Chm)*
Andrew McLean *(CEO)*
Beth Vendice *(Pres-Performance Div)*
Cheryl Green *(Sr VP-Media)*
Ted Roderick *(VP-Bus Dev)*
Chrissy Ferrier *(Dir-Creative & Exec Producer)*
Jill Morris *(Assoc Dir-Media)*
Marcelino Miyares *(Acct Exec-Mercury en Espanol)*

Accounts:
Hoveround Corp. Wheelchairs
RedBrick Health; Minneapolis, MN Corporate Communications, Online Marketing, Public Relations, Social Media

MERCURY WERKS
15851 Dallas Pkwy Ste 1155, Addison, TX 75001
Tel.: (972) 993-3300
Fax: (972) 993-3319
E-Mail: johnm@mercury-werks.com
Web Site: www.mercury-werks.com

Agency Specializes In: Communications, Digital/Interactive, Direct Response Marketing, Email, Internet/Web Design, Media Planning, Search Engine Optimization, Strategic Planning/Research

Chip Gorman *(Sr VP-Insight & Plng & Gen Mgr)*
Mellisa Braden *(VP-Client Partnership)*
Alicia Richardson *(Acct Dir)*
Andi Karnes *(Dir-Print Production)*
Kortni Harris *(Sr Acct Exec-Client Partnership)*
Stacy Krumholz *(Sr Acct Exec)*
Tory Lane *(Sr Acct Exec)*
Lindsey Rosenfeld *(Sr Acct Exec)*
Callie Hurmis *(Acct Exec)*

Accounts:
Arby's Restaurant Group, Inc. (Print Agency of Record) Marketing, Media Planning, Online
AT&T Communications Corp.
Bennigans
Credit Free Life Business Services
Fed EX
Ford
Frito Lay
Hilton Worldwide
Holiday Inn
LensCrafters

MERCURYCSC
(Formerly Mercury Advertising)
22 S Grand Ave, Bozeman, MT 59715
Tel.: (406) 586-2280
Fax: (406) 586-2685
E-Mail: jeff.welch@mercurycsc.com
Web Site: www.mercurycsc.com

Employees: 20

Agency Specializes In: Travel & Tourism

Jeff Welch *(Pres)*
Mike Geraci *(Chief Creative Officer)*
Maclaren Latta *(VP-Consumer Insights)*
Tanya White *(VP-Fin & HR)*
Donnie Clapp *(Dir-Emerging Media)*
Nathan Hanna *(Dir-Art)*
Seth Neilson *(Dir-Creative)*
Jeremy Sandlin *(Dir-Interactive Art)*
Tara Vetrone *(Office Mgr)*
Molly Ambrogi-Yanson *(Mgr-PR & Earned Media)*
Katie Coyle *(Mgr-Insights & Acct)*
Megan Ault Regnerus *(Mgr-Comm)*
Rachel Stevens *(Mgr-Digital Comm)*

Accounts:
First Interstate Bank
Great Falls Clinic
Mackenzie River Pizza Co.
Montana Office of Tourism
Montana Tourism

MEREDITH COMMUNICATIONS
10151 University Blvd 163, Orlando, FL 32817
Tel.: (321) 285-1660
Fax: (321) 226-0246
E-Mail: meredith@creatingwow.com
Web Site: www.creatingwow.com

Agency Specializes In: Email, Internet/Web Design, Search Engine Optimization, Strategic

Planning/Research

Meredith Oliver *(Pres)*
Joe Ceryanec *(CFO & VP)*
Allen C. Oliver *(CFO)*
John Zieser *(Chief Dev Officer & Gen Counsel)*
Tom Harty *(Pres-Meredith Natl Media Grp)*
Paul Karpowicz *(Pres-Meredith Local Media Grp)*

Accounts:
Gallery Homes of Deland Inc Residential Construction Services
Red Door Homes Residential Construction Services
The Tribute Lakeside Golf & Resort Community Residential & Golf Development Services
Wynne Jackson Real Estate Development Services

MEREDITH XCELERATED MARKETING
800 Corporate Pointe, Culver City, CA 90230
Tel.: (424) 672-9500
Web Site: meredithxceleratedmarketing.com

Employees: 80

Agency Specializes In: Advertising, Integrated Marketing, Magazines

Martin Reidy *(Pres & CEO)*
Tony Platt *(Chief Creative Officer)*
Kristi D. VandenBosch *(Chief Digital Officer)*
Georgine Anton *(Exec VP)*
Quentin Walz *(VP-Interactive Sls)*
Dan Rubin *(Exec Dir-Strategy)*

Accounts:
Chrysler
The Home Depot
Hyundai
Kraft
Mitsubishi North America
Procter & Gamble

MERIDIAN - CHILES
921 Beasley St Ste 140, Lexington, KY 40509
Tel.: (859) 252-3350
Fax: (859) 299-7999
Toll Free: (800) 366-4426
Web Site: www.meridianchiles.com

E-Mail for Key Personnel:
President: mes@meridiancomm.com
Creative Dir.: drenaud@meridiancomm.com

Employees: 17
Year Founded: 1975

Agency Specializes In: Advertising, Brand Development & Integration, Consumer Marketing, Event Planning & Marketing, Pets , Public Relations

Mary Ellen Slone *(Pres)*
Charley Brough *(Dir-Media)*
Linda Dickinson *(Mgr-Production)*

Accounts:
Bal Homes
Corporate Centre
Equestrian Events, Inc.
Kentucky Community & Technical College System; Versailles, KY; 2002
Kentucky State University; Frankfort, KY; 2004
Lexington Clinic
Mile Stone Realty Consultants
Whitaker Bank

MERIDIAN CREATIVE ALLIANCE
113 E Church St, Ozark, MO 65721-8313
Tel.: (417) 581-2884
Fax: (417) 581-2906
Toll Free: (800) 955-2884
E-Mail: ideas@meridiancreative.com
Web Site: www.meridiancreative.com

E-Mail for Key Personnel:
President: adguy@meridiancreative.com
Creative Dir.: jd@meridiancreative.com
Media Dir.: lewis@meridiancreative.com

Employees: 4
Year Founded: 1997

Agency Specializes In: Advertising, Automotive, Broadcast, Business-To-Business, Cable T.V., Collateral, Consulting, Corporate Identity, Direct-to-Consumer, Graphic Design, In-Store Advertising, Internet/Web Design, Local Marketing, Media Buying Services, Media Planning, Men's Market, Newspaper, Newspapers & Magazines, Out-of-Home Media, Outdoor, Planning & Consultation, Point of Purchase, Point of Sale, Print, Production, Production (Print), Promotions, Radio, Retail, Sports Market, Strategic Planning/Research, T.V., Trade & Consumer Magazines

Approx. Annual Billings: $25,500,000

Breakdown of Gross Billings by Media: Brdcst.: $19,800,000; Print: $5,700,000

Bob Bryant *(Owner)*
John Dillon *(Partner-Meridian Creative)*
Jim Lewis *(Partner-Meridian Creative)*

Accounts:
Core Group; Springfield, MO Pharmaceuticals; 1997
Peoples Bank of the Ozarks; Nixa, MO Banking Services; 1997
SLS Loudspeakers; Springfield, MO; 1999

THE MERIDIAN GROUP
575 Lynnhaven Pkwy 3rd Fl, Virginia Beach, VA 23452-7350
Tel.: (757) 340-7425
Fax: (757) 340-8379
Toll Free: (800) 294-3840
E-Mail: joe@themeridiangroup.com
Web Site: www.themeridiangroup.com

E-Mail for Key Personnel:
Public Relations: terry@themeridiangroup.com

Employees: 30
Year Founded: 1980

National Agency Associations: AAF

Agency Specializes In: Advertising, Affluent Market, Automotive, Aviation & Aerospace, Brand Development & Integration, Branded Entertainment, Broadcast, Business-To-Business, Co-op Advertising, Consumer Goods, Consumer Marketing, Corporate Communications, Corporate Identity, Crisis Communications, Digital/Interactive, E-Commerce, Email, Event Planning & Marketing, Exhibit/Trade Shows, Financial, Food Service, Health Care Services, Hospitality, Leisure, Logo & Package Design, Luxury Products, Marine, Market Research, Media Buying Services, Media Planning, Media Relations, Media Training, Medical Products, Mobile Marketing, Package Design, Paid Searches, Planning & Consultation, Podcasting, Print, Production (Ad, Film, Broadcast), Production (Print), Public Relations, Publicity/Promotions, Radio, Real Estate, Recruitment, Restaurant, Retail, Search Engine Optimization, Sports Market, Strategic Planning/Research, Trade & Consumer Magazines, Travel & Tourism

Approx. Annual Billings: $33,000,000

Breakdown of Gross Billings by Media: Brdcst.: $5,600,000; Bus. Publs.: $2,240,000; Collateral: $7,000,000; Consulting: $2,800,000; Mags.: $2,000,000; Newsp.: $5,600,000; Pub. Rels.: $2,000,000; Radio & T.V.: $2,800,000; Trade & Consumer Mags.: $1,960,000; Worldwide Web Sites: $1,000,000

Joseph Takach *(Founder & CEO)*
Terry Kelley *(VP)*
David Stearns *(Gen Mgr)*
David Watson *(Dir-Creative)*
Shane Webb *(Dir-Creative)*
Erin Brothers *(Acct Mgr)*

Accounts:
The Reefs Resort & Club PR, Rebranding Campaign, Website Development
Stihl, Inc.; Virginia Beach, VA
Wounded Warrior Project; 2006

MERING & ASSOCIATES
1700 I St Ste 210, Sacramento, CA 95811
Tel.: (916) 441-0571
Fax: (916) 441-1370
E-Mail: info@mering.com
Web Site: www.meringcarson.com

Employees: 50

Agency Specializes In: Advertising, Public Relations

Dave Mering *(Founder & CEO)*
Tammy Haughey *(Acct Dir-Brand Strategy & Mgmt)*
Chris Pagano *(Dir-Media)*
Debi Houston *(Office Mgr)*
Lori Bartel *(Acct Supvr)*
Adam Mason *(Specialist-Search Engine Mktg)*

Accounts:
California Raisins
California Tourism
Disneyland Meetings
Lake Tahoe Visitors Authority
NFL
Sierra at Tahoe Ski Resort
Thunder Valley Casino

Branch

MeringCarson
1010 S Coast Hwy 101 Ste 105, Encinitas, CA 92024
Tel.: (760) 635-2100
Fax: (760) 635-2106
E-Mail: info@meringcarson.com
Web Site: www.meringcarson.com

Agency Specializes In: Sponsorship

Lorie Brewster *(CFO)*
Paul Whitbeck *(Gen Mgr)*
John Mergen *(Exec Dir-Media)*
Bert Hamaoui *(Grp Dir-Media)*
Janelle Okamoto *(Producer-Digital)*
Kristen Haro *(Project Mgr-Social & Digital)*
Catherine Sharp *(Brand Mgr-Global)*
Michelle Misner *(Supvr-Connection)*
Wade Bare *(Acct Exec)*
Christie Pierce *(Media Planner & Buyer-Connections Digital)*

Accounts:
Balboa Park Cultural Partnership Media Planning
CA Speedway
California Raisins
California Travel & Tourism Commission
Central Garden & Pet Company AvoDerm, Media Planning & Buying
New-LDK Ventures (Agency of Record)
Pebble Beach Resorts
Raley's

Red Lion Hotels Brand
San Diego Convention & Visitors Bureau; San Diego, CA (Agency of Record)
San Diego Tourism Authority
Squaw Valley Ski Resort
Stones Gambling Hall (Creative Agency of Record)
New-Tahiti Tourisme North America, Inc. Global Communications
Victorinox Swiss Army Marketing
Visit California (Advertising Agency of Record) Campaign: "Dreamers", Campaign: "Kids at Play"
Walt Disney Parks & Resorts

MERIT MILE COMMUNICATIONS

131 NE 1st Ave Ste 100, Boca Raton, FL 33432
Tel.: (561) 362-8888
E-Mail: info@meritmile.com
Web Site: www.meritmile.com

Employees: 15
Year Founded: 2007

Mark Reino *(CEO)*
John Sternal *(Dir-PR & Social Media)*
Mark Leblanc *(Mgr-Interactive)*

Accounts:
Hearst Corp. B2B; 2012
Microsoft Corp B2B; 2007
Parallels, Inc. B2C; 2011
Swapalease.com; Cincinnati, OH Brand Positioning, Media Outreach, PR, Strategic Message Development; 2012

MERITDIRECT, LLC.

2 International Dr, Rye Brook, NY 10573
Tel.: (914) 368-1000
Fax: (914) 368-1150
E-Mail: hq@meritdirect.com
Web Site: www.meritdirect.com

Employees: 98
Year Founded: 1999

Revenue: $5,000,000

Ralph Drybrough *(Pres)*
Rob Sanchez *(CEO)*
Richard Ackley *(VP-Customer Acq & Retention)*
Blair Barondes *(VP)*
Dan Harding *(VP)*
James Scova *(VP-Data & Media Svcs)*
Frank Willey *(VP-Client Strategy)*
Eric J. Newell *(Sr Dir-Strategy)*

Accounts:
Kiplinger
Microsoft
S&S Worldwide
Taylor Corporation
Uline
United Business Media
Wells Fargo

MERKLE INC.

7001 Columbia Gateway Dr, Columbia, MD 21046
Tel.: (443) 542-4000
Fax: (443) 542-4001
Web Site: www.merkleinc.com/

Employees: 1,000
Year Founded: 1977

Agency Specializes In: Advertising, Brand Development & Integration, Collateral, Communications, Consumer Marketing, Corporate Identity, Direct Response Marketing, Electronic Media, Event Planning & Marketing, Exhibit/Trade Shows, Internet/Web Design, Sponsorship

David Williams *(Chm & CEO)*
William Stoughton *(Partner-Mgmt Consulting Grp)*
Jean Holder *(CFO & Exec VP)*
Matthew Mobley *(CTO & Exec VP)*
Mark A. Weninger *(Chief Creative Officer & Agency Grp Head)*
Patrick Hounsell *(Chief Digital Officer & Exec VP)*
Andy Fisher *(Chief Analytics Officer)*
Adam Lavelle *(Chief Growth Officer-Digital)*
Peter Randazzo *(Chief Agency Tech Officer)*
Owen McCorry *(Exec VP & Gen Mgr-Merkle Health)*
Mike Mojica *(Exec VP & Gen Mgr-Retail & Consumer Goods Practice)*
Dave Paulus *(Exec VP & Gen Mgr)*
Will Bordelon *(Exec VP-Vertical Markets)*
Harry Brakeley *(Exec VP)*
Tony Giordano *(Exec VP-Tech Solutions Grp)*
Matt Naeger *(Exec VP-Digital Strategy)*
Tony Steel *(Exec VP)*
Gerry Bavaro *(Sr VP-Enterprise Solutions Grp)*
Aileen Cahill *(Sr VP-Retail & Consumer Goods)*
David Magrini *(Sr VP-Health Insurance)*
Olaf Tennhardt *(Sr VP-Mktg Tech, Digital Mktg & Data Mgmt)*
Marc Fanelli *(VP & Gen Mgr-Intl Mktg Solutions)*
Dave Boyd *(VP & Client Partner-Retail & Consumer Goods)*
Paul Evers *(Client Partner & VP)*
Larry Blum *(VP-Healthcare & CPG Practices)*
Mary Ann Buoncristiano *(VP-List Brokerage & Acq Svcs)*
Serge Del Grosso *(VP-Media Svcs)*
David Furlong *(VP)*
Steven L. Gregg *(VP-Sls & Mktg)*
Mark Guenther *(VP-Retail & Consumer Goods practice)*
Alex Kooluris *(VP-Retail & Consumer Goods practice)*
Kelly Leger *(VP)*
Alison Monk *(VP-Client Engagement)*
John Padwick *(VP-Travel Vertical)*
Karen Pierce *(VP)*
David Skinner *(VP-Strategic Alliances & Partnerships)*
Justin Stayrook *(VP-Experience Tech)*
Bob Branch *(Sr Dir-Digital Strategy)*
Feng Jia *(Sr Dir-Analytics)*
Rory O'Flaherty *(Sr Dir-Media Svcs)*
Bruce Purple *(Sr Dir-Strategy)*
David Swezey *(Sr Dir-Retail Markets)*
Joe Byers *(Dir-Digital Media)*
Caroline Nash *(Dir-Digital Messaging Partner Mgmt)*
Jay Wells *(Dir-Digital Strategy)*
Amanda Day *(Acct Mgr)*
Sarah Bourdeau *(Mgr-PR & Analyst Rels)*

Accounts:
21st Century
Advanta
Aegon
Aetna
Ally Financial Inc.
Bank of America
Blockbuster
Bristol Myers Squibb
Care
Carestar Financial Group
Catholic Charities USA (Agency of Record) Fundraising Strategy
Charles Schwab
Citizens Bank Marketing
Dell
DirecTV
Easter Seals (Agency of Record) Digital, Display Advertising, Email, Marketing Strategy, Production Management, Web, creative
EmblemHealth Customer Strategy
Feeding America
New-Fiat Chrysler Analytics
Global Fund For Women Creative, Digital, Email Marketing, Program Analysis, Strategy, Web Services
GMAC Insurance
Habitat For Humanity International Account Management, Analytics, Design, Digital, Production, Strategy
HSBC
JPMorgan Chase
KeyBank
Kimberly-Clark CRM
Lifescan
M&T
New-MetLife, Inc. Digital Media
National Jewish Medical & Research Center; 2007
National Multiple Sclerosis Society
New-Neos Therapeutics (Consumer Brand & Digital Agency of Record)
PNC
Salvation Army
Samsung Electronics; 2008
StarKist CRM
Susan G. Komen for the Cure (Integrated Direct Response Agency of Record) Creative, Digital Media, Direct Mail, Direct Marketing, Print, Social Media, Strategy, Susan G. Komen Breast Cancer Foundation, Inc.
T-Mobile US
The United States Navy Memorial Analytics, Caging, Campaign: "Blessing of the Fleets", Creative Design, Print Production, Program Management, Strategy
U.S. Olympic Committee (Agency of Record) Direct Mail Fundraising
Vonage; Holmdel, NJ Direct Campaigns; 2007
Wachovia

Branches

IMPAQT

Foster Plaza 10 680 Andersen Dr, Pittsburgh, PA 15220
Tel.: (412) 733-7100
Fax: (412) 733-1010
Toll Free: (888) 949-4672
Web Site: http://www.merkleinc.com/what-we-do/digital-agency-services/media

Employees: 80

Agency Specializes In: Consulting, Digital/Interactive, Search Engine Optimization

Richard Hagerty *(CEO)*
Kevin Amos *(VP-Tech & Growth Markets)*
Vanessa Cooper *(Acct Grp Dir)*
Ethan Hagerty *(Dir-Bus Dev)*
Zach Simon *(Dir-Performance Media)*
Zhanna Dubinsky *(Mgr-Digital Strategy-Merkle)*

Accounts:
Chase
Mercedes
Office Depot
Penske
Tiffany & Co

Merkle Connect

1050 17th St Ste 2100, Denver, CO 80265
Tel.: (720) 836-2000
Web Site: www.merkleinc.com

Agency Specializes In: Social Media

Tim Berry *(Co-Pres)*
Dave Paulus *(Exec VP-Bus Dev)*
John Roberts *(VP & Grp Dir-Creative)*
Elizabeth Eckard *(Sr Dir-Digital Messaging)*
Craig Howard *(Sr Dir-Tech Svcs)*
Kerri Driscoll *(Dir-Digital Strategy)*
Jonathan Till *(Assoc Dir-Creative)*
Jessica Wheeler *(Sr Acct Mgr)*
Jessica Bolton *(Assoc Acct Mgr)*
Amanda McMurray *(Assoc Acct Mgr)*

Accounts:
Samsung Telecommunications America, LLC

Merkle Inc.
900 E 8th Ave Ste 200, King of Prussia, PA 19406
Tel.: (610) 879-8000
Fax: (610) 879-8010
Web Site: www.merkleinc.com

Employees: 45

Agency Specializes In: Advertising, Brand Development & Integration, Business-To-Business, Collateral, Consulting, Consumer Marketing, Digital/Interactive, Direct Response Marketing, Electronic Media, Financial, Hispanic Market, Internet/Web Design, Planning & Consultation, Production, Telemarketing, Travel & Tourism

John Roberts *(VP, Grp Dir-Creative & Head-Practice)*
Josh Sinel *(VP & Gen Mgr-Social)*
Annemarie Armstrong *(VP & Client Partner)*
Angelina Eng *(VP-Platform Solutions & Activation)*
Melanie Kinney *(VP-Digital Agency Grp)*
Echo Liang *(VP-Quantitative & Digital Analytics)*
Karima Zmerli *(VP-Digital Data)*
Bob Baer *(Sr Dir)*
Anamitra Chaudhuri *(Sr Dir-Insurance & Wealth Mgmt Analytics Practice)*
Eryck Dzotsi *(Sr Dir-SEO)*
Blandine Genix *(Sr Dir-Media Client Svcs)*
Jeffrey Godish *(Sr Dir-Digital Strategy & Customer Experience)*
Frank Tino *(Sr Dir-Production)*
Courtney Caldwell *(Dir-Digital Client Engagement)*
Daniel Parmar *(Dir)*
Jillian Tate *(Dir-Media Client Svcs)*
Kristy LaPlante *(Assoc Dir-Digital Strategy)*
Ricardo Rivera *(Assoc Dir)*
Lauren Polinsky *(Sr Acct Mgr-SEO)*
Amanda McMurray *(Assoc Acct Mgr)*
Ken Geis *(Client Partner-Retail & Consumer Goods)*
Billy Leef *(Mgr-Media Client Svcs)*
Bethany Merchant *(Mgr-Media Svcs)*
Bianca Goins *(Assoc Mgr-Acct Mgmt)*
Mark Systma *(Sr Specialist-Digital Media)*
Gabriel Ho *(Analyst-QSG Digital)*

RKG (The Rimm-Kaufman Group)
701 E Water St, Charlottesville, VA 22902
(See Separate Listing)

MERKLEY+PARTNERS
200 Varick St, New York, NY 10014-4810
Tel.: (212) 805-7500
Fax: (212) 805-7445
E-Mail: reception@merkleyandpartners.com
Web Site: www.merkleyandpartners.com

Employees: 185
Year Founded: 1993

National Agency Associations: 4A's-ADC

Agency Specializes In: Advertising, Sponsorship

Approx. Annual Billings: $800,000,000

Alex Gellert *(CEO)*
Rob Moorman *(CMO)*
Drummond Berman *(Grp Head-Creative)*
Jennifer Bolivar *(Head-Production)*
Erich Hartmann *(Grp Head-Creative)*
Simon Nickson *(Grp Head-Creative)*
Mathilde Benington Hopkins *(Gen Mgr-Media & Interactive)*
Scott Gelber *(Exec Dir-Digital)*
Scott Zacaroli *(Grp Dir-Creative)*
Eric Rand *(Sr Acct Dir)*
Maggi Vale *(Grp Acct Dir-New Bus)*
Heather Hopkins *(Sr Producer-Digital)*
Beth Liss *(Acct Dir)*
Jenna Lowy *(Art Dir)*
Joe Rispoli *(Acct Dir-Mercedes-Benz)*
Adam Arnegger *(Dir-Media Strategy)*
Beverly Don *(Dir-Art Production)*
John Duffy *(Dir-Creative)*
Tim O'Malley *(Assoc Dir-Creative)*
Francesco Deluca *(Sr Acct Supvr-Mercedes-Benz USA)*
Hallie Bates *(Supvr-Digital Media)*
Crystal Deuel *(Jr Copywriter)*
Mina Hirsch *(Media Planner)*
Greg Kissler *(Copywriter)*
Tia Starr *(Media Planner)*
Marie Strycharz *(Copywriter)*

Accounts:
Ad Council Amber Alerts, Buzzed Driving, Campaign: "Party Foul", Fair Housing, Gun Safety, H1N1, Lead Paint, Online Sexual Exploitation; 2000
All Detergent Brand
AlphaOne Marketing Bravo, C-Town Supermarkets; 2014
Armored AutoGroup Inc. A/C Pro, Armor All, STP
Ferrero U.S.A., Inc. Ferrero Rocher, Ferrero Rondnoir, Nutella; 2004
Florida's Natural Growers Fit & Delicious, Florida's Natural Orange Juice; 2014
Johnny Mac Soldiers Fund; 2014
Mercedes-Benz USA; 1999
New-NBTY, Inc. Digital, Ester-C (Lead Creative Agency), Kid's Vitamin, Social Communications
Niconovum Zonnic; 2011
Preen; 2011
smart car; 2011
Sprinter Media Only; 2011
The Sun Products Corporation (Agency of Record) All Detergent, Broadcast, Campaign: "Inside Dirt: The Dirty Truth About Your Clean Laundry", Consumer, Digital, Media, Print, Public Relations, Retail, Social, Wisk, all Free Clear OXI, all OXI Laundry Booster, all Radiant
Sun Products (Agency of Record) Snuggle, Sunlight, Wisk (Media Only); 2009
Teva Pharmaceuticals ProAir, QVAR; 2012
Vanda Pharmaceuticals Fanapt, Hetlioz; 2013

Branch

Merkley + Partners/Healthworks
200 Varick St 12th Fl, New York, NY 10014-4810
Tel.: (212) 366-3500
Fax: (212) 805-7445
Web Site: www.merkleyandpartners.com

Employees: 200
Year Founded: 1995

Agency Specializes In: Health Care Services, Pharmaceutical

Andy Hirsch *(Chm & Exec Dir-Creative)*
Roger Morales *(CFO)*
Abi Aron *(Grp Head-Creative)*
Drummond Berman *(Grp Head-Creative)*
Erich Hartmann *(Grp Head-Creative)*
Simon Nickson *(Grp Head-Creative)*
Scott Gelber *(Exec Dir-Digital)*
Eddie Van Bloem *(Grp Dir-Creative)*
Lisa Mannarelli Puleo *(Grp Acct Dir)*
Joe Rispoli *(Acct Dir-Mercedes-Benz)*
Whitney Bryan *(Dir-Plng)*
Vladimir Golinder *(Dir-Digital Ops & Tech)*
Gary Grossman *(Dir-Brdcst Production)*
Joanna Kalliches *(Dir-Creative)*
Chris Landi *(Dir-Creative)*
Jenna Lowy *(Dir-Art)*
Kate Sinnott *(Assoc Dir-Media)*
Ronna Boyer *(Acct Supvr-All Laundry Detergent)*
Kim Heller *(Supvr-Digital Media)*
Samantha Kaufman *(Supvr-Media)*
Julia Zak *(Supvr-Media)*
Alexandra Castellanos *(Acct Exec)*
Kate Thuma *(Acct Exec)*
Jennifer Hunley *(Sr Acct Planner)*
Hallie Bates *(Media Planner)*
Crystal Deuel *(Jr Copywriter)*
Gregory Kissler *(Jr Copywriter)*
Beth Stirling *(Media Planner)*
Joanna Tuzel *(Media Planner)*
Clemmy Little *(Asst Acct Exec)*

Accounts:
Maybach
Mercedes-Benz Campaign: "Control", Campaign: "Derby", Campaign: "Four Words", Print, S-Class, Soul, Superdome
PSEG
Smart Car Unclutter
Sun Products Corp

MERLIN EDGE INC.
602-12th Ave SW Ste 100, Calgary, AB T2R 1J3 Canada
Tel.: (403) 237-7684
Fax: (403) 237-7745
E-Mail: info@merlinedge.com
Web Site: www.merlinedge.com

Employees: 20
Year Founded: 1993

Laurie Watson *(Pres & Dir-Creative)*
George Koch *(Partner, VP, Editor & Sr Writer)*
Arvind Singh *(Dir-Art & Sr Graphic Designer)*
Tracey Evans *(Sr Project Coord)*

MERLOT MARKETING
4430 Duckhorn Dr, Sacramento, CA 95834
Tel.: (916) 285-9835
Fax: (916) 285-9875
E-Mail: gr8mkting@merlotmarketing.com
Web Site: www.merlotmarketing.com

Employees: 15

Debi Hammond *(Pres & CEO)*
Brenda Forman *(VP-Client Svcs)*
Beth Wenbourne Katz *(Dir-Digital Engagement)*
Patrick Storm *(Dir-PR)*
Kym Preslar *(Office Mgr)*
Whitney Harris *(Specialist-Digital Engagement)*
Lauren Razzano *(Specialist-Digital Engagement)*
Elijah Creel *(Graphic Designer & Coord-Mktg)*
Luis D. Sosa *(Asst Acct Coord-Mktg & PR)*

Accounts:
American Marketing Association, Sacramento Valley
CalChamber
Dacor
Dimension 5 Construction
Madsen Roofing
Water, Inc.

MERRICK TOWLE COMMUNICATIONS
5801-F Ammendale Rd, Beltsville, MD 20705-1264
Tel.: (301) 974-6000
Fax: (240) 264-1292
E-Mail: blawrence@merricktowle.com
Web Site: www.merricktowle.com

Employees: 70
Year Founded: 1985

National Agency Associations: AAF-AMA

Agency Specializes In: Advertising, Collateral, Consulting, Digital/Interactive, Email, Event

Planning & Marketing, Graphic Design, Integrated Marketing, Internet/Web Design, Local Marketing, Media Buying Services, Media Planning, Newspaper, Newspapers & Magazines, Outdoor, Planning & Consultation, Print, Production (Print), Real Estate, Regional, Search Engine Optimization, Urban Market, Web (Banner Ads, Pop-ups, etc.)

Breakdown of Gross Billings by Media: Adv. Specialities: 1%; Brdcst.: 1%; Collateral: 14%; D.M.: 4%; Graphic Design: 5%; Internet Adv.: 9%; Mags.: 16%; Mdsg./POP: 4%; Newsp.: 17%; Outdoor: 5%; Plng. & Consultation: 14%; Worldwide Web Sites: 10%

Jason Knauer *(Dir-Creative)*
Donna Mcgee *(Dir-Production)*
Sean Ruberg *(Dir-Strategy)*
Joe Symoski *(Dir-Art)*
Zach Salwen *(Mgr-Digital)*
Devin Emery *(Designer-Studio)*
Gregg Hutson *(Copywriter)*
Harry Merrick, IV *(Planner-Strategic)*

Accounts:
Beazer Homes; Atlanta, GA
JBG; Chevy Chase, MD
The Tower Companies The Blairs
Vornado

MESH DESIGN

7912 Wrenwood Blvd Ste C, Baton Rouge, LA 70809
Tel.: (225) 248-1111
Fax: (225) 248-1407
E-Mail: info@meshdesign.biz
Web Site: www.meshbr.com

Year Founded: 2003

Agency Specializes In: Brand Development & Integration, Collateral, Corporate Identity, Direct Response Marketing, Graphic Design, Internet/Web Design, Package Design, Radio, Strategic Planning/Research, T.V.

Brian Hanlon *(Owner)*
Taylor Bennett *(Principal)*
Jason Feirman *(Acct Dir & Brand Strategist)*
Brooke Dynes *(Dir-Traffic & Fin)*
Allison McInnis *(Dir-Media & Strategic Plng)*
Christina Persaud *(Acct Exec & Strategist-PR & Mktg)*
Lea Ciskowski *(Acct Exec-Social Media)*
Lacye Beauregard *(Designer)*
David Catoire *(Designer-Video)*

Accounts:
Community Bank of Louisiana Advertising, Creative Execution, Media Placement, Public Relations, Strategic Marketing
Fleurish Productions
Louisiana Workers Compensation Corporation Advertising, Creative Execution, Media Placement, Public Relations, Strategic Marketing
Oldcastle (Agency of Record) Building Construction Products Mfr

MESH INTERACTIVE AGENCY

142 Main St, Nashua, NH 03060
Tel.: (617) 809-4164
E-Mail: billschick@meshagency.com
Web Site: www.meshagency.com/

Employees: 12
Year Founded: 2006

Agency Specializes In: Advertising, Advertising Specialties, Brand Development & Integration, Business Publications, Business-To-Business, Co-op Advertising, Collateral, Communications, Consulting, Consumer Marketing, Corporate Communications, Corporate Identity, Digital/Interactive, Direct Response Marketing, E-Commerce, Electronic Media, Exhibit/Trade Shows, Financial, Graphic Design, Health Care Services, High Technology, In-Store Advertising, Information Technology, Internet/Web Design, Investor Relations, Local Marketing, Logo & Package Design, Magazines, Medical Products, Multimedia, New Product Development, Newspaper, Newspapers & Magazines, Point of Purchase, Point of Sale, Print, Production, Sales Promotion, Sports Market, Strategic Planning/Research, Trade & Consumer Magazines, Travel & Tourism

Approx. Annual Billings: $700,000

Bill Schick *(Exec VP-Digital)*
Jennifer Kamerman *(Dir-Digital Mktg & Agency Dev)*
Linda Lafleur *(Dir-Project Mgmt)*

Accounts:
3D Exchange Application Development, Marketing, Social Media, Web
Avedro Web
RAMP Web
Sequans Social Media, Web Marketing
TheraFit Marketing, Social Media
Traceparts Web

MESSAGE FIRST

230 N 2nd St Ste 2C, Philadelphia, PA 19106
Tel.: (215) 825-7423
E-Mail: hello@messagefirst.com
Web Site: www.messagefirst.com

Agency Specializes In: Graphic Design, Internet/Web Design

Jesse Author *(Pres)*
Kim Goodwin *(VP-Design)*

Accounts:
AT&T Communications Corp. Telecommunication Network Service Providers
Bankrate Inc. Banking & Insurance Services
BMC Software Information Technology Services
Comcast Telecommunication & Television Network Services
Cornell University Educational Institution

MESSINA DESIGN

1425 University Ave Ste B, San Diego, CA 92103
Tel.: (858) 336-3493
Web Site: www.messinadesign.biz

Year Founded: 2002

Agency Specializes In: Advertising, Brand Development & Integration, Collateral, Email, Internet/Web Design, Logo & Package Design, Print

Daniela Messina *(Founder & Creative Dir)*
Christine Virola *(Acct Mgr)*
Madeline Wukusick *(Designer)*

Accounts:
Cerner
Denver Learning Institute
Easyturf
Gordon-Weiss-Schanzlin Vision Institute
Hilton San Diego Bayfront
Innovacyn
Lars Remodeling & Design
OneRoof Energy
San Diego Jewish Academy
University of San Diego

METAPHOR INC.

119 Cherry Hill Rd, Parsippany, NJ 07054
Tel.: (973) 334-1009
Fax: (973) 334-1667
E-Mail: info@metaphorinc.com
Web Site: www.metaphorinc.com

Employees: 15
Year Founded: 1998

Agency Specializes In: Digital/Interactive, Education, Health Care Services, Internet/Web Design, Pharmaceutical

Nick Calandrillo *(Owner)*
Dwayne Hann *(Pres)*
Chris Calandrillo *(VP & Acct Grp Supvr)*

METHOD INC.

972 Mission St 2nd Fl, San Francisco, CA 94103
Tel.: (415) 901-6300
Fax: (415) 901-6310
E-Mail: inquiries@method.com
Web Site: www.method.com

Employees: 70

Agency Specializes In: Advertising, Advertising Specialties, Arts, Brand Development & Integration, Business-To-Business, Consumer Marketing, Corporate Identity, Digital/Interactive, Electronic Media, Entertainment, Identity Marketing, Internet/Web Design, Multimedia, New Product Development, New Technologies, Print, Production, Social Marketing/Nonprofit, T.V., Web (Banner Ads, Pop-ups, etc.)

Jason Prohaska *(Mng Dir)*
David Eveleigh-Evans *(Chief Creative Officer)*
David Rajan *(CTO)*
Paul Cloutier *(Principal)*
Patrick Newbery *(Principal)*
Alex Mileyeva *(Exec Dir-Global Ops)*
Reema Pinto *(Exec Dir-Client Svcs)*
Jon Karlin *(Client Svcs Dir)*
Brennan Wozencroft *(Client Svcs Dir)*
Sieun Cha *(Dir-Creative)*
Kyle Crouse *(Dir-Tech)*
Stuart George *(Dir-Technical)*
Garrett Groszko *(Dir-Interaction Design)*

Accounts:
AIGA Campaign: "AIGA Website"
AOL Corporate Site
Cisco
CNN
Fujitsu
Gucci
MF Global
Microsoft
Promptu Spoken Search
Samsung CenterStage, Digital Installation, Home Appliance
Showtime
SoftKinetic
Sony

Branch

Method

972 Mission St Fl 2, San Francisco, CA 94103
Tel.: (415) 901-6300
Fax: (415) 901-6310
E-Mail: inquiries@method.com
Web Site: method.com

Employees: 35

Alicia Bergin *(Mng Dir)*
Tim Billing *(COO)*
David Eveleigh-Evans *(Chief Creative Officer)*

Patrick Newbery *(Chief Strategy Officer)*
Paul Cloutier *(Principal)*
Athila Armstrong *(Exec Dir-Creative)*
Alex Mileyeva *(Exec Dir-Global Ops)*
Reema Pinto *(Exec Dir-Client Svcs)*
Brennan Wozencroft *(Client Svcs Dir)*
Sieun Cha *(Dir-Creative)*
Angela Tang *(Dir-Interaction Design)*
Steve Wake *(Dir-Creative)*

Accounts:
Adobe
AOL
CNN
Comcast
Fujitsu
Keihl's
Organic Motion
Sony
Visa

METHODIKAL, INC.
77 College St Ste 3E, Burlington, VT 05401
Tel.: (802) 233-9127
Web Site: www.methodikal.net

Agency Specializes In: Advertising, Graphic Design, Internet/Web Design

Seth Drury *(Co-Owner)*
Mike Hannigan *(Co-Owner)*

Accounts:
Vermont Ski Areas Association, Inc.

METRE LLC
116 5th Ave S, La Crosse, WI 54601
Tel.: (608) 782-5508
E-Mail: info@metreagency.com
Web Site: www.metreagency.com

Agency Specializes In: Advertising, Brand Development & Integration, Content, Digital/Interactive, Media Buying Services, Media Planning, Print, Public Relations, Social Media, Strategic Planning/Research

Kerstin Boudreau *(Dir-Res & Comm)*
Justin Garvey *(Dir-Strategy & Analytics)*
Ben Addington *(Acct Mgr)*
Leah Call *(Copywriter)*
Hannah Michlig *(Coord-Res)*
Jacob Redmond *(Coord-Media)*
Amber Schneider *(Coord-Media)*

Accounts:
La Crosse Regional Airport

METROPOLIS ADVERTISING
719 Peachtree Rd Ste 210, Orlando, FL 32804
Tel.: (407) 835-8080
Fax: (407) 517-4419
E-Mail: agency@metropolisadvertising.com
Web Site: www.metropolisadvertising.com

Year Founded: 1996

Agency Specializes In: Advertising, E-Commerce, Environmental, Exhibit/Trade Shows, Graphic Design, Package Design, Print, Public Relations, Search Engine Optimization, Web (Banner Ads, Pop-ups, etc.)

Kevin Kent *(Pres & Dir-Creative)*
Kevin Boynton *(VP & Dir-Creative)*
Alicia Worrell *(VP-Client Svcs)*
Andrew Ontko *(Designer-Web)*

Accounts:
Edyth Bush Charitable Foundation 40th Anniversary Campaign, Website Redesign
Winderweedle, Haines, Ward & Woodman, P.A

MEYER BENNETT CREATIVE
2109 W 5th Ave Ste F, Columbus, OH 43212
Tel.: (614) 485-9913
Web Site: www.meyerbennettcreative.com

Year Founded: 2000

Agency Specializes In: Advertising, Brand Development & Integration, Broadcast, Corporate Identity, Graphic Design, Internet/Web Design, Logo & Package Design, Print, Social Media, Strategic Planning/Research

Bill Meyer *(Partner)*
Robin Meyer *(Partner)*

Accounts:
Nationwide Insurance

MEYERS + PARTNERS
833 W Jackson Blvd Ste 600, Chicago, IL 60607
Tel.: (312) 733-9999
Fax: (312) 226-0526
Web Site: www.meyerspartners.com

E-Mail for Key Personnel:
President: msmeyers@mmeyers.com
Creative Dir.: jgasper@mmeyers.com

Employees: 11
Year Founded: 1983

Agency Specializes In: Advertising, Brand Development & Integration, Business-To-Business, Communications, Consumer Marketing, Corporate Identity, Direct Response Marketing, Health Care Services, High Technology, Internet/Web Design, Logo & Package Design, Media Buying Services, New Product Development, Public Relations, Publicity/Promotions, Strategic Planning/Research, Trade & Consumer Magazines

Approx. Annual Billings: $5,000,000

Breakdown of Gross Billings by Media: Bus. Publs.: 20%; Collateral: 5%; Internet Adv.: 5%; Newsp. & Mags.: 10%; Radio: 10%; Trade & Consumer Mags.: 40%; Worldwide Web Sites: 10%

Michael S. Meyers *(Founder & CEO)*
Jim Gasper *(Partner & Dir-Creative)*
Patrick Rovito *(Mgr-Interactive Dev)*
Amanda Blumeyer *(Acct Exec)*

Accounts:
Chicago Cutting Die; Northbrook, IL
Encyclopedia Britannica
Entergy
Hitachi OMD; Norman, OK
MIB Group; Westwood, MA Medical
National Louis University
TeamQuest
Tecta America
Woodard
World Book
ZipDee

THE MEYOCKS GROUP
6800 Lake Dr Ste 150, West Des Moines, IA 50266-2544
Tel.: (515) 225-1200
Fax: (515) 225-6400
E-Mail: dougjeske@meyocks.com
Web Site: www.meyocks.com/

Employees: 30
Year Founded: 1989

Agency Specializes In: Agriculture, Brand Development & Integration, Business-To-Business, Collateral, Communications, Consumer Marketing, Corporate Identity, Direct Response Marketing, Event Planning & Marketing, Exhibit/Trade Shows, Food Service, Internet/Web Design, Logo & Package Design, Point of Purchase, Point of Sale, Print, Production, Public Relations, Publicity/Promotions, Retail, Sales Promotion, Sponsorship, Strategic Planning/Research

Doug Jeske *(Pres)*
Chad Baker *(VP-Creative)*
Rachel Allinson *(Dir-Creative & Art)*
Ali Kauffman *(Acct Mgr-Hy-Vee Team)*
Deb Mitchell *(Acct Mgr)*
Katie Schetzsle *(Acct Mgr)*
Karlyn Nosbusch *(Media Planner & Buyer)*
Kristi Pauss *(Sr Media Planner & Buyer)*

Accounts:
Delta Dental Plan of Iowa; Ankeny, IA
Dragotec USA (Advertising Agency of Record)
Farm Credit Services of America; Omaha, NE; 1998
Firestone Agricultural Tire Div.; Des Moines, IA
Harrisvaccines; Ames, IA
Hy-Vee Food Stores, Inc.; Des Moines, IA; 1994
Valent BioSciences Corporation; Libertyville, IL

MG LOMB ADVERTISING, INC.
1387 Fairport Rd Ste 700, Fairport, NY 14450
Tel.: (585) 388-5400
Toll Free: (888) 892-5402
Web Site: www.mglomb.com

Year Founded: 1996

Agency Specializes In: Advertising, Brand Development & Integration, Collateral, Corporate Identity, Event Planning & Marketing, Internet/Web Design, Logo & Package Design, Print

Michael Lomb *(Mng Partner & Dir-Creative)*
Daniel Meiling *(Designer-Multimedia)*

Accounts:
Allen-Bailey Tag & Label Inc.

MGA MEDIA GROUP
1345 Ave of the Americas 2nd fl, New York, NY 10105
Tel.: (212) 251-1015
E-Mail: ask@mgamediagroup.com
Web Site: www.mgamediagroup.com

Agency Specializes In: Advertising, Content, Event Planning & Marketing, Media Relations, Public Relations, Social Media

Maria Grazia Andriano *(Pres)*

Accounts:
New-Renaissance Hotels

MGH, INC.
100 Painters Mill Rd Ste 600, Owings Mills, MD 21117-7305
Tel.: (410) 902-5000
Fax: (410) 902-8712
Web Site: www.mghus.com

E-Mail for Key Personnel:
President: amalis@mghadvertising.com

Employees: 90
Year Founded: 1995

Agency Specializes In: Advertising, Alternative Advertising, Arts, Automotive, Bilingual Market, Brand Development & Integration, Broadcast, Business Publications, Business-To-Business,

Cable T.V., Co-op Advertising, Collateral, College, Computers & Software, Consulting, Consumer Goods, Consumer Marketing, Consumer Publications, Corporate Communications, Corporate Identity, Crisis Communications, Customer Relationship Management, Digital/Interactive, Direct Response Marketing, Direct-to-Consumer, Education, Electronic Media, Email, Entertainment, Event Planning & Marketing, Exhibit/Trade Shows, Financial, Food Service, Government/Political, Graphic Design, Guerilla Marketing, Health Care Services, High Technology, Hispanic Market, Hospitality, Identity Marketing, In-Store Advertising, Industrial, Integrated Marketing, Internet/Web Design, Leisure, Local Marketing, Logo & Package Design, Magazines, Market Research, Media Buying Services, Media Planning, Media Relations, Media Training, Men's Market, Merchandising, Mobile Marketing, Multimedia, New Technologies, Newspaper, Newspapers & Magazines, Out-of-Home Media, Outdoor, Over-50 Market, Package Design, Pharmaceutical, Planning & Consultation, Point of Purchase, Point of Sale, Print, Production, Public Relations, Publicity/Promotions, Radio, Real Estate, Restaurant, Retail, Sponsorship, Strategic Planning/Research, T.V., Trade & Consumer Magazines

Approx. Annual Billings: $65,000,000

Breakdown of Gross Billings by Media: Brdcst.: 30%; D.M.: 15%; Graphic Design: 5%; Out-of-Home Media: 5%; Print: 30%; Pub. Rels.: 15%

Andy Malis *(Chm & CEO)*
Shelley Welsh *(CFO & Sr VP)*
John Patterson *(Exec VP & Exec Dir-Creative)*
Terra Hopson *(Exec VP & Dir-Creative)*
Beth Willard *(Exec VP & Dir-Acct Svc)*
Mike Skandalis *(Exec VP)*
Cheryl Peluso *(Sr VP & Acct Svcs Dir)*
Edward Repasky *(Sr VP & Acct Dir)*
Ryan Goff *(Sr VP & Dir-Social Media Mktg)*
Chris McMurry *(Sr VP & Dir-PR & Damage Prevention Accts)*
Sherri Broughton *(VP & Sr Dir-Art)*
Sharon Kane *(VP & Sr Dir-Art)*
Kerry Owens *(VP & Acct Dir-PR)*
Lindsey Halpin *(Acct Dir)*
Allison Randall *(Sr Art Dir-Interactive)*
Kristi Betz *(Dir-PR)*
Deena Callahan *(Dir-HR)*
Katie Cresswell *(Dir-Interactive Ops)*
Kelly Cahill *(Acct Mgr-PR)*
Sara Corbin *(Acct Mgr)*
Shannon Keys *(Acct Mgr)*
Haley Loftus *(Acct Mgr)*
Marah Schmitz *(Acct Mgr)*
Melissa Dobres Segall *(Acct Mgr)*
Ashley Fortney *(Mgr-Digital Media Strategy)*
Kimberly Ritchie *(Mgr-Social Media Mktg)*
Michelle Yang *(Mgr-Campaign)*
Lea Staines *(Acct Supvr)*
Katie Grieco *(Acct Exec-PR)*
Megan Kowalski *(Acct Exec-Social Media Mktg)*
Emily Meier *(Acct Exec-PR)*
Abbie Nowak *(Acct Exec-Social Media)*
Kim Short *(Acct Exec-PR)*
Chris Rumbley *(Media Planner & Media Buyer)*
Joon Kim *(Copywriter)*
Lane Routzahn *(Acct Coord-Social Media Mktg)*
Paul Shiah *(Acct Coord-Acct Svcs)*
Alex Conn *(Coord-Traffic-Acct Svcs)*
T. J. Sanders *(Assoc Strategist-Interactive)*

Accounts:
Adler Display
Alex Cooper Auctioneers, Inc.
American Psychological Association
Anthony & Sylvan Pools Creative, Digital Marketing, Media Planning & Buying
Benari Jewelers Advertising, Marketing
Capitol Vein & Laser Centers
Common Ground Alliance Call811.com; 2008
DASH IN Food Stores Sales Marketing, Social Media
General Dynamics Information Technology
Global Franchise Group
Great American Cookies
The Greene Turtle Franchising Corporation
Hot Dog on a Stick
Indiana 811
M&T Bank
M-Edge Logo, Research Study, Retail Package Design, Search Engine Marketing, Tagline, Website Redesign
Marble Slab Creamery
Marco's Pizza (Agency of Record)
Maryland Department of Tourism
McCormick & Company Campaign: "Baylieve", Campaign: "Baytriotism", Integrated Marketing Campaign, McCormick World of Flavors, OLD BAY Seasoning
Medifast Weight Control Centers Advertising, Marketing
Mid-Atlantic Sports Network Digital, Media, Print, Radio, Television
Miss Shirley's
Miss Utility
National Aquarium; Baltimore, MD
National Consumers League Grassroots Marketing
Nobel Learning Communities
Ocean City Council Advertising, Marketing, Media Buying, Public Relations, Social Media
Old Bay Campaign: "Baytriotism", Events, Marketing, Social Media Marketing
Pretzelmaker
RoamRight Display Marketing, Email Marketing, Online, Search Engine Optimization, Strategic Marketing
Run for Your Lives
Snack Food Association Marketing, Public Relations
State Department Federal Credit Union
Sunshine State One Call of Florida (Agency of Record) Sunshine 811
TEDCO Public Relations
Thera Pearl Marketing, Public Relations
University of Maryland Medical System
Utz Quality Foods
Utz
Vein & Vascular Institute
Visit Baltimore
Wedding Day Diamonds
Wockenfuss Candies Creative, Media Planning & Buying, Social Media
ZIPS Dry Cleaners Creative, Media Planning & Buying, Social Media, Strategic Planning

MGI COMMUNICATIONS

(Formerly KW Advertising)
N56 W13585 Silver Spring Dr., Menomonee Falls, WI 53051
Tel.: (262) 703-0800
Fax: (262) 703-0900
Web Site: www.mgicommunications.com

E-Mail for Key Personnel:
Creative Dir.: filw@kwadvertising.com

Employees: 10
Year Founded: 1980

Agency Specializes In: Agriculture, Automotive, Broadcast, Business Publications, Business-To-Business, Co-op Advertising, Collateral, Consumer Marketing, Corporate Identity, Exhibit/Trade Shows, Food Service, Graphic Design, Health Care Services, Industrial, Internet/Web Design, Logo & Package Design, Media Planning, Medical Products, Newspaper, Newspapers & Magazines, Outdoor, Planning & Consultation, Print, Production, Publicity/Promotions, Radio, Sales Promotion, T.V., Trade & Consumer Magazines

Approx. Annual Billings: $9,375,000

Pierre Payne *(Pres)*
Trish Hastings *(Mgr-Bus Dev)*
Kristi George *(Analyst-Search Engine Mktg)*

Accounts:
Hammond Valve; Milwaukee, WI Commercial & Plumbing Valves; 1990
Milwaukee Valve Company; Milwaukee, WI Industrial & Commercial Valves; 1985
Modine Manufacturing Co.; Racine, WI All Divisions; 1984
Spargo Spa & Salon
Victory Homes (Agency of Record)
Ward Manufacturing; Blossburg, PA WardFlex; 2002

MGM GOLD COMMUNICATIONS

112 W 20th St 7th Fl, New York, NY 10011
Tel.: (212) 645-7323
Fax: (631) 532-1351
E-Mail: adm@mgmgoldcommunications.com
Web Site: www.mgmgoldcommunications.com

Employees: 12
Year Founded: 1980

Agency Specializes In: Advertising, Bilingual Market, Brand Development & Integration, Broadcast, Business-To-Business, Cable T.V., Collateral, Communications, Consulting, Consumer Goods, Consumer Marketing, Consumer Publications, Corporate Identity, Digital/Interactive, Fashion/Apparel, Graphic Design, Health Care Services, Integrated Marketing, Local Marketing, Logo & Package Design, Luxury Products, Magazines, Market Research, Media Buying Services, Media Planning, Multicultural, Multimedia, Newspaper, Newspapers & Magazines, Out-of-Home Media, Outdoor, Over-50 Market, Package Design, Point of Purchase, Point of Sale, Production, Production (Ad, Film, Broadcast), Production (Print), Public Relations, Publicity/Promotions, Radio, Regional, Sales Promotion, Seniors' Market, Syndication, T.V., Trade & Consumer Magazines, Transportation, Travel & Tourism, Viral/Buzz/Word of Mouth, Web (Banner Ads, Pop-ups, etc.)

Approx. Annual Billings: $18,000,000

Breakdown of Gross Billings by Media: Other: 20%; Print: 50%; T.V.: 30%

Mario G. Messina *(Pres & Chief Creative Officer)*

MHA MEDIA

5150 Wilshire Boulevard Ste 200, Los Angeles, CA 90036
Tel.: (323) 461-1100
E-Mail: info@mhamedia.com
Web Site: www.mhamedia.com

Agency Specializes In: Advertising, Brand Development & Integration, Digital/Interactive, Event Planning & Marketing, Public Relations

Marilyn G. Heston *(Pres)*
Nicol Bou Assaf *(Acct Mgr)*

Accounts:
New-Haney
New-The Seafarer Jeans
New-Via Spiga

MHZ DESIGN COMMUNICATIONS INC.

171 E Liberty St Ste 340, Toronto, ON M6K 3P6 Canada
Tel.: (416) 626-1777
Fax: (416) 626-7227
E-Mail: team@mhzdesign.com
Web Site: www.mhzdesign.com

Employees: 15
Year Founded: 1998

Agency Specializes In: Advertising

Angelo Perri *(Mng Partner)*
Carl Schubert *(VP)*
Domenic Vendittelli *(Dir-Creative)*
Pebbles Correa *(Sr Designer)*
Marcella Lio *(Acct Coord)*
Jordan Farrugia *(Coord-Social Media)*

Accounts:
GE Capital (Canada)
Hallmark (Canada)
Liquid Capital
Rogers Communications Inc

MI DIGITAL AGENCY

(Formerly Metter Interactive)
557 Main St, Bethlehem, PA 18018
Tel.: (610) 419-4510
Web Site: www.midigitalagency.com/

Year Founded: 1997

Agency Specializes In: Advertising, Brand Development & Integration, Business-To-Business, Content, Digital/Interactive, Graphic Design, Public Relations, Strategic Planning/Research

Michael Carroll *(Pres)*
Jeff Metter *(VP-Tech)*
David Snyder *(VP-Acct Svcs)*
Juan D. Bolanos *(Sr Designer)*

Accounts:
Connotate, Inc.

THE MICHAEL ALAN GROUP

22 W 38th St, New York, NY 10018
Tel.: (212) 563-7656
Fax: (212) 563-7657
Toll Free: (866) 395-7703
E-Mail: info@michael-alan.com
Web Site: www.michael-alan.com

Employees: 10
Year Founded: 2001

Agency Specializes In: Advertising, Advertising Specialties, Alternative Advertising, Branded Entertainment, Business-To-Business, Cable T.V., Consulting, Consumer Goods, Consumer Marketing, Consumer Publications, Entertainment, Event Planning & Marketing, Exhibit/Trade Shows, Experience Design, Fashion/Apparel, Guerilla Marketing, Local Marketing, Magazines, Mobile Marketing, Newspapers & Magazines, Out-of-Home Media, Outdoor, Production, Promotions, Publicity/Promotions, Search Engine Optimization, Strategic Planning/Research, T.V., Trade & Consumer Magazines, Viral/Buzz/Word of Mouth

Approx. Annual Billings: $3,000,000

Jonathan Margolis *(Pres & CEO)*
Erin Mills *(COO)*
Jill Rudnitzky *(Sr VP)*
Elizabeth Walker *(VP)*
Amy Spielholtz *(Acct Dir)*
David O'Neill *(Dir-Art)*
Allie Lewbel *(Sr Acct Mgr)*
Eva Chung *(Office Mgr)*
Nicole Battista *(Sr Acct Exec)*
Lenetta Pesotini *(Acct Exec)*

Accounts:
Bravo
MTV
Nickelodeon
People Magazine
Saks Fifth Avenue
WE TV

MICHAEL WALTERS ADVERTISING

444 N Wabash Ste 4W, Chicago, IL 60030
Tel.: (312) 467-5550
E-Mail: eschmidt@michaelwaltersadvertising.com
Web Site: www.michaelwaltersadvertising.com

Year Founded: 1998

Agency Specializes In: Above-the-Line, Advertising, Advertising Specialties, Affiliate Marketing, Affluent Market, African-American Market, Agriculture, Alternative Advertising, Arts, Asian Market, Automotive, Aviation & Aerospace, Below-the-Line, Bilingual Market, Brand Development & Integration, Branded Entertainment, Broadcast, Business Publications, Business-To-Business, Cable T.V., Catalogs, Children's Market, Co-op Advertising, Collateral, College, Commercial Photography, Communications, Computers & Software, Consulting, Consumer Goods, Consumer Marketing, Consumer Publications, Content, Corporate Communications, Corporate Identity, Cosmetics, Crisis Communications, Custom Publishing, Customer Relationship Management, Digital/Interactive, Direct Response Marketing, Direct-to-Consumer, E-Commerce, Education, Electronic Media, Electronics, Email, Engineering, Entertainment, Environmental, Event Planning & Marketing, Exhibit/Trade Shows, Experience Design, Fashion/Apparel, Financial, Food Service, Game Integration, Gay & Lesbian Market, Government/Political, Graphic Design, Guerilla Marketing, Health Care Services, High Technology, Hispanic Market, Hospitality, Household Goods, Identity Marketing, In-Store Advertising, Industrial, Infomercials, Information Technology, Integrated Marketing, International, Internet/Web Design, Investor Relations, Legal Services, Leisure, Local Marketing, Logo & Package Design, Luxury Products, Magazines, Marine, Market Research, Media Buying Services, Media Planning, Media Relations, Media Training, Medical Products, Men's Market, Merchandising, Mobile Marketing, Multicultural, Multimedia, New Product Development, New Technologies, Newspaper, Newspapers & Magazines, Out-of-Home Media, Outdoor, Over-50 Market, Package Design, Paid Searches, Pharmaceutical, Planning & Consultation, Podcasting, Point of Purchase, Point of Sale, Print, Product Placement, Production, Production (Ad, Film, Broadcast), Production (Print), Promotions, Public Relations, Publicity/Promotions, Publishing, RSS (Really Simple Syndication), Radio, Real Estate, Recruitment, Regional, Restaurant, Retail, Sales Promotion, Search Engine Optimization, Seniors' Market, Social Marketing/Nonprofit, South Asian Market, Sponsorship, Sports Market, Stakeholders, Strategic Planning/Research, Sweepstakes, Syndication, T.V., Technical Advertising, Teen Market, Telemarketing, Trade & Consumer Magazines, Transportation, Travel & Tourism, Urban Market, Viral/Buzz/Word of Mouth, Web (Banner Ads, Pop-ups, etc.), Women's Market, Yellow Pages Advertising

Approx. Annual Billings: $25,000,000

Breakdown of Gross Billings by Media: Collateral: 6%; Internet Adv.: 10%; Logo & Package Design: 2%; Newsp. & Mags.: 20%; Outdoor: 7%; Radio & T.V.: 50%; Trade Shows: 5%

Ken Lakowske *(Pres-Michael Walters Adv)*
Jim Lake *(VP)*
Jay Gurel *(Acct Svcs Dir)*
Ron Drake *(Dir-Bus Dev)*
Greg Kosinski *(Dir-Creative)*
Meri Vassek *(Dir-Media)*
Wendy Klein *(Acct Mgr)*
Kimm Ladewski *(Acct Supvr)*
Erin O'Reilly *(Coord-Media)*

Accounts:
Adventist Hospital; Bollingbrook, IL; 2002
Alaron; Chicago, IL; 2007
College of Dupage; 2000
College of Lake County; Grayslake, IL; 2007
Comcast SportsNet; Chicago, IL; 2007
Grand Canyon University; AZ; 2007
Olivet Nazarene University Marketing
Paslode; Vernon Hills, IL; 2008
San Joaquin Community Hospital/Adventist Health (Agency of Record) Marketing Communications
Sears Commercial; Hoffman Estates, IL; 2007
Whitehall Jewelers; Chicago, IL; 2007
Woodfield Mall; Schaumburg, IL; 1998

MICHAELSWILDER

7773 W Golden Ln, Peoria, AZ 85345-7977
Tel.: (623) 334-0100
Fax: (623) 334-0200
Toll Free: (800) 423-6468
E-Mail: hcminfo@michaelswilder.com
Web Site: www.michaelswilder.com

Employees: 40
Year Founded: 1989

National Agency Associations: ADM-YPA

Agency Specializes In: Advertising Specialties, Internet/Web Design, Media Buying Services, Recruitment, Search Engine Optimization, Yellow Pages Advertising

Approx. Annual Billings: $17,000,000

Breakdown of Gross Billings by Media: Internet Adv.: 10%; Newsp.: 20%; Yellow Page Adv.: 70%

Shelly Little *(CEO)*
Stacey Shaw *(Sr VP-Client Svcs-S2E Solutions)*
Rick Jorgensen *(Controller)*
Wendy Dimartini *(Client Svcs Dir)*
Steve Nagle *(Dir-New Bus Dev)*
Mike Ryan *(Dir-Creative)*
Laurel Winkelman *(Coord-Client)*

Accounts:
AAA-A Key Mini Storage
American Leak Detection
Arizona Public Service Company
Brundage Management Company, Inc.
City of Glendale
Gold's Gym
Jiffy Lube
Southwest Insurance Benefits
Storage Partners
Storage Solutions
The Tech Group
Western Career College
WesternTool Supply

MICHELSEN ADVERTISING

10855 NW 33rd St, Doral, FL 33172
Tel.: (305) 446-5211
Fax: (305) 446-5442
Web Site: www.michelsenadvertising.com

Agency Specializes In: Advertising, Digital/Interactive, Event Planning & Marketing, Internet/Web Design, Media Buying Services, Media Planning, Print, Public Relations, Strategic Planning/Research

Natalie Baro *(Pres)*
Stephanie Price *(Dir-Media)*
Jennifer Sanchez *(Creative Dir)*
Alexis Cantillo *(Acct Exec)*

Michele Paris *(Coord-Media)*

Accounts:
Humana, Inc.

MICROARTS
655 Portsmouth Ave, Greenland, NH 03840-2246
Tel.: (603) 430-1110
Fax: (603) 431-5111
E-Mail: pgetman@microarts.com
Web Site: www.microarts.com

E-Mail for Key Personnel:
President: pgetman@microarts.com

Employees: 18

Agency Specializes In: Advertising

Michaleen Craig *(Dir-Digital)*
Geoff Cunningham, Jr. *(Dir-Creative)*
Amy Cypres *(Dir-Accts & Strategic Plng)*
Dj Haskins *(Dir-Bus Dev)*
Blythe Langley *(Dir-Design)*
Ann Marie Niswender *(Mgr)*
David O'Shaughnessy *(Sr Designer)*

Accounts:
Bamboo
Business Logic
Chartworth
Firebrand
Ignite
Mount Will- The Peaks

MICROMASS COMMUNICATIONS INC
11000 Regency Pkwy Ste 300, Cary, NC 27518
Tel.: (919) 851-3182
E-Mail: mmc.engageus@micromass.com
Web Site: www.micromass.com

Employees: 50

Agency Specializes In: Event Planning & Marketing, Graphic Design, Strategic Planning/Research, Technical Advertising

Phil Stein *(CFO)*
Jessica Brueggeman *(Sr VP-Health Behavior Grp)*
Rob Peters *(Sr VP-Strategy)*
Kelly Hutchinson *(VP-HR)*
Philip Mann *(Grp Acct Dir)*
Greg Dosmann *(Grp Assoc Dir-Creative)*
Chris Libey *(Assoc Dir-Creative)*
Bonnie Overton *(Assoc Dir-Creative)*
Ethan Messier *(Mgr-Acctg)*
Chad Benditz *(Specialist-Mktg & PR)*

Accounts:
Acremex Metabolic Space Services
Merck's Singulair Medical Services

MICSTURA
12955 Biscayne Blvd Ste 408, Miami, FL 33181
Tel.: (786) 239-7380
E-Mail: ehenriques@micstura.com
Web Site: www.micstura.com

Employees: 7
Year Founded: 2005

Agency Specializes In: Above-the-Line, Advertising, Advertising Specialties, Affiliate Marketing, Affluent Market, African-American Market, Agriculture, Alternative Advertising, Arts, Asian Market, Automotive, Aviation & Aerospace, Below-the-Line, Bilingual Market, Brand Development & Integration, Branded Entertainment, Broadcast, Business Publications, Business-To-Business, Cable T.V., Catalogs, Children's Market, Co-op Advertising, Collateral, College, Commercial Photography, Communications, Computers & Software, Consulting, Consumer Goods, Consumer Marketing, Consumer Publications, Content, Corporate Communications, Corporate Identity, Cosmetics, Crisis Communications, Custom Publishing, Customer Relationship Management, Digital/Interactive, Direct Response Marketing, Direct-to-Consumer, E-Commerce, Education, Electronic Media, Electronics, Email, Engineering, Entertainment, Environmental, Event Planning & Marketing, Exhibit/Trade Shows, Experience Design, Fashion/Apparel, Financial, Food Service, Game Integration, Gay & Lesbian Market, Government/Political, Graphic Design, Guerilla Marketing, Health Care Services, High Technology, Hispanic Market, Hospitality, Household Goods, Identity Marketing, In-Store Advertising, Industrial, Infomercials, Information Technology, Integrated Marketing, International, Internet/Web Design, Investor Relations, Legal Services, Leisure, Local Marketing, Logo & Package Design, Luxury Products, Magazines, Marine, Market Research, Media Buying Services, Media Planning, Media Relations, Media Training, Medical Products, Men's Market, Merchandising, Mobile Marketing, Multicultural, Multimedia, New Product Development, New Technologies, Newspaper, Newspapers & Magazines, Out-of-Home Media, Outdoor, Over-50 Market, Package Design, Paid Searches, Pharmaceutical, Planning & Consultation, Podcasting, Point of Purchase, Point of Sale, Print, Product Placement, Production, Production (Ad, Film, Broadcast), Production (Print), Promotions, Public Relations, Publicity/Promotions, Publishing, RSS (Really Simple Syndication), Radio, Real Estate, Recruitment, Regional, Restaurant, Retail, Sales Promotion, Search Engine Optimization, Seniors' Market, Social Marketing/Nonprofit, South Asian Market, Sponsorship, Sports Market, Stakeholders, Strategic Planning/Research, Sweepstakes, Syndication, T.V., Technical Advertising, Teen Market, Telemarketing, Trade & Consumer Magazines, Transportation, Travel & Tourism, Urban Market, Viral/Buzz/Word of Mouth, Web (Banner Ads, Pop-ups, etc.), Women's Market, Yellow Pages Advertising

Approx. Annual Billings: $250,000

Eduardo Henriques *(Mng Partner)*
Alfredo Haack *(Dir-Art)*

MIDDLEBERG COMMUNICATIONS, LLC
40 W. 25th St 4th Floor, New York, NY 10010
Tel.: (212) 812-5671
Fax: (212) 202-4118
E-Mail: info@middlebergcommunications.com
Web Site: www.middlebergcommunications.com

Employees: 20
Year Founded: 2006

Agency Specializes In: Public Relations, Sponsorship

Don Middleberg *(CEO)*
Roger Ardan *(Mng Dir)*
Jason Stein *(Pres-Laundry Svc)*

Accounts:
Amerifit Nutrition, Inc. AZO; 2007
Animal Planet
BigString Corporation Email Service; 2007
Connotate
Hollander Home Fashions Corporation
Knovation
Kodak Graphic Communications Group
Meredith
Playmaker Systems Branding, Digital, Media Relations, Positioning
Right Guard
Schedulicity
Van Wagner
The Weather Channel

MIDDLETON & GENDRON, INC.
(Acquired by Eric Mower + Associates & Name Changed to M&G/Eric Mower + Associates)

MIDNIGHT OIL CREATIVE
3800 W Vanowen St, Burbank, CA 91505
Tel.: (818) 295-6300
Fax: (818) 847-9599
E-Mail: info@midnightoilcreative.com
Web Site: www.midnightoilcreative.com

Employees: 47

Tom Stillwell *(CEO)*
Jason Covey *(Exec VP)*
John Posta *(Exec Dir-Corp Strategy)*
Kristin Bruno *(Acct Dir)*
Brooke Lawler *(Acct Dir)*
Justin Scott *(Acct Dir)*
Oogie Lee *(Dir-Creative)*
Dino Hainline *(Strategist-Theatrical)*

Accounts:
Acti Vision
Disney
Focus Features
Lucas Arts
NBC Universal
Rockport
Verizon
XBOX 360

MIDWEST MEDIA SERVICES
PO Box 4512, North Liberty, IA 52317
Tel.: (319) 626-3364
Fax: (319) 626-3643
E-Mail: Marketing@midwestmediaservices.com

E-Mail for Key Personnel:
Media Dir.: stevef@midwestmediaservices.com

Employees: 6
Year Founded: 1995

Agency Specializes In: Direct Response Marketing, Graphic Design, Internet/Web Design, Magazines, Newspaper, Newspapers & Magazines, Print, Radio, Recruitment, Transportation

Approx. Annual Billings: $2,600,000

Breakdown of Gross Billings by Media: Internet Adv.: $118,000; Mags.: $1,000,000; Newsp.: $1,250,000; Other: $81,100; Production: $32,400; Radio: $76,000; Trade Shows: $42,500

Steven J. Feldmann *(Dir)*

Accounts:
Cdljobs.com; Coralville, IA
Goodfellow Printing; Iowa City, IA
Heartland Express Inc.; North Liberty, IA Employment Recruiting

MIGHTY 8TH MEDIA, LLC
83 E Main St, Buford, GA 30518
Tel.: (770) 271-3001
Fax: (770) 271-3955
E-Mail: info@m8th.com
Web Site: www.m8th.com

Year Founded: 2005

Agency Specializes In: Advertising, Brand Development & Integration, Collateral, Email, Environmental, Exhibit/Trade Shows, Internet/Web Design, Search Engine Optimization, Social Media

Bradley Sherwood *(Partner & Dir-Creative)*
Jonathan Holmes *(Partner)*
Justin Gillispie *(Dir-Bus Dev)*
Gordon McMahan *(Dir-Accts-Natl)*
Ashley Ripley *(Sr Acct Mgr)*
Beverly Buster *(Office Mgr)*
Britt Pecht *(Acct Mgr)*
Chase Wall *(Strategist-Brand)*
Ben Davis *(Sr Designer)*
Tammy Dock-Brown *(Sr Designer)*

Accounts:
Ray's Restaurants
SparkQuest

MIGHTY ENGINE

219 Cuthbert St Ste 600, Philadelphia, PA 19106
Tel.: (215) 384-1944
E-Mail: hello@themightyengine.com
Web Site: www.themightyengine.com

Year Founded: 2000

Heseung Ann Song *(Pres & CEO)*
Jennifer Krout *(Dir-Ops)*
Steven Sonntag *(Dir-Content)*
Logan Eadon *(Sr Graphic Designer)*

Accounts:
Kolsby Gorden
Stockton & Partners

MIK ADVERTISING & DESIGN, LLC

184 Hunters Ln, Newington, CT 06111
Tel.: (860) 436-6094
E-Mail: info@mikadvertising.com

Employees: 1
Year Founded: 2001

Agency Specializes In: Advertising, Automotive, Brand Development & Integration, Business Publications, Business-To-Business, Catalogs, Collateral, Consulting, Consumer Goods, Consumer Marketing, Consumer Publications, Corporate Communications, Corporate Identity, Digital/Interactive, Direct Response Marketing, Direct-to-Consumer, E-Commerce, Education, Electronic Media, Email, Environmental, Exhibit/Trade Shows, Financial, Government/Political, Graphic Design, Guerilla Marketing, High Technology, Hospitality, Identity Marketing, In-Store Advertising, Industrial, Integrated Marketing, Internet/Web Design, Leisure, Local Marketing, Logo & Package Design, Magazines, Marine, Market Research, Media Buying Services, Media Planning, Media Relations, Medical Products, Mobile Marketing, Multimedia, New Product Development, New Technologies, Newspaper, Newspapers & Magazines, Outdoor, Package Design, Podcasting, Point of Purchase, Point of Sale, Print, Product Placement, Production, Production (Print), Public Relations, Radio, Real Estate, Sales Promotion, Strategic Planning/Research, T.V., Technical Advertising, Trade & Consumer Magazines, Transportation, Travel & Tourism, Viral/Buzz/Word of Mouth, Web (Banner Ads, Pop-ups, etc.)

Approx. Annual Billings: $100,000

Breakdown of Gross Billings by Media: Bus. Publs.: $2,500; Collateral: $8,500; Corp. Communications: $4,000; D.M.: $5,000; Graphic Design: $55,000; Logo & Package Design: $8,000; Outdoor: $2,500; Print: $8,500; Trade & Consumer Mags.: $5,000; Trade Shows: $1,000

John M. Mik *(Owner)*

MILAGRO MARKETING

1141 Ringwood Ct Ste 20, San Jose, CA 95131
Tel.: (408) 324-0106
Fax: (408) 324-1712
E-Mail: info@milagromarketing.com
Web Site: www.milagromarketing.com

Year Founded: 2001

Agency Specializes In: Advertising, Brand Development & Integration, Event Planning & Marketing, Internet/Web Design, Logo & Package Design, Media Planning, Print, Public Relations

Sergio Estrada *(Art Dir)*
David Ocampo *(Creative Dir)*
Carol Ruvalcaba *(Dir-Social Media)*
Isadora Busch *(Strategist-Social Media)*
Andrea Gutierrez *(Designer)*

Accounts:
Dia San Jose

MILE 9

23622 Calabasas Rd Ste 323, Calabasas, CA 91302
Tel.: (818) 876-7100
Fax: (818) 876-7101
E-Mail: info@mile9agency.com
Web Site: www.mile9agency.com

Employees: 15

Agency Specializes In: Advertising, Advertising Specialties, Brand Development & Integration, Broadcast, Cable T.V., Collateral, Corporate Identity, Direct Response Marketing, Experience Design, Guerilla Marketing, Newspapers & Magazines, Out-of-Home Media, Package Design, Radio, Sales Promotion, Social Marketing/Nonprofit, T.V., Viral/Buzz/Word of Mouth

Jeff Smaul *(Pres & Exec Dir-Creative)*
Brad Carraway *(VP-Brand Strategy)*
Izabela Drodge *(Mgr-Admin)*
Kathleen Gurarie *(Acct Exec)*

Accounts:
ABC
ABC Television Opportunity Knocks, Pushing Daisies
Atari
Chevy
ESPN Monday Night Football, SportsCenter
FCS
Fox
Fox Sports Network
FX Channel
K-Swiss Campaign: "Blade Max"
NBC
Nestle
NFL Network
Nike
Speed Channel
Sprint
TCM
Wells Fargo

MILESTONE BROADCAST

33 Flatbush Ave 4th Fl, Brooklyn, NY 11217
Tel.: (212) 647-1212
E-Mail: paul.sladkus@goodnewsbroadcast.com
Web Site: www.goodnewsplanet.com

Employees: 11
Year Founded: 1985

Agency Specializes In: African-American Market, Arts, Asian Market, Content, Electronic Media, Entertainment, Environmental, Event Planning & Marketing, Hispanic Market, Integrated Marketing, Internet/Web Design, Production, Social Media, T.V., Web (Banner Ads, Pop-ups, etc.)

Approx. Annual Billings: $900,000

Breakdown of Gross Billings by Media: Adv. Specialities: $900,000

Paul H. Sladkus *(Founder & Pres)*
Austin Guo-siang Tang *(VP & Dir-Productions & Ops)*
Jerry Alteri *(Dir-Fin)*
Vid Son Doz *(Dir-Art)*
Greg Sullivan *(Dir-Dev)*
Maryann Zimmer *(Counsel)*

Accounts:
IBM
Johnson & Johnson
MSI Computers
Senior Net

MILKSONO LLC

11 Day St Level 1, South Norwalk, CT 06854
Tel.: (203) 851-1100
Web Site: www.milksono.com

Year Founded: 2001

Agency Specializes In: Advertising, Digital/Interactive, Outdoor, Print, Social Media, T.V.

Joseph Sequenzia *(CEO & Mng Partner)*
Maureen Main *(Partner & CFO)*
Deborah Casey *(Partner & Dir-Accounts)*
Kelly Coveny *(Chief Creative Officer)*
Tom Kidwell *(Exec Dir-Creative)*
Dylan Cyr *(Dir-Art)*
Sara Erwin *(Dir-Integrated Art)*
Brendan Abrassart-White *(Assoc Dir-Creative)*
T. J. Garvin *(Sr Acct Mgr)*
Melissa Gladkosky *(Mgr-Production)*
Kristin Kidd *(Acct Exec)*

Accounts:
illycaffe S.p.A.
Liggett Vector Brands Inc. Zoom E-Cigs

MILLENNIAL MEDIA INC.

2400 Boston St 3rd Fl, Baltimore, MD 21224
Tel.: (410) 522-8705
Fax: (410) 558-6268
E-Mail: media@millennialmedia.com
Web Site: www.millennialmedia.com

Employees: 100
Year Founded: 2007

Agency Specializes In: Mobile Marketing

Ernie Cormier *(COO)*
Matt Gillis *(Pres-Platform Bus)*
Alia Lamborghini *(Sr VP-Sls-NA)*
Matt Tengler *(Sr VP-Product)*
Zac Pinkham *(Mng Dir-EMEA)*
Liza Blumenthal *(Reg VP-Northeast Sls)*
Tony Gemma *(Reg VP)*
Bill Assaad *(VP-Fin Plng & Analysis)*
Patrick McCormack *(VP-Publisher Sls)*
Julienne Thompson *(VP-Programmatic Bus)*
Joseph Wilkinson *(VP-IR)*
Kristin Celano *(Head-Advertiser Mktg)*
Calynn Krieger *(Sr Dir-Strategy)*
Suzanne Shaw *(Sr Dir-Platform Mktg)*
Jon Wayman *(Sr Dir-Mobile Strategy)*
Christina Feeney *(Dir-Comm)*
Sarah Jennings *(Dir-Creative)*
Laura Krebill *(Dir-Sls-East)*
Susan Ridley *(Dir-Sls-Programmatic)*
Sara Sulock *(Sr Mgr-Mktg-Global Events)*
Lauren Barron *(Sr Acct Mgr-GMS)*

Emma Benjamin *(Acct Mgr-GMS)*
Kelly Byrne *(Acct Mgr)*
Kasey Sonnefeld *(Project Mgr-Ops)*
Clare Lochary *(Mgr-Comm)*
Lia Roth *(Mgr-Mktg-Platform Mktg)*
Michael Winnick *(Mgr-Programmatic Analytics)*
Kevin Sullivan *(Acct Exec)*
Alyssa Hinger *(Coord-Traffic)*
Jennifer Russo *(Coord-Events & Mktg)*

Accounts:
GoTV Networks; 2007

MILLENNIUM 3 MANAGEMENT INC.

2005 Market St Ste 3125, Philadelphia, PA 19103
Tel.: (215) 751-0140
Fax: (215) 751-0149
E-Mail: info@millennium3management.com
Web Site: m3mpr.com

Employees: 8
Year Founded: 1989

Agency Specializes In: African-American Market, Collateral, Communications, Consulting, Consumer Goods, Consumer Marketing, Corporate Communications, Corporate Identity, Crisis Communications, Event Planning & Marketing, Government/Political, Graphic Design, Internet/Web Design, Media Buying Services, Multicultural, Newspaper, Newspapers & Magazines, Planning & Consultation, Print, Public Relations, Strategic Planning/Research, Travel & Tourism, Urban Market

A. Bruce Crawley *(Pres)*
Anthony Marc Fullard *(Exec VP)*
Jennifer Chapple Ingram *(Asst VP-Client Rels)*

Accounts:
African-American Chamber of Commerce
AmeriHealth Mercy Health Plan
Art Sanctuary
Barnes Foundation
Chester Community Charter School; Chester, PA Education
City of Philadelphia
Domus
Geri-Perk
Heublein
Independence Blue Cross
London Fog
Maramont Corp.
Philadelphia Tribune
School District of Philadelphia

MILLENNIUM BUSINESS COMMUNICATIONS LLC

501 New Karner Rd Ste 3, Albany, NY 12205
Tel.: (518) 694-9935
Fax: (518) 694-9938
E-Mail: info@millenniumbc.net
Web Site: www.millenniumbc.com

Agency Specializes In: Advertising, Brand Development & Integration, Business Publications, Corporate Identity, Direct Response Marketing, Media Relations, Public Relations, Search Engine Optimization, Web (Banner Ads, Pop-ups, etc.)

Joe Madelone *(CEO)*
Henry Nahal *(CTO & Principal)*
Paul Madelone *(Principal)*

Accounts:
The Bette Companies
Embassy Designs Custom Millwork Creations Kitchen Bath & Custom Millwork Designer Services
Fidelis Care New York
Hill & Markes
Salad Creations
Saratoga Care
Silverman Law
Vinnick Construction Co. Inc

MILLENNIUM COMMUNICATIONS, INC.

6900 Jericho Tpke Ste 100LL, Syosset, NY 11791
Tel.: (516) 682-8080
Fax: (516) 682-9090
Web Site: www.millenniumweb.com

Employees: 25

Agency Specializes In: Broadcast, Communications, Digital/Interactive, E-Commerce, Email, Integrated Marketing, Local Marketing, Logo & Package Design, Print, Promotions, Radio, Strategic Planning/Research, T.V., Web (Banner Ads, Pop-ups, etc.)

Revenue: $2,700,000

Patrick Macri *(Pres & CEO)*
Theresa Macri *(CFO)*
David Denara *(CTO)*
Jeffrey Maldavir *(VP-Client Svcs)*
Janine Prestegaard *(Grp Acct Dir-Strategic Plng)*
David Rivera *(Acct Dir)*
Lisa D'Elia *(Dir-Design)*
Angela Florie *(Acct Mgr & Project Mgr-Interactive)*
J. J. Gembinski *(Project Mgr-Interactive)*
Todd Robertson *(Sr Designer)*

Accounts:
Bass
Bimbo Bakeries USA Inc.
Boboli
Cable Vision
Hyatt
JPMorgan Chase & Co.
Kraft
Microsoft
New World Pasta Company Advertising, Campaign: "There's No Yolks and No Other", Digital, No Yolks, Online
Ronzoni
Thomas
Wrigley

MILLENNIUM INTEGRATED MARKETING

150 Dow St, 3rd Fl, Manchester, NH 03101
Tel.: (603) 792-2200
Fax: (603) 792-2201
Toll Free: (877) 873-7445
Web Site: www.mill-im.com

Employees: 10

National Agency Associations: 4A's

Agency Specializes In: Advertising, Advertising Specialties, Affluent Market, Brand Development & Integration, Broadcast, Business Publications, Business-To-Business, Co-op Advertising, Collateral, College, Commercial Photography, Communications, Consumer Marketing, Content, Corporate Communications, Corporate Identity, Crisis Communications, Customer Relationship Management, Digital/Interactive, Education, Email, Event Planning & Marketing, Exhibit/Trade Shows, Experience Design, Graphic Design, Guerilla Marketing, Health Care Services, Identity Marketing, In-Store Advertising, Integrated Marketing, Internet/Web Design, Local Marketing, Magazines, Market Research, Media Buying Services, Media Planning, Media Relations, Mobile Marketing, New Product Development, Newspaper, Outdoor, Paid Searches, Podcasting, Production, Production (Print), Promotions, Public Relations, Publicity/Promotions, Radio, Sales Promotion, Search Engine Optimization, Social Marketing/Nonprofit, Social Media, Sponsorship, Strategic Planning/Research, T.V., Telemarketing, Viral/Buzz/Word of Mouth

Linda Fanaras *(Pres)*
Jessica Chabot *(Client Svcs Dir)*
Mark Dingman *(Dir-Digital Creative)*
Gina DiVenuti *(Mgr-Content Mktg)*
Aiden Redmond *(Mgr-Digital Content)*

Branch

Millennium Integrated Marketing
101 Federal St 19th Fl, Boston, MA 2110
(See Separate Listing)

MILLER ADVERTISING

(Formerly The Richards Organization)
84 Calvert St, Harrison, NY 10528-3213
Tel.: (914) 835-3111
Fax: (914) 835-3698
Toll Free: (800) 4ALLADS
E-Mail: info_wny@milleraa.com
Web Site: www.milleraa.com

Employees: 30
Year Founded: 1982

National Agency Associations: AAF-AD CLUB

Agency Specializes In: Advertising, Business-To-Business, Commercial Photography, Custom Publishing, Direct Response Marketing, Education, Graphic Design, Media Planning, Newspapers & Magazines, Outdoor, Print, Production, Public Relations, Radio, Real Estate, Recruitment, Retail, T.V., Travel & Tourism

Approx. Annual Billings: $22,750,000

Breakdown of Gross Billings by Media: Bus. Publs.: $750,000; Collateral: $1,000,000; D.M.: $250,000; Mags.: $2,000,000; Newsp.: $18,500,000; Outdoor: $50,000; Radio: $130,000; Transit: $70,000

N. Richards *(Acct Supvr)*
T. Wyker *(Acct Exec)*

Accounts:
Benson Commercial Realty
Bowtie Inc. Magazine Publishers (Recruitment)
Calix Network Inc.; Petaluma, CA Recruitment; 1999
Coach Realtors; LI Real Estate; 2007
Community National Bank; NY; 2007
Corcoran Wexlar; NY Real Estate; 1995
Dutchess Boces; NY Recruitment; 2009
Edward Lee Cave, Inc.
Essex Corporation; New York, NY Recruitment
First Realty Group, Inc.
Frances Billingsley Real Estate
Goodstein Realty; FL; NY; VA; 2000
Keller Williams; NY Real Estate; 2008
Kelly Associated; Darien, CT Real Estate
Prudential Affiliates; NY Real Estate; 1995
Prudential Connecticut Realty
Prudential Rand; New City, NY Real Estate; 2000
ReMax; NY Real Estate; 2006
Sotheby's Affiliates; NY; PA; VA Real Estate; 2005
Westchester Realty Affiliates Real Estate
Worcester Public Schools
Zierick Manufacturing

MILLER ADVERTISING AGENCY INC.

71 5th Ave 5th Fl, New York, NY 10003-3004
Tel.: (212) 929-2200
Fax: (212) 727-4734
Toll Free: (800) 229-6574
E-Mail: info@milleraa.com
Web Site: http://www.milleraa.com/

Employees: 125
Year Founded: 1919

Agency Specializes In: Automotive, Financial, Internet/Web Design, Legal Services, Real Estate, Recruitment, Travel & Tourism

Nicole Miller *(Principal)*
Andrew Miller *(VP)*
James T. Curry *(Controller-Fin)*
Vinny Talamo *(Dir-Art)*
Ryan Cohen *(Acct Supvr, Media Planner & Buyer)*
Peggy Robinson *(Acct Exec & Copywriter)*
Tina DiZenzo *(Acct Rep)*

Accounts:
Adelphi University Recruitment
The Chubb Corporation; Warren, NJ
Coach; New York, NY (Recruitment)
Cohen Brothers Realty; New York, NY Developers
Cohen Media Group Film Distribution
Coldwell Banker; Parsippany, NJ Residential Brokerage
Corvias Group Recruitment
Dunbar Armored Recruitment
F.D.I.C.
Federal Bureau of Investigation; Washington, DC
Fordham University Recruitment
Glenwood Management; New Hyde Park, NY
Google Recruitment
Henry Street Settlement; New York, NY
Lily Pulitzer Recruitment
Manfredi Auto Mall; Staten Island, NY
Manfredi Dodge; Brooklyn, NY Auto Dealer
March of Dimes Recruitment
Moran & Co., Chicago, IL Real Estate Development
Morgan Stanley & Co.; New York, NY
MTA; New York, NY Legal, Recruitment & Real Estate
New York City Transit Authority; New York, NY Legal Notices, Recruitment
New York Life
New York State Division of Housing & Urban Renewal; New York, NY
NY Power Authority; New York, NY
NY Public Library Connected Communities Special Program
Princeton Regional School District; Princeton, NJ Recruitment
Queensboro Toyota; Woodside, NY
Sheldon Good & Co.; Chicago, IL Real Estate Auctions
Solow Building Corp.; New York, NY Developer
Starrett Housing Corp.; New York, NY Real Estate
Stribling & Associates; New York, NY Real Estate
U.S. Drug Enforcement Administration
United States Department of Justice Advertising for Seized and Forfeited Properties
Wakefern Food Corp. Recruitment

Branches

Miller Advertising Agency Inc.-Chicago

1 Northfield Plz Ste 300, Northfield, IL 60093-1214
Tel.: (847) 441-2618
Fax: (847) 441-2619
E-Mail: info_il@milleraa.com
Web Site: www.milleraa.com

Employees: 5

Agency Specializes In: Automotive, Real Estate, Recruitment

Steve Brown *(Mng Dir)*
Scott Watson *(CFO)*
Alyssa Hellenbrand-Best *(Dir-Ops)*
Lindsey Sauter *(Mgr-Property)*
Mitch Colstad *(Community Mgr)*
Sarah Hart *(Community Mgr)*
Jaclyn Skjervem *(Community Mgr)*
Shannon Sloat *(Community Mgr)*

Miller Adv.

71 5th Ave, New York, NY 10003
Tel.: (212) 929-2200
Fax: (516) 364-9391
E-Mail: info_li@milleraa.com
Web Site: http://www.milleraa.com/

Employees: 25

Leonard Miller *(Chm)*
Bob Miller *(Pres-New York)*
Jim Reiley *(Dir-IT)*
Olga Volynsky *(Dir-Art)*
Al Lewis *(Mgr-Studio)*
Nesta George *(Asst Controller-Fin)*

Miller Legal Services

2442 N Lincoln Ave, Chicago, IL 60614
Tel.: (773) 388-3393
Fax: (773) 290-2567
E-Mail: info_chicagolegal@milleraa.com
Web Site: www.levinadvertising.com

Employees: 5

Agency Specializes In: Legal Services

Adam B. Levin *(Acct Exec)*

MILLER BROOKS

11712 N Michigan St, Zionsville, IN 46077
Tel.: (317) 873-8100
E-Mail: contact@millerbrooks.com
Web Site: www.millerbrooks.com

Agency Specializes In: Advertising, Brand Development & Integration, Collateral, Content, Logo & Package Design, Public Relations

Barbie Wentworth *(Pres & CEO)*
Rosie O'Hara *(Mng Dir & Dir-PR)*
Kurt Ashburn *(Acct Dir)*
Uriaha Foust *(Dir-Creative)*
Karen Grant *(Dir-Ops)*
Kelly Wiltfong *(Media Planner & Media Buyer)*

Accounts:
D.L. Couch Wallcovering, Inc.

THE MILLER GROUP

1516 S Bundy Dr Ste 200, Los Angeles, CA 90025
Tel.: (310) 442-0101
Fax: (310) 442-0107
E-Mail: tmgconnect@millergroupmarketing.com
Web Site: www.millergroupmarketing.com/

Employees: 20
Year Founded: 1990

National Agency Associations: AAF-THINKLA

Agency Specializes In: Advertising, Advertising Specialties, Brand Development & Integration, Branded Entertainment, Business Publications, Co-op Advertising, Collateral, Communications, Consulting, Consumer Marketing, Digital/Interactive, Direct Response Marketing, Direct-to-Consumer, Education, Integrated Marketing, Local Marketing, Luxury Products, Market Research, Media Planning, Media Relations, Medical Products, Multimedia, New Product Development, Planning & Consultation, Promotions, Public Relations, Strategic Planning/Research

Approx. Annual Billings: $10,000,000

Breakdown of Gross Billings by Media: Brdcst.: 15%; Collateral: 10%; D.M.: 15%; Internet Adv.: 10%; Newsp.: 20%; Outdoor: 15%; Pub. Rels.: 15%

Renee Miller *(Pres & Dir-Creative)*
Gary Bettman *(Sr VP & Producer-Brdcst)*
Jeff Camp *(Acct Dir)*
Scott Steer *(Dir-Branding & Promo)*
Bill Williams *(Planner-Strategic)*
Lena Hopfmann *(Acct Coord)*

Accounts:
7-Eleven
First Federal Bank of California; Santa Monica, CA Financial Sevices
General Electric
Goodwill Industries
Greenlite
Kenwood
RE/MAX of California & Hawaii; Los Angeles, CA; 2004
SynerScope Website
Wolf Range Co

MILLER-REID, INC.

1200 Mountain Creek Rd Ste 480, Chattanooga, TN 37405
Tel.: (423) 875-5868
Fax: (423) 875-6573
E-Mail: info@miller-reid.com
Web Site: www.miller-reid.com

Employees: 7
Year Founded: 1979

Agency Specializes In: Consumer Marketing

Kent Keasler *(Pres)*
Jeanie Camp *(Dir-Media)*
Sam Turner *(Dir-Creative)*

Accounts:
Citizens National Bank; Athens, TN

MILLWARD BROWN INC.

3333 Warrenville Rd, Lisle, IL 60532
Tel.: (630) 505-0066
Fax: (630) 505-0077
Toll Free: (800) 937-0099
E-Mail: info@us.millwardbrown.com
Web Site: www.millwardbrown.com

Employees: 300
Year Founded: 1974

Agency Specializes In: Advertising, African-American Market, Brand Development & Integration, Business-To-Business, Children's Market, Communications, Consumer Marketing, Digital/Interactive, E-Commerce, Entertainment, Fashion/Apparel, Financial, Health Care Services, High Technology, Hispanic Market, In-Store Advertising, Information Technology, Internet/Web Design, Logo & Package Design, New Product Development, Over-50 Market, Pharmaceutical, Point of Purchase, Point of Sale, Print, Public Relations, Retail, Sales Promotion, Seniors' Market, Strategic Planning/Research, T.V., Teen Market, Transportation, Travel & Tourism

Dave Sandberg *(CFO)*
Cheryl Stallworth-Hooper *(CEO-Firefly North America)*
Nick Findlay *(Head-Ops-Global)*
Patty Currie *(Acct Dir-PepsiCo-Global)*
Daren Poole *(Global Brand Dir-Creative Dev)*
Peter Walshe *(Acct Dir-Global)*
Lauren Ariano *(Dir-Client Mgmt)*
Annie Pecoraro *(Dir-Client Mgmt)*
Michelle Weinrich *(Dir-Client Mgmt)*
Aaron Codak *(Mgr-Client Svcs Fin-North America)*
Nigel Hollis *(Sr Analyst-Global)*
Duncan Southgate *(Global Brand Dir-Digital)*

Accounts:

Barclays
Chrysler
Volvo

Branches

Millward Brown
(Formerly Dynamic Logic)
24-48 Bloomsbury Way, Level 2, London, WC1A 2PX United Kingdom
Tel.: (44) 020 7126 5000
Fax: (44) 020 7126 5003
Web Site:
www.millwardbrown.com/footer/contact/united-kingdom

Dale Beaton *(Mng Dir)*
Robin Wood *(CMO)*
David Chantrey *(Chief Strategy Officer-Europe)*
Karen Rivoire *(Chief HR Officer-Millward Brown)*
Tim Wragg *(CEO-Millward Brown Europe)*
Nick Bull *(Sr Dir-Bus Dev)*
Bal Thandi *(Dir-Global Comm & Mktg)*
Raam Tarat *(Project Mgr-Global Comm-BrandZ)*
Stuart Brookes *(Mgr-Bus Dev)*
Isabel Caterer *(Sr Exec-Client)*
Nick Cooper *(Sr Partner)*

Millward Brown
(Formerly Dynamic Logic)
303 2nd St N Tower 3rd Fl, San Francisco, CA 94107
Tel.: (415) 268-1650
Fax: (415) 268-1651
E-Mail: jasonl@millwardbrown.com
Web Site: www.millwardbrown.com

Employees: 22

Jason Lapp *(Exec VP-Growth & Strategy)*
Tristan Gaiser *(VP & Head-West Coast Team-Advertiser Grp)*
Leah Spalding *(VP & Head-West Coast)*
Judy Mahtaban *(VP-Bus Dev)*
Rebecca Szew *(VP-Client Svc)*
Kent Parmington *(Dir-Sls)*
Carla Verder *(Dir-Client & Bus Dev)*
Rachelle Vangene *(Assoc Dir)*
Audrey Lee *(Acct Supvr)*
Alicia Rauser *(Acct Supvr)*

Millward Brown
(Formerly Dynamic Logic)
3333 Warrenville Rd Ste 400, Lisle, IL 60532
Tel.: (630) 505-0066
Fax: (630) 505-0077
Web Site:
www.millwardbrown.com/footer/contact/united-states/illinois

Employees: 18

Ciju Nair *(Principal & Head-Connected Data, Effectiveness & ROI solutions)*
Chris Borchert *(Sr VP-Growth & Strategy)*
Hillary Oestreicher *(VP)*
Lauren Ariano *(Dir-Client Mgmt)*
Sara Beaty *(Dir-Mktg-Media Effectiveness Solutions)*
Crystal Baker *(Sr Client Analyst)*
Heath Greenfield *(Bus Partner-Express & Self-Serve Solutions)*
Michael Pecoraro *(Sr Client Analyst)*
Jessica Sarkisian *(Sr Client Analyst)*

Accounts:
Ford
Group M Agencies
P&G

Millward Brown Australia
Level 11, 181 Miller St North, Sydney, 2060 Australia
Tel.: (61) 2 9927 1111
Fax: (61) 2 9953 1112
E-Mail: info@au.millwardbrown.com
Web Site: www.millwardbrown.com

Ben Dixon *(Mng Dir)*
Sara Law *(Chief Client Officer)*
Cindy Grass *(Head-Talent & Strategy)*
Mark Henning *(Head-Media & Digital, AMAP Reg)*
Britt-Marie Malmberg *(Sr Mgr-ACE)*
Stephen Davies *(Sr Acct Mgr)*
Hayley Phillips *(Sr Acct Mgr)*
David Cardenas *(Sr Acct Coord)*
Cornelia Weyrich *(Client Svc Dir)*

Millward Brown Brazil
Al Santos 2101 - 7 Andar, Sao Paulo, 01419-002 Brazil
Tel.: (55) 11 3069 3601
Fax: (55) 11 3898 2730
E-Mail: valkiria.garre@millwardbrown.com
Web Site: www.millwardbrown.com

Employees: 100

Eduardo Heiji Tomiya *(Mng Dir)*
Valkiria Garre *(Exec Dir)*
Maria Silvia Muniz De Souza *(Acct Dir)*
Marina Fernandez *(Dir-Plng & Svc Area Qualitative)*
Adriana Sousa *(Dir-Digital & Media-Latin America)*
Milton Souza *(Client Svc Dir & Dir-Plng)*
Francisco Bayeux De Araujo *(Reg Mgr-Solutions-Latham)*
Luis Bosisio *(Acct Mgr)*
Flavia Hadad *(Acct Mgr)*
Natalia Marques *(Mgr-HR)*
Viviane Varandas *(Client Svc Dir)*

Millward Brown Canada
4950 Yonge Street Suite 600, Toronto, ON M2N 6K1 Canada
Tel.: (416) 221-9200
Fax: (416) 221-7681
E-Mail: info@us.millwardbrown.com
Web Site: www.millwardbrown.com

Employees: 55
Year Founded: 1985

Agency Specializes In: Brand Development & Integration, Consulting, Consumer Marketing, Planning & Consultation, Strategic Planning/Research

Scott Megginson *(Pres-Canada)*
Aurelio Diluciano *(VP)*
Paul Gareau *(VP)*
Sandra Pinchak *(VP-Res Design & Mgmt)*
David Scott *(VP-Res Ops)*
Cesar Zea *(VP-Client Mgmt)*
Andrea Cheng *(Sr Bus Analyst-Client Svc)*

Millward Brown/Centrum
Paulvan Vlissingen Scraac 10B, 1018 DH Amsterdam, Netherlands
Tel.: (31) 20 556 6666
Fax: (31) 20 556 6555
E-Mail: info@millwardbrown.nl
Web Site: www.millwardbrown.com

Anthonie Onzenoort *(Mng Dir)*
Marcel Spijkerman *(Acct Dir)*
Rob Van Benthem *(Acct Dir)*
Marieke Kok *(Dir-Firefly)*
Hugo Schurink *(Dir-Strategic Growth)*
Cheney Gasparini *(Acct Mgr)*
Vladimir Den Baars *(Client Dir)*

Millward Brown China
Fl 17 Golden Bridge Plz, No 585 Xizang Rd Middle, Shanghai, 200003 China
Tel.: (86) 21 6359 8622
Fax: (86) 21 6359 8682
E-Mail: info@cn.millwardbrown.com
Web Site: www.millwardbrown.com

Employees: 100

Albert Sim *(Mng Dir)*
Adrian Gonzalez *(CEO-Africa, Middle East & Asia Pacific)*
Mark Du *(Acct Dir)*
Maple Feng *(Acct Dir)*
Sherry Liu *(Acct Dir)*
William Wei *(Acct Dir)*
Sijia Lin *(Assoc Dir)*
Jennifer Chen *(Acct Mgr)*
Shuyun Qiu *(Assoc Acct Mgr)*
Jie Yan *(Assoc Acct Mgr)*
Hui Yao *(Assoc Acct Mgr)*

Millward Brown Delfo
Via Guglielmo Silva 36, 20149 Milan, Italy
Tel.: (39) 02 4399 5861
Fax: (39) 02 4385 0520
Web Site: www.millwardbrown.com

Employees: 14

Agency Specializes In: Advertising

Fabio Da Col *(Grp Acct Dir)*
Mario Marchetti *(Dir-Fin)*
Grace Nicolosi *(Dir-Res Mgmt Office-Europe)*
Lisa Rosen *(Dir-Bus Intelligence)*
Shiva Mohammadian *(Acct Mgr)*
Barbara Rolandi *(Acct Mgr)*
Matteo Beccarelli *(Client Svc Dir)*

Millward Brown Denmark
Raadhuspladsen 45-47 5th Fl, 1550 Copenhagen, v Denmark
Tel.: (45) 33 77 10 40
Fax: (45) 33 77 10 50
E-Mail: mbdk@millwardbrown.dk
Web Site:
www.millwardbrown.com/footer/contact/denmark

Employees: 30

Lars Kaa Andersen *(Owner)*
Irene Iversen *(Head-Insights & Ops & Dir)*
Anja Vintrup Kristensen *(Coord-Project Team)*

Millward Brown, Inc.
501 Kings Hwy E, Fairfield, CT 06825-4859
Tel.: (203) 335-5222
Fax: (203) 333-6307
E-Mail: info@us.millwardbrown.com
Web Site: www.millwardbrown.com

Employees: 200

Simon Moody *(Pres-North America)*

Millward Brown Lansdowne
(Formerly Millward Brown IMS)
Millbank House Arkle Road, Sandyford, 18 Dublin, Ireland
Tel.: (353) 1 676 1196
Fax: (353) 1 676 1196
Web Site: www.millwardbrown.com/

Employees: 90

Maureen Van Wijk *(Mng Dir)*

Brendan Beere *(Acct Dir)*
Annemarie Dillon *(Acct Dir)*
Sonya McGuirl *(Acct Dir)*
Ailis Hickey *(Assoc Dir-Res Mgmt)*
Paul Moran *(Assoc Dir)*
Conor Murphy *(Client Svc Dir)*

Accounts:
Diageo
O2
Vodafone

Millward Brown Market Reseach Services
Mahalakshmi Chamber 3rd Fl Mahatma Gandhi Rd, Bengaluru, 560001 India
Tel.: (91) 80 42927000
Fax: (91) 80 42927070
E-Mail: praveen.ramachandra@in.millwardbrown.com
Web Site: www.millwardbrown.com

Employees: 45

Agency Specializes In: South Asian Market

Shishir Varma *(Chief Client Officer-Africa Middle East Asia Pacific)*
Marisha Gupta *(Head-Global Cross Media Hub)*
Praveen Ramachandra *(Reg Head-Acct-Africa Middle East Asia Pacific)*

Millward Brown Mexico
Avenida Tamaulipas 150-1202 Colonia Condesa, Mexico, DF 06140 Mexico
Tel.: (52) 55 3098 1000
Fax: (52) 55 3098 1090
E-Mail: ricardo.barrueta@mx.millwardbrown.com

Ricardo Barrueta *(Dir Gen-North Latam)*
Gonzalo Fuentes *(CEO-Latin America)*
Enrique Gonzalez Sainz *(VP-Client Svc)*
JAMES GALPIN *(Head-Media & Digital-LATAM)*
Jorge Macias *(Head-Mktg Sciences)*
Francisco Javier Rodriguez *(Sr Acct Dir)*
Cindy Salas *(Acct Coord-Project Mgmt Dept)*
Cinthia Catana *(Sr Acct Coord)*

Millward Brown Philippines
8/F Equitable Bank Tower 8751 Paseo De Roxas, Salcedo Village, Makati, 1226 Philippines
Tel.: (63) 2 864 8960
Fax: (63) 2 884 8564
E-Mail: info@ph.millwardbrown.com
Web Site: www.millwardbrown.com

Employees: 45

Nena Barredo *(Mng Dir)*
Jenny Grace Surio *(VP-HR)*
Vicky Abad *(Grp Acct Dir)*
Agnes Manalac *(Grp Acct Dir)*
Marian Villanueva *(Acct Dir)*
Vida Cruz *(Acct Mgr)*
Amily Isturis *(Mgr-HR)*
Robbie Ann Joco *(Mgr-Res)*
Threese Mariano *(Mgr-Qualitative Acct Res)*
Jomanuel Cordova *(Assoc Acct Dir)*
Athena Ariadne Ilagan *(Assoc Acct Dir-Quantitative)*

Millward Brown Portugal
Avenida Eng Duarte Pacheco Torre 1 - 90 Piso, 1070-101 Lisbon, Portugal
Tel.: (351) 213 581 130
Fax: (351) 213 581 148
Web Site: www.millwardbrown.com

Millward Brown Singapore
300 Beach Rd, #35-03 The Concourse, Singapore, 199555 Singapore
Tel.: (65) 6323 2273
Fax: (65) 6323 3182
E-Mail: info@sg.millwardbrown.com
Web Site: www.millwardbrown.com

Employees: 80

Priti Mehra *(Mng Dir)*
Gaurav Hirey *(Chief HR Officer-Africa, Middle East & Asia Pacific)*
Nichola Rastrick *(Mng Dir-South East Asia)*
Yee Mei Chan *(Reg Dir-Mobile Deployment)*
Bhomik Chandna *(Reg Dir-Digital Strategy)*
Richard Heath *(Grp Acct Dir)*
Shobhana Ramachandran *(Grp Acct Dir)*
Eliza Obordo-Claravall *(Acct Dir)*
Jane Ng *(Dir-Client Solutions, South East Asia)*
Lynn Chia *(Acct Mgr)*
Lakshmy Priya *(Mgr-Brand Performance Programs)*

Accounts:
Unilever

Millward Brown SMG/KRC
ul Nowoursynowska 154a, 02-797 Warsaw, Poland
Tel.: (48) 22 545 2000
Fax: (48) 22 545 2100
E-Mail: office@smgkrc.pl
Web Site: www.millwardbrown.com

Krzysztof B. Kruszewski *(Pres)*
Marek Biskup *(Client Svcs Dir)*
Katarzyna Jeczmyk *(Dir-HR)*
Jan M. Kujawski *(Dir-R&D)*
Kuba Antoszewski *(Mgr-PR)*
Paul Ciacek *(Client Svc Dir)*

Millward Brown South Africa
7 Mellis Rd, Bradenham Hall, Gauteng, South Africa
Tel.: (27) 11 202 7000
Fax: (27) 11 202 7032
Web Site: www.millwardbrown.com

Employees: 120

Erik du Plessis *(Chm)*
Charles Foster *(Mng Dir-Africa & Middle East)*
Natalie Otte *(Grp Acct Dir)*
Shreenu Chintamani *(Acct Mgr)*
Katherine Du Plessis *(Acct Mgr)*
Jennifer Axelson *(Mgr-Mktg Science)*
Alexandre De Jubecourt *(Assoc Acct Dir)*
Sonja Myburgh *(Assoc Acct Dir)*
Alwyn Venter *(Assoc Acct Dir)*

Millward Brown Spain
Alcala 474, 28027 Madrid, Spain
Tel.: (34) 91 325 4100
Fax: (34) 91 325 4101
E-Mail: juan.ferrer-vidal@millwardbrown.com
Web Site: www.millwardbrown.com

Employees: 165

Agency Specializes In: Advertising

Pepe Martinez *(Gen Dir)*
Elisabet Contijoch *(Acct Dir)*
Lluis Casas Esterich *(Acct Dir)*
Naroa Marcos Larrinaga *(Acct Dir)*
Elaine Hervello *(Dir-Client)*
Alejandro Turnes Gomez *(Acct Mgr)*
Alexandre Lopez Lorenzo *(Client Mgr)*
Borja Marcos *(Client Dir)*
Bernd Rijks *(Client Svc Dir-Intl Unit)*

Millward Brown Taiwan
7F-1 No 37 Sec 3, Minsheng E Rd, Taipei, Taiwan
Tel.: (886) 2 7710 1200
Fax: (886) 2 7707 1201
E-Mail: info@tw.millwardbrown.com
Web Site: www.millwardbrown.com

Rupam Borthakur *(Mng Dir-HK & Taiwan)*
Joyce Gan *(Head-Client Svcs)*
Grace Chang *(Acct Dir)*
Sumit Kamra *(Assoc Dir)*
Felix Chang *(Acct Mgr)*
Lung-An Kuo *(Assoc Acct Dir)*

Millward Brown Thailand
Level 14 Kamol Sukosol Bldg 317 Silom Road, Bangrak, Bangkok, 10500 Thailand
Tel.: (66) 2 686 6400
Fax: (66) 2 234 6541
E-Mail: info@th.millwardbrown.com
Web Site: www.millwardbrown.com

Employees: 60

Klaas Hommez *(Mng Dir)*
Prashant Kolleri *(Mng Dir-MENA)*
Siriporn Padungsuntorn *(Reg Dir-PM-SEA)*
Pannawat Sirisak *(Acct Dir)*
Anshul Mishra *(Acct Mgr)*
Ramesh Redekar *(Acct Mgr)*
Pawee Sriwareerat *(Acct Mgr)*
Pinyapassh Subhandvadh *(Mgr-Res)*
Punlert Nuansirikosol *(Assoc Acct Dir)*
Yada Sareesavetrat *(Assoc Acct Dir)*

Millward Brown Ulster
Aisling House, 50 Stranmillis Embankment, Belfast, Northern Ireland BT9 5FL United Kingdom
Tel.: (44) 28 9023 1060
Fax: (44) 28 9024 3887
E-Mail: ctoner@ums-research.com
Web Site: www.millwardbrown.com

Employees: 160

Catherine Toner *(Mng Dir)*
Clare Moore *(Acct Dir)*
Glenn Hall *(Dir-Res)*
Alan Lobo *(Dir)*
Dawn Mccartney *(Assoc Dir)*

Millward Brown UK Ltd.
Olympus Avenue Tachbrook Park, Warwick, CV34 6RJ United Kingdom
Tel.: (44) 1926 452233
Fax: (44) 1926 833600
E-Mail: info@uk.millwardbrown.com
Web Site: www.millwardbrown.com

Employees: 500

Agency Specializes In: Planning & Consultation, Strategic Planning/Research

David Chantrey *(Chief Strategy Officer-Europe)*
John Svendsen *(Sr VP & Brand Dir-Media-Global)*
Gordon Pincott *(Global Head-Solutions)*
Mauricio Martinez *(Gen Mgr)*
Vincent Blaney *(Brand Dir-Media & Digital-European)*
Duncan Southgate *(Brand Dir-Digital-Global)*
Peter Walshe *(Acct Dir-Global)*

Millward Brown
2425 Olympic Blvd Ste 240-E, Santa Monica, CA 90404
Tel.: (310) 309-3400
Fax: (310) 309-3401
E-Mail: info@us.millwardbrown.com
Web Site: www.millwardbrown.com

Employees: 25

George Donovan *(Chief Sls Officer)*
Jason Lapp *(Exec VP-Growth & Strategy)*
Michael Perlman *(Sr VP-Media Practice)*
Erika Bzdel *(VP-Growth & Strategy-Natl Accounts)*
Joline Mcgoldrick *(Dir-Res)*

Millward Brown
26555 Evergreen Rd Ste 600, Southfield, MI 48076-4228
Tel.: (248) 351-2888
Fax: (248) 351-2878
E-Mail: peter.teachman@millwardbrown.com
Web Site: www.millwardbrown.com

Stephen DiMarco *(CMO)*
Peter Teachman *(Exec VP)*
Dolly Denyse *(Sr VP-Client & Mktg Dev Team)*
Jason Caine *(VP & Head-Retail & Consumer Goods Sector)*
Kate Ginsburg *(VP-Insights & Analytics)*
Peter Brown *(Dir-Client Mgmt)*
Amelia O'Connor *(Dir-Res)*
Zoe Morin *(Mgr-Sls-Compete PRO & API)*
Erin Harrison *(Client Analyst)*
Aniya Zaozerskaya *(Client Mgr)*

Millward Brown
11 Maidson Ave 12th Fl, New York, NY 10010
Tel.: (212) 548-7200
Fax: (212) 548-7201
E-Mail: info@us.millwardbrown.com
Web Site: www.millwardbrown.com

Agency Specializes In: Brand Development & Integration, Consumer Marketing, Planning & Consultation, Sponsorship

Jean Mostaccio *(Partner-HR Bus & Dir-Talent Strategy)*
Mario Simon *(CEO-Millward Brown Vermeer)*
Michelle Eule *(Sr VP-Res & Client Svcs)*
Susan Hickey *(Sr VP-Mktg & Comm)*
Stefan Sellberg *(Sr VP-Digital Media Grp)*
Joline Mcgoldrick *(VP-Res-Millward Brown Digital)*
Marisa Mcmahon *(VP-Advertiser Grp)*
Matt Rebmann *(VP-Client & Market Dev)*
Lauren Orski *(Sr Dir)*
Joe Shantz *(Sr Dir-Advanced Analytics)*
Travis Coleman *(Dir-Media Practice)*
Stacy Graiko *(Dir-Qualitative Res)*
Jamie Jones *(Dir-Mktg & Comm)*
Ronit Wilkof *(Acct Supvr)*
Christine Nguyen *(Supvr-Res)*
Ann Green *(Sr Partner-Client Solutions)*
Ali Rana *(Grp Sr VP-Emerging Media Lab)*

MIND ECOLOGY
107 Leland St Ste 4, Austin, TX 78704
Tel.: (512) 326-1300
Web Site: www.mindecology.com

Agency Specializes In: Advertising, Content, Internet/Web Design, Media Buying Services, Search Engine Optimization, Social Media

Darren Drewitz *(Founder & Strategist)*
Jed C. Jones *(Pres)*
David Drewitz *(Mng Dir)*
James Ballard *(Dir-Web Concept & Design)*
Amanda Melendrez *(Mgr-Mktg Svcs)*
Sarah OBrien *(Designer-Creative)*

Accounts:
Brinderson Holdings
City of Arlington
Harker Heights Medical Clinic

MIND OVER MARKETS
7 Owl Creek, Santa Fe, NM 87505
Tel.: (505) 989-4004
Fax: (505) 989-4005
E-Mail: irv@mindovermarkets.com
Web Site: www.mindovermarkets.com

Employees: 6
Year Founded: 2003

Agency Specializes In: Advertising, Brand Development & Integration, Business-To-Business, Collateral, Communications, Consulting, Consumer Goods, Consumer Marketing, Consumer Publications, Corporate Communications, Corporate Identity, Environmental, Graphic Design, Health Care Services, Internet/Web Design, Logo & Package Design, New Product Development, Outdoor, Podcasting, Print, Promotions, Public Relations, Publicity/Promotions, RSS (Really Simple Syndication), Radio, Search Engine Optimization, Strategic Planning/Research, T.V., Trade & Consumer Magazines, Travel & Tourism, Web (Banner Ads, Pop-ups, etc.), Women's Market

Carolyn Par *(Principal)*
Irv Weinberg *(Principal)*
David Wolfe *(Specialist-New Media)*

Accounts:
Johnson & Johnson
Mac Recycling
Planet USA
Poochi
Professional Green; Santa Fe, NM Industrial Green Cleaning Products
Resting In The River Organic Farm & Natural Products; Abiquiu, NM Natural Remedies, Natural Skin Care
Santa Fe Community College; Santa Fe, NM Environmental Studies, Teamwork In Action Program
Ski Tacs

MINDENSEMBLE
909 Texas Ave Ste 1403, Houston, TX 77002
Tel.: (713) 824-8583
E-Mail: info@mindensemble.com
Web Site: www.mindensemble.com

Year Founded: 2007

Agency Specializes In: Advertising, Brand Development & Integration, Communications, Digital/Interactive, Product Placement

Rory Doyal *(Co-Founder & Mng Partner)*
Irwina Liaw *(Co-Founder & Dir-Creative)*

Accounts:
The Inn At Dos Brisas

MINDFIRE COMMUNICATIONS INC
102 N Cody Rd, Le Claire, IA 52753
Tel.: (563) 265-5556
Web Site: www.mindfirecomm.com

Year Founded: 2007

Agency Specializes In: Advertising, Brand Development & Integration, Digital/Interactive, Internet/Web Design, Logo & Package Design, Media Relations, Print, Public Relations, Social Media, Strategic Planning/Research

Lynn Manternach *(Co-Owner & Pres)*
Mike Smith *(Owner & Dir-Creative)*
Erik Meade *(Co-Owner)*
Tara Midence *(Media Buyer)*

Accounts:
Mississippi Valley Surgery Center

MINDFRAME, INC.
347 Kellogg Blvd E, Saint Paul, MN 55101-1411
Tel.: (612) 204-0320
E-Mail: info@mindframe.com
Web Site: www.mindframe.com

Employees: 7
Year Founded: 1996

Agency Specializes In: Business-To-Business, Digital/Interactive, E-Commerce, Electronic Media, Graphic Design, High Technology, Internet/Web Design, RSS (Really Simple Syndication)

J.P. Doffing *(Owner)*

Accounts:
American Time and Signal Company
Brock White; Saint Paul, MN Construction Products; 2008
Continuing Ed Express; MN Online Continuing Education; 2006
Discount Steel; MN Metal; 2008
First State Bank of Wabasha
Gopher Sport; Owatonna, MN; 2005
Gopher Sport; Owatonna, MN; 2005
Larkin Hoffman; Bloomington, MN; 2002
Life Time Fitness; Eden Prairie, MN; 2001
National Business Institute; WI Online Learning; 2009
Schroeder Company; Maplewood, MN; 2001
Ultimate Events; MN Tent & Party Rental; 2010

MINDFUL KREATIVE
2244 Walters Rd, Allison Park, PA 15101
Tel.: (412) 492-9501
Fax: (412) 492-9505
Web Site: www.mindfulkreative.com

Agency Specializes In: Advertising, Brand Development & Integration

Melinda Kaiser *(Pres)*
Amy Meyers *(Dir-Media)*
Mary Wrenshall *(Dir-Strategy & Dev)*
Annie Lewis *(Acct Mgr)*
Erin Carlin *(Acct Exec)*

Accounts:
Gateway Health Plan, L.P.

MINDGRUVE, INC.
1018 8th Ave, San Diego, CA 92101
Tel.: (619) 757-1325
Web Site: www.mindgruve.com

Employees: 35
Year Founded: 2001

Agency Specializes In: Affiliate Marketing, Alternative Advertising, Digital/Interactive, Direct Response Marketing, Electronic Media, Email, Guerilla Marketing, Local Marketing, Mobile Marketing, Multimedia, Newspapers & Magazines, Paid Searches, Promotions, Publishing, Search Engine Optimization, Social Media, Viral/Buzz/Word of Mouth, Web (Banner Ads, Pop-ups, etc.)

Mike Hodges *(Pres)*
Chad Robley *(CEO)*
Michael Garten *(Mng Dir)*
Clint Walden *(Exec Dir-Creative)*
Ellyn Rice *(Assoc Dir-Media)*
Marche Kaanehe *(Acct Mgr)*

Accounts:
House of Blues
LiveNation
Opus Bank

Procter & Gamble
Scripps Health

MINDSAILING

400 S 4th St Ste 401-122, Minneapolis, MN 55415
Tel.: (612) 961-9625
E-Mail: info@mindsailing.com
Web Site: www.mindsailing.com

Year Founded: 2011

Agency Specializes In: Advertising, Brand Development & Integration, Communications, Digital/Interactive, Social Media

Julie Mackenzie *(Pres & CEO)*
Heather Saucier *(Partner & Dir-Innovation)*
Chris Farrar *(Dir-Ops)*

Accounts:
Kips Bay Medical, Inc.

MINDSHARE STRATEGIES

9382 Oak Ave, Waconia, MN 55387
Tel.: (952) 442-8850
E-Mail: info@mindshare.bz
Web Site: www.mindshare.bz

Agency Specializes In: Advertising, Collateral, Crisis Communications, Digital/Interactive, Media Relations, Public Relations, Social Media, Strategic Planning/Research

Carleen Herndon *(VP-Bus Dev & Acct Exec)*
Karen Everett *(VP-Ops & Admin)*
Michele Wade *(Acct Exec)*
Nancy LaRoche *(Sr Graphic Designer)*

Accounts:
Satellite Logistics Group

MINDSMACK

311 W 43rd St, New York, NY 10036
Tel.: (732) 348-8785
E-Mail: sales@mindsmack.com
Web Site: www.mindsmack.com

Employees: 40
Year Founded: 1997

Agency Specializes In: Alternative Advertising, Aviation & Aerospace, College, Communications, Consulting, Consumer Marketing, Digital/Interactive, Education, Exhibit/Trade Shows, Fashion/Apparel, Game Integration, Graphic Design, High Technology, Internet/Web Design, Logo & Package Design, Mobile Marketing, Multimedia, New Technologies, Pharmaceutical, Production, Promotions, Public Relations, Real Estate, Restaurant, Search Engine Optimization, Technical Advertising, Teen Market

Samuel Feuer *(Co-Founder)*

Accounts:
CitiGroup
IBM
Pepsi
Yahoo

MINDSPACE

2402 S Rural Rd Ste 201, Tempe, AZ 85282
Tel.: (480) 941-8497
E-Mail: info@mindspace.net
Web Site: www.mindspace.net

Agency Specializes In: Brand Development & Integration, Digital/Interactive, Media Planning, Production, Social Media, Strategic Planning/Research

Brent Shetler *(Principal & Dir-Creative)*
Darren Steele *(Principal & Dir-Strategy)*
Jay Contonio *(Dir)*

Accounts:
GarageFly.com Consumer Services

MINDSPIKE DESIGN LLC

320 E Buffalo St Ste 606, Milwaukee, WI 53202
Tel.: (414) 765-2344
Web Site: www.mindspikedesign.com

Agency Specializes In: Advertising, Digital/Interactive, Event Planning & Marketing, Internet/Web Design, Logo & Package Design, Media Buying Services

Mike Magestro *(Owner & Dir-Creative)*
Calysta Phalen *(Acct Exec-Digital Mktg)*

Accounts:
Renovo Endodontic Studio
Wangard Partners, Inc.
WelcomeToGlendale.com

MINDSTORM COMMUNICATIONS GROUP, INC.

10316 Feld Farm Ln Ste 200, Charlotte, NC 28210
Tel.: (704) 331-0870
Fax: (704) 331-0891
E-Mail: contact@gomindstorm.com
Web Site: www.gomindstorm.com

Employees: 4
Year Founded: 1999

Agency Specializes In: Advertising, Advertising Specialties, Bilingual Market, Brand Development & Integration, Business-To-Business, Collateral, Commercial Photography, Communications, Corporate Identity, Digital/Interactive, Direct Response Marketing, E-Commerce, Electronic Media, Exhibit/Trade Shows, Fashion/Apparel, Graphic Design, Industrial, Internet/Web Design, Local Marketing, Logo & Package Design, Media Buying Services, Medical Products, New Product Development, Outdoor, Point of Sale, Print, Public Relations, Restaurant, Strategic Planning/Research, T.V., Technical Advertising

Revenue: $1,000,000

Jeff Masilun *(Partner & Dir-Creative)*

Accounts:
Best Sweets; Mooresville, NC; 2007
Sagebrush Steakhouse; Mooresville, NC; 2007

MINDVOLT

114B W Market St, Athens, AL 35611
Tel.: (256) 233-8585
E-Mail: info@mindvolt.com
Web Site: www.mindvolt.com

Agency Specializes In: Advertising, Brand Development & Integration, Collateral, Digital/Interactive, Internet/Web Design, Logo & Package Design, Print, Radio, Social Media

Chad Bottcher *(Pres & Dir-Creative)*
Julia Pack *(Dir-Art & Office Mgr)*
Cate Schilloff *(Dir-Art & Mgr-Production)*
Julia Young *(Office Mgr)*

Accounts:
Alabama Boston Terrier Rescue
Altec Industries Inc.
An Original Velvet Elvis
Bone Collector Season 2
Chameleon 360 Sports Training Inc.
Equestrian Safety Products
Open Range Service Group
Time Domain, Corp.
Troy Landry's Choot Em
Wasp Archery

MINDWRITE COMMUNICATIONS, INC.

117 Bernal Rd Ste 70-126, San Jose, CA 95119
Tel.: (408) 224-4024
Web Site: www.mind-write.com

Year Founded: 2005

Agency Specializes In: Brand Development & Integration, Digital/Interactive, Electronic Media, Email, Exhibit/Trade Shows, Graphic Design, Local Marketing, Media Relations, Podcasting, Publicity/Promotions, Strategic Planning/Research

Sandy Fewkes *(Co-Owner)*
Robert Johnson *(Principal)*

Accounts:
Business Practicum
Hyphenated Systems
Rudolph Technologies
Semiconductor International Magazine

MINERVA DESIGN

274 N Goodman St A403, Rochester, NY 14607
Tel.: (585) 442-8800
E-Mail: hello@minervadesign.com
Web Site: www.minervadesign.com

Year Founded: 1995

Agency Specializes In: Advertising, Brand Development & Integration, Digital/Interactive, Graphic Design, Social Media

Mike Minerva *(Owner & Dir-Design)*
Kevin Siebert *(Dir-Digital)*

Accounts:
DNA Imports
HBT Architects

MINISTERS OF DESIGN

1610 20th St NW, Washington, DC 20009
Tel.: (202) 350-0070
Web Site: www.ministersofdesign.com

Year Founded: 2012

Agency Specializes In: Advertising, Brand Development & Integration, Digital/Interactive, Graphic Design, Logo & Package Design, Print, Social Media

Russell Hirshon *(Pres & Dir-Digital Strategy)*
Hazem Abughazaleh *(Dir-Strategic Svcs)*
Sara Lin *(Dir-Design)*
Andrew Pascoe *(Dir-Technical)*
Andrew Reifman *(Designer)*

Accounts:
Fat Pete's Barbecue
Right Proper Brewing Company

MINNOW PROJECT

815 O St, Lincoln, NE 68508
Tel.: (402) 475-3322
Web Site: www.minnowproject.com

Agency Specializes In: Advertising, Brand Development & Integration, Collateral, Digital/Interactive, Event Planning & Marketing, Logo & Package Design, Media Planning, Public Relations, Social Media

Christy Puev *(VP-Ops & Dir-Media)*
Randy Gibson *(Dir-Creative Svcs)*
Scott Shaner *(Dir-Art)*
Ashley Cameron *(Graphic Designer & Designer-Interactive)*

Accounts:
Nebraska Wildlife Federation

MINT ADVERTISING

120 W Main St, Clinton, NJ 08809
Tel.: (908) 238-1500
Fax: (908) 238-1025
Web Site: www.mintadvertising.com

Agency Specializes In: Advertising Specialties, Automotive, Financial, Integrated Marketing

Eric W. Schoenfeld *(Founder & CEO)*
Richard Bodge *(VP-Client Svcs)*
Scott Robinson *(VP-Client Svcs)*
Taylor Mazzarese *(Dir-Art)*
Westley Hackmann *(Sr Acct Mgr)*
Darren Manship *(Acct Supvr)*
Caitlyn Harvey *(Acct Exec)*
Laurie Richter *(Coord-Admin)*

Accounts:
Dominos Pizza Fast Food Services
Honda Automobile Mfr

MINTZ & HOKE COMMUNICATIONS GROUP

40 Tower Ln, Avon, CT 06001-4222
Tel.: (860) 678-0473
Fax: (860) 679-9850
Web Site: www.mintz-hoke.com

Employees: 55
Year Founded: 1971

National Agency Associations: 4A's-PRSA

Agency Specializes In: Advertising, Aviation & Aerospace, Broadcast, Business-To-Business, Cable T.V., Collateral, Communications, Consumer Marketing, Corporate Identity, Digital/Interactive, Direct Response Marketing, Electronic Media, Event Planning & Marketing, Government/Political, Graphic Design, Health Care Services, Industrial, Information Technology, Internet/Web Design, Leisure, Logo & Package Design, Media Buying Services, Multimedia, Newspaper, Newspapers & Magazines, Outdoor, Print, Public Relations, Publicity/Promotions, Radio, Sponsorship, Strategic Planning/Research, Travel & Tourism

Approx. Annual Billings: $60,000,000

Breakdown of Gross Billings by Media: Other: 15%; Print: 25%; Radio & T.V.: 40%; Worldwide Web Sites: 20%

Ron Perine *(Pres & CEO)*
Sara-Beth Donovan *(Sr VP-Media)*
Andrew Wood *(Sr VP-Strategy & Plng)*
Grant Sanders *(VP & Dir-Creative)*
Trevor Dobrowsky *(Assoc Dir-Creative)*
Lisa Geissler *(Assoc Dir-Media)*
Michelle LaPoint *(Assoc Dir-Media)*
Maribeth Magiera *(Mgr-Brdcst Promo & Buyer)*
Heather Gillette *(Acct Supvr)*
Bill Graulty *(Acct Supvr)*
Penny Turton *(Media Planner)*
Christine Matonti *(Coord-Bus Dev)*
Kathleen Morelli *(Sr Program Mgr-Digital)*

Accounts:
American Arbitration Association; 2007
ArtSpace Connecticut
BMW
CertainTeed
CIGNA HealthCare
Connect-ability
Discover Re Reinsurance
DRS; 2007
Electric Boat; Groton, CT Submarines
General Dynamics/Electric Boat
Hartford HealthCare Media
Hartford Steam Boiler
Harvey Building Products
Ingersoll Rand
Legrand
Mohegan Sun Casino
Nielson Sessions Engineered Hardware
OFS Optical Fiber
Pexco
Praxair North American Industrial Gases Oxygen Tank
Prudential Financial
Prudential Retirement
Quinnipiac University
State of Connecticut
UTC Aerospace Systems

MIRABAL & ASSOCIATES

Doral Bank Plz Ste 801-802 101 W Mendez Vigo St, Mayaguez, PR 00680-3890
Tel.: (787) 831-3040
Fax: (787) 831-3045
E-Mail: info@mirabalpr.com
Web Site: www.mirabalpr.com

Employees: 3
Year Founded: 1986

Agency Specializes In: Advertising, Brand Development & Integration, Business-To-Business, Consumer Marketing, Direct Response Marketing, Education, Event Planning & Marketing, Fashion/Apparel, Financial, Food Service, Government/Political, Graphic Design, High Technology, Planning & Consultation, Public Relations, Real Estate, Retail, Strategic Planning/Research, Trade & Consumer Magazines, Travel & Tourism

Approx. Annual Billings: $750,000

Pura I. Mirabal *(Pres)*

Accounts:
GlaxoSmithKline

MIRAGE ADVERTISING

206 Monroe St, Monroeville, PA 15146
Tel.: (412) 372-4181
Fax: (412) 372-4518
E-Mail: support@miragemarcom.com
Web Site: www.miragemarcom.com

Employees: 8
Year Founded: 1988

Agency Specializes In: Advertising, Brand Development & Integration, Corporate Communications, Digital/Interactive, Event Planning & Marketing, Graphic Design, Internet/Web Design, Newspapers & Magazines, Public Relations

Curt Brooks *(Owner & Pres)*
Christine Godzin *(Controller)*
Dave Porter *(Dir-Creative)*
James Schoaf *(Mgr-Web Sys)*

Accounts:
Belizean Dreams Tourism Services
Hopkins Bay Developments
InvestEdge, Inc Technical Services
LogiSync Embedded Hardware Design Provider
Target Drilling Drilling Services

MIRESBALL

2605 State St, San Diego, CA 92103-6419
Tel.: (619) 234-6631
Fax: (619) 234-1807
E-Mail: hello@miresball.com
Web Site: www.miresball.com

E-Mail for Key Personnel:
President: scott@miresbrands.com

Employees: 24
Year Founded: 1985

Agency Specializes In: Automotive, Brand Development & Integration, Collateral, Communications, Consulting, Consumer Marketing, Corporate Identity, Digital/Interactive, Electronic Media, Environmental, Exhibit/Trade Shows, Food Service, Graphic Design, Health Care Services, High Technology, Internet/Web Design, Investor Relations, Leisure, Logo & Package Design, New Product Development, Point of Purchase, Point of Sale, Print, Restaurant, Sports Market, Strategic Planning/Research, Transportation, Travel & Tourism

Approx. Annual Billings: $10,000,000

John Ball *(Partner & Dir-Creative)*
Scott Mires *(Partner & Dir-Creative)*
Holly Houk *(Acct Dir)*
Angela Renac *(Dir-Design)*
Miguel Perez *(Assoc Dir-Creative)*
Katie Gray *(Acct Mgr)*
Deirdre O'Byrne *(Mgr-Traffic)*
Chris Sullivan *(Mgr-IT)*
Beth Folkerth *(Sr Designer)*
Kathya Fredricks *(Sr Designer)*
Gale Spitzley *(Sr Designer)*

Accounts:
Ballast Point Brewing & Spirits
Behr
New-Best Western Hotels & Resorts
CND
Pebble Beach U.S. Open
PIRCH
Shure; 2005
Smithsonian
Taylor Guitars
WalMart

MIRUM GLOBAL

466 Lexington Ave, New York, NY 10017
Tel.: (212) 210-7000
E-Mail: press@mirumagency.com
Web Site: www.mirumagency.com

Year Founded: 2015

Agency Specializes In: Advertising, Content, Digital/Interactive

Stefano Zunino *(Chm)*
Nick Read *(CFO)*
Dave Wallace *(COO)*
John Baker *(CMO)*
Matt Webb *(CTO)*
Dan Khabie *(CEO-North America)*
Jonathan Renker *(VP-Strategy)*
Sarah Kotlova *(Global Head-Agency Svcs)*
Andrew Peterson *(Producer-Digital)*
Peter Amstutz *(Dir-Analytics)*

Accounts:
CBRE
Cyrela
Daum Kakao
Finnair
HSBC
Magazine Luiza
Mazda
Microsoft

Nokia
Petco
Singapore Tourism Board Digital, Production
TD Bank
Walmart
XL

MIRUM MINNEAPOLIS

100 N 6th St Ste 300C, Minneapolis, MN 55403
Tel.: (612) 752-5500
Fax: (612) 752-5501
Web Site: www.jwt.com/mirumminneapolis

National Agency Associations: 4A's

Agency Specializes In: Advertising, Brand Development & Integration, Digital/Interactive

Joyce Zincke *(Mng Dir)*
Julie Koepsell *(Sr VP & Dir-Client Svcs)*

Accounts:
New-Fulton Brewery

MISSION MEDIA, LLC.

616 Water St Ste 225, Baltimore, MD 21202
Tel.: (410) 752-8950
Fax: (410) 752-8951
Toll Free: (800) 760-9008
E-Mail: info@missionmedia.net
Web Site: www.missionmedia.com

Year Founded: 2000

Agency Specializes In: Advertising, Brand Development & Integration, Digital/Interactive, Environmental, Graphic Design, Internet/Web Design, Package Design, Production, Search Engine Optimization, Web (Banner Ads, Pop-ups, etc.)

Joe Loverde *(Owner)*
Laura Langdon *(Pres-North America)*
Todd Harvey *(Principal & Dir-Creative)*
Jay McCutcheon *(VP-Mktg & Dev)*
Amy Toleson *(Dir-Web Dev)*
Mark Kubat *(Assoc Dir-Creative)*
Patrick Lamond *(Assoc Dir-Creative)*
Samia Khan *(Mgr-Resource)*

MISTER FACE

(Formerly Radio Face)
149 5th Ave 13th Fl, New York, NY 10010
Tel.: (212) 375-1250
E-Mail: contact@misterfaceny.com
Web Site: www.misterfaceny.com

Year Founded: 2010

Agency Specializes In: Advertising, Digital/Interactive, Media Buying Services, Web (Banner Ads, Pop-ups, etc.)

Daniel Doebrich *(Mng Partner)*

Accounts:
Domain.Me
Fiat S.p.A. Fiat 500

MISTRESS

2415 Michigan Ave, Santa Monica, CA 90404
Tel.: (213) 841-8103
Web Site: www.mistress.agency

Employees: 51
Year Founded: 2010

Agency Specializes In: Above-the-Line, Advertising, Alternative Advertising, Below-the-Line, Branded Entertainment, Digital/Interactive, Direct Response Marketing, Electronic Media, Experience Design, Game Integration, Guerilla Marketing, In-Store Advertising, Magazines, Mobile Marketing, Multimedia, Outdoor, Print, Product Placement, Production, Social Media, Sponsorship, Strategic Planning/Research, Web (Banner Ads, Pop-ups, etc.)

Boris de Malvinsky *(Co-Founder & Partner)*
Hartmut Heinrich *(Co-Founder & Mng Dir)*
Damien Eley *(Partner-Creative)*
Scott Harris *(Partner-Creative)*
Jens Stoelken *(Partner-Strategy)*
Steve Orenstein *(COO)*
Lixaida Lorenzo *(Creative Dir)*
Tim Cyrol *(Dir-HR)*
Paul OShea *(Dir-Creative)*
Mike Toofer *(Dir-New Bus)*
Ben Beale *(Assoc Dir-Creative)*
Aya Nishimura *(Mgr-Culture)*
Rachel Guest *(Copywriter)*

Accounts:
Brown-Forman Finlandia
Coca-Cola Campaign: "Hiiire", Campaign: "You Only Live NOS", NOS Energy Drink
ESPN Internet Ventures Sports Television Channel
Finlandia Vodka
New-Imax Corp. Global Creative
Levis Jeans & Authentic Clothing For Men & Women
Mattel Inc. Campaign: "Double Loop Stunt", Campaign: "Hot Wheels For Real", Campaign: "Hot Wheels Test Facility", Campaign: "The World's Best Driver", Hot Wheels, Social Media, TV
New-National Nude Day
NOS
PayPal
Red Bull Soft Drink Mfr
Sol Republic Campaign: "Music Made Me Do It"
Spinmaster Games
Take-Two Interactive Software Inc. Custom Computer Programming Services
Ubisoft Inc. Advertising, Assassin's Creed IV: Black Flag, Assassin's Creed Unity, Campaign: "Make History"
VH1 "Hindsight", Campaign: "Love is in the Air", Campaign: "Missed Connection", Dating Naked

MITCHELL & RESNIKOFF

8003 Old York Rd, Elkins Park, PA 19027-1410
Tel.: (215) 635-1000, ext. 212
Fax: (215) 635-6542
E-Mail: rresnikoff@mitch-res.com
Web Site: www.mitch-res.com

E-Mail for Key Personnel:
President: rresinkoff@mitch-res.com

Employees: 13
Year Founded: 1970

National Agency Associations: DMA-MCA

Agency Specializes In: Advertising, Brand Development & Integration, Broadcast, Business-To-Business, Collateral, Communications, Consulting, Corporate Identity, Direct Response Marketing, E-Commerce, Graphic Design, Logo & Package Design, Magazines, Newspapers & Magazines, Out-of-Home Media, Outdoor, Point of Sale, Production, Sales Promotion, Strategic Planning/Research

Approx. Annual Billings: $11,000,000

Ronald B. Resnikoff *(CEO)*
Linda Resnikoff *(Sr VP & Dir-Creative)*
Steven Resnikoff *(VP-Production Svcs)*
John Byrnes *(Exec Dir-Art)*
Lynette Byrnes *(Sr Acct Exec)*

Accounts:
AmeriGas
EP Henry
Freedom Medical
National Gaucher
Penn State-Abington Campus
Perelman Jewish Day School
Savitz
Sterling Trustees
Stone Center
Ted's Pools
USPro Restoration
WealthCloud

MITCHELL COMMUNICATIONS GROUP

2 N College Ave, Fayetteville, AR 72701
Tel.: (479) 443-4673
Web Site: www.mitchcommgroup.com

Employees: 75

National Agency Associations: 4A's-COPF

Agency Specializes In: Automotive, Communications, Digital/Interactive, Financial, Food Service, Hospitality, Retail, Social Media, Sponsorship, Strategic Planning/Research, Travel & Tourism

Sarah Clark *(Pres)*
Elise Mitchell *(CEO)*
Larry Templeton *(CFO)*
Michael Clark *(COO)*
Blake Woolsey *(Exec VP)*
Brett Carrey *(Sr VP & Gen Mgr)*
John Gilboy *(VP-Consumer Insights)*
Anngelica Newland *(VP-Digital Strategy)*
Greg W. Smith *(Sr Dir)*
TJ Pike *(Dir-Consumer Comm)*

Accounts:
New-Kraft
New-Procter & Gamble
New-Sam's Club
Walmart

MITCHELL, LINDBERG & TAYLOR, INC.

4020 E Ponce De Leon Ave, Clarkston, GA 30021
Tel.: (404) 292-4502
Fax: (404) 292-4480
Toll Free: (800) 265-1244
E-Mail: clindberg@mltcreative.com
Web Site: www.mltcreative.com

Employees: 25
Year Founded: 1984

National Agency Associations: AMA

Agency Specializes In: Advertising Specialties, Business-To-Business, Consumer Marketing, Graphic Design, Internet/Web Design

William C. Mitchell *(Partner & Sr Dir-Creative)*
Glenn Taylor *(Partner & Sr Dir-Creative)*
Brian Sheppard *(Dir-Creative-Interactive Media & Specialist-B2B Inbound Mktg)*
Vann Morris *(Dir-Buyer Behavior)*

Accounts:
Acuity Brands, Inc.
Auction Access
AutoTec, LLC
Manheim Auctions

MITHOFF BURTON PARTNERS

123 W Mills Ave Ste 500, El Paso, TX 79901
Tel.: (915) 544-9400
Fax: (915) 544-9426
Toll Free: (877) 335-2322
Web Site: www.mithoffburton.com

E-Mail for Key Personnel:
President: pfraire@mithoffburton.com

Creative Dir.: ccochran@mithoffburton.com
Production Mgr.: dbrooks@mithoffburton.com

Employees: 22
Year Founded: 1931

National Agency Associations: 4A's-AAF-MCA

Agency Specializes In: Advertising, Bilingual Market, Brand Development & Integration, Broadcast, Business-To-Business, Co-op Advertising, Collateral, Communications, Consulting, Consumer Marketing, Consumer Publications, Corporate Communications, Corporate Identity, Digital/Interactive, E-Commerce, Education, Electronic Media, Entertainment, Financial, Graphic Design, Health Care Services, Hispanic Market, Local Marketing, Logo & Package Design, Market Research, Media Buying Services, Media Planning, Media Relations, Medical Products, Newspaper, Newspapers & Magazines, Outdoor, Package Design, Planning & Consultation, Print, Production (Print), Promotions, Public Relations, Publicity/Promotions, Radio, Real Estate, Recruitment, Regional, Social Marketing/Nonprofit, Sports Market, Strategic Planning/Research, T.V., Transportation

Approx. Annual Billings: $65,000,000

Breakdown of Gross Billings by Media: Mags.: $2,600,000; Newsp.: $5,200,000; Other: $23,400,000; Outdoor: $4,550,000; Radio: $5,200,000; T.V.: $24,050,000

Chana Burton *(Owner)*
Peter Fraire *(Pres, COO & Creative Dir)*
Bill Burton, Jr. *(CEO)*
Steffen Poessiger *(VP & Sr Client Svcs Dir)*
Creighton Hermann *(Dir-Digital & Interactive)*
Irma Watson *(Mgr-Acctg)*
Dana Guerra *(Media Planner & Buyer)*

Accounts:
The Ag Conservancy; Tulsa, OK
Border Entertainment of Alaska; Anchorage, AK Blockbuster Video Rental Franchise
Border Entertainment of El Paso; El Paso, TX Blockbuster Video Rental Franchise
Braden Aboud Foundation; El Paso, TX
Camino Real Hotel; El Paso, TX
Cimarron Foundation El Paso Charitable Trust Services; 2003
El Paso Community Foundation
El Paso Diabetes Association; El Paso, TX
El Paso Symphony Orchestra; El Paso, TX
Elamex, SA; El Paso, TX Contract Manufacturer; 1980
Fair Oaks Farms
First American Bank
Foster Sports Entertainment; El Paso, TX; 2008
Franklin Connections; El Paso, TX Supply-Chain Management System
Giant Convenience Stores
Greater El Paso Chamber of Commerce
Handgards; El Paso, TX Food Handling Products
Hunt Building Corp.; El Paso, TX Military Housing Services, Real Estate Development
Hunt Family Foundation; El Paso, TX
Insights - El Paso Science Museum; El Paso, TX
J.M. Smucker Company
JDW Insurance; El Paso, TX Insurance Agency
JP&A Concerts Entertainment; El Paso, TX; 2004
Kemin Industries, Inc.; Des Moines, IA Chemicals
Kemp Smith LLP; El Paso, TX Law Firm
Lacy & Company; El Paso, TX Fine Jewelry
Land Legacy
Lintel; Mexico Commercial Construction
M.D. Anderson Cancer Center; El Paso Region
Medical Center of the Americas; El Paso, TX
Mithoff & Jacks, LLP; Houston, TX Law Firm
Professional Investment Counsel; El Paso, TX; 2000
Rio Grande Cancer Foundation; El Paso, TX
Rocky Mountain Mortgage; El Paso, TX
Rudolph Automotive Group; El Paso, TX Rudolph Honda
Sierra Providence Health Network; El Paso, TX Hospitals
Southwest Dairy Farmers; Sulphur Springs, TX Museum & Dairy Cooperative
St. Francis on the Hill; El Paso, TX Church
Sunland Optical; El Paso, TX; 2004
Sunrise Confections, Inc.; El Paso, TX Candy
Travel Centers of America; El Paso, TX Truck Stops & Convenience Stores
TVO Development; El Paso, TX
West Star Bank; El Paso, TX
Western Refining Company; El Paso, TX
YWCA Paso del Norte Region Non-Profit Services; 2002

MITHUN
(Formerly Campbell Mithun, Inc.)
Campbell Mithun Tower 222 S 9th St, Minneapolis, MN 55402-3389
Tel.: (612) 347-1000
Fax: (612) 347-1515
E-Mail: abaxter@cmithun.com
Web Site: everythingtalks.com/

E-Mail for Key Personnel:
Media Dir.: dhurrelbrink@compasspoint-media.com

Employees: 300
Year Founded: 1933

National Agency Associations: 4A's-AA-ADFED-DMA-PMA

Agency Specializes In: Advertising, Advertising Specialties, Agriculture, Brand Development & Integration, Broadcast, Business Publications, Business-To-Business, Cable T.V., Children's Market, Collateral, Communications, Consumer Goods, Consumer Marketing, Consumer Publications, Corporate Communications, Customer Relationship Management, Digital/Interactive, Direct Response Marketing, Direct-to-Consumer, Experience Design, Fashion/Apparel, Financial, Guerilla Marketing, Health Care Services, Hospitality, Household Goods, In-Store Advertising, Integrated Marketing, Internet/Web Design, Local Marketing, Logo & Package Design, Magazines, Market Research, Media Buying Services, Media Planning, Mobile Marketing, New Product Development, Newspaper, Newspapers & Magazines, Out-of-Home Media, Outdoor, Package Design, Paid Searches, Point of Purchase, Point of Sale, Print, Product Placement, Production (Print), Promotions, Radio, Restaurant, Retail, Search Engine Optimization, Social Marketing/Nonprofit, Social Media, Sponsorship, Strategic Planning/Research, T.V., Trade & Consumer Magazines, Viral/Buzz/Word of Mouth, Women's Market

Breakdown of Gross Billings by Media: Brdcst.: 64%; D.M.: 3%; Internet Adv.: 2%; Mags.: 11%; Newsp.: 5%; Out-of-Home Media: 2%; Radio: 13%

David Carter *(Chief Creative Officer)*
Denis Budniewski *(Exec VP & Dir-Acct Leadership & Growth)*
Melissa Schoenke *(Exec VP)*
Ty Kendig *(Sr VP & Grp Acct Dir)*
Karen Ryan *(Sr VP & Dir-Acct Ops-Team General Mills)*
Charlie LeCrone *(VP & Assoc Dir)*
Kelly Manderfeld *(VP & Assoc Media Dir-Compass Point Media)*
Jeremy Pinches *(Acct Dir)*
Kathy DiToro *(Dir-Integrated Production)*
Patricia Erskine *(Assoc Dir-Media)*
Jay Morrison *(Assoc Dir-Creative)*
Brent Larson *(Sr Mgr-Production Bus)*
Andrea Brazelton *(Supvr-Interactive Media Strategy)*
Jennifer Burdick *(Supvr-Media)*
Erica Cross *(Supvr-Media Strategy)*
Ryan Hatzenbuhler *(Supvr-Interactive Media)*
Megan Nyberg *(Supvr-Media Strategy)*
Andrea Thomson *(Supvr-Media Strategy)*
Melissa Winnig *(Supvr-Media Strategy)*
April Hynes *(Strategist-Media)*
Jana Olson *(Strategist-Media)*
Amanda White *(Strategist-Media)*
Mara Pederson *(Analyst-Media)*
Brittany Swaine *(Analyst-Media)*
Wendy Hansen *(Assoc Creative Dir)*
Kate Pabst *(Assoc Creative Dir)*
Christopher Spong *(Community Mgr)*

Accounts:
ACE Group Insurance; 2010
Airborne Health; 2009
Alvesco; 2010
Ashley Furniture Industries, Inc.
Best Western International Best Western Hotels; 2011
Betty Crocker
BizFillings; 2010
Chipotle; 2010
DOG for DOG
General Mills 8th Continent Soy Milk, Betty Crocker Cake Mix & Frosting, Betty Crocker Warm Delights, Bisquick, Caribou Coffee Bars, Chex Cereal, Chex Snack Mix, Cinnamon Toast Crunch Cereal, Curves Cereal, French Toast Crunch, Frosted Mini Chex, Gardettos Snack Mix, Golden Grahams, Hamburger Helper, Honey Nut Chex, Milk & Cereal Bars, Morning Mix, Nature Valley Granola Bars, Oatmeal Crisp Cereal, PopSecret, Specialty Potatoes; 1968
Johnsonville; 2007
J.R. Watkins Co. (Agency of Record) Creative Advertising
KeyBank; Cleveland, OH Advertising, Brand Planning, Creative, Hassle-Free Account, Local Market Events, Marketing, Media, Mobile, OOH, Print, Social, TV, Web
Minnesota Department of Public Safety Hefty, ZooPals; 2004
National City Bank of Indiana
Nestle - Purina PetCare Purina; 2010
Pandora
Popeyes Louisiana Kitchen "Red Stick Staredown", Campaign: "#LoveThatChicken", Campaign: "Chicken Waffle Tenders", Digital, Red Stick Chicken
Schwan Food Asian Sensations, Edwards Pies, Freschetta, Mrs. Smith Pies, Red B! aron, Tony's, Wolfgang Puck; 2000
Sonovian
SUPERVALU, Inc. Cub Foods
The Toro Company Campaign: "Count on It", Campaign: "Toro Treadmill", Lawn Boy, Snowblowers, TimeCutter Zero-Turn Riding Mower, Toro TimeMaster; 1962
United Way Twin Cities United Way - Twin Cities Chapter; 2005
Wellmark Blue Cross & Blue Shield "What Matters", Broadcast, Campaign: "Blood Pressure", Campaign: "Promises Matter", Campaign: "Reflex", Campaign: "Sample", Digital, Social Media, Website, myWellmark
Wells Fargo Yellow Pages; 1991

Branch

Compass Point Media
510 Marquette Ave, Minneapolis, MN 55402
(See Separate Listing)

MITTCOM LTD.
180 Wells Ave Ste 304, Newton, MA 02459
Tel.: (617) 614-0014
Fax: (617) 597-9996
E-Mail: emittman@mittcom.com

Web Site: www.mittcom.com

Employees: 8

Agency Specializes In: Advertising, Brand Development & Integration, Event Planning & Marketing, Market Research, Media Buying Services, Media Planning, Production, Production (Ad, Film, Broadcast), Production (Print), Promotions, Public Relations, Radio, Sponsorship, Strategic Planning/Research, T.V.

Bruce J. Mittman *(Pres & CEO)*
Glenn Lucas *(Exec VP)*
Aaron Watters *(VP)*
Kimberly Boroyan *(Controller)*
Deborah Delany *(Sr Dir-Art)*
Sara Bloomrose *(Brand Dir)*
Andrew Capobianco *(Dir-Search Engine Mktg)*
Lees Greenberg *(Dir-Ops & Fin)*
Jon Rizzo *(Dir-Video Production)*
Alicia Pensarosa *(Brand Mgr)*

Accounts:
Boch Automotive Enterprises
Boston Militia
ERA Boston Real Estate
Free Masons
Metropolitan
The Phoenix
Simplex
TenXClub

MIXTAPE MARKETING

1509 W Koenig Ln, Austin, TX 78756
Tel.: (512) 981-7155
E-Mail: info@mixtapeagency.com
Web Site: www.mixtapeagency.com

Agency Specializes In: Advertising, Brand Development & Integration, Internet/Web Design, Search Engine Optimization, Social Media, Strategic Planning/Research

Charlie Brown *(Principal)*
Craig Steckbeck *(Creative Dir)*

Accounts:
New-Make Fuzzy Tracks

THE MIXX

350 7th Ave Ste 1403, New York, NY 10001
Tel.: (212) 695-6663
Fax: (212) 695-6664
E-Mail: contact@themixxnyc.com
Web Site: www.themixxnyc.com

Employees: 17
Year Founded: 1996

Agency Specializes In: Business-To-Business, Corporate Identity, Graphic Design, Internet/Web Design, Multimedia, Real Estate, Strategic Planning/Research, Travel & Tourism

Robyn Streisand *(Pres & CEO)*
Lisa Chernin *(Dir-Creative)*

Accounts:
VAL Floors Flooring Contractors

MJE MARKETING SERVICES

3111 Camino del Rio N Ste 100, San Diego, CA 92108
Tel.: (619) 682-3841
Fax: (619) 682-3844
E-Mail: info@mjemarketing.com
Web Site: www.mjemarketing.com

Employees: 10
Year Founded: 1994

Agency Specializes In: Financial, Government/Political, High Technology, Travel & Tourism

Marlee J. Ehrenfeld *(Pres & Dir-Creative)*
Kristen McDade Byrne *(VP-Comm & Pub Affairs)*
Aaron Ishaeik *(Sr Dir-Art)*
Robb Henderson *(Client Svcs Mgr)*
Nancy Mumford *(Specialist-Mktg Comm)*

Accounts:
Angels Foster Families
ASAP 21
Bank of Southern California
Borrego Springs Bank
The Port of San Diego Public Art Program
San Diego County Regional Airport Authority Commemorative Book
San Diego New Car Dealers Association
Think Blue, City of San Diego
UPS

MJR CREATIVE GROUP

(Private-Parent-Single Location)
1114 N Fulton St, Fresno, CA 93728
Tel.: (559) 499-1930
E-Mail: hello@mjrcg.com
Web Site: www.mjrcg.com

Employees: 11
Year Founded: 1995

Agency Specializes In: Advertising, Content, Corporate Identity, Internet/Web Design, Social Media

Revenue: $1,100,000

Michael Rolph *(CEO)*
Jana Bukilica *(CFO)*
Geoff Johnston *(Acct Dir & Producer)*
Jason Bukilica *(Acct Dir)*
Nico Dondlinger *(Dir-Creative & Designer-UI & UX)*
Brian Moore *(Dir-Creative)*
Frank Ruiz *(Dir-Art)*
Bradley Fitzhenry *(Brand Mgr)*
Bekah Franklin *(Designer)*

Accounts:
California Association of Nurseries & Garden Centers Plantable
Front Door Farms

MKG

599 Broadway 4th Fl, New York, NY 10012
Tel.: (212) 620-7770
E-Mail: nyc@thisismkg.com
Web Site: www.thisismkg.com

Year Founded: 2002

Agency Specializes In: Advertising, Digital/Interactive, Event Planning & Marketing, Social Media, Sponsorship

Maneesh K. Goyal *(Founder)*
Tracy Bussan *(Pres)*
David Garlick *(COO)*
Lauren Austin *(Dir-Creative)*
Christine Capone *(Dir-Accts)*
Isabella Rodriguez *(Acct Exec)*

Accounts:
Audi
Delta Air Lines, Inc.
Evian Events & Promotions
J.P. Morgan Asset Management Holdings Inc.

MKTG INC.

343 W Erie St Ste 520, Chicago, IL 60654
Tel.: (312) 202-8901
E-Mail: info@mktg.com
Web Site: www.mktg.com

Agency Specializes In: Advertising, Digital/Interactive, Print, Social Media, Sponsorship, Strategic Planning/Research

Jim Garofalo *(VP-Client Svcs)*
Kevin Collins *(Gen Mgr)*

Accounts:
Dick's Sporting Goods (Event, Community & Experiential AOR)

MKTWORKS, INC.

292 Main St, Cold Spring, NY 10516
Tel.: (845) 265-7000
Fax: (845) 231-4061
E-Mail: info@marketingworksnow.com
Web Site: www.marketingworksnow.com

Employees: 10
Year Founded: 2002

Agency Specializes In: Above-the-Line, Advertising, Advertising Specialties, Affiliate Marketing, Affluent Market, African-American Market, Agriculture, Alternative Advertising, Arts, Asian Market, Automotive, Aviation & Aerospace, Below-the-Line, Bilingual Market, Brand Development & Integration, Branded Entertainment, Broadcast, Business Publications, Business-To-Business, Cable T.V., Catalogs, Children's Market, Co-op Advertising, Collateral, College, Commercial Photography, Communications, Computers & Software, Consulting, Consumer Goods, Consumer Marketing, Consumer Publications, Content, Corporate Communications, Corporate Identity, Cosmetics, Crisis Communications, Custom Publishing, Customer Relationship Management, Digital/Interactive, Direct Response Marketing, Direct-to-Consumer, E-Commerce, Education, Electronic Media, Electronics, Email, Engineering, Entertainment, Environmental, Event Planning & Marketing, Exhibit/Trade Shows, Experience Design, Fashion/Apparel, Financial, Food Service, Game Integration, Gay & Lesbian Market, Government/Political, Graphic Design, Guerilla Marketing, Health Care Services, High Technology, Hispanic Market, Hospitality, Household Goods, Identity Marketing, In-Store Advertising, Industrial, Infomercials, Information Technology, Integrated Marketing, International, Internet/Web Design, Investor Relations, Legal Services, Leisure, Local Marketing, Logo & Package Design, Luxury Products, Magazines, Marine, Market Research, Media Buying Services, Media Planning, Media Relations, Media Training, Medical Products, Men's Market, Merchandising, Mobile Marketing, Multicultural, Multimedia, New Product Development, New Technologies, Newspaper, Newspapers & Magazines, Out-of-Home Media, Outdoor, Over-50 Market, Package Design, Paid Searches, Pharmaceutical, Planning & Consultation, Podcasting, Point of Purchase, Point of Sale, Print, Product Placement, Production, Production (Ad, Film, Broadcast), Production (Print), Promotions, Public Relations, Publicity/Promotions, Publishing, RSS (Really Simple Syndication), Radio, Real Estate, Recruitment, Regional, Restaurant, Retail, Sales Promotion, Search Engine Optimization, Seniors' Market, Social Marketing/Nonprofit, South Asian Market, Sponsorship, Sports Market, Stakeholders, Strategic Planning/Research, Sweepstakes, Syndication, T.V., Technical Advertising, Teen Market, Telemarketing, Trade & Consumer Magazines, Transportation, Travel & Tourism, Urban Market, Viral/Buzz/Word of Mouth, Web (Banner Ads, Pop-ups, etc.), Women's Market,

Yellow Pages Advertising

Marc Sabin *(Exec VP)*
Ron Hill *(Dir-Media)*
Chris Nelson *(Dir-Creative)*
Debbie Darman *(Mgr-Mktg Svcs)*

Accounts:
Hudson Highlands Green Way Triathalon
Hudson River Navigator

MKTX INC
6125 NE Cornell Rd Ste 380, Hillsboro, OR 97124
Tel.: (503) 646-6589
E-Mail: answers@mktx.com
Web Site: www.mktx.com

Year Founded: 1998

Agency Specializes In: Advertising, Brand Development & Integration, Content, Internet/Web Design, Print, Public Relations, Search Engine Optimization, Social Media

Bob Patterson *(Pres)*
Joe Santana *(Dir-Creative)*
Todd Wold *(Dir-Internet Strategies)*
Andrea White *(Acct Mgr)*

Accounts:
Applicos

M.L. ROGERS
(Acquired & Absorbed by Dentsu Aegis)

MLT CREATIVE
4020 E Ponce de Leon Ave, Clarkston, GA 30021
Tel.: (404) 292-4502
Fax: (404) 292-4480
E-Mail: info@mltcreative.com
Web Site: www.mltcreative.com

Employees: 15

Agency Specializes In: Business-To-Business

Glenn Taylor *(Partner & Sr Dir-Creative)*
Billy Mitchell *(Partner, Dir-B2B Mktg Creative & Specialist-Inbound Mktg)*
Brian Sheppard *(Dir-Creative-Interactive Media & Specialist-B2B Inbound Mktg)*
Matt Albert *(Dir-Art)*
Chris Davis *(Dir-Production)*
Vann Morris *(Dir-Buyer Behavior)*
Sonya Stoudemire *(Office Mgr-Bus)*

Accounts:
Airgas
Autotec AuctionACCESS (Web Site)
Manheim Manheim Specialty Auctions

MMB
580 Harrison Ave, Boston, MA 02118
Tel.: (617) 670-9700
Fax: (617) 670-9711
E-Mail: ccaufield@mmb580.com
Web Site: www.mmb580.com

Employees: 60
Year Founded: 2001

Agency Specializes In: Advertising, Automotive, Brand Development & Integration, Broadcast, Business-To-Business, Cable T.V., Collateral, Communications, Consulting, Consumer Marketing, Consumer Publications, Corporate Communications, Corporate Identity, Digital/Interactive, Direct Response Marketing, Electronic Media, Entertainment, Fashion/Apparel, Financial, Graphic Design, Health Care Services, High Technology, In-Store Advertising, Information Technology, Investor Relations, Leisure, Local Marketing, Logo & Package Design, Magazines, Merchandising, New Product Development, Newspaper, Newspapers & Magazines, Out-of-Home Media, Outdoor, Over-50 Market, Pharmaceutical, Planning & Consultation, Point of Purchase, Point of Sale, Print, Production, Radio, Restaurant, Retail, Sponsorship, Sports Market, Strategic Planning/Research, Syndication, T.V., Teen Market, Trade & Consumer Magazines, Travel & Tourism

Jamie Mambro *(Founder, Partner & Exec Dir-Creative)*
Fred Bertino *(Pres & Chief Creative Officer)*
Carrie Parks *(Partner & Dir)*
Lance Smith *(Mng Dir)*
Greg Almeida *(Sr VP, Dir-Creative & Copywriter)*
Travis Robertson *(Sr VP & Dir-Creative & Art)*
Matt Fallon *(Acct Dir)*
Jen Pantano Campbell *(Dir-Art & Designer)*
Mike Hollywood *(Dir-Social Media & PR)*
Leslie Intoppa *(Dir-HR)*
Brian Ratner *(Dir-Digital Art)*
Chris Poulin *(Assoc Dir-Creative)*
Allison Price *(Mgr-Bus Dev)*
Lisa Gapinske *(Acct Exec)*
Liz Albrecht *(Sr Art Dir & Designer)*
Spencer Cook *(Copywriter)*
Brian Hayes *(Copywriter)*

Accounts:
American Funds
Boston Children's Hospital
ESPN
FGX International Foster Grant
Gulf States Toyota; Houston, TX Creative
Hannaford Supermarkets (Agency of Record) Creative Strategy
Ken's Steak House Dressings Campaign: "Guard Rabbit", Salad Dressing
LogMeIn
Ocean State Job Lot
Starkist
Stowe
Thomasville
Toyota Tundra
UNICEF

MMG WORLDWIDE
(Merged with YPartnership & changed name too MMGY Global.)

MMGY GLOBAL
(Formerly MMG Worldwide)
4601 Madison Ave, Kansas City, MO 64112
Tel.: (816) 472-5988
Fax: (816) 471-5395
E-Mail: creid@mmgyglobal.com
Web Site: www.mmgyglobal.com

E-Mail for Key Personnel:
President: creid@mmgyglobal.com
Creative Dir.: scolovin@mmgyglobal.com

Employees: 120
Year Founded: 1981

Agency Specializes In: Advertising, Affiliate Marketing, Brand Development & Integration, Broadcast, Consumer Marketing, Crisis Communications, Customer Relationship Management, Digital/Interactive, E-Commerce, Graphic Design, Hospitality, Integrated Marketing, Internet/Web Design, Media Buying Services, Media Planning, Mobile Marketing, Multicultural, Newspaper, Newspapers & Magazines, Outdoor, Paid Searches, Podcasting, Public Relations, Radio, Restaurant, Search Engine Optimization, Strategic Planning/Research, T.V., Trade & Consumer Magazines, Travel & Tourism, Viral/Buzz/Word of Mouth, Web (Banner Ads, Pop-ups, etc.)

Approx. Annual Billings: $130,000,000

Breakdown of Gross Billings by Media: Bus. Publs.: 2%; Cable T.V.: 5%; Collateral: 8%; Consulting: 4%; Consumer Publs.: 9%; D.M.: 6%; E-Commerce: 11%; Fees: 11%; Internet Adv.: 19%; Logo & Package Design: 2%; Newsp.: 2%; Pub. Rels.: 8%; Spot Radio: 5%; Spot T.V.: 4%; Strategic Planning/Research: 4%

Don Montague *(Chm)*
Calep Howard *(CTO)*
Stewart Colovin *(Exec VP-Creative & Brand Strategy)*
Claire Bishop *(Sr VP-Integrated Media Strategy)*
Lucas Cobb *(VP-Integrated Plng)*
Doug Day *(VP-Field Mktg)*
Bob Frohoff *(VP-Media)*
Alan Kuykendall *(Acct Svcs Dir)*
Chris Pomeroy *(Dir-Strategies & Client Svcs-Global)*
Jessica Cox *(Assoc Dir-Media)*
Justin Farmer *(Assoc Dir-Creative)*
Trey Stanley *(Sr Acct Exec)*
Rachel Arthachinda *(Media Planner-Digital)*
Casey Calhoun *(Media Buyer-Digital)*
Nick Clark *(Coord-eMail Mktg Program)*
Ariel Wituszynski *(Coord-Digital Media)*
Meliah Cranmer *(Media Supvr)*
Caitlin Stephens *(Sr Media Buyer)*

Accounts:
The Alexander Hotel
The Barbados Tourism Authority
Bermuda Tourism Authority (Advertising Agency of Record) Creative, Marketing, Media Planning, Strategy
Bloomington Minnesota CVB
Colorado Tourism Office
Hospitality Sales & Marketing Association International Advertising, Digital Marketing, Public Relations
Kennedy Space Center Visitor Complex
Leading Hotels of the World (Integrated Marketing & Public Relations Agency of Record) Media Relations, Strategic Planning
Lufthansa
Marriott Resorts
National Geographic Expeditions
NH Hotel Group Brand Strategy
Niagara Falls State Park
Occidental Hotels & Resorts (US Public Relations Agency of Record)
Philadelphia CVB
Silversea Cruise Lines
South Dakota Department of Tourism
Springfield Missouri CVB
Terranea Resort
Travel Guard North America
Tucson Visitors Bureau Brand Positioning Strategy
Visit Sarasota County
The WWI Museum

Branches

MMG
919 Fish Hook Cove, Bradenton, FL 34212
Tel.: (941) 932-8599
E-Mail: mgoff@mmgworldwide.com
Web Site: www.mmgyglobal.com

Agency Specializes In: Advertising

Don Montague *(Chm)*
Hugh Mcconnell *(CFO & Exec VP-Ops)*
Calep Howard *(CTO)*
Stewart Colovin *(Exec VP-Creative & Brand Strategy)*
Kerry Cannon *(Mng Dir-Orlando)*
Katie Briscoe *(VP-Client Svcs)*

Steve Cohen *(VP-Insights)*
Craig Compagnone *(VP-Bus Strategy)*
Chris Pomeroy *(Dir-Global Strategies & Client Svcs)*
Allison Way *(Dir-Content Strategy)*

MMGY Global
(Formerly MMG Mardiks)
245 5th Ave 9th Fl, New York, NY 10016
Tel.: (212) 219-7560
Fax: (212) 219-0759
E-Mail: cmardiks@mmgyglobal.com
Web Site: www.mmgyglobal.com

Employees: 12

Agency Specializes In: Leisure, Public Relations, Sponsorship, Travel & Tourism

Julie Freeman *(Exec VP & Mng Dir-PR)*
David Perez *(VP-PR)*
Angela Cavis *(Sr Acct Dir)*
Elyse Eisen *(Acct Dir-PR)*
Lena Williamson *(Office Mgr)*
Nick Schweers *(Sr Acct Exec-PR)*
Trey Stanley *(Sr Acct Exec)*

Accounts:
The Beaches of Fort Myers & Sanibel Community Relations, National Media Relations, Strategic Public Relations Counsel
Champagne Louis de Sacy Strategic Outreach Campaign
Radisson Edwardian
ShermansTravel Media, LLC Travel Deals & Destination Advice; 2008
Travel Portland Media Relations

MMGY Global
(Formerly Ypartnership)
423 S Keller Rd Ste 100, Orlando, FL 32810-6121
Tel.: (407) 875-1111
Fax: (407) 875-1115
E-Mail: pyesawich@mmgyglobal.com
Web Site: www.mmgyglobal.com

Employees: 75
Year Founded: 1983

National Agency Associations: AAF

Agency Specializes In: Advertising, Advertising Specialties, Affluent Market, Brand Development & Integration, Branded Entertainment, Broadcast, Cable T.V., Co-op Advertising, Collateral, Communications, Consumer Marketing, Corporate Identity, Crisis Communications, Digital/Interactive, Direct Response Marketing, Direct-to-Consumer, E-Commerce, Electronic Media, Email, Entertainment, Event Planning & Marketing, Exhibit/Trade Shows, Food Service, Government/Political, Graphic Design, Guerilla Marketing, Health Care Services, Hospitality, Integrated Marketing, Internet/Web Design, Leisure, Local Marketing, Logo & Package Design, Luxury Products, Magazines, Media Buying Services, Media Planning, Media Relations, Media Training, Mobile Marketing, Multicultural, Multimedia, New Product Development, Newspapers & Magazines, Outdoor, Paid Searches, Planning & Consultation, Podcasting, Point of Purchase, Point of Sale, Print, Production (Ad, Film, Broadcast), Production (Print), Promotions, Public Relations, Publicity/Promotions, Publishing, Radio, Real Estate, Regional, Restaurant, Retail, Sales Promotion, Search Engine Optimization, Seniors' Market, Social Media, Sports Market, Strategic Planning/Research, T.V., Trade & Consumer Magazines, Travel & Tourism, Viral/Buzz/Word of Mouth, Web (Banner Ads, Pop-ups, etc.), Women's Market

Kerry Cannon *(Mng Dir)*
Chris Davidson *(Exec VP-Strategy & Client Leadership-Global)*
Kim Lenox *(VP & Grp Dir-Tourism Strategy)*
Steve Cohen *(VP-Insights)*
Chris Pomeroy *(Dir-Strategies & Client Svcs-Global)*
Amy Stepp *(Sr Acct Exec)*
Amber Hallums *(Jr Media Buyer)*

Accounts:
American Association of Nude Recreation
American Hotel & Lodging Association
Bermuda Tourism Authority (Agency of Record) Creative Strategy, Media Buying, Media Planning, Media Strategy, Mobile, Online, Print, Video
Cancun Convention & Visitors Bureau
Colonial Williamsburg Foundation
Grupo HIMA; Puerto Rico Healthcare, Public Relations; 2008
Grupo Posadas Hotels & Resorts; 2007
Honduras Institute of Tourism; 2007
Institute of Certified Travel Agents
Loreto Bay Company (Agency of Record) Resort Communities; 2008
Mexico Tourist Board; 2008
Mobil Travel Guide
Nassau/Paradise Island Promotion Board
Nuevo Leon Ministry of Tourism; Monterrey, Mexico
Saint John's Country Convention & Visitors Bureau
Travel Media Group (Agency of Record) Creative, Digital Media, Marketing, Public Relations
WMS Gaming; Chicago, IL
Wynn Resorts Las Vegas Le Reve

MMI AGENCY
1721 Pease St, Houston, TX 77703
Tel.: (713) 929-6900
Web Site: www.mmiagency.com

Year Founded: 1986

Benjamin Spiegel *(CEO)*
Jung Choi *(Sr VP-Creative)*
Amanda Hansen *(Sr VP-Mktg)*
Charity Poage *(VP-Acct Svcs)*
Kate Thomas *(VP-Delivery)*
Maggie Malek *(Head-PR & Social Media)*
Jay Hickman *(Dir-PR)*
Brandi Lalanne *(Dir-Digital)*
Gus Vaeza *(Dir-Bus Dev)*
Daniel Cadis *(Mgr-Digital)*

Accounts:
American General Life Companies
Direct Energy Broadcast, Campaign: "Reduce Your Use For Good", Company Blog, Power-To-Go Pre-Paid Product, Social Media
MD Andersen Cancer Center
Perry's Steakhouse & Grille
Shell Houston Open

MOB MEDIA
27121 Towne Centre Dr Ste 260, Foothill Ranch, CA 92610
Tel.: (949) 222-0220
Fax: (949) 222-0243
E-Mail: info@mobmedia.com
Web Site: www.mobmedia.com

Employees: 20
Year Founded: 1989

Agency Specializes In: Advertising, Advertising Specialties, Brand Development & Integration, Business-To-Business, Cable T.V., College, Consumer Publications, Direct Response Marketing, Direct-to-Consumer, Education, Electronic Media, Government/Political, Graphic Design, Guerilla Marketing, Local Marketing, Media Buying Services, Media Planning, Multimedia, Newspaper, Newspapers & Magazines, Out-of-Home Media, Outdoor, Print, Production (Ad, Film, Broadcast), Production (Print), Promotions, Public Relations, Radio, T.V., Technical Advertising, Trade & Consumer Magazines, Web (Banner Ads, Pop-ups, etc.)

Jeffrey Monroe *(Pres)*
Paul Otis *(CEO)*
Mitzi Perry *(Mng Dir & VP)*
Ivan Betancourt *(Sr Dir-Art)*
Russ Grace *(Exec Producer-Video-Brdcst)*
Allan Whetzel *(Client Svcs Dir)*
Yves Le Sieur *(Dir-Creative)*
Melissa Husdon *(Project Mgr-Social Media)*
Lisa Bolen *(Mgr-Acctg & HR)*
Michelle Lundblade *(Sr Media Buyer & Planner)*

Accounts:
Academy of Healing Arts
American Career College
Forefront Education Group
FOX Movie Channel
Inland Empire Auto Show
Scientific Telephone Systems
Scripps Networks
Show Biz Productions
Wes-Tec
Woodward Laboratories

MOBEXT
101 Huntington Ave Fl 16, Boston, MA 02199
Tel.: (617) 425-4346
Fax: (617) 425-4101
Web Site: www.mobext.com

Agency Specializes In: Advertising, Mobile Marketing, Technical Advertising

Warren Zenna *(Mng Dir-US & Exec VP)*
Andrew Hoffman *(VP-Mobile Mktg)*
Patricia Lopez *(Mgr-Mobile Mktg)*
Maddy Reavey *(Mgr-Mobile Mktg)*
Stephanie Harrold *(Supvr-Local Brdcst)*

Accounts:
McDonald's Corporation
Shakey's Digital, Mobile, Online Media, Social Media

MOBILE POSSE, INC.
1320 Old Chain Bridge Rd Ste 240, McLean, VA 22101
Tel.: (703) 348-4084
Fax: (703) 639-0662
E-Mail: info@mobileposse.com
Web Site: www.mobileposse.com

Employees: 20
Year Founded: 2005

Agency Specializes In: Advertising, Investor Relations, Mobile Marketing

Jon Jackson *(CEO)*
Steve Sincavage *(CFO)*
Erik Nienaber *(CTO)*
Gregory Wester *(Exec VP-Bus Dev & Gen Mgr-Res & Insights)*
Eric Newman *(VP-R&D)*

Accounts:
STATS LLC; McLean, VA

MOBIUM
(Name Changed to Mobium Integrated Branding)

MOBIUM INTEGRATED BRANDING
(Formerly Mobium)

200 S Michigan Ave, Chicago, IL 60604
Tel.: (312) 422-8950
Fax: (312) 422-5901
E-Mail: info@mobium.com
Web Site: www.mobium.com

E-Mail for Key Personnel:
Creative Dir.: mmcintyre@mobium.com

Employees: 35
Year Founded: 1979

National Agency Associations: 4A's-BMA-TAAN

Agency Specializes In: Above-the-Line, Advertising, Advertising Specialties, Agriculture, Aviation & Aerospace, Below-the-Line, Brand Development & Integration, Business Publications, Business-To-Business, Cable T.V., Collateral, Communications, Computers & Software, Consulting, Content, Corporate Communications, Corporate Identity, Customer Relationship Management, Digital/Interactive, Direct Response Marketing, E-Commerce, Electronic Media, Electronics, Email, Engineering, Event Planning & Marketing, Exhibit/Trade Shows, Financial, Graphic Design, Guerilla Marketing, Health Care Services, High Technology, Industrial, Information Technology, Integrated Marketing, International, Internet/Web Design, Logo & Package Design, Magazines, Market Research, Media Buying Services, Media Planning, Media Relations, Medical Products, Multimedia, New Product Development, Newspaper, Newspapers & Magazines, Out-of-Home Media, Outdoor, Paid Searches, Pharmaceutical, Planning & Consultation, Print, Production, Promotions, Public Relations, Publicity/Promotions, Radio, Real Estate, Sales Promotion, Search Engine Optimization, Social Media, Sponsorship, Strategic Planning/Research, T.V., Technical Advertising, Trade & Consumer Magazines, Viral/Buzz/Word of Mouth, Web (Banner Ads, Pop-ups, etc.)

Approx. Annual Billings: $15,000,000

Jc Addison *(Exec VP)*
Paul Brienza *(Exec VP-Digital)*
Patrick McAuley *(Sr VP-Acct Svcs)*
Mike Speck *(VP-Creative)*
Jay Sharfstein *(Exec Dir-Creative)*
Chris Deyoung *(Dir-Creative)*
Brittany Shifrin *(Acct Supvr)*
Melissa Hefner *(Strategist-Digital Media)*
Kay Anstrom *(Sr Graphic Designer)*

Accounts:
Bemis North America Rigid & Flexible Packaging; 2014
Guest-tek, Ltd. Internet, Voice, WiFi & TV Solutions for Hotels; 2015
IFF Non-Profit Lending & Real Estate Consulting; 2012
Moog, Inc. Motion Control Solutions For Industrial Applications; 2004
National Restaurant Association Trade Show Branding & Communications; 2011
Smalley Steel Rings Industrial Fasteners & Springs; 2014
Teradata Marketing Automation Software; 2014

MOCEAN
2440 S Sepulveda Blvd, Los Angeles, CA 90064
Tel.: (310) 481-0808
E-Mail: info@moceanla.com
Web Site: www.moceanla.com

Employees: 50
Year Founded: 2004

Agency Specializes In: Advertising, Brand Development & Integration, Content

Revenue: $1,100,000

Michael Mcintyre *(Pres)*
Craig Murray *(CEO)*
Greg Harrison *(Sr VP & Dir-Creative)*
Jeremy Keeler *(VP-Home Entertainment, Producer & Writer)*
Pam Postrel *(VP & Dir-Creative-Animation & Family)*
Roshone Harmon *(VP-Revenue Cycle)*
Troy Hutchinson *(Dir-Creative & Writer)*
Scott Goldman *(Dir-Creative)*
Sherri Jacobsen *(Assoc Dir-Creative)*

Accounts:
Discovery
Disney
EA
FX
Google
Hulu
Relativity
Screen Gems
Showtime
Warner Bros
YouTube

MOCK
247 14th St NW, Atlanta, GA 30318
Tel.: (470) 225-6819
E-Mail: hello@mocktheagency.com
Web Site: www.mocktheagency.com

Year Founded: 2008

Agency Specializes In: Advertising, Digital/Interactive, Graphic Design, Outdoor, Radio, T.V.

Donald J. Mock *(Mng Partner & Dir-Creative)*
Rob Broadfoot *(Partner & Dir-Creative)*
Kirby Matherne *(Dir-Art & Graphic Designer)*
Wendy Mixon *(Dir-Art)*
Meghan Stoneburner *(Mgr-Social Media)*

Accounts:
Ruud

MOD & COMPANY
159 Dousman St, Saint Paul, MN 55102
Tel.: (612) 238-3930
E-Mail: info@modandco.com
Web Site: www.modandco.com

Year Founded: 2001

Agency Specializes In: Advertising, Brand Development & Integration, Collateral, Internet/Web Design, Logo & Package Design, Print, Promotions

Luke Soiseth *(Principal, Dir-Editorial & Producer)*
Jana Soiseth *(Principal & Dir-Creative)*
Britt Sax *(Dir-Art)*
Melinda Goodman *(Strategist-Mktg & Res)*
Heidi McIntyre *(Strategist-Mktg & Res)*
Christina LeClaire *(Designer)*
Alison Eiler *(Coord-Mktg)*

Accounts:
Black Gold Farms
Healthy Food Shelves
Minnesota Office of Higher Education
The Shops at West End
Woot Froot

MODCO GROUP
(Formerly KD&E)
102 Madison Ave 10th Fl, New York, NY 10016
Tel.: (212) 243-0242
E-Mail: info@modcogroup.com
Web Site: modcogroup.com

Employees: 50
Year Founded: 1991

National Agency Associations: LAA

Agency Specializes In: Advertising, Aviation & Aerospace, Bilingual Market, Broadcast, Business-To-Business, Collateral, Direct Response Marketing, Entertainment, Exhibit/Trade Shows, Fashion/Apparel, Financial, Health Care Services, High Technology, Hispanic Market, Internet/Web Design, Magazines, Marine, Media Buying Services, Medical Products, New Product Development, Newspaper, Newspapers & Magazines, Out-of-Home Media, Outdoor, Print, Production, Public Relations, Publicity/Promotions, Radio, Retail, Sponsorship, T.V., Trade & Consumer Magazines

Erik Dochtermann *(Founder & COO)*
Sara Rotman *(CEO & Chief Creative Officer)*
Ellie Bamford *(Pres-MODCo Media)*
Gretchen Vater *(Exec Dir-Creative &Dir-Client Svcs)*
Cressida Payavis *(Sr Dir-Art)*
Telina Pedro *(Acct Supvr)*
Julia Claflin *(Supvr-Client Strategy)*
Kimberly Van Schoick *(Supvr-Digital Media)*
Tara Purtill *(Acct Exec)*

Accounts:
2K Games 2K Sports
Alex and Ani
Amanzi Tea
Cache
Coty Be Jeweled, Princess
David's Bridal White by Vera Wang
Elle
Joe Fresh
Kohls Simply Vera Vera Wang
Lagos Inc.
Men's Wearhouse
Pinnacle Care
South Peak Games
Take Two Interactive; New York, NY Playstation & Nintendo Titles; 1999
USAI
Vera Wang
Via Spiga
Zales Vera Wang Love

MODEA
117 Washington St SW, Blacksburg, VA 24060
Tel.: (540) 552-3210
Fax: (540) 552-3223
E-Mail: info@modea.com
Web Site: www.modea.com

Year Founded: 2006

David Catalano *(Co-Founder & Pres)*
Aaron Herrington *(Co-Founder)*
Steve Grant *(Chief Strategy Officer)*
Ted Boezaart *(Gen Mgr)*
Shannon Wright *(Dir-Production Svcs)*

Accounts:
Chiquita
HTC

MODERN BRAND COMPANY
1305 2nd Ave N Ste 103, Birmingham, AL 35203
Tel.: (205) 705-3777
Fax: (205) 705-3778
E-Mail: info@themodernbrand.com
Web Site: www.themodernbrand.com

Employees: 3
Year Founded: 2007

Agency Specializes In: Advertising, Brand Development & Integration, Business-To-Business,

Collateral, Communications, Computers & Software, Corporate Identity, Graphic Design, Identity Marketing, Local Marketing, Logo & Package Design

Approx. Annual Billings: $1,000,000

Breakdown of Gross Billings by Media: Graphic Design: 100%

Michael Bell *(Founder & Partner)*
Bradford Kachelhofer *(Owner)*
Liz Harris *(Dir-PR)*
Jacob Schwartz *(Dir-Creative)*

Accounts:
Media for Health BodyLove

MODERN CLIMATE
800 Hennepin 8th Fl, Minneapolis, MN 55403
Tel.: (612) 343-8180
Fax: (612) 343-8178
E-Mail: info@modernclimate.com
Web Site: modernclimate.com/

Employees: 25
Year Founded: 1998

Agency Specializes In: Brand Development & Integration, Sponsorship

Geoff Bremner *(Pres & CEO)*
Len Eichten *(CFO)*
John Moberg *(COO & CTO)*
Brant Haenel *(Chief Strategy Officer)*
Keith Wolf *(Chief Creative Officer)*
Shane Mechelke *(VP-Tech)*
Justin Campbell *(Dir-Creative)*
Kalei Gaines *(Dir-Engagement)*
Jason Tell *(Chief Knowledge Officer)*

Accounts:
Andersen Windows
Best Buy
Empi
Hearth & Home Technologies
Heggies Pizza Brand Identity, Communications, Digital, Strategic Planning
Intel Corporation
Jamba, Inc.
Post-it PopNotes
Saint Jude Medical
UnitedHealthcare

THE MODERNS
900 Broadway Ste 903, New York, NY 10003
Tel.: (212) 387-8852
Fax: (212) 387-8824
E-Mail: byu@themoderns.com
Web Site: modernsnyc.tumblr.com/

Employees: 9
Year Founded: 1992

Agency Specializes In: Advertising

Janine James *(Pres & Chief Creative Officer)*
Kevin Szell *(Partner & Dir-Design)*
Bumhan Yu *(Designer)*

Accounts:
American Express
Harter; Middlebury, IN

MODUS OPERANDI
6534 W Sunset Blvd, Los Angeles, CA 90028
Tel.: (323) 467-9600
Web Site: www.modop.com

Year Founded: 2011

Agency Specializes In: Advertising, Content, Digital/Interactive, Social Media

Brian Kingston *(Founder, Partner & CFO)*
Dave Mcveigh *(Owner & Exec Dir-Creative)*
Jeff Suhy *(Pres)*
Miles Dinsmoor *(Co-CEO & Partner)*
Charles Lee *(Co-CEO & Head-Production)*
Shannon Clune *(Partner & VP-Accounts)*
Aaron Sternlicht *(Founder Partner & Chief Creative Officer)*
Roy Martin *(VP-Tech)*
Min Kim *(Exec Dir-Creative)*
Danielle Chitwood *(Dir-Social Strategy)*
Matt Delamater *(Dir-Art)*

Accounts:
Belvedere Vodka Campaign: "Know the Difference", Campaign: "The First Lady of Vodka", Digital, Mobile, Social, Web Channels, Website
Electronic Arts Inc. FIFA 13
Golden Road Brewing (Agency of Record)
Nitro City Panama

MOIRE MARKETING PARTNERS
407 N Washington St, Falls Church, VA 22046
Tel.: (703) 237-0045
Fax: (202) 822-0199
E-Mail: info@moiremarketingpartners.com
Web Site: www.moiremarketing.com

Employees: 7
Year Founded: 2001

Agency Specializes In: Brand Development & Integration, Internet/Web Design, Logo & Package Design, Magazines, Media Buying Services, Print, Public Relations, Search Engine Optimization, Strategic Planning/Research, T.V.

Jeff Roberts *(Pres)*
Jim Garzione *(Partner)*
Erin Conron Lum *(Acct Exec)*
Elizabeth Edelson *(Sr Designer)*
Margo Howard *(Sr Designer)*

Accounts:
Akin Gump Strauss Hauer & Feld Legal Services
Cushman & Wakefield Real Estate Services
Paul Weiss Legal Services

MOJO LAB
30 W 3rd Ave Ste 200, Spokane, WA 99201
Tel.: (509) 232-0803
Web Site: www.mojo-lab.com

Year Founded: 2013

Agency Specializes In: Advertising, Digital/Interactive, Graphic Design, Internet/Web Design, Print

Chris Clifford *(Principal)*
Clint Janson *(Principal)*
Kevin Graham *(Editor & Designer)*
Keelin Toal *(Acct Exec & Coord-Traffic)*

Accounts:
Churchills Steakhouse
The Spokane Tribe of Indians
Truckland

MOMENTUM MARKETING
295 Seven Farms Dr, Charleston, SC 29492
Tel.: (843) 377-8450
Fax: (843) 377-8451
E-Mail: info@momentumresults.com
Web Site: momentummarketing.wordpress.com

Agency Specializes In: Advertising, Brand Development & Integration, Graphic Design, Internet/Web Design, Logo & Package Design, Market Research, Media Buying Services, Public Relations, Search Engine Optimization

Pam Hartley *(Founder & Principal)*
Lawrence Greenspon *(VP-Accts)*
Emily Trogdon *(Dir-PR)*
Lauren Turgeon *(Mgr-Events & Sponsorship & Acct Coord)*
Julia Melvin *(Mgr-Social Media Content)*
Gillian Mechling *(Acct Exec)*
Maria Rebula *(Acct Exec)*
Melissa Caloca *(Designer-Creative Svcs)*
John Lee Clair *(Designer-Creative Svcs)*
Rosalyn Caudle *(Acct Coord)*

Accounts:
The Coastal Cupboard
Cupcake DownSouth Campaign: "Sweet"
Indigo Auto Group Desert European Motorcars
Loeber Motors, Inc.
NeSmith Chevrolet 40th Anniversary, Online Promotion, Press, Print, Radio, Social Media
Palmetto Moon
Wonder Works, Inc.

MOMENTUM WORLDWIDE
250 Hudson St, New York, NY 10013
Tel.: (646) 638-5400
E-Mail: info@momentumww.com
Web Site: www.momentumww.com

E-Mail for Key Personnel:
President: chris.weil@momentumww.com

Employees: 2,000
Year Founded: 1987

National Agency Associations: 4A's-AMA-PMA-POPAI

Agency Specializes In: Above-the-Line, Advertising, Advertising Specialties, Affluent Market, African-American Market, Alternative Advertising, Automotive, Below-the-Line, Bilingual Market, Brand Development & Integration, Branded Entertainment, Broadcast, Business-To-Business, Collateral, College, Communications, Computers & Software, Consulting, Consumer Goods, Consumer Marketing, Corporate Communications, Corporate Identity, Cosmetics, Customer Relationship Management, Digital/Interactive, Electronic Media, Electronics, Entertainment, Event Planning & Marketing, Exhibit/Trade Shows, Experience Design, Fashion/Apparel, Financial, Food Service, Game Integration, Gay & Lesbian Market, Government/Political, Graphic Design, Guerilla Marketing, Health Care Services, High Technology, Hispanic Market, Household Goods, Identity Marketing, In-Store Advertising, Integrated Marketing, International, Internet/Web Design, Leisure, Local Marketing, Logo & Package Design, Luxury Products, Magazines, Media Relations, Media Training, Medical Products, Merchandising, Mobile Marketing, Multicultural, Multimedia, Newspaper, Newspapers & Magazines, Out-of-Home Media, Outdoor, Package Design, Pharmaceutical, Planning & Consultation, Podcasting, Point of Purchase, Point of Sale, Print, Product Placement, Production (Print), Promotions, Public Relations, Publicity/Promotions, Recruitment, Restaurant, Retail, Sales Promotion, Search Engine Optimization, Social Marketing/Nonprofit, Sponsorship, Sports Market, Strategic Planning/Research, Sweepstakes, Teen Market, Transportation, Travel & Tourism, Urban Market, Viral/Buzz/Word of Mouth, Women's Market

Chris Weil *(CEO)*
Philippe Touzot *(CFO)*
Luke D'Arcy *(CMO)*
Omid Farhang *(Chief Creative Officer-North*

America)
Jason Alan Snyder *(CTO-North America)*
Kevin McNulty *(Pres-Intl Markets)*
Donnalyn Smith *(Exec VP & Reg Dir-North America)*
Shaun Brown *(VP & Global Acct Dir)*
Aleigh Huston-Lyons *(Strategist)*

Accounts:
Advanced Micro Devices
Allstate Protect It or Lose It
American Express Campaign: "Unstaged"; 1997
Anheuser-Busch Inc. Budweiser, Campaign: "Drink Responsibly", Campaign: "Friends are Waiting", Creative, Media; 1998
Bentley
Coca-Cola Refreshments USA, Inc.; Atlanta, GA Coca-Cola, Sprite; 1996
Comcast Corporation
General Motors Buick
Hyundai
Johnson & Johnson
KRAFT; Chicago, IL & NJ; 2004
Lg Electronics Mobile Campaign: "Jane's Addiction Comes Alive"
Microsoft; 2000
Mondelez International
Nestle
Office Depot; Chicago, IL; 2009
Porsche Cars North America, Inc.
SeaWorld Parks & Entertainment LLC Cove, Discover, KaTonga
Starwood Hotels & Resorts
United Airlines Global Sponsorship Portfolio
United States Army; 2006
UPS; Atlanta, GA Sponsorship & Activation-Sports; 2010
Verizon

Branches

ChaseDesign, LLC
1326 New Seneca Tpk, Skaneateles, NY 13152
Tel.: (315) 685-1120
E-Mail: business@chasedesign.net
Web Site: www.chasedesign.net

Agency Specializes In: Package Design

Lindsay Pittard *(Head-Client)*
Christopher P. Andrews *(Mgr-Design)*
Matt Chadderdon *(Sr Strategist-Client)*
Ronald J. Kingston *(Sr Designer)*
Sean McNaughton *(Sr Designer-Visual Comm)*
Eric Meier *(Designer-Media)*
Stefanie Stoddard *(Exec Sec)*

Accounts:
Procter & Gamble

Momentum
384 Northyards Blvd NW Ste 390, Atlanta, GA 30313-2441
Tel.: (404) 954-8300
Fax: (404) 954-8399
E-Mail: momusat@momentumww.com
Web Site: www.momentumww.com

Employees: 25

National Agency Associations: 4A's

Agency Specializes In: Event Planning & Marketing, Sales Promotion

Matthew Gidley *(Mng Dir)*
Omid Farhang *(Chief Creative Officer)*
Mike Wilhelm *(Sr VP, Gen Mgr & Client Svcs Dir)*
Simone Parravicini *(Sr Dir-Art)*
Jennifer Birkel *(Acct Dir)*
Kyle Burnett *(Acct Dir)*
Sopho Chikvaidze *(Acct Dir)*

Momentum
444 N Michigan Ave Ste 1700, Chicago, IL 60611
Tel.: (312) 245-3500
Fax: (312) 245-3550
Web Site: www.momentumww.com

Employees: 62
Year Founded: 2002

National Agency Associations: 4A's

Agency Specializes In: Event Planning & Marketing, Sales Promotion, Sponsorship

Amy Barnard *(Sr VP & Grp Dir-Bus Leadership)*
Lena Elkhatib *(Assoc Dir-Creative)*
Michael Campione *(Sr Mgr-Bus Leadership)*
Sara Maccaferri *(Acct Mgr-Bus Leadership)*
Robin Lomax *(Mgr-Bus Leadership-Chick-fil-A & Coca-Cola)*
Andrew Stolp *(Mgr-Bus Leadership)*
Melissa Lacey *(Sr Acct Exec)*
Kate Calille *(Acct Exec)*
Tiffany Moten *(Acct Exec)*

Accounts:
Mondelez International, Inc. In-Store Marketing & Promotional, Salad Dressings

Momentum
7930 Clayton Rd Ste 400, Saint Louis, MO 63117
Tel.: (314) 646-6200
Fax: (314) 646-6960
E-Mail: info@momentumww.com
Web Site: www.momentumww.com

Employees: 270
Year Founded: 1987

National Agency Associations: 4A's-AMA-PMA-POPAI

Agency Specializes In: Advertising, Consulting, Digital/Interactive, Entertainment, Event Planning & Marketing, Promotions, Retail, Sales Promotion, Sponsorship, Sports Market

David Bannecke *(Sr VP & Grp Dir-Creative)*
Dina Stoeppler *(Sr VP & Reg Dir-HR)*
Jeff Coburn *(Sr VP & Dir-Creative Strategy)*
Jen Teasdale *(Acct Dir)*
Mary Riggs *(Dir-Brdcst Production & Bus Affairs)*
Greg Sullentrup *(Dir-Creative Svcs)*
Anne Gierse *(Strategist-Shopper Mktg)*

Accounts:
American Express; 1997
AMR Corporation American Airlines
Anheuser-Busch Inc. Budweiser Select 55; 1998
The Coca-Cola Company Dasani, My Coke Rewards, Sprite
Lg Electronics Mobile Campaign: "Jane's Addiction Comes Alive"
Lion Co.
Minute Maid Company
Nike, Inc.
The Procter & Gamble Company Crest, Fixodent, Scope
Seiyu
SSM Health Care Network Branding, Strategy

MONARCH COMMUNICATIONS INC.
343 Millburn Ave Ste 305, Millburn, NJ 07041
Tel.: (973) 912-9101
Fax: (973) 912-0875
E-Mail: ira@moncominc.com
Web Site: www.moncominc.com

Employees: 5

Agency Specializes In: Advertising, Graphic Design, Internet/Web Design, Print

Ira Berkowitz *(Owner)*
Ron Ribaudo *(Dir-Creative)*
April Dies *(Media Buyer-Interactive)*

Accounts:
Advantage Lites & Louvers
Bongrain North America
Care Station Medical Group
Centenary College
Colavita Foods USA
Deidre's House
The Episcopal Church Foundation
Gotham Bank of New York
Hamburger Woolen Company
The Horizon Group
IND-EX Inc.
Landice Treadmills
Mount Pleasant Animal Shelter
New Jersey SEEDS
Pectus Services
Perugina Chocolates
Primary Case Company
Sports Care Services
The Urban Dove
The Valerie Fund
Zero International

MONDO ROBOT
1737 15th St, Boulder, CO 80302
Tel.: (303) 800-2916
E-Mail: info@mondorobot.com
Web Site: www.mondorobot.com

Agency Specializes In: Advertising, Digital/Interactive, Event Planning & Marketing, Logo & Package Design

Chris Hess *(Founder & Dir-Creative)*
Jerimy Brown *(Sr Dir-Art)*
Spencer Schutz *(Sr Dir-Art)*
Justin Johnson *(Dir-Technical)*
Kelly Medema *(Office Mgr)*
Ben Frederick *(Sr Designer-Interaction)*

Accounts:
K2

MONO
1350 Lagoon Ave, Minneapolis, MN 55408
Tel.: (612) 454-4900
Fax: (612) 454-4950
E-Mail: info@mono-1.com
Web Site: www.mono-1.com

Employees: 40
Year Founded: 2004

Agency Specializes In: Automotive, High Technology, Information Technology, Pets , Retail, Sponsorship, Transportation

Michael Hart *(Co-Founder & Co-Chm-Creative)*
Chris Lange *(Co-Founder & Co-Chm-Creative)*
Jim Scott *(Co-Founder & Mng Partner)*
T. Scott Major *(Co-Chm-Creative)*
Joel Stacy *(Co-Chm-Creative)*
Erin Keeley *(CMO)*
Alison Clark *(Grp Acct Dir)*
Jane Delworth *(Grp Acct Dir)*
Paula Biondich *(Dir-Creative)*
John Blackburn *(Dir)*
Dave Bullen *(Dir-Art)*
Julie Vessel *(Dir-Talent)*
Lauren Buckley *(Strategist)*
Kathleen Flanders *(Project Head)*

Accounts:
Advance Auto Parts (Creative Agency of Record) Brand Strategy, Campaign: "That Feeling", Marketing

Animal Planet
Apple iPad
Blu Dot Real Good Experiment
Blue Cross and Blue Shield of Minnesota Campaign: "The Human Doing"
Breaking Bad Television Series
The Gatorade Company Digital, Print, Propel Water, Social, TV, Video
General Mills
Harvard Business School
Honeywell Broadcast, Digital, Lyric Thermostat, OOH, Print, Social
Lucy Activewear Campaign: "#Childspose"
NHL & NBC
OfficeMax
Parsons The New School For Design Campaign: "Soundaffects"
Phillips Distilling Company; Minneapolis, MN (Agency of Record)
The Science Channel
Sesame Workshop; 2004
Smashburger (Agency of Record) Creative, Experiential, Out-of-Home, Print, Radio
Sperry Top-Sider, Inc. Campaign: "Odysseys Await"
Target Campaign: "Cannonball", Campaign: "Everyday Collection", Campaign: "Field Trip", Campaign: "Scoot", Campaign: "Slide", Campaign: "Sunrise", Campaign: "Target Run", Campaign: "Tire Swing", Creative, Grocery & Food Business
Tillamook Cheese (Advertising Agency of Record)
TurboChef Technologies TurboChef Oven
USA Networks; 2005
Virgin Mobile USA, Inc. Do Whatever It Takes, Virgin Unite

THE MONOGRAM GROUP

233 S Wacker Dr Ste 410, Chicago, IL 60606
Tel.: (312) 726-4300
Fax: (312) 726-4300
Web Site: www.monogramgroup.com

Year Founded: 1990

Agency Specializes In: Advertising, Brand Development & Integration, Digital/Interactive, Market Research

Scott Markman *(Pres & Partner)*
Jackie Short *(Partner & Dir-Res)*
Chip Balch *(Dir-Creative)*
Lisa Harris *(Reg Mgr)*

Accounts:
Abbott Laboratories
American Hospital Association
Central Illinois Regional Museum
The Chicago Council on Global Affairs
Chicago Symphony Orchestra
Cole Taylor Bank
Kemper Investments
McDonald's Corporation
Wilson Sporting Goods Co.

MONOPOLIZE YOUR MARKETPLACE

2140 E Southlake Blvd #L812, Southlake, TX 76092
Tel.: (817) 416-4333
Fax: (817) 796-2967
E-Mail: info@mym-essentials.com
Web Site: www.mymessentials.com

Employees: 12
Year Founded: 1994

Agency Specializes In: Digital/Interactive, Internet/Web Design

Rich Harshaw *(Founder & CEO)*
Judi Schaefer *(COO & VP-Client Svcs)*
Bryan Bauman *(COO)*

MONSTER MEDIA, LLC

555 S Lake Destiny Dr, Orlando, FL 32810
Tel.: (407) 478-8163
Web Site: www.monstermedia.net

Employees: 60
Year Founded: 2006

Agency Specializes In: Sponsorship

Revenue: $2,600,000

Chris Beauchamp *(CEO)*
Stephen Randall *(Exec VP-Mobile & Social)*
Kristin Camorata *(Dir-HR)*
Gustavo Marrero *(Sr Mgr-Acct Mgmt)*
Brice Mcpheeters *(Acct Exec-Strategic B2B)*
Stephen Deming *(Designer-Interactive)*

THE MONTELLO AGENCY

9310 Old Kings Rd Ste 1704, Jacksonville, FL 32257
Tel.: (904) 737-0012
Web Site: www.montelloagency.com

Agency Specializes In: Advertising, Collateral, Corporate Identity, Graphic Design, Internet/Web Design, Logo & Package Design, Outdoor, Print, Public Relations, Social Media

Cynthia Montello *(Pres & CEO)*
Howard Montello *(Sls Dir)*

Accounts:
Durbin Crossing
Susan Carter CPA

MONTGOMERY STIRE & PARTNERS INC., ADVERTISING & PUBLIC RELATIONS

111 Veterans Blvd Ste 410, Metairie, LA 70005
Tel.: (504) 525-6789
Fax: (504) 525-6796
E-Mail: fstire@montgomerystire.com
Web Site: www.montgomerystire.com

Employees: 1
Year Founded: 1976

National Agency Associations: Second Wind Limited

Agency Specializes In: Public Relations

Approx. Annual Billings: $2,400,000

Frank E. Stire *(Pres)*

Accounts:
Crown Buick; Metairie, LA
Louisiana Manufactured Housing Association

MONTZINGO ASSOCIATES INC.

5122 Sunrise Ridge Trl, Middleton, WI 53562
Tel.: (608) 798-5099
Fax: (608) 258-3065

Employees: 3
Year Founded: 1975

Agency Specializes In: Advertising, Consulting, Corporate Identity, Medical Products, Travel & Tourism

Approx. Annual Billings: $2,000,000

Breakdown of Gross Billings by Media: Collateral: $1,800,000; Newsp.: $100,000; Radio: $100,000

John D. Montzingo *(Owner)*

Accounts:
Capital City Cleaning
Gleason Associates
McCaughey Properties

MOONLIGHT CREATIVE GROUP, INC.

930 E Blvd Ste B, Charlotte, NC 28203
Tel.: (704) 358-3777
Web Site: www.moonlightcreative.com

Year Founded: 1996

Agency Specializes In: Advertising, Brand Development & Integration, Digital/Interactive, Internet/Web Design, Logo & Package Design, Media Buying Services, Media Planning, Print

Dawn Newsome *(Partner)*
Jesse Weser *(Sr Designer)*

Accounts:
Charlotte Indoor Tennis Club

MOORE & ISHERWOOD COMMUNICATIONS, INC.

156 8th St, New Bedford, MA 02740-6003
Tel.: (508) 996-3946
Fax: (508) 997-2469
Web Site: www.micomm.com

E-Mail for Key Personnel:
President: eisherwood@micomm.com

Employees: 5
Year Founded: 1975

Agency Specializes In: Corporate Identity, Education, Environmental, Government/Political, Graphic Design, Health Care Services, Internet/Web Design, Logo & Package Design, Public Relations, Travel & Tourism

Approx. Annual Billings: $2,500,000

Breakdown of Gross Billings by Media: Bus. Publs.: $200,000; Collateral: $600,000; Mags.: $100,000; Newsp.: $100,000; Production: $500,000; Pub. Rels.: $500,000; Radio & T.V.: $500,000

Elizabeth Isherwood *(Pres)*
Susan Gilmore *(Dir-Art)*

Accounts:
Fall River Office of Economic Development; Fall River, MA
Precix Inc.

MOORE & SCARRY ADVERTISING

12601 Westlinks Dr Ste 7, Fort Myers, FL 33913-8638
Tel.: (239) 689-4000
Fax: (239) 689-4007
Web Site: www.mooreandscarry.com

Employees: 30
Year Founded: 2002

Agency Specializes In: Advertising, Automotive, Brand Development & Integration, Broadcast, Cable T.V., Co-op Advertising, Collateral, Direct Response Marketing, Graphic Design, Infomercials, Magazines, Media Buying Services, Multimedia, Newspaper, Newspapers & Magazines, Outdoor, Planning & Consultation, Print, Production, Radio, Recruitment, Sales Promotion, Strategic Planning/Research, T.V.

Approx. Annual Billings: $29,000,000

Breakdown of Gross Billings by Media: Brdcst.: $10,000,000; Cable T.V.: $3,500,000; Print:

$8,000,000; Production: $1,500,000; Radio: $6,000,000

Tom Kerr *(Co-Owner)*
Paul Caldwell *(Partner)*
Jacquie Miller *(VP & Gen Mgr)*
Karyn Cardona *(Dir-Media)*
Lucero Ruiz *(Dir-Production)*
Jason Zulauf *(Dir-Art)*
Jeremy Baker *(Sr Acct Exec)*
Kevin McDade *(Sr Media Buyer)*

Accounts:
Armstrong Toyota (Agency of Record)
Bob Taylor Chevrolet; Fort Myers, FL; 2005
Bob Taylor Jeep; Fort Myers, FL; 2005
Coggin Automotive Group
Courtesy Autogroup
Nalley Automotive Group
North Point Automotive Group; Little Rock, AR; 2005
Towne Hyundai
Towne Toyota

MOORE COMMUNICATIONS GROUP

2011 Delta Blvd, Tallahassee, FL 32303
Tel.: (850) 224-0174
Fax: (850) 224-9286
E-Mail: jimh@moorecommgroup.com
Web Site: www.moorecommgroup.com

Employees: 25

Agency Specializes In: Advertising, Brand Development & Integration, Communications, Event Planning & Marketing, Government/Political, Integrated Marketing, Internet/Web Design, Local Marketing, Media Relations, Public Relations

Karen B. Moore *(Founder & CEO)*
Richard Moore *(Owner)*
Jamie Fortune *(Mng Dir)*
Jordan Jacobs *(Mng Dir)*
Terrie Glover *(VP)*
Amy Mcilwain *(VP-Social & Digital Strategy)*
Nanette Schimpf *(VP)*
Ayla Anderson *(Sr Dir)*
Courtney Cox *(Acct Exec)*
Adam Montgomery *(Acct Exec)*
Donovan Parisi *(Designer-Web)*
Whitney Pickett *(Coord-Comm)*

Accounts:
American Lung Association of Florida
Florida Chamber of Commerce
Vote Smart Florida

MOORE, EPSTEIN, MOORE

273 Applewood Ctr Place Ste 342, Seneca, SC 29678
Tel.: (864) 719-0048
E-Mail: tmoore@mooreepsteinmoore.com
Web Site: www.mooreepsteinmoore.com

Employees: 15
Year Founded: 1983

Approx. Annual Billings: $21,000,000

Ted Moore *(Partner)*
Marianne Moore *(Exec VP)*

Accounts:
Outback Bowl; Tampa, FL
Southeast Communities
Tampa Bay & Co
Tampa Convention Center

MOOSYLVANIA MARKETING

7303 Marietta, Saint Louis, MO 63143
Tel.: (314) 533-5800
Fax: (314) 533-8056
Web Site: www.moosylvania.com

Employees: 45

Agency Specializes In: Sponsorship

Revenue: $2,800,000

Nick Foppe *(Pres & Mng Partner)*
Norty Cohen *(CEO)*
Rick Zuroweste *(Partner & CMO)*
AnneMarie Greene *(COO)*
Sharon Ayres *(VP-HR)*
Mike Cassimatis *(Dir-Creative)*
Mike Wienke *(Dir-Creative)*
Whitney Voigt *(Acct Mgr)*
Chelsea Fischer-Lodike *(Acct Exec)*
Andrea Jincks *(Asst Acct Exec)*
Lauren Runge *(Asst Acct Exec)*

Accounts:
Capital One
K-Mart
Nestle Purina
Ocean Spray
Over The Moon
Purina
Sapporo USA
Sears Kmart
Solutia
Steaz (Social Agency of Record)
We Car
WOW Green

THE MORAN GROUP LLC

8900 Bluebonnet Blvd, Baton Rouge, LA 70810
Tel.: (225) 769-1059
Toll Free: (800) 375-9986
E-Mail: info@moranadvertising.com
Web Site: www.moranadvertising.com

Agency Specializes In: Advertising, Digital/Interactive, Internet/Web Design, Media Buying Services, Media Planning, Print, Radio, Search Engine Optimization, Social Media, T.V.

Jim Moran *(Owner)*
Pamela LeJeune *(VP)*
Cameron Roberson *(Art Dir)*
Linda Dixon *(Dir-Media)*
Mike Freyder *(Creative Dir)*
Nicholas Robichaux *(Assoc Dir-Creative)*
Alex Ludwig *(Acct Mgr)*
Patrick Box *(Acct Exec-Digital Media)*
Amie Chamberlain *(Sr Media Buyer)*
Stephanie Croteau *(Coord-Digital)*

Accounts:
Fred Haas Toyota World

MORBELLI, RUSSO & PARTNERS ADVERTISING, INC.

2 Sylvan Way Ste 302, Parsippany, NJ 07054
Tel.: (973) 644-9663
Fax: (973) 644-9878
E-Mail: mrp@morbelli-russo.com
Web Site: www.morbelli-russo.com

E-Mail for Key Personnel:
President: mario@morbelli-russo.com
Creative Dir.: steve@morbelli-russo.com

Employees: 10
Year Founded: 1987

Agency Specializes In: Advertising, Advertising Specialties, Bilingual Market, Brand Development & Integration, Broadcast, Business Publications, Business-To-Business, Cable T.V., Children's Market, Collateral, Consumer Goods, Consumer Marketing, Consumer Publications, Corporate Communications, Corporate Identity, Direct Response Marketing, Direct-to-Consumer, E-Commerce, Electronic Media, Email, Exhibit/Trade Shows, Fashion/Apparel, Financial, Food Service, Gay & Lesbian Market, Graphic Design, Health Care Services, In-Store Advertising, Internet/Web Design, Logo & Package Design, Magazines, Market Research, Media Buying Services, Media Planning, Medical Products, Multimedia, New Product Development, Newspaper, Newspapers & Magazines, Out-of-Home Media, Outdoor, Over-50 Market, Package Design, Pharmaceutical, Point of Purchase, Point of Sale, Print, Production, Production (Print), Public Relations, Radio, Restaurant, Retail, Sales Promotion, Search Engine Optimization, Seniors' Market, Social Media, Sports Market, Strategic Planning/Research, T.V., Trade & Consumer Magazines, Transportation, Travel & Tourism, Viral/Buzz/Word of Mouth, Women's Market, Yellow Pages Advertising

Approx. Annual Billings: $105,000,000

Mario J. Morbelli, Jr. *(Owner)*
Steve Russo *(Owner)*
Eric Ortiz *(VP & Supvr-Creative)*
Cristina Murphy *(Sr Dir-Art)*

Accounts:
Admiral Insurance Co.; Cherry Hill, NJ; 1998
Bollinger Insurance; Short Hills, NJ; 1999
Johnson & Johnson; NJ
Summit Medical Group; Summit, NJ
Water-Jel Technologies; Carlstadt, NJ; 2001
WineryPak; NJ; 2006

MORE ADVERTISING

246 Walnut St Ste C, Newton, MA 2460
Tel.: (617) 558-6850
Fax: (617) 558-6851
E-Mail: info@moreadvertising.com
Web Site: www.moreadvertising.com

Agency Specializes In: Advertising, Brand Development & Integration, Digital/Interactive, Event Planning & Marketing, Media Buying Services, Media Planning, Media Relations, Print, Public Relations, Strategic Planning/Research

Donna Latson Gittens *(Founder & Principal)*
Judi Haber *(Principal)*
Bob Boucher *(Dir-Creative)*

Accounts:
Boston Water & Sewer Commission
UMass Amherst

MORE MEDIA GROUP

1427 Goodman Ave, Redondo Beach, CA 90278
Tel.: (310) 937-9663
Fax: (310) 937-9759
E-Mail: billg@moremediagroup.com
Web Site: www.moremediagroup.com

Employees: 6
Year Founded: 2000

Agency Specializes In: Advertising, Advertising Specialties, Affluent Market, Alternative Advertising, Arts, Automotive, Brand Development & Integration, Branded Entertainment, Broadcast, Business Publications, Business-To-Business, Cable T.V., Catalogs, Co-op Advertising, Collateral, Communications, Computers & Software, Consulting, Consumer Goods, Consumer Marketing, Consumer Publications, Content, Corporate Communications, Corporate Identity, Custom Publishing, Customer Relationship Management, Digital/Interactive, Direct Response Marketing, Direct-to-Consumer, E-Commerce, Electronic Media, Electronics, Engineering,

Entertainment, Event Planning & Marketing, Exhibit/Trade Shows, Fashion/Apparel, Financial, Graphic Design, Guerilla Marketing, High Technology, Hispanic Market, Identity Marketing, In-Store Advertising, Industrial, Integrated Marketing, International, Internet/Web Design, Investor Relations, Leisure, Local Marketing, Luxury Products, Magazines, Market Research, Media Buying Services, Media Planning, Media Relations, Media Training, Merchandising, Mobile Marketing, Multimedia, New Product Development, New Technologies, Newspaper, Newspapers & Magazines, Out-of-Home Media, Outdoor, Package Design, Paid Searches, Pharmaceutical, Planning & Consultation, Podcasting, Point of Purchase, Point of Sale, Print, Product Placement, Production, Production (Ad, Film, Broadcast), Production (Print), Promotions, Public Relations, Publicity/Promotions, Publishing, RSS (Really Simple Syndication), Radio, Real Estate, Retail, Sales Promotion, Social Marketing/Nonprofit, Sponsorship, Sports Market, Strategic Planning/Research, Syndication, T.V., Technical Advertising, Trade & Consumer Magazines, Transportation, Viral/Buzz/Word of Mouth, Web (Banner Ads, Pop-ups, etc.)

Approx. Annual Billings: $5,500,000

Breakdown of Gross Billings by Media: Audio/Visual: $2,000,000; E-Commerce: $1,000,000; Exhibits/Trade Shows: $2,500,000

Bill Ganz *(Founder)*

Accounts:
Epson; Long Beach, CA
Fender

MOREHEAD DOTTS RYBAK

2767 Santa Fe St, Corpus Christi, TX 78404
Tel.: (361) 883-6327
E-Mail: info@mdradvertising.com
Web Site: www.mdradvertising.com

Agency Specializes In: Advertising, Brand Development & Integration, Broadcast, Collateral, Digital/Interactive, Email, Event Planning & Marketing, Internet/Web Design, Logo & Package Design, Media Buying Services, Media Planning, Package Design, Print, Public Relations, Radio, Social Media, Strategic Planning/Research, T.V.

Fred Dotts *(Pres & CEO)*
Mo Morehead *(Principal)*
Holly Osborn *(VP-Client Svcs)*
Debra Estrada *(Comptroller)*
Janet Wilems *(Sr Dir-Art)*
Stephanie Cude *(Mgr-Digital Content)*
Lauren Clayton *(Acct Exec)*

Accounts:
Texas A&M International University

MORGAN + COMPANY

4407 Canal St, New Orleans, LA 70119
Tel.: (504) 523-7734
Fax: (504) 523-7737
E-Mail: info@morganandco.com
Web Site: www.morganandco.com

Employees: 10

National Agency Associations: 4A's

Agency Specializes In: Business-To-Business, Digital/Interactive, Education, Entertainment, Exhibit/Trade Shows, Financial, Health Care Services, Hospitality, Local Marketing, Media Relations, Mobile Marketing, Outdoor, Print, Radio, Retail, Social Marketing/Nonprofit, T.V., Travel & Tourism

Revenue: $120,000

Brenda Cole *(CFO)*
Renee Cobb-Stuart *(Dir-Media Buying)*
Eric Fullmer *(Planner-Digital Media)*

Accounts:
Ballista
Cleco
New Orleans Police
Ochsner
Raised Floor Living

MORGAN & MYERS, INC.

N16 W23233 Stone Ridge Dr Ste 200, Waukesha, WI 53188
Tel.: (262) 650-7260
Fax: (262) 650-7261
Web Site: www.morganmyers.com

E-Mail for Key Personnel:
President: toliver@morganmyers.com

Employees: 25
Year Founded: 1982

Agency Specializes In: Advertising, Agriculture, Brand Development & Integration, Business-To-Business, Collateral, Communications, Consulting, Consumer Marketing, Corporate Identity, E-Commerce, Environmental, Financial, Food Service, Government/Political, Graphic Design, Health Care Services, Industrial, Information Technology, Internet/Web Design, Planning & Consultation, Print, Production, Public Relations, Publicity/Promotions, Restaurant, Retail, Sales Promotion, Sponsorship, Strategic Planning/Research, Technical Advertising

Breakdown of Gross Billings by Media: D.M.: 20%; Farm Publs.: 50%; Radio: 10%; Trade & Consumer Mags.: 20%

Tim Oliver *(Pres)*
Max Wenck *(Partner)*
Linda Basse Wenck *(Principal & Dir-Corp Affairs)*
Janine Whipps *(Principal)*
Sherry Cerafoli *(Acct Coord)*
Tonia McBride *(Acct Coord)*

Accounts:
Foremost Farms, USA , Dairy Cooperative; 2004
Foremost Farms, USA
Kraft Agriculture-Related PR, Oscar Mayer; 2007
McDonald's
Monsanto
NCSRP Coalition
Nestle Purina PetCare Company
Novartis
Progressive Agriculture Foundation Creative
West Nile Equine

Branches

Morgan & Myers, Inc.

1005 Stratford Ave, Waterloo, IA 50701-1952
Tel.: (319) 233-0502
Fax: (319) 233-8077
E-Mail: jwhipps@morganmyers.com
Web Site: www.morganmyers.com

Employees: 30
Year Founded: 1986

Agency Specializes In: Agriculture, Business-To-Business, Financial, Food Service, Pets

Janine Stewart *(Principal & Dir-Integrated Comm)*
Linda Basse Wenck *(Principal & Dir-Corp Affairs & Social Responsibility)*
Max Wenck *(Principal & Dir-Agriculture & Pasture-to-Plate Practice)*
Janine Whipps *(Principal)*

Accounts:
Rabobank International

MORNINGSTAR MEDIA GROUP

240 Edward St, Sycamore, IL 60178
Tel.: (815) 899-0150
Web Site: www.morningstarmediagroup.com

Agency Specializes In: Advertising, Brand Development & Integration, Graphic Design, Internet/Web Design, Social Media

Ryan Weckerly *(Pres & CEO)*

Accounts:
Lake Cook Orthopedics

MOROCH PARTNERS

3625 N Hall St Ste 1100, Dallas, TX 75219-5122
Tel.: (214) 520-9700
Fax: (214) 252-1724
E-Mail: contact@moroch.com
Web Site: www.moroch.com

Employees: 250
Year Founded: 1981

National Agency Associations: 4A's

Agency Specializes In: Above-the-Line, Advertising, Advertising Specialties, African-American Market, Arts, Asian Market, Automotive, Below-the-Line, Bilingual Market, Brand Development & Integration, Broadcast, Cable T.V., Catalogs, Co-op Advertising, Collateral, College, Commercial Photography, Communications, Consulting, Consumer Goods, Consumer Marketing, Consumer Publications, Content, Corporate Communications, Corporate Identity, Crisis Communications, Digital/Interactive, Direct Response Marketing, Direct-to-Consumer, Education, Electronic Media, Email, Entertainment, Event Planning & Marketing, Exhibit/Trade Shows, Faith Based, Financial, Food Service, Game Integration, Gay & Lesbian Market, Graphic Design, Guerilla Marketing, Health Care Services, High Technology, Hispanic Market, Household Goods, Identity Marketing, In-Store Advertising, Infomercials, Integrated Marketing, Internet/Web Design, Leisure, Local Marketing, Logo & Package Design, Magazines, Marine, Market Research, Media Buying Services, Media Planning, Media Relations, Media Training, Men's Market, Merchandising, Mobile Marketing, Multicultural, New Product Development, Newspaper, Out-of-Home Media, Outdoor, Package Design, Pharmaceutical, Planning & Consultation, Point of Purchase, Point of Sale, Print, Production, Production (Ad, Film, Broadcast), Production (Print), Promotions, Public Relations, Publicity/Promotions, Radio, Recruitment, Regional, Retail, Sales Promotion, Seniors' Market, Social Marketing/Nonprofit, Social Media, Sponsorship, Sports Market, Strategic Planning/Research, Syndication, T.V., Teen Market, Telemarketing, Trade & Consumer Magazines, Travel & Tourism, Urban Market, Viral/Buzz/Word of Mouth, Web (Banner Ads, Pop-ups, etc.), Women's Market, Yellow Pages Advertising

Thomas F. Moroch *(Owner)*
Rob Boswell *(Pres & COO)*
Glenn Geller *(Mng Partner-Brand Plng Strategy)*
Cristina Vilella *(Partner-Central Div)*
Laura Keene *(CFO)*
Mark Stepanek *(CFO)*
Melinda Yoder *(COO)*
Doug Martin *(Chief Dev Officer)*

Yolanda Alarcon Cassity *(Chief Integration Officer-McDonald's)*
Sam Chadha *(Chief Integration Officer)*
Matt Powell *(Exec Dir-Media)*
Leeann Wells *(Sr Producer-Brdcst)*
Kevin Foreman *(Creative Dir-Digital)*
Bruna Saavedra *(Acct Dir)*
Matt Sitser *(Acct Dir)*
Melissa A. Clark *(Dir-Comm Media)*
Carol Dodson *(Dir-Corp Media)*
Donald Pierce *(Dir-Bus Insights)*
David Soames *(Dir-Creative)*
Dustin Taylor *(Dir-Creative)*
Kathleen Torres *(Dir-Brdcst)*
Stephanie Quante *(Acct Supvr)*
Ashley Stock *(Sr Acct Exec)*
Katie Skarke *(Acct Exec)*
Tim Forman *(Planner-Brand)*
Greg Szmurlo *(Copywriter)*
Emily Green *(Sr Media Planner)*
Sheila Lemon *(Sr Partner)*
Calvin Mellick *(Sr Supvr & Sr Media Planner)*

Accounts:
Baylor Healthcare System
Boost Mobile/Sprint
ClubCorp
The Coca-Cola Company
Dallas Men Against Abuse Campaign: "Be A Man", PSA
Disney
The Joint Chiropractic (Advertising Agency of Record) Campaign: "RELIEF. ON SO MANY LEVELS.", Creative Development, Marketing Planning
Make-A-Wish Foundation of America
McDonald's Restaurants Campaign: "Joywalk", Campaign: "Neil Golden's Birthday", Campaign: "Rhythm Straw", Campaign: "Studio Sessions", Creative, McCafe, Media Planning & Buying, Ohio Valley Co-op Bus, Social, Strategic Planning
Midas, Inc.
Oasis Brands, Inc. Paseo
Pure Fishing
New-Six Flags Theme Park (Media Agency of Record)
Sony Pictures Entertainment, Inc. Columbia TriStar Motion Picture Group
Stage Stores Creative, Media Buying & Planning, Strategy
Visionworks Creative, Media Buying, Strategic Advertising & Communications
Wilsonart International, Inc. (Brand Positioning & Consumer Advertising Agency of Record) Strategic

Branches

MEplusYOU
12404 Park Central Dr Ste 400, Dallas, TX 75251
(See Separate Listing)

Moroch
10809 Executive Ctr Dr Ste Plz 8, Little Rock, AR 72211
Tel.: (501) 225-9537
Fax: (501) 225-9541
E-Mail: info@moroch.com
Web Site: www.moroch.com

Employees: 2

Agency Specializes In: Consumer Marketing

Kamron Moore *(Partner)*
Stephanie Quante *(Acct Supvr)*
Delaine Farr *(Sr Acct Exec)*

Accounts:
Citracal
McDonald's
Midas
Sony Pictures Classic
Universal
Walt Disney Pictures

Moroch
2450 Venture Oaks Way, Sacramento, CA 95833
Tel.: (916) 929-9100
Fax: (916) 929-9108
E-Mail: info@moroch.com

Employees: 10

Agency Specializes In: Consumer Marketing

Robin Doss *(Partner)*
Clay Merrill *(Mgr-Comm)*

Accounts:
McDonald's

Moroch
81 SW 10th St Ste 2200, Fort Lauderdale, FL 33324
Tel.: (214) 560-9700
Fax: (954) 236-3603
E-Mail: action@moroch.com

Employees: 2

Agency Specializes In: Consumer Marketing

Andrea Salazar-Urquiaga *(Acct Supvr)*
Melissa Slattery *(Sr Acct Exec)*

Accounts:
20th Century Fox
Columbia Pictures
McDonald's
Universal
Verizon

Moroch
590 Means St NW, Atlanta, GA 30318
Tel.: (404) 607-8822
Fax: (404) 724-0378
E-Mail: action@moroch.com
Web Site: www.moroch.com

Employees: 20

Agency Specializes In: Consumer Marketing

Pat Kempf *(Co-Founder & Vice Chm)*
Courtney Standerfer *(Acct Dir-McDonald's)*
Andrew Lamar *(Acct Supvr)*
Michelle Velez *(Sr Acct Exec)*

Accounts:
Bimbo Bakeries USA
Citracal
Johnson & Johnson
Lionsgate
McDonald's Campaign: "Rhythm Straw", Coke
Midas
Sony Pictures Classics
TriStar
Verizon

Moroch
3500 N Causeway Blvd Ste 1405, Metairie, LA 70002
Tel.: (504) 833-8399
Fax: (504) 833-7890
E-Mail: info@moroch.com
Web Site: www.moroch.com

Employees: 400

Agency Specializes In: Consumer Marketing

Christina Blanco Dufrene *(Sr Acct Exec)*
Jason Price *(Sr Acct Exec)*
Nancy Rimel *(Acct Exec)*
Jamie Yarnell *(Acct Exec)*
Tanya Leon *(Asst Acct Exec)*

Accounts:
20th Century Fox
McDonald's
Midas
Sony Pictures Classic
Universal
Verizon
Walt Disney Pictures

Moroch
1215 Fern Ridge Pkwy, Saint Louis, MO 63141
Tel.: (314) 878-8311
Fax: (314) 878-8344
Web Site: www.moroch.com

Employees: 6

Cheri Wood *(Sr Acct Dir)*
Diane Glaus *(Acct Dir)*
Joanna Devereaux *(Acct Supvr)*
Alvaro Salinas *(Sr Media Planner & Supvr)*
Shelby Rothman *(Sr Acct Exec)*
Gray Stamulis *(Acct Exec)*

Accounts:
Fertell
First Look Studios
Fox Walden
Gulp
McDonald's Corporation
Overture
Warner Independent Pictures

Moroch
5400 Glenwood Ave Ste G05, Raleigh, NC 27612
Tel.: (919) 881-7880
Fax: (919) 881-7859
E-Mail: action@moroch.com

Employees: 4

Agency Specializes In: Consumer Marketing

Andrea Jonas *(Acct Dir)*
Allicia Giese *(Acct Supvr)*
Anne Hylton *(Acct Supvr)*
Sandy Smith *(Acct Supvr)*
Ashley Zillo *(Acct Supvr)*
Michelle Faison *(Sr Acct Exec)*
Zavious Robbins *(Acct Exec)*

Moroch
115 Gold Ave SW Ste 205, Albuquerque, NM 87102
Tel.: (505) 836-1823

Andi Conner *(Mgr-Print Production)*
Ashley Zillo *(Acct Supvr)*

Moroch
15 Fishers Rd, Pittsford, NY 14534
Tel.: (585) 586-6320
Fax: (585) 586-6353
Web Site: www.moroch.com

Agency Specializes In: Advertising

Cassidy Salomon *(Dir-Media Plng)*
Heidi Baumer *(Sr Acct Supvr)*
Allicia Giese *(Acct Supvr)*
Stephanie Quante *(Acct Supvr)*

Accounts:

McDonald's

Moroch
301 NW 63rd Ste 690, Oklahoma City, OK 73116
Tel.: (405) 848-6800
Fax: (405) 842-3607
E-Mail: action@moroch.com

Employees: 11

Agency Specializes In: Consumer Marketing

Bethany Yingst *(Sr Acct Exec)*
Ashley Quimby *(Acct Coord)*
Lisa Rooks *(Sr Partner)*

Accounts:
Gulp
Mattress Giant
Monster
MRS Bairds
Overhead Doors
Sathways
Tia Rosa

Moroch
402 Main St 5th Fl, Houston, TX 77002
Tel.: (713) 223-2788
Fax: (713) 223-2798
E-Mail: info@moroch.com
Web Site: www.moroch.com

Employees: 10

Agency Specializes In: Consumer Marketing

Nancy Terrell *(Partner)*
Keisha Williford *(Partner)*
Bob Shallcross *(Chief Creative Officer)*
Christopher Calhoon *(Dir-Digital Production)*
Lisa Gomes *(Dir-Media Ops)*
Shannon Morrison *(Mgr-Ops)*
Christy Rogge *(Acct Supvr-Stage Stores)*
Stephanie Ward *(Supvr-Brdcst)*
Carly O'Meara *(Sr Acct Exec)*
Kate Helbing *(Asst Acct Exec)*

Accounts:
Midas International, Inc.

Moroch
901 NE Loop 410 Ste 826, San Antonio, TX 78209-1310
Tel.: (210) 822-4840
Fax: (210) 822-8092
E-Mail: sanantonio@moroch.com
Web Site: www.moroch.com

Employees: 8

Agency Specializes In: Consumer Marketing

Lura Hobbs *(Mng Partner)*
Nancy Terrell *(Partner)*
Cristina Vilella *(Partner-Central Div)*
Keisha Williford *(Partner)*
Laura Keene *(CFO)*
Melinda Yoder *(COO)*
Bill Shearer *(CIO)*
Bob Shallcross *(Chief Creative Officer)*
Brad B. McCormick *(Chief Digital Officer)*
Danielle Krauter *(Grp Dir-Media)*
Russell Parker *(Acct Dir)*
Bruna Saavedra *(Acct Dir)*
Matt Sitser *(Acct Dir)*
Carol Dodson *(Dir-Corp Media)*
Holly Rodriguez *(Dir-Media Plng)*
Alex Archambault *(Mgr-Software Dev)*
Joseph Salazar *(Sr Acct Supvr)*
Angie Banks *(Acct Supvr)*
Erica-Renee Contreras *(Acct Supvr)*
Monique Davila *(Acct Supvr)*
Kendall Gibbs *(Acct Supvr)*
Christy Rogge *(Acct Supvr-Stage Stores)*
Shannon Morrison *(Supvr-Ops)*
Jason Price *(Sr Acct Exec)*
Nancy Rimel *(Acct Exec)*
Sheila Lemon *(Sr Partner)*

Moroch
9020 Stoney Point Pkwy Ste 370, Richmond, VA 23235
Tel.: (804) 320-6376
Fax: (804) 320-6379
E-Mail: action@moroch.com

Employees: 3

Agency Specializes In: Consumer Marketing

Courtney Standerfer *(Acct Dir-McDonald's)*
Andrew Lamar *(Acct Supvr)*

Accounts:
McDonald's

Moroch
3901 Brisco Rd Ste 12, Parkersburg, WV 26104
Tel.: (304) 424-7134
Fax: (304) 424-3609
E-Mail: action@moroch.com
Web Site: www.moroch.com

Employees: 5

Agency Specializes In: Consumer Marketing

Kamron Moore *(Partner)*
Andrea Jonas *(Acct Dir)*
Damon Ketchum *(Acct Dir)*
Andrew Renzi *(Sr Acct Supvr)*
Allicia Giese *(Acct Supvr)*
Stephanie Quante *(Acct Supvr)*
Ashley Zillo *(Acct Supvr)*

Accounts:
Citracal
Focus
Mattress Giant
McDonald's Corporation
Midas
Travel Channel
Uniden
Verizon
Walt Disney

MORONEY & GILL, INC.
245 Park Ave 39th Fl, New York, NY 10167
Tel.: (212) 672-1675
Fax: (212) 792-4001
E-Mail: kmoroney@moroneyandgill.com
Web Site: www.moroneyandgill.com

Employees: 60
Year Founded: 1991

Agency Specializes In: Consulting, Health Care Services, Pharmaceutical

Approx. Annual Billings: $20,000,000

Breakdown of Gross Billings by Media: Adv. Specialities: $10,000,000; Collateral: $10,000,000

Kevin Moroney *(Pres & CEO)*
Vasilio Pitsios *(Mng Dir & Exec Dir Medical & Regulatory Svcs)*

Accounts:
PuraCap Pharmaceutical LLC Advertising, EpiCeram

MORRIS & CASALE INC.
1525 Rancho Conejo Blvd, Thousand Oaks, CA 91320
Tel.: (818) 889-2950
Fax: (805) 480-3870
E-Mail: bill@morriscasale.com
Web Site: www.morriscasale.com

Employees: 10
Year Founded: 2004

Agency Specializes In: Above-the-Line, Advertising, Below-the-Line, Brand Development & Integration, Broadcast, Business Publications, Business-To-Business, Cable T.V., Catalogs, Children's Market, Collateral, College, Commercial Photography, Communications, Computers & Software, Consulting, Consumer Goods, Consumer Publications, Corporate Identity, Cosmetics, Customer Relationship Management, Digital/Interactive, Direct-to-Consumer, E-Commerce, Electronics, Email, Fashion/Apparel, Financial, Food Service, Graphic Design, Health Care Services, High Technology, Household Goods, In-Store Advertising, Infomercials, Integrated Marketing, Internet/Web Design, Logo & Package Design, Market Research, Media Buying Services, Multimedia, New Product Development, New Technologies, Newspaper, Outdoor, Package Design, Podcasting, Point of Purchase, Print, Production, Production (Ad, Film, Broadcast), Production (Print), Public Relations, Publicity/Promotions, Radio, Restaurant, Sales Promotion, Search Engine Optimization, T.V., Telemarketing, Trade & Consumer Magazines, Web (Banner Ads, Pop-ups, etc.)

Breakdown of Gross Billings by Media: Collateral: 10%; Graphic Design: 10%; Print: 15%; Production: 5%; Radio & T.V.: 15%; Strategic Planning/Research: 10%; Trade Shows: 5%; Worldwide Web Sites: 30%

Bill Casale *(Co-Founder)*
Matthew Morris *(Co-Dir-Creative)*

MORRIS CREATIVE GROUP
555 W Jackson Ave Ste 301, Knoxville, TN 37902
Tel.: (865) 637-9869
Fax: (865) 637-9900
Toll Free: (866) 637-9869
E-Mail: info@morriscreative.com
Web Site: www.morriscreative.com

Agency Specializes In: Advertising, Brand Development & Integration, Crisis Communications, Internet/Web Design, Media Relations, Outdoor, Print, Public Relations, Social Media, Strategic Planning/Research

Chuck Morris *(Founder & Principal)*
Kellie Ward *(Dir-Client Svc)*
Sherrie DeMarcus *(Office Mgr)*
Kellie Crye *(Sr Graphic Designer)*
Liz Hoover *(Sr Designer)*

Accounts:
Trinity Health Foundation of East Tennessee

THE MORRISON AGENCY
3500 Piedmont Rd Ste 700, Atlanta, GA 30305
Tel.: (404) 233-3405
Fax: (404) 261-8384
Web Site: www.morrisonagency.com

E-Mail for Key Personnel:
President: bob@morrisonagency.com
Creative Dir.: ron@morrisonagency.com

Employees: 30
Year Founded: 1986

National Agency Associations: 4A's-ICOM

Agency Specializes In: Above-the-Line, Advertising, Below-the-Line, Brand Development & Integration, Business-To-Business, Collateral, Communications, Computers & Software, Consulting, Corporate Communications, Corporate Identity, Crisis Communications, Customer Relationship Management, Digital/Interactive, Education, Engineering, Environmental, Financial, Food Service, Graphic Design, Health Care Services, High Technology, Industrial, Information Technology, Integrated Marketing, International, Internet/Web Design, Investor Relations, Legal Services, Logo & Package Design, Marine, Market Research, Media Planning, Medical Products, Mobile Marketing, Multimedia, New Product Development, New Technologies, Package Design, Production, Real Estate, Restaurant, Social Marketing/Nonprofit, Strategic Planning/Research, Technical Advertising, Travel & Tourism

Approx. Annual Billings: $30,000,000

Jeff Silverman *(COO)*
Kyle Lewis *(Chief Creative Officer & Sr VP)*
Amanda Forgione *(VP & Grp Brand Dir)*
Jennifer Keough Raj *(VP & Grp Brand Dir)*
Sifa Hanson *(Sr Brand Mgr)*
Jennifer Wise *(Sr Brand Mgr)*
Julie Closson *(Brand Mgr)*
Tashia Gregston Rodriguez *(Grp Brand Mgr)*

Accounts:
Aquilex; Atlanta GA Energy Industry Maintenance, Repair & Revitalization
Aviva Health; Atlanta, GA Disease Management & Wellness Programs
CNL; Orlando, FL REITs & Alternative Investments Company
Mitsubishi Electric; Lawrenceville, GA Cooling & Heating Solutions
Movius; Atlanta, GA Mobile Media Solutions
Palmetto Dunes Oceanfront Resort; Hilton Head Island, SC Resort Accomodations & Amenities
Triad Advisors; Atlanta, GA Registered Investment Advisor & Insurance Agency

MORRISON CREATIVE COMPANY INC
907 11th St, Cody, WY 82414
Tel.: (307) 527-4144
Web Site: www.morrisoncreative.com

Agency Specializes In: Advertising, Corporate Identity, Internet/Web Design, Outdoor, Package Design

Scott Morrison *(Pres)*

Accounts:
Hiviz Shooting Systems Creative Agency of Record

MORROW LANE
120 E 23rd St, New York, NY 10010
Tel.: (203) 605-2997
Web Site: www.morrowlane.com

Employees: 15
Year Founded: 2014

Agency Specializes In: Brand Development & Integration, Communications, Content, Digital/Interactive, Direct Response Marketing, E-Commerce, Email, Event Planning & Marketing, Integrated Marketing, Paid Searches, Planning & Consultation, Search Engine Optimization, Social Marketing/Nonprofit, Social Media, Strategic Planning/Research, Viral/Buzz/Word of Mouth, Web (Banner Ads, Pop-ups, etc.)

Jennifer Eident *(CEO & Co-Founder)*

Accounts:
LSTN Headphones

MORSEKODE
7900 International Dr Ste 140, Minneapolis, MN 55425
Tel.: (952) 853-9555
Fax: (952) 853-2250
E-Mail: mark@morsekode.com
Web Site: www.morsekode.com

Employees: 12

Agency Specializes In: Advertising, Brand Development & Integration, Digital/Interactive, Entertainment, Graphic Design, Health Care Services, High Technology, Internet/Web Design, Retail, Strategic Planning/Research

Mark Morse *(Owner & CEO)*
Paul Jongeward *(Partner & VP-Strategy)*
Shad Christensen *(Acct Dir)*
Matt Boswell *(Dir-Art)*
Stephanie Benson *(Sr Acct Mgr)*
Danny Dobrin *(Sr Acct Mgr)*

Accounts:
Salvation Army

MORTAR ADVERTISING
2 Bryant St, San Francisco, CA 94105
Tel.: (415) 772-9907
Fax: (415) 772-9952
E-Mail: heythere@mortaragency.com
Web Site: www.mortaragency.com

Employees: 20
Year Founded: 2002

Agency Specializes In: Advertising, Advertising Specialties, Affluent Market, Alternative Advertising, Brand Development & Integration, Broadcast, Business-To-Business, Collateral, College, Communications, Consulting, Content, Corporate Communications, Digital/Interactive, Direct Response Marketing, Education, Email, Financial, Graphic Design, Guerilla Marketing, Health Care Services, Identity Marketing, Integrated Marketing, Internet/Web Design, Leisure, Market Research, Media Buying Services, Media Planning, Media Relations, Mobile Marketing, Multicultural, New Product Development, Newspapers & Magazines, Outdoor, Planning & Consultation, Print, Production (Ad, Film, Broadcast), Public Relations, Publicity/Promotions, Radio, Real Estate, Social Marketing/Nonprofit, Social Media, Strategic Planning/Research, Travel & Tourism, Viral/Buzz/Word of Mouth, Web (Banner Ads, Pop-ups, etc.)

Approx. Annual Billings: $22,000,000

Mark Williams *(Founder & Mng Partner)*
Ben Klau *(Gen Mgr)*
Jeremy Cook *(Acct Supvr & Producer)*
Scott Burke *(Dir-Brand Dev)*
Lisa Clapper *(Dir-Brand Strategy)*
Brian Scheyer *(Dir-Creative)*
Mary Ann Gratol *(Office Mgr)*
Jennifer Lee *(Copywriter)*

Accounts:
AdBrite Digital Ad Exchange
Antenna Software Mobile Applications
Avinger Medical Devices
Bain Capital Ventures Venture Capital
Big Blue Bus Public Transportation
Budda Amplifiers Music & Entertainment
Carondelet Health Network Campaign: "Be well"
Coast Casinos Entertainment
FrontRow Active Learning Systems Voice Clarification Products
Golden Gate University Education
Isilon Systems Scale-out Storage
Jigsaw Business Contact Directory
Matrix Partners Venture Capital
Mohr Davidow Ventures Venture Capital
Oneshare.com Gift of Stock Ownership
Rydex Investments Asset Management
Samuel Merritt University Education
San Francisco AIDS Foundation Non-Profit

MORTENSON SAFAR KIM
916 E Westfield Blvd, Indianapolis, IN 46220
Tel.: (317) 955-9414
Web Site: mskadvertising.com

National Agency Associations: 4A's

Agency Specializes In: Advertising, Collateral, Corporate Identity, Digital/Interactive, Internet/Web Design, Media Buying Services, Media Planning, Production, Promotions, Social Media, Sponsorship

Shannon Safar *(Pres & Partner)*
Peter Kim *(Partner & Exec Creative Dir)*
Noah Gregg *(Sr Dir-Art)*
Ted Xistris *(Dir-Creative & Copywriter)*
Lamont Chandler *(Dir-Creative & Dir-Art)*
Margaux Oliver *(Office Mgr)*

Accounts:
Hoosier Lottery (Advertising Agency of Record)
Wisconsin State Fair (Agency of Record) Advertising, Creative, Media Buying, Media Planning

Branch

Mortenson Safar Kim
(Formerly Meyer & Wallis, Inc.)
117 N Jefferson St Ste 204, Milwaukee, WI 53202-4615
Tel.: (414) 224-0212
Fax: (414) 224-0420
Web Site: mskadvertising.com

Employees: 25
Year Founded: 1967

National Agency Associations: 4A's-AAF-MCA

Agency Specializes In: Advertising, Brand Development & Integration, Broadcast, Business-To-Business, Collateral, Consumer Marketing, Education, Entertainment, Financial, Health Care Services, Magazines, Media Buying Services, Newspaper, Newspapers & Magazines, Out-of-Home Media, Outdoor, Print, Production, Radio, Real Estate, Retail, Sponsorship, Strategic Planning/Research, T.V.

Chris Mortenson *(Owner & CEO)*
Barb Tice *(CFO)*
Mary Parodo *(Exec VP-Client Svcs)*
Gina August *(Dir-Media)*
Andrew Nordquist *(Dir-Art & Creative)*
Julie Rasmussen *(Assoc Dir-Media)*
Ryan Prom *(Mgr-Acctg)*
Stephanie Winter *(Supvr-Media Buying)*

Accounts:
Anheuser-Busch Creative, Digital Advertising, Michelob Golden Light (Agency of Record), OOH, Point-of-sale Marketing, Social Media, TV
Boy Scouts of America
Horizon Homecare & Hospice
Palermo's Pizza; Milwaukee Frozen Pizza; 2005
QPS Employment Group Branding, Marketing, Strategic Planning, Web Development
Sentry Foods (SuperValu)

MORTON ADVERTISING INC.

875 Ave of the Americas Ste 1111, New York, NY 10001-3507
Tel.: (212) 465-2250
Fax: (212) 465-1575
E-Mail: info@mortonad.com
Web Site: www.mortonad.com

E-Mail for Key Personnel:
President: don@mortonad.com

Employees: 4
Year Founded: 1961

National Agency Associations: MAAN-MCA

Agency Specializes In: Advertising, Business Publications, Business-To-Business, Collateral, Consumer Publications, Direct Response Marketing, Graphic Design, Industrial, Internet/Web Design, Logo & Package Design, Magazines, Print, Publicity/Promotions

Approx. Annual Billings: $800,000

Donald Reisfeld *(Owner)*

Accounts:
Cotronics Corp.; Brooklyn, NY Hi-Temp Industrial Adhesives; 2007
Dreidels Unlimited; Edison, NJ; 1987
E.S. Nacht Co. Inc.; New York, NY Diamond & Estate Jewelry; 1990
Edmund Scientific; Tonawanda, NY Scientific, Educational & Optical Products; 2001
Elective Benefits; Morristown, NJ Insurance
Halcraft USA, Inc.; Mount Vernon, NY Craft Products, Kit & Costume Jewelry Components & Findings; 1976
Historic Newspaper Archives; Rahway, NJ Mail Order; 1990
ID Solutions a Div. of Arch Crown, Inc.; Hillside, NJ RFID Labels; 1998
Infosys Consulting; Fremont, CA Consulting Services; 2005
LaserMetrics a Div. of FastPulse Technology, Inc.; Saddle Brook, NJ Optical Testing Equipment; 2006
Neve Shalom; Metuchen, NJ Conservative Synagogue; 1990
New York Sewing Machine Inc.; North Bergen, NJ Sewing Machines, Parts & Attachments; 1992
Record Press, Inc.; New York, NY Digital Appellate Printers; 2000
Shogun Trading Co., Inc.; New York, NY Pearl Importers & Wholesalers; 1980
Superior Sewing Machine & Supply LLC; New York, NY; 1992
Tri-State Kitchen & Bath, LLC; North Bergen, NJ Kitchen & Bathroom Cabinets; 2006
Westchester & Rockland Society of Pharmacists; White Plains, NY; 2009

MORTON VARDEMAN & CARLSON

200 Broad St Ste 203, Gainesville, GA 30503
Tel.: (770) 536-8921
Fax: (770) 535-2753
Web Site: www.vardeman.com

Employees: 12
Year Founded: 1973

National Agency Associations: Second Wind Limited

Agency Specializes In: Advertising

John Vardeman *(Pres)*
Patrick Ceska *(Partner & Sr Acct Exec)*
Tina Carlson *(Exec VP & Dir-Creative)*
Lisa Aldridge *(Mgr-Production)*
Bryan Nicoll *(Mgr-Internet Programming)*
Jeff Butler *(Acct Exec-PR)*

Accounts:
American Cool Air

MORVIL ADVERTISING & DESIGN GROUP

1409 Audubon Blvd Ste B3, Wilmington, NC 28403
Tel.: (910) 342-0100
Fax: (910) 342-0167
E-Mail: getcreative@morvil.com
Web Site: www.morvil.com

Agency Specializes In: Advertising, Brand Development & Integration, Collateral, Corporate Identity, Digital/Interactive, Graphic Design, Internet/Web Design, Logo & Package Design, Media Buying Services, Media Planning

Jeff Morvil *(Pres & Dir-Creative)*
Harry Hartofelis *(Dir-Art & Designer)*
Kim Bardill *(Dir-Art & Sr Graphic Designer)*
Joy Hall *(Project Mgr & Mgr-Mktg)*
David Southerland *(Mgr-Production & Designer)*

Accounts:
OrthoWilmington
Wilmington Plastic Surgery

MOSAIC MULTICULTURAL

2777 E Camelback Rd Ste 300, Phoenix, AZ 85016
Tel.: (480) 648-7539
Web Site: www.mosaicmulticultural.com

Agency Specializes In: Advertising, Brand Development & Integration, Broadcast, Digital/Interactive, Graphic Design, Internet/Web Design, Media Relations, Promotions, Public Relations, Social Media

Mark Suarez *(Mng Dir & Principal)*
Yadelle Dreyer *(Acct Supvr)*

Accounts:
Southern Arizona McDonalds Operator Association (Agency of Record) General Market, Hispanic

MOSAK ADVERTISING & INSIGHTS

3809 Juniper Trace, Austin, TX 78738
Tel.: (512) 374-2800
E-Mail: info@mosak.com
Web Site: www.mosak.com

Year Founded: 2000

Agency Specializes In: Advertising, Brand Development & Integration, Digital/Interactive, Email, Internet/Web Design, Market Research, Media Planning, Print, Promotions, Social Media

Monique Threadgill *(Founder & Pres)*
Randy Cieslewicz *(CFO)*
Kelly Clancy *(VP-Client Svcs)*
Andy Jones *(VP-Res & Analysis)*
Ralph Yznaga *(Exec Dir-Creative)*
Alicia Bergner *(Grp Dir-Creative)*
Greg Needham *(Grp Dir-Creative)*
Ilaria Bonalumi *(Dir-Media)*

Accounts:
Oklahoma Indian Gaming Association

MOSES INC.

(Formerly Moses Anshell, Inc.)
20 W Jackson St, Phoenix, AZ 85003
Tel.: (602) 254-7312
Fax: (602) 324-1222
E-Mail: hello@mosesinc.com
Web Site: www.mosesinc.com

Employees: 35
Year Founded: 1981

Agency Specializes In: Sponsorship

Chris Fiscus *(VP & Dir-PR)*
Dominic Celico *(VP-Fin)*
Diana Moore *(VP-Admin & HR)*
Karin Valentine *(Grp Acct Dir)*
Caterina Facchinetti *(Dir-Media)*
Matt Fischer *(Dir-Art)*
Brian Jagodnik *(Dir-Art)*
James Shipp *(Dir-Bus Dev)*
Elena Pavlova *(Acct Mgr)*
Katie Johnson *(Copywriter)*

Accounts:
ADA
Arizona Department of Health Services
The Arizona Humane Society; Phoenix, AZ Non-Profit Animal Shelter
Arizona Ready
Arizona Wine Growers Association
BDA Inc.
Bonded Logic
Cenpatico of Arizona
Citizens' Clean Elections Commission
Dos Cabezas WineWorks; Sonoita, AZ
Fender Musical Instruments Corp.
First Things First
The GRAMMY Museum
Grand Canyon University; AZ "Find Your Purpose" Campaign, Ken Blanchard College of Business, Light Rail Train Wrap, Local Television, Outdoor, Radio
Maricopa County WIC
Nintendo
Olympian Labs Branding
Roger Clyne and The Peacemakers
Shutters on the Beach Hotel
Ubisoft
Ultimate Gaming
U.S. Airways

MOST BRAND DEVELOPMENT + ADVERTISING

25 Enterprise Ste 250, Aliso Viejo, CA 92656
Tel.: (949) 475-4050
Fax: (949) 475-4051
E-Mail: john@mostagency.com
Web Site: www.mostagency.com

Employees: 15
Year Founded: 2005

Agency Specializes In: Advertising, Advertising Specialties, Affluent Market, Alternative Advertising, Automotive, Bilingual Market, Brand Development & Integration, Broadcast, Cable T.V., Co-op Advertising, Communications, Consulting, Consumer Goods, Consumer Marketing, Consumer Publications, Corporate Communications, Corporate Identity, Custom Publishing, Customer Relationship Management, Digital/Interactive, Direct Response Marketing, Direct-to-Consumer, E-Commerce, Electronic Media, Email, Financial, Food Service, Graphic Design, Guerilla Marketing, Hispanic Market, Hospitality, Household Goods, Identity Marketing, Information Technology, Integrated Marketing, Internet/Web Design, Leisure, Local Marketing, Logo & Package Design, Magazines, Market Research, Media Buying Services, Media Planning, Media Relations, Mobile Marketing, Multicultural, Multimedia, New Product Development, New Technologies, Newspaper, Out-of-Home Media, Over-50 Market, Package Design, Paid Searches, Planning & Consultation, Podcasting, Point of Sale, Print, Production, Production (Ad, Film, Broadcast), Production (Print), Public Relations, Publicity/Promotions, RSS (Really Simple Syndication), Radio, Real Estate, Regional, Retail, Sales Promotion, Search Engine Optimization, Seniors' Market, Social Marketing/Nonprofit, Social

Media, Strategic Planning/Research, T.V., Teen Market, Trade & Consumer Magazines, Travel & Tourism, Viral/Buzz/Word of Mouth, Web (Banner Ads, Pop-ups, etc.)

Approx. Annual Billings: $69,000,000

Breakdown of Gross Billings by Media: Cable T.V.: 10%; Consulting: 12%; Internet Adv.: 3%; Network Radio: 35%; Network T.V.: 27%; Production: 13%

John G. Most *(Pres & CEO)*
Dave Macleod *(VP & Acct Dir)*
Jodi A. Most *(VP-Mktg)*
Jon Grenier *(Sr Dir-Art)*
Marci Grzelecki *(Dir-Bus Dev)*
Joel Tarman *(Dir-Creative)*
Mike Burkhart *(Assoc Dir-Creative)*
Emily Jiang *(Supvr-Media)*

Accounts:
Move, Inc.; Westlake Village, CA; 2007
National Association of REALTORS; Chicago, IL & Washington, DC Public Awareness Campaign; 1998
National Multiple Sclerosis Society Pacific South Coast Chapter; Carlsbad, CA MS 150 Bike Event; 2005
Pacific West Association of REALTORS; Anaheim, CA Charity Foundation, Member Branding, Public Awareness; 2006
REALTOR.COM; Chicago, IL Website Brand Awareness; 2004
Vroom Foods; Santa Ana, CA Foosh Energy Mints; 2004

MOTHER LTD.

Biscuit Bldg 10 Redchurch St, London, E2 7DD United Kingdom
Tel.: (44) 20 7012 1999
Fax: (44) 20 7012 1989
E-Mail: info@motherlondon.com
Web Site: www.motherlondon.com

Employees: 120

Matthew Clark *(Partner)*
Andy Medd *(Partner-Strategy)*
Ben Heap *(Head-Creative Resource)*
Hermeti Balarin *(Exec Creative Dir)*
Chaka Sobhani *(Creative Dir)*
James Broomfield *(Dir-Strategy)*
Freddy Mandy *(Dir-Creative)*
Sophie Spence *(Strategist)*
Gosia Pawlak *(Designer)*
Stef Calcraft *(Strategy Partner)*
Katie Mackay *(Joint Head-Strategy)*

Accounts:
Acer Aspire S5 Ultrabook, Aspire T3 Ultrabook, Campaign: "Bake it", Campaign: "Cupcakes"
Anheuser-Busch InBev Beck's Sapphire, Campaign: "Le President", Campaign: "Serenade", Campaign: "The Simple Life", Cidre, Green Box Project, Stella Artois Cidre
Arla Campaign: "Balance", Castello
Boots Advertising, Campaign: "Boots Christmas", Campaign: "Smalltown Boy", Campaign: "Ta Dah!", Digital, No7, Offline Creative, Online, Outdoor Media
Cancer Research UK Cinema, Creative, Direct Mail, Events, Fundraising Campaign, National PR, Press Digital, Race For Life, Radio, Social Media
Chipotle Campaign: "Delicious However You Say It"
Comic Relief
Diageo plc Baileys (Global Strategic & Creative Agency), J&B, Pimm's, Quinns, Smirnoff Apple Bite
Elle Magazine Campaign: "Make Them Pay", Campaign: "Rebranding Feminism"
Fox
Foyle Campaign: "It's The Thought That Counts", Retail
Halfords Campaign: "Dedicated Motoring", Campaign: "Tour de Britain", Campaign: "Worst Favour Ever"
Hovis Advertising, Campaign: "Boy on a Bike", Digital, In-Store, Public Relations, Radio, TV, Video-On-Demand
Ikea Beds, Campaign: "Rediscover the Joy of the Kitchen", Campaign: "The Joy of Storage", Campaign: "The Kitchen", Campaign: "The Wonderful Everyday", Campaign: "There's No Bed Like Home", Digital, OOH, Online, Outdoor, Print, Social Media, TV
Jesus (Global Agency of Record) Campaign: "IfoundJesusinLondon", Marketing, Musician
The Kaleidoscope Trust Campaign: "Russian Dolls"
New-LateRooms.com Creative Advertising
Match.com Campaign: "Ukulele", TV
The Ministry of Letters The Singing Alphabet
Mobile first bank Atom Bank Brand Strategy, Creative, Marketing, Strategic
Mondelez International, Inc. Advertising, Campaign: "Putting on the Ritz", Campaign: "This is not a Chocolate Bar", Digital, Green & Black's, In-Store, Jacobs Coffee, Marketing Campaign, OOH, Out-of-Home, Press, Print, Public Relations, Ritz Crisp & Thin, Sampling, TV, Video
Moneysupermarket.com "EpicStrut", CRM, Campaign: "Kid in a Cake Shop", Campaign: "You're So MoneySuperMarket", PR, Radio, Social Media, TV, Vegas
Smirnoff Campaign: "Apple Bite"
Stella Artois Campaign: "The Perfectionists", Campaign: "The Simple Life", Stella Artois Cidre, TV
TMZ
Unilever UK Bertolli, Campaign: "WAG", Cuppa Club, Global Creative, Global Strategic, I Can't Believe It's Not Butter, PG Tips
United Nations Communications
Water.org Creative

Branches

Mother New York

595 11th Ave, New York, NY 10036
Tel.: (212) 254-2800
Fax: (212) 254-6121
E-Mail: press@mothernewyork.com
Web Site: www.mothernewyork.com

Employees: 150

National Agency Associations: 4A's

Agency Specializes In: Advertising, Sponsorship

Paul Malmstrom *(Founder, Owner & Partner)*
Susan Holden *(CFO)*
Gabriel Blido *(Dir-Art)*
Jed Grossman *(Dir-Creative)*
Catherine Nickson *(Office Mgr)*
Bruno Frankel *(Strategist)*
Leopold Billard *(Sr Creative)*

Accounts:
Anheuser-Busch InBev Beck's, Oculto, Online, Outdoor Advertising, Print, Sapphire, Social Media Marketing, Stella Artois Campaign: "Chalice Factory" & Stella Artois Feast on Film 1
Arla
Blue Q
Cablevision Brand Campaign, Campaign: "Bolton", Campaign: "MIDWULS", Optimum, Re-Branding
New-Calvin Klein Inc. "The Full Story", Campaign: "Meet Us", Campaign: "MyCalvins", Campaign: "Raw Texts, Real Stories", Digital
CK One
CNN
Coca-Cola Refreshments USA, Inc. Full Throttle, Powerade
Dell Dell XPS One; 2007
Diageo Tanqueray Gin
New-The Diamond Producers Association Global Strategic Marketing
Dogmatic
Emusic Campaign: "Araabmuzik - Dooms Day"
Frank
General Motors Chevrolet, The Road We're On
Goodfella's The Scoop
Halfords
IKEA Campaign: "One Room Paradise"
Illuminati
James Patterson "Private Vegas" Book, Self Destructing Book
JCPenney
LVMH 10 Cane Rum
Maison Gerard
Microsoft
MillerCoors Beer, Miller Lite Brewers Collection, Milwaukee Best
Mitchum Campaign: "Lies"
Mondelez International, Inc. Campaign: "World Gone Sour", Sour Patch Kids (Agency of Record)
NBC
New Balance
New Balance Life Style Products
Newton Vineyard
New-Philadelphia 76ers, L.P.
Pike Whiskey Campaign: "White Pike Whiskey"
Proust.com Campaign: "It's Fun To Judge"
Reading is Fundamental Campaign: "Book People Unite"
Red Bull
Spike TV
New-Stella Artois
Tanqueray
Target 3.1 Phillip Lim, Campaign: "Little Marina", Kaleidoscopic Fashion Spectacular
TBS; Atlanta, GA
Ten Cane LVMH
Virgin Mobile USA, Inc. Campaign: "An Obvious Deal", Campaign: "BlinkWashing", Campaign: "Retrain Your Brain", Campaign: "Sparah", Campaign: "The Fantastic Tale Of Young Branson", Campaign: "catsies"
Zeebox Campaign: "Ship In A Bottle"

Madre

Petrona Eyle 450 DTO, CJD, C1107 Buenos Aires, Argentina
Tel.: (54) 11 5787 0500
Web Site: madrebuenosaires.com

Agency Specializes In: Advertising

Rafael D'Alvia *(Partner & Gen Dir-Creative)*
Gabriela Scardaccione *(Partner)*
Nicolas Roberts *(Gen Dir-Creative)*
Raul Vasenna *(Dir-Art)*
Sebastian Visco *(Dir-Creative)*

Accounts:
Aerolineas Argentinas
Banco Hipotecario
Coca-Cola Refreshments USA, Inc. PowerAde

MOTIVATED MARKETING

7087 Rivers Ave, North Charleston, SC 29406
Tel.: (843) 856-7322
E-Mail: info@motivatedmarketing.com
Web Site: www.motivatedmarketing.com

Agency Specializes In: Advertising, Brand Development & Integration, Collateral, Digital/Interactive, Graphic Design, Internet/Web Design, Logo & Package Design, Media Buying Services, Search Engine Optimization, Social Media

Chuck Groome *(Dir-Ops)*
Kristin Smith *(Dir-Media)*

Braden Bellack *(Acct Mgr)*
Allie Fox *(Acct Mgr)*
Catherine Kut *(Mgr-Traffic)*
Evan Cincala *(Acct Exec)*
Mark MacGillvray *(Acct Exec)*
Jamie McRae *(Acct Exec)*

Accounts:
Coastal Kids Dental

MOTIVE
620 16th St Ste 200, Denver, CO 80202
Tel.: (303) 302-2100
Web Site: www.thinkmotive.com

Agency Specializes In: Advertising

Krista Nicholson *(VP-Ops & Strategy)*
Tony Phillips *(Sr Dir-Digital Art)*
Drew Wallace *(Sr Dir-Art)*
Taylor Woodard *(Sr Acct Dir)*
Mike Cole *(Acct Dir)*
Jon Peters *(Acct Dir)*
Ryan Eschenbach *(Dir-Art & Designer-Motion)*
Rhenee Bartlett *(Dir-Events)*
Andrew Geppelt *(Dir-Design)*
Eric Ronshaugen *(Dir-Concept)*
Spencer Trierweiler *(Dir-Creative)*
Brad Burns *(Sr Acct Mgr)*
Loveleen Molnar *(Acct Supvr)*
Jenna Brigham *(Acct Exec)*

Accounts:
Boingo Wireless, Inc.
Native Eyewear
PepsiCo Inc. Baja Blast, Campaign: "But Only with Pepsi", Campaign: "Get Hyped for Halftime.", Campaign: "Rebel Spirit", Creative, DewShine, Mountain Dew, SoBe, Pepsi Pass

MOTTIS
(Formerly Kelly MarCom)
131 Charlotte Ave Ste 201, Sanford, NC 27330
Tel.: (919) 718-6506
Fax: (919) 718-6607
E-Mail: contact@mottis.com
Web Site: mottis.com

Employees: 10
Year Founded: 1996

Agency Specializes In: Advertising, Brand Development & Integration, Broadcast, Collateral, Commercial Photography, Communications, Consulting, Corporate Communications, Crisis Communications, Direct Response Marketing, E-Commerce, Email, Event Planning & Marketing, Exhibit/Trade Shows, Experience Design, Identity Marketing, International, Internet/Web Design, Local Marketing, Logo & Package Design, Media Relations, Media Training, Outdoor, Print, Promotions, Public Relations, Radio, Regional, Sponsorship, Sports Market, Strategic Planning/Research, T.V., Telemarketing, Trade & Consumer Magazines

Shelley Kelly *(Pres & CEO)*
Mariryan Starr *(VP & Strategist-Integrated Mktg)*
Shari Becker *(Acct Svc Dir)*
Melinda Walker *(Acct Mgr)*

Accounts:
3M
Butterball, LLC
Chevrolet
CitiFinancial
FedEx
Oracle
Precision Pharma Services
Subaru

MOTUM B2B
376 Wellington St W, Toronto, ON M5V 1E3 Canada
Tel.: (416) 598-2225
Fax: (416) 598-5611
Toll Free: (866) MOTUM-B2B
E-Mail: hwb@hwbinc.com
Web Site: www.motumb2b.com

E-Mail for Key Personnel:
President: rwillingham@motumb2b.com

Employees: 12
Year Founded: 1993

Agency Specializes In: Advertising, Advertising Specialties, Brand Development & Integration, Business-To-Business, Collateral, Communications, Corporate Communications, Corporate Identity, Direct Response Marketing, Electronic Media, Engineering, Graphic Design, Industrial, Information Technology, Internet/Web Design, Logo & Package Design, Magazines, Media Buying Services, New Product Development, Newspapers & Magazines, Planning & Consultation, Print, Production, Public Relations, Strategic Planning/Research, Technical Advertising, Trade & Consumer Magazines, Transportation

Approx. Annual Billings: $3,000,000

Richard Willingham *(Pres & CEO)*
Scott Moore *(VP-Digital Strategy)*
Cheryl Gill *(Controller)*
Lisa Kemerer *(Dir-Creative Svcs)*
Jennifer Reeves *(Dir-Content)*
Mark Whiting *(Dir-Web Dev)*
Leandro Antonio *(Mgr-Integrated Mktg)*
Christina Dong *(Mgr-Digital Mktg)*
Steve Lendt *(Mgr-Analytics & Media)*
Lauren Armstrong *(Specialist-Integrated Mktg)*

Accounts:
Alpha Controls & Instrumentation
BASF Spray Polyurethanes; Wyandotte, MI Chemicals
Toyota Industrial Equipment; Scarborough, ON Fork Lift Trucks; 1999

MOVEMENT PUBLIC RELATIONS
8715 Skyline Dr, Los Angeles, CA 90046
Tel.: (310) 272-5200
Web Site: www.movementpublicrelations.com

Year Founded: 2004

Agency Specializes In: Advertising, Brand Development & Integration, Communications, Public Relations, Strategic Planning/Research

Adam Mischlich *(Pres & CEO)*

Accounts:
LJL Designs (Agency of Record)
Proof of Concept Event Branding, Marketing, Strategic Public Relations

MOVEMENT STRATEGY
4720 Table Mesa Dr Ste F-100, Boulder, CO 80305
Tel.: (303) 442-2542
E-Mail: helloboulder@movementstrategy.com
Web Site: www.movementstrategy.com

Year Founded: 2008

Agency Specializes In: Advertising, Content, Digital/Interactive, Internet/Web Design, Social Media, Strategic Planning/Research

Eric Dieter *(Co-Founder)*
Jason Mitchell *(Pres & CEO)*
Stephen Para *(Chief Growth Officer & Exec VP)*
Christy Pregont *(Creative Dir)*
Nick Hoppe *(Dir-Media Strategy)*
Abid Anwar *(Strategist-Social Media)*
Clay Branch *(Sr Engr-Res)*

Accounts:
USA Today (Social Media Agency of Record)

MOVEO
1 Parkview Plz Ste 150, Oakbrook Terrace, IL 60181
Tel.: (630) 570-4800
Fax: (630) 571-3031
E-Mail: info@moveo.com
Web Site: www.moveo.com

Employees: 40
Year Founded: 1987

National Agency Associations: BMA

Agency Specializes In: Advertising, Brand Development & Integration, Business-To-Business, Collateral, Commercial Photography, Communications, Consulting, Consumer Marketing, Consumer Publications, Corporate Identity, Digital/Interactive, Direct Response Marketing, E-Commerce, Electronic Media, Entertainment, Event Planning & Marketing, Exhibit/Trade Shows, Graphic Design, Health Care Services, High Technology, Infomercials, Internet/Web Design, Logo & Package Design, Medical Products, Multimedia, Newspapers & Magazines, Pharmaceutical, Planning & Consultation, Print, Production, Radio, Sales Promotion, Sponsorship, Strategic Planning/Research, T.V., Technical Advertising, Trade & Consumer Magazines

Brian Davies *(Mng Partner)*
Bob Murphy *(Mng Partner)*
Dave Cannon *(VP-Interactive Svcs)*
Angela Costanzi *(VP-Creative Svcs)*
Sheri Granholm *(VP-Engagement Mgmt)*
Kevin Randall *(VP-Brand Strategy & Res)*
Karla Jackson *(Dir-Creative)*

Accounts:
CareerBuilder
Lincoln Partners; Chicago, IL Investment Banking Firm; 2001
Littelfuse; Des Plaines, IL Circuit Protection, Overcurrent, Overvoltage Protection & Fuses; 2001
Loyola
Mercy Health Partners
Molex; Lisle, IL Electrical Interconnection Devices; 1988
Motorola Solutions, Inc.
Plexus; Appleton, WI Design & Build Firm; 2000
Resurrection Center for Integrative Medicine
Resurrection Health Care
RUSH-Riverside Hospital
Saint James Hospital; Chicago Heights, IL Healthcare
Siemens Building Technologies; Buffalo Grove, IL Building Automation, Fire Safety, HVAC, Security
U.S. Robotics
Wellgroup

MOXIE SOZO
1140 Pearl St, Boulder, CO 80302-5253
Tel.: (720) 304-7210
Fax: (720) 304-7219
E-Mail: info@moxiesozo.com
Web Site: www.moxiesozo.com

Employees: 30

Agency Specializes In: Advertising, Advertising Specialties, Affluent Market, Alternative Advertising, Arts, Automotive, Brand Development & Integration, Branded Entertainment, Broadcast, Business Publications, Business-To-Business, Cable T.V., Catalogs, Children's Market, Co-op Advertising, Collateral, College, Commercial Photography, Communications, Consulting, Consumer Goods, Consumer Marketing, Consumer Publications, Corporate Identity, Cosmetics, Custom Publishing, Direct Response Marketing, Direct-to-Consumer, Education, Electronic Media, Email, Entertainment, Environmental, Event Planning & Marketing, Exhibit/Trade Shows, Fashion/Apparel, Financial, Food Service, Government/Political, Graphic Design, Guerilla Marketing, Health Care Services, Hospitality, Identity Marketing, In-Store Advertising, Integrated Marketing, Internet/Web Design, Investor Relations, Leisure, Local Marketing, Logo & Package Design, Luxury Products, Magazines, Market Research, Media Buying Services, Media Planning, Media Relations, Men's Market, Merchandising, Mobile Marketing, Multicultural, Multimedia, New Product Development, Newspaper, Newspapers & Magazines, Outdoor, Package Design, Planning & Consultation, Point of Sale, Print, Production (Print), Promotions, Publicity/Promotions, Publishing, Radio, Real Estate, Restaurant, Sales Promotion, Search Engine Optimization, Social Marketing/Nonprofit, Sponsorship, Sports Market, Strategic Planning/Research, T.V., Teen Market, Trade & Consumer Magazines, Transportation, Travel & Tourism, Urban Market, Viral/Buzz/Word of Mouth, Web (Banner Ads, Pop-ups, etc.), Women's Market

Eric Nowels *(Dir-Interactive)*
Costa Raptis *(Dir-Client Partnerships)*
Ketan Manohar *(Assoc Dir-Creative & Strategy)*
Tyler Beckwith *(Designer)*
Roxanne Ferguson *(Designer)*
Sophia Sweeney *(Designer)*
Melanie Carol *(Jr Designer)*

Accounts:
LEAP Organics
Left Hand Brewery
Mountain High Ski Resorts
ProBar
Running Times
Smartwool
Stanford University

MOXLEY CARMICHAEL

800 S Gay St Ste 1105, Knoxville, TN 37929
Tel.: (865) 544-0088
Fax: (865) 544-1865
E-Mail: cmmoxley@moxleycarmichael.com
Web Site: www.moxleycarmichael.com

Employees: 16
Year Founded: 1992

Agency Specializes In: Advertising, Crisis Communications, Graphic Design, Integrated Marketing, Internet/Web Design, Media Relations, New Technologies, Public Relations, Strategic Planning/Research

Alan Carmichael *(Pres & COO)*
Cynthia Moxley *(CEO)*
Shaun Fulco *(CFO)*
Scott Bird *(VP)*
Lauren Miller *(Client Svcs Dir)*
Charley Sexton *(Dir-Creative)*
Michelle Henry *(Acct Mgr)*
Amanda Shell Jennings *(Sr Acct Exec)*
Natalie Bailey *(Acct Exec)*
Amanda Shell *(Acct Exec)*

Accounts:
Animal Center
Cherokee
Covenant Health
Gerdau
Home Federal Bank
New-Joseph Construction Marketing, Public Relations
Knoxville Area Urban League
Knoxville Convention Center
Knoxville Symphony Orchestra
Knoxville Utilities Board
Knoxville Zoo
Knoxville's Community Development Corporation
MEDIC Regional Blood Center Blood & Blood Products Provider
Pilot Travel Centers LLC Travel Services
Premier Surgical Associates
Priority Ambulance
South College Educational Services
Summit Medical Group
New-Tennessee Theatre
U.S. Cellular Cellular Battery Providing Services
New-US Nitrogen

MOXXY MARKETING

295 Main St Ste 230, Salinas, CA 93901
Tel.: (831) 975-5002
Fax: (831) 975-5054
Web Site: www.getmoxxy.com

Year Founded: 2009

Agency Specializes In: Advertising, Logo & Package Design, Print, Social Media, Strategic Planning/Research

Terry Feinberg *(Principal)*
Karen Nardozza *(Principal)*
Bryan Rodgers *(Mgr-Design & Production)*

Accounts:
Chicago Vegan Foods
S. B. Nutrition

MOXY OX LLC

195 S Maestri Rd, Tontitown, AR 72762
Tel.: (479) 419-5879
Web Site: www.creative.moxyox.com

Year Founded: 2011

Agency Specializes In: Advertising, Brand Development & Integration, Content, Digital/Interactive, Event Planning & Marketing, Public Relations

Randy Hurban *(CEO)*
Steve McBee *(Partner)*
Matthew Huber *(Head-Ops & Customer Experience)*
Micah Whitfield *(Sls Mgr-Moxy Ox Print & Design for Print)*
Larry Netherton *(Mgr-Production)*

Accounts:
Allergy & Stress Relief Center of Arkansas
Evolved Mommy
K+K Veterinary Supply
Paramount Plumbing, Inc.
Specialized Real Estate Group
Sterling Frisco

MP AGENCY, LLC

(Formerly Martz Parsons)
(d/b/a BIG YAM The Parsons Agency)
7077 E Marilyn Rd Bldg 5, Scottsdale, AZ 85254
Tel.: (480) 998-3154
Fax: (480) 998-7985
Toll Free: (800) 426-3663
Web Site: bigyam.com/contact

E-Mail for Key Personnel:
President: cmartz@martzagency.com

Employees: 12
Year Founded: 1980

National Agency Associations: 4A's-TAAN

Agency Specializes In: Advertising, Advertising Specialties, Automotive, Brand Development & Integration, Broadcast, Business Publications, Business-To-Business, Collateral, Consumer Marketing, Consumer Publications, Corporate Identity, Digital/Interactive, Electronic Media, Engineering, Event Planning & Marketing, Financial, Graphic Design, Health Care Services, High Technology, Internet/Web Design, Logo & Package Design, Magazines, Media Buying Services, Medical Products, New Product Development, Newspaper, Newspapers & Magazines, Out-of-Home Media, Outdoor, Pharmaceutical, Point of Purchase, Print, Production, Public Relations, Publicity/Promotions, Radio, Real Estate, Restaurant, Retail, Sales Promotion, Sports Market, Strategic Planning/Research, T.V., Trade & Consumer Magazines, Travel & Tourism

Revenue: $10,000,000 Fees Capitalized

Marianne Curran *(CEO)*
David Richardson *(Chief Digital Officer)*
Kelly Siegal *(VP-Growth Initiatives)*
John Zello *(Creative Dir)*
Diane Smith *(Dir-PR)*
Richard Haynie *(Assoc Dir-Creative)*
Dennis Lewis *(Assoc Dir-Creative)*
Jenna Smith *(Sr Strategist-Media)*

Accounts:
Alaska Trust Company
Arizona Commerce Authority
New-Blues City Harley-Davidson
The Bob & Renee Parsons Foundation
Estrella
Fennemore Craig
Fort McDowell
Gallagher and Kennedy, P.A
Go AZ Motorcycles
Harley-Davidson of Scottsdale
New-Inov8 Golf (Marketing & Public Relations Agency of Record)
Intercontinental Montelucia Resort & Spa
Mirabel
Montelucia
Ninety Degrees Gray Development
Olympia Group
One Neck
Pacific Links International
New-Parsons Xtreme Golf
Phoenix Children's Hospital
The Reef Residences at Atlantis
RLC Labs
Scottsdale National Golf Club
Southern Highlands Golf Club
Southern Highlands Master-Planned Community; 1998
New-Southern Thunder Harley-Davidson
New-Spooky Fast Custom Finishing
Valley of the Sun YMCA
New-YAM Capital
YAM Properties
Yurbuds Campaign: "The Infinite Loop"

MP&A DIGITAL & ADVERTISING

4804 Courthouse St Ste 3B, Williamsburg, VA 23188
Tel.: (757) 645-3113
Web Site: www.madiganpratt.com

Agency Specializes In: Advertising, Brand Development & Integration, Digital/Interactive, Internet/Web Design, Logo & Package Design, Media Buying Services, Media Planning, Print, Public Relations, Social Media

Madigan Pratt *(Pres)*
Ann Hughes *(Exec VP)*
Amy Kerr *(Dir-PR)*
Matt Roche *(Dir-Search Mktg)*
Harshad Methrath *(Assoc Dir-Creative)*
Stephanie Miller *(Mgr-Social Media & Acct Exec)*
Catherine Smagan *(Acct Supvr)*
Laura Bonfiglio *(Acct Exec)*

Accounts:
New-Bucuti & Tara Beach Resorts (Agency of Record)
Dream Catchers of Williamsburg
The Somerset on Grace Bay

MQ&C ADVERTISING & MARKETING
1611 West Ave, Austin, TX 78701-1531
Tel.: (512) 499-0660
Fax: (512) 469-0803
E-Mail: ck@mq-c.com
Web Site: www.mq-c.com

Employees: 6
Year Founded: 1981

National Agency Associations: AFA

Agency Specializes In: Automotive, Entertainment, Government/Political, Pets , Real Estate, Restaurant, Retail

Ben Morris *(Founder)*
Cindy C. K. Carman *(Owner)*
Manasseh Sarpong *(CFO)*
Linda Rae Sanchez *(Dir-Acct & Creative Svcs)*
Juli Sarich *(Sr Media Buyer)*

Accounts:
Cafe Serranos
Grape Vine Market
Nightmare Factory
The Salvation Army - Austin Area

M.R. DANIELSON ADVERTISING LLC
1464 Summit Ave, Saint Paul, MN 55105
Tel.: (651) 324-5078
Fax: (651) 698-0104
E-Mail: mike@mrdan.com
Web Site: www.mrdan.com

Employees: 8
Year Founded: 1988

Agency Specializes In: Agriculture, Business-To-Business, Consumer Marketing, High Technology, Medical Products

Michael Danielson *(Pres)*
Alexandra Danielson *(Dir-Art & Acct Exec)*
Jodi Germain *(Dir-Art & Designer)*
Kris Kobe *(Dir-Art & Designer)*
Michael Beachy *(Dir-Art & Web Design)*
Jenna Dominik *(Dir-Mktg & Sls)*
Julianna Danielson *(Designer)*

Accounts:
3M Space
Ace Engineering; Minneapolis, MN; 2006
AEC Engineering
Armac Computer
Brainerd Technical
Cannon Equipment; Rosemont, MN; 2006
Ecolab; Saint Paul, MN; 2001
Minnesota Wire & Cable; Saint Paul, MN; 2006

MRC MEDICAL COMMUNICATIONS
12 Lincoln Blvd Ste 201, Emerson, NJ 07630
Tel.: (201) 986-0251
Fax: (201) 986-0361
E-Mail: info@mrcmedical.net
Web Site: www.mrcmedical.net

Employees: 10
Year Founded: 1978

Agency Specializes In: Education, Exhibit/Trade Shows, Graphic Design, Internet/Web Design, Medical Products, Multimedia, Production

David J. Rector *(Chm)*
Susan Rector *(Dir-New Bus Dev)*

Accounts:
FujiFilm
Healthcare Software Solutions
Merck Pharmaceutical; White House Station, NJ; 1997
Proximity
Sony; Park Ridge, NJ; 1988
Stryker; Kalamazoo, MI; 1998

MRM MCCANN
622 3rd Ave, New York, NY 10017-6707
Tel.: (646) 865-6230
Fax: (646) 865-6264
E-Mail: info@mrm.com
Web Site: mrm-mccann.com

Employees: 2,000
Year Founded: 1985

National Agency Associations: 4A's

Agency Specializes In: Above-the-Line, Advertising, Below-the-Line, Broadcast, Business-To-Business, Consulting, Consumer Marketing, Digital/Interactive, Direct Response Marketing, E-Commerce, Electronic Media, Event Planning & Marketing, Health Care Services, Magazines, Pharmaceutical, Telemarketing

Approx. Annual Billings: $1,800,000,000

Bill Kolb *(Chm)*
Sara Bresee *(Grp Mng Dir, Sr VP & Head-Intel Global Acct)*
Martin Garrocho *(Chief Creative Officer)*
Joyce King Thomas *(Chief Creative Officer)*
Marcy Samet *(Exec VP)*
Jan Lemke *(Sr VP & Grp Acct Dir)*
Kate Miller *(Sr VP & Dir-Client Svcs)*
Rebekah Simkus *(VP & Dir-Brand & Audience Strategy)*
Mary Doris-Smith *(Dir-CRM)*
Terri Loux *(Dir-Creative Ops)*
Slobodan Markovic *(Dir-Creative)*
Goran Ocokoljic *(Dir-Creative)*
Caitlin Livengood *(Sr Acct Exec)*
Dara Noble *(Sr Strategist-Social Media)*
Alex Gross *(Designer)*

Accounts:
Applebee's
Bristol-Myers Squibb
Choice Hotels International Digital, Marketing
Dell
Diageo Bulleit, Captain Morgan, Crown Royal, Jose Cuervo, Smirnoff, Zacapa
Ecco Digital
ExxonMobil
General Mills
GM
Intel Intel Core i7, Intel.com
Johnson & Johnson
L'Oreal
Microsoft
Mondelez International, Inc. Philadelphia Brand
Nestle Purina Chef Michael's
New York State Lottery Creative, Digital
OppenheimerFunds, Inc. (Agency of Record) Campaign: "Invest in a Beautiful World"
Purina
Unilever
United States Army Campaign: "At the Ready", Online Creative
Verizon FiOS

North America

MacLaren McCann Canada Inc.
10 Bay St, Toronto, ON M5J 2S3 Canada
(See Separate Listing)

MRM Princeton
105 Carnegie Ctr, Princeton, NJ 08540
(See Separate Listing)

MRM Worldwide New York
622 3rd Ave, New York, NY 10017
Tel.: (646) 865-6230
Fax: (646) 865-6264
E-Mail: info@mrmworldwide.com
Web Site: mrm-mccann.com

Employees: 180

Agency Specializes In: Above-the-Line, Advertising, Branded Entertainment, Consumer Marketing, Corporate Identity, Customer Relationship Management, Digital/Interactive, Direct Response Marketing, E-Commerce, Sponsorship

Michael McLaren *(CEO)*
Jon Burleigh *(CFO)*
Martin O'Brien *(Exec VP-Strategy)*
Sue R.E. Geramian *(Sr VP-Brand Comm-Global)*
Doug Darrigo *(VP & Dir-Creative)*
Randy Beringer *(Sr Dir-Art)*
Brian Hawe *(Mgmt Supvr)*
Cassandra Barboe *(Dir-Art & Designer)*
Tony Jones *(Dir-Creative)*
Darius Shayegi *(Dir-Fin Plng)*
Linda Sorbera *(Dir-HR-Global)*
Charlotte Beckwith *(Acct Supvr)*
Kaisha De La Mare *(Acct Supvr)*
Deepti Reddy *(Sr Acct Exec)*
Amanda Walsh *(Sr Strategist-Social Media)*
Emily Gomez *(Acct Exec)*
Rachael Kenney *(Acct Exec)*
Karinna Schultz *(Acct Exec)*
Erika Gould *(Jr Copywriter)*
Brian Gundich *(Analyst-Fin)*
Erin Hughes *(Exec Bus Dir)*
Joey Jackson *(Sr Production Mgr-Branded Programs)*
Jillian Terry *(Assoc Specialist-Social Media)*

Accounts:
Applebee's
Bristol-Myers Squibb
Dell
ExxonMobil
General Mills
GM
L'Oreal
MasterCard
Microsoft
Nestle

MRM Worldwide
600 Battery St, San Francisco, CA 94111
Tel.: (415) 262-5600
Fax: (415) 262-5400
E-Mail: david.shearer@mrmworldwide.com
Web Site: mrm-mccann.com

Employees: 125

National Agency Associations: 4A's

Agency Specializes In: Above-the-Line, Below-the-Line, Digital/Interactive, Direct Response Marketing, Email, Planning & Consultation,

Production, Sponsorship

Neil Levy *(VP & Grp Dir-Creative)*
Tina Applegate *(Sr Acct Exec)*
Kelly Mcclelland *(Sr Acct Exec)*
Marissa Nichols *(Planner-Strategy)*

Accounts:
Microsoft; Redmond, WA Software; 1999

MRM Worldwide
360 W Maple Rd, Birmingham, MI 48009
Tel.: (248) 203-8000
Fax: (248) 203-8010
E-Mail: info@mrmworldwide.com
Web Site: mrm-mccann.com

Employees: 15

National Agency Associations: 4A's

Agency Specializes In: Above-the-Line, Below-the-Line, Digital/Interactive, Mobile Marketing

Tamy Harms *(Pres)*
Jill Cooley *(Mng Dir)*
Marcy Quinn Samet *(Exec VP & Chief Growth Officer-Global)*
Jack Scheible *(Exec VP & Dir-CX & CRM-Global)*
Teresa Nord *(Sr VP & Dir-Mktg Tech Office)*
Lori Sullivan *(Sr VP & Dir-CRM)*
Sue Geramian *(Sr VP-Brand Comm-Global)*
Shekhar Gowda *(VP & Dir-Tech)*
Michael Matos *(VP & Dir-IT)*
Rebekah Simkus *(VP & Dir-Brand & Audience Strategy)*
Thomas Hillhouse *(Dir-Tech-Global Mktg)*
Mariann Gojcaj *(Assoc Dir-Program Mgmt)*
Nick Gonzalez *(Assoc Dir-Tech)*
William Gard *(Acct Exec)*

Accounts:
Carrera
Dell
General Motors Corporate, Customer Experience Strategy & Planning, Customer Relationship Management, Digital Production, GM Fleet, Web Development
Intel
Microsoft
Nestle

MRM London
76-80 Southwark Street, London, SE1 0PN United Kingdom
Tel.: (44) 20 7837 3737
Fax: (44) 207 153 8153
Web Site: www.mrm-meteorite.com/

Employees: 275
Year Founded: 1983

Agency Specializes In: Above-the-Line, Advertising, Below-the-Line, Consumer Marketing, Customer Relationship Management, Digital/Interactive, Direct Response Marketing, E-Commerce, Email, Identity Marketing

Andrew Appleyard *(Co-Owner & Dir)*
Hugh Bishop *(Chm)*
Havard Hughes *(Head-Pub Affairs)*
Michael Taggart *(Head-Digital & Social)*
Richard Wheat *(Dir)*
Jenny Crossland *(Assoc Dir)*
Chris Tuite *(Assoc Dir-Corp & Consumer)*
Ellis Ford *(Acct Exec)*
Barbara Kaiser *(Acct Exec)*
Tor Williams *(Acct Exec)*

Accounts:
Adviser Home PR
Aegon Ireland Digital, Media Relations, Social Media, Traditional Media
Ashcourt Rowan Plc PR
Banque Havilland S.A. PR
Caracalla 1947 Digital, Social Media PR
Carrera
Diageo
eye2eye Marketing Strategy, Online
Flagstone Investment Management (Lead Public Relations Agency)
General Mills
GenLife Digital Media Strategy, Media Relations, Public Affairs, Social Media Strategy
Hornbuckle Mitchell Media Relations, PR
Kames Capital
MasterCard
Microsoft
Nestle
The Open University
Philadelphia
Positive Solutions PR
Psion
Scottish Friendly Digital Communications, Media Relations
Sunovion Pharmaceuticals Inc.
Thesis Asset Management Plc PR
VocaLink PR
World Vision

MRM Paris
69 Blvd du General Leclerc, 92583 Clichy, France
Tel.: (33) 1 47 59 41 00
Fax: (33) 1 47 59 41 02
E-Mail: contact@mrmworldwide.fr
Web Site: www.mrm-mccann.fr

Employees: 200
Year Founded: 1981

Agency Specializes In: Above-the-Line, Below-the-Line, Consumer Marketing, Digital/Interactive, Direct-to-Consumer

Agnes Puig *(Deputy Dir Gen)*
Dragan Kontic *(CTO, Deputy Gen Mgr & Dir-Customer Mgmt Interaction)*
Michele Ferrebeuf *(Exec VP-McCann Worldgroup Europe)*
Erik Bertin *(Deputy Gen Mgr-Strategy)*
Emmanuel Dayre *(Exec Dir-Creative)*
Pascal Joseph *(Dir-Bus Dev)*

Accounts:
CPW
HP
MasterCard
Microsoft
Nestle
Opel

MRM Worldwide
(Formerly MRM Partners Dialogo)
Via Valtellina 15/17, 20159 Milan, Italy
Tel.: (39) 02 854 2111
Fax: (39) 02 869 0527
E-Mail: michele.sternai@mrmitaly.it
Web Site: mrm-mccann.com

Employees: 28
Year Founded: 1993

Agency Specializes In: Above-the-Line, Below-the-Line, Consumer Marketing, Digital/Interactive, Direct Response Marketing

Michele Sternai *(CEO-Italy)*
Giuliano Bellini *(Dir-Creative)*
Stefano Cairati *(Dir-Creative)*
Alice Pinto *(Project Mgr-Digital)*
Arianna Agazzi *(Mgr-Digital Project-New Bus)*
Loredana Calo *(Client Svc Dir)*

Accounts:
General Motors
L'Oreal
Periodici San Paolo Book Series
Safilo
Unilever

MRM Worldwide
Grosser Hasenpfad 44, 60598 Frankfurt, Germany
Tel.: (49) 69 605 070
Fax: (49) 69 605 07 112
E-Mail: christoph.stadeler@mccann.de
Web Site: mrm-mccann.com

E-Mail for Key Personnel:
President: christoph.stadeler@mccann.de

Employees: 60
Year Founded: 1999

Agency Specializes In: Above-the-Line, Automotive, Brand Development & Integration, Consumer Publications, Corporate Communications, Corporate Identity, Digital/Interactive, Direct Response Marketing, Direct-to-Consumer, E-Commerce, Internet/Web Design

Laurent Jaulin *(CFO)*
Elke Klinkhammer *(Chief Creative Officer)*
Frank Ladner *(CTO)*
Martin Biela *(Exec Dir-Creative)*
Suzana Mitrasinovic *(Acct Dir)*
Cortney Endecott *(Dir-HR)*
Dominik Heinrich *(Dir-Creative)*

Accounts:
BalticMiles Campaign: "Burn the Miles"
GranataPet #SnackBall
Lufthansa A380

Latin America

Dittborn & Unzueta MRM
Avenida Ezdora Goyenechea 3477 8th Fl, Las Condes, Santiago, Chile
Tel.: (56) 2 338 9500
Fax: (56) 2 338 9555
E-Mail: tdittborn@mrm.cl
Web Site: mrm-mccann.com

Employees: 40
Year Founded: 1997

Agency Specializes In: Above-the-Line, Advertising, Below-the-Line, Consumer Marketing, Customer Relationship Management, Digital/Interactive, Direct-to-Consumer, E-Commerce

Marcy Q. Samet *(Chief Growth Officer)*

Accounts:
Mobil1
Ripley

MRM Mexico
Palo Santo 17, Col Lomas Altas, Mexico, DF 11950 Mexico
Tel.: (52) 55 58 59 10
Fax: (52) 55 5096 4342
E-Mail: daniel.boveda@mccann.com.mx
Web Site: mrm-mccann.com

Employees: 45

Agency Specializes In: Above-the-Line, Advertising, Consumer Marketing, Customer Relationship Management, Digital/Interactive, Direct Response Marketing, Direct-to-Consumer, E-Commerce

Asia Pacific

MRM Worldwide Hong Kong

14 Fl Sunning Plaza 10 Hysan Avenue, Causeway Bay, China (Hong Kong)
Tel.: (852) 2808 7888
Fax: (852) 2881 6590
E-Mail: jason.chau@mrmworldwide.com
Web Site: mrm-mccann.com

Employees: 40
Year Founded: 1996

Agency Specializes In: Above-the-Line, Advertising, Below-the-Line, Consumer Marketing, Customer Relationship Management, Direct Response Marketing, E-Commerce

Jonathan Mackay *(Mng Dir & Sr VP)*
Mark Woodcock *(Reg Dir-Data & Analytics)*
Clara Tam *(Client Svcs Dir)*
Zaber Ali *(Dir-Media Svcs)*
Kate Clough *(Dir-Engagement Plng)*
Mairi Hood *(Dir-Digital Analytics)*
Heather Robinson *(Dir-Strategy & Plng)*
Muiji Lee *(Sr Acct Mgr)*

Accounts:
Dell
Intel
Mastercard

MRM Worldwide India

8 Balaji Estate Guru Ravi Dass Marg, Kalkaji, New Delhi, 110019 India
Tel.: (91) 11 2600 2600
Fax: (91) 11 2628 1034
E-Mail: india@mrmworldwide.com
Web Site: mrm-mccann.com

Employees: 50
Year Founded: 1993

Agency Specializes In: Above-the-Line, Advertising, Below-the-Line, Consumer Marketing, Customer Relationship Management, Digital/Interactive, Direct Response Marketing, Direct-to-Consumer, E-Commerce

Manish Sharma *(Mgr-Media Operation)*

MRM Worldwide Singapore

40A Orchard Road #05-01 The MacDonald House, Singapore, 238838 Singapore
Tel.: (65) 6737 9911
Fax: (65) 6739 3453
E-Mail: jen.faucon@ap.mccann.com
Web Site: mrm-mccann.com

Agency Specializes In: Above-the-Line, Advertising, Below-the-Line, Customer Relationship Management, Digital/Interactive, Direct Response Marketing, Direct-to-Consumer, E-Commerce, Email

Nick Handel *(Mng Dir)*
Joan Deni *(Sr VP & Mng Dir-Singapore)*
Aishah Haroon *(Bus Dir)*
Charlene Leung *(Acct Dir)*
Fritzie Plamenco *(Mgr-Digital Dealer Support-General Motors International)*

Accounts:
Unilever Digital, Food Solutions Business

MRM Worldwide

Shin-Aoyama Building E 1-1-1 Minami-Aoyama, Minato-ku, Tokyo, 107-8679 Japan
Tel.: (81) 3 3746 8900
Fax: (81) 3 3746 8901
Web Site: www.mrmjapan.co.jp

Employees: 50
Year Founded: 1987

Agency Specializes In: Above-the-Line, Advertising, Below-the-Line, Consumer Marketing, Customer Relationship Management, Digital/Interactive

Miho Shiozaki *(Pres)*
Rie Otsuka *(Grp Acct Dir-Bus Leadership)*
Kaori Taguchi *(Acct Dir)*
Ryo Murai *(Mgr-Comm Design)*
Mika Tanaka *(Mgr-Localization)*
Yuki Mori *(Acct Supvr)*

Accounts:
Citibank Japan Ltd
Club Createurs Beaute Japan, Inc
GAP Japan K.K
Google Japan Campaign: "AdWords Puzzle", Campaign: "Find the Key to Business Success"
Nestle Japan Ltd
Pfizer Japan Inc
UPS Japan Co., Ltd

MRM Worldwide

61 Dr S S Rao Road, Parel, Mumbai, 400012 India
Tel.: (91) 22 4230 3300
Fax: (91) 22 2300 3147
E-Mail: india@mrmworldwide.com
Web Site: mrm-mccann.com

Employees: 22
Year Founded: 1998

Agency Specializes In: Above-the-Line, Advertising, Consumer Marketing, Customer Relationship Management, Digital/Interactive, Direct-to-Consumer

Manish Sharma *(Mgr-Media Operation)*

MRM PRINCETON

105 Carnegie Ctr, Princeton, NJ 08540
Tel.: (609) 895-0200
Fax: (609) 895-0222
Web Site: mrm-mccann.com

E-Mail for Key Personnel:
Production Mgr.: sdenooyer@gillespie.com

Employees: 175
Year Founded: 1973

National Agency Associations: 4A's-BPA-DMA

Agency Specializes In: Above-the-Line, Advertising, Bilingual Market, Brand Development & Integration, Broadcast, Business Publications, Business-To-Business, Cable T.V., Collateral, Communications, Consulting, Consumer Marketing, Consumer Publications, Corporate Identity, Digital/Interactive, Direct Response Marketing, E-Commerce, Education, Electronic Media, Exhibit/Trade Shows, Financial, Government/Political, Graphic Design, Health Care Services, High Technology, Hispanic Market, Industrial, Infomercials, Information Technology, Internet/Web Design, Legal Services, Logo & Package Design, Magazines, Media Buying Services, Medical Products, New Product Development, Newspaper, Newspapers & Magazines, Out-of-Home Media, Outdoor, Pharmaceutical, Planning & Consultation, Point of Purchase, Point of Sale, Print, Production, Radio, Real Estate, Retail, Sponsorship, Sports Market, Trade & Consumer Magazines, Transportation

Jay Zivotovsky *(Sr VP & Dir-Fin)*
Sue DeNooyer *(Sr VP-Ops)*
Ruby Brown *(Head-Ops)*
Bil Chamberlin *(Sr Dir-Art-MRM worldwide)*
Randi Rosenfeld *(Dir-Social Strategy)*
Scott Hathaway *(Project Mgr-Digital)*
Matthew Paul *(Specialist-Social Media)*
Thomas Visicaro *(Sr Analyst-Client Fin)*

Accounts:
Dell
General Mills
GM
McNeil Consumer Products Flexeril
Microsoft

MRP MARKETING CLOUD

(Formerly Market Resource Partners LLC)
1880 JFK Blvd 19th Fl, Philadelphia, PA 19103
Tel.: (215) 587-8800
Fax: (215) 557-1575
E-Mail: info@mrpfd.com
Web Site: www.mrpfd.com/

Employees: 100

Agency Specializes In: Collateral, Email, Event Planning & Marketing, Exhibit/Trade Shows, High Technology, Market Research, Web (Banner Ads, Pop-ups, etc.)

Revenue: $6,600,000

Kevin Cunningham *(Partner)*
James Regan *(Partner)*
Romano DiToro *(CIO)*
Kristin Carey *(VP-Acct Dev)*
Joseph L. Rotondo *(VP)*

Accounts:
Cisco

MRW COMMUNICATIONS LLC

6 Barker Square Dr # 1, Pembroke, MA 02359-2225
Tel.: (781) 924-5282
Fax: (781) 926-0371
E-Mail: jim@mrwinc.com
Web Site: www.mrwinc.com

E-Mail for Key Personnel:
President: tom@mrwinc.com

Employees: 10
Year Founded: 2003

Agency Specializes In: Advertising, Brand Development & Integration, Business Publications, Business-To-Business, Collateral, Communications, Consumer Marketing, Corporate Identity, Direct Response Marketing, Electronic Media, Exhibit/Trade Shows, Financial, Graphic Design, Health Care Services, High Technology, Industrial, Information Technology, Internet/Web Design, Logo & Package Design, Magazines, Media Buying Services, Medical Products, Newspaper, Newspapers & Magazines, Outdoor, Planning & Consultation, Print, Production, Radio, Retail, Sales Promotion, Strategic Planning/Research, T.V., Technical Advertising, Trade & Consumer Magazines

Approx. Annual Billings: $8,000,000

James J. Watts *(Owner & Mng Partner)*
Thomas Matzell *(Dir-Creative-Copy)*

Accounts:
Bank Five
The Gemini Group
Keurig Coffee Systems
Kronos
Lab Corp; 2005
Lexington Furniture
MSI

Nelco; Woburn, MA Medical Radiation Shielding
Pyramid Hotel Group
Q1 Labs; Waltham, MA Network Security Products
Schwartz Law Offices
StonecroftCapital
United Capital Financial Advisers
Viisage Identity Software Products

MRY
(Formerly Mr. Youth)
11 W 19th St 3rd Fl, New York, NY 10011
Tel.: (212) 274-0470
Fax: (888) 847-5321
Web Site: mry.com/

Employees: 500

Agency Specializes In: Digital/Interactive, Social Media, Sponsorship, Viral/Buzz/Word of Mouth

Matt Britton *(Founder & CEO)*
Kingsley Taylor *(Mng Dir)*
Dan LaFontaine *(CFO & COO)*
Ian Chee *(Chief Strategy Officer)*
Karen Flanagan *(Sr VP & Grp Dir)*
Michelle Excell *(Head-Production)*
Evan Kraut *(Exec Dir-Brand Dev)*
Brian Ragan *(Exec Dir-Experience Design)*
Leo Leone *(Grp Dir-Creative)*
Eli Pakier *(Grp Dir-Strategy)*
Anna Haczkiewicz *(Sr Dir-Art)*
Michael Bollinger *(Grp Acct Dir)*
Stacey Zimmerman *(Grp Acct Dir)*
Stefanie Gunning *(Dir-Creative)*
Eugene Hwang *(Dir-Strategy)*
Mike Ruiz *(Dir-Creative)*
Andrew Walko *(Dir-Art)*
Maya Avrasin *(Assoc Dir-Content Strategy)*
Vinny Squillace *(Assoc Dir-Brand Dev)*
Michael Dolce *(Sr Project Mgr-Digital)*
Vinny Squillance *(Acct Mgr)*
Erin Boyer *(Client Partner)*
Lauren Jack *(Acct Supvr)*
Jacqueline Potter *(Acct Supvr)*
Toni Dawkins *(Assoc Strategist)*
Monica Koh *(Assoc Strategist)*

Accounts:
Adobe Campaign: "Make It With Creative Cloud", Creative
AT&T Campaign: "It Can Wait"
Bayer
Coca Cola
Gillette
JetBlue
Johnson & Johnson
Moleskine Website Redesign
National Grid Digital
New York City Drone Film Festival
Pizza Hut Digital
Reckitt Benckiser Cepacol, Delsym, Digital Marketing, Mucinex
Sidney Frank Importing Company "JagerBonds", Jagermeister
Skype
Spotify
Symantec
T Mobile
Visa Campaign: "Everywhere Initiative", Campaign: "GoInSix", Digital

Branches

MRY
146 Brick Ln, London, E1 6RU United Kingdom
Tel.: (44) 2070636465
Fax: (44) 2070636001
Web Site: www.mry.com

Agency Specializes In: Advertising, Content, Digital/Interactive, Social Media

Gemma Butler *(Dir-Creative-EMEA)*
Gav Gordon-Rogers *(Dir-Creative)*
Aisling Thornton *(Sr Mgr-Community)*
Tony Wright *(Strategist-Social)*

Accounts:
The Glenlivet (CRM Agency of Record)

MRY
2001 The Embarcadero, San Francisco, CA 94133
Tel.: (415) 293-2111
Fax: (888) 666-9741
Web Site: www.mry.com

Agency Specializes In: Advertising, Content, Digital/Interactive, Social Media, Sponsorship

Dan Lafontaine *(CFO & COO)*
David Berkowitz *(CMO)*
David Weinstock *(Chief Creative Officer)*
Evan Kraut *(Chief Growth Officer)*
Clare Hart *(Mng Dir-MRY Europe)*
Kingsley Taylor *(Mng Dir-MRY West)*
Ed Mangis *(Exec Dir-HR)*
Ali Forgeron *(Mgmt Supvr-Neutrogena)*
Parry Rominger *(Acct Exec)*

Accounts:
Del Monte Foods, Inc. (Digital & Social Agency of Record)

MSA ADVERTISING & PUBLIC RELATIONS
475 Park Ave S 6th Fl, New York, NY 10016
Tel.: (212) 532-5151
Fax: (212) 532-5499
Web Site: www.msanewyork.com

Employees: 30
Year Founded: 1951

National Agency Associations: APA

Agency Specializes In: Collateral, Consumer Marketing, Direct Response Marketing, Event Planning & Marketing, High Technology, Logo & Package Design, Newspaper, Outdoor, Print, Public Relations, Radio, Sales Promotion, T.V., Transportation

Approx. Annual Billings: $30,000,000

Paul Greenberg *(Mng Partner)*
Keith Klein *(Chief Creative Officer)*
Ron Spivak *(Sr Dir-Art)*
Sherman Yee *(Sr Dir-Art)*

Accounts:
The All Company
Bristol-Myers Squibb Company
Gamla Digital Imaging
Parliament Wine Company
Sandoz Pharmaceuticals Corporation
TUVRheinland

MSA MARKETING
5511 Capital Ctr Dr Ste 105, Raleigh, NC 27606
Tel.: (919) 463-9680
Web Site: www.thinkmsa.com

Year Founded: 1991

Agency Specializes In: Advertising, Event Planning & Marketing, Internet/Web Design, Market Research, Media Relations, Multimedia, Production, Social Media, Sponsorship

Jan Johnson *(Pres & CEO)*
Kate Geisler *(Acct Exec)*

Accounts:
Meredith College

MSA: THE THINK AGENCY
2530 Meridian Pkwy Ste 200, Durham, NC 27713
Tel.: (919) 463-9680
Fax: (919) 463-9722
Toll Free: (800) 849-2118
Web Site: www.thinkmsa.com

Employees: 55
Year Founded: 1991

Approx. Annual Billings: $12,000,000

Lewis Finch *(Pres)*
Dennis Wipper *(VP & Dir-Creative)*
Nick Burns *(Dir-Art)*
Andrew Lada *(Assoc Dir-Media)*
Cindi August *(Project Mgr-MSA Mktg, Inc.)*
Kate Geisler *(Acct Exec)*
Brooke Beasley *(Coord-Media)*

Accounts:
Inuvo, Inc.
Meredith College Media Planning & Buying
NC Aquariums
NC Public Power
North Carolina Division of Parks & Recreation
North Carolina State Board of Elections
Rex Healthcare
State Fair; Raleigh, NC
The Umstead Hotel and Spa
UNC Healthcare

MSI
(Formerly Marketing Support, Inc.)
200 E Randolph Dr Ste 5000, Chicago, IL 60601
Tel.: (312) 565-0044
Fax: (312) 946-6100
E-Mail: info@agencymsi.com
Web Site: agencymsi.com

Employees: 90
Year Founded: 1962

Agency Specializes In: Advertising, Brand Development & Integration, Broadcast, Business-To-Business, Cable T.V., Catalogs, Co-op Advertising, Collateral, Communications, Consulting, Consumer Goods, Consumer Marketing, Consumer Publications, Corporate Communications, Corporate Identity, Digital/Interactive, Direct Response Marketing, Direct-to-Consumer, E-Commerce, Electronic Media, Event Planning & Marketing, Graphic Design, Guerilla Marketing, Household Goods, Identity Marketing, In-Store Advertising, Industrial, Integrated Marketing, Internet/Web Design, Local Marketing, Logo & Package Design, Luxury Products, Magazines, Market Research, Media Buying Services, Media Planning, Media Relations, Media Training, Men's Market, Merchandising, Mobile Marketing, New Product Development, Newspaper, Newspapers & Magazines, Out-of-Home Media, Outdoor, Package Design, Paid Searches, Pets , Planning & Consultation, Point of Purchase, Point of Sale, Print, Production, Production (Print), Promotions, Public Relations, Publicity/Promotions, Radio, Retail, Sales Promotion, Search Engine Optimization, Social Media, Strategic Planning/Research, Sweepstakes, T.V., Teen Market, Trade & Consumer Magazines,

Women's Market

Approx. Annual Billings: $25,000,000

David L. Weiner *(CEO)*
Dave Gaston *(Exec VP)*
Stacy Gelman *(Exec VP-Ops)*
Gaelen Bell *(VP-Social Mktg & PR)*
Maureen Brennan *(VP-Pub Rels & Social Media)*
Molly Dineen *(Dir-Media)*

Accounts:
ACE Hardware; Oakbrook, IL
Adobe; San Francisco, CA
American Marketing Association; Chicago, IL
Big Apple Bagels; Deerfield, IL
Briggs & Stratton; Milwaukee, WI
Cabela's; Sydney, NE
Fluidmaster; San Juan, CA Repair Parts
The Home Depot; Atlanta, GA Retail Chain
Lochinvar; Lebanon, TN
MB Financial Bank; Rosemont, IL
Sears-KMart; Hoffman Estates, IL Retail Chain
Serta; Hoffman Estates, IL
Tractor Supply Co. Inc.; Brentwood, TN
White-Rodgers Division; Saint Louis, MO Heating & AC Controls

Subsidiary

MSI Advertising
200 E Randolph Dr Ste 5000, Chicago, IL 60305
Tel.: (312) 946-6006
Web Site: www.msiadvertising.com

Employees: 35
Year Founded: 2015

Agency Specializes In: Above-the-Line, Alternative Advertising, Below-the-Line, Broadcast, Business Publications, Cable T.V., Catalogs, Co-op Advertising, Collateral, Consumer Publications, Digital/Interactive, Direct Response Marketing, Electronic Media, Email, Exhibit/Trade Shows, Guerilla Marketing, In-Store Advertising, Infomercials, Local Marketing, Magazines, Multimedia, Newspaper, Newspapers & Magazines, Outdoor, Paid Searches, Podcasting, Point of Purchase, Point of Sale, Print, Production, Production (Print), Promotions, RSS (Really Simple Syndication), Radio, Search Engine Optimization, Shopper Marketing, Social Media, Sponsorship, Sweepstakes, T.V., Telemarketing, Trade & Consumer Magazines, Viral/Buzz/Word of Mouth, Web (Banner Ads, Pop-ups, etc.), Yellow Pages Advertising

Dave Weiner *(Founder)*
Tom Hall *(Principal-Creative)*
Dave Hamel, *(Principal-Strategy)*
Eileen McKnight *(Principal-Media)*

Accounts:
ACE Hardware
Adobe
American Egg Board
American Marketing Association
Beauty Brands
Becker Professional Education
Big Apple Bagels
Boys & Girls Clubs
Briggs & Stratton
Cabelas
Capital Education
Carex
Guitar Center
In-Sink-Erator
MB Financial Bank
NDS
Sears
Serta
Therm Flo
Tractor Supply
Zonatherm

MSM DESIGNZ INC
505 White Plains Rd 2nd Fl Ste 204, Tarrytown, NY 10591
Tel.: (914) 909-5900
Fax: (775) 317-5196
Web Site: www.msmdesignz.com

Agency Specializes In: Advertising, Brand Development & Integration, Internet/Web Design, Print, Social Media

Mario S. Mirabella *(Owner & Dir-Creative)*
Kelsey Belgrave *(Mgr-Social Media)*
Anthony Terlizzi *(Mgr-SEO)*

Accounts:
White Plains Downtown BID

MUDD ADVERTISING
915 Technology Pkwy, Cedar Falls, IA 50613
Tel.: (319) 277-2003
Fax: (319) 277-8176
Toll Free: (800) 367-6833
E-Mail: info@mudd.com
Web Site: www.mudd.com

Employees: 144

National Agency Associations: Second Wind Limited

Agency Specializes In: Automotive

Jim Mudd, Jr. *(Founder)*
Chris Mudd *(Pres & COO)*
Jason Cashman *(Gen Mgr-Sls)*
Gary Kroeger *(Dir-Creative)*
Therese Kuster *(Dir-Digital Ops)*
Ryan Thacher *(Dir-Ops)*
Wayne Wilson *(Reg Mgr)*
Emmalee Albers *(Analyst-Mktg)*
Rachel Johnson *(Brand Sls Mgr-Kia & Hyundai)*

Branch

Mudd Advertising
211 W Wacker Dr 2nd Fl, Chicago, IL 60606
Tel.: (312) 781-0176
Toll Free: (888) 313-3536
E-Mail: info@mudd.com
Web Site: www.mudd.com

Employees: 10

Jim Mudd *(Founder)*
Chris Mudd *(Pres & COO)*
Mary Kay Mudd *(Dir-Mudd360)*
Scott Braun *(Mgr-Digital Assets)*
Corey Langan *(Team Head-Natl Acct)*

MUH-TAY-ZIK HOF-FER
649 Front St, San Francisco, CA 94611
Tel.: (415) 255-6363
Web Site: www.mtzhf.com

Year Founded: 2008

Agency Specializes In: Advertising, Digital/Interactive, Social Media, Sponsorship

John Matejczyk *(Co-Founder & Exec Dir-Creative)*
Matt Hofherr *(Co-Founder & Dir-Strategy)*
Michelle Spear *(Head-Production)*
Michelle Spear Nicholson *(Head-Production)*
Adam Ledbury *(Sr Dir-Art)*
Todd Allen Bois *(Creative Dir)*
Stevan Chavez *(Art Dir)*
Carolina Cruz-Letelier *(Acct Dir)*
Dean Casalena *(Dir-Tech)*
Tony Zimney *(Dir-Creative)*
Nate Gagnon *(Assoc Dir-Creative)*
Courtney Lovell *(Acct Mgr & Project Mgr)*
Kashmir Hyder *(Acct Mgr)*
Veronika Luquin Campbell *(Acct Supvr)*
Zach Rubin *(Client Svc Dir)*

Accounts:
American Automobile Association (Agency of Record) Campaign: "Insurance That's Not Just Insurance"
Audi of America (Social Media Agency of Record) Creative Content
Do.com
E & J Gallo Winery
Golden State Warriors #WeAreWarriors, Campaign: " Ice Bath", Campaign: "Assist", Campaign: "Fast Break", Campaign: "Little Help"
Google, Inc. Google Goggles, Google Mobile
New-Maker Studios Digital, Social
New-The Munchery Campaign: "Dinner Is Home", Digital, Media, OOH, Radio
Netflix Campaign: "Fireplace For Your Home", Campaign: "Spoil Yourself"
New-OXO Media
Zoosk Inc. Campaign: "First Comes Like", Online, TV

MULLEN
(Merged with Lowe & Partners to form Mullen Lowe Group)

MULLEN ADVERTISING & PUBLIC RELATIONS, INC.
(Acquired & Absorbed by The Lavidge Company)

MULLEN LOWE GROUP
(Formerly Mullen)
40 Broad St, Boston, MA 02109
Tel.: (617) 226-9000
Fax: (617) 226-9100
Web Site: www.mullenlowegroup.com

Employees: 375
Year Founded: 1970

National Agency Associations: 4A's

Agency Specializes In: Advertising, Advertising Specialties, Affluent Market, Automotive, Brand Development & Integration, Branded Entertainment, Broadcast, Business Publications, Business-To-Business, Cable T.V., Catalogs, Children's Market, Co-op Advertising, Collateral, Communications, Consulting, Consumer Marketing, Consumer Publications, Corporate Communications, Corporate Identity, Crisis Communications, Digital/Interactive, Direct Response Marketing, Direct-to-Consumer, E-Commerce, Education, Electronic Media, Email, Entertainment, Environmental, Event Planning & Marketing, Exhibit/Trade Shows, Experience Design, Fashion/Apparel, Financial, Government/Political, Graphic Design, Guerilla Marketing, Health Care Services, High Technology, Identity Marketing, In-Store Advertising, Industrial, Infomercials, Information Technology, Integrated Marketing, Internet/Web Design, Legal Services, Leisure, Local Marketing, Logo & Package Design, Luxury Products, Magazines, Marine, Market Research, Media Buying Services, Media Planning, Media Relations, Media Training, Medical Products, Men's Market, Merchandising, Mobile Marketing, Multimedia, New Product Development, New Technologies, Newspaper, Newspapers & Magazines, Out-of-Home Media, Outdoor, Package Design, Paid Searches, Pharmaceutical, Planning & Consultation, Point of Purchase, Point of Sale, Print, Product Placement, Production, Production (Print), Promotions, Public Relations,

Publicity/Promotions, Radio, Real Estate, Recruitment, Restaurant, Retail, Sales Promotion, Search Engine Optimization, Seniors' Market, Sponsorship, Sports Market, Stakeholders, Strategic Planning/Research, Sweepstakes, Syndication, T.V., Technical Advertising, Teen Market, Telemarketing, Trade & Consumer Magazines, Transportation, Travel & Tourism, Urban Market, Women's Market, Yellow Pages Advertising

Alex Leikikh *(CEO)*
Sheila Leyne *(Mng Partner & Exec VP)*
Paul Slack *(COO)*
John Moore *(Chief Media Officer)*
Mark Wenneker *(Chief Creative Officer)*
Naomi Troni *(Chief Growth Officer)*
Jason Black *(Exec VP & Exec Dir-Creative)*
Marc Kempter *(Exec VP & Dir-Acct Mgmt)*
Paul Foulkes *(Sr VP & Exec Dir-Creative)*
Liza Near *(Sr VP & Exec Dir-Integrated Production)*
Kristen Abramo *(Sr VP & Grp Dir-Media-Mediahub)*
Jade Watts *(Sr VP & Grp Dir-Digital)*
Drayton Martin *(Sr VP & Grp Acct Dir)*
Jaclyn Ruelle *(Sr VP & Acct Dir)*
Patrick Acosta *(Sr VP & Dir-Analytics)*
Denise Ambrosio *(Sr VP & Dir-HR)*
Zeke Bowman *(Sr VP & Dir-Brdcst Production)*
Sean Corcoran *(Sr VP & Dir-Digital Media & Social Influence)*
Chere Furman *(Sr VP & Dir-Creative Support Svcs)*
John Kearse *(Sr VP & Dir-Creative)*
Lance Koenig *(Sr VP & Dir-Strategy)*
Christian Madden *(Sr VP & Dir-Creative & Tech)*
Jonathan Ruby *(Sr VP & Dir-Creative)*
John Wolfarth *(Sr VP & Dir-Creative)*
Richard Maloney *(Sr VP)*
David Swaebe *(Sr VP-Comm & Bus Dev)*
Tiffany Stevens *(VP & Exec Producer-Digital)*
Jesse Brandt *(VP & Acct Dir)*
Sue DeSilva *(VP & Creative Dir)*
Brian Leech *(VP, Dir-Art & Assoc Dir-Creative)*
Jon Reil *(VP & Dir-Creative & Art)*
Rachel Allen *(VP & Assoc Dir-Media)*
Jennifer Biagiotti *(VP & Assoc Dir-Media)*
Laurel Boyd *(VP & Assoc Dir-Digital Media)*
Yvonne Leung *(VP & Assoc Dir-Media)*
Kate Melville *(VP & Assoc Dir-Media)*
Brooke Perry *(VP & Assoc Dir-Video Investments)*
Allison Rude *(VP & Assoc Dir-Creative)*
Tammy Skuraton *(VP & Mgr-Creative)*
Kalley Jolly *(VP-PR & Social Influence)*
Trupti Patil *(VP-Strategic Analytics)*
Keith Lusby *(Exec Dir-MediaHub)*
Tim Vaccarino *(Exec Dir-Creative)*
Dave Weist *(Exec Creative Dir)*
Dan Madsen *(Sr Dir-Art)*
Alanna Whelan *(Sr Producer-Digital)*
Courtney Calvert *(Acct Dir)*
Kirk Kelley *(Creative Dir)*
Megan Oxland *(Acct Dir)*
Lisa Della Piana *(Art Dir)*
Jessica Zdenek *(Acct Dir)*
Tom Francesconi *(Dir-Art)*
Mathew Ray *(Dir-Interactive)*
Anna Vlajkovic *(Dir-Plng)*
Blake Winfree *(Dir-Art)*
Tracy Barahona *(Assoc Dir-Digital Media)*
Tony Frusciante *(Assoc Dir-Creative)*
Vanessa Higgins *(Assoc Dir-Media)*
Tracey LeBlanc *(Assoc Dir-Buying-Local Negotiations)*
Nick Mathisen *(Assoc Dir-Creative)*
Andrea Mileskiewicz *(Assoc Dir-Creative)*
Katie Ott *(Assoc Dir-Video Investments)*
Samantha Paul *(Assoc Dir-Digital Media)*
Scott Slagsvol *(Assoc Dir-Creative)*
Tiffany Ahern *(Sr Brand Strategist)*
Ashley Rumery *(Mgr-Copy Editing)*
Katie Tammaro *(Mgr-Comm)*
Molly Bluhm *(Acct Supvr)*
Jeff Branz *(Acct Supvr)*
Bethany Ciampa *(Acct Supvr-PR)*
Tim Connor *(Acct Supvr)*
Ralph Davidson-Palmer *(Acct Supvr)*
Danielle Morrissey *(Acct Supvr)*
Melissa Sabones *(Acct Supvr)*
Michelle Blaser *(Supvr)*
Tiffany Blosser *(Supvr-Media)*
Alex Hale *(Supvr-Media Sciences)*
Shoshana Levine *(Supvr-Digital Media)*
Leo McNeil *(Supvr-Media)*
Thomas Morningstar *(Supvr-Programmatic)*
Lauren Brennan *(Sr Acct Exec)*
Vishal Chandawarkar *(Sr Acct Exec)*
Brittany Topham *(Sr Acct Exec)*
Danielle Dawkins *(Acct Exec)*
Sarah Morgan *(Strategist-Media)*
Kylie Mugg *(Acct Exec)*
Meaghan Quinn *(Acct Exec)*
Beba Rivera *(Acct Exec)*
Justin Rodis *(Acct Exec)*
Emily Schmitt *(Acct Exec)*
Benjamin Verrill *(Acct Exec)*
Anna Bohlin *(Planner-Digital Media)*
Alan Cook *(Designer)*
Nicole Frattura *(Media Planner)*
Steven Frey *(Planner-Digital Media)*
Chris Gilbert *(Copywriter)*
Lauren Meyers *(Media Planner)*
Han Na Jung *(Designer)*
Diego Sarmiento *(Copywriter)*
Sarah Schmid *(Copywriter)*
Evelynne Scholnick *(Copywriter)*
Macie Soler-Sala *(Jr Copywriter)*
Eugene Torres *(Copywriter)*
Kaitlyn Wood *(Media Planner)*
Kate Chartier *(Asst Acct Exec)*
Stephanie Costa *(Asst Acct Exec)*
Kristen Fougere *(Asst Acct Exec)*
Breana Appolonia *(Sr Media Planner)*
Allie Babes *(Sr Media Planner)*
Kathleen Brower *(Asst Media Planner-Digital)*
Kara Buettner *(Sr Media Planner)*
Lindsey Melnyk *(Sr Media Planner & Buyer)*
Ali Sakai *(Asst Media Planner-Digital)*

Accounts:
Adidas Light You Up - New York Projection Video
Airbnb Campaign: "Hollywood & Vines"
Amazon.com, Inc.
American Greetings (Agency of Record) Campaign: "ThankList", Campaign: "World's Toughest Job"
Barnes & Noble Creative, Media
Bose Corporation Direct Response, Media
New-Capital One Campaign: "Biggest Fan", Digital, OOH, Print
CardStore Campaign: "Mother's Day"
Century 21 (Agency of Record) Campaign: "A Flamingo", Campaign: "Breaking Bad", Campaign: "Built-Ins", Campaign: "Frog Fountain", Campaign: "Garden Gnome", Campaign: "Lawn Invasion", Campaign: "Master Suite", Campaign: "Pet Friendly", Campaign: "Playroom", Campaign: "Slightly Haunted", Campaign: "Smarter. Bolder. Faster.", Campaign: "Tryptophan Slow Jam", Campaign: "Vaulted Ceilings", Drone Delivery Pads, Social Creative, Social Media; 2010
Coca-Cola Creative Development, Honest Tea, Strategy
Constant Contact, Inc.
Defense Human Resource Activity Marketing, PR
Department of Defense
EmblemHealth; New York, NY Creative, Media
Ernst & Young
FAGE Total Greek Yogurt Plain
Foxwoods (Agency of Record)
General Motors Brand Marketing, Customer Relationship Management, Digital Marketing, Financial Services, Fleet Services, GM Card, GM Certified Used Vehicles
Google Beat Box, Campaign: "Gomo", Campaign: "New Baby", Galaxy Nexus, Google Play, Nexus 10
Grain Foods Foundation Bread, Integrated Mareketing
Honda Motor Co. 2014 MDX, Acura (Lead Creative Agency), Acura 2016 ILX, Campaign: "Astro", Campaign: "Comedians in Cars Getting Coffee", Campaign: "Love", Campaign: "Made for Mankind", Campaign: "March Memeness"
HSBC
Indeed.com Advertising
JetBlue Airways Corporation Advertising, Campaign: "Air on the Side of Humanity", Campaign: "Celebrity Baggage", Campaign: "Fly It Forward", Campaign: "Getaways Granter", Campaign: "HumanKinda", Campaign: "Never Ending", Campaign: "You Above All", Creative, Digital, Media, Non-Traditional Advertising, Online, Outdoor, Print, Radio, Social, Television, Video, i-people
Lemon Campaign: "King of Pop"
LivingSocial
Mamas & Papas Baby Gear
MassMutual Financial Group (Agency of Record) "Hiking" Spot, "Restaurant" Spot, Campaign: "Vows to Protect", Digital, Good Decisions Campaign; 2006
Match.com
Mullen Point-of-Purchase, Radio, TV
National Geographic Channels "Live From Space", Campaign: "Killing Lincoln Conspiracy", Campaign: "Killing With Kindness", Killing Jesus, Website
Olympus Camera, Olympus PEN E-PL1
OwnerIQ Digital, Media
Qwest/CenturyLink
Reynolds American Media Buying, Vuse
Royal Caribbean Campaign: "Come Seek", Creative
Santander/Sovereign
Shinola Media Agency of Record
Time Warner Inc.
TRESemme Campaign: "Mercedes-Benz Fashion Week"
TruTv
U.S. Cellular Brand Strategy, Creative, Digital, Media, Performance Analytics
US Department of Defense
Viacom Hot in Cleveland, Media, Media Buying, Media Planning, TV Land (Agency of Record), VH1, Younger
Videology
Zappos.com #paywithacupcake, Campaign: "More than Shoes", Campaign: "Streaker", Media Buying & Planning

Branches

Mediahub
40 Broad St, Boston, MA 02109
Tel.: (617) 226-9000
Fax: (617) 226-9100

National Agency Associations: 4A's

John Moore *(Pres)*
Kristen Abramo *(Sr VP & Grp Dir-Media)*
Patrick Acosta *(Sr VP & Dir-Analytics)*
Steve Kalb *(Sr VP & Dir-Video Investments)*
Sean Corcoran *(Exec Dir-Innovation)*
Scott Karambis *(Exec Dir-Comm Plng)*
Keith Lusby *(Exec Dir)*
Erin Swenson Gorrall *(Grp Dir-Plng)*
Liz Fermon *(Supvr-Digital Media)*
Adam Telian *(Supvr-Digital Media)*
Cailin Carson *(Sr Media Buyer)*
Kaitlin Hill *(Sr Media Planner)*
Kelly Hughes *(Sr Media Buyer)*
Tana Rogers *(Assoc Media Dir)*

Accounts:
New-California Avocado Commission Media
Patron Spirits Media Buying, Media Planning, Outdoor, Television

Advertising Agencies

Royal Caribbean Digital, Media Buying, Media Planning, North American Media
Scotts Miracle-Gro Media

Mullen Lowe
(Formerly Mullen)
999 N Sepulveda Blvd, El Segundo, CA 90245
Tel.: (617) 226-9932
Fax: (617) 226-9000
Web Site: www.mullenlowegroup.com

National Agency Associations: 4A's

Agency Specializes In: Advertising, Collateral, Graphic Design, Logo & Package Design, Print, Strategic Planning/Research

Cameron McNaughton *(Mng Dir)*
Lee Newman *(CEO-US)*
Tom Donovan *(Sr VP & Dir-Strategy)*
David Swaebe *(Sr VP-Comm & Bus Dev)*
Margaret Keene *(Exec Dir-Creative)*
Sean Stell *(Sr Dir-Art)*
Jonathan Renteria *(Assoc Dir-Strategic Analytics)*

Accounts:
American Honda Motor Co., Inc. "My Way", Acura, Acura ILX, Campaign: "Bottle", Campaign: "Catch It If You Can", Campaign: "It's That Kind of Thrill", Campaign: "Let the Race Begin", Campaign: "Made for Mankind", Creative, Digital, Marketing, Online, Social Media, TLX, TV
New-California Avocado Commission Campaign: "Hand Grown in California", Creative
The Patron Spirits Company Campaign: "It Doesn't Have to Make Sense to Be Perfect", Global Creative, Out of Home Media, TV

Mullen Lowe
(Formerly Mullen)
600 Battery St, San Francisco, CA 94111
Tel.: (617) 226-9000
Fax: (617) 226-9100
Web Site: www.mullenlowegroup.com

Agency Specializes In: Advertising

Mark Wenneker *(Chief Creative Officer)*
Nicole Neopolitan *(Grp Acct Dir)*
Cortney Calvert *(Acct Dir)*
Paul Foulkes *(Dir-Art)*
Anna Vlajkovic *(Dir-Plng)*
Alli Blender *(Assoc Dir-Media)*
Ryan Anctil *(Assoc Producer-Digital)*

Accounts:
Airbnb Campaign: "Hollywood and Vines"
American Honda Motor Co., Inc. Acura, Campaign: "The Test"
Google Inc. Google Play

Mullen Lowe
(Formerly Mullen)
1 Woodroad Ave, Detroit, MI 48226
Tel.: (313) 596-9002
Fax: (313) 394-0045
Web Site: www.mullenlowegroup.com

Employees: 210

Agency Specializes In: Advertising, Advertising Specialties, Automotive, Brand Development & Integration, Broadcast, Business Publications, Business-To-Business, Cable T.V., Children's Market, Co-op Advertising, Collateral, Communications, Consumer Marketing, Consumer Publications, Corporate Identity, Digital/Interactive, Direct Response Marketing, E-Commerce, Education, Electronic Media, Engineering, Environmental, Exhibit/Trade Shows, Fashion/Apparel, Financial, Food Service, Government/Political, Graphic Design, Health Care Services, High Technology, Information Technology, Internet/Web Design, Investor Relations, Legal Services, Leisure, Logo & Package Design, Magazines, Marine, Media Buying Services, Medical Products, Multimedia, New Product Development, Newspaper, Newspapers & Magazines, Out-of-Home Media, Outdoor, Over-50 Market, Planning & Consultation, Point of Purchase, Point of Sale, Print, Production, Public Relations, Publicity/Promotions, Radio, Recruitment, Retail, Sales Promotion, Seniors' Market, Sports Market, Strategic Planning/Research, Sweepstakes, T.V., Trade & Consumer Magazines, Transportation, Travel & Tourism

Molly Barag *(Sr Acct Exec)*
Peter Martin *(Sr Acct Exec)*
Brittany Topham *(Sr Acct Exec)*
Esther Chung *(Planner-Digital Media)*
Kayla Doyle *(Media Planner)*
Courtney Maestri *(Media Planner)*
Alexa Sellecchia *(Planner-Digital Media)*

Accounts:
General Motors Brand Marketing, Customer Relationship Management, Digital Marketing, Financial Services, Fleet Services, GM Card, GM Certified Used Vehicles
National Geographic Channel

Mullen Lowe
(Formerly Mullen)
101 N Cherry St Ste 600, Winston Salem, NC 27101-4035
Mailing Address:
PO Box 5627, Winston Salem, NC 27113-5627
Tel.: (336) 765-3630
Fax: (336) 774-9550
Web Site: www.mullenlowegroup.com

Employees: 165
Year Founded: 1949

National Agency Associations: 4A's-DMA

Agency Specializes In: Advertising, Advertising Specialties, Agriculture, Automotive, Brand Development & Integration, Broadcast, Business Publications, Business-To-Business, Cable T.V., Children's Market, Co-op Advertising, Collateral, Communications, Computers & Software, Consumer Goods, Consumer Marketing, Consumer Publications, Corporate Communications, Customer Relationship Management, Digital/Interactive, Direct Response Marketing, Direct-to-Consumer, E-Commerce, Education, Electronic Media, Email, Engineering, Environmental, Event Planning & Marketing, Exhibit/Trade Shows, Fashion/Apparel, Financial, Food Service, Government/Political, Graphic Design, Guerilla Marketing, Health Care Services, High Technology, Household Goods, In-Store Advertising, Industrial, Information Technology, Integrated Marketing, International, Internet/Web Design, Investor Relations, Legal Services, Leisure, Local Marketing, Logo & Package Design, Magazines, Marine, Media Buying Services, Media Planning, Medical Products, Mobile Marketing, Multimedia, New Product Development, Newspaper, Newspapers & Magazines, Out-of-Home Media, Outdoor, Over-50 Market, Package Design, Paid Searches, Pharmaceutical, Planning & Consultation, Point of Purchase, Point of Sale, Print, Production, Production (Ad, Film, Broadcast), Production (Print), Promotions, Public Relations, Publicity/Promotions, Radio, Recruitment, Regional, Retail, Sales Promotion, Search Engine Optimization, Seniors' Market, Shopper Marketing, Social Marketing/Nonprofit, Social Media, Sponsorship, Sports Market, Strategic Planning/Research, Sweepstakes, T.V., Trade & Consumer Magazines, Transportation, Travel & Tourism, Viral/Buzz/Word of Mouth

Jennifer Ganshirt *(Co-Founder & Mng Partner)*
Anne Elwell *(Mng Partner, Exec VP & Grp Acct Dir)*
Sam Rand *(Mng Partner)*
Shaun Stripling *(CMO & Sr VP)*
Lauri Bauer *(Sr VP & Grp Dir-Media)*
Matt Belson *(Sr VP & Grp Acct Dir)*
Susanna Gates-Rose *(Sr VP & Dir-Brdcst Production)*
Jennifer Cross *(VP & Acct Dir)*
Seton McGowan *(VP & Assoc Dir-Strategy)*
Margaret Keene *(Exec Dir-Creative)*
Christy Blain *(Grp Dir-Creative)*
Gerald Troutman *(Dir-Print & Supvr-Media)*
Alicia Hamblen *(Dir-Bus Dev & Project Mgmt)*
Matt Mason *(Assoc Dir-Creative)*
Kathryn McLean *(Assoc Dir-Audio & Video Investment)*
Sarah Ross *(Assoc Dir-Media)*
Elizabeth Bragg *(Acct Supvr)*
Elizabeth Surrett *(Acct Supvr)*
Jackie Grano *(Supvr-Alternative Media)*
Megan Handerhan *(Media Buyer-Mediahub)*
Tara Nelson *(Copywriter)*
Cailin Carson *(Sr Media Buyer)*

Accounts:
Asheville Convention & Visitors Bureau Marketing
Auntie Anne's Pretzels; 2013
Buncombe County Tourism Development Authority (Agency of Record) Creative, Media
CenturyLink; 2007
Computer Sciences Corporation (CSC); 2008
CSX Transportation; 2007
Escort Radar; 2011
Gazelle.com; 2013
Hanes Hosiery; 2010
Hanesbrands
ITT Corporation - Xylem; 2011
La Quinta Inns & Suites; Irving, TX; 2007
Lenovo Group Ltd; 2012
Mcgladrey; 2009
McGraw Hill Financial; 2012
Men's Wearhouse; 2009
N.C. Education Lottery (Agency of Record) Creative Advertising, Digital, Event Marketing, Media Buying, Media Planning, Public Relations, Social Media, Strategic Planning, Web Development
New Holland (Agency of Record) Agriculture, Brand Creative, Construction, Direct Marketing, Marketing Communications, Media Buying, Media Planning, Social Media, Strategic Planning
Pep Boys Campaign: "Car Problems Are People Problems", Digital, Direct Mail, Radio, Social Media; 2012
Sprout; 2011
Sylvan Learning Center; 2013
Ulta Beauty (Advertising Agency of Record) Campaign: "All Things Beauty", Creative, Media Content, Strategy
Unilever TRESemme; 2010

Mullen Lowe
386 Park Ave S, New York, NY 10016
Tel.: (646) 762-6700
Web Site: www.mullenlowegroup.com

National Agency Associations: 4A's

Amy Ferguson *(Dir-Creative-JetBlue)*
Julia Neumann *(Dir-Creative-JetBlue)*
Tara Nolan *(Dir-Global Brand & Bus Dev)*
Stephanie Doennecke *(Mgr-Global Comm)*

Accounts:
New-JetBlue
Milk
Unilever

Mullen Lowe
(Formerly Mullen)
The Crane Bldg 40 24th St, Pittsburgh, PA 15222-4600
Tel.: (412) 402-0200
Fax: (412) 402-0160
Web Site: www.mullenlowegroup.com

Employees: 50
Year Founded: 1987

Agency Specializes In: Advertising, Automotive, Brand Development & Integration, Broadcast, Business Publications, Business-To-Business, Cable T.V., Co-op Advertising, Collateral, Communications, Consulting, Consumer Marketing, Consumer Publications, Corporate Identity, Digital/Interactive, Direct Response Marketing, E-Commerce, Education, Electronic Media, Event Planning & Marketing, Exhibit/Trade Shows, Financial, Food Service, Government/Political, Graphic Design, Health Care Services, High Technology, Information Technology, Internet/Web Design, Investor Relations, Leisure, Logo & Package Design, Magazines, Media Buying Services, Media Planning, Medical Products, Multimedia, New Product Development, Newspaper, Newspapers & Magazines, Out-of-Home Media, Outdoor, Over-50 Market, Planning & Consultation, Point of Purchase, Point of Sale, Print, Production, Production (Ad, Film, Broadcast), Public Relations, Publicity/Promotions, Radio, Recruitment, Retail, Sales Promotion, Seniors' Market, Sports Market, Strategic Planning/Research, Sweepstakes, T.V., Trade & Consumer Magazines, Transportation, Travel & Tourism, Web (Banner Ads, Pop-ups, etc.)

Kayla Gorski *(Acct Dir)*
Tish Chajkowski *(Office Mgr)*
Scott Taggart *(Project Mgr & Mgr-Traffic)*
Jennifer Bodford *(Supvr-Media)*
Vishal Chandawarkar *(Sr Acct Exec)*
Kristen Andersen *(Media Planner)*
Jake Bevis *(Media Planner)*
Corinne Smith *(Sr Media Planner)*

Accounts:
GT Advanced Technologies; Nashua, NH
PPG Industries, Inc. Olympic Paints & Stains

Non-U.S. Branch

Mullen Lowe Group
(Formerly Lowe And Partners)
60 Sloane Avenue, London, SW3 3XB United Kingdom
(See Separate Listing)

Branches

303LOWE
(Formerly Lowe Hunt)
Level 2 33 Playfair Street, The Rocks, Sydney, NSW 2000 Australia
Mailing Address:
GPO Box 2005, Sydney, 2000 Australia
Tel.: (61) 2 9006 7000
Fax: (61) 2 9006 7070
Web Site: www.303lowe.com.au

Employees: 140
Year Founded: 1931

Agency Specializes In: Consumer Marketing, Digital/Interactive, Direct Response Marketing, Publicity/Promotions

Nick Cleaver *(CEO)*
Tony Dunseath *(Mng Partner & Dir-Client Svcs)*
Brad Morris *(Mng Partner)*
Derry Simpson *(Head-Strategy & Plng)*
Todd Baker *(Dir-Bus)*
Emad Khayyat *(Creative Dir)*
Scott Pritchett *(Art Dir)*
Emily Woods *(Acct Dir)*
Richard Berney *(Dir-Art & Creative)*
Lindsay Medalia *(Dir-Creative)*
Mike Naylor *(Dir-Bus)*
Sophie O'Sullivan *(Dir-Bus)*
Phil Watson *(Dir-Creative-Digital, Direct & Brand Activation)*
Charnre Terblanche *(Acct Mgr)*
Claire Yow *(Acct Mgr)*
Steven Peles *(Acct Exec)*
Bethany Thompson *(Acct Exec)*
David Biddle *(Copywriter)*
Paula Cardona *(Sr Graphic Designer)*
Daniel Clarke *(Planner)*
Tom Davey *(Designer)*
John Gault *(Copywriter)*
Dan Robinson *(Copywriter)*
Luke Sweet *(Designer)*
Matt Smith *(Sr Art Dir)*

Accounts:
New-The Art Gallery of Western Australia
Ascot Racecourse
Audi Creative, OOH, Online, Press, Print, Q7, TV
Aussie Home Loans Campaign: "Smart to Ask"
The Australian Museum Advertising, Brand Strategy
Budget Direct Advertising, CANSTAR, Campaign: "Captain Risky", Campaign: "Close Call", Car Insurance, Creative, Digital, Home Insurance, Outdoor, Print, Social, TV
Cash Converters
Cerebos
Challenger Campaign: "Balloon", Campaign: "Challenger Consumer"
New-CV Check
Edith Cowan University Campaign: "The ME Project", Campaign: "The Way University Should Be"
Enjo Campaign: "Domestic Goddess"
Fairfax Digital
Football Federation of Australia Hyundai A-League
Fujitsu Air Conditioner
Harley-Davidson Campaign: "Big Bag of Peanuts", Campaign: "Book Club", Campaign: "Test Ride Your New Life"
Hoyts
Hydro Tasmania
IKEA Campaign: "Ouija", Campaign: "Rent"
IMB Building Society
Indeed Communications Strategy, Creative
Interactive Microsite Campaign: "The Me Project"
Johnson & Johnson Baby Products, Personal Care, Splenda
Macquarie University Creative, Media
New-National Art School #SeeInspiration
New-NSW Police
Oovie
P&N Bank Brand Strategy
PepsiCo
Pernod Ricard S.A.
Perth International Arts Festival Campaign: "Totems"
Public Service Campaign: "Driver Distraction", Campaign: "Enjoy The Ride", The Office of Road Safety
Qantas Airways Limited
Red Rock Deli Campaign: "Siren"
Red Rooster Campaign: "Heroes of Hunger", Campaign: "RoosterRaps"
Royal Life Saving Society Campaign: "The Submerged Studio"
South Australia Health Campaign: "Let's Think Positive"
Southern Cross Travel Insurance Campaign: "Wedding"
Transperth
Unilever Cup-A-Soup, Digital Communication, Food, Household Products, Male Body Spray

Adventa Lowe
13 Pymonenka Str., Building 5A, 5th Floor, Kiev, 04050 Ukraine
Tel.: (380) 44 495 2860
Fax: (380) 44 495 2863
Web Site: www.lowe.com.ua

Svetlana Shynkarenko *(Mng Dir)*
Mykhailo Orlov *(Head-Creative Grp & Dir-Art)*
Vladimir Kuchmarenko *(Grp Head-Creative)*
Denis Urusov *(Grp Head-Creative)*
Olga Mamaeva *(Acct Grp Dir)*
Iryna Denyak *(Acct Dir)*
Olya Dobrotskaya *(Acct Dir)*
Elena Komendo *(Sr Acct Mgr)*
Oksana Osadchuk *(Acct Mgr)*

Accounts:
Kyivstar Ukraine Campaign: "Nullkatraz"
Nuts Trio

DLKW Lowe
60 Sloane Ave, London, SW3 3XB United Kingdom
Tel.: (44) 207 584 5033
Fax: (44) 20 7240 8739
E-Mail: info@dlkwlowe.com
Web Site: www.dlkwlowe.com

Employees: 75
Year Founded: 2000

National Agency Associations: IPA

Agency Specializes In: Advertising, Automotive, Food Service, Production (Ad, Film, Broadcast), Social Marketing/Nonprofit, T.V.

Tom Knox *(Chm)*
Erica Hoholick *(Pres)*
Rebecca Morgan *(Mng Partner-Strategy)*
James Pool *(Mng Partner)*
Dave Henderson *(Chief Creative Officer)*
Jeremy Hine *(Pres-EMEA)*
Charlie Hurrell *(Head-Acct Mgmt)*
Trudy Waldron *(Head-Brdcst)*
Zach Watkins *(Creative Dir & Copywriter)*
Kate Banks *(Acct Dir)*
Phil Cockrell *(Creative Dir)*
Jerry Hollens *(Creative Dir)*
Basil Mina *(Creative Dir)*
Chuck Monn *(Art Dir & Grp Creative Dir)*
Stephen Webley *(Creative Dir)*
Paul Wilde *(Acct Dir)*
Amber Casey *(Dir-Creative)*
Ben Mccarthy *(Dir-Art & Creative)*
James Millers *(Dir-Creative)*
David O'Hanlon *(Dir-Global Plng)*
Lovisa Silburn *(Dir-Creative)*
Rose Reynolds *(Acct Mgr)*
Rob Carew *(Designer)*
James Dawkins *(Planner)*
Luiz Filipin *(Copywriter)*
Charles Hodges *(Grp Creative Dir & Copywriter)*
Richard Kelly *(Planner)*
Ayesha Walawalker *(Planner)*
Alexandre Okada *(Global Creative Dir)*

Accounts:
The British Heart Foundation Advertising, Integrated Marketing, Online, Retail, Social Media
Calor Gas Brand Strategy, Communications, Creative, Digital, Mail Channels, Print, TV
Cif Campaign: "Burglary"
Coral Campaign: "Cornerman", Campaign: "Raising the Game", Football Jackpot
Domestos
The Electoral Commission Creative, Digital, Unmissable
GeoLotto Creative, Online, Print, TV

Legoland Windsor Campaign: "Darth", Campaign: "Mini Breaks", Theme Park
Lenovo Group Ltd. (Lead Creative Agency) Advertising, Broadcast, Campaign: "Goodweird", Digital, OOH, Print, TV, Yoga Tablet, Yoga Tablet 2 Pro
Marie Curie Cancer Care Campaign: "Symmetry", Campaign: "The Great Daffodil Appeal "
Microloan Foundation Campaign: "Big Five Christmas", Campaign: "Live Donation Billboard", Campaign: "Pennies for Life", Pennies For Life
NHS Blood & Transplant Campaign: "This Years Must Have Gift"
The Post Office Campaign: "Christmas. Sorted", Campaign: "Holiday", Creative, Digital, Experiential, Online, Outdoor, Press, TV
Remy Cointreau Group OOH, Print, Remy Martin (Global Advertising)
Samaritans Creative
SEAT Campaign: "Extreme Simulator"
Stroke Awareness
Sudocrem Creative
Unilever Adventures, Advertising, Bravery, Broadcast, Cafe Zero, Campaign: "Burglary", Campaign: "Dirt is good", Campaign: "Flavor of Home", Campaign: "For Whatever Life Throws", Campaign: "Set Them Free", Campaign: "Teachers", Campaign: "TubeStrike", Cif, Domestos, Flora, Knorr, Mud, OMO, Online, Outdoor, Persil, Persil Dual Capsules, Sure

Lowe Adventa

1st Volkonskiy pereulok 13 str 2, Moscow, Russia
Tel.: (7) 495 739 0110
Fax: (7) 495 739 4577

Anastacia Demchinskaya *(Acct Dir)*
Ekaterina Ostroglazova *(Acct Dir)*
Tatiana Porvatova *(Acct Dir)*
Nigina Abidova *(Dir-Fin)*
Mikhail Panteleev *(Dir-Creative)*
Olga Chikaleva *(Acct Mgr)*
Lyubov Demko *(Mgr-New Bus)*

Accounts:
ANNA National Center for Violence Prevention Campaign: "Don't Disguise. Call for Help."
Cityoga Campaign: "Yoga Progress Pants"
Greenpeace Campaign: "Put Them In Our Shoes"
Lukoil Campaign: "Predators"

Lowe Age

30 Terbatas Street, Riga, LV 1011 Latvia
Tel.: (371) 67502535
Fax: (371) 728 1077
E-Mail: everita.everte@loweage.lv
Web Site: mullenlowegroup.com/agencies/lowe-age-latvia

Tony Wright *(Chm)*
Hugh Doherty *(CFO)*

Lowe Age

Suvalku Str 2a, LT 03106 Vilnius, Lithuania
Tel.: (370) 5 231 0630
Fax: (370) 5 231 0600
Web Site: www.loweage.lt/index.html

Andrius Verseckas *(Mng Dir)*
Laura Bautrenaite *(Acct Mgr)*

Lowe & Partners

C Marques de Cubas 4, 28014 Madrid, Spain
Tel.: (34) 9178 93350
Fax: (34) 91 555 3622
E-Mail: jr.lopezcortijo@loweworldwide.com
Web Site: www.hello-lola.com

Employees: 70

Year Founded: 1957

National Agency Associations: AEAP

Agency Specializes In: Advertising, Automotive, Consumer Goods, Food Service, Pharmaceutical

Tony Wright *(Chm)*
Dario Albuquerque *(Assoc Dir-Creative)*

Accounts:
Banesto
Buckler
Click Seguros Campaign: "Very Very Amicable Report"
Fight Club Gym Campaign: "Mountain"
Fyne Formacion
Kiss TV Campaign: "All for the Music"
Lesac Campaign: "Soho"
Libero
Mattel Campaign: "Barbie"; "Hot Wheels"; "Scrabble"; "Monster High"
Monkey Week Campaign: "Music Beer"
Nomad Skateboards Campaign: "Very Old School", Campaign: "We Are The Same"
Scrabble
Seat
Shandy Cruzcampo
Signal Campaign: "Brush Day & Night"
TriNa
Unilever Campaign: "Magnum"; "Cornetto"; "Fruttare"; "Cafe Zero"; "Rexona"
Upload Cinema Campaign: "Hikikimori", Campaign: "Internet On A Zip"
Visionlab Campaign: "Gratu-Gratu-Ito-Ito"
Wide Campaign: "Men & Women"

Lowe & Partners

17 Radu Voda Str, Bucharest, 4 Romania
Tel.: (40) 21 301 0000
Fax: (40) 21 301 00 99
Web Site: hello-lola.com

Veronica Savanciuc *(Pres & CEO)*
Hortensia Nastase *(VP-Creative Svcs)*
Dan Costea *(Sr Dir-Art)*
Alexandru Micu *(Sr Dir-Art)*
Manuela Gogu *(Creative Dir)*
Aslinda Khanafi *(Copywriter)*
Alina Balan *(Client Svc Dir)*

Accounts:
Polyclinic Institute of Physico-Chemical Medicine Drinking Awareness
Romanian Red Cross
Stella Artois

Lowe Asia-Pacific

150 Cantonment Road 03 01 03 Cantonment Centre Blk A, Singapore, 089762 Singapore
Tel.: (65) 6849 4888
E-Mail: vikas.mehta@loweandpartners.com
Web Site: www.loweasiapacific.com

Agency Specializes In: Advertising, Brand Development & Integration

Andrew Ho *(Dir-Art)*
Sheng Jin Ang *(Dir-Creative & Art)*
Josephine Lim *(Reg Acct Mgr-Asia Pacific)*
Will Waddington *(Reg CFO-Asia Pacific)*

Accounts:
Clear Eyes Eye Gel Supplier
The Coca-Cola Company Soft Drink & Beverage Mfr & Distr
PETA

Lowe Brindfors

Birger Jarlsgatan 57C, Box 6518, 113 83 Stockholm, Sweden
Tel.: (46) 8 566 255 00
Fax: (46) 8 566 25 700
E-Mail: info@lowebrindfors.se
Web Site: www.lowebrindfors.se/

Annette Gardo *(CEO)*
Calle Sjoenell *(Chief Creative Officer)*
Rikard Linder *(Dir-Art)*
Petter Lublin *(Dir-Art & Creative)*
Patrik Reuterskiold *(Dir-Creative)*
Patrik Westerdahl *(Dir-Art)*
Kristin Tysk *(Acct Mgr)*
Martin Bartholf *(Copywriter)*
Noel Pretorius *(Designer)*

Accounts:
Alcro Paint Manufacturer
Balettakademien Campaign: "The Chewing Gum"
BMW
Electrolux Campaign: "Best in Test"
Ericsson
Folkoperan Campaign: "Julius Caesar"
Forsakringskassan
Friends Anti-Bullying, Campaign: "The Bullying Simulator"
Friskis & Svettis Campaign: "Just As Round"
General Motors
Magnum "The Pleasure Shaker" iAD, Campaign: "Pleasure Hunt 2", Campaign: "Pleasure Hunt 3"
Marbodal
Mini Cooper
Nordiska Kompaniet
Radda Barnen Campaign: "Lottery of Life"
Saab Change Perspective Campaign
Save the Children Sweden
SPP
Sveriges Annonsorer
Swedbank Campaign: "Credit Stress"
Tiger Of Sweden Campaign: "Denim Moves"
Unilever Campaign: "Magnum Pleasure Hunt Across Amsterdam", Campaign: "Pleasure Hunt 2", Magnum Ice Cream
Vattenfall Campaign: "King of the Slope"
Viktor Rydberg Gymnasium Campaign: "Passing Notes"
Yoggi

Lowe Bull

St Andrews Office Park Meadowbrook Lane, Epsom Downs Bryanston, 2021 Johannesburg, South Africa
Tel.: (27) 11 780 6300
Fax: (27) 11 780 6154
Web Site: www.lowebull.co.za

Bruce Anderson *(Exec Dir-Creative)*
Kirk Gainsford *(Exec Dir-Creative)*
Alistair Morgan *(Dir-Creative)*
Tenille Abrahams *(Art Buyer)*
Erik Salamon *(Copywriter)*

Accounts:
Association for Responsible Alcohol Use Breakfast
Axe; 2007
Bibo
Cape Times Biko, Campaign: "Illustrated Newspaper", Campaign: "You can't get any closer to the news"
Cape Town Fish Market Campaign: "Anchor"
Career Times
Castle Milk Stout
Coca-Cola Refreshments USA, Inc. Coke Light
Dulux
English Word Power
Food & Trees for Africa
Fromageries Bel
Good Fellas
GPS Creative Campaign: "Ozzy", Malema
Johnson & Johnson
Organ Donor Foundation Campaign: "Leila", Campaign: "Surfer"
Pentel
Pulp Books

SAB Miller
Stop Rhino Poaching Campaign: "your hair and nails can save the rhino"
Sunlight Anti-bacterial Dishwashing Liquid
Tetrapak
TracTec
Unilever Campaign: "Think Red", Flora Margarine, Sunlight
Universal Music
Wesbank
Wonder Bra
YOU Magazine Consumer Research

Lowe Profero China
36/F Huai Hai Plaza, 1045 Huai Hai Zhong Road, Shanghai, 200023 China
Tel.: (86) 21 3331 5198
Fax: (86) 21 2411 0661
Web Site: mullenlowegroup.com/agencies/lowe-profero-china-shanghai

Fanny Yum *(CEO)*
Jackie Xu Rui *(Mng Dir)*
Tanner Tan *(CFO & COO-Greater China)*
Norman Tan *(Chief Creative Officer-China)*
Zhenjiang Chen *(Sr Dir-Art)*
Qiang Zeng *(Sr Dir-Creative)*
Sean Hung *(Dir-Plng)*
Sue Lu *(Sr Acct Mgr)*

Accounts:
Alipay "Zheng Bang Bang", Creative
Buick
Clarks China Campaign: "Clarks Sponge Street"
The Founder Group
General Motors Corp. Campaign: "Signs Are There For A Reason"
Independent Commission Against Corruption Outdoor, Radio, TV, Website
Johnson & Johnson Johnson's Baby
K-Boxing
Markor Furniture Creative
Plan International Campaign: "Because I am a Girl"
Shanghai General Motors Buick Verano, Campaign: "HUMAN TRAFFIC SIGN"
Unilever Clear, Cornetto, Knorr, Magnum, Rexona, Solero

Lowe GGK
Mariahilfer Strasse 17, A-1060 Vienna, Austria
Tel.: (43) 6645 442 777
Fax: (43) 1 910 10 480
E-Mail: rudi.kobza@loweggk.at
Web Site: www.loweggk.at

Employees: 40
Year Founded: 1972

Rudolf Kobza *(CEO)*
Michael Kapfer-Giuliani *(Mng Dir & COO)*
Dieter Pivrnec *(Exec Dir-Creative)*

Accounts:
A Sterreichische Lotterien
Aktion Mensch Campaign: "The Vision", Exploitation Awareness
Austrian Committee for UNICEF Campaign: "Once Upon a Time"
Austrian Lotteries Ape
Cs Hospice Rennweg Cancer Hospice
CS Nursing & Socialcentre Campaign: "Art Gallery"
Debra Austria Campaign: "Balloon"
Hugyfot
ING Bank
Kronen Zeitung
Life Ball Campaign: "20th Anniversary"
ONV
Palmers Textil Campaign: "Blind Date"
Sea Shepherd Conservation Society
Unilever
Vienna Capitals

Lowe GGK
Mlynske Luhy 88, 821 05 Bratislava, Slovakia
Tel.: (421) 2 592 07611
Fax: (421) 2 592 07677
E-Mail: kontakt@loweggk.sk
Web Site: www.loweggk.sk

Marek Pajtas *(Mng Dir)*
Jozef Cerven *(Art Dir)*
Ondrej Korinek *(Dir-Creative)*
Tatiana Leporis *(Acct Mgr)*
Miroslav Nadobry *(Acct Mgr)*
Marta Sekerkova *(Acct Mgr)*
Ivana Stulcova *(Acct Mgr)*

Accounts:
Audi
Baumit
Electrolux
Facebook
Green Swan
Incon
Kontinuita
Provident Financial

Lowe Ginkgo
Joaquin Nunes 3082, Montevideo, Uruguay
Tel.: (598) 2 771 61 61
Web Site: www.facebook.com/loweginkgo

Gabriel Roman *(Pres)*
Sebastian Mir *(Gen Dir-Creative)*
Bernardo Alvarez *(Dir-Art)*
Gonzalo Lopez Balinas *(Dir-Creative)*
Luis Meyer *(Dir-Art)*
Diego Roman *(Dir-Creative)*

Accounts:
Amnesty International Campaign: "Roberto", Omar
El Pais Health & Beauty Magazine
Fundacion Logros Charity, Organic Vegetable Program
Logros Foundation Campaign: "Made in School"
Penalty Sportswear
Ramasil Unigota Glue
Renault Campaign: "Locked/Unlocked"
S.O.S. Canino Campaign: "A subject that needs your attention"
Unilever Axe Campaign: "Deniers", Knorr Soup

Lowe LDB
66/15 Ananda Coomaraswamy Mawatha (Green Path), Colombo, 3 Sri Lanka
Tel.: (94) 11 584 1741
Fax: (94) 11 268 5218
Web Site: www.lowesrilanka.com

Employees: 53

Lilamani Dias Benson *(Founder)*
Hari Krishnan *(CEO)*
Rimzan Farook *(Head-Media & Bus Dev)*
Dilshara Jayamanne *(Exec Dir-Creative)*
Anusha Fonseka *(Dir-Fin)*
Famil Izzeth *(Sr Acct Exec)*

Mullen Lowe Lintas Group
(Formerly Lowe Lintas)
Express Towers 15th Floor, Nariman Point, Mumbai, 400021 India
Tel.: (91) 22 6636 1577
E-Mail: Krishna.Iyer@loweandpartners.com
Web Site: www.mullenlowelintas.in

E-Mail for Key Personnel:
President: prem.mehta@lowemail.com

Year Founded: 1939

Arun Iyer *(Chief Creative Officer)*
Sriharsh Grandhe *(Exec VP-LinEngage)*
Danny Nathani *(VP)*
Shantanu Sapre *(Exec Dir)*
Russell John *(Sr Dir-Brand Plng)*
Priyank Pant *(Sr Dir-Brand Svcs)*
Mohit Arora *(Dir-Unit Creative)*
Ujjwal Kabra *(Dir-Creative)*
Sarvesh Raikar *(Dir-Unit Creative)*
Parag Shahane *(Dir-Creative-LinTeractive)*
Shweta Iyer *(Sr Mgr-Brand Svcs)*

Accounts:
3M Post-It
ABP News Campaign: "Sab Suntein Hain"
Active Wheel
Aditya Birla Group Campaign: "Children", Kara Skincare Wipes, UltraTech Cement
New-Aero Group
Apollo Hospitals Creative
Arvind Limited Campaign: "Hip Hop Party", Campaign: "Messed up Look", Flying Machine
Axis Bank Campaign: "Priority Banking", Campaign: "Progress on", Home Loan
Bharat Forge Ltd. Creative
Bharat Matrimony Campaign: "Career"
Bharat Petroleum Corporation Ltd.
Bharti Retail Creative, Easy Day
New-Bharti SoftBank
Bigtree Entertainment Pvt Ltd
Birla Cement Campaign: "Wall Care Putty"
Book My Show
New-Cardekho.com
Coca-Cola Refreshments USA, Inc.
Dabur India Limited Campaign: "Ajay Devgan Chatpatae", Campaign: "Happy Face", Hajmola Mint, Real Juice, Vatika-Root Strengthening & Henna Cream Conditioning Shampoos; 2009
Dollar Industries Limited Dollar Bigboss
The Economic Times Creative
ET Now Campaign: "Half Knowledge"
Expedia Inc Campaign: "Rajnee vs Chuck"
Fever 104 FM
Force Motors
FreeCharge Creative
GarudaFood
Go Air Creative
Godrej HIT Campaign: "Kill it Before it Kills You", Hit Anti Roach Gel
Greenply Industries Limited Campaign: "Always Hoenga", Seikh
New-Grofers Brand Campaign
Havells India Ltd Air Fryer, Cables, Campaign: "Bijli Baba", Campaign: "Court Marriage", Campaign: "Fans Forever - Rajesh Khanna", Campaign: "Gym", Campaign: "Old Age Home", Campaign: "Respect Women", Campaign: "Wires That Don't Catch Fire", Coffee Maker, Havells Modular Switches
Hector Beverages
The Hindu Creative
Hindustan Times Campaign: "You Read They Learn - Text book"
Hindustan Unilever Ltd Campaign: "Help a Child Reach 5", Campaign: "Real Joy of Togetherness", Campaign: "Saving Lives", Kissan, Lifebuoy, Surf Excel
HomeShop18
HT Media Limited Campaign: "Toll Free Gurgaon", Crow, Fever 104
HUL Campaign: "Cricket", Campaign: "Kid With Her Friends"
ICICI Bank Limited Prudential Life Insurance
Idea Cellular 3G, Campaign: "Deep Sleep", Campaign: "Get justice", Campaign: "No ullu banaoing. What an Idea, Sirjee!"
Infiniti Retail Limited Wedding
Just Dial
Kissan Squeezo
Lifebuoy Talc
New-Lohiya Group Gold Drop
LT Foods Ltd Campaign: "Pyaar ki Special Bhasha"
Luxor Group Campaign: "Terrorists", Luxor Marker Pens
Mahuaa Media Pvt. Ltd. Creative

Maruti Suzuki India Ltd Campaign: "Go Get the Music", Campaign: "Lost Friends", Campaign: "This Diwali ", Creative, Ertiga, Maruti Alto
Max Bupa Campaign: "Family"
Media Content & Communication Services India Pvt Ltd
Mia Jewellery
Myntra.com Creative
Nestle Eclairs, Polo
Nirula's
OLX Campaign: "Bech De", Creative, Unclutter
One Touch
Pepsodent
New-Policybazaar
Practo
RedBus.in Campaign: "Red Bus Baby"
Rexona
Starsports.com Campaign: "Carry the World Cup", Creative
Suzlon Brand Campaign, Creative
Tanishq Campaign: "A Wedding To Remember", Campaign: "Accessible Tanishq'", Campaign: "Differentiated Wedding Jeweller", Campaign: "Festive Gold Collection"
Tata Group Campaign: "Affordable Diamonds", Campaign: "As Beautiful As Your Work", Campaign: "Crafted to Inspire", Zoya
Tata Tea Campaign: "Jaago Re - Politician ", Campaign: "Power of 49", Campaign: "Shahrukh on Women's Day", Creative
Titan Industries Ltd Campaign: "Eye Sport", Campaign: "First Diamond Ring", Campaign: "Girls Bag", Campaign: "Mature is in", Campaign: "Move On", Campaign: "Move Your Ass", Fastrack, Sunglass, Watch
Unilever
Urban Ladder
U.S. POLO ASSN
Videocon Campaign: "Pollution Free", Direct-to-Home
Woodland Campaign: "Adventure Never Stops", Campaign: "No Ticket to Travel", Campaign: "Tough Naturally"
Zopper Creative

Lowe MENA

11th Fl Shatha Tower, PO Box 500242, Dubai Media City, Dubai, United Arab Emirates
Tel.: (971) 4 369 2848
Fax: (971) 4 368 8257
E-Mail: info@lowemena.com
Web Site: www.lowemena.com

Mounir Harfouche *(CEO)*
Prashant Bhor *(Grp Head-Art & Creative)*
Joseph Makhoul *(Gen Mgr)*
Mohannad Zorba *(Sr Dir-Art)*
Stephanie Pagani *(Acct Dir)*
Mark Lewis *(Dir-Creative)*
Joshua Newnes *(Copywriter)*
Sujay Nanavati *(Reg Bus Dir)*

Accounts:
Abu Dhabi Media Creative, Strategic
Al Rawabi Dairy Company Advertising, Creative, Strategic
Axe
BKP Music Campaign: "Testimonial"
Bloomingdales Campaign: "Get Dizzy Purse", Campaign: "Shirt", Campaign: "Vanishing Fast"
Dubai Multi Commodities Centre (DMCC) Creative, Strategy
Ferrero Nutella, Tic Tac
Galadari Automobiles Co Creative
Galadari Ice Cream Co Creative
HUL Campaign: "She was - He was"
Masafi
Papers Worldwide
Pizza Hut Brand & Tactical Communicatios
Red Bull Campaign: "Art of Motion, Kuwait Rising"
Roads & Transport Authority of Dubai
Unilever Campaign: "Show them the Way"

Lowe Pirella Fronzoni

Via Pantano 26, 20122 Milan, Italy
Tel.: (39) 02 85 721
Fax: (39) 02 85 72 410
E-Mail: agemzaimia@loweworldwide.com

Employees: 60
Year Founded: 1981

National Agency Associations: ASSAP

Agency Specializes In: Advertising

Diego Ricchiuti *(Pres & CEO)*
Ferdinando Galletti *(Dir-Art & Supvr)*
Rosario Giordano *(Copywriter)*

Accounts:
New-CoRePla
Foxy Asso Ultra
Levissima Campaign: "Wild Purity Button"
New-Lindt & Sprungli Lindt
Maxmara
MIBAC Campaign: "The Man Who had Never Drunk a Coffee"
New-Nestle Waters
Pirelli Truck Tyres Campaign: "Umbrellas"
The Post Internazionale
Repubblica
San Pellegrino
SEAT Altea
Toyota
New-Unilever

Lowe Pirella

Via Salaria 222, I-00198 Rome, Italy
Tel.: (39) 06 85 721
Fax: (39) 06 858 778
Web Site: mullenlowegroup.com

Daniele Dionisi *(Grp Head-Creative)*
Angelo Marino *(Dir-Art & Supvr)*
Michele Bellini *(Copywriter)*

Lowe Poland

ul Domaniewska 39, NEFRYT Building, 02-672 Warsaw, Poland
Tel.: (48) 22 312 01 00
Fax: (48) 22 848 8155
Web Site: www.lowewarsaw.com/

Employees: 100

Kinga Grzelewska *(Mng Partner & Exec Dir-Creative)*
Marcin Nowak *(Dir-Creative)*
Aleksandra Wisniewska *(Dir-Client Svc & Bus Dev)*
Anna Jagielska *(Mgr-Print & DTP-Lowe & Partners Worldwide)*

Accounts:
Kino Praha Cinema Campaign: "Erotic Film Festival"
Nidecker SA Nideccy Handmade Umbrellas
Robertkupisz.com
Unilever Knorr
Zerwijmy Lancuchy

Lowe Porta

Avda del Parque 4314 Cuidad Empresaria, Huechuraba, Santiago, Chile
Tel.: (56) 2 750 7700
Fax: (56) 2 750 7702

Agency Specializes In: Advertising

Sergio Andrade *(Art Dir)*
Gonzalo Baeza *(Creative Dir)*
Kiko Carcavilla *(Creative Dir)*
Mariano Perez *(Creative Dir)*
Luis Ramirez *(Art Dir)*
Sebastian Collantes *(Dir-Creative)*
Felipe Abufhele *(Copywriter)*
Alejandro Calleja *(Copywriter)*

Accounts:
Alcoholics Anonymous
Champion Pet Food
Cristal Cero Campaign: "Monster Angelina"
New-Energy Drink
Fundaciaon Vanculos Campaign: "Onion"
Gobierno De Chile Campaign: "Paradero"
Mademsa Campaign: "Mountain"
Opticas Place Vendome Campaign: "Clear Glasses"
TVN Campaign: "Computers"
VTR Campaign: "Mentalista"
Zoologico Metropolitano De Santiago Campaign: "Ranita Darwin"

Lowe Profero

(Formerly Profero)
Centro 3 19 Mandela St, Camden, London, NW1 0DU United Kingdom
Tel.: (44) 20 7387 2000
Fax: (44) 20 7529 8700
E-Mail: wayne.arnold@loweprofero.com
Web Site: www.loweprofero.com

Employees: 250
Year Founded: 1998

National Agency Associations: IAB-IPA

Agency Specializes In: Advertising, Brand Development & Integration, Communications, Digital/Interactive, Internet/Web Design, Media Buying Services, Strategic Planning/Research

Buster Dover *(Mng Dir)*
Phillippa Norrige *(Fin Dir)*
Wayne Arnold *(Chm-Mktg Society Southeast Asia & CEO-Global)*
Dale Gall *(CEO-UK)*
Ross Jenkins *(Global Mng Dir-Performance-London)*
Eloise Smith *(Exec Dir-Creative)*

Accounts:
ASOS
Bayer Schering Pharma
BBC Radio One
BMW (UK) Ltd. Mini; 2008
COI UK
Diageo Global Digital, Smirnoff
HTC 25 Steps to Being a Music Legend, Social Media Strategy
Johnson's Baby
Marks & Spencer AOL One Day Advent Calendar, Campaign: "Pass the Parcel"
Money Dashboard
Pepsi Europe
Pizza Hut Campaign: "Feed A Friend"
Revlon Digital
Seiko
Unilever Persil
Western Union

Lowe Rauf

159 Bangalore Town, Shahrah-e-faisal, Karachi, Pakistan
Tel.: (92) 218 247 332
Web Site: www.lowepakistan.com

Khalid Rauf *(Chm & CEO)*
Aamir Khwaja *(COO)*
Abbas Alam *(Chief Strategy Officer)*
Aamir Rauf *(Chief Digital Officer)*
Murtaza Shakir *(Exec Dir-Creative-Lahore)*
Naved Qureshi *(Acct Mgmt Dir)*
Hunaina Akhai *(Mgr-HR)*

Lowe Scanad

PO Box 34537 5th Fl The Chancery, Valley Road, Nairobi, Kenya
Tel.: (254) 20 271 0021
Fax: (254) 20 271 8772
E-Mail: bharat@scanad.com
Web Site: www.scanad.com

Betty Radier *(Mng Dir)*
Karambir Rai *(Mng Dir)*
Jason Bruckner *(Head-Creative)*
Mark Fidelo *(Head-Creative)*
Francis Karugah *(Head-Bus-Digital)*
Tony Njuguna *(Head-Creative)*
Richard Walker *(Head-Creative)*

Accounts:
Barclays
Daily Nation
Equity
Johnson & Johnson
Ken Gen
National Bank Kenya
NC Bank
Old Mutual
Serena Hotels
Tuzo

Lowe Singapore

150 Cantonment Road #03-01/03 Cantonment Centre Blk A, Singapore, 089762 Singapore
Tel.: (65) 6849 4888
Web Site: www.lowesingapore.com

Year Founded: 1978

Ranjit Jathanna *(Chief Strategy Officer)*
Erick Rosa *(Exec Creative Dir)*
Lisa Glasgow *(Reg Dir-Creative)*
Subarna Prabhakar *(Bus Dir-Global)*
Mei Cheong *(Dir-Bus)*
Andrew Ho *(Dir-Art)*
Loh Seow Khian *(Dir-Art)*
Jasmine Tan *(Dir-Creative Svc)*
Karen Vermeulen *(Dir-Art)*
Jonathan Nienaber *(Reg Mgr-Plng)*
Viraj Swaroop *(Copywriter)*

Accounts:
Asian Advertising Festival Campaign: "Tattoo Artist"
Association of Women for Action & Research
Electrolux
Gender Equality Advocacy Group Campaign: "STOP THE CYCLE"
Kirin Holdings Singapore Pte Ltd
Knorr
Ministry of Community Development, Youth & Sports of Public Guardian Creative, Mental Capacity Act, Social Media Campaign, Strategic Planning
Peta
Rinso Liquid
Samroc Colour Mixing
Save The Children Campaign: "Donate Volume"
Signal Sensitive Toothpaste
Sure Deodorant
Tupperware Brands Corporation Campaign: "Organise Chaos"
Unilever Breeze Excel, Campaign: "Dirt is good", Campaign: "Evolution", Campaign: "Stains Have Evolved", Campaign: "Whiskey", Clear, Lifebuoy Hand Wash, Omo, Persil, Rinso, Surf

Lowe SSP3

Carrera 9, 79A - 19 Piso 6, Bogota, Colombia
Tel.: (57) 1 605 8000
Fax: (57) 1 317 2591
E-Mail: Francisco.Samper@lowe-ssp3.com
Web Site: www.lowe-ssp3.com

Employees: 150

Agency Specializes In: Advertising, Automotive, Consumer Goods, Pharmaceutical

Jose Miguel Sokoloff *(Chief Creative Officer)*
Carlos Camacho *(Exec Creative Dir)*
Jaime Duque *(Exec Dir-Creative-LOWE & SSP3)*
Miguel Angel Grillo *(Creative Dir)*
Silvia Julieta Rodriguez *(Art Dir)*
Andres Estepa *(Dir-Art)*
Duvan Villegas *(Dir-Art)*
Carolina Duque *(Acct Exec)*
Daniel Baloco *(Copywriter)*
Luisito Giraldo *(Copywriter)*
Carolina Mejia *(Planner)*

Accounts:
Arturo Calle Fragrances
Arturo Calle Jeans
Bavaria
Bordados Y Calados Campaign: "Point Card"
Childfund Alliance
Clear
Colombian Ministry of Defence Campaign: "Operation Bethlehem", Campaign: "Operation Christmas", Campaign: "Rivers of Light", Campaign: "Sokoloff", Poster, Radio, TV
Colsubsidio Book Exchange Campaign: "Bounty", Campaign: "Colsubsidio Book Exchange", Campaign: "Come with a story and leave with another."
Colsubsidio English Courses Campaign: "Bang", Campaign: "Beep", Campaign: "Meow", Campaign: "Moo", Campaign: "Ouch", Campaign: "Woof", campaign: "haha"
Copa Airlines Non-Stop Flights To International Destinations
Ditopax Antacid Grills
El Espectador Newspaper
Helm Bank Campaign: "Thief"
Johnson & Johnson
Merck SD Campaign: "Bull Dog", Campaign: "Jack Russell"
Ministry of Defense Campaign: "You Are My Son"
MSD Merck Sharp & Dome Cooper Industrial Strength Disinfectant, Nopikex Repellent
Nopikex Campaign: "Mosquito", Campaign: "Spring"
OMO
Pastas La Muneca Campaign: "Cannibal", Campaign: "HOT WATER"
Pipican
Red Bull Campaign: "Maraca"
Schering Plough Campaign: "Goat"
Unilever Axe, Campaign: "Let Me In", Campaign: "The Anti Dandruff Calendar", Dry Soups, Knorr Soups

Lowe Strateus

Square d'Orleans 80 rue Taitbout, 75439 Paris, Cedex 9 France
Tel.: (33) 1 40 41 56 00
Fax: (33) 1 40 41 56 56
E-Mail: julie.gaye@lowestrateus.com
Web Site: www.lowestrateus.com

Employees: 130
Year Founded: 1989

Agency Specializes In: Advertising, Business Publications, Business-To-Business, Communications, Consulting, Consumer Marketing, Consumer Publications, Corporate Communications, Corporate Identity, Electronic Media, Environmental, Event Planning & Marketing, Financial, Government/Political, Industrial, Information Technology, Internet/Web Design, Legal Services, Media Training, Planning & Consultation, Public Relations, Publicity/Promotions, Strategic Planning/Research

Philippe Adenot *(CEO)*
Gilbert Ballester *(CFO)*
Benoit de Laurens *(VP & Gen Mgr)*
Nicolas Moniaux *(VP & Dir-Ops)*
Amandine Manget *(Grp Head-Institutional Comm)*
Marielle Gatinel *(Acct Dir)*
Anissa Alem *(Mgr-Nespresso Customer)*
Florent Kervot *(Deputy Dir)*

Accounts:
Corbis Motion
Google
KFC France Advertising
La Campagne
Miss Epil
Nestle Nespresso
Primage
Sojasun
Triballat
Unilever

Lowe Swing Communications

92-94 Tzar Assen St, 1463 Sofia, Bulgaria
Tel.: (359) 2 954 9346
Fax: (359) 2 954 1154
Web Site: www.loweswing.com

Employees: 25

Jana Sarandeva *(Owner)*
Stanimira S. Irobalieva *(Acct Dir)*
Martin Markov *(Creative Dir)*
Vladislava Mavrova *(Acct Dir)*
Neda Novachkova *(Acct Dir)*
Alexander Slavov *(Copywriter)*

Accounts:
Flirt Vodka
Mall of Sofia

Lowe Tokyo

(Formerly Lowe & Partners/Standard)
Aoyama Plaza Bldg., 2-11-3, Kita-Aoyama, Minato-Ku, Tokyo, 107-0061 Japan
Tel.: (81) 3 5475 8560
Fax: (81) 3 5475 8551
Web Site: www.lowetokyo.com/

Employees: 100
Year Founded: 1958

National Agency Associations: IAA-JAAA

Richard Nabata *(CEO)*
Masayo Sugimoto *(Dir-Plng)*

Lowe Athens

54 Kapodistriou, Filothei, 15123 Athens, Greece
Tel.: (30) 210 68 77 500
Fax: (30) 210 68 77 599
Web Site: www.loweandpartners.gr

James Nass *(CEO)*
Thanos Vlachopoulos *(CFO & Gen Dir)*
Rena Chrisoulaki *(Dir-Creative)*
Maria Fytrou *(Dir-Production)*
Panagiotis Tzempelikos *(Dir-Creative)*
Dionissis Vagourdis *(Dir-Creative)*

Accounts:
Galaxy 92 FM

Lowe

Rufino Pacific Towers 6784 Ayala Avenue, Makati City, Manila, 1200 Philippines
Tel.: (63) 2 811 1111
Fax: (63) 2 811 0130
E-Mail: francis.trillana@loweworldwide.com
Web Site: www.lowephilippines.com/

Employees: 100

Leigh Reyes *(Pres & Chief Creative Officer)*
Ochie R. Quito *(CFO & VP-Fin)*
Alan Fontanilla *(Mng Dir-Open)*
Mike Trillana *(VP-Bus Ops & Dev)*
Abi Aquino *(Exec Dir-Creative)*
Sonia Pascual *(Sr Dir-Art)*
Gerald Lim *(Acct Dir)*
Rene Dominguez *(Dir-Creative)*

Accounts:
AB Foods
Asia Brewery, Inc Cobra (Agency of Record)
The Doughnut People Campaign: "Weigh While You Pay"
Filinvest Creative, Timberland Heights
Fita Biscuits
Hit Productions Campaign: "Lorem Ipsum"
Johnson & Johnson
Mr. Quickie Shoe Repair
Plana Forma
Red Cross Philippines Campaign: "Red Cross Sos to Sms"
Red Ransom Campaign: "Billy"
Sky Flakes Cereal
SM Eco Bag
SM Prime Holdings Inc
Unilab Active Health Creative
Unilever
Weeds Season 3 DVD

Lowe
195 Empire Tower 28th Floor, South Sathorn Rd, Bangkok, Yamawa Sathorn 10120 Thailand
Tel.: (66) 2 627 7000
Fax: (66) 2670 1061
E-Mail: dan.zonmani@loweandpartners.com
Web Site: www.lowethailand.com//

Employees: 277
Year Founded: 1968

Supavadee Tantiyanon *(CEO)*
Eric Yeo *(Chief Creative Officer)*
Piya Churarakpong *(Exec Dir-Creative)*
Blair Wang *(Sr Acct Mgr)*
Gabriele Espaldon *(Reg Copywriter)*

Accounts:
BIG C Supercenter Public Co
BJC
Cerebos
Chamni's Eye Co. Campaign: "Surgery"
Clear Shampoo
Coca-Cola Refreshments USA, Inc.
Condom Awareness
Dumex
Heineken Thailand
Johnson & Johnson
Krungsri Bank Communication Campaigns, Outdoor, Print, Television
Mercedes-Benz Campaign: "Man Owl"
PlanToys Campaign: "Mom made toys my mood"
SCG Cement
Scholl Sandals
Stock Exchange of Thailand
Sun Products Canada Corporation Sunlight Liquid Detergent
Synmunkong Insurance Car Insurance, Motor Insurance
Thai Airways
Thai Asia Pacific Brewery Co Ltd Digital, Tiger Beer
Thai Health Promotion Foundation
Tiger Cement
Unilever Thai Holding Co., Ltd.; Bangkok Campaign: "100% Lucky Horoscope", Campaign: "Worst Love 1", Campaign: "Worst Love 5", Citra, Close Up, Pepsodent, Sunlight, Surf, Wall's; 1973

Lowe
4th - 6th Floors Victoria Building Jl Sultan Hasanuddin kav No 47-51, Jakarta, 12160 Indonesia
Tel.: (62) 21 725 4849
Fax: (62) 21 725 4850
Web Site: www.loweindonesia.com

Joseph Tan *(CEO)*
Roy Wisnu *(Chief Creative Officer & Copywriter)*
Din Sumedi *(Chief Creative Officer)*
Rizky Wisnu *(Grp Head-Creative & Dir-Art)*
Fanny Pardiansyah *(Grp Head-Creative & Copywriter)*
Reza Maulana *(Sr Dir-Art)*
Raufi Khaerunnisa *(Grp Acct Dir)*
Arief Mardianto *(Creative Dir)*
Vinsensius Seno *(Art Dir)*
Firman Halim *(Dir-Creative)*
Lucianne Putri *(Dir-Art)*
Bayu Adharmacila *(Mgr-Design)*
Dhannisa Nurfira *(Copywriter-Lowe & Partners Worldwide)*

Accounts:
Aulia Foundation Campaign: "Street Singer"
Axis Telecom BTL
Electrolux Washing Machine
Garuda Airlines Creative, Digital Campaign
Johnson & Johnson Baby, Clean & Clear
Lifebuoy Handwash
PT Nestle Confectionery; Jakarta, Indonesia Fox's, KitKat, Polo; 2008
PT Tempo Scan Pacific Neo Rheumacyl Liniment
Pt. Unilever Indonesia Campaign: "Chocolatier", Campaign: "Paddle Pop Max Adventures", Campaign: "Video Game", Cornetto, Lifebuoy, Magnum, Pepsodent Torsion Toothbrush, Vaseline, Wall's
QM Financial Campaign: "Stop the Debt Starter Pack"
Rinso Campaign: "Zoo, Farm"
Sampoerna
UNICEF Screen Off Campaign
Unilever Indonesia Bango, Pureit

Lowe
B2 Husrev Gerede Caddesi, Sehit Mehmet Sok No. 9, Besiktas, Istanbul, Turkey
Tel.: (90) 212 977 7700
Fax: (90) 212 285 0184
Web Site: www.loweistanbul.com/

E-Mail for Key Personnel:
President: nesteren.davutoglu@lowelintas.com

Employees: 70
Year Founded: 1944

Serife Kutlu Kirimli *(VP)*
Cuneyt Ozalp *(Grp Head-Creative)*
Emre Koc *(Dir-Art)*
Asil Yildiz *(Dir-Art)*
Ersan Develier *(Copywriter)*
Emre Lafci *(Copywriter)*
Deniz Yenihayat *(Copywriter)*

Accounts:
Adel Tape
Calve Sauces
Clear Shampoo
Continental Campaign: "SSR Runflat Tires"
Dan Antiquities Shop Campaign: "Next Owner"
Dubai Group Sigorta Kasko
Dun Remix Antiques Shop
Fizy Music Search Engine Campaign: "Music Makes You High"
Johnson & Johnson Johnson's Baby (Baby Care Products), Johnson's PH 5.5 Skin, Face & Hair Products, Neutrogena Lip Moisturizer
Nestle Polo, Polo Ice Gum
Nusret Steakhouse
OMO Detergent
SEAT
SSR Runflat Tires
Turkish Airlines
Unilever Axe Effect Project, Campaign: "Dirt Makes Good Stories", Campaign: "The White Castle", Rexona Man, Rinso Detergent
New-Volkswagen Group

Lowe
6th Floor Oxford House tai Koo Place 979 Kings Road, Quarry Bay, China (Hong Kong)
Tel.: (852) 2895 0669
Fax: (852) 2895 2897
Web Site: www.lowechina.com

Tanner Tan *(CFO & COO)*
Baiping Shen *(Chief Strategy Officer-China)*
Eddie Wong *(Chief Creative Officer)*
Norman Tan *(Exec Dir-Creative)*
Emma Chan *(Grp Dir-Creative)*
Anna Sin *(Acct Dir-Lowe Hong Kong)*
Sue Lu *(Assoc Acct Dir)*

Accounts:
999 Creative
EPS

Lowe Malaysia
2A 2nd Fl Ikano Huset 2 Jalan PJU, 7/2 Mutiara Damansara, 47800 Petaling Jaya, Selangor Malaysia
Tel.: (60) 37 801 6000
Fax: (60) 3 7494 1311
Web Site: www.lowemalaysia.com

Employees: 30

Mazuin Zin *(Mng Dir)*
Ong Bee Lin *(Grp Head-Bus & Gen Mgr)*
Gheetha James *(Head-HR)*
Sailesh Wadhwa *(Dir-Strategy Plng)*
Ilyanna Ayob *(Acct Mgr)*
Hidhir Hussin *(Brand Mgr)*

Accounts:
Ayamas Take-Home Chicken; 2008
Bank Simpanan Nasional Campaign: "Savings Through Responsible Spending", Press
Danone Dumex Marketing
F&N Dairies Tea Pot
Johnson & Johnson
Jotun Group Creative, Jotashield
Kidzcare
Land Rover Land Rover Owners Club
Maybank Fortis; 2007
Perodua
Ridsect
Spritzer Spritzer Tinge
Timeless Commitment Creative, Yogen Fruz
Toyo Tire & Rubber Co., Ltd. Strategic
Unilever Breeze

Lowe
Level 47 Bitexco Financial Tower, 02 Hai Trieu Street, Ho Chi Minh City, Vietnam
Tel.: (84) 8 391 41765
Fax: (84) 8 914 1773
Web Site: www.lowevietnam.com

Martin Copola *(Art Dir)*
Tan Phan *(Art Dir)*
Chau Tran *(Acct Dir)*
Anh Vo *(Acct Dir)*
Nisal Attenayake *(Dir-Art)*
Michael Ton *(Dir-Client Svcs)*
Quynh Lai *(Acct Exec)*
Sajju Ambat *(Planner)*
Phuong Pham *(Planner)*
Phuong Anh Tram *(Copywriter)*

Accounts:
New-5giay.vn
New-Castrol BP

Dutch Lady Campaign: "Our Milk Is Made With Love"
Masan Consumer Corp. Bottled Beverages Portfolio, Integrated Communications, Vinh Hao Mineral Water, WakeUp 247 Energy Drink
Nescafe
New-Nhat Nguyet Trading
Sunlight
Unilever Axe, Campaign: "Dirt is Good", Campaign: "Let Love Rule", Closeup, Creative, OMO, Personal Care, Home Care & Foods
Vinamilk; Vietnam

LoweFriends AS

Kobmagergade 60, DK-1150 Copenhagen, K Denmark
Tel.: (45) 33 18 71 00
Fax: (45) 33 18 71 01
E-Mail: info@lowefriends.dk
Web Site: www.lowefriends.dk

Employees: 60
Year Founded: 1939

Maria Damm Jensen *(CEO)*
Lotte Aagaard *(Partner & Dir-Art)*
Kim Juul *(Partner & Copywriter)*
Jette Nejstgaard *(Mng Dir)*
Mads Kold *(Creative Dir-Digital)*
Hans-Henrik Langevad *(Dir-Creative)*
Rasmus Foght *(Project Mgr & Mgr-Production)*
Toni Ladegaard *(Copywriter)*

Accounts:
Norregade Campaign: "Be happy in your mouth", Campaign: "Goth", Norregade Bolcher

MULLER BRESSLER BROWN

11610 Ash St Ste 200, Leawood, KS 66211
Tel.: (816) 531-1992
Fax: (816) 531-6692
E-Mail: info@mbbagency.com
Web Site: www.mbbagency.com

E-Mail for Key Personnel:
Media Dir.: Jennifer_Nugent@mbbagency.com
Production Mgr.: scott_chapman@mbbagency.com

Employees: 33
Year Founded: 1982

National Agency Associations: 4A's

Agency Specializes In: Advertising, Affluent Market, Automotive, Brand Development & Integration, Collateral, Consumer Goods, Consumer Marketing, Corporate Identity, Digital/Interactive, Financial, Food Service, Graphic Design, Health Care Services, Media Buying Services, Media Planning, Media Relations, Men's Market, Paid Searches, Point of Sale, Print, Production, Production (Ad, Film, Broadcast), Production (Print), Public Relations, Radio, Recruitment, Restaurant, Retail, Search Engine Optimization, Sponsorship, Sports Market, Travel & Tourism, Web (Banner Ads, Pop-ups, etc.)

Jim Brown *(Partner & COO)*
Denny Meier *(CFO)*
Steven Burnett *(Grp Dir-Digital)*
Leah Mountain *(Acct Dir)*
Richole Ogburn *(Sr Acct Mgr)*
Mary Cisetti *(Acct Mgr)*
Bob Waddell *(Acct Supvr)*
Emily Leeper *(Coord-Earned Media)*
Carrie Gill *(Sr Media Planner-Interactive)*
Stacy Sanderson *(Sr Media Planner)*

Accounts:
Children's Hospital of Illinois
Consumer Reports
eBay
Hallmark Hallmark Hall of Fame Division
Kansas Department of Agriculture Creative, Digital, eCommerce
The Mutual Fund Store (Agency of Record) Creative, Marketing, Strategic Direction
OSF Healthcare System; Peoria, IL Home Health, International HR, Operational HQ, Practice Groups Domestic
SFP Database Management, Digital, Digital Analytics, E-mail Marketing, Mobile/Tablet Development, Website Development
St. Teresa's Academy
University of Kansas School of Business (Agency of Record) Campaign: "It's Where Business is Going"

THE MULLIKIN AGENCY

1391 Plz Pl Ste A, Springdale, AR 72764
Tel.: (479) 750-0871
Fax: (479) 750-2685
Web Site: www.mullikinad.com

Agency Specializes In: Advertising, Internet/Web Design, Logo & Package Design, Print, Public Relations, Radio, T.V.

Randy Mullikin *(Pres)*
Julie Magnuson *(VP)*
Zach Burk *(Strategist-Social Media)*

Accounts:
The Eye Center
Pristine Blue

MULLIN/ASHLEY ASSOCIATES, INC.

306 Canon St, Chestertown, MD 21620
Tel.: (410) 778-2184
Fax: (410) 778-6640
Toll Free: (888) 662-4558
E-Mail: info@mullinashley.com
Web Site: www.mullinashley.com

Employees: 15
Year Founded: 1978

National Agency Associations: AANI-Second Wind Limited

Agency Specializes In: Business-To-Business, Health Care Services

Phillip L. Nones *(Pres)*
Marlayn D. King *(Dir-Creative)*
Stephanie Anne Robbins Edwards *(Acct Exec)*
Elizabeth Wojdyla *(Project Strategist)*

Accounts:
Benchworks
The Benedictine School for Exceptional Children
Cambridge International
Celeste Industries
Chestertown Foods
New-Choptank Transport
CPFilms
Eagle Foodservice Equipment; Smyrna, DE; 1992
Fusion UV Systems
Gainco, Inc.; Gainesville, GA Poultry Processing Equipment; 1999
Historical Society of Kent County
Hughes Associates
New-KRM Development Corporation
National Fire Protection Association
New Hanover Regional Medical Center
New-University of Maryland Shore Regional Health
W.L. Gore & Associates, Sealant Technologies Group; Elkton, MD Industrial Sealing Products; 1981
YourScan

MULTICULTURAL MARKETING RESOURCES

150 W 28th St Ste 1501, New York, NY 10001
Tel.: (212) 242-3351
Web Site: www.multicultural.com

Year Founded: 1994

Agency Specializes In: Advertising, Public Relations

Lisa Skriloff *(Pres)*

Accounts:
New-Leo Olper

MULTIPLY COMMUNICATIONS

2800 E 40th St, Minneapolis, MN 55406
Tel.: (612) 877-4500
Web Site: www.multiplycommunications.com

Year Founded: 2002

Agency Specializes In: Advertising, Brand Development & Integration, Collateral, Internet/Web Design, Media Planning, Print, Public Relations

Darren Varley *(Creative Dir)*

Accounts:
Edgewater
Financial Freedom
St. Jude Medical

MUNN RABOT LLC

33 W 17th St Fl 3, New York, NY 10011-5511
Tel.: (212) 727-3900
Fax: (212) 604-9804
Toll Free: (888) 847-0290
Web Site: www.munnrabot.com

E-Mail for Key Personnel:
Creative Dir.: peter@munnrabot.com
Media Dir.: john@munnrabot.com

Employees: 15
Year Founded: 1995

National Agency Associations: 4A's

Agency Specializes In: Advertising, Brand Development & Integration, Broadcast, Business Publications, Cable T.V., Collateral, Consulting, Consumer Marketing, Consumer Publications, Corporate Identity, Digital/Interactive, E-Commerce, Education, Electronic Media, Financial, Health Care Services, Internet/Web Design, Magazines, Media Buying Services, Medical Products, Newspaper, Newspapers & Magazines, Out-of-Home Media, Outdoor, Print, Production, Radio, Social Media, Strategic Planning/Research, T.V., Trade & Consumer Magazines, Travel & Tourism

Approx. Annual Billings: $20,000,000

Breakdown of Gross Billings by Media: Bus. Publs.: 2%; Cable T.V.: 15%; Collateral: 5%; Consumer Publs.: 3%; Internet Adv.: 8%; Mags.: 5%; Newsp.: 20%; Outdoor: 10%; Radio: 15%; T.V.: 15%; Trade & Consumer Mags.: 2%

Orson Munn *(CEO & Partner)*
Rachel Lubertine *(Partner & COO)*
Peter Rabot *(Partner & Dir-Creative)*
Sara Criss *(VP & Mgmt Supvr)*
Garrett Lubertine *(Sr Dir-Art)*
Val Junker *(Dir-IT)*
Robin Peskin *(Dir-Media)*
Clarisa Garcia *(Media Planner)*

Accounts:
Bessemer Trust; New York, NY; 2007
Brigham & Women's Hospital; Boston, MA; 2009

Morgan Stanley Children's Hospital; New York, NY; 1999
New York Institute of Technology; Westbury, NY; New York, NY; 2002
NYU Langone Medical Center Campaign: "Made for New York", Campaign: "Melting Pot", Campaign: "Winter Athletes", Digital, Langone Orthopedics Program, Outdoor, Print
Weill Cornell Physicians Organization; New York, NY; 2005

MUNROE CREATIVE PARTNERS

1435 Walnut St Ste 600, Philadelphia, PA 19102-3219
Tel.: (215) 563-8080
Fax: (215) 563-1270
E-Mail: jmunroe@munroe.com
Web Site: www.munroe.com

E-Mail for Key Personnel:
President: jmunroe@munroe.com

Employees: 28
Year Founded: 1989

Agency Specializes In: Advertising, Collateral, Digital/Interactive, Graphic Design, Production

Approx. Annual Billings: $10,000,000

Frank V. Pileggi *(Partner & Exec VP)*
Michael Cavallaro *(Sr Dir-Art)*
Sara Mcmillan *(Dir-Content Strategy)*
Kathy Valusek *(Dir-Art)*
Lauren Ciallella *(Mgr-Creative)*
Harry Volpe *(Mgr-Production)*
Dave Meyers *(Copywriter)*

Accounts:
Allen & Company
Avon
CETEC
Concord Watches
Cushman & Wakefield
Hill International
JP Morgan Chase
Met Life
Moinian Group
Pennsylvania Business Bank
PJM
SEI Corp.
Strohl Systems
Sunoco
Swiss Army Brands
Turano Baking Company
United Way

Branch

Munroe Creative Partners

711 3rd Ave 16th Fl, New York, NY 10017
Tel.: (212) 284-7683
Fax: (212) 284-7684
E-Mail: jmunroe@munroe.com
Web Site: www.munroe.com

Employees: 15

Agency Specializes In: Advertising, Sponsorship

Judy Munroe *(CEO)*
Earl Gansky *(Partner & CFO)*
Melisa Polazzi *(Sr Dir-Art)*
Darren Stueber *(Sr Dir-Art)*
Emily Blumette *(Assoc Dir-Art)*
Lauren Ciallella *(Mgr-Creative)*
Lauren Gonzalez *(Acct Exec)*

Accounts:
Campbell Soup Company
Clemens Construction Company
ESPN
Furr's Buffet & Furr's Fresh Buffet
Hill International
LibertyPointe Bank
Mercedes Benz of Greenwich
NBC Universal
Pennsylvania Academy of the Fine Arts
The Switzer Group

MUNSON GROUP

4615 Parliament Dr Ste 103, Alexandria, LA 71303
Tel.: (318) 445-5966
Web Site: www.themunsongroup.com

Agency Specializes In: Advertising, Brand Development & Integration, Broadcast, Collateral, Crisis Communications, Internet/Web Design, Outdoor, Public Relations, Radio, T.V.

Robin Cosenza *(Dir-PR)*
Michelle Corley *(Designer)*

Accounts:
16th Judicial District Attorney
Coalition of Community Groups
Hixson Autoplex
LSU Medical School
Washington Economic Development Foundation

MURDOCH MARKETING

217 E 24th St Baker Lofts Ste 220, Holland, MI 49423
Tel.: (616) 392-4893
E-Mail: results@murdochmarketing.com
Web Site: www.murdochmarketing.com

Agency Specializes In: Advertising, Brand Development & Integration, Broadcast, Corporate Identity, Internet/Web Design, Media Planning, Outdoor, Print, Strategic Planning/Research

Eddie Bullinger *(Partner & Dir-Art)*
Nancy Murdoch *(Partner)*
Tom Murdoch *(Partner)*
Stephanie Browne *(Mgr-Content & Client Support)*

Accounts:
Cottage Home

MURPHYEPSON, INC.

151 E Nationwide Blvd, Columbus, OH 43215
Tel.: (614) 221-2885
E-Mail: mail@murphyepson.com
Web Site: www.murphyepson.com

Year Founded: 1989

Agency Specializes In: Advertising, Crisis Communications, Media Relations, Print, Public Relations, Social Media

Kathleen Murphy *(Pres)*
Leah Salyers *(Dir-Art)*
Stephanie Tresso *(Acct Mgr)*
Lindsey Kobelt *(Acct Exec & Copywriter)*

Accounts:
City of Columbus
Finance Fund
Ohio SADD
Southern Gateway

MUSE COMMUNICATIONS

9543 Culver Blvd 2nd Fl, Culver City, CA 90232
Tel.: (310) 945-4100
Fax: (310) 945-4110
E-Mail: info@museusa.com
Web Site: www.museusa.com

E-Mail for Key Personnel:
President: shelley@museusa.com

Employees: 27
Year Founded: 1986

National Agency Associations: 4A's-THINKLA

Agency Specializes In: Advertising, African-American Market, Asian Market, Automotive, Bilingual Market, Brand Development & Integration, Broadcast, Business Publications, Business-To-Business, Cable T.V., Collateral, Communications, Consulting, Consumer Marketing, Corporate Identity, Direct Response Marketing, E-Commerce, Education, Electronic Media, Entertainment, Environmental, Event Planning & Marketing, Financial, Food Service, Government/Political, Graphic Design, Health Care Services, High Technology, Hispanic Market, Internet/Web Design, Leisure, Logo & Package Design, Magazines, Media Buying Services, Merchandising, New Product Development, Newspaper, Newspapers & Magazines, Out-of-Home Media, Outdoor, Over-50 Market, Planning & Consultation, Point of Purchase, Point of Sale, Print, Production, Public Relations, Publicity/Promotions, Recruitment, Restaurant, Retail, Seniors' Market, Sponsorship, Sports Market, Strategic Planning/Research, Syndication, T.V., Teen Market, Travel & Tourism

Shelley Yamane *(Pres & Chief Strategic Officer)*
Jo Melvin Muse *(Chm/CEO-Holly Springs-Mississippi)*
Benton Wong *(Principal)*
Michael McCallum *(Sr Dir-Creative)*
Gina Cadres *(Acct Dir)*
Aireka Muse *(Copywriter)*

Accounts:
American Honda Motor Co., Inc. Honda Automobiles
California State Lottery
Google
Honda Campaign: "Meant For You. Fit For You."
Mattel

MUSTACHE AGENCY

93 St Marks Pl 4th Fl, New York, NY 10009
Tel.: (212) 226-3493
E-Mail: info@mustacheagency.com
Web Site: www.mustacheagency.com

Year Founded: 2010

Agency Specializes In: Advertising, Content, Digital/Interactive, Social Media

John Limotte *(Founder & Exec Dir)*
Jeff Cambron *(Principal & Dir-Mktg)*
Todd Griffin *(Principal & Dir-Accounts & Bus Dev)*
Will Bystrov *(Dir-Creative-Post-Production)*

Accounts:
New-Climate Reality Project Campaign: "World's Easiest Decision"
Skinceuticals
Visit Holland

MUTT INDUSTRIES

215 SE Morrison Studio 2004, Portland, OR 97214
Tel.: (503) 841-5427
E-Mail: info@muttindustries.com
Web Site: www.muttindustries.com

Agency Specializes In: Advertising, Sponsorship

Steve Luker *(Partner & Dir-Creative)*
Scott Cromer *(Partner)*
Cindy Wade *(CFO & Gen Mgr)*
Adam Long *(Dir-Art, Dir & Editor)*
Steven Birch *(Dir-Art)*
Seth Conley *(Dir-Art)*
Erin M. Kelley *(Strategist-Digital)*

Accounts:
Adidas
Ford Motor Company Ford Fiesta, Ford Explorer
GAP 1969 Jeans
Gerber
L.A. Dodgers
NIKE
Paciugo
Tampa Bay Buccaneers

MVC

14724 Ventura Blvd Ste 505, Ventura, CA 91403
Tel.: (818) 282-2698
E-Mail: info@mvcagency.com
Web Site: www.mvcagency.com

E-Mail for Key Personnel:
President: jason@mvcagency.com

Employees: 7
Year Founded: 2000

Agency Specializes In: Advertising, Arts, Bilingual Market, Brand Development & Integration, Broadcast, Business-To-Business, Cable T.V., Catalogs, Collateral, Communications, Consumer Marketing, Consumer Publications, Corporate Communications, Corporate Identity, Cosmetics, Digital/Interactive, Direct-to-Consumer, E-Commerce, Education, Electronic Media, Email, Entertainment, Environmental, Exhibit/Trade Shows, Experience Design, Fashion/Apparel, Food Service, Graphic Design, Health Care Services, Hispanic Market, Identity Marketing, In-Store Advertising, Information Technology, Integrated Marketing, Internet/Web Design, Logo & Package Design, Luxury Products, Magazines, Media Planning, Medical Products, Merchandising, Multicultural, Multimedia, New Technologies, Newspaper, Newspapers & Magazines, Outdoor, Package Design, Planning & Consultation, Podcasting, Point of Purchase, Point of Sale, Print, Production, Production (Ad, Film, Broadcast), Production (Print), Promotions, Publishing, Search Engine Optimization, Social Marketing/Nonprofit, Strategic Planning/Research, T.V., Trade & Consumer Magazines, Transportation, Urban Market, Viral/Buzz/Word of Mouth, Web (Banner Ads, Pop-ups, etc.)

Approx. Annual Billings: $1,000,000

Breakdown of Gross Billings by Media: Collateral: $250,000; Graphic Design: $250,000; Logo & Package Design: $250,000; Video Brochures: $250,000

Jason Pires *(Founder, CEO & Dir-Creative)*
Marioly Molina *(Co-Founder & Dir-Art)*
Nicholas Castelli *(Dir-Mktg)*

Accounts:
Coda Electric
Computer Sciences Corporation; Los Angeles, CA IT
Diesel
Jessica Cosmetics; Los Angeles, CA Cosmetics
Westcoast Ear Nose Throat Medical

MVNP

999 Bishop St 24th Fl, Honolulu, HI 96813-4429
Tel.: (808) 536-0881
Fax: (808) 529-6208
E-Mail: ideas@mvnp.com
Web Site: www.mvnp.com

E-Mail for Key Personnel:
Media Dir.: lkimura@mvnp.com
Production Mgr.: bsoares@mvnp.com

Employees: 92
Year Founded: 1946

National Agency Associations: 4A's

Agency Specializes In: Advertising, Broadcast, Collateral, Direct Response Marketing, Event Planning & Marketing, Internet/Web Design, Multimedia, Public Relations, Publicity/Promotions

Approx. Annual Billings: $28,000,000

Breakdown of Gross Billings by Media: Brdcst.: $1,120,000; D.M.: $840,000; Fees: $5,320,000; Internet Adv.: $1,680,000; Mags.: $3,920,000; Newsp.: $4,480,000; Print: $2,240,000; Production: $1,400,000; Radio: $1,680,000; T.V.: $5,320,000

Nick Ng Pack *(Owner)*
Susie Kim *(Producer-Brdcst)*
Lori Kimura *(Dir-Media)*
Susan Moss *(Dir-HR)*
Kris Tanahara *(Dir-PR)*
Dave Daniels *(Assoc Dir-Creative)*
Mike Wagner *(Assoc Dir-Creative)*

Accounts:
Ala Moana Center; Honolulu, HI; 2001
Alexander & Baldwin; Honolulu, HI; 1971
First Hawaiian Bank; Honolulu, HI; 1969
First Insurance Company of Hawaii, Ltd
General Growth Properties
Hawaii Tourism Authority Campaign: "The Hawaiian Islands"; 2003
Hawaii Visitors & Convention Bureau; 2000
Hawaiian Telcom
Ke Kailani; 2004
Matson Navigation; 1998
McDonald's of Hawaii; Honolulu, HI Quick Service Restaurant; 1997
Starwood Hotels & Resorts French Polynesia; 2000
Starwood Hotels & Resorts Hawaii; Honolulu, HI; 1995

MVP COLLABORATIVE

1751 E Lincoln Ave, Madison Heights, MI 48071
Tel.: (248) 591-5100
Fax: (248) 591-5199
E-Mail: info@mvpcollaborative.com
Web Site: www.mvpcollaborative.com

Employees: 25
Year Founded: 1980

Agency Specializes In: Business-To-Business, Event Planning & Marketing, Planning & Consultation, Public Relations, Publicity/Promotions, Strategic Planning/Research

Karl Siegert *(COO)*
Jeff Kirk *(VP & Acct Dir)*
Crystal Alexander *(Controller)*
Sharon Ricketts *(Exec Acct Dir-Audi of America)*
Allison Piper *(Sr Acct Exec)*

Accounts:
Audi of America, Inc. Experiential Marketing
Pfizer

MW MARKETING GROUP

7831 Meadowood Dr, Hudsonville, MI 49426
Tel.: (616) 308-1572
Fax: (616) 669-0613
E-Mail: info@mw-mg.com
Web Site: www.mwmarketinggroup.com

Employees: 4
Year Founded: 2003

Agency Specializes In: Advertising, Brand Development & Integration, Business Publications, Communications, Consulting, Corporate Communications, Corporate Identity, Direct Response Marketing, Electronic Media, Event Planning & Marketing, Graphic Design, Industrial, Internet/Web Design, Logo & Package Design, Magazines, Media Buying Services, Multimedia, Newspapers & Magazines, Planning & Consultation, Print, Public Relations, Publicity/Promotions, Radio, Sales Promotion, Strategic Planning/Research, T.V., Trade & Consumer Magazines

Mark Weber *(Owner)*

Accounts:
RoMan Manufacturing; Grand Rapids, MI; 2004

MWH ADVERTISING, INC.

47 Hulfish St Ste 400, Princeton, NJ 08542
Tel.: (609) 430-9925
Fax: (609) 945-2298
E-Mail: martin@mwhads.com
Web Site: www.mwhads.com

Employees: 6
Year Founded: 1997

Agency Specializes In: Advertising, Business Publications, Business-To-Business, Collateral, Corporate Communications, Corporate Identity, Digital/Interactive, E-Commerce, Financial, Graphic Design, Internet/Web Design, Logo & Package Design, Media Buying Services, Media Planning, Multimedia, Print, Production, Real Estate, Retail, Strategic Planning/Research, Trade & Consumer Magazines, Web (Banner Ads, Pop-ups, etc.)

Approx. Annual Billings: $2,250,000

Martin W. Hilson *(Owner)*

Accounts:
XL Capital
XL Insurance
XL RE

THE MX GROUP

(Formerly MarketSense)
7020 High Grove Blvd, Burr Ridge, IL 60527-7599
Tel.: (630) 654-0170
Toll Free: (800) 827-0170
E-Mail: sales@themxgroup.com
Web Site: www.themxgroup.com

E-Mail for Key Personnel:
President: amahler@themxgroup.com

Employees: 100
Year Founded: 1988

National Agency Associations: BMA-DMA

Agency Specializes In: Advertising, Below-the-Line, Brand Development & Integration, Business Publications, Business-To-Business, Collateral, Communications, Consulting, Content, Corporate Communications, Corporate Identity, Customer Relationship Management, Digital/Interactive, Direct Response Marketing, Direct-to-Consumer, E-Commerce, Electronic Media, Electronics, Email, Event Planning & Marketing, Exhibit/Trade Shows, Graphic Design, High Technology, Hospitality, Industrial, Information Technology, Integrated Marketing, Internet/Web Design, Logo & Package Design, Market Research, Media Buying Services, Media Planning, Media Relations, Multimedia, Paid Searches, Pharmaceutical, Planning & Consultation, Podcasting, Print, Production, Production (Print), Promotions, Public Relations, Publicity/Promotions, Sales Promotion, Search Engine Optimization, Strategic Planning/Research, Technical Advertising, Telemarketing, Viral/Buzz/Word of Mouth, Web (Banner Ads, Pop-ups, etc.)

Approx. Annual Billings: $13,000,000

Andrew S. Mahler *(Founder & CEO)*
Kevin Coe *(VP-Digital Dev)*
Kellie De Leon *(Acct Dir)*
Alex Fraser *(Sr Acct Mgr)*
Megan Ryan *(Sr Acct Mgr)*
Samantha Krause *(Acct Mgr)*
Laura Prochaska *(Acct Supvr)*
Anna Burns Whalen *(Sr Recruiter)*

Accounts:
Abbott Laboratories; 2006
Anvil International; 2003
Bosch-Rexroth Drives & Controls; 1998
Catamaran; 2011
Cision; 2007
Cox Automotive AutoTrader Group, DealShield, VinSolutions, vAuto; 2006
Dyson Airblade; 2012
GE Intelligent Platforms; 2010
JMC Steel; 2011
MAVERICK Technologies; 2000
Siemens; 2009
Tempur & Sealy Corporation Posturepedic, Stearns & Foster, Tempur-pedic; 2002

MXM
(Formerly Genex)
800 Corporate Pointe Ste 100, Culver City, CA 90230
Tel.: (424) 672-9500
Fax: (310) 736-2001
E-Mail: kristi.vandenbosch@mxm.com
Web Site: meredithxceleratedmarketing.com/

Employees: 150
Year Founded: 1995

Agency Specializes In: Automotive, Business-To-Business, Consulting, Consumer Marketing, Digital/Interactive, E-Commerce, Electronic Media, Entertainment, Financial, Food Service, Graphic Design, Health Care Services, High Technology, Information Technology, Sponsorship

Approx. Annual Billings: $11,500,000

Kristi VandenBosch *(Chief Digital Officer & Sr VP)*
Jeff Anulewicz *(Exec Dir-Strategy)*
Calum Handley *(Exec Dir-Creative)*
Veronica Orzech *(Acct Dir)*
Hillary Jackson Donovan *(Dir-Social Media Engagement)*
Lindsay Gsell *(Dir-Social Engagement)*
Maggie Pitts *(Dir-Engagement & Insights)*
Sonja Spence *(Dir-Engagement & Insights)*
Maria Goycoolea *(Supvr-Engagement & Insights)*
Xiyan Qian *(Sr Media Planner)*

Accounts:
Kimberly-Clark
Lexus
Mamco
Mondelez International, Inc.
Nestle Purina PetCare Digital
Toyota

MXM MOBILE
(Formerly The Hyperfactory (USA) Inc.)
805 3rd Ave 23rd Fl, New York, NY 10022
Tel.: (212) 499-2000
E-Mail: mobile@mxm.com
Web Site: meredithxceleratedmarketing.com

Year Founded: 2001

Agency Specializes In: Advertising, Sponsorship

Dawn Furey *(Mng Dir & Sr VP)*
Mark Bieschke *(CTO)*
Tony Platt *(Chief Creative Officer)*
Rich Berenson *(Chief Bus Dev Officer-MXM)*
Kristi Vandenbosch *(Chief Digital Officer)*
David Brown *(Exec VP)*
Patricia Lyle *(Sr VP & Gen Mgr-MXM Analytics)*
Katherine Kress *(Sr VP & Exec Grp Dir)*
Doug Stark *(Sr VP & Exec Grp Dir)*
Jeff Anulewicz *(Exec Dir-Strategy)*
Calum Handley *(Exec Dir-Creative)*
Howard Hunt *(Exec Dir-Client Svc)*
Scott Lelo *(Dir-Mobile Analytics)*
Steve Pope *(Dir-HR MXM)*

Accounts:
Mondelez International, Inc.

MY BLUE ROBOT
1717 Cypress Trace Dr, Safety Harbor, FL 34695
Tel.: (727) 637-4251
E-Mail: info@mybluerobot.com
Web Site: www.mybluerobot.com

Agency Specializes In: Advertising, Brand Development & Integration, Digital/Interactive, Graphic Design, Internet/Web Design

Chris Nesci *(Pres & Exec Dir-Creative)*
Brook Eschenroeder *(Dir-Creative)*
Christina Rouch *(Dir)*
Rob Stainback *(Dir-Interactive Creative)*
Victoria Casal *(Copywriter-Digital)*

Accounts:
Olian Technologies
Palm Ceia Village Health Market & Cafe
Roy & Shannon Burnett

MY CREATIVE TEAM, INC.
13315 Willow Breeze Ln, Huntersville, NC 28078
Tel.: (704) 464-3679
Fax: (704) 895-0887
Web Site: www.my-creativeteam.com

Year Founded: 2006

Agency Specializes In: Advertising, Email, Internet/Web Design, Media Buying Services, Media Planning, Production (Ad, Film, Broadcast), Public Relations, Social Media

Brant Waldeck *(Partner & Dir-Creative)*
Harry Hoover *(Partner & Strategist-Brand)*
Liz Labunski *(Dir-Art)*
Todd Osborne *(Sr Designer)*

Accounts:
Personna Industrial

MYJIVE INC
1000 NC Music Factory Blvd Ste C7, Charlotte, NC 28206
Tel.: (704) 334-4615
Fax: (888) 726-5909
E-Mail: charlotte@myjive.com
Web Site: www.myjive.com

Agency Specializes In: Advertising, Brand Development & Integration, Content, Digital/Interactive, Internet/Web Design, Media Buying Services, Print, Search Engine Optimization, Social Media, Strategic Planning/Research

Albert Banks *(Partner & Mng Dir)*
Ron Edelen *(Partner & Dir-Design)*
John Howard *(Sr Dir-Interactive Art)*
Kenya Madyun *(Sr Producer-Mktg)*
Michael Chatten *(Dir-Emerging Tech)*
Mark Conachan *(Dir-Creative)*
Brett McCoy *(Dir-Engagement)*
Bonnie Sugrue *(Acct Mgr)*
Elliott Antal *(Mgr-Digital Mktg)*
Brian Conlon *(Mgr-New Bus Dev)*

Accounts:
Project L.I.F.T Digital, Social Media, Traditional
Regal Marine Industries, Inc.

MYN COLLECTIVE
39 W 14th St Ste 408, New York, NY 10011
Tel.: (212) 675-6582
Fax: (888) 383-9112
E-Mail: inquiries@myngroup.com
Web Site: www.myngroup.com

Agency Specializes In: Advertising, Brand Development & Integration, Communications, Digital/Interactive, Media Relations

Michelle Ng *(VP-Creative & Strategic Brand Dev)*
Rose Reynoso *(Acct Exec)*

Accounts:
PU3

MYRIAD TRAVEL MARKETING
6033 W Century, Manhattan Beach, CA 90045
Tel.: (310) 649-7700
E-Mail: lax@myriadmarketing.com
Web Site: www.myriaddestinations.com

Employees: 30
Year Founded: 1987

Agency Specializes In: Advertising, Event Planning & Marketing, Exhibit/Trade Shows, Public Relations, Sales Promotion, Travel & Tourism

Revenue: $25,000,000

Al Merschen *(Pres & CEO)*
Julie Averay *(VP-Representation)*
Michael Price *(VP-Mktg)*
Maria Rivera *(Sr Acct Mgr)*
Mollie Mckenzie *(Acct Mgr)*
Shirley Tu *(Mgr-Mktg)*
Katie Rees *(Acct Exec)*
Lauren Winn *(Acct Exec-Custom Publ)*
Stephanie Morrow *(Acct Coord)*
Mia Seidner *(Coord-Publ)*

Accounts:
Australia's Northern Territory Tourist Office
British Virgin Islands
Costa Mesa CVB
Cunard
EVA Air
Fiji Airways
German National Tourist Office
Hawaii CVB
The Kenya Tourism Board
Kyoto
Macau Government Tourist Organization
Melbourne CVB
Papua New Guinea Tourism
Rio CVB
Samoa Tourism Authority
Seawings UAE
Signature Travel Network
Taiwan Tourism

Branch

Myriad Travel Marketing
501 5th Ave Ste 1101, New York, NY 10017-7805
Tel.: (646) 366-8162
Fax: (646) 366-8170
E-Mail: nyc@myriadmarketing.com
Web Site: www.myriaddestinations.com

Employees: 20

Agency Specializes In: Advertising, Travel & Tourism

Al Merschen *(Mng Partner)*
Michael Price *(VP & Dir-Mktg)*
Julie Averay *(VP-Representation)*
Jennifer Goger Eun *(Acct Mgr)*
Brian Kagan *(Acct Mgr)*
Annalie Baltazar-Rau *(Mgr-Fin)*
Mackenzie Griffin *(Acct Exec)*
Shannon Troy *(Acct Exec)*

Accounts:
Eagle Creek
Signature Travel Network
Voyages

MZ GROUP
(Formerly HC International)
1001 Ave of the Americas Ste 411, New York, NY 10018
Tel.: (212) 813-2975
Web Site: www.mzgroup.com

Employees: 10

Agency Specializes In: Investor Relations

Matthew Hayden *(Mng Partner-North America)*
Ted Haberfield *(Pres-MZ North America)*
Greg Falesnik *(Sr VP)*
Derek Gradwell *(Sr VP-Natural Resources)*
Debra Juhl *(Dir-Ops)*
Pam Smith *(Sr Mgr-Acctg)*

Accounts:
China Green Agriculture Inc.
China Integrated Energy Inc.
Sino Clean Energy Inc.

THE N GROUP
(Formerly Nordensson Group LLC)
283 N Stone Ave # 101, Tucson, AZ 85701-1213
Tel.: (520) 325-7700
Fax: (520) 322-0123
E-Mail: jnordensson@thengroup.com
Web Site: www.thengroup.com

E-Mail for Key Personnel:
President: jnordensson@thengroup.com

Employees: 5
Year Founded: 2005

Agency Specializes In: Financial, Health Care Services, High Technology, Public Relations, Travel & Tourism

Approx. Annual Billings: $2,500,000

Jeff Nordensson *(Pres)*

Accounts:
Adobe Plastic Surgery
American Heart Association
American Red Cross
Arizona Arthritis Center
Bank of Tucson
The Janzen Wahl Group
Pima County Board of Supervisors
Sand & Sea Capital
Sunrise Bank of Albuquerque
Tucson Electric Power
UApresents
Yuma Community Bank

NAARTJIE MULTIMEDIA
(Formerly Basset & Becker Advertising)
1300 6th Ave, Columbus, GA 31901-2275
Tel.: (706) 327-0763
Fax: (706) 323-1147
E-Mail: someone@beginswithN.com
Web Site: naartjiemultimedia.com/

Employees: 10
Year Founded: 1986

Agency Specializes In: Business-To-Business, Exhibit/Trade Shows, Government/Political, Graphic Design, Internet/Web Design, Media Buying Services, Multimedia, Restaurant, Sales Promotion, Travel & Tourism

Approx. Annual Billings: $4,000,000

Breakdown of Gross Billings by Media: Bus. Publs.: $200,000; Cable T.V.: $50,000; Mags.: $50,000; Newsp.: $550,000; Other: $150,000; Outdoor: $125,000; Production: $450,000; Pub. Rels.: $20,000; Radio: $125,000; T.V.: $800,000

Josh Becker *(Acct Exec & Supvr-Production)*

Accounts:
City of Columbus
Columbus Bank & Trust Company; Columbus, GA
Columbus Carpet Mills Store
Columbus Convention & Visitors Bureau; Columbus, GA
Columbus State University
Columbus Technical Institute
Country's Barbeque
McMullen Funeral Home
Part IV Restaurants
Phenix Food Service
Presidential Pathways Travel Assoc.
Ronald McDonald House of West Georgia
Synovus Financial Corp.; Columbus, GA
Valley Hospitality
W.C. Bradley Real Estate; Columbus, GA

NADA GLOBAL
931 S Coast Hwy, Laguna Beach, CA 92651
Tel.: (949) 485-6575
E-Mail: hello@nadaglobal.com
Web Site: www.nadaglobal.com

Year Founded: 2004

Agency Specializes In: Advertising, Brand Development & Integration, Internet/Web Design, Print

Daniel Williams-Goldberg *(Founder & CEO)*
Guady Pleskacz *(Dir-Client Rels)*
Stefanie Williams-Goldberg *(Dir-Strategic Mktg)*
Melanie De Arakal *(Mgr-SEO & Social Media)*
Claire Deberg *(Lead Editor)*

Accounts:
Great Lakes Educational Consulting
Green Apple Lunchbox
HarrisKramer Associates
NTS, Inc.
SB Electrical Services, Inc.

NADI LLC
406 E State St, Rockford, IL 61104
Tel.: (815) 962-7090
E-Mail: contact@nadicreative.com
Web Site: www.nadicreative.com

Year Founded: 2009

Agency Specializes In: Advertising, Brand Development & Integration, Collateral, Corporate Identity, Digital/Interactive, Graphic Design, Internet/Web Design, Package Design, Search Engine Optimization, Social Media

Aaron Hotlen *(Owner)*
Bridget Finn *(Acct Exec)*

Accounts:
City of Rockford
Custom Gear & Machine Inc
Knife-Xpress

NAIL COMMUNICATIONS
63 Eddy St, Providence, RI 02903
Tel.: (401) 331-6245
Fax: (401) 331-2987
E-Mail: jcrisp@nail.cc
Web Site: www.nail.cc

E-Mail for Key Personnel:
Creative Dir.: bgross@nail.cc

Employees: 22
Year Founded: 1998

National Agency Associations: 4A's

Agency Specializes In: Advertising, Automotive, Brand Development & Integration, Broadcast, Business-To-Business, Children's Market, Collateral, Commercial Photography, Communications, Consumer Marketing, Consumer Publications, Corporate Communications, Corporate Identity, Digital/Interactive, Direct Response Marketing, E-Commerce, Electronic Media, Entertainment, Fashion/Apparel, Graphic Design, Health Care Services, High Technology, In-Store Advertising, Industrial, Internet/Web Design, Logo & Package Design, Point of Sale, Production, Public Relations, Radio, Strategic Planning/Research, Teen Market, Travel & Tourism

Approx. Annual Billings: $20,000,000

Jeremy Crisp *(Mng Partner)*
Alec Beckett *(Partner-Creative)*
Jeanette Palmer *(Head-Client Svcs)*
Lizzi Weinberg *(Head-Production)*
Briana Masterson *(Producer-Digital)*
Emily Sherman Bucci *(Sr Acct Mgr)*
Stephen Fitch *(Acct Mgr)*
Myles Dumas *(Sr Designer)*
Dana Haddad *(Designer)*

Accounts:
Aryzta (Agency of Record) Digital, Outdoor, Print, Social, TV
Gore Tex
Just Born Mike & Ike, Website
Lifespan Campaign: "15,000" Winter Olympics 2014
Lightlife Foods Digital, Social Media
Mystic Aquarium Creative
New Balance Campaign: "Nobody Runs Like Boston", Fresh Foam Zante, Online, Out-of-Home Advertising, Social Media
Popcorn, Indiana (Agency of Record) Marketing, Out-of-Home
Rhode Island Community Food Bank
Sea Research Foundation Creative
Spray Cake
Stonyfield Campaign: "#CheatOnGreek", Campaign: "Confessions", Creative, Digital, Marketing, Petite Creme Yogurt, Social
Vibram FiveFingers, YouAreTheTechnology.com

NANCY BAILEY & ASSOCIATES, INC.
220 E 42Nd St, New York, NY 10017
Tel.: (212) 421-6060
Fax: (678) 352-9222
Web Site: www.baileylicensing.com

Employees: 13
Year Founded: 1982

Agency Specializes In: Communications, Consulting, Graphic Design, Local Marketing, Product Placement, Strategic Planning/Research

Nancy Bailey *(Chm)*
Josephine Law *(Mng Dir)*
Oliver Herzfeld *(Chief Legal Officer & Sr VP)*
Rachel Terrace *(Sr VP-Brand Mgmt)*

Lisa Reiner *(Mng Dir-Europe & Asia Pacific)*
Nicole Desir *(VP-Brand Mgmt & Exec Dir-Blueprint)*
Frances Alvarez *(VP)*
Celia Asprea *(VP-HR)*
Debra Restler *(VP-Bus Dev & Mktg)*
Louise French *(Assoc VP-Mktg & Bus Dev-Intl)*

Accounts:
Coppertone
Covergirl
Energizer
Eveready
Febreze
Mr. Clean
Nestle Nesquik
Tide
Travelocity

NANCY J. FRIEDMAN PUBLIC RELATIONS, INC.

35 E 21st St 8th Fl, New York, NY 10010
Tel.: (212) 228-1500
Fax: (212) 228-1517
E-Mail: mail@njfpr.com
Web Site: www.njfpr.com

Employees: 15
Year Founded: 1987

Agency Specializes In: Brand Development & Integration, Crisis Communications, Event Planning & Marketing, Media Relations, Planning & Consultation, Recruitment

Lorraine Rios *(VP-Office Admin)*
Jaclyn Boschetti *(Acct Dir)*
Courtney Long *(Acct Dir)*
Meredith Klinger *(Acct Supvr)*
Elizabeth Janis *(Sr Acct Exec)*
Rachel Kasab *(Sr Acct Exec)*
Alexis Murray-Merriman *(Sr Acct Exec)*
Hannah Nelson *(Sr Acct Exec)*
Christina Cherry *(Acct Exec)*

Accounts:
The Allegria Hotel
Apple Core Hotels
BD Hotels
Borgata Hotel, Casino & Spa; Atlantic City, NJ
The Bowery Hotel
Canoe Bay, Relais & Chateaux; Chetek, WI
New-Canyon Ranch Management, LLC (Agency of Record) Marketing Communications
The Charles Hotel
Condado Palm Inn & Suites
Condado Vanderbilt
Conrad Fort Lauderdale Beach Marketing Communications
The Dermot Company Integrated Marketing
Destination D.C Campaign: "DC Cool", Media
Elysian Hotel
Gansevoort; Las Vegas, NV
Gansevoort Park
Gemma at The Bowery Hotel
Generator Hostels Generator Paris
Grand Hyatt New York
The Hanover Inn
Hotel Gansevoort South Condo Hotel Units
Hyatt Regency Aruba Resort & Casino
The Inn at Little Washington Suites, Restaurant & Cookbooks
iStar (Agency of Record) Marketing Communications, Social Media Strategy
The Jade Hotel; New York, NY Marketing Communications
JW Marriott Desert Springs; Palm Desert, CA
New-Kimpton Taconic Hotel Integrated Marketing Communications
New-Li-Lac Chocolates Integrated Marketing Communications
The Liberty Hotel
London & Partners Campaign: "Autumn Season of Culture", Integrated Marketing Communications
The Marlton
Marmara Collection Marketing Communications, Marmara Park Avenue
Nakkas Marketing Communications
The New York Palace Hotel Strategy
Oasis Collections (Agency of Record) Marketing Communications
The Out NYC (Agency of Record) XL Nightclub
Pier A Harbor House
Pod 39
The Pod Hotel
The Quin Integrated Marketing Communications
Riff Hotels Marketing Communications
The Ritz-Carlton South Beach
Sheraton Hotels & Resorts Worldwide Brand Public Relations
SIXTY SoHo Marketing Communications
Spring Creek Ranch; Jackson Hole, WY
Sunswept Resorts
New-Tribeca Grand (Agency of Record) Integrated Marketing Communications
Visit Savannah Integrated Marketing Communications, Media
Visit St. Pete Clearwater Dali Museum, Domestic Public Relations, Integrated Marketing Communications
The Water Club Hotel
Westin Hotels & Resorts
Wild Walk Marketing Communications
Wilderness Adventure Spa at Spring Creek Ranch; Jackson Hole, WY

NANSEN INC

400 N State St Ste 220, Chicago, IL 60654
Tel.: (312) 279-0760
E-Mail: chicago@nansen.com
Web Site: www.nansen.com

Agency Specializes In: Advertising, Digital/Interactive, Graphic Design

Jonathan Pettersson *(Co-Founder, Pres & VP-North America)*
Markus Bereflod *(Dir-Ops)*
Justin Dauer *(Dir-Creative)*
Joe Grause *(Dir-Bus Dev)*
Jonas Naslund *(Dir-Technical)*
Mark Rowland *(Dir-Strategy)*

Accounts:
SRAM Corporation

NARRATIVE

989 Ave of the Americas, New York, NY 10018
Tel.: (646) 736-2395
E-Mail: info@narrative.is
Web Site: www.narrative.is/

Employees: 16
Year Founded: 2013

Agency Specializes In: Advertising, Alternative Advertising, Brand Development & Integration, Communications, Consumer Marketing, Content, Cosmetics, Digital/Interactive, Electronic Media, Event Planning & Marketing, Fashion/Apparel, Guerilla Marketing, Men's Market, Multicultural, New Product Development, Out-of-Home Media, Outdoor, Publicity/Promotions, Social Media, Sports Market, Strategic Planning/Research, Tween Market, Viral/Buzz/Word of Mouth, Web (Banner Ads, Pop-ups, etc.)

Tricia Clarke-Stone *(Co-Founder & CEO)*
Nathan Phillips *(Chief Creative Officer)*
Ashley Connors *(Dir-Strategy)*

Accounts:
New-JCPenney (Digital & Social Media Agency of Record); 2015
New-Under Armour

THE NARUP GROUP

(Formerly William J. Narup & Co.)
1215 Washington St Ste 208, Winnetka, IL 60091
Tel.: (847) 853-9400
Fax: (847) 853-9404
Web Site: www.narup.com

Employees: 5
Year Founded: 1958

National Agency Associations: IAA-Second Wind Limited

Agency Specializes In: Business-To-Business, Communications, Public Relations

Approx. Annual Billings: $2,500,000

William J. Narup *(Founder)*
Cathy Ann Westhouse *(Specialist-Online Mktg)*

Accounts:
DSM Desotech

NAS RECRUITMENT INNOVATION

9700 Rockside Rd Ste 170, Cleveland, OH 44125
Fax: (216) 468-8115
Toll Free: (866) 627-7327
E-Mail: info@nasrecruitment.com
Web Site: www.nasrecruitment.com

Employees: 300
Year Founded: 1947

National Agency Associations: 4A's

Agency Specializes In: Advertising Specialties, Communications, Exhibit/Trade Shows, Recruitment, Trade & Consumer Magazines

Approx. Annual Billings: $25,000,000

Breakdown of Gross Billings by Media: Newsp. & Mags.: $20,000,000; Other: $5,000,000

Patty Van Leer *(Chief Product Officer & Sr VP)*
Matt Adam *(Exec VP & Strategist-Talent)*
Jennifer R. Henley *(VP-Media Svcs)*
Kristine Rhodes *(VP-Mktg)*
Kevin Hawkins *(Sr Dir-Solutions & Strategy)*
Charles Kapec *(Dir-Creative)*
Tracy Wharton *(Dir-Res)*
David Firestone *(Mgr-Print Svcs)*

Accounts:
Christus Santa Rosa
Mt. Washington Pediatric Hospital
New-United States Army
U.S. Cellular
Wendy's

California

NAS Recruitment Communications

2580 Bonita St, Lemon Grove, CA 91945
Tel.: (216) 468-8151
E-Mail: nas.sd@nasrecruitment.com
Web Site: www.nasrecruitment.com

Employees: 3

Agency Specializes In: Recruitment

Philip Ridolfi *(CEO)*
Patty Van Leer *(Chief Product Officer & Sr VP)*
Matt Adam *(Exec VP & Talent Strategist)*
Jennifer Henley *(VP-Client Svcs)*

NAS Recruitment Communications

11620 Wilshire Blvd., 9th Fl, Los Angeles, CA 90025

Tel.: (323) 930-3580
Fax: (323) 930-3590
Web Site: www.nasrecruitment.com

Employees: 5

Agency Specializes In: Recruitment

Kristine Rhodes *(VP-Mktg)*
Haley Cherba *(Client Relationship Mgr)*

Colorado

NAS Recruitment Communications
6160 S Syracuse Way Ste 100, Greenwood Village, CO 80111
Tel.: (303) 694-3600
Fax: (303) 694-0555
E-Mail: nas.dn@nasrecruitment.com
Web Site: www.nasrecruitment.com

Employees: 5

National Agency Associations: 4A's

Agency Specializes In: Recruitment

Patty Van Leer *(Chief Product Officer & Sr VP)*

Georgia

NAS Recruitment Communications
4462 Bretton Ct Ste 13 Bldg 2, Acworth, GA 30101
Tel.: (770) 425-0887
Fax: (770) 974-8807
E-Mail: info@nasrecruitment.com
Web Site: www.nasrecruitment.com

Employees: 4

National Agency Associations: 4A's

Agency Specializes In: Recruitment

Matthew Adam *(Exec VP)*
Chris Bacon *(Acct Dir)*
Debbie Smith *(Sr Acct Mgr)*

Illinois

NAS Recruitment Communications
111 E Wacker Dr 10th Fl, Chicago, IL 60611
Tel.: (312) 587-1795
Fax: (312) 425-6785
E-Mail: nas.ch@nasrecruitment.com
Web Site: www.nasrecruitment.com

Employees: 1

National Agency Associations: 4A's

Agency Specializes In: Recruitment

Chris Bacon *(Acct Dir)*
Jason Weinhaus *(Dir-Bus Dev)*
Sean Bain *(Strategist-Interactive)*

Missouri

NAS Recruitment Communications
7930 Clayton Rd Ste 400, Saint Louis, MO 63117
Tel.: (314) 646-6950
E-Mail: nas.st@nasrecruitment.com
Web Site: www.nasrecruitment.com

Employees: 2

Agency Specializes In: Recruitment

Ashley Smith *(Acct Mgr)*
Sean Bain *(Strategist-Interactive)*

Canada

NAS Recruitment Communications
1665 W Broadway Ste 670, Vancouver, BC V6J 1X1 Canada
Tel.: (604) 683-4461
Fax: (604) 689-5886
E-Mail: nas.vc@nasrecruitment.com
Web Site: www.nasrecruitment.com

Employees: 3

Agency Specializes In: Communications, Recruitment

Maureen Laventure *(Dir-Canadian Ops)*
Tracy Wharton *(Dir-Res)*
Maela Villarica *(Project Mgr-Strategy)*

NASUTI + HINKLE CREATIVE THINKING
8101-A Glenbrook Rd, Bethesda, MD 20814
Tel.: (301) 222-0010
E-Mail: mail@nasuti.com
Web Site: www.nasuti.com

Employees: 9

National Agency Associations: Second Wind Limited

Agency Specializes In: Fashion/Apparel, Real Estate

Karen Nasuti *(Pres, Partner & Strategist-Brand)*
Woody Hinkle *(Principal & Copywriter)*

Accounts:
American Red Cross
Happy Tails Dog Spa
Hershey Lodge
La Ferme Restaurant
The Madison Hotel
Now Resorts & Spa
One Duval
Pier House Resorts & Spa
Urban Country

NATCOM MARKETING
80 SW 8th St Ste 2230, Miami, FL 33130
Tel.: (786) 425-0028
Fax: (786) 425-0067
E-Mail: Info@natcom-marketing.com
Web Site: www.natcomglobal.com

E-Mail for Key Personnel:
President: bob@natcom-marketing.com

Employees: 10
Year Founded: 1982

National Agency Associations: IAA

Agency Specializes In: Advertising, Advertising Specialties, African-American Market, Aviation & Aerospace, Bilingual Market, Brand Development & Integration, Business Publications, Business-To-Business, Cable T.V., Catalogs, Co-op Advertising, Collateral, Communications, Consulting, Consumer Marketing, Consumer Publications, Corporate Communications, Corporate Identity, Digital/Interactive, Direct Response Marketing, E-Commerce, Email, Event Planning & Marketing, Exhibit/Trade Shows, Financial, Government/Political, Graphic Design, Health Care Services, Hispanic Market, In-Store Advertising, Integrated Marketing, International, Internet/Web Design, Leisure, Local Marketing, Magazines, Market Research, Media Buying Services, Media Planning, Medical Products, Merchandising, Multicultural, Multimedia, New Product Development, New Technologies, Newspaper, Newspapers & Magazines, Out-of-Home Media, Outdoor, Over-50 Market, Pharmaceutical, Point of Purchase, Point of Sale, Print, Production, Production (Ad, Film, Broadcast), Production (Print), Promotions, Public Relations, Publicity/Promotions, Publishing, Radio, Real Estate, Recruitment, Regional, Retail, Sales Promotion, Seniors' Market, Sponsorship, Sports Market, Strategic Planning/Research, Sweepstakes, T.V., Telemarketing, Trade & Consumer Magazines, Travel & Tourism, Web (Banner Ads, Pop-ups, etc.)

Approx. Annual Billings: $15,200,000

Breakdown of Gross Billings by Media: Audio/Visual: $304,000; Brdcst.: $760,000; Bus. Publs.: $760,000; Cable T.V.: $760,000; Collateral: $760,000; Comml. Photography: $152,000; Consulting: $1,520,000; Consumer Publs.: $1,520,000; Corp. Communications: $1,520,000; D.M.: $760,000; E-Commerce: $760,000; Fees: $1,520,000; Graphic Design: $760,000; Internet Adv.: $760,000; Mags.: $760,000; Newsp.: $760,000; Newsp. & Mags.: $760,000; Other: $304,000

Sallie Anne Rodriguez *(Mng Dir)*
Bob Bauer *(Sr VP)*
Marion Marvil Jacques *(Mng Dir-Mktg & Strategic Dev)*
Randy Washburn *(Sr Dir-Media & Res)*
Daniel Batlle *(Dir-Creative)*
Marcia Mata *(Dir-Bus Dev)*
Gustavo Sanin *(Dir-Program Mgmt)*

Accounts:
American Airlines
Andalucia Tourist Board; Spain
Burger King
Chevron
Citibank International; Fort Lauderdale, FL
Department of Homeland Security
Frito Lay; San Juan, PR; 1994

NATIONAL MEDIA SERVICES, INC.
91 Summit Dr, Huntington Bay, NY 11743
Tel.: (646) 216-9867
Fax: (646) 758-8172
E-Mail: eric@nmsooh.com
Web Site: www.nmsooh.com

Employees: 10

Agency Specializes In: African-American Market, Branded Entertainment, Children's Market, College, Exhibit/Trade Shows, Fashion/Apparel, Financial, High Technology, Hispanic Market, Identity Marketing, In-Store Advertising, Integrated Marketing, Media Planning, Mobile Marketing, Multicultural, Multimedia, New Product Development, New Technologies, Out-of-Home Media, Promotions, Publicity/Promotions, Social Marketing/Nonprofit, Social Media, Tween Market, Urban Market, Viral/Buzz/Word of Mouth

Eric Davis *(COO)*
Will Feltus *(Sr VP)*
Evan Tracey *(Sr VP)*
Jessica Sanson *(Dir-HR & Mgr-Acctg & Bus Office)*
Jaime Bowers *(Dir-Digital Adv)*
Tracey Robinson *(Dir-Res & Sr Media Buyer)*
Kristy Kovatch *(Media Buyer)*

NATIONAL PROMOTIONS & ADVERTISING INC.
3434 Overland Ave, Los Angeles, CA 90034
Tel.: (310) 558-8555
Fax: (310) 558-8558
Web Site: www.npa.net

Agency Specializes In: Advertising, Print

Kay Kusumoto *(Sr Acct Exec)*
Brian DeSena *(Acct Exec)*

Accounts:
New-Dr Dubrow

NATIONAL RESPONSE GROUP

80737 Avenida Manzanillo, Indio, CA 92203
Tel.: (760) 772-5888

Employees: 9
Year Founded: 1982

National Agency Associations: DMA

Agency Specializes In: Advertising, Advertising Specialties, Affluent Market, Collateral, Consumer Marketing, Direct Response Marketing, E-Commerce, Email, Financial, Telemarketing, Transportation, Travel & Tourism

Breakdown of Gross Billings by Media: D.M.: 70%; E-Commerce: 15%; Mags.: 10%; Sls. Promo.: 5%

Charles M. Greenberg *(Owner)*
Eric Daniels *(CFO)*
Heidi Greenberg *(VP)*
Joseph A. Richman *(VP-Production)*

Accounts:
California Alumni Association; Berkeley, CA
Coit Services; Burlingame, CA Household Cleaning Services
Franklin Bowles Galleries; San Francisco, CA
Visa USA; San Francisco, CA

NATREL COMMUNICATIONS

119 Cherry Hill Rd, Parsippany, NJ 07054
Tel.: (973) 292-8400
Fax: (973) 292-9101
E-Mail: info@natrelusa.com
Web Site: www.natrelusa.com

Employees: 40
Year Founded: 1999

Agency Specializes In: Brand Development & Integration, Direct Response Marketing, Health Care Services, Logo & Package Design, Medical Products, Pharmaceutical

David Nakamura *(Founder & Partner)*
Nicole Hyland *(CMO & Sr VP)*
Sophy Regelous *(Chief Tech & Ops Officer & Sr VP)*
Tamra Micco *(Sr VP & Dir-Client Svcs)*
Susan Mayer Roher *(Dir-Creative)*
Laura Wisniewski *(Acct Grp Supvr)*

Accounts:
Aptalis Pharma
Corcept Therapeutics
CSL Behring
Entera Health
Essential Pharmaceuticals
icon
Impax Pharmaceuticals
JHP Pharmaceuticals
Pfizer Injectables
PharmaDerm
Sanofi-Aventis
Spiritus
Terumo Medical Corporation

NAVAJO COMPANY

1164 Cadillac Ct, Milpitas, CA 95035
Tel.: (408) 957-3800
Fax: (408) 957-3809
E-Mail: thetribe@navajoco.com
Web Site: navajocompany.com

E-Mail for Key Personnel:
President: wayne@navajoco.com

Employees: 25
Year Founded: 1989

Agency Specializes In: Advertising, Advertising Specialties, Brand Development & Integration, Business Publications, Business-To-Business, Co-op Advertising, Collateral, Communications, Consulting, Corporate Identity, Digital/Interactive, Direct Response Marketing, E-Commerce, Education, Electronic Media, Event Planning & Marketing, Exhibit/Trade Shows, Graphic Design, High Technology, Information Technology, Internet/Web Design, Logo & Package Design, Merchandising, Multimedia, Point of Purchase, Point of Sale, Production, Public Relations, Publicity/Promotions, Sales Promotion, Strategic Planning/Research, Technical Advertising

Wayne Martinez *(Founder & Principal)*
Alan Drummer *(Dir-Creative-Content)*
Michael Scadden *(Acct Exec)*
Gerry Goldschmidt *(Sr Writer)*

Accounts:
Dell Computers
Hewlett Packard
Hitachi
IBM
Netapp
Symantec

NAVIGANT MARKETING / KSR

(Formerly Kelley Swofford Roy, Inc.)
2103 Coral Way Ste 724, Miami, FL 33145
Tel.: (305) 445-9020
Fax: (305) 444-9057
Toll Free: (800) 537-5565
E-Mail: info@navigantmarketing.com
Web Site: navigantmarketing.com

Employees: 12
Year Founded: 1983

National Agency Associations: ADFED-IAA

Agency Specializes In: Advertising, Aviation & Aerospace, Bilingual Market, Brand Development & Integration, Broadcast, Business Publications, Business-To-Business, Cable T.V., Co-op Advertising, Collateral, Communications, Consulting, Consumer Marketing, Consumer Publications, Corporate Communications, Corporate Identity, Direct Response Marketing, E-Commerce, Education, Electronic Media, Event Planning & Marketing, Exhibit/Trade Shows, Financial, Government/Political, Graphic Design, High Technology, Hispanic Market, Internet/Web Design, Legal Services, Leisure, Local Marketing, Logo & Package Design, Magazines, Marine, Media Buying Services, New Product Development, Newspaper, Newspapers & Magazines, Outdoor, Planning & Consultation, Point of Purchase, Point of Sale, Print, Production, Public Relations, Publicity/Promotions, Radio, Real Estate, Sales Promotion, Strategic Planning/Research, T.V., Trade & Consumer Magazines, Transportation, Travel & Tourism

Approx. Annual Billings: $18,800,000

Breakdown of Gross Billings by Media: Collateral: $3,400,000; D.M.: $1,250,000; Internet Adv.: $1,000,000; Newsp. & Mags.: $1,420,000; Pub. Rels.: $3,000,000; Radio & T.V.: $4,500,000; Strategic Planning/Research: $2,200,000; Trade & Consumer Mags.: $1,280,000; Worldwide Web Sites: $750,000

Jesus Salinas *(Controller)*
Jose Wilches *(Mgr-IT)*
William R. Roy *(Sr Partner)*

Accounts:
Charlotte County Visitor's Bureau
Community Partnership for Homeless, Inc.
Firenze Inc.
Florida Department of Transportation; Miami, FL Community Outreach: Highway Transportation; 2002
Jackson Memorial Hospital
MDX - Miami-Dade Expressway Authority
Miami-Dade Mayor's Office of Film & Entertainment
Miami-Dade Transit; Miami, FL Bus Transportation; 2003
Royal Caribbean Cruise Lines
SONY - Latin America

NAVIGATION ADVERTISING LLC

416-B Medical Ctr Pkwy, Murfreesboro, TN 37129
Tel.: (615) 898-1496
Fax: (615) 217-4826
Web Site: www.navigationadvertising.com

Agency Specializes In: Advertising, Digital/Interactive, Graphic Design, Internet/Web Design, Media Buying Services, Media Relations, Print, Public Relations, Social Media, Strategic Planning/Research

Christian Hidalgo *(Owner)*

Accounts:
4X4 Nation
Bill Taylor Bushido School of Karate
Elite Energy Gymnastics & Cheer
Rutherfords Best Doctors
The Sport Source
Stones River Dermatology
Walcom USA

NAYLOR, LLC

(Owned by RLJ Equity Partners, LLC)
5950 NW 1st Place, Gainesville, FL 32607
Tel.: (352) 332-1252
Toll Free: (800) 369-6220
Web Site: www.naylor.com

Employees: 500

Alex Debarr *(Pres & CEO)*
Tim Hedke *(CFO & VP)*
Marcus Underwood *(Chief Innovation Officer)*
Tara Ericson *(Grp VP)*
Jon Meurlott *(Grp VP)*
Jill Andreu *(VP-Content Strategy & Dev)*
Dave Bornmann *(VP-Mktg)*

Accounts:
IBEW 2085
Plumbing, Heating, Cooling Contractors National Association

NCI CONSULTING LLC

820 Matlack Dr Ste 101, Moorestown, NJ 08057
Tel.: (856) 866-1133
Fax: (856) 866-1135
E-Mail: info@nciconsulting.com
Web Site: www.nciconsulting.com

Employees: 11

Agency Specializes In: Health Care Services

John M. Coleman *(COO)*
Susan L. Coleman *(Pres-NCI Consulting)*

NCOMPASS INTERNATIONAL

8223 Santa Monica Blvd, West Hollywood, CA

90064
Tel.: (323) 785-1700
E-Mail: info@ncompassonline.com
Web Site: www.ncompassonline.com

Year Founded: 2003

Agency Specializes In: Advertising, Brand Development & Integration, Environmental, Event Planning & Marketing

Matt Mayer *(Sr VP-Strategic Mktg)*
Brent Koning *(VP & Head-Gaming & Global Partnerships)*
Michaela Keller-McCoy *(VP-Client Svcs)*
Aaron Miller *(VP-Innovation)*
Krista Beckmann-Hsieh *(Sr Dir-Media-Acct Svcs)*
Deanne Saffren *(Sr Acct Dir)*
Milan D. Cronovich *(Grp Acct Dir)*
Valerie Coleman *(Acct Dir)*
Andrew Kloack *(Dir-Production)*
Jeff Schlosser *(Dir-Ops & HR)*
Jamie Annis *(Sr Mgr-Strategic Mktg)*

Accounts:
Activision Publishing, Inc. Call of Duty: XP 2011

NEATHAWK DUBUQUE & PACKETT
1 E Cary St, Richmond, VA 23219-3732
Tel.: (804) 783-8140
Fax: (804) 783-0098
Toll Free: (800) 847-2674
E-Mail: mail@ndp-agency.com
Web Site: ndp.agency

E-Mail for Key Personnel:
President: sdubuque@ndp-agency.com
Creative Dir.: mdavis@ndp-agency.com

Employees: 43
Year Founded: 1984

National Agency Associations: Second Wind Limited

Agency Specializes In: Advertising, Brand Development & Integration, Business-To-Business, Collateral, Communications, Consulting, Corporate Identity, Education, Food Service, Government/Political, Graphic Design, Health Care Services, High Technology, Information Technology, Logo & Package Design, Media Buying Services, Medical Products, Newspaper, Newspapers & Magazines, Out-of-Home Media, Outdoor, Over-50 Market, Point of Purchase, Point of Sale, Print, Production, Public Relations, Publicity/Promotions, Radio, Seniors' Market, T.V., Trade & Consumer Magazines, Transportation, Travel & Tourism

Approx. Annual Billings: $47,000,000 Capitalized

Danny Fell *(Pres & CEO)*
Susan E. Dubuque *(Principal)*
Todd Foutz *(Exec VP & Acct Mgmt Dir)*
Brent Morris *(VP-Media Svcs)*
Michelle Ward *(Controller)*
Jimmy Ashworth *(Exec Dir-Creative)*
Jason Anderson *(Dir-Creative)*
Brenda Cosby *(Dir-Art)*
Rob Reid *(Dir-Media)*
Shaun Amanda Herrmann *(Assoc Dir-Social Media & Acct Supvr)*
Greg Zuercher *(Acct Supvr)*

Accounts:
Advance Auto Parts
American Health Care Association
Big River Grill
Carolinas Health Care System
College of William & Mary-Mason School of Business
Hollins University
HomeTown Bank (Agency of Record)
Hotel Roanoke
The Jefferson Hotel
Kennewick General Hospital, Kennewick, WA Print Advertising
Kindred Healthcare
Levine Children's Hospital
Lifestyle Spirits
Merge Computer Group; Richmond, VA; 1998
Metal Systems Inc (Agency of Record)
The Perfect Fix
Tandus
VCU Health System; Richmond, VA
Virginia Museum of Fine Arts Advertising, Media
Virginia State Police; Richmond, VA Auto Theft Prevention; 1992
Virginians for the Arts; Richmond, VA; 1992
Walden Security
Washington Hospital Center; Washington, DC; 1998

Branches

Neathawk Dubuque & Packett
417 Market St, Chattanooga, TN 37402
Tel.: (423) 752-4687
Fax: (423) 752-3697
Toll Free: (888) 619-8697
E-Mail: maupin@ndpagency.com
Web Site: ndp.agency

Employees: 14

Daniel Fell *(Pres & CEO)*
Todd Foutz *(Exec VP & Acct Mgmt Dir)*
Denise Rushing *(VP & Acct Mgr)*
Brent Morris *(VP-Media Svcs)*
Gay Maupin *(Dir-Ops)*
Jonathan Ariail *(Project Mgr-Digital)*
David Peterson *(Strategist-Digital)*

Accounts:
Harvest Foundation
Kindred Healthcare
Museum of the Confederacy
Roanoke Regional Airport
University System of Georgia
Virginians for the Arts

Neathawk Dubuque & Packett
410 S Jefferson St, Roanoke, VA 24011
Tel.: (540) 345-5403
Fax: (540) 345-5414
Web Site: ndp.agency

E-Mail for Key Personnel:
Creative Dir.: jgriessmayer@ndp-agency.com

Employees: 10

Agency Specializes In: Communications, Education, Financial, Health Care Services, Travel & Tourism

Todd Foutz *(Exec VP)*
Thomas Becher *(Sr VP)*
Jimmy Ashworth *(Exec Dir-Creative)*
Jason Anderson *(Dir-Creative)*
Stefanie Brown *(Acct Exec-Strategic Comm)*

Accounts:
The Economic Development Partnership
ITT Nightvision
Lectrus
New VaConnects
Patcraft Commercial Carpet
Virginia Tech

NEBO AGENCY LLC
1031 Marietta St NW, Atlanta, GA 30318
Tel.: (800) 908-6326
Web Site: www.neboagency.com

Year Founded: 2004

Agency Specializes In: Advertising, Digital/Interactive, Internet/Web Design

Adam Harrell *(Pres & Dir-Creative)*
Brian Easter *(CEO)*
Kimm Lincoln *(VP-Digital Mktg)*
Stacy Sutton Williams *(Sr Dir-Conversion)*
Damon Borozny *(Dir-Project Mgmt)*
Sarah Christiansen *(Dir-Digital Mktg Project Mgmt)*
Asher Emmanuel *(Dir-Video)*
Alice Jaitla *(Dir-Bus Dev)*
Pete Lawton *(Dir-Creative)*
Jennifer Vickery *(Dir-Paid Media)*
Emily Winck *(Dir-Web & Application Dev)*

Accounts:
Baynote
Goody
Mage Solar
Second Wind Dream
TAG Think
WalmartLabs

NEEDLE INC.
14864 S Pony Express Rd, Bluffdale, UT 84065
Tel.: (801) 858-0868
E-Mail: info@needle.com
Web Site: www.needle.com

Year Founded: 2009

Agency Specializes In: Advertising, E-Commerce, Social Media

Morgan Lynch *(Founder & CEO)*
Scott Pulsipher *(Pres & COO)*
Amy Heidersbach *(CMO)*
Christian Matsumori *(VP-Product)*
Stephanie Walsh *(VP-Community Ops)*
Jenna Cason *(Head-Corp Comm)*
Adam Davis *(Dir-Customer Success)*
Matt Wichser *(Dir-Fin)*

Accounts:
Axl's Closet Men's & Women's Fashion Material Clothes Mfr
Creminelli Fine Meats Meat Retailer
Moving Comfort Inc Women's Sports Clothes & Accessories Mfr & Distr
Skullcandy Headphones Earbuds & Gaming Headsets Mfr & Distr
Timex
Urban Outfitters Direct Clothes & Accessories Retailers

NEEDLEMAN DROSSMAN & PARTNERS
902 Broadway 15th Fl, New York, NY 10010
Tel.: (212) 506-0770
Fax: (212) 506-0778
E-Mail: info@needlemandrossman.com

E-Mail for Key Personnel:
Chairman: ndrossman@ndpadvertising.com
President: bneedleman@ndpadvertising.com

Employees: 2

National Agency Associations: 4A's

Agency Specializes In: Advertising

Neil Drossman *(Dir-Creative)*

NEFF + ASSOCIATES, INC.
The Novelty Bldg 15 S Third St 4th Fl, Philadelphia, PA 19106
Tel.: (215) 627-4747
Fax: (215) 923-6333
E-Mail: dn@neffassociates.com

Web Site: www.neffassociates.com

E-Mail for Key Personnel:
President: dn@neffassociates.com

Employees: 12
Year Founded: 1984

Agency Specializes In: Advertising, Brand Development & Integration, Business-To-Business, Cable T.V., Communications, Consumer Goods, Consumer Marketing, Direct Response Marketing, Entertainment, Event Planning & Marketing, Fashion/Apparel, Hospitality, Internet/Web Design, Leisure, Local Marketing, Luxury Products, Media Buying Services, Media Planning, Multimedia, Newspaper, Newspapers & Magazines, Out-of-Home Media, Outdoor, Package Design, Print, Public Relations, Radio, Real Estate, Restaurant, Retail, Sports Market, T.V.

Approx. Annual Billings: $18,500,000

Kelly Wolf *(Exec Dir-PR & Social Media)*
Adam Englehart *(Dir-Art)*
Kylie Flett *(Dir-PR & Social Media)*
Rhea Weaver *(Coord-Media)*

Accounts:
1401 Walnut
Absolut Brand's Plymouth Gin
American Heart Association
Bare Necessities
BG Automotive
Business Clubs America
The Calamari Sisters
City Auto Park
David Cutler Group
Dolce Valley Forge Hotel & Meeting Facilities; 2008
East River Bank
Fashion Bug
Geno's Steaks
NBC-10
Sullivan's Steakhouse
Sweat Fitness
United Tire + Service
Wurzak Hotel Group

NEHMEN-KODNER
431 N Polo Dr, Saint Louis, MO 63105
Tel.: (314) 721-1404
Fax: (314) 721-1404
Web Site: www.n-kcreative.com

E-Mail for Key Personnel:
President: pnehmen@n-kcreative.com
Creative Dir.: gkodner@n-kcreative.com

Employees: 2
Year Founded: 1987

Agency Specializes In: Business Publications, Business-To-Business, Collateral, Consumer Publications, Corporate Identity, Exhibit/Trade Shows, Graphic Design, Internet/Web Design, Logo & Package Design, Point of Purchase, Point of Sale, Print

Peggy S. Nehmen *(Owner, Dir-Art & Graphic Designer)*
Gary A. Kodner *(VP & Gen Mgr)*

Accounts:
Anheuser-Busch
Asthma & Allergy Foundation of St. Louis
Bond Wolfe Architects
BSI Constructors
CAJE Central Agency for Jewish Education
Capaha Bank
Centene
CFK Creative
Clayton School District
Cultural Leadership
Darryl Strawberry Foundation
Eleanor Sullivan
Enterprise Bank
Gateway to Hope
Herzog Crebs LLC
Society of Sacred Heart

NEIGHBOR AGENCY
853 Lincoln Blvd, Venice, CA 90291
Tel.: (310) 633-9311
Web Site: neighboragency.com

Year Founded: 2008

Agency Specializes In: Advertising, Brand Development & Integration, Digital/Interactive, Media Planning, Print, Radio, Social Media

Linda Price *(Owner & Pres)*
Chad Seymour *(Owner & CEO)*
Michelle Esposito *(Grp Acct Dir)*
Jim Wayne *(Dir-Digital)*

Accounts:
Jamba, Inc.
Tillamook Campaign: "Slow and Steady Wins the Taste", Farmstyle Greek

NELSON & GILMORE
1604 Aviation Blvd, Redondo Beach, CA 90278
Tel.: (310) 376-0296
Fax: (310) 374-8995
E-Mail: pnelson@nelsongilmore.com
Web Site: www.nelsongilmore.com

Employees: 11
Year Founded: 1978

Agency Specializes In: Business-To-Business, Corporate Identity, Financial, Real Estate

Wayne Nelson *(CEO)*

Accounts:
AMCAL Multi-Housing
Anastasi Development
The Carlyle
CenterPoint
Century Housing
Flamingo Lakes
Hollywood
Los Suenos
MBK Real Estate Ltd.
The Planning Center
The Ring Group
Rutter Development
Watkoloa

NELSON CREATIVE
10290 Kinross Rd, Roswell, GA 30076
Tel.: (404) 606-3877
Web Site: nelsoncreative.net

Scott Nelson *(Founder & Exec Dir-Creative)*

NELSON SCHMIDT
600 E Wisconsin Ave, Milwaukee, WI 53202
Tel.: (414) 224-0210
Fax: (414) 224-9463
E-Mail: marketing411@n-s.com
Web Site: www.nelsonschmidt.com

Employees: 50
Year Founded: 1971

National Agency Associations: AAF-BMA-MAGNET

Agency Specializes In: Advertising, Advertising Specialties, Aviation & Aerospace, Brand Development & Integration, Business-To-Business, Co-op Advertising, Collateral, Communications, Consumer Marketing, Corporate Communications, Corporate Identity, Crisis Communications, Custom Publishing, Digital/Interactive, Direct Response Marketing, Direct-to-Consumer, E-Commerce, Email, Event Planning & Marketing, Exhibit/Trade Shows, Experience Design, Financial, Graphic Design, Health Care Services, High Technology, Identity Marketing, In-Store Advertising, Industrial, Integrated Marketing, International, Internet/Web Design, Legal Services, Local Marketing, Logo & Package Design, Marine, Market Research, Media Buying Services, Media Planning, Media Relations, Medical Products, Multimedia, Outdoor, Paid Searches, Pharmaceutical, Point of Purchase, Point of Sale, Print, Production, Production (Print), Promotions, Public Relations, Publicity/Promotions, RSS (Really Simple Syndication), Radio, Recruitment, Sales Promotion, Search Engine Optimization, Social Media, Sponsorship, Sports Market, Strategic Planning/Research, T.V., Technical Advertising, Telemarketing, Viral/Buzz/Word of Mouth, Web (Banner Ads, Pop-ups, etc.)

Approx. Annual Billings: $67,000,000

Daniel H. Nelson, Sr. *(Chm)*
Daniel H. Nelson, Jr. *(Pres & CEO)*
Christopher Vitrano *(CMO)*
Cody Pearce *(VP-Acct Plng & Mgmt)*
Scott Penniston *(VP-Media Svcs)*
Ken Hagan *(Exec Dir-Creative)*
Kris Jenson *(Sr Dir-Art)*
Becky Dunton *(Acct Dir)*
Kristen Davis *(Acct Supvr)*
Kari Dunham *(Sr Acct Exec)*

Accounts:
Alliance Laundry Systems
Carts of Colorado
Grammer
Hacienda Pinilla; Costa Rica
Honeywell Campaign: "Universal Pilot Sales Kit", ECC, HBS, S&C
McKesson
Milwaukee Art Museum Friends of Art Acquisition & Exhibition Fund
Polaris Industries, Inc. Global Electric Motorcars, Marketing, Online, Print, Sales, Website
Sony Creative Software
UW Colleges
Vorex Customer Relationship Management, Event Promotions, Integrated Marketing Communications Program, Media Planning & Buying, PR, Website Development
Wisconsin Economic Development Corp. Branding, Campaign: "In Wisconsin", Electronic Newsletter, Strategy, Website

NEMER FIEGER
6250 Excelsior Blvd Ste 203, Minneapolis, MN 55416-2735
Tel.: (952) 925-4848
Fax: (952) 925-1907
E-Mail: jmarie@nemerfieger.com
Web Site: www.nemerfieger.com

E-Mail for Key Personnel:
President: jmarie@nemerfieger.com
Creative Dir.: eloeffler@nemerfieger.com

Employees: 30
Year Founded: 1957

National Agency Associations: ADFED-PRSA-Second Wind Limited

Agency Specializes In: Advertising, Arts, Automotive, Brand Development & Integration, Broadcast, Business Publications, Cable T.V., Co-op Advertising, Collateral, Consulting, Consumer Goods, Consumer Publications, Content, Digital/Interactive, Direct Response Marketing,

Electronic Media, Entertainment, Event Planning & Marketing, Food Service, Graphic Design, Guerilla Marketing, Hospitality, In-Store Advertising, Integrated Marketing, Internet/Web Design, Leisure, Local Marketing, Logo & Package Design, Media Buying Services, Media Planning, Media Relations, Multicultural, Multimedia, Newspaper, Newspapers & Magazines, Out-of-Home Media, Outdoor, Planning & Consultation, Point of Purchase, Point of Sale, Print, Production (Print), Promotions, Public Relations, Publicity/Promotions, Radio, Regional, Restaurant, Sales Promotion, Social Media, Sponsorship, Strategic Planning/Research, T.V., Trade & Consumer Magazines, Travel & Tourism, Web (Banner Ads, Pop-ups, etc.), Women's Market

Approx. Annual Billings: $24,000,000

Breakdown of Gross Billings by Media: Bus. Publs.: 2%; Cable T.V.: 3%; Collateral: 3%; Consumer Publs.: 3%; D.M.: 3%; Event Mktg.: 7%; Graphic Design: 7%; Newsp. & Mags.: 15%; Out-of-Home Media: 3%; Outdoor: 2%; Plng. & Consultation: 5%; Point of Purchase: 3%; Pub. Rels.: 15%; Spot Radio: 7%; Spot T.V.: 20%; Worldwide Web Sites: 2%

J. Marie Fieger *(Pres)*
Jim Fieger *(CEO)*
Tom Whelan *(COO & Exec VP)*
Jon Woestehoff *(CMO)*
Chad Olson *(VP-Entertainment Mktg)*
Paul Spicer *(Controller)*
Barbara Hamilton-Sustad *(Acct Dir)*
Molly Mulvehill Steinke *(Dir-Media Rels)*
Peggy Hayes *(Mgr-Fin Svcs)*
Amy Severson *(Sr Acct Exec)*
Kristin Laursen *(Sr Media Buyer)*

Accounts:
AIA-Minnesota
Bridging, Inc.
Championship Auto Shows; Duluth & Minneapolis, MN
Fine Line Features; Los Angeles, CA Motion Picture Distribution
IMAX MNZoo
Ispiri
Kinetico Minnesota Dealers Association
Loffler Cos
Midtown Global Market; Minneapolis, MN
Minneapolis Aquatennial
Minnesota Street Rod Association
Richfield Visitors Association
Rogue Pictures
Subway Restaurants Des Moines IA, Duluth & Superior MN, Eau Claire & La Crosse WI, Green Bay WI, Marquette MI, Minneapolis & Saint Paul MN, Peoria & Bloomington IL, Rochester MN, Sioux City IA, Sioux Falls SD, Springfield-Champaign IL, Wausau WI
Universal Pictures; Universal City, CA Motion Picture Distribution
Warner's Stellian
White Bear Superstore; White Bear Lake, MN Automotive Sales Services

NEMO DESIGN
(Formerly NEMO)
1875 SE Belmont St, Portland, OR 97214
Tel.: (503) 872-9631
Fax: (503) 872-9641
E-Mail: info@nemodesign.com
Web Site: www.nemodesign.com

Employees: 70
Year Founded: 1999

Agency Specializes In: Advertising, Alternative Advertising, Brand Development & Integration, Branded Entertainment, Broadcast, Catalogs, Environmental, Experience Design, Graphic Design, Guerilla Marketing, In-Store Advertising, Logo & Package Design, Magazines, Men's Market, New Product Development, Production, Production (Ad, Film, Broadcast), Production (Print), Retail, Teen Market, Viral/Buzz/Word of Mouth, Web (Banner Ads, Pop-ups, etc.)

Revenue: $60,000,000

Mark Lewman *(Partner & Dir-Creative)*
Trevor Graves *(Principal & Dir-Bus Dev)*
Jeff Bartel *(Principal)*
Jay Floyd *(Dir-Art & Designer)*
Chris Hotz *(Dir-Design)*
John Stierwalt *(Sr Acct Mgr)*
Ryan Barrett *(Mgr-Mktg)*

Accounts:
Bell Helmets
Hewlett-Packard Blackbird; 2006
Hotel Deluxe
Hotel Max
Lumberjax
Mammoth Mountain Ski Area
MasterCraft Boats
Nike; Beaverton, OR 6.0; 2005
Nike Converse, North American Retail
Oakley
Smith Sport Optic; Ketchum, ID Sunglasses; 2003
Tillamook Country Smoker Design
Voodoo PC

NEO@OGILVY
636 11th Ave, New York, NY 10036
Tel.: (212) 259-5477
Web Site: www.neoogilvy.com

Year Founded: 2006

National Agency Associations: 4A's

Agency Specializes In: Digital/Interactive, Planning & Consultation, Social Media, Sponsorship

Nasreen Madhany *(CEO)*
Brian Geist *(Mng Dir)*
Allegra Kadet *(Mng Dir)*
Pete Meyers *(Mng Dir)*
Patty Sachs *(Mng Dir-IBM Worldwide Media-Global)*
MinSun Collier *(Head-Digital Media)*
Michael Bruckstein *(Grp Dir-Plng)*
Melissa Scott *(Grp Dir-Plng)*
Christine Whited *(Grp Dir-Plng)*
Corey Kahn *(Dir-Search & Programmatic Buying)*
Kim Kozma *(Sr Partner & Dir-Media)*
Pranav Pandit *(Sr Partner & Dir)*
Eric Smith *(Dir-Media)*
Sean Gillespie *(Assoc Dir-Media)*
Roxanne Gross *(Assoc Dir-Media)*
Manny Hernandez *(Assoc Dir-Programmatic)*
Helene Tournesac *(Acct Mgr-Digital)*
Jema Jang *(Supvr-Media)*
Samantha Levine *(Supvr-Search)*
Katherine Streinz *(Supvr-Digital Media)*
Rebecca Bogatin *(Media Planner)*
Juliette Castiel *(Media Planner-Programmatic)*
Lindsay Orosco *(Media Planner)*
Alison Pavlis *(Media Planner)*
Natalie Redberg *(Media Planner-Programmatic)*
Jhanvi Shah *(Media Planner)*
Jenna Hirsch *(Asst Media Planner)*
Dean LeNoir *(Asst Media Planner)*
Emily Verone *(Media Supvr-IT-IBM Team)*

Accounts:
British Airways
Caesars Entertainment Corp. Campaign: "The Winning Hand", Digital
Drinkaware Media Planning & Buying
Eastman Kodak Company
IBM Corporation ibm.com
TD Ameritrade Holding Corporation Digital Media, Tdameritrade.com
Tourism Fiji Media Planning & Buying
UPS

NEO-PANGEA, LLC
26 Penn Ave, Reading, PA 19611
Tel.: (866) 514-9141
Fax: (610) 879-4863
E-Mail: info@neo-pangea.com
Web Site: www.neo-pangea.com

Year Founded: 1999

Agency Specializes In: Advertising, Digital/Interactive, Local Marketing, Mobile Marketing

Brett Bagenstose *(Owner)*
Aaron Beaucher *(Partner & Creative Dir)*

Accounts:
Bell Tower Salon & Spa
Francis Cauffman
Samsung America, Inc.
Vaughan Mills
West Reading Borough

NEPTUNE ADVERTISING
3003 SW College Rd Ste 1071, Ocala, FL 34474
Tel.: (352) 286-7534
Web Site: www.neptuneadvertising.com

Agency Specializes In: Advertising, Brand Development & Integration, Collateral, Email, Graphic Design, Internet/Web Design, Logo & Package Design, Media Planning, Outdoor, Print

John Tripodi *(Creative Dir)*
Grace Anderson *(Strategist-Media)*

Accounts:
Surgical Specialists of Ocala
Zone Health & Fitness

NERLAND AGENCY WORLDWIDE PARTNERS
(Name Changed to Spawn Ideas)

NERLAND CO
2400 N 2nd St Ste 402, Minneapolis, MN 55411
Tel.: (612) 254-2694
E-Mail: contact@nerland.co
Web Site: www.nerland.co

Year Founded: 2004

Agency Specializes In: Advertising, Brand Development & Integration, Digital/Interactive, Internet/Web Design, Social Media

Nathan Nerland *(CEO)*
Angie Churchill *(Chief Experience Officer)*
Jordan Obinger *(Creative Dir)*
Robert Prevost *(Dir-Brand Strategy & PR)*
Katie Smith *(Dir-Mktg)*
Drew Mintz *(Acct Mgr)*

Accounts:
Mojo Fit Studios

NETPLUS MARKETING, INC.
718 Arch St Ste 400S, Philadelphia, PA 19106
Tel.: (610) 897-2380
Fax: (610) 897-2381
E-Mail: info@netplusmarketing.com
Web Site: thinknetplus.com

Employees: 37
Year Founded: 1996

Agency Specializes In: Advertising, Brand Development & Integration, Business-To-Business, Communications, Consulting, Consumer Marketing, Digital/Interactive, Direct Response Marketing, E-Commerce, Electronic Media, Fashion/Apparel, Information Technology, Internet/Web Design, Legal Services, Media Buying Services, Medical Products, Pharmaceutical, Planning & Consultation, Publicity/Promotions, Real Estate, Retail, Sponsorship, Strategic Planning/Research, Technical Advertising, Travel & Tourism

Approx. Annual Billings: $10,000,000

Breakdown of Gross Billings by Media: E-Commerce: 100%

Denise E. Zimmerman *(Co-Founder, Pres & Chief Strategy Officer)*
Robin Neifield *(CEO)*
Sean Flanagan *(Sr Dir-Art)*
Sarah Miller *(Dir-Integrated Media)*
John Shanley *(Dir-Creative)*
Anna Vaughan *(Dir-Admin)*

Accounts:
Alfred Angelo Bridal
Aramark
Armstrong World Industries, Inc
Hanover Direct, Inc.
Harriet Carter
Independence Blue Cross
Phillips Foods, Inc. Interactive Marketing; 2008
Phillips Seafood
Rita's Water Ice Franchise Company
Universal Studios

NETREACH

124 S Maple St 2nd Fl, Ambler, PA 19002
Tel.: (215) 283-2300
Fax: (215) 283-2335
E-Mail: sales@netreach.com
Web Site: www.netreach.com

Employees: 20
Year Founded: 1994

Agency Specializes In: Internet/Web Design

Will Bast *(CEO)*
Stephen Bouikidis *(Exec VP)*

Accounts:
American Collectors Insurance
Binswanger International
Blue Star Marketing
Drexel University
Firstrust Bank
Germantown Academy
The Global Consulting Partnership
Guideposts, Inc.
HealthForumOnline
National Foundation for Celiac Awareness
Pennypack Farm and Education Center
Sunoco Logistics
TMC Corp
Wellness Coaches

NETTRESULTS LLC

4590 MacArthur Blvd, Newport Beach, CA 92660
Tel.: (949) 478-5880
E-Mail: GetPress@nettresults.com
Web Site: www.NettResultsLLC.com

Year Founded: 1999

Agency Specializes In: Advertising, Brand Development & Integration, Consulting, Corporate Communications, Corporate Identity, Crisis Communications, Email, International, Local Marketing, Public Relations

Nick Leighton *(CEO)*

Accounts:
AspenTech
Creative Technology
DB Schenker
Getty Images
GoElectricDrive.com
Honeywell
Marks & Spencer
Microsoft
Motorola
New York Institute of Technology
Palo Alto Networks
TruePosition
TurnItIn
United Nations

NETWAVE INTERACTIVE MARKETING, INC.

600 Bay Ave, Point Pleasant, NJ 08742
Tel.: (732) 701-9797
Fax: (732) 701-9798
E-Mail: info@netwaveinteractive.com
Web Site: www.netwaveinteractive.com

Agency Specializes In: Advertising, Brand Development & Integration, Internet/Web Design, Logo & Package Design, Outdoor, Print, Public Relations, Radio, Social Media

Dave McIndoe *(Founder & Pres)*
Nick Kiefer *(Dir-Creative)*
James Franznick *(Acct Mgr)*
Amy Lucantoni *(Acct Mgr)*
Vin Ferrer *(Mgr-Content)*
Amanda Kerekes *(Mgr-Production)*
Adam McIndoe *(Exec Acct Mgr)*

Accounts:
Ocean County Long Term Recovery Group
Toms River Country Club

NETWORK AFFILIATES INC.

940 Wadsworth Blvd Ste 300, Lakewood, CO 80214
Tel.: (303) 232-2707
Fax: (303) 232-2241
E-Mail: mikeg@netaff.com
Web Site: www.netaff.com

Employees: 70

Agency Specializes In: Legal Services, T.V.

Sales: $28,943,916

Norton C. Frickey *(Pres & CEO)*
Todd Kuhlmann *(CFO & COO)*
Harlan Schillinger *(VP & Dir-Mktg)*
Tammy Kehe *(VP)*
Jeff Buenz *(Sr Acct Mgr)*
Brian Hutchin *(Sr Acct Mgr)*

Accounts:
Brown & Crouppen, P.C.

NEUGER COMMUNICATIONS GROUP

25 Bridge Sq, Northfield, MN 55057
Tel.: (507) 664-0700
Toll Free: (888) 761-3400
E-Mail: info@neuger.com
Web Site: www.neuger.com

Year Founded: 2002

Agency Specializes In: Advertising, Brand Development & Integration, Crisis Communications, Digital/Interactive, Graphic Design, Internet/Web Design, Media Relations, Print, Public Relations, Strategic Planning/Research

David L. Neuger *(Pres & CEO)*
Joanne B. Henry *(Exec VP)*
Richard E. Esse *(VP)*
Penelope D. Hillemann *(VP)*

Accounts:
InnerCity Tennis
Mill City Summer Opera
Minnesota Dental Association
Valley View Farms

NEUMUTH ADVERTISING

3542 International St, Fairbanks, AK 99701
Tel.: (907) 456-8988
Fax: (907) 456-5731
Web Site: na-ak.com/2014

Year Founded: 1989

Agency Specializes In: Advertising, Digital/Interactive, Internet/Web Design, Media Relations, Social Media, Strategic Planning/Research

Steve Neumuth *(CEO)*
Tyler Williams *(Dir-Creative)*
Teresa Fitzgerald *(Mgr-Graphic Design)*

Accounts:
Bridgewater Hotel
MAC Federal Credit Union
Mongold Allstate Insurance
Mt. McKinley Bank
Tanana Valley Clinic

NEVER WITHOUT, LLC

1731 Commerce Dr NW, Atlanta, GA 30318
Tel.: (404) 577-3515
Fax: (404) 577-3514
Web Site: www.neverwithout.net

Year Founded: 2006

Agency Specializes In: Advertising, Brand Development & Integration, Email, Media Buying Services, Media Planning

Mickey Cohen *(Mng Partner)*
Naoya Wada *(Mng Partner-Creative)*
Caroline Johnson *(Assoc Acct Mgr)*
Stephanie Melstrom *(Acct Mgr)*

Accounts:
Alzheimer's Association
AT&T Communications Corp.
Emory University
Kudzu.com
Lancome Paris
Marriott Hotels & Resorts
Moe's Southwest Grill, LLC
Simmons Bedding Company
Toyota Motor Sales, U.S.A., Inc.

NEW AGE MEDIA

pob 245456, Brooklyn, NY 11224
Tel.: (718) 368-9292
Web Site: www.newagemediany.com

Employees: 4
Year Founded: 1998

Agency Specializes In: Branded Entertainment, Cable T.V., Magazines, Multimedia, Newspaper, Newspapers & Magazines, Outdoor, Promotions, Radio, Shopper Marketing, Social Media, T.V., Yellow Pages Advertising

Oleg Frish *(Founder)*

Accounts:
Range Rover USA; 2009

NEW BOSTON CREATIVE GROUP
315 Houston St Ste E, Manhattan, KS 66502
Tel.: (785) 587-8185
Fax: (866) 385-5004
Toll Free: (877) 315-8185
E-Mail: info@newbostoncreative.com
Web Site: www.newbostoncreative.com

Employees: 19
Year Founded: 2006

Agency Specializes In: Advertising, Consulting, Environmental, Internet/Web Design, Print, Search Engine Optimization, Social Media

Susan Religa *(Principal)*
Lisa Sisley *(Principal)*
Shawn Dryden *(Dir-Web Dev)*
Julie Fiedler *(Specialist-Comm)*
Tara Marintzer *(Sr Graphic Designer)*

Accounts:
The Biosecurity Research Institute
Capstone3D Development Group
K-State College of Arts & Sciences
Kansas Press Association Keep Reading! Campaign
Steve's Floral

THE NEW GROUP
4540 SW Kelly Ave, Portland, OR 97239
Tel.: (503) 248-4505
Fax: (503) 248-4506
Web Site: www.thenewgroup.com

Employees: 35
Year Founded: 1993

Agency Specializes In: Brand Development & Integration, Digital/Interactive, E-Commerce, Local Marketing, Mobile Marketing, New Technologies, Strategic Planning/Research

Doug New *(Founder & CEO)*
Steve Marshall *(Owner & Pres)*
Susan Hawkins *(COO)*
George Vakoutis *(Exec Dir-Global Accts)*

Accounts:
Jenny Craig Interactive; 2008
Microsoft

NEW MEDIA SOLUTIONS, INC.
3343 Hwy 190 Ste 333, Mandeville, LA 70471
Tel.: (504) 723-4334
Fax: (800) 537-0141
E-Mail: andy@neworleansadvertising.com
Web Site: www.neworleansadvertising.com

E-Mail for Key Personnel:
President: andy@neworleansadvertising.com

Employees: 2
Year Founded: 1996

Agency Specializes In: Advertising, Co-op Advertising, Consulting, Digital/Interactive, Electronic Media, Graphic Design, Internet/Web Design, Media Buying Services, Print, Travel & Tourism

Approx. Annual Billings: $800,000

Breakdown of Gross Billings by Media: Internet Adv.: $800,000

Andrew Mortensen *(Partner)*

Accounts:
Astor Crown Plaza; New Orleans, LA Hotels; 2010
Aventura Mexicana; Mexico Hotels; 1996
The Cove Eleuthera Hotels; 2013
Hotel Elements; Mexico Hotels; 2007
Hotel Monteleone Hotels; 2010
New Orleans Top Hotels Hotels; 1996
Omni Royal Orleans Hotels; 2010
Royal Sonesta Hotels; 2010

NEW RIVER COMMUNICATIONS, INC.
1819 SE 17th St, Fort Lauderdale, FL 33316
Tel.: (954) 535-0644
Fax: (954) 535-0664
Toll Free: (888) 524-2808
E-Mail: info@newrivercommunications.com
Web Site: www.newrivercommunications.com

Employees: 9
Year Founded: 2000

Agency Specializes In: Advertising, Advertising Specialties, Brand Development & Integration, Business-To-Business, Collateral, Communications, Consumer Marketing, Consumer Publications, Corporate Communications, Corporate Identity, Direct Response Marketing, Faith Based, Graphic Design, Internet/Web Design, Investor Relations, Local Marketing, Logo & Package Design, Media Buying Services, Newspapers & Magazines, Planning & Consultation, Print, Production, Strategic Planning/Research, Telemarketing, Yellow Pages Advertising

Breakdown of Gross Billings by Media: Corp. Communications: 10%; D.M.: 50%; Fees: 10%; Graphic Design: 30%

Larry Montali *(Co-Founder & Dir-Creative-New River Comm)*
Rod Taylor *(Pres-New River Comm & Principal)*
Sean O'Neil *(Sr VP)*
Scott Allbee *(Dir-Art)*
Shaun Petersen *(Acct Supvr)*
Alyse Nelson *(Acct Exec)*

Accounts:
Catholic Charities; New York, NY Humanitarian Aid
Cross International; Pompano Beach, FL International Humanitarian Aid
Goodwill Industries of Detroit
National Parkinson Foundation; Miami, FL Parkinson's Disease Research & Aid
The Salvation Army Disaster Relief, Domestic & Foreign Aid

NEW RULES ADVERTISING
3956 W Poplar Point Ct, Trafalgar, IN 46181
Tel.: (317) 878-9516
Web Site: www.newrulesadvertising.com

Agency Specializes In: Advertising, Internet/Web Design, Print, Radio, Social Media, T.V.

Jim Bullock *(Dir)*

Accounts:
Furniture For Less, Inc.

NEW WEST LLC
950 Breckenridge Ln Ste 140, Louisville, KY 40207
Tel.: (502) 891-2500
Fax: (502) 891-2514
E-Mail: info@newwestagency.com
Web Site: www.newwestagency.com

Employees: 13
Year Founded: 2004

Agency Specializes In: Advertising, Public Relations

Becky Simpson *(CEO)*
Tom Kokai *(COO)*
Phillip Booth *(VP-Graphic Design)*
Maria Ladd *(VP)*
Andrea Brady Hampton *(Dir-PR)*
Greg Mauldin *(Acct Mgr)*
Esther Banegas *(Acct Coord)*
Amber Denham *(Coord-Mktg)*
Donna Wade *(Coord-Mktg)*

Accounts:
African American Forum
American Consulting Engineers
American Eagle Outfitters
APS
Blue Equity
DD Williamson
Dow Corning Carrollton
Elations
GE Appliances
GE Consumer & Industrial
Kentucky Department of Tourism
Lincoln Bicentennial Commission
Louisville International Airport
Louisville Slugger Museum
Louisville Urban League
Papa John's
Rogers Group Investments
San Diego International Airport
UK Healthcare
University of Kentucky Healthcare
University of Louisville Health Care
Women 4 Women

NEWFIRE MEDIA
43 Crystal Lk Dr Ste 200, North Augusta, SC 29841
Tel.: (844) 639-3473
E-Mail: info@newfiremedia.com
Web Site: www.newfiremedia.com

Agency Specializes In: Advertising, Digital/Interactive, Internet/Web Design, Media Buying Services, Social Media

Jeremy Mace *(Pres)*
Susie Adamson *(COO & Strategist)*
Turner Simkin *(CMO)*
Chris Hitchcock *(VP-Bus Dev)*
Josh Whiting *(Creative Dir)*
Keith Pickett *(Dir-Tech)*
Ross McDaniel *(Sr Acct Exec)*

Accounts:
The Krystal Company (Digital Agency of Record)
On The Border
Realtree
TaxSlayer

NEWKIRK COMMUNICATIONS, INC.
1518 Walnut St Ste 900, Philadelphia, PA 19102
Tel.: (215) 735-8150
Fax: (215) 735-8157
Web Site: www.facebook.com/newkirkinc

E-Mail for Key Personnel:
President: ssegal@newkirkinc.com
Creative Dir.: ecohen@newkirkinc.com

Employees: 4
Year Founded: 1968

Agency Specializes In: Advertising, Arts, Brand Development & Integration, Broadcast, Business Publications, Business-To-Business, Collateral, Communications, Consumer Marketing, Corporate Communications, Corporate Identity,

Digital/Interactive, Direct Response Marketing, Direct-to-Consumer, E-Commerce, Email, Exhibit/Trade Shows, Fashion/Apparel, Financial, Graphic Design, Identity Marketing, Internet/Web Design, Legal Services, Local Marketing, Logo & Package Design, Magazines, Media Planning, Medical Products, Mobile Marketing, Newspaper, Newspapers & Magazines, Over-50 Market, Pharmaceutical, Print, Production, Production (Print), Promotions, Radio, Real Estate, Retail, Seniors' Market, Social Marketing/Nonprofit, T.V., Trade & Consumer Magazines, Viral/Buzz/Word of Mouth, Web (Banner Ads, Pop-ups, etc.)

Approx. Annual Billings: $1,000,000

Breakdown of Gross Billings by Media: Brdcst.: $50,000; Bus. Publs.: $500,000; Consumer Publs.: $400,000; Internet Adv.: $50,000

Susan Cohen Segal *(Pres)*
Jennifer Morris *(Mng Dir & VP)*
Edmond Cohen *(Dir-Creative)*

Accounts:
Choral Arts Society of Philadelphia; Philadelphia, PA Professional Concerts; 1998
Core Insurance
The MCS Group
New York Zoological Society; New York, NY Wildlife Conservation Magazine; 1989
Roosevelt Paper Co; Mount Laurel, NJ Distributors & Converters of Printing Papers; 1975
Shelter Structures

NEWLINK GROUP

1111 Brickell Ave Ste 1350, Miami, FL 33131
Tel.: (305) 532-7950
Fax: (305) 532-1845
Web Site: www.newlink-group.com

Year Founded: 1996

Agency Specializes In: Advertising, Communications, Public Relations, Social Media

Claudia De Francisco *(Mng Partner)*
Mauricio De Vengoechea *(Mng Partner-Newlink Political)*
Eduardo Del Rivero *(Mng Partner-Newlink America)*
Rafael Mora *(Mng Partner)*
Maria Pis-Dudot *(Sr VP)*
Miguel Lande *(Mng Dir-North & CCA Reg)*
Angela Camacho *(VP-Reputation Mgmt & Public Affairs)*
Jorge Ramirez Diaz *(VP-Newlink Comm)*
Ian McCluskey *(VP-Reputation Mgmt & Pub Affairs)*

Accounts:
New-Coca-Cola
New-Kunachia Chia+Probiotics (Agency of Record), Communications
Palace Resorts
New-Uber (Latin America Agency of Record) Strategic Communications

NEWMAN GRACE INC.

6133 Fallbrook Ave, Woodland Hills, CA 91367
Tel.: (818) 713-1678
Fax: (818) 999-6314
E-Mail: bhemsworth@newmangrace.com
Web Site: www.newmangrace.com

Employees: 6
Year Founded: 1995

Agency Specializes In: Advertising, Brand Development & Integration, Business Publications, Business-To-Business, Cable T.V., Catalogs, Consulting, Consumer Marketing, Corporate Communications, Corporate Identity, Cosmetics, Custom Publishing, Direct Response Marketing, Graphic Design, Health Care Services, Integrated Marketing, Internet/Web Design, Legal Services, Logo & Package Design, Market Research, Media Planning, Newspaper, Newspapers & Magazines, Over-50 Market, Package Design, Print, Production, Production (Print), Publishing, Radio, Social Marketing/Nonprofit, Sports Market, Strategic Planning/Research, T.V., Technical Advertising, Trade & Consumer Magazines, Travel & Tourism, Web (Banner Ads, Pop-ups, etc.)

Approx. Annual Billings: $3,000,000

Breakdown of Gross Billings by Media: Brdcst.: 10%; Bus. Publs.: 15%; Collateral: 20%; Consulting: 25%; Consumer Publs.: 20%; Internet Adv.: 10%

Brian Hemsworth *(Pres)*
Steven Higginson *(Dir-Art)*

Accounts:
The Campbell Center Non-Profit; 2013
Free Agent BMX Action Sports Equipment; 2003
KHS Bicycles; Rancho Dominguez, CA Bicycles; 1999
Long Valley Media Media & Custom Publishing; 2014
Maria's Italian Kitchen Restaurants; 2003
Mentor Group Investment Bankers; 2012
PayQwick Banking/Pay Systems; 2015
QuoteHero.com Insurance; 2014
SRG CPAs Accountants & Business Consultants; 2013
Vendor Direct Solutions Law Firm Management Services; 2013

NEWMARK ADVERTISING, INC.

15821 Ventura Blvd Ste 570, Encino, CA 91436-2947
Tel.: (818) 461-0300
Fax: (818) 530-4394
E-Mail: agencyinfo@newmarkad.com
Web Site: www.newmarkad.com

Employees: 30
Year Founded: 1968

Agency Specializes In: Broadcast, Business Publications, Business-To-Business, Cable T.V., Collateral, Consumer Marketing, Consumer Publications, Cosmetics, Direct Response Marketing, E-Commerce, Financial, Food Service, Graphic Design, Health Care Services, Hispanic Market, Leisure, Magazines, Medical Products, Newspaper, Newspapers & Magazines, Print, Production, Radio, Retail, Trade & Consumer Magazines, Travel & Tourism

Approx. Annual Billings: $25,000,000

Breakdown of Gross Billings by Media: D.M.: $1,250,000; Fees: $2,500,000; Mags.: $2,500,000; Newsp.: $3,750,000; Production: $3,750,000; Radio & T.V.: $11,250,000

Patty Newmark *(Pres & CEO)*
Virginia Dooley *(Acct Supvr)*
Melissa White *(Acct Supvr)*
Aparna Kulkarni *(Acct Exec)*

Accounts:
Citrix Online Division; Santa Barbara, CA GoToMeeting, GoToMyPC; 2003
Executive Car Leasing; Los Angeles, CA Car & Truck Leasing; 1990
Procter & Gamble; Cincinnati, OH Cover Girl, Crest Whitestrips, Folgers, Iams, Max Factor, Nyquil, Olay; 1998
Stamps.com; Los Angeles, CA Custom Photo Mail Stamps; 2007

THE NEWSMARKET, INC.

708 3rd Ave, New York, NY 10017
Tel.: (212) 497-9022
Fax: (212) 682-5260
Toll Free: (888) 887-0886
E-Mail: info@SynapticDigital.com
Web Site: www.thenewsmarket.com

Employees: 200
Year Founded: 2002

Agency Specializes In: Broadcast, Digital/Interactive, Local Marketing, New Technologies

Krish Menon *(CTO)*
Matthew Thomson *(Mng Dir-The NewsMarket)*
Arup Kar *(Dir-Engrg)*
Delano Pansi *(Dir-Client & Media Solutions)*
Tina Chopra *(Acct Mgr-Asia)*
Cleon Grey *(Designer-User Interface)*

Accounts:
GlaxoSmithKline
GM
Google
IBM
Intel
Kia
Panasonic
UNICEF

Subsidiary

Medialink Worldwide Incorporated

90 Park Ave 20th Fl, New York, NY 10016
Tel.: (646) 259-3001
Fax: (646) 259-3012
E-Mail: info@medialink.com
Web Site: www.medialink.com

Employees: 77
Year Founded: 1986

Agency Specializes In: Digital/Interactive, Viral/Buzz/Word of Mouth

Michael Kassan *(Chm & CEO)*
Dee Salomon *(CMO & Sr VP)*
Matt Spiegel *(Sr VP & Gen Mgr-Mktg & Tech Solutions)*
Daryl Evans *(Sr VP-Mobile, Media & Adv Strategy)*
Howard B Homonoff *(Sr VP)*
Lesley Klein *(Sr VP)*
Neil Carty *(VP-Innovation Strategy)*

Accounts:
Vibrant Media Media, Strategic Communications

NEWTON ASSOCIATES MARKETING COMMUNICATIONS, INC.

527 Plymouth Rd, Plymouth Meeting, PA 19462
Tel.: (610) 964-9300
Fax: (610) 964-9306
E-Mail: info@newtonassociates.com
Web Site: www.newtonassociates.com

E-Mail for Key Personnel:
President: dand@newtonassociates.com

Employees: 5
Year Founded: 1973

Agency Specializes In: Advertising, Aviation & Aerospace, Brand Development & Integration, Broadcast, Business Publications, Business-To-Business, Cable T.V., Catalogs, Collateral, College, Communications, Consulting, Consumer Goods, Consumer Marketing, Consumer Publications, Corporate Communications,

Corporate Identity, Education, Electronics, Email, Engineering, Environmental, Event Planning & Marketing, Exhibit/Trade Shows, Financial, Food Service, Graphic Design, High Technology, Hospitality, Household Goods, Industrial, Integrated Marketing, Internet/Web Design, Local Marketing, Logo & Package Design, Magazines, Marine, Market Research, Media Buying Services, Media Planning, Media Relations, Medical Products, Men's Market, Multimedia, New Product Development, New Technologies, Newspaper, Newspapers & Magazines, Out-of-Home Media, Outdoor, Over-50 Market, Package Design, Pharmaceutical, Point of Purchase, Point of Sale, Print, Product Placement, Production, Production (Print), Public Relations, Publicity/Promotions, Radio, Real Estate, Regional, Retail, Sales Promotion, Search Engine Optimization, Seniors' Market, Social Media, Sports Market, Strategic Planning/Research, T.V., Technical Advertising, Trade & Consumer Magazines, Web (Banner Ads, Pop-ups, etc.)

Approx. Annual Billings: $4,500,000

Breakdown of Gross Billings by Media: Audio/Visual: 2%; Bus. Publs.: 15%; Co-op Adv.: 2%; Collateral: 15%; Comml. Photography: 5%; Consulting: 5%; D.M.: 5%; Exhibits/Trade Shows: 2%; Foreign: 5%; Graphic Design: 5%; Internet Adv.: 2%; Logo & Package Design: 10%; Point of Purchase: 5%; Pub. Rels.: 15%; Strategic Planning/Research: 2%; Worldwide Web Sites: 5%

Daniel Ditzler *(Pres & Dir-Creative)*
Gerry Giambattista *(VP & Dir-Art)*
Kathy Foran *(Dir-Media)*

Accounts:
Artisan Door; Lancaster, PA Garage Doors; 2010
Crown Beverage Packaging North America Beverage Packaging; 2015
Earthres
General Doors; Bristol, PA Garage Doors; 2010
Graham Engineering Corp.; York, PA Manufacturer of Blow Molding Machines; 1998
HLP/Klearfold; New York, NY Visual Packaging; 2009
JL Packaging; Pennington, NJ Packaging; 2010
Jomar; Pleasantville, NJ Blow Molding Machinery
Levelese; Denver, CO Level Instrumentation; 2009
Plastrac Blending Systems; 2015
Teal Electronics Corp.; San Diego, CA Power Quality Solutions; 1997
Time & Parking Controls; Upper Darby, PA Systems Integration; 2010
Tinius Olsen Testing Machine Company, Inc.; Horsham, PA Materials Testing Machinery; 2001

NEXT STEP COMMUNICATIONS INC.
40 Goodwin Rd, Kittery Point, ME 03905-5220
Tel.: (207) 703-0343
Web Site: www.next-step.com

Year Founded: 1996

Agency Specializes In: Advertising, Collateral, Exhibit/Trade Shows, Public Relations

Greg Hannoosh *(Founder & Pres)*
Mitch Hannoosh *(Specialist-Mktg)*

Accounts:
Gloucester Engineering, Co.

NEXUS DIRECT
2101 Parks Ave Ste 600, Virginia Beach, VA 23451
Tel.: (757) 340-5960
Fax: (757) 340-5980
E-Mail: info@nexusdirect.com
Web Site: www.nexusdirect.com

Employees: 30
Year Founded: 2004

Agency Specializes In: Direct Response Marketing, Government/Political, Graphic Design, Package Design

Suzanne Cole Nowers *(Founder & CEO)*
Susan Mann *(Pres)*
Ashley Gundlach *(Grp Acct Dir)*
Keith Adams *(Dir-IT)*
Kara Stolpinski *(Mgr-Interactive Mktg)*

Accounts:
Democratic Senatorial Campaign Committee

NFM GROUP
(Formerly NFM Group Inc.)
200 First Ave, Pittsburgh, PA 15222
Tel.: (412) 325-6400
Fax: (412) 394-6411
E-Mail: info@nfmgroup.com
Web Site: www.nfmgroup.com

E-Mail for Key Personnel:
President: jafoley@nfmgroup.com

Employees: 10
Year Founded: 1987

Agency Specializes In: Advertising, Automotive, Brand Development & Integration, Branded Entertainment, Cable T.V., Co-op Advertising, Consumer Goods, Corporate Communications, Direct-to-Consumer, Event Planning & Marketing, Guerilla Marketing, Hospitality, In-Store Advertising, Market Research, Media Buying Services, Media Planning, Mobile Marketing, Multimedia, Newspaper, Outdoor, Print, Production, Production (Ad, Film, Broadcast), Promotions, Recruitment, Retail, Sales Promotion, Sponsorship, Sports Market, Strategic Planning/Research, T.V.

Approx. Annual Billings: $10,000,000

Preston Ciranni *(Co-Pres)*
John P. Foley *(Co-Pres)*

Accounts:
Canon; New York, NY (Sports Marketing) Cameras; 2000
Giant Eagle; Pittsburgh, PA (Event Marketing); 2000
Lennox Industries
Sports Marketing Consultants; Pittsburgh, PA; 1987

NFUSION GROUP
5000 Plz on the Lake Ste 200, Austin, TX 78746
Tel.: (512) 716-7000
Fax: (512) 716-7001
E-Mail: jellett@nfusion.com
Web Site: www.nfusion.com

Employees: 71

Agency Specializes In: Advertising, Digital/Interactive

Breakdown of Gross Billings by Media: Brdcst.: 3%; Consulting: 10%; Internet Adv.: 50%; Print: 37%

John Ellett *(CEO & CMO)*
Ellen Kolsto *(VP-Plng & Insights)*
Carmen Henderson *(Controller)*
Jessica Skewes *(Sr Producer-Interactive)*
Mason Adams *(Acct Dir)*
Alice Lou *(Acct Dir)*
Jimmy Dyer *(Dir-Art)*
Stephanie Donohoe *(Office Mgr & Coord-Mktg)*
Veronica Stetson *(Acct Mgr)*
Erica Wilson *(Acct Supvr)*
Mary McCanna *(Coord-Search & Social)*
Jeremy Palafox *(Assoc Media Dir)*
Bailey Prosser *(Asst Media Planner)*
Violet Repp *(Sr Media Planner)*

Accounts:
Alert Logic
AMD
Atlantic Broadband
AVEVA, Inc.
BJ's Restaurants
CiCi's Pizza
Comerica
la Madeleine
McCoy's Building Supply Centers
Memorial Hermann Healthcare System
Samsung Electronics America, Inc.
SanDisk Campaign: "Telling Life's Stories From Memory"
Toshiba
Zimmer Spine

NICE SHOES, LLC
352 Park Ave S 16th Fl, New York, NY 10010
Tel.: (212) 683-1704
Fax: (212) 683-9233
E-Mail: info@niceshoes.com
Web Site: www.niceshoes.com

Employees: 50
Year Founded: 1996

Revenue: $1,400,000

Dominic Pandolfino *(Owner & CEO)*
Lez Rudge *(Partner)*
Robert Keske *(CIO)*
Ed Rilli *(Head-Production)*
Justin Pandolfino *(Brand Dir)*
Sean Grace *(Dir-Sls)*
Paul DeKams *(Mgr-Mktg)*

Accounts:
Calvin Klein Jeans
Dusty Festival

NICHOLAS & LENCE COMMUNICATIONS LLC
28 W 44th St Ste 1217, New York, NY 10036
Tel.: (212) 938-0001
Fax: (212) 938-0837
Web Site: www.nicholaslence.com

Agency Specializes In: Advertising, Corporate Identity, Media Relations, Promotions, Public Relations, Strategic Planning/Research

Cristyne Nicholas *(CEO)*
Shin-Jung Hong *(VP)*
Laura Rothrock *(Asst VP-Govt & Community Affairs)*
Nick Nicholas *(Dir-Sports Dev)*
Justine Digiglio *(Acct Mgr & Coord-Publicity)*
Joshua A. Knoller *(Acct Mgr)*

Accounts:
The Central Park Horse Show
Marine Park Golf Course
New Balance Track & Field Armory Center
The Russian Tea Room Restaurant Services
Trump Golf Links at Ferry Point (Public Relations Agency of Record)

NICK BIBKO & ASSOCIATES
360 Main St, Phoenix, NY 13135-2440
Tel.: (315) 695-6251
Fax: (315) 695-6251

E-Mail for Key Personnel:
President: nbibko@webtv.com

Employees: 4
Year Founded: 1989

National Agency Associations: ACA-AMA

Agency Specializes In: Consumer Marketing, Corporate Identity, Education, Exhibit/Trade Shows, Financial, Graphic Design, Health Care Services, Industrial, Investor Relations, Medical Products, Newspaper, Newspapers & Magazines, Outdoor, Planning & Consultation, Public Relations, Radio, T.V., Travel & Tourism

Approx. Annual Billings: $633,000

Breakdown of Gross Billings by Media: Bus. Publs.: $18,990; Cable T.V.: $37,980; Consumer Publs.: $31,650; D.M.: $31,650; Exhibits/Trade Shows: $31,650; Graphic Design: $37,980; Newsp. & Mags.: $158,250; Outdoor: $75,960; Plng. & Consultation: $25,320; Pub. Rels.: $25,320; Radio & T.V.: $158,250

Nicholas R. Bibko *(Owner)*

Accounts:
Dermody, Burke & Brown Certified Public Accountants; 1995
Institute of Industrial Relations; Schenectady, NY Labor & Industrial Relations Programs Throughout New York; 1993
Le Moyne College; Syracuse, NY All University Programs, Center for Business Management Programs (MBA Program), Continuous Learning Programs, Summer Sessions; 1983
Medical Center East; East Syracuse, NY; 1989
Seneca Federal Savings; Baldwinsville, Liverpool & North Syracuse, NY; 1980
Silverman & Silverman CPA's; 1990

NICKEL COMMUNICATIONS LLC

47 S Palm Ave Ste 201, Sarasota, FL 34236
Tel.: (941) 954-0600
Web Site: www.nickelcommunications.com

Year Founded: 2006

Agency Specializes In: Advertising, Digital/Interactive, Public Relations

Kristine Nickel *(Mng Partner)*
Lindsey Nickel *(Partner & Dir-Creative)*

Accounts:
Founders Golf Club

NICKELODEON CREATIVE ADVERTISING

39th Fl 1515 Bdwy, New York, NY 10036
Tel.: (212) 258-7500
Web Site: www.nickcreativeadvertising.com

Agency Specializes In: Advertising, Brand Development & Integration

Sharon Cohen *(Exec VP-Partnership Mktg-Kids & Family Grp-Viacom)*
Kim Rosenblum *(Exec VP-Mktg & Creative-TV Land)*
Doug Cohn *(Sr VP-Music Mktg & Talent, Nickelodeon & Viacom Media Networks)*
Claire Curley *(Sr VP-Digital Content)*
Matthew Evans *(Sr VP-Digital)*
John Paul Geurts *(Sr VP-Creative)*
Jennifer Tracy *(Sr VP-Integrated Mktg)*
Terence Coffey *(VP-Media Plng & Strategy)*
Jaime Dictenberg *(VP-Consumer Mktg)*
Colleen Fitzpatrick *(VP-Music)*
Reena Mehta *(VP-Digital & Multiplatform Programming)*
Adam Weiner *(VP-Project Mgmt)*
Annalisa Ciganko *(Sr Dir-Retail Mktg)*
April McKenzie *(Sr Dir-Integrated Mktg)*
Kristina Caruso *(Dir-Sls & Mktg)*
Courtney Litvack *(Dir-Kids Sponsorships)*
Jacqueline Sendgikoski *(Dir-Art)*
Angelita Sierra *(Dir-Integrated Mktg, Social Media & Activation)*
Eric Van Skyhawk *(Assoc Dir-Creative)*
Jordan Cardinale *(Sr Mgr-Consumer Mktg)*
Rachel Peterson *(Acct Mgr)*
Stephanie Clark *(Mgr-Nickelodeon Creative Adv)*
Jaime Hoerbelt *(Mgr-Integrated Mktg)*
Jessica Lettieri *(Mgr-Digital Integrated Mktg)*
Jessica Prucinsky *(Mgr-Integrated Mktg)*
Lauren Treinen *(Acct Exec)*
Angie Wolfrom *(Acct Exec)*

Accounts:
New-American Legacy Foundation
Energizer Holdings, Inc.
Nationwide Campaign: "Collision"
Nick at Nite
Popeyes
Seven & I Holdings Co Ltd
Target Campaign: "Ballet"
TracFone

NIKI JONES AGENCY

39 Front St, Port Jervis, NY 12771
Tel.: (845) 856-1266
Fax: (845) 856-1268
E-Mail: info@nikijones.com
Web Site: www.nikijones.com

Agency Specializes In: Advertising, Brand Development & Integration, Collateral, Internet/Web Design, Print, Public Relations

Niki Jones *(CEO)*
Stephanie Brynes *(Mgr-Social Media & Copywriter)*
David Stone *(Mgr-Fin)*
Olga Zernholt *(Acct Exec)*
Jennifer Krzynowek *(Sr Graphic Designer)*

Accounts:
Greene-Dreher Sterling Fair
Lackawaxen Township

NIMBLE WORLDWIDE

(Formerly Nimble)
12801 N Central Expy N Central Plz 3, Dallas, TX 75243-1727
Tel.: (972) 788-7600
Fax: (972) 788-7680
E-Mail: bwagner@nimbleworldwide.com
Web Site: www.nimbleworldwide.com

Employees: 10
Year Founded: 1955

Agency Specializes In: Advertising, Advertising Specialties, Brand Development & Integration, Broadcast, Business Publications, Business-To-Business, Cable T.V., Co-op Advertising, Collateral, Communications, Consulting, Consumer Marketing, Consumer Publications, Corporate Identity, Cosmetics, Digital/Interactive, Direct Response Marketing, Education, Electronic Media, Entertainment, Event Planning & Marketing, Fashion/Apparel, Financial, Food Service, Graphic Design, Health Care Services, Hispanic Market, Internet/Web Design, Investor Relations, Leisure, Logo & Package Design, Magazines, Media Buying Services, New Product Development, Newspaper, Newspapers & Magazines, Out-of-Home Media, Outdoor, Planning & Consultation, Point of Purchase, Point of Sale, Print, Production, Public Relations, Publicity/Promotions, Radio, Real Estate, Recruitment, Restaurant, Retail, Sales Promotion, Sponsorship, Sports Market, Strategic Planning/Research, Sweepstakes, Syndication, T.V., Teen Market, Trade & Consumer Magazines, Travel & Tourism

Ed Bardwell *(Founder)*
Matt Kelly *(Controller)*
Kary Nowlin *(Acct Exec-Social Media)*

Accounts:
Cole and Company
The Finer Touch
Hawaiian Falls
Humco
Hyatt Regency Dallas
Luxe Home Interiors
Manek Energy
Peterbilt
Richardson Bike Mart
Safety-Kleen Holdco, Inc.
Westfield

THE NISSEN GROUP

150 Third St SW, Winter Haven, FL 33880
Tel.: (863) 294-2812
Fax: (863) 299-3909
E-Mail: rpalfrey@reni.net
Web Site: thenissengroup.com

E-Mail for Key Personnel:
President: nis@nissenadv.com

Employees: 4
Year Founded: 1971

National Agency Associations: AAF

Agency Specializes In: Advertising, Agriculture, Brand Development & Integration, Broadcast, Business Publications, Business-To-Business, Cable T.V., Collateral, Commercial Photography, Communications, Consulting, Consumer Marketing, Consumer Publications, Corporate Identity, Digital/Interactive, Direct Response Marketing, E-Commerce, Education, Electronic Media, Engineering, Environmental, Event Planning & Marketing, Exhibit/Trade Shows, Financial, Food Service, Government/Political, Graphic Design, Health Care Services, High Technology, Industrial, Information Technology, Internet/Web Design, Legal Services, Leisure, Logo & Package Design, Magazines, Marine, Media Buying Services, Medical Products, Merchandising, Multimedia, New Product Development, Newspaper, Newspapers & Magazines, Out-of-Home Media, Outdoor, Over-50 Market, Pharmaceutical, Planning & Consultation, Point of Purchase, Point of Sale, Print, Production, Public Relations, Publicity/Promotions, Radio, Real Estate, Recruitment, Restaurant, Retail, Sales Promotion, Seniors' Market, Sports Market, Strategic Planning/Research, T.V., Technical Advertising, Trade & Consumer Magazines, Transportation, Travel & Tourism

Approx. Annual Billings: $8,204,000

Breakdown of Gross Billings by Media: Bus. Publs.: $840,000; Cable T.V.: $490,000; Collateral: $850,000; Consumer Publs.: $240,000; D.M.: $250,000; Farm Publs.: $60,000; Newsp.: $1,250,000; Other: $60,000; Outdoor: $220,000; Point of Sale: $149,000; Pub. Rels.: $875,000; Radio: $1,120,000; Syndication: $1,800,000

Joe Jensen *(Owner)*
Jay Hook *(VP-Client Svcs)*

NL PARTNERS

188 State St, Portland, ME 04101
Tel.: (207) 775-5251
Fax: (207) 775-3389
E-Mail: cnichols@nlpartners.com
Web Site: www.nlpartners.com

Employees: 12

Russell Leonard *(Pres)*

Dori Shepard *(Mng Partner)*
Chris Nichols *(Chief Creative Officer)*
John Tiedje *(Sr Dir-Art)*
Heather Bowman *(Acct Mgr & Strategist-Brand)*
Jennifer Cartmell *(Acct Mgr)*
Dan McMillen *(Supvr-Media)*
Jenna Eagleton *(Acct Exec-Subway Restaurants)*

Accounts:
Kennebunk Savings Bank

NM MARKETING COMMUNICATIONS, LLC
706 Waukegan Rd, Glenview, IL 60025
Tel.: (847) 657-6011
Fax: (847) 657-8425
E-Mail: info@nmmarketingbiz.com
Web Site: www.nmmarketingbiz.com

E-Mail for Key Personnel:
President: nmerens@nmmarketingbiz.com
Media Dir.: info@nmmarketingbiz.com

Employees: 7
Year Founded: 1999

National Agency Associations: BMA-PRSA

Agency Specializes In: Advertising, Automotive, Bilingual Market, Brand Development & Integration, Business Publications, Business-To-Business, Catalogs, Collateral, Communications, Consulting, Corporate Communications, Corporate Identity, Customer Relationship Management, Direct Response Marketing, Engineering, Event Planning & Marketing, Exhibit/Trade Shows, Graphic Design, Hispanic Market, Household Goods, Industrial, Information Technology, Integrated Marketing, Internet/Web Design, Logo & Package Design, Magazines, Media Buying Services, Media Planning, Media Relations, Media Training, Medical Products, Multicultural, Multimedia, New Product Development, Newspaper, Planning & Consultation, Print, Production (Print), Public Relations, Publicity/Promotions, Publishing, Sales Promotion, Search Engine Optimization, Sports Market, Strategic Planning/Research, Telemarketing, Transportation, Travel & Tourism

Approx. Annual Billings: $2,000,000

Breakdown of Gross Billings by Media: Consulting: 20%; Event Mktg.: 20%; Exhibits/Trade Shows: 10%; Plng. & Consultation: 20%; Pub. Rels.: 30%

Norwin A. Merens *(Mng Dir)*
Thomas A. Stack *(Mng Dir)*
Paul Lloyd *(Mgr-Project)*

Accounts:
Allied Metal Co.; Chicago, IL Aluminum & Zinc Alloys; 2002
American Foundry Society; Schaumburg, IL Industry Trade Association; 2008
Aspen Industries, Inc.; Bensenville, IL Gas-Vented Fireplace Systems; 2007
Demil Metals, Inc.; Highland Park, IL Ordnance Scrap Metal; 2006
Gas Technology Institute; Des Plaines, IL Commercial Testing & Laboratory Services; 2000
Industrial Innovations, Inc.; Wyoming, MI Lubricating Technologies; 2003
Jessup Manufacturing; McHenry, IL Safety Signage/Tapes; 2007
Laurel Manufacturing; Elk Grove Village, IL Die Castings; 2007
North American Die Casting Association; Wheeling, IL Die Casting Industry Promotion; 2003
Pat Hughes; Chicago, IL Chicago Cubs Radio Broadcaster; 2005
Professional Flooring Installers Association; Itasca, IL Industry Trade Association; 2008
Rangers Die Casting Co.; Lynwood, CA Die Casting; 2008
Rolled Metal Products, Inc.; Alsip, IL Steel Service Centers; 2006
Saporito Finishing Co.; Cicero, IL Metal Finishing, Plating, Aluminum & Magnesium Anodizing; 1999
Tsurumi America, Inc.; Glendale Heights, IL Industrial Pumps; 2004
United Stationers Supply Corporation; Deerfield, IL Office Products Distribution; 2007

NO LIMIT AGENCY
730 N Franklin St Ste 310, Chicago, IL 60657
Tel.: (312) 526-3996
Web Site: www.nolimitagency.com

Year Founded: 2008

Agency Specializes In: Advertising, Brand Development & Integration, Digital/Interactive, Print, Public Relations, Social Media

Michelle Lonnee *(Producer-Digital)*
Ahmad Yilmaz *(Producer-Digital)*
Brian Jaeger *(Dir-Accts)*
Matt Diaz *(Acct Mgr)*
Jackie Minchillo *(Acct Mgr)*
Jonny Egan *(Mgr-Digital)*
Alia Rajput *(Mgr-Social Media)*
Devon Deem *(Acct Exec)*
Logan Perakis *(Acct Exec)*

Accounts:
New-Pita Pit
Smoothie King Franchises, Inc.

NO LIMIT MARKETING & ADVERTISING, INC.
2789 Wrights Rd, Oviedo, FL 32765
Tel.: (407) 928-3412
Web Site: www.nolimitma.com

Agency Specializes In: Advertising, Event Planning & Marketing, Media Buying Services, Production, Public Relations, Social Media

Eric Barber *(Co-Founder & Co-Pres)*
Nick Zivolich *(Co-Founder & Co-Pres)*
Pete Amedure *(Sr Acct Exec)*
Kevin Tanicien *(Acct Exec)*

Accounts:
Adora Clinic
AgeLess MediSpa
Ampli5's Health
Sanchez Law Group
Triquest Clinical Research

NO'ALA STUDIOS
250 S Poplar St, Florence, AL 35630-5713
Tel.: (256) 766-4222
Fax: (256) 766-4106
Toll Free: (800) 779-4222
E-Mail: info@noalastudios.com
Web Site: marketing.noalastudios.com

E-Mail for Key Personnel:
Creative Dir.: dsims@atsa-usa.com

Employees: 7
Year Founded: 1990

Agency Specializes In: Business-To-Business, Co-op Advertising, Collateral, Communications, Consulting, Consumer Marketing, Corporate Identity, Direct Response Marketing, Exhibit/Trade Shows, Gay & Lesbian Market, Graphic Design, Health Care Services, Industrial, Internet/Web Design, Logo & Package Design, Medical Products, Merchandising, New Product Development, Newspapers & Magazines, Outdoor, Point of Purchase, Point of Sale, Print, Production, Public Relations, Publicity/Promotions, Radio, Seniors' Market, Trade & Consumer Magazines, Travel & Tourism

Approx. Annual Billings: $2,000,000

Breakdown of Gross Billings by Media: Bus. Publs.: 15%; Collateral: 20%; D.M.: 5%; Mags.: 25%; Newsp.: 10%; Outdoor: 5%; Point of Purchase: 5%; Radio: 5%; T.V.: 10%

Matt Liles *(COO)*
David Sims *(Publr & Dir-Creative)*
Roy Hall *(Office Mgr)*
Rowan Finnegan *(Designer)*
Justin Hall *(Designer)*

Accounts:
American Association for Geriatric Psychiatry
American Health Care Assoc.
The Atlas Society; Washington, DC
Cavalier Homes, Inc.; Addison, AL; 1998
Coffee Health Group; Florence, AL
Homebuilders Assoc. of Alabama
The University of North Alabama; Florence, AL

NOBLE
2215 W Chesterfield Blvd, Springfield, MO 65807-8650
Tel.: (417) 875-5000
Fax: (417) 875-5051
Toll Free: (800) 662-5390
Web Site: www.noble.net

Employees: 200
Year Founded: 1969

National Agency Associations: AMIN-PMA

Agency Specializes In: Advertising, Brand Development & Integration, Broadcast, Business Publications, Business-To-Business, Children's Market, Collateral, Communications, Consulting, Consumer Goods, Consumer Marketing, Corporate Communications, Corporate Identity, Digital/Interactive, Electronic Media, Email, Event Planning & Marketing, Exhibit/Trade Shows, Food Service, Health Care Services, Hospitality, In-Store Advertising, Integrated Marketing, Internet/Web Design, Logo & Package Design, Market Research, Media Buying Services, Media Planning, Media Relations, New Product Development, Point of Purchase, Point of Sale, Print, Production (Ad, Film, Broadcast), Production (Print), Public Relations, Publicity/Promotions, Radio, Restaurant, Sales Promotion, Search Engine Optimization, Sponsorship, Strategic Planning/Research, Technical Advertising, Trade & Consumer Magazines, Travel & Tourism, Web (Banner Ads, Pop-ups, etc.)

Approx. Annual Billings: $260,000,000

Bob Noble *(Owner)*
Keith Acuff *(CEO)*
Nancy Banasik *(Sr VP-Home & Building)*
LeAnne Garoutte *(Sr VP)*
Joe Langford *(Sr VP-Tech)*
Karen Frost *(VP & Dir-Creative)*
Sandy Haymes *(Producer-Creative)*
Tina Bunge *(Mgr-HR)*

Accounts:
Aramark; Philadelphia, PA; 2004
Garland; Freeland, PA; 2006
Grande Cheese; Brownsville, WI; 2004
Hickory Farms; Maumee, OH; 2000
Ice-O-Matic; Denver, CO; 2006
ITW Brands, Glenview, IL
JM Smucker Company; Orrville, OH; 1996
Manitowoc Foodservice USA; Port Richey, FL; 2004

MasterFoodServices; Vernon, CA; 2000
McCormick; Hunt Valley, MD; 2001
MDC Wallcoverings, Elk Grove Village, IL
Otis Spunkmeyer; San Leandro, CA; 2004
Reckitt Benckiser; Parsipanny, NJ; 1994
Scotsman Ice Systems; Vernon Hills, IL; 2004
TAMKO Building Products; Joplin, MO; 1978
U.S. Foodservice, Rosemont, IL

Branch

Noble
33 W Monroe St Ste 200, Chicago, IL 60603
(See Separate Listing)

NOBLE PACIFIC SEA TO SEA, INC.
19916 Old Owen Rd Ste 229 PMB 229, Monroe, WA 98272-9778
Tel.: (360) 568-5314
Fax: (360) 568-5186
E-Mail: sales@noblepacific.com
Web Site: www.noblepacific.com

Employees: 2
Year Founded: 1993

Agency Specializes In: Advertising, Business-To-Business, Media Buying Services, Newspaper, Newspapers & Magazines, Print, Recruitment

Approx. Annual Billings: $2,000,000

Breakdown of Gross Billings by Media: Newsp.: $2,000,000

Nancy Noble *(Owner)*

Accounts:
The Dwyer Group; Waco, TX Franchise Sales; 1994
IAF Beverage; Dallas, TX Franchise; 2003

NOBLE PEOPLE
(Formerly Ikon3)
13 Crosby St, New York, NY 10013
Tel.: (646) 553-3323
Web Site: noblepeople.co/

Year Founded: 2010

Agency Specializes In: Advertising, Digital/Interactive, Media Buying Services, Media Planning, Search Engine Optimization, Social Media

Todd Alchin *(Partner & Sr Strategist-Creative)*
Jason Clement *(Pres-Los Angeles)*
Matthew Borchard *(Dir-Media)*
William de Lannoy *(Dir-Comm Strategy)*
Christine Trontell *(Dir-Media)*
Hillary Wirth *(Assoc Dir-Media)*
Rishabh Kumar *(Media Planner)*
Johanna Penry *(Media Planner)*

Accounts:
New-Annie's Inc. Media
New-FreshDirect Media Buying and Planning
Honest Tea
New-PayPal
USA Today

NOBOX MARKETING GROUP, INC.
180 NE 39Th St Ste 225, Miami, FL 33137
Tel.: (305) 571-2008
Fax: (305) 520-2001
Web Site: nobox.com/

Employees: 12

Antonio Rodriguez *(Partner & Dir-Tech)*
Margarita Irriszary *(Partner)*
Colin Ranieri *(VP-Fin)*
Cecilia Del Castillo *(Dir-Digital Media)*
Juan Carlos Hernandez *(Dir-Partnerships & Ventures)*
Joa Tous *(Assoc Dir-Creative)*
Marcos J. Alonso *(Acct Mgr)*
Cristina Pullin *(Acct Mgr)*
Maria Sepulveda *(Mgr-Digital Media)*
Linett Cortinas *(Acct Exec)*
Jayleen Nazario *(Strategist-Social Media)*
Jan De La Cruz *(Planner-Strategic)*

Accounts:
AAV4
Discovery Communications, Inc.
Download Day
Golden Ticket
Lexus & USTA
Marriott International, Inc.
Redesign Mozilla.com
Samsung Electronics America, Inc.
Scion Art
Sony Computer Entertainment America LLC Playstation
Verizon

Branch

Nobox Marketing Group, Inc.
Metro Parque #7 1st St Ste 303, Guaynabo, PR 00968
Tel.: (787) 792-7070
Fax: (787) 792-5454
E-Mail: info@nobox.com
Web Site: nobox.com/

Employees: 22
Year Founded: 2002

National Agency Associations: AHAA

Agency Specializes In: E-Commerce, Electronic Media, Hispanic Market, Internet/Web Design

Jayson Fittipaldi *(Pres & Chief Creative Officer)*
Cecilia Del Castillo *(Dir-Media)*
Michelle Juarbe *(Acct Exec)*

Accounts:
Banco Popular Premia Loyalty & Rewards
Copa Airlines
Mozilla Firefox
Toyota Lexus
Verizon

NOISE, INC.
4702 Rue Belle Mer, Sanibel, FL 33957
Tel.: (239) 395-9555
E-Mail: JohnS@Make-Noise.com
Web Site: www.make-noise.com

Employees: 20
Year Founded: 1986

Agency Specializes In: Advertising, Advertising Specialties, Brand Development & Integration, Broadcast, Business Publications, Business-To-Business, Cable T.V., Co-op Advertising, Collateral, Commercial Photography, Communications, Consumer Marketing, Consumer Publications, Corporate Communications, Corporate Identity, Crisis Communications, Digital/Interactive, Direct Response Marketing, Direct-to-Consumer, E-Commerce, Education, Electronic Media, Email, Entertainment, Event Planning & Marketing, Exhibit/Trade Shows, Financial, Food Service, Graphic Design, Health Care Services, Hispanic Market, Hospitality, Identity Marketing, In-Store Advertising, Integrated Marketing, Internet/Web Design, Investor Relations, Leisure, Local Marketing, Logo & Package Design, Luxury Products, Magazines, Marine, Market Research, Media Buying Services, Media Planning, Media Relations, Medical Products, Merchandising, Multimedia, New Product Development, Newspaper, Newspapers & Magazines, Out-of-Home Media, Outdoor, Planning & Consultation, Point of Purchase, Point of Sale, Print, Production, Production (Ad, Film, Broadcast), Production (Print), Public Relations, Publicity/Promotions, Radio, Real Estate, Recruitment, Regional, Restaurant, Retail, Sales Promotion, Social Marketing/Nonprofit, Strategic Planning/Research, T.V., Telemarketing, Trade & Consumer Magazines, Travel & Tourism, Web (Banner Ads, Pop-ups, etc.), Yellow Pages Advertising

Approx. Annual Billings: $7,000,000

Breakdown of Gross Billings by Media: Brdcst.: $1,750,000; Print: $5,250,000

John Sprecher *(Pres-NOISE & Dir-Creative)*
Emily Przybylo *(VP)*
Kathy Rusch *(Dir-Media)*

Accounts:
Trident Vitality Campaign: "Falling Stars"
Visit Milwaukee Campaign: "MKE FUN", Out-Of-Home

Branch

Noise, Inc.
PO Box 869, Sanibel, FL 33957
Tel.: (239) 395-9555
Fax: (239) 395-0876
E-Mail: info@make-noise.com
Web Site: www.make-noise.com

Employees: 15

Agency Specializes In: Advertising, Digital/Interactive, Public Relations, Strategic Planning/Research

John Sprecher *(Pres & Dir-Creative)*
Sonny Mares *(VP & Dir-Hospitality Mktg)*
Emily Przybylo *(VP)*

Accounts:
Florida Repertory Theatre

NOLIN BBDO
3575 Boulevard St-Laurent Suite 300, Montreal, QC H2X 2T7 Canada
Tel.: (514) 939-4100
Fax: (514) 939-4006
E-Mail: info@nolinbbdo.com
Web Site: www.nolinbbdo.com

Employees: 70
Year Founded: 1969

National Agency Associations: CAB

Agency Specializes In: Advertising, Advertising Specialties, Automotive, Bilingual Market, Brand Development & Integration, Broadcast, Business Publications, Business-To-Business, Co-op Advertising, Collateral, Communications, Consumer Marketing, Consumer Publications, Corporate Identity, Digital/Interactive, Direct Response Marketing, E-Commerce, Electronic Media, Event Planning & Marketing, Exhibit/Trade Shows, Graphic Design, Internet/Web Design, Logo & Package Design, Magazines, Media Buying Services, New Product Development, Newspaper, Newspapers & Magazines, Out-of-Home Media, Outdoor, Planning & Consultation, Point of Purchase, Point of Sale, Print, Production, Public Relations, Publicity/Promotions, Radio, Retail,

Sales Promotion, Strategic Planning/Research, T.V., Trade & Consumer Magazines

Approx. Annual Billings: $150,000,000

Breakdown of Gross Billings by Media: Other: 2%; Outdoor: 12%; Print: 23%; Radio: 13%; T.V.: 50%

Stephane Charier *(CEO & Dir-Creative)*
Lyne Clermont *(Acct Dir)*
Steve Pepin *(Art Dir)*
Vlada Zaitzev *(Acct Exec & Jr Producer)*

Accounts:
Bayer
Campbell's Soup
Cascades
Chrysler Canada Automotive-Chrysler, Dodge & Jeep; 1987
New-Dairy Farmers of Quebec
Divcom
Federation des Producteurs de Lait du Quebec Campaign: "Milk, Natural Source of Comfort", Fresh Milk; 1976
FedEx Courier Services; 1992
Frito-Lay Canada Cheetos, Lay's, Tostitos; 1982
Groupe Marcelle
Mercedes Benz Smart
Mitsubishi Motors; 2005
National Theater School
P&G
Pepsi-Cola 7-Up, Diet Pepsi, Mountain Dew, Pepsi; 1996
RBC
Splenda
Walter

NOMADIC AGENCY
7702 E Doubletree Ranch Rd Ste 200, Scottsdale, AZ 85258
Tel.: (480) 270-3000
Web Site: www.nomadicagency.com

Year Founded: 1998

Agency Specializes In: Advertising, Brand Development & Integration, Digital/Interactive, Mobile Marketing, Social Media, Web (Banner Ads, Pop-ups, etc.)

Tim Washburn *(Mng Partner & Exec Dir-Creative)*
Joel Neubeck *(Partner & Exec VP-Tech)*
Dawn Bates *(VP-Strategy)*
Jon Gowar *(VP-Client Svc)*
Dane McNeill *(VP-Ops)*
Max Hamilton *(Dir-Product Engrg)*
Kevin Kaminsky *(Dir-UX)*
Amy Leblanc *(Dir-Project Mgmt)*
Greg Orlowski *(Dir-Creative)*

Accounts:
Disney Cruise Line Inc Campaign: "Magical Cruise Adventure Sweepstakes"

NON-LINEAR CREATIONS INC.
Le Germain Office Tower 110 9th Avenue SW Suite 850, Calgary, AB T2P 0T1 Canada
Tel.: (403) 351-0173
Fax: (403) 263-7624
Toll Free: (866) 915-2997
E-Mail: info@nonlinear.ca
Web Site: www.nonlinearcreations.com

Year Founded: 1994

Agency Specializes In: Advertising, Graphic Design, Information Technology, Internet/Web Design, Multimedia, Social Media, Strategic Planning/Research, Web (Banner Ads, Pop-ups, etc.)

Randy Woods *(Pres)*
Shannon Ryan *(CEO)*
Daniel Roberge *(Pres-Nonlinear Enterprise)*
Allison Simpkins *(Pres-Nonlinear Digital)*
Glen Mcinnis *(VP-Delivery)*
Amanda Shiga *(VP-Digital)*
Shawn Crabtree *(Dir-Enterprise Solutions)*

Accounts:
Stratos Global Satellite Phones & Internet Service Provider

NONBOX
5307 S 92nd St, Hales Corners, WI 53130-1677
Tel.: (414) 425-8800
Fax: (414) 425-0021
E-Mail: info@nonbox.com
Web Site: www.nonbox.com

Employees: 25
Year Founded: 1959

National Agency Associations: BPA-IAN-MCA

Agency Specializes In: Brand Development & Integration, Strategic Planning/Research

Bill Eisner *(Partner)*
Greg Bell *(VP-Client Svcs)*
Jim Palmer *(Mgmt Supvr & Dir-Media Svcs)*
Billy Cannestra *(Dir-Tech)*
Jose Coronado *(Dir-Web Dev)*
Jon Grider *(Dir-Creative)*
Kevin Brown *(Assoc Dir-Creative & Writer)*
Kathy Ruppenthal *(Sr Media Planner & Buyer)*

Accounts:
Saint Pauli Girl Beer
Seymour Duncan (Agency of Record)
Steinhafels Furniture

Branches

Nonbox
319 SW Washington St Mezzanine Level, Portland, OR 97204
Tel.: (503) 227-1638
Fax: (503) 417-8613
E-Mail: info@nonbox.com
Web Site: www.nonbox.com

Employees: 12
Year Founded: 1999

Agency Specializes In: Brand Development & Integration, Strategic Planning/Research

Steve Karakas *(Partner)*
Judy Mann-Jensen *(VP-Media)*
Ian Hamilton *(Dir-Sports Mktg)*

Accounts:
Adidas
Peter Jacobsen Sports

Nonbox
1970 E Osceola Pkwy Ste 47, Orlando, FL 34743
Tel.: (321) 287-4919
Fax: (584) 376-7
E-Mail: scott@nonboxconsulting.com
Web Site: www.nonbox.com/

Employees: 10

BJ Bueno *(Mng Partner)*

NORM MARSHALL & ASSOCIATES
(Formerly NMA Entertainment & Marketing)
11059 Sherman Way, Sun Valley, CA 91352
Tel.: (818) 982-3505
Fax: (818) 503-1936
E-Mail: norm@normmarshall.com
Web Site: www.corbisentertainment.com/normmarshall

Employees: 50

Agency Specializes In: Advertising, Entertainment, Event Planning & Marketing, Fashion/Apparel, Food Service, Publicity/Promotions, Sponsorship

Mark Owens *(Pres)*
Norm Marshall *(CEO)*
Malcolm Brooker *(Sr VP & Dir-Creative)*
Caressa Douglas-Lupold *(Sr VP-Production Resources)*
Julie Meier *(Sr VP)*

Accounts:
Emergen-C
Baskin-Robbins Custom Cakes, Ice Cream, Packaging, Promotions
Capital One
Chevrolet
Dunkin' Donuts Packaging, Promotions
GMC
Heineken USA (Entertainment Marketing Agency of Record) Amstel Light, Dos Equis, Entertainment Marketing, Heineken, Heineken Light, Newcastle Brown Ale, Public Relations, Tecate, Tecate Light
Hostess Cupcakes, Ding Dongs, Ho Ho's, Sno Balls, Suzy Q's, Twinkies
OnStar
Royal Purple Industrial Lubricants, Racing Banners, Synthetic Motor Oil
Ty Nant Sparkling Water
U-Haul Boxes, Moving Trucks, Trailers
USA Today Newspapers
XBOX Home Video Gaming Platform, Packaging

NORMAN DIEGNAN & ASSOCIATES
PO Box 298, Oldwick, NJ 08858
Tel.: (908) 832-7951
Fax: (908) 832-9650
E-Mail: n.diegnan@comcast.net
Web Site: www.diegnan-associates.com

Employees: 5
Year Founded: 1977

National Agency Associations: PRSA

Agency Specializes In: Advertising, Business Publications, Communications, Environmental, Event Planning & Marketing, Exhibit/Trade Shows, Industrial, New Product Development, Newspaper, Public Relations, Publicity/Promotions, Radio, Sales Promotion, T.V., Technical Advertising

Approx. Annual Billings: $1,000,000

Norman Diegnan *(VP)*

Accounts:
Hamon Research-Cottrell
ISHA
Net Talon; Fredericksburg, PA Security Products
Newark Wire Cloth; Newark, NJ
NJ League of Community Bankers; Cranford, NJ

NORTH
1515 NW 19th Ave, Portland, OR 97209
Tel.: (503) 222-4117
Fax: (503) 222-4118
E-Mail: hello@north.com
Web Site: www.north.com

Employees: 24
Year Founded: 1991

Agency Specializes In: Brand Development & Integration, Sponsorship

Approx. Annual Billings: $20,000,000

Mark Ray *(Owner, Chief Creative Officer & Principal)*
Luke Perkins *(Exec Dir-Creative)*
Margaret Alvarez *(Brand Dir)*
Brianna Babb *(Brand Dir)*
Jim Carey *(Dir-Creative)*
Jordan Delapoer *(Dir-Brand Strategy)*
Caroline Lewis *(Dir-Media Strategy)*
Eric Samsel *(Dir-Creative)*
Derek Muller *(Asst Brand Mgr)*

Accounts:
Anchor Brewing Co.
Ann Sacks Tile & Stone Fixtures, Stone, Tile
CLIF Bar
New-Columbia Sportswear Company
Cover Oregon Branding, Communications Campaign
Deschutes Brewery; Bend, OR Landmarks
Downtown Marketing Initiative
Kallista
Keen Footwear
Portland General Electric Power
Right Brain Initiative
Subaru of America
Tillamook
Umqua Bank
Yakima Products
Zuke's Natural Pet Treats

NORTH 6TH AGENCY
18 Harrison St 1st Fl, New York, NY 10013
Tel.: (212) 334-9753
Fax: (212) 334-9760
E-Mail: media@n6a.com
Web Site: www.n6a.com

Year Founded: 2010

Agency Specializes In: Advertising, Communications, Crisis Communications, Event Planning & Marketing, Internet/Web Design, Investor Relations, Media Buying Services, Media Relations

Nina Velasquez *(Sr VP)*
Darline Morel *(Office Mgr)*
Jessica Moody *(Sr Acct Exec)*
Robert Vanisko *(Sr Acct Exec)*
Lauren Epstein *(Acct Exec)*
Carli Griffin *(Acct Exec-PR)*
Rachel Jermansky *(Acct Exec)*

Accounts:
Allied Fiber Assessment Reports, Awareness, Content Development, Events, Marketing, Public Relations Agency of Record, Social Media, Speaking Engagements, Tradeshows
APTelecom
New-Concierge Choice Physicians (Public Relations Agency of Record) Media Relations
New-CredSimple (Public Relations Agency of Record)
New-Handshake (Public Relations Agency of Record) Media Relations, Print, Radio, TV
New-ImagineAir (Public Relations Agency of Record)
Kii Public Relations
Next Glass Media Relations, Messaging Initiatives, Public Relations Agency of Record
Parent Society
New-ResQwalk (Agency of Record) Content Development, Creative, Media Relations, Outreach
Tom Coughlin Jay Fund Foundation "Champions for Children", Counsel, Media Relations, Public Relations Agency of Record, Strategy, Writing & Editorial
New-WhoSay (Public Relations Agency of Record)

NORTH CHARLES STREET DESIGN ORGANIZATION
222 W Saratoga St, Baltimore, MD 21201
Tel.: (410) 539-4040
Fax: (410) 685-0961
E-Mail: info@ncsdo.com
Web Site: www.ncsdo.com

Year Founded: 1972

Agency Specializes In: Advertising, Brand Development & Integration, Communications, Graphic Design, Print

Clifford Lull *(Pres)*
Tracy Raff *(Sr Dir-Art)*
Matthew Swanson *(Dir-Special Projects)*
Ulfras Floyd *(Mgr-Production)*

Accounts:
Barnard College
Bridgewater College
Case Western Reserve University
Connections Academy
The George Washington University Law School
Gettysburg College
Hobart & William Smith Colleges
Lebanon Valley College
Manhattanville College
Mills College
New Jersey Institute of Technology
Rutgers University
Sarah Lawrence College
St. Catherine University
St. John Fisher College
St. John's College
St. Paul's School for Girls
Stanford University
University of Pennsylvania
University of Richmond
University of the South
University of Virginia's College at Wise
Whitman College
Yeshiva University

NORTH FORTY
1501 Boyson Sq Dr Ste 201, Hiawatha, IA 52233
Tel.: (319) 261-1040
Fax: (319) 261-1041
E-Mail: info@nforty.com
Web Site: www.nforty.com

Agency Specializes In: Advertising, Brand Development & Integration, Digital/Interactive, Internet/Web Design, Logo & Package Design, Print, Promotions, Radio, Social Media, T.V.

Muna Matthews *(Dir-Creative Content)*
Jake VandeWeerd *(Dir-Creative Vision)*
Gerard Estella *(Dir-Creative Experience)*

Accounts:
LG Electronics U.S.A., Inc.

NORTH OF NINE COMMUNICATIONS
303 2nd St S Tower Ste 800, San Francisco, CA 94107
Tel.: (415) 268-4800
E-Mail: info@nof9.com
Web Site: www.nof9.com

Year Founded: 2011

Agency Specializes In: Advertising, Brand Development & Integration, Crisis Communications, Media Relations, Social Media

Jennifer Graham Clary *(CEO)*
Tony Hynes *(Partner)*
Josh Lefkowitz *(Sr Dir)*
Allison Kubota *(Mgr)*
Cristina Thai *(Mgr)*
Haley Hirai *(Acct Exec)*

Accounts:
DataSift B-to-B, Business Media, Public Relations, Technology, Thought Leadership

NORTH SHORE PUBLIC RELATIONS INC.
3400 Dundee Rd Ste 300, Northbrook, IL 60062
Tel.: (847) 945-4505
Fax: (847) 945-3755
E-Mail: tony@northshorepr.com
Web Site: www.northshorepr.com

Employees: 3
Year Founded: 2007

Agency Specializes In: Internet/Web Design, Media Training, Newspapers & Magazines, Public Relations

Tony Schor *(Pres)*

Accounts:
Greyson International Inc
PuraMed Bioscience Inc Medicinal & Healthcare Products Marketing

NORTH STAR MARKETING
245 Butler Ave, Lancaster, PA 17601
Tel.: (717) 392-6982
Fax: (717) 392-7463
E-Mail: bsmith@northstar-m.com
Web Site: www.northstar-m.com

Employees: 7
Year Founded: 1989

Agency Specializes In: Advertising, Affiliate Marketing, Affluent Market, Brand Development & Integration, Business-To-Business, Collateral, Communications, Consumer Goods, Consumer Marketing, Consumer Publications, Corporate Communications, Corporate Identity, Crisis Communications, Customer Relationship Management, Digital/Interactive, Direct-to-Consumer, E-Commerce, Electronics, Email, Engineering, Event Planning & Marketing, Exhibit/Trade Shows, Food Service, Game Integration, Graphic Design, Household Goods, Identity Marketing, In-Store Advertising, Industrial, Integrated Marketing, Internet/Web Design, Logo & Package Design, Luxury Products, Market Research, Media Relations, New Product Development, Outdoor, Package Design, Paid Searches, Podcasting, Point of Purchase, Point of Sale, Print, Promotions, Public Relations, Publicity/Promotions, RSS (Really Simple Syndication), Radio, Sales Promotion, Search Engine Optimization, Social Marketing/Nonprofit, Strategic Planning/Research, Trade & Consumer Magazines, Viral/Buzz/Word of Mouth, Web (Banner Ads, Pop-ups, etc.)

Approx. Annual Billings: $3,500,000

Kae Groshong Wagner *(Founder, Pres & CEO)*

Accounts:
Lancaster County

NORTH STAR MARKETING, INC.
1130 10 Rod Rd Ste A205, North Kingstown, RI 02852
Tel.: (401) 294-0133
Fax: (888) 561-2814
E-Mail: northstar@fortheloveofmarketing.com
Web Site: www.fortheloveofmarketing.com

Employees: 11

Agency Specializes In: Advertising, Brand Development & Integration, Collateral, Corporate Identity, Digital/Interactive, Email, Event Planning & Marketing, Internet/Web Design, Logo & Package Design, Media Relations, Media Training, Podcasting, Print, Public Relations, Sales Promotion, Search Engine Optimization, Strategic Planning/Research

April Williams McCrory *(Pres)*
Peter Seronick *(Dir)*

Accounts:
BankNewport
Beyond Grace Salon
Current Carrier
Dr. Robert Leonard
The Employers Association, Inc.
GEM Plumbing
LogicBay
New Territories
Pilgrim Screw
RI Flowers
Tameracq Partners
YWCA of Northern RI

NORTH WOODS ADVERTISING
15 Bldg Ste 1201 15 S 5th St, Minneapolis, MN 55402
Tel.: (612) 340-9999
Fax: (612) 340-0857
E-Mail: info@northwoodsadv.com
Web Site: www.northwoodsadvertising.com

Employees: 10

Agency Specializes In: Food Service, Government/Political

Bill Hillsman *(Pres & Chief Creative Officer)*
Jill Harrison *(Dir-Fin & Bus Mgr)*

Accounts:
Malt-O-Meal Breakfast Cereals

NORTHERN LIGHTS DIRECT
150 N Michigan Ave Ste 800, Chicago, IL 60601
Tel.: (312) 263-8686
Fax: (312) 624-7701
E-Mail: contact@northernlightsdirect.com
Web Site: www.northernlightsdirect.com

Agency Specializes In: Media Buying Services, Media Planning, Production, Search Engine Optimization, T.V.

Ian French *(Pres & Partner)*
Sandy French *(CEO & Partner)*
Luc Bourgon *(Partner & COO)*
Jane French *(Partner & Exec VP-Ops)*
Pippa Nutt *(Sr VP-Online & Canadian Media)*
Vince Heney *(VP & Dir-Creative)*
Rebecca Barr *(VP-Media-US)*
Anna Fowles *(VP-Creative & Production Svcs)*

Accounts:
SickKids Foundation Children Charity Services

NORTHLICH
Sawyer Point Bldg 720 E Pete Rose Way, Cincinnati, OH 45202
Tel.: (513) 421-8840
Fax: (513) 455-4749
E-Mail: info@northlich.com
Web Site: www.northlich.com

E-Mail for Key Personnel:
Creative Dir.: JWarman@northlich.com
Public Relations: rmiller@northlich.com

Employees: 100
Year Founded: 1949

National Agency Associations: 4A's-AMA-ICOM-PRSA

Agency Specializes In: Advertising, Brand Development & Integration, Collateral, Consulting, Consumer Marketing, Corporate Communications, Corporate Identity, Crisis Communications, Education, Financial, Food Service, Government/Political, Graphic Design, Health Care Services, Internet/Web Design, Investor Relations, Medical Products, New Product Development, Pharmaceutical, Planning & Consultation, Production, Public Relations, Publicity/Promotions, Restaurant, Retail, Social Media, Sponsorship, Strategic Planning/Research

Kathy Selker *(Pres & CEO)*
Jonathan Richman *(Partner & Chief Brand Officer)*
Tim McCort *(COO)*
Dan Rapp *(VP & Grp Dir-Creative)*
Liz Adkins *(Acct Dir)*
Brad Wymore *(Mgmt Supvr)*
Jennifer DeSutter *(Assoc Dir-Digital Media)*
Dan Whitmyer *(Assoc Dir-Strategy)*
Cassie Kelly *(Acct Mgr)*
Bryce Anslinger *(Supvr-Content)*
Timothy Fagel *(Strategist-Digital)*
Annie Pryatel *(Strategist)*
Megan Damcevski *(Asst Acct Mgr)*
Terry Dillon *(Assoc Creative Dir)*
Ali Stigler *(Asst Acct Mgr)*

Accounts:
American Greetings
Ashland, Inc. Ashland Distribution Company, Ashland Specialty Chemical Company, Valvoline, Valvoline Instant Oil Change
Birds Eye Foods
Buffalo Wings & Rings; Cincinnati, OH Public Relations
Cardinal Health
Cincinnati Bell Inc.
GiveThemTen.org Campaign: "Scooter"
Jefferson's Bourbon Branding, Digital, Print, Social Media
Kahiki Foods
Macy's
Nestle's
Ohio Department of Health
Ohio Lottery Commission Campaign: "Just Right"
Ohio State University Medical Center (Agency of Record)
Procter & Gamble Company
TriHealth
Western & Southern Financial Group Western & Southern Strength
White Castle System, Inc.
Yum Brands A&W, Long John Silver's; 2005

Branches

Northlich Public Relations
720 E Pete Rose Way Ste 120, Cincinnati, OH 45202-3579
(See Separate Listing)

NORTHLICH PUBLIC RELATIONS
720 E Pete Rose Way Ste 120, Cincinnati, OH 45202-3579
Tel.: (513) 421-8840
Fax: (513) 287-1858
E-Mail: info@northlich.com
Web Site: www.northlich.com

E-Mail for Key Personnel:
President: rmiller@northlich.com

Employees: 25
Year Founded: 1956

National Agency Associations: AMA-PRSA

Agency Specializes In: E-Commerce, Environmental, Financial, Food Service, Government/Political, Health Care Services, High Technology, Internet/Web Design, Investor Relations, Public Relations, Publicity/Promotions, Retail, Teen Market, Viral/Buzz/Word of Mouth

Approx. Annual Billings: $5,400,000

Kerry Broderick *(VP & Grp Dir-Creative)*
Dan Rapp *(VP & Grp Dir-Creative)*
Meredith Ferguson *(VP & Acct Dir)*
Michelle Snook *(VP & Acct Dir)*
Todd Schneider *(Acct Dir)*
Liz Adkins *(Dir-Conversation Plng)*
Timothy Fagel *(Strategist-Digital)*

Accounts:
American Greetings Music and Sound Envelopes
Ashland Inc.; Covington, KY; 2000
Birds Eye Foods
Children's Hunger Alliance
Cincinnati Reds
Cincinnati USA Partnership
Hillenbrand; Batesville, IN; 1997
Long John Silver's / Crispy Breaded Microsite
Ohio Lottery
Ohio State Medical Association
The Ohio State University Medical Center Ross Heart Hospital
Ohio Tobacco Prevention Foundation / Debunkify
Procter & Gamble; Cincinnati, OH
Sona Medspa
TriHealth
United Way
Western & Southern Financial Group Seasoned & Stable, Strength Campaign
White Castle System, Inc. Web Site Redesign

Branch

Northlich-Columbus
580 N 4th St Ste 660, Columbus, OH 43215
Tel.: (614) 573-0910
Fax: (614) 573-0909
Web Site: www.northlich.com

Employees: 10

National Agency Associations: 4A's

Agency Specializes In: Public Relations

Kerry Broderick *(VP & Grp Dir-Creative)*
Dan Rapp *(VP & Grp Dir-Creative)*
Meredith Ferguson *(VP & Acct Dir)*
Michelle Snook *(VP & Acct Dir)*
Laura Gels *(Sr Dir-Art)*
Todd Schneider *(Acct Dir)*
Liz Adkins *(Dir-Conversation Plng)*
Kate McGuire *(Dir-Art)*
Sandy Sullivan *(Mgr-HR)*
Timothy Fagel *(Strategist-Digital)*

Accounts:
American Greetings
Birds Eye
Iams
Kentucky Lottery
Macy's
Ohio Lottery
Ohio Tobacco Prevention Foundation

NORTHLIGHT ADVERTISING
1208 Kimberton Rd, Chester Springs, PA 19425
Tel.: (484) 202-8506
Fax: (484) 202-8510
E-Mail: info@northlightadvertising.com
Web Site: www.northlightadv.com

Employees: 4

Year Founded: 1992

Agency Specializes In: Advertising, Advertising Specialties, Cable T.V., Collateral, Corporate Communications, Corporate Identity, Direct Response Marketing, Exhibit/Trade Shows, Graphic Design, In-Store Advertising, Logo & Package Design, Media Buying Services, Newspaper, Newspapers & Magazines, Outdoor, Planning & Consultation, Point of Sale, Print, Production, Public Relations, Publicity/Promotions, Sales Promotion, Strategic Planning/Research, T.V.

Rick Miller *(Pres & Dir-Creative)*
Max Morressi *(CTO)*
Linda Smith *(VP)*

Accounts:
The Desmond Hotel and Conference Center
Dranoff Properties
Elliott Lewis; Philadelphia, PA
First Priority Bank
The General Warren
Harry's Savoy Grill; Wilmington, DE
McKenzie Brew House
The Ronto Group
Shannondell at Valley Forge
Vaughan & Sautter Builders; Wayne, PA

NORTHSHORE DESIGNERS

3655 Torrance Blvd Ste 361, Torrance, CA 90503
Tel.: (424) 247-1143
Fax: (424) 247-1144
E-Mail: n-shore@pacbell.net
Web Site: www.nshoredesign.com

Employees: 1
Year Founded: 1997

Agency Specializes In: Consumer Marketing, Graphic Design, Retail, Seniors' Market

Approx. Annual Billings: $1,000,000

Breakdown of Gross Billings by Media: Mags.: $250,000; Newsp.: $500,000; Worldwide Web Sites: $250,000

Richard L. Goldstein *(Owner)*

Accounts:
AC Nielsen
Advanced Assets, Inc.
Boys & Girls Clubs of Conejo & Las Virgenes
Brian Testo Associates, LLC
Children's Hospital of Los Angeles
City of Los Angeles
City of Torrance
Crimestopper Security Products; Simi Valley, CA Vehicle Security Systems; 1997
Health Quality Management Co.
Manhattan Beach Education Foundation
Northrop Grumman
Paramount Studios
Planned Parenthood
Rehabilitation Center of Beverly Hills; Beverly Hills, CA; 1997
Rouse Asset Services
Tranzon Asset Strategies
University of Southern California; Los Angeles, CA; 1999

NORTHSTAR DESTINATION STRATEGIES

220 Danyacrest Dr, Nashville, TN 37214
Tel.: (615) 232-2103, ext. 24
Fax: (615) 523-1146
Toll Free: (888) 260-7827
E-Mail: info@northstarideas.com
Web Site: www.northstarideas.com

Employees: 15
Year Founded: 2000

Agency Specializes In: Advertising, Travel & Tourism

Approx. Annual Billings: $8,498,000 Capitalized

Don McEachern *(Pres & CEO)*
Ed Barlow *(VP-Strategic Plng)*
Christi Mceachern *(Exec Dir-Creative)*
Ted Nelson *(Dir-Creative)*
Nan Natcher *(Mgr-Brand Print)*
Eric Steltenpohl *(Mgr-Mktg & Creative)*
Kerry Crawford *(Strategist-Social Media)*
Katie Rahn *(Specialist-Community Mktg)*
Lance Wagner *(Coord-Res)*

Accounts:
Brookings
Fort Kollins
Jackson
McKinney
Moose Jaw
Spanish Fork
Victoria TX
Yarmouth

THE NORTHWEST GROUP

28265 Beck Rd Ste C2, Wixom, MI 48393
Tel.: (248) 349-9480
Fax: (248) 349-9415
E-Mail: nwg@nwestgroup.com
Web Site: www.nwestgroup.com

E-Mail for Key Personnel:
President: Tgraham@nwestgroup.com
Creative Dir.: pvankirk@nwestgroup.com
Production Mgr.: dnelson@nwestgroup.com

Employees: 8
Year Founded: 1959

Agency Specializes In: Advertising Specialties, Brand Development & Integration, Business Publications, Business-To-Business, Collateral, Commercial Photography, Consulting, Corporate Communications, Corporate Identity, Direct Response Marketing, E-Commerce, Electronic Media, Environmental, Event Planning & Marketing, Food Service, Graphic Design, Health Care Services, Industrial, Internet/Web Design, Logo & Package Design, Medical Products, New Product Development, Newspaper, Outdoor, Point of Purchase, Point of Sale, Print, Publicity/Promotions, Sales Promotion, Strategic Planning/Research, Telemarketing

Approx. Annual Billings: $1,000,000

Breakdown of Gross Billings by Media: Bus. Publs.: $50,000; Collateral: $300,000; Comml. Photography: $50,000; D.M.: $150,000; Logo & Package Design: $20,000; Plng. & Consultation: $20,000; Print: $150,000; Production: $250,000; Pub. Rels.: $10,000

Tom Graham *(Owner)*
Kim Petty *(Sr Graphic Designer)*

Accounts:
Awrey Bakeries, Inc.; Livonia, MI
UNIVAL; Ann Arbor, MI
Valeo Transmission

NORTON NORRIS

55 E Jackson Blvd Ste 950, Chicago, IL 60604-4800
Tel.: (312) 262-7400
Fax: (708) 478-1199
E-Mail: vince@nortonnorris.com
Web Site: www.nortonnorris.com

Employees: 12

Agency Specializes In: Advertising, Advertising Specialties, Bilingual Market, Brand Development & Integration, Broadcast, Cable T.V., Collateral, Communications, Consulting, Email, Graphic Design, Guerilla Marketing, Hispanic Market, Identity Marketing, Infomercials, Integrated Marketing, Internet/Web Design, Local Marketing, Market Research, Media Buying Services, Media Planning, Media Relations, Newspaper, Newspapers & Magazines, Outdoor, Paid Searches, Planning & Consultation, Production, Production (Ad, Film, Broadcast), Production (Print), Radio, Recruitment, Search Engine Optimization, Strategic Planning/Research, Syndication, T.V.

Approx. Annual Billings: $3,000,000

Vince Norton *(Owner)*
Jean Norris *(Mng Partner-Trng & Assessment)*
Shannon Gormley *(Dir-Trng)*

Accounts:
Aakers College
Remington College
San Diego Golf Academy
University of Chicago

NORTON RUBBLE & MERTZ ADVERTISING

549 W Randolph St, Chicago, IL 60661
Tel.: (312) 470-6117
Fax: (630) 954-0501
E-Mail: mlopiano@nrmadv.com
Web Site: www.nortonadvertising.com

E-Mail for Key Personnel:
President: sueg@nrmadv.com
Creative Dir.: CKlonowski@nrmadv.com

Employees: 19
Year Founded: 1985

Agency Specializes In: Communications, Consumer Marketing

Approx. Annual Billings: $4,200,000

Laura Herzing *(Sr Dir-Art & Assoc Producer)*
Paul Bjorneberg *(Dir-Quality Assurance)*
Chris Chen *(Dir-Creative)*
Christa Velbel *(Dir-Creative)*
Brian Quinn *(Assoc Dir-Creative)*
Kelly Anderson *(Sr Acct Exec)*
Kirsten Chiopelas *(Acct Exec)*
Justin McLeod *(Copywriter)*

NOSTRUM INC.

401 E Ocean Blvd Ste M101, Long Beach, CA 90802
Tel.: (562) 437-2200
Fax: (800) 684-0424
Toll Free: (800) 540-7414
E-Mail: scollida@nostruminc.com
Web Site: www.nostruminc.com

E-Mail for Key Personnel:
President: scollida@nostruminc.com

Employees: 5
Year Founded: 1981

National Agency Associations: 4A's-AMA-DMA

Agency Specializes In: Advertising Specialties, Business Publications, Business-To-Business, Cable T.V., Catalogs, Co-op Advertising, Collateral, Communications, Consulting, Consumer Marketing, Corporate Communications, Corporate Identity, Digital/Interactive, Direct Response Marketing, Direct-to-Consumer, E-Commerce,

Email, Event Planning & Marketing, Exhibit/Trade Shows, Government/Political, Graphic Design, Health Care Services, Hospitality, In-Store Advertising, International, Internet/Web Design, Local Marketing, Logo & Package Design, Magazines, Media Buying Services, Media Planning, Media Relations, Mobile Marketing, Multimedia, New Technologies, Newspaper, Newspapers & Magazines, Outdoor, Point of Purchase, Point of Sale, Print, Production, Production (Ad, Film, Broadcast), Public Relations, Publicity/Promotions, Radio, Real Estate, Restaurant, Sales Promotion, Seniors' Market, Social Marketing/Nonprofit, Stakeholders, T.V., Trade & Consumer Magazines, Urban Market

Approx. Annual Billings: $1,500,000

Susan G. Collida *(Pres & CEO)*

Accounts:
Long Beach Airport
Long Beach Convention Center
Long Beach Transit
Long Beach Visitors and Convention Bureau

NOT MAURICE
524 Sunset Ave, Venice, CA 90291
Tel.: (310) 356-6177
Fax: (310) 857-6452
E-Mail: contact@notmaurice.com
Web Site: www.notmaurice.com

Year Founded: 2004

Agency Specializes In: Advertising, Content, Email, Graphic Design, Internet/Web Design

Patrick Chevalier *(Dir-Creative)*

Accounts:
Marathon Power
SOS-GAL

NOTIONIST
31368 Via Colinas Ste 105, Westlake Village, CA 91362
Tel.: (818) 292-8787
E-Mail: hello@notionist.com
Web Site: www.notionist.com

Agency Specializes In: Advertising, Brand Development & Integration, Digital/Interactive, Graphic Design, Internet/Web Design, Print, Public Relations, Search Engine Optimization, Social Media

Gerard Bello *(Art Dir)*

Accounts:
New-HMH Contractors Incorporation

NOVA ADVERTISING
3929 Old Lee Hwy Unit 92C, Fairfax, VA 22030
Tel.: (703) 855-9641
E-Mail: askus@novaadvertising.com
Web Site: www.novaadvertising.com

Year Founded: 2009

Agency Specializes In: Advertising, Brand Development & Integration, Internet/Web Design, Search Engine Optimization

Behzad Riazi *(Pres)*
Fred Ostovar *(VP-Bus Dev & Mktg)*
Safa Damouzehtash *(VP-Web Dev)*
Ruth Quan *(Mgr-Referral Generation)*
Dominique Jackson *(Mgr-SEO)*

Accounts:
Allergy & Asthma Care Centers
Floor & Beyond
Pop-A-Lock
Smileville Kids

NOVA CREATIVE GROUP, INC.
571 Congress Park Dr, Dayton, OH 45459-4036
Tel.: (937) 434-9200
Fax: (937) 434-0400
Toll Free: (800) 726-1713
Web Site: www.novacreative.com

Employees: 20
Year Founded: 1980

Agency Specializes In: Advertising, Brand Development & Integration, Business-To-Business, Catalogs, Collateral, Corporate Communications, Corporate Identity, Digital/Interactive, Electronic Media, Email, Environmental, Event Planning & Marketing, Graphic Design, In-Store Advertising, Integrated Marketing, Internet/Web Design, Logo & Package Design, Media Planning, Multimedia, Out-of-Home Media, Package Design, Planning & Consultation, Production (Print), Strategic Planning/Research, Web (Banner Ads, Pop-ups, etc.)

Approx. Annual Billings: $2,000,000

Breakdown of Gross Billings by Media: Collateral: 25%; D.M.: 5%; Graphic Design: 35%; Internet Adv.: 5%; Worldwide Web Sites: 30%

Amy Niswonger *(Dir-Creative)*
Marilyn Shields *(Office Mgr)*
Larry P. Knapp *(Mgr-Relationship)*
Bill Rieger *(Mgr-Relationship)*
Mackenzie Graves *(Specialist-Video & Designer)*

Accounts:
Dayton International Airport
Deceuninck North America
Ferrari North America
Greater Dayton Regional Transit Authority
LexisNexis
Miller-Valentine Group
Ohio Head Start Association, Inc.
University of Dayton
Wright State University

NOVA MARKETING
300 Crown Colony Dr, Quincy, MA 02169
Tel.: (617) 770-0304
Fax: (617) 770-1821
E-Mail: info@novainc.com
Web Site: www.novainc.com

Employees: 15

Agency Specializes In: Consulting, In-Store Advertising, Media Buying Services, Newspaper, Newspapers & Magazines, Point of Purchase, Point of Sale, Retail, Sales Promotion, Strategic Planning/Research

Ken Villanova *(Founder & Pres)*
Alex Mohr *(VP-Multicultural Mktg Grp & Grp Head)*
Pat Iamele *(VP & Dir-Creative)*

Accounts:
AstraZeneca
CapeCod Healthcare
CVS Pharmacy
Foot Action
John Deere
Lightolier
Lowe's
Novartis
Staples
WestingHouse

NOVITA COMMUNICATIONS
277 Broadway Ste 201, New York, NY 10007
Tel.: (212) 528-3160
Fax: (917) 591-7292
Web Site: www.novitapr.com

Agency Specializes In: Advertising, Brand Development & Integration, Digital/Interactive, Graphic Design, Public Relations, Social Media, Strategic Planning/Research

Christine Abbate *(Pres)*
Danielle Mcwilliams *(VP)*
Cherie Bustamante *(VP)*
Kristin Coleman *(Acct Dir)*

Accounts:
New-BKLYN Designs

NOW COMMUNICATIONS
750 W Pender St Ste 710, Vancouver, BC V6C 2T7 Canada
Tel.: (604) 682-5441
Fax: (604) 681-4834
Toll Free: (877) 682-5441
E-Mail: team@nowgroup.com
Web Site: www.nowgroup.com

Employees: 10
Year Founded: 1992

Agency Specializes In: Advertising

Revenue: $25,000,000

Ron Johnson *(Founder & Partner)*
Marie Della Mattia *(Pres & CEO)*
Paul Degenstein *(Chief Creative Officer)*
Rupinder Kang *(Client Svcs Dir)*
Carrie Ann Barlow *(Dir-Media)*
Jim Lowe *(Designer)*

NOWAK ASSOCIATES, INC
6075 E Molloy Bldg 7, Syracuse, NY 13211
Tel.: (315) 463-1001
Fax: (315) 463-7933
Web Site: www.nowakagency.com

Employees: 10
Year Founded: 1951

Agency Specializes In: Digital/Interactive, Market Research, Outdoor, Print, Promotions, Public Relations, Social Media, Strategic Planning/Research, T.V.

Tim Nowak *(Pres)*
Donna Nowak-Hughes *(Exec VP)*

Accounts:
Catholic Funeral & Cemetery Services
Graceland Cemetery
Mental Health Foundation Of West Michigan, Inc.
Nigro Companies
Omni Development Company, Inc.
Omni Housing Development LLC
Onondaga Community College
Rose Dental Association
Sony Corporation of America

Branch

Nowak Associates, Inc
6 Wembley Ct, Albany, NY 12205
Tel.: (518) 452-4200
Fax: (518) 452-4204
Web Site: www.nowakagency.com

Year Founded: 1951

Agency Specializes In: Market Research, Outdoor, Print, Promotions, Public Relations, Social Media, Strategic Planning/Research

Donna Nowak-Hughes *(Exec VP)*

Accounts:
Graceland Cemetery
Nigro Companies
Omni Development Company, Inc.
Sony Corporation of America

NPJ ADVERTISING & PUBLIC RELATIONS, INC.
2201 Wisconsin Ave NW Ste 304, Washington, DC 20007-4105
Tel.: (202) 338-4200
Fax: (202) 338-7077
E-Mail: info@npjadvertising.com
Web Site: www.npjadvertising.com

Employees: 5
Year Founded: 2001

Agency Specializes In: Advertising, African-American Market, Brand Development & Integration, Broadcast, Business-To-Business, Cable T.V., Co-op Advertising, Collateral, Communications, Consulting, Consumer Marketing, Corporate Identity, Cosmetics, Education, Electronic Media, Event Planning & Marketing, Government/Political, Logo & Package Design, Media Buying Services, Multimedia, New Product Development, Newspaper, Out-of-Home Media, Outdoor, Planning & Consultation, Point of Sale, Print, Public Relations, Radio, Retail, T.V.

Approx. Annual Billings: $1,667,500

Breakdown of Gross Billings by Media: Cable T.V.: $55,150; Collateral: $1,107,220; Pub. Rels.: $260,130; Radio: $50,000; T.V.: $195,000

Nathaniel Pope, Jr. *(Owner)*
Andre Carley *(Exec Dir-Art)*

Accounts:
Architect of the Capitol; Washington, DC The United States Capitol Complex; 2004
DC Department of Health; Washington, DC Addiction Prevention; 2005
Flagstar Bank Fort Washington Home Loan Center; Fort Washington, MD Mortgages; 2005
Gallaudet University; Washington, DC CAPSS; 2004
Impact Jacket, LLC; Largo, MD Protective Gear for Motorcycle Riders; 2006
Marlborough Country Club; Upper Marlborough, MD Golf & Country Club; 2008
Mercedes-Benz of Annapolis; Annapolis, MD Retail Sales; 2004
National Center for Fathering, Inc.; Kansas City, MO Non-Profit; 2006
National Organization of Concerned Black Men, Inc.; Philadelphia, PA Non-Profit; 2001
Prince George's Country Government; Upper Marlboro, MD Livable Communities; 2005
Serve DC; Washington, DC Service; 2006

NSG/SWAT
73 Spring St Ste 302, New York, NY 10012
Tel.: (212) 257-1726
E-Mail: info@nsgswat.com
Web Site: www.nsgswat.com

Year Founded: 2011

Agency Specializes In: Advertising, Brand Development & Integration, Graphic Design, Internet/Web Design

Edmund Boey *(Dir-Interactive Art)*
Andrew Tobin *(Dir-Creative)*
Woody Wright *(Acct Mgr)*

Accounts:
Morgans Hotel Group

NSPHERE INC.
100 Franklin St 5th Fl, Boston, MA 02110
Tel.: (617) 933-7500
Fax: (617) 344-8363
Web Site: nsphere.net

Employees: 100
Year Founded: 2002

Agency Specializes In: Electronic Media, Internet/Web Design, Web (Banner Ads, Pop-ups, etc.), Yellow Pages Advertising

Revenue: $17,000,000

Jim Woodroffe *(Co-Founder & CTO)*
Jean-Eric Penicaud *(COO)*
Michael Bach *(CMO)*
Michael Gatzke *(VP-Grab Networks)*
Ed Komo *(VP-Engrg-One Kings Lane)*
James Schortemeyer *(Dir-Res)*
Nick Mammola *(Interim CFO)*

Accounts:
LimoRes.net Limousine Rental Business

NTHREEQ MEDIA LLC
7272 E Indian School Rd Ste 540, Scottsdale, AZ 85251
Tel.: (602) 456-9637
E-Mail: info@n3qmedia.com
Web Site: nthreeq.com

Agency Specializes In: Advertising, Brand Development & Integration, Collateral, Graphic Design, Internet/Web Design, Logo & Package Design, Print, Promotions

Angelina Gonzales *(Founder & Pres)*

Accounts:
Elizabeths Moments of Joy
New Frontier Imaging
Roka Akor

NUCLEUS WORLDWIDE
1600 E Franklin Ave Ste D, El Segundo, CA 90245
Tel.: (424) 256-0290
E-Mail: contact@nucleusworldwide.com
Web Site: www.nucleusworldwide.com

Year Founded: 2009

Agency Specializes In: Advertising, Digital/Interactive, Media Planning, Social Media, Strategic Planning/Research

Jack Mickle *(Founder & CEO)*
Cindy Nguyen *(VP & Grp Dir-Media)*
Dean Van Eimeren *(VP & Dir-Creative)*

Accounts:
Association of Volleyball Professionals Brand Strategy, Campaign: "Dig Deep", Creative Development, Graphics, Marketing Agency of Record, Media

NUEVO ADVERTISING GROUP, INC.
1990 Main St Ste 750, Sarasota, FL 34236
Tel.: (941) 752-4433
Fax: (941) 752-1114
E-Mail: hola@nuevoadvertising.com
Web Site: www.nuevoadvertising.com

Employees: 6
Year Founded: 2004

Agency Specializes In: Advertising, Advertising Specialties, Affluent Market, African-American Market, Alternative Advertising, Arts, Automotive, Bilingual Market, Brand Development & Integration, Branded Entertainment, Broadcast, Business Publications, Business-To-Business, Cable T.V., Catalogs, Children's Market, Co-op Advertising, Collateral, College, Commercial Photography, Communications, Computers & Software, Consulting, Consumer Goods, Consumer Marketing, Consumer Publications, Content, Corporate Communications, Corporate Identity, Cosmetics, Crisis Communications, Custom Publishing, Customer Relationship Management, Digital/Interactive, Direct Response Marketing, Direct-to-Consumer, E-Commerce, Education, Electronic Media, Electronics, Email, Engineering, Entertainment, Environmental, Event Planning & Marketing, Exhibit/Trade Shows, Experience Design, Fashion/Apparel, Financial, Food Service, Game Integration, Gay & Lesbian Market, Government/Political, Graphic Design, Guerilla Marketing, Health Care Services, High Technology, Hispanic Market, Hospitality, Household Goods, Identity Marketing, In-Store Advertising, Industrial, Infomercials, Information Technology, Integrated Marketing, International, Internet/Web Design, Investor Relations, Legal Services, Leisure, Local Marketing, Logo & Package Design, Luxury Products, Magazines, Marine, Market Research, Media Buying Services, Media Planning, Media Relations, Media Training, Medical Products, Men's Market, Merchandising, Mobile Marketing, Multicultural, Multimedia, New Product Development, New Technologies, Newspaper, Newspapers & Magazines, Out-of-Home Media, Outdoor, Over-50 Market, Package Design, Paid Searches, Planning & Consultation, Podcasting, Point of Purchase, Point of Sale, Print, Production, Production (Print), Promotions, Public Relations, Publicity/Promotions, Publishing, Radio, Real Estate, Regional, Restaurant, Sales Promotion, Search Engine Optimization, Seniors' Market, Social Marketing/Nonprofit, Sponsorship, Sports Market, Strategic Planning/Research, Sweepstakes, Syndication, T.V., Technical Advertising, Teen Market, Trade & Consumer Magazines, Travel & Tourism, Urban Market, Viral/Buzz/Word of Mouth, Women's Market, Yellow Pages Advertising

Roseanne Avella-Perez *(Pres)*
Pedro Perez *(VP-Sls & Mktg)*

Accounts:
Bradenton Beauty and Barber Academy (Agency of Record)
Fertility Center & Applied Genetics of Florida, Inc.; Sarasota, FL Branding, Online Marketing, Search Engine Optimization, Website
Florida State Fair; Tampa, FL
Manatee Community College; Bradenton, FL
MiCash; Washington, DC
Owen Motors, Inc
The Playful Parrot
South West Water Management; Brooksville, FL
State College of Florida
Tampa Bay Storm AFL; Tampa, FL
Vera International Group
Waste Management Southwest Florida
WellSpring Pharmaceutical Corporation; Sarasota, FL Package Design; 2010

NUF SAID ADVERTISING
2770 Dagny Way Ste 210, Lafayette, CO 80026
Tel.: (303) 665-8188
Fax: (303) 665-8288
E-Mail: firstname@nufsaid.com
Web Site: www.nufsaid.com

Agency Specializes In: Advertising, Internet/Web Design, Logo & Package Design, Print, Promotions

Rick Chadwick *(Owner)*
Travis Ravsten *(Dir-Creativity)*

Accounts:
The Humane Society of Boulder Valley

THE NULMAN GROUP
18 Commerce St Ste 1817, Flemington, NJ 08822
Tel.: (908) 751-5299
Fax: (908) 751-5621
Toll Free: (888) 440-3367
E-Mail: info@nulmangroup.com
Web Site: www.nulmangroup.com

Employees: 8
Year Founded: 1979

Agency Specializes In: Advertising, Bilingual Market, Brand Development & Integration, Broadcast, Business Publications, Business-To-Business, Cable T.V., Co-op Advertising, Collateral, Consulting, Consumer Marketing, Consumer Publications, Corporate Communications, Corporate Identity, Direct Response Marketing, E-Commerce, Electronic Media, Exhibit/Trade Shows, Fashion/Apparel, Financial, Food Service, Government/Political, Graphic Design, Hispanic Market, In-Store Advertising, Industrial, Infomercials, Internet/Web Design, Logo & Package Design, Magazines, Media Buying Services, Merchandising, Multimedia, Newspaper, Newspapers & Magazines, Out-of-Home Media, Outdoor, Planning & Consultation, Point of Purchase, Point of Sale, Print, Radio, Sales Promotion, Sports Market, Strategic Planning/Research, Trade & Consumer Magazines

Claire Curry *(VP)*
Helen Nardone *(Sr Dir-Art)*
Frank Pish *(Sr Dir-Art)*
Humphrey Wilson *(Acct Exec)*

Accounts:
Arla Foods; Basking Ridge, NJ Imported Cheese; 2000
Buyer's International Group; Los Angeles, CA
Northeastern Fine Jewelry; Albany, NY; 2005

NUMANTRA
(Merged with Agency Entourage to form Agency Entourage LLC)

NURTURE DIGITAL
3617 Hayden Ave Ste 103, Culver City, CA 90232
Tel.: (310) 815-1390
E-Mail: hello@nurturedigital.com
Web Site: www.nurturedigital.com

Year Founded: 2009

Agency Specializes In: Advertising, Content, Digital/Interactive, Media Planning

J.C. Molina *(Creative Dir)*
Nate Smith *(Art Dir)*
Nick Lange *(Dir-Creative)*
Jazmine Rodriguez *(Production Mgr)*
Juan David Rangel *(Mgr-Production)*
Lauren Zelner *(Mgr-Partnership)*
Topher Osborn *(Copywriter)*
Katherine St Lawrence *(Coord-Production)*

Accounts:
Food for Life Baking Co
Pfister, Inc. Clarify Faucet

NURUN/ANT FARM INTERACTIVE
271 17th St NW, Atlanta, GA 30363
Tel.: (404) 591-1600
Fax: (404) 876-7226
E-Mail: atlanta@nurun.com
Web Site: www.nurun.com

Employees: 30

Agency Specializes In: Digital/Interactive, Internet/Web Design

Jacques-Herve Roubert *(CEO)*
Amanda Pressly *(Acct Supvr)*

Accounts:
Asheville Convention & Visitors Bureau
Bombardier Recreational Products
Call of Duty Advanced Warfare
Cingular Wireless LLC
Equifax Consumer Credit Services; 2001
Ferrero
Government of Canada
LVMH
Michelin
Microsoft
P&G
STX

NURUN INC.
740 Notre Dame West Street, Suite 600, Montreal, QC H3C 3X6 Canada
Tel.: (514) 392-1900
Fax: (514) 392-0911
Toll Free: (877) 696-1292
E-Mail: montreal@nurun.com
Web Site: www.nurun.com

Employees: 100

Agency Specializes In: Brand Development & Integration, Communications, Digital/Interactive

Jacques-Herve Roubert *(Pres & CEO)*
Steve Tremblay *(CTO-Global)*
Antoine Pabst *(Pres-France & Gen Mgr-Europe)*
Frederic Leblanc *(Gen Dir-Montreal)*
Gregoire Baret *(Exec VP-Strategy & Experience Design-Montreal)*
Dawn Winchester *(Mng Dir-Global)*
Christophe Attele *(VP-Client Svcs)*
Guy Lemieux *(VP-Fin & Admin)*
Jean Pascal Mathieu *(Exec Dir-Digital Innovation Consulting)*
Jimmy Fecteau *(Dir-Creative)*

Accounts:
Archambault
Bayer Pharmaceuticals
FIAT Group Automobiles
Haverty Furniture Companies; Atlanta, GA; 2008
ING NN
Kerastase International
Lancaster
SNC Lavalin
Sony Italia
TVA Shopping
Videotron Ltd.
W.L. Gore & Associates
Workplace Safety and Insurance Board

NV ADVERTISING
518 N Tampa St Ste 210, Tampa, FL 33602
Tel.: (813) 355-0036
Web Site: www.nvadvertising.com

Year Founded: 2010

Agency Specializes In: Advertising, Collateral, Corporate Identity, Graphic Design, Internet/Web Design, Print, Social Media

Nicole Valentin *(Pres & CEO)*
Melissa Parks *(Sr Media Planner)*

Accounts:
Carolina Office Xchange
ROF Inc

NVS DESIGN INC.
8888 Keystone Crossing Ste 1300, Indianapolis, IN 46220
Tel.: (317) 437-4417
Web Site: www.nvsdesigns.com

Employees: 5

Agency Specializes In: Affiliate Marketing, Alternative Advertising, Branded Entertainment, Catalogs, Co-op Advertising, Consumer Publications, Custom Publishing, Digital/Interactive, Direct Response Marketing, Electronic Media, Email, Experience Design, In-Store Advertising, Local Marketing, Magazines, Mobile Marketing, Multimedia, Newspaper, Newspapers & Magazines, Out-of-Home Media, Outdoor, Print, Production, Production (Print), Promotions, RSS (Really Simple Syndication), Radio, Search Engine Optimization, Social Media, T.V., Viral/Buzz/Word of Mouth, Web (Banner Ads, Pop-ups, etc.), Yellow Pages Advertising

Chad Brittian *(CEO)*
Angelina Craig *(Designer)*
Sarah Weaver *(Acct Coord)*
Alyse McMiller *(Asst Designer)*
Marci Taylor *(Asst Designer)*

Accounts:
G&P Machinery; 2014
Yasmin Stump Law Group P.C.; 2010

NYE & ASSOCIATES
428 Pattie, Wichita, KS 67211
Tel.: (316) 263-5878
Fax: (316) 263-6017
Web Site: www.nyeandassociates.com

Agency Specializes In: Advertising, Event Planning & Marketing, Public Relations, Social Media, Strategic Planning/Research

Lee Clark *(Pres)*
Ruth Johnson *(CEO)*
Jennifer S. Worrell *(Acct Svcs Dir)*
Michael Terry *(Graphic Designer & Designer-Web)*

Accounts:
The Derby Recreation Center
TCG Services

NYLON TECHNOLOGY
350 7th Ave 10th Fl, New York, NY 10001-5013
Tel.: (212) 691-1134
Fax: (212) 691-3477
Web Site: www.nylontechnology.com

Employees: 20
Year Founded: 1997

Agency Specializes In: Digital/Interactive, E-Commerce, Electronic Media, High Technology, Information Technology, Internet/Web Design

James Curran *(Co-Founder & Partner)*
Steve Grushcow *(Co-Founder & Partner)*
Shruti Ganguly *(VP-TV & Video)*
Paul Herrmann *(Dir-Law Firm Mktg)*

Accounts:
Arnold & Porter; Washington, DC
Doctors Without Borders USA

Insurance Information Institute
Sutherland Asbill & Brennan
TV Insider

O2IDEAS, INC.

600 University Pk Pl Ste 200, Birmingham, AL 35209
Tel.: (205) 949-9494
Fax: (205) 949-9449
E-Mail: bill.todd@o2ideas.com
Web Site: www.o2ideas.com

Employees: 68
Year Founded: 1967

Agency Specializes In: Advertising, African-American Market, Brand Development & Integration, Broadcast, Business-To-Business, Cable T.V., Collateral, College, Consulting, Consumer Goods, Consumer Marketing, Consumer Publications, Corporate Communications, Corporate Identity, Crisis Communications, Customer Relationship Management, Digital/Interactive, Direct Response Marketing, Direct-to-Consumer, Education, Electronic Media, Electronics, Email, Event Planning & Marketing, Exhibit/Trade Shows, Experience Design, Faith Based, Financial, Food Service, Guerilla Marketing, Health Care Services, In-Store Advertising, Infomercials, Integrated Marketing, Internet/Web Design, Local Marketing, Logo & Package Design, Magazines, Market Research, Media Relations, Media Training, Medical Products, Merchandising, Mobile Marketing, Multicultural, Multimedia, New Product Development, Newspaper, Newspapers & Magazines, Out-of-Home Media, Outdoor, Package Design, Pets , Planning & Consultation, Point of Purchase, Point of Sale, Print, Production (Print), Promotions, Public Relations, Publicity/Promotions, Radio, Real Estate, Recruitment, Regional, Restaurant, Retail, Sales Promotion, Social Marketing/Nonprofit, Social Media, Sponsorship, Strategic Planning/Research, T.V., Telemarketing, Transportation, Travel & Tourism

Approx. Annual Billings: $81,260,340

Ray Donnelly *(CMO)*
Jenny Burrows *(Sr Dir-Art)*
Amy Baldis *(Art Dir)*
Brian Hippensteel *(Dir-Art)*
Christopher Lee *(Dir-Interactive)*
Marci Sheppard *(Acct Supvr)*
Grace Roberts *(Acct Exec)*
Melissa Stewart *(Acct Exec)*
Joe Crowe *(Jr Copywriter)*
Christel Barnett *(Acct Coord)*

Accounts:
Alabama State University; Montgomery, AL Enrollment
Bewhoyouwannabe; Birmingham, AL
Birmingham Zoo; Birmingham, AL Attraction
Books-A-Million Bookseller
Brookwood Medical Center; Birmingham, AL Health Care
Buffalo Rock Bottling; Birmingham, AL Beverage
Carolina Canners; Cheraw, SC Beverage
Dunkin Donuts;Canton, MA Franchise Recruitment
Electrosteel; Birmingham, AL;Mumbai, India Manufacturing
Gateway Social Services
Hoar Construction Commercial Construction
Hoar Program Management
Honda Manufacturing of Alabama; Lincoln, AL Internal Communications & Public, Community Relations
Honda Manufacturing of Indiana; Greensburg, IN Internal Communications & Public, Community Relations
Joe Muggs Restaurant
Mars Petcare; Franklin, TN Employer Branding
The Mattie C. Stewart Foundation; Birmingham, AL
NaphCare
The Nutro Company; Franklin, TN Employer Branding
Pedorthic Care
Pinnacle Data Systems Data Processing
Protective Life
Real Estate Matrix Real Estate Appraisal
Regions Bank
Samford University; Birmingham, AL Education
ServisFirst Bank; Birmingham, AL Financial
Taylor Morrison; Scottsdale, AZ Employer Branding, Internal Communications
Toys"R"Us Internal Communication
Verizon Wireless; Chicago, IL Wireless

O2KL

3 W 18th St 4th Fl, New York, NY 10011
Tel.: (646) 839-6255
Fax: (646) 839-6254
E-Mail: info@o2kl.com
Web Site: www.o2kl.com

Employees: 18
Year Founded: 2004

Agency Specializes In: Advertising, Advertising Specialties, Affiliate Marketing, Affluent Market, Automotive, Aviation & Aerospace, Below-the-Line, Brand Development & Integration, Broadcast, Business Publications, Business-To-Business, Cable T.V., Children's Market, Collateral, Computers & Software, Consumer Marketing, Consumer Publications, Corporate Communications, Digital/Interactive, Direct Response Marketing, Direct-to-Consumer, E-Commerce, Education, Electronic Media, Email, Environmental, Exhibit/Trade Shows, Health Care Services, High Technology, Hospitality, Industrial, Infomercials, Integrated Marketing, Internet/Web Design, Leisure, Luxury Products, Multimedia, New Technologies, Newspaper, Out-of-Home Media, Outdoor, Over-50 Market, Print, Production, Production (Print), Radio, Real Estate, Sales Promotion, Seniors' Market, Social Marketing/Nonprofit, Social Media, Sweepstakes, T.V., Technical Advertising, Telemarketing, Trade & Consumer Magazines, Transportation, Travel & Tourism, Web (Banner Ads, Pop-ups, etc.)

Approx. Annual Billings: $10,000,000

Breakdown of Gross Billings by Media: Collateral: $1,500,000; D.M.: $3,500,000; E-Commerce: $3,000,000; T.V.: $2,000,000

Tracey Owens *(Owner & Pres)*
John Kopilak *(Owner & Dir-Creative)*
Jim Lurie *(Partner)*
Beth Wolfson *(Acct Dir)*
Bill Bonomo *(Dir-Art)*
Nancy Keiter *(Dir-Art)*
Danny Klein *(Dir-Creative)*
Frank Massenzio *(Dir-Ops)*
Jennifer Vale *(Dir-Client Svc)*

Accounts:
AARP; Washington, DC; 2007
Disney
ESPN

O3 WORLD, LLC

1339 Frankford Ave Ste 3, Philadelphia, PA 19125
Tel.: (215) 592-4739
Fax: (215) 592-4610
E-Mail: info@o3world.com
Web Site: www.o3world.com

Employees: 10
Year Founded: 2005

Agency Specializes In: Above-the-Line, Advertising, Advertising Specialties, Affiliate Marketing, Affluent Market, African-American Market, Alternative Advertising, Arts, Automotive, Aviation & Aerospace, Brand Development & Integration, Branded Entertainment, Broadcast, Business Publications, Business-To-Business, Cable T.V., Catalogs, Co-op Advertising, Collateral, College, Commercial Photography, Communications, Computers & Software, Consumer Goods, Consumer Marketing, Content, Corporate Communications, Corporate Identity, Cosmetics, Customer Relationship Management, Digital/Interactive, Direct Response Marketing, Direct-to-Consumer, E-Commerce, Education, Electronic Media, Electronics, Email, Entertainment, Environmental, Event Planning & Marketing, Experience Design, Fashion/Apparel, Food Service, Game Integration, Gay & Lesbian Market, Graphic Design, Health Care Services, High Technology, Hospitality, Household Goods, Identity Marketing, Industrial, Integrated Marketing, International, Internet/Web Design, Leisure, Local Marketing, Logo & Package Design, Luxury Products, Magazines, Media Relations, Medical Products, Men's Market, Mobile Marketing, Multicultural, Multimedia, New Product Development, New Technologies, Newspaper, Newspapers & Magazines, Package Design, Paid Searches, Pharmaceutical, Planning & Consultation, Podcasting, Point of Purchase, Point of Sale, Print, Product Placement, Production, Production (Ad, Film, Broadcast), Production (Print), Promotions, Public Relations, Publicity/Promotions, Publishing, RSS (Really Simple Syndication), Radio, Real Estate, Recruitment, Regional, Restaurant, Retail, Sales Promotion, Search Engine Optimization, Seniors' Market, Social Marketing/Nonprofit, Sponsorship, Sports Market, Stakeholders, Strategic Planning/Research, Sweepstakes, Syndication, T.V., Technical Advertising, Teen Market, Telemarketing, Trade & Consumer Magazines, Transportation, Travel & Tourism, Urban Market, Viral/Buzz/Word of Mouth, Web (Banner Ads, Pop-ups, etc.), Women's Market, Yellow Pages Advertising

Breakdown of Gross Billings by Media: Worldwide Web Sites: 100%

Keith Scandone *(Partner & CEO)*
Joan McManus *(Controller-Fin)*
Mark Amadio *(Dir-Design)*
Barry Golombek *(Dir-Bus Dev)*
Howard Ross *(Dir-Dev)*
Kate Gattuso *(Strategist-Acct)*
Annmarie Avila *(Designer-UX & UI)*
Connor Hasson *(Designer-UI & UX)*
Blaise Vincz *(Designer-UX/UI)*
Jamie Wlodinguer *(Designer-UI & UX)*

Accounts:
Addis Group Brand Positioning
Banyan Productions; Philadelphia, PA Film Production Company; 2005
Breslow Partners; Philadelphia, PA Full Service Public Relations Firm; 2005
Cooper Spirits International Pravda Vodka, Saint Germain
The Fruit Flowers Franchise
Michael Salove Company, Philadelphia, PA Retail Real Estate Advisor; 2005
Michael Spain-Smith Studio; Philadelphia, PA Photography; 2005
The New York Times Travel Show
Philadelphia Weekly; Philadelphia, PA; 2008
Sage Financial Group; West Conshohocken, PA Wealth Management Firm; 2006
Wireless Philadelphia; Philadelphia, PA Wireless Internet Digital Inclusion Program; 2006
Wyatt Zier, LLC; New York, NY
Zygo Vodka; Rigby, ID Peach Flavored Vodka; 2005

OBERHAUSEN MARKETING & PUBLIC RELATIONS
1000 Lincoln Rd Ste 215, Miami Beach, FL 33139
Tel.: (305) 532-1212
E-Mail: info@obrmarketing.com
Web Site: www.obrmarketing.com

Agency Specializes In: Collateral, Communications, Internet/Web Design, Media Planning, Media Relations, Print, Production, Public Relations, Search Engine Optimization, Social Media

Josh Oberhausen *(Pres)*
Aimet Arill Oberhausen *(Partner)*

Accounts:
Add Inc
Clinton Hotel
Couples Resorts
Hotel Esencia
Pediatric Critical Care of South Florida Marketing Counsel, Pediatric Intensive Care Unit, Public Relations
The Perry South Beach
Skin Type Solutions
South Beach Group Hotels
Velas Resorts
Wynwood Central Marketing, Public Relations

OBERLANDER GROUP
143 Remsen St, Cohoes, NY 12047
Tel.: (518) 720-0050
E-Mail: jober@oberlandergroup.com
Web Site: www.oberlandergroup.com

Agency Specializes In: Advertising, Brand Development & Integration, Corporate Identity, Strategic Planning/Research

Mel Quinlan *(Owner)*
John Oberlander *(Dir-Creative)*
Chad Bradt *(Sr Graphic Designer)*
Karen Paul *(Sr Graphic Designer)*

Accounts:
Alvin Ailey American Dance Theater
Balanchine 100
Jose Limon Dance Company Dance Training Institution
Miami City Ballet (Agency of Record)
NY Business Development Corp. Banking & Financial Services
Saratoga Performing Arts Center Entertainment
Tiashoke Farm Dairy Farming Services
Union/Mount Sinai Educational Services

O'BERRY CAVANAUGH
20 E Main St, Bozeman, MT 59715
Tel.: (406) 522-8075
Fax: (406) 522-8076
E-Mail: upstairs@ocbrand.com
Web Site: www.ocbrand.com

Employees: 9
Year Founded: 2004

Agency Specializes In: Advertising, Business Publications, Business-To-Business, Consumer Marketing, Consumer Publications, Corporate Identity, Digital/Interactive, Direct Response Marketing, E-Commerce, Electronic Media, Event Planning & Marketing, Exhibit/Trade Shows, Graphic Design, Information Technology, Internet/Web Design, Logo & Package Design, Magazines, Media Buying Services, Newspaper, Newspapers & Magazines, Point of Sale, Print, Production, Public Relations, Sports Market, Strategic Planning/Research, Trade & Consumer Magazines, Travel & Tourism, Yellow Pages Advertising

Toni O'Berry *(Owner)*
Cary Silberman *(Dir-Creative)*

Accounts:
Einstein Wireless
Gallatin Valley Food Bank
IMDS
Opal
PureWest
Sun West Ranch
Western Transportation Institute

OBI CREATIVE
2920 Farnam St, Omaha, NE 68131
Tel.: (402) 493-7999
E-Mail: info@obicreative.com
Web Site: www.obicreative.com

Year Founded: 2002

Agency Specializes In: Advertising, Brand Development & Integration, Digital/Interactive, Internet/Web Design, Logo & Package Design, Media Buying Services, Outdoor, Print, Public Relations, Social Media

Mary Ann OBrien *(CEO)*
Kevin Hutchison *(VP-Client Rels & Bus Dev)*
Lana LeGrand *(VP-Ops)*
Paul Berger *(Acct Dir)*
Ann Pedersen *(Dir-Mktg & Strategic Comm)*
Spencer Putnam *(Dir-Ops & Tech)*
Erica Rowe *(Dir-Creative)*
Tj Johnson *(Acct Mgr)*
Morgan McVay *(Acct Mgr)*
Olivia Ruhlman *(Acct Coord)*

Accounts:
Lenovo Group Ltd

OBJECT9
4156 WE Heck Ct, Baton Rouge, LA 70816
Tel.: (225) 368-9899
Fax: (225) 368-9898
E-Mail: info@object9.com
Web Site: www.object9.com

Year Founded: 2000

Agency Specializes In: Advertising

Andy Gutowski *(Owner)*
Jon Cato *(Partner & Strategist)*
Branden Lisi *(Partner & Strategist-Brand)*

Accounts:
DOW LOUISIANA
ENTERGY
EXASERV
Fire & Flavor
Kris Wine
LSU CONTINUING EDUCATION
Realtree Camouflage
Red Stripe
SMIRNOFF
SMIRNOFF ICE
Sunshine Pages

Branch

Object9
1145 Zonolite Rd NE Ste 2, Atlanta, GA 30306
Tel.: (678) 447-2228
Fax: (448) 865-08
E-Mail: info@object9.com
Web Site: www.object9.com

Employees: 3

Agency Specializes In: Advertising, Internet/Web Design

Branden Lisi *(Partner & Strategist-Brand)*
Steffan Pedersen *(Mgr-Digital Mktg)*
Gregg Khedouri *(Strategist-Mktg & Brand)*
Kyle Phillips *(Sr Designer)*

Accounts:
Case-Mate
Diageo
NRG Energy, Inc.

OBJECTDC
8212-A, Vienna, VA 22182
Tel.: (703) 917-0023
E-Mail: Vandana@ObjectDC.com
Web Site: objectdc.com

Employees: 6
Year Founded: 1995

Agency Specializes In: Above-the-Line, Below-the-Line, Collateral, Digital/Interactive, Mobile Marketing, Multimedia, Newspapers & Magazines, Out-of-Home Media, Outdoor, Print, Radio, Social Media, T.V., Web (Banner Ads, Pop-ups, etc.)

Approx. Annual Billings: $2,000,000

Nawaf Soliman *(CEO)*
Vandana Gambhir *(VP-Mktg)*

Accounts:
Dish Network
Georgetown University
World Bank
Ziyad

OBLIQUE DESIGN
1290 Yellow Pine Ave Ste D-4, Boulder, CO 80304
Tel.: (303) 449-8100
E-Mail: info@obliquedesign.com
Web Site: www.obliquedesign.com

Agency Specializes In: Advertising, Brand Development & Integration, Internet/Web Design, Print, Social Media

Janice Ferrante *(Owner)*
Steve Iaconis *(Dir-Mktg & Client Svcs)*
Corrie Arnold *(Acct Mgr)*

Accounts:
A Basic Cremation
Farmacopia
Livewell Longmont
Trip30

O'BRIEN ADVERTISING, INC.
(d/b/a Obrien Advertising)
(Private-Parent-Single Location)
1444 Wazee St Ste 333, Denver, CO 80202
Tel.: (303) 820-2174
Web Site: www.thinkoba.com

Employees: 16
Year Founded: 1994

Agency Specializes In: Advertising, Digital/Interactive, Outdoor, Print, Radio, T.V.

Revenue: $3,400,000

OBSIDIAN PUBLIC RELATIONS
493 S Main St Ste 101, Memphis, TN 38103-6406
Tel.: (901) 572-1042
Fax: (901) 544-7163
E-Mail: insight@obsidianpr.com
Web Site: www.obsidianpr.com

Advertising Agencies

Employees: 10

Agency Specializes In: Crisis Communications, Media Relations, Media Training, Newspapers & Magazines, Strategic Planning/Research

Courtney Liebenrood *(Owner)*
Kerri Guyton *(Client Svcs Dir)*
Crissy Lintner *(Client Svcs Dir)*
Lauren Hannaford *(Acct Mgr)*
Daniel Wade *(Acct Mgr)*
Kelli Eason Brignac *(Acct Exec)*
Ali Glemser *(Specialist-Acct)*
Sarah Lichterman *(Acct Exec)*

Accounts:
Architecture Incorporated Architecture & Planning Firms
The Barnett Group
Madison Hotel

THE O'CARROLL GROUP

300 E McNeese Ste 2B, Lake Charles, LA 70605
Tel.: (337) 478-7396
Fax: (337) 478-0503
E-Mail: pocarroll@ocarroll.com
Web Site: www.ocarroll.com

Employees: 4
Year Founded: 1978

Agency Specializes In: Advertising, Brand Development & Integration, Consulting, Consumer Publications, Corporate Identity, Financial, Graphic Design, Internet/Web Design, Local Marketing, Logo & Package Design, Medical Products, Newspaper, Outdoor, Public Relations, Publicity/Promotions, Radio, Social Media, T.V., Travel & Tourism, Web (Banner Ads, Pop-ups, etc.)

Peter J. O'Carroll, Jr. *(Pres & Dir-Creative)*
Pam Doucet *(Acct Rep)*

Accounts:
ASI Office Systems; Lake Charles, LA Office Equipment & Sales
City Savings Bank; Deridder, LA Bank
Port of Lake Charles; Lake Charles, LA Port & Transportation
Southwest Louisiana Convention & Visitors Bureau; Lake Charles, LA Conventions, Tourism

OCD MEDIA

8 E 36th St 5th Fl, New York, NY 10016
Tel.: (212) 213-6904
Fax: (212) 594-4042
E-Mail: Dadelman@ocdmedia.com
Web Site: ocdmedia.com

Employees: 18
Year Founded: 2003

Agency Specializes In: Advertising, Financial, Food Service, Health Care Services, Media Buying Services, Media Planning, Package Design, Pharmaceutical, Retail, Strategic Planning/Research

David Adelman *(Mng Dir)*
Thomas Stolfi *(Sr VP & Dir-Mgmt)*
Christine Lyons *(VP & Dir-Acct Svcs)*
Alexa Paradis *(Asst Media Planner)*

Accounts:
Alger Mutual Funds B2B Digital Campaign; 2014
Alibaba.com; 2011
Aquavault; 2013
Douglas Elliman Real Estate NY Based Luxury Real Estate; 2014
Globe Equipment ecommerce; 2012
Gutsy Products Gutsy Chewy, Gutsy GoGo; 2014
Independence Care System; 2012
Jackson Hewitt Tax Prep; 2013
The Michael J Fox Foundation Event Promotion; 2014
Municipal Credit Union; 2012
NY Kosher Steak NYkoshersteak.com; 2012
Paradigm Spine Coflex Medical Device; 2014
Reboot; 2012
The Ride The Ride Entertainment Bus; 2014
Synergistic Marketing Thecouponbooksavings.com; 2014
Takeda Pharmaceuticals Amitiza; 2006
Tata Global Beverages Eight O'Clock Coffee, Good Earth Tea, Tetley Tea; 2006
Techsmart Scholarship Sweepstakes; 2014
Warner-Chilcott Atelvia, Femcon, Loestrin; 2006

OCEAN BRIDGE GROUP

1714 16th St, Santa Monica, CA 90404
Tel.: (310) 392-3200
E-Mail: cherrman@oceanbridgegroup.com
Web Site: http://www.oceanbridgemedia.com/

Employees: 20
Year Founded: 2002

Agency Specializes In: Above-the-Line, Advertising, Advertising Specialties, Affiliate Marketing, Affluent Market, African-American Market, Agriculture, Alternative Advertising, Arts, Asian Market, Automotive, Aviation & Aerospace, Below-the-Line, Bilingual Market, Brand Development & Integration, Branded Entertainment, Broadcast, Business Publications, Business-To-Business, Cable T.V., Catalogs, Children's Market, Co-op Advertising, Collateral, College, Commercial Photography, Communications, Computers & Software, Consulting, Consumer Goods, Consumer Marketing, Consumer Publications, Content, Corporate Communications, Corporate Identity, Cosmetics, Crisis Communications, Custom Publishing, Customer Relationship Management, Digital/Interactive, Direct Response Marketing, Direct-to-Consumer, E-Commerce, Education, Electronic Media, Electronics, Email, Engineering, Entertainment, Environmental, Event Planning & Marketing, Exhibit/Trade Shows, Experience Design, Fashion/Apparel, Financial, Food Service, Game Integration, Government/Political, Graphic Design, Guerilla Marketing, Health Care Services, High Technology, Hispanic Market, Hospitality, Household Goods, Identity Marketing, In-Store Advertising, Industrial, Infomercials, Information Technology, Integrated Marketing, International, Internet/Web Design, Investor Relations, Legal Services, Leisure, Local Marketing, Logo & Package Design, Luxury Products, Magazines, Marine, Market Research, Media Buying Services, Media Planning, Media Relations, Media Training, Medical Products, Men's Market, Merchandising, Mobile Marketing, Multicultural, Multimedia, New Product Development, New Technologies, Newspaper, Newspapers & Magazines, Out-of-Home Media, Outdoor, Over-50 Market, Package Design, Paid Searches, Pharmaceutical, Planning & Consultation, Podcasting, Point of Purchase, Point of Sale, Print, Product Placement, Production, Production (Ad, Film, Broadcast), Production (Print), Promotions, Public Relations, Publicity/Promotions, Publishing, RSS (Really Simple Syndication), Radio, Real Estate, Recruitment, Regional, Restaurant, Retail, Sales Promotion, Search Engine Optimization, Seniors' Market, Social Marketing/Nonprofit, Sponsorship, Sports Market, Stakeholders, Strategic Planning/Research, Sweepstakes, Syndication, T.V., Technical Advertising, Teen Market, Trade & Consumer Magazines, Transportation, Travel & Tourism, Urban Market, Viral/Buzz/Word of Mouth, Web (Banner Ads, Pop-ups, etc.), Women's Market

Approx. Annual Billings: $265,000,000

Breakdown of Gross Billings by Media: Corp. Communications: 23%; Internet Adv.: 14%; Network Radio: 15%; Point of Purchase: 2%; Production: 5%; Strategic Planning/Research: 4%; T.V.: 37%

Cary Herrman *(Co-Founder & Pres)*
Ramie Ostrovsky *(Co-Founder & CEO)*
Randi Wilson *(Acct Dir)*
John Shotwell *(Dir-Creative)*

Accounts:
Blue Cow Relaxation Drink; 2008
Bonne Bell; Cleveland, OH Bonne Bell Cosmetics, Lip Smackers
Bruce Foods; New Iberia, LA Bruce's Yams, Cajun Injector, Louisiana Hot Sauce
DenMat; Santa Maria, CA Rembrandt Toothpaste & Oral Care
Donald Trump Organization; New York, NY Trump National Golf Club
French Transit, Ltd.; Burlingame, CA Crystal Body Deodorant
Human Touch, LLC; Long Beach, CA Human Touch
Hyland's Inc.; Los Angeles, CA Hyland's Homeopathic Brands
Ingenuity Products, LLC; Cincinnati, OH Repelle
Merz; Greensboro, NC Mederma
MGM; Santa Monica, CA MGM Television
Sunshine Makers, Inc.; Huntington Harbor, CA Simple Green
Union-Swiss Bio-Oil
University Games; San Francisco, CA Various Games & Toys
Waltman Pharmaceuticals, Inc.; Jackson, MS Zapzyt Acne Treatments
Watkins Manufacturing Corp.; Vista, CA Hot Springs Portable Spas
Woodridge Labs, Inc.; Panorama City, CA Anti-Aging

THE O'CONNOR GROUP

1007 1st St, Roanoke, VA 24016
Tel.: (540) 342-1889
Fax: (540) 342-2059
E-Mail: info@adoconnor.com
Web Site: www.adoconnor.com

Employees: 5
Year Founded: 1993

Agency Specializes In: Advertising

Bill O'Connor *(Pres)*
Brandon O'Conner *(Exec VP)*

Accounts:
Global Metal Finishing
Roanoke County
Woods Rogers

OCREATIVE DESIGN STUDIO

521 Westover St, Oconomowoc, WI 53066
Tel.: (262) 567-1164
Fax: (866) 695-9731
E-Mail: contact@ocreativedesign.com
Web Site: www.ocreativedesign.com

Year Founded: 2003

Agency Specializes In: Advertising, Brand Development & Integration, Graphic Design, Internet/Web Design, Logo & Package Design, Print, Social Media

Andrea Koeppel *(Principal & Dir-Creative)*
Matt Koeppel *(Principal & Dir-Technical)*
Teresa Carlson *(Designer-Multimedia)*

OCTAGON
800 Connecticut Ave 2nd Fl, Norwalk, CT 06854
Tel.: (203) 354-7400
Fax: (203) 354-7401
E-Mail: pressinquires@octagon.com
Web Site: www.octagon.com

E-Mail for Key Personnel:
President: jeff.shifrin@octagon.com

Employees: 825
Year Founded: 1983

National Agency Associations: 4A's

Agency Specializes In: Advertising Specialties, African-American Market, Arts, Below-the-Line, Brand Development & Integration, Branded Entertainment, Business-To-Business, College, Consulting, Consumer Goods, Consumer Marketing, Digital/Interactive, Direct-to-Consumer, Entertainment, Event Planning & Marketing, Experience Design, Graphic Design, Hispanic Market, Hospitality, Identity Marketing, Integrated Marketing, International, Local Marketing, Market Research, Merchandising, Mobile Marketing, Multicultural, Promotions, Sales Promotion, Sponsorship, Sports Market, Strategic Planning/Research, Sweepstakes, Viral/Buzz/Word of Mouth

Phil De Picciotto *(Founder & Pres)*
Rick Dudley *(CEO)*
Simon Wardle *(Chief Strategy Officer)*
Gord Lang *(Chief Growth Officer)*
Jeff Shifrin *(Pres/COO-Mktg Worldwide)*
Andre Schunk *(Sr VP)*
Jeff Ehrenkranz *(Mng Dir-Europe, Mid East & India)*
Joe Sobolewski *(Acct Mgr)*
Debra C. Marciano *(Mgr-Experiential Event)*
Thomas Freda *(Acct Exec-Met-Rx & Pure Protein)*

Accounts:
Ace Group Classic Champions Tour
Allstate
Anheuser-Busch InBev N.V./S.A.
Arsenio Hall
Bank of America
BMW of North America
Castrol
Cisco
Coca-Cola Company
Course of the Force Light Saber Relay
DIRECTV
Emmitt Smith
Erin Burnett
The Home Depot
Jimmie Johnson
Johnson & Johnson
Lion Nathan
Mark Webber
MasterCard International
Michael Phelps
Nancy O'Dell
North Face 100 Endurance Race
The North Face
Novartis
Piers Morgan
SAS Championship Presented by Bloomberg Businessweek
Siemens
Sprint
Sybase Match Play Championship (LPGA)
Walmart NW Arkansas Championship Presented by P&G

Branches:

Octagon
919 3rd Ave 18th Fl, New York, NY 10022
Tel.: (212) 546-7300
Fax: (212) 546-7325
E-Mail: info@octagon.com
Web Site: www.octagon.com

Employees: 15
Year Founded: 2001

National Agency Associations: 4A's

Agency Specializes In: Event Planning & Marketing, Sponsorship, Sports Market

Rick Dudley *(Chm & CEO)*
Simon Wardle *(Chief Strategy Officer)*
Gord Lang *(Chief Growth Officer)*
Jody Katz *(VP)*
Jeff Meeson *(VP-Insights & Strategy)*
Noah Kolodny *(Acct Dir)*
Stephanie Wootton *(Sr Acct Exec)*

Accounts:
Master Card

Octagon
7950 Jones Branch Dr, McLean, VA 22107
Tel.: (703) 905-3300
Fax: (703) 905-4495
Web Site: www.octagon.com

Employees: 60

National Agency Associations: 4A's

Agency Specializes In: Event Planning & Marketing, Sports Market

Phil de Picciotto *(Founder & Pres)*
Rick Dudley *(Chm & CEO)*
Nancy Morton *(CFO)*
Jeff Shifrin *(Pres-Octagon Mktg America)*
David Schwab *(Sr VP & Mng Dir-Octagon First Call)*
Tom George *(Sr VP)*
Sean Nicholls *(Mng Dir-Australia & New Zealand)*
Scott Horner *(Dir-North American Sls & Mktg Grp)*

Octagon
10115 Kincey Ave Ste 210, Huntersville, NC 28078
Tel.: (704) 632-7900
Fax: (704) 632-7901
E-Mail: jim.vergata@octagon.com
Web Site: octagon.com

Employees: 80

National Agency Associations: 4A's

Agency Specializes In: Sponsorship, Sports Market

Rick Dudley *(CEO)*
Jeff Austin *(Mng Dir)*
David Yates *(Mng Dir)*
Jeff Shifrin *(Pres-Octagon Mktg America)*
Jeff Kleiber *(Sr VP-Events & Hospitality)*
Kami Taylor *(Sr VP-Octagon Mktg & Events)*
Chris Higgs *(Mng Dir-Golf & Outdoor Events)*
Jim Vergata *(VP & Gen Mgr)*

Accounts:
Sprint Cup Series; 2000

Octagon
5909 Peachtree Dunwoody Rd Ste 600, Atlanta, GA 30328
Tel.: (678) 587-4940
Fax: (678) 587-4941
Web Site: www.octagon.com

Employees: 7

National Agency Associations: 4A's

Agency Specializes In: Sponsorship, Sports Market

Phil de Picciotto *(Founder & Pres)*
Rick Dudley *(CEO)*
Lisa Murray *(CMO & Exec VP)*
Joan Cusco *(Pres-Spain & Portugal)*
Jeff Shifrin *(Pres-Mktg America)*
Lance Hill *(VP)*
Arlette Fernandez *(Acct Dir)*
Chad Glidewell *(Acct Dir)*
Krystal Anthony *(Sr Acct Exec)*

Accounts:
Home Depot

Octagon
8000 Norman Center Dr Ste 400, Minneapolis, MN 55437
Tel.: (952) 841-9100
Fax: (952) 831-8241
E-Mail: info@octagon.com
Web Site: www.octagon.com

Employees: 4

National Agency Associations: 4A's

Agency Specializes In: Sports Market

Rick Dudley *(Pres & CEO)*
Mike Liut *(Mng Dir)*
Michael Thomas *(CFO)*
Lisa Murray *(CMO & Exec VP)*
Peter Carlisle *(Mng Dir-Olympics & Action Sports)*
Jeff Ehrenkranz *(Mng Dir-Europe, India & Middle East)*
Ben Hankinson *(Dir-Player Representation-USA)*
Stevie Patnode *(Sr Acct Exec-Mktg)*

Octagon
7100 Forest Ave Ste 201, Richmond, VA 23226
Tel.: (804) 285-4200
Fax: (804) 285-4224
Web Site: www.octagon.com

Employees: 7

Agency Specializes In: Sports Market

Phil de Picciotto *(Founder & Pres)*
Qondisa Ngwenya *(Owner)*
Rick Dudley *(Chm & CEO)*
Joan Cusco *(Pres-Octagon Spain)*
Jeff Shifrin *(Pres-Octagon Mktg America)*
Sean Nicholls *(Mng Dir-Australia & New Zealand)*
Jeremy Aisenberg *(VP-Strategic Initiatives)*
Julie Kennedy *(VP-Talent)*
Brian Smith *(VP-HR)*

Accounts:
LPGA

Octagon
560 Pacific Ave, San Francisco, CA 94133
Tel.: (415) 318-4311
Web Site: www.octagon.com

Employees: 10

Agency Specializes In: Sports Market

Michael Thomas *(CFO)*
Sean Nicholls *(Pres-Asia Pacific)*
Peter Carlisle *(Mng Dir-Olympics & Action Sports)*
Michaella Karl *(Client Svcs Dir)*
Ken Landphere *(Dir-Coaches & Team Sports)*
John Thornton *(Dir-Client Mgmt)*
Meg Cerullo *(Mgr-Playbook Integration)*

Octagon

8687 Melrose Ave 7th Fl, Los Angeles, CA 90069
Tel.: (703) 905-3300
Fax: (310) 854-8372
E-Mail: alan.walsh@octagon.com
Web Site: www.octagon.com

National Agency Associations: 4A's

Agency Specializes In: Advertising, Entertainment, Sports Market

Phil de Picciott *(Pres)*
Melissa Woltman *(Acct Dir-Consulting)*
Michael Jacobson *(Dir-Octagon First Call Los Angeles)*

Accounts:
Allyson Felix

Octagon
Octagon House 47 Wierda Road West, Wierda Valley, Sandton, 2146 South Africa
Tel.: (27) 11 506 4400
Fax: (27) 11 883 3011
E-Mail: qondisa.ngwenya@octagon.com
Web Site: europe.octagon.com

Employees: 30

Agency Specializes In: Entertainment, Sports Market

Qondisa Ngwenya *(Owner)*
Kugandrie Moodley *(Head-Sls, Sponsorship & Media)*

Accounts:
Carlsberg
Coni
HSBC
MasterCard
NBA
Nivea
Siemens
Speedo
Tesco
Vodafone

Octagon
Octagon House 81-83 Fullham High St, London, SW6 3JW United Kingdom
Tel.: (44) 207 862 0000
Fax: (44) 207 862 0001
E-Mail: ukwebsite.information@octagon.com
Web Site: europe.octagon.com

Employees: 50

Agency Specializes In: Sports Market

Tim Collins *(Co-Mng Dir)*
Phil Carling *(Mng Dir-Football-Worldwide)*
Jeff Ehrenkranz *(Mng Dir-Europe, Mid East & India)*
Joel Seymour-Hyde *(VP-Strategy EMEI)*
Matt Bailey *(Acct Dir)*
Josh Green *(Dir-Creative)*

Accounts:
Budweiser "Coaches Initiative"
Cisco
Mars
MasterCard
NBA
NFL
Nivea
Siemens
Speedo
Tesco
Vodafone

Octagon
Opernplatz 2, 60313 Frankfurt, Germany
Tel.: (49) 69-1504-1210
E-Mail: info@octagongermany.com
Web Site: octagon.com

Agency Specializes In: Sports Market

Alexander Hermesdorf *(VP-Octagon Germany)*
Marc Brix *(Gen Mgr)*
Tassilo Von Hanau *(Acct Mgr)*
Sebastian Steingraeber *(Sr Acct Exec)*

Octagon
123 Moray St S, Melbourne, VIC 3205 Australia
Tel.: (61) 3 9685 3500
Fax: (61) 3 9686 6660
E-Mail: sean.nicholls@octagon.com
Web Site: octagon.com

Employees: 20

Agency Specializes In: Sports Market

Sean Nicholls *(Pres-Asia Pacific)*

Accounts:
Master Card
XXXX Gold

Octagon Sydney
166 William St, Woolloomooloo, Sydney, NSW 2011 Australia
Tel.: (61) 2 9994 4340
Fax: (61) 2 9994 4027
E-Mail: sean.nicholls@octagon.com

Employees: 20

Agency Specializes In: Sports Market

Sean Nicholls *(Pres-Asia Pacific)*
Fleur Massey *(Sr Acct Dir)*
Simone Errey *(Grp Acct Dir)*
Rene Wright *(Dir-Client Svcs-Athletes & Personalities)*

OCTANE VTM
3650 Washington Blvd, Indianapolis, IN 46205
Tel.: (317) 920-6105
E-Mail: questions@octanevtm.com
Web Site: www.octanevtm.com

Rick Ashley *(Pres & Sr Strategist)*
David Zaritz *(Pres-Publicity Solutions LLC)*
Meredith Ingram *(Dir-Channel Mktg)*
Steve James *(Dir-Creative)*
Bryan Spear *(Dir-Creative)*
Susan Dillman *(Strategist-PR)*
Robert Stahlke *(Strategist-New Bus)*
Randy Stone *(Strategist-Res)*
Karen Neligh *(Project Strategist)*
Lisa Stewart-Johnson *(Project Strategist)*

OCTOBER-DESIGN
PO Box 38046, Cleveland, OH 44138
Mailing Address:
PO Box 38046, Cleveland, OH 44138-0046
Tel.: (440) 793-5065
E-Mail: employment@october-design.com
Web Site: www.october-design.com

Employees: 5
Year Founded: 2002

Agency Specializes In: Advertising, Advertising Specialties, Arts, Brand Development & Integration, Broadcast, Catalogs, Co-op Advertising, Collateral, Commercial Photography, Communications, Computers & Software, Consulting, Consumer Goods, Consumer Marketing, Consumer Publications, Content, Corporate Communications, Corporate Identity, Custom Publishing, Customer Relationship Management, Digital/Interactive, Direct Response Marketing, Direct-to-Consumer, E-Commerce, Electronic Media, Electronics, Email, Financial, Graphic Design, High Technology, Household Goods, Identity Marketing, Information Technology, Integrated Marketing, Local Marketing, Logo & Package Design, Media Buying Services, Media Planning, Media Relations, Merchandising, Mobile Marketing, Multimedia, New Product Development, New Technologies, Outdoor, Package Design, Paid Searches, Planning & Consultation, Point of Purchase, Point of Sale, Print, Product Placement, Production, Production (Print), Promotions, Public Relations, Publicity/Promotions, Publishing, Retail, Sales Promotion, Search Engine Optimization, Social Marketing/Nonprofit, Sponsorship, Sports Market, Strategic Planning/Research, Technical Advertising, Viral/Buzz/Word of Mouth, Web (Banner Ads, Pop-ups, etc.)

Ron White *(Owner)*

Accounts:
AAF
Anchor
Contemporary Gardens
Diet Center
GE
Physician's Weight Loss Centers
Qdoba

OCULUS STUDIOS
948 Manchester St Ste 120, Lexington, KY 40508
Tel.: (859) 955-0622
Web Site: www.oculusstudios.com

Agency Specializes In: Advertising, Digital/Interactive, Internet/Web Design, Logo & Package Design, Print, Radio, Search Engine Optimization

Brock Smith *(Owner)*

Accounts:
Commonwealth Credit Union

ODEN MARKETING AND DESIGN
119 S Main St Ste 300, Memphis, TN 38103
Tel.: (901) 578-8055
Fax: (901) 578-1911
Toll Free: (800) 371-6233
E-Mail: vision@oden.com
Web Site: www.oden.com

Employees: 60
Year Founded: 1971

Agency Specializes In: Consulting, Consumer Marketing, Graphic Design, Internet/Web Design

William F. Carkeet, Jr. *(CEO & Principal)*
Bret A. Terwilleger *(COO & Principal)*
Tina Lazarini Niclosi *(Exec VP & Principal)*
Ashley Livingston *(Assoc VP-Digital Mktg)*
David Fuller *(Sr Dir-Design)*
McRae Lenahan *(Acct Mgr-FedEx Sponsorship Brand Mgmt-FedEx Corporate Identity)*
Kate Stratman *(Brand Mgr-Stewardship)*

ODNEY
1400 W Century Ave, Bismarck, ND 58503
Tel.: (701) 222-8721
Fax: (701) 222-8172
Toll Free: (888) 500-8721
E-Mail: odney@odney.com
Web Site: www.odney.com

E-Mail for Key Personnel:
President: pfinken@odney.com
Creative Dir.: mbruner@odney.com
Media Dir.: cdupaul@odney.com
Production Mgr.: smoser@odney.com
Public Relations: mpiehl@odney.com

Employees: 44
Year Founded: 1985

Agency Specializes In: Advertising, Agriculture, Automotive, Brand Development & Integration, Broadcast, Business-To-Business, Cable T.V., Co-op Advertising, Collateral, College, Communications, Consulting, Consumer Goods, Consumer Marketing, Consumer Publications, Corporate Communications, Corporate Identity, Crisis Communications, Digital/Interactive, Direct Response Marketing, Direct-to-Consumer, E-Commerce, Electronic Media, Engineering, Financial, Food Service, Government/Political, Graphic Design, Health Care Services, High Technology, Hospitality, Industrial, Information Technology, Internet/Web Design, Local Marketing, Logo & Package Design, Market Research, Media Buying Services, Media Planning, Media Relations, Medical Products, Newspaper, Newspapers & Magazines, Outdoor, Over-50 Market, Package Design, Planning & Consultation, Point of Purchase, Point of Sale, Print, Public Relations, Publicity/Promotions, Radio, Restaurant, Retail, Seniors' Market, Social Marketing/Nonprofit, Social Media, Strategic Planning/Research, T.V., Trade & Consumer Magazines, Transportation, Travel & Tourism, Viral/Buzz/Word of Mouth, Web (Banner Ads, Pop-ups, etc.), Women's Market

Approx. Annual Billings: $15,000,000

Breakdown of Gross Billings by Media: Other: 40%; Print: 10%; Radio: 10%; T.V.: 40%

Patrick Finken *(Pres)*
Mike Pierce *(Chief Digital Officer)*
Brekka Kramer *(Gen Mgr)*
Michael Bruner *(Sr Dir-Creative)*
Cindy Dupaul-Vogelsang *(Dir-Media)*
Erin Schwengler *(Mgr-IT)*
Lynette Julson *(Media Planner & Media Buyer)*

Accounts:
Basin Electric Cooperative; Bismarck, ND; 1997
Cass County Electric Cooperative
Denny's
First Western Bank; Minot, ND; 1995
Gate City Bank
North Dakota Tourism Department
SRT Communications
Taco John's Restaurants
Touchstone Energy Cooperatives
Verendrye Electric Cooperative

Branches

Odney Advertising-Minot
21 Main St S, Minot, ND 58701
Tel.: (701) 857-7205
Fax: (701) 837-0955
E-Mail: pfinken@odney.com
Web Site: www.odney.com

Employees: 10
Year Founded: 1988

Agency Specializes In: Brand Development & Integration, Internet/Web Design, Planning & Consultation, Strategic Planning/Research

Michael Pierce *(Chief Digital Officer)*
Brekka Kramer *(Gen Mgr)*
Mike Bruner *(Sr Dir-Creative)*
Cindy DuPaul-Vogelsang *(Dir-Media)*
Shane Goettle *(Dir-Pub Affairs, Govt Rels & Lobbying Svcs)*
Meghann Chamberlain *(Strategist-Digital Media)*
Michael Goulet *(Strategist-Digital)*
Paulette Bullinger *(Media Planner & Buyer)*
Katie Hogfoss *(Media Buyer)*

Odney Advertising-Fargo
102 Broadway, Fargo, ND 58102
Tel.: (701) 451-9028
Fax: (701) 235-9483
E-Mail: pfinken@odney.com
Web Site: www.odney.com

Employees: 50
Year Founded: 1989

Agency Specializes In: Brand Development & Integration, Internet/Web Design, Local Marketing, Planning & Consultation, Strategic Planning/Research

Michael Pierce *(Chief Digital Officer)*
Brekka Kramer *(Gen Mgr)*
Cindy DuPaul-Vogelsang *(Dir-Media)*
Shane Goettle *(Dir-Pub Affairs, Govt Rels & Lobbying Svcs)*
Meghann Chamberlain *(Strategist-Digital Media)*
Michael Goulet *(Strategist-Digital)*
Paulette Bullinger *(Media Planner & Buyer)*
Katie Hogfoss *(Media Buyer)*
Savanna Hill *(Acct Coord)*

Accounts:
Relco

ODONNELL COMPANY
59 Elm St Ste 402, New Haven, CT 6510
Tel.: (203) 764-1000
E-Mail: info@odonnellco.com
Web Site: www.odonnellco.com

Agency Specializes In: Advertising, Brand Development & Integration, Digital/Interactive, Event Planning & Marketing, Media Buying Services, Media Relations, Print, Public Relations, Search Engine Optimization, T.V.

Eileen Odonnell *(Partner & Creative Dir)*
Ruth Lamy *(Sr Art Dir)*

Accounts:
New-Somewhat off the Wall

ODOPOD, INC.
391 Grove St, San Francisco, CA 94102
Tel.: (415) 436-9980
Fax: (415) 436-9984
E-Mail: hello@odopod.com
Web Site: www.odopod.com

Employees: 20
Year Founded: 1980

National Agency Associations: SODA

Agency Specializes In: Advertising, Digital/Interactive, Internet/Web Design

Allison McCarthy *(Dir-Bus Dev)*
Albert Poon *(Dir-Creative)*
Stacy Stevenson *(Dir-Bus Dev)*

Accounts:
Adobe
Coca-Cola Portal
Electronic Arts
Ford
Google
MTV
Nike Skateboarding
Red Bull
Sony
Spike
Target

ODYSSEUS ARMS
332 Pine St Ste 200, San Francisco, CA 94104
Tel.: (415) 466-8990
E-Mail: odysseus@o-arms.com
Web Site: www.o-arms.com

Year Founded: 2011

Agency Specializes In: Advertising, Brand Development & Integration, Digital/Interactive, Social Media, Sponsorship

Libby Brockhoff *(Partner & Creative Dir)*
Franklin Tipton *(Partner)*
Eric Dunn *(Mng Dir)*

Accounts:
Amnesty International USA
New-Capital One
New-E. & J. Gallo Carlo Rossi
New-Foster Farms Corn Dogs, Media
New-NBC Universal

ODYSSEY NETWORKS
The Interchurch Ctr 475 Riverside Dr, New York, NY 10115
Tel.: (212) 870-1030
Fax: (212) 870-1040
E-Mail: info@odysseynetworks.org
Web Site: www.odysseynetworks.org

Year Founded: 1987

Agency Specializes In: Advertising, Print, T.V.

Nick Stuart *(Pres & CEO)*
Deb Mathews *(Dir-Faith Community Rels)*
Venus Zambrana *(Office Mgr)*
Mary Dickey *(Mgr-Publicity & Mktg)*

Accounts:
Tony Blair Faith Foundation Religions Organization

OFF MADISON AVE
5555 E Van Buren St Ste 215, Phoenix, AZ 85008
Tel.: (480) 505-4500
Fax: (480) 505-4501
E-Mail: info@offmadisonave.com
Web Site: www.offmadisonave.com

Employees: 30
Year Founded: 1998

Agency Specializes In: Advertising, Automotive, Broadcast, Business-To-Business, Cable T.V., Children's Market, Collateral, Commercial Photography, Communications, Consulting, Consumer Goods, Consumer Marketing, Corporate Communications, Corporate Identity, Cosmetics, Customer Relationship Management, Digital/Interactive, E-Commerce, Education, Electronic Media, Entertainment, Event Planning & Marketing, Financial, Food Service, Government/Political, Graphic Design, Hospitality, In-Store Advertising, Integrated Marketing, Internet/Web Design, Local Marketing, Logo & Package Design, Market Research, Media Buying Services, Media Planning, Media Relations, Multimedia, New Product Development, Newspaper, Newspapers & Magazines, Out-of-Home Media, Outdoor, Package Design, Paid Searches, Planning & Consultation, Point of Sale, Print, Production, Production (Ad, Film, Broadcast), Promotions, Public Relations, Publicity/Promotions, Radio, Real Estate, Recruitment, Restaurant, Retail, Search Engine Optimization, Seniors'

Market, Social Marketing/Nonprofit, Strategic Planning/Research, T.V., Technical Advertising, Trade & Consumer Magazines, Travel & Tourism, Web (Banner Ads, Pop-ups, etc.), Women's Market

David Anderson *(Co-Founder, Pres & CEO)*
Roger Hurni *(Mng Partner & Chief Creative Officer)*
Patrick Murphy *(Dir-Media)*
Michael Stevens *(Dir-Interactive Svcs & Innovation)*
Doug Anderson *(Assoc Dir-Creative)*
Kelley Dilworth *(Acct Supvr)*
Laura Girard *(Supvr-Media)*
Heather Tweedy *(Strategist-Content)*
Chelsea Beyerman *(Media Planner & Media Buyer)*
Sara Arnold *(Copywriter)*

Accounts:
The Arizona Game and Fish Department
Arizona Indian Gaming Association
Arizona Office of Tourism
The Arizona Organizing Committee
DMS Health Technologies
Fraud Posse
Harkins Theatres
Mobillogix
Nike
SkyMall
Tabarka Studio

Branches

Off Madison Ave

604 Arizona Ave Ste 261, Santa Monica, CA 90401
Tel.: (310) 752-9031
Web Site: www.offmadisonave.com

Agency Specializes In: Advertising, Brand Development & Integration, Content, Digital/Interactive, Public Relations, Social Media

Patrick Murphy *(Dir-Media)*

Accounts:
New-The Arizona Office of Tourism
New-Chipotle Mexican Grill
New-Cox Media
New-Harkins Theatres
New-The National Academy of Sports Medicine

Off Madison Ave

1434 Spruce St Ste 100, Boulder, CO 80302
Tel.: (303) 209-0054
Web Site: www.offmadisonave.com

Agency Specializes In: Advertising, Brand Development & Integration, Content, Digital/Interactive, Public Relations, Social Media

Spike Stevens *(Dir-Interactive Svcs)*

Accounts:
New-The Arizona Office of Tourism
New-Chipotle Mexican Grill
New-Cox Media
New-Harkins Theatres
New-The National Academy of Sports Medicine

OGILVY & MATHER

636 11th Ave, New York, NY 10036
Tel.: (212) 237-4000
Fax: (212) 237-5123
E-Mail: emily.ward@ogilvy.com
Web Site: www.ogilvy.com

Employees: 18,000
Year Founded: 1948

National Agency Associations: 4A's-AAF-ABC-ADMA-APA-BPA-DMA-MCA-NYPAA-TAB-THINKLA

Agency Specializes In: Above-the-Line, Advertising, Advertising Specialties, Affiliate Marketing, Affluent Market, African-American Market, Agriculture, Alternative Advertising, Arts, Asian Market, Automotive, Aviation & Aerospace, Below-the-Line, Bilingual Market, Brand Development & Integration, Branded Entertainment, Broadcast, Business Publications, Business-To-Business, Cable T.V., Catalogs, Children's Market, Co-op Advertising, Collateral, Commercial Photography, Communications, Computers & Software, Consulting, Consumer Goods, Consumer Marketing, Consumer Publications, Content, Corporate Communications, Corporate Identity, Cosmetics, Crisis Communications, Customer Relationship Management, Digital/Interactive, Direct Response Marketing, Direct-to-Consumer, E-Commerce, Education, Electronic Media, Electronics, Email, Engineering, Entertainment, Environmental, Event Planning & Marketing, Exhibit/Trade Shows, Experience Design, Fashion/Apparel, Financial, Food Service, Game Integration, Gay & Lesbian Market, Government/Political, Graphic Design, Guerilla Marketing, Health Care Services, High Technology, Hispanic Market, Hospitality, Household Goods, Identity Marketing, In-Store Advertising, Industrial, Infomercials, Information Technology, Integrated Marketing, International, Internet/Web Design, Investor Relations, Legal Services, Leisure, Local Marketing, Logo & Package Design, Luxury Products, Magazines, Marine, Market Research, Media Buying Services, Media Planning, Media Relations, Media Training, Medical Products, Men's Market, Merchandising, Mobile Marketing, Multicultural, Multimedia, New Product Development, New Technologies, Newspaper, Newspapers & Magazines, Out-of-Home Media, Outdoor, Over-50 Market, Package Design, Paid Searches, Pets , Pharmaceutical, Planning & Consultation, Podcasting, Point of Purchase, Point of Sale, Print, Product Placement, Production, Production (Ad, Film, Broadcast), Production (Print), Promotions, Public Relations, Publicity/Promotions, RSS (Really Simple Syndication), Radio, Real Estate, Recruitment, Regional, Restaurant, Retail, Sales Promotion, Search Engine Optimization, Seniors' Market, Social Marketing/Nonprofit, Social Media, Sponsorship, Sports Market, Stakeholders, Strategic Planning/Research, Sweepstakes, Syndication, T.V., Technical Advertising, Teen Market, Telemarketing, Trade & Consumer Magazines, Transportation, Travel & Tourism, Tween Market, Urban Market, Viral/Buzz/Word of Mouth, Web (Banner Ads, Pop-ups, etc.), Women's Market, Yellow Pages Advertising

Carla Hendra *(Chm-OgilvyRED & Vice Chm-Ogilvy & Mather Worldwide Bd)*
Jeremy Kuhn *(Partner & Grp Acct Dir)*
Ruben Mercadal *(Partner & Sr Producer-Ogilvy New York)*
Christina Montero *(Partner & Acct Dir)*
Martin Lange *(Partner-Global Consulting)*
Nicole Pinochet *(Partner & Exec Grp Dir)*
Corinne Kerns Lowry *(Sr Partner, Mng Dir & Joint Head-Client Svcs)*
Jeff Traverso *(Sr Partner & Mng Dir)*
Lauren Crampsie *(Sr Partner & CMO-Global)*
Corinna Falusi *(Chief Creative Officer)*
Steve Simpson *(Chief Creative Officer-North America)*
Khai Meng Tham *(Chief Creative Officer-Worldwide)*
Brandon Berger *(Chief Digital Officer)*
Jaime Prieto *(Pres-Brand Mgmt-Global)*
Joanna Seddon *(Pres-Global Brand Consulting)*
Pam Alvord *(Sr VP & Exec Grp Dir, Dir-Client Svcs & Brand Activation)*
Russell Messner *(Mng Dir-Global)*
Stephen Weinstein *(VP & Acct Dir)*
Colin Mitchell *(Head-Plng-Worldwide)*
David Sogn *(Head-Mktg Analytics)*
J. Archie Lyons *(Exec Creative Dir)*
Jason Aspes *(Exec Dir-Creative)*
Diane Fakhouri *(Sr Partner & Exec Dir-Learning & Dev-North America)*
Felix Fenz *(Exec Dir-Creative)*
David Fowler *(Sr Partner & Exec Dir-Creative)*
Jenny Gadd *(Exec Dir-Content Production)*
Tommy Henvey *(Exec Creative Dir)*
Steve Howard *(Sr Partner & Exec Dir-Creative)*
Maru Kopelowicz *(Exec Creative Dir)*
Christopher Reardon *(Sr Partner & Exec Dir-Creative-Digital Experience)*
Kristian Baek-Mikkelsen *(Grp Dir-Plng)*
Joan Dufresne *(Sr Partner & Grp Dir-Plng)*
Chris Van Oosterhout *(Sr Partner & Grp Dir-Creative)*
Jen Peterson *(Sr Partner & Grp Dir-Plng)*
Eric Wegerbauer *(Grp Dir-Creative)*
Okan Usta *(Sr Dir-Art)*
Jillian Watkins *(Sr Dir-Art)*
Victoria Azarian *(Sr Partner & Grp Acct Dir)*
Sarah Mills *(Grp Acct Dir)*
Michael Paterson *(Sr Partner & Grp Acct Dir)*
Angela Cona *(Sr Partner & Program Dir-Mktg)*
Ryan Laird *(Acct Dir)*
Michael Lombardi *(Acct Dir)*
Sam Mazur *(Creative Dir)*
Prema Techinamurthi *(Acct Dir)*
Guto Terni *(Creative Dir)*
Alicia Zuluaga *(Producer-Brdcst & Content)*
Ben Levine *(Mgmt Supvr)*
Melissa Peterson *(Mgmt Supvr)*
Aditi Reddy *(Mgmt Supvr)*
Jessica Schaevitz *(Mgmt Supvr)*
Phillip Cho *(Dir-Art & Assoc Dir-Creative)*
Adam Kornblum *(Dir-Social Media & Sr Strategist-Content)*
Darren Wright *(Dir-Creative & Copywriter)*
Sebastian Aresco *(Dir-Project Mgmt)*
Robert Balog *(Dir-Creative)*
Bastien Baumann *(Dir-Creative)*
Justin Bettman *(Dir-Art)*
Chris Childerhouse *(Dir-Creative)*
Milton Correa *(Dir-Creative)*
Chris Curry *(Dir-Creative)*
Tom Elia *(Dir-Creative)*
Doreen Fox *(Sr Partner & Dir-Creative)*
Todd Goodale *(Dir-Creative)*
Gloria Hall *(Sr Partner & Dir-Digital Rights Mgmt)*
Vanessa Hobbs *(Dir-Art)*
Andy Jones *(Sr Partner & Dir-Worldwide Plng-Siemens)*
Jack Low *(Sr Partner & Dir-Creative)*
Terrence Maharaj *(Dir-Global Brand Mgmt & Comml)*
Della Mathew *(Dir-Creative & Art)*
SiMone OppenheiMer *(Sr Partner & Dir-Bus Dev-North America)*
Chris Rowson *(Dir-Creative)*
Andrea Scotting *(Sr Partner & Dir-Creative)*
Leslie Stone *(Dir-Plng Svcs)*
Rich Wallace *(Dir-Creative)*
Tony Whiteside *(Dir-Creative)*
Fred Kovey *(Assoc Dir-Creative & Copywriter)*
Nicky Lorenzo *(Assoc Dir-Creative & Copywriter)*
Justin Via *(Assoc Dir-Creative & Copywriter)*
Matt Doherty *(Assoc Dir-Global Digital Creative Dev)*
Beth Kushner *(Assoc Dir-Creative)*
Emily Boedecker *(Mgr-Print Production)*
Peter Czmielewski *(Mgr-Bus Dev)*
Kelly Brody *(Acct Supvr)*
Jena Choi *(Acct Supvr)*
Samantha Devine *(Acct Supvr)*
Juan Luna *(Acct Supvr)*
Megumi Sasada *(Acct Supvr)*
Emily Zale *(Acct Supvr)*
Andres Aguilar *(Supvr-Creative)*
Joshua Shyu *(Sr Acct Exec)*
Alexander Cho *(Acct Exec)*
Ellissa Corwin *(Acct Exec)*

Aniella Opalacz *(Acct Exec)*
Emily Clark *(Jr Copywriter)*
Michael Franklin *(Copywriter)*
Jaime Jimenez *(Copywriter)*
Holden Rasche *(Copywriter)*
Jake Stanley *(Planner-Strategic)*
Caroline Tan *(Copywriter)*
Jennifer Wagstaff *(Jr Copywriter)*
Erin Wilson *(Designer)*
Melanie Lubin *(Coord-Recruitment)*
Jeffrey L. Bowman *(Sr Partner)*
Aaron Kennedy *(Exec Grp Dir)*
Lucy Lieberman *(Sr Partner & Exec Grp Dir)*
Kurt Lundberg *(Sr Partner & Exec Grp Dir)*
Tanya Neufeld *(Asst Media Planner)*
Danielle Russo *(Asst Producer)*
Mark Weintraub *(Exec Grp Dir-Digital)*
Karl Westman *(Sr Partner Exec Producer-Music)*
Joe Youssef *(Assoc Strategist-Digital)*

Accounts:
Aetna B2B Marketing, CRM, Collateral, Consumer Marketing, Digital Marketing, Email Marketing, Newsletters, Trade Shows
AIU
American Chemistry Council, Inc.
American Express American Express Card, BLUE Card, Campaign: "Retrospective", Campaign: "Talking Tags", Campaign: "The Journey Never Stops", Campaign: "The Membership Effect", Centurion Services, Corporate Card, Delta SkyMiles, Gold Card, Green Card, Membership Rewards, OPEN: Small Business Services, Platinum Card, Travelers Cheques, Tribeca Film Festival (Sponsorship), US Open (Sponsorship); 1963
American Red Cross
BAT
Bayer Healthcare Bayer Healthcare Animal Health, Bayer Healthcare Consumer Care, Bayer Healthcare Medical Care, Bayer Schering Pharma, Consumer Communications, Digital, Global Marketing Services, Medical Education, Professional Communications, Public Relations
Bernas
BlackRock Creative; 2006
BP ARCO/ampm, Amoco, BP Connect, Campaign: "Tested to Perfection", Castrol; 1999
British Airways Campaign: "A Ticket To Visit Mum", Campaign: "Discover yourope"
Cabela's Inc. Creative, Strategy
Castrol Industrial North America Castrol
Caterpillar, Inc. "China Shop", "Gravity", "Lantern Festival", "Sand Castle", "Stack", Campaign: "Built For It", Campaign: "Built for It Trials", Campaign: "Tug of War"
CDW Corporation Campaign: "Client Golf", Campaign: "People Who Get IT", Elves
Cisco Systems; 2002
Citizens Bank (Agency of Record) Campaign: "Janitor", Strategy
The Coca-Cola Company Campaign: "'Put a Smile", Campaign: "Drinkable Billboard", Campaign: "Drinkable Commercial", Coke Zero, Diet Coke, Fanta, Media, PlantBottle, Print, Slender Vender, Sprite Zero, The Wearable Movie
Coca-Cola Refreshments USA, Inc. Campaign: "Big Santa", Campaign: "Bottle Bat", Campaign: "Lost In Timeline", Campaign: "Play Fanta", Campaign: "Share a Coke", Coca-Cola Zero, Diet Coke, Fanta, Georgia Coffee, Global Graphic-Novel Campaign, Minute Maid, Package Design, Powerade, Sprite, Vitaminwater; 2009
Comcast Corp Creative
Cricket Communications, Inc
Depend
DuPont Campaign: "Horizons", Campaign: "Stories of Inclusive Innovation"
Eli Lilly Cialis; 2001
Environmental Defense Fund
ESPN "The Chase", Campaign: "Battle of Nations", Campaign: "The Hype", Digital, Print, Radio, Social, Sprint Cup
E*Trade (Creative Agency of Record) Campaign: "Epic Musical", Campaign: "Talent Scout", Campaign: "Type E"
Europcar
Expedia Campaign: "People Shaped Travel"
Express Scripts
FLOR, Inc.
Ford Motor Co.; 1975
GE Capital
Gillette; 2003
Gome & Youngor
Gudang Garam
Hellmann's Campaign: "1 800-Sandwich"
Holiday Inn
Huggies Brand Digital
IBM (Agency of Record) "IBMblr", A Boy & His Atom, Campaign: "Made With IBM", Campaign: "Sessions", Campaign: "Smarter Cities", Campaign: "Split Second", Campaign: "The World's Smallest Movie", Consulting Services, Digital, Linux, Network Servers, Online, Out-of-Home, Print, Social Outdoor, TV; 1994
IKEA "Morning Anthem", Campaign: "First :59", Campaign: "Together We Eat", General Market, Hispanic Market; 2010
Ink48
InterContinental Hotels Group Campaign: "But I Did Stay at a Holiday Inn Express Hotel Last Night", Campaign: "Journey to Extraordinary", Campaign: "Stay Smart", Holiday Inn Express, Holiday Inn Hotels & Resorts, InterContinental Hotels Group, Priority Club Rewards
International Advertising Association
Jinro & Korail
Johnson & Johnson; 2006
Kaplan University Talent Campaign; 2009
KEB Korea
Kimberly-Clark Adult & Feminine Care, Baby, Campaign: "Drop Your Pants City", Campaign: "Generation Know", Campaign: "Great American Try-On", Campaign: "Guard Your Manhood", Campaign: "I have SAM in My Pants", Campaign: "Underwareness", Child Care, Depend Silhouette Active Fit, Depends, Huggies, Kleenex, Kotex, Lead Creative, Poise Hourglass, Poise Microliners, Social Media, U by Kotex
La Jugueteria
Lenovo Group Campaign: "PC Does What", Lenovo.com, ThinkCenter Desktop Computers, ThinkPad; 2005
LVMH, Inc. Louis Vuitton
Mattel Barbie Girls Dolls, Large Dolls; 1954
Mead Johnson Enfamil; 2006
Merck Gaboxadol, Januvia; 1995
Metlife Insurance
MillerCoors, LLC "Catfight", Miller Genuine Draft, Miller Lite
Motorola Mobility LLC Motorola, Inc.
Narmi Tuning
Nascar (Creative Agency of Record) Campaign: "#whatdriversneed", Campaign: "Battle of Nations", Campaign: "Change", Campaign: "Heroes", Campaign: "Machine", Campaign: "Race to Green", Campaign: "The Chase", Campaign: "The Hype", Campaign: "Twist", Chase for the Nascar Sprint Cup, Digital, Online, Print, Radio, Social, Social Media, Sprint Cup
Nationwide (Creative Agency of Record) Campaign: "Jingle", Campaign: "Make Safe Happen", Campaign: "Nationwide Is On Your Side", Digital, Logo, Out of Home, Print, Super Bowl 2015, TV
Nestle Acqua Penna, Calistoga, Campaign: "Break out the Bunny", Campaign: "National Bunny Ears Day", Campaign: "Robot in Italy", Campaign: "The Life Deliziosa", Campaign: "Wrapper", Ice Mountain, Nesquik, Perrier, San Pellegrino; 1999
Pernod Ricard Glenlivet; 2006
Pfizer
Philips Campaign: "I'd FAQ Me", Campaign: "Like You've Never Felt Before", Campaign: "Odyssey", Campaign: "Stick with Technology", Global Creative, Norelco, Philips Sonicare
Pitney Bowes; 2002
Portfolio Night 7
Remy Cointreau Alcohol
SAP Campaign: "Run Like Never Before", Print, SAP HANA, mysap.com; 1999
S.C. Johnson & Son, Inc. Broadcast, Campaign: "Feel Anticipation", Creative, Glade, Home Cleaning, Home Fragrance, Sparkling Spruce
New-Shout
Siemens (Agency of Record) Campaign: "Answers", Campaign: "Blue Danube", Campaign: "Somewhere In America", TV; 2007
Sportsnet New York New York Jets, New York Mets; 2006
Spotify Campaign: "#thatsongwhen", Marketing, Online, Social Media
Suntory & Sochenbicha
Susan G. Komen for the Cure Corporate & Crisis PR
Synchrony Financial (Agency of Record) Advertising, Broadcast, Campaign: "Engage With Us", Digital, Media, Out-of-Home, Print
Tiffany & Co. (Agency of Record) Advertising, Brand Positioning, CT60 Watch, Campaign: "A New York Minute", Campaign: "Will You?", Digital, Global Creative, Out of Home, Print, Strategic, Video
Time Warner Cable Campaign: "New World", Campaign: "This Stop, Charlotte. Next Stop, Tribeca.", Creative, TWC.com, VoIP
Tourneau, Inc. Tourneau
Tribeca Film Festival
Unilever Home & Personal Care USA Dove Energy Glow Moisturizer, Dove Pro-Age, Dove Ultimate Antiperspirant Deodorant, Vaseline
Unilever Campaign: "Real Beauty", Campaign: "Real Curves", Carb Options, Dove, Hellmann's Real Mayonnaise, Home Basics, Ponds, Ponds Institute, Project Sunlight, Q Tips, Slim-Fast, Suave, TV; 1952
United Parcel Service Campaign: "Motion", Campaign: "United Problem Solvers", Campaign: "Your Wishes Delivered", Creative, Online Push, Print, Social Media, TV
Vietnam Airlines
Wilkies
WiTribe

United States:

A. Eicoff & Co.
401 N Michigan Ave 4th Fl, Chicago, IL 60611-4212
(See Separate Listing)

de la Cruz & Associates
(Formerly de la Cruz Group)
Metro Office Park St 1 No 9 Ste 201, Guaynabo, PR 00968-1705
(See Separate Listing)

The Lacek Group
900 2nd Ave S Ste 1800, Minneapolis, MN 55402
(See Separate Listing)

Neo@Ogilvy
636 11th Ave, New York, NY 10036
(See Separate Listing)

Ogilvy & Mather New York
636 11th Ave, New York, NY 10036
Tel.: (212) 237-4000
Fax: (212) 237-5123
Web Site: www.ogilvy.com

Year Founded: 1948

Agency Specializes In: Sponsorship

David Apicella *(Vice Chm-Creative-Ogilvy North*

America)
Corinna Falusi *(Chief Creative Officer & Sr Partner-Ogilvy & Mather New York)*
Donna Pedro *(Chief Diversity Officer)*
Adam Tucker *(Pres-Ogilvy & Mather Adv)*
Simon Pearce *(Mng Dir-New York)*
Mark Donatelli *(Head-Data Strategy & Plng-Global)*
Colin Mitchell *(Head-Plng-Worldwide)*
Martin Sandberg *(Creative Dir)*
Alfredo Rossi *(Dir-Creative)*
Richard Ryan *(Project Mgr-Production)*
Emily Charlton *(Acct Exec)*
Sara Smoler *(Acct Exec-Bus Dev)*

Accounts:
The Advertising Council Global Warming
American Express Company
The Coca-Cola Company
Dove Men+Care
Environmental Defense Fund Global Warming
Holiday Inn
IBM
New-Tiffany & Co
Time Warner Cable

Ogilvy North America
636 11th Ave, New York, NY 10036
Tel.: (212) 237-4000
Fax: (212) 237-5123
Web Site: www.ogilvy.com

Jennifer Fernbach *(Sr Partner & Mng Dir)*
Steve Simpson *(Chief Creative Officer)*
Donna Pedro *(Chief Diversity Officer)*
Ramiro Sandoval *(VP, Dir-Creative & Dir-Mixed Media-Medical Education)*
Liz Taylor *(Exec Dir-Creative, Digital & Social)*
Scott McClure *(Sr Dir-Art)*
Evan Shumeyko *(Sr Dir)*
Whitney Keenan *(Mgmt Supvr)*
Athena Lynn *(Dir-Project Mgmt)*
Megan Height *(Assoc Dir-Project Mgmt)*
Eddie Burns *(Sr Mgr-Content)*
David Halberstadt *(Sr Mgr-Integrated Content Production Bus)*
Eric Hulsizer *(Sr Mgr-Tech)*
Colleen Castle *(Acct Supvr-Siemens & Plenty)*
Jissette Lopez *(Acct Supvr-Res)*
Kate Prescott *(Acct Supvr)*

Accounts:
American Express
Barclays
Blackrock
CDW
Lenovo ThinkPad
Motorola Solutions, Inc.; 2007
Siemens
Wachovia Creative; 2008

Ogilvy & Mather
3530 Hayden Ave, Culver City, CA 90232
Tel.: (310) 280-2200
Fax: (310) 280-9473
Web Site: www.ogilvy.com

Employees: 100
Year Founded: 1971

National Agency Associations: 4A's

Agency Specializes In: Children's Market, Entertainment, High Technology

Dave Galligos *(Sr VP & Exec Dir-Creative)*
Sarah Howell *(Mng Dir-H&O)*
Heather MacPherson *(Mng Dir-Worldwide)*
Dameon Pope *(VP & Acct Dir-Global Loyalty)*
Lori Proctor *(Mgmt Supvr)*
Rhonda Mitchell *(Dir-Creative Svcs)*
Ben Morris *(Dir-OgilvyWest IT)*
Nicholas Costarides *(Assoc Dir-Creative)*
Jordan Peabody *(Assoc Dir-Talent Mgmt)*
Court Lanio *(Acct Supvr)*
Karla Zientowski *(Acct Supvr)*
Melissa Dean *(Acct Exec)*
Madilene Lake *(Asst Acct Exec)*
Sophie Wolf *(Asst Acct Exec)*

Accounts:
BP America, Inc. AM/PM Mini Markets
Cisco Systems
Mattel Barbie
McIlhenny Co. Tabasco
Qualcomm Snapdragon
Scotch Brite

Ogilvy & Mather
350 W Mart Ctr Dr Ste 1100, Chicago, IL 60654-1866
Tel.: (312) 856-8200
Fax: (312) 856-8207
Web Site: www.ogilvy.com

E-Mail for Key Personnel:
Creative Dir.: joe.sciarrotta@ogilvy.com

Year Founded: 1976

National Agency Associations: 4A's

Agency Specializes In: Sponsorship

Jack Rooney *(Chm & CEO)*
Luissandro Del Gobbo *(Partner & Dir-Creative)*
Marie Goss *(Partner & Dir-Brdcst Bus)*
David Morrissey *(Partner & Dir-Plng)*
Cathy Francque *(Mng Dir)*
Joe Sciarrotta *(Chief Creative Officer-Chicago)*
Dasher Lowe *(Mng Dir-OgilvyOne)*
Kathy Cummings *(VP)*
Mananya Komorowski *(VP)*
Chris Turner *(Sr Partner, Head-Creative Integration & Grp Dir-Creative)*
Antonio Nunez *(Head-Plng)*
Matthew Clay *(Grp Dir-Strategy)*
Maureen Shirreff *(Sr Partner & Grp Dir-Creative)*
Dave Metcalf *(Sr Partner & Grp Acct Dir)*
Bowen Mendelson *(Dir-Creative & Copywriter-Ogilvy Chicago)*
Rachel Robbins Clue *(Dir-Project Mgmt)*
Kathleen Katrenak *(Dir-Client Fin)*
HJ Alicia Nam *(Dir-Art)*
Janna Reddig *(Dir-Plng)*
Giovanni Settesoldi *(Dir-Creative)*
Gabe Usadel *(Dir-Design)*
Isaac Pagan *(Assoc Dir-Creative)*
Grant Weber *(Assoc Dir-Creative)*
Jackie Lapides *(Sr Mgr-Content Production)*
Tina Roth *(Mgr-Creative Recruitment)*
Jordan Mitchell *(Acct Supvr & Strategist-Digital)*
Whitney Burton *(Acct Supvr)*
Christy Chakos *(Acct Supvr)*
Dana Fulena *(Acct Supvr)*
Amy Munin *(Acct Supvr-Global)*
Alex Guglielmo *(Acct Exec-Global)*
Jane Johnsen *(Acct Exec-OgilvyOne Worldwide)*
Libby Welke *(Acct Exec)*
Justin Arvidson *(Asst Acct Exec)*
Rachel Williams *(Asst Acct Exec)*
Anna Ibbotson *(Sr Partner & Exec Grp Dir)*

Accounts:
ACT
Allstate
American Bar Association; Chicago, IL (Agency of Record)
Apes Campaign: "A Project of The Conservation Trust"
Arrow Electronics
Ashford University
Beam Inc Creative, Digital, Pinnacle Vodka, Print, Television
Blackhawks Campaign: "Own The Ice"
BP
British Airways Campaign: "Visit Mum"
Cargill, Inc. Truvia
CDW Corporation Broadcast, Campaign: "Charles Barkley", Campaign: "Futuristic", Campaign: "People Who Get It", Campaign: "Smart Growth", Campaign: "Teammates", Digital, Online, Print, Radio, Social Media, The Dome
Chicago Blackhawks Hockey Team (Agency of Record)
Constellation Brands, Inc. Advertising, Corona Light, Modelo Especial
DHL DHL Holdings, Inc.
The Ernest Hemingway Foundation of Oak Park A Farewell To Arms, For Whom The Bell Tolls, The Old Man and the Sea, Videos
Grainger Branding, Creative
Grant Thornton International
Kimberly-Clark Corp. "Huggies Baby-Making Station", Campaign: "Daddy Test", Campaign: "Little Squirmers", Customer Relationship Management, Huggies, Kotex, Loyalty, Mobile, Print, Pull-Ups, Social, Social Media, Television
KISS FM Radio
New-Morton Salt (Creative Agency of Record) Digital, Public Relations, Social
Sargento Creative, Digital
S.C. Johnson & Son, Inc. Glade
Steppenwolf Theatre Campaign: "Clybourne Park", Campaign: "Man In Love", Campaign: "The March", Campaign: "Thirty Year History", Campaign: "Time Stands Still"
Tyson Foods, Inc. Campaign: "Shine It Forward", Jimmy Dean (Creative Agency of Record), Print, Strategy, TV
Unilever Campaign: "Choose Beautiful", Campaign: "Real Beauty", Dove, Dove Men+Care, Suave
UPS (Agency of Record) Campaign: "Guitar", Campaign: "Mailbox Confessions", TV

Ogilvy Public Relations Worldwide
636 11th Ave, New York, NY 10036
(See Separate Listing)

OgilvyInteractive
636 11th Ave, New York, NY 10036
(See Separate Listing)

OgilvyOne Worldwide
350 W Mart Ctr Dr Ste 1100, Chicago, IL 60654-1866
Tel.: (312) 856-8200
Fax: (312) 856-8420
E-Mail: info@ogilvy.com
Web Site: www.ogilvy.com

Employees: 150
Year Founded: 1976

National Agency Associations: 4A's

Dasher Lowe *(Mng Dir)*
Jessica Kaihoi *(Assoc Dir-Creative)*

Accounts:
Cannes Cyber & Design
Comfort
Dove
Ford
IBM
Nestle
Ou Pont
Tourism NSW

OgilvyOne Worldwide New York
636 11th Ave, New York, NY 10036
Tel.: (212) 237-4000
Fax: (212) 237-5123
Web Site: www.ogilvyone.com

Employees: 5,000
Year Founded: 1972

National Agency Associations: 4A's

Agency Specializes In: Direct Response Marketing

Brian Fetherstonhaugh *(Chm & CEO)*
Gunther Schumacher *(Pres & COO)*
Nick Fuller *(Partner & Dir-Mktg)*
Rebecca Barnard *(Partner & Exec Grp Dir)*
Jerry Smith *(Pres-Asia Pacific)*
Nelly Andersen *(Exec VP-Global Brands)*
Mish Fletcher *(Sr Partner & Mng Dir-Worldwide Mktg)*
Colin Mitchell *(Head-Plng-Worldwide Ogilvy & Mather)*
Evan Shumeyko *(Sr Dir-Engagement Strategy)*
Jan Leth *(Dir-Digital Creative-Worldwide)*
Jonathan Stern *(Dir-Global Digital Strategy & Ops-IBM)*
Jeremy Wilson *(Dir-Creative Strategy)*
Jonathan Rigby *(Assoc Dir-Engagement Plng)*

Accounts:
New-Aetna
American Express
BlackRock
New-Coca-Cola
DuPont
New-E*Trade
IBM (Global Direct Marketing Account); 2004
IHG
Ikea
Nestle USA (Confections & Snacks) Confections & Snacks
Unilever
UPS

OgilvyOne
111 Sutter St 10th Fl, San Francisco, CA 94104
Tel.: (415) 782-4700
Fax: (415) 782-4800
Web Site: www.ogilvy.com

Employees: 85

Roland Deal *(Mng Dir)*
Dasher Lowe *(Mng Dir)*
Chris Heydt *(Assoc Dir-Creative Strategy)*
Jonathan Rigby *(Assoc Dir-Engagement Plng)*
Judy Wu *(Supvr-Digital Media)*
Courtney Cantor *(Strategist-Engagement Strategy)*
Candice Hardie *(Acct Exec)*
Emilia M. Pittelli *(Acct Exec)*
Jason Savino *(Acct Exec)*
Paige Warmus *(Strategist-Engagement)*
Kealin Maloney *(Media Planner)*

Accounts:
InterContinental Hotels Group (Agency of Record)
iShares Brand Advertising
Mobixell

Canada

Ogilvy & Mather
33 Yonge St, Toronto, ON M5E 1X6 Canada
Tel.: (416) 367-3573
Fax: (416) 363-2088
E-Mail: laurie.young@ogilvy.com
Web Site: www.ogilvycanada.com

Employees: 148
Year Founded: 1961

Agency Specializes In: Direct Response Marketing, Multimedia, Public Relations, Sales Promotion

Dennis Stief *(CEO)*
Guy Stevenson *(Mng Dir)*
Laurie Young *(Mng Dir)*
Andy Watson *(CFO)*
Ian MacKellar *(Chief Creative Officer)*
Liz Kis *(Grp Head-Creative)*
Doug Potwin *(Dir-Plng)*

Accounts:
Heart and Stroke Foundation Campaign: "We Create Survivors", Creative, Print
Kimberly-Clark Inc. Broadcast, Campaign: "Share The Care", Kleenex, OOH, Online, Print
Rashers
Unilever Body Wash, Campaign: "Bye-Bye Deep Fryer", Campaign: "Real Beauty", Campaign: "Scratch Card", Dove, Hellmann's, The Dove Self Esteem Fund

Ogilvy Montreal
215 Rue St-Jacques Ste 333, Montreal, QC H2Y 1M6 Canada
Tel.: (514) 861-1811
Fax: (514) 861-0439
Web Site: www.ogilvy-montreal.ca

Employees: 80
Year Founded: 1982

Agency Specializes In: Advertising Specialties

Daniel Demers *(Pres & COO)*
Martin Gosselin *(Partner & VP-Creative)*
Linda Perez *(Mng Dir & VP)*
Paul Bergeron *(VP-Acct Svcs)*
Francine Stockli *(VP-Production)*
Francois Leandre *(Sr Dir-Art)*
Gavin Drummond *(Co-Creative Dir)*
Bernardo Andrada *(Dir-Creative)*
Lina Castrechini *(Acct Supvr)*
Maria Tripodi *(Supvr-HR)*

Accounts:
Canadian Armed Forces
Colorectal Cancer Association of Canada
Health Canada
Mont Tremblant Resort Creative, Tremblant

OgilvyOne Worldwide
33 Yonge St, Toronto, ON M5E 1X6 Canada
Tel.: (416) 363-9514
Fax: (416) 36-3 2088
E-Mail: guy.stevenson@ogilvy.com

Employees: 52
Year Founded: 1978

Agency Specializes In: Direct Response Marketing

Guy Stevenson *(Mng Dir)*
Laurie Young *(Mng Dir)*
Ian MacKellar *(Chief Creative Officer-Ogilvy Toronto)*
Dennis Stief *(CEO-Ogilvy & Mather-Canada)*
Aviva Groll *(Sr Partner & Grp Acct Dir)*
Bhavik Gajjar *(Assoc Dir-Creative)*
Lindsay Renwick *(Strategist-Social Media)*

Accounts:
Cisco
DHL
IBM Canada Limited
MX
Tim Hortons, Inc. Campaign: "The Warmest Tim Hortons in Canada", Online
Unilever United States, Inc. Campaign: "Thought Before Action", Dove

Austria:

Ogilvy & Mather Ges m.b.H.
Bachofengasse 8, 1190 Vienna, Austria
Tel.: (43) 1 90100 0
Fax: (43) 1 901 100 300
E-Mail: florian.krenkel@ogilvy.com
Web Site: www.ogilvy.at

Employees: 60
Year Founded: 1961

Florian Krenkel *(CEO)*

Accounts:
Business Doctors Campaign: "Burnout-Check"
Intakt Campaign: "The Eating-Disorder Spoon"
Kleine Zeitung
Mario Haller Campaign: "The Vintage Edition"
Red Cross Austria Campaign: "The Blood Donation Spray"
Reed Exhibition Companies
Reed Messe Wien Campaign: "Stratos Jump Successful", Model Maker Fair

OgilvyOne Worldwide GmbH
Bachofengasse 8, A-1190 Vienna, Austria
Tel.: (43) 1 90 100 0
Fax: (43) 1 90 100 300
Web Site: www.ogilvy.com

Employees: 60
Year Founded: 1984

Agency Specializes In: Direct Response Marketing

Florian Krenkel *(CEO)*

Accounts:
Austrian Postal Service IPO; 2007
BMW
Cisco Systems
Dove
Glaxo Smith Kline
IBM
SAP

Belgium:

Ogilvy & Mather NV/SA
Cantersteen 47, 1000 Brussels, Belgium
Tel.: (32) 25456500
E-Mail: info@ogilvy.be
Web Site: www.ogilvy.be/

Employees: 60
Year Founded: 1969

Sam De Win *(Exec Dir-Creative-Belgium)*
Brigitte Bourgeois *(Dir-Art-Ogilvy Group Brussels)*
Nathalie Strybos *(Copywriter)*

Accounts:
Amnesty International Belgium Campaign: "#tramnesty"
Beefeater
De Zelfmoordlijn
The European Commission's Directorate For The Environment Biodiversity Awareness, DG Environment
European Parliament Campaign: "Act. React. Impact."
Flemish Pork Syndicate
Ford Motor Company Ford Econetic Range, Ford S-Max, Ford Transit

OgilvyOne Worldwide
Blvd de l'Imperatrice 13 Keizerinlaan, 1000 Brussels, Belgium
Tel.: (32) 2 545 6500
Fax: (32) 2 545 6599
E-Mail: koen.vanimpe@ogilvy.com
Web Site: www.ogilvy.be/

Employees: 80
Year Founded: 1968

National Agency Associations: DMA-EDMA

Agency Specializes In: Advertising

Koen Van Impe *(Mng Dir)*
An Vande Velde *(Mng Dir)*
Isabel Artoos *(Acct Dir)*
Sofie Sermon *(Acct Dir)*
Brigitte Bourgeois *(Dir-Art)*
Nathalie Strybos *(Copywriter)*
Laurien Lelievre-Damit *(Jr Acct Exec)*

Accounts:
Belgian Federal Government Website
Coca-Cola Refreshments USA, Inc.
Electrabel
Ford
Zelfmoord 1813

Croatia:

Imelda Ogilvy
Trg zrtava fasizima 2/4, 10000 Zagreb, Croatia
Tel.: (385) 1480 8500
Fax: (385) 1 4833 658
Web Site: www.agencijaimelda.si

Employees: 17
Year Founded: 2000

Branislav Milosevic *(Dir-Art)*

Accounts:
Morela Optics Homeless Man
Surf Festival Campaign: "Surf"

Cyprus:

Pandora/Ogilvy & Mather
Kennedy Business Center 12-14 Kennedy Ave 1st Fl Ofc 101, Nicosia, Cyprus
Mailing Address:
PO Box 23683, Nicosia, Cyprus
Tel.: (357) 22 767374
Fax: (357) 22 767388
E-Mail: pandora@ogilvy.com.cy
Web Site: www.ogilvy.com.cy

Employees: 30

Agency Specializes In: Strategic Planning/Research

Andreas Mishellis *(Mng Dir)*
Elias Arvanitis *(Head-Acct Mgmt)*
Koula Louca *(Gen Mgr)*

Accounts:
BP
British American Tobacco
DHL
Genesis
Gillette Braun, Gillette Toiletries, Oral B, Right Guard
Hellenic Bank
IBM
Kean
Kenzo
KFC
Kimberly Clark
Mattel
Nike
Purple
SC Johnson
Zita

Czech Republic:

Mather Communications s.r.o.
Prohunu 13, 170 00 Prague, 7 Czech Republic
Tel.: (420) 221 998 555
Fax: (420) 221 998 590
E-Mail: mather@mather.cz
Web Site: www.mather.cz

Year Founded: 1991

Agency Specializes In: Corporate Identity, Digital/Interactive, Graphic Design, Out-of-Home Media, Public Relations, Publicity/Promotions, Radio, Sales Promotion, T.V.

Ondrej Obluk *(Mng Dir)*
Michaela Prochazkova *(COO)*
Tomas Belko *(Dir-Creative)*
Miroslava Pohorska *(Dir-HR)*
Jakub Hodbod *(Sr Strategic Planner)*

Accounts:
Avon
Brown Forman
Czech Insurance Company
Deloitte
Kofola
Mondelez International, Inc.
Prima TV
Radiocom
State Environmental Fund Of The Czech Republic
Tesco
UniCredit Bank
Unilever
UPC
Usti Region
Vichy
VITA
Vodafone

Ogilvy & Mather
Hybesova 18, 602 00 Brno, Czech Republic
Tel.: (420) 543 247 192
Fax: (420) 543 247 188
Web Site: www.ogilvymorava.cz

Employees: 11

Tomas Kadlec *(Acct Mgr-Morava)*
Marek Turon *(Mgr-PR)*
Roman Valla *(Mgr)*

Accounts:
Colorlak
Ford Motor Company, s.r.o. Campaign: "Do it Yourself"
Medicom International
Tondach
Velux

Ogilvy & Mather
Privozni 2A, 170 00 Prague, 7 Czech Republic
Tel.: (420) 2 2199 8111
Fax: (420) 2 2199 8888
E-Mail: boris.stepanovic@ogilvy.com
Web Site: www.ogilvy.cz

Employees: 200
Year Founded: 1992

Agency Specializes In: Direct Response Marketing

Tomas Belko *(Exec Dir-Creative)*
Will Rust *(Exec Dir-Creative-Dubai, Middle East & North Africa)*
Frantisek Mares *(Acct Dir)*
Kristina Matiasova *(Acct Dir)*
Claudiu Dobrita *(Dir-Creative-Mather Adventures)*
Miroslava Pohorska *(Dir-HR)*
Carmen Dobrescu *(Copywriter)*
Marek Linhart *(Copywriter)*
Vasek Sramek *(Designer)*
Ivana Senitkova *(Jr Acct Mgr)*

Accounts:
Chiquita
Clavin Campaign: "Erectile dysfunction remedy", Campaign: "Erection Blister", Ultra
Czech Radio
DPD Campaign: "Destroyed Parcel"
Euro
Ford Campaign: "Do It Yourself"
Forum Darcu Campaign: "Give Properly"
GlaxoSmithKline
IBM
ING Real Estate Development
Jaybeam Limited
Kimberly Clark
Mondelez International, Inc.
Nowaco
Philips
Plensky Prazdroj
Prague Pride
Procter & Gamble
Stock Bozkov Amundsen Vodka
Stock Plze Campaign: "Stalinclaus"
SZIF
Unilever
Xerox Campaign: "Artis Pictus"

OgilvyOne Worldwide
Privozni 2A Grounds, 170 00 Prague, 7 Czech Republic
Tel.: (420) 221 998 777
Fax: (420) 221 998 788
E-Mail: info@ogilvyone.cz
Web Site: www.ogilvy.cz

Agency Specializes In: Direct Response Marketing

Pavel Matejicek *(Mng Dir)*

Accounts:
British Airways
Coop
DHL
IBM
Kimberly Clark
O2
RWE
Uni Credit Bank
Zentiva

Denmark:

OgilvyOne Worldwide
Toldbodgade 55, K-1253 Copenhagen, Denmark
Tel.: (45) 3917 8800
Fax: (45) 3917 8801
Web Site: bl.ogilvy.dk/

Employees: 60
Year Founded: 1983

Agency Specializes In: Direct Response Marketing

Jesper Isholm *(Creative Dir)*
Camilla Ploug *(Art Dir)*
Jakob Staalby *(Creative Dir)*
Ole Rydal *(Dir-Creative)*

Accounts:
Falck
Fernet Branca
IBM
Kjaer Kobenhavn Campaign: "Dawn of Woman"
Mellemfolkeligt Samvirke Campaign: "We will not accept it"
The Undo-It Laser Tattoo Removal Campaign: "Butterfly", Campaign: "Skull"
World Wide Fund For Nature
You See

Finland:

Taivas
Unioninkatu 13, 00130 Helsinki, Finland
Tel.: (358) 9 618 420
Fax: (358) 9 666 326
E-Mail: info@taivas.fi
Web Site: www.taivas.fi/

Employees: 20
Year Founded: 1999

Agency Specializes In: Outdoor

Mikko Helme *(Dir-Strategy)*
Jon Silen *(Office Mgr)*
Kirsti Kurki-Myllymaki *(Copywriter)*
Nina Myllyharju *(Client Svc Dir)*

Accounts:
Finnish Aids Council
The Finnish Evangelical Lutheran Mission Campaign: "Voice To The Voiceless"

France:

cba BE
(Formerly CB'a)
94 Avenue de Villiers, 75017 Paris, France
Tel.: (33) 1 40 54 09 00
Fax: (33) 1 47 64 95 75
E-Mail: info@cba-design.com
Web Site: www.cba-design.com/fr

Employees: 185
Year Founded: 1982

Agency Specializes In: Advertising, Brand Development & Integration, Communications, Consumer Marketing, Cosmetics, Food Service, Graphic Design, Internet/Web Design, Logo & Package Design, Publicity/Promotions

Louis Collinet *(CEO)*
Franck Collin *(Gen Mgr-Activation)*
Anne Malberti *(Gen Mgr-CBA Paris)*

Accounts:
Arteum
Costes
Defi Deco
Minute Maid
Monoprix Bien Vivre
Nestle
Unilever Lipton

Ogilvy & Mather
40 Ave George V, 75008 Paris, France
Tel.: (33) 1 5323 3000
Fax: (33) 1 5323 3030
Web Site: ogilvyparis.fr/

Employees: 280
Year Founded: 1972

Natalie Rastoin *(CEO)*
Gerry Human *(Chief Creative Officer)*
Kurt Novack *(Exec Dir-Creative)*
Maureen Shirreff *(Sr Partner & Grp Dir-Creative)*
Lisa Mcleod *(Sr Dir-Global Art-Ogilvy Paris)*
Myriam Nouicer *(Grp Acct Dir)*
Bastien Baumann *(Art Dir)*
Florian Bodet *(Creative Dir)*
Regis Boulanger *(Art Dir)*
Melisa Chamorro *(Art Dir)*
Daniel Lincoln *(Creative Dir)*
Ben Messiaen *(Bus Dir)*
Clara Noguier *(Art Dir)*
Beatrice Lassailly Ramel *(Creative Dir)*
Stephane Santana *(Art Dir)*
Delphine Watenberg *(Bus Dir-Integrated)*
Bruno Bicalho Carvalhaes *(Dir-Art)*
Benoit de Fleurian *(Dir-Global Brands)*
Nicolas Gagner *(Dir-Art)*
Bruna Gonzalez *(Dir-Art)*
Nicolas Lautier *(Dir-Creative)*
Lynn Roer *(Dir-Event Mgmt & Experiential Design)*
Chris Rowson *(Dir-Creative)*
Stephanie Surer *(Dir-Artistic)*
Sid Tomkins *(Dir-Worldwide Design-IBM)*
Fergus O'Hare *(Assoc Dir-Creative)*
Laure Bayle *(Mgr-TV Production)*
Isabel Schnell *(Acct Supvr)*
Nicolas Boivin *(Acct Exec)*
Kevin Martin *(Acct Exec)*
Dorian Salort *(Acct Exec)*
Alexis Valero *(Acct Exec)*
Laure Borot *(Planner)*
Jeremy Claud *(Copywriter)*
Pauline Desforges *(Planner)*
Alejandra Guerrero *(Copywriter)*
Bipasha Mookherjee *(Copywriter)*
John Stuart *(Planner)*

Accounts:
AIDES Campaign: "Shag Tag"
Allianz
Babolat
Beaute Prestige International Campaign: "On The Docks"
Bertelsmann AG
Coca-Cola Campaign: "3/37 Degrees", Campaign: "A Step From Zero", Campaign: "Balloons", Campaign: "Curves", Campaign: "Do the Toe Tappy", Campaign: "Tale of Contour", Campaign: "Zero Clue", Coke Zero, Creative, Diet Coke, Slender Vender, TV
Epson
Europcar Autoliberte, Campaign: "Crush Hour"
Ferrero Campaign: "The Worst Breath in the World", Tic Tac
Fisher Price Camera Campaign: "Bed"
Ford Campaign: "For those moments you go a little bit off track. Lane departure warning system.", Campaign: "Keyfree Login", Campaign: "OFF-TRACK"
Google Campaign: "First Social Same-Sex Marriage", Google+
Grey Goose Campaign: "Fly Beyond"
IBM Buildings Energy, Campaign: "Smart Cities Art Gallery", Campaign: "Smarter Ideas For Smarter Cities", Food Supply, Food Traceability, Outcomes, Tie, Traffic
Jean Paul Gaultier Perfumes Campaign: "On The Docks"
LVMH Moet Hennessy Louis Vuitton SA Campaign: "Angelina Jolie's Journey to Cambodia", Campaign: "Louis Vuitton Perspectives", Spring Summer Fashion Show
Mattel Hot Wheels, Scrabble
Mondadori Magazines France
Neste
Netflix Digital, Outdoor
P&G Campaign: "Some Things Shouldn't End Before the End"
Perrier Fines Bulles
Tic Tac France Campaign: "Worst Breath in the World"
Tiffany & Co. Creative, Strategic
Unilever Campaign: "Dove Hair: Love Your Curls", Campaign: "Inner Thoughts", Campaign: "Kate's Colour", Campaign: "Legacy", Dove, Dove Men + Care
Vigineo Home Security Campaign: "Because you can't always trust luck.", Campaign: "Ether"
Vittel
New-Water for Africa Campaign: "The Marathon Walker"
WWF Campaign: "Red Tuna"

OgilvyHealthcare
44 avenue George V, 75008 Paris, France
Tel.: (33) 1 53 53 12 30
Fax: (33) 1 53 53 12 31
E-Mail: jeanmarc.mosselmans@ogilvy.com
Web Site: ogilvyparis.fr

Year Founded: 1981

Agency Specializes In: Health Care Services

Jean Luc Bagnara *(Mng Dir)*
Reza Ghaem-Maghzami *(Pres-Ogilvy One)*
Eric Maillard *(Mng Dir-France)*
Dilles Bordure *(Head-Plng)*
Baptiste Clinet *(Exec Dir-Creative)*
Kurt Novack *(Exec Dir-Creative)*
Bruno Bicaiho Carvalhes *(Dir-Creative)*
Paul Kreitmann *(Dir-Creative)*
Olivier Le Lostec *(Copywriter)*

OgilvyOne
136 Avenue des Champs Elysees, 75008 Paris, France
Tel.: (33) 1 40 76 24 24
Fax: (33) 1 4076 2425
E-Mail: violaine.germain@ogilvy.com
Web Site: ogilvyparis.fr

Employees: 118

Gilles Bordure *(CFO)*
Reza Ghaem-Maghami *(Pres/CEO-Paris)*
Natalie Heckel *(Exec Dir & Head-Acct Mgmt)*
Jean-Philippe Chevret *(Gen Mgr)*
Kurt Novack *(Exec Dir-Creative)*
Bruno Bicalho Carvalhaes *(Dir-Art)*
Jacquline Damont *(Dir-Art)*
Hadi Zabad *(Dir-Plng-Coca-Cola)*

Accounts:
Amex
Louis Vuitton Campaign: "Perspectives"

Germany:

Ogilvy & Mather Frankfurt
Darmstadter Landstrasse 112, D-60598 Frankfurt, Germany
Tel.: (49) 69 96225 1706
Fax: (49) 69 96225 1444
E-Mail: info@ogilvy.de
Web Site: www.ogilvy.de

Year Founded: 1950

Agency Specializes In: Business-To-Business, Direct Response Marketing, Public Relations, Sales Promotion, Telemarketing

Tolga Buyukdoganay *(Exec Dir-Creative)*
Felix Fenz *(Exec Creative Dir)*
Uwe Jakob *(Exec Dir-Creative)*
Carola Romanus *(Exec Dir-Client Svc)*
Birgit Van den Valentyn *(Exec Dir-Creative)*
Esra Bueyuekdoganay *(Art Dir)*
Thomas Schwarz *(Creative Dir)*
Matthias Bauer *(Dir-Art)*
Constantin Camesasca *(Dir-Art)*
Sebastian Kamp *(Dir-Art)*
Jessica Neubauer *(Dir-Art)*
Tobias Ostry *(Dir-Art)*
Katharina Haller *(Copywriter)*
David Simons *(Copywriter)*
Christian Urbanski *(Copywriter)*
Yves Rosengart *(Client Svc Dir)*

Accounts:
New-Amnesty International
ANAD
Axel Springer Mediahouse Berlin
C. Josef Lamy
Coca-Cola Germany Campaign: "Make Someone Happy", Campaign: "Mini World", TV
Deutsche Bahn Campaign: "Back Seat Holiday", Campaign: "Travel Symphony", Campaign: "Wanna Ride?", Mobility Logistics
DKV Campaign: "Very Angry Neighbour",

Krankenversicherung
dpa Campaign: "All you need to tell the story"
Europcar Minibus Campaign: "Bike get out"
Fleurop Campaign: "Make Her See It in a Different Way", Campaign: "Sister"
Ford
Foundation for Life Organ Donation Extreme Waiting
The Franciscans Duesseldorf Campaign: "Surviving is an Art"
Fujifilm Chicken, X-S1
Furs Leben Campaign: "Waiting For Seven Years"
German Health Insurance
HMTM Hannover Campaign: "The Absolute Pitch"
Honda Campaign: "Grasshopper"
IKEA Billy Closet, Ikea PS Range
Intervention Center Against Domestic Violence
Lebenshilfe Campaign: "50 Blueprints"
Malteser Ambulance Service Campaign: "Speed Trap", Print
Mattel Campaign: "Electric Socket", Matchbox
Media Markt Campaign: "Banner Shake", Campaign: "Mall of Madness"
Mondelez International, Inc. Campaign: "Help Helmut"
Moto Waganari Campaign: "Touch The Untouchable. Real Virtuality"
MTV Campaign: "Download Bar"
nie wieder bohren Campaign: "Driller Killer"
Nintendo
OREO Campaign: "HELP HELMUT"
Oroverde Campaign: "The Donation Army"
Picture Alliance Campaign: "All You Need To Tell The Story"
Rolling Stone Magazine
SAP Bit.Code
Schoeffel
Sony Playstation Video Game
Sportjugend Hessen
SportScheck Campaign: "Sporty Newsletter", Sporty Vouchers
Stadel Museum Campaign: "The New Stadel"
Sternburg Campaign: "Brewery Vs Police"
Telefonica Campaign: "Urban Mood", O2 Campaign: "Urban Mood"
Transparancy International Campaign: "Splash - Its Time To Wake Up"
Triumph Adler Campaign: "Copies Faster."
Unilever Rama Butter
US Mobile
ZMG Newspaper Marketing Association Campaign: "Lilliputian", Campaign: "Mariachi", Press, The Newspaper Effect
Zurich Campaign: "Welcome Home", Home Insurance

Ogilvy & Mather

Am Handelshafen 2-4, Postfach 19 00 21, 40221 Dusseldorf, Germany
Mailing Address:
Postfach 19 00 21, 40110 Dusseldorf, Germany
Tel.: (49) 211 497 00 0
Fax: (49) 211 497 00 110
E-Mail: ogilvyddf@ogilvy.com
Web Site: www.ogilvy.de

Employees: 220
Year Founded: 1981

Felix Fenz *(Exec Dir-Creative)*
Thomas Schwarz *(Exec Dir-Creative)*
Birgit van den Valentyn *(Exec Dir-Creative)*
Andreas Steinkemper *(Creative Dir)*
Vitali Gahl *(Dir-Art)*
Rouven Maccario *(Dir-Art)*
Jill Keehner *(Coord-Bus-Global)*

Accounts:
Allegro Music School
Amadeu Antonio Foundation Foundation Against Right Wing Radicalism
Ars Vivendi Love Toys
Bill Trainer
The Catholic Church Campaign: "Remember"
Civil Sector Of Euromaidan Campaign: "Silent Scream"
Dove
Dusseldorfer Tafel Campaign: "All You Can't Eat", Campaign: "The World's Largest Advent Calendar"
Ford Campaign: "Mother"
Glaxosmithkline Campaign: "A Guiding Thread for a Better Presentation", Supplement
Metro Group Future Store Initiative Campaign: "Scanner Music"
Mondelez International, Inc. Campaign: "Help Helmut"
Oro Verde Campaign: "Every Tree Has A Story"
Philips "Designed to Play", Campaign: "Philips Click & Style", Click & Style, Creative, Mobile
Porzellanklinik Duesseldorf
Raum D Campaign: "Vivid Memories"
Toom Baumarkt The Gnome Protest

Ogilvy Healthworld GmbH

Am Handelshafen 2-4, 40221 Dusseldorf, Germany
Mailing Address:
Postfach 190024, 40110 Dusseldorf, Germany
Tel.: (49) 211-49700-0
Fax: (49) 211-49700505
Web Site: www.ogilvy.de

Employees: 20
Year Founded: 1986

Agency Specializes In: Advertising, Advertising Specialties, Alternative Advertising, Below-the-Line, Brand Development & Integration, Branded Entertainment, Broadcast, Business Publications, Business-To-Business, Catalogs, Co-op Advertising, Communications, Consulting, Consumer Goods, Consumer Publications, Content, Corporate Communications, Corporate Identity, Cosmetics, Crisis Communications, Custom Publishing, Customer Relationship Management, Direct Response Marketing, Direct-to-Consumer, E-Commerce, Education, Email, Entertainment, Environmental, Event Planning & Marketing, Exhibit/Trade Shows, Food Service, Gay & Lesbian Market, Graphic Design, Guerilla Marketing, Health Care Services, Hospitality, Identity Marketing, In-Store Advertising, Integrated Marketing, International, Internet/Web Design, Local Marketing, Logo & Package Design, Market Research, Media Relations, Medical Products, Men's Market, Merchandising, Mobile Marketing, New Product Development, Outdoor, Over-50 Market, Package Design, Pets , Pharmaceutical, Planning & Consultation, Podcasting, Point of Purchase, Point of Sale, Print, Product Placement, Production (Ad, Film, Broadcast), Promotions, Public Relations, Publicity/Promotions, Radio, Sales Promotion, Seniors' Market, Social Marketing/Nonprofit, Social Media, Sponsorship, Technical Advertising, Teen Market, Telemarketing, Web (Banner Ads, Pop-ups, etc.), Women's Market, Yellow Pages Advertising

Ulrich Tillmann *(Chm)*
Ulrike Aretz *(Mng Dir)*
Helmut Hechler *(CFO)*
Dirk Lapaz *(CFO)*
Michael Kutschinski *(Chief Creative Officer)*
Stephan Vogel *(Chief Creative Officer)*
Mona Tillinger *(Head-HR)*
Tim Stubane *(Exec Creative Dir)*

OgilvyInteractive

Darmstadter Landstrasse 112, 60598 Frankfurt, Germany
Tel.: (49) 69 300 66 0
Fax: (49) 69 300 66 111
E-Mail: info@ogilvy-interactive.de
Web Site: www.ogilvy.de

Agency Specializes In: Digital/Interactive

Martin Alles *(Mng Dir-Ogilvy & Mather Dusseldorf)*
Tim Stubane *(Exec Dir-Creative-Ogilvy & Mather Adv Berlin)*
Birgit Van Den Valentyn *(Exec Dir-Creative-Ogilvy & Mather Adv Berlin)*
Nils-Eric Wolff *(Acct Mgr)*
Florian Avdic *(Sr Planner-Creative)*

Accounts:
American Express
Axe
BMW
Cisco
DHL
Dove
GSK
IBM E-Business
Playstation
SAP
Sony

OgilvyOne GmbH

(Formerly OgilvyOne Worldwide)
Darmstadter Landstrasse 112, 60598 Frankfurt, Germany
Tel.: (49) 69 609150
Fax: (49) 69 618031
E-Mail: info@ogilvy.de
Web Site: www.ogilvy.de

Employees: 600
Year Founded: 1977

Agency Specializes In: Direct Response Marketing

Ulrike Aretz *(Mng Dir)*
Dirk Lapaz *(CFO)*
Michael Kutschinski *(Chief Creative Officer-Deutschland)*
Larissa Pohl *(Chief Strategy Officer)*
Stephan Vogel *(Chief Creative Officer)*
Tim Stuebane *(Exec Dir-Creative-Berlin)*
Birgit Van Den Valentyn *(Exec Dir-Creative)*
Tonja Albert *(Dir-Fin)*
Garth Gericke *(Dir-Art)*
Klaus-Martin Michaelis *(Dir-Art)*
Hayley Chappell *(Copywriter)*

Accounts:
Kontor Records Campaign: "Back to Vinyl"
Moto Waganari Directing Shadows
Nescafe

Greece:

Bold Ogilvy Greece

10 Imathias Str, Gerakas, 15344 Athens, Greece
Tel.: (30) 210 6660000
Fax: (30) 210 61 99486
E-Mail: boldogilvy@ogilvy.com
Web Site: ogilvy.gr/bold-ogilvy

Employees: 106
Year Founded: 1977

Antonis Rapsomanikis *(Founder)*
Theodore Cotionis *(Mng Dir)*
Matina Trigidou *(Acct Dir)*
Tessie Moraiti *(Dir-Art)*
Dimitris Peponis *(Dir-Creative)*
Angelos Petrakis *(Dir-Art)*

Accounts:
Ad Print Festival
Aegean Airlines
Aloe Mint Dental Floss
Amnesty International Campaign: "Waiting"
Cosmote
Dupont Coragen Pesticide Campaign: "Green Worm"

Ford Focus
Mattel Greece Matchbox, Scrabble
Nescafe
Piraeus Bank
Ra/farag Aloe Dent Dental Floss
Sarantis Campaign: "The King's Sneeze"
Seat
Sinomarin

OgilvyOne Worldwide

10 Imathias Street, 15 344 Athens, Greece
Tel.: (30) 210 610 6900
Fax: (30) 210 610 6903
E-Mail: ogilvyone@ogilvyone.gr
Web Site: www.ogilvyone.gr

Employees: 29
Year Founded: 1987

Agency Specializes In: Direct Response Marketing

Christos Latos *(Gen Mgr-Athens)*
Panos Sambrakos *(Exec Dir-Creative)*
George Lyras *(Sr Dir-Art)*
Christina Alifakioti *(Acct Dir)*
Franceska Galafti *(Dir-Creative)*
Yannis Piperakis-Papadakis *(Dir-Digital)*
Dimitris Savvakos *(Dir-Creative)*
Vangelis Tolias *(Dir-Creative-Bold Ogilvy Athens)*
Nikolas Tsakonas *(Acct Mgr)*
Olympia Krampoviti *(Copywriter)*
George Theodorakopoulos *(Copywriter)*

Accounts:
Aegean Airlines
Airtickets
BP
Coca-Cola Refreshments USA, Inc. Sprite
Confidis
Cosmote
DHL
Lenova
Lufthansa
Microsoft
Mondelez International, Inc. Campaign: "Lacta Mobile App", Campaign: "Lacta Surprises", Campaign: "Love in the end", Lacta Chocolate Bar, Transmedia Campaign
Nescafe
Nestle Campaign:"#Tweetingbra", Fitness
OTE Business The Business LIVE
Pasal
Piraeus Bank
Pizza Hut
Sato
Toyota Auris
Vodafone
Zoo Bytes

Ireland:

Ogilvy & Mather

6 Ely Place, Dublin, 2 Ireland
Tel.: (353) 1 669 0010
Fax: (353) 1 669 0019
Web Site: www.ogilvy.com

Year Founded: 1974

Agency Specializes In: Sponsorship

Dave Smyth *(Mng Dir)*
Mike Mesbur *(Dir-Creative)*
Laurence O'Byrne *(Dir-Art)*
Nigel Reddy *(Planner-Strategic)*

Accounts:
First Active
Ford Campaign: "8 Minutes"
Heineken International Campaign: "Golden Explosion"
Irish Life
The Irish Society for the Prevention of Cruelty to Children
ISPCC Campaign: "Confidential", Campaign: "Heart Broken Santa", Campaign: "I can't wait", Campaign: "Missing Children Hotline 116 000", Campaign: "Thank You, Please", Campaign: "The Worst Calls"
Kellogg's
Kraft Foods
Kraft Suchard, Toblerone
Littlewoods Ireland
Lucozade
Peter Mark
Pfizer
Strongbow Campaign: "Golden Explosion"
Style Club

OgilvyOne Worldwide

6 Ely Place, Dublin, 2 Ireland
Tel.: (353) 1 669 0020
Fax: (353) 1 669 0029
E-Mail: info@ogilvy.ie
Web Site: www.ogilvy.com

Employees: 90
Year Founded: 1993

Agency Specializes In: Direct Response Marketing

J. P. Donnelly *(Grp CEO)*
Dave Smyth *(Mng Dir)*
Suzanne Delaney *(Head-Digital)*
Jim Condren *(Dir-Fin)*
Mike Mesbur *(Dir-Creative-OGILVY & MATHER DUBLIN)*

Italy:

Ogilvy & Mather

V Pio Emanuelli 1, 00143 Rome, Italy
Tel.: (39) 06 51 8371
Fax: (39) 06 51 9144
E-Mail: guerino.delfino@ogilvy.com
Web Site: www.ogilvy.it

Employees: 23
Year Founded: 1985

Paolo Iabichino *(Chief Creative Officer)*
Giuseppe Mastromatteo *(Chief Creative Officer)*
Alessandro Fontana *(Head-Social@Ogilvy)*
Alessandro Pierobon *(Gen Mgr)*
Letizia Bozzolini *(Sr Dir-Art)*
Giordano Curreri *(Dir-Client Creative)*
Marco Geranzani *(Dir-Client Creative)*
Alexandre Gabriel Levy *(Dir-New Bus)*
Alessandro Izzillo *(Supvr-Digital Creative)*
Paola Guarneri *(Strategist-Digital-Social@Ogilvy)*

Accounts:
Ford Motor Company
Maxima Amoralia
NaturaSi Organic Shops
Ritual Magazine

Ogilvy & Mather

Viale Lancetti 29, 20158 Milan, Italy
Tel.: (39) 02 60 78 91
Fax: (39) 69018107
E-Mail: guerino.delfino@ogilvy.com
Web Site: www.ogilvy.com

Year Founded: 1962

Agency Specializes In: Advertising

Paolo Iabichino *(Chief Creative Officer)*
Giuseppe Mastromatteo *(Chief Creative Officer)*
Ethiopia Abiye *(Acct Dir)*
Carla Marciano *(Acct Dir)*
Serena Pulga *(Copywriter)*
Giordano Curreri *(Client Dir-Creative)*
Marco Geranzani *(Client Dir-Creative)*

Accounts:
Condenast
Emergency
Ford Campaign: "Democratizing Technology"
New-Nestle Campaign: "The Life Deliziosa", San Pellegrino
Sorgenia Campaign: "Energy Saving"
Wind

OgilvyOne Worldwide

Via le V Lancetti 29, 20158 Milan, Italy
Tel.: (39) 02 60 7891
Fax: (39) 02 69 6485
E-Mail: daniela.marone@ogilvy.com
Web Site: www.ogilvy.it

Employees: 100
Year Founded: 1982

Agency Specializes In: Direct Response Marketing

Accounts:
American Express Campaign: "Gift Machine"
Conde Nast

Lithuania:

Adell Taivas Ogilvy

J Jasinskio Street 16A, 2001 Vilnius, Lithuania
Tel.: (370) 5 252 65 22
Fax: (370) 5 252 65 23
E-Mail: david@ogilvy.lt
Web Site: www.ogilvy.lt

Employees: 90

Marius Poskus *(Head-Design Dept & Dir-Design)*
Dovile Filmanaviciute *(Head-Digital)*
Galmatas Sasnauskas *(Creative Dir)*
Alberto Berton *(Art Dir & Copywriter)*
Simas Baciulis *(Acct Dir)*
Tomas Karpavicius *(Creative Dir)*
Giedrius Kumetaitis *(Art Dir)*
Tadas Cislikauskas *(copywriter)*
Jurga Jacenaite *(Copywriter)*
Lukas Sidlauskas *(Copywriter)*

Accounts:
Baltic Management Institute Campaign: "Before you get one, become one."
Lithuanian Bank Association
Lithuanian National Zoo Snake
Lithuanian Vodka Campaign: "Cheers To What's Lithuanian"
SEB Bank
Svyturys-Utenos Alus Campaign: "Utenos Speechless"
Tele2
Veloklinika Bicycle Repair School
Vilnius Birdie

Netherlands:

Ogilvy & Mather (Amsterdam) B.V.

Pilotenstraat 41, 1059 CH Amsterdam, Netherlands
Tel.: (31) 20 7963300
Fax: (31) 20 7963399
E-Mail: info.amsterdam@ogilvy.com
Web Site: www.ogilvy.nl

Employees: 80
Year Founded: 1921

Annelouk Kriele *(Acct Dir)*
Wayne Ching *(Dir-Creative)*

Henk Nieuwenhuis *(Dir-Creative)*
Ellen Suy *(Dir-Mktg & Ops)*
Geertjan Tromp *(Designer-Visual)*
Sascha Walstra *(Copywriter)*

Accounts:
Allsecur Campaign: "Upside Down", Car Insurance
American Express Campaign: "Extra Card Gold DM"
Amnesty International
BP Campaign: "Bingo at the Pump", Campaign: "Jackpot Fill-Up A04"
British American Tobacco
Coca-Cola Campaign: "Choose to Smile", Campaign:"Choose Happiness"
Deloitte
Ford Ford Focus
Foundation Fortisisland Pampus Campaign: "Dutch Shark Alarm"
Foundation Orange Babies Campaign: "Expectations", Campaign: "The Fight"
IBM Campaign: "Flashing Zebra Crossing", Smarter Planet
Mercedes-Benz Rooftop Stickers
Orange Babies Campaign: "Photo swap"
PPG Coatings Netherlands Campaign: "Stairs"
Wordblind Association Campaign: "A Scary Story"
XS4ALL Internet Services

OgilvyOffice
Pilotenstraat 41, 1059 CH Amsterdam, Netherlands
Tel.: (31) 20 7963400
Fax: (31) 20 7963999
E-Mail: info.amsterdam@ogilvy.com
Web Site: www.ogilvy.nl

Employees: 100
Year Founded: 2000

Darre van Dijk *(Chief Creative Officer)*
Hans Veldhorst *(Chief Strategy Officer)*

Accounts:
Histor Colour Cards

OgilvyOne Worldwide
ul Angorska 13A, 03-913 Warsaw, Poland
Tel.: (48) 22 616 30 70
Fax: (48) 22 672 62 44
Web Site: www.ogilvy.com

Employees: 120
Year Founded: 1989

Agency Specializes In: Direct Response Marketing

Joanna Biernacka *(Dir-Art)*

Accounts:
Finishizer Campaign: "Hitler"
Polish Academy of Science
SOS Children's Villages Campaign: "Disappeared"

Portugal:

Ogilvy & Mather Portugal
Edificio Atrium Saldanha Praa Duque de Saldanha Number 1-4E, Lisbon, 1050 Portugal
Tel.: (351) 21 321 8000
Fax: (351) 213218015
E-Mail: ogilvy.portugal@ogilvy.com
Web Site: www.ogilvy.pt

Year Founded: 1986

Agency Specializes In: Advertising Specialties, Communications, Consumer Marketing

Miguel Core *(Sr Dir-Art)*
Nuno Gomes *(Art Dir & Graphic Designer)*
Jorge Coelho *(Creative Dir)*
Joao Marta *(Art Dir)*
Tiago Prandi *(Dir-Art)*
Marta Videira *(Sr Acct Mgr)*
Maria Antunes Varela *(Acct Mgr)*
Fernando Costa *(Supvr-Creative)*
Catarina Oliveira *(Acct Exec)*
Joao Guimaraes *(Copywriter)*
David Rafachinho *(Sr Designer)*
Edgar Sousa *(Copywriter)*
Catarina Toscano *(Designer)*

Accounts:
Azeite Herdade do Esporao
Cais
Coca-Cola Campaign: "La Cantine"
Cofaco Acores
Correio da Manha
Fino Trato Campaign: "Only For Brave Man", Clube Barba Rija
Institute Of Social Security
Mattel Campaign: "Unfinished Work"
Nestla Portugal Campaign: "Playing Secret Santa on Facebook"
Radio Renascenca
New-Record
Super Bock
TMN St Valentine's Day
WWF Campaign: "Memory Game", Vote Earth!

Romania:

Ogilvy & Mather
86 Grigore Alexandrescu Street, 010627 Bucharest, Romania
Tel.: (40) 21 20 10 100
Fax: (40) 21 20 10 109
E-Mail: manuela.necula@ogilvy.com
Web Site: www.ogilvy.com

Year Founded: 1994

Manuela Necula *(Country Head)*

Accounts:
Anim'Est
SEAT Leon Cupra Campaign: "Slowly Gonzales"
Tarom
Vice Magazine Campaign: "Bishop"

Russia:

SPN Ogilvy Communications Agency
4a Novodanilovskya emb, Moscow, 117105 Russia
Tel.: (7) 812 380 00 07
Fax: (7) 813 380 00 7
E-Mail: info@spnogilvy.ru
Web Site: www.spncomms.com

Employees: 100

Agency Specializes In: Advertising, Alternative Advertising, Automotive, Bilingual Market, Brand Development & Integration, Business Publications, Business-To-Business, Catalogs, Communications, Consulting, Consumer Goods, Consumer Marketing, Consumer Publications, Content, Corporate Communications, Corporate Identity, Cosmetics, Crisis Communications, Digital/Interactive, Electronic Media, Entertainment, Environmental, Event Planning & Marketing, Exhibit/Trade Shows, Financial, Graphic Design, Health Care Services, Hospitality, Identity Marketing, Integrated Marketing, International, Investor Relations, Legal Services, Local Marketing, Logo & Package Design, Luxury Products, Market Research, Media Buying Services, Media Planning, Media Relations, Media Training, Medical Products, Men's Market, Multimedia, Newspaper, Outdoor, Package Design, Planning & Consultation, Point of Purchase, Point of Sale, Print, Product Placement, Production, Promotions, Public Relations, Publicity/Promotions, Radio, Regional, Sales Promotion, Social Marketing/Nonprofit, Social Media, Sponsorship, Stakeholders, Strategic Planning/Research, T.V., Teen Market, Trade & Consumer Magazines, Travel & Tourism, Urban Market, Viral/Buzz/Word of Mouth, Web (Banner Ads, Pop-ups, etc.), Women's Market

Leonid Kolodkin *(Deputy Mng Dir)*
Andrey Barannikov *(Gen Mgr)*
Janna Dembo *(Acct Dir)*
Ksenia Maiboroda *(Acct Dir)*
Svetlana Rytsarskaya *(Acct Dir)*
Natalia Vyatkina *(Acct Dir)*
Ekaterina Boglaeva *(Dir-Bus Intelligence)*
Andrew Priima *(Dir-Bus Dev)*
Elena Kiryanova *(Acct Mgr)*
Anastasia Pakhomova *(Acct Mgr-Pub Affairs)*
Tatyana Merkulova *(Office Dir)*

Accounts:
Advanced Micro Devices
Alfa-Bank
Ford
Grohe
Ikea
LG
Ministry of Public Health & Social Development
Mondelez International, Inc.
Nokia
Novartis Consumer Health Campaign: "Voltexercise"
Porsche
Rostelecom
The Russian Public Relations Association
The Saint Petersburg Administration
Sanofi
Swatch Group
Toyota

Slovakia:

Istropolitana Ogilvy
(Formerly CD Ogilvy & Mather)
Martincekova 17, 821 01 Bratislava, 2 Slovakia
Tel.: (421) 2 582 441 55
Fax: (421) 2 582 441 54
Web Site: www.istropolitana.sk

Year Founded: 1996

Rado Olos *(Head-Creative Team)*
Brano Bezak *(Dir-Creative Team)*
Slavomir Danko *(Dir-Digital & New Bus)*
Peter Darovec *(Dir-Creative)*
Michal Mazan *(Dir-Art)*
Diana Stern *(Dir-Art)*

Accounts:
Avon Mirror
Heineken Campaign: "Congratulations, Nairo"
Piano Media
Union Campaign: "Czech Tourist"
VUB Foundation Campaign: "Last Supper"
Zlaty Bazant Campaign: "World & Slovaks"

Spain:

Bassat, Ogilvy & Mather Comunicacion
Josep Tarradellas 123-2nd Fl, 08029 Barcelona, Spain
Tel.: (34) 93 495 9444
Fax: (34) 93 495 9445
E-Mail: salvador.aumedes@ogilvy.com
Web Site: www.grupobassatogilvy.es/

Year Founded: 1991

Agency Specializes In: Advertising, Communications, Digital/Interactive, Health Care Services, Publicity/Promotions, Sales Promotion

Nuria Padrosinto *(Gen Mgr)*
Camil Roca *(Exec Dir-Creative-Ogilvy Barcelona)*
Nacho Magro *(Dir-Creative)*
Francesc Talamino *(Dir-Creative)*
Manuel Cardenas *(Copywriter)*

Accounts:
Barcelona Music Palace
Beneo
Borges Campaign: "Popitas Zero"
Cardiplus
Caritas Campaign: "A No for Anyone"
Channel 3 Telethon Campaign: "Death should be the end of life. Not cancer"
Chile
Cruzcampo Beer
FCC
Florette Salad Gourmet
Ford Campaign: "Ford's Global CEO Visit to Spain"
Grauvell Campaign: "Punk"
IWC
Josep Carreras Foundation Leukemia Foundation Appeal
La Marata De Tv3 Campaign: "One Life Ends, Six Begin"
Mindshare Campaign: "Accurate Radio Commercial"
Motorola Solutions, Inc.
Panasonic Campaign: "Eiffel", Lumix, Wide-Angle Lenses
Procter & Gamble
Realia
Sony
TMB Campaign: "Christmas Carol", Campaign: "Subtravelling"
TV3 Telethon Campaign: "Regeneration, organs anf tissue transplant", Campaign: "Team Hoyt"

Grupo Bassat, Ogilvy
(Formerly Bassat, Ogilvy & Mather, S.A.)
Maria de Molina 39, 28006 Madrid, Spain
Tel.: (34) 91 451 20 00
Fax: (34) 91 451 21 51
Web Site: www.grupobassatogilvy.es/#/home

Employees: 400
Year Founded: 1981

National Agency Associations: AEAP

Agency Specializes In: Publicity/Promotions

Pedro Urbez *(Exec Dir-Creative)*

Accounts:
Banco Santander
BMW Campaign: "Urban & Sport"
Brugal Campaign: "You are the Origin"
Central Lechera Asturiana Campaign: "I'm Back"
Ford Campaign: "Focus on Football", Campaign: "Smells New", Campaign: "St Valentine's"
Islazul Campaign: "Hotel for Plants"
Mun2 Campaign: "Jenni Season 2 Image"
Once Campaign: "Storks"
Openbank Campaign: "Super Slow Motion"
Popitas

OgilvyInteractive
Maria Molina 39, 28006 Madrid, Spain
Tel.: (34) 91 451 20 00
Fax: (34) 91 451 21 51
Web Site: www.ogilvy.com

Employees: 25

Agency Specializes In: Digital/Interactive, Internet/Web Design

Mamen Lucio *(Gen Dir-Madrid-OgilvyOne)*

OgilvyInteractive
Avda-Josep Tarradellas 123-6, 08029 Barcelona, Spain
Tel.: (34) 93 366 6000
Fax: (34) 93 366 6001
E-Mail: oscar.prats@ogilvy.com
Web Site: ogilvy.es

Year Founded: 1998

Agency Specializes In: Digital/Interactive

Jordi Urbea *(Gen Mgr)*

OgilvyOne Worldwide
Maria de Molina 39, 28006 Madrid, Spain
Tel.: (34) 91 451 20 00
Fax: (34) 91 451 21 51
E-Mail: jesus.valderrabano@ogilvy.com
Web Site: www.ogilvy.es

Employees: 150

Agency Specializes In: Direct Response Marketing

Oscar Prats *(Mng Dir)*
Mamen Lucio *(Gen Dir)*
Jesus Valderrabano *(Gen Dir-BASSAT OGILVY)*
Jesus Luque *(Exec Dir-Creative)*
Javier Arcos *(Dir-Creative)*

Accounts:
Atento
Ginos Restaurant
IBM
ING Direct Campaign: "Take them to School"
Nestle
Seur
Siemens Cerberus
Telefonica de Espana Campaign: "Blow Out this Video"
Terra Networks

OgilvyOne Worldwide
Bolivia 68-70, 08018 Barcelona, Spain
Tel.: (34) 93 495 55 55
Fax: (34) 93 366 60 01
E-Mail: jordi.urbea@ogilvy.com
Web Site: www.ogilvy.es

Year Founded: 1981

Agency Specializes In: Consumer Marketing, Direct Response Marketing, Magazines, Print

Cesar Bardaji *(Grp CEO-Panrico)*
Eugenia Bieto *(Dir Gen-ESADE)*
Agusti Cordon *(Dir Gen-Fira Barcelona)*
Antonio Esteve *(Pres-d' Esteve)*
Joan Cornudella *(CEO-Agrolimen)*
Jordi Urbea *(CEO-OgilvyOne & Ogilvy & Mather Adv-Barcelona)*
Josep Manel Barcelo *(Mng Dir-Bacardi Iberia)*
Montse Abbad *(Dir-the two TVE)*
Pere Bonet *(Dir-Grp Comm-Freixenet)*
Pere Duran *(Dir-Consortium of Barcelona Tourism)*
Silvia Escude *(Dir-Comm & Mktg Svcs-Nestle Espana)*
Pepe Alvarez *(Sec Gen-UGT Catalonia)*

Accounts:
Dufry
FCC
Grupo Eulen
IBM
Nestle
Venca

Sweden:

Ogilvy Advertising
Master Samuelsgatan 56, 114 80 Stockholm, Sweden
Tel.: (46) 8 562 584 00
Fax: (46) 8 562 582 04
E-Mail: info@ogilvy.se

Year Founded: 1898

Stina Jansdotter Oberg *(Head-Health &Wellness & Acct Dir)*
Anna Ostergren *(Head-Production & Acct Mgr)*
Marie Klinte *(Sr Acct Dir)*
Timo Orre *(Dir-Art)*
Kenth Persson *(Dir-Bus)*
Louise Lyth *(Acct Mgr)*
Pia Snibb *(Acct Mgr)*

Accounts:
Abbott
Aga Rangemaster Group
American Express
DHL Europe
Ford Motor Kuga
IBM
Nestle
OK Q8
Unilever
United Nations Sweden
WWF Happy

OgilvyOne Worldwide
Master Samuelsgatan 56, 114 80 Stockholm, Sweden
Tel.: (46) 8 562 58300
Fax: (46) 8 562 58302
E-Mail: info@ogilvy.se

Year Founded: 1995

Agency Specializes In: Direct Response Marketing

Accounts:
Abbott
American Express
DHL / Agency
Delicato
Doxa
Handelsbanken
IBM
Irish Tourist Board
Nestle
Unilever

Switzerland:

Grendene Ogilvy & Mather AG
Bergstrasse 50, 8032 Zurich, Switzerland
Tel.: (41) 44 268 6363
Fax: (41) 44 252 7942
E-Mail: info@ogilvy.ch
Web Site: www.ogilvy.ch

Employees: 25
Year Founded: 1959

Agency Specializes In: Advertising

Barbara Duerst *(Mng Dir)*
Toula Stoffel *(Mng Dir-Healthworld)*
Gaby Zimmerli *(Mng Dir-Ogilvy & Mather Werbeagentur)*
Jonathan Schipper *(Sr Acct Dir)*
Thomas Bolliger *(Dir-Creative-Ogilvy & Mather Werbeagentur)*
Markus Sidler *(Planner-Strategic-Ogilvy & Mather Werbeagentur)*

Accounts:
Nestle Hirz Yogurt

OgilvyHealthcare
Bergstrasse 50, 8032 Zurich, Switzerland
Tel.: (41) 44 268 63 23
Fax: (41) 44 252 79 42
E-Mail: info@ogilvy.ch
Web Site: www.ogilvy.ch

Employees: 26

Agency Specializes In: Business-To-Business, Direct Response Marketing, Health Care Services

Barbara Duerst *(Mng Dir-OgilvyOne & OgilvyInteractive)*
Toula Stoffel *(Mng Dir-Healthworld)*
Gaby Zimmerli *(Mng Dir-Ogilvy & Mather Werbeagentur)*
Jonathan Schipper *(Sr Acct Dir-Ogilvy & Mather Werbeagentur)*
Thomas Bolliger *(Dir-Creative-Ogilvy & Mather Werbeagentur)*
Markus Sidler *(Planner-Strategic-Ogilvy & Mather Werbeagentur)*

OgilvyOne AG
Weberstrasse 21, 8036 Zurich, Switzerland
Tel.: (41) 44 295 9400
Fax: (41) 44 295 9401
E-Mail: info@ogilvyone.ch
Web Site: www.ogilvy.ch/

Employees: 16
Year Founded: 1995

Toula Stoffel *(Mng Dir)*
Gaby Zimmerli *(Mng Dir)*
Barbara Duerst *(Mng Dir-OgilvyOne and OgilvyInteractive)*
Jonathan Schipper *(Sr Acct Dir)*
Thomas Bolliger *(Dir-Creative)*
Markus Sidler *(Planner-Strategic)*

Accounts:
Sanagate Insurance
Zurich Financial Services

Turkey:

Ogilvy & Mather
Harmancy Giz Plaza Harman Sokak M1-2 Levant, 80640 Istanbul, Turkey
Tel.: (90) 212 3398 360
Fax: (90) 212 33 98 300
Web Site: www.ogilvy.com

Employees: 100
Year Founded: 1952

Agency Specializes In: Direct Response Marketing, Media Buying Services, Publicity/Promotions

Emine Cubukcu *(Mng Dir)*
Tolga Buyukdoganay *(Exec Dir-Creative)*
Selim Unlusoy *(Exec Dir-Creative)*
Esra Buyukdoganay *(Dir-Art)*
Ersan Develiler *(Copywriter)*
Aytul Ozkan *(Country Head)*

Accounts:
Bingo Stain Remover
Coca Cola Sprite Zero
InterContinental Hotels Group PLC
KFC
Lider Removals
Molfix
Philips
Turkish Traffic Safety Association
United Parcel Service, Inc.

Ogilvy Healthworld
Harmanci Giz Plaza Haman Sokak M 1-2, 34394 Istanbul, Turkey
Tel.: (90) 212 339 8388
Fax: (90) 212 339 8300
E-Mail: beril.koparal@ogilvy.com
Web Site: www.ogilvy.com.tr

Agency Specializes In: Health Care Services

Savas Zeren *(Mng Dir)*

Ukraine:

Ogilvy & Mather
No 27 Chervonoarmiyska 5, 01004 Kiev, Ukraine
Tel.: (380) 44 230 9520
Fax: (380) 44 230 9560
E-Mail: martin.alles@ogilvy.com.ua
Web Site: http://www.ogilvy.com/

Employees: 75
Year Founded: 1997

Martin Alles *(Mng Dir)*
Victor Ishkov *(Mng Dir-Ukraine)*
Oleksandra Doroguntsova *(Creative Dir)*
Svitlana Korytko *(Acct Dir)*
Irina Pigal *(Producer-TV, Photo, Radio & Digital)*
Alexandra Savonik *(Acct Dir-Ukraine)*
Tatiana Shapoval *(Art Dir)*
Zoriana Kachurak *(Client Svc Dir)*

Accounts:
Audi Allroad
Bank Forum
Bosi.com.ua Campaign: "Shoes Online"
Carlsberg Group Campaign: "Videosnatch"
Chumak Apple
Commerzbank Group Campaign: "Hysteria", Campaign: "Surprise"
GlaxoSmithKline Solpadeine Pain Relief
Hercules Campaign: "Tongues"
IDS Borjomi International Campaign: "The World's Deepest Website"
Leif Wellness Centre
Philips Campaign: "Closer"
Solpadeine
Switch/MTV Network Europe Global Climate Change; 2008

United Kingdom:

Coley Porter Bell
18 Grosvenor Gardens, London, SW1W 0DH United Kingdom
Tel.: (44) 207 824 7700
Fax: (44) 207 824 7701
E-Mail: beautiful@cpb.co.uk
Web Site: www.coleyporterbell.com/

Employees: 45
Year Founded: 1979

Agency Specializes In: Consulting, Graphic Design

Vicky Bullen *(CEO)*
Sarah Cameron *(Head-Mktg)*
Stephen Bell *(Exec Dir-Creative)*
Cathy Madoc-Jones *(Acct Dir)*
Rachel Fullerton *(Dir-Fin)*
Alex Ririe *(Dir-Bus)*
Helen Westropp *(Dir-Bus)*

Accounts:
New-Chivas Brothers Chivas Regal
Co-operative Food "Loved By Us"
Fresh Pak Chilled Foods Campaign: "Gourmet Street Tucker You Can Enjoy at Home"', Packaging, The Hungry Wolf Deli Fillers Branding
Kimberly-Clark Kotex
Lifeplus Campaign: "Lifeplus Range"
Monier
Morrisons Campaign: "Morrisons Savers Foods"
Muller Corner Consumer Awareness, Dessert Inspired, Point Of Sale, Voted By You
Nescafe
Pernod Ricard Beefeater Burrough's Reserve, Olmeca Altos Tequila, Perrier Jouet
Premier Foods Loyd Grossman
TUI Travel Brand Development, Marine Division
Unilever Hellmans
White Knight Laundry Company Campaign: "Laundry your Way", Corporate Identity, Logo, knight's Helmet

Ogilvy & Mather EMEA
10 Cabot Square Canary Wharf, London, E14 4QB United Kingdom
Tel.: (44) 207 345 3000
Fax: (44) 207 345 9000
Web Site: www.ogilvy.com

Charlie Rudd *(CEO)*
Gerry Human *(Chief Creative Officer-London)*
Patou Nuytemans *(Chief Digital Officer-EAME)*
Sasha Orr *(Mng Dir-Mondelez-Worldwide)*
Marina Banks *(Head-Acct Mgmt)*
Andre Laurentino *(Exec Creative Dir-Global)*
Chris Chance *(Dir-Art)*
John Cornwell *(Dir-Comml-Worldwide)*
Dennis Lewis *(Dir-Creative)*
Johnny Watters *(Dir-Creative)*
Simon Lotze *(Assoc Dir-Creative)*

Accounts:
New-Carlsberg Group
Grant Thornton International Brand Campaign
Harveys Furniture Retail
Hellmann's Campaign: "The Greatest Thing Ever Created. Apparently"
Hot Wheels Campaign: "Polka Dot"
NABS
Optegra Advertising, Digital, Global Brand, Strategic Brand Development, Website

Ogilvy & Mather, Ltd.
10 Cabot Sq Canary Wharf, London, E14 4QB United Kingdom
Tel.: (44) 207 345 3000
Fax: (44) 207 345 9000
Web Site: www.ogilvy.co.uk

Employees: 500
Year Founded: 1850

Annette King *(CEO)*
Georgie Stewart *(Mng Partner-Global)*
Jodi Kanger *(Partner-Plng-Global)*
Paul Kenny *(Partner-Plng)*
Rachael Mortimer *(Partner-Plng)*
Laurence Sassoon *(Partner-Bus)*
Stephen Wallace *(Partner-Plng)*
James Barnes Austin *(COO)*
Gerry Human *(Chief Creative Officer)*
Mark Lainas *(Chief Innovation Officer)*
Anthony Wickham *(Chief Digital Officer-Worldwide-Unilever)*
James Whatley *(Head-Social Media)*
Trevallyn Hall *(Sr Dir-Art)*
Larry Ball-Piati *(Acct Dir)*
Justin Cox *(Acct Dir)*
Amelia Knowland *(Bus Dir-Global)*
Olvia Rzepcynski *(Acct Dir)*
Mike Watson *(Art Dir)*
Natalie Young *(Acct Dir)*
Martin Casson *(Dir-Art)*
Sasha Dunn *(Dir-Digital Production)*
Miguel Nunes *(Dir-Art)*
Giles Montgomery *(Copywriter)*
Mike Donaghey *(Assoc Dir-Creative-Ogilvy Group*

UK)
Joseph Grigg *(Acct Mgr)*
Christopher Hall *(Acct Mgr)*
Melanie Vlckers *(Acct Mgr)*
Jordan Down *(Copywriter)*
Will Marsden *(Copywriter)*
Jon Morgan *(Copywriter)*
Jez Groom *(Grp Chief Strategy Officer)*

Accounts:
28 Too Many
Allianz Group Global Advertising
American Express Campaign: "Birds on a Wire"
Amnesty International Campaign: "Fan the Flame", Campaign: "Freedom Candles"
Anglo American Mining Services
Associated British Foods Silver Spoon, Truvia
Bite-Back Shark & Marine Conservation Campaign: "Sharkfin"
BP
Burma Campaign UK
Department of Health Creative
Expedia Campaign: "ARM LEG", Campaign: "Travel Yourself Interesting", Online, Press, Social, TV
Ford Motor Company of Europe C-Max, Campaign: "Good Reviews", Campaign: "Magazines", Campaign: "Vincent", Focus, Kuga
Freedom From Torture Campaign: "Recruitment For Torturers"
Heineken Campaign: "A Taste Supreme", Campaign: "Le Big Swim", Kronenbourg 1664
IBM Campaign: "Smarter Cities", Email Program, Email System, Phone App
Kazam
Kodak Graphic Communications Group Campaign: "Football Stadium", Campaign: "Turtle"
Koninklijke Philips Sonicare
Mattel
Motorola Solutions, Inc.
Mtv Staying Alive Campaign: "Being With You"
Munch Bunch
New-Nestle Nescafe
Perrier
PETA Campaign: "Runway Reversal"
Philips Sound 'You Need to Hear This' Pop-up Store, Campaign: "Cop", Campaign: "Tables You Need To Hear", Campaign: "You Need to Hear This", Carolyn, Citiscape Headphones, Swiss Lips
Pizza Hut Creative
Royal Borough of Greenwich Campaign: "The Power of Small"
Ski
Slimfast
Toblerone
Unilever Burgers, Campaign: "A Mother's Body", Campaign: "Auto Tune", Campaign: "Camera Shy", Campaign: "Dana", Campaign: "Hellmann's Summer Hacks", Campaign: "Legacy", Campaign: "Real Beauty Sketches", Campaign: "Smile", Digital, Dove Bar, Dove Soaps, Hand and Body Lotion, Hellmann's Mayonnaise, Radio, Social Media
Vodafone PR
World Wildlife Fund, Inc. Campaign: "Side by Side", Campaign: "Stop Criminals Making A Killing"
Worn All Over Online Fashion Store

OgilvyOne Business

(Formerly Ogilvy Primary Contact Ltd.)
121-141 Westbourne Ter, London, W2 6JR United Kingdom
Tel.: (44) 01483202949
E-Mail: gareth.richards@ogilvy.com
Web Site: www.ogilvyonebusiness.com/

E-Mail for Key Personnel:
President: gareth.richards@primary.co.uk

Year Founded: 1970

Agency Specializes In: Advertising, Business-To-Business, Corporate Identity, Direct Response Marketing, E-Commerce, Electronic Media, Financial, Graphic Design, High Technology, Information Technology, Internet/Web Design, Media Buying Services

Robin Atkins *(Dir-Creative)*
Geoff Neilly *(Dir-Creative Svcs)*
Gareth Richards *(Grp Partner)*

Accounts:
Air Products
BT
Cyngenta
DuPont
FM Global
Monier
SDL
Tetrapak
UPS

Ogilvy Public Relations Worldwide

10 Cabot Square Canary Wharf, London, E14 4QB United Kingdom
Tel.: (44) 20 7345 3000
Fax: (44) 20 7345 9000
Web Site: www.ogilvy.co.uk

Year Founded: 1982

National Agency Associations: IAA

Agency Specializes In: Business-To-Business, Consumer Marketing, Financial, Government/Political

Rory Sutherland *(Vice Chm)*
Marshall Manson *(CEO)*
Janine Smith *(Dir-Creative & Head-Content)*
Jai Kotecha *(Head-Digital, Social & Content)*
Blair Metcalfe *(Head-Media & Entertainment)*
Quintin Keanie *(Acct Dir)*
Ricky Vazquez *(Dir-Content Strategy)*

Accounts:
2ergo
Ford
Princess Cruises Press, Royal Princess

OgilvyInteractive

10 Cabot Square Canary Wharf, London, E14 4QB United Kingdom
Tel.: (44) 207 345 3000
Fax: (44) 20 7345 3888
Web Site: www.ogilvy.co.uk

Employees: 10
Year Founded: 2000

Agency Specializes In: Digital/Interactive

Rory Sutherland *(Vice Chm)*
Paul O'Donnell *(CEO)*
Brian Jensen *(Mng Partner-Innovation & Co-Dir-Customer Lab)*
Jo Coombs *(Mng Dir)*
Mark Lainas *(Chief Innovation Officer)*
Patou Nuytemans *(Chief Digital Officer-EAME)*
Julia Ingall *(Dir-HR & Talent Mgmt-UK Grp & EMEA)*
Nicole Yershon *(Dir-Innovative Solutions)*
Katie Evans *(Mgr-Talent Acq-UK Talent Team)*
Sara Walpole *(Bus Partner-Talent Acq)*

Accounts:
BP
Kodak Graphic Communications Group

OgilvyOne Worldwide Ltd.

10 Cabot Square Canary Wharf, London, E14 4GB United Kingdom
Tel.: (44) 20 7566 7000
Fax: (44) 20 7345 9000
Web Site: www.ogilvy.co.uk

Year Founded: 1976

Agency Specializes In: Communications, Consumer Marketing

Sam Williams-Thomas *(CEO)*
Anya King *(Mng Partner-OgilvyOne & Head-Acct Mgmt London-OgilvyOne Dnx)*
Mel Stanley *(Mng Partner & Dir-Customer Engagement)*
Tracey Barber *(Mng Partner-Mktg & New Bus)*
Alan Makepeace *(Mng Partner)*
Michael Kutschinski *(Chief Creative Officer)*
Charlie Wilson *(Chief Creative Officer)*
Annette King *(CEO-Ogilvy & Mather UK)*
Nicky Beckett *(Acct Dir)*
Rod Broomfield *(Creative Dir)*
Jon Andrews *(Dir-Creative-Tech)*
Pete Atherton *(Dir-Digital-Global)*
Rob Blackie *(Dir-Social)*
Jason Cascarina *(Dir-Creative)*
Andy Davis *(Dir-Creative)*
Clare Lawson *(Client Svc Dir)*

Accounts:
American Express International Campaign: "Thinking Ahead Retail"
Barclays Wealth Digital
Battersea Dogs and Cats Home Campaign: "Looking for You", Outdoor
British Gas Services Ltd. Content
Bupa Campaign: "Bupa By You"
Co-operative Group Digital, Direct Marketing
Department of Health Digital
Dishoom Vintage Bombay
Fanta
IBM LOTUS T5, Predictions
Inter IKEA Systems B.V. Communications Strategy, Website
InterContinental Hotels Group CRM, Global Media
Kern & Sohn Campaign: "The Gnome Experiment"
Louis Vuitton
Milka
News International Creative
Reckitt Benckiser, Inc. Clearasil
Regus Marketing
Unilever Campaign: "Liptagram", Dove, Flora, Hellman's, Lipton Tea, LiptonBrightness, Persil, Vaseline
Yahoo!

Argentina:

Ogilvy & Mather Argentina

Arevalo 1880, C1414CQL Buenos Aires, Argentina
Tel.: (54) 11 4779 4300
Fax: (54) 11 4323 7001
Web Site: www.ogilvy.com

Year Founded: 2001

Agency Specializes In: Advertising, Below-the-Line, Children's Market

Juan Marcos Besagni *(Creative Dir)*
Natalia Noya *(Acct Dir)*
Georgina Roccatagliata *(Acct Dir)*
Maximiliano Ballarini *(Dir-Digital Creative)*
Valeria Pinto *(Mgr-Audio visual Production)*
Rosario Orfila *(Acct Exec)*

Accounts:
20th Century Fox
AFS Campaign: "More Than One World To Know"
AMIA Campaign: "Attack against oblivion", Campaign: "Mourning Tweet", Campaign: "The Bread of Memory", Jewish Community Centre
Ammar Campaign: "Corner 1", Campaign: "Mom Calling Cards"

Budweiser Campaign: "Poolball"
Casey Neistat
CCU Campaign: "Rugbeer", Coke Zero, Schneider Beer, Sprite
Coca-Cola Campaign: "Big Santa", Campaign: "Friendship Machine"
Colegio Las Lomas Oral
Film Suez / Sawa
Kimberly-Clark Advertising, Belt, Campaign: "Dad's Pregnant", Campaign: "Family Boss", Digital, Huggies, Pull-Ups
Kraft Campaign: "Lucas' Table"
La Virginia
La Voz del Interior Campaign: "'Life Signs"
Panasonic Baby Monitor
Retro Boutique
Salta
Santander Rio
Tang Campaign: "Lucas' Table", Campaign: "Shaker Roller Coaster", Campaign: "Tang Shaker"
Ted Campaign: "Ideas Change This World Spread Them", Campaign: "Spread the Tedx", Campaign: "Tedx Hairdressers"
Tedx Buenos Aires Campaign: "Grupo TEDx"
Unilever Campaign: "Glam Shelf"
Zonacitas.com

OgilvyOne Worldwide
Arevalo 1880, C1414CQL Buenos Aires, Argentina
Tel.: (54) 11 4323 7000
Fax: (54) 11 4323 7003
E-Mail: paula.bernasconi@ogilvy.com
Web Site: www.ogilvy.com

Year Founded: 2000

Agency Specializes In: Direct Response Marketing

Gabriela Macche *(Gen Mgr-Argentina)*
Diego Stephani *(Acct Dir)*
Betina Dagostino *(Acct Supvr)*
Victoria Sanchez *(Acct Exec)*

Brazil:

Ogilvy & Mather
SCN Q 1 Bloco F Salas 811 a 880, 70711-905 Brasilia, DF Brazil
Tel.: (55) 61 3327 8290
Fax: (55) 61 327 1374
Web Site: www.ogilvy.com.br

Daniel De Tomazo *(Dir Gen-Plng)*
Renata Saraiva *(Dir Gen-Ogilvy PR)*
Daniel Tatar *(Dir Gen-OgilvyOne)*
Denise Israel *(Gen Dir)*
Toni Ferreira *(Dir-Digital Media)*
Patricia Fuzzo *(Dir-HR)*
Rafael Rosi *(Dir-RTV)*
Sandra Sour *(Dir-Corp Comm)*
Sergio Amado *(Grp Pres-Ogilvy Brazil)*

Accounts:
Banco do Brasil
Burger King
Coca-Cola Refreshments USA, Inc. Fanta
Forbes Campaign: "Billionaires - Zuckerberg"
Mondelez International, Inc.
Sport Club do Recife Campaign: "Immortal Fans"

Ogilvy & Mather
Av Nacoes Unidas 5777, 05477-900 Sao Paulo, SP Brazil
Tel.: (55) 11 3024 9000
Fax: (55) 11 3023 0444
E-Mail: fernando.musa@ogilvy.com
Web Site: www.ogilvy.com.br

Year Founded: 1933

Fernando Musa *(Chief Executive Officer)*
Daniella Gallo *(Dir Gen-Media)*
Daniela Glicenstajn *(Dir Gen-Svc)*
Denise Israel *(Mng Dir)*
Ricardo Silva *(CFO)*
Anselmo Ramos *(Chief Creative Officer)*
Luis Carlos Franco *(Gen Mgr-Rio de Janeiro)*
Paulo Coelho *(Exec Creative Dir)*
Felix Del Valle *(Exec Creative Dir)*
Ale Koston *(Sr Dir-Integrated Art-Ogilvy Brazil)*
Fabio Natan *(Sr Dir-Art)*
Fabiana Amorim *(Acct Dir)*
Silvio Medeiros *(Art Dir)*
Carla Parretti *(Acct Dir)*
Bruno Perez *(Acct Dir)*
Vinicius Prego *(Art Dir)*
Gonzalo Ricca *(Creative Dir)*
Teco Cipriano *(Dir-Art-Ogilvy Brazil)*
Cristian Mazzeo *(Dir-Creative)*
Giovanni Muratori *(Dir-Art)*
Rafael Rosi *(Dir-RTV)*
Renato Rozenberg *(Dir-Art)*
Ericka Coello *(Acct Exec)*
Juliana Fernandes *(Acct Exec)*
Renato Barreto *(Copywriter)*
Bruno Brux *(Copywriter)*
Omar Caldas *(Copywriter)*
Andre Jardim *(Copywriter)*
Philippe Lacerda *(Copywriter)*
Gabriel Lepesteur *(Copywriter)*

Accounts:
Abramet
Agente Cidadao
Almaden
AnaMaria
Band News
Bar Aurora & Boteco Ferraz
Belcuore Cafe
Billboard Campaign: "Fan Check Machine", Campaign: "The End of the Silent Magazine", Campaign: "The Number One Hits Everyone"
Brand Sports
Burger King Burger, Campaign: "Loving You", Whopper
Cafe Belcuore Artisan Strong Coffee
Castrol
Cempre
Claro Campaign: "Road Letters", Campaign: "Share the Best of Rock at the Speed of Punk Rock.", Campaign: "Unlimited Plans For Endless Conversations"
Coca-Cola Refreshments USA, Inc. Beverages, Campaign: "Crazy Acts of Kindnes", Campaign: "Happiness Refill", Campaign: "Sprite Shower", Christmas Message, Fanta, Sprite
Coroa Hand Tools
Costa do Sauipe
Coteminas
Doctors Without Borders Campaign: "Credits Without Borders"
DuPont
Durex Campaign: "Gulliver"
Flying Horse Campaign: "Infinite energy"
Forbes Campaign: "Billionaire Stickers", Campaign: "Money makes you look younger.", Campaign: "The World Without Billionaires", DALAI LAMA X WARREN BUFFETT, Magazine
GIV
Glaxo Campaign: "Nouveau Cuisine"
Globalbev Campaign: "Catoast", Campaign: "Gif Guy"
GRAACC Campaign: "Bald Cartoons", Campaign: "Donate Your Fame"
GSK Campaign: "Chicken Dog", Campaign: "Official Sponsor Of Exits"
Hellmann's Campaign: "Food Slot", Campaign: "Recipe Receipt", Hellmann's Mayonnaise
IBCC
IBM Campaign: "The Beauty Of Real Time Data", Ei
Intimus
Johnson & Johnson Baby Antibacterial Hand Soap, Campaign: "Palm"
Kodak Graphic Communications Group
L'Occitane
Magazine Luiza Campaign: "Magazineyou", Campaign: "Nespresso. When you need to be awake. From R$ 490,00.", Retail Store, Sofa's Week
Miami Ad School ESPM Campaign: "Let him/her Rest In Peace", Campaign: "Student Saver"
Mondelez International, Inc. Mini Bis Snacks
NGO Agente Cidadao
NGO Life Support Group (GIV) Campaign: "If Prejudice is an Illness, Information is the Cure", Print
Oito Vidas Campaign: "Keyboard Cat"
Philips Blenders, Campaign: "Fruit Mashup", Walita Avance Blender
Red Balloon English School Campaign: "Celeb Grammar Cops", Campaign: "Go, conquer the world.", Campaign: "Kid's Flight Announcement"
New-Rio 2016
So Nutricao Nutritional Reeducation
Sol De Janeiro Campaign: "Tattoo Skin Cancer Check"
Sport Club Recife Campaign: "Immortal Fans"
UNICEF
Unilever Campaign: "Patches", Campaign: "Real Beauty Sketches", Campaign: "Recipe Receipt", Dove, Men Care

Ogilvy & Mather
Praia do Botafogo 228 18th Floor, 22359-900 Rio de Janeiro, RJ Brazil
Tel.: (55) 21 2141 2500
Fax: (55) 21 2551 5449
E-Mail: info@ogilvy.com
Web Site: www.ogilvy.com.br

Employees: 50

Luis Carlos Franco *(Dir Gen-Ogilvy & Mather Rio)*
Felix Del Valle *(Exec Dir-Creative)*
Bruno Cunha *(Dir-Plng)*
Elisa Lustosa *(Mgr-Digital Media)*
Veronica Pepe *(Coord-Studio)*

Accounts:
Air France Advertising
AnaMaria
Burger King
Castrol
Claro
Coca-Cola Refreshments USA, Inc.
Comfort
Dupont
Editora Abril
Fanta
FIESP
GlaxoSmithKline
IBM
Michelin
Nacional Iguatemi
Shopping Grande Rio
Sport Club Recife Campaign: "Immortal fans"
Unilever Campaign: "Beauty Patches", Dove

OgilvyOne Worldwide
Praia do Botafogo 228 18th Floor, 22250-040 Rio de Janeiro, RJ Brazil
Tel.: (55) 21 2131 3100
Fax: (55) 21 2551 5449
E-Mail: luiscarlos.franco@ogilvy.com
Web Site: www.ogilvy.com.br

Employees: 100
Year Founded: 1985

Agency Specializes In: Advertising

Renata Saraiva *(Dir Gen)*
Daniel Tatar *(Gen Dir)*
Aricio Strong *(VP)*

Luis Carlos Franco *(Gen Mgr-Rio de Janeiro)*
Daniel De Tomazo *(Dir-Gen Plng)*
Toni Ferreira *(Dir-Digital Media)*
Patricia Fuzzo *(Dir-HR)*
Daniela Glicenstajn *(Dir-Gen Svcs)*
Sandra Sour *(Dir-Corp Comm)*

Accounts:
Allianz
Claro
DIVA
Google
IBM
Souza Cruz S.A. Free, Pall Mall

SLM/Ogilvy
Rua Cel Genuino 421 10 Andar, 90010-350 Porto Alegre, RS Brazil
Tel.: (55) 51 3228 4847
Fax: (55) 51 3228 5536
E-Mail: slm@slm.com.br
Web Site: www.slm.com.br

Year Founded: 1987

Valdir Loeff *(Pres)*
Karine Brasil *(Dir-Creative)*
Sonia de Souza *(Dir-Accounts)*
Luciano Leonardo *(Dir-Creative & Plng)*

Accounts:
Alcoholics Anonymous
Bertolini
DHZ Construction
FIERGS
Gremio
Grupo Gerdau
Radio Gaucha
Souza Cruz
SPAAN
Sulgas

Colombia:

Ogilvy & Mather
Calle 64 Norte 5BN 146 of 315, Centro Empresa, Cali, Valle del Cauca Colombia
Tel.: (57) 2 664 6694
Fax: (57) 2 664 6695
Web Site: www.ogilvy.com

Year Founded: 1971

Agency Specializes In: Direct Response Marketing

Juan Pablo Alvarez *(Gen Dir-Creative)*
Mauricio Guerrero *(Gen Dir-Creative)*
John Raul Forero *(VP-Creative)*
Miguel Alonso *(Grp Acct Dir)*
Daniel Rincon *(Dir-Creative & Copywriter)*
German Ferrucho *(Dir-Creative)*
Fernando Parra *(Dir-Creative-Coca-Cola)*

Accounts:
Neurobix Campaign: "Remember me"

Ogilvy & Mather
Carrera 13 No 94A-26, Bogota, Colombia
Tel.: (57) 1 651 6363
Fax: (57) 1 651 6363
Web Site: www.ogilvy.com

Employees: 100

Mauricio Guerrero *(Gen Dir-Creative)*
Gaston Potasz *(Gen Dir-Creative)*
Juan Pablo Alvarez *(Exec Dir-Creative)*
Sergio Lizarazo *(Sr Dir-Art)*
Juan Cardenas *(Creative Dir & Copywriter)*
Jhon Chacon *(Creative Dir)*
Armando Nino *(Art Dir)*
Daniel Rincon *(Creative Dir)*
Mauricio Reinoso *(Dir-Art & Designer)*
Lupas Celis *(Dir-Creative)*
Manuel Estrada *(Acct Mgr-Coca-Cola-Colombia)*

Accounts:
Carulla Campaign: "Slice a Recipe", Criterion Knives, Kiwi
Coca-Cola Refreshments USA, Inc. Campaign: "Botella de Hielo", Campaign: "Double Ball", Campaign: "Download Concert", Packaging, Rush Hour Cinema
Colombian Ministry of Environment & Natural Resources
Colombina Campaign: "Splot Photocopier"
The Cupcakery Campaign: "Gaddafi"
Cyzone Anti Acne Cleansing Cream
Daimler Colombia Campaign: "Faces Men", Mercedes Benz Campaign: "Attention Assist", Mercedes Benz Campaign: "Blind Spot Assist" & Mercedes Benz Campaign: "Man"
Snacky Spicy Snacks
Ecofill
Fine Cut Knives Fish
Galderma Benzac, Campaign: "Party"
Getty Images Campaign: "Getty Bear", Royalty Free
Grupo Exito Campaign: "Carulla Cooking School"
Harley-Davidson Cycle Helmets
KIA Motors Campaign: "Rearview Camera Race", Campaign: "Top Models"
Mattel Board Game, Campaign: "Hotwheels Loop", Campaign: "Pictionary Pencil Astronaut"
Pictionary Astronaut
Purina Pet Care Dog Food
Unilever
Uno Stacko
WWF Colombia

Ecuador:

Saltiveri Ogilvy & Mather Guayaquil
Av Amazonas y calle UN de Periodistas Edificio Puerta del Sol, Torre Este Piso 7, Quito, Ecuador
Tel.: (593) 2 226 1220
E-Mail: ricardo.sarmiento@ogilvy.com

Agency Specializes In: Direct Response Marketing

Hugo Saltiveri *(Pres)*
Maximiliano Krause *(Gen Mgr)*
Federico Braga *(Art Dir & Creative Dir)*
Fernando Franco *(Art Dir & Creative Dir)*
Manuel Martin *(Creative Dir)*
Diozen Racines *(Art Dir)*
Luis Miguel Molina *(Copywriter)*
Andres Monge *(Copywriter)*

Accounts:
Colineal Sofas
New-Libreria Edimaster Audio Books for Kids: Fairy Tales

Saltiveri Ogilvy & Mather
Avenida Francisco de Orellana Edificio World Trade Center, Torre A Oficina 1105, Guayaquil, Ecuador
Tel.: (593) 4 263 0350
Fax: (593) 42630595

Employees: 2

Hugo Saltiveri *(Pres)*
Federico Braga *(Creative Dir)*
Fernando Franco *(Art Dir)*
Andres Monge *(Copywriter)*

Accounts:
Colineal

El Salvador:

Ogilvy & Mather El Salvador
(Formerly Molina Bianchi: Ogilvy & Mather)
550 Avenida La Capilla No, Col San Benito, San Salvador, El Salvador
Tel.: (503) 2275 3777
Fax: (503) 2275 3784
Web Site: www.ogilvyelsalvador.com/

Employees: 57
Year Founded: 1995

Enzo Bianchi *(Pres & Mng Dir)*
Enzo Paolo Bianchi Gallegos *(Head-Digital)*
Xiomara Herrera *(Dir-Ogilvy PR)*

Accounts:
Dove
Ellipse Campaign: "Strip Tweet"

Mexico:

Ogilvy & Mather
Montes Urales 505 5th Fl Col Lomas de Chapultepec, 11000 Mexico, DF Mexico
Tel.: (52) 55 5350 1800
Fax: (52) 55 5201 6501
E-Mail: recepcion.mexico@ogilvy.com
Web Site: www.ogilvy.com.mx

Year Founded: 1956

Polo Garza *(CEO)*
Horacio Genolet *(CEO-Ogilvy Grp Mexico)*
Ivan Carrasco *(VP-Creative Svcs)*
Agost Carreno *(VP-Creative Svcs-Ogilvy & Mather Mexico)*
Jose Montalvo *(VP-Creative Svcs)*
Victor Alvarado *(Grp Dir-Creative)*
Miguel Velazquez *(Grp Acct Dir)*
Jaime Vidal *(Grp Acct Dir)*
Jimena Delgadillo *(Acct Dir)*
Lee Galvez *(Creative Dir)*
Jaime Gonzalez *(Acct Dir)*
Sergio Diaz Infante *(Art Dir)*
Carlos Meza *(Creative Dir)*
Gonzalo Villegas *(Art Dir)*
Cesar Agost Carreno *(Dir-Reg Creative-Ogilvy Latin America)*
Alejandro Gama *(Dir-Creative)*
Luis Mata *(Dir-Art)*
Pilar Troconis *(Sr Acct Mgr)*
Sergio Almazan *(Copywriter)*
Daniel Garcia *(Copywriter)*

Accounts:
Alberto Achar Campaign: "Gandhi TV"
American Express Company
AMIS Campaign: "Cross Street"
Axtel
Castrol Campaign: "Pregnancy"
Coca-Cola Campaign: "Drink Happiness", Campaign: "Open Your Heart"
Conapred Campaign: "The Hairfest", Casa de la Amistad, Psychological Abuse, tv
Frida Kahlo Museum Campaign: "Frida Kahlo Museum Graphic Identity"
Gandhi Bookstores Campaign: "Executed", Campaign: "Keep Reading", Campaign: "Love", Campaign: "Politicians", Campaign: "Testimony", Hidden Prize, Metrobook
Glaxosmithkline Campaign: "Lamb", Campaign: "Pizza", Eye-Mo Eye Drops, Tums
Hershey's
Hospital San Jose Ambulance Service, Arnold, Organ Donation
Hot Wheels Campaign: "Big Hot Wheels", Toys
IBM
New-Ilusion
New-Maxim Men's Magazine

Medical Center San Josa Hospital Campaign: "The Life T-Shirts"
Mexican Insurance Institution Association Anti-Drunk Driving, Campaign: "Cross Street"
Museo De Memoria Y Tolerancia Campaign: "Tweetbullets"
Museo Interactivo Infantil
Naturalia Campaign: "Testimonials", Campaign: "Tweetwolf"
Nestle
Opticas Lux Campaign: "Correspondent"
Papalote Museo Del Nino
Pictionary
New-Rewedding Nights
World Wildlife Fund Campaign: "Image Not Found", Campaign: "Threads"

OgilvyOne Worldwide
Montes Urales 505 5th Fl, Col Lomas de Chapultepec, 11000 Mexico, DF Mexico
Tel.: (52) 55 5350 1800
Web Site: www.ogilvy.com

Employees: 300
Year Founded: 1986

Agency Specializes In: Direct Response Marketing

Horacio Genolet *(CEO-Ogilvy Group Mexico)*
Diego Del Villar Acebal *(Acct Dir)*
Diana Rodriguez Abisad *(Sr Acct Exec)*

Accounts:
American Express
Coca-Cola Refreshments USA, Inc.
IBM
Nestle
UPS
Unilever

Trinidad:

Abovegroup
(Formerly Abovegroup Ogilvy)
Corner Fitt & Roberts St, Woodbrook, Port of Spain, Trinidad & Tobago
Tel.: (868) 625 7006
Fax: (868) 624 8220
E-Mail: info@abovegroup.com
Web Site: abovegroup.com/

Employees: 58
Year Founded: 1994

Anthony Inglefield *(Mng Dir)*

Accounts:
Unilever

Uruguay:

Punto Ogilvy & Mather
Plaza Independencia, 831 PH Montevideo, 11100 Uruguay
Tel.: (598) 2 900 6070
Fax: (598) 2 903 0690
E-Mail: punto@punto.com.uy
Web Site: www.puntoogilvy.com.uy

Employees: 25
Year Founded: 1964

Agency Specializes In: Advertising, Production (Print), Public Relations

Elbio Acuna *(Owner)*
Pablo Marques *(CEO)*
Emiliano Vargas *(Exec Dir-Creative)*
Rodrigo Castellanos *(Creative Dir & Copywriter)*
Lucho Lannuzzi *(Acct Dir)*
Jorge Manzano *(Dir-Media)*
Rafael Ramirez *(Dir-Art)*
Camila Alganaraz *(Acct Exec)*

Accounts:
Ades
Berghoof Knives
Canarias
Devoto
New-EL PARIS El Escolar Educational Magazine
Frito-Lay
Gillette
New-Hyundai Motor Company
Motorola Solutions, Inc.
Santander Bank Credit Cards, Personal Loans
Tang

Venezuela:

Ogilvy & Mather
Av La Estancia Centro Banaven Torre D Piso 3, Chuao, Caracas, 1080 Venezuela
Tel.: (58) 212 959 0902
Fax: (58) 212 959 6806
Web Site: www.ogilvy.com

Employees: 27

Agency Specializes In: Advertising

Bobby Coimbra *(Pres & Dir-Creative)*
Gustavo Freytez *(VP-Creative Svcs)*
Alfredo Pardo *(VP-Acct Svcs)*
Luis Aponte *(Gen Mgr)*
Maik Gassan *(Sr Dir-Art)*
Maitane Bilbao *(Acct Dir-Coca-Cola Venezuela)*
Irene Filardy *(Dir-Graphic Production)*
Ingrid Ribeiro *(Dir-PR & Corp Comm)*
Shara Napoli Esteban *(Acct Exec)*

Accounts:
Clight Campaign: "Liquid Fruit"
Dr Scholl's Campaign: "If the smell of your feet is getting to you.", Foot Powder
GlaxoSmithKline Campaign: "Geyser"
Jeep Cherokee Climber
Mattel Campaign: "Do you want to go faster?", Campaign: "Polisher", Hot Wheels
Mondelez International, Inc. Campaign: "Orange"
Sherwin-Williams Campaign: "Pool Paint"

Australia:

BADJAR Ogilvy
Level 12, Royal Domain Centre, 380 St Kilda Road, Melbourne, VIC 3004 Australia
Tel.: (61) 3 9690 1477
Fax: (61) 3 9690 4658
E-Mail: info@badjar.com.au
Web Site: www.ogilvy.com.au/

Employees: 300
Year Founded: 1984

Agency Specializes In: Advertising, Consumer Marketing, Digital/Interactive, Financial, Public Relations

Jo Rozario *(Grp Mng Dir-Ogilvy Melbourne)*
Nicholas Desira *(Grp Head-Creative)*
Gavin MacMillan *(Head-Strategy)*
Brendon Guthrie *(Exec Dir-Creative-Ogilvy Melbourne)*
David Ponce de Leon *(Exec Dir-Creative)*
Sally Hastings *(Sr Dir-Art)*
Kieran Moroney *(Sr Dir-Art)*
Matt Rose *(Grp Acct Dir)*
Candice Koffke *(Acct Dir)*
Cameron Mitchell *(Creative Dir)*
Karsten Jurkschat *(Dir-Art)*
Jesse McCormack *(Dir-Art)*
Rebecca Lawler *(Acct Mgr)*
Michael Beard *(Acct Exec)*
Don Jeffery *(Exec Chm)*

Accounts:
AAMI Applause, Campaign: "Drive Happily Ever After: Rhonda decides!", Campaign: "Gravitron", Campaign: "Not Very Insurancey", Campaign: "Safe Driver Rewards", Campaign: "Who's right for Rhonda?", Claim Assist, Life & Income Protection Insurance
AMI
BMW Campaign: "Luxury Car Tax is a Joke"
FireReady
Foster's Australia Crown Lager
Hooroo Campaign: "That Place"
Laminex Australia (Creative Agency of Record) Campaign: "Peacock & Diamond", Essastone
Mccain Foods Australia Frozen Vegetables
Melbourne Food & Wine Festival Creative, Strategy
MINI Campaign: "Ain't Nuthin Country Bout a Countryman", Campaign: "Throw Another Door on the Mini", Creative, Mini Hatch
Myer Campaign: "Colours of Summer", Campaign: "The Power of Give"
Puma Campaign: "PUMA LOVE RUN", Sporting Event
Victorian Government Summer Fire Campaign
Vintage Cellars
Where Is Maps
Yarra Valley Water
Yellow Pages Campaign: "A Few Stray Hairs"

Ogilvy Sydney
72 Thristia Street, Saint Leonards, NSW 2065 Australia
Tel.: (61) 2 9373 6333
Fax: (61) 2 9373 6399
Web Site: www.ogilvy.com.au

Agency Specializes In: Direct Response Marketing

David Fox *(CEO)*
Shaun Branagan *(Grp Head-Creative)*
Ben Kidney *(Head-Digital-Ogilvy & Mather)*
Craig Page *(Head-Digital)*
Rob Spencer *(Head-Brdcst & Video Production)*
Ryan O'Connell *(Deputy Head-Plng)*
Derek Green *(Exec Dir-Creative)*
Scott Sparks *(Sr Dir-Art)*
Brett Terblanche *(Sr Dir-Art)*
Abi Scott *(Sr Acct Dir)*
Sarah Faraday *(Grp Acct Dir-Ogilvy & Mather)*
Sheridan Turner *(Grp Acct Dir)*
Mike Barry *(Creative Dir)*
Wellison Dassuncao *(Sr Art Dir)*
John Marshall *(Acct Dir)*
Kate Smith *(Acct Dir)*
Rupert Hancock *(Dir-Creative)*
Kate Shearer *(Dir-Art)*
Russell Smyth *(Dir-Creative)*
Duncan Stevens *(Dir-Bus)*
Scott Zuliani *(Dir-Art)*
Ruth Hatch *(Sr Acct Mgr)*
Corina Roat *(Sr Acct Mgr-Ogilvy & Mather)*
Anna Michael *(Acct Mgr)*
Kate Piatek *(Acct Mgr)*
Madelin Robertson *(Acct Mgr)*
Deborah Tran *(Acct Exec)*
Chris Ching *(Copywriter)*
Leigh Bignell *(Exec Bus Dir)*

Accounts:
AAMI Flexi-Premiums
American Express Campaign: "Talking Tags"
Blackmores
Coca-Cola Campaign: "Share a Coke", Campaign: "Tastes Like Halloween", Coke, Copa Coca-Cola 2015, Diet Coke, Digital, Fanta, Life, Media, Mobile, Nestea, Online, Out of Home, Powerade, Sprite, TV, Video, Zero
Dove Campaign: "The Ad Makeover"
Holiday Inn Hotels & Resorts

KFC Campaign: "Stop & Smell the Chicken ", Online Ordering, Tastes So Good, The One Box
Kimberly Clark Campaign: "Perfecting the Hug", Huggies Nappies
Kirin Brewery Company, Ltd
Lion Co Campaign: "Experience Collectors", Digital, Hahn Super Dry, Outdoor
Melbourne Food & Wine
MINI Countryman
Myer
Nestle
NSW Government Campaign: "The Mobile Drug Testing"
Purina
Rabobank
Suncorp insurance GIO, Print, TV
Supercoat
Tourism NSW
Uncle Tobys The Simple Life
Vodafone Campaign: "Discover the New", Creative

China:

Ogilvy & Mather Advertising Beijing

9th Floor Huali Building 58 Jinbao Street, Beijing, 100005 China
Tel.: (86) 10 8520 6688
Fax: (86) 10 8520 6060
Web Site: www.ogilvy.com.cn

Year Founded: 1986

Bill Chan *(Exec Dir-Creative)*
Chong Kin *(Exec Dir-Creative)*
Morris Ku *(Sr Dir-Art)*
Vivian Guo *(Acct Dir)*
Yongqiang Hu *(Dir-Art)*
Jiankai Lu *(Dir-Creative)*
Xingsheng Qi *(Dir-Art)*
Qian Wang *(Dir-Art)*
Jason Cutfourth Cheah *(Assoc Dir-Creative)*
Guilin Bo *(Copywriter)*
Vinci Wang *(Copywriter)*

Accounts:
361 Degrees
BSH
Center For Psychological Research Campaign: "Words can be Weapons"
China Foundation for Poverty Alleviation
China Mobile Campaign: "Wireless City"
Coca-Cola
Dolby
Doss
Fanta
Greenpeace Campaign: "It's Not Just The Tree That Gets The Chop", Chopsticks Posters
IBM Campaign: "Analytics Without The Analytics", Campaign: "Hack Attack eDM"
Jiangsu Government Creative, Digital Media, Public Relations
Johnson & Johnson Campaign: "Diary"
Lee
Lenovo Campaign: "Transformers 3"
Levi's Clothing
Lining
Midea
Motorola Solutions, Inc. RAZR, ROKR
MS Society Campaign: "Simple Tasks - Circle"
Nanjing Youth Olympics
NetEase Lottery NetEase Lottery Branding
The North Face
PETA Campaign: "Peta Skin"
Red Bull Campaign: "The Super Badman"
Shanghai Yuzhi Trade Co.
Siemens Campaign: "Keep Your Kitchen Fresh 1", Campaign: "Keep Your Kitchen Fresh"
Subway Sandwich Retailer
Tencent Holdings
ThinkPad
Tsingtao Alcohol, Anti-Drunk Driving
Vans
VisitBritain Campaign: "Great Names for Great Britain", Online Videos, Social Media
Volkswagen Group of America, Inc. Campaign: "Electric Cafe", Campaign: "Eyes on the road"
Wuliangye
Yili "Attitude Determines Quality" Winter Olympics 2014

Ogilvy & Mather (China) Ltd.

25F The Center 989 Changle Road, Shanghai, 200031 China
Tel.: (86) 21 2405 1888
Fax: (86) 21 2405 1880
E-Mail: michael.lee@ogilvy.com
Web Site: www.ogilvy.com.cn

Year Founded: 1992

Shenan Chuang *(Vice Chm-Greater China)*
Chris Reitermann *(CEO)*
Graham Fink *(Chief Creative Officer)*
Alex Runne *(Chief Strategy Officer-Shanghai)*
Sascha Engel *(Creative Dir & Deputy Head-Digital)*
Juggi Ramakrishnan *(Exec Creative Dir)*
Liwen Fan *(Dir-Art)*
Marc Violo *(Dir-Digital Lab)*
Bamboo Zhuang *(Dir-Creative)*
Mike Pearson *(Assoc Dir-Creative)*
Daisy Xuan *(Assoc Dir)*

Accounts:
361 Degrees Campaign: "Delay the Work Day"
Airbus
American Express
BP
Coca-Cola Bottles, Campaign: "2nd Lives", Campaign: "What if empty Coke bottles were never thrown away?", Caps
Day of Peace
Garmin
Goodyear China Campaign: "A Lifetime Commitment to Safety"
H&M Fashion Mixer
HTC Campaign: "HTC One-Subway"
KFC Digital, Mobile App, TV, Traditional Media
Kimberly-Clark Kotex
Lee Jeans
Li Qun
Michelin
Midea Security Cameras Antique, Car, Safe
Motorola Solutions, Inc.
Nestle
The North Face (VF Asia)
Public Health Bureau of Fengxian, Shanghai
Saky Dental Floss Rod
Shirley Price Eye Care
Tourism Victoria Brand & Consumer Campaigns, Content, Digital
Tsingtao Brewery Group; Qingdao, China Ice Beer, Tsingtao Lager, Tsingtao Light, Tsingtao Pure Draft
Unilever Dove, Pond's
WWF/Traffic China
Yihaodian
Zhejiang Elegant Prosper Garment Co. Brand Strategy Development, Image Consulting & Marketing Communications

OgilvyOne Worldwide

9th Floor Huali Building 58 Jinbao Street, Beijing, 100005 China
Tel.: (86) 10 8520 6688
Fax: (86) 10 8520 6666
E-Mail: chris.reitermann@ogilvy.com
Web Site: www.ogilvy.com

Agency Specializes In: Direct Response Marketing

Angel Chen *(Pres)*
Yi Li *(Chief Data Officer)*
Lily Tung *(Mng Dir-Global Brand Mgmt Beijing)*
Doug Schiff *(Exec Dir-Creative)*
Michael Chu *(Dir-Creative)*
Teonghoe Teng *(Dir-Creative)*
Heng Yee Sin *(Assoc Dir-Creative)*

Accounts:
Dong Feng Peugeot Digital Strategy; 2008
GM Encore Campaign: "Hide 'n' Seek "
IBM China Campaign: "Analytics without the Analytics"
Lenovo ThinkPad
Nescafe Campaign: "Live out your boldness", Digital Campaign
PETA Campaign: "Fur Hurts"
Seat Digital Marketing, Social Media, Website
Volkswagen Campaign: "Eyes on the Road"

OgilvyOne

26F The Center 989 Changle Road, Shanghai, 200031 China
Tel.: (86) 21 2405 1888
Fax: (86) 21 2405 1880
Web Site: www.ogilvy.com.cn

Employees: 300

Agency Specializes In: Direct Response Marketing

Jacco Ter Schegget *(Pres-China)*
Connie Ho *(Grp Acct Dir)*
Stefanie Liew *(Grp Acct Dir)*
Tracy Shang *(Grp Acct Dir)*
Tina Chou *(Dir-Bus)*
Michael Chu *(Dir-Creative)*
Vivian Lan *(Dir-Consulting)*
Alicia Yap *(Dir-Bus)*
Virginia Tang *(Bus Consulting Dir)*
Daqing Wang *(Exec Partner-Creative)*

Accounts:
IKEA China; 2008
New-InterContinental Hotels Group Campaign: "Moments of Joy", Holiday Inn, Hualuxe
Johnson & Johnson Acuvue Define
Lincoln Motor Company Online
Philips
Xing Wei College Marketing Campaigns, Online & Offline Promotions

Hong Kong:

H&O

(Formerly Redworks)
23/F The Centre 99 Queen's Road Central, Hong Kong, China (Hong Kong)
Tel.: (852) 21693916
Fax: (852) 25675304
E-Mail: info@hogarth-ogilvy.com
Web Site: www.hogarth-ogilvy.com

Year Founded: 2006

Agency Specializes In: Advertising, Graphic Design

Adam O'Conor *(CEO)*
Catarina Lio *(Mng Dir)*
Michael Tam *(Pres-China)*
Elsa Wong *(Acct Dir)*
Sandy Ling *(Dir-Ops)*

Accounts:
Municipality of Chengdu

Maxx Marketing Ltd.

7 Floor Manley Tower 828 Cheung Sha Wan Road, Kowloon, China (Hong Kong)
Tel.: (852) 2523 2093
Fax: (852) 2977 5794
Web Site: www.maxx-marketing.com

Michael Kwan *(Founder & Pres)*

Andrew Kwan *(Exec VP)*
Ann Wong *(Exec VP)*
Roniel So *(Sr Mgr-Sls & Mktg-HK, South Asia & Southern China)*
Edmund Wong *(Sr Mgr-Quality Assurance)*
Queensa Ma *(Asst Mgr-Mdsg)*
Toby Fung *(Acct Exec)*
Lourine Jennifer *(Acct Exec-Sls & Mktg-APAC & Middle East)*

Accounts:
20th Century Fox
Grupo Bimbo
Kellogg's
L'Oreal
Nestle
Singapore Airlines
Sony Pictures
Unilever

Maxx Marketing Ltd.

7/F Manley Tower, 828 Cheung Sha Wan Road, Hong Kong, China (Hong Kong)
Tel.: (852) 2523 2093
Fax: (852) 2977 5794
Web Site: www.maxx-marketing.com

Agency Specializes In: Advertising

Michael Kwan *(Founder & Pres)*
Andrew Kwan *(Exec VP)*
Ann Wong *(Exec VP)*
Roniel So *(Sr Mgr-Sls & Mktg-HK, South Asia & Southern China)*
Edmund Wong *(Sr Mgr-Quality Assurance)*
Queensa Ma *(Asst Mgr-Mdsg)*
Steven Tam *(Asst Mgr-Mdsg)*

Accounts:
Coca-Cola
Dannon
Hardee's
Kellogg's
KFC
Nestle
P&G
Pizza Hut
Puma

Ogilvy & Mather Advertising

23rd Floor The Center 99 Queen's Road, Central, China (Hong Kong)
Tel.: (852) 2568 0161
Fax: (852) 2885 3215
Web Site: www.ogilvy.com.cn

Agency Specializes In: Advertising

Gavin Simpson *(Chief Creative Officer)*
Gladys Wong *(Gen Mgr)*
Carey Pearson *(Grp Acct Dir)*
John Koay *(Dir-Creative)*
Jason Pan *(Dir-Art)*
Maria Anastasiou *(Acct Mgr)*
Ava Lee *(Acct Mgr)*
Charlie Tsang *(Acct Exec)*
Arnold Yu *(Acct Exec)*
Richard Sorensen *(Assoc Creative Dir)*
Jo Wong *(Sr Art Dir)*

Accounts:
AIAIAI Headphones Campaign: "Get Inside Your Music", Campaign: "Seven Nation Army", Radiohead
Allied Pickfords Campaign: "Guido Moretti", Campaign: "Roger Penrose"
Beijing Sports Radio Campaign: "Hear it live", Soccer
Capella Niseko; Japan Resort; 2008
Carlsberg Group Campaign: "Anyhour Happy Hour", Kronenbourg 1664
China Environmental Protection Foundation Campaign: "Rabbit"
New-CompareAsia Group
Faber Castell Campaign: "Boat", Campaign: "Duck", Campaign: "Iceberg", Campaign: "Just Add Water"
Genki Sushi Hong Kong
Hong Kong CleanUp
Hong Kong Disneyland Campaign: "Lose Your Head at the Dark Side of Disney"
Hong Kong Shark Foundation Campaign: "Bloody Wedding Invitation"
Huggies Campaign: "Babies on the Go"
New-Jeep
KFC Campaign: "Indescribable Taste", Creative
Lucozade Alert
Mercedes-Benz
Midea Campaign: "Choir"
New-Nike
Orbis HK Campaign: "Don't Look Away", Campaign: "Old Parts For New", Campaign: "Strokes", Campaign: "Trade Away Darkness", Chaotic, Experience Blindness, Knots
Pizza Hut
Shangri-La Hotels & Resorts Internal Communications, It's in Our Nature
Shop ElseWhere
Smart Car
Synergy Distribution Ltd Campaign: "Surprisingly Burgundy", Rio Mints
Volkswagen Campaign: "A Phaeton Journey", Phaeton
WWF Campaign: "Vote Ruby"

Ogilvy & Mather Asia/Pacific

23rd Floor The Center 99 Queen's Road, Central, China (Hong Kong)
Tel.: (852) 2568 0161
Fax: (852) 2535 9920
E-Mail: tim.isaac@ogilvy.com
Web Site: www.ogilvy.com

Year Founded: 1962

Paul Heath *(Chm)*
Adam O'Conor *(CEO)*
Paul Matheson *(Pres-Plng-Asia Pacific)*
Giri Jadhav *(VP)*
Keith Ng *(Sr Dir-Art)*
Bo Deng *(Dir-Creative)*
Gan He *(Dir-Art)*
Jiankai Lu *(Dir-Creative)*
Jocelyn Tse *(Dir-Plng)*
Chenghao Xie *(Dir-Art)*

Accounts:
Beijing Sports Radio Campaign: "Tennis"
Coca Cola
MTR Corporation; Hong Kong
Orbis Hong Kong Campaign: "Trade Away Darkness"
Shangri-La Hotels Weibo
Unilever Asia

Ogilvy & Mather India

139/140 Rukmani Lakshmipathy Salia Marshalls Road, Egmore, Chennai, 600 008 India
Tel.: (91) 44 4436 0360
Fax: (91) 44 4434 4370
Web Site: www.ogilvy.com

Year Founded: 1939

Mridula Joseph *(Controller-Creative)*
Karthik Hariharan *(Sr Dir-Plng & Client Svcs Dir)*
Piyush Pandey *(Exec Chm & Creative Dir-South Asia)*
Hephzibah Pathak *(Brand Dir-Global)*
Rajiv Rao *(Dir-Creative-Natl)*
Binu Varghese *(Dir-Creative)*
Kiran Antony *(Grp Creative Dir)*

Accounts:
AICMED
Cadburys India Ltd 5 Star, Campaign: "No Hard Fillings-Toaster & Toast", Campaign: "O Key & Volume Key"
Deccan Odyssey
Donateeyes.org Campaign: "Invisible Beggar"
Family Book Shop
Federal Bank Advertising, Campaign: "Saathi sahi ho, toh kismat khul jaati hai"
Friendsofbooks.com Campaign: "Dog-Ear"
The Hindu Business Line, Campaign: "Cerebration: Test", Campaign: "It's Time To Test Your Business Quotient", Campaign: "Where Every Story has its Song", Creative, Frontline, November Fest, Sportstar, Stay Ahead of The Times
ITC- Agarwathi
L&T Finance
Lenovo
Ma Foi Randstad Creative
Optic Gallery Campaign: "The Card With A Vision"
Parry Ware
Pernod Ricard India Pvt. Ltd. Campaign: "Anniversary", Campaign: "The King's Life"
Spice Mobile Campaign: "Popkorn Mobile"
Style Spa Creative
Sundaram Finance
TTK Health care Creative, Eva, Woodward's Gripe Water
VGN Developers Creative
Vodafone
WWF India Campaign: "Looks Can Kill"
Yahoo India Campaign: "Carry Heavy Attachments"
Yum Restaurants Campaign: "Beatbox", Campaign: "Meeting"

Ogilvy & Mather

Level 06 5th Fl Bagmane Laurel Bagmane Techpark, C V Raman Nagar, Bengaluru, 560 093 India
Tel.: (91) 80 4436 0360
E-Mail: prateek.srivastava@ogilvy.com
Web Site: www.ogilvy.com

Year Founded: 1981

Kiran Ramamurthy *(Sr VP)*
Talha Nazim *(Sr Dir-Creative)*
Mahesh Parab *(Sr Dir-Creative)*
Sairam Vijayan *(Sr Dir-Creative)*
Ajanta Barker *(Dir-Creative-DG & Digital-Worldwide)*
Sangita Dev *(Dir-Creative)*
Abigail Dias *(Dir-Plng)*
Tithi Ghosh *(Dir-Client Svcs)*
Sanjay Nirmal *(Dir-Creative)*
Vishal Rajpurkar *(Dir-Art)*
Sanket Wadwalkar *(Dir-Art)*
Vidya Unni *(Mgr-Talent & HR)*

Accounts:
Aditya Birla Group Campaign: "Hello Friday Dressing"
New-Anouk
Asian Paints Apex Ultima
Bangalore Traffic Police Campaign: "Angry Husband"
Beyond Carlton
Bingo's Red Chilli Bijli
Breathe Easy
British Nutritions Creative, Slimlife, X-tra Gainer, X-tra Mass, X-tra Whey
Cadbury
CarWale Campaign: "Ask the Experts", Media
IBM BSNL
IDBI Bank Campaign: "Everyone", Creative
Indus Pride
International Business Machines Campaign: "IBM Opens in Qatar"
ITC Limited Bingo Tangles, Bingo Yumitos, Brand Proposition, Campaign: "Bomb", Campaign: "If you eat it, you will share it", Campaign: "Train"

KFC Campaign: "KFC-Bald"
Kohler Creative
Lenovo Group Limited
Motorola Solutions, Inc. Mobile Devices (Agency of Record)
MTR Foods Advertising, Campaign: "Onion", Communications, Masalas, Mobile, Print
The National Association for the Blind
Once Again Campaign: "The Tagging Drive"
RMZ Corp.
SABMiller Fosters
Skoll Breweries Haywards 5000 Soda
Taj Mahal
Titan Industries Ltd. 'Raga Pearls', Campaign: "Bad Eyes - Auto", Campaign: "Bad Eyes - Lorry", Campaign: "Farewell", Campaign: "Flair", Campaign: "Gift of Time", Campaign: "Look Young", Campaign: "Tagging", Campaign: "The Bet", Titan Eye+, Titan Watches
World For All "Building, Noose, Train"

Ogilvy & Mather

Mahavir House 303-304 3rd Floor Mahavir House, Basheer Bagh Cross Roads, Hyderabad, 500 029 India
Tel.: (91) 40 4436 0360
Web Site: www.ogilvy.com

Kunal Jeswani *(Chief Digital Officer-India)*
Kapil Arora *(Pres-Ogilvy North)*
Sarang Wahal *(Sr VP)*
Ramesh Keshavan *(VP)*
Niket Kumar *(VP)*
Prakash Nair *(VP)*
Nobin Dutta *(Controller-Creative)*
Hufrish Birdy *(Exec Dir-Fin)*
Talha Nazim *(Sr Dir-Creative)*
Pradipta Roy *(Client Svcs Dir)*
Sangita Dev *(Dir-Creative)*
Rajiv Rao *(Dir-Creative-Natl)*

Accounts:
Shakhi Newspaper & Television
Vodafone

Ogilvy India

14th Floor Commerz International Business Park Oberoi Garden City, off Western Express Highway, Goregaon, Mumbai, 400 063 India
Tel.: (91) 22 4436 0360
Fax: (91) 22 5034 4370
Web Site: www.ogilvy.com

Employees: 650
Year Founded: 1928

Altaf Hussain *(CFO)*
Prakash Nair *(Sr VP)*
Prem Narayan *(Sr VP-Acct Plng)*
B Ramanathan *(Sr VP)*
Ajay Mehta *(VP)*
Antara Suri *(VP)*
Harshik Suraiya *(Grp Head-Creative)*
Mridula Joseph *(Controller-Creative)*
Parag Patil *(Controller-Creative)*
Kainaz Karmakar *(Exec Creative Dir & Copywriter)*
Anurag Agnihotri *(Exec Creative Dir)*
Sumanto Chattopadhyay *(Exec Dir-Creative)*
Sukesh Kumar Nayak *(Exec Dir-Creative)*
Zenobia Pithawalla *(Exec Dir-Creative)*
Neville Shah *(Grp Dir-Creative-Ogilvy & Mather)*
Srreram Athray *(Sr Dir-Creative)*
Elizabeth Dias *(Sr Dir-Creative)*
Laukik Golatkar *(Sr Dir-Art)*
Talha Bin Mohsin *(Sr Dir-Creative-Ogilvy & Mather)*
Mahesh Parab *(Sr Dir-Creative)*
Sujoy Roy *(Sr Dir-Creative)*
Sameer Sojwal *(Sr Dir-Creative)*
Mangesh Someshwar *(Sr Dir-Creative)*
Farid Bawa *(Art Dir)*
Manasi Kadne *(Sr Creative Dir)*
Dushyant Kumar *(Acct Dir)*
Sukhendu Mukherjee *(Art Dir)*
Chirayu Palande *(Art Dir)*
Minal Phatak *(Creative Dir)*
Rohit Sharma *(Acct Dir)*
Dushyant Jethani *(Mgmt Supvr)*
Pratik Koltharkar *(Mgmt Supvr)*
Shivali Nair *(Mgmt Supvr)*
Ramakrishnan Hariharan *(Dir-Creative & Copywriter)*
Amitabh Agnihotri *(Dir-Creative)*
Ganapathy Balagopalan *(Dir-Plng)*
Makarand Joshi *(Dir-Creative)*
Deelip Khomane *(Dir-Art)*
Vishakha Modak *(Dir-Art)*
Deepankar Mukherji *(Dir-Client Servicing)*
Ashish Naik *(Dir-Art)*
Jitendra Patel *(Dir-Art)*
Shamik Sengupta *(Dir-Creative)*
Manoj Joshi *(Assoc Dir-Film)*
Saurabh Kulkarni *(Assoc Dir-Creative)*
Vishnudas Kunchu *(Assoc Dir-Creative)*
Neha Shetty *(Acct Mgr)*
Puneet Dewli *(Acct Supvr)*
Nikhil George *(Supvr-Copy)*
Arshad Shaikh *(Supvr-Copy)*
Mithila Manhas *(Sr Acct Exec)*
Geetanjali Jaiswal *(Copywriter)*
Nitin Pradhan *(Copywriter)*
Aratrika Rath *(Copywriter)*
Vinay Singh *(Copywriter)*
Kunal Dangarwala *(Grp Acct Mgr)*

Accounts:
A Fidilife Initiative
Adani Wilmar Limited Campaign: "Clap"
Aditya Birla Group
The Akanksha Foundation
Amara Raja Batteries Limited Campaign: "Life Saver"
Amul Macho
Anchor Health & Beauty Care Anchor Toothpaste
Asian Paints Ltd Campaign: "Guide Book", Campaign: "Har Ghar Kuch Kehta Hai"
Asthma Society of India Campaign: "Coughing Rocket"
Bajaj Auto Ltd. Campaign: "Precision Performance", Campaign: "PulsarMania2", Campaign: "Speedlines", Creative, Pulsar, Pulsar 200NS
Bajaj Finserv Ltd
Binani Cement Campaign: "Memories", Campaign: "Parental Love"
Blenders Pride
Board of Control for Cricket in India Campaign: "No One will Escape the Excitement", Carnival, OOH, Radio
Bosch
Brooke Bond Lipton India Ltd BRU, Brooke Bond Bru Gold, Campaign: "Imran Wears Saree", Red Label
Cadbury India Ltd 5Star, Cadbury Bournville, Cadbury Dairy Milk Silk, Cadbury Gems, Cadbury Perk Glucose, Campaign: "Basket ball", Campaign: "Cadbury 5 Star Chomp", Campaign: "Cadbury 5 Star", Campaign: "Condition Serious Hai", Campaign: "Jogging", Campaign: "Joy in Snow", Campaign: "Kuch Meetha Ho Jaye", Campaign: "No Hard Fillings", Campaign: "Not So Sweet", Campaign: "Raho Umarless", Campaign: "Runaway Wedding", Campaign: "Softer, Smoother & Silkier", Perk Double, TV
Cancer Patients Aid Association Campaign: "Chanting Lighter"
Carwale.com
Casper Mosquito Repellents Campaign: "End the terror"
Castrol Turbo
CEAT Campaign: "For All Season", Campaign: "Ladoo", Suv Tyres
Channel V Campaign: "The Seatbelt Crew", VithU
Coca-Cola Refreshments USA, Inc. Campaign: "Hill station", Campaign: "Rasta Clear Hai", Campaign: "Snack time, Fanta time", Campaign: "Valet", Fanta, Sprite
Crossword Bookstores Audio books Campaign: "Lips"
Dhanlaxmi Bank
Diu Tourism
Dove Haircare
The Economist
Essar
The Federal Bank
FeviKwik Campaign: "The First Reusable Piggy Bank", Campaign: "Works Even Faster", Lady in White, Dancing Farmer, Egyptian Warrior
Fiat India Automobiles Ltd Campaign: "An Ode to Driving"
Footloose
Fortune Oil
Fox Crime Campaign: "The Photographs Case", Digital, OOH, TV
Future Generali Campaign: "The Last Message", Smart Life
Future Group
Gangavathiexports Campaign: "Swimming"
GlaxoSmithKline Consumer Healthcare Ltd
Google Campaign: "Mom and Daughter, Dress", Campaign: "PledgeToVote", Campaign: "Reunion", Campaign: "Sugar Free"
Government of Gujarat Tourism
Greenply Industries Campaign: "Magician", Plywood
Hamilton
HCG Campaign: "Put Out The Fire"
Helpchat Brand Marketing, Digital, Outdoor, Print, TV
Hero Indian Super League Campaign: "Come on India, Let's Football"
The Hindu Campaign: "The Hindu", Print, Social Media, TV
Hindustan Pencils Campaign: "Playway", Magician, Wrecking Ball, Cage, Nataraj Pencils
Hindustan Unilever Brooke Bond Sehatmand, Bru Gold, Campaign: "Bru Exotica Brazil", Campaign: "Nutrilock", Campaign: "Roti Reminder", Cold Coffee, Comfort Fabric Conditioners, Fast Moving Consumer Goods, Lifebuoy Handwash, Pond's Age Miracle
Honda Cars India
Hotwheels Campaign: "Carpet", Campaign: "Drawer", Campaign: "Star Treck", Campaign: "Vintage Collection", Safari
HUL Brooke Bond Taj Mahal Tea Bags, Campaign: "Freedom of Choice"
IAPA (Indian Association for Promotion of Adoption & Child Welfare)
IBM Campaign: "Ahead of Demand"
ICICI Bank Limited
IDBI Federal Life Insurance Childsurance
Indian Head Injury Foundation
ITC Limited Bingo Tangles, Khao Ek Bane Anek
JG Hosiery Private Limited Campaign: "ATM", Campaign: "Egg"
Kasturi & Sons Ltd
KFC
Kissan
Kraft India Bournvita, Campaign: "Playing with cheeks", Tang
Kurl-On Mattresses
Landmark Group Creative, Home Centre, Shukran
Lenovo India (Agency of Record) Campaign: "Hands", Campaign: "The Fly", Creative, Ultrabook
Madura Garments Campaign: "Catch a Colour"
New-Make Love Not Scars
Marbles
Mattel Campaign: "Refrigerator", Hot Wheels Safari
Max Life Insurance Campaign: "Aapke Sachche Advisors", Campaign: "Couple", Campaign: "House", Max Life Forever Young Pension Plan, Max Life Guaranteed Life Time Income Plan
Mayur
Mbl Campaign: "Colour Change"
McNroe Consumer Products Pvt. Ltd. Campaign: "Gift", Secret Temptation
Mondelez India Bournville - Sob, Bournvita Li'l Champs, Brand Proposition, Cadbury, Campaign: "Not So Sweet", Campaign: "Traffic",

Advertising Agencies

Gems Surprise Packs With Toys Inside
Mother Dairy Campaign: "Awesome", Campaign: "Maa Jaisa Koi Nahi", Campaign: "That Lifts You", Campaign: "Today", Campaign: "Trophy, Sorry Mom", Real Good, Classics Range
M.P. Jewellers
MP Tourism
MTR Spicy Pickle Campaign: "Run out of Tears"
Mumbai Police Campaign: "Mumbai Ke Liye 1 Minute"
National Skill Development Corporation
Natraj Pencils
Nazraana Jewellery
Nehru Zoological Park
Onida Creative
Operation Smile India Campaign: "Clefttosmile"
Parker Titan
Parle Products Campaign: "Kal ke genius", Campaign: "The Power of Milk", Painting Teaser, Parle-G
Perfetti Van Melle, India Campaign: "Archimedes", Campaign: "Colour Your Tongue", Campaign: "Dhoka Kisne Diya", Campaign: "Ja Pani La", Campaign: "Riddle", Campaign: "Yeh Wala", Center Fresh Actisport, Mentos, Mentos Sour Marbles, Television Campaign, The Candy Tree, Xplode
Pernod Ricard Campaign: "Imperial Blue - Diamond"
Philips Electronics India Ltd Air Fryer, Campaign: "1 Light, 2 Colours", Led Lights
Philips
Pidilite Industries Limited Campaign: "'Judh Jayein Tyohaar Pe", Campaign: "Crazy Chairs", Campaign: "Poshan wala Lotion", Campaign: "Raksha Bandhan", Fevicol, Fevicol Runners, Fevistik, Terminator, White Glue Adhesive
Ponds India Campaign: "Activated Carbon"
New-PostPickle
The Procter & Gamble Company Campaign: "Powercheck"
Ramco Systems
Range Rover
Red Bull
Red FM 93.5
Red Label
Religare Enterprises Campaign: "Parrot", Mutual Fund
Rohan Avriti Campaign: "Surprisingly Private Property"
Royal Stag
Sabin Vaccine Institute
SBI Life Insurance Campaign: "Shaving Blade"
Seagrams 100 Pipers, Campaign: "Lift", Campaign: "Live Concert", Campaign: "Remembered for Good", Imperial Blue
SEBI Campaign: "Regidter your Complaint", Creative
Spice Mobile Campaign: "Hit Me", Smartphones
Star India Campaign: "The Photographs Case", Creative, STAR Gold, STAR Jalsha
Star Sports Campaign: "Star Power"
Tata Motors Campaign: "In Everything It's Gold", Campaign: "The Beast Redifned", Jaguar, Tata Sumo Gold
Tata Sky Ltd Campaign: "Boutique", Campaign: "Karoke", Campaign: "Missed Call", Campaign: "Prison Break", Campaign: "Score", Campaign: "TV is Good", Campaign: "Tata Sky Mobile: Ab TV aap ki pocket main", Campaign: "jhingalala", Everywhere TV, Media, Print, Radio, TV, Tata Sky Plus
Tata Steel
Tata Teleservices Limited Campaign: "Package Advisor"
Tea Board of India Creative
Thinkpot
Titan Industries Ltd. Campaign: "Katrina Kaif"
Usha International Ltd. Sewing Machines
Vedanta Group
Vodafone Group plc Campaign: "Because Fun has No Limit", Campaign: "Blackberry Boys", Campaign: "Blue", Campaign: "Celebrate Bandra", Campaign: "Get Ready for Click", Campaign: "Headquarters", Campaign: "Made For Sharing", Campaign: "Made for You", Campaign: "Secure Connectivity", Campaign: "Win A Place", Crazy Feet, Digital, IPL Campaign, International Calling, M-Pesa, On-Ground, Online, Outdoor, POS, Print, Radio, TV, Unlimited Internet Packs, Zoozoos
Vodafone India Limited Campaign: "International Roaming Rates", Campaign: "Mischief", Campaign: "Soldier", Campaign: "The Self Defense Umbrella", Video
Westside
World For All Campaign: "Train"
WWF India Campaign: "Panda"
Yahoo! Inc.
Yum Restaurant Marketing Pvt. Ltd. Campaign: "College Friends Reunion", Campaign: "KFC Paneer Zinger", Campaign: "So Cheesy, Mouse"

Ogilvy

Tower A 6th to 8th Floor Global Business Park Mehrauli Gurgaon Road, Gurgaon Haryana, 122 002 New Delhi, India
Tel.: (91) 124 4760760
E-Mail: sanjay.thapar@ogilvy.com
Web Site: www.ogilvy.com

Year Founded: 1956

Madhukar Sabnavis *(Vice Chm & Country Head-Discovery & Plng)*
Chandana Agarwal *(Mng Partner-Adv Fun)*
Arindam Sengupta *(Sr VP)*
Vivek Verma *(VP)*
Shakoon Khosla *(Controller-Creative)*
Ajay Gahlaut *(Exec Creative Dir)*
Shubha Menon *(Sr Dir-Creative)*
Boom Suanyai *(Art Dir)*
Umesh Baldaniya *(Dir-Art)*
Musfar Khan *(Dir-Art)*
Gaurav Nautiyal *(Dir-Creative)*
Jossy Raphael *(Dir-Creative)*
Shadab Abidi *(Copywriter)*
Anish Diddee *(Copywriter)*

Accounts:
Angels In My Kitchen
Asian Paints Creative
Cadburys India Ltd
Cancer Patients Aid Association Campaign: "Chanting Lighter"
Castrol EDGE Campaign: "Tested to Perfection"
Cisco
Coca-Cola India Campaign: "Boond Boond Mein Sacchai", Campaign: "Snack-time Fanta-Time", Fanta, Kinley, Sprite
Dabur India Campaign: "new and young avatar", Cinema, Dabur Amla Hair Oil, Print, Sanifresh, Television
Eno Campaign: "Food no coming back."
Fevicol
GlaxoSmithKline Campaign: "Rishta Pakka"
Greenply Industries Campaign: "Forever New", Plywood
Hindustan Unilever Limited Lifebuoy
Indian Railways
Kadambani
KFC India Campaign: "Baat Maan Pyaare", Campaign: "Dips Bucket-Weekend Plan", Campaign: "So Veg So Good", Creative, Curry Crunch, Paneer Zinger, Veg Twister
New-Kohler
Kraft Foods Cadbury 5 Star
Lass Naturals Bosom Blossom
Mattel Toys Hot Wheels
Max Life Insurance Co. Ltd. Campaign: "Btana Zaruri Hai"
Ministry of Tourism Creative, Incredible India
Optic Gallery Campaign: "The card with a vision"
Ozorie Migraine Relief Oil
Pernod Ricard
Philips India Campaign: "Jig Saw", Consumer Lifestyle & Lighting, Creative
Pidilite Industries Fevistik
Pizza Hut Campaign: " Double Date", Campaign: "Size Matters"
Seagram's Imperial Blue
Spice Mobiles
Taco Bell Creative
Tata Group Titan
Titan Industries Ltd
Titan Watches
Unilever Campaign: "Why hide your year?", Lakme Skin Care, Pond's Age Miracle
VLCC; 2009
Vodafone India Ltd Vodafone 3g Cellular Phone Service
Wild Stone India Wild Stone Red
Yahoo

OgilvyOne Worldwide

12 Floor Commerz International Business Park Oberoi Garden City, Off Western Express Highway, Goregaon (East), Mumbai, 400 063 India
Tel.: (91) 22 5034 4600
Fax: (91) 22 4434 4370
Web Site: www.ogilvy.com

Year Founded: 2000

Agency Specializes In: Direct Response Marketing

Sonia Khurana *(Sr VP & Head-Customer Engagement)*
Ashwath Ganesan *(VP & Head-Plng)*
Vipul Salvi *(Exec Creative Dir)*
George Kovoor *(Sr Dir-Creative)*
Aarti Madan *(Acct Dir)*
Sanjana Shirke *(Client Svcs Dir)*
Savita Rijhwani *(Mgmt Supvr)*
Martin Ravva *(Assoc Dir-Creative)*
Sudarshan Shettigar *(Assoc Dir-Creative)*
Mihir Chitre *(Supvr-Copy)*
Lini Antony *(Grp Acct Mgr)*
Hetal Nathwani *(Grp Acct Mgr)*
Aniveshika Prakash *(Grp Acct Mgr)*

Accounts:
American Express Banking Corp
DHL
E.I. DuPont India Pvt.Ltd Campaign: "The Power of Shunya"
Piaggio Digital, Vespa LX 125
Star India campaign: "Photographs Case"

OgilvyOne Worldwide

23rd Floor The Center, 99 Queen's Road, Central, China (Hong Kong)
Tel.: (852) 2568 1177
Fax: (852) 2884 1381
E-Mail: sean.rach@ogilvy.com
Web Site: www.facebook.com/OgilvyHK

Employees: 300
Year Founded: 1980

Agency Specializes In: Communications

Sheilen Rathod *(Mng Dir)*
Christopher Brewer *(Head-Consulting & Customer Strategy)*
Shayne Pooley *(Exec Dir-Creative-Ogilvy Redworks)*
Matthew Nisbet *(Dir-Digital Creative)*

Accounts:
American Express
Hong Kong Jockey Club
IBM Campaign: "Your Storage Riddles Solved"
Indigo Living Digital
Mercedes-Benz Campaign: "New Showroom Locator"
Smartone Campaign: "Call Guard Social Movement"

New-Studio City Macau Digital

OgilvyOne Worldwide
Ogilvy Centre 1 Okhla Industrial Estate Phase III, New Delhi, 11 0020 India
Tel.: (91) 11 513 44600
Web Site: www.ogilvy.com

Year Founded: 2000

Agency Specializes In: Direct Response Marketing

Namrata Balwani *(Sr VP)*
Keerthi Raju *(Acct Dir)*
Kousik Panda *(Assoc Dir-Creative)*
Rahul Gupta *(Acct Supvr)*
Rajnandini Ghosh *(Grp Acct Mgr)*
Jagriti Motwani *(Assoc Partner)*

Accounts:
Sony Campaign: "We All Fall"

Indonesia:

Ogilvy & Mather
Plaza Bapindo Bank Mandiri Tower 26 Fl, PO Box 2580, Sudirman Kav 54-55, Jakarta, 12190 Indonesia
Tel.: (62) 21 526 626 1
Fax: (62) 21 526 626 3
Web Site: www.ogilvy.com

Year Founded: 1971

Agency Specializes In: Direct Response Marketing, Public Relations

Katryna Mojica *(CEO)*
Marianne Admardatine *(Mng Dir)*
Din Sumedi *(Chief Creative Officer)*
Judica Nababan *(Gen Mgr-Ogilvy PR Worldwide & Pulse Comm)*
Ridward Ongsano *(Dir-Creative)*
Yuwono Widodo *(Dir-Creative)*
Aji Bekti *(Assoc Dir-Creative)*

Accounts:
A&W Creative; 2008
DHL
Fanta
Fuji
Jala PRT Clothes
Konimex Pharmaceutical Laboratories Feminax, Paramex
New-Ministry of Tourism Strategic Communications
National Network for Domestic Workers Advocacy
Pasta Gigi Formula
P.T. Astra Honda Motor Motorcycle; 2007
PT Gudang Garam Surya Slims; 2008
PT Unilever Indonesia Tbk
Sara Lee Brylcreem, She; 2008
Unilever Creative, Digital Marketing, Molto Ultra One Rinse, Pond's Age Miracle, Pond's Oil Control, Vaseline Women
UPS Express Delivery
World Economic Forum Communications, East Asia Forum, Public Relations

OgilvyInteractive
Bapindo Plaza Bank Mandiri Tower 25th Floor Jalan Jendral, Sudirman Kav 54-55, Jakarta, 12190 Indonesia
Tel.: (62) 2 1526 6261
Fax: (62) 2 1526 6263
Web Site: www.ogilvy.com

Employees: 200

Agency Specializes In: Digital/Interactive

Gretchen Alcantara Largoza *(Mng Dir)*
Misty Maitimoe *(Deputy Mng Dir)*
Steve Aston *(Gen Mgr-Indonesia)*
Ridward Ongsano *(Dir-Creative)*
Lydia Tarigan *(Dir-Creative)*

Japan:

Ogilvy & Mather Japan K.K.
Yebisu Garden Place Tower 25F 4-20-3 Ebisu, Tokyo, Shibuya-ku 150-6025 Japan
Tel.: (81) 3 5791 8888
Fax: (81) 357918887
E-Mail: info@ogilvy.com
Web Site: www.ogilvy.co.jp

Employees: 300
Year Founded: 1995

Aki Kubo *(Chm)*
Todd Krugman *(Pres)*
Paul Cocks *(CFO)*
Ajab Samrai *(Chief Creative Officer)*
Ricardo Adolfo *(Dir-Creative)*
Federico Garcia *(Dir-Creative)*
Masato Mitsudera *(Dir-Creative)*
Yousuke Ozawa *(Dir-Art)*
Junkichi Tatsuki *(Dir-Art)*
Shinichiro Fukushima *(Copywriter)*
Eugene Gao *(Copywriter)*
Francesca Van Haverbeke *(Copywriter)*
Paul Kemp *(Copywriter)*

Accounts:
Adot ADOT.COM Lights, Campaign: "Words Kill Wars"
Alpine
American Express
BP Castrol Engine Oil
British American Tobacco
Coca-Cola Japan Campaign: "Coca-Cola's Hello"
Condomania
Dell Smartphone
DHL
Diageo
Earpick Groom
Economica Global Image Campaign: "Elevator"
Eli Lilly
Estetica Brasil Beauty
Forever Tree Network Campaign: "Dead"
IBM
Kai Corporation
KENT
Kirschel Foundation
Konica Minolta Campaign: "Dream Printer"
Sawanotsuru Alcohol
Shiro Sake
Sneaker Freaker
Suntory
Takahashi Shuzo Rice Liquor
New-TELL Japan
Tokyo Star Bank
The University Of Tokyo
World Wide Fund for Nature
Yaocho Bar Group

OgilvyOne Worldwide
Yebisu Garden Place Tower 25F 4-20-3 Ebisu, Shibuya-ku, Tokyo, 150-6025 Japan
Tel.: (81) 3 5791 8700
Fax: (81) 3 5791 8701
E-Mail: info@ogilvy.com
Web Site: www.ogilvy.co.jp

Employees: 300
Year Founded: 1998

Agency Specializes In: Direct Response Marketing

Todd Krugman *(Pres-Ogilvy & Mather Japan)*
Mike Busby *(Mng Dir-North Asia-Geometry Global Japan GK)*
Fred Kendall *(Mng Dir-RedWorks Japan K.K.)*
Ichiro Ota *(Mng Dir-Geometry Global Japan)*
Masahiro Saito *(Mng Dir-Ogilvy & Mather Japan GK)*
Leo Shiina *(Grp Dir-Fin-Ogilvy & Mather Japan)*
Hiroko Okita *(Bus Dir-Ogilvy PR Worldwide Japan K.K)*
Abi Sekimitsu *(Dir-Content)*
Kuniyoshi Mabuchi *(Rep Dir)*

Accounts:
Nesae

Korea:

Ogilvy & Mather
27-8 Chamwon-Dong, Seocho-Ku, Seoul, 137-903 Korea (South)
Tel.: (82) 2 513 1400
Web Site: www.ogilvy.co.kr

Employees: 200
Year Founded: 1999

Peter Engelbrecht *(Creative Dir)*

Accounts:
Dove
DuPont
IBM
Lenovo
Motorola Solutions, Inc.
Nike
Olympus Mju
Ponds

Malaysia:

Ogilvy & Mather Advertising
Level 11 Menara Milenium 8 Jalan Damanlela, Bukit Damansara, 50490 Kuala Lumpur, Malaysia
Tel.: (60) 3 2718 8888
Fax: (60) 3 2710 6983
Web Site: www.ogilvy.com.my

Employees: 270

Ken Wertime *(Chm)*
Campbell Cannon *(Mng Partner)*
Shireen Peterson *(Mng Partner)*
Nizwani Shahar *(Mng Partner)*
Teng King *(CFO)*
Gavin Simpson *(Chief Creative Officer)*
Selina Ang *(Exec Dir)*
Tan Chee Keong *(Grp Exec Dir-Creative)*
Liew Heng *(Grp Dir-Fin)*
Nikken Chong *(Sr Dir-Art)*
Arindam Chatterjee *(Reg Dir-Plng)*
Donevan Chew *(Deputy Exec Dir-Creative)*

Accounts:
Aeco Technologies Campaign: "Riot"
Barbie
BERNAS NASIONAL BERHAD Campaign: "Bowls For Humanity"
BMW Malaysia Creative
BP
Cisco Systems Malaysia
Coca-Cola Refreshments USA, Inc.
Colgate Palmolive
Danone Dumex
Dequadin Lozenges
DHL
Diageo
Fitness First
Ford Motor Co.
Ford
GBA Corporation
Gillette

GlaxoSmithKline Campaign: "Settle Disagreements", Campaign: "Traffic Blues", Eno
Goodyear
Heineken Campaign: "The Opener"
Hot Wheels Cops & Robbers
IBM
Kesturi
Kimberly Clark Huggies, Kotex
Lego Singapore Pvt Ltd Campaign: "Caterpillar", Campaign: "Whale"
Mattel Campaign: "Jet Fighter", Campaign: "Quick Draw Battleship", Campaign: "Quick Draw Bear", Campaign: "Quick Draw Fencing", Campaign: "Quick Draw Wins", Nascar, Pictionary
Maxis Communications
Maxis
Mondelez International Cadbury
Motorola Solutions, Inc.
National Geographic Tribal Invasion
Nestle Campaign: "Next Games", Milo, The Energy Within
Padiberas Nasional Berhad Campaign: "Chinese New Year"
Pet World Marketing Prodiet Cat Food
Pizza Hut Campaign: "Cook Out", Campaign: "Defrost"
Pure Seed Florist & Gifts Campaign: "Stamps"
Setiaman Trading
Shoes Shoes Shoes Campaign: "Shoe Dating"

OgilvyOne dataservices

Level 10 Menara Milenium, 8 Jalan Damanlela, Bukit Damansara, 50490 Kuala Lumpur, Malaysia
Tel.: (60) 3 2718 8888
Fax: (60) 3 2710 6983
E-Mail: zayn.khan@ogilvy.com
Web Site: www.ogilvy.com.my

Employees: 200

Agency Specializes In: Direct Response Marketing

Anand Badami *(Grp Mng Dir)*
Teng Hock King *(COO & CFO)*
Rafael Guida *(Exec Creative Dir)*

Accounts:
Maxis
Shell

New Zealand:

Ogilvy New Zealand

22 Stanley St, PO Box 4567, Parnell, Auckland, 1140 New Zealand
Tel.: (64) 9 358 5752
Fax: (64) 9 358 5762
E-Mail: greg.partington@ogilvy.co.nz
Web Site: www.ogilvy.co.nz

Employees: 200

Greg Partington *(Mng Dir)*
Anne Boothroyd *(Grp Head-Creative)*
Richard Loseby *(Grp Head-Creative)*
Darran Wong-Kam *(Grp Head-Creative)*
Martin Hermans *(Sr Dir-Art)*
Sandra Daniel *(Grp Acct Dir)*
Jessica Short *(Acct Dir)*
Chris Childerhouse *(Dir-Creative)*
Graham Dolan *(Dir-Creative-Retail)*
Kelly Coburn *(Sr Acct Mgr-Coke & Powerade)*
Alisha Iyer *(Acct Mgr)*
Paul KimTroy Goodall *(Copywriter)*
Paul Kim *(Copywriter)*

Accounts:
AA Insurance Campaign: "Comprehensive Cover"
Auckland Council
BP
Brothers In Arms Youth Mentoring Campaign: "Just Like Your Dad", Campaign: "Listen"
Castrol
Chapel Bar
Coca-Cola Oceania Campaign: "Train Like You're in the Game", Powerade Campaign: "Train Like You're in the Game"
Environmental Protection Authority Campaign: "Handguns, Grenades, Assault Rifles"
Forest & Bird
General Motors Company
Holden Campaign: "'Quartet"
IBM
KFC
Kimberly-Clark Kleenex Cottonelle
Nestle Purina Campaign: "Fetch", Campaign: "Mighty Dog: Shiny Coat"
New Zealand Rugby Union
NZPork Jack
Papakura District Council
Purina
Rebel Sport Campaign: "Flight"
Sprite
WWF

Philippines:

BCD Pinpoint Direct Marketing Inc.

4th Floor Bloomingdale Bldg 205 Salcedo St, Legaspi Village, Manila, 1227 Philippines
Tel.: (63) 2 795 5999
E-Mail: maxine.bahatan@bcdpinpoint.com
Web Site: www.bcdpinpoint.com

Employees: 30

Louie Yu *(Dir-Accounts)*
Patrick Cua *(Acct Mgr)*
Mina Velando *(Acct Exec)*
Katerina Rara *(Jr Copywriter)*

Accounts:
Biomedis
BMW
James Hardie
The Philippine Daily Inquirer
Shopwise

Ogilvy & Mather (Philippines) Inc.

24 & 25 F Picadilly Star Building, Fort Bonifacio Global City, Taguig City, Manila, Philippines
Mailing Address:
PO Box 1401, Makati, Metro Manila, Philippines
Tel.: (63) 2 238 7000
Fax: (63) 2 885 0026
Web Site: www.ogilvy.com/

Year Founded: 1991

Leah Huang *(Mng Dir)*
Richmond Walker *(Grp Dir-Creative)*
Carla Laus *(Grp Acct Dir)*
Lu-Ann Fuentes *(Bus Dir & Dir-Editorial & Comm Svcs)*
Pamela Mariano *(Acct Dir-PR)*
Mervin Teo Wenke *(Acct Dir)*
Leticia Matias *(Dir-Fin)*
Katherine Calilao *(Sr Acct Mgr)*
Arianne Catacutan *(Sr Acct Mgr)*
Hannah Tejuco *(Mgr-Media Rels)*

Accounts:
BP
Mondelez Philippines Inc Campaign: "TANG RECYCLASS"
Nestle
Nike Campaign: "The Upper Hand"
Ponds
Unilever Campaign: "Real Men Surprise their Dates"

OgilvyOne Worldwide

15th Floor Philamlife Tower 8767 Paseo de Roxas, Makati City Metro, Manila, 1200 Philippines
Tel.: (63) 2 238 7000
E-Mail: elly.puyat@ogilvy.com
Web Site: www.ogilvy.com

Year Founded: 1993

Agency Specializes In: Direct Response Marketing

Isa Garcia-Sicam *(Mng Dir)*
Elly Puyat *(Mng Dir)*
Pamela Mariano *(Acct Dir-PR)*
Mike Sicam *(Dir-Creative)*
Katherine Calilao *(Sr Acct Mgr)*
Frances Cabatuando *(Copywriter)*

Accounts:
Johnson & Johnson BONAMINE, Campaign: "Anne", PR & Digital Campaign

Singapore:

Ogilvy & Mather Advertising

35 Robinson Road 03-01 The Ogilvy Centre, Singapore, 068876 Singapore
Tel.: (65) 6213 7899
Fax: (65) 6213 7760
E-Mail: steven.mangham@ogilvy.com
Web Site: www.ogilvypr.com

Employees: 500
Year Founded: 1958

Ee Rong Chong *(Mng Dir)*
Eugene Cheong *(Chief Creative Officer)*
Chandra Barathi *(Head-Tech)*
Todd Krugman *(Exec Dir-Ogilvy & Mather Japan)*
Melvyn Lim *(Exec Dir-Creative)*
Gwen Raillard *(Exec Dir-Plng)*
Charlie Lowe *(Reg Dir-Strategy)*
Mervyn Rey *(Dir-Creative)*
John-John Skoog *(Dir-Art)*
Fabio Montero *(Copywriter)*
Sonal Narain *(Planner)*
Augustus Sung *(Copywriter)*
Esther Tan *(Copywriter)*
Soohan Han *(Reg Acct Dir)*
Molly Wagman *(Sr Partner & Exec Grp Dir)*

Accounts:
Acres Campaign: "Wedding Cards"
ActionAid Campaign: "Be Positive"
Ajmal Perfumes
American Express Company
Ben & Jerry's
Big Orange Campaign: "Free Sample"
BMW
The Coca-Cola Company #CokeDrones, Campaign: "The Coke Hug Machine"
Comfort
DHL
Dyson
Empire Shopping Gallery
Faber-Castell Campaign: "Don't Miss A Word", Campaign: "The Scream,Terrace Cafe at Night"
Google Campaign: "Chrome Experiment Ramayana"
Green Volunteers Campaign: "Generation Fight Back"
IBM Campaign: "60/60 Exhibit"
International Coastal Cleanup Campaign: "Seafood Tanks"
Mattel Matchbox
Nestle Campaign: "Less Planning, More Playing"
Nhip Cau Dau Tu Campaign: "Box Cutters"
Otsuka Pharmaceutical SOYJOY; 2008
Philips Air Fryer
Prudential
Sea Shepherd Campaign: "Tuna"
Shell Global Solutions

SilkAir PR
Singapore Telecommunications Limited
New-Toys "R" Us Tasks for Toys
New-Twitter
Yum Foods Campaign: "Flame Grilled"

Ogilvy & Mather (Singapore) Pvt. Ltd.

The Ogilvy Centre 35 Robinson Rd 03-01, Singapore, 068876 Singapore
Tel.: (65) 6213 7899
Fax: (65) 6213 7980
E-Mail: andrew.thomas@ogilvy.com
Web Site: www.ogilvy.com

Chris Riley *(Grp Chm)*
Jia Ying Goh *(Sr Dir-Art-Global)*
Sarah Guldin *(Dir-Corp Comm)*
Rachel Koh *(Dir-Creative Svcs)*
John-John Skoog *(Dir-Art)*
Pei Ling Ho *(Sr Copywriter-Global)*

Accounts:
BMW Asia Advertising, Digital Communication
Castrol Castrol Magnatec, Digital, OOH, Print
Coca-Cola Campaign: "Hug Machine", Campaign: "When you Open a Coke You Open Happiness", Hacked Coke Bottle, Happiness From the Skies
The Economist
Eu Yan Sang
Faber Castell Artist's Pen, The Thank You Project
Global Alliance Awareness, Donation Appeal
Global Retweet
KFC Singapore (Agency of Record) Campaign: "Heat-Seekers", Communications, Online, Print, Red Hot chicken
National Heritage Board PR, Singapore Art Museum
New-National Productivity Council Creative
Nike Brand Promotion
Photolibrary
Prudential
Sea Shepherd
SingTel Creative, Digital, In-Store, Mobile, Online, Print, Social Media, TV
Unilever Phone Cleaner
WWF

OgilvyOne Worldwide

35 Robinson Road #03-01, The Ogilvy Centre, Singapore, 068876 Singapore
Tel.: (65) 6213 7899
Fax: (65) 6213 7980
Web Site: www.ogilvy.com

Year Founded: 1985

Agency Specializes In: Direct Response Marketing

Oscar Prats *(Mng Dir)*
Jerry Smith *(Pres-Asia Pacific)*
William Adeney *(VP-Mktg Analytics-Asia Pacific)*
Grace Tan *(Grp Head-Creative)*
Melvyn Lim *(Exec Dir-Creative)*
Catherine Chow *(Dir-Art)*
Andrey Danilov *(Dir-Art)*
Rebecca Kao *(Dir-Mktg Analytics)*
Shawnn Lai *(Dir-Creative)*
Diana Lee *(Dir-Art)*
Xander Lee *(Dir-Creative)*
Sean Liu *(Dir-Art)*

Accounts:
Cisco Systems Lifestyle Marketing
Levi's Asia Pacific Copper Jeans
SingTel
Verticurl

Taiwan:

Ogilvy & Mather Advertising

90 Song Ren Rd, 110 Taipei, Taiwan
Tel.: (886) 2 2758 8686
Fax: (886) 2 2758 6363
E-Mail: danielgh.lee@ogilvy.com
Web Site: www.ogilvy.com.tw

E-Mail for Key Personnel:
President: danielgh.lee@ogilvy.com

Accounts:
7-ELEVEN Campaign: "Telephone Booth"
BP
British American Tobacco
Cathay Life Insurance Creative
Cisco Systems
Diageo Creative, Singleton Whisky
Far East Tone
Franz China Collection
Gillette
Home Era Campaign: "Burning Stamp"
IBM
Intel
Kimberly-Clark Taiwan
Kraft
Mercedes-Benz Taiwan "Old-for-New" Promotion, 120th Anniversary
Minute Maid Campaign: "Big Pulp Theme Park"
Philips Campaign: "Augmented Reality Mugs"
PX Mart Campaign: "Pic Your Food"
Rolex
Ta Chong Bank Campaign: "Dream Ranger"
Taiwan High Speed Rail Campaign: "My Pocket Adventure"
TC Bank Campaign: "Tree of Life"
UWT
Yahoo; Taipei, Taiwan (Agency of Record) Campaign: "Tell your Local Story with Yahoo! Search"

Ogilvy Public Relations

90 Song Ren Road, Hsin Yi Dist, Taipei, 110 ROC Taiwan
Tel.: (886) 2 2758 8686
Fax: (886) 2 2758 8144
E-Mail: fupei.wang@ogilvy.com
Web Site: www.ogilvy.com

Employees: 50

Abby Hsieh *(Mng Dir)*
Fupei Wang *(Mng Dir)*
Freda Wan *(Grp Acct Dir)*
Kelly Chen *(Acct Mgr)*
Maggie Chien *(Acct Mgr)*
Angela Hsu *(Acct Mgr)*
Bernice Chen *(Sr Acct Exec)*
Emily Yi Lin Liu *(Sr Acct Exec)*
Grace Lin *(Assoc Acct Dir)*

Accounts:
Taipei Fubon Commercial Bank
Taipei World Trade Center

OgilvyOne Worldwide

3F 89 Song Ren Road, Taipei, 110 ROC Taiwan
Tel.: (886) 2 7745 1688
Web Site: www.ogilvy.com

Year Founded: 1989

Agency Specializes In: Direct Response Marketing

Eric Chang *(Mng Dir)*
Michael Wang *(VP)*
Veronica Kuo *(Grp Acct Dir)*
Edwardth Fan *(Acct Dir)*
Joyce Shih *(Acct Dir)*
Bell Hou *(Acct Mgr)*
Linda Lee *(Acct Exec)*
Frank Chu *(Assoc Acct Dir)*

Thailand:

Ogilvy & Mather Advertising

14th Flr The Offices at Centralworld 999/9 Rama 1 Rd, Patumwan, Bangkok, 10330 Thailand
Tel.: (66) 2 205 6000
Fax: (66) 2 205 6007
Web Site: www.ogilvy.com

Punnee Chaiyakul *(Chm)*
Phawit Chitrakorn *(Mng Dir)*
Nopadol Srikieatikajohn *(Chief Creative Officer & Art Dir)*
Taewit Jariyanukulpan *(Dir-Creative)*
Krai Kittikorn *(Dir-Creative)*
Torpun Lersin *(Dir-Creative)*
Pat Santaya Saralak *(Dir-Creative)*
Komson Yamshuen *(Dir-Art)*
Puripong Limwanatipong *(Assoc Dir-Creative)*

Accounts:
3M Nexcare Water Proof Bandages
A-Time Traveller Campaign: "Singing Whale"
Accident Prevention Network Campaign: "Speed Kills"
American Express
Amway Campaign: "Flying Book"
Asgatec Electric Leaf Blower LS 2503
Bangkok Hospital
Bug Master Co.
Car Cosmetic Co.
Coca-Cola Refreshments USA, Inc.
DHL
DK Health Product Campaign: "History"
Doggie Do Co.
Don't Drive Drunk Foundation Campaign: "Beer"
Dr. Miang Mental Maths Campaign: "Kidculators"
Dutch Mill Campaign: "D-Plus SUPERWOMAN", Pasteurize
Efficient English Services Campaign: "Nowhere to Run"
Ford
Foundation For Children
Glister Toothpaste
Hanyi Chinese School Campaign: "Flirt"
HHK Intertrade
IBM
Interflora Thailand Co. Campaign: "Therapy"
JBL SFX
The J.C.C. Campaign: "Cut to Build"
Karana Travelgear
Karshine Rain-Off
KFC Special Store Campaign: "We Hear Every Dream"
LA Bicycle
Lamptan
M2F Newspaper
Master Trap
Motorola Solutions, Inc.
Mr. Curtain Campaign: "Bedroom", Campaign: "Keep your privacy"
Nature Gift 711 Ltd Campaign: "Call Her"
Nestle
Nike
Olfa Cutter Campaign: "Cut to Build"
Outdoor Innovation
Pacific Corporation Company Campaign: "Worst Wishes"
PEST Control Service Campaign: "Family Tree: Ant"
Pet Diary Co.
Poly-Brite Campaign: "Super Absorbent"
Real Move Co Ltd
Red Bull Beverage
SGD Inter Trading Campaign: "Carpark"
Shera Sound Proof Windows
Siam City Concrete Co.,Ltd. Campaign: "Take a Side"
Super Rich 1965 Co. Bank Note
T-Holding Co. Campaign: "Cat's Slave"
Thai Health Promotion Foundation Campaign: "Smoking Kid"
Thai Life Insurance Co. Campaign: "Garbage Man", Campaign: "Silence of Love", Campaign:

"Street Concert", Campaign: "Unsung Hero"
Thai Olympic Fiber Cement Co.
ThaiCraft Campaign: "Handicraft Qr Code"
TrueMove Campaign: "Giving"
Uni-President
Uni - Top Trading Campaign: "Stained Drain - Teacup"
Venus Technology Campaign: "Fatal Attraction"
Wematch Consulting Campaign: "I Quit You"
WWF Thailand Campaign: "Forests For Life"

OgilvyInteractive
14th Fl The Offices at Centralworld 999/9 Rama 1 Rd, Patumwan, Bangkok, 10330 Thailand
Tel.: (66) 2 205 6000
Web Site: www.ogilvy.com

Agency Specializes In: Digital/Interactive

Kent Wertime *(Pres-Ogilvy Japan & COO-Ogilvy Asia)*

Vietnam:

Ogilvy & Mather (Vietnam) Ltd.
Centec Tower 12th Floor 72-74 Nguyen Thi Minh Khai Street, District 3, Ho Chi Minh City, Vietnam
Tel.: (84) 8 3821 9529
Fax: (84) 8 821 9549
E-Mail: trongduc.nguyen@ogilvy.com
Web Site: www.ogilvy.com

Nguyen Trong Duc *(COO)*
Todd McCracken *(Chief Creative Officer)*
Juggi Ramakrishnan *(Exec Dir-Creative)*
Tien Bac *(Dir-Creative)*
Joe Harris *(Dir-Art)*
Hoang Sa Nguyen *(Dir-Art)*
Geoff Francis *(Designer)*

Accounts:
Castrol Campaign: "Ferrari"
The Economist Campaign: "Signs"
Gambrinus
Global Alliance Asia-Pacific
HeartBeat Vietnam
The Lien Foundation
The Life Foundation campaign: "Stop The Gendercide"
Megastar Cineplex Campaign: "King Kong"
Nhip Cau Dau Tu Campaign: "Barber"
The Samaritans
Sony Bravia, Cyber-shot, PlayStation
Tamiya
Thien Long

Cote d'Ivoire

Ocean Ogilvy
(Formerly Ocean One)
Avenue C16 Jean Mermoz Villa n66, 01 BP 7759, Abidjan, 01 Cote d'Ivoire
Tel.: (225) 22 40 41 70
Fax: (225) 22 48 78 60
Web Site: www.oceanogilvy.com

Year Founded: 2000

Pascal Ntwali Lurhakumbira *(Grp Head-Creative & Dir-Art)*
Vincent Mwepu Makasa *(Gen Mgr)*
Gladys Francillette *(Dir-Sls-Ivory Coast)*
Solomon A. Samake *(Dir-Creative)*
Eric Tarrero *(Dir-Creative)*
Ivoire Studer *(Jr Brand Mgr)*
M'Boke Nehemie *(Mgr-Online Media)*
Marcel Nze *(Mgr-Media Grp)*

Egypt:

MEMAC Ogilvy
4 Abdel Rahman El Rafei St Mohandessin, Cairo, Egypt
Tel.: (20) 2 748 0202
Fax: (20) 2 748 7236
Web Site: www.memacogilvy.com

Year Founded: 1983

Georges Aoun *(Mng Dir)*
Ossama El-kaoukji *(Chief Creative Officer)*
Mohsen Farid *(Acct Dir-Adv Discipline)*
Nicolas Courant *(Dir-Creative)*
Tarek Lasheen *(Dir-PR)*
Noha Rashid *(Acct Mgr)*

Accounts:
Brand Collective
Cinefeel Campaign: "Armed Robbery in a DVD store"
GOLDEN BOWLING
Reynolds Campaign: "Reynolds Markkit Digital Highlighter"
Rotana Creative, Rotana Cinema, Rotana Masriya
Tavegyl Campaign: "Sleeping with Allergy"

Kenya:

Ogilvy & Mather (Eastern Africa) Ltd.
3rd Fl CVS Plaza Kasuku Road Lenana Road, PO Box 30280, Nairobi, 00100 Kenya
Tel.: (254) 20 271 7750
E-Mail: info@ogilvy.co.ke

Year Founded: 1971

Agency Specializes In: Direct Response Marketing, Publicity/Promotions

Eric Ndavi *(Creative Dir)*
Greg Aldous *(Dir-Creative-Ogilvy & Mather Africa)*
Till Aurousseau *(Dir-Creative)*
Coltan de Save *(Dir-Creative)*
Eunice Gachugu *(Acct Mgr)*
Golda Orwa *(Acct Mgr)*
Irene Wahome *(Mgr-Projects)*
Ben Hunt *(Copywriter)*

Accounts:
Bajaj Auto
Brand Kenya
Coca-Cola Refreshments USA, Inc. Sprite
East African Wildlife Society
Kenyatta International Conference Centre
National Hospital Insurance Fund

Mauritius:

Maurice Publicite Ltd.
5th Fl Cerne House Chaussee St, Port Louis, Mauritius
Tel.: (230) 212 0844
Fax: (230) 212 6276
E-Mail: maupub@intnet.mu
Web Site: www.maupub.com

Employees: 32

Jean Jacques De Robillard *(Mng Dir)*
Maggy Maurel *(Deputy Mng Dir)*
Geraldine Neubert *(Dir)*

Accounts:
IBL Foundation
Mimil Pet Food
Oeudor Ltd.
Thon Tropical

Mozambique:

Ogilvy Mozambique
17 Avenue Agostinho Neto, Maputo, Mozambique
Tel.: (258) 21 490 674
Fax: (258) 21 492 493
E-Mail: ogilvy@ogilvy.co.mz
Web Site: www.ogilvyafrica.com

Employees: 17

Joao dos Santos *(CEO)*
Fernanda Barrento *(Mng Dir)*
Miguel Rego *(Dir-Creative)*
Ines Barbosa *(Acct Mgr-Brand Activation & Events)*

South Africa:

Gloo Design Agency
30 Chiappini Street 3rd Floor, Cape Town, Waterkant 8001 South Africa
Tel.: (27) 214800633
Fax: (27) 214800685
Web Site: www.gloo.co.za

Year Founded: 2005

Agency Specializes In: Digital/Interactive, Internet/Web Design, Media Relations, Public Relations, Strategic Planning/Research

Sean Donnelly *(Grp Mng Dir)*
Paula Hulley *(Deputy Mng Dir)*
Adam Brandt *(Exec Dir-Creative)*
Dallas Du Toit *(Exec Dir-Creative)*
Gregory King *(Dir-Creative)*
Michael Pauls *(Dir-Creative)*
Neill Pretorius *(Dir-Creative)*
Anneke Jacobs *(Copywriter)*
Tiffany Morris *(Copywriter)*

Accounts:
AFB Online Communications
Allan Gray Limited Financial Service Providers
Castle Lager Beer Mfr
Mini Car Dealers
On Digital Media Television Network Services
PUMA Sportswear & Lifestyle Products Mfr & Retailer
SABMiller Africa Castle Milk Stout (Digital Agency of Record)
SAMSUNG Computers & Electronics Mfr
South African Tourism Tour & Travel Agency Services
Virgin Active Online
Yum Brands, Inc.

Go Advertising
The Brand Building 15 Sloane St, Bryanston, Johannesburg, 2021 South Africa
Tel.: (27) 11 709 6986
Fax: (27) 11 709 6985
E-Mail: keith.groves@ogilvy.co.za
Web Site: www.ogilvygo.co.za

Employees: 32

Agency Specializes In: Retail

Keith Groves *(Mng Dir)*
Cindy Rowles *(Acct Dir)*
Charlene Willson *(Acct Dir)*
Rebecca Singh *(Dir-Fin)*
John Fourie *(Client Svc Dir)*

Accounts:
Home Corp.
Ultra Liquors

Ogilvy & Mather South Africa (Pty.) Ltd.
The Brand Building 15 Sloane Street, Bryanston, Johannesburg, South Africa
Mailing Address:
Private Bag x33, Bryanston, 2021 South Africa
Tel.: (27) 11 709 6600
Fax: (27) 11 700 3049
Web Site: www.ogilvy.co.za

E-Mail for Key Personnel:
Creative Dir.: mark.fisher@ogilvy.co.za

Employees: 350
Year Founded: 2000

Matthew Barnes *(Exec Creative Dir)*
Mariana OKelly *(Exec Dir-Creative)*
Georja Romano *(Art Dir)*
Larissa Elliott *(Dir-Art)*
Peter Little *(Dir-Creative)*
Stefan Siedentopf *(Dir-Integrated Strategy)*
Mark Zeller *(Mgr-Mktg & Comm)*
Jedd McNeilage *(Sr Designer)*
Justin Oswald *(Copywriter)*

Accounts:
New-Allan Gray
Cadbury Dairy Milk
DSTV (Nat Geo Wild) Camera, Purse, Shoes
East African Wildlife Society
Facebook
KFC
Kimberly-Clark Worldwide, Inc.
New-MultiChoice
Philips Campaign: "It Looks Bigger", Philips Bodygroom for Men
New-SAB Castle Lite
Suntory Lucozade
T. Santamaria
New-Vodacom
Volkswagen AG Touareg
Yum Brands

Ogilvy Cape Town
41 Sir Lowry Road, Woodstock, Cape Town, 8000 South Africa
Tel.: (27) 21 467 1000
Fax: (27) 21 467 1001
E-Mail: capetown@ogilvy.co.za
Web Site: www.ogilvy.co.za

Employees: 208
Year Founded: 1976

Agency Specializes In: Consumer Marketing, Direct Response Marketing, Retail

Luca Gallarelli *(Mng Dir)*
Greg Tebbutt *(Grp Mng Dir)*
Sergio Lacueva *(Creative Dir)*
Iris Vinnicombe *(Head-Production)*
Chris Gotz *(Exec Dir-Creative)*
Tseliso Rangaka *(Exec Creative Dir)*
Nicholas Wittenberg *(Exec Dir-Creative-Digital Portfolio)*
Ryan Amory *(Acct Dir)*
Monique Kaplan *(Art Dir)*
Tania Barker *(Dir-Creative)*
Benjamin de Villiers *(Dir-Art)*
Jacques Massardo *(Dir-Creative)*
Katie Mylrea *(Dir-Art)*
Reijer Van Der Vlugt *(Dir-Art)*
Matthew Blitz *(Mgr-Creative Content-Ogilvy PR)*
Lauren Baker *(Acct Exec)*
Jonathan Reid-Ross *(Acct Exec)*
Logan Broadley *(Copywriter)*
Nicholas Mills *(Designer)*
Justin Osburn *(Copywriter)*
Oskar Petty *(Copywriter)*
Taryn Sher *(Copywriter)*
Neil white *(Copywriter)*

Accounts:
New-Allan Gray Campaign: "The Letter", Television Commercial
American Swiss
Audi South Africa Campaign: "#AudiA3Exchange"
BATSA
BP Southern Africa
Cadbury Stimorol Infinity
Cape Town Tourism
Car Magazine
Careers 24
Castrol
Clorets
Coca-Cola
Dentyne
District Six Museum
Halls Campaign: "Wire Car"
Heinz South Africa Campaign: "Coming of Age", Heinz Crispy Pocketz, Todays Brands, Wellington Sauce Brands
Jeweller American Swiss
Mondelez International, Inc. Campaign: "Face off", Campaign: "Stimorol Mega Mystery", Stimorol Infinity Gum, Stimorol Sensations
Multichoice DSTV
MWEB
National Sea Rescue Institute Campaign: "Names", Campaign: "Sea Fever", Campaign: "We can't do it alone"
Omnico
PBN Campaign: "Rehabilitation is Possible"
SAB Miller Campaign: "Carling Black Label Cup", Castle Lite
Sea Rescue
South African Breweries Campaign: "Be the Coach", Carling Black Label, Castle Lite
Stimorol Air Rush Campaign: "Gum", Campaign: "I believe I can fly"
Sun International
Sunday Times The Times
Unilever
Volkswagen Group of America, Inc. "Volkswagen Golf R: Terminal Velocity", Amarok, Bluemotion, Campaign: "Eat the Road", Campaign: "Fire Truck", Campaign: "Glass-half-full", Campaign: "Just Because it Works Doesn't Mean it's Fixed", Campaign: "Moments", Campaign: "New Tiguan Explorer Tab", Campaign: "Polo GTI: Date Drive", Campaign: "Turns Post Box Into Recycling Bin", Citi Golf, Crafter, Edible Print, Golf, Golf R, Jetta, Polo, Print Ad, Street Quest, Vivo Launch, Volkswagen Genuine Parts, Volkswagen Touareg
WWF

Ogilvy Healthworld
The Brand Building 15 Sloane Street, Bryanston, Johannesburg, 2152 South Africa
Mailing Address:
The Brand Building 15 Sloane Street, Private Bag x33, Bryanston, 2021 South Africa
Tel.: (27) 11 709 9600
Fax: (27) 11 700 3009
E-Mail: gillian.bridger@ogilvy.co.za
Web Site: www.ogilvy.co.za

Employees: 18
Year Founded: 2000

Agency Specializes In: Advertising, Health Care Services, Pharmaceutical

Gillian Bridger *(Mng Dir)*

Accounts:
Bayer
Janssen-Cilag
Johnson & Johnson
Nestle
Novartis
Nycomed
Pfizer
Reckitt Benckiser
Roche
Sanofi-Synthelabo

Ogilvy Johannesburg (Pty.) Ltd.
The Brand Building 15 Sloane Street, Bryanston, 2152 Johannesburg, 2021 South Africa
Mailing Address:
Private Bag x33, Bryanston, 2021 South Africa
Tel.: (27) 11 709 66 00
Fax: (27) 21 700 3000
E-Mail: julian.ribiero@ogilvy.co.za
Web Site: www.ogilvy.co.za

Employees: 200
Year Founded: 1976

Agency Specializes In: Above-the-Line, Advertising, Advertising Specialties, Affluent Market, Alternative Advertising, Below-the-Line, Bilingual Market, Brand Development & Integration, Branded Entertainment, Business-To-Business, Children's Market, Co-op Advertising, Communications, Corporate Communications, Crisis Communications, Customer Relationship Management, Digital/Interactive, Direct Response Marketing, E-Commerce, Event Planning & Marketing, Identity Marketing, Infomercials, Integrated Marketing, Local Marketing, Mobile Marketing, Point of Purchase, Point of Sale, Print, Promotions, Public Relations, Publicity/Promotions, Social Marketing/Nonprofit, Strategic Planning/Research, Technical Advertising, Viral/Buzz/Word of Mouth

Neo Makhele *(Grp Dir-Strategy)*
Sharleen James *(Acct Dir-Mgmt)*
Robyn Bergmann *(Dir-Creative)*
Bridget Johnson *(Dir-Creative)*
Graham Lamont *(Dir-Creative)*
Mike Martin *(Dir-Creative)*
Irene Styger *(Copywriter)*

Accounts:
AIDS Foundation Fundraising
And Beyond Safaris
Audi Campaign: "Audi Xenon Plus Headlights", Riot
Bookdealers Campaign: "Bookdealers Eyes"
Bose
Business Connexion It Solutions
Castle Lager
Coca-Cola Refreshments USA, Inc. Fanta, Sprite
Greenpeace Environmental, Victoria Radio Series
Harley Davidson
KFC (Kentucky Fried Chicken) Campaign: "Add Hope", Campaign: "Man 1 Rest of the World 0", Campaign: "Old Couple", Campaign: "So Good"
KykNET
MacMillan Campaign: "The Fear - The Last Days of Robert Mugabe"
MNET Campaign: "My Life As A Movie"
Mondelez International, Inc.
Cadbury South Africa Bournville, Dairy Milk, Lunch Bar
Motorola Solutions, Inc.
Multichoice Campaign: "Frozen Faces", Campaign: "Life By Design", Campaign: "MK is 1", Campaign: "MK is", Campaign: "Nothing's Put On", DStv, M-Net HD Channel
Nestle
Pfizer SA
POWA Neighbours
SA Tourism
SAT
Sun International
The Topsy Foundation Selinah

OgilvyInteractive
41 Sir Lowry Road, PO Box 1142, Woodstock, Cape Town, 8000 South Africa
Tel.: (27) 21 467 1000
Fax: (27) 21 467 1401

E-Mail: oglivy@ogilvy.co.za
Web Site: www.ogilvy.com

Year Founded: 1997

Agency Specializes In: Digital/Interactive, E-Commerce, Internet/Web Design, Web (Banner Ads, Pop-ups, etc.)

Patou Nuytemans *(Chief Digital Officer-EAME)*
Chris Gotz *(Exec Dir-Creative)*

Accounts:
Stimorol Sensations
Volkswagen Golf Campaign: "The Answer", Polo Vivo

OgilvyOne Worldwide-Cape Town
41 Sir Lowry Road, Woodstock, Cape Town, 8000 South Africa
Mailing Address:
PO Box 2653, Cape Town, 8000 South Africa
Tel.: (27) 21 467 1000
Fax: (27) 21 467 1101
Web Site: www.ogilvy.co.za

Employees: 220
Year Founded: 1985

Agency Specializes In: Consumer Marketing, Customer Relationship Management, Digital/Interactive, Direct Response Marketing

Shelley Waterhouse *(Mng Partner & Head-OgilvyOne Johannesburg)*
Benedict Evans *(Mng Dir-Digital Portfolio)*
Chris Gotz *(Exec Dir-Creative)*
Kurt Paulse *(Producer-Digital)*
Taryn Coetzee *(Dir-Ops)*

Accounts:
AVIS
Castrol
DStv
KFC
Sprite Zero

ZOOM Advertising
The District 41 Sir Lowry Rd, Woodstock, Cape Town, 8001 South Africa
Tel.: (27) 21 467 1400
Fax: (27) 21 467 1401
E-Mail: stevem@zoomadvertising.co.za
Web Site: www.zoomadvertising.co.za

Year Founded: 1998

Steve Massey *(Mng Dir-Zoom Adv South Africa)*
Deon Robbertze *(Exec Dir-Creative-Zoom & Dir-Creative-Ogilvy Earth)*
Nina Daniel-Gruber *(Exec Dir-Creative)*
Martin Frank *(Exec Dir-Creative)*
Rob Hill *(Grp Dir-Plng-Ogilvy South Africa)*
Sam Maunders *(Bus Dir-Zoom Ad Africa)*
Karen Burns *(Dir-Creative & Design)*
Eastwood Loftus *(Dir-Fin-Zoom Ad Africa)*

Accounts:
BATSA
Cashbuild
The Crazy Store
Delhiem
Hardware Warehouse
Jordan
Namaqua Wines
Outdoor Warehouse
PEP Stores
Sportsman Warehouse
SuperMax

Bahrain:

MEMAC Ogilvy & Mather W.L.L.
Offices 3501 3502 3503 3504 Almoayyed Tower Building 2504, Road 2382 Al Seef District, Manama, 428 Bahrain
Mailing Address:
PO Box 2140, Manama, Bahrain
Tel.: (973) 17 561756
Fax: (973) 17 578757
E-Mail: memacbh@batelco.com.bh
Web Site: www.memacogilvy.com

Employees: 40
Year Founded: 1984

Edmond I. Moutran *(Founder)*
Samar AbdelHuq *(Acct Dir)*
Mustafa Ozkaya *(Acct Dir)*
Pooja Rekhi Sharma *(Sr Mgr-PR)*
Fadi Khouri *(Acct Mgr)*
Tarek Shawki *(Reg Grp Acct Dir)*

Accounts:
American Express
Coca-Cola Sprite
Grohe
Sawa Mninjah
UN Women Campaign: "#Womenshould"
VIVA Media

Kuwait:

MEMAC Ogilvy
Future Trade Zone Shuwaikh Al Argan Building Block A 1st Floor, Safat, Kuwait, Kuwait
Mailing Address:
PO Box 27216, Safat, Kuwait, 13133 Kuwait
Tel.: (965) 461 0371
Fax: (965) 4610 376
E-Mail: nabil.touma@ogilvy.com
Web Site: www.memacogilvy.com

Year Founded: 1991

Edmond Moutran *(Chm & CEO)*
Ossama El-Kaoukji *(Chief Creative Officer)*
Nabil Touma *(Mng Dir-Kuwait)*
Ben Knight *(Exec Dir-Creative)*
Nadim Ghobril *(Grp Dir-IT)*
Eli Bouchaaya *(Dir-Creative)*
George Laham *(Reg Mng Dir-Levant & North Africa)*

Accounts:
Al Rajhi Bank
American Express
Arab Insurance Group
Arqaam Capital
Burgan Bank
Bvlgari
DIFC
Kuwait Petroleum Company
Motorola Solutions, Inc.
Nokia Nokia N9
Rothmans

Lebanon:

MEMAC Ogilvy
Rizkallah & Boutrous Centre Futuroscope Roundabout 8th Floor, Sin-El-Fil, Beirut, Lebanon
Tel.: (961) 1 486 065
Fax: (961) 1 486 064
Web Site: www.memacogilvy.com

Employees: 45
Year Founded: 1994

Naji Boulos *(Mng Dir-Lebanon)*
Moe Minkara *(Exec Dir-Creative-Beirut)*
Malek Badreddine *(Copywriter-Ogilvy & Mather)*

Accounts:
Concord
Grohe Middle East & Africa Public Relations
Lebanese Autism Society Campaign: "Read Autism From A Different Angle"
LG
Lotus Cars
Nissan Campaign: "Suggest an Arrest"

Pakistan:

Ogilvy & Mather
94 Jinnah Cooperative Housing Society, Block 7/8 Tipu Sultan Rd, Karachi, 75350 Pakistan
Tel.: (92) 21 438 9054
Fax: (92) 21 438 9051
Web Site: www.ogilvy.com

Agha Azfar *(CEO)*
Arshad Aslam *(Exec Dir-Creative)*
Zehra Zaidi *(Exec Dir-Creative)*
Zuhair Muhammad *(Grp Acct Dir)*
Abdul Saboor *(Grp Acct Dir)*
Hassan Bangash *(Acct Dir)*
Raheel Hashmi *(Acct Dir)*
Muzakir Ijaz *(Dir-Bus)*
Shazia Khan *(Dir-Plng)*
Zahra Khan *(Assoc Dir-Creative)*
Saadain Lari *(Sr Acct Mgr)*
Maryam Zaeem *(Acct Mgr)*
Usman Asad *(Grp Acct Mgr)*

United Arab Emirates:

MEMAC Ogilvy
Al-Attar Business Tower 24th Fl Sheikh Zayed Rd, PO Box 74170, Dubai, United Arab Emirates
Tel.: (971) 4 3320 002
Fax: (971) 4 3320 003
E-Mail: ronald.howes@ogilvy.com
Web Site: www.memacogilvy.com

Employees: 180
Year Founded: 1987

Edmond I. Moutran *(Chm & CEO)*
Ronald Howes *(Mng Dir)*
Paul Shearer *(Chief Creative Officer)*
Ramzi Moutran *(Exec Creative Dir)*
Paul Smith *(Reg Dir-Creative-Ogilvy & Mather)*
Gary Rolf *(Dir-Art)*
Logan Allanson *(Assoc Dir-Creative)*
Tarek Shawki *(Reg Grp Acct Dir-Memac Ogilvy & Mather-Dubai)*

Accounts:
Adhari Park
Aloha Tuna Campaign: "Feeding Frenzy"
Arab Bank
BP Visco
Coca-Cola Campaign "Cricket Stars", Campaign: "Social Media Guard", Open Up, It's Ramadan, Sprite
Dubai Metro
Dubal
Engagement Citoyen Campaign: "The Return of Dictator Ben Ali"
Golf Digest
Greenpeace
Huawei Technologies
IKEA Campaign: "The Smallest Ikea Store"
New-KAFA Campaign: "Driving Change"
The King Khalid Foundation
National Trading & Developing Campaign: "Fragrance Of Power"
Orbit Showtime Network Sky News HD
Organisation Sawamninjah Creative, Rescue Radio
PlayStation3

Portfolio Night 8 Dubai
Reporters Without Borders Campaign: "Pixelated Truth"
Sawamninjah Campaign: "Rescue Radio"
Tamweel
Trio Time
UN Women Campaign: "Auto-Complete Truth"
Volkswagen Group of America, Inc. Campaign: "Hijacked Rear View Camera", Polo, Touareg
Volvo

OgilvyOne Middle East
Al Attar Business Tower 24th Floor, PO Box 14854, Sheikh Zayed Road, Dubai, United Arab Emirates
Tel.: (971) 4 3327555
Fax: (971) 4 332 8666
E-Mail: nabil.moutran@ogilvy.com
Web Site: www.memacogilvy.com

Employees: 150

Agency Specializes In: Direct Response Marketing

Fahad Osman *(Bus Dir)*
Sally Tambourgi *(Dir-Creative)*
Louise Bolo *(Copywriter)*

Accounts:
The Coca-Cola Company Campaign: "Fanta: World's First Tastable Print Ad", Edible Advertising, Fanta, Minalakhir, Print, Sprite
KAFA
RSA Car Insurance Interactive Print Ad
Unilever N.V.

OGILVY COMMONHEALTH INTERACTIVE MARKETING
430 Interpace Pkwy, Parsippany, NJ 07054
Tel.: (973) 352-1400
Fax: (973) 352-1210
Web Site: www.ogilvychww.com/

Year Founded: 2004

Agency Specializes In: Advertising

Matt Balogh *(CTO)*
Nelson Figueiredo *(VP & Assoc Dir-Tech)*
Gabriela Lardieri *(Sr Acct Exec)*

Accounts:
Ariad
Bristol-Myers Squibb
Novartis
Ortho Biotech
Ortho-McNeil
Pfizer

OGILVY COMMONHEALTH MEDICAL EDUCATION
402 Interpace Pkwy Bldg B, Parsippany, NJ 07054
Tel.: (973) 352-2000
Fax: (973) 352-1160
Web Site: www.ogilvychww.com/

Year Founded: 1971

Agency Specializes In: Advertising, Education

Denise Israel *(Mng Dir)*
Gloria Gibbons *(Pres-EAME)*
Steven Stockton *(Assoc Dir-Medical)*
Meg Mulholland *(Sr Acct Exec)*
Jessica Remo *(Sr Acct Exec)*
Lisa Vonblohn *(Sr Acct Exec)*
Libby Werner *(Sr Acct Exec)*
Jessica Poracky *(Acct Exec)*
Kate Brooks *(Asst Acct Exec)*

Accounts:
Allergan
LifeScan
Ortho-McNeil
Ortho-McNeil Neurologics
PriCara
Shire Pharmaceuticals

OGILVY COMMONHEALTH PAYER MARKETING
422 Interpace Pkwy, Parsippany, NJ 07054
Tel.: (973) 352-1800
Fax: (973) 352-1220
Web Site: www.ogilvychww.com/

Employees: 32

Agency Specializes In: Advertising

Michael Zilligen *(Pres)*
Rich Trezza *(Pres-Payer Mktg & Gen Mgr-Payer Mktg)*
Michele Andrews *(Exec VP-Strategy)*
Courtney Kober *(Acct Supvr)*
Meg Mulholland *(Sr Acct Exec)*
Lisa Vonblohn *(Sr Acct Exec)*
Libby Werner *(Sr Acct Exec)*
Samantha Emmerling *(Acct Exec)*
Jessica Poracky *(Acct Exec)*
Jessica Remo *(Acct Exec)*
Claire Pisano *(Assoc Supvr-Acct Grp)*

Accounts:
AstraZeneca
Genentech
Novartis
Novartis Consumer Health
Reckitt Benckiser

OGILVY COMMONHEALTH SPECIALTY MARKETING
444 Interpace Pkwy Bld B, Parsippany, NJ 07054
Tel.: (973) 352-4100
Fax: (973) 352-1500
Web Site: www.ogilvychww.com/

Year Founded: 2005

Agency Specializes In: Advertising

Jigna Baranello *(VP & Supvr-Acct Grp)*
Amy Graham *(Gen Mgr)*

Accounts:
Antigenics
Ariad Pharmaceuticals
AstraZeneca
Bayer
Genta Corporation
Johnson & Johnson Vision Care
Ortho Biotech Products, LP
PGSM

OGILVY COMMONHEALTH WELLNESS MARKETING
(Formerly Ogilvy Commonhealth Consumer Care)
424 Interpace Pkwy, Parsippany, NJ 07054
Tel.: (973) 352-1000
Fax: (973) 352-1270
Web Site: www.ogilvychww.com/

Year Founded: 1993

Agency Specializes In: Advertising, Pharmaceutical

Darlene Depalma Dobry *(Mng Partner)*
Shaun Urban *(Mng Partner)*
Marc Weiner *(Mng Partner)*
Catherine Goss *(Mng Dir & Sr VP)*
Nora Tsivgas *(Sr VP & Client Svcs Dir)*
Michele Moss *(Sr VP & Dir-Creative)*
Stephen Lubiak *(Sr VP)*
Clare Litz *(VP & Assoc Dir-Creative)*
Rich Adams *(Acct Dir)*
J. P. Maranzani *(Acct Grp Supvr)*
Courtney Kober *(Acct Supvr)*

Accounts:
AstraZeneca
Genentech

OGILVY COMMONHEALTH WORLDWIDE
400 Interpace Pkwy, Parsippany, NJ 07054
Tel.: (973) 352-1000
Fax: (973) 884-2487
Web Site: https://ogilvychww.com/

Year Founded: 1992

National Agency Associations: 4A's

Agency Specializes In: Advertising, Alternative Advertising, Brand Development & Integration, Business-To-Business, Collateral, Communications, Consumer Marketing, Corporate Identity, Customer Relationship Management, Digital/Interactive, Direct Response Marketing, Direct-to-Consumer, Electronic Media, Environmental, Health Care Services, Identity Marketing, Integrated Marketing, Market Research, Media Buying Services, Media Planning, Medical Products, New Product Development, Pharmaceutical, Planning & Consultation, Publicity/Promotions, Sponsorship, Strategic Planning/Research, Sweepstakes, Web (Banner Ads, Pop-ups, etc.)

Catherine Goss *(Mng Dir & Sr VP)*
Robert Saporito *(CFO)*
Chris Andrews *(CIO)*
Scott Watson *(Chief Creative Officer & Exec VP)*
Ritesh Patel *(Chief Digital Officer & Exec VP)*
Katie Piette *(CEO-Paris & Dir-Global Brand Mgmt Worldwide)*
Ross Thomson *(Exec VP & Dir-Creative)*
Nancy Barlow *(Exec VP-Acct Mgmt)*
Meredith Levy *(Sr VP & Mgmt Supvr-Medical Mktg)*
Robert Velasco *(Sr VP & Mgmt Supvr)*
David Danilowicz *(Sr VP & Dir-Creative & UX)*
Elizabeth Paulino *(Sr VP & Dir-Comm & PR)*
Kate Brooks *(Sr VP)*
Jill Lesiak *(VP & Dir-Creative)*
Brenda Rebilas *(VP & Dir-Creative)*
Chandani Rao *(VP & Acct Grp Supvr-Digital)*
Jaclyn Ninos *(Sr Acct Dir)*
Paula Huntzinger *(Dir-HR & Talent Acq)*
Jennifer Ocello *(Assoc Dir-Media)*
Maria Colicchio *(Acct Grp Supvr)*
Sabrina Marshall *(Acct Grp Supvr)*
Amanda Love *(Acct Supvr-Medical Education)*
Meg Mulholland *(Sr Acct Exec)*
Jessica Remo *(Sr Acct Exec)*
Libby Werner *(Sr Acct Exec)*
Alexis Belote *(Media Planner)*
Jeanne Gallione *(Media Planner)*
Amy McGrath *(Asst Controller-Fin Dept)*

Accounts:
AstraZeneca Recentin, Symbicort, Zactima
Rx Club

Units

Ogilvy CommonHealth Specialty Marketing
444 Interpace Pkwy Bld B, Parsippany, NJ 07054
(See Separate Listing)

Ogilvy CommonHealth Medical Media
442 & 426 Interpace Pkwy, Parsippany, NJ 07054
Tel.: (973) 352-1700
Fax: (973) 352-1230

E-Mail: rfrederick@commonhealth.com
Web Site: www.ogilvychww.com/

Employees: 18
Year Founded: 1999

Agency Specializes In: Advertising

Rebecca Frederick *(Pres)*
Shaun Urban *(Mng Partner)*
Gloria Gibbons *(Pres-EAME)*

Accounts:
Bayer Healthcare
Duramed
Johnson & Johnson Ortho McNeil
Novartis Consumer, Ophthalmics, Pharmaceuticals
Ogilvy-Healthcare
PDI
Roche

Ogilvy CommonHealth Medical Education
402 Interpace Pkwy Bldg B, Parsippany, NJ 07054
(See Separate Listing)

Ogilvy CommonHealth Insights & Analytics
440 Interpace Pkwy, Parsippany, NJ 07054
(See Separate Listing)

Ogilvy CommonHealth Interactive Marketing
430 Interpace Pkwy, Parsippany, NJ 07054
(See Separate Listing)

Ogilvy CommonHealth Payer Marketing
422 Interpace Pkwy, Parsippany, NJ 07054
(See Separate Listing)

Ogilvy Commonhealth Wellness Marketing
(Formerly Ogilvy Commonhealth Consumer Care)
424 Interpace Pkwy, Parsippany, NJ 07054
(See Separate Listing)

OGILVY HEALTHWORLD
636 11th Ave, New York, NY 10036
Tel.: (212) 237-4405
Web Site: www.ogilvy.com

Employees: 66
Year Founded: 1999

National Agency Associations: 4A's

Agency Specializes In: Advertising, Health Care Services

Michael Parisi *(Mng Partner)*
Diane Iler-Smith *(Chief Creative Officer & Exec VP)*
Gloria Gibbons *(Pres-Europe)*
Hsiao Liu *(Sr VP & Reg Head-Brand)*
Maria Folks *(VP & Mgmt Supvr)*
Robert Ross *(VP & Assoc Dir-Creative)*
Elizabeth Krieger *(VP & Grp Acct Supvr)*
Fran Davi *(Dir-HR)*
Raghu Desikan *(Dir-Creative)*
Helen Swift *(Assoc Dir)*

Accounts:
GlaxoSmithKline, Inc.
Pfizer

BPG LLC
Level 6 MAF Tower, PO Box 3294, Dubai, United Arab Emirates
Tel.: (971) 4 295 3456
Fax: (971) 4 295 8066
E-Mail: bizdev@batespangulf.com
Web Site: www.batespangulf.com

Satish Mayya *(CEO-BPG Maxus)*
Sanket Jatar *(Gen Mgr)*
Suneesh Menon *(Gen Mgr-BPG Bates)*
Amit Raj *(Gen Mgr-BPG Maxus)*
Fadi Sibai *(Gen Mgr-BPG Maxus)*
Richard Nugent *(Exec Dir-Creative)*
Hazem El Zayat *(Bus Dir-BPG Possible)*
Taghreed Oraibi *(Acct Dir-PR-BPG Cohn & Wolfe)*
Kevin Jones *(Dir-Strategy Plng-BPG Bates)*

Ogilvy Healthworld Barcelona
Avda Josef Tarradellas 123 2, Barcelona, Spain
Tel.: (34) 934955555
Fax: (34) 933666006
Web Site: www.ogilvy.es/#/commonhealth

Year Founded: 1992

Agency Specializes In: Health Care Services

Lourdes de Pablo *(Pres & CEO)*
Enric Gomez *(Dir Gen-Barcelona)*
Joan Mane Godina *(Dir-Medical-Ogilvy Healthworld & Ogilvy CommonHealth)*
Silvia Amodeo *(Project Head-Digital & Acct Supvr)*
Laura Mesa Salvany *(Acct Exec)*

Accounts:
Almirall; Barcelona, Spain Astucor, Silodyx, Sativex, Parapres; 2002
Amgen; Barcelona, Spain Mimpara
Boehringer Ingelheim Oncology; 2010
Esteve; Barcelona, Spain Vitamin-T, Fortasec; 2010
Faes Farma; Madrid, Spain Bilaxten; 2010
Novartis; Barcelona, Spain Certican, Myfortic, Rasilez, Zometa; 2003
Ordesa International; Barcelona, Spain Blemil, Blevit; 2003
Ordesa National; Barcelona, Spain Blemil, Blevit, Symbioram; 2003
Pfizer; Madrid, Spain Enbrel; 2010
Pierre Fabre Pharma; Barcelona, Spain Osteopor, Tardyferon, Permixon, Fabroven, Testopach, Denubil, Diafusor; 1998
Zambon; Barcelona, Spain Zambon; 2010

Ogilvy Healthworld/Copenhagen
Toltbodsgade 55, 1253 Copenhagen, K Denmark
Tel.: (45) 3 917 8812
Fax: (45) 3 917 8811
E-Mail: christine.enemark@ogilvy.dk
Web Site: www.ogilvy.com

Employees: 50

Morten Vestergren Frederiksen *(Mng Dir)*
Ditlev Ahlefeldt-Laurvig *(Head-Global Brand & Head-Adv UK)*
Luise Ingemann *(Acct Mgr)*
Lisbeth Vange *(Acct Mgr)*

Ogilvy Healthworld EAME
121-141 Westbourne Terrace, London, W2 6JR United Kingdom
Tel.: (44) 20 7108 6500
Fax: (44) 20 7108 6501
Web Site: www.ogilvy.com

Year Founded: 1986

Agency Specializes In: Communications, Health Care Services

Matt De Gruchy *(CEO-UK)*
Nadine Oweis *(Deputy Mng Dir)*
Tracey Wood *(Mng Dir-Medical Education)*
Ditlev Ahlefeldt-Laurvig *(Head-Global Brand-Ogilvy CommonHealth Worldwide, Head-Adv UK)*
Adam Lach-Szyrma *(Grp Dir-Creative)*
Liz Baker *(Dir-Editorial)*

Accounts:
Pfizer Dynastat

Ogilvy Healthworld India
Trade World 2nd Floor C Wing, Senapati Bapat Marg, Mumbai, 400013 India
Tel.: (91) 22 4434 4600
Fax: (91) 22 4341 4610
E-Mail: vaishali.iyeri@ogilvy.com
Web Site: www.ogilvy.com

Employees: 10

Kunal Jeswani *(Chief Digital Officer-India)*
Sonia Khurana *(Sr VP & Head-Customer Engagement)*
Sarang Wahal *(Sr VP)*
Neville Shah *(Grp Dir-Creative)*
Talha Bin Mohsin *(Sr Dir-Creative)*
Talha Nazim *(Sr Dir-Creative)*
Yamini Nair *(Dir-Creative)*
Tushar Pal *(Dir-Creative)*

Ogilvy Healthworld Madrid
Maria de Molina 39, 28006 Madrid, Spain
Tel.: (34) 91 451 2000
Fax: (34) 91 451 24 01
Web Site: www.ogilvy.es/#/healthworld

E-Mail for Key Personnel:
President: enrique.alda@healthworld.es

Employees: 40
Year Founded: 1992

Agency Specializes In: Health Care Services

Enric Gomez *(Dir Gen-Barcelona)*
Ana Garcia-Abad *(COO)*
Joan Mane Godina *(Dir-Medical)*
Silvia Amodeo *(Project Head-Digital & Acct Supvr)*
Laura Mesa Salvany *(Acct Exec)*

Accounts:
Almiral; Barcelona, Spain Sativex; 2006
Astellas; Madrid, Spain Eligard; 2006
AstraZeneca; Madrid, Spain Iressa; 2009
Becton Dickinson; Madrid, Spain; 2008
BMS; Madrid, Spain Onglyza, Atripla; 2007
Eli Lilly; Madrid, Spain Cialis; 2002
Ethicon - Johnson & Johnson Medical; Madrid, Spain Surgicel, Echelon, Harmonic; 2006
Fenil; Madrid, Spain; 2006
Janssen; Madrid, Spain Corporate, Eprex, Velcade, Aciphex, Jurnista, Doribax, Priligy, HIV Corporate; 2000
Meda; Madrid, Spain Relifex, Efiret, Bema Fentanilo; 2007
NUMICO; Madrid, Spain Almiron, Aptamil; 2006
Pfizer; Madrid Champix, Oncology, Xalacom, Xalatan, Aromasil, Sutent, Opthalmics, Animal Health, Torisel; 1998
Pharmamar; Madrid, Spain Yondelis; 2005
Roche; Madrid; 2003
SCA Hygienic Products; Madrid, Spain Tena; 2010
Schering Plough; Madrid, Spain Pegintron, Temodal, Bridion, NuvaRing; 2004

Ogilvy Healthworld Payer Marketing
343 Interspace Pkwy, Parsippany, NJ 07054
Tel.: (973) 352-2400
Fax: (973) 352-1290
Web Site: www.ogilvychww.com

Agency Specializes In: Advertising

Michael Zilligen *(Pres)*
Michael Parisi *(Mng Partner)*
Shaun Urban *(Mng Partner)*
Richard Trezza *(Pres-Payer Mktg & Gen Mgr-Payer Mktg)*
Gloria Gibbons *(Pres-EAME)*
Gordon Olsen *(Exec VP & Strategist-Brand)*
Stephen Lubiak *(Sr VP)*
Laura Kohler *(VP & Mgmt Supvr)*

Ogilvy Healthworld-Toronto
33 Yonge St, Toronto, ON M5E 1X6 Canada
(See Separate Listing)

Ogilvy Healthworld UK
121-141 Westbourne Terrace, London, W2 6JR United Kingdom
Tel.: (44) 20 7108 6000
Fax: (44) 20 7108 6001
Web Site: www.ogilvy.com

Employees: 25
Year Founded: 1982

Agency Specializes In: Advertising, Communications, Consulting, Content, Customer Relationship Management, Digital/Interactive, Direct-to-Consumer, Health Care Services, International, Internet/Web Design, Media Relations, Medical Products, Pharmaceutical, Public Relations, Social Media, Stakeholders, Strategic Planning/Research, Viral/Buzz/Word of Mouth, Web (Banner Ads, Pop-ups, etc.)

Miles Young *(Chm & CEO-Ogilvy & Mather)*
Matt de Gruchy *(CEO)*
Gerry Human *(Chief Creative Officer)*
Paul O'Donnell *(Chm-Ogilvy Grp UK & CEO-Ogilvy & Mather EAME)*
Louis Glynn *(Sr Acct Mgr)*

Accounts:
MANFLU LOZZERS, Rebranding

Ogilvy Healthworld
72 Christie St, St Leonards, Sydney, NSW 2065 Australia
Tel.: (61) 2 9492 8000
Fax: (61) 2 9955 9494
Web Site: www.ogilvy.com

Gavin Macmillan *(Head-Brand Strategy)*
Nathan Quailey *(Gen Mgr-Ogilvy Sydney)*
Isabel Cox *(Sr Acct Dir)*
Laurence Pogue *(Sr Producer-Digital)*
John Marshall *(Acct Dir)*
Rachel Newton *(Acct Dir-Digital)*
Jessica Standfield *(Sr Acct Mgr)*
Kate Piatek *(Acct Mgr)*
Anna Michael *(Acct Exec)*
Peter Smith *(Reg Exec Dir-Creative & Innovations-Asia Pacific)*

Ogilvy Healthworld
Ul Angorska 13a, Warsaw, 03-913 Poland
Tel.: (48) 22 672 6006
Fax: (48) 22 672 6244
E-Mail: olga.sobieraj@ogilvy.com
Web Site: www.ogilvy.com

Olga Sobieraj *(CEO)*

Accounts:
Ford
Gas
IBM
Lacta
MIP TV
Nestle
Play a Sports
The Rock
Siemens
Yahoo

Ogilvy Healthworld
Pilotenstraat 41, 1059 CH Amsterdam, Netherlands
Tel.: (31) 20 796 35 00
Fax: (31) 33 494 7600
E-Mail: s.visser@ogilvyhealthworld.nl
Web Site: http://www.ogilvyhealthworld.com/

Employees: 10
Year Founded: 1998

Agency Specializes In: Health Care Services, Sponsorship

Siep Visser *(Owner)*

Accounts:
Boehringer Ingelheim
Novartis Pharma
Pfizer
UCB

Ogilvy Healthworld
215 Rue Saint Jacques Ste 333, Montreal, QC H2Y 1M6 Canada
Tel.: (514) 861-1811
Fax: (514) 861-0439
E-Mail: information@ogilvy.com
Web Site: www.ogilvy-montreal.ca

Employees: 65

Agency Specializes In: Advertising

Denis Piquette *(Pres)*
Nathalie Laplace *(Mng Dir)*

Accounts:
Avon Canada
CISCO
IBM Canada
Metro
Novartis
Parks Canada
Unilever

OgilvyHealthcare
V le V Lancetti 29, 20158 Milan, Italy
(See Separate Listing)

OGILVY HEALTHWORLD-TORONTO
33 Yonge St, Toronto, ON M5E 1X6 Canada
Tel.: (416) 945-2127
Fax: (416) 920-8487
E-Mail: terry.cully@ogilvyhealthworld.ca
Web Site: www.ogilvy.com

Employees: 20
Year Founded: 1985

Agency Specializes In: Advertising, Advertising Specialties, Alternative Advertising, Bilingual Market, Brand Development & Integration, Broadcast, Business-To-Business, Cable T.V., Collateral, Communications, Consulting, Consumer Goods, Consumer Marketing, Corporate Communications, Corporate Identity, Customer Relationship Management, Digital/Interactive, Direct Response Marketing, Direct-to-Consumer, Electronic Media, Email, Exhibit/Trade Shows, Financial, Graphic Design, Health Care Services, High Technology, In-Store Advertising, Information Technology, Integrated Marketing, Internet/Web Design, Local Marketing, Logo & Package Design, Market Research, Media Buying Services, Media Planning, Medical Products, Mobile Marketing, Multimedia, Newspaper, Newspapers & Magazines, Out-of-Home Media, Outdoor, Over-50 Market, Package Design, Paid Searches, Pharmaceutical, Planning & Consultation, Point of Purchase, Point of Sale, Print, Production, Production (Print), Radio, Sales Promotion, Search Engine Optimization, Seniors' Market, Social Marketing/Nonprofit, Social Media, Strategic Planning/Research, T.V., Teen Market, Women's Market

Breakdown of Gross Billings by Media: Adv. Specialities: 80%; Consulting: 5%; Internet Adv.: 15%

Terry Cully *(Mng Dir)*
Tammy Fox *(Client Svcs Dir)*
Jennifer Vigneux *(Acct Dir)*
John Wong *(Acct Dir)*
Sylvie Bidal *(Dir-Creative)*
Diana Kudla *(Mgr-Digital)*
Chagali Kahagalle *(Acct Supvr)*
Andrew Leeson *(Acct Supvr)*
Haydn Liang *(Copywriter-Medical)*
Yelena Markovic *(Copywriter-Medical)*

Accounts:
Amgen; Toronto, Canada Aranesp, Neulasta, Neupogen, Vectibix, Xvega; 2001
GSK; Toronto, Canada Advair, Avamys, Avodart, Twinrix, Malarone, Cervarix; 1985
King Pharma; Toronto, Canada EpiPen; 2008
Unilever; Toronto, Canada Dove Sensitive Skin Bar; 2001

OGILVYHEALTHCARE
V le V Lancetti 29, 20158 Milan, Italy
Tel.: (39) 02 60789 1
Fax: (39) 02 832 41057
Web Site: www.ogilvy.com

Employees: 15
Year Founded: 2003

Agency Specializes In: Above-the-Line, Advertising Specialties, Below-the-Line, Brand Development & Integration, Children's Market, Collateral, Consulting, Cosmetics, Digital/Interactive, Direct-to-Consumer, Education, Food Service, Health Care Services, Medical Products, Multimedia, Pharmaceutical, Women's Market

Approx. Annual Billings: $3,700,000

Breakdown of Gross Billings by Media: Adv. Specialities: 100%

Giorgio Pasqual *(Mng Dir)*
Ombretta Stanchi *(Mgr-Scientific & Acct Mgr)*
Marco Pela *(Sr Designer-UX & Supvr-UX Team)*

Accounts:
Amgen
Astellas
Gilead
Glaxo Smith Kline
Novartis
Roche

O'HALLORAN ADVERTISING, INC.
270 Saugatuck Ave, Westport, CT 06880-6431
Tel.: (203) 341-9400
Fax: (203) 341-9422
Toll Free: (800) 762-0054
E-Mail: rose@ohalloranagency.com
Web Site: www.ohalloranagency.com

Employees: 28
Year Founded: 1971

National Agency Associations: YPA

Agency Specializes In: Advertising, Advertising

Specialties, Brand Development & Integration, Business-To-Business, Consumer Marketing, Direct Response Marketing, Planning & Consultation, Yellow Pages Advertising

Approx. Annual Billings: $20,000,000

Breakdown of Gross Billings by Media: Yellow Page Adv.: 100%

Kevin O'Halloran *(Owner)*

THE O'HARA PROJECT

9 Washington St 2nd Fl, Morristown, NJ 7960
Tel.: (973) 975-0531
E-Mail: info@oharaproject.com
Web Site: www.oharaproject.com

Year Founded: 2011

Agency Specializes In: Advertising, Brand Development & Integration, Collateral, Digital/Interactive, Event Planning & Marketing, Internet/Web Design, Media Buying Services, Media Planning, Public Relations, Social Media

Katherine O'Hara *(Founder)*

Accounts:
New-The Adventure Project Public Relations
Mason Jar Cookie Company
Network Solutions Company

THE OHLMANN GROUP

(Formerly Penny/Ohlmann/Neiman, Inc.)
1605 N Main St, Dayton, OH 45405-4141
Tel.: (937) 278-0681
Fax: (937) 277-1723
E-Mail: info@ohlmanngroup.com
Web Site: www.ohlmanngroup.com

E-Mail for Key Personnel:
President: walter@ohlmanngroup.com
Media Dir.: linda@ohlmanngroup.com
Production Mgr.: cindy@ohlmanngroup.com

Employees: 20
Year Founded: 1949

National Agency Associations: IAN

Agency Specializes In: Advertising, Alternative Advertising, Arts, Broadcast, Business Publications, Business-To-Business, Cable T.V., Catalogs, Co-op Advertising, Collateral, Communications, Consulting, Consumer Goods, Consumer Marketing, Content, Corporate Communications, Corporate Identity, Crisis Communications, Digital/Interactive, Direct Response Marketing, Direct-to-Consumer, E-Commerce, Education, Electronic Media, Email, Event Planning & Marketing, Exhibit/Trade Shows, Food Service, Government/Political, Graphic Design, Health Care Services, High Technology, Identity Marketing, In-Store Advertising, Industrial, Integrated Marketing, Internet/Web Design, Local Marketing, Logo & Package Design, Media Buying Services, Media Planning, Media Relations, Media Training, Medical Products, Merchandising, Multimedia, New Product Development, Newspaper, Newspapers & Magazines, Out-of-Home Media, Outdoor, Over-50 Market, Package Design, Paid Searches, Point of Purchase, Point of Sale, Print, Production, Production (Print), Promotions, Public Relations, Publicity/Promotions, Radio, Real Estate, Regional, Restaurant, Retail, Sales Promotion, Search Engine Optimization, Seniors' Market, Social Marketing/Nonprofit, Sponsorship, Strategic Planning/Research, T.V., Teen Market, Trade & Consumer Magazines, Transportation, Viral/Buzz/Word of Mouth, Women's Market

Approx. Annual Billings: $10,000,000

Walter Ohlmann *(Pres & CEO)*
Linda Kahn *(Sr VP-Media)*
Kim Gros *(Controller)*
Gary Haschart *(Sr Dir-Art)*
Andy Kittles *(Sr Dir-Art)*
Beth Miller *(Dir-PR)*
Mike Blackney *(Mgr-Digital Media)*
Ian Bowman Henderson *(Mgr-Content Mktg)*
Cindy Zwayer *(Mgr-Production)*
David Bowman *(Sr Strategist-Mktg)*
Jesse Reeves *(Copywriter)*

Accounts:
Graceworks Lutheran Services Creative Design, PR, Social Media, Strategic Marketing

OIA MARKETING COMMUNICATIONS

4240 Wagner Rd, Dayton, OH 45440
Tel.: (937) 222-6421
Fax: (937) 222-1642
E-Mail: oia@oia-inc.com
Web Site: www.oia-inc.com

E-Mail for Key Personnel:
President: rick@oia-inc.com

Employees: 5
Year Founded: 1949

Agency Specializes In: Advertising, Automotive, Business Publications, Business-To-Business, Co-op Advertising, Collateral, Communications, Consulting, Consumer Marketing, Consumer Publications, Corporate Identity, Digital/Interactive, Direct Response Marketing, E-Commerce, Education, Electronic Media, Environmental, Exhibit/Trade Shows, Fashion/Apparel, Financial, Government/Political, Graphic Design, Health Care Services, High Technology, Industrial, Information Technology, Internet/Web Design, Logo & Package Design, Media Buying Services, Medical Products, Merchandising, Multimedia, New Product Development, Newspaper, Newspapers & Magazines, Outdoor, Planning & Consultation, Point of Purchase, Point of Sale, Print, Production, Public Relations, Publicity/Promotions, Radio, Sales Promotion, Strategic Planning/Research, Technical Advertising, Trade & Consumer Magazines, Transportation, Yellow Pages Advertising

Approx. Annual Billings: $3,500,000

Richard D. Bloomingdale *(Pres & Gen Mgr)*
Tod Deppe *(VP-Creative)*
Beverly A. Trollinger *(VP-Ops)*
Donald Carone *(Mgr-Bus Dev)*
Holly McDonald *(Mgr-Production & Media)*

OIC

959 E Colorado Blvd Ste 230, Pasadena, CA 91106
Tel.: (626) 229-0931
Fax: (626) 229-9897
E-Mail: info@theoicagency.com
Web Site: theoicagency.com

Employees: 15
Year Founded: 1998

Agency Specializes In: Advertising, Advertising Specialties, Affiliate Marketing, Affluent Market, African-American Market, Arts, Below-the-Line, Brand Development & Integration, Business Publications, Business-To-Business, Collateral, Communications, Computers & Software, Consulting, Consumer Marketing, Content, Corporate Identity, Digital/Interactive, Direct Response Marketing, Direct-to-Consumer, E-Commerce, Electronic Media, Electronics, Email, Event Planning & Marketing, Exhibit/Trade Shows, Game Integration, Gay & Lesbian Market, Graphic Design, High Technology, Identity Marketing, Industrial, Information Technology, Integrated Marketing, International, Internet/Web Design, Leisure, Logo & Package Design, Market Research, Media Buying Services, Media Planning, Men's Market, Multimedia, New Product Development, New Technologies, Outdoor, Package Design, Planning & Consultation, Print, Production (Ad, Film, Broadcast), Promotions, Publicity/Promotions, Regional, Sales Promotion, Search Engine Optimization, Social Marketing/Nonprofit, Social Media, Sports Market, Strategic Planning/Research, Technical Advertising, Teen Market, Telemarketing, Trade & Consumer Magazines, Urban Market, Web (Banner Ads, Pop-ups, etc.)

Approx. Annual Billings: $3,000,000

Joel Raznick *(Co-Founder & Pres)*
Darin Beaman *(Chief Creative Officer)*
Jay Moore *(Grp Acct Dir-Global)*
Ralph DeFelice *(Dir-Interactive)*
Ken Huang *(Dir-Design)*
Amy Hochstein *(Mgr-Web Content)*
Sheila Sumatra *(Mgr-Acctg)*

Accounts:
AMD
Cathay Bank
InfoVista
Intel
LG Electronics
Nestle; Glendale, CA Powerbar; 2007
Oracle America, Inc.; Sunnyvale, CA Hardware/Softwave Services; 2007

OISHII CREATIVE

717 N Highland Ave Ste 18, Los Angeles, CA 90038
Tel.: (323) 932-1626
E-Mail: contact@oishiicreative.com
Web Site: www.oishiicreative.com

Agency Specializes In: Advertising, Brand Development & Integration, Digital/Interactive, Entertainment, Strategic Planning/Research

Ish Obregon *(Co-Founder & Chief Creative Officer)*
Kate Obregon *(Partner)*
Dan Walkup *(Mng Dir & Exec Producer)*
Asja Tobler *(Producer-Brdcst, Print & Brand Strategy)*

Accounts:
E! Entertainment Campaign: "Botched"
EA Sports
NFL Network
Nicktoons
Ovation
The Walt Disney Company

O'KEEFE REINHARD & PAUL

208 S Jefferson St Ste 101, Chicago, IL 60661
Tel.: (312) 226-6144
E-Mail: info@okrp.com
Web Site: www.okrp.com

Year Founded: 2013

National Agency Associations: 4A's

Agency Specializes In: Advertising, Sponsorship

Nick Paul *(Founder & Pres)*
Tom O'Keefe *(Founder & CEO)*
Matt Reinhard *(Chief Creative Officer)*
Scott Mitchell *(Exec Producer)*
Natasha Kesaji *(Acct Svcs Dir)*

Addie Palin *(Acct Dir)*
Jennifer Bills *(Dir-Creative)*
Nate Swift *(Dir-Strategy)*
Britt Whitaker *(Dir-Art/Designer)*
Christina Chonody *(Sr Acct Exec)*
Dana Quercioli *(Copywriter)*

Accounts:
Ace Hardware Corporation (Agency of Record)
New-American Marketing Association
Big Lots (Agency of Record) "Nailing It", Advertising, Broadcast, Campaign: "Black Friday Woman", Campaign: "Cats Only", Campaign: "Pet Focus Group", Campaign: "Pets with Style", Social

OLD MILL MARKETING
Renovators Old Mill, Millers Falls, MA 01349
Tel.: (413) 423-3569
Fax: (413) 423-3800
E-Mail: py@rensup.com
Web Site: www.oldmillmarketing.com/

Employees: 30
Year Founded: 1978

Agency Specializes In: Advertising, Commercial Photography, Consumer Marketing, Consumer Publications, Direct Response Marketing, Exhibit/Trade Shows, Graphic Design, Magazines, Media Buying Services, New Product Development, Newspapers & Magazines, Print, Production, Real Estate, Sales Promotion, Telemarketing, Trade & Consumer Magazines

Claude Jeanloz *(Pres)*

Accounts:
Cufflink Museum, Inc.; Conway, NH; 1997
Enfield Industries, Inc.; Conway, NH; 1992
The Renovator's Supply, Inc.; Millers Falls, MA Mail Order
Vintage Publications; Millers Falls, MA; 1980
Yield House; Conway, NH

O'LEARY AND PARTNERS
5000 Birch St Ste 1000, Newport Beach, CA 92660
Tel.: (949) 833-8006
Fax: (949) 833-9155
E-Mail: drobinson@adagency.com
Web Site: www.olearyandpartners.com

E-Mail for Key Personnel:
President: drobinson@adagency.com
Media Dir.: drobinson@adagency.com

Employees: 55
Year Founded: 1983

National Agency Associations: 4A's

Agency Specializes In: Advertising, Automotive, Brand Development & Integration, Broadcast, Business-To-Business, Co-op Advertising, Collateral, Consumer Marketing, Corporate Communications, Corporate Identity, Digital/Interactive, Direct Response Marketing, Direct-to-Consumer, E-Commerce, Education, Electronic Media, Financial, Food Service, Graphic Design, Hispanic Market, Household Goods, Internet/Web Design, Leisure, Logo & Package Design, Magazines, Media Buying Services, Men's Market, New Product Development, Newspaper, Newspapers & Magazines, Out-of-Home Media, Outdoor, Planning & Consultation, Point of Purchase, Point of Sale, Print, Production, Public Relations, Publicity/Promotions, Radio, Real Estate, Restaurant, Retail, Sales Promotion, Search Engine Optimization, Seniors' Market, Social Media, Sponsorship, Strategic Planning/Research, T.V., Technical Advertising, Teen Market, Transportation, Travel & Tourism, Viral/Buzz/Word of Mouth

Approx. Annual Billings: $85,000,000

Dave Robinson *(CEO)*
John Rutledge *(CFO & Sr VP)*
Eric Spiegler *(Exec Dir-Creative)*
Maria Ramirez *(Mgmt Supvr)*
Josh Zipper *(Dir-Art)*
Matt McNelis *(Assoc Dir-Creative & Copywriter)*
Carol Knaeps *(Mgr-Production)*

Accounts:
AAA Mid-Atlantic
Bimbo Bakeries USA; Fort Worth, TX Entenmann's, Francisco, Orowheat
Circle K
CO-OP Financial Services; Rancho Cucamonga, CA
Fantastic Sam's; Beverly, MA
In-N-Out Burger; Irvine, CA
Lobster ME
Mothers Polish Campaign: "Bottled Water", Campaign: "Deer"
Sage Hill School; Newport Beach, CA
Uniglobe Travel International; Irvine, CA
WD-40 Company 2000 Flushes, 3-in-One, Campaign: "Precision Drop", Carpet Fresh, Lava, Spot Shot, X-14
West Coast Aviation; Newport Beach, CA Aviation Services, Charters; 2004
Wetzel's Pretzels; Pasadena, CA

OLIVE INTERACTIVE DESIGN & MARKETING INC.
401 Congress Ave Ste 1540, Austin, TX 78701-3637
Tel.: (512) 415-5879
Fax: (512) 457-0208
E-Mail: nb@olivedesign.com
Web Site: www.olivedesign.com

Employees: 11
Year Founded: 1997

Agency Specializes In: Advertising, Advertising Specialties, Communications, Consulting, Consumer Marketing, E-Commerce, Electronic Media, Entertainment, Graphic Design, High Technology, Internet/Web Design, Logo & Package Design, Print, Publicity/Promotions, Strategic Planning/Research, Travel & Tourism

Approx. Annual Billings: $1,000,000

Breakdown of Gross Billings by Media: Graphic Design: 10%; Internet Adv.: 90%

Kyla Kanz *(CEO & Strategist-Interactive Mktg-Bus Dev)*

Accounts:
Blue Fish Development Group
Capitol Metro
Conformative Systems
DMX Music
Farouk Systems
Hewlett-Packard
KLRU
KnowledgeBeam
LifeSize Communications
Permeo Technologies
Primus Networks
Technopolis Xchange
Texas Department of Travel & Tourism; 2000
University of Texas

OLIVE PR SOLUTIONS INC
434 W Cedar Ste 300, San Diego, CA 92101
Tel.: (619) 955-5285
E-Mail: info@oliveprsolutions.com
Web Site: www.oliveprsolutions.com

Agency Specializes In: Advertising, Brand Development & Integration, Event Planning & Marketing, Media Relations, Media Training, Social Media, Strategic Planning/Research

Jennifer Borba Von Stauffenberg *(Pres)*
Jaclyn Acree *(Sr Acct Exec)*
Leah Brown *(Sr Acct Exec)*

Accounts:
New-Adelman Fine Art
New-UVA Mobile

OLIVER RUSSELL
217 S 11th St, Boise, ID 83702
Tel.: (208) 344-1734
Fax: (208) 344-1211
E-Mail: info@oliverrussell.com
Web Site: www.oliverrussell.com

Employees: 14
Year Founded: 1991

National Agency Associations: Second Wind Limited

Agency Specializes In: Sponsorship

Russ Stoddard *(Founder & Pres)*
Mike Stevens *(Sr Dir-Art)*
David Cook *(Dir-Creative)*
Jay Saenz *(Dir-Bus Dev)*
Shawna Samuelson *(Sr Acct Exec)*
Adie Bartron *(Acct Exec)*
Mitch Kuhn *(Designer)*

Accounts:
Hewlett Packard
Simplot Co.
YMCA

OLOGIE
447 E Main St, Columbus, OH 43215
Tel.: (614) 221-1107
Fax: (614) 221-1108
Toll Free: (800) 962-1107
E-Mail: bfaust@ologie.com
Web Site: www.ologie.com

Employees: 85
Year Founded: 1987

Agency Specializes In: Advertising, Brand Development & Integration, Business-To-Business, Consulting, Corporate Communications, Corporate Identity, Financial, Multimedia, Print, Retail, Sponsorship

Beverly Bethge *(Owner)*
William Faust *(Mng Partner)*
Kelly Ruoff *(Partner & Chief Creative Officer)*
Bill Litfin *(Chief Digital Officer)*
Mark Love *(Dir-Video)*

Accounts:
Auburn
Belk
Berkeley
Big Lots, Inc.
Dave Thomas Foundation of Adoption
Elon
Gonzaga University
Hartwick College
Northwestern University
PNC
Pratt
University of Arizona
West Virginia University
Xavier University

OLOMANA LOOMIS ISC
(Formerly Loomis Integrated Strategic Communications)
Pioneer Plz Ste 350 - 900 Fort St Mall, Honolulu, HI 96813
Tel.: (808) 469-3250
Fax: (808) 532-8808
Web Site: olomanaloomisisc.com

Agency Specializes In: Advertising, Graphic Design, Internet/Web Design, Media Relations, Print

Carole Tang *(Chm, Pres & CEO)*
Helen L. Cho *(Dir-Integrated Strategies)*
Mika Keauli'i *(Dir-Fin & Media)*
Liane Hu *(Sr Project Mgr-Comm)*
Joshua Shon *(Coord-Comm Project)*

OLSON
420 N 5th St, Minneapolis, MN 55401
Tel.: (612) 215-9800
Fax: (612) 215-9801
E-Mail: business@olson.com
Web Site: www.olson.com

Employees: 450
Year Founded: 1992

Agency Specializes In: Advertising, Advertising Specialties, Automotive, Brand Development & Integration, Broadcast, Business Publications, Business-To-Business, Cable T.V., Children's Market, Collateral, Communications, Consulting, Consumer Marketing, Consumer Publications, Corporate Identity, Digital/Interactive, Direct Response Marketing, E-Commerce, Education, Electronic Media, Entertainment, Event Planning & Marketing, Exhibit/Trade Shows, Fashion/Apparel, Financial, Food Service, Graphic Design, Health Care Services, High Technology, In-Store Advertising, Industrial, Information Technology, Internet/Web Design, Investor Relations, Legal Services, Leisure, Logo & Package Design, Media Buying Services, Medical Products, Merchandising, New Product Development, Newspaper, Newspapers & Magazines, Out-of-Home Media, Outdoor, Pharmaceutical, Planning & Consultation, Point of Purchase, Point of Sale, Print, Production, Public Relations, Publicity/Promotions, Radio, Real Estate, Retail, Sales Promotion, Sponsorship, Sports Market, Strategic Planning/Research, Sweepstakes, T.V., Technical Advertising, Teen Market, Trade & Consumer Magazines, Transportation, Travel & Tourism

Approx. Annual Billings: $93,000,000

Jonathan Lum *(Chief Strategy Officer)*
Kevin McKeon *(Chief Creative Officer)*
Suzy Cox *(Sr VP)*
Greg Heinemann *(Sr VP)*
Jennifer Gove *(VP & Grp Acct Dir)*
Paul Ratzky *(VP & Dir-Digital Strategy)*
Michelle Davis *(VP-Client Svcs)*
Jim Mattson *(VP-Tech)*
David Scamehorn *(VP-1 to 1 Analytics)*
Steve Peckham *(Gen Mgr-Olson Engage)*
Vince Beggin *(Grp Dir-Creative & Brand)*
Nina Orezzoli *(Grp Dir-Creative)*
Matt Pruett *(Grp Dir-Creative)*
Brian Bloodgood *(Sr Dir-Art)*
Liz Gray *(Sr Dir-Brand Strategy)*
Ed Dziedzic *(Grp Acct Dir)*
Ali Goldner *(Acct Dir)*
Alison Stienessen *(Acct Dir)*
Thomas Douty *(Dir-Digital Strategy)*
Tom Lord *(Dir-Creative)*
Scott Muskin *(Dir-Creative)*
Brit Ryan *(Dir-Art)*
David Statman *(Dir-Creative)*
Kimberly Dunn *(Assoc Dir-Connections Strategy)*
Jeffrey Huang *(Assoc Dir-Connections Strategy)*
Vince Keefe *(Assoc Dir-Interactive Strategy)*
Christina Zajic *(Sr Brand Mgr)*
Nicole Leary *(Acct Mgr)*
Allison Hill *(Mgr-Mktg Strategy)*
Crys Puszczykowski *(Acct Supvr)*
Stephanie Shambo *(Acct Supvr)*
Alicia Houselog *(Supvr-Connections Strategy)*
Abra Williams *(Sr Acct Exec)*
Jaxon Trow *(Strategist-Connections)*

Accounts:
Alzheimer's Association Brand/Digital
Amtrak Loyalty/CRM
New-Atlantic Lottery Corp. Digital
Aurora Health Care Brand/Digital
Bauer Hockey Brand/Digital
Baylor College of Medicine Brand/Digital
Belize Tourism Brand/Digital
Best Buy Loyalty/CRM
Bissell Homecare, Inc. (Agency of Record) Creative, Digital Business, Media
Boston Scientific Brand/Digital
New-California Lottery (Digital Agency of Record) Creative, Strategic
Commerce Bank Brand/Digital
Discover Boating Brand, Digital, PR, Social
General Mills Brand, Digital, PR, Social
GoPro
Guaranteed Rate Brand, Digital, PR, Social
Kidrobot Brand/Digital
The Kraft Heinz Company Oscar Mayer, Public Relations, Social
Luxottica Loyalty/CRM
Markwins Beauty Product (Agency of Record) Broadcast, Data Analytics, Digital, Social-Media, Wet n Wild Beauty
Masco Coatings Group BEHR (Public Relations Agency of Record), BEHRPro (Public Relations Agency of Record), KILZ (Public Relations Agency of Record)
McDonald's Brand, Digital, PR, Social
Minneapolis Airport Commission PR/Social
Minnesota State Lottery (Agency of Record) Digital
Minnesota Wild Brand/Digital
New-Ontario Lottery and Gaming Corp. Digital
PepsiCo PR/Social
PF Chang's (Agency of Record) Advertising, Customer Relationship Management, Digital, Loyalty/CRM, Marketing, Media, Public Relations
Quill.com PR/Social
Royal Canin PR/Social
Sears Campaign: "#BacktoWha", Online
Sharp Electronics Corporation Brand, Creative, Design, Digital
Supercuts Digital, National Broadcast, Social Media
Target
The Terminix International Company Limited Partnership (PR & Social Media Agency of Record) "Fantasy Exterminator League", Campaign: "Mosquitonado"
UnitedHealth Group Ovations
University of Minnesota Brand/Digital
Whole Foods Market Brand/Digital
Wm. Wrigley Jr. Company "Make Game Day Awesomer", "Seattle Mix", PR/Social, Skittles, Video

Branches

Olson
(Formerly Dig Communications)
564 W Randolph St, Chicago, IL 60661
(See Separate Listing)

OMAC ADVERTISING
2573 12th St SE, Salem, OR 97302
Tel.: (503) 364-3340
Fax: (503) 364-1870
E-Mail: design@omacadvertising.com
Web Site: www.omacadvertising.com

Agency Specializes In: Advertising, Brand Development & Integration, Collateral, Corporate Identity, Graphic Design, Internet/Web Design, Logo & Package Design, Print, Radio, Social Media

Bill Lovato *(Owner)*
Doris Lovato *(Office Mgr)*
Lynn Laclef *(Designer-Web)*

Accounts:
Stutzmen Environmental

OMEGA GROUP ADVERTISING AGENCY
2906 N State St Ste 215, Jackson, MS 39216
Tel.: (601) 981-4532
E-Mail: info@omegagroup.tv
Web Site: www.omegagroup.tv

Agency Specializes In: Advertising, Graphic Design, Internet/Web Design, Logo & Package Design, Outdoor, Print

Milan Mueller *(Pres)*
Bruce Silva *(Dir-Res)*
Brandon Stam *(Dir-Implementation)*
Jim Harrity *(Mgr-Sls)*

Accounts:
Hometown Medical
Vicksburg Toyota

OMELET
8673 Hayden Pl, Culver City, CA 90232
Tel.: (213) 427-6400
Fax: (213) 427-6401
E-Mail: info@omeletla.com
Web Site: www.omeletla.com

Employees: 30

Agency Specializes In: Advertising, Brand Development & Integration, Graphic Design, Production (Ad, Film, Broadcast), Production (Print), Sponsorship

Ryan Fey *(Co-Founder & Chief Brand Officer)*
Donald A. Kurz *(Chm & CEO)*
Katrin Tenhaaf *(Partner & Head-Client Svcs)*
Charles Croft *(Mng Dir)*
Grant Holland *(Chief Creative Officer)*
Thas Naseemuddeen *(Chief Strategy Officer)*
Sarah Ceglarski *(Sr Dir-Mktg)*
Devin Desjarlais *(Dir-Comm)*
Kate Eglen *(Dir-Art)*
Raul Montes *(Dir-Creative)*
Marcus Wesson *(Dir-Creative)*
Clemente Bornacelli *(Assoc Dir-Creative)*
Jay Mattingly *(Acct Mgr)*
Jasmeet Gill *(Strategist-Brand)*
Katharine Wolff *(Assoc Acct Dir)*

Accounts:
AT&T
Betsy's Best
Brutal Legend
Burn Notice Covert Ops
Coca-Cola
Crash Village
New-Guild Guitars Content, Print, Social Media
New-HauteLook Campaign: "Hot Look"
HBO
Interscope
L.A. Mayor's Office Campaign: "Save the Drop"
Madonna: Celebrate Yourself
Microsoft Campaign: "Honestly", Campaign: "Smoked By Windows"
Moet & Chandon
NBC Universal Bravo TV, Green is Universal
Pinnacle Foods Group LLC Campaign: "Inspired by Chef. Crushed by You.", Gardein, Media, Online, Videos
Red Bull

Shake Things Up
Sony Electronics X Brand
Square Enix Campaign: "Sarif Industries"
Tactical Espionage Training
New-Ubisoft
Walmart

OMNIA AGENCY

115 Harris Ave 2nd Fl, Providence, RI 02903
Tel.: (401) 861-7700
E-Mail: info@omniaagency.com
Web Site: www.omniaagency.com

Year Founded: 2008

Agency Specializes In: Advertising, Brand Development & Integration, Graphic Design, Internet/Web Design, Media Buying Services

Gail Morris *(CFO & Mng Partner)*
Stacey Caputi Liakos *(Mng Partner)*
Teresa Legein *(Acct Mgr)*

Accounts:
The Bread Boss
Busy B's Academy
Coalition for Social Justice
JLS Hair Design
Rhode Island Student Loan Authority
Twin River Casino

OMNIBUS ADVERTISING

546 W Campus Dr, Arlington Heights, IL 60004
Tel.: (847) 255-6000
E-Mail: info@omnibusadv.com
Web Site: www.omnibusadvertising.com

Agency Specializes In: Advertising, Automotive, Broadcast, Identity Marketing, Internet/Web Design, Print, Production (Ad, Film, Broadcast), Production (Print)

John Gugle *(Dir-Art)*
Melissa Johnson *(Dir-Media)*
Kathy Monnich *(Dir-Ops)*
Lynette Frederick *(Acct Mgr)*
Cliff Schoenrade *(Acct Mgr)*
Jeff Stimson *(Acct Mgr)*
Theresa Daniels *(Acct Exec)*
Beth Wolf *(Acct Exec)*

Accounts:
Speedway LLC

OMNICOM GROUP INC.

437 Madison Ave, New York, NY 10022
Tel.: (212) 415-3600
Fax: (212) 415-3530
E-Mail: publicaffairs@omnicomgroup.com
Web Site: www.omnicomgroup.com

Employees: 74,000
Year Founded: 1986

National Agency Associations: 4A's-MCA

Agency Specializes In: Above-the-Line, Advertising, Advertising Specialties, African-American Market, Automotive, Bilingual Market, Brand Development & Integration, Broadcast, Business Publications, Business-To-Business, Cable T.V., Children's Market, Co-op Advertising, Collateral, Communications, Consulting, Consumer Marketing, Consumer Publications, Corporate Communications, Corporate Identity, Crisis Communications, Custom Publishing, Customer Relationship Management, Digital/Interactive, Direct Response Marketing, Direct-to-Consumer, E-Commerce, Electronic Media, Email, Entertainment, Environmental, Event Planning & Marketing, Exhibit/Trade Shows, Experience Design, Financial, Food Service, Government/Political, Graphic Design, Health Care Services, High Technology, Hispanic Market, In-Store Advertising, Information Technology, Integrated Marketing, Internet/Web Design, Investor Relations, Logo & Package Design, Market Research, Media Buying Services, Media Planning, Media Relations, Medical Products, Merchandising, Mobile Marketing, Multicultural, Multimedia, New Product Development, Newspaper, Out-of-Home Media, Package Design, Pharmaceutical, Point of Purchase, Point of Sale, Print, Product Placement, Production (Ad, Film, Broadcast), Promotions, Public Relations, Publicity/Promotions, Radio, Recruitment, Retail, Sales Promotion, Search Engine Optimization, Social Marketing/Nonprofit, Social Media, Sponsorship, Sports Market, Strategic Planning/Research, Sweepstakes, Syndication, T.V., Telemarketing, Trade & Consumer Magazines, Tween Market, Viral/Buzz/Word of Mouth, Web (Banner Ads, Pop-ups, etc.), Women's Market

Revenue: $15,317,800,000

Bruce A. Crawford *(Chm)*
John Wren *(Pres & CEO)*
Philip Angelastro *(CFO & Exec VP)*
Kevin McShane *(Chief Creative Officer)*
Tiffany Warren *(Chief Diversity Officer & Sr VP)*
Dale Adams *(Chm/CEO-Diversified Agency Svcs Div)*
Sunee Paripunna *(CEO-Thailand)*
Michael J. O'Brien *(Gen Counsel & Sr VP)*
Dennis E. Hewitt *(Treas)*
Mark O'Brien *(Exec VP)*
Janet Riccio *(Exec VP)*
Rita Rodriguez *(Exec VP)*
Peter Sherman *(Exec VP)*
Peter Swiecicki *(Sr VP-Fin & Controller)*
Dawn Zhao *(Sr VP-China)*
Kristen Colonna *(Mng Dir-East)*
Leslie Chiocco *(VP-HR & Retirement Benefits)*
Domingo Gonzalez *(Head-Mobile-US Partnerships & Platforms & Dir)*
Tan Li Wei *(Controller-Fin)*
Christena J. Pyle *(Dir-ADCOLOR)*
Nicole Levitt *(Sr Mgr-Talent Acq)*
Bethany Atchison *(Supvr-Digital)*
Zach Shaub *(Supvr-Digital-WB)*
Fatima Teke *(Supvr-Digital)*
Courtney Dalton *(Strategist-Digital)*
Justin Sanit *(Strategist-Digital-Warner Brothers Theatrical Team)*
Dahna Shimony *(Strategist-Digital)*
Andrew Castellaneta *(Asst Controller)*

Accounts:
Hewlett-Packard Company Hewlett-Packard Company, ePrint
Kraft Foods Group Planters Lovers' Mix
Nissan
Philips Electronics North America Corporation
Porsche Cars North America, Inc. Boxster, Cayenne, Cayman, Panamera, Porsche 911, Porsche Cars North America, Inc.

Parent Company of:

Accuen

225 N Michigan Ave 21st Fl, Chicago, IL 60602
Tel.: (312) 324-7000
E-Mail: info@accuenmedia.com
Web Site: www.accuenmedia.com

Kristen Faust *(Mng Dir)*
Michael Fugazzotto *(Mng Dir)*
Bill Neblock *(CFO)*
Ming Wu *(Gen Mgr-US)*
Susan Wallace *(Acct Dir)*
Eleni Antonopoulos *(Dir-Programmatic Solutions)*
Loretta Berghoff *(Dir-US HR)*
Jack Flewett *(Dir-Programmatic Solutions)*
Francois Maturo *(Dir-Programmatic Solutions)*
Laura Peterson *(Dir-Programmatic Media)*
Mary Heppenstall *(Assoc Dir-Programmatic Media)*
Nauman Mirza *(Assoc Dir)*
Melissa Twedell *(Assoc Dir-Fin)*
Chris Wilson *(Assoc Dir-Trading)*
Elaine Liu *(Sr Mgr-Programmatic Solutions)*
Mark Oster *(Sr Mgr-Programmatic Media)*
Ryan Pittrich *(Sr Mgr-Programmatic Solutions)*
Michael Pugh *(Sr Mgr-Programmatic Media)*
Sabrina Bangladesh *(Mgr-Programmatic Media)*
Brenda Chan *(Mgr-Insights)*
Collin Cousineau *(Mgr-Programmatic Media)*
Kimberly Goughnour *(Mgr-Programmatic Media)*
Michael Haben *(Mgr-Programmatic Media)*
Jenn Huck *(Mgr-Programmatic Media)*
Mikelle Laker *(Mgr-Trading)*
Rob Sullivan *(Mgr-Programmatic Media)*
Rosalyn Weathers *(Supvr-Client Solutions)*
Jorge Lopez *(Analyst-Ops)*
Patti Fialek *(Bus Project Mgr)*

Agency 720

500 Woodward Ave, Detroit, MI 48226
(See Separate Listing)

Alma

(Formerly Alma DDB)
2601 S Bayshore Dr 4th Fl, Coconut Grove, FL 33133
(See Separate Listing)

BBDO Worldwide Inc.

1285 Ave of the Americas, New York, NY 10019-6028
(See Separate Listing)

DDB Worldwide Communications Group Inc.

437 Madison Ave, New York, NY 10022-7001
(See Separate Listing)

Diversified Agency Services

437 Madison Ave, New York, NY 10022-7001
(See Separate Listing)

Downtown Partners Chicago

200 E Randolph St 34th Fl, Chicago, IL 60601
(See Separate Listing)

FAME

60 S Sixth St Ste 2600, Minneapolis, MN 55402
(See Separate Listing)

Fathom Communications

437 Madison Ave, New York, NY 10022
(See Separate Listing)

GSD&M

828 W 6th St, Austin, TX 78703
(See Separate Listing)

ICON International Inc.

107 Elm St 4 Stamford Plz, Stamford, CT 06902
(See Separate Listing)

Interbrand & CEE

(Formerly Interbrand Central and Eastern Europe)
Weinsbergstrasse 118a, Cologne, Germany
Tel.: (49) 44 388 7878
Fax: (49) 44 388 7790
Web Site: http://interbrand.com/

Employees: 120
Year Founded: 1972

Agency Specializes In: Brand Development & Integration, Consulting, Corporate Identity, Digital/Interactive, Environmental, Graphic Design, Internet/Web Design, Package Design, Retail

Manfredi Ricca *(Chief Strategy Officer-EMEA & LatAm)*
Gonzalo Brujo *(CEO-EMEA & LatAm)*
Rebecca Robbins *(Dir-Mktg & Bus Dev-EMEA & LatAm)*

Accounts:
ABB; Switzerland
Actelion; Switzerland
BMW Group; Germany BMW, Mini, Rolls-Royce
Bayer; Germany
Beiersdorf; Germany Nivea
Credit Suisse; Switzerland
Deutsche Telecom; Germany
Deutsche Telekom; Germany
Hugo Boss; Germany
Mercedes AMG; Germany
OMV; Austria
Philips; Netherlands
Roche; Switzerland
Schindler; Switzerland
Siemens; Germany
T-Mobile International AG
T-Online International AG
TUI; Germany
Unilever; Germany Knorr
Wrigley; Germany

Interbrand B.V.
Prof WH Keesomlaan 4, 1183 DJ Amstelveen, Netherlands
Tel.: (31) 20 406 5750
Fax: (31) 20 520 5760
E-Mail: amsterdam@interbrand.com
Web Site: www.interbrand.com

Employees: 10

Agency Specializes In: Advertising

Evert Bos *(Sr Dir)*
Dominiek Post *(Jr Strategist)*

Interbrand
Zirkusweg 1, D-20359 Hamburg, Germany
Tel.: (49) 40 355 366 0
Fax: (49) 40 355 366 66
E-Mail: info@interbrand.com
Web Site: www.interbrand.com

Employees: 20

Agency Specializes In: Advertising

Nina Oswald *(Mng Dir-Central & Eastern Europe)*
Jens Grefen *(Dir-Creative-Germany)*
Ildiko Kovacs *(Dir-Strategy)*
Michael Bohm *(Mgr-IT)*
Jorg Schmitt *(Designer)*
Felipe Wagner *(Sr Designer)*
Anne Rehwinkel *(Client Svc Dir)*

Interbrand
4000 Smith Rd, Cincinnati, OH 45209
(See Separate Listing)

Martin/Williams Advertising Inc.
150 S 5th St, Minneapolis, MN 55402-4428
(See Separate Listing)

Novus Media Inc
2 Carlson Pkwy Ste 400, Plymouth, MN 55447
(See Separate Listing)

OMD Worldwide
195 Broadway, New York, NY 10007
(See Separate Listing)

Omnicom Media Group
195 Broadway, New York, NY 10007
(See Separate Listing)

PHD Media UK
The Telephone Exchange 5 N Crescent, Chenies St, London, WC1E 7PH United Kingdom
(See Separate Listing)

PHD
220 E 42nd 7th Fl, New York, NY 10017
(See Separate Listing)

Resolution Media
225 N Michigan Ave, Chicago, IL 60601
(See Separate Listing)

Rodgers Townsend, LLC
1000 Clark Ave 5th Fl, Saint Louis, MO 63102
(See Separate Listing)

TBWA/Worldwide
488 Madison Ave, New York, NY 10022
(See Separate Listing)

Tribal Worldwide
(Formerly Tribal DDB Worldwide)
437 Madison Ave 8th Fl, New York, NY 10022
(See Separate Listing)

Branding Consultants

BrandWizard
130 Fifth Ave, New York, NY 10011
(See Separate Listing)

Interbrand Corporation
130 5th Ave, New York, NY 10011-4306
(See Separate Listing)

Custom Publishing

Specialist
Clifton Heights, Triangle W, Bristol, BS8 1EJ United Kingdom
Tel.: (44) 1 179 25 1696
Fax: (44) 1 179 25 1808
E-Mail: info@specialistuk.com
Web Site: www.specialistuk.com

Employees: 30

National Agency Associations: APA-PPA

Agency Specializes In: Magazines, Pets

Niki Webb *(CEO)*
Philippe Crump *(Dir-Comml)*
A.J. Howe *(Dir-Creative)*
Ross Wilkinson *(Dir-Content)*
Sarah Russell *(Strategist-Content)*

Accounts:
The Co-operative Group
Defra
KwikFit Insurance
Npower
Peugeot
Quick Fit
Sage
Specsavers

Design

The Designory
211 E Ocean Blvd Ste 100, Long Beach, CA 90802-4850
(See Separate Listing)

Interbrand Design Forum
7575 Paragon Rd, Dayton, OH 45459-5316
(See Separate Listing)

Entertainment, Event & Sports Marketing

Harrison & Shriftman LLC
141 W 36th St 12th Fl, New York, NY 10018
(See Separate Listing)

Pierce Promotions
511 Congress St 5th Fl, Portland, ME 04101
(See Separate Listing)

Radiate Group
5000 S Towne Dr, New Berlin, WI 53151
(See Separate Listing)

Health Care-Public Relations

MMG
700 King Farm Blvd Ste 500, Rockville, MD 20850
Tel.: (301) 984-7191
Fax: (301) 921-4405
E-Mail: hwest@mmgct.com
Web Site: www.mmgct.com

Employees: 165
Year Founded: 1987

Agency Specializes In: Communications, Health Care Services, Medical Products, Pharmaceutical

Helen West *(Pres)*
Ann Kottcamp *(COO)*
Kate Clarke *(VP-Fin)*
Jeff Goldfarb *(VP-Oncology, Infectious Diseases & Pub Health Programs)*
Christie Fry *(Dir-Outreach & Recruitment Svcs & Bus Dev)*
Chuck Johnson *(Dir-IT)*
Michael Rosenberg *(Dir-Strategic Dev)*
Carrie Swallow *(Dir-Strategic Dev)*

Interactive Services

Organic, Inc.
600 California St, San Francisco, CA 94108
(See Separate Listing)

Multicultural Marketing

Dieste
1999 Bryan St Ste 2700, Dallas, TX 75201
(See Separate Listing)

Public Relations

Brodeur Partners
399 Boylston St, Boston, MA 02116-2622
(See Separate Listing)

Kreab
(Formerly Kreab Gavin Anderson Worldwide)
Scandinavian House 2-6 Cannon Street, London, EC4M 6XJ United Kingdom
(See Separate Listing)

Retail/Promotional Marketing

The Integer Group, LLC
7245 W Alaska Dr, Lakewood, CO 80226
(See Separate Listing)

TracyLocke
1999 Bryan St Ste 2800, Dallas, TX 75201
(See Separate Listing)

OMNICOM MEDIA GROUP
195 Broadway, New York, NY 10007
Tel.: (212) 590-7020
Web Site: www.omnicommediagroup.com

Employees: 700

National Agency Associations: 4A's

Agency Specializes In: Media Buying Services, Sponsorship

Sheri Rothblatt *(Mng Dir)*
Dale Travis *(Mng Dir)*
David Devonshire *(CFO)*
Kenneth Corriveau *(CIO)*
John Swift *(Pres/CEO-North America Investment)*
Chris Geraci *(Pres-Brdcst-Natl)*
Robert Habeck *(Pres-Global Acct Mgmt-North America)*
Alan Osetek *(Pres-Resolution Media-Global)*
Jonathan Schaaf *(Pres-Digital Investment)*
Kate Stephenson *(Pres-Acct Mgmt-Global)*
Barry Cupples *(CEO-Investment)*
Colin Gottlieb *(CEO-EMEA)*
Lee Smith *(CEO-Platforms)*
Taylor Davis *(Exec VP-Customer Experience)*
Steve Katelman *(Exec VP-Strategic Partnerships-Global)*
Fred Richardson *(Sr VP-Agency Integration)*
P.J Felix *(VP-Fin)*
Kate Corbett *(Grp Dir-HR)*
George Manas *(Grp Dir-Client Strategy & Dev)*
Katherine Orozco *(Grp Acct Dir)*
Ryan Laul *(Dir-Theory)*
Jeff Parkhurst *(Dir-Analytics)*
Vanessa Villanueva *(Dir-Promos)*
Abby Grauman *(Assoc Dir)*
Jaimie Sparber *(Assoc Dir-Digital Media-Lifestyle & Partner Relationship Mgmt)*
Reid Bradley *(Supvr)*
Jenna Lux *(Supvr-Strategy)*
Nicole Rosenberg *(Supvr-Content-The Content Collective)*
Christina Cosmas *(Acct Exec-Outdoor Media Grp)*

Accounts:
Apple Inc.
Ferrero Global Media Buying & Buying, Nutella, Tic Tac
GlaxoSmithKline Global Media Planning & Buying
Hewlett Packard
HTC Media Planning & Buying
Luxottica Group Global Media Planning & Buying
Porsche Global Media Planning & Buying
Security Mentor
Warner Bros. Media Planning & Buying, New Line Cinemas, Time Warner Video

Branches

OMA San Francisco
555 Market St 10th Fl, San Francisco, CA 94105
Tel.: (646) 278-4100

Agency Specializes In: Outdoor

Jennifer Farquhar *(Assoc Dir)*
Renee Ambre *(Acct Supvr)*
Shannon Durkan *(Sr Acct Exec)*

Annalect
195 Broadway 19th Fl, New York, NY 10007
(See Separate Listing)

OMG Atlanta
3500 Lenox Rd Ste 1200, Atlanta, GA 30326
Tel.: (646) 278-4100

Agency Specializes In: Outdoor

Courtney DiCicco *(Sr Acct Exec)*

OMG Chicago
225 N Michigan Ave 21st Fl, Chicago, IL 60601
Tel.: (646) 278-4100

Agency Specializes In: Outdoor

John Rieselman *(Dir-Media)*
Taylor Marshaus *(Asst Acct Exec)*

Accounts:
Nordstrom Media Planning
Porsche Cars North America Media

OMG Los Angeles
5353 Grosvenor Blvd, Los Angeles, CA 90066
Tel.: (646) 278-4100

Agency Specializes In: Outdoor

John Rieselman *(Dir-Media)*
Adam Popkin *(Assoc Dir-Media-OOH)*
Lauren Spinale *(Assoc Dir-OOH-OMD & Outdoor Media Grp)*
Jenna Zellner *(Assoc Dir-Strategy)*
Melissa Abeles *(Acct Supvr)*
Meaghan Necklaus *(Supvr)*
Kim Hung *(Acct Exec)*
Cristina Nette *(Acct Exec)*
Scott Veroda *(Acct Exec)*

OMG New York
195 Broadway, New York, NY 10007
Tel.: (646) 278-4100

Employees: 56

National Agency Associations: 4A's

Agency Specializes In: Outdoor

Dave Yacullo *(Pres & CEO)*
Mike Arden *(Dir-Digital Investment Ops-US)*
Christina Radigan *(Dir-Mktg & Comm)*
Joel Balcita *(Assoc Dir-Outdoor Media Grp)*
Vanessa Hartley *(Assoc Dir)*
Lisa Hentze *(Assoc Dir)*
Gary Pedersen *(Assoc Dir)*
Susan Rezmovic-Cohen *(Assoc Dir)*
Nathalie Lee *(Acct Exec)*

OMG Portland
1001 SW 5th Ave Ste 1230, Portland, OR 97204
Tel.: (646) 278-4100

Agency Specializes In: Outdoor

Stefanie Ryce *(Assoc Dir)*

OMNIFIC
18627 Brookhurst St. #306, Fountain Valley, CA 97208
Tel.: (714) 850-4646
Fax: (714) 850-4650
E-Mail: frontdesk@omnific.com
Web Site: www.omnific.com

Year Founded: 1991

National Agency Associations: AAF

Agency Specializes In: Advertising, Automotive, Bilingual Market, Brand Development & Integration, Branded Entertainment, Broadcast, Business-To-Business, Cable T.V., Co-op Advertising, Communications, Computers & Software, Consulting, Consumer Marketing, Corporate Communications, Corporate Identity, Direct Response Marketing, Direct-to-Consumer, E-Commerce, Education, Electronic Media, Electronics, Email, Entertainment, Event Planning & Marketing, Exhibit/Trade Shows, Faith Based, Food Service, Graphic Design, Guerilla Marketing, Hispanic Market, Identity Marketing, In-Store Advertising, Industrial, Infomercials, Information Technology, Internet/Web Design, Legal Services, Logo & Package Design, Luxury Products, Market Research, Media Buying Services, Media Planning, Media Relations, Mobile Marketing, Multimedia, New Technologies, Newspaper, Newspapers & Magazines, Outdoor, Paid Searches, Podcasting, Point of Purchase, Print, Product Placement, Production, Production (Print), Promotions, Public Relations, Radio, Recruitment, Regional, Restaurant, Retail, Search Engine Optimization, Seniors' Market, Social Marketing/Nonprofit, Social Media, Sponsorship, T.V., Teen Market, Telemarketing, Viral/Buzz/Word of Mouth, Yellow Pages Advertising

Breakdown of Gross Billings by Media: Adv. Specialities: 70%; Audio/Visual: 5%; Brdcst.: 5%; D.M.: 2%; Internet Adv.: 15%; Radio: 3%

Julie Glacy *(Founder & Pres)*
Clifford Randal *(Dir-Creative & Mgr-Ops)*
Don Glacy *(Branch Mgr-Dallas)*

ON IDEAS, INC.
6 E Bay St Ste 100, Jacksonville, FL 32202-5422
Tel.: (904) 354-2600
Fax: (904) 354-7226
E-Mail: info@onideas.com
Web Site: www.onideas.com

Employees: 45
Year Founded: 1983

National Agency Associations: 4A's-PRSA

Agency Specializes In: Advertising, Arts, Brand Development & Integration, Broadcast, Business-To-Business, Cable T.V., Catalogs, Collateral, Communications, Consulting, Consumer Goods, Consumer Marketing, Corporate Communications, Corporate Identity, Crisis Communications, Customer Relationship Management, Digital/Interactive, Direct Response Marketing, Direct-to-Consumer, E-Commerce, Education, Electronic Media, Email, Environmental, Event Planning & Marketing, Exhibit/Trade Shows, Financial, Health Care Services, Household Goods, Identity Marketing, In-Store Advertising, Infomercials, Integrated Marketing, Internet/Web Design, Leisure, Local Marketing, Logo & Package Design, Luxury Products, Market Research, Media Buying Services, Media Planning, Media Relations, Medical Products, Men's Market, Mobile Marketing, Multimedia, Newspaper, Newspapers & Magazines, Out-of-Home Media, Outdoor, Over-50 Market, Package Design, Pets , Planning & Consultation, Point of Purchase, Point of Sale,

Print, Production, Production (Print), Promotions, Public Relations, Publicity/Promotions, Radio, Regional, Restaurant, Retail, Search Engine Optimization, Seniors' Market, Social Marketing/Nonprofit, Social Media, Sponsorship, Strategic Planning/Research, T.V., Travel & Tourism, Viral/Buzz/Word of Mouth, Web (Banner Ads, Pop-ups, etc.), Women's Market

Approx. Annual Billings: $33,000,000

West Herford *(Pres & Partner)*
Thomas J. Bolling *(CEO)*
Frank Costantini *(Partner & Exec Dir-Creative)*
Deonna Carver *(CFO)*
Denise Graham *(Mgmt Supvr)*
Cheryl Parks *(Mgr-Print Production)*
Victoria Grandal *(Coord-New Bus)*

Accounts:
Advanced BioHealing; LaJolla, CA; 2010
Bi-Lo Winn-Dixie (Agency of Record) Commercial, Grocery Retailer, Holiday Storybook; 2005
Catlin Insurance
Catlin; UK Specialty Insurance; 2007
Enterprise Florida
Epstein & Robbins
EverBank
First Federal Bank; Charleston, SC Financial Services; 2005
Halifax Health; Daytona, FL Health Organization; 2007
Jacksonville Jaguars (Agency Of Record) Creative Services, Marketing Strategy, PR/Community Relations Support
Robert Boissoneault Oncology Institute
Veolia Environmental Services North America; Chicago, IL Environmental Services; 2002
Winn-Dixie Campaign: "Stadium Tri-Panel"

ON-TARGET GRAPHICS

PO Box 24124, Santa Barbara, CA 93121
Tel.: (805) 564-2324
Fax: (805) 564-8074
E-Mail: jona@on-targetgraphics.com
Web Site: www.on-targetgraphics.com

E-Mail for Key Personnel:
Creative Dir.: jona@on-targetgraphics.com

Employees: 3
Year Founded: 1994

Agency Specializes In: Corporate Identity, Direct Response Marketing, Exhibit/Trade Shows, Graphic Design, Internet/Web Design, Logo & Package Design, Media Buying Services, Newspapers & Magazines, Pets , Print, Production

Approx. Annual Billings: $1,035,000

Jona Cole Monaghan *(Owner)*

Accounts:
Applebees; FL
Channel Islands National Marine Sanctuary
Four Seasons Biltmore
Perrier; 1999
Santa Barbara Eyeglass Factory; Santa Barbara, CA; 1994
Santa Barbara Maritime Museum
Video Journal of Orthopaedics
Wendy's; 1998

ON-TARGET MARKETING & ADVERTISING

110 Vintage Park Blvd Bldg J Ste 290, Houston, TX 77070
Tel.: (281) 444-4777
E-Mail: info@ontargetagency.com
Web Site: www.ontargetagency.com

Agency Specializes In: Advertising, Brand Development & Integration, Graphic Design, Internet/Web Design

Scott Steiner *(Pres & CEO)*
Tasha Steiner *(COO)*
James Gardner *(Acct Mgr)*
Marlene Migl Satterwhite *(Sr Graphic Designer)*
Lindsey Bub *(Acct Rep)*

Accounts:
The Falls at Imperial Oaks

ONBEYOND LLC

237 Cascade Dr, Fairfax, CA 94930
Tel.: (415) 453-9369
Fax: (415) 453-9042
E-Mail: info@onbeyond.com
Web Site: www.onbeyond.com

Employees: 1
Year Founded: 2003

Agency Specializes In: Advertising, Communications, Consulting, Government/Political, Social Marketing/Nonprofit, Strategic Planning/Research

Revenue: $4,000,000

Breakdown of Gross Billings by Media: Newsp. & Mags.: 100%

Jonathan Polansky *(Owner)*
Sijay James *(Dir-Creative)*

Accounts:
New York State Department of Health
University of California, San Francisco

ONE ADVERTISING

(Name Changed to Sandbox)

ONE EIGHTEEN ADVERTISING

12400 Wilshire Blvd Ste 540, Los Angeles, CA 90025
Tel.: (310) 442-0118
Fax: (310) 442-0141
E-Mail: joinus@oneeighteen.com
Web Site: www.oneeighteen.com

Employees: 20
Year Founded: 2003

National Agency Associations: HSMAI-THINKLA

Agency Specializes In: Advertising, Alternative Advertising, Brand Development & Integration, Business-To-Business, Catalogs, Collateral, Consumer Goods, Corporate Identity, Customer Relationship Management, Direct Response Marketing, Exhibit/Trade Shows, Experience Design, Gay & Lesbian Market, Graphic Design, Guerilla Marketing, Hospitality, Identity Marketing, Internet/Web Design, Local Marketing, Logo & Package Design, Luxury Products, Magazines, Market Research, Newspaper, Newspapers & Magazines, Out-of-Home Media, Outdoor, Package Design, Paid Searches, Planning & Consultation, Print, Production, Production (Print), Radio, Real Estate, Seniors' Market, Strategic Planning/Research, Travel & Tourism, Urban Market, Viral/Buzz/Word of Mouth, Web (Banner Ads, Pop-ups, etc.)

Michael Larson *(Pres)*
Sebastian Souza *(Acct Supvr)*
Abby Beaudin *(Coord-Traffic)*

Accounts:
Audi Pacific
The Counter
Gavina Coffee; Los Angeles, CA; 2003
Martin Resorts
Pacific Porsche
Subaru Pacific
Westfield Shopping Centers
Wood Smith Henning & Berman
Woodside Homes

ONE NET MARKETING INC.

Ste 301-733 Johnson St, Victoria, BC V8W0A4 Canada
Tel.: (250) 483-7411
Web Site: www.onenetmarketing.com

Year Founded: 2006

Agency Specializes In: Advertising, Brand Development & Integration, E-Commerce, Email, Internet/Web Design, Search Engine Optimization, Social Media

Dylan Touhey *(CMO & Principal)*
Michael Tension *(Dir-Art)*
Andy Chan *(Project Mgr-Legal Svcs & Technical)*
Corbin Ching *(Designer-Web & UI)*

Accounts:
FreeMonee Network Inc.
Spirent Axon

ONE SIMPLE PLAN

212 3rd Ave N Ste 320, Minneapolis, MN 55401
Tel.: (612) 767-2403
E-Mail: info@onesimpleplan.com
Web Site: www.onesimpleplan.com

Year Founded: 2007

Agency Specializes In: Advertising, Brand Development & Integration, Corporate Communications, Event Planning & Marketing, Internet/Web Design, Media Relations, Public Relations, Social Media, Strategic Planning/Research

John Feld *(Sr VP & Dir-Acct Mgmt)*
Dane Roberts *(Producer, Mgr-Social Media & Sr Copywriter)*
Andrea Foss *(Mgr-Acct & Project)*
Amanda Buhman *(Acct Mgr)*
Lee Jones *(Mgr-Media Rels)*

Accounts:
Dunn Bros Coffee
Surly Brewing Company

ONE TRIBE CREATIVE LLC

200 S College Ave Ste 140, Fort Collins, CO 80524
Tel.: (970) 221-4254
Web Site: www.onetribecreative.com

Employees: 5

Agency Specializes In: Advertising, Brand Development & Integration, Collateral, Package Design, Search Engine Optimization, Social Media

Revenue: $1,000,000

Paul Jensen *(Owner & Creative Dir)*
Jon Aguilera *(Dir-Design)*
Jaime Whitlock Donnelly *(Dir-Mktg & Comm)*

Accounts:
Denver AntiTrafficking Alliance

ONE TRICK PONY

251 Bellevue Ave 2nd Fl, Hammonton, NJ 8037
Tel.: (609) 704-2660

E-Mail: info@1trickpony.com
Web Site: www.1trickpony.com

Agency Specializes In: Advertising, Brand Development & Integration, Digital/Interactive, Graphic Design, Logo & Package Design, Print, Production, Radio, T.V.

Keith Pizer *(Owner)*
Sharlene Campanella *(Sr Acct Dir)*
Stephen Snyder *(Acct Dir)*
Bill Starkey *(Dir-Creative)*
Mike Mielcarz *(Assoc Dir-Creative)*
Raghav Hardas *(Copywriter)*
Dan Gomba *(Sr Acct Coord)*

Accounts:
Dark Candi
Ditch Plains
Gorilla Coffee
Gotham Sound & Communications, Inc
La Pomme
Leo's Bagels
Union Square Events
Virgin Mobile USA, Inc. Campaign: "Rumors", Virgin Hotel

ONE/X
3535 Hayden Ave, Culver City, CA 90232
Tel.: (310) 289-4422
Fax: (310) 289-4423
Web Site: www.one-x.com

Employees: 7

Agency Specializes In: Advertising, Industrial

Jason Wulfsohn *(Dir)*

Accounts:
Firefly
Infectiguard
Vizio HDTV; 2008

O'NEILL COMMUNICATIONS
280 Interstate North Cir SE, Atlanta, GA 30339
Tel.: (770) 578-9765
Fax: (770) 509-0027
Web Site: www.oneillcommunications.com

Employees: 7

Agency Specializes In: Advertising, Brand Development & Integration, Business-To-Business, College, Communications, Consulting, Consumer Marketing, Corporate Communications, Customer Relationship Management, Digital/Interactive, Event Planning & Marketing, Food Service, Graphic Design, In-Store Advertising, Internet/Web Design, Local Marketing, Magazines, Media Buying Services, Media Relations, Newspaper, Outdoor, Print, Production, Promotions, Public Relations, Publicity/Promotions, Publishing, Search Engine Optimization, Social Media, Strategic Planning/Research

Gordon O'Neill *(Pres)*
Devika Rao *(Editor, Acct Mgr & Writer)*

Accounts:
American Fence Association; Glen Ellyn, IL
Association of Family Practice Physician Assistants; Roswell, GA
Georgia Association of Physician Assistants; Roswell, GA
Southern Museum of Civil War & Locomotive History; Kennesaw, GA

ONEMETHOD INC
445 King Street West Suite 201, Toronto, ON M5V 1K4 Canada
Tel.: (416) 649-0180
E-Mail: ideas@onemethod.com
Web Site: www.onemethod.com

Year Founded: 2001

Agency Specializes In: Advertising, Brand Development & Integration, Digital/Interactive, Mobile Marketing, Social Media, Strategic Planning/Research

Amin Todai *(Pres & Chief Creative Officer)*
Dave Nourse *(Mng Dir & Sr VP)*
Janice Boduch *(VP & Grp Acct Dir)*
Steve Shaddick *(Head-Technical)*
Jonathan Hotts *(Dir-Art)*
Lionel Wong *(Assoc Dir-Creative)*
Raymond Tong *(Project Mgr-Digital)*
Crystal Gibson *(Strategist-Social Media)*
Karen Oakley *(Copywriter)*

Accounts:
Biore
Fortress Real Capital Real Estate Investment Service Providers
Intuit
Nokia Mobile Phones & Accessories Mfr & Distr
Quiznos
Sony
Toronto Raptors
W3 Awards Awards Provider
The Young Onez Raptors Supporters

ONEUPWEB
13561 S W Bayshore Dr Ste 3000, Traverse City, MI 49684
Tel.: (231) 922-9977
Fax: (231) 922-9966
Toll Free: (877) 568-7477
E-Mail: info@oneupweb.com
Web Site: www.oneupweb.com

Employees: 35
Year Founded: 2000

National Agency Associations: AMA-DMA

Agency Specializes In: Digital/Interactive, Internet/Web Design, Media Planning, Mobile Marketing, Paid Searches, Podcasting, RSS (Really Simple Syndication), Search Engine Optimization, Web (Banner Ads, Pop-ups, etc.)

Lisa Wehr *(Pres & CEO)*
Christopher Carol *(Dir-Bus Strategy & Gen Counsel)*
Sara Ariza *(Client Svcs Dir)*
Shawn Finn *(Dir-Paid Strategy)*
Jared Yaple *(Sr Acct Mgr)*
Frederic Hunt *(Project Mgr-Content Mktg)*
Alaina Dodds *(Strategist-Brand)*
Todd Spencer *(Copywriter-SEO & Content Mktg)*

Accounts:
Artnet Worldwide Online Auctions, Pay-Per-Click Campaign; 2007
Brooks Running
Maritz
Muzak, LLC
SHUTTERFLY, INC
Symantec
ThinkGeek
TracFone
Unisys
Victory Motorcycles

ONEWORLD COMMUNICATIONS, INC.
2001 Harrison St, San Francisco, CA 94110
Tel.: (415) 355-1935
Fax: (415) 355-0295
E-Mail: oneworld@owcom.com
Web Site: www.oneworldsf.com

Employees: 20
Year Founded: 1994

Agency Specializes In: Above-the-Line, Advertising, Affluent Market, African-American Market, Agriculture, Alternative Advertising, Arts, Asian Market, Automotive, Below-the-Line, Bilingual Market, Brand Development & Integration, Branded Entertainment, Broadcast, Business Publications, Business-To-Business, Cable T.V., Children's Market, Co-op Advertising, Collateral, College, Commercial Photography, Communications, Computers & Software, Consulting, Consumer Goods, Consumer Marketing, Consumer Publications, Content, Corporate Communications, Corporate Identity, Crisis Communications, Custom Publishing, Digital/Interactive, Direct Response Marketing, Direct-to-Consumer, E-Commerce, Education, Electronic Media, Electronics, Email, Engineering, Entertainment, Environmental, Exhibit/Trade Shows, Experience Design, Fashion/Apparel, Financial, Gay & Lesbian Market, Government/Political, Graphic Design, Guerilla Marketing, Health Care Services, High Technology, Hispanic Market, Hospitality, Household Goods, Identity Marketing, Industrial, Infomercials, Information Technology, Integrated Marketing, International, Internet/Web Design, Investor Relations, Leisure, Local Marketing, Logo & Package Design, Luxury Products, Magazines, Marine, Market Research, Media Buying Services, Media Planning, Media Relations, Media Training, Medical Products, Men's Market, Merchandising, Mobile Marketing, Multicultural, Multimedia, New Product Development, New Technologies, Newspaper, Newspapers & Magazines, Out-of-Home Media, Outdoor, Over-50 Market, Package Design, Paid Searches, Planning & Consultation, Podcasting, Print, Production, Production (Ad, Film, Broadcast), Production (Print), Promotions, Public Relations, Publicity/Promotions, Publishing, Radio, Real Estate, Recruitment, Regional, Restaurant, Retail, Sales Promotion, Search Engine Optimization, Seniors' Market, Social Marketing/Nonprofit, Social Media, South Asian Market, Sponsorship, Sports Market, Stakeholders, Strategic Planning/Research, Syndication, T.V., Technical Advertising, Teen Market, Trade & Consumer Magazines, Transportation, Travel & Tourism, Urban Market, Viral/Buzz/Word of Mouth, Web (Banner Ads, Pop-ups, etc.), Women's Market

Breakdown of Gross Billings by Media: Adv. Specialities: 4%; Comml. Photography: 3%; Exhibits/Trade Shows: 2%; Graphic Design: 6%; Newsp. & Mags.: 10%; Outdoor: 5%; Print: 5%; Pub. Rels.: 5%; Radio: 35%; Strategic Planning/Research: 10%; Worldwide Web Sites: 15%

Jonathan Villet *(Pres & Dir-Creative & Strategic Svcs)*
Norman Buten *(Dir-Creative & Copywriter)*
Fiona McDougall *(Dir-Creative Production)*
Teresa Schnabel *(Dir-Mktg Res)*
Roger Burgner *(Mgr-Production)*
David Wren *(Strategist-MarCom & Copywriter)*
Marguerite Cueto *(Strategist-Mktg)*

Accounts:
California Coastal Commission Environmental Protection
California Department of Consumers Affairs; 2008
California Relay Service Telephone 711; 2010
Sandia Laboratories Energy Research; 2009
State of California Deaf & Disabled Telecommunications Program; 2010
U.S. Department of Agriculture Food Safety; 2006

ONIT MARKETING
1550 Larimer St, #767, Denver, CO 80202

Advertising Agencies

Tel.: (202) 258-0657
Web Site: www.onitmarketing.com

Agency Specializes In: Digital/Interactive, Social Media

Roni Rudell *(Principal)*

Accounts:
Boiron
Kickstand Magazine
SPIRE Denver
The Walnut Room
Yellowman Clothing

ONLINE CORPORATION OF AMERICA
PO Box 1604, Milford, PA 18337
Tel.: (570) 686-2300
Fax: (570) 686-9090
Toll Free: (888) 250-8100
E-Mail: sales@onlinecorp.com
Web Site: www.onlinecorp.com

E-Mail for Key Personnel:
President: ek@onlinecorp.com
Creative Dir.: ecronin@onlinecorp.com

Employees: 30
Year Founded: 1993

Agency Specializes In: Consulting, Electronic Media, Information Technology, Internet/Web Design

Approx. Annual Billings: $3,500,000

Elliott J. Kayne *(CEO)*

ONPOINT IMAGE & DESIGN INC
525 5th Ave, Pelham, NY 10803
Tel.: (914) 738-6066
Fax: (914) 738-6073
Web Site: www.oidny.com

Year Founded: 1997

Agency Specializes In: Advertising, Digital/Interactive, Print, Promotions

Richard Sohanchyk *(Founder & CEO)*
Sandra Correa *(Dir-Art)*

Accounts:
Harrison High School
Pelham Children's Theater
Port Chester High School
Stepinac High School

ONTOGENY ADVERTISING & DESIGN LLC
PO Box 221, Mosinee, WI 54455
Tel.: (715) 570-0181
Fax: (715) 457-2209
Web Site: www.ontogenyadvertising.com

Year Founded: 2009

Agency Specializes In: Advertising, Broadcast, Event Planning & Marketing, Graphic Design, Internet/Web Design, Media Buying Services, Media Planning, Outdoor, Print, Public Relations

Erin Crawford *(Co-Founder & Dir-Creative)*
Leslie Brown *(Co-Founder & Bus Mgr)*

Accounts:
Cedar Creek Mall
Idea Charter School
The Patriot Center

ONTRACK COMMUNICATIONS
68 Broadview Ave Ste 407, Toronto, ON M4M 2E6 Canada
Tel.: (416) 304-0449
Fax: (416) 304-0473
E-Mail: info@ontrackcommunications.ca
Web Site: www.ontrackcommunications.ca

Employees: 3
Year Founded: 1998

Agency Specializes In: Advertising

Tim Mclarty *(Owner)*

Accounts:
TV Listings

OOHOLOGY
40 Executive Dr, Carmel, IN 46032
Tel.: (317) 550-3420
E-Mail: hello@oohology.com
Web Site: www.oohology.com

Agency Specializes In: Advertising, Brand Development & Integration, Digital/Interactive, Internet/Web Design, Print

Rob Miles *(Founder & Designer)*
Sean Breslin *(CEO)*
Chuck Burke *(Partner & COO)*
Kate Morrison *(CMO)*
David Woodmansee *(CTO)*
Kat French *(Dir-Copy)*
Rahman McGinnis *(Dir-Front-End Dev)*
Kelli McFall *(Mgr-Digital Media)*

Accounts:
Collidea
Dr. T. Gerald ODaniel
New-Louisville Slugger Museum & Factory (Agency of Record) Creative Campaigns, Digital, Exhibit Design, Placement, Traditional Media Planning
OpenRange Gun Range
The Parklands of Floyds Fork
Tim Lange

OOTEM, INC.
276 Shipley St, San Francisco, CA 94107
Tel.: (415) 655-1327
Fax: (415) 520-6922
E-Mail: letschat@ootem.com
Web Site: www.ootem.com

Year Founded: 2009

Agency Specializes In: Advertising

Jason Kelley *(Founder & Pres)*
Andrew Davis *(Dir-Creative)*
Todd Ferrell *(Dir-Acctg)*

Accounts:
Eventbrite
The Pkware Solution
Viivo

OOYALA, INC.
800 W El Camino Real Ste 350, Mountain View, CA 94040
Tel.: (650) 961-3400
E-Mail: info@ooyala.com
Web Site: www.ooyala.com

Year Founded: 2007

Agency Specializes In: Advertising, Digital/Interactive, T.V.

Sean Knapp *(Founder & CTO)*
Dave Hare *(Sr VP-Customer Success)*
Sorosh Tavakoli *(Sr VP-Adtech)*
Chris Wong *(Sr VP-Corp & Bus Dev)*
Caitlin Spaan *(VP-Mktg)*
Mike Petro *(Dir-Value Engrg)*

Accounts:
Comedy.com
Dell
Electronic Arts
Endemol
Esurance
Fremantle
General Mills
The Glam Network
Glam
IMG
Red Bull
SAP
Telegraph Media Group
Telegraph
Vans
Voig
Warner Brothers

OPEN. A CREATIVE COMPANY
850 Adelaide St W, Toronto, ON M6J 1B6 Canada
Tel.: (647) 478-6603
E-Mail: hello@openacreativecompany.com
Web Site: www.openacreativecompany.com

Agency Specializes In: Advertising, Digital/Interactive, Strategic Planning/Research

Martin Beauvais *(Partner)*
Christian Mathieu *(Partner-Strategy)*
Tyler McKissick *(Dir-Art)*
Nicolas Rouleau *(Acct Exec)*
Laurabeth Cooper *(Copywriter)*
Samara Luck *(Copywriter)*

Accounts:
Bier Markt Abbey Bier Fest, Campaign: "Bier is Beautiful"
Casey's
Cineplex
ComFree
Damiva Campaign: "Drier Than A British Comedy", Campaign: "Enough Beating Around The Bush"
Environmental Defence
Evergreen Campaign: "Get Dirty", Repositioning
FB Avocat
Food Basics (Agency of Record) Marketing
Frontier Networks
Kamik (Agency of Record) Branding, Messaging
Microsoft
Xbox Campaign: "The Marketers' Anthem"
Okanagan Spring Brewery Campaign: "Stay Pure"
OMAC
Sleeman Breweries Media Campaign, Okanagan Spring, Old Milwaukee, Retail
Smythe Les Vestes
Toys 'R' Us Babies "R" Us, Creative, National Radio

OPENFIELD CREATIVE
1 W 4th St 25th Fl, Cincinnati, OH 45202
Tel.: (513) 621-6736
E-Mail: opendialogue@openfieldcreative.com
Web Site: www.openfieldcreative.com

Year Founded: 2006

Agency Specializes In: Brand Development & Integration, Collateral, Digital/Interactive, Internet/Web Design, Social Media

Josh Barnes *(Co-Founder)*
Brandon Blangger *(Co-Founder)*
Brian Keenan *(Co-Founder)*
Chris Albert *(VP-Creative)*
D. Scott Frondorf *(VP-Strategy)*

Trevor Minton *(VP-Creative)*
Erika Kauffeld *(Acct Mgr)*
Brian Nikonow *(Designer-UX)*

Accounts:
AssetLogic Group, LLC
Detroit Economic Growth, Corp.
Enercrest, Inc.
Fosdick & Hilmer
KC Harvey Environmental, LLC
Okland Construction
Process Plus LLC
Skanska AB

OPFER COMMUNICATIONS INC.
2861 S Meadowbrook Ave, Springfield, MO 65807
Tel.: (800) 966-2400
Fax: (417) 885-0199
Web Site: www.opfer.com

Year Founded: 1988

Agency Specializes In: Advertising, Direct Response Marketing, Direct-to-Consumer, T.V.

Scott Opfer *(Founder & Pres)*
Robert White *(VP & Dir-Creative)*
Scott Reich *(Dir-Photography)*
Natalie Stewart *(Dir-Ops)*
Deborah Hartwig *(Mgr-Production)*
David Middleton *(Specialist-Media)*
Krissy Bernhardi *(Field Producer)*

Accounts:
Amazing Inventions
Bushnell Outdoor Products, Inc.
Forever Lazy
Generac Power Systems Inc.
Huffy Bicycle Company
Paint Zoom, LLC
Patch Perfect
PitchMen
Stamina Products, Inc.

OPPERMANWEISS
55-59 Chrystie Ste 500, New York, NY 10002
Tel.: (212) 226-2324
E-Mail: hello@oppermanweiss.com
Web Site: www.oppermanweiss.com

Agency Specializes In: Advertising, Brand Development & Integration

Julian Shiff *(Mng Dir)*
Conor Firth *(CFO)*
Benjamin Bailey *(Exec Creative Dir)*

Accounts:
New-Chobani LLC

OPTFIRST INC.
1111 Lincoln Rd #400, Miami Beach, FL 33139
Tel.: (305) 428-2539
Web Site: www.optfirst.com

Year Founded: 2001

Agency Specializes In: Search Engine Optimization

John Vincent Kriney *(Pres)*

Accounts:
AAA Miami Locksmiths

OPTIC NERVE DIRECT MARKETING
457 30th St Ste A WWing, San Francisco, CA 94131
Tel.: (415) 647-9462
Fax: (415) 647-1616
E-Mail: james@opticnervedirect.com
Web Site: www.opticnervedirect.com

Employees: 5
Year Founded: 2001

National Agency Associations: DMA

Agency Specializes In: Advertising, Advertising Specialties, African-American Market, Arts, Bilingual Market, Brand Development & Integration, Business Publications, Business-To-Business, Collateral, Communications, Consulting, Consumer Marketing, Consumer Publications, Corporate Communications, Corporate Identity, Direct Response Marketing, Email, Engineering, Exhibit/Trade Shows, Faith Based, Financial, Gay & Lesbian Market, Graphic Design, Health Care Services, Hispanic Market, Integrated Marketing, International, Logo & Package Design, Magazines, Medical Products, Multicultural, New Product Development, Outdoor, Pets , Pharmaceutical, Point of Purchase, Print, Production (Print), Public Relations, Real Estate, Recruitment, Social Marketing/Nonprofit, Strategic Planning/Research, Transportation, Travel & Tourism

Approx. Annual Billings: $1,000,000

Breakdown of Gross Billings by Media: D.M.: 100%

Accounts:
Bohannon Holman; Atlanta, GA Financial Services; 2003
Boys Hope Girls Hope; San Francisco, CA; 2006
Cyclades; Fremont, CA
Exploratorium
Gentiae; San Francisco, CA Pharmaceuticals
Jewish Family & Children's Services
Karikter; San Francisco, CA
Platinum Financial Group
Rotaplast International; San Francisco, CA
SHANTI; San Francisco, CA; 2004
Wells Fargo; San Francisco, CA

OPTIMUM SPORTS
195 Broadway 17th Fl, New York, NY 10007
Tel.: (212) 590-7100
Web Site: www.optimumsports.com

National Agency Associations: 4A's

Agency Specializes In: Media Planning, Media Relations, Sports Market

Tom McGovern *(Mng Dir)*
Josh Farber *(Acct Dir)*
Jared Banks *(Dir)*
Vanessa Berrios *(Supvr)*
Shannon Ford *(Acct Exec)*
Kristen Gray *(Assoc Acct Dir)*

Accounts:
Callaway Golf
Dicks Sporting Goods "Hell Week"
Diet Mountain Dew
Gatorade
Infiniti
Kobalt
Lowe's
Nissan
Reeses
State Farm
Tostitos
Under Armour

OPTO DESIGN
153 W 27th St Ste 1201, New York, NY 10001
Tel.: (212) 254-4470
Fax: (212) 254-5266
E-Mail: hello@optodesign.com
Web Site: optodesign.com

Employees: 7

Agency Specializes In: Advertising, Arts, Collateral, Communications, Corporate Identity, Custom Publishing, Digital/Interactive, Electronic Media, Industrial, Internet/Web Design, Multimedia, Newspaper, Newspapers & Magazines, Print, Publishing, Real Estate, Sports Market

Ron Louie *(Owner)*
John Klotnia *(Partner)*

Accounts:
Aperture Foundation
Business Week
Executive Council
Insight Out of Chaos
The New York Times Company
New York Times Digital
NYU Alumni Magazine
Universe Publishing

OPTS IDEAS
1 Gate Six Rd Ste B203, Sausalito, CA 94965
Tel.: (415) 339-2020
Fax: (208) 342-8482
E-Mail: info@optsideas.com
Web Site: www.optsideas.com

Employees: 15
Year Founded: 1982

Revenue: $2,600,000

Michael Christman *(Owner)*
Lisa Holland *(Pres & Partner)*
Chris Fitzgerald *(Partner)*
Sophia Larroque *(Partner)*

Accounts:
AOL Time Warner
Apple
Ariba
Asera
BarnesAndNoble.com
Hyperion Solutions
Intel
LPL Financial
Microsoft Corporation

OPUS 59 CREATIVE GROUP
250 N Trade St Ste 209, Matthews, NC 28105
Tel.: (704) 847-4959
Web Site: www.opus59.com

Year Founded: 2007

Agency Specializes In: Advertising, Brand Development & Integration, Business-To-Business, Content, Internet/Web Design, Print, Public Relations, Social Media

Derick Wells *(Partner & Dir-Creative)*
Mark Harrison *(Partner)*

Accounts:
Cargill Dow, llc
OrthoCarolina
Premier, Inc.

ORANGE BARREL
3400 SW Blvd, Grove City, OH 43123
Tel.: (614) 294-4898
Fax: (614) 875-1175
Web Site: www.orangebarrelmedia.com

Agency Specializes In: Advertising, Brand Development & Integration

K. Alex Compston *(COO)*
Danielle Williamson *(VP-Sls)*
Mary Vaughn Mahan *(Dir-Sls)*

Eric Forbes *(Asst Mgr-Ops)*
Megan Knott *(Acct Exec)*
Lorin Wolf *(Acct Exec)*
Patrick McCavanagh *(Reg Acct Exec)*

Accounts:
Riverside Methodist Hospital

ORANGE LABEL ART & ADVERTISING

4000 MacArthur Blvd, Newport Beach, CA 92660
Tel.: (949) 631-9900
Fax: (949) 631-8800
E-Mail: info@orangelabeladvertising.com
Web Site: www.orangelabeladvertising.com

Employees: 15
Year Founded: 1972

Agency Specializes In: Advertising Specialties, Business-To-Business, Co-op Advertising, Direct Response Marketing, Hispanic Market, Information Technology, Media Buying Services, New Technologies, Radio, Retail, Strategic Planning/Research, Teen Market

Revenue: $5,000,000

Rochelle Reiter *(Owner & Principal)*
Wesley Phillips *(CEO)*
Colleen Haberman *(Dir-Special Projects)*
Debbie Nagel *(Dir-Ops)*
Alyse Stranberg *(Strategist)*
Kim Chow *(Coord-Media, Acct & Res)*

Accounts:
Allfax
Chapman University
Coordinated Business Systems
Dameron Hospital
Friar Tux Shop
Greenwell Farms
Hawaii Forest & Trail
Irvine Company
James Imaging Systems
Kahoots Feed and Pet
National Merchants Association
Pacific Architectural Millwork
Seattle Talent
Sharp Electronic Corporation
Tulsa Rib Company

ORANGESEED, INC.

901 N 3rd St Ste 305, Minneapolis, MN 55401
Tel.: (612) 252-9757
E-Mail: info@orangeseed.com
Web Site: www.orangeseed.com

Year Founded: 1996

Agency Specializes In: Advertising, Brand Development & Integration, Digital/Interactive, Event Planning & Marketing, Internet/Web Design

Jon Garrett *(Partner & CFO)*

Accounts:
The Chest Foundation
KDV
Twin Cities In Motion
Washburn Center for Children

ORANGESQUARE

1 S Orange Ave Ste 401, Orlando, FL 32801
Tel.: (407) 494-4022
Web Site: www.orangesquare.net

Year Founded: 2007

Agency Specializes In: Advertising, Brand Development & Integration, Collateral, Graphic Design, Internet/Web Design, Logo & Package Design, Media Buying Services, Media Planning, Print, Social Media

Matt Phillips *(Creative Dir & Strategist-Brand)*

Accounts:
TeamGina

ORLOFF WILLIAMS

66 E Santa Clara St 230, San Jose, CA 95113
Tel.: (408) 293-1791
Web Site: www.orloffwilliams.com

Agency Specializes In: Advertising, Brand Development & Integration, Government/Political, Media Buying Services, Media Relations, Print, Public Relations

Mike Bohrer *(Principal)*

Accounts:
New-Insight Realty Co.

THE ORTON GROUP, INC.

204 E 900 S, Salt Lake City, UT 84111-4215
Tel.: (801) 596-2100
Fax: (801) 596-2151
E-Mail: info@ortongp.com
Web Site: www.ortongroup.net

Employees: 7
Year Founded: 1985

National Agency Associations: AAF

Agency Specializes In: Advertising, Automotive, Business-To-Business, E-Commerce, Electronic Media, Financial, Food Service, Government/Political, Graphic Design, Health Care Services, Industrial, Media Buying Services, Public Relations, Travel & Tourism

Approx. Annual Billings: $6,864,000

Breakdown of Gross Billings by Media: Bus. Publs.: $343,200; Collateral: $960,960; D.M.: $686,400; Mags.: $274,560; Newsp.: $686,400; Outdoor: $343,200; Point of Purchase: $137,280; Radio: $686,400; T.V.: $2,745,600

Larry J. Orton *(Pres)*

Accounts:
Beehive Bail Bonds
Blue Stakes of Utah
Bryce Valley Business Association
Cornerstone
Cornerstone Counseling Center
Dave Strong Porsche
Dave Strong Porsche
Energy Foundation
Energy Foundation of Utah
Forseys
Health Department of Utah
Moon Lake Electrical Cooperative
Mt. Wheeler Power
St. George Area Convention & Visitors' Bureau
Strong Audi
Strong Volkswagen
Utah Health Department
WENCO
Wendy's International
Zions Bank
Zions First National Bank

OSBORN & BARR COMMUNICATIONS

Cupples Sta 914 Spruce St, Saint Louis, MO 63102
Tel.: (314) 726-5511
Fax: (314) 726-6350
Toll Free: (888) BELIEF-2
E-Mail: dillons@osborn-barr.com
Web Site: www.osborn-barr.com

E-Mail for Key Personnel:
Creative Dir.: chechikm@osborn-barr.com
Public Relations: mcdowallc@osborn-barr.com

Employees: 140
Year Founded: 1988

National Agency Associations: 4A's-AAF-AD CLUB-PRSA

Agency Specializes In: Advertising, Agriculture, Brand Development & Integration, Broadcast, Business Publications, Business-To-Business, Co-op Advertising, Collateral, Communications, Consulting, Corporate Identity, Crisis Communications, Digital/Interactive, Direct Response Marketing, E-Commerce, Electronic Media, Event Planning & Marketing, Exhibit/Trade Shows, Financial, Government/Political, High Technology, Internet/Web Design, Media Buying Services, Media Training, Newspaper, Newspapers & Magazines, Out-of-Home Media, Outdoor, Planning & Consultation, Point of Purchase, Print, Production, Public Relations, Publicity/Promotions, Radio, Recruitment, Search Engine Optimization, Sponsorship, Strategic Planning/Research, T.V., Technical Advertising

Approx. Annual Billings: $68,000,000

Breakdown of Gross Billings by Media: Internet Adv.: 1%; Mags.: 46%; Network Radio: 3%; Network T.V.: 5%; Newsp.: 29%; Outdoor: 1%; Spot Radio: 15%

Stephen D. Barr *(Chm)*
Michael Turley *(CEO & Partner)*
Rhonda Ries-Aguilar *(Partner & CFO)*
Susan Knese *(Chief Talent Officer & VP)*
Traci Bertz *(Dir-Creative Svcs)*
Eric Nelson *(Dir-Media)*
Fred Thacker *(Mgr)*
Trista Thompson *(Supvr)*
Jennifer Dolan *(Sr Media Planner)*

Accounts:
Merck Animal Health Equine, Cattle, & Swine
Michelin North America; Greenville, SC Agriculture & Compact Line Tires; 2003
Monsanto Co.; Saint Lous, MO; 1988
Monsanto Dairy; Saint Louis, MO; 2006
National Cattlemen's Beef Association
Solutia Inc. Vydyne
Specialty Fertilizer Products; 2005
United Soybean Board; Saint Louis, MO

Branches

Osborn & Barr

304 W 8th St, Kansas City, MO 64105-1513
Tel.: (816) 471-2255
Fax: (816) 471-7477
Toll Free: (888) 235-4332
Web Site: www.osborn-barr.com

Employees: 32
Year Founded: 1999

National Agency Associations: 4A's

Agency Specializes In: Advertising, Advertising Specialties, Agriculture, Brand Development & Integration, Broadcast, Business Publications, Business-To-Business, Co-op Advertising, Collateral, Communications, Consulting, Consumer Marketing, Consumer Publications, Corporate Identity, Direct Response Marketing, Electronic Media, Environmental, Event Planning & Marketing, Exhibit/Trade Shows, Financial, Government/Political, Graphic Design, Internet/Web Design, Logo & Package Design,

Magazines, Media Buying Services, New Product Development, Newspapers & Magazines, Out-of-Home Media, Outdoor, Pets , Planning & Consultation, Point of Purchase, Print, Production, Public Relations, Publicity/Promotions, Radio, Recruitment, Sales Promotion, Sports Market, Strategic Planning/Research, T.V., Technical Advertising, Trade & Consumer Magazines

Steve Barr *(Chm)*
Michael Turley *(CEO & Partner)*
Rhonda Ries-Aguilar *(Partner & CFO)*
Colleen Church-McDowall *(VP & Dir-PR)*
Stuart Knowlan *(Dir-Art)*
Courtney Floresca *(Assoc Dir-Integrated Media)*

Accounts:
Asgrow
Intervet Animal Health
Michelin Ag Tires
Round Up Ready Canola
Specialty Fertilizer Products
USB Check Off
Yield Guard Plus

OSTER & ASSOCIATES, INC.

3525 5th Ave 2nd Fl, San Diego, CA 92103
Tel.: (619) 906-5540
Fax: (619) 906-5541
E-Mail: info@osterads.com
Web Site: www.osterads.com

E-Mail for Key Personnel:
President: bevo@osterads.com
Creative Dir.: bevo@osterads.com
Media Dir.: karino@osterads.com
Production Mgr.: karino@osterads.com
Public Relations: toddl@osterads.com

Employees: 7
Year Founded: 1986

National Agency Associations: AAF-Second Wind Limited

Agency Specializes In: Advertising, Agriculture, Brand Development & Integration, Business Publications, Business-To-Business, Cable T.V., Catalogs, Collateral, Consulting, Consumer Marketing, Consumer Publications, Environmental, Identity Marketing, Local Marketing, Media Buying Services, Media Planning, Media Relations, Media Training, Outdoor, Package Design, Planning & Consultation, Print, Production, Production (Print), Public Relations, Publicity/Promotions, Search Engine Optimization, T.V., Technical Advertising, Trade & Consumer Magazines, Web (Banner Ads, Pop-ups, etc.)

Approx. Annual Billings: $4,000,000

Breakdown of Gross Billings by Media: Bus. Publs.: 10%; Farm Publs.: 15%; Fees: 10%; Mags.: 5%; Production: 30%; Pub. Rels.: 10%; Radio: 10%; T.V.: 10%

Karin Salas *(VP)*
Patrick Pierce *(Mgr-PR)*
Tyler Schirado *(Acct Exec)*
Aryana Aguiar *(Acct Coord)*

Accounts:
Big Bear Mountain
BigBear Mountain Resorts; 2005
Latitude 33 (Agency of Record)
Organics Unlimited; San Diego, CA

O'SULLIVAN COMMUNICATIONS

42 Davis Rd Ste 1, Acton, MA 01720
Tel.: (978) 264-0707
E-Mail: info@ocmarketing.com
Web Site: www.ocmarketing.com

Employees: 5
Year Founded: 1991

Agency Specializes In: Public Relations

Gabe D'Annunzio *(Partner)*
Joseph Bonis *(Exec VP, CFO & Chief Creative Officer)*
Alison Fischer *(Sr VP-Ops)*
Paul Fuzzi *(VP-Manufacturing & Production)*
Martin Yeager *(VP-Publ Tech)*
David Schertz *(Controller)*
Cheryl Forziati *(Sr Dir-Art)*
Neil Fajardo *(Dir-IT)*
Steve Mruskovic *(Dir-Creative Svcs)*
Julie Zangara-Nemetz *(Mgr-Imaging Svcs)*

Accounts:
The City of Lowell
MassTrack
Town of Falmouth

OTEY WHITE & ASSOCIATES

8146 One Calais Ave, Baton Rouge, LA 70808-3155
Tel.: (225) 201-0032
Fax: (225) 761-9000
E-Mail: oteyw@oteywhite.com
Web Site: www.oteywhite.com

Employees: 6
Year Founded: 1981

Agency Specializes In: Automotive, Retail, Sponsorship, Sports Market

Otey L. White, III *(Pres)*
Melanie Cassidy *(VP-Acct Svcs)*
Jennifer Gordon *(Sr Acct Dir)*
Trent Bland *(Dir-Creative & Copywriter)*
Blake Breaux *(Dir-Art)*
Piper Wilson *(Dir-Fin)*
Kylie Collins *(Sr Acct Mgr)*
Jack K. White *(Mgr-Brdcst Production)*
Hanna Gueringer *(Acct Exec)*

Accounts:
Cox Sports
Genuine Parts Company
Junior League of Baton Rouge
Marucci Bat Company
NAPA Auto Parts National
Spectrum
Stonehenge Capital Company
Tiger Athletic Foundation

OTHERWISE INC

1144 W Randolph St, Chicago, IL 60607
Tel.: (312) 226-1144
Fax: (312) 226-3836
E-Mail: info@otherwiseinc.com
Web Site: www.otherwiseinc.com

Agency Specializes In: Advertising, Brand Development & Integration, Corporate Identity, Digital/Interactive, Graphic Design, Internet/Web Design, Package Design, Print, Social Media

Nancy Lerner *(Pres & Chief Strategy Officer)*
David Frej *(Chief Creative Officer & VP)*

Accounts:
Baird & Warner Campaign: "Begin A Whole New Chapter", Campaign: "Grab Life & Get Going", Campaign: "Live On Bank Street", Campaign: "Move In Move Up", Campaign: "Take Care Of Your Heart", Campaign: "Unwrap The Present"

OTTAWAY COMMUNICATIONS, INC.

3250 W Big Beaver Rd Ste 230, Troy, MI 48084
Tel.: (248) 637-4600
Web Site: www.ottaway.net

Agency Specializes In: Advertising, Brand Development & Integration, Event Planning & Marketing, Graphic Design, Logo & Package Design, Media Buying Services, Media Planning, Print, Public Relations, Strategic Planning/Research

Bob Ottaway *(Owner)*

Accounts:
ABC Warehouse
Ann Arbor Automotive Group
Auto Week Magazine
Botsford Hospital
Celani Family Vineyard
Complete Battery Source
Crain Communications, Inc.
Diamond Jacks Riverboat Tours
Farmer Johns Greenhouse
Gorno Ford & Gorno Mazda

OTTO

1611 Colley Ave, Norfolk, VA 23517
Tel.: (757) 622-4050
Fax: (757) 623-4824
E-Mail: info@thinkotto.com
Web Site: http://new.thinkotto.com/

Employees: 30
Year Founded: 2000

National Agency Associations: Second Wind Limited

Mark Edward Atkinson *(Owner)*
Pete Leddy *(Partner & Pres)*
Jaycen Leblanc *(Sr Dir-Art)*
Hunter Spencer *(Sr Dir-Art)*
Sherri Priester *(Dir-Media)*
Diane Lingoni *(Mgr-Production)*
Joe Mishkofski *(Mgr-Studio)*
Kim Gudusky *(Acct Supvr)*
Lynlea Roudel *(Acct Supvr)*

Accounts:
Kingston Plantation
Virginia Beach Economic Development

Branch

Otto

217 77th St, Virginia Beach, VA 23451
Tel.: (757) 622-4050
Fax: (757) 422-8853
E-Mail: info@thinkotto.com
Web Site: http://new.thinkotto.com/

Employees: 17

Pete Leddy *(Partner & Pres)*
Mark Atkinson *(Partner & Dir-Creative)*
Jaycen Leblanc *(Sr Dir-Art)*
Hunter Spencer *(Sr Dir-Art)*
Sherri Priester *(Dir-Media)*
Diane Lingoni *(Mgr-Production)*
Joey Mishkofski *(Mgr-Studio)*

Accounts:
Calvin & Lloyd
Calyber Boatworks
Hilton Virginia Beach
Hope House Foundation
Kingston Plantation
Ocean Beach Club
Tymoff Moss Architects
Virginia Beach

OUR MAN IN HAVANA

333 W 39th St Fl 8, New York, NY 10018-1473

Tel.: (212) 505-3533
Fax: (212) 868-1955
Web Site: ourmaninhavana.com

Employees: 5

Agency Specializes In: Advertising, Print, Production, Production (Print)

Andrew Golomb *(Founder & Exec Dir-Creative)*
Sylve Rosen-Bernstein *(Assoc Dir-Creative & Copywriter)*

Accounts:
Bear Boat
Cointreau
Global Crossing; 2006
Jewish Museum; New York, NY
Mount Gay Rum
Renaissance
Univision

THE OUSSET AGENCY, INC.
20475 Hwy 46 W Ste 180-602, Spring Branch, TX 78070
Tel.: (830) 885-5130
Fax: (830) 885-5140
Toll Free: (866) 268-7738
E-Mail: info@getousset.com
Web Site: www.getousset.com

Employees: 6
Year Founded: 1982

Agency Specializes In: Business-To-Business, Industrial

Revenue: $1,000,000

John M. Ousset *(Co-Founder)*
Margaret A. Ousset *(Co-Founder)*

OUT THERE
110 E 25th St, New York, NY 10010
Tel.: (646) 790-1456
E-Mail: info@outthereww.com
Web Site: www.outthereww.com

Agency Specializes In: Advertising, Brand Development & Integration, Content, Corporate Identity, Digital/Interactive, Internet/Web Design, Media Buying Services, Media Planning, Search Engine Optimization, Social Media

Samantha Fennell *(Mng Dir)*

Accounts:
Farfetch (Media Agency of Record)
Roberto Cavalli (Media Agency of Record)

OUT THERE ADVERTISING
22 E 2nd St, Duluth, MN 55802
Tel.: (218) 720-6002
Fax: (218) 720-5828
Web Site: www.outthereadvertising.com

Year Founded: 1997

Agency Specializes In: Advertising, Digital/Interactive, Logo & Package Design, Print, Public Relations, Social Media

Kimberly Carlson Keuning *(Pres)*
David Lee Minix *(Dir-Art)*
Darlene M. Olby *(Dir-Media)*
Andy Schwantes *(Acct Exec & Strategist-Digital)*

Accounts:
Duluth Childrens Museum
Farfetch (Media Agency of Record)
Orthopaedic Associates
Roberto Cavalli (Media Agency of Record)

OUTER BANKS MEDIA
102 Old Tom St Ste 205, Manteo, NC 27954
Tel.: (252) 256-7116
E-Mail: info@outerbanksmedia.com
Web Site: www.outerbanksmedia.com

Agency Specializes In: Advertising, Brand Development & Integration, Search Engine Optimization, Social Media, Strategic Planning/Research

C. K. Evans *(Pres)*

Accounts:
New-Outer Banks Brewing Station

OUTERNATIONAL INC
49 W 27th St 6th Fl, New York, NY 10001
Tel.: (212) 722-5000
E-Mail: info@outernational360.com
Web Site: www.outernational360.com

Employees: 5
Year Founded: 2007

Agency Specializes In: Above-the-Line, Advertising, Advertising Specialties, Affluent Market, African-American Market, Alternative Advertising, Arts, Automotive, Aviation & Aerospace, Below-the-Line, Bilingual Market, Brand Development & Integration, Broadcast, Business Publications, Business-To-Business, Cable T.V., Catalogs, Co-op Advertising, Collateral, Communications, Consulting, Consumer Goods, Consumer Marketing, Content, Corporate Communications, Corporate Identity, Digital/Interactive, Direct Response Marketing, E-Commerce, Electronic Media, Electronics, Engineering, Entertainment, Environmental, Event Planning & Marketing, Exhibit/Trade Shows, Experience Design, Fashion/Apparel, Financial, Food Service, Game Integration, Gay & Lesbian Market, Government/Political, Graphic Design, Guerilla Marketing, High Technology, Hospitality, Household Goods, Identity Marketing, In-Store Advertising, Industrial, Information Technology, Integrated Marketing, International, Internet/Web Design, Investor Relations, Leisure, Local Marketing, Logo & Package Design, Luxury Products, Magazines, Marine, Market Research, Media Buying Services, Media Planning, Men's Market, Merchandising, Mobile Marketing, Multicultural, Multimedia, New Product Development, New Technologies, Newspaper, Out-of-Home Media, Outdoor, Package Design, Pets , Podcasting, Point of Purchase, Point of Sale, Print, Production, Production (Print), Promotions, Radio, Real Estate, Regional, Restaurant, Retail, Sales Promotion, Social Marketing/Nonprofit, Social Media, Sponsorship, Sports Market, Stakeholders, Strategic Planning/Research, Sweepstakes, T.V., Technical Advertising, Teen Market, Trade & Consumer Magazines, Transportation, Travel & Tourism, Tween Market, Urban Market, Viral/Buzz/Word of Mouth, Web (Banner Ads, Pop-ups, etc.), Women's Market

Approx. Annual Billings: $2,000,000

Breakdown of Gross Billings by Media: Foreign: 10%; Graphic Design: 5%; Internet Adv.: 5%; Logo & Package Design: 10%; Mags.: 10%; Out-of-Home Media: 5%; Point of Sale: 10%; Print: 15%; Strategic Planning/Research: 10%; T.V.: 15%; Worldwide Web Sites: 5%

Victor Mazzeo *(Founder & Pres)*

Accounts:
The Enhance Group; 2008
Melitta Coffee Melitta Cafe Collection Coffee; 2008
Remy Cointreau USA Inc.; 2008
Russian Standard Vodka Imperia Vodka, Russian Standard Platinum Vodka; 2008

OUTLET TAGS COMPANY
16 Unit, 390 Progressive Ave, Toronto, ON M1R 4H9 Canada
Tel.: (416) 716-9814
E-Mail: outlettags@gmail.com
Web Site: outlettags.com

Employees: 15
Year Founded: 2010

Agency Specializes In: Affiliate Marketing, Alternative Advertising, Exhibit/Trade Shows, Outdoor, Production, Production (Print), Promotions

Approx. Annual Billings: $1,000,000

Mohammed El-Karaouni *(Owner)*

Accounts:
Canadian Tire Corp; 2014

OUTLIER SOLUTIONS
213 SW Ash St Ste 205, Portland, OR 97204
Tel.: (971) 533-7223
E-Mail: hello@outlier.com
Web Site: www.outlier.com

Year Founded: 2005

Agency Specializes In: Advertising, Brand Development & Integration, Graphic Design, Internet/Web Design, Public Relations, Social Media

Kathleen Martin *(Mgr-Mktg & Comm)*
Diana Lien *(Graphic Designer & Designer-Interactive)*

Accounts:
Adidas North America Inc

OUTLOOK MARKETING SERVICES, INC.
325 N LaSalle Ste 325, Chicago, IL 60610
Tel.: (312) 873-3424
Fax: (312) 873-3500
E-Mail: info@outlookmarketingsrv.com
Web Site: www.outlookmarketingsrv.com

Agency Specializes In: Advertising, Media Relations, Public Relations, Social Media

Jeff Rappaport *(Owner & CEO)*
Kristin Fayer *(Sr VP)*
Suzette Sexton *(Sr VP)*
Andrea Davis *(VP)*
Stephen Dye *(Acct Mgr)*
Stacy Greenberg *(Mgr-Content)*

Accounts:
Blue Spark Technologies, Inc
Safco Dental Supply Company; Chicago, IL

OUTOFTHEBLUE ADVERTISING
2424 S Dixie Hwy Ste 100, Miami, FL 33133
Tel.: (305) 442-2431
Fax: (305) 442-4815
Web Site: www.3outoftheblue.com

Agency Specializes In: Advertising

Mari Gallet *(Pres & Dir-New Bus Strategies)*
Renny Tirador *(Pres)*
Beni Mendez *(Dir-Creative)*

Accounts:
Business Improvement District Downtown Coral Campaign: "Only Coral Gables"
Celebrity Cruises, Inc.
Medica HealthCare Plans
Pacific National Bank

OUTSIDE LINE
(Acquired by Saatchi & Saatchi)

OUTSIDE THE BOX INTERACTIVE LLC
150 Bay St Ste 706, Jersey City, NJ 07302
Tel.: (201) 610-0625
Fax: (201) 610-0627
E-Mail: theoffice@outboxin.com
Web Site: www.outboxin.com

Employees: 8
Year Founded: 1995

Agency Specializes In: Advertising, Alternative Advertising, Brand Development & Integration, Branded Entertainment, Business-To-Business, Collateral, Communications, Consulting, Consumer Marketing, Corporate Communications, Corporate Identity, Cosmetics, Customer Relationship Management, Digital/Interactive, Direct Response Marketing, Direct-to-Consumer, E-Commerce, Education, Email, Fashion/Apparel, Graphic Design, Identity Marketing, Industrial, Integrated Marketing, Internet/Web Design, Local Marketing, Marine, Multimedia, New Product Development, Pharmaceutical, Planning & Consultation, Print, Production, Production (Print), Retail, Sales Promotion, Search Engine Optimization, Social Marketing/Nonprofit, Social Media, Web (Banner Ads, Pop-ups, etc.)

Frank DeMarco *(Founder & Mng Partner)*
Lauren Schwartz *(Partner)*

Accounts:
Derecktor Shipyards; Bridgeport, CT Luxury Pleasure Craft & Commercial Shipbuilding; 2003
Greenville Colorants; Jersey City, NJ Industrial Brand Awareness; 2008
Original Women; New York, NY Accessories, Apparel, Home; 2005
Society of Illustrators; New York, NY SOI Organization; 2007

OVATION PR & ADVERTISING
Capitol Hill 840 1st St NE 3rd Fl, Washington, DC 20002
Tel.: (202) 248-5003
Web Site: www.ovationpr.net

Agency Specializes In: Advertising, Media Relations, Public Relations, Social Media, Strategic Planning/Research

Tracie Hovey *(CEO)*

Accounts:
Ann Mahoney
Maryland International Film Festival

THE OWEN GROUP
1502 Texas Ave, Lubbock, TX 79401
Tel.: (806) 788-2291
Web Site: www.owengrp.com

Agency Specializes In: Advertising, Event Planning & Marketing, Graphic Design, Logo & Package Design, Media Planning, Print, Public Relations, Radio, T.V.

Mack Owen *(Pres & Dir-Creative)*
Rebecca Owen *(Treas, Corp Sec & Controller)*
Barry Helms *(Art Dir & Designer)*
Teague Dill *(Dir-Social Media)*
Allyson Schell *(Dir-Media)*

Accounts:
Cardinals Sport Center, Inc.
Truck Town Dodge

OWEN MEDIA
4111 E Madison St Ste 39, Seattle, WA 98112
Tel.: (206) 322-1167
E-Mail: info@owenmedia.com
Web Site: www.owenmedia.com

Year Founded: 1997

Agency Specializes In: Advertising, Digital/Interactive, Event Planning & Marketing, Graphic Design, Public Relations

Paul Owen *(Pres)*

Accounts:
Climate Savers Computing
IBM
InfiniBand Trade Association
Transaction Processing Performance Council

OWENS, HARKEY & ASSOCIATES, LLC
3550 N Central Ave Ste 1710, Phoenix, AZ 85012
Tel.: (602) 254-5159
Fax: (602) 253-9380
Web Site: www.owensharkey.com

Year Founded: 1960

Agency Specializes In: Advertising, Brand Development & Integration, Collateral, Crisis Communications, Market Research, Media Buying Services, Media Planning, Search Engine Optimization, Social Media, T.V.

Scott Harkey *(Pres)*
Matt Owens *(CEO)*
Ivan Galaz *(Sr Dir-Art)*
Jos Anshell *(Dir & Brand Strategist)*
Rachel Noyes *(Asst Dir-Creative)*
Pamela Edelstein *(Mgr-PR & Social Media)*
Lynn Costello *(Media Buyer)*
Ashley Elmer *(Coord-Brand Dev)*
Hillary Houghton *(Coord-Social Media)*
Mackenzie Keller *(Coord-PR)*

Accounts:
American Diabetes Association
Mix1 Life, Inc. (Agency of Record)
Nawgan Products Nawgan Beverages (Agency of Record), Power On Beverages (Agency of Record)
No Fear Energy Branding Strategy
PepsiCo Inc.
Turn 4 Wines
WheyUp Branding Strategy
Xango, LLC

OXFORD COMMUNICATIONS, INC.
11 Music Mtn Blvd, Lambertville, NJ 08530
Tel.: (609) 397-4242
Fax: (609) 397-8863
E-Mail: solutions@oxfordcommunications.com
Web Site: www.oxfordcommunications.com

E-Mail for Key Personnel:
President: jmartorana@oxfordcommunications.com
Creative Dir.: cwhitmore@oxfordcommunications.com
Media Dir.: ksuttermann@oxfordcommunications.com

Employees: 50
Year Founded: 1986

National Agency Associations: NJ Ad Club

Agency Specializes In: Advertising, Brand Development & Integration, Consumer Marketing, Direct-to-Consumer, Event Planning & Marketing, Exhibit/Trade Shows, Logo & Package Design, Media Buying Services, Media Planning, Public Relations, Real Estate, Strategic Planning/Research, Travel & Tourism

Approx. Annual Billings: $38,000,000

Breakdown of Gross Billings by Media: Event Mktg.: 5%; Print: 65%; Production: 20%; Strategic Planning/Research: 10%

Tim McAuliffe *(VP-Digital Integration)*
Maria Coyle *(Acct Dir)*
Stefanie Rumpf *(Dir-Comm)*
Sherry Smith *(Acct Mgr-Acct Svcs)*
Sarah Phillips *(Mgr-Social Media Community)*
Jordyn Rudolf *(Mgr-Digital Media)*
Peter Setaro *(Acct Supvr)*

Accounts:
Brookfield Homes; Vienna, VA Builder; 1996
Bucks County Conference & Visitors Bureau; Bensalem, PA; 1996
Bucks County, PA (Agency of Record) Media Planning & Buying, Strategy
Children's Home Society
Kaplan
Mignatti Companies Creative, PR, Waterside Project, Website Development
New Jersey Manufacturers Insurance Company; Ewing, NJ Marketing Campaign
The New Jersey Motor Vehicle Commission Outreach Programs
Quick Chek Food Stores; 2007
The Residences at Two Liberty
Sesame Place; Langhorne, PA Family Oriented Theme Park; 1995
VOXX International
Audiovox Electronics Corp

P & M ADVERTISING
PO Box 60427, Longmeadow, MA 01116
Tel.: (413) 530-6572
E-Mail: mike@pmadvertising.net
Web Site: www.pmadvertising.net

E-Mail for Key Personnel:
President: mike@pmadvertising.net

Employees: 4
Year Founded: 1978

Agency Specializes In: Automotive, Broadcast, Cable T.V., Co-op Advertising, Fashion/Apparel, Food Service, Graphic Design, Infomercials, Legal Services, Media Buying Services, Newspaper, Outdoor, Planning & Consultation, Print, Production, Radio, Restaurant, Retail, Strategic Planning/Research, T.V.

Michael R. Kessler *(Pres)*

Accounts:
Frigo's
Manny's TV & Appliance; Springfield, MA Home Appliance Stores; 1990
Ochoa Day Spa; South Hadley, MA; 1998
Rocky's Ace Hardware Stores; Springfield, MA Hardware Stores; 1997

P2R ASSOCIATES
39201 Schoolcraft Rd Ste B-15, Livonia, MI 48150
Tel.: (248) 348-2464
Fax: (248) 348-2465
E-Mail: contact@p2rassociates.com
Web Site: www.p2rassociates.com

Employees: 50

Agency Specializes In: Business-To-Business, Communications, Corporate Communications, Crisis Communications, Event Planning & Marketing, Media Relations, Strategic Planning/Research

Revenue: $5,000,000

Gordon Cole *(Pres)*
Scott K. Russell *(Dir-Acct Svcs & New Bus Dev)*

Accounts:
Alderney Advisors LLC
China Bridge
Process Development Corp (Agency of Record) Marketing Communications, Media Outreach, Public Relations
Rent-A-Center's
Toyota

PACE ADVERTISING

230 Park Ave S 12th Fl, New York, NY 10003
Tel.: (212) 331-8825
Fax: (212) 885-0570
E-Mail: info@paceadvertising.com
Web Site: www.paceadv.com

Employees: 30
Year Founded: 1949

Agency Specializes In: Advertising, Collateral, Digital/Interactive, Direct Response Marketing, Electronic Media, Email, Health Care Services, Internet/Web Design, Local Marketing, Logo & Package Design, Media Buying Services, Media Planning, Mobile Marketing, Newspaper, Newspapers & Magazines, Out-of-Home Media, Outdoor, Paid Searches, Point of Purchase, Point of Sale, Print, Production, Production (Print), Public Relations, Publishing, RSS (Really Simple Syndication), Real Estate, Social Media, Travel & Tourism, Web (Banner Ads, Pop-ups, etc.)

Cara Faske *(Pres)*
Richard Nulman *(CEO)*
Holly Kingsley *(VP)*
Philip Chadwick *(Dir-Creative Svcs)*
Jane Kramer *(Dir-Creative)*
Erika Cubano *(Acct Exec)*

Accounts:
Dockside
K. Hovnanian Companies
Kohls Partners
Orleans Homebuilders
Pulte Homes
The Setai Group
The Trump Organization; New York, NY Trump International Hotel and Tower Condominiums

PACIFIC COMMUNICATIONS

575 Anton Blvd Ste 900, Costa Mesa, CA 92626-7665
Tel.: (714) 427-1900
Fax: (714) 796-3039
Web Site: www.pacificcommunications.com

Employees: 130
Year Founded: 1992

Agency Specializes In: Advertising, Advertising Specialties, Brand Development & Integration, Co-op Advertising, Communications, Consumer Marketing, Consumer Publications, Corporate Identity, Direct Response Marketing, E-Commerce, Education, Graphic Design, Health Care Services, Internet/Web Design, Logo & Package Design, Magazines, Media Buying Services, Medical Products, Multimedia, New Product Development, Pharmaceutical, Print, Production, Seniors' Market, Strategic Planning/Research

Approx. Annual Billings: $18,000,000

Breakdown of Gross Billings by Media: Bus. Publs.: $3,600,000; Collateral: $3,600,000; D.M.: $900,000; Mags.: $900,000; Newsp.: $1,800,000; Outdoor: $2,700,000; Pub. Rels.: $1,800,000; Radio: $1,800,000; T.V.: $900,000

Craig Sullivan *(Pres)*
Karen Melanson *(Sr VP & Client Svcs Dir)*
Scott Gandy *(VP & Mgmt Supvr)*
Shelley L. Snow *(VP & Mgmt Supvr)*
Zena Alam *(Sr Dir-Art)*
Eleanor Mirasol *(Dir-Media)*
Marlene Magila *(Assoc Dir-Creative)*
Cara Marciano *(Acct Supvr)*
Peter Shin *(Acct Exec)*

Accounts:
Allergan, Inc.; Irvine, CA (Agency of Record) Acular, Acular PF, Alocril, Alphagan, Botox, Branded & Unbranded Patient & Professional Communications, Complete, Event Management, Field Training, Global External Disease & Oncology Franchises, Juvederm, Latisse, Lumigan, Managed Care, Ocuflox, Refresh, Restasis, Sales Tools, Sanctura XR, Strategic Dvelopment, Web Site Development; 1995
Allergan Skin Care; Irvine, CA Azelex & Elimite; 1995
Bausch + Lomb Surgical EnVista Intraocular Lens, Victus Femtosecond Laser Platform
I-Flow Corporation ON-Q Product Line
MAP Pharmaceuticals Levadex, Medical Communications
Prometheus Laboratories Oncology
SkinMedica, Inc. Latisse, Skin Care, Strategy
Spasticity Answers
Thoratec Corp.; Pleasanton, CA Concept Development, Corporate Branding, Promotions, Strategy

PACIFICCOAST ADVERTISING INC.

2516 Via Tejon Ste 207, Palos Verdes Estates, CA 90274
Tel.: (310) 697-3706
Fax: (310) 697-3711
E-Mail: info@pacificcoastadvertising.com
Web Site: www.pacificcoastadvertising.com

Year Founded: 2005

Agency Specializes In: Advertising, Digital/Interactive, Logo & Package Design, Media Buying Services, Media Planning, Outdoor, Print, Radio, Social Media, T.V.

Tracy Bracken *(Pres)*

Accounts:
Cormier Hyundai
Gardena Nissan

PACIFICO INC.

1190 Coleman Ave Ste 110, San Jose, CA 95110
Tel.: (408) 327-8888
Fax: (408) 559-8883
E-Mail: mcurtis@pacifico.com
Web Site: www.pacifico.com

E-Mail for Key Personnel:
Chairman: mcurtis@pacifico.com

Employees: 7
Year Founded: 1977

National Agency Associations: BMA-BPA-PRSA

Agency Specializes In: Advertising, Brand Development & Integration, Broadcast, Business Publications, Business-To-Business, Cable T.V., Collateral, Communications, Consulting, Consumer Marketing, Consumer Publications, Corporate Identity, Digital/Interactive, Direct Response Marketing, E-Commerce, Electronic Media, Engineering, Exhibit/Trade Shows, Financial, Health Care Services, High Technology, Information Technology, Internet/Web Design, Investor Relations, Logo & Package Design, Magazines, Marine, Media Buying Services, Medical Products, Newspaper, Newspapers & Magazines, Outdoor, Point of Purchase, Point of Sale, Print, Production, Public Relations, Publicity/Promotions, Radio, Real Estate, Strategic Planning/Research, T.V., Technical Advertising, Trade & Consumer Magazines, Transportation

Mary P. Curtis *(CEO)*

Accounts:
Planet Magpie
TSMC

PACO COMMUNICATIONS, INC

(d/b/a PACO Collective [Cross-Cultural Marketing])
400 S Green St Unit H, Chicago, IL 60607
Tel.: (312) 281-2040
Fax: (312) 971-5991
E-Mail: ozzie@pacocollective.com
Web Site: www.pacocollective.com

Employees: 40
Year Founded: 2006

Agency Specializes In: Above-the-Line, Advertising, Advertising Specialties, Arts, Automotive, Below-the-Line, Bilingual Market, Brand Development & Integration, Branded Entertainment, Broadcast, Business-To-Business, Cable T.V., Collateral, Communications, Consulting, Consumer Goods, Consumer Marketing, Consumer Publications, Content, Corporate Communications, Corporate Identity, Crisis Communications, Digital/Interactive, Direct Response Marketing, Direct-to-Consumer, Electronic Media, Event Planning & Marketing, Exhibit/Trade Shows, Experience Design, Financial, Graphic Design, Guerilla Marketing, Health Care Services, Hispanic Market, Household Goods, In-Store Advertising, Internet/Web Design, Local Marketing, Logo & Package Design, Media Buying Services, Media Planning, Media Relations, Media Training, Medical Products, Mobile Marketing, Multicultural, Multimedia, New Product Development, Newspapers & Magazines, Out-of-Home Media, Outdoor, Package Design, Pharmaceutical, Planning & Consultation, Print, Production, Production (Print), Promotions, Public Relations, Publicity/Promotions, Publishing, Radio, Regional, Restaurant, Retail, Sales Promotion, Search Engine Optimization, Social Marketing/Nonprofit, Sports Market, Strategic Planning/Research, T.V., Trade & Consumer Magazines, Travel & Tourism

Approx. Annual Billings: $9,500,000

Ozzie Godinez *(Co-Founder & CEO)*
Veronica Villalon Pinela *(VP-Client Svcs)*
Andres Zamudio *(Dir-Creative)*
Allison West *(Acct Mgr)*
Alejandra Chavez *(Sr Acct Supvr)*
Jonathan Moreno *(Sr Acct Exec-PACO Ideation)*
Sonia Sotello *(Sr Acct Exec)*
Diane Jimenez *(Acct Exec-PACO Ideation)*

Accounts:
Amway
Blue Cross Blue Shield (HCSC) Hispanic Agency of Record
Cacique
Chicago Bears Hispanic Agency of Record
ComEd/Exelon

Gift of Hope Total Market Agency of Record
Jackson Park Hospital
RX Outreach Total Market Agency of Record
White Sox Hispanic Agency of Record

PADILLA/CRT
(Formerly Padilla Speer Beardsley)
1101 W River Pkwy Ste 400, Minneapolis, MN 55415-1241
Tel.: (612) 455-1700
Fax: (612) 455-1060
Web Site: www.padillacrt.com

Employees: 200
Year Founded: 1961

National Agency Associations: COPF-PRSA

Agency Specializes In: Advertising, Agriculture, Brand Development & Integration, Business-To-Business, Collateral, Communications, Consulting, Consumer Goods, Consumer Marketing, Consumer Publications, Corporate Communications, Corporate Identity, Crisis Communications, Digital/Interactive, Direct Response Marketing, Electronic Media, Environmental, Event Planning & Marketing, Exhibit/Trade Shows, Financial, Government/Political, Graphic Design, Health Care Services, High Technology, Industrial, Information Technology, Internet/Web Design, Investor Relations, Local Marketing, Logo & Package Design, Magazines, Media Relations, Media Training, Medical Products, Newspapers & Magazines, Planning & Consultation, Point of Purchase, Real Estate, Retail, Sponsorship, Strategic Planning/Research, Viral/Buzz/Word of Mouth

Lynn Casey *(CEO)*
Heath Rudduck *(Chief Creative Officer)*
Matt Kucharski *(Exec VP-Mktg, Branding, Strategic and Crisis Comm & Social Media)*
Marian Briggs *(Sr VP-IR-Corp Comm Strategies)*
Tom Jollie *(Sr VP-Food, Beverage & Branding)*
Riff Yeager *(Sr VP)*
Tina Charpentier *(VP)*
Matt Fairchild *(VP-Tech & Innovation)*
Al Galgano *(VP-IR & Corp Rels)*
Bob McNaney *(VP-Crisis & Critical Issues-Media Coaching)*
Maureen O'Malley Rehfuss *(VP-HR)*
Danielle Engholm *(Sr Dir)*
Amy Fisher *(Sr Dir)*
Stephanie Fox *(Sr Dir-Healthcare Practice)*
David Heinsch *(Sr Dir-Investor & Corp Rels)*
Chris Higgins *(Sr Dir)*
Matt Sullivan *(Sr Dir)*
Carrie Young *(Sr Dir-Corp Brand Identity, Design, Mktg & Comm)*
Brian Prentice *(Dir-Creative)*
Kimberly Huston *(Acct Supvr)*
Catherine Claeys Scott *(Acct Supvr)*
Laudan Fenster *(Sr Acct Exec)*
Laura Krinke *(Sr Acct Exec)*
Chance Prigge *(Sr Acct Exec)*
Molly O'Mara *(Acct Exec)*
Megan Skauge Schulz *(Acct Exec)*
Max Sundermeyer *(Acct Exec-Environmental Sciences Practice)*
Claire Woit *(Acct Exec-Mfg Practice)*
Thea Buri *(Sr Designer)*
Mike Conway *(Sr Designer)*
Len Pollard *(Asst Acct Exec)*
Leanne Stacey *(Sr Project Coord-SMS Research Advisors)*

Accounts:
3M
Allianz Life
Arctic Cat
August Schell Brewing Co. Brand Strategy, Marcomms Program, PR, Social Media
Barnes & Noble College
BASF
Beam Global Spirits (Agency of Record)
Cargill
Charles Schwab
CHF Solutions
Coppertone
Deluxe Corp
Ditch Witch
Entegris
Fabcon
General Mills
Girl Scouts of the USA
Greater Houston Convention and Visitors Bureau Public Relations
Hass Avocado Board
Land O'Lakes
Les Vins Georges Duboeuf
Memorex; Oakdale, MN Campaign: "Memorex Celebrates 50 years with Yo Gabba Gabba!"
Merck
Midwest & Mountain Dental Creative Development, Direct Marketing
Midwest Dental Creative Development, Direct Marketing, PR
National Marrow Donor Association
North Carolina Sweet Potato Commission
Oshkosh Truck Corp.
Patterson Companies, Inc. Crisis & Issues Management
Pentair Inc (Agency of Record)
Prosciutto di Parma
Qumu Go-to-Market Strategy, Marketing Communications, Media Relations
Rec Boat Holdings; Cadillac, MI Digital, Four Winns, Glastron, Marketing Communications, Public Relations, Social Media, Wellcraft
Rockwell Automation
RTI Surgical
Ryan Companies
SAP; Newton Square, PA Media Relations, SAP Consumer Package Goods, SAP Retail, Thought Leadership
Schell Brewing
New-Smart Beer (Agency of Record) Marketing, Organic Golden Ale, Public Relations
Surmodics, Inc. Investor Relations
Synovis
UnitedHealth Group
University of Minnesota
US Highbush Blueberry Council
Valspar
Van Gogh Imports Tap Whisky, Van Gogh Vodka
Vital Images

Branches

Padilla/CRT
(Formerly CRT/tanaka)
617 W 7th St, Los Angeles, CA 90017
Tel.: (310) 659-5380
Fax: (310) 659-5257
Web Site: www.padillacrt.com

Employees: 7

National Agency Associations: COPF

Agency Specializes In: Public Relations

Mark Raper *(Pres)*
Max Martens *(VP & Head-Los Angeles)*
Veronica Hunt *(Sr Acct Exec)*
Ryan Lamont *(Sr Acct Exec-Consumer & Corp Practices)*

Accounts:
Altria
Amadeus North America
Better Business Bureau
Del Monte
HoMedics
Longwood University
Original Farmers Market (Public Relations Agency of Record)
Satmetrix
Virgin Mobile USA, Inc.
Viviscal
ZeroWater

Padilla/CRT
(Formerly CRT/tanaka)
320 W 13th St 7th Fl, New York, NY 10014
Tel.: (212) 229-0500
Fax: (212) 229-0523
Web Site: www.padillacrt.com

Employees: 20

National Agency Associations: COPF

Agency Specializes In: Public Relations, Sponsorship

Edward Hoffman *(Sr VP-Food, Beverage & Nutrition)*
Amy Epstein *(VP-B2B Branding, Mktg & Comm)*
Lisa Kersey *(VP-Health Practice)*
Anastasia Lopez *(VP-Social Media)*
Pablo Olay *(VP)*
Jason Stemm *(VP)*
Nicole Fischer *(Acct Supvr-Consumer, Food & Beverage Practices)*
Laura Petrosky *(Acct Supvr)*
Emily Valentine *(Acct Supvr)*
Kirsten Lesak Greenberg *(Sr Acct Exec)*
Julie Stas *(Sr Acct Exec)*
Tamek Davis *(Acct Exec)*
Michelle Dembo *(Asst Acct Exec)*

Accounts:
Avocados
Cambria Suites
Drugfree.org Medicine Abuse Project
Florida Tomato Committee
Hass Avocado Board Media Relations, Strategic PR
Longwood University
North Carolina Sweet Potato Commission
Rioja

Padilla/CRT
(Formerly CRT/tanaka)
2200 Colonial Ave Ste 10, Norfolk, VA 23517
Tel.: (757) 640-1982
Fax: (757) 640-1984
Web Site: www.padillacrt.com

Employees: 15

National Agency Associations: COPF

Agency Specializes In: Public Relations

Kim Blake *(Acct Supvr)*
Nikki Parrotte *(Sr Acct Exec)*
Liz Rea *(Acct Exec-Food & Beverage Practice)*

Accounts:
American Physical Therapy Association
Federation of Quebec Maple Syrup Producers
Sage

Padilla/CRT
(Formerly CRT/tanaka)
101 W Commerce Rd, Richmond, VA 23224
Tel.: (804) 675-8100
Fax: (804) 675-8183
Web Site: www.padillacrt.com

Employees: 35
Year Founded: 1996

National Agency Associations: COPF

Agency Specializes In: Agriculture, Automotive, Aviation & Aerospace, Brand Development &

Integration, Business-To-Business, Collateral, Communications, Consulting, Consumer Marketing, Consumer Publications, Corporate Identity, Direct Response Marketing, E-Commerce, Education, Electronic Media, Environmental, Event Planning & Marketing, Fashion/Apparel, Financial, Government/Political, Graphic Design, Health Care Services, Industrial, Information Technology, Investor Relations, Leisure, Logo & Package Design, Medical Products, Multimedia, New Product Development, Newspapers & Magazines, Over-50 Market, Pharmaceutical, Planning & Consultation, Point of Purchase, Public Relations, Publicity/Promotions, Recruitment, Sales Promotion, Sponsorship, Sports Market, Strategic Planning/Research, Teen Market, Trade & Consumer Magazines, Transportation, Travel & Tourism

Mark Raper *(Pres)*
Kelly O'Keefe *(Chief Creative Officer & Chief Strategy Officer)*
Scott Davila *(Sr VP)*
Kevin Flores *(VP & Grp Dir-Creative)*
Julie McCracken *(Sr Dir-Corp Practice)*
Christian Munson *(Sr Dir)*
Rebecca Durkin *(Assoc Dir-Creative)*
Maliya Rooney *(Mgr-Production & Traffic)*
Rosalie Morton *(Acct Supvr)*
Laura Petrosky *(Acct Supvr)*
Lauren Llewellyn *(Sr Acct Exec-Corp Practice)*
Rebecca Comstock *(Acct Exec)*
Kelsey Mohring *(Acct Exec)*
Catie Frech *(Asst Acct Exec)*
Toni Austin *(Coord-Bus Dev)*

Accounts:
Abbott Laboratories
New-Afton Chemicals
Agility Healthcare Solutions Public Relations; 2008
Air New Zealand
Allianz
Amadeus GTD
Arctic Cat
Barnes & Noble College
BASF
Be The Match
Bissell Homecare
Bissell
Blueberries
BlueCross BlueShield Minnesota
Bon Secours Health Systems
Bow Tie Cinemas
Cambria Suites
Cargill
Carmax
Charles Schwab & Co.; San Francisco, CA
Cherry, Bekaert & Holland, LLP
Cheyenne Regional Medical Center
Coppertone
Council for Responsible Nutrition National Lifestyle Campaign; 2007
Discovery Channel Stores; Silver Spring, MD
Ditch Witch
DrugFree.org
Federation of Quebec Maple Syrup Producers
Four Winns
General Mills Cheerios
Girl Scouts of the United States of America Crisis Counsel
Glastron
Hass Avocado Board
HoMedics
HTC
KitchenAid
Land O' Lakes Inc
Longwood University
Memorex
Merck
Mosaic
Network Solutions Public Relations
Northern Virginia Hospital Alliance Crisis Communications Training, Crisis Management Counsel
The Partnership at DrugFree.org
Performance Food Group
Philip Morris USA
Rioja
Rockwell Automation
Sage Products
Sands Anderson
SAP
Satmetrix Systems, Inc.
Starbucks
SunTrust Mortgage
Target Stores; Minneapolis, MN; 2000
TIAA-CREF
UnitedHealthcare
VHA, Inc
The Virginia Foundation for Community College Education (VFCCE) Great Expectations
New-Virginia Lottery
Wilsonart International Digital Marketing, Influencer Outreach, PR, Social & Traditional Media, Trade & Consumer Events, Website, Wilsonart HD

Padilla CRT

105 Oronoco St ste 101, Alexandria, VA 22314
Tel.: (703) 894-5460
Web Site: www.padillacrt.com

Agency Specializes In: Advertising, Brand Development & Integration, Business-To-Business, Digital/Interactive, Event Planning & Marketing, Media Relations, Social Media

Emily Valentine *(Acct Supvr)*
Michael Nelson *(Sr Acct Exec)*

PADILLA SPEER BEARDSLEY

(Merged with CRT/Tanaka to Form Padilla/CRT)

PADULO INTEGRATED INC.

The Padulo Buliding Suite 10, St Clair Ave W, Toronto, ON M4V 1K7 Canada
Tel.: (416) 966-4000
Fax: (416) 966-4012
E-Mail: info@padulo.ca
Web Site: www.padulo.ca

Employees: 40
Year Founded: 1985

Agency Specializes In: Broadcast, Collateral, Communications, Direct Response Marketing, Point of Purchase, Print, Publicity/Promotions

Richard Padulo *(Chm & CEO)*
Kamel Mikhael *(CFO)*
Chris Stavenjord *(VP, Dir-Creative & Strategist)*
Naz Jiwa *(VP & Dir-Media)*
Linda Brock *(Dir-Print Production)*
Monica Musil *(Mgr-Client Relationship)*

Accounts:
Brascan
Citi Cards Canada
First Choice Haircutters
Freefone
George
Katz Group Rexall
Retail Council of Canada Campaign: "Voice of Retail", Multimedia
Royal LePage
Simmons
Ten Second Tan
Walmart Project

PAGANO MEDIA

11 Millbrook St, Worcester, MA 01606
Tel.: (508) 595-9200
Fax: (508) 595-9299
E-Mail: kathleen@paganomedia.com
Web Site: www.paganomedia.com

Employees: 6
Year Founded: 1980

Agency Specializes In: Multimedia, Production, Sponsorship

Joe Pagano *(Pres & Dir-Creative)*
Kathleen Pagano *(CEO & Dir-Strategic)*
Jae Hahn *(Dir-New Media)*
Brandon Wood *(Designer-Creative)*

Accounts:
Chadwick Medical Associates
Coolidge Corner Imaging
New Balance, Inc.
Timber Trading Group
University of Massachusetts Memorial Foundation Emergency Care Campaign

PAGE AGENCY

(Formerly BigDigi LLC)
5307 E Mockingbird Ln 5th Fl, Dallas, TX 75206
Tel.: (214) 453-0081
Web Site: page.agency

Employees: 10
Year Founded: 2009

Agency Specializes In: Advertising, Alternative Advertising, Brand Development & Integration, Branded Entertainment, Broadcast, Business Publications, Cable T.V., Co-op Advertising, Collateral, Digital/Interactive, Direct Response Marketing, Internet/Web Design, Outdoor, Paid Searches, Print, Production, Production (Print), Radio, Search Engine Optimization, Social Media, T.V., Web (Banner Ads, Pop-ups, etc.)

Approx. Annual Billings: $450,000

Aaron Page *(Pres)*
Mike Fisher *(Creative Dir)*
Caleb Stephens *(Acct Mgr)*
Patrick O'Neill *(Strategist-Digital)*
Kathryn Wilson *(Sr Planner-Media)*
Colleen Ahern *(Copywriter)*

Accounts:
Big Town Weekends Trade Shows; 2013
Buzzbrews Kitchen Buzzbrews; 2009
Garza & Harris; 2008
GoGreen Geothermal
GoNFFC.com National Fantasy Football Conference; 2015
Maverick Plumbing
Parker University Seminars
Pinecrest Capital Partners; 2014
Platinum Series Homes by Mark Molthan Platinum Series Realty; 2007
Relativity Outdoors; 2011
Renova Health Renova Foot, Renova Hand Centers, Renova Spine Care; 2013

THE PAIGE GROUP

258 Genesee St Ste 204, Utica, NY 13502
Tel.: (315) 733-2313
Fax: (315) 733-1901
E-Mail: info@paigegroup.com
Web Site: www.paigegroup.com

Employees: 13
Year Founded: 1967

National Agency Associations: PRSA

Agency Specializes In: Advertising, Business-To-Business, Consulting, Consumer Marketing, Media Buying Services, Planning & Consultation, Public Relations

Nancy Pattarini *(Pres & CEO)*
Claude Schuyler *(VP & Sr Dir-Creative)*

Christine Shields *(VP & Dir-Media)*
Allison Damiano-DeTraglia *(VP-Acct Svcs)*
Carrie McMurray *(VP-Plng)*
Catherine Manion *(Mgr-Pub & Media Rels)*

Accounts:
Indium Corp. of America
Mohawk Valley Water Authority
Oneida-Herkimer Solid Waste Authority

PAIGE HENDRICKS PUBLIC RELATIONS INC
1255 W Magnolia Ave, Fort Worth, TX 76104
Tel.: (817) 924-2300
Fax: (817) 924-2312
E-Mail: news@phprinc.com
Web Site: www.phprinc.com

Employees: 4

Agency Specializes In: Advertising, Brand Development & Integration, Communications, Corporate Communications, Crisis Communications, Education, Media Relations, Planning & Consultation, Public Relations, Strategic Planning/Research

Jessa Lewis *(Acct Coord-PR)*

PALIO
(Merged with Ignite Health to form Palio+Ignite)

PALIO+IGNITE
(Formerly Palio)
260 Broadway, Saratoga Springs, NY 12866
Tel.: (518) 584-8924
Fax: (518) 583-1560
E-Mail: info@palioignite.com
Web Site: palioignite.com/

Employees: 180
Year Founded: 1999

Agency Specializes In: Advertising, Advertising Specialties, Brand Development & Integration, Broadcast, Business Publications, Business-To-Business, Collateral, Communications, Consumer Marketing, Consumer Publications, Corporate Identity, Digital/Interactive, Direct Response Marketing, Direct-to-Consumer, Electronic Media, Exhibit/Trade Shows, Graphic Design, Health Care Services, Identity Marketing, In-Store Advertising, Infomercials, Integrated Marketing, Internet/Web Design, Local Marketing, Logo & Package Design, Market Research, Media Buying Services, Medical Products, Multimedia, New Product Development, Newspaper, Package Design, Pharmaceutical, Podcasting, Point of Purchase, Print, Product Placement, Production, Production (Ad, Film, Broadcast), Production (Print), Promotions, Public Relations, Publicity/Promotions, Radio, Sales Promotion, Social Marketing/Nonprofit, Social Media, Strategic Planning/Research, T.V., Technical Advertising, Trade & Consumer Magazines, Web (Banner Ads, Pop-ups, etc.)

Kim Johnson *(Pres)*
Cheryl Fielding *(Sr VP & Client Svcs Dir)*
Laura Presicci *(VP & Dir-Creative)*
Peter Hopper *(Sr Dir-Integrated Client Svcs)*
Lori Goodale *(Dir-Corp Rels)*
Jillian Welker *(Dir-Ops)*
Michael Smith *(Sr Strategist-Digital)*

PALLEY ADVERTISING INC.
100 Grove St Ste 403, Worcester, MA 01605-2627
Tel.: (508) 792-6655
Fax: (508) 792-6626
E-Mail: info@palleyad.com
Web Site: www.palleyad.com

E-Mail for Key Personnel:
President: warren@palleyad.com
Public Relations: bonnie@palleyad.com

Employees: 20
Year Founded: 1982

Agency Specializes In: Advertising, Advertising Specialties, Automotive, Brand Development & Integration, Broadcast, Business Publications, Cable T.V., Co-op Advertising, Collateral, Communications, Consulting, Corporate Identity, Direct Response Marketing, Electronic Media, Exhibit/Trade Shows, Financial, Food Service, Graphic Design, Health Care Services, Industrial, Internet/Web Design, Logo & Package Design, Magazines, Media Buying Services, Merchandising, Multimedia, New Product Development, Newspaper, Newspapers & Magazines, Outdoor, Planning & Consultation, Print, Production, Public Relations, Radio, Recruitment, Restaurant, Retail, Sales Promotion, Sports Market, Strategic Planning/Research, T.V., Trade & Consumer Magazines, Yellow Pages Advertising

Breakdown of Gross Billings by Media: Bus. Publs.: 5%; Collateral: 15%; D.M.: 10%; Mags.: 5%; Newsp.: 20%; Radio: 30%; T.V.: 15%

Warren K. Palley *(Owner)*
Joseph Giacobbe *(Gen Mgr)*

Accounts:
Adcare Hospital
Peppercorns Grille & Tavern
Picadilly Pub Restaurant Chain

PALM TREE CREATIVE LLC
210 S Main St, Middletown, CT 6457
Tel.: (888) 830-4769
Web Site: www.palmtreecreative.com

Year Founded: 2004

Agency Specializes In: Advertising, Brand Development & Integration, Digital/Interactive, Graphic Design, Print, Search Engine Optimization

Chris Pritchard *(VP-Accounts)*

Accounts:
New-Computer Tune & Lube
New-Gro Landscape Inc.

PALMER AD AGENCY
466 Geary St Ste 301, San Francisco, CA 94102
Tel.: (415) 771-2327
Fax: (415) 771-1832
Web Site: www.palmeradagency.com

Agency Specializes In: Advertising, Brand Development & Integration, Digital/Interactive, Media Planning, Print, Radio, Social Media, Sponsorship, Strategic Planning/Research

Lois Palmer *(CFO)*
Drew Palmer *(Principal)*
Kristin Amador *(Dir-Media)*
Steven Anacker *(Dir-Creative)*
Jessie Hammer *(Dir-Integrated Production)*
Tyler Palmer *(Acct Exec)*
Tatyana Balte *(Designer)*
John Runk *(Copywriter)*

Accounts:
HubSpot
SouthFace Solar Electric

PANCOM INTERNATIONAL, INC.
3701 Wilshire Blvd Ste 800, Los Angeles, CA 90010-2816
Tel.: (213) 427-1371
Fax: (213) 383-6729
Toll Free: (877) YPanCom
E-Mail: pci@pancom.com
Web Site: www.pancom.com

E-Mail for Key Personnel:
President: youngkim@pancom.com

Employees: 25
Year Founded: 1981

Agency Specializes In: Advertising, Asian Market, Brand Development & Integration, Broadcast, Direct Response Marketing, Event Planning & Marketing, Graphic Design, Media Buying Services, Newspapers & Magazines, Print, Production, Radio, Sponsorship, Strategic Planning/Research, T.V.

Young M. Kim *(Chm & CEO)*
Paul Moon *(Pres & CMO)*
Joseph Choi *(CFO)*
Sharon Hayashi *(VP-Acct Svcs)*
Peter Byun *(Creative Dir)*
Richard Choi *(Acct Dir)*
Esther Chang *(Mgr-Acctg)*
Eunice Cho *(Mgr-Media)*

Accounts:
AT&T Communications Corp.
AXA Advisors
Ford Motor Co.; Los Angeles, CA Automobiles; 1998
Lincoln
The Salvation Army Campaign: "Goods For Us"
Volvo Cars of North America

PANNOS MARKETING
116 S River Rd, Bedford, NH 03110
Tel.: (603) 625-2443
Fax: (877) 630-6115
Web Site: http://www.pannosmarketing.com/

Agency Specializes In: Advertising, Brand Development & Integration, Digital/Interactive, Public Relations, Social Media

James Pannos *(Pres & Principal)*
Rick Kamp *(Sr VP)*
Langdon Andrews *(VP-Fin Institutions Mktg)*
Tara Hershberger *(VP-Media)*
Jay Bellemare *(Dir-Creative)*
Michael Bouchard *(Dir-Web)*

PANORAMA PUBLIC RELATIONS
1500 1st Ave N, Birmingham, AL 35203
Tel.: (205) 328-9334
Fax: (205) 323-0897
E-Mail: info@prview.com
Web Site: www.prview.com

Employees: 6
Year Founded: 1997

Agency Specializes In: Collateral, Crisis Communications, Exhibit/Trade Shows, Graphic Design, Internet/Web Design, Media Training, Multimedia, Print, Production, Sales Promotion

Darlene Rotch *(CEO)*
Michele Dickey *(Dir-PR & Media Rels)*
Greg Robinson *(Specialist-Comm)*

Accounts:
Belk, Inc.

PANTHER MARKETING INC.
16641 N 91st St, Scottsdale, AZ 85260
Tel.: (480) 419-1600

E-Mail: info@panthermarketing.com
Web Site: www.panthermarketing.com

Agency Specializes In: Advertising, Brand Development & Integration, Content, Digital/Interactive, Graphic Design, Internet/Web Design, Public Relations, Search Engine Optimization, Social Media

Gina Weber *(Founder & Pres)*
Margie Mobley *(Art Dir)*

Accounts:
Jeremy Roenick

PAPA ADVERTISING INC

1673 W 8th St, Erie, PA 16505
Tel.: (814) 454-6236
Fax: (814) 464-0796
Web Site: www.papaadvertising.com

Agency Specializes In: Advertising, Brand Development & Integration, Broadcast, Internet/Web Design, Logo & Package Design, Media Buying Services, Media Planning, Public Relations, Social Media

Doug Vizinni *(Sr Dir-Art)*
Jason Keller *(Dir-Interactive Media)*
Elizabeth Papa *(Dir-Art)*

Accounts:
Clarion County Community Bank
EmergyCare, Inc.
Erie Regional Chamber & Growth Partnership
Family Services
Presbyterian Homes Inc.
Reed Manufacturing Company Inc.
Tri State Pain Institute

PAPAGALOS STRATEGIC COMMUNICATIONS

7330 N 16th St B-102, Phoenix, AZ 85020
Tel.: (602) 279-2933
Fax: (602) 277-6448
Web Site: www.papagalos.com

Agency Specializes In: Advertising, Brand Development & Integration, Digital/Interactive, Graphic Design, Logo & Package Design, Media Planning, Promotions, Public Relations, Social Media, Strategic Planning/Research

Nicholas Papagalos *(Principal)*
Ann Papagalos *(VP)*
Gustavo Estrella *(Dir-Art)*
Michelle McGlinn *(Dir-Art)*
Christine Korecki *(Acct Mgr)*

Accounts:
Ares Security Corporation
M Custom Furniture Inc
Pass Training LLC

PAPPAS GROUP

4100 N Fairfax Dr Ste 200, Arlington, VA 22203
Tel.: (703) 349-7221
Fax: (703) 349-7253
E-Mail: info@pappasgroup.com
Web Site: www.pappasgroup.com

Employees: 22

Agency Specializes In: Advertising, Education, High Technology, Sponsorship

Andrea Frederick *(Acct Dir)*
Allison Mataya *(Client Svcs Dir)*
Patricia Rodriguez *(Acct Dir)*
Jeremy Gilman *(Dir-Strategy)*
Stephan Guenette *(Dir-Tech & User Experience)*
Nicole Whiteley *(Planner-Digital Media)*

Accounts:
AARP
American University
Blackboard, Inc.; Washington, DC
City Shop Girl
Corcoran College of Art + Design; Washington, DC
Discovery Channel Future Weapons
Georgetown University School of Continuing Studies
Georgetown University
Hilton Worldwide
International Spy Museum (Agency of Record) Brand Development, Brand Strategy, Media Buying, Media Planning, Social Media
Mazda
Toyota
Volkswagen Credit & Audi Financial Services (Agency of Record)
Voxtec International Inc.

PAPRIKA COMMUNICATIONS

400 Laurier St W Ste 610, Montreal, QC H2V 2K7 Canada
Tel.: (514) 276-6000
Web Site: www.paprika.com

Year Founded: 1991

Agency Specializes In: Advertising, Brand Development & Integration, Environmental, Graphic Design, Package Design, Strategic Planning/Research

Joanne Lefebvre *(Owner)*
Louis Gagnon *(Dir-Creative)*
Jean Doyon *(Acct Mgr)*

Accounts:
Mission Design

PAPROCKI & CO.

865 Adair Ave, Atlanta, GA 30306
Tel.: (404) 308-0019
Fax: (404) 607-1317
E-Mail: joe@paprockiandco.com
Web Site: www.paprockiandco.com

Employees: 6
Year Founded: 2005

Agency Specializes In: Advertising, Agriculture, Automotive, Brand Development & Integration, Broadcast, Business Publications, Business-To-Business, Cable T.V., Co-op Advertising, Collateral, Consulting, Consumer Marketing, Consumer Publications, Electronic Media, Entertainment, Fashion/Apparel, Food Service, Graphic Design, High Technology, Industrial, Information Technology, Leisure, Magazines, Media Buying Services, Merchandising, Newspaper, Newspapers & Magazines, Out-of-Home Media, Outdoor, Point of Sale, Print, Production, Radio, Real Estate, Restaurant, Retail, Sports Market, Strategic Planning/Research, T.V., Travel & Tourism

Approx. Annual Billings: $3,500,000

Breakdown of Gross Billings by Media: Newsp. & Mags.: $3,500,000

Joe Paprocki *(Owner & Dir-Creative)*

Accounts:
American Express
AT&T Broadband
Atlanta Community Food Bank
Atlanta History Center
BlueLinx
Cheap Lubes
ING Financial
Kodak Graphic Communications Group
Lee Jeans
Nikon
Northside Hospital
Sierra Club; Atlanta, GA (Cause Marketing); 1999
Village Real Estate
The Weather Channel
World Wildlife Fund
Zifty.com

PARA AGENCY

1133 Broadway Ste 803, New York, NY 10010
Tel.: (212) 689-1313
Fax: (212) 689-0303
E-Mail: info@paraagency.com
Web Site: www.paraagency.com

Agency Specializes In: Advertising, Brand Development & Integration, Branded Entertainment, Collateral, Consulting, Consumer Marketing, Corporate Communications, Corporate Identity, Digital/Interactive, E-Commerce, Game Integration, Graphic Design, Information Technology, Internet/Web Design, Logo & Package Design, Mobile Marketing, Multicultural, Multimedia, New Technologies, Promotions, Social Marketing/Nonprofit, Social Media

Breakdown of Gross Billings by Media: Graphic Design: 30%; Logo & Package Design: 30%; Worldwide Web Sites: 40%

Amy Cho *(Dir-Creative)*

Accounts:
CBS; New York, NY
Christie's; New York, NY
The Economist; New York, NY
Memorial Sloan-Kettering Cancer Center

PARADIGM MARKETING & CREATIVE

8275 Tournament Dr Ste 330, Memphis, TN 38125
Tel.: (901) 685-7703
Fax: (901) 531-8513
E-Mail: info@2dimes.com
Web Site: www.2dimes.com

Employees: 9
Year Founded: 1992

Agency Specializes In: Advertising, Brand Development & Integration, Collateral, Digital/Interactive, Graphic Design, Internet/Web Design, Logo & Package Design, Outdoor, Print

Charles T. Gaushell *(Founder & Pres)*
Hannah Collins *(Acct Exec & Copywriter)*

Accounts:
Adventia Wellness
Aerial Innovations
Alyzen Medical Physics
AOC Resins
APS Pharmacy
Artisan on 18th
Atlantic Pacific
Boyle Investment
Cypress Realty
EdR-Education Realty Trust
Fogelman Properties
Greenbox Memphis
Highwoods Properties
Holiday Deli
Jesus is the Sweetest
Linkous Construction
Matrix Achievement Solutions
Old Venice
Opus 29
Poag Lifestyle Centers
Pyros Fire Fresh Pizza
RVC Outdoor Destinations

Semmes Murphey
St. Jude Children's Research Hospital
Stonehenge Residential
West 46th
White Oak Development

PARADIGM MEDIA CONSULTANTS, INC.
PO Box 6213, Fishers, IN 46038
Tel.: (317) 436-4801
Fax: (317) 577-0120
E-Mail: deb@paradigmmedia.com
Web Site: www.paradigmmedia.com

Employees: 5
Year Founded: 2002

Agency Specializes In: Broadcast, Cable T.V., Collateral, Consulting, Direct Response Marketing, Education, Infomercials, Media Buying Services, Newspaper, Newspapers & Magazines, Print, Production, Radio, Recruitment, T.V., Transportation

Approx. Annual Billings: $7,000,000

Breakdown of Gross Billings by Media: Brdcst.: $5,000,000; Newsp.: $1,500,000; Production: $500,000

Deb Rishel *(Owner & Pres)*
Bob Newman *(Owner)*
Nicole Miller *(Coord-Inbound Mktg)*

Accounts:
Advanced Career Institute; Visalia, CA Truck Driver Training
Allied Health; Phoenix, AZ; Rialto, CA; Colorado Springs & Denver, CO & Portland, OR Automotive Services, Culinary Arts, Electrician Services, HVAC Services
Ayers Institute; Shreveport, LA HVAC Training, Medical Assistant Training, Pharmacy Tech Training
Career Education Institute; Boston, MA; Henderson, NV Electronic Systems Technician Training, Massage Therapy Training, Medical Assistant Training, Medical Billing & Coding Training, Network Systems Administrator Training, Pharmacy Tech Training
Diesel Driving Academy; Shreveport, LA; Baton Rouge, LA; New Orleans, LA; Lafayette, LA Truck Driver Training
DriverTrak; Denver, CO Driver Recruiting & Placement
Future Truckers of America; Asheboro, NC Truck Driver Training
Georgia Driving Academy; Conyers, GA Truck Driver Training
Napier Truck Driver Training; Middletown, OH Truck Driver Training
New England Technical Institute; Cromwell, Hamden, New Britain & Shelton, CT
New Prime, Inc.; Springfield, MO Truck Transportation
Nu-Way Truck Driver Training Centers; Pontiac, MI; Saint Louis, MO Truck Driver Training
United States Truck Driving School Truck Driver Training
Vertical Alliance Group; Texarkana, AR Internet Company

PARADISE ADVERTISING & MARKETING
150 2nd Ave N Ste 800, Saint Petersburg, FL 33701
Tel.: (727) 821-5155
Fax: (727) 822-3722
E-Mail: info@paradiseadv.com
Web Site: www.paradiseadv.com

E-Mail for Key Personnel:
President: cedar@paradiseadv.com
Creative Dir.: dave@paradiseadv.como
Media Dir.: media@paradiseadv.com

Employees: 15
Year Founded: 2002

Agency Specializes In: Advertising

Approx. Annual Billings: $9,000,000

Breakdown of Gross Billings by Media: Adv. Specialities: $90,000; Audio/Visual: $90,000; Bus. Publs.: $180,000; Cable T.V.: $900,000; Collateral: $900,000; Comml. Photography: $90,000; Consulting: $90,000; D.M.: $180,000; Graphic Design: $450,000; Internet Adv.: $270,000; Logo & Package Design: $90,000; Mags.: $450,000; Newsp.: $450,000; Outdoor: $360,000; Plng. & Consultation: $90,000; Production: $360,000; Promos.: $90,000; Pub. Rels.: $450,000; Radio: $900,000; Sports Mktg.: $90,000; Strategic Planning/Research: $180,000; T.V.: $1,800,000; Transit: $270,000; Worldwide Web Sites: $180,000

Cedar Hames *(CEO & Chief Strategy Officer)*
Nicole Delaney *(Acct Dir)*
Glenn Bowman *(Dir-Creative, Digital, Mobile & Social)*
Pat Cote *(Dir-Media)*
Cris Drago *(Dir-PR)*
Lorin Konchak *(Sr Acct Exec-PR)*

Accounts:
Daytona Beach Area Convention & Visitors Bureau (Advertising Agency of Record)
Halifax Area Advertising Authority Board Advertising Agency of Record
The Naples, Marco Island, Everglades Convention and Visitors Bureau
Naples/Marco Island/Everglades Convention Visitors Bureau
Saint Petersburg-Clearwater International Airport
Space Florida Space Travel

Branch

Paradise Advertising & Marketing-Naples
649 5th Ave S Ste 213, Naples, FL 34102
Tel.: (239) 821-2192
Fax: (239) 263-2824
E-Mail: naples@paradiseadv.com
Web Site: www.paradiseadv.com

Agency Specializes In: Advertising, Brand Development & Integration, Public Relations, Travel & Tourism

Rudy Webb *(VP-Acct Svcs)*
Brian Arndt *(Dir-Creative & Producer)*
Jessica Anderson *(Project Mgr & Producer-Digital)*
Brenda Carter De Treville *(Acct Dir-Mgmt)*
Nicole Delaney *(Acct Dir)*
Glenn Bowman *(Dir-Creative, Digital, Mobile & Social)*
Jessica Mackey *(Dir-Social Media)*
Juliana Dewberry *(Acct Mgr)*
Valorie Callan *(Specialist-Digital Media)*

Accounts:
St. Pete/Clearwater International Airport

PARADOWSKI CREATIVE
349 Marshall Ave Ste 200, Saint Louis, MO 63119
Tel.: (314) 241-2150
E-Mail: info@paradowski.com
Web Site: www.paradowski.com

Year Founded: 1977

Agency Specializes In: Advertising, Digital/Interactive, Social Media

Gus Hattrich *(Pres)*
Josh Byington *(Dir-Dev & Tech)*
Sue Dillon *(Dir-PR)*
Pat Rosner *(Dir-Insights & Plng)*
Kelly Guerra *(Acct Mgr)*

Accounts:
Cutex Nails
Monsanto Campaign: "America's Farmers Advocacy"
State of Missouri

PARADUX MEDIA GROUP
PO Box 81, Eagle Point, OR 97524
Tel.: (541) 727-0627
E-Mail: contact@paraduxmedia.com
Web Site: www.paraduxmedia.com

Year Founded: 2008

Agency Specializes In: Advertising, Corporate Identity, Graphic Design, Internet/Web Design, Logo & Package Design, Print, Public Relations, Radio, Social Media, T.V.

Tisha Oehmen *(COO)*
Cynthia Couch *(Office Mgr-Support)*
Dixie Nunez *(Office Mgr)*
Kelly Congleton *(Sr Graphic Designer)*
Mike Frey *(Chief Visionary Officer)*

Accounts:
Network Time Foundation

PARADYSZ
5 Hanover Sq, New York, NY 10004
Tel.: (212) 387-0300
Fax: (212) 387-7647
Toll Free: (800) 254-0330
Web Site: www.paradysz.com

Year Founded: 2001

Agency Specializes In: Advertising, Media Buying Services

Michael Cousineau *(Co-CEO)*
Chris Paradysz *(Co-CEO)*
Charles Teller *(Exec VP-Relationship Mgmt)*
Jodi Hitzeman *(Media Planner)*

Accounts:
AARP
Autism Speaks

PARAGON ADVERTISING
43 Court St, Buffalo, NY 14202-3101
Tel.: (716) 854-7161
Fax: (716) 854-7163
E-Mail: info@paragonadvertising.com
Web Site: www.paragonadvertising.com

E-Mail for Key Personnel:
Media Dir.: craig@paragonadvertising.com

Employees: 15
Year Founded: 1989

Agency Specializes In: Advertising, Automotive, Brand Development & Integration, Broadcast, Business Publications, Business-To-Business, Cable T.V., Catalogs, Collateral, Consumer Goods, Consumer Marketing, Consumer Publications, Corporate Communications, Corporate Identity, Digital/Interactive, Direct Response Marketing, Direct-to-Consumer, E-Commerce, Electronic Media, Entertainment, Event Planning & Marketing, Exhibit/Trade Shows, Experience Design, Food Service, Gay & Lesbian Market, Government/Political, Graphic Design, Health Care Services, Hospitality, In-Store Advertising,

Industrial, Information Technology, Internet/Web Design, Legal Services, Leisure, Local Marketing, Logo & Package Design, Magazines, Media Buying Services, Media Planning, Medical Products, Merchandising, New Product Development, Newspaper, Newspapers & Magazines, Out-of-Home Media, Outdoor, Over-50 Market, Package Design, Point of Purchase, Point of Sale, Print, Production, Production (Print), Promotions, Public Relations, Publicity/Promotions, Radio, Recruitment, Regional, Restaurant, Retail, Sales Promotion, Search Engine Optimization, Seniors' Market, Sports Market, Strategic Planning/Research, Syndication, T.V., Teen Market, Trade & Consumer Magazines, Transportation, Travel & Tourism, Urban Market

Approx. Annual Billings: $21,000,000

Breakdown of Gross Billings by Media: Cable T.V.: 15%; D.M.: 5%; Internet Adv.: 5%; Network Radio: 5%; Newsp. & Mags.: 5%; Outdoor: 5%; Spot Radio: 30%; Spot T.V.: 30%

Leo Abbott *(Mng Partner)*
Eric Goldberg *(Mng Partner)*
Scott McCandless *(Partner & VP-Mktg & Media)*
Denise McGrady *(VP-Ops)*
Andrea O'Bryant *(Mgr-Production)*

Accounts:
Anderson's Frozen Custard & Roast Beef; Amherst, NY Restaurant Chain
Big L Distributors; Buffalo, NY Windows & Doors
Chef's; Buffalo, NY Restaurant
Confer Plastics; Tonawanda, NY Pool Accessories
Kaleida Health; Buffalo, NY Hospitals; 2006
Lansky Sharpeners; Tonawanda, NY Knife Sharpeners; 2006
Mighty Taco; Amherst, NY Fast Food
O'Brien, Boyd; Buffalo, NY Attorneys; 2002
Otis Bed Manufacturing; Buffalo, NY
Reeds Jewelers; Buffalo, NY Retail
Total Tan; Blasdell, NY
Upstate Niagara Cooperative, Inc. Bison Brand Dairy Products, Upstate Farms Milk; 2007
Valu Home Centers; Buffalo, NY Retail Building Supply/Hardware

PARAGRAPH
417 N 8th St Ste 300, Philadelphia, PA 19123
Tel.: (215) 629-3550
Fax: (215) 629-2897
E-Mail: info@paragraphinc.com
Web Site: www.paragraphinc.com

Employees: 15

Ziv Navoth *(Co-Founder & CEO)*
Bob Aretz *(Pres)*

Accounts:
ARAMARK Campus Dining Services
Bayard's Chocolates
Citation Technologies
Dixon Environmental
Interior Management, Inc.
Jevs Human Services
Larsen MacColl Partners
Liquent
Millmar Paper
NFL Films
Reading Terminal Market

PARAMORE REDD ONLINE MARKETING
(Name Changed to Paramore the digital agency)

PARAMORE THE DIGITAL AGENCY
(Formerly Paramore Redd Online Marketing)
124 12th Ave S, Nashville, TN 37203
Tel.: (615) 386-9012
Web Site: paramoredigital.com

Employees: 26
Year Founded: 2002

Agency Specializes In: Email, Internet/Web Design, Social Media, Strategic Planning/Research, Viral/Buzz/Word of Mouth, Web (Banner Ads, Pop-ups, etc.)

Revenue: $3,800,000

Hannah Paramore *(Pres)*
Amanda Durand Fortune *(VP-Bus Dev)*
Josh Miller *(VP-Production)*
Matt Burch *(Dir-Content)*
Alyson Bennett *(Acct Mgr)*
Stephanie Friedlander *(Mgr-Bus Dev)*

Accounts:
Cracker Barrel
Cumberland University
The Gwinnett Convention and Visitors Bureau, Georgia Digital Strategy, Media, Website
Historic Lexington, Va., Content Development, Digital, Media Strategy, Social Media, Traditional
The Morris County Tourism Bureau, New Jersey Digital Media, Website
Pedestal Foods
Polk County
TBHC Delivers
Tennessee Department of Tourist Development
Winterplace Ski Resort

PARANOID US
1641 Ivar Ave, Hollywood, CA 90028
Tel.: (323) 993-8450
E-Mail: paranoid@paranoidus.com
Web Site: www.paranoidus.com

Year Founded: 2004

Agency Specializes In: Advertising, Web (Banner Ads, Pop-ups, etc.)

Claude Letessier *(Owner & CEO)*
Cathleen O'Conor *(Partner & Exec Producer)*
Persis Koch *(VP & Exec Producer)*
Elizabeth Durkee *(Head-Production)*
Harrison Elkins *(Head-Sls)*
Chris Spanos *(Head-Production)*
Sam Stephens *(Exec Dir-Creative)*
Kris Merc *(Dir-Creative)*
Sophie Mittleman *(Mgr-Mktg)*

Accounts:
Faune
Nike Footwear
Zeitguised Consulting Group

PARDES COMMUNICATIONS, INC.
34 Bernard St, Lexington, MA 02420
Tel.: (781) 652-8059
E-Mail: info@pardescommunications.com
Web Site: www.pardescommunications.com

Agency Specializes In: Business-To-Business, Customer Relationship Management, Public Relations, Retail, Social Marketing/Nonprofit

Diane Pardes *(Pres)*

PARK&CO
4144 N 44th St Ste A-2, Phoenix, AZ 85018
Tel.: (602) 957-7323
Web Site: www.parkandco.com

Agency Specializes In: Advertising, Brand Development & Integration, Event Planning & Marketing, Media Planning, Media Relations, Public Relations, Social Media, Strategic Planning/Research

Park Howell *(Pres)*
Luis Medina *(VP & Creative Dir)*
Jackie Mossay *(Sr Acct Exec)*
Helene Dion *(Acct Exec)*

Accounts:
New-Podius

PARKER ADVERTISING SERVICE, INC.
101 N Pointe Blvd 2nd Fl, Lancaster, PA 17601
Tel.: (717) 581-1966
Fax: (717) 581-1566
Toll Free: (800) 396-3306
E-Mail: laura@parkerad.com
Web Site: www.parkerad.com

E-Mail for Key Personnel:
President: laura@parkerad.com
Creative Dir.: jaca@parkerad.com
Production Mgr.: nathan@parkerad.com

Employees: 2
Year Founded: 1991

Agency Specializes In: Advertising, Advertising Specialties, African-American Market, Alternative Advertising, Aviation & Aerospace, Bilingual Market, Brand Development & Integration, Broadcast, Business Publications, Business-To-Business, Cable T.V., Co-op Advertising, College, Corporate Communications, Direct Response Marketing, Direct-to-Consumer, Electronic Media, Email, Event Planning & Marketing, Exhibit/Trade Shows, Financial, Graphic Design, Health Care Services, High Technology, Hispanic Market, In-Store Advertising, Internet/Web Design, Magazines, Market Research, Media Buying Services, Media Planning, Media Relations, Medical Products, Mobile Marketing, Multicultural, Multimedia, Newspaper, Newspapers & Magazines, Outdoor, Point of Purchase, Point of Sale, Print, Production (Print), Public Relations, Radio, Recruitment, Social Marketing/Nonprofit, Transportation, Web (Banner Ads, Pop-ups, etc.), Women's Market

Approx. Annual Billings: $1,100,000

Jaca White-Spangler *(Owner & Pres)*

Accounts:
Alcon Manufacturing; Sinking Spring, PA; 1990
Capital BlueCross; Harrisburg, PA; 1986
Constellation Power; Baltimore, MD; 2001
ManTech International Corporation; Fairfax, VA; 2002
Mercy Medical System; Baltimore, MD; 2000
NRG Energy, Inc.
NRG Energy, Inc.; 2002
Prime Retail; Baltimore, MD; 1997
Rite Aid Corporation; Camp Hill, PA; 2005

PARKER AVENUE
(Formerly Motivo)
205 E Third Ave Ste 303, San Mateo, CA 94401
Tel.: (650) 348-9889
Fax: (650) 532-0519
E-Mail: adrienne@parkeravenue.biz
Web Site: www.parkeravenue.biz/

Employees: 1
Year Founded: 1998

Agency Specializes In: Advertising, Alternative Advertising, Brand Development & Integration, Broadcast, Business Publications, Business-To-Business, Cable T.V., Collateral, Communications, Computers & Software, Consulting, Consumer Goods, Consumer Marketing, Consumer Publications, Content, Corporate Communications, Corporate Identity, Direct Response Marketing,

Direct-to-Consumer, Electronic Media, Electronics, Email, Environmental, Event Planning & Marketing, Exhibit/Trade Shows, Financial, Food Service, Graphic Design, Guerilla Marketing, Health Care Services, High Technology, Hospitality, Identity Marketing, In-Store Advertising, Industrial, Information Technology, Integrated Marketing, Internet/Web Design, Leisure, Local Marketing, Logo & Package Design, Magazines, Market Research, Media Buying Services, Media Planning, Medical Products, Multimedia, Newspaper, Newspapers & Magazines, Out-of-Home Media, Outdoor, Over-50 Market, Package Design, Paid Searches, Planning & Consultation, Point of Purchase, Point of Sale, Print, Production, Production (Print), Promotions, Radio, Regional, Restaurant, Sales Promotion, Seniors' Market, Strategic Planning/Research, T.V., Technical Advertising, Trade & Consumer Magazines, Transportation, Travel & Tourism, Urban Market, Web (Banner Ads, Pop-ups, etc.)

Adrienne Parker *(Principal & Dir-Creative)*

Accounts:
Santa Maria Medical Center
Silicon Valley Forum

PARKER BRAND CREATIVE SERVICES

2412 Maplewood Dr Ste 1, Sulphur, LA 70663
Tel.: (337) 214-1119
Fax: (225) 208-1707
E-Mail: info@parkerbrandcreative.com
Web Site: www.parkerbrandcreative.com

Agency Specializes In: Advertising, Brand Development & Integration, Broadcast, Digital/Interactive, Event Planning & Marketing, Graphic Design, Logo & Package Design, Media Planning, Outdoor, Print

Michelle Parker *(Owner & Dir-Art)*
Oran Parker *(Co-Owner)*

Accounts:
Infinite Health

PARKER MADISON DIALOG MARKETING

80 E Rio Salado Pkwy Ste 101, Tempe, AZ 85281
Tel.: (602) 254-2440
Fax: (602) 258-9261
Web Site: www.parkermadison.com

Agency Specializes In: Brand Development & Integration, Consumer Marketing

Mark Godfrey *(Owner)*

Accounts:
Trillium Investment Services
Velo Vie LLC Bicycles Mfr

PARKERWHITE INC.

230 Birmingham Dr, Cardiff By The Sea, CA 92007
Tel.: (760) 783-2020
Web Site: www.parkerwhite.com

Agency Specializes In: Advertising, Brand Development & Integration, Collateral, Email, Exhibit/Trade Shows, Internet/Web Design, Media Planning, Package Design, Search Engine Optimization, Social Media

Cindy White *(CEO & Dir-Creative)*
Tyson Misleh *(Acct Grp Dir)*
Ryan Parker *(Mgr-Bus Dev)*
Eric Ng *(Strategist-Digital)*
Keith White *(Strategist-Brand)*

Accounts:
Aperio, Inc.
Zest Anchors, Inc.

PARLEESTUMPF INC

350 S Main St Ste 113, Doylestown, PA 18901
Tel.: (215) 345-7040
Fax: (215) 345-7042
Web Site: www.parleestumpf.com

Agency Specializes In: Advertising, Brand Development & Integration, Corporate Identity, Digital/Interactive, Internet/Web Design, Package Design, Print, Radio, Social Media, T.V.

Todd Parlee *(Pres)*
Luanne Basile *(Coord-Acctg)*
Diane Jaynes *(Coord-Client Svcs)*

Accounts:
Dranoff Properties, Inc.
PrintMail Systems, Inc
Richard Green & Son

PARTNERS + EDELL

(Name Changed to Rain43)

PARTNERS & HARRISON INC

410 Kings Mill Rd Ste 112, York, PA 17401
Tel.: (855) 618-4200
Web Site: www.partnersandharrison.com

Employees: 10
Year Founded: 2012

Agency Specializes In: Advertising, Alternative Advertising, Brand Development & Integration, Branded Entertainment, Broadcast, Business Publications, Cable T.V., Catalogs, Co-op Advertising, Collateral, Custom Publishing, Exhibit/Trade Shows, Experience Design, In-Store Advertising, Internet/Web Design, Local Marketing, Logo & Package Design, Magazines, Media Planning, Multimedia, Newspapers & Magazines, Outdoor, Point of Purchase, Point of Sale, Print, Production, Production (Print), Promotions, Public Relations, Publishing, Social Media, Sponsorship, T.V., Trade & Consumer Magazines, Web (Banner Ads, Pop-ups, etc.), Yellow Pages Advertising

Nick Harrison *(Partner & Dir-Creative)*
Brad Londy *(Partner)*
Rebekah Sweeney *(Dir-Bus Dev)*
David Tull *(Strategist-Brand & Mktg)*

Accounts:
Rejiva

PARTNERS & SPADE

40 Great Jones, New York, NY 10012
Tel.: (646) 861-2827
E-Mail: info@partnersandspade.com
Web Site: www.partnersandspade.com

Year Founded: 2008

Agency Specializes In: Advertising, Brand Development & Integration, Graphic Design, Production (Ad, Film, Broadcast), Publishing

Anthony Sperduti *(Co-Founder & Co-Dir-Creative)*
Andy Spade *(Partner)*
Fernando Music *(Mng Dir)*
Catherine Borod *(Acct Dir)*
Elizabeth Dilk *(Dir-Art)*
Ashley Jones *(Dir-Art)*

Accounts:
New-Harry's
J. Crew Group, Inc.
Normal Campaign: "Ear Tailor", Earphones
Quirky Campaign: "The World's Least Important CEO"
Shinola Campaign: "The Runwell. It's Just Smart Enough", Creative
Target Campaign: "Party Entertaining With Threshold"
Warby Parker Campaign: "Eyeballs Looking For Glasses", Campaign: "The Literary Life"
Whole Foods Market, Inc. "Beef", "Produce", Advertising, Broadcast, Campaign: "America's Healthiest Grocery Store", Campaign: "Values Matter", Creative

PARTNERS CREATIVE

603 Woody St, Missoula, MT 59802
Tel.: (406) 541-2263
Web Site: www.partnerscreative.com

Year Founded: 2000

Agency Specializes In: Advertising, Brand Development & Integration, Media Buying Services, Media Planning, Public Relations, Search Engine Optimization, Social Media, Strategic Planning/Research

Sean Benton *(VP, Dir-Creative & Copywriter)*
Steve Falen *(VP & Dir-Creative)*
Stacy Kendrick *(Client Svcs Dir)*
Tony Ferrini *(Dir-Digital Technologies)*
Lori Warden *(Acct Exec-PR)*

PARTNERS+NAPIER

192 Mill St Ste 600, Rochester, NY 14614-1022
Tel.: (585) 454-1010
Fax: (585) 454-1575
Toll Free: (800) 274-4954
E-Mail: info@partnersandnapier.com
Web Site: www.partnersandnapier.com

E-Mail for Key Personnel:
President: snapier@partnersandnapier.com
Creative Dir.: jgabel@partnersandnapier.com

Employees: 89
Year Founded: 1972

National Agency Associations: 4A's-AMA

Agency Specializes In: Advertising, Education, Health Care Services, Media Buying Services, Media Planning, New Technologies, Planning & Consultation, Sponsorship, Strategic Planning/Research

Jeffery Gabel *(Mng Partner & Chief Creative Officer)*
Courtney Cotrupe *(Mng Dir)*
Scott Chapman *(Exec Dir-Fin)*
Pete VonDerLinn *(Exec Dir-Creative)*
Everol Smith *(Acct Dir)*
Greg Smith *(Dir-Shopper Mktg & Promos)*
Cara Civiletti Mittler *(Acct Supvr)*
Rachel Ballatori *(Asst Acct Exec)*

Accounts:
Bausch + Lomb
BMW Financial Services BMW, MINI; 2014
Bob Evans Foods; 2014
Capital One Financial Corporation
ConAgra Foods Chef Boyardee, PAM, Ro-Tel; 2014
Constellation Brands
Delta Vacations; 2014
Economic Development Board of Singapore; 2015
Excellus BlueCross BlueShield; 2003
Keurig Green Mountain; 2010
Kodak; 1996
Lufthansa Airlines; 2012
Marlow's Tavern; 2008
Mederma (Agency of Record) Advertising, Campaign: "One Word", Digital, Marketing, Online, Print, TV

Merz Pharmaceuticals; 2012
O'Brien & Gere
The Players' Tribune; 2014
Rochester Regional Health System; 2001
Sanmina; 2010
Saputo Dairy Foods USA Friendship Dairies; 2009
ShopKeep; 2015
TECGEN; 2013
WEX; 2014
Wiley Publishing; 2014

Branches

Partners+Napier
11 E 26th St 6th Fl, New York, NY 10010
Tel.: (212) 401-7799
E-Mail: hello@partnersandnapier.com
Web Site: www.partnersandnapier.com

National Agency Associations: 4A's

Agency Specializes In: Advertising, Brand Development & Integration, Digital/Interactive, Media Buying Services, Media Planning, Strategic Planning/Research

Matt Dowshen *(Pres)*
Ted Florea *(Chief Strategy Officer)*
Courtney Cotrupe *(Mng Dir-Rochester)*
Gary Knaak *(Mng Dir-Content Central)*
Jason Marks *(Exec Creative Dir)*
Greg Smith *(Dir-Shopper Mktg)*

Accounts:
Outdoor Advertising Association of America (Creative Agency of Record)
The Players Tribune (Agency of Record)
ShopKeep (Agency of Record) Brand Strategy, Creative
Singapore Economic Development Board Advertising, Creative

PARTNERS+SIMONS
25 Drydock Ave 8th Fl, Boston, MA 02210
Tel.: (617) 330-9393
Fax: (617) 330-9394
Web Site: www.partnersandsimons.com

Employees: 60
Year Founded: 1989

Agency Specializes In: Sponsorship

Trudy Almquist *(CFO & Exec VP)*
Tony Cotrupi *(Principal)*
Anthony Henriques *(Exec VP-Creative)*
Stephanie Rogers *(Exec VP-Media & Tech)*
Patrick McGloin *(Sr VP & Mng Dir-Life Science Bus)*
Steve Lynch *(Sr VP & Grp Dir-Creative)*
Jim Porter *(Sr VP & Grp Acct Dir)*
Kara Tierney *(VP & Acct Dir)*
Margaret Royston *(VP & Dir-Digital & Creative Svcs)*
Brian Bohne *(Sr Producer-Digital)*
Magarita Epshteyn *(Brand Dir)*
Susan Hanson *(Dir-Contact Plng)*
Roy Wetherbee *(Dir-Interactive Tech)*
Eric Buchka *(Acct Supvr)*
Kaitlin Downing *(Supvr-Media)*

Accounts:
Agilent Technologies
American International Group Inc Print, Television
B. Braun Medical Inc Brand Strategies
Blue Cross & Blue Shield of Massachusetts
Blue Cross of Northeastern Pennsylvania (Agency of Record) Branding, Image Development
Horizon Blue Cross Blue Shield of New Jersey
Horizon Healthcare Services, Inc
The Kenneth B. Schwartz Center
Mitralign Animated Videos, Brand Messaging, Website
NinePoint Medical Strategic Planning, Website
Portsmouth Abbey God is Calling
Select Health
Specialty Scripts
Thermo Scientific
Tufts Medical Center (Agency of Record)

THE PARTNERSHIP
3475 Piedmont Rd, Atlanta, GA 30305
Tel.: (404) 880-0080
Fax: (404) 880-0270
Web Site: www.thepartnership.com

Year Founded: 1983

Agency Specializes In: Advertising, Email, Media Buying Services, Media Planning, Mobile Marketing, Print, Radio, Social Media, Sponsorship, T.V.

David Arnold *(Founder & Pres)*
Randall Hooker *(Exec VP & Exec Dir-Creative)*
Stacee Amos *(VP & Acct Dir)*
Tillman Douglas, Jr. *(Acct Dir)*
James Sadler *(Dir-Creative)*
Jonathan MacArthur *(Assoc Dir-Creative)*
Ed Malyon *(Assoc Dir-Creative)*
Lisa Stover *(Mgr-Fin)*

Accounts:
ATC Financial, LLC.
ATC Income Tax
Carhartt, Inc.
Crowne Plaza Hotels & Resorts
The FDIC
Ferrari Maserati of Atlanta
GS Battery
Holiday Inn
InterContinental Hotels & Resorts
Jeremy Clements Racing
Old Fourth Distillery
SkyView Atlanta
Southeastern United Dairy Industry Association
TEDxPeachtree
UHS-Pruitt Healthcare
Whynatte Latte Digital, Traditional Media

PARTNERSHIP ADVERTISING
11 Pinchot Ct Ste 100, Amherst, NY 14228
Tel.: (716) 689-2222
Fax: (716) 689-2468
E-Mail: info@thepartnershipltd.com
Web Site: www.thepartnershipltd.com

E-Mail for Key Personnel:
President: davis@thepartnershipltd.com
Media Dir.: cappellino@thepartnershipltd.com

Employees: 9
Year Founded: 1987

Agency Specializes In: Advertising, Affiliate Marketing, Alternative Advertising, Brand Development & Integration, Broadcast, Business Publications, Cable T.V., Co-op Advertising, Collateral, Communications, Digital/Interactive, Direct Response Marketing, Direct-to-Consumer, E-Commerce, Electronic Media, Event Planning & Marketing, Food Service, Government/Political, Graphic Design, Infomercials, Integrated Marketing, Local Marketing, Logo & Package Design, Marine, Market Research, Media Buying Services, Media Planning, Media Relations, Newspaper, Newspapers & Magazines, Outdoor, Package Design, Planning & Consultation, Point of Purchase, Point of Sale, Print, Production, Production (Print), Promotions, Public Relations, Publicity/Promotions, Radio, Restaurant, Retail, Sales Promotion, Seniors' Market, Social Marketing/Nonprofit, Sponsorship, Sports Market, Strategic Planning/Research, Sweepstakes, T.V., Telemarketing, Trade & Consumer Magazines, Yellow Pages Advertising

Approx. Annual Billings: $6,000,000

Robert E. Davis *(Pres & CEO)*
Mike Stevens *(VP-Acct Svc)*

Accounts:
Atlantic Enterprises; Erie, PA Pizza Hut Franchise
Buffalo Home Show; Buffalo, NY Home Decor, Products & Services
Buffalo/Niagara Golf Show; Buffalo, NY Golf Products & Services
Coca Cola Bottling Company; Buffalo, NY Soft Drinks/Coca Cola Field
Consumer Credit Counseling; Buffalo, NY Finance Counseling
The Daland Corporation; Wichita, KS Pizza Hut Franchise
Dave's Christmas Store; Buffalo, NY Christmas/Holiday Decor
Dave's Deli; Buffalo, NY Fresh Produce & Meats
Five Guys Burgers & Fries; PA Restaurant
Hospitality West; Traverse City, MI Pizza Hut Franchise; 1998
Jones Lang LaSalle
Kenmore Mercy Foundation; Kenmore, NY Fundraising Development
Kosmart Enterprises; Hazleton, PA Pizza Hut Franchise
Lily of France
M&M Mars
Maryland Pizza Hut; Upper Marlboro, MO Pizza Hut Franchise
MBMS; Amherst, NY Banking Management Systems Maintenance
Niagara Frontier Auto Dealers; Buffalo, NY Auto Show
Park School of Buffalo; Snyder, NY College Prep School
Senior Associates; Buffalo, NY Senior Advocacy
The St. Joe Company
Stamm; Buffalo, NY Legal
Staybridge Suites
Tanning Bed; Buffalo, NY Tanning Salon
Vonner Insurance Group; Amherst;, NY Insurance Products
Weinberg Campus; Buffalo, NY Adult Residential Housing
Western New York Dental; Buffalo, NY Dentistry Service Provider

PARTNERSHIP OF PACKER, OESTERLING & SMITH (PPO&S)
122 State St, Harrisburg, PA 17101
Tel.: (717) 232-1898
Fax: (717) 236-6793
E-Mail: contact@pposinc.com
Web Site: www.pposinc.com

E-Mail for Key Personnel:
President: csmith@pposinc.com

Employees: 25
Year Founded: 1980

Agency Specializes In: African-American Market, Agriculture, Bilingual Market, Brand Development & Integration, Broadcast, Business-To-Business, Co-op Advertising, Communications, Consulting, Consumer Marketing, Environmental, Financial, Food Service, Government/Political, Health Care Services, Hispanic Market, Media Buying Services, Medical Products, Multimedia, Pharmaceutical, Planning & Consultation, Public Relations, Publicity/Promotions, Radio, Seniors' Market, Strategic Planning/Research, T.V., Trade & Consumer Magazines

Approx. Annual Billings: $15,000,000

Virginia A. Roth *(Pres)*

Yvonne Evans *(VP-Fin & Ops)*
Jeffrey S. Miller *(VP-Acct Svcs)*
Jennifer Andren *(Dir-Media)*
Cindy Weesner *(Assoc Dir-Media & Mgr-Acct Dev)*
Karen M. Gray *(Assoc Dir-Creative)*

Accounts:
Bank of Lancaster County
Feld Entertainment
Graham Packaging Company, L.P.
Pennsylvania Apple Marketing Board; Harrisburg, PA; 1984
Pennsylvania Association of Colleges & Universities; Harrisburg, PA; 2000
Pennsylvania Housing Finance Agency; Harrisburg, PA; 2003
Pennsylvania Library Association; Harrisburg, PA; 2003
Pennsylvania Waste Industry Association; 2001
Statewide Adoption Network; Harrisburg, PA; 1996

PARTNERSRILEY
(Formerly MelamedRiley Advertising, LLC)
1375 Euclid Ave Ste 410, Cleveland, OH 44115
Tel.: (216) 241-2141
Fax: (216) 479-2429
Toll Free: (800) 222-4045
E-Mail: info@partnersriley.com
Web Site: www.partnersriley.com

E-Mail for Key Personnel:
Creative Dir.: rriley@mradvertising.com
Media Dir.: ddackiewicz@mradvertising.com

Employees: 25
Year Founded: 1930

Agency Specializes In: Advertising, Brand Development & Integration, Broadcast, Business-To-Business, Collateral, Consumer Marketing, Consumer Publications, Corporate Identity, Electronic Media, Graphic Design, Internet/Web Design, Logo & Package Design, Magazines, Media Buying Services, Multimedia, Newspaper, Newspapers & Magazines, Out-of-Home Media, Outdoor, Point of Purchase, Point of Sale, Print, Production, Radio, Strategic Planning/Research, T.V., Trade & Consumer Magazines

Rick Riley *(Owner)*

Accounts:
FMC
Miratec

PASADENA ADVERTISING
51 W Dayton St Ste 100, Pasadena, CA 91105-2025
Tel.: (626) 584-0011
Fax: (626) 584-0907
E-Mail: accts@pasadenaadv.com
Web Site: www.pasadenaadv.com

E-Mail for Key Personnel:
President: suzanne@pasadenaadv.com
Creative Dir.: tony@pasadenaadv.com
Media Dir.: lori@pasadenaadv.com

Employees: 8
Year Founded: 1986

Agency Specializes In: Advertising, Brand Development & Integration, Broadcast, Collateral, Corporate Identity, Entertainment, Environmental, Fashion/Apparel, Graphic Design, Internet/Web Design, Logo & Package Design, Newspaper, Outdoor, Point of Sale, Print, Production, Radio, Real Estate, Restaurant, Retail, T.V.

Approx. Annual Billings: $6,900,000

Breakdown of Gross Billings by Media: Collateral: 25%; Logo & Package Design: 5%; Newsp. & Mags.: 10%; Outdoor: 5%; Point of Purchase: 5%; Print: 15%; Radio & T.V.: 25%; Trade & Consumer Mags.: 5%; Worldwide Web Sites: 5%

Suzanne Marks *(Owner)*
J. Anthony Nino *(Owner)*
Sarah Baker *(Dir-Art)*
David Ensz *(Dir-Creative)*
Kelly La Croix *(Acct Mgr)*

Accounts:
Bob Hope Burbank Airport
Castro Convertibles
Catholic Charities
Delacey Green
FastFrame; Newbury Park, CA Custom Frames; 2005
Hills Department Stores
Hyde Park Entertainment; Santa Monica, CA
Intracorp; Newport Beach, CA (Logo, Brochures & Corporate Identity) Delacey at Green & Waterstone Project; 2004
LifeForm; Calgary, Canada (Packaging Design); 2003
Mayfield Senior High School; Pasadena, CA (Website)
Old Pasadena Management District
Pacific Coast Feather Cushion
Pasadena Unified School District
The Roho Group
TCW
Trust Company of the West (TCW)
West Basin Municipal Water District

PASKILL STAPLETON & LORD
1 Roberts Ave, Glenside, PA 19038-3497
Tel.: (215) 572-7938
Fax: (215) 572-7937
E-Mail: info@psandl.com
Web Site: www.psandl.com

E-Mail for Key Personnel:
Media Dir.: Kristin@psandl.com

Employees: 30
Year Founded: 1988

Agency Specializes In: Education

Approx. Annual Billings: $6,000,000

Jim Paskill *(Principal & Dir-Creative)*
John Stapleton *(Principal & Dir-Ops)*
David W. Black *(VP-Market Res & Consulting)*
Bill Hurlburt *(VP-Interactive Svcs)*
Robert Oxman *(VP-Creative Svcs)*

Accounts:
Drexel University
Embry Riddle Aeronautical University
Emporia State University
Holy Family University
LaSalle University
Malone University
Monmouth University
Neumann College
NJCU
Oakland University
Saint Leo University
Seton Hall University

Branch

Paskill Stapleton & Lord
155 Maple St Ste 208, Springfield, MA 01105-1805
Tel.: (413) 739-5289
Fax: (413) 781-4595
E-Mail: info@psandl.com
Web Site: www.psandl.com

Employees: 4

Agency Specializes In: Education

Jim Paskill *(Principal & Dir-Creative)*
John Stapleton *(Principal & Dir-Ops)*
David Black *(VP-Market Res & Consulting)*
Bill Hurlburt *(VP-Interactive Svcs)*

Accounts:
Saint Bonaventure University
University of Massachusetts Boston
University of Massachusetts Lowell

PASSENGER
5900 Wilshire Blvd 28th Fl, Los Angeles, CA 90036
Tel.: (323) 556-5400
Fax: (323) 556-5490
E-Mail: info@thinkpassenger.com
Web Site: www.thinkpassenger.com

Employees: 40

Agency Specializes In: Business-To-Business, Strategic Planning/Research

Arnaud Gregori *(CFO)*
Jodie Brinkerhoff *(Sr VP-Sls & Client Svcs)*
Kevin Owens *(Sr VP-Product Mgmt & Engrg)*
Sarah Sandberg *(VP-Client Svcs)*
Marc Macellaio *(Sr Dir-Client Dev)*
Rachel Lurie *(Acct Mgr-Client Svcs)*
Deepti Patel *(Acct Mgr)*
Kelly Maltman *(Mgr-Mktg)*
Bahram Nour-Omid *(Exec Chm)*

Accounts:
ABC, Inc.
Adidas
Coca-Cola Refreshments USA, Inc.
FOX
GE
Mercedes-Benz

PASSEY ADVERTISING INC
1124 W Main St, Medford, OR 97501
Tel.: (541) 779-5455
Toll Free: (800) 460-9762
Web Site: www.passeyadvertising.com

Agency Specializes In: Advertising, Digital/Interactive, Internet/Web Design, Logo & Package Design, Outdoor, Print, Radio, T.V.

Randy Passey *(CEO)*

Accounts:
Black Chapman Webber & Stevens

PATHFINDERS ADVERTISING & MARKETING GROUP
3830 Edison Lakes Pkwy, Mishawaka, IN 46545-3400
Tel.: (574) 259-5908
Fax: (574) 259-5978
E-Mail: info@pathfind.com
Web Site: www.pathfind.com

E-Mail for Key Personnel:
President: sball@pathfind.com
Creative Dir.: JBasker@pathfind.com

Employees: 22
Year Founded: 1979

National Agency Associations: AAF-AMA

Agency Specializes In: Advertising, Automotive, Brand Development & Integration, Broadcast, Business-To-Business, Cable T.V., Co-op Advertising, Collateral, Communications, Consulting, Consumer Marketing, Consumer

Publications, Corporate Communications, Corporate Identity, Direct Response Marketing, Electronic Media, Event Planning & Marketing, Exhibit/Trade Shows, Financial, Food Service, Graphic Design, Health Care Services, High Technology, In-Store Advertising, Industrial, Internet/Web Design, Logo & Package Design, Magazines, Media Buying Services, Multimedia, New Product Development, Newspaper, Newspapers & Magazines, Outdoor, Over-50 Market, Pharmaceutical, Planning & Consultation, Point of Purchase, Point of Sale, Print, Production, Public Relations, Publicity/Promotions, Radio, Real Estate, Retail, Sales Promotion, Seniors' Market, Sponsorship, Strategic Planning/Research, Sweepstakes, T.V., Technical Advertising, Trade & Consumer Magazines, Transportation, Travel & Tourism, Yellow Pages Advertising

Vicky Holland *(Pres)*
Stephen R. Ball *(CEO)*
Kathy Mutka *(Acct Dir & Dir-PR)*
Jane Basker *(Dir-Creative)*
Jeff Staley *(Dir-Art)*
Nancy Ball *(Office Mgr)*
Mike Johnson *(Sr Copywriter)*

Accounts:
Crown International
Fifth Third Bank
GC America
Royal Outdoor Products
Supreme

THE PATIENT RECRUITING AGENCY

6207 Bee Caves Rd Ste 288, Austin, TX 78746
Tel.: (512) 345-7788
Fax: (775) 258-0231
Toll Free: (888) 899-7788
E-Mail: lance@tprausa.com
Web Site: www.tprausa.com

Employees: 30
Year Founded: 1999

Agency Specializes In: Advertising, African-American Market, Bilingual Market, Brand Development & Integration, Broadcast, Cable T.V., Communications, Consumer Marketing, Digital/Interactive, Direct Response Marketing, Direct-to-Consumer, Education, Electronic Media, Graphic Design, Health Care Services, Hispanic Market, Integrated Marketing, Internet/Web Design, Local Marketing, Logo & Package Design, Magazines, Market Research, Media Buying Services, Media Planning, Media Relations, Multimedia, New Technologies, Newspaper, Outdoor, Pharmaceutical, Print, Production, Production (Ad, Film, Broadcast), Production (Print), Radio, Recruitment, Regional, Search Engine Optimization, Seniors' Market, Strategic Planning/Research, T.V., Teen Market, Urban Market, Women's Market

Approx. Annual Billings: $12,000,000

Breakdown of Gross Billings by Media: Network Radio: $1,080,000; Network T.V.: $7,920,000; Print: $600,000; Production: $2,400,000

Lance Nickens *(Pres)*
Carl T. Wibbenmeyer *(COO)*
Todd B. Sanders *(CTO)*
Corrie Palm *(Dir-Investigator Svcs)*
Doug Mackie *(Supvr)*

PATRIOT ADVERTISING INC.

535 E Fernhurst Dr Ste 263, Katy, TX 77450
Tel.: (832) 239-5775
Fax: (832) 553-2599
E-Mail: info@patriotadvertising.com
Web Site: www.patriotadvertising.com

Employees: 15
Year Founded: 2005

Agency Specializes In: Advertising, Affiliate Marketing, Affluent Market, African-American Market, Agriculture, Alternative Advertising, Asian Market, Automotive, Aviation & Aerospace, Bilingual Market, Brand Development & Integration, Broadcast, Business Publications, Business-To-Business, Cable T.V., Collateral, College, Commercial Photography, Communications, Consulting, Consumer Goods, Consumer Marketing, Consumer Publications, Corporate Communications, Corporate Identity, Custom Publishing, Digital/Interactive, Direct-to-Consumer, E-Commerce, Electronic Media, Electronics, Email, Engineering, Entertainment, Event Planning & Marketing, Exhibit/Trade Shows, Experience Design, Fashion/Apparel, Financial, Food Service, Government/Political, Graphic Design, Health Care Services, High Technology, Hispanic Market, Hospitality, Identity Marketing, In-Store Advertising, Industrial, Information Technology, Integrated Marketing, International, Internet/Web Design, Legal Services, Local Marketing, Logo & Package Design, Magazines, Marine, Market Research, Media Buying Services, Media Planning, Media Relations, Media Training, Medical Products, Men's Market, Mobile Marketing, Multicultural, Multimedia, New Product Development, New Technologies, Newspaper, Newspapers & Magazines, Outdoor, Over-50 Market, Package Design, Pharmaceutical, Planning & Consultation, Point of Purchase, Point of Sale, Print, Product Placement, Production, Production (Ad, Film, Broadcast), Production (Print), Promotions, Public Relations, Publicity/Promotions, Publishing, Radio, Real Estate, Recruitment, Regional, Restaurant, Retail, Sales Promotion, Search Engine Optimization, Seniors' Market, Social Marketing/Nonprofit, Sports Market, Strategic Planning/Research, T.V., Technical Advertising, Teen Market, Trade & Consumer Magazines, Transportation, Urban Market, Viral/Buzz/Word of Mouth, Web (Banner Ads, Pop-ups, etc.), Women's Market

Tim Runge *(Owner, Pres & CEO)*
Phil Pool *(Dir-New Bus)*
Lisa Bowes *(Sr Acct Mgr & Graphic Designer)*
Todd Fullet *(Acct Mgr)*

Accounts:
Kroger; Houston, TX (Recruitment); 2005
Tyco; Houston, TX

PATTERSON RIEGEL ADVERTISING

200 E Main St Ste 710, Fort Wayne, IN 46802
Tel.: (260) 422-5614
Fax: (260) 422-5875
Web Site: www.pattersonriegel.com

Agency Specializes In: Advertising, Collateral, Corporate Identity, Internet/Web Design, Logo & Package Design, Media Relations, Promotions, Public Relations, Social Media, Strategic Planning/Research

Matthew Henry *(Pres)*
John Foreman *(Mng Dir)*
Kimberly Clark *(Office Mgr)*
Emilie Henry *(Mgr-Media)*
Emilie Murphy *(Mgr-Media)*

Accounts:
Beers Mallers Backs & Salin LLP

PATTISON OUTDOOR ADVERTISING

2285 Wyecroft Rd, Oakville, ON L6L 5L7 Canada
Tel.: (905) 465-0114
Fax: (905) 465-0633
Toll Free: (800) 363-1675
E-Mail: info@pattisonoutdoor.com
Web Site: www.pattisonoutdoor.com

Employees: 350

Kathy Cormier *(VP-Client Svcs)*
Marilyn King *(VP-Production Svcs)*
Herman Bekkering *(Dir-Creative-Natl)*
Scott Gibb *(Dir-Sls-Edmonton & Northern Alberta)*
Nicoletta McDonald *(Dir-Sls-Calgary & Southern Alberta)*
Joanne Sparrow *(Dir-HR)*
Phil Grosse *(Acct Exec)*

PAUL MILES ADVERTISING

25 Jefferson SE, Grand Rapids, MI 49503
Tel.: (616) 459-6692
Fax: (616) 459-5522
E-Mail: ideas@paulmilesadvertising.com
Web Site: www.paulmilesadvertising.com

Agency Specializes In: Advertising, Media Buying Services, Outdoor, Print, Radio, T.V.

Paul H. Miles *(Pres & Creative Dir)*
Valerie Knapp *(Office Mgr)*
Heather TePastte *(Sr Acct Exec)*

Accounts:
Gezon Motors

PAUL WERTH ASSOCIATES, INC.

10 N High St Ste 300, Columbus, OH 43215-3552
Tel.: (614) 224-8114
Fax: (614) 224-8509
E-Mail: contact@paulwerth.com
Web Site: www.paulwerth.com

E-Mail for Key Personnel:
President: swh@paulwerth.com

Employees: 20
Year Founded: 1963

National Agency Associations: COPF

Agency Specializes In: Advertising, Agriculture, Arts, Brand Development & Integration, Business-To-Business, Collateral, College, Commercial Photography, Communications, Consulting, Consumer Goods, Consumer Marketing, Corporate Communications, Corporate Identity, Crisis Communications, Digital/Interactive, Direct Response Marketing, Direct-to-Consumer, Education, Electronic Media, Email, Environmental, Event Planning & Marketing, Exhibit/Trade Shows, Financial, Food Service, Government/Political, Graphic Design, Health Care Services, High Technology, Hispanic Market, Identity Marketing, In-Store Advertising, Integrated Marketing, Internet/Web Design, Local Marketing, Logo & Package Design, Luxury Products, Market Research, Media Relations, Media Training, Multicultural, Multimedia, Pharmaceutical, Planning & Consultation, Podcasting, Print, Promotions, Public Relations, Publicity/Promotions, Publishing, Radio, Real Estate, Restaurant, Retail, Search Engine Optimization, Social Marketing/Nonprofit, Social Media, Strategic Planning/Research

Sandra W. Harbrecht *(Owner)*
Carl West *(CFO)*
Beth Hillis *(VP)*

Accounts:
Advancement Courses Education
Dave Thomas Foundation for Adoption
Findley Davies Human Resources
Huntington National Bank
Innovation Generation Education
Insurance Industry Resource Council
Moody Nolan Architecture
National Safe Boating Council

The Ohio State University Wexner Medical Center
The Ohio State University Education
Orthopaedic Associates of Zanesville Education
White Castle System, Inc.; Columbus, OH

PAULSEN MARKETING COMMUNICATIONS, INC.

(d/b/a Paulsen AgriBranding)
3510 S 1st Ave Cir, Sioux Falls, SD 57105-5807
Tel.: (605) 336-1745
Fax: (605) 336-2305
E-Mail: hello@paulsen.ag
Web Site: www.paulsen.ag/

E-Mail for Key Personnel:
Creative Dir.: msmither@paulsenmarketing.com
Media Dir.: kmoss@paulsenmarketing.com

Employees: 33
Year Founded: 1951

National Agency Associations: NAMA

Agency Specializes In: Agriculture, Brand Development & Integration, Business-To-Business, Collateral, Communications, Corporate Communications, Corporate Identity, Crisis Communications, Digital/Interactive, E-Commerce, Email, Environmental, Exhibit/Trade Shows, Financial, Graphic Design, Health Care Services, Industrial, Integrated Marketing, Internet/Web Design, Logo & Package Design, Media Buying Services, Media Planning, Medical Products, Mobile Marketing, Package Design, Pets , Pharmaceutical, Print, Production, Public Relations, Publicity/Promotions, Radio, Sales Promotion, Search Engine Optimization, Social Media, Strategic Planning/Research, T.V., Yellow Pages Advertising

Approx. Annual Billings: $10,000,000

Breakdown of Gross Billings by Media: Audio/Visual: $500,000; Bus. Publs.: $100,000; Collateral: $250,000; Comml. Photography: $250,000; Consumer Publs.: $100,000; Corp. Communications: $250,000; D.M.: $350,000; E-Commerce: $500,000; Farm Publs.: $1,000,000; Graphic Design: $500,000; Internet Adv.: $750,000; Logo & Package Design: $250,000; Newsp. & Mags.: $250,000; Point of Purchase: $250,000; Point of Sale: $250,000; Print: $700,000; Production: $250,000; Pub. Rels.: $1,000,000; Radio & T.V.: $500,000; Strategic Planning/Research: $1,000,000; Worldwide Web Sites: $1,000,000

Greg Guse *(Exec VP & Analyst-Industry)*
Mark Smither *(VP & Dir-Strategic)*
Mike Dowling *(VP-Creative Svcs)*
Jane Harms *(VP-Fin & HR)*
Marcus Squier *(VP-Client Svcs)*
Sara Steever *(VP-Digital Svcs)*
Kristie Weiberg *(Assoc Dir-Creative)*
Tara Young *(Project Mgr-Digital)*
Joanie Beaner *(Coord-Media)*
Tom Koeller *(Coord-Analytics)*
Sarah Wolfswinkel *(Coord-Production)*

Accounts:
AgStar Financial Services
AgUnited for South Dakota
E.I. Medical Imaging
Ecolab, Inc.
Grain States Soya
Hallmark Cards, Inc. User Created Cards
Kubota Tractor; Torrance, CA Tractors; 1999
Raven Industries
South Dakota Corn Growers Association; Sioux Falls, SD

PAULSONDANIELS

15 N Main St, Chester, CT 06412
Tel.: (860) 322-4593
E-Mail: hello@paulsondaniels.com
Web Site: www.paulsondaniels.com

Year Founded: 2013

Agency Specializes In: Advertising, Corporate Identity, Graphic Design, Internet/Web Design, Public Relations, Strategic Planning/Research

Susan Daniels *(Partner)*
Michelle Parr Paulson *(Partner)*

Accounts:
Simply Sharing

PAUSBACK ADVERTISING

3711 Medford Rd, Durham, NC 27705
Tel.: (919) 656-0727
Web Site: www.pausback.com

Agency Specializes In: Advertising

Don Pausback *(Dir-Creative)*

Accounts:
Ace Hardware Corporation
National Pawn

PAVLOV

(Formerly Concussion, LLP)
707 W Vickery Blvd #103, Fort Worth, TX 76104
Tel.: (817) 336-6824
Fax: (817) 336-6823
Web Site: www.pavlovagency.com/

Employees: 47
Year Founded: 2001

National Agency Associations: AAF

Agency Specializes In: Advertising, Bilingual Market, Broadcast, Business-To-Business, Cable T.V., Collateral, Consumer Goods, Consumer Marketing, Corporate Identity, Direct Response Marketing, Entertainment, Graphic Design, Health Care Services, Hispanic Market, Hospitality, Identity Marketing, In-Store Advertising, Integrated Marketing, Internet/Web Design, Leisure, Local Marketing, Logo & Package Design, Media Buying Services, Media Planning, Media Relations, Multicultural, Newspaper, Newspapers & Magazines, Out-of-Home Media, Outdoor, Package Design, Paid Searches, Print, Public Relations, Publicity/Promotions, Radio, Real Estate, Search Engine Optimization, T.V., Transportation, Travel & Tourism

Approx. Annual Billings: $20,000,000

Allen Wallach *(CEO)*
Scott Kirk *(Grp Acct Dir)*
Morgan Godby *(Dir-Art)*
Jeffrey Heaton *(Dir-Art)*
Khris Kesling *(Dir-Creative)*
Claire Bloxom Armstrong *(Mgr-PR & Social Media)*
Mallory Ellis *(Supvr-Media)*
Megan Dobbertien *(Acct Exec)*
Jordan Goss *(Jr Acct Exec)*
Brenna Jefferies *(Coord-PR & Social Media)*

Accounts:
Cofidis
Dallas/Fort Worth International Airport B-to-C Marketing, PR
Fort Worth Convention & Visitors Bureau
Konami Gaming Campaign: "Gorilla"
Texas Motor Speedway

PAVONE

1006 Market St, Harrisburg, PA 17101-2811
Tel.: (717) 234-8886
Fax: (717) 234-8940
E-Mail: mlorson@pavone.net
Web Site: www.pavone.net

E-Mail for Key Personnel:
President: mpavone@pavone.net

Employees: 70
Year Founded: 1991

National Agency Associations: 4A's-AMA-APC-PRSA

Agency Specializes In: Advertising, Advertising Specialties, Affiliate Marketing, Agriculture, Alternative Advertising, Brand Development & Integration, Broadcast, Business Publications, Business-To-Business, Cable T.V., Collateral, Communications, Consulting, Consumer Goods, Consumer Marketing, Consumer Publications, Corporate Communications, Corporate Identity, Crisis Communications, Custom Publishing, Customer Relationship Management, Digital/Interactive, Direct-to-Consumer, Electronic Media, Event Planning & Marketing, Exhibit/Trade Shows, Experience Design, Food Service, Graphic Design, Guerilla Marketing, Identity Marketing, In-Store Advertising, Integrated Marketing, Internet/Web Design, Local Marketing, Logo & Package Design, Magazines, Market Research, Media Buying Services, Media Planning, Media Relations, Media Training, Mobile Marketing, Multimedia, New Product Development, Newspaper, Newspapers & Magazines, Out-of-Home Media, Outdoor, Package Design, Point of Purchase, Point of Sale, Print, Production, Production (Ad, Film, Broadcast), Production (Print), Promotions, Public Relations, Publicity/Promotions, RSS (Really Simple Syndication), Radio, Restaurant, Retail, Sales Promotion, Search Engine Optimization, Social Marketing/Nonprofit, Social Media, Sponsorship, Sports Market, Strategic Planning/Research, Sweepstakes, T.V., Trade & Consumer Magazines, Viral/Buzz/Word of Mouth, Web (Banner Ads, Pop-ups, etc.)

Approx. Annual Billings: $8,000,000

Breakdown of Gross Billings by Media: Collateral: 5%; Consulting: 5%; Digital/Interactive: 5%; Event Mktg.: 5%; Graphic Design: 10%; Logo & Package Design: 5%; Out-of-Home Media: 5%; Point of Purchase: 5%; Point of Sale: 5%; Print: 5%; Production: 5%; Promos.: 5%; Pub. Rels.: 10%; Radio: 5%; Strategic Planning/Research: 5%; T.V.: 5%; Trade Shows: 5%; Worldwide Web Sites: 5%

Michael R. Pavone *(Pres & CEO)*
Amy Beamer *(COO)*
Joe Barry *(Sr Dir-Art)*
Robinson Smith *(Dir-Design)*
Gabrielle Denofrio *(Sr Designer)*
Keith Seaman *(Designer)*

Accounts:
Campbell's North America Food Service; NJ Campbell's Soup, Pace; 2009
D.G. Yuengling & Son; PA Yuengling Lager, Yuengling Light Lager, Yuengling Lord Chesterfield, Yuengling Porter
The Hershey Company; PA Design; 1995
Mid-Atlantic Dairy Association "Your Milk Comes from a Good Place" Campaign
Pennsylvania Winery Association; PA; 2001
Ram Trucks Campaign: "God Made a Farmer", Super Bowl
Turkey Hill Dairy; PA Campaign: "The Turkey Hill Experience", Turkey Hill Ice Cream, Turkey Hill Iced Tea; 2006

Branch

Varsity
532 N Front St, Wormleysburg, PA 17043
Tel.: (717) 652-1277
Fax: (717) 652-1477
E-Mail: info@varsitybranding.com
Web Site: www.varsitybranding.com

Employees: 52
Year Founded: 2006

National Agency Associations: 4A's

Agency Specializes In: Advertising, Brand Development & Integration, Business-To-Business, Consumer Goods, Consumer Marketing, Corporate Communications, Digital/Interactive, Direct Response Marketing, Faith Based, Financial, Graphic Design, Health Care Services, Logo & Package Design, Market Research, Media Buying Services, Over-50 Market, Real Estate, Seniors' Market, Strategic Planning/Research

Derek Dunham *(VP-Client Svcs)*
Wayne Langley *(VP-Plng & Performance)*
Jodi Christman *(Dir-Interactive)*
Jenn Kehler *(Dir-Media)*
Robinson Smith *(Dir-Design)*
Greg Carney *(Mgr-Integrated Media)*
James Schorn *(Mgr-Resource)*

Accounts:
Army Distaff Foundation
Asbury
Chapel Pointe
Delta Health Technologies
Friendly Senior Living
Homeland Hospice
Homestead Village
Meadowood
Our Lady of Fatima Village
Shannondoah Village Westminster Canterbury
WellSpan
Westminster Ingleside
Westminster Village Muncie

PAXTON COMMUNICATIONS
58 N State St, Concord, NH 03301-4326
Tel.: (603) 228-4933
Fax: (603) 228-3047
E-Mail: chris@paxtoncommunications.net

Employees: 4
Year Founded: 1994

Agency Specializes In: Business-To-Business, Collateral, Consumer Marketing, Corporate Identity, Direct Response Marketing, Education, Graphic Design, Health Care Services, High Technology, Newspaper, Newspapers & Magazines, Print, Radio, Seniors' Market, Technical Advertising

Approx. Annual Billings: $600,000

Christopher C. Cornog *(Owner)*

PAYNE, ROSS & ASSOCIATES ADVERTISING, INC.
206 E Jefferson St, Charlottesville, VA 22902-5105
Tel.: (434) 977-7607
Fax: (434) 977-7610
E-Mail: info@payneross.com
Web Site: www.payneross.com

E-Mail for Key Personnel:
Creative Dir.: jamie@payneross.com
Public Relations: Anne@payneross.com

Employees: 12
Year Founded: 1981

Agency Specializes In: Advertising, Brand Development & Integration, Business-To-Business, Corporate Identity, Event Planning & Marketing, Graphic Design, Internet/Web Design, Logo & Package Design, New Product Development, Planning & Consultation, Public Relations, Publicity/Promotions, Radio, T.V., Web (Banner Ads, Pop-ups, etc.)

Breakdown of Gross Billings by Media: Adv. Specialities: 5%; Exhibits/Trade Shows: 3%; Graphic Design: 20%; Logo & Package Design: 10%; Newsp. & Mags.: 20%; Print: 25%; Pub. Rels.: 10%; Radio & T.V.: 4%; Spot Radio: 1%; Spot T.V.: 2%

Susan Payne *(Owner)*
Lisa Ross *(Owner)*
Matthew Draper *(Exec Dir)*
Hugo Pearl *(Exec Dir)*
Anne Hooff *(Dir-PR)*
Jamie Howard *(Dir-Creative)*

Accounts:
Charlottesville & University Symphony Orchestra
Charlottesville Area Community Foundation Donor Funds; 2001
The Charlottesville Free Clinic
City of Charlottesville Convention & Visitors Bureau
Downtown Business Association of Charlottesville
Klockner Pentaplast of America; Gordonsville, VA Industrial/Plastics; 1996
Meridian Air Group
Piedmont VA Community College
The Virginia Discovery Museum
Virginia Mennonite Retirement Community
Virginia National Bank; 1997

PBJS, INC.
424 2nd Ave W, Seattle, WA 98119
Tel.: (206) 694-6000
E-Mail: info@pbjs.com
Web Site: www.pbjs.com

Employees: 26
Year Founded: 2003

Agency Specializes In: Digital/Interactive, Sponsorship

Stephanie Danese *(CFO)*
Jenny Pigott *(COO)*
Lindsay Rowe *(VP-Client Engagement & Strategy)*
Pat Cockburn *(Dir-Events & Media)*
Suzanne Asprea *(Assoc Dir-Creative)*
Francine Friedman *(Assoc Dir-Creative)*
Anna Beckett *(Acct Exec)*
Melanie Campfield *(Acct Exec)*
Sarajane Belche *(Assoc Producer)*

Accounts:
AT&T Communications Corp.
Boulder Brands Inc.
Center for Information Work
Cranium
Davos
Digital Art Suite
Future of Flight
Microsoft
Thomas Friedman
Wacap

Branches

PBJS
222 Merchandise Mart Plaza Ste 4-150, Chicago, IL 60654
Tel.: (312) 297-1428
Web Site: www.pbjs.com

Don Lee *(Mng Dir & COO)*
George Bunca *(Mng Dir)*
Pia Dierking *(Sr VP)*
John Gilson *(VP-Ops)*
Lindsay Rowe *(VP-Client Engagement & Strategy)*
Marty Cole *(Sr Dir-Creative)*
Kristen Soderman *(Client Svcs Dir)*

Accounts:
General Motors Experiential Marketing
Procter & Gamble

PBN HILL + KNOWLTON STRATEGIES
(Formerly The PBN Company)
1150 18th St NW Ste 325, Washington, DC 20036
Tel.: (202) 466-6210
Fax: (202) 466-6205
E-Mail: blake.marshall@hkstrategies.com
Web Site: www.pbn-hkstrategies.com

Employees: 10

Peter B. Necarsulmer *(Chm)*
Susan A. Thurman *(Pres)*
Myron Wasylyk *(CEO)*
Olga Vorobieva *(CFO)*
Oksana Monastyrska *(Mng Dir-Ukraine)*

Accounts:
Abbott International
Bank of America
Coalition for Intellectual Property Rights
Dell
Enel
Ferrero
Nord Stream
Statoil
Statoil PR
Western NIS Fund
Xerox

PEAK CREATIVE MEDIA
1801 Boulder St Ste 200, Denver, CO 80202-2658
Tel.: (303) 295-3373
Fax: (303) 455-3363
E-Mail: info@peakcreativemedia.com
Web Site: www.peak-creative.com

Employees: 14
Year Founded: 1992

Approx. Annual Billings: $5,000,000

Steve Fitzrandolph *(Owner)*
Wallace Logie *(CFO)*
Mary Kate Dick *(Art Dir)*
Bill Burns *(Dir-Interactive)*
Jennifer Collins *(Dir-New Bus)*
Andrew Nolte *(Dir-Art)*
Kristin Vanderloos *(Dir-Art)*
Molli Gamelin *(Sr Acct Mgr)*

Accounts:
Accanto Systems
AuditWatch
Colorado Association of Home Builders
Denver Botanic Gardens
Denver Zoo
Dex One Corporation
Pinnacol Assurance
Qwest Communications
UDALL
The University of Denver

PEAK SEVEN ADVERTISING
40 SE 5th St Ste 402, Boca Raton, FL 33432
Tel.: (866) 971-4348
Fax: (561) 465-3176
E-Mail: hello@peakseven.com
Web Site: www.peakseven.com

Agency Specializes In: Advertising, Brand Development & Integration, Digital/Interactive,

Internet/Web Design, Logo & Package Design, Print, Search Engine Optimization, Social Media

Darren Seys *(CEO & Creative Dir)*
Kathleen Bernard *(Sr Acct Dir)*
James Mullins *(Dir-Content & Client Svcs Dir)*
Kata Breman *(Dir-Ops)*
Felix Chi *(Dir-Digital)*
Enrico Morales *(Dir-Art)*

Accounts:
iScrap

PEAKBIETY, BRANDING + ADVERTISING

501 E Jackson St Ste 200, Tampa, FL 33602
Tel.: (813) 227-8006
Fax: (813) 228-7898
E-Mail: darcos@peakbiety.com
Web Site: www.peakbiety.com

E-Mail for Key Personnel:
President: gpeak@peakbiety.com

Employees: 10
Year Founded: 1990

National Agency Associations: 4A's-AMA

Agency Specializes In: Advertising, Affluent Market, Brand Development & Integration, Broadcast, Business Publications, Business-To-Business, Cable T.V., Co-op Advertising, Collateral, Communications, Computers & Software, Consumer Marketing, Consumer Publications, Corporate Communications, Corporate Identity, Direct Response Marketing, Education, Electronic Media, Environmental, Event Planning & Marketing, Exhibit/Trade Shows, Financial, Graphic Design, Health Care Services, High Technology, Identity Marketing, In-Store Advertising, Industrial, Information Technology, Integrated Marketing, Internet/Web Design, Leisure, Local Marketing, Logo & Package Design, Magazines, Market Research, Media Buying Services, Media Planning, Medical Products, Merchandising, Newspaper, Newspapers & Magazines, Out-of-Home Media, Outdoor, Over-50 Market, Package Design, Planning & Consultation, Point of Purchase, Point of Sale, Print, Production, Production (Print), Radio, Real Estate, Regional, Restaurant, Sales Promotion, Seniors' Market, Social Marketing/Nonprofit, Sponsorship, Strategic Planning/Research, T.V., Trade & Consumer Magazines, Transportation, Web (Banner Ads, Pop-ups, etc.), Yellow Pages Advertising

Approx. Annual Billings: $5,000,000

Glen C. Peak *(Pres)*
Donette Arcos *(Dir-Media)*
Amy Phillips *(Dir-Creative)*

Accounts:
Eckerd Youth Alternatives; Clearwater, FL
Florida Hospital Waterman; Tavares, FL
Tampa Bay Water
Tampa Electric Company; Tampa, FL Utility; 2009
Thomas & LoCicero; Tampa, FL Attorneys; 2009

PEAR ADVERTISING

108 27th Ave E, Moline, IL 61244
Tel.: (309) 373-1266
Web Site: www.pearad.com

Year Founded: 2008

Agency Specializes In: Advertising, Brand Development & Integration, Event Planning & Marketing, Internet/Web Design, Logo & Package Design, Media Planning, Public Relations, Radio, Social Media, Strategic Planning/Research

Melanie Shields *(Dir-Sls & Mktg)*

Accounts:
Estes Construction
Mel Foster Co
Niabi Zoo
Point Builders, LLC
Ragan Mechanical Contractors, Inc.

PEARL BRANDS

1635 Hendry St, Fort Myers, FL 33901
Tel.: (239) 313-6059
E-Mail: info@pearlbrands.com
Web Site: www.pearlbrands.com

Agency Specializes In: Advertising, Brand Development & Integration, Digital/Interactive, Internet/Web Design, Logo & Package Design, Print

Scott Qurollo *(Pres & Dir-Creative)*
Tom Calabrese *(Creative Dir)*
Katie Siefert *(Acct Dir)*
Becca Merritt *(Designer-Web & Graphic Designer)*

Accounts:
Bayliner Boats Brand Management, National Advertising
University of Florida Alumni Association

PEARL MEDIA LLC

363 Rt 46 W Ste 260, Fairfield, NJ 07004
Tel.: (973) 492-2300
Web Site: pearlmedia.com/

Agency Specializes In: Advertising

Joshua Cohen *(Pres & CEO)*
Anthony Petrillo *(Sr VP-Bus Dev)*
Jesse Sugarman *(Sr VP-Bus Dev)*
Brian Cohen *(VP-Real Estate & Acq)*
Daniel Odham *(VP-Interactive Dev)*
Jay Carella *(Dir-Bus Dev)*
Mike Christensen *(Dir-Bus Dev)*

Accounts:
Chevrolet Campaign: "World's Biggest Arcade Claw Game"
Kumho Tire "Pop-A-Shot"
Lexus Division Lexus CT 200h Hybrid
NBC

PEDERSEN DESIGN LLC

121 Flinn St, Batavia, IL 60510
Tel.: (630) 482-3514
E-Mail: pdd@pedersendesign.com
Web Site: www.pedersendesign.com

Agency Specializes In: Advertising, Brand Development & Integration, Graphic Design, Internet/Web Design, Print

David L. Pedersen *(Owner)*

Accounts:
Music Matters

PEDONE

49 W 27th St Fl 6, New York, NY 10001
Tel.: (212) 488-5140
Fax: (212) 627-3966
E-Mail: mfp@pedone.com
Web Site: www.pedone.com

E-Mail for Key Personnel:
President: walterc@pedone.com

Employees: 22
Year Founded: 1987

National Agency Associations: 4A's-AD CLUB

Agency Specializes In: Advertising, Affluent Market, Brand Development & Integration, Collateral, Consumer Marketing, Corporate Identity, Digital/Interactive, Food Service, Graphic Design, Guerilla Marketing, Health Care Services, In-Store Advertising, Integrated Marketing, Internet/Web Design, Local Marketing, Logo & Package Design, Luxury Products, Market Research, Media Buying Services, Media Planning, New Product Development, Outdoor, Point of Purchase, Point of Sale, Print, Product Placement, Production, Publicity/Promotions, Radio, Restaurant, Retail, Sales Promotion, Social Marketing/Nonprofit, Social Media, Sponsorship, Strategic Planning/Research, T.V., Travel & Tourism

Approx. Annual Billings: $120,000,000

Breakdown of Gross Billings by Media: Internet Adv.: 13%; Mags.: 33%; Network T.V.: 22%; Newsp.: 8%; Out-of-Home Media: 10%; Spot Radio: 4%; Spot T.V.: 10%

Michael Pedone *(Pres & CEO)*
Dieter Gonzales *(CFO)*
Walter Coyle *(Pres-Pedone Media)*
Alyce Panico *(Exec VP & Dir-Media)*
Diane Montpelier *(Dir-Svcs)*
Burgess Bub *(Supvr-Media)*
Yosef McIntosh *(Asst Media Planner)*

Accounts:
Burt's Bees Inc. Burt's Bees Natural Personal Care; 2008
Essie Nail Polish; 2010
Frederick Wildman & Sons Trapiche, Folonari, Paul Jaboulet Aine, Pascal Jolivet, Pol Roger; 2007
Hermes Luxury Products; 2011
Jarlsberg Cheese Products; 2009
Lacoste USA; New York, NY Apparel, Retail Stores; 2005
Laura Mercier Cosmetics; 2011
L'Oreal USA, Inc.; New York, NY Matrix Hair Products, Vichy; 2004
The Mills Corporation
Pentland Corp. Lacoste Footwear; 2005
Sedu Hair Styling; 2009
Swatch Group Ltd. Omega, Swatch, Blancpain, Rado, Hamilton, Longines, Glashutte Originals, Tissot, Mido; 2006
Tonnino Tuna Filets; 2011
William Greenberg Desserts New York, NY; 2008

THE PEDOWITZ GROUP

810 Mayfield Rd, Milton, GA 30009
Tel.: (856) 782-9859
Toll Free: (888) 459-8622
Web Site: www.pedowitzgroup.com

Agency Specializes In: Business-To-Business, Consulting, Direct-to-Consumer, Information Technology, Podcasting, Sales Promotion, Strategic Planning/Research

Jeff Pedowitz *(Pres & CEO)*
Bruce Culbert *(Partner & Principal)*
Debbie Qaqish *(Chief Strategy Officer & Principal)*
Scott Benedetti *(VP-Sls & Revenue Mktg)*
Kevin Joyce *(VP-Mktg Svcs)*
Cherie Pedowitz *(VP-HR)*
Steven Pekarthy *(VP-Western Reg)*
Bill Hooven *(Acct Dir-Technical)*

Accounts:
Deutsche Bank Banking & Financial Services

PEEBLES CREATIVE GROUP
6209 Riverside Dr Ste 200, Dublin, OH 43017
Tel.: (614) 487-2011
Web Site: www.peeblescreativegroup.com

Year Founded: 1997

Agency Specializes In: Advertising, Brand Development & Integration, Digital/Interactive, Graphic Design, Internet/Web Design, Social Media

Doug Peebles *(Pres, CEO & Dir-Strategic)*
Laura Calhoon *(VP)*
Jill Bryan *(Client Svcs Dir)*
Curt Besser *(Dir-Design)*
Lynn Ison *(Dir-Art)*
Chrissy Payne *(Dir-Creative Svcs)*
Angela Warf *(Dir-Art)*
Amy Bethel *(Mgr-Client Svcs)*

Accounts:
Grow Licking County CIC

THE PEKOE GROUP
7 W 45th St, New York, NY 10036
Tel.: (212) 764-0890
Web Site: www.thepekoegroup.com

Year Founded: 2009

Agency Specializes In: Advertising, Brand Development & Integration, Collateral, Digital/Interactive, Internet/Web Design, Media Buying Services, Media Planning, Print, Promotions, Social Media

Amanda Pekoe *(Pres)*
Christopher Lueck *(Dir-Creative)*
Jessica Ferreira *(Mgr-Mktg)*
Jason K. Murray *(Mgr-Design)*
Jennifer Dorso *(Coord-Digital Media)*

Accounts:
Potomac Theatre Project

PENINSULA AGENCY
441 Meeting St Ste 339, Charleston, SC 29403
Tel.: (843) 606-0730
Web Site: www.peninsulaagency.com

Year Founded: 2013

Agency Specializes In: Advertising, Digital/Interactive, Internet/Web Design, Media Buying Services

Blake Weisel *(Dir-Partner Rels)*
Malcolm Wever *(Dir-Client Svcs)*

Accounts:
Juicer Joe
Multiplastics
People Against Rape

PENN GARRITANO DIRECT RESPONSE MARKETING
(Name Changed to Garritano Group)

PENNA POWERS
(Formerly Penna Powers Brian Haynes)
1706 S Major St, Salt Lake City, UT 84115
Tel.: (801) 487-4800
Fax: (801) 487-0707
Toll Free: (800) 409-9346
E-Mail: cpenna@pennapowers.com
Web Site: www.pennapowers.com

E-Mail for Key Personnel:
President: jhaynes@ppbh.com
Creative Dir.: cpenna@ppbh.com

Employees: 40
Year Founded: 1984

Agency Specializes In: Advertising

Revenue: $8,000,000

Chuck Penna *(CEO & Partner)*
David Lloyd Smith *(Mng Partner)*
Mike Brian *(Partner & Strategist-Mktg & New Media)*
Erico Bisquera *(Dir-Creative)*
Traci Houghton *(Dir-Fin & Production)*
Chris Menges *(Dir-Adv)*
Stephanie Miller-Barnhart *(Dir-PR)*
Marc Stryker *(Dir-Media)*

Accounts:
Nevada's Department of Transportation Zero Fatalities Marketing
Utah Department of Highway Safety
Utah Dept. of Transportation

PENNEBAKER
1100 W 23rd St Ste 200, Houston, TX 77008
Tel.: (713) 963-8607
Fax: (713) 960-9680
Web Site: www.pennebaker.com

Year Founded: 1984

Agency Specializes In: Advertising, Corporate Communications, Graphic Design, Logo & Package Design, Market Research, Public Relations, Search Engine Optimization, Web (Banner Ads, Pop-ups, etc.)

Jeffrey McKay *(Owner)*
Halina Dodd *(Principal & Assoc Dir-Creative)*
Susan Pennebaker *(Principal)*
Ward Pennebaker *(Principal)*
Ian Deranieri *(Producer-Digital)*
Richard Byrd *(Dir-Content Strategy)*
Melissa Carson *(Sr Acct Exec)*
Gabby Doss *(Acct Exec)*
Carrie Cash *(Designer)*
Deann Decker *(Sr Designer)*

Accounts:
Tidel Technologies

PENNY/OHLMANN/NEIMAN, INC.
(Name Changed to The Ohlmann Group)

PENTAGRAM DESIGN, INC.
(Private-Parent-Single Location)
204 5th Ave, New York, NY 10010
Tel.: (212) 683-7000
Web Site: www.pentagram.com

Employees: 50
Year Founded: 1986

Agency Specializes In: Advertising, Brand Development & Integration, Print, Sponsorship

Revenue: $3,400,000

Courtney Gooch *(Designer)*

Accounts:
New-Verizon

PENVINE
(Formerly Abelson Group, Inc.)
200 Broadhollow Rd Ste 20, Melville, NY 11747
Tel.: (917) 445-4454
E-Mail: info@penvine.com
Web Site: www.penvine.com

Agency Specializes In: Brand Development & Integration, Communications, Event Planning & Marketing, Local Marketing, Market Research, Media Relations, Media Training, Public Relations, Travel & Tourism

Ilona Andrea Mohacsi *(Dir)*

Accounts:
Convedia
DataMotion; Morristown, NJ PR & Analyst Relations
Dynamax Technologies, Ltd. Public Relations
Ecological
Google
Hook Mobile
Mobile Content Networks, Inc. Public Relations
Mobilians International, Inc.
Msearch Groove
Project Maintenance Institute
Zemoga

PEOPLE IDEAS & CULTURE
250 Lafayette St 2nd Fl, New York, NY 10012
Tel.: (646) 392-9230
Fax: (646) 392-9240
E-Mail: tellmemore@pic-nyc.com
Web Site: www.pic-nyc.com

Year Founded: 2009

National Agency Associations: 4A's

Agency Specializes In: Advertising, Digital/Interactive, Sponsorship

Domenico Vitale *(Founder)*
Enrico Gatti *(Dir-Brand Strategy)*
Christopher Miller *(Strategist-Creative)*

Accounts:
AOL
Ask.com Campaign: "Sixty Million Questions"
Match
Wyndham Hotel Group Campaign: "Wyndham Rewards Wizard - Crystal Ball, Family & Honeymoon", Digital, Radio

PEOPLESCOUT
860 W Evergreen, Chicago, IL 60642
Tel.: (312) 915-0505
Fax: (312) 915-0873
E-Mail: info@peoplescout.com
Web Site: www.peoplescout.com

Employees: 100
Year Founded: 1992

Agency Specializes In: Advertising, Internet/Web Design, Newspaper, Out-of-Home Media, Outdoor, Print, Radio, Recruitment

Approx. Annual Billings: $6,000,000

Breakdown of Gross Billings by Media: Internet Adv.: 12%; Newsp.: 75%; Other: 10%; Radio: 3%

Allison Brigden *(Sr VP-Internal Functions)*
David Ludolph *(VP-Ops)*
Jessie Ostergard Mcgowan *(VP-Acct Ops)*
Patricia Quintero *(VP-Ops)*
Shea Enright *(Dir-Ops)*
Rebecca Howell *(Dir-Ops)*
Thavone Khounthikoumane *(Dir-Ops)*
Ashley Ziya *(Dir-Solutions Dev)*
Kimberely K. Barnes *(Acct Mgr)*

THE PEPPER GROUP
220 N Smith St Ste 406, Palatine, IL 60067
Tel.: (847) 963-0333
Fax: (847) 963-0888
E-Mail: pepper@peppergroup.com
Web Site: www.peppergroup.com

Employees: 12

National Agency Associations: Second Wind Limited

Agency Specializes In: Advertising, Graphic Design, Integrated Marketing

Tim Padgett *(Founder & CEO)*
George Couris *(Pres)*
Denise O'Neil *(VP-Fin Op)*
Todd Underwood *(Dir-Interactive)*
Lynn Ankele *(Coord-Production)*

Accounts:
Hewlett Packard
Mandell Plumbing
PAMCANI

PEPPERS & ROGERS GROUP
1111 Summer St Fl 5, Stamford, CT 06905-5511
Tel.: (203) 989-2200
Fax: (203) 642-5306
Web Site: www.peppersandrogersgroup.com

Employees: 20

Agency Specializes In: Advertising

Don Peppers *(Founder & Partner)*
Martha Rogers *(Founder & Partner)*
Brent Jameson *(Partner)*
Larry Mead *(Partner)*
Jeff Watzka *(Mng Dir)*
Jim Dickey *(VP-Ops & Svc Excellence)*
Alpay Akdemir *(Dir)*
Doug Harrington *(Dir-Consulting)*
Craig Latham *(Dir-Consulting-Ops & Tech)*
Seth McCulloch *(Dir)*

Branches

Peppers & Rogers Group
Dubai Media City, PO Box 502264, Dubai, United Arab Emirates
Tel.: (971) 4 391 13 53
Fax: (971) 4 390 46 98
Web Site: www.peppersandrogersgroup.com

Agency Specializes In: Advertising

Samer M. Abdallah *(Sr Partner & Head-EMEA Strategy Practice)*
Banu Cetin Akca *(Head-Mktg & Knowledge Mgmt)*
Tarek Dagher *(Sr Mgr)*
Mustafa Ibrahim *(Sr Mgr)*
Charbel Kfoury *(Sr Mgr)*
Pradeep Sharma *(Sr Mgr)*
Jad N. Baroudi *(Mgr)*
Firas Kanawati *(Mgr)*
Tarek Karam *(Mgr)*
Cezar Serhal *(Mgr)*

PEPPERSHOCK MEDIA PRODUCTIONS, LLC.
16719 N Idaho Ctr Blvd, Nampa, ID 83687
Tel.: (208) 461-5070
E-Mail: info@peppershock.com
Web Site: www.peppershock.com

Year Founded: 2003

Agency Specializes In: Advertising, Digital/Interactive, Graphic Design, Internet/Web Design, Logo & Package Design, Market Research, Media Buying Services, Podcasting, Production, Radio

Drew Allen *(Owner)*
Rhea Allen *(Pres & CEO)*
Angie Scobby *(Dir-Art & Graphic Designer)*
Brandon Coates *(Acct Mgr)*
Conrad Piper-Ruth *(Assoc Producer-Video)*

Accounts:
Idaho Fraud Awareness Coalition

PEPPERTREE MARKETING
10565 E Blanche Dr, Scottsdale, AZ 85258
Tel.: (480) 216-1214
Fax: (480) 718-7625
E-Mail: info@peppertreemarketing.com
Web Site: www.peppertreeco.com

Agency Specializes In: Advertising, Internet/Web Design, Media Buying Services, Media Planning, Print, Public Relations, Radio, Social Media, Strategic Planning/Research

Sharon Peppers Villegas *(Pres)*

Accounts:
Best Western International, Inc.
Harmon Electric, Inc.
Verde Canyon Railroad

PERCEPTURE
3322 US 22 W Ste 411, Branchburg, NJ 08876
Tel.: (800) 707-9190
Fax: (800) 465-3164
Toll Free: (800) 707-9190
Web Site: www.percepture.com

Agency Specializes In: Business-To-Business, Communications, Internet/Web Design, Local Marketing, Media Relations, Promotions, Public Relations, Strategic Planning/Research

Thor Harris *(Founder & CEO)*
Rene Mack *(Pres)*
Cathleen Johnson *(Mng Dir-Percepture Travel)*
Colleen Conover *(VP)*
Rachel Schmucker *(Exec Coord)*

Accounts:
AERCO
ChevronTexaco
Daimler-Chrysler
Foot Locker
Halocarbon
Ingersoll-Rand Company
Konica Minolta
LG Electronics
Marotta Controls
Williamsburg Area Destination Marketing Committee Public Relations

PEREIRA & O'DELL
215 2nd St, San Francisco, CA 94105
Tel.: (415) 284-9916
Fax: (415) 284-9926
E-Mail: info@pereiraodell.com
Web Site: www.pereiraodell.com

Employees: 100

Agency Specializes In: Digital/Interactive, Integrated Marketing

PJ Pereira *(Founder & Chief Creative Officer)*
Andrew O'Dell *(Partner & CEO)*
Nancy Daum *(CFO & COO)*
Joshua Brandau *(VP-Media Strategy)*
Jeff Ferro *(VP-Production)*
Chris Wilcox *(VP-Partnerships)*
Dave Arnold *(Exec Dir-Creative-NY)*
Abe Cortes *(Art Dir)*
Mona Gonzales *(Acct Dir)*
Robert Lambrechts *(Creative Dir)*
Marisa Quiter *(Acct Dir)*
Henry Arlander *(Co-Dir-Client Svcs)*
Brett Beaty *(Dir-Art)*
Leila Moussaoui *(Dir-Art & Creative)*
Molly Parsley *(Dir-Mktg & Comm)*
Jasmine Summerset *(Dir-Strategy-Media & Distr)*
Ryan Toland *(Co-Dir-Client Svcs)*
Ivy Truong *(Co-Dir-Client Svcs)*
Jake Dubs *(Assoc Dir-Creative & Writer)*
Jaime Szefc *(Mgr-Bus Affairs)*
Pete Fishman *(Supvr-Media Strategy)*
Jessica Zou *(Sr Acct Exec)*
Rose Valderrama *(Acct Exec)*
Simon Friedlander *(Copywriter)*
Rob Lambrects *(Copywriter)*

Accounts:
1-800 CONTACTS, INC. Campaign: "Pirate's Plank"
21st Century Fox Fox Sports 1
The Ad Council Campaign: "I Want To Be Recycled", PR, Social Media Programme
B Honey Cachaca Campaign: "Bee Sutra", Campaign: "Beejob"
Burger King Ice-Cream Cones, TV
Carrots
Coca-Cola Latin America Broadcast, Campaign: "Crossroads", Campaign: "Something Unexpected", Campaign: "The Rumor", Online
Corona Campaign: "Corona Extra Unapp", Campaign: "Grab the Beach Bottle", Corona Beach Break
Creative Circus
Dell, Inc.
Fiat
Fosters Group
New-Godiva Chocolatier Campaign: "It's More Than Just Chocolate"
Guitar Center
HBO Campaign: "Battle for the Iron Throne"
Henkel Campaign: "Choose Them All", Campaign: "Romancing the Joan", Creative, Digital, Mobile, Out of Home, Print, Purex, Renuzit, Social, Soft Scrub, TV
New-Hyatt Regency Lake Tahoe Resort & Casino Campaign: "It's Good Not to Be Home", Digital, Outdoor, Print, Social, TV
Intel Corporation Campaign: "The Beauty Inside", Campaign: "The Inside Experience", Campaign: "The Power Inside"
Intuit
New-Kashi
Keep America Beautiful Campaign: "Give your garbage another life", Campaign: "I Want to Be Recycled", Campaign: "Smile", Campaign: "Superhero"
The Los Angeles Times
Mattel, Inc. Campaign: "Letters In Their Own Words", Scrabble
Muscle Milk
MySpace Web Site Redesign
New Era Campaign: "First Changes Everything"
Qdoba Mexican Grill Inc. (Lead Agency) Creative, Strategy
Realtor.com
Reebok
Snoop Dogg Rolling Words
Terra
Toshiba America, Inc. Campaign: "The Beauty Inside", Campaign: "The Power Inside"
Ubisoft
Women's Professional Soccer
Yahoo! Campaign: "Tap Joint"

Branch

Pereira & O'Dell

5 Crosby St, New York, NY 10013
Tel.: (347) 505-7674
Web Site: www.pereiraodell.com

Agency Specializes In: Advertising, Brand Development & Integration, Broadcast, Digital/Interactive, Social Media, Sponsorship

Cory Berger *(Mng Dir)*
Dave Arnold *(Exec Creative Dir)*
Lauren Geisler *(Sr Dir-Art)*
Nadia Malik *(Acct Dir)*
Jake Dubs *(Assoc Dir-Creative)*
Dave Gordon *(Assoc Dir-Creative)*
Juan Leguizamon *(Assoc Dir-Creative)*
Michael Lewis *(Assoc Dir-Strategy)*
Jay Marsen *(Assoc Dir-Creative)*
Jana Cudiamat *(Acct Exec)*

Accounts:
New-Charter Communications, Inc.
Fox Sports 1 Campaign: "Honor Thy Saturday", Campaign: "Sorry for All the Football", Creative, Online, Print, Social Media, TV
Los Angeles Times
Memorial Sloan-Kettering Cancer Center Inc. Campaign: "More Science. Less Fear", Creative, Online, Outdoor, Print, Radio, TV
The New Era Cap Company (Lead Creative Agency)
Realtor.com Broadcast, Campaign: "Accuracy Matters", Campaign: "Constant Change", Campaign: "Jim", Campaign: "Real Estate in Real Time", Doghouse, Mom
New-Timberland (Global Creative Agency) Digital, Outdoor, Print

PERENNIAL INC.

15 Waulron St, Toronto, ON M9C 1B4 Canada
Tel.: (416) 251-2180
Fax: (416) 251-3560
Toll Free: (877) 617-8315
E-Mail: thinkingretail@perennialinc.com
Web Site: www.perennialinc.com

Employees: 65
Year Founded: 1990

Agency Specializes In: Advertising

Approx. Annual Billings: $9,123,393

Chris Lund *(CEO)*
Derrick Francis *(VP-Design)*
Danny Kyriazis *(VP-Retail Programs-Global)*
Amanda Laverty *(Dir-HR & Ops-Global)*
Sally Lennox *(Dir-Creative)*
Brent Roth *(Dir-Creative)*
Alex Schnobb *(Dir-Creative-Environments)*
G. Murray Stranks *(Dir-Bus)*
Lauren Kerhoulas *(Mgr-Mktg)*
Megan Breese *(Designer-Intermediate Interior)*
Maxine Dion *(Sr Designer-Environmental)*
Denis McCutcheon *(Sr Designer)*
Eliza Tang *(Sr Designer-Graphics)*

Accounts:
Acklands Grainger
Blockbuster
Canadian Tire
Flexsigns
Home Depot
Pep Boys
Purolator
Spencer's
Sunoco Communications
Sunoco Retail

PERFORMANCE MARKETING

1501 42nd St Ste 550, West Des Moines, IA 50266
Tel.: (515) 440-3550
Fax: (515) 440-3561
E-Mail: info@performancemarketing.com
Web Site: www.performancemarketing.com

Employees: 25

Agency Specializes In: Advertising, Brand Development & Integration, Digital/Interactive, Exhibit/Trade Shows, Logo & Package Design, Media Relations, Product Placement, Production, Promotions, Public Relations, Strategic Planning/Research

Jim Swanson *(Partner-Creative)*
Bill Bissmeyer *(VP-Bus Dev & Ops)*
Matt Kite *(Mgr-Natl Tour)*
Patrick Rehling *(Mgr-Tour)*
Mike Dunn *(Acct Exec)*
Kristine White *(Acct Exec)*

PERICH ADVERTISING + DESIGN

117 N 1st St Ste 100, Ann Arbor, MI 48104-1354
Tel.: (734) 769-2215
Fax: (734) 769-2322
E-Mail: periche@perich.com
Web Site: www.perich.com

E-Mail for Key Personnel:
Public Relations: dunawayc@perich.com

Employees: 30
Year Founded: 1987

Agency Specializes In: Advertising, Automotive, Brand Development & Integration, Broadcast, Business Publications, Business-To-Business, Cable T.V., Collateral, Consumer Marketing, Consumer Publications, Corporate Communications, Corporate Identity, Digital/Interactive, Direct Response Marketing, E-Commerce, Electronic Media, Environmental, Event Planning & Marketing, Exhibit/Trade Shows, Fashion/Apparel, Financial, Graphic Design, Health Care Services, High Technology, In-Store Advertising, Internet/Web Design, Leisure, Local Marketing, Logo & Package Design, Magazines, Medical Products, Newspaper, Newspapers & Magazines, Out-of-Home Media, Outdoor, Planning & Consultation, Point of Purchase, Point of Sale, Print, Production, Publicity/Promotions, Radio, Retail, Sales Promotion, Sports Market, Strategic Planning/Research, T.V., Technical Advertising, Trade & Consumer Magazines, Travel & Tourism

Approx. Annual Billings: $30,000,000

Breakdown of Gross Billings by Media: Bus. Publs.: 20%; Collateral: 15%; D.M.: 5%; Fees: 15%; Internet Adv.: 20%; Logo & Package Design: 5%; Newsp. & Mags.: 5%; Production: 5%; Radio & T.V.: 10%

Ernie Perich *(Pres & Dir-Creative)*
Craig Dunaway *(VP & Client Svcs Dir)*
Carol Mooradian *(VP & Dir-Design)*
Dan Sygar *(VP & Assoc Dir-Creative)*
Brad Jurgensen *(VP-Media & Strategic Plng)*
Shirley Perich *(VP)*
Sandy Schewe *(Supvr-Media)*
Natasha Keasey *(Media Planner)*
Matt Mordarski *(Analyst-Interactive Plng & Search)*
Sarah Dolan *(Acct Coord)*

Accounts:
Altair Engineering & Design Software & Services; 2012
Bank of Ann Arbor Financial Services; 2006
Continental Automotive Automotive Parts & Components; 2012
Eagle Ottawa Automotive Leather; 2014
Fuel Leadership Corporate Leadership Events; 2014
Greektown Casino-Hotel Casino & Hotel; 2014
HCR Manorcare Hospice & Home Health Services; 2006
Learning Care Group Child Care & Early Education; 2013
Meritor Auto Industry Supplier; 2014
Mitsubishi Electric; Cypress, CA (Corporate Branding) Corporate Branding; 2004
MTU Diesel Engines; 2009
NuStep Exercise Equipment; 2014
Oakwood Health Foundation Healthcare Services; 2014
Plex ERP for Manufacturing; 2013
St Joseph Mercy Health System Healthcare Services; 2014

PERISCOPE

921 Washington Ave S, Minneapolis, MN 55415
Tel.: (612) 399-0500
Fax: (612) 399-0601
Toll Free: (800) 339-2103
E-Mail: info@periscope.com
Web Site: www.periscope.com

E-Mail for Key Personnel:
President: gkurowski@periscope.com
Creative Dir.: mhaumersen@periscope.com

Employees: 532
Year Founded: 1994

National Agency Associations: 4A's

Agency Specializes In: Advertising, Alternative Advertising, Automotive, Below-the-Line, Brand Development & Integration, Branded Entertainment, Broadcast, Business Publications, Business-To-Business, Cable T.V., Catalogs, Co-op Advertising, Collateral, Commercial Photography, Communications, Consulting, Consumer Goods, Consumer Marketing, Consumer Publications, Corporate Communications, Corporate Identity, Crisis Communications, Digital/Interactive, Direct Response Marketing, Direct-to-Consumer, Electronic Media, Email, Entertainment, Environmental, Event Planning & Marketing, Exhibit/Trade Shows, Experience Design, Financial, Food Service, Government/Political, Graphic Design, Health Care Services, High Technology, Hospitality, Household Goods, Identity Marketing, In-Store Advertising, Industrial, Integrated Marketing, International, Internet/Web Design, Local Marketing, Logo & Package Design, Luxury Products, Magazines, Market Research, Media Buying Services, Media Planning, Media Relations, Medical Products, Men's Market, Mobile Marketing, Multimedia, Newspaper, Newspapers & Magazines, Out-of-Home Media, Outdoor, Over-50 Market, Package Design, Pharmaceutical, Planning & Consultation, Podcasting, Point of Purchase, Point of Sale, Print, Production, Production (Ad, Film, Broadcast), Production (Print), Promotions, Public Relations, Publicity/Promotions, RSS (Really Simple Syndication), Radio, Regional, Restaurant, Retail, Sales Promotion, Search Engine Optimization, Seniors' Market, South Asian Market, Sponsorship, Sports Market, Strategic Planning/Research, T.V., Technical Advertising, Teen Market, Trade & Consumer Magazines, Transportation, Travel & Tourism, Urban Market, Viral/Buzz/Word of Mouth, Web (Banner Ads, Pop-ups, etc.), Women's Market

Breakdown of Gross Billings by Media: D.M.: 8%; Internet Adv.: 14%; Newsp. & Mags.: 12%; Out-of-Home Media: 8%; Radio: 10%; T.V.: 28%; Trade & Consumer Mags.: 20%

Bill Simpson *(Chm & Exec Dir)*
Liz Ross *(Pres & CEO)*
Joe Harrington *(VP & Acct Dir)*
Rob Peichel *(VP & Creative Dir)*
Bob Ballard *(VP & Mgmt Supvr)*
Katie Kelly-Landberg *(VP & Mgmt Supvr)*

Steve Kuklinski *(VP & Mgmt Supvr)*
Lisa McEllistrem *(VP & Mgmt Supvr)*
Bruce Bourne *(VP & Dir-Design)*
Scott Dahl *(VP & Dir-Creative)*
Justin Royer *(VP & Dir-Digital Engagement)*
Anna Lee Ulsrud *(VP-Retail, Experiential & Events)*
Erika Dodge *(Head-Creative & Sr Art Dir-Digital)*
Jen Neis *(Sr Dir-Art)*
Melanie Zaelich *(Sr Dir-Art)*
Patti Hofstad *(Exec Producer-Brdcst)*
Kym Ohna *(Creative Dir)*
Scott Behmer *(Mgmt Supvr-Retail Strategy)*
Shannon Cranbrook *(Dir-Integrated Media Plng & Buying)*
Justin Davis *(Dir-Art)*
Sara Kosiorek *(Dir-Ops)*
Kelsey Soby *(Dir-Mktg & Bus Dev)*
Ryan Schaul *(Sr Acct Mgr)*
Bridget Jewell *(Brand Mgr)*
Dona Brown *(Mgr-HR)*
Pete Engebretson *(Sr Acct Supvr-Media)*
Jordan Bainer *(Acct Supvr)*
Scott Koelfgen *(Acct Supvr)*
Chris Johnson *(Supvr-Digital Media)*
Cindy Redfield *(Supvr-Media)*
Keri Saline *(Supvr-Experiential Production)*
Alyssa Zarembinski *(Sr Acct Exec)*
Natalie Harrison *(Acct Exec)*
Menzie Henderson *(Acct Exec)*
Brooke Lattin *(Acct Exec)*
Patrick Foulks *(Media Planner & Buyer-Digital)*
Amy Kuderer *(Media Planner)*
Grant Powell *(Media Planner)*
Ali Aagaard *(Asst Acct Exec)*
Lee Cerier *(Coord-Community Engagement)*
Kylie Dahl *(Coord-Digital Media)*
Kelsey Eckberg *(Sr Media Planner & Buyer-Digital)*
Sanjay Kalia *(Country Gen Mgr)*
Erica Larsen *(Sr Media Buyer)*

Accounts:
Andersen Windows & Doors; Bayport, NY (Agency of Record); 2009
Arctic Cat; Three River Falls, MN ATV, PG&A, Snowmobiles; 1982
BASF Corporation (Agency of Record); 2014
Brach's Candy (Agency of Record); 2014
Bridgestone Commercial Tire Group; 2002
Bronson Health System (Agency of Record); 2008
Buffalo Wild Wings (Social Media Agency of Record); 2013
Cargill Animal Nutrition
Cargill Animal Nutrition, Nutrena Division; 2010
Cox Communications; Atlanta, GA Business, Contour, Retail; 2002
Del Monte Fresh Creative, Events, Promotions, Social Media; 2012
ExxonMobil (Digital Agency of Record); 2011
Ferrara Candy Co. Campaign: "Bio Class", Campaign: "Dino", Campaign: "Sour Tooth", Digital, Social Media, TV, Trolli
Gillette Children's Specialty Healthcare (Agency of Record) Brand Awareness, Campaign: "Moving Forward"; 2013
The Golf Wearhouse (Agency of Record); 2014
Great Clips (Agency of Record) Campaign: "Ralphpunzel"; 2010
Hearth & Home Technologies (Digital Agency of Record); 2009
JCPenney Digital Design & Email Programs; 2014
Kemps Foods (Creative Agency of Record); 1999
New-Kohl's Corporation
Minnesota Twins Baseball Club (Agency of Record); 2004
Phillips Distilling Company Campaign: "'Be UV", Creative, Online, Photo Sharing Tool, Prairie Organic Vodka, Print, Revel Stoke Spiced Whisky, UV Vodka, Website
Sportsman's Guide (Agency of Record); 2013
Target ISM, National Event Marketing, Photography, Promotions; 1996
TCF Bank (Agency of Record); 2013
Toro Creative-Comml Div; 2013
Treasure Island; Hastings, MN Resort & Casino; 1997
Truvia Digital, Social Media; 2008
UnitedHealth Group Community & State, Employer & Individual, Media Strategy, Medicare & Retirement; 2007
USA Hockey (Agency of Record); 2008
Valspar Industrial Paint & Coatings; 2011
Walgreens Package Design, Retail Architecture; 2012

PERQ LLC
(Formerly Tri-Auto Enterprises, LLC)
7225 Georgetown Rd, Indianapolis, IN 46268
Tel.: (317) 644-5700
Fax: (305) 723-2215
Toll Free: (800) 873-3117
E-Mail: info@perq.com
Web Site: perq.com

Employees: 59
Year Founded: 2001

Agency Specializes In: Automotive, Direct Response Marketing, Newspaper

Jacob Bracken *(Exec VP)*
Paul Champion *(Exec VP-Ops)*
Curt Knapp *(VP-Engrg)*
Stephanie Ragozzino *(VP-Product Mgmt)*
Muhammad Yasin *(Dir-Mktg & Svcs)*
Hillary Orme *(Acct Mgr)*
Claire Strope *(Acct Mgr)*
Ashley Vanscoy *(Acct Mgr)*
Rachel Kilroy *(Sr Product Mgr)*
Josh Medley *(Product Mgr)*
Skip Lyford *(Mgr-Mktg)*
Blake McCreary *(Sr Graphic Designer)*

Accounts:
Automotive Dealers

PERRONE GROUP
(Formerly J.M. Perrone Co., Inc.)
45 Braintree Hill Office Park Ste 201, Braintree, MA 02184
Tel.: (781) 848-2070
Fax: (781) 741-2300
Web Site: www.perronegrp.com

Employees: 120
Year Founded: 1981

Agency Specializes In: Advertising, Business-To-Business, Collateral, Communications, Consulting, Consumer Marketing, Direct Response Marketing, E-Commerce, Education, Graphic Design, Print, Production, Retail, Strategic Planning/Research

Approx. Annual Billings: $18,000,000

Breakdown of Gross Billings by Media: D.M.: 100%

Paul Barry *(Pres)*
Chriss Dibona *(Client Svcs Dir)*
Kelly Minichello *(Dir-Bus Ops)*
Kristen Palmer *(Dir-Creative)*
Kim Molloy *(Acct Mgr)*
Jenny Patridge *(Acct Mgr)*
Hilary Caccamo *(Specialist-Digital Creative)*

Accounts:
Tufts University
University of Portland

PERRY BALLARD INCORPORATED
(Name Changed to FATHOM Works)

PERRY COMMUNICATIONS GROUP, INC.
980 9th St, Sacramento, CA 95814
Tel.: (916) 658-0144
Fax: (916) 658-0155
E-Mail: info@perrycom.com
Web Site: www.perrycom.com

Employees: 17

Agency Specializes In: Communications, Event Planning & Marketing, Government/Political, Media Relations, Social Marketing/Nonprofit

Revenue: $2,100,000

Kassy Perry *(Pres & CEO)*
Julia Spiess Lewis *(Sr VP)*
Leia Ostermann *(Acct Mgr)*
Kristina Davis *(Mgr-Ops)*
Yadira Beas *(Acct Exec)*
Alexis Kagarakis *(Acct Coord)*
Nicole Norton *(Acct Coord)*

Accounts:
Aetna U.S. Healthcare
Alzheimer's Association, California Chapter
Automotive Aftermarket Industry Association Government Affairs, Grassroots Consulting Services, Public Affairs
Bonnie J. Addario Lung Cancer Foundation
California Pharmacists Association
California Rice Commission
CAWA Government Affairs, Grassroots Consulting Services, Public Affairs
Children Now
G.E. Healthcare
Mental Health Association in California
National Homebuyers Fund
REACH Air Medical Services
Sims Recycling Solutions
SMART Coalition
TMJ Society

PERRY DESIGN & ADVERTISING
206 W. Bonita Ave, K2, Claremont, CA 91711
Tel.: (909) 626-8083
Fax: (909) 980-6398
Web Site: perryadvertising.com

Year Founded: 1997

Agency Specializes In: Advertising, Brand Development & Integration, Broadcast, Cable T.V., Co-op Advertising, Communications, Local Marketing, Logo & Package Design, Magazines, Media Buying Services, Media Planning, Newspaper, Newspapers & Magazines, Out-of-Home Media, Outdoor, Print, Production (Ad, Film, Broadcast), Production (Print), Public Relations, Radio, T.V.

Breakdown of Gross Billings by Media: Adv. Specialities: 100%

Janine Perry *(Mng Partner & Dir-Creative)*

Accounts:
The Shoppes at Chino Hills; Chino Hills, CA

PERRY PRODUCTIONS
602 Dusty Ln, Concord, NC 28027
Tel.: (704) 788-2949
E-Mail: design@perryproductions.com
Web Site: www.perryproductions.com

Employees: 5
Year Founded: 1994

Agency Specializes In: Internet/Web Design

Lisa Perry *(Founder)*
Kimberly Strong *(Exec Dir)*
Rachel Wilkes *(Exec Dir)*
Natasha Suber *(Dir-Mktg & Comm)*

Accounts:
Isaacs Group
Kannapolis Construction
LEI Systems
Pfeiffer University
Protec

PERSUASION ARTS & SCIENCES
4600 Vincent Ave S, Minneapolis, MN 55410
Tel.: (612) 928-0626
Web Site: www.persuasionism.com

National Agency Associations: 4A's

Agency Specializes In: Advertising

Mark Johnson *(Founder & Chief Innovation Officer)*
Dion Hughes *(Founder)*
Mary Haugh *(Dir-Bus)*

Accounts:
Best Buy Mobile
Nice Ride Minnesota

PERSUASION MARKETING & MEDIA
13400 Providence Lake Dr, Milton, GA 30004
Tel.: (770) 343-8326
E-Mail: info@persuasionmarketingandmedia.com
Web Site:
www.persuasionmarketingandmedia.com

Year Founded: 2011

Agency Specializes In: Advertising, Brand Development & Integration, Content, Email, Graphic Design, Internet/Web Design, Logo & Package Design, Print, Social Media

Leisa Odom-Kurtz *(Dir-Strategic & Creative)*

Accounts:
Alpine Bakery & Trattoria
Nancy Anderson

PERSUASIVE BRANDS
301 Central Ave 321, Hilton Head Island, SC 29926
Tel.: (843) 564-8001
Fax: (888) 788-0409
E-Mail: info@persuasivebrands.com
Web Site: www.persuasivebrands.com

Employees: 5
Year Founded: 2006

National Agency Associations: AMA

Agency Specializes In: Advertising, Brand Development & Integration, Business-To-Business, Collateral, Computers & Software, Digital/Interactive, Direct Response Marketing, Direct-to-Consumer, E-Commerce, Email, Integrated Marketing, Internet/Web Design, Market Research

Approx. Annual Billings: $1,000,000

Breakdown of Gross Billings by Media: Adv. Specialities: $1,000,000

Lee Smith *(Pres & CEO)*

Accounts:
IDClothing
Team Gear, Inc.

PERSUASIVE COMMUNICATIONS
141 Sullys Trl Ste 9, Pittsford, NY 14534
Tel.: (585) 264-1170
Fax: (585) 264-1177
E-Mail: info@persuasivewebsite.com
Web Site: www.persuasivewebsite.com

Year Founded: 2004

Agency Specializes In: Advertising, Graphic Design, Internet/Web Design, Public Relations

Paul H. Bush *(Pres)*
Michelle Mastrosimone *(Partner & Project Mgr)*

Accounts:
Nathaniel General Contractors
PathStone Corporation
Pierrepont Visual Graphics, Inc.

PETER HILL DESIGN
222 N 2nd St Ste 220, Minneapolis, MN 55401
Tel.: (612) 925-1927
Fax: (612) 925-2179
Web Site: www.peterhilldesign.com

Agency Specializes In: Advertising, Brand Development & Integration, Collateral, Internet/Web Design, Logo & Package Design, Media Relations, Print, Public Relations, Social Media, Strategic Planning/Research

Megan Junius *(Pres & Creative Dir)*
Allison Krogstad *(Art Dir & Designer)*

Accounts:
Barker Hedges
Gruppo Marcucci
Lateralus
Park Dental
Unesco

PETER MAYER ADVERTISING, INC.
318 Camp St, New Orleans, LA 70130-2804
Tel.: (504) 581-7191
Fax: (504) 581-3009
E-Mail: contact@peteramayer.com
Web Site: www.peteramayer.com

E-Mail for Key Personnel:
President: mayerm@peteramayer.com
Creative Dir.: MayerJ@peteramayer.com
Production Mgr.: browns@peteramayer.com

Employees: 200
Year Founded: 1967

National Agency Associations: 4A's

Agency Specializes In: Advertising, Advertising Specialties, Broadcast, Commercial Photography, Communications, Consulting, Consumer Marketing, Consumer Publications, Direct Response Marketing, Electronic Media, Event Planning & Marketing, Gay & Lesbian Market, Graphic Design, Industrial, Internet/Web Design, Medical Products, Newspaper, Planning & Consultation, Print, Production, Public Relations, Publicity/Promotions, Radio, Sponsorship, Sports Market, Strategic Planning/Research, T.V., Trade & Consumer Magazines, Travel & Tourism

Approx. Annual Billings: $150,000,000

Josh Mayer *(Chief Creative Officer)*
David Crane *(VP & Grp Acct Dir)*
Rachael Greer *(VP & Dir-Ops)*
Michelle Edelman *(VP-Strategy & Plng)*
Eddie Snyder *(VP)*
Jay Winn *(VP-Mktg)*
Larry Lovell *(Mgmt Supvr-PR)*
Jeremy Braud *(Dir-Interactive Media)*
Jamie Davenport *(Dir-Art)*
Jordy Luft *(Dir-Media)*
George Morse *(Dir-Art)*
Michael Heid *(Assoc Dir-Creative & Copywriter)*
Jennifer Rockvoan *(Assoc Dir-Project Mgmt)*
Patti Stallard *(Mgr-Proofreading & Copy Editing)*
Veronica Moss *(Acct Supvr)*
Abby Lorenz McClure *(Sr Acct Exec)*
Andrew Bovine *(Acct Exec-Digital)*

Accounts:
Asheville Convention and Visitors Bureau (Agency of Record)
French Market Coffee
GE Capital
Globalstar, Inc.
GNO, Inc.
Hancock Holding Corporation
Louisiana Department of Economic Development
Mellow Mushroom Bacon, Bootleg Bacon Fest
The National World War II Museum
New Orleans Jazz & Heritage Festival
New Orleans Tourism Marketing Corporation
Okaloosa County Tourism Development Council
Piccadilly Restaurant
Sanderson Farms, Inc.
Sazerac
Scott Equipment
Zatarain's Brands, Inc.

THE PETERMANN AGENCY
22 Sherwood Dr, Shalimar, FL 32579
Tel.: (850) 243-5315
E-Mail: info@petermann.com
Web Site: www.petermann.com

Agency Specializes In: Advertising, Collateral, Corporate Identity, Graphic Design, Internet/Web Design, Media Buying Services, Media Planning, Media Relations, Public Relations, Social Media

Richard Petermann *(Mgr-Production)*
Stephen Smith *(Sr Acct Exec)*

Accounts:
Building Homes for Heroes

PETERSGROUP PUBLIC RELATIONS
1905 N Lamar Ste 201, Austin, TX 78705
Tel.: (512) 794-8600
Fax: (512) 794-8622
E-Mail: info@petersgrouppr.com
Web Site: www.petersgrouppr.com

Employees: 17
Year Founded: 1997

Agency Specializes In: Corporate Communications, Crisis Communications, Customer Relationship Management, Exhibit/Trade Shows, Investor Relations, Media Training, Newspaper, Planning & Consultation

Lauren Peters *(Founder & CEO)*
Valorie Lyng *(VP-Bus Ops)*

Accounts:
Dell
Encirq
GE Security
HigherOut Consulting, Recruiting
Hoovers
IBM
Metrowerks
Motorola Solutions, Inc.
Sony Ericsson
Tivoli
Vignette

PETERSON MILLA HOOKS
1315 Harmon Pl, Minneapolis, MN 55403-1926
Tel.: (612) 349-9116
Fax: (612) 349-9141
E-Mail: cryan@pmhadv.com
Web Site: www.pmhadv.com

E-Mail for Key Personnel:

Creative Dir.: dpeterson@pmhadv.com

Employees: 48
Year Founded: 1990

National Agency Associations: 4A's-AAF-AMA

Agency Specializes In: Advertising, Advertising Specialties, Brand Development & Integration, Broadcast, Consumer Marketing, Cosmetics, Fashion/Apparel, Newspapers & Magazines, Out-of-Home Media, Outdoor, Print, Real Estate, Retail, Sponsorship, Strategic Planning/Research, T.V.

Approx. Annual Billings: $60,000,000

Breakdown of Gross Billings by Media: Mags.: 30%; Newsp.: 10%; Out-of-Home Media: 10%; Point of Sale: 10%; T.V.: 40%

Paolo Guerrero *(Sr Dir-Art)*
Ryan Boekelheide *(Grp Acct Dir)*
Nicholas Berglund *(Art Dir)*
Keith Bracknell *(Dir-Tech)*
David Peterson *(Dir-Creative)*
Courtney Vincent *(Assoc Dir-Creative)*
Erica Lachat *(Acct Supvr)*

Accounts:
Childrens Hospital of Minnesota We Speak Kid
J.C. Penney Campaign: "It's May at JCPenney", General Market Creative
Kmart Campaign: "Chopped", Money Can't Buy Style
Kohl's Corporation Advertising, Campaign: "Find Your Yes", Creative, Marketing, TV
Masco Corporation Behr, Broadcast, Campaign: "True to Hue"
OshKosh B'Gosh, Inc.
Sephora; San Francisco, CA

PETRIE CREATIVE
715 W Johnson St Ste 101, Raleigh, NC 27603
Tel.: (919) 607-1902
Web Site: www.petriecreative.com

Agency Specializes In: Advertising, Brand Development & Integration, Corporate Communications, Graphic Design, Print

Michelle Petrie *(Principal & Dir-Creative)*

Accounts:
NCSU Poole College of Management Global Luxury Management

PETROL ADVERTISING
443 N Varney St, Burbank, CA 91502
Tel.: (323) 644-3720
Fax: (323) 644-3730
E-Mail: info@petrolad.com
Web Site: www.petrolad.com

Year Founded: 2003

Agency Specializes In: Advertising, Brand Development & Integration, Digital/Interactive, Graphic Design, Social Media

Alan Hunter *(Owner, Pres & Chief Creative Officer)*
Ben Granados *(Chief Strategy Officer & Exec VP)*
Art Babayan *(VP & Dir-Creative)*
Chris Bayaca *(VP-Media)*
Larry Mcdonald *(VP-Fin)*
Alen Petkovic *(Sr Dir-A V Creative)*
Sam Clarke *(Acct Dir)*
Wendy Ko *(Acct Dir)*
Shane Sternstein *(Assoc Dir-Creative-3D)*

Accounts:
Irrational Games
Turtle Beach

PETRYNA ADVERTISING
487 Bouchard St, Sudbury, ON P3E2K8 Canada
Tel.: (705) 522-5455
Fax: (705) 522-8753
Toll Free: (416) 628-1438
E-Mail: dave@petrynaadvertising.com
Web Site: www.petrynaadvertising.com

Year Founded: 1983

Agency Specializes In: Advertising, E-Commerce, Graphic Design, Internet/Web Design, Market Research, Multimedia, Production, Promotions

David Petryna *(Pres)*
Lori Beaudry *(Sr Dir-Art)*

Accounts:
Sudbury Symphony Orchestra Entertainment Services

PETTUS ADVERTISING, INC.
101 N Shoreline Blvd Ste 200, Corpus Christi, TX 78401-2824
Tel.: (361) 851-2793
Fax: (361) 851-2796
E-Mail: art@pettusadvertising.com
Web Site: www.pettusadvertising.com

Employees: 5
Year Founded: 1934

Agency Specializes In: Advertising

Approx. Annual Billings: $6,000,000

William Pettus *(Acct Supvr)*

Accounts:
American Bank
The Corpus Christi Convention & Visitors Bureau

PG CREATIVE
14 NE 1st Ave Ste 1106, Miami, FL 33132
Tel.: (305) 350-7995
Fax: (305) 350-0946
E-Mail: info@pgcreative.com
Web Site: www.pgcreative.com

Employees: 4
Year Founded: 2002

Agency Specializes In: Advertising, Bilingual Market, Brand Development & Integration, Broadcast, Business Publications, Business-To-Business, Cable T.V., Collateral, Communications, Consumer Marketing, Consumer Publications, Corporate Identity, Direct Response Marketing, Electronic Media, Entertainment, Event Planning & Marketing, Financial, Food Service, Graphic Design, Health Care Services, Hispanic Market, Internet/Web Design, Logo & Package Design, Magazines, Medical Products, Multimedia, Newspaper, Newspapers & Magazines, Outdoor, Point of Purchase, Point of Sale, Print, Public Relations, Radio, Real Estate, Restaurant, Retail, Sports Market, T.V., Trade & Consumer Magazines, Yellow Pages Advertising

Yvi Garcia *(Partner & Dir-Creative)*
Maritza Pensado *(Partner & Dir-Creative)*

Accounts:
Allegrini Amenities
Black & Decker Latin America
CPC Medical Centers
Drug Free Charlotte County
Easy Scripts
Florida Department of Health
Florida Office of Drug Control
Healthsun Health Plans
Imperial County Office of Education
Matusalem & Co.

PGN AGENCY
1504 E 11 Mile Rd, Royal Oak, MI 48067
Tel.: (248) 414-6860
Fax: (248) 414-6868
E-Mail: info@pgnagency.com
Web Site: www.pgnagency.com

Agency Specializes In: Advertising, Corporate Identity, Internet/Web Design, Outdoor, Package Design, Print, Social Media

Pete Doanato *(Pres)*
Jim Samfilippo *(Dir-Art & Designer)*
Laurie Buck *(Mgr-Traffic)*
Dan Dulka *(Sr Strategist-Digital)*

Accounts:
Belle Isle Awning Co, Inc.
Pierino Frozen Foods, Inc.
Royal Oak Heating & Cooling, Inc.

PGR MEDIA, LLC.
34 Farnsworth St 2nd Fl, Boston, MA 02210
Tel.: (617) 502-8400
Fax: (617) 451-0451
E-Mail: info@pgrmedia.com
Web Site: www.pgrmedia.com

Employees: 20

Agency Specializes In: Advertising, Direct Response Marketing, Fashion/Apparel, Health Care Services, Magazines, Newspaper, Print, Radio, Sponsorship, T.V., Trade & Consumer Magazines, Viral/Buzz/Word of Mouth

Pattie Garrahy *(Founder & CEO)*
Fran Lemire *(CFO)*
Dennis Santos *(Exec VP & Mng Dir-NYC)*
Regina Tarquinio *(Exec VP & Mng Dir-Boston)*
McKenzie Larkin *(VP & Dir-Media)*
Jennifer Callahan *(Dir-Interactive)*
Jaci Gary *(Dir-Interactive Media)*
Kirsten Champlin *(Assoc Dir-Media)*
Stephanie Clark *(Assoc Dir-Media)*
Christin DiPisa *(Assoc Dir-Media)*
Alisha Hicks *(Assoc Dir-Media)*
Katie Coffey *(Supvr-Digital Media)*
Desiree Dileso *(Supvr-Media)*
Joe Greenwood *(Sr Planner-Digital Media)*
Katherine E. Murphy *(Coord-Media)*
Alison Dahlquist *(Sr Media Planner & Buyer)*
Ann Marie Kassabian *(Asst Media Planner)*
Colleen Moran *(Sr Media Planner)*
Claire Moriarty *(Sr Media Planner)*

Accounts:
Celebrity & Azamara Cruises
Horizon Blue Cross Blue Shield of New Jersey
Juicy Couture, Inc.; Arleta
Kate Spade LLC; New York, NY
New Balance; Boston, MA Media Buying & Planning

PHASE 3 MARKETING & COMMUNICATIONS
(Formerly Phase 3 Media, LLC.)
3560 Atlanta Indus Dr, Atlanta, GA 30331
Tel.: (404) 367-9898
Fax: (404) 367-9868
Web Site: www.phase3mc.com/

Employees: 42
Year Founded: 2001

Agency Specializes In: Advertising, Digital/Interactive, Graphic Design, Internet/Web

Design, Print

Revenue: $4,100,000

Jenny Harris *(Sr VP & Gen Mgr)*
Troy McGinnis *(Sr VP & Gen Mgr)*
Sherri Jones *(VP & Gen Mgr-Nashville)*
Susan Frost *(VP-Mktg & Creative Svcs)*
Elyse Hammett *(VP-PR-Corp & Lifestyle)*
Darren Hearsch *(VP-Digital Strategy)*
Rich Guglielmo *(Creative Dir)*
Paula Hankins *(Mktg Dir)*
Courtney Israel *(Art Dir)*
Kathryn Ruland *(Acct Dir)*
Jennifer Buchach *(Dir-Natl & Strategic Accts)*
Christina Gonzalez *(Dir-Natl & Strategic Accts)*
Hollie Hagedorn *(Dir-Sls)*
Liz Bloeser *(Mgr-Mktg)*
Kirsten Ott *(Asst Mgr-Mktg)*
Justin Smith *(Sr Graphic Designer)*
Megan Abney *(Team Head & Bus Dev Mgr)*

Accounts:
Radiator Specialty Company

Branches

Brand Fever
342 Marietta St Ste 3, Atlanta, GA 30313
(See Separate Listing)

PHEEDO, INC.
469 9th St Ste 210, Oakland, CA 94607-4041
Tel.: (510) 923-9250
Fax: (510) 923-9255
Web Site: www.pheedo.com

Employees: 22
Year Founded: 2003

Agency Specializes In: Business-To-Business, Entertainment, Financial, Information Technology, Publicity/Promotions

Jane Doe *(Acct Mgr)*

Accounts:
Cisco
CMP
Dell
ESPN
Gawker Media

PHELPS
(Formerly The Phelps Group)
901 Wilshire Blvd, Santa Monica, CA 90401-1854
Tel.: (310) 752-4400
Fax: (310) 752-4444
E-Mail: jp@phelpsagency.com
Web Site: phelpsagency.com

E-Mail for Key Personnel:
President: jp@phelpsagency.com

Employees: 70
Year Founded: 1981

National Agency Associations: 4A's-ICOM

Agency Specializes In: Above-the-Line, Advertising, Affiliate Marketing, Arts, Automotive, Below-the-Line, Bilingual Market, Brand Development & Integration, Broadcast, Business Publications, Business-To-Business, Cable T.V., Catalogs, Co-op Advertising, Collateral, College, Commercial Photography, Communications, Computers & Software, Consulting, Consumer Goods, Consumer Marketing, Consumer Publications, Corporate Communications, Corporate Identity, Cosmetics, Crisis Communications, Custom Publishing, Customer Relationship Management, Digital/Interactive, Direct Response Marketing, Direct-to-Consumer, E-Commerce, Education, Electronic Media, Electronics, Email, Entertainment, Environmental, Event Planning & Marketing, Exhibit/Trade Shows, Experience Design, Fashion/Apparel, Financial, Food Service, Government/Political, Graphic Design, Guerilla Marketing, Health Care Services, High Technology, Hispanic Market, Hospitality, Household Goods, Identity Marketing, In-Store Advertising, Industrial, Information Technology, Integrated Marketing, International, Internet/Web Design, Leisure, Local Marketing, Logo & Package Design, Luxury Products, Magazines, Market Research, Media Buying Services, Media Planning, Media Relations, Media Training, Medical Products, Men's Market, Merchandising, Mobile Marketing, Multicultural, Multimedia, New Product Development, New Technologies, Newspaper, Newspapers & Magazines, Out-of-Home Media, Outdoor, Over-50 Market, Package Design, Paid Searches, Pets , Pharmaceutical, Planning & Consultation, Podcasting, Point of Purchase, Point of Sale, Print, Production, Production (Print), Promotions, Public Relations, Publicity/Promotions, Publishing, RSS (Really Simple Syndication), Radio, Real Estate, Recruitment, Restaurant, Retail, Sales Promotion, Search Engine Optimization, Seniors' Market, Social Marketing/Nonprofit, Social Media, Sponsorship, Strategic Planning/Research, Sweepstakes, T.V., Technical Advertising, Teen Market, Trade & Consumer Magazines, Transportation, Travel & Tourism, Viral/Buzz/Word of Mouth, Women's Market

Approx. Annual Billings: $65,000,000

Breakdown of Gross Billings by Media: Brdcst.: 10%; Bus. Publs.: 10%; Collateral: 4%; D.M.: 5%; Internet Adv.: 38%; Newsp.: 5%; Out-of-Home Media: 9%; Production: 6%; Pub. Rels.: 10%; Sls. Promo.: 3%

Joe Phelps *(Chm & CEO)*
Ed Chambliss *(Pres)*
Kim Haskell *(Partner)*
Francisco Letelier *(VP & Dir-Creative)*
Randy Brodeur *(VP)*
Brad Gantt *(VP-Creative)*
Jonathan Tilley *(Head-Interactive Team)*
Beau Elwell *(Dir-Creative)*
Nitya Polipalli *(Coord-Media)*

Accounts:
American Licorice Company
Dunn-Edwards Paints Commercial & Retail Paints & Supplies; 2002
Hong Kong Tourism Board U.S. (Social Media Marketing Agency of Record)
Junior Blind of America; Los Angeles, CA Non-profit; 1997
New-Learn4Life Brand Strategy, Content Development, Public Relations
New-Los Angeles World Airports
Luxury Link Travel Group (Agency of Record) Branding, Media Relations, Strategic Marketing Planning & Execution
Monrovia Growers Plants, Flowers, Shrubs & Other Landscaping Supplies; 1997
Monrovia Nursery Co
New-Natrol Brand Strategy, Broadcast, Digital, Media Buying, Media Planning, Merchandising, Print, Public Relations, Social Media
Panasonic Broadcast & Television Systems; Cypress, CA Computers, Plasma TV, Pro-Audio, TV Systems; 1986
Panasonic Corporation of America Panasonic
Public Storage Storage Facilities & Management; 2007
New-Ryze Capital Partners Brand Strategy, Content Strategy, Website Development
Santa Monica Place
SoCal Gas
Susquehanna Health (Agency of Record) Brand & Digital Strategy, Brand Development, Media Planning & Buying, Production
Tahiti Tourisme North America; El Segundo, CA Travel & Tourism; 1992
Tetra Pak Campaign: "Milk Unleashed"
Valvoline Instant Oil Change

PHENOMBLUE
2111 S 67th St Ste 110, Omaha, NE 68106
Tel.: (402) 933-4050
E-Mail: connect@phenomblue.com
Web Site: www.phenomblue.com

Agency Specializes In: Alternative Advertising, Education, Financial, High Technology, Social Media, Strategic Planning/Research

Joel Olsen *(CEO)*
Joe Urzendowski *(CFO)*
Brooke Heck *(VP & Head-Practice)*
Jonathan Tvrdik *(VP & Exec Dir-Creative)*
Scott Faith *(VP-Ops)*
Kate Richling *(VP-Comm)*
Gabe Romero *(VP-Sls & Mktg)*

Accounts:
Bellevue University; Bellevue, NE Higher Ed; 2012
BillingTree
CareerBuilder
Ebay, Inc.
GoGo
Hayneedle Home Decor
HDR
Newegg
Omaha Children's Museum; Omaha, NE; 2012
Thrasher

PHENOMENON
5900 Wilshire Blvd 28th Fl, Los Angeles, CA 90036
Tel.: (323) 648-4000
E-Mail: communicate@phenomenon.com
Web Site: www.phenomenon.com/

Agency Specializes In: Advertising, Brand Development & Integration, Digital/Interactive, Integrated Marketing, Strategic Planning/Research

Tim Bateman *(Dir-Creative)*
Aris Tagle *(Dir-Analytics)*
Abigail Weintraub *(Dir-Strategy)*
Ali Martin Carrillo Filsoof *(Assoc Dir-Creative)*
Brian Jones *(Assoc Dir-Creative)*
Yama Rahyar *(Assoc Dir-Creative)*
Lexi Hill *(Sr Brand Mgr)*
William Kim *(Brand Supvr)*
Matt Lee *(Grp Brand Dir)*
Michael Seide *(Brand Mgr)*

Accounts:
The Men's Wearhouse Inc Campaign: "The Walk of Fame"
New-Wilson Sporting Goods Co Brand Campaign, Campaign: "My Wilson"

PHIL & CO.
833 Broadway 3rd Fl, New York, NY 10003
Tel.: (646) 490-6446
E-Mail: info@philandcompany.com
Web Site: www.philandcompany.com

Year Founded: 2008

Agency Specializes In: Advertising, Brand Development & Integration, Graphic Design, Internet/Web Design, Public Relations, Social Media, Strategic Planning/Research

Cliff Sloan *(Co-Founder & Partner)*
Gary Zarr *(Co-Founder & Partner-Strategic Mktg PR Reputation & Crisis Mgmt)*

Sheryl Victor Levy *(Sr Dir-Digital Strategy)*
Collin Arnold *(Dir-Design)*
Elysia Howard *(Dir-Bus Dev)*
Rex Unger *(Sr Acct Mgr)*

Accounts:
The International Baccalaureate
New-United Nations Foundation Advertising, Marketing, Public Relations, Social Media, Strategy, Video, Website

PHILIPS & ASSOCIATES
6172 S Gatehouse Dr, Grand Rapids, MI 49546
Tel.: (616) 942-4717
E-Mail: philvans@aol.com

Employees: 4
Year Founded: 1982

Agency Specializes In: Advertising, Advertising Specialties, Broadcast, Business Publications, Business-To-Business, Cable T.V., Consulting, Consumer Marketing, Consumer Publications, Corporate Identity, E-Commerce, Electronic Media, Entertainment, Exhibit/Trade Shows, Financial, Food Service, Graphic Design, Internet/Web Design, Legal Services, Magazines, Marine, Media Buying Services, Merchandising, Multimedia, Newspaper, Newspapers & Magazines, Outdoor, Planning & Consultation, Print, Production, Public Relations, Restaurant, Strategic Planning/Research, T.V., Trade & Consumer Magazines

Approx. Annual Billings: $1,100,000

Breakdown of Gross Billings by Media: Consulting: $100,000; Mags.: $750,000; Other: $210,000; Radio: $40,000

Philip Van Suilichem *(Owner & Pres)*
Lisa Carnevale *(Sr Mgr-Mktg)*

Accounts:
Creative Dining
Hekman Furniture; Grand Rapids, MI
Lithibar; Holland, MI
Peace Talks; Grand Rapids, MI Mediation Services; 2002
Philips Publishing
Woodland Realty
Woodmark Originals; Archdale, NC Upholstery

PHILIPS HEALTHCARE COMMUNICATIONS, INC.
3000 Minuteman Rd, Andover, MA 01810-1099
Toll Free: (800) 229-6417
E-Mail: phc205@aol.com
Web Site: www.usa.philips.com

Employees: 3
Year Founded: 1989

Agency Specializes In: Medical Products

Approx. Annual Billings: $5,250,000

Breakdown of Gross Billings by Media: Fees: $5,000,000; Production: $250,000

Richard Crane *(Sr VP-Commodity Mgmt)*
Laura Costello *(VP-Reg Sls-Patient Monitoring)*
Ed Gala *(VP-Global Mktg & Comm-Philips Healthcare)*
Pim Preesman *(Head-Fin-Brazil)*
Kimberly Dyett *(Sr Dir-Experiential Mktg & Ops)*
Maureen Santangelo *(Sr Dir-Mktg Ops-North America)*
Tom Bonnell *(Dir-Philips Design Healthcare & Home Healthcare Solutions)*
Kim DeFroscia *(Dir-Mktg & Product Mgmt)*
Greg Eckstein *(Dir-Mktg Ops)*
Bethany Gates *(Dir-Global Learning Svcs)*
Georg Kornweibel *(Dir-Field Mktg)*
Jim Moran *(Dir-Equipment Remarketing)*
Linda Trevenen *(Dir-Channel Mktg-Global)*
Paul Baril *(Sr Mgr-Global Product-Mobile Solutions)*
Paolo Dilda *(Sr Mgr-Mktg-North America)*
Lois Fenimore *(Sr Mgr-Integrated Comm-Global)*
Elizabeth Franks *(Sr Mgr-Field Mktg-Philips Hospital to Home)*
Melinda Freson *(Sr Mgr-Customer Insights & Activation)*
Dhruv Jyoti *(Sr Mgr-Market Support-Diagnostic X-Ray, Surgery & Mammography)*
Sally Lin *(Sr Mgr-Field Mktg)*
Mark Manum *(Sr Mgr-Field Mktg-iXR Cardiology)*
Chris Martin *(Sr Mgr-Internal Comm)*
Damon Matlon *(Sr Mgr-Field Mktg)*
Laura McNally *(Sr Mgr-Mktg Comm-Healthcare Transformation Svcs)*
Cindy Morton *(Sr Mgr-Mktg)*
Abbie Pauley *(Sr Mgr-Mktg Comm)*
Aaron Rees *(Sr Mgr-Field Mktg-CV Ultrasound)*
Carrie Stearns *(Sr Mgr-Mktg)*
Melanie S. Traughber *(Sr Mgr-MR Clinical Science & Applications-Radiation Oncology)*
Jennifer Werner *(Sr Mgr-Internal Comm)*
Stephanie Fox *(Acct Mgr-Imaging Sys)*
Jane Asamoto *(Mgr-Sls & Market CT)*
Robin P. Bassen *(Mgr-Mktg-Customer Svcs)*
Meagan Duffy *(Mgr-Consumer Field Mktg)*
Paul Gallagher *(Mgr-Mktg & Segmentation)*
Brandon M. Judd *(Mgr-Sls & Market Support-Electrophysiology)*
Kimberly Labagnara *(Mgr-Healthcare Channel Mktg)*
Rhunette Lee *(Mgr-CT Technical Comm)*
Eric Raufeisen *(Mgr-Field Mktg)*
Nicole Rutledge *(Mgr-Field Mktg-Customer Events-Ultrasound)*
Jim Sease *(Mgr-Bus Conversion)*
Atul Soni *(Mgr-Healthcare Analytics)*
Katherine Freedman *(Analyst-Bus Bus Info Sys)*
Sweta Patel *(Engr-Product Support-Mktg-PCCI)*

Accounts:
Preventive Cardiovascular Nurse Association; Middleton, WI; 2000

PHILLIPS DESIGN GROUP
25 Drydock Ave, Boston, MA 02210
Tel.: (617) 423-7676
E-Mail: info@phillipsdesigngroup.com
Web Site: www.phillipsdesigngroup.com

Employees: 8

Agency Specializes In: Brand Development & Integration

Kathleen Sterling *(Dir-Mktg)*
Christiane Greeley *(Office Mgr)*
Angela Kowalczyk *(Sr Graphic Designer)*

PHILOSOPHY COMMUNICATION
209 Kalamath St Ste 2, Denver, CO 80223
Tel.: (303) 394-2366
Fax: (601) 767-0682
E-Mail: info@philosophycommunication.com
Web Site: www.philosophycommunication.com

Year Founded: 2001

Agency Specializes In: Advertising, Brand Development & Integration, Digital/Interactive, Event Planning & Marketing, Public Relations, Search Engine Optimization, Social Media

Jennifer Lester *(Co-Founder)*
Jen Miller *(Co-Founder)*
Rosalin Yurga *(Dir-Art & Designer)*
Connie Tran *(Dir-Art)*
Tyler Jacobson *(Acct Mgr-Digital)*
Angela Shugarts *(Acct Mgr)*
Kristen Strombelline *(Mgr-Mktg)*
Dana Lamonaca *(Asst Mgr-Mktg-Global Skincare)*

Accounts:
Littleton
Pour Kids

PHIRE GROUP
111 Miller Ave, Ann Arbor, MI 48104
Tel.: (734) 332-4200
Fax: (734) 332-4300
E-Mail: info@phiregroup.com
Web Site: thephiregroup.com

Agency Specializes In: Advertising, Business-To-Business, Internet/Web Design, Media Planning, Strategic Planning/Research

Jim Hume *(Owner)*
Mike Rouech *(VP-Brand Strategy)*
Rachel Jackson *(Controller-Brand)*
Matthew Crigger *(Dir-Interactive Media)*
Kurt Keller *(Dir-Creative)*
Kristy Smith *(Acct Exec)*

PHIRE MARKETING
1912 Point Breeze Ave, Philadelphia, PA 19145
Tel.: (267) 519-3710
E-Mail: info@phiremarketing.com
Web Site: phiremarketing.com

Year Founded: 2013

Agency Specializes In: African-American Market, Brand Development & Integration, College, Consulting, Consumer Goods, Consumer Marketing, Digital/Interactive, Entertainment, Event Planning & Marketing, Guerilla Marketing, Integrated Marketing, Local Marketing, Multicultural, Paid Searches, Promotions, Publicity/Promotions, Sales Promotion, Search Engine Optimization, Social Media, Sponsorship, Teen Market, Urban Market

Brian McDaniel *(Dir-Mktg)*

Accounts:
Beam Suntory Inc. Courvoisier, Cruzan Rum, Dekuyper
National Black Accountants Association
Phire Music StrictBizz, Phire Music

PHOENIX GROUP
195-1621 Albert St, Regina, SK S4P 2S5 Canada
Tel.: (306) 585-9500
Fax: (306) 352-8240
E-Mail: powersthatbe@thephoenixgroup.ca
Web Site: www.thephoenixgroup.ca

Agency Specializes In: Advertising, Brand Development & Integration, Corporate Communications, Event Planning & Marketing, Graphic Design, Internet/Web Design, Media Buying Services, Media Planning, Social Media, Strategic Planning/Research

Pam Klein *(Pres)*
David Bellerive *(VP-Creative & Interactive)*
Darren Mitchell *(VP-Strategic Dev)*
Rachel Giatras *(Dir-Media & Strategist-Digital Media)*
J. J. Ellams *(Dir-Art)*
Gillian Meyer *(Dir-Art)*
Dustin Panko *(Dir-Creative)*
Ryan Dowdeswell *(Assoc Dir-Creative)*
Laila Haus *(Assoc Dir-Creative)*
Elaine Nyhus *(Acct Planner)*

Accounts:

The Great Western Brewing Company

PHOENIX MARKETING ASSOCIATES

5110 N Central Ave Ste 300, Phoenix, AZ 85012
Tel.: (602) 282-0202
E-Mail: info@phoenixmarketingassociates.com
Web Site: www.phoenixmarketingassociates.com

Agency Specializes In: Advertising, Brand Development & Integration, Collateral, Public Relations, Social Media

Jason Jantzen *(Pres)*
Jim Timony *(VP)*
Laura Strickland *(Mgr-Mktg & Comm)*

Accounts:
10Zig
Ahi Mahi Fish Grill Branding, Online Marketing, Public Relations, Social Media, Website
American Academy of Pediatrics
Arizona Ballroom Champions Advertising, Branding, Event Planning, Marketing, Online Marketing, Public Relations, SEO, Social Media, Website Creation
New-Brian Ronalds
DB Schenker USA
Define Yourself Clothing Branding
New-Dignity Health Foundation East Valley (Marketing & Public Relations Agency of Record) Dancing for Stroke Gala
New-Dignity Health Branding, Public Relations, Social Media, Website Improvements
Duck and Decanter Social Media
El Sol Foods
Hillside Sedona Public Relations, SEO, Social Media
ICG Consulting
New-JDRF Public Relations
Moonshine Whiskey Bar Ad Placement, Graphic Design, Public Relations, Television
Sanfratello's Pizza Public Relations, Social Media
Shari Rowe Public Relations
New-Shona Salon & Spa
UltraStar Cinemas

PHOENIX MARKETING GROUP, INC.

6750 Maple Terr, Milwaukee, WI 53213
Tel.: (414) 531-3187
E-Mail: jradtke@phoenixmgi.com
Web Site: www.phoenixmgi.com

Employees: 4
Year Founded: 1979

Agency Specializes In: Advertising, Advertising Specialties, Brand Development & Integration, Broadcast, Business Publications, Business-To-Business, Collateral, Corporate Identity, Direct Response Marketing, Electronic Media, Financial, Graphic Design, Health Care Services, Information Technology, Internet/Web Design, Logo & Package Design, Media Buying Services, Medical Products, Pharmaceutical, Production, Public Relations, Strategic Planning/Research, Trade & Consumer Magazines

Approx. Annual Billings: $3,000,000

Breakdown of Gross Billings by Media: Bus. Publs.: $900,000; Collateral: $600,000; D.M.: $300,000; Logo & Package Design: $240,000; Print: $300,000; Pub. Rels.: $300,000; Strategic Planning/Research: $150,000; Worldwide Web Sites: $210,000

Charlie Radtke *(VP & Dir-Creative)*

Accounts:
Cardinal Capital Management; Milwaukee, WI; 2003
Generac Power Systems; Waukesha, WI; 1999
Johnson Controls, Inc.; Milwaukee, WI; 1998
P&H Mining Equipment; Milwaukee, WI; 2000
Perlick
Vestica Healthcare; Milwaukee, WI; 2003
Wonderbox Technologies; Milwaukee, WI; 2003

PHOENIX MEDIA GROUP INC.

375 Greenwich St, New York, NY 10013
Tel.: (212) 965-4720
E-Mail: info@phoenixnyc.tv
Web Site: www.phoenixnyc.tv

Year Founded: 2007

Agency Specializes In: Advertising, Brand Development & Integration, Collateral, Multimedia, Print, Production, Search Engine Optimization, Social Media

Chris Phoenix *(Founder, CEO & Exec Producer)*
Mike Miller *(Gen Mgr)*
Jeffrey Man *(Dir-Creative)*
Nicole Ranucci *(Assoc Producer & Mgr-Ops)*

Accounts:
Cctv There is Only We
CLIO Image Awards & WWD

PIA COMMUNICATIONS

5930 Priestly Dr, Carlsbad, CA 92008
Tel.: (760) 930-9244
Web Site: www.piacomm.com

Employees: 15
Year Founded: 2002

Agency Specializes In: Branded Entertainment, Broadcast, Cable T.V., Communications, Consumer Goods, Content, Digital/Interactive, Electronics, Entertainment, Household Goods, Medical Products, Production, Production (Ad, Film, Broadcast), Social Media

Cheryl Pia *(President)*
Mark Kulik *(Chief Financial Officer)*
Cliff Pia *(Chief Creative Officer)*
Steve Roth *(VP-Agency Dev)*

Accounts:
HP Computer Products

PICCIRILLI DORSEY, INC.

502 Rock Spring Rd, Bel Air, MD 21014
Tel.: (410) 879-6780
Fax: (410) 879-6602
E-Mail: hello@picdorsey.com
Web Site: www.picdorsey.com

Year Founded: 2011

Agency Specializes In: Advertising, Graphic Design, Internet/Web Design, Print

Micah Piccirilli *(Partner & Dir-Creative)*
Adam Dorsey *(Partner)*
Deborah Ponder Mance *(Mgr-Mktg)*

Accounts:
Chas Spa and Salon
Reynolds Dentistry
Ritz-Carlton Residences

PIEHEAD PRODUCTIONS LLC

73 Ct St, Portsmouth, NH 03801
Tel.: (603) 431-5983
Fax: (603) 929-9700
E-Mail: engage@piehead.com
Web Site: www.piehead.com

Year Founded: 2001

Agency Specializes In: Advertising, Content, Digital/Interactive, Search Engine Optimization, Social Media

Mark W. Troy *(Founder & CEO)*
Nikki Raffenetti *(Sr VP-Talent & Culture)*
Jeremy Clough *(VP-Digital & Dir-Creative)*
Jason Rivera *(VP-Engagement Strategy)*
Scott Holt *(Dir-Brand Experience)*
Liz Metsch *(Assoc Dir-Design-Brand Experience)*
Kathryn Fink *(Sr Designer)*
Holly Dennett *(Team Head-Engagement Mgmt)*

Accounts:
Community Coffee Company LLC

PIER 8 GROUP

605 James St N 4th Fl, Hamilton, ON L8L 1J9 Canada
Tel.: (905) 529-7312
Fax: (905) 572-6844
Toll Free: (877) 529-7312
E-Mail: bob@pier8group.com
Web Site: www.pier8group.com

Employees: 5
Year Founded: 2004

Bob Mills *(Pres)*
Paul Seccaspina *(CEO-Oraclepoll Research Ltd.)*
Sylvia Toffoletti *(Sr Dir-Art & Designer-Web)*
Judy Mair *(Webmaster & Designer)*
Peter Stevens *(Designer)*

Accounts:
Niagara Smart Gardening
Ontario Works Hamilton
Tourism Hamilton

Subsidiary

Wordsmith Design & Advertising

605 James Street N 4th Floor, Hamilton, ON L8L 1J9 Canada
Tel.: (905) 529-7312
Fax: (905) 572-6844
E-Mail: info@pier8group.com
Web Site: www.pier8group.com

Bob Mills *(Pres & CEO)*

PIERCE COMMUNICATIONS, INC.

208 E State St, Columbus, OH 43215-4311
Tel.: (614) 365-9494
Fax: (614) 365-9564
E-Mail: gene@piercecomm.com
Web Site: www.piercecomm.com

E-Mail for Key Personnel:
President: gene@piercecomm.com

Employees: 5
Year Founded: 1985

Agency Specializes In: Advertising, African-American Market, Education, Environmental, Government/Political, Public Relations

Approx. Annual Billings: $1,500,000

Gene H. Pierce *(Pres & CEO)*
Heather Dalzell *(Dir-Bus Dev)*

Accounts:
Columbus Public Schools
Ohio Council of Retail Merchants

PIERCE-COTE ADVERTISING

911 Main St, Osterville, MA 02655-2015

Tel.: (508) 420-5566
Fax: (508) 420-3314
E-Mail: info@pierce-cote.com
Web Site: www.pierce-cote.com

Employees: 7
Year Founded: 1988

Approx. Annual Billings: $3,000,000

Bradford Schiff *(Pres)*
Diane McPherson *(VP)*
John Migliaccio *(Exec Dir-Creative)*
Lynn O'Brien *(Dir-Art & Designer)*
Mary Stengel *(Dir-Client Svcs & Dir-Media)*

Accounts:
Cape Cod Museum of Art (Agency of Record)
Corjen Construction, Boston
Eastern Bank
Heritage Museums & Gardens; Sandwich, MA Creative, Media Planning, Public Relations, Strategic Marketing
Hospice & Palliative Care of Cape Cod
The Mayfair Hotel, New York
NYLO Hotel, Providence/Warwick
Plimoth Plantation, Plymouth
Rockland Trust Company
Savings Bank Life Insurance (SBLI)

PIERCE CREATIVE
433 G St Ste 202, San Diego, CA 92101
Tel.: (619) 356-0164
E-Mail: hello@piercesd.com
Web Site: www.piercesd.com

Year Founded: 2008

Agency Specializes In: Advertising, Brand Development & Integration, Email, Event Planning & Marketing, Graphic Design, Internet/Web Design, Logo & Package Design, Print

Jon Youngberg *(Owner)*

Accounts:
Allure Restaurant
Balboa Park
Escape Fish Bar

PIERSON GRANT PUBLIC RELATIONS
6301 NW 5th Way Ste 2600, Fort Lauderdale, FL 33309
Tel.: (954) 776-1999
Fax: (954) 776-0290
E-Mail: info@piersongrant.com
Web Site: www.piersongrant.com

Employees: 15
Year Founded: 1995

Agency Specializes In: Advertising, Arts, Communications, Consumer Goods, Crisis Communications, Education, Event Planning & Marketing, Financial, Government/Political, Graphic Design, Health Care Services, Hospitality, Internet/Web Design, Media Relations, Newspaper, Public Relations, Publicity/Promotions, Real Estate, Restaurant, Sponsorship, Strategic Planning/Research, Travel & Tourism

Revenue: $1,400,000

Jane Grant *(Pres)*
Maria Pierson *(CEO)*
Michael Fruchter *(VP-Digital Strategy)*
Daniel Grant *(VP)*
Marielle Sologuren *(VP)*
Diana Hanford *(Acct Dir)*
Noelle Robillard *(Acct Dir)*
Amy Hoffman *(Acct Supvr)*

Accounts:
CNL Bank
Consert
GL Homes
Holy Cross management
Olive Garden
WM

PILCHER CREATIVE AGENCY
8704 W 49th St, Shawnee, KS 66203
Tel.: (913) 396-9962
Web Site: www.pilchermedia.com

Year Founded: 2008

Agency Specializes In: Advertising, Logo & Package Design, Print, Search Engine Optimization, Social Media

Laura Pilcher *(Owner)*

Accounts:
Forward Edge Marketing
Learning2Fly

PILGRIM
(Formerly CCT Advertising)
1441 29th St, Denver, CO 80205
Tel.: (303) 531-7180
Fax: (303) 531-7181
E-Mail: info@thinkpilgrim.com
Web Site: www.thinkpilgrim.com/

Agency Specializes In: Advertising, Sponsorship

Chris Clemens *(Pres)*
Jon Stockdale *(CFO)*
Lynda Calhoun *(Dir-Digital)*
Michael Dusing *(Dir-Digital Art)*
Holly Menges *(Dir-Creative)*

Accounts:
AAA Colorado
Albany County Tourism Board
Colorado Wildlife Council
Grand Junction Visitor & Convention Bureau

PILOT
160 Broadway E Bldg Ste 800, New York, NY 10038
Tel.: (212) 500-6072
E-Mail: sayhi@pilotnyc.com
Web Site: www.pilotnyc.com

Agency Specializes In: Advertising, Brand Development & Integration, Broadcast, Graphic Design, Print

Waverly Damato *(CFO)*
Marybeth Benivegna *(Sr Creative Dir)*
Linda Danner *(Sr Creative Dir)*
Liz Weinstein *(Creative Dir)*
Kyle Orlowicz *(Assoc Dir-Creative)*
Mike Budney *(Assoc Dir-Creative)*

Accounts:
FXX Network Simpsons Marathon
Turner Broadcasting System, Inc.

PINCKNEY HUGO GROUP
760 W Genesee St, Syracuse, NY 13204-2306
Tel.: (315) 478-6700
Fax: (315) 426-1392
E-Mail: marketing@pinckneyhugo.com
Web Site: www.pinckneyhugo.com

E-Mail for Key Personnel:
President: doug@pinckneyhugo.com
Media Dir.: kathleen@pinckneyhugo.com

Employees: 20
Year Founded: 1940

National Agency Associations: 4A's

Agency Specializes In: Advertising, Agriculture, Automotive, Brand Development & Integration, Broadcast, Business Publications, Business-To-Business, Consumer Marketing, Corporate Identity, Direct Response Marketing, Education, Environmental, Fashion/Apparel, Financial, Graphic Design, Health Care Services, Industrial, Internet/Web Design, Logo & Package Design, Medical Products, Multimedia, Newspaper, Newspapers & Magazines, Out-of-Home Media, Outdoor, Print, Production, Public Relations, Radio, Real Estate, Restaurant, Retail, Strategic Planning/Research, T.V.

Kathleen Brogan *(VP-Media Svcs)*
Christopher Pinckney *(Exec Dir-Creative)*
Colleen O'Mara *(Dir-PR)*
Cathy Van Order *(Dir-Production Svcs)*
Scott McNany *(Assoc Dir-Creative)*
Kathryn Duerr *(Sr Mgr-Digital Media)*
Bryan Weinsztok *(Sr Acct Mgr)*
Scott Herron *(Acct Exec)*
Susan Muench *(Media Buyer)*

Accounts:
Alliance Bank
Bush Brothers; Chestnut Hill, TN Beans
Commonfund Mortgage; Syracuse, NY
Fuccillo Automotive Group; Syracuse, NY
Fuccillo Hyundai; Syracuse, NY
Madison County Tourism
MDR Magnetic Resonance Imaging Technology
Metro Mattress (Agency of Record)
Oncenter Complex
Onondaga Community College; Syracuse, NY
Redco Foods Public Relations, Salada Green Tea
Tylenol

PINCKNEY MARKETING, INC.
1920 Abbott St Unit 300, Charlotte, NC 28203
Tel.: (704) 496-7900
E-Mail: info@pinckneymarketing.com
Web Site: www.pinckneymarketing.com

Agency Specializes In: Advertising, Brand Development & Integration, Digital/Interactive, Graphic Design, Internet/Web Design, Logo & Package Design, Media Buying Services, Print, Radio, Strategic Planning/Research

Mike Pinckney *(Owner & CEO)*
Dani Damous *(Head-Acct)*
Daniel Dixon *(Head-Acct)*
Jessica Storms *(Head-Creative)*
Mike Kerlee *(Mgr-Paid Search)*
Andy Doerr *(Sr Graphic Designer)*
Phillip Leide *(Designer-Motion Graphics & Animation)*
Haley Williams *(Sr Acct Head)*

Accounts:
Byrum Heating & AC, Inc.
Dine Out Charlotte
Lettuce Carry
Nissan of Chesapeake

PINDOT MEDIA
(Formerly Ad Ventures, Inc.)
620 Colonial Park Dr, Roswell, GA 30075-3746
Tel.: (770) 640-5225
Fax: (866) 591-7389
Toll Free: (800) 707-0570
E-Mail: info@pindotmedia.com
Web Site: www.pindotmedia.com

E-Mail for Key Personnel:
President: dcogdell@pindotmedia.com

Employees: 13

Year Founded: 1992

National Agency Associations: YPA

Agency Specializes In: Advertising, Business Publications, Business-To-Business, Consumer Marketing, Local Marketing, Mobile Marketing, Newspaper, Print, Social Media, Yellow Pages Advertising

Approx. Annual Billings: $15,000,000

Breakdown of Gross Billings by Media: Internet Adv.: $2,000,000; Print: $13,000,000

Michael Erich *(Dir-Bus Dev)*
Stephanie Tucker *(Sr Acct Mgr)*
Charlotte Wilborn *(Mgr-Bus Analysis & Product Dev)*

PINEAPPLE ADVERTISING

6304 E 102 St S, Tulsa, OK 74133
Tel.: (918) 313-6463
Web Site: www.pickthepineapple.com

Year Founded: 2008

Agency Specializes In: Advertising, Brand Development & Integration, Digital/Interactive, Logo & Package Design, T.V.

Brian Barlow *(Owner)*
Travis Foust *(Media Buyer)*

Accounts:
Keffer Volkswagen
Lake Country Chevrolet
Oxmoor Auto Group

THE PINK COLLECTIVE

7320 Griffin Rd Ste 103a, Davie, FL 33314
Tel.: (800) 614-0251
Web Site: www.thepinkcollective.com

Year Founded: 2009

Agency Specializes In: Advertising, Brand Development & Integration, Event Planning & Marketing, Internet/Web Design, Print, Radio, Social Media, T.V.

Roly Rodriguez *(Pres & Dir-Creative)*
John Moriano *(Mgr-Studio)*
Jennifer Feraco *(Sr Strategist-Acct)*

Accounts:
Baptist Health South Florida

PINNACLE ADVERTISING

16461 Sherman Way Ste 120 Lake Balboa, Los Angeles, CA 91406
Tel.: (818) 779-0077
Fax: (818) 779-0001
E-Mail: info@pinadsmedia.com
Web Site: www.pinadsmedia.com

Employees: 17

Agency Specializes In: Brand Development & Integration, Print, Radio, T.V., Web (Banner Ads, Pop-ups, etc.)

Jack Rostollan *(VP & Grp Acct Dir)*
Justine Cervenka *(Reg Acct Mgr)*

Accounts:
Exonic
Miller Automotive
National Cable & Telecommunications Association PointSmartClickSafe (Educational Campaign)
Samsung
WeatherTech Campaign: "America At Work", Campaign: "You Can't Do That" Super Bowl 2014, Super Bowl 2015

PINNACLE ADVERTISING & MARKETING GROUP

1515 S Federal Hwy Ste 406, Boca Raton, FL 33432
Tel.: (561) 338-3940
E-Mail: info@pinnacleadgroup.com
Web Site: www.pinnacleadvertising.net/

Year Founded: 2011

Agency Specializes In: Advertising, Digital/Interactive, Media Buying Services, Media Planning, Public Relations, Search Engine Optimization, Social Media

Peter Gary *(Founder & CEO)*
Evelyn Lopez *(CFO)*
Mary Martel *(COO)*
Daniel Kinney *(CTO)*
Alicia Abdulla *(Comptroller)*
Glen Calder *(Dir-PR)*
Brian Lenihan *(Dir-Digital Media Strategy)*
Corey Levin *(Sr Acct Mgr)*
Brittany Spiller *(Acct Exec)*

Accounts:
Florida Atlantic University
Florida Panthers Hockey Club, Ltd. IceDen
JM Lexus
Revitamal (Agency of Record) Advertising, Digital Marketing, Public Relations, SEO, Social Media
Waldan International Public Relations

PINNACLE DIRECT

4700 rue de la Savane Ste 102, Montreal, QC H4P 1T7 Canada
Tel.: (514) 344-3382
Fax: (514) 344-5394
Toll Free: (800) 388-0669
E-Mail: pinnacle@pinnacle-direct.com
Web Site: www.pinnacle-direct.com

Employees: 12
Year Founded: 1984

Agency Specializes In: Bilingual Market, Direct Response Marketing

Approx. Annual Billings: $5,000,000

Breakdown of Gross Billings by Media: Collateral: $500,000; D.M.: $4,250,000; Mags.: $250,000

Howard Golberg *(Owner & Pres)*
Patricia Reuter *(VP)*
Blair Evans *(Dir-Creative)*

Accounts:
Quebec Foundation for the Blind

PINTA

60 E 42nd St Ste 5310, New York, NY 10165
Tel.: (212) 367-9800
Web Site: www.PintaUSA.com

Employees: 40
Year Founded: 2013

Agency Specializes In: Above-the-Line, Advertising, Advertising Specialties, Affiliate Marketing, Affluent Market, African-American Market, Agriculture, Alternative Advertising, Arts, Asian Market, Automotive, Aviation & Aerospace, Below-the-Line, Bilingual Market, Brand Development & Integration, Branded Entertainment, Broadcast, Business Publications, Business-To-Business, Cable T.V., Catalogs, Children's Market, Co-op Advertising, Collateral, College, Commercial Photography, Communications, Computers & Software, Consulting, Consumer Goods, Consumer Marketing, Consumer Publications, Content, Corporate Communications, Corporate Identity, Cosmetics, Crisis Communications, Custom Publishing, Customer Relationship Management, Digital/Interactive, Direct Response Marketing, Direct-to-Consumer, E-Commerce, Education, Electronic Media, Electronics, Email, Engineering, Entertainment, Environmental, Event Planning & Marketing, Exhibit/Trade Shows, Experience Design, Faith Based, Fashion/Apparel, Financial, Food Service, Game Integration, Gay & Lesbian Market, Government/Political, Graphic Design, Guerilla Marketing, Health Care Services, High Technology, Hispanic Market, Hospitality, Household Goods, Identity Marketing, In-Store Advertising, Industrial, Infomercials, Information Technology, Integrated Marketing, International, Internet/Web Design, Investor Relations, Legal Services, Leisure, Local Marketing, Logo & Package Design, Luxury Products, Magazines, Marine, Market Research, Media Buying Services, Media Planning, Media Relations, Media Training, Medical Products, Men's Market, Merchandising, Mobile Marketing, Multicultural, Multimedia, New Product Development, New Technologies, Newspaper, Newspapers & Magazines, Out-of-Home Media, Outdoor, Over-50 Market, Package Design, Paid Searches, Pets, Pharmaceutical, Planning & Consultation, Podcasting, Point of Purchase, Point of Sale, Print, Product Placement, Production, Production (Ad, Film, Broadcast), Production (Print), Promotions, Public Relations, Publicity/Promotions, Publishing, RSS (Really Simple Syndication), Radio, Real Estate, Recruitment, Regional, Restaurant, Retail, Sales Promotion, Search Engine Optimization, Seniors' Market, Shopper Marketing, Social Marketing/Nonprofit, Social Media, South Asian Market, Sponsorship, Sports Market, Stakeholders, Strategic Planning/Research, Sweepstakes, Syndication, T.V., Technical Advertising, Teen Market, Telemarketing, Trade & Consumer Magazines, Transportation, Travel & Tourism, Tween Market, Urban Market, Viral/Buzz/Word of Mouth, Web (Banner Ads, Pop-ups, etc.), Women's Market, Yellow Pages Advertising

Mike Valdes-Fauli *(Pres & CEO)*
Joe Gutierrez *(Mng Dir & Head-Strategic Plng)*
Lauren Cortinas *(Mng Dir)*
Alex Barreras *(Dir-Creative)*
Giancarlo Russo *(Mgr-Creative & Digital Svcs)*
Paula Cornelia Fernandez-Salvador *(Acct Exec)*
Camila Gadala-Maria *(Acct Exec)*
Amanda Gadaleta *(Acct Exec)*
Edgar Otero-Chaparro *(Acct Exec)*

Accounts:
American Express
beIN Sports
Facebook
Flipboard
Florida Marlins
Fox
Pfizer
Spotify
T-Mobile
TD Bank
UFC (Hispanic Agency of Record) Creative Public Relations, Marketing, Social Media

PINTA USA LLC

1111 Lincoln Rd Ste 800, Miami Beach, FL 33139
Tel.: (305) 615-1111
Web Site: www.pintausa.com

Agency Specializes In: Advertising, Communications, Digital/Interactive, Media Buying Services, Media Planning, Promotions, Public

Relations, Social Media, Strategic Planning/Research

Michael Valdes-Fauli *(Pres & CEO)*
Lauren Cortinas *(Mng Dir)*
Alex Barreras *(Creative Dir)*

Accounts:
UFC (Hispanic Agency of Record)

PIONEER NATIONAL ADVERTISING, INC.

4093 12th St Cut Off SE, Salem, OR 97302-1741
Tel.: (503) 364-3346
Fax: (503) 581-6819

E-Mail for Key Personnel:
President: bryan@ostlund.com

Employees: 10
Year Founded: 1959

Agency Specializes In: Agriculture

Approx. Annual Billings: $1,000,000

Bryan Ostlund *(Pres)*
Lisa Ostlund *(Treas & Sec)*

PIPITONE GROUP

3933 Perrysville Ave., Pittsburgh, PA 15214
Tel.: (412) 321-0879
Fax: (412) 321-2217
E-Mail: info@pipitonegroup.com
Web Site: www.pipitonegroup.com

Employees: 32

Agency Specializes In: Advertising, Brand Development & Integration, Communications, Digital/Interactive, Strategic Planning/Research

Revenue: $2,000,000

Scott Pipitone *(CEO)*
Jeff Piatt *(Chief Creative Officer & Principal)*
Augie Aggazio *(VP-Interactive)*
Arnie Begler *(VP-Strategy)*
Scott Witalis *(VP-Client Mktg)*
Kim Tarquinio *(Mgr-Acct Svcs)*

Accounts:
Campos Inc
CENTRIA
Northside Leadership Conference

PISTON AGENCY

1111 6th Ave 6th Fl, San Diego, CA 92101
Tel.: (619) 308-5266
Fax: (619) 238-8923
Web Site: www.pistonagency.com

Employees: 50
Year Founded: 2001

Agency Specializes In: Advertising, Sponsorship

John Hartman *(Co-Founder & Pres)*
Megan Black *(VP-Paid & Organic Media)*
Obele Brown-West *(VP-Acct Mgmt)*
Morgan Vawter *(VP-Analytics & Optimization)*
David Schafer *(Exec Dir-Creative)*
Richard Chavez *(Sr Dir-SEO)*
Colin Ayres *(Creative Dir)*
Jessica D'Elena-Tweed *(Dir-Creative)*
Nick Smith *(Assoc Dir-Media)*
Kelly Pugh *(Supvr-Media)*

Accounts:
AAA
AARP
Avoya Travel Creative, Digital, Media, Print
Bare Escentuals, Inc.
BareMinerals
Cars.com Digital
Exclusive Resorts, LLC
Inspirato
Intuit
Mitsubishi
Mophie
San Diego Chargers Creative Services, Digital Media, In-Stadium Signage, TV Spot, Tickets; 2015
Shiseido
SkullCandy
Sunglass Hut
TVG
Yakult

PITA COMMUNICATIONS LLC

40 Cold Spring Rd, Rocky Hill, CT 06067
Tel.: (860) 293-0157
Fax: (860) 241-1066
E-Mail: info@pitacomm.com
Web Site: www.pitagroup.com

E-Mail for Key Personnel:
President: kim@pitacomm.com
Creative Dir.: paul@pitacomm.com
Media Dir.: keith@pitacomm.com
Production Mgr.: darci@pitacomm.com
Public Relations: jenny@pitacomm.com

Employees: 20
Year Founded: 1996

National Agency Associations: AMA-PRSA

Agency Specializes In: Advertising, African-American Market, Bilingual Market, Brand Development & Integration, Broadcast, Business Publications, Business-To-Business, Collateral, Communications, Consulting, Consumer Marketing, Corporate Communications, Corporate Identity, Digital/Interactive, Direct Response Marketing, E-Commerce, Electronic Media, Event Planning & Marketing, Exhibit/Trade Shows, Financial, Graphic Design, Health Care Services, High Technology, Hispanic Market, Internet/Web Design, Logo & Package Design, Magazines, Media Buying Services, Outdoor, Over-50 Market, Planning & Consultation, Print, Production, Public Relations, Publicity/Promotions, Radio, Real Estate, Recruitment, Seniors' Market, Sports Market, Strategic Planning/Research, Travel & Tourism

Approx. Annual Billings: $1,650,000

Kim Sirois Pita *(Founder)*
Marje Medzela *(Exec Dir-Client Svcs)*
Sandy Frayler *(Acct Svcs Dir)*
Kristen Ehrlich *(Dir-Creative Svcs)*
Steve Latronica *(Dir-Interactive Dev)*
Lisa Santoro *(Dir-Design)*
Karen Murray *(Mgr-Fin)*
Kim Decarlo *(Acct Exec)*
Darlene Sargent *(Sr Designer)*
John Centore *(Coord-Mktg)*
Mark Bonnot *(Sr Developer-Interactive)*

Accounts:
Aetna

PITBULL CREATIVE

1983 Woodsdale Rd, Atlanta, GA 30324
Tel.: (404) 403-2201
Web Site: www.pitbullcreative.net

Year Founded: 2001

Agency Specializes In: Advertising, Digital/Interactive, Graphic Design, Internet/Web Design, Logo & Package Design, Print, Radio

Constantine Pitsikoulis *(Chief Creative Officer)*

Accounts:
Georgia State University
L-3 Communications Holdings Inc.

THE PITCH AGENCY

8825 National Blvd, Culver City, CA 90232
Tel.: (424) 603-6000
E-Mail: contact@thepitchagency.com
Web Site: www.thepitchagency.com

Employees: 28
Year Founded: 2007

Rachel Spiegelman *(Pres)*
Jon Banks *(CEO)*
Xanthe Wells *(Chief Creative Officer)*
Rob Goldenberg *(Exec Dir-Creative)*
Chris Kyriakos *(Exec Dir-Integrated Production)*
Dave Foster *(Grp Acct Dir)*
David Dubois *(Art Dir)*
Audrey Jersin *(Acct Dir)*
Andrew Lopez *(Acct Dir)*
Max Pollak *(Dir-Art)*
Yesenia Diaz *(Acct Exec-La-Z-Boy)*
Nissa Gutierrez *(Acct Exec)*
Katie Roberts *(Copywriter)*

Accounts:
Asics
Bonefish Grill (Agency of Record) Marketing
Burger King (Lead Creative Agency) "Watch Like A King", Broadcast, Campaign: "Bringing Back The Yumbo", Campaign: "NCAA March Madness", Campaign: "Smile", Kids Meal Box, Social Media, Television
Citrix Campaign: "Dr. Looselips", Campaign: "High Stakes", Campaign: "The Tactless Attorney", GoToMeeting, Sharefile
Closet Factory
Haggen, Inc. (Agency of Record) Digital, Experiential, In-Store, Media, Outdoor, Print, Radio, Social, Strategic Positioning, Television
Konami (Agency of Record)
Living Spaces Furniture Brand Identity, Logo Redesign
Maaco; Charlotte, NC Campaign: "Twestimate", Digital, Experiential, Print, Radio
Meineke Car Care Centers, Inc. "Brakes/:10", "Fluids/:10", "General Car Care/:30", "Oil/:30", "Transmissions/:10", Brand Awareness, Broadcast, Campaign: "Drive A Little Smarter", Customer Experience, Digital, Print, Radio, Social Media
Netflix
Pepsi Wild Cherry Pepsi
Pinkberry
San Manuel Indian Bingo and Casino (Agency of Record) Campaign: "All Thrill", Strategic Brand Repositioning
Santa Barbara Museum of Natural History
Weingart Center

PIVOT COMMUNICATION

777 29th St Ste 400, Boulder, CO 80303
Tel.: (303) 499-9291
Fax: (303) 474-3025
E-Mail: info@pivotcomm.com
Web Site: www.pivotcomm.com

Year Founded: 1998

Agency Specializes In: Advertising, Email, Event Planning & Marketing, Internet/Web Design, Media Relations, Media Training, Multimedia, Newspapers & Magazines, Planning & Consultation, Public Relations

Patrick Hyde *(Owner)*
Laura Holloway *(Partner)*
Carole Carroll *(Office Mgr)*

Claire Autruong *(Sr Specialist-Comm)*
Melissa Brooks *(Specialist-Comm)*
Katherine Wartell *(Specialist-Comm)*

Accounts:
BI Inc
The Boomer Group Employment Services
Castle Country Assisted Living Senior Home Care Services
Correctional Counseling, Inc.
EPOCH
Experience Factor
Peak PACE Soultions
Pedal to Properties License Designation Real Estate Services

PIVOT MARKETING
1052 Virginia Ave, Indianapolis, IN 46203
Tel.: (317) 536-0047
Web Site: www.pivotmarketing.com

Agency Specializes In: Advertising, Brand Development & Integration, Internet/Web Design, Public Relations, Social Media

Jenn Hoffman *(Pres)*
Melissa Martin *(Art Dir)*
Ryan Abegglen *(Dir-Creative)*
Joshua Cook *(Dir-Art)*
Jordan Hunt *(Acct Mgr)*
Union Williams *(Acct Exec)*

Accounts:
Bosma Enterprises
Curran Architecture
Hooverwood
Muegge
Newfangled Confections
The Skillman Corporation

PIVOT+LEVY
1505 Westlake Ave N 4th Fl Ste 495, Seattle, WA 98109
Tel.: (206) 285-6191
Fax: (206) 285-6130
E-Mail: info@pivotandlevy.com
Web Site: www.pivotandlevy.com

Employees: 5
Year Founded: 1977

Revenue: $2,000,000

Terry Stoeser *(Founder & Principal)*
Laura Blue *(Dir-Bus Solutions)*
Matt Trinneer *(Dir-Creative)*
Paul Allen *(Mgr-Ops & Client Svcs)*

Accounts:
Benefit IQ
BW Container Systems
CKC
Columbia Hospitality

PIXEL LOGIC, INC.
Pixelogic Bldg 283 Matadero Rd, San Juan, PR 00920
Tel.: (787) 200-6914
E-Mail: info@pixelogicpr.com
Web Site: www.pixelogicpr.com

Year Founded: 2008

Agency Specializes In: Advertising, Digital/Interactive, Email, Social Media

Josvan Perez Morales *(Partner)*
Juan C. Sanchez *(Partner & Sr Strategist-Client)*
Melvin Espinal *(Dir-Creative)*

Accounts:
Toyota Motor North America, Inc. Scion

PIXEL PROSE MEDIA, LLC
Corbin Ave, Los Angeles, CA 91306
Tel.: (818) 900-4028
E-Mail: info@pixelprosemedia.com
Web Site: www.pixelprosemedia.com

Year Founded: 2010

Agency Specializes In: Advertising, Brand Development & Integration, Graphic Design, Media Relations, Social Media

Mick Mars Robinson *(Co-Founder, Co-CEO & Dir-Creative)*
Janet A. Dickerson *(Co-Founder & Co-CEO)*

Accounts:
Highmark Foundation

PIXELS & DOTS LLC
3181 Linwood Ave, Cincinnati, OH 45208
Tel.: (513) 405-3687
E-Mail: info@pixelsanddots.com
Web Site: www.pixelsanddots.com

Year Founded: 2001

Agency Specializes In: Advertising, Brand Development & Integration, Digital/Interactive, Internet/Web Design, Logo & Package Design, Paid Searches, Print, Search Engine Optimization, Social Media

Angela Davis *(CEO & COO)*
Monte Davis *(VP-Sls)*

Accounts:
New-Incite!

PJA
12 Arrow St, Cambridge, MA 02138-5105
Tel.: (617) 492-5899
Fax: (617) 661-1530
E-Mail: gstraface@agencypja.com
Web Site: www.agencypja.com

Employees: 50
Year Founded: 1988

Agency Specializes In: Business-To-Business, Health Care Services, High Technology, Sponsorship

Philip Johnson *(CEO)*
Robert Davis *(Sr VP-Digital Mktg)*
Janet Carlisle *(VP-Client Svcs)*
Nicole Ciacciarelli *(VP-Fin)*
Greg Straface *(VP-Bus Dev)*
Aaron DaSilva *(Exec Dir-Creative)*
Nathan Clapp *(Dir-Art)*
Brian Bernier *(Assoc Dir-Creative)*
Matt Dowling *(Assoc Dir-Media-Integrated)*

Accounts:
Agilysys, Inc Campaign: "Hollywood Premiere", Social Media, rGuest
Boston Scientific
Brother International Corporation
Chase Sapphire
EMC
GE healthcare
Infor; Alpharetta, GA Business Software
Juniper Networks, Inc.
Novell
TE Connectivity Campaign: "How Fiber Comes Alive"
Trend Micro
Westlake Ace Hardware
Yahoo

Branches

PJA Advertising + Marketing
214 Grant Ave Ste 450, San Francisco, CA 94108
Tel.: (415) 200-0800
Fax: (415) 200-0801
Web Site: www.agencypja.com

Employees: 8
Year Founded: 1988

Agency Specializes In: Business-To-Business, Health Care Services, High Technology

Phil Johnson *(CEO)*
Daniel Grace *(Mng Dir & Sr VP)*
Robert Davis *(Exec VP-Strategy)*
Anne Carney *(Producer-Digital)*
Beth Catto *(Acct Dir)*
Peggy Groppo *(Acct Dir-Media)*
Tammy Bondanza *(Dir-Media)*
Evan McDaniel *(Dir-Tech)*
Matt Dowling *(Assoc Dir-Integrated Media)*
Christina Inglese *(Acct Supvr)*

Accounts:
Brother International; Bridgewater, NJ (Agency of Record) All-in-Ones, Marketing, Media Strategy, Planning & Buying, On & Offline Advertising, Printers
Corning Life Sciences Campaign: "Every Lab Needs a Falcon", Digital
Limelight Networks, Inc.
Yahoo

Philip Johnson Associates
214 Grant Ave Ste 450, San Francisco, CA 94108-4628
Tel.: (415) 200-0800
Fax: (415) 200-0801
E-Mail: mlong@agencypja.com
Web Site: www.agencypja.com

Employees: 25

Hugh Kennedy *(Partner & Exec VP-Plng)*
Robert Davis *(Exec VP-Strategy)*
Daniel Grace *(Sr VP & Mng Dir-PJA West)*
Aaron DaSilva *(VP & Exec Dir-Creative)*
Matt Magee *(VP-Digital Strategy)*
Greg Straface *(VP-Bus Dev)*
Beth Catto *(Acct Dir)*
Tammy Bondanza *(Dir-Media)*
Leslie Simpson *(Dir-Talent & Community)*
Tessa Sandler *(Acct Supvr)*

Accounts:
Akamai
Chase
Cognizant
EMC
IBM
iCAD
Infor
Life Technologies Corporation Life Science Technologies
Juniper
LRN
Novell
PTC
SSA Global
TAC
Trendmicro
Yahoo

PK NETWORK COMMUNICATIONS
11 E 47th St 4th Fl, New York, NY 10017-7915
Tel.: (212) 888-4700
Fax: (212) 688-8832

E-Mail: pat@pknetwork.com
Web Site: www.pknetwork.com

E-Mail for Key Personnel:
President: pat@pknetwork.com
Creative Dir.: matt@pknetwork.com
Media Dir.: tara@pknetwork.com
Production Mgr.: maura@pknetwork.com

Employees: 12
Year Founded: 1989

Agency Specializes In: Advertising, Advertising Specialties, Brand Development & Integration, Broadcast, Business Publications, Business-To-Business, Cable T.V., Collateral, Communications, Consulting, Consumer Publications, Corporate Identity, Digital/Interactive, Entertainment, Event Planning & Marketing, Exhibit/Trade Shows, Graphic Design, High Technology, Information Technology, Internet/Web Design, Logo & Package Design, Media Buying Services, Merchandising, Multimedia, New Product Development, Newspaper, Newspapers & Magazines, Planning & Consultation, Print, Production, Public Relations, Publicity/Promotions, Radio, Restaurant, Sales Promotion, Sports Market, Strategic Planning/Research, Sweepstakes, T.V., Technical Advertising, Trade & Consumer Magazines

Approx. Annual Billings: $2,000,000

Patricia A. Kehoe *(Founder & Pres)*
Maura Kehoe *(VP)*
Tara Kehoe *(VP-Media)*
Matt Collins *(Dir-Creative)*

Accounts:
Bottlerocket
Cancer Research & Treatment Fund
ESPN
Expo TV
MediaCom Communication Corp.; 1999
Time Warner
YES Networks

PL&P ADVERTISING
200 NE 44th St, Fort Lauderdale, FL 33334-1442
Tel.: (954) 567-1455
Fax: (954) 567-1197
E-Mail: agency@plpadv.com
Web Site: www.plpadv.com

Employees: 6
Year Founded: 1974

National Agency Associations: ADFED

Agency Specializes In: Advertising, Advertising Specialties, Arts, Automotive, Aviation & Aerospace, Bilingual Market, Brand Development & Integration, Branded Entertainment, Broadcast, Business Publications, Business-To-Business, Cable T.V., Catalogs, Children's Market, Co-op Advertising, Collateral, Communications, Consulting, Consumer Marketing, Consumer Publications, Corporate Communications, Corporate Identity, Cosmetics, Custom Publishing, Direct Response Marketing, Direct-to-Consumer, E-Commerce, Education, Electronic Media, Entertainment, Environmental, Event Planning & Marketing, Exhibit/Trade Shows, Financial, Food Service, Government/Political, Graphic Design, Health Care Services, High Technology, Hispanic Market, Hospitality, In-Store Advertising, Industrial, Infomercials, Information Technology, Integrated Marketing, Internet/Web Design, Investor Relations, Leisure, Logo & Package Design, Magazines, Media Buying Services, Media Planning, Multicultural, Multimedia, New Product Development, Newspaper, Newspapers & Magazines, Out-of-Home Media, Outdoor, Over-50 Market, Package Design, Pharmaceutical, Planning & Consultation, Point of Purchase, Point of Sale, Print, Production, Production (Print), Public Relations, Publicity/Promotions, Radio, Real Estate, Recruitment, Restaurant, Retail, Sales Promotion, Seniors' Market, Strategic Planning/Research, T.V., Trade & Consumer Magazines, Transportation, Travel & Tourism, Web (Banner Ads, Pop-ups, etc.), Yellow Pages Advertising

Breakdown of Gross Billings by Media: Collateral: 20%; Logo & Package Design: 10%; Plng. & Consultation: 20%; Print: 25%; Pub. Rels.: 5%; Radio & T.V.: 10%; Trade Shows: 5%; Worldwide Web Sites: 5%

Alfred A. Padron *(Owner)*
Mercy Padron *(Mgr-Traffic)*

Accounts:
After School Programs, Inc.; Margate, FL Educational Childcare Programs for Elementary Schools; 2003
Broward Center for the Performing Arts; Fort Lauderdale, FL Theater; 2001
Broward Coalition on Aging; Fort Lauderdale, FL Services for the Elderly; 2008
Fenstersheib & Associates; Hallandale, FL Legal Services; 2006
First Choice; Hollywood, FL Employee Research & Screening Services; 2001
Global Debt Solutions; Boca Raton, FL Worldwide Debt Collection Services; 2002
Harmony Elder Services Inc.; Plantation, FL Elderly Care Services; 2003
Leadership Broward Foundation; Fort Lauderdale, FL Civic & Community Services; 2009
Mental Health Advocates; Boca Raton, FL Mental Health Services; 2008
Minto Communications;LLC
Motionpoint; Boca Raton, FL E-Commerce; 2000
Pelican Grand; Fort Lauderdale, FL Leisure Services; 2003
Penn Dutch Food Centers; Hollywood & Margate, FL Grocery Stores; 1996
The Rector Group; Fort Lauderdale, FL Business & Corporate Planning; 2002
Synergy Solutions; Southwest Ranches, FL Grant Writing; 2005
U.S. Record Search; Coral Springs, FL Research & Investigations; 1998
WhoCanISue.com; Boca Raton, FL Legal Help Information Service; 2009
World Fuel Services; Doral, FL Aviation & Marine Fuel Services; 2001

PL COMMUNICATIONS
417 Victor St, Scotch Plains, NJ 07076
Tel.: (908) 889-8884
Fax: (908) 889-8886
Toll Free: (800) 569-8882
E-Mail: paul@plcommunications.com
Web Site: www.plcommunications.com

Employees: 6

Agency Specializes In: Advertising, Collateral, Communications, Corporate Identity, Digital/Interactive, Event Planning & Marketing, Exhibit/Trade Shows, Internet/Web Design, Multimedia, Public Relations, Publicity/Promotions, Web (Banner Ads, Pop-ups, etc.)

Paul Lavenhar *(Principal)*
Mary Jean Murphy *(Dir-Mktg)*

Accounts:
Admiral Insurance
Alta Services
Capacity Coverage of NJ
Garden State Surgical Center
General Office Interiors
Selective Insurance

PLACE CREATIVE COMPANY
187 S Winooski Ave, Burlington, VT 05401
Tel.: (802) 660-2051
Web Site: www.placecreativecompany.com

Year Founded: 2001

Agency Specializes In: Advertising, Brand Development & Integration, Collateral, Internet/Web Design, Package Design

Keri Piatek *(Owner & Dir-Design)*
David Speidel *(Partner)*
Brianne Lucas *(Acct Dir)*
Ann Kiley *(Sr Designer)*
Nick Lamper *(Designer)*
Jordan Meserole *(Sr Designer)*
Michael Niggel *(Sr Designer)*

Accounts:
Hotel Vermont
Vermont Smoke & Cure

THE PLACEMAKING GROUP
505 14th St 5th Fl, Oakland, CA 94612
Tel.: (510) 835-7900
Fax: (510) 768-0044
E-Mail: info@placemakinggroup.com
Web Site: www.placemakinggroup.com

Employees: 12

Agency Specializes In: Advertising, Brand Development & Integration, Corporate Communications, Corporate Identity, Crisis Communications, Digital/Interactive, Direct Response Marketing, Direct-to-Consumer, Email, Event Planning & Marketing, Identity Marketing, Integrated Marketing, Internet/Web Design, Logo & Package Design, Media Relations, Media Training, Multimedia, Podcasting, Production (Ad, Film, Broadcast), Production (Print), Public Relations, Publicity/Promotions, Search Engine Optimization, Strategic Planning/Research, Viral/Buzz/Word of Mouth

Dennis Erokan *(Pres)*
Irvin Hamilton *(Sr VP)*
Barbara Irias *(VP)*
Jannah Lyon *(Dir-Creative)*
Dianne Newton-Shaw *(Acct Mgr)*
Miraim Schaffer *(Acct Mgr)*

Accounts:
1-800-Radiator
Alameda Landing
American Iron & Steel Institute (AISI)
Claremont Rug Company
Emeryville Redevelopment
FloorTec Inc.
HFS Consultants
Michael Coleman Film
Napa Downtown Association
Scott Cole & Associates
SportStars Magazine
Thornton Group
WebSat

PLAID SWAN
2728 Asbury Rd Cove Bldg Ste 650, Dubuque, IA 52001
Tel.: (563) 556-1633
Web Site: www.plaidswan.com

Agency Specializes In: Advertising, Internet/Web Design, Media Planning, Public Relations, Strategic Planning/Research

Vicki Dirksen *(Partner & Principal)*
Betsy McCloskey *(Principal)*

Accounts:
Council Bluffs Convention & Visitors Bureau
Eberhardt Villages Inc
Mystique Casino

PLAN A ADVERTISING

3722 Shipyard Blvd Ste C, Wilmington, NC 28403
Tel.: (910) 769-1730
Fax: (910) 769-1732
E-Mail: info@planaad.com
Web Site: www.planaad.com

Year Founded: 2013

Agency Specializes In: Advertising, Broadcast, Collateral, Digital/Interactive, Internet/Web Design, Logo & Package Design, Media Planning, Print, Radio, Social Media

Angi Israel *(Mng Partner)*
Max Gamble *(Creative Dir)*
Joel White *(Acct Mgr)*
Laura Kinkead *(Acct Mgr)*

Accounts:
Orange Leaf

PLAN B (THE AGENCY ALTERNATIVE)

116 W Illinois St 2W, Chicago, IL 60654
Tel.: (312) 222-0303
Fax: (312) 222-0305
Toll Free: (866) 317-5262
E-Mail: justask@thisisplanb.com
Web Site: www.thisisplanb.com

Employees: 20
Year Founded: 1998

National Agency Associations: AMA

Agency Specializes In: Advertising, Advertising Specialties, Automotive, Brand Development & Integration, Business Publications, Business-To-Business, Communications, Consumer Goods, Corporate Identity, Digital/Interactive, Direct Response Marketing, Direct-to-Consumer, Email, Food Service, Graphic Design, Health Care Services, Identity Marketing, In-Store Advertising, Integrated Marketing, Logo & Package Design, Men's Market, Multimedia, Paid Searches, Pharmaceutical, Point of Purchase, Print, Product Placement, Production (Print), Regional, Restaurant, Retail, Sales Promotion, Search Engine Optimization, Social Marketing/Nonprofit, Social Media, T.V.

Approx. Annual Billings: $14,000,000

Breakdown of Gross Billings by Media: Adv. Specialities: $500,000; Corp. Communications: $1,000,000; Event Mktg.: $250,000; Internet Adv.: $3,000,000; Logo & Package Design: $500,000; Other: $250,000; Print: $3,000,000; Strategic Planning/Research: $2,000,000; T.V.: $1,500,000; Worldwide Web Sites: $2,000,000

Ric Van Sickle *(Partner & COO)*
Clay Cooper *(Partner & Client Svcs Dir)*
Don Weaver *(Exec Dir-Creative)*
Joe Popa *(Grp Dir-Creative)*
Molly Gannon Yant *(Acct Dir)*
Terry Mertens *(Dir-Creative)*
Tom Millman *(Dir-Creative)*

Accounts:
Azteca Foods, Incorporated
Butterball, LLC New Product Development; 2006
Jaguar Land Rover North America CRM; 2010
Keiser Corporation (Advertising Agency of Record) Digital, Print, Social
Northern Trust Bank Interactive Branding; 2010
Papermate Pens Writing Utensils; 2009
New-TITLE Boxing Club
Virgin Healthcare Individual Healthcare Products, Virgin/Humana One
Volvo Cars of North America Campaign: "Truly Cool", Volvo XC60; 2008
Wilson Tennis Wilson Tennis Equipment

PLAN LEFT LLC

604 Gallatin Ave Ste 209, Nashville, TN 37206
Tel.: (615) 649-0690
Fax: (615) 649-0667
Web Site: www.planleft.com

Year Founded: 2012

Agency Specializes In: Advertising, Brand Development & Integration, Digital/Interactive, Graphic Design, Logo & Package Design, Media Buying Services, Print, Social Media

Matthew Smith *(Pres & CEO)*
Michael Bailey *(Dir-Creative)*
Katie Marcario *(Brand Mgr & Specialist-Social Media)*
Joshua Smith *(Mgr-Production)*

Accounts:
Hillhouse Naturals

PLANET CENTRAL

16740 Birkdale Commons Pkwy Ste 206, Huntersville, NC 28078
Tel.: (704) 875-9028
Fax: (704) 875-9763
E-Mail: barry.wilson@planetcentral.com
Web Site: www.planetcentral.com

Agency Specializes In: Advertising

Barry Wilson *(Pres & Partner)*
Dawn Dantzler *(Sr VP-Strategy)*
Jennifer Lawrence *(VP & Acct Dir)*
Melissa Ryder *(Sr Acct Exec)*
Addison Prophet *(Acct Exec)*
Jamie Brown *(Asst Acct Exec)*

Accounts:
The French Culinary Institute

Branch

Planet Central

9 S 5th St, Richmond, VA 23219
Tel.: (704) 875-9749
Fax: (804) 726-9438
E-Mail: terry.fink@planetcentral.com
Web Site: www.planetcentral.com

Employees: 25
Year Founded: 1999

Agency Specializes In: Above-the-Line, Advertising, Below-the-Line, Broadcast, Business Publications, Cable T.V., Collateral, Consumer Publications, Digital/Interactive, Direct Response Marketing, Electronic Media, Email, Guerilla Marketing, In-Store Advertising, Local Marketing, Magazines, Mobile Marketing, Multimedia, Newspapers & Magazines, Out-of-Home Media, Outdoor, Paid Searches, Point of Purchase, Point of Sale, Print, Production, Production (Print), Promotions, Radio, Search Engine Optimization, Social Media, Sponsorship, Sweepstakes, T.V., Trade & Consumer Magazines, Web (Banner Ads, Pop-ups, etc.)

Barry Wilson *(Pres)*
Amanda Vandenbroek *(VP & Acct Supvr)*
Lauren Chavis *(VP-Media)*
John Hoar *(VP-Creative)*
Deirdre Hughes *(VP-Fin)*
Kelly Thornton *(VP-Digital Design)*
Mandy Thornton *(VP-Digital Design)*
Julie Maurer *(Asst Media Buyer)*

Accounts:
Atley Pharmaceuticals
Dominion Resources
New-ES Foods Pre-Packaged Kids Meals; 2010
New-Gold's Gym Fitness Centers; 2013
New-Park Sterling Bank Financial Services; 2012
New-Portrait Innovations Retail Portrait Studios; 2002
Raycom Sports
New-Tilson Home Corp. New Home Construction; 2000
Uno Chicago Grill
Wilmington Trust

PLANET PROPAGANDA, INC.

605 Williamson St, Madison, WI 53703
Tel.: (608) 256-0000
Fax: (608) 256-1975
E-Mail: info@planetpropaganda.com
Web Site: www.planetpropaganda.com

Employees: 25
Year Founded: 1989

Agency Specializes In: Advertising, Communications, Digital/Interactive, Graphic Design, Media Relations, Print

Revenue: $1,700,000

Ben Hirby *(Partner & Dir-Digital Creative)*
Kevin Longino *(Dir-Art)*
Brian Hucek *(Assoc Dir-Creative & Writer)*
Andrea Slotten *(Mgr-Studio)*
Jeremy Cesarec *(Strategist-Digital Mktg)*
Brandi Duncan *(Designer-Production)*
Erin Fuller *(Sr Designer)*
Katie Garth *(Designer)*
Sam West *(Assoc Acct Dir)*

Accounts:
Grammicci Spring
Organic Valley
Replogle Globes Website

PLANIT

500 E Pratt St 10th Fl, Baltimore, MD 21202
Tel.: (410) 962-8500
Fax: (410) 962-8508
E-Mail: info@planitagency.com
Web Site: www.planitagency.com

Employees: 40

Agency Specializes In: Advertising, Public Relations, Sponsorship

Edward E. Callahan *(Co-Founder & Strategist-Creative)*
Jack Spaulding *(Exec Dir-Strategic Plng)*
Andy Abbot *(Sr Producer-Digital)*
Maxwell Connors *(Assoc Producer-Digital)*
Rosie Riashy *(Producer-Digital)*
Brenda Showell *(Acct Dir)*
Rich Fulks *(Dir-Ops)*
Joe Glorioso *(Dir-Art)*
Trish McClean *(Dir-Acct Plng)*
Sarah Quackenbush *(Dir-Client Engagement)*
Rich Reiter *(Dir-Creative)*
Phil Reisinger *(Assoc Dir-Creative)*
Kristin Schields *(Acct Supvr)*
Kacey Bidnick *(Sr Acct Exec)*
Mary Anderson *(Specialist-Digital Media)*
Sarah Cannon *(Acct Exec)*
Scott LaRue *(Acct Exec)*
Taylor Callinan *(Designer-Production)*
Jeff Long *(Acct Planner)*

Cody Davidow *(Assoc Acct Exec)*

Accounts:
Advertising Association of Baltimore AIGA
AGCO
The AMES Companies, Inc (Agency of Record) Build Awareness, Digital Media, Integrated Marketing, Public Relations, Social Media, TV
New-Association of Pool & Spa Professionals (Agency of Record) Campaign: "Escape", Consumer Awareness, Consumer Campaign, Digital Media, Marketing, Microsite, Print Advertisements, Public Relations
Baltimore Area Acura Dealers Association Tier 2 Strategic Marketing
Baltimore Office of Promotion & The Arts
Barclays Bank
Chevy Chase Bank
CitiFinancial
CollabraSpace
DeWALT
DICK'S Sporting Goods
FILA
Island Def Jam Records
M-Edge Accessories
Marriott International
Maryland Automobile Insurance Fund
McCormick Foods
Merritt Properties Interactive, Public Relations; 2008
Remedi SeniorCare Name Change/Website
Royal Building Products' Exteriors & Distribution division
Susan G. Komen Maryland Campaign: "Onestepcloser", Digital Advertising, Public Relations, Race for the Cure, Radio, Social Media, Strategy, TV, Theme, Website
Under Armour
Universal Music Group
Venable LLP
XL Health

PLASTIC MOBILE
(Acquired by Havas Worldwide)

PLASTIC MOBILE
171 E Liberty St Ste 204, Toronto, ON M6K 3P6 Canada
Tel.: (416) 538-8880
E-Mail: contact@plasticmobile.com
Web Site: www.plasticmobile.com

Year Founded: 2007

Agency Specializes In: Advertising, Mobile Marketing, Social Media, Technical Advertising

Melody Adhami *(Pres & COO)*
Maggie Adhami-Boynton *(VP-Ops)*
Sadaf Mohammad *(Mgr-HR)*
Nedame Hanson *(Coord-HR)*

Accounts:
Air Miles Air Miles Goes The Extra Mile

PLATFORM MEDIA GROUP
1111 NOrth Las Palmas Ave, Los Angeles, CA 90038
Tel.: (323) 337-9042
E-Mail: heshelman@platformgrp.com
Web Site: www.platformgrp.com

Employees: 3
Year Founded: 2006

Agency Specializes In: Advertising

Margot Lewis *(Pres & Dir-Creative)*
Henry Eshelman *(Mng Dir)*

Accounts:
Marriott International, Inc. Hospitality Services; 2014

PLATTFORM ADVERTISING
(Name Changed to Keypath Education)

PLATYPUS ADVERTISING + DESIGN
N29 W23810 Woodgate Ct W Ste 100, Pewaukee, WI 53072
Tel.: (262) 522-8181
Fax: (262) 522-8180
E-Mail: dan@platypus-ad.com
Web Site: www.platypus-ad.com

Employees: 17
Year Founded: 1987

Agency Specializes In: Automotive, Brand Development & Integration, Broadcast, Business-To-Business, Collateral, Corporate Identity, Direct Response Marketing, Exhibit/Trade Shows, Graphic Design, Health Care Services, Industrial, Internet/Web Design, Media Buying Services, Outdoor, Print, Production, Radio, Retail, Sports Market, Strategic Planning/Research, T.V., Travel & Tourism

Approx. Annual Billings: $18,000,000

Dan Trzinski *(Pres)*
Mary Adamczak *(Sr Dir-Art)*
Tim Chiappetta *(Sr Dir-Art-Motion Graphics)*
Walter Grace *(Sr Dir-Art)*
Martin Defatte *(Dir-Web Dev)*
Gary Haas *(Assoc Partner & Dir-Creative)*
Kathy Sorcan *(Dir-Media)*
Nancy Wilkes *(Dir-PR)*

Accounts:
A&A Manufacturing Cable & Hose Carriers & Bellows; 2001
Noah's Ark
Pneumatech/ConservAir Compressed Air Equipment; 1997
WISN Television Station Promotion; 1988
Zebra Technologies; 2005

PLAY ADVERTISING
1455 Lakeshore Rd Ste 208 S, Burlington, ON L7S 2J1 Canada
Tel.: (905) 631-8299
Fax: (905) 631-8335
Toll Free: (800) 360-2355
E-Mail: info@playadvertising.com
Web Site: www.playadvertising.com

Employees: 10
Year Founded: 1997

Agency Specializes In: Advertising

Brian Torsney *(Pres)*
Lee Field *(Grp Acct Dir)*
Neil Woodley *(Creative Dir)*
Jean Katchanoski *(Dir-Production)*
Donna Sampson *(Specialist-Media)*
Carm Cicconi *(Designer)*
Susan Elsley *(Sr Writer)*

Accounts:
Dundas Valley Golf Club
FirstOntario Credit Union
Mackesy Smye Lawyers

PLAYGROUND GROUP INC
18 Bridge St Ste 2D, Brooklyn, NY 11201
Tel.: (718) 797-9529
E-Mail: info@playgroundgroup.com
Web Site: www.playgroundgroup.com

Employees: 2

Agency Specializes In: Advertising, Brand Development & Integration, Content, Corporate Identity, Email, Game Integration, Internet/Web Design, Multimedia, Package Design, Point of Purchase

Noah Gaynin *(CEO & Dir-Creative)*

Accounts:
24 Hour Fitness
The Academy of Television Arts & Sciences Entertainment Services
AcroSports
American Land Conservancy
AXN
Cazabba Marketing
Cleaire
Devious Media
GameTrust
Katazo
Timbuk 2

PLAYWIRE MEDIA
(Formerly Intergi)
1000 E Hillsboro Blvd Ste 201, Deerfield Beach, FL 33441
Tel.: (954) 418-0779
Fax: (954) 252-2561
Web Site: playwiremedia.com/

Employees: 20
Year Founded: 2007

Agency Specializes In: Advertising, Entertainment, Game Integration, Publishing, Web (Banner Ads, Pop-ups, etc.)

Steven Berger *(Pres)*
Jayson Dubin *(CEO)*
Tanya Brown *(VP-Global Revenue)*
Julia Loranger *(Sls Dir-West Coast)*
Kaci Sanchez *(Mgr-Accts Receivable & Collections)*
Caroline Anderson *(Coord-Publr Rels)*
Christina Vosilla *(Coord-Publr Rels)*

Accounts:
Sony Online Entertainment Online Entertainment Services
World Of Warcraft

PLETH
2010 Reynolds St, Batesville, AR 72501
Tel.: (888) 276-0848
Web Site: www.pleth.com

Year Founded: 2004

Agency Specializes In: Advertising, Brand Development & Integration, Digital/Interactive, Graphic Design, Internet/Web Design, Media Buying Services, Media Planning, Print, Social Media, Strategic Planning/Research

Gregory Smart *(Owner)*
Stephen Smart *(Co-Owner)*

Accounts:
3D Precision Enterprises
Davis Dubose Knight Forestry & Real Estate
Natalies Cafe
Volt Industrial Plastics, Inc.
Wilson Gardens

PLONTA CREATIVE, LLC
255 E Fireweed Ln Ste 109, Anchorage, AK 99503
Tel.: (907) 263-9327
Web Site: www.plontacreative.com

Year Founded: 2011

Agency Specializes In: Advertising, Event Planning & Marketing, Internet/Web Design, Social Media

Shannon Plonta-Reeves *(CEO)*

Accounts:
Skinny Raven Sports

PLOWSHARE GROUP, INC.
One Dock St, Stamford, CT 6902
Tel.: (203) 425-3949
Fax: (203) 425-3950
Web Site: www.plowsharegroup.com

Year Founded: 1994

Agency Specializes In: Advertising, Broadcast, Logo & Package Design, Media Buying Services, Media Planning, Print, Radio, T.V.

Jeff Boal *(Founder & Pres)*
Tom Derreaux *(Sr VP-Campaign Mgmt & Media Monitoring)*
Mark Pajewski *(VP & Dir-Media)*
Wendy Moniz *(VP-Campaign Mgmt & Bus Dev)*
Karl Maruyama *(Sr Dir-Art)*
Lisa Silva *(Dir-Art & Graphic Designer)*
Joe Piazza *(Dir-Art)*
Annmarie O'Malley *(Office Mgr)*
Catherine Jones *(Mgr-Fin & Acct Exec)*
Katie Kellogg *(Sr Campaign Mgr)*

PLUME21
511 W Mercer Pl, Seattle, WA 98119
Tel.: (206) 805-8821
Web Site: www.plume21.com

Year Founded: 2009

Agency Specializes In: Advertising, Brand Development & Integration, Communications, Digital/Interactive, Environmental, Graphic Design, Media Relations, Public Relations, Social Media, Strategic Planning/Research

Thomas Lamprecht *(Chief Creative Officer)*
Kristina Muller-Eberhard *(Exec Dir-Creative)*

Accounts:
T-Mobile US Telecommunication Services

PLUS
162 W 21 St 4th Fl, New York, NY 10011
Tel.: (212) 473-3800
Web Site: www.weareplus.com

Employees: 20
Year Founded: 2001

Agency Specializes In: Above-the-Line, Below-the-Line, Branded Entertainment, Digital/Interactive, In-Store Advertising, Mobile Marketing, Production, Social Media, T.V., Web (Banner Ads, Pop-ups, etc.)

Jeremy Hollister *(Co-Founder)*
Judy Wellfare *(Co-Founder)*
Amy Hollis *(Producer-Acct Svcs)*

Accounts:
Bastille 1789 Campaign: "A Strange Adventure"
Kiehl's
MAC Cosmetics MAC
Starwood Hotels & Resorts Worldwide, Inc. "Keyless Key", SPG, St Regis, Starwood; 2011

PLUS ULTRA ADVERTISING
355 E Manchester Blvdl, Inglewood, CA 90301
Tel.: (310) 672-7587
E-Mail: info@pultrae.com
Web Site: www.pultrae.com

Employees: 8
Year Founded: 2015

Agency Specializes In: Cable T.V., Digital/Interactive, Guerilla Marketing, Local Marketing, Production, Social Media, T.V., Telemarketing, Web (Banner Ads, Pop-ups, etc.)

Lakpathy Wijesekara *(Partner)*

Accounts:
New-Boyd Funeral Homes; 2015
New-Indo Hair Human Hair Wigs; 2015

PM DIGITAL
5 Hanover Sq, New York, NY 10004
Tel.: (212) 387-0300
Fax: (212) 387-7647
Toll Free: (800) 254-0330
Web Site: www.pmdigital.com

Employees: 285
Year Founded: 2001

Agency Specializes In: Advertising, Affiliate Marketing, Digital/Interactive, Direct Response Marketing, Email, Local Marketing, Mobile Marketing, Paid Searches, Promotions, Search Engine Optimization, Social Media, Sweepstakes, Web (Banner Ads, Pop-ups, etc.)

Roy DeYoung *(Sr VP-Creative Strategy)*
Valerie Davis *(VP)*
Mary Beth Keetly *(VP-Mktg)*
Tim Lippa *(VP-Paid Digital Media)*
Josh Grashin *(Sr Dir)*
Amy Barnes *(Client Svcs Dir)*
Allie Peay *(Client Svcs Dir)*
Thomas Burke *(Dir-Search Strategy)*
Lauren Edmonds *(Dir-Search Engine Mktg)*
Tiffany Goik *(Dir-Mktg)*
John Lynch *(Dir-Bus Dev)*
Megan O'Connor *(Dir-Paid Media)*
Felicia Passaro *(Dir)*
Stephen Reinfurt *(Dir-Art)*
Marc Friedman *(Sr Acct Mgr)*
Laurel Gillespie *(Sr Acct Mgr)*

Accounts:
Burt's Bees Inc.
Keurig, Inc.
Martha Stewart Living Omnimedia, Inc.
The North Face, Inc.
Steven Madden Ltd
Travelzoo Inc

PM PUBLICIDAD
1776 Peachtree St NW, Atlanta, GA 30309
Tel.: (404) 870-0099
Fax: (404) 870-0321
E-Mail: eperez@pmpublicidad.com
Web Site: www.pm3.agency

Employees: 26
Year Founded: 2003

National Agency Associations: AHAA

Agency Specializes In: Advertising, Automotive, Bilingual Market, Brand Development & Integration, Cable T.V., Consulting, Consumer Goods, Direct Response Marketing, Experience Design, Hispanic Market, International, Mobile Marketing, Multicultural, New Product Development, Podcasting, Point of Sale, Promotions, Sponsorship, Sports Market, Strategic Planning/Research, Viral/Buzz/Word of Mouth

Approx. Annual Billings: $15,000,000

Breakdown of Gross Billings by Media: Adv. Specialities: $3,000,000; D.M.: $1,000,000; Event Mktg.: $2,500,000; Fees: $1,500,000; Plng. & Consultation: $500,000; Radio: $1,000,000; Sports Mktg.: $2,000,000; T.V.: $3,500,000

Eduardo Perez *(Pres)*
Myrna DeJesus *(Sr VP-Plng)*
Patricia Ramon *(Controller)*
Hernan Feuermann *(Exec Creative Dir)*
Freddy Fajardo *(Sr Dir-Art)*
Adrian Cano *(Creative Dir)*

Accounts:
Cox Communications; Atlanta, GA Cable TV, Digital Phone Services, High Speed Internet; 2007
Cox Communications; Las Vegas, NV Cable TV, Digital Phone Services, High Speed Internet; 2011
Cox Communications; Phoenix, AZ Cable TV, Digital Phone Services, High Speed Internet; 2008
Cox Communications; San Diego, CA Cable TV, Digital Phone Services, High Speed Internet; 2008
Getloaded; Richmond, VA Online Freight Matching Service; 2011
NAPA Auto Parts; Atlanta, GA Aftermarket Automotive Parts & Accessories
NAPA Auto Parts; Atlanta, GA Automotive Aftermarket Parts & Accessories; 2003

PMA INC.
550 S Oleander Dr, Palm Springs, CA 92264
Tel.: (760) 778-1313
Web Site: www.pmaadvertising.com

Agency Specializes In: Advertising, Digital/Interactive, Event Planning & Marketing, Print, Public Relations, Social Media

Paul Mahoney *(Founder & CEO)*
Tina Arnot *(Dir-Art)*

Accounts:
New-Crystal Ridge

PMG WORLDWIDE, LLC
2821 W 7th St 270, Fort Worth, TX 76107
Tel.: (817) 420-9970
E-Mail: info@pmg.com
Web Site: www.pmg.com

Agency Specializes In: Advertising, Brand Development & Integration, Search Engine Optimization, Social Media, Sponsorship

George Popstefanov *(Founder & Pres)*
Price Glomski *(Exec VP-Digital Strategy)*
Nick Drabicky *(Head-Strategy)*
David Gong *(Dir-Strategic Accts)*
Hayley Rhodes *(Designer)*

Accounts:
New-Beats Electronics LLC

PMS ADVERTISING, INC.
2429 Randall Rd, Carpentersville, IL 60110
Tel.: (847) 426-6900
Web Site: www.pmsadv.com

Agency Specializes In: Advertising, Graphic Design, Media Planning, Public Relations, Radio

Pat Szpekowski *(Pres)*
Dan Szpekowski *(VP)*

Accounts:

EAC Shuttle

PNEUMA33
61533 American Loop Ste 12, Bend, OR 97702
Tel.: (888) 608-3878
E-Mail: connect@pneuma33.com
Web Site: www.pneuma33.com

Year Founded: 2011

Agency Specializes In: Advertising, Brand Development & Integration, Graphic Design, Internet/Web Design, Print

James Kramer *(Principal & Dir-Strategy)*
Anna Kramer *(VP & Creative Dir)*
Nathan Wright *(Art Dir-Creative)*
Anne-Marie Daggett *(Dir-Mktg)*

Accounts:
Summers Wood Floor Co

POCKET HERCULES
510 1st Ave N Ste 210, Minneapolis, MN 55403
Tel.: (612) 435-8313
Fax: (612) 435-8318
E-Mail: jack@pockethercules.com
Web Site: www.pockethercules.com

Employees: 16

Agency Specializes In: Brand Development & Integration

Tom Camp *(Co-Founder)*
Jason Smith *(Partner)*
Jack Supple *(Chief Creative Officer)*
Stephen Dupont *(VP-PR & Content Mktg)*
Aaron Emery *(Dir-Art & Designer)*
Curtis Aj Ward *(Dir-Art)*
Chue Zeng Yang *(Dir-Art)*
Amy Oberbroeckling *(Specialist-PR)*

Accounts:
Key Surgical
Lakemaid Beer
Pearl Izumi
The Prairie Club
Rapala
Shimano Fishing
Sufix
Tiny Footprint Coffee
Vedalo HD

THE POD ADVERTISING
502 E Pk Ave, Tallahassee, FL 32301
Tel.: (850) 597-8374
E-Mail:
ideasbloomcreative@thepodadvertising.com
Web Site: www.thepodadvertising.com

Year Founded: 2011

Agency Specializes In: Advertising, Brand Development & Integration, Event Planning & Marketing, Graphic Design, Internet/Web Design, Media Buying Services, Print, Social Media

Samantha Strickland *(CEO)*
Brian Ramos *(CMO & Principal)*
Kristin Bass-Petersen *(Dir-Production)*
Jeremy Lawrence *(Sr Graphic Designer)*

Accounts:
TLFCU Youth Accounts
United Solutions Company

THE PODESTA GROUP
1001 G St NW Ste 900 E, Washington, DC 20001
Tel.: (202) 393-1010
Fax: (202) 393-5510
E-Mail: mail@podesta.com
Web Site: www.podesta.com

Employees: 75
Year Founded: 1988

Agency Specializes In: Crisis Communications, Government/Political, Media Relations, Media Training, Public Relations

Kimberley Fritts *(CEO)*
Randall Gerard *(Principal)*
Izzy Klein *(Principal)*
Lauren Maddox *(Principal)*
Mike Quaranta *(Principal)*
Stephen Rademaker *(Principal)*
Will Bohlen *(VP)*
Rachelle Johnson *(VP)*
Jordan Valdes *(VP)*
Heather Feinstein *(Dir-Special Projects)*

Accounts:
AMBER Ready Inc Public Safety Services
Coalition For Competitive Insurance Rates Insurance Services
Hawker Britton
Kreab Gavin Anderson
PLM Group

POINT A MEDIA INC.
2908 Westward Dr, Nacogdoches, TX 75964
Tel.: (936) 568-9200
Fax: (936) 568-9230
Web Site: www.pointamedia.com

Agency Specializes In: Advertising, Brand Development & Integration, Internet/Web Design, Media Planning, Outdoor, Print, Radio, Social Media, T.V.

Angela Wiederhold *(Owner)*
Dana Britton *(Designer)*

Accounts:
Axley & Rode LLP
Silver Spring
Wingate Architectural Millwork, Co.

POINT B
1001 Euclid Ave, Atlanta, GA 30307
Tel.: (404) 888-1700
Fax: (404) 888-1704
E-Mail: babuka@pointbagency.com
Web Site: www.pointbagency.com

Employees: 12
Year Founded: 1988

Agency Specializes In: Advertising, Broadcast, Collateral, Communications, Corporate Communications, Digital/Interactive, Email, Identity Marketing, Local Marketing, Media Relations, Multimedia, Outdoor, Print, Product Placement, Promotions, Public Relations, Publishing, Radio, Recruitment, Strategic Planning/Research, T.V.

Brian Armstrong *(Mng Dir)*
Annalisa Johnson *(Controller-Firmwide)*
Kristen Lenci *(Sr Dir)*
Ben Burke *(Dir-Practice & Retail)*
Leslie Gilbert *(Dir-Talent Acq)*
Jeff Hazeltine *(Dir-Fin)*
Maridelle Morrison *(Dir-Natl Recruiting)*

Accounts:
Best Gloves
Jenkins Clinic

POINT B COMMUNICATIONS
750 N Orleans St Ste 550, Chicago, IL 60654-5040
Tel.: (312) 867-7750
Fax: (312) 867-7751
E-Mail: info@pointbcommunications.com
Web Site: www.pointbcommunications.com

E-Mail for Key Personnel:
President: rgrusin@pointbcommunications.com
Media Dir.: jkallen@pointbcommunications.com
Production Mgr.:
clahucik@pointbcommunications.com

Employees: 15
Year Founded: 1974

Agency Specializes In: Advertising, Arts, Business-To-Business, Catalogs, Co-op Advertising, Collateral, Communications, Consumer Goods, Corporate Identity, Digital/Interactive, Direct-to-Consumer, Email, Entertainment, Exhibit/Trade Shows, Gay & Lesbian Market, Graphic Design, Hospitality, Household Goods, Identity Marketing, Industrial, Integrated Marketing, Internet/Web Design, Leisure, Logo & Package Design, Luxury Products, Media Buying Services, Media Planning, Multimedia, New Product Development, Newspaper, Newspapers & Magazines, Out-of-Home Media, Outdoor, Package Design, Point of Purchase, Print, Production, Production (Ad, Film, Broadcast), Production (Print), Radio, Regional, Restaurant, Social Marketing/Nonprofit, Strategic Planning/Research, Travel & Tourism

Approx. Annual Billings: $18,000,000

Breakdown of Gross Billings by Media: Cable T.V.: 1%; Collateral: 20%; D.M.: 20%; In-Store Adv.: 1%; Internet Adv.: 15%; Logo & Package Design: 5%; Mags.: 20%; Mdsg./POP: 1%; Newsp.: 5%; Outdoor: 3%; Point of Sale: 1%; Radio: 5%; Sls. Promo.: 3%

Robert Grusin *(Pres)*
Jessica Stone-Grusin *(VP)*
Tim Grob *(Controller)*
Carol Holderfield *(Sr Dir-Art)*
Cary Lahucik *(Dir-Ops)*
John Sieruta *(Assoc Dir-Creative)*

Accounts:
The Drake Hotel; Chicago, IL
Grand Traverse Resort & Spa; Traverse City, MI
Home Depot; Atlanta, GA
Hotel Orrington; Evanston, IL
Lake Geneva Convention and Visitors Bureau
Nara Restaurant; Chicago, IL
Noble Fool Theatricals; Saint Charles, IL
Pacifica Hotels; Santa Barbara, CA
Pheasant Run Resort; Saint Charles, IL
Scudder Financial
Sonesta Hotels & Resorts; Boston, MA
Umstead Resort; NC
Whirlyball; IL

THE POINT GROUP
5949 Sherry Ln Ste 1800, Dallas, TX 75225-8084
Tel.: (214) 378-7970
Fax: (214) 378-7967
E-Mail: mail@thepointgroup.com
Web Site: www.thepointgroup.com

Employees: 40
Year Founded: 1996

Agency Specializes In: Advertising, Brand Development & Integration, Business-To-Business, Collateral, Communications, Consulting, Corporate Identity, Direct Response Marketing, Electronic Media, Exhibit/Trade Shows, Financial, Food Service, Graphic Design, High Technology, Information Technology, Internet/Web Design, Media Buying Services, Newspaper, Newspapers & Magazines, Outdoor, Planning & Consultation,

Point of Purchase, Print, Production, Public Relations, Publicity/Promotions, Real Estate, Restaurant, Retail, Strategic Planning/Research, T.V., Trade & Consumer Magazines

Approx. Annual Billings: $69,000,000 Capitalized

David Kniffen *(Chm & CEO)*
Brenda Hurtado *(Pres & COO)*
Martha Cook *(VP)*
Malcolm Miller *(VP)*
Kimberly Stoilis *(VP)*
Cassie Bunch *(Dir-Digital & Traditional Media)*
Mitch Friedman *(Dir-Creative)*
Billy Hayes *(Dir-IT)*
Seth Sekhon *(Asst Acct Exec)*

Accounts:
St Luke's Hospitals

Branch

The Point Group
1990 Post Oak Blvd Ste 240, Houston, TX 77056
Tel.: (713) 622-7174
Fax: (713) 622-0579
E-Mail: marketing@thepointgroup.com
Web Site: www.thepointgroup.com

Employees: 7

David Kniffen *(Chm & CEO)*
Brenda Hurtado *(Pres & COO)*
Donna Lassen *(CFO)*
Kimberly Stoilis *(VP)*
Scott Tims *(Acct Supvr)*

Accounts:
Accure
Accuro Healthcare Solutions
The Jones Company
Snelling
Victory Park
W Hotels & Residences

POINT TO POINT INC.
23240 Chagrin Blvd Ste 200, Beachwood, OH 44122
Tel.: (216) 831-4421
Fax: (216) 831-3099
E-Mail: mgoren@pointtopoint.com
Web Site: www.pointtopoint.com

E-Mail for Key Personnel:
President: mgoren@p2pcom.com

Employees: 21
Year Founded: 1981

Agency Specializes In: Above-the-Line, Advertising, Affluent Market, Below-the-Line, Brand Development & Integration, Broadcast, Business Publications, Business-To-Business, Collateral, Communications, Consulting, Consumer Marketing, Corporate Communications, Corporate Identity, Digital/Interactive, Direct Response Marketing, E-Commerce, Electronic Media, Game Integration, Graphic Design, Guerilla Marketing, Health Care Services, High Technology, Hospitality, Industrial, Integrated Marketing, International, Internet/Web Design, Local Marketing, Logo & Package Design, Market Research, Media Buying Services, Media Planning, Medical Products, Merchandising, Mobile Marketing, Newspaper, Outdoor, Over-50 Market, Paid Searches, Planning & Consultation, Print, Publicity/Promotions, Radio, Retail, Seniors' Market, Sponsorship, Strategic Planning/Research, T.V., Technical Advertising, Trade & Consumer Magazines, Web (Banner Ads, Pop-ups, etc.)

Approx. Annual Billings: $15,000,000

Mark Goren *(CEO)*
Greg Thomas *(Chief Creative Officer)*
Jessica Endress *(VP & Acct Dir)*
Jason Hoehnen *(VP & Acct Dir)*
Mark Cerame *(VP-Engagement & Connection Strategy)*
Jennifer Ristic *(VP-PR & Social Media)*
Reggie Tabora *(Dir-Interactive Creative)*
Jason Craig *(Acct Mgr)*
Kate Kinison *(Sr Media Planner & Buyer)*

Accounts:
American Architectural Manufacturers Association; Schaumburg, IL
Schindler Elevator
Sherwin-Williams

POINTER ADVERTISING LLC
204 Longneedle Ct, Raleigh, NC 27603
Tel.: (919) 250-8321
Fax: (919) 661-8065
Web Site: www.pointeradvertising.com

Year Founded: 2006

Agency Specializes In: Advertising, Digital/Interactive, Graphic Design, Internet/Web Design, Logo & Package Design, Print, Public Relations, Search Engine Optimization, Social Media

Lindsat Michael *(Owner)*

Accounts:
Artsplosure
Baubles-n-Bling
Bell Howell
Casteel Chiropractic
ConsumerDNA

POINTER PR LLC
1026 1st Ave W, Seattle, WA 98119
Tel.: (206) 390-0204
E-Mail: mark@pointerpr.com
Web Site: www.pointerpr.com

Employees: 1

Agency Specializes In: Communications, Media Relations, Media Training, Planning & Consultation, Public Relations

Mark S. Peterson *(Principal)*

Accounts:
Marchex
Poptent
Swim Across America
Wave Broadband

POINTROLL INC.
3200 Horizon Dr Ste 120, King of Prussia, PA 19406-2680
Tel.: (800) 203-6956
Fax: (267) 285-1141
Toll Free: (800) 203-6956
E-Mail: sales@pointroll.com
Web Site: www.pointroll.com

Employees: 350
Year Founded: 2000

Agency Specializes In: Digital/Interactive, Internet/Web Design

Mario Diez *(CEO)*
Hal Trencher *(Sr VP-Sls)*
Frank Petersen *(VP-HR)*
Kerry Sacks *(Sr Dir-Acct Mgmt)*
Emily Wilkes *(Brand Mktg Mgr)*
Maura P. Dailey *(Dir-Brand Mktg)*
Scott Reynolds *(Dir-Product Mgmt)*
Kyle Garis *(Sr Project Mgr-Digital-Cofactor)*
Jennifer Hunsicker *(Project Mgr-Digital)*
William Orthman *(Project Mgr-Digital)*
Eric DiMatteo *(Assoc Mgr-Digital Project)*
Christopher Hawkins *(Assoc Mgr-Digital Project)*

Accounts:
1-800 Communications
1-800-Contacts
1-800-Mattress
20th Century Fox
20th Century Fox Home Entertainment, Inc.; 2008
A&E
A1 Wireless
ABC
Absolut
Active Buddy
Adidas
Affinity
AIG
ACE Aviation Holdings Inc.
Air Jamaica
Airline Network
Pernod Ricard UK
Allstate
Always There
American Airlines
American Express
AmeriTrade
Amerix
Amgen
AstraZeneca
AT&T Communications Corp.
Sanofi-Aventis Research & Development
Avis
Banco do Brasil
Bank of America
Bankrate
BBC
Bell South
Bermuda Tourism
Biogen
Black & Decker
Blockbuster
BlueCross
Borland
Bosch
Bose
BreastCancer.Org
Bristol Myers Squibb
British Airways
Broadcom
Buell Motorcycles
Business Filings
Business Week
CableVision
Cadence
Campbell's
Canon
Car & Driver
Carfax
Cartoon Network
Central TAFE
Cisco
Citibank
CitiGroup
Coca-Cola Refreshments USA, Inc.
Colgate Palmolive
Combe
Comcast
Comedy Central
Computers4Sure
Conoco
Coors Brewing Company
Covers.com
Cyber World Group
Cypress
DAC
Chrysler LLC
Datek
David's Bridal
DeBeers

Dell
Department of Engraving
Discount Tire
Discover
Disney
Dow Corning
Dr Pepper
East West Mortgage
Eastpointe Mortgage
Energizer
Entrust
Ernst & Young
Expedia
Experian
Federated Stores
Fiat
Fidelity Investments
FindLaw
Florist.com
Food Network
Ford Motor Company
Forest Labs
Fox Broadcasting
Fox Films
FTD
Fujifilm
FX Networks
Gallup Interactive
Garbko
Gateway
Genentech
General Mills
General Motors
Gevalia
Gillette
GlaxoSmithKline
GOL Transportes
GPS Store
H&R Block
Haagen-Dazs
Hallmark
Harman Kardon
Harrahs
Heavenly Treasures
Heineken
Hertz
HGTV
Home Depot
Honda
HotJobs
HP-Compaq
HSBC
Hyatt
Hyundai
IBM
Icon Fitness
Ikea
Illinois Tourism
In Demand
Infiniti
ING Direct
Intel
Intercontinental Hotels
Ireland
Jaguar
Johnson & Johnson
JPMorgan Chase
Kaiser Permanente
Keebler
Kelloggs
Kia Motors
King World
Knex
KPMG
Kraft
LanChile
Lancome
Last Minute Travel
Lexus
Lifetime TV
Lincoln
LL Bean
Lockheed Martin
LoJack
L'Oreal
Lowes
Majesco
Marriott
Massachusetts Tourism
Mazda
Mercedes-Benz
Merck
Mercury
Merrill Lynch
Metro Dealers
MGM
Microsoft
Miller Brewing Co.
Miramax Films
Moore Business School
Mortgage America
Motive Product Group
Nabisco
Nacmias Brothers
Nestle
NetLedger
New Line Cinema
NextCard
Nike
Nissan
Nortel
Novell
ONDCP
One Great Family
Ontario Tourism
Oracle
Orbitz Worldwide, Inc.
Overstock
Overture
Panasonic
Paper Mate
Paramount Pictures
Paris Hotel
PBS
Pepperidge Farm
Pepsi
Pfizer
Pharmacia
Philadelphia Tourism
Phillip Morris
The Picture People
Pier One
Pizza Hut
Polaroid
Porsche
Pressplay
Procrit
Procter & Gamble
Proflowers.com
Progressive
Puerto Rico Government
Purina
QDS
Quaker
Qwest
R&K
Radisson
Rayovac
Raytheon
RBC Mortgage
RCN
River Bell
Roche
Rogers Wireless
Royal Caribbean
SBC
Schering Plough
Singapore Airlines
Sirius XM Radio Inc.
Morgan Stanley Smith Barney LLC
Snapple
Solage
Sonic Restaurants
Sony
Southwest Airlines
SpeedTV
Sport & Health Clubs
Sprint
Staples
Starwood
State Farm
Subway
Success Course
Oracle America, Inc.
Sunsilk Marketing
Syfy
Synopsys
Talk.com
TeleCash
Texas Instruments
Thermador
Thrifty
Toll Brothers
Toshiba
Toyota
Travelocity
Trilegiant
Tropicana
Tylenol
Unilever
United States Air Force
United States Navy
Universal Home Videos
Universal Pictures
USA Network
Verio
VeriSign
Verizon
Vermont Castings
VH-1
Viack
VIP Honda
Visa
Wachovia Bank
Warner Brothers
Waypoint Bank
Weight Watchers

Branches

PointRoll Inc.

535 Madison Ave, New York, NY 10022
Tel.: (212) 725-6319
Fax: (212) 867-3412
E-Mail: info@pointroll.com
Web Site: www.pointroll.com

Employees: 40

Agency Specializes In: Advertising, Digital/Interactive

Mitchell Kreuch *(Sr VP-Revenue Ops)*
Joe Sullivan *(VP-Product)*
Mike Dillon *(Acct Dir-Automotive)*
Robin Schwartz *(Sls Dir-Southeast Reg)*
Jason Swider *(Dir-Sls)*
Emily Wilkes *(Mgr-Brand Mktg)*
Kevin Brickley *(Acct Exec)*
Daniel Chang *(Acct Exec)*
Kenneth Cunningham *(Acct Exec)*
Jaimie Kusher *(Acct Exec)*
Gabrielle Lubart *(Acct Exec)*

PointRoll Inc.

213 W Institute Pl, Chicago, IL 60610
Tel.: (312) 640-2640
Fax: (312) 640-2636
Web Site: www.pointroll.com

Evan Cowitt *(VP-West Coast Sls)*
Jenny Johnson *(Dir-Sls)*
Dan Mouradian *(Dir-Creative Tech)*
Natalie Strickler *(Dir-Sls)*
Angela Grimes *(Acct Mgr-Midwest-Cofactor)*
Danielle Pontarelli *(Acct Exec)*

PointRoll Inc.

340 E Big Beaver Rd Ste 150, Troy, MI 48083
Tel.: (248) 680-7111
Fax: (248) 680-9905
E-Mail: info@pointroll.com
Web Site: www.pointroll.com

Employees: 1

Mario Diez *(CEO)*
Emily Wilkes *(Brand Mktg Mgr)*
Kristin Cammarota *(Dir-Sls)*
Katie Warren *(Dir-Sls)*
April Biddle *(Mgr-Mktg Ops)*

Accounts:
Embassy Suites Resorts
Intel Skills Tests

POLARIS FINANCIAL TECHNOLOGY LIMITED
(Formerly Polaris Software Lab Limited)
Polaris House 244 Anna Salai, 600 006 Chennai, India
Tel.: (91) 44 3987 4000
Fax: (91) 44 2852 3280
Web Site: www.polarisft.com

Employees: 10,974

Revenue: $359,355,557

Uppili Srinivasan *(Partner & COO)*
Shashi Mohan *(Partner, CIO, CTO & Exec VP)*
Pankaj Modi *(Partner, Sr VP-Global Delivery & Ops & Head-Capital Markets)*
Sanjeev Gulati *(Chief Client Officer)*
Venkatesh Srinivasan *(CEO-Intellect Treasury & Capital Markets)*
K. Srinivasan *(Exec VP & Head-Geography-Growth Markets-IMEA)*
Anil Verma *(Dir)*
Vikas Misra *(Bus Head-Enterprise Solution & Mainframe)*

Accounts:
Enterprise Content Management
IBM Mainframe
Oracle
PACE

Subsidiary

Polaris Enterprise Solutions Limited
Polaris House, 249 Polaris Towers Udyog Vihar, Gurgaon, Haryana 122001 India
Tel.: (91) 124 391 6300
Fax: (91) 124 2345 059
E-Mail: info@polarisesl.com
Web Site: www.polarisesl.com

Dipak Bishnoi *(Partner & Head-Global Deliveries)*
Amitava Pathak *(Sr VP & Head-Retail Products)*
Himanshu Bhardwaj *(VP)*
Mohit Oberoi *(Dir)*

U.S. Subsidiaries

Intellect Design Arena Inc
(Formerly Polaris Software Lab India Ltd.)
2730 Sidney St Ste 200, Pittsburgh, PA 15203
Tel.: (412) 297-0050
Fax: (412) 297-0052
Toll Free: (800) 682-7332
Web Site: www.intellectseec.com/

Employees: 130
Year Founded: 1988

Ravindra Koka *(Partner & CTO-Intellect SEEC)*
S. Swaminathan *(Partner-Intellect Design Arena & Grp CFO)*
Laila Beane *(CMO & Head-Consulting)*
Manish Maakan *(CEO-iGTB)*
Lakshan Desilva *(Sr VP & Head-Solution Mgmt & Presales-Global)*
Bharath Venkatachari *(Sr VP & Head-India Dev Centers)*
Ron Steiger *(VP & Product Mgr-Claims)*
Sriram Narasimhan *(VP & Head HR)*

Accounts:
Bankers Life & Casualty Company
ICICI Prudential Life Insurance

Polaris Software Lab India Limited
Woodbridge Pl 517 Rte 1 S Ste 2103, Iselin, NJ 08830
Tel.: (732) 590-8100
Fax: (732) 404-1188
Web Site: polarisft.com

Employees: 2,000

Suresh Kamath *(Pres)*
Shashi Mohan *(Partner, CIO, CTO & Exec VP)*
Pankaj Modi *(Partner, Sr VP-Global Delivery & Ops & Head-Capital Markets)*
Vikas Misra *(Partner & Head-Bus-Enterprise Solutions)*
T V Sinha *(Partner & Head-Insurance & Portals Deliveries-Global)*
Pranav Pasricha *(CEO-IntellectSEEC)*
K Srinivasan *(Exec VP & Head-Geography-Growth Markets-IMEA)*
Rama Sivaraman *(Global Head-Ops-Polaris Fin Tech Limited)*

Accounts:
HP
IBM
Microsoft
Oracle

POLARIS PUBLIC RELATIONS, INC.
One Yonge St, S-1801, Toronto, ON M5E 1W7 Canada
Tel.: (416) 597-1518
Fax: (416) 597-9127
E-Mail: info@polarisprinc.com
Web Site: www.polarisprinc.com

Employees: 1

Agency Specializes In: Collateral, Communications, Corporate Communications, Event Planning & Marketing, Internet/Web Design, Media Relations, Newspaper, Product Placement, Public Relations, Social Marketing/Nonprofit, Strategic Planning/Research

Shelley Pringle *(Principal)*
Denny Allen *(Specialist-Media Trng)*
Chris Atkinson *(Strategist-Digital)*
Randy Milanovic *(Specialist-Online Mktg)*

Accounts:
Active International Canada Content Marketing, Inbound Marketing, Media Relations, PR, Strategy
Bay Shore Home Health
CIBC
Ericsson
Hallmark Canada
JAN Kelley Marketing
Nestle Canada

POLARIS RECRUITMENT COMMUNICATIONS
13 E Central Ave Ste 100, Miamisburg, OH 45342
Tel.: (937) 847-1100
Fax: (937) 847-1101
E-Mail: info@polarisrc.com
Web Site: www.polarisrc.com

E-Mail for Key Personnel:
President: danprice@polarisrc.com

Employees: 7
Year Founded: 2001

Agency Specializes In: Advertising, Advertising Specialties, Cable T.V., Collateral, Direct Response Marketing, Electronic Media, Health Care Services, Internet/Web Design, Magazines, Newspaper, Newspapers & Magazines, Out-of-Home Media, Outdoor, Radio, Recruitment

Approx. Annual Billings: $4,000,000

Breakdown of Gross Billings by Media: Adv. Specialities: $200,000; Cable T.V.: $80,000; Collateral: $400,000; Consulting: $200,000; E-Commerce: $200,000; Exhibits/Trade Shows: $80,000; Newsp. & Mags.: $2,640,000; Radio: $200,000

Michael Langham *(Dir-Creative Svcs)*
Gina Wolfe *(Acct Mgr)*
Diana Fry *(Coord-Recruitment)*

Accounts:
Ivy Tech State College
Marian General Hosptial
Masonic Health Care

POLLER & JORDAN ADVERTISING AGENCY, INC.
PO Box 166249, Miami, FL 33116-6249
Tel.: (305) 992-0705
Fax: (305) 598-9078
E-Mail: info@advertisingmiami.com
Web Site: www.advertisingmiami.com

Employees: 6
Year Founded: 1972

Agency Specializes In: Advertising, Advertising Specialties, African-American Market, Automotive, Aviation & Aerospace, Bilingual Market, Brand Development & Integration, Business Publications, Business-To-Business, Children's Market, Co-op Advertising, Collateral, Consulting, Consumer Marketing, Consumer Publications, Direct Response Marketing, E-Commerce, Education, Electronic Media, Financial, Graphic Design, Health Care Services, High Technology, Hispanic Market, Internet/Web Design, Legal Services, Logo & Package Design, Magazines, Marine, New Product Development, Newspaper, Newspapers & Magazines, Outdoor, Point of Purchase, Print, Production, Public Relations, Publicity/Promotions, Radio, Retail, Sales Promotion, Seniors' Market, T.V., Trade & Consumer Magazines

Breakdown of Gross Billings by Media: Bus. Publs.: 10.11%; D.M.: 8.89%; Internet Adv.: 23.44%; Mags.: 4.44%; Newsp.: 13.34%; Other: 11.11%; Pub. Rels.: 2%; Radio: 10%; Spot T.V.: 16.67%

Robert Poller *(Co-Owner)*
Shari Goldstein *(Dir-PR)*
Kelly Williams *(Dir-Art)*

Accounts:
Arthur Murray; Miami, FL; 1989
Kelly Tractor Co.; FL Machinery

POLLINATE
919 SW Taylor 3rd Fl, Portland, OR 97205
Tel.: (800) 679-9720
E-Mail: luckyday@pollinate.com
Web Site: www.pollinate.com

Year Founded: 2008

Agency Specializes In: Advertising, Brand Development & Integration, Broadcast, Digital/Interactive, E-Commerce, Graphic Design, Media Planning, Package Design, Social Media, Strategic Planning/Research

Levi Patterson *(Co-Founder)*
Ben Waldron *(Partner)*
Simeon Roane *(Exec Dir-Creative)*
Dana Rierson *(Sr Dir-Art)*
Bob Vandehey *(Dir-Creative)*
Rob Rosenthal *(Assoc Dir-Creative)*
Kate Malinoski *(Acct Mgr)*
Yuki Tanaka *(Supvr-Media)*

Accounts:
Byron Winery
New-Eddie Bauer
New-First Republic Bank
Louis Vuitton Moet Hennessy Group
New-New Seasons Markets
Newton Vineyard
New-Oregon Lottery
Sur La Table, Inc.
Wilson Sporting Goods Co.

POLYCREATIVE

2308 E 10th Ave B, Tampa, FL 33605
Tel.: (727) 518-4397
E-Mail: info@polycreative.com
Web Site: www.polycreative.com

Agency Specializes In: Cable T.V., Content, Digital/Interactive, E-Commerce, Internet/Web Design, Media Buying Services

Erik Cattelle *(Owner)*

Accounts:
Headshot Days Web Designing Services
The Inventors Business Center Marketing Services
Meadows Medical Solutions & Physical Therapy Healthcare Services

POMEGRANATE, INC

228 Park Ave S Ste 38570, New York, NY 10003
Tel.: (212) 520-1911
E-Mail: east@pom8.com
Web Site: www.pom8.com

Year Founded: 2008

Agency Specializes In: Advertising, Digital/Interactive

Grant Powell *(CEO & Partner)*
Sarah Douglass *(Coord-Sls & Mktg)*

Accounts:
Canon Inc.
Engagement Media Technologies Digital
Google Inc.
Nestle USA, Inc.
Porsche Cars North America, Inc.
Robert Bosch GmbH
Toyota Motor Corporation

THE POMERANTZ AGENCY LLC

914 Bay Rdg Rd Ste 180, Annapolis, MD 21403
Tel.: (410) 216-9447
E-Mail: info@pomagency.com
Web Site: www.pomagency.com

Agency Specializes In: Advertising, Brand Development & Integration, Content, Internet/Web Design, Print, Social Media, Strategic Planning/Research

Kathy Greenspan *(Owner & Dir-Strategic & Creative)*
Cliff Massey *(Controller)*
Leslie Brady *(Acct Dir)*

Accounts:
DP Solutions
Integrated Security Technologies

PONDELWILKINSON INC.

1880 Century Park E Ste 350, Los Angeles, CA 90067
Tel.: (310) 279-5980
Fax: (310) 279-5988
E-Mail: investor@pondel.com
Web Site: www.pondel.com

Employees: 15
Year Founded: 1981

Agency Specializes In: Financial, Health Care Services, High Technology, Industrial, Information Technology, Investor Relations, Public Relations, Sponsorship

Evan Pondel *(Pres)*
Roger S. Pondel *(CEO)*
Laurie Berman *(Mng Dir)*
George Medici *(Sr VP)*
E. E. Wang *(Sr VP)*
Judy Lin Sfetcu *(VP)*
Matt Sheldon *(VP)*
Caroline Dillingham *(Mgr-Social Media & Digital Strategy)*
Nancy Hines *(Mgr-Acctg)*

Accounts:
Advanced Refining Concepts
APP Pharmaceuticals, Inc.; Schaumburg, IL
Autobytel
Corinthian Colleges
FEI Corporation
First California Financial Group, Inc.
Hardesty, LLC
NetSol Technologies, Inc. Investor Relations
QAD
Somaxon Pharmaceuticals, Inc.
Superior Industries International, Inc.
UTI

PONDER IDEAWORKS

20291 Ravenwood Ln, Huntington Beach, CA 92646
Tel.: (714) 801-4113
Fax: (714) 968-3327
E-Mail: claudia@ponderideaworks.com
Web Site: www.ponderideaworks.com

Employees: 3
Year Founded: 1991

National Agency Associations: THINKLA

Agency Specializes In: Advertising, Advertising Specialties, African-American Market, Agriculture, Asian Market, Bilingual Market, Brand Development & Integration, Broadcast, Business Publications, Business-To-Business, Cable T.V., Children's Market, Collateral, Communications, Consulting, Consumer Marketing, Consumer Publications, Corporate Identity, Digital/Interactive, Direct Response Marketing, E-Commerce, Education, Electronic Media, Entertainment, Event Planning & Marketing, Exhibit/Trade Shows, Fashion/Apparel, Food Service, Government/Political, Graphic Design, Health Care Services, High Technology, Hispanic Market, Information Technology, Internet/Web Design, Legal Services, Leisure, Logo & Package Design, Magazines, Media Buying Services, Medical Products, Merchandising, Multimedia, New Product Development, Newspaper, Newspapers & Magazines, Out-of-Home Media, Outdoor, Planning & Consultation, Point of Purchase, Point of Sale, Print, Production, Public Relations, Publicity/Promotions, Radio, Restaurant, Retail, Sales Promotion, Strategic Planning/Research, T.V., Technical Advertising, Teen Market, Trade & Consumer Magazines, Travel & Tourism

Approx. Annual Billings: $3,200,000

Breakdown of Gross Billings by Media: Brdcst.: 40%; Collateral: 10%; Consulting: 20%; Other: 5%; Print: 15%; Worldwide Web Sites: 10%

Claudia Ponder *(CEO)*

Accounts:
Adult Day Services of Orange County; Huntington Beach, CA
Department of Alcohol and Drug Prevention (State of Calif); Sacramento, CA Drug Prevention; 2002
Experian; Orange, CA Credit Information; 1997
Literacy in the Media; Los Angeles, CA; 2002
New Horizons
PeopleSoft
Sonoma State University CHIIP; Sacramento, CA
State of California EDD; Sacramento, CA

POOLE COMMUNICATIONS

108 N 3rd St Ste 100, Hannibal, MO 63401
Tel.: (573) 221-3635
Toll Free: (800) 900-3635
Web Site: www.poolecommunications.com

Year Founded: 1984

Agency Specializes In: Advertising, Internet/Web Design, Print, Public Relations, Radio

Sally Poole *(Pres & CEO)*

Accounts:
Cason, Huff & Schlueter Insurance

POOLHOUSE

23 W Broad St Ste 404, Richmond, VA 23220
Tel.: (804) 876-0335
E-Mail: info@poolhousedigital.com
Web Site: http://poolhouse.co/

Agency Specializes In: Advertising, Digital/Interactive, Media Buying Services, T.V.

Natalie Boyse *(Acct Exec)*

Accounts:
Joni Ernst

POP

1326 5th Ave Ste 800, Seattle, WA 98101
Tel.: (206) 728-7997
Fax: (206) 728-1144
E-Mail: pr@pop.us
Web Site: www.popagency.com

Agency Specializes In: Digital/Interactive

Bill Predmore *(Founder & CEO)*
Tony Hoskins *(Founder & Partner)*
Kaci Clot *(Sr VP-Corp Strategy)*
Erin West *(VP-Client Svcs)*
Tom Moran *(Exec Dir-Creative)*
Erica Fransen *(Acct Dir)*
Lance Williams *(Mktg Dir)*
Melissa Herron *(Dir-Strategy)*
Eric Rak *(Assoc Dir-Creative)*
Jeff Paredes *(Sr Analyst-Technical)*

Accounts:
Amazon.com
Brown-Forman
EA Games

Epson
Google
Microsoft
National Geographic
Nintendo
Target
Ubisoft

POP-DOT MARKETING

111 W Wilson St Ste 11, Madison, WI 53703
Tel.: (608) 371-9767
E-Mail: info@popdotmarketing.com
Web Site: www.popdotmarketing.com

Year Founded: 2013

Agency Specializes In: Advertising, Brand Development & Integration, Digital/Interactive, Logo & Package Design, Media Planning, Outdoor, Print, Public Relations, Social Media, Strategic Planning/Research

Jason Fish *(Founder, CEO & Sr Strategist-Creative)*
Kate Ewings *(Partner & Strategist-Brand)*
Allison Kattreh *(Coord-Digital & Social Media)*

Accounts:
Beaulieu America Creative Services, Marketing, Strategy
Fit Moms Transformation Center
New-HotelRED (Agency of Record)
New-Madison & Rayne (Marketing Agency of Record) Brand Strategy, Creative
Madison Womens Expo
New-True Studio (Agency of Record) Branding, Marketing
New-The Wise (Marketing Agency of Record)

POP LABS, INC

7850 Parkwood Cir Ste B3, Houston, TX 77270
Toll Free: (877) 500-1399
E-Mail: gene@poplabs.com
Web Site: www.poplabs.com

Employees: 40
Year Founded: 2001

Agency Specializes In: Digital/Interactive, Graphic Design, High Technology, Internet/Web Design, Media Buying Services, Media Relations, Multimedia, Paid Searches, RSS (Really Simple Syndication), Search Engine Optimization, Web (Banner Ads, Pop-ups, etc.)

Approx. Annual Billings: $5,000,000

Gene McCubin *(Founder & Pres)*
Craig Tippit *(Dir-Search Mktg)*
Erin Womack *(Dir-Ops)*
Keshia Curvey *(Coord-Client Svcs)*
Anthony Shields *(Team Head-New Bus Dev)*

Accounts:
iEnergy Branding, Integrated Marketing, Print & Collateral Materials, Web Design; 2010
Jack's Carpet Social Media, Web Site, email; 2007
Pisco Porton Brand Development; 2011
South Texas Dental PPC, Social Media, Web Site, email; 2008

POPULAR CREATIVE LLC

851 Elmwood St, Shreveport, LA 71104
Tel.: (318) 655-4875
Web Site: www.popular-creative.net

Agency Specializes In: Advertising, Brand Development & Integration, Graphic Design, Internet/Web Design, Strategic Planning/Research

Todd Miller *(Co-Founder & Art Dir)*
Paul Mccallister *(Co-Founder & Creative Dir)*

Accounts:
Sweet Tee Shreveport

PORCARO COMMUNICATIONS

433 W 9th Ave, Anchorage, AK 99501-3519
Tel.: (907) 276-4262
Fax: (907) 276-7280
E-Mail: porcaro@gci.net
Web Site: www.porcarocommunications.com

E-Mail for Key Personnel:
President: mikep@gci.net

Employees: 15
Year Founded: 1982

Agency Specializes In: Advertising, Communications

Approx. Annual Billings: $10,000,000

Michael F. Porcaro *(Owner)*
Mark Hopkin *(Pres)*
John Hume *(Sr Dir-Art)*
Daryl Hoflich *(Dir-Creative)*
Scott Banks *(Sr Acct Mgr)*
Janis Plume *(Mgr-Traffic & Production)*

Accounts:
Alaska Railroad
Alaska Railroad Corp.
ASRC Energy Services
Bidsync
The Endurance
GCI; Anchorage, AK Local Service, Long Distance, Cellular, Internet & Cable Communications; 1997
Lite Speed
Panoramas
Petro Marine; Seward, AK Maritime Fuel Service
Shell Oil Company
Tech Head

Branches

Wian

(Formerly Porcaro Vancouver)
504-221 West Esplanade, Vancouver, BC V7M 3J3 Canada
Tel.: (604) 985-2400
Fax: (604) 986-8166
E-Mail: hello@wianbranding.com
Web Site: wianbranding.com/

Employees: 7

Agency Specializes In: Advertising

Sandra Fong *(Mng Partner)*
Coromoto Diaz *(Sr Dir-Art & Designer)*

Accounts:
Alaska Railroad Corporation
Baywest Management
BC Ferries
Finning
HSBC
Kodak Graphic Communications Group
New Gold

PORETTA & ORR, INC.

450 East St, Doylestown, PA 18901
Tel.: (215) 345-1515
Fax: (215) 345-6459
E-Mail: brudnokb@porettaorr.com
Web Site: www.porettaorr.com

Employees: 40
Year Founded: 1989

Agency Specializes In: Direct Response Marketing, Event Planning & Marketing, Exhibit/Trade Shows, Health Care Services, Medical Products, Pharmaceutical

Barbara Orr *(Owner & Exec VP)*
Joseph Poretta *(Pres)*
Rick Counihan *(VP-Client Svcs & Ops)*
Jack Murnane *(Acct Mgr)*
Beverly Brudnok *(Mgr-Bus Dev & Acct Exec)*
John McKeon *(Sr Designer)*

Accounts:
Abbott
AstraZeneca
Gate Pharmaceutical
Johnson & Johnson
Merck & Co. (International)
MSD Pharmaceuticals Private Limited
Reliance
Sanofi-Aventis Research & Development
Shire Vyvanse
TAP

PORTE ADVERTISING, INC.

462 7th Ave 6th Fl, New York, NY 10018
Tel.: (212) 354-6906
Fax: (212) 354-5727
E-Mail: jayheyman@porteadvertising.com
Web Site: www.porteadvertising.com

Employees: 2
Year Founded: 1993

Agency Specializes In: Brand Development & Integration, Collateral, Direct Response Marketing, Public Relations

Jay H. Heyman *(Co-Owner)*
Paul C. Mesches *(Co-Owner)*

Accounts:
Bankruptcy Services
Energetics Unlimited Personal & Corporate Exercise Programs; 1996
Paradigm Vision Video Conferencing
Wetson Restaurant Group; New York, NY Dallas BBQ, Tony's Di Napoli Restaurant; 1998

POSITIONCLICK CORPORATION

99 Chauncy St Ste 910, Boston, MA 02111
Tel.: (617) 500-3458
Web Site: www.positionclick.com

Employees: 275
Year Founded: 2005

Agency Specializes In: Collateral, Digital/Interactive, Direct Response Marketing, Electronic Media, Email, In-Store Advertising, Local Marketing, Mobile Marketing, Paid Searches, Point of Purchase, Point of Sale, Product Placement, Search Engine Optimization, Web (Banner Ads, Pop-ups, etc.), Yellow Pages Advertising

Approx. Annual Billings: $3,000,000

Eric Melin *(Co-Founder & CEO)*

Accounts:
99brokers Business Brokerage; 2012
Beer Bites, LLC Bar Snacks; 2012
Lingerie Planet, Inc. Lingerie; 2011
PopuTrust, LLC People Search; 2013

POSNER MILLER ADVERTISING

(Formerly Posner Advertising)
71 5th Ave, New York, NY 10003
Tel.: (212) 727-4790
Fax: (212) 480-3440
Toll Free: (800) 664-3817

E-Mail: info@posneradv.com
Web Site: http://www.posnermiller.com/

E-Mail for Key Personnel:
President: pposner@posneradv.com

Employees: 30
Year Founded: 1959

Agency Specializes In: Advertising, Brand Development & Integration, Business-To-Business, Collateral, Communications, Consulting, Consumer Marketing, Corporate Communications, Corporate Identity, Digital/Interactive, Direct Response Marketing, E-Commerce, Education, Electronic Media, Electronics, Email, Exhibit/Trade Shows, Gay & Lesbian Market, Graphic Design, Health Care Services, Identity Marketing, Integrated Marketing, Internet/Web Design, Logo & Package Design, Magazines, Media Buying Services, Media Planning, Media Relations, Medical Products, Mobile Marketing, Outdoor, Over-50 Market, Package Design, Print, Production, Promotions, Public Relations, Publicity/Promotions, Real Estate, Recruitment, Sales Promotion, Search Engine Optimization, Seniors' Market, Strategic Planning/Research, T.V., Transportation, Travel & Tourism, Urban Market, Viral/Buzz/Word of Mouth

Approx. Annual Billings: $35,000,000

Breakdown of Gross Billings by Media: Brdcst.: $1,050,000; Bus. Publs.: $1,150,000; Fees: $3,600,000; Internet Adv.: $10,600,000; Mags.: $1,220,000; Newsp.: $14,800,000; Outdoor: $1,010,000; Production: $1,570,000

Peter Posner *(Pres)*
Bob Posner *(Principal)*
Tamir Bourla *(Sr Acct Dir)*
Andrew Dimond *(Sr Acct Dir)*
Harry Tropp *(Media Dir)*

Accounts:
Bays Water Development
Capella Hotels and Resorts
Fisher Brothers
LG
LG Commercial
Mandl Schools
Prudential Douglas Elliman

POSSIBLE STORMS
6138 Franklin Ave #320, Los Angeles, CA 90028
Tel.: (323) 898-4778
Web Site: possiblestorms.com

Agency Specializes In: Above-the-Line, Advertising, Advertising Specialties, Affiliate Marketing, Affluent Market, African-American Market, Agriculture, Alternative Advertising, Arts, Asian Market, Automotive, Aviation & Aerospace, Below-the-Line, Bilingual Market, Brand Development & Integration, Branded Entertainment, Broadcast, Business Publications, Business-To-Business, Cable T.V., Catalogs, Children's Market, Co-op Advertising, Collateral, College, Commercial Photography, Communications, Computers & Software, Consulting, Consumer Goods, Consumer Marketing, Consumer Publications, Content, Corporate Communications, Corporate Identity, Cosmetics, Crisis Communications, Custom Publishing, Customer Relationship Management, Digital/Interactive, Direct Response Marketing, Direct-to-Consumer, E-Commerce, Education, Electronic Media, Electronics, Email, Engineering, Entertainment, Environmental, Event Planning & Marketing, Exhibit/Trade Shows, Experience Design, Faith Based, Fashion/Apparel, Financial, Food Service, Game Integration, Gay & Lesbian Market, Government/Political, Graphic Design, Guerilla Marketing, Health Care Services, High Technology, Hispanic Market, Hospitality, Household Goods, Identity Marketing, In-Store Advertising, Industrial, Infomercials, Information Technology, Integrated Marketing, International, Internet/Web Design, Investor Relations, Legal Services, Leisure, Local Marketing, Logo & Package Design, Luxury Products, Magazines, Marine, Market Research, Media Buying Services, Media Planning, Media Relations, Media Training, Medical Products, Men's Market, Merchandising, Mobile Marketing, Multicultural, Multimedia, New Product Development, New Technologies, Newspaper, Newspapers & Magazines, Out-of-Home Media, Outdoor, Over-50 Market, Package Design, Paid Searches, Pets , Pharmaceutical, Planning & Consultation, Podcasting, Point of Purchase, Point of Sale, Print, Product Placement, Production, Production (Ad, Film, Broadcast), Production (Print), Promotions, Public Relations, Publicity/Promotions, Publishing, RSS (Really Simple Syndication), Radio, Real Estate, Recruitment, Regional, Restaurant, Retail, Sales Promotion, Search Engine Optimization, Seniors' Market, Shopper Marketing, Social Marketing/Nonprofit, Social Media, South Asian Market, Sponsorship, Sports Market, Stakeholders, Strategic Planning/Research, Sweepstakes, Syndication, T.V., Technical Advertising, Teen Market, Telemarketing, Trade & Consumer Magazines, Transportation, Travel & Tourism, Tween Market, Urban Market, Viral/Buzz/Word of Mouth, Web (Banner Ads, Pop-ups, etc.), Women's Market, Yellow Pages Advertising

Simon Rohrer *(Dir)*
Frances Vine *(Dir)*

Accounts:
Walk the Night LLC; 2011

POSTERSCOPE
2 Park Ave., 24th Fl, New York, NY 10016
Tel.: (917) 621-3250
Fax: (562) 695-1310
E-Mail: connie.garrido@posterscope.com
Web Site: www.posterscopeusa.com

National Agency Associations: 4A's

Agency Specializes In: Media Buying Services, Sponsorship

Joanne Zmood *(Mng Dir & Exec VP)*
Paula Stokes *(CFO)*
James Davies *(Chief Strategy Officer-UK & USA)*
Helma Larkin *(CEO-US)*
Martin Porter *(Sr VP & Dir-Client Mgmt)*
Jessica Freely *(VP & Dir)*
Mary Schaetzle *(VP & Dir-Media Investments & Client Svcs)*
Nathaniel Chambers *(Assoc Dir-Planning)*
Sarah Podziomek *(Assoc Dir)*
Mindy Zonis *(Assoc Dir)*
Maisie Wong *(Acct Supvr)*
Stephen Angelovich *(Supvr)*
Nicole Mattsson *(Supvr-Integrated Plng-Out of Home)*
Winnie Weir-Johnson *(Supvr-Client Delivery)*
Leland Chen *(Assistant Media Planner)*
Nick Echeverria *(Assistant-Media Investment)*
Lauren Formisano *(Associate-Production)*
Shari Kram *(Associate-Consumer Insights)*
Mary O'Brien *(Asst Media Planner)*
Brittany Pietrosh *(Assoc Media Planner)*
Gregory Pinkus *(Assistant-Media Planning)*

Accounts:
Adidas
Coca-Cola Refreshments USA, Inc.
General Motors Chevy Colorado

POTRATZ PARTNERS ADVERTISING INC.
31 Lafayette St, Schenectady, NY 12305
Tel.: (518) 631-5505
Toll Free: (866) 840-5714
Web Site: www.exclusivelyautomotive.com

Employees: 13
Year Founded: 2001

Agency Specializes In: Advertising, Automotive, Digital/Interactive, Media Buying Services, Production

Approx. Annual Billings: $8,518,000

Breakdown of Gross Billings by Media: Brdcst.: $600,000; Cable T.V.: $1,000,000; Comml. Photography: $138,000; Consulting: $200,000; D.M.: $600,000; Event Mktg.: $200,000; Fees: $2,000,000; Graphic Design: $180,000; Internet Adv.: $300,000; Newsp.: $2,000,000; Radio: $1,300,000

Paul D. Potratz, Jr. *(Owner)*
Dan Allen *(VP-Creative Svcs)*
Samantha Cunningham Zawilinski *(VP-Acct Svcs)*
Michelle Campbell *(Mgr-Performance)*
Paul Chamberlain *(Mgr-Performance)*
Brian Hart *(Mgr-Performance)*
Stefanie Markiewicz *(Mgr-Performance)*
Jose Romero *(Mgr-Mktg Comm)*
James Lewis-Van Vorst *(Sr Graphic Designer)*

POTTS MARKETING GROUP LLC
1115 Leighton Ave Ste 1-B, Anniston, AL 36207
Tel.: (256) 237-7788
Fax: (256) 237-8818
Web Site: www.pottsmarketing.com

Agency Specializes In: Advertising, Brand Development & Integration, Graphic Design, Internet/Web Design, Public Relations

Tom Potts *(Pres)*
Bill Adams *(Creative Dir)*

Accounts:
New-Foothills Community Partnership

POTTS MUELLER
116 W Illinois St Fl 6E-A, Chicago, IL 60654
Tel.: (312) 955-0199
E-Mail: potts@pottsmueller.com
Web Site: www.pottsmueller.com

Agency Specializes In: Advertising, Brand Development & Integration, Event Planning & Marketing, Media Relations, Public Relations, Social Media

Denise Potts Mueller *(Dir-PR)*

Accounts:
New-Garnier Men Indonesia

POUTRAY PEKAR ASSOCIATES
344 W Main St, Milford, CT 06460
Tel.: (203) 283-9511
Fax: (203) 283-9514
Web Site: ingredientmarketingsolutions.com/

Employees: 8
Year Founded: 1963

Agency Specializes In: Business-To-Business, Communications, Cosmetics, Food Service, Pharmaceutical

Approx. Annual Billings: $2,700,000

Carol Pekar *(Owner)*
William Poutray *(Owner)*

Rosemary DeFeo *(Dir-Media)*

Accounts:
Accurate Ingredients; NY Food Ingredients; 2004
Advanced Food Systems
Beudemheim Inc.; Plainview, NY
CNI
Kemira Specialty Inc.; Northvale, NJ
Land O' Lakes Ingredients Solutions Ingredient Solutions
Virginia Dare Extracts; Brooklyn, NY; 1997

POWELL CREATIVE

1616 17th Ave S, Nashville, TN 37212
Tel.: (615) 385-7736
E-Mail: info@powellcreative.com
Web Site: www.powellcreative.com

Agency Specializes In: Advertising, Brand Development & Integration, Collateral, Graphic Design, Internet/Web Design, Logo & Package Design

Wayne Powell *(Pres & Sr Dir-Creative)*
Scott Spencer *(VP & Dir-Creative)*
Rose Wilson *(Office Mgr)*
Amy Rochelle *(Mgr-Interactive)*
Stephen Lackey *(Acct Coord)*

Accounts:
The Governors Golf Club

POWER CREATIVE

11701 Commonwealth Dr, Louisville, KY 40299-2358
Tel.: (502) 267-0772
Fax: (502) 267-1727
Web Site: www.powercreative.com

E-Mail for Key Personnel:
President: dpower@powercreative.com
Creative Dir.: vholcomb@powercreative.com
Media Dir.: tlucas@powercreative.com

Employees: 130
Year Founded: 1976

National Agency Associations: PRSA-Second Wind Limited

Agency Specializes In: Advertising, Brand Development & Integration, Business-To-Business, Catalogs, Co-op Advertising, Collateral, Commercial Photography, Consumer Publications, Corporate Identity, Digital/Interactive, E-Commerce, Email, Exhibit/Trade Shows, Graphic Design, High Technology, In-Store Advertising, Industrial, Internet/Web Design, Logo & Package Design, Magazines, Media Buying Services, Media Planning, Merchandising, Multimedia, Newspapers & Magazines, Out-of-Home Media, Outdoor, Point of Purchase, Point of Sale, Print, Production, Production (Print), Promotions, Public Relations, Radio, Sales Promotion, Sponsorship, Strategic Planning/Research, T.V., Trade & Consumer Magazines, Web (Banner Ads, Pop-ups, etc.)

Approx. Annual Billings: $92,000,000

Breakdown of Gross Billings by Media: Collateral: 18%; Comml. Photography: 24%; Internet Adv.: 5%; Logo & Package Design: 8%; Point of Purchase: 7%; Point of Sale: 4%; Print: 2%; Pub. Rels.: 2%; Radio & T.V.: 2%; Sls. Promo.: 18%; Trade & Consumer Mags.: 9%; Worldwide Web Sites: 1%

M. David Power *(Pres & CEO)*
Andy Stillwagon *(CMO)*
Debra Cooley *(Sr VP-Fin)*
Christine Stark *(Sr VP-Acct Svcs-GE Appliances)*
Dave Pender *(VP & Dir-Creative)*
Mark Bird *(VP-Architectural Mktg)*
Adam Loewy *(Acct Dir)*
Carla Terwilleger *(Dir-Dev)*
Leah Mattingly *(Supvr-Media)*
Emily Craig Mueller *(Acct Exec)*

Accounts:
Bentwood Kitchens; Lancaster, TX; 2008
Churchill Downs Inc.
Commonwealth Bank & Trust; Louisville, KY; 2005
CRS Processing; Louisville, KY; 2009
Fluid Management; Wheeling, IL; 2009
GE Appliances
GE Aviation; Cincinnati, OH; 2005
General Electric Consumer Products; Louisville, KY Appliances, Lighting; 1976
Lennox International Heating & Air Conditioning; 1999
Lexmark; Lexington, KY Printers; 2000
UTC Fire & Security; Bradenton, FL Security and Fire Systems
Zeon Chemicals, LP; Louisville, KY Raw Materials; 2002

THE POWER GROUP

1409 S Lamar Ste 1500, Dallas, TX 75215
Tel.: (214) 693-2146
Web Site: www.thepowergroup.com

Agency Specializes In: Advertising, Crisis Communications, Event Planning & Marketing, Media Training, Social Media

Amy Power *(Pres & CEO)*
Jordan Liberty *(Dir-PR)*
Samantha Davis *(Dir-Dev)*
Lauren Leger *(Mgr-Digital Strategy)*
Kelly Ervine *(Acct Exec)*
Chelsea Sproles *(Acct Exec)*
Abbey Pennington *(Acct Exec)*

Accounts:
New-Cotton Patch Cafe
New-Dive Coastal Cuisine
New-Promised Land Dairy

POWER MEDIA GROUP INC.

17960 Sierra Hwy Ste 100, Santa Clarita, CA 91351
Tel.: (818) 714-2140
Fax: (661) 430-5491
Toll Free: (800) 901-5272
E-Mail: info@powermediagroup.com
Web Site: www.powermediagroup.com

Year Founded: 2001

Agency Specializes In: Internet/Web Design, Market Research, Media Buying Services, Outdoor, Print, Radio, Strategic Planning/Research, Telemarketing

Patricia Gracia *(Founder & Pres)*
Ricardo Pleitez *(Coord-IT)*

Accounts:
Creativa Interior-Primor Beds & Curtains Distr
El Aviso Magazine Publishing Services

POWERHOUSE FACTORIES

1111 St Gregory St, Cincinnati, OH 45202
Tel.: (513) 719-6417
Web Site: www.powerhousefactories.com

Year Founded: 2004

Agency Specializes In: Advertising, Brand Development & Integration, Social Media

Ben Nunery *(Co-Founder & Principal)*
Sean Dana *(Dir-Creative)*
Nathan Dye *(Dir-Content)*
Katy Garibay *(Dir-Word of Mouth Mktg)*
Darius Kemp *(Dir-Mktg & Innovation Strategy)*
Lauren Hoffman *(Sr Strategist-Influencer Mktg)*
Josh Flynn *(Strategist)*
Christine Hoffman *(Specialist-Influencer Mktg)*

Accounts:
Land O'Frost Content Strategy, Media Planning & Buying, Social Media Marketing
Tire Discounters, Inc.
WhiteWave Foods Company

POWERPACT, LLC

355 Lexington Ave 12th Fl, New York, NY 10017
Tel.: (877) 361-5700
Web Site: www.powerpact.com

Agency Specializes In: Advertising

Amanda Martin *(Assoc Dir-Art)*

Accounts:
American Diabetes Association
Betty Crocker Products
Capital One Bank (Europe) PLC
Gift Card Hall
Green Giant
Ikea North America Services LLC
Land O'Lakes, Inc.
LG Electronics USA Inc Digital Marketing
Mott's Holdings, Inc.
The Procter & Gamble Company
Sempra Energy
Virgin Vines
Yoplait USA, Inc.

POWERS ADVERTISING

17502 Brentwood Ct, Fort Myers, FL 33967
Tel.: (239) 244-7167
Web Site: www.powersadvertising.com

Agency Specializes In: Advertising, Advertising Specialties, Affluent Market, Alternative Advertising, Automotive, Aviation & Aerospace, Bilingual Market, Brand Development & Integration, Broadcast, Business Publications, Business-To-Business, Cable T.V., Catalogs, Collateral, Commercial Photography, Communications, Consulting, Consumer Goods, Consumer Marketing, Consumer Publications, Content, Corporate Communications, Corporate Identity, Cosmetics, Crisis Communications, Digital/Interactive, Direct Response Marketing, Direct-to-Consumer, E-Commerce, Electronic Media, Email, Event Planning & Marketing, Faith Based, Food Service, Government/Political, Graphic Design, Guerilla Marketing, Hispanic Market, Hospitality, Identity Marketing, In-Store Advertising, Information Technology, Integrated Marketing, Internet/Web Design, Leisure, Local Marketing, Logo & Package Design, Luxury Products, Marine, Market Research, Media Buying Services, Media Planning, Media Relations, Medical Products, Men's Market, Mobile Marketing, Multimedia, New Product Development, New Technologies, Newspaper, Newspapers & Magazines, Outdoor, Over-50 Market, Package Design, Paid Searches, Pets , Pharmaceutical, Planning & Consultation, Podcasting, Point of Purchase, Print, Production, Production (Ad, Film, Broadcast), Production (Print), Promotions, Public Relations, Publicity/Promotions, RSS (Really Simple Syndication), Radio, Regional, Retail, Search Engine Optimization, Seniors' Market, Social Marketing/Nonprofit, Social Media, Strategic Planning/Research, T.V., Technical Advertising, Teen Market, Trade & Consumer Magazines, Transportation, Travel & Tourism, Urban Market, Web (Banner Ads, Pop-ups, etc.), Women's Market, Yellow Pages Advertising

Rebekah Powers *(Owner)*

Accounts:
PTS Office Automation

POWERS AGENCY
1 W 4th St 5th Fl, Cincinnati, OH 45202-3623
Tel.: (513) 721-5353
Fax: (513) 721-0086
E-Mail: info@powersagency.com
Web Site: www.powersagency.com

E-Mail for Key Personnel:
President: cpowers@powersagency.com
Creative Dir.: lgraf@powersagency.com
Media Dir.: jbking@powersagency.com
Public Relations: dlally@powersagency.com

Employees: 35
Year Founded: 1986

National Agency Associations: PRSA

Agency Specializes In: Advertising, Advertising Specialties, Automotive, Brand Development & Integration, Broadcast, Business Publications, Business-To-Business, Cable T.V., Children's Market, Consumer Marketing, Consumer Publications, Corporate Identity, Digital/Interactive, Direct Response Marketing, E-Commerce, Electronic Media, Entertainment, Event Planning & Marketing, Exhibit/Trade Shows, Financial, Graphic Design, Health Care Services, Information Technology, Internet/Web Design, Magazines, Media Buying Services, Medical Products, New Product Development, Newspapers & Magazines, Outdoor, Pharmaceutical, Print, Public Relations, Restaurant, Retail, Strategic Planning/Research, T.V., Telemarketing, Yellow Pages Advertising

Charles W. Powers *(Chm)*
Lori Powers *(Pres, CEO & Chief Creative Officer)*
Krista Taylor *(CMO)*
Dan Pinger *(Dir-Consulting)*
Amy Hibbard *(Acct Coord)*
Robert Wilson *(Asst Media Buyer)*

Accounts:
AssureRx
Biggs
Castellini Group of Companies; 2005
Check n Go
The Clovernook Center for the Blind; Fairfield, OH Opportunities for the Blind; 1997
Drees Homes; Cincinnati, OH Real Estate Development; 1998
Frisch's Restaurants; Cincinnati, OH Big Boy Restaurants; 1997
Mercedes Benz of West Chester; 2005
Mercedes-Benz of Cincinnati; Cincinnati, OH Car Dealer; 1992
Mercy Health Partners; Cincinnati, OH Health Care System; 1997
Penn Station East Coast Subs
Pfizer Pharmaceuticals; 2001
Western & Southern Financial Group Masters & Women's Open
YMCA of Greater Cincinnati; 2001

Branch

Pinger PR at Powers
1 W 4th St 5th Fl, Cincinnati, OH 45202-3623
(See Separate Listing)

THE POWERS THAT BE LLC
320 West Nine Mile Rd Ste B, Ferndale, MI 48220
Tel.: (313) 909-3780
E-Mail: info@tptbagency.com
Web Site: www.tptbagency.com

Agency Specializes In: Advertising, Digital/Interactive, Media Planning, Social Media

Louis Bilotta *(Jr Copywriter)*

Accounts:
New-BraunAbility
New-Guernsey Farms Dairy

POZA CONSULTING SERVICES
1119 Colorado Ave Ste 18, Santa Monica, CA 90401
Tel.: (310) 458-4637
Fax: (310) 264-0850
E-Mail: info@pozaconsulting.com
Web Site: www.pozaconsulting.com

Employees: 2
Year Founded: 1990

Agency Specializes In: Bilingual Market, Brand Development & Integration, Children's Market, Consulting, Consumer Marketing, Hispanic Market, Strategic Planning/Research

Approx. Annual Billings: $400,000

Ines Poza *(Owner)*

PP+K
(Formerly Pyper Paul + Kenney, Inc.)
1102 N Florida Ave, Tampa, FL 33602
Tel.: (813) 496-7000
Fax: (813) 496-7003
E-Mail: hr@uniteppk.com
Web Site: www.uniteppk.com/

Employees: 34
Year Founded: 2004

Agency Specializes In: Above-the-Line, Advertising, Advertising Specialties, Affiliate Marketing, Affluent Market, African-American Market, Agriculture, Alternative Advertising, Arts, Asian Market, Automotive, Aviation & Aerospace, Below-the-Line, Bilingual Market, Brand Development & Integration, Branded Entertainment, Broadcast, Business Publications, Business-To-Business, Cable T.V., Catalogs, Children's Market, Co-op Advertising, Collateral, College, Commercial Photography, Communications, Computers & Software, Consulting, Consumer Goods, Consumer Marketing, Consumer Publications, Content, Corporate Communications, Corporate Identity, Cosmetics, Crisis Communications, Custom Publishing, Customer Relationship Management, Digital/Interactive, Direct Response Marketing, Direct-to-Consumer, E-Commerce, Education, Electronic Media, Electronics, Email, Engineering, Entertainment, Environmental, Event Planning & Marketing, Exhibit/Trade Shows, Experience Design, Fashion/Apparel, Financial, Food Service, Game Integration, Gay & Lesbian Market, Government/Political, Graphic Design, Guerilla Marketing, Health Care Services, High Technology, Hispanic Market, Hospitality, Household Goods, Identity Marketing, In-Store Advertising, Industrial, Infomercials, Information Technology, Integrated Marketing, International, Internet/Web Design, Investor Relations, Legal Services, Leisure, Local Marketing, Logo & Package Design, Luxury Products, Magazines, Marine, Market Research, Media Buying Services, Media Planning, Media Relations, Media Training, Medical Products, Men's Market, Merchandising, Mobile Marketing, Multicultural, Multimedia, New Product Development, New Technologies, Newspaper, Newspapers & Magazines, Out-of-Home Media, Outdoor, Over-50 Market, Package Design, Paid Searches, Pets , Pharmaceutical, Planning & Consultation, Podcasting, Point of Purchase, Point of Sale, Print, Product Placement, Production, Production (Ad, Film, Broadcast), Production (Print), Promotions, Public Relations, Publicity/Promotions, Publishing, RSS (Really Simple Syndication), Radio, Real Estate, Recruitment, Regional, Restaurant, Retail, Sales Promotion, Search Engine Optimization, Seniors' Market, Social Marketing/Nonprofit, Sponsorship, Sports Market, Stakeholders, Strategic Planning/Research, Sweepstakes, Syndication, T.V., Technical Advertising, Teen Market, Telemarketing, Trade & Consumer Magazines, Transportation, Travel & Tourism, Urban Market, Viral/Buzz/Word of Mouth, Web (Banner Ads, Pop-ups, etc.), Women's Market, Yellow Pages Advertising

Revenue: $40,000,000

Tom Kenney *(Partner & Exec Creative Dir)*
Rebecca Cardin *(Bus Mgr & Controller)*
Liz Phelps *(Exec Dir-Media)*
Simon Duggan *(Dir-Photography)*
Samuel Keene *(Dir-Digital)*
Paul Prato *(Dir-Creative)*
Kyle Matos *(Acct Supvr)*
Jessica Marcucci *(Acct Exec)*

Accounts:
American Society for Prevention of Cruelty to Animals(ASPCA); New York, NY; 2008
Big Boy
Big Dog Mower Co (Agency of Record) Brand Awareness
Bright House Networks LLC Broadcast, Campaign: "Burned", Campaign: "Coming Home", Campaign: "Connecting Friends", Campaign: "First Dance"
Florida Aquarium; 2006
Freilli Motorsports
General Motors Hummer
Grand-Am Road Racing; Daytona Beach, FL; 2008
HITCH (Agency of Record) Crowdsourcing
Jailhouse Fire Hotsauce; 2006
LEGOLAND Florida Resort (Media Agency of Record) Digital Media, Strategic Media, Traditional Media
Lennar Homes Tampa (Agency of Record) Brand Strategy, Communications, Creative, Digital, Marketing, Media Buying, Media Planning, Public Relations, Social Media
Metropolitan Ministries; Tampa, FL; 2007
Tires Plus; 2006
Touch Vodka; 2006
Visit Tampa Bay (Agency of Record) Creative
YMCA

PR-BS
9735 Tavernier Dr, Boca Raton, FL 33496
Tel.: (561) 756-4298
Fax: (561) 883-3867
E-Mail: gary@pr-bs.net
Web Site: www.pr-bs.net

Employees: 1

Agency Specializes In: Broadcast, Corporate Communications, Crisis Communications, Event Planning & Marketing, Investor Relations, Media Buying Services, Media Planning, Print, Production (Print), Public Relations

Gary Schweikhart *(Co-Founder & Pres)*

Accounts:
Cranes BeachHouse Hotel Hotels/Tourism Services

PR CAFFEINE
2438 E 117th St Ste 100, Burnsville, MN 55337
Tel.: (612) 254-6300
E-Mail: info@prcaffeine.com
Web Site: www.prcaffeine.com

Agency Specializes In: Advertising, Digital/Interactive, Search Engine Optimization, Social Media

Ryan Berkness *(Founder & CEO)*
Bonnie Rae Backer *(Dir-Admin)*

Accounts:
New-Berkness Swiss
New-Car Buyer's Advocate
New-KSI Swiss
New-PetTronix
New-Titus Contracting

PRADINUK ADVERTISING

102-326 Wardlaw Ave, Winnipeg, MB R3L 0L6 Canada
Tel.: (204) 982-0700
Fax: (204) 947-5500
E-Mail: info@pradinuk.com

E-Mail for Key Personnel:
President: ronp@pradinuk.com

Employees: 4
Year Founded: 1979

Agency Specializes In: Advertising, Consulting, Public Relations

Approx. Annual Billings: $1,200,000

Denise Fyse *(Mgr-Admin)*

Accounts:
Winnipeg Convention Center; Winnipeg, Canada

PRAIRIE DOG/TCG

811 Wyandotte St, Kansas City, MO 64105-1608
Tel.: (816) 822-3636
Fax: (816) 842-8188
E-Mail: jhobbs@pdog.com
Web Site: www.pdog.com

Employees: 45

Agency Specializes In: Advertising, Health Care Services

Phil Smith *(Owner)*
Jerry Hobbs *(Mng Dir & Exec VP)*
Rachel Lupardus *(CFO & COO)*
Ross Wuetherich *(Grp Dir-Creative)*
Lisa Smith *(Acct Mgr)*
Donna Summers *(Fin Mgr)*
Tina Wheeler *(Mgr-Ops)*
Marie Baldwin *(Designer-Digital)*
Diane Roussin-Long *(Designer)*
Carrie Baer *(Coord-Client Rels)*

Accounts:
Anne Arundel Medical Center; Annapolis, MD
Baptist Health; Jacksonville, FL
Billings Clinic; Billings, MT
Capital Regional Medical Center; Tallahassee, FL
Elmhurst Memorial Healthcare; Elmhurst, IL
Fremont Area Medical Center; Fremont, NB
Garden Grove Hospital; Garden Grove, CA
Golden Valley Memorial Hospital; Clinton, MO
HCA East Division; Ft. Lauderdale, FL
HCA Midwest; Kansas City, MO
SwedishAmerican Health System; Rockford, IL
Texas Institute for Surgery
Triad Hospitals, Inc.
Trident Health System
Tulane Medical Center; New Orleans, LA
Ukiah Valley Medical Center; Ukiah, CA
Unity Health System
University of Connecticut Health
Western Missouri Medical Center

PRAXIS COMMUNICATIONS, INC.

2600 Philmont Ave Ste 111, Huntingdon Valley, PA 19006-5307
Tel.: (215) 947-2080
Fax: (215) 947-2256
E-Mail: advice@praxisagency.com
Web Site: www.praxisagency.com

E-Mail for Key Personnel:
President: agladish@praxcom.com
Creative Dir.: jlofurno@praxcom.com

Employees: 5
Year Founded: 1979

Agency Specializes In: Advertising, Brand Development & Integration, Business-To-Business, Collateral, Communications, Consulting, Corporate Identity, Direct Response Marketing, Exhibit/Trade Shows, High Technology, Industrial, Internet/Web Design, Newspapers & Magazines, Planning & Consultation, Print, Production, Public Relations, Strategic Planning/Research, Technical Advertising, Trade & Consumer Magazines, Travel & Tourism

Approx. Annual Billings: $5,000,000

Breakdown of Gross Billings by Media: Collateral: 15%; D.M.: 10%; Other: 5%; Plng. & Consultation: 10%; Print: 15%; Pub. Rels.: 15%; Strategic Planning/Research: 10%; Trade Shows: 5%; Worldwide Web Sites: 15%

Alan W. Gladish *(Owner)*
Tricia Barrett *(VP-Ops)*
James E Blair *(Dir-Internet Mktg)*
Leif Fifer *(Dir-Art)*
Janet LoFurno *(Dir-Creative)*
David Allen *(Mgr-Engrg)*
Ronnie Henrick *(Mgr-Interactive Media)*

Accounts:
Brooks Instrument, LLC; Hatfield, PA Flow Control Instrumentation; 1994
Extreme Broadband Engineering; Englishtown, NJ Cable Components; 2004
Financial Group Plus, LLC; PA Accounting Services; 1987
Kingsbury, Inc.; Philadelphia, PA Bearing & Lubrication Systems; 1992
Printers Trade; Philadelphia, PA Trade Printing; 1999
Vacuum Furnace Systems, Corp.; Souderton, PA Vacuum Furnaces for Commercial Heat Treating; 1997

PREACHER

119 W 8th St, Austin, TX 78701
Tel.: (512) 489-0200
E-Mail: info@preacher.co
Web Site: www.preacher.co

Year Founded: 2014

National Agency Associations: 4A's

Agency Specializes In: Advertising, Brand Development & Integration, Digital/Interactive, Event Planning & Marketing

Krystle Loyland *(Founder & CEO)*
Rob Baird *(Founder & Chief Creative Officer)*
Seth Gaffney *(Founder & Chief Strategy Officer)*
Taryn Kealani *(Art Dir)*
Eric Pieper *(Art Dir)*
Carson Mobley *(Strategist)*
Joe Hartley *(Copywriter)*

Accounts:
New-Tommy John

PRECISION ADVERTISING

5530 Pare St Ste 201, Montreal, Quebec H4P 2M1 Canada
Tel.: (514) 343-4949
Fax: (877) 743-4949
E-Mail: info@precisioncg.com
Web Site: www.precisioncg.com

Employees: 12
Year Founded: 1997

Agency Specializes In: Advertising, Brand Development & Integration, Digital/Interactive, Event Planning & Marketing, Exhibit/Trade Shows, Graphic Design, Internet/Web Design, Print, Public Relations, Social Media

Glen Eisenberg *(Pres)*
Jen Larry *(VP-Strategy & Ops)*
Richard Mondoux *(Controller)*
Jake Jones *(Dir-Art)*
Yves Sauriol *(Designer-Motion)*
Robyn Kessler *(Acct Coord)*
Catherine Lemay *(Acct Coord)*
Megan Covens *(Jr Planner-Strategic)*

Accounts:
ASM
Conrad C
Essilor
Neostrata
WestGroupe

PREJEAN CREATIVE, INC.

216 La Rue France, Lafayette, LA 70508
Tel.: (337) 593-9051
Web Site: www.prejeancreative.com

Year Founded: 1997

Agency Specializes In: Advertising, Collateral, Corporate Identity, Digital/Interactive, Logo & Package Design, Package Design

Kevin Prejean *(Owner & Dir-Creative)*
Art Young *(Dir-Content Dev)*

PRESIDIO STUDIOS

9719 Seneca Trl S, Lewisburg, WV 24901
Tel.: (304) 647-5656
Fax: (530) 451-9716
Toll Free: (888) 308-9650
E-Mail: info@presidiostudios.com
Web Site: www.presidiostudios.com

Agency Specializes In: Advertising, Broadcast, Content, Graphic Design, Internet/Web Design, Print

Timothy Luce *(Owner)*

Accounts:
Pocahontas County CVB

PRESTON KELLY

222 First Ave NE, Minneapolis, MN 55413
Tel.: (612) 843-4000
Fax: (612) 843-3900
E-Mail: iconicideas@prestonkelly.com
Web Site: www.prestonkelly.com

E-Mail for Key Personnel:
President: ckelly@prestonkelly.com

Employees: 45
Year Founded: 1950

National Agency Associations: 4A's-WORLDWIDE PARTNERS

Agency Specializes In: Advertising, Below-the-Line, Brand Development & Integration, Broadcast, Business Publications, Business-To-Business, Cable T.V., Children's Market, Collateral, Communications, Consumer Goods, Consumer Marketing, Consumer Publications, Digital/Interactive, Direct Response Marketing, Electronic Media, Fashion/Apparel, Financial, Graphic Design, Guerilla Marketing, Health Care Services, Household Goods, Integrated Marketing, International, Internet/Web Design, Legal Services, Leisure, Local Marketing, Luxury Products, Magazines, Market Research, Media Planning, Media Relations, Medical Products, Men's Market, Mobile Marketing, Newspaper, Newspapers & Magazines, Out-of-Home Media, Outdoor, Paid Searches, Planning & Consultation, Point of Purchase, Point of Sale, Print, Production, Production (Ad, Film, Broadcast), Production (Print), Public Relations, Publicity/Promotions, Radio, Regional, Restaurant, Retail, Search Engine Optimization, Social Marketing/Nonprofit, Social Media, Sponsorship, Sports Market, Strategic Planning/Research, T.V., Trade & Consumer Magazines, Travel & Tourism, Viral/Buzz/Word of Mouth, Women's Market

iconic ideas: An Iconic Idea is a meaningful symbol or concept consumers adopt to instantly identify and share your brand. Imagine the competitive advantage you'd have if every time a consumer saw or heard a message from you: Click! They connected your brand with a distinctive emotion or idea. An iconic idea is an instant embodiment of your brands DNA. Honest and authentic. Differentiating and clear. An iconic idea not only connects consumers with brands and product lines, it engages, focuses and inspires entire organizations. This can accelerate your marketplace momentum. Increase your service performance. And put internal staff and external partners on the same page. Iconic ideas work.

Approx. Annual Billings: $56,000,000

Breakdown of Gross Billings by Media: Digital/Interactive: 26%; Out-of-Home Media: 9%; Print: 7%; Radio: 22%; Strategic Planning/Research: 14%; T.V.: 22%

Chuck Kelly *(CEO)*
Chris Preston *(Principal, Exec VP & Dir-Creative)*
Katia Holmes *(VP & Acct Dir)*
Mark Jenson *(VP & Acct Dir)*
Peter Tressel *(VP & Dir-Creative & Digital)*
Dawn Leuer *(Controller)*
Anne Taylor *(Art Dir)*
Melissa Tresidder *(Art Dir)*
Scott Dahlgren *(Dir-Media & Connections)*
Beth Elmore *(Dir-Production Svcs)*
Yuliya Crevier *(Assoc Dir-Digital)*
Denise Loidolt *(Supvr-PR)*
Jaime Westlund *(Sr Media Planner & Buyer)*

Accounts:
Baker Tilly; Minneapolis, MN Accounting & Business Services; 2009
Caringbridge; Eagan, MN; 2013
Central Research Laboratories; Red Wing, MN Business to Business; 1952
Edina Realty; Edina, MN Billboard, Online; 2012
Elkay Manufacturing Company (Agency of Record)
Greater Twin Cities YMCA Campaign: "Another Reason Y", Campaign: "Cement Shoes", Health & Wellness; 2001
Gundersen Health System Campaign: "Baby", Campaign: "Camping", Campaign: "Therapy Dog"
HealthPartners; Bloomington, MN Group Health Insurance; 2007
InSinkErater; Racine, WI Campaign: "Stop the Raccoons", Digital Display Advertising, Social Media, Television; 2013
Mall of America; Bloomington, MN Entertainment, Fashion, Travel & Tourism, Retail; 2004
Medtronic, Moundsview, MN Cardiac Rhythm Disease Management, Neuro; 2011
National Marrow Donor Program; Minneapolis, MN Non-profit Bone Marrow Resource; 2008
Physicians Mutual Insurance Co Health & Life Insurance; 2008
Roundy's Supermarkets Inc.; Milwaukee, WI Grocery, Retail; 2005
SuperAmerica; Woodbury, MN; 2013

PRICE & PARTNERS, INC.
112 Krog St Ste 7, Atlanta, GA 30307
Tel.: (404) 428-9972
Web Site: www.priceandpartners.com

Agency Specializes In: Advertising, Digital/Interactive, Graphic Design, T.V.

Chris Shaw *(Dir-Interactive)*
Mary Tviet *(Dir-Interactive Creative)*
Molly Carter Gaines *(Strategist-Social Media)*

Accounts:
The Coca-Cola Company
Merigold Hunting Club, LLC

THE PRICE GROUP, INC.
1801 Broadway, Lubbock, TX 79401-3015
Tel.: (806) 763-5033
Fax: (806) 763-8030
E-Mail: phil.price@pricegroupinc.com
Web Site: www.pricegroupinc.com

E-Mail for Key Personnel:
President: phil.price@pricegroupinc.com
Creative Dir.: scott.zajicek@pricegroupinc.com
Media Dir.: pam.sharpe@pricegroupinc.com
Production Mgr.: mike.meister@pricegroupinc.com

Employees: 23
Year Founded: 1972

National Agency Associations: AAF

Agency Specializes In: Advertising, Agriculture, Arts, Automotive, Brand Development & Integration, Broadcast, Business Publications, Business-To-Business, Cable T.V., Co-op Advertising, Collateral, College, Consulting, Consumer Publications, Corporate Communications, Corporate Identity, Crisis Communications, Direct Response Marketing, Education, Electronic Media, Engineering, Entertainment, Environmental, Event Planning & Marketing, Exhibit/Trade Shows, Financial, Food Service, Government/Political, Graphic Design, Health Care Services, High Technology, Hospitality, Identity Marketing, In-Store Advertising, Industrial, Information Technology, Internet/Web Design, Legal Services, Local Marketing, Logo & Package Design, Media Buying Services, Media Planning, Media Relations, Medical Products, Multimedia, Newspaper, Newspapers & Magazines, Out-of-Home Media, Outdoor, Over-50 Market, Package Design, Planning & Consultation, Point of Purchase, Point of Sale, Print, Production, Promotions, Public Relations, Publicity/Promotions, Radio, Real Estate, Recruitment, Regional, Restaurant, Seniors' Market, Social Marketing/Nonprofit, Sponsorship, Strategic Planning/Research, Technical Advertising, Trade & Consumer Magazines, Transportation, Travel & Tourism, Web (Banner Ads, Pop-ups, etc.), Women's Market

Approx. Annual Billings: $13,000,000

Amanda Patterson *(VP & Controller)*
Pam Sharpe *(VP & Dir-Media)*
David Barnett *(Dir-Tech)*
Natalia Lawson *(Acct Exec)*

Accounts:
All Saints Episcopal School
American Cancer Society; Lubbock
American State Bank
Ballet Lubbock
Lubbock Chamber of Commerce
Lubbock Club
Lubbock Economic Development Association
Lubbock Power & Light
Lubbock Symphony Orchestra
Orlando's Italian Restaurant
Plains Cotton Coop Association
Raider Ranch
Rentrak Media Planning & Buying
Scoggin Dickey Buick, Chevrolet, Hummer, Saab
Sears Methodist Retirement System; Abilene, TX
Silent Wings Museum Foundation
Texas Tech Alumni Association
Texas Tech University College of Visual & Performing Arts
Tom Martin
Watson; Hobbs, NM Buick, Chevrolet, Hyundai, Pontiac
Zia Park & Black Gold Casino

PRICEWEBER MARKETING COMMUNICATIONS, INC.
10701 Shelbyville Rd, Louisville, KY 40243
Tel.: (502) 499-9220
Fax: (502) 491-5593
Web Site: www.priceweber.com

Employees: 60
Year Founded: 1968

National Agency Associations: 4A's-CSPA-DMA-PRSA-Second Wind Limited

Agency Specializes In: Advertising, Advertising Specialties, Alternative Advertising, Automotive, Brand Development & Integration, Branded Entertainment, Broadcast, Business Publications, Business-To-Business, Cable T.V., Co-op Advertising, Collateral, Commercial Photography, Communications, Consumer Marketing, Consumer Publications, Corporate Communications, Corporate Identity, Crisis Communications, Digital/Interactive, Direct Response Marketing, E-Commerce, Electronic Media, Email, Event Planning & Marketing, Exhibit/Trade Shows, Financial, Graphic Design, Guerilla Marketing, Health Care Services, High Technology, In-Store Advertising, Industrial, Integrated Marketing, International, Internet/Web Design, Local Marketing, Logo & Package Design, Luxury Products, Magazines, Marine, Media Buying Services, Media Planning, Media Relations, Medical Products, Merchandising, New Product Development, New Technologies, Newspaper, Newspapers & Magazines, Out-of-Home Media, Outdoor, Over-50 Market, Pharmaceutical, Planning & Consultation, Point of Purchase, Point of Sale, Print, Promotions, Public Relations, Publicity/Promotions, Radio, Real Estate, Retail, Sales Promotion, Search Engine Optimization, Sponsorship, Sports Market, Strategic Planning/Research, Sweepstakes, T.V., Technical Advertising, Trade & Consumer Magazines, Transportation, Travel & Tourism, Web (Banner Ads, Pop-ups, etc.)

Approx. Annual Billings: $52,000,000

Tony Beard *(Pres & Chief Creative Officer)*

Fred Davis *(CEO)*
Jeremy Schell *(Partner, Chief Digital Officer & VP)*
Mike Nickerson *(CMO)*
Clinton Hunter *(Exec VP & Grp Dir)*
Mel Bryant *(Brand Dir-Plng & Grp Dir-Creative)*
Jennifer Cline *(Acct Dir)*
Steve Kozarovich *(Acct Dir)*
J. C. Thorpe *(Dir-Creative)*
Brad Caraway *(Assoc Dir-Creative)*
Molly Owens *(Media Planner & Media Buyer)*
Lauren Cox *(Assoc Media)*

Accounts:
American Trucking Associations; Alexandria, VA Trucking Associations; 2003
Brown-Forman Beverages Worldwide Bolla Wines, Canadian Mist Whiskey, Early Times Kentucky Whiskey, Fontana Candida Wines, Korbel Champagne & Brandy, Michel Picard Wines, Old Forester Bourbon, Pepe Lopez Tequila; 1968
Cummins Inc.; Columbus, IN Diesel Engines; 1968
Godiva Chocolatier; New York, NY; 2006
Meritor
RJ Reynolds Tobacco; Winston-Salem, NC Tobacco Products; 1983
The Valvoline Co., Industrial Division; Lexington, KY Lubricants; 1995
Wabash National Trailer; Lafayette, IN; 2006

PRIMA INTEGRATED MARKETING
(Acquired by Publicis Groupe SA & Name Changed to Prima Arc)

PRIMACY
(Formerly Acsys Interactive)
157 New Britain Ave, Farmington, CT 06032
Tel.: (860) 679-9332
Web Site: www.theprimacy.com

Year Founded: 1994

Agency Specializes In: Advertising, Digital/Interactive, Mobile Marketing, Social Media

Stan Valencis *(Pres)*
Patrick Phalon *(Sr VP & Dir-Creative)*
Michael Stutman *(Sr VP-Strategy)*
Andy Berling *(VP-Bus Dev)*
Amy Hooper *(VP-Project Mgmt)*
Melissa Tait *(VP-Tech)*
Jeremy Walker *(VP-Digital Mktg)*
Mandy Davis *(Dir-Mktg-Media)*
Kurt Gannon *(Assoc Dir-User Experience)*
Brittany Beebe *(Acct Supvr)*

Accounts:
Amica Life Insurance Company
The Hartford
Mass Mutual
Otis Elevator Company
Saint Michael's College
Sikorsky
Timex
Yale-New Haven Hospital

PRIMARY DESIGN INC
57 Wingate St 4th Fl, Haverhill, MA 01832
Tel.: (978) 373-1565
Web Site: www.primarydesign.com

Employees: 5

Agency Specializes In: Advertising, Brand Development & Integration, Digital/Interactive, Email, Event Planning & Marketing, Logo & Package Design, Media Buying Services, Media Planning, Print

Revenue: $1,200,000

John Schroeder *(Pres & CEO)*
Christine Hardiman *(Sr Dir-Project)*
David Vadala *(Art Dir & Mgr-Studio)*
Liz Fedorzyn *(Sr Art Dir)*
Jamie Randazzo *(Creative Dir)*
Michael Hinde *(Sr Graphic Designer)*
Lynne Rempelakis *(Designer-Production)*

Accounts:
HomeStart Inc

PRIME ACCESS
(Acquired by Global Advertising Strategies)

PRIME ACCESS
55 Broad St 8th Fl, New York, NY 10004
Tel.: (212) 868-6800
Web Site: www.prime-access.com

Year Founded: 2012

Agency Specializes In: Advertising, Brand Development & Integration, Communications, Digital/Interactive, Media Planning

Chip Weinstein *(CEO)*
Margarita Peces *(Partner-Creative Brand)*
Harrisen Kim *(VP-Creative Svcs)*
John Church *(Dir-Creative)*
Christopher A. Davis *(Acct Supvr)*
Alex Blyakher *(Sr Graphic Designer-Studio)*
Olga Omelchenko *(Sr Designer)*

Accounts:
Novo Nordisk, Inc.

PRIME ADVERTISING
111 Gordon Baker Rd Ste 428, North York, ON M2H 3R1 Canada
Tel.: (416) 591-7331
Fax: (416) 591-7342
E-Mail: julileung@primead.com
Web Site: www.primead.com

Employees: 20
Year Founded: 1988

Agency Specializes In: Advertising

John Leung *(Pres)*
Juliana Leung *(VP)*
Timothy Sham *(Acct Exec)*
Ayushman Sharma *(Acct Exec)*

Accounts:
Telus

PRIME L.A
6525 Sunset Blvd Ste G2, Hollywood, CA 90028
Tel.: (323) 962-9207
Fax: (323) 962-7647
E-Mail: info@primela.com
Web Site: www.primela.com

Agency Specializes In: Advertising, Entertainment, Event Planning & Marketing, Financial, Infomercials, Merchandising, Public Relations

Suzi Bruno *(Founder & Pres)*

Accounts:
Adler Leather Furniture Rental Services
Boston Scientific Corporation
Broadway Jewelry Plaza
Crystal Promotions
Life Link International
North American Products
Xenon Entertainment

THE PRIME TIME AGENCY
1313 25th Ave, Gulfport, MS 39501
Tel.: (228) 863-8892
Fax: (228) 863-0236
E-Mail: primetime@theprimetimeagency.com
Web Site: www.theprimetimeagency.com

Agency Specializes In: Advertising, Brand Development & Integration, Broadcast, Collateral, Internet/Web Design, Logo & Package Design, Media Planning, Print, Public Relations, Social Media

Ted Riemann *(Owner & Dir-Creative)*
John Seymour *(Dir-Art)*
Shannon Bickett *(Office Mgr)*
Kerry Stoddard *(Acct Exec)*

Accounts:
Center for Health Management
Charter Bank
Harrison County Development Commission
Harrison County Tourism Commission
Haynes Electric, Inc.
Memorial Hospital at Gulfport
Mississippi Development Authority
Palace Casino Resort
Riemann Family Funeral Homes

PRIME VISIBILITY
1156 Ave of the Americas Ste 301, New York, NY 10036
Tel.: (866) 774-6381
E-Mail: hello@primevisibility.com
Web Site: www.primevisibility.com

Year Founded: 1998

Agency Specializes In: Advertising, Brand Development & Integration, Collateral, Email, Internet/Web Design, Logo & Package Design, Print, Search Engine Optimization, Social Media, Strategic Planning/Research

Pamela Nelson *(Sr Dir-Analytics & Reporting)*
Andrea Snyder *(Sr Dir-Digital Svcs)*
Christine Borg *(Sr Acct Dir)*
Sean Cashman *(Dir-Strategy & Fin Vertical)*
David Neuman *(Mgr-Social Media)*
Kathy Sanders *(Mgr-Copywriting Grp)*

Accounts:
Aio Wireless
Kidde Fire Fighting
Nutricap Labs

PRIMEDIA, INC.
350 5th Ave 59th Fl, New York, NY 10119
Tel.: (212) 601-1960
Fax: (212) 222-2357
Toll Free: (800) 796-3342
Web Site: www.primediany.com/

Year Founded: 1993

Richard Rutigliano *(Pres)*
Carl F. Salas *(Treas & Sr VP)*
Rachel Joyce *(Mgr-Mktg)*
Elizabeth O'Sullivan *(Media Buyer)*

Accounts:
Amex
Benchmark Hospitality
CDC
Fortis
Inmarkets

THE PRIMM COMPANY
112 College Pl, Norfolk, VA 23510-1992
Tel.: (757) 623-6234
Fax: (757) 622-9647
Toll Free: (800) 292-0299

E-Mail: office@primmco.com
Web Site: www.primmco.com

E-Mail for Key Personnel:
President: ron@primmco.com

Employees: 9
Year Founded: 1974

National Agency Associations: AAF

Agency Specializes In: Advertising, Automotive, Broadcast, Business-To-Business, Cable T.V., Co-op Advertising, Corporate Identity, Direct Response Marketing, Education, Electronic Media, Financial, Food Service, Government/Political, Graphic Design, Industrial, Internet/Web Design, Legal Services, Media Buying Services, Multimedia, Outdoor, Print, Production, Public Relations, Publicity/Promotions, Radio, Restaurant, Retail, Sales Promotion, Strategic Planning/Research, T.V., Yellow Pages Advertising

Approx. Annual Billings: $6,000,000

Breakdown of Gross Billings by Media: Cable T.V.: $400,000; Collateral: $110,000; D.M.: $70,000; Graphic Design: $75,000; Logo & Package Design: $35,000; Newsp.: $400,000; Out-of-Home Media: $400,000; Outdoor: $110,000; Production: $1,210,000; Radio: $800,000; Spot T.V.: $2,390,000

Ronald J. Primm *(Chm & Dir-Creative)*
Tiffany Curran *(Pres)*
Emily Primm *(CFO & VP)*
Steve Spencer *(Dir-Art)*
Stephanie Lee Elgin Dudley *(Mgr-Production)*
Sean Burke *(Specialist-Social Media)*
Dave Flanagan *(Strategist-Mktg & Adv)*
Sharon Oakley *(Specialist-Online Mktg)*

Accounts:
Eggleston Service

PRINCETON LYONS GRAPHICS LLC
51 Westcott Rd, Princeton, NJ 08540
Tel.: (609) 947-5641
Fax: (609) 497-1657
E-Mail: pel@lyonsgraphics.com
Web Site: www.lyonsgraphics.com

Employees: 2
Year Founded: 1977

Agency Specializes In: Corporate Identity, Education, Graphic Design, Health Care Services, Medical Products, Print

Approx. Annual Billings: $120,000

Breakdown of Gross Billings by Media: Collateral: $15,000; D.M.: $90,000

Patrick E. Lyons *(Dir-Comm)*

PRINCETON MARKETECH
2 Alice Rd, Princeton Junction, NJ 08550
Tel.: (609) 936-0021
Fax: (609) 936-0015
E-Mail: bzyontz@princetonmarketech.com
Web Site: www.princetonmarketech.com

E-Mail for Key Personnel:
President: bzyontz@princetonmarketech.com
Creative Dir.: renee@princetonmarketech.com

Employees: 4
Year Founded: 1987

Agency Specializes In: Business-To-Business, Collateral, Communications, Consulting, Consumer Marketing, Corporate Communications, Corporate Identity, Direct Response Marketing, E-Commerce, Electronic Media, Event Planning & Marketing, Financial, Graphic Design, High Technology, Internet/Web Design, Logo & Package Design, New Product Development, Planning & Consultation, Point of Purchase, Point of Sale, Production, Sales Promotion

Bob Zyontz *(Pres)*

Accounts:
Chase Business Banking; Columbus, OH Direct Mail & Marketing Communications for Customers & Prospects; 2008
Chase Commercial Bank Marketing; Chicago, IL Executive White Papers for C-Level Executives; 2006
Chase Commercial Bank Marketing; Chicago, IL Executive White Papers for C-Level Executives; 2006
Harleysville National Bank; Harleysville, PA Commercial, Private Banking Solutions, Retail; 2006

PRINCETON PARTNERS, INC.
205 Rockingham Row, Princeton, NJ 08540
Tel.: (609) 452-8500
Fax: (609) 452-7212
E-Mail: webmaster@princetonpartners.com
Web Site: www.princetonpartners.com

E-Mail for Key Personnel:
President: tsullivan@princetonpartners.com
Public Relations: rmanno@princetonpartners.com

Employees: 50
Year Founded: 1965

National Agency Associations: MAGNET

Agency Specializes In: Advertising, Advertising Specialties, African-American Market, Agriculture, Asian Market, Automotive, Aviation & Aerospace, Bilingual Market, Brand Development & Integration, Broadcast, Business Publications, Business-To-Business, Cable T.V., Children's Market, Collateral, Communications, Consulting, Consumer Marketing, Consumer Publications, Corporate Communications, Corporate Identity, Cosmetics, Digital/Interactive, Direct Response Marketing, E-Commerce, Education, Electronic Media, Engineering, Entertainment, Environmental, Event Planning & Marketing, Exhibit/Trade Shows, Fashion/Apparel, Financial, Food Service, Government/Political, Health Care Services, High Technology, Hispanic Market, In-Store Advertising, Industrial, Information Technology, Internet/Web Design, Investor Relations, Leisure, Local Marketing, Marine, Medical Products, Merchandising, Multimedia, New Product Development, Newspapers & Magazines, Outdoor, Over-50 Market, Pharmaceutical, Planning & Consultation, Point of Purchase, Point of Sale, Production, Public Relations, Real Estate, Recruitment, Restaurant, Retail, Sales Promotion, Seniors' Market, Sports Market, Strategic Planning/Research, Technical Advertising, Teen Market, Transportation, Travel & Tourism

Approx. Annual Billings: $12,000,000

Breakdown of Gross Billings by Media: Adv. Specialities: $3,000,000; Audio/Visual: $1,000,000; Consulting: $2,000,000; Corp. Communications: $1,000,000; Event Mktg.: $3,000,000; Point of Purchase: $300,000; Point of Sale: $200,000; Promos.: $1,000,000; Pub. Rels.: $200,000; Trade Shows: $300,000

Jeff Chesebro *(Pres)*
Thomas Sullivan *(CEO)*
Sheila Smith *(VP & Dir-Media)*
Paul Federico *(Dir-Creative)*
Leslie Glick *(Dir-Media)*
Robert Groves *(Mgr-Media)*
Jan Sullivan *(Mgr-HR)*

Accounts:
Activity Works
Adva
America Living Well
Capital Health
Directravel
Dome-Tech Solar
FMC Biopolymer
Greenwich Exterminating
Integrity Health
JLG
Pacer
PNC Bank
Sherwin Williams
Sun National Bank
Western Industries; Parsippany, NJ Residential & Commercial Pest Control
Yale Materials Handling Corporation; Greenville, NC International Lift Truck Marketer

PRINCIPOR COMMUNICATIONS
429 N St SW Ste S804, Washington, DC 20024
Tel.: (202) 595-9008
Fax: (202) 595-9008
E-Mail: info@principor.com

Year Founded: 2002

John Jordan *(Owner)*

Accounts:
Disability Management Employer Coalition (DMEC) Trade Assoc.; San Diego, CA Disability Management Processes
Fidelis
Nucleus Solutions Technology; Arlington, VA Technology to Improve Workplace Productivity
Office of Community Services
Passfaces

PRISMATIC
(Formerly FDG CREATIVE)
745 N Magnolia Ave #301, Orlando, FL 32803
Tel.: (407) 895-0029
Fax: (407) 895-0017
Web Site: helloprismatic.com

Employees: 7

Agency Specializes In: Advertising, Brand Development & Integration, Catalogs, Collateral, College, Consulting, Direct-to-Consumer, Education, Environmental, Exhibit/Trade Shows, Graphic Design, Integrated Marketing, Internet/Web Design, Local Marketing, Logo & Package Design, Multimedia, Package Design, Print, Publishing, Social Marketing/Nonprofit

Approx. Annual Billings: $660,000

Breakdown of Gross Billings by Media: Adv. Specialities: $30,000; Collateral: $100,000; Graphic Design: $300,000; Logo & Package Design: $30,000; Worldwide Web Sites: $200,000

Stephanie Darden *(Pres & Dir-Creative)*
James Dahlgren *(Dir-Interactive Design)*
Ashley Heafy *(Dir-Art)*
Maurix Suarez *(Dir-Emerging Media & Dev)*
Trinity Tesler *(Project Head)*

PRODIGAL MEDIA COMPANY
42 Mcclurg Rd, Boardman, OH 44512
Tel.: (330) 707-2088
Fax: (330) 707-2089
Toll Free: (877) 776-3442
E-Mail: inquiries@prodigalmedia.com
Web Site: prodigalcompany.com

Employees: 15
Year Founded: 1994

Agency Specializes In: Advertising, Brand Development & Integration, Business-To-Business, Cable T.V., Collateral, Commercial Photography, Communications, Consumer Marketing, Corporate Communications, Corporate Identity, Digital/Interactive, Direct Response Marketing, E-Commerce, Email, Exhibit/Trade Shows, Graphic Design, Health Care Services, Identity Marketing, Industrial, Integrated Marketing, Internet/Web Design, Investor Relations, Local Marketing, Logo & Package Design, Market Research, Media Buying Services, Media Planning, Media Relations, Medical Products, Multimedia, Newspaper, Newspapers & Magazines, Package Design, Paid Searches, Planning & Consultation, Point of Sale, Print, Production, Production (Print), Promotions, Public Relations, Publicity/Promotions, Radio, Regional, Retail, Sales Promotion, Search Engine Optimization, Social Marketing/Nonprofit, Strategic Planning/Research, T.V., Trade & Consumer Magazines, Viral/Buzz/Word of Mouth, Women's Market, Yellow Pages Advertising

Approx. Annual Billings: $10,000,000

Jeff Hedrich *(Pres & Strategist-Brand)*
Vince Bevacqua *(Exec VP)*
Maggie Courtney-Hedrich *(VP-Bus Dev)*
Adrienne Sabo *(Assoc Dir-Creative)*
Tony Marr *(Mgr-Digital Audio & Video)*
Shari Pritchard *(Mgr-Production & Sr Designer)*
Jill Jenkins *(Acct Exec)*
Juliana Seelman *(Designer-Multimedia)*
Evan Sobinovsky *(Designer-Interactive)*

Accounts:
Sheely
Sony Campaign: "Sony In Voice Of Poland"

THE PRODUCERS, INC.
4742 N 24th St Ste 340, Phoenix, AZ 85016
Tel.: (602) 264-7100
Fax: (602) 264-6600
E-Mail: jvfly@theproducersinc.com
Web Site: www.theproducersinc.com

E-Mail for Key Personnel:
Creative Dir.: edwin@pros1.com

Employees: 6
Year Founded: 1977

Agency Specializes In: Business-To-Business, Direct Response Marketing, High Technology

Judi Victor *(Chm & CEO)*
Jeanette Long *(Mgr-Mktg)*

Accounts:
BUSRide Magazine
General Dynamics
Hamilton Telecommunications
Heartland Payment Systems
Honeywell, Inc.
Hypercom, Inc.
Iridium LLC
Marine Spill Response Corporation
Motorola Solutions, Inc.
Seeley International

PRODUCT MARKETING GROUP, INC.
978 Douglas Ave Ste 100, Altamonte Springs, FL 32714-5205
Tel.: (407) 774-6363
Fax: (407) 774-6548
E-Mail: bwine@productmarketingfl.com
Web Site: www.productmarketingfl.com

Employees: 5
Year Founded: 1985

Agency Specializes In: Advertising, Advertising Specialties, Aviation & Aerospace, Collateral, Corporate Communications, Education, Engineering, Event Planning & Marketing, Financial, Food Service, Government/Political, Health Care Services, In-Store Advertising, Internet/Web Design, Local Marketing, Medical Products, Point of Purchase, Point of Sale, Public Relations, Real Estate, Restaurant, Travel & Tourism

Approx. Annual Billings: $1,500,000

Breakdown of Gross Billings by Media: Adv. Specialities: $100,000; Brdcst.: $50,000; Bus. Publs.: $100,000; Collateral: $500,000; Consulting: $50,000; D.M.: $100,000; E-Commerce: $100,000; Event Mktg.: $50,000; Exhibits/Trade Shows: $50,000; Fees: $100,000; Newsp.: $50,000; Outdoor: $50,000; Point of Purchase: $100,000; Radio: $50,000; T.V.: $50,000

Beverly B. Winesburgh *(Pres & Principal)*

Accounts:
Gerard J. Pendergast Architect
Orlando Sanford International Airport; Sanford, FL; 2004
Sanford Economic Development Council
Seminole County Medical Society
Seminole County Property Appraiser; Sanford, FL; 1998
Universal Energy Corp.

PROFILES, INC.
3000 Chestnut Ave Ste 201, Baltimore, MD 21211
Tel.: (410) 243-3790
Fax: (410) 243-3792
E-Mail: info@profilespr.com
Web Site: www.profilespr.com

Employees: 15

Agency Specializes In: Advertising, Crisis Communications, Event Planning & Marketing, Media Relations, Strategic Planning/Research

Amy Burke Friedman *(Pres)*
Jamie Watt Arnold *(Sr VP)*
Christina Camba *(Acct Exec)*
Mitch Case *(Acct Exec)*
Leanna Bernhard *(Jr Acct Exec)*

Accounts:
The National Aquarium
RA Sushi; Los Angeles, CA
Zuckerman Spaeder LLP; Washington, DC

PROFITFUEL, INC.
(Acquired by & Name Changed to Yodle)

PROGRESS
99 E River Dr, East Hartford, CT 06108
Tel.: (860) 528-1100
Web Site: www.progress-digital.com

Agency Specializes In: Advertising, Brand Development & Integration, Content, Digital/Interactive, Email, Search Engine Optimization, Social Media

Eduardo Pelegri-Llopart *(VP-Tech)*
Mark Troester *(Sr Dir-Product Mktg & Enterprise Application Dev)*

Accounts:
Blue Back Dental
Coordinated Systems Inc
IGX Global
Iron Duck
PIC Aviation
Prestone Products Corp.

PROJECT 2050
28 W 25th St, New York, NY 10010
Tel.: (646) 290-8700
Fax: (646) 336-6220
E-Mail: fearless@p2050.com
Web Site: www.p2050.com

Agency Specializes In: African-American Market, Asian Market, Bilingual Market, Hispanic Market, Teen Market

Phil Colon *(Pres)*
Angela Arambulo *(Dir-Art & Consulting)*
Giuseppe D'Alessandro *(Strategist)*

Accounts:
Boost Mobile
Ea Sports
Jarritos
Latina
New Era
Nike
Target
Timberland
Vibe
Virgin Entertainment Group
Voto Latino

PROJECT ROW
19903 12th Ave NW, Seattle, WA 98177
Tel.: (206) 399-1821
Web Site: www.project-row.com

Employees: 7
Year Founded: 2015

Agency Specializes In: Broadcast, Collateral, Digital/Interactive, Direct Response Marketing, Local Marketing, Magazines, Mobile Marketing, Newspaper, Newspapers & Magazines, Out-of-Home Media, Outdoor, Print, Production, Production (Print), Radio, Social Media, T.V., Viral/Buzz/Word of Mouth, Web (Banner Ads, Pop-ups, etc.)

Kelsey Berow *(Co-Founder & CEO)*

Accounts:
In Concert with Good; 2015

PROJECT: WORLDWIDE
3600 Giddings Rd, Auburn Hills, MI 48326
Tel.: (248) 475-2500
Web Site: www.project.com

Employees: 1,900

Revenue: $275,000,000

Robert G. Vallee, Jr. *(Chm & CEO)*
Laurence Vallee *(Pres)*
David Drews *(CFO)*
Joost Dop *(CEO-EMEA)*
Ben Taylor *(CEO-Asia Pacific)*
Peter Lambousis *(Sr VP-Corp Strategy)*
Brian Martin *(Sr VP-Mktg & Comm)*
Ben Casey *(VP-Digital Engagement Mktg)*

Holdings

Argonaut Inc.
576 Folsom St, San Francisco, CA 94105
(See Separate Listing)

G7 Entertainment Marketing

4000 Centre Pointe Dr, La Vergne, TN 37086
(See Separate Listing)

George P. Johnson Company, Inc.
3600 Giddings Rd, Auburn Hills, MI 48326-1515
(See Separate Listing)

Juxt
(Formerly Juxt Interactive, Inc.)
576 Folsom St, San Francisco, CA 94105
(See Separate Listing)

Motive
620 16th St Ste 200, Denver, CO 80202
(See Separate Listing)

Partners+Napier
192 Mill St Ste 600, Rochester, NY 14614-1022
(See Separate Listing)

The Pitch Agency
8825 National Blvd, Culver City, CA 90232
(See Separate Listing)

Shoptology Inc
7800 N Dallas Pkwy Ste 160, Plano, TX 75024
(See Separate Listing)

Spinifex Group
14/32 Ralph Street, Alexandria, NSW 2015 Australia
Tel.: (61) 283321300
Fax: (61) 293192232
Web Site: www.spinifexgroup.com

Agency Specializes In: Advertising, Digital/Interactive

Glen Joseph *(Chm)*
Dhani Sutanto *(Dir-Creative)*

Accounts:
Acura Automobile Mfr
CISCO Hardware & Software Development Services
Events NSW Campaign: "VIVID MCA - Painting the Building"
IBM Australiasia Information Technology Services
Nissan Ellure Automobile Mfr
QAFCO Fertiliser Mfr
Streets Campaign: "Magnum Infinity"
Unilever Magnum
Vodafone Telecommunications Services

School
645 Walnut Street, Boulder, CO 80302
Tel.: (720) 390-6000

Year Founded: 2013

Max Lenderman *(CEO)*
Joseph Corr *(Principal & CTO)*

Accounts:
Bolthouse Farms
Nike
United Nations
Vail Film Festival (Agency of Record) Digital, Print, Radio, Sponsorship Activation

Raumtechnick
Plieninger Strasse 54, 73760 Ostfildern, Germany
Tel.: (49) 7158 98740
Web Site: raumtechnik.com/

Achim Reinhuber *(Sr VP & Mng Dir)*

Accounts:
Audi
BMW
Maquet Getinge Group
Mercedes-Benz
Siemens
WMF

PROLIFIC CREATIVE AGENCY
2510 E 15th St Ste 201, Tulsa, OK 74104
Tel.: (918) 615-9610
Web Site: www.prolificcreative.com

Agency Specializes In: Advertising, Brand Development & Integration, Digital/Interactive, Internet/Web Design, Print

James Schellhorn *(CEO & Dir-Creative)*
Ian Russell *(Dir-Art)*
Kholter Hunt *(Acct Mgr)*
Taylor Foley *(Mgr-Production)*
Savannah Haddock *(Acct Exec)*

Accounts:
Kazar Audio Video

PROM KROG ALTSTIEL INC.
1009 W Glen Oaks Ln Ste 107, Mequon, WI 53092-3382
Tel.: (262) 241-9414
Fax: (262) 241-9454
E-Mail: info@pkamar.com
Web Site: pkamar.publishpath.com

E-Mail for Key Personnel:
President: bruce@pkamar.com

Employees: 12
Year Founded: 1986

Agency Specializes In: Advertising, Advertising Specialties, Agriculture, Automotive, Aviation & Aerospace, Brand Development & Integration, Broadcast, Business Publications, Business-To-Business, Cable T.V., Co-op Advertising, Collateral, Commercial Photography, Communications, Consulting, Consumer Marketing, Consumer Publications, Corporate Identity, Digital/Interactive, Direct Response Marketing, E-Commerce, Education, Electronic Media, Engineering, Event Planning & Marketing, Exhibit/Trade Shows, Fashion/Apparel, Financial, Food Service, Graphic Design, Health Care Services, High Technology, Industrial, Information Technology, Internet/Web Design, Investor Relations, Leisure, Logo & Package Design, Magazines, Marine, Media Buying Services, Medical Products, Merchandising, Multimedia, New Product Development, Newspaper, Newspapers & Magazines, Out-of-Home Media, Outdoor, Pharmaceutical, Planning & Consultation, Point of Purchase, Point of Sale, Print, Production, Public Relations, Publicity/Promotions, Radio, Recruitment, Restaurant, Retail, Sales Promotion, Sports Market, Strategic Planning/Research, Sweepstakes, T.V., Technical Advertising, Trade & Consumer Magazines, Transportation, Travel & Tourism

Approx. Annual Billings: $21,000,000

Breakdown of Gross Billings by Media: Adv. Specialities: 3%; Audio/Visual: 5%; Bus. Publs.: 5%; Co-op Adv.: 2%; Collateral: 8%; Consulting: 2%; D.M.: 5%; E-Commerce: 2%; Exhibits/Trade Shows: 5%; Farm Publs.: 5%; Fees: 8%; Graphic Design: 3%; Internet Adv.: 5%; Logo & Package Design: 2%; Mdsg./POP: 2%; Other: 2%; Plng. & Consultation: 5%; Point of Purchase: 2%; Print: 5%; Production: 2%; Promos.: 2%; Pub. Rels.: 5%; Sls. Promo.: 2%; Strategic Planning/Research: 2%; Trade & Consumer Mags.: 3%; Trade Shows: 3%; Video Brochures: 2%; Worldwide Web Sites: 3%

Bruce Prom *(Owner)*
Vicki Lee *(VP & Dir-Media & Client Svcs)*
Bill Elverman *(Dir-PR)*
George Wamser *(Production Mgr-Art)*
Sandy Mercier *(Acct Exec)*
Joy LeClair *(Media Planner & Media Buyer)*

Accounts:
Caleffi North America; Milwaukee, WI Solar Water Heating; 2006
Cartridge World Refillable ink cartridges; 2012
Mels Pig Roast; Cedarburg WI Annual Charity Event; 2012
Richard Wolf Endoscopic devices; 2012
ROYDAN; Manitowoc, WI Software; 2012
Viega North America; Bedford, MA Radiant Hydronic Heating Systems; 2001
Waymar Orthopedic Technologies, Inc; Mequon, WI Orthopedic Surgery & Rehab Equipment; 2005
Yacht Club at Sister Bay; Sister Bay, WI Luxury Resort; 2009

PROMEDIA GROUP
4106 Reas Ln, New Albany, IN 47150
Tel.: (812) 948-6214
E-Mail: info@promediagroup.com
Web Site: www.promediagroup.com

Employees: 12

Agency Specializes In: Advertising, Brand Development & Integration, Internet/Web Design, Print

Revenue: $2,000,000

Dan Williamson *(CEO)*
Mary Ram *(Mng Partner)*
Christin Higgins *(Dir-Media)*
Vicki Williamson *(Office Mgr)*

Accounts:
City of Jefferson Indiana
ERL Marine

PROMO DIGITAL
(Acquired by Ogilvy & Mather & Name Changed to Promo Interactive)

THE PROMOTION FACTORY
5 E 19th St 6th Fl, New York, NY 10003
Tel.: (212) 217-9065
E-Mail: info@thepromofact.com
Web Site: www.thepromofact.com

Agency Specializes In: Advertising, Entertainment, Event Planning & Marketing, Fashion/Apparel, Luxury Products, Media Buying Services, Media Planning, Media Relations, Public Relations, Social Media, Sponsorship, Strategic Planning/Research

Venanzio Ciampa *(Pres)*
Kaitlin Derkach *(Acct Dir)*
Alexandre Corda *(Dir-Digital Mktg)*
Britt Berg *(Sr Acct Exec)*

Accounts:
Buccellati
Girard-Perregaux
JeanRichard

PROOF ADVERTISING
114 W 7th St Ste 500, Austin, TX 78701
Tel.: (512) 345-6658
Fax: (512) 345-6227
Web Site: www.proof-advertising.com

Employees: 70
Year Founded: 1989

National Agency Associations: 4A's

Agency Specializes In: Advertising, Brand Development & Integration, Business-To-Business, Co-op Advertising, Collateral, College, Computers & Software, Digital/Interactive, Hospitality, In-Store Advertising, Leisure, Local Marketing, Logo & Package Design, Media Buying Services, Point of Purchase, Point of Sale, Real Estate, Restaurant, Sales Promotion, Sponsorship, Trade & Consumer Magazines, Travel & Tourism

Approx. Annual Billings: $60,000,000

Lynn Dobson *(CFO)*
Carolyn Fisher *(Grp Dir-Media)*
Sparky Witte *(Grp Acct Dir)*
Rob Story *(Dir-Art & Assoc Dir-Creative)*
Heather Hager *(Supvr-Interactive Media)*
Roy Eagan *(Acct Exec)*
Tiffany Han *(Media Planner & Buyer-Digital)*
Nina Rodriguez *(Media Planner & Buyer)*
Emily Scruggs *(Media Planner & Buyer-Digital)*
Mackenzie Rachal *(Asst Acct Exec)*
Jared Sisson *(Asst Acct Exec)*
Mathieu Gregoire *(Asst Media Planner & Buyer)*
Robb Lampman *(Sr Media Planner & Buyer)*

Accounts:
3M; Austin, TX Electrical Products, Visual, Fiber Optics & Telecom; 1989
BancVue B2B Media, Consumer-Driven Digital, Grassroots Media Strategy, Kasasa, Partnerships, Planning & Buying, Sponsorships, Traditional
Baylor University; 2003
ERA Real Estate Business-to-Business, Consumer Marketing
Extraco Banks; Waco, TX Financial Services; 2008
Honeywell Aerospace
Huawei Device USA
Hyatt Hotels Corporation
Hyatt Resorts
San Antonio Convention & Visitors Bureau
San Antonio Tourism
Stubb's Bar-B-Q (Agency of Record) Anytime Sauces, Cooking Sauces, Creative, Digital, Media Buying, Media Planning, Print, Social
Subway Restaurants Creative, Marketing, Quick Service Restaurants, Strategy; 2005
United States Army; 2006

PROOF INTEGRATED COMMUNICATIONS

1110 Vermont Ave NW 12th Fl, Washington, DC 20005
Tel.: (202) 530-4700
Fax: (202) 530-4500
E-Mail: info@proofic.com
Web Site: www.proofic.com

Year Founded: 2009
National Agency Associations: 4A's

Agency Specializes In: Advertising, Brand Development & Integration, Collateral, Crisis Communications, Digital/Interactive, Graphic Design, Market Research, Media Planning, Print, Social Media

Matt Lieppe *(Chief Creative Officer)*
Michael Beno *(Chief Client Officer)*
Tyler Pennock *(Mng Dir-Digital Health Strategy)*
Ladon Roeder *(Exec Dir-Creative)*
Ethan Farber *(Sr Dir-Digital Strategy)*
Steve King *(Sr Dir-Digital Strategy)*
Stephanie Hu *(Dir-Analytics Products)*
Luke Peterson *(Dir-Analytics Products)*
Nick Hartman *(Assoc Dir-Creative)*

Accounts:
Chase Bank
The Coca-Cola Company
Federation Equestre International
Ford Motor Company
Intel Corporation
Nevada Tourism Digital
The Procter & Gamble Company
Sony Corporation of America

Proof Integrated Communications

(Formerly Proof Interactive Communications)
230 Park Ave S, New York, NY 10003-1502
Tel.: (212) 614-6000
Fax: (212) 598-6966
E-Mail: info@proofic.com
Web Site: www.proofic.com

Employees: 25
National Agency Associations: 4A's

Agency Specializes In: Electronic Media, Graphic Design, Internet/Web Design, Production

Tyler Pennock *(Mng Dir-Digital Health Strategy)*
Ethan Farber *(Sr Dir-Digital Strategy)*
Steve King *(Sr Dir-Digital Strategy)*
Elizabeth Penniman *(Sr Dir-Creative-Production)*
Jody Lange *(Dir-Creative)*
Dan McGiffin *(Dir-Creative)*
Luke Peterson *(Dir-Analytics Products)*
Nick Hartman *(Assoc Dir-Creative)*
Jose Rodriguez *(Assoc Dir-Creative)*

PROPAGANDA GLOBAL ENTERTAINMENT MARKETING

2 Bis Rue De La Maison Rouge, 1207 Geneva, Switzerland
Tel.: (41) 22 339 90 80
Fax: (41) 22 339 90 89
E-Mail: switzerland@propagandagem.com
Web Site: www.propagandagem.com

Employees: 12
Year Founded: 1991

Agency Specializes In: Advertising Specialties, Brand Development & Integration, Branded Entertainment, Event Planning & Marketing, Exhibit/Trade Shows, Integrated Marketing, Media Planning, Media Relations, Product Placement, Publicity/Promotions, T.V.

Ruben Igielko-Herrlich *(Owner)*
Sophie Joller *(Office Mgr-Global)*
Vanessa Adams *(Mgr-Bus Dev)*

Accounts:
Audi
Bang & Olufsen
Campari
Casio
Diesel
Lacoste
Lamborghini
MV Augusta
Nokia
Panasonic
Pro Chili
Rimowa
Santa Margherita
Tag Heuer

Branches

Propaganda Americas

11264 Playa Ct, Culver City, CA 90230
Tel.: (310) 202-2300
Fax: (310) 397-2310
E-Mail: usa@propagandagem.com
Web Site: www.propagandagem.com

Employees: 15

Agency Specializes In: Sponsorship

Daphne Briggs *(VP)*
Brett Newman *(Dir-Production-TV)*

PROPANE STUDIO

1160 Battery St Ste 350, San Francisco, CA 94111
Tel.: (415) 550-8692
E-Mail: newbusiness@propanestudio.com
Web Site: www.propanestudio.com

Year Founded: 2003

Agency Specializes In: Advertising, Brand Development & Integration, Digital/Interactive, Integrated Marketing, Mobile Marketing, Planning & Consultation, Social Media

Marylee George *(COO)*
Neil Chaudhari *(Principal & Dir-Strategy)*
Rahul Odedra *(Exec Dir-Creative)*

Accounts:
Charles Schwab
Ghiradelli
Hitachi
Kaiser Permanente
Macy's, Inc.
VW / AUDI

PROPELLER

1428 Brickell Ave 6th Fl, Miami, FL 33131
Tel.: (305) 400-7985
Fax: (305) 400-7990
Web Site: www.flypropeller.com

Employees: 35
Year Founded: 1991

Agency Specializes In: Above-the-Line, Advertising, Advertising Specialties, Affluent Market, Alternative Advertising, Arts, Aviation & Aerospace, Brand Development & Integration, Business Publications, Business-To-Business, Cable T.V., Co-op Advertising, Collateral, Communications, Consumer Goods, Consumer Marketing, Consumer Publications, Corporate Identity, Customer Relationship Management, Digital/Interactive, Direct Response Marketing, Direct-to-Consumer, E-Commerce, Electronic Media, Email, Environmental, Event Planning & Marketing, Exhibit/Trade Shows, Financial, Graphic Design, Guerilla Marketing, Health Care Services, Identity Marketing, In-Store Advertising, Integrated Marketing, International, Internet/Web Design, Investor Relations, Leisure, Local Marketing, Logo & Package Design, Luxury Products, Magazines, Marine, Market Research, Media Buying Services, Media Planning, Media Relations, Medical Products, Mobile Marketing, Multimedia, New Product Development, Newspaper, Newspapers & Magazines, Outdoor, Package Design, Paid Searches, Pharmaceutical, Planning & Consultation, Podcasting, Point of Purchase, Point of Sale, Print, Production, Production (Ad, Film, Broadcast), Promotions, Public Relations, Publicity/Promotions, Radio, Real Estate, Restaurant, Retail, Sales Promotion, Search Engine Optimization, Sponsorship, Stakeholders, Strategic Planning/Research, Sweepstakes, T.V., Trade & Consumer Magazines, Travel & Tourism, Viral/Buzz/Word of Mouth, Web (Banner Ads, Pop-ups, etc.)

Approx. Annual Billings: $5,000,000

Dan Merrell *(Co-Founder, Pres & CEO)*

Sue Beddingfield *(VP)*
Laura Beth Stubblefield *(Sr Dir-Media & Comm)*
Brian Lange *(Dir-Strategic Partnerships)*
Jared Henderson *(Mgr-Mktg)*
Sam Santamaria *(Mgr-Mktg)*

Accounts:
Guggenheim Investments Inc.
Hawks Gate Resort
M & M Aerospace Hardware Inc.
The National Parkinsons Foundation
Occidental Hotels & Resorts
Primetime Race Group
Quantum Builders
Silver Hill Financial

PROPERVILLAINS
(Formerly Leap LLC)
45 Bromfield St Fl 11, Boston, MA 02108
Tel.: (617) 721-7749
Web Site: propervillains.agency

Year Founded: 2012

Agency Specializes In: Advertising, Brand Development & Integration, Crisis Communications, Digital/Interactive, Outdoor, Package Design, Print, Public Relations, Radio, Social Media

Jeff Monahan *(Co-Founder, Strategist & Writer)*
Meghan Gardner *(Partner & Dir-PR)*

Accounts:
Wovenware (Public Relations Agency of Record)

PROPHET
3340 Peachtree Rd, Atlanta, GA 30326
Tel.: (404) 812-4130
Web Site: www.prophet.com

Agency Specializes In: Advertising, Brand Development & Integration, Graphic Design, Strategic Planning/Research

Brad White *(Partner)*
Mat Zucker *(Partner)*
Robert Huey *(Dir-Fin & Controller)*
Hector Pottie *(Assoc Partner & Dir-Creative-London)*
Laurie Santos *(Dir-Firm Ops)*
David Brabbins *(Assoc Partner)*
Alan Casey *(Assoc Partner)*
Jessica Everett *(Assoc Partner)*
Mike Fleming *(Assoc Partner)*
Jason Stabile *(Assoc Partner)*

Accounts:
Bayerische Motoren Werke Aktiengesellschaft
Cisco Systems, Inc.
GE Healthcare
Johnson & Johnson
McDonald's Corporation
Zurich Financial Services AG

PROPHIT MARKETING
154 N Broadway St, Green Bay, WI 54303
Tel.: (920) 435-4878
E-Mail: info@prophitmarketing.com
Web Site: www.prophitmarketing.com

Agency Specializes In: Advertising, Digital/Interactive, Graphic Design, Internet/Web Design, Print

Lisa Pritzl *(Dir-Process Mgmt & Art Dir)*
Emily Katers *(Mgr-Process)*
Meredith Bartos *(Coord-Events)*

Accounts:
Festival Foods

PROPOINTE
2401 Rosecrans Ave Ste 380, El Segundo, CA 90245-1495
Mailing Address:
PO Box 2395, El Segundo, CA 90245-1495
Tel.: (310) 337-0542
Fax: (310) 695-6065
Toll Free: (888) 337-0542
E-Mail: ask@propointe.com
Web Site: www.propointe.com

E-Mail for Key Personnel:
President: rsinger@propointe.com

Employees: 7
Year Founded: 1988

Agency Specializes In: Advertising, Business-To-Business, Co-op Advertising, Consulting, Consumer Marketing, Customer Relationship Management, Digital/Interactive, Direct Response Marketing, Direct-to-Consumer, E-Commerce, Email, Financial, Guerilla Marketing, In-Store Advertising, Internet/Web Design, Local Marketing, Restaurant, Retail, Telemarketing

Approx. Annual Billings: $2,400,000

Breakdown of Gross Billings by Media: Consulting: 10%; D.M.: 40%; Internet Adv.: 20%; Local Mktg.: 30%

Robert Singer *(Principal)*

PROSPECTMX
210 W Grant St, Lancaster, PA 17603
Toll Free: (877) 312-7331
Web Site: www.prospectmx.com

Year Founded: 2007

Agency Specializes In: Affiliate Marketing, Consulting, Internet/Web Design, Paid Searches, Search Engine Optimization

Steve Young *(Co-Founder & CFO)*
Joshua Cranmer *(VP-Mktg)*
Ashley Walter *(Dir-Ops)*
Scott Rehnberg *(Mgr-Relationship Mktg)*
Vinson Sensenig *(Mgr-Relationship)*

Accounts:
MES Inc. Engineering & Consulting Services

PROTAGONIST LLC
360 W 31st St Ste 1000, New York, NY 10001
Tel.: (212) 677-7450
Fax: (212) 253-8265
E-Mail: info@beaprotagonist.com
Web Site: www.beaprotagonist.com

Year Founded: 2008

Agency Specializes In: Advertising, Brand Development & Integration, Digital/Interactive, Print, Sponsorship, T.V.

Tom Cotton *(Partner)*
Jordan Rednor *(Partner)*
Sophia Donohue *(Client Svcs Dir)*
Wyndham Stopford *(Dir-Creative)*
Kirandeep Sumal *(Acct Supvr)*
Isabel Stanish *(Jr Copywriter)*

Accounts:
Zicam LLC (Advertising Agency of Record) Digital, Social Marketing, Traditional

PROTERRA ADVERTISING
5055 Keller Springs Rd Ste 560, Addison, TX 75001
Tel.: (972) 732-9211
Fax: (972) 732-7687
E-Mail: sandyr@proterraadvertising.com
Web Site: http://proterrausa.com/

Employees: 8
Year Founded: 1993

Agency Specializes In: Above-the-Line, Advertising, Advertising Specialties, African-American Market, Alternative Advertising, Below-the-Line, Bilingual Market, Brand Development & Integration, Branded Entertainment, Broadcast, Business-To-Business, Cable T.V., Collateral, College, Commercial Photography, Communications, Consulting, Consumer Goods, Consumer Marketing, Content, Corporate Communications, Corporate Identity, Cosmetics, Customer Relationship Management, Digital/Interactive, Direct Response Marketing, Direct-to-Consumer, E-Commerce, Education, Electronic Media, Electronics, Email, Entertainment, Environmental, Event Planning & Marketing, Exhibit/Trade Shows, Experience Design, Financial, Food Service, Graphic Design, Guerilla Marketing, Health Care Services, Hispanic Market, Hospitality, Household Goods, In-Store Advertising, Infomercials, Information Technology, Integrated Marketing, Internet/Web Design, Leisure, Local Marketing, Logo & Package Design, Magazines, Market Research, Media Buying Services, Media Planning, Media Relations, Medical Products, Mobile Marketing, Multicultural, Multimedia, New Product Development, New Technologies, Newspaper, Newspapers & Magazines, Out-of-Home Media, Outdoor, Package Design, Planning & Consultation, Point of Purchase, Point of Sale, Print, Product Placement, Production, Promotions, Public Relations, Publicity/Promotions, Radio, Regional, Restaurant, Retail, Sales Promotion, Search Engine Optimization, Seniors' Market, Social Marketing/Nonprofit, Sponsorship, Sports Market, Strategic Planning/Research, Sweepstakes, T.V., Teen Market, Trade & Consumer Magazines, Transportation, Travel & Tourism, Urban Market, Viral/Buzz/Word of Mouth, Web (Banner Ads, Pop-ups, etc.)

Approx. Annual Billings: $29,500,000

Breakdown of Gross Billings by Media: Brdcst.: $4,500,000; D.M.: $10,000,000; Print: $15,000,000

Danny Sanchez *(Founder & CEO)*
Larry Sanchez *(Pres & Dir-Small Bus Mktg)*
Lisa De Leon *(Pres)*
Maren Minchew *(Dir-Digital Experiences & PR)*
Sandy Rivera *(Office Mgr)*
Laura Barron *(Acct Exec)*
Josh Salganik *(Strategist-SEO)*

Accounts:
The Adolphus; Dallas, TX
American Airlines Center; Dallas, TX; 2000
AT&T Communications Corp.; Dallas, TX; 1995
CHUBB Insurance; Chicago, IL; 2005
GE Financial; Schaumburg, IL; 2005
Hit Entertainment (Barney); Dallas, TX; 2003
LA Fitness; Irvine, CA
Mattress Firm
State Farm Auto Insurance; Bloomington, IL; 1995
Visionworks of America, Inc.

PROTOBRAND
1818 Pine St 4th Fl, Philadelphia, PA 19103
Tel.: (215) 735-6621
E-Mail: k2k@comcat.com
Web Site: www.protobrand.com

Agency Specializes In: Market Research

Ric Lipman *(Owner)*

Accounts:
3M
AT&T Communications Corp.
Bristol Myers-Squibb
Coca-Cola Refreshments USA, Inc.
General Mills
Helene Curtis
IBM
Johnson & Johnson
Kelloggs
Nabisco Foods
Pfizer
Procter & Gamble
Quaker Oats
Schering-Plough
United States Army

PROTOTYPE ADVERTISING, INC
1035 Avalon Dr, Forest, VA 24551
Tel.: (434) 846-2333
Fax: (434) 846-2339
Web Site: www.prototypeadvertising.com

Employees: 50
Year Founded: 2002

Agency Specializes In: Advertising, Email, Graphic Design, Print

Todd Allen *(Owner)*
Josh Oppenheimer *(Pres & Principal)*
Lori Keys *(Exec VP)*
David Norcross *(VP-Sls)*
Klint Holland *(Sr Dir-Web)*
Todd Hacker *(Dir-Video)*
Megan Norcross *(Dir-Comm)*

Accounts:
Banker Steel Company, LLC.
Delta Power Equipment Corp.
Famous Footwear
Jacobsen Ltd.
Tech Global Inc.
University of Pittsburgh

PROVE AGENCY
12910 Culver Blvd Ste D, Los Angeles, CA 90066
Tel.: (310) 737-8600
Web Site: prove.it/

Employees: 30
Year Founded: 2010

Agency Specializes In: Advertising, Brand Development & Integration, Digital/Interactive, Direct Response Marketing, Electronic Media, High Technology, Internet/Web Design, Planning & Consultation, Strategic Planning/Research

Approx. Annual Billings: $5,000,000

Vincent Cevalte *(Acct Dir-Digital)*
Jamie Stevenson *(Acct Dir)*
Jenna Doherty *(Dir-Digital Production)*
Joy Go *(Dir-Search Optimization & Strategy)*
Kyle Mitrione *(Acct Mgr)*
Matthew Poldberg *(Mgr-SEM)*

Accounts:
GE GE Lightening

PROVERB
195 W Springfield St, Boston, MA 02118-3406
Tel.: (617) 266-0965
Web Site: www.thetruthmadesimple.com

Employees: 15

Agency Specializes In: Brand Development & Integration, Communications, Digital/Interactive, Product Placement, Strategic Planning/Research

Daren Bascome *(Owner)*
Christine Needham *(Mng Partner & Dir-Client Svcs)*
Sarah Mushtaq *(Dir-Art & Graphic Designer)*
Tamika Reid *(Jr Designer)*

Accounts:
Boston Public Schools Awareness Campaign, BPS Arts Expansion Initiative
Bump Water Brand-Building

PROVIDENCE MARKETING GROUP
9151 Lerum Ln, Pepin, WI 54759
Tel.: (715) 442-2078
Web Site: www.providencemarketinggroup.net

Agency Specializes In: Advertising, Media Buying Services, Public Relations, Social Media, Strategic Planning/Research

Jeff Bergmann *(Pres)*
Luke Hartle *(VP-Content & Distr)*
Glenn Walker *(VP)*

Accounts:
Heartland Wildlife Institute
Mystery Ranch (Marketing Agency of Record) Media Planning, Public Relations
Pradco Outdoor Brands
Siberian Coolers (Marketing Agency of Record) Public Relations

PROXIMITY CHICAGO
410 N Michigan Ave, Chicago, IL 60611
Tel.: (312) 595-2779
Fax: (312) 595-2682
Web Site: proximityworld.com

Year Founded: 2008

Agency Specializes In: Advertising, Digital/Interactive, Graphic Design, Internet/Web Design, Social Media, Technical Advertising

Fred Koblinger *(CEO-PKP BBDO)*
Katie Summy *(Sr VP & Client Svc Dir)*
Kamil Redestowicz *(Dir-Digital Creative)*

Accounts:
Blackberry CRM
Hewlett-Packard Company
Johnson & Johnson
Marriott International, Inc.
Mercedes-Benz USA Inc.
Mondelez International, Inc.
PepsiCo Inc.
The Procter & Gamble Company
Volkswagen Group of America, Inc.
WBEZ Campaign: "2032 Membership Drive", Campaign: "Do It. For Chicago", Campaign: "Interesting People Make Interesting People", Campaign: "We Want Listeners Tomorrow. Go Make Babies Today"

PROXIMO MARKETING STRATEGIES
348 McLaws Cir Ste 3, Williamsburg, VA 23185
Tel.: (757) 741-8098
Toll Free: (888) 325-8159
Web Site: www.proximomarketing.com

Year Founded: 2012

Agency Specializes In: Advertising, Brand Development & Integration, Digital/Interactive, Graphic Design, Internet/Web Design, Social Media

Will Melton *(Founder & Strategist-Digital Mktg)*
Katelin Cosner *(Dir-Bus Dev)*
Brittany Shaffer *(Dir-Social Media)*
Scott George *(Mgr-Ops)*

Accounts:
DXV American Standard
Guardian Point
Natasha House
Norfolk Plumbing

PRUITT HUMPHRESS POWERS & MUNROE, INC.
25 Saint Marks Rivers Edge Dr, Saint Marks, FL 32355
Tel.: (850) 925-1050
Fax: (850) 925-1054
E-Mail: phpm@polaris.net
Web Site: www.phpm.com

Employees: 5
Year Founded: 1971

Agency Specializes In: Business Publications, Business-To-Business, Communications, Corporate Identity, Direct Response Marketing, Graphic Design, Industrial, Media Buying Services, New Product Development, Newspapers & Magazines, Print, Production, Public Relations, Strategic Planning/Research, Technical Advertising

Approx. Annual Billings: $2,500,000

Breakdown of Gross Billings by Media: Graphic Design: 50%; Trade & Consumer Mags.: 50%

R. Michael Pruitt *(Pres & CEO)*
Savoy Brown *(Dir-Art)*
Glenda Pruitt *(Mgr-Ops)*

PS
1133 Broadway Ste 923, New York, NY 10010
Tel.: (212) 367-0908
Fax: (212) 202-5450
E-Mail: info@psnewyork.com
Web Site: www.insideps.com/

Agency Specializes In: Advertising, Brand Development & Integration, Corporate Identity, Digital/Interactive, Internet/Web Design, Logo & Package Design, Web (Banner Ads, Pop-ups, etc.)

Penny Hardy *(Partner & Dir-Creative)*
Vivi Feng *(Designer)*

Accounts:
Ecotones
Elysian Landscapes
H3
Steven Harris Architects
Taisoo Kim Partners

PUBLIC COMMUNICATIONS, INC.
One E Wacker Dr Ste 2450, Chicago, IL 60601
Tel.: (312) 558-1770
Fax: (312) 558-5425
E-Mail: ideas@pcipr.com
Web Site: www.pcipr.com

Employees: 45
Year Founded: 1963

Agency Specializes In: Public Relations, Publicity/Promotions

Craig Pugh *(Pres)*
Jill L. Allread *(CEO)*
Pamela Oettel *(CFO & COO)*
Remi Gonzalez *(Sr VP)*
Leigh Wagner *(Sr VP)*
Johnathon Briggs *(VP)*
Sara Conley *(VP)*

Ruth A. Mugalian *(VP)*
Grant Fuller *(Dir-Digital Strategy)*
Charlie Rice-Minoso *(Asst Acct Exec)*

Accounts:
Adler School of Professional Psychology
AIDS Foundation of Chicago (Agency of Record)
American Board of Medical Specialties
American Society for Clinical Pathology
British School of Chicago
ProCure Treatment Centers, Inc; Bloomington, IN

THE PUBLIC RELATIONS & MARKETING GROUP

156 N Ocean Ave, Patchogue, NY 11772
Tel.: (631) 207-1057
Fax: (631) 337-4190
Web Site: www.theprmg.com

Year Founded: 2002

Agency Specializes In: Advertising, Brand Development & Integration, Event Planning & Marketing, Government/Political, Graphic Design, Internet/Web Design, Media Relations, Public Relations, Social Media

John C. Zaher *(Founder, Pres & CEO)*
Laura Larson *(Creative Dir)*

Accounts:
New-Ben's Kosher Delicatessen Restaurant & Caterers

PUBLICIS & HAL RINEY

(Name Changed to Riney)

PUBLICIS GROUPE S.A.

133 Ave des Champs-Elysee, 75008 Paris, France
Tel.: (33) 1 44 43 70 00
Fax: (33) 1 44 43 75 25
E-Mail: contact@publicisgroupe.com
Web Site: www.publicisgroupe.com

Employees: 45,001
Year Founded: 1926

National Agency Associations: EAAA

Agency Specializes In: Advertising

Revenue: $7,670,804,400

Jean-Yves Naouri *(COO)*
Dan Connolly *(CEO-Level Studios)*
Arthur Sadoun *(CEO-Publicis Worldwide)*
Joseph A. LaSala, Jr. *(Gen Counsel)*
Jean-Michel Etienne *(Grp CFO & Exec VP)*
Olivier Altmann *(Sr VP-Comm & Admin)*
Olivier Fleurot *(Sr VP)*
Jean-Michel Bonamy *(VP-IR & Strategic Fin Plng)*
Stephane Estryn *(Dir-Mergers & Acq)*
Carlos Mera *(Dir-Creative)*
Lea Rissling *(Dir-Art)*

Accounts:
Allstate
American Express
AstraZeneca
AT&T Communications Corp.
Audi
New-AXA
BMW
Carrefour SA Global Advertising
New-CitiGroup, Inc. Global Media
Club Med
Coca-Cola Great Britain
Dassault Systems
Ferrero Media
Heineken (Lead Global Agency)
Intel
JCPenney
Kellogg's
Kraft Foods
Kraft Cadbury (Media Buying Agency)
Lancome
L'Oreal USA, Inc.
Marriott
Nestle Nescafe
Nike
Nissan
Novartis
O2
Oracle
Orange Poland Smart Offer
Pernod Ricard
Philip Morris
Polo Ralph Lauren
Procter & Gamble Crest, Oral B, Tampax
Renault Campaign: "Renault Tv", Campaign: "Twizy Launch Party"
Rokkan Aer Lingus
Sanofi
New-Sears Holdings Corp. Digital, Sears (Agency of Record)
Shell Oil
Siemens
Sony Ericsson
Telefonica
Toyota
Wal-Mart
Walt Disney Home Video, Gaming & Movie Studio
Zurich Financial

Austria

Publicis

Kettenbruckengasse 16, A-1040 Vienna, Austria
Tel.: (43) 1 588 09 0
Fax: (43) 1 588 09 111
E-Mail: office@publicis.at
Web Site: www.publicis.at

Employees: 80

Agency Specializes In: Advertising, Automotive, Consumer Goods, Consumer Marketing, Consumer Publications

Elisabeth Pelzer *(Mng Dir & Head-Austrian Hub Ops)*

Accounts:
Cafe Hawelka
CUBE
Fanta
General Motors Company Campaign: "Zafira Echoes", Chevrolet
HP
Innovatives Osterreich
LG
Maggi
Magna
NOM
Pfizer
Renault Megane CC
STIHL Leaf Blowers
UNHCRUN
Verkehrsburo
Wein Enegie
Zewa

Belgium

Duval Guillaume

Uitbreidingstraat 2-8, B-2600 Antwerp, Belgium
Tel.: (32) 3 609 09 00
Fax: (32) 3 609 09 19
E-Mail: info@duvalguillaume.com
Web Site: www.duvalguillaume.com

Employees: 200

Agency Specializes In: Advertising, Communications, Digital/Interactive, Financial, Recruitment

Jonas Caluwe *(Art Dir)*
Elke Janssens *(Acct Dir-Intl)*
Ervin Ramrattan *(Art Dir)*
Ad Van Ongeval *(Dir-Art)*
Piet Wulleman *(Dir-Strategy)*
Diane Deherdte *(Office Mgr)*
Jef Leysen *(Acct Mgr)*

Accounts:
Arla Foods Apetina (Global Lead Agency)
AXA Campaign: "Maxi Prepaid: Going to like by likes"
Belagom
New-British Broadcasting Corporation Save The Hoff
Carlsberg Breweries
Castello
Coca-Cola Campaign: "Fishing & Knitting", Campaign: "Hypnosis", Campaign: "Open Happiness", Campaign: "Petanque", Campaign: "You have 70 seconds", Coke Zero
De Opvoedingslijn Childrens' Choir
Dexia Employment Benefits Banking, Financial Services, Insurance
Febelfin
Manpower Human Resource Services
Newspaperswork
Nutricia
Organ Donor Foundation
Plan Belgium
Reborn to Be Alive
Sara Lee
Smirnoff
TNT A Dramatic Surprise on a Quiet Square, Campaign: "Belgian Arrival", Campaign: "Push to add drama", Campaign: "TNT: A dramatic surprise on an ice-cold day", Campaign: "We Know Drama"
Vallformosa

Publicis

Koolmijnenkaai 62 Quai Des Charbonnages, 1080 Brussels, Belgium
Tel.: (32) 2 645 3511
Fax: (32) 2 646 3456
E-Mail: info@publicis.be
Web Site: publicis-brussels.tumblr.com

Employees: 47
Year Founded: 1953

Alain Janssens *(Mng Partner & Dir-Creative)*
Johan Parmentier *(Mng Partner)*
Seb De Roover *(Head-Digital)*
Tom Berth *(Creative Dir)*
Jeannette Westerhout *(Bus Dir)*
Geert De Rocker *(Dir-Creative)*
Eric Piette *(Copywriter)*

Accounts:
3M Campaign: "Library"
Avvocati Senza Frontiere
BNP Paribas Fortis Campaign: "Life Moves Forward"
Carrefour Carrefour Express
Fortis Bank
Maggi
Minute Maid
Nescafe
Perfect Wash
Post-It
Renault Campaign: "From 0 to 62 MPH in 6 seconds.", Megane RS
Reporters Without Borders Talking Ad
Responsible Young Drivers Campaign: "Driving Test", Campaign: "Texting & driving test"
Wonderbra

Advertising Agencies

Bosnia & Herzegovina

M.I.T.A.
Trg Solidarnofpi 2A, 71000 Sarajevo, Bosnia & Herzegovina
Tel.: (387) 33 768 895
Fax: (387) 33 768 875
E-Mail: alna@mita.ba
Web Site: www.mita.ba

Employees: 20

Agency Specializes In: Media Buying Services

Ejub Kucuk *(CEO)*
Azra Pilav *(Media Dir)*
Elma Kadric *(Dir-Digital)*
Melissa Sefer Licin *(Dir-PR)*

Bulgaria

Publicis Marc
Abacus Business Center, 118 Bulgaria Blvd., 1618 Sofia, Bulgaria
Tel.: (359) 24340710
Fax: (359) 29159015
E-Mail: contacts@publicis-marc.bg
Web Site: www.publicis.bg

Agency Specializes In: Advertising, Brand Development & Integration

Nikolai Nedelchev *(Mng Dir)*
Kalina Petkova *(Deputy Mng Dir)*
Anna Georgieva *(Art Dir)*
Sergei Georgiev *(Dir-Art)*
Milena Ivanova *(Dir-Art)*
Karl Betz *(Acct Mgr)*
Darina Ivanova *(Acct Mgr)*
Simona Popova *(Acct Mgr)*
Rumen Kirov *(Copywriter)*

Accounts:
Olineza Olineza Chili Sauce, Sweating Dog
Renault
Tema

Croatia

Publicis d.o.o.
Heinzelova 33, 10000 Zagreb, Croatia
Tel.: (385) 1 23 09 100
Fax: (385) 1 23 09 101
E-Mail: office@publicis.hr
Web Site: www.publicis.com

Employees: 40

Damir Brcic *(CEO)*

Accounts:
Garnier
Heineken
HP
Renault
T-Mobile US

Cyprus

Marketway Ltd.
Marketway Building, 20 Karpenisiou Street, 1077 Nicosia, Cyprus
Tel.: (357) 22 391000
Fax: (357) 22 391150
E-Mail: marketway@marketway.com.cy

Employees: 42

Naya Koutroumani *(Head-Creative)*
Christos Christodoulou *(Dir-Art & Studio)*
Alessio Criscuoli *(Dir-Art)*
Stella Violari *(Dir-PR)*
Amalia Chiromeridou *(Mgr-New Bus Dev)*

Accounts:
Cybarco
Green Dot
Hannibal Veg Restaurant
Izi Kill
La Vache Qui Rit
Lantis Developments
Lantis Solar
Muskita Aluminium
Super Home Center
Tabasco Campaign: "Extremely Hot"
Thanos Hotels
Top Kinisis
Toyota Campaign: "Cake Girl", Campaign: "Don't shoot and drive.", Instagram, Lexus
Vavlitis Hotels

Czech Republic

Publicis
Jankovcova 1114-1123, 170 00 Prague, 7 Czech Republic
Tel.: (420) 234 711 111
Fax: (420) 234 711 199
E-Mail: publicis@publicis.cz
Web Site: www.publicis.cz

Employees: 60

Michal Winkler *(Mng Dir)*
Ekaterina Gavricheva *(Dir-Bus Dev)*
Marek Gult *(Dir-Creative)*
Jakub Hanzlicek *(Dir-Creative)*
Mahulena Poliakova *(Dir-PR)*
Petr Neumann *(Client Svc Dir)*

Accounts:
Allianz
Axman Production
British Airways
CITI
Clarion
Elite Rent
Garnier Fructis
Hewlett-Packard
Janssen-Cilag
L'Oreal Natea
Mactrend
Rent Point
Rowenta
Sanofi Aventis
Sanofi Synthelabo
Tefal

Denmark

Reputation
Bredgade 15, DK-1260 Copenhagen, Denmark
Tel.: (45) 3338 5070
Fax: (45) 3338 5071
E-Mail: info@reputationcph.com
Web Site: www.reputationcph.com

Employees: 36

Mikkel Jonsson *(Owner)*
Alexander Peitersen *(Owner)*
Christian Madsen *(Partner & Dir-Client Svcs)*
Charlotte Gautier *(Acct Dir)*
Betina Foss *(Acct Mgr)*
Peter Rude Torp *(Office Mgr-Reputation)*

Accounts:
Copenhagen Business School
Huset i Magstraede
Lundbeck
Max Factor
Nycomed
P & G
Radiometer
Sanofi-Aventis
Storebaelt
UCB Pharma
World OutGames

France

BOZ Paris
22 rue de Courcelles, 75008 Paris, France
Tel.: (33) 1 44 95 99 00
Fax: (33) 1 44 95 99 19
E-Mail: eric@boz.fr
Web Site: www.boz.fr

Employees: 30

Carole Wassermann *(Dir Gen)*
Eric Deschamps *(Dir-Creative)*
Yves Le Gars *(Dir-Medico-Mktg)*
Valerie Landon *(Dir-Medical & Multichannel Strategy)*
Barbara Baudier *(Acct Mgr)*

Carre Noir
24 rue Salmon de Rothschild, 92288 Suresnes, Cedex France
Tel.: (33) 1 57 32 85 00
Fax: (33) 1 42 94 06 78
E-Mail: main02@carre-noir.fr
Web Site: www.carrenoir.com

Employees: 150

Agency Specializes In: Advertising

Christophe Fillatre *(Pres)*
Clementine Segard *(Grp Acct Dir-Branding & Design)*
Gregoire Betoulaud *(Dir-Creative)*
Didier Colpaert *(Dir-Creative)*
David Hausman *(Dir-Creative)*
Claire Morel *(Dir-Artistic)*
Gorana Garevski *(Assoc Dir)*
Sibyl Roux *(Acct Mgr-Brand Design & Pkg)*

Phonevalley
131 Ave Charles de Gaulle, Neuilly, 92200 Paris, France
Tel.: (33) 1 42 80 57 22
Fax: (33) 1 42 80 60 48
E-Mail: contact@phonevalley.com
Web Site: www.phonevalley.com

Employees: 60

Agency Specializes In: Mobile Marketing

Patrick Herrmann *(CTO)*
Olivier Le Garlantezec *(Mng Dir-Europe)*
Emilie Berenguer *(Sr Acct Dir)*
Franck Corcuff *(Dir-Production)*

Accounts:
Air France-KLM Group
Colgate Palmolive
Doctors Without Borders
Mercedes Benz
Mondadori
Paramount
The PhoneHouse
T-Online
Universal
Virgin

Publicis Activ Annecy
(Formerly Publicis Alpes)
Park Nord Les Pleiades no26, BP 434, 74370 Metz-Tessy, France
Tel.: (33) 4 50 52 64 94
Fax: (33) 4 50 52 65 91
E-Mail: agence@publicisactive-alpes.fr
Web Site: www.publicisactiv-lyon.fr

Employees: 9

Alexandre Collomb *(Exec Mng Dir)*
Yves Dauteuille *(Dir-Creative)*
Cyril Flautat *(Dir-Artistic)*
Christoph Gros *(Dir-Artistic)*
Geraldine Audibert *(Sr Acct Mgr)*

Publicis Activ Strasbourg
(Formerly Publicis Koufra)
1 rue du Dome, 67000 Strasbourg, France
Tel.: (33) 3 88 14 35 36
Fax: (33) 3 88 14 35 00
E-Mail: franck.barennes@publicisactiv.com
Web Site: www.publicisactiv-bordeaux.fr

Employees: 25

Viviane Beoletto *(Assoc Dir)*

Publicis Conseil
133 Champs-Elysees, 75008 Paris, 08 France
Tel.: (33) 1 444 37000
Fax: (33) 1 4443 7525
Web Site: www.publicisgroupe.com

Employees: 100

Publicis Dialog
133 Avenue des Champs Elysees, CEDEX, 75008 Paris, France
Tel.: (33) 1 44 43 78 00
Fax: (33) 1 44 43 78 77
Web Site: www.publicis-dialog.fr

Employees: 150
Year Founded: 1998

Agency Specializes In: Direct Response Marketing, Event Planning & Marketing, Sales Promotion

Thierry Brule *(Deputy Dir Gen)*
Christian Verger *(CEO-France)*
Nicolas Zunz *(VP-Publicis France)*
Nabila Rakibi *(Acct Dir)*
Rick Sherfey *(Dir-Strategic Plng-Europe)*
Matthieu Droulez *(Sr Art Dir)*

Accounts:
New-AXA Group
Cap Gemini
Fidelity
HP
Kenzo Mode Campaign: "Kenzo Website"
La Halle Campaign: "The Sac Shopper"
McDonald's
Nestla Sencha Shizuoka
Nicolas
Oasis
Pampryl
PlayStation Campaign: "We are the Players, we are Playstation"
Renault Campaign: "Renault Ingots Operation"
Sanofi Ipraalox Campaign: "Frequent heartburn?"

Publicis Et Nous
33 rue des Jeuneurs, 75012 Paris, France
Tel.: (33) 1 55 35 90 90
Fax: (33) 1 55 35 90 91
Web Site: www.publicisgroupe.com

Employees: 35

Isabelle Pignon-Mashola *(CIO-EMEA)*
Peggy Nahmany *(VP & Dir-Comm)*
Dominique Le Bourhis *(Grp Treas & VP)*
Thomas Barbusse *(Controller-Intl Fin)*
Sabrina Pittea *(Coord-Comm)*
Marco Gennari *(Grp Controller-FP&A)*
Nicolas Laungani *(Grp Controller-Fin-FP&A Dept)*
Denis Rageot *(Grp Controller-Fin-FP&A Dept)*

Accounts:
Club Med
MGI Luxury Group Ebel Watches

Publicis Soleil
44 Blvd Longchamp, 13001 Marseilles, France
Tel.: (33) 4 91 10 79 70
Fax: (33) 4 91 10 79 95
Web Site: www.publicisgroupe.com

Employees: 45

Benoit Filliat *(Dir-Artistic)*
Julien Meurisse *(Copywriter)*

Accounts:
Aqualung
La Provence Newspaper

Publicis.Net
133 Ave des Champs Elysees, 75002 Paris, France
Tel.: (33) 1 55 34 44 44
Fax: (33) 1 55 34 44 20
E-Mail: contact@publicisnet.fr
Web Site: www.publicis.com

Employees: 60

Agency Specializes In: Internet/Web Design

Fabienne Regna-Marius *(Controller-Mgmt)*

Accounts:
BNP Paribas
Coca-Cola Refreshments USA, Inc.
Dim
Disneyland Resort Paris
Giorgio Armani
Hygena
L'Oreal
Lancaster
Lesieur
Orange
Petit Bateau
Renault
SFR Ckoiceholdup
Voyages SNCF

Germany

Pixelpark AG
Bergmannstrasse 72, 10961 Berlin, Germany
Tel.: (49) 3050580
Fax: (49) 3050581400
E-Mail: info@pixelpark.com
Web Site: www.publicispixelpark.de

Employees: 377
Year Founded: 1991

Dirk Kedrowitsch *(COO)*
Christian Jungbluth *(Gen Mng Dir-Fin)*
Ralf Niemann *(Gen Mng Dir-Client Svcs)*
Gotz Teege *(Gen Mng Dir-Strategy)*

Subsidiaries

Publicis Pixelpark
(Formerly Pixelpark Bielefeld GmbH)
Walther-Rathenau-Strasse 33, D-33602 Bielefeld, Germany
Tel.: (49) 521 98780 0
Fax: (49) 521 98780 49
E-Mail: presse@pixelpark.com
Web Site: www.publicispixelpark.de

Employees: 52

Agency Specializes In: Communications, E-Commerce

Stefan Schopp *(Mng Dir)*
Olav A. Waschkies *(Mng Dir)*
Roland Vanoni *(Chief Creative Officer-Deutschland)*
Jorg Puphal *(Mng Dir-Erlangen)*
Christian Jungbluth *(Gen Mgr-Deutschland)*
Andreas Brunsch *(Exec Creative Dir)*
Timm Weber *(Exec Dir-Creative-Hamburg)*
Katharina Lohse *(Bus Dir)*
Gotz Teege *(Gen Mng Dir)*

Accounts:
Allianz
Boehringer Ingelheim
Deutsche Post
Drager Campaign: "Fire Quencher"
Lesen Und Schreiben Campaign: "Life Of Fear"

Publicis Pixelpark
Implerstr 11, 81371 Munich, Germany
Tel.: (49) 899040070
Fax: (49) 4.99E+11
E-Mail: kontakt.muenchen@publicis.de
Web Site: www.publicispixelpark.de

Agency Specializes In: Advertising, Corporate Communications, Digital/Interactive, Event Planning & Marketing, Public Relations

Olaf Wolff *(Mng Dir)*
Mathias Wundisch *(Mng Dir-Munich)*
Joel Flammann *(Gen Mgr-Deutschland)*
Stephan Ganser *(Exec Dir-Creative-Munich)*
Madeleine Schleemilch *(Sr Dir-Art)*
Michele Imhof *(Dir-Art)*

Accounts:
European Aeronautic Defence & Space Company EADS N.V.
Lupine Lighting Systems
One Earth - One Ocean
Siemens Aktiengesellschaft

Greece

Publicis Hellas
3-5 Menandrou Street, Kifissia, 14561 Athens, Greece
Tel.: (30) 210 628 1000
Fax: (30) 210 628 1009
E-Mail: info@publicis.gr

Employees: 50

Nicky Acrioti *(CEO)*
Panagiotis Kokkoris *(Dir-IT)*
Maria Argyropoulou *(Client Svc Dir)*
Angelina Desilla *(Client Svc Dir)*
Aris Sterodimas *(Sr Accountant)*

Accounts:
British American Tobacco
Coca-Cola Refreshments USA, Inc.
Garnier
Hewlett Packard
Mattel
Nestle
Sanofi-Synthelabo

Sara Lee
Whirlpool

Italy

Carmi & Ubertis Design S.R.L.
2 Via Savio Alessandro, 15033 Casale Monferrato, Italy
Tel.: (39) 014271686
Fax: (39) 014 276 444
Web Site: www.carmieubertis.it

Employees: 21

Agency Specializes In: Advertising

Alessandro Ubertis *(Owner)*
Elio Carmi *(Dir-Creative)*

Carre Noir Turino
Corso Re Umberto 87, 10128 Turin, Italy
Tel.: (39) 011 56 21 937
Fax: (39) 011 53 86 11
E-Mail: ilaria.scardovi@carrenoir.it
Web Site: www.carrenoir.com

Employees: 20

Agency Specializes In: Advertising, Brand Development & Integration, Branded Entertainment

Beatrice Mariotti *(Chief Creative Officer & VP)*

Accounts:
Agile

Publicis Networks
Via Riva Villa Santa 3, 20145 Milan, Italy
Tel.: (39) 02 310 37 1
Fax: (39) 02 349349 00
E-Mail: publicis@publicis.it
Web Site: www.publicis.it

Employees: 100

Bruno Bertelli *(Exec Creative Dir)*
Cristiana Boccassini *(Exec Creative Dir)*
Federica Fragapane *(Acct Dir)*
Giada Salerno *(Acct Dir)*
Alessandro Candito *(Dir-Art & Supvr-Creative)*
Francesco Epifani *(Dir-Art & Supvr)*
Sophian Bouadjera *(Dir-Art)*
Paolo Bartalucci *(Copywriter)*

Accounts:
Campari Group
Jagermeister Campaign: "#BETHENIGHTMEISTER"
Club Med
Coca-Cola Campaign: "Never Extinguish", Campaign: "Visions"
Garnier
Heineken Campaign: "Navigate The Sub", Campaign: "Reach the Sunrise"
Leroy Merlin Household,Garden and Pets
Nestla Italiana Campaign: "Trolley"
Rai
Renault
Security Service Campaign: "Following Eyes"
Sony Ericsson
Tavola Campaign: "Caravan"
Whirlpool
Yovis Viaggio Campaign: "The Great Escape"

Publicis S.R.L.
Via A Riva di Villasanta 3, 20145 Milan, Italy
Tel.: (39) 02 31037 1
Fax: (39) 02 3493 4898 (Mgmt)
E-Mail: publicis@publicis.it
Web Site: www.publicis.it

Employees: 115

Agency Specializes In: Advertising

Bruno Bertelli *(CEO & Exec Dir-Creative)*
Cristiana Boccassini *(Exec Dir-Creative)*
Alessandro Candito *(Dir-Art & Supvr-Creative)*
Francesco Epifani *(Dir-Art & Supvr)*
Renzo Mati *(Assoc Dir-Creative)*
Michele Picci *(Assoc Dir-Creative)*
Giorgio Garlati *(Supvr-Creative)*
Aureliano Fontana *(Assoc Creative Dir)*
Anna Varisco *(Client Svc Dir)*

Accounts:
ANIA
Coca-Cola Refreshments USA, Inc. Burn, Never Extinguish
Farmland Dairies LLC Panna Chef
Fornet
Ilva De Sorono
Malu Parmalat
Nestle Italiana
Procter & Gamble
Renault Italia
Whirlpool Europe

Publicis
Via Tata Giovanni 8, 00154 Rome, Italy
Tel.: (39) 06 570201
Fax: (39) 06 5745 708
E-Mail: publicis@publicis.it
Web Site: www.publicis.it

Employees: 40

Agency Specializes In: Advertising

Cristiana Boccassini *(Exec Dir-Creative)*
Giada Salerno *(Acct Dir)*
Jacopo Menozzi *(Dir-Art)*
Michele Picci *(Assoc Dir-Creative)*
Marco Vigano *(Supvr-Creative)*
Emanuele Viora *(Assoc Creative Dir)*

Accounts:
Burn Energy Drink Campaign: "Never Extinguish"
Heineken Campaign: "Dream Island", Campaign: "Sunrise", Global Creative

Luxembourg

Mikado S.A.
38 route d'Esch, 1470 Luxembourg, Luxembourg
Tel.: (352) 45 75 45 1
Fax: (352) 45 75 45 75
E-Mail: contact@mikado.lu
Web Site: www.mikado.lu

Employees: 15

Jean Luc Mines *(Chm)*
Patrick Bertrand *(Dir-Art)*
Aurelie Bertrand *(Sr Acct Mgr)*

Accounts:
Astra
Baloise
Bureau Moderne
Chambre des Metiers
Clearstream
Cloos S.A.
Commerzbank
Enterprise des Postes et Telecommunications
Europe Online
Ministere du Logement
United Trust
Utopolis
Ville de Luxembourg
Zardonni

Netherlands

Compasso Mundocom
Van Der Hooplaan 241, 1185 LN Amstelveen, Netherlands
Tel.: (31) 20 517 1580
Fax: (31) 20 517 1581
E-Mail: info@mailcm.nl
Web Site: www.compassomundocom.nl

Employees: 45

Agency Specializes In: Print, Production

Manon Van Otegem *(Acct Dir)*

Accounts:
Dayzers
Estee Lauder International
Fiat
L'Oreal
Lancia
Mercedes Benz
Nederlandse Staatsloterij
Novib
Sectorfondsen Zorg en Welzijn
Ticketbox

Publicis Dialog
Prof WH Keesomlaan 12, 1183 DJ Amstelveen, Netherlands
Mailing Address:
Postbus 205, 1180 AE Amstelveen, Netherlands
Tel.: (31) 20 406 14 00
Fax: (31) 20 406 14 01
E-Mail: info@publicis.nl
Web Site: www.publicis.nl

Employees: 50

Marcel Hartog *(Exec Dir-Creative)*

Accounts:
British Airways
Club Med
Greenpeace
Hartstichting
Hewlett-Packard
KLM
Nestle
NS International
Plenty Easypull Campaign: "Your helping hand for minor out-of-home accidents."
Red Cross
Saatchi & Saatchi X

Publicis
Prof WH Keesomlaan 12, 1183 DJ Amstelveen, Netherlands
Mailing Address:
PO Box 205, 1180 AE Amstelveen, Netherlands
Tel.: (31) 20 406 12 00
Fax: (31) 20 406 1300
E-Mail: info@publicis.nl
Web Site: www.publicis.nl

Employees: 65
Year Founded: 1996

Marcel Hartog *(Exec Dir-Creative)*
Steef Nijhof *(Dir-Creative & Art)*

Accounts:
ALS Foundation Netherlands Campaign: "ALS", Campaign: "I Have Already Died.", Campaign: "Theodoor"
Bloemen.nl Campaign: "Screwed"
Bnp Paribas Campaign: "Dow Jones"

Club Med
Coca-Cola Light Nederland
Dutch Fund For Victims Campaign: "Mugged"
Dutch Heart Foundation
Ericsson Telecommunicatie
Ernst & Young
Flowers.nl Campaign: "Screwed"
Kika
L'Oreal Garnier
Mauritshuis
Ministerie van Economische Zaken
Plenty Campaign: "Camper"
Procter & Gamble
Randstad Campaign: "Big Boss is Watching You"
Royal Dutch Army
SCA Hygiene Products Campaign: "Edet Soft. Origami"
Stivoro
T-Mobile US
United Biscuits

Poland

Publicis Sp. z.o.o.

Al Jana Pawla II 80, 01-175 Warsaw, Poland
Tel.: (48) 22 535 65 50
Fax: (48) 22 535 65 60
E-Mail: publicis@publicis.pl
Web Site: www.publicis.pl

Employees: 100

Marek Gargala *(Mng Dir)*
Maciej Lissowski *(COO)*
Dagmara Gadomska *(Acct Dir)*
Micha Kisielewski *(Creative Dir)*
Adam Miecznikowski *(Acct Dir)*
Micha Oleksow *(Art Dir)*

Accounts:
Coca-Cola Refreshments USA, Inc.
Dacia
Ferrero
France Telecom S.A.
Garnier
Groupe SEB
Grupa L'Oreal
Hewlett Packard
Nobody Child Foundation
Renault
Sanofi Aventis
Sensomat.pl
Whirlpool

Portugal

Publicis Publicidade Lda.

Rua Goncalves Zarco 14, 1449-013 Lisbon, Portugal
Tel.: (351) 21 303 5100
Fax: (351) 21 303 5200
E-Mail: publicidade@publicis.pt
Web Site: www.publicis.com

Employees: 20
Year Founded: 1959

Teresa Bastos *(CEO)*
Joana Arez *(Exec Dir-Creative)*
Susana Doutor *(Dir-Customer Svc)*
Ricardo Ferreira *(Dir-Art)*
Pedro Ribeiro *(Dir-Production & Grafica Administrative)*

Accounts:
Dia
Nestle Buitoni, Chocolates
Procter & Gamble Campaign: "Snoring Playback", Vicks
Renault Twizy Campaign: "'Don't Dream And Drive", Campaign: "Silence Drive"

Romania

Publicis

8 Luminei Street, Bucharest, 2 Romania
Tel.: (40) 21 407 5600
Fax: (40) 21 407 5649
E-Mail: front.desk@publicis.ro
Web Site: www.publicis.com

Employees: 50

Jorg Riommi *(Chief Creative Officer)*
Miruna Macri *(Art Dir & Designer)*
Cristian Anton *(Art Dir)*
Miruna Sandulescu *(Acct Dir)*
Lucian Cernat *(Dir-Art)*
Ciprian Frunzeanu *(Dir-Digital Art)*
Mihai Tigleanu *(Dir-Art)*
Erik Vervroegen *(Dir-Creative-Intl)*
Ana Chreih *(Sr Acct Mgr)*
Oana Radu *(Sr Acct Mgr)*
Oana Popescu *(Acct Mgr)*
Liana Negrea *(Sr Acct Exec)*
Andreea Popa *(Copywriter)*
Marius Tudor *(Copywriter)*
Raluca Bararu *(Sr Art Dir)*
Dan Frinculescu *(Grp Creative Dir)*

Accounts:
ACR
AdPrint Festival by Luerzer's Campaign: "Fly Pack, Plan, Burger, Bang"
The Alternative School Creative Thinking
New-Art Safari
Beretta
Bucharest City Police Campaign: "Old Man"
Carrefour Campaign: "broccoli"
Dacia
L'Oreal Cosmetics
Martini
New-National Library of Romania
New-New Zealand Rugby House All Blacks: Jonah Lomu
Nissan Qashqai
Nutrivet
Oral-B Campaign: "Bad breath?"
P&G Campaign: "Dinner"
Pegas Bicycles Campaign: "The Internet Of The People"
Phoenixy Gusto Snacks
Renault Cars, Renault Fluence
Riello Romania Beretta Heating System
Romanian Traffic Police Campaign: "Your Last Journey", Campaign: "seatbelt song"
Varta Campaign: "Apocalypse", Campaign: "Indestructible flashlight.", Campaign: "When your home shows its dark side."
Whirlpool Campaign: "Bring back your sportswear with the Whirlpool Sports Washer."

Slovenia

MMS Marketinske Komunikacije, D.O.O.

(Formerly Publicis Studio Pet d.o.o.)
Ameriska ulica 8, 1000 Ljubljana, Slovenia
Tel.: (386) 12343500
Fax: (386) 12343501
E-Mail: info@publicis.si
Web Site: www.publicis.si

Employees: 42

Nina Huremovic *(Acct Mgr)*
Spla Petac *(Client Svc Dir)*

Accounts:
Hempel
Jazz Kamp Kranj
Mercator
Mobitel
Nova KBM
Renault
Sberbank
Si.mobil

Spain

Carre Noir Barcelona

Duana 3-2, Barcelona, 08003 Spain
Tel.: (34) 933 016 500
Fax: (34) 933 020 323
Web Site: www.carrenoir.es

Employees: 6

Agency Specializes In: Brand Development & Integration, Branded Entertainment, Consulting, Consumer Goods, Corporate Identity, Package Design, Retail

Joan Ricart *(CEO)*
Els Neirinckx *(Dir-Art)*

Accounts:
Armonia Cosmetica Natural
Coca-Cola Refreshments USA, Inc. Powerade Plus
Lacer
Nestle
Sanofi

Publicis

C/ Ramirez De Arellano 21, 28043 Madrid, Spain
Tel.: (34) 91 555 84 11
Fax: (34) 91 556 16 37 (Mgmt)
E-Mail: info@publicis.es
Web Site: www.publicis.es

Employees: 123
Year Founded: 1992

Miguel Angel Furones *(Pres)*
Bitan Franco *(Exec Dir-Creative)*
Sito Morillo *(Exec Dir-Creative)*
Nuria Pradera *(Acct Dir)*
Anthony Caseiro *(Dir-Art)*
Rosario Garcia *(Acct Supvr)*
Pablo Murube *(Copywriter)*

Accounts:
BIC Campaign: "BIC Idea"
Carrefour
Dacia
Daikin Campaign: "Lonely days for them", Campaign: "Poker"
Db Apparel Intimates Campaign: "Books", Campaign: "Glamour"
FAD Campaign: "Dance Music Not For Dancing"
Grupo Lecta Campaign: "Paper Camera"
Grupo Mahou San Miguel Campaign: "Freedom To Willix"
Hiviajes Campaign: "Caribbean"
La Primitiva Lottery Campaign: "We Don't Dream Cheap"
Ministerio De Defensa Campaign: "Life Simulator"
Norgine Campaign: "Hitler"
Randstad Campaign: "Lake"
Renault Campaign: "Earth"
Telefonica
VisionLab Campaign: "Software Terms"

Switzerland

Publicis Dialog Zurich

Stradelhofer Strasse 25, CH-8001 Zurich, Switzerland
Tel.: (41) 44 711 7211
Fax: (41) 44 711 7272
Web Site: www.publicis.ch

Nastja Burger *(Partner-Fin)*

Edgar Edgar Magyar *(CFO)*
Muriel Aste *(Head-Acct Unit)*
Ester Elices *(Head-Strategy)*
Gina Armellino *(Brand Dir)*
Christian Brutsch *(Brand Dir)*
Daniel Ahrens *(Dir-Creative & Art)*
Lorenz Clormann *(Dir-Creative & Art)*

Publicis
Stadelhofer Strasse 25, 8001 Zurich, Switzerland
Tel.: (41) 44 711 7211
Fax: (41) 44 711 7272
E-Mail: management@publicis.ch
Web Site: www.publicis.ch

Employees: 110

Curdin Janett *(CEO)*
Ralph Halder *(Exec Dir-Creative)*
Tom Muller *(Dir-Art)*
Grischa Rubinick *(Dir-Creative)*
Andreas Hornung *(Copywriter)*
Thomas Schob *(Copywriter)*
Urs Schrepfer *(Copywriter)*

Accounts:
Assugrin Campaign: "Belt Holes"
Bardill Sport
Bernina Store
Calanda
Du Kulturmedien Campaign: "Tomi Ungerer"
DU Magazine
Dusch-WC Center Shower Toilet
Endress + Hauser Campaign: "Yoghurt Challenge"
Energie Experten Campaign: "Finger Hero"
Equal Pay Day
Federico Naef
Jura Elektroapparate Campaign: "Jura Court"
Jura Campaign: "Roger"
Laurent Herzog Campaign: "Bella Bionda"
Le Delizie Di Capua Campaign: "Chastity Belt"
Lk International Campaign: "Heli"
L'Oreal Campaign: "Black", Campaign: "Hide Yesterday", Garnier Fructis
Lundbeck Campaign: "Lean on me, Digital Loneliness"
Ma-Bel Pfister Campaign: "Living in a Mailbox"
Nestle NESCafe
Neue Zuricher Zeitung
Orange Communications Campaign: "Orange Me Groom", Campaign: "Orange Young: Freedom Colors"
Orell Facessli Campaign: "Books.Ch"
Renault Nissan Suisse SA; Urdorf Corner Poster, Kaleos
Rowenta
Sauber Motorsport Campaign: "The Letter"
Swiss International Air Lines Campaign: "Start"
The Swiss Red Cross Campaign: "Bottle"
Swisscom Mobile AG; Bern Telecommunications
UBS
Youcinema Snackbar
zai Campaign: "Zai Ski St. Moritz"
Zurich Women's Center

United Kingdom

August Media
Zetland House, Scrutton Street, London, EC2A 4HJ United Kingdom
Tel.: (44) 2077493300
E-Mail: hello@augustmedia.com
Web Site: www.augustmedia.com

Year Founded: 2005

Agency Specializes In: Advertising, Brand Development & Integration, Magazines, Social Media

Mark Lonergan *(Co-Owner & Mng Dir)*
Sarah Bravo *(Dir-Editorial)*
Steven Hunter *(Dir)*
Jules Rogers *(Dir-Creative)*

Accounts:
Golfbreaks.com Digital, E-Commerce

Bartle Bogle Hegarty Limited
60 Kingly Street, London, W1B 5DS United Kingdom
(See Separate Listing)

Chemistry Communications Group, Plc
(Formerly Publicis Chemistry)
Oxford House, 76 Oxford St, London, W1D 1BS United Kingdom
Tel.: (44) 20 7935 7744
Fax: (44) 20 7487 5351
E-Mail: catherine.turner@publicis.co.uk
Web Site: www.publicischemistry.com

Employees: 160

Agency Specializes In: Digital/Interactive, Email, Media Relations, Outdoor, Radio, Sales Promotion

Emma Rush *(Mng Dir)*
Dylan Williams *(Chief Strategy Officer & Chief Innovation Officer-Global)*
Kevin Allen *(Chief Strategy Officer)*
Philomena Gray *(Grp Dir-HR-UK & Nordics)*
Laura Holme *(Dir-New Bus-Publicis)*
Philippa Bolton *(Client Svc Dir)*

Accounts:
Aviva
Baileys The Baileys Lounge
Benecol
Diageo GB
Dove
Everything Everywhere Digital Communications, Direct Mail, Retail
Gatwick Airport Mobile, Online, Social Media
Gu Advent Calendar
Kraft
Norwich Union
Orange
Plenty
Royal Mail Group Bbusiness-to-Business CRM, Campaign: "The MailMen", Digital, Direct Marketing, MarketReach, Media Buying, Media Planning, Out of Home, Print
SCA Bodyform
Topshop A Bag For Lives
Velvet
Visa

Freud Communications
55 Newman St, London, W1T 3EG United Kingdom
Tel.: (44) 20 3003 6300
Fax: (44) 20 3003 6303
Web Site: www.freuds.com

Employees: 300

Matthew Freud *(Chm)*
Andrew McGuinness *(CEO)*
Caroline Wray *(Mng Dir-Consumer)*
Giles Pocock *(Dir-Partnership)*
Paola Nicolaides *(Assoc Dir)*
Jennifer Summers *(Sr Acct Mgr-Insight)*

Accounts:
ASDA
COI
Comic Relief
Comparethemarket.com PR
The Department of Energy & Climate Change Campaign: "Change-4Life", PR
Department of Health Public Health Campaigns
Diageo
Food Network Consumer PR
Iglo Group Consumer
Kerry Foods
Mars Digital, Galaxy
nike
Pepsico
Pizza Hut
SKY
Universal
Visa
Walkers
Warburtons

Poke
5th Floor 82 Baker Street, London, W1U 6AE United Kingdom
Tel.: (44) 20 7830 3030
Fax: (44) 0207 749 5383
E-Mail: hello@pokelondon.com
Web Site: www.pokelondon.com

Employees: 60
Year Founded: 2001

Agency Specializes In: Advertising, Advertising Specialties, Arts, Automotive, Content, Cosmetics, Digital/Interactive, Electronics, Internet/Web Design, RSS (Really Simple Syndication)

Nick Farnhill *(Founder & Mng Partner)*
Christina Marks *(Head-Client)*
Nicolas Roope *(Exec Creative Dir)*
Angus Mackinnon *(Grp Dir-Creative)*
Jake Cooper *(Dir-Creative)*
Malin Hanus *(Dir-Creative)*
Hannah Ormsby *(Designer)*

Accounts:
Albion Bakery
BakerTweet
Diesel Campaign: "DIESEL EYEWEAR SS12", Campaign: "Fit Your Attitude"
French Connection UK
Manchester City
Manifesto
Oasis
Orange Gold Spots
Orange RockCorps
Orange Campaign: "Phone Fund", GlastoTag, Mobile Phones, Spot the Bull Campaign, talkingpoint.orange.co.uk, www.mobmates.co.uk
Peoples Policies
Skype Outside
Turnbull & Asser Creative, Design, Global Digital Communications, Strategy
Yahoo!

Publicis Blueprint
12 Dorset Street, London, W1U 6QS United Kingdom
Tel.: (44) 207 830 3979
Fax: (44) 207 462 7931
E-Mail: info@publicis-blueprint.co.uk
Web Site: www.publicis-blueprint.co.uk

Employees: 120

Geri Richards *(CEO)*
Stuart Gillespie *(Sr Dir-Art)*
Jane Ditcham *(Grp Acct Dir)*
Sue Higgs *(Dir-Creative)*
Steve Nicholls *(Dir-Creative)*
Joshua Norbury *(Dir-Art & Creative)*
Paul Bennett *(Copywriter-Adv)*

Accounts:
New-BHS
Cath Kidston
Confused.com Campaign: "Lab"
Heathrow Traveller Customer Magazine
Inmarsat

Orange
Vue Entertainment Vue Magazine

Publicis UK

82 Baker St, London, W1U 6AE United Kingdom
Tel.: (44) 20 7935 4426
Fax: (44) 20 7487 5351
E-Mail: will.hamilton@publicis.co.uk
Web Site: publicis.london/

Employees: 500
Year Founded: 1972

National Agency Associations: IPA

Agency Specializes In: Advertising, Consumer Marketing, Direct Response Marketing, Electronic Media, Print

Guy Wieynk *(CEO-UK Group & Nordics)*
Karen Buchanan *(CEO)*
Will Arnold-Baker *(Mng Partner)*
Dylan Williams *(Global Chief Strategy & Innovation Officer)*
Phil Dowgierd *(Mng Dir-Digital)*
Trent Patterson *(Head-Acct Mgmt & Bus Dir-Global)*
Darren Savage *(Head-Strategy)*
David Prideaux *(Exec Dir-Creative)*
Philomena Gray *(Grp Dir-HR-UK & Nordics)*
Jo Finch *(Sr Dir-Art)*
Stuart Pond *(Sr Acct Dir)*
Katie Edwards *(Bus Dir-Grp)*
Paul Manson *(Creative Dir)*
Rochelle Parry *(Bus Dir)*
Troy Parsonson *(Acct Dir)*
Rami Amaral *(Dir-Strategy)*
Kevin Colquhoun *(Dir-Art)*
Valerie Daverat *(Dir-Medical & Publicis Life Brands)*
Steve Glenn *(Dir-Creative-European)*
Dan Kennard *(Dir-Art)*
Josh Norbury *(Dir-Creative & Art)*
Ed Robinson *(Dir-Creative)*
Noel Sharman *(Dir-Creative)*
Darran Snatchfold *(Dir-Plng)*
Dave Sullivan *(Dir-Creative)*
Pavlos Themistocleous *(Dir-Creative-Digital)*
Alexandra Webb *(Sr Acct Mgr)*
Debbie Burke *(Mgr-Traffic)*
Anthony Harris *(Strategist)*
Steve Moss *(Copywriter)*
Ben Smith *(Copywriter)*
Dave Stansfield *(Designer)*
Mark Teece *(Copywriter)*

Accounts:
Airbus
The Army Recruiting Group Campaign: "Do More. Be More"
Barratt Developments
Beefeater Campaign: "This is My London"
New-BHS
Bongrain
The British Army Campaign: "Do More. Be More.", Campaign: "Message on a Mountain", campaign: "No Ordinary Career"
Circle Sports
Circle
Coca-Cola Campaign: "Coming Together", Campaign: "Taste The Possibilities", Coke Zero, Digital, In-Store, Outdoor, Print, TV
Coffee Mate
Confused.com Brian, Brian the Robot, Campaign: "shoelace", Creative, Digital, PR, Radio, Rebrand Campaign
Debra Brand Relaunch
Depaul Trust Campaign: "Don't Let Their Stories End On The Streets", Campaign: "Ihobo 1.1", Campaign: "There's Another Side to the Story", Cardboard Box Business, Outdoor, The Depaul Box Company
Dupaul iPhone
Easyjet Campaign: "A Royal Place In The Pun"
European Aeronautic Defence & Space Co. EAD N.V.; 2008
Ferrero Advertising, Ferrero Rocher
Galiform Plc
Garnier Ambre Solaire, Belle Color, Blonding, Body, Fructis, Fructis Style, Lumia, Movida, Nutrisse, Synergie
The Glenlivet Campaign: "Master Your Senses", Print, The Glenlivet Alpha
Hoola Hoops
Jigsaw Autumn & Winter Collection, In Store Activation
Malibu Rum
McVitie's Group AM, Core, Go-Ahead!, Jaffa Cakes, Penguin, Quirks
Nescafe Gold Blend, Green Blend, Original 3 in 1
Nestle Coffee-Mate, Maggi, Nestle Waters, Nesvita, Purina
PayPal Campaign: "Easy as Pie", Campaign: "Options", Outdoor, TV
Pernod Ricard Chivas Brothers, Malibu
Phileas Fogg Campaign: "They're not Crisps They're Phileas Fogg"
The Pilion Trust
Plenty Kitchen Roll Campaign: "Nonna Knows Best"
Procter & Gamble Bounty, Campaign: "At Least You Don't Have to Worry About Your Smile", Campaign: "Merry Beeping Christmas from Oral-B", Charmin, Oral-B, Pepto Bismol, Puffs, Tempo, Vicks
Renault Advertising, Avantime, CRM, Campaign: "Fate", Campaign: "Rabbits", Campaign: "Rain, Kiss My Glass", Campaign: "What Is Va Va Voom?", Campaign: "You Do the Maths", Clio, Dacia, Digital, Espace, Kangoo, Laguna, Marketing, Marque, Megane, Press, Renault 4+, Renault to Go, Scenic, TV, Through the Line, Twizy, Vel Satis, Wind Roadster, Windows, ZE Range
Rexnord Holdings, Inc.
SCA Campaign: "Apartment", Campaign: "As Life Unfolds", Campaign: "Plenty the Big One Launch", Drypers, Libero, Lotus, Plenty
SMA
T-Mobile US
Tata Steel
Tefal
The Territorial Army
Tourism Ireland Campaign: "Jump into Ireland"
Troicare
UBS Campaign: "Braille"
Virgin Unite
Zurich

Turner Duckworth Design

Voysey House Barley Mow Passage, W4 4PH London, United Kingdom
(See Separate Listing)

U.S. Branch

Turner Duckworth

831 Montgomery St, San Francisco, CA 94133
Tel.: (415) 675-7777
Fax: (415) 675-7778
E-Mail: info@turnerduckworth.com
Web Site: www.turnerduckworth.com/

Employees: 15

Agency Specializes In: Sponsorship

Chris Garvey *(Dir-Creative)*
Sarah Moffat *(Dir-Creative)*
Rebecca Williams *(Dir-Design)*
Melissa Chavez *(Designer)*
Nicole Jordan *(Designer)*
Brian Labus *(Designer)*
Jesse Recor *(Designer)*

Accounts:
The Coca-Cola Company Coca-Cola, Diet Coke
Coca-Cola Refreshments USA, Inc. Campaign: "Coca-Cola Arctic Home", Diet Coke Crop Packaging, Diet Coke logo
D&AD
New-Georgia-Pacific Brawny Man
Levi Strauss & Co. Campaign: "Levi's Visual Identity System"

ZenithOptimedia

24 Percy Street, London, W1T 2BS United Kingdom
(See Separate Listing)

Bahrain

Publicis-Graphics

Shaikh Mubarak Bldg 203 Rm 502 5th Floor, PO Box 1004, 30 Government Road, Manama, Bahrain
Tel.: (973) 22 87 37
Fax: (973) 17 22 43 98
E-Mail: graphics@batelco.com.bh
Web Site: www.publicisgraphics.com

Eddy Ghosn *(Gen Mgr)*

Egypt

Publicis-Graphics

3 El Mansour Mohamed St 5th Fl Ste 502, Zamalek, 11211 Cairo, Egypt
Tel.: (20) 2 7353 994
Fax: (20) 2 7357 536
E-Mail: pg@pgcairo.com
Web Site: www.publicisgraphics.com

Salma Aclimandos *(Acct Dir)*
Yousra Allam *(Acct Mgr)*

Israel

Geller Nessis Publicis

(Formerly Geller Nessis D'Arcy)
7 Bejerano Bros Str, Ramat Gan, Israel
Tel.: (972) 36 25 4777
Fax: (972) 36 25 4778
E-Mail: michala@geller-nessis.co.il

Employees: 17
Year Founded: 1983

Agency Specializes In: Above-the-Line, Advertising, Advertising Specialties, Below-the-Line, Business-To-Business, Digital/Interactive, Graphic Design

Orly Reuveni *(Acct Dir)*
Asaf Tamir *(Copywriter)*

Accounts:
ClubMed
Nestle Campaign: "The Hottest ice cream ever", Ice Cream
Sprite
Union Bank

Jordan

Publicis Graphics

10 Saeed Abu Javer St Um Uthaina, Po Box 17992, Amman, 11195 Jordan
Tel.: (962) 655 28174
Fax: (962) 655 28175
E-Mail: info@publicisgraphics.com.jo
Web Site: www.publicisgraphics.com

Accounts:
Crest
Ferrero
Kafa
Lacoste
Merito
Nestle
Oral-B
PZ Cussons
RIO more
Sohat
Total

Qatar

Publicis-Graphics
Villa No 20 Al Kanan Street, PO Box 22582, Al Mirqab, Doha, Qatar
Tel.: (974) 44 435 7663
Fax: (974) 435 7702
E-Mail: info@pgqatar.com
Web Site: www.publicisgraphics.com

Employees: 20

Khalil Ayass *(Mng Dir)*
Carla Chaaya Aramouni *(Acct Dir)*

Saudi Arabia

Publicis-Graphics
Jewelry Centre Tahlia Road, 21462 Jeddah, Saudi Arabia
Mailing Address:
PO Box 7222, Jeddah, 21462 Saudi Arabia
Tel.: (966) 2 665 7514
Fax: (966) 2 665 6423
E-Mail: ibeyhum@pgjeddah.com
Web Site: www.publicisgraphics.com

Tarek Chehab *(Dir-Acct)*
Mohamad Ghaziri *(Dir-Acct)*
Amr Sallam *(Planner-Strategic)*

Publicis-Graphics
1st Floor Mutabagani Headqarters Bldg, Tahlia Street, Riyadh, 11515 Saudi Arabia
Mailing Address:
PO Box 58523, Riyadh, 11515 Saudi Arabia
Tel.: (966) 1 465 2707
Fax: (966) 1 416 4411
E-Mail: publicis-graphics@pgjeddah.com
Web Site: www.publicisgraphics.com

Employees: 40

Emad Ibrahim *(Sr Dir-Art)*
Faisal Aleisawi *(Acct Dir)*
Riad Chehab *(Client Svcs Dir)*
Tarek Chehab *(Acct Dir)*
Khaled Saab *(Dir-Creative)*
Arafat Okal *(Mgr-Studio & Traffic)*
Nizamuddin Syed *(Mgr-Events & Traffic)*
Mohamad Ali Farchoukh *(Sr Acct Exec)*
Jehad Sayed *(Sr Graphic Designer)*

Accounts:
Alinma Bank
Hewlett Packard
L'Oreal
Nestle

United Arab Emirates

Publicis-Graphics
Office Tower 10th Fl Ste 1036, Al Ghurair Ctr, Dubai, 11853 United Arab Emirates
Mailing Address:
PO Box 11853, Deira, Dubai, United Arab Emirates
Tel.: (971) 4 222 2231
Fax: (971) 4 222 6360
E-Mail: pgdubai@publicisgraphics.ae
Web Site: www.publicisgraphics.com

Employees: 100
Year Founded: 1973

Agency Specializes In: Graphic Design

Edmond Ghosn *(Gen Mgr)*
Radhika Gandhi *(Acct Dir)*
Dipti Mathur *(Client Svcs Dir)*
Shant Arabsessian *(Sr Acct Exec)*
Dalia Bekdache *(Jr Acct Exec)*
Maher Abouzeid *(Grp Gen Mgr-Lower Gulf)*

Accounts:
Al Islami
British Airways
Burger King
Chiquita
Ferrero
HP
Hugo Boss
L'Oreal
Lacoste
Nestle Nido
Oral-B
Panasonic
Petromin Oils
Sanofi-Aventis
Saraya
Sharp
Sohat
United Sugar Company

South Africa

Arc South Africa
(Formerly Prima Arc)
Dunkley House 32 Barnet Street Gardens, Cape Town, South Africa
Tel.: (27) 214684000
Fax: (27) 214684010
E-Mail: info@arcww.co.za
Web Site: www.arcww.co.za

Employees: 50
Year Founded: 1996

Agency Specializes In: Advertising, Customer Relationship Management, Digital/Interactive, E-Commerce, Internet/Web Design, Mobile Marketing, Production, Search Engine Optimization, Social Media, Strategic Planning/Research

Peter Farrell *(Mng Dir)*
Desmond Buchler *(Sr Dir-Art)*
Gavin Schilder *(Dir-Art & Mgr-Studio)*
Annatjie Du Plessis *(Dir-Ops)*
Keith Lindsay *(Dir-New Bus)*
Driekie Van Biljon *(Dir-Art)*
Estelle Du Toit *(Sr Acct Mgr)*
Jane Muggleston *(Sr Acct Mgr)*
Dale Lawrence *(Mgr-Print Production)*
Agafar Mabie *(Mgr-Campaign)*

Accounts:
Adidas
BMW
DirectAxis. Insurance & Financial Service Providers
MINI
Shell Energy & Petrochemicals Mfr
Virgin Active

Publicis Johannesburg Pty. Ltd.
140a Kelvin Drive Morningside Manor, Sandton, 2000 South Africa
Tel.: (27) 11 519 1800
Fax: (27) 11 519 1900
E-Mail: tyoung@publicis.co.za
Web Site: www.publicisgroupe.com

Employees: 60
Year Founded: 1997

National Agency Associations: ACA

Kevin Tromp *(Grp CEO)*
Cuanan Cronwright *(Assoc Dir-Creative & Copywriter)*
Tracy Young *(Mgr-HR)*
Zakiyya Vahed *(Acct Exec)*
Natalie Katz *(Planner-Strategic)*

Accounts:
Hewlett-Packard
L'Oreal Ambre Solaire, Cacharel, Lancome, Plenitude, Polo, Ralph Lauren; 1993
Nestle Cremora, Klim, Maggi, Make-A-Litre, Nescafe, Ricoffy; 1993
Purina
Renault South Africa Campaign: "Numbers 28's", Laguna, Megane, Passenger Cars, Safrange; 1996
The Salvation Army Campaign: "Blankets for the Living"
Sanofi
Softsheen Carson
Whirlpool & KIC South Africa Major Domestic Appliances; 1996

Canada

Nurun Inc.
740 Notre Dame West Street, Suite 600, Montreal, QC H3C 3X6 Canada
(See Separate Listing)

Branches

Nurun/Ant Farm Interactive
271 17th St NW, Atlanta, GA 30363
(See Separate Listing)

Nurun/China Interactive
162 Yong Nian Rd, 3rd Fl, Shanghai, 200025 China
Tel.: (86) 21 5383 4038
Fax: (86) 21 5383 4050
E-Mail: china@nurun.com
Web Site: www.nurun.com

Julie Marchesseault *(CEO-China)*
Annabella Yang *(VP-Asia Pacific)*
Lily Huang *(Acct Dir)*
Eyrie Yang *(Assoc Dir-Creative)*
Peggy Li *(Acct Mgr)*
Cynthia Zheng *(Sr Acct Exec)*
Foye Deng *(Sr Designer-Web)*
Dami Hu *(Sr Designer-Web)*

Accounts:
Australia Wool Innovation
Chivas Regal
Danone Group Digital
FAW-VW-Audi
Helena Rubenstein China
JCDecaux Shanghai
Malibu
Pepsico (China)
Pernod Ricard Martell Noblige Cognac; 2008
Philips Electronics
Procter & Gamble Braun, Gillette, Olay, Pantene, Pringles, Safeguard, Vidal Sassoon; 2007

Nurun France
CET Centre Jean Monnet CS 61428, Longlaville CEDEX, 54400 Longwy, France
Tel.: (33) 3 82 24 00 00
Fax: (33) 3 82 24 00 10
E-Mail: france@nurun.com
Web Site: nurun.com

Employees: 16

Agency Specializes In: Advertising

Antoine Pabst *(CEO-France & Gen Mgr-Europe)*
Laure Garboua Tateossian *(Exec VP & Gen Mgr)*
Stephane Bartolomucci *(Dir-HR)*
Pauline Girardey *(Planner-Strategic)*

Nurun France
31 bis rue des Longs Pres, 92514 Boulogne-Billancourt, Cedex France
Tel.: (33) 1 58 17 59 00
Fax: (33) 1 58 17 59 01
E-Mail: france@nurun.com
Web Site: www.nurun.com

Employees: 300

Agency Specializes In: Digital/Interactive, Electronic Media, Internet/Web Design

Antoine Pabst *(CEO-France & Gen Mgr-Europe)*
Arthur Sadoun *(CEO-Global)*
Laure Garboua Tateossian *(Exec VP & Gen Mgr)*
Melanie Cumbo *(Acct Dir)*
Safeer Bandali *(Acct Mgr)*
Julie Bernard *(Project Mgr-Digital)*
Victoria Bocquet *(Mgr-Dev & New Bus)*
Laure-Elise Tran *(Acct Supvr)*

Accounts:
Blackberry Campaign: "Shareman"
Groupe Danone
Groupe L'Oreal
Lacoste Campaign: "Unconventional Talents in Nyc"
Yves Saint Laurent Campaign: "Yves Saint Laurent Experience"

Nurun Inc.
96 Spadina Ave 9th Fl, Toronto, ON M5V 2J6 Canada
Tel.: (416) 591-6000
Fax: (416) 591-6100
E-Mail: toronto@nurun.com
Web Site: www.nurun.com

Employees: 50

Agency Specializes In: Advertising, Digital/Interactive

Jenna Yim *(Gen Mgr)*
Mark Aning *(Dir-Tech)*
Blair Coughtrey *(Dir-Delivery Mgmt)*
Gail Leija *(Dir-Interaction Design)*
Amy Shea *(Assoc Dir-Creative)*
Angela Chow *(Mgr-HR)*
Thomas Ko *(Mgr-Dev)*
Flora Li *(Sr Designer)*

Accounts:
AGF
Bolton Services
Home Depot Canada
IMAX Corporation
Lancaster
Michelin North America
Nestle Italia
Snickers
Wisk

Nurun Inc.
18 E 16th St 7th Fl, New York, NY 10003
Tel.: (212) 524-8100
Fax: (212) 524-8101
Web Site: www.nurun.com

Agency Specializes In: Brand Development & Integration, Communications, Internet/Web Design

Jim Yang *(Chief Strategy Officer)*
Antoine Pabst *(CEO-France & Gen Mgr-Europe)*
Sebastian Cavanagh *(Exec VP & Gen Mgr)*
Laure Tateossian *(Exec VP & Gen Mgr)*
Sylvio Rancourt *(Exec VP-Nurun & Quebec)*
Albert Poon *(Exec Dir-Design)*

Accounts:
Kerastase US
Matrix
MedPointe Pharma

Nurun Spain
Entenza 94 Office 1, 08015 Barcelona, Spain
Tel.: (34) 93 238 8110
Fax: (34) 93 415 3048
E-Mail: barcelona@nurun.com
Web Site: www.nurun.com

Employees: 6
Year Founded: 2001

Agency Specializes In: Advertising, Consumer Marketing, Food Service, International, Multicultural

Sebastian Cavanagh *(Exec VP & Gen Mgr)*
Gonzalo Corchon Duaygues *(Dir-Dev)*
Julio Estepa *(Dir-Fin)*
Marisa Gonzalez Lafuente *(Dir-Bus Svcs)*
Isabel Martin *(Acct Mgr-Digital)*
Dario Diaz Gonzalez *(Project Mgr-Digital)*
Maria Bosch *(Acct Exec-Digital)*
Camino Martinez *(Strategist-Digital Mktg)*
Sara Moreno *(Sr Designer-Visual)*

Accounts:
Chupa Chups International
Codorniu Wines
Smint
Vichy Spain

Ove Design & Communications Ltd.
111 Queen Street East, Suite 555, Toronto, ON M5C 1S2 Canada
Tel.: (416) 423-6228
Fax: (416) 423-2940
E-Mail: start@ovedesign.com
Web Site: www.ovedesign.com

Employees: 25

Agency Specializes In: Internet/Web Design

Michel Viau *(Pres & CEO)*
Admira Nezirevic *(Mng Dir-Client Svc)*
Melissa Westerby *(Acct Dir)*
Peter Baker *(Dir-Design)*
Derek Wessinger *(Dir-Design)*
Ash Pabani *(Assoc Dir-Creative)*
Noor Malik *(Acct Coord)*
Joel Adrian Werner *(Acct Coord)*

Accounts:
Bank of Montreal
Body & Soul Fitness Corp.
CSI Global Education
Dundee Realty Corp.
George Weston Limited
Harris Bank
Hospitals of Ontario Pension Plan
Loblaw Companies Ltd.
Onex Corporation
Sun Life Financial
Sunoco Inc

Publicis Brand/Design
111 Queen St E Ste 200, Toronto, ON M5C 1S2 Canada
Tel.: (416) 925-7733
Fax: (416) 925-7341
Web Site: www.publicis.ca

Agency Specializes In: Advertising

Brett McIntosh *(CMO)*
Duncan Bruce *(CEO-Canada)*
Tracey Tobin *(VP & Brand Dir)*
Leonard Wise *(VP & Brand Dir)*
Lukasz Dolowy *(Grp Acct Dir)*
Bobby Malhotra *(Brand Dir)*
Emily Steeves *(Acct Dir)*
Lisa Hsieh *(Acct Supvr)*
Rachel Levman *(Acct Supvr)*
John Sime *(Acct Supvr)*
Stephanie Chan *(Sr Acct Exec)*

Publicis Dialog & Interactive-Montreal
3530 Boulvard Saint-Laurent Bureau 400, Montreal, QC H2X 2V1 Canada
Tel.: (514) 285-1414
Fax: (514) 842-5907
E-Mail: infomtl@publicis.ca
Web Site: www.publicis.ca

Employees: 100

Agency Specializes In: Digital/Interactive

Alain Tadros *(COO)*
Brett McIntosh *(VP)*
Lindsey Ash *(Dir-HR & Admin Svcs)*
Nicolas Baillargeon *(Dir-Art)*
Dom Bulmer *(Copywriter)*

Accounts:
New-Napa Autopro

Publicis Dialog
111 Queen St E Ste 200, Toronto, ON M5C 1S2 Canada
Tel.: (416) 925-5260
Fax: (416) 925-7341
Web Site: www.publicis.ca

Employees: 300

Brett McIntosh *(Mng Partner & VP)*
Shawna Miller *(VP & Brand Dir)*
Tracey Tobin *(VP & Brand Dir)*
Nicolas Massey *(VP & Dir-Creative)*
Alister Adams *(VP-Digital)*
Jessica Balter *(Grp Acct Dir)*
Lukasz Dolowy *(Grp Acct Dir)*
Bobby Malhotra *(Brand Dir)*
Lindsey Ash *(Dir-HR & Admin)*

Publicis Montreal
3530 Blvd St- Laurent St 400, Montreal, QC H2X 2V1 Canada
Tel.: (514) 285-1414
Fax: (514) 842-5907
E-Mail: info@publicis.ca
Web Site: www.publicis.ca

Employees: 115
Year Founded: 1996

Yves Gougoux *(Chm)*
Alain Tadros *(Pres)*
Lucy Goode *(VP & Dir-Strategic Plng)*
Anne-Marie Blouin *(Dir-Creative)*
Antoine Dasseville *(Dir-Art)*
Patrick McConnell *(Dir-Production)*

Advertising Agencies

Carl Robichaud *(Dir-Creative)*

Accounts:
Belron Canada Campaign: "Mafioso"
Brunet Campaign: "Myriam", TV
Centraide of Greater Montreal Campaign: "Alcoholic", Campaign: "Giving Brightens lives", Campaign: "Thug"
Chrysler Campaign: "Bear", Campaign: "The Rock", RAM Trucks
Coca Cola
Hewlett Packard
Jeep Campaign: "Legendary Fun.", Wrangler
Kia Canada; 2002
Labatt USA LLC Alexander Keiths, Bud Light, Labatt's Blue
L'Oreal Canada; 1996
Mira Foundation Campaign: "Work-Home Maze"; 1997
Mira Guide Dog Association Campaign: "Colours"
Musee des Beaux-arts de Montreal
National Defense
Nestle Campaign: "The Dog"
Purina
Rogers Communications
Subway Restaurants

Publicis NetWorks
111 Queen Street East Ste 200, Toronto, ON M5C 1S2 Canada
Tel.: (416) 925-7733
Fax: (416) 925-7341
E-Mail: andrew.bruce@publicis.ca
Web Site: www.publicis.ca

Employees: 300

Brett McIntosh *(CMO)*
Tracey Tobin *(VP & Brand Dir)*
Lucy Goode *(VP & Dir-Strategic Plng)*
Alister Adams *(VP-Digital)*
Bobby Malhotra *(Brand Dir)*
Lindsey Ash *(Dir-HR & Admin)*
Melina Tessier *(Supvr-Accts)*
Marie Jo B. Massy *(Planner-Content)*
Laetitia Rampazzo *(Coord-Council)*

Accounts:
Rogers

Publicis Toronto
111 Queen St E Ste 200, Toronto, ON M5C 1S2 Canada
Tel.: (416) 925-7733
Fax: (416) 925-7341
E-Mail: email@publicis.ca
Web Site: www.publicis.ca

E-Mail for Key Personnel:
President: srancourt@publicis.ca
Creative Dir.: dbruce@publicis.ca

Employees: 300
Year Founded: 1975

Bryan Kane *(Pres)*
Scott Pinkney *(VP & Exec Dir-Creative)*
Michael Murray *(VP & Creative Dir)*
Christine McNab *(VP & Client Partner-Rogers)*
Max Valiquette *(VP-Strategic Plng)*
Tim Kavander *(Grp Dir-Creative)*
Christian Martinez *(Sr Dir-Art)*
Siobhan Quinn *(Producer-Brdcst)*
Mark Spalding *(Dir-Art & Assoc Dir-Creative)*

Accounts:
Canada Post
City of Toronto
HP
Kia Canada Inc.; 2002
Lennox
Livegreen
Nestle Canada Campaign: "Strange Animal", Nescafe; 1997
Purina
Rogers Communications Inc. Campaign: "The Movies"
Toronto Blue Jays

United States

Big Fuel Communications LLC
11 W 19th St, New York, NY 10011
(See Separate Listing)

Burrell
233 N Michigan Ave Ste 2900, Chicago, IL 60601
(See Separate Listing)

DigitasLBi
(Formerly Digitas Inc.)
33 Arch St, Boston, MA 02110
(See Separate Listing)

Discovery USA
(Formerly Williams-Labadie Advertising)
Merchandise Mart Plz Ste 550, Chicago, IL 60654
Tel.: (312) 220-1500
Fax: (312) 222-2530
E-Mail: info@discoverychicago.com
Web Site: www.discoveryworldwide.com

Employees: 65
Year Founded: 1990

National Agency Associations: 4A's

Agency Specializes In: Health Care Services, Medical Products

Don Young *(Grp Mng Dir)*
Ed Cowen *(Exec VP & Head-Practice-Medical Comm)*
Kristin M. Keller *(Exec VP-Client Engagement)*
Suzanne Richards *(VP & Grp Dir-Creative)*
Evan Young *(VP & Dir-Creative)*
Steve Clark *(Acct Dir)*
Robin Corralez *(Dir-HR)*
Jesse Jodrey *(Acct Coord)*

Accounts:
Abbott Medical Optics, Inc.; Santa Ana, CA
Astellas Pharma USA
Oscient
Oscient Pharmaceuticals
Prometheus
Prometheus Laboratories
SciClone Pharmaceuticals
Smith & Nephew AMO, NPWT

Fallon Worldwide
901 Marquette Ave Ste 2400, Minneapolis, MN 55402
(See Separate Listing)

Kekst & Co.
437 Madison Ave, New York, NY 10022
(See Separate Listing)

Leo Burnett Worldwide, Inc.
35 W Wacker Dr, Chicago, IL 60601-1723
(See Separate Listing)

Media Vest
1675 Broadway, New York, NY 10019
Tel.: (212) 468-4000
Fax: (212) 468-4110
E-Mail: questions@mediavestww.com
Web Site: www.mediavestww.com

Employees: 900
Year Founded: 1998

Agency Specializes In: Media Buying Services, Planning & Consultation

Andrea Cancro *(Mng Dir & Exec VP)*
Dan Donnelly *(Mng Dir & Exec VP)*
Francis Pessagno *(Mng Dir & Exec VP)*
Allison Kallish *(Mng Dir & Sr VP)*
Dan Kern *(Mng Dir & Sr VP)*
Deborah Marquardt *(Mng Dir & Sr VP)*
Richard Hartell *(Pres-Strategy)*
Coleen Kuehn *(Pres-Client Leadership)*
Melissa Shapiro *(Pres-Investment)*
Pam Zucker *(Pres-Marketplace Ignition & Innovation)*
Robin Steinberg *(Exec VP-Publ & Dir-Digital-Investment & Activation)*
Larry Davis-Swing *(Sr VP & Head-Analytics-North America)*
Jeff Fischer *(Sr VP & Grp Dir-Branded Content)*
Kate Hogan *(Sr VP & Grp Dir-Client)*
Brad Liebow *(Sr VP & Grp Dir-Client-Wal-Mart)*
Ian Maidman *(Sr VP & Grp Dir-Client)*
Jaclyn Marino *(Sr VP & Grp Dir-Client-Mondelez)*
Matthew Nalecz *(Sr VP & Grp Dir-Digital)*
Norm Chait *(Sr VP & Dir-OOH Investment & Activation)*
Erin Kienast *(Sr VP & Dir-Innovation & Activation)*
Vanessa Newkirk *(Sr VP & Dir-Digital)*
Kerry O'Sullivan *(Sr VP & Dir-Media Res)*
Joseph Rose *(Sr VP & Dir-Analytics)*
Oleg Korenfeld *(Sr VP-Adv Tech & Platforms)*
Elisabeth Ryan *(VP & Grp Dir-Client)*
Vincent Sauvagnargues *(VP & Grp Dir-Media)*
Lauren Stein *(VP & Grp Dir-Client)*
George Coppola *(VP & Dir-Connections)*
Allison Duray *(VP & Dir-Ops)*
Colleen Durkin *(VP & Dir-Activation)*
Julie Goldstein *(VP & Dir-Activation)*
Jasen Kelly *(VP & Dir-Shopper Mktg)*
Michelle Lee *(VP & Dir-Connections)*
Josie Lyons *(VP & Dir)*
Kristin Marquart *(VP & Dir-Connections)*
Julie Masser *(VP & Dir-Investment & Activation)*
Jeanette Millan *(VP & Dir-Activation)*
Anthony So *(VP & Dir-Search Mktg)*
Jennifer Sobel *(VP & Dir-Talent Acq)*
Roxanna Tirado *(VP & Dir)*
Doreen Szeto *(VP & Strategist-Human Experience)*
Kristina Goldberg *(VP-Programmatic)*
Rose Ahn *(Dir-Digital)*
Anne Marie Courtney *(Dir-Activation)*
Arielle Heller *(Dir-Connections-Comcast Corporate)*
Jill Kerszko *(Dir-Digital Media)*
Rinku Mahbubani *(Dir-Digital)*
Jesse Markward *(Dir-Digital)*
Zachary Noren *(Dir-Digital)*
Steven Rodriguez *(Dir-Connections)*
Tom Xenos *(Dir-Res)*
Gordon Bach *(Assoc Dir-Digital)*
Courtney Betley *(Assoc Dir-Connections)*
Arlene DeSousa *(Assoc Dir)*
Andrew Frischman *(Assoc Dir-Digital)*
Adriane Genova *(Assoc Dir-Media)*
Liam Herlihy *(Assoc Dir-Connections Plng & Strategy)*
Danielle Hildebrandt *(Assoc Dir-Connections)*
Denise Hooper *(Assoc Dir-Connections)*
Patricia Kim *(Assoc Dir-Media)*
Keith Klein *(Assoc Dir-Out-of-Home & Non-Traditional Media)*
Tess Konter *(Assoc Dir-Activation)*
Andy Llerena *(Assoc Dir)*
Mollie Moschberger *(Assoc Dir-Local Activation)*
Lauren Rodas *(Assoc Dir-Technical Activation & Analytics Grp)*
Jennifer Rodriguez *(Assoc Dir-Activation)*
Chad Rosenwasser *(Assoc Dir)*
Neil Sorrentino *(Assoc Dir)*
Sarah Teachout *(Assoc Dir-Activation)*
Dalila Velez *(Assoc Dir-Connections)*

Allison Furai *(Mgr-Mobility)*
Alexandra Gladden *(Mgr-Connections)*
Ashley Hertz *(Mgr-Activation)*
Carmen Loo *(Mgr-Digital Activation)*
Erika Lutz *(Mgr-Mobility-P&G-Starcom MediaVest Group)*
Millicent Macon *(Mgr-Connections)*
Leo Mikinberg *(Mgr-Programmatic)*
Brandon Muller *(Mgr-Connections, Plng & Res)*
Alison Nolen *(Mgr-Connections)*
Julia Rosenbloom *(Mgr-Connections)*
Chelsea Schild *(Mgr-Programmatic-Social Media)*
Adrian Sutherland *(Mgr-Strategy & Activation-Coca Cola)*
Andrea Liao *(Supvr-Integrated Brand Strategy)*
Kelly Zapalik *(Supvr-Starcom USA)*
Anjali Nebhnani *(Strategist-Human Experience)*
Falon Alexandra *(Planner-Strategic)*
Jason Tennenbaum *(Media Planner)*
Kelly Andrews *(Sr VP Dir-Data & Analytics)*

Accounts:
1-800-Contacts
Aflac (Lead Media Agency) Buying, Planning
American Honda Motor Co., Inc.
Avaya; 2006
Avon Products
Bloomin' Brands, Inc. (Agency of Record) Media Buying, Media Planning, Offline Media, Online Media
Bristol-Myers Squibb
Brown-Forman Corporation (Global Media Agency)
The Coca-Cola Company
Coca-Cola Refreshments USA, Inc.
Comcast Corporation Cable, Theme-Park, Xfinity; 2006
Cox Communications, Inc. (Agency of Record) Campaign: "TV Just for Me.", Contour, Media, Residential Services, TV
Disney Channel
Earthlink
Eisai
Heineken USA Inc. Campaign: "Mega Football Ad we didn't actually make.", Desperados, Dos Equis, Heineken, Heineken Light, Media Buying, Newcastle
Honda Acura, Media Planning & Buying
Keurig Green Mountain (Media Agency of Record) US Media Planning, US Media Strategy
Mars, Incorporated
Mars Petcare
Microsoft Corporation Bing, Internet Explorer, Microsoft, Microsoft Corporation, Microsoft Office, Windows 7, XBox, XBox 360
Mondelez International Belvita, Bubblicious, Chiclets, Chips Ahoy!, Dentyne, Dentyne Ice, Dentyne Pure, Digital Buying, Green & Black's, Halls, Media, Media Planning & Buying, Nabisco, Nabisco 100 Calorie, Newtons, Nilla, Oreo, Oreo Cakesters, Print Buying, Ritz, SnackWell's, Sour Patch Kids, Stride, Swedish Fish, TV, Toblerone, Trident, Trident Layers, Triscuit, Wheat Thins
Novartis Corporation
Post Foods, LLC Alpha-Bits, Cocoa Pebbles, Fruity Pebbles, Grape Nuts, Great Grains, Honey Bunches of Oats, Honey-Comb, Post Bran Flakes, Post Foods, LLC, Post Raisin Bran, Post Selects, Post Shredded Wheat, Post Trail Mix Crunch, Waffle Crisp
Procter & Gamble Company Aussie, Clairol, Gillette, Olay, Vidal Sassoon
Procter & Gamble Cosmetics CoverGirl, CoverGirl Clean, CoverGirl Lash Blast, CoverGirl Shine Blast, CoverGirl Simply Ageless, CoverGirl Wetslicks AmazeMint, Covergirl Exact Eyelights, Covergirl Lip Perfection, Covergirl Naturelux, Covergirl Outlast, Covergirl Queen, Covergirl Shadowblast, Covergirl.com, Procter & Gamble Cosmetics
Procter & Gamble Prestige Quiksilver (fragrance), Roxy (fragrance)
PUR Media
Sam's Club
Samsung America, Inc.
Sprint Corporation Media
Starwood Hotels & Resorts Worldwide
TD Ameritrade Media; 2008
Touchstone Energy
Travelers Media Planning & Buying
UBS
Wal-Mart Stores, Inc. Media
Wendy's
Yahoo U.S. Online & Offline Media

Medicus Life Brands
1675 Broadway 5th Fl, New York, NY 10019-5820
(See Separate Listing)

Moroch Partners
3625 N Hall St Ste 1100, Dallas, TX 75219-5122
(See Separate Listing)

MRY
(Formerly Mr. Youth)
11 W 19th St 3rd Fl, New York, NY 10011
(See Separate Listing)

MSLGROUP
(Formerly Manning Selvage & Lee, Inc.)
375 Hudson St, New York, NY 10014
(See Separate Listing)

Optimedia International US Inc.
375 Hudson St 7th Fl, New York, NY 10014
(See Separate Listing)

PBJS, Inc.
424 2nd Ave W, Seattle, WA 98119
(See Separate Listing)

Performics
180 N LaSalle Ste 1100, Chicago, IL 60601
Tel.: (312) 739-0222
Fax: (312) 739-0223
E-Mail: info@performics.com
Web Site: www.performics.com

Employees: 140

Scott Shamberg *(Pres-US)*
Michael Kahn *(CEO-Worldwide)*
Joe Reinstein *(Exec VP-Integrated Svcs)*
Beatriz Fernandez de Bordons *(Sr VP-Performance Media)*
Matt Miller *(Sr VP-Strategy & Analytics)*
Jennifer Kaiser *(VP & Grp Dir)*
Tessa Binney *(VP & Grp Acct Dir)*
Brad Beiter *(VP-Performance Content)*
Leo Dalakos *(VP-Client Svcs)*
Jeff Licciardi *(VP-Local)*
Katie Bogda *(Dir-Mktg Comm)*
Nicole Duncan *(Dir-Media)*
Teresa Hsu *(Dir-Media)*
Dan Malachowski *(Dir-Mktg)*
Heather Kollme *(Sr Mgr-Media)*
Ami Shah *(Sr Mgr-Media)*
Nicole Maley *(Assoc Mgr-Media)*
Victoria Mioduszewski *(Assoc Mgr-Media-Client Solutions)*
Laura Zalewski *(Assoc Mgr-Media)*

Accounts:
Apple
Kohl's
Redbox

Publicis Dialog Boise
168 N 9th St Ste 250, Boise, ID 83702
Tel.: (208) 395-8300
Fax: (208) 395-8333
E-Mail: lynda.bruns@publicis-usa.com
Web Site: www.publicisna.com

Employees: 15
Year Founded: 1985

National Agency Associations: 4A's

Agency Specializes In: Digital/Interactive, Sponsorship

Kevin Sweeney *(CFO & Exec VP-North America)*
Julie Levin *(CMO-North America)*
Carla Serrano *(Chief Strategy Officer)*
Tim Kavander *(Exec VP & Dir-Creative)*
Bill Newbery *(Grp Dir-Creative)*
Christal Gammill *(Acct Dir)*
Lindsey Ash *(Dir-HR & Admin-Publicis Canada)*
Kurt Olson *(Dir-Creative)*

Publicis Dialog
6500 Wilshire Blvd Ste 1900, Los Angeles, CA 90048
Tel.: (323) 782-5160
Fax: (323) 782-5161
Web Site: www.publicis.com

Employees: 10

National Agency Associations: CSPA-DMA

Agency Specializes In: Brand Development & Integration

Mary Puls *(Exec VP)*

Publicis Healthcare Communications Group
One Penn Plz 5th Fl, New York, NY 10019
(See Separate Listing)

Publicis Indianapolis
200 S Meridian St Ste 500, Indianapolis, IN 46225-1076
Tel.: (317) 639-5135
Fax: (317) 639-5134
E-Mail: tom.hirschauer@publicis-usa.com
Web Site: http://www.publicisna.com

Employees: 50

Agency Specializes In: Advertising, Brand Development & Integration, Broadcast, Business-To-Business, Collateral, Consumer Marketing, Electronic Media, Financial, Graphic Design, Health Care Services, Magazines, Newspaper, Outdoor, Print, Public Relations, Sponsorship, T.V., Travel & Tourism

Jeff Huser *(Dir-Creative)*
Sara O'Neill *(Dir-Creative)*

Publicis New York
(Formerly Publicis Kaplan Thaler)
1675 Broadway, New York, NY 10019
(See Separate Listing)

Publicis Seattle
(Formerly Publicis West)
424 2nd Ave W, Seattle, WA 98119-4013
Tel.: (206) 285-2222
Fax: (206) 273-4219
Web Site: publicisseattle.com

Employees: 200

Agency Specializes In: Advertising, Sponsorship

Scott Foreman *(CEO)*
Jason Sullivan *(Mng Dir & Exec VP)*
Andrew Christou *(Chief Creative Officer & Exec*

VP)
Britt Peterson Fero *(Chief Strategy Officer)*
Corey Bartha *(Exec VP & Head-Integrated Production)*
Jason Lucas *(Exec VP & Exec Dir-Creative)*
Lori Davis *(Exec VP & Exec Bus Dir)*
Adam Thomason *(VP & Grp Acct Dir)*
Adam Oliver *(Head-Production)*
Steve Williams *(Grp Dir-Creative & Writer)*
Jason Fong *(Sr Dir-Art)*
Julia Luplow *(Sr Dir-Art)*
Simson Chantha *(Art Dir)*
Garth Knutson *(Acct Dir)*
Maria Schoonover *(Acct Dir)*
Nick Schuitemaker *(Acct Dir)*
Baeu Bernstein *(Dir-Creative)*
Steve johnston *(Dir-Creative)*
Stacy Milrany *(Dir-Creative & Art)*
Rob Kleckner *(Assoc Dir-Creative)*
Andrew Starmer *(Acct Supvr)*
Nicole McKeown *(Sr Strategist-Digital-T-Mobile)*
Marie Matuszewski *(Strategist)*
Derek Anderson *(Assoc Creative Dir)*

Accounts:
American Girl LLC Campaign: "Together We Make the Holidays"
Brand Drops
Bumbershoot Creative
Cinerama
Citi
Coca-Cola Refreshments USA, Inc.
Coinstar
Dish Network; Englewood, CO
Eddie Bauer Lead Creative
Garnier
Hewlett-Packard
New-KinderCare
Knowledge Universe (Agency of Record) Before- and After- School Programs, Champions, KinderCare Learning Centers
New-Kraft Heinz
Les Schwab Campaign: "RV Weekend", Campaign: "Stranded Nanny", Television
Nestle
NYC Bicycle Safety Coalition
P & G
Power Bar
Sara Lee Ball Park, Creative
T-Mobile US Campaign: "#KimsDataStash", Campaign: "One-Up", Campaign: "Pets Unleashed", Campaign: "The Simple Choice", My Faves, Super Bowl 2015, T-Mobile@Home, TV, Whenever Minutes
UBS
UNICEF
United Way
Visit Seattle (Advertising Agency of Record) Creative Development, Marketing Strategy, Media Buying, Media Planning
Zurich

Publicis USA
4 Herald Sq 950 6th Ave, New York, NY 10001
(See Separate Listing)

Razorfish New York
375 Hudson St, New York, NY 10014
(See Separate Listing)

Resultrix
The Plz 10800 NE 8th St Ste 220, Bellevue, WA 98004
(See Separate Listing)

Riney
(Formerly Publicis & Hal Riney)
2001 The Embarcadero, San Francisco, CA 94133-5200
(See Separate Listing)

Rokkan
300 Park Ave S, New York, NY 10010
(See Separate Listing)

Rosetta
(Formerly Rosetta Marketing Group, LLC)
100 American Metro Blvd, Hamilton, NJ 08619
(See Separate Listing)

Saatchi & Saatchi
375 Hudson St, New York, NY 10014
(See Separate Listing)

Sapient Corporation
131 Dartmouth St, Boston, MA 02116
(See Separate Listing)

Starcom MediaVest Group
35 W Wacker Dr, Chicago, IL 60601-1723
(See Separate Listing)

VivaKi
2001 The Embarcadero, San Francisco, CA 94133
Tel.: (415) 369-6300
Web Site: www.vivaki.com

Year Founded: 2008

Agency Specializes In: Advertising, Digital/Interactive

Luca Montani *(CEO)*
Dave Marsey *(Mng Dir & Exec VP)*
Michael Wiley *(Mng Dir)*
Shirley Xu-Weldon *(Sr VP-Analytics & Strategic Solutions)*
Shelby Farmer *(Client Svcs Mgr)*
Rina Nagashima *(Campaign Mgr-AOD)*

Accounts:
Ebay Inc.
Taco Bell Corp.

VivaKi
35 W Wacker Dr, Chicago, IL 60601
(See Separate Listing)

Winner & Associates
2029 Century Park E Ste 1750, Los Angeles, CA 90067
Tel.: (818) 385-1900
Fax: (310) 432-7771
E-Mail: winner@winnr.com

Employees: 25

Agency Specializes In: Consulting

Charles Winner *(Founder)*
Sonia Freedman *(CFO)*
Justyn Winner *(Gen Counsel & Exec VP)*
Bob Rawitch *(Exec VP)*
Vickie Allande-Fite *(Sr VP)*
Phyllis Gibson *(Sr VP)*
J.P. Ellman *(VP)*
Madeline Fries *(VP)*
Iris Gelt Warner *(VP)*
Heather Tremblay *(Dir-Media Rels)*

Accounts:
El Paso Electric
Exxon Corporation
ExxonMobil
FlexJet
InterGen Energy
Los Angeles Turf Club
Los Angeles World Airports

Argentina

Publicis Graffiti
Azopardo 1315, C1107 ADW Buenos Aires, Argentina
Tel.: (54) 11 5556 3500
E-Mail for Key Personnel:
President: ebaca@grafitti.com.ar

Employees: 50
Year Founded: 1985

Agency Specializes In: Advertising, Automotive, Consumer Goods, Financial, Food Service, Graphic Design, Household Goods, Multimedia, Pharmaceutical, Production, Production (Ad, Film, Broadcast), Production (Print), T.V., Travel & Tourism

Fabio Mazia *(Exec Creative Dir)*
Tomas Fitz-simon *(Acct Dir)*
Estefania Pecora *(Art Dir)*
Laura Visco *(Creative Dir)*
Leandro Ezquerra *(Copywriter)*
Vidhi Shah *(Copywriter)*

Accounts:
Carrefour Campaign: "Low Pages"
Movistar Campaign: "Tweet & Coach"
Renault Campaign: "Stupid Art"

Brazil

DPZ-Duailibi, Petit, Zaragoza, Propaganda S.A.
Cidade Jardim Ave 280, Sao Paulo, SP 01454-900 Brazil
Tel.: (55) 11 3068 4000
Fax: (55) 11 3085 4298
E-Mail: mail@dpz.com.br
Web Site: http://dpzt.com.br/

Employees: 230
Year Founded: 1968

Agency Specializes In: Graphic Design

Roberto Duailibi *(Partner)*
Mauricio Tortosa *(Chief Strategy Officer)*
Elvio Tieppo *(Gen Dir-Svc)*
Rafael Urenha *(Exec Dir-Creative)*
Cristina Haynes *(Acct Dir)*
Denise Poerner Nogueira *(Acct Dir)*
Fernanda Petinati *(Acct Dir-Media)*
Ana Paula Alencar *(Dir-Media)*
Marcello Barcelos *(Dir-Creative)*
Edwartt Lopes *(Dir-Art)*
Marina Wajnsztejn *(Dir-Plng)*
Diego Zaragoza *(Dir-Creative)*
Debora Bolssonaro *(Mgr-Svc)*

Accounts:
Amado Sao Paulo Bar E Restaurante Soy Burger
Anzen Wax Center
Azul
Bombril Campaign: "Ketchup", Fort Insect Repellent, Lysoform Disinfectant, Mon Bijou, Stain Remover, Vantage Stain Remover
Campari
CNI
Dersa
Duratex
Giraffas
Itau Personnalite
Itau Unibanco Itaucard Credit Card
Itautec; 1982
Jurema
Nestle Neston
Papaiz

Sadia; 1968
Senac
Souza Cruz S.A. Carlton, Hollywood
Stilgraf Print Production
Sunset Rent A Car
Triathon Gym Military Training Class
Vantage
Vivo Cellular; 2000
Vivo

Publicis Brasil Communicao
Av Juscelino Kubitschek 1909, 12th Floor N Tower, Sao Paulo, 04551060 Brazil
Tel.: (55) 11 3169 9000
Fax: (55) 11 4560 9001
Web Site: www.publicis.com.br/

Employees: 390
Year Founded: 2003

National Agency Associations: ABAP (Brazil)

Agency Specializes In: Brand Development & Integration, New Product Development, Sales Promotion

Hugo Rodrigues *(CEO)*
Tato Bono *(Head-Production)*
Erik Vervroegen *(Exec Creative Dir)*
Kevin Zung *(Exec Creative Dir)*
Gabriela Borges *(Acct Dir-Sanofi Brands)*
Anderson Kiss *(Art Dir)*
Giuliana Macedo *(Acct Dir)*
Daniel Schiavon *(Art Dir)*
Germano Weber *(Art Dir)*
Cristiane Zuben *(Acct Svcs Dir)*
Alexandre Goncalves *(Dir-Art)*
Rodrigo Guaxupe *(Dir-Art)*
Vitor Hildebrand *(Dir-Art)*
Juliana Laporta *(Dir-Strategic Plng)*
Rodrigo Gigante Machado *(Dir-Art)*
Luiz Tosi *(Dir-Svc)*
Daniella Martins *(Acct Mgr)*
Alex Adati *(Copywriter)*
Felipe Barbosa *(Copywriter)*
Rafael Barreiros *(Copywriter)*
Fred Gerodetti *(Copywriter)*
Ana Mattioni *(Copywriter)*
Kiko Mattoso *(Copywriter)*
Rodrigo Strozenberg *(Copywriter)*

Accounts:
Arno Campaign: "Save your patterns.", Campaign: "Ugly Parents"
Fundacao Pro-Sangue Campaign: "Your Donation Can Save Lives"
Groupe Seb Arno Turbo Silence Fan, Campaign: "Bandits", Campaign: "Maximum Wind Power", Campaign: "Ugly Parents, Beautiful Kids 1", Fan
Habib Moto-Reindeer
L'officiel III Campaign: "Blurred Eyes - Birthday"
L'Oreal
Nestle Campaign: "Getting Home", Campaign: "Only a Dog", Purina
Procter & Gamble Campaign: "Green", Campaign: "Post-It Notes", Campaign: "Search / Ribs", Oral-B, Toothpaste, Vick Inhaler, Vick Pyrena, Vick Syrup
Sangue Corinthiano
Sanofi Aventis Campaign: "Dermacyd Teen Code", Targifor Batt, Targifor: Old car
Santa Cruz Wine Store
SBT Campaign: "What Not to Wear TV Show: Bad Choices / Earrings"
Sony AXN, Campaign: "CSI Clues/Kiss Mark", Campaign: "Homework", TV Channel
New-TVSBT

Publicis Brasil Communicao
Praca X 15 fl 8, 20040 020 Rio de Janeiro, Brazil
Tel.: (55) 21 3981 0300
Fax: (55) 21 2558 3100
Web Site: www.publicis.com.br

Employees: 55
Year Founded: 2003

Agency Specializes In: Brand Development & Integration, Consumer Marketing, New Product Development, Sales Promotion

Dan Ribiero *(Creative Dir)*
Daguito Rodrigues *(Creative Dir)*
Andrea Veronezi *(Dir-Media)*

Accounts:
Arno Turbo Silence Fan
AXN Campaign: "AXN TV BOXES"
Brainstorm Campaign: "Shop Poster"
Lost VI
Mackenzie University
Oral-B Essential Floss Campaign: "Don't let it escape"
Targifor C
Varilux Multifocal Lens
Vick

Chile

Publicis Chile SA
Apoquindo 3000 Piso 8, 755-0306 Santiago, Chile
Tel.: (56) 2 757 3000
Fax: (56) 2 208 6727
E-Mail: agencia@publicis.cl
Web Site: www.publicis.cl

Employees: 90

David Hunt *(Mng Dir-Digital)*
Nestor Cifuentes *(Dir-Art)*
Michael Honeyman *(Dir-Creative)*
Jose Miguel Videla *(Dir-Creative)*
Joaquin Ceron *(Copywriter)*
Sebastian Vega *(Copywriter)*

Accounts:
Elly Lilly Cialis
New-Favorita Tissues
Garnier Garnier Hair Dye
GMO
Japi Jane Campaign: "Sauna"
L'Oreal Campaign: "Tetris Baby", Campaign: "Tetris Party", Garnier Anti dark Circle
MAGGI
Mckay Campaign: "Gift Machine"
MOVISTAR
NESCAFE
Nestle
SURA
Volkswagen Amarok

Colombia

Publicis-CB
Calle 82 No 6-51, 11001 Bogota, Colombia
Tel.: (57) 1 634 1810
Fax: (57) 1 611 5187
E-Mail: publiciscb@publiciscb.com.co
Web Site: www.publiciscolombia.com

Employees: 97

Rodrigo Tarquino *(Chief Creative Officer)*
Camilo Carvajal *(Gen Dir-Creative)*
Ricardo Beltran *(Dir-Creative)*
Paul Duque *(Dir-Plng)*
Guillermo Gonzalez *(Dir-Creative)*
Fabio Mendoza *(Dir-Creative)*
Maria Camila Marquez *(Acct Exec)*
Nicolas Camargo *(Copywriter)*

Accounts:
Bridgestone
Davivienda
Fundamor
Harley-Davidson
Hp
Neko
Nestle Campaign: "The 9,242 Km Direct Mail"
Procter & Gamble
Purina Pet Care De Colombia Purina Dog Chow
Renault Campaign: "A Scroll Dodging Obstacles", Campaign: "A postcard that brands"
Sanofi Aventis
Sofasa
Telefonica

Mexico

Olabuenaga Chemistri
Prado Norte 125 Piso 2, Lomas de Chapultepec, Mexico, DF 11000 Mexico
Tel.: (52) 55 5249 4200
Fax: (52) 55 5249 4292
E-Mail: och@och.com.mx

Employees: 100
Year Founded: 1951

Agency Specializes In: Advertising, Automotive, Aviation & Aerospace, Brand Development & Integration, Consulting, Consumer Marketing, Cosmetics, Direct Response Marketing, E-Commerce, Electronic Media, Financial, Food Service, Magazines, Newspapers & Magazines, Out-of-Home Media, Pharmaceutical, Planning & Consultation, Point of Purchase, Point of Sale, Print, Production, Public Relations, Publicity/Promotions, Radio, Retail, Sales Promotion, Strategic Planning/Research, T.V., Telemarketing, Travel & Tourism, Yellow Pages Advertising

Ceci Garnica *(Grp Dir-Creative)*
Gabriela Ortiz *(Grp Dir-Creative)*
Diego Armas *(Sr Acct Dir)*
Belen Moy Campos *(Acct Dir)*
Fernanda Gonzalez *(Producer-Digital)*
Gabriela Fenton *(Dir-New Bus)*
Aldo Gonzalez Figueroa *(Dir-Creative)*
Edson Gonzalez *(Dir-Integrated Art)*

Accounts:
Cerveceria Cuauhtemoc Moctezuma Tecate Beer
Cinepolis
Heineken Campaign: "It's Easy Being a Man", Digital, Radio, Spanish-language, Tv
Mars; 1987
Milenio
Pepsi
Vive!
Wal-Mart

Publicis Arredondo de Haro
Prolongacion Paseo de la Reforma, 1015 5 piso Col Desarrollo, Mexico, DF CP 01310 Mexico
Tel.: (52) 5 9177 5600
Fax: (52) 55 91775603
E-Mail: lillian.mezher@publicisah.com
Web Site: www.publicis.com

Alejandro Cardoso *(Pres/CEO-Latin America)*
Juan Carlos Tapia *(VP-Customer Svc)*
Alfredo Alquicira *(Grp Dir-Creative)*
Alejandro Garcia *(Art Dir)*
Hector Fernandez Maldonado *(Creative Dir)*
Atria Medina *(Acct Dir)*
Mark Nakamichi *(Acct Dir)*
Ivan Pedraza *(Creative Dir)*
Lauro Quintanar *(Art Dir)*
Tonatiuh Torres Cornejo *(Art Dir)*
Karla Alvarez *(Dir-Customer Svc)*
Luis Madruga *(Dir-Creative)*
Juan Carlos Rached *(Dir-Customer Svc)*

Marjorie Vardo *(Dir-Art)*
Erik Vervroegen *(Dir-Intl Creative-Publicis Worldwide)*
Alfredo Ramos *(Assoc Dir-Creative)*
Nancy Martinez Aguilar *(Copywriter)*
Javier Olmos *(Copywriter)*
Alan Ramirez *(Copywriter)*
Jessica Apellaniz *(Grp Creative Dir)*

Accounts:
Banamex
Best Day Travel
BMW Bike, Campaign: "Injured Letters", Mini, The Word Blocker
CEMDA Mexican Environmental-Law Center Campaign: "Help Save Us"
Consejo de Promocion Turistica de Mexico
CPTM Campaign: "Mexico Taxi Project"
Daiichi Sankyo Campaign: "Weeble Wobble Motel"
DIF Zapopan
Garnier Campaign: "Joke"
Gerber
Gruma Maseca, Mission
Grupo Reforma
Home Depot
Ideasmusik Campaign: "Beard"
L'Oreal
Mexican Transplant Association
Mexico Tourism Board Campaign: "Mexico Taxi Project"
Mini Cooper Campaign: "Misplaced Airbag", Campaign: "Restroom Assistant", Campaign: "Words can hurt"
Mini
Nestle Campaign: "Eye", Maggi Mini Sauce, Nescafe
P&G
Paralife Foundation Campaign: "I Will Work for Free"
Purina
Renault Campaign: "Kangoo Compressor"
Rioja
Telcel Campaign: "Stupidphone"

Panama

Publicis Fergo, S.A.

Calle 50 y Calle 67 San Francisco Building 3rd Fl, Panama, Panama
Mailing Address:
PO Box 0832-2490 WTC, Panama, Panama
Tel.: (507) 270 88 11
Fax: (507) 270 88 92
E-Mail: info@publicisfergo.com

Employees: 51
Year Founded: 1960

Agency Specializes In: Consumer Marketing, Event Planning & Marketing, Exhibit/Trade Shows, Public Relations

Alejandro Cardoso *(CEO-Latin America)*
Carmen Julia Corrales *(CEO-Publicis Panama)*

Accounts:
AES Panama S.A. Energy
Corporacion El Sol
Grupo Silaba Fiat, Hummer, Kia Motor
Heineken
Nestle Central America Region & Panama Biscuits, Cereal Partners Worldwide, Maggi, Purina Pet Care
Optica Sosa y Arango Optics
Sanofi-Aventis
Telefonica Mobiles Panama Movestar

Trinidad & Tobago

Publicis Caribbean

Albion Court 61 Dundonald Street, Port of Spain, Trinidad & Tobago
Tel.: (868) 627 4040
Fax: (868) 624 9529
E-Mail: patrick@publiciscaribbean.com
Web Site: www.publiciscaribbean.com/

Employees: 26

Patrick Johnstone *(CEO)*
James Amow *(Dir-Creative)*
Keisha Sirjuesingh *(Acct Exec)*
Paul Amar *(Sr Graphic Designer)*
Charisse Thavenot *(Reg Acct Dir)*

Uruguay

Publicis Impetu

Colonia 922 Piso 8, 11100 Montevideo, Uruguay
Tel.: (598) 2 902 05 44
Fax: (598) 2 902 19 42
E-Mail: publicisimpetu@publicisimpetu.com.uy
Web Site: www.publicisimpetu.com.uy

Employees: 30

Agency Specializes In: Advertising, Cosmetics, Financial, Food Service, Production (Print)

Esteban Barreiro *(Gen Dir-Creative)*
Maria Jose Caponi *(Acct Dir)*
Diego Besenzoni *(Dir-Art)*
Mauricio Minchilli *(Acct Mgr)*
Alejandra Hermida *(Sr Acct Exec)*

Accounts:
Alejandra Forlan Foundation
Banco Comercial
Ford
La Mayor
La Republica Campaign: "App Iphone"
L'Oreal
Maristar
Movistar
Nestle El Chana Coffee
Nike 10K, Free 5.0 Shoe
Nuevo Siglo Cable Television Services, Campaign: "Cows"

Venezuela

Publicis 67

Av Casanova Centro Comercial, Torre Norte Piso 11, Plaza Venezuela, Caracas, 1060 Venezuela
Tel.: (58) 212 400 4500
Fax: (58) 212 400 4580
E-Mail: antonio.betancourt@publicis.com.ve

Employees: 100
Year Founded: 1967

Agency Specializes In: Advertising

Fabian Bonelli *(Chief Creative Officer)*
Gerardo Pernia *(Chief Creative Officer)*
Demian Campos *(Dir-Creative & Art)*
Yoryi Cantor *(Dir-Creative)*
Noraida Otazo *(Dir-Creative-Publicis Venezuela)*
Jose Castro *(Graphic Designer-Adv)*
Elias Isea *(Copywriter)*

Accounts:
Accion Solidaria Aids Fundations
Amnesty International
Black&Decker
Bridgestone Hollydays
Chartpak Campaign: "Moon"
Civil Association Volunteers for animals
Ecological Movement of Venezuela
Escuela De Futbol Santa Campaign: "Street Robbery"
Firestone
Fundaseno Campaign: "Doctor's Appointment", Campaign: "Letters"
Getty Images
The History Channel
Nestle Campaign: "Jacket"
Renault
Solidarity Action World Day Against HIV
Telefonica Campaign: "Subway"

Asia/Pacific

Publicis Asia/Pacific Pte. Ltd.

80 Anson Road #33-00, Fuji Xerox Twrs, Singapore, 079907 Singapore
Tel.: (65) 6 836 3488
Fax: (65) 6836 3588
E-Mail: angel.cruz@publicis.com.sg
Web Site: www.publicis.com

Employees: 100

Ajay Thrivikraman *(Chief Creative Officer-South East Asia)*
Ambba Kuthiala *(Gen Mgr & Reg Bus Dir)*
Rakesh Hinduja *(Reg Dir-Bus)*
Sharon Tan *(Reg Dir-Bus)*
Sidhaesh Subrah *(Grp Acct Dir)*
Jess Seow *(Acct Dir)*
Erik Vervroegen *(Dir-Intl Creative-Publicis Worldwide)*
Rica Facundo *(Sr Mgr-Acct & Social Media)*
Anita Belani *(Acct Mgr)*
Chi Kuan Tham *(Acct Mgr)*
Dione Mayuko Harrison *(Sr Reg Acct Mgr)*
Prachi Partagalkar *(Reg Grp Acct Dir)*

Accounts:
Burger King Singapore Campaign: "Bk Coupon Generator"
Crisis Relief
Excelcom Indonesia
Korea Telecom
MiniNurse
Procter & Gamble Vicks Cough Drops
Purefoods
Vicks Campaign: "Bring Voice Back"

Australia

Publicis Australia

Bond Store 3 30 Windmill St, Walsh Bay, Sydney, NSW 2000 Australia
Tel.: (61) 2 9258 9000
Fax: (61) 2 9258 9001
Web Site: www.publicis.com.au

Employees: 300

Andrew Baxter *(CEO)*
Iona Macgregor *(Chief Strategy Officer)*
Ryan Bernal *(Grp Acct Dir)*
Lindsay Donaldson *(Dir-Ops)*
Justin Gurney *(Dir-Plng)*
Sebastian Vizor *(Dir-Art)*
Jenn Butler *(Mgr-Fin & Comml)*
Oskar Westerdal *(Copywriter)*

Accounts:
Axa
Burn Energy Drink
The Coca-Cola Company Ride; 2008
Hahn
J. Boag & Son James Boag's Pure
James Boag's Draught
LG
Lion Co. Campaign: "Spill Proof Beer", Campaign: "Super In. Super Out.", Campaign: "The Sirens of Bass Strait", James Boag's Premium
Nestle Campaign: "Caution", Campaign: "Maxibon bumps Magnum off its royal pedestal", Drumsticks, Maggi Fusian; 2007

Qantas
Tourism NT Campaign: "Do the NT", Digital, Print, TV Commercials
Toyota Campaign: "Thermo"
Virgin Group Ltd

Publicis Australia
Level 3 164 Grey Street, PO Box 3204, South, Brisbane, QLD 4101 Australia
Tel.: (61) 73121 6666
Fax: (61) 73121 6777
Web Site: www.publicis.com.au

Employees: 75

Rob Kent *(Mng Dir)*
Andy Geppert *(Sr Dir-Art)*
Joanna Millington *(Acct Dir)*
Karyn Stroet *(Acct Dir)*
Louisa Taliacos *(Acct Dir)*
Ryan Petie *(Dir-Creative)*
Sarah-Jane Ewing *(Sr Acct Mgr)*
Sarah McCabe *(Acct Mgr)*
Mel Porter *(Acct Mgr)*
Georgia Pratt *(Acct Mgr)*
James Walker *(Mgr-Fin)*

Accounts:
ACT For Kids Campaign: "Twinkle Twinkle"
Air Asia
Bio-Organics
Golden Casket Lottery Instant Scratch-its
Powerball
Queensland Rail Campaign: "Crosses", TattsBet, Tourism Queensland
RID Campaign: "The RID Amazon DT Challenge"
Subway Campaign: "I got it made"
Sunshine Coast
UNiTAB
VW

Publicis Australia
Level 6 Freshwater place, Melbourne, VIC 3006 Australia
Tel.: (61) 3 9685 3444
Fax: (61) 3 9685 3434
E-Mail: mrelbourne.reception@publicis.com.au
Web Site: www.publicis.com.au

Employees: 60

Georgie Pownall *(Gen Mgr)*
David Schaak *(Dir-Art)*

Accounts:
Darrell Lea Campaign: "Everyone's Darrell Lea"
New-Monde Nissin Corporation
Mondelez Cadbury, Caramello Nibbles
Nestle Connoisseur Ice Cream
Nike
Peters Campaign: "Maxiblokes", Maxibon
Tourism Victoria Campaign: "Play Melbourne"
Toyota Campaign: "Legendary Moments"

China

King Harvests
2F No.400 Gulin Road, Pufa Creation Park, Shanghai, 200235 China
Tel.: (86) 2164840551
Fax: (86) 21 64839813
E-Mail: info@kingharvests.com
Web Site: www.kingharvests.com

Employees: 100

Laura Lee, *(Mng Dir & Dir-Creative)*
Larry Ong *(Exec Dir-Creative)*
Jing Liu *(Sr Acct Dir)*
Guangye Zhang *(Dir-Art)*
Stella Lee *(Sr Acct Mgr)*
Kai Gu *(Sr Acct Exec)*

Accounts:
Bosch
Haier
Sanyo
Siemens

Publicis (Beijing)
Rm 1510 15/F Zhuzong Tower No 25 Dong San Huan Zhong Rd, Chaoyang District, Beijing, 100020 China
Tel.: (86) 10 6594 5180
Fax: (86) 10 6594 5168

Employees: 104
Year Founded: 1996

Robert Fuchs *(Mng Dir)*
Chris Duffy *(CEO-Beijing)*
David Gompel *(CEO-Greater China)*
David Hunt *(Mng Dir-Greater China)*
Wee-Hoon Tan *(Head-Plng)*
Brian Yang *(Exec Dir-Creative)*

Accounts:
Airbus
Hewlett Packard
Mengnlu
Nestle Dreyer's Grand Ice Cream; 2008
Tencent
Tinghsin Group
UBS
United Continental Holdings
Western Union

Publicis Guangzhou
Publicis House Guangdong Guest House, 603 JieFang BeiRd, 510180 Guangzhou, China
Tel.: (86) 20 8310 0500
Fax: (86) 20 8310 0502
Web Site: www.publicisgroupe.com

Employees: 30

Chenghua Yang *(CEO)*
Bill Wang *(Mng Dir)*
Julie Marchesseault *(Exec VP & Gen Mgr-Publicis NURUN)*
David Hunt *(Mng Dir-Digital)*
Swee Chen Low *(Head-Creative & Gen Mgr)*
Sheena Jeng *(Dir-Creative)*
Heidi Zhang *(Dir-Strategic Plng)*

Accounts:
Wechat

Publicis Shanghai
6/F Building A 98 Yan Ping Road, Shanghai, 200042 China
Tel.: (86) 21 2208 3888
Fax: (86) 21 540 33903
Web Site: www.publicisgroupe.com

Employees: 120

C. H. Yang *(CEO)*
Sheena Jeng *(Chief Creative Officer)*
David Hunt *(Mng Dir-Digital)*
Jean-baptiste Comte-Liniere *(Exec Dir-Creative)*
Will Tao *(Creative Dir)*
Xia Wang *(Art Dir)*
Hui Yao *(Art Dir)*
Zoe Zhao *(Art Dir)*
Bastien Grisolet *(Dir-Art)*
Leo Lee *(Dir-Creative)*
Tracy Zhang *(Dir-HR-Shared Service Center, China & Hong Kong)*
Angela Ann Arches-Antonio *(Assoc Dir-Creative)*

Accounts:
3M 3M Lint Roller
Cerebos Campaign: "Naked", Campaign: "Poker"
Dongfeng Citroen Creative
New-Greenpeace
Haier Co., Ltd
Pernod Ricard Ballantine's, Creative, TVC; 2007
Ricoh Campaign: "Self-Portait", Campaign: "Young at Heart"
Shanghai Jahwa United Co. Liushen
Taipei Women's Rescue Foundation Charity Campaign: "Rescue child prostitute"
Zhe Jiang Xin Hua Compassion Education Foundation Campaign: "Fire Fly"

Hong Kong

Luminous Experiential MSLGROUP
(Formerly Luminous Experiential Marketing Communications)
14/F East Exchange Tower, 38 Leighton Road, Causeway Bay, China (Hong Kong)
Tel.: (852) 2214 2688
Fax: (852) 2850 8777
Web Site: www.luminous-asia.com

Employees: 40

Antony Spanbrook *(Owner)*
Dave Low *(Mng Dir)*
Tamsyn Barker *(Gen Mgr-Singapore)*
Beth Griffiths *(Acct Dir)*
Monique Ng *(Dir-Production)*
Julie Yeung *(Sr Acct Mgr)*
Ginia Choi *(Sr Graphic Designer)*
Rachel Lui *(Assoc Producer)*

Accounts:
Audi
Cathay Pacific
Deutsche Bank
PricewaterhouseCoopers
Prudential

Publicis Hong Kong
23/F 1063 Kings Road, Quarry Bay, Hong Kong, China (Hong Kong)
Tel.: (852) 2590 5888
Fax: (852) 2856 9905
E-Mail: Laurie.kwong@publicis-asia.com
Web Site: www.publicis.com

Employees: 98

Daniel Cullen *(Gen Mgr)*
Mark Birman *(Exec Dir-Creative)*
Thierry Halbroth *(Exec Dir-Creative)*
Sebastien Vacherot *(Exec Dir-Creative)*
Ray Chan *(Grp Dir-Creative)*
Nicoletta Stefanidou *(Grp Dir-Creative)*
Alex Ng *(Sr Dir-Art)*
Eva Ng *(Dir-Plng)*
Kerwin Choy *(Copywriter)*
Jean Ng *(Copywriter-English)*
Apitchaya Borvornsettanan *(Reg Bus Dir)*

Accounts:
Anthisan
Brand Golden Bird's Nest, In-Store, Print, Television
Citibank
CLP
Duracell Creative
L'Oreal
Marriott International
MGM Grand Macau
Pacsafe Campaign: "Pacsafe Wire Mesh"
New-Sadia
Sca Tissue Campaign: "Boxer", Citrus Blossom Tissue, Tempo Citrus Blossom "Relaxing Crabby Claw"
Society for Community Organization

Tefal
Tempo Creative
Tena Creative, Public Relations
Western Union Asia Pacific, Branding

India

MarketGate Consulting

507-A 5th Fl Kakad Chambers Dr, Annie Besant Road Worli, Mumbai, 400018 India
Tel.: (91) 9930222556
Fax: (91) 24926634
E-Mail: info@market-gate.com
Web Site: www.market-gate.com

Employees: 7
Year Founded: 2005

Agency Specializes In: Brand Development & Integration, Consulting, Strategic Planning/Research

Shripad Nadkarni *(Founder & Dir)*
Rama Jeswani *(VP)*
Varun Khanna *(VP)*
Sameer Walzade *(Assoc VP)*

Accounts:
Colgate
Dabur
General Motors
GlaxoSmithKline
Godrej
HSBC
Madura Garments
Mahindra & Mahindra
Radio Mirchi Viacom

MSL Group India

(Formerly Hanmer MSL)
Rehem Mansion - 1 3rd Floor 42 Shahih Bhagat Singh Road, Colaba, Mumbai, 400 001 India
Tel.: (91) 22 6633 5969
Fax: (91) 22 6633 5979
Web Site: india.mslgroup.com/contact-us

Employees: 150

Pankaj Desai *(Sr VP-MSLGroup)*
Glen Dsouza *(Sr VP)*
Parveez Modak *(Sr VP)*
Ketan Pote *(Acct Dir)*
Monica Srivastava *(Acct Dir)*
N. Dhanshekar Iyer *(Dir-Fin & Ops-MSLGROUP)*
Mukesh Tharali *(Sr Mgr-HR)*
Nikita Crasta *(Sr Acct Mgr)*
Aziz Khan *(Acct Mgr)*
Shrinivas Alley *(Mgr-HR)*
Sanoj Ramakrishnan *(Asst Mgr-HR)*
Rinu Jha *(Assoc Acct Dir)*

Accounts:
ABB Brand Building, Corporate Reputation Management, Crisis & Issues Management, Strategic Communications
Big Bazaar Creative, Engagement Solutions, Strategy
Biocon Public Relations, Strategic Communications
Changi Airport Group
Coca-Cola India Communications
Courtyard by Marriott Brand Building, Corporate Reputation Management, Crisis & Issues Management, Strategic Communications
CREDAI Bengaluru Public Relations, Strategic Communications
eBay India Social Media Engagement Campaign
FINO Brand Building, Corporate Reputation Management, Crisis & Issues Management, Strategic Communications
GM India
History channel Public Relations, Strategic Communications
HTC Public Relations, Strategic Communications
ING Vysya Life Insurance
The Institute of Neurosciences - Kolkata Creative, Engagement Solutions, Strategy
Investors' Clinic Creative, Engagement Solutions, Strategy
J & K Bank Brand Building, Corporate Reputation Management, Crisis & Issues Management, Strategic Communications
JM Financial
JW Marriott Bengaluru Creative, Engagement Solutions, Strategy
Kinetic Group
Lenovo Smart Phones Computer, Film, Mobile, Tv
LG Electronics
MCX
Monster Energy Drink
Neo Sports Neo Cricket, Public Relations, Strategic Communications
ParentCircle Brand Awareness, Communication Strategy
PC Chandra Jewellers Experiential, PR, Social Media
PNB Metlife Insurance
Raymond Group Creative Communications, Engagement Solutions, Strategic Advisory
Sheth Developers & Realtors Strategic Counsel
Singapore Tourism Board PR, Social Media
Sobha Developers
Sony India Campaign: "The Rise of Mobile Photography", Sony Xperia Z1
STAR Movies Campaign: "Bringing Bond Back"
Steelcase
Tata Motors
United Technologies
Usha International Corporate Reputation, Product Communications
V-Guard Industries Core Communications
Videocon D2H
Volkswagen
Whirlpool Creative, Engagement Solutions, Strategy
World Gold Council
Zoom; 2008

Publicis Ambience Mumbai

Viva Ctr 126 Mathuradas Mills Compound, N M Joshi Marg Lower Parel (W), Mumbai, 400 013 India
Tel.: (91) 22 2482 9000
Fax: (91) 22-2660 3292
E-Mail: Nakul.Chopra@publiciindia.com

Paritosh Srivastava *(COO)*
Bobby Pawar *(Chief Creative Officer-South Asia & Dir)*
Sunanda Chadha *(Sr VP)*
Chandan Jha *(VP)*
Shikha Sud *(Grp Head-Creative & Copywriter)*
Amod Dani *(Exec Dir-Creative)*
Akshay De *(Art Dir)*
Umesh Rawool *(Creative Dir)*
Shruti Srivastava *(Art Dir)*

Accounts:
Adam Extra Long Condoms
Ambuja Cements Ltd
Autocop
Bharti Axa Bharti Axa General Insurance, Bharti Axa Life Insurance, Campaign: "Dedicated Claims Handler", Creative
BrandSTIK Campaign: "Giant Storage", USB Flash Drives
Citi Bank Campaign: "200 Years", Campaign: "Diwali Happier", Campaign: "Holidays"
Garnier Color Naturals
Gokuldas Intimatewear Pvt Ltd Campaign: "Fabulous, As I Am"
HUL Campaign: "Reinvent", Lakme Poptints
JK Helene Curtis Park Avenue Beer Shampoo
Jyothy Laboratories Ltd. Campaign: "Sad Faces", Creative, Henko
Kansai Nerolac Paints Ltd Digital, High-Definition
Libero Babycare Range
Musafir.com Campaign: "Mela", Creative
Nerolac Campaign: "Umbrella", Excel
Park Avenue Beer Shampoo, Campaign: " Beer Head", Campaign: "A cooling effect", Campaign: "Man Hair", Creative
Procter & Gamble Campaign: "Thorn", Creative, Oral B, Vicks
Rajhans Nutriments Creative
Renault Creative, Duster
Rhythm House
Rotaract Club of Mumbai Shivaji Park
Schmitten Campaign: "What's Theirs is Theirs'
TBZ Creative
Tempo Hand Sanitizer
Tencent Inc. Campaign: "3 Idiots", Campaign: "Ajeeb Shajeeb Morning"
V-Guard Industries Ltd
Videocon D2H Creative Duties
VIP Luggage Creative Duties; 2010
Vu Technologies Campaign: "Theatre of Sound"
World Gold Council & Reliance Money Campaign: "My Gold Plan"

Publicis Beehive

(Formerly Beehive Communications)
701-A Poonam Chambers Dr Annie Besant Road, Worli, Mumbai, 400 018 India
Tel.: (91) 22 660 86800
Fax: (91) 22 666 11337
E-Mail: sanjit@beehivecommunications.com
Web Site: www.beehivecommunications.com

Employees: 130

Agency Specializes In: Brand Development & Integration, Digital/Interactive, Media Buying Services, Media Planning

B. Sanjit Shastri *(CEO)*

Accounts:
Aptech Ltd
CCNG
Centuary Mattresses Campaign: "Party Blower"
Chambor Campaign: "Rouge Plump"
Enkay Telecom
Everest Roofing Systems
Food Express
General Motors
Genting Hong Kong Limited
Gujarat Tourism
Hard Rock Cafe
HImachal Tourism
India Bulls Finance
Indscot Beverages
Intercraft Trading Campaign: "Chambor of Secrets"
Jubilant Retail
Kesari Travel Company
Korea Tourism
Krispy Kreme Doughnuts
MAAC
Mahesh Tutorials
Malaysia Tourism
Mantri Developers
MT Educare Ltd.
Resort World Sentosa
Royal Palms Leisure
Shiro
Survana TV
Taurus Mutual Fund
Thai Airways
Total Mall
Tourism Malaysia World Music Festival
VCI Hospitality
Venus Drugs & Cosmetics Campaign: "Spike Hold Calendar"
Vijay Sales Campaign: "Generations"

Publicis India Communications Pvt. Ltd.

126 Mathuradas Mills Compound N M Joshi Marg, Off Senapati Bapat Marg Lower, 400 013

Mumbai, India
Tel.: (91) 22 2482 9000
Fax: (91) 22 2482 9096
E-Mail: publicis@publicisindia.com
Web Site: www.publicis.com

Employees: 160

Bobby Pawar *(Chief Creative Officer & Mng Dir-South Asia)*
Nakul Chopra *(CEO-South Asia)*
Atin Wahal *(VP-Client Svcs)*
Ullas Chopra *(Head-Creative)*
Amod Dani *(Exec Dir-Creative)*
Shahrukh Irani *(Creative Dir)*
Suravi Pradhan *(Client Svcs Dir)*
Ashish Khazanchi *(Dir-Natl Creative-Ambience Publicis)*

Accounts:
Ahilya Pharmaceuticals
Ambuja Cement Campaign: "Arjun Deewar", Creative
Angel Broking Ltd Campaign: "We For You"
Apollo Tyres Ltd
Asbah
Beam Inc
Bookstalk Audiobooks Campaign: "William Shakespeare"
Brandstik Solutions USB Flash Drives
Citibank Campaign: "Qrossword"
DC Design
Diageo
Dr. Morepen
Emami
Enamor Campaign: "Fabulous, as I am"
Expedia Inc. Campaign: "French Flirting"
HDFC Mutual Fund Campaign: "Dear Dad", HDFC Debt Fund for Cancer Cure
Helpage India
HP Mini Notebooks, Travel Batteries
International Olive Council
Kansai Nerolac Paints Nerolac - Healthy Home Paints, Nerolac HD Impression
Kennel1
Kimaya Impex Campaign: "Shit Car"
LAADLI Campaign: "Temple"
Lakme
L'Oreal Garnier
Maruti Suzuki India Ltd. Campaign: "Festival", Campaign: "Made All Distances Smaller", Campaign: "Make Bonds Stronger"
Micro Technologies Vehicle Security Systems
Movie Junction Campaign: "Eyes"
Nerolac
Nestle India Campaign: "Gifts", Campaign: "Rich and Creamy", Creative, Foods & Dairy Business, Maggi, Nescafe, Nescafe Sunrise, Nestea
OK Products OK Chewing Gum
Omax Elevators
Osmania Fine Printing Works
Premier Roadstar
Procter & Gamble
Pronto Couriers
Rajkot Traffic Police Campaign: "Prison"
Rotaract Club Of India Shivaji Park
Rotaract Club of Mumbai Shivaji Park
SH Kelkar & Company Creative
Siciliano Pizza
Srushti Herbal & Allied Products Stabnil Headache Balm
Supermax Personal Care Razor Blades
Talentube.com
TATA Broadband
Vacha Trust
Vicks Campaign: "Thorns"
Volkswagen Campaign: "Think Blue Beetle"
VU Television Campaign: "Bravery-Stupidity", Campaign: "Speaker"
WeChat Marketing
Yog Sutra

Publicis India Communications Pvt. Ltd.

Vatika Triangle 6th Fl Sushant Lok, Phase I Block A, Gurgaon, 122 002 India
Tel.: (91) 124 412 1000
Fax: (91) 124 412 1020
Web Site: www.publicis.com

Employees: 75

Nakul Chopra *(CEO-South Asia)*
Hemant Misra *(CEO-Publicis Capital)*
Sreekumar Balasubramanian *(Sr VP)*
Sougata Kundu *(Client Svcs Dir)*
Deepak Sharma *(Art Dir)*
Amir Siddiqui *(Acct Dir)*
Natwar Singh *(Art Dir)*
Joy Mohanty *(Dir-Natl Creative)*
Sunny Johnny *(Assoc Dir-Creative)*
Pranjal Bordoloi *(Copywriter)*
Rajesh Chandra *(Copywriter)*

Accounts:
Adam Condoms
Cleartrip Campaign: "Goa to Delhi"
Fly Trap
New-GLOW Fabric Softner
Hewlett-Packard Campaign: "Peephole", Pen Drive
IFFCO Tokyo General Insurance
India Picture Stock Image Provider
MakeMyTrip Creative
Nestle Campaign: "Project Cradle", Maggi Hungrooo, Sauce
People for Animal Campaign: "Tiger"
The Pioneer Climate Change Conference
Procter & Gamble Co
New-SpiceJet Creative
Steadfast Paper Shredders
Tood Campaign: "Bachelor's Shoe Rack"

Publicis iStrat

603 Mahatta Towers B-1 Community Center, Janak Puri, New Delhi, 110058 India
Tel.: (91) 11 25511354
Fax: (91) 11 25613701
Web Site: www.istrat.in

Employees: 50

Agency Specializes In: Digital/Interactive, E-Commerce, Search Engine Optimization, Social Media

Sonya Sahni *(Chief Strategy Officer)*
Aniruddha Deb *(VP & Head-Bus)*
Richa Chhabra *(Acct Mgr)*
Geetika Sarpal *(Acct Mgr)*
Yamini Sharma *(Acct Mgr-Client Svcs)*
Vikash Gupta *(Mgr-Design Team)*
Madhurima Purokayastha *(Mgr-Digital Mktg & Bus Dev)*
Kapil Thairani *(Sr Acct Exec-Project Mgmt)*
Sanjay Chejara *(Sr Media Planner)*

Accounts:
Alpha G:Corp
The Confederation of Indian Industries
Dupont
Fabindia Creative
Hero Corp
Hindware
Maruti Suzuki
Nestle

Bangladesh

Protishabda Communications

26 Kemal Ata Turk Ave 3rd Floor, Banani Commercial Area, Dhaka, 1213 Bangladesh
Tel.: (880) 2 881 8082
Fax: (880) 2881 7524

Employees: 25

Agency Specializes In: Advertising

Shakil Wahed *(Owner)*
Rakibul Hassan *(Sr Acct Exec)*

Indonesia

Publicis Indonesia

Samudera Indonesia Building 5th Floor Jl Jend S Parman Kav 35, Slipi, Jakarta, 11480 Indonesia
Tel.: (62) 21 548 0719
Fax: (62) 21 548 0870
Web Site: www.publicis.co.id

E-Mail for Key Personnel:
President: henry.saputra@publicis-metro.com

Employees: 90
Year Founded: 1972

National Agency Associations: PPPI

Ben Lightfoot *(CEO)*
Kike Gutierrez *(Chief Creative Officer)*
Benny Perry Napitupulu *(Dir-Art-Malaysia)*
Marco Widjaja *(Dir-Creative)*

Accounts:
Actavis Indonesia Dumocalcin
BMW
Change.org
Greenpeace Indonesia
The Jakarta Post
Jaringan Advokasi Tambang
Jatam
L'Oreal Campaign: "Urban Hero", Garnier Men
Neo Rheumacyl
Nestle Coffee Mate, Dancow
Periplus Bookshops Digital, In-Store
Procter & Gamble Vicks F44
PT URC Indonesia
Qanpas
TIKI Indonesia

Japan

Beacon Communications K.K.

JR Tokyo Maguro Building 3-1-1 Kami-Osaki, Shinagawa-ku, Tokyo, 141-0021 Japan
Tel.: (81) 3 5437 7200
Fax: (81) 3 5437 7211
E-Mail: tokyo.prbeacon@beaconcom.co.jp
Web Site: www.beaconcom.co.jp

Employees: 350
Year Founded: 2001

National Agency Associations: ABC-IAA-JAAA-JMAA

Nicolas Menat *(Pres)*
Sayori Kato *(Exec Dir-HR)*
Yuhei Takeyama *(Sr Dir-Art)*
Taketo Igarashi *(Creative Dir)*
Ai Yamaguchi *(Art Dir)*
Kazz Ishihara *(Dir-Creative)*
Marie Kobayashi *(Acct Supvr)*
Daisuke Kimura *(Designer)*
Kuniaki Yamamoto *(Copywriter)*
Yasuo Matsubara *(Assoc Creative Dir)*

Accounts:
AIFUL Corp.; 2002
AR Drone Campaign: "Flying Banner"
BMW Japan
Ebara Foods Industry, Inc. Campaign: "Funfair in Your Mouth"
Electronic Arts K.K.
GlaxoSmithKline K.K.
Herman Miller Japan
Human Lab
Lenovo Campaign: "DO.NEXT"

Max Factor K.K. Illume, Muse, SK-II
Merial Japan Frontline Plus, Pet Medications
Mondelez
Nike Japan Campaign: "Play the Real Thing", Football, Nike Five, Sportswear
Nikon Corporation Campaign: "Tears"
Norton Campaign: "Stuff that Matters"
One Eight Promotion Campaign: "Pinch Pinup"
Parrot Campaign: "Flying Banner"
Procter & Gamble Far East Ltd. Ariel, Attento, Braun Oral-B, Campaign: "International Flight Mouth", Campaign: "Life & Dirt", Campaign: "Mom's First Birthday", Campaign: "Transform Audition", Crest Spin Brush, Eukanuba, Herbal Essences, Iams, Joy, Pampers, Rejoy, Vidal Sassoon, WELLA, Whisper; 1983
Puma
Second Harvest Japan
Skymark Airlines Co., Ltd.
Sumitomo 3M Ltd.
Symantec Anti-virus Software, Campaign: "Boy in Love", Campaign: "She Said Daddy", Campaign: "Stuff that Matters", Campaign: "Writer's Story"
Tumi Japan
Wada Elementary School Campaign: "Ribbond Birds"
Whirlpool Campaign: "Corporate Identity"
Wide Corporation

Carre Noir Tokyo

10 F JR Tokyu Meguro Building, 3-1-1 Kami-Osaki Shinagawa-ku, 141-0021 Tokyo, Japan
Tel.: (81) 3 5719 8905
Fax: (81) 3 5719 8919
Web Site: www.carrenoir.com

Beatrice Mariotti *(VP & Dir-Creative)*

Malaysia

Publicis (Malaysia) Sdn. Bhd.

M1 Mezanine Fl Wisme LYL, 46100 Petaling Jaya, Selangor Malaysia
Tel.: (60) 3 7952 2222
Fax: (60) 3 7952 2220
E-Mail: dean.branhan@publicis.com.my

Employees: 80

Angeline Tung *(Gen Mgr)*
Monica Chen *(Exec Dir-Creative)*
May Ling Yong *(Assoc Dir-Creative)*

Accounts:
Nestle Lactogen
Sanofi Aventis Campaign: "Change for Life", Campaign: "It's Time to Love Your V", Digital, Essentiale, Lactacyd, POSM, Print

Philippines

Publicis JimenezBasic

14/F Solaris One Bldg 130 Dela Rosa St, Legaspi Village, Makati, Philippines
Tel.: (63) 2 811 5098
Fax: (63) 2 325 0291
E-Mail: ask@publicisjimenezbasic.com.ph
Web Site: www.publicis.com

Don Sevilla, III *(Exec Dir-Creative)*
Brandie Tan *(Exec Creative Dir)*
Beng Calma *(Grp Acct Dir)*
Nino Gupana *(Copywriter & Creative Dir)*
J P Cuison *(Assoc Creative Dir & Dir-Art)*
Lec Flores *(Dir-Creative)*
Paulo Famularcano *(Assoc Dir-Creative)*
Niki Francisco *(Acct Mgr)*
Catherine Falla *(Acct Supvr)*
Iofer Mijares *(Copywriter)*

Accounts:
Cebu Pacific
Globe Telecom
Greenwich Pizza Campaign: "Tavola"
Innovetelle
Manila Bulletin Binatilyo
Monde Nissin Corp Lucky Me
Nutriasia UFC Banana Catsup
New-Summit Publication
This Is My Philippines
Unilab Alaxan, Allerts, Solmux

Publicis Manila

4F Herco Center 114 Benavides Street Legaspi Village, Makati, 1229 Philippines
Tel.: (63) 28 12 54 66
Fax: (63) 2810 5784
Web Site: www.publicis.com

E-Mail for Key Personnel:
Chairman: Matec.Villanueva@publicis-manila.com

Employees: 105
Year Founded: 2003

Matec Villanueva *(CEO)*
Alexander Joshua Marquez *(Acct Dir)*
Hannah Poblador *(Acct Dir)*
Cara Soto *(Dir-Strategic Plng)*
Nei Apologista *(Assoc Dir-Bus Unit)*
Pamy Velilla-Hernandez *(Assoc Dir-Bus Unit)*
Joseph Carlo Ramos *(Sr Acct Mgr)*
Christine Maris Cardema *(Acct Mgr)*
Mica Valencia *(Acct Mgr)*

Accounts:
ABS-CBN Mobile
Animal Welfare Coalition
Asia Brewery Inc. Creative, Tanduay Black
Nestle Philippines Campaign: "Youmeoke", Milo Powdered Drink, NesCafe, Nido Milk

Singapore

Publicis Singapore

80 Anson Road, #33-00 Fuji Xerox Twrs, Singapore, 079907 Singapore
Tel.: (65) 6836 3488
Fax: (65) 6836 2588
Web Site: www.publicis.com

Employees: 100

Lou Dela Pena *(CEO)*
Ajay Thrivikraman *(Chief Creative Officer-South East Asia)*
Tattoo Yar *(Grp Head-Creative)*
Sharon Tan *(Gen Mgr)*
Troy Lim *(Exec Creative Dir)*
Jon Loke *(Exec Creative Dir)*
Justine Lee *(Grp Dir-Creative)*
Xiulu Chua *(Art Dir)*
Erik Vervroegen *(Dir-Intl Creative-Publicis Worldwide)*
Tay Kok Wei *(Dir-Art)*
Dean Bramham *(Reg CEO-Southeast Asia)*

Accounts:
100 Plus Campaign: "Outdo yourself"
AAAA Singapore
New-Axa Campaign: "Born to Protect", OOH
Beyond Social Services Campaign: "Rearranging Lives"
Bitexco Financial Centre
BMW Group
CDL Group
Citibank
Expedia Branding, Creative
Fraser & Neave Campaign: "Singapore to Istanbul"
Garnier Skincare
L'Oreal Garnier Men
Love & Co. Campaign: "True love wins"
Procter & Gamble Campaign: "Vicks Voice of Indonesia", Oral-B
New-Sadia Content Marketing, Social Media
Samaritans of Singapore Campaign: "Hidden Pain"
Scoot
Wink Hostel Campaign: "Don't Waste it. Share it at Wink"

Thailand

Publicis (Thailand) Ltd.

Empire Tower 47th Fl, 195 S Sathorn Rd, Yannawa, 10120 Bangkok, Thailand
Tel.: (66) 2 659 5959
Fax: (66) 2 659 5968
Web Site: www.publicis.com

Employees: 70

Louis-Sebastien Ohl *(CEO)*
June Saowanee Rattanasomboonsuk *(Mng Dir)*
Mikki Brunner *(VP & Reg Dir-Creative)*
Vancelee Teng *(Exec Dir-Creative)*
Bruno Biondi *(Dir-Acct Mgmt)*
Manop Janwantanagul *(Mgr-Fee & Compensation)*

Accounts:
Airbus Group Communication, Creative, Marketing
L'Oreal
Mentos

PUBLICIS HEALTHCARE COMMUNICATIONS GROUP

One Penn Plz 5th Fl, New York, NY 10019
Tel.: (212) 771-5500
Fax: (212) 468-4021
E-Mail: info@publicishealthcare.com
Web Site: www.publicishealthcare.com

Employees: 25
Year Founded: 2003

National Agency Associations: 4A's

Agency Specializes In: Health Care Services, Medical Products

Nicholas Colucci *(Pres & CEO)*
Matt McNally *(Pres & Chief Media Officer-Global)*
Rick Keefer *(Chief Dev Officer-Global)*
Alexandra von Plato *(Pres-North America)*
Lyn Falconio *(Exec VP & Bus Dir-Worldwide)*
Andrea Palmer *(Sr VP)*
Alex Goldman *(VP & Dir)*
Rachel Krouse *(VP & Dir)*
Sarah Bast *(VP)*
Austin Smith *(VP-Talent Mgmt-Global)*
Adrian Sansone *(Gen Mgr)*
Amanda Lawson *(Dir-Media)*
Kerri Stumpo *(Dir-Digital Media)*
Kaitlin Russomano *(Assoc Dir-Media)*
Michelle AuBuchon *(Mgr-Internal Comms)*
Heidi Frank *(Acct Supvr)*
Casey Johnson *(Acct Supvr)*
Lily Nathanson *(Supvr-Media)*
Mac Haertl *(Media Planner)*
Sam Welch *(Grp Pres-Global)*

Accounts:
AstraZeneca

Branches

Publicis Life Brands Resolute

(Formerly Publicis Healthcare Communications)
Pembroke Building Kensington Village, Avonmore Road, London, W14 8DG United Kingdom
Tel.: (44) 20 7173 4000
Fax: (44) 20 7173 4101
Web Site: www.publicislifebrandsresolute.com

Employees: 80

National Agency Associations: IAA

Agency Specializes In: Health Care Services

Anna Korving *(Mng Dir)*
Shaheed Peera *(Exec Dir-Creative)*
Katie Elderton-Brown *(Grp Acct Dir)*
Neil Croker *(Creative Dir)*
Megan Howard *(Client Svcs Dir)*
Emma Knott *(Acct Dir)*
Martin Fell *(Dir-Creative Svcs)*
Greg Porter *(Mgr-Ops)*
Louisa Garnier *(Copywriter)*
Paul Williams *(Sr Art Dir)*

Accounts:
Takeda Campaign: "The Boy I Used to Know"

Publicis Touchpoint Solutions
(Formerly Publicis Selling Solutions)
1000 Floral Vale Blvd Ste 400, Yardley, PA 19067-5570
Tel.: (215) 525-9800
Fax: (609) 219-0118
Toll Free: (800) 672-0676
Web Site: www.touchpointsolutions.com

Employees: 50
Year Founded: 1995

Agency Specializes In: Health Care Services, Pharmaceutical

Kathy Delaney *(Chief Creative Officer-Global-Publicis Healthcare Comm Group)*
Matt McNally *(Pres-Publicis Health Media)*
Nick Colucci *(CEO-Publicis Healthcare Comm Grp)*
Eileen J. May *(Sr VP-Contact Center Ops)*
Mark Stevens *(Sr VP-Strategy & Comml Effectiveness)*
Susan Beach *(VP-Sls & Bus Dir-Natl)*
Archie Robinson *(Gen Mgr)*
Christina DiBiase *(Dir-Natl Bus)*
Nora Zartler *(Dir-Comml Bus)*
Bob Bagnell *(Rep-Pharmaceutical Sls)*
Elaine Bixby *(District Bus Mgr)*
Joel Buchanan *(District Mgr-Sls)*

Accounts:
Orexo AB Zubsolv
Reckitt Benckiser Pharmaceuticals

PUBLICIS KAPLAN THALER
(Name Changed to Publicis New York)

PUBLICIS NEW YORK
(Formerly Publicis Kaplan Thaler)
1675 Broadway, New York, NY 10019
Tel.: (212) 474-5000
Fax: (212) 474-5702
Web Site: www.publicisna.com

Year Founded: 1997

National Agency Associations: 4A's

Agency Specializes In: Advertising, Branded Entertainment, Children's Market, Corporate Identity, Cosmetics, Entertainment, Faith Based, Financial, Health Care Services, Integrated Marketing, Pharmaceutical, Promotions, Real Estate, Retail, Sponsorship, Viral/Buzz/Word of Mouth

Breakdown of Gross Billings by Media: E-Commerce: 2%; Newsp. & Mags.: 20%; Other: 10%; Outdoor: 5%; Radio: 8%; T.V.: 55%

Linda Kaplan Thaler *(Chm)*
Andrew Bruce *(Pres & CEO)*
Tricia Kenney *(Chief Comm Officer)*
Katie Bury *(Exec VP & Gen Mgr)*
Jim Kotulka *(Exec VP & Exec Dir-Creative)*
Brian Lefkowitz *(Exec VP & Exec Creative Dir)*
Carlos Figueiredo *(Exec VP & Dir-Creative)*
Eric Green *(Exec VP & Dir-Experience Design)*
Frank Bele *(Sr VP & Exec Dir-Creative)*
Kate Carleton *(Sr VP & Grp Acct Dir-Global)*
Brian Fernandez *(Sr VP & Grp Acct Dir)*
Susie Lodise *(Sr VP & Grp Acct Dir)*
Rich Stoffer *(Sr VP & Grp Acct Dir)*
Jill Danenberg *(Sr VP & Dir-Creative)*
Ben Royce *(Sr VP & Dir-Search)*
Tamara Neufeld Brown *(VP & Grp Acct Dir)*
Robert Camilleri *(VP & Dir-Global Ops)*
George Logothetis *(VP & Dir-Creative)*
Maurice Riley *(VP & Dir-Strategy)*
Xavier Rodon *(VP-Creative & Dir)*
Heather Stiteler *(VP, Assoc Dir-Creative & Copywriter)*
Michelle Encizo *(VP & Assoc Dir-Project Mgmt)*
Larry Kirschner *(VP & Assoc Dir-Creative & Copy)*
Matthew Stein *(VP & Assoc Dir-Creative)*
Tommy Troncoso *(VP & Assoc Dir-Creative)*
Rico Cipriaso *(VP-Digital)*
Jason Graff *(Exec Dir-Creative)*
Geneika Lewis *(Sr Acct Dir)*
Trac Nguyen *(Sr Producer-Interactive)*
Steve Rechtman *(Sr Producer-Interactive)*
Rodrigo Bistene *(Art Dir)*
Solomon Ganz *(Acct Dir)*
Carine Johannes *(Acct Dir)*
Vanessa Kopec *(Acct Dir)*
Sean McNeal *(Acct Dir-Digital)*
Nadia Blake *(Dir-Brdcst Production)*
Doug Loffredo *(Dir-Art)*
James Rothwell *(Dir-Creative)*
Alexandre Abrantes *(Assoc Dir-Creative & Copywriter)*
Jeroen de Korte *(Assoc Dir-Creative & Copywriter)*
David Drayer *(Assoc Dir-Creative)*
Eubin Kim *(Assoc Dir-Creative)*
Alyssa Ruiz *(Sr Mgr-Community & Strategist-Social)*
Zachary Cyrus *(Acct Supvr-Digital)*
Sarah Gore *(Acct Supvr)*
Jia Zheng *(Sr Strategist-Digital)*
Sara Jaye-Esposito *(Acct Exec)*
Sara Knee *(Strategist)*
Ben Neenan *(Acct Exec)*
Kristin Pulaski *(Acct Exec)*
Desiree Yanes *(Acct Exec)*
Fernando Carrion *(Copywriter)*
Kay Loftus *(Asst Acct Exec)*
Josephine Maeng *(Asst Acct Exec)*
Catherine Nolli *(Asst Acct Exec)*
Jessica Poolt *(Acct Coord)*

Accounts:
Abbott Laboratories Campaign: "The Mother 'Hood", Digital, Online, Similac
Advertising Council BoostUp.org, PSA, Print, Understood.org, stopalcoholabuse.gov; 2007
Aflac Incorporated (Lead Creative Agency) Aflac Duck, Boat, Campaign: "Eureka! One Day Pay", Campaign: "Physical Therapy", Campaign: "Rounds", Insurance; 1998
Animal New York
Anti-Defamation League Campaign: "Imagine a World Without Hate", Campaign: "Imagine"; 2012
AXA; 2011
Bristol-Myers Squibb Eliquis; 2003
Cartier; 2009
Citigroup Citi Global, Retail Banking, CitiGold Card, Citi Institutional Client Group, Citi Cards.com, Fxpro, ThankYou Rewards, Women & Co.; 2007
Doctors of the World More Than A Costume
Dow Jones Wall Street Journal; 2011
Edmunds.com , Inc Campaign: "Ask the Car People", TV; 2011
Hanesbrands Champion; 2007
Loreal Paris Garnier, Lancome, L'Oreal, Biotherm, SoftSheen-Carson, Matrix; 1981
L'Oreal USA, Inc.
Merck Miralax, Dr. Scholl's, Gardasil, Pneumovax, Suvorexant, Zostavax; 2011
Nestle Buitoni, Campaign: "Pocket Like It's Hot", Coffee-mate, Dolce Gusto, Hot Pockets, Lean Pockets, Nescafe; 2007
Pfizer Celebrex, Lyrica; 2003
Procter & Gamble Bounty, Campaign: "Halloween Treats Gone Wrong", Campaign: "Keep It Clean", Campaign: "ScopeBacon", Campaign: "Thanks to Crest Their Teeth Are Covered", Campaign: "The Effects of Halloween Candy", Campaign: "The Power of Dad", Cascade, Charmin, Crest, Dawn, Fibersure, Glide, Metamucil, Oral-B, Pepto, PlusC, Prilosec OTC, Puffs, Scope Mouthwash, Swiffer, VapoRub, Vicks DayQuil, Vicks Nyquil, Vicks ZQuil; 1964
Red Lobster (Lead Creative Agency)
Rosetta Stone; 2011
Sanofi Pasteur Consumer (Creative Agency of Record); 2007
Scope
Shire Intuniv; 2006
Sleepy's Campaign: "Making the world a better place to sleep", Campaign: "Our First Place", Campaign: "Welcome Home", Creative, Digital, OOH, Radio, TV
TriHonda Dealer Group Lead Creative
UBS Global Financial Services, Wealth Management, Investment Banking; 1998
Wendy's International Inc. Campaign: "Know It All", Campaign: "Now That's Better", Campaign: "To Be With You", Pretzel Bacon Cheeseburger, Radio, TV, Video; 2009
Zurich Financial; 2008

PUBLICIS USA
4 Herald Sq 950 6th Ave, New York, NY 10001
Tel.: (212) 279-5550
Fax: (212) 279-5560
Web Site: www.publicisna.com

Employees: 950
Year Founded: 1952

National Agency Associations: 4A's

Agency Specializes In: Advertising, Advertising Specialties, Communications, Digital/Interactive, Direct Response Marketing, Event Planning & Marketing, Hispanic Market, Investor Relations, Public Relations, Sales Promotion, Sponsorship

Julie Levin *(CMO-North America)*
Andy Bird *(Chief Creative Officer)*
Dawn Winchester *(Chief Digital Officer-North America)*
Andrew Bruce *(CEO-North America)*
David Corr *(Exec VP & Exec Dir-Creative)*
Linda Joselow *(Exec VP & Grp Acct Dir-Publicis Kaplan Thaler)*
Don Blashford *(Exec VP & Acct Dir-Worldwide)*
Angela Pasqualucci *(Exec VP & Acct Dir-BAL Worldwide)*
Mark Hider *(Exec VP)*
Eric Moncaleano *(Sr VP & Exec Dir-Creative)*
Lisa Hersh *(Sr VP & Grp Acct Dir)*
Emily Shahady *(Sr VP & Grp Acct Dir-Cadillac)*
Dan Cohen *(Sr VP & Creative Dir)*
Emma Barcoe *(Sr VP & Dir-Strategy)*
Victor Basile *(Sr VP & Dir-Print & Art Production)*
Tanvir Hannan *(Sr VP & Dir-Strategic Res & Analytics)*
Mark Ronquillo *(Sr VP & Dir-Creative-Publicis Adv)*
Jeremy Bowles *(Mng Dir-Global)*
Darielle Smolian *(VP & Sr Producer-Art)*
Tanya Hill *(VP & Acct Dir)*
Jennifer Tyler *(VP & Producer)*
Michael Reilly *(VP & Mgmt Supvr)*
Jana Jarosz *(VP & Dir-Creative & Art)*
Betsy Liegey *(VP & Dir-Strategic)*
Alex Yenni *(VP & Dir-Digital Strategy)*

Jackie Panepinto *(VP & Sr Mgr-Traffic)*
Mitja Petrovic *(Gen Mgr & Dir)*
Tyler Beck *(Dir-Consumer Insights)*
Krystal Chellis *(Dir-HR)*
Victor Zeiris *(Assoc Dir-Creative & Writer-Beauty Grp)*
Brooke Miller *(Assoc Dir-Bus Dev)*
Nelson Fortier *(Sr Mgr-Mktg & Dev)*
Van Nguyen *(Acct Mgr-Publicis Groupe)*
Jody Menna *(Mgr-HR)*
Robert Robbins *(Mgr-Print Production)*
Lauren Kowalsky *(Acct Supvr-Integrated)*
Amanda Gallucci *(Content Strategist)*

Accounts:
Ad Council (Pro Bono)
Anheuser-Busch InBev Beck's
Cadillac
CitiGroup; 2007
The Coca-Cola Company Coca-Cola, Vault
Coinstar
Crest Sensitivity
General Mills campaign: "Magic Brownies"
General Motors Company Cadillac (Global Creative Agency of Record), Cadillac CT6, Campaign: "Arena", Campaign: "Dare Greatly", Campaign: "The Daring: No Regrets"
Heineken Campaign: "#DMDS", Campaign: "The Experiment"
Hewlett Packard
L'Oreal U.S.A. Biolage, Garnier Fructis, Garnier Lumia, Garnier Nutrisse, Lancome, Matrix, Professional Division, SoftSheen-Carson
Merck Miralax, OTC Brands
Nestle USA, Inc.; Glendale, CA Hot Pockets, Libby's Nestea, Nescafe, PowerBar
Pfizer, Inc. Celebrex
Procter & Gamble Bounty, Campaign: "Oath of Office", Campaign: "Waitress", Charmin, Creative, Crest, DayQuil, Intrinsa, Metamucil, NyQuil, Oral-B Pulsonic, Pepto Bismol, Prilosec, Puffs, Tampax, ThermaCare, VapoRub, ZzzQuil
Ray-Ban
Sanofi SA
T-Mobile USA "Subtitles with Joel McHale", Campaign: "Bike Race", Campaign: "Jump"
TruGreen
UBS Campaign: "Everywhere is Art", Stephen Wiltshire Billboard
UNICEF
Walt Disney Company The Walt Disney Company
Whirlpool Corp

Branches

MSL Seattle
(Formerly Publicis Consultants)
424 2nd Ave W, Seattle, WA 98119-4013
Tel.: (206) 285-5522
Fax: (206) 272-2497
Web Site: northamerica.mslgroup.com

E-Mail for Key Personnel:
President: steve.bryant@publicis-pr.com

Employees: 239

National Agency Associations: COPF

Agency Specializes In: Business-To-Business, Children's Market, Event Planning & Marketing, Exhibit/Trade Shows, Food Service, Health Care Services, Pharmaceutical, Public Relations, Publicity/Promotions, Restaurant, Teen Market

Lisa Kelly *(Sr VP & Grp Dir-Mgmt)*
Greg Eppich *(Sr VP)*
Vicki Nesper *(Sr VP)*
Patty Tazalla *(Acct Supvr)*
Tessa Weber *(Sr Acct Exec)*
Jennifer Egurrola Leggett *(Acct Exec)*

Accounts:
DuPont Crop Protection
Mori Building Company
T-Mobile US Campaign: "Alter Ego"

Publicis Dialog Boise
168 N 9th St Ste 250, Boise, ID 83702
Tel.: (208) 395-8300
Fax: (208) 395-8333
E-Mail: lynda.bruns@publicis-usa.com
Web Site: www.publicisna.com

Employees: 15
Year Founded: 1985

National Agency Associations: 4A's

Agency Specializes In: Digital/Interactive, Sponsorship

Kevin Sweeney *(CFO & Exec VP-North America)*
Julie Levin *(CMO-North America)*
Carla Serrano *(Chief Strategy Officer)*
Tim Kavander *(Exec VP & Dir-Creative)*
Bill Newbery *(Grp Dir-Creative)*
Christal Gammill *(Acct Dir)*
Lindsey Ash *(Dir-HR & Admin-Publicis Canada)*
Kurt Olson *(Dir-Creative)*

Publicis Hawkeye
(Formerly hawkeye)
2828 Routh St Ste 300, Dallas, TX 75201
(See Separate Listing)

Publicis Indianapolis
200 S Meridian St Ste 500, Indianapolis, IN 46225-1076
Tel.: (317) 639-5135
Fax: (317) 639-5134
E-Mail: tom.hirschauer@publicis-usa.com
Web Site: http://www.publicisna.com

Employees: 50

Agency Specializes In: Advertising, Brand Development & Integration, Broadcast, Business-To-Business, Collateral, Consumer Marketing, Electronic Media, Financial, Graphic Design, Health Care Services, Magazines, Newspaper, Outdoor, Print, Public Relations, Sponsorship, T.V., Travel & Tourism

Jeff Huser *(Dir-Creative)*
Sara O'Neill *(Dir-Creative)*

Publicis Seattle
(Formerly Publicis West)
424 2nd Ave W, Seattle, WA 98119-4013
Tel.: (206) 285-2222
Fax: (206) 273-4219
Web Site: publicisseattle.com

Employees: 200

Agency Specializes In: Advertising, Sponsorship

Scott Foreman *(CEO)*
Jason Sullivan *(Mng Dir & Exec VP)*
Andrew Christou *(Chief Creative Officer & Exec VP)*
Britt Peterson Fero *(Chief Strategy Officer)*
Corey Bartha *(Exec VP & Head-Integrated Production)*
Jason Lucas *(Exec VP & Exec Dir-Creative)*
Lori Davis *(Exec VP & Exec Bus Dir)*
Adam Thomason *(VP & Grp Acct Dir)*
Adam Oliver *(Head-Production)*
Steve Williams *(Grp Dir-Creative & Writer)*
Jason Fong *(Sr Dir-Art)*
Julia Luplow *(Sr Dir-Art)*
Simson Chantha *(Art Dir)*
Garth Knutson *(Acct Dir)*
Maria Schoonover *(Acct Dir)*
Nick Schuitemaker *(Acct Dir)*
Baeu Bernstein *(Dir-Creative)*
Steve johnston *(Dir-Creative)*
Stacy Milrany *(Dir-Creative & Art)*
Rob Kleckner *(Assoc Dir-Creative)*
Andrew Starmer *(Acct Supvr)*
Nicole McKeown *(Sr Strategist-Digital-T-Mobile)*
Marie Matuszewski *(Strategist)*
Derek Anderson *(Assoc Creative Dir)*

Accounts:
American Girl LLC Campaign: "Together We Make the Holidays"
Brand Drops
Bumbershoot Creative
Cinerama
Citi
Coca-Cola Refreshments USA, Inc.
Coinstar
Dish Network; Englewood, CO
Eddie Bauer Lead Creative
Garnier
Hewlett-Packard
New-KinderCare
Knowledge Universe (Agency of Record) Before- and After- School Programs, Champions, KinderCare Learning Centers
New-Kraft Heinz
Les Schwab Campaign: "RV Weekend", Campaign: "Stranded Nanny", Television
Nestle
NYC Bicycle Safety Coalition
P & G
Power Bar
Sara Lee Ball Park, Creative
T-Mobile US Campaign: "#KimsDataStash", Campaign: "One-Up", Campaign: "Pets Unleashed", Campaign: "The Simple Choice", My Faves, Super Bowl 2015, T-Mobile@Home, TV, Whenever Minutes
UBS
UNICEF
United Way
Visit Seattle (Advertising Agency of Record) Creative Development, Marketing Strategy, Media Buying, Media Planning
Zurich

PUBLICITY MATTERS
14644 McKnew Rd, Burtonsville, MD 20866
Tel.: (301) 385-2090
E-Mail: matt@publicitymatters.net
Web Site: www.publicitymatters.net

Agency Specializes In: Internet/Web Design, Media Relations, Print, Public Relations, Publicity/Promotions

Matt Amodeo *(Pres)*

Accounts:
Active Duty Fitness for Women
Andrea Kirby's Sports Media Group
Big Apple Circus
Dreyer's (Edy's) Grand Ice Cream
Fresco Designs
Gold's Gym International
McDonald's
Old Hickory Grille
One To One Fitness Centers
Silver Eagle Group Media Relations
SMG Worldwide

PULSAR ADVERTISING, INC.
8383 Wilshire Blvd Ste 334, Beverly Hills, CA 90211
Tel.: (323) 302-5110
Fax: (323) 966-4907
E-Mail: agonzalez@pulsaradvertising.com
Web Site: www.pulsaradvertising.com

E-Mail for Key Personnel:

President: agonzalez@pulsaradvertising.com

Employees: 35
Year Founded: 1992

Agency Specializes In: Advertising, Bilingual Market, Brand Development & Integration, Consumer Marketing, Corporate Identity, Digital/Interactive, E-Commerce, Event Planning & Marketing, Internet/Web Design, Logo & Package Design, Planning & Consultation, Public Relations

Approx. Annual Billings: $17,000,000

Alberto Gonzalez *(Founder, Pres & Exec Dir-Creative)*
James Wright *(Partner)*
Andy Ankowski *(Dir-Creative & Copywriter)*
Peter Kavelin *(Dir-Art)*
Raymond Shea *(Dir-Acct Plng)*
Morgan Daniels *(Assoc Dir-Creative)*
Alex Herrmann *(Mgr-Creative Studio)*
Ashley Fagelbaum *(Acct Supvr)*

Accounts:
Arlington County Commuter Assistance
Foothill Transit
LAX
Metrolink
The Metropolitan Transportation Authority
San Francisco HealthPlan
Virginia Department of Transportation

Branches

Pulsar Advertising, Inc.
1023 15th St NW Ste 800, Washington, DC 20005
Tel.: (202) 775-7456
Fax: (202) 775-7459
E-Mail: kcarlson@pulsaradvertising.com
Web Site: www.pulsaradvertising.com

Employees: 5

Agency Specializes In: Advertising, Transportation

Katherine Carlson *(Mng Dir)*
Scott Baker *(Sr Acct Exec)*
Josh Opat *(Acct Exec)*

Accounts:
Arlington Metro
Bart
Green Earth Technologies
Summer Winds
Virginia Department of Taxation
Virginia Department of Transportation

Pulsar Advertising, Inc.
830 E Main St Ste 2310, Richmond, VA 23219
Tel.: (804) 225-8300
Fax: (804) 225-8347
E-Mail: info@pulsaradvertising.com
Web Site: www.pulsaradvertising.com

Employees: 8

Agency Specializes In: Advertising, Transportation

Jim Wright *(Partner)*

Accounts:
Virginia Department of Transportation

PULSE MARKETING & ADVERTISING LLC
3344 W 143rd Terr, Leawood, KS 66224
Tel.: (913) 205-9958
E-Mail: info@pulsemarketing.biz
Web Site: www.pulsemarketing.biz

Year Founded: 2005

Agency Specializes In: Advertising, Broadcast, Collateral, Corporate Identity, Logo & Package Design, Media Buying Services, Outdoor, Public Relations, Social Media, Strategic Planning/Research

David O'Brien *(Principal & Dir-Creative)*
Ryan Duffy *(Dir-Creative & Copywriter)*
Jim Potoski *(Dir-PR & Copywriter)*
Cherie Dean *(Dir-Creative & Digital)*

Accounts:
American Fallen Warriors Memorial Foundation

PULSECX
(Formerly Roska Healthcare Advertising)
211B Progress Dr, Montgomeryville, PA 18936-9618
Tel.: (215) 699-9200
Fax: (215) 699-9240
Web Site: www.pulsecx.com/

Employees: 45
Year Founded: 1981

National Agency Associations: DMA

Agency Specializes In: Advertising, Advertising Specialties, Brand Development & Integration, Business Publications, Business-To-Business, Consumer Marketing, Digital/Interactive, Direct Response Marketing, E-Commerce, Electronic Media, Financial, Graphic Design, Health Care Services, High Technology, Industrial, Information Technology, Internet/Web Design, Logo & Package Design, Media Buying Services, Medical Products, New Product Development, Newspapers & Magazines, Out-of-Home Media, Pharmaceutical, Print, Strategic Planning/Research

Approx. Annual Billings: $41,000,000

Jay H. Bolling *(CEO)*
Kurt Mueller *(Chief Innovation Officer)*
Mary L. Lacquaniti *(Sr Dir-Mktg & HR)*
Nancy Walsh *(Acct Dir)*
Glenn Hauler *(Dir-Creative-Copy)*
Brian Phillips *(Dir-Creative)*
Nichole Engle *(Acct Supvr)*

Accounts:
Astellas Creative, Myrbetriq

PULSEPOINT
(Formerly Datran Media LLC.)
345 Hudson Street 5th Floor, New York, NY 10014
Tel.: (212) 706-9781
Fax: (212) 706-9758
Web Site: www.pulsepoint.com

Year Founded: 2001

Agency Specializes In: Advertising, Email, Local Marketing

Sloan Gaon *(CEO)*
Darline Jean *(COO)*
Mitchell Eisenberg *(Gen Counsel, Sec & Sr VP-Corp Dev)*
Jack Dempsey Southerland, III *(Sr VP-Programmatic Solutions)*
Andrew Stark *(Sr VP-Content Solutions)*
Lindsay Boesen *(VP-Mktg)*
Anthony Stewart *(Head-Acct Mgmt & Sr Dir-Programmatic & Strategic Partnerships)*
Garrett Ryan Taylor *(Dir-Programmatic Partnerships)*
Ricardo Velez, Jr *(Mgr-Programmatic Ops)*

Accounts:
BabytoBee Health Care Centers
Beltone Hearing Health Services
eDiets Health & Fitness Centers
eHarmony Social Media
NASCAR.COM Races & Track Events
Only Nature Pet Store Pet Food Supplier
PGATOUR.com News & Entertainment Services
PulsePoint, Inc.
Sony Electronic Products Mfr & Distr
TaxBrain Online Income Tax Preparation Services

PUMPED INC
14 NE 1st Ave Ste 904, Miami, FL 33132
Tel.: (305) 371-3955
E-Mail: hello@pumpedinc.com
Web Site: www.pumpedinc.com

Year Founded: 2005

Agency Specializes In: Advertising, Brand Development & Integration, Digital/Interactive, Search Engine Optimization, Social Media, Sponsorship

Cynthia Lagos *(Dir-Art)*
Carlos F. Pena *(Chief Branding Officer)*

Accounts:
Liberty Extraction & Drying

PUMPHOUSE CREATIVE INC.
(Formerly PrintElectric, Inc.)
PO Box 140886, Dallas, TX 75214
Tel.: (214) 655-6832
Fax: (214) 889-3100
E-Mail: mark@pumphousecreative.com
Web Site: www.pumphousecreative.com

Employees: 4
Year Founded: 1997

Agency Specializes In: Advertising, Brand Development & Integration, Business-To-Business, Communications, Event Planning & Marketing, Exhibit/Trade Shows, Food Service, Graphic Design, Logo & Package Design, Newspaper, Outdoor, Point of Purchase, Point of Sale, Print, Production

Approx. Annual Billings: $600,000

Bruce McElroy *(Dir)*

Accounts:
Consilient Restaurants QSR; 2004
Regogo Racing Vintage Automobile Racing; 2012
Rockers vs Mods Motorsport Events; 2007
Snookies Restaurants QSR; 2010
Society Petroleum Engineers Oil & Gas; 1997

PUMPHREY MARKETING, INC.
4853 Galaxy Pkwy Ste A, Cleveland, OH 44128-5939
Tel.: (216) 464-9687
Fax: (216) 292-4205
Web Site: www.pumphreymktg.com

E-Mail for Key Personnel:
President: davep@pumphreymktg.com
Media Dir.: lenore@pumphreymktg.com
Production Mgr.: denise@pumphreymktg.com

Employees: 8
Year Founded: 1975

Agency Specializes In: Brand Development & Integration, Business-To-Business, Collateral, Communications, Corporate Communications, Corporate Identity, Direct Response Marketing, E-Commerce, Electronic Media, Engineering, Exhibit/Trade Shows, Graphic Design, High Technology, Industrial, Internet/Web Design, Logo

& Package Design, Media Buying Services, Multimedia, Planning & Consultation, Print, Production, Public Relations, Publicity/Promotions, Sales Promotion, Technical Advertising, Web (Banner Ads, Pop-ups, etc.)

Approx. Annual Billings: $4,500,000

Breakdown of Gross Billings by Media: Bus. Publs.: 20%; Collateral: 15%; Fees: 1%; Internet Adv.: 12%; Logo & Package Design: 3%; Plng. & Consultation: 6%; Print: 2%; Production: 5%; Pub. Rels.: 6%; Sls. Promo.: 30%

David C. Pumphrey *(Pres)*
Denise M. Orosz *(VP)*
Lenore R. Sienkiewicz *(Client Svcs Dir)*
Phil Brindley *(Acct Mgr)*

PURDIE ROGERS, INC.

5447 Ballard Ave NW, Seattle, WA 98107
Tel.: (206) 628-7700
Fax: (206) 628-2818
Web Site: www.purdierogers.com

Year Founded: 1990

Agency Specializes In: Advertising, Broadcast, Cable T.V., Collateral, Digital/Interactive, Direct Response Marketing, Electronic Media, Email, Exhibit/Trade Shows, In-Store Advertising, Media Buying Services, Mobile Marketing, Multimedia, Newspapers & Magazines, Out-of-Home Media, Outdoor, Paid Searches, Planning & Consultation, Point of Purchase, Point of Sale, Print, Production (Print), Promotions, Public Relations, Radio, Search Engine Optimization, Social Media, T.V., Trade & Consumer Magazines, Viral/Buzz/Word of Mouth, Web (Banner Ads, Pop-ups, etc.)

Approx. Annual Billings: $8,000,000

George Purdie *(Principal)*
Andy Rogers *(Principal)*
Marybeth Turk *(Sr Acct Dir)*
Ben Morris *(Dir-Data Analytics)*
Martin Pieracci *(Dir-Art)*
Scott Rockwell *(Dir-Interactive)*
Barnett Turk *(Dir-Creative)*

Accounts:
Caldera Spas; 2010
Corona Clipper; 2008
Fiberon Decking; 2010
Hanwha Solar Hanwha SolarOne; 2010
Parex USA Parex, TEIFS, LaHabra, El Rey; 2004

PURE BRAND COMMUNICATIONS, LLC

2401 Larimer St, Denver, CO 80205-2122
Tel.: (303) 297-0170
Fax: (303) 845-9588
E-Mail: info@pure-brand.com
Web Site: www.pure-brand.com

Employees: 18
Year Founded: 2003

National Agency Associations: 4A's

Agency Specializes In: Advertising

Revenue: $4,600,000

Dan Igoe *(Co-Owner & Mng Partner)*
Gregg Bergan *(Owner & Chief Creative Officer)*
Stacey Rose Knox *(Acct Dir)*
Jerry Stafford *(Dir-Art)*
Alisa Anderson *(Project Mgr-Mktg & PR)*
Tessa Watts *(Strategist-Mktg)*

Accounts:
NCM Fathom
Special Olympics

Branches

Pure Brand Communications

200 E 8th Ave Ste 203, Cheyenne, WY 82001-1440
Tel.: (307) 634-5871
Fax: (307) 634-5873
Web Site: www.pure-brand.com

Employees: 3

National Agency Associations: 4A's

Janis Tharp *(Sr Acct Mgr-PR)*

PURE MATTER

30 E Santa Clara St Ste 240, San Jose, CA 95113
Tel.: (408) 297-7800
Fax: (408) 297-7055
E-Mail: info@purematter.com
Web Site: www.purematter.com

Employees: 10

Courtney Smith *(Co-Owner & Chief Creative Officer)*
Bryan Kramer *(CEO)*
Ryan Campbell *(Client Svcs Dir)*

Accounts:
American Cancer Society
Blach Construction
Cisco Systems
Commonwealth Central Credit Union
Coremetrics Inc
Filice Insurance
Ireland San Filippo
Real Tie Innovations
San Vitum Health
Satelitte Healthcare
Stone Publishing

PUREI

12 E Wilson St, Batavia, IL 60510
Tel.: (630) 406-7990
Fax: (630) 406-7993
Web Site: www.purei.com

Employees: 10
Year Founded: 2000

Agency Specializes In: Advertising, Agriculture, Alternative Advertising, Arts, Automotive, Aviation & Aerospace, Brand Development & Integration, Broadcast, Cable T.V., Catalogs, Collateral, Commercial Photography, Communications, Computers & Software, Consulting, Consumer Goods, Consumer Publications, Corporate Communications, Corporate Identity, Cosmetics, Customer Relationship Management, Digital/Interactive, Direct Response Marketing, E-Commerce, Education, Electronic Media, Electronics, Email, Engineering, Entertainment, Environmental, Exhibit/Trade Shows, Experience Design, Fashion/Apparel, Financial, Food Service, Government/Political, Graphic Design, Health Care Services, Hospitality, Household Goods, Identity Marketing, In-Store Advertising, Industrial, Infomercials, Information Technology, Integrated Marketing, Internet/Web Design, Investor Relations, Legal Services, Leisure, Logo & Package Design, Magazines, Marine, Media Planning, Medical Products, Merchandising, Mobile Marketing, Multimedia, New Technologies, Newspaper, Newspapers & Magazines, Outdoor, Package Design, Paid Searches, Planning & Consultation, Point of Purchase, Print, Production, Production (Ad, Film, Broadcast), Production (Print), Public Relations, Radio, Recruitment, Restaurant, Retail, Sales Promotion, Search Engine Optimization, Social Marketing/Nonprofit, Social Media, Sports Market, Stakeholders, Strategic Planning/Research, T.V., Trade & Consumer Magazines, Transportation, Travel & Tourism, Web (Banner Ads, Pop-ups, etc.)

Approx. Annual Billings: $2,000,000

Len Davis *(Pres)*
Darin Barri *(Partner)*
Michael Wallace *(Partner)*
Debbie Wager *(Dir-Art & Designer)*
Kelly Yee *(Mgr-Ops)*
Jessie Black *(Designer-Motion Graphics)*
Benjamin Ouart *(Sr Graphic Designer)*
Jim Titus *(Sr Engr-Production, R&D)*

Accounts:
Bison Gear & Engineering Corporation
New-Seattle's Best Coffee; 2014

PUREMOXIE

134 Linden St, Oakland, CA 94607
Tel.: (510) 371-7990
E-Mail: contact@pure-moxie.com
Web Site: www.pure-moxie.com

Agency Specializes In: Advertising, Brand Development & Integration, Digital/Interactive, Media Planning, Outdoor, Print, Radio, Social Media, Sponsorship, T.V.

Antonio Patric Buchanan *(Co-Founder & CEO)*
Wendy Taylor-Tanielian *(Pres)*
Paris Mitzi Hinson *(Co-CEO)*
Tami Brewer *(Sr VP-Digital Svcs)*
Paul D. Cragin *(Sr VP-Analytics)*

Accounts:
Spicy Vines

PURERED

(Formerly GA Communications Inc.)
2196 W Park Ct, Stone Mountain, GA 30087
Tel.: (770) 498-4091
Fax: (770) 498-0691
Toll Free: (800) 562-4091
Web Site: www.purered.net

Employees: 200
Year Founded: 1968

Agency Specializes In: Advertising, Advertising Specialties, Broadcast, Business-To-Business, Collateral, Commercial Photography, Consulting, E-Commerce, Internet/Web Design, Media Buying Services, Point of Sale, Print, Production, Retail, Sponsorship

Approx. Annual Billings: $24,000,000

Michael Minasi *(CEO)*
J. Greg Latham *(CFO)*
Kevin Kincaid *(Sr VP)*
Perry Hunter *(VP & Grp Dir-Creative)*
Karin Klapak *(VP-Digital Mktg)*
David Mimbs *(VP)*
Hob Pusey *(VP-Ops)*
Justin Carll *(Dir-Strategy & Bus Dev)*
Julia Fraser *(Dir-Digital Accts)*
Elizabeth Newman *(Dir-Accts)*
Kurt Nebiker *(Assoc Dir-Creative-Digital Mktg)*
Michael Dawkins *(Specialist-Mktg)*
Shannon Josey *(Specialist-Adv Content Mgmt)*
Jon Shelton *(Sr Designer)*

Accounts:
Safeway Inc.
SP Richards
SuperValu

PureRED Creative
5243 Royal Woods Pkwy Ste 200, Atlanta, GA 30084
Tel.: (770) 491-3353
Fax: (770) 491-6614
Web Site: www.purered.net

Employees: 25

Agency Specializes In: Internet/Web Design, Production, Strategic Planning/Research

Greg Latham *(CFO)*
David Mimbs *(VP)*
Mike Hynson *(Gen Mgr)*
Kent Fleming *(Dir-Digital Svcs)*
Corky Pratt *(Dir-Studio Creative)*
Phillip Smith *(Dir-Digital Creative)*
Sonny Thomas *(Dir-Creative)*
Elisabeth Legrande *(Assoc Dir-Creative)*
Jeffrey Lewis *(Assoc Dir-Creative)*
Alexander Santiago *(Assoc Dir-Creative)*

Accounts:
Russell Brands LLC
Safeway Inc.
Wal-Mart

PUROHIT NAVIGATION
111 S Wacker Dr Ste 4700, Chicago, IL 60606-4303
Tel.: (312) 341-8100
Fax: (312) 341-8119
E-Mail: purohit@purohitnavigation.com
Web Site: www.purohitnavigation.com/

Employees: 50
Year Founded: 1985

Agency Specializes In: Advertising, Brand Development & Integration, Business-To-Business, Collateral, Communications, Consumer Marketing, Corporate Identity, Education, Graphic Design, Health Care Services, Internet/Web Design, Logo & Package Design, Medical Products, Pharmaceutical, Planning & Consultation, Print, Production, Recruitment, Sales Promotion, Strategic Planning/Research

Approx. Annual Billings: $85,000,000 Capitalized

Kim Hogen *(Exec VP & Controller)*
Monica Noce Kanarek *(Exec VP-Creative)*
Anshal Purohit *(Exec VP-Strategic Dev)*
Melanie Fiacchino *(Sr Dir-Art)*
Jim Cherrier *(Dir-HR)*
Todd Treleven *(Dir-Creative & Art)*
Jen Scattereggia *(Assoc Dir)*
Andrea Clerk *(Acct Supvr)*

Accounts:
Abbott Laboratories
Allergan Inc.
American Orthopaedic Association
APP Pharmaceuticals, Inc.; Schaumburg, IL
Eisai
Eloquest
Ferndale Laboratories, Inc.
Galderma
Monogram Biosciences, Inc.
Phenogen
US Oncology, Inc.
WaferGen

PURPLE BOTTLE MEDIA
1525 SE 41st Ave, Portland, OR 97214
Tel.: (503) 208-5886
E-Mail: info@purplebottlemedia.com
Web Site: www.purplebottlemedia.com

Year Founded: 2011

Agency Specializes In: Advertising, Brand Development & Integration, Digital/Interactive, Internet/Web Design, Print, Social Media, Strategic Planning/Research

Jeremy Davis *(Dir-Creative & Digital Strategy)*
Daniel McGinn *(Dir-IT)*

Accounts:
Reel Cameras

PURPLE DIAMOND
32 Jordan St, Beverly, MA 1915
Tel.: (978) 927-0626
Web Site: www.purplediamondmarketing.com

Agency Specializes In: Advertising, Brand Development & Integration, Collateral, Internet/Web Design, Media Buying Services, Radio, Social Media, T.V.

Charlene St. Jean *(Owner)*

Accounts:
Womens Toolbox

PURPLE GROUP
2845 N. Kedzie Ave., Chicago, IL 60618
Tel.: (773) 394-9660
Web Site: www.purplegrp.com

Agency Specializes In: Advertising, Communications, Digital/Interactive, Event Planning & Marketing, Internet/Web Design, Promotions, Public Relations, Search Engine Optimization, Social Media, Strategic Planning/Research

Laritza Lopez *(Pres)*
Esau Melendez *(Dir-Film & Video & Producer)*
Annet Miranda *(Acct Exec)*

Accounts:
Gear Up Get Ready

PURPOSE ADVERTISING
79 S Main St, Barnegat, NJ 08005
Tel.: (609) 312-7922
E-Mail: info@purposeadvertising.com
Web Site: www.purposeadvertising.com

Year Founded: 2010

Agency Specializes In: Advertising, Content, Internet/Web Design, Outdoor, Print, Radio, Search Engine Optimization, Social Media, Strategic Planning/Research, T.V.

Michael Sweigart *(Pres, CEO, COO & CMO)*
Steven Myszka *(Mgr-Internet Mktg)*

Accounts:
AIGA San Francisco
Contemporary Closets
Dr Young Orthodontic & Cosmetic Services
Encore Garage
The Jeep Store
L&M Contractors
Sea Breeze Ford
Seaview Auto
Sinfonia d'Amici
The Tokyo Ballet

PUSH
101 Ernestine St, Orlando, FL 32801-2317
Tel.: (407) 841-2299
Fax: (407) 841-0999
E-Mail: frontdesk@pushhere.com
Web Site: www.pushhere.com

Employees: 35
Year Founded: 1996

National Agency Associations: AAF-PRSA-TAAN

Agency Specializes In: Advertising, Advertising Specialties, Arts, Brand Development & Integration, Broadcast, Business Publications, Business-To-Business, Cable T.V., Collateral, Communications, Consulting, Consumer Marketing, Consumer Publications, Corporate Communications, Corporate Identity, Digital/Interactive, Direct Response Marketing, Electronic Media, Entertainment, Event Planning & Marketing, Exhibit/Trade Shows, Graphic Design, Guerilla Marketing, Health Care Services, Hospitality, In-Store Advertising, Integrated Marketing, Internet/Web Design, Leisure, Local Marketing, Logo & Package Design, Magazines, Market Research, Media Buying Services, Media Planning, Media Relations, Men's Market, Mobile Marketing, Multimedia, Newspaper, Newspapers & Magazines, Out-of-Home Media, Outdoor, Paid Searches, Planning & Consultation, Point of Purchase, Point of Sale, Print, Production, Production (Ad, Film, Broadcast), Production (Print), Public Relations, Publicity/Promotions, Radio, Real Estate, Recruitment, Restaurant, Retail, Sales Promotion, Search Engine Optimization, Sports Market, Strategic Planning/Research, T.V., Trade & Consumer Magazines, Travel & Tourism, Viral/Buzz/Word of Mouth, Web (Banner Ads, Pop-ups, etc.), Women's Market

Breakdown of Gross Billings by Media: Fees: 62%; Other: 28%; Production: 10%

John Ludwig *(CEO)*
Chris Robb *(Partner & Chief Brand Officer)*
Mark Unger *(Partner & Dir-Digital & Design)*
Ron Boucher *(Dir-Creative)*
David Whaite *(Dir-Design)*
Andy MacMillin *(Assoc Dir-Creative)*
Lauren Ekey *(Sr Acct Exec)*
Susan Zeigler *(Sr Media Planner & Media Buyer)*
Saya Arakawa *(Jr Media Planner & Buyer)*

Accounts:
Orlando Regional Healthcare; Orlando, FL Arnold Palmer Hospital For Children, MD Anderson Cancer Center, Orlando Regional Medical Center, Winnie Palmer Hospital For Women; 2003
Tavistock Property
New-Visit Florida

PUSH CRANK PRESS
131 N Foster, Dothan, AL 36302
Tel.: (334) 790-9785
Web Site: www.pushcrankpress.com

Agency Specializes In: Advertising, Brand Development & Integration, Collateral, Corporate Identity, Logo & Package Design, Print, Social Media, Strategic Planning/Research

Mike Riddle *(Partner)*
Corey Gibbons *(Dir-Studio)*
Russell Wiggins *(Dir-Design)*

Accounts:
Wiregrass Museum of Art
WoodStrong

PUSH10, INC.
123 N 3rd St 2nd Fl, Philadelphia, PA 19106
Tel.: (215) 375-7735
E-Mail: info@push10.com
Web Site: www.push10.com

Year Founded: 2006

Agency Specializes In: Advertising, Brand Development & Integration, Graphic Design, Logo & Package Design, Print, Social Media

Sabrina Pfautz *(Partner)*
Greg Henry *(Pres-Push10 Design Studios)*
Emily Schilling *(Graphic Designer & Designer-Web)*

Accounts:
Blaschak Coal Corp.
Manifesta

PUSH22
22 W Huron St, Pontiac, MI 48342
Tel.: (248) 335-9500
Fax: (248) 335-7848
E-Mail: info@push22.com
Web Site: www.push22.com

Year Founded: 2004

Agency Specializes In: Advertising, Brand Development & Integration, Broadcast, Digital/Interactive, Media Planning, Media Relations, Print, Social Media

Dave Sarris *(Partner)*
Mike Verville *(Partner)*
Deborah Diers *(Dir-Media)*
Paul Ryder *(Dir-New Bus)*
Rob Wilkie *(Dir-Creative)*
Todd Malhoit *(Assoc Dir-Creative)*
Melissa Milostan *(Sr Acct Exec)*
Marisa Salvaggio *(Acct Exec)*
Christine Spahr *(Acct Exec)*

Accounts:
Faurecia USA Holdings, Inc.

PUSHTWENTYTWO
22 W Huron St, Pontiac, MI 48342
Tel.: (248) 335-9500
Fax: (248) 335-7848
E-Mail: info@push22.com
Web Site: push22.com/

Employees: 15

Agency Specializes In: Advertising, Automotive, Brand Development & Integration, Broadcast, Business Publications, Business-To-Business, Cable T.V., Communications, Corporate Communications, Corporate Identity, Digital/Interactive, Email, Engineering, Health Care Services, Hospitality, Integrated Marketing, Internet/Web Design, Media Buying Services, Multimedia, Newspaper, Newspapers & Magazines, Outdoor, Podcasting, Point of Sale, Print, Radio, Search Engine Optimization, Social Media, Trade & Consumer Magazines, Web (Banner Ads, Pop-ups, etc.)

David Sarris *(Partner)*
Michael Verville *(Partner)*
Scott Auch *(Sr Dir-Art)*
Deborah Diers *(Dir-Media)*
Paul Ryder *(Dir-New Bus)*
Rob Wilkie *(Dir-Creative)*
Melissa Milostan *(Sr Acct Exec)*
Alison Grabowski *(Acct Exec)*
Andrea Quinn *(Acct Exec)*
Christine Spahr *(Acct Exec)*
Collin Magin *(Copywriter)*

Accounts:
Champion Homes; Troy, MI Factory Build Homes; 2005
Key Global Automotive; MI; 2009
Lafayette Place Lofts
OSRAM
RE FormsNet; 2008

Walbridge

PWB MARKETING COMMUNICATIONS
2750 South State St, Ann Arbor, MI 48104
Tel.: (734) 995-5000
E-Mail: dialogue@pwb.com
Web Site: www.pwb.com

Employees: 6

Agency Specializes In: Advertising, Brand Development & Integration, Logo & Package Design, Media Planning, Print, Social Media, Strategic Planning/Research

Steve Peterson *(Chm)*
Sean Hickey *(COO)*
Arlene Mueller *(Principal)*
Keith Kopinski *(Sr Dir-Art)*
Ron Bizer *(Dir-Design)*
Marcy Jennings *(Dir-Acct Strategy)*
Tammy Mayrend *(Dir-Search & Social Media)*

Accounts:
Maya Heat Transfer Technologies

PYPER YOUNG
235 Central Ave, Saint Petersburg, FL 33701
Tel.: (727) 873-1210
Web Site: www.pyperyoung.com

Year Founded: 2012

Agency Specializes In: Advertising, Brand Development & Integration, Broadcast, Collateral, Digital/Interactive, Internet/Web Design, Media Planning, Package Design, Print, Social Media

Tracy Young *(Co-Founder & Acct Dir)*
Kelly Pyper *(Co-Founder & Dir-Media)*
Brian Carlock *(Exec VP & Sr Dir-Creative)*
Wendy Payton *(Acct Mgr)*

Accounts:
Museum of Fine Arts of St. Petersburg Florida Inc.

PYRO BRAND DEVELOPMENT
8750 N Central Expy Ste 1050, Dallas, TX 75231-6436
Tel.: (214) 891-7600
Fax: (214) 891-5055
E-Mail: info@pyrobranddevelopment.com
Web Site: www.pyroagency.com

Employees: 5
Year Founded: 1994

Agency Specializes In: Advertising, Automotive, Brand Development & Integration, Logo & Package Design, New Product Development, Newspapers & Magazines, Point of Sale, Print, Restaurant

John Beitter *(Founder & Principal)*
Benji Vega *(Dir-Creative)*
Karen Dougherty *(Planner-Brand)*

Accounts:
American Heritage Billiards
Business First Bank (Agency of Record) Advertising, Rebranding
Dallas CVB
Great Gatherings
Home Interiors & Gifts
The National Association of Mortgage Brokers
WFAA TV

PYTCHBLACK
1612 Summit Ave Ste 415, Fort Worth, TX 76102
Tel.: (817) 570-0915
Web Site: www.pytchblack.com

Year Founded: 2013

Agency Specializes In: Advertising, Brand Development & Integration, Digital/Interactive, Graphic Design, Logo & Package Design, Outdoor, Radio, Social Media, T.V.

Andrew Yanez *(Owner)*
Amy Yanez *(Dir-Media)*

Accounts:
Righteous Foods
WilliamsTrew Sothebys

PYXL, INC.
2099 Thunderhead Rd Ste 301, Knoxville, TN 37922
Tel.: (865) 690-5551
Web Site: www.thinkpyxl.com

Year Founded: 2000

Agency Specializes In: Advertising, Digital/Interactive, Graphic Design, Public Relations, Social Media

Brian Winter *(Founder)*
Josh Phillips *(Pres)*
Creed Huckaby *(Mng Dir)*
Ramona Koplan *(Dir-Bus Ops)*
Kervie Mata *(Dir-Design Methodology)*
Tim Wirtz *(Dir-Strategic Dev)*
Brenna DeLeo *(Mgr-HR)*

Accounts:
Carpathia Hosting, Inc.

Q LTD.
109 Catherine St, Ann Arbor, MI 48104
Tel.: (734) 668-1695
Fax: (734) 668-1817
E-Mail: tom@qltd.com
Web Site: www.qltd.com

Employees: 13
Year Founded: 1981

Agency Specializes In: Advertising, Brand Development & Integration, Collateral, Communications, Corporate Identity, Education, Event Planning & Marketing, Exhibit/Trade Shows, Internet/Web Design, Logo & Package Design, Print, Transportation

Jeff Callendar *(Mng Dir)*
Christine Golus *(Mng Dir)*
Elizabeth Miersch *(Editor-in-Chief & Dir-Equinox Editorial)*
Patricia Greve *(Office Mgr)*
Paul Koch *(Strategist-Creative)*
Katie Chang *(Designer)*
Lisa Marie Norton *(Sr Designer)*

Accounts:
SIGGRAPH

Q STRATEGIES
832 Georgia Ave Ste 300, Chattanooga, TN 37402
Tel.: (423) 602-9645
Fax: (423) 486-9402
Web Site: www.qstrategies.com

Year Founded: 2013

Agency Specializes In: Advertising, Communications, Content, Crisis Communications, Media Relations, Public Relations, Social Media, Strategic Planning/Research

Tom Griscom *(Partner & Strategist)*

Christina Siebold *(Partner & Strategist)*
Kelly Allen *(Acct Exec)*
Cynthia Fagan *(Acct Exec)*

Accounts:
TechTown

Q2 MARKETING GROUP
(Acquired & Absorbed by The Borenstein Group, Inc.)

QD SOLUTIONS, INC.
5316 Hwy 290 W Ste 450, Austin, TX 78735
Tel.: (512) 892-7690
Fax: (512) 892-7695
E-Mail: results@qdsglobal.com
Web Site: www.qdsglobal.com

Employees: 8
Year Founded: 1998

Agency Specializes In: Brand Development & Integration, Broadcast, Cable T.V., Collateral, Consulting, Consumer Marketing, Consumer Publications, Corporate Identity, Graphic Design, Health Care Services, Logo & Package Design, Magazines, Media Buying Services, Medical Products, Newspaper, Newspapers & Magazines, Pharmaceutical, Planning & Consultation, Print, Production, Radio, Strategic Planning/Research, T.V.

Approx. Annual Billings: $3,000,000

James Dodson *(Pres)*
Alexandra Tirado *(VP-Project Mgmt)*
Theodore Hennessy *(Sr Dir-Art)*
Lauren Digiovanni *(Asst Project Mgr)*

Accounts:
Amgen; Thousand Oaks, CA
INC Research; Raleigh, NC
PPD, Inc; Morrisville, NC
Quintiles, Inc; Morrisville, NC
Shire-Movetis

QUAINTISE, LLC
4400 N Scottsdale Rd Ste 9567, Scottsdale, AZ 85251
Tel.: (602) 820-4563
Fax: (480) 773-7516
E-Mail: info@quaintise.com
Web Site: www.quaintise.com

Year Founded: 2002

Agency Specializes In: Advertising, Public Relations

Raquel Baldelomar *(Founder & Mng Dir)*
Calvin Naito *(VP-PR)*
Jill Bernstein *(Dir-Content Mktg)*
Mark Cornelius *(Dir-Design)*
Matthew Dinnerman *(Dir-Strategy)*
Stephanie Holbrook *(Dir-Social Media)*
Kevin Munk *(Dir-Art)*
John Nguyen *(Dir-Bus Dev)*
Cortney Tucker *(Dir-Art)*
Courtney Kolling *(Sr Acct Exec)*

Accounts:
Arizona Heart Institute
Laser Nail Center
Luxury Travel Magazine

QUAIS CONSULTING
(Acquired by VML & Name Changed to VML Quais)

QUAKER CITY MERCANTILE
114-120 S 13th St, Philadelphia, PA 19107
Tel.: (215) 922-5220
Fax: (215) 922-5228
Web Site: quakercitymercantile.com/

Employees: 60
Year Founded: 1988

Agency Specializes In: Advertising, Brand Development & Integration, Consumer Marketing, Corporate Identity, Direct Response Marketing, Entertainment, Event Planning & Marketing, Fashion/Apparel, Graphic Design, Logo & Package Design, New Product Development, Point of Purchase, Print, Publicity/Promotions, Retail, Sponsorship, T.V.

Steven Grasse *(Founder)*
Bernadette Potts-Semel *(Sr Acct Dir)*
Molly Lux *(Acct Dir)*
Annelie Kahn *(Dir-Art & Designer)*
Ron Short *(Dir-Art & Designer)*
Justin Pittney *(Dir-Creative)*
Clare McKenna *(Sr Acct Mgr)*
Elise Conway *(Acct Mgr)*
Ketura Tone *(Acct Mgr)*
Breanne Furlong *(Mgr-Social Media)*
Max Gordon *(Designer)*
Danni Sinisi *(Designer)*
Dayna Levin *(Coord)*

Accounts:
Diageo Plc
Evil Empire
Guinness Broadcast, Campaign: "In Pursuit of More", Online
Lilly Pulitzer
Narragansett Brewing Company Design
Prince
Sailor Jerry
William Grant & Sons Hendrick's Gin

QUALLSBENSON LLC
272 Water St Ste 3F, New York, NY 10038
Tel.: (212) 810-6998
Web Site: www.quallsbenson.com

Year Founded: 2010

Agency Specializes In: Advertising, Graphic Design, Internet/Web Design, Logo & Package Design, Social Media

Troy Benson *(Partner)*
Joe Qualls *(Partner)*

Accounts:
AST Group

QUALLY & COMPANY, INC.
1187 Wilmette Ave, Ste 160, Wilmette, IL 60091-2719
Tel.: (847) 975-8247
E-Mail: iva@quallycompany.com
Web Site: www.quallycompany.com

Employees: 18
Year Founded: 1979

Agency Specializes In: Advertising, Brand Development & Integration, Consulting, Corporate Identity, Graphic Design, Integrated Marketing, New Product Development, Point of Purchase

Approx. Annual Billings: $11,800,000

Michael Iva *(Owner)*

QUANGO
4380 SW Mcadam Ave Ste 380, Portland, OR 97239
Tel.: (503) 968-0825
E-Mail: info@quangoinc.com
Web Site: quangoinc.com

Agency Specializes In: Advertising, Brand Development & Integration, Graphic Design, Identity Marketing, Logo & Package Design, Multimedia, Print, Search Engine Optimization, Social Media

Sean Henderson *(Pres)*
Wes Sieker *(VP-Bus Dev)*
Xochitl Ocampo *(Controller)*
Doug Daniels *(Dir-Art)*
Tobias Sugar *(Dir-Creative)*
Trisha Lester *(Acct Exec)*
Casey Koehler *(Copywriter)*
Andrew Parnell *(Sr Designer-Interaction)*
Aaron Ransley *(Web Developer)*

Accounts:
Adobe
Dell Ultrabook
Intel

QUANTASY, INC.
9543 Culver Blvd, Culver City, CA 90232
Tel.: (310) 945-4111
E-Mail: info@quantasy.com
Web Site: www.quantasy.com

Year Founded: 2011

Agency Specializes In: Advertising, Brand Development & Integration, Social Media

Will Campbell *(CEO)*
Ron Gillyard *(Chief Growth Officer)*
Danilo Roque *(Producer-Interactive)*
Alicia Herczeg *(Dir-Digital Strategy)*
Hong Le *(Dir-Tech)*

Accounts:
American Honda Motor Co., Inc. CR-V Moments Campaign
Li-Ning Content, Online, Social, WayofWade.com
Wells Fargo & Company

QUANTUM COMMUNICATIONS
33 LePere Dr, Pittsford, NY 14534
Tel.: (585) 248-8250
Fax: (866) 527-5351
Toll Free: (800) 662-5943
E-Mail: info@quantumcommunications.net
Web Site: www.quantumcommunications.net

E-Mail for Key Personnel:
President: bwarner@quantumcommunications.net

Employees: 3
Year Founded: 1983

Agency Specializes In: Advertising, Automotive, Brand Development & Integration, Broadcast, Cable T.V., Commercial Photography, Consulting, Corporate Identity, E-Commerce, Graphic Design, In-Store Advertising, Infomercials, Internet/Web Design, Logo & Package Design, Media Buying Services, Media Planning, Newspaper, Planning & Consultation, Production (Ad, Film, Broadcast), Radio, T.V.

Donalee Moulton *(Principal)*
Lynne Bowen-Lowe *(VP-Bus Dev)*

Accounts:
Ametek Power Instruments
RMR Computers
Rochester Instruments

Advertising Agencies

QUARRY INTEGRATED COMMUNICATIONS
1440 King Street North, Saint Jacobs, ON N0B 2N0 Canada
Tel.: (519) 664-2999
Web Site: www.quarry.com

Employees: 100
Year Founded: 1973

National Agency Associations: ICA

Agency Specializes In: Advertising, Agriculture, Brand Development & Integration, Business-To-Business, Communications, Corporate Identity, Digital/Interactive, Graphic Design, Health Care Services, High Technology, Integrated Marketing, Internet/Web Design, Outdoor, Pharmaceutical, Public Relations, Radio, Search Engine Optimization, Social Media, Strategic Planning/Research

Alan Quarry *(Chm)*
Ken Whyte *(Pres)*
Glen Drummond *(Chief Innovation Officer)*
Bob Wilbur *(Sr VP-Agri Food)*
Mandey Moote *(Mng Dir-Client Results)*
Maurice Allin *(VP)*
Norm Clare *(VP-Mktg Tech Strategy)*
Sarah Harwood *(VP-Strategy)*
David Whyte *(Media Planner)*

Accounts:
BlackBerry; 1998

U.S. Branch

Quarry Integrated Communications USA
4819 Emperor Blvd Ste 400, Durham, NC 27703-5420
Tel.: (919) 941-2020
Fax: (919) 941-2021
E-Mail: rferguson@quarry.com
Web Site: www.quarry.com

Agency Specializes In: Advertising, Brand Development & Integration, Business-To-Business, Digital/Interactive, Health Care Services, Integrated Marketing, Internet/Web Design, Pharmaceutical, Public Relations, Search Engine Optimization, Social Media, Sponsorship

Frances Ranger *(VP-Strategy)*
Antonia Matthews *(Head-Practice-Inbound Mktg)*
Kristi Drum *(Dir-Client Svc & Life Sciences)*
Dave Burt *(Sr Head-Imaging)*

Accounts:
FedEx
Nortel
Novartis

QUATTRO DIRECT LLC
1175 Lancaster Ave, Berwyn, PA 19312
Tel.: (610) 993-0070
Fax: (610) 993-0057
E-Mail: scohen@quattrodirect.com
Web Site: www.quattrodirect.com

Agency Specializes In: Direct Response Marketing, Email

Dan Boerger *(Partner & Mng Dir)*
Tom McNamara *(Partner & Mng Dir)*
Robert Bingaman *(VP-Creative Svcs)*
Julie Herbster *(VP-Digital Strategy)*
Colette Croce *(Acct Dir)*
Mary Edwards *(Acct Dir)*
Amy McDonald *(Acct Dir)*
Stephanie Natale *(Acct Dir)*
Camille Vallinino *(Acct Dir)*
Tom Flynn *(Dir-Project Mgmt)*
Eric Hellberg *(Dir-Production)*
Mike Magargal *(Dir-UX)*
Brendon Gildea *(Acct Mgr)*
Rebecca Kousisis *(Acct Mgr)*

Accounts:
AARP
Cor Cell
GMAC Mortgage
The Hartford / AARP Automobile Insurance
Verizon Telecommunications

THE QUELL GROUP
2282 Livernois Rd, Troy, MI 48083
Tel.: (248) 649-8900
Fax: (248) 649-8988
E-Mail: info@quell.com
Web Site: www.quell.com

Employees: 15

National Agency Associations: APRC-IABC-PRSA

Agency Specializes In: Advertising, Automotive, Brand Development & Integration, Business-To-Business, Collateral, Communications, Consulting, Consumer Marketing, Consumer Publications, Content, Corporate Communications, Corporate Identity, Crisis Communications, Customer Relationship Management, Digital/Interactive, Electronic Media, Email, Environmental, Event Planning & Marketing, Exhibit/Trade Shows, Financial, Food Service, Government/Political, Graphic Design, Health Care Services, Identity Marketing, Integrated Marketing, International, Internet/Web Design, Local Marketing, Logo & Package Design, Magazines, Market Research, Media Buying Services, Media Planning, Media Relations, Media Training, Medical Products, Mobile Marketing, New Product Development, Newspaper, Newspapers & Magazines, Outdoor, Package Design, Paid Searches, Pharmaceutical, Planning & Consultation, Podcasting, Print, Promotions, Public Relations, Publicity/Promotions, RSS (Really Simple Syndication), Restaurant, Strategic Planning/Research, Trade & Consumer Magazines, Viral/Buzz/Word of Mouth, Web (Banner Ads, Pop-ups, etc.)

Mike Niederquell *(Pres & CEO)*
Rudy Pokorny *(Dir-Art)*
Justin Rose *(Dir-Creative)*
Brian Bleau *(Acct Supvr)*
Aron Lawrence *(Designer-Interactive)*
Melissa Beauchamp *(Asst Acct Exec)*

Accounts:
On-Site Specialty Cleaning & Restoration; Fraser, MI
Schuler Incorporated
Studio 2 Dental Design; Kentwood, MI

QUENZEL & ASSOCIATES
12801 University Dr Ste 1 - 4, Fort Myers, FL 33907
Tel.: (239) 226-0040
Web Site: www.quenzel.com

Agency Specializes In: Advertising, Internet/Web Design

Earl Quenzel *(Partner)*
Robert Mehler *(VP-Bus Dev)*
Sean Breckley *(Acct Dir)*

Accounts:
Best Trip Choices Tour & Travel Management Services
Denmark Interiors Furniture & Accessories
John R Woods Realtor Branding & Advertising
Lighthouse Waterfront Restaurant Seafood & Steak Restaurant
Pink Shell Beach Resort & Spa
TriMix Gell Health Care Services

THE QUEST BUSINESS AGENCY, INC.
2150 W 18th St Ste 202, Houston, TX 77008
Tel.: (713) 956-6569
Fax: (713) 956-2593
E-Mail: info@tqba.com
Web Site: www.tqba.com

E-Mail for Key Personnel:
President: alanv@tqba.com

Employees: 9
Year Founded: 1981

National Agency Associations: AMA-BPA

Agency Specializes In: Above-the-Line, Advertising, Advertising Specialties, African-American Market, Agriculture, Aviation & Aerospace, Below-the-Line, Bilingual Market, Brand Development & Integration, Broadcast, Business Publications, Business-To-Business, Cable T.V., Collateral, College, Communications, Computers & Software, Consulting, Consumer Goods, Consumer Marketing, Corporate Communications, Corporate Identity, Customer Relationship Management, Direct Response Marketing, Direct-to-Consumer, E-Commerce, Education, Electronic Media, Electronics, Email, Engineering, Environmental, Event Planning & Marketing, Exhibit/Trade Shows, Financial, Graphic Design, Health Care Services, High Technology, Hispanic Market, Identity Marketing, In-Store Advertising, Industrial, Information Technology, Internet/Web Design, Local Marketing, Logo & Package Design, Magazines, Market Research, Medical Products, Merchandising, Multicultural, Multimedia, New Product Development, New Technologies, Newspaper, Newspapers & Magazines, Out-of-Home Media, Outdoor, Planning & Consultation, Point of Purchase, Point of Sale, Print, Production, Promotions, Public Relations, Publicity/Promotions, Recruitment, Sales Promotion, Sports Market, Strategic Planning/Research, T.V., Technical Advertising, Telemarketing, Trade & Consumer Magazines, Transportation

Approx. Annual Billings: $16,440,010 Fees Capitalized

Breakdown of Gross Billings by Media: Bus. Publs.: $2,201,003; D.M.: $8,736,501; Mags.: $5,502,506

Alan D. Vera *(Owner)*

Accounts:
The Dow Chemical Company; Midland, MI Oil & Gas; 2008
Shell Energy North America; Houston, TX Merchant Energy Services; 2008
Shell Global Solutions; Houston, TX Operations Optimization Consulting Services; 1994
Suez Energy Resources North America; Houston, TX Electric Power & Related Services; 2008

QUEST GROUP
225 W Main St, West Point, MS 39773
Tel.: (662) 494-0244
E-Mail: info@getquest.com
Web Site: www.getquest.com

Agency Specializes In: Advertising, Digital/Interactive, Event Planning & Marketing, Logo & Package Design, Media Relations, Media Training, Print, Public Relations, Social Media, Strategic Planning/Research

Cierra Hodo *(Partner)*
Max Reed *(Producer-Creative)*
Crystal Storey *(Specialist-PR)*

Accounts:
Emerson Animal Clinic
Jamison, Money, Farmer & Co.
Sally Kate Winters
Superior Catfish

QUESTUS
675 Davis St, San Francisco, CA 94111
Tel.: (415) 677-5700
Fax: (415) 677-9517
E-Mail: sales@questus.com
Web Site: www.questus.com

Employees: 70
Year Founded: 1998

Agency Specializes In: Advertising, Digital/Interactive, Internet/Web Design, Web (Banner Ads, Pop-ups, etc.)

Approx. Annual Billings: $13,000,000

Jeff Wagener *(VP & Dir-Creative)*
Debbie Dumont *(VP-Client Svcs)*
Scott Fiaschetti *(VP-Insights & Strategy)*
Kris Rohman *(Gen Mgr)*
Matthew Hussey *(Acct Dir)*
Audrey Kell *(Dir-Art)*
Chelsea Martell *(Assoc Dir-Creative)*
Patryk Tenorio *(Acct Supvr)*
Kristy Noryko *(Generalist-HR)*

Accounts:
Almay
American Suzuki Motor Corporation Hayabusa
Avery - Martha Stewart Home Office
BET
Capital One
Discovery Communications
ESPN
Expedia
Fox Digital
General Mills Gold Medal Flour, Total Cereal, Yoplait Smoothie
Hubzu
The New York Times
News Corporation
Target
United Healthcare
Universal Orlando
Verizon
VEVO

Branch

Questus
250 Hudson St, New York, NY 10013
Tel.: (646) 442-5755
Fax: (212) 533-3210
E-Mail: sales@questus.com
Web Site: www.questus.com

Employees: 50
Year Founded: 1998

Agency Specializes In: Advertising, Sponsorship

Jordan Berg *(Co-Founder & Co-Pres)*
Jeff Rosenblum *(Co-Founder)*
Jeff Wagener *(VP & Dir-Creative)*
Scott Fiaschetti *(VP-Insights & Strategy)*
Edward Lu *(VP-Fin)*
Debble Tung *(VP-Acct Svcs)*
Joshua Hearn *(Sr Dir-Art)*
Larry Miller *(Dir-Bus Dev)*

Accounts:
Avery Martha Stewart Home Office
Capital One
Expedia
Flyover
General Mills Gold Medal Flour, Total Cereal, Yoplait Smoothie
Holt Renfrew
Marriot Inc.
Pernod Ricard
Starbucks
Suzuki Motorcycles
Universal Orlando
Verizon NFL

QUEUE CREATIVE
410 S Cedar St Ste F, Lansing, MI 48912
Tel.: (517) 374-6600
Fax: (517) 374-4215
E-Mail: lori@queueadvertising.com
Web Site: www.queueadvertising.com

Employees: 5
Year Founded: 2004

Agency Specializes In: Advertising, Advertising Specialties, Arts, Automotive, Brand Development & Integration, Broadcast, Business Publications, Business-To-Business, Cable T.V., Co-op Advertising, Collateral, College, Commercial Photography, Communications, Consulting, Consumer Goods, Corporate Communications, Corporate Identity, Direct Response Marketing, Education, Electronic Media, Email, Event Planning & Marketing, Exhibit/Trade Shows, Financial, Government/Political, Graphic Design, Health Care Services, Hospitality, Identity Marketing, Industrial, Infomercials, Integrated Marketing, Internet/Web Design, Local Marketing, Logo & Package Design, Market Research, Media Planning, Media Relations, Media Training, Medical Products, Men's Market, Multimedia, Newspaper, Newspapers & Magazines, Out-of-Home Media, Outdoor, Package Design, Planning & Consultation, Point of Purchase, Print, Production, Production (Ad, Film, Broadcast), Production (Print), Public Relations, Publicity/Promotions, Radio, Regional, Retail, Sales Promotion, Seniors' Market, Social Marketing/Nonprofit, Sponsorship, Strategic Planning/Research, T.V., Technical Advertising, Trade & Consumer Magazines, Women's Market

Breakdown of Gross Billings by Media: Brdcst.: 50%; Consulting: 10%; Graphic Design: 30%; Outdoor: 10%

Lori Cunningham *(Mng Partner)*
Annette Louise *(Office Mgr)*

Accounts:
Paramount Coffee Company; Lansing, MI; 2005

QUEUE CREATIVE MARKETING GROUP LLC
29 S Lasalle Ste 930, Chicago, IL 60603
Tel.: (312) 564-6000
Fax: (847) 364-0270
Toll Free: (800) 935-1073
Web Site: www.in-queue.com

E-Mail for Key Personnel:
President: rvangalis@in-queue.com

Employees: 30
Year Founded: 1983

National Agency Associations: NAMA

Agency Specializes In: Advertising, Advertising Specialties, Agriculture, Automotive, Brand Development & Integration, Broadcast, Business Publications, Business-To-Business, Cable T.V., Children's Market, Collateral, Communications, Consulting, Consumer Marketing, Consumer Publications, Corporate Communications, Corporate Identity, Digital/Interactive, Direct Response Marketing, E-Commerce, Food Service, Graphic Design, High Technology, Hispanic Market, In-Store Advertising, Industrial, Internet/Web Design, Local Marketing, Logo & Package Design, Magazines, Media Buying Services, Merchandising, Multimedia, New Product Development, Newspaper, Newspapers & Magazines, Outdoor, Over-50 Market, Pharmaceutical, Point of Purchase, Point of Sale, Print, Production, Publicity/Promotions, Radio, Restaurant, Retail, Sales Promotion, Strategic Planning/Research, Sweepstakes, T.V., Teen Market, Trade & Consumer Magazines

Approx. Annual Billings: $2,500,000

Chris Wilhelm *(VP & Creative Dir)*
Jon Britt *(Dir-Art)*
Claire Mykrantz *(Mgr-Social Media Community)*
Jen Rumbaugh *(Acct Supvr)*
Monica Rowley *(Acct Exec-Digital)*

Accounts:
La Belle Vie
Mrs. Field's Cookies
North American Salt
Prairie Hills Motorsport Club
YoCrunch Yogurt
Zoo Atlanta

QUIET LIGHT COMMUNICATIONS
220 E State St, Rockford, IL 61104
Tel.: (815) 398-6860
Web Site: www.quietlightcom.com

Agency Specializes In: Advertising, Brand Development & Integration, Corporate Identity, Event Planning & Marketing, Internet/Web Design, Media Buying Services, Media Planning, Public Relations, Social Media, Strategic Planning/Research

Mike Leonard *(Pres)*
Terry Schroff *(CEO)*
Don Peach *(VP-Bus Dev & Ops)*
Vinnie Caiozzo *(Art Dir)*
Diana Hamblock *(Art Dir)*
Patrick McDonough *(Creative Dir)*
Kevin Miller *(Acct Mgr)*
Jeanne Turner *(Mgr-PR)*
Ellen Grall *(Acct Exec)*

Accounts:
Puratos

QUIGLEY-SIMPSON
11601 Wilshire Blvd 7th Fl, Los Angeles, CA 90025
Tel.: (310) 996-5800
Fax: (310) 943-1414
E-Mail: info@quigleysimpson.com
Web Site: www.quigleysimpson.com

Employees: 98
Year Founded: 2002

National Agency Associations: DMA-ERA

Agency Specializes In: Advertising, African-American Market, Automotive, Bilingual Market, Brand Development & Integration, Broadcast, Cable T.V., Children's Market, Communications, Consulting, Consumer Marketing, Cosmetics, Digital/Interactive, Direct Response Marketing, Education, Electronic Media, Entertainment, Financial, Government/Political, High Technology, Hispanic Market, Infomercials, Leisure, Media Buying Services, Media Planning, Mobile Marketing, Multicultural, Multimedia, New Product Development, New Technologies, Pets , Pharmaceutical, Planning & Consultation, Podcasting, Production, Radio, Seniors' Market, Sponsorship, Strategic Planning/Research, T.V.,

Travel & Tourism

Gerald Bagg *(Co-Chm)*
Renee Hill-Young *(Co-Chm)*
Angela Zepeda *(CEO)*
Alissa Stakgold *(Mng Dir)*
Shannon Adams *(VP & Assoc Dir-Brdcst)*
Pat Asher *(Dir-Digital Media)*
Sariah Dorbin *(Dir-Creative)*
Victoria Chang *(Assoc Dir-Brdcst)*
Nicole Ellingson *(Assoc Dir-Creative)*
Dyan Ullman *(Mgr-HR & Talent)*
Mary Louise Mendoza *(Media Buyer)*

Accounts:
Breville
Chase Card Services Credit Card
ChildFund International
Gillette
JP Morgan Chase Amazon.com Credit Card, British Airways Credit Card, Chase Sapphire Card, Continental Airlines World Card, Continental Airlines Presidential Plus Card, Freedom Card, United Mileage Plus Card
Magic Jack
Magic Jack
Mars Dove Ice Cream, M&Ms, Snickers Ice Cream, Uncle Ben's Rice
Pinnacle Foods Duncan Hines, Mrs. Paul's, Van De Kamps, Vlasic
Procter & Gamble Actonel, Always, Bella & Birch, Bounce, Bounty, Braun, Cascade, Charmin, Cheer, Clairol, Covergirl, Crest, Dawn, Downy, Enablex, Eukanuba, Febreze, Folgers, Gain, Head & Shoulders, Herbal Essences, Iams Cat & Dog, Luvs, Mr. Clean, Olay, Oral-B, Pampers, Pantene, Parent's Choice, Pepto-Bismol, Prilosec, PuR, Puffs, Secret, Swiffer, Tampax, Thermacare, Tide, Vicks
RetailMeNot, Inc Campaign: "Spend Less. Shop More", Campaign: "We're Out to Save the World (Some Money)", Creative, Media Planning & Buying, RetailMeNot.com
Shutterfly, Inc.
Warner Brothers

QUILLIN ADVERTISING
8080 W Sahara Ave Ste A, Las Vegas, NV 89117
Tel.: (702) 256-5511
Fax: (702) 838-9899
E-Mail: info@quillinlv.com
Web Site: www.quillinlv.com

Year Founded: 2002

Agency Specializes In: Advertising, Public Relations, Social Media

Tim Quillin *(Pres)*
Sharry Quillin *(CFO & Specialist-Media)*
Benjamin Burns *(Dir-Creative Strategy)*
Cindy Pino *(Dir-PR)*
Estie MacAlister *(Office Mgr & Coord-Media)*
Antonia Genov *(Mgr-Social Media)*
Julia Gilmour *(Strategist-Social Media)*
Melanie Shafer *(Acct Exec-PR)*
Michael Speciale *(Media Planner & Media Buyer)*

Accounts:
Drivers Talk Radio

QUINLAN & COMPANY
385 N French Rd Ste 106, Amherst, NY 14228-2096
Tel.: (716) 691-6200
Fax: (716) 691-2898
E-Mail: info@quinlanco.com
Web Site: www.quinlanco.com

Employees: 18
Year Founded: 1987

Agency Specializes In: Advertising, Broadcast, Business Publications, Business-To-Business, Cable T.V., Collateral, Communications, Consulting, Consumer Goods, Consumer Marketing, Consumer Publications, Corporate Communications, Direct Response Marketing, Direct-to-Consumer, E-Commerce, Electronic Media, Exhibit/Trade Shows, Graphic Design, Industrial, Internet/Web Design, Investor Relations, Logo & Package Design, Magazines, Media Buying Services, Media Planning, Newspaper, Newspapers & Magazines, Out-of-Home Media, Outdoor, Planning & Consultation, Point of Purchase, Print, Production, Public Relations, Publicity/Promotions, Radio, Social Marketing/Nonprofit, Social Media, T.V., Technical Advertising, Transportation, Yellow Pages Advertising

Gary W. Miller *(Pres & CEO)*
Beverly Dipalma *(VP & Dir-Creative)*
Julia Vona *(VP)*
Jessica Chapman *(Acct Dir)*
Malorie Benjamin *(Dir-Media)*
Katie Mohr *(Acct Mgr)*
Grace Gerass *(Coord-Digital Content)*
Sarah Miller *(Coord-PR)*

Accounts:
Apple Rubber Products Inc.
Northwest Savings Bank
Sahlen Packing Company
Trocaire College

QUINLAN MARKETING COMMUNICATIONS
550 Congressional Blvd Ste 350, Carmel, IN 46032
Tel.: (317) 573-5080
Fax: (317) 573-5088
E-Mail: info@quinlanmarketing.com
Web Site: www.quinlanmarketing.com

E-Mail for Key Personnel:
President: johnm@quinlanmktg.com
Media Dir.: phyllisw@quinlanmktg.com
Production Mgr.: amyd@quinlanmktg.com

Employees: 22
Year Founded: 1937

National Agency Associations: BPA

Agency Specializes In: Advertising, Business-To-Business, Consumer Marketing, Corporate Identity, Event Planning & Marketing, Exhibit/Trade Shows, Graphic Design, Industrial, Internet/Web Design, Market Research, Media Planning

Breakdown of Gross Billings by Media: Collateral: 60%; Event Mktg.: 25%; Mags.: 15%

John C. Mccaig *(Pres & Dir-Creative)*
Jay Koenig *(Sr Dir-Art)*
Linda Fosnight *(Dir-Admin)*
Jason Lester *(Dir-Art)*
Jackie Donaldson *(Acct Exec)*
Phyllis Wilkinson *(Acct Exec)*

Accounts:
Aces Power Marketing; Carmel, IN Energy Risk Management; 2007
Allison Transmission Holdings, Inc.; Indianapolis, IN Automatic Transmissions; 1993
Kiwi Tek; Carmel, IN Medical Coding Software; 2002
Townsend; Parker City, IN Wind Energy, Vegetation Management; 2009
Twin Disc Inc.; Racine, WI Power Transmission Equipment
Umbaugh & Associates; Indianapolis, IN; 2006

QUINN & HARY MARKETING
PO Box 456, New London, CT 06320
Tel.: (860) 444-0448
Fax: (860) 447-9419
E-Mail: results@quinnandhary.com
Web Site: www.quinnandhary.com

Year Founded: 2002

Agency Specializes In: Advertising, Brand Development & Integration, Communications, Event Planning & Marketing, Integrated Marketing, Internet/Web Design, Strategic Planning/Research

David Quinn *(Pres)*
Nicole Montgomery *(Gen Counsel)*
Ann Ziker *(VP-Advancement)*
Peter Hary *(Dir-Creative)*

Accounts:
City of New London PR
L&M Physicians Physician Practice Services
Smith Insurance Insurance Services
St. Thomas More School Educational Services
triVIN Inc. Motor Vehicle Processing Services

QUINN FABLE ADVERTISING
115 E 55th St, New York, NY 10022
Tel.: (212) 974-8700
Fax: (212) 974-0554
E-Mail: info@quinnfable.com
Web Site: www.quinnfable.com

Employees: 40
Year Founded: 1988

Approx. Annual Billings: $55,000,000

Kathy Fable *(Pres & CEO)*
Julie Curtis *(Exec VP-Tech Svcs)*
Tim Shaw *(Creative Dir)*
Susanne Dunlap *(Assoc Dir-Creative)*
Ashley Lagzial *(Acct Exec)*

Accounts:
AT&T Communications Corp.
Church & Dwight
Daily News
Dapper Baby
Harvard Maintenance
Microsoft
MIO TV
Mondelez International, Inc.
Next Decade Entertainment

QUINN GROUP
727 W Garland, Spokane, WA 99205
Tel.: (509) 327-6688
Web Site: www.quinngroup.com

Agency Specializes In: Advertising, Internet/Web Design, Media Buying Services, Media Planning, Promotions, Public Relations, Radio, T.V.

Bonnie Quinn *(Owner)*
Vic Holman *(Dir-Creative)*
Sean Lumsden *(Acct Mgr & Copywriter)*
Kathi Kull *(Mgr-Fin & Acct Coord-Quinn Grp Adv & Mktg)*
Ryan Throckmorton *(Strategist-Creative)*
Shelby Ryan *(Media Buyer & Coord-Traffic)*

Accounts:
Fairmount Memorial Association

QUINTESSENTIAL PR
8913 W Olympic Blvd 104, Beverly Hills, CA 90211
Tel.: (310) 770-4764
Fax: (310) 657-3245
E-Mail: info@quintessentialpr.com
Web Site: www.quintessentialpr.com

Agency Specializes In: Advertising, Brand Development & Integration, Public Relations

Allyona Sevanesian *(Owner)*

Accounts:
New-InSite Properties

QUISENBERRY
211 W 2nd Ave, Spokane, WA 99201
Tel.: (509) 325-0701
Web Site: www.quisenberry.net

Agency Specializes In: Advertising, Brand Development & Integration, Digital/Interactive, Graphic Design, Internet/Web Design, Media Buying Services, Media Planning, Outdoor, Print, Radio

Carl Heidle *(Sr Dir-Art)*
Teresa Meyer *(Dir-Media & Acct Planner)*
Molly Kernan *(Dir-Fin)*
Monte Mindt *(Dir-Creative)*
Patty Kilcup *(Mgr-PR)*
Jordan Quisenberry *(Mgr-Production)*

Accounts:
Washington State University Athletics

R&R PARTNERS
900 S Pavilion Center Dr, Las Vegas, NV 89144
Tel.: (702) 228-0222
Fax: (702) 939-4383
E-Mail: info@rrpartners.com
Web Site: www.rrpartners.com

E-Mail for Key Personnel:
Media Dir.: FWhitwell@rrpartners.com
Public Relations: derquiaga@rrpartners.com

Employees: 200
Year Founded: 1974

National Agency Associations: 4A's

Agency Specializes In: Brand Development & Integration, Broadcast, Communications, Event Planning & Marketing, Government/Political, Health Care Services, Internet/Web Design, Media Buying Services, Production, Public Relations, Publicity/Promotions, Sponsorship, Strategic Planning/Research, Travel & Tourism

Mary Ann Mele *(Pres & Chief Brand Officer)*
Billy Vassiliadis *(CEO & Principal)*
Bob Henrie *(Partner & Principal)*
Fletcher Whitwell *(Sr VP & Grp Mng Dir-Media & Measurement)*
James King *(CFO & Principal)*
Randy Snow *(Chief Strategic Officer & Principal)*
Morgan Baumgartner *(Gen Counsel & Dir-Nevada Govt-Pub Affairs)*
Rob Dondero *(Exec VP)*
Ron Eagle *(Sr VP-PR)*
Todd Gillins *(VP-Res)*
Michelle Mader *(VP-Mktg Ops)*
Arnie DiGeorge *(Exec Dir-Creative)*
Coleman Engellenner *(Grp Dir-Media)*
Chris Evans *(Grp Dir-Media)*
David Weissman *(Sr Dir-PR)*
Ron Rubin *(Grp Acct Dir)*
Rebekah Bell *(Acct Dir)*
Courtney Bonnici *(Dir-R&R Partners Foundation)*
Ron Lopez *(Dir-Creative)*
Mark Naparstek *(Dir-Creative)*
Kameron Paries *(Dir-Art)*
Lindsey Hill Patterson *(Dir-Media)*
Peg Boltz *(Assoc Dir-Creative)*
Cyler Pennington *(Assoc Dir-Social Media)*
Kristine Rasgorshek *(Assoc Dir-Media)*
Emily Jones *(Project Mgr-Digital)*
Alyson Ashbock *(Acct Supvr)*
Jessica Murray *(Acct Supvr-PR)*
Jill Blanchette *(Supvr-Bus Dev)*
Kevin Brigman *(Media Planner & Media Buyer)*
Kevin Geary *(Media Planner & Media Buyer)*
Jill Glavich *(Media Planner & Media Buyer)*
Cory Lloyd *(Media Planner & Media Buyer)*
Kenny Utler *(Media Planner & Media Buyer)*
Fran Barr *(Corp Dir-HR)*
Ali Johnson *(Asst Media Planner & Buyer)*
Michaela Meade *(Sr Media Planner & Buyer)*
Brandi Skrtich *(Sr Supvr-Media)*
Jeremy Thompson *(Corp Dir-Social Media)*

Accounts:
American Coalition for Clean Coal Electricity
The Animal Foundation, Las Vegas "Pet Cat", "Pet Dog"
Beggars banquet
Boeing
Caesars Entertainment Corporation Bally's Las Vegas, Flamingo Las Vegas, Harrah's Entertainment, Inc.
Excalibur
Intermountain Healthcare, Inc.
The Krewellavator
Las Vegas Convention & Visitors Authority; Las Vegas, NV Campaign: "Cee Lo's Escape", Campaign: "How to Vegas", Campaign: "Protect the Moment", Campaign: "Transformation", Campaign: "What Happens Here, Stays Here", Las Vegas Tourism, LasVegas.com, Newspaper Advertising, Outdoor, Rebranding, Social Media, TV, What Happens Here, Stays Here Campaign
MGM Resorts International Aria, MGM Resorts International
Nevada Power Company; Las Vegas, NV Power Services; 1998
Nevada Resort Association; Las Vegas, NV Consolidated Lobbying Efforts, Public Realtors
Nevada Tourism (Public Relations)
Norwegian Cruise Line
NV Energy Inc.
RE/MAX International, Inc. RE/MAX International, Inc., Remax.com
Southern Nevada Water Authority Conservation; 2007
Springs Preserve Campaign: "Around The Corner"
Utah Department of Health
Utah Department Of Highway Safety
Utah Transit Authority
Western Digital
Western Union
Wynn Resorts

Branches

R&R Partners
615 Riverside Dr, Reno, NV 89503-5601
Tel.: (775) 323-1611
Fax: (775) 323-9021
E-Mail: vendors@rrpartners.com
Web Site: www.rrpartners.com

Employees: 25
Year Founded: 1982

National Agency Associations: 4A's

Agency Specializes In: Public Relations, Strategic Planning/Research, Travel & Tourism

Bob Henrie *(Partner & Principal)*
Morgan Baumgartner *(Gen Counsel & Dir-Nevada Govt & Pub Affairs)*
Sarah Catletti *(Sr Acct Exec)*

Accounts:
Nevada Commission On Tourism; Carson City, NV

R&R Partners
1700 E Walnut Ave, El Segundo, CA 90245
Tel.: (310) 321-3900
Web Site: www.rrpartners.com

National Agency Associations: 4A's

Agency Specializes In: Sponsorship

John Wells *(Sr VP & Grp Mng Dir-Brand Mgmt)*
David Ellis *(Sr VP-Strategic Consulting)*
Carlos Arambula *(VP-Hispanic Mktg)*
Brian Hoar *(VP-Dev)*
Coleman Engellenner *(Grp Dir-Media)*
Lauren Crilley *(Acct Dir)*
Tony Caruso *(Assoc Dir-Media)*
Erin McCleskey *(Sr Acct Exec)*
James Esco *(Media Planner & Media Buyer)*
Alyssa Cohen *(Media Planner & Buyer)*
Michael Catalano *(Sr Media Planner)*
Mandi Enger *(Asst Media Planner & Buyer)*
Astrid Raimondo *(Corp Dir-Engagement)*

R&R Partners
837 E S Temple, Salt Lake City, UT 84102-1304
Tel.: (801) 531-6877
Fax: (801) 531-6880
E-Mail: info@rrpartners.com
Web Site: www.rrpartners.com

Employees: 20
Year Founded: 1987

National Agency Associations: 4A's

Agency Specializes In: Public Relations

Bob Henrie *(Partner & Principal)*
Cathie DeNaughel *(Mng Dir & VP)*
Steve Wright *(Grp Acct Dir)*
Shannon Bukovinsky *(Dir-Media)*
Mike Zuhl *(Dir-Govt & Pub Affairs)*
Tiffeny Yen *(Supvr-Ops)*

Accounts:
Intermountain Health Care Health Plans
OCTA Orange County Transit Authority
Utah Transit Authority

R&R Partners
101 N First Ave Ste 2900, Phoenix, AZ 85003
Tel.: (480) 317-6040
Fax: (480) 804-0033
E-Mail: info@rrpartners.com
Web Site: www.rrpartners.com

Employees: 15
Year Founded: 1987

National Agency Associations: 4A's

Agency Specializes In: Public Relations, Strategic Planning/Research

Billy Vassiliadis *(CEO & Principal)*
Jim King *(CFO & Principal)*
Cindy Dreibelbis *(Exec Dir & Principal)*
Erik Sandhu *(Sr VP-Fin & Ops)*
Matt Silverman *(Mng Dir-Phoenix & VP)*
Lou Flores *(Dir-Creative)*
AJ Montgomery *(Brand Mgr)*
Billy Kelly *(Supvr-Brand)*
Sarah Leidy *(Media Planner & Media Buyer)*
Karen Rulapaugh *(Corp Dir-Media)*

Accounts:
CIGNA
COX Cable
Cox Communications
The Landmark at Cirrolin
National Bank of Arizona
Rio Salado Town Lake Foundation
Valley Metro Regional Public Transit Authority; Phoenix, AZ Campaign: "Valley Metro Notes"

R&R Partners
101 Constitution Ave NW Ste L110, Washington, DC 20001
Tel.: (202) 289-5356
Fax: (202) 289-3792
Web Site: www.rrpartners.com

National Agency Associations: 4A's

Agency Specializes In: Advertising

Bob Henrie *(Partner & Principal)*
Sean Tonner *(Pres-Denver)*
Steven Horsford *(Mng Dir-Washington & Sr VP-Strategic Integration & Partnerships)*
Suzanne Hofmann Erickson *(VP-Govt & Pub Affairs)*
Rob Mason *(VP-Engagement)*
Mark Meissner *(Sr Dir-Strategic Comm)*
Kweku Boafo *(Dir-Intl Affairs)*

R/GA
350 W 39th St, New York, NY 10018-1402
Tel.: (212) 946-4000
Fax: (212) 946-4010
E-Mail: web@rga.com
Web Site: www.rga.com

Year Founded: 1977

National Agency Associations: 4A's

Agency Specializes In: Brand Development & Integration, Digital/Interactive, E-Commerce, Electronic Media, Internet/Web Design

Robert Greenberg *(Founder, Chm & CEO)*
Robin Forbes *(Mng Dir & Sr VP)*
Chapin Clark *(Mng Dir & VP)*
Alex Schneider *(Mng Dir/VP-Portland)*
Matt Tepper *(Mng Dir & VP-CRM)*
Ameer Youssef *(VP & Grp Mng Dir)*
Marc Maleh *(Mng Dir)*
Joe Tomasulo *(CFO & Exec VP)*
Ivan Arbitman *(CIO)*
Daniel Diez *(CMO-Global & Exec VP)*
Barry Wacksman *(Chief Strategy Officer-Global)*
Richard Mellor *(Chief HR Officer & Exec VP)*
Chris Colborn *(Global Chief Design & Innovation Officer & Exec VP)*
Sue Davidson *(Mng Dir-Analytics & Accountability & Sr VP)*
Dave Edwards *(Sr VP & Mng Dir-Bus Dev-US)*
Chloe Gottlieb *(Sr VP & Exec Dir-Creative-New York)*
Jay Zasa *(Sr VP & Exec Dir-Creative-Campaigns)*
Anthony Romano *(Sr VP-Client Svcs)*
Tony Effik *(VP & Mng Dir-Media & Connections)*
Alex Morrison *(VP & Mng Dir-R/GA Content Studio)*
Jess Greenwood *(VP-Content & Partnerships)*
Michael Lowenstern *(VP-Digital Adv)*
George Nguyen *(Head-Grp Plng)*
Thomas Bossert *(Exec Dir-Creative & Brand Dev & Grp Dir)*
Paul Dery *(Exec Dir-Creative)*
Eric Jannon *(Exec Dir-Creative)*
Erin Lynch *(Grp Exec Dir-Creative)*
Chris Northam *(Exec Dir-Creative)*
Tom Quaglino *(Exec Creative Dir)*
Saulo Rodrigues *(Exec Dir-Creative)*
David Womack *(Exec Dir-Creative-Experience Design)*
Carlos Almonte *(Grp Dir-Production)*
Kyle Bunch *(Grp Dir-Mobile & Social Platforms)*
Jason Chan *(Grp Dir-Mobile & Social Platforms)*
Sung Park *(Grp Dir-Media & Connections)*
Mike Rigby *(Exec Brand Dir-Global Creative & Grp Dir)*
Shawn Zupp *(Grp Acct Dir)*
Christine Claxton *(Acct Dir)*
Alex Thoma *(Acct Dir)*
Olivia Widjaya *(Acct Dir)*
Geetika Agrawal *(Dir-Creative)*
Keith Byrne *(Dir-Creative)*
Chris Cima *(Dir-Creative)*
Andrew Eaton *(Dir-Creative)*
Nancy Espinal *(Dir-Bus Affairs)*
Lee Gordon *(Dir-Experience Design)*
Tristan Kincaid *(Dir-Creative)*
Diallo Marvel *(Dir-Creative)*
Aaron Pollick *(Dir-Creative-Nike)*
Dave Surgan *(Dir-Mobile & Social Platforms)*
Megan Trinidad *(Dir-Creative)*
Dylan Viner *(Dir-Plng)*
Niels West *(Dir-Creative)*
Jason Fund *(Assoc Dir-Plng)*
Eduardo Quadra *(Assoc Dir-Creative)*
Ethan Schmidt *(Assoc Dir-Creative & Copy)*
Ben Waldman *(Assoc Dir-Creative)*
Chase Bibby *(Mgr-Analytics)*
Samantha Friedberg *(Acct Supvr)*
Julia Reingold *(Supvr-Media)*
Allie Walker *(Strategist)*
Trevor Eld *(Grp Exec Dir-Creative)*

Accounts:
Adam Tensta Campaign: "One Copy Song"
The Advertising Council, Inc. Campaign: "Horn of Africa Relief", Campaign: "Love Has No Labels"
American Eagle
Aston Martin Campaign: "Aston Martin"
Audible, Inc. Branding, Creative
Avaya
Bacardi Cherry Noir Vodka, Digital, Grey Goose
Barnes & Noble
Beats Electronics LLC Advertising, Beats by Dre, Campaign: "Hear What You Want", Campaign: "Jungle", Campaign: "Out-Nike Nike", Campaign: "Straight to the Gym", Campaign: "The Game Before The Game"
Capital One Financial Corporation
Chapstick Campaign: "On Everyone's Lips"
Converse The Sampler
Equinox Campaign: "The Pursuit"
E*Trade Broadcast, Campaign: "Beards", Campaign: "Fast Food", Campaign: "Opportunity Is Everywhere", Digital, Television
Getty Images Campaign: "The Watermark Project"
Giorgio Armani Campaign: "Drops for Life Mobile App", Campaign: "Drops for Life"
The Goldman Sachs Group, Inc.
Google Campaign: "Google Wallet"
HBO
Hewlett-Packard
IBM
JC Penney Digital Marketing, E-Commerce
New-Jet.com, Inc. TV
Johnson & Johnson Donate a Photo
The Los Angeles Lakers
Mastercard Campaign: "Ask Buck", Campaign: "Check In to the Ballgame", Campaign: "Miyamo", Campaign: "World's Fastest Demos - First Date", Food Truck Feast, Global Digital
McCormick & Company Campaign: "Dinnertising", Creative, Grill Mates, Lawry's, Media Planning, Old Bay, Platform Development, US Digital
Microsoft Windows
New-MLB Advanced Media, LP. Los Angeles Dodgers
New York Red Bulls
Newcastle Brown Ale
Nike Campaign: "Black Mamba", Campaign: "Nike+ Fuelband", Campaign: "OneNike", Campaign: "Social Response Lab", EPIC, Nike Basketball, Nike Plus, Nike Running, Nike SB App, Nike Women, Nike iD, Nike+ GPS, Nike.com, The Film Room, Zoom
Nokia Campaign: "Success Redefined"
Pepsi
Perfetti Van Melle Mentos
Pfizer Advil, Digital Creative
Qol Devices Alvio
Rip Curl Campaign: "Mirage"
Samsung Electronics Campaign: "Life of the Extreme", Campaign: "TextsFromMom", Campaign: "The Match Part 1, Campaign: "The Match Part 2, Campaign: "The Match", Campaign: "WinnerTakesEarth", Galaxy 11, Galaxy Note Edge, Gear S2, Samsung Smart Home
Samsung Telecommunications America Campaign: "Samsung Holiday Dreams", Digital
Subaru Digital
Sunglass Hut
Target
Unilever Rexona 36 Day Challenge
Verizon Campaign: "Thanksgetting", Digital, Fios
Volvo Digital, Global Strategy

Branches

R/GA London
15 Rosebery Ave, London, EC1R 4AB United Kingdom
Tel.: (44) 2070713330
Fax: (44) 2070713310
E-Mail: web@rga.com
Web Site: www.rga.com

Employees: 48

Agency Specializes In: Advertising, Digital/Interactive

Jim Moffat *(Mng Dir & Exec VP)*
James Temple *(Mng Dir, VP & Exec Dir-Creative)*
Matt Lodder *(Mng Dir & VP)*
George Prest *(VP & Exec Creative Dir-Global Unilever)*
Lucio Rufo *(Head-Visual Design & Grp Dir-Creative)*
Ryan Wareham *(Exec Dir-Production)*
Simon Wassef *(Grp Dir-Strategy)*
Charlie Smith *(Acct Dir)*
Owen Roberts *(Dir-Creative)*
Daniel Williams *(Dir-Creative)*
John Wilson *(Client Partner)*
Ruth Dwyer *(Mgr-Facilities-Europe)*
Kat Hahn *(Assoc Creative Dir)*

Accounts:
BBC Digital Strategy
Beats By Dre Campaign: "Beats by Dre x Cesc Fabregas: Hear What You Want", Campaign: "Hear What You Want - Cesc Fabregas", Campaign: "Meet The Pills", Campaign: "The Game Before The Game"
Diageo Baileys (Digital Agency of Record), Campaign: "Here's To Us", Campaign: "Here's to Getting Together", Campaign: "Here's to Staying in", Digital
Dyson (Digital Agency of Record)
Getty Images Brand Advertising, Campaign: "The Watermark Project", Digital
ghd Community for Stylists
Google
Heineken
McDonald's
Nike Digital, European Football, Pro-Direct Soccer Zone App
Nokia Nokia Digital Retail
O2 Priority Moments
Unilever Axe, Campaign: "Do:More", Citra, Dawn, Digital Campaign, Magnum, Rexona, Signal (Global Digital), Simple, St Ives, Sunsilk, Sure
Virgin Atlantic In Flight Entertainment System

R/GA Los Angeles
5636 Tujunga Ave, North Hollywood, CA 91601
Tel.: (818) 623-2062
Fax: (818) 623-2063
Web Site: www.rga.com

Employees: 1

National Agency Associations: 4A's

Agency Specializes In: Advertising, Sponsorship

Josh Mandel *(Mng Dir & VP)*
Ami Lewis *(Sr Dir-Art)*
Daniel Soares *(Sr Dir-Art)*
Shane Chastang *(Brand Dir)*
Zach Hilder *(Creative Dir)*
Eze Blaine *(Dir-Digital Creative)*
Will Esparza *(Dir-Creative)*
Poppy Thorpe *(Assoc Dir-Strategy)*
James Stephens *(Grp Brand Dir)*
Kristina Litvin *(Jr Dir-Art & Designer-Visual)*

Accounts:
Avaya
Beats Electronics LLC Campaign: "Beats by Dre x Cesc Fabregas: Hear What You Want", Campaign: "DestroyBadSound", Campaign: "Hear what you want", Campaign: "Re-Established 2014", Campaign: "The Game Before The Game"
Loreal Paris
Netflix, Inc. Campaign: "Watch Together", Online
Nokia

R/GA San Francisco
35 S Park, San Francisco, CA 94107
Tel.: (415) 624-2000
Fax: (415) 624-2010
Web Site: www.rga.com

Employees: 55
Year Founded: 2008

National Agency Associations: 4A's

Agency Specializes In: Advertising, Digital/Interactive, Sponsorship

Bob Greenberg *(Founder, Chm & CEO)*
Paola Colombo *(Mng Dir & VP)*
Jennifer Remling *(Sr VP-Talent)*
Robyn Freye *(Mng Dir-Bus Dev & VP)*
Kelli Robertson *(Mng Dir-Plng)*
Paulo Melchiori *(Exec Dir-Creative)*
Derek Hockman *(Acct Dir)*

R/GA Sao Paulo
Av. Nacoes Unidas 12.551 - 12 andar, Brooklin Novo, Sao Paulo, Brazil
Tel.: (55) 11 4503 9862
Web Site: www.rga.com

Fabiano Coura *(Mng Dir & VP)*
Maria Eduarda Di Pietro *(Sr Dir-Art)*
Juliana Amorim *(Mgr-HR)*
Gabriel Berta *(Designer-Visual)*
Marcio Garcia *(Team Head-Technical)*
Anderson Leite *(Team Head-Technical)*

Accounts:
Tim Campaign: "Tim Beta"

R/GA
217 N Jefferson 5th Fl, Chicago, IL 60661
Tel.: (312) 276-5300
Web Site: www.rga.com

National Agency Associations: 4A's

Agency Specializes In: Advertising, Brand Development & Integration, Digital/Interactive, Social Media, Sponsorship

Jeff Brecker *(Mng Dir & VP)*
Dinesh Goburdhun *(Exec Dir-Creative & Specialist-Design)*
Eric Jannon *(Exec Dir-Creative)*
Chris Northam *(Exec Dir-Creative)*
Michael Morowitz *(Sr Dir-Technical)*
Christine Robertson *(Acct Supvr)*
Tyler Moore *(Planner)*

Accounts:
Abercrombie & Fitch Co.
Beef Checkoff Creative, Media Planning & Buying
Capital One Financial Corporation

R/GA
405 N Lamar Blvd, Austin, TX 78703
Tel.: (512) 322-3968
Web Site: www.rga.com

National Agency Associations: 4A's

Agency Specializes In: Advertising, Brand Development & Integration, Digital/Interactive, Internet/Web Design, Social Media, Sponsorship

Candice Hahn *(VP & Mng Dir)*
Daniel Diez *(CMO-Global)*
Chapin Clark *(Exec VP & Mng Dir-Copywriting-New York)*
Chloe Gottlieb *(Sr VP & Exec Dir-Creative-New York)*
Daniel Jurow *(Sr VP-Production-Global)*
Kyle Bunch *(Mng Dir-Social)*
Katrina Bekessy *(Dir-Tech & Design)*

Accounts:
Fossil, Inc.

R/WEST
1430 SE 3rd Ave 3rd Fl, Portland, OR 97214
Tel.: (503) 223-5443
Fax: (503) 223-5805
E-Mail: info@r-west.com
Web Site: www.r-west.com

Agency Specializes In: Advertising, Brand Development & Integration, Public Relations, Social Media, Strategic Planning/Research

Sarah Simmons *(Partner & Pres-Portland)*
Heather Villanueva *(VP & Dir)*
Taylor Siolka *(Assoc Dir-Creative)*
Stephanie Howe *(Brand Mgr)*
Jackie Hensel *(Supvr-Media)*
Ian Johnson *(Designer)*
Nicole Farin *(Acct Coord)*

Accounts:
FLIR One Campaign: "Meet The Heat"
Franciscan Estate
OHSU Knight Cancer Institute

R+M
15100 Weston Pkwy Ste 105, Cary, NC 27513
Tel.: (919) 677-9555
Fax: (919) 677-9511
E-Mail: info@rmagency.com
Web Site: www.rmagency.com

Employees: 8
Year Founded: 1992

Agency Specializes In: Brand Development & Integration

Beverly Murray *(Founder & CEO)*
Greg Norton *(Pres)*
Susan McDonnell *(VP-Brand Culture + Pit Boss)*
Susan Nettles *(VP-Brand Culture + Pit Boss)*
Chris Holleman *(Exec Dir-Interactive)*
Brett Hartsfield *(Dir-Art)*
Deb Roper *(Mgr-Ops & Production)*
Lauren Brown *(Strategist-Brand)*

Accounts:
Art of Safety
Camp Kanata
CareAnyware Creative, Market Planning, Strategic Brand Counsel
SoliClassica

R2C GROUP
(Formerly Respond2 Cmedia)
207 NW Park Ave, Portland, OR 97209
Tel.: (503) 222-0025
Fax: (503) 573-1941
E-Mail: info@r2cgroup.com
Web Site: www.r2cgroup.com

Employees: 135
Year Founded: 1998

Agency Specializes In: Advertising, Consumer Marketing, Digital/Interactive, Direct Response Marketing, Infomercials, Internet/Web Design, Media Buying Services, T.V.

Approx. Annual Billings: $225,000,000

Breakdown of Gross Billings by Media: D.M.: $210,000,000; Production: $10,000,000; Worldwide Web Sites: $5,000,000

David Savage *(Mng Partner & Chief Client Officer)*
Mark Toner *(CMO)*
Bryan Noguchi *(Sr VP & Dir-Media)*
Lester McCord *(VP & Grp Dir)*
Kyle Eckhart *(VP-Client Dev)*
Clayton Scott *(Dir-Online Media)*
Erik Stachurski *(Dir-Fin)*
Caitlin Virgin *(Coord-Media)*
Tonya Walshe *(Sr Media Buyer)*

Accounts:
Adobe
Bare Escentuals
Bare Minerals
Blinds.com Broadcast, Marketing Campaign, Media, Media Buying, TV Brand Strategy, TV Creative, TV Production
Blockbuster Online
ChristianMingle.com Campaign: "The Power of Two, United in Faith"
Columbia House
Direct Response TV
Estee Lauder
General Mills
Home Depot
johnnycarson.com
Nautilus Bowflex
Philips
Procter & Gamble
Provide Commerce (TV Agency of Record) Analytics, Brand Strategy, Creative, Media Buying, Media Planning, ProFlowers, Shari's Berries
TaxACT (Agency of Record) Campaign: "DIY America", Creative, Media
Total Gym

Branch

Marketing & Media Services, LLC
(d/b/a MMSI)
931 Jefferson Blvd Ste 1001, Warwick, RI 02886
Tel.: (401) 737-7730
Fax: (401) 737-6465
Toll Free: (888) 298-7730
Web Site: www.mmsipi.com

E-Mail for Key Personnel:
President: sally@mmsipitv.com

Employees: 25
Year Founded: 1985

National Agency Associations: DMA

Agency Specializes In: Advertising, Advertising Specialties, Affiliate Marketing, Alternative Advertising, Bilingual Market, Broadcast, Cable T.V., Co-op Advertising, Digital/Interactive, Direct Response Marketing, Hispanic Market, Integrated Marketing, Internet/Web Design, Media Buying

Services, Outdoor, Over-50 Market, Seniors' Market, Syndication, T.V., Travel & Tourism, Web (Banner Ads, Pop-ups, etc.)

Sally E. Dickson *(Pres)*
Anthony J. Ferranti *(Exec VP)*
Kaila Vallee *(Client Svcs Dir)*
Michael Bellamy *(Mgr-Acctg)*

R2INTEGRATED
400 E Pratt St, Baltimore, MD 21202
Tel.: (410) 327-0007
Fax: (410) 327-4082
E-Mail: info@r2integrated.com
Web Site: www.r2integrated.com

Employees: 200
Year Founded: 2003

Agency Specializes In: Brand Development & Integration, Digital/Interactive, E-Commerce, Event Planning & Marketing, Financial, Internet/Web Design, Search Engine Optimization, Strategic Planning/Research, Technical Advertising

Revenue: $40,000,000

Matt Goddard *(CEO)*
Chris Chodnicki *(Partner & CTO)*
Walter Starr *(CFO & VP-Fin)*
Dennis Totah *(Exec VP-Ops-US)*
Nick Christy *(Sr VP-Enterprise Tech)*
Sarah Hampton *(VP-Ops)*
Mike Jensen *(VP-Production-West Reg)*
Page Sands *(VP-Social Mktg)*
Steve Hill *(Sr Dir-Brand Strategy)*
Kara Alcamo *(Dir-Search Mktg)*
Lindsay McGettigan *(Dir-Mktg Strategy & Insights)*
Natalie Staines *(Dir-Mktg)*
Caroline Hook *(Sr Acct Mgr)*
Michael Kirby *(Sr Acct Strategist)*

Accounts:
Aramark
BUNN
Forbes Inc. Publishing Services
Hershey's
Microsoft
National Aquarium (Digital Agency of Record) Content Marketing, Website
Under Armour

Branches

CatapultWorks
(Formerly Catapult Direct)
300 Orchard City Dr Ste 131, Campbell, CA 95008
(See Separate Listing)

Make Me Social
310 Commerce Lake Dr, Saint Augustine, FL 32095
(See Separate Listing)

RABBLE + ROUSER INC
3401 Blake St, Denver, CO 80205
Tel.: (303) 399-8499
Web Site: www.rabbleandrouser.com

Year Founded: 2005

Agency Specializes In: Advertising, Brand Development & Integration, Content, Digital/Interactive, Logo & Package Design, Print, Radio, Social Media, Strategic Planning/Research, T.V.

Scott Schroeder *(CEO & Principal)*
Lee Payne *(VP-Client Svcs)*
Chris Armijo *(Dir-Interactive Creative)*
Marsha Capen *(Dir-Editorial)*
Patrick Hefner *(Dir-Application Dev)*
Shum Prats *(Dir-Creative)*
Dianna Benavidez *(Project Mgr-Digital)*
Tony Felice *(Strategist-Digital)*

Accounts:
Farm Credit System

RABINOVICI & ASSOCIATES
20815 NE 16th Ave Ste B10, Miami, FL 33179-2124
Tel.: (305) 655-0021
Fax: (305) 655-0811
E-Mail: mail@rabinovicionline.com
Web Site: www.rabinovicionline.com

Employees: 10
Year Founded: 2000

National Agency Associations: AHAA

Agency Specializes In: Hispanic Market, Sponsorship

Ester Rabinovici *(Mng Partner)*
Samuel Rabinovici *(VP)*
Dominik Niceva *(Creative Dir)*
Jose Luis Bures Valiente *(Dir-Art & Specialist-Print Production)*
Miguel Angel Chala *(Dir-Strategy & Bus Dev)*
Felipe Restrepo *(Dir-Art)*
Andy Sikorski *(Sr Acct Exec)*
Andrea Damico *(Copywriter)*

Accounts:
Accord Flooring
American Pipe and Tank
Bancafe
Bancoldex
Cremalleras Rey
Dow
Eastman Kodak
Ernst & Julio Gallo
Grupo Bimbo
Hill & Knowlton
Jarden
Laboratorios Roche
Mazda
Microsoft
Motorola Solutions, Inc. Latin American Interactive Initiatives, NPI
Occidental Resorts
RSA
Segurexpo de Colombia S.A.
Sony Music
Sunbeam Corp.
Unilever
Wacom

RADAR STUDIOS
401 W Ontario St Ste 300, Chicago, IL 60654
Tel.: (312) 266-2900
Fax: (312) 266-2960
Web Site: www.radarstudios.com

Agency Specializes In: Advertising, Digital/Interactive, Production

Don Hoeg *(Co-Founder)*
Eve Cross *(Head-Production)*
Jack Conte *(Dir)*
Sam Macon *(Dir)*
Pix Talarico *(Dir)*
Matthew Nowak *(Designer)*
Greg Somerlot *(Sr Editor-Creative)*

Accounts:
Ferrara Candy Company, Inc.

RADARWORKS
3101 Western Ave Ste 555, Seattle, WA 98121
Tel.: (206) 441-6657
Fax: (206) 441-4107
E-Mail: info@radarworks.com
Web Site: www.radarworks.com

Employees: 33
Year Founded: 1995

Agency Specializes In: Above-the-Line, Advertising, Advertising Specialties, Affluent Market, Alternative Advertising, Below-the-Line, Brand Development & Integration, Business Publications, Business-To-Business, Catalogs, Collateral, Communications, Computers & Software, Consulting, Consumer Goods, Consumer Marketing, Consumer Publications, Corporate Communications, Digital/Interactive, Direct Response Marketing, Direct-to-Consumer, Electronic Media, Electronics, Email, Event Planning & Marketing, Exhibit/Trade Shows, Experience Design, Financial, Graphic Design, Health Care Services, High Technology, Household Goods, Identity Marketing, Integrated Marketing, Internet/Web Design, Local Marketing, Logo & Package Design, Magazines, Media Buying Services, Media Planning, Multimedia, New Product Development, New Technologies, Newspaper, Newspapers & Magazines, Out-of-Home Media, Outdoor, Package Design, Paid Searches, Planning & Consultation, Point of Sale, Production, Production (Print), Publicity/Promotions, Regional, Search Engine Optimization, Social Marketing/Nonprofit, Sponsorship, Strategic Planning/Research, T.V., Trade & Consumer Magazines, Travel & Tourism

Ray Araujo *(Owner)*
Julie Foster *(VP & Dir-Media)*
Lou Maxon *(Exec Dir-Creative)*
Brea Stevens *(Sr Acct Dir)*
Erik Franklin *(Dir-Event Svcs)*
April Duron *(Sr Acct Mgr)*
Megan Hamlin Betz *(Sr Project Mgr-Interactive)*
Bradley Holschen *(Project Mgr-Interactive)*
Paul Wickler *(Mgr-Social Media)*
Ashley Meadows *(Specialist-Social Media & Copywriter)*

Accounts:
Acer America Corporation Campaign: "Star Trek Into Darkness"
Amazon.com, Inc.
C&K Markets
Cairncross & Hempelmann, P.S.
City National Bank
City of Bellevue
Downtown Seattle Association
Expedia
King & Mackovak Lasik Centers
McCaw Hall
Pride Foundation
Seattle Center
Susan G. Komen for the Cure
Vertafore Inc.
Washington CASH

Branch

Radarworks
6100 Wilshire Blvd Ste 1500, Los Angeles, CA 90048-5107
Tel.: (323) 965-5091
Fax: (323) 965-5092
Web Site: www.radarworks.com/

Employees: 7

Agency Specializes In: Advertising

Tom Whitman *(Sr VP & Dir-Flip)*
Julie Foster *(VP & Dir-Media)*

Jack Sichterman *(Exec Dir-Creative)*
Jocelyne Horstmann *(Sr Strategist-Media)*
Sam Ortiz *(Coord-Event)*

Accounts:
Acer America Corporation
Amazon.com, Inc.
Susan G. Komen for the Cure

RADIATE GROUP
5000 S Towne Dr, New Berlin, WI 53151
Tel.: (312) 324-8980
Fax: (312) 324-8960
Web Site: www.radiategroup.com

Agency Specializes In: Entertainment, Sports Market

Marc Smathers *(Exec VP)*

Accounts:
Nokia

Division

GMR Entertainment
220 E 42nd St, New York, NY 10017
Tel.: (212) 515-1915
Fax: (212) 515-1945
Web Site: www.gmrmarketing.com

Agency Specializes In: Above-the-Line, Alternative Advertising, Brand Development & Integration, Branded Entertainment, Consulting, Entertainment, Event Planning & Marketing, Experience Design, Integrated Marketing, Product Placement, Production

Stephen Knill *(Exec VP-Music & Entertainment)*
Alex Beer *(Sr VP-Client Mgmt)*
Vince O'Brien *(Sr VP-Global Sports & Entertainment Consultancy)*
Cameron Wagner *(Sr VP)*
Stephen Coakley *(VP-Client Mgmt)*
Heather Gaecke *(VP-HR)*
Casey Gartland *(VP-Music & Entertainment)*
Jeff Handler *(VP-Sports Mktg)*
Suzanne Boyd *(Sr Acct Dir)*
Amy Switzer *(Acct Dir)*

Accounts:
A&E Television
Nokia
Time Warner Cable

THE RADIO AGENCY
(Formerly Radio Direct Response)
1400 N Providence Rd Ste 4000, Media, PA 19063
Tel.: (610) 892-7300
Fax: (610) 892-1899
Toll Free: (800) 969-AMFM
E-Mail: info@radiodirect.com
Web Site: www.radiodirect.com

Employees: 10
Year Founded: 1993

National Agency Associations: DMA

Agency Specializes In: Advertising, Broadcast, Consulting, Consumer Marketing, Corporate Identity, Direct Response Marketing, Electronic Media, Infomercials, Integrated Marketing, Media Buying Services, Promotions, Radio, Sales Promotion

Breakdown of Gross Billings by Media: Radio: 100%

Mark Lipsky *(Pres & CEO)*
Vince Raimondo *(VP-Mktg)*
Barbra Tabnick *(VP-Acct Svcs)*

RADIO FACE
(Name Changed to Mister Face)

RADIO LOUNGE - RADIO ADVERTISING AGENCY
12926 Dairy Ashford Ste 120, Sugar Land, TX 77478
Tel.: (281) 494-4680
E-Mail: babbott@radioloungeusa.com
Web Site: www.radioloungeusa.com

Agency Specializes In: Advertising, African-American Market, Alternative Advertising, Brand Development & Integration, Business Publications, Communications, Consumer Marketing, Digital/Interactive, Direct Response Marketing, Electronic Media, Hispanic Market, Media Buying Services, Media Planning, Media Relations, Men's Market, Production (Ad, Film, Broadcast), RSS (Really Simple Syndication), Radio, Strategic Planning/Research, Syndication, Urban Market, Viral/Buzz/Word of Mouth, Women's Market

Approx. Annual Billings: $400,000

Ray Schilens *(Pres & CEO)*

RADIOVISION LP
531 W Main St, Denison, TX 75020
Tel.: (903) 337-4200
Fax: (903) 337-4296
Toll Free: (800) 326-3198
Web Site: www.radiovisioninc.com

Employees: 35

Agency Specializes In: Automotive, Brand Development & Integration, Digital/Interactive, Electronic Media, Internet/Web Design, Media Buying Services, Media Planning, Outdoor, Print, Production, Production (Ad, Film, Broadcast), Promotions, Radio, Sales Promotion, Search Engine Optimization, Social Media, Strategic Planning/Research, T.V.

Shelley McBride *(Owner & Mng Partner)*
Joe Pollaro *(Owner & Partner)*
Lisa Melvin *(CFO)*
H. Lee Fuqua *(Dir-Mktg)*
Dayla Rice *(Acct Mgr)*

Accounts:
Randall Reed Planet Ford

RADIUS ADVERTISING
10883 Pearl Rd Ste 100, Strongsville, OH 44136
Tel.: (440) 638-3800
Fax: (440) 638-3109
E-Mail: info@radiuscleveland.com
Web Site: www.radiuscleveland.com

Year Founded: 2003

Agency Specializes In: Advertising, Brand Development & Integration, Broadcast, Collateral, Corporate Identity, Digital/Interactive, Internet/Web Design, Promotions, Public Relations, Social Media

Randy Pindor *(Pres)*
Marty Allen *(Dir-Studio Production)*
Bill Bender *(Dir-Media Mktg)*
Russ Hirth *(Dir-Creative)*
Lori Marefka *(Acct Supvr)*
Matthew Bender *(Acct Exec)*

Accounts:
Bike Brite

RADIX COMMUNICATIONS, INC.
3399 S Lakeshore Dr, Saint Joseph, MI 49085
Tel.: (269) 982-7400
Fax: (269) 982-7405
E-Mail: position@radixcom.net
Web Site: www.radixcom.net

Employees: 30
Year Founded: 1965

Agency Specializes In: Collateral, Consumer Marketing, Consumer Publications, Industrial, Point of Purchase, Sponsorship

Carl Mosher *(Pres)*

Accounts:
Gast Manufacturing Corp.; Benton Harbor, MI Air Pumps & Motors
Sears Roebuck; Hoffman Estates, IL
Whirlpool Corporation; Benton Harbor, MI KitchenAid, Major Appliances

RADONICRODGERS COMMUNICATIONS INC.
418 Hanlan Road Building B Unit 19, Vaughan, ON L4L4Z1 Canada
Tel.: (416) 695-0575
Fax: (416) 695-0576
Toll Free: (800) 585-3029
E-Mail: info@radonicrodgers.com
Web Site: www.radonicrodgers.com

Agency Specializes In: Catalogs, Exhibit/Trade Shows, Guerilla Marketing, Internet/Web Design, Media Buying Services, Media Planning, Strategic Planning/Research

Ross Rodgers *(Co-Founder & Partner)*
Edward Radonic *(Mng Partner & Dir-Mktg)*
Jarold Muino *(Sr Designer)*

Accounts:
Attractions Ontario Association (Advertising Agency of Record) Social Media, Website
CIT Tours Travel & Tour Agencies

RAGAN CREATIVE STRATEGY & DESIGN
261B Victoria St, Kamloops, BC V2C 2A1 Canada
Tel.: (250) 851-0229
Fax: (250) 851-9840
E-Mail: info@ragan.ca
Web Site: www.ragan.ca

Employees: 6
Year Founded: 1993

Agency Specializes In: Advertising, Brand Development & Integration, Consulting, Corporate Identity, Graphic Design, Integrated Marketing, Internet/Web Design, Local Marketing, Logo & Package Design, Magazines, Media Buying Services, Media Planning, Newspaper, Outdoor, Package Design, Paid Searches, Planning & Consultation, Point of Purchase, Point of Sale, Print, Production, Production (Print), Publishing, Radio, Search Engine Optimization, Social Media, Strategic Planning/Research, T.V., Web (Banner Ads, Pop-ups, etc.)

Ralph Ragan *(Owner)*

Accounts:
Cahilty Lodge
Fire Place Centre
Four Points Sheraton; Kamloops, BC
Kamloops Golf Consortium; 2007
MJB Lawyers
Sun Rivers Resort
Talking Rock Golf Resort

Advertising Agencies

RAIN
4 Greenleaf Woods Ste 301, Portsmouth, NH 03801
Tel.: (603) 498-5864
Fax: (603) 430-0142
E-Mail: steve@rainbiz.com
Web Site: www.rainbiz.com

Employees: 7

Agency Specializes In: Financial, High Technology, Travel & Tourism

Revenue: $1,000,000

Will Hall *(Exec Dir-Creative)*
Christijan Draper *(Dir-UX)*
Chelsey Ellison *(Designer)*
Jamie Hunter *(Sr Designer)*
Greg Rorem *(Designer-UX)*

Accounts:
Bottom Line Technology
Bottomline Technologies Banking Campaign
Hancom Federal Credit Union
Interactive Super Computing
Microsoft
NaviSite
New Forma
New Hampshire Credit Union League
Rhode Island Credit Union League
The United Way

RAIN AGENCY
1104 NW 15th Ste 200, Portland, OR 97209
Tel.: (503) 944-6235
E-Mail: info@rainagency.com
Web Site: www.rainagency.com

Agency Specializes In: Advertising

David Savinar *(Pres)*

Accounts:
Dole Foods
Johnson & Johnson
Terrain Land Development

RAIN43
(Formerly Partners + Edell)
445 King Street W Ste 301, Toronto, ON M5V 1K4 Canada
Tel.: (416) 361-1804
Fax: (416) 203-8002
E-Mail: info@rain43.com
Web Site: www.rain43.com

Employees: 24

Agency Specializes In: Advertising

Laura Davis-Saville *(VP & Dir-Strategic Plng)*
Edge Watson *(Controller)*
Shawna Dressler *(Dir-HR & Ops)*
Ryan Speziale *(Dir-Art)*
Madison Turner *(Dir-Art)*
Paisley McNair *(Acct Supvr)*
Mike Albrecht *(Copywriter)*
Liam Brown *(Planner-Strategic)*
Andrew Payne *(Copywriter)*
Jeremy Richard *(Copywriter)*
Heather Osbourne *(Acct Coord)*

Accounts:
Bridgepoint Health
Castrol
Hado Labo
Ontario Toyota Dealer Advertising Association
Toyota

RAINMAKER ADVERTISING
7237 Tangleglen Dr, Dallas, TX 75248
Tel.: (214) 827-0770
Fax: (972) 992-3934
E-Mail: talk2us@rainmakeradv.com
Web Site: www.rainmakeradv.com

Agency Specializes In: Advertising, Brand Development & Integration, Content, Internet/Web Design, Logo & Package Design, Search Engine Optimization

Christopher J. Miller *(Owner)*

Accounts:
Dallas Medical Center
Town of Addison

RAINMAKER COMMUNICATIONS
650 Castro St Ste 120 220, Mountain View, CA 94041
Tel.: (925) 296-6104
E-Mail: info@rainmakercommunications.com
Web Site: www.rainmakercommunications.com

Agency Specializes In: Corporate Communications, Local Marketing, Public Relations, Strategic Planning/Research

Molly Davis *(Co-Founder & Partner)*
Stacy Pena *(Co-Founder)*
Adam Soffe *(Acct Dir)*

Accounts:
Cisco
Devine Capital Partners
Girls Leadership Institute
Opus Capital
Oracle
SAP
Symantec
Vontu
WAVC
Workday
Zendesk

RAINS BIRCHARD MARKETING
(Formerly Rains Marketing)
1001 SE Water Ave Ste 420, Portland, OR 97214
Tel.: (503) 297-1791
Fax: (503) 297-2282
Web Site: www.rainsbirchardmarketing.com

E-Mail for Key Personnel:
President: gary@rainsmarketing.com
Creative Dir.: jon@rainsmarketing.com

Employees: 8
Year Founded: 1987

National Agency Associations: PRSA

Agency Specializes In: Business-To-Business, Collateral, Commercial Photography, Consulting, Corporate Identity, E-Commerce, Exhibit/Trade Shows, Financial, Graphic Design, High Technology, Industrial, Internet/Web Design, Logo & Package Design, Media Buying Services, Planning & Consultation, Print, Public Relations, Strategic Planning/Research, Technical Advertising, Transportation

Approx. Annual Billings: $2,600,000 Capitalized

Breakdown of Gross Billings by Media: Consulting: 11%; Graphic Design: 24%; Print: 35%; Pub. Rels.: 15%; Worldwide Web Sites: 15%

Jon Rains *(Owner & Dir-Creative)*
Ryan Svensson *(Acct Mgr)*
Justin Mitchel *(Designer)*

Accounts:
ConMet; Portland, OR Brake Drums; 2003
High Purity Standards; Charleston, SC Analytical Standards; 2005

RAKA
33 Penhallow St., Portsmouth, NH 03801
Tel.: (603) 436-7770, ext. 122
E-Mail: kmorales@rakacreative.com
Web Site: www.rakacreative.com

Year Founded: 2004

Agency Specializes In: Advertising, Alternative Advertising, Arts, Brand Development & Integration, Business-To-Business, Children's Market, Collateral, College, Communications, Computers & Software, Consumer Goods, Consumer Marketing, Corporate Communications, Corporate Identity, Digital/Interactive, E-Commerce, Electronic Media, Environmental, Financial, Food Service, Graphic Design, Health Care Services, Hospitality, Household Goods, Identity Marketing, Information Technology, Integrated Marketing, Internet/Web Design, Leisure, Logo & Package Design, Luxury Products, Medical Products, Men's Market, Mobile Marketing, Multimedia, New Technologies, Print, Restaurant, Retail, Search Engine Optimization, Social Marketing/Nonprofit, Social Media, Viral/Buzz/Word of Mouth, Web (Banner Ads, Pop-ups, etc.), Women's Market

Breakdown of Gross Billings by Media: Audio/Visual: 10%; E-Commerce: 10%; Internet Adv.: 20%; Logo & Package Design: 5%; Print: 5%; Worldwide Web Sites: 50%

Daniel Marino *(Partner & Dir-Creative)*
Duncan Craig *(Partner)*
Zang Garside *(Partner)*
Brian Dekoning *(Dir-Inbound Mktg)*
Jessica Hayes *(Dir-Sls)*
Amahl Majack *(Mgr-Inbound Content)*
Sam Nute *(Specialist-Inbound Mktg)*
Leigh Spader *(Designer)*
Jonathan Steinberg *(Sr Designer)*

RALLY
1218 3rd Ave Ste 300 Seattle Twr, Seattle, WA 98101
Tel.: (206) 219-0029
Web Site: www.rallygroup.com

Agency Specializes In: Advertising, Brand Development & Integration, Digital/Interactive, Social Media, Strategic Planning/Research

Kelly Parriott *(Pres & Partner)*
Keith Goldberg *(Partner, Chief Creative Officer & Exec Dir-Creative)*
Jeff Roberts *(Mng Dir-Client Svcs)*
Michelle Flessner *(Sr Acct Dir)*
Thomas King *(Dir-Digital Creative)*
Sandy Towry *(Dir-Ops)*

Accounts:
Cracker JackD
Speakman (Advertising & Digital Agency of Record)

RALSTON & ANTHONY ADVERTISING
875 N Michigan Ave, Chicago, IL 60611
Tel.: (800) 520-8760
Fax: (800) 510-8760
E-Mail: info@ralstonandanthony.com
Web Site: www.ralstonandanthony.com

Agency Specializes In: Advertising, Broadcast, Digital/Interactive, Event Planning & Marketing, Internet/Web Design, Media Relations, Media Training, Print, Promotions, Social Media

Christopher Skraba *(Founder & Pres)*

Accounts:
CheckGear

THE RAMEY AGENCY LLC
3100 N State St Ste 300, Jackson, MS 39216
Tel.: (601) 898-8900
Fax: (601) 898-8999
Toll Free: (800) 594-0754
E-Mail: cray@tra.net
Web Site: www.rameyagency.com

E-Mail for Key Personnel:
President: jgarner@tra.net
Creative Dir.: BPotesky@tra.net
Media Dir.: ttanner@tra.net

Employees: 38
Year Founded: 1985

Agency Specializes In: Advertising, Brand Development & Integration, Broadcast, Business Publications, Business-To-Business, Collateral, Communications, Consulting, Consumer Marketing, Consumer Publications, Corporate Communications, Corporate Identity, Direct Response Marketing, E-Commerce, Event Planning & Marketing, Exhibit/Trade Shows, Financial, Graphic Design, In-Store Advertising, Investor Relations, Leisure, Local Marketing, Logo & Package Design, Magazines, Media Buying Services, Newspaper, Newspapers & Magazines, Outdoor, Planning & Consultation, Point of Purchase, Point of Sale, Print, Production, Public Relations, Publicity/Promotions, Radio, Retail, Sales Promotion, Sponsorship, Strategic Planning/Research, Trade & Consumer Magazines, Travel & Tourism

Approx. Annual Billings: $32,000,000

Breakdown of Gross Billings by Media: Bus. Publs.: $3,200,000; Collateral: $8,000,000; Consumer Publs.: $6,400,000; Foreign: $1,600,000; Logo & Package Design: $1,600,000; Plng. & Consultation: $3,200,000; Pub. Rels.: $3,200,000; Radio & T.V.: $4,800,000

Jack Garner *(Pres)*
Chris Ray *(Partner & CEO)*
Jim Garrison *(Partner & COO)*
Bob Potesky *(Partner & Exec Creative Dir)*
Terry Tanner *(Sr VP & Dir-Media)*
Kristine Jacobs *(VP, Grp Acct Dir & Dir-Strategic Plng)*
Wynn Saggus *(VP & Grp Acct Dir)*
Kathy Potts *(VP & Acct Mgmt Dir)*
Wes Williams *(VP & Dir-Creative)*
Crystal Coleman *(Sr Dir-Art)*
Sherry Messemore *(Mgr-Acctg)*
Jana Brady *(Acct Exec)*
Anne Lauren Fratesi *(Acct Exec-Social Media)*

Accounts:
The Alluvian
Bank of the Ozarks
BankPlus; Madison, MS Financial Services
C Spire Creative Agency of Record
The Catfish Institute
ClimateMaster Geothermal,
Culinary Institute of America
Dassault Systems
Entergy Corp
Meyer Corporation
Mississippi Tourism
Saint Charles Cabinetry
Stephens Inc.; Little Rock, AR Investment Bankers
Viking Range Corp.; Greenwood, MS High-End Residential Kitchen Equipment

RAMSEY MEDIAWORKS LLC
PO Box 279, Joplin, MO 64802
Tel.: (417) 782-3694
Fax: (417) 781-1968
Toll Free: (800) 209-8536
Web Site: www.ramseymediaworks.com

Year Founded: 2002

Agency Specializes In: Advertising, Email, Exhibit/Trade Shows, Internet/Web Design, Logo & Package Design, Outdoor, Print

Julie Ramsey *(Pres)*
Todd Ramsey *(Principal)*
Nathan Horton *(Dir-Creative)*
Jimi Adams *(Sr Designer)*

Accounts:
Andrus Transportation
The Empire District Electric Company
I3 Tech Group

RANCH7 CREATIVE, LLC
738 Wilson St, Santa Rosa, CA 95401
Tel.: (707) 526-1080
Web Site: www.ranch7.com

Year Founded: 2002

Agency Specializes In: Advertising, Brand Development & Integration, Graphic Design, Internet/Web Design, Logo & Package Design, Social Media

Laurie Gibbs *(Partner & Dir-Editorial)*
Kate Brouillet *(Mgr-Studio)*

Accounts:
City of Santa Rosa
James Randi Educational Foundation

RAND ADVERTISING
6 Tibbetts Dr, Lincoln, ME 04457
Mailing Address:
PO Box 505, Lincoln, ME 04457
Tel.: (207) 794-8071
E-Mail: info@randadvertising.com
Web Site: www.randadvertising.com

Employees: 2
Year Founded: 1988

Agency Specializes In: Advertising Specialties, Business-To-Business, Commercial Photography, Event Planning & Marketing, Graphic Design, Internet/Web Design, Local Marketing, Logo & Package Design, Point of Sale, Print, Public Relations, Publicity/Promotions, Travel & Tourism

Connie Rand *(Co-Owner)*
Lee Rand *(Co-Owner)*

Accounts:
C.B. Kenworth
Clay Funeral Home
Eagle Lodge & Camps
Thornton Brothers

THE RANDALL BRANDING
1329 E Cary St Ste 200, Richmond, VA 23219
Tel.: (804) 767-4979
Web Site: www.randallbranding.com

Employees: 7

Agency Specializes In: Advertising, Brand Development & Integration, Internet/Web Design, Logo & Package Design, Print, Radio, Social Media

Jesse Randall *(Pres & Chief Creative Officer)*
Megan Chandler *(Dir-Art & Graphic Designer)*
Colleen Festa *(Dir-Art & Graphic Designer)*
Jessica Hildebrand *(Dir-Client Rels)*

Accounts:
Atlantic Constructors
B&B Printing
The Baby Jogger Company
Childrens Home Society of Virginia
Dominion Riverrock
e2 Events
Early Mountain Vineyards
New-Good Run Research
The Growers Exchange
New-Harman Eye Center
Lifestyle Home Builders
Linda Nash Ventures LLC
MicroAire Surgical Instruments Inc.
PartnerMD
New-Rountrey & Collington
RTS Labs
Scribekick
TechTrader
Three One One Productions
Timmons Group
New-TMI Consulting Marketing
New-VCU
Virginia Museum of Fine Arts
Virginia Physicians for Women
New-Work & Think

THE RANKIN GROUP, LTD.
17821 E 17th St Ste 270, Tustin, CA 92780-2137
Tel.: (714) 832-4100
Fax: (714) 282-8825
E-Mail: rankin@rankin-group.com
Web Site: www.rankin-group.com

Employees: 4
Year Founded: 1983

National Agency Associations: BMA-PRSA

Agency Specializes In: Advertising, Advertising Specialties, Automotive, Aviation & Aerospace, Brand Development & Integration, Business-To-Business, Co-op Advertising, Collateral, Commercial Photography, Communications, Consulting, Consumer Marketing, Digital/Interactive, Direct Response Marketing, E-Commerce, Electronic Media, Engineering, Environmental, Exhibit/Trade Shows, Graphic Design, High Technology, Industrial, Information Technology, Internet/Web Design, Logo & Package Design, Medical Products, Multimedia, New Product Development, Pharmaceutical, Planning & Consultation, Point of Purchase, Point of Sale, Public Relations, Publicity/Promotions, Sales Promotion, Strategic Planning/Research, Technical Advertising, Telemarketing

Ernest Rankin *(Pres)*
Marcie May *(VP-Ops)*

Accounts:
TEAC

RAPP
437 Madison Ave 3rd Fl, New York, NY 10022
Tel.: (212) 817-6800
Fax: (212) 590-8400
E-Mail: tara.vetro@rapp.com
Web Site: www.rapp.com

Employees: 2,000
Year Founded: 1965

Agency Specializes In: Automotive, Broadcast, Business-To-Business, Consumer Marketing, Digital/Interactive, Direct Response Marketing, Electronic Media, Financial, Health Care Services, High Technology, Infomercials, Internet/Web

Design, Media Buying Services, Pharmaceutical, Planning & Consultation, Print, Production, Sponsorship, Strategic Planning/Research, T.V., Telemarketing

Approx. Annual Billings: $2,411,800,000 Capitalized

Alexei Orlov *(CEO)*
Ricardo Pomeranz *(Chief Digital Officer)*
Marco Scognamiglio *(Pres-EMEA & APAC & Exec VP-Global Clients-Worldwide)*
John Singer *(Sr VP & Head-US Healthcare Practice)*
Rik Haslam *(Sr VP & Exec Dir-Creative)*
Paul Blockey *(Sr VP & Dir-Experience Strategy & Design)*
Marie-Angie Vassallo *(VP & Grp Acct Dir)*
Joseph Nowicki *(VP & Dir-Decision Sciences)*
Nic Climer *(Exec Dir-Creative)*
Shiona McDougall *(Exec Dir-Plng)*
Sid Brown *(Acct Dir)*
Erica Stevens *(Dir-Art & Designer)*
Louise Coulson *(Dir-Mktg & Sls)*
Jeff Goodnow *(Dir-Brdcst Production)*
Andreas Luchini *(Dir-Art)*
Melissa Murphy *(Dir-Mktg)*
Joey Monteverde *(Assoc Dir-Creative & Copywriter)*
Meghan Hayden *(Mgr-Creative Svcs)*
Alison Condon *(Acct Supvr)*
Amanda Foderaro *(Supvr-Mgmt)*
Nicole Bronstein *(Acct Exec)*
Stephanie McClain *(Acct Exec)*

Accounts:
AMC Entertainment Direct Marketing & CRM
Bacardi
Barnes & Noble
Best Buy
Coty Sally Hansen & Licensed Guess, Halle Berry, Beckham & Playboy
Direct Energy
DirecTV
Disney
DSG International
Express Scripts Direct Marketing, Interactive, Public Relations; 2008
Exxon/Mobil
GlaxoSmithKline Plc
The Guide Dogs for the Blind Association
Hewlett-Packard
Humana, Inc. Health Insurance
Hyatt Hotels
Johnson & Johnson
Kaiser Permanente
Mercedes-Benz
Merck
National Football League
Nestle Digital, Gerber
Novartis
Pepsi
Pfizer Campaign: "Anti-Counterfeit"
Royal Caribbean Cruises
Time Warner Cable
Toyota Campaign: "Handraiser"
Toys R Us
Travelocity
Viagra Campaign: "Exhibit I: A Couterfeit Epidemic"
Wm. Wrigley Jr. Company 5 Gum
XM Satellite Radio

North America

Critical Mass Inc.
402 11th Ave SE, Calgary, AB T2G 0Y4 Canada
(See Separate Listing)

Kern
(Formerly The Kern Organization)
20955 Warner Center Ln, Woodland Hills, CA 91367-6511
(See Separate Listing)

Rapp Dallas
7850 N Belt Line Rd, Irving, TX 75063
Tel.: (972) 409-5400
Web Site: www.rapp.com

Agency Specializes In: Sponsorship

Greg Brent *(VP-Tech)*
Addison Deitz *(VP-Bus Dev)*
Charles Henderson *(VP-Client Growth & New Bus)*
Suellen Anderson *(Dir-Program Mgmt)*
Cody Hudson *(Dir-Solutions)*
Jackie Kaufman *(Sr Mgr-Print Production)*
Heather Mathews *(Supvr-Client Svcs)*
Christine Pope *(Specialist-Creative Tech)*

Accounts:
Bank of America

Rapp Los Angeles
222 N Sepulveda Blvd Ste 500, El Segundo, CA 90245-5644
Tel.: (310) 563-7200
Fax: (310) 563-7297
E-Mail: hello@rappusa.com
Web Site: www.rapp.com

Employees: 100

Agency Specializes In: Consumer Marketing, Direct Response Marketing, Sponsorship

Greg Andersen *(Mng Dir)*
Jessica Kernan *(Chief Strategy Officer-North America)*
Pahzeet Liebermann *(VP & Grp Acct Dir)*
Alang'o Otieno *(VP-Customer Experience Analytics)*
Matt Johnson *(Head-Activation & Media-West Coast)*
Nick Platt *(Exec Dir-Creative)*
Scott Alexander *(Mgmt Supvr)*
Richard Tseng *(Assoc Dir-Creative)*
Laura Orsini *(Acct Supvr)*

Accounts:
Hasbro, Inc.
Mattel

TrackDDB
(Formerly Rapp Worldwide)
33 Bloor Street 17th Fl, Toronto, ON M4W 3H1 Canada
Tel.: (416) 972-7700
Fax: (416) 972-7701
Web Site: trackddb.com

Employees: 15

Ian Haworth *(Chm & Chief Creative Officer-Global)*
Paul Tedesco *(Mng Dir & VP)*
Barb Williams *(Exec Dir-Creative)*
Carla Rimando *(Dir-Art)*
Eric Grimes *(Copywriter)*

Accounts:
Canadian Blood Services
Marrow Network
OneMatch Stem Cell

United Kingdom

Haygarth Group
28-31 High Street, Wimbledon Village, London, SW19 5BY United Kingdom
Tel.: (44) 20 8971 3300
Fax: (44) 20 8947 3700
Web Site: www.haygarth.co.uk

Employees: 102
Year Founded: 1984

National Agency Associations: DMA

Agency Specializes In: Direct Response Marketing, Event Planning & Marketing, Exhibit/Trade Shows, Planning & Consultation, Public Relations, Publicity/Promotions

Sophie Daranyi *(CEO)*
Marcus Sandwith *(Mng Dir)*
Steve Rogers *(Grp Dir-Creative)*
Bob Blandford *(Dir-Creative)*
Suzy Ray *(Dir-New Bus & Mktg)*
Sue Jenvey *(Assoc Dir)*

Accounts:
Beefeater Digital Campaign
Budgens Brand Marketing, Strategic Brand Development
Dairy Crest
Filofax
Gillette
Johnson & Johnson Campaign: "Apply Within", K-Y Jelly
Londis Brand Marketing, Strategic Brand Development
London Designer Outlet Experiential, PR
Mywalit Events, Public Relations
Organic UK Campaign: "Organic. Naturally different"
Palm Inc. Palm Pre
Premier Foods PLC Lloyd Grossman, Sharwood's
Rachel's Dairy
SCA Bodyform, Velvet
Vodafone Freebees, Pay As You Go handsets, Retail Campaign

RAPP CDS EMEA LIMITED
(Formerly HLB Ltd.)
1 Riverside Manbre Road, London, W6 9WA United Kingdom
Tel.: (44) 20 8735 7350
Fax: (44) 20 8735 7351
E-Mail: infohlb@wwavrc.co.uk

Employees: 350

Agency Specializes In: Direct Response Marketing

Marco Scognamiglio *(CEO-UK)*

Rapp London
1 Riverside Manbre Road, London, W6 9WA United Kingdom
Tel.: (44) 208 735 8000
Fax: (44) 208 735 7501
Web Site: rapp.com/

Employees: 400
Year Founded: 1976

Agency Specializes In: Automotive, Consumer Marketing, Corporate Identity, Cosmetics, Direct Response Marketing, Event Planning & Marketing, Exhibit/Trade Shows, Financial, Government/Political, Pets , Public Relations, Publicity/Promotions

Chris Freeland *(CEO-UK)*
Ian Maynard *(Mng Dir-RAPP Media)*
Simon Cheshire *(Head-Digital Design)*
Jason Andrews *(Exec Creative Dir)*
Ben Golik *(Grp Exec Dir-Creative)*
Rob Reason *(Exec Dir-Plng)*
Rich Donovan *(Creative Dir)*
Jon Leney *(Creative Dir)*
Clare Wilson *(Creative Dir)*
Sid Gordon *(Dir-Creative)*
Paul Holman *(Dir-Bus)*
Simon Kavanagh *(Assoc Creative Dir)*

Accounts:
Abbott
AkzoNobel Business-to-Business, Cuprinol, Customer Relationship Marketing, Dulux Trade, Global Digital Strategy, Hammerite, Polycell
AstraZeneca
Bayer
Cancer Research UK Charities, Direct Mail Campaign; 1998
The Co-operative Bank
Comparethemarket.com
Google
GSK
Habitat
Hastings Direct Direct Marketing, Media Planning & Buying
Hertz
International Fund for Animal Welfare Turtle Survival Awareness
Ladbrooks
Merck
Mothercare CRM Advertising
Niagara Healthcare Media
Otsuka
PayPal Digital
Pfizer Pharmaceutical; 2001
Procter & Gamble UK; 2002
SCA Hygiene
Scottish & Newcastle
Scottish Power Marketing
Sony Consumer Products Small Electrical Goods; 1996
Specialist Holidays Group Media Planning & Buying
UNICEF Campaign: "Any Reason"
Virgin Media
Wanadoo
World Wildlife Fund Charities; 2003

Rapp UK
Leith Assembly Rooms 43 Constitution Street, Edinburgh, EH6 7BG United Kingdom
Tel.: (44) 131 553 9444
Fax: (44) 131 553 9440
Web Site: www.rapp.com

Employees: 30
Year Founded: 1993

Agency Specializes In: Consumer Marketing, Direct Response Marketing

Tania Feeley *(Mng Partner)*
James Griffiths *(Mng Partner)*
John Perkins *(Mng Dir)*
John Markham *(CTO)*
Marco Scognamiglio *(CEO-UK)*
Ian Maynard *(Mng Dir-RAPP Media)*
Natalie Green *(Dir-Bus)*
Mike Wells *(Dir-Digital)*
Nick Friend *(Sr Acct Mgr)*
Carolyn Stebbings *(Exec Mng Partner-Data)*

Accounts:
Gleneagles Above-The-Line Communications, Direct Mail, Email Marketing, Hotel Collateral, Strategic Marketing
Standard Life

Rapp UK
Olympic House The Birches, East Grinstead, West Sussex RH19 1EH United Kingdom
Tel.: (44) 1342 33 6300
Fax: (44) 1342 33 6301
E-Mail: hello@uk.rapp.com
Web Site: www.rapp.com

Employees: 400

Agency Specializes In: Consumer Marketing, Information Technology

John Perkins *(Mng Dir)*
Samantha Nolan *(Sr VP & Acct Mgmt Dir)*
Suzanne Hilliar *(Head-HR & People Dev)*
Nina Cornish *(Acct Dir)*
Tom Nowell *(Acct Dir)*
Amy Thomas *(Acct Dir)*
Ellie-May Brooks *(Sr Acct Mgr)*
Elijah Lyons *(Sr Acct Mgr)*

Accounts:
AIG
AOL
Bacardi-Martini
BBC Worldwide
Best Western
British Airways
Diageo
John Lewis Partnership
The Open University DM Business, Media Planning & Buying
Orange
Pfizer
Virgin Media Digital, Direct Customer Marketing, Direct Response Acquisition, Radio, TV
Yell.com

Latin America

Rapp Argentina
Reconquista 723 2 Piso, 1003 Buenos Aires, Argentina
Tel.: (54) 11 5554 7277
Fax: (54) 11 5554 7299
E-Mail: info@rappcollins.com.ar
Web Site: www.rappargentina.com.ar

E-Mail for Key Personnel:
President: mrainuzzo@rappcollins.com.ar

Employees: 15
Year Founded: 1986

Agency Specializes In: Consumer Marketing, Direct Response Marketing

Pedro Morrone *(Partner)*
Connie Demuru *(Mng Dir-Argentina & Uruguay)*
Agustina Antig *(Acct Exec)*
Manuela Marconi *(Acct Exec)*

Accounts:
AB&P
Adlatina.com
Alba
Calsa
Coca-Cola Refreshments USA, Inc.
Esso
Heineken
Hospital Universidad Austral
IAE Universidad Austral

Rapp Brazil
Av Juscelino Kubetischek 1726, 4 e 5 andares Itam Bibi, CEP 04543-00 Sao Paulo, SP Brazil
Tel.: (55) 11 3077 1300
Fax: (55) 11 3077 1333
E-Mail: sofia.tost@rappbrasil.com.br
Web Site: www.rapp.com

Year Founded: 1987

Agency Specializes In: Consumer Marketing, Direct Response Marketing, Sales Promotion

Ricardo Pomeranz *(Chief Digital Officer)*
Abaete de Azeredo *(Pres/CEO-Latin America)*
Andre Pasquali *(VP-Creative)*
Felipe Andrade *(Grp Head-Creative)*
Rodrigo Noventa *(Grp Head-Creative)*
Camila Paioli Cardoso *(Acct Dir)*
Fernanda Moraes *(Acct Dir)*
Mauro Pinheiro *(Acct Dir)*
Thiago Barreto *(Dir-Art & Supvr-Creative)*
Tatiana Pacheco *(Client Svc Grp Dir)*

Accounts:
Banco Itaas Campaign: "Itaas Fun Trade"
FedEx
Itau Bank
Natura
Pepsi
Philips Walita
Sadia
Sodexo
Telefonica
TVA
Whirlpool
Zodiac

RappDigital Brazil
Av Juscelino Kubitschek, CEP 01453-000 Sao Paulo, SP Brazil
Tel.: (55) 11 3077 1300
Fax: (55) 11 3077 1333
E-Mail: rh@rappdigital.com.br
Web Site: www.rapp.com

Employees: 35
Year Founded: 2000

Agency Specializes In: Digital/Interactive, Direct Response Marketing, Planning & Consultation

Ricardo Pomeranz *(Chief Digital Officer)*
Marcos Bittencourt Bittencourt *(Exec VP)*
Mauro Letizia *(VP-Digital Creative)*
Felipe Andrade *(Grp Head-Creative)*
Everson Bastos *(Sr Dir-Art)*
Renato F. Moreira Costa *(Acct Dir)*
Mauro Pinheiro *(Acct Dir)*
Thiago Barreto *(Dir-Art & Supvr-Creative)*
Andre Bercelli *(Dir-Art)*
Andre Monteiro *(Mgr-IT)*
Branca Sant'Anna *(Supvr-Performance Media)*
Flavia Ito *(Asst-Media)*
Tatiana Pacheco *(Client Svc Grp Dir)*

Accounts:
Credicard
Editora Moderna
Itau Bank
Nestle
Nokia
Petrobas
Pfizer
Philips
Roche
Telefonica
Unibanco AIG

Asia Pacific

Rapp Australia
Level 3 46-52 Mountain Street, Ultimo, Sydney, NSW Australia
Tel.: (61) 2 8260 2222
Fax: (61) 2 82602777
Web Site: rapp.com.au/

Employees: 35
Year Founded: 1981

Agency Specializes In: Consumer Marketing, Sales Promotion

Simone Blakers *(Mng Dir-Sydney)*
Craig Bailey *(Dir-Creative)*
Emily Somers *(Dir-Art)*
Scott R. Holliday *(Designer)*
Ron Prince *(Designer-Digital)*
Tricia Tan *(Sr Bus Mgr)*

Rapp Malaysia
D601-D605 6th Floor Block D Kelana Square 17 Jalan SS7/26, 47301 Petaling Jaya, Malaysia
Tel.: (60) 3 7806 5799
Fax: (60) 3 7806 3489
E-Mail: yewaiye.lim@rapp.com.my
Web Site: www.rapp.com.my

Employees: 70

Lim Wai Yee *(COO)*
Edward Ong *(Exec Dir-Creative)*
Jeff Ooi *(Dir-Creative)*

Accounts:
BMW; 2007
Enrich Malaysia Airlines
GlaxoSmithKline; 2007
Johnson & Johnson Johnson & Johnson Baby Care
Merican Muay Thai Gym
Panasonic
Prince Court Medical Centre; 2007
Wyeth Pfizer

Rapp Melbourne
7 Electric Street, Richmond, VIC 3121 Australia
Tel.: (61) 3 9429 4766
Fax: (61) 3 9254 3640
Web Site: www.rapp.com

Agency Specializes In: Consumer Marketing, Direct Response Marketing, Sales Promotion

Tess Doughty *(Mng Dir)*
Steve Crawford *(Exec Dir-Creative)*
Craig Bailey *(Dir-Creative)*
Murray Bransgrove *(Dir-Creative)*
Scott Smith *(Dir-Creative)*
Emily Somers *(Dir-Art)*
Ryan Najelski *(Copywriter)*
Ron Prince *(Designer-Digital)*
Adam Smith *(Copywriter)*

Accounts:
Australian Red Cross Blood Service
Australian Unity
PZ Cussons

Rapp New Zealand
(Formerly WOW Rapp New Zealand)
80 Greys Ave Level 2, Auckland, 1010 New Zealand
Mailing Address:
PO Box 1872, Auckland, New Zealand
Tel.: (64) 93541376
Fax: (64) 9 306 0974
Web Site: rapp.co.nz

Employees: 45

Agency Specializes In: Consumer Marketing, Direct Response Marketing, Sales Promotion

Claudia MacDonald *(Mng Partner)*
Robert Limb *(Mng Dir)*
Jake Siddall *(Dir-Art)*
Tim Wood *(Dir-Creative)*
Harriet Arbuckle *(Acct Exec)*
Sokpart Pao *(Copywriter)*

Accounts:
AMI Insurance
Auckland City Mission
Bendon Lingerie
Fairfax Sundays Newspapers
Freedom Air
Hasbro
Hutchwilco
HWI
Kraft Foods Chocolates
Lion Nathan Wines
Mother Earth Foods
New World
Nokia
Phillips Electronics
Sky TV
Stihl
Wattie's

Rapp Tokyo
3-1-1 Higashi-Ikebukuro, Tokyo, 150-0012 Japan
Tel.: (81) 3-5789-6060
Web Site: www.rapp.com

Agency Specializes In: Direct Response Marketing

Marc Kremer *(Gen Mgr)*
Mariya Sokolova *(Assoc Strategist)*

Europe

AID-Analyse Informatique de Donnees
4 Rue Henri le Sidamer, 78000 Versailles, France
Tel.: (33) 1 3923 9300
Fax: (33) 1 3923 9301
E-Mail: info@aid.fr
Web Site: www.aid.fr

Employees: 40
Year Founded: 1972

Agency Specializes In: Consumer Marketing, Direct Response Marketing

Anne Gayet *(Dir-Data Mining)*
Cindy Galpin *(Project Mgr-E-mailing & Web Mktg)*
Ana Meaude *(Key Acct Dir)*

Accounts:
Barclays
EDF
HP
Keolis
Martell
Peugeot
Renault
SCA
Sony Style
Zapa

Rapp Amsterdam
Prof WH Keesomlaan 4, 1183 DJ Amstelveen, Netherlands
Mailing Address:
PO Box 373, 1180 AJ Amstelveen, Netherlands
Tel.: (31) 20 406 5858
Fax: (31) 20 406 5850
E-Mail: info@rapp.nl
Web Site: www.rapp.com

E-Mail for Key Personnel:
Creative Dir.: gerard.teuben@rappcollins.nl

Employees: 35

Pieter Ottevanger *(Acct Dir)*
Guus Van Vorstenbosch *(Dir-Creative)*

Accounts:
Air France/KLM
Avero Achmea
DZV
Fifteen
IFAW Campaign: "The Elephant March"
KLM International
Nestle Purina Felix, Gourmet, Pet Food
Rabobank Netherlands Banking Products, Rabo Journal, Rabobank Company News, Varie; 1995
Randstad
Robeco Investment Products; 2000
Zilveren Kruis Achmea Health Insurance, ZK Active; 2000

Rapp Paris
55 Rue de Amsterdam, 75008 Paris, Cedex 08 France
Tel.: (33) 1 533 257 57
Fax: (33) 1 53 32 63 55
E-Mail: info@ddblive.com
Web Site: www.rapp.com

Employees: 100
Year Founded: 1972

Agency Specializes In: Direct Response Marketing

Antony Roy *(Dir-Strategies)*
Muriel Verger *(Dir-Comm-PR)*

Accounts:
Canal + Campaign: "The Great Embed"
Fairtrade
Sony Monolith, Playstation

WWAV
Stationsweg 2, Postbus 2024, 3445 AA Woerden, Netherlands
Tel.: (31) 348 435 930
Fax: (31) 348 435 939
E-Mail: info@wwav.nl
Web Site: www.wwav.nl

Employees: 35

Agency Specializes In: Consumer Marketing, Direct Response Marketing

Angelique Verkleij *(Partner & Dir)*
Marie-Claire De Waal *(partner)*
Martijn De Groot *(Dir-Art)*
Guido Liebregts *(Dir-Art)*
Erik van Benten *(Dir-Procurement & Quality)*
Heidi Marchal *(Sr Acct Mgr)*
Wike Van Dieen *(Sr Acct Mgr)*
Ard Lok *(Strategist-Acct)*
Peter Heinen *(Copywriter)*

Accounts:
Astma Fonds
Centraal Bureau Fondsenwerving
Cliniclowns
Dierenbescherming
Edukans
Evangelische OmroepStichting AAP
ICCO
KWF
Kerkinactie
Natuurmonumenten
Oxfam Novib
Samenwerkende Hulporganisaties SHO
Stop AIDS Now!
Vluchtelingenwerk
Vogelbescherming

RARE
(Acquired & Absorbed by Arcane)

RATTLE ADVERTISING
16 Broadway, Beverly, MA 01915-4457
Tel.: (978) 998-7890
Fax: (978) 998-7880
E-Mail: info@rattlethemarket.com
Web Site: www.rattlethemarket.com

Employees: 10
Year Founded: 2001

Agency Specializes In: Bilingual Market, Brand Development & Integration, Broadcast, Business-To-Business, Cable T.V., Children's Market, Co-op Advertising, Collateral, Communications,

Consulting, Consumer Marketing, Consumer Publications, Corporate Communications, Corporate Identity, Digital/Interactive, Direct Response Marketing, E-Commerce, Education, Electronic Media, Entertainment, Exhibit/Trade Shows, Fashion/Apparel, Financial, Food Service, Government/Political, Graphic Design, Health Care Services, High Technology, In-Store Advertising, Information Technology, Internet/Web Design, Leisure, Local Marketing, Logo & Package Design, Magazines, Media Buying Services, Medical Products, New Product Development, Newspaper, Newspapers & Magazines, Out-of-Home Media, Outdoor, Planning & Consultation, Point of Purchase, Point of Sale, Print, Production, Public Relations, Publicity/Promotions, Radio, Real Estate, Restaurant, Retail, Sales Promotion, Strategic Planning/Research, T.V., Technical Advertising, Trade & Consumer Magazines, Transportation, Travel & Tourism

Sally Murphy *(Owner)*

Accounts:
Boston Harbor Cruises; Boston, MA Codzilla Thrill Boat Ride; 2007
Boston Main Streets Foundation
BTS Asset Management; Lexington, MA (Agency of Record) Corporate Identity, Marketing, Rebranding
Enterprise Bancorp Rewards Checking
Fairmont Copley Plaza Hotel; 2003
Giant Screen Cinema Association
Giant Screen Films
The Kittery Outlets
Kittery Trading Post
LEGO KidsFest
Peabody Essex Museum
Samuels & Associates; Boston, MA Real Estate; 2005
Signature Healthcare Beth Israel Deaconess Medical Center, Broadcast, Lead Agency, Media Buying, Media Planning, Online, Outdoor, Print
Wise Construction
York Hospital; ME; 2003

RAWLE MURDY ASSOCIATES, INC.
960 Morrison Dr, Charleston, SC 29403
Mailing Address:
PO Box 1117, Charleston, SC 29402-1117
Tel.: (843) 577-7327
E-Mail: contact@rawlemurdy.com
Web Site: www.rawlemurdy.com

Employees: 22
Year Founded: 1975

National Agency Associations: Second Wind Limited

Agency Specializes In: Above-the-Line, Advertising, Advertising Specialties, Affiliate Marketing, Affluent Market, African-American Market, Agriculture, Alternative Advertising, Arts, Asian Market, Automotive, Aviation & Aerospace, Below-the-Line, Bilingual Market, Brand Development & Integration, Branded Entertainment, Broadcast, Business Publications, Business-To-Business, Cable T.V., Catalogs, Children's Market, Co-op Advertising, Collateral, College, Commercial Photography, Communications, Computers & Software, Consulting, Consumer Goods, Consumer Marketing, Consumer Publications, Content, Corporate Communications, Corporate Identity, Cosmetics, Crisis Communications, Custom Publishing, Customer Relationship Management, Digital/Interactive, Direct Response Marketing, Direct-to-Consumer, E-Commerce, Education, Electronic Media, Electronics, Email, Engineering, Entertainment, Environmental, Event Planning & Marketing, Exhibit/Trade Shows, Experience Design, Faith Based, Fashion/Apparel, Financial, Food Service, Game Integration, Gay & Lesbian Market, Government/Political, Graphic Design, Guerilla Marketing, Health Care Services, High Technology, Hispanic Market, Hospitality, Household Goods, Identity Marketing, In-Store Advertising, Industrial, Infomercials, Information Technology, Integrated Marketing, International, Internet/Web Design, Investor Relations, Legal Services, Leisure, Local Marketing, Logo & Package Design, Luxury Products, Magazines, Marine, Market Research, Media Buying Services, Media Planning, Media Relations, Media Training, Medical Products, Men's Market, Merchandising, Mobile Marketing, Multicultural, Multimedia, New Product Development, New Technologies, Newspaper, Newspapers & Magazines, Out-of-Home Media, Outdoor, Over-50 Market, Package Design, Paid Searches, Pets , Pharmaceutical, Planning & Consultation, Podcasting, Point of Purchase, Point of Sale, Print, Product Placement, Production, Production (Ad, Film, Broadcast), Production (Print), Promotions, Public Relations, Publicity/Promotions, Publishing, RSS (Really Simple Syndication), Radio, Real Estate, Recruitment, Regional, Restaurant, Retail, Sales Promotion, Search Engine Optimization, Seniors' Market, Social Marketing/Nonprofit, Social Media, South Asian Market, Sponsorship, Sports Market, Stakeholders, Strategic Planning/Research, Sweepstakes, Syndication, T.V., Technical Advertising, Teen Market, Telemarketing, Trade & Consumer Magazines, Transportation, Travel & Tourism, Tween Market, Urban Market, Viral/Buzz/Word of Mouth, Web (Banner Ads, Pop-ups, etc.), Women's Market, Yellow Pages Advertising

Bruce D. Murdy *(Pres)*
Sandy Corson *(VP & Dir-Fin & Admin)*
Michele Crull *(VP & Dir-Mktg & Ops)*
John Kautz *(VP & Dir-Brand Leadership)*
Lindsey Miller *(Acct Supvr)*

Accounts:
Big Canoe
CARTA (Charleston Area Regional Transportation Authority); 1999
The Ford Plantation
Lennar Charleston
Lennar Charlotte
Melrose Resort
Patriot's Point Development Authority; Mt. Pleasant, SC; 2005
Questis Portfolio Partners, LLC
The Reserve at Lake Keowee
South Carolina State Ports Authority; Charleston, SC Container & Break Bulk Port Services
Terminix Services
The Virginian

RB OPPENHEIM ASSOCIATES + DIGITAL OPPS
2040 Delta Way, Tallahassee, FL 32303
Tel.: (850) 386-9100
Fax: (850) 386-4396
Web Site: www.rboa.com

Agency Specializes In: Advertising, Brand Development & Integration, Digital/Interactive, Graphic Design, Media Buying Services, Media Relations, Print, Public Relations, Search Engine Optimization

Rick Oppenheim *(CEO)*
Gabrielle Shaiman *(Acct Exec)*

Accounts:
New-Smashburger

RBMM
7007 Twin Hills Ave Ste 200, Dallas, TX 75231
Tel.: (214) 987-6500
Fax: (214) 987-3662
Web Site: rbmm.com

Employees: 25
Year Founded: 1979

Agency Specializes In: Advertising, Arts, Brand Development & Integration, Business Publications, Business-To-Business, Catalogs, Collateral, College, Commercial Photography, Computers & Software, Consumer Goods, Consumer Marketing, Corporate Communications, Corporate Identity, Cosmetics, Digital/Interactive, Direct Response Marketing, Direct-to-Consumer, Education, Electronic Media, Email, Entertainment, Environmental, Exhibit/Trade Shows, Food Service, Graphic Design, Health Care Services, Hospitality, Identity Marketing, In-Store Advertising, Information Technology, Integrated Marketing, Logo & Package Design, Luxury Products, Medical Products, New Product Development, Package Design, Planning & Consultation, Point of Purchase, Point of Sale, Print, Production (Print), Real Estate, Restaurant, Retail

Approx. Annual Billings: $20,000,000

Brian Boyd *(Principal)*
Steve Gibbs *(Principal)*
Stan Richards *(Principal)*
Yvette Wheeler *(Principal)*
Jeff Barfoot *(Mng Principal)*
Philip Smith *(Principal Designer)*

Accounts:
Atmos Energy Corporation; Dallas, TX; 2002
Auntie Annes
Austin College; Sherman, TX; 2008
Baylor Health Care System; Dallas, TX; 2003
Dr. Pepper Bottling; Irving, TX; 2001
Dresser Incorporated; Addison, TX; 2008
ExxonMobil; Dallas, TX; 2004
Freddy's Frozen Custard; Wichita, KS; 2009
G.P. Putnam Sons; New York, NY Publisher; 1992
Greyhound
The Home Depot; Atlanta, GA; 1994
Nokia; Irving, TX; 1997
NRG Energy, Inc.; 2001
Texas A&M; Bryan, TX; 2006
UCLA Health Systems
Wake Forest University; Winston-Salem, NC; 2008
Zeno

RCI
550 Heritage Dr Ste 200, Jupiter, FL 33458
Tel.: (561) 686-6800
Fax: (561) 686-8043
Web Site: www.rcirecruitmentsolutions.com

Employees: 90
Year Founded: 1985

Agency Specializes In: Communications, Publicity/Promotions, Recruitment

Approx. Annual Billings: $11,700,000

Michael C. Moore *(Chm & CEO)*
Pat Matarese *(Pres, CFO & Dir)*
Aaron Greider *(VP-Sls)*
Samantha Moore *(VP-Client Svcs)*
Tonya Greene *(Dir-Natl Recruitment)*
Melody Storms *(Dir-Strategic Plng & Dev)*
Maryanna Choinski *(Mgr-Production)*
Ashleigh Roth *(Mgr-Direct Sourcing)*

Accounts:
Adidas Group
Daiichi Sankyo
EMBARQ
The Fresh Market
NSK Steering Systems
Sprint

University of Massachusetts Lowell; Lowell, MA
Continuing Education
Verizon
ZEP Industries

RCP MARKETING
(d/b/a Rc Video And Audio;Source One Signs)
(Private-Parent-Single Location)
1756 Lakeshore Dr, Muskegon, MI 49441
Tel.: (231) 759-3160
Fax: (231) 755-5569
Web Site: www.rcpmarketing.com

Employees: 30
Year Founded: 1981

Agency Specializes In: Advertising, Logo & Package Design, Media Planning, Social Media

Revenue: $6,400,000

Amy Atkinson *(Pres)*
Randy Crow *(CEO)*
Tim Achterhoff *(VP)*
Jane Savidge *(VP)*
Michael Davis *(Dir-Web & Interactive)*
Nicole Oquist *(Dir-Design)*
Jon Baarda *(Sr Acct Mgr)*
Carly Crow *(Acct Mgr)*
Melissa Blackmer *(Acct Coord)*
Katie Schneider *(Acct Coord)*

Accounts:
MS Metal Solutions

RDA INTERNATIONAL
100 Vandam St 1st Fl, New York, NY 10013
Tel.: (212) 255-7700
E-Mail: info@rdai.com
Web Site: www.rdai.com

Employees: 64

Agency Specializes In: Advertising, Brand Development & Integration, Communications, Consumer Goods, Cosmetics, Customer Relationship Management, Digital/Interactive, Entertainment, Hospitality, Integrated Marketing, Internet/Web Design, Leisure, Logo & Package Design, Luxury Products, Media Planning, Multimedia, New Technologies, Print, Production, Sponsorship, Strategic Planning/Research, Viral/Buzz/Word of Mouth

Approx. Annual Billings: $80,000,000

Michael Racz *(CEO & Principal)*
Kate List *(Acct Dir)*
Jennifer Murphy *(Acct Dir)*
Anthony Bagliani *(Dir-Creative)*
Joshua Borden *(Dir-Art)*
Elena Drobova *(Dir-Creative)*
Mara Erickson *(Acct Supvr)*
Allison Stern *(Acct Supvr)*
Molly Thomas *(Acct Exec)*
Andres Foldvari *(Copywriter)*
Jessica Galoforo *(Sr Media Planner)*

Accounts:
Sony Electronics; 1999

RDG ADVERTISING
6655 S Tenaya Way Ste 200, Las Vegas, NV 89113
Tel.: (702) 367-3649
E-Mail: info@rdglv.com
Web Site: www.rdglv.com

Agency Specializes In: Advertising, Brand Development & Integration, Event Planning & Marketing, Graphic Design, Internet/Web Design, Media Training, Public Relations

Angelo Ramirez *(Pres)*
Paula Cleveland *(Acct Svcs Dir)*

Accounts:
MGM Grand Hotel, LLC

RDW GROUP INC.
125 Holden St, Providence, RI 02908-4919
Tel.: (401) 521-2700
Fax: (401) 521-0014
E-Mail: info@rdwgroup.com
Web Site: www.rdwgroup.com

E-Mail for Key Personnel:
President: jpontarelli@rdwgroup.com
Creative Dir.: jpatch@rdwgroup.com
Media Dir.: mpinto@rdwgroup.com

Employees: 140
Year Founded: 1986

Agency Specializes In: Advertising, Advertising Specialties, Aviation & Aerospace, Brand Development & Integration, Broadcast, Business Publications, Business-To-Business, Cable T.V., Collateral, Commercial Photography, Communications, Consulting, Consumer Marketing, Consumer Publications, Corporate Identity, Digital/Interactive, Direct Response Marketing, E-Commerce, Environmental, Event Planning & Marketing, Exhibit/Trade Shows, Food Service, Government/Political, Graphic Design, Health Care Services, High Technology, Industrial, Internet/Web Design, Logo & Package Design, Magazines, Media Buying Services, Medical Products, Multimedia, New Product Development, Newspaper, Newspapers & Magazines, Outdoor, Pharmaceutical, Planning & Consultation, Print, Production, Public Relations, Publicity/Promotions, Radio, Real Estate, Recruitment, Sales Promotion, Sports Market, Strategic Planning/Research, Sweepstakes, T.V., Technical Advertising, Trade & Consumer Magazines, Travel & Tourism

Approx. Annual Billings: $117,000,000 Capitalized

Breakdown of Gross Billings by Media: Brdcst.: $1,170,000; Cable T.V.: $2,340,000; Collateral: $17,550,000; Fees: $10,530,000; Network T.V.: $8,190,000; Newsp.: $18,720,000; Outdoor: $2,340,000; Production: $19,890,000; Pub. Rels.: $8,190,000; Spot Radio: $9,360,000; Spot T.V.: $4,680,000; Trade & Consumer Mags.: $11,700,000; Trade Shows: $1,170,000; Worldwide Web Sites: $1,170,000

Jay G. Conway *(Partner & Sr VP)*
Philip Loscoe, Jr. *(Partner & Sr VP)*
Martha Lindman *(Partner & Art Dir)*
Dante Bellini, Jr. *(Exec VP)*
Angela Yang *(VP-Social Media & Strategy)*
Jeffrey Patch *(Exec Dir-Creative)*
Marla Pinto *(Dir-Media)*
Claudette Coyne *(Assoc Dir-Media)*
Will Andersen *(Acct Mgr)*
Tara Bonvehi *(Mgr-Digital Production)*
Robert Forcino *(Mgr-Production)*
Kaitlyn Delaney *(Coord-Social Media)*

Accounts:
Blue Cross/Blue Shield of Rhode Island; 1998
Cornell University Johnson School
Eversource
Harvard University MBA Program
Honeywell Safety Products
The International Monetary Fund
Oxford University Press
The World Bank

Branches

RDW Group, Inc.
32 Franklin St, Worcester, MA 01608-1900
Tel.: (401) 521-2700
Fax: (508) 755-3059
E-Mail: info@rdwgroup.com
Web Site: www.rdwgroup.com

Employees: 10
Year Founded: 1986

Agency Specializes In: Advertising, Advertising Specialties, Aviation & Aerospace, Brand Development & Integration, Broadcast, Business Publications, Business-To-Business, Cable T.V., Collateral, Commercial Photography, Communications, Consulting, Consumer Marketing, Corporate Identity, Digital/Interactive, Direct Response Marketing, E-Commerce, Environmental, Event Planning & Marketing, Exhibit/Trade Shows, Food Service, Government/Political, Graphic Design, Health Care Services, High Technology, Industrial, Internet/Web Design, Logo & Package Design, Magazines, Media Buying Services, Medical Products, Multimedia, New Product Development, Newspaper, Newspapers & Magazines, Outdoor, Pharmaceutical, Planning & Consultation, Print, Production, Public Relations, Publicity/Promotions, Radio, Real Estate, Recruitment, Sales Promotion, Sports Market, Strategic Planning/Research, Sweepstakes, T.V., Technical Advertising, Trade & Consumer Magazines, Travel & Tourism

Alen Yen *(Pres, Partner & Dir-Creative)*
Jay Conway *(Partner & Sr VP)*
Phil Loscoe *(Partner & Sr VP)*
Dave Monti *(Partner & Sr VP)*
Sarah Johnson *(Dir-Social Media)*
Marla Pinto *(Dir-Media)*
Dee Dee Edmondson *(Sr Acct Exec-PR)*
Elizabeth Sweitzer *(Acct Exec)*

Accounts:
The Colleges of Worcester Consortium
MCLE (Massachusetts Continuing Legal Education Assoc.)
Old Sturbridge Village
Rhode Island Builders Assoc

REA MEDIA GROUP
423 E 9th St, Tucson, AZ 85705
Tel.: (520) 622-2190
Web Site: www.reamediagroup.com

Agency Specializes In: Advertising, Brand Development & Integration, Internet/Web Design, Media Buying Services, Media Planning, Outdoor, Print, Public Relations, Radio

Raul Aguirre *(Pres & CEO)*
Marisol Flores-Aguirre *(Dir-Media & Promos)*

Accounts:
Donate Life

REACH + ACQUIRE
(Formerly Jonsson Media Group)
16485 Laguna Canyon Rd, Ste 110, Irvine, CA 92618
Tel.: (949) 682-9829
Web Site: www.reachandacquire.com

Year Founded: 2011

Agency Specializes In: Advertising, Content, Digital/Interactive, Internet/Web Design, Media Planning, Social Media, Strategic Planning/Research

Cameron Jonsson *(Founder & CEO)*
Kelly Hoang *(Controller)*

Brianna Jonsson *(Dir-Mktg)*
Jarred Romley *(Dir-Content Strategy & Design)*
Neil Spencer *(Strategist-Content)*
Keith Born *(Analyst-Performance Media)*
Saish Kotecha *(Jr Designer)*

Accounts:
Neon Carrot Events

READY SET ROCKET
636 Broadway Ste 1200, New York, NY 10012
Tel.: (212) 260-2636
E-Mail: info@readysetrocket.com
Web Site: www.readysetrocket.com

Employees: 30
Year Founded: 2009

Agency Specializes In: Advertising, Digital/Interactive, Electronic Media, Email, Experience Design, Internet/Web Design, Mobile Marketing, Multimedia, Paid Searches, Point of Purchase, Point of Sale, Production, Search Engine Optimization, Social Media, Strategic Planning/Research

Approx. Annual Billings: $5,000,000

Aaron Harvey *(Co-Founder & Partner)*
Lauren Nutt Bello *(Partner & VP-Client Svcs)*
Jonelle Chandler *(Dir-UX Art & Producer)*
Gareth Price *(Dir-Technical)*
Cole Sletten *(Assoc Dir-Creative)*
Kitty Tsang *(Mgr-Digital Mktg)*
Peter Lacerenza *(Jr Copywriter)*

Accounts:
New-Accion
New-Ann Taylor
New-Deutsche Bank Deutsche Asset & Wealth Management
New-Diesel
New-Edison Properties Manhattan Mini Storage
New-Hugo Neu Flex Spaces at Kearny Point
New-Johnson & Johnson Tylenol
New-J.P. Morgan
Kenneth Cole Productions, Inc. Banner, Campaign: "Man Up for Mankind", Mankind, Media, Strategy
New-Live Nation
New-Marriott
New-Meredith Corporation
New-Michael Kors
New-Parlux Jay Z Gold, Nude by Rihanna
New-Perfumania
New-Seagram's Gin
New-Univision

READY366
33 E 17th St Union Sq, New York, NY 10003
Tel.: (212) 488-5366
Fax: (212) 228-2474
E-Mail: newday@ready366.com
Web Site: www.ready366.com

Employees: 20

Agency Specializes In: Brand Development & Integration, Environmental, Graphic Design, Industrial, Package Design, Strategic Planning/Research

Susan Palombo *(Founder & Pres)*
Kate Burgess *(Dir-Strategy)*
John Witherow *(Dir-Creative)*
Mary Salazar-Toth *(Mgr-Client)*
Justin Gamero *(Sr Strategist-Client)*
Anna Marmorstein *(Strategist-Client & Social Media)*
Alex Azzi *(Designer)*
Marissa Caputo *(Designer)*
Raymond Mawst *(Jr Designer)*

Accounts:
Cegadim Dendrite
Coca-Cola Refreshments USA, Inc.
Diageo
Frito Lay
Hershey's; Hershey, PA
Intel
LEE
Novartis; Basel, Switzerland
Pfizer
Zyrtec

REAL BRANDING LLC
(Name Changed to Anthem Worldwide)

REAL FRESH CREATIVE
8600 Foundry St, Savage, MD 20763
Tel.: (301) 604-1444
Fax: (410) 497-1103
E-Mail: projects@realfreshcreative.com
Web Site: www.realfreshcreative.com

Agency Specializes In: Advertising, Graphic Design, Internet/Web Design, Logo & Package Design, Print

Kayle Tucker Simon *(Owner)*

Accounts:
Conscious Corner
Home Box Office, Inc. Treme
Roots Market

REAL INTEGRATED
(Formerly Solomon Friedman Advertising)
40900 Woodward Ave Ste 300, Bloomfield Hills, MI 48304-2256
Tel.: (248) 540-0660
Fax: (248) 540-2124
Web Site: realintegrated.com/

E-Mail for Key Personnel:
Media Dir.: susanne@realintegrated.com

Employees: 45
Year Founded: 1954

Agency Specializes In: African-American Market, Automotive, Business-To-Business, Cable T.V., Co-op Advertising, Collateral, Consulting, Consumer Marketing, Consumer Publications, Corporate Identity, Entertainment, Financial, Food Service, Internet/Web Design, Logo & Package Design, Magazines, Media Buying Services, Newspaper, Outdoor, Point of Purchase, Point of Sale, Print, Public Relations, Publicity/Promotions, Radio, Retail, Sales Promotion, Sports Market, Strategic Planning/Research, T.V., Telemarketing, Transportation

Approx. Annual Billings: $33,270,000

Breakdown of Gross Billings by Media: Mags.: $332,700; Newsp.: $20,295,800; Other: $997,000; Radio: $5,655,900; T.V.: $5,988,600

John Ozdych *(Pres & Dir-Creative)*
Lisa Anderson *(CFO)*
Roger Honet *(Pres-Co-op Svcs)*
Deanna Deshaw *(Dir-Production)*
Susanne Schumacher *(Dir-Integrated Media)*
Ron Lee *(Assoc Dir-Creative & Copywriter)*
Matt Totsky *(Assoc Dir-Creative)*
Denise Nasierowski *(Sr Acct Exec)*
Eric Jagoda *(Specialist-Digital Media)*
Brandon Moner *(Designer-UI & Web)*
Connor Artman *(Team Head-Digital)*
Rachel Mortensen *(Assoc Producer)*
Ryan Peck *(Team Head-Social Media)*

Accounts:
The Henry Ford
KFC Dealer Groups 13 Co-Ops
MGM Grand Detroit
Michigan Opera Theatre
North American Bancard
University of Michigan - Dearborn

REAL PIE MEDIA
280 S Beverly Dr Ste 300, Beverly Hills, CA 90212
Tel.: (310) 385-0500
Web Site: www.realpie.com

Agency Specializes In: Advertising, Brand Development & Integration, Digital/Interactive, Internet/Web Design, Social Media

Kirk Skodis *(Founder & Dir-Creative)*
Rob Flemming *(Exec VP-Digital Mktg)*
Robin Kapustin *(Dir-Interactive Art)*

REALITY2 LLC
11661 San Vicente Blvd Ste 900, Los Angeles, CA 90049
Tel.: (310) 826-5662
Fax: (310) 826-5606
E-Mail: farida@reality2.com
Web Site: www.reality2.com

E-Mail for Key Personnel:
President: farida@reality2.com
Creative Dir.: jorge@reality2.com

Employees: 10
Year Founded: 1976

National Agency Associations: THINKLA

Agency Specializes In: Brand Development & Integration, Business-To-Business, Collateral, Communications, Consumer Marketing, Direct Response Marketing, E-Commerce, Entertainment, Hispanic Market, Internet/Web Design, Logo & Package Design, Point of Purchase, Strategic Planning/Research

Approx. Annual Billings: $5,000,000

Breakdown of Gross Billings by Media: Collateral: $1,500,000; Print: $2,000,000; Radio & T.V.: $500,000; Worldwide Web Sites: $1,000,000

Farida Fotouhi *(Pres)*
Jorge Alonso *(Partner)*
Cesar Martin *(Dir-Digital & Print Production)*

Accounts:
AccessIT Digital Cinema; 2005
First Federal Bank
Gerawan Farms
iDcentrix; El Segundo, CA Security Technology; 2006
Jarrin Printing
Larta; Los Angeles, CA Technology Services; 2003
Pavement Recycling Systems; Riverside, CA; 2007
Peninsula Hotel
Point Research Corporation
SNL Financial

REALLY GOOD COPY CO.
92 Moseley Ter, Glastonbury, CT 06033-3714
Tel.: (860) 659-9487
Fax: (860) 659-9487
E-Mail: copyqueen@aol.com
Web Site: www.reallygoodcopy.com

E-Mail for Key Personnel:
President: copyqueen@aol.com

Employees: 2
Year Founded: 1981

Agency Specializes In: Advertising, Broadcast, Business-To-Business, Catalogs, Collateral,

Consumer Marketing, Corporate Communications, Direct Response Marketing, Direct-to-Consumer, Health Care Services, Industrial, Over-50 Market, Point of Purchase, Promotions, Public Relations, Publicity/Promotions, Viral/Buzz/Word of Mouth

Donna Donovan *(Pres)*

Accounts:
American Aerospace Corp. Aerospace Subcontractor; 2008
Danbury Hospital Joint Replacement Ctr Medical
Guardair Corp. Industrial Maintenance Products; 2013
The Hartford Insurance Group Financial Products/Services
Lighthouse Depot Mail Order Catalog; 2009
National Living Organ Donors Foundation nonprofit; 2013
Plow & Hearth Mail Order Catalog

REALM ADVERTISING
Palisades Office Park 5901 Peachtree Dunwoody Rd Ste A550, Atlanta, GA 30328
Tel.: (404) 255-5811
Fax: (404) 255-5828
E-Mail: info@realmco.com
Web Site: realmco.com

Employees: 20

Agency Specializes In: Advertising, Brand Development & Integration, Event Planning & Marketing, Strategic Planning/Research

Jeff Gray *(Owner)*
Jeff Chasten *(Pres & Mng Partner)*
Linda Ross *(Partner)*
Michael Stewart *(Partner-Client Svcs)*
Chuck Allen *(VP & Dir-Change Comm)*
Eric Berrios *(VP-Client Svcs)*
Jim Marion *(Copywriter)*

Accounts:
Chick-fil-A
Cox Enterprises
Fiesta Gas Grills
Georgia Ports Authority
Novelis
UPS

REALTIME MARKETING GROUP
61 SE 4th Ave, Delray Beach, FL 33483
Tel.: (561) 450-6966
Web Site: www.realtimemg.com

Year Founded: 2009

Agency Specializes In: Advertising, Search Engine Optimization, Social Media, Technical Advertising

Terra Spero *(Founder & Mng Partner)*
Tom Spero *(Mng Partner)*
Irin Akter *(Dir-Creative)*

Accounts:
Core Institute
Cut 432
Frankel & Cohen, LLC
JCD Sports Group
Lavish Nail Spa; Wilton Manors, FL
Pompano Beach CRA Digital Branding, Social Strategy
Rosin Eyecare
Zavee

REALTIME MEDIA, INC.
40 Morris Ave Ste 300, Bryn Mawr, PA 19010-3300
Tel.: (484) 385-2900
Fax: (610) 337-2300
E-Mail: rtmcontact@rtm.com
Web Site: www.rtm.com

Employees: 30
Year Founded: 1993

Agency Specializes In: Advertising, Business-To-Business, Consumer Marketing, Digital/Interactive, Direct Response Marketing, Internet/Web Design, Publicity/Promotions, Sales Promotion, Sweepstakes

Approx. Annual Billings: $7,500,000

Tara Armstrong *(Sr VP-Ops)*
Toby Bodner *(Dir-Strategy & Bus Dev)*
Amy Sullivan *(Dir-Project Mgmt)*
Maura Klondar *(Acct Exec-Digital)*
Logan J. McGee *(Jr Designer)*

Accounts:
Allergan
AOL, LLC
AstraZeneca
AT&T Communications Corp.
Casio
Circuit City
ESPN
Garnier
GlaxoSmithKline
Harper Collins
Home Depot
Lipton
MasterCard
Maybelline
National Geographic
NBA
Old Navy
Philadelphia Eagles
Smirnoff
Sony
United States Postal Service

REALWORLD MARKETING
8098 N Via De Nogocio, Scottsdale, AZ 85258
Tel.: (480) 296-0160
Web Site: realworldinc.com

Agency Specializes In: Automotive, Brand Development & Integration, Broadcast, Digital/Interactive, Media Buying Services, Print, Production (Ad, Film, Broadcast)

Jay Wilson *(Chm & CEO)*
Leah Wilson *(Pres)*
Syringa Ortega *(VP-Client Svcs)*
Matt Page *(Editor-Video & Designer-Motion)*
Ginny Michaelson *(Dir-Media & Acct Exec)*
Jenny Lang *(Dir-Bus Dev)*
Jenni Ryan *(Dir-Ops)*
Jennifer Delatorre *(Mgr-Traffic)*
Andrew Cranmer *(Sr Specialist-Paid Media)*

Accounts:
Honda

REARVIEW
PO Box 440518, Kennesaw, GA 30160
Tel.: (678) 574-7261
Fax: (678) 574-7258
E-Mail: contact@rvadv.com
Web Site: www.rvadv.com

Employees: 10
Year Founded: 1998

Agency Specializes In: Advertising, Affluent Market, Arts, Brand Development & Integration, Broadcast, Business-To-Business, Collateral, Consumer Marketing, Corporate Communications, Cosmetics, Customer Relationship Management, Digital/Interactive, E-Commerce, Email, Environmental, Event Planning & Marketing, Exhibit/Trade Shows, Gay & Lesbian Market, Graphic Design, High Technology, In-Store Advertising, Integrated Marketing, Internet/Web Design, Leisure, Local Marketing, Logo & Package Design, Luxury Products, Magazines, Media Planning, Multimedia, Newspaper, Newspapers & Magazines, Out-of-Home Media, Outdoor, Over-50 Market, Package Design, Paid Searches, Point of Purchase, Print, Production (Ad, Film, Broadcast), Real Estate, Regional, Restaurant, Sales Promotion, Search Engine Optimization, Seniors' Market, Trade & Consumer Magazines, Travel & Tourism, Web (Banner Ads, Pop-ups, etc.), Women's Market, Yellow Pages Advertising

Approx. Annual Billings: $1,750,000

Breakdown of Gross Billings by Media: Graphic Design: 20%; Local Mktg.: 20%; Logo & Package Design: 20%; Print: 20%; Worldwide Web Sites: 20%

Alex Danaila *(Mng Partner)*
Jennifer Papadatos *(Mng Partner)*
Nick Mracek *(Sr Designer)*

Accounts:
Ashton Woods Homes; 2006
HomeAid Atlanta; Atlanta, GA Charity; 2006
Manheim Drive

REASON PARTNERS, INC.
2 Berkeley St Ste 304, Toronto, ON M5A 4J5 Canada
Tel.: (416) 929-9190
Fax: (415) 929-7923
Web Site: reasonpartners.com/

Year Founded: 1987

Peter Holmes *(CEO & Dir-Creative)*

Accounts:
Canada Trust
Credit Canada Campaign: "Get Out From Under", Print Ads
George Richards
Krinos Foods
Nettlemax
Second Cup Coffee Co.
The Weather Network

REBEL INDUSTRIES
10573 Pico Blvd #290, Los Angeles, CA 90064
Tel.: (323) 833-8378
Fax: (509) 692-1523
E-Mail: info@rebelindustries.com
Web Site: www.rebelindustries.com

Employees: 7
Year Founded: 1999

Agency Specializes In: Affluent Market, Alternative Advertising, Automotive, Below-the-Line, Brand Development & Integration, Branded Entertainment, Collateral, College, Consulting, Consumer Marketing, Content, Corporate Identity, Custom Publishing, Digital/Interactive, Entertainment, Event Planning & Marketing, Experience Design, Fashion/Apparel, Food Service, Graphic Design, Guerilla Marketing, Integrated Marketing, Internet/Web Design, Local Marketing, Luxury Products, Men's Market, Mobile Marketing, Multicultural, New Technologies, Promotions, Publishing, Sponsorship, Teen Market, Urban Market, Viral/Buzz/Word of Mouth

Revenue: $5,000,000

Josh Levine *(Founder & CEO)*
Rose Chhun *(Mgr-Experiential Mktg)*

Cassandra Santana *(Mgr-Social Media)*
Mark Faicol *(Acct Exec)*

Accounts:
Absolut
Dr. Pepper
E. & J. Gallo Winery Experiential, Shellback Rum
EA Sports
ESPN The Magazine
FIJI Water
MGM Studios
Piedmont Distillers Experiential, Junior Johnson's Midnight Moon Moonshine
Reebok
Warner Bros

REBRANDERY
100 Hope St, Stamford, CT 6906
Tel.: (203) 633-4444
Fax: (203) 633-4444
E-Mail: hello@rebrandery.com
Web Site: www.rebrandery.com

Year Founded: 2013

Agency Specializes In: Advertising, Brand Development & Integration, Content, Digital/Interactive, Internet/Web Design, Search Engine Optimization, Strategic Planning/Research, T.V.

F. Robb Caster *(Chief Strategy Officer)*
Timothy Berger *(Dir-Internet Mktg)*
E. Seth Panman *(Dir-Video Production)*
Laurence Sheinman *(Dir-Digital Mktg)*

Accounts:
Adam Colberg

REBUILD NATION
2990 W Grand Blvd Ste 408, Detroit, MI 48202
Tel.: (855) 725-3628
E-Mail: info@rebuildnation.com
Web Site: www.rebuildnation.com

Year Founded: 2012

National Agency Associations: 4A's

Agency Specializes In: Advertising, Content, Event Planning & Marketing, Internet/Web Design, Media Buying Services, Search Engine Optimization

Joshua Gershonowicz *(Owner)*
Steve DeAngelis *(Partner & VP-Strategy)*
Laurie Blume *(Dir-Creative)*
Kari Ryan *(Dir-Social Media)*
Kobie Solomon *(Dir-Creative)*
Stephanie Potash *(Sr Acct Mgr)*
Pam Lenning *(Mgr-Primary Production)*
Noah Bakst *(Strategist-Bus)*

Accounts:
Downtown Royal Oak

RECESS CREATIVE LLC
635 W Lakeside Ave Ste 101, Cleveland, OH 44113
Tel.: (216) 400-7187
Fax: (216) 274-9196
Web Site: www.recesscreative.com

Agency Specializes In: Advertising, Brand Development & Integration, Content, Digital/Interactive, E-Commerce, Internet/Web Design, Media Buying Services, Media Planning, Search Engine Optimization, Social Media

Chris Jungjohann *(COO & Mng Partner)*
Tim Zeller *(Chief Creative Officer & Mng Partner)*
Chad Milburn *(Partner)*
A. J. Jimenez *(Art Dir)*
Grace Johnson *(Art Dir)*
Bill Karbler *(Acct Dir)*
Tony Pichotta *(Creative Dir)*
Annie Callahan *(Dir-Search)*
Kristin Ferguson *(Acct Exec)*
Angelina Rosati *(Acct Exec)*

Accounts:
Cub Cadet

RECRUITSAVVY
330 Franklin Tpke, Mahwah, NJ 07430
Tel.: (201) 529-2270
Fax: (201) 684-1156
E-Mail: inquires@recruitsavvy.com
Web Site: www.recruitsavvy.com

Employees: 16
Year Founded: 1996

Agency Specializes In: Advertising, Collateral, Consulting, Electronic Media, Newspaper, Recruitment

Approx. Annual Billings: $1,000,000

Breakdown of Gross Billings by Media: Internet Adv.: $200,000; Print: $800,000

Michael Wilder *(Pres)*
Melissa Gasparis *(Dir-Trng)*
Deborah Devries *(Acct Exec)*
Holly Goldin *(Acct Exec)*
Maureen Kayal *(Acct Exec)*
Michelle Londono *(Acct Exec)*
Ellen Murphy *(Acct Exec)*
Sylvia Reiss *(Acct Exec)*
Debi Dinucci *(Exec Recruiter)*
Donna Halvorsen *(Exec Recruiter)*
Suzanne Marotti *(Exec Recruiter)*

Accounts:
AXA Advisors
Boston Generating
Comprehensive Behavioral Healthcare
Eisai, Inc.
Geneva
Konica Minolta Business Solutions
State Farm Insurance Group
Teledyne LeCroy
United Rentals, Inc.

RED BROWN KLE
840 N Old World Third St Ste 401, Milwaukee, WI 53203
Tel.: (414) 272-2600
Fax: (414) 272-2690
Toll Free: (888) 725-2041
E-Mail: brown@redbrownkle.com
Web Site: www.redbrownkle.com

Employees: 7
Year Founded: 2000

National Agency Associations: 4A's

Agency Specializes In: Advertising, Business-To-Business, Consumer Marketing, Hospitality, Integrated Marketing, Leisure, Medical Products, Multicultural

Carl Brown *(Owner & Pres)*
Wade Kohlmann *(VP-Strategy & Client Svc)*
Lynn Schoenecker *(Sr Dir-Art)*
Brad Schultz *(Sr Dir-Art)*
Kurt Kleman *(Dir-Creative)*
Nicholas Shera *(Dir-Scientific Svcs & Medical Writing)*
Carrie Drzadinski *(Acct Supvr)*
Melanee Talsky *(Acct Supvr)*
Kristin Terpeza *(Sr Copywriter-Medical & Healthcare Mktg)*
Sarah Zweifel *(Acct Exec)*
Claire Ryan *(Coord-Production)*

Accounts:
Harley-Davidson; Milwaukee, WI

RED CIRCLE AGENCY
251 1st Ave N Ste 400, Minneapolis, MN 55401
Tel.: (612) 372-4612
E-Mail: info@redcircleagency.com
Web Site: www.redcircleagency.com

Agency Specializes In: Strategic Planning/Research

Chad Germann *(Founder, Pres & CEO)*
Angel Suarez *(Exec VP)*
Christy Kendall *(Dir-Creative)*
Bonn Banwell *(Dir-Creative)*
Tara Ezzell *(Dir-Casino Strategy)*
Deborah McPartland *(Dir-Media)*
John Schultz *(Dir-Digital Strategy)*
Dean Shavor *(Assoc Dir-Creative)*
Heidi Umhoefer *(Sr Acct Supvr)*
Andy McPartland *(Acct Exec)*

Accounts:
Chicken Ranch Casino
Fortune Bay Resort Casino
Grand Casino
Ho-Chunk Casinos
Kentucky Downs
Meskwaki Bingo Casino Hotel
Mille Lacs Band of Ojibwe
Red Lake Indian Tribe
Seven Clans Casino
Shoshone Rose Casino

RED CROW MARKETING INC.
1320 N Stewart, Springfield, MO 65802
Tel.: (417) 889-1658
Web Site: www.redcrowmarketing.com

Year Founded: 2004

Agency Specializes In: Advertising, Graphic Design, Internet/Web Design, Production (Ad, Film, Broadcast), Strategic Planning/Research

Ron Marshall *(Owner)*
Erin Goodman *(Media Buyer)*

Accounts:
Branson Creek Sports
Chesterfield Eye Works
Christian Health Care
Core
DOE Eat Place
Houlihans
Turner Reid
Tuscany

RED DELUXE BRAND DEVELOPMENT
85 Union Ave, Memphis, TN 38103
Tel.: (901) 522-9242
Fax: (901) 522-9890
E-Mail: engage@reddeluxe.com
Web Site: www.reddeluxe.com

Employees: 14
Year Founded: 2002

National Agency Associations: AAF

Agency Specializes In: Brand Development & Integration, Broadcast, Business-To-Business, Collateral, Communications, Consulting, Consumer Marketing, Consumer Publications, Corporate Communications, Corporate Identity, Digital/Interactive, Education, Financial,

Advertising Agencies

Government/Political, Graphic Design, Health Care Services, In-Store Advertising, Internet/Web Design, Leisure, Local Marketing, Logo & Package Design, Magazines, Media Buying Services, Medical Products, Newspaper, Newspapers & Magazines, Out-of-Home Media, Outdoor, Point of Sale, Print, Radio, Real Estate, Restaurant, Retail, Seniors' Market, Strategic Planning/Research, T.V., Trade & Consumer Magazines, Travel & Tourism

Stinson Liles *(Co-Founder & Principal)*
Martin Wilford *(Co-Founder & Principal)*
Kim Gurley *(Dir-Art)*
Sam Keasler *(Assoc Dir-Creative)*
Geri Holmes *(Office Mgr)*

Accounts:
American Lung Association; New York, NY Fighting for Air Campaign, Out-of-Home, Print, Public Service Announcement, Radio, Television
American Red Cross Africa Ads
The Elizabeth Glaser Pediatric AIDS Foundation Communications Strategy, Rebrand
NBA Grizzlies
Red Cross Brand Spot

RED DOOR INTERACTIVE, INC.

350 10th Ave Set 1100, San Diego, CA 92101
Tel.: (619) 398-2670
Fax: (619) 398-2671
E-Mail: dobiz@reddoor.biz
Web Site: www.reddoor.biz

E-Mail for Key Personnel:
President: rcarr@reddoor.biz

Employees: 60
Year Founded: 2002

National Agency Associations: PRSA

Agency Specializes In: Advertising, Business-To-Business, Communications, Consulting, Consumer Marketing, Cosmetics, Customer Relationship Management, Digital/Interactive, Direct Response Marketing, Direct-to-Consumer, E-Commerce, Electronic Media, Email, Information Technology, Internet/Web Design, Media Buying Services, Out-of-Home Media, Social Media, Strategic Planning/Research, Teen Market, Web (Banner Ads, Pop-ups, etc.)

Approx. Annual Billings: $14,000,000

Breakdown of Gross Billings by Media: Consulting: $1,000,000; Digital/Interactive: $2,000,000; E-Commerce: $1,000,000; Internet Adv.: $5,000,000; Plng. & Consultation: $1,000,000; Strategic Planning/Research: $1,000,000; Worldwide Web Sites: $3,000,000

Reid Carr *(Pres & CEO)*
Amy Carr *(Exec VP-HR)*
Dennis Gonzales *(VP-Ops)*
Erika Werner *(VP-Client Svcs)*
Andrew Batten *(Dir-Digital Analytics & Optimization)*
Patrick Cinco *(Dir-Creative)*
John Faris *(Dir-Cross Channel Mktg)*
Charles Wiedenhoft *(Dir-Strategy)*
Jordan Kasteler *(Sr Mgr-SEO)*
Nancy Cymerman *(Sr Copywriter-Interactive)*
Shannon Robinson *(Strategist-SEO)*
Justin Gabbert *(Analyst-Digital)*

Accounts:
Caldera Spas Email Marketing, Search Engine Optimization, Search Engine Marketing, Social Commerce
Charlotte Russe; San Diego, CA Charlotte Russe Social Media; 2009
CND Shellac
Cox Communications; San Diego, CA Broadband Cable Services; 2009
OneRoof Energy (Digital Agency of Record) Online Marketing, Strategic Planning
Overstock; Salt Lake City, UT e-tailer; 2008
Paychex Benefit Technologies; San Diego, CA Benetrac; 2003
Rubio's; San Diego, CA Fast-Casual Restaurant; 2005
Shea Homes; Walnut, CA New Homes; 2010
Souplantation & Sweet Tomatoes Restaurants
Sutter Home Winery
Zodiac Pool Care; Vista, CA Baracuda, Nature2, Polaris, Zodiac

RED DOT DESIGN, LLC

112 5th St W, Des Moines, IA 50265
Tel.: (515) 279-0712
E-Mail: info@reddotad.com
Web Site: www.reddotad.com

Agency Specializes In: Advertising, Brand Development & Integration, Collateral, Digital/Interactive, Graphic Design, Internet/Web Design, Print, Public Relations, Radio, Social Media, T.V.

Jason Ploog *(Principal)*
Todd Schatzberg *(Principal)*
Pam Gillaspey *(Dir-Strategy)*
Philip Schriver *(Designer)*

Accounts:
CoOpportunity Health
Splashlight

RED FLANNEL

218 Schanck Rd 2nd Fl, Freehold, NJ 07728
Tel.: (732) 761-8998
Fax: (732) 761-9424
E-Mail: request@redflannelgroup.com
Web Site: www.redflannelgroup.com

E-Mail for Key Personnel:
President: bob@redflannelgroup.com
Creative Dir.: jim@redflannelgroup.com

Employees: 6
Year Founded: 1984

Agency Specializes In: Advertising, Brand Development & Integration, Business Publications, Business-To-Business, Cable T.V., Collateral, College, Communications, Consulting, Consumer Marketing, Corporate Communications, Corporate Identity, Direct Response Marketing, E-Commerce, Education, Electronic Media, Event Planning & Marketing, Exhibit/Trade Shows, Financial, Graphic Design, Health Care Services, High Technology, In-Store Advertising, Industrial, Information Technology, Internet/Web Design, Investor Relations, Logo & Package Design, Magazines, Medical Products, New Product Development, Newspaper, Newspapers & Magazines, Outdoor, Package Design, Pharmaceutical, Planning & Consultation, Point of Purchase, Point of Sale, Print, Production, Production (Print), Promotions, Public Relations, Radio, Sales Promotion, Strategic Planning/Research, Trade & Consumer Magazines, Transportation

Approx. Annual Billings: $1,000,000

Breakdown of Gross Billings by Media: Graphic Design: $400,000; Logo & Package Design: $200,000; Newsp. & Mags.: $150,000; Plng. & Consultation: $50,000; Radio & T.V.: $200,000

Robert K. Flanagan *(Owner)*
James J. Redzinak *(VP & Dir-Creative)*
Christine Stanzione *(Dir-Mktg)*

Accounts:
Congoleum; Mercerville, NJ; 2003
Freehold Radiology; Freehold, NJ; 1998
Prudential; Newark, NJ; 1997
Technol; Eatontown, NJ; 2003

RED FUSE COMMUNICATIONS, INC.

3 Columbus Cir, New York, NY 10019
Tel.: (212) 210-3873
Web Site: www.redfuse.com

Agency Specializes In: Advertising, Brand Development & Integration, Digital/Interactive, Public Relations, Sponsorship

Stephen Forcione *(CEO)*
Frank Sicilia *(CIO)*
Les Levine *(CFO-Red Fuse Comm)*
Roger DiPasca *(Mng Dir-Shopper Comm-Global)*
Adam Konowitz *(Mng Dir-KC, Prague & Tokyo)*
Alice Dure *(Sr Partner & Head-Digital Practice)*
Ellen Pace *(Head-Client-Global)*
Gloria de la Guardia *(Exec Creative Dir)*
Randy Diaz *(Art Dir)*
Luis Garcia *(Client Svcs Dir-North America)*
Ashlea Noonan *(Acct Dir)*
Christine Rousseau *(Acct Dir-Global)*
Barbara Hamilton *(Dir-Creative-Global)*
Rosanne Johnson *(Dir-Digital)*
Mariana Warfield *(Dir-Digital Strategy-LATAM)*
Tracey Zimmerman *(Dir-Plng)*
Antonio Arias *(Assoc Dir-Creative)*
Lizbeth Cabal-Perez *(Mgr-Media Buying)*
Fernanda Giacomelli *(Acct Supvr)*
Jared Hall *(Supvr-Media)*
Justina Yeboah *(Supvr-Digital)*
Chris Konstantinidis *(Acct Exec-Global)*
Borja Eizmendi *(Copywriter)*
Jason Oke *(Reg Mng Dir-Asia)*
Esete Workneh *(Sr Media Planner)*

Accounts:
Colgate Palmolive Campaign: "Turning Packaging into Education", Colgate Total
The Speed Stick Handle It

RED HOT JOE

11700 Preston Rd Ste 660, Dallas, TX 75230-2710
Tel.: (214) 403-9412
E-Mail: info@redhotjoe.com
Web Site: www.redhotjoe.com

Year Founded: 2008

Agency Specializes In: Advertising, Digital/Interactive, Internet/Web Design, Radio, T.V.

Kristy Hutchins *(VP)*
Tim Hutchins *(Dir-Creative)*

RED HOUSE GROUP INC

(Name Changed to Able&Co)

RED HOUSE MEDIA LLC

1001 Kingwood St Studio 218, Brainerd, MN 56401
Tel.: (218) 454-3210
Web Site: www.redhousemedia.com

Year Founded: 2004

Agency Specializes In: Advertising, Brand Development & Integration, Internet/Web Design, Outdoor, Print, Public Relations, Radio, Social Media

Aaron Hautala *(Owner & Creative Dir)*
Beth Hautala *(VP)*
Dain Erickson *(Dir-Art)*
Heidi Lake *(Dir-Media)*

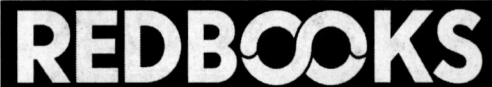

Bryan Petersen *(Mgr-Creative Ops)*

Accounts:
Lexington Manufacturing

RED ID AGENCY
1717 McKinney Ave Ste 700, Dallas, TX 75202
Tel.: (877) 954-9907
Web Site: www.redidagency.com

Year Founded: 2008

Agency Specializes In: Advertising, Collateral, Graphic Design, Internet/Web Design, Logo & Package Design, Media Buying Services, Media Planning, Print, Public Relations, Radio

Teresa Nguyen *(Founder & Pres)*

Accounts:
RoboKind Robotics

RED LEAF
4601 Excelsior Blvd Ste 503, Minneapolis, MN 55416
Tel.: (952) 303-4285
Fax: (952) 303-4286
E-Mail: info@redleafdesign.com
Web Site: www.redleafdesign.com

Year Founded: 2004

Agency Specializes In: Advertising, Catalogs, Digital/Interactive, Identity Marketing, Print

Irma Navarro-Hankins *(Owner & Designer)*

Accounts:
Interior Surface Solutions

RED LION
111 Queen St E Ste 400, Toronto, Ontario M5C 1S2 Canada
Tel.: (416) 603-6500
Web Site: www.redlioncanada.com

Agency Specializes In: Advertising, Digital/Interactive, Social Media, Strategic Planning/Research

Matthew Litzinger *(Pres & Chief Creative Officer)*
John Schofield *(Mng Dir-Strategy)*
Kaitlin Doherty *(Acct Dir)*
Christine McArthur *(Brand Dir)*
Jacoub Bondre *(Dir-Tech)*
Stephen Sandian *(Dir-Art)*
Abigail Berkley *(Acct Exec)*
Kyle Carpenter *(Copywriter)*
Duncan Collis *(Designer)*
Shannon Elizabeth Murphy *(Copywriter)*
Amy Mielke *(Coord)*

Accounts:
Havergal College (Advertising Agency of Record) Marketing
itravel2000.com (Agency of Record) Creative Development, Digital, Out of Home, Print, Radio, Strategic
New-Paymi (Agency of Record) Brand Positioning
Responsible Gambling Council
Tbooth (Agency of Record) Creative, Strategic Planning

RED MARKETING COMMUNICATIONS
3832 Mtn Shadows Rd, Calabasas, CA 91301
Tel.: (818) 599-5448
Web Site: www.redminds.com

Year Founded: 2004

Agency Specializes In: Advertising

Art Nagano *(Co-Founder & Partner-Creative)*
Ed Ball *(Partner-Creative)*
Linda Jackson *(Sr VP)*

Accounts:
Abbott Medical Optics, Inc.
The CDM Company, Inc.
Jemma Wynne Jewelers
Royal Household Products, Inc
Staar Surgical Company
Triage Entertainment

RED MOON MARKETING
4100 Coca-Cola Plz Ste 215, Charlotte, NC 28211
Tel.: (704) 366-1147
Fax: (704) 366-2283
E-Mail: jim.bailey@redmoonmkt.com
Web Site: www.redmoonmkt.com

E-Mail for Key Personnel:
President: jim.bailey@redmoonmkt.com

Employees: 25
Year Founded: 1988

Agency Specializes In: Advertising, Advertising Specialties, African-American Market, Automotive, Brand Development & Integration, Broadcast, Business-To-Business, Cable T.V., Children's Market, Co-op Advertising, Collateral, Commercial Photography, Communications, Consulting, Consumer Marketing, Corporate Communications, Corporate Identity, Crisis Communications, Digital/Interactive, Direct Response Marketing, E-Commerce, Education, Electronic Media, Entertainment, Event Planning & Marketing, Exhibit/Trade Shows, Food Service, Graphic Design, Guerilla Marketing, Hispanic Market, Hospitality, Identity Marketing, In-Store Advertising, Internet/Web Design, Leisure, Local Marketing, Logo & Package Design, Luxury Products, Media Buying Services, Merchandising, Mobile Marketing, Multimedia, New Product Development, Outdoor, Planning & Consultation, Point of Purchase, Point of Sale, Print, Production, Promotions, Public Relations, Publicity/Promotions, Radio, Restaurant, Retail, Sales Promotion, Social Marketing/Nonprofit, Sponsorship, Sports Market, Strategic Planning/Research, Sweepstakes, T.V., Teen Market, Telemarketing, Trade & Consumer Magazines, Transportation, Travel & Tourism, Viral/Buzz/Word of Mouth

Approx. Annual Billings: $15,000,000

Breakdown of Gross Billings by Media: Bus. Publs.: $650,000; Event Mktg.: $1,950,000; Graphic Design: $2,600,000; Logo & Package Design: $650,000; Mdsg./POP: $650,000; Sls. Promo.: $1,300,000; Sports Mktg.: $5,900,000; Strategic Planning/Research: $1,300,000

James Bailey *(Pres & CEO)*
Eddie Burklin *(CFO)*
Greg Luehrs *(Sr VP)*
Greg Mercer *(Sr VP-Acct Svcs)*
Jimmy Harte *(VP)*
Tiffany Moeller *(Dir-Art)*
Andrea Kall *(Sr Acct Mgr)*
Chase Gregory *(Acct Exec)*
Mason McVerry *(Acct Exec)*
Krista Nuzum *(Acct Exec)*
Haley Randazzo *(Acct Exec)*
Sarah Scott *(Acct Exec)*
Michael Skipper *(Acct Exec)*
Nigel Standish *(Acct Exec)*

Accounts:
Better Bakery, LLC; Valencia, CA Gourmet Pretzels, Marketing Communication, Public Relations, Retail Packaging, Sales, Trade Promotions
BKT Experiential
Brown Forman; Louisville, KY Spirits; 2004
Charlotte Bobcats; Charlotte, NC NBA Team; 2003
Cinnabon; Atlanta, GA Cinnamon Pretzels; 2004
Circle K; Charlotte, NC Retail; 2005
Consolidated Theatres; Charlotte, NC Movies; 2005
Fetzer Vineyards
Harris-Teeter Stores; Charlotte, NC Hunter Dairy, Rancher Meat, VIC Card; 2002
Jack Daniels
Merita
MolliCoolz: Sacramento, CA Ice Cream; 2006
Powerade
YMCA of Greater Charlotte; Charlotte, NC Health & Wellness; 2002

THE RED PEAK GROUP
560 Broadway Ste 506, New York, NY 10012
Tel.: (212) 792-8930
Fax: (212) 792-8931
E-Mail: jfox@redpeakgroup.com
Web Site: www.redpeakgroup.com

Year Founded: 1983

Agency Specializes In: Advertising, Event Planning & Marketing, Hospitality, Internet/Web Design, Promotions, Recruitment, Sponsorship, Strategic Planning/Research, Travel & Tourism

Susan Cantor *(Pres)*
Murray Schwartz *(Partner)*
James Fox *(CEO-Red Peak Branding)*
Gavin Manley *(Head-Bus Dev)*
Denise Beatty *(Sr Acct Dir)*
Jillian Booty *(Grp Acct Dir)*
Michelle Caganap *(Grp Acct Dir)*
Steve Lipman *(Dir-Production)*
Megan Meagher *(Dir-Strategy)*
Catherine Mevs *(Dir-Strategy)*

Accounts:
Acer Marketing
The City of Santa Clara, California Brand Identity, Brand Positioning, Marketing
HUB Campaign: "LifeCycle"
Intel Campaign: "Intel Clear", Microprocessor Design & Mfr
Nuts.com

RED PEG MARKETING
727 N Washington St, Alexandria, VA 22314
Tel.: (703) 519-9000
Fax: (703) 519-9290
E-Mail: info@redpegmarketing.com
Web Site: www.redpegmarketing.com

Employees: 40

Agency Specializes In: Sponsorship

Approx. Annual Billings: $20,000,000

Brad Nierenberg *(Pres & CEO)*
Andrew Connell *(Sr VP-Client Svc)*
Martin Codd *(VP-Ops)*
Michael McCanna *(Sr Dir-Art)*
Daniel Brienza *(Dir-Creative)*
Matt Sincaglia *(Strategist-Brand)*
Sara Khalatbari *(Coord-Digital & Social)*

Accounts:
Chevrolet
Geico
National Guard
Texas On Tour

RED PEPPER, INC.
110 29th Ave N Ste 100, Nashville, TN 37203

Tel.: (615) 320-9335
Fax: (615) 320-3890
Toll Free: (800) 490-9335
Web Site: http://redpepper.land/

Employees: 20

Agency Specializes In: Advertising

Tim McMullen *(Founder & Exec Dir-Creative)*
Sarah Bina *(Dir-Art & Graphic Designer)*
Eva DePaulis *(Dir-Media)*
Darcy Ferrara *(Dir-Fin)*
Cat Garnett *(Dir-Comm & Res)*
Rachael Schendel *(Dir-Creative)*
Yancey Kenna *(Strategist-Social Media)*
Matt Walkley *(Sr Designer-UI & UX)*
Erin Sephel *(Coord-Social Media)*

Accounts:
Averitt
John Deere Boots
Kirkland's Inc Pinning Parlor
Magnolia
Music City Moves
New-Slack Campaign: "Euphoria", Digital, Outdoor
Trevecca Nazarene University

Branch

Red Pepper, Inc
113 S Perry St Ste 200, Lawrenceville, GA 30045
Tel.: (678) 749-7483
Fax: (678) 749-7584
Toll Free: (800) 490-9335
E-Mail: joni@redpepperland.com
Web Site: http://redpepper.land/

Employees: 5

Dave Mcmullen *(Principal)*

Accounts:
Brand Vaughn Lumber
Gwinnet Convention & Visitors Bureau

RED POPPY MARKETING LLC
2318 Main St Ste 2, Stratford, CT 06615
Tel.: (203) 377-4922
Web Site: www.redpoppymarketing.com

Agency Specializes In: Advertising, Brand Development & Integration, Collateral, Content, Graphic Design, Internet/Web Design, Public Relations, Social Media, Strategic Planning/Research

Heather B. Habelka *(Pres)*

Accounts:
Reverse The Course
ShopFunder LLC

RED RACER ADVERTISING
5646 Milton St Ste 800, Dallas, TX 75206
Tel.: (214) 494-8400
Fax: (214) 494-8410
E-Mail: info@redraceradv.com
Web Site: www.redraceradv.com

Year Founded: 2009

Agency Specializes In: Advertising, Brand Development & Integration, Broadcast, Content, Digital/Interactive, Media Planning, Print, Promotions, Social Media, Strategic Planning/Research

Scott Crowell *(Pres)*
Amy Crowell *(Mng Partner)*

Accounts:
Specialty Blends

RED RAG & BULL
2319 Colfax Ave Ste 204, Denver, CO 80206
Tel.: (303) 503-9246
E-Mail: info@redragandbull.com
Web Site: www.redragandbull.com

Year Founded: 2013

Agency Specializes In: Advertising, Brand Development & Integration, Content, Digital/Interactive, Logo & Package Design, Social Media

Jordan Sher *(Founder & Dir-Content)*
Troy Jones *(Dir-Creative)*

Accounts:
Savvisdirect
Symmetry
Trek Travel

RED ROCKET MEDIA GROUP
9351 Eastman Park Dr, Windsor, CO 80550
Tel.: (970) 674-0079
Fax: (970) 237-3412
Toll Free: (888) 674-0079
E-Mail: jennifer@redrocketmg.com
Web Site: www.redrocketmg.com

Employees: 10
Year Founded: 2001

Agency Specializes In: Advertising, Advertising Specialties, Brand Development & Integration, Business Publications, Business-To-Business, Catalogs, Collateral, Commercial Photography, Communications, Consulting, Consumer Goods, Consumer Marketing, Consumer Publications, Content, Corporate Communications, Corporate Identity, Digital/Interactive, Direct-to-Consumer, E-Commerce, Electronic Media, Email, Exhibit/Trade Shows, Experience Design, Graphic Design, Identity Marketing, Internet/Web Design, Local Marketing, Logo & Package Design, Market Research, Media Buying Services, Media Planning, Media Relations, Multimedia, Newspapers & Magazines, Package Design, Paid Searches, Planning & Consultation, Point of Sale, Print, Production, Production (Print), Public Relations, RSS (Really Simple Syndication), Radio, Search Engine Optimization, Strategic Planning/Research, Trade & Consumer Magazines, Transportation, Viral/Buzz/Word of Mouth, Web (Banner Ads, Pop-ups, etc.), Yellow Pages Advertising

Approx. Annual Billings: $300,000

Breakdown of Gross Billings by Media: Collateral: 30%; Consulting: 10%; Exhibits/Trade Shows: 10%; Logo & Package Design: 15%; Worldwide Web Sites: 35%

Chadd Bryant *(Owner)*
Eric Spikes *(Partner)*
Kengi Her *(Sr Designer)*

RED ROCKET STUDIOS
4700 LB McLeod Ste B2, Orlando, FL 32811
Tel.: (407) 895-9358
Fax: (407) 895-9468
Web Site: www.redrocketstudios.com

Agency Specializes In: Advertising, Brand Development & Integration, Collateral, Internet/Web Design, Media Planning, Print, Promotions, Public Relations

David Reagan *(Founder)*
Tim Lauterbach *(Partner & Exec Producer)*
Jeff Campese *(Partner & Dir-Creative)*
John E. Hubbard *(Dir-Launch)*

Accounts:
Movember Foundation
Nautique Boats
Orlando, Inc.

RED ROOK ROYAL
451 Parks Cir, Gentry, AR 72734
Tel.: (479) 301-1972
Web Site: www.redrookroyal.com

Year Founded: 2008

Agency Specializes In: Advertising, Brand Development & Integration, Graphic Design, Internet/Web Design, Print, Public Relations

Will Dockery *(Founder & Dir-Creative)*

Accounts:
Decatur Medi Clinic
Deeper Youth Conference
Farmington Church of Christ
Howlers

RED SIX MEDIA
319 3rd St, Baton Rouge, LA 70801
Tel.: (225) 615-8836
E-Mail: info@redsixmedia.net
Web Site: www.redsixmedia.com

Agency Specializes In: Advertising, Brand Development & Integration, Graphic Design, Internet/Web Design, Logo & Package Design

Matt Dardenne *(Co-Owner & Dir-Creative)*
Kristen Morrison *(Co-Owner & Acct Mgr)*
Joe Martin *(Creative Dir)*
James Spencer *(Dir-Interactive)*
Michael Duke *(Jr Copywriter)*

Accounts:
Cancer Services of Greater Baton Rouge

RED SPOT INTERACTIVE
1001 Jupiter Park Dr. #124, Jupiter, FL 33458
Tel.: (800) 401-7931
Web Site: www.redspotinteractive.com

Employees: 50
Year Founded: 2010

Agency Specializes In: Collateral, Digital/Interactive, Email, Local Marketing, Print, Search Engine Optimization, Web (Banner Ads, Pop-ups, etc.)

Approx. Annual Billings: $5,000,000

Jimmy Rhoades *(CTO)*
Matt Tompkins *(Sr Dir-Product Dev & Search Engine Mktg)*
Ryan Lehrl *(Dir-Sls)*

RED SQUARE GAMING
202 Government St, Mobile, AL 36602
Tel.: (251) 476-1283
E-Mail: hello@redsquaregaming.com
Web Site: www.redsquaregaming.com

Year Founded: 2013

Agency Specializes In: Advertising, Brand Development & Integration, Content, Digital/Interactive, Email, Internet/Web Design, Media Buying Services, Media Planning,

Sponsorship, Strategic Planning/Research

Sarah Jones *(Pres)*
Andy Layton *(Head-Copy & Assoc Dir-Creative)*
Wade Stringfellow *(Sr Dir-Art)*
Sam Solomon *(Sr Producer-Interactive)*
Alanna Moman-Rawden *(Acct Dir)*
Caleb Moore *(Dir-Production)*
Robyn Steadham *(Mgr-Production)*
Jay Schmidt *(Sr Acct Exec)*
Shelby Shockley *(Acct Exec)*
Philip Laue *(Copywriter)*

Accounts:
Hard Rock Hotel & Casino Las Vegas

RED TETTEMER O'CONNELL & PARTNERS
(Formerly Red Tettemer & Partners)
1 S Broad St 24th Fl, Philadelphia, PA 19107
Tel.: (267) 402-1410
Fax: (267) 402-1458
E-Mail: ranchforeman@redtettemer.com
Web Site: rtop.com

Employees: 96

Agency Specializes In: Entertainment, Logo & Package Design, Retail, Sponsorship, Travel & Tourism

Steve Red *(Pres & Chief Creative Officer)*
Carla Mote *(Mng Partner)*
Steve O'Connell *(Partner & Exec Dir-Creative)*
Perry Morris *(Mng Dir)*
Hilary Craven *(CMO)*
Jessica O'Conor *(VP & Grp Acct Dir)*
Todd Taylor *(VP & Dir-Creative)*
Jeremy Gilberto *(Sr Dir-Art)*
Ron Villacarillo *(Dir-Creative & Art Dir)*
Matt Dimmer *(Dir-Creative)*
Ari Garber *(Dir-Creative)*
Kelly Goldenberg *(Dir-Media)*
Matthew Gould-Lucht *(Dir-Art)*
Michelle Maben *(Dir-Art)*
Ben Levy *(Assoc Dir-Creative & Copywriter)*
Michelle Mitchell *(Acct Mgr)*
Chelsea Dubin *(Acct Exec)*
Adam Leaventon *(Strategist-Connection)*
Josh Sirulnik *(Strategist)*
Uri Weingarten *(Strategist)*
Jordan Breindel *(Copywriter)*
Kristen Meade *(Media Planner)*
Tedd Wood *(Copywriter)*

Accounts:
Airheads Campaign: "The World Needs More Airheads"
Big Ten Network Campaign: "Big Ten Mini-Mascots"
California Association of REALTORS (Agency of Record) Campaign: "Biker", Campaign: "Champions of Home & Ripple", Campaign: "Cool Shirt", Campaign: "Long Story", Digital & Social, Media Planning & Buying
Century 21 Real Estate LLC Campaign: "Smarter. Bolder. Faster.", Campaign: "Wedding", Digital, OOH, Print, TV
Citadel "truth tube"
Dial Corporation "Gorgeous Man", Camp Dirt, Dial For Men, Digital, Renuzit, Right Guard, TV, In Store & Event Marketing
Dockers (Social Agency of Record) Campaign: "Dad Jam", Campaign: "Stop Dad Pants", Digital, Social Media
Fox Networks Group Social & Digital
Front Burner Brands (Agency of Record) GrillSmith, Melting Pot
Henkel Consumer Goods Dial for Men, Right Guard
New-The Honest Kitchen
New-Kellogg Company Morningstar Farms
New-Mitchell & Ness Nostalgia Co. "Gentlemen of Streetwear", Hi Crown Fitted Cap, Hi Crown Fitted Line
NBC Universal Social
Peach Street Distillers Campaign: "Tub Six-Shooter"
Planet Fitness "Planet of Triumphs", "Thank-o-Matic 5,000,000", Campaign: "Gymtimidation", Campaign: "Hot", Campaign: "Pilatatumba", Clunk-a-Lunk, Creative, Digital, Online, Social
Renuzit Air Fresheners Campaign: "Gorgeous Man"
Rival Bros Branding, OOH, Packaging
SEPTA Transit Authority
New-Speck
Sprout Channel Social
Swarovski North America Limited Inc. Advertising, Social/Digital
New-T. Rowe Price Group Inc.
TuB Gin Consumer Activations, Digital, Experiential, OOH, Social, Video
Under Armour Campaign: "What's Beautiful", Finding Undeniable, Social Media, Ultimate Intern, Under Armour Women
Visit Philly Digital, OOH, Print, Video
William Grant & Sons "A Celebration of Summer Solstice", Ancho Reyes Liquer (Agency of Record), Global Creative, Rekya Vodka, Social, Videos

RED THE AGENCY
(Formerly Red Communications)
10235 111th St Ste 6, Edmonton, AB T5K 2V5 Canada
Tel.: (780) 426-3627
Fax: (780) 426-3620
E-Mail: ddarwent@redtheagency.com
Web Site: www.redtheagency.com

Employees: 19
Year Founded: 2001

Lori Billey *(Founder, CEO & Partner)*
Randy Cronin *(Partner & Dir-Strategy)*
Cass Williamson *(CFO)*
Chris Phillips *(Dir-Media)*
Craig Redmond *(Dir-Creative)*
Christy Yaseyko *(Dir-Art)*
Alison Schatz *(Acct Mgr & Project Mgr)*
Katie Rolheiser *(Copywriter)*
Jonathan Manning *(Assoc Creative Dir)*

Accounts:
Airco Charters
New-Alberta Symphony Orchestra
Edmonton Airports
Edmonton Oil Kings Hockey Team; 2007
Goodwill Industries
Government of Alberta
Greenboro Homes
Hinton Wood Products
The Mongolie Grill
Natural Health Practitioners
Northlands
OK Tire
Red Deer River Watershed Alliance
Servus Place
Telkomsel
University of Calgary - EVDS

RED URBAN
1100 33 Bloor Street East, Toronto, ON M4W3H1 Canada
Tel.: (416) 324-6330
E-Mail: hello@redurban.ca
Web Site: www.redurban.ca

Agency Specializes In: Advertising, Digital/Interactive, Graphic Design, Market Research, Planning & Consultation

Steve Carli *(Pres)*
Christina Yu *(Exec VP)*
Samantha Brightling *(Acct Dir)*
Caroline Kilgour *(Dir-Client Svcs)*
Meagan Patry *(Art Dir)*
Alicia Outschoorn *(Dir-Art)*
Cooper Evoy *(Copywriter)*

Accounts:
New-Hudson's Bay Company (HBC) Campaign: "Country of Adventurers"
Subaru
Volkswagen Canada Campaign: "Butcher", Campaign: "Drive Until", Campaign: "Golf GTD", Campaign: "Somebody That I Used to Know", Car Dealers, Jetta, Passat, Volkswagen Golf

RED212
5509 Fair Lane, Cincinnati, OH 45227
Tel.: (513) 772-1020
Fax: (513) 772-6849
E-Mail: annechambers@red212.com
Web Site: www.red212.com/

Employees: 18
Year Founded: 2001

Agency Specializes In: Advertising

Anne Chambers *(CEO)*
Richard Walker *(Partner, COO & Dir-Production)*
Donivan Perkins *(Partner & Exec Dir-Creative)*
Kristin Schwandner *(Partner & Client Svcs Dir)*
Rob Lunsford *(Dir-Digital Mktg)*
Lauren Harmon *(Acct Supvr)*
Amy Cullion Klunk *(Acct Supvr)*
Alexandra Lincoln *(Analyst-Digital Mktg)*

Accounts:
Chiquita Fresh Express
Olay
Prilosec OTC
Procter & Gamble Febreze, Olay Skincare Products, Swiffer
Scotts Ortho

RED7 AGENCY
174 Meeting St, Charleston, SC 29401
Tel.: (844) 733-7337
E-Mail: hello@red7agency.com
Web Site: red7.agency/

Employees: 16
Year Founded: 2015

Agency Specializes In: Broadcast, Business Publications, Cable T.V., Catalogs, Co-op Advertising, Collateral, Custom Publishing, Digital/Interactive, Direct Response Marketing, Electronic Media, Email, Exhibit/Trade Shows, Experience Design, Game Integration, Guerilla Marketing, In-Store Advertising, Infomercials, Local Marketing, Magazines, Mobile Marketing, Multimedia, Newspaper, Newspapers & Magazines, Out-of-Home Media, Outdoor, Paid Searches, Podcasting, Point of Purchase, Point of Sale, Print, Product Placement, Production, Production (Print), Promotions, Publishing, RSS (Really Simple Syndication), Radio, Search Engine Optimization, Shopper Marketing, Social Media, Sponsorship, Sweepstakes, Syndication, T.V., Trade & Consumer Magazines, Viral/Buzz/Word of Mouth, Web (Banner Ads, Pop-ups, etc.), Yellow Pages Advertising

Red7 is a strategic, analytics driven, creative agency that builds global brands and rich customer experiences using a method called measurable marketing. The agency partners with both Business-to-Consumer and Business-to-Busiess clients to create smarter marketing solutions that drive measurable success in all digital and traditional channels.

Jason Wilder *(Pres)*
Gary Carter *(EVP & Creative Dir)*
JoDee Anderson *(EVP-PR)*
Tracy Mikulec *(EVP-Digital Services)*

Accounts:
Agit Global
The DarkRoom
Honeywell Fire Protection, Industrial Safety; 2008
Intova Waterproof Cameras; 2010
Ntt Data IT Systems; 2010
SixAxis ErectaStep, RollaStep, SafeRack, YellowGate; 2012

RED7E
637 W Main St, Louisville, KY 40202-2987
Tel.: (502) 585-3403
Fax: (502) 582-2043
Toll Free: (800) 656-7272
Web Site: www.red7e.com

E-Mail for Key Personnel:
President: danb@red7e.com
Production Mgr.: laurab@red7e.com

Employees: 20
Year Founded: 1974

Agency Specializes In: Brand Development & Integration, Consumer Marketing, Education, Entertainment, Faith Based, Financial, Health Care Services, Strategic Planning/Research

Dan Barbercheck *(Pres & Exec Dir-Creative)*
Jim Hoyland *(COO & VP)*
Karl Feige *(Dir-Art)*
Sarah McCool *(Dir-Digital)*
James Williamson *(Dir-Creative)*
Mary Zdobylak *(Mgr-Traffic)*
Wally Dahman *(Sr Art Dir & Assoc Creative Dir)*

Accounts:
Baptist Hospital Northeast; Lagrange, KY Health Care; 2000
Hillerich & Bradsby Co.; Louisville, KY Sports Equipment; 2001
Hilliard Lyons Brokerage; Louisville, KY Investment Managers; 1994
Jefferson County Public Schools; Louisville, KY; 1999
Kentucky Farm Bureau; Louisville, KY Property & Casualty Insurance; 2003
Western Baptist Hospital; Paducah, KY; 2001

REDBEAN SOCIETY
44 W 28th St 8th Fl, New York, NY 10001
Tel.: (646) 794-4130
Fax: (646) 219-2248
E-Mail: jbird@redbeansociety.com
Web Site: www.redbeansociety.com

Agency Specializes In: Brand Development & Integration, Hispanic Market, Media Planning

Jackie Bird *(CEO)*

Accounts:
American Express
Chocolate Cortez Chocolate Mfr
MTV
Sony
Tavern Direct Food Products Producer
Wrigleys

REDBEARD
378 5th St, Hollister, CA 95023
Tel.: (831) 634-4633
Fax: (831) 634-4626
E-Mail: info@redbeard.com
Web Site: www.redbeard.com

Employees: 12
Year Founded: 1990

Agency Specializes In: Advertising

Gregg Hoffman *(Pres)*
Michael Albright *(Dir-Creative)*
Marie Hoffman *(Dir-Comm)*
Sam Rivera *(Designer)*

Accounts:
The Aimbridge Group
Justice Federal Credit Union

REDBIRD COMMUNICATIONS
201-4489 Viewmont Ave, Victoria, BC V8Z 5K8 Canada
Tel.: (250) 479-3806
Fax: (250) 479-3896
E-Mail: info@redbirdonline.com
Web Site: www.redbirdonline.com

Employees: 8
Year Founded: 2001

Agency Specializes In: Advertising

Carol Vincent *(Pres)*
Gary Linford *(VP-Dev & Admin)*
Carolyn Walker *(Mgr-Production)*

Accounts:
Merridale Cider

REDCHAIR BRANDING
158 Locke St S Unit 2, Hamilton, ON L8P 4A9 Canada
Tel.: (905) 528-6032
Web Site: www.redchairbranding.com

Employees: 10
Year Founded: 1999

National Agency Associations: Second Wind Limited

Agency Specializes In: Brand Development & Integration, Education, Graphic Design, Health Care Services, Hospitality, Integrated Marketing, Internet/Web Design, Print, Recruitment, Sports Market, Strategic Planning/Research, Travel & Tourism

Approx. Annual Billings: $246,211

Accounts:
Alberici Constructors
All Staff Business Recruiting Services
Ball Construction
Casino Windsor
City of Stratford Stratford Tourism
CRICH (St. Mike's) Centre for Research on Inner-City Health
CritiCall Ontario
Integra Technologies BlackHawk, Flange Trak, RCP Services
Longo's
Medtronic of Canada Medtronic Hospitality Suite
Nerds on Site
OMAC-Mortgages
Western New York

REDDING COMMUNICATIONS LLC
1325 N Main St, High Point, NC 27262
Tel.: (336) 887-3090
Web Site: www.reddingcom.com

Year Founded: 2003

Agency Specializes In: Advertising, Brand Development & Integration, Collateral, Graphic Design, Internet/Web Design, Logo & Package Design, Outdoor, Print, Radio, Strategic Planning/Research

Don Redding *(Owner & CEO)*
Geary Potter *(VP-New Bus Dev)*
Heather Redding *(VP-Fin)*
Patrick McQueen *(Sr Art Dir)*
Lindsey Fairrington *(Designer)*

Accounts:
Alight Foundation
Columbia Forest Products
Cone Health Network
Cornerstone HR Group
Costco

REDENGINE DIGITAL
1485 Chain Bridge Rd Ste 305, McLean, VA 22101
Tel.: (703) 556-8489
Web Site: www.redenginedigital.com

Year Founded: 2001

Agency Specializes In: Advertising, Digital/Interactive, Social Media

Liz Murphy *(Founder)*
Brian Rogel *(Assoc Dir-SEO & SEM)*
Austin Buckley *(Sr Acct Mgr)*
Joseph McLaughlin *(Acct Mgr & Sr Strategist-Digital)*

Accounts:
American Diabetes Association

REDFONT MARKETING GROUP
8410 Pit Stop Ct Ste 142, Charlotte, NC 28027
Tel.: (800) 920-8090
E-Mail: info@redfontmarketing.com
Web Site: www.redfontmarketing.com

Agency Specializes In: Advertising, Event Planning & Marketing, Internet/Web Design, Print, Public Relations, Social Media

Jim Quick *(Pres & Creative Dir)*
Patrick Pearson *(VP)*

Accounts:
ABBA
St Joseph Pregnancy Resource Clinic

REDHEAD COMPANIES
6011 University Blvd Ste 210, Ellicott City, MD 21043
Tel.: (410) 465-1282
Fax: (410) 461-2446
E-Mail: info@redheadcompanies.com
Web Site: http://marketing.redheadcompanies.com/

Employees: 20

Agency Specializes In: Advertising, Digital/Interactive

Scott Koerwer *(Partner)*
Paula Dwyer *(VP & Acct Grp Supvr)*
Charles Freeman *(Dir-Creative)*
Juliet Gilden *(Acct Supvr)*
Carey Christie *(Designer)*

Accounts:
Howard Bank

REDHEAD MARKETING & PR
PO Box 3522, Park City, UT 84060
Tel.: (435) 901-2071

Web Site: www.redheadmarketingpr.com

Year Founded: 2010

Agency Specializes In: Advertising, Brand Development & Integration, Collateral, Content, Email, Event Planning & Marketing, Internet/Web Design, Media Training, Public Relations

Hilary Reiter *(Principal)*
Tracie Heffernan *(Acct Dir-New York Office)*

Accounts:
Destination PC
Flower Studio on Main
Glenn Wright for House District 54
InteliCon
Sage Mountain Animal Rescue
Summit County Attorney David Brickey
Summit County Treasurer Corrie Forsling
Terahertz Device Corporation
Wasatch & Wool

REDHYPE
248 N Laurens St, Greenville, SC 29601
Tel.: (864) 232-2000
Web Site: www.redhype.com

Year Founded: 2009

Agency Specializes In: Advertising, Brand Development & Integration, Collateral, Digital/Interactive, Email, Graphic Design, Internet/Web Design, Logo & Package Design, Print, Social Media

Marie Dunn-Blough *(Pres & Chief Creative Officer)*
Michael Smith *(Art Dir)*
Jeremy Washington *(Dir-Social Media & Graphic Designer)*
Brooks Brackett *(Sr Graphic Designer)*
Lindsey Hayes *(Designer-Multimedia)*
Mika Hearn *(Coord-Graphic)*
Lauren Tedeschi *(Asst-Creative)*

Accounts:
Bringfido.com
Carolina Ballet Theatre
Highland Homes Inc.
Institute for Integrated Healthcare
Maxim Medical
Miracle Hill Ministries
SureTek Medical

REDINGTON INC.
49 Richmondville Ave Ste 108, Westport, CT 06880
Tel.: (203) 222-7399
Fax: (203) 222-1819
E-Mail: info@redingtoninc.com
Web Site: www.redingtoninc.com

Employees: 7

Agency Specializes In: Investor Relations

Thomas Redington *(Pres)*
Deirdre Abbotts *(Mgr-Ops)*

Accounts:
Adeona
Alexza
Carrington Laboratories
ContraFect Corporation
Crucell N.V. Protein Manufacturing
Digital Angel
Dynavax
Elan
Galapagos
Lpath
Pipex Pharma
XTL Bio
Ziopharm Oncology

REDMOND DESIGN
1460 Madison Ave, Memphis, TN 38104
Tel.: (901) 728-5464
Web Site: www.redmonddesign.com

Agency Specializes In: Advertising, E-Commerce, Email, Logo & Package Design, Outdoor, Print, Promotions, Radio, T.V., Web (Banner Ads, Pop-ups, etc.)

Jerry Dean Redmond Jr. *(Principal & Sr Dir-Design)*
Phalange Calvin *(VP-Jackson Ops)*
Ashley Redmond *(Acct Exec)*
David Veal *(Acct Exec)*

Accounts:
Byas Funeral Home, Inc.
M. J. Edwards Funeral Home
Memphis City Schools

REDRATTLER CREATIVE
118 Broadway St Ste 630, San Antonio, TX 78205
Tel.: (210) 460-0012
E-Mail: getbit@redrattlercreative.com
Web Site: www.redrattlercreative.com

Agency Specializes In: Advertising, Brand Development & Integration, Collateral, Content, Internet/Web Design, Logo & Package Design, Print, Search Engine Optimization

Accounts:
Bill Miller BBQ

REDROC AUSTIN
11044 Research Blvd A-525, Austin, TX 78759
Tel.: (512) 506-8808
Fax: (512) 506-9229
E-Mail: getreal@redrocaustin.com
Web Site: redrocadvertising.com

Year Founded: 1997

Agency Specializes In: Advertising, Event Planning & Marketing, Graphic Design, Internet/Web Design

Ernest Corder *(Pres & Chief Creative Officer)*
Brady Woodall *(VP-Acct Svcs)*
David W. Ciccoccioppo *(Dir-Creative)*
Kim Corder *(Dir-Acctg)*
Molly Crum *(Acct Mgr)*
Erin Ivy *(Acct Mgr)*
Daisy Kong *(Acct Mgr)*
Lorie Person *(Acct Coord)*

Accounts:
Armadillo Christmas Bazaar
Texas School of Bartenders

REDROCKET CONNECT LLC
1095 Forsyth Ln, Galena, OH 43021
Tel.: (317) 294-9869
Web Site: www.redrocketconnect.com

Agency Specializes In: Advertising, Brand Development & Integration, Internet/Web Design, Media Buying Services, Print, Promotions, Public Relations, Search Engine Optimization

Greg Henderson *(Principal & Dir-Client Svcs)*
Sara Moseley *(Dir-Brand Voice)*
Tracey Parsons *(Dir-Strategy & Social Media)*
Megan Shroy *(Dir-PR)*
Doug Wright *(Dir-Interactive)*
Marsha Young *(Dir-Media)*

Accounts:
VineBrook Homes
The WaterWorks

REDSCOUT LLC
28 W 25th St 10th Fl, New York, NY 10010
Tel.: (646) 336-6028
Fax: (646) 336-6122
E-Mail: will@redscout.com
Web Site: www.redscout.com

Employees: 50

National Agency Associations: 4A's

Agency Specializes In: Brand Development & Integration, Social Media

Margo Husted *(CFO)*
Daniel Wadia *(Mng Dir-New York)*
Jaime Klein Daley *(Grp Dir-Strategy)*
Leah Hoxie *(Dir-Strategy)*
Noah Waxman *(Dir-Strategy)*
Kyla Wagman *(Strategist)*
Arian Franz *(Sr Graphic Designer)*

Accounts:
ABC Family
Activision Publishing
American Express
Diageo
Domino's
Frito-Lay, Inc. Lay's
Gawker Media LLC
Hyatt
Kate Spade
New-Kenneth Cole Productions, Inc. Campaign: "The Courageous Class"
LinkedIn
PepsiCo Inc. Pepsi
Petco Campaign: "The Power of Together"

Branch

Redscout LLC
99 Osgood Pl 2nd Fl, San Francisco, CA 94133
Tel.: (415) 644-5278
Web Site: www.redscout.com

National Agency Associations: 4A's

Alex Cripe *(Dir-Strategy)*
Ali Hartwell *(Strategist)*

REDSTONE COMMUNICATIONS INC.
10031 Maple St, Omaha, NE 68134
Tel.: (402) 393-5435
Fax: (402) 393-2139
E-Mail: info@redstonespark.com
Web Site: www.redstoneweb.com

E-Mail for Key Personnel:
President: pwebb@redstonespark.com

Employees: 25
Year Founded: 1983

National Agency Associations: AAF-AMA-DMA-PRSA

Agency Specializes In: Advertising, Agriculture, Automotive, Brand Development & Integration, Broadcast, Business Publications, Business-To-Business, Cable T.V., Co-op Advertising, Collateral, Communications, Consumer Marketing, Corporate Identity, Direct Response Marketing, Electronic Media, Entertainment, Financial, Food Service, Government/Political, Graphic Design, Health Care Services, High Technology, Information Technology, Internet/Web Design, Logo & Package Design, Media Buying Services, Multimedia, Newspapers & Magazines, Outdoor, Production, Public Relations, Radio, Restaurant,

Retail, Seniors' Market, T.V., Trade & Consumer Magazines

Stacy Vance *(Owner & CFO)*
Jim Svoboda *(Owner)*
Claudia Martin *(Chm & Partner)*
Steve Armbruster *(Partner & Dir-Creative)*
Gail Seaton *(Partner & Acct Svc Dir)*
Shawna Eves *(Mgr-Traffic & Print Production)*
Amanda Dunning-Peterson *(Specialist-Online & Sr Media Buyer)*

Accounts:
College of Saint Mary
Cox Communications; Omaha, NE Cable Television Services
Metropolitan Utilities District

REED ADVERTISING
13 Emory Pl, Knoxville, TN 37917
Tel.: (865) 523-4075
Fax: (865) 523-4824
E-Mail: sales@reedadvertising.com
Web Site: www.reedadvertising.com

E-Mail for Key Personnel:
President: jim@reedadvertising.com

Employees: 5
Year Founded: 1985

National Agency Associations: Second Wind Limited

Agency Specializes In: Advertising, Automotive, Brand Development & Integration, Broadcast, Business-To-Business, Co-op Advertising, Collateral, Communications, Consulting, Consumer Marketing, Corporate Identity, Exhibit/Trade Shows, Financial, Graphic Design, Health Care Services, Industrial, Leisure, Logo & Package Design, Magazines, Media Buying Services, Newspaper, Outdoor, Planning & Consultation, Point of Purchase, Point of Sale, Print, Production, Publicity/Promotions, Radio, Recruitment, Sales Promotion, Strategic Planning/Research, T.V., Trade & Consumer Magazines, Travel & Tourism

Approx. Annual Billings: $1,400,000

Breakdown of Gross Billings by Media: Bus. Publs.: $320,000; Collateral: $815,000; D.M.: $95,000; Newsp.: $170,000

Jim Reed *(Owner)*
Dot Reed *(Controller)*
Catherine Doak *(Dir-Art)*
Joe McChesney *(Dir-Creative)*

REED & ASSOCIATES MARKETING
3517 Virginia Beach Blvd, Virginia Beach, VA 23452
Tel.: (757) 962-7375
Fax: (757) 962-3364
E-Mail: info@reedandassociatesmarketing.com
Web Site: www.reedandassociatesmarketing.com

Year Founded: 2007

Agency Specializes In: Advertising, Media Buying Services, Media Planning, Outdoor, Production, Public Relations, Radio, T.V.

Dave Reed *(Co-Founder & Pres)*
Ashley N. Knepper *(Co-Founder & VP)*
Mike Reed *(Partner)*
Jessica Dahl *(Coord-PR & Social Media)*
Allison Haberkorn *(Coord-Mktg)*

Accounts:
Window World, Inc

REED SENDECKE KREBSBACH
(d/b/a RS+K)
701 Deming Way, Madison, WI 53717-1937
Tel.: (608) 827-0701
Fax: (608) 827-0702
E-Mail: info@rsandk.com
Web Site: www.rsandk.com

Employees: 17

Agency Specializes In: Advertising

Kay Krebsbach *(Pres)*
Laurie Wilkinson *(CFO)*
Stan Reed *(Principal)*
Man Disalvo *(Exec VP)*
Jun Trackray *(VP)*
Scot Kemp *(Dir-Design)*
Gregory Parker *(Designer)*
Kay Sakiya *(Designer-Production)*
Patti Kessler *(Coord-Media)*

Accounts:
Blain Supply
Gilson Inc
MGE
Thermo Fisher Scientific
Thermo Scientific Instruments

REESE
1875 Morgantown Rd, Reading, PA 19607
Tel.: (610) 378-1835
Fax: (610) 378-1676
E-Mail: info@reeseadv.com
Web Site: www.reeseadv.com

Employees: 12
Year Founded: 1981

Agency Specializes In: Advertising, Brand Development & Integration, Broadcast, Business Publications, Business-To-Business, Cable T.V., Collateral, Communications, Consulting, Consumer Goods, Consumer Marketing, Consumer Publications, Corporate Communications, Corporate Identity, Customer Relationship Management, Digital/Interactive, Direct Response Marketing, Direct-to-Consumer, E-Commerce, Electronic Media, Email, Engineering, Event Planning & Marketing, Exhibit/Trade Shows, Faith Based, Fashion/Apparel, Financial, Food Service, Graphic Design, Guerilla Marketing, Health Care Services, Household Goods, Industrial, Integrated Marketing, Internet/Web Design, Legal Services, Leisure, Local Marketing, Logo & Package Design, Magazines, Market Research, Media Buying Services, Media Planning, Media Relations, Media Training, Medical Products, Mobile Marketing, Multimedia, Newspaper, Newspapers & Magazines, Out-of-Home Media, Outdoor, Package Design, Paid Searches, Planning & Consultation, Point of Purchase, Point of Sale, Print, Production, Production (Print), Promotions, Public Relations, Publicity/Promotions, RSS (Really Simple Syndication), Radio, Regional, Retail, Sales Promotion, Search Engine Optimization, Social Marketing/Nonprofit, Social Media, Sports Market, Strategic Planning/Research, T.V., Trade & Consumer Magazines, Travel & Tourism, Web (Banner Ads, Pop-ups, etc.)

Approx. Annual Billings: $7,000,000

Matt Golden *(Co-Owner & Mng Partner)*
Greg Purcell *(Co-Owner & Mng Partner)*
Chrissy Faller *(Dir-PR)*
Alan Kline *(Dir-Creative)*
Ken Ravel *(Supvr-Creative)*
Meredith Rightmire Youtz *(Acct Exec)*

Accounts:
Berks Economic Partnership; Reading, PA Economic Development; 2004
Berks Eye Physicians & Surgeons; Wyomissing, PA LASIK Eye Surgery; 2009
Berks Fire Water Restorations; Reading, PA Disaster Recovery; 2010
Caron Foundation; Wernersville, PA Drug & Alcohol Rehab
Citrix Online; Hoboken, NJ Voice Over IP; 2006
Enersys, Inc.; Reading, PA Industrial Batteries; 2006
Penn National Gaming; Wyomissing, PA Casino Web Sites; 2011
Rentokil; Reading, PA Citrugard Termite Control; 2011
Vossloh North America; Reading, PA Railroad Components; 2009
Vossloh Track Materials; Reading, PA; 2009

THE REFINERY
US Bank Bldg 14455 ventura blvd 3rd fl, Sherman Oaks, CA 91423
Tel.: (818) 843-0004
E-Mail: outreach@therefinerycreative.com
Web Site: www.therefinerycreative.com

Agency Specializes In: Advertising, Brand Development & Integration, Digital/Interactive, Print

Adam Waldman *(Owner)*
Brett Winn *(Partner & Creative Dir)*
Nancy Julson *(Acct Mgr)*
Rowena Rosenberg *(Acct Exec)*

Accounts:
New-20th Century Fox
New-ABC
New-CBS
New-Fox Broadcasting
New-Screen Gems
New-Sony Pictures Entertainment
New-Universal
New-Walt Disney Studios
New-Warner Bros
New-The Weinstein Company

REFLECTIVE DIGITAL SOLUTIONS
PO Box 217, Swepsonville, NC 27359
Tel.: (919) 913-5806
E-Mail: eboyer@reflectivedigital.com
Web Site: www.reflectivedigital.com

Employees: 1
Year Founded: 2007

Agency Specializes In: Advertising, Alternative Advertising, Business Publications, Cable T.V., Collateral, Graphic Design, Internet/Web Design, Logo & Package Design, Print, Real Estate, Web (Banner Ads, Pop-ups, etc.)

Eric Boyer *(Coord-Mktg & Graphic Designer)*

RE:FUEL
(Formerly Alloy Media + Marketing)
151 W 26th St 12th Fl, New York, NY 10001
Tel.: (212) 401-0070
Toll Free: (866) 360-9688
E-Mail: info@refuelnow.com
Web Site: www.refuelagency.com

Employees: 203
Year Founded: 2000

Agency Specializes In: Broadcast, Direct Response Marketing, Internet/Web Design, Newspaper, Newspapers & Magazines, Out-of-Home Media, Promotions

Approx. Annual Billings: $105,000,000

Andrew Sawyer *(CFO)*
David Cirinelli *(VP-Bus Dev-Military)*

Timothy Gerstmyer *(VP-Digital Networks & Solutions)*
Alison Holmes *(VP-Mktg & Comm)*
Phillip Carroll *(Dir-Creative Svcs)*
Mike Quigley *(Dir-Digital Adv Ops)*
Taissa Bokalo *(Mgr-Tracking)*
Mallory Dewitt *(Sr Acct Exec)*
Jan Dorrance *(Sr Acct Exec)*
Amber Vanorman *(Acct Exec)*
Nancy Alborea *(Media Buyer)*

Accounts:
Amazon
Kimberly-Clark
Pinacle Foods
Procter & Gamble
Spin Master

Branches

re:fuel
(Formerly Hustle Promotions)
10 Abeel Rd, Cranbury, NJ 08512
Tel.: (609) 655-8878
Toll Free: (800) 849-0998
Web Site: refuelagency.com

Agency Specializes In: Outdoor, Promotions, Social Media, Sponsorship

Chris Cassino *(COO)*
John Weipz *(VP-Media & Promos)*
Phil Carroll *(Dir-Creative Svcs)*
Kerry Locklear *(Dir-Sampling)*
Nicole Fama *(Mgr-Media Ops)*
Michael Cardinale *(Coord-Fulfillment)*

Accounts:
Amazon.com
Bad Panda Entertainment

RE:GROUP, INC.
213 W Liberty St, Ann Arbor, MI 48104-1398
Tel.: (734) 213-0200
Fax: (734) 327-6636
E-Mail: regroup@regroup.us
Web Site: www.regroup.us

Employees: 35
Year Founded: 1996

National Agency Associations: IFAA-MMA-WOMMA

Agency Specializes In: Above-the-Line, Advertising, Alternative Advertising, Automotive, Aviation & Aerospace, Below-the-Line, Bilingual Market, Brand Development & Integration, Broadcast, Business-To-Business, Cable T.V., Co-op Advertising, Collateral, Communications, Consulting, Consumer Marketing, Consumer Publications, Corporate Communications, Corporate Identity, Digital/Interactive, Direct Response Marketing, Direct-to-Consumer, Education, Electronic Media, Email, Exhibit/Trade Shows, Fashion/Apparel, Financial, Food Service, Graphic Design, Health Care Services, High Technology, Identity Marketing, In-Store Advertising, Integrated Marketing, International, Internet/Web Design, Local Marketing, Logo & Package Design, Market Research, Media Buying Services, Media Planning, Medical Products, Merchandising, Mobile Marketing, New Technologies, Newspapers & Magazines, Outdoor, Over-50 Market, Package Design, Paid Searches, Pharmaceutical, Point of Purchase, Point of Sale, Print, Production, Production (Print), Promotions, Public Relations, Publicity/Promotions, RSS (Really Simple Syndication), Radio, Real Estate, Regional, Restaurant, Retail, Sales Promotion, Search Engine Optimization, Seniors' Market, Social Marketing/Nonprofit, Sponsorship, Strategic Planning/Research, T.V., Trade & Consumer Magazines, Transportation, Travel & Tourism, Viral/Buzz/Word of Mouth, Women's Market

Approx. Annual Billings: $23,000,000

Janet Muhleman *(Pres)*
Carey Jernigan *(VP-Bus Dev & PR)*
Nick Conflitti *(Sr Dir-Art)*
Rhonda Huie *(Dir-Creative)*
Sharon Costantini *(Office Mgr)*
Pat Cuda *(Sr Partner-Media)*
Julia Shi *(Assoc Strategist-Digital)*

Accounts:
Ben & Jerry's Franchise Frozen Desserts, Ice Cream; 2001
DTE Energy Gas & Electric Utilities; 2012
G.J. Garner Home Builder; 2014
Goodwave FAVE: Fruit and Vegetable Juice; 2013
HealthPlus of Michigan; Flint, MI Health Insurance; 2009
New-Library of Congress
Millicare Franchise; 2014
Molly Maid Franchise; 2014
Osram Opto Semiconductors; 2012
Pet Supplies Plus Franchise; 2013
Right at Home In-home Care; 2012
Taubman Malls; 2014
New-Tilted Kilt (Agency of Record)

REID/O'DONAHUE & ASSOCIATES INC.
(Merged with LWT Communications to form Stamp Idea Group, LLC)

REILLY ADVERTISING
64 Windy Hill Rd, Cohasset, MA 02025
Tel.: (781) 383-2133
Fax: (781) 383-2947
E-Mail: jreilly@reillyadv.com

Employees: 3
Year Founded: 1987

Agency Specializes In: Advertising, Brand Development & Integration, Co-op Advertising, Consumer Marketing, Consumer Publications, Corporate Identity, Direct Response Marketing, Entertainment, Graphic Design, Internet/Web Design, Leisure, Logo & Package Design, Magazines, Media Buying Services, Newspaper, Newspapers & Magazines, Point of Purchase, Public Relations, Real Estate, Restaurant, Retail, Sales Promotion, Strategic Planning/Research, T.V., Travel & Tourism

Approx. Annual Billings: $2,500,000

James A. Reilly *(Pres)*

Accounts:
Cape Cod Melody Tent; Hyannis, MA; 1991
Commonwealth Coop Bank; Boston, MA; 2003
DeScenza Diamonds; Boston, MA; 2002
South Shore Music Circus; Cohasset & Hyannis, MA; 1987

RELEVANT 24
(Acquired by Publicis Groupe S.A.)

RELEVANT 24
46 Plympton St, Boston, MA 02118
Tel.: (617) 674-2059
Web Site: www.relevant24.com

Agency Specializes In: Advertising, Brand Development & Integration, Content, Public Relations

Lane Murphy *(Co-Founder & Pres)*
Marci Gallucci *(Co-Founder & CEO)*
Jordi Chapdelaine *(Exec VP-Bus Dev)*
Christine Peterson *(Sr Acct Mgr & Producer-Digital)*
Tyler Price *(Dir-Creative)*
Divya Bahl *(Sr Acct Mgr)*
Aleks Fonseca *(Strategist-Digital)*

Accounts:
Bud Light
National Geographic Channel

REMEDY
121 W Wacker Dr Ste 2250, Chicago, IL 60601
Tel.: (312) 377-3410
Fax: (312) 377-3420
E-Mail: info@remedychicago.com
Web Site: www.remedychicago.com

Employees: 20

Agency Specializes In: Brand Development & Integration

Carol McCarthy *(Owner & Pres)*
Deanna Stallsmith *(Chief Creative Officer)*
Denise D'Angelo Nora *(VP-Client Svcs)*
Donna Schatz *(VP-Ops & Talent)*
Karen Rafeedie *(Dir-Creative)*
Chrissi Cowhey *(Assoc Dir-Design)*

Accounts:
Edward Hospital & Health Services
Herman Miller Healthcare (Agency of Record)
Swedish Covenant Hospital

REMER INC. CREATIVE MARKETING
205 Marion St, Seattle, WA 98104
Tel.: (206) 624-1010
Fax: (206) 467-2890
E-Mail: info@remerinc.com
Web Site: www.remerinc.com

Employees: 12
Year Founded: 1993

Agency Specializes In: Advertising, Alternative Advertising, Brand Development & Integration, Broadcast, Business-To-Business, Co-op Advertising, Collateral, Communications, Consumer Marketing, Corporate Communications, Corporate Identity, Direct Response Marketing, Event Planning & Marketing, Exhibit/Trade Shows, Identity Marketing, In-Store Advertising, Integrated Marketing, Internet/Web Design, Media Buying Services, Media Planning, Mobile Marketing, Multimedia, Newspapers & Magazines, Out-of-Home Media, Outdoor, Package Design, Paid Searches, Planning & Consultation, Production, Production (Ad, Film, Broadcast), Production (Print), Promotions, Public Relations, Publicity/Promotions, Radio, Retail, Sales Promotion, Search Engine Optimization, Sponsorship, Sports Market, Strategic Planning/Research, T.V., Trade & Consumer Magazines, Viral/Buzz/Word of Mouth, Web (Banner Ads, Pop-ups, etc.)

Approx. Annual Billings: $6,600,000

David Remer *(CEO & Dir-Creative)*
Andrea Jones *(Sr VP-Strategy & Client Svcs)*
Christopher Harwood *(Assoc Dir-Creative & Copywriter)*

Accounts:
Fastrax
Getty Images
Little League International
Lucid Systems
McKinstry

REMERINC
205 Marion St, Seattle, WA 98104
Tel.: (206) 624-1010
Fax: (206) 467-2890
E-Mail: info@remerinc.com
Web Site: www.remerinc.com

Employees: 15
Year Founded: 1993

Agency Specializes In: Advertising, Digital/Interactive, Internet/Web Design, Media Relations, Mobile Marketing, Strategic Planning/Research

Approx. Annual Billings: $7,900,200

Dave Remer *(CEO & Dir-Creative)*
Andrea Jones *(Sr VP-Strategy & Client Svcs)*
Chris Harwood *(Assoc Dir-Creative & Copywriter)*

Accounts:
ABC Video Broadcasting Services
Alaska USA Federal Credit Union
Back to Basics
Boys & Girls Clubs of King County
ESPN Video Broadcasting Services
Getty Images Entertainment Services
iWitness
Rover.com
Starbucks Coffee Products Retailer

REMIXED
113 E Pine St, Orlando, FL 32801
Tel.: (407) 283-7369
E-Mail: info@r3mx.com
Web Site: www.r3mx.com

Agency Specializes In: Advertising, Brand Development & Integration, Collateral, Digital/Interactive, Internet/Web Design, Logo & Package Design, Print, Social Media

Douglas Berger *(Co-Founder & Partner)*
Simon Jacobsohn *(Co-Founder & Partner)*

Accounts:
Unified Sounds

RENEGADE COMMUNICATIONS
(Formerly Renegade)
10950 Gilroy Rd Ste J, Hunt Valley, MD 21031
Tel.: (410) 667-1400
Fax: (410) 667-1482
E-Mail: info@renegadecommunications.com
Web Site: www.renegadecommunications.com

Employees: 50
Year Founded: 1988

Agency Specializes In: Advertising, Brand Development & Integration, Business-To-Business, Cable T.V., Collateral, College, Communications, Consulting, Consumer Goods, Consumer Marketing, Corporate Communications, Corporate Identity, Digital/Interactive, Direct Response Marketing, E-Commerce, Email, Faith Based, Fashion/Apparel, Financial, Government/Political, Infomercials, Integrated Marketing, Internet/Web Design, Logo & Package Design, Planning & Consultation, Podcasting, Print, Production, Production (Print), Public Relations, Radio, Search Engine Optimization, Seniors' Market, Social Marketing/Nonprofit, Social Media, Sports Market, Strategic Planning/Research, T.V., Viral/Buzz/Word of Mouth

Approx. Annual Billings: $62,000,000 Capitalized

Paul Field *(Chief Strategy Officer)*
Chris Beutler *(Chief Innovation Officer)*
Bill Ferguson *(Sr VP & Dir-Acct Mgmt)*
Marie Gooch *(VP-Trng & Dev)*
Brian Stetson *(Exec Dir-Production)*
Kory McCann *(Sr Dir-Strategic Partnerships)*
Ken Hall *(Dir-Creative & Digital)*
Chris Roederer *(Dir-Production)*
Mark Krasselt *(Mgr-Creative Production)*

Accounts:
Black & Decker
Comcast Corporation
Cox Communications, Inc.
McCormick & Company, Incorporated
Motorola Solutions, Inc.
Rommel Ace Hardware Stores, Brand Awareness, Harley-Davidson Dealerships
Time Warner Cable

RENEGADE, LLC
437 5th Ave, New York, NY 10016
Tel.: (646) 838-9000
Fax: (646) 486-7800
Web Site: www.renegade.com

E-Mail for Key Personnel:
Creative Dir.: JVinick@renegademarketing.com

Employees: 60
Year Founded: 1994

National Agency Associations: WOMMA

Agency Specializes In: Advertising, Advertising Specialties, Asian Market, Broadcast, Business-To-Business, Collateral, Consumer Marketing, Corporate Identity, Digital/Interactive, Direct Response Marketing, Electronic Media, Event Planning & Marketing, Exhibit/Trade Shows, Food Service, High Technology, Hispanic Market, Information Technology, Internet/Web Design, Logo & Package Design, Media Buying Services, Merchandising, Newspapers & Magazines, Out-of-Home Media, Pharmaceutical, Print, Production, Public Relations, Publicity/Promotions, Radio, Sales Promotion, Strategic Planning/Research, Technical Advertising, Teen Market

Drew Neisser *(Founder & CEO)*
Linda Cornelius *(COO)*
Anne Rothschild *(Dir-Creative)*
Stephanie Isaacs *(Acct Svc Dir)*
Amy Nielsen *(Copywriter)*

Accounts:
HSBC; New York, NY; 2003
Jenny Craig
NCAA
RR Donnelley
Time Warner Business Class PerkZone

RENMARK FINANCIAL COMMUNICATIONS, INC.
1550 Metcalfe Ste 502, Montreal, QC H3A 1X6 Canada
Tel.: (514) 939-3989
Fax: (514) 939-3717
E-Mail: info@renmarkfinancial.com
Web Site: www.renmarkfinancial.com

Employees: 25
Year Founded: 1999

Agency Specializes In: Corporate Communications, Exhibit/Trade Shows, Financial, Internet/Web Design, Investor Relations, Media Planning, Media Relations, Radio, T.V.

Henri Perron *(Pres)*
John Boidman *(VP)*
Stephanie Lavoie *(VP-HR)*
Barry Mire *(VP)*
Barbara Komorowski *(Sr Acct Mgr)*

Accounts:
Agnico-Eagle Mines Limited; Toronto, Canada
Enerplus Corporation Road Show
First Quantum Minerals Ltd
Noranda Income Fund
Thompson Creek Metals Company Inc.; Toronto, Canada Road Show
TomaGold Corporation Investor Relations, Media

REPEQUITY
(Formerly Virilion, Inc.)
1211 Connecticut Ave NW Ste 250, Washington, DC 20036
Tel.: (202) 654-0800
Fax: (202) 654-0839
Web Site: www.repequity.com

Year Founded: 1997

Agency Specializes In: Children's Market, Computers & Software, Digital/Interactive, Electronic Media, Game Integration, Government/Political, Internet/Web Design, Web (Banner Ads, Pop-ups, etc.)

Tripp Donnelly *(Founder & CEO)*
Kyong Choe *(CFO)*
Eric Gilbertsen *(VP-Digital Strategy)*
Jim Huang *(Sr Dir-SEO)*
Sarah Knoepfler *(Dir-Search Mktg)*
Erica Finet *(Mgr-Search Engine Mktg)*
Melissa Cahoon *(Sr Acct Exec)*
Mary Beth Mitesser *(Acct Exec)*

Accounts:
Auto Alliance www.DiscoverAlternatives.com
Business Software Alliance Cyber Tree House
Ebay Government Relations
Georgetown University McDonough School of Business
HSBC
Pulp Business
Unicef
US Fund for UNICEF www.unicefusa.org
WEEI

REPUBLICA
The Republica Bldg, Miami, FL 33145
Tel.: (786) 347-4700
Fax: (305) 443-1631
E-Mail: info@republica.net
Web Site: www.republica.soy

Employees: 93
Year Founded: 2006

Agency Specializes In: Advertising Specialties, African-American Market, Brand Development & Integration, Hispanic Market, Media Buying Services, Media Relations, Media Training, Multicultural, Public Relations, Publicity/Promotions, Sponsorship

Approx. Annual Billings: $14,500,000

Jorge A. Plasencia *(Owner, Chm & CEO)*
Tony Arner *(CFO)*
Carlos Guzman *(CMO & Exec VP)*
Milton Lebron *(VP-Creative Svcs)*
Ignacio Martel *(Dir-Art)*
Anna del Rio Chong *(Sr Acct Mgr-Comm)*
Natalie Rodriguez *(Acct Exec)*

Accounts:
Adrienne Arsht Philanthropy/Arts; 2008
Alliance International; 2014
BankUnited; 2011
Baptist Health Healthcare; 2010
Bill & Melinda Gates Foundation; 2010
Boehringer Ingelheim Pharmaceuticals Inc.; 2013
Codina Partners Real Estate; 2013
Four Seasons Hotels & Resorts
Google Technology; 2012

Goya Foods Latin Foods; 2010
Hispanic Association on Corporate Responsibility - HACR; 2009
National Museum of the American Latino Commission Government; 2011
The National Pork Board (Agency of Record) Community Relations, Media, National Multicultural Marketing, Public Relations, Research, Social Media, Strategy
NBC Universo Creative
NBCUniversal Advertising, Brand Strategy, Broadcast, Community Relations, Consumer, Creative, Digital, Marketing, Promotions
Nielsen Research Services; 2007
Pernod Ricard Americas Travel Retail - PRATR (Agency of Record) Spirits; 2008
Sedano's Supermarkets Grocery; 2008
Square; 2014
Strong Women Strong Girls Nonprofit; 2012
Target Retail; 2013
Telemundo Network Inc. Creative
TOUS; 2014
Toyota
Universal Orlando Resort Advertising, Hispanic Marketing, Theme Parks; 2009
World Fuel Services

THE REPUBLIK

211 Rigsbee Ave, Durham, NC 27701
Tel.: (919) 956-9400
Fax: (919) 956-9402
E-Mail: inquiries@therepublik.net
Web Site: www.therepublik.net

E-Mail for Key Personnel:
President: rswest@therepublik.net
Creative Dir.: dsmith@therepublik.net
Media Dir.: dfry@therepublik.net
Production Mgr.: dbrightwell@therepublik.net

Employees: 15
Year Founded: 2001

National Agency Associations: AAF

Agency Specializes In: Advertising, Advertising Specialties, Automotive, Bilingual Market, Brand Development & Integration, Broadcast, Business Publications, Business-To-Business, Cable T.V., Co-op Advertising, Collateral, Commercial Photography, Communications, Consulting, Consumer Marketing, Consumer Publications, Corporate Communications, Corporate Identity, Digital/Interactive, Direct Response Marketing, E-Commerce, Education, Electronic Media, Entertainment, Environmental, Event Planning & Marketing, Exhibit/Trade Shows, Fashion/Apparel, Financial, Food Service, Government/Political, Graphic Design, Health Care Services, High Technology, In-Store Advertising, Industrial, Information Technology, Internet/Web Design, Investor Relations, Legal Services, Leisure, Logo & Package Design, Magazines, Marine, Media Buying Services, Medical Products, Merchandising, Multimedia, New Product Development, Newspaper, Newspapers & Magazines, Out-of-Home Media, Outdoor, Planning & Consultation, Point of Purchase, Point of Sale, Print, Production, Public Relations, Publicity/Promotions, Radio, Real Estate, Recruitment, Restaurant, Retail, Sales Promotion, Strategic Planning/Research, T.V., Technical Advertising, Trade & Consumer Magazines, Travel & Tourism, Yellow Pages Advertising

Approx. Annual Billings: $5,000,000

Breakdown of Gross Billings by Media: Adv. Specialities: 2%; Audio/Visual: 1%; Brdcst.: 6%; Bus. Publs.: 2%; Cable T.V.: 2%; Co-op Adv.: 1%; Collateral: 2%; Comml. Photography: 1%; Consulting: 4%; Consumer Publs.: 2%; Corp. Communications: 2%; D.M.: 4%; E-Commerce: 2%; Event Mktg.: 1%; Exhibits/Trade Shows: 2%; Foreign: 3%; Graphic Design: 6%; In-Store Adv.: 3%; Internet Adv.: 5%; Logo & Package Design: 2%; Mdsg./POP: 2%; Newsp. & Mags.: 4%; Out-of-Home Media: 2%; Outdoor: 2%; Point of Purchase: 2%; Point of Sale: 2%; Print: 2%; Radio: 5%; Sls. Promo.: 3%; Strategic Planning/Research: 10%; Trade & Consumer Mags.: 8%; Transit: 1%; Worldwide Web Sites: 4%

Robert Shaw West *(Chm & CEO)*
Mark Scoggins *(Producer-Creative)*
Michael Bustin *(Dir-Strategic Dev)*
Luke Modesto Rayson *(Dir-Art)*
Matt Shapiro *(Dir-Art)*
Rachel Wells *(Dir-Analytics)*
Sam Stejskal *(Specialist-PR)*
Sarah Thornton *(Strategist-Brand)*
Dwayne Fry *(Chief Strategic Officer)*

Accounts:
21c Museum Hotels
Alliance Architecture
The Army's Army; Fayetteville, NC The Army's Army; 2008
Dixie Bones; Woodbridge, VA BBQ Post 401, Dixie Bones; 2009
DunnWell Dunwell; 2008
Fayetteville Area Convention & Visitors Bureau
FHI (Agency of Record)
First Flight Venture Center
Giorgios Hospitality Group City Kitchen, Kalamaki, Kipos, Parizade, Village Burger
I-95 Cooperative
LexisNexis LexisNexis Practice Management, Firm Manager, PC Law, Time Matters; 2009
POM Sonamba; 2010
Rec Boat Holdings 'Scarab Power Boats', Digital, Print, Radio
Red Door Company Marketing Strategy, Sales
Seagrove Area Potters Association; Seagrove, NC Logo, Seagrove, Website; 2010
Spiffy

REPUBLIK PUBLICITE + DESIGN INC.

1435 St-Alexandre Ste 220, H3A 2G4 Montreal, QC Canada
Tel.: (514) 390-8844
Fax: (514) 390-8848
E-Mail: info@republik.ca
Web Site: www.republik.ca

Employees: 7
Year Founded: 1998

Agency Specializes In: Above-the-Line, Advertising, Advertising Specialties, Affluent Market, Alternative Advertising, Arts, Automotive, Aviation & Aerospace, Below-the-Line, Bilingual Market, Brand Development & Integration, Broadcast, Business Publications, Children's Market, Co-op Advertising, Collateral, Communications, Consulting, Consumer Goods, Consumer Marketing, Consumer Publications, Corporate Communications, Corporate Identity, Digital/Interactive, Direct Response Marketing, Direct-to-Consumer, E-Commerce, Electronic Media, Email, Entertainment, Environmental, Event Planning & Marketing, Financial, Food Service, Government/Political, Graphic Design, Guerilla Marketing, Health Care Services, Hospitality, Household Goods, In-Store Advertising, Integrated Marketing, International, Internet/Web Design, Leisure, Local Marketing, Logo & Package Design, Luxury Products, Magazines, Market Research, Media Buying Services, Media Planning, Medical Products, Men's Market, Merchandising, Mobile Marketing, Multicultural, Multimedia, New Product Development, Newspaper, Newspapers & Magazines, Out-of-Home Media, Outdoor, Over-50 Market, Package Design, Paid Searches, Pharmaceutical, Planning & Consultation, Podcasting, Point of Purchase, Point of Sale, Print, Product Placement, Production, Production (Ad, Film, Broadcast), Production (Print), Promotions, Publicity/Promotions, Radio, Real Estate, Regional, Restaurant, Retail, Sales Promotion, Search Engine Optimization, Social Marketing/Nonprofit, Social Media, Strategic Planning/Research, T.V., Teen Market, Telemarketing, Trade & Consumer Magazines, Transportation, Travel & Tourism, Tween Market, Urban Market, Viral/Buzz/Word of Mouth, Web (Banner Ads, Pop-ups, etc.), Women's Market

Approx. Annual Billings: $1,000,000

Vincent Fortin *(Partner & Acct Dir)*
Vincent Fortin-Laurin *(Partner & Acct Dir)*
Jean-Philippe Shoiry *(Partner & Strategist-New Media)*

Accounts:
AMQ/CMA Quebec Medical Association; 2011
Blakes; Montreal, QC & Toronto, ON Lawyers; 2005
Campagna Motors TRX & V13R Vehicles; 2011
Children's Wish Foundation; 2012
GARDA Security; 2008
Glutenberg/BSG Gluten-free Beers; 2012
Hydro-Quebec; Montreal, QC Hydro; 2000
Integrim; Montreal, QC Digital Information; 2009
Loranger Marcoux; Montreal, QC Lawyers; 2008
LUSH
MD Physician Services Financial & Administrative Services; 2011
Moet Hennessy (Creative Digital Agency of Record) Belvedere, Glenmorangie, Hennessy, Social Media, Veuve Clicquot
Orchestre Symphonique de Longueuil; Longueuil Symphony Orchestra; 2007
Ordre des Pharmaciens du Quebec; 2012
Regie du Cinema Cinema Quebec Government Agency; 2010
Reves d'enfants Foundation; 2012
Sani Marc Sanitizing Product Distributor; 2012

REPUTATION INK

1303 N Main St Ste 108, Jacksonville, FL 32206
Tel.: (904) 374-5733
E-Mail: info@rep-ink.com
Web Site: www.rep-ink.com

Agency Specializes In: Advertising, Public Relations, Strategic Planning/Research

Michelle King *(Pres & Principal)*
Heather Kingry *(VP-Content)*
Kristi A. Dosh *(VP-PR)*
Allison Banko *(Sr Acct Exec)*

Accounts:
New-Nocatee Community
New-The PARC Group
New-Stellar

REPUTATION PARTNERS

105 W Adams St Ste 2220, Chicago, IL 60603
Tel.: (312) 222-9887
Fax: (312) 222-9755
E-Mail: info@reputationpartners.com
Web Site: www.reputationpartners.com

Employees: 12

National Agency Associations: COPF

Agency Specializes In: Communications, Crisis Communications, Media Relations, Media Training, Strategic Planning/Research

Revenue: $1,500,000

Nicholas Kalm *(Founder, Pres & CEO)*
Jane G. Devron *(Co-Founder & Sr VP)*
Courtney Harper *(Sr VP)*

Jamie Veal *(VP)*
Ashley Dennison *(Acct Dir)*
Brendan Griffith *(Acct Dir)*
Lynn Sheka *(Acct Dir)*

Accounts:
PulteGroup
WPS Health Insurance

RESEARCH DEVELOPMENT & PROMOTIONS
(d/b/a RDP)
360 Menores Ave, Coral Gables, FL 33134
Tel.: (305) 445-4997
Fax: (305) 445-4221
E-Mail: info@rdppromotions.com
Web Site: www.rdppromotions.com

Employees: 6

Agency Specializes In: Advertising, Food Service

Robert N. Del Pozo *(Owner & Pres)*
Richard G. Amundsen *(Exec VP)*
Victoria Goldstein-Macadar *(VP-PR)*
Peter Ekstein *(Dir-Creative)*
Mary Keel *(Supvr-Bus Dev & Acct Supvr)*

Accounts:
American Airlines
Bacardi USA
CBS/Telemundo
Coca-Cola Refreshments USA, Inc.
Conrad Hilton Hotel
J. Schlitz Brewing
Merrick Festival
Pfizer
Unilever

RESERVOIR
5721 Monkland, Montreal, QC H4A 1E7 Canada
Tel.: (514) 489-1534
Fax: (514) 483-6692
E-Mail: production@reservoirmontreal.com
Web Site: www.reservoir.ca

Employees: 10

Agency Specializes In: Graphic Design, Integrated Marketing, Publicity/Promotions, Strategic Planning/Research

Simon Boulanger *(Partner)*
Mitch Cayouette *(Sr Dir-Art)*
Renee Hudon *(Dir-Artistic)*
Philippe De L'Etoile *(Acct Mgr)*

RESH MARKETING CONSULTANTS, INC.
22 Surrey Ct, Columbia, SC 29212-3140
Tel.: (803) 798-0009
Fax: (803) 798-3413
E-Mail: info@resh.com
Web Site: www.resh.com

Employees: 5
Year Founded: 1979

Agency Specializes In: Broadcast, Cable T.V., Co-op Advertising, Communications, Consulting, Consumer Marketing, Consumer Publications, Direct Response Marketing, E-Commerce, Electronic Media, Exhibit/Trade Shows, Graphic Design, Industrial, Infomercials, Internet/Web Design, Magazines, Media Buying Services, Newspaper, Newspapers & Magazines, Outdoor, Planning & Consultation, Point of Purchase, Print, Production, Public Relations, Publicity/Promotions, Radio, Real Estate, T.V., Travel & Tourism

Hal Von Nessen *(Principal)*

Accounts:
Colony Builders
Keystone Homes
Rymarc Homes

RESOLUTION MEDIA
225 N Michigan Ave, Chicago, IL 60601
Tel.: (312) 980-1600
Fax: (312) 980-1699
Web Site: www.resolutionmedia.com

Employees: 85

National Agency Associations: 4A's

Agency Specializes In: Search Engine Optimization, Sponsorship

Alan Osetek *(Pres-Global)*
Jeff Campbell *(Sr VP & Mng Dir-Central)*
Viji Davis *(VP-Mktg)*
Kate DuBois *(Reg Dir-Midwest)*
Kris McDermott *(Acct Dir)*
Kieran Dunn *(Dir-Bus Dev)*
Ted Schuster *(Dir-Adv)*
Jonavan Smith *(Dir-Fin)*
Sakinah Charbeneau *(Assoc Dir-Mktg)*
Nicole Jaureguy Gardner *(Assoc Dir-Adv & Acct)*
Brooke Handwerker *(Assoc Dir-Client Strategy & Dev)*
Rachel Aguiar *(Mgr-Mktg)*
Casey Sheehan *(Acct Supvr)*
Miles Betley *(Supvr-Adv Solutions)*
Annie Condron *(Supvr-SEO Content)*
Meaghan Murphy *(Supvr-Adv)*
Ellen Potapov *(Supvr-Social Media)*
Marly Schuman *(Supvr-Social Media)*
Will Longhini *(Sr Strategist-Adv)*
Ariel Evans *(Strategist-Social Media-Adv Solutions)*
Rebecca Mensing *(Strategist-Social Media)*
Alexandra Stolarski *(Strategist-Social Media)*
Luise Walter *(Strategist)*
Andrew Heisler *(Coord-Social)*
Elizabeth Saathoff *(Coord-Adv)*
Kate Tummelson *(Coord-Mktg)*
Daanish Chishti *(Assoc Acct Dir)*
Natalie Ezeta *(Assoc Acct Dir)*
Lindsey Nelson *(Assoc Acct Dir)*
Bergen Rebello *(Assoc Acct Dir)*

Accounts:
The Gatorade Company
The Hertz Corporation
Hewlett-Packard
HTC Corporation
Levi's
Lowe's
Pepsi
State Farm
Unilever Search Engine Marketing, Search Engine Optimization
Visa

Branches

Resolution Media
195 Broadway 20th Fl, New York, NY 10017
Tel.: (312) 980-1600
E-Mail: Info@ResolutionMedia.com
Web Site: www.resolutionmedia.com

Employees: 31

Jeff Campbell *(Co-Founder & VP)*
Amman Badlani *(Dir-SEO)*
Lillian Chuo *(Dir)*
Chris Longo *(Dir)*
Jennifer Chiang *(Assoc Dir-Paid Search)*
Jacinta Gandy *(Assoc Dir-Social)*
Jessica Bader *(Acct Mgr-Search)*
Julie Lubin *(Supvr-Adv-Paid Search)*
Jonathan Yantz *(Supvr-Social Media)*

Accounts:
Briggs & Stratton
FedEx
Hertz
HP
Lowe's
McDonald's
Pier 1imports
State Farm Insurance

RESOUND CREATIVE
8400 S Kyrene Rd Ste 125, Tempe, AZ 85284
Tel.: (480) 351-4857
E-Mail: gimme@resoundcreative.com
Web Site: www.resoundcreative.com

Agency Specializes In: Advertising, Brand Development & Integration, Content, Graphic Design, Internet/Web Design

Mike Jones *(Mng Partner & Strategist-Brand)*
Jeff Watson *(Dir-Content Strategy)*
Kayla Izard *(Specialist-Mktg)*
Matt Le *(Designer)*
Luke Miller *(Acct Rep)*
Douglas Morales *(Web Developer)*

Accounts:
DollarDays International, LLC

RESOURCE
(Merged with Ammirati)

RESOURCE/AMMIRATI
400 N Michigan Ave Ste 600, Chicago, IL 60611
Tel.: (312) 801-7100
E-Mail: inquiry@resource.com
Web Site: www.resourceammirati.com

Agency Specializes In: Advertising, Brand Development & Integration, Business-To-Business, Digital/Interactive, Social Media

Deirdre Egan *(Mng Dir)*

Accounts:
New-Kohl's Corporation

Branch

Resource/Ammirati
(Formerly Ammirati)
19 Union Sq W 11th Fl, New York, NY 10003
Tel.: (212) 925-2111
E-Mail: inquiry@resource.com
Web Site: www.resourceammirati.com

Employees: 200

Agency Specializes In: Advertising, Brand Development & Integration, Identity Marketing, Shopper Marketing, Social Media, Sponsorship, Web (Banner Ads, Pop-ups, etc.)

Matthew Ammirati *(Chm-Creative)*
Gabriel Miller *(Pres & Partner)*
Kristen Rumble *(Partner & Exec VP-Brand Strategy)*
Todd Wender *(Partner & Exec Dir-Creative)*
Mike Frame *(CFO)*
Giles Hendrix *(Exec Dir-Interactive)*
Andrew Haynes *(Dir-Art)*
Kent Sednaoui *(Dir-New Bus)*
Nicole Zizila *(Dir-Creative)*
Steven Zizila *(Dir-Creative)*
Ola Abayomi *(Acct Mgr)*

Accounts:
Birchbox Advertising, Brand Awareness,

Broadcast, Campaign: "A Better Way to Beautiful", Campaign: "Open for Beautiful", Campaign: "There's a Better Way", Creative
North American Breweries Campaign: "Blue Gold", Campaign: "Get Undomesticated", Creative, Labatt Beer, Labatt Blue, Print, Seagram's Escapes, Traditional Broadcast

RESOURCE COMMUNICATIONS GROUP

6404 International Pkwy Ste 1550, Plano, TX 75093
Tel.: (972) 447-9000
Fax: (972) 447-9002
E-Mail: rcg@rescomm.com
Web Site: www.rescomm.com

E-Mail for Key Personnel:
President: tgold@rescomm.com
Production Mgr.: jgold@rescomm.com

Employees: 7
Year Founded: 1990

Agency Specializes In: Advertising, Business-To-Business, Collateral, Education, Health Care Services, Internet/Web Design, Newspapers & Magazines, Outdoor, Production (Print), Real Estate, Recruitment, Seniors' Market, Web (Banner Ads, Pop-ups, etc.)

Approx. Annual Billings: $4,000,000

Breakdown of Gross Billings by Media: Bus. Publs.: $200,000; Collateral: $80,000; D.M.: $40,000; Internet Adv.: $200,000; Newsp.: $3,400,000; Outdoor: $40,000; Radio & T.V.: $40,000

Tamara Gold *(Mgr & Principal)*

Accounts:
Center For Advanced Legal Studies
First National Bank; Omaha, NE
Pinnacle Partners in Medicine
SKIFE Medical Center

RESPOND2 CMEDIA

(Name Changed to R2C Group)

RESPONSE LLC

100 Crown St, New Haven, CT 6510
Tel.: (203) 776-2400
E-Mail: info@thepowertoprovoke.com
Web Site: www.thepowertoprovoke.com

Agency Specializes In: Advertising, Brand Development & Integration, Content, Digital/Interactive, Print, Social Marketing/Nonprofit

Carolyn Walker *(Partner & CEO)*
Kim DeMartino *(VP-Client Svcs)*
Ashley Marshall *(Sr Designer)*

Accounts:
New-Stony Creek Brewery

RESPONSE MARKETING GROUP LLC

8730 Stony Point Pky Ste 250, Richmond, VA 23235-1969
Tel.: (804) 747-3711
Fax: (804) 225-0500
E-Mail: mail@rmg-usa.com
Web Site: www.rmg-usa.com

Employees: 15
Year Founded: 1993

Agency Specializes In: Advertising, Brand Development & Integration, Business-To-Business, Corporate Communications, Internet/Web Design, Logo & Package Design, Media Buying Services, Merchandising, New Product Development, Pharmaceutical, Print, Production, Public Relations, Publicity/Promotions, Sales Promotion, Strategic Planning/Research, Trade & Consumer Magazines

Approx. Annual Billings: $10,400,000

Breakdown of Gross Billings by Media: Adv. Specialities: $920,000; Audio/Visual: $460,000; Consulting: $460,000; E-Commerce: $460,000; Event Mktg.: $460,000; Graphic Design: $460,000; Logo & Package Design: $1,288,000; Print: $1,196,000; Production: $1,288,000; Radio & T.V.: $920,000; Trade & Consumer Mags.: $2,488,000

David Klineberg *(Partner & VP-Strategy)*
Brian Long *(Chief Creative Officer)*

Accounts:
Carpenter
Stainmaster

RESPONSE MEDIA, INC.

3155 Medlock Bridge Rd, Norcross, GA 30071-1423
Tel.: (770) 451-5478
Fax: (770) 451-4929
E-Mail: postmaster@responsemedia.com
Web Site: www.responsemedia.com

Employees: 55
Year Founded: 1979

National Agency Associations: DMA

Agency Specializes In: Bilingual Market, Business-To-Business, Direct Response Marketing, Electronic Media, Fashion/Apparel, Financial, High Technology, Hispanic Market, New Product Development, Out-of-Home Media, Pharmaceutical, Sales Promotion, Strategic Planning/Research

Approx. Annual Billings: $33,000,000

Breakdown of Gross Billings by Media: D.M.: $25,000,000; Internet Adv.: $3,000,000; Other: $5,000,000

Josh Perlstein *(CEO)*
Douglas Breuer *(COO)*
Keith Perlstein *(CTO)*
Michael McMackin *(VP-Fin & HR & Controller)*
Michelle Rainbow *(VP-Media & Campaign Mgmt)*
Diane Widerstrom *(VP-Integrated Svcs)*
Vencilla Ejaz *(Sr Acct Mgr)*

Accounts:
Abbott
Advanstar Communications
Advanta
Aegon
AIG
Alaska Tourism
American Airlines
American Diabetes Association
American General
American Red Cross
AT&T Communications Corp.
Bank of America
AT&T Southeast
Blair Corp.; Warren, PA; 1982
Brown & Williamson
Cadillac
Canine Health Foundation
Capitol One, NEBS; Boston, MA Business to Business Catalog
Charter Communications
Chicago Council on Foreign Affairs
Children's Book of the Month Club
ChildFund International
CitiFinancial
Colgate Palmolive
Colonial Penn
Compaq Computer Corp.
Compuware
Butterball, LLC
Countrywide
Cox Business Services
Disney
Drs. Foster & Smith
DS Waters of America, Inc.
E*Trade
Epson
Exact Software
First Union
Fredericks of Hollywood
GEICO Insurance
Georgia Power
Georgia Tourism
Grandparents.com
Habitat for Humanity
Heinz
Honda
i2
IBM
Iridium
JCPenney
JCPenney Portrait Studios
JD Edwards
Jensen Tools
Juno; NY; 1996
Kraft General Foods
Lexus
Marriott Hotels
Merck
Metropolitan Life Insurance
Microsoft
Minnesota Tourism
Moen
National Parkinson Association
Nestle
Omaha Steaks; 2001
One Step Ahead
Peachtree Software
Pfizer
Philips Petroleum
Physicians Mutual Insurance Company
PlaceWare/Live Meeting
Procter & Gamble
Rational Software
Renaissance Cruise Lines
Royal Caribbean
Saab
The Salvation Army
Sanofi-Synthelabo
SHUTTERFLY, INC
Sprint
Staples Direct Catalog
Stork Avenue
SunTrust
Swiss Colony
Sycom
Thompson Cigar
Time Warner/AOL
Unilever
United Way
Verizon
Wachovia
West Marine
Westinghouse
Yves Rocher; 2001

RESPONSE MINE INTERACTIVE

(Formerly Response Mine)
3390 Peachtree Rd Ste 800, Atlanta, GA 30326
Tel.: (404) 233-0370
Fax: (404) 233-0302
E-Mail: contact@responsemine.com
Web Site: www.responsemine.com

Employees: 70
Year Founded: 2001

Agency Specializes In: Advertising, Advertising Specialties, Consumer Marketing,

Digital/Interactive, Graphic Design, Internet/Web Design

Ken Robbins *(Founder & Pres)*
David Secrest *(Partner-Mktg & VP-Ops)*
Brent Wheeler *(Sr VP)*
Ryan Woolley *(Sr VP-Digital Mktg Svcs)*
Andrew Baum *(VP-Partner Mktg)*
Mark Hamilton *(VP-Fin)*
Richard E. Skaggs *(Member)*

Accounts:
American Home Shield
Carter's/Osh Kosh B'Gosh Digital Marketing; 2010
Laser Spine Institute Digital Marketing
LD Products
Liberty Medical
Navy Federal Credit Union
Rooms To Go Digital Marketing; 2004
The Scooter Store
Terminex
TryuGreen

THE RESPONSE SHOP, INC.
7486 La Jolla Blvd Ste 164, La Jolla, CA 92037
Tel.: (858) 735-7646
Fax: (858) 777-5418
E-Mail: marla@responseshop.com
Web Site: www.responseshop.com

Employees: 12
Year Founded: 2000

National Agency Associations: DMA

Agency Specializes In: Advertising, African-American Market, Bilingual Market, Broadcast, Business-To-Business, Cable T.V., Consulting, Consumer Marketing, Consumer Publications, Direct Response Marketing, Electronic Media, Entertainment, Financial, Hispanic Market, Infomercials, Internet/Web Design, Media Buying Services, Newspaper, Over-50 Market, Pets , Pharmaceutical, Print, Radio, Seniors' Market, T.V., Teen Market, Telemarketing, Trade & Consumer Magazines, Travel & Tourism

Marla Hoskins *(Founder & Pres)*
Sam Auster *(Pres-Auster Productions)*
Jean B. Hall *(Copywriter)*
Peter Hochstein *(Copywriter)*

Accounts:
1-800 Pet Meds
1800Medicine; Irvine, CA Diabetes Supplies
AARP; Washington, DC Membership
AOL, LLC; Dulles, VA Internet Service; 2003
Cheapoair.com; New York, NY
The Chicago Tribune Daily Newspaper; 2002
eFax.com
eHealthInsurance, Inc.
FreeCreditReport.com; Irvine, CA Credit Monitoring Service; 2002
The Hacker Group; Bellevue, WA; 2005
IntuitWebsites.com; Mountainview, CA
JustListed.com
Real Health Laboratories; 2001
Reynolds Handi-Vac
Time-Life Music; Alexandria, VA Music Compilations; 2004
Trendwest Resorts; Redmond, WA Time Share Sales; 2002
TurboTax; San Diego, CA TurboTax Federal Free Edition
Unitrin Direct; Vista, CA Auto Insurance; 2004
Wyndham Vacation Ownership; Orlando, FL Time-Share Sales; 2003

RESPONSORY
(Formerly Johnson Direct)
250 Bishops Way, Brookfield, WI 53005
Tel.: (262) 782-2750
Toll Free: (800) 710-2750
E-Mail: info@responsory.com
Web Site: www.responsory.com

Employees: 13
Year Founded: 1999

National Agency Associations: DMA

Agency Specializes In: Advertising, Automotive, Brand Development & Integration, Business Publications, Business-To-Business, Collateral, Communications, Consulting, Consumer Marketing, Corporate Identity, Cosmetics, Direct Response Marketing, Education, Financial, Graphic Design, Health Care Services, High Technology, Industrial, Information Technology, Internet/Web Design, Medical Products, Over-50 Market, Pharmaceutical, Point of Sale, Public Relations, Seniors' Market, Trade & Consumer Magazines, Travel & Tourism, Yellow Pages Advertising

Approx. Annual Billings: $21,000,000

Breakdown of Gross Billings by Media: D.M.: $21,000,000

Grant A. Johnson *(Pres & CEO)*
Mara J Frier *(COO)*
Denise B. Hearden *(VP-Digital)*
Maria Johnson *(VP)*
Lisa Robbins *(VP-Client Svcs)*
Robert Trecek *(Dir-Bus Dev)*
Becky Behrendt *(Acct Exec)*

Accounts:
ASQ Quality-Association
Blue Cross Blue Shield of Kansas Health Insurance
BMO Harris Banking
Kleen Test Products Contract Manufacturing
Security Health Plan Health Insurance

RESULTRIX
(Acquired by Publicis Groupe S.A.)

RESULTS DIRECT MARKETING
555 N Woodlawn Ste 300, Wichita, KS 67208-3683
Tel.: (316) 689-8555
Fax: (316) 689-8111
Toll Free: (877) 689-8555
Web Site: www.resultsdm.com

Employees: 15
Year Founded: 1998

National Agency Associations: DMA-Second Wind Limited

Agency Specializes In: Automotive, Direct Response Marketing, Print, Production, Retail

Buddy Kuhn *(Pres)*
Peter Janssen *(VP)*
Matt Weber *(VP)*
Andrea Hollingsworth *(Dir-Fin)*
Maia Briggs *(Mgr-Mktg)*
Kim Lawrence *(Mgr-Production)*
Cinda York *(Mgr-Mktg Svcs)*
Christina Duncan *(Coord-Mktg)*

Accounts:
BG Boltons Restaurant
Citibank
Color Tyme
Corporate Lodging
Jiffy Lube International
Kansas Aviation Museum
Plains Captial McAfee Mortgage
Rainbow Rentals
Rapid Rentals
Rent-A-Center
Reserve National Insurance Company
Shell Oil

RESULTS, INC., ADVERTISING AGENCY
777 Terrace Ave, Hasbrouck Heights, NJ 07604-0822
Tel.: (201) 288-7888
Fax: (201) 288-5112
E-Mail: info@resultsinc.com
Web Site: www.resultsinc.com

Employees: 10
Year Founded: 1954

Agency Specializes In: Advertising, Brand Development & Integration, Broadcast, Business Publications, Business-To-Business, Cable T.V., Collateral, Commercial Photography, Communications, Consulting, Consumer Marketing, Consumer Publications, Corporate Identity, Digital/Interactive, Direct Response Marketing, Direct-to-Consumer, E-Commerce, Event Planning & Marketing, Financial, Infomercials, Internet/Web Design, Logo & Package Design, Media Buying Services, New Product Development, Newspaper, Newspapers & Magazines, Out-of-Home Media, Outdoor, Pharmaceutical, Point of Purchase, Point of Sale, Print, Production, Public Relations, Publicity/Promotions, Radio, Real Estate, Recruitment, Retail, Seniors' Market, T.V., Trade & Consumer Magazines

Approx. Annual Billings: $9,200,000

Breakdown of Gross Billings by Media: Brdcst.: 10%; Cable T.V.: 5%; Collateral: 5%; Internet Adv.: 25%; Newsp. & Mags.: 40%; Outdoor: 5%; Pub. Rels.: 5%; Spot Radio: 5%

David I. Green *(Pres & CEO)*

Accounts:
Advanced Realty Group
Bergman
Builder Marketing Services
Hovnanian Industries; Tinton Falls, NJ Real Estate
Kennedy Funding; Hackensack, NJ Private Lender
Mack Cali Realty Corp
NJ Retina
Silver Arches Capitol Partners

THE RETAIL MARKETING GROUP, INC.
1875 Lockeway Dr Ste 706, Alpharetta, GA 30004
Tel.: (770) 903-1108
Fax: (770) 903-1129
Toll Free: (800) 364-5230
E-Mail: marv@rmgweb.net
Web Site: www.retailmarketinggroup.com

Employees: 7
Year Founded: 1993

Agency Specializes In: Direct Response Marketing, Print, Production, Strategic Planning/Research

Approx. Annual Billings: $6,000,000

Breakdown of Gross Billings by Media: D.M.: $2,400,000; Newsp.: $3,600,000

Marv Beneteau *(Owner)*
Suzanne Beneteau *(Mgr)*

RETELE COMPANY
15 Division St, Greenwich, CT 06830
Tel.: (203) 629-1261
E-Mail: dgamanos@aol.com
Web Site: www.reteleco.com

Employees: 3
Year Founded: 1986

Agency Specializes In: Advertising, Brand Development & Integration, Business-To-Business, Communications, Consumer Publications, Exhibit/Trade Shows, Food Service, Internet/Web Design, Local Marketing, Logo & Package Design, Magazines, Media Buying Services, Medical Products, New Product Development, Newspaper, Newspapers & Magazines, Out-of-Home Media, Outdoor, Planning & Consultation, Print, Production, Publicity/Promotions, Radio, Real Estate, Restaurant, Retail, Sales Promotion, T.V., Transportation, Travel & Tourism

Dean C. Gamanos *(Pres)*

Accounts:
Ayhans Mediterranean Brands; Long Island, NY Salad Dressings
Carousel: Stamford, CT Balloons, Propane
Greenwich Wine Society Wine Club
Just Bulbs; New York, NY Lighting
Kellari Taverna; New York, NY Restaurant
Rick's Fix-It Home Repairs
Rosie O'Grady; New York, NY Food Services
Thatcher Courier Systems; New York, NY Business Services
Westchester Wine School; NY Wine Education
Wine Wise Beverage Retailer
Yates Scapes Landscape Design

RETHINC ADVERTISING

4714 N 44th St, Phoenix, AZ 85018
Tel.: (480) 268-9588
Fax: (480) 268-9877
Web Site: www.rethincadvertising.com

Agency Specializes In: Advertising, Brand Development & Integration, Digital/Interactive, Graphic Design, Media Buying Services, Outdoor, Print, Promotions, Radio, Social Media

Ed Olsen *(Pres)*
Stephanie Riley *(Principal)*
Andrew Gibson *(Coord-Social Media & Mktg)*

Accounts:
Fort McDowell Casino

RETHINK

700-470 Granvill St, Vancouver, BC V6C 1V5 Canada
Tel.: (604) 685-8911
Fax: (604) 685-9004
E-Mail: tomshepansky@rethinkcanada.com
Web Site: www.rethinkcanada.com

Employees: 60
Year Founded: 1999

Ian Grais *(Founder & Creative Dir-Natl)*
Aaron Starkman *(Partner & Dir-Creative)*
Max May *(Partner)*
Mitch McKamey *(Partner)*
Ailsa Brown *(Acct Dir)*
Dan Culic *(Acct Dir)*
Marjo Durand *(Acct Dir)*
Laura Rioux *(Producer-Brdcst)*
Chris Staples *(Creative Dir)*
Chelsea Stoelting *(Acct Dir)*
Sarah Vingoe *(Producer-Brdcst)*
Bob Simpson *(Dir-Creative & Writer)*
Irene Pau *(Dir-Art)*
Nicolas Quintal *(Dir-Creative & Art)*
Mike Dubrick *(Assoc Dir-Creative)*
Joel Holtby *(Assoc Dir-Creative)*
Lisa Nakamura *(Assoc Dir-Creative)*
Haley Kriksic *(Acct Mgr)*
Albane Rousselot *(Acct Mgr)*
Leah Gregg *(Strategist-Content)*
Arrabelle Stavroff *(Copywriter)*

Accounts:
2K Sports
A&W Campaign: "Better Beef", Creative, TV
Alzheimer Society of British Columbia Campaign: "Brain Scan"
BC Adventure
New-BC Centre for Disease Control
BC Lions
Bladeworks Fencing Society
Broke Bike Alley
Bulk Cat Litter Warehouse
The Canadian Fairtrade Network
Canadian Institute of Diversity & Inclusion "Hello, My Name is Vladimir", "Luge" Winter Olympics 2014, #NotForGay
Canadian Men's Health Foundation Advertising, Brand Strategy, Creative
Children of the Street Society
Chris Tarry Campaign: "Rest of the Story"
Coast Capital Savings
Credit Counselling Society of British Columbia Campaign: "Cut Credit Business Card"
Dogwood Initiative Campaign: "Oil Poster"
Funktion
Greenpeace
Hip Baby
New-ImmunizeBC
La Charcuterie
Langara College
Lavalife Campaign: "Clickchange"
Leukemia & Lymphoma Society of Canada
Masterfile.com
Metro News Campaign: "Cabbage"
Molson Coors Canada (Lead Agency) Campaign: "Guyet", Campaign: "I Am Canadian", Campaign: "Seed Coaster", Campaign: "The Beer Fridge: Project Indonesia", Coors Light, Molson Canadian, Rickards, Social, TV
Mr. Lube
Muskoka Brewery Campaign: "Muskoka Mode iPhone App"
Muskoka Beer
NAIT
Norburn Model Aircraft Supply
Offsetters Ice Cube Tray
Orkin PCO Services
Pacific National Exhibition
Palladin Security
Panorama Hair
Pastry Training Centre
Peer 1 Web Hosting
Plastic Pollution Coalition
Playland Campaign: "Fear Made Fun", Campaign: "Pigeon", Campaign: "Seeing Cars"
Realizer
Science World "Science of Sports", Campaign: "Apparitions", Campaign: "Now You Know", Campaign: "Positively Painful", Creative, Online, Print, TV
Scotts Miracle-Gro Company (Agency of Record) Advertising, Brand Strategy, Miracle-Gro, Ortho, Scotts
Shaw Campaign: "You won't miss a thing"
New-Slack Display, Print
Slice
Soma
Sparrow Guitars
Splashdown Waterpark Campaign: "Woman"
Sport Chek Campaign: "What are You Sweating for?", Creative
Vancouver Canadians
Vancouver Orphan Kitten Rescue Association
Vancouver Police Department
Variety
Victoria Bug Zoo
Vonnegut Dollhouse
Wanderlust
Wayne Kozak Stationary
YWCA

Branch

Rethink

110 Spadina Ave Ste 200, Toronto, ON M5V 2K4 Canada
Tel.: (416) 583-2178
Web Site: www.rethinkcanada.com

Employees: 20

Andy Macaulay *(Mng Partner)*
Maxine Thomas *(Partner & Head-Strategy)*
Dre Labre *(Partner & Creative Dir)*
Aaron Starkman *(Partner & Dir-Creative)*
Scott Lyons *(Acct Dir)*
Chris Staples *(Creative Dir)*
Eric Arnold *(Dir-Art)*
Joel Holtby *(Dir-Art)*
Felipe Mollica *(Dir-Art)*
Rob Tarry *(Dir-Creative)*
Morgan Tierney *(Assoc Dir-Creative)*
Kai De Bruyn Kops *(Acct Mgr)*
Lynn Summers *(Acct Exec)*
Sean O'Connor *(Copywriter)*

Accounts:
Canadian Cancer Society
Canadian Fair Trade Network
Historica Canada
Justin Poulsen
Metro Canada Campaign: "Available anywhere. Download the Metro app today.", Campaign: "Pocket Sized"
Molson Coors Canada (Agency of Record) Beer Fridge, Campaign: "Wake Up", Canadian & Rickard's Brands (Agency of Record)
Parissa
Science World
Sheridan College
Toronto Star (Agency of Record)
Uber

RETHINK CREATIVE GROUP

401 Pebble Way, Arlington, TX 76006
Tel.: (571) 264-0522
Web Site: rethinkcreative.org

Year Founded: 2013

Agency Specializes In: Advertising, Affluent Market, Brand Development & Integration, Business-To-Business, College, Consulting, Content, Corporate Identity, Digital/Interactive, Direct-to-Consumer, E-Commerce, Electronic Media, Email, Event Planning & Marketing, Faith Based, Graphic Design, Guerilla Marketing, Identity Marketing, Integrated Marketing, Internet/Web Design, Logo & Package Design, Media Buying Services, Men's Market, Package Design, Planning & Consultation, Print, Production (Ad, Film, Broadcast), Promotions, Public Relations, Publicity/Promotions, RSS (Really Simple Syndication), Radio, Regional, Sales Promotion, Social Marketing/Nonprofit, Social Media, Strategic Planning/Research, T.V., Teen Market, Web (Banner Ads, Pop-ups, etc.), Women's Market

David Valentine *(CEO)*

Accounts:
Adelbert's Brewery
jobipedia; 2015
Veritas Life Adventures; 2015

RETHINK MEDIA GROUP

729 Monroe St, Quincy, IL 62301
Tel.: (217) 222-2288
Fax: (217) 222-2286
Web Site: www.rethinkmediagroup.net

Agency Specializes In: Advertising, Internet/Web Design, Media Planning, Print, Radio, Strategic Planning/Research, T.V.

Corie Royer *(Co-Owner)*

Susan Till *(Co-Owner)*

Accounts:
Merkel Metal Recycling & Container Service

RETNA MEDIA INC.
2100 W Loop S Ste 900, Houston, TX 77027
Tel.: (917) 727-1540
E-Mail: info@retnamedia.com
Web Site: www.retnamedia.com

Agency Specializes In: Advertising, Brand Development & Integration, Broadcast, Digital/Interactive, Direct Response Marketing, Email, Logo & Package Design, Package Design, Web (Banner Ads, Pop-ups, etc.)

Fritz Colinet *(Exec Dir-Creative)*

Accounts:
Cafe Centosette Food Services
The Latino Click LLC. Entertainment Services

RETZ ADVERTISING + DESIGN
(Formerly retzcanter)
8051 Cazenovia Rd, Manlius, NY 13104
Tel.: (315) 579-0999
Web Site: retzad.com/

Employees: 3
Year Founded: 1992

Agency Specializes In: Brand Development & Integration, Business-To-Business, Catalogs, Collateral, Consumer Marketing, Corporate Identity, Education, Email, Financial, Graphic Design, Health Care Services, High Technology, Industrial, Internet/Web Design, Logo & Package Design, Medical Products, Multimedia, Newspaper, Package Design, Real Estate, Retail, Strategic Planning/Research

Donald Retz *(Owner & Dir-Creative)*
John Taborosi *(Dir-Bus Dev & Ops)*

Accounts:
Oberdorfer Aluminum Foundry

REUBEN RINK
939 Burke St Ste A, Winston Salem, NC 27101
Tel.: (336) 724-1766
E-Mail: info@reubenrink.com
Web Site: www.reubenrink.com

Agency Specializes In: Advertising, Broadcast, Digital/Interactive, Print, Social Media, Strategic Planning/Research

J. G. Wolfe *(Owner & Pres)*
Penny Booze *(Controller)*
Linda Darnall *(Creative Dir)*
Keith Hutchens *(Sr Art Dir)*
Kit Falvey *(Dir-Client Svcs)*
Randy Jones *(Dir-Content Dev)*
Jay McLain *(Dir-Digital Art)*
Martha Murphy *(Dir-PR)*
Amanda Marshall *(Mgr-Acct Relationship)*
Michelle Samuel *(Acct Coord)*

Accounts:
Piedmont Wind Symphony

REVANA DIGITAL
(Formerly Webmetro)
(d/b/a Multivest)
160 E Via Verde Ave Ste 100, San Dimas, CA 91773-3901
Tel.: (909) 599-8885
Toll Free: (866) 922-4632
E-Mail: info@revana.com
Web Site: www.revanadigital.com

Employees: 40
Year Founded: 1995

National Agency Associations: AMA

Agency Specializes In: Advertising, Affiliate Marketing, Bilingual Market, Business-To-Business, Consulting, Content, Digital/Interactive, Direct Response Marketing, Direct-to-Consumer, E-Commerce, Electronic Media, Email, Hispanic Market, Information Technology, Integrated Marketing, Internet/Web Design, Local Marketing, Market Research, Media Planning, New Technologies, Sponsorship, Web (Banner Ads, Pop-ups, etc.)

Approx. Annual Billings: $26,000,000

Breakdown of Gross Billings by Media: E-Commerce: $1,000,000; Internet Adv.: $25,000,000

Martin Longo *(CTO)*
Patrick Burke *(VP-Program Sls)*
Jonathan Gray *(VP-Mktg & Bus Dev)*
Karen Helweg *(VP-User Engagement)*
Arnold Sandoval *(VP-Client Strategy)*
Jennifer Taylor-Scordia *(VP-Client Strategy)*
Laura Ward *(VP-Ops & Tech)*
Ryan Adams *(Exec Dir-Program Sls)*
Barbara Wingle *(Exec Dir-Strategic Mktg & Analytics)*
Jessie Mamey *(Sr Dir-Media)*
Casey Chapouris *(Client Svcs Dir)*
Barbra Balog *(Dir-Program Sls)*
Zanya Medrano *(Dir-Program Sls)*
Russ Mensik *(Team Head & Sr Mgr-eMarketing)*

Accounts:
American Management Association; New York, NY Management Training; 2006
Hair Club Email, Interactive Media, Landing Page Optimization, Online Acquisition Strategy, Search Engine Marketing
Honest Florist
Public Storage; Los Angeles, CA Self Storage

REVEL
3303 Lee Pkwy, Dallas, TX 75219
Tel.: (214) 397-0202
Fax: (214) 397-0203
E-Mail: info@revelunited.com
Web Site: www.revelunited.com

Employees: 3
Year Founded: 2006

Agency Specializes In: Advertising, Affluent Market, Brand Development & Integration, Broadcast, Business Publications, Business-To-Business, Children's Market, Collateral, Commercial Photography, Consulting, Consumer Marketing, Corporate Identity, Gay & Lesbian Market, Graphic Design, Health Care Services, Hispanic Market, Identity Marketing, Integrated Marketing, International, Internet/Web Design, Logo & Package Design, Luxury Products, Magazines, Medical Products, Multimedia, Newspaper, Newspapers & Magazines, Outdoor, Package Design, Paid Searches, Planning & Consultation, Point of Purchase, Point of Sale, Print, Production (Print), Radio, Regional, Restaurant, Retail, Strategic Planning/Research, T.V., Technical Advertising, Trade & Consumer Magazines, Transportation, Women's Market

Approx. Annual Billings: $8,600,000

Breakdown of Gross Billings by Media: Consulting: 20%; Radio & T.V.: 80%

Horacio Cobos *(Exec Dir-Creative)*

Accounts:
Baylor Health Care System; Dallas, Texas; 2006
deBoulle; Dallas, TX Jewelry; 2006
Global Smoothie Supply Inc; Dallas, Texas Frutissimo Brand; 2008
Maggie Moo's Ice Cream & Treatery Creative
Marble Slab Creamer Creative
Morrison & Cox
Sound Isolation Company: Charlotte NC; 2007

REVEL ADVERTISING
429 N Boonville, Springfield, MO 65806
Tel.: (417) 368-6966
E-Mail: howdy@reveladvertising.com
Web Site: www.reveladvertising.com

Year Founded: 2010

Agency Specializes In: Advertising, Brand Development & Integration, Internet/Web Design, Print

Chris Jarratt *(Partner & Dir-Creative)*
Amanda Smith *(Dir-Art)*
Shanda Trautman *(Dir-Accounts)*

Accounts:
Missouri State Bears

REVEL INTERACTIVE
559 Gunnison Ave, Grand Junction, CO 81501
Tel.: (970) 444-2084
E-Mail: info@revelinteractive.com
Web Site: www.revelinteractive.com

Agency Specializes In: Advertising, Email, Search Engine Optimization, Social Media

Kayla Wagner *(Founder & Pres)*
Alexandra Kassel *(Dir-Digital Mktg)*
Chelsea Rae Maxwell *(Dir-Client Strategy)*
Christina Brennan *(Mgr-Campaign)*
Rachel Greenrod *(Mgr-Digital Mktg)*
Paige Hall *(Coord-Digital Mktg)*

Accounts:
Nicole Miller

REVEL UNITED
3303 Lee Pkwy Ste 102, Dallas, TX 75219
Tel.: (214) 397-0202
Web Site: www.gorevelunited.com

Year Founded: 2006

Agency Specializes In: Advertising, Brand Development & Integration

Horacio Cobos *(Exec Dir-Creative)*

Accounts:
Baylor Scott & White Health Campaign: "Changing Health Care. For Life"
Great American Cookies
MaggieMoo's Ice Cream & Treatery
Marble Slab Creamery

REVERB COMMUNICATIONS INC.
18711 Tiffeni Dr Ste K, Twain Harte, CA 95383
Tel.: (209) 586-1495
Fax: (209) 586-1855
E-Mail: info@reverbinc.com
Web Site: www.reverbinc.com

Employees: 15

Agency Specializes In: Brand Development & Integration, Collateral, Hospitality, Market Research, Media Buying Services, Package

Design, Public Relations, Recruitment, Sales Promotion, Sponsorship

Doug Kennedy *(Owner)*
Tracie Snitker *(Pres)*
Abby Oliva *(Dir-PR)*
Douglass Perry *(Dir-PR)*
Danitra Alomia *(Sr Mgr-PR)*

Accounts:
3D Chat
Artfire Films
Frima
Harmonix
Majesco Entertainment Company
Pangea Software
Playlogic Entertainment Inc Video Game Publisher
Playlogic Entertainment Inc Entertainment Software Publisher
ZEN Studios Online Gaming Services

REVISION
32 E 31St St, New York, NY 10016
Tel.: (212) 889-0005
Fax: (212) 889-0006
E-Mail: moreinfo@revisionnyc.com

Employees: 15
Year Founded: 1993

Agency Specializes In: Business Publications, Collateral, Communications, Corporate Identity, Digital/Interactive, Entertainment, Fashion/Apparel, Internet/Web Design, Logo & Package Design, Media Buying Services, Outdoor, Planning & Consultation, Print, Public Relations, Sales Promotion, Strategic Planning/Research, Trade & Consumer Magazines, Travel & Tourism

Approx. Annual Billings: $38,000,000

Breakdown of Gross Billings by Media: Mags.: 40%; Newsp. & Mags.: 10%; Outdoor: 5%; Radio: 20%; T.V.: 25%

Alan Blum *(Pres)*
Lori Theisen *(Mng Dir)*

Accounts:
Countess Mara

REVIVEHEALTH
Ste 214, Nashville, TN 37203
Tel.: (615) 742-7242
Web Site: www.thinkrevivehealth.com

Agency Specializes In: Advertising, Brand Development & Integration, Digital/Interactive, Internet/Web Design, Public Relations, Search Engine Optimization, Social Media

Brandon Edwards *(CEO)*
Chris Bevolo *(Exec VP)*
Chris Boyer *(Sr VP-Digital)*
Mark Willis *(Sr VP)*
Katherine Brick *(VP)*
Katie Clark *(Mgr-Mktg)*
Ashley Merchant *(Sr Acct Supvr)*
Libby Werner *(Acct Supvr)*
Carolyn Edwards *(Sr Acct Exec)*
Ashley Webb *(Acct Exec)*

Accounts:
New-Arcadia Healthcare Solutions (Agency of Record)
New-Athenahealth Inc
New-Connecture
New-Kyruus
New-Livongo Health
New-Lucro
New-Pamplona Capital Partners (Strategic Marketing Communication Agency of Record)
New-T-System, Inc.

REVLOCAL
4009 Columbus Rd SW Ste 222, Granville, OH 43023
Tel.: (740) 281-5016
E-Mail: info@revlocal.com
Web Site: www.revlocal.com

Year Founded: 2011

Agency Specializes In: Advertising, Content, Digital/Interactive, Graphic Design, Paid Searches, Search Engine Optimization

Marc Hawk *(Pres)*
Aaron Boggs *(Exec VP)*
Lauren Keegan *(Mgr-Bus Dev)*

Accounts:
New-The Golf Depot

REVOLUTION
(Name Changed to Revolution Marketing LLC)

REVOLUTION MARKETING LLC
(Formerly rEvolution)
600 W Chicago Ave, Chicago, IL 60654
Tel.: (312) 529-5850
Fax: (312) 529-5851
E-Mail: info@revolutionworld.com
Web Site: www.revolutionworld.com

Employees: 65
Year Founded: 2001

National Agency Associations: PMA

Agency Specializes In: Above-the-Line, Advertising, Below-the-Line, Brand Development & Integration, Business-To-Business, Communications, Consulting, Consumer Marketing, Electronic Media, Event Planning & Marketing, Experience Design, Guerilla Marketing, Hospitality, In-Store Advertising, Integrated Marketing, Internet/Web Design, Local Marketing, Media Buying Services, Media Planning, Media Relations, Point of Purchase, Point of Sale, Promotions, Public Relations, Publicity/Promotions, Radio, Social Marketing/Nonprofit, Social Media, Sponsorship, Sports Market, Strategic Planning/Research, Sweepstakes, Teen Market, Urban Market, Viral/Buzz/Word of Mouth, Web (Banner Ads, Pop-ups, etc.)

John Rowady *(Founder & Pres)*
Larry Mann *(Exec VP)*
Dan Lobring *(Mng Dir-Comm)*
Terry Moon *(Mng Dir-Acctg & Fin)*
Scott Kohler *(Dir-Media Svcs)*
Melinda Markley *(Dir-Media)*
David Hood *(Client Svcs Mgr)*

Accounts:
Chipotle
Continental Tire (Sponsorship Marketing Agency of Record)
ESPN
Frosted Flakes
Goose Island
IndyCar
Mizuno
Nat Geo
Northwestern Mutual
Polaris Industries Broadcast, Digital Advertising, Media Buying, Media Planning, Media Strategy, Off-Road Vehicles (Media Agency of Record)
Principal Financial Group
Red Bull
Travelers

REVOLVE
Suite 225 200 Waterfront Drive, Bedford, NS B4A 4J4 Canada
Tel.: (902) 835-3559
Fax: (902) 835-6971
E-Mail: info@revolve.ca
Web Site: www.revolve.ca

Agency Specializes In: Digital/Interactive, Internet/Web Design, Mobile Marketing, Print, Radio, Social Marketing/Nonprofit, Social Media, Strategic Planning/Research, T.V., Web (Banner Ads, Pop-ups, etc.)

Phil Otto *(CEO)*
Mat Allen *(Partner & Dir-Creative)*
Robin Cook *(Dir-Media & Sr Brand Strategist)*
Wayne Mendes *(Dir-Fin)*
Katie Bellefontaine *(Mgr-Production)*
Mike Bardsley *(Strategist-Brand)*
Alyson Sanders *(Strategist-Brand)*
Jonny Stevens *(Strategist-Brand)*
Jon Burke *(Designer-Web)*
Nicola Hancock *(Brand Strategist, Media Planner & Buyer)*

Accounts:
Ace Hardware
Atlantic Lottery Lottery Service Providers
Brain Candy Toys
Tour For Kids Bicycle Camp

REVSHARE
32836 Wolf Store Rd, Temecula, CA 92592
Tel.: (951) 302-2091
Fax: (951) 302-0579
E-Mail: info@revshare.com
Web Site: www.revshare.com

Employees: 60
Year Founded: 1989

Tom Moyes *(CFO)*
Brendan Condon *(CEO-Media Properties Holdings)*
Alan Levien *(VP-IT)*
Stephanie Hanson *(Dir-Media Plng)*
Sonia Martinez *(Dir-IS & Project Mgmt)*
Joseph Spillman *(Dir-Media Ops)*
Angela Healey *(Coord-Ad Sls & Office Mgr)*
Sarah Beecher *(Mgr-Multimedia Production)*
Candace Kraus *(Mgr-Sls Dev)*

Accounts:
Ebay

REX DIRECT NET, INC.
100 Springdale Rd A3 Ste 253, Cherry Hill, NJ 08003
Tel.: (856) 489-9581
Fax: (201) 221-7733
Toll Free: (888) 572-3244
E-Mail: contactus@rexdirectnet.com
Web Site: www.rexdirectnet.com

Employees: 20
Year Founded: 2001

Agency Specializes In: Affiliate Marketing, Affluent Market, African-American Market, Business-To-Business, Children's Market, College, Consumer Goods, Cosmetics, Digital/Interactive, Direct-to-Consumer, E-Commerce, International, Internet/Web Design, Market Research, Men's Market, Planning & Consultation, Teen Market, Web (Banner Ads, Pop-ups, etc.), Women's Market

Jennine T. Rexon *(Founder)*
Vito Tonkonog *(VP-Generation & Pay-Per-Call)*
Jason Stanley *(Mgr-Ops)*

REX PUBLIC RELATIONS
1632 S Denver Ave, Tulsa, OK 74119
Tel.: (918) 599-0029
Fax: (918) 599-0039
Web Site: www.rexpr.com

Employees: 7

Agency Specializes In: Brand Development & Integration, Communications, Event Planning & Marketing, Graphic Design, Media Relations, Public Relations, Strategic Planning/Research

Marnie Ducato *(VP-Comm)*

Accounts:
Tulsa Airport Authority Transport Services

REYNOLDS & ASSOCIATES
2041 Rosecrans Ave, El Segundo, CA 90245
Tel.: (310) 324-9155
Fax: (310) 324-9186
E-Mail: info@reynoldsand.com
Web Site: www.reynoldsla.com

E-Mail for Key Personnel:
President: cwreynolds@reynoldsand.com
Creative Dir.: rross@reynoldsand.com
Production Mgr.: kshaver@reynoldsand.com

Employees: 13
Year Founded: 1991

National Agency Associations: 4A's-THINKLA

Agency Specializes In: Advertising, Bilingual Market, Brand Development & Integration, Broadcast, Business Publications, Business-To-Business, Children's Market, Co-op Advertising, Collateral, Communications, Consulting, Consumer Marketing, Corporate Identity, Digital/Interactive, Direct Response Marketing, E-Commerce, Event Planning & Marketing, Exhibit/Trade Shows, Financial, Graphic Design, High Technology, Hispanic Market, Industrial, Information Technology, Internet/Web Design, Leisure, Logo & Package Design, Magazines, Media Buying Services, New Product Development, Newspaper, Newspapers & Magazines, Out-of-Home Media, Outdoor, Point of Purchase, Point of Sale, Print, Production, Public Relations, Publicity/Promotions, Radio, Restaurant, Retail, Sales Promotion, Seniors' Market, Strategic Planning/Research, Sweepstakes, T.V., Trade & Consumer Magazines, Transportation, Travel & Tourism

Charles W. Reynolds, Jr. *(Pres)*
Margie Gostyla *(Exec VP)*
Catherine Braybrooke *(Acct Dir)*
Leticia Brunner *(Media Dir)*
Robert H. Ross *(Dir-Creative)*
Kat Shaver *(Dir-Production Svcs)*

THE REYNOLDS GROUP
400 Trabert Ave, Atlanta, GA 30309
Tel.: (404) 888-9348
Fax: (404) 888-9349
E-Mail: info@thereynoldsgroupinc.com
Web Site: www.thereynoldsgroupinc.com

Employees: 14

Kelly Norris *(VP)*
Julia Baker *(Dir-Ops-Atlanta)*
Michelle Flood *(Dir-Mktg-Baking Paper & Plastic)*
Kelley McLaughlin *(Sr Acct Mgr)*
Erica Hinchman *(Acct Mgr)*
Brooke Lane *(Acct Mgr)*
Breckenridge Rochow *(Acct Mgr)*
Lacey Outten *(Acct Supvr)*
Lauren Lestin *(Supvr-PR)*
Caroline Plyler Haye *(Sr Acct Coord)*

Accounts:
Abattoir
Open Hand
Podponics
Sage & Swift Gourmet Catering
Serpas True Food
Spa Sydell
Star Provisions
Troubadour

RFB COMMUNICATIONS GROUP
600 S Magnolia Ave Ste 300, Tampa, FL 33606
Tel.: (813) 259-0345
Fax: (813) 250-2816
E-Mail: info@rfbcommunications.com
Web Site: www.rfbcommunications.com

Employees: 6

Agency Specializes In: Crisis Communications, Media Relations, Public Relations

Suzie Boland *(Founder & Pres)*
Jill Moore *(Acct Exec)*

Accounts:
STAR Technology Enterprise Technology & Manufacturing Services

R.H. BLAKE, INC.
26600 Renaissance Pkwy, Cleveland, OH 44128-5773
Tel.: (216) 595-2400
Fax: (216) 595-2410
Web Site: www.rhblake.com

E-Mail for Key Personnel:
President: brb@rhblake.com

Employees: 6
Year Founded: 1976

Agency Specializes In: Business-To-Business, Environmental, Industrial, Medical Products, Pharmaceutical, Technical Advertising

Approx. Annual Billings: $2,000,000

Breakdown of Gross Billings by Media: Bus. Publs.: $400,000; Collateral: $900,000; D.M.: $100,000; Production: $300,000; Pub. Rels.: $100,000; Sls. Promo.: $200,000

Bruce Blake *(Pres)*
Bradley Urbon *(Sr Acct Mgr)*
Colleen McKenna *(Mgr-Production)*

Accounts:
Sly, Inc.; Strongsville, OH

RHEA + KAISER
Naperville Financial Ctr 400 E Diehl Rd Ste 500, Naperville, IL 60563-1342
Tel.: (630) 505-1100
Fax: (630) 505-1109
E-Mail: info@rkconnect.com
Web Site: www.rkconnect.com

E-Mail for Key Personnel:
President: dmartin@rkconnect.com
Creative Dir.: rlanda@rkconnect.com

Employees: 60
Year Founded: 1978

National Agency Associations: AMA-NAMA-PRSA

Agency Specializes In: Advertising, Agriculture, Brand Development & Integration, Business-To-Business, College, Communications, Consulting, Consumer Marketing, Digital/Interactive, Direct Response Marketing, Event Planning & Marketing, Health Care Services, Internet/Web Design, Media Buying Services, Media Planning, Pets , Public Relations, Publicity/Promotions, Social Media, Sponsorship, Strategic Planning/Research

Breakdown of Gross Billings by Media: Collateral: 4.8%; D.M.: 1.5%; Fees: 23.1%; Other: 5.2%; Out-of-Home Media: 1.2%; Print: 19.2%; Pub. Rels.: 6.9%; Radio: 24%; T.V.: 14.1%

Diane Martin *(Pres & CEO)*
Martyn Dean *(Sr VP & Exec Dir-Creative)*
Andrea Bonney *(VP & Grp Acct Dir)*
Jack Vos *(Dir-Creative)*
Kelsey Brummel *(Acct Mgr)*
Justin Kenny *(Acct Mgr-PR)*
Katie Kaiser *(Acct Supvr)*
Mary Hull *(Supvr-Production)*
Denise Mazurek *(Supvr-Production)*
Pete Hlavach *(Strategist-Digital)*
Brittany Lantry *(Asst-Media)*

Accounts:
Bayer CropScience BIO Brands, Crop Protection Products, Fungicide, Herbicide, Insecticide; 1985
Cotton Council International Commodity Promotion; 2011
DePaul University Student Recruitment & Brand Positioning; 2006
FFA Student Organization; 2001
GROWMARK, Inc. Ag Services & Supplies Cooperative, FS; 1981
Northwestern Memorial Hospital
Novus International Animal Nutrition
Sandvik Mining & Construction Mining & Construction Equipment; 2007
Valley Irrigation Agricultural Irrigation Systems; 2007

RHINO MARKETING WORLDWIDE
550 Post Oak Blvd Ste 450, Houston, TX 77027
Tel.: (713) 681-6711
Fax: (713) 681-5220
Web Site: www.rhinoworldwide.com

Year Founded: 1994

Agency Specializes In: Advertising, Brand Development & Integration, Market Research, Media Planning, Sponsorship, Strategic Planning/Research

Thomas Hensey *(Mng Partner)*
Brian Dubiski *(Partner-Strategic Bus Dev)*

Accounts:
Keller Williams Realty

RHINOFORCE
3990 Oldtown Ave Ste A115, San Diego, CA 92110
Toll Free: (888) 674-4664
Web Site: www.rhinoforce.com

Agency Specializes In: Advertising, Affiliate Marketing, Alternative Advertising, Business-To-Business, Consumer Marketing, Direct-to-Consumer, Local Marketing

Alfred Liwanag *(Dir)*

Accounts:
mobitary.com

RHYCOM STRATEGIC ADVERTISING
Corporate Woods Bldg 27 10975 Grandview Ste 650, Overland Park, KS 66210
Tel.: (913) 451-9102
Fax: (913) 451-9106
E-Mail: info@rhycom.com
Web Site: www.rhycom.com

E-Mail for Key Personnel:
President: rrhyner@rhycom.com

Employees: 10
Year Founded: 1999

Agency Specializes In: Advertising, Brand Development & Integration, Business Publications, Business-To-Business, Collateral, Communications, Consulting, Consumer Marketing, Consumer Publications, Corporate Identity, Direct Response Marketing, E-Commerce, Event Planning & Marketing, Graphic Design, Information Technology, Logo & Package Design, Magazines, Media Buying Services, Merchandising, New Product Development, Outdoor, Pharmaceutical, Planning & Consultation, Point of Purchase, Point of Sale, Print, Production, Public Relations, Publicity/Promotions, Radio, Sales Promotion, Strategic Planning/Research, Technical Advertising, Trade & Consumer Magazines

Approx. Annual Billings: $3,000,000

Breakdown of Gross Billings by Media: Bus. Publs.: 10%; Collateral: 20%; Exhibits/Trade Shows: 5%; Fees: 5%; Graphic Design: 10%; Radio: 20%; Strategic Planning/Research: 10%; Trade & Consumer Mags.: 20%

Rick Rhyner *(Pres)*
Pam Williams *(Dir-Media & Client Svcs)*

Accounts:
Sheridans Frozen Custard Corp
New-Toner Jewelers Broadcast Advertising, Interactive, Website
Vince & Associates Clinical Research
Xenotech

RHYMES ADVERTISING & MARKETING

(Formerly Rhymes and Company Advertising)
5909 W Loop S Ste 145, Bellaire, TX 77401
Tel.: (713) 871-8980
Fax: (713) 871-0855
E-Mail: felix@rhymes.com
Web Site: www.rhymes.com

Employees: 4
Year Founded: 1981

National Agency Associations: AAF

Agency Specializes In: Advertising, Affluent Market, Alternative Advertising, Arts, Automotive, Brand Development & Integration, Broadcast, Business Publications, Business-To-Business, Cable T.V., Catalogs, Children's Market, Co-op Advertising, Collateral, Communications, Computers & Software, Consumer Goods, Consumer Marketing, Consumer Publications, Corporate Identity, Digital/Interactive, Direct Response Marketing, Direct-to-Consumer, Electronic Media, Electronics, Entertainment, Event Planning & Marketing, Fashion/Apparel, Financial, Food Service, Government/Political, Graphic Design, Guerilla Marketing, Health Care Services, High Technology, Hospitality, Identity Marketing, In-Store Advertising, Industrial, Infomercials, Integrated Marketing, Internet/Web Design, Legal Services, Leisure, Local Marketing, Logo & Package Design, Luxury Products, Magazines, Market Research, Media Buying Services, Media Planning, Medical Products, Men's Market, Merchandising, Multimedia, New Technologies, Newspaper, Newspapers & Magazines, Out-of-Home Media, Outdoor, Over-50 Market, Package Design, Point of Purchase, Point of Sale, Print, Product Placement, Production, Production (Print), Promotions, Public Relations, Publicity/Promotions, Radio, Real Estate, Recruitment, Regional, Restaurant, Retail, Sales Promotion, Seniors' Market, Social Marketing/Nonprofit, South Asian Market, Sponsorship, Stakeholders, Strategic Planning/Research, T.V., Telemarketing, Trade & Consumer Magazines, Transportation, Travel & Tourism, Viral/Buzz/Word of Mouth, Women's Market

Felix Rhymes *(Pres)*

RHYMES AND COMPANY ADVERTISING

(Name Changed to Rhymes Advertising & Marketing)

RHYTHMONE

(Formerly Burst!)
8 New England Executive Pk, Burlington, MA 01803
Tel.: (781) 272-5544
Fax: (781) 852-5163
Web Site: http://www.rhythmone.com/

Employees: 150

John Babcock *(Sr VP-Sls)*
Chuck Moran *(VP-Mktg)*
Liz Hegarty *(Sr Dir-Bus Dev)*
Jenny Caleo *(Dir-Exchange Supply)*
Kim Hale *(Dir-Sls)*
Brittany Dickson *(Mgr-Media Partnerships)*
Bess Renfer *(Mgr-Mobile Solutions)*
Scott Hanson *(Acct Exec-Digital)*
Jay Rich *(Acct Exec)*

Accounts:
RedOrbit

Branch

RhythmOne

(Formerly Burst Media)
1156 Ave Of The Americas Ste 301, New York, NY 10168
Tel.: (917) 621-8618
Fax: (212) 759-8334
Web Site: http://www.rhythmone.com/

Employees: 85

Agency Specializes In: Advertising, Digital/Interactive, Internet/Web Design, New Technologies

Katie Paulsen *(VP-Influencer Mktg)*
Liz Hegarty *(Sr Dir-Bus Dev)*
Caitlin Quaranto *(Sr Dir-Social Influencer Programs)*
Catharine Anderson Dyer *(Dir-Northeast Sls-Burst Media & Rhythm)*
Chris Ryan *(Dir-Sls)*
Melody Brunell *(Sr Mgr-Adv Ops)*
Brittany Dickson *(Mgr-Media Partnerships)*
Jay Rich *(Acct Exec)*
Ted Tubekis *(Acct Exec)*

Accounts:
EveryZing
Pawspot

THE RIBAUDO GROUP

(Formerly Benjamin & Ribaudo Advertising Inc.)
594 Broadway Ste 1206, New York, NY 10012
Tel.: (212) 465-2496
Fax: (212) 465-2497
E-Mail: victor@theribaudogroup.com
Web Site: www.theribaudogroup.com

Employees: 15

Agency Specializes In: Advertising, Advertising Specialties, Brand Development & Integration, Catalogs, Co-op Advertising, Collateral, Commercial Photography, Communications, Consulting, Consumer Goods, Consumer Publications, Corporate Identity, Custom Publishing, Direct Response Marketing, Email, Fashion/Apparel, Food Service, Graphic Design, In-Store Advertising, Internet/Web Design, Logo & Package Design, Magazines, Merchandising, New Product Development, Newspaper, Newspapers & Magazines, Out-of-Home Media, Outdoor, Point of Purchase, Point of Sale, Print, Production, Production (Ad, Film, Broadcast), Production (Print), Publishing, Radio, Real Estate, Restaurant, Retail, Trade & Consumer Magazines, Transportation, Web (Banner Ads, Pop-ups, etc.)

Approx. Annual Billings: $8,000,000

Victor Ribaudo *(Owner)*
Rich Buyer *(Partner & Dir-Web & Graphic Svcs)*

Accounts:
American Manufacturers Mall
Davinci Imported Pasta
The Food Emporium; Montvale, NJ Supermarket
The Great Atlantic & Pacific Tea Co., Inc.; Montvale, NJ Supermarkets
World Finer Foods; Bloomfield, NJ DaVinci & Reese

RIBECK & CO.

570 Mt Pleasant St, West Rockport, ME 04865
Tel.: (207) 390-0078
E-Mail: fred@ribeckdesign.com
Web Site: www.ribeckdesign.com/

Employees: 3
Year Founded: 1977

Agency Specializes In: Fashion/Apparel, Food Service, Medical Products, Outdoor, Publicity/Promotions

Fred Ribeck *(Owner)*

Accounts:
Duck Trap River Smoked Seafood; Lincolnville, ME
Port Clyde Foods; Rockland, ME
Sun Yacht Charters; Camden, ME Sailboat Charters

RICE ADVERTISING & DESIGN

4532 A Bonney Rd, Virginia Beach, VA 23462
Tel.: (757) 497-1455
Web Site: www.radvb.com

Year Founded: 2002

Agency Specializes In: Advertising, Brand Development & Integration, Graphic Design, Media Planning, Outdoor, Print, Public Relations, Radio, Social Media, T.V.

Craig Rice *(Pres)*

Accounts:
Votenza

RICH MEDIA WORLDWIDE

930 Washington Ave 5th Fl, Miami Beach, FL 33139
Tel.: (305) 672-9980
Fax: (305) 672-8720
E-Mail: inquiry@rmworldwide.com
Web Site: www.realvu.com

Employees: 5
Year Founded: 2001

Agency Specializes In: Advertising, Advertising Specialties, Business-To-Business,

Digital/Interactive, E-Commerce, Electronic Media, Internet/Web Design, Leisure, Media Buying Services, Production, Sales Promotion, T.V.

Approx. Annual Billings: $1,600,000

Breakdown of Gross Billings by Media: Fees: $1,000,000; Other: $600,000

Dave Chidester *(Partner)*
Alan James Edwards *(COO)*
Igor Tchibirev *(CTO)*
Sam K King *(Mgr-Publr Rels)*

Accounts:
Crowne Plaza; Miami, FL Hotel; 2002
David Copperfield; Los Angeles, CA Dream Portal; 2001
Hilton Worldwide Hotel; 2003
Hyatt; Orlando, FL Hotel; 2002
Marriott; Orlando, FL Hotel; 2002
Wilhemina; New York, NY Models; 2002

RICHARDS
(Formerly Richards Communications)
8350 Whispering Pines Dr, Russell, OH 44072-9591
Tel.: (216) 514-7800
E-Mail: jrichards@richardsgo.com
Web Site: www.richardsgo.com

Employees: 6
Year Founded: 1981

Agency Specializes In: Advertising Specialties, Asian Market, Automotive, Bilingual Market, Brand Development & Integration, Broadcast, Business Publications, Business-To-Business, Cable T.V., Catalogs, Co-op Advertising, Collateral, Communications, Consulting, Consumer Goods, Consumer Marketing, Consumer Publications, Content, Corporate Communications, Corporate Identity, Custom Publishing, Customer Relationship Management, Digital/Interactive, Direct Response Marketing, Direct-to-Consumer, E-Commerce, Electronic Media, Electronics, Email, Engineering, Environmental, Event Planning & Marketing, Exhibit/Trade Shows, Graphic Design, Guerilla Marketing, Health Care Services, Identity Marketing, In-Store Advertising, Industrial, Infomercials, Integrated Marketing, International, Internet/Web Design, Investor Relations, Local Marketing, Logo & Package Design, Magazines, Market Research, Media Buying Services, Media Planning, Media Relations, Media Training, Medical Products, Merchandising, Mobile Marketing, Multicultural, Multimedia, New Product Development, New Technologies, Newspaper, Newspapers & Magazines, Out-of-Home Media, Outdoor, Over-50 Market, Package Design, Paid Searches, Pharmaceutical, Planning & Consultation, Podcasting, Point of Purchase, Point of Sale, Print, Product Placement, Production, Production (Print), Promotions, Public Relations, Publicity/Promotions, Radio, Retail, Sales Promotion, Search Engine Optimization, Seniors' Market, Social Marketing/Nonprofit, South Asian Market, Strategic Planning/Research, Sweepstakes, T.V., Trade & Consumer Magazines, Yellow Pages Advertising

Jared Richards *(VP)*
Bob Bohach *(Assoc Dir-Creative)*

Accounts:
ABB Inc.
Honeywell International; Morristown, NJ
MetroHealth Hospital Systems; Cleveland, OH
Spectrum Orthopaedics
University Hospitals

RICHARDS/CARLBERG
1900 W Loop S Ste 1100, Houston, TX 77027
Tel.: (713) 965-0764
Fax: (713) 965-0135
E-Mail: chuck_carlberg@richardscarlberg.com
Web Site: www.richardscarlberg.com

Employees: 25
Year Founded: 1948

National Agency Associations: 4A's-AAF

Agency Specializes In: Advertising, African-American Market, Asian Market, Automotive, Bilingual Market, Brand Development & Integration, Broadcast, Business-To-Business, Cable T.V., Co-op Advertising, Collateral, Communications, Consumer Marketing, Consumer Publications, Corporate Communications, Corporate Identity, Digital/Interactive, Direct Response Marketing, Electronic Media, Event Planning & Marketing, Exhibit/Trade Shows, Financial, High Technology, Hispanic Market, In-Store Advertising, Industrial, Internet/Web Design, Local Marketing, Logo & Package Design, Media Buying Services, Merchandising, Multimedia, New Product Development, Newspaper, Newspapers & Magazines, Out-of-Home Media, Outdoor, Point of Purchase, Point of Sale, Print, Production, Public Relations, Publicity/Promotions, Radio, Restaurant, Retail, Sales Promotion, Sponsorship, Strategic Planning/Research, Sweepstakes, T.V., Trade & Consumer Magazines, Yellow Pages Advertising

Approx. Annual Billings: $45,000,000

Gayl Carlberg *(Co-Principal & Dir-Creative)*
Chuck Carlberg *(Principal-Brand Creative)*
Karen Holland *(Brand Dir-Creative & Art)*
Lindsey Renee Durham *(Dir-Art)*
Andrea Marban *(Brand Mgr)*
Travis Morin *(Brand Mgr)*

Accounts:
Aggreko LLC
Buffalo Bayou Partnership
Darden Restaurants Olive Garden
End Hunger Network
HomeVestors of America; Dallas, TX Home Buying Services, Reselling Services; 2005
Houston Airport Systems
Houston Chronicle Newspaper & Interactive Online Services
Mahindra
People's Trust Federal Credit Union
RiceTec Rice Select
The Rose
Signature Home Theater
Snelson Oilfield Lighting
The Sterling Group
Stop Trashing Houston
University of Saint Thomas

THE RICHARDS GROUP, INC.
2801 N Central Expwy, Dallas, TX 75204
Tel.: (214) 891-5700
Fax: (214) 265-2933
E-Mail: Diane_Fannon@richards.com
Web Site: www.richards.com

Employees: 705
Year Founded: 1976

National Agency Associations: ABC

Agency Specializes In: Advertising, Advertising Specialties, Affluent Market, African-American Market, Automotive, Aviation & Aerospace, Bilingual Market, Brand Development & Integration, Branded Entertainment, Broadcast, Business Publications, Business-To-Business, Cable T.V., Children's Market, Co-op Advertising, Collateral, College, Communications, Consulting, Consumer Goods, Consumer Marketing, Consumer Publications, Corporate Communications, Corporate Identity, Cosmetics, Crisis Communications, Customer Relationship Management, Digital/Interactive, Direct Response Marketing, Direct-to-Consumer, E-Commerce, Education, Electronic Media, Electronics, Email, Entertainment, Event Planning & Marketing, Exhibit/Trade Shows, Experience Design, Fashion/Apparel, Financial, Food Service, Game Integration, Government/Political, Graphic Design, Guerilla Marketing, Health Care Services, Hispanic Market, Hospitality, Household Goods, In-Store Advertising, Integrated Marketing, Internet/Web Design, Investor Relations, Leisure, Local Marketing, Logo & Package Design, Luxury Products, Magazines, Marine, Market Research, Media Buying Services, Media Planning, Media Relations, Media Training, Medical Products, Men's Market, Mobile Marketing, Multicultural, Multimedia, New Product Development, New Technologies, Newspaper, Newspapers & Magazines, Out-of-Home Media, Outdoor, Over-50 Market, Package Design, Paid Searches, Planning & Consultation, Point of Purchase, Point of Sale, Print, Product Placement, Production, Production (Print), Promotions, Public Relations, Publicity/Promotions, Radio, Real Estate, Recruitment, Regional, Restaurant, Retail, Sales Promotion, Search Engine Optimization, Seniors' Market, Social Marketing/Nonprofit, Social Media, Sponsorship, Sports Market, Strategic Planning/Research, Sweepstakes, Syndication, T.V., Trade & Consumer Magazines, Transportation, Travel & Tourism, Urban Market, Viral/Buzz/Word of Mouth, Women's Market

Approx. Annual Billings: $1,360,000,000

Cassie Ladd *(Partner)*
Rhonda Contreras *(Principal)*
James Hering *(Principal)*
Dale Hruby *(Principal)*
Mary Price *(Principal-Brand Media)*
Stan Richards *(Principal)*
Jimmy Bonner *(Dir-Art & Grp Head-Creative)*
Rob Baker *(Grp Head-Creative)*
Sue Batterton *(Grp Head-Creative)*
Glenn Dady *(Head-Creative Grp)*
Mike Malone *(Grp Head-Creative)*
Carl Warner *(Grp Head-Creative)*
Nora De los Rios *(Grp Dir-Media)*
Jacquie Gonzalez *(Grp Dir-Media)*
Shannon Haydel *(Grp Dir-Media)*
Jaquie Hoyos *(Grp Dir-Media)*
Mike Latour *(Sr Dir-Art)*
Dominic Al-Samarraie *(Creative Dir)*
Henry Castleton *(Art Dir)*
Derek Darst *(Acct Dir-Brand Mgmt)*
Brian Linder *(Creative Dir)*
Paul Nelson *(Producer-Brdcst)*
Andy Younker *(Producer-Brdcst)*
Mike Bales *(Dir-Creative & Writer)*
David Eastman *(Dir-Creative & Copywriter)*
Chris Smith *(Dir-Creative & Writer)*
Andrew Bui *(Dir-Art)*
David Canright *(Dir-Creative)*
Dan Case *(Dir-Art)*
Andy Coulston *(Dir-Art)*
Lynda Hodge *(Dir-Creative)*
David Morring *(Dir-Creative)*
Kevin Reid *(Dir-Art)*
Kristen Scialo *(Dir-Art)*
Dave Stone *(Dir-Art)*
Judy Wright *(Dir-Creative & Art)*
Monica Abbracciamento *(Brand Mgr)*
Ann Bills *(Brand Mgr)*
Rosalie Bonner *(Brand Mgr)*
Kate Fuller *(Brand Mgr-New Bus)*
Drew Ingram *(Brand Mgr)*
Jeffrey Lefkovits *(Brand Mgr)*
Kevyn Montesi *(Brand Mgr)*
Charlotte Brooke *(Supvr-Brand Media)*
Lucie Prann *(Supvr-Brdcst Negotiating)*
Tyler Norton *(Strategist-Social Media)*
Cory O'Brien *(Strategist-Digital)*

Chris Cannon *(Copywriter)*
Jamie Harms *(Media Planner-Brand)*
Jeff Hodgson *(Copywriter)*
Sarah Jackson *(Media Buyer)*
Andria Kushan *(Copywriter)*
Dave Longfield *(Copywriter)*
Wendy Mayes *(Copywriter)*
Drew Simel *(Planner-Brand)*

Accounts:
New-Advocates United; 2015
American Signature, Inc. (Agency of Record) Branding Strategy, Creative, Digital, Social Media
Anderson Erickson Dairy; Des Moines, IA Independent Dairy; 2006
Atlanta Falcons; Flowery Branch, GA NFL Team; 2007
The Auto Club Group "Emma", AAA, Campaign: "Expect something more" Super Bowl 2014
Behringer; Addison, TX Real Estate Investment Services; 2005
Biltmore; Asheville, NC Vanderbilt 8,000 Acre Estate; 2007
Blue Plate Mayonnaise; 2010
Carroll Shelby's Chili; Leesburg, TX Custom Chili Kit; 2010
Central Market; San Antonio, TX Gourmet Grocery Chain; 2009
Chick-fil-A, Inc (Agency of Record) Advertising, Campaign: "Eat Mor Chikin", Creative, Quick Service Restaurant Chain; 1994
Chrysler Group Broadcast, Campaign: "Beautiful Lands", Campaign: "Renegades", Campaign: "Wisdom", Dodge, Jeep Renegade, Super Bowl 2015; 2009
Dallas Symphony Orchestra; Dallas, TX Orchestra; 2010
New-Dr Pepper Snapple Group; 2015
Dymatize Nutrition Sports Nutritional Supplement
Fiat Chrysler Automobiles "The Fiat 500X Blue Pill", 500X SUV, Alfa Romeo, Fiat, Jeep, Ram, Super Bowl 2015; 2011
Fleet Laboratories; Lynchburg, VA Boudreaux's Butt Paste, Pedia-Lax, Personal Care & Health Care, Summer's Eve; 2010
New-FNH USA; 2015
FRAM; Danbury, CT Oil, Air & Fuel Filters; 2009
GameStop Corp. Assassin's Creed, Campaign: "Going To Gamestock", Campaign: "We're All Players", Halo, Video Game Retailer; 2006
Gander Mountain; Minneapolis, MN Camping, Boating & Outdoor Retailer; 2002
GoRVing; Reston, VA RV Travel Coalition; 2002
H-E-B; San Antonio, TX "Barbie", "Slogans", "Toga", "Wise", Advertising, Food Retailer; 1998
The Home Depot; Atlanta, GA Campaign: "Home Depot is More Than a Store. You Can Do it. We Can Help", Home Improvement Retailer, Magazine Ads, Newspaper, Radio, TV; 1993
The Maids Residential Cleaning Company; 2002
MD Anderson Cancer Center; Houston, TX Cancer Treatment & Research Center; 1996
Miraca Life Sciences
Motel 6; Carrolton, TX Budget Motel Chain; 1986
National Vision, Inc America's Best Contacts & Eyeglasses (Agency of Record), Campaign: "Owl", Creative, Digital, Eyeglass World (Agency of Record), Media Buying, Media Planning, Public Relations, Strategy Development
NatureSweet; San Antonio, TX Tomatoes; 1998
NorthStar Anesthesia; Fort Worth, TX Anesthesia; 2010
New-Omni Hotels & Resorts; 2015
Orkin, Inc.; Atlanta, GA Residential & Commercial Pest Control Services; 2007
Pier 1 Imports; Fort Worth, TX Home Furnishing & Accessories Retailer; 2010
Prestone, Danbury, CT Antifreeze, Campaign: "Beastly", Campaign: "New Prestone", Campaign: "Parking Lot", Campaign: "Patented"; 2009
QuikTrip; Tulsa, OK Gas & Convenience Stores; 2002
Ram Trucks Broadcast, Campaign: "Courage Is Already Inside", Campaign: "Roots and Wings", Campaign: "The Pack", Commercial Vehicles, Dakota, Digital, Print, Ram Light & Heavy Duty Truck, Social Media, TV; 2009
RiceSelect Specialty Rice & Pasta Products; 2012
Rockwell Collins; Cedar Rapids, IA Communication & Aviation Electronics; 2008
Ruth's Hospitality Group
SAIC; San Diego, CA; 2008
The Salvation Army; Alexandria, VA; 2006
Schwab Trading Services (Creative Agency of Record)
Sea Island; Sea Island, GA Resort; 2011
Sewell Automotive Group; Dallas, TX Automotive Dealer; 2002
Shamrock Farms; Phoenix, AZ Dairy; 2005
Southern Methodist University; Dallas, TX; 2002
Stuller; Lafayette, LA Jewelers' Resource; 2009
Sub-Zero; Madison, WI Luxury Refrigeration; 2001
SuddenLink; Saint Louis, MO Cable Broadband Provider; 2008
T-Mobile US; Richardson, TX Telecommunications Network; 2001
Texas Scottish Rite Hospital for Children Campaign: "Giving Children Back Their Childhood", Campaign: "Moments", Digital, OOH, Print, Radio, Television
TGI Friday's; Carrollton, TX Casual Dining Restaurants, Creative, Media; 2011
The Tire Rack; South Bend, IN Automotive Products Distributor; 2007
TXU Energy; 2011
Wawa; Wawa, PA Convenience Stores; 2004
Wolf Campaign: "Reclaim the Kitchen", Luxury Cooking Appliances, Online; 2001
New-Zephyr Gin; 2015
New-ZiegenBock; 2015

Branches

Richards/Lerma
7007 Twin Hills Ste 300, Dallas, TX 75231-6437
(See Separate Listing)

Richards Partners
8750 N Central Expy Ste 1100, Dallas, TX 75231-6430
(See Separate Listing)

Latitude
8750 N Central Expwy Ste 1200, Dallas, TX 75231
(See Separate Listing)

RBMM
7007 Twin Hills Ave Ste 200, Dallas, TX 75231
(See Separate Listing)

RICHARDS/LERMA
7007 Twin Hills Ste 300, Dallas, TX 75231-6437
Tel.: (214) 891-4100
Web Site: www.richardslerma.com

Employees: 70
Year Founded: 2008

Agency Specializes In: Above-the-Line, Advertising, Below-the-Line, Bilingual Market, Brand Development & Integration, Broadcast, Cable T.V., Collateral, Communications, Consulting, Consumer Goods, Custom Publishing, Digital/Interactive, Direct Response Marketing, Electronic Media, Email, Event Planning & Marketing, Hispanic Market, In-Store Advertising, Integrated Marketing, Internet/Web Design, Local Marketing, Magazines, Market Research, Media Buying Services, Media Planning, Mobile Marketing, Multimedia, Newspaper, Newspapers & Magazines, Out-of-Home Media, Outdoor, Paid Searches, Planning & Consultation, Point of Purchase, Point of Sale, Print, Production, Production (Ad, Film, Broadcast), Promotions, Public Relations, Publicity/Promotions, Radio, Regional, Social Media, Sponsorship, Sweepstakes, Syndication, T.V., Technical Advertising, Trade & Consumer Magazines, Viral/Buzz/Word of Mouth, Web (Banner Ads, Pop-ups, etc.)

Approx. Annual Billings: $75,000,000

Pete Lerma *(Founder & Principal)*
Aldo Quevedo *(Principal & Creative Dir)*
Melissa Garcia *(Principal & Dir-Ops)*
Salma Gottfried *(Principal-Brand Mgmt)*
Stan Richards *(Principal)*
Miguel Moreno *(Brand Dir-Creative)*
Stephanie Hoefken *(Dir-PR)*
Nancy Morkovsky *(Dir-Brand Plng)*
Diana Diaz *(Brand Mgr)*
Wendy Hernandez *(Brand Mgr)*
Isabella Naranjo *(Brand Mgr)*

Accounts:
Advance Auto Parts Hispanic Advertising; 2009
Chrysler Dodge Jeep, Hispanic Advertising & Marketing, RAM Trucks; 2010
FRAM Hispanic Advertising; 2008
The Home Depot Hispanic Advertising & Marketing; 2010
Pizza Patron Creative, Digital, Product Development, Public Relations, Social Media
Prestone Hispanic Advertising; 2009
Salvation Army Hispanic Advertising; 2011
T-Mobile US Hispanic Advertising; 2009
United Way Hispanic Advertising; 2012

RICHTER7
280 S 400 W Ste 200, Salt Lake City, UT 84101
Tel.: (801) 521-2903
Fax: (801) 359-2420
E-Mail: email@richter7.com
Web Site: www.richter7.com

E-Mail for Key Personnel:
President: dnewbold@richter7.com
Public Relations: tbrown@richter7.com

Employees: 37
Year Founded: 1971

National Agency Associations: AMIN

Agency Specializes In: Advertising, Advertising Specialties, Brand Development & Integration, Broadcast, Business-To-Business, Collateral, Communications, Consumer Marketing, Consumer Publications, Corporate Identity, Digital/Interactive, Direct Response Marketing, Financial, Graphic Design, Health Care Services, Internet/Web Design, Leisure, Media Buying Services, Medical Products, Merchandising, New Product Development, Newspaper, Outdoor, Package Design, Point of Sale, Print, Public Relations, Radio, Social Media, Strategic Planning/Research, T.V., Transportation, Travel & Tourism, Web (Banner Ads, Pop-ups, etc.)

Approx. Annual Billings: $42,000,000

Breakdown of Gross Billings by Media: Brdcst.: $10,000,000; Collateral: $5,000,000; D.M.: $1,000,000; Internet Adv.: $1,000,000; Other: $23,000,000; Outdoor: $2,000,000

Tal Harry *(Partner & Exec VP-Digital Mktg)*
Walt McRoberts *(VP & Dir-Media Svcs)*
Mark Bangerter *(Sr Dir-Art & Designer-Experiential)*
Celia Willette *(Dir-Bus Dev & Client Strategy)*
Jennifer Gordon *(Acct Mgr)*
Peter Brown *(Mgr-Social Media & PR)*

Accounts:
Apple Beer
BD Medical; Salt Lake City, UT Health Technology; 2007
Cocoa Metro Campaign: "Bunker", Campaign: "Flask"
Hogle Zoo; Salt Lake City, UT Entertainment, Zoorassic Park Campaign; 2002
Jackson Hole Resort Lodging; Jackson, WY Property Management; 1998
Questar
Salt Lake Community College; Salt Lake City, UT; 2007
Salt Lake County
Siemens Hearing Instruments
Utah Aikikai
Utah Commission on Marriage
Utah Highway Safety Office Campaign: "Eye Chart"
Utah's Hogle Zoo Campaign: "Hogle Zoo Zoorassic Park"
Workers Compensation Fund of Utah; Salt Lake City, UT Insurance; 1994
Zions Bancorporation; Salt Lake City, UT Financial Institution; 1997

RICOCHET PARTNERS, INC.
521 SW 11th Ave Ste 400, Portland, OR 97205
Tel.: (503) 220-0212
Fax: (503) 220-0213
Web Site: www.ricochetpartners.com

Employees: 10

Agency Specializes In: Brand Development & Integration, Consulting, Integrated Marketing, Local Marketing, Media Relations, New Product Development, Sponsorship

Peter Charlton *(Co-Founder & Chief Creative Officer)*
Jeanne McKirchy-Spencer *(Chm & Chief Strategy Officer)*
Catherine Cousins-McLeod *(VP-Acct Svcs)*
Kevin Chase *(Sr Dir-Art & Technical)*
Ron Spencer *(Dir-Digital Media Production)*
Zara Friedland *(Jr Project Mgr)*

Accounts:
eb5
Holcim US; 2008

RIDGE MARKETING & DESIGN LLC
91 S Maple Ave, Basking Ridge, NJ 7920
Tel.: (908) 340-4480
E-Mail: info@ridgemarketing.com
Web Site: www.ridgemarketing.com

Year Founded: 2004

Agency Specializes In: Advertising, Brand Development & Integration, Collateral, Corporate Identity, Digital/Interactive, Internet/Web Design, Public Relations, Search Engine Optimization, Social Media

Rob Quincy *(Pres & Creative Dir)*
Andrea Quincy *(COO)*
Jim Lodise *(Creative Dir)*
Tracy Grace *(Acct Mgr)*

Accounts:
Hiperos

RIEGNER & ASSOCIATES, INC.
18481 W 10 Mile Rd, Southfield, MI 48075-2621
Tel.: (248) 569-4242
Fax: (248) 443-0690
Web Site: www.riegner.com/

Employees: 15

Bryan Riegner *(Pres)*
Bernie Riegner *(CFO)*
Dave Weber *(Dir-Creative)*

Accounts:
Detroit Diesel Corp.

RIESTER
802 N 3rd Ave, Phoenix, AZ 85003
Tel.: (602) 462-2200
Fax: (602) 307-5811
E-Mail: astiles@riester.com
Web Site: www.riester.com

E-Mail for Key Personnel:
President: triester@riester.com

Employees: 70
Year Founded: 1989

Agency Specializes In: Advertising, Bilingual Market, Brand Development & Integration, Broadcast, Business-To-Business, Cable T.V., Children's Market, Communications, Consumer Marketing, Corporate Identity, Cosmetics, Digital/Interactive, Direct Response Marketing, E-Commerce, Education, Electronic Media, Entertainment, Environmental, Event Planning & Marketing, Fashion/Apparel, Financial, Food Service, Government/Political, Graphic Design, Health Care Services, High Technology, Hispanic Market, Information Technology, Internet/Web Design, Investor Relations, Marine, Media Buying Services, Medical Products, New Product Development, Newspaper, Newspapers & Magazines, Out-of-Home Media, Pets , Pharmaceutical, Planning & Consultation, Print, Production, Public Relations, Publicity/Promotions, Radio, Real Estate, Restaurant, Retail, Sales Promotion, Seniors' Market, Sponsorship, Sports Market, Strategic Planning/Research, T.V., Technical Advertising, Trade & Consumer Magazines, Transportation, Travel & Tourism

Breakdown of Gross Billings by Media: Cable T.V.: 20%; Outdoor: 8%; Print: 12%; Pub. Rels.: 9%; Radio: 12%; Spot T.V.: 35%; Trade Shows: 1%; Worldwide Web Sites: 3%

Timothy W. Riester *(Pres & CEO)*
Alan Perkel *(Chief Digital Officer & Principal)*
Kurt Krake *(Exec Dir-Media)*
Stephanie Fleming *(Acct Dir)*
Christina Borrego *(Dir-PR)*
Tricia Kashima *(Dir-Media)*
Ben Dveirin *(Assoc Dir-Creative)*
Mike Ross *(Assoc Dir-Creative)*
Kari Brill *(Sr Media Planner & Buyer)*

Accounts:
Arizona Department of Commerce
California Department of Conservation Division of Recycling; 2001
FDA Anti-Smoking Campaign
Gilead Sciences
Hormel Foods Herdez
Idahoan Foods Campaign: "Idahoan On Your Table"
La Victoria (Agency of Record) peppers, salsa, taco sauce
McDonald's; 1991
Medicis Pharmaceutical Company
MidFirst Bank of Oklahoma & Arizona
MidFirst Bank
PacifiCorp
Pfizer
Scottsdale Convention & Visitor's Bureau
Sun Valley Dairy Campaign: "Happiness", Digital, Mobile Advertising, Social, Television, VOSKOS
The Thunderbird Graduate School of International Management
Veterinary Pet Insurance
Voskos Greek Yogurt Campaign: "Farm"
Zeltiq Coolsculpting

Branches

Riester-Robb
132 W Pierpont Ave Ste 300, Salt Lake City, UT 84101-1102
Tel.: (801) 532-7333
Fax: (801) 532-6029
E-Mail: info@riester.com
Web Site: www.riester.com

Employees: 25
Year Founded: 1938

National Agency Associations: AMIN

Agency Specializes In: Advertising

Skip Branch *(Partner)*
Bryan Ojala *(Exec Dir-CPG Grp)*
Tricia Kashima *(Dir-Media)*
Troy Pottgen *(Dir-Creative)*
David J. Kovacs *(Assoc Dir-Content Strategy)*
Mike Ross *(Assoc Dir-Creative)*
Briana Jimenez *(Mgr-Integration)*
Lindsay Cheatham *(Supvr-Integration)*
Angie Vollmers *(Media Buyer & Planner)*
Bernadette Smith *(Writer-Digital Content)*
Kari Brill-Torrez *(Sr Media Planner & Buyer)*
Monica Meyerand *(Sr Media Planner)*

Accounts:
Park City Chamber of Commerce/Convention & Visitors Bureau (Advertising Agency of Record)

Riester Robb
1960 E Grand Ave Ste 260, El Segundo, CA 90245
(See Separate Listing)

RIESTER ROBB
1960 E Grand Ave Ste 260, El Segundo, CA 90245
Tel.: (310) 392-4244
Fax: (310) 392-2595
Web Site: www.riester.com

Employees: 10
Year Founded: 1995

National Agency Associations: THINKLA

Agency Specializes In: Advertising, Brand Development & Integration, Broadcast, Business Publications, Business-To-Business, Cable T.V., Children's Market, Collateral, Consulting, Consumer Marketing, Consumer Publications, Direct Response Marketing, E-Commerce, Financial, Hispanic Market, Logo & Package Design, Magazines, Media Buying Services, New Product Development, Newspaper, Newspapers & Magazines, Out-of-Home Media, Outdoor, Planning & Consultation, Point of Purchase, Point of Sale, Print, Production, Publicity/Promotions, Radio, Real Estate, Restaurant, Retail, Sales Promotion, Strategic Planning/Research, T.V., Trade & Consumer Magazines

Approx. Annual Billings: $20,000,000

Breakdown of Gross Billings by Media: Cable T.V.: $5,500,000; Mags.: $1,000,000; Network T.V.: $1,000,000; Newsp.: $1,500,000; Outdoor: $1,000,000; Point of Purchase: $3,000,000; Spot Radio: $2,000,000; Spot T.V.: $5,000,000

Timothy W. Riester *(Pres & CEO)*
Bryan Ojala *(Exec Dir-Consumer Package Goods Grp)*
Christina Borrego *(Dir-PR & Multicultural Svcs)*
Troy Pottgen *(Dir-Creative)*

Ben Dveirin *(Assoc Dir-Creative)*
Leslie Sonnenklar *(Assoc Dir-PR)*
Angie Vollmers *(Media Buyer & Planner)*
Kari Brill-Torrez *(Sr Media Planner & Buyer)*

Accounts:
California Department of Conservation
MegaMex Foods, LLC
Sun Valley Dairy Voskos

RIGER ADVERTISING AGENCY, INC.
53 Chenango St, Binghamton, NY 13902
Tel.: (607) 723-7441
Fax: (607) 723-7623
E-Mail: agency@riger.com
Web Site: www.riger.com

E-Mail for Key Personnel:
Creative Dir.: rstiene@riger.com
Media Dir.: lvankuren@riger.com
Production Mgr.: pcronk@riger.com

Employees: 12
Year Founded: 1950

National Agency Associations: 4A's-AAF-BPA-MCA

Agency Specializes In: Advertising, Brand Development & Integration, Broadcast, Business Publications, Business-To-Business, Cable T.V., Co-op Advertising, Collateral, Communications, Consumer Marketing, Consumer Publications, Corporate Identity, Direct Response Marketing, E-Commerce, Education, Electronic Media, Engineering, Exhibit/Trade Shows, Financial, Food Service, Graphic Design, Health Care Services, High Technology, Industrial, Internet/Web Design, Investor Relations, Legal Services, Leisure, Logo & Package Design, Magazines, Marine, Media Buying Services, Medical Products, Merchandising, Multimedia, New Product Development, Newspaper, Newspapers & Magazines, Out-of-Home Media, Outdoor, Point of Purchase, Point of Sale, Print, Production, Public Relations, Publicity/Promotions, Radio, Recruitment, Restaurant, Retail, Sales Promotion, Strategic Planning/Research, T.V., Trade & Consumer Magazines, Travel & Tourism, Yellow Pages Advertising

Mark Bandurchin *(Mng Partner)*
Steve Johnson *(Mng Partner)*
Rob Stiene *(Dir-Creative)*
Barbara Butler *(Office Mgr)*
Laurie Van Kuren *(Mgr-Media & Acct Svcs)*
Karen Frobel *(Specialist-Print Production)*
Jamie Jacobs *(Acct Exec)*

Accounts:
Binghamton University; Binghamton, NY
Board of Cooperative Educational Services (BOCES); Binghamton, NY
CFCU Community Credit Union; Ithaca, NY
East Stroudsburg University
Economic Development Alliance of Broome County; Johnson City, NY
ESSA Bank & Trust; Stroudsburg, PA
First Heritage Federal Credit Union; Painted Post, NY
GHS Federal Credit Union
Sanofi Pasteur
Sanofi Pasteur
Tioga State Bank
United Health Services; Binghamton, NY

RIGHT ANGLE
119 E Main St, Lafayette, LA 70501
Tel.: (337) 235-2416
Fax: (337) 237-5445
E-Mail: info@rightangleadv.com
Web Site: www.rightangleadv.com

Year Founded: 1987

Agency Specializes In: Advertising, Advertising Specialties, Alternative Advertising, Brand Development & Integration, Broadcast, Business Publications, Cable T.V., Catalogs, Co-op Advertising, Collateral, Communications, Consulting, Consumer Publications, Content, Corporate Communications, Corporate Identity, Crisis Communications, Custom Publishing, Digital/Interactive, Direct Response Marketing, Electronic Media, Email, Event Planning & Marketing, Exhibit/Trade Shows, Graphic Design, Identity Marketing, In-Store Advertising, Infomercials, Integrated Marketing, Internet/Web Design, Local Marketing, Logo & Package Design, Magazines, Market Research, Media Buying Services, Media Planning, Media Relations, Media Training, Mobile Marketing, Multimedia, New Product Development, Newspaper, Newspapers & Magazines, Out-of-Home Media, Outdoor, Package Design, Paid Searches, Planning & Consultation, Print, Production, Production (Ad, Film, Broadcast), Production (Print), Promotions, Public Relations, Publicity/Promotions, Publishing, Radio, Regional, Sales Promotion, Search Engine Optimization, Social Marketing/Nonprofit, Social Media, Strategic Planning/Research, T.V., Technical Advertising, Trade & Consumer Magazines, Viral/Buzz/Word of Mouth, Web (Banner Ads, Pop-ups, etc.)

Cheryl Taylor Bowie *(Pres)*
Blake Lagneaux *(Sr Dir-Art)*
Amanda Poehler *(Dir-Art)*
Donna LeJeune *(Office Mgr)*

Accounts:
Camp Bon Coeur

THE RIGHT LIST
20a North West Blvd Ste 290, Nashua, NH 03053
Toll Free: (800) 697-5977
Web Site: www.therightlist.com

Employees: 52

Agency Specializes In: Alternative Advertising, Broadcast, Digital/Interactive, Direct Response Marketing, Electronic Media, Email, Exhibit/Trade Shows, Local Marketing, Mobile Marketing, Multimedia, Print, Promotions, Search Engine Optimization, Social Media, Telemarketing, Trade & Consumer Magazines, Viral/Buzz/Word of Mouth, Web (Banner Ads, Pop-ups, etc.)

Approx. Annual Billings: $4,000,000

John Foster *(Sr VP-Mktg)*

Accounts:
InfoUSA
Norwegian Cruise Line

RILEY HAYES ADVERTISING
333 S First St, Minneapolis, MN 55401
Tel.: (612) 338-7161
Fax: (612) 338-7344
E-Mail: info@rileyhayes.com
Web Site: www.rileyhayes.com

Employees: 35
Year Founded: 1991

Tom Hayes *(Founder & CEO)*
Kerry Krepps *(Partner & Dir-Creative)*
Dan Hoedeman *(VP & Dir-Acct Mgmt & Digital)*
Eric Weiss *(VP & Dir-Creative)*
Steve Wendling *(VP & Dir-Media)*
Dave Plamann *(Dir-Fin)*
Tony Ticknor *(Dir-Technical)*
Margaret Hamamoto *(Acct Supvr)*
Maria Lloyd *(Supvr-Media)*
Natalie Judd *(Acct Exec)*

Accounts:
3M
Delta SkyMiles "TheGiftBackProject"
Dunwoody College of Technology (Advertising Agency of Record)

RINEY
(Formerly Publicis & Hal Riney)
2001 The Embarcadero, San Francisco, CA 94133-5200
Tel.: (415) 293-2001
Fax: (415) 293-2620
Web Site: www.riney.com

Employees: 253
Year Founded: 1986

National Agency Associations: 4A's-AAF

Agency Specializes In: Advertising, Brand Development & Integration, Sponsorship, T.V.

Approx. Annual Billings: $821,200,000

Breakdown of Gross Billings by Media: Cable T.V.: $35,000,000; Fees: $71,300,000; Internet Adv.: $3,700,000; Network T.V.: $188,900,000; Newsp.: $164,200,000; Out-of-Home Media: $6,500,000; Production: $43,800,000; Radio: $63,700,000; Sports Mktg.: $6,000,000; Spot T.V.: $131,600,000; Trade & Consumer Mags.: $106,500,000

Julie Liss *(Chief Strategy Officer)*
Kevin Roddy *(Chief Creative Officer)*
Alex Palomo *(Assoc Creative & Art Dir)*
EJ Slody *(Dir-Creative)*
Katie Edson *(Sr Acct Exec)*

Accounts:
24-Hour Fitness
AAA of Northern California, Nevada & Utah
Beam Global Spirits
Beneful
Hewlett-Packard; Cupertino, CA; 1998
Office of National Drug Control Policy Partnership for a Drug-Free America

RIPLEY-WOODBURY MARKETING COMMUNICATIONS, INC.
3516 Bravata Dr, Huntington Beach, CA 92649
Tel.: (714) 846-2550
Fax: (714) 846-2514
E-Mail: info@rwmarketing.com
Web Site: www.rwmarketing.com

E-Mail for Key Personnel:
President: ManleyW@rwmarketing.com

Employees: 6
Year Founded: 1946

National Agency Associations: THINKLA

Agency Specializes In: Business-To-Business

Approx. Annual Billings: $1,000,000

Manley H. Woodbury *(Pres)*
Terry Tsujioka *(Acct Exec & Copywriter)*

Accounts:
Advanced UV UV Water Treatment Systems
Ancra Cargo Restraint Products
CoMatrix Telephone Systems
Dura Coat Products Coil & Spray Coatings
InSync Information Technology Consultants
Lantronix Network Enabling Technologies
Lantronix
Orthodyne Electronics
Space Control; Walnut Creek, CA Self-Storage Management Software

Syagen Technology High-Throughput Molecular Analyzers
Telatemp Corp.; Fullerton, CA Temperature Monitoring Devices
Thermal Dynamics

RISDALL MARKETING GROUP

550 Main St, New Brighton, MN 55112-3271
Tel.: (651) 286-6700
Fax: (651) 631-2561
Toll Free: (888) RISDALL
E-Mail: info@risdall.com
Web Site: www.risdall.com

E-Mail for Key Personnel:
President: ted@risdall.com
Creative Dir.: kevin@risdall.com
Production Mgr.: kelly@risdall.com

Employees: 60
Year Founded: 1972

National Agency Associations: IAN

Agency Specializes In: Brand Development & Integration, Business Publications, Business-To-Business, Collateral, Corporate Identity, Direct Response Marketing, E-Commerce, Education, Environmental, Exhibit/Trade Shows, Financial, Food Service, Graphic Design, Health Care Services, High Technology, Industrial, Internet/Web Design, Legal Services, Leisure, Logo & Package Design, Medical Products, New Product Development, Pharmaceutical, Point of Purchase, Print, Public Relations, Publicity/Promotions, Real Estate, Sports Market, Strategic Planning/Research, Technical Advertising

Approx. Annual Billings: $200,000,000

Breakdown of Gross Billings by Media: Brdcst.: 1%; Bus. Publs.: 22%; Cable T.V.: 1%; Collateral: 10%; Consumer Publs.: 8%; D.M.: 7%; Graphic Design: 4%; Internet Adv.: 6%; Logo & Package Design: 4%; Newsp.: 2%; Pub. Rels.: 2%; Sls. Promo.: 2%; Worldwide Web Sites: 31%

Ted Risdall *(Chm & Pres-Risdall Mktg Grp)*
John Risdall *(Vice Chm & CEO)*
Tina Karelson *(Partner)*
Mariann Hohe *(Chief Strategy Officer)*
Glenna Dibrell *(Sr VP & Acct Supvr)*
Sara Dziedzic *(VP-Bus Dev)*
Matt Bergen *(Dir-Interactive Creative)*
Rick Johnson *(Dir-Web Dev)*
Pete Proper *(Dir-Art)*
Maggie Tompkins *(Sr Acct Exec)*
Tyler Morey *(Acct Exec)*
Lauren Westling *(Acct Exec)*

Accounts:
Abe Tech Website
ACE Solid Waste
The Ackerberg Group Branding & Website Design
Advanced Carpet Restoration
Advanced Dental Specialists Website re-design and development
Affinity Plus Federal Credit Union Outdoor, Radio, TV, Website
Agosto
AgStar Website Redesign
Airborne Athletics Media Relations
All Star Construction Search Engine Optimization
Allina Health Screen To Prevent, Website
Amazing Cosmetics Brand Management
American Anti-Aging Society, Inc.; 2008
American Composers Forum
American Dental Partners Brand & Website
American Family Dental
American Friends of the Alexander Von Humboldt Foundation Website Design & Development
American Guidance Service (AGS)
American Marketing Association
American Pest Solutions
Anderberg
Antique Car Run, Inc.
API Outsourcing
Applied Technology Consultants; Minneapolis, MN Intranet U
Archway
Armor Security, Inc.
ASFI
Assurity River Group Digital Marketing
ATEK Companies Public Relations; 2007
Barbara Greving Studio Brand Development & Commercial Web Site
Barn Light Electric
Bd's Mongolian Grill (Agency of Record)
Be a Bombshell Cosmetics Branding & Marketing
Beisswenger Hardware
Bella Semplice Brand Management
Bentinho Massaro Strategy & Branding
Big Brother Big Sister of the Greater Twin Cities
Blue Book Publications
Boss Insurance Group
Boulder Creek Stone Products
Brave New Workshop
Buerkle Automotive Branding, Positioning, Strategy
Calabrio Inc.; 2008
Calypso
CardioVascular Centers & Hypertension Diagnostics Branding, Collateral, Messaging, Public Relations, Signage Development
Carlson Wagonlit Travel
Carol Pletcher
Cash For Junk Cars, Inc. Website Design & Ecommerce
Caveo Technologies
Central Medical, Inc.
Cherry Blooms
Chippewa Valley Technical College Advertising Planning, Media Placements
CieloStar
Citizens' Council for Health Freedom Creative services
City of New Brighton
CocoLaPalm Resort
Codex Corporation PR
Cold Steel, Inc.; Ventura, CA; 2002
College of St. Scholastica
Colorado Symphony Website Development & Design
Comm-Works Branding
Como Park Animal Hospital Online Marketing
Concur Technologies, Inc.
Condre Storage Marketing, Sales
Conservation Beyond Borders PR, Web Design & Development
Conwed Plastics Website, PPC & SEO
Corespine Technologies
Coretrate
Country Jam; 2008
Crenlo, Inc.; Rochester, NY Metal Fabrication; 2000
Crown College PPC, SEO, Social Media
CURRENT Restaurant Integrated Marketing, Public Relations, Special Events
Customer Driven Realty, LLC
CVS Flags Website
Dalco Enterprises, Inc.
Davanni's Pizza & Hot Hoagies Media Planning
David Fong's Integrated Marketing, Public Relations, Special Events
Decker Publications
Deerwood Orthodontics Website Redesign & Dev
Dejen Digital LLC
Delkor Systems Inc. Print Advertising
Deluxe Corp.; Saint Paul, MN Check Printers; 2000
Dental Services Group Marketing Strategy, Online Visibility Analysis
Dental Solutions
Despatch Industries
Destiny Candle Investment Branding & Marketing
Devicix, LLC
Direct Marketing Group
Distinctive Orthodontics
Donatelle
DuAll Investments Website & Online Marketing
Earthexchange Charitable Foundation E-mail Program Development, Landing Page, Special Event Planning
Eden Prairie Chamber Online Marketing
Eemax, Inc. Animation, PR, Production, Video Writing
Eemax University Website
Electrosonic
Elkay Manufacturing Information Architecture, User Interface Design
Empi, Inc.; Saint Paul, MN Medical Products; 2002
Empi; Saint Paul, MN Medical Products; 1996
Endurance Financial Federal Credit Union
The Energy Conservatory Public Relations
Event Sales
Fairview Health Services; Minneapolis, MN; 2001
Farmington Area Public Schools
FasTest SEO, Website Redesign
FemMed, Inc.
First Advisors Financial Planning
Flexo Impressions Website Development
FloatPro LLC Packaging, Web
Friend of a Friend, LLC UBS Website Design
Gareth Stevens Publishing
Gemini; Cannon Falls, MN Letters, Logos & Plaques
George Sawyer
Glacier Companies; 2008
Good Look Ink Public Relations, Strategic Marketing
Gopher Sport Video Development
Great Northwest Insurance; 2008
Greene Holcomb & Fisher LLC
Groveland Capital Creative, Website Design
Gun Vault
Habitech; Plano, TX Furniture
Health Recovery Center SEO, Website Redesign
Healthways Walkadoo Digital Marketing, Print
Hearing Components (Comply Foam) Public Relations; 2007
Help Me Grow
Hennepin County
Hickory Tech
Holly Mordini Beauty Marketing
HomeValu Interiors Social Media Monitoring
Hopkins Rotary; 2008
Hospitals Without Borders Web Site; 2007
Huckleberry
Ibody Science
Innovative Tools & Technologies Inc Digital Marketing
International Medica Foundation Public Relations
IXfactor Web Site; 2007
Jacobs Incentive Travel
JAIN Dental Direct Mail Advertising, Outdoor
JKW Translations
John Kappler; 2008
Khuraira Cosmetics
Kozlaks/Kozys
Labels 2 Learn (Agency of Record) Public Relations
Lakeview Clinic
Leadership Catalysts SEO, Social Media
Liberty Diversified Brand Strategy, Marketing
LifeScience Alley; 2007
Little Blind Spot
Lixivian Social Media
Locator Technologies Sales, Website Development; 2008
Lumens Integration Inc.
Lund Food Holdings, Inc.; 2008
Magnum Research, Inc.; Minneapolis, MN Sporting Goods
Mall of America Camp Snoopy
Manchester Square Group
Manny's Private Car Service
McKinley Group Inc.
McNally Smith College of Music
Mechdyne Brand Development, Public Relations, Search Engine Marketing
Med Supports
Medafor
Medication Management Systems
Medicom Digital

Medspira (Agency of Record) Strategic Public Relations & Communications
Memoir of Me, Inc.
Meridian Behavioral Health Marketing, Website
Meritas
Meritex
Metro Dentalcare
Metropolitan State University Public Relations, Website Redesign
Micron Metalworks; Blaine, MN Metal Fabrication
Midwest Dental Online Marketing Services
Mikki Williams Online Marketing, Website Development
Miltona Turf Tool Specialists, Website
Minnesota Angel Network
Minnesota Foreign Trade Zone
Minnesota Health & Housing Alliance; 2007
Minnesota Hospital Association Strategy, Website Redesign
Minnesota Inventors Congress Public Relations
Minnesota Masonic Charities; 2008
Minnesota Organization on Fetal Alcohol Syndrome Web-Based Record Management System; 2007
Minnesota Youth Soccer Association
MN Valley Testing Laboratories Client Portal Development
Mounds View Public Schools Mobile, Website
New Mountain Learning Marketing Collateral
North Oaks Golf Club Public Relations; 2007
Northwest Graphic Supply
Northwest Youth & Family Services Collateral Development
Northwestern College
Novologix
The Occasions Group; 2008
OmniLingua Worldwide, LLC Search Engine Marketing
Opportunity Partners
Optical Solutions; Minneapolis Telecommunications; 2000
OutsourceOne, Inc.
P2 Inc.
Par Aide (Agency of record)
Parkway Lawn; 2008
Pathway Health Services Website & Application Development, Website Redesign
Pellegrene Ferrell & Associates Soap Tunes; 2008
Peter's Auto Body; 2008
Peters Body Shop; 2008
P.H.T. Systems Inc
PJW Automotive
The Plus Group
PRA Location Services PR, Web Development
Premier Card Solutions
Priority Courier Express Sales Materials, Website Redesign
ProfitSee Brand Development, Marketing
Progressive Marketing Products, Inc.; Brea, CA Manufacturer of Mounts
PS Finance
Pur Minerals
QBF Website Redesign
Rainbow Pest Experts; 2007
Rainbow Treecare
Ramsey County Residential Media Planning, Strategy
Ramsey/Washington County Resource Recover Project Website Development
Raymedica; Minneapolis, MN Medical Products; 2001
RE/MAX North Central Public Relations
Redwood Dental Group
Renaissance Learning DNN Consulting
Restoration Professionals
Rice Lake Weighing Systems SEO, Website Redesign
Risdall Financial
Robert Hill Law Marketing, Website Development & Design
Ron Clark Construction & Design
Rotary Club of Minneapolis
Rustic Ridge Pillow & Hospitality Supply Co.
SafeNet Consulting Brand Strategy & Positioning
Safety Call Online Marketing, Website Development
Sail Away Cafe Integrated Marketing, Public Relations, Special Events
Sanimax
Schmidt; 2008
Schoonover Bodyworks, Inc. Website Development
Schussler Creative Event Management
Sealed Mindset Digital Marketing, Video Production, Website Redesign
Senior Abilities Unlimited LLC Market Research
Sentient Consultants
Shield Technologies; 2007
Shoreview Area Housing Initiative Print Collateral, Website Redesign
Shriners Public Relations, Social Media
Simply Neat Organizing
SkyWater Search Partners Marketing
Smith Foundry Co.; Minneapolis, MN Castings
Smith System Manufacturing, Inc.; Plano, TX Office & School Furniture
Snow Sneak Peek
Snuff Mill Consulting Branding, Fundraising, Website Design
Solboe Productions, LLC
Solid Waste Management Coordinating Board; 2007
Spanlink
Spectacle Shoppe
SpectraCell Laboratories Inc PR
Spineology; 2008
Stylmark Brand Messaging, Trade Industry Presentation
Tailwind Voice & Data Branding, Messaging
Tech Logic Print
Tevera Branding & Public Relations; 2007
Tolomatic, Inc. Search Engine Optimization
Tooth Doctor for Kids
TopLine Federal Credit Union
Transport Distribution Services Inc Marketing Evaluation & Strategy
TravelMaps
Tristan Publishing
Truck Writers
True Capitalism
Trust Point Website Development
Turck (Agency of Record) Digital Marketing, Print Advertising, Public Relations, Strategy, Trade Show Support
Twin Cities Originals
Twin City Fan
Ubiquio
UniPunch
United Business Mail; 2008
United Scientific Digital Marketing, Print
University of Minnesota College of Science and Engineering Technological Leadership Institute, Website
University of Minnesota Neurology Department
The University of Texas at Tyler Email Marketing Campaign
UpSize Magazine; 2008
U.S. Toy Company
Venture Academy PR
Vertical Storage Inc. Marketing Strategy, Online Visibility
Viking Industrial Center Analysis, Online Marketing, Strategy; 2008
Viksnins Harris & Padys Collateral
VINMonitor Public Relations, Website Design
Vision-Ease Lens Design, Production, Public Relations, Strategy
Vista Technologies Stereolithography
Visual Impact
Wayne D. Jorgenson PR
Waytek, Inc. Online Marketing Planning, SEO
Western National Insurance Group
Wheelhouse Logo
White Bear Lake Area Schools
Whitewater Unified School District; WI; 2008
Wildlife Research Center
Winthrop & Weinstine
Winthrop Resources Brand Strategy, Public Relations
Work Effects Brand Strategy
World Youth Orchestra & Choir
Yeadon Fabric Domes, LLC
Zam Network; 2008
ZetaSys Dental
Zinpro
ZIRC

Branches

Risdall Public Relations

(Formerly Risdall McKinney Public Relations)
550 Main St, New Brighton, MN 55112
Tel.: (651) 286-6700
Fax: (651) 631-2561
E-Mail: rmpr@risdall.com
Web Site: www.risdallpublicrelations.com

Employees: 55

Agency Specializes In: Public Relations

Joel Swanson *(Pres)*
Glenna Dibrell *(Sr VP & Acct Supvr)*
Dave Folkens *(VP)*
Andrea Goodall *(VP)*
Tina Karelson *(Exec Dir-Creative)*
Rochelle Snyder *(Sr Acct Exec)*
Michelle Peterson *(Acct Coord)*

Accounts:
Archway
Awnings today
Industrial Fabrics Association International Awnings Today Consumer Campaign; 2007
Masonic Cancer Center
Mentro Dental
Meritex
Minnesota Childrens Museum
Vision Ease Lens

RISE INTERACTIVE

1 S Wacker Dr Ste 300, Chicago, IL 60606
Tel.: (312) 281-9933
E-Mail: mark.benoit@riseinteractive.com
Web Site: www.riseinteractive.com

Employees: 20
Year Founded: 2004

National Agency Associations: AMA-BMA

Agency Specializes In: Business-To-Business, Computers & Software, Consulting, Consumer Goods, Consumer Marketing, Digital/Interactive, Direct-to-Consumer, E-Commerce, Email, Internet/Web Design, Local Marketing, Paid Searches, Planning & Consultation, Search Engine Optimization, Social Media, Web (Banner Ads, Pop-ups, etc.)

Approx. Annual Billings: $2,000,000

Breakdown of Gross Billings by Media: Internet Adv.: 95%; Other: 5%

Jon Morris *(Founder & CEO)*
Scott Conine *(VP-Bus Ops)*
Howard Diamond *(VP-Digital Strategy)*
Brian Speck *(Controller)*
Irene Fogelson *(Dir-Acct Strategy)*
Sean Roach *(Dir-Product Dev & Innovation)*
Michael Wall *(Dir-Digital Strategy)*
Lou Amodeo *(Assoc Dir-Creative)*
Mark Benoit *(Assoc Dir-Digital Strategy)*
Ashmita Chatterjee *(Assoc Dir)*
Carl Petersen *(Assoc Dir-Fin Svcs)*
Josh Arntz *(Assoc Mgr-Digital Mktg)*
Heather Sellitto *(Assoc Mgr-Digital Mktg)*
Matthew Kent *(Sr Acct Exec)*

Accounts:

Allstate Motor Club; Chicago, IL Motor Club Services
Blue Cross Blue Shield of Michigan
Careerbuilder.com
Classic Residence by Hyatt; Chicago, IL Adult Communities
DeVry
Miami Children's Hospital Digital, Social Media
Northshore University HealthSystem
Ulta Beauty

RITCHEY ASSOCIATES, INC.

2859 Central St Ste 135, Evanston, IL 60201
Tel.: (312) 282-8124
E-Mail: deborah@raonline.com

E-Mail for Key Personnel:
President: deborah@raonline.com

Employees: 4
Year Founded: 1984

National Agency Associations: AMA-BMA-CIMA

Agency Specializes In: Advertising, Advertising Specialties, Affluent Market, Brand Development & Integration, Business-To-Business, Collateral, Communications, Consulting, Corporate Communications, Corporate Identity, Digital/Interactive, Direct Response Marketing, Direct-to-Consumer, Email, Event Planning & Marketing, Exhibit/Trade Shows, Financial, Graphic Design, Health Care Services, High Technology, Integrated Marketing, Internet/Web Design, Local Marketing, Logo & Package Design, Luxury Products, Market Research, Medical Products, New Product Development, Planning & Consultation, Podcasting, Print, Promotions, Real Estate, Sales Promotion, Search Engine Optimization, Social Media, Travel & Tourism, Web (Banner Ads, Pop-ups, etc.), Women's Market

Approx. Annual Billings: $2,000,000

Breakdown of Gross Billings by Media: Collateral: 10%; Corp. Communications: 10%; D.M.: 10%; Internet Adv.: 15%; Other: 15%; Promos.: 15%; Strategic Planning/Research: 10%; Worldwide Web Sites: 15%

Deborah Ritchey *(Pres)*

Accounts:
BMW
Four Seasons
Motorola Solutions, Inc.

RITTA

568 Grand Ave, Englewood, NJ 07631
Tel.: (201) 567-4400
Fax: (201) 567-7330
E-Mail: info@ritta.com
Web Site: www.ritta.com

E-Mail for Key Personnel:
President: kay@ritta.com

Employees: 20
Year Founded: 1978

Agency Specializes In: Advertising, Advertising Specialties, Affluent Market, African-American Market, Alternative Advertising, Arts, Automotive, Bilingual Market, Brand Development & Integration, Broadcast, Business Publications, Business-To-Business, Cable T.V., Catalogs, Collateral, Communications, Consulting, Consumer Goods, Consumer Marketing, Consumer Publications, Corporate Communications, Corporate Identity, Cosmetics, Custom Publishing, Customer Relationship Management, Direct Response Marketing, Direct-to-Consumer, E-Commerce, Education, Electronic Media, Electronics, Email, Entertainment, Event Planning & Marketing, Exhibit/Trade Shows, Experience Design, Fashion/Apparel, Financial, Graphic Design, Guerilla Marketing, Health Care Services, High Technology, Hispanic Market, Household Goods, Identity Marketing, In-Store Advertising, Infomercials, Integrated Marketing, Internet/Web Design, Legal Services, Leisure, Local Marketing, Logo & Package Design, Luxury Products, Magazines, Media Planning, Medical Products, Mobile Marketing, Multicultural, Multimedia, New Product Development, New Technologies, Newspaper, Newspapers & Magazines, Out-of-Home Media, Outdoor, Over-50 Market, Package Design, Pharmaceutical, Planning & Consultation, Point of Purchase, Point of Sale, Print, Production, Production (Ad, Film, Broadcast), Production (Print), Promotions, Publicity/Promotions, Radio, Regional, Retail, Sales Promotion, Social Marketing/Nonprofit, Sports Market, Strategic Planning/Research, T.V., Trade & Consumer Magazines, Transportation, Travel & Tourism, Viral/Buzz/Word of Mouth, Web (Banner Ads, Pop-ups, etc.), Women's Market

Approx. Annual Billings: $3,200,000

Kay Ritta *(Owner)*
Koryn Schermer *(CEO)*
Kevin Janosz *(COO)*
Jacqueline Millstein *(Chief Creative Officer & Dir-Creative)*
Nick Gelens *(Mgr-Publ)*
Steve Scheiner *(Mgr-Print Production)*
Paula Silva *(Acct Supvr)*
Victoria List *(Copywriter)*

Accounts:
Bergen Performing Arts Center; Englewood, NJ; 2004
BMW of North America; Woodcliff Lake, NJ Luxury Automobiles; 1986
Englewood Hospital & Medical Center; Englewood, NJ Medical Center; 1999
Rider Insurance; Springfield, NJ Motorcycle Insurance; 2004
Samsung Electronics; Ridgefield Park, NJ; 1999

RIVER COMMUNICATIONS, INC.

333 Westchester Ave, White Plains, NY 10604
Tel.: (914) 686-5599
Fax: (914) 686-5558
E-Mail: ideas@riverinc.com
Web Site: www.riverinc.com

Employees: 12
Year Founded: 1988

Agency Specializes In: Communications, Corporate Communications, Internet/Web Design, Local Marketing, Media Relations, Public Relations

Revenue: $2,600,000

James F. Tobin *(Founder & CEO)*
Troy Mayclim *(Sr VP)*
Maureen Richardson *(Sr VP)*

Accounts:
Ritchie Capital Management
State Street Global Advisors

RIVERS AGENCY

215 Henderson St, Chapel Hill, NC 27514
Tel.: (919) 932-9985
Fax: (919) 932-1413
Toll Free: (888) 784-8477
Web Site: www.riversagency.com

Agency Specializes In: Advertising, Email, Graphic Design, Internet/Web Design, Logo & Package Design, Public Relations, Search Engine Optimization, T.V.

Lauren Rivers *(CEO)*
Sarah Owens *(Sr Dir-Art)*
Mary Gunn *(Dir-Art)*
Claire Blevins *(Assoc Dir-Art)*

Accounts:
Cree Bulbs

RIZEN CREATIVE

314 S 9th St Ste 200, Boise, ID 83702
Tel.: (208) 938-5583
Fax: (208) 939-5162
E-Mail: hello@rizencreative.com
Web Site: www.rizencreative.com

Year Founded: 2002

Agency Specializes In: Advertising, Digital/Interactive, Internet/Web Design, Logo & Package Design, Media Buying Services, Media Planning, Media Relations, Public Relations, Social Media, Strategic Planning/Research

Jeremy James *(Dir-Art & Sr Graphic Designer)*
Linda Handlos *(Acct Exec)*

Accounts:
Boise Convention & Visitors Bureau

RIZK ADVERTISING

8101 W 123rd St, Palos Park, IL 60464
Tel.: (708) 357-1717
E-Mail: info@rizkadvertising.com
Web Site: www.rizkadvertising.com

Agency Specializes In: Advertising, Digital/Interactive, Graphic Design, Internet/Web Design, Logo & Package Design, Print, Social Media, T.V.

Rob Rizk *(Founder & Dir-Creative)*

Accounts:
Country Squire Foods

RJ PALMER LLC

(Merged with TargetCast tcm to form Assembly)

RK PROMOTIONS & ADVERTISING INC.

723 Downing Place, Geneva, IL 60134
Tel.: (630) 262-1616
Fax: (630) 262-1616
E-Mail: rkpromotions@comcast.net

Employees: 1
Year Founded: 1991

Agency Specializes In: Advertising, Advertising Specialties, Affluent Market, Broadcast, Business Publications, Business-To-Business, Cable T.V., Co-op Advertising, Collateral, Commercial Photography, Consulting, Consumer Goods, Consumer Marketing, Consumer Publications, Corporate Identity, Custom Publishing, Direct Response Marketing, Email, Exhibit/Trade Shows, Graphic Design, Household Goods, Integrated Marketing, Internet/Web Design, Magazines, Media Buying Services, Media Planning, Men's Market, Multimedia, Newspaper, Outdoor, Paid Searches, Planning & Consultation, Print, Production (Ad, Film, Broadcast), Production (Print), Promotions, Public Relations, Radio, Retail, Search Engine Optimization, T.V., Women's Market

Approx. Annual Billings: $500,000

Robert Kaspar *(Owner)*

RK VENTURE
(Formerly Vaughn Wedeen Kuhn)
120 Morningside SE, Albuquerque, NM 87108
Tel.: (505) 243-4000
Fax: (505) 247-9856
Web Site: www.rkventure.com

Employees: 15
Year Founded: 1982

Agency Specializes In: Advertising, Pets

Richard Kuhn *(Owner & Exec Creative Dir)*
Becky Hahs *(Sr Dir-Art & Designer)*
Nick Tauro, Jr. *(Dir-Brdcst Creative & Writer)*
Pablo Garcia *(Office Mgr)*
Dianne De Leon *(Mgr-Accts & Client Svcs)*
Mario Moreno *(Specialist-Production)*
Lee Gallegos *(Coord-Social Media)*

Accounts:
ABQ Uptown
Arch of Leadership
AT&T Broadband
Atkinson & Company
Avalon Trust Company
Bresnan Communications
Citi
Comcast
Cox Communications
Cystic Fibrosis Foundation
The Daniels Company
Denish, Kline & Associates
LA Metro Website
Mesa Del Sol
New Mexico State Fair Campaign: "Lynette At The Fair"
NMDOT "ENDWI" App, Campaign: "Aftermath", Campaign: "BKLUP", Campaign: "DNTXT", Campaign: "Medical Evidence", DWI Campaign
RCN Telecom Services, LLC Broadcast, Direct Mail, Marketing, Mobile, Online, Outdoor, Print, Social Media
Santa Fe Baby Fund
Santa Fe CVB
Ultramain Systems, Inc.

RKG (THE RIMM-KAUFMAN GROUP)
701 E Water St, Charlottesville, VA 22902
Tel.: (434) 970-1010
Fax: (434) 973-7765
E-Mail: info@rimmkaufman.com
Web Site: www.rimmkaufman.com

Employees: 170
Year Founded: 2003

Agency Specializes In: Advertising, Digital/Interactive, Paid Searches, Production (Ad, Film, Broadcast), Search Engine Optimization, Social Media

Adam Audette *(Pres)*
George Gallate *(CEO)*
Dalton Dorne *(CMO)*
George Michie *(Chief Marketing Scientist)*
Ryan Gibson *(Exec VP-Mktg Strategy)*
Matthew Mierzejewski *(Exec VP-Client Svc & Delivery)*
Attila Szabo *(VP-Software Dev)*
Jody O'Donnell *(Dir-SEO Technical)*

Accounts:
Beall's Department Stores, Inc.
CareerBuilder, LLC
Eddie Bauer, Inc.
Express
Herman Miller, Inc.
Jones New York
NutriSystem, Inc.
Zale Corporation

RKG (THE RIMM-KAUFMAN GROUP)
(Acquired by Merkle Inc.)

RKR MARKETING & ADVERTISING
(Private-Parent-Single Location)
43176 Business Pk Dr Ste 108, Temecula, CA 92590
Tel.: (951) 694-4400
Fax: (951) 694-4757
E-Mail: info@rkrmarketing.com
Web Site: www.rkrmedia.com

Employees: 12
Year Founded: 2001

Agency Specializes In: Advertising, Brand Development & Integration, Broadcast, Collateral, Internet/Web Design, Logo & Package Design, Media Buying Services, Print, Promotions, Public Relations

Revenue: $1,200,000

Judy Zulfiqar *(CEO)*
Jacob Myers *(Creative Dir)*
Cyndi Lemke *(Dir-Sls & Mktg)*
Michele Brewer *(Office Mgr)*
Miquella Zulfiqar *(Mgr-Production)*
Cheri Alston *(Coord-Sponsorship)*

Accounts:
LeMaster Computer Services

RLR ADVERTISING INC.
102 Sound Ct, Northport, NY 11768
Tel.: (631) 925-5590
Fax: (631) 925-5591
E-Mail: admin@rlradv.com
Web Site: www.rlradv.com

E-Mail for Key Personnel:
President: admin@rlradv.com
Creative Dir.: art@rlradv.com
Production Mgr.: support@rlradv.com

Employees: 3
Year Founded: 1986

Agency Specializes In: Recruitment

Robert L. Ruehle, Sr. *(Pres & CEO)*
Wendy Ann Ruehle *(Exec VP)*

RLS GROUP
2468 Atlantic Blvd, Jacksonville, FL 32207
Tel.: (904) 399-3943
Fax: (904) 410-4913
Web Site: www.rls-group.com

Agency Specializes In: Advertising, Brand Development & Integration, Event Planning & Marketing, Graphic Design, Internet/Web Design, Logo & Package Design, Public Relations, Radio, T.V.

Jill Storey *(Co-Owner & VP)*
Rob Storey *(Pres)*

Accounts:
Two Smart Cookies

R.M. BARROWS, INC. ADVERTISING & PUBLIC RELATIONS
847 N. Humboldt St #207, San Mateo, CA 94401
Tel.: (650) 344-4405
E-Mail: barrows@barrows.com
Web Site: www.barrows.com

Employees: 1
Year Founded: 1980

Agency Specializes In: Automotive, Bilingual Market, Broadcast, Business Publications, Business-To-Business, Cable T.V., Collateral, Consulting, Consumer Marketing, Consumer Publications, Corporate Identity, Cosmetics, Digital/Interactive, Direct Response Marketing, E-Commerce, Education, Electronic Media, Entertainment, Event Planning & Marketing, Financial, Food Service, Government/Political, Graphic Design, Health Care Services, High Technology, Hispanic Market, Industrial, Infomercials, Information Technology, Internet/Web Design, Logo & Package Design, Magazines, Media Buying Services, Medical Products, New Product Development, Newspaper, Newspapers & Magazines, Out-of-Home Media, Outdoor, Pharmaceutical, Planning & Consultation, Print, Production, Public Relations, Publicity/Promotions, Radio, Real Estate, Recruitment, Restaurant, Retail, Strategic Planning/Research, T.V., Trade & Consumer Magazines, Travel & Tourism, Yellow Pages Advertising

Robert M. Barrows *(Pres)*

Accounts:
Cyber Sizzle USA
Paladin Medical; San Carlos, CA; 2006
Publicitytour.info
searchingforbigfoot.com; Redwood City, CA Bigfoot Expedition, Bigfoot TV Projects, Books, Movies; 2006
The Video Enhanced Grave Marker; Burlingame, CA; 2006

RMD ADVERTISING
6116 Cleveland Ave, Columbus, OH 43231
Tel.: (614) 794-2008
Fax: (614) 794-0476
E-Mail: ditzhazy@rmdadvertising.com
Web Site: www.rmdadvertising.com

Employees: 15
Year Founded: 1992

Agency Specializes In: Advertising, Brand Development & Integration, Broadcast, Business Publications, Cable T.V., Co-op Advertising, Collateral, Consulting, Consumer Goods, Consumer Marketing, Consumer Publications, Corporate Communications, Corporate Identity, Crisis Communications, Customer Relationship Management, Digital/Interactive, Direct Response Marketing, Direct-to-Consumer, Email, Experience Design, Food Service, Guerilla Marketing, Household Goods, Identity Marketing, In-Store Advertising, Industrial, Integrated Marketing, Internet/Web Design, Logo & Package Design, Media Buying Services, Media Planning, Media Relations, Media Training, Merchandising, Multimedia, Newspaper, Point of Purchase, Point of Sale, Print, Production (Print), Promotions, Public Relations, Publicity/Promotions, Radio, Retail, Sales Promotion, Strategic Planning/Research, T.V., Trade & Consumer Magazines, Viral/Buzz/Word of Mouth

Approx. Annual Billings: $2,100,000

Donn Ditzhazy *(Mng Partner & Dir-Creative)*
Sue Reninger *(Mng Partner-Brand Strategy)*
Amanda Soule *(Acct Mgr)*
Alexandra Koury *(Acct Exec)*
Samantha C. Anderson *(Coord-Special Projects)*

Accounts:
Bil-Jac Foods
New-Brio Tuscan Grille
Crunchtables
Dei Fratelli Canned Tomato Products; 2008
Graeter's Ice Cream; Cincinnati, OH; 2015
New-Joel Silverman Public Relations, Social Media
Klosterman Baking Company

Le Tour de France Bicycle Brand Strategy, Public Relations
Panera Bread; Columbus, OH; 1999
Rudolph Foods Pork Rinds; 2008
S&F Foods
Tandoor Chef
T.G.I. Friday's
Watershed Distillery; Columbus, OH BtoB Awareness, PR, Social Media

RMI MARKETING & ADVERTISING

436 Old Hook Rd 2nd Fl, Emerson, NJ 07631
Tel.: (201) 261-7000
Fax: (201) 261-4970
E-Mail: jm@rmi-inc.com
Web Site: www.rmi-inc.com

Employees: 20
Year Founded: 1973

National Agency Associations: AD CLUB

Agency Specializes In: Advertising, Advertising Specialties, Automotive, Aviation & Aerospace, Brand Development & Integration, Business-To-Business, Co-op Advertising, Collateral, Consumer Marketing, Corporate Identity, Cosmetics, Direct Response Marketing, E-Commerce, Education, Entertainment, Environmental, Event Planning & Marketing, Exhibit/Trade Shows, Fashion/Apparel, Financial, Food Service, Graphic Design, Health Care Services, High Technology, In-Store Advertising, Industrial, Internet/Web Design, Investor Relations, Local Marketing, Logo & Package Design, Magazines, Marine, Merchandising, Multimedia, New Product Development, Newspaper, Newspapers & Magazines, Pharmaceutical, Point of Purchase, Point of Sale, Print, Production, Publicity/Promotions, Real Estate, Restaurant, Retail, Sales Promotion, Trade & Consumer Magazines, Transportation, Travel & Tourism

Approx. Annual Billings: $17,000,000

Breakdown of Gross Billings by Media: Adv. Specialities: 10%; Corp. Communications: 10%; E-Commerce: 10%; Exhibits/Trade Shows: 10%; Graphic Design: 10%; Internet Adv.: 10%; Point of Purchase: 10%; Point of Sale: 10%; Print: 10%; Sls. Promo.: 10%

Jonathan Morgan *(VP)*

Accounts:
Adidas
Barnes & Noble; New York, NY
Bowker
Carrera
CellularOne
Citibank; New York, NY
CMP; Manhasset, NY
DSTi; New York, NY
Jaguar Cars
Kaman Music Corporation; Bloomfield, CT
Liberty Helicopters; Linden, NJ Charter Services & Scenic Tours; 1998
Mercedes-Benz
Monari Federzoni
New Jersey Foster Parents
OR-Live
Ovation Guitars
Ricoh Corporation; West Caldwell, NJ
SGS Testing; Fairfield, NJ
SLP3D; New Hartford, CT
Volvo Cars of North America
Yamaha Corporation
Yamaha Music Corp.; CA

RMR & ASSOCIATES, INC.

5870 Hubbard Dr, Rockville, MD 20852-6425
Tel.: (301) 230-0045
Fax: (301) 230-0046
E-Mail: rsachs@rmr.com
Web Site: www.rmr.com

E-Mail for Key Personnel:
President: rsachs@rmr.com

Employees: 10
Year Founded: 1987

Agency Specializes In: Advertising, Brand Development & Integration, Business-To-Business, Collateral, Consumer Marketing, Corporate Identity, Direct Response Marketing, Event Planning & Marketing, Exhibit/Trade Shows, Graphic Design, High Technology, Information Technology, Internet/Web Design, Logo & Package Design, Media Buying Services, Print, Production, Public Relations, Publicity/Promotions, Strategic Planning/Research, Technical Advertising

Robyn M. Sachs *(Owner & Pres)*
Jim Cavender *(Dir-Art)*
William J. Holleran *(Dir-Creative & Content)*
Seth Menishon *(Coord-Media Res)*

Accounts:
Digital Intelligence Systems Corporation
iCore Networks

R.N. JOHNSON & ASSOCIATES CREATIVE MARKETING

113 E Van Buren St, Woodstock, IL 60098
Tel.: (815) 337-4461
E-Mail: gj@rnjohnson.com
Web Site: www.rnjohnson.com

E-Mail for Key Personnel:
Creative Dir.: gj@rnjohnson.com

Employees: 4
Year Founded: 1950

Agency Specializes In: Advertising, Brand Development & Integration, Business Publications, Business-To-Business, Collateral, Corporate Identity, Digital/Interactive, Electronic Media, Email, Graphic Design, Guerilla Marketing, Integrated Marketing, Internet/Web Design, Newspapers & Magazines, Search Engine Optimization, Strategic Planning/Research

Approx. Annual Billings: $574,000

Breakdown of Gross Billings by Media: Bus. Publs.: $87,300; Collateral: $142,960; D.M.: $113,040; Newsp. & Mags.: $87,300; Plng. & Consultation: $46,560; Worldwide Web Sites: $96,840

Gregory R. Johnson *(Pres & Dir-Creative)*

Accounts:
City of Crystal Lake
Dorian-Gray Retirement Planning, Inc.
Elgin Visual & Performing Arts Center
JA Frate Transport Company
Microtech Machine Company
Numerical Precision Inc.

RNO1, LLC

274 Redwood Shores Pkwy, Redwood City, CA 94065
Tel.: (650) 268-9783
E-Mail: letschat@rno1.com
Web Site: www.rno1.com

Year Founded: 2008

Agency Specializes In: Advertising, Brand Development & Integration, Digital/Interactive, Logo & Package Design, Print, Social Media

Michael Gaizutis *(Principal)*

Accounts:
G-Form, LLC
JJ law

ROBBINS KERSTEN DIRECT

(Formerly KerstenDirect)
855 E Collins Blvd, Richardson, TX 75081
Tel.: (972) 664-1115
Fax: (972) 664-1120
Toll Free: (800) 222-6070
E-Mail: connect@robbinskersten.com
Web Site: robbinskersten.com/

Employees: 94
Year Founded: 1978

Agency Specializes In: Affiliate Marketing, Bilingual Market, Communications, Customer Relationship Management, Digital/Interactive, Direct Response Marketing, Faith Based, Internet/Web Design, Media Planning, Newspapers & Magazines, Print, Search Engine Optimization, Social Marketing/Nonprofit, Strategic Planning/Research, Telemarketing

Robin Riggs *(Chief Creative Officer)*
Max Bunch *(Sr VP-Consulting & Client Svc)*
Amanda Wasson *(Sr VP-Digital Strategy)*
Eddy Camas *(VP-Client Svc)*
Kevin Eagan *(VP-Production Svcs)*
Andrew Laudano *(VP-Client Svcs)*
Kristen McCool *(VP-Client Svcs)*

Accounts:
American Bible Society Fundraising
Braille Institute of America Fundraising
National Ovarian Cancer Coalition Fundraising
National Park Foundation Digital Fundraising
Ronald Reagan Presidential Foundation Fundraising
Speroway (Agency of Record)
Susan G. Komen For The Cure Digital Fundraising

ROBERT FLEEGE & PARTNERS

340 Howland Dr, Columbus, OH 43230
Tel.: (614) 270-9043
Fax: (614) 478-9734
E-Mail: robban@fleege.com
Web Site: www.fleege.com

Employees: 1
Year Founded: 2000

Agency Specializes In: Advertising, Automotive, Business-To-Business, Cable T.V., Entertainment, Event Planning & Marketing, Exhibit/Trade Shows, Graphic Design, High Technology, Magazines, Media Buying Services, Newspaper, Newspapers & Magazines, Out-of-Home Media, Outdoor, Print, Production, Technical Advertising, Trade & Consumer Magazines, Transportation, Yellow Pages Advertising

Approx. Annual Billings: $250,000

Breakdown of Gross Billings by Media: Cable T.V.: 15%; Collateral: 10%; Outdoor: 60%; Print: 15%

Robert Robban Fleege *(Dir-Art, Copywriter & Graphic Designer)*

Accounts:
Adams Suzuki
Columbus Funnybone
San Francisco International Auto Show; Sausalito, CA SF Auto show; 1996
Seattle Sutton
Veale Properties; Santa Rosa, CA Outdoor Media; 1998
Zephyr Ventilation; San Francisco, CA Range Hoods & Appliances; 1997

ROBERT J. BERNS ADVERTISING LTD.
2250 E Devon Ave Ste 235, Des Plaines, IL 60018
Tel.: (847) 699-9527
Fax: (847) 296-8678
E-Mail: robertjbernsadvertising@comcast.net
Web Site: robertjbernsadvertising.com/

E-Mail for Key Personnel:
President: mberns8861@aol.com

Employees: 2
Year Founded: 1968

Agency Specializes In: Direct Response Marketing, Newspapers & Magazines, Publicity/Promotions

Approx. Annual Billings: $5,000,000

Mark Berns *(Dir-Art)*

Accounts:
Cummins Allison Corp.; Mt. Prospect, IL; 1975
Marketing Resource Group

ROBERT MARSTON & ASSOCIATES, INC.
485 Madison Ave, New York, NY 10022
Tel.: (212) 371-2200
Fax: (212) 755-4598
E-Mail: mars@marstonpr.com
Web Site: marstonsc.com

Employees: 35

Agency Specializes In: Communications, Crisis Communications, Health Care Services, Internet/Web Design, Local Marketing, Media Relations, Media Training, Medical Products, Public Relations, Publicity/Promotions

Revenue: $2,900,000

Michael J. Cargill *(Principal)*
Lori M. Gosset *(Principal)*
Lara Markenson *(Sr Dir)*

Accounts:
Abbott Laboratories
American Textile Manufacturers
Anheuser-Busch Companies, Inc
ConAgra
Control Data Corporation
Eastman Kodak
Genworth Financial
The Interactive Advertising Bureau

ROBERT SHARP & ASSOCIATES
3615 Canyon Lake Dr Ste 1, Rapid City, SD 57702
Tel.: (605) 341-5226
Fax: (605) 341-7390
E-Mail: info@thesharpagency.com
Web Site: www.robertsharpassociates.com

Agency Specializes In: Advertising, Event Planning & Marketing, Internet/Web Design, Logo & Package Design, Media Buying Services, Media Planning, Print, Public Relations, Social Media, Strategic Planning/Research

Robert Sharp *(Pres & CEO)*
Tony Dodd *(VP & Dir-Web Dev & Creative)*
Stacey Sharp *(VP)*
Ian Sharp *(Acct Mgr)*

Accounts:
Sturgis Motorcycle Rally

ROBERTS + LANGER DDB
437 Madison Ave 8th Fl, New York, NY 10022
Tel.: (646) 289-7300
Fax: (212) 593-1286
Web Site: www.robertsandlanger.com

E-Mail for Key Personnel:
President: stone@robertsntarlow.com

Employees: 50
Year Founded: 2004

National Agency Associations: 4A's

Agency Specializes In: Consumer Marketing, Cosmetics, Fashion/Apparel, Sponsorship

Approx. Annual Billings: $175,000,000

Andy Langer *(Chief Creative Officer)*
Lynn Mercado *(Exec VP & Grp Head-Creative)*
Torrey Plank *(Sr VP & Grp Acct Dir)*
Karen Snook *(Sr VP & Grp Acct Dir)*
Christina Cooley *(Sr VP & Creative Dir-Aveeno Beauty)*
Jessica Tamberlame *(Sr VP & Acct Dir-Global)*
Kimberly Broatch *(VP & Acct Dir)*
Andrea Haber *(VP-Brdcst Bus & Mgr-Talent)*
Nancy Dao *(Dir-Art)*
Claire Elizabeth Murphy *(Dir-Digital Creative)*
Aimee Drob *(Acct Exec)*
Michelle Linares *(Acct Exec)*
Stacey Parkes *(Assoc Creative Dir)*

Accounts:
Aveeno
Barnes & Noble, Inc. 4 NOOK, Advertising, Campaign: "A Book Is A Gift Like No Other", Campaign: "You Never Know Who You'll Meet at Barnes & Noble", TV
Hunter Douglas Blinds & Shades
Johnson & Johnson Baby Products, Inc.; New Brunswick, NJ
Johnson & Johnson Corporate Campaign: "Anthem", K-Y Lubricating Jelly, Lubriderm, Neutrogena, Rembrandt
Kraft
Neutrogena Corporation
Polo/Ralph Lauren; New York, NY Accessories, Eyewear, Footwear, Men's, Women's, & Children's Apparel, Polo.com, TV Production

ROBERTS COMMUNICATIONS INC.
64 Commercial St, Rochester, NY 14614-1010
Tel.: (585) 325-6000
Fax: (585) 325-6001
E-Mail: criby@robertscomm.com
Web Site: www.robertscomm.com

E-Mail for Key Personnel:
President: bmurtha@robertscomm.com
Creative Dir.: bkielar@robertscomm.com

Employees: 65
Year Founded: 1971

National Agency Associations: 4A's-DMA-PRSA

Agency Specializes In: Advertising, Business Publications, Business-To-Business, Co-op Advertising, Collateral, Consulting, Corporate Identity, Direct Response Marketing, Financial, Graphic Design, Health Care Services, High Technology, Industrial, Information Technology, Internet/Web Design, Investor Relations, Logo & Package Design, Newspaper, Newspapers & Magazines, Outdoor, Planning & Consultation, Point of Purchase, Point of Sale, Print, Production, Public Relations, Publicity/Promotions, Sales Promotion, Sponsorship, Strategic Planning/Research, Trade & Consumer Magazines

Approx. Annual Billings: $60,000,000

Katrina Busch *(Pres)*
William Murtha *(CEO)*
Bruce Kielar *(Chief Creative Officer & Exec VP)*
Brian Rapp *(VP & Dir-Creative)*
Kristin Bridenbaugh *(Acct Dir)*
Kelley Redmond *(Dir-Art)*
Tina Clark *(Mgr-Digital & Social Media Strategy)*
Rachel Spence *(Supvr-Creative)*
Jessica DeMinco *(Sr Acct Exec)*
Rachel Melendez *(Sr Acct Exec)*
Jeanne Metcalfe *(Sr Acct Exec)*
Alyssa Davis *(Copywriter)*

Accounts:
Blue Cross Blue Shield of Minnesota
New-Council Rock Wealth Advisory Group (Agency of Record) Advertising, Public Relations
CricKet
The Deaf Wellness Center
Dorschel Automotive Group; Rochester, NY (Agency of Record) Digital, Marketing, Merchandising, Online Advertising, Print, Public Relations, Radio, Social Media, Television
eHealth Global
ESL Federal Credit Union; Rochester, NY; 2000
New-Finger Lakes Health Systems Agency
New-Freshop, Inc. (Agency of Record) Digital Advertising, Public Relations
New-Heritage Christian Services Advertising, Direct Marketing, Social Media
New-ITT Enidine Digital, Public Relations
The Lifetime Healthcare Companies
MasterCard International; New York, NY Employee Communications; 1997
Nixon Peabody LLP
Paychex
Red Cross of Western New York
Xerox Corporation; Rochester, NY Campaign: "Jazz Festival"

ROBERTS CREATIVE GROUP
107 S Magnolia St, Laurel, MI 39440
Tel.: (601) 425-0054
Web Site: www.robertscreative.com

Agency Specializes In: Advertising, Brand Development & Integration, Collateral, Digital/Interactive, Event Planning & Marketing, Outdoor, Public Relations, Radio, Social Media

Eric Roberts *(CEO)*
Crystal Gordon *(Head-Designer)*
Zac Freundt *(Dir-Art)*
Matt Flowers *(Acct Exec)*
Chris Eskridge *(Designer)*
Nathan Farley *(Designer)*
Krista Moylan *(Copywriter)*

Accounts:
Magnolia Wireless

ROBERTSON & MARKOWITZ ADVERTISING & PR
108 E Montgomery Crossroads, Savannah, GA 31406
Tel.: (912) 921-1040
Fax: (912) 921-0333
Web Site: www.robmark.com

Agency Specializes In: Advertising, Event Planning & Marketing, Graphic Design, Internet/Web Design, Logo & Package Design, Media Planning, Media Relations, Public Relations, Radio, Strategic Planning/Research

Lisa Markowitz-Kitchens *(Pres)*
Ted Robertson *(CEO)*
Diane Butler *(Office Mgr & Media Buyer)*
Mandy Bradshaw *(Specialist-Social Media & Acct)*
Cassie Hanuscak *(Sr Graphic Designer)*

Accounts:
Chatham Orthopaedic Associates

ROBERTSON & PARTNERS
(Formerly Robertson Wood Advertising)

6061 S Fort Apachee Rd Ste 100, Las Vegas, NV 89148
Tel.: (702) 947-7777
Fax: (702) 262-9037
E-Mail: info@rw-west.com
Web Site: robertson.partners/

Employees: 20
Year Founded: 1977

National Agency Associations: AAF

Agency Specializes In: Advertising, Brand Development & Integration, Broadcast, Business Publications, Business-To-Business, Cable T.V., Co-op Advertising, Collateral, Consumer Marketing, Consumer Publications, Corporate Identity, Direct Response Marketing, Electronic Media, Entertainment, Exhibit/Trade Shows, Food Service, Graphic Design, Health Care Services, High Technology, Hispanic Market, Internet/Web Design, Logo & Package Design, Media Buying Services, Newspaper, Newspapers & Magazines, Outdoor, Planning & Consultation, Point of Purchase, Point of Sale, Print, Production, Public Relations, Publicity/Promotions, Radio, Real Estate, Restaurant, Retail, T.V., Travel & Tourism

Approx. Annual Billings: $21,000,000

Scott Robertson *(Pres)*
Louise Robertson *(Partner & Dir-Interactive Svcs)*
Paul Fitzgerald *(Partner-East Div)*
George Davey *(CFO)*
Joshua Griffin *(Pres-Govt Affairs)*
Piper Overstreet *(VP-Pub Affairs)*
Loralee Humphries *(Controller & Dir-HR)*

Accounts:
Summerlin THHC; Las Vegas, NV

ROBINSON & ASSOCIATES INC
201 S Spring St Ste 600, Tupelo, MS 38804
Tel.: (662) 844-2654
Fax: (662) 841-5627
Web Site: www.robinson-advertising.com

Agency Specializes In: Advertising, Brand Development & Integration, Event Planning & Marketing, Logo & Package Design, Media Buying Services, Media Planning, Outdoor, Promotions, Public Relations, Radio

Tom Robinson *(Chm & CEO)*
Ty Robinson *(Pres & COO)*
Sally Kepple *(VP)*
Lacy Luckett *(VP-Client Svcs)*
Donna Shelton *(Dir-Admin)*
Raymond Jourdan *(Acct Supvr)*
Natasha Pierre-Louis *(Acct Exec)*
Jessica Crawley *(Media Buyer & Coord)*

Accounts:
BancorpSouth, Inc.
Franks Franks Jarrell & Wilemon
Tommy Morgan Realtors

ROBINSON CREATIVE INC.
Southlake Town Sq 286 Grand Ave Ste 238, Southlake, TX 76092
Tel.: (817) 748-5057
Fax: (817) 416-7833
E-Mail: info@robinsoncreativeinc.com
Web Site: www.robinsoncreativeinc.com

Employees: 10
Year Founded: 1998

Agency Specializes In: Collateral, Identity Marketing, Multimedia, Print, Production (Print), Promotions

Ben Robinson *(Founder & Pres)*
Terri J. Cooper *(Dir-Interior Design)*
Kat Hood *(Dir-Art)*
Esther Lee *(Dir-Art)*
Andrew Librizzi *(Dir-Audio & Visual)*
Sam Musso *(Acct Exec-Los Angeles)*
Donna Bradle *(Coord-Mktg)*
Renee Whitehead *(Coord-Mktg)*

ROCK CANDY MEDIA
5900 Balcones Dr Ste 205, Austin, TX 78731
Tel.: (512) 291-7626
Fax: (512) 233-5193
E-Mail: info@rockcandymedia.com
Web Site: www.rockcandymedia.com

Year Founded: 2009

Agency Specializes In: Advertising, Brand Development & Integration, Internet/Web Design, Media Buying Services, Media Planning, Print

Annie Liao Jones *(Principal)*
Samuel Kimelman *(VP-Strategy)*

Accounts:
Algebraix Data
AmbitIT
Austin Urology Institute
Austin Wine and Cider Website, logo
DigitHaus
National Instruments
ShoreTel Sky Offline, Online, Strategic Marketing
Texas Disposal Systems Garden-Ville, Marketing, Social Media

ROCKET 55
800 Washington Ave N Ste 671, Minneapolis, MN 55401
Tel.: (612) 315-2399
Web Site: www.rocket55.com

Employees: 15
Year Founded: 2007

Agency Specializes In: Advertising, Affluent Market, African-American Market, Agriculture, Arts, Asian Market, Automotive, Aviation & Aerospace, Bilingual Market, Business-To-Business, Children's Market, College, Commercial Photography, Computers & Software, Consumer Goods, Consumer Marketing, Content, Cosmetics, Customer Relationship Management, Digital/Interactive, Direct-to-Consumer, Education, Electronics, Engineering, Entertainment, Environmental, Faith Based, Fashion/Apparel, Financial, Food Service, Gay & Lesbian Market, Government/Political, Health Care Services, High Technology, Hispanic Market, Hospitality, Household Goods, Industrial, Information Technology, International, Internet/Web Design, Investor Relations, Legal Services, Leisure, Local Marketing, Luxury Products, Marine, Medical Products, Men's Market, Merchandising, Multicultural, New Technologies, Over-50 Market, Pets , Pharmaceutical, Planning & Consultation, Real Estate, Recruitment, Restaurant, Retail, Search Engine Optimization, Seniors' Market, Social Media, South Asian Market, Sports Market, Stakeholders, Teen Market, Transportation, Travel & Tourism, Tween Market, Urban Market, Web (Banner Ads, Pop-ups, etc.), Women's Market

Steve Ayres *(Founder & CEO)*
Caitlin Tvrdik *(Dir-Mktg)*
Paige Craig *(Mgr-Social Media)*
Mike Delsing *(Sr Designer-Interactive)*

Accounts:
Hearth & Home Technologies; 2012
Schneiderman's Furniture; 2012

ROCKET POP MEDIA
2530 W Main ST, Richmond, VA 23220
Tel.: (804) 644-2525
Web Site: www.rocketpopmedia.com

Year Founded: 2001

Agency Specializes In: Advertising, Digital/Interactive, Internet/Web Design, Social Media

Scott Dickens *(Pres)*
Cara Dickens *(VP & Producer)*
Brendan Howard *(Strategist-New Media)*
Chris Crews *(Copywriter)*

Accounts:
Carter & Spence

ROCKET RED
1700 Pacific Ave Ste 250, Dallas, TX 75201
Tel.: (972) 776-0022
Fax: (972) 776-0023
E-Mail: gayden@gorocketred.com
Web Site: www.gorocketred.com

Employees: 10
Year Founded: 1995

National Agency Associations: AMA

Agency Specializes In: Above-the-Line, Advertising, Advertising Specialties, Affiliate Marketing, Alternative Advertising, Aviation & Aerospace, Brand Development & Integration, Branded Entertainment, Business-To-Business, Co-op Advertising, Collateral, Communications, Consumer Goods, Consumer Marketing, Corporate Communications, Corporate Identity, Digital/Interactive, Direct Response Marketing, Direct-to-Consumer, Email, Entertainment, Environmental, Event Planning & Marketing, Exhibit/Trade Shows, Experience Design, Game Integration, Government/Political, Graphic Design, Guerilla Marketing, Health Care Services, High Technology, Hospitality, In-Store Advertising, Integrated Marketing, Internet/Web Design, Local Marketing, Logo & Package Design, Market Research, Media Planning, Media Relations, Merchandising, Mobile Marketing, Multicultural, Multimedia, New Product Development, New Technologies, Newspaper, Out-of-Home Media, Outdoor, Planning & Consultation, Print, Production (Ad, Film, Broadcast), Production (Print), Promotions, Public Relations, Publicity/Promotions, RSS (Really Simple Syndication), Real Estate, Retail, Sales Promotion, Search Engine Optimization, Social Marketing/Nonprofit, Sports Market, Strategic Planning/Research, Sweepstakes, Viral/Buzz/Word of Mouth, Web (Banner Ads, Pop-ups, etc.)

Approx. Annual Billings: $4,000,000

Breakdown of Gross Billings by Media: Audio/Visual: 5%; Consulting: 35%; Corp. Communications: 25%; D.M.: 10%; Exhibits/Trade Shows: 25%

George Deeb *(Mng Partner)*
Gayden Day *(Principal & Exec Dir-Creative)*
Raynaldo Alvarez *(Dir-Art)*
Jillian Ripple Lines *(Dir-Client Svcs)*
Steve Ringer *(Dir-Creative)*
Jourdan Day *(Acct Exec)*

Accounts:
Dallas Executive Airport
Lund International
North Texas Tollway Authority
Technollo

ROCKET SCIENCE

700 Larkspur Landing Cir Ste 199, Larkspur, CA 94939
Tel.: (415) 464-8110
Fax: (415) 464-8114
E-Mail: request@rocketscience.com
Web Site: www.rocketscience.com

Employees: 11
Year Founded: 1996

Agency Specializes In: Consulting, Exhibit/Trade Shows, Media Relations, Product Placement, Public Relations, Strategic Planning/Research

Revenue: $5,000,000

Michael Ward *(Partner & Dir-Creative)*
Ryan Palombo *(Dir-Art)*
Rich Mullikin *(Strategist-PR)*

Accounts:
Avira Gmbh
Ekahau, Inc.

ROCKETCREATIVE

6097 Mapleton Dr, New Albany, OH 43054
Tel.: (847) 387-8088
Fax: (602) 795-7715
E-Mail: info@rocketcreative.com
Web Site: www.rocketcreative.com

Employees: 2
Year Founded: 2004

Agency Specializes In: Advertising, Business-To-Business, Commercial Photography, Corporate Communications, Event Planning & Marketing, Exhibit/Trade Shows, Graphic Design, International, Internet/Web Design, Print, Public Relations, Publicity/Promotions

Scott Ritter *(Owner & Dir-Creative)*
Cara Mormino *(VP)*

ROCKETLAWNCHAIR

(Formerly Integre Advertising by Design)
N8 W22323 Johnson Dr Ste D, Waukesha, WI 53186
Tel.: (262) 544-8800
Fax: (262) 544-8801
E-Mail: juliec@rocketlc.com
Web Site: rocketlawnchair.com/

Employees: 15

Dean Bressler *(Partner & Dir-Creative)*
Julie Cosich *(Dir-Client Integration)*
Wendy Westadt *(Mgr-Traffic & Production)*
Valerie Becknell *(Strategist-Acct)*

Accounts:
GE Healthcare
Rite-Hite
Spacesaver Corporation

ROCKEY & ROCKWELL ADVERTISING, INC.

1934 Old Gallows Rd, Ste 350, Vienna, VA 22182
Tel.: (703) 734-1500
Fax: (703) 734-7811
E-Mail: info@rockeyrockwell.com
Web Site: www.rockeyrockwell.com

Employees: 20
Year Founded: 1994

Agency Specializes In: Advertising, Direct Response Marketing, Internet/Web Design, Media Buying Services, Public Relations

Stephanie Rockey *(Owner & Pres)*

Accounts:
Hendrick Honda; Woodbridge, VA

ROCKFISH INTERACTIVE

(Acquired by WPP plc)

THE ROCKFORD GROUP

216 Congers Rd Bldg 2, New City, NY 10956
Tel.: (845) 624-1322
Fax: (845) 624-1435
E-Mail: michael@rockfordgroup.com
Web Site: www.rockfordgroup.com

Employees: 4

Agency Specializes In: Advertising, Advertising Specialties, Alternative Advertising, Automotive, Brand Development & Integration, Broadcast, Business Publications, Business-To-Business, Cable T.V., Catalogs, Collateral, Communications, Consumer Goods, Consumer Marketing, Corporate Communications, Corporate Identity, Cosmetics, Digital/Interactive, Direct Response Marketing, Direct-to-Consumer, Electronic Media, Email, Event Planning & Marketing, Government/Political, Guerilla Marketing, Health Care Services, Identity Marketing, Infomercials, Integrated Marketing, Internet/Web Design, Leisure, Local Marketing, Logo & Package Design, Luxury Products, Magazines, Marine, Market Research, Media Buying Services, Media Planning, Media Relations, Medical Products, Men's Market, Mobile Marketing, Multimedia, New Product Development, New Technologies, Newspaper, Newspapers & Magazines, Out-of-Home Media, Outdoor, Over-50 Market, Paid Searches, Pets , Planning & Consultation, Print, Product Placement, Production, Production (Ad, Film, Broadcast), Production (Print), Public Relations, Publicity/Promotions, Radio, Regional, Retail, Sales Promotion, Social Marketing/Nonprofit, Social Media, Sponsorship, T.V., Trade & Consumer Magazines, Tween Market, Viral/Buzz/Word of Mouth, Web (Banner Ads, Pop-ups, etc.)

Breakdown of Gross Billings by Media: Graphic Design: 10%; Internet Adv.: 20%; Radio: 60%; Worldwide Web Sites: 10%

Michael Zack *(Pres)*

Accounts:
Nissan
Paul Conte Cadillac
United House Wrecking

ROCKIT SCIENCE AGENCY

7520 Perkins Rd Ste 330, Baton Rouge, LA 70808
Tel.: (225) 709-9490
E-Mail: info@rockitscienceagency.com
Web Site: www.rockitscienceagency.com

Employees: 50
Year Founded: 2000

Agency Specializes In: Advertising, Brand Development & Integration, Business-To-Business, Digital/Interactive, Direct Response Marketing, Graphic Design, Media Planning, Outdoor, Print, Public Relations

Brad Bongiovanni *(Pres & Chief Creative Officer)*
Brent A. Sims *(Principal & Strategist-Brand)*
Amy Crawford *(VP-Strategic Ops)*
Stephen Bowling *(Dir-Interactive)*
Grant Hurlbert *(Dir-Creative)*
Theresa Thao Nguyen *(Acct Exec)*
Kyle Baker *(Designer-Interactive)*

Accounts:
Baton Rouge General Medical Center
Blue Cross & Blue Shield
Bruce Foods Corporation
Pernix Therapeutics Holdings, Inc.
Rave Cinemas, LLC
Ritter Maher Architects
St.Elizabeth's Medical Center
Tipton Associates

RODGERS TOWNSEND, LLC

1000 Clark Ave 5th Fl, Saint Louis, MO 63102
Tel.: (314) 436-9960
Fax: (314) 436-9961
Web Site: www.rodgerstownsend.com

Employees: 118
Year Founded: 1996

National Agency Associations: 4A's

Agency Specializes In: Advertising, Digital/Interactive, Direct Response Marketing, Sponsorship

Tim Rodgers *(Co-Founder & CEO)*
Michael McCormick *(Chief Creative Officer)*
Erik Mathre *(Sr VP & Dir-Creative)*
Crystal Merritt *(VP & Acct Plng Dir)*
Jonathan Hansen *(Sr Dir-Art)*
Marianne Daniels *(Bus Mgr-Brdcst & Producer)*
Carrie Muehlemann *(Dir-Talent & Rels)*
Cheryl Sparks *(Dir-Production)*
J. Chambers *(Assoc Dir-Creative)*

Accounts:
AB InBev
Ardent Outdoors Creative, Fishing Reels & Accessories, Media Buying
AT&T Communications Corp. Campaign: "Smart Grid Holiday Dimensional"
Circus Flora
Con-Way
Enterprise Holdings
The Hartford Campaign: "Melissa", Campaign: "Play On: Office Dance", Online, Paralympic TV
Humane Society
LouFest LouFest Poster Series
Magic House Campaign: "Born"
Maritz, Inc.; Saint Louis, MO Corporate Branding, Travel, eMaritz; 2001
Mayflower Print Campaign
Missouri Baptist
Nawgan; Saint Louis, MO Campaign: "One Brainy Beverage", Creative
Outreach International Campaign: "Outreach Box Labels"
PBS
Pleats Cleaners
The Saint Louis Arts & Education Council
Saint Louis Children's Hospital; Saint Louis, MO; 2000
Saint Louis Post Dispatch; Saint Louis, MO; 2002
Saint Louis Rams; Saint Louis, MO Football; 1999
Spectrum/Spectracide Terminate; Saint Louis, MO AccuShot Sprayer, Campaign: "Tame the Wild", Cutter, Hot Shot, Peters, Spectracide, Terminate; 1999
WhiteWave Foods Products

THE ROGERS AGENCY

524 Liverpool Ct, Chesapeake, VA 23322
Tel.: (757) 546-8288
Web Site: www.therogersagency.com

Employees: 4
Year Founded: 2004

Agency Specializes In: Advertising, Affluent Market, African-American Market, Automotive, Brand Development & Integration, Broadcast, Cable T.V., Co-op Advertising, Communications,

Consulting, Consumer Goods, Consumer Marketing, Digital/Interactive, Electronic Media, Graphic Design, Hispanic Market, Household Goods, Infomercials, Internet/Web Design, Legal Services, Local Marketing, Logo & Package Design, Market Research, Media Buying Services, Media Planning, Media Relations, Media Training, Mobile Marketing, Multimedia, Outdoor, Over-50 Market, Paid Searches, Planning & Consultation, Production, Production (Ad, Film, Broadcast), Radio, Regional, Search Engine Optimization, Seniors' Market, Social Media, Strategic Planning/Research, T.V., Urban Market, Web (Banner Ads, Pop-ups, etc.), Women's Market

David Rogers *(Pres)*
Mitzi Andrews *(Dir-Creative)*
Rebekah Hughes *(Designer-Web & Graphic Designer)*

Accounts:
Tysinger Automotive Audi, Hyundai, Mercedes Benz, Smart; 2008

ROKKAN
(Acquired by Publicis Groupe S.A.)

ROKKAN
300 Park Ave S, New York, NY 10010
Tel.: (212) 835-9300
Fax: (212) 251-9393
E-Mail: info@rokkan.com
Web Site: www.rokkan.com

Employees: 100
Year Founded: 2000

Agency Specializes In: Advertising, Advertising Specialties, Brand Development & Integration, Communications, Content, Digital/Interactive, Email, Internet/Web Design, Mobile Marketing, New Product Development, Out-of-Home Media, Package Design, Planning & Consultation, Production, Production (Ad, Film, Broadcast), Public Relations, Social Media, Sponsorship, Strategic Planning/Research, Web (Banner Ads, Pop-ups, etc.)

John Noe *(CEO & Mng Partner)*
Charles Bae *(Mng Partner & Chief Creative Officer)*
Chung Ng *(Mng Partner)*
Brian Carley *(Chief Creative Officer & Sr VP)*
Jim Blackwelder *(CTO)*
Matthew Garcia *(Sr VP-Client Svcs)*
Sean Miller *(Sr VP-Strategy)*
Joe Tao *(Sr VP-Production)*
Bryan Le *(VP & Creative Dir)*
Kaitlyn Brenner *(VP-Client Partnership)*
Joe Meanor *(VP-Client Partnership)*
Anthea Tang *(VP-Client Partnership)*
Lindsay Williams *(VP-Media & Analytics)*
Ariel Hammer *(Sr Dir-Art)*
Jeff Samson *(Dir-Creative)*
Billy Veasey *(Dir-Creative)*
Pete Michaud *(Acct Supvr)*
Diana Friedman *(Sr Acct Exec)*
Mikel McCavana *(Assoc Strategist)*

Accounts:
2K Games 2kgames.com
Aer Lingus
American Express
Anthem Inc Campaign: "ABCs of Disease", Digital, Social Media
Bethesda
Dishonored Campaign: "Part"
Canyon Creek Ranch
Chipotle
Citi
Coca-Cola North America Campaign: "Share a Coke with Humanity"
General Mills
The Humane Society of the United States Campaign: "Same Day Pups: Puppy Drone Delivery", Creative, Media, Video
Hyatt
Hyundai
JetBlue Campaign: "Jetblue.com", Campaign: "Share a Coke with Humanity", Digital
Longhorn Steakhouse Campaign: "Winter Wondersteak", Online, Social Media
NestlePurina Pet Care Fancy Feast
Princess Cruises
Tag Heuer Content Online, Social Media

ROMADS
1560 N Sandburg Terr Ste 3608, Chicago, IL 60610
Tel.: (312) 587-7919
Fax: (312) 643-1846
E-Mail: johnr@romads.com
Web Site: www.romads.com

Employees: 1
Year Founded: 2005

Agency Specializes In: Recruitment

Approx. Annual Billings: $700,000

John M. Romanyak *(Pres)*
Angela Phillips *(Acct Mgr)*

ROME & COMPANY
233 E Wacker Dr Apt 4011, Chicago, IL 60601-5116
Tel.: (312) 938-1013
Fax: (312) 938-1081
E-Mail: mail@romecreative.com
Web Site: www.romecreative.com

E-Mail for Key Personnel:
President: jerry@romecreative.com
Public Relations: mail@romecreative.com

Employees: 8
Year Founded: 1984

Agency Specializes In: Advertising, Automotive, Brand Development & Integration, Business-To-Business, Collateral, Communications, Consulting, Consumer Marketing, Consumer Publications, Corporate Communications, Corporate Identity, Direct Response Marketing, E-Commerce, Exhibit/Trade Shows, Graphic Design, Health Care Services, Information Technology, Internet/Web Design, Leisure, Local Marketing, Logo & Package Design, Magazines, Multimedia, New Product Development, Newspaper, Newspapers & Magazines, Out-of-Home Media, Over-50 Market, Package Design, Planning & Consultation, Point of Purchase, Point of Sale, Print, Sales Promotion, Seniors' Market, Strategic Planning/Research, Trade & Consumer Magazines, Transportation, Travel & Tourism, Web (Banner Ads, Pop-ups, etc.)

Breakdown of Gross Billings by Media: Collateral: 15%; Graphic Design: 30%; Newsp. & Mags.: 20%; Print: 5%; Worldwide Web Sites: 30%

Jerry Roman *(Pres)*

Accounts:
Cars.com; Chicago, IL (Affliate Marketing, Newspaper, Website & Collateral); 2003
Joseph Henry Jeweler; Chicago, IL (Print); 2005
The Lodging Unlimited; Chicago, IL (Brochures & Collateral); 2000
See More Shopping; Chicago, IL

ROMJUE ADVERTISING & CO
913 Gulf Breeze Pky Ste 15A, Gulf Breeze, FL 32561
Tel.: (850) 916-2822
Fax: (850) 916-2829
Web Site: www.romjueadvertising.com

Agency Specializes In: Advertising, Internet/Web Design, Media Buying Services, Media Planning, Outdoor, Radio, Social Media, Strategic Planning/Research, T.V.

Trudy Romjue *(Pres & CEO)*

Accounts:
Northwest Florida Regional Airport

RON FOTH ADVERTISING
8100 N High St, Columbus, OH 43235-6400
Tel.: (614) 888-7771
Fax: (614) 888-5933
E-Mail: ronfothsr@ronfoth.com
Web Site: www.ronfoth.com

Employees: 35
Year Founded: 1975

Agency Specializes In: Brand Development & Integration, Consumer Marketing, Fashion/Apparel, Food Service, Media Buying Services, Retail, Sponsorship, Sports Market

Breakdown of Gross Billings by Media: Bus. Publs.: 3%; Collateral: 6%; D.M.: 2%; Mags.: 5%; Newsp.: 7%; Outdoor: 1%; Point of Purchase: 3%; Radio: 30%; T.V.: 43%

Ron Foth *(Pres & CEO)*
David Henthorne *(Sr VP & Creative Dir)*
Robert Fradette *(Sr VP & Dir-Media)*
Larry Row *(Sr VP & Dir-Media)*
Ron Foth, Jr. *(Sr VP-Creative)*
Missy Weiss *(VP & Acct Mgr)*
Marty Nowak *(VP-Production)*
Mike Foth *(Acct Dir-Svcs)*
Todd King *(Dir-Art)*
Gene Roy *(Dir-Art)*
Dana Ford *(Strategist-Social Media)*

Accounts:
The California Academy of Sciences Campaign: "Bees"
Columbus Zoo & Aquarium Campaign: "Baby Babble", Polar Friend
Lake Erie
MGM Resorts International (Agency of Record) Beau Rivage Resort & Casino, Digital, Gold Strike Casino Resort, Outdoor, Print, Radio, Social Media, Television
Nutramax Laboratories
Oak Street Mortgage; Indianapolis, IN; 2003
Ohio Travel & Tourism
Safelite AutoGlass Creative, Social
Safeway
New-Santa Monica Travel & Tourism (Agency of Record) Brand Refresh, Brand Strategy, Brand direction, Integrated Marketing, International Advertising, Logo, Media Buying, Media Planning
The Wendy's Company Fast Food; 1999

THE RON TANSKY ADVERTISING & PUBLIC RELATIONS
3140 Woodgreen Ct, Thousand Oaks, CA 91362
Tel.: (805) 241-8688
E-Mail: rtansky@aol.com
Web Site: rontansky.com

E-Mail for Key Personnel:
President: rtansky@aol.com

Employees: 2
Year Founded: 1976

Agency Specializes In: Advertising, Alternative Advertising, Brand Development & Integration, Business Publications, Business-To-Business, Co-op Advertising, Collateral, Communications, Consulting, Consumer Marketing, Cosmetics, Electronics, Environmental, High Technology, Household Goods, Industrial, Leisure, Magazines, Marine, Media Relations, New Product Development, Newspaper, Pharmaceutical, Point of Purchase, Public Relations, Publicity/Promotions, Radio, Sales Promotion, Technical Advertising, Trade & Consumer Magazines

Approx. Annual Billings: $1,000,000

Ron Tansky *(Dir-Creative)*

RONI HICKS & ASSOCIATES
11682 El Camino Real Ste 200, San Diego, CA 92130
Tel.: (858) 947-2700
Fax: (858) 947-2701
E-Mail: jwheeler@ronihicks.com
Web Site: www.ronihicks.com

E-Mail for Key Personnel:
President: jwheeler@ronihicks.com

Employees: 22
Year Founded: 1979

Agency Specializes In: Advertising, Brand Development & Integration, Business-To-Business, Collateral, Communications, Consumer Marketing, Corporate Communications, Corporate Identity, Direct Response Marketing, Electronic Media, Event Planning & Marketing, Graphic Design, Integrated Marketing, Internet/Web Design, Logo & Package Design, Media Buying Services, Media Planning, Media Relations, Mobile Marketing, Production (Ad, Film, Broadcast), Public Relations, Real Estate, Sales Promotion, Search Engine Optimization, Social Media, Strategic Planning/Research, Web (Banner Ads, Pop-ups, etc.)

Approx. Annual Billings: $6,000,000

Jane Carey Wheeler *(Owner)*
Diane Gaynor *(Partner & Exec VP)*
Todd Ochsner *(VP-Brand Strategy)*
Erica Mendelson *(Dir-Pub affairs)*
Kira Young *(Dir-Media)*
Jo Depiano *(Office Mgr)*

Accounts:
Black Mountain Ranch Real Estate Developments; 2010
Brehm Communities Real Estate Developments; 1993
JMI Properties Real Estate Developments; 2009
Newland Communities Real Estate Developments; 1997
Rancho Mission Viejo Real Estate Developments; 1998

RONIN ADVERTISING GROUP
400 University Dr Ste 200, Coral Gables, FL 33134-7114
Tel.: (305) 444-6868
Fax: (305) 859-9776
Web Site: www.roninadv.com

Employees: 55

National Agency Associations: AFA

Agency Specializes In: Advertising, Food Service, Health Care Services, Hospitality, Real Estate, Retail, Sports Market

Karen Ableman *(Pres)*
John Swisher *(Chief Creative Officer)*
Paul Norton *(Dir-SEO)*
Maria Venegas *(Dir-Creative)*
Bianca Zeiler *(Dir-Creative Strategy)*
GiGi DiFazio *(Mgr-Print Production)*
Jonathan Gosper *(Jr Acct Exec)*

Accounts:
Millennium Place Boston Brochure, Website
Millennium Tower San Francisco

ROOFTOP COMMUNICATIONS
2526 St Paul St, Baltimore, MD 21218
Tel.: (410) 243-5550
Fax: (410) 243-5569
E-Mail: billh@rooftopcommunications.com
Web Site: www.rooftopcommunications.com

Employees: 11
Year Founded: 2004

Agency Specializes In: Brand Development & Integration, Direct Response Marketing, Internet/Web Design, Public Relations

Barbara Brotman Kaylor *(CEO & Acct Mgmt Supvr)*

Accounts:
Ashford Kent
Baldwin & Co.
Delsey Luggage
Priority Partners
Pure Face
Spring Swing

ROOKS ADVERTISING LLC
6958 Professional Pkwy E, Sarasota, FL 34240
Tel.: (941) 747-2021
Fax: (941) 747-2629
E-Mail: contact@rooksadvertising.com
Web Site: rooksadvertising.com

Agency Specializes In: Advertising, Brand Development & Integration, Graphic Design, Internet/Web Design, Logo & Package Design, Media Buying Services, Print, Public Relations, Radio, Social Media

David Rooks *(Pres)*
Linda Day *(Copywriter-Adv)*

Accounts:
Your Trainers Group

ROOM 214, INC.
3390 Valmont Rd Ste 214, Boulder, CO 80301
Tel.: (866) 624-1851
Fax: (303) 865-3759
E-Mail: info@room214.com
Web Site: www.room214.com

Year Founded: 2004

Agency Specializes In: Advertising, Brand Development & Integration, Content, Digital/Interactive, Internet/Web Design, Social Media

Jason Cormier *(Co-Founder)*
Keely Cormier *(Client Svcs Dir)*
Erica Griffiths *(Producer-Digital)*
Maya Shaff *(Acct Dir)*
Libby Turner *(Acct Dir)*
Jen Casson *(Dir-Creative Svcs)*
Ben Castelli *(Dir)*
Michael Kwolek *(Dir-Res)*
Jess Castanuela *(Acct Mgr)*
Leah Lesko *(Acct Supvr)*
Scott Shelton *(Gen Specialist)*

Accounts:
Verizon Wireless

ROOSTER
200 Varick St, New York, NY 10014
Tel.: (212) 380-3284
E-Mail: info@roosternewyork.com
Web Site: www.roosternewyork.com

Year Founded: 2010

Agency Specializes In: Advertising, Internet/Web Design, T.V.

Sebastian Eldridge *(CEO & Partner)*
Gavin McInnes *(Chief Creative Officer)*

Accounts:
Vans, Inc.

ROSBERG FOZMAN ROLANDELLI ADVERTISING
4745 Sutton Park Ct Ste 804, Jacksonville, FL 32224
Tel.: (904) 329-3797
Fax: (904) 329-1207
E-Mail: mike@rfrad.com
Web Site: www.rfrad.com

Employees: 5

Agency Specializes In: Advertising, Affluent Market, Collateral, Corporate Identity, Leisure, Luxury Products, Real Estate

Richard Rosberg *(Owner)*
Mike Fozman *(Partner & Dir-Creative)*

Accounts:
East West Communities
Universal Health Systems
VyStar Credit Union

ROSE COUNTRY ADVERTISING & PUBLIC RELATIONS
11904-113th Ave, Edmonton, AB T5G 3C2 Canada
Tel.: (780) 451-5670
Fax: (780) 452-2890
E-Mail: info@rcadvertising.ca
Web Site: www.rcadvertising.ca

Employees: 3
Year Founded: 1981

Brian Stecyk *(Owner)*
Ted Tennison *(Partner)*

ROSEN
1631 NE Broadway Ste 615, Portland, OR 97232
Tel.: (503) 224-9811
E-Mail: info@rgrosen.com
Web Site: rosenconvergence.com

E-Mail for Key Personnel:
President: richard@rgrosen.como

Employees: 1
Year Founded: 1990

National Agency Associations: AMA-DMA

Agency Specializes In: Brand Development & Integration, Consulting, Direct Response Marketing, Identity Marketing

Approx. Annual Billings: $1,200,000

Breakdown of Gross Billings by Media: Collateral: 5%; Consulting: 5%; D.M.: 40%; E-Commerce: 15%; Mags.: 20%; Newsp.: 5%; Plng. &

Consultation: 8%; Radio: 2%

Richard G. Rosen *(Pres & CEO)*
Jane C. Rosen *(Partner & Chief Creative Officer)*
Carrie Schave *(Mgr-Mktg)*

Accounts:
Anthem Health Plans of Virginia
First Tech Credit Union; 2004
GE Capital
Genworth Financial
MetLife
Modern Solution
Ricoh Americas

ROSENBERG ADVERTISING

12613 Detroit Ave, Lakewood, OH 44107
Tel.: (216) 529-7910
Fax: (216) 529-7915
Web Site: www.rosenbergadv.com

Agency Specializes In: Advertising, Corporate Identity, Digital/Interactive, Internet/Web Design, Logo & Package Design, Media Planning, Outdoor, Print, Radio, Social Media

David Rosenberg *(Pres)*
Melissa Sattler *(Partner & Dir-Creative Svcs)*
Austin Rosenberg *(Partner)*
Kara McKenna *(Sr Dir-Art)*
Marisa Himes *(Dir-Ops)*
Dave Simon *(Dir-Creative)*
Connie Ramser *(Sr Acct Mgr)*
Nellie Calanni *(Strategist-Social Media)*

Accounts:
MacroPoint
NFP Structured Settlements

ROSENPLOT DESIGN LLC

PO Box 1083, Bloomington, IN 47402
Tel.: (812) 822-2077
Fax: (812) 822-1179
Web Site: www.rosenplotdesign.com

Year Founded: 2000

Agency Specializes In: Advertising, Brand Development & Integration, Graphic Design, Internet/Web Design, Logo & Package Design, Print, Social Media, T.V.

Jennifer Rosenplot *(Graphic Designer & Copywriter)*

Accounts:
The Salvation Army

ROSETTA

(Formerly Rosetta Marketing Group, LLC)
100 American Metro Blvd, Hamilton, NJ 08619
Tel.: (609) 689-6100
Fax: (609) 631-0184
E-Mail: info@rosetta.com
Web Site: www.rosetta.com

Employees: 1,100
Year Founded: 1998

Agency Specializes In: Advertising, Business-To-Business, Communications, Consumer Marketing, Digital/Interactive, Direct Response Marketing, Financial, Health Care Services, Internet/Web Design, Leisure, Media Buying Services, Pets , Pharmaceutical, Retail, Search Engine Optimization, Sponsorship, Strategic Planning/Research, Travel & Tourism

Revenue: $60,000,000

David Worth *(Mng Partner-Global Strategic Plng & Exec VP)*
Ned Elton *(Mng Partner)*
Maria DePanfilis *(Partner-Analytics & Optimization)*
Joe Lozito *(CTO)*
Ram Sarma *(Sr VP-Tech)*
Andrew Hsu *(Creative Dir)*
Bob Strickland *(Creative Dir)*
Kim McFetridge *(Dir-HR)*
Katie Meyler *(Dir-Project Mgmt Healthcare)*
Lisa Gallo *(Assoc Partner-PMO Healthcare)*

Accounts:
AARP
Abbott
Allergan
Amgen
AOL
AstraZeneca
BlackBerry
Bristol-Myers Squibb
Campmor
CapitalOne
Citizens
Crane & Co.
David's Bridal Retail
Disney
Fleisher's Campaign: "Grass-Fed and Organic Meats"
Genentech
Gillette
Hallmark
Helzberg Diamonds Interactive
Hewlett Packard
HSBC
Johnson & Johnson
Jos. A. Bank
KeyCorp
KraftMaid Cabinetry
Marriott Travel & Leisure
Merrill Lynch
Microsoft
MSC Direct
National City
Nationwide Insurance Digital-Media Buying, Financial Services
NBC Universal
Novartis
OfficeMax
Otsuka
Pfizer
Pirelli Tire North America Interactive
Renaissance Hotels
Rogers Communications (Agency of Record)
Samsung Electronics
Shire
Special Olympics New Jersey Brand Positioning, Digital Media, Marketing Strategy, Social Media, Web Site
Sprint Nextel
Sunglass Hut
T-Mobile US Communications, Media & Technology
Things Remembered
UCB Healthcare
United States Mint
Valvoline CRM/loyalty, Creative Services, Interactive, Online Reputation Management And Analytics, SEO, Social Media, Technology Development
Vitamix

Branches

Rosetta

(Formerly Level, a Rosetta Co.)
4800 Morabito Pl, San Luis Obispo, CA 93401
Tel.: (805) 781-0546
Fax: (805) 781-0547
Web Site: www.rosetta.com

Employees: 160
Year Founded: 1995

Agency Specializes In: Sponsorship

Dan Connolly *(CEO)*
Frank Garavaglia *(Sr VP-Project Mgmt & Ops Lead Rosetta West)*
Evelyn Kim *(Sr VP-Bus Dev)*
Griselda Fernandez *(VP-Paid, Owned & Earned Media & Assoc Partner)*
Isabella Kanjanapangka *(Acct Supvr, Sr Acct Exec & Producer)*
Shawna Jackson *(Acct Dir)*
Lisa Charlebois *(Dir-Creative)*
Nicole Mercier *(Dir-People Svcs)*
Cale Thompson *(Dir-Paid, Owned & Earned Media)*
Garrett Colburn *(Assoc Dir-Mktg Strategy)*
Jason Kiselstein *(Acct Supvr)*
Danielle Beerson *(Acct Exec)*

Rosetta

2 N Riverside Plz, Chicago, IL 60606
Tel.: (312) 568-7010
Web Site: www.rosetta.com

Agency Specializes In: Digital/Interactive, Search Engine Optimization, Web (Banner Ads, Pop-ups, etc.)

Nick Hahn *(Mng Partner)*
Ted Thompson *(Partner & Sr VP)*
Jeanne Ryan *(Partner)*
Eli Grant *(VP-Growth Ops)*
Cale Thompson *(Dir-Paid, Owned & Earned Media)*
Ray Lansigan *(Assoc Partner-Mktg Strategy)*
Erika Papaccioli *(Assoc Partner-Rosetta Consulting)*

Rosetta

99 Hudson St, New York, NY 10013
Tel.: (646) 502-3100
Fax: (646) 502-3199
Web Site: www.rosetta.com

Employees: 150

Tod Rathbone *(Partner & Sr VP-Strategic Plng)*
Scott Reese *(Partner & Exec Dir-Creative)*
David Worth *(Exec VP-Global Strategic Plng)*
Katherine Battle *(Sr VP-Strategic Plng)*
Drew Kurth *(Sr VP-East Reg)*
Jon Winsell *(Sr VP-Strategic Plng)*
Michael Chang *(VP-Project Mgmt)*
Danielle Winter *(Acct Exec)*

Accounts:
Amgen
Fleisher's Campaign: "Lust for Better Meat", Grass-fed & Organic Meat
High Point Insurance
Merck

Rosetta

3700 Park East Dr Ste 300, Cleveland, OH 44122
Tel.: (216) 896-8900
Fax: (216) 896-8991
Web Site: www.rosetta.com

Employees: 80
Year Founded: 1989

Agency Specializes In: Digital/Interactive, Sponsorship

Paul Elliott *(Mng Partner-Consumer Products & Retail)*
Mike Chenelle *(Partner)*
Shawn Cornelius *(Partner)*
Dan O'Neil *(Partner-Fin Svc)*
John Pompeii *(Partner)*
Mark Eckman *(Exec VP-Delivery & Ops)*

Caroline Emmet *(Dir)*
Dominic Litten *(Dir-Paid, Owned & Earned Media)*
Katie Chioran *(Acct Exec)*
Brittany Slattery *(Specialist-Corp Comm)*
Noelle Pennyman *(Sr Assoc Specialist-Social Mktg)*

Accounts:
Borders
Citizens Bank Online
Coach
Marriott
National City Bank
Nationwide
Vita-Mix Corp. Content Strategy, Creative Design, Interactive, Marketing, Search Engine Optimization, Website Development

ROSETTA MARKETING GROUP, LLC
(Acquired by Publicis Groupe S.A. & Name Changed to Rosetta)

ROSKA DIRECT
(Name Changed to PulseCX)

ROSS ADVERTISING, INC.
60 E Magnolia Blvd, Burbank, CA 91502
Tel.: (818) 955-5155
Fax: (818) 955-9944
Web Site: rossadvertisinginc.com

E-Mail for Key Personnel:
President: dross@rossadv.com
Media Dir.: vhenderson@rossadv.com

Employees: 7
Year Founded: 1986

Agency Specializes In: Broadcast, Direct Response Marketing, Education, Entertainment, Food Service, Media Buying Services, Medical Products, Production, Radio, Restaurant, Retail, T.V.

Approx. Annual Billings: $12,500,000

Breakdown of Gross Billings by Media: Cable T.V.: $50,000; Newsp.: $60,000; Radio: $480,000; Spot T.V.: $11,910,000

David L. Ross *(Pres)*
Rick Perry *(VP)*

Accounts:
Celibre Medical
Danmer Custom Shutters
Hollywood Piano
Law Offices of J. Russell Brown; Los Angeles, CA Motorcycle Injury Law; 1988
Lotus Clinical Research
Othro Mattress
Spotloan

THE ROSS GROUP
6511 Hayes Dr, Los Angeles, CA 90048
Tel.: (323) 935-7600
Fax: (323) 935-7603
E-Mail: mary@thereelroosgroup.com
Web Site: www.thereelrossgroup.com

Employees: 7
Year Founded: 1988

Agency Specializes In: Arts, Brand Development & Integration, Branded Entertainment, Business-To-Business, Communications, Consulting, Consumer Marketing, Consumer Publications, Corporate Communications, Corporate Identity, Cosmetics, Crisis Communications, Customer Relationship Management, Email, Entertainment, Event Planning & Marketing, Fashion/Apparel, Identity Marketing, Integrated Marketing, Leisure, Local Marketing, Luxury Products, Magazines, Media Buying Services, Media Planning, Media Relations, Multimedia, New Product Development, Newspaper, Newspapers & Magazines, Package Design, Planning & Consultation, Product Placement, Production (Ad, Film, Broadcast), Production (Print), Promotions, Public Relations, Publicity/Promotions, Retail, Sales Promotion, Sponsorship, Strategic Planning/Research, T.V., Travel & Tourism, Women's Market

Approx. Annual Billings: $1,600,000

Breakdown of Gross Billings by Media: Local Mktg.: $500,000; Pub. Rels.: $1,100,000

Mary Hall Ross *(Owner)*
Andrea Romero *(Acct Exec)*

Accounts:
Blanton's Bourbon
Buffalo Trace
Christopher Guy
Jean Fares Couture

ROTH ADVERTISING, INC.
PO Box 96, Sea Cliff, NY 11579-0096
Tel.: (516) 674-8603
Fax: (516) 674-8606
E-Mail: charles@rothadvertising.com
Web Site: www.rothadvertising.com

Employees: 2
Year Founded: 1971

Agency Specializes In: Advertising, Business-To-Business, Catalogs, Consulting, Consumer Marketing, Consumer Publications, Direct Response Marketing, Direct-to-Consumer, Education, Email, Exhibit/Trade Shows, Faith Based, Graphic Design, Internet/Web Design, Media Buying Services, Media Planning, Media Relations, Newspapers & Magazines, Planning & Consultation, Print, Production, Public Relations, Publicity/Promotions, Publishing, Social Marketing/Nonprofit, Strategic Planning/Research, Trade & Consumer Magazines

Approx. Annual Billings: $908,000

Breakdown of Gross Billings by Media: Adv. Specialities: $5,000; Bus. Publs.: $75,000; Consumer Publs.: $458,000; Exhibits/Trade Shows: $5,000; Print: $365,000

Daniel J. Roth *(Owner)*

Accounts:
American Mental Health Foundation; New York, NY Books; 1999
Baylor University Press; Waco, TX Books; 2009
Cardinal Cooke Guild; New York, NY Newsletter; 1988
Catholic Book Publishers Association; Rockford, IL "Spirit of Books" Catalog, Catholic Bestseller List; 1990
Catholic Media Publishers Association; San Antonio, TX "Spirit of Books" Catalog, Catholic Bestseller List; 1990
Catholic Press Association; Chicago, IL CPA Book Awards; 2009
Knights of the Holy Sepulchre; New York, NY Newsletter; 2004
Nassau County Psychological Association; Merrick, NY Newsletter; 1974
New City Press; Hyde Park, NY Books; 1998
Paulist Press; Mahwah, NJ Direct Mail List Management; 2004
Templeton Press; West Conshohocken, PA Books; 2008
Westminster John Knox Press; Louisville, KY Books; 2002

ROTH PARTNERS LLC
507 Claflin Ave, Mamaroneck, NY 10543
Tel.: (917) 543-9333
Web Site: www.rothpartnersllc.com

Year Founded: 2010

Agency Specializes In: Advertising, Brand Development & Integration, Digital/Interactive, Multicultural, Public Relations, Social Marketing/Nonprofit, Strategic Planning/Research

Rick Roth *(Founder & CEO)*
Martyn Straw *(Sr Dir-Strategy)*
Skip Allocco *(Dir-Creative & Exec Producer)*
Araminta Atherton *(Dir-Art & Design)*
Ross Sutherland *(Dir-Creative)*

Accounts:
Graco baby Media Planning & Buying, Public Relation, Shopper Marketing
Infosys Creative
The National Association for the Specialty Food Trade
Newell Rubbermaid Graco
True Citrus Inc.
Walter Surface Technologies Business-to-Business

ROTTER GROUP INC.
256 Main St 2nd Fl, Huntington, NY 11743
Tel.: (631) 470-7803
Fax: (631) 420-7807
E-Mail: srotter@rottergroup.com
Web Site: rottercreativegroup.com

E-Mail for Key Personnel:
President: srotter@rotterkantor.com

Employees: 22
Year Founded: 1965

National Agency Associations: THINKLA

Agency Specializes In: Advertising, Broadcast, Cable T.V., Children's Market, Consulting, Consumer Marketing, Consumer Publications, Digital/Interactive, Electronics, Entertainment, Fashion/Apparel, Internet/Web Design, Leisure, Magazines, Media Buying Services, Newspapers & Magazines, Print, Production, Production (Print), Public Relations, Radio, Restaurant, Strategic Planning/Research, T.V., Teen Market, Trade & Consumer Magazines, Tween Market

Breakdown of Gross Billings by Media: Cable T.V.: 55%; Consulting: 10%; Internet Adv.: 10%; Mags.: 5%; Network T.V.: 20%

Steve H. Rotter *(Chm & Chief Creative Officer)*
Steve Stetzer *(Pres)*

Accounts:
Blip Toys
Disney
Giochi Preziosi Toys
jakks pacific
University Games

Branch

Rotter Group Inc.
2670 Solana Way, Laguna Beach, CA 92651
Tel.: (949) 715-3814
Fax: (949) 715-3814
E-Mail: srotter@rottergroup.com
Web Site: rottercreativegroup.com

Employees: 5

Agency Specializes In: Advertising

Steve Rotter *(Owner)*

Accounts:
Blip
Chaotic
Disney
Estes/Cox
Giochi Preziosi
Playmates Toys; Costa Mesa, CA Disney Princess, Teenage Mutant Ninja Turtles; 2000
Smith Tinker
Toy Island
UniversityGames
Wham-O!

ROUNDHOUSE

537 SE Ash St Ste 401, Portland, OR 97214
Tel.: (503) 287-0398
E-Mail: info@roundhouseagency.com
Web Site: www.roundhouseagency.com

Year Founded: 2001

Agency Specializes In: Advertising, Digital/Interactive, Print, Radio, Sponsorship, Strategic Planning/Research

Joe Sundby *(Founder & Exec Dir-Creative)*
Dan Walsh *(Partner & Mng Dir)*
Mako Miyamoto *(Sr Dir-Art)*
Mary French *(Acct Dir)*
Bryan Houlette *(Creative Dir)*
Megan Amberson *(Dir-Brand Strategy)*

Accounts:
Adidas
Microsoft
Pluralsight
Red Bull
Redington

ROUNDHOUSE MARKETING & PROMOTION, INC.

560 E Verona Ave, Verona, WI 53593
Tel.: (608) 497-2550
Fax: (608) 497-2598
E-Mail: info@roundhouse-marketing.com
Web Site: www.roundhouse-marketing.com

Employees: 20

Agency Specializes In: Brand Development & Integration, Graphic Design, Point of Sale, Print, Promotions

Robert Carr *(Owner)*
Mike Mahnke *(Sr Acct Mgr)*
Casey Moen *(Sr Acct Mgr)*
Stefanie Kelly *(Acct Exec)*
Christina Steel *(Acct Exec)*

Accounts:
Batteries Plus
Boca
Claussen
Kohler
Kraft
Lunchables
Microsoft Xbox (Social Media)
Smucker's
Springs
Sterling
Verizon

ROUNDPEG

1003 E 106th St, Indianapolis, IN 46280
Tel.: (317) 569-1396
Fax: (317) 569-1389
Web Site: www.roundpeg.biz

Employees: 5
Year Founded: 2002

Agency Specializes In: Logo & Package Design, Public Relations, Web (Banner Ads, Pop-ups, etc.)

Lorraine Ball *(Owner & Dir-Creative)*
Lisa Paschke *(Partner & Gen Mgr)*
Anne Boyle *(Partner & Dir-Strategy)*
Darryl West *(Dir-Engrg)*
Melissa Phillips *(Mgr-Bus Dev)*
Alison Klein *(Specialist-Content Mktg)*
Eric Heinemann *(Sr Partner)*

ROUTE 1A ADVERTISING

2633 W 8th St, Erie, PA 16505
Tel.: (814) 461-9820
Fax: (814) 461-0594
E-Mail: info@route1a.com
Web Site: www.route1a.com

Year Founded: 2002

Agency Specializes In: Advertising, Internet/Web Design, Print, T.V.

Mike Flack *(Pres)*
Damon Kleps *(Dir-Art)*
Jamie Potosnak *(Dir-Creative)*
Amy Vanscoter *(Acct Exec)*

Accounts:
Rocky Boots
Saint Vincent Health Center

ROUTE2 ADVERTISING

112 E Line St Ste 312, Tyler, TX 75702
Tel.: (903) 504-5921
Web Site: www.route2advertising.com

Year Founded: 2011

Agency Specializes In: Advertising, Brand Development & Integration, Graphic Design, Internet/Web Design, Logo & Package Design, Radio

Mike Hill *(Owner & Dir-Creative)*

Accounts:
Bronco Oilfield Services
Centaur Arabian Farms
Cork Food & Drink
Green Bug
Karis Resources
Mann Tindel & Thompson
Matt Begley & Bitter Whiskey
Mentoring Minds, Lp.
Pure Relaxation
Ricks On the Square
Stillbent
Texas Rose Festival

THE ROXBURGH AGENCY INC

245 Fischer Ave B4, Costa Mesa, CA 92626
Tel.: (714) 556-4365
E-Mail: hello@roxburgh.com
Web Site: www.roxburgh.com

Agency Specializes In: Advertising, Brand Development & Integration, Event Planning & Marketing, Internet/Web Design, Outdoor, Print, Social Media, Strategic Planning/Research

Claudia Roxburgh *(Founder & Pres)*
Barbara Drummond *(Sr VP)*
Barbara Paulsen *(VP-Fin & Admin)*
Alicia Toth *(Dir-Creative Resources)*
Austin Hartigan *(Acct Exec)*
Tami Newcomb *(Acct Exec)*

Accounts:
Woodbridge Pacific Group

ROYALL MEDIA, INC.

45 Rockefeller Plz Ste 2000, New York, NY 10111
Tel.: (646) 727-0943
E-Mail: info@royalladv.com
Web Site: www.royalladv.com

Agency Specializes In: Advertising, Brand Development & Integration, Print, Strategic Planning/Research

William Royall *(Founder, Owner & Pres)*

Accounts:
Florida Hospital
Rockefeller Business Group Centers

RP3 AGENCY

7316 Wisconsin Ave Ste 450, Bethesda, MD 20814
Tel.: (301) 718-0333
Fax: (301) 718-9333
E-Mail: info@rp3agency.com
Web Site: www.rp3agency.com

Year Founded: 2009

National Agency Associations: 4A's

Agency Specializes In: Advertising, Brand Development & Integration, Digital/Interactive, Internet/Web Design, Print, Sponsorship

Beth Johnson *(Pres & Principal)*
Jim Lansbury *(Principal & Chief Creative Officer)*
Maggie Bergin *(Exec Dir-Acct Leadership & Integrated Production)*
Christina Pantelias Raia *(Dir-Strategic Plng)*
Amanda Antosh *(Mgr-Social Media)*
Katherine Lopes *(Acct Coord)*

Accounts:
Darcars
Washington Area Women's Foundation Website

RPA

RPA

2525 Colorado Ave, Santa Monica, CA 90404
Tel.: (310) 394-4000
Fax: (310) 633-7099
E-Mail: info@rpa.com
Web Site: www.rpa.com

Employees: 500
Year Founded: 1986

National Agency Associations: 4A's-THINKLA

Agency Specializes In: Advertising, Advertising Specialties, Affluent Market, Arts, Automotive, Brand Development & Integration, Broadcast, Business-To-Business, Cable T.V., Co-op Advertising, Collateral, Consumer Goods, Consumer Marketing, Corporate Communications, Corporate Identity, Customer Relationship Management, Digital/Interactive, Direct Response Marketing, E-Commerce, Electronic Media, Electronics, Email, Entertainment, Event Planning & Marketing, Financial, Food Service, Game Integration, Graphic Design, Health Care Services, High Technology, Household Goods, Integrated Marketing, Internet/Web Design, Leisure, Luxury

Products, Magazines, Market Research, Media Buying Services, Mobile Marketing, New Technologies, Newspaper, Newspapers & Magazines, Out-of-Home Media, Outdoor, Point of Purchase, Point of Sale, Print, Product Placement, Production, Radio, Restaurant, Retail, Sales Promotion, Search Engine Optimization, Social Media, Sponsorship, Sports Market, Strategic Planning/Research, T.V., Trade & Consumer Magazines, Transportation, Travel & Tourism, Viral/Buzz/Word of Mouth

RPA is a leading independent advertising agency. The agency builds momentum for brands by offering clients truly integrated campaigns that resonate throughout its disciplines, which include traditional advertising, interactive, and direct and event marketing.

Approx. Annual Billings: $1,200,000,000

Gerry Rubin *(Co-Founder)*
Larry Postaer *(Co-Chm)*
Peter Imwalle *(COO & Exec VP)*
Gary Paticoff *(Chief Production Officer & Sr VP)*
Jason Sperling *(Sr VP & Exec Dir-Creative)*
David Measer *(Sr VP & Grp Dir-Strategic Plng)*
Kirt Danner *(Sr VP & Grp Acct Dir)*
Cathleen Campe *(Sr VP & Dir-Audience Investment)*
Mike Margolin *(Sr VP & Dir-Audience Strategy)*
Lark Baskerville *(Sr VP)*
Tim Leake *(Sr VP-Growth & Innovation)*
Adam Blankenship *(VP & Grp Acct Dir)*
Eric Davis *(VP & Grp Acct Dir)*
Jeffery Moohr *(VP & Grp Acct Dir)*
Selena Pizarro *(VP-Exec Producer)*
Ken Pappanduros *(VP, Dir-Creative & Copywriter)*
Chuck Blackwell *(VP & Dir-Creative & Art)*
Maria Del Homme *(VP & Dir-Bus Affairs)*
Alicia Dotter Marder *(VP & Dir-Creative)*
Aaron Dodez *(VP & Assoc Dir-Digital Mktg)*
Leo Borges *(Sr Dir-Art)*
Marcella Coad *(Sr Dir-Art)*
Matthew Pullen *(Sr Dir-Art)*
Perrin Anderson *(Creative Dir)*
J Barbush *(Creative Dir)*
Erin Costello *(Sr Art Dir)*
Joshua McCrary *(Jr Art Dir)*
Hobart Birmingham *(Dir-Creative)*
Laura Crigler *(Dir-Art)*
Stephen Chow *(Assoc Dir-Creative-Art)*
Jennifer Ross *(Assoc Dir-Bus Affairs)*
Jeni Stewart *(Assoc Dir-Creative)*
Rosalyn Bugg *(Sr Digital Producer)*
Jason Bateman-Nadler *(Mgr-Digital Mktg)*
Marco Fantone *(Mgr-Product Info)*
Brooks Perry *(Mgr-Digital Mktg)*
Alison Bickel *(Acct Supvr)*
Kim Caldwell *(Acct Supvr)*
Jacob Gentry *(Acct Supvr)*
Joey Hanson *(Acct Supvr)*
Birgitta Johnson *(Acct Supvr)*
Gabrielle Brownstein *(Supvr-Natl Investments)*
Joanna Kennedy *(Supvr-Digital Content Strategy)*
Sari Rowe *(Supvr-Art Production)*
Robbie Thai *(Supvr-Digital Mktg)*
Tyler Sweeney *(Sr Specialist-Digital Content Strategy)*
Matthew Boyer *(Acct Exec)*
Jason Barrett *(Copywriter)*
Josh Hepburn *(Copywriter)*
Christina Contreras *(Asst Acct Exec-Integrated)*
Annie Boyle *(Coord-Brdcst Production)*
Steve Oak *(Coord-Digital Mktg)*
Amanda Womack *(Coord-Social Media)*
Jaime Villalva *(Sr Art Dir)*

Accounts:
AMPM (Agency of Record) Creative, Digital, Social Media, Strategic
Apartments.com (Agency of Record) Campaign: "Change your apartment. Change the world.", Campaign: "Contest", Campaign: "Rentless Future"
ARCO; La Palma, CA (Agency of Record) "TOP TIER", Brand Positioning, Campaign: "Embarassing", Campaign: "Mishap", Campaign: "Treat", Campaign: "Try It", Gasoline, Online, Outdoor, Radio, ampm Convenience Stores; 2005
BP ARCO
Delano Las Vegas campaign: "Defiantly Inspired"
Farmers Insurance Campaign "University of Farmers", Campaign: "15 Seconds of Smart", Multimedia, TV; 2010
Honda Motor Co. #hugfest, Accord, Advertising, Broadcast, CR-V, Campaign: "#FirstHonda", Campaign: "#StartSomething Special: Mairead & Kevin's Wedding", Campaign: "Better/Launch", Campaign: "DNT TXT & DRV", Campaign: "Efficiency", Campaign: "Fans of You Too", Campaign: "Fit For You", Campaign: "Happy Honda Days", Campaign: "Honda Loves You Back", Campaign: "Hugs" Super Bowl 2014, Campaign: "It's Here", Campaign: "Man and His Car", Campaign: "Million Mile Joe", Campaign: "Music Festival", Campaign: "NaughtyOrNice-a-tron", Campaign: "One More Thing to Love About Today,", Campaign: "Owners Manual", Campaign: "Skeletor", Campaign: "Stampede", Campaign: "Start Something Special", Campaign: "Summer Cheerance", Campaign: "Surprising Monsters Calling Home", Campaign: "The Power of Dreams", Campaign: "Today Is Pretty Great - Performance", Civic, Creative, Fit, HR-V SLF, Honda, Honda Summer Clearance, HondaHAIR, Insight, Media, Odyssey, Online, Pilot, Print, Radio, Ridgeline, Social Media; 1974
Intuit Small Business; Mountain View, CA CPA IPA Advertising, Campaign: "Freedom", Campaign: "Glennda", Campaign: "Just Dogs", Campaign: "Small Business Big Game", GoldieBlox, QuickBooks Online Accountant, Quicken, Super Bowl 2014, TurboTax; 2011
La-Z-Boy; Monroe, MI Campaign: "As the Room Turns", Campaign: "Live Life Comfortably", Campaign: "Movie Set", Campaign: "Photo Shoot"; 2007
Los Angeles Clippers Branded Entertainment, Campaign: "Be Relentless", Campaign: "Together We Will", Creative, Digital & Social Marketing, Media Buying, Media Planning, OOH, Print, Strategy
Mandalay Bay Resort & Casino Campaign: "Resortist", Outdoor, Print; 2008
Newport Beach Film Festival; Newport Beach, CA Campaign: "5 Years Under the Influence", Campaign: "Bedtime Story", Campaign: "Mandible"; 2009
Tempur Sealy (Agency of Record) Campaign: "Moms: You're Important", Creative, Digital, Social Marketing, Strategy, Tempur-Pedic
XO Mints Campaign: "The Ugly Couple Song", Online

RPM ADVERTISING

222 S Morgan St, Chicago, IL 60607
Tel.: (312) 455-8600
Fax: (312) 455-8617
Toll Free: (800) 475-2000
Web Site: www.rpmadv.com

Employees: 94
Year Founded: 1994

Agency Specializes In: Advertising, Advertising Specialties, Agriculture, Automotive, Aviation & Aerospace, Brand Development & Integration, Broadcast, Business Publications, Business-To-Business, Cable T.V., Children's Market, Co-op Advertising, Collateral, Commercial Photography, Communications, Consulting, Consumer Marketing, Consumer Publications, Corporate Identity, Cosmetics, Digital/Interactive, Direct Response Marketing, E-Commerce, Education, Electronic Media, Engineering, Entertainment, Environmental, Event Planning & Marketing, Exhibit/Trade Shows, Fashion/Apparel, Financial, Food Service, Gay & Lesbian Market, Government/Political, Graphic Design, Health Care Services, High Technology, Hispanic Market, Industrial, Infomercials, Information Technology, Internet/Web Design, Investor Relations, Legal Services, Leisure, Logo & Package Design, Magazines, Marine, Media Buying Services, Medical Products, Merchandising, Multimedia, New Product Development, Newspaper, Newspapers & Magazines, Outdoor, Pharmaceutical, Planning & Consultation, Point of Purchase, Point of Sale, Print, Production, Public Relations, Publicity/Promotions, Radio, Real Estate, Recruitment, Restaurant, Retail, Sales Promotion, Seniors' Market, Sports Market, Strategic Planning/Research, Sweepstakes, Syndication, T.V., Technical Advertising, Teen Market, Telemarketing, Trade & Consumer Magazines, Transportation, Travel & Tourism, Yellow Pages Advertising

Approx. Annual Billings: $42,000,000

Breakdown of Gross Billings by Media: Collateral: 2%; D.M.: 5%; Mags.: 5%; Newsp.: 30%; Outdoor: 5%; Point of Purchase: 3%; Radio: 20%; T.V.: 30%

Sarah Russell *(Sr VP & Acct Dir)*
Wendy Sergot *(VP & Acct Dir)*
Jennifer Guli *(VP-Strategy & Plng)*
Jennifer Wiza *(VP-Strategy & Plng)*
Alexis Novitski *(Acct Dir)*
Bradley Gordee *(Assoc Dir-Creative)*
Cathy Saia *(Acct Exec)*

Accounts:
Fields Auto Group
Harrah's Entertainment
Hollywood Casinos
Horseshoe Casinos
Percipia (Agency of Record) Advertising, Digital, Print, Video
Sheraton Casino & Hotel
Stafford Air & Space Museum (Agency of Record)
Volvo Cars of North America, Inc.- Central Region; Chicago, IL Automotive
Wyndham Worldwide

RPM/Las Vegas

7251 W Lake Mead Blvd Ste 300, Las Vegas, NV 89128
Tel.: (702) 562-4060
Fax: (702) 562-4001
E-Mail: platzow@rpmadv.com
Web Site: www.rpmadv.com

Larry Bessler *(Chief Creative Officer)*
Timothy A. Jones *(Sr Dir-Art)*
Alexis Novitski *(Acct Dir)*
Amy Wybo *(Dir-Creative)*
John Mondlock *(Assoc Dir-Creative)*
Sheila Charapata *(Acct Supvr)*
Tiffany Froy *(Acct Supvr)*
Anastasia Guletsky *(Copywriter)*
Elizabeth Lawal *(Media Buyer)*
Nathaniel Stetzler *(Asst Acct Exec)*

RS ENTERPRISES

PO Box 496, Gig Harbor, WA 98335
Tel.: (253) 265-8666
E-Mail: rse@rsenter.com
Web Site: www.rsenter.com

E-Mail for Key Personnel:
President: russ@rsenter.com

Employees: 3
Year Founded: 1989

Agency Specializes In: Consulting, Consumer Marketing, Electronic Media, Internet/Web Design, Pets , Publicity/Promotions

Russell Holster *(Dir)*

Accounts:
Petstation; Seattle, WA; 1994
Supermall; Seattle, WA; 1996

RSC MARKETING & ADVERTISING
(Formerly Mosaic Marketing Communications)
5737 Kanan Rd Ste 232, Agoura Hills, CA 91301
Tel.: (818) 597-0080
Fax: (818) 597-0081
Web Site: www.rscmarketing.com/

Employees: 1
Year Founded: 1984

National Agency Associations: THINKLA

Agency Specializes In: Advertising, Alternative Advertising, Automotive, Brand Development & Integration, Broadcast, Cable T.V., Co-op Advertising, Collateral, Communications, Consulting, Consumer Marketing, Direct Response Marketing, E-Commerce, Electronics, Entertainment, Event Planning & Marketing, Experience Design, Fashion/Apparel, Financial, Food Service, Graphic Design, In-Store Advertising, Internet/Web Design, Local Marketing, Logo & Package Design, Luxury Products, Magazines, Media Buying Services, Media Planning, Media Relations, Newspaper, Newspapers & Magazines, Out-of-Home Media, Outdoor, Over-50 Market, Package Design, Planning & Consultation, Point of Purchase, Point of Sale, Print, Production, Production (Ad, Film, Broadcast), Production (Print), Promotions, Public Relations, Publicity/Promotions, Radio, Real Estate, Regional, Restaurant, Retail, Sales Promotion, Search Engine Optimization, Social Marketing/Nonprofit, Sponsorship, Strategic Planning/Research, Sweepstakes, T.V., Web (Banner Ads, Pop-ups, etc.)

Approx. Annual Billings: $1,500,000

Breakdown of Gross Billings by Media: Cable T.V.: $750,000; Collateral: $75,000; Newsp. & Mags.: $500,000; Production: $75,000; Radio: $100,000

Bob Charney *(Pres)*

Accounts:
Neftin Westlake Cars; Thousand Oaks, CA Mazda Dealership, Volkswagen Dealership; 1996
Silver Star Mercedes-Benz; Thousand Oaks, CA Mercedes-Benz Dealership; 1995
Silver Star Motor Car Co.; Thousand Oaks, CA Cadillac, Hummer, LandRover, Lexus, Saab; 1996

RSQ
(Formerly Red Square)
54 Saint Emanuel St, Mobile, AL 36602
Tel.: (251) 650-0118
Fax: (251) 476-1582
E-Mail: wave@rsq.com
Web Site: www.rsq.com

Employees: 77
Year Founded: 1977

National Agency Associations: 4A's-MCA

Agency Specializes In: Advertising, Automotive, College, Education, Financial, Health Care Services, Public Relations, Restaurant

Breakdown of Gross Billings by Media: Brdcst.: 40%; Internet Adv.: 10%; Outdoor: 10%; Print: 20%; Production: 20%

Rich Sullivan, Jr. *(Pres & Exec Dir-Creative)*
Sarah Jones *(Pres)*
Elena Freed *(COO & Exec VP)*
Wally Hitchcock *(Assoc Dir-Creative)*
Shar'Day Porter *(Sr Media Planner & Media Buyer)*
Kate Hannon *(Jr Media Buyer)*

Accounts:
Bertram Yachts Sport Fishing Yachts
Bienville Capital Management Financial Services
FIN Branding Group, LLC E-Cigarettes
First Community Bank; Mobile, AL Financial Services
Foosackly's Chicken Fingers; Mobile, AL Quick Serve Restaurants
Full Sail University Education
Hibbett Sports Retail
Hilton Hotels & Resorts Hospitality
Kent State University
Mobile Bay CVB Campaign: "Mobile Bay-Secretly Awesome"
PCI Gaming; Atmore, AL Gaming
Shoe Station; Mobile, AL Retail
Syracuse University Education
U-J Chevrolet; Mobile, AL Retail
University of Alabama; Tuscaloosa, AL Education

Branch

Red Square Gaming
202 Government St, Mobile, AL 36602
(See Separate Listing)

RT&E INTEGRATED COMMUNICATIONS
(Formerly Reese, Tomases & Ellick, Inc. (RT&E))
768 Mount Moro Rd Ste 27, Villanova, PA 19085-2007
Tel.: (484) 380-3541
Web Site: www.rteideas.com

E-Mail for Key Personnel:
President: chousam@rteideas.com

Employees: 33
Year Founded: 1957

National Agency Associations: AMIN

Agency Specializes In: Advertising, Brand Development & Integration, Broadcast, Business-To-Business, Collateral, Communications, Consulting, Consumer Marketing, Corporate Identity, Digital/Interactive, Direct Response Marketing, Financial, Graphic Design, Health Care Services, High Technology, Internet/Web Design, Media Buying Services, Medical Products, New Product Development, Out-of-Home Media, Outdoor, Point of Purchase, Print, Public Relations, Publicity/Promotions, Sales Promotion, Strategic Planning/Research, Transportation, Travel & Tourism, Viral/Buzz/Word of Mouth

Approx. Annual Billings: $35,000,000

Breakdown of Gross Billings by Media: Cable T.V.: $1,750,000; Collateral: $3,500,000; D.M.: $3,500,000; E-Commerce: $1,400,000; Internet Adv.: $1,750,000; Newsp.: $1,400,000; Other: $1,400,000; Out-of-Home Media: $1,750,000; Promos.: $3,150,000; Pub. Rels.: $3,500,000; Radio: $1,400,000; Trade & Consumer Mags.: $7,000,000; Worldwide Web Sites: $3,500,000

Dave Meredith *(Mgr-Interactive)*

Accounts:
AGS Chemicals
AstraZeneca
DuPont; Wilmington, DE; 1987
GE Asset Intelligence; Devon, PA; 1999
GE Trailer Fleet Services; Devon, PA; 2000
Invista
Overture Ultimate Home Electronics
Southco, Inc.; Concordville, PA; 2003
Surveillance Data Inc
W.L. Gore & Associates; Newark, DE; 2002
WHYY Inc.; Wilmington, DE; Philadelphia, PA; 2000
YMCA of Delaware-Central Branch; Wilmington, DE; 2002

RUBY PORTER MARKETING & DESIGN
2504 Oakmont Way Ste A, Eugene, OR 97401
Tel.: (541) 683-3064
Fax: (541) 255-4970
Web Site: www.rubyporter.com

Year Founded: 2008

Agency Specializes In: Advertising, Brand Development & Integration, Collateral, Digital/Interactive, Internet/Web Design, Logo & Package Design, Print, Search Engine Optimization, Social Media

Ashely Duke *(Dir-Ops)*
Robert Steck *(Dir-Tech)*
Lee Bliven *(Dir-Managed Svcs)*
Charles LaBorn *(Dir-Application Dev)*
Christopher Hayes *(Mgr-SEO & Social Media)*

Accounts:
Echo Electuary

RUCKUS MARKETING, LLC
261 W 35th St 10th Fl, New York, NY 10001
Tel.: (646) 564-3880
Web Site: www.ruckusmarketing.com

Agency Specializes In: Advertising, Brand Development & Integration, Internet/Web Design, Media Buying Services, Strategic Planning/Research

Alex Friedman *(Co-Founder & Pres)*
Brian Faust *(VP-Tech)*
Dave Gilliland *(Dir-Creative)*
Ryan Gerhardt *(Copywriter)*
Lauren Harvey *(Sr Designer-Creative)*

Accounts:
Byoutik
Undies.com
View N Me
Westville

RUECKERT ADVERTISING
638 Albany Shaker Rd, Albany, NY 12211
Tel.: (518) 446-1091
Fax: (518) 446-1094
Toll Free: (800) 200-5236
E-Mail: info@rueckertadvertising.com
Web Site: www.rueckertadvertising.com

Employees: 6

Dean Rueckert *(Pres-PR)*
Edward Parham *(VP-PR)*
Steven Cass *(Comptroller)*
Linda Mather *(Dir-Mktg)*
Jason Rueckert *(Dir-Art)*
Chris Rueckert *(Acct Exec)*

Accounts:
The Anderson Group
Breeze-Eastern Corporation
Cillis Builders
Colonial Insurance Agency, LLC
Computer Professionals International
DocSTAR
Eastern Heating & Cooling

Eastwyck Village Marketing, Website Redesign
Fireman's Association of the State of New York Campaign: "Is there a FIRE in you?", Digital, Marketing, Radio, Social Media, TV, Website
First National Bank of Scotia
Freihofer's Run for Women
Horizon Wind
IP Logic
Junior League of Albany
The Michaels Group
MicroKnowledge
MM Hayes Companies
National Park Service
New York State Public Service Commission
Riverview Center
State Telephone Company Website
Sylvan Learning Centers
US Department of Energy
Wingate Inn Lake George

RUMBLETREE

216 Lafayette Rd, North Hampton, NH 03862
Tel.: (603) 433-6214
Fax: (603) 433-6269
E-Mail: info@rumbletree.com
Web Site: www.rumbletree.com

Employees: 10

Agency Specializes In: Advertising, Brand Development & Integration, Collateral, Corporate Communications, Email, Internet/Web Design, Media Buying Services, Media Planning, Public Relations, Social Media, Strategic Planning/Research

Charlie Yeaton *(Pres & Dir-Creative)*
Jessica Dufoe Kellogg *(Dir-Client Ops)*
Kelley Angulo *(Acct Mgr)*
Brianne Cox *(Acct Coord)*

Accounts:
Etchex Laser Engraving
First Colebrook Bank
Frisbie Memorial Hospital
Les Fleurs
New Hampshire Lodging & Restaurant Association (Agency of Record)

RUMOR ADVERTISING

455 N 400 W, Salt Lake City, UT 84103
Tel.: (801) 355-5510
Fax: (801) 355-0603
Web Site: www.rumoradvertising.com

Agency Specializes In: Advertising, Brand Development & Integration, Broadcast, Internet/Web Design, Logo & Package Design, Package Design

Shane OToole *(Pres)*
Tyler Sohm *(VP-Creative & Brand Experience)*
Julie Wilder *(VP-Media Svcs)*
Josh Wangrud *(Dir-Art)*

Accounts:
Brighton Ski Resort

RUNWAY 21 STUDIOS INC.

15010 N 78th Way Ste 206, Scottsdale, AZ 85260
Tel.: (480) 998-2195
Fax: (480) 348-8508
Web Site: www.runway21studios.com

Year Founded: 2002

Agency Specializes In: Advertising, Brand Development & Integration, Digital/Interactive, Graphic Design, Logo & Package Design, Print, Radio, Social Media, T.V.

Brad Michaelson *(Pres, CEO & Creative Dir)*
Julie Schilly *(Dir-Design & Social Media)*
Mike Baine *(Dir-Digital Media)*

Accounts:
Arizona State University Arizona Ready for Rigor
Kassman Orthopedics
Pei Wei Asian Diner
Phoenix Suns

RUNYON SALTZMAN & EINHORN

1 Capitol Mall 4th Fl Ste 400, Sacramento, CA 95814
Tel.: (916) 446-9900
Fax: (916) 446-3619
E-Mail: contact@rs-e.com
Web Site: www.rs-e.com

E-Mail for Key Personnel:
Creative Dir.: pnorris@rs-e.com
Media Dir.: smcmenamy@rs-e.com
Production Mgr.: ttafoya@rs-e.com
Public Relations: cholben@rs-e.com

Employees: 56
Year Founded: 1960

Agency Specializes In: Advertising, African-American Market, Alternative Advertising, Asian Market, Bilingual Market, Brand Development & Integration, Consumer Marketing, Corporate Communications, Corporate Identity, Crisis Communications, Government/Political, Graphic Design, Hispanic Market, Internet/Web Design, Local Marketing, Logo & Package Design, Market Research, Media Buying Services, Media Planning, Media Relations, Media Training, Multimedia, Point of Purchase, Point of Sale, Production, Production (Ad, Film, Broadcast), Production (Print), Promotions, Public Relations, Publicity/Promotions, Strategic Planning/Research

Revenue: $5,000,000

Chris Holben *(Pres & Dir-PR)*
Jane Einhorn *(Sr VP)*
Paul McClure *(VP & Dir-Adv)*
Kelley Kent *(Dir-Media)*
Harriet Saks *(Dir-Info Sys)*
Cathy Grewing *(Office Mgr)*
Lauren Morgan *(Mgr-HR)*
Elizabeth Corbitt *(Acct Supvr)*
Nicole Jarred *(Acct Supvr)*
Alicia Leupp *(Acct Supvr-Social Mktg)*
Rosemary O'Brien *(Strategist-Media Rels)*

Accounts:
Best Foundation Tunnel Tail Web
California Department Of Public Health
California State Fair
JACO Environmental
WHA Television

RUPERT

3668 Albion Pl N, Seattle, WA 98103
Tel.: (206) 420-8696
E-Mail: reachpeople@thisisrupert.com
Web Site: www.thisisrupert.com

Year Founded: 2010

Agency Specializes In: Advertising, Graphic Design, Internet/Web Design

Noah Tannen *(Founder & Pres)*
Matty Harper *(Dir-Creative)*
Jesselle Benson *(Acct Mgr)*

Accounts:
Seattle's Best Coffee

RUSS REID COMPANY, INC.

2 N Lake Ave Ste 600, Pasadena, CA 91101-1868
Tel.: (626) 449-6100
Fax: (626) 449-6190
Toll Free: (800) 275-0430
E-Mail: info@russreid.com
Web Site: www.russreid.com

E-Mail for Key Personnel:
President: tharrison@russreid.com
Creative Dir.: rgehrke@russreid.com

Employees: 220
Year Founded: 1964

Agency Specializes In: Direct Response Marketing, Government/Political, Hispanic Market, Public Relations

Approx. Annual Billings: $112,990,000 (Fees Capitalized)

Breakdown of Gross Billings by Media: Cable T.V.: $1,274,000; D.M.: $71,090,000; Fees: $27,400,000; Internet Adv.: $462,000; Newsp. & Mags.: $3,701,000; Radio: $1,033,000; T.V.: $8,030,000

Alan Hall *(Pres & CEO)*
Stacey Girdner *(Chief People Officer & VP)*
Lisa Scott Benson *(Exec VP-Strategy, Insights & Integration)*
Lori Burns *(Sr VP)*
Kevin White *(Sr VP-Media)*
Lois Ephraim *(VP & Dir-Creative)*
Andrew Olsen *(VP-Client Svcs)*
Renay Galati *(Sr Dir-Production & Ops)*
Karen C. Erren *(Client Svcs Dir)*
John Wilkinson *(Acct Dir)*
Kerri Bormacoff *(Dir-HRIS & Payroll Svcs)*

Accounts:
American Cancer Society
American Red Cross
Association of Gospel Rescue Missions
Azusa Pacific University
Christian Blind Mission
Detroit Rescue Mission Ministries
Goodwill Syndication
Habitat for Humanity International
Heart and Stroke Foundation
Helping Up Mission
Hospital for Sick Children Foundation
Operation Smile
Paralyzed Veterans of America
The Planetary Society
Ronald McDonald House
Saint Jude Children's Research Hospital
St. Joseph's Indian School
Starlight Starbright Children's Foundation
World Vision Canada Campaign: "Back to School Appeal"
World Vision

RUSSELL HERDER

222 S 9th St, Minneapolis, MN 55402
Tel.: (612) 455-2360
Fax: (612) 333-7636
Toll Free: (800) 450-3055
E-Mail: info@russellherder.com
Web Site: www.russellherder.com

E-Mail for Key Personnel:
President: ddomagala@russellherder.com

Employees: 30
Year Founded: 1984

National Agency Associations: 4A's

Agency Specializes In: Brand Development & Integration, Business-To-Business, Consumer Marketing, Digital/Interactive, Education, Exhibit/Trade Shows, Financial,

Government/Political, Health Care Services, Internet/Web Design, Leisure, Logo & Package Design, Marine, Media Buying Services, New Product Development, Planning & Consultation, Print, Production, Publicity/Promotions, Radio, Strategic Planning/Research, Travel & Tourism

Brian Herder *(Owner)*
Carol Russell *(CEO)*
Traci Holbrook *(Mgr-Admin Support)*
Matt Mudra *(Strategist-Digital)*
Jodie Oliver *(Copywriter)*
Jessica Tijerina *(Sr Media Buyer & Planner)*
Heather Hejna *(Acct Coord)*

Accounts:
American Association of Medical Colleges; Washington, D.C. Creative, Digital, PR, Strategic Planning
Association of American Colleges
East Africa Medical Foundation Creative, Digital, PR, Strategic Planning

Branch

Russell Herder
315 E River Rd, Brainerd, MN 56401-3503
Tel.: (218) 829-3055
Fax: (218) 829-2182
Toll Free: (800) 450-3055
Web Site: www.russellherder.com

Employees: 10
Year Founded: 1998

National Agency Associations: 4A's

Agency Specializes In: Advertising

Brian Herder *(Owner)*
Carol Russell *(CEO)*

Accounts:
Agricultural Utilization Research Institute
Betty Crocker
Nasseff Specialty Center
Seaswirl Boats
St. Paul Heart Clinic
Twin Cities Human Resource Association

RUSSELL-RISKO AGENCY
(Formerly Adspeak Marketing Communications)
919 Truman Ct, Warrington, PA 18976
Tel.: (215) 343-6565
Web Site: www.russellrisko.com

Employees: 6
Year Founded: 2000

Agency Specializes In: Advertising, Advertising Specialties, Affluent Market, Alternative Advertising, Aviation & Aerospace, Brand Development & Integration, Business Publications, Business-To-Business, Catalogs, Co-op Advertising, Collateral, Commercial Photography, Communications, Consulting, Consumer Publications, Content, Corporate Communications, Corporate Identity, Custom Publishing, Customer Relationship Management, Digital/Interactive, Direct Response Marketing, E-Commerce, Electronic Media, Electronics, Email, Engineering, Environmental, Event Planning & Marketing, Exhibit/Trade Shows, Financial, Graphic Design, Health Care Services, High Technology, Identity Marketing, In-Store Advertising, Industrial, Information Technology, Integrated Marketing, International, Internet/Web Design, Investor Relations, Local Marketing, Logo & Package Design, Magazines, Market Research, Media Buying Services, Media Planning, Media Relations, Medical Products, Mobile Marketing, Multimedia, New Technologies, Newspaper, Newspapers & Magazines, Outdoor, Over-50 Market, Package Design, Paid Searches, Pharmaceutical, Planning & Consultation, Point of Purchase, Point of Sale, Print, Production, Production (Ad, Film, Broadcast), Production (Print), Promotions, Public Relations, Publicity/Promotions, Publishing, RSS (Really Simple Syndication), Real Estate, Regional, Sales Promotion, Search Engine Optimization, Social Marketing/Nonprofit, Social Media, Stakeholders, Strategic Planning/Research, Technical Advertising, Trade & Consumer Magazines, Web (Banner Ads, Pop-ups, etc.), Yellow Pages Advertising

Approx. Annual Billings: $250,000

Breakdown of Gross Billings by Media: Bus. Publs.: 15%; Collateral: 10%; E-Commerce: 5%; Exhibits/Trade Shows: 5%; Graphic Design: 10%; Internet Adv.: 20%; Logo & Package Design: 5%; Pub. Rels.: 10%; Strategic Planning/Research: 5%; Video Brochures: 5%; Worldwide Web Sites: 10%

Russell Risko *(Principal & Dir-Creative)*
Bob Bannar *(Editor-Copy-Media Rels)*
Ilena Di Toro *(Specialist-Media Rels & Publicity)*
Carol Macrini *(Sr Graphic Designer)*

RUSSO PARTNERS LLC
12 W 27th St 4th Fl, New York, NY 10001
Tel.: (212) 845-4200
Fax: (212) 845-4260
E-Mail: tony.russo@russopartnersllc.com
Web Site: www.russopartnersllc.com

Tony Russo *(Chm & CEO)*
Robert Flamm *(Sr VP)*
Matt Middleman *(VP)*
Lena Evans *(Asst VP)*
Andreas Marathovouniotis *(Acct Supvr)*
Darren Chia *(Acct Coord)*

Accounts:
Advanced Cell Technology, Inc.
Arena Pharmaceuticals

RUSTMEDIA
307 Broadway, Cape Girardeau, MO 63701
Tel.: (573) 388-3460
E-Mail: info@rustmedia.com
Web Site: www.rustmedia.com

Agency Specializes In: Advertising, Brand Development & Integration, Digital/Interactive, Graphic Design, Search Engine Optimization, Social Media

Jeff Rawson *(Dir-Creative)*
Matt Melton *(Mgr-Ops)*
Cheryl Sullivan *(Mgr-Insta Print)*
Tim Westray *(Mgr-Hub)*
John Hodges *(Acct Exec)*
Alynda Smithey *(Acct Exec)*
Jean Hampton *(Designer)*
Amber Overbey *(Designer)*
Kate Schaefer *(Sr Designer)*

Accounts:
Chateau Girardeau

RUSTY GEORGE CREATIVE
(Private-Parent-Single Location)
732 Broadway Ste 302, Tacoma, WA 98402
Tel.: (253) 284-2140
Fax: (253) 284-2142
E-Mail: info@rustygeorge.com
Web Site: www.rustygeorge.com

Year Founded: 2001

Agency Specializes In: Advertising, Brand Development & Integration, Digital/Interactive, Logo & Package Design

Rusty George *(Principal)*
Carlos Lozano *(Art Dir)*
Crissy Pagulayan *(Acct Mgr)*
Kitura George *(Mgr-Ops)*
Jacquelyn Marcella *(Mgr-Traffic)*

Accounts:
MC Delivery

RUXLY CREATIVE
1019 Kane Concourse Ste 202, Bay Harbor Islands, FL 33154
Tel.: (305) 397-8065
E-Mail: info@ruxly.com
Web Site: www.ruxly.com

Year Founded: 2006

Agency Specializes In: Advertising

Brandon Kaplan *(Pres)*

Accounts:
Bacardi
Columbia University School of International Public Affairs
E-ZPass
Latam Airlines
The New York Wheel
The Windsor

RX COMMUNICATIONS GROUP LLC
445 Park Ave 10th Fl, New York, NY 10022
Tel.: (917) 322-2568
Web Site: www.rxir.com

Employees: 10

Melody Carey *(Founder & Pres)*
Rhonda Chiger *(Owner & Co-Pres)*
Lisa Janicki *(CFO)*
Paula Schwartz *(Sr VP-IR)*
Eric Goldman *(VP)*
Amber Bielecka *(Specialist-Healthcare Comm)*

Accounts:
Catalyst Pharmaceutical Partners, Inc.
TetraLogic Pharmaceuticals

RYACTIVE
13824 Campus Drive, Oakland, CA 94605
Tel.: (415) 320-7922
E-Mail: contact@ryactive.com
Web Site: www.ryactive.com/

Employees: 12
Year Founded: 2007

Agency Specializes In: Advertising, Advertising Specialties, Affluent Market, African-American Market, Alternative Advertising, Arts, Asian Market, Automotive, Aviation & Aerospace, Bilingual Market, Branded Entertainment, Cable T.V., Children's Market, Consumer Goods, Consumer Marketing, Cosmetics, E-Commerce, Electronic Media, Electronics, Entertainment, Fashion/Apparel, Gay & Lesbian Market, Government/Political, Health Care Services, High Technology, Hispanic Market, Hospitality, Information Technology, Leisure, Local Marketing, Luxury Products, Men's Market, Multimedia, New Technologies, Over-50 Market, Pharmaceutical, Product Placement, Production (Ad, Film, Broadcast), Promotions, Regional, Restaurant, Seniors' Market, Social Media, South Asian Market, Sports Market, T.V., Teen Market, Tween Market, Urban Market, Viral/Buzz/Word of Mouth, Women's Market

Approx. Annual Billings: $5,250,000

RYAN JAMES AGENCY
3692 Nottingham Way, Hamilton Square, NJ 08690
Tel.: (609) 587-0525
E-Mail: info@ryanjamesagency.com
Web Site: www.ryanjamesagency.com

Year Founded: 2008

Agency Specializes In: Advertising, Brand Development & Integration, Internet/Web Design, Media Planning, Social Media

Ryan James Csolak *(Pres & Dir-Creative & Accounts)*
Erica Boland *(Dir-Art)*
Kristine Lee *(Acct Mgr)*
Ariel McArdle *(Acct Mgr)*
Chrissy Volk *(Acct Coord)*

Accounts:
Blue Raccoon Home Furnishings
Heartland Payment Systems, Inc.
Millennium Broadway Hotel
Thinkform Architects
Tommy Hilfiger USA

RYAN MARKETING PARTNERS, LLC
270 Farmington Ave Ste 171 The Exchange, Farmington, CT 06032
Tel.: (860) 678-0078
Fax: (860) 678-0220
E-Mail: patr@ryanmarketing.com
Web Site: www.ryanmarketing.com

Employees: 10
Year Founded: 1996

Agency Specializes In: Advertising, Brand Development & Integration, Collateral, Communications, Consumer Publications, Corporate Identity, Direct Response Marketing, E-Commerce, Electronic Media, Event Planning & Marketing, Graphic Design, Internet/Web Design, Logo & Package Design, Magazines, Media Buying Services, Merchandising, Multimedia, Newspapers & Magazines, Point of Purchase, Point of Sale, Print, Production, Public Relations, Publicity/Promotions, Radio, Strategic Planning/Research, Technical Advertising

Approx. Annual Billings: $2,500,000

Lindsay Ryan *(Mng Partner)*
Ben Roberts *(Dir-Creative)*
Tara Rimetz *(Project Mgr & Coord-Social Media)*

Accounts:
Arrow Pharmacy
Centennial Inn
Deer Valley
ESPN
Herbasway
Mohegan Sun; CT
Northeast Energy Partners; CT; 2008
Shelco Filters; Middletown, CT; 2008
Stanley

S&A COMMUNICATIONS
(Formerly S & A Cherokee)
Westview at Weston 301 Cascade Pointe Ln, Cary, NC 27513
Tel.: (919) 674-6020
Fax: (919) 674-6027
Toll Free: (800) 608-7500
E-Mail: sayhey@sacommunications.com
Web Site: www.sacommunications.com/

Agency Specializes In: Crisis Communications, Digital/Interactive, Event Planning & Marketing, Market Research, Media Relations, Public Relations, Publishing, Search Engine Optimization

Chuck Norman *(Owner & Principal)*
Ron Smith *(Owner & Principal)*
Deneen Winters Bloom *(Client Svcs Dir)*
Teresa Kriegsman *(Dir-Digital Strategy & Design)*
Glenn Gillen *(Sr Acct Mgr)*
Jessica Johnson *(Acct Exec-Auto Remarketing & SubPrime Auto Finance News)*
Amanda Raxlin *(Acct Exec)*

Accounts:
Atiz Innovation; Los Angeles, CA PR, Scandock - Scans from smartphones
MetroGistics Vehicle Transportation Services
Mid-South Engineering Creative Strategy, Marketing, Website
Precision Tune Auto Care Communication, Digital Strategies, Marketing
RallyPoint Sport Grill Creative Services, Digital, Marketing, Public Relations
TribeSpring Design & Marketing Communications, PR

S&D MARKETING ADVERTISING
1873 S Bellaire St Ste 1600, Denver, CO 80222
Tel.: (303) 785-3220
E-Mail: info@sd-advertising.com
Web Site: www.sd-advertising.com

Agency Specializes In: Advertising, Brand Development & Integration, Digital/Interactive, Social Media

Ronda Dorchester *(Pres)*
Lorie Sadler *(Pres)*
Anne Marie Hukreide *(VP-Client Svcs)*
Wade Blacketor *(Controller)*
Ann Marthews *(Sr Dir-Integrated Svcs)*
Bruce Holmes *(Sr Mgr-Production)*
Jill Lovett *(Sr Acct Mgr)*
Kathleen Berry *(Acct Supvr)*
Jenna Schwab *(Sr Coord-Client Svcs)*

Accounts:
Adaptive Spirit

S2 ADVERTISING
533 N Nova Rd Ste 213B, Ormond Beach, FL 32174
Tel.: (386) 254-6898
Fax: (386) 672-3304
E-Mail: graphics@s2advertising.com
Web Site: www.s2advertising.com

Employees: 5
Year Founded: 1992

National Agency Associations: AAF

Agency Specializes In: Advertising, Affluent Market, Arts, Business-To-Business, Co-op Advertising, Collateral, Communications, Consulting, Custom Publishing, Exhibit/Trade Shows, Fashion/Apparel, Graphic Design, High Technology, In-Store Advertising, Industrial, Integrated Marketing, Internet/Web Design, Legal Services, Leisure, Logo & Package Design, Luxury Products, Magazines, Marine, Market Research, Media Buying Services, Media Planning, Medical Products, Newspaper, Out-of-Home Media, Package Design, Print, Production, Production (Ad, Film, Broadcast), Production (Print), Restaurant, Social Marketing/Nonprofit, Sports Market, Trade & Consumer Magazines, Travel & Tourism, Web (Banner Ads, Pop-ups, etc.)

Approx. Annual Billings: $1,500,000

Breakdown of Gross Billings by Media: Bus. Publs.: 35%; Consumer Publs.: 40%; Fees: 20%; Other: 5%

Chris Scali *(Owner)*

S2 FINANCIAL MARKETING
(Name Changed to Blue Flame Thinking)

S3
718 Main St, Boonton, NJ 07005
Tel.: (973) 257-5533
Fax: (973) 257-5543
E-Mail: info@theS3agency.com
Web Site: thes3agency.com/home

Employees: 25
Year Founded: 2001

Agency Specializes In: Above-the-Line, Advertising, Advertising Specialties, Affiliate Marketing, Affluent Market, African-American Market, Agriculture, Alternative Advertising, Arts, Asian Market, Automotive, Aviation & Aerospace, Below-the-Line, Bilingual Market, Brand Development & Integration, Branded Entertainment, Broadcast, Business Publications, Business-To-Business, Cable T.V., Catalogs, Children's Market, Co-op Advertising, Collateral, College, Commercial Photography, Communications, Computers & Software, Consulting, Consumer Goods, Consumer Marketing, Consumer Publications, Content, Corporate Communications, Corporate Identity, Cosmetics, Crisis Communications, Custom Publishing, Customer Relationship Management, Digital/Interactive, Direct Response Marketing, Direct-to-Consumer, E-Commerce, Education, Electronic Media, Electronics, Email, Engineering, Entertainment, Environmental, Event Planning & Marketing, Exhibit/Trade Shows, Experience Design, Fashion/Apparel, Financial, Food Service, Game Integration, Gay & Lesbian Market, Government/Political, Graphic Design, Guerilla Marketing, Health Care Services, High Technology, Hispanic Market, Hospitality, Household Goods, Identity Marketing, In-Store Advertising, Industrial, Infomercials, Information Technology, Integrated Marketing, International, Internet/Web Design, Investor Relations, Legal Services, Leisure, Local Marketing, Logo & Package Design, Luxury Products, Magazines, Marine, Market Research, Media Buying Services, Media Planning, Media Relations, Media Training, Medical Products, Men's Market, Merchandising, Mobile Marketing, Multicultural, Multimedia, New Product Development, New Technologies, Newspaper, Newspapers & Magazines, Out-of-Home Media, Outdoor, Over-50 Market, Package Design, Paid Searches, Pharmaceutical, Planning & Consultation, Podcasting, Point of Purchase, Point of Sale, Print, Product Placement, Production, Production (Ad, Film, Broadcast), Production (Print), Promotions, Public Relations, Publicity/Promotions, Publishing, RSS (Really Simple Syndication), Radio, Real Estate, Recruitment, Regional, Restaurant, Retail, Sales Promotion, Search Engine Optimization, Seniors' Market, Social Marketing/Nonprofit, Sponsorship, Sports Market, Stakeholders, Strategic Planning/Research, Sweepstakes, Syndication, T.V., Technical Advertising, Teen Market, Telemarketing, Trade & Consumer Magazines, Transportation, Travel & Tourism, Urban Market, Viral/Buzz/Word of Mouth, Web (Banner Ads, Pop-ups, etc.), Women's Market, Yellow Pages Advertising

Denise Blasevick *(CEO)*
Adam Schnitzler *(Chief Creative Officer)*
Michael Kolatac *(Assoc Dir-Creative)*
Stefanie Fernandez *(Acct Supvr)*

Tracey Jeffas *(Acct Supvr)*
Jaime Hamel *(Strategist-Digital)*
Samantha Banner *(Acct Coord)*
Jazmine Rodriguez *(Acct Coord)*

Accounts:
BMW Motorrad USA Creative, Media
BMW of North America
Designs By Lolita
Eight O'Clock Coffee
Emmi Cheeses, Fondues, Yogurts
ERA Franchise Systems
Good Earth Tea
RCI
Safilo USA
Sanofi
Spyker PR, Spyker B6 Concept
SRSsoft Digital
Turtle Back Zoo
Wyndham Worldwide Corporation

S360S

PO Box 38809, Baltimore, MD 21231
Tel.: (410) 599-4672
Fax: (410) 732-2683
E-Mail: info@s360s.com
Web Site: www.s360s.com

Employees: 7

Agency Specializes In: Advertising, Brand Development & Integration, Branded Entertainment, Business-To-Business, Communications, Consumer Goods, Consumer Marketing, Content, Education, Entertainment, Environmental, Event Planning & Marketing, International, Leisure, Luxury Products, Marine, Market Research, Mobile Marketing, Outdoor, Publicity/Promotions, Sponsorship, Women's Market

Beth Perry *(Pres)*

SAAL ADVERTISING INC

6528 Constitution Dr, Fort Wayne, IN 46804
Tel.: (260) 432-7225
Toll Free: (866) 722-5123
E-Mail: saal@saal.net
Web Site: saal.net/

Agency Specializes In: Advertising, Brand Development & Integration, Internet/Web Design, Logo & Package Design, Print, Radio, T.V.

Walt Steffen *(Pres)*
Wesley DeKoninck *(Dir-Digital Mktg)*
Anna McClain *(Dir-Art)*

Accounts:
Nancy Mann Design

SAATCHI & SAATCHI

375 Hudson St, New York, NY 10014
Tel.: (212) 463-2000
Fax: (212) 463-2367
Web Site: www.saatchi.com

Employees: 6,709
Year Founded: 1970

National Agency Associations: 4A's-AAF-ABC-APA-BPA-MCA-TAB-THINKLA

Agency Specializes In: Sponsorship

Cliff Francis *(Deputy Chm)*
Jay Benjamin *(Chief Creative Officer & Exec VP)*
Talia Handler *(Exec VP & Grp Acct Dir)*
Julie Bowers *(Exec VP-Acct Svcs)*
Deborah Botkin *(VP & Dir-Creative Ops)*
Laura Mulloy *(Exec Dir-Creative)*
Mark Reichard *(Exec Dir-Creative)*
Mark Scholler *(Exec Dir-Creative)*
Helen Shin *(Sr Dir-Art)*
Chris Belmore *(Acct Dir)*
Paige Gruman *(Mgmt Supvr)*
John Doris *(Dir-Content Production)*
Frank Fusco *(Dir-Creative)*
Johnnie Ingram *(Dir-Creative)*
Billy Leyhe *(Dir-Creative)*
Luca Lorenzini *(Dir-Creative-Global)*
Paul Melter *(Dir-Fin Reporting)*
Iain Nevill *(Dir-Creative)*
Luca Pannese *(Dir-Creative-Global)*
John Payne *(Dir-Creative)*
Kira Shalom *(Dir-Creative)*
Amy Still *(Dir-Digital)*
James Tucker *(Dir-Creative)*
Emily Woolf *(Dir-Strategic Plng)*
Brad Soulas *(Assoc Dir-Creative & Writer)*
Lauren McCrindle *(Assoc Dir-Creative)*
Mark Potoka *(Assoc Dir-Creative)*
Taylor Doyle *(Acct Supvr)*
Courtney Scott *(Acct Supvr)*
Tani Yee *(Acct Supvr)*
Sharon Yun *(Supvr-Integrated Media)*
Ted Walker *(Acct Exec)*
Nick Elliot *(Copywriter)*
Thalia Forbes *(Copywriter)*
Kevin Harrington *(Planner-Strategic)*
Brian Ritter *(Planner-Strategic)*
Gina Song *(Asst Media Planner)*

Accounts:
Avaya, Inc.
The Brother/Sister Sol
Centers For Disease Control & Prevention VERB
Charter Communications Campaign: "Camping", Campaign: "Game Night", Campaign: "Kid", Campaign: "Mom", Campaign: "Sunday Football", Campaign: "Tweens", Spectrum Network
Chase Freedom Cards (Creative Agency of Record), Sapphire Credit Card (Creative Agency of Record), TV
Coors Brewing Company "Smooth Musings", Keystone Light
CrossRoads Community Campaign: "Mouth Watering Copycat"
Fruit Gushers
General Mills, Inc. Campaign: "3rd Shift", Campaign: "Bigger Is Better", Campaign: "Breakfast Avalanche", Campaign: "Don't Fight Your Instincts", Campaign: "Fruit Rollups", Campaign: "Get Zem Going.", Campaign: "Gracie" Super Bowl 2014, Campaign: "Just Checking", Campaign: "Must be the Honey", Campaign: "Nana", Campaign: "Prize", Campaign: "The House of Haagen-Dazs", Campaign: "The Yoplait Greek Taste-Off,", Cheerios, Chew Treats, Cocoon, Creative Advertising, Digital, Fiber One Cereal, Fiber One Snack Bars, Fruit by the Foot, Go-Gurt, Green Giant, Haagen-Dazs, Healthy Weight Commitment Foundation, Honey Nut Cheerios, Lucky Charms, Multigrain Cheerios, Nature Valley, Old El Paso, PR, Progresso Soups, Social, Toaster Strudel, Total, Total Protein, Totino's, Wheaties, Yoplait; 2010
Goodwill Campaign: "Donate Stuff. Create Jobs", Digital, Outdoor, Print, Radio
Harlem School of the Arts
Heineken USA Campaign: "Born Bold", Campaign: "One Bold Night", Social Media, TV, Tecate (Agency of Record), Tecate Light (Agency of Record)
Intel Campaign: "Anthem"
International Multifoods Corporation Pillsbury
The J.M. Smuckers Co. Folgers
Kraft Foods Capri Sun, Kool-Aid
Lenovo Campaign: "Do Devil - Your Sketch", Campaign: "Seize the Night", Day in the Life: Band, Digital Marketing, Do Devil: Demolition Derby, Ray Li, TV Advertising, ThinkPad, YOGA 2 Pro, Yoga Tablet; 2011
Luvs Campaign: "Car Simulator", Campaign: "Music Lesson", Campaign: "Pacifier", Campaign: "Sanitize", Campaign: "Storytime"
Martin Luther King Jr. National Memorial Project Foundation (Ad Council)
Mead Johnson Enfamil
MGD 64
MillerCoors Campaign: "#TheOriginal", Campaign: "Big Ass Fish", Campaign: "Great Taste, Less Filling", Campaign: "Little Extra", Keystone, Lead Creative, MGD64, Miller 64, The Internship; 2007
Mondelez International, Inc. Campaign: "Bear", Campaign: "Fun Audit", Campaign: "Smile. It's Kool-Aid", Capri Sun, Digital, Print, TV
Novartis Campaign: "Embers", Campaign: "You Look Dumber When Your Mouth's Open - Classroom Craft", Theraflu, Triaminic
Pampers Campaign: "Miracles"
Pfizer, Inc. Chantix
Procter & Gamble Pet Care Iams
Procter & Gamble Ariel Actilift, Campaign: "Ariel Fashion Shoot - Blogger Outreach", Campaign: "Breastfeeding", Campaign: "Car Simulator", Campaign: "Drop a dooty", Campaign: "Duracell Quantum Powers The San Francisco 49ers", Campaign: "Duracell Quantum Powers The Seattle Seahawks", Campaign: "Miracle Stain", Campaign: "Music Lesson", Campaign: "Pacifier", Campaign: "Pop of Fresh/Blue Yellow", Campaign: "Power Your Game", Campaign: "Sanitize", Campaign: "Save it? Or wash it in Tide?", Campaign: "Season of the Whiff", Campaign: "Storytime", Campaign: "The Beautymonsters", Campaign: "Tide Pods - Pop", Campaign: "Troy's Hair", Campaign: "Trust Your Power", Campaign: "Trust the Power Within", Creative, Dawn, Digital, Duracell, Duracell Quantum, Fashion Shoot, Head & Shoulders, Luvs, Olay, Old Spice, Tide Stain Savers, Tide Total Care, Tide to Go
Prop 8
Reynolds Packaging Group; TX
Rockefeller Center
T-Mobile US
Toyota Campaign: "Connections", Campaign: "Good Move", Toyota Camry, Yaris
Walmart Campaign: "Greenlight a Vet", Campaign: "I Am a Factory", Campaign: "Lights On" Winter Olympics 2014, Campaign: "Love", Campaign: "Work is a Beautiful Thing", Holiday Advertising
Wendy's International; Dublin, OH; 2007

United States

Saatchi & Saatchi Latin America

(Formerly Nazca Saatchi & Saatchi)
800 Brickell Ave Ste 400, Miami, FL 33131
Tel.: (305) 351-2900
Fax: (305) 351-2899
E-Mail: jac@nazca.com
Web Site: www.saatchi.com

Employees: 40

Javier Campopiano *(Chief Creative Officer-Latin America & Multicultural USA)*

Saatchi & Saatchi Healthcare Innovations

1000 Floral Vale Blvd 4th Fl, Yardley, PA 19067
Tel.: (215) 497-8400
Fax: (215) 497-9535
Web Site: saatchihealth.com/pa

Employees: 62

National Agency Associations: 4A's

Agency Specializes In: Health Care Services

JD Cassidy *(Mng Dir)*
Jane Cullen *(VP-Strategic Plng)*

Jennifer Mcalpin *(Dir-Editorial Svcs)*
Anna Binninger *(Mgr-Fin)*

Accounts:
AstraZeneca
Pfizer

Saatchi & Saatchi Los Angeles

3501 Sepulveda Blvd, Torrance, CA 90505
Tel.: (310) 214-6000
Fax: (310) 214-6160
Web Site: www.saatchila.com

Employees: 342
Year Founded: 1975

National Agency Associations: 4A's-THINKLA

Agency Specializes In: Above-the-Line, Advertising, Alternative Advertising, Below-the-Line, Brand Development & Integration, Broadcast, Collateral, Communications, Consulting, Consumer Marketing, Content, Digital/Interactive, Event Planning & Marketing, Graphic Design, Guerilla Marketing, Integrated Marketing, Internet/Web Design, Logo & Package Design, Media Buying Services, Media Planning, Mobile Marketing, New Technologies, Newspapers & Magazines, Out-of-Home Media, Outdoor, Planning & Consultation, Print, Production, Production (Print), Public Relations, Publicity/Promotions, Radio, Retail, Sales Promotion, Sponsorship, Strategic Planning/Research, T.V., Web (Banner Ads, Pop-ups, etc.)

Kurt Ritter *(Chm/CEO-West Coast)*
Lalita Koehler *(Exec Dir-Integrated Production)*
John Lisko *(Exec Dir-Comm)*
Al Reid *(Exec Dir)*
Dawn Wager *(Grp Dir-Comm)*
Philip Samartan *(Sr Dir-Art)*
Erica Baker *(Grp Acct Dir-Integrated)*
Drew Corpman *(Grp Acct Dir-Integrated)*
Steve Sluk *(Grp Acct Dir)*
Cathy Weaver *(Grp Acct Dir)*
Dianne Gee *(Acct Dir)*
Alex Newson *(Acct Dir)*
Cliff Atkinson *(Dir-Comm-Interactive)*
Erich Funke *(Dir-Creative)*
Kayla Green *(Dir-Digital Strategy)*
Chris Nicholls *(Dir-Comm)*
John Payne *(Dir-Creative)*
Chris Pierantozzi *(Dir-Creative)*
Phil Teeple *(Dir-Brand Integration)*
Janet Waters *(Dir-Media)*
Tal Wagman *(Assoc Dir-Creative & Copywriter)*
Breanne Carpenter *(Assoc Dir-Comm)*
Gaurika Chadha *(Assoc Dir-Interactive Comm)*
Biba Millstein *(Assoc Dir-Bus Affairs)*
Verner Soler *(Assoc Dir-Creative)*
Christopher Thornton *(Assoc Dir-Media)*
Karen Mahoney *(Sr Mgr-Brdcst Bus)*
Scott Finders *(Mgr-Bus Strategy)*
Alison Gunn *(Acct Supvr)*
Lauren Messina *(Acct Supvr)*
Michelle Tello *(Acct Supvr)*
Lulu Cao *(Supvr-Comm)*
Ryan Seiter *(Acct Exec)*
Craig Schultz *(Media Planner)*

Accounts:
New-Amanda Foundation Campaign: "Digital Pawprint"
Duracell
General Mills, Inc. Total
Kraft Foods Group Capri Sun, Kool-Aid
Mondelez International Trident, Trident Layers
Operation Hope (Pro Bono)
Square Enix
Surfrider Foundation Ocean Armor
Toyota Dealer Associations
Toyota Motor Sales, U.S.A., Inc. (Advertising Agency of Record) "RAV4 Genie", 4Runner, Avalon, Campaign: "200 Foot Journey", Campaign: "Anthem", Campaign: "Endeavour Pull", Campaign: "Father's Day Redo", Campaign: "Father's Day Reunion", Campaign: "How Great I Am", Campaign: "It's Reinvented", Campaign: "Joyride", Campaign: "More Connected", Campaign: "My Bold Dad", Campaign: "No Room For Boring" Super Bowl 2014, Campaign: "Play Now", Campaign: "Prius Goes Plural", Campaign: "Spelling Bee", Campaign: "The Camry Effect", Campaign: "The Great Road", Campaign: "To Be a Dad", Campaign: "Toyota Tacoma VS", Campaign: "Ultimate Journey", Campaign: "Wish Granted", Campaign: "Yaris - Its a Car", Camry, Corolla, FJ Cruiser, Highlander, Land Cruiser, Lexus ES Series, Lexus GS Series, Matrix, Online, Prius/HSD, RAV4, Sequoia, Shareathon, Sienna, Super Bowl 2015, Super Bowl Teaser, Swagger Wagon, TV, Tacoma, Toyota Camry Solara, Toyota Sienna, Toyota.com, Tundra, Tundra Endeavour, Venza, Yaris
Toyota Motor North America, Inc.
YMCA

Saatchi & Saatchi New York

375 Hudson St, New York, NY 10014-3660
Tel.: (212) 463-2000
Fax: (212) 463-9855
Web Site: www.saatchiny.com

Employees: 515
Year Founded: 1980

Agency Specializes In: Above-the-Line, Advertising, Affluent Market, Alternative Advertising, Automotive, Brand Development & Integration, Business-To-Business, Cable T.V., Children's Market, Co-op Advertising, Consumer Goods, Consumer Marketing, Digital/Interactive, Direct-to-Consumer, E-Commerce, Environmental, Fashion/Apparel, Government/Political, Guerilla Marketing, Health Care Services, Hispanic Market, Household Goods, In-Store Advertising, Internet/Web Design, Investor Relations, Leisure, Luxury Products, Magazines, Men's Market, Mobile Marketing, Multicultural, New Technologies, Over-50 Market, Pets , Pharmaceutical, Point of Purchase, Print, Product Placement, Public Relations, Restaurant, Sponsorship, T.V., Teen Market, Travel & Tourism, Urban Market, Viral/Buzz/Word of Mouth, Women's Market, Yellow Pages Advertising

Jay Benjamin *(Chief Creative Officer)*
Michele Daly *(Chief Creative Talent Officer)*
Jay Ferguson *(Exec VP & Grp Acct Dir)*
Carolyn Cho *(Sr VP & Grp Acct Dir-Global)*
Lynn Rossi *(Sr VP & Grp Acct Dir)*
Caitlin Pavelle *(VP & Acct Dir)*
Margie Millero *(VP & Dir-Mgmt)*
A. Chris Moreira *(Exec Dir-Creative)*
Helen Shin *(Sr Dir-Art)*
Connor Bryant *(Acct Dir)*
Matilda Kahl *(Art Dir)*
Lisandro Ancewicz *(Dir-Art)*
Billy Leyhe *(Dir-Creative)*
Luca Lorenzini *(Dir-Creative-Global)*
Tiffany Pan *(Dir-Art)*
Chris Skurat *(Dir-Creative)*
Jamie Daigle *(Assoc Dir-Bus Dev)*
Mark Potoka *(Assoc Dir-Creative)*
Justin Roth *(Assoc Dir-Creative)*
Erin Wendel *(Assoc Dir-Creative)*
Ciara Monchek *(Acct Supvr)*
Carly Wallace *(Acct Supvr)*
Ted Walker *(Acct Exec)*
Callum Spence *(Copywriter)*
Rees Steel *(Copywriter)*

Accounts:
Brotherhood/Sister Sol "Talk About The Talk"
Charter Communications Spectrum Network
Evolve Campaign: "The Bill of Rights for Dumbasses"
Gay Men's Health Crisis "Celibacy Challenge"
General Mills, Inc. Betty Crocker/Snacks Div., Big G Cereal Div., Campaign: "Body Language", Campaign: "Buzz Meets Grumpy Cat", Campaign: "Caught in the Act", Campaign: "Don't Fight Your Instincts", Campaign: "Go-Gurt. Whatever It Takes To Get It All.", Campaign: "Hephaestus", Campaign: "Our Gluten Free Story", Campaign: "Real Estate", Cheerios, Chew Treats, Frozen Baked Goods, Go-Gurt, Haagen-Dazs, Healthy Weight Commitment Foundation, Home Baked Classics, Honey Nut Cheerios, Lucky Charms Marshmallow Only, Meals Division, Pancakes, Pillsbury, Pillsbury USA Division Refrigerated Dough, Progresso Light Soups, Toaster Scrambles, Toaster Strudel, Totinos Pizza, Totinos Pizza Rolls, Waffle Sticks, Waffles, Wheaties, Yoplait, Yoplait-Columbo Div.; 1923
GLAAD "Celibacy Challenge"
Harlem School of the Arts
Martin Luther King, Jr. National Memorial Foundation Project (Pro Bono); 2002
Mead Johnson
Novartis Buckley's, Lamisil/Lamasilk, TheraFlu, Triaminic
NYS Department of Economic Development; New York, NY "I Love NY' Campaign; 2007
Overturn Prop 8
Pampers Campaign: "Hush Little Baby"
The Procter & Gamble Co (Agency of Record) Beauty Care Division, Campaign: "Keep Love Strong", Campaign: "MOMS, DON'T SWEAT THE SMALL STUFF", Campaign: "Naptime", Campaign: "Shopping", Creative, Eukanuba, Fabric & Home Care Division, Fixodent, Iams, Luvs, Scope, Tide, Tide 2X Ultra; 1921
The Procter & Gamble Company (Beauty Care Division) Head & Shoulders, Olay Personal Care Cleansing Products, Olay Skin Care Products, Safeguard
The Procter & Gamble Company (Pampers & Luvs) Kandoo Body Wash, Kandoo Handsoap, Kandoo Wipes, Luvs Baby Wipes, Luvs Diapers, Pampers Baby Dry, Pampers Baby Wipes, Pampers Baby Wipes Baby Fresh, Pampers Baby Wipes Calming, Pampers Baby Wipes Clean N Go, Pampers Baby Wipes Sensitive, Pampers Baby Wipes Skin Soothing Moisture, Pampers Baby Wipes Swipers, Pampers Baby Wipes Unscented, Pampers Diapers, Pampers Easy Ups Trainers, Pampers New Prodcts, Pampers Splashers Swimpants, Pampers Swaddlers, Pampers Swaddlers Sensitive, Underjames Nightwear by Pampers; 2002
Procter & Gamble (Food & Beverage Div)
Reynolds Packaging Group; Richmond, VA Reynolds Bake Cups, Reynolds Bright Ideas, Reynolds Freezer Paper, Reynolds Handi-Vac, Reynolds Hot Bags, Reynolds Oven Bags, Reynolds Parchment Paper, Reynolds Pot Lux, Reynolds Wrap, Reynolds Wrap Release Non-Stick Foil; 1996
Toyota Dealers Association; CT; NJ; NY; PA; 1978

Saatchi & Saatchi X

605 Lakeview Dr, Springdale, AR 72764
Tel.: (479) 575-0200
Fax: (479) 725-1136
Web Site: www.saatchix.com

Employees: 250
Year Founded: 1997

National Agency Associations: 4A's

Agency Specializes In: Advertising, Consumer Goods, Digital/Interactive, Experience Design, Food Service, In-Store Advertising, International, Package Design, Point of Purchase, Regional, Retail, Shopper Marketing

Jim Cartwright *(Mng Dir & Exec VP)*
David Schumacher *(CFO)*
Jessica Hendrix *(Pres-USA)*
Frank Flurry *(Dir-Production)*

Accounts:
P&G
Sam's Club
Tracfone
Wal-Mart Stores, Inc.; Bentonville, AR

Saatchi & Saatchi X
222 Merchandise Mart Plz, Chicago, IL 60654
Tel.: (312) 977-4900
Web Site: www.saatchix.com

Employees: 30
Year Founded: 1997

National Agency Associations: 4A's

Agency Specializes In: Advertising, Consumer Goods, Digital/Interactive, Experience Design, Food Service, In-Store Advertising, International, Package Design, Point of Purchase, Regional, Retail, Shopper Marketing, Sponsorship

Josh Rateliff *(VP & Mng Dir)*
Chris Gray *(VP-Shopper Psychology, Shopper Insights & Head-Plng Team)*
Samantha Sanda *(Acct Dir)*
Amanda Danish *(Dir-Plng & Insights)*
Kim Wagner *(Acct Supvr)*
Paul Porter *(Jr Strategist)*

Accounts:
Mead Johnson
P&G
Pepsico

Saatchi & Saatchi X
375 Hudson St, New York, NY 10014-3660
Tel.: (212) 463-2000
Fax: (212) 463-2438
Web Site: www.saatchix.com

Employees: 25
Year Founded: 1997

Agency Specializes In: Advertising, Consumer Goods, Digital/Interactive, Experience Design, Food Service, In-Store Advertising, International, Package Design, Point of Purchase, Regional, Retail, Shopper Marketing

Jessica Appelgren *(VP-Comm)*
Daniel Jacobs *(Sr Dir-Strategy)*
Julie Quick *(Dir-Plng)*

Accounts:
Diageo
Elizabeth Arden
Wendy's Merchandising

Saatchi & Saatchi
5285 SW Meadows Rd Ste 232, Lake Oswego, OR 97035
Tel.: (503) 333-9088
Fax: (503) 431-2448
E-Mail: info@saatchi.com
Web Site: www.saatchi.com

Employees: 5

Agency Specializes In: Advertising, Integrated Marketing, Media Planning, Sponsorship, Strategic Planning/Research

Kostas Karanikolas *(Exec Dir-Creative-Global)*
Wes Alexander *(Dir-Mgmt)*
Michael Crutchfield *(Dir-North America Design & Creative)*
Kirk Guthrie *(Exec Head-HR & Talent)*

Team One USA
(Formerly Team One Advertising)
13031 W Jefferson Blvd, Los Angeles, CA 90094-7039
(See Separate Listing)

Saatchi & Saatchi Wellness
375 Hudson St 13th Fl, New York, NY 10014
(See Separate Listing)

Canada

Saatchi & Saatchi
2 Bloor St E Ste 600, Toronto, ON M4W 1A8 Canada
(See Separate Listing)

Belarus

Primary Saatchi & Saatchi
Kazarmenny Lane 4 Office 1, Minsk, 220030 Belarus
Tel.: (375) 17 328 62 12
Fax: (375) 17 206 5946
E-Mail: prochakov_r@saatchi.by

Employees: 25

Agency Specializes In: Advertising

Ruslan Prochakov *(Mng Dir)*
Eugeny Yunov *(Dir-Creative)*

Belgium

Saatchi & Saatchi Brussels
Ave Rogierlaan 20, 1030 Brussels, Belgium
Tel.: (32) 2 247 1711
Fax: (32) 2 247 17 71
E-Mail: marc.michils@saatchi.be
Web Site: www.saatchi.be

Employees: 38

Roland Minnoy *(CFO)*
Alexander Chaban *(Dir-Creative)*
Arnold Hovaert *(Dir-Art)*
Jonathan Moerkens *(Sr Acct Mgr)*
Damien Veys *(Copywriter)*
Jan Teulingkx *(Deputy Exec Dir-Creative-EMEA)*

Accounts:
Amcor
Ansell
Antwerp Zoo Campaign: "The Smartest Ape in the World"
Ariel
Atlas Copco
BIVV
Carrefour
Ciba Vision
Duvel Beer
European Commission Campaign: "Ex-Smokers are Unstoppable", Campaign: "Quit Smoking With Barca", Directorate-General Health & Consumers
FC Barcelona Campaign: "Quit Smoking with Barca"
Fostplus
Head & Shoulders
International Paper
Lazer Helmets
Novartis
Novy
Nucleair Forum Campaign: "Clear About Nuclear"
Pampers
Pay Fair
Samsonite Campaign: "Arrivals", Campaign: "Enjoy Every Second", Campaign: "Samsonite Vs. The World", Campaign: "Travel Lighter to Go Further"
Senseo
Sony
Toyota
University of Gent
Visa
ZOO Campaign: "The World's Smartest Ape"

Czech Republic

Saatchi & Saatchi
Jankovcova 23, 170 00 Prague, 7 Czech Republic
Tel.: (420) 234 721 222
Fax: (420) 234 721 234
E-Mail: michaela.gillova@saatchi.cz
Web Site: saatchi.com/cs-cz

Employees: 30

Agency Specializes In: Advertising

Tomas Lobel *(Mng Dir)*
Ondrej Hubl *(Dir-Creative)*
Katerina Kovarovicova *(Mgr-Traffic)*

Accounts:
BIOspotrebitel.cz
Bugsy's bar
Ceska sporitelna
Emirates Airlines
Mitsubishi Motors
Novartis
Procter & Gamble
Quelle
Radio 1
T-Mobile US Campaign: "Christmas With T-Mobile - Baloon"
Visa

Denmark

Saatchi & Saatchi
Esplanaden 34A 1 sal, 1263 Copenhagen, K Denmark
Tel.: (45) 33 937980
Fax: (45) 33 938180
E-Mail: saatchi@saatchi.dk
Web Site: saatchi.com/da-dk

Employees: 40
Year Founded: 1987

Agency Specializes In: Advertising

Jason Mendes *(Exec Dir-Creative)*
Charlotta Tibbelin *(Acct Dir)*
Regner Lotz *(Dir-Creative)*
Annette Piilgaard *(Dir-Bus)*
Paul McHugh *(Acct Mgr)*
Diana Wellendorf *(Acct Mgr)*
Rikke Wichmann-Bruun *(Reg Mng Dir-Automotive)*

Accounts:
Bell
Coca-Cola Refreshments USA, Inc. Campaign: "Gangster", Campaign: "Stableboy"
Gori
P&G Campaign: "Ariel Big Stain"
Sony Ericsson
Toyota

Egypt

Saatchi & Saatchi
19 Soliman Abaza Street, Mohandesseen, Cairo,

Egypt
Tel.: (20) 23 335 3205
Fax: (20) 23 761 3618
E-Mail: wael.hussein@saatchieg.com
Web Site: www.saatchi.com

Employees: 30
Year Founded: 1990

Agency Specializes In: Advertising

Shirine Aoun *(Client Svcs Dir)*
Ibrahim Ashur *(Dir-Art)*
Naila Fateen *(Dir-Art)*
Ahmed Nabil *(Dir-Creative)*
Sherif Nashed *(Dir-Creative)*
Raja Rizkallah *(Dir-Art)*
Hanaa Messiha *(Office Mgr)*
Ahmed Gad *(Mgr-IT)*
Wael Nazeem *(Client Svc Dir)*

Accounts:
Kraft Cadbury Campaign: "Bear & Gorilla", Creative, MORO
Procter & Gamble
Toyota

France

Saatchi & Saatchi
53 Boulevard Ornano, 93200 Paris, France
Tel.: (33) 1 48 13 40 00
Fax: (33) 1 48 13 99 99
E-Mail: info@saatchi.fr
Web Site: www.saatchiduke.com

Employees: 100
Year Founded: 1928

National Agency Associations: AACC-IAA

Agency Specializes In: Consumer Marketing

Oli Osmond *(Acct Dir-Digital)*
Olivier Gamblin *(Dir-Art & Supvr-Art)*
Eric Auvinet *(Dir-Art)*
Vincent Berard *(Dir-Artistic)*
Philippe Rachel *(Dir-Art)*
Florian Roussel *(Dir-Art)*
Romain Sadoul *(Asst Dir-Fin)*
Laurie Mogarra *(Copywriter)*

Accounts:
Association France Alzheimer
Babybel
Chantelle
Courrier International
Doctors of the World Campaign: "How Do You Treat Tooth Decay ?"
Fixodent
Fluocaril
France Alzheimer Campaign: "Hands"
French National Olympic Committee Support the French Olympic Team Campaign, Television
GDF SUEZ
Lexus
Nexans
Procter & Gamble Pampers
Reporters Without Borders
RSF
Saint Gobain
Toyota Avensis, Campaign: "Averages", Campaign: "My Dad My Hero", GT86, Yaris
Transitions
Volkswagen Campaign: "Fluffy"

Germany

Saatchi & Saatchi
Uhlandstrasse 2, 60314 Frankfurt am Main, 60038 Germany
Tel.: (49) 69 714 20
Fax: (49) 69 714 2346
E-Mail: info@saatchi.de
Web Site: www.saatchi.de

Employees: 100
Year Founded: 1970

Agency Specializes In: Advertising

Dirk Gobel *(COO)*
Thomas Kanofsky *(Exec Dir-Creative)*
Daniel Grether *(Grp Dir-Creative)*
Vitor Mainho *(Art Dir-Integrated)*
Jorg Riommi *(Creative Dir)*
Jean-Pierre Gregor *(Dir-Integrated Creative)*
Irina Popp *(Copywriter)*

Accounts:
Ariel
Avis Autovermietung
Deutsche Telekom AG Campaign: "Share 2014", T-COM
Diakonie Frankfurt
Dinosaur Museum Senckenberg Campaign: "Big Bone"
EE
Kobold
Pampers Cruisers
Psychothriller Campaign: "The Locker-Shocker"
Taxi Frankfurt Campaign: "Karaoke Stunt"
Toyota Campaign: "AYGO. Pissing around", Campaign: "Four Passangers", Campaign: "The World's Smallest Newspaper", Campaign: "Tight Curve"
The United Nations Food and Agriculture Organization
Visa International
Volvo Car Germany
Vorwerk Campaign: "Vacuum Love"
Your's Irish Bar Campaign: "Karaoke S.O.S."

Hungary

Saatchi & Saatchi
Alvinci Ut 16, 1022 Budapest, Hungary
Tel.: (36) 1 345 9300
Fax: (36) 1 345 9399
E-Mail: Kinga.Meszaros@saatchi.hu
Web Site: www.saatchi.com

E-Mail for Key Personnel:
President: zoltan.paksy@saatchi.hu
Creative Dir.: janos.debreceni@saatchi.hu

Employees: 50
Year Founded: 1990

Agency Specializes In: Advertising

Kinga Meszaros *(Mng Dir)*
Tunde Egrine Matisz *(Dir-PR)*
Reka Oravecz *(Sr Acct Mgr)*

Israel

BBR Saatchi & Saatchi
6 Hachilason Street, Ramat Gan, 52522 Israel
Tel.: (972) 3 755 2626
Fax: (972) 3 755 2727
E-Mail: info@bbr.co.il
Web Site: www.saatchi.com

Agency Specializes In: Advertising

Yossi Lubaton *(CEO)*
Dorit Gvili *(VP-Production & Content)*
David Kosmin *(VP-Plng-Saatchi & Saatchi Israel)*
Hagai Liran *(VP, Acct)*
Nadav Pressman *(Exec Creative Dir)*
Shony Rivnay *(Exec Creative Dir)*
Shirley Bahar *(Sr Dir-Art)*
Amir Ariely *(Creative Dir)*
Ale Feldman *(Art Dir)*
Niv Herzberg *(Art Dir)*
Shiran Jerochim *(Art Dir)*
Idan Levy *(Creative Dir)*
Aia Bechor *(Dir-Art)*
Tomer Gidron *(Dir-Creative)*
Vicki Tseitlin *(Acct Mgr)*
Yogev Atoon *(Acct Supvr)*
Lee Bryn *(Acct Supvr)*
Daniela Livni *(Acct Supvr)*
Yogev Weiss *(Acct Supvr)*
Naomi Ashkenzi *(Supvr-Plng)*
Ori Ben Dror *(Acct Exec)*
Reni Bracha *(Acct Exec)*
Stav Hershkovitz *(Acct Exec)*
Omri Sela *(Acct Exec)*
Orit Bar-Niv *(Copywriter)*
Ran Even *(Copywriter)*
Lora Goichman *(Planner-Strategic)*
Tal Hirschberg *(Copywriter)*
Becky Malakov *(Copywriter)*
Lior Shoham *(Copywriter)*
Eran Spanier *(Copywriter)*

Accounts:
102 FM Tel Aviv Radio
ACE
Almah Chewing Gum
American Express Campaign: "The Young Professionals Project"
Ariel Campaign: "Banana Pudding", Campaign: "Dolce De Leche"
Beit Lohamei Haghetaot
Bekol Campaign: "Fading Music", Campaign: "Sonar Invasion"
Carlsberg Campaign: "Uncompromising Quality"
Carmel Wine
CMYK Magazine Campaign: "Advertising magazine in Israel: Big Idea"
Coca Cola Company Campaign: "Refresh It", Sprite
Coffee Shot
Delek Motors Campaign: "Speaks for Itself", Ford Transit
Direct Insurance
Eden Mineral Water
Elite Coffee Campaiagn: "Sweetening The News", Campaign: "The Personal Billboard"
First Hug Hibuk Rishon's
Ford Campaign: "Don't Be The Minivan Guy", Campaign: "Magazine", Campaign: "Mirror", Ford Explorer, Ford Focus, Print Ad, S-Max
Free Pollard
Ghetto Fighters
Government Of Kosovo
Haier
HOT Cable TV
The Impossible Brief Campaign: "Blood Relations"
Kitchen Aid
Kosovo Government
Life Dental Floss
Masenko Campaign: "The Trail of Perfume"
Mazda 3, 5
The Men's Helpline for Domestic Violence
Moulinex
Newpan Campaign: "Secretary"
Orange
Otrivin
Pampers & Magisto
The Parents Circle Families Forum (PCFF) Campaign: "We Don't Want You Here"
The Peres Center For Peace Campaign: "Blood Relations", Public Affairs Initiative
Procter & Gamble Laundry Detergent
Rav-Bariach
Shapa Campaign: "The Mailboosters"
Shazam
Shikun & Binui Green Energy Awareness
New-Shvurim
Splendid Chocolate Campaign: "Cassette Tape"
Strauss Group Achla, Campaign: "75 Years Old and Still Hip", Chocolate, Cow Chocolate,

Advertising Agencies

Splendid
Superpharm Campaign: "Colors of Passion", Campaign: "The Touch Counter"
Tefal
TNT Clothing
Tzimaon
The University Veterinarian Hospital Campaign: "The Bandaged Animal Statues"

Italy

Saatchi & Saatchi Healthcare

Corso Monforte 52, 20122 Milan, Italy
Tel.: (39) 02 77012
Fax: (39) 02 7701 3420
E-Mail: info@saatchi.it
Web Site: www.saatchi.com

Employees: 26

Agency Specializes In: Health Care Services

Oscar Rovelli *(CFO)*
Fabrizio Caprara *(Chm-Italy & Dir-Mktg-EMEA)*
Giuseppe Caiazza *(CEO-France & Italy & Head-Automotive Bus Europe)*
Adriano Aletti *(Mng Dir-Shopper Mktg)*
Maria Rosa Musto *(Gen Mgr-Milan)*
Camilla Pollice *(Gen Mgr-Rome)*
Agostino Toscana *(Exec Dir-Creative)*
Antonio Gigliotti *(Dir-Creative)*
Alessandro Orlandi *(Dir-Creative)*
Philip Mattei *(Strategist-Digital)*

Accounts:
Carlsberg
Cheerios
Head & Shoulders
New Zealand Post
Pampers
Port Salut
T-Mobile US
Tooheys New
Toyoto
VISA

Saatchi & Saatchi

Via Nazionale 75, 00187 Rome, Italy
Tel.: (39) 06 362 201
Fax: (39) 06 324 0254
E-Mail: info@saatchi.it
Web Site: www.saatchi.com

Employees: 55
Year Founded: 1988

Agency Specializes In: Advertising

Giuseppe Caiazza *(CEO-France & Italy & Head-Automotive Bus Europe)*
Agostino Toscana *(Exec Dir-Creative)*
Manuel Musilli *(Dir-Creative)*
Alessandro Orlandi *(Dir-Creative)*
Ilaria Lorenzetti *(Acct Supvr)*

Accounts:
CoorDown Campaign: "DammiPiuVoce", Down Syndrome
Enel SpA Enel
Luxotica
New-Procter & Gamble Fixodent
Toyota (GB) PLC

Saatchi & Saatchi

Corso Monforte 52, 20122 Milan, Italy
Tel.: (39) 02 77011
Fax: (39) 02 781196
E-Mail: fabrizio.caprara@saatchi.it
Web Site: www.saatchi.com

Employees: 70
Year Founded: 1988

Agency Specializes In: Consumer Marketing

Andrea Salvaneschi *(Sr Dir-Art & Creative)*
Sandro Amabili *(Acct Dir)*
Giulio Frittaion *(Art Dir)*
David Denni *(Dir-Art, Supvr & Designer)*
Alessio Bianconi *(Dir-Art)*
Fabio D'Alessandro *(Dir-Art)*
Alessandro Orlandi *(Dir-Creative)*
Michele Sartori *(Dir-Art)*
Francesca Bertocco *(Acct Mgr)*
Giordano Mantegna *(Acct Mgr)*
Ilaria Lorenzetti *(Acct Supvr)*
Marta Policastri *(Copywriter)*
Alice Scornajenghi *(Copywriter)*
Paola Rolli *(Deputy Dir-Creative)*

Accounts:
Acqua Vitasnella
Agenzia delle Entrate Campaign: "Parasites"
Alpitour World
Alternative Europee
Banca Intessa
Bastard
Boehringer Ingelheim OTC Products Bisolvon Linctus, Guttalax Drops & Pearls & Silomat
Calzedonia Campaign: "25 Years Together"
Carrefour Market Campaign: "Back to 1961", Campaign: "The Sunburnt", Les Cosmetiques
Club Med; 2013
Conferenza Episcopale Italiana Campaign: "This Is Not A Movie", Italian Catholic Church
Coor Down Campaign: "Dear Future Mom", Campaign: "Integration Day"
Deutsche Telekom Campaign: "Angry Birds Live"
Dompe Campaign: "The Rarest Ones"
Enel Campaign: "Hammer"
FAO International Campaign Against Hunger
Galbani International Cheeses
Il Ponte Del Sorriso Campaign: "Casting"
Italian Culture Week
Leroy Merlin
Lexus Campaign: "120 Heartbeats", Campaign: "Trace Your Road", GS Hybrid, IS Hybrid
Medici Senza Frontiere Social Campaign
Ministry of Health
Mondadore
Nonna Betta
Presidenza Del Consiglio Dei Ministri Human Rights 50th Anniversary, Organ Donation Campaigns, Pre-Registration at University
Procter & Gamble Italia Ariel, Campaign: "Saving Aslan", Campaign: "The Best Italian Recipe", Demak'Up, Fixodent, Head & Shoulders, Kukident, Oil of Olay, Pampers, Spic & Span
Renault Italia Cefe, Clio, Dealers, Laguna, Safrane
Rotoloni Regina
Sofidel Campaign: "Message In A Roll"
Top Digital
Toyota (GB) PLC Auris, Auris Hybrid, Campaign: "Advanced World", Campaign: "Ananchronis", Campaign: "Shopping", Campaign: "The Alternative", Campaign: "The Station Wagon ", Campaign: "What target Wants", Toyota IQ
The Vatican Charity Foundation Campaign: "This is Not a Movie"

Latvia

Adell Saatchi & Saatchi

15 Elizabetes Street, Riga, 1010 Latvia
Tel.: (371) 67 320 263
Fax: (371) 67 830 507
E-Mail: varis.l@saatchi.lv
Web Site: www.saatchi.com

Employees: 24

Agency Specializes In: Advertising

Varis Lazo *(Owner)*
Jelena Lavrane *(Copywriter)*

Accounts:
Novartis

Lebanon

Saatchi & Saatchi

Quantum Tower 9th Floor Charles Malek Avenue Saint Nicolas St, 20714714 Beirut, Achrafieh Lebanon
Tel.: (961) 1 204 060
Fax: (961) 1 202 157
E-Mail: eli_khoury@saatchi.com.lb
Web Site: www.saatchi.com

E-Mail for Key Personnel:
Creative Dir.: creative@saatchi.com.lb
Media Dir.: media_planning@saatchi.com.lb

Agency Specializes In: Advertising

Shady Kaddoum *(Assoc Dir-Creative)*

Accounts:
Kunhadi

Namibia

DV.8 Saatchi & Saatchi

84 Frans Indongo St, Windhoek, Namibia
Mailing Address:
PO Box 9485, Windhoek, Namibia
Tel.: (264) 61 239 757
Fax: (264) 61 250 899
E-Mail: ideas@dv8.com.na

Employees: 16

Agency Specializes In: Advertising

Accounts:
Tafel Lager

Netherlands

Saatchi & Saatchi Leo Burnett

(Formerly Saatchi & Saatchi)
Danzigerkade 23C, 1013 AP Amsterdam, Netherlands
Mailing Address:
PO Box 308, 1180 AH Amstelveen, Netherlands
Tel.: (31) 20 543 15 43
Fax: (31) 20 543 1543
E-Mail: saatchi@saatchi.nl
Web Site: www.saatchi-amsterdam.nl

Employees: 25
Year Founded: 1950

Agency Specializes In: Advertising

Marcel Holscher *(Mng Partner)*
Jan Uitendaal *(CFO)*
Arjan Kabtijns *(CEO-Publicis Grp Nederland)*
Campbell McLean *(Acct Dir)*
Tim Bishop *(Dir-Art)*
Rick Coolegem *(Dir-Creative)*
Tim ten Dam *(Dir-Art)*
Maarten Dobbelaar *(Dir-Creative)*

Accounts:
Head & Shoulders
Marktplaats.nl Campaign: "It Squeaks"
Parkinson Vereniging
Samsung Samsung Motion Sync Vacuum Cleaner
Time Out
Topgear Magazine Campaign: "Your New Ride"

Nigeria

SO&U Saatchi & Saatchi
2 Oyetula Street Off Ajanaku Street via Thomas Ajufo Street Opebi, Ikeja, Lagos, Nigeria
Mailing Address:
PO Box 14376, Opebi Ikeja, Lagos, Nigeria
Tel.: (234) 1 774 1754
Fax: (234) 1 554 6334
Web Site: www.sou.com.ng

E-Mail for Key Personnel:
President: utchayanoruo@sousaatchi.com
Creative Dir.: utchayanoruo@sousaatchi.com

Employees: 15
Year Founded: 1990

Agency Specializes In: Communications

Udeme Ufot *(Mng Dir)*
Olalekan Oladunwo *(Sr Dir-Art)*
Amen Salami *(Art Dir)*
Anthony Ekun *(Dir-Creative)*
Ayotunde Ishola *(Dir-Art)*
Olusegun Korode *(Copywriter)*
Sola Kosoko *(Copywriter)*
Seyi Owolawi *(Copywriter)*
Damola Adedamola *(Deputy Dir-Creative)*
Ken Orimalade *(Deputy Creative Dir)*

Accounts:
Access
Central Bank of Nigeria
Exxon Mobile
Guinness Nigeria
HP
Multilinks Telcom
Oando
New-Orijin Beer
P&G

Norway

Saatchi & Saatchi A/S
Storgata 33, 0184 Oslo, Norway
Tel.: (47) 23 32 70 00
Fax: (47) 23 32 70 01
E-Mail: jorgen@saatchi.no
Web Site: www.saatchi.no

E-Mail for Key Personnel:
President: jon@saatchi.no
Creative Dir.: jorgen@saatchi.no

Employees: 16
Year Founded: 1987

Agency Specializes In: Advertising

Jon Fredrik Sandengen *(CEO)*
Eiliv Gunleiksrud *(Dir-Creative, Digital & Design)*
Linus Hjellstrom *(Dir-Art)*
Ola Bagge Skar *(Dir-Production Art)*
Oyvind Waage *(Dir-Creative)*
Mads Ronold *(Mgr-Digital Content)*
Fanny Vaager Brekke *(Copywriter)*

Accounts:
Alvor
Department Of Renovation, Oslo
New-Nidar AS Smash
Ovingshotellet
Toyota Campaign: "Toyota Yaris Launch", Campaign: "Try My Hybrid"

Poland

Saatchi & Saatchi
Ul Domaniewska 42, 02-672 Warsaw, Poland
Tel.: (48) 22 345 21 00
Fax: (48) 22 345 21 01
E-Mail: marek.zoledziowski@saatchi.pl
Web Site:
https://www.facebook.com/SaatchiPoland/

Employees: 100
Year Founded: 1990

Agency Specializes In: Graphic Design, Print, T.V.

Krysztof Pudlak *(CFO)*
Kamila Gorska *(Acct Dir-Central Europe)*
Blanka Lipinska *(Dir-Creative)*
Johan Pasternak *(Dir-Art)*
Anna Drozda *(Acct Mgr)*
Michal Pawlowski *(Deputy Dir-Creative)*

Accounts:
Carlsberg
Carrefour
Deutsche Telekom Campaign: "Christmas Surprise With Mariah Carey"
E.Wedel Campaign: "Wave"
New-GlaxoSmithKline Consumer Healthcare
Lexus
Novartis Campaign: "Hachoo!"
Otrivin
Polish Red Cross Campaign: "Friend Request"
New-Run With Heart Foundation
Schneider Electric
Toyota Campaign: "Lamp", Campaign: "The 4x4 you can always count on", Land Cruiser
Voltaren Campaign: "For Freedom Of Movement, Ball"

Romania

Saatchi & Saatchi
Central Business Park Cladirea D+E Parter Calea Serban Voda nr 133, Sector 4, 040205 Bucharest, Romania
Tel.: (40) 31 7300 600
Fax: (40) 31 7300 601
E-Mail: saatchi@saatchi.ro
Web Site: www.saatchi.com

Employees: 100

Radu Florescu *(Mng Dir)*
Calin Ionescu *(Grp Dir-Creative)*
John Pallant *(Reg Dir-Creative-Europe, Middle East & Africa)*
Laura Iane *(Co-Dir-Creative)*
Alexandru Malaescu *(Dir-Art)*
Marius Tianu *(Dir-Creative)*
Liliana Voinescu *(Sr Mgr-Pub Projects)*
Cristian Scurtu *(Copywriter)*

Accounts:
A.A.C.A.R. Horia Motoi Campaign: "Repetition"
Alpha Bank
Carlsberg
Chio
Enel Campaign: "Plant the Bill"
Greenpeace
Novartis
Ori Diamonds Campaign: "Eternity"
Sony Ericsson
Toyota/Lexus
Toyota Campaign: "Wolf"
United Way
Vibrocil
Visa Europe
Voltaren

Russia

Saatchi & Saatchi Russia
Bolshoy Levshinky 6/2 bld 1, 119034 Moscow, Russia
Tel.: (7) 495 739 8777
Fax: (7) 495 739 8778
Web Site: www.saatchi.com

Oleg Panov *(Sr Dir-Art)*
Dima Zhukov *(Sr Dir-Art)*
Charlie Brooke *(Art Dir)*
Oksana Mosokha *(Dir-Art)*
Anna Stashkevich *(Dir-Art)*

Accounts:
Ariel
Intermediagroup JSC
Jaguar Magazine
Mtv Networks Entertainment Campaign: "Save April First!"
Novartis International AG
Olay
Otrivin
Sochnaya Dolina
Vibrocil Campaign: "Horror"
Viciunai
Voltaren Pain Relief Gel

Slovenia

Saatchi & Saatchi
Poslovna Stavba Slovenijales III Nadstopje, Dunajska Cesta 22, 1000 Ljubljana, Slovenia
Tel.: (386) 1 23 43 550
Fax: (386) 1 23 43 551
E-Mail: mitja.petrovic@saatchi.si
Web Site: www.saatchi.si

Employees: 30

Matej Kodric *(Dir-Creative)*

Accounts:
Little Buddha
Toyota Yaris

South Africa

Saatchi & Saatchi
The Foundry Ebenezer Road, Greenpoint, Cape Town, 8001 South Africa
Mailing Address:
PO 694, Cape Town, 8000 South Africa
Tel.: (27) 21 413 7500
Fax: (27) 21 425 7550
E-Mail: ian.young@saatchi.co.za
Web Site: www.saatchi.com

Employees: 100

Agency Specializes In: Advertising

Jonathan Beggs *(Chief Creative Officer)*
John Pallant *(Reg Dir-Creative-Europe, Middle East & Africa)*
Tyrone Beck *(Creative Dir)*
Andrew Chandler *(Art Dir)*
Harriet Stockwell *(Dir-Art)*
Mimi Cooper *(Assoc Dir-Creative)*
Hilda-Mari Cronje *(Copywriter)*
Alice Gnodde *(Copywriter-M&C Saatchi)*

Accounts:
Dynafi
Eskom Campaign: "15 Watts"
Kalahari Ads Digital, Through the Line
KWV
New-Momentum
Novartis Excedrin, Fenivir, Lamisil, Mebucaine, Theraflu, Voltaren
Operation Smile Campaign: "Art of Distraction", Campaign: "Fix A Smile Birthday Calendar"
Osram Energy Saving Light Bulbs
PharmaDynamics Campaign: "Phil", Campaign: "Sneezing Sucks"

Pioneer Foods Campaign: "Recipe Book"
Sasko Flour
Sports Illustrated
Tuffy Campaign: "Garbage Truck", Campaign: "Landfill Monster", Campaign: "The Lazy Man's Guide to Saving the World"
The Volunteer Wildfire Service Campaign: "Hedgehog"
Wordsworth Bookstore Campaign: "20,000 Leagues Under the Sea", Campaign: "Lord of the Flies", Campaign: "Words Worth Reading"
Young Designer's Emporium

Saatchi & Saatchi
28 Roos Street ext 29, Fourways, Johannesburg, 2195 South Africa
Mailing Address:
PO Box 650831, Benmore, Johannesburg 2010 South Africa
Tel.: (27) 11 548 6000
Fax: (27) 11 548 6001
Web Site: www.saatchi.com

Employees: 50
Year Founded: 1975

National Agency Associations: ACA

Grant Meldrum *(Mng Dir-Johannesburg & Africa Network)*
Alison Stansfield *(Reg Dir-Creative-IMEA)*
Charlotte Grey *(Acct Dir)*
Carla Le Roux *(Dir-Creative)*
Keshia Meyerson *(Dir-Art)*
Yvonne Hall *(Assoc Dir-Creative)*
Myka Hecht-Wendt *(Designer-Interactive)*
Madre Roothman *(Copywriter-Digital)*

Accounts:
49M Above-the-Line, National Energy Efficiency Initiative
Eskom
Mondelez Cadbury
Novartis Otrivin Nasal Spray, Voltaren
PharmaDynamics
Procter & Gamble Ariel
Red Pepper Audio Books Campaign: "Gulliver"
Tuffy

Spain

Saatchi & Saatchi
Calle Goya 24 4a Planta, 28001 Madrid, Spain
Tel.: (34) 91 151 20 00
Fax: (34) 91 151 20 01
E-Mail: miguel.roig@saatchi.es
Web Site: www.saatchi.com

Employees: 60
Year Founded: 1978

National Agency Associations: AEAP

Agency Specializes In: Direct Response Marketing, Public Relations

Mauricio Duque *(Sr Dir-Art-Del Campo Saatchi & Saatchi Spain)*
Fernando Dominguez *(Copywriter-Del Campo Saatchi & Saatchi)*

Accounts:
Procter & Gamble Campaign: "Dressing Gown", Campaign: "First Timers"
Reporters Without Borders
Toyota Road Safety Awareness

Sweden

Saatchi & Saatchi
Drukningtatam 95A, 11360 Stockholm, Sweden
Tel.: (46) 8 5057 1700
Fax: (46) 8 5057 1750
E-Mail: jd@saatchi.se
Web Site: www.saatchi.se

Employees: 23

Agency Specializes In: Advertising

Gustav Egerstedt *(Exec Dir-Creative-Saatchi & Saatchi Stockholm)*
Elin Johansson *(Acct Dir & Planner)*
Victor Bergabo *(Art Dir)*
Jonas Bjorlin *(Acct Dir)*
Jonas Frank *(Art Dir)*
Maria Lindskog Klasen *(Acct Dir)*
Olov Lagerkvist *(Art Dir)*
Marie Nodbrink *(Acct Mgr)*
Petter Esbjornsson *(Copywriter)*
Amalia Pitsiava *(Copywriter)*

Accounts:
A Glass of Water
Ariel
Australian Koala Foundation
B-Reel
Boxer
Canal +
Carlsberg
ELMSTA 3000 Horror Fest Campaign: "Hillbilly Horror"
Gainomax
The Gillette Company
Lambi
LG Sweden Door-in-Door, OLED-TV, Online, Social Media
Norrmejerier Jokk Juice
Norwegian
Orkla
Out of Office Ad
Popaganda Music Festival Campaign: "The Live Quiz Release"
Procter & Gamble Nordic Ariel Actilift Detergent, Campaign: "Ariel Fashion Shoot", Gillette
Sma Brytare Campaign: "A small bread baked with barley"
SPP
Stockholm Art Week Campaign: "Stockholm is your Canvas"
Stockholm Pride
Stockholm Public Transport
Toyota Campaign: "An ordinary car"
Viasat Campaign: "Speed"

Switzerland

Saatchi & Saatchi Zurich
Raffelstrasse 32, CH-8045 Zurich, Switzerland
Tel.: (41) 442981818
Fax: (41) 442400344
Web Site: www.saatchi-ch.com

Agency Specializes In: Advertising

Andrea Pedrazzini *(CEO-Switzerland & Head-Global Client-GSK)*
Jason Romeyko *(Exec Dir-Creative)*
Fred Doms *(Sr Dir-Art)*
Melanie Bisseret-Foucher *(Acct Dir-GSK Equity Brands-Global)*
Gustavo Figueiredo *(Dir-Creative)*
Magdalena Kubacka *(Dir-Digital)*
Lorna Steele *(Sr Acct Mgr)*
Cassy Ymar *(Sr Acct Mgr)*
Guendalina Gennari Curlo *(Acct Mgr-Global)*
Katya Ivashchenko *(Acct Mgr)*
Matthieu Lespes *(Acct Mgr)*

Accounts:
Seat Campaign: "End of the World", Seat Leon Formula Racing
United Nations Children's Fund Stop Violence against Girls

Saatchi & Saatchi
Place du Temple 15, 1227 Carouge, Switzerland
Tel.: (41) 22 307 2727
Fax: (41) 22 307 2770
Web Site: www.saatchi-ch.com

Employees: 50

Agency Specializes In: Advertising

Pascal Schaub *(Mng Dir & Dir-Strategy-Zurich)*
Marc Chandler *(VP & Sr Dir-Art)*
Juerg Aemmer *(Exec Creative Dir)*
John Pallant *(Reg Dir-Creative-EMEA)*
Andrea Pedrazzini *(Grp Acct Dir)*
Sarah Lambert *(Acct Dir)*
Gustavo Figueiredo *(Dir-Creative)*
Gisele Gentil *(Acct Mgr)*
Natascha Imfeld *(Copywriter)*
Marine Quere *(Copywriter)*

Accounts:
Association of Swiss Pay Card Providers
Baboo
Bel Babybel, Cantadou, La Vache Qui Rit
Ciba Vision
CPW
Emirates Airlines
Fenistil Gel
Fiat
Group E
Henniez
Koala.ch
Novartis Anti Inflammatory Pills, Campaign: "Transformers", Fenistil Skin Care Gel, Fenistil: Mosquito, Lamisil, Otrivin Nasal Spray, Theraflu, Voltaflex, Voltaren
Procter & Gamble
New-Swisscom
UN Cares Campaign: "Stigma"
Voltarol

Turkey

Saatchi & Saatchi Istanbul
Adnan Saygun Cad Kelaynak Sok No 1/1, Ulus Besiktas, 34340 Istanbul, Turkey
Tel.: (90) 212 283 16 00
Fax: (90) 212 280 16 52
E-Mail: info@saatchiistanbul.com
Web Site: saatchiistanbul.com/tr-tr

Employees: 60

Agency Specializes In: Advertising

United Arab Emirates

Saatchi & Saatchi
27 28 & 29 Beach Villas Jumeira Beach Rd, Jumeira 1, Dubai, United Arab Emirates
Mailing Address:
PO Box 23252, Dubai, United Arab Emirates
Tel.: (971) 4 344 4346
Fax: (971) 4 344 1477
E-Mail: info@saatchime.com
Web Site: www.saatchi.com

Employees: 50

Agency Specializes In: Advertising

Adil Khan *(CEO-MENA)*
Colman Sheil *(Exec Creative Dir-Saatchi & Saatchi X Dubai)*
Ion Cojocaru *(Art Dir)*
Ghaled Ghorayeb *(Acct Dir)*

Hema Patel *(Acct Dir)*
Sneha Sathe *(Art Dir)*
Ahmed Bahaa *(Dir-Art)*
Khaled Ibrahim *(Dir-Art)*
Raja Rizkallah *(Dir-Art)*
Hamid Naqvi *(Acct Mgr)*
Nihal Salim *(Acct Mgr)*
Akshaya Sikand *(Acct Mgr)*
Andy Daniluc *(Copywriter)*
Wayne Fernandes *(Copywriter)*
Sam Hughes *(Copywriter)*
Doug Mackay *(Copywriter)*
Jeton Morina *(Copywriter)*
Simon Raffaghello *(Copywriter)*

Accounts:
ADCB
Anais Association
Ariel Campaign: "White Singlet Vs Red Tights"
Arla Campaign: "Betty Botter"
Barry Kirsch Production
Cadbury In-Store, Online
Federal Foods
General Mills
New-Good Night
Mall of the Emirates & Atlantis
Mondelez International, Inc. Campaign: "Inspiring Swiss", Toblerone
Novartis
New-P&G
Red Bull
Roads & Transport Authority (RTA) Campaign: "Test Ride The Bus", Creative, Dubai Metro Marketing Campaign; 2009
SAMBA
Unicef

United Kingdom

Outside Line
80 Charlotte Street, London, W1A 1AQ United Kingdom
Tel.: (44) 20 7462 7400
E-Mail: admin@outsideline.co.uk
Web Site: www.outsideline.co.uk

Employees: 50

Agency Specializes In: Communications, Content, Digital/Interactive, Planning & Consultation, Public Relations

Adam Alexandroni *(Dir-Content)*
Clare Ruck *(Dir-Ops & Fin)*
Lynda Tomlinson *(Production Mgr-Content & Experiential)*

Accounts:
Andy Murray Sports Entertainment Services
Arla Foods Social Media, Wing-Co
British Gas Gas & Electricity Maintenance Services
Cravendale Campaign: "Always On', In-store, LOVE Cravendale, Online Display, Outdoor, PR, Social Media, Websites
Lurpak Bake Club Website, Bakery Products Mfr, Campaign: "FoodBeats"
Sure for Men Deodorant Mfr

Saatchi & Saatchi EMEA Region Headquarters
80 Charlotte Street, London, W1A 1AQ United Kingdom
Tel.: (44) 207 636 5060
Fax: (44) 207 462 7896
Web Site: www.saatchi.co.uk

Employees: 500

Agency Specializes In: Advertising

John Pallant *(Reg Dir-Creative)*
Marion Cohen *(Dir-Art)*
Julia Franks *(Dir-New Bus)*
Richard Huntington *(Dir-Strategy-London)*

Accounts:
Mattessons
Olay

Saatchi & Saatchi London
80 Charlotte Street, London, W1A 1AQ United Kingdom
Tel.: (44) 2076365060
Fax: (44) 2076378489
Web Site: www.saatchi.co.uk

Employees: 500
Year Founded: 1970

National Agency Associations: IAA

Agency Specializes In: Advertising

Adam Collins *(Mng Partner)*
Charles Pym *(Mng Partner)*
Katrien De Bauw *(COO)*
David Hackworthy *(Chief Strategy Officer)*
Richard Huntington *(Chief Strategy Officer)*
Larissa Vince *(Chief Growth Officer)*
Rob Burleigh *(Exec Dir-Creative-Global)*
Kostas Karanikolas *(Exec Dir-Creative-Global)*
Jamie Vickery *(Grp Acct Dir)*
Mark Slack *(Art Dir & Copywriter)*
Katrina Bain *(Acct Dir)*
Allan Stevenson *(Art Dir)*
Lucy Titterington *(Creative Dir-Digital)*
Olly Farrington *(Dir-Art & Creative & Copywriter)*
Adam Chiappe *(Dir-Creative)*
Matt Kandela *(Dir-New Bus-Worldwide)*
Mark Norcutt *(Dir-Creative)*
Laurence Quinn *(Dir-Creative)*
Ben Robinson *(Dir-Art)*
Jason Romeyko *(Dir-Creative-Intl)*
Amy Wright *(Sr Acct Mgr-Integrated)*
Emily Mason *(Mgr-Bus Dev)*
Simon Dilks *(Sr Designer)*
Antony Gough *(Designer)*
Jose Hernandez *(Copywriter)*
Mike Whiteside *(Copywriter)*

Accounts:
New-Amigo Campaign: "Sausages & Chip", Richmond, TV, Video-on-Demand
New-Bathstore Campaign: "Bathrooms Matter", Creative
New-The Big Issue Brand
Carlsberg Campaign: "A Life Well Lived", San Miguel
New-Chelsea F.C. Chelsea Football Club Get me a Sponsor
Deutsche Telekom EE, T-Mobile
Diageo Campaign: "Paint it Black"
Direct Line Insurance Advertising, Campaign: "Break In", Campaign: "Roger", Digital, Print, Social Media, TV
European Youth Campaign
Everything Everywhere Campaign: "Bufferface", Campaign: "Bus", Campaign: "Conga", Campaign: "Numa"
New-General Mills Global Creative, Haagen-Dazs
H. J. Heinz Company
HomeAway, Inc. Advertising, TV
HSBC Campaign: "Anyone's Game", Premier & Wealth Proposition, Rugby Sevens, Sponsorship
Kerry Foods Campaign: "peacekeeper", Digital, Richmond, Wall's & Mattessons, Wall's Sausages
Kidscape
Luminous Campaign: "Work Smart, Not Hard"
Marie Curie Creative, Digital Communications
Mattesons Campaign: "Hank", Campaign: "Miss Marvins"
Mondelez International, Inc. Campaign: "Vending Gig"
Nike Foundation Aisha's Story, Girl Hub
OK Go I'm Not Through
Olay Campaign: "Childs VIew"
Operation Black Vote
Premier Foods Ambrosia, Batchelors, Bisto, Campaign: "power brands", Hovis, Loyd Grossman, Mr Kipling, Oxo, Sharwood
Procter & Gamble Campaign "Love, Sleep & Play", Campaign: "Dressing Gown", Pampers
New-Rekorderlig Cider
T-Mobile US Campaign: "Giving Britain what Britain loves", PAYG, T-Mobile G1, The T-Mobile Parking Ticket, Wedding, Welcome Back
Toyota Motor Europe Campaign: "Fall in Love With Driving Again", Campaign: "Gadget Guy", Campaign: "Go Fun Yourself", Campaign: "The Real Deal", Campaign: "Who's Driving", Toyota Aygo, Toyota GT86, Yaris, Yaris Hybrid
Uservoice Campaign: "Similar Stories"
Visa Campaign: "Bolt Vs London", Campaign: "Grandad Tourismo", Campaign: "Ready", Creative, Football Evolution, Visa Europe, Visa International
Weight watchers Broadcast, Campaign: "Helping Men Lose Weight", Campaign: "Here to Help", Campaign: "Losing Weight For Parents", Campaign: "Weight Loss For Busy People", Digital Creative

Saatchi Masius
(Formerly Team Saatchi)
23 Howland Street, London, WNT 4AY United Kingdom
Tel.: (44) 207 436 6636
Fax: (44) 207 462 7756
E-Mail: sophie.hooper@teamsaatchi.co.uk
Web Site: saatchimasius.co.uk

Employees: 18

Agency Specializes In: Advertising, Digital/Interactive

Surrey Garland *(Creative Dir)*
Mel Harvey *(Art Dir)*
Jamie Webb *(Acct Dir)*
Martin Hill *(Dir-Digital)*
Joe Luffman *(Dir-Design)*
Joanna Cutmore *(Office Mgr)*
Tomasz Bartkowiak *(Designer)*
Adam Crowley *(Graphic Designer-Interactive & Motion)*
Richard Warren *(Copywriter)*

Accounts:
Edwardian Group London
The May Fair Hotel Campaign: "May Fair Affair", Online, Print
Olympus
Scoff & Banter

Argentina

Del Campo Nazca Saatchi & Saatchi
Bogota 973, Martinez, CP 1640 Buenos Aires, Argentina
Tel.: (54) 11 4836 0800
Fax: (54) 11 4836 0800
E-Mail: pdelcampo@dcnazca.com.ar
Web Site: www.delcamposaatchi.com/

Employees: 100

Agency Specializes In: Advertising, Automotive, Aviation & Aerospace, Food Service, Multimedia, Print, Production (Print)

Pablo Del Campo *(Chm)*
Jose M. Reobasco *(CFO)*
Javier Campopiano *(Chief Creative Officer)*
Raffaella Scarpetti *(Head-Production)*
Rafael Santamarina *(Exec Dir-Creative)*

Ariel Serkin *(Exec Creative Dir)*
Fernando Lanuza *(Sr Dir-Art)*
Claudio Amoedo *(Exec Producer)*
Andy Fogwill *(Exec Producer)*
Agustin Suarez *(Creative Dir)*
Ana Bogni *(Art Dir)*
Mariano Cafarelli *(Acct Dir)*
Sebastin Duccoli *(Creative Dir)*
Ezequiel De Luca *(Dir-Art)*
Hernan Garcia Dietrich *(Dir-Art)*
Mauricio Duque *(Dir-Art)*
Ammiel Fazzari *(Dir-Creative)*
Javier Agena Goya *(Dir-Art)*
Fernando Militerno *(Dir-Creative)*
Javier Pizarro *(Dir-Art)*
Mariano Serkin *(Dir-Creative)*
Nicolas Vara *(Dir-Creative)*
Juan Comba *(Acct Mgr)*
Adrian Aspani *(Mgr-Production)*
Koko Puch *(Mgr-Print Production)*
Maximiliano Beltran *(Acct Exec)*
Manuela Sorzana *(Acct Exec)*
Italo Canepa *(Copywriter)*
Nicolas Diaco *(Copywriter)*
Virginia Feito *(Copywriter)*
Juan Manuel Seillant *(Copywriter)*
Bruno Tortolano *(Designer)*
Diego Feldman *(Reg Acct Dir)*

Accounts:
Anheuser-Busch Inbev Alcohol, Andes Beer, Campaign: "Hagglers", Campaign: "Message in a Bottle", Campaign: "Miraculous Hen", Campaign: "Norte Photoblocker", Campaign: "The Fairest Night of All", Campaign: "The Great Escape", Norte Beer
Arcor Campaign: "Recipes in 140 Characters"
Beldent Gum Campaign: "Almost Identical"
BGH Air Conditioners, Big Noses, Campaign: "Big Steal", Campaign: "Dads in Briefs", Campaign: "Mr. Miyagi" / "Julia" / "Keanu", Campaign: "Musical Microwaves", Campaign: "My Home is an Oven", Quick Chef Music, Silent Air
Cablevision
Changyou
Coca-Cola Refreshments USA, Inc. Campaign: "The Cheering Truck", Cepita, Coke, Coke Light, Coke Zero, Fanta, Powerade, Sprite
CTI Movil
Fibertel
Flash
General Mills Ariel, La Saltena Pastas, La Saltena Tapas, Tide
Head & Shoulders
Hospital Aleman
Islazul Campaign: "Back to Happy Shopping"
Kraft Foods
Labatt USA LLC
Leica Campaign: "Leica No Instagram"
Milka
Petrobras
Playstation 3
Procter & Gamble Ariel, Gillette, Olay, Pampers, Razor, Tide
Sony Campaign: "Einstein", Campaign: "Famous Pictures", Campaign: "We're all Players", Cyber-Shot, PlayStation
Telmex: CTI
New-Toyota Aygo X-Cite, Digital, Outdoor, Print, TV
VH1 Campaign: "I Will Survive"
Volkswagen Group of America, Inc. Audi

Bermuda

AAC Saatchi & Saatchi
29 Front Street, Hamilton, HM 11 Bermuda
Mailing Address:
PO Box HM 1188, Hamilton, HM EX Bermuda
Tel.: (441) 295 2626
Fax: (441) 292 0473
E-Mail: info@aac.bm
Web Site: www.aac.bm

E-Mail for Key Personnel:
President: remmerson@aac.bm
Media Dir.: steven@aac.bm

Employees: 17
Year Founded: 1961

Agency Specializes In: Collateral, Corporate Identity, Direct Response Marketing, Event Planning & Marketing, Media Buying Services, Public Relations, Strategic Planning/Research

Peter Hebberd *(VP & Gen Mgr)*
Corinne Frith *(Sr Acct Dir)*
Donna Mingledorff *(Sr Graphic Designer)*
Peter O'Flaherty *(Sr Graphic Designer)*
Lisza Rawlins *(Sr Graphic Designer)*

Accounts:
Applied Computer Technologies
Corrado Benu Interior Design
Endurance Specialty Insurance
Furniture Flair
The Harbourmaster Fine Luggage, Leather Goods
IAC Marketing Committee RIMS Conference Coordination
International Bonded Courier
OIL Insurance
Pembroke Tile & Stone
Renaissance Re
Saltus Grammar School
Tokyo Millenium Re

Brazil

F/Nazca Saatchi & Saatchi
Av Republica do Libano, 253 Ibirapuera, Sao Paulo, 04501-000 Brazil
Tel.: (55) 11 3059 4800
Fax: (55) 11 3059 4948
E-Mail: ffernandes@fnazca.com.br
Web Site: www.fnazca.com.br

Employees: 253

Fabio Fernandes *(CEO & Dir-Creative-Brazil)*
Saulo Sanches *(Grp Acct Dir)*
Cecilia Guerriero *(Art Dir)*
Pedro Prado *(Dir-Creative & Copywriter)*
Andre Cais *(Dir-Media)*
Rodrigo Cotellessa *(Dir-Art)*
Mauricio B. De Almeida *(Dir-Media)*
Isabelle de Vooght *(Dir-Art)*
Carlos di Celio *(Dir-Creative)*
Juliana Hasegawa *(Dir-Integrated Production)*
Pedro Hefs *(Dir-Art)*
Keka Morelle *(Dir-Art)*
Ricardo Pocci *(Dir-Creative & Art)*
Jota Russo *(Dir-Tech)*
Harisson Santos *(Dir-Art)*
Rafael Cappelli *(Acct Mgr)*
Luiz Ortega *(Project Mgr-Digital-AmBev Skol)*
Andrea Almeida *(Mgr-Svc)*
Luana Gallizzi *(Mgr-Media)*
Julianna Carvalho *(Acct Supvr)*
Andre Brandao *(Copywriter)*
Leandro Dolfini *(Copywriter)*
Adriana Leite *(Copywriter)*
Andreia Nascentes *(Art Buyer)*
Jose Porto *(Planner)*
Isaac Serruya *(Copywriter)*

Accounts:
50graus
ActionAid Campaign: "Calendar"
Alpargatas Broadcast, Campaign: "Baby Carriage", Campaign: "It's Runderful", Campaign: "Signs", Campaign: "Skate", Digital, Mizuno, OOH, Point-of-Sale, Print, TV
Ambev Campaign: "Carnival Website", Campaign: "Morcegos", Campaign: "Mountain", Campaign: "Poltrona Skol Design", Campaign: "Prepare for the War", Campaign: "Roundy", Campaign: "Underwater", Skol, Skol Beats, Skol Beats Senses, Skol Beer, Skol Folia
Anheuser-Busch InBev N.V.
APABO Campaign: "Eyes Give Life"
Associacao Cultural Videobrasil Campaign: "Good Morning, Good Afternoon, Good Night"
ATL
BITC
Carrefour Campaign: "Virou.gr Package", Supermarket
CCRJ Campaign: "Rituals Teeth"
Claro
Electrolux Campaign: "Best Mother's Day present", Campaign: "Explosion", Electrolux DT52X
Fundacao SOS Mata Atlantica
Google Chrome
Honda Motor Company Campaign: "Drivemixer", Campaign: "Flipbook", Campaign: "Urban Species", Fit Twist, Honda City 2015, Honda HR-V, POS, Radio
HSBC Bank Brasil SA
Leica Gallery Sao Paulo Campaign: "100", Campaign: "Legend Leica II 1932", Campaign: "Reincarnated", Campaign: "Soul", Leica Institucional, Leica camera
Lenovo Group Limited
Mead Johnson Nutrition Company
Mondelez International, Inc.
Mondelez International
Nike 600K Challenge, Campaign: "Addictabilitation Clinic", Campaign: "Addiction", Campaign: "Before and After", Corinthians, New Jersey Launch, Republic Document Kit, Sports Retailer, Sportswear
NIS Group Co., Ltd Campaign: "Miojo Day"
Nissin Campaign: "Miojo Day Project"
NYC Ballet
O GLOBO
Operacao Sorriso Campaign: "Stay Apes"
Operation Smile
Pan-American Association of Eye Banks Campaign: "Eyes"
Petrobras Campaign: "Abduction", Oil
Pinacoteca Do Estado De Sao Paulo Campaign: "Curiosism", Campaign: "Robot Cat"
Pinacoteca of the State of Sao Paulo
Play TV Radio, Television
The Procter & Gamble Company Olay
SESC Campaign: "Good Morning, Good Afternoon, Good Night"
Skol Campaign: "Carnival Website", Campaign: "Mountain", Campaign: "Prepare for the War", Skol Beer
Sos Atlantic Forest Foundation Campaign: "Egg X Chicken", Environmental Awareness, Photography Competition
SOS Mata Atlantica Campaign: "Google Images", Campaign: "SOS Google Search"
Suplicy Coffees
T-Mobile US
Trident
Unicef
Unimed-Rio Campaign: "Life doesn't stop giving. So don't stop taking.", Campaign: "The Beach"

F/Nazca Saatchi & Saatchi
Praia de Flamengo 200 19th Floor, Rio de Janeiro, RJ 22210-030 Brazil
Tel.: (55) 21 3284 3700
Fax: (55) 21 2205 1148
Web Site: www.fnazca.com.br

Fabio Fernandes *(CEO & Dir-Creative-Brazil)*

Accounts:
LG
Revista Piaui

Honduras

Mass Nazca Saatchi & Saatchi
Colonia Palmira Avenue Republica de Venezuela 2130, 1396, Tegucigalpa, Honduras
Tel.: (504) 238 2000
Fax: (504) 2238-2100
E-Mail: fernando@mass.hn
Web Site: www.saatchi.com

Employees: 60
Year Founded: 1986

Agency Specializes In: Above-the-Line, Advertising, Advertising Specialties, Alternative Advertising, Below-the-Line, Business Publications, Co-op Advertising, Communications, Computers & Software, Consumer Marketing, Corporate Communications, Corporate Identity, Crisis Communications, Digital/Interactive, Direct-to-Consumer, Graphic Design, Hispanic Market, In-Store Advertising, Integrated Marketing, Internet/Web Design, Local Marketing, Logo & Package Design, Media Buying Services, Media Planning, Media Training, Men's Market, Multimedia, Outdoor, Package Design, Point of Purchase, Point of Sale, Production, Promotions, Public Relations, Publishing, Social Marketing/Nonprofit, Social Media, Strategic Planning/Research, Teen Market, Urban Market, Women's Market

Harold Rodriguez *(Dir-Creative)*

Accounts:
BAC Honduras; Honduras Bank & Financial Services
Bank of America Corp.
Credomatic; Honduras Credit Cards
DIMASA Ford; Honduras Ford Automobile Dealer
Jetstereo; Honduras Consumer Electronics
Motomundo; Honduras Motorcycles
Nestle; Honduras Maggi, Nido, Anchor, Nestfruta, Gerber, Nestum, Purina, Nescafe
Reckitt Benckiser; Honduras Durex Condoms;Vanish Cleaning Products
SKY; Honduras Cable TV
SONY Corp; Honduras Consumer Products
Sony
Texaco Inc.
Ultra Motors
Ultramotor; Honduras Yamaha Motorcycles and Equipment

Peru

Quorum Nazca Saatchi & Saatchi
Avenue Angamos Oeste 1218, Miraflores, Lima, 18 Peru
Tel.: (51) 1 421 2313
Fax: (51) 1 441 4893
E-Mail: rrachi@quorum1.com.pe
Web Site: www.saatchi.com

Employees: 40
Year Founded: 1984

National Agency Associations: APAP (Portugal)

Mauricio Paez *(CEO)*
Juan Durrieu *(Creative Dir)*
Rodrigo Melgar *(Creative Dir)*
Guillermo Ramos *(Dir-Art)*
Oscar Tamayo *(Dir-Creative)*
Andres Villalobos *(Dir-Art)*
Daniel Biasevich *(Copywriter)*
Alejandro Fang *(Copywriter)*
Xavier Lagos *(Copywriter)*
Daniel Saavedra *(Copywriter)*

Accounts:
Brahma
Fenix Led Flashlight
Nissan Frontier Campaign: "Just like your Frontier"
Papa John's Pizza Delivery
Procter & Gamble Ariel, Old Spice, Safeguard, Whitewater; 1999
Tatoo Adventure Gear
Telepizza Campaign: "Magnet Demo"
Transperuana Insurance Company Micro Insurance
Volunteer Firemen Company Campaign: "Living Room"

Puerto Rico

Badillo Nazca Saatchi & Saatchi
1504 Ave Franklin D Roosevelt, San Juan, PR 00920-2700
Mailing Address:
PO Box 11905 Caparra Heights Station, San Juan, PR 00922-1905
Tel.: (787) 622-1000
Fax: (787) 793-0307
E-Mail: julio.semidei@badillopr.com
Web Site: www.saatchi.com

E-Mail for Key Personnel:
President: erastof@badillo-pr.com

Employees: 25

National Agency Associations: 4A's

Agency Specializes In: Advertising, Hispanic Market

Erasto Freytes *(Pres)*
Fernando Toledo *(CFO)*
Juan Carlos Jalvo Rodriguez *(Chief Creative Officer)*
Candida Massielle Asencio *(Sr Dir-Art)*
Mariano German-Coley *(Dir-Creative)*
Ilia Marquez *(Copywriter)*

Accounts:
Bel
Claro
Diageo/Guinness
Emirates Airline
FreshMart Campaign: "Backwards", Campaign: "Jalapea'o"
General Mills
Head & Shoulders
Mead Johnson
Novartis
Ofi Arte Store
Peurto Rico United Way Campaign: "Children Against Bullets"
Procter & Gamble Campaign: "33", Olay
Puerto Rico Horror Film Fest
Staedtler / OFI Arte Store
Toyota Campaign: "Friends", Campaign: "Letter", Campaign: "Mob Guy", Rav 4, Tacoma
Whirlpool ECO-Fridge
Yaris Campaign: "Creature"

Trinidad

Lonsdale Saatchi & Saatchi
8 & 10 Herbert Street, St Clair, Port of Spain, Trinidad & Tobago
Mailing Address:
PO Box 1251, Port of Spain, Trinidad & Tobago
Tel.: (868) 622 6480
Fax: (868) 628 0210
E-Mail: info@lonsdalesaatchi.com
Web Site: www.lonsdalesaatchi.com

E-Mail for Key Personnel:
President: Kenrick@lonsaatch.com

Employees: 75
Year Founded: 1953

Agency Specializes In: Communications, Consumer Marketing, Internet/Web Design, Public Relations

Kenrick Attale *(Owner)*
Julie Harris *(Head-Creative Svcs & Dir-Strategic Plng)*
Paul Benson *(Dir-Art)*
Nicole Noel *(Dir-Art)*
Kevin Reis *(Assoc Dir-Creative)*
Gina Jardim *(Mgr-Fin Production)*
Alison Mair *(Sr Acct Exec)*
Marilyn Morrison *(Sr Graphic Designer)*
Reina Rodriguez-Cupid *(Copywriter)*

Accounts:
3M
Absolut Vodka
Blue Waters
BrydenPi
Carib Brewery
Carreras
City Motors
Hi Lo Food Stores
Kitchen Aid
LIAT
Marketing & Distribution
Nipdec
Parts World
Payless Shoe Stores
Tracmac
Whirlpool

Venezuela

AW Oveja Negra Saatchi & Saatchi
Edificio ABA 4th Fl, Las Mercedes, Caracas, Venezuela
Tel.: (58) 212 400 4430
Fax: (58) 212 400 4486
E-Mail: info@saatchi-ve.com
Web Site: www.saatchi.com

Employees: 40
Year Founded: 1976

Eduardo Chibas *(Owner)*
Gloria Chibas *(Pres)*
Lenin Perez *(Chief Creative Officer)*
Jorge Gonzalez *(Gen Mgr)*

Accounts:
Cerveceria Regional Cerveza Zulia
Digitel Telecommunications
Excelsior Gama
General Mills Venezuela Diablitos Underwood, Rica-Deli, Underwood Pasta Sauce
Kraft Foods Trident
Leones de Caracas Baseball Club
Procter & Gamble Ariel, Pampers

Indonesia

Perwanal Saatchi & Saatchi
Menara Jamsostek South Tower 22nd Fl, JL Jend Gatot Subroto Kav 38, Jakarta, 12930 Indonesia
Tel.: (62) 21 5297 1500
Fax: (62) 21 5297 1501
Web Site: www.saatchi.com

Employees: 50

Dini Makmum *(CEO-Saatchi & Saatchi Advertising)*
Alex Tagaroulias *(Exec Creative Dir)*
Eddu Enoary Eigven *(Dir-Art)*

Accounts:
AirAsia
Novartis Campaign: "Voltaren Pain Relief Gel: Equality"
Toyota Indonesia
Virgin Group Ltd

Australia

Saatchi & Saatchi Australia

70 George Street, The Rocks, Sydney, NSW 2000 Australia
Tel.: (61) 2 8264 1111
Fax: (61) 2 9235 0617
E-Mail: corrina.bartley@saatchi.com.au
Web Site: www.saatchi.com

Employees: 180

National Agency Associations: AFA

Agency Specializes In: Advertising, Brand Development & Integration, Communications, Consumer Marketing, Direct Response Marketing, E-Commerce, Internet/Web Design, Logo & Package Design, Print, Production, Retail, Sales Promotion, Sports Market, Strategic Planning/Research

Catherine Harris *(Mng Partner-Transformation)*
Alison Miegel *(CFO)*
Maria Casas *(Head-Social)*
Mike Spirkovski *(Exec Dir-Creative)*
Kate Gooden *(Sr Producer-Brdcst)*
Pierre-Antoine Gilles *(Art Dir)*
Steve Carlin *(Dir-Creative)*
Samantha Russo *(Acct Mgr-OPSM)*
Elliot Walsh *(Designer)*
Flavio Fonseca *(Sr Art Dir)*
Jess Hughes *(Grp Bus Dir)*

Accounts:
Aerius
Air Tahiti Nui
Award Advertising School Campaign: "Prepare Yourself"
Bank of Melbourne (Lead Creative Agency)
BankSA (Lead Creative Agency)
Capi Campaign: "Hard to Make. Easy to Drink", Creative
Electric Art
Emirates Airlines
Fox Sports
General Mills
Iams Dog Food
Lexus Campaign: "Brand", Campaign: "Drive By - Downtown"
Mead Johnson
Mondelez International, Inc. Cadbury, Cadbury Coco, Campaign: "Joyville", Campaign: "Marvellous Performance", Dominoes, Marvellous Creations, Sour Patch, The Natural Confectionery Company
Woolworth Campaign: "Joyville"
Monteith's Cider
NIB Creative, Online Media, Print, TV
Novartis
OPSM Campaign: "Penny The Pirate", Prescription Sun
Panasonic Campaign: "Enjoy Fresher Air", Nanoe Automotive Air Conditioning
Pitzy Folk CAPI Sparkling, Campaign: "Natural"
Procter & Gamble Olay
RSPCA Pro Bono Advertising
Service NSW
Sony Sony Alpha A-55 Camera, Sony Cyber-Shot, Sony Nex-5 Camera
St George Bank Aussies Homebuying, Campaign: "Start Something", Creative
Sydney Writers Festival
Toyota 4WD Range, Campaign: "A Great Way To Raise A Family", Campaign: "Bad in Dad", Campaign: "Calling All The Heroes", Campaign: "Eco Friendly Billboards", Campaign: "FJ Napkins", Campaign: "Unbreakable Drivers", Camry Atara, Camry RZ, Country Border Security, HiLux, Nothing Soft Gets In, TV, Toyota Prado

Team Saatchi/Saatchi & Saatchi Healthcare

70 George Street, The Rocks, Sydney, NSW 2000 Australia
Tel.: (61) 2 8264 1111
Fax: (61) 2 9235 0617
Web Site: www.saatchi.com.au

Employees: 160

Agency Specializes In: Health Care Services

Toby Aldred *(Mng Partner)*
Ben Court *(Mng Partner)*
Maria Casas *(Head-Social)*
Mike Spirkovski *(Exec Dir-Creative)*
Charmaine Andrew *(Dir-New Bus & Comm)*
Craig Chester *(Dir-Creative)*

Accounts:
Boxer Gold
Emarald
Merck Sharp & Dohme Campaign: "Topsy Turvy", Demazin
Sanofi-Aventis
Soni
Toohays New
Toyota

Greater China

Saatchi & Saatchi

36/F Central International Trade Centre Tower C, 6A Jianguomen Wai Avenue, Beijing, 100022 China
Tel.: (86) 10 6563 3600
Fax: (86) 10 6563 3601
E-Mail: charles_sampson@saatchi.com.cn
Web Site: www.saatchi.com

Agency Specializes In: Advertising

Michael Lee *(CEO-China)*
Tian It Ng *(Exec Creative Dir)*
Kevin Chiu *(Grp Dir-Creative)*
Sharrow Lam *(Dir-Creative)*
Zimo Li *(Dir-Creative)*

Accounts:
CCTV
China National Cereals, Oils & Foodstuffs Corporation Le Conte, Lolas, Merveille
China Telecom Campaign: "Row"
Greenpeace
Hewlett-Packard PC, The DV3 Movie Pro PC
Huawei Mediapad
Huiyuan
IKEA Campaign: "Big Dreams, Small Space"
Lenovo
Lexus China; 2007
Mazda ATL, BTL, CX-7, Digital, Mazda 6
Mengniu; China Ice Cream, White Milk
Novartis Campaign: "Liberty"
Rebecca Campaign: "Curly", Wigs
Sands China Creative

Saatchi & Saatchi

29 F Lippo Plaza, 222 Huai Hai Zhong Road, Shanghai, 200021 China
Tel.: (86) 21 5396 5586
Fax: (86) 21 5396 6196
E-Mail: justin.billingsley@saatchi.com.cn
Web Site: www.saatchi.com/

Irene Shum *(Mng Dir)*
Michael Lee *(CEO-China)*
Fan Ng *(Exec Dir-Creative)*
Kenny Choo *(Reg Dir-Creative-Olay & Safeguard)*
Bill Ho *(Dir-Integrated Creative)*
Chris Shi *(Dir-Creative)*
Guojing Yang *(Assoc Dir-Creative)*

Accounts:
Beijing Happy Valley
CCTV
China Alliance For Low Carbon Action Campaign: "The Wrath Of Coal"
China Mobile
Citroen DS (Creative Agency of Record)
Greenpeace Campaign: "Paper Cuts Life"
Mead Johnson
Mondelez International, Inc.
Nippon
PPTV Brand Strategy, Creative
Procter & Gamble
Robam Home Appliances Brand Strategy, Creative
Safeguard
Siemens China
Suntory China Suntory Premium Draft; 2008

Saatchi & Saatchi

2-5F Gold Sun Building 109 Ti Yu Xi Road, Guangzhou, 510620 China
Tel.: (86) 20 3879 1228
Fax: (86) 20 3879 2430
E-Mail: polly_chu@saatchi.com.cn
Web Site: www.saatchi.com

Employees: 202

Agency Specializes In: Advertising

Pully Chau *(CEO)*
Carol Lam *(Mng Partner & Chief Creative Officer)*
Fan Ng *(Exec Dir-Creative)*
Richard Tong *(Dir-Creative-Integrated Design)*

Accounts:
Amway
BBK Electronics
Beijing Happy Valley
New-ChangYou
China Mobile
Double A International
E Fund Management
Johnson & Johnson
Kerry Oils & Grains
Kingdee Group Marketing Communications Campaign, Print, TVC, Website
MeadJohnson Alacta Sustagen, Enfa
New-Ping Concert Of The Wind
Procter & Gamble Ariel, Campaign: "Chocolate Bunny", Crest, Head & Shoulders, Oil of Olay, Safeguard
Seiko

Hong Kong

Saatchi & Saatchi

27/F Tai Tung Building Fleming Road, Wanchai, China (Hong Kong)
Tel.: (852) 2 582 3333
Fax: (852) 2511 2246
Web Site: www.saatchi.com

Employees: 30
Year Founded: 1982

Paul Ho *(Grp Dir-Creative-Shopper)*
Andrea Khou *(Sr Dir-Creative)*
Ringo Fai *(Dir-Digital Plng-Saatchi & Saatchi South China)*
Steven Yip *(Sr Project Mgr-Digital)*

Accounts:
Green Peace Campaign: "Water Purifier Kid"
Ritz-Carlton

India

Saatchi & Saatchi Direct
37/6 Aga Abbas Ali Road off Ulsoor Road, Bengaluru, 560 042 India
Tel.: (91) 80 4149 9181
Fax: (91) 80 4149 9181
Web Site: www.saatchi.com

Agency Specializes In: Direct Response Marketing

Malavika Harita *(CEO)*
Chandan Mahimkar *(Chief Creative Officer-Design)*
Devraj Basu *(Sr VP & Gen Mgr)*
Priyanka Chatterjee *(VP)*
Savita Iyer *(Assoc Dir-Plng-AAIK)*
Michell Anthony *(Asst Mgr-HR)*

Accounts:
Procter & Gamble Ariel, Campaign: "Colour & Style"

Saatchi & Saatchi
Urmi Estate Tower A 15th Floor 95 Ganpatrao Kadam Marg, Lower Parel, Mumbai, 400 013 India
Tel.: (91) 22 3001 9444
Fax: (91) 22 2287 2215
Web Site: www.saatchi.com

Anil S. Nair *(CEO & Mng Partner)*
Malavika Harita *(CEO-Focus Network)*
Ashutosh Karkhanis *(Exec Creative Dir)*
Sandeep Poyekar *(Dir-Creative)*

Accounts:
Cairn
Carlsberg Creative
Eko
Exide Life Insurance Company Limited
General Mills Betty Crocker Dessert Mixes, Green Giant frozen vegetables, Haagen Dazs Ice Cream, Multigrain & Gold Atta, Nature Valley granola bars, Parampara, Pillsbury Cake Mixes, Pillsbury Chakki Fresh
HCL Campaign: "Carpet Seller", Campaign: "Change", ME Tablets
Hero Motocorp
IndiaFirst Life Insurance
Jockey
Lenovo
Mead Johnson
Novartis Otrivin Cold Tab
Pepperfry.com
Pillsbury Mass Foods Campaign: "Soft Khao, Soft Raho"
Procter & Gamble Ariel, Campaign: "Cricketer's Wife", Campaign: "Good Morning Baby", Campaign: "Precious Saree", Campaign: "Punch", Head & Shoulders, Olay, T-Shirt
Reliance
Renault India
Shamiana
Springwel Mattresses Campaign: "Sleep Exchange"
Vedanta
Vip Industries Ltd
Wave Infratech Marketing

Japan

Saatchi & Saatchi Fallon Tokyo
4-9-3 Jingumae, Shibuya-ku, Tokyo, 150-0001 Japan
Tel.: (81) 3 6438 1255
Fax: (81) 3 6438 1223
Web Site: www.ssftokyo.co.jp

Employees: 40

Naoki Ishikawa *(CFO)*
Luca Grelli *(Exec Dir-Creative)*
Maiko Itami *(Client Svcs Dir)*
Kenji Moriuchi *(Art Dir)*
Takei Yoshishige *(Creative Dir)*
Dominic Byrnes *(Dir-Digital)*
Darren Rogers *(Dir-Integrated Comm)*
Nick Ashley *(Planner)*

Accounts:
Godiva Japan
Reebok Easytone Shoes
Toot
New-Toyota Motor Campaign: "Dream Car of the Day"

Malaysia

Saatchi & Saatchi Arachnid
A-16-1 Tower A Northpoint Offices Midvalley City, 1 Medan Syed Putra Utara, 59200 Kuala Lumpur, Malaysia
Tel.: (60) 322878831
Fax: (60) 322878932
Web Site: www.arachnid.com.my

Agency Specializes In: Advertising

Weng Keong Chin *(Mng Dir)*
Chin Weng Keong *(Mng Dir)*
David Soo *(Gen Mgr)*
Gavin Teoh *(Sr Acct Dir)*
Loong Sheng Mae *(Sr Acct Mgr)*
Adeline Quek *(Sr Acct Mgr)*
Ayuni Jamal *(Acct Mgr)*
Yuet-mee Leow *(Sr Planner-Digital & Planner)*
Sue Lynn Chin *(Assoc Acct Dir)*
Sylvia Wong *(Assoc Acct Dir)*

Accounts:
Durex Malaysia 360-Degree Integrated Campaigns, Creative
PETRONAS Dagangan Berhad
Petronas Lubricants International Digital, Web

Saatchi & Saatchi
Unit 7 2 Level 7 CP Tower 11 Section 16 11, Jalan Damansara, 46350 Petaling Jaya, Malaysia
Tel.: (60) 3 7964 8000
Fax: (60) 3 7955 6131
Web Site: www.saatchi.com

Employees: 75
Year Founded: 1989

Agency Specializes In: Advertising

Adrian Sng *(Mng Dir)*
Shannon Cullum *(CEO-Singapore, Malaysia & Indonesia)*
Ian Lee *(Grp Head-Creative)*
Loong Sheng Mae *(Sr Acct Mgr)*
Sylvia Wong *(Assoc Acct Dir)*

Accounts:
Asia Pacific Breweries Tiger Beer
Bank Simpanan Nasional
CPW Nestle
Guinness
KDU
Paramount Corporation Berhad
Penguin Books
Procter & Gamble Safeguard Antibacterial Soap
UMW-Toyota

Mauritius

P&P Link Saatchi & Saatchi
D Seetulsingh St, Port Louis, Mauritius
Tel.: (230) 211 4429
Fax: (230) 211 4428
E-Mail: pnplink@intnet.mu
Web Site: www.saatchi.com

Employees: 20

Agency Specializes In: Advertising

Pria Thacoor *(Owner)*

Accounts:
Fortis Clinique Darne
Unicorn

New Zealand

Saatchi & Saatchi
Level 3 123-125 The Strand Parnell, Auckland, 1010 New Zealand
Mailing Address:
PO Box 801, Auckland, 1140 New Zealand
Tel.: (64) 9 3555 000
Fax: (64) 9 3796 149
Web Site: www.saatchi.com

Employees: 100
Year Founded: 1984

National Agency Associations: IAA

Agency Specializes In: Advertising

Nicola Bell *(CEO)*
George Mackenzie *(Mng Dir)*
Matt Sellars *(Grp Head-Creative)*
Watchara Tansrikeat *(Sr Dir-Art)*
Rachael Williams *(Sr Acct Dir)*
Emily Drake *(Art Dir)*
Katja Green *(Acct Dir)*
Jason Kennedy *(Acct Dir)*
Terry Williams-Willcock *(Creative Dir-Digital)*
Paul Wilson *(Bus Dir)*
Brad Collett *(Dir-Art)*
Slade Gill *(Dir-Creative-New Zealand)*
Amya Karaitiana *(Dir-Art)*
Murray Streets *(Dir-Strategy)*
Amanda Brittain *(Sr Acct Mgr)*
Janisa Parag *(Sr Strategist-Brand)*
Nic Turner *(Acct Exec)*
Ross Davis *(Designer)*
Rob Flynn *(Designer)*
Chris Leskovsek *(Designer)*
Dave Sylvester *(Copywriter)*

Accounts:
ASB Bank 1000km Tennis Court, Campaign: "Robot", Campaign: "Succeed On"
New-Atamira Dance Company
Breast Cancer Research Trust
Coca-Cola Amatil Baker Halls, Campaign: "Grab Life by the Bottle", Deep Spring, L&P, Pump
DB Breweries Amstel, Campaign: "TUI 11-11-11", Heineken, Monteith's, SOL Beer, Tiger Beer; 2007
Tui Brewery Limited Campaign: "Always Something Brewing", Campaign: "Catch A Million", Campaign: "Half Time Distractions", Campaign: "TUI - Planking", TUI Cricket Box
L&P Sour Campaign : "Hold onto Summer"
Light 'n' Tasty
New Zealand Defence Force - NZ Navy
NZ Electoral Commission
Procter and Gamble
Rodney District Council
Royal New Zealand Air Force Campaign: "NZ Air Force - Step Up", Step Up
Sanitarium Health Food Company Campaign: "Dream Day"
Sealord Group Limited Campaign: "Smoked salmon billboard", Campaign: "Smoked: Just Like Our New Manuka Salmon"
Telecom Mobile
Telecom New Zealand Campaign: "Telecom Prepaid 'Snap'", Campaign: "Waiting is Over", Ultra Mobile
Toyota Campaign: "Call of the Wild", Campaign:

"FJ Cruiser - Top to Bottom", Campaign: "FJ Top to Bottom", Campaign: "Feels Good Inside", Campaign: "Hilux - Roadkill", Campaign: "Hilux - Tougher Than You Can Imagine", Campaign: "Impossibly Tough", Camry, Corolla, Tougher Than You Can Imagine, iQ
Tui Beer Campaign: "Catch A Million"
Unilever Campaign: "Don't freak. It'll be back", Marmite
Women's Refuge Campaign: "An Auction to Remember", Campaign: "Valentine's Day"

Saatchi & Saatchi
101-103 Courtenay Pl, Te Aro, Wellington, 6011 New Zealand
Mailing Address:
PO Box 6540, Wellington, New Zealand
Tel.: (64) 4 385 6524
Fax: (64) 4 385 9678
E-Mail: toby.talbot@saatchi.com
Web Site: www.saatchi.com

Employees: 22

Agency Specializes In: Advertising

Corey Chalmers *(Exec Dir-Creative-New Zealand)*
Derek Lockwood *(Dir-Design-Worldwide)*
Jordan Sky *(Dir-Creative)*

Accounts:
New-ASB Bank
DB Breweries Heineken, Tui
Toyota
Wellington Zoo

Philippines

Ace Saatchi & Saatchi
Saatchi House 2296 Don Chino Roces Avenue Parso Tamo Extension, Kayamanan C, Makati, Philippines
Tel.: (63) 2 857 4900
Fax: (63) 2 814 2100
E-Mail: rey_icasas@acesaatchi.com.ph
Web Site: www.acesaatchi.com.ph

Employees: 160
Year Founded: 1949

Agency Specializes In: Advertising

Mio Chongson *(COO)*
Gigi Garcia *(VP & Client Svcs Dir)*
Andrew Petch *(Exec Dir-Creative)*
Vino Yanuario *(Art Dir)*
Angeline Manahan *(Acct Mgr)*
Barbara Escueta *(Acct Supvr)*

Accounts:
2211 Works
Cebuana Lhuillier
Eagle Cement Campaign: "Construction Reinforcements"
Kraft Cadbury Philippines Campaign: "Sing for Joy", Campaign: "Tiger Energy Playground", Tiger Biscuits
Lucerne Campaign: "Newspaper Wristwatch"
Mead Johnson Nutrition
The North Face
Pampers Diapers Campaign: "ZZZ Radio"
PJ Lhuillier Campaign: "Sisters Remeet"
PLDT Gabay Guro Campaign: "Anna Banana", Surveillance Camera
Procter & Gamble #FlakerDate, Antibacterial Soap, Ariel Detergent, Campaign: "Fashion Laundry", Campaign: "ZZZ Radio - Pampers", Head & Shoulders, Olay Campaign: "Reverse Ageing Compacts", Safeguard Soap, Soap
Toyota Anti Drink Driving, Campaign: "Text ECG", Land Cruiser
Vespa

Singapore

Saatchi & Saatchi Asia Pacific
3D River Valley Road #03-01, Clarke Quay, 179023 Singapore, Singapore
Tel.: (65) 6339 4733
Fax: (65) 6339 3916
Web Site: www.saatchi.com

Agency Specializes In: Recruitment

Steve Walls *(Head-Plng-Singapore)*
Celevel Ranoco-Butler *(Gen Mgr)*
Dominic Stallard *(Chief Creative Dir & Exec Creative Dir)*
Anthony Tham *(Exec Dir-Creative)*
Bobee Chua *(Acct Dir)*
Paul Copeland *(Creative Dir)*
Kimmy De Leon *(Art Dir)*
Evelyn Tan *(Acct Dir)*
Tania Neubronner *(Acct Mgr)*
Andrea Cid *(Copywriter)*
Stephanie Gwee *(Copywriter)*
Arvid Lithander *(Copywriter)*
Mariuze Jino Moreto *(Copywriter)*

Accounts:
Acer Global Creative
Doctor's Associates, Inc.
Lenovo
Lexus
Pampers Worldwide Digital
The Procter & Gamble Company
Singapore Airlines Creative, Scoot
The World Toilet Organization Campaign: "Brown Friday"

Thailand

Saatchi & Saatchi
25/F Sathorn City Tower 175 S Sathorn Rd Khwaeng Thungmahamek, Khet Sathorn, Bangkok, 10120 Thailand
Tel.: (66) 2 640 4700
Fax: (66) 2 679 5210
E-Mail: oranat_asanasen@saatchith.com
Web Site: www.saatchi.com

Employees: 80
Year Founded: 1988

Mark Cochrane *(CEO)*
Golf Nuntawat Chaipornkaew *(Exec Dir-Creative-Thailand)*
Shayne Chomchinda *(Art Dir)*
Bongkoch Khunvithaya *(Acct Dir)*
Graham Painter *(Creative Dir)*
Chotika Parinnayok *(Art Dir)*
Papop Chaowanapreechana *(Copywriter)*
Orathai Maneechot *(Planner)*
Tanongsak Tannoprat *(Copywriter)*

Accounts:
AJE Group Big Cola, Campaign: "Think Big", Global Brand Campaign
Electrolux Campaign: "Power"
Energy Policy & Planning Office Energy Saving; 2008
Garena Campaign: "I Am the One", Campaign: "Messi's Arrival", Content, FIFA Online 3, Website
New-GrabTaxi Campaign: "Super Easy Life"
Huawei Technologies Co., Ltd. Honor 3C, Marketing
Mead Johnson
Ocean Life Insurance
PTT Retail Management Creative, Jiffy Stores, Jiffy Super Fresh Markets, Pearly Tea
Syn Mun Kong Car Insurance
Thanachart Bank Creative, Digital, In-Store, Outdoor, Print, Social Media, TV
Virgin Active

SAATCHI & SAATCHI WELLNESS
375 Hudson St 13th Fl, New York, NY 10014
Tel.: (212) 463-3400
Web Site: www.saatchiwellness.com

National Agency Associations: 4A's

Agency Specializes In: Brand Development & Integration, Communications, Local Marketing, Sponsorship, Web (Banner Ads, Pop-ups, etc.)

Kathy Delaney *(Chief Creative Officer)*
Michelle Kelly *(Sr VP & Grp Acct Dir)*
Tina McDonald *(Sr VP & Grp Acct Dir)*
Steve Pytko *(Sr VP & Dir-Brdcst Production)*
Jason Levy *(Sr VP-Experience Strategy & Innovation)*
Teri Fitzpatrick *(VP & Acct Dir)*
Olena Kushch *(VP & Acct Dir)*
Carolyn Gargano *(VP & Assoc Dir-Creative)*
Bob Buzas *(Dir-Art)*
Harry Dorrington *(Dir-Creative)*
Carol Fiorino *(Dir-Creative)*
Erica Martinez *(Dir-Plng)*
Angela Dawson *(Acct Supvr)*
Ed Grasso *(Strategist-Engagement)*
Oliver Adriance *(Copywriter)*
Beth Mart *(Copywriter)*
Chelsea Resnick *(Acct Coord)*

Accounts:
Abbott Laboratories Humira
Allegra
New-Allergan
Ambien CR
Amitiza
AstraZeneca
Coalition to Stop Gun Violence Advertising
Crossroads Campaign: "Street Fare"
Eli Lilly
Frontline
NexGard Chewables
Nexium
NuvaRing
Plavix
Transitions
Viramune

SABA AGENCY
(d/b/a Creative Concepts)
(Private-Parent-Single Location)
5329 Office Ctr Ct Ste 220, Bakersfield, CA 93309
Tel.: (661) 326-0393
Fax: (661) 326-0398
Toll Free: (877) 742-8023
Web Site: www.sabaagency.com

Employees: 12
Year Founded: 1989

Agency Specializes In: Advertising, Internet/Web Design, Logo & Package Design, Print

Revenue: $1,400,000

Tom Saba *(Pres & CFO-Ops)*
Cathy Berthiaume *(Dir-Creative Svcs)*
Charlie Mckay *(Mgr-Social Media & Graphic Designer)*
Jeri Merlo *(Mgr-Sls)*
Tom Thompson *(Sr Acct Exec)*
Debbe Haley *(Acct Exec)*
Ian Perry *(Acct Exec)*

Accounts:
Commute Kern

SABRE MARKETING (EAST) LLC

90 S Newtown St Rd Ste 10, Newtown Square, PA 19073
Tel.: (610) 353-5611
Fax: (610) 353-5614
E-Mail: info@sabreonline.com
Web Site: www.sabreonline.com

Employees: 5

Agency Specializes In: Advertising, Health Care Services

Grant Rowe *(Pres-Sabre Marketing Services)*

Accounts:
Campbell's
Pepperidge Farm
V8

SACHS MEDIA GROUP
114 S Duval St, Tallahassee, FL 32301
Tel.: (850) 222-1996
Fax: (850) 224-2882
E-Mail: contact@sachsmedia.com
Web Site: sachsmedia.com

Employees: 20
Year Founded: 1996

National Agency Associations: COPF

Agency Specializes In: Advertising, Digital/Interactive, Government/Political, Local Marketing, Media Relations, Public Relations, Social Marketing/Nonprofit, Web (Banner Ads, Pop-ups, etc.)

Revenue: $1,900,000

Ronald L. Sachs *(Owner)*
Michelle Lagos Ubben *(Partner, COO & Dir-Campaigns & Branding)*
Ryan Banfill *(Partner & Sr VP)*
Vicki Johnson *(Sr VP)*
Ryan Cohn *(VP-Social & Digital Ops)*
Lisa Garcia *(VP-Ops & Campaigns)*
Jon Peck *(VP-PR)*
Erin Pace *(Dir-Design)*
Beth Watson *(Sr Acct Mgr)*
Marilyn Siets *(Deputy Sr Mgr-Fin)*
Herbie Thiele *(Deputy Dir-Pub Affairs)*

Accounts:
Amateur Athletic Union Crisis Communications, PR
Automated Healthcare Solutions
Bing Energy, Inc.; Tallahassee, FL (Agency of Record)
Florida Department of Veterans' Affairs Logo, Mobile Application, Outreach Campaign, Radio, Rebranding, Social Media Campaign, Website
National Hurricane Center Campaign: "Get Ready, America!"
National League of Cities
National Safe Driving Initiative Campaign: "Drive for Life"
National Solar Power; Melbourne, FL (Agency of Record)
Nestle Waters of North America
Nopetro; Tallahassee, FL (Agency of Record)

SACRED COW
2525 S Lamar Blvd Ste 5, Austin, TX 78704
Tel.: (512) 289-5522
Web Site: www.sacredcowadvertising.com

Agency Specializes In: Advertising

Rich Tlapek *(Grp Dir-Creative)*

Accounts:
CBS Sports
The Charles Schwab Corporation
Deere & Company
Nissan North America, Inc.
Pier 1 Imports, Inc.
Sony Corporation PlayStation
Toyota Motor North America, Inc.
United HealthCare Services, Inc.

SACUNAS
(Formerly Sacunas, Inc.)
835 Sir Thomas Ct, Harrisburg, PA 17109
Tel.: (717) 652-0100
E-Mail: info@sacunas.net
Web Site: www.sacunas.net

E-Mail for Key Personnel:
President: nsacunas@sacunas.net
Creative Dir.: dbarbush@sacunas.net

Employees: 12
Year Founded: 1990

National Agency Associations: AMA-PRSA

Agency Specializes In: Brand Development & Integration, Business-To-Business, Collateral, Communications, Corporate Communications, Corporate Identity, Electronic Media, Email, Engineering, Graphic Design, Health Care Services, Identity Marketing, Industrial, Integrated Marketing, Market Research, Newspapers & Magazines, Public Relations, Strategic Planning/Research, Transportation

Nancy H. Sacunas *(Pres & CEO)*
DeAnna Halewski *(VP)*
Todd Scott *(Dir-PR Svcs)*
Julia Mosemann *(Copywriter-Digital)*

Accounts:
AudaExplore Insurance Industry Data Services; 2014
CoventryCares from Health America Health Insurance; 2012
Lane Corrugated & Plastic Steel Pipe; 2011
Michael Baker International Engineering Services; 2011
PennDOT Transportation Services; 2000
TE Connectivity - AD&M Division Electronics; 2009
TE Connectivity - Industrial Division Electronics; 2012
URS Commuter Services; 2010

SAESHE ADVERTISING
1055 W Seventh St Ste 2150, Los Angeles, CA 90017-2577
Tel.: (213) 683-2100
Fax: (213) 683-2103
E-Mail: info@saeshe.com
Web Site: www.saeshe.com

E-Mail for Key Personnel:
President: lkwon@saeshe.com

Employees: 20
Year Founded: 1992

Agency Specializes In: Advertising, Advertising Specialties, Asian Market, Bilingual Market, Brand Development & Integration, Business Publications, Business-To-Business, Cable T.V., Children's Market, Co-op Advertising, Collateral, Commercial Photography, Communications, Consulting, Consumer Marketing, Consumer Publications, Digital/Interactive, Direct Response Marketing, E-Commerce, Education, Electronic Media, Engineering, Entertainment, Event Planning & Marketing, Exhibit/Trade Shows, Food Service, Government/Political, Graphic Design, Health Care Services, Industrial, Internet/Web Design, Magazines, Media Buying Services, Multimedia, Newspaper, Newspapers & Magazines, Out-of-Home Media, Outdoor, Planning & Consultation, Print, Production, Public Relations, Publicity/Promotions, Radio, Sales Promotion, Seniors' Market, Sports Market, Strategic Planning/Research, T.V., Technical Advertising, Teen Market, Telemarketing, Trade & Consumer Magazines, Travel & Tourism, Yellow Pages Advertising

Approx. Annual Billings: $6,000,000

Lawrence Kwon *(Pres)*
Kiyoshi Morihara *(VP)*
Roy Seow *(Dir-Creative)*
Lauren Halley *(Acct Exec)*
Tess Tan *(Media Planner & Media Buyer)*
Diego A. Chavez *(Acct Coord-PR)*
Annie Hui *(Acct Coord)*
Jade Kelley *(Acct Coord)*

Accounts:
Allianz Life Insurance
Blue Cross of California
CalRecycle Campaign: "Check Your Number"
Los Angeles County Dept. of Health Services
Los Angeles World Airports
Macy's
Malaysia Tourism Board
Netscreen
Thai Airways International; El Segundo, CA; 1994
US Bank

SAGE COMMUNICATIONS
1651 Old Meadow Rd Ste 500, McLean, VA 22102-4321
Tel.: (703) 748-0300
Fax: (703) 564-0101
E-Mail: info@aboutsage.com
Web Site: www.aboutsage.com

Employees: 35

Revenue: $5,000,000

David Gorodetski *(Co-Founder, COO & Exec Dir-Creative)*
Larry Rosenfeld *(CEO)*
Pava Cohen *(Pres-Govt Grp)*
Mike Shaughnessy *(Sr VP & Client Svcs Dir)*
Robert Derby *(Sr VP)*
Catherine Melquist *(Sr VP-Satellite Div)*
Karen O'Shaughnessy *(VP & Dir-Media)*
Bayard Brewin *(VP-Strategic Svcs)*
Duyen Truong *(VP-PR)*
Scott Greenberg *(Dir-Mktg)*
Brian Kelley *(Dir-PR Group)*

Accounts:
Accelera Solutions
Alarm.com
American Systems
AT&T Communications Corp.
DC Jazz Festival
Discover.com
Dynamics Research Corporation
Federal Trade Commission
H3 Solutions Marketing Strategy, Media Relations, Messaging, PR, Social Media
LaserLock Technologies Integrated Marketing, Public Relations
ManTech International
The National Cherry Blossom Festival
National Institutes of Health
St. Jude Research Hospital
Talent Curve Brand Awareness, Social Media

Branches

Brotman Winter Fried Communications
1651 Old Meadow Rd Ste 500, McLean, VA 22102
(See Separate Listing)

Longbottom Communications
2343 N. Vernon St, Arlington, VA 22207

Tel.: (703) 528-5490
E-Mail: penelope@aboutlongbottom.com
Web Site: longbottomcommunications.com

Agency Specializes In: Brand Development & Integration, Collateral, Communications, Corporate Communications, Corporate Identity, Event Planning & Marketing, Internet/Web Design, Magazines, Media Relations, Newspaper, Newspapers & Magazines, Social Media, Web (Banner Ads, Pop-ups, etc.)

Penelope Longbottom, *(Pres)*
Patrick Boyle *(Mng Partner)*
Steven Sands *(Assoc Dir-Creative)*
Jennifer Hoil *(Acct Mgr)*

SAGE COMMUNICATIONS PARTNERS, LLP.

1500 John F Kennedy Blvd, Philadelphia, PA 19102
Tel.: (215) 209-3037
Fax: (215) 209-3078
Web Site: www.sage-communications.com

Agency Specializes In: Social Marketing/Nonprofit

Sharon Gallagher *(Co-Founder & Partner)*
Barbara Beck *(Principal)*
Bridget Kulik *(Sr Strategist-Comm)*

Accounts:
Commerce Bank
The John Templeton Foundation
The National Philanthropic Trust

SAGE ISLAND

1638 Military Cutoff Rd, Wilmington, NC 28403
Tel.: (910) 509-7475
Fax: (910) 509-3181
Web Site: www.sageisland.com

Agency Specializes In: Advertising, Collateral, Email, Graphic Design, Internet/Web Design, Logo & Package Design, Print, Search Engine Optimization, Social Media

Mike Duncan *(CEO & Dir-Creative)*
Mike Kujawski *(CTO & VP)*
Donnie Bullers *(Controller)*
Kim Lannou *(Production Mgr)*

Accounts:
Dolphin Shores
Fundamentec
Landfall Realty
PolyQuest
SnowSports Industries America
The Surfboard Warehouse
Warehouse Skateboards
Wilmington Dermatology Center

SAGEFROG MARKETING GROUP, LLC

62 E Oakland Ave, Doylestown, PA 18901
Tel.: (215) 230-9024
Fax: (215) 230-9039
E-Mail: info@sagefrog.com
Web Site: www.sagefrog.com

Agency Specializes In: Advertising, Brand Development & Integration, Collateral, Consulting, Direct Response Marketing, Event Planning & Marketing, Exhibit/Trade Shows, Identity Marketing, Internet/Web Design, Local Marketing, Public Relations, Sales Promotion, Search Engine Optimization, Strategic Planning/Research

Suzanne Morris *(Mng Partner & Head-Creative)*
Mark Schmukler *(Mng Partner)*
Margretta Feuer *(Mgr-PR & Sr Acct Exec)*
Katie Schmidt *(Mgr-Online Mktg)*
Jennifer Buchholz *(Sr Acct Exec)*
Menden Kalan *(Sr Acct Exec)*
Jennifer Peters *(Sr Acct Exec)*
Kevin Schluth *(Acct Exec)*

Accounts:
Amphibian Ark
Bristol-Myers Squibb
Cornerstone Dental Labs
Dermavviduals USA
Healogix
Novo Nordisk
Particle Sciences Discovery
Penn Pharma Americas; South Wales, UK (Agency of Record)
Penn Pharma CDMO
Pine Run Health Center

SAGEPATH INC.

3475 Piedmont Rd NE Ste 1525, Atlanta, GA 30305
Tel.: (404) 926-0078
Fax: (404) 631-6407
E-Mail: contact@sagepath.com
Web Site: www.sagepath.com

Year Founded: 1999

Agency Specializes In: Advertising, Media Relations, Mobile Marketing, Social Media

Stan Thompson *(VP-Ops)*
Eva Taylor *(Acct Dir)*
Paul Tilbian *(Acct Dir)*
Paul Abrelat *(Dir-Digital Solutions)*
Patrick Aguilar *(Dir-User Experience)*
Gregory Clark *(Sr Designer)*
Jessica Respass *(Sr Project Manager)*

Accounts:
The Home Depot, Inc.
RaceTrac Petroleum, Inc.
The World of Coca-Cola

SAGMEISTER & WALSH

206 W 23rd St 4th Fl, New York, NY 10011
Tel.: (212) 647-1789
Fax: (212) 647-1788
E-Mail: info@sagmeister.com
Web Site: www.sagmeisterwalsh.com/

Agency Specializes In: Advertising, Graphic Design

Jessica Walsh *(Partner)*
Stefan Sagmeister *(Designer)*
Pedro Sanches *(Designer)*
Zipeng Zhu *(Designer)*

Accounts:
EDP Renovaveis S.A.
Frooti
Institute of Contemporary Art in Philadelphia Campaign: "Now is better"
Parle Agro

SAHARA COMMUNICATIONS, INC.

1607 Saint Paul St, Baltimore, MD 21202
Tel.: (410) 576-7245
Fax: (410) 547-8322
E-Mail: info@saharainc.net
Web Site: www.saharainc.net

Year Founded: 2002

Agency Specializes In: Advertising, E-Commerce, Email, Internet/Web Design, Public Relations

Sandy Harley *(Pres & CEO)*

Accounts:
The Journey Home

SAHLMAN WILLIAMS, INC.

(Name Changed to At The Table Public Relations)

SAIBOT MEDIA INC.

(Formerly Saibot Technologies Inc.)
5455 N Federal Hwy, Boca Raton, FL 33487
Tel.: (877) 724-2686
Toll Free: (877) 724-2686
E-Mail: adam@saibotny.com
Web Site: www.saibotmedia.com

Employees: 12
Year Founded: 1999

Agency Specializes In: Advertising, Advertising Specialties, Affiliate Marketing, Affluent Market, Alternative Advertising, Arts, Automotive, Brand Development & Integration, Business-To-Business, College, Commercial Photography, Computers & Software, Consulting, Consumer Goods, Consumer Marketing, Content, Corporate Communications, Corporate Identity, Cosmetics, Customer Relationship Management, Digital/Interactive, Direct-to-Consumer, E-Commerce, Education, Electronic Media, Electronics, Email, Engineering, Entertainment, Environmental, Fashion/Apparel, Financial, Food Service, Government/Political, Health Care Services, Hospitality, Household Goods, Identity Marketing, Industrial, Integrated Marketing, Internet/Web Design, Legal Services, Leisure, Local Marketing, Luxury Products, Marine, Market Research, Media Buying Services, Media Planning, Media Relations, Media Training, Medical Products, Men's Market, Mobile Marketing, New Product Development, New Technologies, Over-50 Market, Paid Searches, Pets , Pharmaceutical, Planning & Consultation, Public Relations, RSS (Really Simple Syndication), Real Estate, Regional, Restaurant, Retail, Search Engine Optimization, Social Media, Strategic Planning/Research, Syndication, Technical Advertising, Transportation, Travel & Tourism, Tween Market, Urban Market, Viral/Buzz/Word of Mouth, Women's Market, Yellow Pages Advertising

Breakdown of Gross Billings by Media: Internet Adv.: 70%; Worldwide Web Sites: 30%

Adam Furman *(Pres & CEO)*

Accounts:
AtakTrucking.com; NJ Construction Materials; 2007
DiamondBladeDealer.com; NY Concrete Blades, Core Bits, Diamond Blades; 2007
WhichDraft; Montclair, NJ; 2009

SAIBOT TECHNOLOGIES INC.

(Name Changed to Saibot Media Inc.)

SAINT BERNADINE MISSION COMMUNICATIONS INC

228 E Georgia Main Fl, Vancouver, British Columbia V6A 1Z7 Canada
Tel.: (604) 646-0001
E-Mail: info@stbernadine.com
Web Site: www.stbernadine.com

Year Founded: 2004

Agency Specializes In: Advertising, Broadcast, Corporate Identity, Digital/Interactive, Graphic Design, Internet/Web Design, Package Design, Strategic Planning/Research

Mike Krafczyk *(Partner)*
Andrew Samuel *(Partner)*
David Walker *(Partner)*
Patricia Janecek *(Acct Mgr)*

Accounts:
Cori Creed
Famoso

SAINT-JACQUES VALLEE TACTIK
1600 boul Rene-Levesque W 10th Fl, Montreal, QC H3H 1P9 Canada
Tel.: (514) 935-6375
Fax: (514) 935-9479
E-Mail: info.svyr@svyr.ca
Web Site: www.svyr.ca

E-Mail for Key Personnel:
President: louis-eric_vallee@svyr.ca

Employees: 50
Year Founded: 1934

Agency Specializes In: Advertising

Pierre Nolin *(VP & Dir-Creative)*
Guy Bastien *(VP-Fin & Admin)*
Elyse Boulet *(VP-Acct Svcs)*
Ariane-Andree Beaudet *(Dir-Consulting Grp)*

Accounts:
Colgate Palmolive; 1993
Le Club des Petits Dejeuners du Quebec; 1996
LG Electronics
Loto Quebec Campaign: "Anamorphosis"
Molson Canada; 2000
Reno Depto

SALES DEVELOPMENT ASSOCIATES, INC.
7850 Manchester Rd, Saint Louis, MO 63143-2710
Tel.: (314) 862-8828
Fax: (314) 862-8829
Toll Free: (800) 462-6866
E-Mail: patb@sdastl.com
Web Site: www.sdastl.com

Employees: 14
Year Founded: 1989

Agency Specializes In: Advertising, Business-To-Business, Direct Response Marketing, Telemarketing

Patricia Biggerstaff *(Pres)*
Jennifer Balossi *(Acct Mgr)*
Melissa Chambers *(Acct Exec)*

Accounts:
ISK BioTech; Memphis, TN; 1990
Varco Pruden Buildings, Inc.; Memphis, TN; 1998

SALLY JOHNS DESIGN
1040 Washington St, Raleigh, NC 27605
Tel.: (919) 828-3997
Fax: (919) 828-4999
Toll Free: (866) 501-7957
Web Site: https://www.sallyjohnsdesign.com/

Agency Specializes In: Advertising, Brand Development & Integration, Broadcast, Digital/Interactive, Graphic Design, Internet/Web Design, Media Planning, Print, Public Relations, Strategic Planning/Research

Sally Johns *(Creative Dir & Acct Mgr)*

Accounts:
Rex Healthcare Foundation

SALTWORKS
PO Box 522023, Salt Lake City, UT 84152
Tel.: (801) 879-4928
Web Site: www.saltworksdigital.com

Year Founded: 2004

Agency Specializes In: Advertising, Brand Development & Integration, Content, Digital/Interactive, Graphic Design, Internet/Web Design, Print, Radio, Search Engine Optimization, Social Media

Doug Burton *(Co-Founder & Exec Creative Dir)*
Sheila Burton *(Co-Founder & Dir-Bus Dev)*
Michael Landon *(Dir-Tech)*

Accounts:
Granger School of Music

SAM BROWN INC.
7 Maplewood Dr, Newtown Square, PA 19073
Tel.: (610) 353-4545
Fax: (610) 353-5462
E-Mail: laura@sambrown.com
Web Site: www.sambrown.com

Employees: 15

Agency Specializes In: Advertising, Pharmaceutical

Laura M. Liotta *(Pres)*
Darrel Kachan *(Sr Writer)*
Jamie Lacey-Moreira *(Team Head-Corp Biotech)*
Michele Parisi *(Team Head-West Coast)*
Kristin Paulina *(Team Head-Healthcare Svcs)*

Accounts:
Ascenta Therapeutics
Ception
EnteroMedics Inc
GlaxoSmithKline
MEDA
Together RX Access

SAMANTHA SLAVEN PUBLICITY
8285 W Sunset Blvd 10, West Hollywood, CA 90046-2419
Tel.: (323) 650-5155
Fax: (323) 927-1738
E-Mail: samantha@samanthaslaven.com
Web Site: www.samanthaslaven.com

Employees: 2

Agency Specializes In: Brand Development & Integration, Fashion/Apparel, Media Relations, Product Placement, Production, Public Relations, Strategic Planning/Research

Samantha Slaven *(Owner)*

Accounts:
ABS by Allen Schwartz watches
Tsubo Footwear Designers

SAMBA ROCK
90 SW 3rd St, Miami, FL 33130
Tel.: (858) 480-7625
Web Site: www.sambarock.co

Employees: 2
Year Founded: 2015

Agency Specializes In: Above-the-Line, Advertising, Advertising Specialties, Affluent Market, Agriculture, Alternative Advertising, Arts, Automotive, Aviation & Aerospace, Below-the-Line, Bilingual Market, Brand Development & Integration, Branded Entertainment, Business-To-Business, Children's Market, Collateral, College, Commercial Photography, Communications, Computers & Software, Consulting, Consumer Goods, Consumer Marketing, Consumer Publications, Content, Corporate Communications, Corporate Identity, Cosmetics, Custom Publishing, Customer Relationship Management, Digital/Interactive, Direct Response Marketing, Direct-to-Consumer, E-Commerce, Education, Electronic Media, Electronics, Email, Engineering, Entertainment, Environmental, Experience Design, Fashion/Apparel, Financial, Game Integration, Government/Political, Graphic Design, Guerilla Marketing, Health Care Services, High Technology, Hispanic Market, Hospitality, Household Goods, Identity Marketing, In-Store Advertising, Industrial, Infomercials, Integrated Marketing, International, Internet/Web Design, Investor Relations, Legal Services, Leisure, Local Marketing, Logo & Package Design, Magazines, Marine, Market Research, Media Buying Services, Media Planning, Medical Products, Men's Market, Merchandising, Mobile Marketing, Multicultural, Multimedia, New Product Development, New Technologies, Newspaper, Newspapers & Magazines, Out-of-Home Media, Outdoor, Over-50 Market, Package Design, Paid Searches, Pharmaceutical, Planning & Consultation, Point of Purchase, Point of Sale, Print, Production, Production (Ad, Film, Broadcast), Production (Print), Publishing, Real Estate, Recruitment, Regional, Restaurant, Retail, Sales Promotion, Search Engine Optimization, Seniors' Market, Shopper Marketing, Social Marketing/Nonprofit, Sports Market, Stakeholders, Strategic Planning/Research, T.V., Technical Advertising, Teen Market, Trade & Consumer Magazines, Transportation, Travel & Tourism, Tween Market, Urban Market, Viral/Buzz/Word of Mouth, Web (Banner Ads, Pop-ups, etc.), Women's Market

Valter Klug *(Founder & Creative Director)*

Accounts:
The Little Chalet Restaurant; 2015
Medical App; 2015

SAMPSON/CARNEGIE, CO., INC.
1419 E. 40th St, Cleveland, OH 44103
Tel.: (216) 881-2556
Fax: (216) 881-5252
Toll Free: (800) 277-5301
Web Site: www.sampsoncarnegie.com/

Employees: 6
Year Founded: 1992

National Agency Associations: AAF-MCAN

Agency Specializes In: Advertising, Affluent Market, Alternative Advertising, Brand Development & Integration, Broadcast, Business-To-Business, Cable T.V., Collateral, Consulting, Consumer Marketing, Content, Corporate Communications, Corporate Identity, Crisis Communications, Digital/Interactive, E-Commerce, Electronic Media, Email, Engineering, Entertainment, Food Service, Graphic Design, High Technology, Identity Marketing, Internet/Web Design, Local Marketing, Logo & Package Design, Magazines, Media Buying Services, Media Planning, Multimedia, New Product Development, Newspaper, Newspapers & Magazines, Outdoor, Over-50 Market, Point of Sale, Print, Production, Public Relations, Publicity/Promotions, Radio, Real Estate, Regional, Restaurant, Retail, Sales Promotion, Search Engine Optimization, Seniors' Market, Strategic Planning/Research, T.V., Trade & Consumer Magazines, Viral/Buzz/Word of Mouth

Approx. Annual Billings: $1,560,000

Breakdown of Gross Billings by Media: Audio/Visual: 20%; Bus. Publs.: 17%; Cable T.V.: 29%; Fees: 14%; Spot T.V.: 20%

Peter Sampson *(Pres & Dir-Creative)*
Bailey Williams *(Strategist-Digital)*

Accounts:
Austin's Restaurants; Cleveland, OH Custom Concept Restaurants; 2000
Bacon Veneer Company Wood Veneer Manufacturing; 1994
Busch Funeral & Cremation Services Funeral & Cremation Services; 1992
Don's Lighthouse Grille Custom Concept Restaurant; 1992
Don's Pomeroy House Custom Concept Restaurant; 1992
Don's Restaurants
Eby's Evergreen Plantation Christmas Tree Farm; 1997
Rimkus Consulting Group Engineering & Consulting; 2001
Smith & Bull, LLC; Akron, OH Racing Gear; 2008

SAN DIEGO MEDIA CONNECTIONS

10755 Scripps Poway Pkwy, San Diego, CA 92131
Tel.: (858) 832-1470
Fax: (858) 759-7075
E-Mail: bob@sdmediaconnections.com
Web Site: www.sandiegomediaconnections.com

Employees: 2
Year Founded: 2004

Agency Specializes In: Advertising, Broadcast, Cable T.V., Co-op Advertising, Consulting, Direct Response Marketing, Electronic Media, Entertainment, Health Care Services, Hispanic Market, In-Store Advertising, Local Marketing, Market Research, Media Buying Services, Media Planning, Media Relations, Mobile Marketing, Newspaper, Newspapers & Magazines, Outdoor, Planning & Consultation, Print, Production (Print), Radio, Strategic Planning/Research, T.V., Women's Market

Approx. Annual Billings: $3,500,000

Breakdown of Gross Billings by Media: Brdcst.: $3,250,000; Print: $250,000

Lisa Flanders *(Pres)*

Accounts:
All Pro Bail Bonds; San Diego, CA; 2006
Alvarado Hospital; San Diego, CA; 2008
Coin Mart; Chula Vista, CA; 2005
Courtesy Chevrolet; San Diego, CA; 2007
Encompass Clinical Research; 2007
Furniture Heaven; San Diego, CA; 2005
KRC Rock; San Diego, CA; 2006
Mapleton Super Storage; Salt Lake City, UT; 2006
Mulloy's Fine Jewelry; Carlsbad, CA; 2005
Plackers; San Diego, CA; 2007
Stones Unlimited; Carlsbad, CA; 2005

THE SAN JOSE GROUP

233 N Michigan Ave 24 Fl, Chicago, IL 60601
Tel.: (312) 565-7000
Fax: (312) 565-7500
E-Mail: sanjose@sjadv.com
Web Site: www.thesanjosegroup.com

Employees: 57
Year Founded: 1981

Agency Specializes In: Advertising, Bilingual Market, Brand Development & Integration, Broadcast, Collateral, Communications, Consulting, Consumer Marketing, Corporate Identity, Direct Response Marketing, E-Commerce, Electronic Media, Event Planning & Marketing, Hispanic Market, Internet/Web Design, Logo & Package Design, Planning & Consultation, Public Relations, Retail, Sponsorship, Strategic Planning/Research, Travel & Tourism

Approx. Annual Billings: $58,000,000

George L. San Jose *(Pres & Chief Creative Officer)*
Mark Revermann *(VP-Insights & Integration)*
Adriana Escarcega *(Acct Dir)*
Seth Patterson *(Dir-HR & Talent Acq)*
Allison Narvaez *(Mgr-Convergent Mktg)*
Nancy Casales *(Sr Acct Exec)*
Angelica Martinez *(Acct Exec-PR)*

Accounts:
Abbott Laboratories
Abbott Nutrition Glucerna
American Cancer Society
Echo, Inc
Exelon
H&R Block Inc.
Hispanic Christian Churches Association
Hormel Foods Corp. SPAM, Buffalo Salsa Picante, Hormel, Dona Maria Mole, Herdez
HyCite Corporation Royal Prestige
Illinois Bureau of Tourism
MGM Grand
Shire U.S. Intuniv, Vyvanse
Sunovion Pharmaceuticals, Inc Xopenex, Alvesco
Tribeca Flashpoint Media Arts Academy (Agency of Record) Media
United States Cellular Corporation

SANBORN ADVERTISING

2102 Rio Dr, Rapid City, SD 57702
Tel.: (605) 390-3914
E-Mail: info@sanbornads.com
Web Site: www.sanbornads.com

Agency Specializes In: Advertising, Graphic Design, Internet/Web Design, Logo & Package Design, Media Relations, Outdoor, Promotions, Public Relations, Radio, T.V.

Michael Sanborn *(Owner)*
Brandt Heinemann *(Partner)*
Amy Nichols *(Producer-Digital)*
Scott Ellis *(Dir-Digital)*
Steve Kutsch *(Dir-Creative)*
Jesse Scheller *(Dir-Art)*
Delaney Nye *(Assoc Dir-Creative)*
Scott Wallace *(Assoc Dir-Creative)*
Shaun Cammack *(Mgr-IT & Specialist-Production)*

Accounts:
1-2-3 Roofing & Seamless Gutters

SANDBOX

(Formerly One Advertising)
70 Richmond Street East Main Floor, Toronto, ON M5C 1N8 Canada
Tel.: (416) 862-8181
Fax: (416) 862-9553
Web Site: sandboxww.ca/

Employees: 25
Year Founded: 1993

National Agency Associations: 4A's

Agency Specializes In: Advertising

Jill King *(Pres)*
Ted Boyd *(CEO)*
Niall Shaw *(CTO)*
Rebecca Ho *(Acct Dir)*
Jacob Gawrysiak *(Dir-Creative)*
Michel Lang *(Dir-Creative)*
Charlotte DiLecce *(Acct Supvr)*
Amy Jacobs *(Copywriter)*

Accounts:
3M
Dairy Farmers of Canada
Fountain Tire
H&R Block
LCBO
Milk
Ministry of Small Business & Entrepreneurship
Molson Coors Canada Campaign: "The Most Interesting Man In The World", Dos Equis, Heineken, Newcastle Brown, OOH, Radio, Strongbow
Ontario Government
Owens Corning Digital, Social Media
Second Cup (Agency of Record) Retail & Branding
Workopolis

SANDERSWINGO

SANDERS/WINGO ADVERTISING, INC.

221 N Kansas Ste 900, El Paso, TX 79901
Tel.: (915) 533-9583
Fax: (915) 533-3601
E-Mail: swresults@sanderswingo.com
Web Site: www.sanderswingo.com

Employees: 38
Year Founded: 1958

National Agency Associations: 4A's-Second Wind Limited

Agency Specializes In: African-American Market

Our purpose: Unconventional ideas that turn brands into cultural icons. Sanders/Wingo has built a national reputation for strategic insight and exceptional solutions. Today's new reality changes every day. Mainstream has become multicultural. Urban culture drives trends and transcends old boundaries of color and geography. Sanders/Wingo has produced high-resonance campaigns for clients in diverse categories and business sectors. Combining real-world insight with global-caliber business practices, Sanders/Wingo turns brands into institutions and short-term objectives into long-term accomplishment.

Robert V. Wingo *(Chm)*
Leslie Wingo *(Pres & CEO)*
Trenzio Turner *(Mng Partner & Sr VP)*
Scott McAfee *(Mng Partner)*
Kerry Jackson *(Partner & Exec VP)*
Antoine Harris *(Sr Dir-Art)*
Sam Bonds *(Creative Dir)*
Elizabeth Powell *(Dir-Bus Dev)*
Corey Seaton *(Dir-Creative)*
Hilary Fox *(Acct Supvr)*

Accounts:
AT&T Communications Corp. Campaign: "Our Song", Campaign: "Stronger"
CINTRA US
El Paso Convention & Visitors Bureau
GECU
KFC
Mini Cooper
MINI USA
Ocean Alexander

Subsidiary

SANDERSWINGO

Sanders/Wingo
2222 Rio Grande Bldg C 3rd Fl, Austin, TX 78705
Tel.: (512) 476-7949
Fax: (512) 476-7950
Web Site: www.sanderswingo.com

Employees: 50
Year Founded: 2001

National Agency Associations: 4A's

Agency Specializes In: Advertising, Sponsorship

Our purpose: Unconventional ideas that turn brands into cultural icons. Sanders/Wingo has built a national reputation for strategic insight and exceptional solutions. Today's new reality changes every day. Mainstream has become multicultural. Urban culture drives trends and transcends old boundaries of color and geography. Sanders/Wingo has produced high-resonance campaigns for clients in diverse categories and business sectors. Combining real-world insight with global-caliber business practices, Sanders/Wingo turns brands into institutions and short-term objectives into long-term accomplishment.

Trenzio Turner *(Mng Partner & Sr VP)*
Scott McAfee *(Partner)*
Rodney Northern *(Sr VP & Dir-Client Svc)*
Dee Anne Heath *(Sr VP-The Knowledge Grp)*
Rhonda Dore *(VP & Grp Dir-Creative)*
Elizabeth Powell *(Dir-Bus Dev)*
Corey Seaton *(Dir-Creative)*
Carter Pagel *(Assoc Dir-Creative & Copywriter)*
Elizabeth Mcdermott *(Assoc Dir-Media)*
Hilary Fox *(Acct Supvr)*
Scott Rostohar *(Copywriter)*
Austin Bingham *(Acct Coord)*

Accounts:
American Heart Association
AT&T Campaign: "Our Song"
Block Buster
Burger King
Del Sol
GECU
Mini Cooper
Ocean Alexander
Shell
Texas Gas
UTEP

SANDIA ADVERTISING
510 N Tejon St, Colorado Springs, CO 80903
Tel.: (719) 473-8900
Web Site: www.sandiaadvertising.com

Agency Specializes In: Advertising, Collateral, Digital/Interactive, Print, Public Relations, Social Media

Bernard Sandoval *(Pres)*
Shari Gore *(Media Dir)*
Stacey Long *(Designer-Creative)*

Accounts:
Flying Horse
Johannes Hunter Jewelers
La Casita Mexican Grill
Lazer TroKar
PepsiCo Inc.
United States Olympic Committee
Wright & McGill Co.

SANDLOT STUDIOS
Chandler & 40th, Phoenix, AZ 85048
Tel.: (602) 366-5589
Web Site: www.sandlotstudios.com

Year Founded: 2000

Agency Specializes In: Advertising, Brand Development & Integration, Collateral, Internet/Web Design, Print, Production, Web (Banner Ads, Pop-ups, etc.)

Vikki Green *(Owner & Dir-Creative)*

Accounts:
Altar Insurance, Inc
Biltmore Business Partners
The Harp Foundation
KatzDesignGroup
Washington State Parks Foundation

SANDY HULL & ASSOCIATES
1143 Cedar View Dr, Minneapolis, MN 55405
Tel.: (612) 605-3966
Fax: (612) 605-0603
Toll Free: (866) 656-8103
Web Site: www.sandyhull.com

Employees: 10

Agency Specializes In: Advertising, Business-To-Business, Computers & Software, Consumer Marketing, Corporate Identity, Digital/Interactive, Direct Response Marketing, Direct-to-Consumer, E-Commerce, Education, Email, Engineering, Environmental, Faith Based, Graphic Design, Guerilla Marketing, Health Care Services, Identity Marketing, Industrial, Information Technology, Integrated Marketing, Internet/Web Design, Local Marketing, Logo & Package Design, Marine, Market Research, Medical Products, Mobile Marketing, Over-50 Market, Paid Searches, Print, Production (Print), RSS (Really Simple Syndication), Regional, Seniors' Market, Social Marketing/Nonprofit, Social Media, Sponsorship, Web (Banner Ads, Pop-ups, etc.), Women's Market, Yellow Pages Advertising

Approx. Annual Billings: $250,000

Breakdown of Gross Billings by Media: Collateral: 50%; Fees: 50%

Sandra Sweatt Hull *(Principal & Strategist-Mktg)*

Accounts:
Dolphin Journeys; Kona, HI Tourism
Foundation of International Freedom; Houston, TX Educational Services
Teleprovision; Minneapolis, MN Telecommunications

SANGAM & ASSOCIATES
3435 Wilshire Blvd Ste 2880, Los Angeles, CA 90010
Tel.: (213) 252-6320
Fax: (213) 252-9055
E-Mail: info@sang-am.com
Web Site: www.sang-am.com

Employees: 15
Year Founded: 1995

Agency Specializes In: Asian Market

Jaime Lee *(VP)*
Jong-Oh Kim *(Head-Acct Svc Team)*

Accounts:
Asiana Airlines; Seoul, Korea Airlines Travel; 1994
DAE SANG; Seoul, Korea Food Products
Hanmi Bank

SANGER & EBY
501 Chestnut St, Cincinnati, OH 45203
Tel.: (513) 784-9046
Web Site: www.sangereby.com

Agency Specializes In: Advertising, Brand Development & Integration, Content, Digital/Interactive, Print, Social Media

Kat Jenkins *(VP-Strategic Plng)*
Alyssa Weidenhamer *(Dir-Client Svcs)*
Katie Pohlman *(Designer)*

Accounts:
New-Macy's Inc.

SANTY INTEGRATED
8370 E Via de Ventura Ste K-100, Scottsdale, AZ 85258
Toll Free: (888) 679-3685
E-Mail: dsanty@santy.com
Web Site: www.santy.com

Agency Specializes In: Brand Development & Integration, Sponsorship

Dan Santy *(Pres & CEO)*
Maria Dillon *(Client Svcs Dir)*
Sagar Patel *(Dir-Digital)*
Adam Pierno *(Dir-Brand Strategy & Plng)*
Katie Rubel *(Acct Mgr)*
Jonathan Carroll *(Specialist-Search Mktg)*
Amanda Fellows *(Acct Coord)*
Hannah Tooker *(Coord-Social Media)*
Nicole Luna *(Sr Media Planner & Buyer)*

Accounts:
Cactus Bowl Media Buying, Media Planning, Planning, Strategic Consultation
Calbee North America Harvest Snaps
Carefree RV Resorts
Catholic Education Arizona
China Mist Iced Tea (Agency of Record) Content Strategy, Creative, Digital Marketing, Public Relations, Social Media
Delta Air Lines, Inc. Social Listening
Fiesta Bowl Media Buying, Media Planning, Planning, Strategic Consultation
Health Guard
Hospice of the Valley
Northrop Grumman
Paradise Bakery & Cafe
Peter Piper, Inc.
Philosophy
Pizza Properties
Real Mex Restaurants, Inc. Brand Strategy, Chevy's Fresh Mex (Agency of Record), Digital, El Torito (Agency of Record), Media Buying, Media Planning, Mobile Media, Social Media Advertising, TV, Traditional Print Media
Southwest Pizza

SAPIENT CORPORATION
(Acquired by Publicis Groupe S.A.)

SAPIENT CORPORATION
131 Dartmouth St, Boston, MA 02116
Tel.: (617) 621-0200
Fax: (617) 621-1300
E-Mail: info@sapient.com
Web Site: www.sapient.com

Employees: 13,000
Year Founded: 1991

Agency Specializes In: Information Technology

Revenue: $1,305,232,000

Alan J. Herrick *(Co-Chm, Pres & CEO)*
William Kanarick *(CMO & Sr VP)*
Gaston Legorburu *(Chief Creative Officer-Worldwide & Exec Dir)*
Joseph S. Tibbetts, Jr. *(Mng Dir-Asia Pacific, CFO-*

Global & Sr VP)
Christopher Davey *(Mng Dir-Worldwide Commerce, Sr VP & Head-Content Mgmt Practice)*
Christian Oversohl *(Sr VP & Mng Dir-Asia Pacific)*
Rajdeep Endow *(Mng Dir-India & Head-Global Delivery)*
Frank Schettino *(VP & Head-Culture)*
David Depew *(VP)*
Lisa Kile *(Dir-Program Mgmt)*
Dean Ridlon *(Dir-IR)*
Mary L. Stewart *(Dir-Internal Comm)*

Accounts:
Bertucci's Corporation Bertucci's Brick Oven Pizzeria, Bertucci's Corporation
BP
Chrysler Group; Auburn Hills, MI Digital
Cisco
Coca-Cola Refreshments USA, Inc. Powerade
Hawaiian Airlines
Hilton Worldwide
Honda Jet
Honda Jet
Intuit
Kaiser Permanente
KeyCorp
Library of Congress
Logan's Roadhouse Creative, Digital, Social
Public Storage
Sony Electronics
Star Alliance
Sunglass Hut
Times Online
UK Department of Health
Verizon
VisitBritain
Webster Bank Brand Communications, Marketing, Media Planning & Buying, Online Creative, Print, Research, Strategy Development, Website Development

Branches

Sapient Atlanta
3630 Peachtree Rd NE, Atlanta, GA 30326
Tel.: (770) 407-3400
Fax: (770) 407-3401
E-Mail: info@sapient.com
Web Site: www.sapient.com

Employees: 103

National Agency Associations: 4A's

Alan Herrick *(Co-Chm & CEO)*
Chris Davey *(Mng Dir, Sr VP & Head-Global Customer Engagement Platform)*
William Kanarick *(CMO & Sr VP)*
Gaston Legorburu *(Chief Creative Officer & Exec Dir)*
Chip Register *(CEO-Sapient Consulting)*
Teresa Bozzelli *(Sr VP & Mng Dir-Sapient Govt Svcs)*
Christian Oversohl *(Sr VP & Mng Dir-APAC)*
Laurie Maclaren *(Sr VP-People & Internal Ops)*
Frank Schettino *(VP & Head-Culture)*
Melissa Read *(Head-Global Social Insights)*

Sapient Boston
131 Dartmouth St 3rd Fl, Boston, MA 02116
Tel.: (617) 621-0200
Fax: (617) 621-1300
E-Mail: info@sapient.com
Web Site: www.sapient.com

Employees: 300

National Agency Associations: 4A's

Stacy Simpson *(Chief Comm Officer)*
Alan Wexler *(Pres-SapientNitro)*
Alan Pafenbach *(Exec Dir-Creative)*
Lisa Walczak *(Sr Mgr-Interactive Program Mgmt)*
Cassie Olson *(Sr Media Planner)*

Accounts:
Coca-Cola Refreshments USA, Inc.
Foot Locker
Powerade
Unilever

Sapient Chicago
30 W Monroe 12th Fl, Chicago, IL 60603
Tel.: (312) 458-1800
Fax: (312) 696-0325
E-Mail: info@sapient.com
Web Site: www.sapient.com/

Employees: 10

National Agency Associations: 4A's

Alan Herrick *(Chm, Pres & CEO)*
Chris Davey *(Mng Dir, Sr VP & Head-Global Customer Engagement Platform)*
William Kanarick *(CMO & Sr VP)*
Gaston Legorburu *(Exec Dir & Chief Creative Officer)*
Alan Wexler *(Pres-SapientNitro)*
Chip Register *(CEO-Sapient Consulting)*
Christian Oversohl *(Sr VP & Mng Dir-APAC)*
Laurie Maclaren *(Sr VP-People & Internal Ops)*
Frank Schettino *(VP & Head-Culture)*
Raju Patel *(VP)*
Andrew Schultz *(Dir & Gen Mgr)*
Jamie Anderson *(Dir-Brand Strategy & Customer Experience)*

Accounts:
FatWire Software
Google
HP
Oracle America, Inc.
SAP

Sapient Corporation
2911 Grand Ave, Miami, FL 33133
Tel.: (305) 253-0100
Fax: (305) 253-0013
E-Mail: info@sapient.com
Web Site: www.sapient.com

Employees: 200

Agency Specializes In: Advertising, Digital/Interactive, Financial, Food Service

Alan J. Herrick *(Co-Chm & CEO)*
Gaston Legorburu *(Chief Creative Officer-Worldwide & Exec Dir)*
Joey Wilson *(VP-Mktg Strategy)*
Boyd Kanawisher *(Sr Dir-Enrollment)*
Chanel Abislaiman *(Acct Dir)*
Malissa Martin *(Acct Dir)*
Boris Stojanovic *(Dir-Creative Production Studio)*

Accounts:
American Cancer Society
BP
New-Carnival Cruise Lines Digital Strategy
Citi Credit Cards
Citibank
CitiFinancial
Coca-Cola Refreshments USA, Inc.
CVS Health
Dow Jones
Healthy Choice
Hilton Worldwide
Janus
Joe's Stone Crab
JP Morgan
Mars
NBC
Nissan USA
PepsiCo, Inc. Gatorade / Gatorade G
Rock & Roll Hall of Fame
Sony Electronics
Verizon Terremark
Verizon
Viacom
Wall Street Journal
Webster Bank

Sapient Houston
1111 Bagby St Ste 1950, Houston, TX 77002
Tel.: (713) 493-6880
Fax: (617) 621-1300
E-Mail: info@sapient.com
Web Site: www.sapient.com

Employees: 7,000

National Agency Associations: 4A's

Alan Herrick *(Chm, Pres & CEO)*
William Kanarick *(CMO & Sr VP)*
Gaston Legorburu *(Chief Creative Officer & Exec Dir)*
Alan Wexler *(Pres-SapientNitro)*
Chip Register *(CEO-Sapient Consulting)*
Christian Oversohl *(Sr VP & Mng Dir-APAC)*
Mark Crosno *(VP-Bus Dev Global Markets)*
Masud Haq *(VP)*
Rashed Haq *(VP-Energy Commerce)*
Siddharth Bahl *(Dir)*
Charles Ford *(Dir-Bus Consulting Svcs)*

Accounts:
The Premise
VisitBritain.com
Yahoo

Sapient Miami/Falls
2911 Grand Ave Ste 100, Miami, FL 33133
Tel.: (305) 253-0100
Fax: (305) 253-0013
E-Mail: info@sapient.com
Web Site: www.sapient.com/

Employees: 40

National Agency Associations: 4A's

Agency Specializes In: Sponsorship

Matthew Atkatz *(Exec Dir-Creative)*
Robert Kleman *(Exec Dir-Creative-SapientNitro)*
Tiffany Ramirez *(Mgr & Sr Producer)*
Allison Bistrong *(Brand Dir-Mktg)*
Jason Levine *(Creative Dir)*
Brian Jones *(Assoc Dir-Creative)*

Accounts:
Share Happy
Visit Florida Campaign: "Flock To Florida"

Sapient Washington DC
1515 N Courthouse Rd, Arlington, VA 22201
Tel.: (703) 908-2400
Fax: (703) 908-2401
E-Mail: info@sapient.com
Web Site: www.sapient.com/

Employees: 400

National Agency Associations: 4A's

Alan Herrick *(Chm, Pres & CEO)*
Chris Davey *(Mng Dir, Sr VP & Head-Global Customer Engagement Platform)*
Chip Register *(CEO-Sapient Consulting)*
Christian Oversohl *(Sr VP & Mng Dir-APAC)*
Laurie Maclaren *(Sr VP-People & Internal Ops)*
Nathan Brewer *(VP)*
Bill Annibell *(Dir-Tech)*

Steve Heinzman *(Dir-Bus Ops)*

Accounts:
Compuware
Demandware
Google
HP
Oracle America, Inc.
redhat
SAP
UNICA

Sapient
(Formerly Sapient New York-One Penn Plaza)
40 Fulton St 2nd Fl, New York, NY 10138
Tel.: (212) 206-1005
Fax: (212) 206-8510
E-Mail: info@sapient.com
Web Site: www.sapient.com

Employees: 200

National Agency Associations: 4A's

Matthew Forsyth *(Asst Gen Counsel & VP)*
Hilding Anderson *(Dir-Res & Insights)*
Sheryl Baff *(Dir-Mktg-Sapient Global Markets)*
Ryan Jones *(Mgr-Search Strategy & Analytics)*
Angicel Morales *(Acct Supvr)*

Accounts:
The Coca-Cola Company

SapientNitro USA, Inc.
40 Fulton St, New York, NY 10038
(See Separate Listing)

Subsidiary

Sapient Securities Corporation
131 Tartmouth 3rd Fl, Boston, MA 02116
Tel.: (617) 621-0200
Fax: (617) 621-1300
E-Mail: info@sapient.com
Web Site: www.sapient.com

Employees: 300

Alan Herrick *(Co-Chm & CEO)*
William Kanarick *(CMO & Sr VP)*
Gaston Legorburu *(Chief Creative Officer-Worldwide & Exec Dir)*
Chip Register *(CEO-Sapient Consulting)*
Alan Wexler *(CEO-SapientNitro)*
Chris Davey *(Sr VP, Mng Dir-Global Commerce & Head-Content Mgmt)*
Laurie Maclaren *(Sr VP-People & Internal Ops)*
Teresa Bozzelli *(VP & Mng Dir-Sapient Government Svcs)*
Frank Schettino *(VP & Head-Culture)*

Non-U.S. Subsidiaries

Sapient Canada Inc.
(d/b/a Sapient Toronto)
129 Spadina Ave Ste 500, Toronto, ON M5V 2L3 Canada
Tel.: (416) 645-1500
Fax: (416) 645-1501
E-Mail: info@sapient.com
Web Site: www.sapient.com

Employees: 250

Andrew Kirby *(VP-Client Svcs)*
Michael Howatson *(Exec Creative Dir)*

Sapient Corporation Private Limited
(d/b/a Sapient Delhi)
The Presidency Mehrauli-Gurgaon Road Sector 14, Gurgaon, Haryana 122 001 India
Tel.: (91) 124 2808 018
Fax: (91) 124 2808 015
Web Site: www.sapient.com/en-us/contact-us/global-offices/asia/gurgaon.html

Ashok Sethi *(CIO)*
Sumit Sharma *(VP)*
Manu Vaish *(VP)*
Neha Pathak *(Head-PR-India)*
Ravi Shankar *(Head-Global Capability-Commerce)*
Surjo Dutt *(Creative Dir)*
Saurabh Das *(Dir)*
Sandeep Gupta *(Dir)*
Gaurav Maheshwari *(Dir-Program Mgmt)*
Ruchir Pande *(Dir-Program Mgmt)*
Sandeep Tripathi *(Assoc Strategist-CMS Developer Content)*

Branch

Sapient Corporation Pte. Ltd. - Noida
(d/b/a Sapient Noida)
Green Blvd Tower C 3rd & 4th Fl, Plot No B 9A Sector 62, Noida, 201 301 India
Tel.: (91) 120 479 5000
Fax: (91) 120 479 5001
E-Mail: info@sapient.com
Web Site: www.sapient.com

Alan Herrick *(Co-Chm, Pres & CEO)*
Rajdeep Endow *(Mng Dir-India & Head-Global Deliver-SapientNitro)*
Sanjay Menon *(VP)*
Sumit Sharma *(VP)*
Manu Vaish *(VP)*
Salil Swarup *(Head-Hybris Specialized Grp & Dir)*
Ravi Shankar *(Head-Global Capability-Commerce)*
Shefali Agrawal *(Dir-Program Mgmt)*
Ritika Basu *(Reg Head-Delivery & Dir)*
Ruchir Pande *(Dir-Program Mgmt)*
Brinda Bhalla *(Sr Mgr)*

Accounts:
Yahoo

Sapient Limited
(d/b/a Sapient London)
Eden House 8 Spital Square, London, E1 6DU United Kingdom
Tel.: (44) 2077864500
Fax: (44) 2077864600
E-Mail: info@sapient.com
Web Site: www.sapient.com/en-us/contact-us/global-offices/europe/london.html

Employees: 400

Neil Dawson *(Chief Strategy Officer-Europe-SapientNitro)*
Nigel Vaz *(Chief Strategy Officer)*
Geoff Whitehouse *(Head-PR & Analyst Rels)*
Mark Hunter *(Exec Dir-Creative)*
Trefor Thomas *(Exec Dir-Creative)*
Justin Barnes *(Dir-Creative-SapientNitro)*
Daniel Harvey *(Dir-Experience Design)*
Lillian Shieh *(Dir-Experience Strategy)*

Accounts:
Britain's Beer Alliance Advertising, Campaign: "There's a Beer for That", Marketing, TV
British Airways (Digital Agency of Record) Social Media
GlaxoSmithKline
Global Brewers Initiative Advertising, Let There Be Beer
HTC Digital, One M9 Smartphone, Online, Print
INVISTA Digital, Global Brand Strategy, LYCRA(R), Print, Social
Ladbrokes Creative
Save the Children Digital Transformation
New-Tesco Mobile

Sapient Munich
Arnulfstrasse 60, 80335 Munich, Germany
Tel.: (49) 89 552 987 0
Fax: (49) 89 552 987 100
E-Mail: info.de@sapient.com
Web Site: www.sapient.com

Employees: 150

Christian Oversohl *(Sr VP & Mng Dir-Asia Pacific)*
Markus Ruhl *(VP-Legal & Asst Gen Counsel)*

Branch

Sapient GmbH - Dusseldorf
(d/b/a Sapient Dusseldorf)
Hammer St 19, D 40219 Dusseldorf, Germany
Tel.: (49) 211540340
Fax: (49) 21154034600
E-Mail: info@sapient.com
Web Site: www.sapient.com/de-de/Contact-Us/Global-Offices/Dusseldorf.html

Employees: 100

Christian Oversohl *(Sr VP & Mng Dir-APAC)*
Annett Spies *(Dir-Legal)*

Accounts:
California - The Game
The Premise
Share Happy
Visitbritain.com
Where's Roger
Yahoo

Sapient
(Formerly SapientNitro)
161 Fitzroy Street, Saint Kilda, Melbourne, VIC 3182 Australia
Tel.: (61) 3 9537 0488
Fax: (61) 3 9537 0866
Web Site: www.sapient.com

Year Founded: 1991

Stephen Forth *(Mng Dir)*
Scarlett Lok *(Head-Client Svcs)*
Natalie Hocking *(Sr Acct Dir)*
Ralph Barnett *(Dir-Creative)*
Sarah Chernishov *(Dir-Art)*
Gerard Blanton *(Assoc Dir-Creative)*
John Shard *(Mgr-Natl Studio)*
Amanda Windus *(Planner-Strategy)*

Accounts:
AEIOU Autism Therapy
Australian Grown
BCF Campaign: "Scared Fish"
Betstar
Cenovis Campaign: "Get On With the Good Stuff", Digital, In-Store, Media Integration, Monster Girl, Ninja Boy, TV
Chum
Comvita
Earphone Bully
Foot Locker Campaign: "Foot Locker Art Prize"
G6 Hospitality LLC
Hush Puppies
Kmart
Nikon
Primus Telecom
RACQ Online, Press, Radio, TV
Tourism Queensland 1 Day in Paradise - Trailer
Velocity
Virgin Blue Airlines

SAPIENTNITRO USA, INC.

40 Fulton St, New York, NY 10038
Tel.: (212) 560-5700
Fax: (212) 560-5701
E-Mail: info@sapient.com
Web Site: www.sapientnitro.com/en-us.html#home

E-Mail for Key Personnel:
Creative Dir.: douglas.spitzer@sapientnitro.com

Employees: 300
Year Founded: 1998

National Agency Associations: 4A's

Agency Specializes In: Advertising Specialties, Broadcast, Cable T.V., Children's Market, Co-op Advertising, Consumer Marketing, Consumer Publications, Event Planning & Marketing, Fashion/Apparel, Leisure, Logo & Package Design, Magazines, Media Buying Services, Merchandising, Newspaper, Newspapers & Magazines, Out-of-Home Media, Outdoor, Planning & Consultation, Print, Production, Radio, Retail, Sponsorship, Sports Market, T.V.

Chris Davey *(Mng Dir, Sr VP & Head-Worldwide Commerce & Content Mgmt Practice)*
Kim Douglas *(VP & Mng Dir)*
Scott Wickstrom *(Mng Dir & VP)*
Alyssa Altman *(Mng Dir)*
William Kanarick *(CMO & Sr VP)*
Gaston Legorburu *(Chief Creative Officer-Worldwide & Exec Dir)*
Ron Shamah *(Sr VP)*
Julie Atherton *(VP & Grp Head-Strategy)*
Andrew Choban *(Head-Social Media Engagement)*
Jeff Stokvis *(Head-Omni-Channel Mktg Strategy)*
Andy Greenaway *(Exec Dir-Creative-Asia & Pac)*
Christian Waitzinger *(Exec Dir-Creative)*
Marie Rockett *(Sr Dir-Art)*
Cesar Santos *(Sr Dir-Art)*
Naomi Hirst *(Sr Acct Dir)*
Amy Daneke *(Acct Dir-Intl)*
Justin Barnes *(Dir-Creative)*
Sean Black *(Dir-Media, Innovation & Strategic Partnerships)*
Matthew Cirri *(Dir-Media-North America)*
Adina Dahlin *(Dir-Mktg Strategy & Analysis)*
Andrew Goldstein *(Dir-Creative)*
George Haenisch *(Dir-Strategy & Bus Dev)*
Amy Junger *(Dir)*
Jordan Lipton *(Dir-Creative)*
David Serrano *(Dir-Client Svcs)*
Lee Ekstrom *(Assoc Dir-Creative)*
Kirk Gustafson *(Assoc Dir-Creative-Experience Design)*
Susan Phuvasitkul *(Assoc Dir-Creative & Copy)*
Giancarlo Pisani *(Assoc Dir-Creative)*
Crystal Aria *(Sr Mgr-Mktg Strategy & Analysis)*
Bryan Caynor *(Sr Mgr-Office Svcs)*
John Duffield *(Sr Mgr-Interactive Program Mgmt)*
Brian Miller *(Sr Mgr-Consumer Intelligence)*
Kelly Buchanan *(Mgr-Interactive Program Mgmt)*
Tina Markowitz *(Mgr-Social Media)*
Laura Pieretti *(Mgr-Program Mgmt)*
Michelle Shahar *(Mgr-Info Architecture)*
Stephanie Terhaar *(Mgr-Interactive Program Mgmt)*
Lawrence Williford *(Mgr-UX Design)*
Angela Sun *(Acct Supvr)*
Mary Elizabeth Zumba *(Acct Supvr)*
Dan Parness *(Supvr-Media)*
Jenny Garcia *(Sr Associate, Interactive Program Mgmt)*
Darren McColl *(Chief Brand Strategy Officer-Global)*
Muchi Salazar *(Sr Assoc-Media)*

Accounts:
Activision Publishing, Inc.; Santa Monica, CA Call of Duty, Digital Marketing Strategy, Modern Warfare 3, Skylanders Spyro's Adventure
ADT Digital Marketing, online
Bacardi Limited Broadcast, Campaign: "Fly Beyond", Digital, Grey Goose (Social Agency of Record), Print
Bertucci's Corporation Bertucci's Brick Oven Pizzeria
Borgata Hotel Casino & Spa
Burger King Holdings Inc.
Chrysler Group LLC (Agency of Record) Chrysler, Dodge, Interactive Duties, Jeep, Online Advertising, Ram Truck, Site Design & Development
Citigroup Inc.
Citizens Bank Online
Coca-Cola Refreshments USA, Inc. 2012 London Olympics Sponsorship, Campaign: "Vitaminwater Uncapped", Powerade
Conagra
Dove
Dunkin' Donuts "Digital Menu Board"
Foot Locker, Inc. Campaign: "Foot Locker Art Prize"
Hyatt
Invista Lycra
Kids Foot Locker; New York, NY Active Wear; 1998
Lady Foot Locker; New York, NY Active Wear; 1998
LeBron James
Mars, Inc. Interactive, Internet
Metlife Campaign: "MetLife Central"
Metropolitan Life Metlifecentral
New Balance Campaign: "In-store Digital Sales Experience"
Nike
Project Rockit Campaign: "Earphone Bully"
Rolling Stone
Singapore Airlines
Sprint Sprint.com
Sunglass Hut
Unilever
Vail Resorts Epic Discovery, EpicMix 2011, EpicMix Season 2
Vodafone

Branches

Campfire
313 Church St, New York, NY 10013
(See Separate Listing)

The Community
(Formerly La Comunidad)
6400 Biscayne Blvd, Miami, FL 33138
(See Separate Listing)

SapientNitro Atlanta
500 North Park Town Center 1100 AbernathyRd NE, Atlanta, GA 30328
Tel.: (770) 407-3400
Fax: (770) 407-3401
Web Site: www.sapient.com

David Hewitt *(VP)*
Graham Engebretsen *(Head-Brand Experiences & Business Strategy)*
John McHale *(Exec Dir-Creative)*
Reed Coss *(Dir-Creative)*
David Jacobson *(Dir-Mktg Strategy & Analysis)*
Richard Kim *(Dir-Tech)*

Accounts:
New-Coca-Cola
The End It Movement Campaign: "Trafficking In Traffic"
First Data Corporation (Agency of Record) Brand Identity
New-Fisher Island Campaign: "The Island Immersion Room ", Campaign: "The Palazzo del Sol Experience"
Whole Foods

SapientNitro iThink
Av Engenheiro Luis Carlos Berrini 901, 2 Andar, Sao Paulo, Brazil
Tel.: (55) 11 3201 7400
Web Site: www.sapientnitro.com/en-us.html#home

Employees: 60

Agency Specializes In: Digital/Interactive

Raffael Mastrocola *(Mng Dir)*
Marcelo Tripoli *(Chief Creative Officer-Latam Reg)*
Carlos Borges *(VP-Strategy)*
Flavia Denser *(Acct Dir)*
Tiago Lucci *(Dir-Creative)*
Paula Salvarani Rocha *(Acct Mgr)*

Accounts:
Boehringer
Castrol
Disney
Google
Johnson & Johnson
Kraft
Nestle
PepsiCo
Skol
Vivo/Telefonica

SapientNitro
158 Cecil St 03-01, Singapore, 069545 Singapore
Tel.: (65) 6671 4933
Fax: (65) 6225 7025
Web Site: www.sapient.com

Agency Specializes In: Advertising, Digital/Interactive

Christian Oversohl *(Sr VP & Mng Dir-APAC)*
Virginie Pontruche *(Sr Acct Dir)*
Emily Duder *(Acct Dir)*
Tyler Munoz *(Client Svcs Dir)*
Simon Collins *(Dir-Mktg Strategy & Analysis)*
Sebastian Troen *(Dir-Bus Dev)*
Haikel Zaini *(Dir-Art)*
Andrew Trimboli *(Sr Mgr-Content Strategy)*
Ari Widjanarko *(Sr Mgr-Strategy)*
Rajiv Babu *(Mgr-Tech)*

Accounts:
GlaxoSmithKline Panadol-Global Digital Agency of Record

Second Story, Inc.
714 N Fremont St No 200, Portland, OR 97227
Tel.: (503) 827-7155
E-Mail: info@secondstory.com
Web Site: www.secondstory.com

Employees: 30

Agency Specializes In: Advertising, Internet/Web Design

David Beauvais *(Dir-Bus Dev)*
Chris DeWan *(Dir-Design)*
Thomas Wester *(Dir-Innovation)*

Accounts:
AIGA
Occidental College
Whole Foods Digital

SAPUTO DESIGN, INC.
870 Hampshire Rd Ste D, Westlake Village, CA 91361
Tel.: (805) 494-1847
Fax: (805) 777-9101
E-Mail: info@saputodesign.com
Web Site: www.saputodesign.com

Employees: 10
Year Founded: 1998

Agency Specializes In: Automotive, Catalogs, Corporate Communications, Graphic Design, Health Care Services, Hospitality, In-Store Advertising, Logo & Package Design, Medical Products, Package Design, Point of Purchase, Point of Sale, Print, Travel & Tourism

Thomas Saputo *(Pres & Exec Dir-Creative-Saputo Design)*

Accounts:
Amgen, Inc.; Thousand Oaks, CA
Pleasant Holidays, LLC; Thousand Oaks, CA

SARD VERBINNEN & CO.
630 3rd Ave 9th Fl, New York, NY 10017
Tel.: (212) 687-8080
Fax: (212) 687-8344
Web Site: www.sardverb.com

Agency Specializes In: Crisis Communications, Investor Relations, Media Relations

George Sard *(Chm & CEO)*
David Harris *(Mng Dir & CFO)*
Matt Benson *(Mng Dir)*
Jonathan Gasthalter *(Mng Dir)*
Brooke Gordon *(Mng Dir)*
Matt Reid *(Mng Dir)*
Bob Rendine *(Mng Dir)*
James Tully *(Mng Dir-New York)*
Marc Minardo *(VP & Dir-Digital Comm Grp)*

Accounts:
Danaher Corp Public Relations
New-DraftKings
Fisher Communications
Forest Laboratories, Inc.; New York, NY
FXI-Foamex Innovations
Infinium Capital Management
Integrated Device Technology, Inc.; San Jose, CA
Spectrum Brands
Takata Communications
Univision Communications Inc. Corporate Communications

SARKISSIAN MASON
135 W 26th St 5 Fl, New York, NY 10001
Tel.: (212) 625-8212
Fax: (212) 625-8211
E-Mail: info@sarkissianpartners.com
Web Site: www.sarkissianpartners.com

Employees: 20
Year Founded: 1999

Agency Specializes In: Branded Entertainment, Digital/Interactive, E-Commerce, Electronic Media, Game Integration, Graphic Design, Internet/Web Design, Print, Production (Ad, Film, Broadcast), Strategic Planning/Research, T.V.

Approx. Annual Billings: $3,000,000

Patrick Sarkissian *(CEO)*
Alex Shrage *(Gen Counsel)*
Rachael Pierson *(Acct Exec & Producer)*
Ashley Waller *(Office Mgr)*

Accounts:
Boeing
Bose
Champion Enterprises Holdings, LLC
Classic BMW
CNN
Dedon Blades of Grass
Ferragamo
HBO
Lego
Lexus
LVMH Makeup Forever
Mazda
Mazda Interactive Tours
Mazda6
Nike Mash Up
Revlon
Target
Venetian Hotels
Zappos Couture.Zappos.com

SASQUATCH
(Formerly Sasquatch - Advertising, Brand Strategy, Interactive, Design)
5331 SW Macadam Ave Ste 348, Portland, OR 97239
Tel.: (503) 222-2346
Fax: (503) 222-2492
E-Mail: kenc@sasquatchagency.com
Web Site: www.sasquatchagency.com

Employees: 12
Year Founded: 1996

National Agency Associations: AMIN

Agency Specializes In: Above-the-Line, Advertising, Affluent Market, Alternative Advertising, Brand Development & Integration, Broadcast, Business-To-Business, Cable T.V., Catalogs, Collateral, Communications, Consulting, Consumer Goods, Consumer Marketing, Consumer Publications, Corporate Identity, Crisis Communications, Digital/Interactive, Electronic Media, Entertainment, Environmental, Fashion/Apparel, Financial, Graphic Design, Guerilla Marketing, Hospitality, Identity Marketing, Integrated Marketing, International, Internet/Web Design, Legal Services, Leisure, Logo & Package Design, Luxury Products, Magazines, Media Buying Services, Media Planning, Media Relations, Men's Market, Multimedia, Newspaper, Newspapers & Magazines, Out-of-Home Media, Outdoor, Package Design, Paid Searches, Planning & Consultation, Point of Purchase, Point of Sale, Print, Production, Production (Print), Public Relations, Radio, Real Estate, Social Marketing/Nonprofit, Social Media, Sports Market, Strategic Planning/Research, Trade & Consumer Magazines, Transportation, Travel & Tourism, Viral/Buzz/Word of Mouth, Web (Banner Ads, Pop-ups, etc.), Women's Market

Approx. Annual Billings: $6,500,000

Breakdown of Gross Billings by Media: Brdcst.: 12%; Cable T.V.: 15%; Collateral: 10%; Graphic Design: 10%; Internet Adv.: 8%; Logo & Package Design: 5%; Mags.: 25%; Newsp.: 10%; Outdoor: 5%

Ken Chitwood *(Partner, Acct Dir & Dir-Media)*
Danny Pettey *(Head-PR & Social Media)*
Kristin Casaletto *(Sr Dir-Design)*
Jack Chitwood *(Dir-Tech)*
Nick Greener *(Dir-Social Media)*
Devin Brown *(Project Mgr & Asst Acct Exec)*
Wes Barnhart *(Acct Supvr)*
Jessica Vowell *(Acct Exec)*
Sandi Mcgrogan *(Designer)*
Kevin Murphy *(Designer-Production)*
Katie Grimshaw *(Asst Acct Exec)*
Scott Horlbeck *(Coord-Social Media)*

Accounts:
Gerber Legendary Blades; Portland, OR Outdoor Gear; 2008
GSI Outdoors; Spokane, WA Sporting Goods; 2008
Heathman Lodge; Vancouver, WA Hotel; 1997
Original S.W.A.T. Footwear; Modesto, CA Law Enforcement/Military Footwear; 2005
River Rock Casino; Geyserville, CA Resort & Casino; 2007
Skammania Lodge; Stevenson, WA Resort; 2005
White Sierra; San Jose, CA Outerwear, Clothing; 2009
Wiley X Sunglasses; Livermore, CA Eyewear; 2006

SATURDAY BRAND COMMUNICATIONS
1310 S Tryon St Ste 110, Charlotte, NC 28203
Tel.: (704) 919-0034
E-Mail: info@heysaturday.com
Web Site: www.heysaturday.com

Agency Specializes In: Advertising, Brand Development & Integration, Digital/Interactive, Internet/Web Design, Media Buying Services, Public Relations, Publicity/Promotions, Search Engine Optimization, Social Media, Strategic Planning/Research

Tim Dillingham *(Creative Dir)*

Accounts:
New-NoDa Brewing Company

SATURDAY MFG INC.
1717 Ingersoll Ave Bay 121, Des Moines, IA 50309
Tel.: (515) 440-0014
Web Site: www.saturdaymfg.com

Year Founded: 2009

Agency Specializes In: Advertising, Brand Development & Integration, Collateral, Corporate Identity, Print

Brian Sauer *(Art Dir)*
Scott Lewellen *(Copywriter)*

Accounts:
Thelmas Treats

SAVAGE INITIATIVE
3502 Windsor Rd, Wall Township, NJ 07719
Tel.: (732) 280-6912
Fax: (732) 280-6913
E-Mail: info@savageinitiative.com
Web Site: www.savageinitiative.com

Employees: 1
Year Founded: 1997

Agency Specializes In: Advertising

Approx. Annual Billings: $150,000

Shawn N. Savage *(Owner & Designer)*

Accounts:
CoilWorld Magazine
The Lifestyle Company
Permeable Technologies Inc.

SAVAGE SOLUTIONS, LLC
4118 W Minnesota Ct, Franklin, WI 53132
Tel.: (414) 732-4946
Fax: (414) 423-0678
E-Mail: csavage@savage-solutions.com
Web Site: www.savagesolutionsllc.com

E-Mail for Key Personnel:
President: csavage@savage-solutions.com
Creative Dir.: jhiggins@savage-solutions.com
Public Relations: ksavage@savage-solutions.com

Employees: 6
Year Founded: 2005

National Agency Associations: PRSA

Agency Specializes In: Advertising, Brand Development & Integration, Co-op Advertising, Collateral, Computers & Software, Consulting, Consumer Goods, Consumer Marketing, Corporate Communications, Crisis Communications, Custom Publishing, Digital/Interactive, Direct Response

Marketing, Direct-to-Consumer, E-Commerce, Electronic Media, Email, Graphic Design, Guerilla Marketing, Health Care Services, In-Store Advertising, Integrated Marketing, Local Marketing, Magazines, Media Buying Services, Media Planning, Media Relations, Media Training, Mobile Marketing, Multimedia, New Product Development, New Technologies, Newspaper, Newspapers & Magazines, Outdoor, Package Design, Point of Purchase, Point of Sale, Print, Product Placement, Production, Production (Ad, Film, Broadcast), Production (Print), Promotions, Public Relations, Publicity/Promotions, Publishing, Radio, Retail, Sports Market, T.V., Transportation, Web (Banner Ads, Pop-ups, etc.)

Approx. Annual Billings: $500,000

Kelly Savage *(Owner & Pres-Savage Total Services Inc.)*
Cory C. Savage *(Pres)*
Mark Hungsberg *(Sr Dir-Art)*
Jackie Michl *(Producer-Digital)*
Joel Hermanson *(Assoc Dir-Creative)*
Lara Eucalano *(Copywriter & Specialist-Social Media)*
Michael Farrell *(Designer-Web)*
Matt Bougie *(Project Coord-Digital)*

Accounts:
RipRoad; New York, NY; 2008

THE SAWTOOTH GROUP
141 West Front St., Red Bank, NJ 07701
Tel.: (732) 945-1004
E-Mail: info@sawtoothgroup.com
Web Site: www.sawtoothgroup.com

E-Mail for Key Personnel:
Creative Dir.: kbridges@sawtoothgroup.com

Employees: 75
Year Founded: 1988

Agency Specializes In: Advertising, Brand Development & Integration, Broadcast, Cable T.V., College, Consumer Goods, Consumer Marketing, Consumer Publications, Digital/Interactive, Education, Experience Design, Financial, Food Service, Health Care Services, Hospitality, Integrated Marketing, Leisure, Magazines, Media Planning, Newspaper, Newspapers & Magazines, Out-of-Home Media, Outdoor, Pets , Planning & Consultation, Print, Production, Production (Ad, Film, Broadcast), Production (Print), Radio, Real Estate, Search Engine Optimization, Social Marketing/Nonprofit, Social Media, Sponsorship, Strategic Planning/Research, T.V., Trade & Consumer Magazines, Travel & Tourism, Women's Market

Sawtooth Group believes that to discover the truth and genuinely connect with consumers, they must literally become the consumers. That's why they immerse themselves in your brand. It's the Sawtooth Way.

Approx. Annual Billings: $150,000,000

Bill Schmermund *(Partner & CEO)*
Kristi Bridges *(Partner & Exec Dir-Creative)*
Jay Quilty *(Partner-Client Svcs)*
Tzeitel Haviland *(Dir-Media)*
Susan Von Brachel *(Assoc Dir-Creative)*
Jennifer Mulligan *(Media Planner)*
Lauren DiMatteo *(Sr Media Planner)*
Lisa Milewski *(Assoc Media Dir)*

Accounts:
Beech-Nut
Blue Buffalo
Continuum Cancer Centers of New York
The Dwelling Place of New York
Freixenet
Lawry's
Lunch Break
McCormick & Company, Inc
Old Bay
PNC
Rewind
Signature Brands
Thai Kitchen

Division

Sawtooth Health
100 Woodbridge Ctr Dr Ste 102, Woodbridge, NJ 07095
Tel.: (732) 636-6600
Fax: (732) 602-4212
Web Site: www.sawtoothgroup.com

Year Founded: 2007

Bill Schmermund *(CEO & Partner-Sawtooth Grp)*
Kristi Bridges *(Partner & Exec Dir-Creative)*
Jay Quilty *(Partner-Client Svcs)*
Tzeitel Haviland *(Dir-Media)*
Lisa Milewski *(Assoc Dir-Media)*
Dawn Morris *(Assoc Dir-Creative)*
Jenny Mulligan *(Assoc Dir-Media)*
Allison Gibbons *(Mgr)*
Lauren Mondoro *(Supvr-Media)*
Seth Ferris *(Sr Specialist-Digital & Art)*
Rebecca Mencel *(Sr Specialist-Digital Media)*

Accounts:
1-800-DOCTORS
Beach Nut
Coldwell Banker
Horizon
Lawrys
McCormick
PNC
Willow Stream

SAWYER AGENCY
1002 Milwaukee Ave, Los Angeles, CA 90042
Tel.: (323) 739-0049
E-Mail: info@sawyeragency.com
Web Site: www.sawyeragency.com

Agency Specializes In: Advertising, Digital/Interactive, Graphic Design, Internet/Web Design, Logo & Package Design, Print

Accounts:
Natural Resources Defense Council

SAWYER STUDIOS INC.
36 W 25th St 12th Fl, New York, NY 10010
Tel.: (212) 645-4455
E-Mail: info@asawyer.com
Web Site: www.sawyerentertainment.com

Agency Specializes In: Advertising, Digital/Interactive, Internet/Web Design, Media Planning, Print, Public Relations, Social Media

Arnie Sawyer *(Founder & CEO)*
Zachary Soreff *(Partner)*
Courtney Jones *(Dir-Bus & Agency Dev)*
Lexi deVogelaere *(Acct Mgr)*
Steven Hopkinson *(Acct Mgr)*
Adam Paulen *(Acct Supvr)*
Jared Shaffer *(Designer)*

Accounts:
New-Drafthouse Films
New-Focus Features
New-HBO
New-Magnolia Pictures
New-Vimeo

SAY IT LOUD
1121 N Mills Ave, Orlando, FL 32803
Tel.: (407) 898-7299
E-Mail: 411@sayitloud.us
Web Site: www.sayitloud.us

Agency Specializes In: Advertising, Brand Development & Integration

Troy Branson *(Acct Svcs Dir)*
Cortney Smith *(Acct Coord & Coord-Production)*

Accounts:
UCF Tv

SAY IT WITH WORDS
32068 Waterside Ln, Westlake Village, CA 91361-3622
Tel.: (818) 991-1587
E-Mail: nfinkel@siww.net
Web Site: www.siww.net

E-Mail for Key Personnel:
President: nfinkel@siww.net

Employees: 4
Year Founded: 1982

National Agency Associations: DMA

Agency Specializes In: Advertising, Brand Development & Integration, Business Publications, Business-To-Business, Collateral, Communications, Consumer Marketing, Corporate Communications, Corporate Identity, Customer Relationship Management, Direct Response Marketing, Direct-to-Consumer, E-Commerce, Event Planning & Marketing, Financial, Guerilla Marketing, Identity Marketing, In-Store Advertising, Infomercials, Integrated Marketing, Local Marketing, Over-50 Market, Planning & Consultation, Point of Purchase, Product Placement, Production (Print), Promotions, Public Relations, Publicity/Promotions, Search Engine Optimization, Seniors' Market, T.V., Women's Market, Yellow Pages Advertising

Approx. Annual Billings: $160,000

Naomi Finkel *(Owner & Dir-Creative)*

Accounts:
The Costco Connection; Isiquah, WA; 2006
JEMEC Management Consulting; Thousand Oaks, CA Leadership Management Consulting; 2003
Jonathan Greenfield Financial
Live-Light Bariatric Surgery
LTC Properties; Westlake Village, CA Assisted Living & Nursing Properties; 2008
Mark Kennedy Financial
New West Symphony League
Rotary Club of Westlake Village; CA; 2008

SAYLES & WINNIKOFF COMMUNICATIONS
1201 Broadway Ste 904, New York, NY 10001
Tel.: (212) 725-5200
Fax: (212) 679-7368
E-Mail: info@sayleswinnikoff.com
Web Site: www.sayleswinnikoff.com

Employees: 10

Year Founded: 2003

Agency Specializes In: Advertising, Public Relations

Alan Winnikoff *(Owner & Co-Principal)*
Carina Sayles *(CEO)*
Geena Pandolfi *(Acct Exec)*

Accounts:
Dimensional Branding Group
Glynwood Center
Igloo Diamonds
Koobli
Mental Health Association of NYC
National Engineer's Week Foundation
RIOT Media
Sonar Entertainment Television Programming; 2008

SBC ADVERTISING
333 W Nationwide Blvd, Columbus, OH 43215
Tel.: (614) 255-2333
Fax: (614) 255-2600
Web Site: www.sbcadvertising.com

E-Mail for Key Personnel:
President: ddennis@sbcadvertising.com
Creative Dir.: nwiderschein@sbcadvertising.com
Media Dir.: phnidka@sbcadvertising.com

Employees: 125
Year Founded: 1969

National Agency Associations: PRSA

Agency Specializes In: Advertising, Advertising Specialties, African-American Market, Automotive, Bilingual Market, Brand Development & Integration, Broadcast, Business-To-Business, Children's Market, Co-op Advertising, Collateral, Communications, Consumer Marketing, Digital/Interactive, Direct Response Marketing, E-Commerce, Education, Event Planning & Marketing, Fashion/Apparel, Financial, Food Service, Health Care Services, High Technology, Hispanic Market, In-Store Advertising, Industrial, Information Technology, Internet/Web Design, Investor Relations, Local Marketing, Logo & Package Design, Magazines, Media Buying Services, Merchandising, New Product Development, Newspaper, Newspapers & Magazines, Out-of-Home Media, Outdoor, Pets , Planning & Consultation, Point of Purchase, Point of Sale, Print, Production, Public Relations, Radio, Restaurant, Retail, Sales Promotion, Sponsorship, Strategic Planning/Research, T.V., Trade & Consumer Magazines

Approx. Annual Billings: $100,000,000

Neil Widerschein *(Partner & Chief Creative Officer)*
Matt Wilson *(COO & Gen Mgr)*
Paul Hnidka *(Sr VP & Dir-Media)*
Jim Livecchi *(Sr VP-B2B Mktg)*
Ken Brown *(VP & Acct Dir)*
Pete Fantine *(VP-Bus Analytics & Acct Dir)*
Lance Dooley *(Dir-Creative)*
Andy Knight *(Dir-Creative)*
Leon Yourkiewicz *(Assoc Dir-Creative)*
Valerie Wunder *(Acct Supvr-PR)*
Jessica Rowland *(Acct Exec)*

Accounts:
AAA
AARP
Abrasive Technology
AJWright
Barbasol
Bed, Bath & Beyond
Butler Animal Health Supply
BuyBuy Baby
Channellock, Inc.
Cranel Imaging
Elmer's Products
Genie Garage Doors
Huntington Bank
IGS Energy
Johnson Diversey
Krazy Glue
North American
Ohio Tuition Trust Authority (Agency of Record)
Overhead Door Corporation (Agency of Record)
Plaskolite, Inc.
Schottenstein Zox & Dunn
Solo Foodservice
Subway
Surescripts
Thirty-One Gifts
Tyco Fire & Building Products
Ultimate Software
Value City Furniture
Wayne-Dalton
Whirlpool
White Castle System, Inc.
Worthington Industries

SCALES ADVERTISING
2303 Wycliff St, Saint Paul, MN 55114
Tel.: (651) 641-0226
Fax: (651) 641-1031
E-Mail: general@scalesadvertising.com
Web Site: www.scalesadvertising.com

Employees: 63
Year Founded: 1972

Agency Specializes In: Advertising, Catalogs, Corporate Identity, Direct Response Marketing, Package Design, Point of Purchase, Trade & Consumer Magazines

Jill Gapinski *(VP-Ops)*
Jim Finnegan *(Head-Production)*
Jeff Richards *(Acct Dir)*
Duane Dickhaus *(Dir-Creative)*
John Dyrhaug *(Dir-Creative)*
Corby Bodenburg *(Mgr-Digital Media)*
Anna Shefveland *(Mgr-HR)*
Lindsay Lajiness *(Sr Acct Exec)*

Accounts:
3M Fire Protection
C.H. Robinson
Capital Safety
Cuddeback
EcoXpress Couriers Courier Services
Hayward Pool Products
Rage Broadheads Archery & Hunting Broadheads Mfr
Wagner SprayTech
Yeti Coolers

SCATENA DANIELS COMMUNICATIONS INC.
2165 San Diego Ave, San Diego, CA 92110
Tel.: (619) 232-0222
Fax: (619) 501-9758
E-Mail: info@scatenadaniels.com
Web Site: www.scatenadaniels.com

Agency Specializes In: Advertising, Communications, Event Planning & Marketing, Media Relations, Public Relations, Social Media

Arika Anderson Daniels *(Founder & Partner)*
Denise Scatena *(Founder & Partner)*
Sandra De La Torre *(Acct Exec)*
Ann Marie Price *(Acct Exec)*

Accounts:
Coastal Animal Hospital Advanced Veterinary Technology, House Call Services, Modern Medicine
Community HousingWorks Brand Message Development, Media Outreach
Cranial Technologies Medical Services
Elizabethan Desserts; Encinitas, CA Media Relations, Social Media
Home Start, Inc.
I Love A Clean San Diego
Mama's Kitchen Charitable Organization, Strategy
Marshall Faulk Foundation Training Services
National Comedy Theatre Media Relations, Social Media Outreach Strategy
Old Town Chamber of Commerce
Planned Parenthood of the Pacific Southwest Strategic Leadership
San Diego Festival of Science & Engineering BIOCOM
The San Diego REPertory Theatre Entertainment Services
San Diego State University School of Journalism & Media Studies
SecondWave Recycling
New-Susan G. Komen San Diego (Public Relations Agency of Record) Media Relations

SCENARIODNA
41 E 11th St, New York, NY 10003
Tel.: (917) 364-9742
E-Mail: marielena@scenariodna.com
Web Site: www.scenariodna.com

Employees: 15
Year Founded: 2001

Agency Specializes In: Brand Development & Integration, Branded Entertainment, College, Communications, Consulting, Consumer Goods, Consumer Marketing, Fashion/Apparel, Integrated Marketing, Leisure, Luxury Products, Market Research, New Technologies, Planning & Consultation, Strategic Planning/Research

Tim Stock *(Partner)*
Marie Lena Tupot *(Partner)*

Accounts:
American Greetings; 2006
Mercedes Benz
MillerCoors
Nestle
Toyota
Unilever

SCHAEFER ADVERTISING CO.
(Formerly Blanchard Schaefer Advertising & Public Relations)
1228 S Adams St, Fort Worth, TX 76104
Tel.: (817) 226-4332
Fax: (817) 860-2004
E-Mail: info@schaeferadvertising.com
Web Site: www.schaeferadvertising.com

Employees: 11
Year Founded: 1985

National Agency Associations: AAF-AMA-PRSA

Agency Specializes In: Advertising, Brand Development & Integration, Broadcast, Business-To-Business, Cable T.V., Co-op Advertising, Collateral, Commercial Photography, Consumer Marketing, Consumer Publications, Corporate Identity, Cosmetics, Direct Response Marketing, Electronic Media, Exhibit/Trade Shows, Health Care Services, Internet/Web Design, Legal Services, Logo & Package Design, Magazines, Medical Products, Newspaper, Newspapers & Magazines, Out-of-Home Media, Outdoor, Pharmaceutical, Planning & Consultation, Point of Purchase, Point of Sale, Print, Production, Public Relations, Publicity/Promotions, Radio, Recruitment, Restaurant, Retail, Sales Promotion, Strategic Planning/Research, T.V., Teen Market, Trade & Consumer Magazines, Transportation

Approx. Annual Billings: $11,000,000

Todd Lancaster *(VP & Dir-Creative)*
Kim McRee *(VP-Acct Svc)*
Maren Gibbs *(Project Mgr-Production)*
Erin Naterman *(Acct Supvr)*
Charlie Howlett *(Sr Designer)*

Accounts:
The Coffee Bean & Tea Leaf
Emcare
Frame Saver
JPS Health Network Health System; 2003
Lone Star Film Society (Agency of Record)
Pegasus Logistics
Rental One
Supply Depot

SCHAEFER MEDIA & MARKETING

1659 Central Ave Ste 201, Albany, NY 12205
Tel.: (518) 533-9870
Fax: (518) 514-1383
Web Site: www.schaefer-media.com

Agency Specializes In: Advertising, Brand Development & Integration, Corporate Identity, Graphic Design, Media Buying Services, Outdoor, Print, Radio, T.V.

John Schaefer *(Principal)*
Derek Rogers *(Art Dir)*

Accounts:
Exit 9 Wine & Liquor Warehouse
Mayfair Jewelers
Security Plumbing & Heating Supply

SCHAFER CONDON CARTER

1029 W Madison, Chicago, IL 60607
Tel.: (312) 464-1666
Fax: (312) 464-0628
E-Mail: gen@schafercondoncarter.com
Web Site: www.schafercondoncarter.com

E-Mail for Key Personnel:
Creative Dir.: tim@sccadv.com
Production Mgr.: Scott@sccadv.com

Employees: 60
Year Founded: 1989

Agency Specializes In: Advertising, Brand Development & Integration, Business-To-Business, Collateral, Communications, Consulting, Food Service, Logo & Package Design, New Product Development, Planning & Consultation, Print, Public Relations, Restaurant, Sponsorship, Trade & Consumer Magazines

Approx. Annual Billings: $50,000,000

Breakdown of Gross Billings by Media: Other: 20%; Print: 40%; Radio: 20%; T.V.: 20%

Mark Schafer *(Chm)*
David Selby *(Pres & Mng Partner)*
Tim Condon *(CEO)*
Mike Grossman *(Mng Partner-SCC & Grossman PR)*
Greg Wenstrup *(COO)*
Gwen Friedow *(VP-Brand Plng)*
Kristin Glunz *(Acct Dir)*
Erika Bye *(Dir-Digital Media)*
Michael Dorich *(Dir-Creative)*
Paige Robinson *(Sr Acct Exec)*
Laoise Rubio *(Sr Acct Exec)*
Laura Koziel *(Sr Strategist-Media)*
Colleen Gerth *(Acct Exec)*
Emily Finlay *(Asst Planner-Brand)*

Accounts:
Allen Edmonds
Armour-Eckrich Meats
Azteca Foods; Chicago, IL Azteca Brand Tortillas, Buena Vida Fat Free Tortillas
Beam Global Spirits
Campbell Soup Co
Chicago Cubs
ConAgra Foodservice; 2007
First Midwest Bank; Itasca, IL
Giordano's Enterprises Inc; Loop, IL Campaign: "Hungry"
GoodFoods Group (Agency of Record); 2008
Growing Lean
Ideal Industries, Inc.
John Morrell Food Group
Land O'Lakes (Agency of Record)
National Pork Board
New Chapter Organics
Procter & Gamble
Rotary International
Social Market Analytics
Solo Cup Company; Chicago, IL Disposable Tableware
Terlato Wines International; Lake Bluff, IL
Uncle Dougie's
Winona Capital Management Brand Planning, Marketing Creative Services
Women's Food Service Forum

SCHEFFEY INC

350 New Holland Ave, Lancaster, PA 17602
Tel.: (717) 569-8274
Fax: (717) 569-8276
E-Mail: info@scheffey.com
Web Site: www.scheffey.com

Agency Specializes In: Advertising, Brand Development & Integration, Broadcast, Corporate Identity, Email, Graphic Design, Internet/Web Design, Media Buying Services, Media Planning, Media Relations, Media Training, Outdoor, Print, Public Relations, Social Media, Strategic Planning/Research

Scott Scheffey *(Pres & Dir-Strategic)*
Douglas Hershey *(VP & Creative Dir)*
Hope Graby *(Dir-PR & Mgr-Client)*
Lisa Campbell *(Dir-Strategic)*
Kelly Rozick *(Mgr-Client)*
Bryan Coe *(Strategist-Digital Mktg)*
Lisa Lysle *(Media Buyer)*
Gwen Hossler *(Coord-Ops)*
Kristen Thomas *(Coord-Project)*

Accounts:
Avant Garden Decor
Inclinator Company of America

SCHIEFER MEDIA INC

20361 Irvine Ave Ste B-1, Newport Beach, CA 92660
Tel.: (949) 336-1700
Fax: (949) 335-4601
Web Site: www.schiefermedia.com

Agency Specializes In: Advertising, Brand Development & Integration, Media Buying Services, Media Planning, Print, Public Relations, Social Media

James Schiefer *(Pres)*
Alyce Strapp *(Dir-Media)*
Dawn Selleck *(Office Mgr)*
Paul Schiefer *(Sr Acct Exec)*
Michele Raffanello *(Media Buyer-Integrated & Planner)*
Ellen Scott *(Media Planner-Integrated & Buyer)*

Accounts:
MagnaFlow (Media Agency of Record)

SCHIFINO LEE ADVERTISING

511 W Bay St Ste 400, Tampa, FL 33606
Tel.: (813) 258-5858
Fax: (813) 254-1146
E-Mail: info@schifinolee.com
Web Site: www.schifinolee.com

Employees: 20
Year Founded: 1993

Agency Specializes In: Digital/Interactive, Graphic Design, Media Buying Services, Public Relations

Ben Lee *(Owner & Principal)*
Howard Beauchamp *(Sr Dir-Art)*
Pat Floyd *(Sr Dir-Digital Art)*
Roxie M. Clements *(Sr Acct Dir)*
Ann E. Sinclair *(Dir-Art)*
Jim Flemister *(Mgr-Production)*
Kendra Mahon *(Acct Exec)*
Michael Looper *(Copywriter)*

Accounts:
AT&T Business
Catalina Marketing
DeBartolo Holdings LLC
Elder Automotive Group
elogic
Eva Dry
Gasparilla Interactive Festival (Agency of Record)
Greyster
Jaguar
Lazydays RV Supercenter
Tampa Bay Sports Commission Campaign: "New Now"
TMA
Vigo Alessi Alessi Labels
WellCare Health Plans Lead Generation, Medicare Advantage Plans, Online Enrollment

SCHNEIDER+LEVINE PR+COMMUNICATIONS

(Formerly SnL Communications)
1700 Sawtelle Blvd Ste 111, Los Angeles, CA 90025
Tel.: (310) 996-0239
Fax: (310) 996-0249
Web Site: www.slpr.co

Employees: 10
Year Founded: 1988

Agency Specializes In: Advertising, Promotions, Public Relations

Staci Levine *(Partner)*
Karen Schneider *(Partner)*
Ramsay Horn *(Sr Acct Exec)*
Shayna Cooperstone *(Coord-PR)*

Accounts:
MEK Denim Fitting Hand-Crafted

SCHOLLNICK ADVERTISING

2828 Metairie Ct, Metairie, LA 70002
Tel.: (504) 838-9615
Fax: (504) 833-8638
E-Mail: info@schollnickadvertising.com
Web Site: www.schollnickadvertising.com

Year Founded: 1981

Karen Shuey *(CFO & Gen Mgr)*
Eileen Levy *(Dir-Creative)*

Accounts:
Pizza Hut

SCHOOL OF THOUGHT

544 Pacific Ave 3rd Fl, San Francisco, CA 94133
Tel.: (415) 433-4033
E-Mail: admissions@schoolofthought.com
Web Site: www.schoolofthought.com

Year Founded: 2008

Agency Specializes In: Advertising, Digital/Interactive, Media Buying Services, Media Planning, Print, Radio, Social Media

Joseph Newfield *(Co-Founder & Dir-Creative)*
Tom Geary *(Partner & Exec Dir-Creative)*
Rachel Newell *(Acct Dir)*
Kaity Ferretti *(Dir-Art)*
Stacia Hanley *(Dir-Media)*
Faruk Sagcan *(Dir-Art)*
Danielle Detrick *(Office Mgr)*
Brenna Murphy *(Mgr-Bus Dev)*
Diana Wolff *(Acct Supvr)*
Ryan Gelow *(Sr Strategist-Media)*

Accounts:
Intrepid Travel Creative
LeapMotion
Meyenberg Goat Milk
Milliman
Naked Energy Bars
North Lake Tahoe
Red Bull North America, Inc.
Rumble Entertainment
San Francisco Department of the Environment (Agency of Record) Experiential, Out-of-Home, SEO, Social Advertising
The Walt Disney Company
WebEx

SCHRAMM MARKETING GROUP

11 Penn Plz 5th Fl, New York, NY 10001-2003
Tel.: (212) 983-0219
Fax: (212) 983-0524
Web Site: www.schrammnyc.com/

Employees: 2

Joe Schramm *(Mng Partner)*
Rafael Eli *(COO)*

Accounts:
The Hispanic Television Summit
Soccer United Marketing

SCHROEDER ADVERTISING, INC.

412 Tenafly Rd, Englewood, NJ 07631-1733
Tel.: (201) 568-4500
Fax: (201) 568-3028
E-Mail: lyn@schroederinc.net
Web Site: www.schroederinc.net

Employees: 5
Year Founded: 1978

Agency Specializes In: Advertising, Brand Development & Integration, Collateral, Consumer Marketing, Consumer Publications, Corporate Identity, Graphic Design, Internet/Web Design, Logo & Package Design, Print, Production, Public Relations, Trade & Consumer Magazines

Approx. Annual Billings: $1,775,000

Breakdown of Gross Billings by Media: Collateral: $100,000; Fees: $75,000; Logo & Package Design: $50,000; Mags.: $1,050,000; Pub. Rels.: $50,000; Worldwide Web Sites: $450,000

Lyn Schroeder *(Pres)*

Accounts:
Cross River Design; Annandale, NJ Landscape Architects; 2004
Delia Inc.; Wallingford, CT High-End Kitchen Appliances; 1989
Diverscity.net Web Entertainment Site; 2000
etable.net; New York, NY Online Food Magazine; 2000
Greystone & Company; New York, NY Mortgage Banking; 2003
Greystone Healthcare Corp.; Tampa, FL Nursing Homes & Rehab Centers; 2004
Greystone Home Collection; New York, NY & Los Angeles, CA Accessories, Antiques, Furniture, Textiles; 2002
Jim Thompson Thai Silk Co.; Atlanta, GA; Bangkok, Thailand Thai Silk Fabric; 1996
Paul Mathieu
Roche Bobois

SCHUBERT COMMUNICATIONS, INC.

112 Schubert Dr, Downingtown, PA 19335-3382
Tel.: (610) 269-2100
Fax: (610) 269-2275
Web Site: www.schubertb2b.com/

E-Mail for Key Personnel:
President: jschubert@schubert.com
Creative Dir.: rcarango@schubert.com
Public Relations: chenneghan@schubert.com

Employees: 18
Year Founded: 1978

National Agency Associations: PRSA

Agency Specializes In: Advertising, Brand Development & Integration, Business-To-Business, Communications, Consulting, Industrial, Internet/Web Design, Logo & Package Design, Print, Public Relations, Publicity/Promotions, Strategic Planning/Research, Technical Advertising

Approx. Annual Billings: $5,000,000

Breakdown of Gross Billings by Media: Bus. Publs.: $1,250,000; Collateral: $750,000; D.M.: $500,000; Internet Adv.: $500,000; Pub. Rels.: $1,250,000; Worldwide Web Sites: $750,000

Joseph F. Schubert *(Founder & CEO)*
Rich Carango *(Pres & Dir-Creative)*
Christopher D. Raymond *(VP-Interactive Svcs)*
Peggy Schubert *(Mgr-Fin)*
Chris Henneghan *(Strategist-Brand)*
Eileen Haines *(Coord-Media)*

Accounts:
Avanti Markets, Inc Interactive Marketing, Strategic Marketing
Datastrip
Hale Products; Conshohocken, PA; 1997
Houghton International Inc.
Sensaphone Email Marketing, Public Relations, Strategic Marketing Services

SCHUM & ASSOCIATES

1438 Cedar Ave, McLean, VA 22101-3514
Tel.: (703) 448-8150
Fax: (703) 448-8479
E-Mail: schum@schum.com
Web Site: www.schum.com/contact/contact_index.htm

Employees: 6
Year Founded: 1981

Agency Specializes In: Advertising

Guy Schum *(Pres & Dir-Creative)*
Diane L. Schum *(Acct Exec)*

Accounts:
AGC (Associated General Contractors Association of America)
American Institutes for Research
Art Directors Club of Metropolitan Washington
Barbara Maude's Bakery
Clark Construction
The College of William & Mary
Focus Technologies, Inc.
George Washington University
GridWise Alliance
ILEX Construction & Woodworking
The John Akridge Company
Medical Research Laboratories (MRL)
Patrick Henry College
Rudd, Inc.
Urban Land Institute
The Washington Post

SCHUPP COMPANY, INC.

401 Pine St, Saint Louis, MO 63102-2731
Tel.: (314) 421-5200
Fax: (314) 421-5554
E-Mail: info@schuppco.com
Web Site: www.schuppco.com

E-Mail for Key Personnel:
President: mschupp@schuppco.com

Employees: 25
Year Founded: 1993

Agency Specializes In: Advertising, Brand Development & Integration, Broadcast, Business-To-Business, Children's Market, Consumer Marketing, Consumer Publications, Corporate Identity, Entertainment, Financial, Graphic Design, High Technology, Internet/Web Design, Logo & Package Design, New Product Development, Point of Purchase, Point of Sale, Print, Production, Radio, Sales Promotion, Sports Market, Strategic Planning/Research, T.V., Trade & Consumer Magazines

Breakdown of Gross Billings by Media: Mags.: 15%; Newsp.: 10%; Outdoor: 10%; Radio: 30%; T.V.: 35%

Emily Gruninger *(Acct Dir)*
Linda Schumacher *(Dir-Brdcst & Mgr-IT)*
Jessen Wabeke *(Assoc Dir-Creative)*
Cindy Patrick *(Office Mgr & Mgr-Facilities)*
Sarah Bieber *(Acct Supvr)*
Lindsey Thielen *(Acct Exec)*

Accounts:
The Medicine Shoppe International; 2004
MillerCoors; Milwaukee, WI; 2001
The Saint Louis Blues; Saint Louis, MO; 1997

SCITECH MARKETING

161 Ash St, Spencer, MA 01562
Tel.: (508) 826-5900
Web Site: scitechmarketing.com

E-Mail for Key Personnel:
President: jim@sctgrp.com
Creative Dir.: dennis@sctgrp.com
Media Dir.: laura@sctgrp.com
Public Relations: mike@sctgrp.com

Employees: 3
Year Founded: 2008

Agency Specializes In: Advertising, Advertising Specialties, Automotive, Aviation & Aerospace, Brand Development & Integration, Broadcast, Business Publications, Business-To-Business, Co-op Advertising, Collateral, Commercial Photography, Communications, Corporate Communications, Corporate Identity, Direct Response Marketing, E-Commerce, Electronic Media, Engineering, Environmental, Event Planning & Marketing, Exhibit/Trade Shows, Graphic Design, Health Care Services, High Technology, Industrial, Information Technology, Internet/Web Design, Logo & Package Design, Magazines, Marine, Media Buying Services, Medical Products, Multimedia, New Product Development, Newspaper, Newspapers & Magazines, Outdoor, Pharmaceutical, Print, Production, Public Relations, Radio, Strategic

Planning/Research, Technical Advertising

C. Michael Toomey *(Pres)*

SCOPE CREATIVE AGENCY

3401 Chester Ave Ste G, Bakersfield, CA 93301
Tel.: (661) 412-2265
Web Site: www.wearescope.com

Agency Specializes In: Advertising, Broadcast, Corporate Identity, Digital/Interactive, Graphic Design, Print

Tessa Bender *(Editor & Copywriter)*
Jean-Luc Slagle *(Dir-Creative)*

Accounts:
Barber Honda
Chain Cohn Stiles
IES Electrical Construction
Taft College

SCOPPECHIO

(Formerly Creative Alliance)
437 W Jefferson St, Louisville, KY 40202
Tel.: (502) 584-8787
Fax: (502) 589-9900
Toll Free: (800) 525-0294
E-Mail: Toni.Clem@Scoppechio.com
Web Site: www.scoppechio.com/home

Employees: 150
Year Founded: 1987

Agency Specializes In: Advertising, Brand Development & Integration, Broadcast, Corporate Communications, Corporate Identity, Digital/Interactive, Education, Entertainment, Event Planning & Marketing, Exhibit/Trade Shows, Government/Political, Graphic Design, Health Care Services, In-Store Advertising, Integrated Marketing, Internet/Web Design, Local Marketing, Logo & Package Design, Media Buying Services, Merchandising, New Product Development, Out-of-Home Media, Outdoor, Package Design, Point of Purchase, Print, Production, Public Relations, Publicity/Promotions, Radio, Restaurant, Shopper Marketing, Sponsorship, Travel & Tourism

Approx. Annual Billings: $185,776,910

Toni Clem *(Pres & COO)*
Jerry Preyss *(CEO)*
Thomas Hewitt Gilmore *(CMO)*
Joe Adams *(Exec VP & Sr Designer)*
Carrie Crawford Frazier *(VP & Acct Dir)*
Andy Vucinich *(VP & Dir-Creative)*
Denny Leffler *(VP-HR)*
Rico Nieto *(VP-Multicultural Mktg)*
Edward King *(Sr Dir-Art)*
Charlotte Reed *(Sr Acct Dir)*
Matthew Wolford *(Dir-Digital Art)*
Jordan Kassel *(Mgr-Mktg Comm)*
Katy O'Toole *(Acct Supvr)*
Trevor Howie *(Supvr-Media)*
Holly Wood *(Supvr-Media)*
Katherine Eckert *(Sr Acct Exec)*
Nicholas Hayward Bennett *(Acct Exec)*
Lacey Bobo *(Acct Exec)*
Shelby Nicole Fonda *(Acct Exec)*
Jessica Lauren Blanchard *(Copywriter)*

Accounts:
New-Baptist Health Kentucky (Agency of Record) Creative, Digital, Media, Public Relations, Strategic Planning
Churchill Downs, Inc.
Community Health Systems; Nashville, TN; 2006
Einstein Noah Restaurant Group, Inc.
General Electric Company
KCTCS; Lousiville, KY
Kentucky Department of Tourism
Kentucky Humane Society; Louisville, KY; 2005
KentuckyOne Health
KFC Corporation (Hispanic Agency of Record) Broadcast, Campaign: "Finger Lickin' Good", Campaign: "Para Chuparse Los Dedos", Digital, OOH, Radio
LG&E
Long John Silver's; Louisville, KY "Think fish", Campaign: "Final Frontier", Campaign: "Marinated Pork", Campaign: "Methane"; 2001
NPC International, Inc.
Pizza Hut, Inc. Account Planning, Creative Services, Digital, Local Restaurant Marketing, Merchandising, Print Media Planning & Placement; 2011
Thorntons Inc. (Agency of Record)

SCORCH AGENCY

3010 Locust St Ste 102, Saint Louis, MO 63103
Tel.: (314) 827-6360
Fax: (314) 667-3367
Web Site: www.scorchagency.com

Year Founded: 2009

Agency Specializes In: Advertising, Digital/Interactive, Email, Environmental, Graphic Design, Internet/Web Design, Outdoor, Package Design, Search Engine Optimization, Social Media

Chris Buehler *(Founder & CEO)*
Bryan Roach *(Dir-Creative)*
Erin Edwards *(Acct Mgr)*
Scott Locker *(Mgr-Bus Dev)*
Mindy Bollegar *(Designer-Interactive)*
Sarah Hamilton *(Designer)*
Zach Pickett *(Designer)*
Danielle Varella *(Designer)*
Anjelica Aquilino *(Jr Art Dir)*

Accounts:
Axius Financial
Dos Lunas Tequila
HiGear Innovations
Hotel Maison DeVille
The Shell Building

THE SCOTT & MILLER GROUP

816 S Hamilton St, Saginaw, MI 48602-1516
Tel.: (989) 799-1877
Fax: (989) 799-6115
Toll Free: (888) 791-1876
E-Mail: smg@scottandmiller.com
Web Site: www.scottandmiller.com

Employees: 14
Year Founded: 1964

National Agency Associations: BMA

Agency Specializes In: Advertising, Advertising Specialties, Brand Development & Integration, Broadcast, Business-To-Business, Collateral, Communications, Corporate Communications, Corporate Identity, Direct Response Marketing, Electronic Media, Event Planning & Marketing, Exhibit/Trade Shows, Graphic Design, Identity Marketing, Internet/Web Design, Logo & Package Design, Media Buying Services, Newspaper, Newspapers & Magazines, Out-of-Home Media, Outdoor, Package Design, Planning & Consultation, Point of Purchase, Print, Production, Production (Print), Promotions, Public Relations, Sales Promotion, Strategic Planning/Research, Trade & Consumer Magazines

Approx. Annual Billings: $2,800,000

Breakdown of Gross Billings by Media: Adv. Specialities: 2%; Audio/Visual: 3%; Bus. Publs.: 5%; Collateral: 70%; D.M.: 8%; Graphic Design: 5%; Logo & Package Design: 3%; Other: 2%; Point of Purchase: 2%

Rusty Beckham *(Pres)*
Vogue Nowels *(Dir-Creative)*
David Dutton *(Acct Mgr & Sr Copywriter)*
John Polson *(Acct Mgr & Sr Copywriter)*
Gale Schrotenboer *(Office Mgr)*

Accounts:
The Dow Chemical Company; Midland, MI Internal & External Communications, Products & Services; 1964
Flexible Packaging Association; Linthicum, MD Collateral Literature, Advertising, Corporate Branding; 2006
Innotek; Houston, TX Trade Publication Advertising; 2007
Johnson Carbide Products; Saginaw, MI Catalogs, Ads, Web Site Development; 1971
Legend Valve; Shelby Township, MI Trade Publication Advertising, Collateral Materials; 2004

SCOTT COOPER ASSOCIATES, LTD.

215 Coachman Place E, Syosset, NY 11791
Tel.: (631) 249-9700
E-Mail: info@scottcooper.com
Web Site: www.scottcooper.com

Employees: 11
Year Founded: 1990

National Agency Associations: Second Wind Limited

Agency Specializes In: Brand Development & Integration, Business-To-Business, Collateral, Communications, Consumer Marketing, Corporate Identity, Digital/Interactive, Direct Response Marketing, Event Planning & Marketing, Graphic Design, High Technology, Internet/Web Design, Logo & Package Design, Medical Products, New Product Development, Print, Public Relations, Strategic Planning/Research, Trade & Consumer Magazines

Approx. Annual Billings: $5,000,000

Breakdown of Gross Billings by Media: Bus. Publs.: $500,000; Collateral: $1,700,000; D.M.: $1,000,000; Pub. Rels.: $1,000,000; Trade & Consumer Mags.: $500,000; Worldwide Web Sites: $300,000

Scott Cooper *(Owner)*
Jessica Aiello *(Acct Supvr)*

Accounts:
Canon USA; Lake Success, NY
Samsung
Viridian Energy
Windstream

SCOTT, INC. OF MILWAUKEE

(d/b/a Scott Advertising)
1031 N Astor St, Milwaukee, WI 53202-3324
Tel.: (414) 276-1080
Fax: (414) 276-3327
Web Site: www.scottadv.com

E-Mail for Key Personnel:
President: chuck@scottadv.com
Creative Dir.: chris@scottadv.com
Media Dir.: jane@scottadv.com
Production Mgr.: lynda@scottadv.com

Employees: 32
Year Founded: 1961

National Agency Associations: MCA

Agency Specializes In: Advertising, Brand Development & Integration, Business Publications, Business-To-Business, Catalogs, Corporate

Communications, Corporate Identity, Customer Relationship Management, Direct Response Marketing, Electronic Media, Email, Event Planning & Marketing, Exhibit/Trade Shows, Food Service, Graphic Design, Hospitality, In-Store Advertising, Industrial, Integrated Marketing, Internet/Web Design, Leisure, Logo & Package Design, Market Research, Media Buying Services, Media Planning, Media Relations, Merchandising, New Product Development, Package Design, Planning & Consultation, Point of Purchase, Point of Sale, Promotions, Public Relations, Publicity/Promotions, Restaurant, Sales Promotion, Social Media, Sponsorship, Strategic Planning/Research, Trade & Consumer Magazines, Web (Banner Ads, Pop-ups, etc.)

Approx. Annual Billings: $6,785,785

Breakdown of Gross Billings by Media: D.M.: 4%; E-Commerce: 1%; Event Mktg.: 1%; Exhibits/Trade Shows: 5%; Graphic Design: 15%; Internet Adv.: 12%; Logo & Package Design: 7%; Plng. & Consultation: 4%; Point of Sale: 9%; Pub. Rels.: 1%; Sls. Promo.: 11%; Strategic Planning/Research: 8%; Trade & Consumer Mags.: 13%; Worldwide Web Sites: 9%

Charles E. Reynolds *(Pres)*
Kelly Ruschman *(VP)*
Jim Westerman *(VP)*
Jon Haven *(Sr Dir-Art)*
Christopher Conway *(Dir-Art)*
Jane Harris *(Dir-Media)*
Kerri Brodie *(Acct Mgr)*
Jeff Krueger *(Acct Coord)*

Accounts:
Clear Springs Foods, Inc.; ID Fish, Trout, Specialty Seafood; 2004
Custom Culinary; Lombard, IL Bases, Sauces & Gravies; 2009
Hillshire Brands
J.R. Simplot Co.; Boise, ID Foodservice; 2010
JM Smucker's
Kureha America Inc.-Seaguar; New York, NY Fishing Line; 2005
Sara Lee Food Services; Cincinnati, OH Premium Meats & Bakery; 2002
Server Products, Inc.; Menomonee Falls, WI Food Service Equipment

SCOTT-MCRAE ADVERTISING INC.

701 Riverside Pk Pl Ste 100, Jacksonville, FL 32204-3343
Tel.: (904) 354-4900
Fax: (904) 354-4600
E-Mail: info@smag.com
Web Site: www.scottmcraeadvertising.com

Employees: 7
Year Founded: 1968

National Agency Associations: AAF

Agency Specializes In: Advertising, Media Buying Services

David Hodges *(Pres)*
Jeff Curry *(CFO & Exec VP)*
Monica Hillin *(VP-HR)*
Joni McIntyre *(VP-IT Svcs)*
Joe Humphrey *(Dir-Used Vehicle-North Florida Platform)*
Joanne Ackman *(Mgr-Risk)*
Larry Burd *(Mgr-Compliance)*
Cheryl Coward *(Mgr-Benefits)*
Joe Davenport *(Mgr-Wholesale & Corp Buyer)*
Torben Reichhardt *(Mgr-Svc)*

Accounts:
Bark on Park Posters
Countryside Ford Campaign: "Amp", Campaign: "Ego", Campaign: "Envy"
Dolphin Reef
Duval Ford
FCA Jacksonville Campaign: "Field of Dreams"
Hawthorn Estates
Jacksonville Automotive Dealers Association
Jacksonville Zoo
Second Harvest North Florida Campaign: "Food Fight", More Filling Animation

SCOTT PHILLIPS & ASSOCIATES

101 W Grand Ave Ste 405, Chicago, IL 60610
Tel.: (312) 943-9100
Web Site: www.sphillips.com

Employees: 2

Agency Specializes In: Public Relations, Sponsorship

Scott Phillips *(Founder & Pres)*

Accounts:
Adolph Coors Company
American Osteopathic Association
Baskin-Robbins Ice Cream
Bekins Van Lines, LLC
Citicorp Diners Club Inc
Cragin Federal Bank for Savings
Gateway, Inc.
Mesirow Financial Holdings, Inc.
Oracle America, Inc.
SkyTel Communications, Inc.
Telular Corporation

SCOTT THORNLEY + COMPANY

384 Adelaide St W 1st Fl, Toronto, ON M5V 1R7 Canada
Tel.: (416) 360-5783
Fax: (416) 360-4040
E-Mail: info@stcstorytellers.com
Web Site: www.stcstorytellers.com/

Employees: 20

Agency Specializes In: Direct Response Marketing, Graphic Design, Internet/Web Design, Sales Promotion, Strategic Planning/Research

Jennifer Nebesky *(Acct Dir)*
Henry Zaluski *(Assoc Dir-Creative)*
Rocky Manserra *(Mgr-Production)*
Matt Milne *(Acct Exec)*

Accounts:
Canadian Council for the Arts
CBC's The Hour
Malivoire Wine
MTI
Ontorio Innovation Trust
Qnx Software Systems Campaign: "Seamless Connectivity"
Raywal
Rogers Wireless
Zerofootprint

SCOUT BRANDING CO.

216 29th St S, Birmingham, AL 35233
Tel.: (205) 324-3107
Fax: (205) 324-1994
Web Site: www.scoutbrand.com

Employees: 11
Year Founded: 2006

Agency Specializes In: Advertising, Brand Development & Integration, Graphic Design, Social Media

Paul Crawford *(Owner)*
Dalton Smith *(Partner & COO)*
Anna Bird *(Dir-Art & Designer)*
Carlee Sanford *(Client Svcs Mgr)*
Ryan Meyer *(Designer)*
Peyton Hare *(Coord-Client Svcs)*

Accounts:
Alabama Gas Corporation
America's First Federal Credit Union
Balch & Bingham
Baptist Health Systems, Inc
Blowout Boutique
Bridgeworth Financial, LLC.
Britt Little Horn
Children's Health System
Christian & Small LLP
Clarus Consulting Group
Hare, Wynn, Newell & Newton
Harp Law
J&J Industries
Jay Electric
Kansas Child & Family Services
League of Southeastern Credit Unions
Mannington Residential
Marketry
Navigate Affordable Housing Partners
Oasis Women's & Children's Counseling Center
Ollie Irene
Physician Strategy Group
Princeton Baptist Medical Center
Regions
Southeastern Environmental Center
St. John & Associates
United States Postal Service
Westervelt Communities
Women's Fund

SCOUT MARKETING

3391 Peachtree Rd Ste 105, Atlanta, GA 30326
Tel.: (404) 917-2688
Web Site: findscout.com

Employees: 50
Year Founded: 1999

Agency Specializes In: Advertising, Advertising Specialties, Brand Development & Integration, Business-To-Business, Collateral, Communications, Consumer Goods, Consumer Marketing, Consumer Publications, Corporate Identity, Cosmetics, Customer Relationship Management, Direct Response Marketing, Direct-to-Consumer, Electronic Media, Email, Exhibit/Trade Shows, Health Care Services, Household Goods, Identity Marketing, In-Store Advertising, Infomercials, Integrated Marketing, Internet/Web Design, Leisure, Luxury Products, Market Research, Media Buying Services, Media Relations, Medical Products, Pharmaceutical, Point of Purchase, Point of Sale, Print, Promotions, Strategic Planning/Research, T.V., Trade & Consumer Magazines, Web (Banner Ads, Pop-ups, etc.), Women's Market

Jennifer Brekke *(Co-Founder & CEO)*
Bob Costanza *(Co-Founder & Exec Dir-Creative)*
Mark Goldman *(Pres)*
Allen Stegall *(Principal & Exec Dir-Strategy)*
Cheryl Maher *(Sr VP & Client Svcs Dir)*
Zebbie Gillispie *(VP & Dir-Digital Creative)*
Jessica Levin *(Dir-Analytics & Social Strategy)*
Elizabeth Hawkins *(Mgr-Search Mktg)*
Valerie Sherpa *(Mgr-Traffic)*
Shannon Brooks *(Supvr-Creative Svcs)*
Molly Davis *(Acct Exec)*

Accounts:
Advanced Biohealing
Alimera Sciences
Astra Tech
Azur Pharma
Elan
Farm Rich
Flowers Foods, Inc. Cobblestone Bread Co.

Advertising Agencies

(Agency of Record), Marketing, Nature's Own (Agency of Record), Wonder (Agency of Record)
Invista Antron, STAINMASTER
SeaPak
Teva Pharmaceuticals
Tolmar Inc
Uncle Maddio's Pizza Joint (Advertising & Marketing Agency of Record) Advertising, Marketing, Strategic Planning

SCPF
1688 Meridian Ave Ste 200, Miami Beach, FL 33139
Tel.: (305) 674-3222
Fax: (305) 695-2777
E-Mail: scpf.admin@scpf.com
Web Site: www.scpf.com

Employees: 20
Year Founded: 1996

National Agency Associations: 4A's

Agency Specializes In: Sponsorship

Ignasi Puig *(CEO & Partner)*
Alex Orellana *(Acct Grp Dir)*
Nicolle Cure *(Acct Exec)*
Veronica Vainrub *(Sr Acct Planner)*

Accounts:
Banco Santander Internacional; 2011
IKEA Hispanic Market; 2009
Olympus Campaign: "Stunt Man"; 2012
New-Pull & Bear

SCRATCH
67 Mowat Ave Ste 240, Toronto, ON M6K 3E3 Canada
Tel.: (416) 535-0636
Fax: (416) 535-1431
E-Mail: itch@scratchmarketing.com
Web Site: www.scratchmarketing.com

Year Founded: 2004

Agency Specializes In: Advertising, Brand Development & Integration, Digital/Interactive, Event Planning & Marketing, Media Planning, Print, Public Relations, Radio, Social Media, Web (Banner Ads, Pop-ups, etc.)

David Riabov *(Founder, Pres & Partner)*
Elan Packer *(Partner)*
Robert Wise *(Partner)*
Kevin Manklow *(Dir-Creative)*
Razi Saju *(Dir-Digital)*
Desiree Beaubien *(Jr Graphic Designer)*

Accounts:
Jinko Solar Branding Assignment
Pepsi
Sherwood Windows Group Rebranding

SCREAM AGENCY
1501 Wazee St Unit 1B, Denver, CO 80202
Tel.: (303) 893-8608
E-Mail: info@screamagency.com
Web Site: www.screamagency.com

Agency Specializes In: Advertising, Brand Development & Integration, Public Relations

Lora Ledermann *(Owner & Creative Dir)*
Amy Mikkola *(Acct Exec)*

Accounts:
New-Dot-Ski

SCREAMER CO.
107 Leland St Ste 3, Austin, TX 78704
Tel.: (512) 691-7894
Fax: (512) 691-7895
E-Mail: info@screamerco.com
Web Site: screamerco.com

Year Founded: 2006

Agency Specializes In: Advertising, Brand Development & Integration, Graphic Design, Media Buying Services, Media Planning, Public Relations

Scott Creamer *(Founder & Dir-Creative)*
Dan Wehmeier *(Acct Mgr)*

Accounts:
Dell Children's Medical Center of Central Texas
ORF Brewing

SCREEN STRATEGIES MEDIA
11150 Fairfax Blvd Ste 505, Fairfax, VA 22030
Tel.: (703) 272-7300
E-Mail: screenstrategiesmedia@gmail.com
Web Site: www.screenstrategiesmedia.com

Agency Specializes In: Consulting, Media Buying Services, Media Planning, Strategic Planning/Research

Rachael Jones *(Owner & Media Dir)*
Kyle Osterhout *(Owner)*
Caroline Bahng *(Dir-Media)*

Accounts:
Planned Parenthood

SCREENPUSH INTERNATIONAL INC
5455 Wilshire Blvd Ste 2127, Los Angeles, CA 90036
Tel.: (323) 372-1289
E-Mail: info@screenpush.com
Web Site: www.screenpush.com

Year Founded: 2009

Agency Specializes In: Advertising, Brand Development & Integration, Digital/Interactive, Event Planning & Marketing, Social Media

Joe Kavanaugh *(Mng Partner-Client Relations & Strategy)*
Joshua Otten *(Mng Partner-Ops & Strategy)*
Devin Buttner *(Partner-Tech Ops & Dev)*
Mark Shaw *(VP-Bus Dev)*
Annette Delkash *(Dir-Bus Dev-EU)*
Joel Otten *(Dir-Targeted Adv & SMI)*
Angelica Rosales *(Dir-Social Mktg)*

Accounts:
Association of Volleyball Professionals

SCRIBBLERS' CLUB
288 Frederick St, Kitchener, ON N2H 2N5 Canada
Tel.: (519) 570-9402
Fax: (519) 570-3849
E-Mail: info@scribblersclub.com
Web Site: http://www.scribblersclub.com/

Employees: 6
Year Founded: 1990

Agency Specializes In: Brand Development & Integration, Business Publications, Business-To-Business, Exhibit/Trade Shows, Graphic Design, Internet/Web Design, Logo & Package Design, Market Research, New Product Development, Print

Eric Sweet *(Pres & Chief Creative Officer)*
Robin Parsons *(Dir-Creative)*

Accounts:
Arriscraft International
Cascades Paper
CKE Restaurants
Dianolite
Intelligent Air
Just Fix It
Kalaya
MetsaBoard
Mod Pod
Montclair
Mudd Puppy Chase
Reaud Technologies
Snapple
Spatique
Wedding Path

SCRIPT TO SCREEN LLC
200 N Tustin Ave Ste 200, Santa Ana, CA 92705
Toll Free: (855) 853-8910
E-Mail: newbusiness@scripttoscreen.com
Web Site: www.scripttoscreen.com

Year Founded: 1986

Agency Specializes In: Digital/Interactive, Media Relations, Production (Ad, Film, Broadcast), Strategic Planning/Research

Ken Kerry *(Co-Founder & Exec Dir-Creative)*
Barbara L. Kerry *(Chm & CEO)*
Mick Koontz *(COO)*
Alex Dinsmoor *(Chief Strategy Officer & Exec VP)*
Joanie Laxson *(VP & Exec Producer)*
Mike Ramsey *(VP-Production)*

Accounts:
New-Tracy Anderson's Metamorphosis
New-Trainer Headphones

SDB CREATIVE
3000 N Garfield Ste 185, Midland, TX 79705
Tel.: (432) 218-6736
E-Mail: info@sdbcreativegroup.com
Web Site: www.sdbcreativegroup.com

Year Founded: 2005

Agency Specializes In: Advertising, Content, Email, Graphic Design, Internet/Web Design, Radio, Search Engine Optimization, Social Media, T.V.

Shane Boring *(Pres)*
Dedee Boring *(VP)*
Kelsie Rasure *(Mgr-Inbound Program)*

Accounts:
Medical Center Pharmacy

SDI MARKETING
200-65 International Blvd Ste, Toronto, ON M9W 6L9 Canada
Tel.: (416) 674-9010
Fax: (416) 674-9011
E-Mail: info@sdimarketing.com
Web Site: www.sdimarketing.com

Employees: 50

Agency Specializes In: Advertising

Geoff Conant *(Partner & Sr VP)*
Oliver Gleeson *(Corp Counsel & VP)*
Andy Harkness *(Sr VP-Sports Mktg)*
Adam Armit *(Acct Mgr)*
Laura Paladino *(Mgr-HR)*
Julia Ludwig *(Acct Coord)*
Erin McClean *(Acct Coord)*
Heather Osborne *(Acct Coord)*
Ali Pettersen *(Acct Coord)*
Meaghan Trueland *(Acct Coord)*

Accounts:
Procter & Gamble

SEAL IDEAS
(Name Changed to The Flatland)

SEAN TRACEY ASSOCIATES
401 State St Ste 3, Portsmouth, NH 03801-4030
Tel.: (603) 427-2800
E-Mail: info@seantracey.com
Web Site: www.seantracey.com

Employees: 8
Year Founded: 1985

Agency Specializes In: Advertising, Brand Development & Integration, Branded Entertainment, Broadcast, Direct Response Marketing, Fashion/Apparel, Financial, Health Care Services, Hispanic Market, In-Store Advertising, Infomercials, Market Research, Men's Market, Multimedia, Newspapers & Magazines, Print, Production, Production (Ad, Film, Broadcast), Production (Print), Radio, Retail, Sports Market, T.V., Trade & Consumer Magazines, Women's Market

Approx. Annual Billings: $25,000,000

Sean Tracey *(Dir-Creative & Brand Strategist)*
Amy Greenlaw *(Acct Mgr)*

Accounts:
BayCoast Bank Financial; 2010
R.C. Bigelow Company; Fairfield, CT Beverage; 2002
Sugar Hill Retirement Community Real Estate; 2010
Town & Country Federal Credit Union; Portland, ME Financial; 2007
Wentworth-Douglass Hospital Healthcare; 2009
Woodsville Guaranty Savings Bank; 2012

THE SEARCH AGENCY
11150 W Olympic Blvd Ste 600, Los Angeles, CA 90064-1823
Tel.: (310) 582-5700
Fax: (310) 452-2422
E-Mail: info@thesearchagency.com
Web Site: www.thesearchagency.com

Employees: 90

Agency Specializes In: Search Engine Optimization

Carl Dunham *(Founder & CTO)*
David Hughes *(CEO)*
Peter Harrington *(CFO)*
David Rahmel *(Exec VP-SEO)*
Steve Levitt *(Sr VP-Bus Dev & Mktg)*
David Waterman *(Sr Dir-Digital Mktg & SEO Strategy)*
Matt Grebow *(Sr Grp Dir-Search Mktg)*

Accounts:
Microsoft
Yahoo!

SECOND STORY, INC.
(Acquired by SapientNitro USA, Inc.)

SECRET LOCATION
80 Mitchell Avenue Unit 3, Toronto, ON M6J 1B9 Canada
Tel.: (416) 545-0800
E-Mail: contact@thesecretlocation.com
Web Site: www.thesecretlocation.com

Year Founded: 2007

Agency Specializes In: Advertising, Digital/Interactive, Integrated Marketing, Multimedia, Strategic Planning/Research, Technical Advertising

James Milward *(Founder & Exec Producer)*
Pietro Gagliano *(Partner & Dir-Creative)*
Ryan Andal *(VP & Dir-Technical)*
Ashley Choi *(Dir-Art)*
Marshall Lorenzo *(Dir-Art)*
Kyle Zborowski *(Dir-Art)*

Accounts:
ACE Aviation Holdings Inc. Tour & Travel Agency Services
New-Crowdrise
Dodge Car Dealers
Infiniti Car Dealers
Kraft Foods Soft Drink & Beverage Mfr
New-LOS ANGELES PHILHARMONIC ASSOCIATION
Nissan Car Dealers
The Sevens What are the sevens.com
TeenNick Entertainment Service Providers
Teletoon Campaign: "Humans Vs Vampires"
Trend Hunter Inc Trend Spotting & Cool Hunting Community Services

SECRET WEAPON MARKETING
1658 10th St, Santa Monica, CA 90404
Tel.: (310) 656-5999
Fax: (310) 656-6999
E-Mail: pat@secretweapon.net
Web Site: www.secretweapon.net

Employees: 25
Year Founded: 1997

Agency Specializes In: Advertising Specialties, Brand Development & Integration, Broadcast, Cable T.V., Newspaper, Outdoor, Print, Production, Radio, Sponsorship, Strategic Planning/Research, T.V.

Approx. Annual Billings: $200,000,000

Breakdown of Gross Billings by Media: Cable T.V.: $30,000,000; Network T.V.: $60,000,000; Radio: $30,000,000; Spot T.V.: $80,000,000

Dick Sittig *(Founder & Dir-Creative)*
Patrick Adams *(Mng Dir)*
Joanne O'Brien *(Grp Acct Dir)*
Brock Anderson *(Acct Dir)*
Gerardo Guillen *(Dir-Art)*
Leah Dieterich *(Assoc Dir-Creative)*
Elizabeth Guise *(Office Mgr & Mgr-Facilities)*

Accounts:
Honda Campaign: "Happy Honda Days"
Southern California Honda Dealers Broadcast, Campaign: "All Dressed In Blue", Campaign: "Sleigh Wash", Creative, Digital, Social Media
Valley Honda Dealer Association Creative

SEE INSIGHT
55 Ivan Allen Jr Blvd Ste 350, Atlanta, GA 30308
Tel.: (404) 481-2672
Web Site: www.see-insight.com

Employees: 65
Year Founded: 1979

National Agency Associations: MAGNET-PRSA

Agency Specializes In: Advertising, Arts, Automotive, Brand Development & Integration, Broadcast, Business-To-Business, Cable T.V., Children's Market, Co-op Advertising, Collateral, College, Communications, Consulting, Content, Corporate Communications, Corporate Identity, Customer Relationship Management, Digital/Interactive, Direct Response Marketing, Direct-to-Consumer, E-Commerce, Education, Electronic Media, Email, Environmental, Experience Design, Fashion/Apparel, Financial, Graphic Design, Guerilla Marketing, Health Care Services, Hispanic Market, Identity Marketing, In-Store Advertising, Integrated Marketing, Internet/Web Design, Local Marketing, Logo & Package Design, Marine, Market Research, Media Buying Services, Media Planning, Medical Products, Multicultural, Multimedia, Newspaper, Newspapers & Magazines, Out-of-Home Media, Outdoor, Package Design, Paid Searches, Pharmaceutical, Planning & Consultation, Point of Purchase, Point of Sale, Print, Production, Production (Ad, Film, Broadcast), Production (Print), Public Relations, Publicity/Promotions, Radio, Regional, Restaurant, Retail, Sales Promotion, Social Media, Strategic Planning/Research, T.V., Teen Market, Transportation, Tween Market, Urban Market, Viral/Buzz/Word of Mouth, Web (Banner Ads, Pop-ups, etc.), Women's Market

Approx. Annual Billings: $100,000,000

Jeff Peters *(Exec VP-Insight & Innovation)*

Accounts:
Buffets, Inc Branding & Communications, Creative, Direct Point-Of-Sale, Print, Radio, Television
Church's Chicken Restaurants; Atlanta, GA Media Buying, Media Planning; 2008
The Coca-Cola Company
Coca-Cola Refreshments USA, Inc.; Atlanta, GA; 2000
General Mills
Hardywood Park Craft Brewery Campaign: "It's Hard To Be Modest"
J Mack Robinson College of Business at Georgia State University; Atlanta, GA; 1998
Jim Beam
Levi Strauss & Co; San Francisco, CA; 2009
Ovation Brands; Greer, SC Buffets, Ryan's, Trader Joe's
Tree Zero; Atlanta, GA; 2009
Tresemme - Alberto Culver; Chicago, IL; 2009

SEE YA GROUP
6830 NW 77th Ct, Miami, FL 33166
Tel.: (786) 708-1792
E-Mail: info@seeyagroup.com
Web Site: www.seeyapr.com

Agency Specializes In: Advertising, Brand Development & Integration, Digital/Interactive, Graphic Design, Logo & Package Design, Print, Social Media

Nathalie Maass *(CEO)*

Accounts:
Lifestyle Miami

SEED BRANDING STUDIO
3330 NE 190 St, Aventura, FL 33180
Tel.: (305) 987-0876
Web Site: www.seedbrandingstudio.com

Year Founded: 2008

Agency Specializes In: Above-the-Line, Affiliate Marketing, Alternative Advertising, Below-the-Line, Branded Entertainment, Broadcast, Business Publications, Cable T.V., Catalogs, Co-op Advertising, Collateral, Consumer Publications, Digital/Interactive, Electronic Media, Email, Exhibit/Trade Shows, Experience Design, Game Integration, Guerilla Marketing, In-Store Advertising, Local Marketing, Magazines, Mobile Marketing, Multimedia, Newspaper, Newspapers & Magazines, Out-of-Home Media, Outdoor, Paid

Searches, Podcasting, Point of Purchase, Point of Sale, Print, Product Placement, Production, Production (Print), Promotions, RSS (Really Simple Syndication), Radio, Search Engine Optimization, Shopper Marketing, Social Media, Sponsorship, Sweepstakes, Syndication, T.V., Telemarketing, Trade & Consumer Magazines, Viral/Buzz/Word of Mouth, Web (Banner Ads, Pop-ups, etc.), Yellow Pages Advertising

Gabriela Borja *(Dir-Mktg)*

Accounts:
Bremen Motors BMW, Mercedes Benz Trucks, Moni Cooper
Ceiba Groupe Luxury Real Estate Development
Colour Republic Floral Farm
Del Sur Foods Authentic Hispanic Foods
Lennox Hotel Luxury Hospitality
Paramount Transport Construction, Logistics, Transport

SEED CREATIVE
PO Box 523, Marietta, GA 30061
Tel.: (678) 528-1592
Web Site: www.seed-creative.com

Employees: 5
Year Founded: 2002

Agency Specializes In: Above-the-Line, Advertising, Advertising Specialties, Affiliate Marketing, Affluent Market, African-American Market, Agriculture, Alternative Advertising, Arts, Asian Market, Automotive, Aviation & Aerospace, Below-the-Line, Bilingual Market, Brand Development & Integration, Branded Entertainment, Broadcast, Business Publications, Business-To-Business, Cable T.V., Catalogs, Children's Market, Co-op Advertising, Collateral, College, Commercial Photography, Communications, Computers & Software, Consulting, Consumer Goods, Consumer Marketing, Consumer Publications, Content, Corporate Communications, Corporate Identity, Cosmetics, Crisis Communications, Custom Publishing, Customer Relationship Management, Digital/Interactive, Direct Response Marketing, Direct-to-Consumer, E-Commerce, Education, Electronic Media, Electronics, Email, Engineering, Entertainment, Environmental, Event Planning & Marketing, Exhibit/Trade Shows, Experience Design, Faith Based, Fashion/Apparel, Financial, Food Service, Game Integration, Gay & Lesbian Market, Government/Political, Graphic Design, Guerilla Marketing, Health Care Services, High Technology, Hispanic Market, Hospitality, Household Goods, Identity Marketing, In-Store Advertising, Industrial, Infomercials, Information Technology, Integrated Marketing, International, Internet/Web Design, Investor Relations, Legal Services, Leisure, Local Marketing, Logo & Package Design, Luxury Products, Magazines, Marine, Market Research, Media Buying Services, Media Planning, Media Relations, Media Training, Medical Products, Men's Market, Merchandising, Mobile Marketing, Multicultural, Multimedia, New Product Development, New Technologies, Newspaper, Newspapers & Magazines, Out-of-Home Media, Outdoor, Over-50 Market, Package Design, Paid Searches, Pets , Pharmaceutical, Planning & Consultation, Podcasting, Point of Purchase, Point of Sale, Print, Product Placement, Production, Production (Ad, Film, Broadcast), Production (Print), Promotions, Public Relations, Publicity/Promotions, Publishing, RSS (Really Simple Syndication), Radio, Real Estate, Recruitment, Regional, Restaurant, Retail, Sales Promotion, Search Engine Optimization, Seniors' Market, Shopper Marketing, Social Marketing/Nonprofit, Social Media, South Asian Market, Sponsorship, Sports Market, Stakeholders, Strategic Planning/Research, Sweepstakes, Syndication, T.V., Technical Advertising, Teen Market, Telemarketing, Trade & Consumer Magazines, Transportation, Travel & Tourism, Tween Market, Urban Market, Viral/Buzz/Word of Mouth, Web (Banner Ads, Pop-ups, etc.), Women's Market, Yellow Pages Advertising

Approx. Annual Billings: $250,000

Ryan Vickerman *(Dir-Creative)*

Accounts:
Governors Gun Club; 2011

SEED FACTORY MARKETING
692 10th St NW 2nd Fl, Atlanta, GA 30318
Tel.: (404) 996-4041
E-Mail: grow@seedfactorymarketing.com
Web Site: seedfactorymarketing.com

Employees: 10
Year Founded: 2012

Agency Specializes In: Alternative Advertising, Broadcast, Digital/Interactive, Guerilla Marketing, Infomercials, Mobile Marketing, Multimedia, Outdoor, Print, Product Placement, Social Media, Trade & Consumer Magazines, Viral/Buzz/Word of Mouth

Angie Maddox *(Mng Partner & Dir-PR)*
Mark Sorenson *(Partner & Dir-Creative)*
Chris Barber *(Partner-Social & SEO)*
Julie French *(Partner-Media)*
Rick Ender *(Dir-Healthcare)*

Accounts:
ArborGuard
Atlanta Humane Society
High Museum of Art Atlanta
Moda Aids Awareness Campaign; 2013
Navicent Health Campaign: "Everything About Us Is All About You", Campaign: "Kindness"
Werner Co

SEED STRATEGY, INC.
740 Ctr View Blvd, Crestview Hills, KY 41017
Tel.: (859) 594-4769
Fax: (859) 594-4767
E-Mail: contact@seedstrategy.com
Web Site: www.seedstrategy.com

Agency Specializes In: Advertising, Brand Development & Integration, Branded Entertainment, Communications, New Product Development, Strategic Planning/Research

Susan Jones *(Pres & CEO)*
Chad Buecker *(COO)*
Robert Cherry *(Chief Creative Officer)*
Tracy Kelly *(Sr VP-Ops)*
John McSherry *(Sr VP-Ops)*
David Hayes *(VP-Ops, R&D)*
Gretchen Mahan *(Strategist)*
Jamila Watson *(Strategist-Insights)*

Accounts:
Sara Lee Corporation
Silk Soymilk
Wrigley Eclipse Gum

SEER INTERACTIVE
1028 N 3rd St, Philadelphia, PA 19123
Tel.: (215) 967-4461
Fax: (215) 873-0744
Web Site: www.seerinteractive.com

Year Founded: 2002

Agency Specializes In: Advertising, Search Engine Optimization

Wil Reynolds *(Founder)*
Brett Fratzke *(Acct Mgr-PPC)*
Brandon Wensing *(Acct Mgr-Analytics)*
Mallory Oliver *(Mgr-Mktg)*
Ali Freezman *(Acct Exec)*
Ally Malick *(Team Head-PPC)*
Adam Melson *(Team Head-SEO)*
Alisa Scharf *(Team Head-SEO)*

Accounts:
AWeber Communications Email Marketing Software Providers
The University of Pennsylvania Educational Institution
Wine Enthusiast Companies Wine Mfr & Distr

THE SEIDEN GROUP
708 3rd Ave 13th Fl, New York, NY 10017
Tel.: (212) 223-8700
Fax: (212) 223-1188
E-Mail: mseiden@seidenadvertising.com
Web Site: www.seidenadvertising.com

Employees: 43
Year Founded: 1995

Agency Specializes In: Advertising, Brand Development & Integration, Consulting, New Product Development, Planning & Consultation, Sponsorship

Approx. Annual Billings: $90,000,000

Shari Bronson *(Grp Mng Dir)*
Steve Feinberg *(Chief Creative Officer)*
Patrick Lupinski *(Mng Dir-Seiden & Friends)*
Eva Ng *(Controller)*
Meredith Cohen *(Dir-Production)*
Brittany Moore *(Acct Supvr)*
Corey Klar *(Media Planner-Integrated)*
Katie Freedman *(Assoc Acct Exec)*
Jeremy Cohen *(Assoc Strategist)*
Tim Hurley *(Jr Graphic Designer)*
Andrea Lynch *(Assoc Strategist)*
Rachel Metter *(Grp Sr Strategist)*
Eric Pearson *(Sr Assoc Dir-Strategy)*

Accounts:
BD Medical Diabetes Care
Polytechnic University
RediClinic
Shire
Weight Watchers
YMCA,New York

SEITER & MILLER ADVERTISING, INC.
(Name Changed to SMA NYC)

SELECTNY
401 Broadway, New York, NY 10013
Tel.: (212) 367-5600
Fax: (212) 929-5678
E-Mail: info.newyork@selectny.com
Web Site: www.selectny.com

Employees: 260
Year Founded: 1993

National Agency Associations: 4A's

Agency Specializes In: Advertising, Brand Development & Integration, Communications, Cosmetics, Sponsorship

Wolfgang Schaefer *(Chief Strategy Officer)*
Gabriel Eid *(Exec Dir-Creative)*
Nichelle Sanders *(Grp Acct Dir)*
Michelle Fogarty *(Dir-Digital Strategy)*
Simona Gaudio *(Dir-Client Svcs & Digital)*
Steve Whittier *(Dir-Digital & Integrated Creative)*
Anita Asante *(Assoc Dir-NEW Bus-NEW YORK)*

Olivier Van Doorne *(Office Mgr)*
Corinne Figliuzzi *(Mgr-Community)*
Kelly Dye *(Planner-Strategic)*

Accounts:
Artistry
Coty, Inc.
Davidoff Cool Water, Fragrances
Elie Tahari
Fredrick Fekkai Campaign: "Most Privileged Hair in the World"
Glow By JLo Fragrance
Joop Fragrance & Fashion
Just Cavalli Women's Fragrance
Miss Sixty
Nautica
Sebastian Professional
Seiko
St. John Knits International, Inc. (Agency of Record) Brand Positioning, Campaign: "Golden Coast Glamour", Creative, Social Media
Stage Stores Inc. (Lead Agency) Social Media, Traditional Media
Stetson Fragrance Shania Twain Fragrance
Still by Jennifer Lopez
Swarovski Jewelry
Taylor Swift (Elizabeth Arden) Taylor Swift Incredible Things Fragrance; 2014
Timex
Wella

Branches

SelectNY.Paris
94 Rue Saint Lazare, Esc A 7eme etage, 75009 Paris, France
Tel.: (33) 1 53 01 95 00
Fax: (33) 1 53 01 95 15
E-Mail: info.paris@selectny.com
Web Site: www.selectny.com

Employees: 16
Year Founded: 1996

Agency Specializes In: Communications

April Alegre *(Dir-Art)*
Julian Bowyer *(Dir-Strategic Plng)*
Romina Corchia *(Dir-Art)*
Tiffany Fontaine *(Dir-Art)*
Caroline Le Hir *(Dir-Artistic)*
Alexandra Mercuri *(Dir-Art)*
Laure Roucaute *(Dir-Art)*
Estelle Simounet *(Dir-Artistic)*
Fabrice Policella *(Assoc Dir-Creative)*
Liam Fearn *(Copywriter)*

SelectNY.Koblenz GmbH
Schlossstrasse 1, Koblenz, 56068 Germany
Tel.: (49) 261 972 610
Fax: (49) 261 972 6111
E-Mail: info.koblenz@selectny.com
Web Site: www.selectlp.com

Employees: 45
Year Founded: 1991

Agency Specializes In: Communications, Trade & Consumer Magazines

Herwig Preis *(Founder & CEO)*
Christian Schroeder *(Owner)*

Accounts:
Chopard Casmir, Casran (Lancaster Group), Madness, Mirabai, Pure Wish, Wish
Coty Group 100% Pure Chipie
Darjeeling Lingerie (Chantelle Group)
Douglas Cosmetics
Fortant de France Wines
Swarovski
Vivienne Westwood Boudoir (Lancaster Group), Libertine
Wolford (Starcknaked)

SelectNY.Hamburg GmbH
Hohelustchaussee 18, Hamburg, 20253 Germany
Tel.: (49) 40 45 02 19 0
Fax: (49) 40 45 02 19 10
E-Mail: info.hamburg@selectNY.com
Web Site: www.selectlp.com

Employees: 65
Year Founded: 1992

Agency Specializes In: Communications, Cosmetics, Fashion/Apparel

Christian Schroeder *(Owner)*
Gerhard Aretz *(Gen Mgr)*
Marion V. Appuhn *(Sr Dir-Art)*
Natasha Haack *(Acct Dir)*
Daniel Krauss *(Dir-Plng)*
Will Matthews *(Dir-Creative)*
Christine Ratsch *(Dir-Creative)*
Daniel Waziri *(Dir-Art)*
Martina Etemadieh *(Client Svc Dir)*

Accounts:
Calvin Klein
Chopard
Davidoff
Hilfiger Fragrances
Lancaster
Wella AG Cosmetics, Hair Care

SelectNY.Berlin GmbH
Chaussee Strasse 123, Berlin, 10115 Germany
Tel.: (49) 30 34 34 630
Fax: (49) 30 34 34 63 63
E-Mail: info.berlin@selectny.com

Employees: 45
Year Founded: 2000

Agency Specializes In: Communications

Wolfgang Schaefer *(Chief Strategy Officer)*
Alex Mittag *(Dir-Client Svc)*

Accounts:
Aktion Mensch Social Services
DKMS
Rezidor SAS
Unilever
WWF - Fund for Nature

THE SELLS AGENCY, INC.
401 W Capitol Ave Ste 400, Little Rock, AR 72201-3414
Tel.: (501) 666-8926
Fax: (501) 663-0329
E-Mail: info@sellsagency.com
Web Site: www.sellsagency.com

Employees: 20

Agency Specializes In: Advertising, Financial, Health Care Services

Revenue: $5,000,000

Mike Sells *(Owner & CEO)*
Jon Hodges *(VP & Exec Dir-Creative)*
Rachel Arnold *(Dir-Fin)*
Elizabeth Luttrell *(Dir-Art)*
Gaea Miller *(Dir-Fin)*
Joel Richardson *(Dir-Art)*
Mark Schulte *(Dir-Creative)*
Lauren Bradbury *(Acct Exec)*
Kristen Burgeis *(Acct Exec)*
Allison Drennon *(Acct Exec)*
Lauren Griffin *(Acct Exec-Mktg, Special Projects & Bus Dev)*
Thad James *(Designer-Interactive)*
Melissa Tucker *(Copywriter)*
Heather Royal *(Jr Media Buyer)*

Accounts:
ARVEST Bank Group
Carlton-Bates
Conway Regional Health System
Fayetteville, AR Tourism
TAC Air

Branch

The Sells Agency, Inc.
124 W Meadow Ste 100, Fayetteville, AR 72701-5229
Tel.: (479) 695-1760
Fax: (479) 695-2428
E-Mail: info@sellsagency.com
Web Site: sellsagency.com

Employees: 3

National Agency Associations: AAF-APA-BMA

Agency Specializes In: Advertising, Aviation & Aerospace, Brand Development & Integration, Broadcast, Business-To-Business, Cable T.V., Consulting, Corporate Communications, Corporate Identity, Customer Relationship Management, Digital/Interactive, Direct-to-Consumer, Electronic Media, Email, Financial, Health Care Services, Hospitality, Information Technology, Integrated Marketing, Leisure, Local Marketing, Logo & Package Design, Magazines, Media Buying Services, Media Planning, Media Training, Mobile Marketing, Multimedia, Newspaper, Newspapers & Magazines, Out-of-Home Media, Outdoor, Paid Searches, Planning & Consultation, Print, Production (Ad, Film, Broadcast), Production (Print), Promotions, Public Relations, Publicity/Promotions, Radio, Recruitment, Strategic Planning/Research, T.V., Travel & Tourism, Web (Banner Ads, Pop-ups, etc.)

Mike Sells *(Owner & CEO)*
Jon Hodges *(Sr Dir-Art)*
Drew Finkbeiner *(Dir-Northwest Arkansas)*
Greg Harrison *(Dir-Media)*
Mark Schulte *(Dir-Creative)*
Amber Coldicott *(Office Mgr)*
Kristen Burgeis *(Acct Exec)*
Emily Canada *(Acct Exec-PR)*
Allison Drennon *(Acct Exec)*
Thad James *(Designer-Interactive)*
Stacey Roberts *(Exec-PR)*

Accounts:
Acxiom
ArCom Systems
Arkansas Tech University
Arvest Bank Group
Carlton-Bates
First State Bank
Mercy Medical Center; Rogers, AR
TAC Air

SELMARQ
6813 Fairview Rd Ste C, Charlotte, NC 28210
Tel.: (704) 365-1455
Fax: (704) 365-1458
E-Mail: info@selmarq.com
Web Site: www.selmarq.com

Employees: 3
Year Founded: 1983

National Agency Associations: BMA

Agency Specializes In: Advertising, Advertising

Specialties, Automotive, Bilingual Market, Brand Development & Integration, Business Publications, Business-To-Business, Collateral, Communications, Consulting, Corporate Communications, Corporate Identity, Direct Response Marketing, E-Commerce, Engineering, Event Planning & Marketing, Food Service, Graphic Design, Industrial, Internet/Web Design, Logo & Package Design, Magazines, Media Buying Services, New Product Development, Planning & Consultation, Print, Public Relations, Publicity/Promotions, Recruitment, Restaurant, Sales Promotion, Strategic Planning/Research, Technical Advertising, Trade & Consumer Magazines

Jeff Rothe *(Pres)*
Michele Clark *(Dir-Creative)*
Andrea Miller *(Office Mgr)*
Andrea Rothe *(Office Mgr)*

Accounts:
Brixx
Hersey Meters
Sonoco
World Affairs Council of Charlotte

SELPH COMMUNICATIONS
PO Box 572425, Salt Lake City, UT 84157
Tel.: (801) 541-6067
Fax: (801) 401-7175
E-Mail: wayne@wayneselph.com

E-Mail for Key Personnel:
President: wayne@wayneselph.com

Employees: 2
Year Founded: 2004

Agency Specializes In: Advertising, Cable T.V., Communications, Consumer Goods, Consumer Marketing, Corporate Identity, E-Commerce, Electronic Media, Environmental, Food Service, Local Marketing, Media Buying Services, Planning & Consultation, Restaurant, Strategic Planning/Research, Trade & Consumer Magazines

Approx. Annual Billings: $2,025,000

Breakdown of Gross Billings by Media: Brdcst.: $500,000; Consulting: $350,000; Consumer Publs.: $120,000; Fees: $223,000; Graphic Design: $285,000; Newsp. & Mags.: $375,000; Outdoor: $147,000; Trade Shows: $25,000

Wayne Selph *(Owner)*
Diania Dickerson *(Sr Media Planner & Sr Media Buyer)*

THE SELTZER LICENSING GROUP
1180 Ave of the Americas 3rd Fl, New York, NY 10036
Tel.: (212) 244-5548
Web Site: www.seltzerlicensing.com

Year Founded: 1998

Agency Specializes In: Advertising, Brand Development & Integration

Sherry Halperin *(Partner)*
Cheryl Rubin *(Exec VP-Brand Licensing)*
Ricardo Yoselevitz *(Dir-Brand Licensing & Bus Dev)*
Charles Africa *(Sr Mgr-Market Insights)*
Megan Hoyt *(Acct Exec)*
Stu Seltzer *(Specialist-Brand Licensing, Partnership Mktg & Strategic Alliance)*

Accounts:
Bertolli
Cheer's
Fox Studios
Good Humor
Klondike
Nautilus, Inc
Popsicle Playwear Ltd.
Safeway, Inc.
Star Trek
Unilever United States, Inc. Skippy, Breyer's, Suave

SENAREIDER
4005 Broadway Ste C, San Antonio, TX 78209
Tel.: (210) 930-3339
Web Site: www.senareider.com

Agency Specializes In: Advertising, Digital/Interactive, Internet/Web Design, Media Buying Services, Media Planning, Package Design, Public Relations, Radio, Social Media, Strategic Planning/Research

Mayra Urteaga *(Mgr-Acctg)*

Accounts:
Maroon Consultants

SENSIS
811 Wilshire Blvd Ste 2050, Los Angeles, CA 90017-2642
Tel.: (213) 341-0171
Fax: (323) 861-7436
Toll Free: (866) 434-2443
E-Mail: info@sensisagency.com
Web Site: www.sensisagency.com

Agency Specializes In: Advertising, Digital/Interactive, Sponsorship

Jose Villa *(Pres)*
Abdi Zadeh *(Mng Dir)*
Karla Fernandez Parker *(Mng Dir-Texas)*
Avi Bachar *(VP-Fin & Admin)*
Javier San Miguel *(Grp Dir-Creative)*
Lois Mogrove *(Acct Dir)*
Romina Bongiovanni *(Dir-Earned Media)*
Wade Butcher *(Dir-Project Mgmt)*
Ken Deutsch *(Dir-Media)*
Ken Yapkowitz *(Dir-Tech)*
Daniel De La Torre *(Acct Exec)*

Accounts:
AARP
Cooperative of American Physicians
DIRECTV
FDA Center for Tobacco Products Public Health Education Campaigns
First 5 Santa Barbara County
Fox Entertainment
L.A. Care Health Plan
Metrolink
National Society of Hispanic MBAs Logo, Public Relations, Social Media
Porto's Bakery
Santa Clara Family Health Plan Website
Sempra Energy
Southern California Public Radio
Tadin Herb & Tea
The Trevor Project
Union Bank
United Healthcare
U.S. Army
U.S. Coast Guard Academy; New London, CT

Branch

K. Fernandez and Associates, LLC
2935 Thousand Oaks #6, San Antonio, TX 78247
(See Separate Listing)

SEO INC.
2720 Loker Ave W Ste G, Carlsbad, CA 92010
Tel.: (760) 929-0039
Fax: (760) 929-8002
E-Mail: info@seoinc.com
Web Site: www.seoinc.com

Employees: 65

Agency Specializes In: Search Engine Optimization

Garry Grant *(CEO)*
Arnaud Lemaire *(VP-Sls)*
Jerrold Burke *(Dir-Paid Search)*
Paola Ramirez *(Acct Mgr)*

Accounts:
AT&T Communications Corp.
Avalon Communities
Camp Bow Wow
Microsoft

SEQUEL RESPONSE, LLC
6870 Washington Ave S, Eden Prairie, MN 55344
Tel.: (952) 564-6930
Fax: (952) 944-4028
Web Site: www.sequelresponse.com

Agency Specializes In: Advertising

Tom Rothstein *(Pres & Partner)*
Jay Carroll *(Partner & CMO)*
Vicki Erickson *(VP-Ops)*
James LaHaise *(Sr Dir-Art)*
Paula Heimerl *(Dir-Estimating & Acct Mgr)*
Scott Anderson *(Dir-Database Mktg)*
James Fussy *(Dir-Database Mktg & Analytics)*
Erik Koenig *(Dir-Mktg)*
Carrie Dunn *(Acct Mgr)*

Accounts:
LifeLock Inc.
Specialty Insurance Agency, Inc.
Springs Window Fashions LLC
WPS Health Insurance

SERENDIPIT
4450 N 12th St Ste 238, Phoenix, AZ 85014
Tel.: (602) 283-5209
E-Mail: info@serendipitconsulting.com
Web Site: www.serendipitconsulting.com

Agency Specializes In: Advertising, Brand Development & Integration, Digital/Interactive, Event Planning & Marketing, Internet/Web Design, Public Relations, Social Media

Melissa DiGianfilippo *(Partner)*
Alexis Krisay *(Partner)*
Wes Krisay *(Creative Dir)*
Shawn Byrne *(Dir-Digital Mktg)*

Accounts:
Amazingmail
B3 Strategies
Boys & Girls Clubs of Metro Phoenix
New-Crave
New-Donley Service Center
Fuchsia Spa
Galicia Fine Jewelers
Merge Architectural Group
New-Miller Russell Associates
Orangetheory Fitness East Bay
Phoenix Spine Surgery Center
Safeguard Security and Communications, Inc.
Stonemont Financial
Strong Tower Real Estate Group
Sublime

SERIF GROUP
250 Walton Ave Ste 160, Lexington, KY 40502
Tel.: (859) 271-0701

E-Mail: info@serifgroup.com
Web Site: www.serifgroup.com

Year Founded: 1999

Agency Specializes In: Advertising, Graphic Design, Internet/Web Design, Logo & Package Design, Print, Social Media

Bill Powell *(Owner)*
Jackie Powell *(Co-Owner)*

Accounts:
Shaun Ring
Shield Works

SERINO COYNE LLC

1515 Broadway 36th Fl, New York, NY 10036-8901
Tel.: (212) 626-2700
Fax: (212) 626-2799
E-Mail: info@serinocoyne.com
Web Site: www.serinocoyne.com

Employees: 95
Year Founded: 1977

Agency Specializes In: Advertising, Broadcast, Collateral, Consumer Marketing, Direct Response Marketing, Entertainment, Event Planning & Marketing, Graphic Design, Integrated Marketing, Internet/Web Design, Logo & Package Design, Magazines, Media Planning, Newspaper, Newspapers & Magazines, Out-of-Home Media, Outdoor, Print, Production, Production (Print), Radio, Retail, Sponsorship, Strategic Planning/Research, T.V.

Greg Corradetti *(Pres)*
Leslie Barrett *(VP-Bus Engagement)*
Tom Callahan *(VP-Creative Strategy)*
Jim Glaub *(VP-Content & Community)*
Michele Groner *(VP-Strategy & Plng)*
Kim Hewski *(VP-Res & Customer Relationship)*
Scott Yambor *(VP-Media Svcs)*
Suzanne Tobak *(Sr Dir-Events)*
Steve Gordon *(Dir-Visual Assets)*
Grace Zoleta *(Asst Dir-Acctg)*
Whitney Creighton *(Assoc Dir-Comm)*
Zack Kinney *(Assoc Dir-Creative & Brdcst)*
Patrick Mediate *(Mgr-Social Media)*
Sofia Nisnevich *(Mgr-Client Receivables)*
Anna Pitera *(Mgr-Mktg)*
Diana Salameh *(Mgr-Mktg)*
Jacqui Kaiser *(Supvr-Digital Media)*

Accounts:
13
The 25th Annual Putnam County Spelling Bee
42nd Street
700 Sundays
A Catered Affair
A Chorus Line
A Little Night Music
ABKCO
The Addams Family
All About Me
All Shook Up
American Express
American Idiot
An Evening With Patti Lupone & Mandy
Banana Shpeel
Bare
Beauty & The Beast
Big Apple Circus
Blithe Spirit
The Bowery Presents
Brigadoon
Brighton Beach/Memoirs/Broadway Bound
Broadway.com
Cablevision
Chitty Chitty Bang Bang
Clear Channel
Company
The Country Girl
Cry Baby
Curtains
Dame Edna, Back with a Vengeance
The Davidsohn Group
Disney on Broadway
Dracula
Drumstruck
Enron
Equus
Fantastics
The Farnsworth Invention
Fiddler on the Roof
Frankel/ Green Theatrical Management
Fuerza Bruta
Glory Days
God of Carnage
Good Vibrations
The Graduate
Grease
Grease (Tour)
Grey Gardens
Hairspray
The Homecoming
Hoopz
The Immigrant
Impressionism
In The Next Room/ The Vibrator Play
Jersey Boys - Toronto
Jersey Boys
Jersey Boys (Tour)
Joe Turners Come & Gone
The League of American Theaters & Producers
Leap of Faith
Legally Blonde
Legally Blonde (Tour)
Legends
Lend Me A Tenor
Les Miserables
The Light in the Piazza
Lincoln Center Theater
The Lion King
The Lion King (North American Tour)
The Little House on the Prairie (Tour)
The Little Mermaid
Live Nation Theatricals
Lone Star Love
Mambo Kings
Mamma Mia!
Mamma Mia! (Tour)
Mandy Patinkin: Dress Casual
Mary Poppins-Los Angeles
Mary Poppins-North American Tour
Mary Poppins
Metropolitan Opera
Minsky's
Movin' Out
MSG Network
Nederlander Productions
Next To Normal
November
Passing Strange
The Phantom of the Opera
The Phantom of the Opera (Tour)
The Producer Circle Co.
The Producers
Promises Promises
The Public Theater
Race
Richard Frankel Productions
Rochard Frankel Productions
Rock of Ages
Season of Savings
Second Stage Theatre
Shorenstein-Hays/Nederlander Theatres; San Francisco, CA
Shubert Group Sales
Shubert Organization
Soccer Mom
South Pacific
South Pacific (Tour)
Spamalot
Spamalot (Tour)
Spiderman
Spring Awakening
Spring Awakening (Tour)
Steel Magnolias
Stomp
Symphonie Fantasticque
Tale of Two Cities
Tarzan
Tele-Charge
Theatre Direct, Inc.
Thoroughly Modern Millie
The Two & Only
UBU Repertory Co.
Vanities
The Vibrator Play
The Wedding Singer
Whoopi Goldberg on Broadway
Wicked - San Francisco
Wicked Toronto
Wicked
Wicked (Tour)
The Wiz

Branches

Serino Coyne LLC

1050 Battery St, San Francisco, CA 94111-1209
Tel.: (415) 309-0687
Fax: (415) 984-6134
Web Site: www.serinocoyne.com

Year Founded: 2003

Agency Specializes In: Advertising, Broadcast, Collateral, Consumer Marketing, Direct Response Marketing, Entertainment, Event Planning & Marketing, Graphic Design, Integrated Marketing, Internet/Web Design, Logo & Package Design, Magazines, Media Planning, Newspaper, Newspapers & Magazines, Out-of-Home Media, Outdoor, Print, Production, Production (Print), Radio, Retail, Strategic Planning/Research, T.V.

Caroline Thompson *(Dir-Natl Accounts)*
Denise Brown *(Supvr-Client Acctg)*
Tee Panton *(Coord)*

Accounts:
Jersey Boys
Wicked-San Francisco

SEROKA

N17 W24222 Riverwood Dr, Waukesha, WI 53188
Tel.: (262) 523-3740
Fax: (262) 523-3760
E-Mail: information@seroka.com
Web Site: www.seroka.com

Employees: 15
Year Founded: 1981

Agency Specializes In: Advertising, Affluent Market, Brand Development & Integration, Catalogs, Collateral, Communications, Computers & Software, Consulting, Consumer Marketing, Consumer Publications, Corporate Communications, Corporate Identity, Crisis Communications, Customer Relationship Management, Digital/Interactive, Direct Response Marketing, Direct-to-Consumer, Email, Event Planning & Marketing, Exhibit/Trade Shows, Faith Based, Financial, Graphic Design, Health Care Services, High Technology, Identity Marketing, Industrial, Information Technology, Internet/Web Design, Leisure, Logo & Package Design, Luxury Products, Market Research, Media Relations, Medical Products, New Technologies, Newspapers & Magazines, Outdoor, Pharmaceutical, Podcasting, Point of Sale, Production, Production (Ad, Film, Broadcast), Promotions, Public Relations, Radio, Sales Promotion, Search Engine

Optimization, Seniors' Market, Strategic Planning/Research, T.V., Technical Advertising, Transportation, Travel & Tourism, Web (Banner Ads, Pop-ups, etc.)

Revenue: $1,300,000

Patrick H. Seroka *(Pres & CEO)*
Scott Serok *(Principal)*
John Seroka *(VP)*
Amy Hansen *(Dir-PR & Client Svcs)*
Jeff Joyner *(Dir-Creative)*

SERPENTE & COMPANY, INC.
1 Eves Dr Ste 158, Marlton, NJ 08053
Tel.: (856) 797-5701
Fax: (856) 797-6939
E-Mail: jserpente01@hotmail.com
Web Site: www.serpenteandco.com

E-Mail for Key Personnel:
President: jserpente01@hotmail.com

Employees: 3
Year Founded: 2005

Agency Specializes In: Direct Response Marketing

Joseph Serpente *(Pres)*

Accounts:
ABTS
AC Linen
American Cryogas Industries
American Financial Corp.
Arco Chemical
Atlantic City Country Club
Classic Cake Company
Collective Savings Bank
College Money
Cominex
Conrail
Debugit Franchise Assoc.
Detrex
Divorce Center
Harbor Linen
Italian Bistro; 1994
KMS Laboratories
Mab Paints
Metro Dealers
National Penn Bank
Parke Bank

SERVICE MEDIA PAYANT INC.
417 Saint Pierre, Montreal, QC H2Y 2M4 Canada
Tel.: (514) 842-6666
Fax: (514) 842-4753
E-Mail: dmarcil@servicemp.ca
Web Site: www.servicemp.ca

Employees: 3
Year Founded: 1989

Agency Specializes In: Advertising, Media Buying Services, Media Planning

Manon Vincent *(Owner)*

Accounts:
Benjamin Moore Paint
Government of Qubec
Mobilia Furniture

SET CREATIVE
12 W 27th St Fl 6, New York, NY 10001
Tel.: (646) 738-7000
Fax: (212) 213-9431
E-Mail: hello@setcreative.com
Web Site: www.setcreative.com

Employees: 120
Year Founded: 2009

Agency Specializes In: Advertising, Digital/Interactive, Event Planning & Marketing, Exhibit/Trade Shows

Alasdair Lloyd-Jones *(Pres & Chief Strategy Officer)*
Sabina Teshler *(CEO)*
Louis Carlton *(Exec Dir-Studio)*
Israel Kandarian *(Exec Dir-Creative-North America)*
Christina Danton *(Dir-Design)*
Darin Dougherty *(Dir-Design)*
Whitney Connolly *(Acct Mgr)*
Michael Scherer *(Project Mgr-Special Projects)*
Christine Alex *(Mgr-Production)*
Dan Olson *(Strategist-Brand)*
Tatom Masagatani *(Designer-Mechanical)*

Accounts:
New-Arc'teryx
New-BMW
New-Google Glass
New-Jordan
Nike, Inc.
New-Red Bull
New-Uniqlo

SEVELL+SEVELL, INC.
939 N High St, Columbus, OH 43201
Tel.: (614) 341-9700
Fax: (614) 341-9701
E-Mail: sevell@sevell.com
Web Site: www.sevell.com

Agency Specializes In: Advertising, Logo & Package Design, Multimedia, Print, Web (Banner Ads, Pop-ups, etc.)

Beverly Sevell *(Co-Owner)*
Steve Sevell *(Owner)*
Steven Kropp *(Designer-Web)*

Accounts:
1 Source, Inc.
American Eagle Fulfillment, Inc.
American Heritage Home Renovations
Floyd Browne Group
Geneflow, Inc.
SMPS Columbus
Strategic Health Resources

THE SEVENTH ART, LLC
900 Broadway, New York, NY 10003
Tel.: (212) 431-8289
Fax: (212) 431-8492
E-Mail: info@the7thart.com
Web Site: www.theseventhart.com

Employees: 20

Agency Specializes In: Advertising

Michel Mein *(Founder & CEO)*
Rebecca Van De Sande *(Brand Dir)*
Manon Zinzell *(Brand Dir)*
Blaire Alfonso *(Dir-Creative)*
Mar I. Reeser Del Rio *(Dir-Studio)*
Brian Watson *(Dir-Art)*
Lindsey Stein *(Coord-Mktg)*

Accounts:
The Charles
Exteel
Isla Moda
The Mandarin Oriental
Plaza Hotel
Riverhouse
St. Regis
Time Warner Center
Trump Chicago
The W Hotel
White Elephant

SEVENTH POINT
4752 Euclid Rd, Virginia Beach, VA 23462-3823
Tel.: (757) 473-8152
Fax: (757) 473-9825
Toll Free: (800) 951-6226
E-Mail: info@seventhpoint.com
Web Site: www.seventhpoint.com

Employees: 28

Agency Specializes In: Advertising, Automotive, Brand Development & Integration, Broadcast, Business-To-Business, Cable T.V., Co-op Advertising, Communications, Consulting, Consumer Marketing, Corporate Communications, Corporate Identity, Digital/Interactive, Direct Response Marketing, Electronic Media, Entertainment, Event Planning & Marketing, Graphic Design, Health Care Services, Industrial, Information Technology, Internet/Web Design, Logo & Package Design, Magazines, Media Buying Services, New Product Development, Newspaper, Out-of-Home Media, Point of Sale, Print, Production, Public Relations, Publicity/Promotions, Strategic Planning/Research, T.V., Transportation, Travel & Tourism

Approx. Annual Billings: $27,500,000

Breakdown of Gross Billings by Media: Brdcst.: 53%; Internet Adv.: 10%; Other: 18%; Print: 19%

Chris Calcagno *(Pres, Principal & Dir-Creative)*
Mike Carosi *(VP-Ops)*
Doreen Collins *(VP-Fin)*
Leslie Lemons *(Media Dir)*
Gabriel Cohen *(Dir-Integrated Media)*
Crystal Henderson *(Mgr-Acctg)*
Jeremy Fern *(Specialist-Higher Ed & Acct Exec)*
Kyleigh Fitzgerald *(Coord-Mktg & Accts)*

Accounts:
Amerigroup Corporation; Virginia Beach, VA Healthcare Services; 2002
Building Beyond Boundaries
Checkered Flag Motorcar Company
TowneBank; Portsmouth, VA Banking & Financial Services; 1998
Troy University; Troy, AL Higher Education Services; 2002
Wheeler Interests Logo & Tagline

SEXTON & CO.
4429 South Atchison Circle, Aurora, CO 80015
Tel.: (303) 246-0366
Fax: (303) 997-7330
E-Mail: jerry@sextonandcompany.com
Web Site: www.sextonandcompany.com

Employees: 5
Year Founded: 1996

National Agency Associations: BMA

Agency Specializes In: Advertising, Brand Development & Integration, Business-To-Business, Consulting, Consumer Marketing, Corporate Communications, Corporate Identity, Digital/Interactive, E-Commerce, Electronic Media, Event Planning & Marketing, Exhibit/Trade Shows, Government/Political, Graphic Design, Health Care Services, High Technology, Infomercials, Integrated Marketing, Internet/Web Design, Local Marketing, Logo & Package Design, Media Buying Services, Medical Products, Multimedia, New Technologies, Planning & Consultation, Production, Public Relations, Publicity/Promotions, Sales Promotion, Search Engine Optimization, Social Marketing/Nonprofit, Social Media, Strategic Planning/Research, T.V., Travel & Tourism

Jerry Sexton *(Founder & Owner)*

Accounts:
DI Graphics; Denver, CO Online Marketing
Farm Mart; Englewood, CO Farm Supplies; 1992
Grease Monkey; Greenwood Village, CO Auto Services, Website, Video; 2009
PRO Hardware; Denver, CO; 1953
Vac-Tron Online Marketing

SFW AGENCY
(Formerly Sales Factory Woodbine)
210 S Cherry St, Winston Salem, NC 27101-5231
Tel.: (336) 333-0007
Fax: (336) 333-9177
Web Site: www.sfwresults.com

Employees: 20
Year Founded: 1985

National Agency Associations: 4A's-Second Wind Limited

Agency Specializes In: Brand Development & Integration, Broadcast, Business-To-Business, Collateral, Consumer Marketing, Corporate Identity, Education, Event Planning & Marketing, Fashion/Apparel, Graphic Design, Health Care Services, Logo & Package Design, Magazines, Newspaper, Out-of-Home Media, Planning & Consultation, Point of Purchase, Point of Sale, Radio, Retail, Sponsorship, Strategic Planning/Research, T.V.

Ged King *(CEO)*
Juan Hernandez *(VP-Insights & Strategy)*
Ashley Dillon *(Acct Dir)*
Victoria Kearns *(Acct Dir)*
David Geren *(Dir-Strategy)*
Alex Snart *(Dir-Art)*
Kellie Cutrer *(Mgr-Email Mktg)*
Linda Rosa *(Mgr-Studio Production)*
Jon Lamphier *(Copywriter)*
Shayla Stockton *(Asst Acct Exec)*
Leonard Hilty *(Acct Coord)*
Brittany Matters *(Coord-Bus Dev)*

Accounts:
Anthos Flowering Bulbs Campaign: "Dig, Drop, Done. Identity"
Corona Tools
Ekornes Home Furnishings
First Community Bancshares Inc.; Bluefield, VA (Agency of Record)
High Point Convention & Visitors Bureau Brand Identity, Marketing
High Point Regional Health System
iBulb Marketing Programs
Lowe's Home Improvement; Mooresville, NC
Tanglewood Park Campaign: "Tree"

SGW
219 Changebridge Rd, Montville, NJ 07045-9514
Tel.: (973) 299-8000
Fax: (973) 299-7937
Toll Free: (800) SSDWIMC
Web Site: www.sgw.com

Employees: 45
Year Founded: 1979

National Agency Associations: BPA-PRSA

Agency Specializes In: Advertising, Brand Development & Integration, Digital/Interactive, Graphic Design, Media Buying Services, Public Relations

Frank P. Giarratano *(COO & CMO)*
Cesare Pari *(Sr VP & Dir-Creative)*
Kris Scelba *(VP-Acct Svcs)*
Bill Ward *(VP-Automotive Svcs)*
Debbie Carrillo *(Mgr-Billing)*
Diana Westenberger *(Sr Acct Coord)*

Accounts:
Delta Dental of New Jersey
Enritsu
Muscle Maker Grill
Saint Peter's University Hospital
Signature Information Solutions
Teledyne LeCroy
University of Medicine & Dentistry of NJ

SHABLE & ASSOCIATES
(Acquired & Absorbed by BrandExtract, LLC)

SHADOW PR
30 W 21St St, New York, NY 10010
Tel.: (212) 972-0277
Fax: (212) 918-9296
E-Mail: info@shadowpr.com
Web Site: www.shadowpr.com

Employees: 20
Year Founded: 2007

Agency Specializes In: Entertainment, Fashion/Apparel, Media Relations, Social Media

Brad Zeifman *(Co-CEO)*
Michelle Davidson *(Partner)*
Alexandra Lasky *(VP)*
Randee Braham *(Assoc VP)*
Brian Vaughan *(Acct Mgr)*
Sara Lieberman *(Acct Exec)*
Rachel Litzinger *(Acct Exec)*
Danielle Marmel *(Acct Exec)*
Sabrina Meyer *(Jr Acct Exec)*

Accounts:
Butter
DKNY Hosiery
Donna Karan
The Estate
Hollywood Roosevelt
The Light Group
Nylon Magazine
Rent the Runway Brand's Celebrity Outreach, Broadcast Media, Event Activations, Online, Print
Tenjune
Thompson Beverly Hills
Windmark Recording

SHAKER RECRUITMENT ADVERTISING & COMMUNICATIONS, INC.
The Shaker Bldg 1100 Lk St, Oak Park, IL 60301
Tel.: (708) 383-5320
Fax: (800) 848-3297
Toll Free: (800) 323-5170
E-Mail: info@shaker.com
Web Site: www.shaker.com

Employees: 203
Year Founded: 1951

Agency Specializes In: Advertising, Communications, Recruitment, Sponsorship

Approx. Annual Billings: $69,000,000

Breakdown of Gross Billings by Media: Collateral: 7%; Internet Adv.: 25%; Other: 3%; Out-of-Home Media: 1%; Print: 60%; Radio & T.V.: 4%

Catherine Shaker Breit *(Exec VP-Client Svcs)*
Derek Briggs *(VP-Fin Svcs)*
Gerald Digani *(VP-Health Care)*
Ellen Paige *(VP-Client Svcs)*
Joseph G. Shaker *(VP)*
Mike Temkin *(VP-Strategic Plng & Dev)*
Tony Lepore *(Dir-Brand Strategy)*
Denise Polanski *(Dir-Creative)*
Tracy Wascoe Noer *(Sr Acct Mgr)*
Bruce Felts *(Rep-Bus Dev)*

Branches

Shaker Recruitment Advertising & Communications, Inc.
1408 N Westshore Blvd Ste 508, Tampa, FL 33607-3844
Tel.: (813) 704-2988
Toll Free: (888) 323-1170
E-Mail: south@shaker.com
Web Site: www.shaker.com

Employees: 7

Agency Specializes In: Advertising, Advertising Specialties, Recruitment

Joseph G. Shaker *(Pres)*
Jerry Digani *(VP-Health Care)*
Mike Temkin *(VP-Strategic Plng & Dev)*

Accounts:
Coca-Cola Refreshments USA, Inc.
Cognos ERP
Morton's ERP

SHAMIN ABAS PUBLIC RELATIONS
222 Lakeview Ave Ste 101, West Palm Beach, FL 33401
Tel.: (561) 366-1226
Fax: (561) 366-4015
E-Mail: info@shaminabaspr.com
Web Site: www.shaminabaspr.com

Employees: 5

Agency Specializes In: Advertising, Entertainment, Fashion/Apparel, Financial, Local Marketing, Public Relations, Technical Advertising

Shamin Abas *(Founder & Pres)*
Kelly Downey *(Assoc Partner & Dir-Palm Beach)*
Elizabeth Feigenbaum *(Jr Acct Exec)*

SHAMLIAN CREATIVE
105 W 3rd St, Media, PA 19063
Tel.: (610) 892-0570
E-Mail: info@open-inc.com
Web Site: www.shamliancreative.com

Agency Specializes In: Advertising, Brand Development & Integration, Content, Corporate Identity, Graphic Design, Internet/Web Design, Media Planning, Print, Social Media, Sponsorship, Strategic Planning/Research

Fred Shamlian *(Founder & Dir-Creative)*
Joshua Phillips *(Sr Designer)*

Accounts:
Tuckers Tavern

THE SHAND GROUP
1482 E Valley Rd Ste 474, Santa Barbara, CA 93108
Tel.: (805) 969-1068
Fax: (805) 969-0046
E-Mail: results@theshandgroup.com
Web Site: www.theshandgroup.com

Employees: 20

Agency Specializes In: Advertising

Bobby Shand *(Pres)*
Chris Weakley *(Partner & Mng Dir)*
Angelique Rothermel *(VP-Strategic Plng)*

Kathy Lynch *(Dir-Fin)*
Chi Tung *(Acct Mgr-Global)*
Lingtong Li *(Acct Exec)*
Rehan Shaikh *(Acct Exec)*

Accounts:
Centurion
Platinum Guild International USA

SHARAVSKY COMMUNICATIONS

4128 Dana Ln, Lafayette Hill, PA 19444-1320
Tel.: (610) 834-5499
E-Mail: alans@sharavsky.com
Web Site: www.sharavsky.com

E-Mail for Key Personnel:
President: alans@sharavsky.com

Employees: 7
Year Founded: 1993

Agency Specializes In: Advertising, Brand Development & Integration, Business-To-Business, Collateral, Consumer Marketing, Education, Entertainment, Health Care Services, Internet/Web Design, Newspaper, Out-of-Home Media, Pharmaceutical, Print, Radio, T.V.

Alan Sharavsky *(Pres, Chief Creative Officer & Chief Strategy Officer)*
Todd Broder *(Dir-Broderville Pictures & Exec Producer)*
Randy Friter *(Bus Dir)*

Accounts:
Broderville Pictures
Frontline Technologies
Lippincott Publishing
McNeil Consumer Healthcare; Fort Washington, PA Over-the-Counter Supplements & Medications; 2001
Mercy Health System
Nickelodeon
Philadelphia Industrial Development Corporation: Philadelphia, PA Portfol Loan Tracking Software; 2005
Temple University Health Systems

SHARK COMMUNICATIONS

255 S Champlain Ste 7, Burlington, VT 05401-5261
Tel.: (802) 658-5440
Fax: (802) 658-0113
E-Mail: info@sharkcomm.com
Web Site: www.sharkcomm.com

E-Mail for Key Personnel:
President: pete@sharkcomm.com
Production Mgr.: rick@sharkcomm.com

Employees: 10
Year Founded: 1986

Agency Specializes In: Advertising, Bilingual Market, Brand Development & Integration, Business Publications, Business-To-Business, Catalogs, Collateral, Communications, Consulting, Consumer Marketing, Consumer Publications, Corporate Communications, Corporate Identity, Digital/Interactive, Direct-to-Consumer, E-Commerce, Graphic Design, Guerilla Marketing, High Technology, In-Store Advertising, Information Technology, Integrated Marketing, Internet/Web Design, Leisure, Logo & Package Design, Magazines, Medical Products, Newspaper, Newspapers & Magazines, Outdoor, Point of Purchase, Print, Public Relations, Radio, Search Engine Optimization, Strategic Planning/Research, T.V., Trade & Consumer Magazines, Travel & Tourism, Web (Banner Ads, Pop-ups, etc.)

Approx. Annual Billings: $3,500,000

Breakdown of Gross Billings by Media: Collateral: $1,050,000; D.M.: $175,000; Mags.: $350,000; Newsp.: $1,050,000; Point of Purchase: $175,000; Radio: $350,000; T.V.: $350,000

Peter Jacobs *(Dir-Creative & Strategic)*

Accounts:
Brookline Bank; Boston, MA Energy Systems, Marketing
Dinse Knapp & McAndrew
Eastern Funding NYC
First Ipswich Bank
Green Mountain College
Shearer Chevrolet
State of Vermont; Montpelier, VT Captive Insurance, Department of Economic Development, Global Trade Office

SHARP COMMUNICATIONS

415 Madison Ave 24th Fl, New York, NY 10017
Tel.: (212) 829-0002
E-Mail: info@sharpthink.com
Web Site: www.sharpthink.com

E-Mail for Key Personnel:
President: jb@sharpthink.com

Employees: 20
Year Founded: 2001

National Agency Associations: 4A's-AMA-COPF

Agency Specializes In: Advertising, Brand Development & Integration, Broadcast, Collateral, Corporate Identity, Digital/Interactive, Direct Response Marketing, Event Planning & Marketing, Exhibit/Trade Shows, Internet/Web Design, Logo & Package Design, Outdoor, Print, Public Relations

Approx. Annual Billings: $3,000,000

Robert L. Ireland, Jr. *(Partner & Mng Dir-Creative)*
Anri Seki *(VP & Sr Dir-Design)*
Elizabeth Hewitt *(VP & Acct Dir)*
Jaret Posmentier *(VP & Acct Dir)*
Jessica Alter *(Acct Supvr)*
Meghan Ficarelli *(Acct Supvr)*
Sarah Kingsley *(Sr Acct Exec-PR)*

Accounts:
Abigail Kirsch
Art Miami
Artexpo New York
BASF
Benjamin Moore (PR, Social Media & Event Services Agency of Record) Campaign: "Annual Color of the Year", Digital Media
Cosentino
DNA Information
East Side House Settlement
Ferrari
Florida International Fine Art Fair
Kobrand Lincourt Vineyards, St Francis Vineyards
Legrand North America Adorne Collection, Corporate Communications
Lincoln Center Chamber Music Society
LOTS
NYC Department of Parks
Pier Sixty
Pret A Manger Brand Marketing, Media Relations, PR, Pret Foundation, Special Events & Support
Randall's Island Sports Foundation
Simon Pearce
Sotheby's
Tourneau PR
Trium Global EMBA (NYU/LSC/HEC)
The V Foundation for Cancer Research

SHASHO JONES DIRECT INC.

267 W 25th St, New York, NY 10001
Tel.: (212) 929-2300
Fax: (212) 929-5630
E-Mail: glenda@sjdirect.com
Web Site: www.sjdirect.com

E-Mail for Key Personnel:
President: glenda@sjdirect.com

Employees: 3
Year Founded: 1991

National Agency Associations: DMA

Agency Specializes In: Advertising, Advertising Specialties, Brand Development & Integration, Consumer Marketing, Cosmetics, Direct Response Marketing, Fashion/Apparel, Graphic Design, Health Care Services, Internet/Web Design, Merchandising, Planning & Consultation, Production, Retail, Strategic Planning/Research

Approx. Annual Billings: $1,000,000

Glenda Shasho Jones *(Pres & CEO)*

Accounts:
AT&T Communications Corp.
Barrie Pace
Casual Living
Chadwicks, Clifford & Wills
Columbia House
The Discovery Channel
Discovery Kids
Disney
FootSmart
Garnet Hill
Jos. A. Bank
SellSmart; AZ Real Estate

SHAW & TODD, INC.

205 Rockingham Row, Princeton, NJ 08540-5759
Tel.: (609) 436-0251
E-Mail: mmelia@shawtodd.com
Web Site: www.shawtodd.com

E-Mail for Key Personnel:
President: mmelia@shawtodd.com
Creative Dir.: jpropper@shawtodd.com

Employees: 6
Year Founded: 1980

National Agency Associations: BMA-NJ Ad Club

Agency Specializes In: Advertising, Brand Development & Integration, Business Publications, Business-To-Business, Collateral, Communications, Corporate Identity, Digital/Interactive, Education, Electronic Media, Engineering, Exhibit/Trade Shows, Graphic Design, High Technology, Industrial, Internet/Web Design, Logo & Package Design, Magazines, Market Research, Media Buying Services, Media Planning, Multimedia, New Product Development, New Technologies, Newspapers & Magazines, Print, Production, Production (Print), Promotions, Public Relations, Search Engine Optimization, Technical Advertising, Trade & Consumer Magazines

Approx. Annual Billings: $5,500,000

Mary Melia *(Owner)*
Keith Todd *(VP-Acct Svc & Media)*

Accounts:
BioTek; Winooski, VT Microplate Instrumentation
Diagnostica Stago; Parsippany, NJ Laboratory Equipment
Enterix; Edison, NJ Cancer Screening Products
ITC; Edison, NJ Advance Diagnostic Solutions
Tamron; Commack, NY Optical Lenses

SHAZAAAM LLC

41216 Vincenti Court, Novi, MI 48375
Tel.: (248) 366-0388
E-Mail: getpr@shazaaam.com

Web Site: www.shazaaam.com

Agency Specializes In: Advertising, Brand Development & Integration, Crisis Communications, Media Relations, Media Training, Public Relations, Social Media

Adrienne Lenhoff *(Pres)*

Accounts:
New-Annette Ferber Collections

SHEEHY & ASSOCIATES
2297 Lexington Rd, Louisville, KY 40206-2818
Tel.: (502) 456-9007
Fax: (502) 456-1895
E-Mail: info@sheehy1.com
Web Site: www.sheehy1.com

E-Mail for Key Personnel:
President: davec@sheehy1.com
Media Dir.: kristyc@sheehy1.com
Production Mgr.: bobi@sheehy1.com

Employees: 50
Year Founded: 1957

Agency Specializes In: Financial, Health Care Services, Media Buying Services, Restaurant, Retail, Travel & Tourism

Approx. Annual Billings: $50,000,000

Breakdown of Gross Billings by Media: Mags.: 5%; Newsp.: 9%; Radio: 28%; T.V.: 58%

Dave Carter *(Pres & Dir-Creative)*
Robert C. Iler *(Exec VP & Sr Producer)*
Deb Timmons *(Exec VP & Dir-Agency Resources)*
Jan Kellogg *(Sr VP)*
Dennis Weedman *(Sr Dir-Art)*
Shelby Nichols *(Assoc Dir-Media & Mgr-Digital Media)*
Leslie Kill *(Assoc Dir-Media)*
Rich Machin *(Assoc Dir-Creative)*
Meredith Snook Wilkins *(Sr Acct Mgr)*
Alyson Middleton *(Media Planner & Media Buyer)*
Lauren Bradley *(Asst-Media)*
Harley Gilman *(Asst-Media)*
Kasey Kinney *(Asst-Media)*

Accounts:
Arby's Cooperatives; Charlotte, Lexington, Greenville, KY Fast Food
Kroger Supermarkets
Omaha Woodmen Life Insurance Society Woodmen of the World

SHEEPSCOT CREATIVE
SE Hawthorne Blvd, Portland, OR 97214
Tel.: (503) 310-3745
E-Mail: info@sheepscotcreative.com
Web Site: www.sheepscotcreative.com

Year Founded: 2010

Agency Specializes In: Advertising, Brand Development & Integration, Communications, Event Planning & Marketing, Graphic Design, Print, Social Media

Dave Weich *(Pres)*
Alison Hallett *(Acct Dir)*
Michael Kosmala *(Strategist)*

Accounts:
Josephine Community Libraries, Inc.
Oregon Cultural Trust

SHEILA DONNELLY & ASSOCIATES
116 W 23rd St Ste 500, New York, NY 10011
Tel.: (212) 851-8425
Fax: (212) 851-8425
E-Mail: info@sheiladonnelly.com
Web Site: www.sheiladonnelly.com

Employees: 10
Year Founded: 1987

Agency Specializes In: Brand Development & Integration, Consulting, Customer Relationship Management, Event Planning & Marketing, Hospitality, Local Marketing, Media Relations, New Product Development, Promotions, Publicity/Promotions, Real Estate, Sales Promotion, Travel & Tourism

Revenue: $1,100,000

Sheila Donnelly Theroux *(Founder & Pres)*
Joel Ann Rea *(Mng Dir-East Coast & Dir-Creative)*
Jeong Ku Hwang *(Acct Mgr)*
Kathy Ho *(Acct Exec)*
Megan Mulcahy *(Acct Exec)*

Accounts:
51 Buckingham Gate
Montage Beverly Hills
Montage Hotels & Resorts
The Opposite House
The Pierre
The Residences At W Hollywood The Penthouses
Swire Hotels

SHELTON GROUP
12400 Coit Rd Ste 650, Dallas, TX 75251
Tel.: (972) 239-5119
Fax: (972) 239-2292
E-Mail: koliver@sheltongroup.com
Web Site: www.sheltongroup.com

Employees: 40

Agency Specializes In: Advertising, Investor Relations

Suzanne Shelton *(Mng Partner-Strategic Comm)*
Leanne K. Sievers *(Exec VP-IR)*
Matt Kreps *(Mng Dir-IR)*
Brett L. Perry *(Mng Dir-IR)*
Lee Ann Head *(VP-Res)*
Beverly Twing *(Sr Acct Mgr)*

Accounts:
Diodes Inc.; 2008
Inphi Corporation
Lots of Little Accessories; Dallas, TX; 2008
Multiquip EZ Grout Hog Crusher
NTRglobal North American Division; 2007
Oscar Fierro Designs; 2008
Pixelworks, Inc.; San Jose, CA
Reflex Photonics (Agency of Record)
Stone Core Films; Dallas, TX; 2008
Vimicro International Corporation
Wasting Water Is Weird Campaign: "Bathroom", Campaign: "Car Wash", Campaign: "Dishwasher"
WJ Communications

SHEPHERD
1301 Riverplace Blvd Ste 1100, Jacksonville, FL 32207
Tel.: (877) 896-8774
Web Site: www.shepherdagency.com

Year Founded: 1984

Agency Specializes In: Advertising, Brand Development & Integration, Digital/Interactive, Outdoor, Print, Public Relations

Robin Shepherd *(Founder & Pres)*
Keith Lowe *(Jr Art Dir)*
Damon Williams *(Art Dir & Assoc Creative Dir)*
Andrew Kraft *(Dir-Ops)*
BeckyLynn Schroeder *(Acct Exec)*
Marina Martin *(Acct Coord)*
Amanda Langenbach *(Jr Designer)*

Accounts:
CSX Corporation
Hoptinger Pub
Merial

THE SHEPPARD
201 N Westmoreland Ave Ste 130, Los Angeles, CA 90004
Tel.: (323) 200-2164
Toll Free: (877) 572-3561
E-Mail: info@thesheppard.com
Web Site: www.thesheppard.com

Agency Specializes In: Advertising

Matthew Sheppard *(CEO)*
Suzanne Sheppard *(Client Svcs Dir)*
Heather Spilsbury *(Acct Dir)*
Andy Chase *(Dir-Media)*
Ric Din *(Dir-Bus)*
Brook Lee *(Dir-Creative)*
Yoshie Kurkowski *(Mgr-Hospitality & Event)*

SHEPPARD LEGER NOWAK INC.
1 Richmond Sq, Providence, RI 02906-5139
Tel.: (401) 276-0233
Fax: (401) 276-0230
E-Mail: sln@slnadv.com
Web Site: www.slnadv.com

E-Mail for Key Personnel:
President: nowak@slnadv.com
Creative Dir.: sheppard@slnadv.com
Media Dir.: leger@slnadv.com
Public Relations: mayoh@slnadv.com

Employees: 6
Year Founded: 1997

Agency Specializes In: Advertising, Brand Development & Integration, Business Publications, Business-To-Business, Collateral, Communications, Corporate Identity, E-Commerce, Electronic Media, Engineering, Exhibit/Trade Shows, Graphic Design, High Technology, Industrial, Information Technology, Internet/Web Design, New Product Development, Print, Public Relations, Publicity/Promotions, Retail, Sales Promotion, Strategic Planning/Research, Technical Advertising, Trade & Consumer Magazines

Approx. Annual Billings: $6,000,000

Breakdown of Gross Billings by Media: Collateral: $600,000; Fees: $4,800,000; Pub. Rels.: $600,000

Daniel Sheppard *(Owner & Dir-Creative)*
Edward G. Nowak, Jr. *(Pres)*
Robert Mayoh *(VP-PR & Acct Svc)*
Marina Dippel *(Dir-Social Media Svcs)*
Michelle Aguiar *(Office Mgr)*

Accounts:
Accu-Time Systems
Matco-Norca
Rogers Corporation

SHERMAN COMMUNICATIONS & MARKETING
427 N Harvey Ave, Oak Park, IL 60302
Tel.: (708) 445-8598
Fax: (708) 445-8568
E-Mail: jason@shermancm.com
Web Site: www.shermancm.com

Employees: 4

Agency Specializes In: Advertising, Brand Development & Integration, Communications, Digital/Interactive, Email, Integrated Marketing, Media Relations, Public Relations

Jason Sherman *(Pres)*

Accounts:
The American Academy of Art Educational Services
Attorneys' Title Guaranty Fund Insurance Services
Neighborhood Housing Services of Chicago
RE/MAX International
Seko
University of Chicago Children's Hospital

SHERRY MATTHEWS ADVOCACY MARKETING

200 S Congress Ave, Austin, TX 78704-1219
Tel.: (512) 478-4397
Fax: (512) 478-4978
Toll Free: (877) 478-4397
E-Mail: somebody@sherrymatthews.com
Web Site: www.sherrymatthews.com

Employees: 50
Year Founded: 1983

Agency Specializes In: African-American Market, Asian Market, Broadcast, Children's Market, Communications, Corporate Identity, Direct Response Marketing, Education, Environmental, Event Planning & Marketing, Exhibit/Trade Shows, Government/Political, Graphic Design, Health Care Services, Hispanic Market, Internet/Web Design, Media Buying Services, Medical Products, Newspaper, Newspapers & Magazines, Out-of-Home Media, Outdoor, Print, Production, Public Relations, Radio, Real Estate, Strategic Planning/Research, T.V., Transportation, Travel & Tourism

Approx. Annual Billings: $20,000,000

Breakdown of Gross Billings by Media: Mags.: $800,000; Newsp.: $350,000; Other: $500,000; Outdoor: $750,000; Print: $2,400,000; Production: $5,750,000; Pub. Rels.: $700,000; Spot Radio: $3,400,000; Spot T.V.: $5,350,000

Sherry Matthews *(Founder & CEO)*
Charles Webre *(Partner-Creative)*
Wardaleen Belvin *(CFO)*
Rich Terry *(Sr VP & Creative Dir)*
Karen Purcell *(Sr VP & Dir-Media)*
Janet Lea *(Sr VP)*
Rob Buck *(Dir-Creative)*
Marilyn Carter *(Dir-Creative Svcs)*
Gretchen Hicks *(Dir-Design)*
Wally Williams *(Dir-Creative)*

Accounts:
Capital Metropolitan Transportation Authority
Childrens Health Insurance Program
Medair
Partnership For A Drug Free Texas; Austin, TX; 1997
Street Smart Campaign: "Pedestrian Faces"
Texas Department of Health; Austin, TX Abstinence Education, Diabetes, Immunizations, Toxic Substances; 1993
Texas Department of Transportation; Austin, TX Campaign: "Don't Mess With Texas", Happy Hour FAIL, Traffic Safety; 1997
Texas Health & Human Services Commission Children's Health Insurance Program; 1999

SHIFT CREATIVE GROUP

316 E Broad St, Cookeville, TN 38501
Tel.: (931) 303-4605
E-Mail: info@shiftcreativegroup.com
Web Site: www.shiftcreativegroup.com

Agency Specializes In: Advertising, Brand Development & Integration, Digital/Interactive, Graphic Design, Print, Social Media

Stu McLaughlin *(Producer-Bus Dev)*

Accounts:
Blue Tiger USA
Fitzgerald Glider Kits

SHIFT, INC.

24 Vardy St Ste 202, Greenville, SC 29601
Tel.: (864) 235-8821
E-Mail: info@shiftisgood.com
Web Site: www.shiftisgood.com

Year Founded: 2005

Agency Specializes In: Advertising, Internet/Web Design, Search Engine Optimization, Social Media

Mike Harrison *(Pres & Strategist)*
Craig Carney *(Sr VP-Sls)*
Andrea Wolinetz *(VP-Partnerships)*
Frank Allgood *(Dir-Client Comm)*
Meredith Martin *(Mgr-PR)*
Gary Upham *(Sr Designer)*

Accounts:
Automation Engineering Corporation
U by Kotex

SHINE ADVERTISING

612 W Main St Ste 105, Madison, WI 53703
Tel.: (608) 442-7373
Fax: (608) 442-7374
E-Mail: hello@shinenorth.com
Web Site: shineunited.com

E-Mail for Key Personnel:
President: chanke@shinenorth.com
Creative Dir.: mkriefski@shinenorth.com

Employees: 34
Year Founded: 2001

Agency Specializes In: Above-the-Line, Advertising, Affiliate Marketing, Below-the-Line, Brand Development & Integration, Broadcast, Children's Market, Collateral, College, Consulting, Consumer Goods, Consumer Marketing, Consumer Publications, Content, Digital/Interactive, Direct Response Marketing, Direct-to-Consumer, E-Commerce, Education, Electronic Media, Electronics, Email, Entertainment, Graphic Design, Household Goods, Identity Marketing, Integrated Marketing, International, Internet/Web Design, Leisure, Logo & Package Design, Luxury Products, Magazines, Market Research, Men's Market, Newspapers & Magazines, Out-of-Home Media, Outdoor, Package Design, Planning & Consultation, Print, Promotions, Regional, Restaurant, Retail, Sales Promotion, Search Engine Optimization, Strategic Planning/Research, Sweepstakes, T.V., Trade & Consumer Magazines, Urban Market, Viral/Buzz/Word of Mouth, Web (Banner Ads, Pop-ups, etc.), Women's Market

Revenue: $3,000,000

Curt Hanke *(Founder, CEO & Sr Strategist)*
John Krull *(Partner, VP & Dir-Creative)*
Audelino Moreno *(Sr Dir-Art)*
Ginny Bronesky Stuesser *(Dir-Media)*
Kelly Mlsna *(Acct Supvr)*
Emily Kothe *(Sr Acct Exec)*
Corrisa Bielefeldt *(Acct Exec)*
Megan Ciurczak *(Sr Acct Planner)*

Accounts:
Kaplan Inc. SCORE! Educational Centers

SHINE UNITED LLC

202 N Henry St, Madison, WI 53703
Tel.: (608) 442-7373
E-Mail: hello@shineunited.com
Web Site: www.shineunited.com

Year Founded: 2001

Agency Specializes In: Advertising, Brand Development & Integration, Digital/Interactive, Graphic Design, Media Relations, Package Design, Print, Public Relations, Social Media, T.V.

Curt Hanke *(Founder, CEO & Chief Strategist)*
Mike Kriefski *(Founder, COO & Exec Dir-Creative)*
John Krull *(Partner, VP & Dir-Creative)*
Audelino Moreno *(Sr Dir-Art)*
James Breen *(Assoc Dir-Creative & Copywriter)*
Corisa Bielefeldt *(Sr Acct Exec)*
Emily Kothe *(Sr Acct Exec)*
David Byrne *(Sr Planner-Media)*
Megan Ciurzak *(Sr Acct Planner)*

Accounts:
New-Aguila Ammunition (US Agency of Record) Marketing Communications
Amazon.com
Carver Yachts
New-Erbert & Gerbert's Sandwich Shops (Agency of Record) Digital, Radio, Social, Television
Harley-Davidson
Kohler Co
LaCrosse Footwear, Inc. (Lead Creative Agency) Advertising, Digital, Marketing, Print, TV
Mizuno Running & Golf
Moxie Cycling Co. Brand Strategy, Marketing
Nordic Consulting
Park Bank Brand Strategy, Digital, Marketing, Media Planning & Buying, PR, Promotion, Social Media, Traditional Media
New-W. L. Gore & Associates, Inc. Digital Advertising, GORE-TEX, Print Advertising, Social Media
Wente Family Estates & Food Network Brand Strategy, Creative, Digital, Entwine, Social Media
Winston Fly Rods
Wisconsin Cheese Group
Wisconsin Milk Marketing Board, Inc.

SHINY ADVERTISING

(Formerly Essentia Creative)
1800 Wawaset St, Wilmington, DE 19806
Tel.: (302) 384-6494
Fax: (302) 384-7645
E-Mail: connect@shiny.agency
Web Site: shiny.agency

Year Founded: 2005

Agency Specializes In: Advertising, Brand Development & Integration, Digital/Interactive, Print, Social Media

Katy Thorbahn *(Partner & Mng Dir)*
John Avondolio *(Partner & Dir-Client Engagement)*
Shannon Stevens *(Partner & Dir-Creative)*
Joe Johnson *(Sr Acct Mgr)*

Accounts:
SIG Combibloc

THE SHIPYARD

(Formerly People to my Site)
580 North 4th St Ste 500, Columbus, OH 43215
Tel.: (800) 295-4519
E-Mail: Info@TheShipyard.com
Web Site: www.theshipyard.com/

Employees: 25

Agency Specializes In: Broadcast, Consulting, Media Buying Services, Promotions, Public Relations, Strategic Planning/Research

Jennifer Ridenour *(COO)*
Michelle Gastin *(Mgr-Digital Mktg)*
Sarah Cowden *(Sr Specialist-Social Media)*
Fernando Bergas-Coria *(Acct Exec)*

Accounts:
Lexus
Nationwide Childrens Hospital
The Scotts Company

SHIRLEY/HUTCHINSON CREATIVE WORKS

707 N Franklin Ste 100, Tampa, FL 33602
Tel.: (813) 229-6162
Fax: (813) 229-6262
Toll Free: (866) 479-1548
E-Mail: john@shirleyhutchinson.com
Web Site: www.shirleyhutchinson.com

E-Mail for Key Personnel:
President: john@shirleyhutchinson.com
Creative Dir.: jim@shirleyhutchinson.com

Employees: 5
Year Founded: 1988

Agency Specializes In: Advertising, Advertising Specialties, Brand Development & Integration, Business-To-Business, Collateral, Consumer Marketing, Corporate Identity, Direct Response Marketing, Financial, Food Service, Graphic Design, Internet/Web Design, Leisure, Logo & Package Design, Media Buying Services, Outdoor, Point of Purchase, Point of Sale, Print, Public Relations, Radio, Restaurant, Sales Promotion, Strategic Planning/Research, Sweepstakes, T.V., Yellow Pages Advertising

Approx. Annual Billings: $1,500,000

John Shirley *(Principal)*
Sahil Patel *(Dir-Office Admin)*

SHOESTRING

PO Box 616, Gardiner, ME 04345
Toll Free: (888) 835-6236
E-Mail: heroes@shoestringagency.org
Web Site: shoestring.agency

Year Founded: 2001

Agency Specializes In: Advertising, Brand Development & Integration, Graphic Design, Internet/Web Design, Media Relations, Strategic Planning/Research

Hannah Brazee Gregory *(Founder & Chief Creative Officer)*
Kyle Gregory *(Mng Dir & Principal)*
Eric Hoffsten *(Sr Dir-Art & Designer)*

Accounts:
Lincoln Crossing Recreational Foundation
The National Board of Legal Specialty
Yad Chessed

THE SHOP

(Formerly True Action Network)
495 Broadway 4th Fl, New York, NY 10012
Tel.: (212) 965-2800
E-Mail: contact@theshop.com
Web Site: www.the-shop.com

Agency Specializes In: Email, Graphic Design, Media Planning, Mobile Marketing, Search Engine Optimization, Social Media, Strategic Planning/Research

Brian Bolten *(Head-Strategy)*
John S. Couch *(Head-Creative)*
Brian Sannicandro *(Grp Dir-Mktg)*

Accounts:
Aeropostale Men & Women Clothes & Accessories Mfr
Calvin Klein Men & Women Clothes & Accessories Mfr
Haggar Clothing Co Dress & Apparel Mfr & Distr
Levi Strauss Jeans & Authentic Cloths Mfr
Mondelez International, Inc.
Pepperidge Farm E-Commerce Site, Goldfish, Goldfish My Way

SHOPPER MARKETING GROUP ADVERTISING INC.

(Formerly EMG - Ethnic Marketing Group, Inc.)
24412 McBean Pkwy Ste 123, Valencia, CA 91355
Tel.: (661) 295-5704
Fax: (661) 295-5771
Web Site: www.smg-roi.com/

Employees: 17
Year Founded: 1991

National Agency Associations: AHAA

Agency Specializes In: Above-the-Line, Advertising, Automotive, Below-the-Line, Bilingual Market, Brand Development & Integration, Branded Entertainment, Broadcast, Business-To-Business, Cable T.V., Catalogs, Children's Market, Co-op Advertising, Collateral, Communications, Consumer Goods, Consumer Marketing, Corporate Identity, Customer Relationship Management, Direct Response Marketing, Direct-to-Consumer, Entertainment, Experience Design, Financial, Guerilla Marketing, Health Care Services, Hispanic Market, In-Store Advertising, Infomercials, Internet/Web Design, Local Marketing, Logo & Package Design, Magazines, Market Research, Media Buying Services, Media Planning, Media Relations, Media Training, Men's Market, Mobile Marketing, Multicultural, New Product Development, Newspaper, Newspapers & Magazines, Out-of-Home Media, Outdoor, Over-50 Market, Package Design, Point of Sale, Print, Product Placement, Production, Production (Ad, Film, Broadcast), Production (Print), Promotions, Public Relations, Publicity/Promotions, Radio, Restaurant, Sales Promotion, Sponsorship, Sports Market, Sweepstakes, T.V., Teen Market, Trade & Consumer Magazines, Women's Market

Mario Echevarria *(CEO & Mng Partner)*

Accounts:
Boar's Head
Foresters; Canada Insurance; 2008
Ocean Spray
Shasta
Tupperware Brands Corporation; Orlando, FL; 1992
Weber Stephen Products Co.; Chicago, IL Weber BBQ Grills; 2000

SHOPTOLOGY INC

7800 N Dallas Pkwy Ste 160, Plano, TX 75024
Tel.: (469) 287-1200
E-Mail: info@goshoptology.com
Web Site: www.goshoptology.com

Year Founded: 2013

Agency Specializes In: Advertising, Digital/Interactive

Charlie Anderson *(CEO)*
Dino De Leon *(Sr VP & Head-Creative)*
Ken Madden *(Sr VP & Head-Engagement)*
Julie Quick *(Sr VP & Head-Insights & Strategy)*
David Huang *(Sr Mgr-Production)*
Joshua Narofsky *(Copywriter)*

Accounts:
Mozido

SHOREPOINT COMMUNICATIONS, LLC

160 Lehigh Ave Ste B, Lakewood, NJ 08701
Tel.: (732) 961-7936
Fax: (732) 961-7939
Web Site: www.shorepointcomm.com

Agency Specializes In: Advertising, Brand Development & Integration, Content, Digital/Interactive, Graphic Design, Internet/Web Design, Logo & Package Design, Media Buying Services, Print, Social Media

David Francis *(CEO & Dir-Creative)*
Melissa Caryn *(Dir-Social Media & PR)*
Deb Kovacs *(Dir-Art)*
Jon Weiss *(Dir-Mktg & Bus Dev)*

Accounts:
Hippocratic Solutions
Manahawkin Urgent Care

SHOTWELL DIGITAL

1042 S Olive St, Los Angeles, CA 90015
Tel.: (831) 325-6250
Web Site: www.shotwelldigital.com

Agency Specializes In: Advertising, Brand Development & Integration, Digital/Interactive, Graphic Design, Search Engine Optimization

Matt Moss *(Acct Dir)*
Scott Wilson *(Dir-Creative)*

Accounts:
Purps

SHOUT OUT LLC

PO Box 50552, Knoxville, TN 37950
Tel.: (865) 219-3564
E-Mail: info@shoutoutllc.com
Web Site: www.shoutoutllc.com

Year Founded: 2008

Agency Specializes In: Advertising, Brand Development & Integration, Corporate Identity, Internet/Web Design, Logo & Package Design, Media Relations, Outdoor, Print, Public Relations, Radio

Brooks A. Brown *(Founder & Principal)*

Accounts:
Debbie Lambert Real Estate Sales
FedSavvy Educational Solutions

SHOUTLET, INC.

1 Erdman Pl Ste 102, Middleton, WI 53717
Tel.: (608) 833-0088
Fax: (608) 833-9029
E-Mail: sales@shoutlet.com
Web Site: www.shoutlet.com

Employees: 9
Year Founded: 2002

Agency Specializes In: Advertising, Brand Development & Integration, Business Publications, Business-To-Business, Collateral, Communications, Consulting, Consumer Marketing, Consumer Publications, Corporate Identity, Direct Response Marketing, Education,

Electronic Media, Exhibit/Trade Shows, Government/Political, Graphic Design, High Technology, Industrial, Internet/Web Design, Logo & Package Design, Merchandising, Pharmaceutical, Planning & Consultation, Point of Purchase, Point of Sale, Print, Production, Sales Promotion, Sports Market, Strategic Planning/Research, Trade & Consumer Magazines

Mark Herrington *(CEO)*
Greg Gerik *(VP-Product Mktg & Indus Solutions)*
David Prohaska *(VP-Mktg)*
Chad Bryant *(Acct Dir)*
Melissa Johnson *(Dir-Strategic Mktg)*
Emily Zei *(Mgr-Product Mktg)*

Accounts:
New-24 Hour Fitness
New-3M
Arroweye
New-Best Buy
New-Canon
Classic Media
Ebay
New-Fox Sports
Headrush (Pro Bono)
New-Hot Topic
M7
MI7
Milwaukee's Best
New-Norwegian Cruise Line
Optima Batteries
Pentair
Rayovac
Remington
Southern Herb
Susan G. Komen Breast Cancer Foundation (Pro Bono)
WiCell Research Institute
Wrigley Orbit
Yamaha

SHOW MEDIA, LLC

383 5th Ave.2nd Fl, New York, NY 10016
Tel.: (212) 883-8783
Fax: (212) 883-0959
E-Mail: info@showmedia.com
Web Site: www.showmedia.com

Agency Specializes In: Advertising, Event Planning & Marketing, Out-of-Home Media

Laurence Hallier *(Founder & CEO)*
Jonathan Goodrich *(CTO & Sr VP)*
Blake Knight *(VP & Gen Mgr)*
Ron Parkinson *(VP-Ops)*
Taryn Borst *(Office Mgr)*
Steve Chatham *(Acct Exec)*

Accounts:
Nestle S.A. Purina

SIC 'EM ADVERTISING INC.

1840 Gateway Dr Ste 200, San Mateo, CA 94404-4029
Tel.: (650) 569-3940
Fax: (650) 569-3943
E-Mail: info@sic-em.com
Web Site: www.sic-em.com

Employees: 10
Year Founded: 1986

Approx. Annual Billings: $3,000,000

James Mercado *(Co-Founder, Principal & Dir-Creative)*
David Zeitman *(Strategist-Brand)*

Accounts:
AOL Voice Services
McAfee Software
McGraw Insurance
N Computing
Newcastle Brown Ale
Oracle America, Inc.
Pacific Specialty Insurance

SICOLAMARTIN

(Name Changed to Y&R Austin)

SID LEE

75 Queen Street Ofc 1400, Montreal, QC H3C 2N6 Canada
Tel.: (514) 282-2200
Fax: (514) 282-0499
E-Mail: info@sidlee.com
Web Site: www.sidlee.com

Employees: 550
Year Founded: 1993

Agency Specializes In: Advertising, Bilingual Market, Brand Development & Integration, Communications, Digital/Interactive, Direct Response Marketing, Graphic Design, In-Store Advertising, Internet/Web Design, Logo & Package Design, Outdoor, Print, Publicity/Promotions, T.V.

Bertrand Cesvet *(Owner)*
Julie Provencal *(Partner & VP-Accts & Global Client Integration)*
Kris Manchester *(Exec Dir-Creative)*
Andrew Bernardi *(Sr Dir-Art)*
Audree Couture *(Acct Dir)*
Myriam Veilleux *(Acct Dir)*
Brian Gill *(Dir-Creative)*
Emilie Thibault *(Coord-Creative)*

Accounts:
Absolut Vodka (Agency of Record) Campaign: "Make the Holidays Pop", Campaign: "Transform Today", Digital, Experiential Marketing, Social Media
Adidas Adidas F50, Campaign: "All in for #MyGirls", Campaign: "The Cautionary Tale of Ebenezer Snoop", Campaign: "Unite All Originals", Originals
Aeroplan
AFC Ajax NV Campaign: "The Ajax Experience"
Art Directors Club
BelairDirect
Bombardier Business Aircraft Challenger, Learjet
Burger King Canada Campaign: "Fries King"
Cirque du Soleil
Club Med (Agency of Record) Creative, Strategic
Danone
Dentyne Campaign: "Diner"
Dom Perignon Campaign: "Foldout"
Enercare Brand Awareness, Digital, Radio, TV
Gaz Metro
Italian Trade Commission (Agency of Record) Branding, Campaign: "Made in Italy", Consumer, Content, Creative, Digital, Social Media
Keurig Canada Campaign: "Brewhaha", Keurig 2.0 System
New-Le Chateau TV
Maison Birks Branding
MGM Resorts International
PC Financial Campaign: " That's Just Good Banking"
Postmedia (Agency of Record) Campaign: "Postmedia Reimagined", Digital, Print
Red Bull
RONA Inc. Campaign: "A Win For Us", Campaign: "Customize Your Holidays", Creative, Marketing
Samsung Electronics Digital
Sobey's (IGA)
Societe des alcools du Quebec
Suzuki
Tourism Montreal Campaign: "MTLMOMENTS"
Ubisoft
Uniprix
Videotron Campaign: "Pineapple Juice", Campaign: "Vidaotron Flagship"
Warner Bros Games Campaign: "Batman Arkham City"
Wines from France

Branches

SID LEE

12, rue du Sentier, 75002 Paris, France
Tel.: (33) 1 44 88 83 90
E-Mail: jdelpuech@sidlee.com
Web Site: www.sidlee.com

Johan Delpuech *(Mng Partner-Paris)*
Sylvain Thirache *(Exec Dir-Creative, Mgr & Partner-Paris)*
Stephane Soussan *(Creative Dir-Paris)*
Therese Jonsson *(Dir-Art)*
Joelle Paquette *(Mgr-PR & Comm)*
Sarah Patier *(Strategist)*

Accounts:
BNP Paribas
Coca-Cola Refreshments USA, Inc. Vitamin Water
Gaite Lyrique
INQ
Kronenbourg Campaign: "The French Blah Blah"
Love2recycle
Tourisme Montreal
Ubisoft Assassin's Creed 3, Assassin's Creed IV: Black Flag, Campaign: "Defy History", Campaign: "Rise"
Warner Brothers

SID LEE

55 Mill Street Building 5, Suite 500, Toronto, ON M5A 3C4 Canada
Tel.: (416) 421-4200
Web Site: www.sidlee.com

Vito Piazza *(Pres-Sid Lee Toronto & Calgary & Partner)*
Eric Alper *(Partner & Exec VP-Client Svcs)*
Matt Di Paola *(Mng Dir-Digital Innovation)*
Claudia Roy *(VP & Exec Producer-Global)*
Jared Stein *(VP-Bus Growth & Dev)*
Jeffrey DaSilva *(Exec Dir-Creative)*
Tom Koukodimos *(Exec Dir-Creative)*
Oliver Brooks *(Dir-Art)*
Amanda Buchanan *(Dir-User Experience)*
Nicolas LeBlanc *(Dir-Artistic)*
Mike Richardson *(Copywriter)*

Accounts:
Birks & Mayors Strategic Development
Blue Goose
Coca Cola Canada Campaign: "Taste"
Google Canada
Italian Trade Commission
Maple Leafs Sports & Entertainment
Marks
PC Financial
Post Media
Subway Restaurants Canada (Creative Agency of Record) Digital, In-Store, Strategy
TJX Canada
Toronto FC Campaign: "It's a Bloody Big Deal"
Toronto Raptors Campaign: "#WeTheNorth"
Unilever Canada Axe Canada (Agency of Record), Campaign: "#Selfmaker", Creative

SID LEE

Waterorenplein 4-A, Amsterdam, 1051 Netherlands
Tel.: (31) 020662303
E-Mail: info@sidlee.com
Web Site: www.sidlee.com

Mac Macdonald *(Pres & Partner-SID LEE Amsterdam)*

Alex Pasini *(Partner & Dir-Creative)*
J. Darden Longenecker *(Exec VP-Ops)*
Yann Mooney *(Exec Dir-Creative)*
Henrik Leichsenring *(Sr Dir-Art)*
Ali Ronca *(Acct Dir)*
Christy Colon *(Acct Mgr)*
Joelle Paquette *(Mgr-PR & Comm)*
Laura Van Der Heiden *(Acct Exec)*
Jette Van Der Made *(Coord-Fin)*

Accounts:
Absolut Campaign: "Transform today", Nights by Absolut
Adidas Holiday Hookup
Heineken Starvision

Sid Lee
12-16 Vestry St, New York, NY 10013
(See Separate Listing)

SID PATERSON ADVERTISING, INC.
650 5th Ave, New York, NY 10019
Tel.: (212) 725-9600
Fax: (212) 779-7291
E-Mail: info@spadvertising.com
Web Site: www.spadvertising.com

E-Mail for Key Personnel:
President: sid@spadvertising.com

Employees: 30
Year Founded: 1963

Agency Specializes In: Advertising, Automotive, Broadcast, Business-To-Business, Cable T.V., Co-op Advertising, Collateral, Corporate Identity, Direct Response Marketing, Entertainment, Event Planning & Marketing, Fashion/Apparel, Financial, Food Service, Hispanic Market, Infomercials, Internet/Web Design, Media Buying Services, Media Planning, Newspaper, Newspapers & Magazines, Out-of-Home Media, Outdoor, Print, Production, Radio, Real Estate, Recruitment, Restaurant, Retail, T.V., Travel & Tourism

Approx. Annual Billings: $20,000,000

Breakdown of Gross Billings by Media: Newsp. & Mags.: $9,000,000; Outdoor: $1,000,000; Radio & T.V.: $10,000,000

Sid Paterson *(Pres)*
Tom Avitabile *(Sr VP & Dir-Creative)*
Jack Bloom *(Sr VP)*
Burt Thomas *(Controller)*
Pat Asaro *(Dir-Media)*
Lorenzo Concepcion *(Dir-Art)*
Michael Rudman *(Mgr-Production)*

Accounts:
Bay Ridge Auto Dealers Chrysler, Dodge, Honda, Hyundai, Infiniti, Jeep, Kia, Lexus, Lincoln, Mercury, Mitsubishi, Nissan, Subaru, Suzuki, Toyota, Volvo
Free Country; New York, NY Outerwear; 2002
Homeguard; Stamford, CT Home Service Warranty; 1997
IDT Pennytalk (Phone Cards); 2007
Mercedes-Benz; 2002
Northeast Dental (Dental Insurance); 2007
PCNY USA; Staten Island, NY General Contractors & Builders; 1999
Perma-Sol; Hoboken, NJ Environmental Cleaning Solutions; 2002
Power Express Mortgage Bankers
Power Outlets; Long Island, NY Appliance, Television Retailers; 2001
Sher Institute of Reproductive Medicine; 2007
Sonoma-Loeb Wines; New York, NY; 2003
Tribeca Summit (Condominiums); 2007
UJA; New York, NY (Special Projects); 2005
Valvoline Auto Centers; Boston, MA; 2007
WarranTech; Bedford, TX Extended Automotive & Home Service Contracts

SIDDALL, INC.
1 Capitol Sq 830 E Main St 24th Fl, Richmond, VA 23219
Tel.: (804) 788-8011
Fax: (804) 788-8893
E-Mail: contactus@siddall.com
Web Site: www.siddall.com

E-Mail for Key Personnel:
Creative Dir.: shindman@siddall.com
Media Dir.: lthompson@siddall.com

Employees: 15
Year Founded: 1975

Agency Specializes In: Advertising, Brand Development & Integration, Broadcast, Business-To-Business, Collateral, Communications, Consumer Publications, Corporate Communications, Corporate Identity, Crisis Communications, Direct Response Marketing, E-Commerce, Environmental, Event Planning & Marketing, Financial, Government/Political, Graphic Design, Guerilla Marketing, Health Care Services, Leisure, Market Research, Media Buying Services, Media Planning, Media Relations, Newspapers & Magazines, Out-of-Home Media, Outdoor, Pharmaceutical, Planning & Consultation, Production (Print), Promotions, Public Relations, Radio, Real Estate, Retail, Social Marketing/Nonprofit, Strategic Planning/Research, T.V., Trade & Consumer Magazines, Transportation, Travel & Tourism

Approx. Annual Billings: $18,250,196

Breakdown of Gross Billings by Media: Fees: $13,624,000; Internet Adv.: $497,758; Newsp.: $530,181; Outdoor: $320,215; Production: $1,173,000; Radio: $1,149,669; T.V.: $258,863; Trade & Consumer Mags.: $696,510

John N. Siddall *(CEO)*
Roberta McDonnell *(COO, Sr VP & Exec Dir-Production)*
Bettina Roda *(Controller)*
Dennis Lock *(Mgr-Graphic Arts)*
Kira Siddall *(Strategist-Social Media-Bus Dev)*

Accounts:
Children's Hospital; Richmond, VA
Claris Financial
Fairfax County Economic Development Authority; 1978
Rocketts Landing; Richmond, VA; 2006
State Fair of Virginia
Virginia Department of Transportation
Virginia Eye Institute
Whitman, Requardt & Associates

SIDES & ASSOCIATES, INC.
222 Jefferson St Ste B, Lafayette, LA 70501-3267
Tel.: (337) 233-6473
Fax: (337) 233-6485
Toll Free: (800) 393-6473
E-Mail: media@sides.com
Web Site: www.sides.com

Employees: 20
Year Founded: 1976

National Agency Associations: 4A's

Agency Specializes In: Consumer Marketing, Government/Political

Approx. Annual Billings: $6,980,000

Larry Sides *(Pres)*
Kathy Ashworth *(Exec VP)*
Jeffrey Eichholz *(VP)*
Bridget Mires *(VP-Media)*

Accounts:
Department of Health & Hospitals
The Emerald Companies
FEMA
McDonald's

SIEGEL+GALE
625 Ave of the Americas 4th Fl, New York, NY 10011
Tel.: (212) 453-0400
Fax: (212) 453-0401
E-Mail: newyork@siegelgale.com
Web Site: www.siegelgale.com

Employees: 175
Year Founded: 1969

Agency Specializes In: Advertising, Brand Development & Integration, Business-To-Business, Communications, Consulting, Corporate Identity, Financial, Graphic Design, Internet/Web Design, Sponsorship, Strategic Planning/Research

Approx. Annual Billings: $50,000,000

David Srere *(Co-Pres, CEO & Chief Strategy Officer)*
Howard Belk *(Co-CEO & Chief Creative Officer)*
Margaret Molloy *(CMO-Global & Head-Bus Dev)*
Jason Cieslak *(Pres-Pacific Rim-Leadership)*
Britt Bulla *(Dir-Strategy)*
Nikolas J. Contis *(Dir-Naming, Brand Dev & Leadership-Global)*
Lori Cummings *(Dir-Project Mgmt)*
Daniel Katz Golden *(Dir-Strategy)*
Russ Meyer *(Dir-Strategy & Insights-Global)*
Thomas Mueller *(Dir-Digital, Leadership & Simplification-Global)*
Brian Rafferty *(Dir-Res Insights-Global)*
Anneliese Atwell *(Strategist)*
Marc Desmond *(Strategist)*
Preanka Hai *(Strategist)*
Joe Zhou *(Strategist)*
Jennifer Dorland *(Assoc Strategist)*

Accounts:
3M
AARP
Adecco Group Campaign: "Accounting Principals"
Agility
American Express
Ameya Preserve
Anthem
AT&T Communications Corp.
Bayor
Berklee College of Music
Boise
Buena Vista Home Entertainment
Caterpillar
Chubb
Citicorp
CNBC
Comcast
CooperVision, Inc.
Dell
Disney
Dolce
Dow Chemical
DuPont
Eaton Corporation
ESPN
Eurotel
The Four Seasons Hotel Group
Free Library of Philadelphia
General Electric
Genworth
Harley Davidson
Hewlett Packard Enterprise Brand Identity, Brand Strategy, Campaign: "Accelerating Next"
IBM
Independence Blue Cross Logo Redesign

Ingersoll-Rand
Internal Revenue Service
ITFC
Johnson & Johnson
The Legal Aid Society
Manhattan Transit Authority
Mastercard
McAfee
Microsoft
The National Basketball Association
Neustar
Novartis
Robert Wood Johnson Foundation
SAP
Saudi Aramco
Sony Playstation
United Health Group
Verizon Wireless
YMCA of the USA

Branch

Siegel+Gale

10960 Wilshire Blvd Ste 400, Los Angeles, CA 90024-3702
Tel.: (310) 312-2200
Fax: (310) 312-2202
E-Mail: losangeles@siegelgale.com
Web Site: www.siegelgale.com

Employees: 25

Agency Specializes In: Advertising, Automotive, Brand Development & Integration, Broadcast, Business-To-Business, Collateral, Communications, Consulting, Corporate Communications, Corporate Identity, Digital/Interactive, E-Commerce, Entertainment, Financial, Graphic Design, Health Care Services, High Technology, Industrial, Information Technology, Internet/Web Design, Logo & Package Design, Medical Products, Pharmaceutical, Planning & Consultation, Strategic Planning/Research

Jason Cieslak *(Pres-Pacific Rim)*
Glisten McCrary *(VP-Bus Dev)*
Alyson Schonholz *(Grp Dir-Strategy, Insights, Brand Dev & Digital)*
Nikolas Contis *(Dir-Naming, Brand Dev & Leadership-San Francisco)*
Lisa Kane *(Dir-Strategy)*
Matthias Mencke *(Dir-Creative)*
David Pulaski *(Dir-Res)*
Simon Frost *(Strategist)*

Accounts:
3M
American Express
Clean Energy Fuels Corp Logo, Strategy, Visual Identity
Dell
McAfee
Pulse
Yahoo

SIGMA GROUP

10 Mountainview Road, Upper Saddle River, NJ 07458-1933
Tel.: (201) 261-1123
Fax: (201) 261-0399
E-Mail: media@sigmagroup.com
Web Site: www.sigmagroup.com

E-Mail for Key Personnel:
President: vchronis@sigmagroup.com
Media Dir.: jkim@sigmagroup.com
Production Mgr.: ACosta@sigmagroup.com

Employees: 60
Year Founded: 1986

National Agency Associations: Second Wind Limited

Agency Specializes In: Brand Development & Integration, Cable T.V., Consumer Marketing, Corporate Identity, Cosmetics, Digital/Interactive, Direct Response Marketing, Electronic Media, Entertainment, Event Planning & Marketing, Exhibit/Trade Shows, Graphic Design, Health Care Services, High Technology, Industrial, Infomercials, Internet/Web Design, Logo & Package Design, Media Buying Services, New Product Development, Newspapers & Magazines, Out-of-Home Media, Outdoor, Pharmaceutical, Point of Purchase, Point of Sale, Print, Production, Public Relations, Radio, Sales Promotion, Sponsorship, Sports Market, Strategic Planning/Research, T.V., Technical Advertising, Trade & Consumer Magazines, Travel & Tourism, Yellow Pages Advertising

Diane DeCastro *(VP & Sr Grp Acct Dir)*
Patricia Paris *(Grp Dir-HR)*
Christine McPartlan *(Sr Dir-Art)*
Kerri Koppel *(Dir-Media)*
Timothy Stapleton *(Dir-Creative)*
Celine Morton *(Mgr-Digital Media Campaign)*
Linsey Schwetje *(Mgr-Bus Dev)*
Tiffany Farhat *(Sr Grp Supvr)*

Accounts:
Famous Footwear
Helen of Troy Limited Brut, Infusium 23, Pert Plus
Hunter Douglas
Huntington Learning Center Customer Engagement, Digital Strategy, Direct Marketing, Media Planning and Buying
I&R Ultra Service
Mastercard
Nielsen Bainbridge
Panasonic Core Trainer
Panasonic Corporation of North America Handheld PCs, Toughbook Computers; 2001
Panasonic Massage Chair
Panasonic Projector
PR Newswire
Rita's Italian Ice Creative Development, Media Planning & Buying, Strategy
Siemens
Terramar

SIGMA MARKETING GROUP LLC

1 Cambridge Pl 1850 Winton Rd S, Rochester, NY 14618-3923
Tel.: (585) 473-7300
Fax: (585) 473-0300
E-Mail: mshann@sigmamarketing.com
Web Site: www.sigmamarketing.com

Employees: 76
Year Founded: 1985

National Agency Associations: DMA

Agency Specializes In: Automotive, Business-To-Business, Co-op Advertising, College, Consulting, Consumer Marketing, Customer Relationship Management, Digital/Interactive, Direct Response Marketing, Direct-to-Consumer, E-Commerce, Education, Financial, Graphic Design, Health Care Services, High Technology, Hospitality, Information Technology, Integrated Marketing, Internet/Web Design, Market Research, New Product Development, Pharmaceutical, Planning & Consultation, Print, Production, Retail, Strategic Planning/Research, Telemarketing, Viral/Buzz/Word of Mouth

Approx. Annual Billings: $11,000,000

Stefan Willimann *(CEO)*
Martha Bush *(Sr VP-Strategy & Solutions)*
Andrew Lucyszyn *(VP-Digital)*
Marty Maynard *(VP-Client Engagement Grp)*
Vida Tamoshunas *(VP-Mktg Analytics)*
Nikki DellaPenta *(Head-Client Dev)*
David Haka *(Dir-Acctg)*
Michelle Tahara *(Analyst-Fin)*

Accounts:
AAA; 2008
Assurant; 2005
Avaya; 2003
Citizens Bank; 1995
Dollar/Thrifty Auto Group
Eastman Kodak; 2003
Key Bank; 1997
MetLife
Monro Muffler; 2005
MVP; 2008
Nationwide; 2004
Shredit; 2007
Xerox; 1995

SIGNAL INC.

7780 Brier Creek Pkwy Ste 415, Raleigh, NC 27617
Tel.: (919) 474-0330
Fax: (919) 474-0440
Toll Free: (877) 404-0330
E-Mail: info@signalinc.com
Web Site: www.signalinc.com

Employees: 11

Agency Specializes In: Advertising, Content, Digital/Interactive, Graphic Design, Internet/Web Design, Package Design

Revenue: $4,572,175

Ricky Haynes *(Pres)*
Rick Haynes *(CEO)*
Dave Grinnell *(Partner)*
Jim Ellis *(VP & Acct Dir)*
John Gibson *(Dir-Creative)*
Adam Howard *(Dir-Interactive)*
Patrick Jones *(Dir-Art)*
April Kilpatrick *(Dir-Art)*
Robert Locklear *(Dir-IT)*
Meghann Porter *(Dir-Digital Mktg)*
Chris Robinson *(Dir-Web Dev)*
Melissa Herboth *(Assoc Dir-Creative)*
Kelly Borberg *(Copywriter)*

Accounts:
Wake Audubon Society

SIGNAL OUTDOOR ADVERTISING

7616 Southland Blvd Ste 114, Orlando, FL 32809
Tel.: (407) 856-7079
Fax: (407) 856-7039
E-Mail: rickn@signaloutdoor.com
Web Site: www.signaloutdoor.com

Employees: 24
Year Founded: 1998

Agency Specializes In: Advertising, Out-of-Home Media, Outdoor

Approx. Annual Billings: $25,000,000

Breakdown of Gross Billings by Media: Out-of-Home Media: 100%

Ray Moyers *(COO)*
Rick Newcomer *(VP-Sls & Mktg)*
Toni Short *(Dir-New Bus Initiatives)*
Carlene Parsons *(Office Mgr)*
Steven Smith *(Mgr-Ops)*
Bill Thatcher *(Mgr-Sls)*
Mary Pozzi *(Acct Exec)*

Accounts:

HART; Tampa, FL Bus Advertising Shelters
LYNX; Orlando, FL Bus Advertising Shelters
Miami Dade Transit; Miami, FL Bus Bench Advertising

Branches

Signal Outdoor Advertising
68 Southfield Ave Bldg 2 Ste 100, Stamford, CT 06902
Tel.: (203) 328-3763
Fax: (203) 328-3764
Web Site: www.signaloutdoor.com

Rick Newcomer *(VP-Sls & Mktg)*
Norman Macdonald *(Gen Mgr-CT)*
Katie Nickerson *(Gen Mgr)*
A. Marie Sullivan *(Dir-HR)*
Kathy D'Errico *(Acct Exec)*
Ken Radigan *(Acct Exec)*
Maritza Rodriguez *(Acct Exec)*
Molly Sliwinski *(Acct Exec)*
Valencia Walton *(Acct Exec)*
Kirk Watters *(Acct Exec)*

Signal Outdoor Advertising
6011 Benjamin Rd Ste 104, Tampa, FL 33634
Tel.: (813) 249-6309
Fax: (813) 249-6340
Web Site: www.signaloutdoor.com

Employees: 20

Rick Newcomer *(VP-Sls & Mktg)*
Norman Macdonald *(Gen Mgr-CT)*
Katie Nickerson *(Gen Mgr)*
A. Marie Sullivan *(Dir-HR)*
Vincent Mark Ciambruschini *(Mgr-Market)*
Judi Hughes *(Mgr-Market-Tampa Florida)*
Lynn Terlaga *(Reg Gen Mgr-NY, NJ, CT)*

Accounts:
Bluecross Blueshield Insurance
Dunkin Donuts
Krispy Kreme
Mastercard
Moe's
Target
Weather Express

SIGNAL POINT MARKETING+DESIGN
607 E 6th Ave, Post Falls, ID 83854
Tel.: (208) 777-8942
E-Mail: tom@signalpt.com
Web Site: www.signalpointgraphics.com

Employees: 5
Year Founded: 1997

Agency Specializes In: Advertising, Agriculture, Brand Development & Integration, Business Publications, Catalogs, Consumer Goods, Corporate Identity, Cosmetics, Graphic Design, Identity Marketing, Logo & Package Design, Magazines, New Product Development, Newspaper, Newspapers & Magazines, Package Design, Pharmaceutical, Point of Purchase, Point of Sale, Print, Production, Restaurant, Trade & Consumer Magazines, Travel & Tourism

Approx. Annual Billings: $850,000

Breakdown of Gross Billings by Media: Collateral: 10%; Consumer Publs.: 5%; Graphic Design: 30%; Logo & Package Design: 10%; Mags.: 10%; Plng. & Consultation: 20%; Print: 15%

Thomas Latham *(Principal)*

Accounts:
Coeur d 'Alene Cellars
Herbal Fortress
LifeStream
Timber Rock Wine

SIGNALFIRE, LCC
1624 Hobbs Dr, Delavan, WI 53115
Tel.: (262) 725-4500
Fax: (262) 725-4499
Web Site: www.signalfire.us

Year Founded: 2002

Agency Specializes In: Advertising, Brand Development & Integration, Content, Graphic Design, Internet/Web Design, Media Relations, Print, Public Relations, Search Engine Optimization, Social Media

Matthew Olson *(Pres)*
Nick Zaharias *(Mng Dir)*
Jodi Heisz *(Dir-Art)*

Accounts:
Continental Plastic, Corp
Door County Coffee & Tea Company
DP Electronic Recycling
Franklin Development Trust, Inc.
The Martin Group Inc
Voyager Capital Management, LLC

SIGNATURE ADVERTISING
1755 Kirby Pkwy Ste 200, Memphis, TN 38120
Tel.: (901) 754-2200
Fax: (901) 754-9118
E-Mail: info@signatureadvertising.com
Web Site: www.signatureadvertising.com

Employees: 50
Year Founded: 1994

Agency Specializes In: Advertising

Mark Henry *(Pres & CEO)*
Brian Tisdale *(Acct Svcs Dir)*
Kevin Miller *(Dir-Creative)*
Karen Parks *(Dir-Creative Svcs)*
Marya Green *(Sr Acct Mgr)*
Cathy Reece *(Sr Art Dir)*

Accounts:
Fed Ex
HomeWood Suites
Landau
Tru Green ChemLawn

THE SIGNATURE AGENCY
1784 Heritage Center Dr, Wake Forest, NC 27587
Tel.: (919) 878-8989
Fax: (919) 878-3939
Toll Free: (800) 870-8700
E-Mail: info@signatureagency.com
Web Site: www.signatureagency.com

Employees: 10
Year Founded: 1987

Agency Specializes In: Advertising, Agriculture, Brand Development & Integration, Business Publications, Business-To-Business, Collateral, Communications, Consulting, Corporate Communications, Corporate Identity, Custom Publishing, Direct Response Marketing, Education, Electronic Media, Environmental, Exhibit/Trade Shows, Graphic Design, Health Care Services, Industrial, Integrated Marketing, Internet/Web Design, Logo & Package Design, Medical Products, Package Design, Pharmaceutical, Planning & Consultation, Production (Print), Public Relations, Publicity/Promotions, Sales Promotion, Strategic Planning/Research

Sidney Reynolds *(Owner)*
Anne Shelton *(VP)*

Accounts:
614 Dental Spa Dentistry Services
AgCarolina Financial Financial Services
AgRenaissance Field Management Software
nContact Medical Devices
ONUG Communications Engineering
Witherspoon Rose Culture Nursery

SIGNATURE BRAND FACTORY
(Formerly Signature Advertising)
409 Canal St, Milldale, CT 06467-0698
Tel.: (860) 426-2144
Fax: (860) 426-2149
E-Mail: Todd@sig-brand.com
Web Site: www.signaturebrandfactory.com/

Year Founded: 1990

National Agency Associations: Second Wind Limited

Agency Specializes In: Advertising, Aviation & Aerospace, Brand Development & Integration, Corporate Identity, Medical Products, Strategic Planning/Research, Technical Advertising

Jerry Reardon *(Pres & CEO)*
Jeremy Russell *(VP & Head-Digital Creative)*
Rapahel Coto *(Dir-Creative)*
Steve Whinfield *(Sr Mgr-Production)*
Tricia Santoro Pina *(Mgr-Production)*

Accounts:
Disney
Time Warner

SIGNATURE COMMUNICATIONS
417 N 8th St Ste 401, Philadelphia, PA 19123
Tel.: (215) 922-3022
Fax: (215) 922-3033
E-Mail: ideas@signatureteam.com
Web Site: www.signatureteam.com

Employees: 12

Agency Specializes In: Brand Development & Integration, Broadcast, Collateral, Corporate Communications, Corporate Identity, Digital/Interactive, Direct Response Marketing, Exhibit/Trade Shows, Internet/Web Design, Media Buying Services, Out-of-Home Media, Outdoor, Point of Purchase, Point of Sale, Print, Production, Radio, Sales Promotion, Strategic Planning/Research

Bob Brown *(Owner)*
Tony DeMarco *(CEO & Dir-Creative)*
Anthony Rosowski *(VP)*
Peter Schmitz *(Sr Dir-Art)*
Amy Merola *(Art Dir)*
John Gifford *(Dir-Digital Creative)*
Leslie Hamada *(Dir-Mktg)*
Marissa O'Hara *(Planner-Media & Acct Mgmt)*

Accounts:
Banom
Crozer-Keystone Health System
Greater Wildwoods Tourism Improvement & Development Authority (GWTIDA)
Motorola Solutions, Inc.
Sirius
StonCor Group, Inc.
Voxx International

SIGNATURE CREATIVE, INC.
(Private-Parent-Single Location)
1513 N Gardner St, Los Angeles, CA 90046
Tel.: (323) 850-1162

E-Mail: hello@signaturecreative.com
Web Site: www.signaturecreative.com

Employees: 15
Year Founded: 2005

Agency Specializes In: Advertising, Brand Development & Integration, Broadcast, Digital/Interactive, Package Design, Print, Social Media, Strategic Planning/Research

Revenue: $3,600,000

Olivier Courbet *(Sr Dir-Interactive Art)*

Accounts:
The Sunset Strip

SIGNET INTERACTIVE LLC
4545 Post Oak Pl Dr Ste 150, Houston, TX 77027
Tel.: (281) 822-2824
Web Site: www.signetinteractive.com

Year Founded: 2011

Agency Specializes In: Advertising, Content, Digital/Interactive, Email, Search Engine Optimization, Social Media

Meredith Nudo *(Editor-Interactive Mktg)*
Ashley Mathis *(Acct Dir)*
Kristin Baker *(Dir-Ops)*
Derek Lanphier *(Dir-Creative Dev)*
Kristin Lanphier *(Dir-Ops)*
Joelle Eid *(Mgr-Interactive Community)*
Andy Rich *(Sr Designer)*

Accounts:
Carrie Ann
Universal Pegasus

SILTANEN & PARTNERS
353 Coral Cir, El Segundo, CA 90245
Tel.: (310) 986-6200
Fax: (310) 986-6214
E-Mail: newbusiness@siltanenpartners.com
Web Site: www.siltanen.com

Employees: 60
Year Founded: 1999

National Agency Associations:

Agency Specializes In: Automotive, Children's Market, Consumer Marketing, Electronics, Entertainment, Fashion/Apparel, Game Integration, Real Estate, Restaurant, Retail, Sponsorship, Technical Advertising

Rob Siltanen *(Owner & CEO)*
Tim Murphy *(Pres & Partner)*
Ruth Amir *(CMO & Dir-New Bus)*
Mike Braue *(Client Svcs Dir)*
Kelly Saffrey *(Acct Dir)*
Joe Hemp *(Dir-Creative)*
Isabelle Stehley *(Dir-Print Svcs)*
Christina Lee *(Assoc Dir-Project Mgmt)*
Susan Chu *(Acct Mgr & Project Mgr)*

Accounts:
Amazon Fire smartphone, Kindle Fire
Coldwell Banker Real Estate LLC Campaign: "Catch", Campaign: "Home's Best Friend", Campaign: "Your Home", Creative, Full Service; 2011
Epson America, Inc. Creative; 2011
Panda Express Full Service & Digital, Gaming; 2007
Skechers Campaign: "Man Vs.Cheetah", Campaign: "Mr. Quiggly", Campaign: "The Hall", Fitness/Performance Lines, GOrun 2, Relaxed Fit, Super Bowl 2015; 2011
VTech Electronics Creative, VTech Kids (Agency of Record)
YMCA; Los Angeles, CA Advertising/Promotions, Pro Bono

THE SILVER AGENCY
109 N Twr Ave Ste 200, Centralia, WA 98531
Tel.: (360) 736-8065
E-Mail: info@silveragency.com
Web Site: www.silveragency.com

Agency Specializes In: Advertising, Internet/Web Design, Logo & Package Design, Print, Radio, Search Engine Optimization, Social Media, T.V.

Chad Taylor *(CEO)*

Accounts:
Steel Partners Inc
Water Doctor

SILVER COMMUNICATIONS, INC.
35 E 21st St 7th Fl, New York, NY 10010
Tel.: (203) 445-6329
Fax: (212) 387-7875
E-Mail: info@silvercomm.com
Web Site: www.silvercomm.com

Employees: 10
Year Founded: 1956

National Agency Associations: DMA-MCA

Agency Specializes In: Business-To-Business, Consumer Marketing, Graphic Design

Approx. Annual Billings: $3,000,000

Gregg Sibert *(Owner & Dir-Creative)*

Accounts:
The Bank of New York BNY ConvergEX Group
Baron Capital Management
Baron Funds
Clearbrook Financial
Forest Laboratories, Inc.
ING Barings
Loeb & Troper
Multex.com
Nielsen Media Research
Prime Charter Ltd.
Townsend Analytics
UBS

SILVER CREATIVE GROUP
50 N Main St, South Norwalk, CT 06854
Tel.: (203) 855-7705
Web Site: www.silvercreativegroup.com

Year Founded: 2004

Agency Specializes In: Advertising, Brand Development & Integration, Corporate Identity, Exhibit/Trade Shows, Internet/Web Design, Logo & Package Design, Print

Paul Zullo *(Mng Dir)*
Donna Bonato *(Principal & Dir-Creative)*
Katelyn Avery *(Acct Mgr)*
Jonathan Burke *(Designer)*

Accounts:
Heavenly Bites

THE SILVER TELEGRAM
320 Pine Ave Mezzanine Ste, Long Beach, CA 90802
Tel.: (562) 495-6045
E-Mail: info@thesilvertelegram.com
Web Site: www.thesilvertelegram.com

Agency Specializes In: Advertising, Brand Development & Integration, Event Planning & Marketing, Public Relations, Social Media

Ronjini M. Joshua *(Owner & Acct Dir)*
Erica McCarthy *(Acct Mgr)*
Karen Sorenson *(Sr Acct Exec)*
Lauren Provence *(Acct Exec)*
John Yoon *(Acct Exec)*

Accounts:
New-3Dsimo

SILVERCREST ADVERTISING
15357 Magnolia Blvd Ste 223, Sherman Oaks, CA 91403
Tel.: (818) 336-4800
Fax: (818) 804-3473
E-Mail: info@sca-mail.com
Web Site: www.silvercrestadvertising.com

Year Founded: 2011

Agency Specializes In: Advertising, Media Planning

William Rodriguez *(Founder & Pres)*
Ryan Gesler *(CTO)*

Accounts:
House Doctors & House Medic Marketing
The Johnny Rockets Group, Inc.

SILVERLIGN GROUP INC.
54 N Central Ave Ste 200, Campbell, CA 95008
Tel.: (408) 792-3010
Fax: (408) 792-3014
Web Site: www.ebayenterprise.com

Agency Specializes In: Brand Development & Integration, Integrated Marketing

Marc Fleishhacker *(Mng Dir)*
Billy Seabrook *(Chief Creative Officer)*
Grady Baker *(Client Svcs Dir)*

Accounts:
Cisco
Denon
Dockers; 2007
Driscoll's
Ebay
Expedia
Levi's
Marantz
Mark Logic
Openwave
PG&E
ReplayTV
Target Corp.
Vera Wang
Vitaminwater
West Elm
Williams-Sonoma

SILVERMAN MEDIA & MARKETING GROUP, INC.
2829 Merrick Rd Ste 115, Woodbury, NY 11710
Tel.: (516) 781-1668
Fax: (516) 679-1614
E-Mail: smmgsports@aol.com
Web Site: www.silverman-media.com

Employees: 1
Year Founded: 1996

Agency Specializes In: Advertising

Revenue: $1,600,000

Ira H. Silverman *(Pres)*

Accounts:
Ann Liguori Productions, Inc.
Grandstand Sports & Memorabilia; New York, NY
H & K Steel Sculptures
Huntington Hospital
Karp Auto Group
Major League Lacrosse (MLL)
MetroStar Music
Miggle Toys; Chicago, IL
Sound and Video Creations, Inc.
StarGames

SIMANTEL

1435 18th St Ste 144, Saint Louis, MO 63104
Tel.: (314) 865-0265
Web Site: www.simantel.com

Year Founded: 1980

Agency Specializes In: Advertising, Advertising Specialties, Agriculture, Arts, Brand Development & Integration, Broadcast, Business-To-Business, Cable T.V., Collateral, Communications, Corporate Communications, Corporate Identity, Digital/Interactive, Direct Response Marketing, Engineering, Event Planning & Marketing, Exhibit/Trade Shows, Financial, Graphic Design, Health Care Services, Identity Marketing, Industrial, Integrated Marketing, International, Internet/Web Design, Local Marketing, Logo & Package Design, Magazines, Market Research, Media Buying Services, Media Relations, Newspaper, Newspapers & Magazines, Out-of-Home Media, Outdoor, Paid Searches, Planning & Consultation, Print, Production, Production (Ad, Film, Broadcast), Production (Print), Public Relations, Publicity/Promotions, Sales Promotion, Search Engine Optimization, Social Marketing/Nonprofit, Social Media, Strategic Planning/Research, Trade & Consumer Magazines, Transportation, Travel & Tourism, Web (Banner Ads, Pop-ups, etc.)

Kevin McConaghy *(Principal)*
Maggie Whalen *(VP & Exec Dir-Creative)*
Tim Leesman *(VP & Client Svcs Dir)*
Misty Dykema *(VP & Dir-Strategic Svcs)*
Barry Littlejohn *(Acct Dir)*
Tanya Simpson *(Dir-Ops)*
Andrew Tuma *(Dir-Digital)*
Erin Kennedy *(Sr Acct Mgr)*
Nicki Urban *(Acct Mgr)*
Kate Vick *(Sr Project Mgr-Digital)*
Olivia Moore *(Designer)*

Accounts:
AFB International; St. Charles, MO Branding, Creative Print, Electronic Advertising, Website
Ameren; 2007
Caterpillar; 1985
EGLI; 2011
Illinois Mutual; 1997
LG Seeds; 2002
National Precast Concrete Association; 2012

THE SIMON GROUP, INC.

1506 Old Bethlehem Pike, Sellersville, PA 18960-1427
Tel.: (215) 453-8700
Fax: (215) 453-1670
E-Mail: marcom@simongroup.com
Web Site: www.simongroup.com

E-Mail for Key Personnel:
President: msimon@simongroup.com
Production Mgr.: dbrennan@simongroup.com
Public Relations: bsmith@simongroup.com

Employees: 14
Year Founded: 1986

National Agency Associations: PRSA

Agency Specializes In: Advertising, Aviation & Aerospace, Brand Development & Integration, Business-To-Business, Catalogs, Collateral, Communications, Computers & Software, Consulting, Corporate Identity, Digital/Interactive, Direct Response Marketing, E-Commerce, Electronic Media, Electronics, Email, Engineering, Environmental, Exhibit/Trade Shows, Graphic Design, Health Care Services, High Technology, Industrial, Information Technology, Internet/Web Design, Logo & Package Design, Magazines, Media Buying Services, Media Planning, Media Relations, Medical Products, New Product Development, New Technologies, Paid Searches, Pharmaceutical, Planning & Consultation, Point of Purchase, Point of Sale, Print, Product Placement, Production, Production (Print), Public Relations, Publicity/Promotions, Sales Promotion, Search Engine Optimization, Strategic Planning/Research, Technical Advertising, Trade & Consumer Magazines

Dave Lesser *(Pres)*
Marty Simon *(CEO)*
Karen Burke *(VP-Fin)*
Beth Smith *(VP)*
Mark Matyas *(Dir-Creative)*
Jena Warren *(Acct Mgr & Strategist-Digital Mktg)*
Mary Kaye Yerkes *(Office Mgr)*
Joanna Puglisi-Barley *(Mgr-PR)*
Christina Sanchez *(Coord-PR-Special Projects)*
Karen Stayer *(Coord-Media)*

Accounts:
Aitech Defense Systems; Chatsworth, CA Embedded Systems; 2005
Amphenol Industrial; Sidney, NY Interconnect Components & Systems; 2001
Applied Energy Systems
DELO Industrial Adhesives Public Relations
Elma Electronic; Ivyland, PA Integrated Real-Time & Embedded Systems; 2004
Elsys Instruments (Agency of Record) Public Relations, Social Media Presence
Enersys, Inc.; Reading, PA DC Power Solutions; 1995
Fox Electronics; Fort Myers, FL Crystals, Oscillators; 1995
IEE (Agency of Record) Marketing Communications Campaign
Ingersoll Rand Industrial Technology; Davidson, NC Air Solutions, Campaign: "It's in the Air"; 2005
LCR Electronics; Norristown, PA Filters/Motion Control; 2008
Measurement Specialties
Megger Creative Development, Online Advertising
Men Micro
Metabo Corp.; West Chester, PA Power Tools; 2001
Woodstream Corporation (Agency of Record) Creative, FiShock, Marketing Communications, Zareba

SIMON GROUP MARKETING COMMUNICATIONS, INC.

2121A Dewey Ave, Evanston, IL 60201
Tel.: (847) 424-9910
Fax: (847) 424-9918
E-Mail: mail@simongroup.biz
Web Site: www.simongroup.biz

Employees: 5
Year Founded: 1980

Agency Specializes In: Advertising, Brand Development & Integration, Business Publications, Business-To-Business, Catalogs, Collateral, Communications, Consulting, Consumer Goods, Consumer Marketing, Corporate Communications, Corporate Identity, Cosmetics, Customer Relationship Management, Direct Response Marketing, Direct-to-Consumer, E-Commerce, Email, Engineering, Entertainment, Exhibit/Trade Shows, Financial, Food Service, Graphic Design, High Technology, Identity Marketing, In-Store Advertising, Industrial, Integrated Marketing, Internet/Web Design, Legal Services, Logo & Package Design, Media Buying Services, Media Relations, New Product Development, Newspaper, Newspapers & Magazines, Outdoor, Package Design, Planning & Consultation, Point of Purchase, Point of Sale, Print, Production, Public Relations, Publicity/Promotions, Restaurant, Sales Promotion, Search Engine Optimization, Social Media, Strategic Planning/Research, Technical Advertising, Trade & Consumer Magazines

Approx. Annual Billings: $500,000

Seth Bender *(Partner)*

THE SIMONS GROUP

303 E Wacker Dr #1109, Chicago, IL 60601
Tel.: (312) 252-8900
Web Site: www.thesimonsgroup.com

Agency Specializes In: Affiliate Marketing, Business Publications, Digital/Interactive, Direct Response Marketing, Electronic Media, Exhibit/Trade Shows, Experience Design, Local Marketing, Magazines, Mobile Marketing, Newspaper, Newspapers & Magazines, Print, Search Engine Optimization

Dina Barabash *(Specialist-PR & Media)*

SIMONS MICHELSON ZIEVE, INC.

1200 Kirts Blvd Ste 100, Troy, MI 48084
Tel.: (248) 362-4242
Fax: (248) 362-2014
Web Site: www.smz.com

E-Mail for Key Personnel:
Creative Dir.: jklayman@smz.com
Media Dir.: aklein@smz.com
Production Mgr.: kfinley@smz.com
Public Relations: ngrandberry@smz.com

Employees: 43
Year Founded: 1929

National Agency Associations: ADCRAFT-DMA

Agency Specializes In: Advertising, Arts, Brand Development & Integration, Broadcast, Business-To-Business, Cable T.V., Collateral, Communications, Consumer Marketing, Corporate Communications, Corporate Identity, Entertainment, Event Planning & Marketing, Fashion/Apparel, Financial, Food Service, Graphic Design, In-Store Advertising, Infomercials, Integrated Marketing, Internet/Web Design, Leisure, Local Marketing, Market Research, Media Buying Services, Media Planning, Media Relations, Medical Products, New Product Development, Newspaper, Newspapers & Magazines, Out-of-Home Media, Outdoor, Point of Purchase, Point of Sale, Print, Production, Production (Print), Promotions, Public Relations, Publicity/Promotions, Radio, Restaurant, Retail, Search Engine Optimization, Sponsorship, Sports Market, Strategic Planning/Research, T.V., Trade & Consumer Magazines, Yellow Pages Advertising

Approx. Annual Billings: $52,000,000

Breakdown of Gross Billings by Media: Bus. Publs.: 2%; Cable T.V.: 3%; Collateral: 5%; Consumer Publs.: 3%; Fees: 10%; Mdsg./POP: 10%; Newsp.: 5%; Outdoor: 5%; Production: 10%; Spot Radio: 17%; Spot T.V.: 20%; Yellow Page Adv.: 10%

James Michelson *(Pres)*
Pam Renusch *(Exec VP & Grp Acct Dir)*
Joel Bienenfeld *(VP & Dir-Production)*

Louie Katsaros *(VP & Acct Supvr)*
Michael Corbeille *(Exec Dir-Creative)*
Kelsey Sedlmeyer *(Jr Art Dir)*
Amy Klein *(Dir-Media)*
Terri Peirce *(Dir-Media Buying)*
Nicci Lymburner *(Acct Mgr)*
Juanita Hursey *(Mgr-Traffic)*
Trish Cowan *(Copywriter)*
Karen Martinez *(Acct Coord)*
Barb Campagna *(Sr Supvr-Graphics)*

Accounts:
Automation Alley; Troy, MI Technology Sector Membership Organization; 1998
Botsford Hospital
CBS Detroit/CW 50 Television Stations; 2011
City Creek Center; Salt Lake City, UT Mixed-Use Retail Development; 2011
Community Choice Credit Union Marketing
Detroit Metro Convention & Visitors Bureau (Agency of Record)
Detroit Red Wings
Detroit Tigers; Detroit, MI Major League Baseball Team; 2004
Fisher Theatre/Netherlander Company LLC; Detroit, MI Entertainment; 1990
Grand Hotel (Agency of Record) Creative Strategy, Integrated Marketing
Group 10 Management (Agency of Record) Airlines Parking, Digital Advertising, Qwik Park, Traditional, U.S. Park
Joe Muer Seafood (Advertising Agency of Record)
Lipari Foods; Warren, MI Consumer Packaged Goods; 2010
Mackinac Island Tourism (Creative Agency of Record) Marketing Communications
The Mall at Patridge Creek; Macomb, MI Regional Shopping Malls; 2006
MCUL
Michigan Bureau of State Lottery; Detroit, MI Lottery Games; 1996
Michigan Dental Association; Lansing, MI; 2001
Michigan Lottery Classic Lotto 47, Daily 3, Daily 4, Fantasy 5, Instant Games, Keno, Mega Millions, Michigan Lottery, Millionaire Raffle, Powerball
The Parade Company Event Marketing; 2008
SecureWatch 24 (SW24); New York, NY Commercial & Residential Security; 2011
Stamford Town Center; Stamford, CT Retail Shopping Mall; 2010
Stony Point Fashion Park; Richmond,VA Open-Air Mall; 2010
SVS Vision Retail Optical Centers; 2008
Taubman Centers; Bloomfield, MI Ice Palace Holiday Experience; 2007
Woodward Dream Cruise Classic Cars; 2008
Wright & Filippis Designed Brochures, Internal & External Communications, Marketing, Media, Newsletters, Radio Spots, Research, Signage, Videos, Website

SIMPLE TRUTH COMMUNICATION PARTNERS
314 W Superior St Ste 300, Chicago, IL 60654
Tel.: (312) 376-0360
Fax: (312) 376-0366
Web Site: www.yoursimpletruth.com/

Employees: 35
Year Founded: 1996

Agency Specializes In: Advertising Specialties, Brand Development & Integration, Business-To-Business, Collateral, Communications, Consulting, Corporate Identity, Education, Financial, Graphic Design, Health Care Services, Logo & Package Design

Approx. Annual Billings: $6,000,000

Breakdown of Gross Billings by Media: Collateral: 40%; Graphic Design: 20%; Logo & Package Design: 10%; Print: 10%; Promos.: 10%; Strategic Planning/Research: 10%

Rhonda Kokot *(Mng Partner)*
Susan Bennett *(Partner & Exec Dir-Creative)*
Mark Drozd *(Partner & Exec Dir-Creative)*
Mande Mischler *(Acct Dir)*
Steve Batterson *(Assoc Dir-Brand Voice)*
Jonah Doftert *(Acct Supvr)*
Lauren Hewitt *(Sr Acct Exec)*
Candice Caldwell *(Copywriter)*
Samantha Feld *(Designer)*
Scott Gundersen *(Sr Designer)*

Accounts:
Allstate Insurance; Northbrook, IL Casualty, Property; 1999
Chicago History Museum; Chicago, IL; 2006
Sunrise Senior Living; McLean, VA Senior Living Services; 2003
United Airlines; Elk Grove Village, IL; 1997

SINGLE THROW INTERNET MARKETING
1800 Route 34 #303, Wall Township, NJ 07719
Tel.: (866) 233-4810
Fax: (732) 612-1072
Web Site: www.singlethrow.com

Agency Specializes In: Email, Search Engine Optimization, Social Media, Viral/Buzz/Word of Mouth, Web (Banner Ads, Pop-ups, etc.)

Larry Bailin *(CEO)*
Jim Farrell *(CFO & Partner)*
Jennifer Patterson *(VP-Ops)*
Scott Dailey *(Dir-Strategic Dev)*
Danielle Butera *(Mgr-Ops)*
Chelsea Sullivan *(Sr Coord-Mktg)*

Accounts:
Acer Computers
Bel Brands USA Babybel, Laughing Cow
Hillshire Brands
Kiwi Shoe Care
Kozy Schack Enterprises LLC
Nakoma Products LLC Endust
Scholastic

SINGLETON & PARTNERS, LTD.
740 W Superior Ave, Cleveland, OH 44113
Tel.: (216) 344-9966
Fax: (216) 344-9921
E-Mail: singletonpartners@adelphia.net
Web Site: www.singletonpartners.com

Employees: 20

Agency Specializes In: Broadcast, Communications, Education, Event Planning & Marketing, Government/Political, Local Marketing, Media Planning, Multicultural, Multimedia, Planning & Consultation, Production, Public Relations

Renee Singleton *(Pres & CEO)*
Joyce Brown *(VP & Dir-Corp Mktg Div)*
Janda Singleton-Johnson *(VP & Dir-Social Mktg Div)*
Whitney Clayton *(Specialist-Interactive Comm & Res)*

Accounts:
Adoption Network Cleveland
Cuyahoga County Library
Greater Cleveland Partnership
Greater Heights Academy
Karamu House
Ohio Tourism Division
Popeyes Chicken & Biscuits

SINUATE MEDIA, LLC.
2001 E Lohman Ave Ste 110-323, Las Cruces, NM 88001
Tel.: (443) 992-4691
E-Mail: hello@sinuatemedia.com
Web Site: www.sinuatemedia.com

Employees: 6

Agency Specializes In: Corporate Communications, Event Planning & Marketing, Exhibit/Trade Shows, Guerilla Marketing, Internet/Web Design, Mobile Marketing, Podcasting, Social Marketing/Nonprofit, Viral/Buzz/Word of Mouth

Leah Messina *(Founder & CEO)*

Accounts:
Baltimore Book Festival
Bandon
BioSecurity Technologies
DeWalt
Doncaster Salli Ward
Harp
Heather Fulkoski Acupuncture
Horizon Media
Jolles
KidsPeace
Meyer Jabara Hotels
Posh Restaurant & Supper Club
Washington Hospital Center

SIQUIS, LTD.
1340 Smith Ave Ste 300, Baltimore, MD 21209-3797
Tel.: (410) 323-4800
Fax: (410) 323-4113
E-Mail: info@siquis.com
Web Site: www.siquis.com

Employees: 50
Year Founded: 1986

National Agency Associations: AMA-Second Wind Limited

Agency Specializes In: Advertising, Affluent Market, Brand Development & Integration, Broadcast, Business-To-Business, Cable T.V., Catalogs, Children's Market, Co-op Advertising, Collateral, College, Commercial Photography, Communications, Computers & Software, Consumer Marketing, Consumer Publications, Corporate Communications, Corporate Identity, Cosmetics, Direct Response Marketing, Education, Email, Exhibit/Trade Shows, Fashion/Apparel, Financial, Graphic Design, High Technology, Internet/Web Design, Logo & Package Design, Magazines, Media Buying Services, Media Planning, Men's Market, Newspaper, Newspapers & Magazines, Out-of-Home Media, Outdoor, Point of Purchase, Point of Sale, Production, Production (Ad, Film, Broadcast), Production (Print), Publishing, Radio, Social Marketing/Nonprofit, Sports Market, Strategic Planning/Research, T.V., Trade & Consumer Magazines, Transportation, Web (Banner Ads, Pop-ups, etc.), Women's Market

Approx. Annual Billings: $56,000,000

Breakdown of Gross Billings by Media: Collateral: 6%; D.M.: 25%; Internet Adv.: 2%; Logo & Package Design: 7%; Newsp. & Mags.: 24%; Out-of-Home Media: 3%; Point of Sale: 2%; Production: 1%; Radio: 30%

David Melnick *(Pres)*
Anita Kaplan *(CEO)*
Marc Rosenstein *(CFO & Sr VP)*
Debbie Norris *(VP & Dir-Media)*
Moira DiJulio *(VP-Direct Response)*
Ron Thompson *(Dir-Creative)*
Alex Ferrari *(Acct Exec)*
Gail Spiva *(Sr Media Planner & Buyer)*

Accounts:

Ankota
Curve Appeal Jeans
Dolfin Swimwear; Sinking Spring, PA
E-Z Pass
Goldwell; Linthicum, MD
Gorilla Glue
Green Bull Ladders
The Greene Turtle
Grinnell Paving Stones
Isis
Isis Outdoorwear
Montgomery Parks
Postal Outfitters; Metarie, LA
Renfro Legwear
Samuel Parker Clothiers
Simpson Race Products; New Braunfels, TX

SIR ISAAC

81 Washington St Ste 203, Salem, MA 1970
Tel.: (978) 594-8023
E-Mail: info@sirisaac.com
Web Site: www.sirisaac.com

Year Founded: 2008

Agency Specializes In: Advertising, Collateral, Corporate Identity, Internet/Web Design, Package Design, Print, Radio, T.V.

Ross Dobson *(Founder & Pres)*
Alison Avezzie Hanchett *(Art Dir)*
Angela Doran *(Creative Dir)*
Amber Richardson *(Acct Exec)*

Accounts:
Champion Seed
HarborOne Bank
MedSentry
Mission of Hope International

SIRE ADVERTISING

109 Monroe St, Selinsgrove, PA 17870
Tel.: (570) 743-3900
Fax: (570) 743-3901
E-Mail: info@sireadvertising.com
Web Site: www.sireadvertising.com

Year Founded: 2002

Agency Specializes In: Advertising, Broadcast, Collateral, Internet/Web Design, Logo & Package Design, Print, Public Relations

Shawn Felty *(Pres & Dir-Creative)*
Katelyn Snyder *(Graphic Designer & Designer-Web)*

Accounts:
JD Feaster Earthworks
Lycoming Bakery

SIRIUS STUDIOS

3805 H St, Eureka, CA 95503
Tel.: (707) 443-9836
Web Site: www.sirius-studios.com

Agency Specializes In: Advertising, Graphic Design, Radio, T.V.

Alan Olmstead *(Owner)*

Accounts:
Almquist Lumber Co.
Amulet Manufacturing Co, Inc.
Arcata Recycling Center
Dalianes Worldwide Travel Service
Eureka Brake & Automotive
Eureka Glass Company, Inc.
Humboldt County Environmental Health
Humboldt Finest
Low's Furniture Co, Inc.
Nelson Floor Company
North Coast Bakery
North Coast Co-op
Northern Mountain Supply
Northern Redwood Federal Credit Union
Philips Camera & Studio

SITEK MARKETING/COMMUNICATIONS

704 Westbrooke Terrace Dr, Ballwin, MO 63021
Tel.: (636) 861-0509

Employees: 5
Year Founded: 1999

Tim Sitek *(Owner & Pres)*

Accounts:
Colliers Turley Martin Tucker; Saint Louis, MO Commercial Real Estate; 1999
McEnry Automotion; Saint Louis, MO

SITEWIRE

740 S Mill Ave Ste 210, Tempe, AZ 85281
Tel.: (480) 731-4884
Fax: (480) 731-4822
E-Mail: info@sitewire.net
Web Site: www.sitewire.com

Employees: 60
Year Founded: 1999

National Agency Associations: AMA-SEMPO

Agency Specializes In: Advertising, Affiliate Marketing, Below-the-Line, Consulting, Digital/Interactive, Direct Response Marketing, E-Commerce, Electronic Media, Internet/Web Design, Media Planning, Paid Searches, Search Engine Optimization, Strategic Planning/Research, Web (Banner Ads, Pop-ups, etc.)

Approx. Annual Billings: $14,000,000

Sandy Catour *(CFO & COO)*
Joyce Clark *(Controller)*
Patricia Tompkins *(Sr Dir-Art)*
Jessica Radich *(Acct Dir)*
Steve Koch *(Dir-Social Customer Care)*
Liz Magura *(Dir-Art)*
Samantha Rosenbach *(Acct Mgr)*
Anthony Mills *(Mgr-Analytics)*
Karen Strickland *(Mgr-IT & Ops)*
Kimberley Hand *(Sr Strategist-Social Media)*

Accounts:
Avnet
Flight Centre
Golf Channel / Golf Now
The Irvine Company; Irvine, CA Fashion Island, Irvine Apartment Communities
Loctite
PGI
Sophos
Thrive Foods

SITUATIO NORMAL

7 N Willow St Ste 8A, Montclair, NJ 07042
Tel.: (763) 300-1132
E-Mail: info@situationormal.com
Web Site: www.situationormal.com

Year Founded: 2010

Agency Specializes In: Advertising, Brand Development & Integration, Graphic Design, Media Buying Services, Media Planning, Print, Social Media, Sponsorship

Robert Tagliareni *(Founder & Creative Dir)*

Accounts:
Fresh Neck
Papi Wine

SITUATION INTERACTIVE

1372 Broadway 20th Fl, New York, NY 10018
Tel.: (212) 982-3192
Web Site: www.situationmarketing.com

Employees: 13
Year Founded: 2004

Agency Specializes In: Advertising, Brand Development & Integration, Communications, Digital/Interactive, E-Commerce, Email, Entertainment, Internet/Web Design, Promotions, Search Engine Optimization

Revenue: $1,500,000

Damian Bazadona *(Pres)*
Jeremy Kraus *(Exec Dir-Client Svcs)*
Lisa Cecchini *(Dir-Media & Insights)*
Christina Ferrara *(Dir-Art & Sr Designer)*
Peter Yagecic *(Dir-Tech)*
John Howells *(Assoc Dir-Creative)*
Katryn Geane *(Acct Supvr)*
Mollie Shapiro *(Acct Exec)*
Rachel Harpham *(Media Planner)*

Accounts:
Brooklyn Academy of Music
DreamWorks Animation SKG, Inc.
The Metropolitan Opera
NewYork.com
Radio City Entertainment
Universal Studios, Inc.
The Walt Disney Company

SIX DEGREES

1217B N Orange Ave, Orlando, FL 32804
Tel.: (407) 730-3178
Web Site: www.sixdegreeshigher.com

Year Founded: 2007

Agency Specializes In: Advertising, Brand Development & Integration, Communications, Digital/Interactive

Michael Young *(Principal & Dir)*
Jason Kucharski *(VP-Creative & Dir)*
Elizabeth Buccianti *(Dir-PR)*
Thomas Pena *(Dir-Art)*

Accounts:
Farina & Sons
Slocum Platts Architects

SIX POINT CREATIVE WORKS

9 Hampden St, Springfield, MA 1103
Tel.: (413) 746-0016
E-Mail: hello@sixpointcreative.com
Web Site: www.sixpointcreative.com

Agency Specializes In: Advertising, Brand Development & Integration, Event Planning & Marketing, Logo & Package Design, Media Buying Services, Outdoor, Print, Public Relations, Social Media, Strategic Planning/Research

Meghan Lynch *(Pres & CEO)*
David Wicks *(Chief Creative Officer)*
Marsha Montori *(Strategist-Creative)*

Accounts:
Bay Path University Womens Leadership Conference

SIXDI INC

(Formerly Teshler Inc)

11024 Arroyo Canyon, Austin, TX 78736
Tel.: (512) 288-2984
Fax: (512) 394-9259
E-Mail: info@sixdi.com
Web Site: www.sixdi.com

Employees: 6
Year Founded: 1999

Agency Specializes In: Advertising, Advertising Specialties, Affiliate Marketing, Brand Development & Integration, Broadcast, Business-To-Business, Cable T.V., Catalogs, Commercial Photography, Communications, Consulting, Consumer Marketing, Content, Corporate Communications, Crisis Communications, Customer Relationship Management, Digital/Interactive, Direct-to-Consumer, Education, Electronic Media, Electronics, Financial, Food Service, Government/Political, Graphic Design, Health Care Services, High Technology, Identity Marketing, In-Store Advertising, Industrial, Infomercials, Integrated Marketing, Internet/Web Design, Investor Relations, Luxury Products, Market Research, Medical Products, New Product Development, New Technologies, Newspaper, Outdoor, Pharmaceutical, Planning & Consultation, Point of Purchase, Point of Sale, Print, Production, Production (Ad, Film, Broadcast), Production (Print), Radio, Real Estate, Regional, Sales Promotion, Stakeholders, Strategic Planning/Research, Technical Advertising, Trade & Consumer Magazines, Web (Banner Ads, Pop-ups, etc.)

Approx. Annual Billings: $2,000,000

Yuri Teshler *(Owner)*
Jeanne Teshler *(COO & Head-Production & Writing Teams)*

Accounts:
Charles & Colvard Ltd Jewels Mfr

SIXSPEED
4850 W 35th St, Minneapolis, MN 55416
Tel.: (952) 767-3464
Web Site: www.six-speed.com

Year Founded: 2009

Agency Specializes In: Advertising, Digital/Interactive, Event Planning & Marketing

Andi Dickson *(Principal)*
Becky Zenk *(Acct Dir)*
Erik Oelke *(Dir-Art)*
Nick Rudie *(Assoc Dir-Creative)*
Tom Beckel *(Sr Acct Mgr)*
Chris Hergott *(Acct Mgr)*
Mara Castillo *(Mgr-Creative Resourse & Traffic)*
Andrew Ellingson *(Assoc Producer)*

Accounts:
Red Bull Crashed Ice
Red Bull Mississippi Grind
Red Bull Night of the Taurus
Skier's Choice Moomba (Agency of Record), Supra (Agency of Record)

SIZMEK
(Formerly DG MediaMind)
750 W John Carpenter Fwy Ste 400 & 700, Irving, TX 75039
Tel.: (972) 581-2000
E-Mail: info@sizmek.com
Web Site: www.sizmek.com

Employees: 379
Year Founded: 1999

Agency Specializes In: Digital/Interactive, Internet/Web Design

Revenue: $63,775,000

Neil Nguyen *(Pres & CEO)*
Ken Saunders *(CFO)*
Ricky Liversidge *(CMO)*
Greg Smith *(CTO)*
Andrew Bloom *(Sr VP-Strategic Bus Dev)*
Jack Reynolds *(Corp VP-HR)*
Jaime Singson *(Dir-Product Mktg)*
Kim Walter *(Dir-HR Ops)*
Olivia Silvestri *(Sr Mgr-Client Svcs)*
Brittany Porcek *(Sls Mgr)*
Amy Holt *(Mgr-HR-Talent Acq Programs)*
Krista Spreitzer *(Mgr-Sls)*
Andrea Tapia *(Coord-Client Svc)*

Accounts:
Siemens AG

Sizmek
6601 Center Dr W Ste 350, Los Angeles, CA 90045
Tel.: (323) 202-4050
Web Site: www.sizmek.com

Ricky Liversidge *(CMO)*
Greg Smith *(CTO)*
AJ Vernet *(VP-Global Accts NAM & Social)*
Ray Erickson *(Dir-Video & Rich Media Sls)*

Sizmek
401 Park Ave S 5th Fl, New York, NY 10016
Tel.: (646) 202-1320
Web Site: www.sizmek.com

Liz Ritzcovan *(Chief Revenue Officer)*
Andrew Bloom *(Sr VP-Strategic Bus Dev)*
Rachel Walkden *(Sr VP-Global Ops)*
Mike Caprio *(VP-Global Product Sls & Gen Mgr)*
Jennifer Chen *(VP-Global Media Solutions & Gen Mgr-Vantage)*
Stella M. Araya-Weil *(VP-Global Holdings)*
Canaan Schladale-Zink *(VP-Sls-Americas)*
Steve Woolway *(Gen Mgr-Peer39)*

Sizmek
(Formerly MediaMind)
Level 10 77 King St, Sydney, NSW 2000 Australia
Tel.: (61) 2 8243 0000
Fax: (61) 2 9475 1041
Web Site: sizmek.com/regional/sizmek/apac

Carolyn Bollaci *(Reg VP-ANZ)*
Jordan Khoo *(VP-APAC)*
Scott Ries *(Dir-Technical Svcs)*
Marc Hiscock *(Client Svcs Mgr)*
Hassan Seoud *(Acct Mgr-Creative)*
Camille Cooper *(Mgr-Sls)*
Sara Cheng *(Team Head-Creative Acct Mgmt)*

Accounts:
Ford
Mastercard
McDonald's
Mediacom
Mindshare
Nike
Sony
Toyota
Vodafone
Zenith

Sizmek
(Formerly MediaMind)
WG Plein 233, 1054 SC Amsterdam, Netherlands
Tel.: (31) 20 6839 857
Fax: (31) 84 8337727
E-Mail: info@mediamind.com
Web Site: www.sizmek.com

Employees: 5

Guy Makmel *(Mng Dir)*
Olliver Kahle *(Client Svcs Mgr)*
Richard Tan *(Client Svcs Mgr)*
Sjoerd Elsinga *(Mgr-Creative & Technical Svcs)*
Bator Engelsman *(Mgr-Creative Svcs)*
Brayan Van Bronckhorst *(Mgr-Ops)*

Accounts:
Microsoft

Sizmek
(Formerly MediaMind)
101 West Grand Ave 3rd Fl, Chicago, IL 60606
Tel.: (312) 755-0506
Web Site: www.sizmek.com

Employees: 3

Gregory Smith *(CTO)*
Joe Tripodo *(Assoc VP-Ops-North America)*
Heidi Aguilar *(Assoc Sls Dir)*
Olivia Silvestri *(Sr Client Svcs Mgr)*

SJ COMMUNICATIONS
25251 Paseo De Alicia Ste 200, Los Angeles, CA 92653
Tel.: (818) 881-3889
Fax: (818) 332-4212
E-Mail: info@sjcommunications.com
Web Site: www.sjcommunications.com

Agency Specializes In: Brand Development & Integration, Business-To-Business, Entertainment, Event Planning & Marketing, Government/Political, Media Relations, Production, Public Relations, Strategic Planning/Research, Travel & Tourism

Krysty O'Quinn Ronchetti *(Founder & CEO)*

Accounts:
Angel Fire Resort
Ski New Mexico
Sunset Strip Business Association
Universal Music Publishing Group
Virgin Entertainment Group

SJI ASSOCIATES, INC.
1001 6th Ave 23rd Fl, New York, NY 10018
Tel.: (212) 391-7770
Fax: (212) 391-1717
E-Mail: suzy@sjiassociates.com
Web Site: www.sjiassociates.com

Employees: 20

Agency Specializes In: Collateral, Digital/Interactive, In-Store Advertising, Internet/Web Design, Logo & Package Design, Out-of-Home Media, Outdoor, Point of Purchase, Print, Publicity/Promotions

Suzy Jurist *(Owner)*
Dan O'Shea *(Partner)*
Matthew Birdoff *(Dir-Art)*
Dave Brubaker *(Dir-On-Air Creative)*
David O'Hanlon *(Dir-Art)*
Jay Weiser *(Dir-Tech & Production)*
Anthony K. Guardiola *(Mgr-PrePress Production)*
Carole Mayer *(Sr Copywriter & Designer)*
Marie Coons *(Sr Designer)*
Andrew Zimmerman *(Sr Designer)*

Accounts:
DC Comics
HBO Go
Nikon
PBS Kids

Univision

SK+G ADVERTISING LLC

8912 Spanish Ridge Ave, Las Vegas, NV 89148
Tel.: (702) 478-4000
Fax: (702) 478-4001
E-Mail: contactus@skg.global
Web Site: skg.global/

Employees: 120
Year Founded: 1999

Agency Specializes In: Advertising, Alternative Advertising, Brand Development & Integration, Broadcast, Business Publications, Business-To-Business, Cable T.V., Collateral, Communications, Consumer Marketing, Consumer Publications, Corporate Communications, Corporate Identity, Customer Relationship Management, Digital/Interactive, Direct Response Marketing, Direct-to-Consumer, Electronic Media, Entertainment, Event Planning & Marketing, Experience Design, Fashion/Apparel, Food Service, Government/Political, Graphic Design, Guerilla Marketing, Hospitality, Identity Marketing, Integrated Marketing, Internet/Web Design, Leisure, Logo & Package Design, Luxury Products, Magazines, Media Buying Services, Media Planning, Media Relations, Media Training, Mobile Marketing, Multimedia, Newspaper, Newspapers & Magazines, Out-of-Home Media, Outdoor, Package Design, Paid Searches, Planning & Consultation, Point of Purchase, Point of Sale, Print, Production, Production (Ad, Film, Broadcast), Production (Print), Public Relations, Publicity/Promotions, Radio, Real Estate, Restaurant, Retail, Search Engine Optimization, Social Marketing/Nonprofit, Social Media, Sponsorship, Strategic Planning/Research, T.V., Trade & Consumer Magazines, Transportation, Travel & Tourism, Viral/Buzz/Word of Mouth, Web (Banner Ads, Pop-ups, etc.)

Approx. Annual Billings: $95,000,000

John Schadler *(Mng Partner)*
Jim Gentleman *(Sr VP-Acct Mgmt & Strategy)*
Norm Craft *(VP-Acct Mgmt)*
Joan Jungblut *(VP-Media)*
Ralph Pici *(Head-Strategic Brand Mktg, Digital, Social, Mobile & Ecommerce)*
Michele Madole *(Dir-PR)*
Kim Nasuta *(Dir-HR)*
Brian Veasey *(Dir-Bus Dev)*
Matt Maynard *(Sr Mgr-Digital Media)*
Estela Castro-Garcia *(Mgr-Digital Media)*
Nikki Neu *(Strategist-Social Media & Acct Exec-PR)*
Melissa Gonzalez *(Acct Exec)*
Patricia Goode *(Acct Exec-Digital)*
Patty Halabuk *(Acct Exec-Trialogue Direct)*
Khara Scheppmann *(Acct Exec)*
Mary Christian *(Art Buyer)*
Rebecca Koonce *(Asst Acct Exec)*
Anne Genseal *(Grp Media Dir)*

Accounts:
ABA Interior Design; Las Vegas, NV Interior Design Services; 2001
Agassi Graf Holdings; Las Vegas, NV; 2009
Allegiant Media Buying & Planning
Andre Agassi Foundation
Baha-Mar Brand Strategy, Creative, Media Planning & Buying, Web Development; 2005
Belterra Resort Casino; Vevay, IN; 2002
Borgata Hotel Casino & Spa Borgata; 2002
Lumiere Place; Saint Louis, MO Casino, Hotel & Spa; 2007
Mandarin Oriental; Las Vegas, NV
MGM Resorts International; Las Vegas, NV; 2002
Nevada Cancer Institute; Las Vegas, NV; 2002
Orient-Express properties
River City Casino; Saint Louis, MO; 2008
Silverton Casino Lodge Hotel; Las Vegas, NV; 2008
New-SLS Las Vegas (Advertising Agency of Record)
Solaire Resort & Casino Manila Creative Development
Tropicana Las Vegas; Las Vegas, NV Casino Hotel; 2011

SKADADDLE MEDIA

2658 Bridgeway Ste 203, Sausalito, CA 94965
Tel.: (415) 332-5577
Fax: (415) 332-5544
E-Mail: info@skadaddlemedia.com
Web Site: www.skadaddlemedia.com

Employees: 5

Agency Specializes In: Advertising

Todd Lieman *(Founder, Pres & Chief Creative Officer)*
Lisa Kolb *(Dir-Creative)*

Accounts:
Airstream Campaign: "Live Riveted"
MBT Footwear
Mutual of Omaha; Omaha, NE
Wherever The Need

SKAGGS CREATIVE

414 Broadway, New York, NY 10013
Tel.: (212) 966-1603
Fax: (212) 966-1604
Web Site: www.skaggscreative.com

Year Founded: 1998

Agency Specializes In: Advertising, Digital/Interactive

Jonina Skaggs *(Co-Founder & Dir-Art)*
Bradley Skaggs *(Mng Partner)*
Jana Papiernikova *(Designer)*

SKAR ADVERTISING

(Formerly Smith, Kaplan, Allen & Reynolds, Inc.)
111 S 108th Ave, Omaha, NE 68154-2699
Tel.: (402) 330-0110
Fax: (402) 330-8791
Toll Free: (866) 330-0112
E-Mail: skar@skar.com
Web Site: www.skar.com

Employees: 36
Year Founded: 1949

National Agency Associations: APA

Agency Specializes In: Advertising

Approx. Annual Billings: $25,000,000

Breakdown of Gross Billings by Media: Bus. Publs.: $500,000; Mags.: $4,500,000; Newsp.: $2,500,000; Other: $5,000,000; Outdoor: $1,000,000; Radio: $4,500,000; T.V.: $7,000,000

Mike Collins *(Owner)*
Joleen Smith David *(Partner, Pres & Dir-PR)*
Greg Ahrens *(Partner, VP & Co-Dir-Creative)*
Mark Carpenter *(Partner & VP-Creative Strategy & Production Svcs)*
Mike Duman *(Partner & Co-Dir-Creative)*
Lavon Eby *(Exec VP)*
Jenn Bunnell *(Dir-Media)*
Sierra Frauen *(Media Planner & Media Buyer)*
Lauren Anderson *(Coord-Media)*
Megan Reid *(Coord-Media)*

Accounts:
Butterball, LLC Chef Boyardee, Gulden's Mustard, Hunts Ketchup
ETMC Regional Healthcare System
League of Letters
Metropolitan Plastic & Reconstructive Surgery
Nebraska Lottery (Agency of Record) Brand Awareness, Campaign: "Find Your Game. Find Your Fun.", Campaign: "Millionaire Tips", Campaign: "Pick 5 Aliens", Strategic Marketing
The Salvation Army
Sue Bee Honey

SKDKNICKERBOCKER

1818 N St NW Ste 450, Washington, DC 20036
Tel.: (202) 464-6900
Fax: (202) 464-4798
Web Site: www.skdknick.com

Agency Specializes In: Email, Market Research, Publicity/Promotions, Strategic Planning/Research

Bill Knapp *(Owner)*
Kerri Lyon *(Mng Dir)*
Jim Mulhall *(Mng Dir)*
Karen Olick *(Mng Dir)*
Amy Brundage *(Sr VP)*
Nell McGarity Callahan *(Sr VP-Pub Affairs)*
Anna Bell F. Gall *(Sr VP-Pub Affairs)*
Marcela Salazar *(Sr VP)*
Kelley McCormick *(Mng Dir-Washington, DC)*
Hilary B. Rosen *(Mng Dir-Washington)*
Sally Francis *(VP)*

Accounts:
Association of American Railroads Line-Haul Railroad Provider & Maintenance
New-Planned Parenthood Crisis
Respect for Marriage Coalition DOMA, PR
Sean Eldridge

SKINNY

(Acquired by Vitro & Name Changed to Vitro NY)

SKIVER

3434 Via Lido 2nd Fl, Newport Beach, CA 92663
Tel.: (949) 450-9998
Web Site: www.skiver.com

Employees: 17
Year Founded: 2001

Agency Specializes In: Advertising, Broadcast, Collateral, Digital/Interactive, Graphic Design, Media Buying Services, Media Planning, Print, Social Media, Sponsorship, Strategic Planning/Research

Jeremy Skiver *(CEO)*
Sean Hardwick *(Partner, Mng Dir & Exec VP)*
Rob Pettis *(Exec Dir-Creative)*
Derek Hall *(Acct Dir)*
Sequoyah Genova *(Dir-Ops)*
Chris Van Dusen *(Dir-Digital Strategy)*
Mike Devries *(Asst Acct Exec)*

Accounts:
4 Copas Tequila
Boy Scouts of America
Electra
Hooters of America Branding, Campaign: "Step Into Awesome"
Infinium Spirits
Kangaroo Express
Landmark
Mercedes Benz Laguna Niguel & Foothill Ranch
Oakley Elements
One Hope Wines
Pau Maui Vodka
Puerto Los Cabos
T-Mobile
Targus Protect What's Inside
Viewsonic

Western Digital

Branch

Skiver
11 Piedmont Ctr 7th Fl, Atlanta, GA 30305
Tel.: (678) 920-1268
Web Site: www.skiver.com

Employees: 17
Year Founded: 2001

Agency Specializes In: Advertising, Broadcast, Collateral, Digital/Interactive, Graphic Design, Media Buying Services, Print, Social Media, Strategic Planning/Research

Jeremy Skiver *(CEO)*
Sean Hardwick *(Partner, Mng Dir & Exec VP)*
Rob Pettis *(Exec Dir-Creative)*
Chris Van Dusen *(Dir-Digital Strategy)*

Accounts:
4 Copas Tequila
Boy Scouts of America
Electra
Hooters Step Into Awesome Campaign
Infinium Spirits
Kangaroo Express
Landmark
Mercedes-Benz Laguna Niguel & Foothill Ranch
Oakley Elements
One Hope Wines
Pau Maui Vodka
Puerto Los Cabos
T-Mobile
Targus Protect What's Inside
Viewsonic
Western Digital

SKM GROUP
6350 Transit Rd, Depew, NY 14043
Tel.: (716) 989-3200
Fax: (716) 989-3220
E-Mail: info@skmgroup.com
Web Site: www.skmgroup.com

Employees: 25
Year Founded: 1986

National Agency Associations: DMA-Second Wind Limited

Approx. Annual Billings: $13,000,000

Breakdown of Gross Billings by Media: Brdcst.: 5%; Bus. Publs.: 10%; Cable T.V.: 5%; Collateral: 5%; Consulting: 5%; D.M.: 30%; Fees: 14%; Internet Adv.: 5%; Network Radio: 5%; Network T.V.: 5%; Newsp.: 2%; Outdoor: 2%; Point of Sale: 5%; Print: 2%

Bryan LeFauve *(COO)*
Micky Farber *(Sr VP-Acct Svcs & Direct Mktg)*
Jill Fecher *(VP-Acct Svcs)*
Michael Brown *(Sr Dir-Art)*
Jason Hughes *(Creative Dir)*
Julie Desmond Schechter *(Acct Dir-Direct Mktg)*
Lisa Dojnik *(Dir-Art)*
Michael Downey *(Dir-Art)*
Jamie Garcia *(Dir-Art)*
Rob Murphy *(Dir-Creative)*
Lauren Cius *(Assoc Dir-Creative)*
Tara Erwin *(Mgr-PR)*
James Gillan *(Mgr-Strategic Branding)*
Jonathan Koziol *(Mgr-Traffic)*
Mary Usen *(Mgr-Production)*
Ashley Lewis *(Acct Supvr-New Bus Dev)*
Kimberly McCarthy *(Sr Acct Exec)*
Katie Johnson *(Acct Exec)*
Amanda Waggoner *(Acct Exec)*
Greg Bauch *(Copywriter)*

Accounts:
American Benefits Consulting; New York, NY Insurance; 2001
Holiday Valley
Identifix; Roseville, MN Direct Mail, Interactive, Marketing Communication, Media & Public Relations
InterBay Funding; Philadelphia, PA Commercial Lending; 2002
NYSERDA; Albany, NY Energy Conservation; 2005
PNM; Albuquerque, NM Utility Service; 2005
Tops Markets LLC B-Quick

SKM MEDIA GROUP
6001 Broken Sound Pkwy NW Ste 510, Boca Raton, FL 33487
Tel.: (877) 859-9055
E-Mail: sales@skmmediagroup.com
Web Site: www.skmmediagroup.com

Employees: 26
Year Founded: 2008

Agency Specializes In: Digital/Interactive, Direct Response Marketing, Electronic Media, Email, Local Marketing, Print, Production (Print), Promotions

Approx. Annual Billings: $15,000,000

Vito Didio *(VP-Email Mktg)*

Accounts:
Allstate Campaign Management, Customer Profiling & Analysis, Direct Mail, Lead Generation & Distribution, Marketing Platform Development, Microsite Landing Pages, Multi Agent Ordering, Print Fulfillment, Targeted Data; 2010

SKSW
(Name Changed to Hadeler Krueger)

SKY ADVERTISING, INC.
14 E 33 St 8th Fl, New York, NY 10016
Tel.: (212) 677-2500
Fax: (212) 677-2791
Toll Free: (888) 752-9664
E-Mail: info@skyad.com
Web Site: www.skyad.com

E-Mail for Key Personnel:
President: info@skyad.com

Employees: 15
Year Founded: 1989

Agency Specializes In: Internet/Web Design, Newspaper, Newspapers & Magazines, Real Estate, Recruitment, Sponsorship, Trade & Consumer Magazines

Approx. Annual Billings: $10,000,000

Mike Tedesco *(COO & Exec VP)*
Phil Kaminowitz *(Sr VP)*
Marcia Leventhal *(Sr VP)*
Roberta Schreiner *(Sr VP)*
Ivy Ching *(VP & Sr Acct Dir)*
Jimmy Cintron *(VP-Ops)*
Martin Castro *(Sr Dir-Art)*
Giovanni Escot *(Sr Dir-Interactive Art)*
Jamie Davids *(Sr Acct Exec)*
Chris Sexton *(Sr Acct Exec)*

Accounts:
The Brooklyn Hospital Center
Century 21 Real Estate LLC
Columbia University; 1990
Louis Vuitton N.A.
Metropolitan Museum of Art
The Rockefeller University

Branches:

Sky Advertising-Chicago
159 N Marion St Ste 292, Oak Park, IL 60301-1032
Tel.: (708) 707-2070
E-Mail: perry@skyad.com
Web Site: www.skyad.com

Employees: 100

Agency Specializes In: Advertising

Bill Steely *(Pres)*
Janine Jones *(CFO)*
Mike Tedesco *(Chief Creative Officer & Exec VP)*
Roberta Schreiner *(Sr VP)*
Jimmy Cintron *(VP-Ops)*
Martin Castro *(Sr Dir-Art)*
Amelia Guarneri *(Dir-Interactive Svcs)*
Melissa Trout *(Acct Mgr)*
Vincent Morgan, Jr. *(Mgr-Bus Dev)*
Chris Sexton *(Sr Acct Exec)*

Accounts:
Better Homes
Century 21
Coldwell Bankers
Columbia University
Housing Works
Kaplan University
Lisi
P&G
Presbyterian Homes
Solo
Sotheby's

SKYCASTLE MEDIA, LLC
3701 Sacramento St, San Francisco, CA 94118
Tel.: (888) 776-3893
E-Mail: info@skycastlemedia.com
Web Site: www.skycastlemedia.com

Year Founded: 2005

Agency Specializes In: Advertising, Brand Development & Integration, Content, Digital/Interactive, Public Relations, Social Media

Tracy Oliver *(Principal)*

Accounts:
Crystal Mountain Therapies

SKYLINE MEDIA GROUP
5823 Mosteller Dr, Oklahoma City, OK 73112
Tel.: (405) 286-0000
Fax: (405) 286-3086
E-Mail: info@skylinemediainc.com
Web Site: www.skylinemediainc.com

Employees: 15

Agency Specializes In: Direct Response Marketing, Outdoor, Point of Purchase, Print, T.V., Web (Banner Ads, Pop-ups, etc.)

Thomas C. Stalcup *(Principal & Dir-Creative)*
Michael S. Fowler *(Dir-Ops)*
Todd E. Clark *(Assoc Dir-Creative)*
Michael Thompson *(Mgr-Traffic & Media Buyer)*
Gloria S. Hart *(Mgr-Media)*

SKYPINE CREATIVE
2061 NW 2nd Ave Ste 107, Boca Raton, FL 33431
Tel.: (561) 361-7050
E-Mail: hello@skypinecreative.com

Web Site: www.skypinecreative.com

Agency Specializes In: Advertising, Brand Development & Integration, Collateral, Corporate Identity, Email, Graphic Design, Internet/Web Design, Logo & Package Design, Print, Social Media

Thiago Pinheiro *(Creative Dir)*

Accounts:
Nommerz

SKYWORLD INTERACTIVE

444 Washington St, Woburn, MA 02180
Tel.: (781) 438-7300
Fax: (781) 569-1401
E-Mail: seminars@skyworld.com
Web Site: www.skyworld.com

Employees: 20
Year Founded: 1995

Agency Specializes In: Digital/Interactive, Internet/Web Design

Michael Ratner *(Pres & CEO)*
Bill McClure *(Mng Partner)*

Accounts:
Acuvue
AOL
ESPN
HBO
National Geographic
One Beacon Insurance

SKYYA COMMUNICATIONS

16680 N Manor Rd, Minneapolis, MN 55346
Tel.: (952) 949-1371
Fax: (952) 955-6017
E-Mail: info@skyya.com
Web Site: www.skyya.com

Agency Specializes In: Advertising, Business-To-Business, Communications, Corporate Communications, Entertainment, Mobile Marketing, Planning & Consultation, Public Relations, Strategic Planning/Research

Susan Donahue *(Founder & Partner)*
Derek Peterson *(CEO & Mng Partner)*
Megan Jean Kathman *(Sr Acct Exec)*
Rebecca Kufrin *(Sr Acct Exec)*
Jeremy Ertl *(Acct Exec)*

Accounts:
Bluelounge
Dotcom-Monitor Network & Website Monitoring Services Provider
ET Water
Globalstar Mobile Satellite Voice & Data Services Provider
iCentera
Speaklike

SLACK AND COMPANY

(Formerly Slack Barshinger & Partners, Inc.)
233 N Michigan Ave Ste 3050, Chicago, IL 60601
Tel.: (312) 970-5800
Fax: (312) 970-5850
Toll Free: (800) 888-6197
E-Mail: info@slackandcompany.com
Web Site: www.slackandcompany.com

Employees: 55
Year Founded: 1988

National Agency Associations: AMA-BMA-DMA-PRSA-WOMMA

Agency Specializes In: Advertising, Brand Development & Integration, Business Publications, Business-To-Business, Co-op Advertising, Collateral, Communications, Consulting, Corporate Communications, Corporate Identity, Digital/Interactive, Direct Response Marketing, E-Commerce, Electronic Media, Electronics, Event Planning & Marketing, Exhibit/Trade Shows, Financial, Food Service, Government/Political, Graphic Design, High Technology, Industrial, Information Technology, Internet/Web Design, Investor Relations, Logo & Package Design, Media Buying Services, Multimedia, New Product Development, Newspaper, Newspapers & Magazines, Out-of-Home Media, Outdoor, Planning & Consultation, Point of Purchase, Point of Sale, Print, Production, Public Relations, Publicity/Promotions, Radio, Sales Promotion, Sponsorship, Strategic Planning/Research, Technical Advertising, Trade & Consumer Magazines

Gary Slack *(Chm)*
Ron Klingensmith *(Chief Creative Officer, Partner & Exec VP)*
Kelley Fead *(Partner, Exec VP, Head-Brand Practice & Dir-Creative)*
K. Rich Dettmer *(Partner, Exec VP & Dir-Digital Strategy)*
Matt Finizio *(VP & Dir-Creative)*
Tony McDermott *(VP & Dir-Media)*
Mike Ritt *(VP & Assoc Dir-Creative)*
Margaret McIntyre *(VP-Brand Strategy & Insights)*
Josh Schober *(Sr Dir-Art)*

Accounts:
AEM
ArcelorMittal Steel USA Inc.
BAI
Cascades
Case Construction Equipment
Dow Corning
Elevance Renewable Sciences
Gates Corporation
General Electric Company
Ingredion
Institute of Food Technologists
Jones Lang LaSalle
Kaufman Hall
Navman Wireless
Scot Forge
Society of Actuaries
Spraying Systems Co.

SLACK BARSHINGER & PARTNERS, INC.

(Name Changed to Slack and Company)

SLANT MEDIA LLC

263 C King St, Charleston, SC 29401
Tel.: (843) 722-2221
E-Mail: info@slantmedia.net
Web Site: www.slantmedia.net

Year Founded: 2004

Agency Specializes In: Advertising, Brand Development & Integration, Digital/Interactive, Graphic Design, Multimedia

Christopher Cecil *(Founder & Dir-Creative)*
Esme Melchior *(Mgr-Mktg)*

Accounts:
Rush 3 Studio

SLAUGHTER GROUP

2031 11th Ave S, Birmingham, AL 35205
Tel.: (205) 871-9020
Fax: (205) 252-2691
E-Mail: info@slaughtergroup.com
Web Site: www.slaughtergroup.com

Employees: 25
Year Founded: 1980

Agency Specializes In: Brand Development & Integration, Graphic Design

Approx. Annual Billings: $30,000,000

Terry D. Slaughter *(Owner)*
John D. Carpenter *(Exec VP-Brand Dev)*
Christine Dehart Mcfadden *(Brand Mgr-Content)*
Weston Markwell *(Mgr-Digital Content & Designer)*

Accounts:
Alys Beach
Momentum Textiles; Irvine, CA; 1994
Regions Bank
Royal Cup Coffee; Birmingham, AL; 1992

SLEIGHT ADVERTISING INC

15405 Weir St, Omaha, NE 68154
Tel.: (402) 334-3530
Fax: (402) 334-3447
E-Mail: info@sleightadvertising.com
Web Site: www.sleightadvertising.com

Employees: 20

Agency Specializes In: Advertising, Graphic Design, Internet/Web Design, Media Buying Services, Media Planning, Print, Public Relations, Radio, Social Media, T.V.

Revenue: $6,000,000

Iris Sleight *(Pres)*
Andrew Sleight *(CEO & Creative Dir)*
Kristi Kooima *(Client Svcs Dir)*
Trevor Hudson *(Dir-Bus Dev)*
Jeff Armstong *(Assoc Dir-Creative)*
Brooke Brockman *(Sr Acct Mgr)*
Stephanie Bowling *(Graphic Designer & Designer-Web)*

Accounts:
Assure Womens Center
Centris Federal Credit Union Campaign: "Mortgage of Bliss"
DSS Coin & Bullion
Kristin's Kids
New Midland Marble & Granite
Zio's Pizzeria Campaign: "Man on the Street", Campaign: "Worth The Trip"

SLIGHTLY MAD

81 Scudder Ave, Northport, NY 11768
Mailing Address:
P.O. Box 711, Northport, NY 11768
Tel.: (631) 271-2971
Web Site: www.weareslightlymad.com

Employees: 10
Year Founded: 2008

Agency Specializes In: Advertising, Alternative Advertising, Broadcast, Corporate Communications, Corporate Identity, Digital/Interactive, Environmental, Logo & Package Design, Mobile Marketing, Print, Radio, Strategic Planning/Research, T.V.

Approx. Annual Billings: $3,000,000

Paul Levine *(Pres & Dir-Strategic)*
Dawn Amato *(Partner & Chief Creative Officer)*
Dawn Amato Rudolph *(Chief Creative Officer)*
Jennifer Wassenbergh *(Dir-Growth & Dev)*
Ekiel Arrington *(Mgr-Res)*
Hanna Kalkova *(Mgr-Interactive Mktg)*

Accounts:
Boston Classical Orchestra; Boston, MA; 2011

Catholic Health Services; New York, NY Health Care; 2011
CCI; NY; 2008
CWP; NY Financial Services; 2009
E-Z SAVE; NY Shopping Club; 2010
Grecian Corner Cafe; NY Restaurant; 2008
LAB-AIDS; NY Education; 2010
LIVS; NY Veterinary Specialty Hospital; 2008
Longislandbiz2biz; NY Business Networking Community Services; 2008
North Fork Potato Chips; NY; 2011
NYVF; NY Non Profit; 2008
Shadowbox Design Management Events & A/V installation; 2013
St. Charles Hospital; NY Healthcare; 2009
Staller Associates; New York, NY Real Estate; 2011
Taylor Mason; Philadelphia, PA Entertainment Services; 2008

SLINGSHOT, LLC

208 N Market St Ste 500, Dallas, TX 75202
Tel.: (214) 634-4411
Fax: (214) 634-5511
Web Site: www.slingshot.com

E-Mail for Key Personnel:
President: owenh@davidandgoliath.com
Creative Dir.: DavidC@davidandgoliath.com

Employees: 100
Year Founded: 1995

Agency Specializes In: Advertising, African-American Market, Aviation & Aerospace, Bilingual Market, Brand Development & Integration, Broadcast, Business Publications, Business-To-Business, Co-op Advertising, Collateral, Communications, Consulting, Consumer Marketing, Consumer Publications, Corporate Identity, Digital/Interactive, E-Commerce, Electronic Media, Engineering, Entertainment, Exhibit/Trade Shows, Financial, Food Service, Health Care Services, High Technology, Hispanic Market, Information Technology, Internet/Web Design, Leisure, Logo & Package Design, Magazines, Marine, Media Buying Services, Medical Products, Merchandising, New Product Development, Newspaper, Newspapers & Magazines, Out-of-Home Media, Outdoor, Planning & Consultation, Point of Purchase, Point of Sale, Print, Production, Radio, Restaurant, Retail, Sales Promotion, Sponsorship, Sweepstakes, Syndication, T.V., Technical Advertising, Teen Market, Trade & Consumer Magazines, Transportation, Travel & Tourism

Approx. Annual Billings: $80,000,000

Karen Stanton *(CFO)*
David Young *(COO)*
Paul W. Flowers *(Pres-CIRCA 46)*
Tony Balmer *(VP-Client Svcs)*
Clay Coleman *(Sr Dir-Art)*
Ann Vorlicky *(Exec Producer)*
Lauren Mosier *(Assoc Dir)*

Accounts:
American Heart Association
Borden Dairy
Texas Governor's Office of Economic Development & Tourism Campaign: "It's Like A Whole Other Country", Digital, Experiential, Print, Social Media, TV, Tourism Marketing
Weight Watchers

SLOT RIGHT MARKETING

533 2nd St, Encinitas, CA 92024
Tel.: (760) 798-2899
E-Mail: info@slotright.com
Web Site: www.slotright.com

Year Founded: 2010

Agency Specializes In: Advertising, Digital/Interactive, Media Buying Services, Media Planning, Social Media

Joe Koller *(Founder)*
Quinn Pham *(Mng Partner)*

Accounts:
Aston Martin
Dearfoams
Focus Features
Freestyle Digital Media
Infiniti Global
Splendid Soho

SLS ADVERTISING CO

1453 3rd St 320, Santa Monica, CA 90401
Tel.: (323) 362-6757
E-Mail: hello@slsadco.com
Web Site: www.slsadco.com

Year Founded: 2013

Agency Specializes In: Advertising, Brand Development & Integration, Graphic Design, Print

Joe Simpson *(Principal)*
Freda Neff *(VP)*

Accounts:
Nurse Jamie

SMA NYC

(Formerly Seiter & Miller Advertising, Inc.)
121 E 24th St, New York, NY 10010
Tel.: (212) 843-9900
Fax: (212) 843-9901
Web Site: www.smanyc.com/

Employees: 25
Year Founded: 1990

National Agency Associations: 4A's-AD CLUB-AWNY-BMA

Agency Specializes In: Aviation & Aerospace, Education, Financial, Health Care Services, High Technology, Restaurant, Technical Advertising

Approx. Annual Billings: $50,000,000

Breakdown of Gross Billings by Media: Brdcst.: 20%; Cable T.V.: 20%; Consumer Publs.: 15%; Internet Adv.: 20%; Newsp.: 10%; Out-of-Home Media: 5%; Radio: 10%

Bob Rose *(Pres)*
Stefan Danielski *(Principal & Dir-Creative)*
Martin Schneider *(Principal & Dir-Creative)*
Tom Hadlock *(Sr Dir)*
William Tong *(Acct Dir)*
Ellen McKnight *(Dir-Media Plng)*
Phil Sievers *(Dir-Bus Dev)*

Accounts:
Almac Clinical Services
BDO Accounting Firm; 2010
Kyocera Document Solutions

SMACK MEDIA

4913 Smith Canyon Ct, San Diego, CA 92130
Tel.: (858) 735-2711
Web Site: www.smackmedia.com

Agency Specializes In: Advertising, Brand Development & Integration, Media Buying Services, Media Planning, Media Relations, Public Relations, Social Media, Strategic Planning/Research

Elisette Carlson *(Founder)*
Morgan Gonzalez *(VP)*
Natasha LaBeaud Anzures *(Sr Acct Mgr)*
Joanna Murphy *(Sr Acct Mgr)*

Accounts:
Alpha Warrior
currexSole Public Relations
Trigger Point
University of San Diego

SMACKET CREATIVE

PO Box 681, Spring Grove, IL 60081
Tel.: (847) 665-9540
Web Site: www.smacket.com

Year Founded: 2012

Agency Specializes In: Advertising, Brand Development & Integration, Internet/Web Design, Search Engine Optimization, Social Media

Don Petsche *(Mng Dir)*

Accounts:
Divorce Financial Experts
Partners in Development

SMAK

326 W Cordova St, Vancouver, BC V6B 1E8 Canada
Tel.: (604) 343-1364
E-Mail: letschat@smak.ca
Web Site: www.smak.ca

Employees: 12
Year Founded: 2003

Agency Specializes In: Guerilla Marketing, Internet/Web Design, Media Relations

Nikki Hedstrom *(Pres)*
Clay Dube *(Acct Dir-Natl)*
Ravina Bains *(Acct Mgr)*
Ashley Meikle *(Acct Coord)*

Accounts:
BC Hydro
Dairy Farmers of Canada
TELUS

SMAK STRATEGIES

3840 Broadway St Apt 27, Boulder, CO 80304
Tel.: (303) 859-3317
Web Site: www.smakstrategies.com

Agency Specializes In: Advertising, Digital/Interactive, Graphic Design, Print, Public Relations, Search Engine Optimization, Social Media

Maria Hennessey *(Founder & Pres)*
Scott Kaier *(Acct Dir)*

Accounts:
Allied Feather & Down Media Relations, Public Relations, Strategic Communications
Armpocket
BackJoy Orthotics, LLC
EvoFit
Harbinger
HumanX
Kari Traa
North American Handmade Bicycle Show (PR Agency of Record) Communications, Marketing, Media, Social Media
Potable Aqua
Redhed (Public Relations Agency of Record)
Sweet Protection
Ultimate Direction (Public Relations Agency of Record) Media Relations, Strategic

Communications

SMALL ARMY
300 Massachusetts Ave, Boston, MA 02115
Tel.: (617) 450-0000
Fax: (617) 450-0010
E-Mail: info@smallarmy.net
Web Site: www.smallarmy.net

Employees: 20
Year Founded: 2002

Agency Specializes In: Advertising, Brand Development & Integration, Collateral, Direct Response Marketing, Email, Graphic Design, Local Marketing, Media Buying Services, Media Planning, New Technologies, Strategic Planning/Research

Jeff Freedman *(Founder & CEO)*
Dana Ferruzzi *(Dir-Art)*
Heather Pidgeon *(Dir-Media)*
Christian Williams *(Assoc Dir-Creative)*
Brianna Lonergan *(Sr Mgr-Relationship)*
Jennifer Giampaolo *(Asst Acct Exec)*
Sylvain Lucarelli *(Asst Producer)*
Tim Maclean *(Contract Recruiter)*

Accounts:
Boston Body Worker
Boston Globe
OneBeacon Insurance Group New Jersey Skylands Insurance

S.MARK GRAPHICS FLORIDA INC.
500 NE 9th Ave, Fort Lauderdale, FL 33301
Tel.: (954) 523-1980
Fax: (954) 523-1986
E-Mail: design@smark.com
Web Site: www.smark.com

Employees: 2
Year Founded: 1984

Agency Specializes In: Collateral, Corporate Identity, Direct Response Marketing, Graphic Design, Internet/Web Design, Logo & Package Design

Nick Scalzo *(VP & Dir-Creative)*

SMART MARKETING ADVERTISING AGENCY
100 Old Smith Mill Rd, Anderson, SC 29625
Tel.: (864) 224-6002
Fax: (864) 751-4183
Web Site: www.thinksmartmarketing.net

Agency Specializes In: Advertising, Email, Internet/Web Design, Logo & Package Design, Outdoor, Print, Radio, Search Engine Optimization, Social Media

Tonya Thomason *(Owner)*

Accounts:
Med Central Health Resource
Trinity Dental Center

SMARTLITE
4800 N Federal Hwy Ste 200A, Boca Raton, FL 33431
Tel.: (561) 416-0220
Fax: (561) 416-0260
Toll Free: (877) 768-5483
E-Mail: efernon@smartliteusa.com
Web Site: www.smartliteusa.com

Employees: 18
Year Founded: 2000

Agency Specializes In: Advertising, Alternative Advertising, Collateral, Consumer Goods, Consumer Marketing, Graphic Design, Identity Marketing, In-Store Advertising, Local Marketing, Logo & Package Design, Out-of-Home Media, Outdoor, Print, Production (Print), Retail, Transportation

Don Berger *(Dir-Sls)*
Scott Bloom *(Dir-Sls)*
Ed Conyers *(Dir-Sls)*
Ron Dunton *(Dir-Sls)*
Kathy Elias *(Dir-Sls)*
Patrick Mcauley *(Dir-Sls)*
Michalitsa Moshos *(Dir-Sls)*
Kim Salandra *(Dir-Sls)*
Melanie Vanopdorp *(Dir-Sls)*

Accounts:
Warner Brothers

SMG MULTICULTURAL
35 W Wacker Dr, Chicago, IL 60601
Tel.: (312) 220-5300
Fax: (312) 220-6561
Web Site: www.starcomusa.com

Year Founded: 2007

National Agency Associations: 4A's

Agency Specializes In: Advertising

Mark Pavia *(Pres & Mng Dir-Digital)*
Kathy Kline *(Mng Dir & Sr VP)*
Monica Gadsby *(CEO-Latin America & US Multicultural)*
Marla Skiko *(Exec VP & Dir-Digital Innovation)*

Accounts:
ESPN, Inc.
The Procter & Gamble Company
Samsung

SMITH
(Formerly Ascentium-MWR)
518 W Riverside Ave, Spokane, WA 99201-0504
Tel.: (509) 455-4300
Fax: (509) 747-9211
Toll Free: (800) 242-2330
E-Mail: contact@smith.co
Web Site: www.smith.co

Employees: 42
Year Founded: 1980

Agency Specializes In: Advertising, Collateral, Communications, Digital/Interactive, High Technology, Sponsorship, Strategic Planning/Research

Approx. Annual Billings: $33,000,000 Capitalized

Colleen Lillie *(CFO)*
James Kim *(Chief Strategy Officer)*
Mark Cavanaugh *(Acct Dir)*
Christina Williams *(Acct Mgr)*
Sarah Sposari *(Sr Program Mgr)*

Accounts:
AT&T Mobility
Electronic Arts
Henry Weinhards Organic
Microsoft
T-Mobile US
Windows

SMITH ADVERTISING AND DESIGN
23 Collingwood Cres, Winnipeg, MB R2J 3L3 Canada
Tel.: (613) 231-7123
Fax: (613) 231-5828
E-Mail: dave@getsmith.com
Web Site: www.getsmith.com

Employees: 1
Year Founded: 1993

SMITH & DRESS LTD.
432 W Main St, Huntington, NY 11743
Tel.: (631) 427-9333
Fax: (631) 427-9334
E-Mail: dress2@att.net
Web Site: www.smithanddress.com

Abby Dress *(Founder & Partner)*

SMITH & JONES
(Name Changed to Idea Agency)

SMITH & JONES
297 River St, Troy, NY 12180
Tel.: (518) 272-2400
Web Site: www.smithandjones.com

Agency Specializes In: Advertising, Brand Development & Integration, Internet/Web Design, Print

Mark Shipley *(CEO)*
Rachel Digman *(Comptroller)*
Dave Mercier *(Sr Dir-Art)*
Mia Barbera *(Acct Svcs Dir)*
Dave Borland *(Acct Dir)*
Alan Beberwyck *(Dir-Content)*
Sharon Lawless *(Dir-Print Production)*
Dave Vener *(Dir-Mktg)*
Braden Russom *(Acct Mgr)*
Lynn White *(Mgr-Production)*
Caitlin Ryan *(Strategist-Media)*

Accounts:
Columbia Memorial Hospital
DataGen Healthcare Analytics Public Relations
New-Portneuf Medical Center (Agency of Record) Creative, Strategic Marketing

SMITH & SURRENCY, LLC
(Name Changed to Digital Edge)

SMITH ASBURY INC
225 N Lima St Ste 6, Sierra Madre, CA 91024
Tel.: (626) 836-3300
Fax: (626) 836-5500
E-Mail: info@smithasbury.com
Web Site: www.smithasbury.com

Agency Specializes In: Advertising, Advertising Specialties, Affluent Market, Alternative Advertising, Arts, Bilingual Market, Brand Development & Integration, Broadcast, Business Publications, Business-To-Business, Catalogs, Collateral, Communications, Consulting, Consumer Goods, Consumer Marketing, Consumer Publications, Content, Corporate Communications, Corporate Identity, Crisis Communications, Custom Publishing, Digital/Interactive, Direct Response Marketing, E-Commerce, Electronic Media, Electronics, Email, Engineering, Environmental, Exhibit/Trade Shows, Experience Design, Financial, Food Service, Government/Political, Graphic Design, Health Care Services, Household Goods, Identity Marketing, Industrial, Information Technology, Integrated Marketing, International, Internet/Web Design, Legal Services, Local Marketing, Logo & Package Design, Magazines, Media Planning, Media Relations, Medical Products, Mobile Marketing, Multicultural, Multimedia, New Product Development, Newspaper, Newspapers & Magazines, Planning &

Consultation, Podcasting, Production (Ad, Film, Broadcast), Production (Print), Promotions, Public Relations, Publicity/Promotions, Publishing, RSS (Really Simple Syndication), Regional, Restaurant, Retail, Social Marketing/Nonprofit, Sports Market, Strategic Planning/Research, Sweepstakes, Technical Advertising, Teen Market, Trade & Consumer Magazines, Urban Market, Viral/Buzz/Word of Mouth, Web (Banner Ads, Pop-ups, etc.)

Approx. Annual Billings: $520,000

Breakdown of Gross Billings by Media: Bus. Publs.: $20,000; Collateral: $100,000; Consulting: $100,000; Exhibits/Trade Shows: $70,000; Graphic Design: $50,000; Newsp. & Mags.: $20,000; Pub. Rels.: $80,000; Worldwide Web Sites: $80,000

Greg Asbury *(CEO)*

Accounts:
Clifford Swan Investment Counsel
Merrill Lynch Global Wealth Management

SMITH BROTHERS AGENCY, LP
116 Federal St, Pittsburgh, PA 15212
Tel.: (412) 359-7200
Fax: (412) 391-3562
E-Mail: michael.b@smithbrosagency.com
Web Site: www.smithbrosagency.com

Employees: 70
Year Founded: 2001

National Agency Associations: 4A's-AMA-ANA

Agency Specializes In: Above-the-Line, Advertising, Advertising Specialties, Affluent Market, Alternative Advertising, Automotive, Below-the-Line, Brand Development & Integration, Branded Entertainment, Broadcast, Business Publications, Business-To-Business, Children's Market, Collateral, College, Communications, Consumer Goods, Consumer Marketing, Consumer Publications, Content, Corporate Communications, Corporate Identity, Cosmetics, Digital/Interactive, Direct Response Marketing, Direct-to-Consumer, E-Commerce, Education, Electronic Media, Email, Entertainment, Event Planning & Marketing, Experience Design, Fashion/Apparel, Financial, Food Service, Graphic Design, Guerilla Marketing, Health Care Services, High Technology, Household Goods, Identity Marketing, In-Store Advertising, Infomercials, Integrated Marketing, Internet/Web Design, Local Marketing, Logo & Package Design, Luxury Products, Market Research, Media Buying Services, Media Planning, Men's Market, Mobile Marketing, Multimedia, New Product Development, New Technologies, Newspaper, Newspapers & Magazines, Out-of-Home Media, Outdoor, Package Design, Paid Searches, Pets , Pharmaceutical, Planning & Consultation, Point of Purchase, Point of Sale, Print, Product Placement, Production (Ad, Film, Broadcast), Promotions, Public Relations, Publicity/Promotions, Radio, Real Estate, Regional, Restaurant, Retail, Sales Promotion, Search Engine Optimization, Shopper Marketing, Social Marketing/Nonprofit, Social Media, Sponsorship, Sports Market, Strategic Planning/Research, Sweepstakes, T.V., Technical Advertising, Trade & Consumer Magazines, Travel & Tourism, Tween Market, Viral/Buzz/Word of Mouth, Web (Banner Ads, Pop-ups, etc.), Women's Market

Breakdown of Gross Billings by Media: Adv. Specialities: 5%; Brdcst.: 5%; Bus. Publs.: 5%; Collateral: 5%; D.M.: 5%; Event Mktg.: 5%; Graphic Design: 5%; Internet Adv.: 15%; Logo & Package Design: 5%; Newsp. & Mags.: 10%; Outdoor: 10%; Pub. Rels.: 10%; Radio & T.V.: 15%

Lindsey Smith *(Founder & Co-Chief Creative Officer)*
Bronson Smith *(Owner)*
Michael Bollinger *(Pres)*
David Heidenreich *(Partner & VP-Engagement)*
Steve Hay *(VP-Client Svcs)*
Jamie Sylves *(Assoc Dir-PR & Social Media)*
Nora DiNuzzo *(Mgr-Bus Dev)*
Jackie Mavin *(Sr Acct Exec)*

Accounts:
New-The Art Institutes (Agency of Record) National Marketing, Print, Social, Television, Video
Bigelow Tea
Del Monte 9 Lives; 2005
First National Bank
Heinz; 2006
Jamba Energy Drink Display, Outdoor, PR, Social Media, Television, Traditional & Online Creative
The J.M. Smucker Company Creative, Sahale Snacks, Social
Nestle USA, Inc. Creative, Digital, Drumstick, Frosty Paws, Nescafe Dolce Gusto, Skinny Cow, Social Media, Strategy, Wonka Ice Cream (Digital Agency of Record); 2009
New-PPG Industries Inc. Creative, Digital, Olympic Paints & Stains (Agency of Record), Print, Social Media, Television
New-Putney Vet
Red Bull Red Bull Editions
Sister Schubert's
Skinny Cow Ice Cream
STOUFFER'S Digital, Display, New Product Introductions, Online Marketing Creative and Development, Social Media Initiatives, Strategic Planning, Web Site Updates
New-UPMC
Wonka Ice Cream (Digital Agency of Record)

SMITH/JUNGER/WELLMAN
920 Abbot Kinney Blvd, Venice, CA 90291-3311
Tel.: (310) 392-8625
Fax: (310) 392-0159
E-Mail: sandy@smithjungerwellman.com
Web Site: www.smithjungerwellman.com

Employees: 6
Year Founded: 1978

National Agency Associations: THINKLA

Agency Specializes In: Advertising, Brand Development & Integration, Business-To-Business, Collateral, Communications, Consulting, Consumer Marketing, Corporate Identity, Direct Response Marketing, Entertainment, Event Planning & Marketing, Financial, Graphic Design, High Technology, Internet/Web Design, Leisure, Logo & Package Design, Magazines, Newspaper, Newspapers & Magazines, Outdoor, Planning & Consultation, Print, Production, Public Relations, Publicity/Promotions, Radio, Real Estate, Sports Market, T.V., Trade & Consumer Magazines

Todd Stein *(Principal)*
Stacy Watkins *(VP-Acct Svcs)*
Courtney Skelton *(Controller)*

Accounts:
The Bridges at Rancho Sante Fe; Rancho Santa Fe, CA Private Golf Course Community; 2000
Calabasas Commerce Center
Desert Princess
First Interstate Tower
Marina City Club Towers
Mauna Kea Hotel
Monterra Ranch
San Juan Oaks Golf Club
Sherwood Country Club; Thousand Oaks, CA Private Golf Course; 1988
Sunrise Apartments

SMITH MILLER MOORE, INC.
6219 Balcom Ave Ste 101, Encino, CA 91316-7209
Tel.: (818) 708-1704
Fax: (818) 344-7179
E-Mail: info@smithmillermoore.com
Web Site: www.smithmillermoore.com

E-Mail for Key Personnel:
President: patti@smithmillermoore.com

Employees: 6
Year Founded: 1978

Agency Specializes In: High Technology

Approx. Annual Billings: $2,000,000

Patti Smith *(Pres & CEO)*
Marlene Moore *(VP)*

Accounts:
Deposition Sciences Optical Coatings
Hood Tech Vision UAV Payloads
L-3 Applied Optics Center Optics
Opto Diode Corp. Photodetectors from UV to IR
OSI OptoElectronics Photodiodes, LEDS, Optical Assemblies
Photron Inc. High Speed Cameras
Precision Glass & Optics Complete Optical Solutions
Sensors Unlimited - UTC Aerospace Systems Shortwave Infrared Cameras & Systems
Sierra-Olympic infrared Cameras & Systems
Spectra Physics Lasers
Toshiba Imaging Systems High Def and UltraHD Cameras
Wilco Imaging, Inc.; San Diego, CA

SMITH, PHILLIPS & DI PIETRO
1440 N 16th Ave, Yakima, WA 98902
Tel.: (509) 248-1760
Fax: (509) 575-7895
E-Mail: rwphillips@spdadvertising.com
Web Site: www.spdadvertising.com

Employees: 6
Year Founded: 1932

Agency Specializes In: Broadcast, Business Publications, Collateral, Consumer Publications, Financial, Food Service, Graphic Design, Health Care Services, Logo & Package Design, Media Buying Services, Newspaper, Outdoor, Public Relations, T.V., Trade & Consumer Magazines, Travel & Tourism

Approx. Annual Billings: $3,600,000

Breakdown of Gross Billings by Media: Brdcst.: 30%; Event Mktg.: 5%; Graphic Design: 10%; Logo & Package Design: 5%; Mdsg./POP: 10%; Newsp.: 25%; Radio: 15%

Bob Dipietro *(Partner, Dir-Creative & Acct Mgr)*
Robert W. Phillips *(Partner, Acct Mgr & Dir-Creative)*
Trina Nixon *(Dir-Art & Designer)*
Rhonda Karnitz *(Office Mgr)*
Darcie Hanratty *(Acct Coord-Traffic & Print Media Buying)*

Accounts:
Central Washington Sportsmen Show; 1990
Central Washington State Fair; 1965
Columbia River Circuit Finals Rodeo; 1998
Comprehensive Mental Health; 2013
Snipes Mountain; 1995
Tri-Cities Sportsman Show; Tri-Cities, WA; 1992
United Way Central Washington
Yakima Bait Co.; Yakima, WA Fishing Lures; 1984
Yakima Federal Savings & Loan; 1986

SMITH WALKER DESIGN
19625 62nd Ave S Ste C 109, Kent, WA 98032
Tel.: (253) 872-2111
Fax: (253) 872-2140
Toll Free: (866) 542-4198
E-Mail: jeff@smithwalkerdesign.com
Web Site: www.smithwalkerdesign.com

E-Mail for Key Personnel:
Creative Dir.: robin@smithwalkerdesign.com

Employees: 6

Agency Specializes In: Advertising, Business-To-Business, Catalogs, Collateral, Commercial Photography, Content, Corporate Communications, Corporate Identity, Direct-to-Consumer, Electronic Media, Engineering, Exhibit/Trade Shows, Graphic Design, High Technology, Industrial, Internet/Web Design, Logo & Package Design, Marine, Multimedia, New Product Development, Package Design, Point of Purchase, Point of Sale, Print, Production, Production (Print), Technical Advertising, Web (Banner Ads, Pop-ups, etc.)

Jeffrey Smith *(Pres & Dir-Creative)*
Robin Walker *(Partner & Dir-Art)*

Accounts:
Fatigue Technology Inc
Samson Rope Technologies; Ferndale, WA
SeaMetrics

SMITHGIFFORD
106 W Jefferson St, Falls Church, VA 22046
Tel.: (703) 532-5992
Fax: (703) 532-8011
E-Mail: msmith@smithgifford.com
Web Site: www.smithgifford.com

Employees: 10
Year Founded: 2002

Agency Specializes In: Advertising, Automotive, Brand Development & Integration, Broadcast, Cable T.V., Children's Market, Collateral, Consumer Marketing, Corporate Identity, Education, Electronic Media, Entertainment, Financial, Food Service, Graphic Design, Health Care Services, High Technology, Industrial, Information Technology, Internet/Web Design, Logo & Package Design, Magazines, Medical Products, Newspaper, Newspapers & Magazines, Outdoor, Pharmaceutical, Planning & Consultation, Print, Radio, Real Estate, Restaurant, Retail, Strategic Planning/Research, T.V., Technical Advertising, Transportation, Travel & Tourism

Approx. Annual Billings: $20,000,000

Breakdown of Gross Billings by Media: Brdcst.: $9,000,000; Cable T.V.: $5,400,000; Graphic Design: $900,000; Logo & Package Design: $900,000; Newsp. & Mags.: $1,800,000; Production: $2,000,000

Matt Smith *(CEO & Sr Partner)*
Suzanne Smith *(Chief Creative Officer)*
Trisha Holman *(Acct Dir)*
Lisa Biskin *(Dir-Creative-Copy)*
Fred Krazeise *(Dir-Social Media & Inbound Mktg)*
Caitlin Scott *(Asst Acct Mgr)*

Accounts:
American Trucking Association; Washington, DC; 2006
Browns Car Stores; Washington, DC Auto Dealers
Falls Church News Press; Falls Church, VA; 2004
Inova Health System Campaign: "Join the Future of Health", Campaign: "Thank You Flowers"
Roy Rogers Restaurant; Frederick, MD
Voxeant

SMIZER PERRY
68 Pepperbox Rd, Waterford, CT 06385-3512
Tel.: (860) 437-8877
Fax: (860) 437-8407
E-Mail: info@smizerperry.com
Web Site: www.smizerperry.com

Employees: 6

Karl Smizer *(Owner & Dir-Creative)*

Accounts:
Forrester Research
GDEB
Guthrie
Life
MMS
NLMS
Pfizer
Saybrook
Starbak
TBH
This & That
WinZip Computing

SMM ADVERTISING
(Formerly AMH&E Marketing)
811 W Jericho Tpke Ste 109 E, Smithtown, NY 11787
Tel.: (631) 434-3330
Fax: (631) 265-5185
Toll Free: (800) 223-9227
E-Mail: info@smmadvertising.com
Web Site: www.smmadvertising.com

Employees: 25
Year Founded: 1973

National Agency Associations: 4A's-AMA

Agency Specializes In: Advertising, Aviation & Aerospace, Brand Development & Integration, Business-To-Business, Cable T.V., Collateral, Commercial Photography, Consumer Goods, Consumer Marketing, Corporate Communications, Digital/Interactive, Direct Response Marketing, E-Commerce, Education, Electronics, Exhibit/Trade Shows, Financial, Graphic Design, Industrial, Integrated Marketing, Internet/Web Design, Local Marketing, Logo & Package Design, Market Research, Media Buying Services, Media Planning, Media Relations, Media Training, Medical Products, New Product Development, Package Design, Paid Searches, Pets , Production, Production (Ad, Film, Broadcast), Production (Print), Public Relations, Radio, Real Estate, Recruitment, Retail, Sales Promotion, Social Marketing/Nonprofit, Sports Market, Strategic Planning/Research, Sweepstakes, Technical Advertising, Teen Market, Transportation, Travel & Tourism, Web (Banner Ads, Pop-ups, etc.)

Charlie MacLeod *(CEO)*
Judith Bellem *(Principal & Dir-Acct Svcs)*
Robert Mattson *(Exec VP)*
Judy Debiase *(VP-Creative Tech)*
Jennifer Schmitt *(Dir-Media & Acct Exec)*
Jan Krsanac *(Dir-Mktg)*
Cathy Murphy *(Office Mgr)*

Accounts:
Climatronics Corporation
Metro Solar
Reliance Steel & Aluminum; Los Angeles, CA; 2006

SMS
Weymouth Rd., Landisville, NJ 08326
Mailing Address:
P.O. Box 600, Minotola, NJ 08341
Tel.: (856) 697-1257
Web Site: www.smsmktg.com

Agency Specializes In: Advertising

Robert Norton *(Pres)*
David Thornbury *(CEO)*
Nora Bush *(CFO)*
Joanne Adams *(Exec VP-Data Ops)*
Robin Neal *(Exec VP)*
Tom Walsh *(Exec VP)*
Monique Adams *(Sr VP)*
Dolores Ryan Babcock *(Sr VP)*
Cyndi Lee *(Sr VP-List Mgmt)*
James Orleman *(Sr Dir-IT)*

Accounts:
Shimadzu Scientific Instruments, Inc.; Columbia, MD

SMUGGLER
38 W 21st St 12th Fl, New York, NY 10010
Tel.: (212) 337-3327
Fax: (212) 337-9686
Web Site: www.smugglersite.com

Agency Specializes In: Commercial Photography, Entertainment, T.V.

Fergus Brown *(Co-Mng Dir)*
Lisa Rich *(COO)*
Heather Rabbatts *(Mng Dir-Smuggler Entertainment London)*
Tor Fitzwilliams *(Dir-Sls East Coast)*
Madelaine Guppy *(Dir-Sls)*
Brent Novick *(Dir-Sls West Coast)*
Jacqui Wilkinson *(Dir-Sls & Strategy)*
Euan Rabbatts *(Counsel-In House)*

Accounts:
Coco Cola Campaign: "Future Flame", Soft Drink Supplier
Converse Apparel & Other Purchasing Store, Campaign: "History Made in the Making"
Daimler Vehicle Innovations Campaign: "Unbig", Smart Car
ESPN Media Services
Ford New & Used Car Dealers
Honda Campaign: "Woodsman"
LG Home Appliances & Electronic Products Retailer
Nike Airborne, Jordan Brand
Prey 2
Prudential "Sunrise"
Puma Shoe Purchasing Store
Smirnoff "Crazy Nights"
Southwest Airlines Co
Toyota "Connections"
Xbox Campaign: "Dust to Dust", Gears of War 3

SNAP AGENCY
735 Florida Ave S, Plymouth, MN 55426
Tel.: (763) 220-8347
Fax: (952) 400-3568
E-Mail: go@snapagency.com
Web Site: www.snapagency.com

Year Founded: 2010

Agency Specializes In: Advertising, Email, Internet/Web Design, Search Engine Optimization, Social Media

George Lee *(Pres & CEO)*
Spenser Baldwin *(VP & Gen Mgr)*
Tim Brown *(Dir-Art & Designer-Interaction)*
Jake Butzer *(Dir-Bus Dev)*
Danielle Eisenbacher *(Dir-Production)*
Morgan Molitor *(Acct Mgr & Project Mgr)*
Mike Frahm *(Mgr-Content)*
Abby Olson *(Copywriter-SEO)*

Accounts:

OrthoCor Medical

SNAPPCONNER PR
1258 W 104th S Ste 301, South Jordan, UT 84095
Tel.: (801) 994-9625
Fax: (801) 456-7893
Web Site: www.snappconner.com

Agency Specializes In: Product Placement, Public Relations, Publicity/Promotions, Strategic Planning/Research, Technical Advertising

Cheryl Snapp Conner *(Founder)*
Vic Conner *(Owner)*
A. Cory Maloy *(Exec VP)*
Thomas C. Post *(Sr VP-Content Strategy)*
Lauren Solomon *(Sr VP-Image & Brand Dev)*
Mark Fredrickson *(VP)*
Amy Osmond Cook *(Mgr-Content)*

Accounts:
Accend Group Financial Services
Acentra
Advent Systems Technological Development Services
AxisPointe
Broadcast International
CenturyLink Utah
Eleventh Avenue
Fishbowl
Footnote
Forte
Franchise Foundry
I-O Corporation Technological Services
Interbank FX Brokerage & Online Trading Services
Mountain West Venture Capital Network
MountainWest Capital Network
NaviTrust
NCSI Educational Services
Neutron Interactive
Red Sky Solutions
SageCreek Partners Marketing Services
Salt Lake Broadway Entertainment Services
Sendside Communication Services
Shout TV
Silver Fern
Spera
Tempus Global Data (Public Relations Agency of Record)
Tree House Interactive
Utah Technology Council
Vucci Technology Solutions Provider
Wendia

SNITILY CARR
(See Under Firespring)

THE SNYDER GROUP
9255 Doheny Rd, Los Angeles, CA 90069
Tel.: (310) 858-0444
Fax: (310) 858-6999
E-Mail: art@snyder-group.com
Web Site: www.snyder-group.com

Employees: 2
Year Founded: 1990

Art Snyder *(Founder)*

Accounts:
ABS
Meridith Baer & Associates
Patron

SO CREATIVE
1610 Silber Rd, Houston, TX 77055
Tel.: (713) 863-7330
Fax: (713) 880-4676
E-Mail: inquiry@socreatives.com
Web Site: www.socreatives.com

Agency Specializes In: Advertising, Brand Development & Integration, Digital/Interactive, Media Buying Services, Media Planning, Outdoor, Print, Public Relations, Social Media, Strategic Planning/Research

Sherri Oldham *(Pres)*
Brandon McGrath *(Coord-Acct Svcs)*

Accounts:
Avondale
Evolve Data Center Solutions LLC

THE SOAP GROUP
PO Box 7828, Portland, ME 04112
Tel.: (888) 697-0509
Fax: (207) 772-2066
Toll Free: (888) 697-0509
E-Mail: advocate@thesoapgroup.com
Web Site: www.thesoapgroup.com

Agency Specializes In: Advertising, Broadcast, Business-To-Business, Environmental, Internet/Web Design, New Technologies, Print, Public Relations

John Rooks *(Founder & Pres)*
Bob Rooks *(Partner & Dir-Technical Environmental Svcs)*

Accounts:
Brighter Planet
Carbon Canopy
Mines Action Canada
Mwobs
NativeEnergy
Nelma
Reverb Gaming
White Lotus Home Chemical-Free Mattresses & Furniture

SOAR COMMUNICATIONS
PO Box 581138, Salt Lake City, UT 84158
Tel.: (801) 656-0472
E-Mail: info@soarcomm.com
Web Site: www.soarcomm.com

Employees: 3
Year Founded: 2004

Agency Specializes In: Collateral, Communications, Financial, Graphic Design, Local Marketing, Media Relations, Outdoor, Sales Promotion, Sports Market, Strategic Planning/Research

Chip Smith *(Pres & CEO)*
Maura Lansford *(Acct Exec)*

Accounts:
Bergans of Norway Public Relations
Bikes 4 Kids Utah
Outdoor Retailer (Agency of Record)
Precision Travel Werx
Primawear
Road Warrior Sports Public Relations
Trips for Kids

SOCIAL CONTROL
5655 Lindero Canyon Rd Ste 425, Westlake Village, CA 91362
Tel.: (747) 222-7123
Web Site: socialcontrol.com

Employees: 16
Year Founded: 2009

Agency Specializes In: Alternative Advertising, Digital/Interactive, Electronic Media, Experience Design, Game Integration, Mobile Marketing, Production, Social Media, Sponsorship, Sweepstakes, T.V., Viral/Buzz/Word of Mouth, Web (Banner Ads, Pop-ups, etc.)

Approx. Annual Billings: $20,000,000

Seth Silver *(CEO)*
Miri Nadler *(Dir-Content Mktg)*

Accounts:
MedPost Urgent Cares Health Care; 2014
Western Union Financial Services; 2014

SOCIAL DISTILLERY
2401 E 6th St Ste 3038, Austin, TX 78702
Tel.: (512) 401-3172
E-Mail: info@socialdistillery.com
Web Site: www.socialdistillery.com

Year Founded: 2011

Agency Specializes In: Advertising, Content, Market Research, Social Media

Kristen Sussman *(Founder & Pres)*
Leigh Pankonien *(VP)*
Ariele Rosch *(Art Dir)*
Ryan Johnston *(Dir-Content)*
Lana Marshall *(Dir-Creative)*
Josh Shepherd *(Dir-Strategy)*
Amanda Hoang *(Acct Mgr-Social Media)*
Mercer Moore *(Acct Mgr)*
Sarah Rose *(Mgr-Community)*
Hailey Whidden *(Acct Coord)*

Accounts:
Jive Software, Inc. Office Hero Campaign

SOCIAL HOUSE INC
309 E 8th St Ste 402, Los Angeles, CA 90014
Tel.: (213) 935-8050
E-Mail: hello@socialhouseinc.com
Web Site: www.socialhouseinc.com

Employees: 15
Year Founded: 2010

Agency Specializes In: Advertising, Content, Social Media, Strategic Planning/Research

Norel C. Mancuso *(Pres & CEO)*
Jon Foshee *(Dir-Art)*
Wade Parkins *(Dir-Content)*
Michael Tanenbaum *(Dir-Analytics)*
Stephanie Pagano *(Sr Acct Mgr)*
Marcos Castillo *(Mgr-Social Media)*
Jillian Fairman *(Mgr-Social Media)*
Audrey Ma *(Mgr-Community)*
Jake Hirsch *(Coord-Strategy & Analyst)*

Accounts:
PepsiCo Inc.

SOCIAL INFLUENT
(Formerly The Bernard Group)
6836 Bee Caves Rd Ste 274, Austin, TX 78746
Tel.: (512) 827-9395
Web Site: http://www.socialinfluent.com/

Employees: 75
Year Founded: 1998

Agency Specializes In: Brand Development & Integration, Event Planning & Marketing, Exhibit/Trade Shows, Investor Relations, Local Marketing, Media Training, Strategic Planning/Research, Web (Banner Ads, Pop-ups, etc.)

Revenue: $2,400,000

Tom Price *(Partner)*

Accounts:
Difusion Technologies inc
Neterion, Inc.
Safe Scribe
Violin Scable memory
Wildfire Films, LLC

SOCIALFLY, LLC

225 W 39th St Ste 803, New York, NY 10018
Tel.: (917) 300-8298
E-Mail: info@socialflyny.com
Web Site: www.socialflyny.com

Agency Specializes In: Advertising, Media Relations, Public Relations, Social Media

Stephanie Abrams *(Founder & CEO)*
Courtney Spritzer *(Founder & COO)*
Jennifer Fiorenza *(VP)*
Alanna Pithis *(Acct Dir)*
Caroline Quigley *(Acct Mgr)*
Gregory Cartin *(Copywriter)*

Accounts:
New-Treat House
New-Wala Swim

SOCKEYE CREATIVE

240 N Broadway Ste 301, Portland, OR 97209
Tel.: (503) 226-3843
Fax: (503) 227-1135
E-Mail: hello@sockeyecreative.com
Web Site: sockeye.tv

Employees: 12

Agency Specializes In: Digital/Interactive, Identity Marketing, Print, Sponsorship

Andy Fraser *(Co-Founder & Pres)*
Peter Metz *(Co-Founder & Dir-Creative)*
Steve Potestio *(VP-HR)*
Shelley Stevens *(Grp Acct Dir)*
Tim Sproul *(Dir-Creative)*
Jason Maurer *(Writer & Strategist)*
Julian Gese *(Designer)*
Dan Ohlsen *(Designer-Digital)*

Accounts:
New-Adidas
Columbia Sportswear Company
Keen
New-Mirth Provisions
New-The Oregonian Newspaper
Port of Portland

SODA & LIME LLC

7083 Hollywood Blvd Ste 549, Los Angeles, CA 90028
Tel.: (323) 875-3820
E-Mail: info@sodaandlime.com
Web Site: www.sodaandlime.com

Year Founded: 2014

Agency Specializes In: Advertising, Brand Development & Integration, Content, Digital/Interactive, Social Media

Bonner Bellew *(Founder & CEO)*
Mandi Gum *(Sr Art Dir)*
Joshua Wells *(Creative Dir)*
Zachary Dodge *(Dir-Strategic Partnerships)*
Garrett Yamasaki *(Assoc Dir-Creative)*

Accounts:
Breakout Gaming
Koral
Lootsie
Matuse
Study Buddy
World Wrestling Entertainment, Inc.

SODAPOP MEDIA LLC

808 Office Park Cir Ste 400, Lewisville, TX 75057
Tel.: (214) 390-3700
E-Mail: info@sodapopmedia.com
Web Site: www.sodapopmedia.com

Year Founded: 2004

Agency Specializes In: Advertising, Corporate Identity, Digital/Interactive, Graphic Design, Internet/Web Design, Logo & Package Design, Social Media

James Faulkner *(Principal & Dir-Creative)*

Accounts:
American Heart Association
Frito-Lay
Orthofix
Retirement Advisors Of America, Inc.
Special Delivery

SOHO SQUARE

636 11th Ave, New York, NY 10036
Tel.: (212) 237-7646
E-Mail: alda@sohosq.com
Web Site: www.sohosq.com

Year Founded: 2003

Agency Specializes In: Advertising

Shashank Lanjekar *(Sr VP & Head-Plng)*
C Ravikumar *(Sr Dir-Creative)*
Alexa Christon *(Acct Exec)*

Accounts:
Avon Products
Franklin Templeton Asset Mgmt
H &R Johnson India Ltd
The Himalaya Drug Company Neem Face Scrub
Piaggio Campaign: "Life by Vespa", Vespa
Sprint Xohm; 2008
Wachovia Direct-Mail Card Creative
Yahoo! Inc.

Branch

Soho Square London

20 Soho Square, London, W1A 1PR United Kingdom
Tel.: (44) 20 7345 3000
Fax: (44) 20 7345 9000
E-Mail: graeme.robertson@sohosq.com
Web Site: www.sohosq.com

Steve Lepley *(CFO)*
Nick Strauss *(Head-Plng)*
James Wheatley *(Head-Social)*
Roland Hafenrichter *(Exec Dir-Creative)*
Sally Fitzgerald *(Dir-Design)*
Jukka Kettunen *(Dir-Creative-Digital Media)*
Giles Horton *(Copywriter)*

Accounts:
Avon Global Business
Barclays Capital
Barclays Wealth
Dogs Trust
Kenwood
Media Trust
Samsung
Walpole

SOKAL MEDIA GROUP

11000 Regency Pkwy Ste 402, Cary, NC 27518
Tel.: (919) 872-9410
Fax: (919) 872-9415
Web Site: www.sokalmediagroup.com

Year Founded: 2010

Agency Specializes In: Advertising, Email, Internet/Web Design, Mobile Marketing, Print, Public Relations, Radio, Search Engine Optimization, Social Media, T.V.

Mark Sokal *(Owner & CEO)*
April Safar *(CFO)*
Bryan Fisher *(Gen Mgr)*
Randy A. Mason *(Gen Mgr)*
Emily Simpson Sabol *(Dir-Art)*
Mitchell Smith *(Dir-Digital Media)*
Derek Thompson *(Mgr-Internet Mktg)*
Chelsy Hill *(Media Buyer)*
Erin Dehart Burroughs *(Coord-Media)*
Heather Thornton *(Coord-Media)*

Accounts:
New-Crystal Auto Mall (Agency of Record) Advertising, Creative, Digital, Marketing, Media, Strategic Planning
New-The Faulkner Organization (Agency of Record) Creative, Digital, Media, Strategic Planning
Hendrick Toyota
Midstate Toyota

SOLEM & ASSOCIATES

1 Daniel Burnham Ct Ste 205-C, San Francisco, CA 94109
Tel.: (415) 788-7788
Fax: (415) 788-7858
E-Mail: solem@solem.com
Web Site: www.solem.com

Employees: 6
Year Founded: 1977

Agency Specializes In: Communications, Crisis Communications, Faith Based, Government/Political, Graphic Design, Media Relations, Production, Strategic Planning/Research

Revenue: $1,200,000

Don Solem *(Pres)*
Anne Jeffrey *(Exec VP)*
Jon Kaufman *(Exec VP)*
Dave Hyams *(Sr VP)*
Kirk Cowgill *(Sr Acct Exec)*

SOLEMENE & ASSOCIATES

4400 Williamsburg Rd, Dallas, TX 75220-2059
Tel.: (214) 357-7325
Fax: (214) 357-7347
E-Mail: wasa@prodigy.net

E-Mail for Key Personnel:
President: wasa@prodigy.net

Employees: 4
Year Founded: 1973

Agency Specializes In: Advertising, Automotive, Broadcast, Event Planning & Marketing, Government/Political, Hispanic Market, Investor Relations, Multimedia, Out-of-Home Media, Outdoor, Package Design, Point of Sale, Production, Promotions, Public Relations, Publicity/Promotions, Radio, Restaurant, T.V., Transportation

Approx. Annual Billings: $1,000,000

Breakdown of Gross Billings by Media: Brdcst.: $100,000; Event Mktg.: $350,000; Outdoor:

$200,000; Production: $100,000; Pub. Rels.: $250,000

William A. Solemene *(Pres)*
Margaret Pugh *(Dir-PR)*

Accounts:
Dallas Military Ball; Dallas, TX (Civic/Charitable Event & Public Relations Activity); 1997
Dallas Veterans Day Parade (Advertising & Public Relations) Dallas Veterans Day; 1999
Downey Communications; Washington, DC Publications & Marketing Support; 1975

SOLSTICE ADVERTISING LLC

3700 Woodland Dr Ste 300, Anchorage, AK 99517
Tel.: (907) 258-5411
Fax: (907) 258-5412
E-Mail: info@solsticeadvertising.com
Web Site: www.solsticeadvertising.com

Year Founded: 2005

Agency Specializes In: Advertising, Graphic Design, Internet/Web Design, Media Planning, Public Relations

Lincoln Garrick *(Pres)*
Laura Tauke Pribyl *(Dir-Art)*
Jackie Bartz *(Copywriter)*
Elyse Delaney *(Copywriter)*
Robert Manley *(Copywriter)*

THE SOLUTIONS GROUP INC.

(Formerly Alexander & Richardson)
161 Washington Valley Rd Ste 205, Warren, NJ 07059-7121
Tel.: (732) 302-1223
Fax: (732) 356-9574
E-Mail: info@thesolutionsgroupinc.com
Web Site: www.thesolutionsgroupinc.com

Employees: 20
Year Founded: 1985

Agency Specializes In: Advertising

Peter Ferrigno *(CEO)*
Bill Gordy *(Partner & Chief Strategy Officer)*
Douglas Longenecker *(VP-Client Svcs)*
Christine Cutri *(Acct Dir)*
Kyleann Ledebuhr *(Dir-Creative)*
Jacqueline Zeiman *(Dir-Mktg Strategy)*
Shilpa Ramesh *(Acct Mgr & Mgr-Social Media)*
Sara Pomykacz *(Acct Mgr)*

Accounts:
AAI Development Services
Accutest Laboratories
Amersham Biosciences
Coldwell Banker
MetLife
Somerset Hills YMCA

SOLVE

112 N 3rd St 3rd Fl, Minneapolis, MN 55401
Tel.: (612) 677-2500
E-Mail: info@solve-ideas.com
Web Site: www.solve-ideas.com

Agency Specializes In: Advertising, Brand Development & Integration, Media Planning, Social Media, Sponsorship

Hans Hansen *(Co-Founder & Exec Dir-Creative)*
John Colasanti *(CEO)*
Ryan Murray *(Acct Dir)*
Andrew Pautz *(Acct Dir)*
Jarrod Gustin *(Dir-Art)*
Eric Husband *(Dir-Creative)*
Roman Paluta *(Dir-Bus Dev)*
Nick Smasal *(Dir-Design)*
Parker Mullins *(Acct Mgr)*
Kurt Stafki *(Mgr-Social Media)*
Joe Stefanson *(Copywriter)*

Accounts:
Abu Dhabi Commercial Bank Out of Home, Print, Videos
Annie's Homegrown
Applegate
Bentley Motors (Agency of Record) Communications Strategy
Best Buy
Cascadian Farm Campaign: "Bee Friendlier"
The Epilepsy Foundation Of Minnesota
New-Founders Brewing Company (Agency of Record)
General Mills Bee Friendlier, Cascadian Farm (Agency of Record), Marketing
GiveBack.org
Greg LeMond Bicycles, Brand Positioning, Digital, Social
Honest Tea
Lactalis Group (North American Agency of Record) Black Diamond, Consumer Communications, Creative, Design, Galbani, Strategic Positioning
Medifast, Inc.
Optum Pro Cyling
Orbea Bicycles
Organic Valley Campaign: "Bringing The Good", Campaign: "Mud Pie"
Porsche Cars North America Bentley, Catalogs, Consumer Engagement
President Cheese Campaign: "Life Well Paired"
Rudi's Organic Bakery
Shopko (Agency of Record)
True Value Company Media Planning, Media Strategy

SOLVERIS MARKETING AND COMMUNICATIONS, LLC

7 Peter Cooper Rd Ste 12G, New York, NY 10010
Tel.: (732) 801-0401
E-Mail: info@solveris1.com
Web Site: www.solveris1.com

Agency Specializes In: Advertising, Collateral, Digital/Interactive, Internet/Web Design, Logo & Package Design, Print, Social Media

Tony Sarcone *(Owner & Partner-Strategy & Client Rels)*

Accounts:
Carney Security Inc
FlowPay Corporation
MylittleO
Ozzzz's Sleep Aid for Children
RetailConnections LLC

SONICBIDS

500 Harrison Ave Fl 4 Ste 404R, Boston, MA 02118
Tel.: (617) 502-1300
Fax: (617) 482-0516
E-Mail: sales@sonicbids.com
Web Site: www.sonicbids.com

Employees: 40
Year Founded: 2002

Agency Specializes In: Internet/Web Design, Promotions

Revenue: $8,000,000

Eric Shea *(Mgr-Music Network)*

Accounts:
BMI
Converse
Diesel Gap
Filter Magazine
Guitar Hero
Harpoon
Jansport

SONNHALTER

633 W Bagley Rd, Berea, OH 44017-1356
Tel.: (216) 242-0420
Fax: (216) 242-0414
Web Site: www.sonnhalter.com

E-Mail for Key Personnel:
President: jsonnhalter@sonnhalter.com
Creative Dir.: sbessell@sonnhalter.com

Employees: 9
Year Founded: 1976

National Agency Associations: BMA-PRSA

Agency Specializes In: Advertising, Business Publications, Business-To-Business, Collateral, Corporate Identity, Direct Response Marketing, E-Commerce, Event Planning & Marketing, Graphic Design, Industrial, Internet/Web Design, Logo & Package Design, Media Buying Services, New Product Development, Print, Production, Public Relations, Publicity/Promotions, Sales Promotion

Approx. Annual Billings: $7,000,000

C. John Sonnhalter *(Founder)*
Matt Sonnhalter *(Pres)*
Terri Sonnhalter *(VP-Fin)*
Rosemarie Ascherl *(Dir-PR)*
Scott Bessell *(Dir-Creative)*
Sandra Bucher *(Mgr-Media)*
Robin Heike *(Mgr-Production)*
Rachel Kerstetter *(Engineer-PR)*

Accounts:
Brennan Industries; Solon, OH Hydraulic & Pneumatic Fittings; 1986
Buyers Products Snow & Ice Control Products, Truck Accessories; 2002
Council Tool; Lake Waccamaw, SC Striking Tools; 1998
General Pipe Cleaners Drain Cleaning Equipment; 2014
Gerber Plumbing Fixtures: Toilets, Faucets, Drains; 2012
KNIPEX; Chicago, IL Hand Tools; 2011
Nook Industries Linear Motion Solutions; 2014
Osborn Metal Finishing: Brushes, Buffs & Abrasives; 2012
Precision Machined Products Association Trade Association for Precision Machine Companies; 2002
Presrite Corporation Forging; 1979
Protection Services Inc. Traffic Control Products; 2004
UniCarriers Americas; 2011
United Conveyor Corporation Ash Handling Solutions; 2008
VIEGA; Wichita, KS Plumbing, Heating & Pipe Joining Products; 2011

SONSHINE COMMUNICATIONS

975 N Miami Beach Blvd, North Miami Beach, FL 33162
Tel.: (305) 948-8063
Fax: (305) 948-8074
E-Mail: info@sonshine.com
Web Site: www.sonshine.com

Year Founded: 1993

Agency Specializes In: Advertising, Graphic Design, Internet/Web Design, Media Relations, Strategic Planning/Research

Bernadette Morris *(Pres & CEO)*
Colin Morris *(Mng Dir & COO)*

Ricardo Reyes *(Assoc VP & Dir-Creative)*
Simone Cook *(Acct Coord)*

Accounts:
The City of Miami Gardens
Community Health of South Florida Inc
Florida Department of Transportation Marketing, Media
Jacq's Organics
Kaiser Family Foundation
Neighborhood Housing Services of South Florida
US Marshals Service

SOPEXA USA
250 Hudson St Ste 703, New York, NY 10013-1437
Tel.: (212) 477-9800
Fax: (212) 473-4315
E-Mail: contact@sopexa.com
Web Site: www.sopexa.com

Employees: 24
Year Founded: 1964

Agency Specializes In: Bilingual Market, Brand Development & Integration, Co-op Advertising, Collateral, Communications, Consulting, Consumer Marketing, Corporate Identity, Direct Response Marketing, E-Commerce, Event Planning & Marketing, Exhibit/Trade Shows, Graphic Design, Internet/Web Design, Logo & Package Design, Merchandising, New Product Development, Planning & Consultation, Point of Purchase, Point of Sale, Public Relations, Publicity/Promotions, Restaurant, Sales Promotion, Strategic Planning/Research, Travel & Tourism

Approx. Annual Billings: $11,000,000 (US, Canada, Mexico)

Breakdown of Gross Billings by Media: D.M.: 5%; Internet Adv.: 10%; Other: 5%; Pub. Rels.: 25%; Radio: 2%; Sls. Promo.: 25%; T.V.: 10%; Trade & Consumer Mags.: 13%; Trade Shows: 5%

Pauline Oudin *(Mng Dir)*
Olivier Moreaux *(Mng Dir-Americas)*
Julie Bucaille *(Controller-Fin)*
Benjamin Bourinat *(Dir-PR)*
Alice Loubaton *(Sr Mgr-Trade Rels)*
Valerie Gerard *(Sr Acct Mgr-Svc & Bus Dev)*
Emily Mackay *(Sr Acct Mgr-Svcs)*

Accounts:
Avocados from Mexico
BNIC PR, Social Media Strategy
Bordeaux Wine Bureau; Bordeaux, France; 1993
New-Cafe de Costa Rica Public Relations
Cognac
European Union; Brussels, Belgium European Authentic Foods (EAT), Rhone/Alsace/Jerez; 2004
Fancy Food Show (French Pavillion); New York, NY; 1996
French Cocktail Hour; Paris, France; 2004
French Ministry of Agriculture; Paris, France; 2001
French National Wine Council/ONIVINS ("Wines From France"); Paris, France; 1989
Provence Wine Council; Les Arcs sur Argens, France; 1999
New-Saint James Rum Global Public Relations
Southwest Wines
Wines of France

Branch

Sopexa
Trident House, 46-48 Webber Street, London, SE1 8QW United Kingdom
Tel.: (44) 207 312 3600
Fax: (44) 207 312 3636
Web Site: http://www.sopexa.com/en/agency/uk

Anne Burchett, *(Mng Dir)*

Accounts:
Sogevinus Barros, Burmester, Calem, Kopke, Public Relations

SORENSON ADVERTISING
491 N Bluff St, Saint George, UT 84770
Tel.: (877) 727-2650
Fax: (800) 867-5127
Toll Free: (877) 727-2650
E-Mail: info@sorensonadvertising.com
Web Site: www.sorensonadvertising.com

Agency Specializes In: Advertising, Brand Development & Integration, Digital/Interactive, Media Buying Services, Outdoor, T.V.

Erik Sorenson *(Pres & CEO)*
Brad Demille *(Controller)*
Ladd Egan *(Dir-PR)*
Jessica Merrill *(Dir-Media)*
Corey Ostler *(Dir-Art)*
Brynley Shumway *(Office Mgr)*
Steven Hess *(Mgr-Social Media)*
Katelyn Boulton *(Acct Coord)*
Joy Davis *(Coord-PR)*

Accounts:
Baja Broadband

SOUBRIET & BYRNE
45 West 21th St. Ste 3A, New York, NY 10018
Tel.: (212) 929-3734
Fax: (212) 391-6491
Web Site: www.sba-nyc.com

Agency Specializes In: Advertising, Graphic Design, Production, Promotions

Philip Byrne *(Pres & Dir-Creative)*
Carmen Soubriet *(Partner & Dir-Creative)*
Iordanka Katardjieva *(Dir-Media)*
Loren Osborn *(Dir-Art)*

Accounts:
Austrian Airlines
EL AL Campaign: "Vacations"
Finnair
Franklin Templeton Investments
Guardian Investments
KLM
Morphoses
Netherlands Board of Tourism
Sector Spider SPDR

SOURCE COMMUNICATIONS
433 Hackensack Ave 8th Fl, Hackensack, NJ 07601-6319
Tel.: (201) 343-5222
Fax: (201) 343-5710
E-Mail: info@sourcead.com
Web Site: www.sourcead.com

E-Mail for Key Personnel:
President: lrothstein@sourcead.com
Creative Dir.: dkoye@sourcead.com

Employees: 50
Year Founded: 1984

National Agency Associations: AMA-DMA

Agency Specializes In: Advertising, Broadcast, Business-To-Business, Cable T.V., Co-op Advertising, Collateral, Communications, Consumer Marketing, Consumer Publications, Direct Response Marketing, Electronics, Event Planning & Marketing, High Technology, In-Store Advertising, Internet/Web Design, Local Marketing, Media Buying Services, Newspaper, Newspapers & Magazines, Out-of-Home Media, Outdoor, Point of Purchase, Point of Sale, Print, Production, Radio, Restaurant, Retail, Sales Promotion, Social Marketing/Nonprofit, Sponsorship, Sports Market, Strategic Planning/Research, T.V., Trade & Consumer Magazines, Transportation, Travel & Tourism

Lawrence Rothstein *(Pres & Mng Partner)*
Barry Bluestein *(Mng Partner & COO)*
Ray Katz *(Mng Partner-Source 1 Sports)*
Janine Perkal *(VP, Acct Dir & Strategist-Mktg & Adv)*
Jason Bacharach *(VP & Acct Dir)*
Erica Hayman *(VP & Acct Dir)*
Rich Degni *(VP & Dir-Creative)*
Linda Frankel *(Dir-Media)*
Tony Maffei *(Supvr-Brdcst)*
Brian Marchesani *(Acct Exec)*
Bonnie Appel *(Sr Media Buyer)*

Accounts:
Amtrak; Washington D.C. Acela Express, Metroliner, Passenger Railroad; 2000
Sony; San Diego, CA; 2009
Subway Sandwich Shops; NY Sandwiches; 2005
Subway Sandwich Shops; Philadelphia, PA Sandwiches; 2008
Wise; Atlanta, GA Snack Foods; 2004

Branch

Source Communications
2592 Coronado Pl, Vista, CA 92081
Tel.: (858) 655-7465
Web Site: www.sourcead.com

Employees: 5

Agency Specializes In: Advertising

Janine Perkal *(VP, Acct Dir & Strategist-Mktg & Adv)*
Anne Battistoni *(Acct Dir)*
Barbara Urban *(Acct Dir)*

SOURCE OUTDOOR GROUP
210 Washington St NW, Gainesville, GA 30024
Tel.: (770) 535-6028
Web Site: www.sourceoutdoorgroup.com

Agency Specializes In: Advertising, Communications, Media Relations, Outdoor

Aaron McCaleb *(Pres & CEO)*

Accounts:
iEntertainment Network, Inc.

SOURCELINK
500 Pk Blvd Ste 415, Itasca, IL 60143
Tel.: (847) 238-5400
Fax: (847) 238-0216
Toll Free: (866) 947-6872
Web Site: www.sourcelink.com

Employees: 600
Year Founded: 1999

Agency Specializes In: Advertising

Approx. Annual Billings: $110,000,000

Don Landrum *(CEO)*
Keith Chadwell *(COO)*
Dan Jackson *(Pres-Carolina)*
Jim Wisnionski *(Pres-Mktg Solutions Grp & Corp CIO)*
Rich Pocock *(VP-Svcs)*

Brent Tartar *(VP-Sls)*
Jeff White *(Dir-Customer Experience)*
Dan Browne *(Product Mgr-MultiTrac)*
Frances Avgerinos *(Mgr-Technical Solutions)*
Marek Goczal *(Mgr-Dev)*
Maria Dennis *(Acct Exec)*

Accounts:
Blood Bank Acquisition, Retention Efforts

Branches

SourceLink
3303 W Tech Rd, Miamisburg, OH 45342
Tel.: (937) 885-8000
Fax: (937) 885-8010
Toll Free: (800) 305-9414
Web Site: www.sourcelink.com

Employees: 120
Year Founded: 1998

Agency Specializes In: Direct Response Marketing

Casey Hendrick *(COO)*
Cindy Randazzo *(Chief Strategy Officer & VP)*
Jim Wisnionski *(Corp CIO & Pres-Mktg Solutions Grp)*
Rich Pocock *(VP-Svcs)*
Brent Tartar *(VP-Sls)*
Jennifer Earley *(Mgr-Production)*
Andy Gradolph *(Mgr-Strategic Relationship)*
Tammy Dixon *(Sr Acct Exec)*

SourceLink
10866 Wilshire Blvd Ste 700, Los Angeles, CA 90024-4354
Tel.: (310) 208-2024
Fax: (310) 208-5681
E-Mail: productdevelopment@msdbm.com
Web Site: www.sourcelink.com

E-Mail for Key Personnel:
President: ESchlaphoff@msdbm.com

Employees: 25
Year Founded: 1991

National Agency Associations: DMA

Agency Specializes In: Automotive, Business-To-Business, Consulting, Consumer Marketing, Direct Response Marketing, E-Commerce, Financial, Health Care Services, High Technology, Information Technology, Internet/Web Design, Strategic Planning/Research, Travel & Tourism

Cindy Randazzo *(Chief Strategy Officer & VP)*
Dan Jackson *(Pres-South Carolina)*
Chris Hamlin *(VP-Enterprise Mktg Solutions)*
Brent Tartar *(VP-Sls)*
Rick Berman *(Dir-Bus Dev)*

SourceLink
1224 Poinsett Hwy, Greenville, SC 29609
Tel.: (864) 233-2519
Fax: (864) 678-2146
Web Site: www.sourcelink.com

Employees: 100

Agency Specializes In: Advertising

Rick Norman *(CTO)*
Steven Bowles *(Dir-Bus Dev-Document & Statement Solutions Grp)*
Jon Cheek *(Dir-Production Ops)*
Ian Franklin *(Dir-Bus Dev)*
Noel Hendley *(Dir-Bus Dev)*
Cindy Miller *(Dir-Bus Dev)*
Debbie Thurston *(Dir-Client & Data, IT Svcs)*
Channing Laughridge *(Acct Mgr)*
Chip Lindrum *(Mgr-IS)*
Amy Moore *(Mgr-Strategic Relationship)*

SourceLink
5 Olympic Way, Madison, MS 39110
Tel.: (601) 898-8700
Fax: (601) 898-8724
Web Site: www.sourcelink.com

Employees: 125

Agency Specializes In: Advertising

Phil Graben *(COO)*
Chris Hamlin *(VP-Enterprise Mktg Solutions)*
Craig Blake *(Dir-Bus Dev)*
John Salerno *(Dir-Bus Dev)*
Mike Wilkins *(Dir-Bus Dev)*
Tracey Miller *(Mgr-Strategic Relationship)*

SOUTH COMPANY
1028 Hayne Ave SW, Aiken, SC 29801
Tel.: (803) 226-0284
Web Site: www.south-company.com

Agency Specializes In: Advertising, Event Planning & Marketing, Logo & Package Design, Print, Public Relations, Social Media, Strategic Planning/Research

Cynthia South *(Pres)*
Mike Thomas *(Mng Partner)*
Ron Turner *(Dir-Creative)*
Rebecca Vigne *(Dir-PR)*
Chris Wolf *(Dir-Dev)*
Haley Pope *(Jr Acct Exec)*

Accounts:
Dekoda Watson
Top Notch Express Car Wash

SOUTH END MEDIA
PO Box 286, Concord, NH 3302
Tel.: (603) 228-4243
E-Mail: info@southendmedia.com
Web Site: www.southendmedia.com

Agency Specializes In: Advertising, Internet/Web Design, Media Planning, Print, Radio, T.V.

Kurt Muhlfelder *(Owner)*

Accounts:
Capital Well Co, Inc.

THE SOUTHER AGENCY, INC.
518 E Main St, Spartanburg, SC 29302-1927
Tel.: (864) 583-2959
Fax: (864) 583-1309
E-Mail: info@southeragency.com
Web Site: www.southeragency.com

E-Mail for Key Personnel:
President: lsouther@aol.com
Production Mgr.: HParsons@aol.com

Employees: 5
Year Founded: 1981

National Agency Associations: AAF

Agency Specializes In: Advertising, Business-To-Business, Cable T.V., Co-op Advertising, Corporate Identity, Direct Response Marketing, Event Planning & Marketing, Exhibit/Trade Shows, Financial, Graphic Design, Legal Services, Logo & Package Design, Magazines, Media Buying Services, New Product Development, Newspaper, Newspapers & Magazines, Out-of-Home Media, Outdoor, Planning & Consultation, Point of Purchase, Point of Sale, Print, Production, Public Relations, Publicity/Promotions, Radio, Restaurant, Retail, Sales Promotion, Seniors' Market, Strategic Planning/Research, T.V., Trade & Consumer Magazines

Approx. Annual Billings: $1,000,000

Breakdown of Gross Billings by Media: Newsp.: $250,000; Radio: $250,000; T.V.: $500,000

Larry Souther *(Pres)*

Accounts:
Jim Smith & Associates; Spartanburg, SC Commercial Real Estate
Oak Creek Retirement Village; Burlington, NC; 1999
SABAC
Sharon Village Retirement Apartments; Charlotte, NC; 1999
Spartanburg Methodist College; Spartanburg, SC; 1997
Spartanburg Residential Development Corp. (Non-Profit); 2003
Spartanburg Water System; Spartanburg, SC; 1995
White Oak Estates; Spartanburg, SC Retirement Centers; 1997
Wilkins Communications Network Christian Radio Network; 2003

SOUTHWARD & ASSOCIATES, INC.
10 S Riverside Plz Ste 1950, Chicago, IL 60606-3801
Tel.: (312) 207-0600
Fax: (312) 207-6940
Web Site: www.southward.com

E-Mail for Key Personnel:
President: fsouthward@southward.com
Production Mgr.: rmoffit@southward.com

Employees: 7
Year Founded: 1961

National Agency Associations: NARB-Second Wind Limited

Agency Specializes In: Brand Development & Integration, Business-To-Business, Collateral, Communications, Corporate Identity, E-Commerce, Electronic Media, Exhibit/Trade Shows, Financial, Graphic Design, Industrial, Internet/Web Design, Travel & Tourism

Approx. Annual Billings: $4,600,000

Fred Southward *(Owner)*
Merry K. Elrick *(VP)*
Peggy M. O'Brien *(Dir-Creative)*

Accounts:
American Osteopathic Association
American Society of Home Inspectors
Community Savings Bank; Chicago, IL
DH Thompson
Howard Johnson's; Skokie, IL
Unique Indoor Comfort; Elmhurst, IL
William T. Glasgow, Inc.; Orland Park, IL

SOUTHWEST STRATEGIES LLC
401 B St Ste 150, San Diego, CA 92101
Tel.: (858) 541-7800
Fax: (858) 541-7863
Web Site: www.swspr.com

Agency Specializes In: Advertising, Crisis Communications, Event Planning & Marketing, Graphic Design, Media Relations, Media Training, Social Media, Strategic Planning/Research

Alan Ziegaus *(Chm)*

Chris Wahl *(Pres)*
Jennifer Ziegaus Wahl *(CEO)*
Elizabeth A. Hansen *(VP)*
Jessica Luternauer *(Sr Dir-Pub Affairs)*
Kimberly Olive Colla *(Dir-Pub Affairs)*
Wesley Jones *(Mgr-Pub Affairs)*

Accounts:
New-Coast Income Properties
New-General Dynamics/NASSCO
New-H. G. Fenton Company

THE SOUZA AGENCY
2547 Housley Rd, Annapolis, MD 21401-6751
Tel.: (410) 573-1300
Fax: (410) 573-1305
E-Mail: clients@souza.com
Web Site: www.souza.com

Year Founded: 1983

Agency Specializes In: Advertising, Advertising Specialties, African-American Market, Brand Development & Integration, Business Publications, Business-To-Business, Collateral, Communications, Consulting, Consumer Marketing, Corporate Identity, Digital/Interactive, Direct Response Marketing, E-Commerce, Entertainment, Event Planning & Marketing, Exhibit/Trade Shows, Graphic Design, Internet/Web Design, Local Marketing, Logo & Package Design, New Product Development, Newspapers & Magazines, Outdoor, Print, Public Relations, Real Estate, Restaurant, Sports Market, Strategic Planning/Research, Travel & Tourism, Yellow Pages Advertising

Anthony Souza *(Founder)*
Roseanne Souza *(Mng Dir & Dir-Creative)*

Accounts:
Aramark Corporation
Chesapeake Beach Resort & Spa; Chesapeake Beach, MD; 2005
Planet Five, LLC.

SOVRN
(Formerly Sovrn Creative, Inc.)
1101 W Grove St 201, Boise, ID 83702
Tel.: (208) 345-6064
E-Mail: contact@thesovrn.com
Web Site: thesovrn.com/

Year Founded: 2008

Agency Specializes In: Advertising, Corporate Identity, Graphic Design, Multimedia

Brian Cottier *(Partner, Dir-Creative & Designer)*
Philip McLain *(Partner & Designer)*
Joe Rice *(Partner)*
Nicole Cahill *(Dir-Art & Designer)*
Travis Dryden *(Dir-Strategy & Content)*
Tom Jensen *(Dir-Technical)*
Chris Beaudoin *(Designer-Motion)*

Accounts:
Bill Coffey Musician
Mettle for Men Beauty Care Products Mfr
Populas Furniture & Appliances Store

SPACE150
212 3rd Ave N Ste 150, Minneapolis, MN 55401
Tel.: (612) 332-6458
E-Mail: space@space150.com
Web Site: www.space150.com

Employees: 112
Year Founded: 2000

Agency Specializes In: Brand Development & Integration, Content, E-Commerce, Graphic Design, Media Buying Services, Media Planning, New Product Development, Sponsorship, Strategic Planning/Research

David Denham *(Pres & Chief Strategy Officer)*
Marc Jensen *(Mng Partner & CTO)*
Dutch Thalhuber *(COO)*
Matt Benka *(Exec VP-Acct Svc)*
Greg Swan *(VP-PR & Emerging Media)*
Brock Davis *(Grp Dir-Creative)*
Alex Dubrovsky *(Assoc Dir-Creative)*
Barrett Haroldson *(Assoc Dir-Creative)*
Ben Schmidt *(Assoc Dir-Creative)*

Accounts:
3M Company
American Eagle 77kids, Campaign: "Rock to School"
American Express
Best Buy
Buffalo Wild Wings Inc. Digital Strategy
Cakes.Com
Cambria campaign: "Every Dream Leads you Somewhere"
Cascadian Farm
Dairy Queen Orange Julius
Discovery
Forever21 (Agency of Record) Digital Billboard, Holographic Runway
General Mills
Imation Corp Imation, Memorex, XtremeMac
Land Securities
New-Link Snacks, Inc. Campaign: "Is Space Beast?", Jack Link's
Quiksilver/ROXY
RuMe Brand Strategy, Media, PR
Starz Entertainment
Style Caster
Target Corp
TDK
Xcel Energy Inc Brand Strategy, Content Strategy, Creative Design, User-experience

SPAR, INCORPORATED
501 Coolidge St PO Box 52831, New Orleans, LA 70121
Tel.: (504) 849-6410
Fax: (504) 849-6555
E-Mail: lcasteix@sparadvertising.com
Web Site: www.sparadvertising.com

E-Mail for Key Personnel:
Creative Dir.: lcasteix@sparadvertising.com

Employees: 7
Year Founded: 1965

Agency Specializes In: Advertising, Advertising Specialties, Brand Development & Integration, Graphic Design, In-Store Advertising, Logo & Package Design, Media Buying Services, Package Design, Point of Purchase, Point of Sale, Production (Print), Sales Promotion

Breakdown of Gross Billings by Media: Adv. Specialities: 15%; In-Store Adv.: 2%; Logo & Package Design: 45%; Out-of-Home Media: 2%; Outdoor: 25%; Point of Purchase: 2%; Point of Sale: 9%

Bill Bartels *(Vice Chm)*
Todd Bryce *(Sr VP-Customer & Retail Ops)*
John Fermann *(VP-Bus Dev)*
Jim Misurelli *(VP-Bus Dev)*
Lane Casteix *(Gen Mgr & Dir-Creative)*
Greg Page *(Client Svcs Dir)*
Sharlene Sheppard *(Client Svcs Dir)*
Husam Mufti *(Dir-Info Sys)*
Cheryl Rapp *(Dir-HR)*
Jessica Murdock *(Client Svcs Mgr)*
James Piland *(Client Svcs Mgr)*
Kindra Reck *(Client Svcs Mgr)*
Lisa M. Wells *(Acct Exec)*
Donna Vignali *(Client Svc Dir)*

Accounts:
Bacardi USA, Inc.; Metairie, LA , Spirits
Bellabrew; Metairie,LA
Buffalo Trace Distillery; Frankfort, KY
Diageo; TX; Addison, TX , Spirits
Gemini Spirits & Wine; Chicago, IL
National Children's Study, Tulane University; New Orleans, LA
Pernod Ricard; Dallas, TX Spirits
Republic National Distributing Company; New Orleans, LA , Spirits; 1965
Sazerac Co. Inc.; New Orleans, LA , Spirits Rectifier; 1965

SPARK
2309 W Platt St, Tampa, FL 33609
Tel.: (813) 253-0300
E-Mail: miller@spark.us
Web Site: www.spark.us

Employees: 39
Year Founded: 2001

Agency Specializes In: Advertising, Brand Development & Integration

Tony Miller *(CEO)*
Elliott Bedinghaus *(VP-Creative)*
Richard Cassey *(VP-Engagement)*
Nashira Babooram *(Dir-Media)*
Amy Do *(Dir-Social Media)*
Michelle Kaloger *(Dir-Ops)*
Dylan Melcher *(Dir-Photography)*
Gabriel DeLorenzi *(Sr Brand Mgr)*
Amanda Story *(Mgr-PR & Bus Dev)*
David Gonzalez *(Designer)*

Accounts:
All Children's Hospital
AVI-SPL
Coppertail Brewing Co.
The Dali Museum
The Epicurean Hotel
HARLEY-DAVIDSON Automobiles
Helicon Foundation Repair Services
MarineMax
Reeves Import Motorcars
Sweetbay Supermarket
Visit Florida

SPARK
(Name Changed to Lehigh Mining & Navigation)

SPARK MEDIA
153 Gateway Dr, Macon, GA 31210
Tel.: (478) 254-2263
Web Site: www.sparkmediacreative.com

Agency Specializes In: Advertising, Content, Digital/Interactive, Internet/Web Design, Media Buying Services, Print, Social Media

Scott Park *(Principal & Dir-Creative)*
Caralyn Moore *(Mgr-Social Media & Assoc Producer)*
Oliver Lukacs *(Sr Editor-DP)*

Accounts:
Galles Chevrolet
Moultrie Technical College This Changes Everything

SPARK STRATEGIC IDEAS
6230 Fairview Rd Ste 430, Charlotte, NC 28210
Tel.: (704) 995-1787
E-Mail: ignite@sparksi.com
Web Site: www.sparksi.com

Agency Specializes In: Advertising

Anne Marie Holder *(CEO)*
Patty Reuss *(Mng Dir)*
Brian Koch *(Dir-Creative)*
Thom Ransom *(Specialist-Media-Digital)*

Accounts:
Dean & Deluca
Girl Scouts, Hornets' Nest Council
Smashburger

SPARK44
3830 Clarington Ave, Culver City, CA 90232
Tel.: (310) 853-1850
Web Site: www.spark44.com

Year Founded: 2011

National Agency Associations: 4A's

Agency Specializes In: Advertising, Communications, Digital/Interactive

Sophie Ford Masters *(Bus Dir-UK)*
Bruce Dundore *(Dir-Creative-North America)*
M. Ryan Moore *(Dir-Creative)*
Jim Kowalski *(Assoc Dir-Creative)*
Allison Jabaley *(Mgr-Retail Mktg)*
Kate Krigbaum *(Acct Supvr)*
Elliot Darvick *(Sr Strategist-Social)*
Hazel Aliaga *(Acct Exec)*
Kerwin Jonathan *(Acct Exec)*
Heather Hoffman *(Analyst-Performance-Digital Strategy)*

Accounts:
Jaguar Land Rover North America LLC Advertising, Campaign: "British Intelligence", Campaign: "British Villains", Campaign: "How Alive Are You?", Campaign: "Rare and Meant to Be", Campaign: "Rendezvous" Super Bowl 2014, F-Type, Global Strategic & Creative, Print Advertising, XJ & XF Models

SPARKFACTOR
1644 N Honore St Ste 200, Chicago, IL 60622
Tel.: (773) 292-8000
Fax: (773) 486-7037
E-Mail: info@sparkfactor.com
Web Site: www.sparkfactor.com

Agency Specializes In: Advertising, Brand Development & Integration, Corporate Identity, Digital/Interactive, Graphic Design, Internet/Web Design, Logo & Package Design, Outdoor, Print, Social Media

George Lowe *(Owner)*
Kate Alpert *(Client Svcs Dir)*
Andrea Garcia *(Mgr-Digital Engagement)*
Vishnu Boray *(Designer)*

Accounts:
Howard Street
Mayne Stage

SPARKLOFT MEDIA
601 SW Oak St, Portland, OR 97205
Tel.: (503) 610-6113
E-Mail: contact@sparkloftmedia.com
Web Site: www.sparkloftmedia.com

Agency Specializes In: Advertising, Crisis Communications, Event Planning & Marketing, Media Buying Services, Social Media

Aaron Babbie *(VP)*
Jurek Lipski *(Acct Dir)*

Accounts:
New-Brand USA (Digital Content Creation & Social Community Management Agency of Record)

SPARKPLUG MARKETING & COMMUNICATIONS INC.
57 Lascelles Blvd, M5P 2C9 Toronto, ON Canada
Tel.: (416) 488-8867
E-Mail: gayle@sparkplug.ca
Web Site: www.sparkplug.ca

Employees: 10
Year Founded: 1995

Agency Specializes In: Above-the-Line, Advertising, Brand Development & Integration, Business-To-Business, Catalogs, Children's Market, College, Communications, Computers & Software, Consumer Goods, Consumer Marketing, Corporate Communications, Corporate Identity, Digital/Interactive, Direct Response Marketing, Direct-to-Consumer, Email, Market Research, Media Planning, New Product Development, Out-of-Home Media, Print, Production (Print), Radio, Social Marketing/Nonprofit, Strategic Planning/Research, T.V., Teen Market, Women's Market

Gayle Akler *(Pres & Chief Strategic Officer)*
Stuart Solway *(Dir-Creative & Writer)*

SPARKS & HONEY
437 Madison Ave 3rd Fl, New York, NY 10022
Tel.: (212) 894-5100
Fax: (212) 590-8100
E-Mail: info@sparksandhoney.com
Web Site: www.sparksandhoney.com

Year Founded: 2012

Agency Specializes In: Advertising, Brand Development & Integration, Content, Social Media

Terry Young *(Founder & CEO)*
Paul Butler *(COO)*
Sarah Davanzo *(Chief Strategy Officer)*
Mike Lanzi *(Chief Client Officer)*
Camilo LaCruz *(Exec VP & Head-Content)*
Imari Oliver *(VP & Dir-Creative Strategy)*
Dena Brody *(Acct Dir-Global)*
Tim Ettus *(Dir-Ops)*
Nick Ayala *(Strategist-Cultural)*
Wesley Luna-Smith *(Jr Strategist-Cultural)*

Accounts:
New-AT&T
New-Humana
Hyatt Hotels Corporation
Jarden Corp.
Life is Good
New-PepsiCo
New-Unilever
New-Visa

SPARKS EXHIBITS & ENVIRONMENTS
(Formerly Sparks Marketing Group, Inc.)
2828 Charter Rd, Philadelphia, PA 19154-2111
Tel.: (215) 676-1100
Fax: (215) 676-1991
Toll Free: (800) 925-7727
E-Mail: info@sparksonline.com
Web Site: www.sparksonline.com

Employees: 313
Year Founded: 1966

Agency Specializes In: Event Planning & Marketing, Exhibit/Trade Shows, Retail

Approx. Annual Billings: $20,300,000

Jeffrey K. Harrow *(Chm)*
Matt Wood *(Pres)*
Robert Ginsburg *(CEO & CFO)*
Dax Callner *(Sr VP-Strategy)*
Jane Hawley *(Sr VP)*
David Lentz *(Sr VP-Creative Strategy & Brand Plng)*
Cynthia McArthur *(VP-Strategic Accts)*
Joy Mossholder *(VP-Bus Dev)*

Accounts:
Boston Scientific
GE
Google I/O
HP Discover
JC Penney
Juicy Couture
LG Electronics
McKesson
Neutrogena
Owens Corning
Safilo
Sampan
SAP
Splendid
Stride Rite
Verizon Wireless
Villanova University

SPARKS GROVE
3333 Piedmont Rd NE Ste 800, Atlanta, GA 30305-1811
Tel.: (404) 961-9900
Fax: (404) 961-9890
Web Site: www.sparksgrove.com

Employees: 27

Agency Specializes In: Alternative Advertising, Brand Development & Integration, Branded Entertainment, Consulting, Consumer Goods, Corporate Identity, Custom Publishing, Digital/Interactive, Direct Response Marketing, Direct-to-Consumer, E-Commerce, Email, Entertainment, Environmental, Experience Design, Game Integration, Graphic Design, Guerilla Marketing, Health Care Services, Hospitality, Identity Marketing, Internet/Web Design, Leisure, Logo & Package Design, Luxury Products, New Product Development, Podcasting, Production (Print), RSS (Really Simple Syndication), Search Engine Optimization, Sponsorship, Strategic Planning/Research, Travel & Tourism, Viral/Buzz/Word of Mouth, Web (Banner Ads, Pop-ups, etc.)

Approx. Annual Billings: $4,000,000

Alex Bombeck *(Pres)*
Minsoo Pak *(VP & Chief Creative Officer)*
Scott Bryan *(VP)*
Elizabeth Searcy *(VP)*
Rob Sherrell *(VP)*
Lange Taylor *(VP)*
Heather Regna *(Exec Dir-Client Svcs)*
David Huntington *(Creative Dir)*
Anne Shoulders *(Dir)*
Michael Valverde *(Dir-Mktg & Bus Dev)*
Amanda Hilyer *(Coord-Traffic)*

Accounts:
AT&T Communications Corp.
BMW Car Club of America
Coca-Cola Refreshments USA, Inc.
Delta Air Lines (Business to Business Agency of Record) Business-to-Business
Premiere Global Services

SPARXOO
514 N Franklin St Ste 202, Tampa, FL 33602
Tel.: (813) 402-0208
E-Mail: info@sparxoo.com
Web Site: www.sparxoo.com

Employees: 4
Year Founded: 2007

National Agency Associations: AMA

Agency Specializes In: Advertising, Consulting, Consumer Marketing, Digital/Interactive, E-Commerce, Electronic Media, Entertainment, Event Planning & Marketing, Gay & Lesbian Market, Guerilla Marketing, Identity Marketing, Internet/Web Design, Logo & Package Design, Luxury Products, Magazines, Paid Searches, Planning & Consultation, Publicity/Promotions, Publishing, Search Engine Optimization, Social Marketing/Nonprofit, Social Media, Sports Market, Strategic Planning/Research, Viral/Buzz/Word of Mouth

Approx. Annual Billings: $500,000

Breakdown of Gross Billings by Media: Graphic Design: 17%; In-Store Adv.: 33%; Strategic Planning/Research: 50%

David Capece *(Founder & CEO)*
Katherine Parsons *(Head-Strategy)*
Nicholas Ferry *(Acct Dir-Strategic)*
Grace Northern *(Acct Dir-Strategic)*
Ryan Krail *(Dir-Creative)*

Accounts:
Chase Bank; Wilmington, DE Market Research
Clean Plates; New York, NY Clean Plates Guide
Do Good Real Estate; Wilmington, NC Local Marketing
Fox Sports; Los Angeles, CA Web Development
Habitat for Humanity; Atlanta, GA Brand Development
Turner Broadcasting; Atlanta, GA

SPAULDING COMMUNICATIONS, INC.
619 E College Ave Studio A, Decatur, GA 30030
Tel.: (404) 270-1010
Fax: (404) 270-1020
E-Mail: info@spauldingcommunications.com
Web Site: www.spauldingcommunications.com

Year Founded: 2002

Agency Specializes In: Collateral, Email, Internet/Web Design, Logo & Package Design, Media Relations, Production, Sales Promotion, Strategic Planning/Research, T.V.

Matt Spaulding *(Pres & Sr Strategist)*
Reyes Rosheuvel *(Sr Dir-Art)*
Alice Murray *(Sr Strategist-Media Rels)*

Accounts:
American Seating
Cifial
Intercontinental
Rheem
Zeftron

SPAWN IDEAS
(Formerly Nerland Agency Worldwide Partners)
510 L St, Anchorage, AK 99501-3532
Tel.: (907) 274-9553
Fax: (907) 274-9990
Web Site: www.spawnak.com

Employees: 29
Year Founded: 1975

National Agency Associations: 4A's-AAF-AMA-PRSA

Agency Specializes In: Advertising, Alternative Advertising, Brand Development & Integration, Broadcast, Collateral, Communications, Consumer Marketing, Corporate Communications, Corporate Identity, Crisis Communications, Digital/Interactive, Direct Response Marketing, Electronic Media, Health Care Services, In-Store Advertising, Integrated Marketing, Internet/Web Design, Local Marketing, Logo & Package Design, Media Buying Services, Media Planning, Media Relations, Media Training, Multimedia, Newspaper, Newspapers & Magazines, Out-of-Home Media, Outdoor, Planning & Consultation, Point of Purchase, Point of Sale, Print, Production, Production (Ad, Film, Broadcast), Production (Print), Promotions, Public Relations, Publicity/Promotions, Radio, Recruitment, Retail, Sales Promotion, Social Marketing/Nonprofit, Sports Market, Strategic Planning/Research, T.V., Web (Banner Ads, Pop-ups, etc.), Yellow Pages Advertising

Karen King *(Pres & CEO)*
Lisa King *(CFO & VP)*
Graham Biddle *(Dir-Creative)*
Andy Zanto *(Assoc Dir-Creative)*
Alonna Brorson *(Acct Supvr)*
Colleen Cronin *(Acct Supvr)*
Codie Costello *(Supvr-Bus Dev)*
Geneva Turrini *(Acct Coord)*

Accounts:
The Alaska Club Health Club Network; 1994
Alaska KMcDonalds
Alyeska Pipeline Service Company
BP Exploration; AK Oil Industry
City of Anchorage
Fairbanks Memorial Hospital Healthcare
Major Marine Broadcast, Digital, Media Planning & Buying, Print, Social, Trade Planning & Buying
Midas Alaska Automotive; 2000
Ocean Beauty Seafoods; Seattle, WA Seafood
Rasmuson Foundation
State of Alaska DOT & PF; Anchorage, AK Transportation; 1999
Ted Stevens International Airport Transportation

SPEAK
205 E Main St, Hillsboro, OR 97123
Tel.: (503) 946-6463
Fax: (866) 774-9578
E-Mail: info@speakagency.com
Web Site: speakagency.com/

Year Founded: 2007

Agency Specializes In: Advertising, Brand Development & Integration, Content, Event Planning & Marketing, Internet/Web Design, Logo & Package Design, Print, Social Media

Jason Anthony *(Principal)*
Paul Sandy *(Partner & Creative Dir)*
Kristen Errera *(Partner & Dir-Acct Svcs)*
Josh Rhodes *(Dir-Strategy & Bus Dev)*
Brad Grace *(Assoc Dir-Creative)*
Deb Norloff *(Copywriter)*
Dan Obrien *(Copywriter)*
Dee Heron *(Sr Designer)*
Kathy Dipaolo *(Sr Designer)*
Patrick Woolworth *(Designer)*

Accounts:
Clarks Bistro & Pub

SPEAKEASY DIGITAL MARKETING
800 Jackson St Ste B-100, Dallas, TX 75202
Tel.: (214) 628-9700
Fax: (214) 628-9696
E-Mail: speak@yourspeakeasy.com
Web Site: www.yourspeakeasy.com

Year Founded: 2012

Agency Specializes In: Advertising, Content, Promotions, Social Media

Mike Orren *(Pres)*
Lindsay Jacaman *(Chief Revenue Officer)*
Sarah Magee *(Mng Dir-Ops & Strategy)*
Kimberly Jones *(Acct Dir)*
Erin Davis *(Dir-Creative)*
Dan Sturdivant *(Dir-Speakeasy Consulting)*
Andrews Cope *(Mgr-Content & Acct Mgr)*
Emma Margaux Miller *(Acct Mgr)*
John Stalle *(Acct Mgr)*
Bryn Townsend *(Acct Mgr)*
Laura Hall *(Specialist-Digital Media & Social Media Mktg)*

Accounts:
The Dallas Morning News Co.
Heart of Dallas

SPEARHALL ADVERTISING & PUBLIC RELATIONS
2150 West Washington St Ste 402, San Diego, CA 92110
Tel.: (619) 683-3700
Fax: (858) 586-7009
E-Mail: shelly@spearhall.com
Web Site: www.spearhall.com

Employees: 2
Year Founded: 1980

Shelly Hall *(Owner)*
Tiffany Dugan *(VP-Sls & Mktg)*

Accounts:
Golf Fest New York
Golf Fest San Diego
Golf Fest Vegas
Mammoth Mountain Chalets
Montesoro
Panera Bread
San Diego Arts Festival
Village Pines

SPECIFIC MEDIA INC.
4 Park Plz Ste 1500, Irvine, CA 92614
Tel.: (949) 861-8888
Fax: (949) 861-8990
E-Mail: info@specificmedia.com
Web Site: www.specificmedia.com

Year Founded: 1999

Agency Specializes In: Advertising, Media Planning

Russell Vanderhook *(Co-Founder & Sr VP)*
Fabrizio Blanco *(CTO)*
Jason Knapp *(Chief Product Officer)*
Drew Bordages *(Gen Counsel, Sec & Sr VP)*
Craig Benner *(Sr VP-Sls-US)*
Erin Madorsky *(Sr VP-Sls)*
John Chung *(VP-Sls-Lakes Reg)*
Michael Muse *(Acct Mgr)*
Hilary Jaschke *(Acct Exec)*
Christina Stocker *(Acct Exec)*

SPECK COMMUNICATIONS
3200 Main St Ste 1.2, Dallas, TX 75226
Tel.: (214) 370-9927
Web Site: www.speckcommunications.com

Year Founded: 2008

Agency Specializes In: Advertising, Brand Development & Integration, Collateral, Corporate Identity, Digital/Interactive, Internet/Web Design, Logo & Package Design, Media Buying Services, Media Planning, Print

Dan Curtis *(Pres)*
Carey Morgan *(Acct Dir)*
Rebekkah French *(Dir-Creative)*
Jena Jessen *(Dir-Art)*

Grayson Cagle *(Acct Exec)*
Melody Curtis *(Strategist-Mktg)*

Accounts:
The Witte Museum

SPECTRUM INTERACTIVE MEDIA LLC
419 Lafayette St 2nd Fl, New York, NY 10003
Tel.: (888) 234-0118
Fax: (212) 228-6139
E-Mail: info@spectrumim.com
Web Site: www.spectrumim.com

Agency Specializes In: Digital/Interactive, Email, Internet/Web Design, Market Research, Media Buying Services, Media Planning, Mobile Marketing, Search Engine Optimization

Nigel Milne *(Mng Dir)*
Stephen Holmes *(Dir-Sls & Mktg)*
Sara Siskin *(Mgr-Social Media)*

Accounts:
Rock Sake Alcoholic Beverage Mfr

SPECTRUM MARKETING, INC.
48 Jackson Dr, Stony Point, NY 10980
Tel.: (212) 244-4915
E-Mail: info@spectrummktg.com
Web Site: www.spectrummktg.com

Employees: 6
Year Founded: 1971

National Agency Associations: BMA

Agency Specializes In: Advertising, Public Relations, Sales Promotion

Keith R. Albert *(Pres)*
Jason Gustetic *(Exec VP-Client Svcs)*

Accounts:
Storz

SPENCER ADVERTISING AND MARKETING
3708 Hempland Rd, Mountville, PA 17554
Tel.: (717) 569-6544
Fax: (717) 569-5244
Web Site: www.thinkspencer.com

Employees: 15

Kevin Clarkin *(VP-Acct Svcs)*
Dan Hooven *(Dir-Creative)*
Megan Balmer *(Acct Exec)*
Clayton Margerum *(Copywriter)*
Alexander Tufarolo *(Copywriter)*

Accounts:
Mannington Resilient Floors
Pennsylvania Turnpike Commission Communications, Marketing, PR

SPERO MEDIA
295 Madison Ste 1808, New York, NY 10017
Tel.: (212) 688-8999
Web Site: www.speromedia.com

Agency Specializes In: Advertising, Direct Response Marketing, Education, Entertainment, Internet/Web Design, Local Marketing, Media Relations, Outdoor, Print, Production, Radio, Retail, Sponsorship, Sports Market, T.V.

Harry Spero *(Pres)*
April Cotton *(Dir-Integrated Strategy)*
Rayanne Mulieri *(Acct Mgr & Mgr-Promotions)*
Morielle Albo *(Acct Mgr, Media Buyer & Planner)*

Brittany Cole *(Acct Mgr)*

Accounts:
Crazy Eddie
Emerald Funding
Goen Seminars
Liberty Funding
US Open Series

SPHERE ADVERTISING
940 Tate Blvd SE Ste 107, Hickory, NC 28602
Tel.: (828) 855-3288
Web Site: www.sphereadv.com

Year Founded: 2009

Agency Specializes In: Advertising, Brand Development & Integration, Graphic Design, Internet/Web Design, Logo & Package Design, Media Buying Services, Print, Promotions, Radio, T.V.

Chad Shehan *(Owner)*
Jeff Sigmon *(Owner)*

Accounts:
Bumgarner Camping

SPHERICAL COMMUNICATIONS
58 E 11th St 8th Fl, New York, NY 10003
Tel.: (917) 558-7396
E-Mail: info@sphericalcommunications.com
Web Site: www.sphericalcommunications.com

Year Founded: 2011

Agency Specializes In: Advertising, Brand Development & Integration, Digital/Interactive, Internet/Web Design, Social Media

Adam J. Wallace *(Founder, CEO & Head-Strategy)*
Raymond Spaddy *(Dir-Digital & Content Mktg)*

Accounts:
Travel Tripper

SPIKE ADVERTISING INC.
27 Kilburn St, Burlington, VT 05401
Tel.: (802) 951-1700
Fax: (802) 951-1705
E-Mail: tools@spikeadvertising.com
Web Site: www.spikeadvertising.com

Employees: 10
Year Founded: 1998

Agency Specializes In: Collateral, Internet/Web Design, Logo & Package Design, Print, Production (Ad, Film, Broadcast), Production (Print), Radio, T.V., Web (Banner Ads, Pop-ups, etc.)

Ken Millman *(Pres & Chief Creative Officer)*
Andre Razo *(Dir-Creative)*

Accounts:
Creative Workforce Solutions
Jameison Insurance Agency
Langrock Sperry & Wool
Timberlane Dental Group
University of Vermont Extension
Vermont Agency of Transportation
Vermont Children's Trust Foundation

SPIKER COMMUNICATIONS, INC.
PO Box 8567, Missoula, MT 59807
Tel.: (406) 721-0785
Fax: (406) 728-8915
E-Mail: spikers@spikercomm.com
Web Site: www.spikercomm.com

E-Mail for Key Personnel:
President: wspiker@spikercomm.com
Production Mgr.: aceland@spikercomm.com

Employees: 10
Year Founded: 1983

Agency Specializes In: Advertising, Aviation & Aerospace, Brand Development & Integration, Broadcast, Business Publications, Business-To-Business, Cable T.V., Collateral, Commercial Photography, Communications, Consulting, Consumer Marketing, Consumer Publications, Corporate Communications, Corporate Identity, Direct Response Marketing, Education, Electronic Media, Entertainment, Environmental, Event Planning & Marketing, Exhibit/Trade Shows, Financial, Food Service, Government/Political, Graphic Design, Health Care Services, Internet/Web Design, Leisure, Local Marketing, Logo & Package Design, Magazines, Media Buying Services, Medical Products, New Product Development, Newspaper, Newspapers & Magazines, Out-of-Home Media, Outdoor, Over-50 Market, Planning & Consultation, Point of Sale, Print, Production, Public Relations, Publicity/Promotions, Radio, Real Estate, Recruitment, Restaurant, Seniors' Market, Sports Market, Strategic Planning/Research, T.V., Teen Market, Trade & Consumer Magazines, Transportation, Travel & Tourism

Chris Spiker *(Owner & Partner)*
John Wes Spiker *(Pres & Dir-Creative)*
Heather Phillips *(Mgr-Production & Graphic Designer)*
Anita Cleland *(Mgr-Production)*

Accounts:
Clearcreek Tahoe
First Security Bank; Missoula, MT Financial Services; 1989
Rocky Mountain Log Homes; Hamilton, MT; 1983
SnowBowl; Missoula, MT Ski Resort; 1983
Stock Farm; Hamilton, MT Development; 1995

SPIN ADVERTISING
2008 E Stadium Blvd, Ann Arbor, MI 48104
Tel.: (734) 213-5326
Fax: (888) 334-6485
E-Mail: info@spin-advertising.com
Web Site: www.spin-advertising.com

Agency Specializes In: Advertising, Brand Development & Integration, Digital/Interactive, Internet/Web Design, Logo & Package Design, Media Planning, Outdoor, Print, Search Engine Optimization

Adrienne Cormie *(Partner & Exec Dir-Creative)*
Thomas Cormie *(Partner-Mktg & Media)*

Accounts:
Bennett Optometry

SPIN CREATIVE STUDIO
2420 Alcott St, Denver, CO 80211
Tel.: (303) 534-5244
E-Mail: info@spincreativestudio.com
Web Site: http://www.spindenver.com/

Agency Specializes In: Advertising, Brand Development & Integration, Digital/Interactive, Media Buying Services, Media Planning, Outdoor, Print, Radio, Strategic Planning/Research, T.V.

Brigette Schabdach *(CEO)*
Kalli Skov *(Mng Dir)*
Erin Groce *(Acct Exec)*
Travis Bartlett *(Sr Designer)*
Kelsey Fagan *(Designer)*
Libby Lingle *(Acct Coord)*

Accounts:
ANSR Group
Green Apple Supply
The USA Pro Challenge (Advertising Agency of Record) Creative Development, Strategy

SPIN RECRUITMENT ADVERTISING
712 Bancroft Rd Ste 521, Walnut Creek, CA 94598
Tel.: (925) 944-6060
Fax: (925) 944-6063
E-Mail: info@spinrecruitment.com
Web Site: www.spinrecruitment.com

Employees: 8

Agency Specializes In: Advertising, Brand Development & Integration, Collateral, Communications, Exhibit/Trade Shows, Newspapers & Magazines, Print, Recruitment

Traci Dondanville *(Owner)*
Stephanie Fong *(VP)*

Accounts:
City of Oakland; Oakland, CA
Dignity Health Medical Foundation
Kaiser Permanente
Oroweat; South San Francisco, CA

SPIRE AGENCY
15950 N Dallas Pkwy Ste 400, Dallas, TX 75248
Tel.: (214) 393-5200
E-Mail: info@spireagency.com
Web Site: www.spireagency.com

Year Founded: 2008

Agency Specializes In: Advertising, Collateral, Digital/Interactive, Event Planning & Marketing, Exhibit/Trade Shows, Logo & Package Design, Social Media

Steve Gray *(Owner & Partner)*
Kimberly Tyner *(Owner & Partner)*
Rebekah Ellis *(Acct Mgr)*

Accounts:
Texas Capital Bank

SPIRO & ASSOCIATES MARKETING, ADVERTISING & PUBLIC RELATIONS
12651 McGregor Blvd Unit 4-402, Fort Myers, FL 33919
Tel.: (239) 481-5511
Fax: (239) 481-5852
Web Site: www.spiroandassociates.com

E-Mail for Key Personnel:
President: cspiro@spiroandassociates.com

Employees: 12
Year Founded: 1988

National Agency Associations: AAF

Agency Specializes In: Advertising, Automotive, Brand Development & Integration, Broadcast, Business Publications, Business-To-Business, Cable T.V., Children's Market, Co-op Advertising, Collateral, Consulting, Consumer Publications, Corporate Identity, Direct Response Marketing, E-Commerce, Event Planning & Marketing, Financial, Government/Political, Graphic Design, Health Care Services, Internet/Web Design, Leisure, Logo & Package Design, Magazines, Marine, Media Buying Services, Medical Products, Multimedia, New Product Development, Newspaper, Newspapers & Magazines, Out-of-Home Media, Outdoor, Point of Purchase, Point of Sale, Print, Production, Public Relations, Publicity/Promotions, Radio, Real Estate, Retail, Seniors' Market, Strategic Planning/Research, T.V., Trade & Consumer Magazines, Travel & Tourism, Yellow Pages Advertising

Breakdown of Gross Billings by Media: Co-op Adv.: 7%; Internet Adv.: 5%; Mags.: 21%; Newsp.: 37%; Out-of-Home Media: 5%; Radio: 10%; T.V.: 15%

Christopher T. Spiro *(CEO)*
Rachel Martin Spiro *(VP)*
Heideman Heidman *(Sr Dir-Art)*
Lynsey Yuknus *(Sr Dir-Art)*
Robert Armstrong *(Dir-Creative)*
Thomas Calabrese *(Dir-Creative)*
Gail Gubelman *(Designer-Indus Art)*

Accounts:
BlackHawk
Blind Pass Condominiums; Sanibel, FL Vacation Rentals; 2000
Levitt and Sons
The Oaks
Raso Realty, Inc
Royal Shell Vacations; Captiva & Sanibel, FL Condominium & Private Home Vacation Rentals; 1998
Seasons
Spiro Associates
Tradition

SPITBALL LLC
60 Broad St, Red Bank, NJ 07701
Tel.: (732) 345-9200
E-Mail: ideas@spit-ball.com
Web Site: www.spit-ball.com

Agency Specializes In: Advertising, Brand Development & Integration, Graphic Design, Internet/Web Design, Logo & Package Design, Media Planning, Package Design

Anthony Torre *(Partner & CMO)*
Steve Bailey *(Partner & Creative Dir-Spitball Adv)*
Ben Douglass *(Dir-Art)*
Dana Vulpis *(Acct Exec & Media Planner)*

Accounts:
Affordable Housing Alliance
Downtown Somerville Alliance
Engineering & Land Planning Associates
Lil Cutie Pops
Morph Wheels
Reproductive Medicine Associates of New Jersey

SPLASH COMMUNICATIONS, LLC
47 W Valverde Rd, Corrales, NM 87048
Tel.: (310) 399-9336
Fax: (505) 404-1128
E-Mail: info@splashcom.com
Web Site: www.splashcom.com

Employees: 1
Year Founded: 1971

Agency Specializes In: Advertising, Advertising Specialties, Aviation & Aerospace, Brand Development & Integration, Business-To-Business, Collateral, Communications, Consulting, Consumer Goods, Consumer Marketing, Corporate Communications, Corporate Identity, Digital/Interactive, Direct Response Marketing, Electronic Media, Electronics, Exhibit/Trade Shows, Financial, Graphic Design, Health Care Services, High Technology, Hospitality, Industrial, Internet/Web Design, Leisure, Logo & Package Design, Luxury Products, Magazines, Multimedia, Newspaper, Newspapers & Magazines, Out-of-Home Media, Outdoor, Package Design, Planning & Consultation, Print, Production, Production (Print), Radio, Real Estate, Restaurant, Retail, Seniors' Market, Technical Advertising, Trade & Consumer Magazines, Travel & Tourism

Approx. Annual Billings: $500,000

Breakdown of Gross Billings by Media: Collateral: 10%; Consulting: 55%; Graphic Design: 15%; Logo & Package Design: 20%

Steven J. Levine *(Owner)*

SPLASH MEDIA GROUP
5040 Addison Cir Ste 400, Addison, TX 75001
Tel.: (972) 392-6700
Web Site: www.splashmedia.com

Agency Specializes In: Advertising, Content, Digital/Interactive, Media Buying Services, Search Engine Optimization, Social Media

Jim Mckinnis *(Pres & Chief Creative Officer)*
John Dankovchik *(CEO)*
Steve Campanini *(Chief Comm Officer)*

Accounts:
New-ZTE USA

SPLASHWRENCH
PO Box 150208, Cape Coral, FL 33915
Tel.: (239) 206-4487
Web Site: www.splashwrench.com

Year Founded: 2010

Agency Specializes In: Advertising, Collateral, Graphic Design, Internet/Web Design, Logo & Package Design, Media Buying Services, Print, Radio, Search Engine Optimization, Social Media

James George *(Mng Dir)*
Patricia George *(Strategist-Mktg)*

Accounts:
Brewfest Event
Browtopia Press Release
Columbus Properties LP
The Deli Fort Myers
The Morgan House
Ninos Thick & Thin
Slow Food Southwest Florida
US Sports Therapy

THE SPLINTER GROUP
605 W Main St 201, Carrboro, NC 27510
Tel.: (919) 969-0979
Fax: (919) 969-0971
E-Mail: hello@thesplintergroup.net
Web Site: www.thesplintergroup.net

Year Founded: 2000

Agency Specializes In: Advertising, Graphic Design, Public Relations, Social Media

Lane Wurster *(Partner & Dir-Creative)*
Steve Balcom *(Gen Mgr)*
Bronwyn Gruet *(Designer)*

Accounts:
Buns
Burlington Aviation
Carolina Brewery
Daisy Cakes
Etix

SPM COMMUNICATIONS
2030 Main St Ste 325, Dallas, TX 75201
Tel.: (214) 379-7000
Fax: (214) 379-7007
E-Mail: info@spmcommunications.com
Web Site: www.spmcommunications.com

Employees: 20

Agency Specializes In: Public Relations

Suzanne Miller *(Founder & Pres)*
Mary Kate Jeffries *(VP)*
Kristen Kauffman *(VP-Editorial)*
Ann Hinshaw *(Dir)*
Jeannine Brew *(Acct Supvr)*
Ruchy Sharda *(Supvr-Media Analytics)*

Accounts:
New-Austin Footwear Labs (Public Relations Agency of Record)
New-Boulder Organic Foods (Public Relations Agency of Record)
Bruegger's Bagels
Chipotle Mexican Grill
Eraclea
I and love and you (Public Relations Agency of Record) Media
Joe's Crab Shack
Main Event Entertainment
Michaels Stores, Inc
New-Newk's Eatery
Petmate
Pollo Tropical
Romano's Macaroni Grill
Salata
Stubb's Legendary Bar
Taco Cabana
Van's International Foods

Branch

MediaLine PR
2030 Main St 3rd Fl, Dallas, TX 75201
(See Separate Listing)

SPM MARKETING & COMMUNICATIONS
15 W Harris Ave Ste 300, La Grange, IL 60525-2498
Tel.: (708) 246-7700
Fax: (708) 246-5184
E-Mail: harken@spmadvertising.com
Web Site: www.spmadvertising.com

Employees: 45
Year Founded: 1983

Agency Specializes In: Advertising, Brand Development & Integration, Broadcast, Cable T.V., Collateral, Communications, Consumer Marketing, Corporate Communications, Corporate Identity, Electronic Media, Health Care Services, Internet/Web Design, Media Buying Services, Newspapers & Magazines, Out-of-Home Media, Outdoor, Over-50 Market, Print, Production, Public Relations, Radio, Strategic Planning/Research

Approx. Annual Billings: $63,000,000

Lawrence W. Margolis *(Mng Partner)*
Patti Winegar *(Mng Partner)*
Nancy E. Miller *(CFO)*
Dan Miers *(Chief Strategy Officer)*
Robert A. Konold *(Sr VP & Grp Dir-Creative)*
Donna L. Greene *(VP & Acct Dir)*
Mike Lynn *(VP & Dir-Integrated Media)*
Rick Korzeniowski *(Exec Dir-Creative)*
Cathy Felter *(Acct Dir)*

Accounts:
Meridian Health; Wall, NJ
Rush University Medical Center & Affiliates; Chicago, IL
University of Kansas Hospital; Kansas City, KS

SPOKE AGENCY
32 Britain St Ste 400, Toronto, ON M5A 1R6 Canada
Tel.: (416) 646-2340
Fax: (416) 646-2344
E-Mail: talktous@spokeagency.com
Web Site: www.spokeagency.com

Year Founded: 2009

Agency Specializes In: Advertising, Digital/Interactive, Media Buying Services, Public Relations, Social Media

Jeff Greenspoon *(CEO)*
Kai Exos *(Chief Creative Officer)*
Karen Lo *(Dir-Art)*
Marshall Cole *(Designer)*
Tiffany Delve *(Designer)*
Ria Medalla *(Media Planner)*
Chantelle Ennis-Charoo *(Assoc Producer)*

Accounts:
FanXchange
ING Direct
Nickelodeon/Nick

SPOKE MARKETING
3145 Locust St, Saint Louis, MO 63103
Tel.: (314) 827-0600
Toll Free: (866) 925-5719
E-Mail: info@wearespoke.com
Web Site: spokemarketing.com

Year Founded: 2008

Agency Specializes In: Advertising, Brand Development & Integration, Digital/Interactive

Brian Schwartz *(Co-Founder)*
Mike Egel *(Partner)*
Jay Yerxa *(Dir-Art)*
Sarah Eikmann *(Mgr-Traffic)*

Accounts:
Lashly & Baer, P.C.
The Omni Club

SPOKE8 MARKETING
(Name Changed to InVerve Marketing)

SPONGE, LLC
1165 N Clark St, Chicago, IL 60610
Tel.: (312) 397-8828
E-Mail: info@spongechicago.com
Web Site: www.spongechicago.com

Employees: 5
Year Founded: 2007

Agency Specializes In: Brand Development & Integration, Identity Marketing, Strategic Planning/Research

Paul Brourman *(Founder, CEO & Chief Creative Officer)*
Larry Butts *(Dir-Art)*

Accounts:
Grazie, Inc. App Development, Branding, Marketing, Software Product Launch; 2013
McDonald's Digital Experience Development/Content; 2014
The PrivateBank B2B, Consumer Marketing/Campaigns; 2012

SPOON+FORK
419 Lafayette St, New York, NY 10003
Tel.: (646) 723-3324
E-Mail: hungry@spoonandforkstudio.com
Web Site: www.spoonandforkstudio.com

Employees: 4
Year Founded: 2003

Agency Specializes In: Brand Development & Integration, Corporate Identity, Package Design

Pritsana Kootint-Hadiatmodjo *(Founder & Dir-Creative)*
Chez Bryan Ong *(Founder & Dir-Creative)*
Jennifer Chou *(Designer)*

Accounts:
Heathcliff (Creative Agency) Web Site; 2009

SPORTSBRANDEDMEDIA INC.
8 Rockwin Rd, Rockville Centre, NY 11570
Tel.: (516) 705-4366
Fax: (516) 377-1243

Employees: 8

Agency Specializes In: Brand Development & Integration, Branded Entertainment, Consulting, Entertainment, Event Planning & Marketing, Game Integration, Integrated Marketing, Market Research, Media Relations, Product Placement, Production, Social Media, Sponsorship, Sports Market

Approx. Annual Billings: $1,000,000

Breakdown of Gross Billings by Media: Production: $300,000; Sports Mktg.: $600,000; Strategic Planning/Research: $100,000

John Meindl *(Founder & Pres)*
Sarah Thomas *(Sr Acct Mgr)*

Accounts:
H2H
Sky Race World Cup
The World Cup Project

SPORTSMARK MANAGEMENT GROUP, LTD.
(d/b/a Sportsmark)
781 Lincoln Ave Ste 380, San Rafael, CA 94901
Tel.: (415) 461-5801
Fax: (415) 461-5804
E-Mail: solutions@sportsmark.com
Web Site: www.sportsmark.com

Employees: 40
Year Founded: 1989

Agency Specializes In: Event Planning & Marketing

David Elmore *(Founder)*
Steve Skubic *(CEO)*
Patrick Dawson *(Dir-Production & Design)*
Stephanie Lee *(Sr Acct Mgr)*

Accounts:
Adidas
ArcelorMittal
Bank of America
Bell Canada
British Airways
CBS
Chevron
Cisco
National Football League Campaign: "NFL House"
Office Depot
Omega
Sony
Yahoo

THE SPOT MEDIA GROUP
600 N Hartley St Ste 140, York, PA 17404
Tel.: (717) 852-7768
Fax: (717) 718-3762

E-Mail: info@thespotmediagroup.com
Web Site: www.thespotmediagroup.com

Agency Specializes In: Advertising, Collateral, Graphic Design, Internet/Web Design, Media Buying Services, Print

Dave Maday *(Owner & Pres)*
Maria Mancuso *(COO)*

Accounts:
Industrial & Commercial Electrical Contractor

SPOT ON
213 Fordham St, Bronx, NY 10464
Tel.: (718) 885-3434
Web Site: www.spotonny.com

Agency Specializes In: Advertising, African-American Market, Alternative Advertising, Bilingual Market, Broadcast, Cable T.V., Co-op Advertising, Direct-to-Consumer, Electronic Media, Entertainment, Graphic Design, Hispanic Market, Infomercials, Internet/Web Design, Logo & Package Design, Media Buying Services, Multimedia, Package Design, Production, Production (Ad, Film, Broadcast), Social Media, Teen Market, Urban Market, Women's Market

Approx. Annual Billings: $300,000

Stephen Franciosa, Jr. *(Dir & Exec Producer)*
Frank Mosca *(Dir & Exec Producer)*
Jarett Bellucci *(Dir)*
John Morena *(Dir)*
Christopher Walters *(Dir)*
Rebecca Rosado *(Mgr-Production)*
Richard Goldstien *(Acct Exec)*
Alex Tavis *(Acct Exec)*

Accounts:
Special Olympics Campaign: "R Word"

SPOT SAVVY, LLC
235 E 22nd St Ste 15J, New York, NY 10010
Tel.: (347) 689-3340
Fax: (347) 599-2941
Toll Free: (888) 447-2889
E-Mail: e.stephenson@spotsavvy.com
Web Site: www.spotsavvy.com

Employees: 4
Year Founded: 2006

Agency Specializes In: Advertising, Affiliate Marketing, African-American Market, Alternative Advertising, Brand Development & Integration, Broadcast, Business-To-Business, Cable T.V., Commercial Photography, Consumer Goods, Consumer Marketing, Corporate Communications, Digital/Interactive, Direct Response Marketing, Exhibit/Trade Shows, Hispanic Market, Household Goods, Industrial, Integrated Marketing, Investor Relations, Local Marketing, Media Buying Services, Mobile Marketing, Over-50 Market, Pharmaceutical, Production, T.V.

Approx. Annual Billings: $1,000,000

Breakdown of Gross Billings by Media: Brdcst.: 80%; Comml. Photography: 20%

Edward Stephenson *(Pres)*
Scott Whitney *(CEO)*

Accounts:
Occulus Innovative Sciences; Petaluma, Ca Microcyn; 2009
Virtela; Greenwood Village, Co Network Solutions; 2009

SPOTCO
114 W 41st St 18th Fl, New York, NY 10036
Tel.: (212) 262-3355
Fax: (212) 399-0563
E-Mail: spot@spotnyc.com
Web Site: www.spotnyc.com

Employees: 70
Year Founded: 1996

Agency Specializes In: Advertising, Environmental, Graphic Design, Print, Radio, T.V., Web (Banner Ads, Pop-ups, etc.)

Drew Hodges *(Founder & CEO)*
Ilene Rosen *(Pres)*
Tom Greenwald *(Chief Strategy Officer)*
Robert Jones *(Acct Dir)*
Jay Cooper *(Dir-Creative-Brand)*
Darren Cox *(Assoc Dir-Creative-Design)*
Rachel Weiss *(Acct Mgr-Mktg)*
Kyle Fox *(Mgr-Digital Media)*
Denise Preston *(Mgr-Fin)*

Accounts:
Chicago
Cirque du Soleil Zumanity
Cirque du Soleil-Wintuk
Guthrie Theater
The Last Ship
The Weinstein Company Nine

SPRAGUE NELSON, LLC.
119 Braintree St Ste 702, Boston, MA 02134
Tel.: (617) 782-6300
E-Mail: tim@spraguenelson.com
Web Site: www.spraguenelson.com

Employees: 5
Year Founded: 2005

Agency Specializes In: Advertising, Brand Development & Integration, Collateral, Content, Corporate Identity, Digital/Interactive, Direct Response Marketing, Email, Exhibit/Trade Shows, Internet/Web Design, Local Marketing, Logo & Package Design, Media Buying Services, Media Planning, Print, Radio, Sales Promotion, Search Engine Optimization, Social Media, Sports Market, Strategic Planning/Research, T.V., Trade & Consumer Magazines, Web (Banner Ads, Pop-ups, etc.)

Approx. Annual Billings: $1,500,000

Jay Nelson *(Dir-Creative & Writer)*
Tim Sprague *(Dir-Creative & Art)*

Accounts:
Atari
Battleship Cove
Bay State College
Central Bank
Emmanuel College
Lawyers Concerned for Lawyers
Mac-Gray

SPRING ADVERTISING
301-1250 Homer St, Vancouver, BC V6B 1C6 Canada
Tel.: (604) 683-0167
Fax: (888) 607-8264
E-Mail: grow@springadvertising.com
Web Site: www.springadvertising.com

Employees: 20

Agency Specializes In: Digital/Interactive, Print, Radio, T.V.

Richard Bergin *(Partner & Client Svcs Dir)*
Rob Schlyecher *(Partner & Creative Dir)*
James Filbry *(Art Dir, Assoc Creative Dir & Copywriter)*
Jeremy Grice *(Assoc Partner & Assoc Dir-Creative)*
Caitlin Taylor *(Acct Coord)*

Accounts:
1010 Tires
Backbeat Studio Campaign: "Guerilla kick"
Brothers Landscaping Campaign: "Turf Business cards"
Capilano
The Comic Shop Campaign: "Sounds"
Four Seasons Campaign: "This Is Your Time"
Happy Planet
John Casablancas Institute
Lakota Campaign: "Back Pain"
Make Vancouver Campaign: "Scribble Slate"
NAL Sound
RainCity Housing Campaign: "Bench"
New-Seven & I Holdings Co. 7-Eleven
Tease Hair Salon
Tourism Burnaby Social Media Campaign
Urban Barn Campaign: "Lift", No Assembly Required 1
Vinyl Records Campaign: "Nirvana, Beatles, Bob Marley, Michael Jackson"
Xdress.com

SPRING, O'BRIEN & CO. INC.
30 West 26th St, 4th Fl, New York, NY 10010
Tel.: (212) 620-7100
Fax: (212) 620-7166
E-Mail: flair@spring-obrien.com
Web Site: www.spring-obrien.com

E-Mail for Key Personnel:
President: chris@spring-obrien.com
Creative Dir.: robert@spring-obrien.com
Media Dir.: jimc@spring-obrien.com
Production Mgr.: larryb@spring-obrien.com

Employees: 40
Year Founded: 1982

National Agency Associations: MCA

Agency Specializes In: Business-To-Business, Information Technology, Public Relations, Real Estate, Travel & Tourism

Approx. Annual Billings: $32,500,000

Breakdown of Gross Billings by Media: Cable T.V.: 10%; Collateral: 10%; Internet Adv.: 10%; Mags.: 25%; Newsp.: 20%; Production: 5%; Pub. Rels.: 15%; Trade Shows: 5%

Chris Spring *(Owner)*
Robert Steward *(Exec VP)*
Lauren Kaufman *(Sr VP)*
John T. Mulqueen *(Dir-Editorial)*
Martin Elder *(Mgr-Media Rels)*
Jil Krusemann *(Asst Acct Exec)*

Accounts:
Air Tahiti
Alexander & Roberts Media Relations, PR, Promotions, Strategic Partner Development
Auerbach Grayson & Co
The China National Tourist Office
East West Partners
Fidessa
Harbor View Hotel
Insight Cuba Print, Online & Broadcast Relations, Public Relations Program; 2003
International Business Wales
Las Palmas
Lost Iguana Resort & Spa
MedjetAssist PR
Miletus Trading
Morocco Tourism Board
Mountain Travel Sobek Media Relations Campaign, Public Relations

OnePipe Equities
OneTravel.com Brand Awareness, Media Relations, PR, Promotions, Strategic Partner Development
Perillo Tours
Punta Mita Resort; Mexico
Scout Real Estate Capital
Tourism Victoria
TraderPlanet.com
Visit South Walton
New-Wales Government Media Relations, Promotions, Public Relations
Yampu Latin America Tours

SPRINGBOX, LTD.

706 Congress Ave Ste A, Austin, TX 78701
Tel.: (512) 391-0065
Fax: (512) 391-0064
E-Mail: info@springbox.com
Web Site: www.springbox.com

E-Mail for Key Personnel:
President: adam@getspringbox.com
Public Relations: press@getspringbox.com

Employees: 60
Year Founded: 2004

Agency Specializes In: Advertising, Business-To-Business, Digital/Interactive, E-Commerce, Electronic Media, High Technology, Internet/Web Design, Media Buying Services

Approx. Annual Billings: $1,000,000

Breakdown of Gross Billings by Media: E-Commerce: 10%; Internet Adv.: 40%; Worldwide Web Sites: 50%

Maria Saavedra *(COO)*
Megan Coffey *(Chief Creative Officer)*
Trevor Kale *(Chief Engagement Officer)*
Michael Swail *(VP-Fin & Ops)*
Megan Berryman *(Dir-Creative)*
Tom Hudson *(Dir-Tech)*
Jennifer Thomas *(Mgr-Bus Dev)*

Accounts:
ClearCube; Austin, TX Blade PCs; 2004
Dell, Inc.

SPROKKIT

818 W 7th St, Los Angeles, CA 90017
Tel.: (213) 626-2076
Fax: (231) 232-3739
E-Mail: info@sprokkit.com
Web Site: www.sprokkit.com

Employees: 11
Year Founded: 2003

Agency Specializes In: Business Publications, Business-To-Business, Communications, Digital/Interactive, E-Commerce, Exhibit/Trade Shows, Financial, Graphic Design, Integrated Marketing, International, Internet/Web Design, Multimedia, Print, Real Estate, Restaurant, Social Media, Web (Banner Ads, Pop-ups, etc.)

Breakdown of Gross Billings by Media: Audio/Visual: 10%; Collateral: 15%; Consulting: 10%; E-Commerce: 10%; Event Mktg.: 5%; Exhibits/Trade Shows: 10%; Graphic Design: 10%; Other: 5%; Print: 15%; Worldwide Web Sites: 10%

Morgan J. Arnold *(CEO)*
Lexie Ruh Rhodes *(COO)*
Piper Baron *(Acct Dir)*
Tiffany Munoz *(Acct Mgr)*

Accounts:
Captain D's
Carl's Jr.; Carpinteria, CA
Champion Broadband
CKE Restaurants Inc.
Del Taco LLC; Lake Forest, CA
Denny's
Dunkin' Donuts
Fox Digital Media
Hardee's
Mathnasium; Los Angeles, CA Math Tutoring
Mimi's Cafe LLC; Tustin, CA
Pacific National Group Inc.; Irwindale, CA

SPROUT MARKETING

2825 E Cottonwood Pkwy Ste 450, Salt Lake City, UT 84121
Tel.: (801) 748-1500
Web Site: www.sproutmarketing.com

Agency Specializes In: Advertising, Brand Development & Integration, Market Research, Public Relations

Bruce Kennedy Law *(Owner)*
Jason Gillespie *(Mgr-Mktg)*

Accounts:
CityDeals.com Online Discount Coupon Retailer
ContentWatch Inc. Internet Management Services
Mercato Partners Consumer Business Services
Olympus Capital Housing Loan Provider
S5 Wireless Communications Services & Products
Sorenson Communications Communications Services & Products
Studies Weekly Textbook Publishers

SPRY CREATIVE

1535 W Loop S Ste 250, Houston, TX 77027
Tel.: (832) 433-7770
Web Site: www.sprycreativegroup.com

Agency Specializes In: Advertising, Brand Development & Integration, Content, Corporate Communications, Digital/Interactive, Logo & Package Design, Outdoor, Print, Social Media, Strategic Planning/Research

Jarred King *(Principal)*
Mary Shekari *(Principal)*

Accounts:
Neighbors Emergency Center

SPYDERLYNK

9559 S Kingston Ct Ste 200, Englewood, CO 80112
Tel.: (303) 790-0108
E-Mail: info@spyderlynk.com
Web Site: www.spyderlynk.com

Employees: 10

Agency Specializes In: Advertising, Brand Development & Integration, Mobile Marketing

Nicole Skogg *(Founder & CEO)*
Matt Brown *(CTO)*
Colin Daniel Quinn *(VP-Bus Dev & Sr Acct Mgr)*
Ashley Angeli *(Dir-Accts)*

Accounts:
Aveda Corporation
The Coca-Cola Company Coke Zero
Conde Nast Campaign: "Glamour Magazine Friends"
Hewlett-Packard Company
Toyota Motor Corporation

SPYGLASS BRAND MARKETING

1639 Hennepin Ave S, Minneapolis, MN 55403
Tel.: (612) 486-5959
E-Mail: info@spyglasscreative.com
Web Site: www.spyglasscreative.com

Year Founded: 2001

Agency Specializes In: Advertising, Brand Development & Integration, Graphic Design, Logo & Package Design

Molly Rice *(Founder, Pres & Partner)*
Andy Slothower *(Owner)*
Jeff Busch *(CEO & Mng Dir)*
Ben Lang *(Dir-Digital Strategy)*
Tim Palm *(Dir-Creative)*

Accounts:
eLumen

SQ1

(Formerly Square One, Inc.)
1801 N Lamar Ste 375, Dallas, TX 75202
Tel.: (214) 749-1111
Fax: (214) 379-8499
Web Site: sq1.com

Employees: 90
Year Founded: 1995

National Agency Associations: 4A's

Agency Specializes In: Advertising, Brand Development & Integration, Broadcast, Business-To-Business, Cable T.V., Co-op Advertising, Collateral, Consulting, Consumer Goods, Consumer Marketing, Consumer Publications, Corporate Communications, Corporate Identity, Digital/Interactive, Direct-to-Consumer, Electronic Media, Entertainment, Event Planning & Marketing, Experience Design, Fashion/Apparel, Food Service, Gay & Lesbian Market, Graphic Design, Guerilla Marketing, High Technology, Hispanic Market, Hospitality, Household Goods, Identity Marketing, In-Store Advertising, Integrated Marketing, Local Marketing, Logo & Package Design, Luxury Products, Magazines, Market Research, Media Buying Services, Media Planning, Merchandising, Mobile Marketing, Multicultural, Multimedia, New Product Development, Newspaper, Newspapers & Magazines, Out-of-Home Media, Outdoor, Package Design, Paid Searches, Planning & Consultation, Podcasting, Point of Sale, Print, Production, Radio, Restaurant, Retail, Sales Promotion, Sponsorship, T.V., Trade & Consumer Magazines

Approx. Annual Billings: $186,000,000

Judge Graham *(Pres)*
Ernie Capobianco *(CEO)*
John Holmes *(Partner)*
Gabe Winslow *(Partner)*
Justin Broderick *(Sr VP-Magnetic Experiences)*
Marian Leonard *(VP-Shopper Mktg)*
Brittany Ecker *(Acct Dir)*
James Squires *(Dir-Creative)*
Gregg Guzman *(Assoc Dir-Plng)*
Jenna Crane *(Acct Supvr)*
Jourdan Wilkerson *(Acct Supvr)*
Laura Kramer *(Sr Acct Exec)*
Libby Smith *(Sr Acct Exec)*
Sean Frazier *(Planner-Digital Media)*

Accounts:
American Olean
Brinker International On the Border (Digital Agency of Record), Strategy
Carolina Turkey; 2005
Crayola LLC
Daltile
Dickeys Barbecue
Dr Pepper
Jiffy Lube Website
Potters House
Tic Tangle

Washington Dental Service

SQ1
(Acquired by Ansira)

SQUARE ONE MARKETING
1993 Albany Ave, West Hartford, CT 06117
Tel.: (860) 232-7300
Fax: (860) 232-7303
E-Mail: driley@squareone-marketing.com
Web Site: www.squareone-marketing.com

E-Mail for Key Personnel:
President: driley@squareone-marketing.com

Employees: 2
Year Founded: 2003

Agency Specializes In: Advertising, Arts, Brand Development & Integration, Broadcast, Business Publications, Business-To-Business, Cable T.V., Catalogs, Co-op Advertising, Collateral, College, Commercial Photography, Communications, Computers & Software, Consulting, Consumer Goods, Consumer Marketing, Consumer Publications, Content, Corporate Communications, Corporate Identity, Digital/Interactive, Direct Response Marketing, Direct-to-Consumer, E-Commerce, Education, Electronic Media, Email, Event Planning & Marketing, Exhibit/Trade Shows, Fashion/Apparel, Financial, Gay & Lesbian Market, Graphic Design, Health Care Services, High Technology, Hospitality, Household Goods, Identity Marketing, In-Store Advertising, Industrial, Information Technology, Integrated Marketing, Internet/Web Design, Investor Relations, Leisure, Local Marketing, Logo & Package Design, Magazines, Media Buying Services, Media Planning, Medical Products, Merchandising, Mobile Marketing, Multimedia, New Product Development, Newspaper, Newspapers & Magazines, Out-of-Home Media, Outdoor, Over-50 Market, Package Design, Pharmaceutical, Planning & Consultation, Point of Purchase, Point of Sale, Print, Production, Production (Ad, Film, Broadcast), Production (Print), Promotions, Public Relations, Publicity/Promotions, Radio, Real Estate, Recruitment, Restaurant, Retail, Sales Promotion, Search Engine Optimization, Social Media, Sports Market, Strategic Planning/Research, T.V., Technical Advertising, Trade & Consumer Magazines, Transportation, Travel & Tourism, Web (Banner Ads, Pop-ups, etc.), Yellow Pages Advertising

Approx. Annual Billings: $2,000,000

David Riley *(Pres & Dir-Creative)*
Brittany Ecker *(Acct Supvr)*
Laura Kramer *(Acct Exec)*
Libby Smith *(Acct Exec)*

Accounts:
City of Meriden, CT
Colony Tools & Safety Products for Contractors

SQUARE TOMATO
900 1st Ave South Ste 411, Seattle, WA 98134
Tel.: (206) 264-0644
E-Mail: info@sqtomato.com
Web Site: www.sqtomato.com

E-Mail for Key Personnel:
Creative Dir.: frank@sqtomato.com

Employees: 12

Agency Specializes In: Advertising, Advertising Specialties, Agriculture, Asian Market, Bilingual Market, Brand Development & Integration, Broadcast, Business Publications, Business-To-Business, Cable T.V., Co-op Advertising, College, Computers & Software, Consumer Marketing, Corporate Communications, Corporate Identity, Cosmetics, Digital/Interactive, Electronics, Email, Engineering, Entertainment, Exhibit/Trade Shows, Fashion/Apparel, Financial, Food Service, Game Integration, Graphic Design, Guerilla Marketing, Health Care Services, High Technology, Hospitality, Identity Marketing, In-Store Advertising, Industrial, Integrated Marketing, International, Internet/Web Design, Leisure, Local Marketing, Luxury Products, Magazines, Market Research, Media Buying Services, Medical Products, Men's Market, Newspapers & Magazines, Outdoor, Print, Production, Production (Print), Promotions, Publishing, Radio, Recruitment, Restaurant, Retail, Social Marketing/Nonprofit, Sports Market, Strategic Planning/Research, T.V., Technical Advertising, Trade & Consumer Magazines, Transportation, Travel & Tourism, Viral/Buzz/Word of Mouth

Approx. Annual Billings: $1,600,000

Breakdown of Gross Billings by Media: Fees: $400,000; Graphic Design: $200,000; Print: $500,000; Worldwide Web Sites: $500,000

John Lin *(Mng Dir)*
Frank Clark *(Dir-Creative)*
Nikki Levine *(Dir-Art)*

Accounts:
AllSports
The Bravern
Corbis Corbis, Veer, Greenlight, Corbis Entertainment
Healthy Paws Pet Insurance
Kari Gran
Mrs. Cook's Gene Juarez

Branch

Square Tomato
833 Broadway 2nd Fl, New York, NY 10003
Tel.: (646) 820-0228
Web Site: www.sqtomato.com

Year Founded: 2012

Agency Specializes In: Alternative Advertising, Digital/Interactive, Direct Response Marketing, Email, Experience Design, Game Integration, Magazines, Newspapers & Magazines, Out-of-Home Media, Outdoor, Point of Purchase, Print, Promotions, Social Media, Web (Banner Ads, Pop-ups, etc.)

John Juan Lin *(Mng Dir)*

Accounts:
Corbis Corbis Images, Veer; 2012
Healthy Paws
Mrs. Cook's
Teavana

SQUAT NEW YORK
210 W 35th St 4th Fl, New York, NY 10001
Tel.: (917) 551-6777
E-Mail: info@squatdesign.com
Web Site: www.squatny.com

Agency Specializes In: Advertising, Brand Development & Integration, Graphic Design, Internet/Web Design, Logo & Package Design, Print, Social Media

Shiri Kornowski *(Dir-Creative)*
Melanie Boellinger *(Mgr-Production)*
James Tucci *(Strategist-Market)*
Cheungyoon Kim *(Sr Designer)*
Sonia Rahardja *(Copywriter)*

Accounts:
Pereg Gourmet Quinoa

SQUEAKY WHEEL MEDIA
640 W 28th St, New York, NY 10001
Tel.: (212) 994-5270
Fax: (212) 994-5271
E-Mail: info@squeaky.com
Web Site: www.squeaky.com

Employees: 20
Year Founded: 2001

National Agency Associations: AAF-AD CLUB-AMA-AWNY

Agency Specializes In: Advertising, Brand Development & Integration, Business-To-Business, Catalogs, Collateral, Communications, Consulting, Content, Corporate Communications, Corporate Identity, Digital/Interactive, Direct-to-Consumer, E-Commerce, Email, Fashion/Apparel, Financial, Graphic Design, Guerilla Marketing, Identity Marketing, International, Internet/Web Design, Logo & Package Design, Luxury Products, Mobile Marketing, Multicultural, Multimedia, Paid Searches, Podcasting, Print, Promotions, Publicity/Promotions, Recruitment, Sales Promotion, Search Engine Optimization, Social Marketing/Nonprofit, Sponsorship, Urban Market, Viral/Buzz/Word of Mouth, Web (Banner Ads, Pop-ups, etc.), Women's Market

Approx. Annual Billings: $3,000,000

Breakdown of Gross Billings by Media: E-Commerce: $400,000; Graphic Design: $600,000; Worldwide Web Sites: $2,000,000

Anthony Del Monte *(Founder)*
Mailet Lopez *(Co-Founder)*
Mahmud Ferdous *(Dir-Tech)*
Mona Kanwar *(Dir-Bus Dev)*
Drake Yang *(Dir-Creative)*
Luis Garay *(Mgr-Mktg)*
Dana Festejo *(Designer)*
Olivia Joel *(Designer)*
Jonathan Levi *(Designer)*

Accounts:
Chelsea Premium Outlets; Roseland, NJ
DKNY/Estee Lauder; New York, NY Delicious Night, Uncoverthecity.com; 2007
Elizabeth Arden; New York, NY www.elizabetharden.com; 2007
I Had Cancer Campaign: "A Support Community"
Lexus; New York, NY Campaign: "Lexus CT 200h", Microsite; 2007
New York Live Arts

SQUEAKYWHEEL PROMOTIONS
75 S Broadway Ste 400, White Plains, NY 10601
Tel.: (914) 304-4277
E-Mail: info@squeakywheelpromotions.com
Web Site: www.squeakywheelpromotions.com

Employees: 10

Agency Specializes In: Promotions, Public Relations

Jackie Saril *(Principal)*

Accounts:
Black Bird
Brugal Rum
Celebrifantasy
Gold Flakes Supreme
Monticello Motor Club
Morpheus Media
Ronco
Singha Beer

The Snocone Stand Inc
Social Diva
Swing Juice
UpTown Magazine

SQUID INK CREATIVE
200 W Douglas Ave Ste 230, Wichita, KS 67202
Tel.: (316) 260-3805
Web Site: www.squidinkcreative.com

Year Founded: 2009

Agency Specializes In: Advertising, Graphic Design, Internet/Web Design, Logo & Package Design

Mark Karlin *(Partner & CFO)*
Brad Painchaud *(Dir-Bus Dev)*
Derek Pletcher *(Dir-Creative)*
Mark Maack *(Mgr-Web Svcs)*
Lizzy Weber *(Mgr-Studio)*

Accounts:
Wichita Force Football
Wichita Thunder

SQUIRES & COMPANY
3624 Oak Lawn Ave Ste 200, Dallas, TX 75219
Tel.: (214) 939-9194
E-Mail: info@squirescompany.com
Web Site: www.squirescompany.com

Agency Specializes In: Advertising, Brand Development & Integration, Corporate Identity, Digital/Interactive, Internet/Web Design, Print, Promotions

Jimmy Squires *(Pres)*
Michael Beukema *(Sr Art Dir)*
Ryan Bailey *(Art Dir)*
Jamie Lucas *(Acct Dir)*
Geoff German *(Creative Dir)*
John Richardson *(Dir-Tech)*
Ben Harwell *(Assoc Dir-Tech)*
Mike Williams *(Production Mgr)*
Shana Donica *(Office Mgr)*
Jaclyn Williamson *(Designer)*

Accounts:
Jones Energy, Ltd
Permian Basin Petroleum Association

S.R. VIDEO PICTURES, LTD.
23 S Route 9W, Haverstraw, NY 10927
Tel.: (845) 429-1116
Fax: (845) 429-1117
E-Mail: mks1000@aol.com
Web Site: www.sr-video.com

Employees: 12
Year Founded: 1989

Agency Specializes In: Advertising, Advertising Specialties, Automotive, Bilingual Market, Broadcast, Business-To-Business, Cable T.V., Children's Market, Co-op Advertising, Commercial Photography, Consulting, Consumer Marketing, Corporate Identity, Digital/Interactive, Entertainment, Event Planning & Marketing, Food Service, Health Care Services, High Technology, In-Store Advertising, Industrial, Infomercials, Local Marketing, Logo & Package Design, Media Buying Services, Medical Products, Multimedia, New Product Development, Outdoor, Point of Purchase, Point of Sale, Production, Real Estate, Recruitment, Restaurant, Retail, Sales Promotion, Sports Market, T.V., Telemarketing

Approx. Annual Billings: $5,500,000

Breakdown of Gross Billings by Media: Adv. Specialities: $250,000; Brdcst.: $2,750,000; Cable T.V.: $1,750,000; T.V.: $750,000

Mitch Saul *(Owner)*

Accounts:
Atlantic Cooling Systems
Dagastino Irrigation
Davis Sport Shop
Debany Financial Group
Fellows, Hymowitz Law Firm
The Media Group; Long Island City, NY Color Match, Dura Lube
Nanuet Diamond Exchange Diamonds & Gold; 1996
Ocean Properties, Ltd.; Delray Beach, FL Hotel; 1992

SRB COMMUNICATIONS
1819 L St NW 7th Fl, Washington, DC 20036
Tel.: (202) 775-7721
Fax: (202) 777-7421
Web Site: www.srbcommunications.com

Agency Specializes In: Advertising, Brand Development & Integration, Event Planning & Marketing, Multimedia, Production (Print), Publicity/Promotions, Social Media, Strategic Planning/Research

Sheila Brooks *(Founder, Pres & CEO)*
Cecelia Smith-Budd *(CFO)*
Calvin Washington *(Dir & Mgr-Production)*
David Brigham *(Mgr-Ops)*

Accounts:
Washington Suburban Sanitary Commission

SRCPMEDIA
201 N Union St Ste 200, Alexandria, VA 22314
Tel.: (703) 683-8326
Fax: (703) 683-8826
E-Mail: srcpmedia@srcpmedia.com
Web Site: www.srcpmedia.com

Agency Specializes In: Consulting, Digital/Interactive, Media Planning, Media Training

Greg Stevens *(Founder)*
Ben Burger *(Partner)*
Paul Curcio *(Partner)*
Eric Potholm *(Partner)*
Jay Payne *(VP-Creative Svcs)*
Charlie Liebschutz *(Assoc VP)*
Betsy Vonderheid *(Dir-Media)*

Accounts:
Wal-Mart

SRI ADVERTISING
16200 Ventura Blvd, Encino, CA 91436
Tel.: (323) 851-2008
Fax: (818) 793-0351
E-Mail: susan@sriadvertising.com
Web Site: www.sriadvertising.com

Employees: 3
Year Founded: 1994

Agency Specializes In: Industrial, Newspaper, Newspapers & Magazines

Approx. Annual Billings: $750,000

Breakdown of Gross Billings by Media: Bus. Publs.: 25%; D.M.: 25%; Newsp.: 50%

Susan Isaacs *(Pres)*
Gary Terarutyunyan *(Dir-Art)*
Lisa Isaacs *(Acct Mgr)*

SRPR, INC.
2841 1/2 Avenel St, Los Angeles, CA 90039
Tel.: (323) 644-9725
Fax: (760) 567-4321
E-Mail: inquiries@shevrushpr.com
Web Site: www.shevrushpr.com

Year Founded: 2005

Agency Specializes In: Advertising, Communications, Consumer Goods, Direct Response Marketing, Financial, Health Care Services, Internet/Web Design, Legal Services, Local Marketing, Media Relations, New Technologies, Pharmaceutical, Product Placement, Public Relations, Retail, Trade & Consumer Magazines

Shev Rush *(Founder & CEO)*
Brenda Patterson *(Mng Dir)*
J. Eric Fisher *(Coord-Client Support)*

Accounts:
Bellatore, LLC.
Brulant
Estancia
Hoge, Fenton Jones & Appel, Inc.
Nixon Peabody, LLP
PW Johnson Wealth Management

SS+K AGENCY
88 Pine St 30th Fl, New York, NY 10005
Tel.: (212) 274-9500
E-Mail: contact@ssk.com
Web Site: www.ssk.com

National Agency Associations: 4A's

Agency Specializes In: Brand Development & Integration, Market Research, Social Media, Sponsorship

Lenny Stern *(Co-Founder)*
Brad Kay *(Pres & Partner)*
Bobby Hershfield *(Partner & Chief Creative Officer)*
Mark Kaminsky *(Partner)*
Rebecca Matovic *(Partner)*
John Swartz *(Sr VP & Dir-Production & Innovation)*
Jennifer Barr *(VP & Acct Dir)*
Makena Cahill *(VP & Acct Dir)*
Will Flood *(VP)*
Alyssa Wilson Georg *(Sr Dir-Art)*
Armando Flores *(Creative Dir & Copywriter)*
Anthony DeBery *(Dir-Creative Svcs)*
Kat Lam *(Assoc Dir-Creative)*
Francesca Chabrier *(Copywriter)*
Melissa Feldsher *(Acct Planner)*
Step Schultz *(Copywriter)*
Steven Young *(Copywriter)*

Accounts:
AFL-CIO Work Connects Us All
American Student Assistance Advertising, Campaign: "20SomethingProblems", Digital Strategy, PR, Production, Social Media
Comcast Corporation Internet Essentials, Marketing
Creative Artists Agency, Inc.
E*Trade Social Media
Fairlife Digital, Social Media
FreshDirect (Advertising Agency of Record) Creative, Digital, Experiential, Outdoor, Social
FWD.US Campaign: "The New Colossus"
HBO "Awkward Family Viewing", Campaign: "Appreciation", Campaign: "Faithful Dad", Campaign: "Unconditional Love", Campaign: "What's He In", Campaign: "Your Body, Your Choice", HBO Go
Honest Tea The Honest Store
Jackson Hewitt (Creative Agency of Record) Brand Positioning, Branding, Campaign: "Cashier",

Campaign: "Waitress", Campaign: "Working Hard for the Hardest Working", Customer Engagement, Direct Mail, Public Relations, Radio, Tax Preparation Service, Television Advertisements
New-Jet.com, Inc. #JetSpree, Social
JW Marriott (Lead Creative Agency)
Kraft Campaign: "Mio Speakers"
Massachusetts Teachers Assn
Mr. Pizza Campaign: "True Origins of Pizza"
The New Yorker Campaign: "Train", Marketing
Pfizer
Share Our Strength, Inc.
Smile Train Campaign: "Dreaming of Midnight", Campaign: "Power of a Smile", Campaign: "Serious Baby"
Tommy John

SSCG MEDIA GROUP

220 E 42nd St, New York, NY 10017
Web Site: www.sscgmedia.com

National Agency Associations: 4A's

Agency Specializes In: Customer Relationship Management, Digital/Interactive, Media Buying Services, Multimedia, Strategic Planning/Research

Debbie Renner *(Mng Partner)*
Johanna Jarvis *(Sr VP & Dir-Multichannel Media)*
Gwen Canter *(VP & Dir-Multichannel Media)*
Juliet Lee *(VP & Dir-Multichannel Media)*
Trish Natale *(VP & Dir-Multichannel Media)*
Kerrie Sovelove *(VP & Dir-Multichannel Media & Ops)*
Lisa Healy *(VP & Assoc Dir-Multichannel Media)*
Rebecca Straney *(Planner-Multichannel Media)*

Accounts:
Acorda
Alcon
Amgen
Bayer
Celgene
Davita Labs
EMD Serono
Genentech
Gilead
Greenstone LLC
Incyte
Mallinckrodt
MedImmune
Noven
Novo Nordisk
Otsuka
Pfizer
Quest Diagnostics
Roche
Salix
Shire
Takeda
Teva
Watson Pharmaceuticals

ST. CLAIRE GROUP

716 Adams St Ste C, Carmel, IN 46032
Tel.: (317) 816-8810
Fax: (317) 816-8820
E-Mail: bob@stclairegroup.com
Web Site: www.stclairegroup.com

E-Mail for Key Personnel:
President: bob@stclairegroup.com

Employees: 14
Year Founded: 1992

Agency Specializes In: Brand Development & Integration, Business-To-Business, Communications, Health Care Services, Medical Products, Strategic Planning/Research

Approx. Annual Billings: $18,000,000

Breakdown of Gross Billings by Media: Bus. Publs.: 5%; Collateral: 20%; Event Mktg.: 5%; Exhibits/Trade Shows: 5%; Fees: 10%; Graphic Design: 4%; Mags.: 5%; Newsp.: 10%; Outdoor: 1%; Radio: 10%; Strategic Planning/Research: 5%; T.V.: 20%

Greg Bausch *(VP & COO-St. Claire Medical Grp)*
Laura Roman *(VP & Acct Supvr)*

Accounts:
Hoosier Energy
St. Vincent Heart Center of Indiana

THE ST. GREGORY GROUP, INC.

9435 Waterstone Blvd, Cincinnati, OH 45249
Tel.: (513) 769-8440
Fax: (513) 769-1640
E-Mail: pmartin@stgregory.com
Web Site: www.stgregory.com

E-Mail for Key Personnel:
President: pmartin@stgregory.com
Creative Dir.: rfaust@stgregory.com
Media Dir.: mbauer@stgregory.com
Production Mgr.: bill@stgregory.com

Employees: 19
Year Founded: 1982

Agency Specializes In: Advertising, Automotive, Bilingual Market, Broadcast, Business-To-Business, Cable T.V., Co-op Advertising, Collateral, Communications, Consumer Goods, Consumer Marketing, Consumer Publications, Corporate Identity, Direct Response Marketing, Direct-to-Consumer, Electronic Media, Exhibit/Trade Shows, Fashion/Apparel, Financial, Government/Political, Graphic Design, Health Care Services, High Technology, Hispanic Market, In-Store Advertising, Industrial, Internet/Web Design, Leisure, Local Marketing, Logo & Package Design, Magazines, Media Buying Services, Media Planning, Medical Products, Multimedia, Newspaper, Newspapers & Magazines, Outdoor, Package Design, Point of Purchase, Point of Sale, Print, Production, Production (Ad, Film, Broadcast), Production (Print), Publicity/Promotions, Radio, Real Estate, Regional, Retail, Sales Promotion, Social Marketing/Nonprofit, Sports Market, Strategic Planning/Research, T.V., Trade & Consumer Magazines, Transportation

Patrick Martin *(Pres)*
Martin Bauer *(VP)*
Russ Faust *(VP-Creative Svcs)*
Lori Martin *(Dir-Creative)*

Accounts:
Audi Cincinnati East
Borcherding Buick GMC
Busam Subaru
Busan Nissan
Central Indiana Honda Dealers
Cincinnati-Northern Kentucky Honda Dealers
DiaPharma
Fenton
Great Traditions Land Development Corp.
Greater Michiana Honda Dealers
Hart Productions; Cincinnati, OH Consumer Show Producer
Indianapolis Acura Dealers
Jack's Glass
K-Cor
Kentuckiana Honda Dealers
Maserati of Cincinnati
Merchant's Bank
Northwest Ohio Honda Dealers
Porsche of the Village
Stafford Jewelers
TD Retail Card Services
Tri-State Sight
Volvo of the Village/Volvo of Cincinnati

ST. JACQUES MARKETING

60 Washington St Ste 101, Morristown, NJ 07960
Tel.: (973) 829-0858
Fax: (973) 624-3836
Toll Free: (800) 708-9467
E-Mail: philip@stjacques.com
Web Site: www.stjacques.com

Employees: 25
Year Founded: 1991

Agency Specializes In: Advertising, Business-To-Business, Co-op Advertising, Collateral, Communications, Consumer Marketing, Corporate Communications, Corporate Identity, Digital/Interactive, Direct Response Marketing, In-Store Advertising, Integrated Marketing, Internet/Web Design, Local Marketing, Logo & Package Design, Market Research, Media Buying Services, Media Planning, Mobile Marketing, Multimedia, Newspapers & Magazines, Package Design, Paid Searches, Print, Promotions, Real Estate, Search Engine Optimization, Social Marketing/Nonprofit, Social Media, Trade & Consumer Magazines, Web (Banner Ads, Pop-ups, etc.)

Philip St. Jacques *(Pres & Partner)*
Michael St. Jacques *(CEO)*
William Hill *(CFO)*
Meredith Solis *(VP-Acct Mgmt)*
Mike Gold *(Dir-Creative)*
Kristine Kieswer *(Dir-Content)*
Meredith Gilroy *(Sr Mgr-Qualification)*
Erin Hudecek *(Acct Exec)*
Carla Mercurio *(Acct Exec)*
Lindsey Trella *(Sr Designer)*

Accounts:
7-Eleven Convenience Stores; 2009
Boys & Girls Club Charitable Services
Century 21 Residential Real Estate
Coldwell Banker Commercial Commercial Real Estate
Jack in the Box Hamburger Restaurants; 2008
Kiddie Academy Educational Child Care
Supercuts Salon; 2008
T-Mobile US; 2007
Yum Brands! Restaurant Group

ST. JOHN & PARTNERS

5220 Belfort Rd Ste 400, Jacksonville, FL 32256-6017
Tel.: (904) 281-2500
Fax: (904) 281-0030
E-Mail: sjp@sjp.com
Web Site: www.sjp.com

Employees: 85
Year Founded: 1984

National Agency Associations: 4A's

Agency Specializes In: Advertising, Arts, Automotive, Brand Development & Integration, Branded Entertainment, Broadcast, Business-To-Business, Cable T.V., Co-op Advertising, Collateral, Consulting, Consumer Goods, Consumer Publications, Corporate Communications, Corporate Identity, Crisis Communications, Digital/Interactive, Direct Response Marketing, Direct-to-Consumer, Electronic Media, Email, Environmental, Event Planning & Marketing, Food Service, Government/Political, Graphic Design, Guerilla Marketing, Health Care Services, High Technology, Identity Marketing, In-Store Advertising, Information Technology, Integrated Marketing, Internet/Web Design, Legal Services, Leisure, Local Marketing, Logo & Package Design, Magazines, Market

Research, Media Buying Services, Media Planning, Media Relations, Media Training, Mobile Marketing, New Product Development, New Technologies, Newspaper, Newspapers & Magazines, Out-of-Home Media, Outdoor, Package Design, Paid Searches, Planning & Consultation, Point of Purchase, Point of Sale, Print, Product Placement, Production, Promotions, Public Relations, Publicity/Promotions, Radio, Real Estate, Recruitment, Regional, Restaurant, Retail, Sales Promotion, Search Engine Optimization, Social Marketing/Nonprofit, Social Media, Sponsorship, Sports Market, Stakeholders, Strategic Planning/Research, Sweepstakes, T.V., Trade & Consumer Magazines, Travel & Tourism, Viral/Buzz/Word of Mouth, Women's Market

Approx. Annual Billings: $120,000,000 Fees Capitalized

Breakdown of Gross Billings by Media: Internet Adv.: 6%; Mags.: 1%; Newsp.: 6%; Outdoor: 2%; Radio: 10%; T.V.: 75%

Dan St. John *(Chm & CEO)*
Jeff McCurry *(Pres & COO)*
Peter Herbst *(VP & Exec Creative Dir)*
Shane Santiago *(VP & Dir-Digital)*
Celia Weeks *(VP & Dir-HR)*
Laura Brown *(Dir-Print Production)*
Shawn Parks *(Assoc Dir-Media)*
Alexa Orndoff *(Acct Mgr-Digital)*
Lyndsay Rossman *(Acct Supvr-PR)*
Lauren Collie *(Sr Strategist-Media)*
Kristen Bankert *(Copywriter)*

Accounts:
American Health Care Association Care Conversations Mobile Site
Daytona International Speedway
The Florida Lottery; Tallahassee, FL Campaign: "Big Zax Snak", Campaign: "Cocka-doodle-do", Campaign: "Dress Up", Campaign: "Lucky For Life-Jake", State Lottery; 2009
Florida Prepaid College Board (Agency of Record) Creative Advertising, Digital, Social Media
Jacksonville Chamber of Commerce (Cornerstone); Jacksonville, FL Economic Development; 2001
PARC Management, LLC; Jacksonville, FL Amusement Parks; 2007
State of Florida Department of the Lottery Cash 3, Fantasy 5, Florida Lotto, Mega Money, Play 4, Powerball, Scratch Offs
Terrell Hogan; Jacksonville, FL Law Firm; 2001
Wounded Warrior Project Helicopters Poster, Rocket Launcher Poster
Zaxby's Franchising, Inc.; Athens, GA Campaign: "Zaxby's TV - Hotness", Restaurant Chain; 2002

ST8MNT INC.
1585 Mallory Ln Ste 201, Brentwood, TN 37027
Tel.: (615) 818-0329
Fax: (615) 818-0347
E-Mail: info@st8mnt.com
Web Site: www.st8mnt.com

Agency Specializes In: Advertising, Brand Development & Integration, Broadcast, Collateral, Digital/Interactive, Environmental, Internet/Web Design, Package Design, Print

Bethany Newman *(Owner & Pres)*
Josh Newman *(Principal & Dir-Creative)*
Alex Pavkov *(Mgr-Production)*
Austin Hale *(Sr Designer)*

Accounts:
Randa Solutions

STAATS FALKENBERG & PARTNERS INC.
PO Box 1466, Austin, TX 78767
Tel.: (512) 579-3800
Fax: (512) 579-3801
E-Mail: info@staats.com
Web Site: www.staats.com

E-Mail for Key Personnel:
President: howard@staats.com
Creative Dir.: david@staats.com

Employees: 10
Year Founded: 1985

National Agency Associations: AD CLUB

Agency Specializes In: Advertising, Advertising Specialties, Brand Development & Integration, Business-To-Business, Collateral, Communications, Consulting, Corporate Communications, Crisis Communications, Graphic Design, Internet/Web Design, Logo & Package Design, Market Research, Media Planning, Production (Ad, Film, Broadcast), Production (Print), Public Relations, Publicity/Promotions, Search Engine Optimization, Social Marketing/Nonprofit, Strategic Planning/Research, Trade & Consumer Magazines

Howard Falkenberg *(Pres)*

Accounts:
Aldi Development Partners, LLC
HealthTronics, Inc.
Marlin Atlantis
USIndigo LLC
White Construction Company

STACKPOLE & PARTNERS ADVERTISING
222 Merrimac St, Newburyport, MA 01950
Tel.: (978) 463-6600
Fax: (978) 463-6610
E-Mail: contact@stackpolepartners.com
Web Site: www.stackpolepartners.com

E-Mail for Key Personnel:
Creative Dir.: creative@stackpolepartners.com
Media Dir.: media@stackpolepartners.com

Year Founded: 1984

Agency Specializes In: Above-the-Line, Advertising, Alternative Advertising, Automotive, Below-the-Line, Brand Development & Integration, Broadcast, Business Publications, Business-To-Business, Cable T.V., Co-op Advertising, Commercial Photography, Communications, Consulting, Consumer Publications, Corporate Communications, Corporate Identity, Custom Publishing, Customer Relationship Management, Digital/Interactive, Direct Response Marketing, Direct-to-Consumer, Education, Electronic Media, Email, Engineering, Environmental, Event Planning & Marketing, Exhibit/Trade Shows, Financial, Graphic Design, Guerilla Marketing, High Technology, Industrial, Internet/Web Design, Legal Services, Local Marketing, Logo & Package Design, Magazines, Market Research, Media Buying Services, Media Planning, Medical Products, Multimedia, New Technologies, Newspaper, Newspapers & Magazines, Out-of-Home Media, Outdoor, Package Design, Planning & Consultation, Podcasting, Point of Purchase, Point of Sale, Print, Production, Production (Ad, Film, Broadcast), Production (Print), Promotions, Public Relations, Publicity/Promotions, Publishing, RSS (Really Simple Syndication), Radio, Retail, Sales Promotion, Search Engine Optimization, T.V., Transportation, Viral/Buzz/Word of Mouth, Web (Banner Ads, Pop-ups, etc.)

Approx. Annual Billings: $8,400,000

Peter Stackpole *(Pres)*
Erin Bilenchi *(Dir-Media)*
Nicole Bless *(Dir-Art)*
Alison Fruh *(Dir-Fin & Ops)*
Trev Stair *(Dir-Creative)*
Clara Lubansky *(Acct Mgr)*

Accounts:
Agenta Consulting
Andover Bank
Beacon Recovery Group; Boston, MA; 2000
Bridgewater Savings Bank; Bridgewater, MA; 2005
Coady Law; Boston, MA; 1999
DOAR Litigation Consulting; Lynnbrook, NY; 2004
Fiduciary Trust
First & Ocean Bank
First Trade Union Bank
Georgetown Savings Bank; Georgetown, MA; 2005
Holland & Knight
HUB Technologies
LexisNexis; Dayton, OH; 1996
Llesiant; Austin, TX; 2005
Lowell General Hospital
Matthew Bender; New York, NY; 1995
Merchants Leasing; Hooksett, NH; 2003
North American Systems
Nutter McClennen & Fish; Boston, MA; 2004
Riker, Danzig, Hyland, Perretti; Morristown, NJ; 2002
Rudman Winchell; Bangor, ME Corporate Identity System, Marketing Communications Strategy, New Brand Architecture, New Logo Design, Web Site
Shephard's; Colorado Springs, CO; 1995
Skinder-Strauss Associates
St. Marys Credit Union
Thomson Interactive Media
UFP Technologies; Georgetown, MA; 1999
Watertown Savings Bank; Watertown, MA; 2002
Wolters Kluwer; Chicago, IL; 2006

STADIUM AGENCY
W 2nd St, Perrysburg, OH 43551
Tel.: (419) 304-5684
Web Site: www.stadiumfirm.com

Year Founded: 2013

Agency Specializes In: Advertising, Internet/Web Design, Social Media

Steven Kluber *(Head-Sls)*
Larry Mauter *(Specialist-Ecommerce)*

Accounts:
Charles E. Boyk Law Offices LLC
Toledo City Paper

STALKER ADVERTISING & PUBLIC RELATIONS LLC
24853 S 194th St, Queen Creek, AZ 85142
Tel.: (419) 340-2977
E-Mail: info@stalkeradvertising.com
Web Site: www.stalkeradvertising.com

Agency Specializes In: Advertising, Brand Development & Integration, Corporate Identity, Digital/Interactive, Internet/Web Design, Outdoor, Print, Public Relations, Search Engine Optimization, T.V.

Sharon Kalinowski *(Principal)*

Accounts:
Golden Retriever Rescue Resource

STAMATS
615 5th St SE, Cedar Rapids, IA 52406-1888
Tel.: (319) 364-6167
Fax: (319) 365-5421
Toll Free: (800) 553-8878
E-Mail: info@stamats.com
Web Site: www.stamatscommunications.com

E-Mail for Key Personnel:
President: guy.wendler@stamats.com

Year Founded: 1923

National Agency Associations: AMA-DMA

Agency Specializes In: Brand Development & Integration, Communications, Consulting, Direct Response Marketing, Faith Based, Internet/Web Design, Planning & Consultation, Production, Strategic Planning/Research

Guy H. Wendler *(Pres & CEO)*
Robert A. Sevier *(Sr VP)*
William S. Stamats *(VP & Gen Mgr)*
Tony Dellamaria *(VP & Grp Publr-Comml Buildings)*
Kim Leonard *(VP-Info Svcs)*
Jen Visser *(Sr Strategist-Digital)*

Accounts:
California State Polytechnic University
Florida International University
Physicians' Clinics of Iowa, P.C.
Saint Anthony Hospital; Chicago, IL
Seimens

STAMEN DESIGN

2017 Mission St Ste 300, San Francisco, CA 94110
Tel.: (415) 558-1610
Fax: (415) 651-9485
E-Mail: info@stamen.com
Web Site: www.stamen.com

Employees: 12
Year Founded: 2001

Agency Specializes In: Digital/Interactive, Internet/Web Design

Eric Rodenbeck *(Founder, CEO & Dir-Creative)*
Shawn Allen *(Partner & Dir-Interaction)*
Bill Conneely *(Gen Mgr)*
Julie Bottrell Delbuck *(Dir-Ops)*
Michael Neuman *(Dir-Design)*
Beth Schechter *(Mgr-Education & Outreach)*
Heather Grates *(Designer-Visual)*

Accounts:
Adobe Kuler Application Software Development Services
Global Business Network Business Consulting Services
INdigital Telecommunication Services
Quokka Sports Sports Entertainment Services
Yahoo! Nikon Stunning Gallery Online Photo Management Services

STAMP IDEA GROUP, LLC

(Formerly LWT Communications)
111 Washington Ave, Montgomery, AL 36104
Tel.: (334) 244-9933
Fax: (334) 244-7713
Toll Free: (888) 244-9933
E-Mail: stamp@stampideas.com
Web Site: stampideas.com

E-Mail for Key Personnel:
President: allred@lwtcom.com

Employees: 29
Year Founded: 1959

National Agency Associations: AAF

Agency Specializes In: Education, Real Estate, Retail, Travel & Tourism

Approx. Annual Billings: $16,000,000

David Allred *(Partner)*
Jim Leonard *(Partner-Strategic Mktg, Copywriting & Creative Oversight)*
Bruce Reid *(Partner)*
Leah Evans *(Mgr-Ops)*
Roberta Pinkston *(Supvr-Media)*
Colin Campbell *(Project Coord-Interactive)*

Accounts:
Abec Resorts
AIM: Abstinence in Motion Project
Alabama River Clean Water Partnership
Aronov Marketing Cooperative
Columbus Cultural Arts Alliance
Kaufman Gilpin McKenzie Thomas Weiss, P.C.
Kelley Bartlett Conservancy
Knud Nielsen
The Locker Room
Tuskegee Airmen Memorial Fund

STAN ADLER ASSOCIATES

333 7th Ave, New York, NY 10001
Tel.: (212) 863-4100
Fax: (212) 863-4141
E-Mail: stan@stanadler.com
Web Site: www.stanadler.com

Employees: 35
Year Founded: 1980

Approx. Annual Billings: $5,000,000

Joella Autorino *(Acct Dir & Dir-New media)*
Stan Adler *(Dir-Creative)*
Maura Ryan *(Dir-Bus Dev-Fin Svcs)*
Claudia Meyers *(Mgr-PrePress)*
Laura Samet *(Mgr-Print Production)*
Amanda Boulton *(Sr Designer)*
Betty Hinchman *(Sr Writer)*
Andrew Lin *(Sr Designer-Production)*

Accounts:
Acadia Realty Trust
Davis
Deutsche Asset Management
Dreyfus; New York, NY Financial Services; 1993
Farm Family
Melanoma Research Foundation
Morgan Stanley; New York, NY Financial Services; 2001
UBS
Wells Fargo

STANDARD TIME

163 S La Brea Ave, Los Angeles, CA 90036
Tel.: (310) 822-7200
Web Site: www.standardtimela.com

Agency Specializes In: Advertising, Brand Development & Integration, Broadcast, Digital/Interactive, Social Media

John Cochran *(CEO)*
Jake Levin *(Head-Digital Creative)*
Michael Sharp *(Exec Creative Dir)*
Celine Nahas *(Sr Dir-Art)*
Andrea Carrillo Iglesias *(Dir-Art & Designer)*
Joshua Kopeika *(Assoc Dir-Creative)*
Spencer Somers *(Assoc Dir-Creative)*
Laura Wimer *(Assoc Dir-Creative)*
Alex Stevens *(Sr Graphic Designer)*

Accounts:
Ole Smoky Moonshine (Agency of Record) Campaign: "C'mon Live a Little"
Olloclip

STANTON & EVERYBODY

1424 4th Ave Ste 828, Seattle, WA 98101
Tel.: (206) 224-4242
Web Site: www.stantonandeverybody.com

Lisa Dahlby *(Project Mgr & Acct Supvr)*

STANTON PUBLIC RELATIONS & MARKETING

880 3rd Ave, New York, NY 10022
Tel.: (212) 366-5300
Fax: (212) 366-5301
E-Mail: info@stantonprm.com
Web Site: www.stantonprm.com

Employees: 20
Year Founded: 1995

Agency Specializes In: Business-To-Business, Communications, Crisis Communications, Media Relations, Public Relations, Sponsorship

Alex Stanton *(CEO)*
Tom Faust *(Mng Dir)*
Charlyn Lusk *(Mng Dir)*
Katrin Carola Lieberwirth *(VP)*
George Sopko *(VP)*
Kerri Donner *(Mgr-Comm)*
Scott Lessne *(Sr Acct Exec)*
Olivia Ludington *(Asst Acct Exec)*

Accounts:
Berkline (Agency of Record)
Carl Marks Advisory Group Public Relations
Conning & Company Communications, Media Relations, Public Relations
Delos Insurance Company Insurance Services
Drexel University External Communications
Pine Brook Road Partners (Agency of Record)
Seedko Financial
Sun Capital Partners Inc
Wall Street Access

STAPLEGUN

204 N Robinson Ste 2000, Oklahoma City, OK 73102
Tel.: (405) 601-9430
Fax: (405) 708-6349
Web Site: www.staplegun.us

Agency Specializes In: Advertising, Media Planning, Social Media

Brent McCutchen *(Owner)*
Philip Baker *(CEO-Creative)*
Matthew Grice *(Sr VP)*
Brandon Inda *(Dir-Corp Tech)*
Ryan McNeill *(Dir-DP)*
Chad Osko *(Dir-Digital & Social Media)*
Sean Ferguson *(Assoc Dir-Creative)*
Nicholas Archibald *(Acct Exec)*
Jeanette Schreiber *(Writer-Technical)*

Accounts:
A+ Oklahoma Schools
CJ Dental
Griffin's Foods Ltd.
SandRidge Energy, Inc.

STAPLES MARKETING

(Name Changed to AFFIRM)

STAR MARKETING INC

3532 Katella Ave Ste 205, Los Alamitos, CA 90720
Tel.: (562) 799-1555
Web Site: www.starmarketing.com

Year Founded: 1987

Agency Specializes In: Advertising, Brand Development & Integration, Collateral, Print, Public Relations, Strategic Planning/Research

Chris Sandberg *(Pres)*

Accounts:
ABS Auto Auctions
Active Sales Co. Inc.
Amsino
Design Guild Moulding
Lakin Tire
Norfox
Norman Fox & Co
Rent What Inc.
Sew What, Inc.
Volcanic Red Coffees

STAR7
289 Pilot Rd Ste B, Las Vegas, NV 89119
Tel.: (702) 253-1551
Fax: (702) 253-7993
E-Mail: info@star7vegas.com
Web Site: www.star7vegas.com

Employees: 7
Year Founded: 1993

Agency Specializes In: Advertising, Brand Development & Integration, Business-To-Business, Collateral, Direct Response Marketing, Entertainment, Graphic Design, Local Marketing, Media Buying Services, Outdoor, Public Relations, Social Marketing/Nonprofit

Approx. Annual Billings: $2,500,000

Breakdown of Gross Billings by Media: Brdcst.: $250,000; Bus. Publs.: $750,000; Collateral: $875,000; Consumer Publs.: $250,000; Other: $125,000; Pub. Rels.: $250,000

Cary Duckworth *(Owner)*

Accounts:
The Alexander Dawson School at Rainbow Mountain; Las Vegas, NV Private Schooling; 2008
Audi Henderson; Henderson, NV Automobiles; 2007
Bank of Nevada
Epicurean Charitable Foundation
Findlay Chevrolet; Las Vegas, NV Automobiles; 2006
Findlay Volkswagen; Henderson, NV Automobiles; 2006
Lamborghini Las Vegas
The Smith Center for Performing Arts; Las Vegas, NV Performing Arts Center; 2006
Supreme Court of Nevada
The Village at Lake Las Vegas

STARCOM MEDIAVEST GROUP
35 W Wacker Dr, Chicago, IL 60601-1723
Tel.: (312) 220-3535
Fax: (312) 220-6530
Web Site: usa.starcomww.com/

Employees: 900
Year Founded: 1997

National Agency Associations: 4A's-WOMMA

Agency Specializes In: Media Buying Services, Planning & Consultation, Sponsorship

Danielle Gonzales *(Mng Dir & Exec VP)*
Andrew Kasprzycki *(Mng Dir & Exec VP)*
Karla Knecht *(Mng Dir & Exec VP)*
Patrick O'Connor *(CFO)*
Jonathan Hoffman *(Pres-Experience Design)*
Laura Krajecki *(Pres-Global Human Experience Strategy)*
John Sheehy *(Pres-Global Ops)*
Lisa Weinstein *(Pres-Global Digital, Data & Analytics)*
Laura Desmond *(CEO-Global)*
Monica Gadsby *(CEO-SMG US Multicultural-Latin America)*
Chris Nolan *(CEO-Australia)*
David N. Gould *(Exec VP & Mng Dir-Digital-Global)*
Lisa Hurwitz *(Exec VP & Mng Dir-P&G)*
Mark Pavia *(Mng Dir-Digital & Exec VP)*
Alycia Mason *(Exec VP & Grp Dir)*
Valerie Beauchamp *(Exec VP & Dir-Global Bus Dev)*
Warren Griffiths *(Exec VP & Dir-Global Digital-SMG Global Digital Investments)*
Tracey Scheppach *(Exec VP & Dir-Innovations-VivaKi)*
Becky Walden *(Exec VP & Dir-Global Network Clients)*
Kevin Gallagher *(Exec VP-Local Activation)*
Matt Kain *(Exec VP-Global Network Client Ops)*
Lena Petersen *(Exec VP-Product & Partnership-Global)*
Kate Sirkin *(Exec VP-Res)*
Jill Vannatta *(Exec VP)*
Gina Jacobson *(Sr VP & Grp Dir)*
Jill Sylvester *(Sr VP & Grp Dir-Tech & Ops Solutions)*
Magen Hanrahan *(Sr VP & Media Dir)*
Dan Bruinsma *(Sr VP & Dir-Activation)*
Juan Davila *(Sr VP & Dir-Content Mktg-LIQUIDTHREAD Americas)*
Kathy Dillon *(Sr VP & Dir)*
Victor Garcia *(Sr VP & Dir-Americas Bus Dev)*
Nicole Hayes *(Sr VP & Dir)*
Erin Houg *(Sr VP & Dir-Digital)*
Helen Katz *(Sr VP & Dir-Res)*
Adam Kruse *(Sr VP & Dir-Global)*
Moira Lisowski *(Sr VP & Dir-Digital-Kraft)*
Gina Mazzorana *(Sr VP & Dir-Global Integrated Product-P&G)*
Michelle McGowan *(Sr VP & Dir-Corp Comm)*
John Melone *(Sr VP & Dir-Sprint)*
Rosemary Miller *(Sr VP & Dir-Ops)*
Tracey Paull *(Sr VP & Dir-Digital Media)*
Trina Potter *(Sr VP & Dir-Media)*
Kati Sciortino *(Sr VP & Dir-Human Experience Strategy)*
Shelley Watson *(Sr VP & Dir-Activation)*
Jeff Dow *(Sr VP-Digital Strategy & Analytics-Global)*
Harvin Furman *(Sr VP-COE Digital Acceleration)*
Kevin Lange *(Sr VP-Social Media)*
Chad Maxwell *(Sr VP-Audience & Measurement Solutions)*
Ravi Moorthy *(Sr VP-USA)*
Steve Murtos *(Sr VP)*
Bryan Simkins *(Sr VP-Tech & Activation Grp)*
Kim Yates *(Sr VP-Strategy & Idea Design-Kraft Foods)*
Mercedes Ritchey *(VP, Head-Integrated Agency & Dir-Comm Plng)*
Peteris Freimanis *(VP & Brand Dir)*
Jeff Hughes *(VP & Media Dir)*
Desiree Benson *(VP, Dir-Human Experience & Strategist)*
Courtney Ballantini *(VP & Dir-Media)*
Cecilia Bizon *(VP & Dir-Media)*
Daryl Blanco *(VP & Dir)*
Darcy Bowe *(VP & Dir-Media)*
Beth Bradley *(VP & Dir-Human Experience Strategy)*
Katy Carlin *(VP & Dir)*
Kira Clifton *(VP & Dir)*
Cindy DeLeon *(VP & Dir-Strategy)*
Tracy Reimers Donahue *(VP & Dir-Media)*
Brooke Gilbertson *(VP & Dir-Client Ops)*
Sarah Greenspan *(VP & Dir)*
Katharine Greis *(VP & Dir-Bus Dev)*
Ross Grimes *(VP & Dir-Media)*
Adrienne Gutierrez *(VP & Dir-Media)*
Jonathan Haynes *(VP & Dir-Analytics)*
Zach Isaacs *(VP & Dir)*
Stacy Karabuykov *(VP & Dir-Media)*
Elizabeth Leonard *(VP & Dir-Digital)*
Amanda Lombardi *(VP & Dir)*
Marissa Lutz *(VP & Dir-Media)*
Diane Marshall *(VP & Dir)*
Dan Matarelli *(VP & Dir)*
Brooke McCaughrin *(VP-Strategy & Dir-Media)*
Ann Poulose *(VP & Dir-Media)*
Jeff Razniewski *(VP & Dir-Media)*
Colleen Robson *(VP & Dir-Client Ops)*
Kerry Ross *(VP & Dir-Media)*
Susan Seams *(VP & Dir-Strategy)*
Timothy Sobieszczyk *(VP & Dir)*
Gumala Steele *(VP & Dir)*
Cristina Torres *(VP & Dir)*
Helen McCormack *(VP & Assoc Dir-Media)*
Grant Anderson *(VP & Reg Acct Dir)*
Sabrina Pierrard *(VP-Human Experience Strategy-Global)*
Dorthea Fenner *(Head-Digital Ops)*
Kendall Hidalgo *(Acct Dir-Global)*
Anthony Thomas *(Acct Dir)*
Cara Wetters *(Media Dir)*
Amy Adams *(Dir-Digital Activation)*
Chris Aubin *(Dir-Reg Mktg & Multicultural)*
Dana Belanger *(Dir-Experience Strategy)*
Becky Blomquist *(Dir-Digital)*
Donna Booth *(Dir-Human Experience Centers-Global)*
Lauren Brand *(Dir-Media)*
Dianne Brewer *(Dir)*
Candace Calandriello *(Dir-Strategy Media)*
Emily Carlisle *(Dir)*
Antonio Casanova *(Dir-SEO)*
Alison Ciccione *(Dir-Media)*
Damien Evans *(Dir-Investment-Global)*
William Ferrell *(Dir-Data & Analytics-Melbourne)*
Maureen Glure *(Dir-Media)*
Mark Griffin *(Dir)*
Lauren Hadley *(Dir-Integrated Insights)*
Katrina Laney *(Dir-Media Strategy & Activation)*
Michael Leger *(Dir-Human Experience-Anheuser-Busch InBev)*
Sarah Louise Marren *(Dir-Media)*
Jennifer Mathis *(Dir-Media)*
Colleen Meenan *(Dir)*
Nicole Newsome *(Dir-Media)*
Dan O'Brien *(Dir-Strategy)*
Brad Passo *(Dir-Digital Activation)*
Seema Patel *(Dir-Youth Human Experience Center-Global)*
Jacob Rice *(Dir-Search Engine Mktg-SEO & PPC)*
Doug Salo *(Dir-Media-Natl Video & Print Activation-Bank Of America Acct)*
Sterling Sanders *(Dir-Global Design, Global Growth, Bus Dev & Design)*
Alichia Sawitoski *(Dir-Digital)*
Jack Sullivan *(Dir-Media)*
Samantha Tenicki *(Dir)*
Marnie Tyler *(Dir-Media)*
Jennifer Vianello *(Dir-Bus Dev-Global)*
Courtney Weg *(Dir-Bus Strategy)*
Emily Yale *(Dir-Programmatic)*
Joel Yeomans *(Dir)*
Nicole Bahls *(Assoc Dir-Media-P&G)*
Amy Barrett *(Assoc Dir-Kraft)*
Jessica Bartucci *(Assoc Dir)*
Megan Boveri *(Assoc Dir-Media)*
Jennafer Bridgemann Ocenas *(Assoc Dir-Tech & Ops Solutions)*
Nadine Brown *(Assoc Dir-Bus Ops)*
Rebecca Carpenter *(Assoc Dir)*
Rebecca Chodroff *(Assoc Dir)*
Elle Cordes *(Assoc Dir)*
Lindsey Cox *(Assoc Dir)*
Stacie Cwik *(Assoc Dir-Media-Human Experience-Deliver)*
Alyssa D'Anna *(Assoc Dir)*
Lee Dunbar *(Assoc Dir)*
Lindsay Eckert *(Assoc Dir)*
Leslie Engel *(Assoc Dir-TAAG Analytics)*
Kathryn Ericksen *(Assoc Dir-Publ Activation Grp)*
Megan Fesl *(Assoc Dir-TAAG)*
Carly Fisher *(Assoc Dir-Media-Digital)*
Erika Flogstad *(Assoc Dir-Media)*
Sara Ford *(Assoc Dir-Media)*
Micah Fortenberry *(Assoc Dir-Ops)*
Meghan Garrity *(Assoc Dir-Media)*
Aileen Gattuso *(Assoc Dir-Media)*
Michael Gilloon *(Assoc Dir)*

Leigh Godin *(Assoc Dir)*
Meghan O'Keefe Gorman *(Assoc Dir)*
Morgan Gorskey *(Assoc Dir-Media)*
Mara Grigg *(Assoc Dir)*
Ed Hausser *(Assoc Dir-Media)*
Jess Heitner *(Assoc Dir-Media)*
Kendall Hidalgo *(Assoc Dir-Media)*
Stephanie Howard *(Assoc Dir-Media)*
Bob Hunt *(Assoc Dir-Samsung)*
Evan Jackson *(Assoc Dir)*
Kathleen Jagielo *(Assoc Dir-Media)*
Jon Jarog *(Assoc Dir-Media)*
Erin Kellan *(Assoc Dir-Media)*
Caitlin Krois *(Assoc Dir-Digital, Kraft Foods)*
Lisa Kuenning *(Assoc Dir-Media)*
Adriane Lepore *(Assoc Dir)*
Jordan Levinson *(Assoc Dir-Activation)*
Allison Livermore *(Assoc Dir-Media)*
Kelsey Lofstrand *(Assoc Dir)*
Kelly Loscher *(Assoc Dir-Best Buy)*
Amanda Ludwig *(Assoc Dir)*
Julie Malaniuk *(Assoc Dir-Media)*
Kristin Mann *(Assoc Dir-Strategy)*
Sara Markey *(Assoc Dir)*
Kathryn Mathews *(Assoc Dir)*
Gerard McKee *(Assoc Dir-Media-Define & Design-ESPN Team)*
Christie McNamara *(Assoc Dir)*
Katherine Miles *(Assoc Dir-Media)*
Melissa Mitchell *(Assoc Dir)*
Joslyn Moya *(Assoc Dir)*
Merideth Murray *(Assoc Dir-Media)*
Jade Nelson *(Assoc Dir)*
Susan Niemczyk *(Assoc Dir)*
Morgan Otte *(Assoc Dir-Media)*
Diana Patterson *(Assoc Dir-Media)*
Kylea Pohl *(Assoc Dir)*
Bethany Purdy *(Assoc Dir-Ops-Global)*
Matthew Reder *(Assoc Dir-Media)*
Gabby Rodriguez *(Assoc Dir-Media)*
Mandy Rogers *(Assoc Dir-Media)*
Audra Rosen *(Assoc Dir)*
Paola Rovelo *(Assoc Dir)*
Michael Ryan *(Assoc Dir-Media)*
Ryan Schuster *(Assoc Dir)*
Whitney Sewell *(Assoc Dir)*
Ryan Shaw *(Assoc Dir-Integrated Mktg Comm)*
Anne Siebert *(Assoc Dir-Media-Publ COE)*
John Smith *(Assoc Dir)*
Bill Stanton *(Assoc Dir-Media)*
Katie Tangri *(Assoc Dir)*
Stephen Teller *(Assoc Dir-Innovations & Bus Intelligence)*
Cheryl Trauernicht *(Assoc Dir-Media & Digital)*
Angela Ventimiglia *(Assoc Dir)*
Kent Weaver *(Assoc Dir)*
Mike Witham *(Assoc Dir)*
Craig Wojtak *(Assoc Dir)*
Ryan Worthy *(Assoc Dir-Media)*
Barbara Zaucha *(Assoc Dir-Integrated Insights)*
Jason Atwood *(Mgr)*
Megan Barnicle *(Mgr-Search)*
Samantha Belbin *(Mgr-Connections-P&G)*
Brianne Boles-Marshall *(Mgr-Media-Procter & Gamble)*
Daniel Callahan *(Mgr-Design Support & Competitive Reporting)*
Tara DeFreytas *(Mgr-Digital Media)*
Sara Dougadir *(Mgr-Connections)*
Grant Dudgeon *(Mgr-Data & Analytics)*
Kate Feeley *(Mgr)*
Scott Franzer *(Mgr-Digital-P&G Programmatic)*
Alden Golab *(Mgr-Audience & Measurement Solutions)*
Katie Griffith *(Mgr-Connections)*
Kate Hinz *(Mgr-Connections)*
Kelly Kantarski *(Mgr-Programmatic)*
Tom Pfeil *(Mgr-Analytics)*
Chris Powers *(Mgr-Activation)*
Crissy Rea-Bain *(Mgr-Connections)*
Sharika Sheaffer *(Mgr-Media)*
Allison Zilbershatz *(Mgr-Dev & Production)*
Tim Quirsfeld *(Supvr & Analyst-Digital Media)*
Sydney Allen *(Supvr-Digital Media)*
Stephanie Arno *(Supvr-Video Drive)*
Katie Back *(Supvr-Multicultural Media)*
Jillian Ben-Ezra *(Supvr-Media)*
Erika Benford *(Supvr-Digital)*
Kelley Bond *(Supvr-Media)*
Isaiah Bradford *(Supvr-Print Platform Media)*
Brittney Brenner *(Supvr-Digital Media)*
Eliza Burns *(Supvr-Media)*
Jacalyn Ceglinski *(Supvr-Digital Media)*
Betsy Chaklos *(Supvr-Digital Media)*
Tyler Crawford *(Supvr-Strategy & Digital Media)*
Julie Dazzo *(Supvr-Media-P&G Femcare Total)*
Cullen Deady *(Supvr-Media Plng-P&G)*
Michel DePaola *(Supvr-Media-Activation)*
Laura Drugan *(Supvr)*
Lauren East *(Supvr-Media)*
Melissa Elegant *(Supvr-Media)*
Amanda Emerson *(Supvr-Media-Spark SMG Hispanic, Kao Brands, Daisy & CiCi's)*
Cortez Ervin *(Supvr)*
Maggie Erzinger *(Supvr-Digital Media)*
Lauren Fisher *(Supvr-Media-Kraft Natl Brdcst Media)*
Brittnee Fitzgerald *(Supvr-Media)*
Tom Foreman *(Supvr-Experience Design)*
Betsy Frisby *(Supvr-Digital Media)*
Robbie Fuss *(Supvr-Media)*
Drew Gascon *(Supvr-Media)*
Ashley Geib *(Supvr-Media)*
Nanah Han *(Supvr-Media)*
Derek Heathcote *(Supvr-Media)*
Margaret Hemphill *(Supvr-Media)*
Jamie Hirzel *(Supvr-Comm)*
Crystal Hubert *(Supvr-Media)*
Russell Humes *(Supvr-Media)*
Alexis Hymen *(Supvr-Digital & Brdcst Media)*
Brad Impson *(Supvr)*
Ellen Jepsen *(Supvr-Media)*
Kirsten Kamerman *(Supvr-Media)*
Michele Kim *(Supvr-Media)*
Tommy Kircher *(Supvr)*
Madeline Kirklighter *(Supvr-Kellogg, Strategic Plng & Ops-US & Latin America)*
Chelsie Koenig *(Supvr-Shopper Mktg)*
Laura Krain *(Supvr-Human Experience & Media)*
Lindsey Kroll *(Supvr-Media)*
Alexandra Lampros *(Supvr-Media)*
Heather Lanham *(Supvr-Media)*
Jacqueline Lee *(Supvr-Media)*
Liz Mack *(Supvr-Media)*
Elizabeth Marino *(Supvr-Media)*
Caitlin Mathews *(Supvr-Digital Media)*
Daniella McConnell *(Supvr-Media Strategy-Mars Multicultural)*
Sara McGee *(Supvr-Media)*
Kassie Mclaughlin *(Supvr-Media Strategy)*
Angela McPhillips *(Supvr-Media)*
Jessica Mickles *(Supvr)*
Beth Cieminski O'Meara *(Supvr-Media)*
Haley Oberon-Levoff *(Supvr-Digital Media)*
Nadine Oddi *(Supvr-P&G Prestige Luxury Strategic Plng & Buying)*
Elizabeth Orlando *(Supvr-Media)*
Danielle Ortega *(Supvr-Media)*
Paul Cuong Pham *(Supvr-Media)*
Andrea Piszczor *(Supvr-Bus Dev)*
Elizabeth Potter *(Supvr-Media)*
Chris Prinz *(Supvr-Media)*
Jessica Rosul *(Supvr-Media)*
Becky Sandholm *(Supvr-Best Buy Media)*
Laura Sauer *(Supvr-Media)*
Matthew Schons *(Supvr-Media)*
Amy Scott *(Supvr)*
Abbey Sherrard *(Supvr-Digital Strategy)*
Jon Siegan *(Supvr-Media)*
Ryan Sitzmann *(Supvr-Video Activation)*
Jackie Slagle *(Supvr-Media)*
Kelly Sorensen *(Supvr-Human Experience)*
Morgan Standley *(Supvr-Media)*
Dana Staton *(Supvr)*
Shannon Stiles *(Supvr-Media-Natl Video)*
Kelsey Sullivan *(Supvr-Media)*
Kaelin Sweeney *(Supvr-Human Experience)*
Maria Tocco *(Supvr-Media)*
Nicole Travis *(Supvr-Media)*
Carolyn Vanoer *(Supvr-Media)*
Ellie Weed *(Supvr-Media)*
Jenna Weeks *(Supvr-Media)*
Tiffany Wilder *(Supvr-Media)*
Soojin Youn *(Supvr-Media-Kraft)*
Tia DeVito *(Strategist-Media & Planner-Procter & Gamble)*
Gwen Daniels *(Strategist-Human Experience)*
Meredith Hayford *(Strategist-Human Experience)*
Robert Madera *(Specialist-Media)*
Meghan McManus *(Sr Analyst-Programmatic Acct)*
Scott Cooper *(Analyst-Paid Search & Social Media)*
September Forsyth *(Media Buyer)*
Kate Gillespy *(Acct Planner)*
Juan Huerta *(Media Planner)*
Leah Krantzler *(Media Planner)*
Brian Pankauskas *(Analyst-Programmatic Acct)*
Claire Sindlinger *(Analyst-Programmatic & Bidded Media)*
Eric Toepper *(Media Buyer-Local)*
Joel Vinas *(Analyst-Ops)*
Heather Chan *(Assoc)*
Kali Cottone *(Assoc Media Dir-Electronic Arts)*
Dorcas Dvorak *(Sr Media Buyer)*
Matthew Fisher *(Assoc Media Dir)*
Camila Juricic *(Assoc Media Dir)*
Celeste Kalouria *(Assoc-Digital Media)*
Nicole Karol *(Assoc-Media)*
Tim Kirkpatrick *(Assoc Media Dir)*
Stephanie Knoeck *(Assoc Media Dir)*
Hilary Lassof *(Assoc-Media)*
Laurie McClure *(Sr Media Buyer)*
Carrie McCroskey *(Assoc Media Dir)*
Natalya Namts *(Assoc Media Dir-Digital-MARS Petcare)*
Conner Rohwer *(Assoc-Media)*
Chirag Sanghvi *(Sr Engr-Advance Analytics-Spark SMG)*
Brianna Sudrla *(Assoc-Media)*
Thomas Temmerman *(Assoc-Media)*
Missy Warner *(Assoc Media Dir)*
Maddie Watkins *(Assoc-Tech & Ops Solutions)*

Accounts:
Ally Financial Inc.
American Honda Motor Co., Inc. Acura
Anheuser-Busch Companies, Inc.
Anthem Media Planning/Buying
Asics (Global Media Agency) Analytics, Data, Media Buying, Media Planning
Avis Budget Group Campaign: "It's Your Space"
Bank of America Corporation Bank of America Corporation, Bank of America Investment Services, Merrill Lynch, U.S. Trust
Bank of America Home Loans
Best Buy Campaign: "Showrooming", Campaign: "Twas", Campaign: "Your Ultimate Holiday Showroom", Media Buying and Planning
BlackBerry
Bristol Myers Squibb
The Coca-Cola Company Fanta, Full Throttle, Media Buy, Sprite
Comcast Cable, E! Entertainment TV, The Style Network, Theme-Park
Darden Restaurants, Inc. Media, Olive Garden
Emirates Group; 2008
New-Etihad Airways
The Festival of Media Asia Pacific
Hallmark Cards, Inc. Hallmark Cards, Inc., Hallmark Gold Crown, Hallmark.com, Keepsake
Harley-Davidson, Inc.
Heineken Campaign: "GITG", Media
Holden
Honda Motor Co. Acura, Media, Media Buying & Planning
Jim Beam Brands Co. Basil Hayden's, Canadian Club, Courvoisier, Knob Creek, Maker's Mark
Kashi Company GOLEAN, Good Friends Cinna-Raisin Crunch, Good Friends and Kashi, Heart to Heart, Honey Puff, Nuggets and Flakes, Kashi All Natural Frozen Entrees, Kashi Frozen Pizzas, Kashi Granola, Kashi Pilaf, Kashi TLC, Mighty Bites, Mountain Medley, Organic Promise,

Strawberry Field, TLC Chewy Trail Mix, Vive Digestive Wellness Cereal
New-Kashi
Kellogg Company Pop Tarts
New-Kraft Heinz Company Classico Sauces, Heinz Ketchup, Media Buying, Media Planning, Ore-Ida
McCormick & Company
Miller Brewing Co.; Milwaukee, WI; 1982
National Basketball Association Media Buying, Media Planning
Pitney Bowes Media strategy
The Procter & Gamble Company Always, Campaign: "Like a Girl", Clairol, Head & Shoulders Old Spice, Media, Media Buying, Secret, Swiffer, ThermaCare, Tide, Venus Embrace, Vidal Sassoon
Samsung America, Inc.
Samsung Electronics Campaign: "Galaxy And The Golden Egg", Campaign: "Project Teamwork", Media Buying; 2007
Turner Broadcasting (Media Buying) CNN, Cartoon Network, Digital, Ground Floor, Out of Home, Print, TBS, TNT, TV, Turner Movie Classics, Turner Sports
Twitter
V.F. Corporation Lee, Media Buying, Media Planning, Nautica, North Face Parkas, Timberland Pro Boots, Wrangler Jeans
New-Visa, Inc. (Global Media Agency of Record)
Wal-Mart
Walgreen Company Walgreen Company, Walgreens.com
New-Wendy's Media Buying
Wm. Wrigley Jr. Company Campaign: "Top Chef Just Desserts", Media Buying

SMG Performance Marketing
35 W Wacker Dr, Chicago, IL 60601
Tel.: (312) 220-3535
Web Site: www.smvgroup.com/our-brands

Agency Specializes In: Advertising, Brand Development & Integration, Digital/Interactive, Direct Response Marketing

LisaAnn Rocha *(Mng Dir & Sr VP)*
Dan Matarelli *(VP)*
Alichia Sawitoski *(Dir-Digital)*
Jack Thornburg *(Mgr-SEO)*
Brittany Legan *(Supvr-Digital Media)*

Accounts:
National Safety Council Media Buying, Media Planning
Starbucks Corporation

Liquid Thread
35 West Wacker Dr, Chicago, IL 60601
Tel.: (312) 220-3591
Web Site: www.liquidthread.com/

National Agency Associations: 4A's

Eric Levin *(Sr VP & Grp Dir-Brand Content)*
Erin Vogel *(Sr VP-Digital Experience & Dir-Strategy)*
Shirley Xu-Weldon *(Sr VP-Analytics & Strategic Solutions-VivaKi)*
Katrina Frank *(VP & Dir)*
Jonathan Haynes *(VP & Dir-Analytics)*
Lizzie Levin *(VP & Dir-Dev & Production)*
Allison Owens *(Mgr-Comm Plng & Producer)*
Debbie Kaplan *(Dir-Brand Content)*
Michelle Siegel Silverblatt *(Assoc Dir-Media-Liquid Thread)*
Elizabeth Potter *(Supvr-Media)*

Liquid Thread
1675 Broadway, New York, NY 10019
Tel.: (212) 468-4000
Web Site: www.liquidthread.com

Employees: 50

National Agency Associations: 4A's

Brent Poer *(Pres & Dir-Global Creative)*
Jill Griffin *(Sr VP & Mng Dir-Content Solutions & USA Ops)*
Elissa Harman *(Sr VP & Exec Creative Dir-Content)*
Paul Furia *(Sr VP & Grp Dir)*
Margee Hocking *(Sr VP & Grp Dir-Brand Content)*
Jason Stermer *(VP & Grp Dir-Brand Content)*
Lizzie Levin *(VP & Dir-Dev & Production)*
Nicole Mollen *(VP & Dir)*
Colleen Marks *(Dir-Content)*
Melissa Hillard *(Assoc Dir-Brand Content & Storytelling)*
Laura Pekarek *(Mgr-Brand Content)*

Accounts:
Coke
Delta Faucet
Kraft
Mars
Procter & Gamble
Walmart
Wendy's

MediaVest USA
6500 Wilshire Blvd Ste 1100, Los Angeles, CA 90046
Tel.: (323) 658-4500
Fax: (323) 658-4592
E-Mail: brent.poer@mediavestww.com
Web Site: www.smvgroup.com

National Agency Associations: 4A's-THINKLA

Agency Specializes In: Media Buying Services, Sponsorship

Jennifer Karayeanes *(Mng Dir & Exec VP)*
Nancy Tortorella *(Mng Dir & Exec VP)*
Liz Ryan *(Sr VP & Grp Dir-Client)*
Melissa Campbell *(Sr VP & Grp Client Dir)*
Jason Dailey *(Sr VP-Precision Mktg-Search & Social)*
Melissa Norton *(VP & Reg Dir-Media)*
David Avalon *(VP & Dir-Digital)*
James Lee *(VP & Dir-Bus Integration & Digital Strategy)*
Rebecca Mann *(VP & Dir-Connections)*
Wesley Orlick *(VP & Dir-Media)*
Kate Vivalo *(Dir-Ops)*
Keri Zuckerman *(Dir-Digital)*
Melissa Andraos *(Assoc Dir-Digital)*
Connie Chiu *(Assoc Dir-Digital)*
Antonia Dillon *(Assoc Dir-Programmatic)*
Denise James *(Assoc Dir-Programmatic)*
Emily Kaufman *(Assoc Dir-Media-Digital Strategy)*
Christopher Lawrence *(Assoc Dir)*
Jaime Millman *(Assoc Dir-Media)*
Richard Oh *(Assoc Dir-Media)*
Charisse Oraa *(Assoc Dir-Digital)*
John Papadopoulos *(Assoc Dir-Honda)*
Nicole Scott *(Assoc Dir-Programmatic)*
Amanda Dixon *(Mgr-Digital Media)*
Laura Kakos *(Mgr-Programmatic)*
Lauren Kime *(Mgr-Connections)*
Rebecca Mansfield *(Mgr-Programmatic)*
Damon Parry *(Mgr-Connections)*
Joshua Rogers *(Mgr-Programmatic)*
Diana Song *(Mgr-Strategy)*
Mark Thomas *(Mgr-Connections)*
Zachary Zaban *(Mgr-Social Media & ECommerce)*
Erika Sekse Lutz *(Supvr-Activation-P&G)*
Franchesca Silvestre *(Media Planner-Digital & Buyer)*

Accounts:
Bristol Myers Squibb
CBS Films Media Buying & Planning
Comcast Corporation
Mars North America; 2004
Mattel Brands Barbie, HotWheels, Matchbox, Scrabble, Uno
TriHonda Dealer Group Media Planning & Buying

Relevant 24
46 Plympton St, Boston, MA 02118
(See Separate Listing)

SMG/P&G
35 W Wacker Dr, Chicago, IL 60601
Tel.: (312) 220-3535
Fax: (312) 220-6530
E-Mail: laura.desmond@smvgroup.com
Web Site: www.smvgroup.com

National Agency Associations: 4A's

Agency Specializes In: Advertising

Laura Desmond *(CEO)*
Iain Jacob *(Pres-Dynamic Markets)*
John Sheehy *(Pres-Global Ops)*
John Antoniades *(CEO-MENA)*
Monica Gadsby *(CEO-SMG US Multicultural-Latin America)*
Ali Nehme *(Mng Dir-Digital)*
Sue Frogley *(Dir-Comml-Global)*

Accounts:
AllState
Coca-Cola Refreshments USA, Inc.
Emirates
GM
Kellogg's
Mondelez International, Inc.
Procter & Gamble
The Walt Disney Company

SMG United
1675 Broadway, New York, NY 10019
Tel.: (212) 468-4000
Web Site: www.smvgroup.com

Employees: 3,000

National Agency Associations: 4A's

Agency Specializes In: Advertising

Mercedes Ritchey *(VP, Head-Integrated Agency & Dir-Comm Plng)*
Nicole Accordino *(VP & Dir-Connections)*
Patrick Talty *(Gen Mgr-New Minnesota Stadium)*
Colleen Leahy *(Dir-Consumer Experience)*

Accounts:
Procter & Gamble Tide

Spark Communications
222 Merchandise Mart Plz Ste 550, Chicago, IL 60654-1032
(See Separate Listing)

Starcom Latin America Regional Headquarters
806 Douglas Rd Ste 700, Coral Gables, FL 33134-3129
Tel.: (305) 648-2122
Fax: (305) 529-8893
E-Mail: diana.garcia@mia.starcomworldwide.com
Web Site: www.smvgroup.com

Employees: 40

Agency Specializes In: Media Buying Services, Sponsorship

Victor Garcia *(Mng Dir & Sr VP)*
Mike Amour *(Pres-Asia Pacific)*

Lisa Weinstein *(Pres-Global Digital, Data & Analytics)*
Laura Desmond *(CEO-Global)*
Monica Gadsby *(CEO-SMG US Multicultural-Latin America)*
Bertilla Teo *(CEO-Greater China)*
Brian Terkelsen *(CEO-MediaVest USA)*
Borja Beneyto *(VP & Reg Dir-Digital-Latin America)*
Sue Frogley *(Dir-Comml-Global)*

Accounts:
Allstate
Altria
Coca-Cola Refreshments USA, Inc.
Emirates
Kellogg's
Mars Inc
Miller
Mondelez International, Inc.
P&G
Samsung Campaign: "2111", Campaign: "Vina Del Samsung Multiview"
The Walt Disney Company

Starcom MediaVest- GM Team

(Formerly Starcom MediaVest)
150 W Jefferson Ste 400, Detroit, MI 48226
Tel.: (313) 237-8200
Fax: (313) 237-8490
E-Mail: dennis.donlin@gm-planworks.com
Web Site: www.smvgroup.com

Employees: 200

Agency Specializes In: Media Buying Services, Sponsorship

Ken Taylor *(Pres)*
Nicole Martin *(VP & Grp Dir-Data & Analytics)*
Sara Atsalakis *(VP & Dir-Tech & Activation Grp-LATAM)*
Leah Herbert *(VP & Dir-Learning & Dev)*
Kelly Lariviere *(Dir-Strategy)*
Sonia Morales *(Assoc Dir)*
Jennifer Walton *(Assoc Dir-Budget Ops)*
Theresa Horvath *(Supvr-Ops)*
Christina Jankauskas *(Sr Media Buyer-Print & On-line & Supvr)*
Heather Kortes *(Supvr-Media)*
Kathleen Malo *(Media Buyer)*
Adowa Watson *(Planner-Kraft Ops)*
Jenn Wolff *(Sr Media Planner)*

Accounts:
Ally Bank
Ally Financial, Inc.
Beam, Inc. Starbucks Coffee
ESPN, Inc.
Harley-Davidson, Inc.

Starcom MediaVest Group

175 Bloor St E N Tower 10th Fl, Toronto, ON M4W 3R9 Canada
Tel.: (416) 928-3636
Fax: (416) 927-3202
E-Mail: lauren.richards@smvgroup.com
Web Site: www.smvgroup.com

Agency Specializes In: Media Buying Services, Media Planning

Alexandra Panousis *(CEO)*
Anne Myers *(COO)*
Steve Cotten *(VP & Grp Dir)*
Randy Carelli *(VP, Grp Acct Dir & Dir-Digital)*
Dane Gyoker *(Mgr-Digital Media)*
Eugenia Kung *(Mgr-Strategy)*
Jenna Eager *(Supvr-Digital Solutions)*
Melody Daly *(Specialist-Media)*
Jessica Biagioni *(Planner-Strategy)*

Accounts:
New-Crayola Canada Media
Emirates
Express Creative
Kelloggs
Kraft
Samsung Samsung Galaxy Note
TD Bank Group Media Strategy & Buying

Starcom MediaVest Group

1675 Broadway, New York, NY 10019
(See Separate Listing)

Starcom Medios

Avenida Apoquindo 3000, Las Condes Piso 7, Santiago, 6760341 Chile
Tel.: (56) 236 25803
Fax: (56) 236 25959

Employees: 20

Agency Specializes In: Media Buying Services

Rodrigo Almonacid *(Dir-Media)*
Andrea Paz Retamales *(Dir)*
Nicolas Maulen Parada *(Coord & Supvr-Digital)*
Jose Caceres *(Media Planner)*
Hector Diaz *(Planner-Digital Media)*
Alejandra Arenas Moya *(Media Planner)*
Daniela Ortega *(Media Planner)*
Haylin Alvarado Pizarro *(Planner-Digital Media)*
Alex Poblete Vasquez *(Media Planner)*
Loreto Leiva Vega *(Media Planner)*

Accounts:
Cosmeticos Avon

Starcom USA

35 W Wacker Dr, Chicago, IL 60601
Tel.: (312) 220-3535
Fax: (312) 220-6530
E-Mail: lisa.donohue@starcomworldwide.com
Web Site: www.smvgroup.com

Employees: 100

National Agency Associations: 4A's

Agency Specializes In: Media Buying Services, Media Planning

Rob Davis *(Mng Dir & Exec VP)*
Andrew Kasprzycki *(Mng Dir & Exec VP)*
Lisa Bradner *(Mng Dir & Sr VP)*
Amanda Richman *(Pres-Investment & Activation)*
Phil Geyskens *(Exec VP & Mng Dir-Data & Analytics)*
Kelly Andrews *(Exec VP & Dir-Data & Analytics)*
Tracey Scheppach *(Exec VP & Dir-Innovations)*
Alison Moriarty *(Sr VP & Grp Dir-HR)*
Paul DeJarnatt *(Sr VP & Dir)*
Tim Libby *(Sr VP & Dir-Digital)*
Adam Rattner *(Sr VP & Dir-Bus Dev)*
Harvin Furman *(Sr VP-COE Digital Acceleration)*
Pat McCormick *(VP & Dir-Data & Analytics)*
Dan Mitz *(VP & Dir)*
Sue Seams *(VP & Dir-Strategy)*
Jennifer Kern *(Grp Dir-Strategy)*
Alison Reveille *(Dir)*
Christopher Chin *(Assoc Dir)*
Karen Umeki Muscolino *(Assoc Dir-Media)*
Jessica Rafalski *(Assoc Dir-Human Experience-Define)*
Ray House *(Mgr-Comm)*
Clare Bieker *(Supvr-Media Strategy-Anheuser Busch InBev)*
Elizabeth Chaklos *(Supvr-Digital Media)*
Jenna Goffman *(Supvr-Media)*
Sean Mills *(Supvr-Human Experience & Media)*
Maggie Stewart *(Supvr-Media)*
Ryan Cook *(Specialist-Tech & Ops)*

Accounts:
Advance Auto Parts Media
Airbnb Media Strategy, U.S. Activation
Allstate
American Egg Board Media Planning & Buying
Bank of America Corporation Media; 2008
Beam Global Spirits & Wine, Inc.; Deerfield, IL
BlackBerry
Bon-Ton Stores Media Buying & Planning
CBS Films Display, Media Buying and Planning, Search, Social
Choose Chicago Media Buying, Media Planning
Del Monte Foods Nature's Recipe
Disney Alice in Wonderland (Media Agency)
ESPN
Esurance Media Buying
Hallmark
Kellogg Co. Pop-Tarts, Special K
The Kraft Heinz Company Media, Oscar Mayer
LEGO LEGO Star Wars
Mars North America Mars, Wrigley
Mattel American Girl
Microsoft
MTV Content Development, MTV Other
Novartis Global Media
Pringles Media
Procter & Gamble Campaign: "The WorldS First Live Beauty Ad", Noxzema
Samsung
U.S. Cellular Digital
Walt Disney Company
Wm. Wrigley Jr. Company; Chicago, IL

Starcom Worldwide

5200 Lankershim Ste 600, North Hollywood, CA 91601
Tel.: (818) 753-7200
Fax: (818) 753-7350
E-Mail: connect@starcomworldwide.com
Web Site: www.smvgroup.com

Year Founded: 2002

National Agency Associations: 4A's

Agency Specializes In: Media Buying Services, Sponsorship

Kathy Ring *(Pres & COO)*
Sasha Wolfe *(Sr VP & Grp Dir)*
Jennifer Lewis *(VP & Dir-Media)*
Cindy Ransier *(VP & Dir)*
Jake Rice *(VP & Dir-Digital Media & Analytics)*
Sarah Doughty *(Assoc Dir-Comm Plng)*
Jade Ku *(Assoc Dir-Media)*
Lauren Macht *(Assoc Dir-Media)*
Natasha Prada *(Assoc Dir-Media)*
Steven Zint *(Assoc Dir-Media)*
Tina Gumbrecht *(Office Mgr)*
Kaity Swanekamp *(Mgr-Tech & Activation Grp)*
Juli Suk *(Supvr-Media)*

Accounts:
ABC Cable Network Group
Allstate Insurance Company
Del Monte
Electronic Arts Media
Guitar Center (Media Agency of Record) Analytics, Media Buying, Media Planning, Strategy
Hanesbrand Inc.
Mart
Mattel Barbie, Hot Wheels, Media
Universal Orlando Resort
Walt Disney Company Disney Channels Worldwide, The Walt Disney Company

Tapestry Partners

35 W Wacker Dr, Chicago, IL 60601
Tel.: (312) 220-3535
Fax: (312) 220-6561
E-Mail: monicam.gadsby@tapestrypartners.com
Web Site: www.tapestrypartners.com

National Agency Associations: 4A's

Agency Specializes In: Media Buying Services, Media Planning, Sponsorship

Lia Silkworth *(Mng Dir & Exec VP)*
Dana Bonkowski *(Sr VP & Dir-Media)*
Sayuri Alvarez *(Dir-Media)*
Amanda Williamson *(Dir-Strategy-Tapestry)*
Benjamin Aguirre, Jr. *(Assoc Dir-Media-Multicultural-Multiple Client Accts)*
Agnieszka Kwiecien *(Assoc Dir-Media-Samsung, Novartis)*
Alejandra Gonzalez *(Supvr)*

Accounts:
ACH Foods Mazola, Media Buying & Planning; 2008
Advance Auto Parts (Multicultural Media Planning & Buying)
AllState Corporation; 2007
Americatel
Applebee's
Bank of America
Best Buy
Burger King Corp. Media
ESPN Deportes
GM
Hanes
Kellogg's
Kraft
Miller
Minute Maid
Nintendo
Phillip Morris
Procter & Gamble
Toys R Us
U.S. Cellular
Walgreens

MediaVest Worldwide
Via San Quintino 28, 10121 Turin, Italy
Tel.: (39) 011 560 1980
Fax: (39) 011 560 1725
E-Mail: i.gannio@starcomitalia.com
Web Site: www.smvgroup.com

Agency Specializes In: Media Buying Services

Olivia Reposo *(Controller-Fin)*
Michele Rossi *(Dir-Digital)*
Fabio Tattilo *(Dir-Media)*
Paola Bariani *(Supvr-Digital)*
Alessandro Monchiero *(Planner-Digital Media)*
Clizia Monguzzi *(Planner-Digital Media)*
Francesca Santoro *(Asst Planner-Digital)*

Starcom Denmark
Solbjergvej 3 3 sal, 2000 Frederiksberg, Denmark
Tel.: (45) 3520 0080
Fax: (45) 3 520 0099
E-Mail: cdalgaard@starcom.dk
Web Site: denmark.starcomww.com/

Agency Specializes In: Media Buying Services

Stine Halberg *(CEO-Vivaki Denmark)*
Louise Bak Schou *(Bus Dir)*
Mette Knak *(Mgr-Brdcst)*
Marco S Nielsen *(Mgr-Digital)*

Starcom Media Worldwide Estrategia
Goya 22 1 Fl, 28001 Madrid, Spain
Tel.: (34) 911 872 100
Fax: (34) 91 204 4599
Web Site: www.smvgroup.com

Employees: 50

Agency Specializes In: Media Buying Services, Media Planning

Pilar Ulecia *(Mng Dir)*
Miguel Garcia *(CEO-Southern Europe)*
Marta Ruiz-Cuevas *(CEO-Spain)*
Bertilla Teo *(CEO-Greater China)*
Rita Gutierrez *(Mng Dir-Barcelona)*
Marta Brondo *(Acct Dir)*
Ana Escriva *(Acct Dir)*
Santiago Cordon *(Dir-Customer Svc)*

Starcom Mediavest Group Moscow
Usievitcha U1 20/1, Moscow, 125190 Russia
Tel.: (7) 495 969 2010
Fax: (7) 095 969 2004
E-Mail: teliseeva@starcomworldwide.ru
Web Site: www.smvgroup.com

Employees: 110

Agency Specializes In: Media Buying Services

Jeff Chalmers *(CEO-SMG Russia)*
Svetlana Gusarova *(Sr Media Planner)*
Ekaterina Ubushaeva *(Sr Media Planner)*

Accounts:
Procter & Gamble Campaign: "Fashion Academy", Campaign: "Pampers Good Night Babies"
VimpelCom

Starcom MediaVest
16 Sir John Rogersons Quay, Dublin, 2 Ireland
Tel.: (353) 1 649 6445
Fax: (353) 1 649 6446
E-Mail: richard.law@starcommediavest.ie
Web Site: www.smvgroup.com

Employees: 32

Agency Specializes In: Media Buying Services

Michael Clancy *(Mng Dir)*
Alan Cox *(CEO-Core Media)*
Aiden Green *(Dir)*

Accounts:
AIB
Altria
Coca-Cola Refreshments USA, Inc.
Emirates
ESB Group Media
Kelloggs
Kraft
Murphys Campaign: "When It Rains It Pours"
O2
P&G
Supervalu Media
The Walt Disney Company

Starcom MediaVest
Whitfield House 89 Whitfield St, London, W1T 4HQ United Kingdom
Tel.: (44) 20 7190 8000
Fax: (44) 20 7190 8001
E-Mail: marketing@smvgroup.co.uk
Web Site: www.starcomuk.com/

Employees: 350
Year Founded: 1991

Agency Specializes In: Media Buying Services

Pippa Glucklich *(Co-CEO)*
Steve Parker *(Co-CEO)*
Chris Camacho *(Mng Partner-Precision Mktg)*
Adam Foley *(Mng Partner)*
Nicola Harvey *(Mng Partner)*
Matt Blackborn *(Pres-Investment & Diversification)*
Jodie Stranger *(Pres-Global Network Clients)*
Iain Jacob *(CEO-EMEA)*
Robin Clarke *(Mng Dir-Sports-EMEA)*
Ben Cronin *(Mng Dir-UK)*
Eva Powell *(Head-Strategy)*
Duff Borer *(Bus Dir)*
Liam Brennan *(Dir-Digital Strategy)*
Frank Durrell *(Dir-Digital Strategy & Tech-Global Network Clients)*
Jim Kite *(Dir-Strategic Dev-EMEA)*
Kieran Parsley *(Dir-Fin)*
Max Doherty *(Assoc Dir-Programmatic)*
Adam Hancox *(Assoc Dir-Programmatic)*

Accounts:
Bauer Media Media Planning & Buying
Betway
BlackBerry
Burger King Media Planning & buying, Repositioning
Buyagift Digital, International PPC
Capital One
Cineworld TV
Dreams Beds, Media, Paid Search Media; 2010
EasyProperty Media Buying, Media Planning
Etihad Airways Partner Global Media, Media Planning
Europcar Global Digital, Media
Flybe
Ford Retail Media
Hailo Media Planning & Buying
Heineken UK Bulmers, Bulmers Cider Bold Black Cherry, Bulmers Cider Pressed Red Grape, Campaign: "In the Beginning", Digital, Foster's Media Planning & Buying, Media, Outdoor, Print, Strongbow Cider, Strongbow Dark Fruit
New-Lidl Buying, Digital Buying, Media, Outdoor, Planning, Press, TV
McCormick Digital, Media
Metro Media Planning & Buying
Mondelez International, Inc.
NFL
Otrivine Campaign: "#snotwhatisaid"
P&O Ferries Media Buying, Media Planning
Royal London Group Digital, Media Buying, Media Planning, Outdoor, TV
RSA
Samsung Content Strategy
Spotify UK Buying
Tata Global Beverages Campaign: "Find Sydney", Media Planning & Buying, Tetley
Travelodge Digital, Media
Uswitch Media Planning & Buying
Yahoo Digital, Social

Starcom Middle East & Egypt Regional Headquarters
Dubai Media City Bldg No 11, PO Box 7534, Dubai, United Arab Emirates
Tel.: (971) 4 367 6401
Fax: (971) 4 367 2585
Web Site: www.smvgroup.com

Agency Specializes In: Media Buying Services

John Antoniades *(CEO-MENA)*
Rayan Hajjar *(Mng Dir-Client-P&G MENA)*
Brayden J. Ainzuain *(Dir-Digital Media)*
Fadi Zaidan *(Dir-Media)*
Zaid Barrishi *(Sr Mgr-Digital Media)*
Wassim Jammal *(Sr Mgr-Media)*
Sara S *(Mgr-Media Plng)*
Alain Brahamcha *(Client Mng Dir)*
Tarek Daouk *(Reg Mng Dir-MediaVest MENA)*
Layal Hassi *(Sr Media Planner-Digital)*

Accounts:
Ariel
BlackBerry
Emirates Airline
Honda Motor Co., Ltd.
MAF Leisure & Entertainment
Mango
Mars, Incorporated
Procter & Gamble Co. Olay
Samsung
Snickers

Sunbulah Group Media Buying, Media Planning

Starcom Motive Partnership London
24-27 Great Pulteney St, London, W1F 9NJ United Kingdom
Tel.: (44) 207 453 4444
Fax: (44) 207 427 2401
Web Site: www.starcomww.com

Employees: 350

Agency Specializes In: Media Buying Services

Chris Allen *(Mgr-TV)*

Accounts:
Samsung

Starcom Norway
Tollbugt 17, PO Box 504, Sentrum, 0105 Oslo, Norway
Mailing Address:
Postboks 1769, Vika, 0122 Oslo, Norway
Tel.: (47) 9063 7700
Fax: (47) 2283 0921
E-Mail: firmapost@starcom.no
Web Site: www.starcom.no

Agency Specializes In: Media Buying Services

Ingrid Holstad *(CFO)*
Simen Lund Svindal *(Controller-Fin)*
Catharine Mitlid *(Dir-Strategy)*
Dag Ormasen *(Dir-Buying)*
Endre Lovaas *(Mgr-Experience)*
Nina Bielke Ronningen *(Mgr-Client Svcs)*
Karen Bistrup *(Planner-Digital)*
Cecilie Ciekals *(Planner-Performance)*
Michelle Raye Vera Cruz Angeles *(Jr Controller)*
Ingvild Kvamme *(Client Svc Mgr)*
Hege Eirin Lysnes *(Client Svc Dir)*
Havar Sesseng *(Client Svc Dir)*

Accounts:
Ruter Analyses, Media, Negotiations

Starcom Sp. z o.o.
ul Sobieskiego 104, 00-764 Warsaw, Poland
Tel.: (48) 22 493 99 99
Fax: (48) 22 489 99 00
E-Mail: info@starcom.com.pl
Web Site: www.starcompoland.com/en

E-Mail for Key Personnel:
President: jakub_benke@starcom.com.pl

Employees: 90

Agency Specializes In: Media Buying Services

Anna Sakowicz *(Chief Digital Officer-Poland)*

Starcom Worldwide
Szepvolgyi Business Park Cepulet Building 1V Emelet Floor, 1037 Budapest, Hungary
Tel.: (36) 1 801 3300
Fax: (36) 1 801 3399
Web Site: www.smvgroup.com

Employees: 20

Agency Specializes In: Media Buying Services, Media Planning

Tunde Horvath *(Dir-Media)*

Starcom
Beethoven 15, Planta 5, 08021 Barcelona, Spain
Tel.: (34) 933 9677 00
Fax: (34) 933 967 727
Web Site: www.smvgroup.com

Employees: 35

Agency Specializes In: Media Buying Services, Media Planning

Miguel Garcia *(CEO-SMG Iberia)*
Rita Gutierrez *(Mng Dir-Barcelona)*
Jesus De La Torre *(Acct Grp Dir)*
Marta Brondo *(Acct Dir)*
Ana Escriva *(Acct Dir)*
Santiago Cordon *(Dir-Client Svcs-BARCELONA)*
Oscar Perez Garrido *(Dir-Negotiation & Purchase)*
Marta Herrera *(Dir-Comm Plng & Bus Dev)*
Oscar Perez *(Dir-Trading)*
Guillermo Barbera Galiana *(Acct Supvr)*
Yuson Sim Uo *(Acct Supvr)*

Asia Pacific

SMG Convonix
506/B Navbharat Estate Zakaria Bunder Road, Sewri (W), Mumbai, 400015 India
Tel.: (91) 22 2411 2836
Fax: (91) 22 2415 4831
Web Site: www.convonix.com

Employees: 200

Agency Specializes In: Paid Searches, Search Engine Optimization, Social Media

Vishal Sampat *(CEO)*
Sarfaraz Khimani *(COO)*
Suchit Sikaria *(Sr VP-SEO & Head-Bus-West & South)*
Surajendu Sinha *(VP & Head-Bus-West & South)*
Varun Chawla *(VP-Search Mktg)*
Atul Gawand *(VP-HR)*
Rahul Gupte *(VP-Ops & ORM)*
Natasha Kapoor *(VP)*
Pallav Jain *(Dir-Bus Dev)*

Accounts:
Aditya Birla Group
Budweiser
Cadbury Dairy Milk Creative, Digital Strategy
Club Mahindra
CoverFox.com Media
Dabur India (Media Agency of Record) Media Buying, Media Planning
DBS
Jet Airways Media
New-Jumboking Vada Pav (Media Agency of Record)
Kodak
Kotak Mahindra Group
Lodha Group Digital, Media, SEO, Search Marketing
Reliance Industries
Taj Hotels
Tata Motors

Starcom Beijing
Rm 1507 15/F Bright China Chang An Tower One, 7 Jianguomen Nei Ave, Beijing, 100005 China
Tel.: (86) 10 8519 9699
Fax: (86) 10 8519 9688
Web Site: www.smvgroup.com

Agency Specializes In: Media Buying Services

Benjamin Yeow *(Dir-Digital Ops-Asia)*

Accounts:
Anheuser-Busch InBev Media
BMW China Media, Mini
Mars Inc. Campaign: "M&M'S Celebrity Glitz", Doublemint, Mars, Wrigley
Samsung

Starcom Guangzhou
2&3A/F SanXin Plz No 33 W Huangpu Ave, Guangzhou, 510620 China
Tel.: (86) 20 3820 1900
Fax: (86) 20 3820 1891
E-Mail: ann.chan@gz.starcommedia.com
Web Site: www.smvgroup.com

Agency Specializes In: Media Buying Services

Victor Villar *(Sr VP & Mng Dir-PG Ops)*
Todd Wilson *(Sr VP & Mng Dir-P&G Asia)*
Anuj Dahiya *(Head-Digital-P&G China)*
Ann Chan *(Gen Mgr-Guangzhou)*
Sarika Tulsyan *(Reg Dir-Digital-P&G Asia)*
Terry Ni *(Dir-Plng)*
Caterina Camerata Scovazzo *(Dir-Strategy-Shanghai)*
Cher Wu *(Dir-Digital)*
Joe Zhao *(Dir-Bus)*
Jamie Brownlee *(Assoc Dir-Digital)*

Accounts:
Guangdong Development Bank Media Planning & Buying
Procter & Gamble Gillette, Oral B

Starcom Hong Kong
Room 602-605 1063 King's Road, Quarry Bay, China (Hong Kong)
Tel.: (852) 2539 1683
Fax: (852) 2567 4552
Web Site: www.smvgroup.com

Year Founded: 1999

Agency Specializes In: Media Buying Services

Alfred Cheng *(Reg Dir)*
Kristine Banzon *(Assoc Dir & Mgr-Media)*

Accounts:
Air New Zealand
Longchamp
Maxim's Cakes Campaign: "Let's Celebrate", Media, OOH, Print
Mead Johnson Campaign: "Mommys Pal App"
Novartis
P&G Media, Pantene
Richemont Group
Samsung
UBS
Warner Brothers

Starcom Melbourne
Level 6 Building 3 6 Riverside Quay, Southbank, Melbourne, VIC 3006 Australia
Tel.: (61) 3 9673 7000
Fax: (61) 3 86964803
Web Site: www.starcomaustralia.com//

Year Founded: 1983

Agency Specializes In: Media Buying Services

David Angell *(Mng Dir)*
Peter Toone *(Gen Mgr)*
Dianne Richardson *(Exec Dir)*
Kate Gangitano *(Acct Dir)*
Naomi Johnston *(Client Svcs Dir)*
Sally Phelps *(Bus Dir)*
Jordan Smith *(Acct Dir)*
Jason Tonelli *(Dir-Digital)*

Accounts:
AAMI Media
Apia
Autobarn Media Buying
Diageo Media Buying

InvoCare
Lion Dairy & Drinks
Mars Petcare Campaign: "Puppy Love"
Optus Media, My Plan
Seek.com.au Media
Treasury Wine Estates
Vitasoy
Warner Music Australia Media

Starcom Shanghai
3/F 900 HuaiHai Middle Rd, Shanghai, 200020 China
Tel.: (86) 21 6133 8518
Fax: (86) 21 6133 8519
Web Site: www.smvgroup.com

Agency Specializes In: Media Buying Services

Bertilla Teo *(CEO-Greater China)*
Ann Chan *(Gen Mgr-Guangzhou)*
Benny Lam *(Gen Mgr-Shanghai)*
Caterina Camerata *(Dir-Strategy)*
Jeffrey Tan *(Dir-Natl Res & Insights-China)*

Accounts:
Coca-Cola Refreshments USA, Inc. Campaign: "Share a Coke", Media

Starcom Worldwide Southeast Asia HQ
137 Telok Ayer St #06-01, Singapore, 068602 Singapore
Tel.: (65) 6435 7101
Fax: (65) 6538 8967
Web Site: www.smvgroup.com

Agency Specializes In: Media Buying Services

Patricia Goh *(Mng Dir)*
Ranganathan Somanathan *(COO)*
Mike Amour *(Pres-Asia Pacific)*
Ken Mandel *(Pres-Global Client Network Practice-Asia Pacific)*
Rajesh Mahtani *(Head-Growth & Strategy-South East Asia)*
Elaine Poh *(Exec Dir-Creative)*

Accounts:
Altria
Avenza (Agency of Record)
Bank of America Merrill Lynch
Emirates
Far East Organisation Media
New-Heineken Media Buying
IG Markets Singapore Media
Kelloggs
Kraft
Mars & Wrigley Media
New-National Productivity Council Media
P&G
Samsung
Singapore GP Media
Tiger Airways
Zespri International Limited (Agency of Record)

Starcom Worldwide
24F Tower 2 Enterprise Center 6766 Ayala Avenue Corner, Paseo de Roxas, Makati, 1200 Philippines
Tel.: (63) 2 884 8053
Web Site: www.smvgroup.com

Agency Specializes In: Media Buying Services

Joanna Mojica *(Mng Dir)*
Veron Agustin *(Gen Mgr)*
Liam Capati *(Gen Mgr)*
Hope Binay *(Dir-Media)*
Oliver Salazar *(Dir-Media-Samsung)*
Jed Maynard Manuel *(Mgr-Out-of-Home Media)*
Andre Abad *(Planner-OOH & Buyer)*
Rein Comentan *(Sr Media Planner & Buyer)*
Karl Faustino *(Sr Media Planner & Sr Media Buyer)*
Jayson Galvez *(Sr Media Planner & Buyer)*
Euf Nunez *(Sr Media Planner & Buyer)*
Jomariz Trillana *(Sr Media Planner & Buyer)*

Accounts:
Altria
Goldilocks Media Planning & Buying
Mars Mars, Wrigley
Unilab

Starcom Worldwide
Bond Store 2 28 Windmill St Walsh Bay, Sydney, NSW 2000 Australia
Tel.: (61) 2 8666 8000
Fax: (61) 2 8666 8001
Web Site: www.smvgroup.com

Employees: 50
Year Founded: 1978

Agency Specializes In: Media Buying Services

Toby Barbour *(Mng Dir)*
Chris Nolan *(CEO-Starcom MediaVest Grp)*
Tracey Weinreb *(Dir-Natl Performance)*
Patrick Whitnall *(Dir-Strategy-Natl)*
Alex Concannon *(Strategist-Bus Integration-Data & Analytics)*

Accounts:
InvoCare
Just Car Insurance
Mars Mars, Wrigley
P&G
Riedel Through the Line
Samsung Media
Virgin Mobile Social Media

Starcom Worldwide
Level 6 307 Queen Street, Brisbane, QLD 4000 Australia
Tel.: (61) 7 3329 1000
Fax: (61) 7 3329 1100
Web Site: www.smvgroup.com

Year Founded: 1981

Agency Specializes In: Media Buying Services

Caleb Watson *(Gen Mgr)*

Accounts:
AV Jennings Queensland
MAX Employment

STARMARK INTERNATIONAL, INC.
210 S. Andrews Ave., Fort Lauderdale, FL 33301
Tel.: (954) 874-9000
Fax: (954) 874-9010
Toll Free: (888) 280-9630
E-Mail: ideas@starmark.com
Web Site: www.starmark.com

Employees: 30
Year Founded: 1978

National Agency Associations: 4A's-DMA

Agency Specializes In: Brand Development & Integration, Business-To-Business, Collateral, Communications, Consulting, Consumer Marketing, Corporate Communications, Direct Response Marketing, E-Commerce, Electronic Media, Environmental, Exhibit/Trade Shows, Financial, Government/Political, Health Care Services, High Technology, Information Technology, Internet/Web Design, Logo & Package Design, Marine, New Product Development, Point of Purchase, Print, Public Relations, Sales Promotion, Strategic Planning/Research, Telemarketing, Trade & Consumer Magazines, Travel & Tourism

Approx. Annual Billings: $43,000,000

Breakdown of Gross Billings by Media: Brdcst.: $1,720,000; D.M.: $10,320,000; Graphic Design: $4,730,000; Mags.: $4,300,000; Newsp.: $860,000; Other: $6,450,000; Outdoor: $860,000; Pub. Rels.: $3,440,000; Video Brochures: $1,720,000; Worldwide Web Sites: $8,600,000

Jacqui Hartnett *(Pres)*
Peggy Nordeen *(CEO)*
Lisa Hoffman *(CMO)*
Lisa Hoffman-Linero *(CMO)*
Chuck Malkus *(Chief Strategy Officer)*
Jeremy Schwartz *(VP-Digital Mktg)*
Sue Kane *(Controller)*
Lisa Levy *(Acct Mgr)*
Diana Wright *(Acct Mgr)*
Jeff Titelius *(Mgr-Digital Svcs)*
Kristen Martinez *(Acct Supvr)*

Accounts:
Boca Resort & Club
Broward Center
Greater Fort Lauderdale Convention & Visitors Bureau Campaign: "Defrost Your Swimsuit", Campaign: "Hello Sunny"
Nova Southeastern University

STARMEDIA GROUP
(Formerly Starmedia Communications)
1285 Rue Hodge, Montreal, QC H4N 2B6 Canada
Tel.: (514) 447-4873
E-Mail: request@starmedia.ca
Web Site: www.starmedia.ca

Employees: 9
Year Founded: 2001

Agency Specializes In: Advertising, Advertising Specialties, Alternative Advertising, Aviation & Aerospace, Brand Development & Integration, Branded Entertainment, Business-To-Business, Catalogs, Collateral, Communications, Consumer Goods, Corporate Communications, Digital/Interactive, E-Commerce, Entertainment, Event Planning & Marketing, Graphic Design, Logo & Package Design, Media Buying Services, Media Planning, Multimedia, Planning & Consultation, Print, Production, Production (Ad, Film, Broadcast), Promotions, Public Relations, Publishing, RSS (Really Simple Syndication), T.V., Web (Banner Ads, Pop-ups, etc.)

Approx. Annual Billings: $800,000

Alex Cholella *(Owner)*

Accounts:
Bodog
Cosmoprof North America
Moroccan Oil
Scharf Group

THE STARR CONSPIRACY
(Formerly Starr Tincup)
122 S Main St, Fort Worth, TX 76104
Tel.: (817) 204-0400
Fax: (817) 878-4347
Web Site: thestarrconspiracy.com/

Employees: 17

Agency Specializes In: Advertising, Affiliate Marketing, Brand Development & Integration, Business-To-Business, Communications, Consulting, Consumer Marketing, Content, Corporate Communications, Corporate Identity, Digital/Interactive, Graphic Design, Identity

Marketing, International, Internet/Web Design, Local Marketing, Logo & Package Design, Market Research, Media Buying Services, Media Planning, Planning & Consultation, Production (Ad, Film, Broadcast), Promotions, Social Marketing/Nonprofit, Social Media, Web (Banner Ads, Pop-ups, etc.)

Approx. Annual Billings: $12,000,000

Breakdown of Gross Billings by Media: D.M.: $8,000,000; Print: $3,000,000; Production: $1,000,000

Mark Mitchell *(Partner)*
Steve Smith *(Partner)*
Jonathan Goodman *(Mng Dir-The Starr Conspiracy Intelligence Unit)*
Jonathan Irwin *(Dir-Art)*
George Larocque *(Principal Analyst & Dir-Go To Market Svcs)*
Matt Tatum *(Dir-Bus Dev)*
Craig Calloway *(Acct Mgr)*
Heather Tolksdorf *(Acct Mgr)*
Marc Stewart *(Strategist-Digital Media)*

STARWORKS GROUP

5 Crosby St 6th Fl, New York, NY 10013
Tel.: (646) 336-5920
E-Mail: newyork@starworksny.com
Web Site: www.starworksgroup.com

Year Founded: 2000

Agency Specializes In: Advertising, Brand Development & Integration, Content, Digital/Interactive, Event Planning & Marketing, Graphic Design, Internet/Web Design, Public Relations

Patrick Butler *(CFO)*
George MacPherson *(VP-PR)*
Liana Graves *(Sr Acct Dir)*
Mark Holcomb *(Acct Dir)*
Leigh Brill *(Acct Dir)*
Jaime David *(Dir-Fashion PR)*
Keegan Obrien *(Dir-Digital Media & Mktg)*
Jessica Sciacchitano *(Mgr-PR)*

Accounts:
AllSaints

STASZAK COMMUNICATIONS

16462 Martincoit Rd, Poway, CA 92064
Tel.: (858) 674-7409
Fax: (858) 630-2737
E-Mail: teresa@staszakcom.com
Web Site: www.staszakcom.com

Employees: 2
Year Founded: 2002

Agency Specializes In: Advertising, Brand Development & Integration, Broadcast, Cable T.V., Collateral, Communications, Consulting, Consumer Marketing, Consumer Publications, Corporate Identity, Direct Response Marketing, Engineering, Event Planning & Marketing, Exhibit/Trade Shows, Graphic Design, Health Care Services, High Technology, Information Technology, Internet/Web Design, Logo & Package Design, Magazines, Media Buying Services, Newspaper, Newspapers & Magazines, Out-of-Home Media, Outdoor, Pharmaceutical, Planning & Consultation, Print, Production, Publicity/Promotions, Radio, Recruitment, Strategic Planning/Research, T.V., Trade & Consumer Magazines, Yellow Pages Advertising

Teresa Staszak *(Mng Dir)*

Accounts:
Broadcom
Palomar Pomerado Health
Qualcomm
Quintech Solutions, Inc.

STATIK DIGITAL AGENCY

500 Everett Mall Way SE Ste 213, Everett, WA 98208
Tel.: (425) 243-4712
Web Site: www.statik-digital.com

Agency Specializes In: Advertising, Brand Development & Integration, Digital/Interactive, Graphic Design, Internet/Web Design, Print, Radio, Search Engine Optimization, Social Media, T.V.

Jon Knight *(Dir-Creative)*

Accounts:
Eslick

STATION FOUR

100 N Laura St Ste 602, Jacksonville, FL 32202
Tel.: (904) 399-3219
E-Mail: info@stationfour.com
Web Site: www.stationfour.com

Year Founded: 2007

Agency Specializes In: Advertising, Content, Digital/Interactive, Internet/Web Design, Logo & Package Design, Print, Social Media

Chris Lahey *(Owner)*
Chris Olberding *(CEO & Partner-Creative)*
Dan Croft *(VP-Bus Strategy)*
Michael Turner *(VP-Digital Strategy)*
Sean Tucker *(Assoc Dir-Creative)*
Ashley Durham *(Project Mgr-Mktg)*
Michael Docster *(Strategist-Digital Mktg)*
Karen Foligno *(Designer)*
Sabreena Katz *(Designer)*
Jared Rypkema *(Copywriter)*

Accounts:
Jacksonville Downtown Art Walk
Safariland Campaign: "Safariland Patrol Bikes"

STATTNER COMMUNICATIONS INC.

3001 Sherbrooke St W Ste 102, Montreal, QC H3Z 2X8 Canada
Tel.: (514) 747-5536
Fax: (514) 747-5584
E-Mail: ilene@stattner.com
Web Site: www.stattner.com

Employees: 2
Year Founded: 1993

Agency Specializes In: Advertising

Jeff Stattner *(Pres)*
Ilene Stattner *(VP)*

Accounts:
BCP
Canada Direct
Dairy Farmers of Canada
Dascal Group
KBSP
OSL

STEADYRAIN, INC.

716 Geyer Ave Ste 400, Saint Louis, MO 63104-4073
Tel.: (314) 446-0733
Fax: (314) 446-0734
E-Mail: info@steadyrain.com
Web Site: www.steadyrain.com

Employees: 50
Year Founded: 1999

Agency Specializes In: Advertising, E-Commerce, Internet/Web Design, Social Marketing/Nonprofit, Social Media, Technical Advertising

Thompson Knox *(Pres)*
Joe Marcallini *(VP-Internet Strategy)*
David Kidd *(Dir-Digital Mktg)*
Matt Ocello *(Strategist-Internet)*

Accounts:
FTL Finance
Kaldi's Coffee Roasting Company
McDonald's Corporation

STEAK

32 Avenue Of The Americas 16th Fl, New York, NY 10013-2473
Tel.: (646) 556-6585
Fax: (917) 591-9389
E-Mail: hello@steakdigital.com
Web Site: www.steakgroup.com/uk

Employees: 70
Year Founded: 2005

National Agency Associations: IAB

Agency Specializes In: Advertising Specialties, Affiliate Marketing, Consulting, Consumer Goods, Consumer Marketing, Digital/Interactive, Direct Response Marketing, Direct-to-Consumer, E-Commerce, Electronic Media, Email, Integrated Marketing, International, Internet/Web Design, Media Buying Services, Media Planning, Multimedia, New Technologies, Paid Searches, RSS (Really Simple Syndication), Search Engine Optimization, Strategic Planning/Research, Viral/Buzz/Word of Mouth, Web (Banner Ads, Pop-ups, etc.)

Rob Connolly *(CEO)*
Gabriel Charles *(Acct Dir)*

Accounts:
American Student Assistance Campaign: "#20SomethingProblems", Media Strategy & Buying
Canon
Expedia
Scotts Miracle-Gro
Toyota
Trump

STEALTH CREATIVE

1617 Locust St, Saint Louis, MO 63103
Tel.: (314) 480-3606
Fax: (314) 361-2086
E-Mail: info@stealthcreative.com
Web Site: www.stealthcreative.com

Agency Specializes In: Advertising, Digital/Interactive, Internet/Web Design, Search Engine Optimization

Julie Seff *(Pres & VP-Bus Strategy)*
Marie Schmich *(VP & Dir-Media)*
David Nimock *(VP-Acct Svcs)*
Ann Higby *(Dir-PR)*
Michael Kleckner *(Sr Acct Exec)*
Brian Reinhardt *(Strategist-SEM & Copywriter)*
Caitlin Oppland *(Coord-Mktg)*

Accounts:
AGCO Corporation

STEARNS 208 MARKETING LLC

PO Box 2221, Saint Cloud, MN 56302
Tel.: (218) 321-4175

Web Site: www.stearns208.com

Employees: 5

Agency Specializes In: Digital/Interactive, Electronic Media, Email, Local Marketing, Mobile Marketing, Paid Searches, Print, Search Engine Optimization, Social Media, Viral/Buzz/Word of Mouth, Web (Banner Ads, Pop-ups, etc.)

Cody Murphy *(Pres)*

Accounts:
Share Memories, LLC; 2014

STEBBINGS PARTNERS

427 John L Dietsch Blvd, Attleboro Falls, MA 02763-1000
Tel.: (508) 699-7899
Fax: (508) 699-7897
E-Mail: info@stebbings.com
Web Site: www.stebbings.com

Employees: 10
Year Founded: 1970

National Agency Associations: BPA

Agency Specializes In: Advertising, Brand Development & Integration, Business Publications, Business-To-Business, Commercial Photography, Consumer Marketing, Consumer Publications, Corporate Identity, Electronic Media, Graphic Design, High Technology, Internet/Web Design, Logo & Package Design, Media Buying Services, Newspaper, Newspapers & Magazines, Planning & Consultation, Print, Production, Public Relations, Publicity/Promotions

David Stebbings *(CEO & Partner)*
Dawn S. Lunn *(Partner & CFO)*
Terrence Joyce *(Dir-Bus Dev)*
Paul Shelasky *(Dir-CVS Studio)*

Accounts:
A.T. Cross
Brookfield Engineering
E. A. Dion
Euro-Pro
Samsonite

STEEL ADVERTISING & INTERACTIVE

6414 Bee Cave Rd, Austin, TX 78746
Tel.: (866) 783-3564
Toll Free: (800) 681-8809
E-Mail: ideas@steelbranding.com
Web Site: www.steelbranding.com

Year Founded: 2000

Agency Specializes In: Advertising, Internet/Web Design, Medical Products, Pharmaceutical, Web (Banner Ads, Pop-ups, etc.)

Kirsten Cutshall *(Pres)*
Cheryl Habbe *(Partner & Dir-Order & Reason)*
Amy Bailey *(VP-PR)*
Deanna Krischke *(VP-Bus Dev)*
Katherine Boschert *(Producer-Interactive)*
Denise Waid *(Creative Dir)*
Andrea Wallace *(Acct Supvr & Dir-Bus Dev)*
Samantha McCanless *(Mgr-Ops)*
Sarah Noel *(Acct Supvr)*
Kara Banff *(Media Buyer)*

Accounts:
ACS Learning
Advanced Micro Devices
AMD
Amelia Bullock Realtors
Convio
Dell
The Greensheet
Siemens

STEELE & ASSOCIATES, INC.

125 N Garfield, Pocatello, ID 83204
Tel.: (208) 233-7206
Fax: (208) 233-7384
Web Site: steelebranding.com/

E-Mail for Key Personnel:
President: jsteele@steele-associates.com

Employees: 7
Year Founded: 1979

National Agency Associations: AAF-Second Wind Limited

Agency Specializes In: Advertising, Agriculture, Automotive, Brand Development & Integration, Co-op Advertising, Collateral, Communications, Consulting, Consumer Marketing, Corporate Identity, Direct Response Marketing, Event Planning & Marketing, Exhibit/Trade Shows, Financial, Graphic Design, Health Care Services, High Technology, Industrial, Internet/Web Design, Logo & Package Design, Magazines, Media Buying Services, Medical Products, Merchandising, New Product Development, Newspaper, Newspapers & Magazines, Out-of-Home Media, Outdoor, Point of Purchase, Point of Sale, Print, Production, Public Relations, Publicity/Promotions, Radio, Real Estate, Restaurant, Retail, Sales Promotion, Strategic Planning/Research, T.V., Trade & Consumer Magazines, Travel & Tourism, Yellow Pages Advertising

Approx. Annual Billings: $2,300,000

James F. Steele *(CEO)*
Scott Elliott *(Dir-Creative)*
Mike Lyon *(Dir-Art)*
Amy Cordell *(Coord-Production & Media Buyer)*

Accounts:
AMI Semiconductors; 1988
Farm Bureau Insurance Company of Idaho; 1998
FMC Corporation; 1998
Idaho State University; 1994
J.R. Simplot Co.; Pocatello, ID Minerals & Chemicals; 1981
Regional Development Alliance; 2000

STEELE ROSE COMMUNICATIONS

12085 Morehead, Chapel Hill, NC 27517
Tel.: (919) 240-5803
Web Site: www.steelerosecom.com

Agency Specializes In: Advertising, Brand Development & Integration, Crisis Communications, Digital/Interactive, Media Training, Public Relations, Social Media

Karen Barnett *(Pres)*

Accounts:
New-Rethinkingthebox

STEELE+

2500 Northwinds Pkwy Ste 190, Atlanta, GA 30009
Tel.: (770) 772-3600
Fax: (770) 772-3601
Web Site: www.steeleplus.com

Employees: 9
Year Founded: 2003

Agency Specializes In: Advertising

Christopher Steele *(Owner)*
Scott Coleman *(Pres)*
Scott Estep *(Exec VP & Dir-Media)*
Donna McKinley *(Exec VP & Dir-Production)*

Accounts:
Environmental Stoneworks
Georgia Pacific
Lexmark

STEENMAN ASSOCIATES

2811 245th Pl SE Sammamish, Seattle, WA 98075
Tel.: (425) 427-9692
Fax: (425) 427-9693
E-Mail: info@steenmanassociates.com
Web Site: www.steenmanassociates.com

Ed Steenman *(Owner)*

Accounts:
Auburn Volkswagen

STEIN + PARTNERS BRAND ACTIVATION

(Merged with IAS b2b Marketing to Form Stein IAS)

STEIN IAS

(Formerly Stein + Partners Brand Activation)
432 Park Ave S, New York, NY 10016-8013
Tel.: (212) 213-1112
Fax: (212) 779-7305
Web Site: www.steinias.com

Employees: 100
Year Founded: 1984

Agency Specializes In: Advertising, Brand Development & Integration, Broadcast, Business-To-Business, Cable T.V., Collateral, Computers & Software, Consumer Marketing, Content, Corporate Identity, Customer Relationship Management, Digital/Interactive, Direct Response Marketing, E-Commerce, Education, Electronic Media, Email, Entertainment, Event Planning & Marketing, Financial, High Technology, Industrial, Information Technology, Integrated Marketing, Internet/Web Design, Magazines, Market Research, Media Planning, Multimedia, New Product Development, New Technologies, Newspaper, Newspapers & Magazines, Out-of-Home Media, Outdoor, Paid Searches, Planning & Consultation, Point of Sale, Print, Production, Production (Print), Promotions, Publicity/Promotions, Publishing, Radio, Real Estate, Sales Promotion, Search Engine Optimization, Social Marketing/Nonprofit, Social Media, Sponsorship, Strategic Planning/Research, T.V., Trade & Consumer Magazines, Travel & Tourism, Web (Banner Ads, Pop-ups, etc.)

Approx. Annual Billings: $25,000,000

Marianne Moore *(Partner & Chief Strategy Officer)*
Ted Kohnen *(CMO)*
Barrie Rubinstein *(Exec Dir)*
Jason Abbate *(Dir-Interactions)*
Danny Santos *(Dir-Creative Svcs)*
Steve Affat *(Assoc Dir-Integrated Mktg)*
Mike Azzara *(Sr Strategist-Content)*

Accounts:
ADP
ASME
Atos
BP Castrol
CenturyLink
Chicago Board Options Exchange (Agency of Record) Campaign: "Execute success", Campaign: "Faces", Online, Outdoor, Print, Radio
Chief Executive Group Brand Strategy, Creative, Digital Services, Go-To-Market Planning, Marketing Communications Services, Positioning
Crisp Media Campaign: "Certifiably Better"

Curiosityville
KPMG
Nespresso
Pearsons
Wolters Kluwer

STEIN ROGAN + PARTNERS
(Name Changed to Stein IAS)

STEINER SPORTS MARKETING
145 Huguenot St, New Rochelle, NY 10801-6454
Tel.: (914) 307-1000
Fax: (914) 632-1102
E-Mail: generalinfo@steinersports.com
Web Site: www.steinersports.com

Employees: 100

Agency Specializes In: Sports Market

Brandon Steiner *(Founder & CEO)*
Kelvin Joseph *(COO)*
Steven Costello *(Exec VP)*
Sean Mahoney *(Exec VP)*
Mara Steiner *(VP-HR)*
Brooks Cowan *(Dir-Sls)*
Eric Levy *(Dir-Pur)*
Tina Cancellieri *(Mgr-Ops)*

Accounts:
Citibank
Mastercard
New York Yankees Memorabilia

STELLAR ENGINE
67 W St Ste 401, Brooklyn, NY 11222
Tel.: (718) 541-6658
E-Mail: hello@stellar-engine.com
Web Site: www.stellar-engine.com

Year Founded: 2011

Agency Specializes In: Advertising, Brand Development & Integration, Content, Social Media

Ehren Gresehover *(Co-Founder & Dir-Creative)*
Tammy Oler *(Co-Founder & Dir-Strategy)*
Mac Rogers *(Copywriter & Producer)*
Shaun B. Fauntleroy *(Community Mgr)*

Accounts:
Skittles

STELLARHEAD
45 Main St Ste 1010, Brooklyn, NY 11201
Tel.: (646) 374-4984
E-Mail: info@stellarhead.com
Web Site: www.stellarhead.com

Year Founded: 2010

Agency Specializes In: Advertising, Brand Development & Integration, Consulting, Content, Digital/Interactive, Event Planning & Marketing, Mobile Marketing, Production, Public Relations, Social Media

Laurel Harris *(Founder, Pres & Exec Producer)*
Doris Fayez *(Controller)*
Joe Feinstein *(Dir-Bus Dev)*
Beth Gibeley *(Dir-Bus Dev)*
Nikki Sodaro *(Coord-Design & Production)*

Accounts:
Terex Corporation

STEP ONE CREATIVE
317 W 1st St Ste 101, Oswego, NY 13126
Tel.: (315) 342-2554
Fax: (315) 216-4652
E-Mail: info@steponecreative.com
Web Site: www.steponecreative.com

Year Founded: 1996

Agency Specializes In: Advertising, Brand Development & Integration, Collateral, Event Planning & Marketing, Logo & Package Design, Media Planning, Print, Public Relations, Social Media

Mark Proud *(Dir-Creative)*
Shelby Stepien *(Specialist-Design & Plng)*

Accounts:
Eagle Beverage Co, Inc.
Heritage Gunworks
Oswego County Opportunities Inc.
Oswego law firm Amdursky, Pelky, Fennell & Wallen
Oswego's Sports Photography
Pathfinder Bank's Oswego Hockey Classic
Tri-Oswego
US Naval Sea Cadets - Rochester Division

STEPHAN ADVERTISING AGENCY, INC.
807 N Waco St Ste 11, Wichita, KS 67203-3971
Tel.: (316) 265-0021
Fax: (316) 264-1825
E-Mail: dstephan@msvads.com

Employees: 4
Year Founded: 1963

National Agency Associations: AMA

Agency Specializes In: Financial, Food Service, Health Care Services, Retail

Approx. Annual Billings: $1,250,000

Breakdown of Gross Billings by Media: Bus. Publs.: $62,500; D.M.: $25,000; Mags.: $37,500; Newsp.: $250,000; Outdoor: $50,000; Radio: $412,500; T.V.: $412,500

Donald K. Stephan *(Pres)*

STEPHAN & BRADY, INC.
1850 Hoffman St, Madison, WI 53704-2541
Tel.: (608) 241-4141
Fax: (608) 241-4246
E-Mail: gwhitely@stephanbrady.com
Web Site: www.stephanbrady.com

Employees: 45
Year Founded: 1952

Agency Specializes In: Advertising, Brand Development & Integration, Business-To-Business, Collateral, Consumer Marketing, Corporate Identity, Digital/Interactive, Direct Response Marketing, E-Commerce, Event Planning & Marketing, Food Service, Integrated Marketing, Internet/Web Design, Logo & Package Design, Market Research, Media Buying Services, Media Planning, Media Relations, Media Training, Package Design, Point of Purchase, Point of Sale, Print, Promotions, Public Relations, Sales Promotion, Strategic Planning/Research, Web (Banner Ads, Pop-ups, etc.)

Breakdown of Gross Billings by Media: Brdcst.: 9%; Consumer Publs.: 10%; Fees: 19%; Mags.: 10%; Newsp.: 8%; Other: 2%; Outdoor: 1%; Production: 16%; Pub. Rels.: 22%; Worldwide Web Sites: 3%

George Whitely *(Pres & CEO)*
Marki Landerud *(Acct Dir)*
Laura Krogstad *(Dir-Media)*
Nicole Jenkins *(Sr Acct Exec)*
Jessica Scholz *(Asst Acct Exec)*
Megan McDowell *(Coord-PR & Social Media)*
Kate Salkin *(Sr Designer-Interactive)*

Accounts:
Archer Daniels Midland (ADM)
Badgerland Farm Credit Services; Baraboo, WI
Church Mutual Insurance Co.; Merrill, WI
Emmi-Roth Kase USA, Ltd.
Gordon Flesch Co.; Madison, WI Office Equipment & Supplies
Jones Dairy Farm
Newry Capital Group, LLC
Research Products
Virchow, Krause & Co.; Madison, WI
Wisconsin Milk Marketing Board; Madison, WI Consumer, Trade Relations, Food Service & Dairy Research Public Relations
Wisconsin Public Service; Green Bay, WI
Wisconsin Special Olympics; Madison, WI

STEPHAN PARTNERS, INC.
233 Spring St Ste 801, New York, NY 10013
Tel.: (212) 524-8583
Fax: (212) 524-8501
E-Mail: info@stephanpartners.com
Web Site: www.stephanpartners.com

E-Mail for Key Personnel:
President: george@stephanpartners.com
Creative Dir.: carol@stephanpartners.com

Employees: 7
Year Founded: 1995

Agency Specializes In: Advertising, Affiliate Marketing, Business-To-Business, Collateral, Communications, Consulting, Consumer Goods, Corporate Identity, Digital/Interactive, Direct Response Marketing, E-Commerce, Email, Event Planning & Marketing, Exhibit/Trade Shows, Financial, Graphic Design, Internet/Web Design, Magazines, Media Buying Services, New Product Development, Out-of-Home Media, Print, Production, Public Relations, Publicity/Promotions, Sales Promotion, Search Engine Optimization, Stakeholders, Strategic Planning/Research, Telemarketing

Breakdown of Gross Billings by Media: Bus. Publs.: $4,560,000; Mags.: $120,000; Newsp.: $120,000; Other: $1,900,000; T.V.: $3,000,000

George N. Stephan *(Mng Dir)*
Carolyne Berkeley *(Dir-Customer Insights)*
Carol Bokuniewicz *(Dir-Creative-Branding)*
Jeff Bretl *(Dir-Creative & Direct Mktg)*
Bob Feinberg *(Dir-Creative-Direct Mktg)*
Steve Meltzer *(Dir-Creative-Integrated Comm)*
Jim Parry *(Dir-Creative-Adv)*

Accounts:
Clinique
Financial Times
Maggie Maternity
MCEnergy
MTV Networks
Orlando CVB
Rodale
Spectrum Resorts
Time Warner
Wall Street Journal
Wenner Media

STEPHEN HALES CREATIVE INC
2230 N University Pkwy Ste 7D, Provo, UT 84604
Tel.: (801) 373-8888
E-Mail: info@halescreative.com
Web Site: www.halescreative.com

Agency Specializes In: Advertising, Brand Development & Integration, Collateral, Corporate

Identity, Digital/Interactive, Graphic Design, Internet/Web Design, Logo & Package Design, Print

Stephen A. Hales *(CEO & Dir-Creative)*
Kelly Nield *(Sr Dir-Art)*
Spencer Hales *(Designer)*

Accounts:
Americas Freedom Festival
Brigham Young University
Deseret Book Co.
Excel Eye Center
HyClone
LDS Living
Nuestra Gente
ProSteel
Selnate International
Tahitian Noni International

STEPHENS & ASSOCIATES ADVERTISING, INC.
7400 W 132nd St Ste 100, Overland Park, KS 66213
Tel.: (913) 661-0910
Fax: (913) 661-0967
Toll Free: (800) 466-0910
Web Site: www.stephens-adv.com/

E-Mail for Key Personnel:
President: chuck@stephens-adv.com

Employees: 30
Year Founded: 1980

National Agency Associations: DMA

Agency Specializes In: Agriculture, Business-To-Business, Collateral, Pets , Pharmaceutical, Point of Purchase, Trade & Consumer Magazines

Chuck Stephens *(Pres & CEO)*
Jennifer Brocker *(Chief Creative Officer)*
Cathy McCormick *(Chief Strategy Officer)*
Boo Larsen *(Client Svcs Dir)*
Susan Wright *(Acct Dir)*
Ted Glickman *(Dir-PR)*
Patricia Thomblison *(Dir-Medical)*
Carol Stuart *(Mgr-Production)*
Aimee Sims *(Acct Coord)*

Accounts:
Capitol Resources
Care Credit; Anaheim, CA
Summit VetPharm

STEPHENS DIRECT
417 E Stroop Rd, Kettering, OH 45429
Tel.: (937) 299-4993
Fax: (937) 299-9355
E-Mail: info@stephensdirect.com
Web Site: www.stephensdirect.com

Employees: 22
Year Founded: 1981

Agency Specializes In: Business-To-Business, Collateral, Consumer Marketing, Direct Response Marketing, Event Planning & Marketing, Financial, Media Buying Services, Merchandising, Point of Sale, Print, Production, Retail, Sales Promotion, Sweepstakes

Phillip Stephens, II *(Pres & COO)*
Ken Ott *(Mng Dir-Art)*
Beth Sjostrom *(VP-Creative Svcs)*
Sharon Doty *(Project Mgr & Mgr-Production Coordination)*
Amy Shahandeh *(Acct Exec)*
Chris Bruggeman *(Copywriter)*
Amanda Brown *(Coord-Production)*
Jennifer Ball *(Client Svc Dir)*

Accounts:
GE Capital
Right State

THE STEPHENZ GROUP, INC.
75 E Santa Clara St Ste 900, San Jose, CA 95113-1319
Tel.: (408) 286-9899
Fax: (408) 286-9866
Toll Free: (800) 535-1055
E-Mail: info@stephenz.com
Web Site: www.stephenz.com

E-Mail for Key Personnel:
President: bzenz@stephenz.com
Creative Dir.: spaulson@stephenz.com
Production Mgr.: lchau@stephenz.com

Employees: 28
Year Founded: 1981

Agency Specializes In: Advertising, Brand Development & Integration, Business-To-Business, Collateral, Corporate Communications, Digital/Interactive, Direct Response Marketing, Electronic Media, Exhibit/Trade Shows, Graphic Design, Guerilla Marketing, High Technology, Identity Marketing, Integrated Marketing, Internet/Web Design, Logo & Package Design, Media Buying Services, Media Planning, Media Relations, Mobile Marketing, Multimedia, Point of Sale, Public Relations, Strategic Planning/Research, Web (Banner Ads, Pop-ups, etc.)

Approx. Annual Billings: $68,000,000

Barbara E. Zenz *(Pres & CEO)*
Barbara Sater *(VP-Strategic Svcs)*
Stephanie Paulson *(Exec Dir-Creative)*
Phillip Kim *(Assoc Dir-Creative-Design)*
Judie Jordan *(Mgr-Bus Dev)*
Scott Brendel *(Sr Acct Exec)*

Accounts:
AMD; 2005
Applied Materials
ATI; 2006
ELO Touchsystems; 2007
Epson America, Inc.
Gilead Sciences; 1999
Hewlett Packard, Home Products Div
Hitachi
IBM
Intermec
Neterion
NuGen Technologies Inc. (Agency of Record)
Samsung Semiconductor
Samsung; 2000
San Jose State University
Shore Tel; 2007
Symmetricom Inc. (Agency of Record)
TE Connectivity
Visa

STERLING CROSS COMMUNICATIONS
12416 90th Pl N, Maple Grove, MN 55369
Tel.: (763) 496-1499
Web Site: www.sterlingcrossgroup.com

Agency Specializes In: Brand Development & Integration, Communications, Digital/Interactive, Direct-to-Consumer, Electronic Media, Email, Internet/Web Design, Media Relations, Media Training, New Product Development, Podcasting, Public Relations, RSS (Really Simple Syndication), Strategic Planning/Research, Viral/Buzz/Word of Mouth

Mary Lower *(Owner & Pres)*
Mykl Roventine *(Dir-Social Media & Web Svcs)*

Accounts:
BajaSol
Curry Up
Dakota
DuraTech Industries (Haybuster) GP-50 Grain Processor
Tripl3Caff
Truffles
Twin Cities Community Gospel Choir

STERLING MEDIA NORTHWEST
PO Box 906, North Bend, OR 97420
Tel.: (541) 982-3098
Web Site: www.sterlingmedianw.com

Year Founded: 2009

Agency Specializes In: Advertising, Brand Development & Integration, Logo & Package Design, Media Buying Services, Public Relations, Radio, Social Media

Michelle Sargent *(Partner & Designer-Creative Mktg)*

Accounts:
Carrie Grant Photography
South Coast Orthopaedics & Associates
South Coast Orthopaedics Physical Therapy
South Coast Surgery Center
Yellow Cab Taxi

STERLING RICE GROUP
1801 13th St Ste 400, Boulder, CO 80302
Tel.: (303) 381-6400
Fax: (303) 444-6637
E-Mail: email@srg.com
Web Site: www.srg.com

Employees: 125
Year Founded: 1984

Agency Specializes In: Advertising, Agriculture, Brand Development & Integration, Broadcast, Business-To-Business, Cable T.V., Children's Market, Communications, Consulting, Consumer Goods, Consumer Marketing, Corporate Identity, Cosmetics, Digital/Interactive, Direct-to-Consumer, Education, Financial, Food Service, Graphic Design, Health Care Services, Household Goods, Identity Marketing, Integrated Marketing, Internet/Web Design, Local Marketing, Logo & Package Design, Magazines, Media Buying Services, Media Planning, Medical Products, New Product Development, Newspaper, Newspapers & Magazines, Outdoor, Over-50 Market, Package Design, Planning & Consultation, Print, Production (Ad, Film, Broadcast), Production (Print), Radio, Regional, Restaurant, Retail, Seniors' Market, Social Marketing/Nonprofit, Sponsorship, Strategic Planning/Research, T.V., Teen Market, Trade & Consumer Magazines, Transportation, Travel & Tourism, Web (Banner Ads, Pop-ups, etc.), Women's Market

Ed Rzasa *(Mng Partner)*
Mike Walters *(Mng Partner)*
Sheila Rosen *(Partner & Mng Dir)*
Jeff Curry *(Partner & Grp Dir-Creative)*
Susan Peck *(Partner & Grp Dir-Media)*
Jennifer Jones *(Partner & Dir-Design Strategy)*
Daniel Burak *(Mng Dir)*
Patrick Campbell *(Assoc Dir-Creative)*
Jessica Altus *(Sr Mgr-Integrated Production)*
Rob Renegar *(Mgr-Insights)*
Jon Sharpton *(Supvr-Digital Media)*
Jill Holmstrom *(Sr Strategist)*
Marissa Strobel *(Sr Planner-Digital Media)*

Accounts:
Almond Board of California
Annie's Homegrown

Arrow Electronics
Bernina
Boulder Brands Inc.
Bush Brothers Baked Beans
Cascadian Farms
The Children's Hospital
ConAgra
Culture of Giving
Efficas
Fantastic Foods
Fisher Biosciences
Fitness Holdings International
Frito-Lay, Inc.
Frontier Airlines
General Mills
Johnson & Johnson
Kellogg's
Level 3 Communications
MillerCoors
Mondelez International, Inc.
National Pork Producers Council
Noodles & Company
Oscar Mayer
Pepperidge Farm
PepsiCo
PPG Industries
Prairie Grove Farms
Quaker Oats
Rocky Mountain Cancer Centers
Rubbermaid
Shell Oil
The State of Colorado Campaign: "Making Colorado"
Trinidad Benham Corporation
UBS Financial Services
US Potato Board
White Wave Foods Horizon Organic
Yogi Tea

STERN ADVERTISING, INC.

950 Main Ave, Cleveland, OH 44113
Tel.: (216) 464-4850
Fax: (216) 464-7859
E-Mail: billstern@Sternadvertising.com
Web Site: www.sternadvertising.com

Employees: 78
Year Founded: 1954

Agency Specializes In: Advertising, African-American Market, Brand Development & Integration, Broadcast, Cable T.V., Co-op Advertising, Collateral, Consumer Marketing, Fashion/Apparel, Graphic Design, Health Care Services, Newspaper, Outdoor, Point of Purchase, Point of Sale, Print, Radio, Restaurant, Retail

William J. Stern *(Owner)*
Steve Romanenghi *(Exec VP & Exec Dir-Creative)*
Doug Cohen *(Exec VP & Acct Mgmt Dir)*
Kerry Ford *(VP & Grp Dir-PR)*
Brendan Riley *(VP & Mgmt Supvr)*
Lynne Trivelli *(VP & Assoc Dir-Media)*

Accounts:
Cleveland Museum of Art; 2012
Jared the Galleria of Jewelry Jewelry Retailer; 1988
Kay Jewelers Jewelry Retailer; 1988
McDonald's Restaurants; Oak Brook, IL; 1981
Southwest General Health Center Hospital; 2008
Sterling Jewelers, Inc.
Third Federal Savings & Loan; Cleveland, OH Banking Services; 2003

STERN PR MARKETING

16508 Taylor St, Omaha, NE 68116
Tel.: (402) 212-7489
Web Site: www.sternpr4less.com

Year Founded: 2004

Agency Specializes In: Advertising, Corporate Communications, Email, Graphic Design, Internet/Web Design, Media Relations, Public Relations, Search Engine Optimization, Social Media

Susan Stern *(Owner)*

Accounts:
Beef Additive Alert
Resurrection Evangelical Lutheran Church

STEVE CHIRELLO ADVERTISING

121 S 1st St, Fulton, NY 13069
Tel.: (315) 592-9778
Fax: (315) 598-2474
Web Site: www.chirello.com

Year Founded: 1996

Agency Specializes In: Advertising, Internet/Web Design, Logo & Package Design, Media Planning, Public Relations

Steve Chirello *(Owner)*

Accounts:
Foster Funeral Home

THE STEVEN STYLE GROUP

106 W 32nd St Ste 600, New York, NY 10001
Tel.: (212) 465-1290
Fax: (212) 465-1299
E-Mail: information@stylegroup.com

Employees: 5

Agency Specializes In: Advertising

Steven Style *(Founder & Pres-Arts & Sensory Evolution)*

Accounts:
ATON
BDI Marketing
Body Wisdom Media
Cold Tree Press
ELAN Home Systems
Escient
Hillside Candy GoNaturallyT; 2008
Hirschfeld Properties LLC
Nace Link Network
Scott A. Jones
Silver Dolphin
Uncle Jimstone's Educational Adventures
Uncle John's Bathroom Reader

STEVENS ADVERTISING

190 Monroe Ave NW Ste 200, Grand Rapids, MI 49503
Tel.: (616) 942-2801
Fax: (616) 942-2804
E-Mail: creative@stevensinc.com
Web Site: www.stevensinc.com

Employees: 10
Year Founded: 1921

Agency Specializes In: Advertising, Brand Development & Integration, Broadcast, Business-To-Business, Cable T.V., Co-op Advertising, Collateral, Communications, Consulting, Consumer Marketing, Consumer Publications, Corporate Identity, Direct Response Marketing, Education, Electronic Media, Entertainment, Exhibit/Trade Shows, Fashion/Apparel, Financial, Food Service, Graphic Design, Internet/Web Design, Logo & Package Design, Magazines, Media Buying Services, Medical Products, Multimedia, Newspaper, Newspapers & Magazines, Out-of-Home Media, Outdoor, Planning & Consultation, Point of Purchase, Point of Sale, Print, Production, Radio, Restaurant, Retail, Strategic Planning/Research, T.V., Trade & Consumer Magazines, Travel & Tourism, Yellow Pages Advertising

Mike Muller *(Owner)*
Allen Crater *(Pres)*
Charla Proctor *(Dir-Art)*
Diane Rivard *(Dir-Media)*
Daniel Spicer *(Dir-Creative)*
Lisa Decker *(Acct Exec)*

Accounts:
Advantage Health
American Education Group Fusion Academy Brochure
Bill & Paul's Sporthaus; Grand Rapids, MI
CLC Network
Crystal Mountain Resort; Thompsonville, MI
Elite Plastic Surgery
Exempla Healthcare
Maple Island Log Homes
The Sharpe Collection

STEVENS & TATE MARKETING

1900 S Highland Ave Ste 200, Lombard, IL 60148
Tel.: (630) 627-5200
Fax: (630) 627-5255
E-Mail: info@stevens-tate.com
Web Site: www.stevens-tate.com

Agency Specializes In: Advertising, Internet/Web Design, Logo & Package Design, Print, Social Media

Mark Beebe *(Owner & Partner)*
Dan Gartlan *(Pres)*
Debbie Szwast *(Acct Svcs Dir)*
Tom Furie *(Dir-Bus)*
Jeanne O'Neill *(Dir-Media)*
Maria Pelley *(Dir-Art)*
Nicole Wagner *(Dir-Mktg)*
Walt Mutschler *(Mgr-Creative)*
Kelsey Nihiser *(Acct Exec)*
Paul Schappel *(Sr Art Dir)*

Accounts:
Carstens, Inc. Campaign: "A Roo For You", WALKAroo, WALLAroo(C)
Genieco, Inc. (Agency of Record) Gonesh Incense, Marketing, Online, Social Media
Illinois Food Retailers Association Campaign: "Connect, Learn, Advance"
K. Hovnanian Homes

STEVENS STRATEGIC COMMUNICATIONS, INC.

Gemini Towers, Ste 500, 1991 Crocker Rd, Westlake, OH 44115-1900
Tel.: (440) 617-0100
Fax: (440) 614-0529
E-Mail: estevens@stevensstrategic.com
Web Site: www.stevensstrategic.com

E-Mail for Key Personnel:
President: estevens@stevensstrategic.com

Employees: 12
Year Founded: 1973

National Agency Associations: AAF-MCA

Agency Specializes In: Advertising, Automotive, Aviation & Aerospace, Brand Development & Integration, Broadcast, Business Publications, Business-To-Business, Co-op Advertising, Collateral, Communications, Consulting, Consumer Marketing, Corporate Communications, Corporate Identity, Direct Response Marketing, Education, Engineering, Environmental, Event Planning & Marketing, Exhibit/Trade Shows, Financial, Food Service, Graphic Design, Health Care Services,

High Technology, In-Store Advertising, Industrial, Internet/Web Design, Investor Relations, Local Marketing, Logo & Package Design, Magazines, Media Buying Services, Medical Products, Merchandising, New Product Development, Planning & Consultation, Point of Purchase, Point of Sale, Print, Production, Public Relations, Publicity/Promotions, Real Estate, Restaurant, Retail, Sales Promotion, Seniors' Market, Social Media, Sports Market, Strategic Planning/Research, Sweepstakes, Telemarketing, Trade & Consumer Magazines, Transportation, Travel & Tourism

Edward Stevens *(Chm & CEO)*
David Walker *(Pres)*
Steve Toth *(Sr Dir-Art)*
Jennie Ford *(Dir-Digital Mktg)*
Meredith Traxler *(Office Mgr)*
Nandi Thorn *(Supvr-Health Care)*
Jim Difrangia *(Acct Exec)*

Accounts:
American Association of Automatic Door Manufacturing
American Greetings
Ametek
AmTrust
Council of Smaller Enterprises (COSE)
Cuyahoga Community College
Cuyahoga County Public Library
Eriez
FII
Ghent Manufacturing
Ingenuity Cleveland
Lancaster Colony
Materion
Medical Mutual of Ohio
National Safety Apparel
Neighborhood Centers Association
Ohio Semitronics
Ross Enviornmental

STEVENSON ADVERTISING

16521 13th Ave W, Lynnwood, WA 98037
Tel.: (425) 787-9686
Fax: (425) 787-9702
E-Mail: brett@stevensonadvertising.com
Web Site: www.stevensonadvertising.com

Employees: 17
Year Founded: 1990

Agency Specializes In: Advertising, Automotive, Broadcast, Business-To-Business, Cable T.V., Co-op Advertising, Consumer Publications, Corporate Identity, Custom Publishing, Direct Response Marketing, Graphic Design, Guerilla Marketing, Internet/Web Design, Logo & Package Design, Magazines, Market Research, Media Buying Services, Media Planning, Multimedia, Newspaper, Newspapers & Magazines, Production, Production (Print), Public Relations, Publicity/Promotions, Publishing, Radio, Seniors' Market, Strategic Planning/Research, T.V., Trade & Consumer Magazines

Approx. Annual Billings: $4,000,000

Breakdown of Gross Billings by Media: Bus. Publs.: $1,000,000; Radio & T.V.: $3,000,000

Brett Stevenson *(Pres & CEO)*
Kathy Balcom *(VP-Sls-Eastern WA)*
Tim Grand *(VP-Sls & Media)*
Merri Hanson *(VP-Bus Dev)*
Laura Miranda *(Controller)*
Shawn Sergev *(Dir & Mgr-Video Production)*
Mary Beth Manley *(Specialist-SEO & Designer-Web)*

Accounts:
Campbell & Company
Cascade Natural Gas
Larson Automotive Group
The Rock Wood Fired Kitchen
Senior Housing Assistance Group (SHAG)
Vern Fonk Insurance

STEWARD MARKETING, LLC

9595 Six Pines Ste 8210, The Woodlands, TX 77380
Tel.: (832) 955-1056
Fax: (832) 442-5842
Toll Free: (877) 541-2718
E-Mail: info@stewardmarketing.com
Web Site: www.stewardmarketing.com

Employees: 11
Year Founded: 2002

National Agency Associations: AMA

Agency Specializes In: Advertising, Advertising Specialties, Bilingual Market, Brand Development & Integration, Broadcast, Business Publications, Business-To-Business, Cable T.V., Collateral, Communications, Consulting, Consumer Marketing, Consumer Publications, Corporate Identity, Digital/Interactive, Direct Response Marketing, E-Commerce, Electronic Media, Engineering, Event Planning & Marketing, Graphic Design, Health Care Services, High Technology, Hispanic Market, Industrial, Information Technology, Internet/Web Design, Logo & Package Design, Magazines, Medical Products, Multimedia, Newspaper, Newspapers & Magazines, Outdoor, Over-50 Market, Planning & Consultation, Print, Public Relations, Radio, Real Estate, Seniors' Market, Strategic Planning/Research, Technical Advertising, Trade & Consumer Magazines, Travel & Tourism

Approx. Annual Billings: $10,000,000

James P. Alexander *(Pres & CEO)*
Bart Darling *(Dir-Creative)*

STIEGLER, WELLS, BRUNSWICK & ROTH, INC.

(d/b/a SWB&R)
3865 Adler Pl, Bethlehem, PA 18017-9000
Tel.: (610) 866-0611
Fax: (610) 866-8650
Web Site: www.swbrinc.com

E-Mail for Key Personnel:
President: ernie.stiegler@swbinc.com
Creative Dir.: alan.zerbe@swbinc.com
Media Dir.: debbie.drake@swbinc.com
Production Mgr.: donna.sinko@swbinc.com
Public Relations: henry.raab@swbinc.com

Employees: 35
Year Founded: 1969

National Agency Associations: 4A's-INBA

Agency Specializes In: Advertising, Arts, Automotive, Aviation & Aerospace, Bilingual Market, Brand Development & Integration, Business Publications, Business-To-Business, Cable T.V., Children's Market, Co-op Advertising, Collateral, College, Communications, Consulting, Consumer Goods, Consumer Marketing, Consumer Publications, Corporate Communications, Corporate Identity, Crisis Communications, Customer Relationship Management, Digital/Interactive, Direct Response Marketing, Direct-to-Consumer, E-Commerce, Education, Electronic Media, Electronics, Email, Engineering, Entertainment, Event Planning & Marketing, Exhibit/Trade Shows, Financial, Graphic Design, Guerilla Marketing, Health Care Services, High Technology, Identity Marketing, In-Store Advertising, Industrial, Infomercials, Information Technology, Integrated Marketing, International, Internet/Web Design, Investor Relations, Local Marketing, Logo & Package Design, Magazines, Market Research, Media Buying Services, Media Planning, Media Relations, Medical Products, Mobile Marketing, Multimedia, New Product Development, Newspaper, Newspapers & Magazines, Out-of-Home Media, Outdoor, Package Design, Paid Searches, Pharmaceutical, Planning & Consultation, Podcasting, Point of Purchase, Point of Sale, Print, Product Placement, Production, Production (Print), Promotions, Public Relations, Publicity/Promotions, Radio, Regional, Sales Promotion, Search Engine Optimization, Social Marketing/Nonprofit, Social Media, Sponsorship, Stakeholders, Strategic Planning/Research, Sweepstakes, Technical Advertising, Telemarketing, Trade & Consumer Magazines, Transportation, Viral/Buzz/Word of Mouth, Yellow Pages Advertising

Approx. Annual Billings: $35,000,000

Breakdown of Gross Billings by Media: Internet Adv.: 20%; Mags.: 50%; Newsp.: 20%; Radio: 10%

Scott Friedman *(Pres & COO)*
Ernie R. Stiegler *(CEO)*
Thomas Roth *(CFO)*
Henry R. Raab *(VP-PR)*
Donna R. Sinko *(VP-Production)*
Kathy Morrow-Voelker *(Co-Dir-Creative)*
Mike Walbert *(Dir-Strategic Comm)*

Accounts:
BDP International; Philadelphia, PA Global Logistics; 1997
Crayola; Easton, PA Art Products; 1984
Garlock Sealing Technologies; Palmyra, NY Bore Oil Seals, Klozure Oil Seals; 2007
Mack Financial Services; Greensboro, NC Financial Support Options for Mack Truck Customers; 2009
Mack Trucks, Inc.; Greensboro, NC Heavy & Medium-Duty Trucks; 1997
Masco Bath; Moorestown, NJ Bath & Shower Products; 2008
Perminova; La Jolla, CA Cardiovascular and Surgery Information Management Systems; 2012
Senco; Cincinnati, OH Contractor Power Tools
Sika Corporation; Lyndhurst, NJ Specialty Construction Chemicals & Products; 2004
Stemco; Longview, TX Supplies Wheel & Components to Heavy Duty Truck Markets; 2009

STILLWATER AGENCY

1919 Williams St Ste 201, Simi Valley, CA 93065
Tel.: (888) 519-5149
Web Site: www.stillwateragency.com

Year Founded: 2013

Agency Specializes In: Advertising, Email, Media Buying Services, Print, Radio, Search Engine Optimization, Social Media, T.V.

Lance Wilson *(Pres)*
Al Alfieri *(CEO)*
Sophia Wilson *(COO)*
Peter Gregory *(VP-Digital Mktg)*
David McBride *(Dir-Major Accounts)*
Jeb Orsini *(Coord-Mktg)*

Accounts:
Brake Performance

STILT MEDIA

250 Catalonia Ste 805, Miami, FL 33134
Tel.: (305) 230-4827
Web Site: www.stiltmedia.com

Year Founded: 2013

Agency Specializes In: Advertising, Brand Development & Integration, Collateral, Email, Graphic Design, Internet/Web Design, Logo & Package Design, Print, Search Engine Optimization

Guigo Simoes *(Founder & COO)*
Rafael Tano *(Dir-Digital Mktg)*
Giorgio Caniggia *(Mgr-Social Media)*
Patrick Maggio *(Mgr-Social Media)*

Accounts:
Anatomy at 1220

STIMULUS ADVERTISING & WEB DESIGN
1000 Jefferson St Unit 2B, Lynchburg, VA 24502
Tel.: (434) 455-7188
Web Site: www.stimulusadvertising.com

Year Founded: 2008

Agency Specializes In: Advertising, Brand Development & Integration, Corporate Communications, E-Commerce, Internet/Web Design, Logo & Package Design, Print, Public Relations, Search Engine Optimization, Social Media

Lynn Kirby *(Owner)*
Mark Davis *(Assoc Project Mgr & Copywriter)*
Banner Kidd *(Assoc Producer-Adv)*

Accounts:
Bedford Tourism
Benchmark ProTech
Dominion Seven Architects, PLC

STIMULUS BRAND COMMUNICATIONS
1 Currier Way, Ewing, NJ 8628
Tel.: (609) 538-1126
Web Site: www.stimulusbrand.com

Year Founded: 2002

Agency Specializes In: Advertising, Brand Development & Integration, Broadcast, Event Planning & Marketing, Graphic Design, Media Buying Services, Media Planning, Public Relations, Radio, Social Media

Tom McManimon *(Owner, Principal & Dir-Creative)*

Accounts:
Inglis

STINKDIGITAL
20 Jay St Ste 404, Brooklyn, NY 11201
Tel.: (212) 633-9600
E-Mail: hello@stinkdigital.com
Web Site: www.stinkdigital.com

Year Founded: 2009

Agency Specializes In: Advertising, Internet/Web Design, Production (Ad, Film, Broadcast)

Mark Pytlik *(CEO & Mng Dir)*
Chris Mele *(Mng Dir)*
Stefan Dufgran *(Head-UX & Strategist-Digital)*
Ben Hughes *(Exec Dir-Creative)*
Alex Sturtevant *(Exec Producer-New Bus)*
Sean Manion *(Producer-Interactive)*
Satu Pelkonen *(Dir-Art)*

Accounts:
Diesel SpA
Google
Luxottica
Miu Miu
Pitchfork
Red Bull
Sony "Move", Sony Action Cam
New-Spotify
New-Twitter

STIR ADVERTISING & INTEGRATED MARKETING
252 E Highland Ave, Milwaukee, WI 53202
Tel.: (414) 278-0040
Fax: (414) 278-0390
E-Mail: brianb@stirstuff.com
Web Site: www.stirstuff.com

E-Mail for Key Personnel:
President: brianb@stirmarketing.com
Creative Dir.: stevek@stirmarketing.com
Media Dir.: SuzieL@stirmarketing.com

Employees: 8
Year Founded: 2000

National Agency Associations: PRSA-Second Wind Limited

Agency Specializes In: Advertising, Automotive, Brand Development & Integration, Broadcast, Business Publications, Business-To-Business, Cable T.V., Collateral, Communications, Consulting, Consumer Marketing, Consumer Publications, Corporate Communications, Corporate Identity, Direct Response Marketing, Electronic Media, Event Planning & Marketing, Financial, Government/Political, Graphic Design, Health Care Services, In-Store Advertising, Internet/Web Design, Leisure, Local Marketing, Logo & Package Design, Magazines, Marine, Media Buying Services, Medical Products, New Product Development, Newspaper, Newspapers & Magazines, Out-of-Home Media, Outdoor, Planning & Consultation, Point of Purchase, Point of Sale, Print, Production, Public Relations, Publicity/Promotions, Radio, Recruitment, Retail, Sales Promotion, Strategic Planning/Research, Sweepstakes, T.V., Trade & Consumer Magazines, Travel & Tourism

Approx. Annual Billings: $5,000,000

Brian Bennett *(Owner & Pres)*
Bill Kreese *(Partner & Exec Dir-Creative)*
Matt McNulty *(Dir-Art)*
Lori Lanza *(Mgr-Media)*
Megan Hemmelgarn *(Acct Supvr-PR)*
Renee Solveson *(Sr Acct Exec)*
Caroline Wittenberg *(Acct Exec)*
Erin Keefe *(Asst Acct Exec)*

Accounts:
Associated Bank Print, Rebranding
AXIS Automation PR
Bank Mutual Corp (Advertising & Marketing Agency of Record) Creative Services, Media Buying, Public Relations, Web Development
Blue Co Brands Rebranding, Website Design
Cousins Subs Campaign: "Bait", PR, Rebranding, Web Design
Dr. Comfort (Agency of Record) Creative, Media Buying, Public Relations
GE Healthcare
Halloin Murdock Designing, PR, Website
Milwaukee Area Technical College Digital, Direct Marketing, Social Media
Milwaukee Bucks
Milwaukee/NARI Design, Website
New-Rural Mutual Insurance Company (Agency of Record)
Sargento Cheese Branding Development
United Performing Arts Fund Branding, Collateral Design
WISPARK Brand Development, Drexel Town Square, Website

STOCKHOLM DESIGN
15200 Sunset Blvd Ste 213, Los Angeles, CA 90272
Tel.: (310) 454-0004
Fax: (310) 943-1484
E-Mail: agency@stockholmdesign.com
Web Site: www.stockholmdesign.com

Employees: 10
Year Founded: 1997

Agency Specializes In: Automotive, Communications, Consulting, Digital/Interactive, Fashion/Apparel, Financial, Government/Political, Health Care Services, In-Store Advertising, Legal Services, Production, Retail

Markus Hammarberg *(Founder & CEO)*
Joakim Olsson *(VP & Sr Dir-Art)*

Accounts:
FOX
HBO
Lionsgate Films
Millennium
Warner Bros

STOLTZ MARKETING GROUP
913 W. River St., Ste 410, Boise, ID 83702
Tel.: (208) 388-0766
Fax: (208) 388-0764
E-Mail: kens@stoltzgroup.com
Web Site: www.stoltzgroup.com

E-Mail for Key Personnel:
President: kens@stoltzgroup.com
Creative Dir.: davec@stoltzgroup.com

Employees: 15
Year Founded: 1996

Agency Specializes In: Advertising, Affluent Market, Agriculture, Aviation & Aerospace, Brand Development & Integration, Broadcast, Business Publications, Business-To-Business, Cable T.V., Catalogs, Collateral, Communications, Consulting, Consumer Marketing, Corporate Identity, Digital/Interactive, Direct Response Marketing, E-Commerce, Electronic Media, Email, Environmental, Exhibit/Trade Shows, Food Service, Graphic Design, In-Store Advertising, Information Technology, Integrated Marketing, Internet/Web Design, Leisure, Logo & Package Design, Luxury Products, Magazines, Multimedia, Newspaper, Newspapers & Magazines, Out-of-Home Media, Outdoor, Package Design, Planning & Consultation, Point of Purchase, Point of Sale, Print, Production, Public Relations, Publicity/Promotions, Radio, Real Estate, Regional, Retail, Sales Promotion, Search Engine Optimization, Social Marketing/Nonprofit, Social Media, Strategic Planning/Research, T.V., Trade & Consumer Magazines, Web (Banner Ads, Pop-ups, etc.)

Approx. Annual Billings: $15,000,000

Breakdown of Gross Billings by Media: Brdcst.: $2,250,000; Bus. Publs.: $1,500,000; Collateral: $5,250,000; Consulting: $3,750,000; Fees: $2,250,000

Ken Stoltz *(Pres)*
Julie Stevens *(CFO)*
Kate Holgate *(Sr Dir-Art)*
Jay Bowen *(Sr Acct Dir)*
Bill Doty *(Producer-Digital Media)*
Jill Watterson *(Client Svcs Dir)*
Ward Duft *(Dir-Creative)*
Tony Hart *(Dir-Art)*
Dan Stone *(Mgr-PR & Copywriter)*
Brian Harrison *(Strategist-Digital)*
Joe Eck *(Coord-Production & Media)*

Accounts:
AIRE; Boise, ID Boats, Rafts; 2005
Atlas Holdings LLC Private Equity; 2009
Blue Cross of Idaho Health Insurance; 2011
Castor & Pollux Organix Brand Pet Food; 2011
Fresh Betty Spaghetti QSR; 2010
Idaho Wheat Commission; 2002
Idahoan Foods; Lewiston, ID Potato Products; 1996
The Pacific Companies Multifamily Housing Development; 2013
RedBuilt Engineered Wood Products; 2009
Soundview Paper Paper Products; 2011

THE STONE AGENCY
312 W Millbrook Rd Ste 225, Raleigh, NC 27609
Tel.: (919) 645-0799
E-Mail: jennym@thestoneagency.com
Web Site: thestoneagency.com

Walter Peel *(CFO)*
Jackie D'Antonio *(VP-Strategy)*
Kermit Rainman *(Exec Dir-Faith Driven Consumer)*
Luis Garcia-Gadea *(Dir-Art)*
Pearce Godwin *(Dir-Targeting Strategy)*
Leonard O Goenaga *(Dir-Digital Engagement)*
Carri Bojara *(Acct Supvr)*
Jackie Cole *(Acct Supvr)*
Jorge Manuel Acosta *(Specialist-Digital Engagement)*
Jack Ruhle *(Coord-Comm)*

STONE WARD
225 E Markham St Ste 450, Little Rock, AR 72201-1629
Tel.: (501) 375-3003
Fax: (501) 375-8314
E-Mail: info@stoneward.com
Web Site: www.stoneward.com

E-Mail for Key Personnel:
President: mward@stoneward.com
Creative Dir.: lstone@stoneward.com
Media Dir.: dreid@stoneward.com
Production Mgr.: bfowler@stoneward.com
Public Relations: bscisson@stoneward.com

Employees: 45
Year Founded: 1984

National Agency Associations: AMIN

Agency Specializes In: Brand Development & Integration, Broadcast, Business-To-Business, Co-op Advertising, Collateral, Consumer Marketing, Corporate Identity, Digital/Interactive, Exhibit/Trade Shows, Food Service, Graphic Design, Health Care Services, Information Technology, Internet/Web Design, Logo & Package Design, Media Buying Services, Planning & Consultation, Point of Purchase, Print, Production, Public Relations, Publicity/Promotions, Radio, Restaurant, Sponsorship, T.V., Transportation, Travel & Tourism

Approx. Annual Billings: $19,000,000

Breakdown of Gross Billings by Media: Fees: $6,460,000; Production: $7,030,000; Pub. Rels.: $2,090,000; Radio & T.V.: $950,000; Worldwide Web Sites: $2,470,000

Millie Ward *(Owner)*
John Rogers *(CFO & Treas)*
Bill Jennings *(Sr Dir-Art)*
Bill Brookshire *(Dir-Creative)*
Kyle Floyd *(Dir-Creative)*
Kandace Gerber *(Dir-Art)*
Emily Reeves *(Dir-Digital Innovation & Insight Plng)*
Tommy Walker *(Dir-Brdcst Production)*

Accounts:
Arkansas BlueCross BlueShield
Arkansas Department of Economic Development; Little Rock, AR; 1995
Arkansas Electric Cooperative Corp. Branding, Marketing
BancorpSouth
Baptist Health; Little Rock, AR Health Care System; 1998
Blue Cross and Blue Shield of Arkansas
Bridge2Rwanda
Energy Efficiency Arkansas
New-No Barriers (Agency of Record) Creative, Marketing Strategy, Public Relations, Social Media
Simmons First National Bank
SnapOn
SportClips
Terminix; Memphis, TN Termite & Pest Control; 1997
U.S. Soccer Federation

STONEARCH
710 S 2nd St 7th Fl, Minneapolis, MN 55401
Tel.: (612) 200-5000
E-Mail: info@stonearchcreative.com
Web Site: www.stonearchcreative.com

Agency Specializes In: Advertising, Brand Development & Integration, Content, Digital/Interactive, Education, Social Media, Strategic Planning/Research

Judy Kessel *(Founder & Chm)*
Jessica Boden *(Pres)*
Jerrold Gershone *(CEO)*
Phil Hoch *(Creative Dir)*
Amy Asbury *(Dir-Agency Partnerships)*
Cassie Benowitz *(Dir-Strategy)*
Nikki Cron *(Dir-Client Svcs)*
Sue Katula *(Dir-Content)*
Katie Uphus *(Dir-Ops)*

Accounts:
New-LifeScience Alley
Medela Inc Medela Breastfeeding (Agency of Record)
New-Vital Images Brand Awareness

STONER BUNTING ADVERTISING
322 N Arch St Fl 1, Lancaster, PA 17603-2991
Tel.: (717) 291-1491
Fax: (717) 399-8197
E-Mail: info@stonerbunting.com
Web Site: www.stonerbunting.com

Employees: 30
Year Founded: 1984

Agency Specializes In: Advertising, Automotive, Brand Development & Integration, Broadcast, Business Publications, Business-To-Business, Cable T.V., Co-op Advertising, Collateral, Communications, Consulting, Consumer Marketing, Consumer Publications, Corporate Identity, Electronic Media, Exhibit/Trade Shows, Graphic Design, Leisure, Logo & Package Design, Magazines, Multimedia, New Product Development, Newspaper, Newspapers & Magazines, Out-of-Home Media, Outdoor, Planning & Consultation, Point of Purchase, Point of Sale, Print, Production, Radio, Retail, Sales Promotion, Strategic Planning/Research, T.V., Trade & Consumer Magazines, Travel & Tourism

Approx. Annual Billings: $35,000,000

Breakdown of Gross Billings by Media: Collateral: 10%; D.M.: 10%; Mags.: 25%; Newsp.: 10%; Outdoor: 5%; Point of Purchase: 10%; Radio: 10%; T.V.: 20%

Dan Nguyen *(Owner & Pres)*
Jim Roosa *(Mng Dir & VP)*
Christine Vulgaris *(CFO)*
Allison Schiding *(Strategist-Creative)*

Accounts:
Armstrong
Bonton
Brooks Brothers
The Container Store
Harry & David
HDI Railing Systems
Invista; Wilmington, DE
Jiffy Lube
The Lancaster Chamber of Commerce & Industry
Landry's Restaurants Inc.
Royal China
Stainmaster
Sunglass Hut
Talbots

STOREBOARD MEDIA
441 Lexington Ave 14th Fl, New York, NY 10017
Tel.: (212) 682-3300
E-Mail: sales@storeboards.net
Web Site: www.storeboards.net

Employees: 10
Year Founded: 1982

Agency Specializes In: Graphic Design, Media Buying Services, Print, Retail, Strategic Planning/Research

Revenue: $4,000,007

Douglas B. Leeds *(Chm & CEO)*
Rick Sirvaitis *(Pres)*
Charlie Williams *(Exec VP)*
Melissa Gerard *(Sr Acct Dir)*
Jim McDonald *(Acct Dir)*
Caroline Kelso *(Dir-Ops)*
Jill Olson *(Office Mgr)*

Accounts:
Alberto Culver
Kerr Drug; 2008
Kraft Foods

STOREYMANSEAU, LLC
603 Upper Straw Rd, Hopkinton, NH 03229
Tel.: (603) 856-7647
E-Mail: info@storeymanseau.com
Web Site: www.storeymanseau.com

Year Founded: 2000

Agency Specializes In: Advertising, Brand Development & Integration, Collateral, Graphic Design, Internet/Web Design, Media Buying Services, Media Relations

Laurie Storey-Manseau *(Principal)*

Accounts:
Sanel Auto Parts Co.

STORY WORLDWIDE
48 W 25th St, New York, NY 10010
Tel.: (212) 481-3452
E-Mail: josh.golden@storyworldwide.com
Web Site: www.storyworldwide.com

Employees: 160
Year Founded: 2005

Agency Specializes In: Advertising, Business Publications, Digital/Interactive, Internet/Web Design, Production (Ad, Film, Broadcast), Viral/Buzz/Word of Mouth, Web (Banner Ads, Pop-ups, etc.)

Approx. Annual Billings: $45,000,000

Kirk Cheyfitz *(CEO)*
Charles Coxe *(Sr VP-Narrative)*
Jacqueline Brini *(VP-Strategy & Plng)*
Heidi Waldusky *(Exec Dir-Creative)*
Hali Bodenstein *(Acct Dir)*
Ali Kohut *(Dir-Recruiting)*
Meredith Hariton Vona *(Dir-Media)*
Shrivika Ramaswamy *(Acct Supvr)*
Samantha Cranston *(Sr Acct Exec)*
Anna Gerz *(Strategist-Social)*

Accounts:
Blue Man Group E-commerce, Entertainment; 2011
Brown-Forman Finlandia, Maximus; 2011
Cisco Technology; 2011
Folio Society Campaign: "Beautiful Books"
General Mills Green Giant, Hamburger Helper, Total; 2010
Jaeger Fashion; 2011
Johnson & Johnson One Touch; 2007
Lexus Automotive; 2005
Medtronic; 2010
SEI Financial Services & Technology; 2011
Starz Entertainment, Original Programming; 2012
Unilever Bertolli, I Can't Believe It's Not Butter, Knorr; 2006

Branches

Story Worldwide
87 Wall St, Seattle, WA 98121
Tel.: (206) 336-3001
Fax: (206) 336-3030
Web Site: www.storyworldwide.com

Employees: 15

Simon Kelly *(CEO-North America)*
Heidi Waldusky *(Exec Dir-Creative)*
Mitchell Wexler *(Acct Dir)*
Dave Carlyle *(Dir-IT-Seattle)*
Kelly Rudhe *(Office Mgr-Accts Payable)*
Carrie Blocher *(Production Mgr-Seattle)*
Stephanie Mansey *(Acct Supvr)*
Shrivika Ramaswamy *(Acct Supvr)*
Courtney Kelly *(Sr Acct Exec)*

Accounts:
Empire Cinemas
The Independent
Lexus

Story Worldwide
20 Marshall St Ste 220, South Norwalk, CT 06854
Tel.: (203) 831-8700
Fax: (203) 299-0068
Web Site: www.storyworldwide.com

Employees: 50
Year Founded: 1997

Agency Specializes In: Advertising, Brand Development & Integration, Business-To-Business, Children's Market, Consumer Marketing, Cosmetics, Digital/Interactive, Direct Response Marketing, E-Commerce, Information Technology, Internet/Web Design, Media Buying Services, Sales Promotion, Sponsorship, Strategic Planning/Research, Sweepstakes

Kirk Cheyfitz *(CEO)*
Jacqueline Brini *(Sr VP-Strategy & Plng)*
Nicole Ogoff *(Exec Dir-Client Svcs)*
Nils D'Aulaire *(Dir-Creative-New York City)*
Ash Oat *(Assoc Dir-Creative)*
Kaitlin Brennan *(Copywriter)*
Beth Griffenhagen *(Copywriter)*
Clark Mitchell *(Sr Editor-Creative)*

Accounts:
BIC Products
Coty Beauty
Country Cork
Detroit
Holland America Line
Johnson & Johnson
Klondike
Lexus
Lulu Guinness Handbags & Accessories
Nestle Waters North America
Oasis Stores
Playtex
Red Door Spa Holdings
Sheffield
Unilever I Can't Believe It's Not Butter
UPS
VF Corporation
Wish-Bone

STRADA ADVERTISING, LLC.
(d/b/a Strada Advertising)
(Private-Parent-Single Location)
1221 S Clarkson St Ste 400, Denver, CO 80210
Tel.: (303) 407-1976
E-Mail: hello@stradaadvertising.com
Web Site: www.stradaadvertising.com

Employees: 12
Year Founded: 2001

Agency Specializes In: Advertising, Brand Development & Integration, Broadcast, Collateral, Digital/Interactive, Internet/Web Design, Print

Revenue: $2,300,000

Amy Levi *(Pres & Dir-Creative)*

Accounts:
MeadWestvaco
Mesa del Sol

STRADEGY ADVERTISING
642 S 4th St Ste 400, Louisville, KY 40202
Tel.: (502) 339-0991
E-Mail: info@stradegyadvertising.com
Web Site: www.stradegyadvertising.com

Agency Specializes In: Advertising, Digital/Interactive, Print, Strategic Planning/Research

Jane Pfeiffer *(Owner)*
Chris Becker *(Dir-Mktg & Strategic Plng)*
Doris Irwin *(Dir-Media)*
Jenna Morales *(Acct Mgr)*
Bill Cherep *(Mgr-Traffic)*
Shelby Blevins *(Strategist-Digital)*
Katelyn Hellige *(Acct Exec)*
Theresa Schuler *(Acct Exec)*
Daphne Fisher *(Media Buyer)*
Monica Cunningham *(Acct Coord)*
Hannah Fisher *(Acct Coord)*
Mary Holfelner *(Acct Coord)*
Caroline Peck *(Acct Coord-Bus Dev)*

Accounts:
Ashley Armor
Ashley Furniture HomeStore Wine & Design
Heine Brothers Now Open
Peoples Trust & Savings Bank
Qdoba Mango Salad
University of Louisville Hospital
The Vint Julep

STRAHAN ADVERTISING
1940 Old Tustin Ave, Santa Ana, CA 92705
Tel.: (714) 547-6383
Fax: (714) 547-5463
E-Mail: info@strahanad.com
Web Site: www.strahanad.com

Employees: 7
Year Founded: 1979

Agency Specializes In: Advertising, Business-To-Business, Food Service

Timothy D. Strahan *(Pres)*
Paula Williams *(Sr Acct Supvr)*

Accounts:
Fisher Manufacturing
Montague
World-Wide Advantage

STRAIGHT NORTH, LLC.
1001 W 31st St Ste 100, Downers Grove, IL 60515
Tel.: (630) 366-8150
Fax: (630) 366-8151
Toll Free: (866) 779-7675
Web Site: www.straightnorth.com

Employees: 30

Agency Specializes In: Brand Development & Integration, Collateral, Commercial Photography, Consulting, Graphic Design, Multimedia, Print, Strategic Planning/Research, Web (Banner Ads, Pop-ups, etc.)

David M. Duerr *(Chm & CEO)*
Kevin Duffy *(Pres & Chief Creative Officer)*
Scott Hepburn *(Gen Mgr-Charlotte Office)*
Michael E. Char *(Dir-Sls & Mktg)*
Korey Kashmer *(Mgr-Internet Mktg)*

Accounts:
Amdocs
Bank Consulting Group
CookTek
Dremel
Edward Hospital
Flexible Benefit Services Corporation
IPC International
JSH&A / Starbucks
Millennium Trust Company
Officite
Segall Bryant & Hamill
Tennex
Tensor Group

STRATA-MEDIA, INC.
1 Spectrum Pointe Dr Ste 130, Lake Forest, CA 92630-2283
Tel.: (714) 771-0667
Fax: (714) 538-6127
E-Mail: info@strata-media.com
Web Site: www.strata-media.com

Employees: 5
Year Founded: 1995

Agency Specializes In: Collateral, Corporate Identity, Event Planning & Marketing, Exhibit/Trade Shows, Financial, Graphic Design, Print, Production

Kimberly Hansen *(Dir-Art)*

Accounts:
Greater New Port Physicians
Heritage Point Financial
Idev
Kerr Sybron Dental
Micro Vention
Nobel Biocare
Optivest
Quality Systems, Inc.
Think Mortgage
WealthPointe

STRATACOMM, LLC
1615 L St NW, Washington, DC 20036
Tel.: (202) 289-2001
Fax: (202) 289-1327
Web Site: www.stratacomm.net

Year Founded: 1995

Agency Specializes In: Communications, Digital/Interactive, Event Planning & Marketing, Public Relations, Sponsorship

Bill Buff *(Mng Partner)*
John F. Fitzpatrick *(Co-Mng Partner)*
Sharon Hegarty *(Mng Dir)*
Randy Best *(CFO)*
Jacqueline Bengel *(VP)*
Shannon Blair *(VP-Admin)*
Bryon Johnston *(VP)*
Kristin Ford-Glencross *(Acct Dir)*
Jennifer Heilman *(Acct Dir)*
Kenneth Gayles *(Sr Acct Exec)*
Marcia Robinson *(Asst Office Mgr)*

Accounts:
Federal Motor Carrier Safety Administration
Nissan North America, Inc.
Norfolk Southern

STRATEGIA INC.
320 W Ohio St Ste 300, Chicago, IL 60654
Tel.: (312) 574-0077
E-Mail: hello@strategiamedia.com
Web Site: www.strategiainc.com

Agency Specializes In: Advertising, Brand Development & Integration, Digital/Interactive, Internet/Web Design, Logo & Package Design, Print, Search Engine Optimization, Social Media

Peter Switzer *(Dir-Res)*

Accounts:
Chris Nybo
Fuller House Bar

STRATEGIC
70 W 36th St, New York, NY 10018
Tel.: (212) 869-3003
Fax: (212) 204-1200
E-Mail: info@strategicagency.com
Web Site: thestrategicagency.com

Employees: 50

Agency Specializes In: Advertising

Peter Stern *(Pres)*
Tony Andrea *(Exec VP)*
Chad Mancini *(VP & Grp Acct Dir)*
Jason Calabrese *(Grp Acct Dir-Under Armour & North American Breweries)*
Timothy Archibald *(Acct Supvr)*
Brenna Dykta *(Acct Supvr)*
Darby Nelson *(Acct Supvr)*
Emily Lewicki *(Acct Exec)*
James Nicholson *(Acct Exec)*
Lauren Szewczyk *(Coord-Ops)*

Accounts:
Capital One Bank
Capital One Bank (USA), N.A.
GlaxoSmithKline
Hershey's
The History Channel
Labatt Blue
Labatt USA LLC
Lipton
OfficeMax
Stella Artois

STRATEGIC AMERICA
6600 Westown Pkwy Ste 100, West Des Moines, IA 50266-7708
Tel.: (888) 898-6400
Fax: (515) 224-4181
E-Mail: mschreurs@strategicamerica.com
Web Site: www.strategicamerica.com

E-Mail for Key Personnel:
President: jschreurs@strategicamerica.com
Creative Dir.: GElkin@strategicamerica.com
Media Dir.: jstuber@strategicamerica.com
Public Relations: lmsolo@strategicamerica.com

Employees: 90
Year Founded: 1980

National Agency Associations: 4A's

Agency Specializes In: Advertising, Brand Development & Integration, Broadcast, Business Publications, Business-To-Business, Cable T.V., Co-op Advertising, Collateral, Commercial Photography, Communications, Consulting, Consumer Marketing, Consumer Publications, Corporate Identity, Digital/Interactive, Direct Response Marketing, E-Commerce, Education, Electronic Media, Entertainment, Event Planning & Marketing, Exhibit/Trade Shows, Financial, Food Service, Government/Political, Graphic Design, Health Care Services, High Technology, Industrial, Information Technology, Internet/Web Design, Leisure, Logo & Package Design, Magazines, Media Buying Services, Merchandising, Newspaper, Newspapers & Magazines, Out-of-Home Media, Outdoor, Planning & Consultation, Point of Purchase, Point of Sale, Print, Production, Public Relations, Publicity/Promotions, Radio, Restaurant, Retail, Sales Promotion, Sponsorship, Sports Market, Strategic Planning/Research, T.V., Trade & Consumer Magazines, Travel & Tourism

Approx. Annual Billings: $51,100,000

John C. Schreurs *(Pres & COO)*
Michael R. Schreurs *(CEO)*
Bruce Ganzer *(VP-Creative)*
Nathan Johnson *(VP-Mktg Svcs)*
Dave Miglin *(VP-Interactive Svcs)*
Kelcey Stoehr *(Sr Dir-Art)*
Bryce Thomson *(Acct Grp Dir)*
Ben Handfelt *(Dir-Media Rels)*
Carol Van Der Hart *(Dir-Media)*
Carrie Thomson *(Assoc Dir-Media)*
Gregory Welch *(Assoc Dir-Creative)*
Randy Driesen *(Sr Acct Mgr)*
Sarah Snider *(Sr Acct Mgr)*
Carole Curtis *(Acct Mgr-Media)*
Aubrie Glen *(Acct Mgr-Client Svcs)*
Rob Schreurs *(Acct Mgr)*
Joey Taylor-Moon *(Mgr-Interactive Svcs)*
Patti Barbalato *(Sr Acct Supvr)*
Sheryl Rinker *(Sr Acct Supvr)*
Caleb Bailey *(Media Buyer & Specialist-Digital)*
Glenda Lynch *(Media Buyer)*
Savana Dale *(Acct Coord)*
Taylor Rookaird *(Acct Coord-PR)*
Gabrielle Broderick *(Asst Acct Mgr)*
Tracey Schwarz *(Sr Media Planner & Buyer)*

Accounts:
Department of Natural Resources; Des Moines, IA
Farm Bureau Financial Services
Hunter Douglas
The Iowa Lottery; Des Moines, IA Media Buying; 1983
Kohler
Marsh & McLennan
Nationwide Mutual Insurance Company
Nationwide
Service Experts, Inc.
The Wendy's Company

STRATEGIC DOMAIN, INC.
336 West 37th St, New York, NY 10018
Tel.: (212) 812-1900
Fax: (212) 924-4393
E-Mail: info@strategicdomain.com
Web Site: www.strategicdomain.com

E-Mail for Key Personnel:
President: mperoff@strategicdomain.com

Employees: 18
Year Founded: 1998

Agency Specializes In: Advertising, Business-To-Business, Consulting, Consumer Goods, Consumer Marketing, Corporate Communications, Corporate Identity, Digital/Interactive, Direct-to-Consumer, E-Commerce, Email, Graphic Design, Health Care Services, Integrated Marketing, Internet/Web Design, Logo & Package Design, Market Research, Medical Products, New Technologies, Paid Searches, Pharmaceutical, Planning & Consultation, Publicity/Promotions, Search Engine Optimization, Social Media, Strategic Planning/Research, Web (Banner Ads, Pop-ups, etc.)

Breakdown of Gross Billings by Media: Graphic Design: 5%; Internet Adv.: 30%; Promos.: 5%; Strategic Planning/Research: 30%; Worldwide Web Sites: 30%

Michael Peroff *(Mng Partner)*

Accounts:
Benjamin Moore; Montvale, NJ; 2007
Eisai; Teaneck, NJ; 2005
EUSA; Langhorne, PA; 2003
National Community Pharmacists Association; Alexandria, VA; 2002
Novartis; East Hanover, NJ; 1998
Ortho-McNeil Women's Health Products
Ortho-McNeil/Johnson & Johnson; Raritan, NJ; 1999
Orthofix International; McKinney, TX; 2006
Pfizer; New York, NY; 2005
Pharmacist e-Link; New York, NY; 2002
Salix Pharma; Raleigh, NC; 2003
Sanofi-Aventis; Bridgewater, NJ; 2007
Unicef; New York, NY; 2009

STRATEGIC MARKETING INC.
8895 N Military Trl Ste 202B, Palm Beach Gardens, FL 33410-6284
Tel.: (561) 688-8155
Fax: (561) 688-8156
E-Mail: tmurphy@thinkstrategic.com
Web Site: www.thinkstrategic.com

Year Founded: 1992

Agency Specializes In: Corporate Identity, Direct Response Marketing, Internet/Web Design, Logo & Package Design, Market Research, Media Planning, Public Relations, Radio, Strategic Planning/Research, T.V.

Terry Murphy *(Pres)*
Barbara Mannino *(Sr Acct Mgr)*
Natalie Harmon *(Acct Mgr)*

Accounts:
Capitol Carpet & Tile Flooring Materials Retailer
Events & Adventures of Long Island
Stanley Steemer Floor Cleaning Materials Provider

STRATEGIC MEDIA, INC.
2857 Executive Dr, Clearwater, FL 33762
Tel.: (727) 531-7622
Web Site: www.strategic-webdesign.com/

Employees: 10
Year Founded: 1995

Agency Specializes In: Alternative Advertising, Event Planning & Marketing, Experience Design, Guerilla Marketing, Internet/Web Design, Local Marketing, Mobile Marketing, Out-of-Home Media

Approx. Annual Billings: $1,200,000

Breakdown of Gross Billings by Media: Out-of-Home Media: 60%; Worldwide Web Sites: 40%

Chuck Nelms *(Pres & CEO)*
Michael Finegold *(Dir-Ops)*
Elizabeth Holland *(Media Buyer)*
Michelle Irvin *(Media Buyer)*
Andrea Massar *(Media Buyer)*

STRATEGICAMPERSAND INC.
250 Bloor St E Ste 1440, Toronto, ON M4W 1E6 Canada
Tel.: (416) 961-5595
Fax: (416) 961-7955
Toll Free: (877) 222-1653
E-Mail: info@stratamp.com
Web Site: www.stratamp.com

Employees: 30
Year Founded: 1991

Agency Specializes In: Advertising, Corporate Communications, Direct Response Marketing, Integrated Marketing, Internet/Web Design, Media Relations, Multimedia, New Technologies, Public Relations

Gayle Robin *(Founder, Partner & Pres)*
Miles Pollock *(Partner)*
Anita Wong *(VP-PR)*
Janice Young *(Controller)*
Illya Noble *(Dir-Art)*
Andrea Clarke Berry *(Mgr-PR-Cisco Canada)*
Ashleigh Mair *(Coord-PR)*
Meaghan Van Kuik *(Coord-Mktg)*

Accounts:
Nikon
OpenTable (Canada Agency of Record) Public Relations, Social Media
Sony

STRATEGIES, A MARKETING COMMUNICATIONS CORPORATION
13681 Newport Ave Ste 8 Ste 616, Tustin, CA 92780
Tel.: (714) 957-8880
Fax: (714) 957-8880
E-Mail: mail@strategiesadpr.com
Web Site: www.strategiesadpr.com

Employees: 8
Year Founded: 1991

Agency Specializes In: Advertising, Brand Development & Integration, Business-To-Business, Collateral, Consulting, Direct Response Marketing, Health Care Services, High Technology, Medical Products, Print, Production, Public Relations, Strategic Planning/Research

Breakdown of Gross Billings by Media: Collateral: 20%; D.M.: 10%; E-Commerce: 10%; Graphic Design: 20%; Pub. Rels.: 23%; Strategic Planning/Research: 15%; Trade & Consumer Mags.: 2%

Linda White *(Founder)*
Tara Stoutenborough *(Owner)*
Kathryn Thompson *(Controller)*
Oscar Wright *(Sr Dir-Art)*
Deborah Jones *(Client Svcs Dir)*
Lindsay Thompson *(Sr Acct Exec)*

Accounts:
HireRight Inc.; Irvine CA Pre-Employment Background Screening Provider; 2001
Rosemount Analytical; Irvine, CA Industrial Process Analytical Equipment; 1992
VACO Los Angeles Financial Services Talent Agency; 2010

STRATEGIS
12 Welch Ave Ste 7, Stoughton, MA 02072
Tel.: (781) 297-9200
Web Site: http://strategis.is/

Employees: 8
Year Founded: 1999

Dolores Gonsalves *(Co-Owner, CFO, Gen Mgr & Strategist)*
Akeem Mason *(Dir-Creative)*
George Irish *(Sr Strategist-Mktg)*

STRATEGY+STYLE MARKETING GROUP
25 Lenape Dr, Montville, NJ 07045
Tel.: (973) 588-3979
Web Site: www.strategyplusstyle.com

Year Founded: 2010

Agency Specializes In: Advertising, Consulting, Digital/Interactive, Media Relations, Public Relations

Karen E. Fluharty *(Partner)*
Sue Helondovitch *(VP-PR)*
Stephen Babula *(Mgr-Creative Svcs)*
Kerrie Levy *(Acct Exec)*
Ashley Waitts *(Sr Graphic Designer)*
Mary Alexander *(Coord-Fin)*

Accounts:
Foothills Mall
Helzberg's Diamond Shops, Inc.
Legends Outlets Kansas City
The Shops at Northfield Stapleton
The Shops at Skyview Center

STRATMARK
(Name Changed to Robbins Kersten Direct)

STRAWBERRYFROG
60 Madison Ave, New York, NY 10010
Tel.: (212) 366-0500
Fax: (212) 366-0521
E-Mail: inquiries@strawberryfrog.com
Web Site: www.strawberryfrog.com

Employees: 80

Agency Specializes In: Graphic Design, Sponsorship

Scott Goodson *(Co-Founder & Chm)*
Karin Drakenberg *(Co-Founder & Exec VP)*
Susan Bueser *(CFO)*
Christine Piper *(Head-Client Svc & Grp Acct Dir)*
Craig Love *(Exec Creative Dir)*
Shayne Millington *(Dir-Creative)*
Tom Jackson *(Copywriter)*

Accounts:
Afya Foundation
Albania Campaign: "Go Your Own Way", Digital, Public Relations, Short Films, Social Media
Aquatine Group Advertising, Aqua-Tine, Branding, Campaign: "We Love Smokers", Digital, Marketing, Social Media, Website
Beam Global Spirits & Wine Campaign: "Cage Your Angel", Campaign: "Make History", Campaign: "Parallels", Global Creative, Jim Beam - Creative Duties, Jim Beam Black, Red Stag
Emirates Airlines Boeing 777, Campaign: "Anthem", Campaign: "Hello Tomorrow"
European Wax Center Campaign: "Skin that's simply instagrammable", Campaign: "Waxing For All", Digital, National Marketing, Outdoor, Poster, Print, Radio, Social, Social Media
Fortune Magazine
Frito-Lay, Inc. Sabra, Stacy's Pita Chips, True North; 2008
Harrisdirect Financial Services; 2005
Heineken Heineken
Impact Beverage LLC Brand Strategy, Digital, HeadOn (Strategic & Creative Branding Agency of Record), In-Store, Media, Print, TV
Jim Beam Campaign: "Make History", Campaign: "Parallels"
Jockey
LG Campaign: "Prison Break", LG Optimus G
Mahindra Campaign: "The Girl Epidemic"
Morgan Stanley
Nanhi Kali K.C. Mahindra Education Trust Campaign: "The Girl Epidemic"
Nature's Variety Campaign: "Long Live Pets", Media, Social
New Balance
Procter & Gamble Campaign: "O Canada, Baby!", Pampers, Pampers Hello Baby Pregnancy Calendar App
Smart USA
SunTrust Banks, Inc. (Agency of Record) Advertising, Creative, Marketing, Strategic
Wasa NA

STREAM ADVERTISING LLC
401 S Catlin, Missoula, MT 59801
Tel.: (406) 317-1345
Web Site: www.streamadv.com

Agency Specializes In: Advertising, Media Buying Services, Media Planning, Strategic Planning/Research

Cher Shermer *(Pres)*

Accounts:
Blue Ribbon Auto Inc
V-Tec Auto Repair

STREAM COMPANIES
255 Great Valley Pkwy Ste 150, Malvern, PA 19355
Tel.: (610) 644-8637
Fax: (610) 540-6433
Toll Free: (888) 449-7443
Web Site: www.streamcompanies.com

Employees: 25
Year Founded: 1997

Agency Specializes In: Digital/Interactive, Radio, T.V.

Jason Brennan *(Co-Founder)*
David Regn *(Co-Founder)*
Brian Baker *(Chief Client Officer & Exec VP)*
William Parlaman *(VP-Digital Mktg)*
Dave Mazzoni *(Dir-Creative)*
Amol Waishampayan *(Dir-Digital Creative)*
Michelle Gordon *(Acct Exec & Specialist-Social Media)*

Accounts:
Automotive Training Center
Fred Beans Family of Dealerships
Kremer Eye Center
Lynnes Auto Group
McCafferty Auto Group
Nissan 24

STREET CANCE MARKETING

Advertising Agencies

COMMUNICATIONS
234 W Florida St, Milwaukee, WI 53202-5729
Tel.: (414) 765-0333
Fax: (414) 765-1207
E-Mail: hello@streetcance.com
Web Site: www.streetcance.com

E-Mail for Key Personnel:
President: daves@street-cance.com

Employees: 10
Year Founded: 1981

Agency Specializes In: Business-To-Business, Health Care Services

Approx. Annual Billings: $15,000,000

Cassie Miletich *(Dir-Media)*
Chris Tiedje *(Mgr-Digital & Creative Svcs)*
John J. Cance *(Copywriter)*

Accounts:
Marklin Scale Model Trains
Rietschle Thomas

STREET FACTORY MEDIA
2942 Pleasant Ave S, Minneapolis, MN 55408
Tel.: (651) 248-1406
E-Mail: info@streetfactorymedia.com
Web Site: www.streetfactorymedia.com

Year Founded: 2001

Agency Specializes In: Advertising, Guerilla Marketing

Aurora Bell *(Dir-Integrated Projects)*
Corey Spoden *(Dir-Ops)*

Accounts:
Burt's Bees Inc.

STREET LEVEL STUDIO
250 Waukegan Ave, Highwood, IL 60040
Tel.: (847) 432-5150
Web Site: www.streetlevelstudio.com/

Joe Davis *(Owner)*
Tanya Fretheim *(Acct Svcs Dir & Project Mgr)*

Accounts:
Emerald Spa
FreightQuote.com
Gabe's Backstage Lounge
Life Fitness
Mercury Plastics
Tap Pharmaceuticals
WLG, Inc.

STREICKER & COMPANY INC.
37 Eastern Ave, East Providence, RI 02914
Tel.: (401) 435-0200
E-Mail: advertise@streicker.com
Web Site: www.streicker.com

Employees: 4
Year Founded: 1977

National Agency Associations: MCA

Agency Specializes In: Advertising, Business-To-Business, Collateral, Corporate Communications, Corporate Identity, Direct Response Marketing, Exhibit/Trade Shows, Fashion/Apparel, Graphic Design, Health Care Services, High Technology, Industrial, Logo & Package Design, Marine, Medical Products, New Product Development, Outdoor, Print, Public Relations, Publicity/Promotions, Strategic Planning/Research, Trade & Consumer Magazines, Web (Banner Ads, Pop-ups, etc.)

Approx. Annual Billings: $2,000,000

Paul W. Streicker *(Pres)*
Chris Roe *(Dir-Art)*

Accounts:
Bruin Plastics Co. Laminates; 1986
Conference Exchange; 2004
Cottrell Paper Co. Insulating Paper; 1986
DeWAL Industries; 2005
Evans Co. Miniature Stampings Miniature Stampings; 1983
Gehring Textiles Inc; 2001
J&M Diamond Tool Co. Diamond Inserts; 1991
Safety Flag Co. of America High Visibility Safety Products; 1976
Sentry Battery Corp; 1998

STRENG DESIGN & ADVERTISING
244 W River Dr, Saint Charles, IL 60174
Tel.: (630) 584-3887
Fax: (630) 584-1695
E-Mail: hello@strengdesign.com
Web Site: www.strengdesign.com

Agency Specializes In: Advertising, Brand Development & Integration, Graphic Design, Internet/Web Design, Package Design, Print

Rick Streng *(Owner)*
Peter Schwartz *(VP)*
Will Sosa *(Dir-Art)*
Steve Clevenger *(Mgr-Production)*
Stacia Ellermeier *(Mgr-Social Media & Sr Designer)*
John McKillip *(Mgr-Web Project)*
Derrik Engel *(Designer-Digital Media)*

Accounts:
Big Apple Bagels

STRIDE ADVERTISING
592 Helen Dr, Ripon, CA 95366
Mailing Address:
PO Box 389, Ripon, CA 95366
Toll Free: (888) 536-8220
E-Mail: svink@strideadvertising.com
Web Site: www.strideadvertising.com

Agency Specializes In: Advertising, College, Education, Government/Political, Media Buying Services, Multimedia, Newspaper, Outdoor, Real Estate, Recruitment, Restaurant, Retail, Social Media, Web (Banner Ads, Pop-ups, etc.)

Approx. Annual Billings: $572,000

Sam Vink *(Owner)*

Accounts:
United States Government Help Wanted, Recruitment

STRIDE CREATIVE GROUP
305 St Paul St, Burlington, VT 5401
Tel.: (802) 652-4855
Fax: (802) 652-4856
Web Site: www.stridecreative.com

Year Founded: 2004

Agency Specializes In: Advertising, Brand Development & Integration, Email, Internet/Web Design, Logo & Package Design, Media Planning, Outdoor, Print, Search Engine Optimization, Social Media

Terri Parent *(Principal)*
Catherine McIntyre *(Principal)*
Kate Dodge *(Acct Mgr)*

Accounts:
Lake Champlain Chocolates
Physicians Computer Company
Sojourn
Vermont Tech

STRIKE MARKETING
906 Rutland St, Houston, TX 77008
Tel.: (713) 343-9000
Web Site: www.strikemg.com

Agency Specializes In: Advertising, Brand Development & Integration, Event Planning & Marketing, Public Relations, Strategic Planning/Research

Joe Pogge *(CEO & Principal)*
Thomas Goggins *(Sr Acct Exec)*
Adam Bruchas *(Acct Exec)*
Kyndal Goza *(Jr Acct Mgr)*

Accounts:
Choice Leather Furniture
Ecofest
Mountain View Regional Hospital
Spirit International, Inc.

STRONG
201 Office Park Dr Ste 220, Birmingham, AL 35223
Tel.: (205) 313-4000
Web Site: www.strongautomotive.com

Employees: 45
Year Founded: 1977

Agency Specializes In: Advertising, Affluent Market, African-American Market, Asian Market, Automotive, Bilingual Market, Brand Development & Integration, Cable T.V., Co-op Advertising, Consulting, Consumer Marketing, Content, Digital/Interactive, Direct Response Marketing, Direct-to-Consumer, Email, Graphic Design, In-Store Advertising, Internet/Web Design, Local Marketing, Logo & Package Design, Luxury Products, Market Research, Media Buying Services, Media Planning, Men's Market, Multimedia, Newspaper, Newspapers & Magazines, Outdoor, Over-50 Market, Paid Searches, Planning & Consultation, Point of Purchase, Point of Sale, Print, Production, Production (Ad, Film, Broadcast), Production (Print), Promotions, Radio, Regional, Sales Promotion, Search Engine Optimization, Seniors' Market, Social Marketing/Nonprofit, Social Media, Strategic Planning/Research, T.V., Web (Banner Ads, Pop-ups, etc.), Women's Market

Bill Marefka *(VP & Sr Acct Dir)*
Josh Bradish *(VP-Dealer Direct)*
Scott Rossi *(VP-Digital Svcs)*
Sheila Grandy *(Dir-Media)*
Gayle Rogers *(Dir-Interactive)*
Kristin Thompson *(Sr Acct Exec)*
Megan Cesnick *(Acct Exec)*
Joy Cummings *(Acct Coord)*
Mary-Kate Laird *(Coord-Interactive)*
Mindy Dent *(Asst-Digital Mktg)*
Casey Quattlebaum *(Sr Media Buyer-Adv)*

Accounts:
Limbaugh Toyota

STRONGVIEW SYSTEMS, INC.
1300 Island Dr Ste 200, Redwood City, CA 94065
Tel.: (650) 421-4200
Fax: (650) 421-4201
Web Site: www.strongview.com

Employees: 25

Agency Specializes In: Brand Development & Integration, Consumer Publications, Email, Local Marketing, Social Marketing/Nonprofit

Revenue: $1,900,000

Tim McQuillen *(Founder & CIO)*
Bill Wagner *(CEO)*
Bill Griffin *(CFO)*
Dave Frankland *(Chief Strategy Officer)*
Steve Melamed *(Chief Sls Officer)*
Rob Brosnan *(Sr VP-Strategy)*
Tal Nathan *(Sr VP-Client Svcs)*
John Cadigan *(VP-Ops)*
Mike Gentile *(Dir-Creative)*

Accounts:
IHG
McAfee
T. Rowe Price
Viacom
Zecco Holdings, Inc.

STROTHER COMMUNICATIONS
222 S 9th St Fl 41, Minneapolis, MN 55402
Tel.: (612) 288-2400
Fax: (612) 288-0504
Web Site: www.scgpr.com

Employees: 20
Year Founded: 1992

Agency Specializes In: Public Relations

Approx. Annual Billings: $2,000,000

Patricia Henning Strother *(Pres)*
Patrick Strother *(CEO & Chief Creative Officer)*
Trevor Nolte *(Sr Dir-Art)*
Joy Wagner *(Dir-Creative)*
Randy West *(Dir-Bus Dev)*
Carol Payne *(Acct Mgr)*
Jeron Udean *(Acct Mgr)*

Accounts:
Smead Manufacturing; Hasting, MN

STRUCK
(Formerly StruckAxiom)
159 W Broadway Ste 200, Salt Lake City, UT 84101
Tel.: (801) 531-0122
Fax: (801) 531-0123
E-Mail: infoslc@struck.com
Web Site: www.struck.com

Employees: 50
Year Founded: 2003

National Agency Associations: SODA

Agency Specializes In: Advertising, Alternative Advertising, Brand Development & Integration, Branded Entertainment, Broadcast, Cable T.V., Collateral, Corporate Identity, Digital/Interactive, Electronic Media, Email, Event Planning & Marketing, Exhibit/Trade Shows, Experience Design, Graphic Design, Guerilla Marketing, In-Store Advertising, Internet/Web Design, Logo & Package Design, Media Buying Services, Media Planning, Media Relations, Multimedia, Newspapers & Magazines, Out-of-Home Media, Outdoor, Paid Searches, Point of Purchase, Point of Sale, Print, Production, Production (Ad, Film, Broadcast), Production (Print), Social Media, Sponsorship, Strategic Planning/Research, T.V., Viral/Buzz/Word of Mouth, Web (Banner Ads, Pop-ups, etc.)

Approx. Annual Billings: $17,000,000

Matt Anderson *(CEO & Exec Dir-Creative)*
Ethan Huegly *(CFO)*
Brent Watts *(Exec Dir-Creative)*
Jeremy Chase *(Client Svcs Dir)*
Dustin Davis *(Dir-Creative)*
Chris George *(Dir-Art)*
Scott Sorenson *(Dir-Creative)*
David Bunnell *(Assoc Dir-Creative)*
Cacia Harris *(Acct Mgr-Media)*
Machel Devin *(Acct Supvr)*

Accounts:
Glasses.com; 2013
Jack in the Box Inc Digital, Redesign, Website
Lennar Homes Digital Creative; 2013
Nickelodeon Nick Animation Studios; 1998
Sage Sage1, Sage2; 2015
Utah Office of Tourism (Agency of Record) Campaign: "Mighty 5", Creative

Branches

Struck
(Formerly StruckAxiom)
24 NW First Ave Ste 270, Portland, OR 97209
Tel.: (503) 517-2526
E-Mail: infola@struck.com
Web Site: www.struck.com

Employees: 12

Agency Specializes In: Sponsorship

Matt Anderson *(Exec Dir-Creative)*
Katherine Kizer Cochran *(Dir-Production)*
Matt Gitchell *(Dir-Technical)*
John Gross *(Dir-Mktg & Client Dev)*
Abe Levin *(Dir-Digital Design)*
Jennifer Luecht *(Mgr-Mktg)*
Ben Peters *(Strategist-Digital)*
Cody Simmonds *(Strategist)*
Jimmy Carson *(Copywriter)*
Joanna Papaleo *(Designer-Interactive)*
Regina Geltosky *(Sr Designer-Interactive)*

STUDE-BECKER ADVERTISING LLC
332 Minnesota St Ste E100, Saint Paul, MN 55101
Tel.: (651) 293-1393
Fax: (651) 223-8050
E-Mail: mike@stude-becker.com
Web Site: www.stude-becker.com

Employees: 8
Year Founded: 1998

Agency Specializes In: Direct Response Marketing, Financial, Health Care Services

Approx. Annual Billings: $3,200,000

Breakdown of Gross Billings by Media: Collateral: $1,600,000; Mags.: $1,600,000

Michael Dunn *(Owner & Partner)*
Steve Peterson *(Partner)*
Jason Daum *(Dir-Digital Media)*
Dean Olson *(Dir-Art)*
Robert Stude *(Dir-Art)*
Susan Donohue *(Copywriter)*

Accounts:
3M; Saint Paul, MN; 1998
Datasciences International
Universal Hospital Services Inc.

STUDIO 2 ADVERTISING
1641 Broad St, Greensburg, PA 15601
Tel.: (724) 836-2220
Fax: (724) 836-2060
E-Mail: info@studio-2.com
Web Site: www.studio-2.com

Employees: 5
Year Founded: 1976

Agency Specializes In: Industrial, Retail

Approx. Annual Billings: $1,000,000

Breakdown of Gross Billings by Media: D.M.: $200,000; Mags.: $100,000; Newsp.: $200,000; Pub. Rels.: $300,000; Radio: $100,000; T.V.: $100,000

Roger Strayer *(VP & Controller)*
Ron McElhaney *(Dir-Bus Dev)*
Norman Orlandi *(Dir-Creative)*
Lisa Razza *(Dir-Art)*

Accounts:
Basic Carbide
Cambria Rowe Business College
Howard Hanna Real Estate Services
Kennywood
Magnetics
Mon Valley Hospital

STUDIO A ADVERTISING
203 N Main St, Mishawaka, IN 46544-1410
Tel.: (574) 259-5555
Fax: (574) 258-6107
E-Mail: customerservice@studioaadvertising.com
Web Site: www.studioaadvertising.com

Employees: 20
Year Founded: 1980

Agency Specializes In: Broadcast, Production

Approx. Annual Billings: $5,000,000

Rick Singleton *(Pres)*
Bob Singleton *(Sr Mgr)*
Angela Huff *(Mgr-Quality Assurance)*
Marcia La Forest *(Mgr-Customer Fin Rels)*
Tee Singleton *(Corp Office Mgr)*

STUDIO BRAND COLLECTIVE
1824 Spring St Ste 201, Houston, TX 77007
Tel.: (832) 350-8458
E-Mail: hello@studiobrandcollective.com
Web Site: www.studiobrandcollective.com

Year Founded: 2012

Agency Specializes In: Advertising, Brand Development & Integration, Event Planning & Marketing, Public Relations, Social Media

Karee Laing *(Chief Creative Officer & Principal)*
Radica McKenzie *(Dir-Ops)*
Melissa Sanders *(Dir-Creative Svcs)*
Elizabeth Tenorio *(Assoc Dir-Design)*
Ashley Brasset *(Mgr-Studio)*
Alicia McGINNIS *(Mgr-Mktg & Brand Dev)*
Victoria Korbin *(Acct Exec-Brand Mktg)*

Accounts:
ModMade Goods

STUDIO CENTER
161 Business Park Dr, Virginia Beach, VA 23462
Tel.: (757) 286-3080
Fax: (757) 622-0583
Toll Free: (866) 515-2111
Web Site: www.studiocenter.com

Year Founded: 1966

Agency Specializes In: Advertising, Digital/Interactive, Internet/Web Design, Print, Search Engine Optimization, T.V.

William Prettyman *(CEO)*

Jessica Lasorsa *(Dir-Casting)*
Mark Wildenhaus *(Dir-Creative)*

Accounts:
New-Genworth Financial Inc.

STUDIO D MARKETING COMMUNICATIONS
9374 Olive Blvd Ste 104, Saint Louis, MO 63132
Tel.: (314) 810-2711
Web Site: www.studiodmarcom.com

Employees: 4
Year Founded: 2013

Agency Specializes In: Advertising, Content, Internet/Web Design, Media Planning, Media Relations, Public Relations, Social Media, Strategic Planning/Research

Revenue: $2,000,000

Scott Dieckgraefe *(Founder & Pres)*
Kate Alstadt *(Mgr-Social Media)*
Terri Waters *(Mgr-PR)*
Tom Taylor *(Specialist-Mktg Comm)*

Accounts:
The 7th Grade Poetry Foundation; 2014
Cambridge Engineering Commercial & Industrial Unit Heater Mfr; 2013
Coventry Capital Wealth Management Services; 2013
Frontenac Bank
KRJ Architects Architectural Planning Services; 2013
Unico Systems Residential & Heating & Cooling Equipment; 2013

STUDIO303INC.
3233 Volterra Way, Myrtle Beach, SC 29579
Tel.: (843) 903-4760
Fax: (843) 903-4342
Web Site: www.studio303inc.com

Employees: 2
Year Founded: 2000

Agency Specializes In: Advertising, Graphic Design

Deanne Johnson *(Owner)*

Accounts:
Grand Strand Urology
Loris Healthcare System
Prudential Realty

STUDIOTHINK
1301 E 9th St, Cleveland, OH 44114
Tel.: (216) 574-9533
Fax: (216) 621-9910
E-Mail: info@studiothink.net
Web Site: www.studiothink.net

Year Founded: 2004

Agency Specializes In: Advertising, Brand Development & Integration, Digital/Interactive, Email, Graphic Design, Internet/Web Design, Logo & Package Design, Print, Public Relations, Strategic Planning/Research

Christine Lobas *(Founder, CEO & Mng Partner)*
Mark Stornes *(Partner)*
Stephen Meyer *(Sr Dir-Art)*
Ryan Shull *(Dir-Interactive)*
Jana Vanadia *(Dir-Creative)*
Beverly Vance *(Dir-Ops)*

Accounts:
Earnest Machine Products Co.
Truven Health Analytics

STUN CREATIVE
5757 Wilshire Blvd Ste 600, Los Angeles, CA 90036
Tel.: (323) 460-4035
Fax: (323) 460-4562
E-Mail: contact_la@stuncreative.com
Web Site: www.stuncreative.com

Employees: 60
Year Founded: 2000

Agency Specializes In: Advertising, Broadcast, Cable T.V., Sponsorship

Mark Feldstein *(Principal)*
Doug Ryan *(VP-Post production)*
Sara Cahill *(Exec Dir-Creative)*
Joseph Kiely *(Exec Dir-Creative)*
Stephen Kirklys *(Art Dir)*
Jessica Wolensky *(Acct Dir)*
John Chuldenko *(Copywriter)*

Accounts:
California Pizza Kitchen (Creative Advertising Agency of Record)
New-Fandango
New-SGN Cookie Jam
ShoeDazzle
Sundance Channel Entertainment Services
Unilever Campaign: "Real Strength", Dove Men + Care
Virgin America Campaign: "Twin Tested"

STYLE ADVERTISING
3617 8th Ave S, Birmingham, AL 35222
Tel.: (205) 933-8893
Fax: (205) 933-8897
Web Site: www.styleadvertising.com

Agency Specializes In: Advertising, Communications, Public Relations

Bill Stoeffhaas *(Owner & Partner)*
Audrey Pannell *(Dir-PR & Social Media)*
Wes Trammel *(Dir-Creative)*
Kirsten Ebert *(Strategist-PR & Digital Media)*

Accounts:
Fortun Foods Inc

SUASION COMMUNICATIONS GROUP
599 Shore Rd, Somers Point, NJ 08244
Tel.: (609) 653-0400
Fax: (609) 653-6483
Toll Free: (800) 222-0461
E-Mail: info@suasionmarketing.com
Web Site: www.suasionmarketing.com

E-Mail for Key Personnel:
President: sschmidt@smithokeefe.com
Creative Dir.: sal@smithokeefe.com

Employees: 6
Year Founded: 1998

National Agency Associations: PRSA-Second Wind Limited

Approx. Annual Billings: $5,000,000

Susan Adelizzi-Schmidt *(Pres)*
Lisa Baylinson *(Creative Dir)*

Accounts:
French Creek
The HERO Campaign
Michael Donahue Builders
Suasion

SUB ROSA
27 W 24th St Ste 501, New York, NY 10010
Tel.: (212) 414-8605
Fax: (646) 349-1685
E-Mail: lastname@wearesubrosa.com
Web Site: www.wearesubrosa.com

Agency Specializes In: Advertising, Brand Development & Integration, Graphic Design, Production (Ad, Film, Broadcast)

Michael Ventura *(CEO)*
Matt Lower *(Gen Mgr)*
Josh Davis *(Dir-Media Arts)*
Esther Downton *(Dir-Production)*
Mark James Foster *(Dir-Art)*
Kristopher Kowal *(Dir-Activation)*

Accounts:
Absolut Vodka
Axe
New-Coca-Cola
Diesel
Ecko
Estee Lauder Cosmetics
General Electric Campaign: "Garages"
Kiehls Cosmetics Brand Retailers
Levi's
L'Oreal Cosmetics Producers
Mountain Dew Soft Drinks
Pantone "Make It Brilliant", Brand Strategy, Content Creation, Creative, Print, Social
Pepsi
POPSUGAR Inc Campaign: "We Search, We Find, We ShopStyle", Creative, ShopStyle
Sony BMG

SUBMIT EXPRESS INC.
502 S Verdugo Dr Ste 200, Burbank, CA 91502
Tel.: (818) 567-3030
Fax: (818) 567-0202
Toll Free: (877) 737-3083
E-Mail: feedbacks@submitexpress.com
Web Site: www.submitexpress.com

Employees: 40

Agency Specializes In: Above-the-Line, Advertising, Advertising Specialties, Affiliate Marketing, Affluent Market, African-American Market, Agriculture, Alternative Advertising, Arts, Asian Market, Automotive, Aviation & Aerospace, Below-the-Line, Bilingual Market, Brand Development & Integration, Branded Entertainment, Broadcast, Business Publications, Business-To-Business, Cable T.V., Catalogs, Children's Market, Co-op Advertising, Collateral, College, Commercial Photography, Communications, Computers & Software, Consulting, Consumer Goods, Consumer Marketing, Consumer Publications, Content, Corporate Communications, Corporate Identity, Cosmetics, Crisis Communications, Custom Publishing, Customer Relationship Management, Digital/Interactive, Direct Response Marketing, Direct-to-Consumer, E-Commerce, Education, Electronic Media, Electronics, Email, Engineering, Entertainment, Environmental, Event Planning & Marketing, Exhibit/Trade Shows, Experience Design, Fashion/Apparel, Financial, Food Service, Game Integration, Gay & Lesbian Market, Government/Political, Graphic Design, Guerilla Marketing, Health Care Services, High Technology, Hispanic Market, Hospitality, Household Goods, Identity Marketing, In-Store Advertising, Industrial, Infomercials, Information Technology, Integrated Marketing, International, Internet/Web Design, Investor Relations, Legal Services, Leisure, Local Marketing, Logo & Package Design, Luxury Products, Magazines, Marine, Market Research, Media Buying Services, Media Planning, Media Relations, Media Training, Medical Products, Men's Market, Merchandising, Mobile Marketing,

Multicultural, Multimedia, New Product Development, New Technologies, Newspaper, Newspapers & Magazines, Out-of-Home Media, Outdoor, Over-50 Market, Package Design, Paid Searches, Pharmaceutical, Planning & Consultation, Podcasting, Point of Purchase, Point of Sale, Print, Product Placement, Production, Production (Ad, Film, Broadcast), Production (Print), Promotions, Public Relations, Publicity/Promotions, Publishing, RSS (Really Simple Syndication), Radio, Real Estate, Recruitment, Regional, Restaurant, Retail, Sales Promotion, Search Engine Optimization, Seniors' Market, Social Marketing/Nonprofit, South Asian Market, Sponsorship, Sports Market, Stakeholders, Strategic Planning/Research, Sweepstakes, Syndication, T.V., Technical Advertising, Teen Market, Telemarketing, Trade & Consumer Magazines, Transportation, Travel & Tourism, Urban Market, Viral/Buzz/Word of Mouth, Web (Banner Ads, Pop-ups, etc.), Women's Market, Yellow Pages Advertising

Angelina Zarokian *(VP)*
Shaun An *(Dir-Bus Dev)*
Thushara Herath *(Mgr-Ops)*
Sean Sarian *(Sr Acct Exec)*

Accounts:
Affinity
Amgen
CIT
Dollar
Purina Mills

SUBURBIA ADVERTISING

590 Beaver Lk Rd RR3, Victoria, BC V9E 2J7 Canada
Tel.: (250) 744-1231
Fax: (250) 744-1232
Web Site: suburbiastudios.com

Employees: 13
Year Founded: 1988

National Agency Associations: MAGNET

Agency Specializes In: Advertising Specialties, Affiliate Marketing, Environmental, Point of Purchase, Point of Sale, Retail

Mary-Lynn Bellamy-Willms *(Partner & CEO)*
Jacquie Arnatt *(Partner & Gen Mgr)*
Russ Willms *(Partner & Sr Dir-Art)*
Virginia Boggie *(Partner & Client Svcs Dir)*
Jeremie White *(Partner & Dir-Design)*
Bruce Meikle *(Assoc Dir-Creative)*
Jacquie Henning *(Acct Mgr)*
Coralie Jeffery *(Acct Mgr)*
Bonney King *(Mgr-Production)*

Accounts:
Bay House Group
Coastal Community Credit Union
Hillside Shopping Center
Hotel Grand Pacific
Planet Organic Natural Foods Grocery Store
Upper Canada Mall

Branch

Suburbia Advertising

3-1363 56th St, Delta, BC V4L 2P7 Canada
Tel.: (604) 943-6414
Fax: (604) 943-5516
E-Mail: virginia@suburbiaadvertising.com
Web Site: suburbiastudios.com

Agency Specializes In: Brand Development & Integration, Consumer Marketing, Retail

Jacquie Arnatt *(Partner & Gen Mgr)*
Russ Willms *(Partner & Sr Dir-Art)*
Virginia Boggie *(Partner & Client Svcs Dir)*
Bruce Meikle *(Assoc Dir-Creative)*
Coralie Jeffery *(Acct Mgr)*
Bonney King *(Mgr-Production)*

Accounts:
BC Cancer Foundation Vancouver Island
Canada Bread Company, Ltd
Planet Organic Markets
Upper Canada Mall
Willowbrook Shopping Centre
Woodgrove Shopping Centre

SUCCESS ADVERTISING HAWAII

66 Queen St Ste 1602, Honolulu, HI 96813
Tel.: (808) 536-7222
Fax: (808) 536-7277
Web Site: www.successhi.com

Employees: 4
Year Founded: 2001

Beth Busch *(Pres)*
Julius Pecson *(Dir-Production & Admin)*
Nainoa Afa'Ese-Wong *(Acct Exec)*

Accounts:
Job Quest
Workforce

SUCCESS COMMUNICATIONS GROUP

26 Eastmans Rd, Parsippany, NJ 07054
Tel.: (973) 535-9300
Fax: (973) 992-7543
Toll Free: (800) 848-4323
E-Mail: vdoyle@successcomgroup.com
Web Site: successcomgroup.com/

Employees: 40
Year Founded: 1990

Agency Specializes In: Recruitment

Approx. Annual Billings: $30,000,000

Breakdown of Gross Billings by Media: Internet Adv.: 35%; Newsp.: 60%; Other: 5%

Tom Marguccio *(VP & Dir-Creative)*
Tina Davis *(VP-Acct Svcs)*
Sue Katalinas *(VP-Sls)*
Kurt Praschak *(VP-PR)*
Elissa Jannicelli *(Client Svcs Dir)*
Donna Zolla *(Acct Dir)*
Regina Liu *(Sr Acct Mgr & Strategist-Digital)*
Russ Zaborowski *(Assoc Creative Dir)*

Accounts:
AstraZeneca
Deloitte
Pizza Hut

Branches

Success Communications Group

(Formerly Success Advertising)
1545 Hotel Circle S Ste 145, San Diego, CA 92108
Tel.: (619) 299-3858
Fax: (619) 299-3118
Toll Free: (800) 557-8904
E-Mail: mbeere@successcomgroup.com
Web Site: successcomgroup.com/

David Deverell *(Exec VP)*
Jonathan Friedman *(Exec VP)*
Tina Davis *(VP-Acct Svcs)*
Mike Gatta *(VP-Natl Dev)*
Darlene Hannan *(Client Svcs Dir)*
Russ Zaborowski *(Assoc Dir-Creative)*
Regina Liu *(Sr Acct Mgr & Strategist-Digital)*
Chris Krautheim *(Acct Mgr)*
Gina Gentile *(Acct Exec)*

Success Advertising

26 Eastmans Rd, Parsippany, NJ 07054
Tel.: (973) 992-7800
Fax: (973) 597-5136
Toll Free: (800) 848-4323
E-Mail: vdoyle@successadv.com
Web Site: www.successcomgroup.com

Employees: 51
Year Founded: 1961

National Agency Associations: PRSA

Agency Specializes In: Planning & Consultation, Public Relations, Recruitment, Strategic Planning/Research

Michael Cherenson *(Exec VP)*
Tom Marguccio *(VP & Dir-Creative)*
Russ Zaborowski *(Assoc Dir-Creative)*

Accounts:
Aldi Foods
American College of Cardiology
Lennar Homes
Los Almos
Sears Home Improvement Center
Sovereign Bank
Walmart
Wawa

Success Advertising

345 7th Ave Ste 2502, New York, NY 10001
Tel.: (212) 244-8811
Fax: (212) 244-8871
E-Mail: jdiamant@successcomgroup.com
Web Site: successcomgroup.com

Employees: 7

Agency Specializes In: Recruitment

Joe Diamant *(VP)*

SUDLER & HENNESSEY

4700 De La Savane Ste 200, Montreal, QC H4P 1T7 Canada
Tel.: (514) 733-0073
Fax: (514) 733-8668
E-Mail: judith.st-pierre@sudler.com
Web Site: www.sudler.com

E-Mail for Key Personnel:
Media Dir.: sheila_gittelman@sudler.com

Employees: 20
Year Founded: 1980

Agency Specializes In: Bilingual Market, Cosmetics, Health Care Services, Medical Products, Pharmaceutical

Debbie Burton *(Assoc Dir-Creative)*
Dijana Loncaric *(Acct Exec)*

Accounts:
Abbott
Novartis
Pfizer
Sanofi-Aventis Research & Development

SUDLER & HENNESSEY WORLDWIDE HEADQUARTERS

230 Park Ave S, New York, NY 10003-1566
Tel.: (212) 614-4100
Fax: (212) 598-6907
Web Site: www.sudler.com

Year Founded: 1941

National Agency Associations: 4A's

Agency Specializes In: Advertising, Brand Development & Integration, Communications, Education, Internet/Web Design, Media Planning, Multicultural, Planning & Consultation, Promotions, Sales Promotion, Sponsorship, Strategic Planning/Research

Jed Beitler *(Chm & CEO)*
Louisa Holland *(Co-CEO-Americas)*
John Marchese *(Exec VP & Client Svcs Dir)*
Tim O'Grady *(VP & Grp Acct Supvr)*
Cathy Robins *(Dir-Global Strategic Comm)*
Gabrielle Allidi *(Acct Grp Supvr)*
Alison Eiffe *(Acct Supvr)*
Maggie Cribbin *(Sr Acct Exec)*
Addie Blackburn *(Sr Media Planner)*

Accounts:
Pfizer, Inc. Viracept

Branches

IntraMed Educational Group
230 Park Ave S 5th Fl, New York, NY 10003-1502
Tel.: (212) 614-3800
Fax: (212) 614-6960
E-Mail: ruben.gutierrez@intramedgroup.com
Web Site: www.intramedgroup.com

Employees: 113
Year Founded: 1972

Agency Specializes In: Health Care Services

Ruben Gutierrez *(Mng Dir)*
Kathy Bronshtein *(Chief Compliance Officer & Exec VP)*
Alissa Sklaver *(Exec VP & Client Svc Dir)*
Jason Bogdan *(VP & Sr Program Dir)*
Jessica Greenberg *(VP & Sr Program Dir)*
Ashley Woerner *(Sr Mgr-Speaker Bureau)*
Alison Mozak *(Mgr-Speaker Bureau)*
Larysa Szkambara *(Coord-Traffic)*
Kristin D'Amato *(Sr Program Dir)*
Jessica Distasi *(Sr Program Dir)*
Kecia Marsh *(Sr Program Dir)*
Melissa Semanik *(Sr Program Dir)*
Alysha Torres-Ricketts *(Sr Coord)*
Robert Vetter *(Sr Program Dir)*

Precept Medical Communications
4 Connell Dr Bldg IV Ste 601, Berkeley Heights, NJ 07922-2705
Tel.: (908) 288-0100
Fax: (908) 288-0123
Web Site: www.preceptmedical.com

National Agency Associations: 4A's

Agency Specializes In: Medical Products

Donna Michalizysen *(Mng Partner)*
Lee Howell *(Exec VP & Dir-Medical Affairs)*
Maura Trent *(Exec VP & Supvr-Mgmt)*
Denise Dugan *(Sr VP & Mgmt Supvr)*
Glenn Thorpe *(VP & Sr Program Dir)*
Nick Ferenz *(Dir-Medical)*
Peggy Bergh *(Sr Program Dir)*

Australia/New Zealand

Sudler & Hennessey Sydney
The Denison Level 8 65 Berry St, North, Sydney, NSW 2060 Australia
Tel.: (61) 2 9931 6111
Fax: (61) 2 9931 6162
E-Mail: sudlersydney@sudler.com
Web Site: www.sudler.com

Employees: 35
Year Founded: 1974

National Agency Associations: AFA

Agency Specializes In: Health Care Services

Rob Rogers *(Co-CEO-Americas)*
Alex Macmanus *(Dir-Bus)*
Akash Dave *(Sr Acct Exec)*

Accounts:
Astra Zeneca
Inghams Chickens
Lilly
Novartis; 1996
Novo Nordisk
Roche

Canada

Sudler & Hennessey
4700 De La Savane Ste 200, Montreal, QC H4P 1T7 Canada
(See Separate Listing)

France

Sudler & Hennessey Frankfurt
Dornhof Str 44 46, 63263 Neu-Isenburg, Germany
Tel.: (49) 6102 7993 333
Fax: (49) 6102 7993 101
E-Mail: roger.stenz@sudler.com
Web Site: www.sudler.com

Employees: 25
Year Founded: 1976

Agency Specializes In: High Technology, Pharmaceutical

Yvonne Jackson *(Head-Global Client-WPP & Dir-Strategic Plng & New Bus Dev)*

Accounts:
Astellas
Bayer
Berlin Chemie
Chiron Behring
Intramed
Merck Darmstadt

Italy

IntraMed Communications Milan
Via Bertieri 4, I-20146 Milan, Italy
Tel.: (39) 02 345 451
Fax: (39) 02 3310 6875
Web Site: www.sudler.com

Employees: 20
Year Founded: 1992

Agency Specializes In: Health Care Services, Pharmaceutical

Rita Pugliese *(Acct Dir)*
Federica Candia *(Sr Acct Mgr)*

Accounts:
AstraZeneca
Boehringer Ingelheim
CSL Behring; King of Prussia, PA
Danone
Dompe
Eli Lilly
Janssen-Cilag
Novartis
Pfizer

Sudler & Hennessey European Headquarters
Via Traiano 7, I-20149 Milan, Italy
Tel.: (39) 02 349 721
Fax: (39) 02 349 1698
E-Mail: shmilan@it.sudler.com
Web Site: www.sudler.com

Employees: 200

Agency Specializes In: Pharmaceutical

Lia Treichler *(COO, CFO-Italy & Dir-Client Procurement-EMEA)*
Brian Kelly *(Chief Strategy Officer)*
Max Jackson *(CEO-EMEA & APAC)*
Jennifer Lambert *(Head-Bus Dev-EMEA & Asia Pac)*

Accounts:
Abbott
Bayer
Bristol-Meyers
Lundbeck
Merck Sharpe & Dohme
Novartis
Nycomed
Pfizer
Schering

Sudler & Hennessey Milan
Via Bertieri 4, I-20146 Milan, Italy
Tel.: (39) 02 349 721
Fax: (39) 02 349 1698
E-Mail: maurizio.mioli@sudler.com
Web Site: www.sudler.com/

Employees: 130
Year Founded: 1982

Agency Specializes In: Health Care Services, Pharmaceutical

Alessio Carli *(Exec VP & Mng Dir)*
Giovanni De Pretto *(Mng Dir & Exec VP)*

Accounts:
Anifa
Gaba
Italian Government (Ministry of Health)
Nabi Biopharmaceuticals
Schering Plough

United Kingdom

Sudler & Hennessey Ltd.-London
11 - 33 St Johns Street, London, EC1M 4AA United Kingdom
Tel.: (44) 207 307 78 00
Fax: (44) 207 307 78 11
E-Mail: sudlerlondon@sudler.com
Web Site: www.sudler.com

Employees: 50
Year Founded: 1979

Agency Specializes In: Health Care Services

David Higgins *(Mng Dir)*
Lee Williams *(Exec Dir-Creative)*
Kirstie Pereira *(Sr Acct Dir)*
Jemma Nathan *(Acct Dir-S&H Medical Comm)*
Norbert Brunhuber *(Dir-Client Strategy)*
Nick Hembury *(Dir-Creative Svcs)*
Tamena Bashir *(Acct Mgr)*
Rebecca Foster *(Acct Mgr)*
Stephanie Mills *(Acct Mgr)*

Accounts:
Alk Abello
Bristol Myers Squibb
Colgate Oral Pharmaceuticals
Novo Nordisk Activelle
Pfizer

SUGAR PINE MEDIA
150 E Cypress Ave, Redding, CA 96002
Tel.: (530) 241-3737
Fax: (530) 210-2546
E-Mail: info@sugarpinemedia.com
Web Site: www.sugarpinemedia.com

Year Founded: 2011

Agency Specializes In: Advertising, Brand Development & Integration, Digital/Interactive, Internet/Web Design, Logo & Package Design, Print, Public Relations, Radio, Social Media

Rocky Slaughter *(Co-Founder & CEO)*

Accounts:
Segway of Healdsburg
Shasta Regional Community Foundation

SUGARTOWN COMMUNICATIONS
1486 Sugartown Rd, Paoli, PA 19301
Tel.: (610) 296-7870
Fax: (610) 296-7023
E-Mail: info@sugartowncommunications.com
Web Site: www.sugartowncommunications.com

Year Founded: 2007

Agency Specializes In: Advertising, Brand Development & Integration, Content, Graphic Design, Internet/Web Design, Media Buying Services, Media Planning

Joan Ford Goldschmidt *(Founder & Pres)*
Betsy Bryce *(Controller)*

Accounts:
Bittersweet Farm

SUISSEMADE
1616 Westgate Cir, Brentwood, TN 37027
Tel.: (615) 844-6188
Fax: (615) 844-6189
E-Mail: info@suissemade.com
Web Site: www.suissemade.com

Agency Specializes In: Advertising, Digital/Interactive, Internet/Web Design, Print

Daniel Whisnant *(Owner & Sr Designer)*

Accounts:
Italian Gun Grease
Viking

SUKLE ADVERTISING, INC.
(d/b/a Sukle Advertising & Design)
2430 W 32nd Ave, Denver, CO 80211
Tel.: (303) 964-9100
Fax: (303) 964-9663
E-Mail: info@sukle.com
Web Site: www.sukle.com

Employees: 10
Year Founded: 1995

Mike Sukle *(Owner)*
Michon Schmidt *(Mgr & Producer-Brdcst)*
Jeff Euteneur *(Assoc Dir-Creative)*
Pedro Saldarriaga *(Assoc Dir-Creative)*
Dana Cohen *(Acct Svc Dir)*
Sarah Nelson *(Acct Mgr)*
Martha Campbell *(Project Mgr & Mgr-Traffic)*
Elizabeth Hoopes *(Acct Supvr)*
Dan Schultz *(Acct Planner)*

Accounts:
Deep Rock Water
Denver Water Campaign: "Use Even Less"
GoLite
SCARPA
WYDOH The Line
WYDOH Through with Chew
Wyoming Department of Health Campaign: "Need Someone"

SULLIVAN BRANDING
(Formerly CS2 Advertising)
175 Toyota Plz Ste 100, Memphis, TN 38103
Tel.: (901) 526-6220
Fax: (901) 526-6221
Web Site: www.sullivanbranding.com

E-Mail for Key Personnel:
Media Dir.: whigh@sullivanbranding.com

Employees: 40
Year Founded: 1987

Agency Specializes In: Advertising, Advertising Specialties, Brand Development & Integration, Broadcast, Business Publications, Business-To-Business, Cable T.V., Co-op Advertising, Collateral, Communications, Consumer Marketing, Consumer Publications, Corporate Identity, Digital/Interactive, Direct Response Marketing, Education, Electronic Media, Entertainment, Environmental, Event Planning & Marketing, Exhibit/Trade Shows, Financial, Food Service, Graphic Design, Health Care Services, High Technology, Industrial, Internet/Web Design, Leisure, Logo & Package Design, Magazines, Media Buying Services, Medical Products, Merchandising, New Product Development, Newspaper, Newspapers & Magazines, Out-of-Home Media, Outdoor, Point of Purchase, Point of Sale, Print, Production, Public Relations, Publicity/Promotions, Radio, Real Estate, Recruitment, Restaurant, Retail, Sales Promotion, Sports Market, Strategic Planning/Research, Sweepstakes, T.V., Technical Advertising, Trade & Consumer Magazines, Travel & Tourism

Approx. Annual Billings: $18,000,000

Robert F. Vornbrock *(Exec VP & Dir-Client Dev)*
Chris O'Brien *(Grp Dir-Creative)*
Karen McKenzie *(Acct Dir)*
Justin Achelpohl *(Dir-Art)*
Don MacDougall *(Assoc Dir-Creative)*
Kenny Patrick *(Assoc Dir-Creative)*
Jordan Jackson *(Acct Mgr)*
Jackie Messmer *(Acct Mgr)*
Tim Laughlin *(Mgr-Digital Delivery)*
Jen Clarke *(Strategist-Digital)*
Laura Poff *(Acct Exec)*
Jo High *(Media Buyer)*
Brady Purnell *(Media Planner)*
Helena Kooi *(Acct Coord)*
Margaret Watford *(Acct Coord)*

Accounts:
Memphis Convention & Visitors Bureau
Methodist Healthcare

Branch

Sullivan Branding LLC
(Formerly White/Thompson, LLC)
1808 Patterson St, Nashville, TN 37203
Tel.: (615) 321-1033
Fax: (615) 321-1038
Toll Free: (888) 795-4260
Web Site: www.sullivanbranding.com

Employees: 16
Year Founded: 1983

National Agency Associations: TAAN

Agency Specializes In: Advertising, Automotive, Consulting, Consumer Marketing, Health Care Services, Logo & Package Design, Strategic Planning/Research

David Dasenbrock *(VP & Media Acct Planner)*
Ashley Ramsey *(Acct Dir)*
Chris Vogel *(Acct Dir-Digital)*
Kristen Counce *(Dir-Media)*
Lucie Bardone *(Sr Acct Mgr)*
Brady Purnell *(Media Buyer)*
Jacob Estrada *(Coord-Media)*

SULLIVAN CREATIVE SERVICES, LTD.
6C Hills Ave, Concord, NH 03301
Tel.: (603) 228-0836
E-Mail: carol@sullivancreative.com
Web Site: www.sullivancreative.com

Employees: 4
Year Founded: 1987

Agency Specializes In: Advertising, Brand Development & Integration, Business Publications, Business-To-Business, Catalogs, Collateral, College, Communications, Computers & Software, Consulting, Corporate Communications, Corporate Identity, Direct Response Marketing, Education, Electronic Media, Email, Engineering, Environmental, Exhibit/Trade Shows, Financial, Graphic Design, High Technology, Identity Marketing, Integrated Marketing, Internet/Web Design, Local Marketing, Logo & Package Design, Market Research, Media Buying Services, Media Planning, Media Relations, Newspapers & Magazines, Outdoor, Print, Production (Print), Public Relations, Publicity/Promotions, Search Engine Optimization, Social Marketing/Nonprofit, Strategic Planning/Research, Technical Advertising, Trade & Consumer Magazines, Travel & Tourism

Pamela E. Sullivan *(Pres & Dir-Creative)*
Carol Fusaro *(VP & Acct Mgr)*

Accounts:
Concord Group Insurance
Landmark Services
League of NH Craftsmen
Nashua Transit System
New London Hospital
NH Open Doors

SULLIVAN HIGDON & SINK INCORPORATED
255 N Mead St, Wichita, KS 67202-2707
Tel.: (316) 263-0124
Fax: (316) 263-1084
Toll Free: (800) 577-5684
E-Mail: info@shscom.com
Web Site: www.wehatesheep.com

Employees: 90
Year Founded: 1971

National Agency Associations: 4A's-AAF-AMA-AMIN-BMA-PRSA

Agency Specializes In: Advertising, Advertising Specialties, Aviation & Aerospace, Brand Development & Integration, Broadcast, Business Publications, Business-To-Business, Collateral, Communications, Consumer Marketing, Corporate Identity, Direct-to-Consumer, E-Commerce, Entertainment, Financial, Food Service, Health Care Services, High Technology, Internet/Web Design, Media Buying Services, Media Planning,

Medical Products, Men's Market, Point of Sale, Public Relations, Travel & Tourism

Breakdown of Gross Billings by Media: Bus. Publs.: 1%; Collateral: 1%; D.M.: 5%; Fees: 13%; Internet Adv.: 1%; Mags.: 10%; Newsp.: 12%; Outdoor: 1%; Print: 14%; Radio: 6%; T.V.: 36%

John January *(Co-CEO)*
Brock Campbell *(VP-Brand Mgmt)*
Lathi de Silva *(VP-Reputation Mgmt)*
Jim Vranicar *(VP-Connections Plng)*
Jeff Wendling *(Producer-Digital)*
Donna Montgomery *(Dir-Make It Happen)*
Bart Wilcox *(Assoc Dir-Creative & Copywriter)*
Kelly Birch *(Brand Mgr-Contact)*
Kelsey Rawson *(Brand Mgr)*
Jenna Reid *(Brand Mgr)*
Ashley Yearout *(Brand Mgr-Contact)*
Darrin Hephner *(Mgr-Mktg Implementation)*
Nemmy Matiru *(Mgr-Acctg)*
Becca Heeke *(Asst Brand Mgr)*
Devin Brown *(Designer)*
Abby Kallenbach *(Designer)*
Bailey Cernohous *(Coord)*
Hannah Kern *(Coord-Project)*

Accounts:
Aerion Corp. (Agency of Record)
American Century Investments; Kansas City, MO; 2007
Borden Cheese & Dairy
Cache Valley Dairy (Agency of Record)
CareFusion
Cargill Meat Solutions; Wichita, KS; 2002
Dairy Farmers of America; Kansas City, MO Borden Cheese (Agency of Record), Cache Valley Dairy Butter & Cheese (Agency of Record); 2008
The Engine Alliance
Intrust Bank; Wichita, KS; 2008
Kansas Health Foundation; Wichita, KS
Lycoming; Williamsport, PA; 2003
Merial
Pizza Hut; Dallas, TX
Pratt & Whitney
Shatto Milk Company
Spirit Aerosystems; Wichita, KS; 2005
Swiss Re
Turbine Engine Components Technologies Corp; Thomasville, GA
Westar Energy; Topeka, KS; 2004

Branches:

Sullivan Higdon & Sink Incorporated
2000 Central, Kansas City, MO 64108-2022
Tel.: (816) 474-1333
Fax: (816) 474-3427
Toll Free: (800) 809-0884
E-Mail: info@shscom.com
Web Site: www.wehatesheep.com

Employees: 39
Year Founded: 1997

National Agency Associations: 4A's

Tom Bertels *(Mng Partner-Wichita)*
Randall Mikulecky *(Mng Partner)*
Brock Campbell *(VP & Grp Dir-Brand Mgmt)*
Tony Robinson *(VP & Dir-Fin)*
Jim Vranicar *(VP-Connections Plng)*
Diane Galante Young *(Acct Dir)*
Raven Hubbard *(Brand Mgr)*
Emily Moon *(Brand Mgr)*
Melissa Racer *(Sr Head-MarComm)*

Accounts:
Aerion Corporation
American Century Investments
Blue Cross and Blue Shield
Cache Valley Dairy (Agency of Record)
CareFusion
Cargill Meat Solutions
Dairy Farmers of America Borden's
H&R Block Inc
INTRUST Bank
Merial Limited; Duluth, GA
North Kansas City Hospital
Pizza Hut Franchises
Pratt & Whitney
Quest Diagnostics
Sargent Aerospace & Defense
Sonic Corp. Below-the-Line, In-Store Communications, Local-Store Marketing, Merchandising
Water Partners

Sullivan Higdon & Sink Incorporated
6801 Whittier Ave Ste 301, McLean, VA 22101-4549
Tel.: (703) 752-7845
Fax: (703) 752-7849
E-Mail: info@shscom.com
Web Site: www.wehatesheep.com

Employees: 15
Year Founded: 2003

National Agency Associations: AAF-AMIN-BMA-PRSA

Agency Specializes In: Advertising, Public Relations

Scott McCullers *(VP-Pub Affairs-Washington)*

Accounts:
Sargent; Tucson, AZ (Agency of Record)

SULLIVAN PERKINS
2811 McKinney Ave Ste 320, Dallas, TX 75204-8566
Tel.: (214) 922-9080
Fax: (214) 922-0044
E-Mail: info@sullivanperkins.com
Web Site: www.sullivanperkins.com

Employees: 20
Year Founded: 1984

Agency Specializes In: Brand Development & Integration

Mark Perkins *(Pres & CEO)*
Tricia Magel *(Sr Mgr-Client Svcs)*
Joel Lapidus *(Acct Mgr)*
Ly Phan *(Acct Mgr)*
Somere Sanders *(Acct Mgr)*
Brian Bevolo *(Mgr-Production)*
Carly Lemay *(Acct Exec)*
Brett Baridon *(Sr Graphic Designer)*

Accounts:
BNSF Railway Company; Fort Worth, TX Transportation; 2003
Kosmos Energy Oil & Gas; 2011
Lake Austin Spa Resort; Austin, TX Destination Hospitality; 2000
Southwestern Medical Foundation Philanthropy; 2014
VHA Healthcare; 2014

SUMMERFIELD ADVERTISING INC.
939 N High St Ste 207, Columbus, OH 43201
Tel.: (614) 221-4504
E-Mail: information@summerfieldadvertising.com
Web Site: www.summerfieldadvertising.com

Year Founded: 2004

Agency Specializes In: Advertising, Brand Development & Integration, Collateral, Corporate Communications, Digital/Interactive, Internet/Web Design, Search Engine Optimization, Social Media

Laura Steinmaus *(VP & Dir-Accounts)*
Cory Oakley *(Dir-Art)*
Mirsada Tinjak *(Dir-Art)*
Dave Demarchi *(Client Dir, Assoc Dir-Creative & Copywriter)*
Diane Shields *(Strategist-Brand & Copywriter)*

Accounts:
United Schools Network

THE SUMMIT GROUP
117 W 400 S, Salt Lake City, UT 84101
Tel.: (801) 595-1155
Fax: (801) 595-1165
Web Site: www.summitslc.com

Year Founded: 1981

Agency Specializes In: Advertising, Brand Development & Integration, Collateral, Digital/Interactive, Guerilla Marketing, Internet/Web Design, Print, Public Relations, Radio, T.V.

Todd Wolfenbarger *(Owner & Partner)*
James Rabdau *(Partner)*
Frank Izurieta *(Client Svcs Dir)*
Kat Falcone *(Dir-Media)*
Jordan Howe *(Acct Supvr)*
Suzi Adams *(Media Buyer)*
Tiffany Caldwell *(Media Buyer)*

Accounts:
AAA
Mountain Jones Waldo
SelectHealth
Subway Restaurant PR
T-Mobile

SUMMIT MARKETING
425 N New Ballas Rd, Saint Louis, MO 63141-7091
Tel.: (844) 792-2013
Toll Free: (866) 590-6000
E-Mail: info@summitmarketing.com
Web Site: www.summitmarketing.com

Employees: 390
Year Founded: 1996

National Agency Associations: DMA

Agency Specializes In: Advertising

Michelle Noyes *(Chief Dev Officer)*
Joanne Leightner *(Controller)*
Jeff Triplett *(Controller)*
Tom Kaminski *(Acct Dir)*
Elizabeth Kleve *(Assoc Dir-Creative)*
Jennifer Viscomi *(Sr Acct Mgr)*
Alice Angulo *(Acct Mgr)*
Leah Godfrey *(Strategist-Interactive)*
Brian Smith *(Acct Exec-Natl)*

Accounts:
Allstate
American Heart Association
Arch Chemicals
Bank One Corporation
Brunswick Bowling Centers
Cingular
CNO Financial Group, Inc.
The Coca-Cola Company
GEICO Insurance
Kellogg's
Lowe's
McDonald's
Motorola Solutions, Inc.
The Salvation Army
Starlight Theatre

Branches

Summit Group
(Formerly Summit Marketing)
1100 Cir 75 Pkwy Ste 1200, Atlanta, GA 30339
Tel.: (770) 303-0400
Fax: (770) 303-0450
E-Mail: info@summitmg.com
Web Site: www.summitmg.com

Employees: 60
Year Founded: 1996

Agency Specializes In: Advertising, Sponsorship

Amy Rabideau *(Dir-Pur)*
Jennifer Hardy *(Acct Mgr)*
Susan Camp *(Mgr-IT)*
Anna Cheney *(Sr Acct Exec)*
Samantha Sullivan *(Acct Exec)*
Sarah Wittkop *(Asst Acct Exec)*
David Kirkland *(Grp Pres)*

Summit Group
(Formerly Summit Marketing)
960 Maplewood Dr, Itasca, IL 60143
Tel.: (630) 775-2700
Fax: (630) 775-0132
Web Site: www.summitmg.com

Employees: 70

Agency Specializes In: Advertising

Dan Renz *(CEO)*
Rusty Allen *(CFO & COO)*
Miller Cari *(VP-Strategy & Plng)*
Dana Bernard *(Dir-HR)*
Tiffani Durckel *(Acct Mgr)*
Janelle Touma *(Mgr-Mktg)*
Debbie Yedlin *(Sr Acct Exec)*
Colleen Krause *(Acct Exec)*
Brocky Proxmire *(Acct Exec)*
Jenna Kalina *(Acct Coord)*

Summit Group
(Formerly Summit Marketing Group)
11961 Tech Rd, Silver Spring, MD 20904
Tel.: (301) 625-0800
Fax: (301) 625-0820
Toll Free: (866) 237-0400
E-Mail: info@summitmg.com
Web Site: www.summitmg.com

Employees: 50

Agency Specializes In: Advertising

Tom Murphy *(Dir-Natl Accounts)*
Stephen Brien *(Sr Acct Exec)*
Sandi Dutton *(Sr Acct Exec)*

Summit Marketing
4930 Sabal Lk Cir, Sarasota, FL 34238
Tel.: (941) 927-8027
Fax: (941) 927-5890
E-Mail: sarasota@summitmarketing.com
Web Site: www.summitmarketing.com

Agency Specializes In: Advertising

Michelle Noyes *(Chief Dev Officer)*
Jake Tritton *(VP-Client Dev-Charitable Organizations)*
Pat Monteleone *(Sr Dir-Analytics & Insights)*
Lisa Heinemann *(Dir-Production)*
Julie Barnickol *(Mgr-Production Svcs)*
Sue Jolly *(Sr Acct Exec)*
Kevin Bryant *(Acct Exec-Natl)*
Christopher Howard *(Acct Exec-Natl)*

Accounts:
American Heart Association
American Red Cross
Arch Chemicals
Brunswick
Coca-Cola Refreshments USA, Inc.
Kellogg's

Summit Marketing
10916 Strang Line Rd, Lenexa, KS 66215
Tel.: (913) 888-6222
Fax: (913) 495-9822
Toll Free: (800) 843-7347
E-Mail: kansascity@summitmarketing.com
Web Site: www.summitmarketing.com

Employees: 80

Agency Specializes In: Advertising, Sponsorship

Michelle Noyes *(Chief Dev Officer)*
Jake Tritton *(VP-Client Dev-Charitable Organizations)*
Susan Yockey *(Dir-Strategic Fundraising Client Svcs)*
Janell Conner *(Acct Mgr)*
Julie Barnickol *(Mgr-Production Svcs)*
Kim Gasper *(Sr Acct Exec)*
Kevin Bryant *(Acct Exec-Natl)*

Accounts:
Allstate
American Heart Association
American Red Cross
Applebee's International
Arch Chemicals
Comcast
Geico
Grainger
Iron Workers Union
Keebler
Kellogg's
Kroger
McDonald's

SUMNER GROUP
223 W Main Ave Ste F, Gastonia, NC 28052-4104
Tel.: (704) 865-4613
Fax: (704) 853-1776
Toll Free: (800) 331-4613
E-Mail: info@sumnergroup.com
Web Site: www.sumnergroup.com

E-Mail for Key Personnel:
Creative Dir.: anthony@sumnergroup.com
Media Dir.: mfry@sumnergroup.com
Production Mgr.: jwestfall@sumnergroup.com

Employees: 11
Year Founded: 1987

Agency Specializes In: Advertising, Advertising Specialties, African-American Market, Arts, Automotive, Broadcast, Business-To-Business, Cable T.V., Co-op Advertising, Collateral, Direct Response Marketing, Education, Event Planning & Marketing, Exhibit/Trade Shows, Financial, Graphic Design, Hispanic Market, Internet/Web Design, Legal Services, Local Marketing, Logo & Package Design, Magazines, Market Research, Media Buying Services, Media Planning, Media Relations, Newspaper, Newspapers & Magazines, Outdoor, Planning & Consultation, Point of Purchase, Point of Sale, Print, Production, Public Relations, Publicity/Promotions, Radio, Regional, Retail, Sales Promotion, Social Marketing/Nonprofit, Sports Market, Strategic Planning/Research, Syndication, T.V., Telemarketing, Travel & Tourism, Viral/Buzz/Word of Mouth, Web (Banner Ads, Pop-ups, etc.), Women's Market, Yellow Pages Advertising

Approx. Annual Billings: $2,000,000 Capitalized

Breakdown of Gross Billings by Media: Bus. Publs.: 5%; Collateral: 40%; D.M.: 10%; Mags.: 10%; Newsp.: 10%; Radio: 5%; T.V.: 20%

Jacque Sumner *(Owner & Pres)*
Michael Sumner *(Owner & VP-Client Svcs)*
John Endres *(Dir-Internet Svcs)*
Anthony Rodriguez *(Dir-Creative)*
Ben Davis *(Acct Rep-Sls)*

Accounts:
Cancer Services of Gaston County
CareFirst Animal Hospital
Carolina Commerce Bank; Gastonia, NC; 2006
CarolinaEast Health System Public Awareness
Douglas R. Harris Jewelers
Harris Jewelers
Karl Truman
Patterson & Adams
Schiele Museum
Watson Insurance; Gastonia, NC Campaign: "Go Watson", Marketing

SUN & MOON MARKETING COMMUNICATIONS, INC.
Fl 6 12 E 41st St, New York, NY 10017-7202
Tel.: (212) 686-9600
Fax: (212) 686-9601
E-Mail: mkirch@sunandmoonmktg.com
Web Site: www.sunandmoonmktg.com

E-Mail for Key Personnel:
President: mkirch@sunandmoonmktg.com
Creative Dir.: jhorn@sunandmoonmktg.com
Production Mgr.: dhuang@sunandmoonmktg.com

Employees: 15
Year Founded: 1994

Agency Specializes In: Business Publications, Business-To-Business, Collateral, Communications, Corporate Identity, Event Planning & Marketing, Exhibit/Trade Shows, Financial, Graphic Design, Internet/Web Design, Logo & Package Design, Newspapers & Magazines, Outdoor, Print, Production, Real Estate, Sales Promotion, Strategic Planning/Research, Trade & Consumer Magazines

Approx. Annual Billings: $4,300,000

Breakdown of Gross Billings by Media: Collateral: $1,892,000; Fees: $516,000; Mags.: $1,118,000; Newsp.: $774,000

Madelyne F. Kirch *(Pres)*
Terri Vaccarino *(Sr VP & Client Svcs Dir)*
Jessica Sand *(Dir-Creative)*
Scott Silverman *(Dir-Interactive & Assoc Creative Dir)*
Rachel Charlo-Powers *(Mgr-Mktg)*
Christine Ricciardella *(Mgr-Media)*

Accounts:
Beacon Capital Partners; New York, NY
Capstone Equities; NY
Coldwell Banker Developments; NY
Cushman & Wakefield; New York, NY
DCD Capital; New York, NY; Washington, DC
GFI Capital; NY
RMC Development Corp; NJ
S.L. Green Realty Corp; New York, NY
Taconic Investment Partners; NY Real Estate
Trinity Real Estate; New York, NY Commercial Real Estate Holdings

SUNDANCE MARKETING, LLC
430 Sundance Trail, Webster, NY 14580

Tel.: (585) 670-0347
E-Mail: lsagona@sundance-marketing.com
Web Site: www.sundance-marketing.com

Agency Specializes In: Advertising, Communications, Print

Laurie Sagona *(Pres)*
Mary Pavone *(Dir-Media)*

Accounts:
Helendale Dermatology

SUNDIN ASSOCIATES, INC.
34 Main St 3rd Fl, Natick, MA 01760
Tel.: (508) 650-3972
Fax: (508) 650-3881
E-Mail: info@sundininc.com
Web Site: www.sundininc.com

E-Mail for Key Personnel:
President: roger@sundlininc.com

Employees: 10
Year Founded: 1976

Agency Specializes In: Financial

Approx. Annual Billings: $12,000,000

Breakdown of Gross Billings by Media: Cable T.V.: $600,000; Collateral: $3,600,000; Logo & Package Design: $1,200,000; Newsp.: $3,600,000; Plng. & Consultation: $1,800,000; Production: $600,000; Radio: $600,000

Roger W. Sundin, Jr. *(Founder & COO)*
Kristin Sundin Brandt *(Pres)*
Ed O'Donnell *(Exec VP)*
Bill Orsini *(Sr Dir-Art)*
Lisa Segarra *(Dir-Art)*

Accounts:
Adams Cooperative Bank
Barre Savings Bank
Cooperative Central Bank
Framingham Cooperative Bank
Millbury Savings Bank
New England Financial Marketing Association
The Provident Bank
Ryan's Hope for a Cure Charitable Foundation
St. Anne's Credit Union

SUNDOG
2000 44th St SW 6th Fl, Fargo, ND 58103
Tel.: (701) 235-5525
Fax: (701) 235-8941
Web Site: www.sundoginteractive.com

Employees: 73
Year Founded: 1977

National Agency Associations: Second Wind Limited

Agency Specializes In: Brand Development & Integration, Broadcast, Corporate Identity, Financial, Graphic Design, Health Care Services, Public Relations, Restaurant, Retail, Strategic Planning/Research

Approx. Annual Billings: $18,000,000

Brent Teiken *(CEO)*
Eric Dukart *(COO)*
Johnathon Rademacher *(CTO)*
Matt Gustafson *(Exec VP-Fin & Admin)*
Ron Lee *(VP-Client Svcs)*
Jonathan Gilbertson *(Mgr-Client Success)*

Accounts:
Bobcats

SUNRISE ADVERTISING
700 Walnut St Ste 500, Cincinnati, OH 45202
Tel.: (513) 333-4100
Fax: (513) 333-4101
E-Mail: info@sunriseadvertising.com
Web Site: www.sunriseadvertising.com

E-Mail for Key Personnel:
Creative Dir.: JBrowning@sunriseadvertising.com

Employees: 20
Year Founded: 2003

Agency Specializes In: Advertising, Brand Development & Integration, Broadcast, Cable T.V., Co-op Advertising, Collateral, Communications, Consulting, Consumer Marketing, Consumer Publications, Corporate Communications, Electronic Media, Investor Relations, Local Marketing, Newspapers & Magazines, Product Placement, Production, Radio, Restaurant, Search Engine Optimization, Social Media, Sponsorship, T.V.

Brian McHale *(Owner & CEO)*
Tim Hogan *(Exec Dir-Creative)*
Cynthia D'Alessandro *(Grp Acct Dir)*
Bill Brassine *(Dir-Media)*
Chris Fryburger *(Dir-Bus Dev)*
Todd Jessee *(Dir-Creative)*
Mike Grueter *(Assoc Dir-Media)*
Angella Eidell *(Acct Exec)*
Emily Sowders *(Acct Exec)*

Accounts:
Papa John's
Skyline Chili; Cincinnati, OH; 1998

SUNSTAR
211 N Union St Ste 240, Alexandria, VA 22314-2643
Tel.: (703) 299-8390
Fax: (703) 299-8393
Web Site: www.sunstarstrategic.com

Employees: 20

National Agency Associations: CIPR-COPF

Agency Specializes In: Communications, Corporate Communications, Investor Relations, Market Research, Media Relations, Media Training, Newspaper, Strategic Planning/Research

Revenue: $3,000,000

Kathryn Morrison *(Pres & CEO)*
Dan Sondhelm *(Partner & Sr VP)*
Seuk Kim *(Partner & VP)*
Melissa Murphy *(Partner & VP)*
Bob Tebeleff *(Partner & VP)*
Hibre Teklemariam *(Partner & VP)*
Sue Bryant *(Partner & Mgr-Ops)*
Robert Brummond *(CFO & Dir-Ops)*

Accounts:
AFBA 5Star Fund, Inc.

SUPER GENIUS LLC
343 WEst Erie St Ste 520, Chicago, IL 60654
Tel.: (773) 732-1165
E-Mail: info@supergeniusllc.com
Web Site: www.supergeniusinc.com

Agency Specializes In: Advertising, Alternative Advertising, Brand Development & Integration, Branded Entertainment, Consumer Marketing, Content, Digital/Interactive, Entertainment, Event Planning & Marketing, Integrated Marketing, Internet/Web Design, Local Marketing, Mobile Marketing, Retail, Urban Market

Approx. Annual Billings: $2,000,000

Breakdown of Gross Billings by Media: Adv. Specialities: $2,000,000

Mat Burnett *(Founder & Partner)*
Bill Connell *(Founder & Partner)*
Craig Motlong *(Exec Dir-Creative)*

Accounts:
Nike
Nokia

SUPER TOP SECRET
244 Edison St, Salt Lake City, UT 84111
Tel.: (801) 906-0256
E-Mail: hello@wearetopsecret.com
Web Site: www.wearetopsecret.com

Agency Specializes In: Advertising, Digital/Interactive, Graphic Design

Jared Strain *(Founder & Partner)*
Ryan Martindale *(Partner & Exec Dir-Creative)*
Ryan Potter *(Partner & Dir-Interactive)*
Aaron Sather *(Partner & Dir-Creative)*
Rheda Fouad *(Partner)*
Kassandra Scribner *(Designer-UI & UX)*

Accounts:
Microsoft Corporation
Ride Snowboards
Rossignol Snowboards Decade of Momentum
Siege Audio Company

SUPERCOOL CREATIVE
1556 N La Brea Ave Ste 100, Los Angeles, CA 90028
Tel.: (323) 466-1090
E-Mail: supercool@supercoolcreative.com
Web Site: www.supercoolcreative.com

Year Founded: 2005

Agency Specializes In: Advertising, Brand Development & Integration, Business-To-Business, Consulting, Content, Digital/Interactive, Social Media, T.V.

David Murdico *(Partner & Dir-Creative)*
Robert McBane *(CFO)*
Vince Murdico *(Dir-Digital Strategy & Consulting)*

Accounts:
Dickies
Pizza Hut, Inc.
T-Mobile US

SUPEROXYGEN, INC.
10599 Wilshire Blvd Ste 212, Los Angeles, CA 90024
Tel.: (310) 948-1534
E-Mail: raycampbell@superoxygen.com
Web Site: www.superoxygen.com

Employees: 10
Year Founded: 2002

Agency Specializes In: Graphic Design, Internet/Web Design, Public Relations

Revenue: $1,500,000

Ray Campbell *(Dir-Creative)*

Accounts:
CompareTheCandidates.com; Los Angeles, CA Political Networking
Darren Seaton & Associated; San Jose, CA Consulting Services
Golf Steady Inc.

Kabateck Brown Kellner; Los Angeles, CA Legal Services
LetYourVoiceBeSeen.com; Los Angeles, CA Onlice Social Networking
Los Angeles Child Development Center
Los Angeles County Library; Los Angeles, CA Book Donation
Miken Clothing; Los Angeles, CA Clothing
Nissan Motors
Procter & Gamble
PropulsionX; Los Angeles, CA Automotive
Random Snowboards
Saatchi & Saatchi Advertising
Shallman Communications
Toyota Motor Sports
Walmart
Winner Mandabach

SURDELL & PARTNERS, LLC

3738 S 149th St, Omaha, NE 68144
Tel.: (402) 501-7400
Fax: (402) 553-1170
E-Mail: pjung@surdellpartners.com
Web Site: www.surdellpartners.com

Employees: 25
Year Founded: 2005

National Agency Associations: 4A's

Revenue: $5,500,000

Pat Jung *(Co-Owner)*
Dan Surdell *(Co-Owner)*
Bill Nordin *(Chief Creative Officer)*
Adam Kanzmeier *(Dir-Strategic Consulting & Customer Data)*
Dave Dotzler *(Specialist-Digital Imaging)*

Accounts:
Bright Futures Foundation
Kohls
Nebraskaland Magazine
Pace Communications

SURGE COMMUNICATIONS

(Name Changed to adHOME Creative)

SURPRISE ADVERTISING

369 Capisic St, Portland, ME 04102
Tel.: (207) 879-4560
Fax: (207) 879-4565
Web Site: www.surpriseadvertising.com

Year Founded: 1989

Agency Specializes In: Advertising, Collateral, Graphic Design, Internet/Web Design, Logo & Package Design, Public Relations, Radio

Sam Surprise *(Pres)*

Accounts:
NAPA Auto Parts

SUSAN BLOND, INC.

50 W 57th St Fl 14, New York, NY 10019
Tel.: (212) 333-7728
Fax: (212) 262-1373
E-Mail: info@susanblondinc.com
Web Site: www.susanblondinc.com

Employees: 17
Year Founded: 1987

Agency Specializes In: Advertising, Event Planning & Marketing, Fashion/Apparel, Financial, Graphic Design, Health Care Services, Magazines, Production (Ad, Film, Broadcast), Restaurant, Web (Banner Ads, Pop-ups, etc.)

Susan Blond *(Pres)*
Noreen Perry *(Office Mgr)*
Samantha DeFalco *(Coord-New Bus Dev)*

Accounts:
Avianne & Co.
Sean Paul

SUSAN DAVIS INTERNATIONAL

1101 K St NW Ste 400, Washington, DC 20005
Tel.: (202) 408-0808
Fax: (202) 408-1231
E-Mail: info@susandavis.com
Web Site: www.susandavis.com

Employees: 30

Agency Specializes In: Advertising, Brand Development & Integration, Communications, Crisis Communications, Education, Entertainment, Environmental, Exhibit/Trade Shows, Government/Political, Graphic Design, Health Care Services, Hospitality, Local Marketing, Promotions, Public Relations, Real Estate, Social Marketing/Nonprofit, Sponsorship, Sports Market, Strategic Planning/Research, Travel & Tourism

Susan A. Davis *(Chm)*
Frank Cilluffo *(Mng Dir)*
Tom E. Davis *(VP)*
Lisa T. Miller *(VP)*
Aliza Bran *(Assoc Acct Exec)*

Accounts:
Army Historical Foundation Digital Media, PSA, Print, Radio
Capitol Communicator Media Relations, Publicity
Caring for Military Families: The Elizabeth Dole Foundation
Employer Support of the Guard and Reserve
The Institute of Museum & Library Services Media Relations, Strategic Communications
Institute of Museums and Library Sciences
Isha Foundation
LUNGevity Foundation
Marine Corps Heritage Foundation Media Relations
National Harbor
National Museum of Women in the Arts
The Navy League
Thoth Awards Event Management
US Department of Defense
Vietnam Veterans Memorial Fund Communications Campaign
Washington Tennis & Education Foundation Event Management

SUSAN MAGRINO AGENCY

352 Park Ave S, New York, NY 10010
Tel.: (212) 957-3005
Fax: (212) 957-4071
E-Mail: info@smapr.com
Web Site: www.smapr.com

Employees: 30
Year Founded: 1992

Agency Specializes In: Brand Development & Integration, Event Planning & Marketing, Public Relations, Sponsorship

Susan Magrino *(Founder & CEO)*
Allyn Magrino *(Pres & COO)*
Leigh Ann Ambrosi *(Exec VP)*
Molly Peterson *(VP-Home & Design)*
Courtney Iselin *(Sr Dir-Travel)*
Amy Hoadley *(Sr Acct Dir-Travel & Real Estate)*
Annie Taplin *(Acct Dir)*
Katie Lee Pollack *(Dir-Digital Mktg)*
Pam Steigmeyer *(Mgr-Corp Svcs)*
Vanessa Morin *(Sr Acct Supvr)*
Jaclyn York *(Sr Acct Exec)*

Accounts:
30 Park Place Four Seasons Private Residences New York
Babeth's Feast
Bedell Cellars
Castle Hill Inn
Champagne Nicolas Feuillatte
CIRCA Consumer Support, Marketing, Media, PR
The Cromwell
DoubleTree by Hilton
Fairmont Scottsdale Princess
Fontainebleau Miami Beach PR
Geoffrey Beene
Grace Bay Club; 2007
Hakkasan New York
Hammacher Schlemmer Redesign
Hyatt Regency New Orleans
Hyatt Union Square New York
Lavazza Public Relations
Le Meridien Hotels & Resorts
The LINQ
Loews Regency Hotel
Marie France Van Damme
Martha Stewart Living Omnimedia, Inc.; New York, NY
New-Matthew Kenney Cuisine
Meyer Davis Studios Marketing, PR
Nicolas Feuillatte
Obica Public Relations
New-Obrascon Huarte Lain (Public Relations Agency of Record) Mayakoba Residences, Promotions
The One Group One Hospitality, STK Restaurants
OWN
Paramount Hotel
The Plaza PR
Pure Home
The Ranch at Live Oak Malibu PR
The Residences at Baha Mar (Public Relations Agency of Record)
The Rittenhouse Hotel
Rottet Studio
Six Senses Hotels Resorts Spas
SpongeBath
Sri panwa Public Relations
Stew Leonard's
Sugar Beach Residences
Turnberry Isle Miami
Vineyard Vines
William Grant PR
New-Willis Tower
Windsor Brand Messaging, Press; 2007

SUSSMAN AGENCY

29200 Northwestern Hwy Ste 130, Southfield, MI 48034
Tel.: (248) 353-5300
Fax: (248) 353-3800
Web Site: www.sussmanagency.com

Agency Specializes In: Advertising, Internet/Web Design, Print, T.V.

Joell Hart *(Sr Dir-Art)*
Kimberly Bizon *(Dir-Web & Interactive)*
Chris Culpepper *(Dir-Media-Natl)*
David Doolittle *(Dir-Creative)*
Stephanie Beer Howcroft *(Assoc Dir-Media)*
Rose Russell *(Mgr-Media Continuity)*

Accounts:
Art Van Furniture, Inc.

SUTHERLAND WESTON MARKETING COMMUNICATIONS

6 State St Ste 102, Bangor, ME 04401
Tel.: (207) 945-9999
Fax: (207) 945-3636
E-Mail: info@sutherlandweston.com
Web Site: www.sutherlandweston.com

Agency Specializes In: Advertising, Event Planning

Advertising Agencies

& Marketing, Graphic Design, Internet/Web Design, Logo & Package Design, Media Relations, Public Relations, Search Engine Optimization, Social Media, Strategic Planning/Research

Cary Weston *(Pres)*
Elizabeth Sutherland *(Partner)*
Pauline Higgins *(Fin Dir & Office Mgr)*
Jillian Piehler *(Dir-Mktg)*
Lily Fryer *(Acct Mgr)*
Amanda Anderson *(Mgr-Web Dev)*
Ric Tyler *(Mgr-Media Svcs)*

Accounts:
City of Calais
Maine Potato Board

THE SUTTER GROUP

4384 Lottsford Vista Rd, Lanham, MD 20706-4817
Tel.: (301) 459-5445
Fax: (301) 459-9129
E-Mail: info@sutter-group.com
Web Site: www.sutter-group.com

Employees: 7
Year Founded: 1987

Agency Specializes In: Automotive, Brand Development & Integration, Business Publications, Business-To-Business, Direct Response Marketing, E-Commerce, Event Planning & Marketing, Exhibit/Trade Shows, Graphic Design, Internet/Web Design, Logo & Package Design, Print

Karen Sutter *(Pres)*
John Sutter *(COO)*
John Cassella *(Dir-Creative)*
Rebecca Lombardo *(Dir-Mktg & Bus Dev)*

Accounts:
Spoiled Rotten

SVM PUBLIC RELATIONS & MARKETING COMMUNICATIONS

(Formerly Stauch Vetromile)
2 Charles St 3rd Fl N, Providence, RI 02904
Tel.: (401) 490-9700
Fax: (401) 490-9707
E-Mail: info@svmmarcom.com
Web Site: www.svmmarcom.com

Employees: 16
Year Founded: 1971

Agency Specializes In: Advertising, Brand Development & Integration, Business-To-Business, Communications, Computers & Software, Consulting, Consumer Marketing, Corporate Communications, Corporate Identity, Crisis Communications, Digital/Interactive, Direct Response Marketing, Event Planning & Marketing, Exhibit/Trade Shows, Graphic Design, Health Care Services, High Technology, Information Technology, Integrated Marketing, Internet/Web Design, Local Marketing, Logo & Package Design, Magazines, Media Buying Services, Media Planning, Media Training, Package Design, Print, Production, Production (Ad, Film, Broadcast), Production (Print), Promotions, Public Relations, Strategic Planning/Research

Robert W. Vetromile *(Pres)*
Jill Colna *(VP-PR)*
Cari Thorpe *(Controller)*
Rachelle Costa *(Dir-Admin)*
Laura Nelson *(Dir-PR)*
Jeff Lavery *(Acct Supvr-PR)*
Jill Anderson *(Sr Acct Exec-PR)*
Kathryn Kelly *(Sr Acct Exec)*
Sarah Anderson *(Acct Exec)*

Accounts:
Astea International
WorldCare Clinical

SWAFFORD & COMPANY ADVERTISING

820 Washinton Ave Ste D, Santa Monica, CA 90403
Tel.: (310) 451-0611
Fax: (310) 553-9639
E-Mail: info@swafford.net
Web Site: www.swafford.net

Employees: 10
Year Founded: 1947

National Agency Associations: MCA

Agency Specializes In: Advertising, Travel & Tourism

John Swafford *(Pres)*

Accounts:
Doubletree Hotels
Fess Parkers Doubletree Resort
Hilton Worldwide Garden Inn

SWAN ADVERTISING

9121 W Russell Rd Ste 116, Las Vegas, NV 89148
Tel.: (702) 876-1559
Fax: (702) 876-4699
Web Site: www.swanadvertising.com

Agency Specializes In: Advertising, Logo & Package Design, Outdoor, Print, Radio, T.V.

Steve Swan *(Pres-Swan Resource Svcs)*
Hernan Valencia *(Dir-Creative)*
Anna Swan *(Office Mgr)*
Maureen McDougall *(Acct Exec)*
Dottie Korkosz *(Media Buyer)*

Accounts:
Findlay Toyota

SWANSON RUSSELL ASSOCIATES

1222 P St, Lincoln, NE 68508-1425
Tel.: (402) 437-6400
Fax: (402) 437-6401
E-Mail: sra@sramarketing.com
Web Site: www.swansonrussell.com

E-Mail for Key Personnel:
President: stever@sramarketing.com
Creative Dir.: brianb@sramarketing.com
Media Dir.: kayw@sramarketing.com
Public Relations: jeffp@sramarketing.com

Employees: 115
Year Founded: 1962

National Agency Associations: APA-MCA

Agency Specializes In: Agriculture, Business-To-Business, Consumer Marketing, Health Care Services, Outdoor

Johan Apel *(Pres & CEO)*
Dave Hansen *(Partner)*
Brent Schott *(Sr VP & Grp Acct Dir)*
Kay Wigle *(Sr VP & Dir-Media)*
Greg Wiley *(Sr VP & Dir-Creative Dev)*
Katie Sands *(VP & Acct Dir)*
Dave Christiansen *(VP & Dir-Creative)*
Joe Maguire *(VP & Dir-Creative)*
Mike Babel *(VP & Mgr-Fin)*
Jim Brestel *(VP & Mgr-Info Svcs)*
Tony Sattler *(VP & Mgr-Interactive Strategy)*
Ashley Rolf *(Dir-Art)*
Ryan Holt *(Assoc Dir-Art)*
Rachel Hrabik *(Acct Mgr)*
Taryn Liess *(Assoc Acct Mgr)*
Andrea Tremayne *(Mgr-Database Mktg)*
Jenna Sutterfield *(Asst Mgr-Traffic)*
Patrick Finnegan *(Acct Supvr)*
Stuart Adams *(Media Planner)*
Laura Hirschman *(Coord-PR)*
Stephanie Riekhof *(Assoc Acct Supvr)*

Accounts:
AcuSport Corporation; Bellefontaine, OH Distributor of Outdoor and Shooting Sports Products.; 2007
Becker Underwood; Ames, IA Specialty Colorants & Bio-Agronomic Products; 1999
Blue Blood Brewery
Cannon Safe Inc Creative Services, Database, Interactive services, Marketing Communications, Media Relations, Public Relations, Strategic Planning
The Fertilizer Institute 4R Nutrient Stewardship, NutrientStewardship.com, Program Branding
FMC
New-Global Roundtable for Sustainable Beef Marketing Communications
Golf Course Builders of America Association; Lincoln, NE; 2000
Hodgdon Powder Co; Kansas City, MO Black Powder; 1995
Humminbird; Eufaula, AL Electronic Fishfinders; 2004
Hunting & Shooting Heritage Foundation; Newton, CT Shooting Sports Industry Support Organization; 2001
Leupold; Beaverton, OR Sporting Optics; 1998
LinPepCo
Minn Kota; Racine, WI Transon & Bow-Mount Tolling Motors; 1998
NC+ Hybrids; Lincoln, NE Hybrid Seed Producer; 1988
Nebraska Bankers Association; Lincoln, NE; 1997
Nebraska's Tourism Commission Tourism PR
Nosler
Omaha Hilton
Omaha Public Relations Society of America
Pro Lift
Profile Products, LLC; Buffalo Grove, IL Soil Amendments Manufacturer; 1998
Propane Education & Research Council
Runza Restaurants; Lincoln, NE Fast Food Chain; 2000
ScentBlocker
SCUBAPRO Marketing
ShoreLand'r; Ida Grove, IA Boat Trailers & Marine Accessories; 1999
Turfco; Minneapolis, MN Turf & Landscape Renovation Equipment; 2000
University of Arkansas for Medical Sciences (Advertising Agency of Record)
Weatherby Foundation International; Turlock, CA Hunting Preservation & Wildlife Conservation Foundation; 1998
Woolrich Inc.; Woolrich, PA Outdoor Apparel; 2002

Branch

Swanson Russell Associates

14301 FNB Pkwy Ste 312, Omaha, NE 68154-5299
Tel.: (402) 393-4940
Fax: (402) 393-6926
E-Mail: sra@swansonrussell.com
Web Site: www.swansonrussell.com

Employees: 30
Year Founded: 1985

Agency Specializes In: Agriculture, Business-To-Business, Health Care Services, Outdoor, Pets , Recruitment

Steve Johnson *(VP & Acct Dir)*
Karl Ploeger *(Acct Dir)*

Randy Shnackenberg *(Mgr-Production)*
Judy Pickens *(Media Planner)*
Kaila Shirey *(Media Buyer)*
Chris Johnson *(Sr Designer-Interactive)*
Brenda Warren *(Sr Media Buyer)*

Accounts:
AGCO
AGP - Projects; Omaha, NE Agricultural Cooperative; 1994
BlueCross BlueShield; Omaha, NE Insurance Provider; 2007
Bullet Weights
Cannon
Corona
Global Animal Management, Inc.
Humminbird
Intervet/Schering-Plough Animal Health; Union, NJ Animal Health Products; 1994
Laboratory Management Partners, Inc. Communications
Mercy Hospital; Iowa City, IA Community Hospital; 1998
New-Omaha Convention & Visitors Bureau Collateral, Digital, Direct Mail, Mobile App, Print, TV, Video, Website
Physicians Mutual; Omaha, NE Insurance; 2004
Purina Mills
Quarry Oaks
Rain Bird
Vermeer
Wolfe Eye Clinic; Marshalltown, IA Private Practice Physicians Group; 2007

SWASH LABS
209 E University Dr, Denton, TX 76209
Tel.: (940) 808-0071
Web Site: www.swashlabs.com

Year Founded: 2011

Agency Specializes In: Advertising, Brand Development & Integration, Content, Digital/Interactive, Graphic Design, Media Buying Services, Media Planning, Package Design, Print, Social Media

Josh Berthume *(CEO & Dir-Creative)*
Diana Fonner *(Dir-Ops)*
Scott Garrison *(Dir-Plng & Media)*
Joan Wells *(Dir-Artistic)*
Kevin Edger *(Mgr-Digital Media)*

Accounts:
Iteach Texas
Mellow Mushroom Denton
Mellow Mushroom Flower Mound
Mellow Mushroom Mckinney
Mellow Mushroom San Antonio

SWEDA ADVERTISING
120 N Abington Rd, Clarks Green, PA 18411
Tel.: (570) 586-0777
E-Mail: info@sweda-advertising.com
Web Site: www.sweda-advertising.com

Agency Specializes In: Advertising, Internet/Web Design, Logo & Package Design, Media Planning, Outdoor, Print, Radio, T.V.

George Sweda *(Owner & Pres)*
Robyn Ziska *(Dir-Media)*
Jill Lewis *(Office Mgr)*
Emily Dwyer *(Strategist-Brand)*

Accounts:
Griffin Pond Animal Shelter
Tobyhanna Army Depot Federal Credit Union
Veterinary Referral & Emergency Center

SWEENEY
19106 Old Detroit Rd, Cleveland, OH 44116
Tel.: (440) 333-0001
Fax: (440) 333-0005
E-Mail: info@sweeneypr.com
Web Site: www.sweeneypr.com

Employees: 4
Year Founded: 1986

Agency Specializes In: Advertising, Advertising Specialties, Affluent Market, Alternative Advertising, Automotive, Brand Development & Integration, Business Publications, Business-To-Business, Catalogs, Children's Market, Co-op Advertising, Collateral, College, Communications, Consulting, Consumer Goods, Consumer Marketing, Consumer Publications, Corporate Communications, Corporate Identity, Crisis Communications, Customer Relationship Management, Digital/Interactive, Direct Response Marketing, Direct-to-Consumer, Education, Electronic Media, Email, Environmental, Event Planning & Marketing, Exhibit/Trade Shows, Experience Design, Faith Based, Fashion/Apparel, Financial, Food Service, Graphic Design, Guerilla Marketing, Health Care Services, Hospitality, Household Goods, Identity Marketing, In-Store Advertising, Industrial, Integrated Marketing, Internet/Web Design, Local Marketing, Logo & Package Design, Luxury Products, Magazines, Market Research, Media Planning, Media Relations, Media Training, Medical Products, Men's Market, Merchandising, Mobile Marketing, Multimedia, New Product Development, New Technologies, Newspaper, Newspapers & Magazines, Outdoor, Over-50 Market, Package Design, Paid Searches, Pets , Pharmaceutical, Planning & Consultation, Podcasting, Point of Purchase, Point of Sale, Print, Product Placement, Production, Promotions, Public Relations, Publicity/Promotions, RSS (Really Simple Syndication), Radio, Restaurant, Retail, Sales Promotion, Search Engine Optimization, Seniors' Market, Social Marketing/Nonprofit, Social Media, Sponsorship, Strategic Planning/Research, T.V., Technical Advertising, Teen Market, Trade & Consumer Magazines, Viral/Buzz/Word of Mouth, Web (Banner Ads, Pop-ups, etc.), Women's Market

Jennifer Manocchio *(Pres)*
Kelly Erickson *(Office Mgr)*
Elizabeth Kwolek *(Acct Supvr)*
Leah Evanovich *(Acct Exec)*
Rebecca Wrenn *(Acct Exec)*

Accounts:
Alta House; Cleveland, OH Recreation Center; 2005
Centers for Dialysis Care (Agency of Record)
Diabetes Daily; Cleveland, OH Online Network; 2009
Gasco Affiliates; Oldsmar, FL Precision Calibration Gas, Equipment & Accessories; 2007
Housekeeping Channel; Boise, ID Housecleaning Services; 2006
Legacy Innovation; Cleveland, OH Cabinets, Countertops, Mantels; 2001
Magic American/Homax; Bellingham, WA Cleaning Products, Pest Control Products; 2005
The Plaza Group; Houston, TX Petrochemicals; 2007
Weiman Products; Gurnee, IL Home Cleaning Products; 2008
Westfield Shoppingtowns; Los Angeles, CA Shopping Centers; 2005
Yube; Foxboro, MA Modular Furniture; 2010

Branch

SWEENEY
201 N Front St Ste 904, Wilmington, NC 28401
Tel.: (910) 772-1688
Fax: (910) 772-1689
E-Mail: info@sweeneypr.com
Web Site: www.sweeneypr.com

Employees: 2

Jennifer Manocchio *(Pres)*
Rachel Kaylor *(Dir-Digital & Social Media)*
Morgan Lang *(Acct Exec)*

Accounts:
Prone2Paddle Product Messaging, Public Relations, Tradeshow Marketing

SWEENEY CREATIVE
(Formerly Sweeney & Farrow)
640 Farnham Dr, Richmond, VA 23236-4111
Tel.: (804) 873-0165
Fax: (813) 603-9790
E-Mail: stan@sweeneycreative.com
Web Site: www.sweeneycreative.com

Employees: 2
Year Founded: 1987

Agency Specializes In: Advertising, Agriculture, Arts, Automotive, Aviation & Aerospace, Brand Development & Integration, Broadcast, Business Publications, Business-To-Business, Cable T.V., Catalogs, Children's Market, Co-op Advertising, Collateral, Commercial Photography, Communications, Consumer Goods, Consumer Marketing, Consumer Publications, Corporate Identity, Cosmetics, Direct Response Marketing, Direct-to-Consumer, Electronic Media, Environmental, Event Planning & Marketing, Exhibit/Trade Shows, Financial, Food Service, Gay & Lesbian Market, Government/Political, Graphic Design, Guerilla Marketing, Health Care Services, Hospitality, Industrial, Internet/Web Design, Investor Relations, Leisure, Local Marketing, Logo & Package Design, Magazines, Marine, Media Buying Services, Medical Products, Merchandising, Multimedia, New Product Development, Newspaper, Newspapers & Magazines, Out-of-Home Media, Outdoor, Over-50 Market, Package Design, Pharmaceutical, Point of Purchase, Point of Sale, Print, Production, Production (Print), Public Relations, Publicity/Promotions, Publishing, Radio, Real Estate, Recruitment, Restaurant, Retail, Sales Promotion, Seniors' Market, Sports Market, T.V., Trade & Consumer Magazines, Transportation, Travel & Tourism

Breakdown of Gross Billings by Media: Audio/Visual: 5%; Bus. Publs.: 5%; Collateral: 10%; Exhibits/Trade Shows: 5%; Graphic Design: 10%; Logo & Package Design: 10%; Newsp.: 13%; Pub. Rels.: 2%; Radio: 15%; Trade Shows: 5%; Worldwide Web Sites: 20%

Accounts:
Albermarle Eye Centers; Nags Head, NC Eye Care; 2009
Blue Chip Structures Equine Buildings
Captain Max King Marine; VA Beach, VA Marine Dealership; 2009
Carano Dental; Lancaster, PA; 2005
CJW Medical Center; Richmond, VA Healthcare, Sports Medicine; 2005
Clean-Works Building Maintenance
Eastern Land; Annville, PA Land Development; 2010
Econ Electrical; Richmond, VA Electrical; 2009
Hershey Farms Hotel; Lancaster, PA Hotel; 2009
The Hodges Touch; Richmond, VA Painting Company
Lancaster Medical Society; Lancaster, PA Medical Society; 2011
Mathews Visitors Center; Mathews, VA Tourism; 2006
Northern Neck Treasures; Irvington, CA Tourism; 2010

Palco; Lancaster, PA Healthcare; 2010
Rider Insurance Motorcycle Insurance
RigidPly Rafters Inc. Building Materials
SweeneyMatz CPA; Fort Lauderdale, FL CPA; 1995
Wellness Counseling; Lancaster, PA Counseling
White House Apple Products; Winchester, PA Apple Products; 1989
YellowFin Va; Virginia Beach, VA Boats; 2010

SWEENEYVESTY

95 Morton St Ground Fl, New York, NY 10014
Tel.: (212) 905-3345
Fax: (212) 905-3349
Web Site: www.sweeneyvesty.com

Year Founded: 1987

Agency Specializes In: Advertising, Automotive, Brand Development & Integration, Communications, Content, Crisis Communications, Digital/Interactive, Entertainment, Event Planning & Marketing, Fashion/Apparel, Financial, Game Integration, Graphic Design, Hospitality, Information Technology, Integrated Marketing, Investor Relations, Local Marketing, Logo & Package Design, Luxury Products, New Product Development, Production (Ad, Film, Broadcast), Publicity/Promotions, Publishing, Retail, Sales Promotion, Sponsorship, Travel & Tourism, Web (Banner Ads, Pop-ups, etc.)

Brian Sweeney *(Chm)*
Jane Vesty *(CEO & Dir)*
Carla Hofler *(Exec VP & Gen Mgr-Intl)*
Greg Fahey *(Gen Mgr-Auckland)*

Accounts:
Saatchi & Saatchi New Zealand
New-Wallse (Public Relations Agency of Record) Media Relations

SWELL

77 Franklin St, New York, NY 10013
Tel.: (646) 397-9355
E-Mail: info@swellny.com
Web Site: www.swellny.com

Agency Specializes In: Advertising, Brand Development & Integration, Content, Digital/Interactive, Internet/Web Design, Search Engine Optimization, Social Media, Strategic Planning/Research, T.V.

Tarik Malak *(Founder & Chief Creative Officer)*
Eduardo Meza *(Dir-Design)*
William Miesmer *(Sr Acct Mgr & Sr Mgr-Brand Strategy)*
Matthew Payne *(Project Mgr-Digital)*
Chelsea Chun *(Mgr-New Bus Dev)*
Yasir Haque *(Mgr-Social Media & SEO)*
Eamon Monaghan *(Mgr-Digital Production)*

Accounts:
Kapitall Inc

SWELLSHARK

55 W 39th St, 18th Fl, New York, NY 10018
Tel.: (212) 993-7227
E-Mail: Contact@SwellShark.com
Web Site: www.swellshark.com

National Agency Associations: 4A's

Mary Perhach *(Pres)*
Nick Pappas *(CEO)*
Emily Knapp *(Head-Content & Media Strategy)*
John Hlatky *(Grp Acct Dir)*
Daniel Schaeffer *(Dir-Digital Media)*
Olivia Barone *(Mgr-Community)*
Brooke Capps *(Strategist-Content & Creative)*

Accounts:
Applegate Farms
Beech-Nut
Harry's
Hudson Whiskey
Shinola Detroit
Uniqlo
William Grant & Sons

SWIFT AGENCY

1714 NW Overton St, Portland, OR 97209
Tel.: (503) 227-8305
E-Mail: hello@swift.co
Web Site: www.swift.co

Year Founded: 2007

Agency Specializes In: Advertising, Customer Relationship Management, Digital/Interactive, Media Buying Services, Search Engine Optimization, Social Media

Paul Wille *(Pres & Chief Performance Officer)*
Liz Valentine *(CEO)*
Maren Elliott *(COO)*
Alicia McVey *(COO)*

Accounts:
New-Black Diamond
New-HTC Corp.
New-Nestle USA SweeTARTS (Digital Agency of Record)
New-Nike
New-Starbucks

SWIFT SMART SOLUTIONS

717 N Forest Ave 200N, Lake Forest, IL 60045
Tel.: (847) 283-0272
Web Site: swiftsmartsolutions.com

Year Founded: 1997

Agency Specializes In: Communications, Event Planning & Marketing, Publicity/Promotions

Vicky Swift *(Pres)*
Mark Owen *(Partner & Exec VP)*
Duffy Swift *(Partner & Exec VP)*
Jamie Haberkorn *(Dir-Learning & Dev)*
Jessica Nichols *(Mgr-Learning & Dev)*
Jen Roberts *(Acct Exec)*

Accounts:
Abbott Healthcare Services
Astellas
Baxter
Genzyme Healthcare Services
Lundbeck

SWIM CREATIVE

415 E Superior St, Duluth, MN 55802
Tel.: (218) 722-1404
E-Mail: contact@swimcreative.com
Web Site: www.swimcreative.com

Year Founded: 2005

Agency Specializes In: Advertising, Brand Development & Integration, Digital/Interactive, Logo & Package Design, Print, Social Media

Patrice Bradley *(CEO & Dir-Creative)*
David Sadowski *(Partner & Dir-Brand Strategies)*
Cody Paulson *(Sr Dir-Design)*
Ben Luoma *(Dir-Interactive Media)*
Kevin Cain *(Office Mgr)*
Amber Ooley *(Strategist-Media)*
Talyn Riedesel *(Copywriter)*

Accounts:
Fryberger Buchanan Smith & Frederick P.A

SWIRL ADVERTISING

101 Montgomery St Ste 200, San Francisco, CA 90404
Tel.: (415) 276-8300
Fax: (415) 276-8301
E-Mail: info@swirl.net
Web Site: swirl.net/

E-Mail for Key Personnel:
President: Matt@swirl.net

Employees: 62
Year Founded: 1997

National Agency Associations: 4A's

Agency Specializes In: Advertising, Advertising Specialties, Affiliate Marketing, Agriculture, Alternative Advertising, Automotive, Below-the-Line, Bilingual Market, Brand Development & Integration, Branded Entertainment, Broadcast, Business Publications, Business-To-Business, Cable T.V., Co-op Advertising, Collateral, College, Commercial Photography, Communications, Computers & Software, Consulting, Consumer Goods, Consumer Marketing, Consumer Publications, Corporate Communications, Corporate Identity, Customer Relationship Management, Digital/Interactive, Direct Response Marketing, Direct-to-Consumer, E-Commerce, Education, Electronics, Email, Entertainment, Environmental, Event Planning & Marketing, Exhibit/Trade Shows, Experience Design, Fashion/Apparel, Financial, Food Service, Gay & Lesbian Market, Graphic Design, Guerilla Marketing, Health Care Services, High Technology, Hispanic Market, Identity Marketing, In-Store Advertising, Integrated Marketing, International, Internet/Web Design, Leisure, Local Marketing, Logo & Package Design, Magazines, Media Buying Services, Media Planning, Media Relations, Men's Market, Mobile Marketing, Multicultural, Multimedia, New Product Development, New Technologies, Newspaper, Newspapers & Magazines, Out-of-Home Media, Outdoor, Over-50 Market, Paid Searches, Planning & Consultation, Point of Purchase, Point of Sale, Print, Product Placement, Production, Production (Print), Promotions, Publicity/Promotions, Radio, Real Estate, Restaurant, Retail, Sales Promotion, Search Engine Optimization, Seniors' Market, Social Marketing/Nonprofit, South Asian Market, Sponsorship, Sports Market, Strategic Planning/Research, Sweepstakes, T.V., Teen Market, Telemarketing, Trade & Consumer Magazines, Transportation, Travel & Tourism, Viral/Buzz/Word of Mouth, Women's Market

Martin Lauber *(Founder & CEO)*
John Berg *(Mng Partner)*
Greg Fischer *(Exec VP-Media Svcs)*
Greg Riley *(Exec VP-Strategy)*
Wayne Esplana *(Controller)*
Kevin McCarthy *(Exec Dir-Creative)*
Whitney Ward *(Sr Dir-Art)*
Ryan Lincks *(Grp Acct Dir)*
Wendy Shay *(Grp Acct Dir)*
Stacy Simon *(Acct Dir)*
Heather Jenkin *(Assoc Dir-Media & Sr Supvr-Media)*
Amy Law *(Assoc Dir-Creative)*
Jules Murphy *(Assoc Dir-Creative)*
Christina Torres *(Assoc Dir-Media)*
Julia Hatfield *(Acct Mgr)*
Lauren Viruete *(Acct Mgr)*
Conor Ryan *(Acct Supvr)*
Lesley Harman *(Strategist-Media)*
Jessica Hollenbacher *(Strategist-Media)*
Kathryn Poh *(Strategist-Media)*
Lesley Watson *(Strategist-Media)*

Accounts:

511
Bay Club
The Clorox Company
Coinstar Inc (Agency of Record)
eBay, Inc.
eBay Motors
Walmart Digital

SWITCH

6600 Manchester Ave, Saint Louis, MO 63139
Tel.: (314) 206-7700
Fax: (314) 206-4570
E-Mail: switch@theswitch.us
Web Site: www.liberateyourbrand.com

Employees: 130
Year Founded: 1982

National Agency Associations: 4A's

Agency Specializes In: Sponsorship

Approx. Annual Billings: $50,000,000

John Nickel *(Pres)*
Jason Mendenhall *(Exec VP-Cloud)*
Jeff Oberschelp *(Exec VP)*
Terry Hobbs *(Sr VP)*
Nicole Phillips *(VP-Bus Dev & Acct Mgmt)*
Josh Kell *(Exec Creative Dir)*
Craig Kammien *(Sr Dir-Creative)*
James Campbell *(Dir-Creative)*
Chris Douglas *(Dir-Digital)*
Scott McRae *(Dir-Tech)*
Rebecca Reardon *(Dir-Creative)*
John Roth *(Acct Exec)*

Accounts:
Anheuser-Busch InBev N.V./S.A.
Budweiser
Coca-Cola
Covidien Health Care
Elsevier
Glaceau/Vitaminwater
Muscle Milk

SWITCHBACK PUBLIC RELATIONS & MARKETING INC.

10075 W River St Ste 206, Truckee, CA 96161
Tel.: (530) 550-2252
Fax: (530) 582-4202
E-Mail: info@switchbackpr.com
Web Site: www.switchbackpr.com

Employees: 11
Year Founded: 1999

Brinn Talbot *(Owner & Pres)*
Melissa Williams *(Dir)*
Anna Mia Koenig *(Acct Mgr)*

Accounts:
Canyon Springs of Truckee
Cass House Inn & Restaurant
Chase International
Dragonfly
Royal Gorge Cross Country
Ruby Mountain Helicopter Skiing
Tahoe Board of Realtors
Truckee Chamber of Commerce
West End Bistro
Wine, Walk & Shop

SWIZZLE COLLECTIVE

1601 W 6th St, Austin, TX 78703
Tel.: (512) 590-0091
Web Site: www.swizzlecollective.com

Agency Specializes In: Advertising, Brand Development & Integration, Graphic Design, Print, Social Marketing/Nonprofit

Noah Davis *(Partner)*

Accounts:
New-Presidium Group

SWOOP INC.

125 Cambridgepark Dr, Cambridge, MA 02140
Toll Free: (877) 848-9903
Web Site: www.swoop.com

Year Founded: 2011

Agency Specializes In: Advertising

Ron Elwell *(Founder & CEO)*
Simeon Simeonov *(Founder & CTO)*
Rick Albert *(Pres & Partner)*
Scott Rines *(Exec VP & Gen Mgr)*
William V. Powers *(Exec VP-Strategic Dev)*
Katie Carr *(VP-Sls)*

Accounts:
Boulder Brands Inc.
General Mills, Inc.
Groupe Danone S.A.

SYMMETRI MARKETING GROUP, LLC

500 N Michigan Ave Ste 1600, Chicago, IL 60611
Tel.: (312) 222-2500
Fax: (312) 222-2560
Web Site: www.symmetrimarketing.com

Year Founded: 2003

Agency Specializes In: Advertising, Brand Development & Integration, Business-To-Business, Collateral, Digital/Interactive, Internet/Web Design, Search Engine Optimization, Social Media

Meredith Darbyshire *(Acct Dir)*
Joshua Gardner *(Acct Dir)*
Kristina Musial *(Acct Dir)*
Kristen Paladino *(Acct Dir)*
Ken Martino *(Assoc Dir-Creative)*
Winston Tsao *(Mgr-Tech)*
Jenna Fletcher *(Sr Acct Exec)*
Courtney Christ *(Sr Specialist-Digital Mktg)*
Megan King *(Sr Graphic Designer)*

Accounts:
Accurate Perforating
Dentsply

SYNAPTIC DIGITAL

(Acquired by Definition 6)

SYNAPTIC DIGITAL

708 3rd Ave, New York, NY 10017
Tel.: (212) 682-8300
E-Mail: learnmore@synapticdigital.com
Web Site: www.synapticdigital.com

Agency Specializes In: Content, Financial, Media Planning, Media Relations, T.V.

Laura Pair *(Mng Dir)*
Krish Menon *(CTO)*
Rich Quigley *(VP-Client Svcs & Strategist-Brdcst)*
Julia Heath *(VP)*
Rebecca Reissman *(VP-Client Solutions)*
Michael Reina *(Mgr-IT & Sr Engr-Network)*

Accounts:
Adidas Apparel Mfr
Bridgestone Tyre Mfr
Clairol Professional Beauty Care Products Mfr & Distr
Dove Chocolate Discoveries Chocolate Food Retailer
General Motors Automobile Mfr
GlaxoSmithKline
Google
Honeywell Engineering Services
Intel
Philips Electrical & Electronic Products Mfr

SYNCAPSE CORP.

20 Duncan St Suite 301, Toronto, ON M5H 3G8 Canada
Tel.: (416) 593-3773
E-Mail: syncapseto@syncapse.com
Web Site: www.syncapse.com

Agency Specializes In: Consumer Goods, Financial, Restaurant, Retail, Social Media, Strategic Planning/Research

Sarah Johnston *(Mng Dir-Toronto & Sr VP-Brand Partnerships)*
Sarah Long *(Mng Dir-NY & VP)*
David Blumer *(Sr Head-Strategy)*

Accounts:
BlackBerry Mobile Phone & Accessories Mfr & Distr
Cellularsouth Mobile Phones & Accessories Dealer
Edelman Global Public Relations Service Provider
OMD Media Communications

SYNDCTD

1506 N Gardner St Fl 2, Los Angeles, CA 90046
Tel.: (323) 378-5802
E-Mail: info@syndctd.com
Web Site: www.syndctd.com

Year Founded: 2012

Agency Specializes In: Advertising, Content, Digital/Interactive, Graphic Design, Logo & Package Design, Media Buying Services, Outdoor, Print, Radio, T.V.

Phil Camino *(Mng Partner)*
Aaron Turkel *(Dir-Strategy)*
Alex Moroch *(Sr Mgr-Growth & Dev)*
Simone Wicks *(Mgr-Creative Svcs)*
Hannah Barnes *(Specialist-Social Media)*

Accounts:
Arnette, Ltd.
Circle of Confusion
Diamond Carter
Embrace Entertainment Group Inc
Forks over Knives
Harman-Kardon Inc.
Hybritivity
Icracked
Las Vegas Monorail
Mad Decent
Madame Tussauds
Maestro Dobel
Marc Friedland
Pingup
Red Bull North America, Inc.
Rockwell Table Stage
Sea Life

SZEN MARKETING

34145 Pacific Coast Hwy #607, Dana Point, CA 92629
Tel.: (949) 248-0200
Fax: (413) 502-1688
E-Mail: info@szen.us
Web Site: www.szen.us

Year Founded: 2007

Agency Specializes In: Advertising, Brand Development & Integration, Business-To-Business, Collateral, Communications, Consulting, Consumer Goods, Consumer Marketing, Corporate

Communications, Corporate Identity, Fashion/Apparel, Graphic Design, Hospitality, Integrated Marketing, Internet/Web Design, Leisure, Logo & Package Design, Luxury Products, Market Research, New Product Development, Package Design, Strategic Planning/Research

Approx. Annual Billings: $1,600,000

Breakdown of Gross Billings by Media: Consulting: $1,600,000

Gary Szenderski *(Owner)*

T. J. SACKS & ASSOCIATES

445 Park Ave 9th Fl, New York, NY 10022
Tel.: (212) 787-0787
Fax: (212) 787-0790
E-Mail: tjsacks@tjsacks.com
Web Site: www.tjsacks.com

Agency Specializes In: Advertising, Fashion/Apparel, Food Service, Health Care Services, Industrial, Leisure, Retail, Social Marketing/Nonprofit, Travel & Tourism, Web (Banner Ads, Pop-ups, etc.)

Temi J. Sacks *(Pres)*

Accounts:
The Biondo Group
Cassin & Cassin LLP
Creata International
Diamond Rose Jewelry
Life Options Institute
MultiPet
National Products Ltd
Quantum Workplace

T3 (THE THINK TANK)

1801 N Lamar Blvd, Austin, TX 78701
Tel.: (512) 499-8811
Fax: (512) 499-8552
E-Mail: info@t-3.com
Web Site: www.t-3.com

E-Mail for Key Personnel:
President: gayg@t-3.com
Creative Dir.: jays@t-3.com

Employees: 145
Year Founded: 1989

Agency Specializes In: Advertising, Advertising Specialties, Automotive, Brand Development & Integration, Broadcast, Business Publications, Business-To-Business, Catalogs, Collateral, Commercial Photography, Communications, Consulting, Consumer Marketing, Consumer Publications, Content, Corporate Communications, Corporate Identity, Customer Relationship Management, Digital/Interactive, Direct Response Marketing, E-Commerce, Education, Electronic Media, Email, Entertainment, Event Planning & Marketing, Fashion/Apparel, Financial, Food Service, Government/Political, Graphic Design, Health Care Services, High Technology, Hospitality, Information Technology, Integrated Marketing, Internet/Web Design, Leisure, Logo & Package Design, Magazines, Market Research, Media Buying Services, Media Planning, Media Relations, Medical Products, Merchandising, Mobile Marketing, Multimedia, New Product Development, New Technologies, Newspaper, Newspapers & Magazines, Out-of-Home Media, Outdoor, Pharmaceutical, Planning & Consultation, Point of Purchase, Point of Sale, Print, Production, Production (Print), Public Relations, Publicity/Promotions, Radio, Recruitment, Retail, Sales Promotion, Social Marketing/Nonprofit, Social Media, Sponsorship, Sports Market, Strategic Planning/Research, T.V., Technical Advertising, Teen Market, Trade & Consumer Magazines, Travel & Tourism, Viral/Buzz/Word of Mouth, Web (Banner Ads, Pop-ups, etc.)

Approx. Annual Billings: $15,000,000

Gay Warren Gaddis *(Founder & CEO)*
Lee Gaddis *(Chm)*
Mary Arnold *(CFO)*
Keith Johnston *(COO)*
Jay Suhr *(Chief Creative Officer & Sr VP)*
Ben Gaddis *(Chief Innovation Officer)*
Jennifer Mollo *(Exec Dir-Client Rels)*
Chris Wooster *(Exec Dir-Creative)*
Jill Runyon *(Grp Acct Dir)*
Dillon Nugent *(Client Svcs Dir)*
Leah Heck *(Dir-Internal Dev)*
Oscar Llarena *(Dir-Experience)*
Keith Tanski *(Dir-Strategy)*
Hawk Thompson *(Dir-Content Strategy)*
Andrea Ehringer *(Acct Supvr)*
Eric Kwiatkowski *(Acct Supvr)*
Angela Yang *(Sr Strategist-Social Media)*
Erik Dezendorf *(Assoc Acct Dir)*

Accounts:
7-Eleven, Inc. (Digital Agency of Record) Mobile, Social
ConocoPhillips Lubricants; Houston, TX Interactive
Gogo Inflight Internet (Agency of Record) Strategy, Creative & Media
Marimekko Marketing Strategy
Microsoft; Seattle, WA E-Mail, Online Media Services & Web Site; 2003
Mobile Loaves & Fishes
Pegasystems Inc. Campaign: "Pega Can -- Can Salesforce?", Online, Print
Pfizer
United Parcel Service; Atlanta, GA Interactive & DM
Which Wich (Agency of Record) Digital Experience, Strategy

Branches

T3 (The Think Tank)

126 5th Ave 15th Fl, New York, NY 10011
Tel.: (212) 404-7045
Fax: (212) 404-7049
E-Mail: info@t-3.com
Web Site: www.t-3.com

Employees: 13
Year Founded: 2002

Agency Specializes In: Advertising, Advertising Specialties, Brand Development & Integration, Broadcast, Business Publications, Business-To-Business, Collateral, Commercial Photography, Communications, Consulting, Consumer Marketing, Consumer Publications, Corporate Communications, Corporate Identity, Digital/Interactive, Direct Response Marketing, E-Commerce, Electronic Media, Entertainment, Event Planning & Marketing, Exhibit/Trade Shows, Financial, Food Service, Government/Political, Graphic Design, Health Care Services, High Technology, Infomercials, Information Technology, Internet/Web Design, Legal Services, Leisure, Logo & Package Design, Magazines, Media Buying Services, Medical Products, Merchandising, Multimedia, New Product Development, Newspaper, Newspapers & Magazines, Out-of-Home Media, Outdoor, Pharmaceutical, Planning & Consultation, Point of Purchase, Point of Sale, Print, Production, Public Relations, Publicity/Promotions, Radio, Recruitment, Retail, Sales Promotion, Sponsorship, Sports Market, Strategic Planning/Research, T.V., Technical Advertising, Trade & Consumer Magazines, Travel & Tourism

Joe Volpicelli *(Sr VP & Exec Dir-Creative)*
Matt Diiorio *(Grp Acct Dir)*
Jill Runyon *(Acct Dir)*
Adrienne Chalfant *(Assoc Acct Dir)*

Accounts:
JPMorgan Chase
Microsoft Corporation MSN.com
UPS UPS My Choice, UPS Regifter

T3 (The Think Tank)

576 Folsom St, San Francisco, CA 94105
Tel.: (415) 983-0815
Fax: (415) 362-6967
Web Site: www.t-3.com

Employees: 25

Agency Specializes In: Sponsorship

Tamara Weinman *(Mng Dir)*
Andrew Tedjo *(Sr Media Planner)*

Accounts:
Microsoft

TABER CREATIVE GROUP

1693 Eureka Rd Ste 200, Roseville, CA 95661
Tel.: (916) 771-6868
Fax: (916) 771-5848
E-Mail: info@tabercreative.com
Web Site: www.tabercreative.com

Year Founded: 1997

Agency Specializes In: Advertising, Brand Development & Integration, Corporate Identity, Digital/Interactive, Internet/Web Design, Logo & Package Design, Print, Social Media, Strategic Planning/Research

Kirk Taber *(Principal & Dir-Client Svcs)*
Michele M. Taber *(Dir-Creative & Dir-Digital Mktg Svcs)*
Andrea Faria *(Media Buyer)*

Accounts:
Titan School Solutions

TACO TRUCK CREATIVE

3172 Lionshead Ave, Carlsbad, CA 92010
Tel.: (760) 517-8800
E-Mail: hello@tacotruckcreative.com
Web Site: www.tacotruckcreative.com

Employees: 10
Year Founded: 2013

Agency Specializes In: Advertising, Brand Development & Integration, Content, Digital/Interactive, Print, Social Media, Strategic Planning/Research, T.V.

Ernie Koury *(Pres & Partner)*
Travis Graham *(Partner & Dir-Creative)*
Dave Huerta *(Partner & Dir-Creative)*
Todd Haring *(Client Svcs Dir)*
Jamie Apodaca *(Dir-Production)*
Joshua Forstot *(Dir-Innovation & Strategy)*
Lauren Tibbals *(Acct Mgr)*

Accounts:
Callaway Golf Company
Golf Now
Rondo Pools

TACTICAL MAGIC

1460 Madison Ave, Memphis, TN 38104
Tel.: (901) 722-3001
Fax: (901) 722-2144

Web Site: www.tacticalmagic.com

Year Founded: 2001

Agency Specializes In: Brand Development & Integration, Communications, Direct Response Marketing, Email, Outdoor, Package Design, Print, Radio, Search Engine Optimization, T.V.

Mary Hallowell *(CFO)*
Brian Borgman *(Dir & Designer)*
Susan Adler Thorp *(Strategist-PR & Media)*

Accounts:
Eyewear Gallery
Fulmer Helmets Inc

TAFT & PARTNERS

1 Palmer Sq E, Princeton, NJ 08542
Tel.: (609) 683-0700
E-Mail: info@taftandpartners.com
Web Site: www.taftandpartners.com

Employees: 20
Year Founded: 1983

Agency Specializes In: Advertising, Advertising Specialties, Alternative Advertising, Branded Entertainment, Business-To-Business, Collateral, Communications, Computers & Software, Consulting, Consumer Goods, Consumer Marketing, Corporate Communications, Corporate Identity, Crisis Communications, Digital/Interactive, Direct Response Marketing, Direct-to-Consumer, E-Commerce, Education, Email, Environmental, Event Planning & Marketing, Experience Design, Game Integration, Government/Political, Graphic Design, Health Care Services, High Technology, Hospitality, Household Goods, Identity Marketing, Industrial, Information Technology, Integrated Marketing, Internet/Web Design, Investor Relations, Logo & Package Design, Market Research, Media Planning, Media Relations, Medical Products, Mobile Marketing, New Technologies, Package Design, Pharmaceutical, Podcasting, Print, Promotions, Public Relations, Publishing, RSS (Really Simple Syndication), Search Engine Optimization, Social Marketing/Nonprofit, Social Media, Sports Market, Stakeholders, Strategic Planning/Research, Syndication, Technical Advertising, Transportation, Urban Market, Women's Market

Approx. Annual Billings: $5,000,000

Breakdown of Gross Billings by Media: Adv. Specialities: 100%

Pete Taft *(Founder & CEO)*
Mara Connolly *(Co-Owner & Exec VP)*
Elliot Bloom *(Principal-Consulting)*
Susan Nicholas *(Principal)*
Rachel Darwin *(Mgr-Comm)*
John Reuland *(Mgr-Comm)*
Lisa Williams *(Coord-Ops)*

TAG

(Formerly tag idea revolution)
10 Disera Drive, Suite 260, Thornhill, ON L4J 0A7 Canada
Tel.: (905) 940-1948
Fax: (905) 940-4489
E-Mail: tag@tagagency.ca
Web Site: tagagency.ca/

Employees: 30

Agency Specializes In: Advertising, Alternative Advertising, Commercial Photography, Consumer Marketing, Corporate Communications, Digital/Interactive, Direct Response Marketing, Event Planning & Marketing, Food Service, Graphic Design, Guerilla Marketing, In-Store Advertising, Integrated Marketing, Internet/Web Design, Logo & Package Design, Media Buying Services, Media Planning, Merchandising, Mobile Marketing, Package Design, Planning & Consultation, Print, Production, Production (Ad, Film, Broadcast), Production (Print), Strategic Planning/Research, Web (Banner Ads, Pop-ups, etc.)

Fabio Orlando *(Founder & Chief Creative Officer)*
Matt Orlando *(Pres)*
Michael Reneau *(Exec Dir)*
Danica Wolch *(Acct Dir)*
Jonas Tarstan *(Dir-HR)*
Chloe Lackman *(Acct Mgr)*
Dan Graham *(Mgr-Studio)*
Frank Morales *(Mgr-Production)*
Jeff Robbins *(Sr Strategist-Digital)*

Accounts:
Bausch & Lomb
Cuispro
First Choice Haircutters
High Liner Foods
Honda Canada
Ricoh Campaign: "Imagine. Change", Online, Print Advertising, Search Engine Marketing
Swiss Herbal Remedies

TAG ONLINE INC.

6 Prospect Village Plz 1st Fl, Clifton, NJ 07013
Tel.: (973) 783-5583
Fax: (973) 783-5334
E-Mail: staff@tagonline.com
Web Site: www.tagonline.com

E-Mail for Key Personnel:
President: amy@tagonline.com

Employees: 7
Year Founded: 1993

Agency Specializes In: Advertising, Brand Development & Integration, Business-To-Business, Communications, Consulting, Digital/Interactive, E-Commerce, Electronic Media, Graphic Design, High Technology, Information Technology, Internet/Web Design

Breakdown of Gross Billings by Media: Consulting: 25%; Worldwide Web Sites: 75%

Amy Gideon *(Pres)*
Andrew Gideon *(CTO & VP)*
Valerie Paik *(VP-Bus Dev)*
Joe Brozyniak *(Designer-Web)*

Accounts:
Art Plus - Corporate Art Consultants
BCG Advisors, Inc.
Crystal Plaza
Dietz & Associates, LLC Architects
Federal Magistrate Judge Association
Finazzo Cossolini O'Leary Meola & Hager, LLC
Manhattan District Attorney's Office
National Organization of Investment Professionals
Savastano Kaufman & Company
Vaslas Lepowsky Hauss & Danke LLP

TAG WORLDWIDE

75 Spring St 3rd Fl, New York, NY 10012
Tel.: (212) 625-6250
Fax: (212) 625-6260
Web Site: www.tagworldwide.com

Employees: 2,000
Year Founded: 2000

Agency Specializes In: Brand Development & Integration, Communications

Revenue: $2,500,000

John Paulson *(CEO)*
Stuart Trood *(CFO)*
Todd Handcock *(CEO-Asia Pacific)*
Ajit Kara *(CEO-Americas)*
Peter Zillig *(CEO-TAG Europe)*
Michael Rubin *(Project Mgr-Digital)*
Michael Pschirer *(Acct Exec-Print Procurement)*
Edwin Melendez *(Sr Designer-Print & Digital Production)*

Accounts:
Diageo
Hilton
O2
R&A
Reebok
Zurich

TAGLINE MEDIA GROUP

1655 N Swan Rd, Tucson, AZ 85712
Tel.: (520) 207-8910
Web Site: www.taglinegroup.com

Agency Specializes In: Advertising, Brand Development & Integration, Collateral, Internet/Web Design, Logo & Package Design, Media Buying Services, Public Relations, Social Media

Debra Weisel *(Principal)*
Leanna Kruszewski *(Dir-Art)*
Susy Wash *(Office Mgr)*
Christina White *(Designer-Web)*

Accounts:
Boreale Law

TAGTEAM BUSINESS PARTNERS LLC

2189 Silas Deane Highway Ste 11, Rocky Hill, CT 6067
Tel.: (860) 436-3900
Fax: (860) 436-3904
Web Site: www.tagteambp.com

Agency Specializes In: Advertising, Business-To-Business, Digital/Interactive, Media Buying Services, Media Planning, Print, Social Marketing/Nonprofit, T.V.

Mark Zurzola *(Owner)*
Larry Piretti *(VP)*

Accounts:
New-Connecticut Lighting Centers

TAIGMARKS INC.

223 S Main St Ste 100, Elkhart, IN 46516
Tel.: (574) 294-8844
Fax: (574) 294-8855
E-Mail: tm@taigmarks.com
Web Site: www.taigmarks.com

Employees: 15
Year Founded: 1967

National Agency Associations: AMA

Agency Specializes In: Advertising, Brand Development & Integration, Event Planning & Marketing, Health Care Services, Industrial, Leisure, Logo & Package Design, Magazines, Medical Products, Multimedia, Point of Sale, Print, Production, Public Relations, Radio, Sales Promotion, Sweepstakes, T.V., Trade & Consumer Magazines, Transportation

Steve Taig *(Pres)*
Rob Hartzler *(Dir-Art)*
Mike Knaack *(Dir-PR)*

Jeff Prugh *(Dir-Art)*
Sue Truckowski *(Dir-Art)*
Daniel Carter *(Acct Mgr)*
Craig Hosterman *(Acct Mgr)*
Jennifer Lantz *(Office Mgr)*
Deb Smith *(Mgr-Production)*

Accounts:
Ziggity Systems, Inc.; Middlebury, IN Poultry Watering Systems

TAILFIN
1246 Virginia Ave NE, Atlanta, GA 30306
Tel.: (404) 872-9798
Fax: (404) 872-9707
E-Mail: info@tailfin.com
Web Site: www.tailfin.com

Year Founded: 1999

Agency Specializes In: Advertising, Brand Development & Integration, Digital/Interactive, Event Planning & Marketing, Internet/Web Design, Logo & Package Design, Media Planning, Promotions, Search Engine Optimization, Social Media

Lola Carlisle *(Owner & Exec Dir-Creative)*
Kris Cottrell *(Sr Dir-Art & Designer-Web)*
Jose Estrada *(Dir-Art & Designer)*
Ashley McAlpin *(Dir-Art)*
Chelsea Schmidt *(Acct Mgr)*
Lynn Strickland *(Mgr-Fin)*

Accounts:
Piedmont Healthcare

TAILORED MARKETING INC.
401 Wood St Ste 1400, Pittsburgh, PA 15222
Tel.: (412) 281-1442
Fax: (412) 281-3335
E-Mail: taylor@tailoredmarketing.com
Web Site: www.tailoredmarketing.com

Employees: 3
Year Founded: 2000

National Agency Associations: PAF

Agency Specializes In: Advertising, Advertising Specialties, Affiliate Marketing, Affluent Market, Brand Development & Integration, Broadcast, Business-To-Business, Catalogs, Collateral, Communications, Consulting, Corporate Communications, Corporate Identity, Event Planning & Marketing, Exhibit/Trade Shows, Financial, Graphic Design, Guerilla Marketing, Internet/Web Design, Leisure, Logo & Package Design, Media Buying Services, Mobile Marketing, Multimedia, New Technologies, Outdoor, Package Design, Planning & Consultation, Print, Production (Print), Promotions, Public Relations, Publicity/Promotions, Radio, Real Estate, Sales Promotion, Search Engine Optimization, Social Marketing/Nonprofit, Social Media, Sponsorship, Sports Market, Strategic Planning/Research, Sweepstakes, Travel & Tourism

Approx. Annual Billings: $500,000

Taylor Abbett *(Owner)*
Kerri Lozano *(Dir-Art)*
Tj Dapper *(Mgr-Style & Class)*

TAKE 5 SOLUTIONS
2385 NW Executive Center Dr Ste 200, Boca Raton, FL 33431
Tel.: (561) 819-5555
Fax: (561) 819-0245
Toll Free: (866) 861-8862
E-Mail: Sales@Take5S.com
Web Site: www.take5s.com

Employees: 20
Year Founded: 2003

National Agency Associations: DMA

Agency Specializes In: Above-the-Line, Advertising, Advertising Specialties, Affiliate Marketing, Affluent Market, African-American Market, Agriculture, Alternative Advertising, Arts, Asian Market, Automotive, Aviation & Aerospace, Below-the-Line, Bilingual Market, Brand Development & Integration, Branded Entertainment, Broadcast, Business Publications, Business-To-Business, Cable T.V., Catalogs, Children's Market, Co-op Advertising, Collateral, College, Commercial Photography, Communications, Computers & Software, Consulting, Consumer Goods, Consumer Marketing, Consumer Publications, Content, Corporate Communications, Corporate Identity, Cosmetics, Crisis Communications, Custom Publishing, Customer Relationship Management, Digital/Interactive, Direct Response Marketing, Direct-to-Consumer, E-Commerce, Education, Electronic Media, Electronics, Email, Engineering, Entertainment, Environmental, Event Planning & Marketing, Exhibit/Trade Shows, Experience Design, Fashion/Apparel, Financial, Food Service, Game Integration, Gay & Lesbian Market, Government/Political, Graphic Design, Guerilla Marketing, Health Care Services, High Technology, Hispanic Market, Hospitality, Household Goods, Identity Marketing, In-Store Advertising, Industrial, Infomercials, Information Technology, Integrated Marketing, International, Internet/Web Design, Investor Relations, Legal Services, Leisure, Local Marketing, Logo & Package Design, Luxury Products, Magazines, Marine, Market Research, Media Buying Services, Media Planning, Media Relations, Media Training, Medical Products, Men's Market, Merchandising, Mobile Marketing, Multicultural, Multimedia, New Product Development, New Technologies, Newspaper, Newspapers & Magazines, Out-of-Home Media, Outdoor, Over-50 Market, Package Design, Paid Searches, Pharmaceutical, Planning & Consultation, Podcasting, Point of Purchase, Point of Sale, Print, Product Placement, Production, Production (Ad, Film, Broadcast), Production (Print), Promotions, Public Relations, Publicity/Promotions, Publishing, RSS (Really Simple Syndication), Radio, Real Estate, Recruitment, Regional, Restaurant, Retail, Sales Promotion, Search Engine Optimization, Seniors' Market, Social Marketing/Nonprofit, South Asian Market, Sponsorship, Sports Market, Stakeholders, Strategic Planning/Research, Sweepstakes, Syndication, T.V., Technical Advertising, Teen Market, Telemarketing, Trade & Consumer Magazines, Transportation, Travel & Tourism, Urban Market, Viral/Buzz/Word of Mouth, Web (Banner Ads, Pop-ups, etc.), Women's Market, Yellow Pages Advertising

Approx. Annual Billings: $2,000,000

Alex Radetich *(CEO)*
Beth Meyer *(CFO)*
Bill DeLisi *(CIO & CTO)*
Richard D. Gluck *(Exec VP-Sls)*
Don Morris *(VP-Sls)*
Josh Silver *(VP-Adv Ops)*
Michael Angelis *(Dir-Sls)*
Tara Eliel-Finger *(Dir-List Mgmt)*
Sasha Valdes *(Dir-Multicultural Mktg)*
Paul Richman *(Mgr-Strategic Sls)*

TALK, INC.
PO Box 987, Wilmington, NC 28402
Mailing Address:
PO BOX 987, Wilmington, NC 28402-0987
Tel.: (910) 371-9770
Fax: (970) 371-9776
Toll Free: (877) 395-5051
E-Mail: newbiz@talkinc.com
Web Site: www.talkinc.com/

Employees: 6
Year Founded: 1990

Agency Specializes In: Advertising, Advertising Specialties, Event Planning & Marketing, Graphic Design, Health Care Services, Public Relations, Publicity/Promotions, Real Estate

Debbie Elliott *(Pres & Dir-Creative)*

Accounts:
Big Sky Design
Butterball, Inc. America's Iconic Turkey
SEAHEC
Springdale Outdoor

TAMBOURINE
2941 W Cypress Creek Rd 2nd Fl, Fort Lauderdale, FL 33309
Tel.: (954) 975-2220
Fax: (954) 301-0460
E-Mail: hello@tambourinecreative.com
Web Site: www.tambourine.com

Agency Specializes In: Advertising, Brand Development & Integration, Digital/Interactive, Social Media

Rafael Cardozo *(Pres)*
Judykay Janney *(Controller-Fin)*
Brian Ferrell *(Dir-Bus Dev)*
Adriana Suao *(Dir-Client Svcs)*
Mekell Helle *(Sr Mgr-Client Success)*
Ana Leon *(Mgr-Client Success & Jr Acct Exec)*
Christina Davis *(Mgr-Client Success)*
Rachel Peters *(Mgr-Client Success)*
Kristin Berlehner *(Designer-Web)*

Accounts:
Caribbean Hotel & Tourism Association
Four Seasons Hotels & Resorts
Marriott Key West Beachside Hotel
Nevis Tourism Authority
St. Maarten Tourist Bureau

TAMM + KIT
(Formerly Tamm Communications Inc.)
250 The Esplanade Berkeley Hall Ste 402, Toronto, ON M5A 1J2 Canada
Tel.: (416) 304-0188
Fax: (416) 304-0488
Toll Free: (877) 679-4909
E-Mail: info@tammandkit.com
Web Site: www.tammandkit.com

Employees: 22
Year Founded: 1998

Agency Specializes In: Advertising, Broadcast, Collateral, Corporate Communications, Electronic Media, Newspapers & Magazines, Outdoor, Print, Recruitment, Social Marketing/Nonprofit

Ciabh McEvenue *(Mng Dir)*
Eric Bargenda *(Dir-Design)*
Susan Tse *(Acct Mgr)*
Jessica Lai *(Mgr-Media Svcs)*
Joshua Dueck *(Strategist-Media & Media Buyer)*
Daniel Adams *(Sr Designer-Graphic & Motion)*
Catherine Caple *(Sr Graphic Designer)*
Richard Thirumaran *(Designer-Web & Digital)*
Pamela Saikaly *(Coord-Studio)*

Accounts:
Best Buy
Casino Niagara

Conexus
Dynatec
OLG
Pet Valu
Shoppers Drug Mart
The Source
St. Joseph's Hospital

TANDEM ASSOCIATES

350 Sentry Pkwy Bldg 610, Blue Bell, PA 19422
Tel.: (610) 397-1833
Fax: (610) 397-1891
Web Site: www.tandemassociates.com

E-Mail for Key Personnel:
President: mplamondon@tandemassoc.com

Employees: 8
Year Founded: 1994

Agency Specializes In: Brand Development & Integration, Broadcast, Collateral, Consulting, Consumer Goods, Consumer Marketing, Corporate Identity, Direct-to-Consumer, Event Planning & Marketing, Food Service, Graphic Design, Guerilla Marketing, Household Goods, In-Store Advertising, Internet/Web Design, Local Marketing, Logo & Package Design, Market Research, Media Buying Services, Media Planning, New Product Development, Newspapers & Magazines, Planning & Consultation, Point of Purchase, Point of Sale, Print, Production (Ad, Film, Broadcast), Promotions, Publicity/Promotions, Radio, Regional, Sales Promotion, Search Engine Optimization, Sports Market, Strategic Planning/Research, T.V., Trade & Consumer Magazines, Viral/Buzz/Word of Mouth

Approx. Annual Billings: $5,000,000

Breakdown of Gross Billings by Media: Collateral: $200,000; Event Mktg.: $300,000; Mags.: $250,000; Other: $600,000; Plng. & Consultation: $500,000; Promos.: $500,000; Radio: $400,000; Strategic Planning/Research: $1,500,000; T.V.: $750,000

Mark Plamondon *(Pres)*
Jean Ritchie *(VP & Acct Dir)*

Accounts:
Alpo Petfoods
Capital Blue Cross
Cold Eeze Cough Drops; Philadelphia, PA; 2008
Gerber Baby Products
Just Born Candy
Mrs Webbs Specialty Foods; Philadelphia, PA; 2008
Procter & Gamble
St. Joseph's University; Philadelphia, PA; 2005
Tastykake
W.L. Gore; MD; 2006

TANEN DIRECTED ADVERTISING

12 S Main St Ste 401, Norwalk, CT 06854-2980
Tel.: (203) 855-5855
Fax: (203) 855-5865
E-Mail: ilene@tanendirected.com
Web Site: www.tanendirected.com

E-Mail for Key Personnel:
President: ilene@tanendirected.com

Employees: 11
Year Founded: 1985

National Agency Associations: DMA

Agency Specializes In: Business-To-Business, Collateral, Direct Response Marketing, Faith Based, Financial, Internet/Web Design, Logo & Package Design, Print, Production, Radio

Ilene Cohn Tanen *(Pres)*
Christophe Bardot *(Dir-Print Design)*
Caron Dickinson *(Dir-Production Design)*
Christy Sagalyn *(Dir-Bus Dev)*
Vincent Zito, Jr. *(Copywriter)*

Accounts:
Bausch & Lomb; Wilmington, MA
Best Doctors; Boston, MA
Citigroup; New York, NY
First Investors; Houston, TX
Interleukin Genetics; Waltham, MA
MasterCard International; Purchase, NY
The New York Times; New York, NY
Pepsico; Purchase, NY
Pitney Bowes; Stamford, CT
Subway; Milford, CT

TANGELO

2444 Times Blvd Ste 300, Houston, TX 77005
Tel.: (713) 229-9600
Fax: (866) 899-4956
Web Site: www.tangeloideas.com

Agency Specializes In: Advertising, Brand Development & Integration, Broadcast, Direct Response Marketing, Email, Print, Product Placement, Search Engine Optimization, Viral/Buzz/Word of Mouth, Web (Banner Ads, Pop-ups, etc.)

David Hoyt *(Principal & Exec Dir-Creative)*
Bo Sims *(Acct Dir)*
Daren Guillory *(Dir-Creative)*
Christina Snyder *(Acct Supvr)*

TANIS COMMUNICATIONS

800 W El Camino Real Ste 180, Mountain View, CA 94040
Tel.: (650) 731-0554
Web Site: www.taniscomm.com

Agency Specializes In: Advertising, Brand Development & Integration, Communications, Internet/Web Design, Media Relations, Print, Public Relations, Social Media, Strategic Planning/Research

Nikki Tanis *(President)*
Robin Vaitonis *(Exec VP)*
Allison Niday *(Sr VP-PR)*
Paul Gaither *(Acct Dir)*
Nicole Conley *(Dir-Media Rels)*

Accounts:
Crossbar Inc.

TANK

55 Prince St, Montreal, QC H3C2M7 Canada
Tel.: (514) 373-3333
Fax: (514) 373-3377
E-Mail: info@tank.ca
Web Site: www.tank.ca

Employees: 50

Agency Specializes In: Advertising, Graphic Design, Media Buying Services, Social Media

Benoit Pilon *(Founder, Partner, Chief Creative Officer & VP)*
Marc Lanouette *(Pres)*
Mathieu Cloutier *(Partner, VP & Gen Mgr)*
Julie Simon *(Grp Acct Dir)*
Antoine Halle *(Dir-Interactive Art)*
Jean-Francois Da Sylva-Larue *(Copywriter)*
Marie-Eve Belanger *(Coord-Creation)*
Alexandre Gadoua *(Sr Creative Dir)*

Accounts:
Abbott Laboratories, Limited Ensure
Audi Campaign: "Let Your Inner Child Play"
Fujitsu Campaign: "What The Hell"
New-Interac
Pfizer Champix
New-Reitmans Creative, Strategy
Saputo, Inc.
Transcontinental Media
Uniprix Inc.

TAPIA ADVERTISING

PO Box 64021, Colorado Springs, CO 80962
Tel.: (719) 233-4553
Web Site: www.tapiaadvertising.com

Agency Specializes In: Advertising, Crisis Communications, Event Planning & Marketing, Internet/Web Design, Media Relations, Print, Public Relations, Radio, Social Media, T.V.

Mike Tapia *(Pres)*
Phil Tapia *(VP)*

Accounts:
QwikCare MD

TAPROOT CREATIVE

2057 Delta Way, Tallahassee, FL 32303
Tel.: (850) 309-1900
Fax: (850) 309-1902
E-Mail: holla@taprootcreative.com
Web Site: www.taprootcreative.com

Year Founded: 2005

Agency Specializes In: Advertising, Graphic Design, Logo & Package Design, Media Buying Services, Media Planning, Public Relations, Search Engine Optimization, Social Media

Sean Doughtie *(Pres & CEO)*

Accounts:
New-Knight Creative Communities Institute

TARA, INK.

1666 Kennedy Causeway Ste 703, Miami Beach, FL 33141
Tel.: (305) 864-3434
Fax: (305) 864-3432
E-Mail: info@taraink.com
Web Site: www.taraink.com

Employees: 12

Agency Specializes In: Advertising, Collateral, Crisis Communications, Digital/Interactive, Email, Entertainment, Event Planning & Marketing, Graphic Design, Hospitality, Identity Marketing, Integrated Marketing, Internet/Web Design, Local Marketing, Media Relations, Media Training, Product Placement, Production (Ad, Film, Broadcast), Public Relations, Real Estate, T.V.

Tara Solomon *(Founder & Partner)*
Nick D'Annunzio *(Principal)*
Jake Pierce *(Mgr-Social Media & Editor-Copy)*
Jose Frances *(Dir-Bus Dev)*
Jenn Sobel *(Dir-Promos)*
Sami Aponte *(Acct Coord)*

Accounts:
Discovery Miami Beach
Esteban Cortazar
Giorgio Armani
Haven
Hermes
HIGHBAR at DREAM South Beach; Miami Beach, FL
History Channel
The Light Group
Marni

Melissa & Doug; Wilton, CT
Miami Boutique Hotels Program
Mitchell Group OMIC Skincare
Naomi Campbell Retrospective
The Plum Network Event Coordination, Plum Miami Magazine
Poko Pano
Saab
Saturday Tommy Hilfiger Party
The Smithsonian
Stian Roenning/Alexis Mincolla
Superdry Media Relations, Product Placement
Tapas y Tintos
TUI Lifestyle
Vanity Fair/Tommy Hilfiger Art Basel Party

TARGET
90 Water Street on the Park, Saint John's, NL A1C 1A4 Canada
Tel.: (709) 739-8400
Fax: (709) 739-9699
E-Mail: ads@targetmarketing.ca
Web Site: www.targetmarketing.ca

E-Mail for Key Personnel:
President: nodea@targetmarketing.ca

Employees: 45
Year Founded: 1980

National Agency Associations: CAB

Agency Specializes In: Advertising, Brand Development & Integration

Noel O'Dea *(Pres, Dir-Strategic & Creative Plng)*
Matt Tucker *(Head-Digital)*
Jacqueline Morrissey *(Exec Dir-Media)*
Ernie Brake *(Acct Dir)*
Jane Hall *(Acct Dir)*
Catherine Kelly *(Acct Mgmt Dir)*
Jef Combdon *(Dir-Media)*
Gaye Broderick *(Mgr-HR)*
Cindy Wadden *(Mgr-Production Svcs)*
Allison Daley *(Acct Exec)*

Accounts:
ACE Aviation Holdings Inc.
Air Canada Jazz
Brock University
Canadian Helicopters Limited
Canadian Sea Turtle Network
Fronteer
Ganong Chocolate
Government of Newfoundland & Labrador Department of Tourism, Culture & Recreation
Irving Oil C-Stores, Gasoline, Heating
Larsen Wiener News Network
Maple Leaf Foods Campaign: "Wiener News Network"
McCain Foods; Canada
Newfoundland & Labrador Tourism Campaign: "Secret Place", Tourism
Quidi Vidi Brewing Company
Stella Burry Foundation
Unilever Eversweet Margarine, Imperial Margarine
Universal Barber Shop

TARGET + RESPONSE INC.
420 N Wabash Ave Ste 201, Chicago, IL 60611-3569
Tel.: (312) 321-0500
Fax: (312) 321-0051
Web Site: www.target-response.com

Employees: 14
Year Founded: 1987

Agency Specializes In: Direct Response Marketing, Direct-to-Consumer, Internet/Web Design, Newspapers & Magazines, Radio, Web (Banner Ads, Pop-ups, etc.), Yellow Pages Advertising

Approx. Annual Billings: $15,000,000

Breakdown of Gross Billings by Media: Other: 25%; Radio: 75%

Mike Battisto *(Pres)*
Mike Collins *(Dir-Client Svcs)*
Michelle Draus *(Dir-Media Sls)*

TARGET MARKETING & COMMUNICATIONS INC.
90 Water St, Saint John's, NL A1C 1A4 Canada
Tel.: (709) 739-8400
Fax: (709) 739-9699
E-Mail: info@targetmarketing.ca
Web Site: www.targetmarketing.ca

Agency Specializes In: Advertising

TARGETBASE
7850 N Belt Line Rd, Irving, TX 75063-6098
Tel.: (972) 506-3400
Fax: (972) 506-3505
Toll Free: (866) 506-7850
E-Mail: customer.value@targetbase.com
Web Site: www.targetbase.com

E-Mail for Key Personnel:
President: david.scholes@targetbase.com

Employees: 200
Year Founded: 1979

National Agency Associations: DMA

Agency Specializes In: Advertising, Brand Development & Integration, Children's Market, Consulting, Consumer Marketing, Digital/Interactive, Direct Response Marketing, Entertainment, Financial, Graphic Design, Health Care Services, Infomercials, Information Technology, Internet/Web Design, Leisure, Medical Products, Pharmaceutical, Planning & Consultation, Point of Purchase, Point of Sale, Production, Retail, Sponsorship, Strategic Planning/Research, T.V., Telemarketing, Travel & Tourism

David J. Scholes *(Chm)*
Mark Wright *(Pres & CEO)*
Genine Balliet *(Chief People Officer-People Solutions)*
Kimberley Walsh *(Exec VP-Creative)*
Julie Petroski *(VP & Grp Dir-Creative)*
Barron T. Evans *(VP-Customer Strategy)*
Doug Horstman *(VP-Delivery)*
Lindsey Pults *(VP-Client Svcs)*
Ann Barrick *(Mgr-Library Svcs)*
Anil Varghese *(Chief Security Officer)*
Mark Zahorik *(Chief Delivery Officer-Tech)*

Accounts:
Acura
American Honda Motor Co.
AT&T Mobility LLC
Fisher-Price
Gatorade
GlaxoSmithKline Pharmaceuticals
John Deere; 2007
Oral-B
Procter & Gamble Consumer Packaged Goods
U.S. Oncology
United Healthcare

Branch

Targetbase
202 CentrePort Dr Ste 400, Greensboro, NC 27409
Tel.: (336) 665-3800
Fax: (336) 665-3855
E-Mail: customer.value@targetbase.com
Web Site: www.targetbase.com

Employees: 257

Agency Specializes In: Sponsorship

Mark Wright *(Pres & CEO)*
Genine Balliet *(Chief People Officer-People Solutions)*
Kimberley Walsh *(Exec VP & Exec Dir-Creative)*
Bill Cole *(Sr VP-Analytics)*
Thomas Begin *(VP-Strategy)*
Ilene Harper *(VP-Strategy)*

Accounts:
GlaxoSmithKline, Inc. VESIcare (co-marketed with Astellas Pharma)

Subsidiary

Targetbase Claydon Heeley
The Glassmill 1 Battersea Bridge Rd, London, SW11 3BZ United Kingdom
Tel.: (44) 20 7924 3000
Fax: (44) 20 7294 3096

Employees: 35

Agency Specializes In: Direct Response Marketing, Sales Promotion

Emma Rush *(CEO)*
Shona Forster *(Head-Plng)*
Louise Morgan *(Head-Client Svcs)*
Michael Quinn *(Dir-Creative)*

Accounts:
COI Communications
Red Cross
RNLI
Three
TV Licensing

TARGETCOM, LLC
(Name Changed to Civilian)

TARGETED RESPONSE ADVERTISING
3001 Bridge way Ave Ste K313, Sausalito, CA 94965
Tel.: (415) 332-7916
Fax: (415) 332-7980
Web Site: www.tours.com

Employees: 7
Year Founded: 1982

Agency Specializes In: E-Commerce, Electronic Media, Internet/Web Design, T.V., Travel & Tourism

Approx. Annual Billings: $7,000,000

Breakdown of Gross Billings by Media: Newsp.: $4,000,000; Other: $1,000,000; T.V.: $2,000,000

Joe King *(Founder & Chm)*
Maria Polk *(Pres)*
Paul Vuksich *(Gen Counsel)*
Marijo Douglass *(Exec VP-Fin)*
Lark Gould *(Dir-Content-Travel-Intel, Tours.com & Sightseeing.com)*
Deborah Reinow *(Dir-Bus Dev-Global)*
Megan Siegel *(Mgr-Social Media)*
Bradshaw Rovens *(Specialist-Student Bus Dev)*
Paul du Quenoy *(Corp Exec VP)*

Accounts:
Ames; Duluth, GA; 1982
Hilti; Tulsa, OK Recruitment Advertising; 1982
Management Resources Systems; San Francisco,

CA Recruitment Advertising; 1982
Sightseeing.com; San Francisco, CA Web Development; 1995

TARTAGLIA COMMUNICATIONS
PO Box 5148, Somerset, NJ 08875-5148
Tel.: (732) 545-1848
Fax: (732) 545-1816
E-Mail: info@tartagliacommunications.com
Web Site: www.tartagliacommunications.com

Agency Specializes In: Corporate Communications, Crisis Communications, Event Planning & Marketing, Media Relations, Public Relations

Dennis Tartaglia *(Founder & Pres)*

Accounts:
New-Alzheimer's Drug Discovery Foundation Melvin R. Goodes Prize
American Board of Addiction Medicine Medical Speciality Board
American Hospital Association
Berkeley Initiative for Transparency in the Social Sciences Communications
Gordon & Betty Moore Foundation Public Relations
National Multiple Sclerosis Society
New Jersey Health Foundation
New York Hospital Queens
Raritan Bay Medical Center
Unilever UK Foods
Veterans Health Administration

TARTAN MARKETING
10467 93rd Ave N, Maple Grove, MN 55369
Tel.: (763) 391-7575
Fax: (763) 391-7576
Toll Free: (877) 321-7575
E-Mail: info@tartanmarketing.com
Web Site: www.tartanmarketing.com

E-Mail for Key Personnel:
President: jim@tartanmarketing.com

Employees: 14
Year Founded: 1989

Agency Specializes In: Advertising, Brand Development & Integration, Business-To-Business, Collateral, Communications, Consulting, Corporate Identity, Digital/Interactive, Direct Response Marketing, Electronic Media, Financial, Food Service, Graphic Design, Health Care Services, High Technology, Industrial, Internet/Web Design, Logo & Package Design, Planning & Consultation, Point of Sale, Print, Production (Print), Promotions, Public Relations, Restaurant, Sales Promotion, Strategic Planning/Research

James J. Maclachlan *(Pres)*
Margie Maclachlan *(CEO)*
Angie Zebell *(Sr Dir-Art)*
Tom Dierberger *(Dir-Content)*
Lynn Lewis *(Acct Supvr)*
Kris Pierro *(Acct Supvr)*

Accounts:
Cargill Foods; MN Cargill Oils, Cargill Salt, Horizon Milling, Progressive Baker; 1999
Cargill Kitchen Solutions; 2005
EcoLab
Emerson
Prime Therapeutics
Wolters Kluwer

TASTE ADVERTISING, BRANDING & PACKAGING
33175 Temecula Pkwy Ste A-617, Temecula, CA 92592-7310
Tel.: (951) 302-3909
Fax: (951) 693-5252
E-Mail: info@tasteads.com
Web Site: www.tasteads.com

Employees: 6
Year Founded: 1985

Agency Specializes In: Advertising, Advertising Specialties, Alternative Advertising, Bilingual Market, Brand Development & Integration, Broadcast, Business-To-Business, Catalogs, Co-op Advertising, Collateral, Commercial Photography, Consumer Goods, Consumer Marketing, Direct Response Marketing, Direct-to-Consumer, Electronic Media, Email, Exhibit/Trade Shows, Food Service, Graphic Design, In-Store Advertising, Integrated Marketing, Internet/Web Design, Logo & Package Design, Media Buying Services, Media Planning, Multimedia, Newspaper, Newspapers & Magazines, Outdoor, Package Design, Point of Purchase, Production, Production (Ad, Film, Broadcast), Production (Print), Restaurant, Retail, Sales Promotion, Search Engine Optimization, Strategic Planning/Research, Trade & Consumer Magazines, Web (Banner Ads, Pop-ups, etc.)

Jeff Hood *(Partner & Dir-Creative)*

Accounts:
Aquamar, Inc Website Development
Chicken of the Sea

TATTOO PROJECTS
508 W 5th St Ste 225, Charlotte, NC 28202-1985
Tel.: (704) 900-7150
E-Mail: business@tattooprojects.com
Web Site: www.tattooprojects.com

Employees: 12

Agency Specializes In: Advertising, Communications, Content, Digital/Interactive, Entertainment, Internet/Web Design, Mobile Marketing, Print, Radio, Strategic Planning/Research, T.V., Viral/Buzz/Word of Mouth

Approx. Annual Billings: $4,500,000

Buffy McCoy Kelly *(Pres & Dir-Creative)*
Rudy Banny *(CEO)*
Justin Rentzel *(Sr Dir-Art)*
Chad Brophy *(Assoc Dir-Creative & Writer)*
Ryan McShane *(Acct Supvr)*
Katie Czyzewicz *(Acct Exec)*
Joe Bucher *(Writer-Digital Media)*
Liam Soren *(Copywriter)*

Accounts:
Cozi.com
Floorcare International
New-GreenWorks Tools Communications, Marketing
Hoover/ TTI Floorcare International; Cleveland, OH Hoover Max Extract, Hoover Max Multicyclonic, Hoover Windyunnel Air, Hoover Air Purifiers, Dirt Devil; 2008
Jeff Gordon Children's Foundation Communications, Marketing
John Deere
New-Land Design Communications, Marketing
New-MilkSplash Communications, Marketing
New-Outlaw Screws Communications, Marketing
Remington Firearms
New-Ronald McDonald House of Charlotte Communications, Marketing
Sheetz Inc. (Agency of Record) Broadcast, Campaign: "Quality Just Got a Kick in the Beanz", Digital, Social Media
Through the Looking Glass
UNC Charlotte: Charlotte, NC Branding, Communications, Marketing; 2006
Victory Motorcycles Brand Communications, Broadcast, Communications, Marketing, Out-of-home, Point of sale, Print

TAUBE/VIOLANTE, INC.
37 N Ave Ste 202, Norwalk, CT 06851
Tel.: (203) 849-8200
Fax: (203) 846-6675
E-Mail: admin@taube-violante.com
Web Site: www.taube-violante.com/

E-Mail for Key Personnel:
President: gtaube@snet.com
Creative Dir.: sue@taube-violante.com

Employees: 8
Year Founded: 1955

Agency Specializes In: Business Publications, Business-To-Business, Collateral, Consulting, Consumer Marketing, Corporate Identity, Direct Response Marketing, Engineering, Graphic Design, High Technology, Industrial, Internet/Web Design, Logo & Package Design, Media Buying Services, Medical Products, New Product Development, Pharmaceutical, Point of Sale, Print, Public Relations, Publicity/Promotions, Sales Promotion, Strategic Planning/Research, Technical Advertising, Trade & Consumer Magazines

Revenue: $600,000

Sue Taube *(Owner)*
George S. Taube *(Pres)*

Accounts:
Keystone Electronics Corp.; Astoria, NY Electronic Components & Hardware
Precision Tube; North Wales, PA Tubing & Fabricated Parts
Rema Dri-Vac Corp.; Norwalk, CT Return Systems
Ventronics; Kenilworth, NJ Components, External Power Sources

TAXI
495 Wellington St W Ste 102, Toronto, ON M5V 1E9 Canada
Tel.: (416) 342-8294
Fax: (416) 979-7626
E-Mail: info@taxi.ca
Web Site: www.taxi.ca

Employees: 120
Year Founded: 1992

Agency Specializes In: Digital/Interactive, Graphic Design, Internet/Web Design, Print, Radio, T.V.

Paul Lavoie *(Chm)*
Jane Hope *(Vice Chm)*
Rob Guenette *(CEO)*
Mike Leslie *(Mng Dir)*
Ben Tarr *(Co-Mng Dir)*
Andrew Packwood *(CFO)*
Mark Tomblin *(Chief Strategy Officer)*
Joanne Arfo *(VP & Head-HR & Comm-Global)*
Ben Feist *(VP-Tech)*
Sean McDonald *(VP-Brand Experience)*
Russell Stedman *(Gen Mgr)*
Jeff Maceachern *(Exec Dir-Creative)*
Tony Hird *(Sr Dir-Art)*
Ben Gillibrand *(Grp Acct Dir)*
Tom Greco *(Creative Dir)*
Jessica Lax *(Acct Dir)*
Alana Mcmillan *(Acct Dir)*
Damien Boyes *(Dir-Interaction Design)*
Justine Feron *(Dir-Strategy)*
Irfan Khan *(Dir-Creative)*
James Sadler *(Dir-Creative)*
Mike Blackmore *(Assoc Dir-Creative)*
Bhreigh Gillis *(Acct Mgr)*
David Stuart Airey *(Mgr-Recruitment)*
Hassan Chaudry *(Mgr-Compliance & SOX)*
Keeley O'Hara *(Mgr-Creative Resource)*

Martin Charron *(Copywriter)*
Colin Brown *(Sr Art Dir)*

Accounts:
Advertising and Design Club of Canada Campaign: "The Working Dead"
Alt Hotel
Boston Pizza International, Inc. (Agency of Record) #BPTrophymodel, Campaign: "Finger Cooking", Campaign: "Last Words", TV
Burger King Restaurants of Canada Angry Whopper, Campaign: "Happy Bleeps", Creative
Campbell Soup Co. Go Line of Microwavable Soup Pouches
Canadian Tire Corporation Limited "Ice Truck", Campaign: "House of Innovation", Windshield Wipers
Casino Rama Brand Communications, Strategic Planning
Castor Design Gigashelf
Covenant House
Crosby Molasses
Dundee Wealth Management
Edward Pond Campaign: "Edward Ponds Creative Chef"
Flatties & Drummies Wings
Fleetwood Archery
Hazco Blueprint
Heineken Canada Incorporated
Hockey Hall Of Fame Campaign: "Jimmie Cook"
Kraft Foods Group, Inc. Campaign: "Mio Swish", Gevalia, Kool-Aid, Kraft Peanut Butter, Maxwell House, Mio, Nabob
The Lifesaving Society BC & Yukon Campaign: "Gravestone Kickboard"
McCain
Microsoft Campaign: "Battle for Beauty", Internet Explorer 9
Pfizer Campaign: "Coach", Celebrex, Viagra, Zithromax
Pilsner
Pothole Season
Revlon
Tiff
Top Cuts Campaign: "Laundry"
Town Shoes/The Shoe Company
WVRST

Branches

TAXI Calgary
805 10th Avenue SW Suite 500, Calgary, AB T2R 0B4 Canada
Tel.: (403) 269-8294
Fax: (403) 269-7776
E-Mail: info@taxi.ca
Web Site: calgary.taxi.ca

Employees: 12

Agency Specializes In: Advertising

Andrew Packwood *(CFO)*
Ben Feist *(VP-Tech)*
Matt Shoom-Kirsch *(VP-Client Ops-North America)*
Jeff Maceachern *(Exec Dir-Creative)*
Shelley Raymond *(Brand Dir-TAXI-North America)*
Matt Bielby *(Dir-Creative & Writer)*
Stephanie Fennell *(Dir-HR-Global)*
Ben Tarr *(Dir-Bus Dev & Integration)*
Dave Watson *(Dir-Creative Design-North America)*

Accounts:
AMA Insurance
Aviva
Blue Shield
Carling
Dairy Farmers,Canada
Koodo
Pfizer
Plan B
Reversa
Tim Hortons
Vancouver Aquarium
WestJet

Taxi 2
49 Spadina Ave Ste 403, Toronto, ON M5V2J1 Canada
Tel.: (416) 598-4750
Fax: (416) 598-9754
Web Site: taxi.ca

Daniel Shearer *(Gen Mgr)*
Jeff MacEachern *(Exec Dir-Creative)*
Karlee Bedford *(Acct Dir)*
Alyssa Graff *(Dir-Art)*
Jason Kerr *(Dir-Art)*
Shawn James *(Assoc Dir-Creative)*
Daniel Sherrington *(Acct Mgr)*
Dana Ciani *(Copywriter)*
Marc Levesque *(Copywriter)*
Miryam Weinstein *(Copywriter)*

Accounts:
New-Campbell Company of Canada Ltd Campaign: "We All Soup", Digital, TV
Koodo Mobile
Leon's Furniture Limited (Agency of Record)
New-Moosehead (Agency of Record) Alpine Lager, Creative, Hop City, Moose Light, Moosehead Lager, Strategic
Movember.com Campaign: "David's Big Problem"
New-SiriusXM
Topcuts Campaign: "When it's bad, it's all they see."
WVRST Campaign: "WVRST Sausage Party Invite"

TAXI New York
230 Park Ave S, New York, NY 10003
Tel.: (212) 414-8294
Fax: (212) 414-8444
E-Mail: david.jenkins@taxi-nyc.com
Web Site: taxi.ca/contact/offices/new-york/

Employees: 20
Year Founded: 2004

Agency Specializes In: Sponsorship

David Jenkins *(Pres)*
Rob Guenette *(CEO)*
Frank Sanni *(Head-Plng)*
Reid Miller *(Exec Dir-Creative)*
David Niblick *(Sr Producer & Art Buyer)*

Accounts:
Art Directors Club; New York, NY; 2004
Audible.com Campaign: "Romance"
Capital One Financial Corp.
Clear Channel Outdoor Campaign: "united4th"
Coors Brewing Killian's Irish Red, Molson Canadian
Grandparents.com; 2007
Heineken Campaign: "99 Bottles", Newcastle Brown Ale
Johnson & Johnson Children's Motrin, Motrin
Microsoft - MSN; Redmond, WA; 2004
Mohegan Sun Creative
MoMA
Mondelez International, Inc. Campaign: "Croc Block", Campaign: "Manuel", Creative, Gevalia, MiO
National Hockey League
Outdoor Advertising Association of America Digital Out-of-Home
Outdoor Life Network
Rail Europe Group
Revlon Creative
Rover

TAXI Vancouver
515 Richards St, Vancouver, BC V6B 2Z5 Canada
Tel.: (604) 683-8294
Fax: (604) 683-6112
E-Mail: pr@taxi.ca
Web Site: vancouver.taxi.ca

Employees: 27

Ben Tarr *(Mng Dir)*
Meghan Hawes *(Grp Acct Dir)*
Caroline MacGregor *(Grp Acct Dir)*
Matt Bielby *(Creative Dir)*
Nick Cronk *(Acct Dir)*
Quinn Ingham *(Acct Dir)*
Jack Dayan *(Dir-Plng)*
Tony Hird *(Assoc Dir-Creative & Art)*
Jeremy Harrison *(Acct Mgr)*
Sebastien Wilcox *(Copywriter)*

Accounts:
Aviva
BC Hydro (Agency of Record) Offtober
BrainTrust
Crofton House School
Hard Rock Casino
Hughes Carwash Campaign: "Bacon Underwear", Campaign: "Nose Hairs", Campaign: "Rabies Shot", Campaign: "The Internet"
Kiwi Collection
Metropolis
Opus Hotel Campaign: "Pink Bells"
RBC Centre
Vancouver Aquarium 4D Theatre, Campaign: "45 hill climbing ability. Volkswagen Amarok.", Campaign: "Urinal Pregnancy Test", Ocean Wise Program

TAXI
1435 Rue Saint Alexandre Bureau 620, Montreal, QC H3A 2G4 Canada
Tel.: (514) 842-8294
Fax: (514) 842-6552
E-Mail: pr@taxi.ca
Web Site: www.taxi.ca

Employees: 70

Agency Specializes In: Advertising

Jack Dayan *(Co-Mng Dir)*
Pascal de Decker *(Gen Mgr & Exec Dir-Creative)*
Tony Hird *(Sr Dir-Art)*
Nicolas Rivard *(Sr Dir-Art)*
Matt Bielby *(Dir-Creative & Writer)*
Nikki Jobson *(Assoc Dir-Creative)*
Manuela Paoletta *(Mgr-HR & Talent)*
Martin Charron *(Copywriter)*

Accounts:
Bombardier
Groupe Le Massif Le Massif de Charlevoix Ski Area
McCain
Microsoft
Quebec's Contemporary Music Society
Sun Products Canada Corp. (Agency of Record) Creative

TAYLOE GRAY KRISTOF LLC
221 N 2nd St, Wilmington, NC 2840
Tel.: (800) 620-8480
E-Mail: team@tg-k.com
Web Site: www.tg-k.com

Year Founded: 2009

Agency Specializes In: Advertising, Brand Development & Integration, Digital/Interactive, Graphic Design, Media Buying Services, Media Planning, Print

Nathan Tayloe *(Partner & COO)*
Andrew Gray *(Partner & Chief Technology Officer)*
Bryan Kristof *(Partner & CMO)*

Accounts:
New-Defiant Whisky

TAYLOR & POND CORPORATE COMMUNICATIONS
2970 5th Ave Ste 120, San Diego, CA 92103-5995
Tel.: (619) 297-3742
Fax: (619) 297-3743
E-Mail: tpcorp@tpcorp.com
Web Site: www.taylorpond.com

Employees: 6
Year Founded: 1995

Agency Specializes In: Consulting, Internet/Web Design

Approx. Annual Billings: $1,500,000

Breakdown of Gross Billings by Media: D.M.: $750,000; Other: $750,000

Cindy Pond *(Pres & CEO)*
Milo Richardson *(COO)*
Siri Fomsgaard *(VP-Client Success)*
Jacquie Johnson *(VP-Bus Dev)*

Accounts:
Acuraclassic.com
Bbeaute
Children's Primary Care Medical Group
Creative Nail Design
Gila Rut
Good Feet
Herbalife
Horizon Store
NYX Cosmetics (Digital Agency of Record)
Tango Wine Company
Tervita Corporation
University of San Diego Alumni Association
womenssportsnet.com Women's Fitness, Women's Health, Women's Sports

TAYLOR MADE MEDIA
(Name Changed to Think Mint Media)

TAYLOR WEST ADVERTISING
503 Avenue A, San Antonio, TX 78215
Tel.: (782) 805-0320
Fax: (210) 805-9371
E-Mail: info@taylorwest.com
Web Site: www.taylorwest.com

Employees: 15
Year Founded: 1978

Agency Specializes In: Advertising, Brand Development & Integration, Consulting, Consumer Goods, Consumer Marketing, Corporate Identity, Digital/Interactive, Financial, Graphic Design, Hospitality, Integrated Marketing, Internet/Web Design, Local Marketing, Media Buying Services, Media Planning, Newspaper, Newspapers & Magazines, Outdoor, Paid Searches, Planning & Consultation, Print, Production, Production (Print), Promotions, Social Media, Trade & Consumer Magazines, Web (Banner Ads, Pop-ups, etc.)

Rebecca Berzewski *(Acct Dir)*
Demica Rodriguez *(Sr Acct Exec)*
Meghan Varner *(Jr Acct Exec)*

Accounts:
Hotel Valencia - Riverwalk; San Antonio, TX
Hotel Valencia - Santana Row; San Jose, CA
IBC Bank; Laredo, TX
Valencia Group; San Antonio, TX

TBA GLOBAL
535 N Brand Blvd Ste 800, Glendale, CA 91203-3300
Tel.: (818) 226-2800
Fax: (818) 226-2801
E-Mail: losangeles@tbaglobal.com
Web Site: www.tbaglobal.com

Employees: 116
Year Founded: 1993

Agency Specializes In: Branded Entertainment, Business-To-Business, Consumer Marketing, Event Planning & Marketing

Robert Geddes *(Owner)*
Cindy Bell *(Sr VP-Meeting Svcs)*
Joseph Delorenzo *(VP-Production & Ops)*
Christine Kiesling *(VP-Client Engagement & Strategy)*
Susan Schneiderman *(VP-Client Svcs)*
Tina-marie Wassman *(VP-Event Mgmt)*
Liz Jones *(Client Svcs Dir)*
Mackenzie Staffier *(Dir-Client Engagement & Mktg)*
Karen Jackson *(Planner-Meeting)*
Melissa Touchtone *(Planner-Meeting)*

Accounts:
Amnesty International USA (Agency of Record)
Mighty Fingers
The Western Union Company (Agency of Record)

TB &C

TBC INC.
900 S Wolfe St, Baltimore, MD 21231
Tel.: (410) 347-7500
Fax: (410) 986-1299
E-Mail: webmaster@tbc.us
Web Site: www.tbc.us

E-Mail for Key Personnel:
Creative Dir.: ac@tbc.us
Media Dir.: eborkowski@tbc.us
Production Mgr.: gpasha@tbc.us

Employees: 100
Year Founded: 1974

Agency Specializes In: Advertising, Advertising Specialties, Affluent Market, Alternative Advertising, Arts, Brand Development & Integration, Broadcast, Business Publications, Business-To-Business, Children's Market, Collateral, College, Communications, Consumer Goods, Consumer Marketing, Content, Corporate Communications, Corporate Identity, Crisis Communications, Customer Relationship Management, Digital/Interactive, Direct Response Marketing, Direct-to-Consumer, E-Commerce, Education, Electronic Media, Electronics, Email, Event Planning & Marketing, Exhibit/Trade Shows, Fashion/Apparel, Financial, Food Service, Government/Political, Graphic Design, Guerilla Marketing, Health Care Services, High Technology, Hispanic Market, Hospitality, Household Goods, Identity Marketing, In-Store Advertising, Integrated Marketing, International, Internet/Web Design, Leisure, Local Marketing, Logo & Package Design, Luxury Products, Magazines, Media Buying Services, Media Planning, Media Relations, Media Training, Men's Market, Mobile Marketing, Multimedia, Newspaper, Newspapers & Magazines, Out-of-Home Media, Outdoor, Over-50 Market, Package Design, Paid Searches, Planning & Consultation, Point of Purchase, Point of Sale, Print, Production, Production (Ad, Film, Broadcast), Production (Print), Promotions, Public Relations, Publicity/Promotions, Publishing, Radio, Real Estate, Recruitment, Regional, Restaurant, Retail, Sales Promotion, Search Engine Optimization, Seniors' Market, Shopper Marketing, Social Marketing/Nonprofit, Social Media, South Asian Market, Sponsorship, Sports Market, Strategic Planning/Research, T.V., Trade & Consumer Magazines, Transportation, Travel & Tourism, Viral/Buzz/Word of Mouth, Web (Banner Ads, Pop-ups, etc.), Women's Market, Yellow Pages Advertising

Allan Charles *(Chm & Chief Creative Officer)*
Howe Burch *(Co-Pres)*
Brad Meerholz *(Sr VP & Dir-Design)*
Casey Rhoads *(VP & Acct Dir)*
Erin Borkowski *(VP & Dir-Media)*
Lainie Troutman *(Mgr-Print Production)*
Jeff Whitehead *(Mgr-IT)*
Selena Pigrom *(Supvr-Media)*
Abbie Pedroni *(Asst Acct Exec)*
Kallie Fischer *(Acct Coord)*
Karen Peraza *(Acct Coord)*

Accounts:
Business Health Services; 2014
Connections Academy; 2011
CVS MinuteClinic; 2004
Dogtopia; 2013
Hair Cuttery; 2008
Haribo USA; 2010
Lincoln Financial; 2011
Nava Health & Vitality Centers; 2013
Smyth Jewelers; 2014
Tessco/Ventev; 2012
Tessco; 2012
University of Maryland University College; 2013
Visit Baltimore; 2012
Washington Gas Energy Services; 2013

Direct Marketing Division

TBC Direct, Inc.
900 S Wolfe St, Baltimore, MD 21231
Tel.: (410) 347-7500
Fax: (410) 986-1299
E-Mail: webmaster@tbc.us
Web Site: www.tbc.us

Employees: 76
Year Founded: 1974

Agency Specializes In: Advertising, Direct Response Marketing

Brad Meerholz *(Sr VP & Dir-Design)*
Jason Middleton *(Sr VP & Dir-Creative)*
Jen Beck *(Sr VP-Strategy & Acct Mgmt)*
Patty Stachowiak *(Sr VP-Fin & Ops)*
Erin Borkowski *(VP & Dir-Media)*
Allison Cannavino *(Acct Dir)*
Laura Jones *(Acct Supvr)*
Meghan Litsinger *(Acct Supvr)*
Lara Franke *(Supvr-PR)*
Anne Wineholt *(Supvr-Media)*
Ali Deluca *(Sr Acct Exec)*
Kerry Weir *(Acct Exec)*

Public Relations

TBC, Inc./PR Division
900 S Wolfe St, Baltimore, MD 21231
(See Separate Listing)

TBD
1000 NW Wall St Ste 201, Bend, OR 97701
Tel.: (541) 388-7558
Fax: (541) 388-7532
E-Mail: info@tbdagency.com

Web Site: www.tbdagency.com

Employees: 15
Year Founded: 1997

National Agency Associations: Second Wind Limited

Agency Specializes In: Advertising, Advertising Specialties, Affluent Market, Alternative Advertising, Arts, Automotive, Brand Development & Integration, Broadcast, Business-To-Business, Cable T.V., Catalogs, Collateral, Communications, Consumer Goods, Consumer Marketing, Consumer Publications, Corporate Communications, Corporate Identity, Digital/Interactive, Direct Response Marketing, Education, Email, Entertainment, Environmental, Exhibit/Trade Shows, Financial, Food Service, Government/Political, Graphic Design, Health Care Services, Hospitality, Identity Marketing, In-Store Advertising, Integrated Marketing, Internet/Web Design, Local Marketing, Logo & Package Design, Magazines, Market Research, Media Buying Services, Media Planning, New Product Development, Newspaper, Newspapers & Magazines, Out-of-Home Media, Outdoor, Package Design, Planning & Consultation, Point of Purchase, Point of Sale, Print, Public Relations, Publicity/Promotions, Radio, Real Estate, Social Marketing/Nonprofit, Social Media, Sports Market, Strategic Planning/Research, T.V., Trade & Consumer Magazines, Travel & Tourism, Viral/Buzz/Word of Mouth, Women's Market

Approx. Annual Billings: $3,900,000

Breakdown of Gross Billings by Media: Event Mktg.: $125,000; Fees: $1,650,500; Logo & Package Design: $120,000; Mags.: $217,000; Newsp.: $691,000; Out-of-Home Media: $125,000; Outdoor: $30,000; Plng. & Consultation: $175,000; Point of Sale: $150,000; Radio: $180,000; Strategic Planning/Research: $125,500; T.V.: $196,000; Worldwide Web Sites: $115,000

Rene Mitchell *(Partner & Client Svcs Dir)*
Angela Reid *(Dir-Creative & Writer)*
Jeanie Morton *(Office Mgr)*
Kevin Smyth *(Acct Mgr)*
Randy Dean *(Mgr-Acctg)*
Alice LeBlond *(Mgr-Production)*
Dennis Foster *(Designer-Production)*

Accounts:
21st Amendment Brewery; San Francisco, CA Craft Brewery; 2009
American Licorice; Bend, OR Candy; 2009
Avant Assessment; Eugene, OR Language Assessment; 2010
BendFilm; Bend, OR Film Festival; 2006
Brooks Resources; Bend, OR Real Estate Development; 2000
IronHorse; Prineville, OR Real Estate; 2005
North Rim; Bend, OR Real Estate; 2003
Northwest Crossing; Bend, OR Mixed Use Development; 2004
Odell Brewery; Fort Collins, CO Craft Brewery; 2003
Old Mill District; Bend, OR Shipping, Living & Entertainment District; 2008
Swiss Water Decaffeinated Coffee; Burnaby, BC Decaffeinated Coffee; 2008
Thesys; Anaheim, CA Hybrid Online / Classroom Approach to Learning; 2010

TBWA/WORLDWIDE
488 Madison Ave, New York, NY 10022
Tel.: (212) 804-1300
Fax: (212) 804-1333
Web Site: www.tbwa.com

Employees: 11,000
Year Founded: 1970

National Agency Associations: 4A's-ABC-AMA-DMA

Agency Specializes In: Social Media

Tom Carroll *(Chm)*
Troy Ruhanen *(Pres & CEO)*
James Vincent *(Co-Pres-Intl)*
Chris Garbutt *(Pres-Global Creative & Chief Creative Officer)*
Ed Castillo *(Chief Strategy Officer-New York)*
Duncan Milner *(Chief Creative Officer)*
Emmanuel Andre *(Pres-Intl)*
Keith Smith *(Pres-Intl)*
Perry Valkenburg *(Pres-Intl & Global Ops)*
Jean-Marie Prenaud *(Mng Dir-Worldwide)*
Bradley Apelgren *(VP-Global Client Fin)*
Jerry Gentile *(Grp Dir-Creative)*
Chuck Monn *(Grp Dir-Creative)*
Stan Fiorito *(Grp Acct Dir)*
Hugo Murray *(Grp Acct Dir)*
Katie Hollenkamp *(Dir-Global Bus Integration-Nissan United)*
Kyla Jacobs *(Dir-Bus Dev-Global)*
Baker Lambert *(Dir-Global Data)*
Carol Madonna *(Dir-Svcs)*
Teresa Rad *(Dir-Art Production)*
Brett Wiliiams *(Dir-Global Network-Nissan United)*
Mike Yagi *(Dir-Creative)*
Raphael Milczarek *(Assoc Dir-Creative)*
Alexa Payton *(Mgr-New Bus)*

Accounts:
Absolut Creative
Adidas 2014 Fifa World Cup
Airbnb, Inc.
Apple Inc.; Los Angeles, CA Campaign: "Assistant", Campaign: "Beatles Covers", Campaign: "Learn", Campaign: "Share The Fun", iPad, iPhone Siri, iPod Touch, iTunes
BNY Mellon Digital, Global Creative, Print, TV
Grammy Awards
Johnson & Johnson
Nissan Motor Company "Taxi of Tomorrow", Campaign: "#HailYes", Campaign: "Innovation Garage", Communications Strategy, Datsun, Digital, Nissan Leaf, Nissan NV200, Sentra, Singing Sockets, Video
The Procter & Gamble Company
Singapore Airlines (Creative Agency of Record)

UNITED STATES

Being
488 Madison Ave, New York, NY 10022
Tel.: (212) 804-1300

Brett Edgar *(Grp Acct Dir)*
Samira Ansari *(Dir-Creative)*

Accounts:
Kraft Campaign: "A Gift From Nature", Campaign: "Go-tivations", Campaign: "Harness The Power of Peanut", Campaign: "Zesty Guy"
Mondelez International Campaign: "Air Chase", Campaign: "Chili Pot", Campaign: "Let's Get Zesty", Campaign: "Must! Have! Wheat Thins", Campaign: "Trap Door", Wheat Thins, Zesty Italian Salad

eg+ Worldwide
(Formerly E-Graphics)
200 E Randolph St Ste 3620, Chicago, IL 60601
Tel.: (312) 729-4500
E-Mail: chicago@egplusww.com
Web Site: egplusww.com/

E-Mail for Key Personnel:
Public Relations: rbrown@agency.com

Employees: 55
Year Founded: 1995

Agency Specializes In: Digital/Interactive, E-Commerce, Internet/Web Design, Media Buying Services, Search Engine Optimization, Social Media, Web (Banner Ads, Pop-ups, etc.)

George Ashbrook *(Mng Dir)*
Paul Fothergill *(CFO)*
Mark Rhys Thomas *(Chief Strategy Officer)*
Jason Van Praagh *(CTO)*
Tetsuo Shimada *(Pres/CEO-Japan)*
Myles Peacock *(Pres-Americas & Head-Global Brand)*
Natalie Fernandez *(Reg Dir-Project Mgmt-Americas)*
Pasquale Bortone *(Dir-Studio)*

Accounts:
Aon
Barrie Pace
Energizer
Fisher Price
Hilton Worldwide
HP; Chicago, IL
Jones Lange LaSalle
Red Hat
Sears

TBWA California
5353 Grosvenor Blvd, Los Angeles, CA 90066
Tel.: (310) 305-5000
Fax: (310) 330-56000

John Moyers *(Mng Dir & Exec VP-Shopper Arts Network)*
Barbara Overlie *(CFO)*
Nick Barham *(Chief Strategy Officer)*
Stephen Butler *(Chief Creative Officer)*
Walter Smith *(Mng Dir-Global)*
Fabio Costa *(Exec Dir-Creative)*
Jerry Gentile *(Grp Dir-Creative)*
Lee Clow *(Dir-Media Arts-Global)*
Jennifer Costello *(Dir-Plng)*
Craig Werwa *(Dir-Social Media & Digital)*
Raphael Milczarek *(Assoc Dir-Creative)*
Kirk Williams *(Assoc Dir-Creative)*

Accounts:
Ball Park
Pepsi
Pioneer

TBWA Chiat Day Los Angeles
5353 Grosvenor Blvd, Los Angeles, CA 90066
Tel.: (310) 305-5000
Fax: (310) 305-6000
Web Site: tbwachiatdayla.com

Employees: 500
Year Founded: 1968

National Agency Associations: 4A's-ABC-AMA-DMA-THINKLA

Agency Specializes In: Advertising, Sponsorship

Lee Clow *(Chm)*
Peter Bracegirdle *(Mng Dir)*
Neal Grossman *(COO)*
Stephen Butler *(Chief Creative Officer)*
Jon Castle *(Pres-Nissan United)*
Dick Sitting *(Sr VP)*
Jerico Cabaysa *(Mng Dir-Gatorade)*
Andrew Dauska *(Mng Dir-Nissan)*
Javier Malagon *(Head-Creative-Mexico)*
Brent Anderson *(Exec Creative Dir)*
Fabio Costa *(Exec Dir-Creative)*
Eric Grunbaum *(Exec Dir-Creative)*
Jerry Gentile *(Grp Dir-Creative)*
Scott MacMaster *(Grp Dir-Plng)*
Bernice Chao *(Sr Dir-Integrated Art)*

Liz Levy *(Sr Dir-Art)*
Andrew Reizuch *(Sr Dir-Art)*
Kirsten Rutherford *(Sr Dir-Art)*
Kelly Bayett *(Creative Dir)*
Sarah Lamberson *(Brand Dir)*
Romain Naegelen *(Brand Dir-Global)*
Jennifer Nottoli *(Acct Dir-Global)*
Annie Reyes *(Bus Dir-Global Cross)*
Peter Bassett *(Dir-Production)*
Joerg Bruns *(Dir-Creative)*
Micky Coyne *(Dir-Creative)*
Linda Daubson *(Dir-Bus Affairs)*
Renato Fernandez *(Dir-Creative-Worldwide)*
Rebecca Ginos *(Dir-Art)*
Jayanta Jenkins *(Dir-Creative-Global)*
Vaino Leskinen *(Dir-Mobile)*
Tito Melega *(Dir-Creative-Americas)*
Kate O'Connor *(Dir-Art)*
Matt Paterno *(Dir-Art)*
Mark Peters *(Dir-Creative)*
Martin Ramos *(Dir-Global Plng)*
Mark Sheldrake *(Dir-Creative-Global)*
Drew Stalker *(Dir-Creative)*
Rohit Thawani *(Dir-Digital Strategy & Social Media)*
Abigail Weintraub *(Dir-Plng)*
Craig Werwa *(Dir-Social Media & Digital)*
Mike Yagi *(Dir-Creative)*
Nick Ciffone *(Sr Copywriter)*
Mike Blanch *(Assoc Dir-Creative)*
Mariota Essery *(Sr Art Dir)*
Jason Locey *(Assoc Dir-Creative)*
Mimi Hirsch *(Sr Mgr-Bus Affairs)*
Patrick Jones *(Brand Mgr)*
Erika Buder *(Asst Brand Mgr)*
Ryan Moore *(Acct Supvr-Gatorade-Global)*
Emilie Arrive *(Sr Strategist-Digital)*
Ashley Pratt *(Acct Exec)*
Parker Adame *(Copywriter)*
Lifang He *(Planner-Global Strategic)*
Parker Grant *(Sr Art Dir)*

Accounts:
Adidas Campaign: "All In for Mygirls", Creative, Online, PR, Retail, TV
Airbnb (Lead Creative Agency) Campaign: "Belong Anywhere", Campaign: "HostWithPride", Campaign: "Is Mankind?", Campaign: "Never a Stranger", Lead Creative, TV
Apple Inc. iMac, iPhone, iPod
Best Friends Animal Society Campaign: "No-Kill Los Angeles", Pro Bono
Buffalo Wild Wings (Advertising Agency of Record) Campaign: "Fantasy Football Rich", Campaign: "Football Rich", Creative, Radio, TV
New-Disney Consumer Products
Gatorade Broadcast, Campaign "We Love Sweat", Campaign: "50 Years Fueling The Champion Within", Campaign: "50", Campaign: "Be Like Mike", Campaign: "Burn Some to Earn Some", Campaign: "Dream Like Mike", Campaign: "Groove Like Mike", Campaign: "Hard Work", Campaign: "Jordan Coaches", Campaign: "Made In NY", Campaign: "Moving the Game Forward", Campaign: "My Way", Campaign: "One More", Campaign: "Sweat It to Get It", Campaign: "We Are All-Stars", Gatorade REPLAY, Online, Print, Signage, Sweat It to Get It, TV
GlaxoSmithKline
Hillshire Brands (Creative Agency of Record) Ball Park, Campaign: "Slow Roast Shuffle", Hillshire Farm, Lunch & Dinner Offerings, Online, Simple Sweets
Jameson Campaign: "Hawk"
Johnson & Johnson Campaign: "For All You Love"
Let There Be Dragons
MillerCoors LLC Campaign: "Snowflake", Campaign: "Wonderful World", Miller Lite, Miller Lite (Creative Agency of Record), Strategy, TV
New-Netflix
Nissan Motor Co., Ltd. "Hill Climb,", Advertising, Altima, Armada, Campaign: "Cold Shoulder", Campaign: "Commute", Campaign: "Dealership", Campaign: "Door Trip", Campaign: "Factory of Life", Campaign: "Father", Campaign: "GT Academy", Campaign: "Heisman House", Campaign: "Impress with Sentra", Campaign: "My Versa Road Trip", Campaign: "Sidelines", Campaign: "Spread Your Joy", Campaign: "The Briefcase", Campaign: "Tough Love", Campaign: "With Dad", Frontier, GT Academy Season 2, GT-R, Leaf, Maxima, Murano, NV Cargo, NV Passenger, NV200, Nissan 370Z, Nissan Cube, Nissan Juke, Online, Pathfinder, Quest Mini Van, Rogue, Sentra, Super Bowl 2015, Titan, Versa, Versa Note, Xterra
Nixon (Agency of Record) Communication Planning
NKLA
Pacific Standard Time Campaign: "Celebrate the Era", Campaign: "Ice Cube Celebrates the Eames"
Pedigree
PepsiCo Campaign: "Disappearing Sanders", Campaign: "King's Court", Campaign: "Made in NY", Campaign: "NEXT: Party", Campaign: "Test Drive 2", Campaign: "Test Drive", Campaign: "Unbelievable David Beckham", Campaign: "Zero-Calorie In Disguise", Diet Pepsi, Gatorade: "Pump up the G", Pepsi, Pepsi Edge, Pepsi Max, Pepsi Refresh Project
Pernod Ricard Campaign: "Hawk"
Southwest Airlines Co. Ad Campaign, Brand Message, Campaign: "Some Nights", Campaign: "Welcome Aboard"
Stacy's Campaign: "That's the Stacy's Way"
Stephen Kessler Campaign: "Still Alive"
New-Twitter, Inc. Campaign: "Post Season"
Visa Campaign: "Go World" in 2008", Campaign: "Make It Epic", Campaign: "Ned's Journey", Check Card, Online & Social Media, TV advertising; 2007

TBWA Chiat Day New York

488 Madison Ave, New York, NY 10022
Tel.: (212) 804-1032
Fax: (212) 804-1200
Web Site: www.tbwachiatdayny.com/

Employees: 300

National Agency Associations: 4A's-ABC-AMA-DMA

Agency Specializes In: Sponsorship

Rob Schwartz *(CEO & Dir-Creative)*
Neal Grossman *(COO)*
Chad Hopenwasser *(Head-Integrated Production)*
Carole Smila *(Head-Project Mgmt & Creative Svcs)*
Aki Spicer *(Head-Digital & Content Strategy)*
Walt Connelly *(Exec Dir-Creative-Global)*
Oke Muller *(Grp Dir-Plng)*
Natalie Puccio *(Grp Dir-Plng)*
Carrie Lipper *(Grp Acct Dir)*
Ben Muldrew *(Grp Acct Dir)*
Mike Popowski *(Grp Acct Dir)*
Amy Farias *(Acct Dir)*
Ed Rogers *(Acct Dir)*
James Cheung *(Dir-Creative-China)*
Leigh Davidson *(Dir-Plng)*
Chris King *(Dir-Search & Digital Strategy)*
Julie Maciver *(Dir-Plng)*
Steve Mendonca *(Dir-Art)*
Doug Menezes *(Dir-Digital Design)*
Melatan Riden *(Dir-Design & Art)*
Beth Ryan *(Dir-Creative)*
Joe Shands *(Dir-Creative)*
Anastasia Garcia *(Mgr-Social Content)*
Jared Cohen *(Sr Strategist-Digital)*
Daniel Sanders *(Copywriter)*
Craig Schlesinger *(Copywriter)*
Kiyotaka Sumiyoshi *(Designer-Motion Graphics)*
Brittni Phillips *(Assoc-Media Arts Production)*
Olivia Whyte *(Assoc Producer)*

Accounts:
Accenture
Activision Blizzard Campaign: "Zombie Labs", Creative, Guitar Hero
adidas America, Inc.
American Management Association
Amway Corporation Creative, Nutrilite
Apple, Inc. iMac
beIN Brand Identity, Campaign: "Change the Game", Campaign: "Remote Control"
BIC
New-Brooklyn Film Festival
Cablevision; 2007
Dial Combat, Renuzit, Soft Scrub
Frito-Lay, Inc. Stacy's Pita Chips
G6 Hospitality LLC
GlaxoSmithKline, Inc. Alli, Commit, Nicoderm CQ, Nicorette Gum, Nicorette Mini Lozenge, Zyban
New-GoDaddy (Lead Creative Agency)
Grupo Jumex
Hearts on Fire Global Creative
Home Depot
Jameson
Keep A Child Alive Campaign: "Digital Death"
Kraft Foods Inc. Campaign: "Dictionary", Campaign: "Heart Health", Campaign: "Science", Digital, Planters "Nut-rition" Nuts, Social
Level Vodka
Mars, Incorporated Combos, Milky Way, Twix PB
McDonald's Corporation Baby, Campaign: "Symbols"
Michelin MICHELIN Premier tire
MJZ
Mondelez International, Inc.
Nicorette (Agency of Record)
Nissan "Landing Gear", Campaign: "Nissan Leaf Gas Powered Everything", Campaign: "Value of Zero", Versa
Pedigree
PepsiCo. Campaign: "'Unbelievable David Beckham", Campaign: "Love Every Sip", Creative, Diet Pepsi, Equation, Gatorade, Pepsi, Pepsi Max, Pepsi Next, Pepsi Refresh Everything
Pernod Ricard Campaign: "'Iron Horse", Campaign: "ABSOLUT Blank", Campaign: "Jameson Pub Paintings", Campo Viejo Wines, Creative, Digital, In-Store Marketing, Jameson Irish Whiskey, Kahlua (Global Communications Agency), Kenwood Vineyards, Martel Cognac, Royal Salute Scotch Whiskey, Social-Media Marketing, Tall Tales Campaign
Roche Pharmaceuticals
Sara Lee
Seagram's
Skittles Campaign: "Facebook Fist"
New-Sport Chek (Lead Agency)
Starburst Dog, Fruit Chews; 2007
Sunseeker Global Digital Marketing
Thomson Reuters (Lead Creative Agency)
The Travelers Companies, Inc. (Lead Creative Agency) Campaign: "Bakery", Campaign: "Charging Station", Campaign: "Growing Up", TV
Twix
Visa USA

TBWA Digital Arts Network

488 Madison Ave, New York, NY 10022
Tel.: (212) 804-1300
Web Site: digitalartsnetwork.com/#lsi450627ci0q

Agency Specializes In: Content, Digital/Interactive, E-Commerce, Mobile Marketing, Production, Search Engine Optimization, Social Media

Joanne Lao *(Mng Dir)*
Luke Eid *(Pres-Digital Arts Network)*
Morgan McAlenney *(Sr VP-Digital)*
Juuso Myllyrinne *(VP & Head-Strategy-Digital Arts Network)*
Tuomas Peltoniemi *(Head-Digital & Dir-Technical)*
Ida Mak *(Grp Acct Dir)*
Christina Suen *(Assoc Acct Dir)*

Accounts:
Wrangler Campaign: "Mileage"

TBWA Los Angeles
5353 Grosvenor Blvd, Los Angeles, CA 90066-6913
Tel.: (310) 305-5000
Fax: (310) 305-6000
Web Site: tbwa.com

Employees: 125

Agency Specializes In: Direct Response Marketing

David Colon *(COO)*
Nick Barham *(Chief Strategy Officer)*
Elena Hale *(Chief Strategy Officer)*
Brent Anderson *(Exec Dir-Creative)*
Fabio Costa *(Exec Dir-Creative)*
Eric Grunbaum *(Exec Dir-Creative)*
Jerry Gentile *(Grp Dir-Creative)*
Chuck Monn *(Grp Dir-Creative)*
Jayanta Jenkins *(Dir-Creative-Global)*
Chris Ribeiro *(Dir-Creative)*
Rohit Thawani *(Dir-Digital Strategy & Social Media)*

Accounts:
Adidas
Canon
Nissan
Samsonite
Sony Playstation Video Game Counsel

TBWA/Media Arts Lab
12539 Beatrice St, Los Angeles, CA 90066
Tel.: (310) 305-4400
Fax: (310) 305-4499
Web Site: www.mediaartslab.com

Employees: 200

National Agency Associations: 4A's

Agency Specializes In: Broadcast, Production (Ad, Film, Broadcast), Sponsorship

Lee Clow *(Chm & Dir-Media Arts)*
Erica Hoholick *(Pres)*
David Colon *(COO)*
Duncan Milner *(Chief Creative Officer)*
Eric Grunbaum *(Exec Dir-Creative)*
Danny Duran *(Sr Dir-Integrated Art)*
Masaya Asai *(Dir-Art & Assoc Dir-Creative)*
Guto Araki *(Dir-Creative)*
Kyungran Chang *(Dir-Art)*
Antoine Choussat *(Dir-Creative)*
Anders Gustafsson *(Dir-Creative)*
JD Jurentkuff *(Dir-Creative)*
Gabe Mcdonough *(Dir-Music)*
Helen O'Neill *(Dir-Art Production)*
Mollie Partesotti *(Dir-Brand Strategy)*
Karine Shahar *(Dir-HR)*
Kevin Tenglin *(Dir-Creative)*
Pierre Wendling *(Dir-Interactive Production)*
Robert Westphal *(Dir-Art)*
Chaz Whitworth *(Dir-Art)*
David Zorn *(Dir-Creative)*
Benjamin Bartels *(Assoc Dir-Creative & Art)*
Alain Briere *(Assoc Dir-Creative)*
Justin Walsh *(Assoc Dir-Creative)*
Erin Toerner *(Acct Supvr)*
Jenna Ritter *(Acct Exec)*
Heather Weiss *(Designer)*
Lauren Alejo *(Asst Acct Exec)*
Claire Skillin *(Asst Acct Exec-Global)*

Accounts:
Airtel
Apple Inc. Apple Watch, Campaign: "Assistant", Campaign: "Basically", Campaign: "Beatles Covers", Campaign: "Beijing", Campaign: "Berlin", Campaign: "Chicken Fat", Campaign: "Closer", Campaign: "Designed by Apple in California", Campaign: "Dreams", Campaign: "FaceTime Every Day", Campaign: "For The Colorful", Campaign: "Goals", Campaign: "History of Sound", Campaign: "Hollywood", Campaign: "If it's not an iPhone. It's not an iPhone", Campaign: "Intention", Campaign: "Labor Day", Campaign: "Learn", Campaign: "Life", Campaign: "Loved", Campaign: "Make Music with iPad", Campaign: "Mayday", Campaign: "Metal Mastered", Campaign: "Misunderstood", Campaign: "Music Every Day", Campaign: "Our Signature", Campaign: "Parenthood", Campaign: "Pencil", Campaign: "Photos Every Day", Campaign: "Plastic Perfected", Campaign: "Rise", Campaign: "Shaping the Future of Filmmaking", Campaign: "Share The Fun", Campaign: "Shot on iPhone 6", Campaign: "Stickers", Campaign: "Strength", Campaign: "The Notebook People Love", Campaign: "The Song", Campaign: "Up", Campaign: "Us", Creative, MacBook Air, iPad, iPhone 4S, iPhone 5, iPhone 5C, iPhone 5s, iPhone 6, iPhone 6 Plus, iPod
AT&T Communications Corp.
Conservation International Campaign: "Nature is Speaking", Social
iPod Nano

TBWA North America
488 Madison Ave, New York, NY 10022
Tel.: (212) 804-1300
Fax: (212) 804-1200
Web Site: www.tbwa.com

Employees: 250

Denis Streiff *(CFO)*
Doug Melville *(Chief Diversity Officer)*
Emmanuel Andre *(Pres-Intl)*
John Hunt *(Dir-Creative-Worldwide)*

Accounts:
Absolut

TBWA/WorldHealth
488 Madison Ave 5th Fl, New York, NY 10022
Tel.: (212) 804-1000
Fax: (212) 804-1462
Web Site: www.tbwaworldhealth.com

Agency Specializes In: Health Care Services

Herve Brunette *(Pres)*
Stan Fiorito *(Mng Dir)*
R. Shane Kennedy *(Mng Dir)*
Steve Morris *(Mng Dir)*
Nick Barham *(Chief Strategy Officer)*
Adam Goldman *(Dir-HR)*
Blanca Stephens *(Dir-HR)*
Erika Buder *(Brand Mgr-Sports Mktg)*

Accounts:
Bristol-Myers Squibb
GlaxoSmithKline
Johnson & Johnson
NuvaRing
Pfizer
Roche
TEDMED Digital

Zimmerman Advertising
6600 N Andrews Avenue, Fort Lauderdale, FL 33309-3064
(See Separate Listing)

CANADA

Juniper Park/TBWA
(Formerly Juniper Park)
33 Bloor Street East 14th Fl, Toronto, ON M4W 3H1 Canada
Tel.: (416) 413-7301
Fax: (416) 972-5486
Web Site: www.juniperpark.com

Employees: 100

Agency Specializes In: Brand Development & Integration

Jill Nykoliation *(CEO)*
Alan Madill *(Chief Creative Officer)*
Barry Quinn *(Chief Creative Officer)*
Calvin Daniels *(Head-Client Svcs)*
David Toto *(Gen Mgr)*
Geoff Wilton *(Sr Acct Dir)*
Steven Tiao *(Art Dir & Designer)*
Wendi Hamilton *(Producer-Brdcst)*
Christina Gliha *(Dir-Creative)*
Susie Lee *(Dir-Creative)*
Andy Linardatos *(Dir-Creative)*
Mark Pileggi *(Dir-Ops-Digital)*
Mary Romas *(Mgr-HR)*

Accounts:
Canadian Journalists For Free Expression Campaign: "Cover Up - Anna", Campaign: "Information is Ammunition"
Chicago Tribune
CIBC Creative
Circle 21 Campaign: "Extra Ordinary"
Del Monte Foods Campaign: "Bursting With Life", Community Engagement, Digital Advertising, PR, Print, TV
Delta Hotels
EOS
IFEX Campaign: "International Day to End Impunity Logo"
Lay's
New-Miller Lite
Mines Action Canada
Miss Vickies
New York Fries Campaign: "Farmhand", Campaign: "Fashion Kitty", Campaign: "Knockoff", Campaign: "Premium Dog"
New-Nissan
Ontario Electronic Stewardship Campaign: "Old Computer"
Pepsico Toronto Pearson International Airport Campaign: "Tweet-a-Carol" & Toronto Pearson International Airport Campaign: "Wi-Fi Art", Tropicana Campaign: "Good Morning, Morning" & Tropicana Campaign: "Manifesto", Tropicana Farmstand
New-Petro-Canada
New-Pfizer
Red Cross
SFYS
Smart Food
The Source Campaign: "Backyard Monster Superstar"
Virgin Mobile Campaign: "Mod Club", Creative
YWCA

TAM-TAM/TBWA
1470 Peel St Tower A Ste 700, Montreal, QC H3A 1T1 Canada
Tel.: (514) 285-1470
Fax: (514) 285-0014
E-Mail: tamtam@tamtamtbwa.com
Web Site: www.tamtamtbwa.com

E-Mail for Key Personnel:
President: bmittelhammer@tamtamtbwa.com
Creative Dir.: hchoquette@tamtamtbwa.com

Employees: 30
Year Founded: 1986

Agency Specializes In: Business-To-Business, Communications, Direct Response Marketing, Graphic Design, Internet/Web Design, Media

Buying Services, Publicity/Promotions, Strategic Planning/Research

Brigitte Mittelhammer *(Owner)*
Martin Sansregret *(Pres)*
Yvon Gosselin *(VP-Media)*
Annie Vincent *(Art Dir)*
Dominique Beaulieu *(Media Planner)*
Josianne Dauteuil *(Copywriter)*

Accounts:
Apple
ArcelorMital Mines Canada
Chambre de la securite financiere
Communauto
Comoplast Solideal
Dos Equis
Fondation de l'hopital Maisonneuvre-Rosemont
Fondation Melio
Fondation Mobilys
Gatorade
Hydro Solution
Industries Lassonde Inc.
Investissement Quebec
KPMG
La grande guignolee des medias Campaign: "La grande guignolee des medias"
Missing Children's Network
Nissan Canada
Petro Canada
Univroue

AUSTRIA

TBWA Wien
Heiligenstaedter Strasse 31/401/3, A-1190 Vienna, Austria
Tel.: (43) 1 316 00 0
Fax: (43) 1 316 00 10
E-Mail: Christian.schmid@tbwa.at
Web Site: www.tbwa.at

Employees: 40

Doris Danner *(Reg Dir)*
Tanja Trombitas *(Copywriter)*

Accounts:
Gaulhofer Campaign: "Soundproof Windows"
Georg S. Mayer Campaign: "Direct Mailing With Padlock"
Global 2000 Campaign: "Plastic Fish"
IAA Austrian Chapter Campaign: "The Call for the Call for Entries"
Opel Campaign: "The Most Credible Testimonial in the World"
Technisches Museum Vienna Campaign: "Work In Progress"

BELGIUM

Headline Publishing Agency
Vorstermanstraat 14A, 2000 Antwerp, Belgium
Tel.: (32) 3 260 08 30
Fax: (32) 3 257 35 30
E-Mail: anne.thys@headlinepublishing.be
Web Site: www.headlinepublishing.be

Employees: 10

Agency Specializes In: Print, Production (Print)

Anne Thys *(Mng Dir)*
Valerie De Vooght *(Acct Mgr)*
Wouter Heymans *(Mgr-Digital Publ)*
Marijke Aps *(Supvr-Acct & Editorial)*
Ann De Beukelaer *(Supvr-Acct & Editorial)*
Sophie Coppens *(Acct Exec)*

Accounts:
Audi Magazine
Care Magazine
Century 21 Magazine
Toyota
Umicore

TBWA Brussels
Kroonlaan 165 Avenue de la Couronne, 1050 Brussels, Belgium
Tel.: (32) 2 679 7500
Fax: (32) 2 679 7510
E-Mail: kris.govaerts@tbwa.be
Web Site: www.tbwagroup.be

Employees: 150

Agency Specializes In: Advertising

Kris Govaerts *(CEO)*
Jan Macken *(Exec Dir-Creative)*
Jeroen Bostoen *(Creative Dir)*
Karen Smessaert *(Client Svcs Dir)*
Menno Buyl *(Dir-Art)*
Gert Pauwels *(Dir-Creative-Online & Brand Activation)*
Geert Verdonck *(Dir-Creative)*
Wilfrid Morin *(Copywriter)*
Nicolas De Bauw *(Client Svc Dir)*

Accounts:
Alken-Maes Campaign: "Adopt A Keg"
Alpro
BIVV Campaign: "A Friendly Crash"
Bpost Campaign: "Live Webshop"
Bru
Brussels Airlines
Henkel
Het Nieuwsblad
Instan Net
KBC Bank Campaign: "Today's Youth For Yesterday's Youth"
Knack
Maes
Marcassou
McDonald's
MINI Belux Campaign: "Fan the flame"
Natural Gas
Nissan
Nivea
Olvarit Campaign: "Baby Fitness"
Pedigree
PepsiCo Campaign: "Like Machine", Pepsi
PlayStation Benelux
PlayStation Playstation GT5 Game
Telenet Campaign: "Hymn", Campaign: "Large football jerseys"
Van Marcke
Vitelma

TBWA Group
Kroonlaan Ave de la Couronne 165, 1050 Brussels, Belgium
Tel.: (32) 2 679 7500
Fax: (32) 2 679 7510
E-Mail: koert.impens@tbwagroup.be
Web Site: www.tbwagroup.be/

Employees: 200

Agency Specializes In: Advertising

Jan Macken *(Exec Dir-Creative-TBWA BELGIUM)*
Gert Pauwels *(Creative Dir-Online & Brand Activation)*
Geert Feytons *(Dir-Art-TBWA Brussels)*
Jochen De Greef *(Client Svc Dir)*

Accounts:
Flemish League against Cancer Campaign: "Sticking Their Tongues Out at Cancer", TV, Website
Hansaplast
Inclusie Invest
KBC Campaign: "Gap In The Market"
Lotto
McDonald's
Nissan
Pearle
PlayStation
UNICEF

TEQUILA Agency.com
Rue Haute-Hoogstraat 139, 1000 Brussels, Belgium
Tel.: (32) 2 523 19 11
Fax: (32) 2 523 83 11
E-Mail: info.website@tequila.be

Employees: 200

Agency Specializes In: Direct Response Marketing

Luc Perdieus *(Mng Dir)*
Peter Loiseaux *(Dir-Creative)*
Emilie Demoor *(Acct Mgr)*

BOSNIA

LUNA TBWA Sarajevo
Fra Andjela Zvizdovica 1, 71000 Sarajevo, Bosnia & Herzegovina
Tel.: (387) 33 295 158
Fax: (387) 33 295 158
E-Mail: luna@lunatbwa.ba
Web Site: www.lunatbwa.ba

Employees: 2

Mair Oruc *(Mng Partner)*
Branko Vekic *(Exec Dir-Creative)*
Ramona Ulemak *(Acct Mgr)*
Dejan Balaban *(Mgr-PR)*

Accounts:
GlaxoSmithKline
Henkel
Mars
Microsoft

BULGARIA

TBWA Sofia
44 Buzludja Street, Sofia, 1463 Bulgaria
Tel.: (359) 2 9530050
Fax: (359) 2 9530113
Web Site: www.tbwa.com

Year Founded: 1995

Venelin Sainov *(Dir-Creative)*
Georgi Tsekov *(Dir-S/s)*

CZECH REPUBLIC

TBWA Praha
Frantiska Krizka 1/362, 170 00 Prague, 7 Czech Republic
Tel.: (420) 220 412 501
Fax: (420) 220 412 502
Web Site: www.tbwa.cz

Employees: 40

Agency Specializes In: Advertising

Radek Drad *(Mng Dir-TBWA Praha)*
Petr Bucha *(Dir-Creative)*

Accounts:
Absolut
Adidas

Amnesty
Apple
BDF
Bellinda
CMSS
Dove
Heineken
Henkel
Kitekat
Michelin
Nivea
Pedigree
Syoss
Tchibo
Twix
Visa

DENMARK

TBWA Copenhagen

Bredgade 6, 3.sal, 1123 Copenhagen, K Denmark
Tel.: (45) 39 27 88 99
Fax: (45) 39 27 03 99
E-Mail: info@tbwa.dk
Web Site: www.tbwa.dk

Employees: 30

Agency Specializes In: Advertising, Advertising Specialties, Communications, Graphic Design, International, Logo & Package Design, Mobile Marketing, Print, Social Media

Tobias Lykke Aggergaard *(Exec Dir-Creative)*
Jeppe Kuld *(Art Dir)*
Tobias Lovschall-Wedel *(Copywriter)*
Mikkel Moller *(Sr Creative)*

Accounts:
Adidas
Alis
Apple
BMW
Bornholm Brewery Campaign: "Label Design", Organic Juice
Findus
Kelda
Metro International Campaign: "Accidentally On Purpose"
Nissan
Pedigree
PlayStation
Roche Diagnostics
Singapore Airlines
Twix
WWF

TBWA Interactive

Bredgade 6 3 sal, 1260 Copenhagen, Denmark
Tel.: (45) 39 27 88 99
Fax: (45) 39 27 09 99
E-Mail: info@tbwa.dk
Web Site: www.tbwa.dk

Agency Specializes In: Internet/Web Design

Claes Rasmussen *(CEO)*

Accounts:
Adidas
Apple
Findus
Kelda
Nissan
Novo
Pedigree
Roche Diagnostics
Singapore Airlines
Wexer

ESTONIA

TBWA Estonia

Pamu mnt 139a, 11317 Tallinn, Estonia
Tel.: (372) 665 95 50
Fax: (372) 665 95 51
E-Mail: mail@tbwa.ee
Web Site: www.tbwa.ee

Employees: 12

Erko Karing *(Mng Dir-TBWA & Guvatrak)*
Urmas Reinmaa *(Copywriter)*

Accounts:
Directo
Tallink
The Tallinn Children's Hospital Foundation
Tuborg

FINLAND

TBWA PHS

Fredrikinkatu 42, 0010 Helsinki, Finland
Tel.: (358) 9 17 17 11
Fax: (358) 9 17 18 11
E-Mail: info@tbwa.fi
Web Site: www.tbwa.fi

Employees: 227

Petteri Kilpinen *(CEO-TBWA & Helsinki Oy)*
Vesa Tujunen *(Exec Dir-Creative)*
Sarita Nieminen *(Acct Dir)*
Jaana Haapala *(Dir-Strategic)*
Eino Korkala *(Dir-Art)*
Juuso Kalliala *(Copywriter)*
Heidi Taina *(Copywriter)*
Tomi Winberg *(Copywriter)*

Accounts:
16400 Hannibal, Scream
Adidas Campaign: "Adidas Window Shopping", Neo
Atria Finland Ltd Campaign: "Atria Dinner"
Brandarit
Canal+
CFP
Instru Optiikka
Instrumentarium "Optician: Turbine"
Katsomo
MTV Campaign: "Lion Hunters", Campaign: "MTV3 Max: Man's Road"
Nissan Nordic Europe Campaign: "Rumble"
Optician Instrumentarium
Otavamedia
Panda
Paulig Muki
Pfizer Viagra
Posti
Radio Nova Campaign: "Rehearsals"
Sponda
Veikkaus Football Betting, Keno

FRANCE

/Auditoire

9 rue du Helder, 75310 Paris, Cedex France
Tel.: (33) 1 56 03 57 03
Fax: (33) 1 56 03 57 00
E-Mail: ccourtin@auditoire.fr
Web Site: www.auditoire.com

Employees: 13

Agency Specializes In: Event Planning & Marketing

Cyril Giorgini *(CEO)*
Philippe Castanet *(Mng Partner & Gen Coord-World Innovation Summit for Education)*
Herve Pommier *(CFO)*
Stephanie Berger *(Acct Dir)*
Valerie Bouyssou *(Dir-Projects)*
Amaury Germe *(Dir-Dev)*
Fabienne Guillet *(Mgr-Pur & Ops)*
Natalie Lundgren *(Mgr-Strategic Partnerships-WISE)*

Accounts:
Alstom
Areva
AstraZeneca
Mazars
Nissan
Orange
Pfizer
Renault
SNCF

BDDP & Fils

146 rue du Faubourg Poissonniere, 75010 Paris, France
Tel.: (33) 1 53 21 28 00
Fax: (33) 1 53 21 28 80
E-Mail: welcome@bddpetfils.fr
Web Site: www.bddpetfils.fr

Employees: 70

Laurence Petolat-Vivares *(CEO)*
Francois Blachere *(COO)*
Marco De La Fuente *(VP)*
Nadege Adatte *(Sr Dir-Art)*
Jules Le Barazer *(Art Dir)*
Christian Baujard *(Dir-Strategic Plng)*
Perrine Collin *(Dir-Comm)*
Aurore De Sousa *(Dir-Artistic)*
Olivier Moine *(Dir-Creative)*
Fabien Nunez *(Dir-Artistic)*

Accounts:
Abbe Pierre
Air Liberte
Arte Tv
Aviva
BMW
Credit Foncier
DNF
Eclat Du Cadre Framing Company
Foundation Abbe Pierre Help The Homeless
French Anti Tobacco Association
Harlequin Editions Mira Books
Kleber
L'Assurance Maladie
Les Echos Campaign: "The Decision Maker"
Maisons du Monde
Marks & Spencer
Michelin
Microsoft
Mobitel
Office National Marocain Du Tourisme Campaign: "The Snow"
Samsung
Solidarites International Campaign: "Water & Ink", Water Talk
Thomas Cook
Viagara

Being

50/54 rue du Silly, 92513 Boulogne-Billancourt, France
Tel.: (33) 1 49 09 72 23
E-Mail: antoine.lesec@tbwa-consultingdesign.com
Web Site: www.being.fr

Employees: 200

Agency Specializes In: Advertising

Thierry Buriez *(Dir-Creative)*
Nicolas Couagnon *(Dir-Creative)*
Remy Fournigault *(Dir-Art)*
Agathe Lunel *(Dir-Art)*

Antoine Montes *(Dir-Art)*
Elsa Yvinec *(Acct Mgr)*
Jeremy Jamet *(Copywriter)*
Arnaud Lecarpentier *(Copywriter)*
Joris Vigouroux *(Copywriter)*

Accounts:
Absolut Vodka
Asta Philpot Foundation Campaign: "Beyond Appearances - Diversity Song"
Bergere de France The Knitted Coupon
Come4 Campaign: "The Lover"
Deezer Campaign: "Now nothing will stop the music", Campaign: "The Hand"
Hansaplast Footcare
L'Opinion Newspaper
Nissan Creative
Qatar Tourism Authority
Run For AJD
Schneider Electric Campaign: "A Very Hot Afternoon"

E-Graphics
162-164 rue de Billancourt, BP 411, 92103 Boulogne-Billancourt, France
Tel.: (33) 1 49 09 25 07
Fax: (33) 1 49 09 27 06
E-Mail: info@e-graphics.fr
Web Site: www.e-graphics.fr

Agency Specializes In: Advertising, Print, Production (Print)

Jean-Christophe Aussel *(Pres & CEO)*
Eric Lecam *(Deputy Dir Gen)*
Pascal Mariani *(CEO-France)*
Catherine Caussade *(Dir-Admin & Fin)*
Jean-Christophe Ghirardi *(Mgr-IT)*

EG Plus Worldwide
(Formerly E-Graphics)
50/54 rue de Silly, 92100 Boulogne-Billancourt, France
Tel.: (33) 1 49 09 25 25
Fax: (33) 1 49 09 27 06
E-Mail: paris@egplusww.com
Web Site: egplusww.com/

Employees: 200

Agency Specializes In: Print

Jean-Christophe Aussel *(Pres & CEO)*
Frederic Elkoubi *(Head-Digital)*
Stanislas Lenoir *(Acct Mgr)*
Stephane Maissa *(Mgr-Digital Tech & Multimedia)*

Accounts:
McDonald's
Nissan

/EXCEL
2-6 Boulevard Poissonniere, 75009 Paris, France
Tel.: (33) 1 56 02 35 60
Fax: (33) 1 56 02 35 99
E-Mail: courrier@excel.fr
Web Site: www.excel.fr

Agency Specializes In: Event Planning & Marketing

Francois Couignoux *(VP)*
Cecile Coldefy-Lefort *(Acct Dir-Digital)*
Olivier Ducasse *(Dir-Comml)*
Lyoko Miyoshi *(Assoc Dir)*
Nathalie Jacquin *(Sr Acct Mgr)*
Lucile Malnoury *(Acct Mgr)*
Lydia Jasinski *(Mgr-Sls Admin)*

Accounts:
APF
Caritas France
Efrei
Eutelsat
Handicap International
Insa
Lacub
Lancome
ONA
Supelec

Qualicontact
Espace Clichy 38 av Mozart, 92110 Clichy, France
Tel.: (33) 1 41 40 40 00
Fax: (33) 1 41 40 40 29
E-Mail: info@qualicontact.com
Web Site: www.qualicontact.com

Employees: 80

Agency Specializes In: Telemarketing

Rino Vaccaro *(Pres)*
Amandine Ponssard *(Acct Dir)*
Nathalie Lefrancois *(Mgr-Production)*

Accounts:
Medicine Monde

TBWA/Compact
239 route de Saint-Simon, Immeuble Sirius C BP 1248, 31047 Toulouse, Cedex 1 France
Tel.: (33) 5 61 19 02 02
Fax: (33) 5 61 190 200
E-Mail: olivier.odoul@alsetcachou.com
Web Site: www.tbwa-compact.com

Employees: 50

Agency Specializes In: Advertising

Fabienne Cros-Rouquet *(Gen Dir)*
Isabelle de Colonges *(Gen Dir)*
Claire De Tinguy *(Grp Dir-Strategy)*
Patrice Moraud *(Dir-Creative)*
Cecile Pitton *(Dir-Artistic)*
Serge Sentenac *(Dir-Creative)*

TBWA Corporate
50-54 rue de Silly, 92100 Boulogne-Billancourt, France
Tel.: (33) 1 49 09 25 25
Fax: (33) 1 49 09 26 26
E-Mail: newbusiness@tbwa-corporate.com
Web Site: www.tbwa-corporate.com

Employees: 150

Agency Specializes In: Corporate Identity

Pierre-Andre Cuny *(Dir-Art & Creative)*
Jean-Charles Davin *(Dir-Creative)*
Julien Delarasse *(Dir-Artistic)*

Accounts:
Altran
ArcelorMittal
SNCS

TBWA Europe
50/54 rue de Silly, BP 411, 92100 Boulogne-Billancourt, France
Tel.: (33) 1 49 09 80 00
Fax: (33) 1 49 09 81 57

Cesar Croze *(Deputy Mng Dir)*
Cecile Moreau *(Deputy Mng Dir)*
Jean-Francois Reiser *(Mng Dir-Intl)*
Nick Baum *(VP-Europe)*
Luc Bourgery *(Gen Mgr-TBWA/PARIS)*
Soraya Cottin *(Acct Dir)*
Lara De Nattes *(Acct Dir)*
Menka Harjani *(Acct Dir-Intl)*
Shirley Hunter *(Acct Dir-Intl)*
Aurelie Delorme *(Dir-Sls)*
Quiterie Barreau *(Acct Mgr)*

TBWA/G1
162-164 rue de Billancourt, 92100 Boulogne-Billancourt, France
Tel.: (33) 1 49 09 70 10
Fax: (33) 1 49 09 81 87
Web Site: www.tbwa-france.com

Ewan Veitch *(Pres)*
Maxime Boiron *(Pres-France)*
Celina Eude *(Acct Dir)*
Joerg Bruns *(Dir-Creative)*
Marianne Fonferrier *(Dir-Creative)*
Kiminori Suzuki *(Dir-Art)*
Ela Tengirsek *(Copywriter)*
Karen Lebel *(Sr Accountant-TBWA Paris)*

Accounts:
Nissan West Europe SAS Campaign: "Brothers", Campaign: "Built to Thrill", Campaign: "Control", Campaign: "Emerg-E", Campaign: "Feel the Surge", Campaign: "Ghost Train", Campaign: "Go Get It", Campaign: "Hijack", Campaign: "Juke Stay Awake", Campaign: "Nissan Juke", Campaign: "Pre-Launch", Campaign: "Since now", Campaign: "Sporty", Campaign: "Teaser", Campaign: "The Match", Campaign: "Urban Thrill Rides", Digital, Google Send-to-Car, Human Fly, Juke, Murano, Nissan Leaf, Nissan Micra, Nissan Pulsar, Outdoor, Print, Qashqai+2, Self-Healing iPad, X-Trail

TBWA Paris
162-164 rue de Billancourt, BP 411, 92103 Boulogne-Billancourt, France
Tel.: (33) 1 49 09 70 10
Fax: (33) 1 48 25 04 19
E-Mail: vincent.garel@tbwa-paris.com
Web Site: www.tbwa-france.com

Employees: 400

Guillaume Pannaud *(Pres)*
Hugues Cholez *(Creative Dir)*
Jean-Marie Prenaud *(Pres-Global Clients)*
Anne Vincent *(VP)*
Julien Etheredge *(Head-Acct-Intl)*
Antoine Gauquelin *(Editor & Designer)*
Faustin Claverie *(Exec Dir-Creative)*
Marc Fraissinet *(Exec Dir)*
Anne-Laure Brunner *(Grp Acct Dir)*
Ingrid Varetz *(Art Dir)*
Damien Blanquart *(Art Dir)*
Matthieu Darrasse *(Art Dir)*
Chloe Doisneau *(Acct Dir-McDonald's Happy Meal Europe, Global, US & AMPEA)*
Cedric Moutaud *(Art Dir)*
Fabien Duval *(Dir-Art & Copywriter)*
Benoit Leroux *(Dir-Creative & Copywriter)*
Jean-Francois Goize *(Dir-Creative)*
Phillipe Taroux *(Dir-Art & Creative)*
Teddy Notari *(Brand Mgr)*
Morgane Lejeau *(Mgr-Adv)*
Barbara Chevalier *(Art Buyer)*
Romain Duler *(Copywriter)*
Mehdi Hamzaoui *(Copywriter)*
Stephane Kaczorowski *(Copywriter)*
Jean-Denis Pallain *(Copywriter)*

Accounts:
Action against Hunger Campaign: "#ProtectAidWorkers", Campaign: "One Bullet"
Action Contre La Faim Campaign: "Justice for Muttur", Campaign: "One Bullet"
AIDES Campaign: "Guns", Campaign: "Woody"
Amnesty International France Campaign: "Independence", Campaign: "Pens", Campaign: "The arms trade kills 500,000 civilians a year.

Help us regulate it", Campaign: "We will never let money hide reality from us.", Death Penalty Candles
New-Cine-ma difference
Decompressing
Fontyou
Hansaplast Ear Plugs
Infiniti FX Cross-Over, Outdoor, Press
L'Opinion Newspaper
Mapa Spontex
Martell House
McCain Campaign: "Just Au Four"
McDonald's Billboard, Campaign: "Baby", Campaign: "Dentist", Campaign: "Entretien", Campaign: "Error in your favor", Campaign: "Killer", Campaign: "McFarmer vs McTimber", Campaign: "Pictogram", Campaign: "Yoga", Print, Spicy Chicken Sandwich
Michelin North America, Inc. Campaign: "24 Hours: A Matter of Seconds", Campaign: "France-Great Britain", Campaign: "Italy-Germany", Campaign: "USA-Japan", CrossClimate
Nissan Motor Corp 4x4, Campaign: "Nissan Wedding", Cube, Murano, Note car, Qashqai+2, Symmetry
Novotel
OPI
Pedigree Treats
Pernod Ricard Absolut, Purity
Service Civique
SNCF Campaign: "Incivility - Cigarette", Campaign: "Mission Paris Deauville", Campaign: "Take a look at Brussels", Campaign: "The Most serious game ever"
Sony PlayStation Campaign: "Ski Run Map", Campaign: "Touch Both Sides", Grand Tourismo 4, PlayStation 2, Playstation Vita
Spontex Campaign: "Easy Max"
New-U stores
UGC Campaign: "More Movies More Emotions"
New-voyages-sncf.com Campaign: "The banner contest for psychopaths", Campaign: "The easy way"

Textuel La Mine

146 rue du Fauburg Poissonniere, 75010 Paris, France
Tel.: (33) 1 53 15 75 75
Fax: (33) 1 53 15 75 70
E-Mail: ksentenac@textuel.fr
Web Site: www.lamine.com/

Employees: 25

Agency Specializes In: Digital/Interactive, Electronic Media, Internet/Web Design

Flora Maurice *(CFO)*
Laurence Vignon *(VP)*
Stanislas Pajot *(Gen Mgr)*
Francois Vogel *(Gen Mgr)*
Karine Sentenac *(Deputy Gen Mgr-Strategy & Dev)*

Accounts:
Champion.fr
Infolignes
Leroy Merlin
Nivea
Unilever

GERMANY

Heimat Werbeagentur GmbH

Segitzdamm 2, 10969 Berlin, Germany
Tel.: (49) 3061652
Web Site: www.heimat-berlin.com

Agency Specializes In: Advertising

Matthias Storath *(Mng Dir & Exec Dir-Creative)*
Guido Heffels *(Mng Dir)*
Christina Muller *(Acct Dir)*
Maik Richter *(Acct Dir)*
Alexander Strauss *(Creative Dir)*
Albert Chan *(Dir-Art)*
Stefano de Lucia *(Dir-Art)*
Ove Gley *(Dir-Creative)*
Kai Heuser *(Dir-Creative)*

Accounts:
Adidas AG Campaign: "The biggest Champions League Final of all time", The Face of the Marathon
A.T.U Autoteile Unger
CNN
The Coca-Cola Company
Fonic Campaign: "The Man Who always Tells the Truth"
Hornbach Baumarkt AG Campaign: "Act against Ugliness", Campaign: "Festival", Campaign: "Gothic Girl", Campaign: "Let there be Spring.", Campaign: "Made Out Of Tanks", Campaign: "No one feels it like you do", Campaign: "Symphony", Campaign: "The Infinite House"
MINI Worldwide
Otto Campaign: "Strange Encounters"
Samsung Samsung S4, Staring Contest
New-Siemens Home Appliances
Swisscom Campaign: "Hanging Up", Campaign: "Nico", Campaign: "The S5 Pulse Challenge", Campaign: "Tina"
Turner Broadcasting System, Inc. CNN, Campaign: "The CNN Ecosphere"
Watchever The Returned Campaign: "Obituaries"

TBWA Germany, Berlin

Rosenstrasse 16-17, 10178 Berlin, Germany
Tel.: (49) 30 443 2930
Fax: (49) 30 443 293399
E-Mail: roberta.bantel@tbwa.de
Web Site: www.tbwa.de

Employees: 60

Ulrich Proeschel *(VP-Bus Dev-Europe)*

Accounts:
Absolute Vodka Campaign: "MADE Captured", Campaign: "Scratch'n Cut"
Adidas Campaign: "Tomorrow starts now"
Apple Ipod
Kraft Tassimo Hot Beverage Maker; 2009
McDonald's Coffee House, Fast Food, McCafe
Pernod Ricard Deutschland Art Exhibition, Campaign: "Made ScratchN Cut", Campaign: "Tyra Banksy"
Sony Playstation
Volkswagen Campaign: "The Beetle Test-O-Meter"

TBWA/Germany

Bernhard Nocht Ste 113, D-20359 Hamburg, Germany
Tel.: (49) 40 36 90 70
Fax: (49) 40 36 90 71 11
Web Site: www.tbwa.de

Employees: 100

Peter Kopecky *(CFO)*
Alexander Milstein *(COO-TBWA Germany & Mng Dir-TBWA Worldwide)*
Tobias Schiwek *(Mng Dir-Digital)*
Ulrich Proeschel *(VP-Bus Dev-Europe)*
Winfried Bockius *(Dir-Fin-Germany & Switzerland)*
Markus Neckar *(Dir-Creative)*
Astrid Severin *(Mgr-HR)*
Beatrix Bruckmann *(Client Svc Dir)*
Gilles Frapaise *(Client Svc Dir)*

Accounts:
Deutscher Diabetiker Bund
Merck Femibion, Flexagil, Nasivin; 2008

TBWA Germany

Hanauer Landstrasse 182b, 60314 Frankfurt, Germany
Tel.: (49) 69 15 21 0
Fax: (49) 69 15 21 579
Web Site: www.tbwa.de

Ulrich Proeschel *(VP-Bus Dev)*
Sandra Birkemeyer *(Sr Dir-Art)*
Astrid Severin *(Mgr-HR)*
Beatrix Bruckmann *(Client Svc Dir)*
Kristina Debiel *(Client Svc Dir)*

TBWA Germany

Schanzenstrasse 54a, 40549 Dusseldorf, Germany
Tel.: (49) 211 864 35 0
Fax: (49) 211 864 35 117
E-Mail: rossita.markowitz@tbwa.de
Web Site: www.tbwa.de

Employees: 160

Agency Specializes In: Advertising

Peter Kopecky *(CFO)*
Jorg Herzog *(Exec Dir-Creative)*
Sandra Birkemeyer *(Sr Dir-Art)*
Winfried Bockius *(Dir-Fin-Germany & Switzerland)*
Mitra Ketabi *(Dir-Art)*
Frank Olma *(Dir-Creative)*
Nina Wolke *(Dir-Art)*
Astrid Severin *(Mgr-HR)*
Bastian Goldschmidt *(Planner-Strategic)*
Matthias Hardt *(Copywriter)*
Kristina Debiel *(Client Svc Dir)*
Gilles Frapaise *(Client Svc Dir)*

Accounts:
Henkel AG & Co. KGaA Campaign: "Gliss Strong Hair - SCISSOR", Campaign: "Love Letter To Mum", Campaign: "Re-new Effect", Campaign: "Sidolin Streak Free", Perwoll
Intersnack Knabber-Gebaeck GmbH & Co.KG Campaign: "Backpack", Campaign: "Flying Bags"
Maruyasu Campaign: "Big Sushi Rolls"
Men Perfect Campaign: "Old Men Kurt"
Nissan Motor Corp. Campaign: "Nissan Micra Balcony", Campaign: "Thunderstorm", Nissan Micra, Qashqai, Tiida
Schwarzkopf Campaign: "Men Perfect", Campaign: "Tree"
Syoss Campaign: "White Flower"
Teekanne GmbH "Tea Bubbles"

HUNGARY

TBWA Budapest

Szuret utca 15, H-1118 Budapest, Hungary
Tel.: (36) 1 279 2800
Fax: (36) 1 279 2801
E-Mail: office@tbwa.hu
Web Site: www.tbwa.hu

E-Mail for Key Personnel:
Production Mgr.: krisztina.varga@tbwa.hu

Employees: 30

Doris Danner *(Mng Dir)*
Henrietta Deri *(Acct Dir & Planner)*
Tamasi Brigitta *(Dir-Fin)*
Torday Gabor *(Dir-Creative)*

Accounts:
Accor Hotels
Adidas
Henkel
Mars
Michelin
NIssan

Nivea
Ringier
Tchibo
Tetrapak
Tigaz

IRELAND

Cawley Nea TBWA Advertising
41A Blackberry Lane, Rathmines, Dublin, 6 Ireland
Tel.: (353) 1 496 6920
Fax: (353) 1 496 6923
E-Mail: info@cawleynea-tbwa.ie
Web Site: www.cawleynea-tbwa.ie

Employees: 50

Agency Specializes In: Advertising

Chris Cawley *(Chm)*
Deirdre Waldron *(Mng Dir)*
Paula Kelly *(Grp Acct Dir)*
Chelsey O'Connor *(Art Dir)*
Martin Cowman *(Dir-Creative)*
Johan Sand *(Dir-Technical)*
Niall Staines *(Dir-Digital Art)*
Cian Tormey *(Dir-Art)*
Enda Mac Nally *(Copywriter)*

Accounts:
Adidas
Bank of Ireland Mortgages
Barnardos
BDF Beiersdorf
BMW Ireland
C&C Ireland
Calyx
Dulux
Electric Ireland Campaign: "Tweet Cafe"
ESB
Goodbody
HP
Irish Pride
The Irish Times Campaign: "The Story of Why"
Jameson Ireland
Mars North America
McDonald's Campaign: "Eurosaver Change", The Day Before Payday
Nivea
O'Briens
Playstation
PostTS
Warner Music Ireland

ITALY

B Fluid
(Formerly TEQUILA Italia)
Via Leto Pomponia 3/5, 20146 Milan, Italy
Tel.: (39) 02 8053 219
Fax: (39) 02 8698 4041
E-Mail: contatto.tequila@tequila-it.com
Web Site: www.b-fluid.it

Employees: 25

Agency Specializes In: Direct Response Marketing

Marco Nieri *(Mng Partner)*
Massimo Casini *(Dir-Digital Bus Unit)*
Massimo Gnocchi *(Dir-Creative)*
Marco Molla *(Dir-Art)*
Domenico Servello *(Dir-Art)*
Monica Schipani *(Acct Mgr)*
Francesca Mazzucchelli *(Acct Exec)*

Accounts:
Labatt USA LLC
Costa Crociere
San Carlo
Unicredit Group
Unieuro

TBWA Italia
Via Leto Pomponio 3-5, 20146 Milan, Italy
Tel.: (39) 02 499 851
Fax: (39) 02 499 852 09
E-Mail: marco.fanfani@tbwa.it
Web Site: www.tbwa.it

Employees: 90

Nicola Lampugnani *(Exec Dir-Creative)*
Francesco Pedrazzini *(Sr Dir-Art)*
Giulia Gianfaldoni *(Acct Dir)*
Anna Di Cintio *(Dir-Art)*
Francesco Napoleone *(Dir-Creative-The Integer Group)*
Anna Palama *(Dir-Creative)*
Gina Ridenti *(Dir-Creative)*
Elisabetta Iulita *(Acct Exec)*

Accounts:
adidas AG
Apple Computer (UK) Ltd.
Art Director's Club
Bayer Campaign: "Hole Golf"
Eni Corporate Campaign: "Rethink Energy"
Glaxosmithkline Campaign: "One Year Without Smoking"
Google Campaign: "Design the Future of Your Brand With Youtube"
Henkel
Humanitas Campaign: "Smok-INK"
Industrial Strange Clubwear Campaign: "Market"
La Gazzetta dello Sport
L'Oreal S.A.
Mcdonalds Campaign: "Mcitaly Press Conference Invitation"
Medusa Film Spa Campaign: "Midnight in Paris Moleskine"
Nissan Campaign: "Boost 190", Campaign: "One Track Mind"
Rizzoli-Corriere della Sera Media Group S.p.A. (RCS Media Group)
Sieropositivo.it

TBWA Roma
Via Flaminia Vecchia 495, 00191 Rome, Italy
Tel.: (39) 06 332 268 1
Fax: (39) 06 332 226 836
Web Site: www.tbwa.it

Agency Specializes In: Advertising

Roberto Geremia *(CFO)*
Geo Ceccarelli *(Gen Mgr-Roma)*
Nicoletta Levi *(Gen Mgr)*
Matteo Desogus *(Art Dir & Graphic Designer)*
Marina Belli *(Dir-Strategic Plng)*
Fabrizio Caperna *(Dir-Creative)*
Anna Di Cintio *(Dir-Art)*
Fabrizia Marchi *(Dir-Client)*
Rossana Tocchi *(Dir-Creative)*
Silvia Capuzzi *(Mgr-PR-TBWA/Italia Grp)*
Matteo Consonni *(Client Svc Dir-New Bus)*

Accounts:
Verdeoro Campaign: "Lost World Cup"

LATVIA

TBWA Latvija
Brivibas Str 40-40A, LV-1050 Riga, Latvia
Tel.: (371) 750 5310
Fax: (371) 750 5311
E-Mail: office@tbwa.lv
Web Site: www.tbwa.lv

Employees: 2

Alda Staprans Mednis *(Owner)*
Oskars Laksevics *(Mng Dir)*
Inta Brunina *(Dir-Art)*
Pauls Kesteris *(Dir-Creative)*
Daina Cakste *(Sr Acct Mgr)*

NETHERLANDS

ARA Groep
Kratonkade 3, 3024 ES Rotterdam, Netherlands
Mailing Address:
Postbus 6217, 3002 AE Rotterdam, Netherlands
Tel.: (31) 10 405 7277
Fax: (31) 10 405 7378
E-Mail: info@ara.nl
Web Site: www.ara.nl

Employees: 100
Year Founded: 1975

Agency Specializes In: Consumer Marketing, Digital/Interactive, Direct Response Marketing, Recruitment

Paul Kroef *(Mng Dir)*
Andy Mosmans *(CMO)*
Jaap Toorenaar *(Dir-Creative)*
Leo Berends *(Mgr-Mktg Svcs)*
Paul Cruse *(Mgr)*

Accounts:
Dr. Vanderhoog
Fair Trade
Hetergak Golf Bananen
Koninklijke Luchtmacht
MN Services
NRG
Quick, Baker & McKenzie
RVD
Super Boer
TPG Post
Zwitserleven

Bovil DDB
Dillenburgstraat 5E, 5652 AM Eindhoven, Netherlands
Tel.: (31) 40 252 6499
Fax: (31) 40 255 0671
E-Mail: info@bovilddb.com
Web Site: www.bovil.nl/en

E-Mail for Key Personnel:
Public Relations: michiel.scheerin@bovilddb.com

Employees: 24

Agency Specializes In: Advertising

Shaun Northrop *(Partner & Dir-Creative)*
Michiel Scheeren *(Mng Dir)*
Debbie Van Dorst *(Acct Dir)*
Sandra Van de Velde *(Sr Acct Mgr)*
Erik Luyk *(Acct Mgr)*
Noor Van Hout *(Office Mgr)*
Claudia Vermeulen *(Acct Mgr)*
Cristina Torrijos Sanchez *(Mgr-Ops)*

Accounts:
Aprico
Brunswick
Entre Duex
Fresh Park Venlo
Phillips
Zon Fruit & Vegetables

Brain Box
Mozartlaan 27c, 1217 CM Hilversum, Netherlands
Tel.: (31) 35 628 1870
Fax: (31) 35 6285047
E-Mail: info@brain-box.nl
Web Site: www.brain-box.nl

Employees: 8

Agency Specializes In: Communications

Max Kerremans *(Mng Dir)*
Elisabeth Aeilkema *(Office Mgr)*
Johan Sponselee *(Coord)*

Downtown Action Marketing

General Vetter Straat 82, 1059 BW Amsterdam, Netherlands
Tel.: (31) 20 589 8787
Fax: (31) 20 589 8788
E-Mail: simon.neefjes@tbwa.nl
Web Site: www.tbwa.nl

Employees: 200

Agency Specializes In: Event Planning & Marketing

Helene Hoogeboom *(Mng Dir)*

HFMBOVACO

(Formerly Bovaco)
Lloydkwartier Kratonkade 3, 3024 Rotterdam, Netherlands
Tel.: (31) 010 405 72 20
Fax: (31) 70 363 6136
E-Mail: info@hfm-bovaco.nl
Web Site: www.hfmbovaco.nl

Employees: 45
Year Founded: 1988

Agency Specializes In: Advertising

Paul Kroef *(Mng Dir)*
Rene Wijers *(Dir-Art)*
Wietze Bosma *(Mgr-Media)*
Rob De Groot *(Mgr-Overhead)*
Rinske Wilod Versprille *(Mgr-Ops)*
Frank Van Venrooij *(Copywriter)*

HVR

Parkstraat 83, 2514 JG Hague, Netherlands
Tel.: (31) 70 346 3616
Fax: (31) 10 427 4137
E-Mail: info@hvrgroup.nl
Web Site: www.hvrgroup.nl

Employees: 11

Agency Specializes In: Public Relations

Patrick Dekkers *(Mng Partner)*
Henk Buis *(Partner)*
Peter Knoers *(Sr Partner)*

TBWA Company Group

GENERAAL VETTERSTRAAT 82, 003120 BW Amsterdam, Netherlands
Tel.: (31) 20 571 5300
Fax: (31) 20 571 5600
E-Mail: simon.neefjes@tbwa.nl
Web Site: www.tbwa.nl

Employees: 240

Simon Neefjes *(CEO)*
Patritia Pahladsingh *(Mng Partner)*
Gert Jan Timmer *(Mng Partner)*
Rik Ledder *(Mng Dir)*
Yacco Vijn *(Mng Dir-Creative)*
Valerie Dekeuwer *(Client Svcs Dir)*
Roos Munten Ronner *(Acct Dir)*
Esther Brouwer *(Dir-Client Svc-Albert Heijn)*
Brenda Rangel *(Sr Acct Mgr)*
Eline Croes *(Acct Mgr)*
Christian Van Der Ven *(Acct Mgr)*
Jeroen Konings *(Brand Mgr)*
Anne Van Der Meulen *(Acct Exec)*
Valerie De Groot *(Jr Project Mgr)*

Accounts:
Heineken
Holland Casino
Kayak.com Advertising, Creative
KPN
Nivea
Unox

TBWA Designers Company

Generaal Vetterstraat 82, 1059 BW Amsterdam, Netherlands
Tel.: (31) 20 571 5300
Fax: (31) 20 571 5600
E-Mail: simon.neefjes@tbwa.nl
Web Site: www.tbwa.nl

Employees: 300

Agency Specializes In: Logo & Package Design

Rik Ledder *(Mng Dir)*
Yacco Vijn *(Mng Dir-Creative)*
Valerie Dekeuwer *(Client Svcs Dir)*
Marianne Herweijer *(Client Svcs Dir)*
Danielle Jonk *(Acct Dir)*
Roos Munten Ronner *(Acct Dir)*
Maurice Van Susante *(Acct Dir)*
Esther Brouwer *(Dir-Client Svc-Albert Heijn)*
Klaas Knol *(Dir-Operational)*
Brenda Rangel *(Sr Acct Mgr)*
Marielle Scholten *(Sr Acct Mgr)*
Eline Croes *(Acct Mgr)*
Valerie De Groot *(Jr Project Mgr)*

Accounts:
Adidas
Alberthein
Heineken

TBWA Neboko

General Vetterstraat 82, 1059 BW Amsterdam, Netherlands
Tel.: (31) 20 571 5500
Fax: (31) 020 571 5501
E-Mail: info@neboko.nl
Web Site: www.tbwa.nl

Employees: 100

Simon Neefjes *(CEO)*
Matthijs Slot *(Partner & Creative Dir)*
Ernst Jan van Rossen *(Partner & Dir-Creative)*
Rik Ledder *(Mng Dir)*
Martijn Amendt *(Grp Acct Dir)*
Jasper Roks *(Art Dir)*
Rogier Verbeek *(Art Dir)*
Jojanneke Wenneker *(Acct Mgr)*
Floris Cornelissen *(Copywriter)*
Matthijs Schoo *(Copywriter)*
Rene Van Der Hoofd *(Copywriter)*

Accounts:
New-AXA Bike security
Delta Lloyd Campaign: "de Optimist"
Gamma Campaign: "Gardening"
Healthcity
Heineken Campaign: "Barman", Campaign: "The Switch", Social Networks
IDFA Campaign: "There is More to the Story"
KPN Campaign: "Multiscreen", Interactive Television
McDonald's Campaign: "Dutch Weeks", Merry Christmas
Pearle Opticians Campaign: "Captcha"
Poopy Cat Campaign: "Poopy Cat Dolls"
Unilever Campaign: "Cup-a-Soup Extra"

Thabasco

Hereweg 95, 9721-AA Groningen, Netherlands
Tel.: (31) 50 319 9566
Fax: (31) 50 314 5576
E-Mail: info@thabasco.nl
Web Site: www.thabasco.nl

Hein Scholma *(Partner & Dir-Creative)*

Accounts:
Adformatie
Arriva
Dagblad Van Het Noorden
Diaghilev
John Smith
Marketing Groningen
Nike
Nima
Salland
Stichting Oude Groninger Kerken

POLAND

Data Solutions

Ul Bastionowa 37, 61-663 Poznan, Poland
Tel.: (48) 61 6 250 250
Fax: (48) 61 6 250 251
E-Mail: kontakt@datasolutions.pl
Web Site: www.datasolutions.pl

Employees: 30

Agency Specializes In: Technical Advertising

Marek Kosakowski *(Mng Dir)*
Michat Laskowski *(Dir-IT Dev)*
Gabriela Siemieniuch *(Dir-Strategic Plng)*

Accounts:
Cafe Prima
Citroen
Ferrero
Imperial Tobacco
Kompania Piwowarska
Navo
Nestle
Nivea
Pampers
Samsung
Winiary
Yes
Zelmer

E-Graphics

Ul Rzymowskiego 34, 02-697 Warsaw, Poland
Tel.: (48) 22 457 05 80
Fax: (48) 22 457 05 81
E-Mail: warsaw@egplusww.com
Web Site: egplusww.com

Agency Specializes In: Print

Christian Lainer *(Sr VP-Europe)*
Pawel Piatek *(Jr Acct Exec)*
Magdalena Nowak-Vincent *(Client Svc Dir)*

TBWA Group Poland

ul Rzymowskiego 34, 2-697 Warsaw, Poland
Tel.: (48) 22 457 05 00
Fax: (48) 22 457 06 00
Web Site: www.tbwa.pl

Alena Suszycka *(Mng Dir)*
Agata Ziolo *(Acct Dir)*
Krzysztof Filipczyk *(Dir-Art)*
Arkadiusz Pawlik *(Dir-Creative)*
Martyna Wasowicz *(Acct Mgr)*
Ewelina Bryzek *(Mgr-HR)*
Anna Maciagowska *(Mgr-HR)*
Aleksandra Osko *(Mgr-Bus Dev)*

Hanna Broza *(Client Svc Dir)*
Marta Szufranowicz *(Jr Planner-Strategic)*

TBWA PR
ul Rzymowskiego 34, 02-697 Warsaw, Poland
Tel.: (48) 22 457 06 80
Fax: (48) 22 541 50 01
E-Mail: tbwa@tbwa.pl
Web Site: www.tbwa.pl/

Employees: 10

Joanna Andrzejewska *(Mng Dir)*
Arkadiusz Pawlik *(Dir-Creative)*
Agnieszka Billik *(Sr Acct Mgr)*
Aleksandra Osko *(Mgr-Bus Dev)*
Hanna Broza *(Client Svc Dir)*

Accounts:
Corex
Gellwe
Hartmann
Krakow City Park
Media Markt
Media Saturn Holding
Metsa Tissue
Saturn
Tiger
Warsaw Destination Alliance

TBWA Warszawa
Ul Rzymowskiego 34, 02-697 Warsaw, Poland
Tel.: (48) 22 457 05 00
Fax: (48) 22 457 0600
E-Mail: tbwa@tbwa.pl
Web Site: www.tbwa.pl

Employees: 200

Krzysztof Filipczyk *(Dir-Art)*
Arkadiusz Pawlik *(Dir-Creative)*
Agnieszka Billik *(Sr Acct Mgr)*
Martyna Wasowicz *(Acct Mgr)*
Ewelina Bryzek *(Mgr-HR)*
Hanna Broza *(Client Svc Dir)*
Marta Szufranowicz *(Jr Planner-Strategic)*

Accounts:
AXA
BE
Chappi
Cracow Municipality
Danone
Henkel AG & Co. KGaA
L'Oreal S.A.
Nissan West Europe SAS
Nivea
Samsung
Twix
Unimil
Wawa
Whiskas

PORTUGAL

TBWA Lisbon
Avenida de Liberdade 38 6th Fl, 1250-145 Lisbon, Portugal
Tel.: (351) 21 322 3200
Fax: (351) 21 322 3222
E-Mail: leandro.alvarez@tbwa.pt
Web Site: www.tbwa.pt

Employees: 40
Year Founded: 1979

Leandro Alvarez *(Pres & Chief Creative Officer)*
Filipa Soares *(Head-Strategic Plng)*
Julliano Bertoldi *(Sr Dir-Art)*
Joao Franca Martins *(Sr Dir-Art)*
Isaac Afonso *(Art Dir)*
Joana Heitor *(Acct Dir)*
Joao Ribeiro *(Dir-Creative)*
Joana Margalha *(Acct Mgr)*
Marina Zambujo *(Acct Supvr)*

Accounts:
IKEA Campaign: "Happiness", Campaign: "Occupy IKEA", Print
Master Foods
McDonald's Corporation
McDonald's Restaurants Limited Campaign: "Dog"
Pfizer
Publico Campaign: "Angry Outdoors", Campaign: "Ussr"
Sony
Victoria

ROMANIA

TBWA Merlin
Calea Rahavei nr 196A et 3 sect 5, Bucharest, 050908 Romania
Tel.: (40) 21 212 43 12
Fax: (40) 21 335 09 93
E-Mail: cristian.munteanu@tbwamerlin.ro
Web Site: www.comunicatedepresa.ro/tbwamerlin/

Employees: 36

Cristina Frusinoiu *(CFO)*
Laura Nedelschi *(Dir-Creative)*
Catalin Negreanu *(Dir-PR)*
Alexandru Stanescu *(Dir-SOA)*

Accounts:
McDonald's

SERBIA

LUNA TBWA Belgrade
Milovana Marinkoviaa 3, 11000 Belgrade, Serbia
Tel.: (381) 11 3980 343
Fax: (381) 11 3971 883
E-Mail: ivana.rudic@lunatbwa.rf
Web Site: www.tbwa.com

Employees: 25

Agency Specializes In: Advertising

Bojan Joksimovic *(Mng Dir)*
Milos Ilic *(Chief Creative Officer)*
Ana Nikolic *(Acct Dir)*
Natasa Savin *(Acct Dir)*
Jovana Zivkovic *(Jr Acct Mgr)*

Accounts:
VIFA

SLOVENIA

Luna TBWA
Koprska Ulica 106A, SL-10000 Ljubljana, Slovenia
Tel.: (386) 1 200 41 70
Fax: (386) 1 200 41 71
E-Mail: spela.oblak@luna.si
Web Site: www.luna.si

Employees: 30

Agency Specializes In: Advertising

Spela Oblak *(Mng Dir)*
Janez Rakuscek *(Exec Dir-Creative)*
Peter Razpotnik *(Reg Dir-Fin-TBWA Adriatic)*

Accounts:
Si.mobil Orto Mobile Phones

SPAIN

TBWA Espana
Alfonso XI 12, 28014 Madrid, Spain
Tel.: (34) 915 311 465
Fax: (34) 915 230 640

Felix Munoz *(Mng Dir)*
Guillermo Gines *(Gen Dir-Creative)*
Juan Sanchez *(Gen Dir-Creative)*
Penelope Martos *(Sr Dir-Art)*
Luis Munne *(Creative Dir & Copywriter)*
Eduardo Ustarroz *(Art Dir)*
Fran Lopez *(Dir-Creative)*
Alireza Mohammadian *(Dir-Client Acct Svcs-McDonalds)*
Vicente Rodriguez *(Dir-Creative)*
Daniel Ubach *(Dir-Art)*
Jesus Fuertes *(Planner)*
Elena Gonzalez *(Copywriter)*

Accounts:
Aliados Foundation Campaign: "Peep-Show"
New-ANICOLS Campaign: "Signslator"
Cambridge Institute
Cambridge University Press Campaign: "Sponges"
Chelino Fashion & Love Campaign: "The New Designer Nappy"
McDonald's Campaign: "A Call to Yourself", Campaign: "Wifi&Fries", Campaign: "Writer"
Mondo Sonoro
Road Safety
Sony Computer Entertainment America LLC Campaign: "I Like To Play", Campaign: "INFAMOUS", Campaign: "Injection", Campaign: "Mouse and cheese", PSP, Sony Playstation
Vichy Campaign: "Bald", Campaign: "Together Forever 3"

TBWA Espana
Paseo de Gracia 56 2nd Floor, 8007 Barcelona, Spain
Tel.: (34) 93 272 3636
Fax: (34) 93 272 3600
Web Site: www.tbwa.es

E-Mail for Key Personnel:
Creative Dir.: jteixido@tbwa-europe.com

Employees: 25

Agency Specializes In: Advertising, Consumer Marketing, Food Service, New Technologies

Ramon Sala *(Exec Dir-Creative)*
Roger Cano *(Creative Dir)*
Ferran Mestre *(Art Dir)*
Joan Vidal *(Copywriter & Dir-Creative)*
Marc Navarro *(Dir-Art)*
Enrique De Los Arcos *(Copywriter)*
Carlos Navarro *(Copywriter)*

Accounts:
Absolut Vodka
Adidas Campaign: "All In or Nothing", Campaign: "The Past Doesn't Count"
Alia2 Campaign: "Superheroes Do Not Exist"
Apple Inc.
Association For The Right To Die With Dignity Campaign: "The worst end"
Caixa Catalunya
Canon
Chupa Chups Campaign: "Gum"
Diset
ESPANA
Henkel
L'Oreal
McDonald's A call to yourself, Campaign: "Glasses"
Mondo Sonoro Campaign: "Music comes alive in Mondo Sonoro"
Nissan

Nivea
Sony Campaign: "I like to play", PSP, Playstation
Spontex
Vichy Catalan Campaign: "The most unexpected launch. Vichy Catalan Now in a Can."
Whiskas

SWEDEN

TBWA Stockholm

Wallimgatam 2, 111 60 Stockholm, Sweden
Tel.: (46) 8 41 00 40 00
Fax: (46) 8 41 00 40 01

Employees: 35

Carl Dalin *(Co-Founder, Partner & Dir-Art)*
Per Olholt *(Sr Acct Dir)*
Cecilia Bauman *(Acct Dir)*
Sanna Lengholm *(Dir-Art)*
Johannes Ivarsson *(Copywriter)*
Karl Wikstrom *(Planner)*
Robert Schelin *(Client Svc Dir)*

Accounts:
Adressandring Campaign: "Love Swing"
Apple
Aria
Canal Digital Campaign: "You Killed Kenny"
Fortum
Henkel
Mars North America
Michelin
Moderna Museet Campaign: "Ad Piece"
Nissan
Nivea
Oddset
Peter M
Renault Campaign: "Strongest Man"
Svensk Fjarrvarme Campaign: "The Robot"
Svenska Spel Campaign: "Let Europe Watch"
SVS
Tom Tom

Waterswidgren/TBWA AB

Blasieholmsgatan 5, Stockholm, 111 48 Sweden
Tel.: (46) 8 4106 3080
Fax: (46) 8 6600422
Web Site: www.tbwa.se

Robert Schelin *(Acct Dir)*

Accounts:
The Swedish Cancer Society

SWITZERLAND

TBWA Health A.G.

Seefeldstrasse 19, 8008 Zurich, Switzerland
Tel.: (41) 44 913 32 22
Fax: (41) 44 913 32 23
E-Mail: info@tbwa.ch
Web Site: www.tbwa.ch

Employees: 40

Agency Specializes In: Health Care Services

Bettina Klossner *(Dir-Art)*
Wanda Michel *(Dir-Art)*
Mischa Muller *(Dir-Art)*
Simon Rehsche *(Dir-Strategy)*
Werner Schellenberg *(Dir-Art)*
Cyrill Wirz *(Dir-Creative)*
Beax Hartwig *(Mgr-HR)*
Martin Schmidlin *(Jr Copywriter)*
Sara Steinmann *(Copywriter)*
Stephan Lanz *(Client Svc Dir)*
Jasmine Segginger *(Jr Planner-Strategic)*
Petra Zehnder *(Client Svc Dir)*

Accounts:
Kalixan
McDonald's
Medinova
Pfizer
The Swiss Pharmacist Assoc

TBWA Switzerland A.G.

Seefeldstrasse 19, 8008 Zurich, Switzerland
Tel.: (41) 44 913 3131
Fax: (41) 44 913 3132
E-Mail: info@tbwa.ch
Web Site: www.tbwa.ch

Employees: 50
Year Founded: 1967

Agency Specializes In: Internet/Web Design, Public Relations

Matthias Kiess *(CEO)*
Chan I. Au *(Art Dir)*

Accounts:
Apple Computers
Mars Switzerland Campaign: "Dog Leash", Pedigree Dog Food
McDonald's Campaign: "Saving is Game"
Micro Mobility Systems
Micro X-treme Scooters
Pet Health Association Campaign: "Cat, Dog"
Pro Juventute Campaign: "147 Helpline for Children", Campaign: "Boy"
RoadCross Campaign: "Don't Drink & Drive"
Sony Playstation
Toi Toi

UKRAINE

TBWA Ukraine

13 Pymonenka St forum Business City office 7B/33, Kiev, 04050 Ukraine
Tel.: (380) 4 44 96 09 16
Fax: (380) 4 44 96 09 17
E-Mail: office@tbwa.com.ua
Web Site: www.tbwa.com.ua

Alexander Shyrokov *(Mng Partner)*

Accounts:
Canon
Dilmah
Henkel
Nissan
Visa

UNITED KINGDOM

Maher Bird Associates

82 Charing Cross Road, London, WC2H OBA United Kingdom
Tel.: (44) 207 309 7200
Fax: (44) 207 309 7201
Web Site: www.mba.co.uk

Employees: 50

Graham Kerr *(Chm & Exec Dir-Creative)*
James Middlehurst *(Mng Partner)*
Paul Munce *(Mng Partner)*
James Devon *(Dir-Plng)*
Paul Zetlin *(Dir-Fin)*

Accounts:
The AA
Accor Hotels
Embraer
Everest Direct Marketing
Ibis Hotel
Mercedes Benz
Mercure
Novotel
Rosetta Stone Christmas Marketing Campaign

TBWA/London

76-80 Whitfield Street, London, W1T 4EZ United Kingdom
Tel.: (44) 207 573 6666
Fax: (44) 207 573 6667
Web Site: www.tbwa-london.com

Employees: 142

Agency Specializes In: Advertising

Nick Allsop *(Partner-Creative)*
Adam Stagliano *(Chief Strategy Officer-Intl)*
Josh Tenser *(Head-Product & Innovation)*
Gary Smith *(Grp Dir-Fin)*
Mark Cochrane *(Sr Acct Dir)*
Nick Tidball *(Art Dir & Creative Dir)*
Jason Fletcher *(Creative Dir)*
Frankie Garlick *(Acct Dir-Global)*
Dan Kenny *(Art Dir)*
Olivia Logue *(Acct Dir)*
Simon Morris *(Art Dir)*
David Owen *(Acct Dir)*
Paul Weinberger *(Creative Dir)*
Martin Jon Adolfsson *(Dir-Innovation & Interactive Creative)*
Andrew Gosling *(Dir-Creative Svcs)*
Daniel Quercioli *(Dir-Art)*
Justin Martin *(Sr Acct Mgr)*
Tom Gong *(Copywriter)*
Darren Rosenberg *(Copywriter)*
Daniel Todd *(Sr Designer)*
Dean Webb *(Copywriter)*

Accounts:
Absolut
Adidas Adidas D Rose 3.5, Adidas Football, Campaign: "Jump", Campaign: "Original Artist"
Advertising Association
Airbnb Campaign: "Share Economy"
Albert Kennedy Trust Campaign: "What Might Have Been"
Apple
Ataxia
BEKO Above the Line, Content Generation, Digital, Online Advertising, Optimisation, Social Media, Website Design
The Big Issue Foundation
Bonds Campaign: "'Hello Boys", Campaign: "G'Day Boys", Wonderbra
Coco de Mer Online
Dove Transport for London
Drinkaware Campaign: "Have the Conversation", Creative
Elastoplast
Electrolux Campaign: "Menu De Cannes"
Electronic Arts CRM, Data, Digital, Fifa, Mass Effect, Need for Speed, Social
E.ON
Four Seasons Hotels and Resorts CRM, Digital, Experiential Marketing, Marketing Communications
Fruitasia
Galaxy
GlaxoSmithKline Aquafresh, Campaign: "Captain Aquafresh", Campaign: "The crowd is my only drug.", Global Creative, NiQuitin
Gossard
Heineken Alcohol, Campaign: "Commemorative Plate"
Jungle Sound Studios
Lidl #SchoolOfChristmas, Brand Advertising, Campaign: "#LidlSurprises", Campaign: "Shop A Lidl Smarter", Campaign: "The Little Present", Digital, In-Store, Marketing, Outdoor, Print, Public Relations, Social, TV
Mars North America Pedigree
Mars Twix

McDonald's
Muller Dairy Muller Light, Wunderful Stuff, Yoghurt
Nissan 360 Wrap, Campaign: "Built to Thrill", Campaign: "Feel the Surge", Campaign: "Turn Every Drive into a Ride With Google Send-to-Car Technology", Nissan Juke, Nissan Leaf, NissanConnect, Outdoor, Qashqai, TV
Paul Belford Ltd
Peace One Day Campaign: "Frozen Bullets"
SCA Global Advertising, Tena
Sony UK Above the Line, Bravia, PlayStation 3
Sotheby's Advertising, Lead Global Agency, Marketing
Starburst
Tracker
Tussaud's Group
Whiskas
Wrigley Blue Skittles, Campaign: "Like The Rainbow", Skittles

TBWA/Manchester
St Paul's 781 Wilmslow Road, Didsbury Village, Manchester, M20 2RW United Kingdom
Tel.: (44) 161 908 8600
Fax: (44) 161 908 8601
E-Mail: enquiries@tbwamanchester.co.uk
Web Site: www.tbwamanchester.com/

Employees: 120

Fergus Mccallum *(CEO)*
Jason Chadwick *(Dir-Art)*
Gary Fawcett *(Dir-Creative)*
Ant Harris *(Dir-Art)*
Rhys Hughes *(Dir-Middleweight Art)*
Adam Richardson *(Dir-Art)*
Danny O'Keeffe *(Jr Copywriter)*
Laura Horne *(Jr Acct Exec)*

Accounts:
Alice Campaign: "Madness Returns"
BP Wild Bean Cafe
CSL Campaign: "Perfect Match", Easter Campaign
Eurocamp TV
Harvey Nichols
Henshaws Society Campaign: "Judo"
Manchester Airports Group
Merlin Entertainments
Nissan
PZ Cussons Campaign: "Magical", Campaign: "Wash posh", Digital Banners, Imperial Leather, Outdoor, Print
Seven Seas Campaign: "Good Inside"
Smyths Toys Brand Awareness, Campaign: "Hey, let's play!"
Westland Horticulture Campaign: "Hungry Birds", Unwins Seeds
New-Yours Clothing

TBWAPW
(Formerly TBWA Paling Walters)
76-80 Whitfield Street, London, W1T 4EZ United Kingdom
Tel.: (44) 207 840 7444
Fax: (44) 207 840 7445
Web Site: www.tbwa-pw.com

Employees: 45
Year Founded: 1980

Agency Specializes In: Advertising, Advertising Specialties, Brand Development & Integration, Communications, Consulting, Consumer Marketing, Corporate Identity, E-Commerce, Health Care Services, Internet/Web Design, Logo & Package Design, Medical Products, New Product Development, Pharmaceutical

Andy Hayley *(Mng Dir)*
Steve Morris *(Mng Dir)*
Amelia Torode *(Chief Strategy Officer)*
Beth Moore *(Head-Strategy)*
Diana Janicki *(Exec Dir-Creative)*
Catherine Ellis *(Grp Acct Dir)*
Lucie Crook *(Acct Dir)*
Emma Fitton *(Dir-Fin)*
Victoria Clark *(Planner)*

Accounts:
Bausch & Lomb
Bayer Rennie Ascencia, Canesten
Bristol-Myers Squibb Abilify
GSK NPD, Serevent, Serifide
GSK Consumer Health Corosodyl, Flixonase, Imigran, Niqutin CQ, Nytol, Panadol, Solpadiene, Zovirax
Johnson & Johnson Consumer Health Benylin, Calpol, Sudafed
Pfizer Ltd. Lipitor, Viagra
Roche/Bayer Xeloda, Xenical

TBWA/UK Group
76-80 Whitfield St, London, W1T 4EZ United Kingdom
Tel.: (44) 20 7573 6666
Fax: (44) 20 7573 6782
Web Site: www.tbwa-london.com

Employees: 175

Peter Souter *(Chm & Chief Creative Officer)*
Adam Stagliano *(Chief Strategy Officer-Intl)*
Andrew Gosling *(Head-Creative Svcs)*
Poppy Manning *(Head-Brdcst)*
Herdeep Natt *(Head-Data Strategy)*
Chris Spenceley *(Head-Client Svcs)*
Gary Smith *(Grp Dir-Fin)*
Walter Campbell *(Dir-Creative)*
Ryan Wain *(Dir-Bus Dev)*
Oliver Forder *(Brand Head-Global)*
Peter Knowland *(Brand Head-Global)*
Mike Wortley *(Brand Head-Global)*

Accounts:
Absolut
adidas
Apple
Beiersdorf Elastoplast
Chivis
E-On
Galaxy
Haagen-Dazs
Mars North America
Michelin
National Express
Nissan
Nivea
Pedigree
Singapore Airlines
Sony PlayStation

NAMIBIA

TBWA/Paragon
House 40 Eros Route, Windhoek, Namibia
Mailing Address:
PO Box 11602, Klein, Windhoek, Namibia
Tel.: (264) 61 219954
Fax: (264) 61 220319
E-Mail: info@tbwa.com.na
Web Site: www.tbwa.com.na

Employees: 25

Agency Specializes In: Advertising

Gladys Mubapatasango *(Mng Dir)*
Desmond Amunyela *(Exec Dir-Bus Dev)*
Stanley Nick Katzao *(Exec Dir-Paragon Seafood Products)*
Lazarus Jacobs *(Dir-Paragon Investment Holdings)*
Amber Kamber *(Mgr-Fin-Paragon Seafood Products)*
Anton Theart *(Mgr-Ops)*

Accounts:
Duty Free
Kutako
Paragon
Redorange
Windhoek Observer

NIGERIA

TBWA Concept Unit
37 Ladipo Bateye GRA Ikeja, Lagos, Nigeria
Tel.: (234) 1 470 2467
Fax: (234) 1 545 5515
E-Mail: enquires@tbwaconcept.com
Web Site: www.tbwaconcept.com

Agency Specializes In: Direct Response Marketing

Saheed Rasheed *(Head-Fin)*
Agnes Layode *(Exec Dir-Ops & Corp Svcs)*
Adebajo Adekunle *(Sr Dir-Art)*
Ranti Atunwa *(Dir-Creative)*
Lawrence Chikeme *(Dir-Art)*
Osibo Imhoitsike *(Dir-Bus)*
Emeka Ebeniro *(Mgr-Plng & Strategy)*

Accounts:
ARM
Chicken Inn
Creamy Inn
Harp
Nigerite
Pizza Inn
SPARK
Satzenbrau
Smart Investor
Smirnoff Ice
Society For Family Health
Swan
Swift Broadband

SOUTH AFRICA

Magna Carta
38 Wierda Road West The Hunt, Ground Floor, Johannesburg, South Africa
Mailing Address:
PO Box 785381, Sandton, South Africa
Tel.: (27) 11 784 2598
Fax: (27) 11 783 4735
E-Mail: info@magna-carta.co.za
Web Site: www.magna-carta.co.za

Employees: 70

Agency Specializes In: Public Relations

Annemarie McKay Ichikowitz *(Deputy Mng Dir)*
Lisa Dawson Cape *(Mng Dir-Town)*
Ima Martin Essien Peter *(Acct Dir)*
Tanya Lobegeier *(Acct Dir)*
Tshepiso Molefi *(Acct Dir)*
Zayd Nakwa *(Sr Acct Mgr)*
Jacques De Bie *(Sr Head-Bus Unit)*

Accounts:
Adidas
Barloworld
Deneys Raitz Law Firm
Engen
Fusion
Medscheme
Motorola Solutions, Inc.
Pepsi
Pfizer
Simba
Standard Bank
Standbic Bank
Vodacom

TBWA Durban
Colchester Essex Gardens Nelson Road, Westville Kwa Zulu Natal, Durban, 3630 South Africa
Tel.: (27) 31 267 6690
E-Mail: justin.mccarthy@tbwa.co.za
Web Site: www.tbwa-africa.com

Employees: 130

Agency Specializes In: Advertising

James Porter *(Chm)*
Justin Wright *(Grp Dir-Creative)*
Sharon Cvetkovski *(Producer-Stills & Art Buyer)*
Vanessa Maselwa *(Acct Dir)*

Accounts:
Doom Fogger Campaign: "Roachville"
Spar

TBWA Hunt Lascaris Cape Town
(Formerly TBWA Fusion)
The Foundry Level 5 Cardiff Street, Greenpoint, Cape Town, 8001 South Africa
Mailing Address:
PO Box 6078, 8012 Roggebaai, South Africa
Tel.: (27) 21 417 5700
Fax: (27) 21 425 8482
Web Site: www.tbwa-africa.com

Employees: 20

Agency Specializes In: Advertising

Carl Willoughby *(Creative Dir)*
Damian Bonse *(Dir-Creative)*
Kyle Cockeran *(Copywriter)*

Accounts:
Beegle Micro Tracker
Celio Promotion
Ceres Africa Fruit Juice; 2012
Initial Hygiene Services
Rentokil Initial; 2011
Shatterprufe Windscreens; 2010
Truworths Investor Relations; 2011
Western Cape Government Gov Initiatives; 2010

TBWA Hunt Lascaris (Durban)
Southend Essex Gardens 1 Nelson Road, 3631 Durban, 3630 South Africa
Tel.: (27) 31 267 6600
Fax: (27) 31 266 2566
E-Mail: eira.sands@tbwa.co.za
Web Site: www.tbwa-africa.com

Employees: 130

James Porter *(Chm)*
Ivan Moroke *(Grp Mng Dir)*
Danni Vos Dixon *(Mng Dir)*
Alan Edgar *(Exec Dir-Creative)*
Eira Sands *(Dir-New Bus & Trng)*
Lee Naidoo *(Copywriter)*

Accounts:
Beiersdorf
Build It
Dunlop
Illovo Sugar
Spar

TBWA Hunt Lascaris (Johannesburg)
3 Sandown Valley Crescent, Sandown, Johannesburg, 2196 South Africa
Mailing Address:
3 Sandown Valley, Johannesburg, 2146 South Africa
Tel.: (27) 11 322 3100
Fax: (27) 11 883 7624
E-Mail: jhdr@tbwa.co.za
Web Site: www.tbwa-africa.com

Employees: 150

Derek Bouwer *(CEO)*
Danni Vos Dixon *(Mng Dir)*
Peter Khoury *(Chief Creative Officer)*
Bridget Langley *(Grp Acct Dir)*
Mike Groenewald *(Creative Dir)*
Charles Pantland *(Creative Dir)*
Debbie Pienaar *(Acct Dir)*
Nicola Taylor *(Art Dir)*
Shane Forbes *(Dir-Art)*
Melanie Moore *(Dir-Art)*
Kerry Moralee *(Dir-Art)*
Sifiso Nkabinde *(Dir-Art)*
Craig Walker *(Mgr-Production)*

Accounts:
Apex Awards Campaign: "For the rest of you there's an Apex"
Appletiser Campaign: "it's thirsty work"
New-Artline
Beacon Allsorts Campaign: "Look-a-like"
BIC
City Lodge Campaign: "Alarm"
Doctors Without Borders
Doom Fogger Campaign: "Gets to where they live", Campaign: "Wall of Shoes"
Drive Alive Campaign: "Drive Alive 3D"
E-Graphics
Endangered Wildlife Trust "Blue Swallow", Campaign: "As Close as You'll Get"#, Campaign: "Northern White Rhino", Campaign: "Riverine Rabbit", Campaign: "The Last Ones Left"
Environmental Wildlife Trust
Epic Foods Canola
Famous Brands Campaign: "Sad Sandy"
Flight Centre Campaign: "English"
Guardian Media Group
International Organisation for Migration
Kenilworth Clinic
Mail & Guardian Campaign: "Freedom is Knowing"
Mars Pedigree
Nampak Campaign: "Write It In Your Own Voice"
Neotel
Netsurit
Nissan Almera
Papersmith & Son
PRASA
The Rhino Stamp Project
SBSA Jazz
Sharklife Conservation Group Campaign: "Shark-Finning Sundial"
Southern African Counter-Trafficking Assistance Programme
Standard Bank
Stanlib
Steers Fast Food
Steers South Africa
StopRhinoPoaching.com
Student Flights Campaign: "Grandma", Campaign: "Grandpa", Campaign: "Travel Before it's Not Fun Anymore"
Telkom
Tiger Brands Campaign: "Write it in Your Own Voice"
Tigers Brands Campaign: "Brother & Sister", Campaign: "Bust You Out", Campaign: "Couple", Campaign: "Doom", Campaign: "Jungle Energy Bars", Campaign: "Little Girl", Campaign: "Mommy's Boy", Campaign: "Mother's Favourites", Campaign: "Mother-In-Law"
The Zimbabwean Campaign: "The Voiceless", Newspaper

TBWA South Africa Group
3 Sandown Valley Crescent Sandton, PO Box 785203, Johannesburg, 2196 South Africa
Tel.: (27) 11 322 3218
Fax: (27) 27 11 322 3177
Web Site: www.tbwa-africa.com

Employees: 250

Derek Bouwer *(CEO)*
Eunene Levine *(Mng Dir)*
Reinher Behrens *(Mng Dir-Accounts-Global)*
Marie Jamieson *(Exec Dir-Africa & Dir-Intl Strategy)*
Debbie Pienaar *(Grp Acct Dir)*
Caroline Mogotsi *(Acct Dir)*
Graham Cruikshanks *(Dir-Africa Ops)*
Mike Groenewald *(Dir-Creative)*
Andrew Stewart Francis *(Reg Mgr)*

Accounts:
Liberty
Standard Bank
Tiger Brands

TEQUILA Durban Marketing Services
Colchester Essex Gardens Nelson Road, Westville, Durban, 3630 South Africa
Tel.: (27) 31 267 6690
Fax: (27) 31 267 6691

Employees: 10

Agency Specializes In: Direct Response Marketing

Praveen Inderpersadh *(Mng Dir)*
Eunene Levine *(Mng Dir)*
Kabelo Moshapalo *(Exec Dir-Creative)*
Christine Holcroft *(Sr Acct Dir)*

Accounts:
National Portland Cement
South African Breweries

ISRAEL

Yehoshua TBWA
1 Nirim Street, Tel Aviv, 67060 Israel
Tel.: (972) 3 636 1818
Fax: (972) 3 636 1800
Web Site: www.ytbwa.co.il

Employees: 140

Etai Levi *(VP-Acct Mgmt)*
Amit Stoler *(Exec Dir-Creative)*
Noga Kara *(Creative Dir)*
Mia Kerman *(Creative Dir)*
Gil Goren *(Dir-Creative)*
Natalie Liliav *(Dir-Digital Art)*
Dinat Zisner Catz *(Dir-Art)*
Nava Ben Moshe *(Copywriter)*

Accounts:
Adidas
Assuta Privet Hospital
Betili
Boiron Oscillococcinum
Brimag Campaign: "Beko: Heavy duty 9 kilo load washing machine"
Diners Club International Ltd
Fattal Hotels Pope
JCDecaux
Kidum school Campaign: "QR Code"
LG Campaign: "Filthy Corners", Campaign: "Set Your Picture Free", Hom-Bot Square, Pocket Photo
Maccabi Healthcare Service
McDonald's
Muller
Neviot Campaign: "Workout"
Sloggi
Toyota Campaign: "Cheers!"

KAZAKHSTAN

TBWA Central Asia

Tole Bi 83, Almaty, 050012 Kazakhstan
Tel.: (7) 3272 598 925
Fax: (7) 3272 598 925
Web Site: www.tbwa.kz

Agency Specializes In: Advertising

Lyutsiya Lindt *(CEO)*
Ruslan Kassymov *(Mng Dir)*
Juan Pablo Valencia Montero *(Art Dir Creative Dir & Copywriter)*
Nurlan Satarov *(Art Dir)*
Erlan Soltanov *(Acct Dir)*
Asem Kiyalova *(Dir-Art & Graphic Designer)*
Erzhan Mamazhanov *(Dir-IT)*
Marat Sattarov *(Dir-Art)*
Yulia Shevchik *(Dir-Art)*
Yuriy Pavlikov *(Mgr-Production)*
Ekaterina Belyashina *(Client Svc Dir)*

Accounts:
Avtotravel.com
Bausch & Lomb Campaign: "Coffins Brown Coffin"
Bref
Cafe Malina
Exoderil
Home Dacor Campaign: "Violet"
National Center For Problems Of Healthy Lifestyle Development Campaign: "Help", Campaign: "Ruslan"
Orient De Luxe Campaign: "Red Towel"
Persil Expert Campaign: "Reading the wrong story"
Pizza Hut
Rotomac Microtech Fineline Pen
Sandoz
Tendinol 35

TURKEY

TBWA Istanbul

ATA Center Ahi Evren Cad No 1 Kat G2, Maslak, 34398 Istanbul, Turkey
Tel.: (90) 212 335 74 00
Fax: (90) 212 328 0973
E-Mail: ctopcuoglu@tbwa-instanbul.com
Web Site: www.tbwa.com.tr

Ilkay Gurpinar *(Chief Creative Officer)*
Ozan Can Bozkurt *(Grp Head-Creative)*
Zeynep Karakasoglu *(Head-Creative)*
VJ Anand *(Exec Dir-Creative)*
Guler Balta *(Brand Dir)*
Volkan Karakasoglu *(Creative Dir)*
Ayse Senunver *(Brand Dir)*
Ipek Turkili *(Acct Mgr)*
Nazli Atasoy *(Copywriter)*
Emre Gokdemir *(Copywriter)*
Mehmet Guney *(Copywriter)*
Asli Topcu *(Copywriter)*

Accounts:
Acupuncture Care Center Campaign: "Hamburger"
Adidas
Akbank
Amnesty International
Anadolu Sigorta
Avea
Bay Insaat Campaign: "Colorful Man"
BMW Campaign: "Head Up Display"
Bronzi Solarium
Cellex-C
Esemmat Bug Killer Spray, Campaign: "Human Feast", Esemmat Insect Killer
Fiat
Henkel
IF Istanbul Campaign: "IF Istanbul Corporate Identity"
IKEA
Inlingua Language Courses
Kanukte Flower&Event Campaign: "Hide the Guilt"
Mobotix
Monapa
Mor Cati
Motorola Solutions, Inc.
Nissan Nissan Rear View Camera, Qashqai
Pera Boya Wood Protector
Pinar Light Mayonnaise, Milk
Radikal Campaign: "The 'Fading News"
Resfest
Second Chance
Selpak Tissue Campaign: "Always by Your Side"
Seyahatname.com
Shutterstock
Step Carpet
Tepe Dental Floss
Tivibu
TTNET
Vog Socks
Whiskas
YKM

UNITED ARAB EMIRATES

TBWA Raad

Twin Towers Suites 2101 & 2102 21st Floor Baniyas Street, Deira, Dubai, United Arab Emirates
Tel.: (971) 4 222 6667
Fax: (971) 4 222 6566
E-Mail: ramzi@tbwaraad.com
Web Site: www.tbwaraad.com

Employees: 90

Milos Ilic *(Chief Creative Officer)*
Walid Kanaan *(Chief Creative Officer)*
Rohan Young *(Exec Creative Dir)*
Amira Ibrahim *(Sr Acct Dir)*
Saad Gharzeddine *(Grp Acct Dir)*
Manuel Borde *(Creative Dir)*
Joe Lahham *(Client Svcs Dir)*
Alexander Pineda *(Creative Dir)*
Malek Atassi *(Dir-Creative)*
Deger Cotelioglu *(Dir-Creative)*
Sandeep Fernandes *(Dir-Creative)*
Ian Guimaraes *(Dir-Art)*
Felipe Sona *(Dir-Art)*
Breda Plavec *(Assoc Dir-Creative)*
Natasha Monteiro *(Sr Acct Mgr-Adv & Integrated Mktg)*
Vivian Hawat *(Acct Mgr)*
Bryan Chin-Yu Chou *(Acct Exec)*
Guilherme Grossi *(Copywriter)*
Clayton Needham *(Sr Designer-Digital)*

Accounts:
Abu Dhabi Film Festival Campaign: "Cele- brate Film", Creative, Media
The American University of Beirut Medical Center
Arabian Automobiles Campaign: "Accidental Test Drive"
Beiersdorf AG
Career Junction
Cartoon Network Animation Academy Campaign: "The Wait Is Over"
Combat
DAC Disinfectant
Dubai Events & Establishment Dubai Shopping Festival, Dubai Summer Surprises, Eid al Fitr, Marketing Communications, Modhesh World, National Day, NewYear, Ramadan, Strategy
The Fridge Concert Venue & Music Production House
Galaxy
Gulf Scrabble Championships Campaign: "Battle Captcha"
Hasbro
Henkel Corporation Campaign: "Aargh! ", Combat Cockroach Gel
Khaleej Times Campaign: "The Opinionated Banner"
Mars Pedigree & Whiskas Dubai Pet Show
Music Production House
Niayomi
Nissan Middle East FZE Lane Departure Warning, Nissan 370Z, Nissan Patrol, Pathfinder GPS (Live the DVD Experience Campaign), Cinema, Television, Tiida, Xterra
Nokia Corporation
Persil
Red Tomato Pizza Campaign: "Fridge Magnet"
Royal Opera House Muscat
Sae Institute Dubai
New-SOS Children's Villages International Happy No Mother's Day

AUSTRALIA

Whybin TBWA

80 Gipps Street, Pyrmont, Sydney, NSW 2009 Australia
Tel.: (61) 2 8584 5500
Fax: (61) 2 8584 5555
Web Site: www.whybintbwagroup.com.au

Scott Whybin *(Chm & Reg Exec Dir-Creative-Australia & New Zealand)*
Paul Bradbury *(CEO & Partner)*
Peter Fitzhardinge *(Mng Dir)*
Mike Napolitano *(Gen Mgr)*
Gary McCreadie *(Exec Creative Dir)*
Warrick Nicholson *(Art Buyer & Sr Producer)*
Clive Blackstone *(Sr Art Dir)*
Lucy Kavanagh *(Producer-Digital)*
Suzanne Keen *(Creative Dir)*
Erin Kelly *(Acct Dir)*
Richie Taaffe *(Acct Dir)*
Dave Brady *(Dir-Creative)*
Craig Brooks *(Dir-Creative)*
Alex Stickler *(Sr Acct Mgr)*
Leigh Arbon *(Acct Supvr)*
Avish Gordhan *(Copywriter)*
Warwick Heathwood *(Planner)*
Andrew Roberts *(Sr Designer)*

Accounts:
Adidas
Amorim
Apple
Coopers Campaign: "Coopers Clear Cut Competition"
Country Energy
David Jones Campaign: "It's in You", Campaign: "Power", Creative, Strategic Marketing
EBay
Electronic Arts CRM
Fairfax
Helga's
Heritage Bank + Visa
Insurance Australia Group Limited Campaign: "Balloon", Campaign: "NRMA Car Creation", Campaign: "Nrma Motion Activated Poster"
Knauf Insulation
Luxbet Creative
Mars Petcare Campaign: "Dog-A-Like", Campaign: "Pedigree Adoption Drive", Campaign: "Underdog Day"
Medibank Campaign: "Go Beyond The Tax Break"
M.J.Bale Campaign: "Grazed on Greatness"
Nicabate Pre-Quit
Nissan Australia Campaign: "Nissan 370 Zen to Z"
NRMA Insurance Campaign: "Crashed Car Showroom", Campaign: "Differentiation Makes a Massive Difference", Print, TVC
Origin Campaign: "Half Off", Creative, Digital, Outdoor, Print, TV
Pedigree Campaign: "The Pedigree Adoption drive"
Pfizer Campaign: "Lip Licker"
Presto Creative
RaboDirect Campaign: "Stealing Your Dreams"
SGIO
Stihl Campaign: "Get Real. Get Outside"

The Sydney Morning Herald
Tabcorp
Taronga Western Plains Zoo
Tourism New Zealand Campaign: "Inspired by Wellington", Creative, Digital, Global Brand Strategy, Media
Trade Me Campaign: "New or Used"
Unilever Above the Line, Activations, Cornetto, Magnum, Shopper Marketing, Splice
Wyeth

Whybin TBWA

288 Coventry Street, South, Melbourne, VIC 3205 Australia
Tel.: (61) 3 9690 8555
Fax: (61) 3 9690 5892
E-Mail: admin@mytbwa.com.au
Web Site: www.whybintbwagroup.com.au

Employees: 45

Scott Whybin *(Chm & Reg Exec Dir-Creative-Australia & New Zealand)*
Kimberlee Wells *(CEO)*
Paul Bradbury *(CEO-Sydney & Partner)*
Michael Napolitano *(Mng Dir)*
Margot Ger *(Head-Brdcst & Content Production)*
Tony Hall *(Head-Print Production)*
Peter Kirwan *(Sr Dir-Art)*
Matthew Stoddart *(Sr Dir-Art)*
Damiano Dipietro *(Sr Acct Dir)*
Jo Hardy *(Sr Acct Dir)*
James Bilaver *(Grp Acct Dir)*
Janine Wertheim *(Sr Producer-Brdcst & Content)*
Matt Chiodo *(Acct Dir)*
Tara Ford *(Creative Dir)*
Mark Jones *(Sr Art Dir)*
Daniel Pizzato *(Art Dir)*
Kees Kalk *(Dir-Strategic Plng)*
Damian Royce *(Dir-Creative)*
Guy Munro *(Assoc Dir-Digital-Whybin TBWA)*
Karolina Nanowski *(Acct Mgr)*
Oliva Rourke *(Acct Mgr)*
Jeremy Wilson *(Acct Mgr)*
Rob Hibbert *(Sr Copywriter)*
Paul Arena *(Planner)*
Pat Sofra *(Designer)*
Jim Taylor *(Copywriter)*

Accounts:
2 Degrees Mobile
3AW
Adidas
The Age Campaign: "JUST A CABBIE", Forever Curious
Amorim
ANZ Bank ATM, Campaign: "Bull & Bears", Campaign: "Connectivity - Airplane Asia", Campaign: "GAYTM", Campaign: "Get job ready with ANZ Everyday Banking", Creative, Credit Cards Business, goMoney
Apple
Betstar Campaign: "Eagle", Campaign: "Lucky Country", Campaign: "No Hard Sell", Creative
New-Carsales.com (Lead Creative Agency) Brand Marketing, Creative
Comte
Fairfax
Goodman Fielder
ICAN
McCain Healthy Choice Campaign: "Choose Tasty"
Mecury Energy
Medibank BAMM! THWONG! SPROING! PHROOMP! WEEEE, Creative
Minds for Minds Trust Campaign: "Meeting of the Minds"
Nissan Campaign: "#VJUKE ", Campaign: "More", Campaign: "Queenslander", Campaign: "See Everything", Dualis Hatch, Make a Big Load Feel Small, Nissan GT-R, Nissan JUKE, Nissan Patrol, Nissan Pulsar
Old Mout Cider Campaign: "Old Mout Free Cider Trial"
New-Origin Energy Ltd
PetRescue Campaign: "Who says you can't choose your family?"
RACV
STIHL 21 Trillion Inch', Campaign: "Wireless Hotspot"
Visa
Wyeth

CHINA

TBWA Asia Pacific

16 & 17/F Cambridge House Taikoo Place, 979 King's Road, Quarry Bay, China (Hong Kong)
Tel.: (852) 2573 3180
Fax: (852) 2573 1897
Web Site: www.tbwa.com.hk

Employees: 70

Alain Rhone *(COO)*
Edmund Choe *(Chief Creative Officer-Singapore & Southeast Asia-TBWA/Grp Asia)*
Robin Nayak *(Chief Strategy Officer-Singapore & South East Asia)*
Terence Ling *(Head-Plng-Hong Kong)*
Philippa Fox *(Reg Dir-Comm)*
Rupert Taylor *(Dir-Art & Creative & Writer)*

Accounts:
Absolut
adidas
AIA Group Creative
Apple Computers & Equipment
Beiersdorf
Greenpeace
Haagen-Dazs
Hankook Tyres
Levi's
Masterfoods/Mars Twix
McDonald's
Michelin
Nissan
Nivea
Pepsi
Pernod Ricard
Samsonite
Simplot
Singapore Airlines
SK Telecom
TA Orange
TU Media
VISA

TBWA Beijing

Room 1121 Tower 03 GuangHualu SOHO No 22 GuangHua Lu, ChaoYang District, Beijing, 100022 China
Tel.: (86) 10 5909 3888
Fax: (86) 10 5909 3887
Web Site: tbwa.com.cn

Employees: 70

Edmund Choe *(Chief Creative Officer-Singapore & Southeast Asia)*
Xinyu Wang *(Gen Mgr-BEING Shanghai)*
Joseph Wong *(Gen Mgr-E-Graphics Shanghai)*
Yoyo Wu *(Acct Dir)*
Wanda Wang *(Dir-HR-TBWA/Shanghai)*
Kiddy Wang *(Copywriter)*

Accounts:
Absolu Purity
New-Baobeihuijia
Citizen Brand Marketing, Brand Positioning, Communications Campaigns, Creative, Insights
Mondelez International, Inc.

TBWA Greater China

Unit 605 Jianwai SOHO Ofc Tower B No 39 Dong San Huan Zhong Lu, 100022 Beijing, China
Tel.: (86) 10 5869 6188
Fax: (86) 1058695881
Web Site: projeqt.com

Nils Andersson *(Pres & Chief Creative Officer)*
Hiroaki Mori *(COO)*
Milo Chao *(Chief Strategy officer)*
Antoine Gouin *(Mng Dir-Auditore-China)*
Joseph Wong *(Gen Mgr-E-Graphics Shanghai)*
Gordon Shu *(Exec Dir-Creative)*
Joe Zhou *(Sr Dir-Creative)*
Zhifeng Wang *(Sr Acct Mgr)*
Julie Keying Jiang *(Sr Acct Exec)*

Accounts:
AIA International
Pfizer-Wyeth GOLD
Renault Above the Line, Creative, Digital, Retail Activation, Strategic

TBWA Hong Kong

16/F Cambridge House, Taikoo Place, Hong Kong, China (Hong Kong)
Tel.: (852) 2833 2033
Fax: (852) 2834 5877
E-Mail: general@tbwa.com.hk
Web Site: www.tbwa.com/

Employees: 80

Joanne Lao *(CEO)*
Kin Hui *(Partner-Creative)*
Edmund Choe *(Chief Creative Officer)*
Terence Ling *(Head-Plng)*
Esther Wong *(Exec Dir-Creative)*
Jacqueline Hung *(Sr Dir-Art)*
Jock Auld *(Acct Supvr-Infiniti-Global)*
Chika Tsang *(Sr Art Dir)*

Accounts:
AIA Group Creative
AIDS Concern Campaign: "Don't Be Haunted By Your Sexual Past"
CSL Campaign: "funifies", OOH, Playground, Print, Retail, Street Activation, TV, one2free
New-Lee Jeans Campaign: "Life is Our Canvas"
Levi Strauss Campaign: "Summer Hotline"
Mentholatum Whitening Hand Veil Campaign: "Pigeon"
New-Staccato Above-the-Line, Creative, Digital, Social strategies, Strategic
Wyeth Campaign: "See The World At Home"

TBWA Shanghai

9F 71 West Suzhou Road, Shanghai, 200041 China
Tel.: (86) 21 3353 1166
Fax: (86) 21 3353 1025
Web Site: tbwa.com.cn

Joanne Lao *(CEO)*
Brian Swords *(Mng Dir)*
Franck Besson *(VP-APMEA)*
Gordon Shu *(Exec Creative Dir)*
Don Huang *(Grp Dir-Creative)*
Joe Zhou *(Sr Dir-Creative)*
Kenny Huang *(Sr Art Dir)*
Shell Ni *(Producer-Digital)*
Yvonne Ye *(Creative Dir)*
Rachel Woolley *(Assoc Dir-Plng)*
Gill Wang *(Acct Mgr)*
Ada Yang *(Acct Mgr)*
Zizi Shi *(Sr Art Dir)*

Accounts:
adidas AG Adidas Originals, Campaign: "#thisisme", Campaign: "All in for My Girls", Campaign: "TGIF"
Apple
Bawang Group Creative, Zhuifeng

China Unicom
Costa
General Electric Campaign: "Future Folklore", Campaign: Works Everyday
Hisense Group Strategic Communications & Creative-Television Group
Levis
Martell
McDonald's China Campaign "Nian", Campaign: "It's Good to Get Together", Campaign: "Real. Good."
Mr. Zhao Pesticides
Nivea
Pedigree
Pepsi
Pernod Ricard Absolut, Ballantine's, Glenlivet, Helan Mountain, Martell Noblige Cognac, Purfeel, Royal Salute, TCX
Pfizer Nutrition Creative, ENERCAL Plus, ILLUMA, Wyeth Gold
Porsche; 2008
Quaker
Schindler
New-Siemens (China Lead Agency) Brand Development, Creative
Skittles
Standard Chartered Bank
Visa

INDIA

TBWA India Corporate
Unit 1 Ground Floor Tower B Millenium Plaza, Susahnt Lok Gurgaon, New Delhi, 122002 India
Tel.: (91) 124 432 6666
Fax: (91) 124 432 6677
E-Mail: hr@tbwaindia.com
Web Site: www.tbwaindia.com

Employees: 45

Xavi Bech de Careda *(Chief Strategy Officer)*
Subho Sengupta *(Exec VP)*
Nipun Goomer *(Assoc VP-Acct Mgmt)*
Asha Dsouza *(Client Svcs Dir)*
Valerian Dsouza *(Dir-Creative)*
Shirin Johari *(Dir-Creative)*
Venkateshwarlu Kumarshetty *(Mgr-Production)*
Shweta Dhamija *(Acct Supvr)*
Riddhi Jani *(Assoc Acct Dir)*

Accounts:
adidas
Apple Inc. Campaign: "New & faster", MacBook Air
Dabur India Pvt. Ltd
Dr. Devi Chandiramani Campaign: "Gynaecologist"
GSK
Haier India Communication, Creative, Digital, Media Agency of Record, Outdoor, Print, TV/Radio
Michelin Tires
Mkv Household Products Campaign: "Elephant Combs Logo Design"
munishverma.net
Nissan Motors India Pvt Ltd Campaign: "Powerful Presence"
Pedigree
Tata Group Campaign: "Singing Practice"
Visa Leave the Queue
Yatra.com Campaign: "Tyre Tracks"

TBWA India
G11/12 Paragon Centre Opp Century Mills P.B. Marg, Mumbai, 400013 India
Tel.: (91) 22 43546666
Fax: (91) 22 43546677
E-Mail: nirmalya@tbwaindia.com
Web Site: www.tbwaindia.com

Employees: 60

Nirmalya Sen *(Mng Dir)*
Manosh Mukherjee *(CFO & Grp COO)*
Xavi Bech De Careda *(Chief Strategy Officer)*
Aejaz Khan *(Exec VP-West)*
Sayed Naushad *(Sr Dir-Plng)*
Ritesh Challagali *(Grp Acct Dir)*
Natasha Lalwani *(Acct Dir-India)*
Anand Dalvi *(Dir-Art)*
Shivam Ingale *(Dir-Art)*
Shirin Johari *(Dir-Creative)*
Rajshekar Patil *(Dir-Creative)*
Arnab Ray *(Acct Mgr)*
Nireeksha Shetty *(Brand Mgr)*
Trisha Satra *(Acct Supvr)*
Amrita Chatterji *(Acct Exec)*
Nirvi Shah *(Acct Exec)*

Accounts:
Henkel Pril
IDFC MUTUAL FUND
J G Hosiery Creative, Undergarments
Kuoni Travel Group India Creative, SOTC
Loop Mobile (Agency of Record)
Marvel Realtors
MKV Households Campaign: "Elephant"
Munishverma.net
Nissan Motor Company Campaign: "Big League", Datsun
Peninsula Land Limited Creative
Raymond
Samsonite South Asia Private Limited American Tourister, Creative, Samsonite
Singapore Airlines Campaign: "Understanding Your Needs"

TBWA India
No 62 1st Fl 3rd St, Abhiramapuram, 600018 Chennai, India
Tel.: (91) 44 5211 2800
Fax: (91) 4442112806
E-Mail: arindam@tbwaindia.com
Web Site: www.tbwaindia.com

Employees: 15

Ranjeet Lekhi *(Head-Production & Studio Svcs-Natl)*
Suresh Kumar *(Dir-Fin)*
Nikhil Vijan *(Sr Acct Exec)*

Accounts:
Hygrevar Home and Hearth
Inbisco India Creative, Kopiko
Sify Technologies Consumer Business, Enterprise Business, Software Business
Star Health & Allied Insurance
Star Insurance

TBWA India
A - 1 Tower 4th Fl Golden Enclave, Airport Rd, Bengaluru, 560 017 India
Tel.: (91) 80 4042 9000
Fax: (91) 8040429100
E-Mail: vishal@tbwaindia.com
Web Site: www.tbwaindia.com

Employees: 17

Reena Singh *(Assoc VP-Key Accounts)*
Sangita Shirali *(Dir-Creative)*
Pratul Gaur *(Grp CFO)*

Accounts:
Ascendas Park Square Mall
Spar
Zoiro Campaign: "Scarecrows"

TBWA India
Millenium Plaza Ground Floor Tower 'B' Sushant Lok-I Sector-27, Gurgaon, New Delhi, 122 002 India
Tel.: (91) 12 4432 6666
Fax: (91) 12 4432 6677
E-Mail: delhi@tbwaindia.com
Web Site: www.tbwaindia.com

Employees: 50

Nitin Naresh *(Mng Dir)*
Manosh Mukherjee *(CFO & Grp COO)*
Anirban Sen *(Exec Dir-Creative)*
Siddharth Deo *(Grp Dir-Creative)*
Manisha Das *(Acct Dir)*
Akshat Tewari *(Acct Dir)*
Divita Joshi *(Mgr-Social Media Mktg)*
Ritu Srivastava *(Asst Mgr-HR)*

Accounts:
Adidas
Buzzz Entertainment Campaign: "Darth Vader"
Cigna TTK Health Insurance Company Limited Creative
Dabur India Dabur Badam Tail; 2009
Facebook Campaign: "Use Your Like Wisely"
History Channel
IFDC (Infrastructure Development Finance Company) Mutual Funds Financial Institution; 2010
India Today Group Mail Today Newspaper
Michelin
National Geographic
Nissan Motors India Pvt. Ltd. (Agency Of Record) Campaign: "Moves Like Music", Campaign: "Parking Space", Evalia
Pedigree
SBI
Standard Chartered Bank Campaign: "Here for Good", Campaign: "Naam Vs Kaam", Outdoor, Pan-India Campaign, Print, Radio
Twinings
V-Guard; 2009
Yebhi.com Campaign: "Cyrus", Campaign: "Try n Buy", Creative Duties

INDONESIA

TCP-TBWA Indonesia
Mulia Business Park T Garden, Jakarta, 12780 Indonesia
Tel.: (62) 21 797 6233
Fax: (62) 21 7976234
Web Site: tbwa.com/

Rudy Jusnifa *(Partner)*
Desi Apriani *(Sec)*
Fajar Ibrahim *(Grp Head-Creative)*
Steve Dodds *(Dir)*
Wisnu Satya Putra *(Planner-Strategic)*
Denny Eko Prasetyo *(Grp Planner-Strategic)*

Accounts:
Heinz ABC Campaign: "Posterasi"
Mitsubishi Motors; Indonesia Colt, Colt T120 SS, Tiff
PT Bentoel International Investama Terbuka Star Mild; 2008
PT Johnson Home Hygiene Products Autan, Baygon Lavender
PT Multi Bintang Indonesia Bintang Zero, Bir Bintang
TelkomVision Customer Acquisition Program, Marketing

JAPAN

TBWA/Hakuhodo
1-13-10 Shibaura, Tokyo, Minato-ku 105-0023 Japan
Tel.: (81) 3 5446 7200
Web Site: www.tbwahakuhodo.co.jp

Employees: 295

Year Founded: 1955

Ichiro Zama *(Pres & CEO)*
Chris Iki *(COO)*
Miki Matsui *(Chief Creative Officer)*
Kenta Ikoma *(Creative Dir & Copywriter-Hakuhodo Creative Vox)*
Yo Kimura *(Art Dir)*
Yoshihiro Kono *(Art Dir)*
Yuki Tokuno *(Art Dir)*
Kayako Asano *(Dir-PR)*
Yoshiki Okayasu *(Dir)*
Masakazu Kobayashi *(Acct Supvr)*
Sayaka Ohno *(Acct Supvr)*
Mamiko Hikichi *(Acct Exec)*
Taisuke Kudo *(Acct Exec)*
Masato Goto *(Copywriter)*
Naoto Ichikawa *(Copywriter)*
Hideyuki Tanaka *(Media Planner)*

Accounts:
Adidas "Temperature Discount", Adidas Baseball, Adidas Football, Adidas Tennis, Campaign: "Passion Planetarium", SKYCOMIC
American Home Insurance
Aquafresh
COGOO - Clean City Organization Campaign: "Saddle Blossoms"
Electrolux "43dB Symphony", "Ergothree Play"
Green Label Campaign: "Marionettebot"
Kodansha Campaign: "Social Bookmark"
Kracie Foods
McDonald's Holdings Co. (Japan), Ltd. (Media Planning Agency of Record) "Hiru Mac", "Value Lunch", Creative, Digital
Michelin
Miwa Lock
NGO Campaign: '"Saddle Blossoms"
Nissan Campaign: "City of Stormtroopers", Campaign: "Delicious Road Trip", Campaign: "Distracted", Campaign: "My Car Forever", Dualis, Nissan Juke, Tiida
Procter & Gamble Ariel, Campaign: "Cheers for You Project"
Protoleaf The Soil Restaurant
Quiksilver, Inc. True Wetsuits
Relations Inc. COGOO, Campaign: "Turntable Rider"
Renault
Suntory Holdings Limited Campaign: "3D on the Rocks"
United Arrows Green Label Relaxing Campaign: "Marionettebot", Mannequins

MALAYSIA

TBWA ISC Malaysia

15th Floor Block B HP Towers 12 Jalan Gelenggang, 50490 Kuala Lumpur, Malaysia
Tel.: (60) 3 2080 8200
Fax: (60) 3 2092 4130
E-Mail: info@tbwamy.com
Web Site: www.tbwa.com

Employees: 85

Yeong Hoong Meng *(CFO)*
Jeff Hong *(Head-Creative Svcs)*
Neel Majumder *(Exec Creative Dir)*
Jules Yap *(Sr Dir-Art)*
Loh Mun Yee *(Acct Dir)*
Ivan Teh *(Acct Mgr)*
Sam Lai *(Designer)*
Shen Thuu *(Designer)*

Accounts:
Bursa Malaysia Berhad
Dasein Academy of Art Campaign: "Sunflower"
Energizer Malaysia
General Electric Campaign: '"Moving The Star"
General Mills Haagen-Dazs
JTI
Malaysia Society of Transplantation Campaign: "Organ Donation"
Malaysian Society of Transplantation Campaign: "Live On"
New-McDonald
MPOC
Munchy's Confections
Newell Rubbermaid
Nippon Paint (Creative Agency of Record) Advertising, Product Marketing, Social
Organ Donation Drive
Ovation Vocal Specialist Campaign: "Folk"
Panasonic Viera Plasma & LCD TVs
Papermate Liquid Paper Campaign: "Right The Wrong"
Samsonite
SSL Healthcare
Standard Chartered Bank
Tourism Malaysia
Visa

TEQUILA Myalo

15th Floor Block B HP Towers, Bukit Damansara, 50490 Kuala Lumpur, Malaysia
Tel.: (60) 3 2092 5130
Fax: (60) 3 2093 6130

Agency Specializes In: Direct Response Marketing

Quah Yean Nie *(Dir-PR)*

Accounts:
OSK Investment Bank Malaysia Campaign: "OSK investment challenge"

NEW ZEALAND

TBWA Whybin Limited

11 Mayoral Dr Wellesley St, P O Box 7040, Auckland, 1010 New Zealand
Tel.: (64) 9 366 6266
Fax: (64) 9 366 6110
E-Mail: david.walden@tbwatequila.co.nz
Web Site: www.whybintbwa.co.nz

Employees: 75

Todd McLeay *(CEO)*
Dave King *(Chief Creative Officer)*
David McIndoe *(Head-Plng)*
Nick Bulmer *(Grp Acct Dir)*
Sarah Goldring *(Grp Acct Dir)*
Amanda Green *(Acct Dir)*
Jonathan McMahon *(Dir-Creative)*

Accounts:
2 Degree Mobile
2degrees Telecommunications
APN
Beat Bowel Cancer Aotearoa Campaign: "Bums Are Full Of Surprises - Kiss"
Bell Tea & Coffee Campaign: "Rolling Sleeves", Creative, Strategic
CAANZ
EFFIE Awards
Knauf Insulation
Mercury Energy Campaign: "Good Energy Taxi", Transparent Newspaper
Minds for Minds Campaign: "Meeting of the Minds"
Nissan Specialist Service
NZ Girl
Playstation
Radio Network
Shine
Sony
Sovereign Campaign: "Life's Choice"
Tourism New Zealand Book of New Zealand, Campaign: "The New Newzealand.Com", The Hobbit: The Desolation of Smaug
Visa International
Visa Campaign: "Welly on a Plate"

PHILIPPINES

TBWA Santiago Mangada Puno

1195 Chino Races Ave Corner Yakal Street, Makati City, 1203 Manila, Philippines
Tel.: (63) 2 508 7809
Fax: (63) 2 813 0137
Web Site: www.tbwa-smp.com

Employees: 82

Melvin M. Mangada *(Chief Creative Officer)*
Joey David *(Exec Dir-Creative)*
Marci Reyes *(Exec Dir-Creative)*
Nolan Fabular *(Art Dir)*
Bryan Siy *(Dir-Creative)*
Jake Tesoro *(Dir-Creative)*
C.J. de Silva *(Assoc Dir-Creative)*
Nino Reyes *(Assoc Dir-Creative)*
Maxine Lozada *(Acct Mgr)*

Accounts:
Abmarac Campaign: "Snow"
Adidas Campaign: "Signature Shots"
Ayala Land Inc Campaign: "Koi Fish Feed"
Bench Fix Hairstyling Products
Boysen Knox-out Paint
Cara Welfare Philippines Campaign: "Beggar", Campaign: "Rescue Pets"
Caramba
Digital Filipino Campaign: "Bing"
Earth Day Network Philippines
Energizer Battery Campaign: "Gift of Life"
Eyebank Campaign: "Touching Words Card"
Globe
Kentucky Fried Chicken Campaign: "Fully Loaded Meal"
Lakihan Mo Logo Night Campaign: "Logo 15"
New-Nissan
Nuvali
Peerless Lion Corporation
Penshoppe
The Red Whistle
Save Palawan Movement Campaign: "Underground River"
Shokubutsu Hana
Team Manila
TGI Friday's Campaign: "Unlimited Mojitos"

SINGAPORE

TBWA Singapore

No 5 Kadayanallur Street, Singapore, 069183 Singapore
Tel.: (65) 6225 5288
Fax: (65) 6224 8983
Web Site: www.tbwa.com

Ara Hampartsoumian *(Mng Dir)*
Alrick Dorett *(COO & CFO)*
Kevin Sim *(Grp Head-Creative)*
Beth Kennedy *(Exec Dir)*
Laurent Pastorelli *(Sr Dir-Art)*
Jane Fraser *(Reg Dir-Mktg & Comm-Asia Pacific)*
Mandy Wong *(Grp Acct Dir)*
Peter Etheridge *(Acct Dir)*
Lawrence Hu *(Art Dir)*
Joyce Wong *(Acct Dir)*
Hagan de Villiers *(Dir-Creative)*
Mel Du Toit *(Dir-Creative)*
Natalie Gruis *(Dir-Strategic Plng)*
Aaron Tan *(Sr Art Dir)*

Accounts:
Airbnb, Inc. Campaign: "A Different Paris", Campaign: "Welcome to Airbnb"
APA Publications Campaign: "Say what?!"
Asia Square Campaign: "When you're in the perfect work environment."
Grupo Modelo S.A. de C. V. Asian, Campaign: "Let

the World Wait", Corona, Corona Calendar
JobsDB Creative, Digital, Dream Big, Marketing, Online, Outdoor, Print, Rebranding, TV
Lend Lease Retail Investments Campaign: "Universe"
Martell VSOP
MGPA Singapore Commercial Property - Singapore Square
Michelin
Moda Pacifica
NTUC Enterprise Brand Proposition, Branding, Creative
NTUC FairPrice Branding, Creative, Strategic Communication
Okamoto Condoms Campaign: "Nightcap", Campaign: "Okamoto Freedom Project"
Pernod Ricard
Singapore Airlines A380 Airbus, Campaign: "Audiobooks", Campaign: "The Lengths We Go To", Campaign: "understanding your needs"
Soo Kee Jewellery
Tangs Stores Singapore Above-the-Line Communications, Campaign: "Lump", Outdoor, Print

SOUTH KOREA

TBWA Korea
7-12F J-Tower 538 Sinsa Dong, Kangnam Gu, Seoul, 135-889 Korea (South)
Tel.: (82) 2 501 8888
Fax: (82) 2 501 9568
E-Mail: sangkyu.lee@tbwakorea.com
Web Site: www.tbwakorea.com

Employees: 170

Keith D. Smith *(Chm)*
Chul-Joong Kang *(Pres)*
Sungsoo Han *(Exec Mng Dir)*
Woong Hyun Park *(Exec Dir-Creative)*
Heejeong Choi *(Acct Supvr)*
Kim Mj *(Acct Exec)*

Accounts:
Cesco Creative
CJ Entertainment Domestic Market, Movies; 2009
Daelim e-Comfort Land, e-Pyunhansesang; 2007
Daum Communications
Green Umbrella Child Fund Campaign: "Footprint"
Happycall Frying Pans
Hyundai Card S
Levi's
Nivea
Pernod-Ricard Chivas Regal, Royal Salute
SK Telecom Consumer Branding, SK Broadband, T Brand
Standard Chartered Campaign: "Good Hearted Library Project"

THAILAND

Creative Juice G1
161/1 SG Tower 2nd Floor Soi Mahadle Kluang 3 Rajdamri Road, Lumpini Pat, Bangkok, 10330 Thailand
Tel.: (66) 26 5052 40
Fax: (66) 26 5052 51
E-Mail: business@creativejuicebangkok.com
Web Site: www.creativejuicebangkok.com

Employees: 129

Witawat Jayapani *(Chm)*
Kambhu Hutasankas *(Exec Dir-Creative)*

Accounts:
3M Filtrete Air Purifier, Glass Cleaner, Scotch Packaging Tape
Bangkok Insurance
Board of Trade of Thailand Campaign: "Thai Anti Corruption"
D7 Coffee
Dcash Dcash Max Speed
Dtac Campaign: "Moving Wifi"
Effective Microorganism
EMRO Asia Co., Ltd
Etiqa MotorTakaful.com Safe Tracks
F&N eXtra
GE Money
MMP Corporation Campaign: "Chicken", M Wrap
Naradee Trading Co. Campaign: "Coffee"
Office Depot Campaign: "Vase"
Panapat Healthcare Campaign: "Chicken"
The Pizza Company Delivery Service; 2008
RUUMZ
Siam Inter Multimedia Campaign: "Sports Talk Bubble"
Siam Tamiya
Singha Beer
Tamiya Toys Model Kits, Tamiya Business Card
Thai Airways
Thailand Yellow Pages
Tourism Authority of Thailand
Wrangler Jeans
Yellow Pages

TBWA Thailand
1st-2nd Fl Golden Pavilion Bldg 153/3 Soi Mahardlekluang 1 Rajdamri Rd, Pathumwan, 10330 Bangkok, Thailand
Tel.: (66) 2 687 7400
Fax: (66) 2 679 8598
E-Mail: info@tbwathailand.com
Web Site: www.tbwathailand.com

Employees: 145

Chaipranin Visudhipol *(Chm)*
Chakrit Tachanaparak *(Mng Dir)*
Narong Tresuchon *(Mng Dir-Bus-Intl)*
Prakit Kobkijwattana *(Exec Creative Dir)*
Rit Prompicharn *(Exec Dir-Creative)*
Anupong Aramboot *(Art Dir)*
Phakphoom Nopvaranon *(Art Dir)*
Wasawad Panichpairoj *(Art Dir)*
Yuwarat Surattanasathitkul *(Art Dir)*
Susita Lueksuengsukoom *(Copywriter)*
Vasinee Poungngern *(Copywriter)*
Rotrob Ramakomut *(Assoc Creative Dir)*

Accounts:
Bondex
Chia Tai
FB Battery
Friends of the Asian Elephant
Haw Par Tiger Balm Thailand Campaign: "Pen"
Kryoga Campaign: "Spine"
Land & Houses
McDonald's McDelivery Campaign: "Anytime Anywhere", Happy Meals Smiling Boxes
Michelin
Nissan
Protecta Kote Campaign: "Swinmming Pool"
PTT Group
Sanita International Co., Ltd
SCG Experience Campaign: "Dog"
Siam Furakawa Campaign: "Fb Energy Drink"
Standard Chartered

Vietnam

TBWA/Vietnam
Unit 302 Satra Dong Khoi, Ho Chi Minh City, Vietnam
Mailing Address:
60 Nguyen Dinh Chieu Ste #603, Ho Chi Minh City, Vietnam
Tel.: (84) 8 3824 5315
Fax: (84) 8 3824 5318
E-Mail: info@tbwa.com.vn
Web Site: www.tbwa.com.vn

Employees: 20

Tom Guerin *(Mng Dir)*
Tan Nguyen *(Head-Digital & Acct Dir)*
Hugh Southall *(Exec Dir-Creative)*
Khanh Mai *(Sr Dir-Art)*
Justin Cao *(Art Dir)*
Huong Ngo *(Art Dir)*
Thanh Tam Thai *(Art Dir)*
Lien Dinh *(Dir-Creative)*
Fanindra Jain *(Assoc Dir-Creative)*
Trang Ngo *(Copywriter)*

Accounts:
ATI Vietnam Digital Communications, Marketing, Media Planning
H2O Pro Lures Campaign: "Cat"
H.J. Heinz & CO. Heinz Ketchup, Lea & Perrins Worcestershire
IVIVU.com Campaign: "Let Yourself Out"
Lures
MegaStar Media
MobiFone
Saigon Sports Academy Marketing & Communications Development, Saigon Heat
VISA Campaign: "I Fight for Vietnam"
X-Men

ARGENTINA

Savaglio TBWA
Honduras 5952, Buenos Aires, Argentina
Tel.: (54) 11 5252 9100
Fax: (54) 43114004
E-Mail: info@tbwa.com.ar
Web Site: www.tbwa.com.ar

Employees: 50

Agency Specializes In: Advertising, Automotive, Consumer Goods, Food Service

Pablo Poncini *(Partner & CEO-TBWA/Buenos Aires)*
Guillermo Castaneda *(Exec Creative Dir)*
Cecilia Astengo *(Sr Dir-Art)*
Carlota Gabrielli *(Acct Dir)*
Fernando Serra *(Dir-Creative-TBWA Buenos Aires)*
Andre Soares *(Dir-Art)*
Joao Oliveira *(Copywriter-TBWA Buenos Aires)*

Accounts:
adidas AG
Asdra
Atma Hairdryers Campaign: "Salon hair at home"
BMW
Campari
Consejo Publicitario Argentino
ECOSOL Campaign: "Panels"
GlaxoSmithKline Brasil Ltda.
International Day of Persons with Disabilities
Mars Campaign: "The Tv Star that saved Dogs"
Medicus Campaign: "Swimming Pool", Health Insurance
Newsan Atma Light Bulbs
Nissan North America, Inc. Campaign: "Celltruck"
Pedigree
Persona Campaign: "Lemon"
Prime Campaign: "Striptease"
Samsonite Campaign: "Flying Luggage"
Telecom Campaign: "World Icon"

CHILE

TBWA Frederick
Avda Italia #850 2 Fl, Providencia, Santiago, Chile
Tel.: (56) 2 540 6700
Fax: (56) 2 540 6701
Web Site: projeqt.com/tbwacl/tbwa-frederick

E-Mail for Key Personnel:
Creative Dir.: Eduardo_Frederick@tbwachile.cl

Employees: 50

Agency Specializes In: Advertising, Automotive, Consumer Goods, Consumer Marketing, Food Service, Sports Market

Eduardo F. Aldunate *(Partner, VP & Head-Gen Brand)*
Gabriel Jefferies *(Gen Dir-Accounts & Plng)*
Eduardo Novion *(Gen Dir-Creative)*
Carlos Rosales *(Editor-Creative)*
Rodrigo Pacheco *(Art Dir)*
Felipe Ortiz *(Dir-Art)*
Claudio Ureta *(Dir-Art)*
Seba Urrutia *(Dir-Art)*
Carlos Velasco *(Dir-Art)*
Enrique Zuniga *(Dir-Creative)*
Waton Frederick *(Copywriter)*

Accounts:
Agorex Campaign: "Once Together Nothing Can Break Them Apart"
Aquafresh
BIC
BMW
Costa
Dercomaq Campaign: "Man"
Dog Adoption
Energizer
Foundation Coanil
Heineken
Japi Jane Campaign: "Poolman", Campaign: "Short stories for adults"
Komatsu Campaign: "Tooth"
Mini Coop
Opticas GMO
Pedigree
TAM Airlines Campaign: "The best food in the sky."
Todo Mejora Foundation
Wines of Chile

COLOMBIA

TBWA/Colombia Suiza de Publicidad Ltda
Diagonal 97 # 17/60 Edificio Centro Empresarial, 3rd Floor, 11001 Bogota, DC Colombia
Tel.: (57) 1 635 6090
Fax: (57) 1 611 2006
Web Site: projeqt.com/

Employees: 45

Jaime Cueto *(Chief Creative Officer)*
Cristian Ovalles *(Creative Dir & Copywriter)*
Roger Acosta *(Creative Dir)*
Luis Casadevall *(Dir-Creative)*
Miguel Angel Moreno *(Dir-Creative)*
Paulo Zamora *(Dir-Art)*
Rafael de Nicolas *(Exec Chm)*

Accounts:
Banco de Alimentos de Bogota Campaign: "Dinner"
Cine Colombia Campaign: "Much Bigger"
Cruz Roja Colombiana Campaign: "Blood saves"
Mega Sala Cine Colombia Campaign: "Indiana, Gandalf, Madhatter"
New-UNE Telecomunicaciones

COSTA RICA

TBWA Costa Rica
Guachipelin Escazu, 3312-1000 San Jose, Costa Rica
Tel.: (506) 205 4080
Fax: (506) 205 4088
E-Mail: mcordero@tbwacr.com

Ricardo Cordero Oreamuno *(Gen Mgr)*
Byron Balmaceda *(Dir-Creative)*
Gabriela Soto *(Brand Mgr)*

Accounts:
Lego Campaign: "Crocodile"

GUATEMALA

TBWA/Guatemala
23 Calle 15-14 Zone 13, Guatemala, 1013 Guatemala
Tel.: (502) 2313 6300
Fax: (502) 2385 3802
Web Site: tbwa.com.gt

Martin Sica *(Gen Dir-Creative)*
Raoul Herrera *(Gen Mgr)*
Levin Mendez *(Dir-Art)*

Accounts:
Radio Faro Cultural
Universidad Del Valle de Guatemala Campaign: "Decide Today, Who You Will be Tomorrow"

TEQUILA Guatemala
7A Avenida 14-44 Zona 9, Oficina 25, Nivel 2, Guatemala, 01009 Guatemala
Tel.: (502) 2385 9645
Fax: (502) 2361 3175
E-Mail: info@tequila-guatemala.com
Web Site: www.tequila-guatemala.com

Employees: 12

Agency Specializes In: Direct Response Marketing

Guillermo Diaz *(Owner)*
Cesar Cifuentes *(Dir-Creative)*
Tequila Guatemala *(Dir)*

Accounts:
AgExport

MEXICO

Teran TBWA
Monte Pelvoux 210 4 Piso, Lomas de Chapultepec, 11000 Mexico, DF Mexico
Tel.: (52) 555 209 3100
Fax: (52) 555 209 3176
Web Site: www.terantbwa.com.mx

E-Mail for Key Personnel:
President: jateran@terantbwa.com.mx

Year Founded: 1947

Begona Rubio Ferraez *(Exec Dir)*
Octavio Lopez Vargas *(Exec Dir-Digital)*
Ileana Ramirez *(Grp Acct Dir)*
Begona Lasso *(Acct Dir)*
Daniel Gurrola *(Dir-Creative)*
Sergio Riva Palacio Valdes *(Dir-Digital Creative)*
Guadalupe Ramirez *(Dir-HR)*
Michele Wiener *(Copywriter-Digital & Creative)*

Accounts:
Absolut Vodka
Adidas
Apple
Bayer
Domino's Pizza Campaign: "The Waiting, Reinvented"
EL Palacio de Hierro Campaign: "Plenitud"
GlaxoSmithKline
GNP Car Insurance Campaign: "Car Microphone", Campaign: "We See More than a Sedan"
Henkel
Jumex
Modelo Especial Campaign: "Legend", Campaign: "Special among the great"
Nissan Campaign: "Bateria", Campaign: "You've Changed"
Profuturo
Volaris Airlines
Volaris Campaign: "Vegas"

PERU

TBWA Peru
San Ignacia de Loyola 150, Miraflores, Lima, 18 Peru
Tel.: (51) 1 243 1200
Fax: (51) 1 243 4200
E-Mail: pdufour@tbwaperu.com
Web Site: www.tbwaperu.com

Employees: 45

Agency Specializes In: Advertising

Pilar Dufour *(Dir Gen)*
Giancarlo Cardenas *(Art Dir)*
Sara Cervantes *(Acct Dir)*
Alex Rodriguez *(Art Dir)*
Jorge Santibanez *(Creative Dir)*
Jose Espinosa *(Dir-Trademark)*
Luis Delgado Garrido *(Copywriter)*

Accounts:
Aquamatic Fresh Scents Detergent Campaign: "Nose-Pins"
CrediScotia
Hansaplast
Magazine
Playboy Enterprises, Inc Playboy Retardant Lubricated Condoms
New-Vitis

URUGUAY

TEQUILA Esece
Ellauri 1232, 11300 Montevideo, Uruguay
Tel.: (598) 2707 4277
Fax: (598) 2707 8291
E-Mail: info@tequilaesece.com
Web Site: www.tequilaesece.com

Employees: 25

Agency Specializes In: Direct Response Marketing

Florencia Scheitler *(Owner & Dir)*

Accounts:
Bacardi
Beiersdorf
Colgate
Ipusa
Nestle
Saman

SAUDI ARABIA

TBWA Raad
Salama Center, Prince Sultan Street, Jeddah, Saudi Arabia
Tel.: (966) 14 667 8999
Fax: (966) 2 616 5966
Web Site: www.tbwaraad.com

Ralph Khoury *(CFO)*
Rafic Kamaleddine *(Chief Strategy Officer)*
Noah Khan *(Head-Digital Arts Network)*
Nassim Nasr *(Gen Mgr-Integer ME)*
Mohamed Anwar *(Mgr-DM)*

Accounts:

adidas
Apple
Beko
McDonald's
Pedigree
Qatar National Broadband Network Company Communications Strategy
Samsonite
Singapore Airlines
Standard Chartered
Visa

TC CREATIVES LLC

6301 De Soto Ave, Woodland Hills, CA 91367
Tel.: (443) 615-0545
E-Mail: info@tc-creatives.com
Web Site: www.TC-Creatives.com

Year Founded: 2015

Agency Specializes In: Advertising, Advertising Specialties, Affluent Market, African-American Market, Arts, Brand Development & Integration, Business-To-Business, Catalogs, Children's Market, College, Commercial Photography, Communications, Computers & Software, Consulting, Consumer Goods, Consumer Marketing, Content, Corporate Identity, Cosmetics, Custom Publishing, Direct-to-Consumer, E-Commerce, Electronic Media, Electronics, Email, Entertainment, Event Planning & Marketing, Exhibit/Trade Shows, Fashion/Apparel, Financial, Food Service, Graphic Design, Guerilla Marketing, Health Care Services, High Technology, Hospitality, Household Goods, Identity Marketing, In-Store Advertising, Industrial, Information Technology, Integrated Marketing, International, Internet/Web Design, Investor Relations, Legal Services, Leisure, Local Marketing, Logo & Package Design, Luxury Products, Magazines, Market Research, Media Buying Services, Media Planning, Media Relations, Media Training, Men's Market, Merchandising, Mobile Marketing, Multimedia, New Technologies, Newspaper, Newspapers & Magazines, Out-of-Home Media, Over-50 Market, Package Design, Paid Searches, Planning & Consultation, Point of Sale, Print, Product Placement, Production, Production (Ad, Film, Broadcast), Production (Print), Promotions, Public Relations, Publicity/Promotions, Publishing, Radio, Real Estate, Restaurant, Retail, Sales Promotion, Search Engine Optimization, Seniors' Market, Shopper Marketing, Social Marketing/Nonprofit, Social Media, Sports Market, Strategic Planning/Research, T.V., Technical Advertising, Teen Market, Telemarketing, Trade & Consumer Magazines, Travel & Tourism, Tween Market, Urban Market, Viral/Buzz/Word of Mouth, Web (Banner Ads, Pop-ups, etc.), Women's Market

Tiffiney Cornish *(Owner)*

Accounts:
F. Gary Gray Website; 2015

TCAA

4555 Lk Forest Dr Ste 550, Cincinnati, OH 45242-3792
Tel.: (513) 956-5550
Fax: (513) 956-5558
Web Site: www.tcaausa.com

E-Mail for Key Personnel:
Creative Dir.: bill@ccaa.com

Employees: 15
Year Founded: 1996

Agency Specializes In: Advertising, Automotive, Broadcast, Cable T.V., Co-op Advertising, Direct Response Marketing, Exhibit/Trade Shows, Graphic Design, Hispanic Market, Local Marketing, Magazines, Newspaper, Newspapers & Magazines, Outdoor, Point of Sale, Print, Production, Publicity/Promotions, Radio, Retail, Sales Promotion, Sports Market, T.V.

Approx. Annual Billings: $60,397,000

Breakdown of Gross Billings by Media: Cable T.V.: $11,449,000; Newsp. & Mags.: $6,400,100; Other: $1,851,100; Production: $4,000,000; Radio: $1,998,900; T.V.: $34,697,900

Dan Connors *(COO)*
Mike Schrader *(VP-Creative & Dir)*
Will Wilson *(VP-Digital Mktg)*
Kathleen Davis *(Dir-Media)*
Willy Sorrell *(Dir-Art)*
Scott Atkinson *(Mgr-Interactive Media)*
Nina Feldman *(Media Buyer-TV, Radio & Digital)*
Burke Barlow *(Acct Rep-Northern)*

Accounts:
Cincinnati Region Toyota Dealers Association, KY, MI; OH; TN Automobiles; 1996
New England Toyota Dealers Association
TMMNA (Toyota Motor Manufacturing North America); Erlanger, KY North American Headquarters, Suppliers & Public Relations; 1999
WWTDA (Western Washington Toyota Dealers Association); WA Automobiles; 2000

TCREATIVE, INC.

2789 Wrights Rd Ste 1021, Oviedo, FL 32765
Tel.: (407) 628-1772
Fax: (407) 650-2677
Web Site: www.tcreative.com

Agency Specializes In: Advertising, Brand Development & Integration, Graphic Design, Social Media

Tim Holcomb *(Founder & Pres)*
Anne Marie Rose *(VP)*
Mark Hansen *(Dir-Production)*
Chris Salg *(Dir-Creative)*
Megan Glaser *(Acct Exec)*
Ashley Thompson *(Acct Exec)*

Accounts:
Toasted Restaurants
Tornatore's Cafe and Pizzeria (Agency of Record) Branding, Marketing

TCS ADVERTISING

37 W 1070 S Ste 201, Saint George, UT 84770
Tel.: (435) 674-2846
Fax: (435) 674-5753
Web Site: www.tenneyclemons.com

Agency Specializes In: Advertising, Graphic Design, Internet/Web Design, Media Buying Services, Print, Promotions, Public Relations, Radio, Social Media, T.V.

Brian J. Tenney *(Owner)*
Jeremey Forsberg *(Dir-Art)*

Accounts:
Janice Brooks
Ms. K's Fine Jewelry
True Natural Bodybuilder

TCS MEDIA, INC.

2333 Chinook Trl, Maitland, FL 32751-4079
Tel.: (407) 252-1026
Fax: (407) 264-6310
E-Mail: tom@tcsmedia.com
Web Site: www.tcsmedia.com

Employees: 1
Year Founded: 2003

Agency Specializes In: Advertising, Advertising Specialties, Business Publications, Business-To-Business, Catalogs, Collateral, Consulting, Corporate Identity, Digital/Interactive, Direct Response Marketing, E-Commerce, Electronic Media, Email, Exhibit/Trade Shows, Graphic Design, Internet/Web Design, Local Marketing, Logo & Package Design, Magazines, Market Research, Media Buying Services, Media Planning, Medical Products, Multimedia, New Product Development, Newspaper, Newspapers & Magazines, Pharmaceutical, Print, Production, Public Relations, Publishing, Real Estate, Sales Promotion, Search Engine Optimization, Sports Market, Trade & Consumer Magazines, Travel & Tourism, Web (Banner Ads, Pop-ups, etc.)

Tom Vittetow *(Owner)*

Accounts:
Athletes For America; Orlando, FL (Web Site & Print); 2004
Chris Thompson Realty; Hopetown, Bahamas (Web Site & Print); 2005

T.D. WANG ADVERTISING GROUP, LLC

(Name Changed to TDW+Co)

TDA_BOULDER

(Formerly TDA Advertising & Design)
1435 Arapahoe Ave, Boulder, CO 80302-6307
Tel.: (303) 247-1180
Fax: (303) 247-1214
E-Mail: info@tdaboulder.com
Web Site: www.tdaboulder.com

E-Mail for Key Personnel:
President: thomas@tdaboulder.com

Employees: 15
Year Founded: 1989

National Agency Associations: 4A's

Agency Specializes In: Advertising, Sponsorship

Jonathan Schoenberg *(Co-Owner & Creative Dir & Copywriter)*
Michael Nesmith *(Art Dir)*
Jeremy Seibold *(Creative Dir)*
Christi Tucay *(Acct Dir)*
Barrett Brynestad *(Dir-Art)*
Samantha Johnson *(Dir-Media)*
Colleen Callahan *(Acct Supvr)*
Robin Leighty *(Supvr-Media)*
Abby Parsons *(Acct Exec)*
Mary Kathryn Daugherty *(Media Planner & Media Buyer)*
Daniel Colburn *(Copywriter)*
Tim Kelly *(Copywriter)*

Accounts:
Bawx Campaign: "An Empty Box Full of Possibilities"
Blackburn Bike Accessories; Van Nuys, CA
Burton Snowboards
New-Castor & Pollux Natural Petworks
Charles Medley Distillers Kentucky (Agency of Record)
Cheribundi
The Chill Foundation Online, Print
Daiya Foods (Advertising Agency of Record) Campaign: "Hard to Notice", Digital, Outdoor, Packaging Design, Print, Unconventional Advertising
Deschutes Brewery (Agency of Record)
Elephant Journal Campaign: "Rainbows"
FirstBank "Anywhere Account", Broadcast, Campaign: "Bargain Dummy", Campaign: "Bathroom Break", Campaign: "Be Smart", Campaign: "Bus", Campaign: "Deflate

Mortgages", Campaign: "ED", Campaign: "Easy Should Be Easy", Campaign: "Elders", Campaign: "Eugene", Campaign: "Free", Campaign: "Get Back to the Real World", Campaign: "Legacy", Campaign: "Manure Bill", Campaign: "Pedi", Campaign: "Rules", Campaign: "Start and Grow Today", Digital, Media, Mobile App, Online, Outdoor, Person to Person Transfers Service, Print, Radio, Social; 2008
French's French's French Fried Onions, French's Mustard, French's Worcestershire Sauce, Non-Traditional, Package Design, Print
General Mills
Hapa Sushi Campaign: "Ergonomically Designed", Campaign: "Pairing Menu", Restaurant
New-Hispanic Democrats for Trump
Interbike International Bicycle Expo Online, Print
Justin's Nut Butter; Boulder, CO Footwear
Merrick Pet Care, Inc. (Advertising Agency of Record) Campaign: "The best dog ever deserves Merrick", Campaign: "Wolf Tested", Digital, Print
Newton Running Company Advertising Agency of Record, Digital, Marketing, Running Shoes
Noodles & Company; Broomfield, CO Brand Repositioning, Campaign: "Your World Kitchen", Creative, Digital, In-Store Advertising, Media, Print, Radio, Social Media Marketing
Outdoor Research; Seattle, WA
Patagonia
Regis University Creative, Media, Online, Outdoor, Print, Radio, Strategy, Transit Advertising
Sir Richard's Condom Company Campaign: "Sluts Unite", Campaign: "Suggested Retail", TV
TriNet Group, Inc.
USA Networks

TDG COMMUNICATIONS

93 Sherman St, Deadwood, SD 57732
Tel.: (605) 722-7111
Fax: (605) 722-7112
E-Mail: info@tdgcommunications.com
Web Site: www.tdgcommunications.com

Agency Specializes In: Advertising, Corporate Identity, Internet/Web Design, Logo & Package Design, Media Planning, Print, Public Relations, Social Media

Monte Amende *(Dir-Creative)*
Dan Daly *(Dir-PR)*
Jack Hughes *(Dir-Web Dev)*
Chad Blair *(Acct Exec)*

Accounts:
Keystone Chamber of Commerce

TDH MARKETING COMMUNICATIONS INC.

8153 Garnett Dr, Dayton, OH 45458
Tel.: (937) 438-3434
Fax: (937) 438-3453
E-Mail: kim@tdh-marketing.com
Web Site: www.tdh-marketing.com

Employees: 30
Year Founded: 1994

Agency Specializes In: Advertising, Brand Development & Integration, Digital/Interactive, Identity Marketing, Internet/Web Design, Public Relations

Tim Hull *(Pres & CEO)*
Janet Bismark *(Acct Dir-Mgmt)*
Pam Green *(Dir-Art)*
Laura Child *(Acct Mgr)*

Accounts:
Generation Dayton
Ideal Company
Ohio Masonic Home
Orthopaedic Institute of Dayton
Quebe Holdings
Shook Construction

TDW+CO

(Formerly T.D. Wang Advertising Group, LLC)
409 Maynard Ave S, Seattle, WA 98104
Tel.: (206) 623-6888
Fax: (206) 623-6889
E-Mail: info@tdwang.com
Web Site: www.tdwandco.com

Employees: 30
Year Founded: 2004

Agency Specializes In: Advertising, Brand Development & Integration, Consulting, Digital/Interactive, Event Planning & Marketing, Media Planning, Outdoor, Print, Radio, Strategic Planning/Research, T.V., Web (Banner Ads, Pop-ups, etc.)

Rebecca Deng *(Acct Dir)*
Victoria Wong *(Assoc Dir-Ops)*
Serena Li *(Sr Acct Exec)*
Howard Tran *(Sr Graphic Designer)*
Jorge Aviles *(Acct Coord-Experiential)*
Henry Lin *(Acct Coord)*

Accounts:
Allstate
Comcast
Pacific Gas and Electric Company
Pepsi Bottling Group
Port Of Seattle
Prudential
Seattle Seahawks
Starbucks
Verizon "Year of the Horse", Campaign: "Get A Bag Full of Luck and Fortune"
Wells Fargo
Western Union

TEAM EPIPHANY

1235 Broadway 4th Fl, New York, NY 10001
Tel.: (347) 990-1010
E-Mail: info@teamepiphany.com
Web Site: www.teamepiphany.com

Year Founded: 2004

Agency Specializes In: Advertising, Brand Development & Integration, Digital/Interactive, Public Relations, Search Engine Optimization, Social Media, Sponsorship, Strategic Planning/Research

Lisa Chu *(Mng Dir)*
Coltrane Curtis *(Mng Dir)*
Douglas Brundage *(VP-Strategy)*
Valerie Chiam *(Sr Dir-PR)*
Jarrett Cobbs *(Sr Dir-Strategy)*
Thembi Wesley *(Sr Dir-Events)*
Jane Kim *(Sr Acct Dir)*
Susan Morgan *(Sr Acct Dir)*
Jeffrey Weber *(Art Dir)*
Alexandra Covington *(Sr Acct Mgr)*
Nia Tran *(Sr Acct Mgr)*

Accounts:
Cadillac
New-Heaven Hill Distilleries, Inc. Campaign: "#Since2001", Hpnotiq

TEAM ONE USA

(Formerly Team One Advertising)
13031 W Jefferson Blvd, Los Angeles, CA 90094-7039
Tel.: (310) 437-2500
Fax: (310) 322-7565
E-Mail: info@teamone-usa.com
Web Site: www.teamone-usa.com

E-Mail for Key Personnel:
Public Relations: meg.seiler@teamone-usa.com

Employees: 290
Year Founded: 1987

National Agency Associations: 4A's-AAF-AMA-PRSA-THINKLA

Agency Specializes In: Advertising, Affluent Market, Alternative Advertising, Automotive, Brand Development & Integration, Branded Entertainment, Broadcast, Business Publications, Catalogs, Collateral, Communications, Consulting, Consumer Goods, Corporate Communications, Corporate Identity, Customer Relationship Management, Digital/Interactive, Direct Response Marketing, Email, Entertainment, Event Planning & Marketing, Experience Design, Financial, Graphic Design, Hospitality, In-Store Advertising, Internet/Web Design, Leisure, Logo & Package Design, Luxury Products, Magazines, Media Buying Services, Media Planning, Media Training, Merchandising, Mobile Marketing, Multimedia, New Product Development, Newspaper, Newspapers & Magazines, Out-of-Home Media, Outdoor, Package Design, Paid Searches, Planning & Consultation, Point of Purchase, Point of Sale, Print, Production, Production (Print), Promotions, Public Relations, Publicity/Promotions, Radio, Sales Promotion, Search Engine Optimization, Social Marketing/Nonprofit, Social Media, Sponsorship, Strategic Planning/Research, Syndication, T.V., Travel & Tourism, Viral/Buzz/Word of Mouth

Kurt Ritter *(Chm)*
Julie Michael *(Pres)*
Michael Webb *(CFO)*
Chris Graves *(Chief Creative Officer)*
Mark Miller *(Chief Strategy Officer)*
Chris D'Rozario *(Exec Dir-Creative)*
Alastair Green *(Exec Dir-Creative)*
Paul Silverman *(Exec Dir)*
Craig Crawford *(Grp Dir-Creative)*
Jen Grant *(Grp Dir-Strategy)*
Monica Mellier *(Grp Dir-Media)*
Jason Stinsmuehlen *(Grp Dir-Creative)*
Steve Hanlon *(Sr Dir-Art)*
Jim Ryan *(Grp Acct Dir)*
John Coelho *(Acct Dir)*
John Dohrmann *(Creative Dir)*
Amy Gershwin *(Producer-Brdcst)*
Meredith Gruen *(Acct Dir)*
Amy Oars *(Acct Dir)*
Ian Phillips *(Acct Dir)*
Jon Ruppel *(Creative Dir)*
Adrienne Feldman *(Mgmt Supvr)*
Damian Areyan *(Dir-Experiential Mktg & Sponsorships)*
Allison Citino *(Dir-Comm)*
Rebecca Foster *(Dir-Media)*
Phil Glist *(Dir-Creative)*
James Hendry *(Dir-Creative)*
Phil Henson *(Dir-Creative)*
Heather Hogan *(Dir-Mktg)*
Quoc Lu *(Dir-Art)*
Kathryn McFarlane *(Dir-Creative)*
Amanda Abrams *(Assoc Dir-Creative & Copywriter)*
Dustin Arnold *(Assoc Dir-Creative)*
Jim Darling *(Assoc Dir-Creative)*
Michael Nnadi *(Assoc Dir-Interactive Production)*
Amanda Taft *(Assoc Dir-Media)*
Amanda Delay *(Mgr-Talent)*
Malika Jones *(Mgr-Brdcst Traffic)*
Patrick Jagodzinski *(Acct Supvr-Digital)*
Robin Meselson *(Acct Supvr)*
Trina Sethi *(Acct Supvr)*
Melissa Lam *(Supvr-Interactive Media)*
Scott Miller *(Supvr-Transportation)*
Alison Barendse *(Acct Exec-Digital-Lexus)*
Andrew Crawford *(Acct Exec)*
Lindsay Rich *(Acct Exec)*

Sherie Hodges *(Media Planner)*
Robert Johnston *(Designer)*
Lucia Matioli *(Designer)*
Patrick O'Rourke *(Copywriter)*
Mike Rozycki *(Copywriter)*
Brett Landrum *(Asst Acct Exec)*

Accounts:
2K "Ready or Not", Broadcast, Campaign: "The Aftermath", Campaign: "The Bureau: XCOM Declassified", Evolve
American Express Co. Premium Travel Marketing, Cruise Privileges Program & Private Jet Travel
Bombardier Inc Flexjet; 2008
CBS Watch! Magazine
EDITION Hotels
New-Electronic Arts, inc.
Flexjet, Inc.
FocusDriven.org Awareness Campaign, Campaign: "Candlelight memorial", Campaign: "LOL", Campaign: "OMG", Social Media
General Mills, Inc. Haagen-Dazs
HappyBombs
Heal the Bay
Lexus Dealer Association
Lexus Division (Agency of Record) "December to Remember", Broadcast, Campaign: "#LexusInstafilm", Campaign: "Blend Out", Campaign: "Christmas Train", Campaign: "Color Shift", Campaign: "Crowd", Campaign: "Different Routes", Campaign: "It Got Better", Campaign: "Lexus Design Disrupted", Campaign: "Magic Box", Campaign: "Teleporter", Campaign: "Temptation", Campaign: "The Lexus Fashion Workshop", Campaign: "Tori 500", Digital, Hispanic, L/Studio, LX 570 SUV, Lexus ES, Lexus IS, Lexus IS F Sport, Lexus LS, Lexus NX, Lexus RX, OOH, Print, TV
Marriott International
Nestle USA, Inc.
The Ritz-Carlton Hotel Advertising
Toyota Motor Sales, U.S.A., Inc. Campaign: "LexusInstaFilm", Campaign: "RC Illusion", Lexus CT, Lexus ES Series, Lexus GS Series, Lexus GX Series, Lexus IS Series, Lexus LX Series, Lexus RX Series, Super Bowl 2015

Branches

Team One USA
(Formerly Team One Advertising)
1 Tower Ste 3120 Oak Brook Cerrace, Oak Brook, IL 60181
Tel.: (630) 684-0317
Fax: (630) 684-0324
E-Mail: info@teamone-usa.com
Web Site: www.teamone-usa.com/

Employees: 6

Agency Specializes In: Advertising

Steve Bava *(Dir-Mgmt)*
Adam Bright *(Dir-Digital Art)*
Aaron Jacob *(Dir-Art)*
Dan Unger *(Mgr-Central Area Lexus Dealer Association)*
Abby Jacobs *(Asst Acct Exec-LDA ERM)*
Alex Boggs *(Reg Acct Dir)*
Ashley Chen *(Asst Media Planner)*

TEAMNASH, INC.
4 Jonathan Dr, East Hampton, NY 11937
Tel.: (646) 497-0297
E-Mail: results@teamnash.com
Web Site: www.teamnash.com

Employees: 6
Year Founded: 1995

National Agency Associations: DMA-DMCNY

Agency Specializes In: Advertising, Broadcast, Cable T.V., Consulting, Consumer Goods, Consumer Marketing, Corporate Communications, Cosmetics, Customer Relationship Management, Direct Response Marketing, Direct-to-Consumer, Education, Financial, Infomercials, Internet/Web Design, New Product Development, Newspapers & Magazines, Over-50 Market, Planning & Consultation, Search Engine Optimization, Seniors' Market, Strategic Planning/Research

Approx. Annual Billings: $6,300,000

Breakdown of Gross Billings by Media: Brdcst.: $350,000; Co-op Adv.: $270,000; Consulting: $1,200,000; D.M.: $3,500,000; E-Commerce: $100,000; Internet Adv.: $210,000; Newsp. & Mags.: $45,000; Plng. & Consultation: $625,000

Edward Nash *(Owner)*

Accounts:
Costa REIT; Baltimore, MD Land Investment Trust, 2004
Del Pacifico; Esterillios, Costa Rica Luxury Retirement & Vacation Resort; 2004
Dialog Productions; Istanbul, Turkey Acting & Speech Education; 2003
Dialogo Education; Istanbul, Turkey Acting & Executive Speaking; 2008
Healthwise Coffee; Valencia, CA Continuity
Jergens; Cincinnati, OH Retail Promotion; 2007
JWT; Los Angeles, CA Mature Market Direct Mail
LifebankUSA; Cedar Knolls, NJ Umbilical Cord Blood Banking Services; 2004
Moviebeam; Burbank, CA Video Rental Services; 2004
Revitacel; Washington, DC Beauty Products
Simon & Schuster; NY Language Courses

TECHNETIUM
(Acquired & Absorbed by BMDM)

TEEHAN+LAX
460 Richmond St W Ste 301, Toronto, ON M5V 1Y1 Canada
Tel.: (416) 340-8666
Fax: (416) 340-0777
E-Mail: us@teehanlax.com
Web Site: www.teehanlax.com

Employees: 25

Agency Specializes In: Advertising, Digital/Interactive, Email, Internet/Web Design

Kyra Aylsworth *(Product Mgr & Planner)*

Accounts:
Air Jamaica
Air Miles
Bell Canada Campaign: "Bell Social Portrait"
BMW
Digital Signage
Driving.Ca
Hover.com
Image Spark
JPMorgan
New Balance
OurFaves.Com
The Star.com
SunChips.com
TELUS-Gift Guide
TELUS
Virgin Mobile Canada Digital

TEENAGE RESEARCH UNLIMITED
222 Merchandise Mart Ste 250, Chicago, IL 60654
Tel.: (312) 951-4100
Fax: (321) 951-4845
E-Mail: info@tru-insight.com
Web Site: www.teenresearch.com

Employees: 28

Agency Specializes In: Social Media

Jill Kilcoyne *(Dir-Ops)*
Lisa Moes *(Dir-Res)*
Joanna Folz *(Sr Mgr-Res)*
Caroline Grant-Waddell *(Sr Acct Mgr)*

Accounts:
Hewlett-Packard
Kraft
Microsoft
MTV
MySpace
Pepsi-Cola

TEGO MEDIA
PO Box 5551, Scottsdale, AZ 85261
Tel.: (800) 878-0340
Web Site: www.tego.com

Year Founded: 2007

Agency Specializes In: Advertising, Advertising Specialties, Affluent Market, African-American Market, Bilingual Market, Brand Development & Integration, Communications, Consumer Marketing, Digital/Interactive, Direct Response Marketing, Direct-to-Consumer, Electronic Media, High Technology, Hispanic Market, Integrated Marketing, Luxury Products, Media Planning, Media Relations, Men's Market, Over-50 Market, Production, Production (Ad, Film, Broadcast), Publishing, Seniors' Market, Social Marketing/Nonprofit, Strategic Planning/Research, Technical Advertising, Teen Market, Tween Market, Urban Market, Women's Market

Tiffany Phillips *(Dir-Comm)*

TELESCO CREATIVE GROUP
1868 Niagara Fls Blvd Ste 200, Tonawanda, NY 14150
Tel.: (716) 525-1311
Web Site: www.telescocreativegroup.com

Agency Specializes In: Advertising, Brand Development & Integration, Broadcast, Internet/Web Design

Mike Telesco *(Pres & Creative Dir)*
Greg Meadows *(Creative Dir)*

Accounts:
New-Osteria 166
New-Town Square for Aging

TELL YOUR STORY
20 N Wacker Dr Ste 3330, Chicago, IL 60606
Tel.: (847) 921-3925
E-Mail: info@tellyourstoryinc.com
Web Site: tellyourstoryinc.com

Employees: 10

Agency Specializes In: Business Publications, Publishing

George Rafeedie *(Founder)*

Accounts:
USG Corporation

TEMPO CREATIVE, INC.
13951 N Scottsdale Rd Ste 213, Scottsdale, AZ 85254-3402
Tel.: (480) 659-4100

Fax: (480) 659-9180
Toll Free: (800) 816-9850
E-Mail: info@tempocreative.com
Web Site: www.tempocreative.com

Employees: 12
Year Founded: 2001

Agency Specializes In: Advertising, Brand Development & Integration, Collateral, Content, E-Commerce, Email, Graphic Design, In-Store Advertising, Internet/Web Design, Local Marketing, Logo & Package Design, Market Research, Multimedia, Newspapers & Magazines, Package Design, Point of Sale, Print, Public Relations, Search Engine Optimization, Strategic Planning/Research, Web (Banner Ads, Pop-ups, etc.)

Josh Dolin *(Founder)*
Joy Donaldson *(VP-Client Svcs)*
Charmon Stiles *(VP-Sls & Mktg)*

Accounts:
Cold Stone Creamery; Scottsdale, AZ; 2003
The MC Companies; Scottsdale, AZ
Novara Clinical Research; Mesa, AZ
Sierra Title Service; Phoenix, AZ
Trimble Consulting; Tempe, AZ
Valley Physical Therapy Services; Scottsdsale, AZ
Weight Loss Institute of Arizona; Tempe, AZ

TEN
(Formerly AgencyNet)
330 SW 2nd St Bldg 111, Fort Lauderdale, FL 33312
Tel.: (954) 524-8800
E-Mail: biz@agencyten.com
Web Site: www.agencyten.com

Employees: 30
Year Founded: 1996

National Agency Associations: SODA

Agency Specializes In: Digital/Interactive, Food Service, Radio, Sports Market, T.V.

Betsy DeCarlo *(Pres)*
Melanie Newson *(Sr Dir-Art)*
Lauren Kahn *(Dir-Database Mgmt, Partnership & Agency)*
Lindsay Valero *(Dir-Accts)*

Accounts:
American Heart Association
Anvil Knitwear
Bacardi
BBC America
Bombay Sapphire
Citizen Watch
Clinton Foundation
Dewar's
Ford
INdemand
Martini
Pencils of Promise
Ruby Tuesday
Saint-Gobain
Teach for America
Universal
US Airforce
Wishcloud Campaign: "There's Something Not Right About Jane"

TEN FAST FEET
218 3rd Ave N, Nashville, TN 37201
Tel.: (615) 345-4231
Web Site: www.tenfastfeet.com

Agency Specializes In: Advertising, Brand Development & Integration, Digital/Interactive, Internet/Web Design, Logo & Package Design, Media Buying Services, Print, Social Media

Accounts:
Superior Orthotics & Prosthetics

TENET PARTNERS
(Formerly CoreBrand)
122 W 27th St 9th Fl, New York, NY 10001
Tel.: (212) 329-3030
Fax: (212) 329-3031
E-Mail: esluder@tenetpartners.com
Web Site: tenetpartners.com

E-Mail for Key Personnel:
President: jgregory@corebrand.com

Employees: 30
Year Founded: 1973

Agency Specializes In: Brand Development & Integration, Business-To-Business, Collateral, Communications, Consulting, Corporate Communications, Corporate Identity, Financial, Graphic Design, Internet/Web Design, Investor Relations, Logo & Package Design, Sponsorship, Strategic Planning/Research

James Gregory *(Chm)*
Hampton Bridwell *(CEO)*
Beth Flom *(Partner-Strategy)*
David Garcia *(Partner-Design)*
Brad Puckey *(Partner-CoreBrand Analytics)*
Renee Malfi *(Acct Dir)*
Annick Wydooghe *(Dir-Concept Dev)*
Janice Bissell *(Acct Mgr)*
Lindsay Beltzer *(Mgr-Mktg Comm)*
Larry Oakner *(Sr Partner-Engagement & Strategy)*

Accounts:
AmerisourceBergen
APM Terminals
AT&T, Inc.
Broadridge
Chubb
Cisco Systems
Colgate-Palmolive
Delphi
Dupont
ExxonMobil
Found Animals
The Hartford
ING
Johnson & Johnson
Lincoln Financial
Long Beach Airport
Mastercard Worldwide
Paramount Citrus
Samsung
Sensient Technologies Corporation
Target
Transamerica
Union Pacific
Virginia Commonwealth

TENTHWAVE DIGITAL, LLC
31 W 27th 12th Fl, New York, NY 10001
Tel.: (212) 933-9221
Fax: (646) 607-2471
E-Mail: press@tenthwave.com
Web Site: www.tenthwave.com

Year Founded: 2011

Agency Specializes In: Advertising, Brand Development & Integration, Digital/Interactive, Internet/Web Design, Search Engine Optimization, Social Marketing/Nonprofit

Eric Schwamberger *(Partner, CMO & Chief Content Officer)*
Mike Mazar *(Partner & Creative Dir)*
Rob Kaplan *(Partner)*
Craig Wishner *(Sr VP-Strategic Accts)*
Chris Bragas *(VP-Fin)*
Gunny Scarfo *(VP-Strategy)*
Lauren D'Aloisio *(Dir-Art)*
Leighann Farrelly *(Dir-Social Media)*
Nat Thomson *(Dir-Strategy)*
Ben Zeidler *(Dir-Res & Analytics)*
Olivia Nanda *(Acct Mgr)*
Samuel Edwards *(Strategist-Online Media)*

Accounts:
Alford & Hoff
The Bank of New York Mellon Corporation
Beam Global Spirits & Wines
Cancer Care, Inc.
Duncan Hines
EA Sports
eBay Campaign: "Buy It New, Buy It Now"
Facebook, Inc.
Google
Pinnacle Foods Corporation Birds Eye
Skype
Snyder's-Lance, Inc. Social Media
United Nations Federal Credit Union
VSP Vision Care

TENZING COMMUNICATIONS
615 Wellington St, London, ON N6A 3R6 Canada
Tel.: (519) 642-4404
Fax: (519) 642-4856
E-Mail: gary@gotenzing.com
Web Site: www.gotenzing.com

Employees: 17
Year Founded: 1989

Gary Lintern *(Pres)*
Henry Wong *(VP-Creative & Dir)*
J. C. Molina *(Sr Dir-Art)*
Michelle Clement Homonylo *(Dir-Client Rels)*
Dan Rempel *(Dir-Electronic Environments)*
Christine Wong *(Designer)*

Accounts:
Aercoustics Engineering
Bite Tv
CMHA, Ontario
Hydrogenics
OSRAM Sylvania
Soapstones
Transition Science
Wera Tools

TEQUILA COMMUNICATION & MARKETING INC.
3556 boul Saint Laurent Bureau Ste 200, Montreal, QC H2X 2V1 Canada
Tel.: (514) 849-8005
Fax: (514) 849-9500
E-Mail: tequila@tequila.ca
Web Site: www.tequila.ca

Employees: 20

Agency Specializes In: Advertising

Bernard Berthiaume *(Partner-Strategy & Mgmt)*
Diane Bazinet *(Sr Acct Exec)*

Accounts:
Hyundai

THE TERRI & SANDY SOLUTION
1133 Bdwy Ste 928, New York, NY 10010
Tel.: (917) 261-6792
Web Site: www.terrisandy.com

National Agency Associations: 4A's

Agency Specializes In: Advertising, Print, Sponsorship, T.V.

Sandy Greenberg *(Co-Founder & Co-Pres)*
Terri Meyer *(Co-Founder & Co-Pres)*
Tony Scopellito *(Mng Dir)*
Lauren Gelfman *(Acct Dir-Integrated)*
Drew Schwartz *(Acct Dir-Integrated)*
Cheryl Bailey *(Dir-Strategic Plng)*
Juan Pablo Gomez *(Dir-Art)*
Dani Barish Blevins *(Acct Supvr)*
Todd Condie *(Copywriter)*

Accounts:
Freshpet Campaign: "So Good, You could Eat it", Digital Pre-Roll, Display Banners, Online, Print, Social Media, TV
Gerber
JDate Campaign: "Get Chosen"
Just Born, Inc. "Peanut Chews", Campaign: "Brothers", Campaign: "Express Your Peepsonality", Digital, Goldenberg's, Peeps, TV
People Magazine (Agency of Record) 40th Anniversary, Digital, Print, Royals, Sexiest Man Alive, TV
New-Phonak (Global Lead Agency of Record)
New-Walt Disney Co

TERRY HINES & ASSOCIATES
2550 N Hollywood Way Ste 600, Burbank, CA 91505
Tel.: (818) 562-9433
E-Mail: info@terryhines.com
Web Site: www.terryhines.com

Employees: 20
Year Founded: 1959

Agency Specializes In: Advertising, Entertainment, Publicity/Promotions

Approx. Annual Billings: $8,500,000

Kathryn Findling *(Exec VP-Brand Partnerships)*
Melanie Erichsen *(Acct Dir)*

Accounts:
Buena Vista Pictures Marketing; Burbank, CA Motion Pictures
Fine Line Features Motion Pictures
Hollywood Pictures; Burbank, CA
Lions Gate Films; New York, NY
New Line Cinema; Los Angeles, CA Motion Pictures
Sony Pictures Classics; New York, NY
TNT; Atlanta, GA
Touchtone Pictures; Burbank, CA
Universal Pictures; Universal City, CA Motion Pictures
Walt Disney Pictures; Burbank, CA

TERZETTO CREATIVE
PO Box 188, Barboursville, WV 25504
Tel.: (304) 654-0875
Web Site: www.terzettocreative.com

Agency Specializes In: Advertising, Event Planning & Marketing, Internet/Web Design, Logo & Package Design, Media Buying Services, Promotions

Laura Dial *(Partner & Creative Dir)*
Jenny Lancaster *(Partner & Dir-Client)*
John Lancaster *(Partner & Dir-Multimedia)*

Accounts:
Mid-Atlantic Telehealth Resource Center

TESSER INC.
121 2nd St Top Fl, San Francisco, CA 94105
Tel.: (415) 541-9999
Fax: (415) 541-9699
Toll Free: (800) 310-4400
E-Mail: info@tesser.com
Web Site: www.tesser.com

Agency Specializes In: Advertising, Brand Development & Integration, Business-To-Business, Collateral, Corporate Identity, Graphic Design, Internet/Web Design, Outdoor, Package Design, Print, Sponsorship

Tre Musco *(Owner)*
Donna Motta *(Client Dir & Dir-Studio Svcs)*
Brent White *(Dir-Design)*
Dana Zipser *(Dir-Bus Dev & Mktg)*
Aly Holmes *(Coord-Mktg & Project Coord)*

Accounts:
ArmorAll
Ben & Jerry's Homemade, Inc.
Chevys Fresh Mex
Chili's
Dairy Queen Corporate Store
Del Taco LLC
Domino's Pizza, Inc.
Figaro's Pizza
The Gap, Inc.
Haagen-Dazs
IHOP Cafe
KFC Corporation
Malibu Rum
Spinner

TETHER, INC.
316 Occidental Ave S Ste 400, Seattle, WA 98104
Tel.: (206) 518-6300
E-Mail: info@tetherinc.com
Web Site: www.tetherinc.com

Agency Specializes In: Advertising, Brand Development & Integration, Content, Graphic Design

Bill Allen *(Creative Dir-Interactive)*
Steve Barrett *(Creative Dir)*
Dodi Monahan *(Acct Dir)*
Hart Rusen *(Creative Dir-Adv)*
Matt Schmunk *(Dir-Creative)*
Dan Smith *(Dir-Design)*
Nancy Urner *(Dir-Ops)*

Accounts:
New-Luvo
New-Safariland Campaign: "Fit is Everything", GLS Pro-Fit
Tully's Coffee Brand Refresh Strategy, Marketing

TEVIOT CREATIVE
1650 W End Blvd, Minneapolis, MN 55416
Tel.: (763) 259-5778
E-Mail: hello@teviotcreative.com
Web Site: www.teviotcreative.com

Agency Specializes In: Advertising, Brand Development & Integration, Digital/Interactive, Internet/Web Design, Print

Craig Hall *(Mng Dir)*

Accounts:
Carlson Rezidor Hotel Group
Regis Corporation

TEXAS CREATIVE
334 N Pk Dr, San Antonio, TX 78216
Tel.: (210) 828-8003
E-Mail: info@texascreative.com
Web Site: www.texascreative.com

Agency Specializes In: Advertising, Brand Development & Integration, Collateral, Digital/Interactive, Internet/Web Design, Media Buying Services, Media Planning, Outdoor, Print, Social Media

Brian Eickhoff *(Pres & Sr Dir-Creative)*
Jamie Allen *(COO & Principal)*
Josh Norman *(Exec VP & Dir-Creative)*
Jane Hollimon *(Acct Exec)*
Rebecca Kellogg *(Acct Exec)*
Kevin Eickhoff *(Asst Acct Exec)*
Carlene Calkins *(Asst Media Buyer)*

Accounts:
Tobin Center for the Performing Arts

TEXTOPOLY, INC.
170 Columbus Ave Ste 280, San Francisco, CA 94133
Tel.: (949) 281-7201
Toll Free: (877) 806-3596
E-Mail: hello@xtopoly.com
Web Site: www.xtopoly.com

Employees: 6
Year Founded: 2005

Agency Specializes In: Advertising, Consulting, Mobile Marketing

Approx. Annual Billings: $1,000,000

Breakdown of Gross Billings by Media: Consulting: $1,000,000

Naushad Huda *(CEO)*

TG MADISON
(Acquired by Chemistry Communications Inc. & Name Changed to Chemistry Atlanta)

THACHER INTERACTIVE LLC
41 Grove St 4th Fl, New York, NY 10014
Tel.: (917) 497-3569
E-Mail: hello@thacherinteractive.com
Web Site: www.thacherinteractive.com

Year Founded: 2010

Agency Specializes In: Advertising, Brand Development & Integration, Content, Digital/Interactive, Internet/Web Design, Promotions, Search Engine Optimization, Social Media

Zachary Thacher *(Principal)*
Dave Giles *(Dir-Creative)*
Alex Twersky *(Strategist-Digital)*

Accounts:
Duncan Hines

THAT AGENCY
410 Evernia St Ste 118, West Palm Beach, FL 33401-5431
Tel.: (561) 832-6262
Fax: (561) 832-7707
E-Mail: info@thatagency.com
Web Site: www.thatagency.com

Employees: 12

Agency Specializes In: Advertising, Advertising Specialties, African-American Market, Agriculture, Asian Market, Automotive, Aviation & Aerospace, Bilingual Market, Brand Development & Integration, Broadcast, Business Publications, Business-To-Business, Cable T.V., Children's Market, Co-op Advertising, Collateral, Commercial Photography, Communications, Consulting, Consumer Marketing, Consumer Publications, Corporate Communications, Corporate Identity, Cosmetics, Digital/Interactive, Direct Response Marketing, E-Commerce, Education, Electronic Media,

Engineering, Entertainment, Environmental, Event Planning & Marketing, Exhibit/Trade Shows, Fashion/Apparel, Financial, Food Service, Gay & Lesbian Market, Government/Political, Graphic Design, Health Care Services, High Technology, Hispanic Market, In-Store Advertising, Industrial, Infomercials, Information Technology, Internet/Web Design, Investor Relations, Legal Services, Leisure, Local Marketing, Logo & Package Design, Magazines, Marine, Media Buying Services, Medical Products, Merchandising, Multimedia, New Product Development, Newspaper, Newspapers & Magazines, Out-of-Home Media, Outdoor, Over-50 Market, Pharmaceutical, Planning & Consultation, Point of Purchase, Point of Sale, Print, Production, Public Relations, Publicity/Promotions, Radio, Real Estate, Recruitment, Restaurant, Retail, Sales Promotion, Seniors' Market, Sports Market, Strategic Planning/Research, Sweepstakes, Syndication, T.V., Technical Advertising, Teen Market, Telemarketing, Trade & Consumer Magazines, Transportation, Travel & Tourism, Yellow Pages Advertising

Approx. Annual Billings: $2,000,000

Breakdown of Gross Billings by Media: Internet Adv.: $1,000,000; Print: $500,000; Worldwide Web Sites: $500,000

Bill Teubner *(Pres)*
Michelle Sternbauer *(Exec VP & Acct Dir)*
Casey Kurlander *(Specialist-Social Media Mktg)*
Ronald Busky *(Copywriter)*
Taylor De Luca *(Copywriter)*
Joey Wolff *(Copywriter)*

Accounts:
ACP Jets; West Palm Beach, FL Aircraft; 2005
Bacardi; Washington, DC (Interactive); 2001
Braman Motorcars (Digital Agency of Record) BMW, Bentley, Braman Audi, Content, Mini, Porsche, Rolls Royce, Social Media, Video, Website Strategies
FedEx; Miami, FL E-Business Solutions; 2000
Florida Environmental Pest Management Digital Marketing, Website
Natura Wines Design, Website
Warsteiner Brewery Design, Pilsener Pursuit

THE1STMOVEMENT
1010 E Union St Ste 120, Pasadena, CA 91106
Tel.: (626) 689-4993
Fax: (626) 628-1991
E-Mail: info@the1stmovement.com
Web Site: www.the1stmovement.com

Employees: 20

Agency Specializes In: Digital/Interactive, Sponsorship

Ming Chan *(CEO)*
Bryan Encina *(Head-Technical)*
Jennifer DePauw *(Sr Dir-Ops)*
Tadeo Gonzalez *(Sr Producer-Interactive)*
Kim Hughes *(Acct Dir)*
Brian Midwin *(Dir-Fin)*
Stephanie Guerrero *(Mgr-Fin Support)*
Cody Moiseve *(Sr Designer-Interactive)*

Accounts:
Adobe
AOL
Cardinal Health
E! Online
Gulfstream Aviation
Microsoft
Pentax Imaging Co. Campaign: "Adventure is Everywhere", Digital
Qwest
Rambus
Style Network
TravelStore Digital
VertiFlex
Virgin Records
WOW - Women of Wrestling (Digital Agency of Record) Design, Strategy

THEFRAMEWORKS
755 W Big Beaver Rd Ste 100, Troy, MI 48084
Tel.: (248) 250-9948
E-Mail: info@theframeworks.com
Web Site: www.theframeworks.com

Agency Specializes In: Advertising, Brand Development & Integration, Digital/Interactive

Rosalba Clay *(Sr Acct Dir)*
Nick Francis *(Dir-Creative-Casual Films)*
Travis Smith *(Sr Acct Mgr)*
Amy Walters *(Sr Acct Mgr)*
Melissa Ivey *(Acct Mgr)*
Cheuk Man Lam *(Sr Project Mgr-Digital)*
Rose Stewart *(Designer)*
Marina Munro *(Jr Designer)*

Accounts:
Toshiba Global Commerce Solutions

THELEN
703 W St Germain, Saint Cloud, MN 56301
Tel.: (320) 253-6510
E-Mail: info@thelenideas.com
Web Site: www.thelenideas.com

Agency Specializes In: Advertising, Email, Graphic Design, Internet/Web Design, Logo & Package Design, Outdoor, Print, Public Relations, Radio, Strategic Planning/Research

Ronn Paulson *(Pres)*
Samantha Bohn *(Dir-Art)*
Mary Ellen Kerber *(Acct Exec)*

Accounts:
Red Star Yeast

THELMA LAGER & ASSOCIATES
3015 Glendale Blvd, Los Angeles, CA 90039-1832
Tel.: (323) 664-2177
Fax: (323) 663-6429

Employees: 2
Year Founded: 1964

National Agency Associations: AAF

Agency Specializes In: Advertising, Children's Market, Direct Response Marketing, E-Commerce, Magazines, Merchandising, Planning & Consultation, Print, Publicity/Promotions

Thelma Lager *(Owner)*

Accounts:
Arm's Reach Concepts, Inc.; 1997
Chase Foundation Child Life Services; 1994

THERAPY
2010 S Westgate Ave, Los Angeles, CA 90025
Tel.: (310) 917-1507
Fax: (310) 917-1562
Web Site: therapystudios.com

Employees: 14
Year Founded: 2005

Agency Specializes In: Advertising, Advertising Specialties, Brand Development & Integration, Broadcast, Cable T.V., Communications, Corporate Communications, Electronic Media, Infomercials, Internet/Web Design, Media Buying Services, Production, Publicity/Promotions, Strategic Planning/Research, T.V.

Approx. Annual Billings: $2,000,000

Breakdown of Gross Billings by Media: Spot T.V.: 100%

Wren Waters *(Owner)*
Allegra Bartlett *(Head-Production)*
Juliana Watson *(Office Mgr)*
Sana Bawania *(Assoc Producer)*

Accounts:
Coca-Cola Refreshments USA, Inc.
Fox Broadcasting VFX Design
Kia
Kleenex Tissues
Mercedes Benz
NASCAR Race
Pioneer Navigation System
Time Warner Cable
Volkswagen Group of America, Inc.
Walmart Superstore

THIEL DESIGN LLC
(Private-Parent-Single Location)
325 E Chicago St Ste 2, Milwaukee, WI 53202
Tel.: (414) 271-0775
Web Site: www.thiel.com

Employees: 13
Year Founded: 1975

Agency Specializes In: Advertising, Brand Development & Integration, Digital/Interactive, Print, Social Media

Revenue: $2,500,000

Susan Hoffman *(Principal & Dir-IT)*
Norene Thiel *(Principal & Dir-Ops)*
Keith Walters *(Principal & Strategist)*
Tom Campbell *(Dir-Creative)*
Bennett Counsell *(Mgr-Mktg)*
Ryan Robers *(Mgr-Interactive Media)*
Andrea Walters *(Acct Exec & Sr Designer)*
Lydia Driscoll *(Designer-Production)*
Pete Tonn *(Sr Designer)*
Bill Zalenski *(Sr Designer)*

Accounts:
RC Insurance Services

THIELEN IDEACORP
(Merged with The Astone Agency to form Astone Thielen & Rebranded as Catalyst Marketing Company)

THINK AGENCY
214 N Westmonte Dr Ste 3019, Altamonte Springs, FL 32714
Tel.: (407) 875-1999
Web Site: www.thinkagency.com

Agency Specializes In: Advertising, Brand Development & Integration, Internet/Web Design, Logo & Package Design, Print, Public Relations

Dennis Claypoole *(Pres)*
Jerry Eisen *(Partner & VP)*
Doug Adams *(Partner)*
Chris Davis *(Dir-Web & Application Dev)*
Johnny Greene *(Dir-Production)*
Mike Miller *(Dir-Content Mktg)*
Julie Kalt *(Copywriter)*

Accounts:
Atlas Roofing
Jackson Hewitt Tax Service Inc.

THINK COMMUNICATIONS GROUP, LLC

5948-A Easton Rd, Pipersville, PA 18947
Tel.: (215) 766-8868
Fax: (215) 766-8869
Web Site: www.thinkcommunicationsgroup.com

Year Founded: 2002

Agency Specializes In: Advertising, Brand Development & Integration, Collateral, Digital/Interactive, Print, Strategic Planning/Research

Pamela Ronca-Shumskas *(Principal & Dir-Creative)*
Julie Baines *(Principal-Client Svcs)*
Mark Morano *(Sr Dir-Art)*
Katie Devery *(Sr Acct Exec)*

Accounts:
Helios Creative

THINK CREATIVE INC.

1001 Virgina Dr, Orlando, FL 32803
Tel.: (407) 896-5757
E-Mail: info@thinkcreativeinc.com
Web Site: www.thinkcreativeinc.com

Year Founded: 2000

Agency Specializes In: Advertising, Brand Development & Integration

Mark Freid *(Pres-Creative & Dir-Strategic)*
Briana Lang *(Sr Dir-Art)*
Diane Levine *(Assoc Dir-Creative)*
Kim Capps *(Acct Mgr)*
Jenna Radomsky *(Project Mgr & Acct Coord)*

Accounts:
Chepenik Financial
Competitor Gym Orlando

THINK, INC.

2818 Smallman St, Pittsburgh, PA 15222
Tel.: (412) 281-9228
Fax: (412) 281-9243
E-Mail: info@thinkcreativity.com
Web Site: www.thinkcreativity.com

Employees: 15
Year Founded: 1997

Agency Specializes In: Advertising, Advertising Specialties, Brand Development & Integration, Business Publications, Business-To-Business, Cable T.V., Co-op Advertising, Communications, Consulting, Consumer Marketing, Consumer Publications, Corporate Communications, Corporate Identity, Direct Response Marketing, E-Commerce, Event Planning & Marketing, Exhibit/Trade Shows, In-Store Advertising, Industrial, Local Marketing, Media Buying Services, Multimedia, Newspapers & Magazines, Outdoor, Print, Production, Public Relations, Publicity/Promotions, Radio, Recruitment, Sales Promotion, Strategic Planning/Research, T.V., Telemarketing, Trade & Consumer Magazines

Brian Tedeschi *(Owner)*
Melissa Goda *(Acct Mgr-New Bus Dev)*

Accounts:
Brusters Real Ice Cream
Columbia Gas of Pennsylvania; Pittsburgh, PA LIHEAP; 2003
Fantastic Sams; Pittsburgh, PA Hair Cut & Color Services; 2001
Herr Voss Stamco; Pittsburgh, PA Industrial; 2004
Iron Star Roasting Company
National Guard Youth Challenge Program
Mountaineer ChalleNGe Academy
Nicholson
PPG; Pittsburgh, PA Industrial; 2003
Sheetz; Altoona, PA (Recruitment); 1999
Washington Hospital; Washington, PA (Branding); 2003

THINK MINT MEDIA

(Formerly Taylor Made Media)
2433 Dollarton Hwy Ste 215, North Vancouver, BC V7H 0A1 Canada
Tel.: (604) 985-6877
Fax: (604) 985-6873
Web Site: thinkmint.media/welcome

Employees: 12
Year Founded: 1995

Agency Specializes In: Advertising, Media Buying Services, Media Planning

Joyce Taylor-Bauer *(Pres)*
Suzette Bayrock *(Mng Dir & VP)*
Brandi Bailey *(VP & Dir-Media)*
Brandi Pratt *(VP & Dir-Media)*
Jane Nesbitt *(Sr Acct Dir)*
Hardish Garson *(Acct Dir)*
Teri Banks *(Mgr-Acctg & Mgr-Admin)*

Accounts:
Junxion Strategy
Mercedes Vancouver Group
REMAX of Western Canada
Vancouver Aquarium 4D Theatre

THINK NOCTURNAL LLC

8 Continental Dr Unit E, Exeter, NH 03833
Mailing Address:
Box 505, Portsmouth, NH 03802-0505
Tel.: (603) 512-1186
Fax: (603) 686-5477
E-Mail: info@thinknocturnal.com
Web Site: www.thinknocturnal.com

Employees: 2

Scott Buchanan *(Principal & Strategist-Creative)*

Accounts:
Eastern Air Devices
Electrocraft

THINK SHIFT

(Formerly BCG Communications)
A-120 Donald Street, Winnipeg, MB R3C 4G2 Canada
Tel.: (204) 989-4323
E-Mail: info@thinkshiftinc.com
Web Site: www.thinkshiftinc.com/

Employees: 27
Year Founded: 1993

National Agency Associations: Second Wind Limited

Agency Specializes In: Advertising, Brand Development & Integration, Digital/Interactive, Event Planning & Marketing, Media Planning, Public Relations

David Lazarenko *(Pres)*
Kristen Jones *(Dir-HR)*
Gareth Moore *(Dir-Web Dev)*
Mike Thiessen *(Dir-Interactive)*
Alex Varricchio *(Dir-Mktg)*
Geeta Chopra *(Acct Exec)*
Denise Darling *(Designer-Motion)*
Grant Geard *(Designer-Interaction)*
Rick Sellar *(Sr Designer-Interaction)*
Jenny-Lynn Sheldon *(Designer-Interaction)*

Accounts:
Banville & Jones Wine Merchants
Bee Maid
Canterra Feeds
Canterra Seeds
Cargill
Comcast
Ernst David International Inc.
Front Runner
GHY International
Qualico
Ray
Tolaini Wines
Tradition Game Bird Program
Wawanesa
Westeel Storage Solutions Marketing

Branch

Think Shift

310 SW 4th Ave Ste #510, Portland, OR 97204
Tel.: (503) 789-1338
E-Mail: balajik@thinkshiftinc.com
Web Site: www.thinkshiftinc.com

National Agency Associations: 4A's

Balaji Krishnamurthy, *(Chm)*

THINK TANK PR & MARKETING

727 N 1st St Ste 340, Saint Louis, MO 63102
Tel.: (314) 621-8265
Fax: (314) 621-8267
E-Mail: info@thinktankprm.com
Web Site: www.thinktankprm.com

Year Founded: 2006

Agency Specializes In: Advertising, Brand Development & Integration, Event Planning & Marketing, Internet/Web Design, Print, Public Relations, Search Engine Optimization, Social Media

Trish Cheatham *(CEO)*

Accounts:
New-Ritual Craft Vapor Liquid

THINKCREATIVE

304 W College Ave, Tallahassee, FL 32301
Tel.: (850) 656-7050
E-Mail: info@thinkcreative.com
Web Site: www.thinkcreative.com

Employees: 10
Year Founded: 1995

Agency Specializes In: Brand Development & Integration, Consulting, Web (Banner Ads, Pop-ups, etc.)

Revenue: $2,000,000

Mark Marsiglio *(Pres & CEO)*
Hayley Hay *(Sr Acct Mgr)*

Accounts:
FSU.com
Hitachi Data Systems

THINKHOUSE, LLC

20 Connelly Rd, Huntington, NY 11743
Tel.: (917) 805-0480
Web Site: www.thinkhouse.com

Year Founded: 2007

Agency Specializes In: Advertising, Brand

Development & Integration, Digital/Interactive, Internet/Web Design, Logo & Package Design, Media Buying Services, Media Planning, Social Media

Joyce Berlin Bank *(Owner, Mng Dir & Dir-Mktg)*
Adam Bank *(Dir-Creative)*

Accounts:
Vita Coco "#MakeTheNaturalSwitch", Campaign: "Let Nature Do Its Thing", Digital, PR, Social
WindowTex

THINKING GIANT
207 E 32nd St 4th Fl, New York, NY 10016
Tel.: (646) 216-8944
E-Mail: info@thinkinggiant.com
Web Site: www.thinkinggiant.com

Agency Specializes In: Advertising, Digital/Interactive, Graphic Design, Internet/Web Design, Social Media

Deon Douglas *(Partner)*
Sashea Lawson *(Partner)*
Joey Stafford *(VP)*

Accounts:
SoulSeeKa

THINKMODO, INC.
1 Little W 12th St, New York, NY 10014
Tel.: (212) 231-1080
E-Mail: connect@thinkmodo.com
Web Site: www.thinkmodo.com

Year Founded: 2011

Agency Specializes In: Advertising, Brand Development & Integration

James Percelay *(Co-Founder, Creative Dir & Producer)*
Michael Krivicka *(Co-Founder & Producer)*

Accounts:
20th Century Fox Devil's Due Movie - Devil Baby Campaign
AMC Campaign: "Zombie Experiment"
British Broadcasting Corporation
New-CarLister.co
Carrie Campaign: "Telekinetic coffee shop surprise"
Cosmo
New-Fantastic Four
Film District Campaign: "Elevator Murder Experiment", Dead Man Down
Forbes, Inc.
Hasbro Inc
New-Marvel
MGM Campaign: "Carrie"
Namecheap
The New York Times
Oakley Campaign: "Bubba Hover"
Sony Pictures
Whil Meditation

THINKSO CREATIVE LLC
115 W 30th St Studio 709, New York, NY 10001
Tel.: (212) 868-2499
Fax: (212) 868-2498
E-Mail: info@thinkso.com
Web Site: www.thinksocreative.com

Agency Specializes In: Advertising, Brand Development & Integration, Communications, Identity Marketing, Internet/Web Design, Publishing

Brett Traylor *(Owner)*
Elizabeth Amorose *(Partner)*
Diana Peraita *(Designer)*
Brian Tri *(Designer)*
Tyler Fortney *(Sr Designer-Digital)*
Michelle Kurz *(Jr Designer)*
Kim Mickenberg *(Sr Writer)*

Accounts:
The Armchair Activist
Comprehensive Care Management
Conran
Cross-Cultural Solutions
FOX Interactive Media
Global Health Council
The Mount Sinai Medical Center
On-Ramps
PMFM, Inc.
Quadriad
RDA Interactive
Ripco Real Estate
Stadion
Topdot Mortgage
TPK
Travel zoo
UBS
United Airlines
United Hospital Fund
Weissman School of Arts & Sciences
Western Reserve Life

THIRD DEGREE ADVERTISING
501 N Walker Ave, Oklahoma City, OK 73102
Tel.: (888) 871-3729
Fax: (405) 235-3021
Web Site: www.thirddegreeadv.com

Employees: 18
Year Founded: 1995

National Agency Associations: Second Wind Limited

Agency Specializes In: Brand Development & Integration, Broadcast, Business-To-Business, Corporate Identity, Direct Response Marketing, Education, Electronic Media, Exhibit/Trade Shows, Financial, Government/Political, Health Care Services, Integrated Marketing, Internet/Web Design, Logo & Package Design, Medical Products, Outdoor, Planning & Consultation, Print, Radio, Strategic Planning/Research, Trade & Consumer Magazines

Approx. Annual Billings: $5,000,000

Roy Page *(CEO)*
Amanda Lowery *(Exec VP)*
Holly Arter *(Dir-Media)*
Megan Miranda *(Dir-Creative Strategy)*
Natalie Geis Powers *(Dir-Client Strategy & Ops-RDU)*
Kande Hein *(Mgr-Accts)*
Katelyn Drake *(Strategist-Client)*
Kaylee Goyer *(Designer)*
Caroline Grice *(Acct Coord)*

Accounts:
Allegiance Credit Union; OK; 2002
Amarillo Community Federal Credit Union; TX; 2004
American Airlines Federal Credit Union; Dallas, TX Financial Services; 2007
Association of Central Oklahoma Governments; OK Clean Air Initiative, Clean Cities Initiative, Stormwater Program; 2001
Central OK Habitat for Humanity; OK; 2000
CompOne; OK; 2004
Delta Federal Credit Union; Atlanta, GA Financial Services; 2007
Focus Federal Credit Union; OK; 2003
GOLFUSA; OK; 2004
InterGenetics; Oklahoma City, OK Genetic Testing Services; 2003
Lyric Theatre; Oklahoma City, OK; 2002
New York Credit Union League; Syracuse, NY Financial Services; 2007
Oklahoma Blood Institute; Oklahoma City, OK; 2002
Oklahoma City County Health Department; OK Anti-Syphilis Campaign; 2002
Oklahoma City University; 2003
Oklahoma Medical Research Foundation; Oklahoma City, OK; 2001
Oklahoma RedHawks
Oklahoma University College of Engineering; OK; 2000
Oklahoma University Health Sciences Center; 2001

THIRD RAIL CREATIVE
112 E 7th St, Austin, TX 78701
Tel.: (512) 358-9907
Fax: (512) 857-1323
E-Mail: power@thirdrailcreative.com
Web Site: www.thirdrailcreative.com

Agency Specializes In: Advertising, Brand Development & Integration, Collateral, Outdoor, Print, T.V., Web (Banner Ads, Pop-ups, etc.)

Mark Scholes *(Owner)*
Bryan Branam *(Acct Dir)*
Kristen Williams *(Sr Acct Exec)*

Accounts:
American Society for the Prevention of Cruelty to Animals

THIRD WAVE DIGITAL
1841 Hardeman Ave, Macon, GA 31201
Tel.: (478) 750-7136
Fax: (478) 750-7139
Toll Free: (888) 578-7865
E-Mail: info@thirdwavedigital.com
Web Site: www.thirdwavedigital.com

Year Founded: 1997

Agency Specializes In: Advertising, Corporate Communications, Exhibit/Trade Shows, Internet/Web Design, Print

Bart Campione *(Pres)*
Myron Bennett *(Dir-Creative Svcs)*
Amy Thomas *(Dir-Svcs)*
Troy Jones *(Mgr-Technical)*
Carla Schwab *(Mgr-Bus Ops)*
Sonja Tillman *(Coord)*

Accounts:
Mercer University Interactive Campus Maps, Marketing
Young Harris College Interactive Campus Maps, Marketing

THIRDEYE DESIGN
9 Ferry Wharf Ste 5D, Newburyport, MA 1950
Tel.: (978) 499-7948
E-Mail: info@thirdeyedesign.com
Web Site: www.thirdeyedesign.com

Agency Specializes In: Advertising, Brand Development & Integration, Collateral, Corporate Identity, Email, Internet/Web Design, Logo & Package Design, Outdoor

Joni Toher *(Principal & Creative Dir)*

Accounts:
Duraflex

THIRSTY BOY
223 N Water St, Milwaukee, WI 53202
Tel.: (414) 273-1700
E-Mail: tbeast@thirstyboy.com
Web Site: www.thirstyboy.com

Year Founded: 2008

Agency Specializes In: Advertising, Brand Development & Integration, Internet/Web Design, Print, Social Media

Steve Koeneke *(Owner)*
Travis Knutson *(Partner & Dir-Interactive)*
Brittany Jackson *(Partner)*
Lucas Fitzpatrick *(Dir-Art)*
Christine Ledezma *(Office Mgr)*

Accounts:
CounterPoint Capital
Sub-Zero & Wolf

THIS IS RED
216 Blvd of the Allies 6th Fl, Pittsburgh, PA 15222
Tel.: (412) 288-8800
Fax: (412) 281-2800
E-Mail: newbusiness@thisisredagency.com
Web Site: www.thisisredagency.com

Year Founded: 2010

Agency Specializes In: Advertising, Digital/Interactive

Jeff Myers *(Principal-Creative & Strategy)*
Tamara Swanson *(Dir-Ops)*
Klay Abele *(Designer-Motion)*
Jeff St. Mars *(Designer-Production)*
Alisha Johns *(Assoc Strategist-Creative)*

Accounts:
Zardetto Prosecco

THOMA & THOMA CREATIVE SERVICES, INC.
(Private-Parent-Single Location)
1500 Rebsamen Park Rd, Little Rock, AR 72202
Tel.: (501) 664-5672
Fax: (501) 664-5650
Web Site: www.thomathoma.com

Employees: 13
Year Founded: 1989

Agency Specializes In: Advertising, Brand Development & Integration, Content, Digital/Interactive, Internet/Web Design, Media Planning, Public Relations, Search Engine Optimization, Social Media

Revenue: $2,000,000

Martin Thoma *(Principal)*
Melissa Thoma *(Principal)*
Beverly Hall *(Controller)*
Brian Hodges *(Art Dir)*
Wade McCune *(Dir-Creative)*
Stephanie Drangle *(Production Mgr)*
John Mark Adkison *(Mgr-Inbound Mktg)*
Suzanne Sage *(Sr Acct Exec)*

Accounts:
Little Rock Athletic Club

THOMAS BOYD COMMUNICATIONS
117 N Church St, Moorestown, NJ 08057
Tel.: (856) 642-6226
Fax: (856) 642-6336
Web Site: www.thomasboyd.com

Employees: 8
Year Founded: 1998

Agency Specializes In: Advertising, Brand Development & Integration, Communications, Crisis Communications, Education, Event Planning & Marketing, Exhibit/Trade Shows, Identity Marketing, Local Marketing, Media Relations, Media Training, Newspaper, Public Relations, Strategic Planning/Research

Pam Boyd *(Co-Founder & Pres)*
Liz Thomas *(Co-Founder & CEO)*
Lori Palmer *(Sr Dir-Client Svcs)*
Caitlin Dunican Latko *(Sr Acct Exec)*
Deanna Vallejo *(Acct Coord)*

THOMAS PUCKETT ADVERTISING
1710 Bannie Ave, Las Vegas, NV 89102
Tel.: (702) 383-0005
E-Mail: info@thomaspuckett.com
Web Site: www.thomaspuckett.com

Year Founded: 2002

Agency Specializes In: Advertising, Brand Development & Integration, Digital/Interactive, Strategic Planning/Research

Tom Puckett *(Sr Dir-Creative)*
Melissa Landsman Puckett *(Dir-Media)*

Accounts:
Applied Information Sciences
Aristocrat Technologies
Colliers International
Comprehensive Cancer Centers of Nevada
Oasis Casino Management Systems
Providence Master Planned Community
Southern Nevada Medical Industry Coalition
UNLV

THOMAS TABER & DRAZEN
(Acquired & Absorbed by Gyro Denver)

THOMPSON ADVERTISING, INC.
5121 SW Mallard Point, Lees Summit, MO 64082
Tel.: (816) 366-0199
Web Site: www.thompsonadvertisinginc.com

Agency Specializes In: Brand Development & Integration, Business-To-Business, Corporate Identity, Direct Response Marketing, E-Commerce, Email, Internet/Web Design, Market Research, Media Planning, Multimedia

June Reed *(Mgr-Production)*
Stephanie Butler *(Jr Dir-Creative)*

Accounts:
AmeriTech Leasing,Inc. Lease & Lease Financing Services
ChataBING Online Communication Services
Custom Line Art Professional Illustrators
Dustless Technologies Dust Control Products
Love-Less Ash Company Vacuum Products
Maxam Equipment Asphalt Equipment & Asphalt Plant
Midland Marble & Granit Granite & Marble
Mountain View Apartments Construction Services
Nu Look of KC Inc. Car Wash Services

THE THOMPSON AGENCY
1908 Dilworth Rd E, Charlotte, NC 28203
Tel.: (704) 488-9654
Fax: (704) 333-8815
Toll Free: (866) 828-6135
E-Mail: joe@thethompsonagy.com
Web Site: www.thethompsonagy.com

Employees: 2
Year Founded: 1976

Agency Specializes In: Collateral, Communications, Corporate Identity, Direct Response Marketing, Exhibit/Trade Shows, Graphic Design, Health Care Services, Internet/Web Design, Logo & Package Design, Media Buying Services, Media Planning, Multimedia, Newspaper, Outdoor, Point of Sale, Print, Publicity/Promotions, Radio, Seniors' Market, Social Marketing/Nonprofit, Sports Market, T.V., Trade & Consumer Magazines

Approx. Annual Billings: $500,000

Breakdown of Gross Billings by Media: D.M.: $50,000; Graphic Design: $250,000; Other: $100,000; Worldwide Web Sites: $100,000

Stuart Thompson *(Owner)*

Accounts:
Altavista Wealth Management
BETCO, Inc.; Statesville, NC Mini-Storage Buildings; 1995
Florence Crittenton Services; Charlotte, NC Problem Pregnancy Programs for Single Women; 1990
Time Warner Cable; Charlotte, NC Cable Television; 1994

THORNBERG & FORESTER
78 5th Ave Fl 6, New York, NY 10011
Tel.: (212) 367-0858
Fax: (212) 367-8128
Web Site: www.thornbergandforester.com

Year Founded: 2007

Agency Specializes In: Advertising, Digital/Interactive, Graphic Design, Production

Scott Matz *(Co-Founder & Dir)*
Morgan Goldberg *(Head-Digital & Designer)*
Javier Gonzalez *(Head-Production)*
Jorge Peschiera *(Dir-Creative)*
Kyle Miller *(Assoc Dir-Creative)*
Keith Endow *(Designer)*

Accounts:
Architectural Digest Fisker Karma Experience
Dansko Campaign: "Word of Feet"

THREAD CONNECTED CONTENT
(Formerly Go East)
403 Hayward Ave N, Saint Paul, MN 55128
Tel.: (651) 702-2900
Fax: (651) 702-2929
E-Mail: connect@nowthreading.com
Web Site: nowthreading.com/

Agency Specializes In: Brand Development & Integration, Graphic Design, Logo & Package Design, Mobile Marketing

Ric Pace *(Owner)*
Heidi Broberg *(Sr Dir-Art)*
Dan Sundquist *(Producer-Digital)*
Tim Deis *(Dir-Principal Ops & Fin)*
Breanne Hagen *(Acct Mgr)*
Jana Solberg *(Project Mgr-Digital)*
Kelly Lind *(Acct Exec)*

Accounts:
Beyond Borders Film Festival Entertainment Services
United Family Medicine Health Care Services

THREE ATLANTA
359 E Paces Ferry Rd Ste 300, Atlanta, GA 30305
Tel.: (404) 266-0899
Fax: (404) 266-3699
E-Mail: jhouk@3atlanta.com
Web Site: www.3atlanta.com

Employees: 34

Year Founded: 1982

National Agency Associations: AMIN

Agency Specializes In: Sponsorship

Jackson Houk *(Mng Partner)*
Jeff Cole *(VP & Dir-Creative)*
Brad Ramsey *(VP-Creative & Dir)*
Art Reid *(VP-Adv)*
Heather Taylor *(VP-Media)*
Jonathon McKenzie *(Assoc Dir-Media & Digital)*
Megan Sauerland *(Acct Mgr)*
Michael Frizzell *(Assoc Creative Dir)*

Accounts:
Atlanta Brewing Co.
The Atlanta Journal-Constitution ajcjobs.com
Children's Healthcare of Atlanta
I2 Telecom
Kimberley-Clark
MedAssets
Shaw Industries Campaign: "Missing"
Simmons Bedding Co.; Atlanta, GA Mattresses
UPS
Waffle House
Yamaha

THREE LAKES MARKETING

2303 RR 620 S Ste 135-214, Austin, TX 78734
Toll Free: (888) 842-0292
E-Mail: info@threelakesmarketing.com
Web Site: www.threelakesmarketing.com

Employees: 4
Year Founded: 2004

Agency Specializes In: Advertising, Advertising Specialties, Brand Development & Integration, Business Publications, Business-To-Business, Children's Market, Co-op Advertising, Collateral, Communications, Consulting, Consumer Goods, Consumer Marketing, Content, Corporate Communications, Corporate Identity, Customer Relationship Management, Digital/Interactive, Direct Response Marketing, E-Commerce, Electronic Media, Entertainment, Event Planning & Marketing, Exhibit/Trade Shows, Fashion/Apparel, Graphic Design, Health Care Services, High Technology, In-Store Advertising, Information Technology, Integrated Marketing, Internet/Web Design, Leisure, Local Marketing, Logo & Package Design, Magazines, Medical Products, Merchandising, Mobile Marketing, New Product Development, New Technologies, Newspaper, Outdoor, Pharmaceutical, Planning & Consultation, Point of Purchase, Point of Sale, Print, Promotions, Publicity/Promotions, RSS (Really Simple Syndication), Real Estate, Restaurant, Sales Promotion, Seniors' Market, Strategic Planning/Research, Sweepstakes, T.V., Technical Advertising, Telemarketing, Travel & Tourism, Viral/Buzz/Word of Mouth, Web (Banner Ads, Pop-ups, etc.)

Approx. Annual Billings: $325,000

Breakdown of Gross Billings by Media: Consulting: $175,000; Worldwide Web Sites: $150,000

Greg Elisha *(Owner)*
Vale Farrar *(Product Mgr)*

THRESHOLD INTERACTIVE

13160 Mindanao Way, Marina Del Rey, CA 90292
Tel.: (310) 577-9800
Fax: (310) 577-9844
E-Mail: cheristy.bunyan@thresholdinteractive.com
Web Site: www.thresholdinteractive.com

Employees: 24
Year Founded: 2003

Agency Specializes In: Advertising, Alternative Advertising, Arts, Automotive, Brand Development & Integration, Branded Entertainment, Consumer Goods, Digital/Interactive, E-Commerce, Entertainment, Fashion/Apparel, Graphic Design, Internet/Web Design, Leisure, Logo & Package Design, Luxury Products, Market Research, Media Planning, Mobile Marketing, Search Engine Optimization, Social Marketing/Nonprofit, Sponsorship, Strategic Planning/Research, Travel & Tourism, Viral/Buzz/Word of Mouth

Approx. Annual Billings: $5,000,000

Breakdown of Gross Billings by Media: Adv. Specialities: 50%; Internet Adv.: 50%

John Montgomery *(CEO & Chief Innovation Officer)*
Scott Williamson *(Mng Dir)*
Chris Sherman *(Acct Dir)*
Rita Sweeney *(Acct Dir)*
Lance Christensen *(Sr Acct Exec)*
Amanda Gottesman *(Coord-Social Media)*

Accounts:
Disney
Fox Television
Honda
Nestle USA, Inc. Butterfinger, Digital, Hot Pockets, Social
Nestle Waters North America; Stamford, CT
Paramount Farms
Sony

THUG, LLC

2189 NW Wilson St, Portland, OR 97210
Tel.: (503) 213-4370
E-Mail: info@thugdesign.com
Web Site: www.thugdesign.com

Year Founded: 2001

Agency Specializes In: Advertising, Graphic Design

Damon Sullivan *(CEO)*
Sean Dunnahoo *(Mng Partner & Strategist-UX)*
Colin Bay *(Partner-Res)*
Mark Rose *(Chief Strategy Officer)*
Patrick Anderson *(Client Svcs Dir)*
Mark Mellor *(Dir-Art)*
Antonio Tatum *(Dir-Creative)*

Accounts:
Wessar International Ltd

THUNDER FACTORY

335 Powell St, San Francisco, CA 94102
Tel.: (973) 579-7227
Fax: (415) 956-0604
Web Site: www.thunderfactory.com

Year Founded: 2000

Agency Specializes In: Brand Development & Integration, Collateral, Corporate Communications, Direct Response Marketing, E-Commerce, Event Planning & Marketing, Exhibit/Trade Shows, Internet/Web Design, Public Relations, Strategic Planning/Research

Stacy Phelan *(Acct Dir)*

Accounts:
Extra Space Storage
Factiva
Johnson & Johnson
Match.com
Maveron
McKesson Corp.
Omni-ID
ValleyCrest
World Health

Branches

Thunder Factory Los Angeles

20301 Ventura Blvd Ste 219, Woodland, CA 91364
Tel.: (415) 992-3280
Web Site: www.thunderfactory.com

Employees: 8

Accounts:
AIA
AOL Inc.
Attributor
Avery Dennison RIS
Cabela's
Cingular Wireless LLC

Thunder Factory New York

59 W 19th St Ste 4B, New York, NY 10011
Tel.: (212) 537-4020
Fax: (212) 965-8363
E-Mail: patrick@thunderfactory.com
Web Site: www.thunderfactory.com

Patrick Di Chiro *(Founder, Chm & CEO)*
Stacy Phelan *(Acct Dir)*

Accounts:
AIA
AOL Inc.
Cingular Wireless LLC

TIBEREND STRATEGIC ADVISORS

35 W 35th St 5th Fl, New York, NY 10001-2205
Tel.: (212) 827-0020
Fax: (212) 827-0028
Web Site: www.tiberendstrategicadvisors.com

Employees: 5
Year Founded: 1989

Agency Specializes In: Advertising, Collateral, Crisis Communications, Event Planning & Marketing, Financial, Identity Marketing, Investor Relations, Media Relations, Planning & Consultation, Print, Recruitment, Strategic Planning/Research, Web (Banner Ads, Pop-ups, etc.)

Gregory Q. Tiberend *(Pres & CEO)*
Jason Rando *(COO & Exec VP)*
Joshua Drumm *(Sr VP-IR)*
Andrew W. Mielach *(VP)*
Claire H. Sojda *(Acct Supvr)*
Tirth Patel *(Sr Acct Exec-Healthcare IR)*
Amy Wheeler *(Sr Acct Exec)*

Accounts:
Accera
Antares Pharma
Archimedes
AspenBio Pharma, Inc Investor & Public Relations
BioBehavioral Diagnostics
BioNanomatri

TIC TOC

4228 N Central Expwy Ste 200, Dallas, TX 75206
Tel.: (214) 416-9300
Fax: (214) 259-3185
E-Mail: info@tictoc.com
Web Site: www.tictoc.com

Employees: 25
Year Founded: 1974

Agency Specializes In: Sales Promotion,

Sweepstakes

Amy Burrows *(VP-Client Svcs-Custom Premiums Team)*
Scott Harris *(VP-Sls)*
Michael Ramsey *(VP-Client Svcs)*
Alex Watson *(VP-Sls Incentive Mktg)*
Katy McDowell *(Controller)*
Dan Gittemeier *(Dir-Sls)*
Maria Koch *(Dir-Art)*
Chris Razaki *(Dir-Sls)*
Renee Shreeves *(Dir-Admin & Operation)*
Melodi Rouhani *(Acct Mgr)*
Gaby Grimaldo *(Acct Exec)*
Christy Kaliser *(Acct Exec)*

Accounts:
Black Berry
Disney
Frito
Hersheys
Nokia
Pepsi
Pepsico
Tropicana
Walmart

TIDAL SHORES INC.
(Formerly AO Media & Communications)
PO Box 70207, Houston, TX 77270
Tel.: (713) 806-6789
Toll Free: (877) 545-8324
E-Mail: service@tidalshore.com
Web Site: www.tidalshore.com/

Employees: 9
Year Founded: 1990

Agency Specializes In: Advertising, Advertising Specialties, African-American Market, Agriculture, Asian Market, Automotive, Aviation & Aerospace, Bilingual Market, Brand Development & Integration, Broadcast, Business Publications, Business-To-Business, Cable T.V., Children's Market, Co-op Advertising, Collateral, Commercial Photography, Communications, Consulting, Consumer Marketing, Consumer Publications, Corporate Communications, Corporate Identity, Cosmetics, Digital/Interactive, Direct Response Marketing, E-Commerce, Education, Electronic Media, Engineering, Entertainment, Environmental, Event Planning & Marketing, Exhibit/Trade Shows, Fashion/Apparel, Financial, Food Service, Gay & Lesbian Market, Government/Political, Graphic Design, Health Care Services, High Technology, Hispanic Market, In-Store Advertising, Industrial, Infomercials, Information Technology, Internet/Web Design, Investor Relations, Legal Services, Leisure, Local Marketing, Logo & Package Design, Magazines, Marine, Media Buying Services, Medical Products, Merchandising, Multimedia, New Product Development, Newspaper, Newspapers & Magazines, Out-of-Home Media, Outdoor, Over-50 Market, Pharmaceutical, Planning & Consultation, Point of Purchase, Point of Sale, Print, Production, Public Relations, Publicity/Promotions, Radio, Real Estate, Recruitment, Restaurant, Retail, Sales Promotion, Seniors' Market, Sports Market, Strategic Planning/Research, Sweepstakes, Syndication, T.V., Technical Advertising, Teen Market, Telemarketing, Trade & Consumer Magazines, Transportation, Travel & Tourism, Yellow Pages Advertising

Doria R. Goldman *(Owner & Pres)*
Mary Lieser *(Acct Mgr)*

TIER10 MARKETING
13825 Sunrise Valley Dr Ste 150, Herndon, VA 20171
Tel.: (703) 552-4140
Web Site: tier10.com

Agency Specializes In: Advertising, Automotive, Digital/Interactive, Strategic Planning/Research

David Boice *(Owner & Partner)*
Rebecca Fortier *(Controller-Fin)*
Olivia Devereux *(Dir-Media)*
Katie Hibson *(Dir-Mktg)*
Regina Washington *(Dir-HR)*

Accounts:
Cadillac Car Dealers
Gateway Acura Association (Agency of Record) Marketing
Honda Dealers Association (Agency of Record) 2012 Civic

TIERNEY COMMUNICATIONS
The Bellevue 200 S Broad St, Philadelphia, PA 19102-3803
Tel.: (215) 790-4100
Fax: (215) 790-4363
Web Site: hellotierney.com

E-Mail for Key Personnel:
President: mausten@tierneyagency.com
Creative Dir.: phardy@tierneyagency.com
Media Dir.: gsiano@tierneyagency.com
Public Relations: salbertini@tierneyagency.com

Employees: 142
Year Founded: 1942

National Agency Associations: 4A's

Agency Specializes In: Advertising, Advertising Specialties, Brand Development & Integration, Broadcast, Business Publications, Business-To-Business, Cable T.V., Collateral, Communications, Consulting, Consumer Marketing, Consumer Publications, Corporate Communications, Corporate Identity, Crisis Communications, Digital/Interactive, Direct Response Marketing, E-Commerce, Education, Entertainment, Environmental, Event Planning & Marketing, Exhibit/Trade Shows, Financial, Food Service, Government/Political, Health Care Services, Information Technology, Internet/Web Design, Investor Relations, Leisure, Logo & Package Design, Magazines, Media Buying Services, Media Planning, Media Training, Medical Products, Newspaper, Newspapers & Magazines, Out-of-Home Media, Outdoor, Print, Production, Public Relations, Radio, Real Estate, Sales Promotion, Sponsorship, Strategic Planning/Research, T.V., Trade & Consumer Magazines, Transportation, Travel & Tourism

Mary Stengel Austen *(Pres & CEO)*
Debra C. Griffin *(CFO & Exec VP)*
Molly Watson *(COO)*
Steven Albertini *(Exec VP & Gen Mgr)*
Cathy Mazurek *(Sr VP & Controller)*
Peg Finucan *(Sr VP & Dir-Integrated Production)*
Teri Gerbec *(Sr VP & Dir-Creative)*
Rick Radzinski *(Sr VP & Dir-Mgmt)*
Shelly Hammon *(Sr VP & Assoc Dir-Media)*
Heather Nally *(Acct Dir)*
Andrew Cahill *(Dir-Creative & Writer)*
Kyle Erickson *(Assoc Dir-Creative)*
Valerie Gentieu *(Supvr-Media)*
Mariya Taukule *(Supvr-Digital Media)*
Francesca Gunning *(Sr Acct Exec-PR)*
Rebecca Masterbone *(Sr Acct Exec)*
Emily Cohen *(Media Planner)*
Sarah Fadule *(Media Planner)*
Emily Smeraldo *(Copywriter)*
Zachrey Thornbury *(Copywriter)*
Clark Bower *(Asst Media Planner)*
Amanda Paola *(Asst Media Planner)*

Accounts:
ACM
Cooper University Hospital; Camden, NJ; 2008
Fox Chase Cancer Center; Philadelphia, PA; 2008
General Motors Buick, Cadillac, Chevrolet, Consumer Outreach, GMC Products, Influencer Engagement, Public Relations, Social & Traditional Media
Independence Blue Cross; Philadelphia, PA; 2000 iSelect Campaign: "Olympic Games Bandwagon"
Kings Food Markets, Inc.
New York Restoration Project Print, Radio, TV, Tree, Not a Tree
PA Department of Transportation; Harrisburg, PA; 2008
PA Department of Treasury; Harrisburg, PA; 2008
PECO; 1988
Pennsylvania's Department of Community & Economic Development Marketing, Social Media Outreach, Strategic Planning, Tourism Destination
PWDC (CareerLink); Philadelphia, PA; 2001
TD Bank; Mount Laurel, NJ Campaign: "Bank Human, Again", Campaign: "Chained", Campaign: "Human Truths", MillionTreesNYC, Online, Print, TV; 1996
Temple University Health System; Philadelphia, PA
New-The Toronto-Dominion Bank
Verizon Wireless Consumer Outreach, Events, Influencer Management, Media Relations, PR, Philadelphia Tri-State Advertising, Social Media; 1938
WPVI-TV Inc.; Philadelphia, PA

TILLMAN, ALLEN, GREER
1305 Lakes Pkwy Ste 119, Lawrenceville, GA 30043
Tel.: (770) 236-8703
Fax: (770) 236-8803
E-Mail: info@tillmanallengreer.com
Web Site: www.tillmanallengreer.com

E-Mail for Key Personnel:
President: kelly@tillmanallengreer.com
Creative Dir.: sam@tillmanallengreer.com

Employees: 20
Year Founded: 1998

National Agency Associations: Second Wind Limited

Agency Specializes In: Brand Development & Integration, Business Publications, Business-To-Business, Consulting, Corporate Identity, Education, Magazines, Public Relations, Publicity/Promotions, Strategic Planning/Research, Travel & Tourism

Breakdown of Gross Billings by Media: Cable T.V.: 5%; Collateral: 25%; Consulting: 25%; D.M.: 15%; Pub. Rels.: 20%; Radio: 10%

David Greer *(CEO & Sr Strategist-Mktg)*
Dana Urrutia *(Publr-Gwinnett Magazine & Mgr-PR-TAG Mktg)*
Jonathan Maloney *(Dir-Art)*
Carolyn Blackwell *(Copywriter)*

Accounts:
The Brand Banking Company
Gwinnett Chamber of Commerce
Gwinnett Technical College
Richardson Housing Group

TILTED CHAIR CREATIVE
640 Tillery St, Austin, TX 78702
Tel.: (512) 814-8458
E-Mail: sit@tiltedchaircreative.com
Web Site: www.tiltedchaircreative.com

Agency Specializes In: Advertising, Brand Development & Integration, Internet/Web Design

Jake Rector *(Partner & Strategist-Media)*
Hua Liu *(Dir-Art & Designer)*

Jamie Rodriguez *(Dir-Art & Designer)*
Annie Lin *(Dir-Art)*
Nina Sanchez *(Dir-Art)*
Annie Markovich *(Strategist-Bus Dev & Digital & Copywriter)*
Mike Ihnat *(Copywriter)*

Accounts:
The Piazza Center

TIME ADVERTISING

50 Victoria Ave, Millbrae, CA 94030-2645
Tel.: (650) 259-9388
Fax: (650) 259-9339
E-Mail: timead@timead.com
Web Site: www.timead.com

E-Mail for Key Personnel:
President: baronsuen@timead.com
Creative Dir.: stung@timead.com
Media Dir.: bho@timead.com

Employees: 20
Year Founded: 1987

Agency Specializes In: Advertising, Asian Market, Broadcast, Consulting, Consumer Marketing, Graphic Design, Media Buying Services, Newspapers & Magazines, Outdoor, Print, Production, Production (Ad, Film, Broadcast), Sponsorship, Web (Banner Ads, Pop-ups, etc.), Yellow Pages Advertising

Approx. Annual Billings: $6,500,000

Breakdown of Gross Billings by Media: Fees: $400,000; Newsp. & Mags.: $2,600,000; Outdoor: $150,000; Print: $210,000; Production: $980,000; Radio & T.V.: $2,060,000; Worldwide Web Sites: $100,000

Sherman Tung *(Partner)*
Amy Yip *(Acct Dir)*
Karina Yip *(Acct Dir)*
Bonnie Ho *(Media Planner)*

Accounts:
AT&T Communications Corp.
Brands
California Department of Consumer Affairs
California Department of Health Services
California Lottery Lotto; 1999
Charles Schwab
China Travel Services
Citibank
City of Millbrae
Hong Kong Association of Northern California
Hong Kong Tourism Board
Kaiser Permanente; Oakland, Pasadena, CA; 1995
KTSF 26
Lincoln Financial
MetLife Financial Services
Ritz Tours
Taiwan Tourism Board
Ulferts Center
United Commercial Bank; San Francisco, CA; 2001

TIMEZONEONE

65 E Wacker Pl Ste 1000, Chicago, IL 60601
Tel.: (312) 436-0851
Web Site: www.timezoneone.com

Agency Specializes In: Advertising, Brand Development & Integration, Corporate Communications, Direct Response Marketing, Graphic Design, Identity Marketing, Logo & Package Design, Sponsorship, T.V., Web (Banner Ads, Pop-ups, etc.)

Daniel Thomas *(CEO)*
Ellen Farrar *(VP-Client Engagement)*
Raewyn Topp *(Strategist-Brand)*

Accounts:
Ronald McDonald House

TIMMONS & COMPANY, INC.

1753 Kendarbren Dr Ste 622, Jamison, PA 18929-1049
Tel.: (267) 483-8220
Fax: (215) 340-5861
E-Mail: info@timmonsandcompany.com
Web Site: www.timmonsandcompany.com

Employees: 16
Year Founded: 1974

Agency Specializes In: Advertising, Advertising Specialties, Communications, Consumer Publications, Corporate Identity, Direct Response Marketing, Electronic Media, Event Planning & Marketing, Exhibit/Trade Shows, Graphic Design, Internet/Web Design, Logo & Package Design, Magazines, Media Buying Services, Newspaper, Newspapers & Magazines, Outdoor, Point of Purchase, Print, Production, Public Relations, Publicity/Promotions, Strategic Planning/Research, Trade & Consumer Magazines, Yellow Pages Advertising

Rich Timmons *(Founder)*
Frank Bradley *(VP-Acct Svcs)*
Ana Ferreira *(Dir-Creative)*
Jon Trout *(Mgr-Bus Dev)*
Jill Whiskeyman *(Sr Acct Exec)*
Craig Anderson *(Sr Graphic Designer)*
Robert Moreschi *(Copywriter)*

Accounts:
Agere Systems
First National Bank
Gallus, Inc.
National Medical Services
Vulcan Spring & Mfg. Co.

TINA THOMSON

130 W 25th St Ste 6A, New York, NY 10001
Tel.: (646) 792-1600
E-Mail: info@tinathomson.com
Web Site: www.tinathomson.com

Agency Specializes In: Advertising, Brand Development & Integration, Public Relations, Social Media

Judy Lee *(Asst Acct Exec)*

Accounts:
New-Hada Labo Tokyo

TINAGLIA ADVERTISING

7931 S Broadway Ste 340, Littleton, CO 80122
Tel.: (303) 779-9100
E-Mail: jennifert@teamtinaglia.com

Employees: 6
Year Founded: 1987

Agency Specializes In: Advertising, Broadcast, Business-To-Business, Collateral, Corporate Identity, Direct Response Marketing, Event Planning & Marketing, Financial, Graphic Design, Internet/Web Design, Leisure, Logo & Package Design, Newspaper, Newspapers & Magazines, Outdoor, Point of Purchase, Point of Sale, Print, Production, Radio, Retail, Sports Market, T.V.

Approx. Annual Billings: $1,600,000

Jennifer Tinaglia *(VP-Acctg)*

Accounts:
Bansek & Company; Englewood, CO CPA Firm; 2000
Bonfils Blood Center
Clear Channel/SFX
Denver Tent Company; Denver, CO Commercial Tent Products; 1995
International Management Group; Cleveland, OH Sports Celebrities & Professional Sports Events; 1988
NSN Network Services; Avon, CO Satellite Network Integrator; 1989
The Soccer Stop; Englewood, CO Soccer Specialty Retailer; 2003
SPL International; Denver, CO Match Pak Golf Accessories; 1984
Tiger Woods Foundation; Los Alamitos, CA Professional Golfer's Charitable Organization; 2000
USTA; White Plains, NY; 1998

TINSLEY ADVERTISING

2000 S Dixie Hwy Ste 201, Miami, FL 33133
Tel.: (305) 856-6060
Fax: (305) 858-3877
E-Mail: jim@tinsley.com
Web Site: www.tinsley.com

E-Mail for Key Personnel:
President: jim@tinsley.com
Media Dir.: scott@tinsley.com

Employees: 57
Year Founded: 1974

National Agency Associations: AMA

Agency Specializes In: Advertising, Affluent Market, Alternative Advertising, Automotive, Aviation & Aerospace, Brand Development & Integration, Broadcast, Business Publications, Business-To-Business, Cable T.V., Co-op Advertising, Collateral, Consulting, Consumer Goods, Consumer Marketing, Consumer Publications, Corporate Identity, Digital/Interactive, Direct-to-Consumer, E-Commerce, Electronic Media, Exhibit/Trade Shows, Food Service, Gay & Lesbian Market, Graphic Design, Guerilla Marketing, Health Care Services, Hispanic Market, Hospitality, Integrated Marketing, International, Internet/Web Design, Leisure, Logo & Package Design, Luxury Products, Marine, Market Research, Media Buying Services, Media Planning, Medical Products, New Product Development, Newspaper, Newspapers & Magazines, Out-of-Home Media, Outdoor, Over-50 Market, Package Design, Pharmaceutical, Podcasting, Point of Purchase, Point of Sale, Print, Production (Ad, Film, Broadcast), Production (Print), Promotions, Publishing, RSS (Really Simple Syndication), Radio, Real Estate, Restaurant, Retail, Search Engine Optimization, Seniors' Market, Sports Market, Strategic Planning/Research, T.V., Trade & Consumer Magazines, Transportation, Travel & Tourism, Web (Banner Ads, Pop-ups, etc.)

Rick Balter *(COO)*
John Underwood *(CMO)*
Dorn Martell *(Exec VP & Dir-Creative)*
Scott Sussman *(Sr VP & Dir-Media)*
Casey Lunsford *(VP & Controller)*
Korryn Warner *(Sr Dir-Art)*
Julian Samper *(Dir-Art)*
Rick Blitman *(Assoc Dir-Creative)*
Sofie Vilar-Frary *(Supvr-Acctg)*

Accounts:
Airbus
American Motors Dealer Association
Bascom Palmer Eye Institute Ophthalmic Care Hospitals
The Beacon Council Miami-Dade Economic Development
Cabi Developers; Aventura, FL Everglades on the Bay, The Capital at Brickell
City Furniture Campaign: "Habitat"

Commodore
Dade County Fair & Expo
New-Eau Palm Beach Resort & Spa (Creative Agency of Record)
The Florida Keys & Key West Big Pine Key, Islamorada, Key Largo, Key West, Marathon
Gulf Bay Group of Companies Cannes, Cap d'Antibes, Fiddler's Creek
Karisma Hotels Resorts
Marco Beach Ocean Resort
Massey-Yardley Dealerships Chrysler, Dodge, Jeep
National Marine Manufacturers Association The Miami International Boat Show
The Palm Beach Post La Palma, Palmbeachpost.com, The Pennysaver
Paramount Pictures
Samuel Getz Private Jewelers & Designers
SuperClubs Resorts; The Bahamas, Brazil, Curacao, Dominican Republic, Jamaica Breezes, Grand Lido, Hedonism, Rooms on the Beach, Starfish
Toys 4 Tots Pro Bono Children's Charity
University of Miami
USA Broadcasting

TINY REBELLION

(Formerly dw+h)
1316 Third St Ste 301, Santa Monica, CA 90401
Tel.: (424) 238-8000
E-Mail: press@tiny-rebellion.com
Web Site: www.tiny-rebellion.com/#/home

Employees: 30
Year Founded: 1987

Agency Specializes In: Brand Development & Integration, Consumer Marketing, Direct Response Marketing, Internet/Web Design, Media Buying Services, Print, Production, Radio, T.V.

Lucas Donat *(CEO & Chief Creative Officer)*
Amir Haque *(Partner & Sr Strategist)*
Christy Ferguson *(Mng Dir-Client Svcs)*
Jennifer Parke *(Exec Dir-Creative)*
Mary Kedzior *(Mgmt Supvr)*
Barton Bodell *(Dir-Mktg)*
Jill Burgeson *(Dir-Strategy)*
Hal Carlson *(Dir-Media Svcs)*
Austin Ripmaster *(Dir-Mktg)*
David Blacker *(Assoc Dir-Creative)*
Nick Liebeskind *(Assoc Dir-Creative)*

Accounts:
21st Century Insurance (Agency of Record) Broadcast, Creative, Digital Advertising
Bolthouse Farms Food Porn Index
FOX
Hotwire.com; San Francisco, CA Discount Travel Services; 2006
LegalZoom.com Legal Document Services; 2007
Movie Link
Nutrisystem (Agency of Record)
OpenSky.com
TrueCar Inc. (Agency of Record) Campaign: "DogsInCars", Campaign: "True Love", Campaign: "True Thrill", Digital, Marketing, Public Relations, Social, TV
ZipRecruiter (Creative Agency of Record) Campaign: "Find The Right One", Campaign: "One-Click", Campaign: "Right Resume", Online, TV

TIPPIT & MOO ADVERTISING

3336 Richmond Ave Ste 300, Houston, TX 77098
Tel.: (713) 527-7600
E-Mail: info@tippitandmoo.com
Web Site: www.tippitandmoo.com

Year Founded: 2011

Agency Specializes In: Advertising, Print, Promotions, Public Relations, Radio, Social Media, Strategic Planning/Research, T.V.

Cathy Lopez Negrete *(Pres)*
Javier Gonzalez-Herba *(Exec Dir-Creative)*
Gabriel Flores *(Dir-Creative)*
Doug Kline *(Dir-Creative)*
Jorge Leza *(Dir-Creative)*
Mauren Boneta *(Assoc Dir-Creative)*
Patrick Lopez Negrete *(Acct Exec)*
Ari Diozon *(Copywriter)*

Accounts:
Fiesta Mart, Inc
Gabbanelli Accordions
InComm
Michaels Stores
Professional Sports Partners
Sonic Drive-Ins
Universal Technical Institute
WorldFest
Zadok Jewelers

TIPTON COMMUNICATIONS

323 E Main St, Newark, DE 19711
Tel.: (302) 454-7901
Fax: (302) 454-7903
E-Mail: info@tiptoncommunications.com
Web Site: www.tiptoncommunications.com

Employees: 20
Year Founded: 2006

Agency Specializes In: Advertising, Communications, Digital/Interactive, Public Relations

Revenue: $2,000,000

Daniel R. Tipton *(Pres)*
Michelle Beuscher *(Dir-Hospital Certifications)*
Jessica Bryant *(Dir-Mktg & Comm-New England)*
Karen L. White *(Dir-Creative)*
Moira Owens *(Sr Mgr-Magnet Writing)*
Elaine Hughes *(Mgr-Mktg Comm)*
Nicole Fullerton *(Specialist-Comm)*

Accounts:
4tell
Autism Delaware
Bank of America
Junior Achievement
Lions Eye Bank
New Castle County Chamber of Commerce PR
University of Delaware

TITAN

100 Park Ave, New York, NY 10022
Tel.: (212) 644-6200
Fax: (212) 644-2010
Web Site: www.titan360.com

Employees: 700
Year Founded: 2001

Approx. Annual Billings: $27,200,000

Don Allman *(Pres & CEO)*
Craig Abolt *(CFO, Chief Admin Officer & Exec VP)*
David Etherington *(Chief Strategy Officer & Exec VP)*
Jamie Lowe *(Chief Sls Officer-Titan)*
Mike Collins *(VP & Gen Mgr)*
Greg Ald *(VP & Mgr-Sls-Natl)*
Roman Kosinov *(VP-Digital Ops)*
Emily Glenewinkel *(Mgr-Sls & Mktg Strategy)*
Amanda Rosenberg *(Mgr-Natl Acct)*
Steve Rosenberg *(Sr Acct Exec-Natl)*
Peter Menchaca *(Acct Exec)*

Accounts:
ABC
Anheuser Busch
AOL/Time Warner
AT&T Communications Corp.
Cingular
Delaware River Port Authority Out-of-Home
Southeastern Pennsylvania Transportation Authority (SEPTA); Philadelphia, PA
Timberland

Branches

Titan Worldwide

195 State St 4th Fl, Boston, MA 02109
Tel.: (781) 356-2009
Fax: (617) 227-0166
E-Mail: info@titan360.com
Web Site: www.titan360.com

Employees: 13

Dave Etherington *(Chief Strategy Officer & Exec VP)*
Mary Hamilton *(Sr VP-HR & Admin)*
Eileen Crossin *(Gen Mgr-NY)*
Eoin McCann *(Gen Mgr)*
Tisha Duke *(Acct Mgr-Natl)*
Cindy Medrano *(Office Mgr)*
Natalia Allison *(Mgr-Mktg)*
Michelle Elman *(Mgr-Inventory Control)*
Kevin Haskell *(Mgr-Import Sls)*
Ginger Griffin *(Sr Acct Exec)*
David Rohrer *(Sr Acct Exec)*
Michael Shearin *(Sr Acct Exec)*
Kevin Chow *(Acct Exec)*
Emily Glenewinkel *(Strategist-Sls & Mktg)*
Lauren Guidi *(Acct Exec)*
Steve McCarthy *(Acct Exec)*
Stephanie Costas *(Coord-Inventory Control)*
Julian Hill *(Coord-Mktg)*

Titan Worldwide

55 Dwight Pl, Fairfield, NJ 07004
Tel.: (973) 439-5621
Fax: (973) 439-5744
Web Site: www.titan360.com

Employees: 40

Don Allman *(Pres & CEO)*
Craig Abolt *(CFO, Chief Admin Officer & Exec VP)*
Dave Etherington *(Chief Strategy Officer & Exec VP)*
Jamie Lowe *(Chief Sls Officer & Exec VP)*
Scott Goldsmith *(Chief Comml Officer & Exec VP)*
Mary Hamilton *(Sr VP-HR)*
Miko Rahming *(Sr VP-Innovation & Creative Svcs)*

Titan

(Formerly Titan Worldwide)
879W 190th St Ste 265, Gardena, CA 90248
Tel.: (310) 630-0445
Fax: (310) 630-0469
Web Site: www.titan360.com

Employees: 20

Cindy Medrano *(Office Mgr)*
Lauren Tatasciore *(Office Mgr)*
Natalia Allison *(Mgr-Mktg)*
Jackie Callo *(Mgr-Natl Accts)*
Michelle Elman *(Mgr-Inventory Control)*
Kevin Haskell *(Mgr-Import Sls)*
Chelsea Cunningham *(Sr Acct Exec)*
David Rohrer *(Sr Acct Exec)*
Lauren Guidi *(Acct Exec)*
Bridget Lewis *(Acct Exec)*
Steve mcCarthy *(Acct Exec)*
Alex Murray *(Acct Exec)*

Titan

Advertising Agencies

121 S Broad St Ste 1200, Philadelphia, PA 19107
Tel.: (215) 281-1980
Fax: (215) 281-1990
Web Site: www.titan360.com

Employees: 27

Agency Specializes In: Outdoor

Chris Pezzello *(VP & Gen Mgr)*
Jon Roche *(VP & Gen Mgr)*
Neville Bharucha *(Sr Acct Mgr)*
Matt Clark *(Mgr-Sls)*
Stephanie Dancey *(Acct Exec)*
Megan Gawlak *(Acct Exec)*
Emily Protheroe *(Acct Exec)*

Accounts:
Drexel University
Horizon Wireless

Titan Outdoor
(d/b/a Titan 360)
4636 E Marginal Way S Ste B-100, Seattle, WA 98134
Tel.: (206) 762-2531
Fax: (206) 762-2532

Agency Specializes In: Sponsorship

Dave Etherington *(Chief Strategy Officer & Exec VP)*
Mary Hamilton *(Sr VP-HR & Admin)*
Pamela Quadros *(VP & Gen Mgr)*
Justin Burkholder *(Acct Mgr-Natl)*
Tisha Duke *(Acct Mgr-Natl)*
Robert Levine *(Acct Mgr-Natl)*
Jeff Thaw *(Acct Mgr-Titan Air-Natl)*
Emily Glenewinkel *(Mgr-Sls & Mktg Strategy)*
Kevin Haskell *(Mgr-Import Sls)*
Noemi Bonilla *(Sr Acct Exec)*
Chelsea Cunningham *(Sr Acct Exec)*
Ginger Griffin *(Sr Acct Exec)*
Kevin Chow *(Acct Exec)*

Accounts:
McDonald's
Mercury Advertising
OMG
Seattle Founders
Watermark Credit Union
Wells Fargo

Titan Worldwide
186 City Road, London, EC1V 2NT United Kingdom
Tel.: (44) 207 250 7800
E-Mail: info@titanoutdoor.co.uk
Web Site: www.titan360.com

David Etherington *(Chief Strategy Officer & Exec VP)*

TIVOLI PARTNERS
2115 Rexford Rd Ste 215, Charlotte, NC 28211-5453
Tel.: (704) 295-6800
Fax: (704) 295-6819
Web Site: www.tivolipartners.com

Employees: 6
Year Founded: 1998

Agency Specializes In: Advertising, Brand Development & Integration, Business-To-Business, Corporate Identity, Digital/Interactive, Direct Response Marketing, Financial, High Technology, Newspaper, Print, Production, Public Relations, Strategic Planning/Research, Trade & Consumer Magazines

Approx. Annual Billings: $20,500,000 Capitalized

Lisa Bell *(Owner & Chief Creative Officer)*
Steven Bell *(VP-Ops)*
Stacie Lowry *(VP-Client Svcs & Digital Ops)*

Accounts:
PrintStock
Robinson, Bradshaw & Hinson Legal Services; 2004
Sherpa
Wachovia

TIZIANI & WHITMYRE, INC.
Sharon Commerce Ctr 2 Commercial St, Sharon, MA 02067
Tel.: (781) 793-9380
Fax: (781) 793-9395
E-Mail: info@tizinc.com
Web Site: www.tizinc.com

E-Mail for Key Personnel:
Creative Dir.: fmartins@learytiziani.com
Media Dir.: gmaggiolino@learytiziani.com
Production Mgr.: csullivan@learytiziani.com
Public Relations: jnero@learytiziani.com

Employees: 20
Year Founded: 1991

National Agency Associations: BMA

Agency Specializes In: Advertising, Advertising Specialties, Brand Development & Integration, Business Publications, Business-To-Business, Collateral, Digital/Interactive, Direct Response Marketing, E-Commerce, Electronic Media, Environmental, Exhibit/Trade Shows, Food Service, Graphic Design, High Technology, Industrial, Information Technology, Internet/Web Design, Logo & Package Design, Media Buying Services, Medical Products, New Product Development, Newspapers & Magazines, Planning & Consultation, Point of Sale, Print, Production, Public Relations, Publicity/Promotions, Sales Promotion, Strategic Planning/Research, Technical Advertising, Trade & Consumer Magazines

Breakdown of Gross Billings by Media: Bus. Publs.: 20%; Collateral: 30%; Consulting: 5%; Plng. & Consultation: 5%; Pub. Rels.: 30%; Worldwide Web Sites: 10%

Richard Whitmyre *(Owner)*
Robert O. Tiziani *(CEO)*
Don Goncalves *(Sr VP)*
Fred Martins *(VP & Dir-Creative)*
John Nero *(VP-PR & Integrated Svcs)*
Scott Segel *(Controller)*
Lydia Mello *(Dir-Media & TW Networks)*
Jennifer Guimond *(Mgr-Client Svcs)*
Craig S. Sullivan *(Designer)*

Accounts:
Advanced Instruments; Norwood, MA Instrumentation for Clinical & Life Science Laboratories; 2001
Federal Electronics
Hollingsworth & Vose Co.; East Walpole, MA Non-Woven Fabrics
Howard Leight/Sperian Hearing Protection
Invensys Business Solutions; Foxboro, MA Manufacturing Systems
Invensys plc; London, UK Energy Management Systems, Manufacturing Systems; 2001
Schneeberger, Inc.; Bedford, MA Linear Motion Systems
Spectro Analytical Instruments; Fitchburg, MA

TJM COMMUNICATIONS
2441 SR 426 Ste 1061, Oviedo, FL 32708
Tel.: (407) 265-1823
Fax: (407) 977-5009
E-Mail: treva@tjmcommunications.com
Web Site: www.tjmcommunications.com

Year Founded: 2001

Agency Specializes In: Advertising, Advertising Specialties, Business Publications, Communications, Corporate Communications, Corporate Identity, Entertainment, Event Planning & Marketing, Food Service, Public Relations, Publicity/Promotions, Sports Market, Travel & Tourism

Treva J. Marshall *(Pres)*
Joel Kaiman *(Acct Supvr)*

Accounts:
57 Main Street Wine Company
SUN STREAM Hotels & Resorts
Walt Disney World Swan & Dolphin Hotel
ZORA

TKO ADVERTISING
700 N Lamar Ste 200 B, Austin, TX 78703
Tel.: (512) 472-4856
Fax: (512) 472-6856
E-Mail: thinkbig@tkoadvertising.com
Web Site: http://tkoadvertising.com/

Year Founded: 1995

Agency Specializes In: Advertising

Raul Garza *(Co-Founder & Dir-Creative)*
Todd Alley *(Dir-Creative)*
Jonathan Davis *(Dir-Art)*
Tricia Gruett *(Dir-Art)*
Christina Dunk *(Acct Mgr)*
Jim Champion *(Mgr-Ops)*
Noe Perez *(Designer-Web)*

TLG MARKETING
6700 E Pacific Coast Hwy, Long Beach, CA 90803
Tel.: (562) 537-6936
Web Site: www.tlgmarketingconsultants.com

Employees: 4
Year Founded: 2006

Agency Specializes In: Advertising, Automotive, Brand Development & Integration, Broadcast, Cable T.V., Consulting, Consumer Goods, Crisis Communications, Digital/Interactive, E-Commerce, Education, Email, Engineering, Entertainment, Financial, Government/Political, Graphic Design, Health Care Services, In-Store Advertising, Industrial, Internet/Web Design, Legal Services, Local Marketing, Logo & Package Design, Magazines, Media Buying Services, Media Training, Mobile Marketing, Multimedia, Newspaper, Newspapers & Magazines, Print, Promotions, Publishing, RSS (Really Simple Syndication), Radio, Real Estate, Restaurant, Retail, Search Engine Optimization, Social Media, T.V., Technical Advertising, Travel & Tourism, Web (Banner Ads, Pop-ups, etc.)

Approx. Annual Billings: $500,000

Travis LaRiviere *(Dir-Creative)*

Accounts:
AOI Tea Company Japanese Green Tea; 2010
Excel Laser Vision Institute Lasik Eye Surgery; 2007
Lanzone Morgan, LLP Legal Services; 2008
Long Beach Water Department Water Conservation; 2011

TLG MULTICULTURAL COMMUNICATIONS

(Name Changed to Turnstile)

TM ADVERTISING

3030 Olive St, Dallas, TX 75219-7690
Tel.: (972) 556-1100
Fax: (972) 830-2619
E-Mail: contactus@tm.com
Web Site: www.tm.com

Employees: 200
Year Founded: 1934

National Agency Associations: 4A's-AAF

Agency Specializes In: Advertising, Automotive, Bilingual Market, Brand Development & Integration, Broadcast, Business Publications, Business-To-Business, Cable T.V., Co-op Advertising, Communications, Consumer Marketing, Digital/Interactive, Direct Response Marketing, E-Commerce, Electronic Media, Event Planning & Marketing, Fashion/Apparel, Financial, Food Service, Graphic Design, High Technology, Information Technology, Internet/Web Design, Leisure, Logo & Package Design, Magazines, Media Buying Services, Multimedia, New Product Development, Newspaper, Out-of-Home Media, Planning & Consultation, Point of Purchase, Point of Sale, Print, Production, Radio, Restaurant, Retail, Sales Promotion, Sponsorship, Strategic Planning/Research, Transportation, Travel & Tourism

Approx. Annual Billings: $430,000,000

Breakdown of Gross Billings by Media: Collateral: 1%; D.M.: 1%; Mags.: 15%; Newsp.: 13%; Other: 4%; Out-of-Home Media: 3%; Point of Purchase: 1%; Radio: 7%; T.V.: 55%

Becca Weigman *(CEO)*
Lisa Bennett *(Chief Creative Officer & Partner-Creative)*
Scott Savarese *(CFO)*
Shep Kellam *(Sr VP & Grp Dir-Creative)*
Susan Scull *(Sr VP & Acct Mgmt Dir)*
Terri Bauer *(Sr VP & Dir-HR)*
Marc Mintle *(VP & Dir-Creative)*
April Steinbach *(VP & Dir-Creative)*
Sherri Moody *(VP & Mgr-Media Ops)*
Chris Bettin *(Grp Dir-Creative)*
Emily Stanford *(Acct Dir)*
Dan Dougherty *(Assoc Dir-Creative)*
Jason Niebaum *(Assoc Dir-Creative)*
Kendra Wilson *(Assoc Dir)*
Katie Gurry-Brown *(Mgr-Digital Media)*
Sam Wagnon *(Coord-Bus Dev)*
Sullivan Franklin-Mitchell *(Assoc Media Planner)*
Lauren Treu *(Sr Media Planner)*

Accounts:
AA.com
American Advertising Federation Dallas Campaign: "Mural"
American Heart Association
AMR Corporation; Fort Worth, TX American Airlines
Best Friends Animal Society
Captain D's Campaign: "Long Goodbye", Campaign: "When You Love Seafood This Much, It's Gotta Be D's!"
Craft Brewers Alliance, Inc.
Craft Brewers Alliance, Inc. Liquid Goodness Campaign, Long Hammer IPA, Online, Out-of-Home, Point of Purchase, Print
Dallas Film Society; Dallas, TX 2011 Dallas International Film Festival, Marketing
Dex Media Inc Campaign: "The Wheel", Superpages Mobile App
The DFW Interactive Marketing Association
Discover Network
Pacific Gas & Electric Company Campaign: "Your Energy Plus Ours"
Superpages.Com
New-Universal Studios
Verizon Superpages.com, Yellow Pages

TMA+PERITUS

33 E Main St Ste 451, Madison, WI 53703
Tel.: (608) 234-4880
Fax: (715) 849-3900
E-Mail: abrown@tmaperitus.com
Web Site: www.tmaperitus.com

Employees: 15
Year Founded: 1983

Agency Specializes In: Advertising, Brand Development & Integration, Direct Response Marketing, Event Planning & Marketing, Magazines, Merchandising, Newspaper, Pets , Public Relations, Radio, Sales Promotion, Strategic Planning/Research, T.V.

Thomas Marks *(Pres)*
Kathy Marks *(Mng Partner)*
Kurt Huber *(Sr Dir-Art)*

Accounts:
A&B Process Services
BizFilings
Cenflex
M3 Insurance Solutions
SAA Design Group Website
Toole Design Group Website
Urban Land Interests Navigation, Website
Wisconsin Potato & Vegetable Growers Association Logo

TMC COMMUNICATIONS, LLC

245 Park Ave 24th Fl, New York, NY 10167
Tel.: (212) 792-5673
Fax: (212) 792-5674
E-Mail: Thomas.Clohesy@TMCCommunications.com
Web Site: www.tmccommunications.com

Employees: 2
Year Founded: 1997

Agency Specializes In: Communications, Financial, Identity Marketing, Investor Relations, Local Marketing, Media Training, Product Placement, Public Relations, Strategic Planning/Research

Nazan Clohesy *(Partner)*
Thomas Clohesy *(Mng Dir)*

Accounts:
LIFE Biosystems

TMH AGENCY

3700 Toone St Ste 1458, Baltimore, MD 21224
Tel.: (301) 503-2576
Web Site: www.tmhagency.com

Year Founded: 2014

Agency Specializes In: Advertising, Digital/Interactive, Graphic Design, Media Buying Services, Media Planning, Public Relations, Radio, Search Engine Optimization, Social Media, T.V.

Therese M. Hessler *(Pres & CEO)*
Ashley Winters *(Production Mgr & Graphic Designer)*

Accounts:
Antwerpen Motor Cars Ltd

TMINUS1 CREATIVE, INC.

122 John Robert Thomas Dr, Exton, PA 19341
Tel.: (610) 280-7005
Fax: (610) 280-7009
E-Mail: info@tm1c.com
Web Site: www.tm1c.com

Year Founded: 2011

Agency Specializes In: Advertising, Collateral, Corporate Identity, Internet/Web Design

Terry Scullin *(Owner)*
Beth Thren *(VP & Sr Dir-Art)*
Jackie Bofinger *(Sr Dir-Art)*
Alena McCullough *(Dir-Art)*
Tara Ott *(Dir-Art)*
Colleen Gardner *(Sr Acct Mgr)*
Marcia Schneider *(Office Mgr)*

Accounts:
Agilent Technologies, Inc.

TMP WORLDWIDE ADVERTISING & COMMUNICATIONS, LLC

125 Broad St 10th Fl, New York, NY 10004
Tel.: (646) 613-2000
Fax: (646) 613-0649
Toll Free: (800) 867-2001
E-Mail: info@tmp.com
Web Site: www.tmp.com

Employees: 535
Year Founded: 1967

Agency Specializes In: Above-the-Line, Advertising, Below-the-Line, Brand Development & Integration, Communications, Digital/Interactive, Event Planning & Marketing, Exhibit/Trade Shows, Government/Political, Health Care Services, High Technology, Mobile Marketing, Multicultural, Recruitment, Viral/Buzz/Word of Mouth, Web (Banner Ads, Pop-ups, etc.)

Approx. Annual Billings: $266,844,000

Michelle Abbey *(Pres & CEO)*
Emerson Moore *(Gen Counsel & Sr VP)*
Sherry Jacobson *(Exec VP)*
Matt Lamphear *(Exec VP-Digital Products & Strategy)*
Ron Blum *(Sr VP-Western & Mid-West Reg)*
Louis Vong *(VP-Digital Strategy)*
Devon Watson *(Acct Dir-Digital Adv)*

Accounts:
AstraZeneca
AT&T Communications Corp.
Boeing
Corning; Taiwan
Edward Jones
The Health Service Executive
Internal Revenue Service Strategic Media
Kaiser Permanente; San Francisco, CA
KPMG
Northrop Grumman
Pitt County Memorial Hospital
SAP
United States Patent & Trademark Office
VistaPrint N.V.
Yukon-Kuskokwim Health Corporation; Bethel, AK

Branches

Blaze Advertising

17 Fullarton Road, Kent Town, SA 5067 Australia
Tel.: (61) 8 81301900
Fax: (61) 8 8130 1999
Web Site: www.blazeadvertising.com.au

Leanne Krstevski *(Mng Dir-Natl)*
Casey Aimer *(Head-Digital)*
Peter Grzesch *(Gen Mgr)*
Julie Harding-Aimer *(Acct Dir)*
Liv Pultar *(Acct Dir)*

Jessica Saethang *(Acct Dir)*
Simone Gur *(Sr Acct Mgr)*
Nathan Salter *(Sr Acct Mgr)*
Vicki Cogan *(Acct Mgr)*
Ali Lowe *(Acct Mgr)*
Bernice Gibbs *(Client Svc Dir)*

TMP Worldwide/Advertising & Communications
200 714-1 St SE, Calgary, AB T2G 2G8 Canada
Tel.: (403) 266-7061
Fax: (403) 269-4022
E-Mail: Wayne.burns@tmp.com
Web Site: www.tmp.com

Employees: 20

Agency Specializes In: Electronic Media, Recruitment

Tracy Clark *(Reg VP)*
Tracy Kapteyn *(VP-Product Svcs & Support)*
Carol Choquette *(Mgr-Mktg & North American Sls Ops)*
Steve Popowich *(Acct Exec)*

TMP Worldwide/Advertising & Communications
36 Lombard St 3rd Fl, Toronto, ON M5A 7J3 Canada
Tel.: (416) 861-8679
Fax: (416) 861-1171
E-Mail: wayne.burns@tmp.com
Web Site: www.tmp.com

Employees: 20

Agency Specializes In: Electronic Media, Recruitment

Wayne Burns *(Sr VP-Canada)*
Colette O'Neill Taylor *(Sr VP-Canada)*
Carline O'Meally *(Reg VP & VP-Ops)*
Helen Tom *(VP-Creative Ops)*
Stephen Wright *(Sr Dir-Art)*
Fiona Byrne *(Acct Dir)*
Deanne Dawkins *(Acct Dir)*
Kristin Langford *(Acct Mgr & Project Mgr)*
Sharon Taylor *(Sr Project Mgr-Digital)*
Jordan Hoeller *(Sr Acct Exec)*

TMP Worldwide/Advertising & Communications
1453 Sainte-Alexandre St Ste 850, Montreal, QC H3A 2G4 Canada
Tel.: (514) 288-9004
Fax: (514) 288-8464
E-Mail: wayne.burns@tmp.com
Web Site: www.tmp.ca

Employees: 15

Agency Specializes In: Electronic Media, Recruitment

David Gardner *(Dir-Strategy)*

TMP Worldwide/Advertising & Communications
330 N Brand Blvd Ste 1050, Glendale, CA 91203
Tel.: (818) 539-2000
Fax: (917) 522-3817
Toll Free: (800) 443-0817
E-Mail: info@adcomms.tmp.com
Web Site: www.tmp.com

Employees: 50

Agency Specializes In: Electronic Media, Recruitment

John Julio *(VP-Client Strategy-Digital Adv)*
Jessica Meehan *(Sr Acct Dir)*
Bekki Chapman *(Acct Dir-Media Strategist & Analyst)*
Latoya Hamilton *(Acct Dir)*
Meg Hays *(Acct Dir)*
Jennie Matice *(Acct Dir)*

TMP Worldwide/Advertising & Communications
150 Spear St, San Francisco, CA 94105
Tel.: (415) 820-7800
Fax: (415) 820-0540
Web Site: www.tmp.com

Agency Specializes In: Electronic Media, Recruitment

Michelle Abbey *(Pres & CEO)*
Jason Day *(CFO)*
Emerson Moore *(Gen Counsel & Sr VP)*
Yazad Dalal *(Exec VP-Asia)*
Daniel Prin *(Exec VP-Europe)*
Chris Stynes *(Sr VP)*
Christophe Fourleignie *(VP & Mng Dir-France)*
Darren Harris *(Head-Client Strategy-UK)*
Jan Nicolay Anthon *(Gen Mgr-Germany)*

TMP Worldwide/Advertising & Communications
255 Alhambra Cir Ste 760, Coral Gables, FL 33134
Tel.: (305) 704-4788
E-Mail: info@tmp.com
Web Site: www.tmp.com

Employees: 15

Agency Specializes In: Electronic Media, Recruitment

Michelle Abbey *(Pres & CEO)*
Emerson Moore *(Gen Counsel & Sr VP)*
Ron Blum *(Sr VP-Western & Mid-West Reg)*
Donna Star *(Sr VP-North Reg)*
Eric Douglas *(Reg VP-Digital)*
Sylvia Kuck *(Reg VP)*
Alec Drummond *(VP-Mktg & Internal Comm-Global)*
Deb Johnson *(VP-Client Strategy)*
Jaime Kertes *(Acct Dir)*
Jenny Steinberg *(Dir-Client Strategy)*

Accounts:
Edward Jones
Kaiser Permanente
SAP-Global Solutions
Solid Energy

TMP Worldwide/Advertising & Communications
47 Perimeter Ctr E Ste 350, Atlanta, GA 30346-2001
Tel.: (770) 280-4811
Fax: (770) 395-6868
E-Mail: info@tmp.com
Web Site: www.tmp.com

Employees: 100

Agency Specializes In: Electronic Media, Recruitment

Courtney Saunders *(Sr VP)*
Sylvia Kuck *(Reg VP)*
Maureen Schroer *(Sr Acct Dir-Natl)*
Dawn Powell *(Acct Dir)*
Lauren Rosner *(Acct Dir)*
Joelle Chauncey *(Dir-Art)*
Lourann Norris *(Dir-Client Strategy)*

Dan Warnick *(Dir-Ops-US)*

TMP Worldwide/Advertising & Communications
444 N Michigan Ave Ste 3100, Chicago, IL 60611-3903
Tel.: (312) 467-9350
Fax: (312) 321-5896
Toll Free: (800) 321-1159
E-Mail: info@tmp.com
Web Site: www.tmp.com

Employees: 75

Agency Specializes In: Electronic Media, Recruitment

Matt Lamphear *(Exec VP-Digital Strategy & Mktg)*
Jennifer Sheffield *(Sr VP-Ops)*
Donna Star *(Sr VP-North Reg)*
Sylvia Kuck *(Reg VP)*
Peter Carr *(VP-Client Strategy)*
Brian Di Bartolomeo *(VP-Client Strategy)*
Kurt Dudycha *(VP-Client Strategy)*
Sheila Spinner *(VP-Bus Dev)*
Jp Decesare *(Dir-Bus Dev)*
Teccara Carmack *(Strategist-Digital)*
Abigail DiFazio *(Planner & Analyst)*

TMP Worldwide/Advertising & Communications
115 E Spring St Ste 600, New Albany, IN 47150
Tel.: (812) 945-9780
Fax: (812) 945-9809
Toll Free: (800) 356-8350
E-Mail: info@tmp.com
Web Site: adcomms.tmp.com

Employees: 12

Agency Specializes In: Direct Response Marketing, Recruitment

Jason Day *(CFO)*
Sylvia Kuck *(Reg VP)*
Jim Stein *(VP & Gen Mgr)*
Matt Mroczka *(VP-Digital Strategy & Client Dev)*
Latoya Hamilton *(Acct Dir)*
Meg Hays *(Acct Dir)*
Jennie Matice *(Acct Dir)*
Jenny Steinberg *(Dir-Client Strategy)*

TMP Worldwide/Advertising & Communications
One Cherry Hill One Mall Dr Ste 610, Cherry Hill, NJ 08002
Tel.: (856) 532-2301
E-Mail: info@tmp.com
Web Site: adcomms.tmp.com

Employees: 3

Agency Specializes In: Communications, Direct Response Marketing, Recruitment

Donna Star *(Sr VP-North Reg)*
Kevin Regan *(VP-Digital Strategy)*
Paulina Stankiewicz *(Project Mgr-Digital)*

TMP Worldwide/Advertising & Communications
720 3rd Ave, Seattle, WA 98104
Tel.: (415) 820-7834
Fax: (206) 494-0009
E-Mail: chris.stynes@tmp.com
Web Site: www.tmp.com

Employees: 7

Agency Specializes In: Electronic Media,

Recruitment

Jason Day *(CFO)*
Emerson Moore *(Gen Counsel & Sr VP)*
Yazad Dalal *(Exec VP-Asia)*
Daniel Prin *(Exec VP-Europe)*
Christophe Fourleignie *(VP & Mng Dir-France)*
Louis Vong *(VP-Digital Strategy)*
Jan Nicolay Anthon *(Gen Mgr-Germany)*

TMR AGENCY
1046 S Florida Ave, Lakeland, FL 33803-1118
Tel.: (863) 583-0081
Fax: (863) 583-0049
Web Site: www.tmragency.com/

Employees: 15

Agency Specializes In: Financial, Health Care Services, Retail

Donovan Tinsley *(Pres)*
Mark Jerkins *(VP-Acct Svcs & Media Rels)*
Christine Murphy *(Office Mgr)*
Mary Breidenbach *(Mgr-Production)*

Accounts:
Lakeland Chamber of Commerce
Lilly O'Toole & Brown Law Firm

TODD ALLEN DESIGN
200 Nibco Pkwy Ste 200, Elkhart, IN 46516
Tel.: (574) 295-8866
Fax: (574) 293-2579
E-Mail: tadesign@tadesign.com
Web Site: www.tadesign.com

Agency Specializes In: Advertising, Corporate Identity, Digital/Interactive, Media Planning, Public Relations, Strategic Planning/Research

Todd Allen *(Pres & Exec Dir-Creative)*
Phil Goodhew *(Sr Dir-Art)*
James Korn *(Dir-Art)*

Accounts:
IU Health Goshen

TOGGLE WEB MEDIA DESIGN
535 5th Ave, New York, NY 10017
Tel.: (212) 658-1105
E-Mail: info@toggleweb.com
Web Site: toggleweb.com

Employees: 13
Year Founded: 2014

Agency Specializes In: Advertising, Arts, Brand Development & Integration, Business-To-Business, Computers & Software, Consulting, Consumer Goods, Consumer Marketing, Content, Corporate Identity, Digital/Interactive, Direct-to-Consumer, E-Commerce, Education, Electronics, Email, Engineering, Entertainment, Fashion/Apparel, Financial, Government/Political, Graphic Design, Guerilla Marketing, High Technology, Hospitality, Household Goods, Identity Marketing, Industrial, Integrated Marketing, Internet/Web Design, Investor Relations, Legal Services, Logo & Package Design, Luxury Products, Market Research, Media Relations, Multimedia, New Technologies, Paid Searches, Pharmaceutical, Production (Print), Promotions, Public Relations, Publicity/Promotions, Real Estate, Recruitment, Restaurant, Retail, Search Engine Optimization, Social Marketing/Nonprofit, Social Media, Strategic Planning/Research, Travel & Tourism, Web (Banner Ads, Pop-ups, etc.)

Robert Steinerman *(Dir-Mktg)*

Accounts:
New-Kaplan Email Marketing Strategy, Web Design; 2014

TOM, DICK & HARRY CREATIVE
(Formerly Tom, Dick & Harry Advertising)
350 W Erie 2nd Fl, Chicago, IL 60654
Tel.: (312) 327-9500
Fax: (312) 327-9501
E-Mail: hello@tdhcreative.com
Web Site: tdhcreative.com/

Employees: 21
Year Founded: 2002

National Agency Associations: BMA

Agency Specializes In: Advertising, Affluent Market, Agriculture, Arts, Automotive, Below-the-Line, Brand Development & Integration, Broadcast, Business-To-Business, Cable T.V., Catalogs, Collateral, College, Communications, Computers & Software, Consumer Goods, Consumer Marketing, Corporate Communications, Corporate Identity, Digital/Interactive, Direct-to-Consumer, Electronics, Entertainment, Event Planning & Marketing, Exhibit/Trade Shows, Faith Based, Financial, Food Service, Graphic Design, Guerilla Marketing, Health Care Services, Hospitality, Identity Marketing, In-Store Advertising, Internet/Web Design, Leisure, Luxury Products, Media Planning, Media Relations, Men's Market, Multimedia, New Technologies, Newspaper, Out-of-Home Media, Package Design, Planning & Consultation, Point of Purchase, Point of Sale, Print, Production (Ad, Film, Broadcast), Production (Print), Promotions, Public Relations, Radio, Retail, Sales Promotion, Search Engine Optimization, Social Media, Sponsorship, Sports Market, T.V., Teen Market, Trade & Consumer Magazines, Transportation, Travel & Tourism, Viral/Buzz/Word of Mouth, Web (Banner Ads, Pop-ups, etc.), Women's Market

Approx. Annual Billings: $30,000,000

Breakdown of Gross Billings by Media: Adv. Specialities: 100%

David Yang *(Co-Founder, Owner & Partner-Creative)*
Bob Volkman *(Co-Founder & Partner-Creative)*
Don Brashears *(Co-Mng Partner)*
Mary Scordo *(Acct Dir)*
Amy Markley *(Dir-Creative)*
Thomas Richie *(Dir-Creative)*
Jared El-Mofty *(Assoc Dir-Creative)*

Accounts:
Aircell; Itasca, IL Airline Broadband Services; 2009
Bally Total Fitness; Chicago, IL Health Club; 2008
Baxter Credit Union; Vernon Hills, IL Financial Services; 2004
Canyon Ranch; Tucson, AZ Luxury Spa; 2008
Discover Financial Services; Riverwoods, IL Student Credit Cards; 2008
ELCA Mission Investment Fund; Chicago, IL Financial Products; 2007
Fox Sports; Chicago, IL TV Network; 2007
Korte Construction Co.; Saint Louis, MO; 2003
Lurie Children's Hospital; Chicago, IL Branding Campaign
Lutheran Church in America; Chicago, IL ELCA; 2007
National PTA; Chicago, IL; 2008
The Private Bank; Chicago, IL; 2009
Shure; Niles, IL Microphones; 2008
Snack Alliance; Vancouver, BC Rice Works Crisps; 2007
Special Olympics Speechless
University of Chicago; Chicago, IL Odyssey Scholarship; 2008

TOM SCOTT COMMUNICATION SHOP
1020 W Main St Ste 320, Boise, ID 83702
Tel.: (208) 373-4991
Fax: (208) 322-1393
E-Mail: cynthia@tscsagency.com
Web Site: tomscott.agency

Agency Specializes In: Advertising, Collateral, Graphic Design, Media Buying Services, Media Planning, Media Relations, Print, Public Relations, Strategic Planning/Research, T.V.

Tom Scott *(Owner)*
Cynthia Gibson *(Acct Svcs Dir)*
Julie Houston *(Dir-Media)*

Accounts:
Capital City Public Market

THE TOMBRAS GROUP
630 Concord St, Knoxville, TN 37919-3305
Tel.: (865) 524-5376
Fax: (865) 524-5667
E-Mail: jwelsch@tombras.com
Web Site: www.tombras.com

E-Mail for Key Personnel:
President: charlie@tombras.com

Employees: 125
Year Founded: 1946

National Agency Associations: 4A's-SEMPO

Agency Specializes In: Advertising, African-American Market, Alternative Advertising, Automotive, Bilingual Market, Brand Development & Integration, Broadcast, Business Publications, Business-To-Business, Cable T.V., Co-op Advertising, Collateral, College, Consulting, Consumer Goods, Consumer Marketing, Consumer Publications, Content, Corporate Communications, Corporate Identity, Digital/Interactive, Direct-to-Consumer, E-Commerce, Education, Electronic Media, Email, Entertainment, Exhibit/Trade Shows, Experience Design, Financial, Food Service, Game Integration, Government/Political, Graphic Design, Guerilla Marketing, Health Care Services, High Technology, Hispanic Market, Hospitality, Industrial, Integrated Marketing, International, Internet/Web Design, Leisure, Local Marketing, Logo & Package Design, Luxury Products, Magazines, Marine, Market Research, Media Buying Services, Media Planning, Men's Market, Mobile Marketing, Multicultural, Newspaper, Newspapers & Magazines, Out-of-Home Media, Outdoor, Package Design, Paid Searches, Pharmaceutical, Planning & Consultation, Podcasting, Point of Sale, Print, Product Placement, Production, Production (Print), Promotions, Publicity/Promotions, Radio, Real Estate, Recruitment, Regional, Restaurant, Retail, Sales Promotion, Search Engine Optimization, Social Marketing/Nonprofit, Social Media, Sponsorship, Sports Market, Strategic Planning/Research, Syndication, T.V., Technical Advertising, Trade & Consumer Magazines, Transportation, Travel & Tourism, Urban Market, Viral/Buzz/Word of Mouth, Web (Banner Ads, Pop-ups, etc.), Women's Market, Yellow Pages Advertising

Approx. Annual Billings: $90,000,000

Dooley Tombras *(Exec VP & Dir-Digital & Strategic Plng)*
David Jacobs *(Sr VP & Dir-Innovation & Strategy)*
Jay Sokolow *(Sr VP)*
Joye Riddle *(VP & Assoc Dir-Media)*
Kevin VanValkenburgh *(VP-Connections Plng)*
Brian Feeney *(Sr Dir-Art)*
Mark Grieco *(Grp Acct Dir)*
Nathan Carver *(Dir-Art)*
Jonathan Gardner *(Dir-Technical)*
Michael Novia *(Dir-Digital Design)*

Keith Thomason *(Dir-Art)*
Melinda Bowles *(Project Mgr-Digital)*
Chris Randall *(Acct Supvr)*
Deborah Redfield *(Sr Media Buyer, Planner & Acct Exec)*
Lauren Heimert *(Acct Exec-PR)*
Cynthia Wells *(Sr Media Buyer & Planner)*

Accounts:
American Cancer Society Campaign: "Gala"
Augusta Convention & Visitor's Bureau; Augusta, GA Tourism; 2008
Axis Boats Brochure, Sports; 2011
Bristol Motor Speedway; Bristol, TN NASCAR Track; 2002
Custom Foods; Knoxville, TN Restaurant Services; 1985
Daimler Trucks North America Transportation, Truck Bucks; 2011
Douglas J AVEDA Institute Digital Marketing, Public Relations, Social Media, Website
East Tennessee Children's Hospital Campaign: "Hopscotch", Healthcare
Eastman Chemical Co.; Kingsport, TN Chemicals, Fibers & Plastics; 1993
Ekornes (Global Digital Agency of Record)
ESPN Events; 2013
Farm Bureau of Tennessee; Columbia, TN Insurance; 2006
Food City Grocery Store; 2009
General Electric Consumer Products
Haywood County Tourism Development Agency; Maggie Valley, NC Tourism; 2003
Home Federal Bank Financial Services; 2010
Kentucky Speedway Sports; 2010
KentuckyOne Health
Lowe's Motor Speedway; Charlotte, NC NASCAR; 2002
Malibu Boats Sports; 2011
McDonald's Co-Op; Knoxville, TN Quick Service Restaurant; 1970
MoonPie (Agency of Record)
National Highway Traffic Safety Administration; Washington, DC #JustDrive, Campaign: "Dark of Night", Campaign: "If You're Texting, You're Not Driving", Campaign: "Texting While Driving", Campaign: "U Drive. U Text. U Pay", Click It, Or Ticket, Drive Sober or Get Pulled Over; 2000
Nissan North America Infiniti InTouch - Content Marketing Agency of Record, NissanConnect - Content Marketing Agency of Record
Ole Smoky Moonshine (Social Media Agency of Record)
New-Orangetheory Fitness (Creative Agency of Record) Brand Creative, Digital, Media Buying, Media Planning, Social Media, Strategic Planning
O'Reilly Auto Parts; Springfield, MO Retail Auto Parts; 2001
Regional Eye Center; Kingsport, TN Eye Care; 1995
Robertshaw Industrial Products; Knoxville, TN Remote Monitoring Equipment; 2001
Smoky Mountain Convention & Visitors Bureau; Maryville, TN Campaign: "A Helping Hand", Campaign: "Low Impact Vacation", Tourism; 1993
Tellico Village; 2011
Tennessee Department of Transportation
Tennessee Rural Health Associates; Columbia, TN Insurance; 1998
Tennessee Valley Authority; Knoxville, TN Utility; 2001
University of Tennessee Men's Athletic Department; Knoxville, TN Football, Basketball, Baseball, Website; 1994
Weigel's Farm Stores Convenience Stores; 2009

TOMSHEEHAN WORLDWIDE
645 Penn St, Reading, PA 19601-3408
Tel.: (610) 478-8448
Fax: (610) 478-8449
E-Mail: info@tomsheehan.com
Web Site: www.tomsheehan.com

E-Mail for Key Personnel:
President: tomsheehan@tomsheehan.com

Employees: 7
Year Founded: 1989

Agency Specializes In: Advertising, Asian Market, Automotive, Brand Development & Integration, Business Publications, Business-To-Business, Co-op Advertising, Collateral, College, Communications, Consulting, Consumer Publications, Corporate Communications, Corporate Identity, Direct Response Marketing, E-Commerce, Education, Electronic Media, Email, Engineering, Entertainment, Environmental, Event Planning & Marketing, Exhibit/Trade Shows, Financial, Food Service, Government/Political, Graphic Design, Health Care Services, High Technology, Hospitality, Identity Marketing, In-Store Advertising, Industrial, Information Technology, Integrated Marketing, International, Internet/Web Design, Investor Relations, Legal Services, Leisure, Local Marketing, Logo & Package Design, Magazines, Market Research, Media Planning, Media Relations, Medical Products, New Product Development, New Technologies, Newspaper, Newspapers & Magazines, Out-of-Home Media, Outdoor, Over-50 Market, Pharmaceutical, Planning & Consultation, Point of Purchase, Point of Sale, Print, Production, Production (Print), Public Relations, Publicity/Promotions, Radio, Real Estate, Recruitment, Regional, Restaurant, Sales Promotion, Search Engine Optimization, Seniors' Market, Social Media, Sports Market, Stakeholders, Strategic Planning/Research, Technical Advertising, Trade & Consumer Magazines, Transportation, Travel & Tourism, Web (Banner Ads, Pop-ups, etc.), Yellow Pages Advertising

Approx. Annual Billings: $1,300,000

Scott Boie *(VP & Strategist-Healthcare)*
Sandra Reber *(Supvr-Creative Svcs)*

Accounts:
Berk-Tek; New Holland, PA Network Cabling; 1993
Carpenter Technology; Reading, PA Alloys & Engineered Products; 1999
Eye Consultants of Pennsylvania; Wyomissing, PA; 2008
Indian River Medical Center; Vero Beach, FL; 2011
Kaiser Aluminum; Laguna, CA Engineered Materials; 2001
Krozer Keystone Health System; Chester, PA; 2011
Munroe Regional Medical Center; Ocala, FL Health Care; 2009
Penn State University; Wyomissing, PA Continuing Education Services, Undergraduate Services; 1996
Reading Hospital & Medical Center; Reading, PA Health Care
Shriners Hospitals for Children; Tampa, FL Health Care; 2009
Sovereign Bank; Reading, PA Financial Services; 2004
Teleflex; Limerick, PA; 2000
Vail Valley Medical Center; Vail, CO Health Care; 2004
Winter Haven Hospital; Winter Haven, FL Health Care; 2009

TONIC
Gold & Diamond Park, Phase 2, Bldg 3, Fl 2, PO Box 117668, Barsha, Dubai, United Arab Emirates
Tel.: (971) 14 341 3868
Fax: (971) 971143413869
Web Site: www.tonicinternational.com

Khaled Gadhallah *(Founder, Partner & Chief Creative Officer)*
Arnaud Verchere *(Founder & Head-Strategy)*
Scott Clephane *(Partner & Dir-Creative-Tonic Branding)*
Stuart Harris *(Partner & Dir-Creative-Tonic Branding)*
Wael Bitter *(Gen Mgr-Branding & Adv-Dubai)*
Cristiano Tonnarelli *(Exec Dir-Creative)*
Valerio Mangiafico *(Sr Dir-Art)*
Francesca Meloni *(Bus Dir)*
Antra Patel *(Dir-Creative)*
Usman Saleemi *(Dir-Digital Art)*
Anton Marais *(Copywriter)*

Accounts:
BAFCO Office Furniture
Burger King
Forever 21
IFFCO
NBF
Petzone
Pfizer Nutrition
PZ Cussons
SinAr Line
TDIC
Windows Live
Yas Waterworld Online, Outdoor, Print, Radio, Social Media

TONIC BLUE COMMUNICATIONS
200 E Evergreen Ave, Mount Prospect, IL 60056
Tel.: (847) 749-3900
Fax: (847) 255-2328
Web Site: www.tonicblue.com

Employees: 15
Year Founded: 1968

Agency Specializes In: Graphic Design, Internet/Web Design, Public Relations

Jim Chamerlik *(Partner)*
Angelina Monaco *(Acct Exec-Sls & Bus Dev)*
Mee Na Davis *(Designer-UI & UX Web)*

TOOLHOUSE INC.
2925 Roeder Ave, Bellingham, WA 98225
Tel.: (360) 676-9275
Fax: (360) 676-8976
Toll Free: (877) 676-9275
E-Mail: info@toolhouse.com
Web Site: www.toolhouse.com

Employees: 25
Year Founded: 1995

Agency Specializes In: Digital/Interactive, Electronic Media, Internet/Web Design

Approx. Annual Billings: $4,000,000

Rand Lien *(Chm)*
Elizabeth Lien *(VP & Controller)*
Kari Obrist *(VP-Project Svcs)*
Kevin Stock *(VP-Tech)*
Rosie Rayborn *(Mgr-Acctg)*
Heidi Kenyon *(Copywriter & Strategist-Content)*
Lindsey Dostart Nieshe *(Coord-Production)*

Accounts:
Intuit Corporation
Novartis

TOP FLIGHT MEDIA
4801 Lindle Rd, Harrisburg, PA 17111
Tel.: (800) 729-5021
E-Mail: info@topflightmedia.com
Web Site: www.topflightmedia.com

Agency Specializes In: Advertising, Brand

Development & Integration, Media Buying Services, Public Relations, Social Media, Strategic Planning/Research

Darren Smith *(Pres)*
Frank Arendt *(Dir-Creative)*
Cristela Tschumy *(Dir-Art)*
Craig Rhodes *(Mgr-Ops)*
Diane McConnell *(Acct Exec)*
Christie Hill *(Coord-Multimedia)*
Tom Downing *(Sr Designer-Interactive)*

Accounts:
DS Wood Bats
Destination Gettysburg
Gettysburg Hotel
GoHunt PA
Havahart
Hershey Harrisburg Craft Beer Country
PA Says No More
Pennsylvania Housing Finance Agency
Pennsylvania Statewide Adoption & Permanency Network #MeetTheKids
Summer in The City

TOP FLOOR TECHNOLOGIES

2725 S Moorland Rd, New Berlin, WI 53151
Tel.: (262) 364-0010
Fax: (262) 364-0015
E-Mail: sfell@topfloortech.com
Web Site: www.topfloortech.com

Employees: 25

Agency Specializes In: Digital/Interactive, Internet/Web Design, Market Research, Media Buying Services, Search Engine Optimization, Web (Banner Ads, Pop-ups, etc.)

Jim Bernthal *(Owner & Pres)*
Shane Fell *(VP-Bus Dev)*
Jennifer Hall *(Mgr-Recruiting)*

Accounts:
Grill The Monkey

TOPIN & ASSOCIATES, INC.

(Acquired by HCB Health)

TOPIN & ASSOCIATES, INC.

(Name Changed to HCB Health Chicago)

THE TOPSPIN GROUP

415 Executive Dr, Princeton, NJ 08540
Tel.: (609) 252-9515
Fax: (609) 252-9294
E-Mail: bryan@topspingroup.com
Web Site: www.topspingroup.com

Employees: 10

Agency Specializes In: Advertising

Andy Judson *(Mng Partner & Acct Svcs Dir)*
Tom Manzione *(Mng Partner & Dir-Creative)*
Chris Connolly *(Supvr-Production)*

Accounts:
American Montessori School
Best Friends Pet Resorts
Good Earth Coffee
Johnson & Johnson McNeil Splenda, Viactiv
Princeton Montessori School
Quickie Manufacturing Mop & Broom Producer

TORCH GROUP

30675 Solon Rd Ste 102, Cleveland, OH 44139-2942
Tel.: (440) 519-1822
Fax: (440) 519-1823
E-Mail: info@torchgroup.com
Web Site: www.torchgroup.com

E-Mail for Key Personnel:
President: rtorch@torchgroup.com

Employees: 8
Year Founded: 1990

Agency Specializes In: Brand Development & Integration, Business-To-Business, Consulting, Consumer Marketing, E-Commerce, Food Service, New Product Development, Planning & Consultation, Recruitment, Sales Promotion, Strategic Planning/Research

Breakdown of Gross Billings by Media: Collateral: 5%; D.M.: 5%; Fees: 75%; Mags.: 5%; Newsp.: 5%; Point of Purchase: 5%

Ronald S. Torch *(Pres, CEO & CMO)*

Accounts:
Alcoa
American Family Insurance
BabySwede
Cleveland Clinic
COSE; Cleveland, OH
First Energy
Fleetmatics
Forest City Commercial
Invacare Corporation
Owens Corning
Parker Hannifin
Progressive Insurance
Scotts Miracle-Gro Company
Smucker's
SS&G Financial Services; Cleveland, OH
Sterling Jewelers
Sun Trust Bank

TORQUE

167 N Racine, Chicago, IL 60607
Tel.: (312) 421-7858
Fax: (312) 421-7866
Web Site: torque.digital/contact

Employees: 10
Year Founded: 1992

National Agency Associations: Second Wind Limited

Eric Masi *(Pres & Exec Dir-Creative)*
Jennifer Masi *(Principal & Dir-Client Svcs)*
Kevin Masi *(Principal & Dir-Strategy)*
Ron Aichholzer *(Dir-Internet Dev & Acct Mgr)*
Sandra Yon *(Office Mgr & Mgr-Acctg)*
Javad Khadivi *(Designer-Mixed Media & Motion)*
Lena Masek *(Designer-Digital)*
Ben Ludwig *(Sr Designer-Interactive)*

Accounts:
Borders
Hallmark
Priester Aviation
Stephen Hamilton Photographics

TOTAL BS MEDIA

121 S Grand Ave, Bozeman, MT 59715
Tel.: (415) 743-0467
Web Site: http://www.totalbsmedia.com/

Agency Specializes In: Advertising, Brand Development & Integration, Content, Digital/Interactive, Email, Print, Public Relations, Search Engine Optimization, Social Media

Sarah Hunter *(Founder & CEO)*

Accounts:
Kale
Owl

TOTALCOM MARKETING, INC.

922 20th Ave, Tuscaloosa, AL 35401-2307
Tel.: (205) 345-7363
Fax: (205) 345-7373
E-Mail: home@totalcommarketing.com
Web Site: www.totalcommarketing.com

E-Mail for Key Personnel:
President: jwarren@totalcommarketing.com

Employees: 12
Year Founded: 1983

National Agency Associations: Second Wind Limited

Agency Specializes In: Advertising, Automotive, Brand Development & Integration, Broadcast, Business Publications, Business-To-Business, Cable T.V., Co-op Advertising, Collateral, College, Communications, Consulting, Consumer Goods, Consumer Marketing, Consumer Publications, Corporate Communications, Corporate Identity, Direct Response Marketing, Electronic Media, Email, Engineering, Environmental, Exhibit/Trade Shows, Financial, Graphic Design, Health Care Services, Industrial, Integrated Marketing, Internet/Web Design, Legal Services, Leisure, Local Marketing, Logo & Package Design, Magazines, Media Buying Services, Media Planning, Media Relations, Medical Products, Newspaper, Newspapers & Magazines, Out-of-Home Media, Outdoor, Over-50 Market, Package Design, Pets , Planning & Consultation, Point of Purchase, Point of Sale, Print, Production, Production (Print), Promotions, Public Relations, Publicity/Promotions, Radio, Real Estate, Regional, Retail, Seniors' Market, Social Media, Strategic Planning/Research, T.V., Trade & Consumer Magazines, Travel & Tourism

Approx. Annual Billings: $8,000,000

Jimmy E. Warren *(Owner & Pres)*
Nancy Siniard *(Mng Partner)*
Molly Bailey *(Sr Dir-Art)*
Candice Butterfield *(Sr Dir-Art)*
Jeff Hinkle *(Sr Dir-Art)*
Lori Moore *(Sr Acct Mgr)*

Accounts:
Bank of Tuscaloosa; Tuscaloosa, AL; 1985
Benchmark Chrysler Jeep; Birmingham, AL; 1992
CB&S Bank; Russellville, AL; 2005
Citizen's Baptist Medical Center; Talladega, AL
Cullman Chrysler Dodge; Cullman, AL; 1996
DCH Regional Healthcare System; Tuscaloosa, AL; 1989
Hudson Poole Jewelers; Tuscaloosa, AL; 2003
Hunt Refining Company; Tuscaloosa, AL; 2000
Hunter Homes; Huntsville, AL; 2000
Huntsville Madison Home Builders Association; Huntsville, AL; 2009
Jackson Hospital; Montgomery, AL; 2005
Leigh Automotive; Tuscaloosa, AL; 2009
Redstone Village; Huntsville, AL; 2006
Thibodaux Medical Center; Thibodaux, LA; 2009
Warrior Roofing; Tuscaloosa, AL; 2000

Branch

Totalcom, Inc.

708 Ward Ave, Huntsville, AL 35801
Tel.: (256) 534-6383
Fax: (256) 534-6443
E-Mail: nsiniard@totalcommarketing.com
Web Site: www.totalcommarketing.com

Employees: 10
Year Founded: 1986

Agency Specializes In: Advertising, Automotive, Brand Development & Integration, Broadcast, Business Publications, Business-To-Business, Cable T.V., Co-op Advertising, Collateral, Communications, Consulting, Consumer Goods, Consumer Marketing, Consumer Publications, Corporate Communications, Corporate Identity, Custom Publishing, Direct Response Marketing, Electronic Media, Email, Event Planning & Marketing, Fashion/Apparel, Graphic Design, Health Care Services, Hospitality, Household Goods, In-Store Advertising, Industrial, Integrated Marketing, Leisure, Local Marketing, Media Planning, Media Relations, Medical Products, Men's Market, New Product Development, Newspapers & Magazines, Outdoor, Over-50 Market, Paid Searches, Pharmaceutical, Point of Purchase, Print, Production, Production (Ad, Film, Broadcast), Production (Print), Public Relations, Radio, Regional, Retail, Seniors' Market, Sports Market, Strategic Planning/Research, T.V., Trade & Consumer Magazines, Travel & Tourism, Women's Market, Yellow Pages Advertising

Nancy Siniard *(Mng Partner)*
Candice Butterfield *(Sr Dir-Art)*
Jeff Hinkle *(Sr Dir-Art)*
Laura Lineberry *(Sr Dir-Art)*
Molly Bailey *(Dir-Art)*
Christy Moody *(Dir-Art)*
Lori Moore *(Sr Acct Mgr)*
Elizabeth Webb *(Media Buyer)*

Accounts:
Alexander's Jewelry; Huntsville, AL Antique, Estate & Designer Jewelry; 1989
Benchmark Automotive Group; Birmingham, AL Chrysler, Jeep & Dodge Dealership; 1992
CB&S Bank; Russellville, AL; 2006
Cullman Dodge; Cullman, AL
Redstone Village; Huntsville, AL Lifecare Retirement Community; 2004
Sunshine Mills; Red Bay, AL Pet Foods; 1989

TOTH BRAND & IMAGING
520 Broadway Ste 7, New York, NY 10012
Tel.: (212) 219-2892
Fax: (212) 219-3438
Web Site: www.toth.com

Agency Specializes In: Advertising

Mike Toth *(Pres & Chief Creative Officer)*

Accounts:
Nautica Enterprises, Inc.

TOTH BRAND IMAGING
215 First St, Cambridge, MA 02142
Tel.: (617) 252-0787
Fax: (617) 252-0838
E-Mail: letters@toth.com
Web Site: www.toth.com

E-Mail for Key Personnel:
President: mtoth@toth.com
Creative Dir.: jreeves@toth.com

Employees: 40
Year Founded: 1982

Agency Specializes In: Fashion/Apparel, Sponsorship

Approx. Annual Billings: $75,000,000

Breakdown of Gross Billings by Media: Bus. Publs.: 5%; Mags.: 70%; Newsp.: 5%; Outdoor: 20%

Jack Sharry *(CFO & COO)*
Maggie Smith *(Sr VP & Dir-Brand & Mktg)*
Quinn Lindgren *(Sr Dir-Art)*
Tyrone Sayers *(Grp Acct Dir)*
Holly Wheeler *(Acct Dir)*
Katie Hinchey *(Project Mgr-Digital)*
Sonia Hyojin Byun *(Assoc Strategist-Digital)*

Accounts:
New-Coach
Hyatt Hotels Campaign: "There's a Place for You", Campaign: "Welcome to a Different Place", Digital, Hyatt Place, Online, Outdoor, Radio
New-J.Crew
Johnston & Murphy Shoes
Keds Corp.; Lexington, MA; 1999
New-L.L.Bean
New-Nautica
New York & Co.; 2008
New-Ralph Lauren
Riders
New-Timex
Tommy Hilfiger
New-Wrangler Western & Specialty
Wrangler Advanced Comfort Jeans, Campaign: "Real. Comfortable. Jeans"

Branches

Toth Brand & Imaging
520 Broadway Ste 7, New York, NY 10012
(See Separate Listing)

TOUCHDOWN MEDIA
40 Bridge St, Metuchen, NJ 08840
Tel.: (848) 248-4198
Fax: (732) 321-6933
E-Mail: rahul@touchdown-media.com
Web Site: www.touchdown-media.com

Year Founded: 2003

Niteka Mokal *(Dir-PR & Media Svcs)*
Daisy Walia *(Mgr-Grassroots & Events)*

Accounts:
Airtel; New Delhi, India; 2008
Daawat Rice; New Delhi, India; 2004
Dish Network; Denver, CO; 2005
Kawan Foods; Malaysia; 2005
PNC Bank; Pittsburgh, PA; 2008
South Asian Spelling Bee; Metuchen, NJ; 2008
Tetley
Warner Bros. Pictures; Burbank, CA; 2008
Western Union; Montvale, NJ; 2005
Yashraj Films; New York, NY; 2004

TOUCHPOINT AGENCY
202-1353 Ellis St, Kelowna, BC V1Y 1Z9 Canada
Tel.: (250) 860-8651
Fax: (250) 860-0780
E-Mail: info@touchpoint-agency.com

Employees: 8
Year Founded: 1993

Accounts:
The Lakes; 2007
Ocorp Development; 2007
The Ridge At McKenzie; 2007

TOUCHPOINTS MARKETING, LLC
2550 Belle Chasse Hwy Ste 220, Gretna, LA 70053
Tel.: (504) 361-1804
Fax: (504) 361-1808
E-Mail: info@touchpointsmarketing.net
Web Site: www.touchpointsmarketing.net

Agency Specializes In: Retail, Travel & Tourism

Katie Gravolet *(Pres)*
Ben Gravolet *(VP-Creative & Strategy)*
Joshua Thompson *(Dir-Creative)*
Karen Ferrara *(Mgr-Production & Traffic)*
Anne Prados Leonard *(Supvr-Acct Svc)*

TOUT ADVERTISING LLC
622 Main St, Rapid City, SD 57701
Tel.: (605) 716-5696
Fax: (605) 718-0995
Web Site: www.toutadvertising.com

Year Founded: 2003

Agency Specializes In: Advertising, Brand Development & Integration, Collateral, Graphic Design, Internet/Web Design, Media Buying Services, Print, Promotions, Radio, Social Media

Zachary Reynolds *(Specialist-Bus Dev)*

Accounts:
Nucleo Fitness

TOWER MARKETING
600-E Eden Rd Ste A, Lancaster, PA 17601
Tel.: (717) 517-9103
Fax: (717) 517-9104
E-Mail: info@tower-communications.com
Web Site: www.towermarketing.net/

Employees: 4
Year Founded: 1996

Agency Specializes In: Advertising, Advertising Specialties, Brand Development & Integration, Business-To-Business, Communications, Consulting, Consumer Marketing, Corporate Communications, Corporate Identity, Digital/Interactive, Direct Response Marketing, E-Commerce, Electronic Media, Event Planning & Marketing, Graphic Design, Information Technology, Internet/Web Design, Logo & Package Design, Point of Sale, Print, Sports Market, Technical Advertising

Approx. Annual Billings: $1,000,000

Breakdown of Gross Billings by Media: Adv. Specialities: $100,000; Collateral: $150,000; Consulting: $100,000; E-Commerce: $200,000; Graphic Design: $200,000; Internet Adv.: $100,000; Print: $150,000

Michael K. Matus *(CEO & Dir-Creative)*
Zachary Rupert *(Dir-Art)*
Kelly Howard *(Specialist-Content Mktg)*
Robert Huska *(Designer)*
Alyssa Gailey *(Coord-Digital Mktg)*
Jackie Woodson *(Coord-Digital Mktg)*

TPRB ADVERTISING
3401 Louisiana St Ste 100, Houston, TX 77002
Tel.: (713) 828-1042
E-Mail: rbrightwell@tprbadvertising.com
Web Site: www.tprbadvertising.com

Year Founded: 2003

Agency Specializes In: Advertising, Brand Development & Integration, Collateral, Digital/Interactive, Event Planning & Marketing, Print, Radio, Social Media

Terry Puster *(Pres)*
Russell Brightwell *(Partner, Exec VP & Dir-Creative)*

Accounts:
OMK Tube

TRACTENBERG & CO.

116 East 16th St, New York, NY 10003
Tel.: (212) 929-7979
E-Mail: info@tractenberg.com
Web Site: www.tractenbergandco.com

Year Founded: 1999

Agency Specializes In: Advertising, Event Planning & Marketing, Public Relations, Social Media

Jacquie Tractenberg *(Pres)*
Susan Biegacz *(VP)*
Sarah Parker *(Assoc VP)*
Gizem Ozcelik *(Acct Dir)*

Accounts:
New-Jigsaw

TRACTION

617 E Michigan Ave, Lansing, MI 48912
Tel.: (517) 482-7919
Web Site: www.projecttraction.com

Agency Specializes In: Advertising, Brand Development & Integration

Camron Gnass *(Owner & Creative Dir)*
Terry Sieting *(Art Dir)*

Accounts:
New-Capital City Film Festival

TRACTION CORPORATION

1349 Larkin St, San Francisco, CA 94109
Tel.: (415) 962-5823
Fax: (415) 962-5815
E-Mail: info@tractionco.com
Web Site: www.tractionco.com

E-Mail for Key Personnel:
Creative Dir.: theo@tractionco.com

Employees: 50
Year Founded: 2001

Agency Specializes In: Above-the-Line, Advertising, Affluent Market, Alternative Advertising, Arts, Automotive, Below-the-Line, Brand Development & Integration, Branded Entertainment, Broadcast, Business-To-Business, Cable T.V., Children's Market, Co-op Advertising, Collateral, College, Communications, Computers & Software, Consulting, Consumer Goods, Consumer Marketing, Consumer Publications, Content, Corporate Communications, Corporate Identity, Cosmetics, Digital/Interactive, Direct Response Marketing, Direct-to-Consumer, E-Commerce, Education, Electronic Media, Electronics, Email, Engineering, Entertainment, Environmental, Event Planning & Marketing, Experience Design, Fashion/Apparel, Financial, Food Service, Graphic Design, Guerilla Marketing, High Technology, Hospitality, Household Goods, Identity Marketing, In-Store Advertising, Information Technology, Integrated Marketing, International, Internet/Web Design, Leisure, Local Marketing, Logo & Package Design, Luxury Products, Magazines, Market Research, Media Buying Services, Media Planning, Men's Market, Mobile Marketing, Multimedia, New Product Development, New Technologies, Newspaper, Newspapers & Magazines, Out-of-Home Media, Outdoor, Over-50 Market, Package Design, Paid Searches, Planning & Consultation, Podcasting, Point of Purchase, Point of Sale, Print, Production, Production (Ad, Film, Broadcast), Production (Print), RSS (Really Simple Syndication), Radio, Recruitment, Regional, Restaurant, Retail, Search Engine Optimization, Social Marketing/Nonprofit, Stakeholders, Strategic Planning/Research, Sweepstakes, T.V., Technical Advertising, Teen Market, Trade & Consumer Magazines, Travel & Tourism, Urban Market, Viral/Buzz/Word of Mouth, Web (Banner Ads, Pop-ups, etc.), Women's Market

Approx. Annual Billings: $15,000,000

Adam Kleinberg *(CEO)*
Luigi Imperatore *(CFO)*
Paul Giese *(Dir-Tech)*
Ward Evans *(Assoc Dir-Creative)*
Michael Ballard *(Mgr-Mktg)*
Brandon Herrera *(Acct Supvr)*
Eve Wakeland *(Acct Supvr)*

Accounts:
Adobe; San Jose, CA Software; 2004
Apple; Cupertino, CA Consumer Electronics; 2005
Bank of America; 2007
California Bank & Trust
Charles Schwab Investing Services; 2015
Dolby; San Francisco, CA; 2014
Healthy Pet Pet Products; 2014
New-Lenovo Group Ltd Campaign: "Users Happen"
Robert Half International Inc. Staffing Services; 2010

TRACTION FACTORY

735 W Wisconsin Ave, Milwaukee, WI 53233
Tel.: (414) 944-0900
Web Site: www.tractionfactory.com

Year Founded: 2010

Agency Specializes In: Advertising, Brand Development & Integration, Collateral, Digital/Interactive, Event Planning & Marketing, Media Relations, Package Design, Print, Radio

Scott Bucher *(Pres)*
Peter Bell *(Creative Dir)*
Shannon Egan *(Dir-Accts)*
Laura Anderson *(Acct Exec)*

Accounts:
ALS Association Wisconsin Chapter
City on a Hill
The Delta Diner
Harley-Davidson, Inc.
Horny Goat Brewing Co
Milwaukee Fire Rescue
Mitchell1
Snap-on Incorporated

TRACTORBEAM

325 S Central Expy, Dallas, TX 75201
Tel.: (214) 747-5400
Fax: (214) 747-2716
E-Mail: info@tractorbeam.com
Web Site: www.tractorbeam.com

E-Mail for Key Personnel:
President: peter@tractorbeam.com

Employees: 10
Year Founded: 1997

Agency Specializes In: Brand Development & Integration, Fashion/Apparel

Eric Benanti *(Partner)*
Peter Benanti *(Principal)*
Matt George *(Dir-Creative)*
Lindsey Henrie *(Strategist-Brand)*

Accounts:
Billy Jealousy
LG Electronics
Samsung
Wyndham Hotel; Dallas, TX; 2001

TracyLocke

TRACYLOCKE

1999 Bryan St Ste 2800, Dallas, TX 75201
Tel.: (214) 259-3500
Web Site: www.tracylocke.com

Employees: 540
Year Founded: 1913

National Agency Associations: 4A's-PMA-POPAI

Agency Specializes In: Advertising, Digital/Interactive, Media Buying Services, Media Planning, Mobile Marketing, Package Design, Promotions, Shopper Marketing, Sponsorship, Sports Market, Strategic Planning/Research

Everything We Do Is BUY DESIGN (TM) Creating Commerce-Driving Content (TM) has been our timeless mission for the last 100 years. Combining our knowledge and understanding of how and why people buy with our unique approach to creativity, we are able to constantly re-imagine retail. Our clients call what we do groundbreaking. We call it BUY DESIGN (TM). Our results driven approach has earned us industry recognition. Most notably, PROMO Magazine Agency of the Year in 2011, numerous Reggie and EFFIE Awards, and TL is perennially ranked in the top five of The HUB Shopper Marketing Agency Survey.

Michael Lovegrove *(Pres & Chief Creative Officer)*
Hugh Boyle *(CEO)*
Mike Bartlett *(Mng Partner)*
James Verna *(Mng Partner)*
Stewart Campbell *(CFO)*
Jim Sexton *(CMO)*
Tyler Murray *(Chief Strategy Officer)*
Maria Zanghetti *(Exec VP-Network Ops)*
Shaun Coulter *(Gen Mgr-West)*
Kryslyn Burks *(Grp Acct Dir & Assoc Gen Mgr)*
Cindy Bruemmer *(Dir-Media Svcs)*
Jonathan Jeter *(Dir-Tech Svcs)*
Michael Kelly *(Dir-Comm)*
Bradford Barron *(Assoc Dir-Creative)*
Anthony Franzino *(Assoc Dir-Design)*
Cesar Ortega *(Mgr-New Bus)*
Christie Johansen *(Acct Supvr)*
Tessa Bennett *(Supvr-Media)*
Carlie Wofford-Chen *(Supvr-Digital Media)*
Katie Cockerham *(Sr Acct Exec)*
Ashley McCormick *(Sr Acct Exec)*
Akiran Assi *(Acct Exec)*
Benjamin Larkin *(Sr Analyst)*
Ashlyn Beadel *(Media Buyer)*
Kelley Fulmer *(Media Planner)*
Kelsey Smith *(Asst Acct Exec)*
Ashley Montgomery *(Asst Media Planner)*

Accounts:
24 Hour Fitness Worldwide Inc.
7-Eleven; 2003
AB-InBev
Absolut Vodka
Chase
Dallas Convention & Visitors Bureau
Dicks Sporting Goods
DonQ Rum
Downtown Dallas Inc.
Gatorade; 1982
Goody Goody Liquor
Harmon
Hewlett-Packard; 2008
Johnson & Johnson
Lipton
L'Occitane
Merck
PepsiCo Inc. In-Store Executions
Perfetti Van Melle
Pizza Hut Design, Digital Strategy, Triple-Cheese Covered Stuffed Crust
Playstation
Reebok Merchandising, Retail

Samsung Electronics America, Inc.
S.C. Johnson & Son, Inc. Campaign: "Great Expectations", Digital, Public Relations, Shopper Marketing, Social Media
Smoothie King
Unilever/Lipton; 2007
YUM!; 1993

Branches

TracyLocke
131 Danbury Rd, Wilton, CT 06897
Tel.: (203) 762-2400
E-Mail: bethann.kaminkow@tracylocke.com
Web Site: www.tracylocke.com

Employees: 500
Year Founded: 1913

National Agency Associations: 4A's-PMA-POPAI

Agency Specializes In: Advertising, Collateral, Communications, Consumer Goods, Consumer Publications, Customer Relationship Management, Graphic Design, Integrated Marketing, Internet/Web Design, Media Buying Services, Merchandising, Production (Print), Publicity/Promotions, Retail, Sponsorship, Strategic Planning/Research

Stewart Campbell *(CFO)*
Jim Sexton *(CMO-Global)*
Michael Lovegrove *(Chief Creative Officer)*
Sanford Stein *(VP & Exec Dir-Creative)*
Maria Zanghetti *(VP)*
Phil Camarota *(Exec Dir-Creative)*
Kaitlyn Urbanetti *(Acct Exec)*
Nitin Budhiraja *(Sr Designer)*
Michael Bartlett *(Client Svc Dir)*
James Verna *(Client Svc Dir)*

Accounts:
24 Hour Fitness
7-Eleven
Absolut Vodka
Chase
Dallas Convention & Visitors Bureau
Dick's Sporting Goods
DonQ Rum
Downtown Dallas Inc.
Gatorade
Goody Goody Liquor
Harmon
Hewlett-Packard
L'Occitane
Lipton
Merck
PepsiCo
Perfetti Van Melle
Pizza Hut
Playstation
Reebok
Samsung
Smoothie King
T-Mobile US
YUM!

TracyLocke
437 Madison Ave, New York, NY 10012
(See Separate Listing)

TracyLocke
609 SW 8th St Ste 325, Bentonville, AR 72712
(See Separate Listing)

TRADEMARK ADVERTISING
12748 Kingston Pike Ste 104, Knoxville, TN 37934
Tel.: (865) 966-1690
Fax: (865) 966-1691
Web Site: www.trademarkads.com

Agency Specializes In: Advertising, Brand Development & Integration, Corporate Identity, Internet/Web Design, Print, Radio, Social Media

Travis Morin *(Pres)*
George Corley *(CEO & Dir-Web Svcs)*
David Clark *(Strategist-Creative & Acct Exec)*
Jr Hertwig *(Acct Exec)*
Cevin Thornbrugh *(Designer)*

Accounts:
Daniel Paul Chairs

TRADEMARK PRODUCTIONS
309 S Main St, Royal Oak, MI 48067
Tel.: (248) 582-9210
Web Site: www.tmprod.com

Year Founded: 1998

Agency Specializes In: Advertising, Internet/Web Design, Public Relations, Search Engine Optimization, Social Media

Dwight Zahringer *(CEO)*
Tyler Fraser *(Creative Dir)*

Accounts:
New-Whole Life Balance

TRAFFIC BUILDERS INC.
11524 Blankenbaker Access Dr Ste 104, Louisville, KY 40299
Tel.: (502) 266-9790
Fax: (502) 753-4498
E-Mail: info@trafficbuildersusa.com
Web Site: www.trafficbuildersusa.com

Agency Specializes In: Direct Response Marketing, Email, Environmental, Package Design, Planning & Consultation, Promotions, Strategic Planning/Research

Chuck Patton *(Owner)*
Tricia Patton *(Mng Partner)*
Nick Simon *(Chief Innovation Officer)*
Cindy Snyder *(Gen Mgr)*
Denise Homsher *(Sr Mgr-Data)*
Melissa Buonadonna *(Mgr-Fulfillment)*
Sharon Hardesty *(Mgr-Ops)*

Accounts:
Burnsville Toyota Automobile Services
Carlson Toyota Automobile Services
Denny Hecker's Toyota
Gary Force Toyota Automobile Services
Labadie Toyota Automobile Services
Maplewood Toyota Automobile Services
Rudy Luther Toyota Automobile Services
Swope Toyota Automobile Services
Walser Toyota Automobile Services
Walters Toyota Automobile Services

TRAFFIK
8821 Research Dr, Irvine, CA 92618
Tel.: (949) 679-6820
Web Site: www.traffikonline.com

Employees: 12

Agency Specializes In: Advertising, Corporate Identity, E-Commerce, Graphic Design, Integrated Marketing, Internet/Web Design, Multimedia, Print, Radio, Search Engine Optimization

Anthony Trimino *(Chief Creative Officer & Principal)*
Brent Shoji *(Exec Dir)*
Shane Kimsey *(Acct Dir)*
Julian Trimino *(Dir-Creative)*
Jeremy Troutt *(Dir-Art)*
Amanda Samaan *(Sr Acct Exec)*
Lucy Nguyen *(Acct Exec)*
Casey Lombardo *(Copywriter)*
Jackie Rooney *(Sr Graphic Designer)*

TRAFFIQ
462 7th Ave, New York, NY 10018
Tel.: (212) 792-2294
Fax: (212) 792-2293
E-Mail: info@traffiq.com
Web Site: www.traffiq.com

Year Founded: 2006

Agency Specializes In: Advertising, Digital/Interactive, Media Buying Services, Media Planning

Approx. Annual Billings: $40,000,000

Breakdown of Gross Billings by Media:
Digital/Interactive: 100%

Richard Halle *(CFO)*
W. Aaron Bowlds *(Gen Counsel)*
Mark J. Lamark Lanene *(Sr VP)*
Joe Pellitteri *(Sr VP)*
Bartolome Soriano *(Sr VP-Production)*
Tony Bulugaris *(VP-Ops)*
Laura Cole *(VP-Mktg)*

Accounts:
Aetrex
Curacao Tourism Campaign: "Dare to Explore", Digital Advertising Agency of Record
Halstead Property
Havas Digital
Jiffy Lube
MSG Networks
Piedmont Healthcare
Wegmans
Whole Foods Market
Xeomin

TRAILER PARK
(Name Changed to Deep Focus)

TRANSLATION LLC
(Formerly Translation Consulting & Brand Imaging)
145 W 45th St 12th Fl, New York, NY 10036
Tel.: (212) 299-5505
Fax: (212) 299-5513
E-Mail: info@translationllc.com
Web Site: www.translationllc.com

Employees: 50

Agency Specializes In: Sponsorship

TRANSWORLD ADVERTISING, INC.
3684 N Wickham Rd Ste C, Melbourne, FL 32935
Tel.: (321) 259-7737
Fax: (321) 259-2473
E-Mail: tburcham@transworldadvertising.com
Web Site: www.transworldadvertising.com

E-Mail for Key Personnel:
President: tburcham@transworldadvertising.com

Employees: 11
Year Founded: 1981

Agency Specializes In: Recruitment

Teri Burcham *(Pres)*
W. Chris Burcham *(VP-Client Svcs)*

TRAPEZE COMMUNICATIONS
300-1005 Broad St, Victoria, BC V8W 2A1 Canada

Tel.: (250) 380-0501
Fax: (250) 382-0501
E-Mail: info@trapeze.ca
Web Site: www.trapeze.ca

Employees: 12
Year Founded: 1997

Agency Specializes In: Advertising

Richard Fischer *(Owner & Dir)*
Valerie Nathan *(Owner & Dir-Creative)*
Martin Aveyard *(Sr Dir-Art & Co-Dir-Creative)*
Laura Gordon Mitchell *(Sr Dir-Art)*
Jennifer Mitchelmore *(Acct Dir)*
Erynn Saunders *(Dir-Art)*
Art Perreault *(Acct Mgr)*
Amy Steen *(Sr Designer-Web)*
Ryann Salik *(Project Specialist)*

Accounts:
The Bay Centre
BC College Presidents Association
BMX World Championships
Broadmead Community Care
Cooper Pacific
Crumsby's
Mondelez International, Inc. TASSIMO
PacificSport
Spinnakers
Tourism Victoria
Victoria Foundation
WIINK

TRAVEL SPIKE, LLC
3300 Highlands Pkwy Ste 120, Smyrna, GA 30082
Tel.: (404) 835-2704
Fax: (501) 421-0771
Web Site: www.travelspike.com

Employees: 20

Agency Specializes In: Education, Email, Internet/Web Design, Media Buying Services, Media Planning, Multimedia, Public Relations, Strategic Planning/Research, Travel & Tourism

Ryan Bifulco *(Founder & CEO)*
Matt Weisberger *(Pres & COO)*
Howard Koval *(Exec VP-Bus Dev)*
Alison Cox *(Sr Mgr-Ad Ops)*

Accounts:
Eldorado
Four Seasons Hotel
Lufthansa
Spirit
Starwood Hotels & Resorts Worldwide Inc
Tourist Office of Portugal
Wyoming

TRAVERS COLLINS & COMPANY
(Acquired & Absorbed by The Martin Group, LLC.)

TRAY CREATIVE
2244 NW Market St Ste A, Seattle, WA 98109
Tel.: (206) 420-3972
Web Site: www.traycreative.com

Year Founded: 2009

Agency Specializes In: Advertising, Brand Development & Integration, Content, Digital/Interactive, Event Planning & Marketing, Internet/Web Design, Logo & Package Design, Media Buying Services, Print

Ralph Allora *(Principal & Dir-Mktg)*
Bridget Perez *(Principal & Dir-Creative)*
James Pope *(Sr Designer)*

Accounts:
Caffe Vita
MarketLinc
Urbanadd

TREEFROG MARKETING AND COMMUNICATIONS
8 N 2nd St 2nd Fl Ste C, Lafayette, IN 47901
Tel.: (765) 588-5808
Fax: (765) 588-5807
Web Site: www.treefrogmarketing.com

Year Founded: 2000

Agency Specializes In: Advertising, Brand Development & Integration, Graphic Design, Internet/Web Design, Logo & Package Design, Strategic Planning/Research

Kelly Rice *(Owner & Sr Strategist-Mktg)*
Vanessa Isenbarger *(Sr Dir-Art)*
Megan Kendall *(Mgr-Content)*

Accounts:
Redefining Spaces LLC

TREETREE
444 N Front St Unit 101, Columbus, OH 43215
Tel.: (614) 291-7944
E-Mail: info@treetreebranding.com
Web Site: www.treetreebranding.com

Agency Specializes In: Advertising, Brand Development & Integration, Digital/Interactive, Event Planning & Marketing, Print

Becca Apfelstadt *(CEO)*
Rachel Hillman *(Grp Acct Dir)*

Accounts:
New-Girl Scouts of Ohio's Heartland

TREFOIL GROUP
735 N Water St Ste 200, Milwaukee, WI 53202
Tel.: (414) 272-6898
Fax: (414) 272-6979
E-Mail: info@trefoilgroup.com
Web Site: www.trefoilgroup.com

Employees: 13
Year Founded: 1991

Agency Specializes In: Advertising, Brand Development & Integration, Collateral, Communications, Digital/Interactive, Direct Response Marketing, Internet/Web Design, Local Marketing, Logo & Package Design, Market Research, Public Relations, Social Marketing/Nonprofit, Strategic Planning/Research

Revenue: $2,000,000

Mary Scheibel *(Founder & Principal)*
John Scheibel *(CEO)*
Vince Halaska *(VP-Digital Ops)*
Nancy Woltzen *(Client Svcs Dir)*
Christopher Kent *(Acct Exec)*
Jessica Spooner *(Acct Exec)*

Accounts:
ARI
DME
Dream It. Do It. Website

TREISTER MURRY AGENCY
1130 Washington Ave 1st Fl N, Miami Beach, FL 33139-4600
Tel.: (305) 531-5720
Fax: (305) 531-5740
E-Mail: info@tma-pr.com
Web Site: www.tma-pr.com

Employees: 2

Agency Specializes In: Public Relations

Richard H. Murry *(Founder)*

TRELLIS MARKETING, INC
127 Doncaster Rd, Kenmore, NY 14217
Tel.: (716) 873-7199
Fax: (716) 873-3897
E-Mail: cmccracken@trellismarketing.com
Web Site: www.trellismarketing.com

Employees: 5

Agency Specializes In: Above-the-Line, Advertising, Advertising Specialties, Affiliate Marketing, Affluent Market, African-American Market, Arts, Asian Market, Automotive, Below-the-Line, Bilingual Market, Brand Development & Integration, Branded Entertainment, Broadcast, Business Publications, Business-To-Business, Cable T.V., Catalogs, Children's Market, Collateral, College, Commercial Photography, Communications, Computers & Software, Consulting, Consumer Goods, Consumer Marketing, Consumer Publications, Content, Corporate Communications, Corporate Identity, Crisis Communications, Custom Publishing, Customer Relationship Management, Digital/Interactive, Direct Response Marketing, Direct-to-Consumer, E-Commerce, Education, Electronic Media, Electronics, Email, Engineering, Entertainment, Environmental, Event Planning & Marketing, Exhibit/Trade Shows, Experience Design, Fashion/Apparel, Financial, Food Service, Game Integration, Gay & Lesbian Market, Government/Political, Graphic Design, Guerilla Marketing, Health Care Services, High Technology, Hispanic Market, Hospitality, Household Goods, Identity Marketing, In-Store Advertising, Industrial, Infomercials, Information Technology, Integrated Marketing, International, Internet/Web Design, Investor Relations, Legal Services, Leisure, Local Marketing, Logo & Package Design, Luxury Products, Magazines, Marine, Market Research, Media Buying Services, Media Planning, Media Relations, Media Training, Medical Products, Men's Market, Merchandising, Mobile Marketing, Multicultural, Multimedia, New Product Development, New Technologies, Newspaper, Newspapers & Magazines, Out-of-Home Media, Outdoor, Over-50 Market, Package Design, Paid Searches, Pharmaceutical, Planning & Consultation, Point of Purchase, Point of Sale, Print, Product Placement, Production, Production (Ad, Film, Broadcast), Production (Print), Promotions, Public Relations, Publicity/Promotions, Publishing, Radio, Real Estate, Recruitment, Regional, Restaurant, Retail, Sales Promotion, Search Engine Optimization, Seniors' Market, Social Marketing/Nonprofit, Sponsorship, Sports Market, Stakeholders, Strategic Planning/Research, Sweepstakes, Syndication, T.V., Technical Advertising, Teen Market, Telemarketing, Trade & Consumer Magazines, Transportation, Travel & Tourism, Urban Market, Viral/Buzz/Word of Mouth, Web (Banner Ads, Pop-ups, etc.), Women's Market, Yellow Pages Advertising

Approx. Annual Billings: $3,000,000

Breakdown of Gross Billings by Media: Local Mktg.: 100%

Catharine McCracken *(Owner)*
Patrick McCracken *(Dir-Media)*
Travis Carlson *(Assoc Dir-Creative)*
Kristin Derby *(Sr Designer)*
Gina Marinelli *(Coord-Special Projects)*

Accounts:
California Closets Marketing
DeLacy Ford
Fichte Endl & Elmer Eyecare Creative, LASIK & Cataract Surgeries, Media, Television Commercials
William Bernhardi

TRENDYMINDS INC
531 East Market St, Indianapolis, IN 46204
Tel.: (317) 926-1727
Fax: (317) 926-1728
Web Site: www.trendyminds.com

Employees: 16

Agency Specializes In: Advertising, Brand Development & Integration, Crisis Communications, Graphic Design, Internet/Web Design, Media Relations, Promotions, Public Relations, T.V., Viral/Buzz/Word of Mouth

Trevor Yager *(Pres & CEO)*
Tyler Murray *(COO & Sr VP)*
Jon Immel *(VP-Digital & Interactive)*
Spencer Dell *(Assoc VP-Client Svc)*
Brian Puffer *(Acct Dir)*
Trena Trowbridge *(Office Mgr)*
Reese Henderson *(Acct Supvr)*
Ian Nixon *(Acct Supvr)*
Nick Pasotti *(Acct Supvr)*
Brittany Yancey *(Acct Exec)*
Jordan Brewer *(Designer)*

Accounts:
New-City of Indianapolis
New-Eli Lilly and Company
New-Harrison College
New-Indiana University Health
Kevin Harvick Entertainment Services
New-Liberty Mutual
Pearson Education Educational Services
New-Salesforce

TREVOR PETER COMMUNICATIONS LTD
488 Wellington St W Ste 100, Toronto, ON M5V 1E3 Canada
Tel.: (416) 275-9102
Web Site: www.trevorpeter.com

Year Founded: 2008

Agency Specializes In: Advertising, Digital/Interactive, Graphic Design, Public Relations, Social Media

Chris Cook *(Pres)*
Dan Mittelman *(Client Svcs Dir)*
Marta Hooper *(Dir-Creative)*

Accounts:
Carlsberg Canada (Creative Agency of Record)

TRI-AUTO ENTERPRISES, LLC
(Name Changed to PERQ LLC)

TRI-MEDIA INTEGRATED MARKETING TECHNOLOGIES INC.
(Formerly Azzam Jordan)
305 Washington Ave Ste 305, Baltimore, MD 21204
Tel.: (410) 825-1800
Fax: (410) 825-3997
Web Site: www.tri-media.com

Employees: 14
Year Founded: 1991

Agency Specializes In: Automotive, Brand Development & Integration, Health Care Services, Logo & Package Design, Real Estate, Travel & Tourism

Albert Lannantuono *(Founder, Pres & CEO)*
Sergey Peregud *(Dir-Tech)*

Accounts:
Animal Planet
AOL
The Art Institutes
AUA Foundation
CBS Digital
Chesapeake Urology
Discovery
EatSmart
Jet Blue Airways
Kraft
The Learning Channel
LivingSocial
Observation Baltimore
Padrinos
Snyders of Hanover Eat Smart Naturals, Grande, Jay's Foods, Kruncher's
Tate
Township Land Company
TV One
Walmart
White House/Black Market

TRI-STATE ADVERTISING CO., INC.
(Name Changed to TSA Communications, Inc.)

TRIAD BUSINESS MARKETING
10670 N Central Expy Ste 300, Dallas, TX 75231
Tel.: (214) 953-6223
Fax: (214) 953-3101
E-Mail: tp@triadbusinessmarketing.com
Web Site: www.triadbusinessmarketing.com

E-Mail for Key Personnel:
President: tp@triadbusinessmarketing.com
Creative Dir.: jgardner@triadbusinessmarketing.com

Employees: 10
Year Founded: 1994

Agency Specializes In: Advertising, Agriculture, Business Publications, Business-To-Business, Collateral, Consulting, Corporate Communications, Corporate Identity, Digital/Interactive, Direct Response Marketing, Environmental, Exhibit/Trade Shows, Financial, Graphic Design, Health Care Services, High Technology, Industrial, Internet/Web Design, Investor Relations, Logo & Package Design, Magazines, Marine, Media Buying Services, Medical Products, Multimedia, New Product Development, Planning & Consultation, Point of Purchase, Point of Sale, Print, Production, Public Relations, Publicity/Promotions, Radio, Real Estate, Sales Promotion, Strategic Planning/Research, Technical Advertising, Trade & Consumer Magazines

Approx. Annual Billings: $6,300,000

Breakdown of Gross Billings by Media: Audio/Visual: $490,000; Bus. Publs.: $1,690,000; Comml. Photography: $1,142,000; D.M.: $964,000; Internet Adv.: $347,000; Local Mktg.: $126,000; Pub. Rels.: $568,000; Worldwide Web Sites: $973,000

Tom Prikryl *(Pres & CEO)*
Ed Giddens *(Sr Dir-Art)*
Julie Gardner *(Dir-Creative)*
Waynette Ray *(Dir-Fin & Ops)*
Jessica Weiss *(Dir-Art)*

Accounts:
Alcoa Fastening Systems; Waco, TX Specialty Fastening Systems; 1995
Alcoa Installation Systems; Kingston, NY Specialty Assembly Tooling Systems; 1995
Alcoa Oil & Gas; Houston, TX Aluminum Alloy Drill Pipe, Risers; 2009
Double E; Dallas, TX Oilfield Production Tools; 2002
Michigan Peat; Houston,TX Peat-Based Growing Medium; 1995

TRIAD RETAIL MEDIA, LLC
100 Carillon Pkwy, Saint Petersburg, FL 33716
Tel.: (727) 231-5041
Web Site: www.triadretail.com

Employees: 30
Year Founded: 2005

Agency Specializes In: Digital/Interactive, Sponsorship

Revenue: $2,300,000

David Haase *(Pres-eBay & US Retailers)*
Ana V. Toro *(Sr VP-Ops & HR & Gen Mgr)*
Eric Meth *(Sr VP-Programmatic Sls)*
Bernadette Van Osdal *(Sr VP-Sls NA-eBay Adv)*
Justin Merkey *(Reg VP-Central-eBay Adv)*
Dan Schock *(Reg VP-Ad Sls-eBay)*
Matthew Romano *(VP-Platform Strategy)*
Jack Spielberg *(VP-eBay Audience Platform)*
Ashley Singer *(Sr Acct Dir-Programmatic-eBay-East)*
Sasha Bartnovsky *(Dir-Platform Solutions)*
Martin Berman *(Dir-Programmatic Sls)*
Paula Hunsche *(Dir-Sls-Walmart)*
Leigh Anne Pederson *(Dir-Adv Tech Strategy)*
Beth Provencher *(Dir-Strategic Sls & eBay Adv Sls)*
Kim Hiebert *(Assoc Dir-Art)*
Kelsey Bohannan *(Acct Mgr-eBay)*
Bobby Munchel *(Acct Mgr-Programmatic)*
Jack Watters *(Acct Mgr)*
Casey Rode *(Mgr-Programmatic Ops)*
Katie Thomaides *(Mgr-Programmatic Ops)*
David Virenius *(Mgr-Programmatic Ops & Yield)*
Elizabeth Cappello *(Acct Exec-eBay)*
Jessica Felice *(Media Buyer-Programmatic)*
Ryan Fletcher *(Media Planner)*
Jennifer LaRue *(Planner-Digital Media)*
Christine Miller *(Planner-Digital Media)*
Brande Palmer *(Media Planner)*
Janada Scott *(Planner-Digital Media)*

Accounts:
CVS Health
Dell
eBay App Advertising
Toys"R"Us
Walmart

TRIBE
2100 Riveredge Pkwy Ste 710, Atlanta, GA 30328
Tel.: (404) 256-5858
Fax: (404) 256-0355
E-Mail: elizabeth@tribeinc.com
Web Site: www.tribeinc.com

Employees: 7

Agency Specializes In: Corporate Communications, Corporate Identity, Women's Market

Elizabeth Cogswell Baskin *(CEO & Exec Dir-Creative)*
Cassondra Berardicurti *(Dir-Art)*
David Lamarca *(Dir-Tech)*
Brittany Silberman *(Acct Mgr)*
Matt Maggart *(Mgr-Traffic)*
Stephen Burns *(Copywriter)*

Accounts:
Cetera Financial

Coca-Cola Refreshments USA, Inc.
Home Depot Culture
InterContinental Hotels Group
Intimacy
Mannington Floors
Northside Hospital
Porsche
UPS

TRIBU
7334 Caribou St, San Antonio, TX 78238
Tel.: (210) 209-9209
E-Mail: hello@wearetribu.com
Web Site: www.wearetribu.com

Year Founded: 2003

Agency Specializes In: Advertising, Brand Development & Integration, Collateral, Digital/Interactive, Graphic Design, Internet/Web Design, Logo & Package Design, Media Buying Services, Outdoor, Social Media

Sara S. Helmy *(CEO)*
Lindsay Miller *(Dir-Art & Graphic Designer)*
Logan Lebouef *(Project Mgr & Strategist-Content)*
Andrew Hoing *(Strategist-Content)*
Michelle Lok *(Strategist-Content)*
Chelsea Mojica *(Graphic Designer & Designer-Website)*

Accounts:
Firstmark Credit Union
Logro Farms
Travis Park

TRICOM ASSOCIATES
1750 New York Ave NW, Washington, DC 20006
Tel.: (703) 276-2772
E-Mail: info@tricomassociates.com
Web Site: www.tricomassociates.com

Agency Specializes In: Advertising, Government/Political, Public Relations, Social Media

Scott Treibitz *(Pres)*
Marco Trbovich *(Sr VP)*
Andrea Garvue *(Acct Exec)*

Accounts:
New-American Federation of Teachers

TRICOMB2B
109 N Main St Ste 700, Dayton, OH 45402
Tel.: (937) 890-5311
E-Mail: info@tricomb2b.com
Web Site: www.tricomb2b.com

Employees: 30
Year Founded: 1984

Agency Specializes In: Business-To-Business

John Buscemi *(Principal)*
Chris Eifert *(Principal)*
Jocelyn Hodson *(Dir-PR)*
Melissa Lorenz *(Dir-Strategic Accts)*
Patrick McMullen *(Dir-Mktg Tech)*
John Nagy *(Dir-Creative Strategy)*
Jon Berry *(Mgr-Content Dev)*
Amy Shroyer *(Acct Exec)*
Stacey Alspaugh *(Designer-Production)*
Kara Cox *(Coord-Traffic)*

Accounts:
Forte Marketing, PR
Rittal Corporation

TRIER AND COMPANY
649 Mission St 5th Fl, San Francisco, CA 94103
Tel.: (415) 285-6147
E-Mail: info@triercompany.com
Web Site: www.triercompany.com

Agency Specializes In: Advertising, Brand Development & Integration, Event Planning & Marketing, Media Relations, Media Training, Public Relations, Social Media

Beth Trier *(Founder & Mng Dir)*

Accounts:
New-Genband
New-Strobs USA

TRIFECTA
3080 Harrodsburg Rd Ste 101, Lexington, KY 40503
Tel.: (859) 652-3361
Fax: (859) 554-0524
E-Mail: info@trifectaky.com
Web Site: www.trifectaky.com

Year Founded: 2010

Agency Specializes In: Advertising, Brand Development & Integration, Content, Graphic Design, Internet/Web Design, Print

Kevin O'Dea *(Owner & Designer)*
Jonathan Moore *(Owner)*
Adam Trumbo *(Mgr & Writer-Content)*

Accounts:
Good Foods Market & Cafe

TRIGGER COMMUNICATIONS & DESIGN
200 1725 10 Ave SW, Calgary, AB T3C 0K1 Canada
Tel.: (403) 265-0812
Fax: (403) 264-2705
E-Mail: info@ideasthattrigger.com
Web Site: www.ideasthattrigger.com

E-Mail for Key Personnel:
Media Dir.: Holly.Popiel@triggerco.com

Employees: 30
Year Founded: 1980

National Agency Associations: CAB-CBP-CDNPA

Agency Specializes In: Communications

Brenda Belcher *(Mng Dir)*
Teresa Leung *(Sr Art Dir)*
Jennifer Fines *(Dir-Bus)*
Kelly Rakhara *(Mgr-Tech Dev)*
Mariana Aramburu *(Acct Supvr)*
Dean Rud *(Strategist-Digital)*
Jordan Finlayson *(Copywriter)*

Accounts:
AMI Autoglass Insurance
BrokerLink
Calgary Zoo Campaign: "One Page. One Ink. One Goal."
The Mustard Seed
RBC Asset Management Inc.
University of Calgary
New-Zombie Walk

TRIGGERFISH MARKETING
200 Townsend St Ste 45, San Francisco, CA 94107
Tel.: (415) 671-4699
Fax: (866) 510-8706
Toll Free: (877) 831-7432
Web Site: www.triggerfish.com

Scott Gregory *(Pres)*

Accounts:
3PAR, Inc.
Barnett Cox & Associates
Black Bag Advertising
Hoffman Lewis
Rauxa Direct
Tee Bee Dee

TRILIX MARKETING GROUP, INC.
615 3rd St Ste 300, Des Moines, IA 50309
Tel.: (515) 221-4900
Fax: (515) 221-0000
E-Mail: info@trilixgroup.com
Web Site: www.trilixgroup.com

Employees: 22
Year Founded: 1981

National Agency Associations: AMA-NAMA-PRSA

Agency Specializes In: Advertising, Agriculture, Automotive, Brand Development & Integration, Business-To-Business, Co-op Advertising, Collateral, Communications, Consulting, Consumer Marketing, Corporate Communications, Direct Response Marketing, E-Commerce, Education, Environmental, Event Planning & Marketing, Exhibit/Trade Shows, Government/Political, Graphic Design, Health Care Services, High Technology, Information Technology, Internet/Web Design, Investor Relations, Local Marketing, Logo & Package Design, Media Buying Services, Medical Products, Merchandising, New Product Development, Newspapers & Magazines, Outdoor, Pharmaceutical, Planning & Consultation, Point of Purchase, Print, Production, Public Relations, Publicity/Promotions, Radio, Recruitment, Retail, Sales Promotion, Sports Market, Strategic Planning/Research

Approx. Annual Billings: $5,000,000

Todd Senne *(Owner & Pres)*
Ron Maahs *(Partner & CEO)*
Brett Adams *(Partner & CMO)*
Yancy De Lathouder *(Dir-Interactive)*
Abe Goldstien *(Dir-Creative Svcs)*
Brent Wirth *(Dir-Creative)*
Paul Burger *(Assoc Dir-Interactive)*

Accounts:
Drake University; Des Moines, IA; 2002
EarthPark; Des Moines, IA Environmental Education; 2004
Great Ape Trust; Des Moines, IA Great Ape Preservation & Research; 2003
Greater Des Moines Partnership
Iowa Pork Producers Association; Clive, IA Pork Consumption Promotion & Producer Education; 1997
McWane Companies; Birmingham, AL Clowe Valve, Kennedy Valve, M&H Valve; 2003
McWane Industries, Inc
NCMIC Group, Inc.; West Des Moines, IA Insurance; 1995
Newsham Choice Genetics
Stine Seed Company; Adel, IA Agricultural Seed; 2003

TRILLION CREATIVE LLC
382 Springfield Ave Ste 408, Summit, NJ 7901
Tel.: (908) 219-4703
Fax: (347) 620-9513
E-Mail: hello@trillioncreative.com
Web Site: www.trillioncreative.com

Year Founded: 2013

Agency Specializes In: Advertising, Brand Development & Integration, Event Planning & Marketing, Graphic Design, Internet/Web Design,

Logo & Package Design, Package Design, Print

Lou Leonardis *(Partner & Dir-Creative)*
Larissa Montecuollo *(Partner & Dir-Creative)*

Accounts:
Aquamate
Cheeky Bites
Madison Avenue Chiropractic Group
Purvi Padia

TRILOGY INTERACTIVE LLC
1936 University Ave Ste 191, Berkeley, CA 94704
Tel.: (510) 548-8800
Fax: (510) 548-8981
E-Mail: info@trilogyinteractive.com
Web Site: www.trilogyinteractive.com

Employees: 40

Agency Specializes In: Advertising Specialties, Brand Development & Integration, Email, Internet/Web Design, Media Relations, New Technologies, Strategic Planning/Research

Brent Blackaby *(Co-Founder & Principal)*
Stacey Bashara *(Partner)*
Larry Huynh *(Partner)*
Josh Ross *(Partner)*
Randy Stearns *(Partner)*

Accounts:
Arizona Economic Council
ASAE & Center for Association Leadership
Barbara Boxer Social Welfare Services
Blue Green Alliance Environmental Movement Services
Brooke Ellison Project
Democratic Governors Association Training Services
Dick Durbin Health Care Reform Services
Fostering Connections Child Health Care & Reform Services
Gillibrand Health Care Services
Health Access Foundation
Media Matters
NALEO
Patty Murray Public Services
PICO National Network

TRIMENTION ADVERTISING
555 Washington Ave, Miami Beach, FL 33139
Tel.: (305) 858-3155
Fax: (305) 858-3154
E-Mail: sales@trimentionadvertising.com
Web Site: trimention.com

Employees: 14

Agency Specializes In: Hispanic Market

John Grove *(Founder, Partner-Trimention Global Comm & Sr Dir-Creative)*
Guillermo Heredia *(Mng Partner)*
Danica Wingate *(Sr Acct Exec & Strategist-Brand)*

Accounts:
Alma
Conrad Hotels
Eastern Air Lines Communications, Strategic Marketing
Hilton Worldwide
Jim Beam
Johnson & Johnson
Microsoft
Samsung
Sony

TRINET INTERNET SOLUTIONS, INC.
108 Discovery, Irvine, CA 92618
Tel.: (949) 442-8900
Fax: (949) 442-8905
E-Mail: info@trinetsolutions.com
Web Site: www.trinetsolutions.com

E-Mail for Key Personnel:
President: john.carley@trinetsolutions.com
Production Mgr.: danielle.berry@trinetsolutions.com
Public Relations: alexis@trinetsolutions.com

Employees: 50
Year Founded: 1995

Agency Specializes In: Affiliate Marketing, Arts, Automotive, Brand Development & Integration, Broadcast, Business-To-Business, Children's Market, Consulting, Consumer Goods, Consumer Marketing, Corporate Identity, Cosmetics, Customer Relationship Management, Digital/Interactive, Direct Response Marketing, E-Commerce, Education, Electronic Media, Electronics, Email, Entertainment, Fashion/Apparel, Graphic Design, Health Care Services, High Technology, Hispanic Market, Hospitality, Integrated Marketing, Internet/Web Design, Leisure, Local Marketing, Luxury Products, Medical Products, Men's Market, Mobile Marketing, Multicultural, Multimedia, New Technologies, Over-50 Market, Paid Searches, Pharmaceutical, Podcasting, Promotions, Publicity/Promotions, RSS (Really Simple Syndication), Real Estate, Recruitment, Restaurant, Retail, Sales Promotion, Search Engine Optimization, Seniors' Market, Social Marketing/Nonprofit, Strategic Planning/Research, Teen Market, Travel & Tourism, Urban Market, Viral/Buzz/Word of Mouth, Women's Market

John Carley *(CEO)*
Bill Porter *(CFO)*
Ron Weber *(COO)*
Jing Liao *(Sr VP-HR)*
Steve Apfelberg *(VP-Mktg)*
Matt Wulkan *(Dir-Channel Mktg & Partner Programs)*

Accounts:
Coca-Cola Refreshments USA, Inc.
IMAX
MAZDA
PricewaterhouseCoopers
Red Cross
Safety Syringes
The Salvation Army
SAP
Sony
Warner Bros.
Whole Foods

TRIO GROUP NW
(Formerly TRIO advertising. design. solutions)
239 SW 41st St, Renton, WA 98057
Tel.: (206) 728-8181
Fax: (206) 728-1334
Web Site: www.triogroupnw.com

Employees: 10
Year Founded: 2003

Agency Specializes In: Education, Government/Political

Jeff Quint *(Owner)*
Dennis Brooks *(Pres)*

Accounts:
City of Seattle
Metro Parks Tacoma-Meadow Park GC Tacoma Open Golf/Footgolf Tournaments
Renton Technical College Student Handbook, Video, Web App
Seattle City Light Budget Billing, Meter Read, Utility Discount Program; 2010
Seattle Public Utility
WA State Parks Boater Safety

TRIPLEINK
60 S 6th St Ste 2800, Minneapolis, MN 55402
Tel.: (612) 342-9800
Fax: (612) 342-9745
Toll Free: (800) 632-1388
E-Mail: info@tripleink.com
Web Site: www.tripleink.com

E-Mail for Key Personnel:
President: cthudson@tripleink.com

Employees: 11
Year Founded: 1991

Agency Specializes In: Advertising, Agriculture, Asian Market, Bilingual Market, Business-To-Business, Collateral, Communications, Corporate Communications, Cosmetics, Digital/Interactive, Fashion/Apparel, Financial, Health Care Services, Hispanic Market, Hospitality, International, Internet/Web Design, Medical Products, Multicultural, Multimedia, Pharmaceutical, Radio, T.V.

Breakdown of Gross Billings by Media: Audio/Visual: 5%; Collateral: 75%; Print: 5%; Radio & T.V.: 5%; Worldwide Web Sites: 10%

Stephanie Cooper *(VP & Dir-Translation Svcs)*
Uta Moncur *(Dir-Tech Svcs)*

TRIPTENT INC
400 W 14th St 3rd Fl, New York, NY 10014
Tel.: (212) 255-3600
Web Site: www.triptent.com

Agency Specializes In: Advertising, Digital/Interactive, Graphic Design, Production, Radio, Sponsorship

Joe Masi *(CEO)*
Colleen Kelly *(Mng Dir & Partner)*
John Paul *(Exec Creative Dir)*
Alex Lose *(Dir-Content)*

Accounts:
New-Kohl's
Unilever

TRISECT, LLC
130 S Jefferson St 5th Fl, Chicago, IL 60661
Tel.: (312) 733-1303
Fax: (312) 733-5883
Web Site: www.trisectagency.com/

Agency Specializes In: Advertising, Brand Development & Integration, Digital/Interactive, Media Buying Services, Production, Promotions, Sponsorship

Tim Nelson *(Pres)*
Matt Witt *(Exec VP-Digital Integration)*
Craig Miller *(VP & Grp Dir-Creative)*
Gauri Kapoor *(VP & Acct Plng Dir)*
Erin Sarofsky *(Exec Creative Dir)*
John Filipkowski *(Creative Dir)*
Danielle Simon *(Dir-Strategic Plng)*
Julian Gallo *(Assoc Dir-Creative)*
Dana Matsuo *(Sr Acct Exec)*
Jeanette Polanin *(Sr Acct Exec)*
Jake Cooper *(Acct Exec)*
Martha Ramette *(Acct Exec-ConAgra Foods)*

Accounts:
ConAgra Foods Campaign: "Child Hunger Ends Here", Consumer Promotion
DeVry University National Student Programs
Healthy Choice
Kawasaki Heavy Industries (U.S.A.), Inc.

Campaign: "Lone Ranger", KX Dirt, KX motocross, Ninja, Online, Teryx4
Kimberly-Clark Corporation Cottonelle, Print, Scott, Scott Naturals, TV, Viva
Mike's Hard Lemonade Co. TV
Paper Mate
Sharpie
Uni-Ball
US Cellular Inc.

TROIKA DESIGN GROUP

6715 Melrose Ave, Hollywood, CA 90038
Tel.: (323) 965-1650
Fax: (323) 965-7885
E-Mail: chuck@troika.tv
Web Site: www.troika.tv

Employees: 40
Year Founded: 2001

Agency Specializes In: Advertising Specialties, Brand Development & Integration, Multimedia, Syndication, T.V.

Kristen Olsen *(Gen Mgr)*
Dale Everett *(Dir-Creative)*
Gil Haslam *(Dir-Creative)*
Seton Kim *(Dir-Creative)*
Reid Thompson *(Dir-Creative)*
Heidi Netzley *(Mgr-Bus Dev)*
Scott Tinter *(Mgr-Production)*
Joshua Kohl Hegmann *(Coord-IT)*
Jessica Raymo *(Coord-Production)*
Andrew Thao *(Coord-Production)*

Accounts:
Animal Planet
Comcast
The CW
DIRECTV
Discovery Communications, Inc.
Disney Interactive Media Group
EA Sports
Electronic Arts Inc.
ESPN SportsCenter
Fox Entertainment Group, Inc.
HBO Sports
HGTV
Los Angeles Lakers
NBC Sports Network
Time Warner Cable SportsNet & Deportes

TROLLBACK + COMPANY

490 Broadway, New York, NY 10012
Tel.: (212) 529-1010
Fax: (212) 529-9540
Web Site: www.trollback.com

Employees: 10

Agency Specializes In: Advertising, Broadcast, Entertainment, Graphic Design, Multimedia, Print, T.V.

Revenue: $5,000,000

Jakob Trollback *(Pres & Dir-Creative)*
Elliott Chaffer *(VP-Creative)*
Thomas Edwards *(Art Dir)*
Mitch Monson *(Dir-Creative & Client Partner)*
Brian Bowman *(Dir-Creative)*
Betsy Jones *(Mgr-Ops)*

TRONCONE + PARTNERS

(Formerly CBK Group)
61 Berea Rd, Walden, NY 12586
Toll Free: (855) 562-9203
Web Site: tronconepartners.com

Employees: 10

National Agency Associations: Second Wind Limited

Revenue: $30,000,000

Carol Romeo *(Owner)*
Bill Troncone *(Pres & Dir-Creative)*

Accounts:
Cerebral Palsy of North Jersey Redesign
Linnea Worldwide Inc.
Riskclick
The U.S. Virgin Islands

TRONE BRAND ENERGY, INC.

(Formerly Trone Inc.)
1823 Eastchester Dr Ste A, High Point, NC 27265
Tel.: (336) 886-1622
Fax: (336) 886-2334
E-Mail: trone@trone.com
Web Site: www.tronebrandenergy.com

Employees: 65
Year Founded: 1982

National Agency Associations: AMIN

Agency Specializes In: Advertising, Affluent Market, Alternative Advertising, Automotive, Brand Development & Integration, Broadcast, Business-To-Business, Cable T.V., Children's Market, Co-op Advertising, Collateral, Consulting, Consumer Goods, Consumer Marketing, Corporate Communications, Corporate Identity, Crisis Communications, Customer Relationship Management, Digital/Interactive, Direct Response Marketing, Direct-to-Consumer, Education, Email, Entertainment, Event Planning & Marketing, Exhibit/Trade Shows, Fashion/Apparel, Financial, Government/Political, Graphic Design, Guerilla Marketing, Health Care Services, High Technology, Household Goods, Identity Marketing, Industrial, Information Technology, Integrated Marketing, Internet/Web Design, Leisure, Local Marketing, Logo & Package Design, Luxury Products, Magazines, Market Research, Media Buying Services, Media Planning, Media Relations, Media Training, Medical Products, Men's Market, Merchandising, Multicultural, Multimedia, New Product Development, Newspaper, Newspapers & Magazines, Out-of-Home Media, Outdoor, Package Design, Paid Searches, Pets, Pharmaceutical, Planning & Consultation, Point of Purchase, Point of Sale, Print, Production, Production (Print), Promotions, Public Relations, Publicity/Promotions, RSS (Really Simple Syndication), Radio, Regional, Retail, Sales Promotion, Search Engine Optimization, Social Media, Sponsorship, Stakeholders, Strategic Planning/Research, T.V., Technical Advertising, Trade & Consumer Magazines, Travel & Tourism, Viral/Buzz/Word of Mouth, Women's Market

Approx. Annual Billings: $24,000,000

Doug Barton *(Pres & Partner)*
Martin Buchanan *(Partner & Exec Dir-Creative)*
Kevin Murphy *(Partner-Strategy & Res)*
Rick Morgan *(CFO)*
Gary Towning *(Sr VP-Digital Strategy & Svcs)*
Robin Yontz *(VP & Dir-Creative)*
Melissa Hintz *(Media Dir)*
Laura Judy *(Acct Mgr-Fin)*
Carolyn Sigmon *(Media Planner & Media Buyer)*

Accounts:
Al Capone; 2012
AVDC; 2012
Boy Scouts of America, Old North State; 2008
Greenies; 2006
Greensboro Imaging; 2005
High Point Bank; 2011
Home Meridian International; 2011
Ingersoll Rand (Agency of Record) Marketing, Power Tool Line, Product Launches
Mars Wisdom Panel; 2012
Michelin; 2011
North Carolina Department of Commerce, Division of Tourism, Film and Sports Development
North State Communications
OraStrip; 2012
Royal Canin; 2011
Servantage; 2011
Shreve & Co; 2012
Standard Process
Susie's Hope
Syngenta Professional Products Avid, Banner Maxx, Barricade, Bonzi, Daconil, Demand, Heritage, Primo Maxx, Reward, SecureChoice
Velcera; 2010
Veterinary Pet Insurance
VPI; 2010

TRONE INC.

(Name Changed to Trone Brand Energy, Inc.)

TRONIC STUDIO

54 W 21st St Ste 705, New York, NY 10010
Tel.: (212) 255-1777
Fax: (212) 255-8415
Web Site: www.tronicstudio.com

Agency Specializes In: Brand Development & Integration, Broadcast, Digital/Interactive, Electronic Media, Entertainment, Internet/Web Design, Media Planning

Jesse Seppi *(Co-Founder & Dir)*
Toby Sowers *(Partner & Exec Producer)*

Accounts:
Hewlett-Packard Computer Hardware Mfr
Take 2 Video Games Distr

TROZZOLO COMMUNICATIONS GROUP

811 Wyandotte St, Kansas City, MO 64105-1608
Tel.: (816) 842-8111
Fax: (816) 842-8188
E-Mail: info@trozzolo.com
Web Site: www.trozzolo.com

Employees: 40
Year Founded: 1989

Agency Specializes In: Advertising, Brand Development & Integration, Broadcast, Business Publications, Business-To-Business, Collateral, Communications, Consumer Goods, Consumer Marketing, Corporate Communications, Corporate Identity, Crisis Communications, Custom Publishing, Digital/Interactive, Direct-to-Consumer, Entertainment, Event Planning & Marketing, Graphic Design, Health Care Services, Identity Marketing, Integrated Marketing, Legal Services, Local Marketing, Magazines, Media Relations, Media Training, Medical Products, Multimedia, Newspaper, Newspapers & Magazines, Planning & Consultation, Promotions, Public Relations, Regional, Social Marketing/Nonprofit, Sports Market, Strategic Planning/Research

Revenue: $42,000,000

Angelo R. Trozzolo *(Pres & CEO)*
Rachel Lupardus *(CFO & COO)*
Paul Behnen *(Sr VP & Exec Dir-Creative)*
Corey Shulda *(Dir-Art)*
Lisa Phillips *(Mgr-Pro Practices)*
Tina Wheeler *(Mgr-Ops-Prairie Dog)*
Natalie Long *(Acct Supvr)*
Sarah Quinlivan *(Acct Supvr)*
Jenny Stasi *(Acct Supvr)*
Kayla Blevins *(Sr Acct Exec)*
Emily Drape *(Acct Exec)*

Accounts:

Alliance Benefit Group
Avila University
Buffalo Funds
Chuy's
Highwoods Properties Inc
Missouri Bank & Trust; Kansas City, MO
Sly James Firm; Kansas City, MO
St. Joseph Chamber Of Commerce
Sys-Tek Companies; Blue Springs, MO
Valencia Group; Houston, TX Hotel Sorella Country Club Plaza, PR

Branch

Prairie Dog/TCG
811 Wyandotte St, Kansas City, MO 64105-1608
(See Separate Listing)

TRUE ACTION NETWORK
(Acquired by EBay, Inc. & Name Changed to The Shop)

TRUE NORTH INC.
630 Third Ave 12th Fl, New York, NY 10017
Tel.: (212) 557-4202
Fax: (212) 557-4204
E-Mail: info@truenorthinc.com
Web Site: www.truenorthinc.com

Employees: 45
Year Founded: 1994

Agency Specializes In: Advertising, Advertising Specialties, Alternative Advertising, Below-the-Line, Business-To-Business, Consumer Marketing, Customer Relationship Management, Digital/Interactive, Direct Response Marketing, Direct-to-Consumer, E-Commerce, Email, Entertainment, Financial, Game Integration, Graphic Design, Integrated Marketing, Internet/Web Design, Media Buying Services, Media Planning, Mobile Marketing, Multimedia, New Technologies, Paid Searches, Point of Purchase, Print, Production, Promotions, Radio, Search Engine Optimization, Social Marketing/Nonprofit, Social Media, Sponsorship, Sports Market, Teen Market, Travel & Tourism, Tween Market, Viral/Buzz/Word of Mouth

Approx. Annual Billings: $30,000,000

Breakdown of Gross Billings by Media: Collateral: $1,000,000; D.M.: $2,000,000; Internet Adv.: $25,000,000; Worldwide Web Sites: $2,000,000

Tim Taylor *(COO)*
John Como *(Client Svcs Dir)*
Annika Bryntse *(Dir-Media Svcs)*
Dan Levine *(Dir)*
Rehan Iqbal *(Assoc Dir-Media)*
Garen Karnikian *(Assoc Dir-Analytics)*
Elisa Tam *(Coord-Media Ops)*

Accounts:
Adlens (Agency of Record) Data Analytics, Media Buying, Media Planning, Social Media
American Mint Collectibles (Direct Mail); 2002
ASPCA; New York, NY Sustainer Donor Acquisition; 2010
Citigroup; New York, NY; 1997
Club ABC Tours; Bloomfield, NJ Tour & Vacation Packages (Online Search Media Planning & Buying, E-Mail, Landing Pages); 2009
Doctors Without Borders; New York, NY Campaign: "Right Now", Sustainer Donor Acquisition; 2011
Goldman Sachs; New York, NY Collateral, Private Banking Statements; 1994
Medco; Franklin Lakes, NJ Pharmaceutical Health Services (Microsite, E-Mail, Direct Mail); 2010
Newsweek Daily Beast Co. Subscription Acquisition (Search Planning, Buying, Online Display, Direct Mail, Partnership Marketing); 1998
Quorum Financial; Purchase, NY Financial Services (Marketing Pages, Collateral & Annual Report)
Royal Mail
ThomasNet.com; New York, NY Event Marketing (Online & Collateral), Search Media; 2004
Toys "R " Us; Wayne, NJ Geoffrey's Birthday Club (Web Site, Online Games); 2008
Welcome Collection

Branch

True North Interactive
417 Montgomery St Ste 900, San Francisco, CA 94104
(See Separate Listing)

TRUMPET LLC
2803 St Philip St, New Orleans, LA 70119
Tel.: (504) 525-4600
Fax: (504) 525-4620
E-Mail: hello@trumpetgroup.com
Web Site: www.trumpetgroup.com

Employees: 30
Year Founded: 1997

Agency Specializes In: Advertising, Brand Development & Integration, Branded Entertainment, Broadcast, Business-To-Business, Cable T.V., Collateral, Communications, Consulting, Consumer Goods, Consumer Marketing, Content, Corporate Communications, Corporate Identity, Digital/Interactive, Entertainment, Food Service, Graphic Design, Guerilla Marketing, Health Care Services, Hospitality, Identity Marketing, In-Store Advertising, Internet/Web Design, Leisure, Local Marketing, Logo & Package Design, New Product Development, Newspapers & Magazines, Outdoor, Package Design, Planning & Consultation, Print, Publicity/Promotions, Restaurant, Retail, Sales Promotion, Sports Market, Strategic Planning/Research, T.V., Travel & Tourism

Approx. Annual Billings: $26,000,000

Breakdown of Gross Billings by Media: Cable T.V.: 1%; Fees: 32%; Internet Adv.: 1%; Mags.: 2%; Newsp.: 5%; Other: 1%; Out-of-Home Media: 8%; Production: 28%; Spot Radio: 6%; Spot T.V.: 5%; Trade & Consumer Mags.: 11%

Jude Chauvin *(Partner, CFO & COO)*
Jenny McGuinness *(Partner & Dir-Project Mgmt)*
Malcolm Schwarzenbach *(Partner & Dir-Brand Study)*
Scott Couvillon *(Principal)*

Accounts:
Future Proof
HUB International Insurance, Risk Management Products & Services
Lia Molly Sweater Designs
Louisiana Economic Development Campaign: "Pick Your Passion", Tourism
Renaissance Hotels
Saute Your Way
St. Charles Vision
Startup New Orleans
Tobacco Free Living State Anti-Smoking Campaign
University of New Orleans

TRUNGALE EGAN + ASSOCIATES
8 S Michigan Ave Ste 2310, Chicago, IL 60603
Tel.: (312) 578-1590
Web Site: www.trungaleegan.com

Agency Specializes In: Advertising, Brand Development & Integration, Collateral, Digital/Interactive, Internet/Web Design, Package Design, Public Relations, Social Media

Bill Egan *(Pres)*
Brad Feldmar *(Exec VP)*
David Fields *(Sr Dir-Art)*
Megan Barry *(Dir-Art)*
Dave Cermak *(Dir-Creative)*
Matthew Henkle *(Dir-Mktg & Tech)*

Accounts:
Annex Wealth Management
Nepsis Capital Management

TRUSCOTT ROSSMAN
124 W Allegan St Ste 800, Lansing, MI 48933
Tel.: (517) 487-9320
Fax: (517) 487-5080
Web Site: www.truscottrossman.com

Year Founded: 2011

Agency Specializes In: Advertising, Crisis Communications, Digital/Interactive, Public Relations

John Truscott *(Principal & Pres)*
Kelly Rossman-McKinney *(Principal & CEO)*
Shaun Wilson *(Sr VP)*

Accounts:
New-Michigan Chamber of Commerce

THE TRUTH AGENCY
454 N Broadway 2nd Fl, Santa Ana, CA 92701
Tel.: (714) 542-8778
Web Site: www.thetruthagency.com/

Employees: 15

Approx. Annual Billings: $20,000,000

Michelle Bohlman *(Dir-Acct Svcs)*
Michael Aranda *(Acct Exec)*

Accounts:
Auction.com
Samsung

TRY J ADVERTISING
6030 Avenida Encinas Ste 210, Carlsbad, CA 92011
Tel.: (855) 314-0199
E-Mail: contact@tryjadvertising.com
Web Site: www.tryjadvertising.com

Agency Specializes In: Advertising, Brand Development & Integration, Digital/Interactive, Event Planning & Marketing, Media Buying Services, Media Planning, Outdoor, Public Relations, Social Media

Dale Weston *(Dir-Comm)*

Accounts:
Lexus Carlsbad
Lexus Escondido

TSA COMMUNICATIONS, INC.
(Formerly Tri-State Advertising Co., Inc.)
307 S Buffalo St, Warsaw, IN 46580-4304
Tel.: (574) 267-5178
Fax: (574) 267-2965
Web Site: www.tsacommunications.com

Employees: 8
Year Founded: 1948

National Agency Associations: AFAA-BPA

Agency Specializes In: Advertising, Agriculture, Business Publications, Business-To-Business, Co-op Advertising, Collateral, E-Commerce, Electronic Media, Email, Engineering, Health Care Services, Industrial, Internet/Web Design, Media Buying Services, Media Planning, Paid Searches, Print, Production, Production (Print), Public Relations, Publicity/Promotions, Sales Promotion, Search Engine Optimization, Technical Advertising, Trade & Consumer Magazines, Yellow Pages Advertising

Clayton R. Kreicker *(Pres)*
T.J. Hartman *(Sr VP)*
April Menzie *(Dir-Creative)*
Cindy Ronk *(Mgr-Traffic)*

Accounts:
ABC Metals, Inc.; Logansport, IN Cut Length & Edge Roll Facilities, Nonferrous Alloys, Precision Slitting; 2008
Abresist Corp.; Urbana, IN Abrasion Resistant Linings
Alstom Power, Inc.; Lisle, IL Size Reduction & Thermal Processing Manufacturing Equipment
American Newlong; Indianapolis, IN Bag Closing Equipment
Aristo Machines, Inc.; Indianapolis, IN Tube End Forming Equipment
Assmann Corp of America; Garrett, IN Polyethylene Tanks & Containers for Corrosive Chemical & Waste Applications
Best Metal Finishing; Osgood, IN Metal Finishing & Plating
Carver Inc.; Wabash, IN Hydraulic Laboratory Presses
Cleveland Track Material Inc.; Cleveland, OH Railroad Trackwork, Cylindrical Fabrications
Elgin Fastener Group; Versailles, IN Industrial Fasteners
Flint & Walling; Kendallville, IN Water Pumps & Equipment; 1998
Indiana Phoenix; Avilla, IN Concrete Delivery Trucks, Water Trucks, Rock Spreaders
Innovative Processing Solutions; Louisville, KY Aggregate Engineering Services
ITW-GALEWRAP; Douglasville, GA Oriented Stretch Film & Automotive Equipment
LMC Workholding; Logansport, IN International Power Chucks & Cylinders, Workholding Devices
Manchester Tool & Die; North Manchester, IN Tube & Forming Equipment
Mier Products, Inc.; Kokomo, IN Driveway Alarms, Siren & Instrument Enclosures
Mitchell, Inc.; Elkhart IN Rubber Cutting & Trimming Machines; 1996
Swager Communications, Inc. Construction Services, Tower Erection, Tower Manufacturing
Topp Industries; Rochester, IN Stump & Sewage Basins, Risers & Covers, Fiberglass Lift Stations, Triple Garage Basin Systems & Landscape Rocks
TransFlo Corp.; Fort Wayne, IN Pneumatic Conveying Equipment
Transhield, Inc.; Elkhart, IN Engineered Shrink Wrap Covers
Warsaw Chemical Co.; Warsaw, IN Car Wash Detergent, Waxes, Sanitary Maintenance Supplies
Warsaw Machinery, Inc. Plastics, Woodworking
Wilkens-Anderson Co.; Chicago, IL Laboratory Equipment
Worksaver, Inc.; Litchfield, IL Farm Tractor Accessories

TSAICOMMS
112 NW Maywood Dr Ste B, Portland, OR 97210
Tel.: (971) 327-0628
Fax: (971) 327-0629
E-Mail: info@tsaicomms.com
Web Site: www.tsaicomms.com

Employees: 2
Year Founded: 2002

Agency Specializes In: Asian Market, Consumer Marketing, Multicultural

Approx. Annual Billings: $300,000

Lillian A. Tsai *(Founder)*

Accounts:
ESCO Corp
Nike

TSN ADVERTISING
301 Arizona Ave Ste 250, Santa Monica, CA 90401
Tel.: (888) 496-4850
E-Mail: contact@tsnadvertising.com
Web Site: www.tsnadvertising.com

Agency Specializes In: Advertising, Brand Development & Integration

Eric Zdenek *(CEO)*
MacKenzie Miller *(VP)*

Accounts:
New-Chumash
New-Jersey Mike
New-flipps

TUCCI CREATIVE INC
5967 E Fairmount, Tucson, AZ 85712
Tel.: (520) 296-7678
Fax: (520) 546-4598
E-Mail: graphics@tuccicreative.com
Web Site: www.tuccicreative.com

Year Founded: 1995

Agency Specializes In: Advertising, Internet/Web Design, Media Planning, Print, Public Relations, Radio, Social Media

Mark Tucci *(Owner & Dir-Creative)*
Cristina Ball *(Office Mgr)*
Briana Scott *(Mgr-Creative & Media Buyer)*
Tonya Tucci *(Coord-Mktg)*

Accounts:
Arico Plumbing
Gersons Used Building Materials
Hodges Eye Care
Homestyle Galleries
Joyful Hearts Yoga
La Contessa Boutique
Tucson Subaru

TULLY-MENARD, INC.
3148 Featherwood Ct, Clearwater, FL 33759
Tel.: (727) 298-8301
Fax: (727) 298-8301
E-Mail: joetully@tullymenard.com
Web Site: www.tullymenard.com

Employees: 4
Year Founded: 1960

Agency Specializes In: Advertising, Advertising Specialties, Automotive, Broadcast, Business-To-Business, Cable T.V., Co-op Advertising, Consumer Marketing, Electronic Media, Event Planning & Marketing, In-Store Advertising, Media Buying Services, Newspaper, Outdoor, Planning & Consultation, Point of Purchase, Point of Sale, Print, Production (Ad, Film, Broadcast), Production (Print), Public Relations, Radio, Real Estate, Restaurant, Retail, T.V., Women's Market

Approx. Annual Billings: $3,000,000

Breakdown of Gross Billings by Media: Collateral: $150,000; Newsp.: $150,000; Outdoor: $450,000; Radio: $1,200,000; T.V.: $1,050,000

Accounts:
The Colonnade Restaurant
The Florida Strawberry Festival
Hyde Park Builders Inc.
Kentucky Fried Chicken; Tampa, FL Restaurant Chain; 1960
The Radio Archives

TUNGSTEN CREATIVE GROUP
510 W 7th St, Erie, PA 16502
Tel.: (814) 871-4100
Fax: (814) 871-4103
E-Mail: info@atomic74.com
Web Site: www.atomic74.com

Agency Specializes In: Advertising, Graphic Design, Internet/Web Design

Jody Farrell *(Partner)*
Joe Weunski *(Partner)*
Oto Hlincik *(Dir-Web)*
Sheila Hultgren *(Production Mgr)*
Nick Kosanovich *(Mgr-Web Projects)*
Jen Winkler *(Sr Designer)*
Holly Stefanko *(Media Buyer)*

Accounts:
Asbury Woods
Erie Insurance Arena
Hamot Health Foundation

TURCHETTE ADVERTISING AGENCY LLC
9 Law Dr, Fairfield, NJ 07004
Tel.: (973) 227-8080
Fax: (973) 227-8342
E-Mail: mgavin@turchette.com
Web Site: www.turchette.com

Employees: 10
Year Founded: 1950

Agency Specializes In: Advertising, Advertising Specialties, Brand Development & Integration, Broadcast, Business Publications, Business-To-Business, Cable T.V., Collateral, Consumer Marketing, Corporate Identity, Cosmetics, Direct Response Marketing, Education, Event Planning & Marketing, Exhibit/Trade Shows, Financial, Graphic Design, Health Care Services, Internet/Web Design, Logo & Package Design, Magazines, Media Buying Services, Medical Products, New Product Development, Newspaper, Newspapers & Magazines, Out-of-Home Media, Outdoor, Pharmaceutical, Planning & Consultation, Point of Purchase, Point of Sale, Print, Production, Public Relations, Publicity/Promotions, Radio, Real Estate, Retail, Sports Market, Strategic Planning/Research, Sweepstakes, Trade & Consumer Magazines

Approx. Annual Billings: $11,000,000

Breakdown of Gross Billings by Media: Collateral: $440,000; Fees: $880,000; Graphic Design: $1,650,000; Newsp. & Mags.: $6,600,000; Outdoor: $330,000; Print: $550,000; Production: $550,000

Michael Gavin *(Chm)*
James Gorab *(Pres)*
Deborah Gavin *(Sr VP)*
Rhona Siciliano *(Asst VP & Dir-Media)*
Richard Kozial *(Dir-Creative)*

Accounts:
Cortegra
Financial Services Inc. (FSI)

James Alexander Corporation; Blairstown, NJ
New-Rondaxe (Agency of Record) Brand Development, Interactive Marketing, Public Relations
World Wide Packaging

TUREC ADVERTISING ASSOCIATES, INC.
9272 Olive Blvd, Saint Louis, MO 63132
Tel.: (314) 993-1190
Web Site: www.turec.com/

Employees: 12
Year Founded: 1976

Revenue: $1,900,000

Ben Turec *(Pres)*
Tony Diguida *(VP)*
Sharon Huber *(Dir-Media)*
Renee Maier *(Dir-Creative)*
Mary Schellerup *(Supvr-Media)*
Andrea Lawson *(Sr Media Buyer & Planner)*
Tracie Sanderlin *(Coord-Traffic)*

Accounts:
Casino Queen

TURKEL BRANDS
2871 Oak Ave, Coconut Grove, FL 33133-5207
Tel.: (305) 476-3500
Fax: (305) 448-6691
E-Mail: mshapiro@turkelbrands.com
Web Site: turkelbrands.com/

E-Mail for Key Personnel:
President: rschaps@turkel.info
Creative Dir.: bturkel@turkel.info
Public Relations: mshapiro@turkel.info

Employees: 35
Year Founded: 1983

Agency Specializes In: Advertising, Bilingual Market, Brand Development & Integration, Broadcast, Business-To-Business, Cable T.V., Co-op Advertising, Collateral, Communications, Consumer Marketing, Corporate Identity, Digital/Interactive, Direct Response Marketing, Electronic Media, Fashion/Apparel, Financial, Graphic Design, Health Care Services, High Technology, Hispanic Market, In-Store Advertising, Information Technology, Internet/Web Design, Leisure, Local Marketing, Magazines, Medical Products, Newspapers & Magazines, Out-of-Home Media, Outdoor, Pharmaceutical, Print, Production, Public Relations, Radio, Real Estate, Restaurant, Retail, Strategic Planning/Research, T.V., Trade & Consumer Magazines, Travel & Tourism

Roberto S. Schaps *(Pres)*
Bruce Turkel *(CEO)*
Sara Saiz *(Mng Dir)*
Francisco Nazar *(Sr VP-Mktg)*
Marlisa Shapiro *(Dir-Comm)*
Zoila Cardoso *(Mgr-Fin)*
Allison Filella *(Mgr-Mktg)*
Eblis Parera *(Mgr-IT)*

Accounts:
Beacon Council
Coconut Grove Trust
Country Club of Miami
Crandon Golf
DMAI
Greater Miami Convention & Visitors Bureau
Jackson Memorial Hospital
Kissimmee-St. Cloud Convention & Visitors Bureau; 2003
Metcare
Mississippi Gulf Coast
Partnership for a Drug Free America, Miami Coalition
Salvadoran American Humanitarian Foundation Human Development Programs
University of Miami Center for Non-Profit Management
Women's Emergency Network

TURN INC.
835 Main St., Redwood City, CA 94063
Tel.: (650) 353-4399
E-Mail: support@turn.com
Web Site: www.turn.com

Year Founded: 2006

Agency Specializes In: Advertising, Brand Development & Integration, Digital/Interactive, Media Planning

Bruce Falck *(CEO)*
Mark Liao *(CFO)*
Maureen Little *(Sr VP)*

Accounts:
New-3 Day Blinds

TURNER DUCKWORTH DESIGN
Voysey House Barley Mow Passage, W4 4PH London, United Kingdom
Tel.: (44) 20 8994 7190
Fax: (44) 20 8994 7192
E-Mail: moira@turnerduckworth.co.uk
Web Site: www.turnerduckworth.com

Employees: 20

Agency Specializes In: Advertising, Affluent Market, Aviation & Aerospace, Brand Development & Integration, Children's Market, Consumer Goods, Content, Cosmetics, Food Service, Internet/Web Design, Logo & Package Design, Multimedia, New Product Development, New Technologies, Package Design, Pharmaceutical, Print, Production, Production (Print), Social Marketing/Nonprofit, T.V., Transportation, Travel & Tourism

Joanne Chan *(Head-Client Svcs)*
Adam Duncan *(Dir-Fin)*
Paula Talford *(Dir-Creative)*
Monica Annesanti *(Sr Acct Mgr)*
Kate Elkins *(Acct Mgr)*
Jamie Pearce *(Acct Mgr)*
Roz Johnston *(Mgr-Comml)*
Jessie Froggett *(Designer)*
Gavin Hurrell *(Designer)*
Matt Lurcock *(Sr Designer)*
Jamie Nash *(Sr Designer)*
Mathilde Solanet *(Designer)*
David Thompson *(Designer)*

Accounts:
Amie
Burger King Brand Strategy, Global Brand Positioning
Carlsberg Campaign: "Tuborg Bottle"
Chivas Brothers Campaign: "The Glenlivet Classic Range Packaging Redesign"
Coca-Cola Refreshments USA, Inc. Diet Coke
D&AD Campaign: "D&Ad In Book And Nomination Awards"
Dockers
Fat Bastard
Honest Tea CocoaNova
Kettle Foods Campaign: "Kettle Ridge Crisps"
Levi Strauss Campaign: "Levis Visual Identity System", HIV/AIDS Video
Lilt Tropical Fruit Drink
Metallica Album Cover; 2008
Neal's Yard Remedies
Palm
Pencil Rankings
Popchips
S.A. Brains
SETI Institute
VSOP Blended Alcohol Drink
Waitrose Good To Go
Zebra Hall

TURNING POINT ADVISORS
310 East Blvd, C10, Charlotte, NC 28203
Tel.: (704) 763-0560

Year Founded: 2002

Approx. Annual Billings: $400,000

Julie Nance *(Pres)*
Barbara J. Hartung *(Principal)*
Thomas P. Long *(Principal)*

TURNPOST CREATIVE GROUP
17330 Wright S Ste 200, Omaha, NE 68130
Tel.: (402) 345-5959
Web Site: www.turnpost.com

Year Founded: 1993

Agency Specializes In: Advertising, Brand Development & Integration, Communications, Graphic Design, Internet/Web Design, Print

Jeff Reiner *(Pres)*
Stuart Lundgren *(Principal)*
Jamie Massey *(Dir-Art)*
Michelle Reagan *(Dir-Art)*
Catherine Kraemer *(Copywriter)*

Accounts:
Benaissance
Elliott Equipment Company Inc.
Travel & Transport Inc.

TURNSTILE
(Formerly TLG Multicultural Communications)
145 Corte Madera Town Center, Corte Madera, CA 94925
Tel.: (415) 927-1010, ext. 201
E-Mail: diana@turnstile-sf.com
Web Site: www.turnstile-sf.com

Employees: 8
Year Founded: 2003

National Agency Associations: AHAA

Agency Specializes In: Hispanic Market, Sponsorship

Approx. Annual Billings: $6,000,000

Diana Putterman *(Pres)*
Ellen Young *(Dir-Media)*

Accounts:
Applied Materials
Comcast
Pebble Beach Company
SunRay Park & Casino
Twin pine Casino

TURNSTILE INC.
12900 Senlac Dr Ste 100, Dallas, TX 75234
Tel.: (214) 210-6000
Fax: (214) 210-5970
Web Site: www.turnstileinc.com

Agency Specializes In: Advertising, Digital/Interactive, Print

John Seeker *(Owner)*

Accounts:
New-Six Flags

TURTLEDOVE CLEMENS, INC.
1230 SW 1st Ave Ste 200, Portland, OR 97204-3200
Tel.: (503) 226-3581
Fax: (503) 273-4277
E-Mail: jay@turtledove.com
Web Site: www.turtledove.com

Employees: 12
Year Founded: 1941

National Agency Associations: APA-ICOM-MCA

Agency Specializes In: Advertising, Communications, Consumer Marketing, Food Service, Graphic Design, Health Care Services, Leisure, Planning & Consultation, Public Relations, Restaurant, Travel & Tourism

Jay Clemens *(Owner)*
Stuart Sammuelson *(VP)*
Jeff Bernius *(Sr Dir-Art)*
Brooke Jones *(Dir-Production)*
Sandra Carpenter *(Acct Mgr)*
Ken Howard *(Mgr-Interactive)*

Accounts:
Adult-Care.org
Clackamas County Tourism
Clackamas Heritage Partners
Kitchen Kaboodle
Portland Metro RV Dealers
Timberline Lodge
Wendys Family Restaurants
Wendy's Northwest Region
Willamette Valley Visitors Association

TUXEDO AGENCY
3414 Ave du Parc Ste 202, Montreal, QC H2X 2H5 Canada
Tel.: (514) 664-5722
E-Mail: info@agencetuxedo.com
Web Site: www.agencetuxedo.com

Year Founded: 2010

Agency Specializes In: Advertising, Brand Development & Integration, Content, Digital/Interactive, Event Planning & Marketing, Graphic Design, Package Design, Print, Public Relations, Social Media

Dominic Tremblay *(Founder & Pres)*
Ludwig Ciupka *(Co-Founder & VP-Creation)*
Laurent Guez *(Co-Founder & VP-Environmental Design)*
Caroline Pilon *(VP-Strategy & Client Svcs)*
Caroline Grutman *(Head-Production)*
Sabrina Del *(Acct Dir)*
Ollie Miles *(Assoc Dir-Creative)*
Rachelle Houde Simard *(Mgr-Digital & Comm)*
Nathan Nardin *(Team Head-Environment Design)*

Accounts:
Dermablend Professional Leg & Body Tattoo Primer, Vichy
L'Oreal USA, Inc. Campaign: "Forget Flawless", Campaign: "Your Skin Deserves Better", Online, Print, Vichy

TV, INC.
2465 Northside Dr Ste 1704, Clearwater, FL 33761
Tel.: (310) 985-1229
Fax: (727) 474-5606
Toll Free: (800) 326-5661
Web Site: www.tvinc.com

Employees: 12
Year Founded: 1987

Agency Specializes In: Advertising Specialties, Affiliate Marketing, Asian Market, Branded Entertainment, Business-To-Business, Consulting, Consumer Marketing, Digital/Interactive, Direct Response Marketing, Direct-to-Consumer, Household Goods, Infomercials, Integrated Marketing, Local Marketing, Newspaper, Production, Radio, T.V.

William Thompson *(Owner, Pres & CEO)*
Kenneth Forsman *(Mng Dir)*

Accounts:
Gary Null & Associates

Branch

TV, Inc.
Gronhogen 1409D SE-380 65 Oland, Stockholm, 1409D Sweden
Tel.: (46) 485 661 212
Fax: (46) 485 661 1212
Web Site: www.tvinc.com

Agency Specializes In: Advertising

William Thompson *(Pres & CEO)*
Kenneth Forsman *(Gen Mgr)*

Accounts:
Ameri-Life Insurance
Auri Car Polish
Bose Electronics
EvansPro Group
The Fat Loss Coach
Ginzu Knives
Keystone Camera
Level Best Golf
Lumina Bicycle Helmet
M&M Mars
Medalist Golf Club

TVGLA
(Formerly The Visionaire Group)
5340 Alla Rd Ste 100, Los Angeles, CA 90066
Tel.: (310) 823-1800
Fax: (310) 823-1822
E-Mail: info@tvgla.com
Web Site: www.tvgla.com

Year Founded: 2007

Agency Specializes In: Media Buying Services, Mobile Marketing

Dimitry Ioffe *(Founder & CEO)*
Brian Pettigrew *(Pres)*
Ryan Kite *(VP-Strategic Svcs)*
Catherine Lance Bones *(Controller)*
Julie Gargan *(Exec Dir-Creative)*
Armando Llenado *(Exec Dir-Creative)*
Shannon Turner *(Sr Acct Dir)*
Amy Ruud *(Sr Producer-Digital)*
Lin Chang *(Dir-Strategic Mktg)*
Larry Davidson *(Dir-Tech)*
Jorge Cantero *(Assoc Dir-Creative)*
Tara Ferguson *(Community Mgr)*

Accounts:
Bates Motel
Cirque Du Soleil
New-Club W Broadcast, Campaign: "WINEing", Digital
Dreamworks Animation Campaign: "Kung Fu Panda 2"
Fox Searchlight
New-Gruppo Campari Appleton Estate, Content, Digital Marketing, Jamaica Rum, Skyy Vodka, Social Media, Spirits, Wild Turkey
The History Channel
Kia
Lionsgate
Mattel
NBC
Pepsi International
Realtor
Showtime
Sony
Universal Pictures
Walt Disney Pictures
Watchmen Motion Comic Entertainment
X-Men Origins Entertainment

TWENTY FOUR SEVEN, INC.
425 NE 9th Ave, Portland, OR 97232
Tel.: (503) 222-7999
Fax: (503) 222-7919
Toll Free: (888) 247-9365
E-Mail: info@twentyfour7.com
Web Site: www.twentyfour7.com

Employees: 20
Year Founded: 1995

Agency Specializes In: Advertising, Strategic Planning/Research

Revenue: $13,700,000

Jennifer Brothers *(Gen Mgr)*
David Patterson *(Dir-Project Mgmt & Engrg)*
Steven Shaw *(Dir-Design)*
Katie Puent *(Office Mgr)*
Kris Wigger *(Project Mgr & Acct Exec)*
Ray Wilson *(Mgr-Project)*
Kyle Kendrick *(Designer)*

Accounts:
Apple
Giorgio Armani
Nike
Starbucks

Branch

Twenty Four Seven
250 Hudson St 11th Fl \@ Sandbox, New York, NY 10013
Tel.: (212) 300-6222
Web Site: www.twentyfour7.com/

Employees: 18

Agency Specializes In: Advertising

Lora Churcher *(Sr Brand Mgr)*

TWENTYTEN GROUP
450 - 375 Water S, Vancouver, BC V6B 5C6 Canada
Tel.: (604) 569-0480
Fax: (604) 569-0492
E-Mail: info@twentytengroup.com
Web Site: www.twentytengroup.com

Year Founded: 2010

Agency Specializes In: Advertising, Brand Development & Integration, Broadcast, Communications, Merchandising, Public Relations, Sponsorship

Andrea J. Shaw *(Founder & Mng Partner)*
Catherine Locke *(Partner)*
Carley Fitzpatrick *(Office Mgr)*
Colin Jarvis *(Assoc Partner)*
Bridget Martin *(Assoc Partner)*
Alyson Schmidt *(Assoc Partner)*
Mark Soder *(Assoc Partner)*
Mike Spicer *(Assoc Partner)*

Accounts:
Canada Games Council Sponsorship, Strategic Marketing
Canada Sevens Strategic Marketing, World Rugby Sevens Series (Agency of Record)
Canadian Olympic Committee
Intrawest ULC
John Furlong
KidSport National Marketing, Strategic Marketing
Rugby Canada World Rugby Sevens Series (Agency of Record)
Snow Sport Consortium
Whistler Blackcomb Holdings Inc.

TWEYEN INC

171 W Wing St Ste 201, Arlington Heights, IL 60005
Tel.: (847) 749-0143
Fax: (847) 749-3016
Web Site: www.tweyen.com

Year Founded: 2000

Agency Specializes In: Advertising, Collateral, Corporate Identity, Internet/Web Design, Package Design

Sean Reilly *(Pres)*
Emily Calvillo *(Dir-Creative)*
Ryan Gamble *(Sr Designer)*
Beth Granitz *(Jr Designer)*

Accounts:
Serta Mattress Company
Stack-On Products Co. Inc.
WorldPoint

TWG COMMUNICATIONS

101 Worthington St E Ste 433, North Bay, ON P1B 1G5 Canada
Tel.: (705) 472-1861
Fax: (705) 472-2343
E-Mail: webcontact@twgcommunications.com
Web Site: www.twgcommunications.com

Employees: 12
Year Founded: 1996

Agency Specializes In: Advertising

Theodosis Margaritis *(Partner & VP-Strategic Mktg)*
William Ferguson *(Partner & Dir-Creative)*
Marnie Ferriera *(Dir-Art & Graphic Designer)*
David Wolfe *(Acct Mgr & Writer)*
Donna Backer *(Acct Mgr)*

Accounts:
ATV Ontario
CMA
College Boreal
Destination Muskoka
KIJIJI
Maple Leaf Foods
Motorola Canada
Northeastern Ontario Tourism (Agency of Record)
One Kids Place
Petro Canada
Procter & Gamble
Shell Canada
Veet
Wood Works

TWIN ADVERTISING

7 S Main St, Pittsford, NY 14534
Tel.: (585) 662-5905
Web Site: www.twinadvertising.com

John Galbraith *(Pres-Twin Partners, Inc)*
Trish Wilgar *(Acct Dir)*

Accounts:
Design Pool & Spa

TWINOAKS

5100 Legacy Dr, Plano, TX 75024
Tel.: (469) 814-1247
Web Site: www.thetwinoaks.com

Employees: 25
Year Founded: 2011

Agency Specializes In: Business Publications, Co-op Advertising, Collateral, Consumer Publications, Exhibit/Trade Shows, Experience Design, In-Store Advertising, Local Marketing, Newspapers & Magazines, Point of Purchase, Point of Sale, Production, Production (Print), Shopper Marketing, Social Media, Sweepstakes, Trade & Consumer Magazines

Steve DeVore *(Mng Partner)*
Cameron Clement *(VP & Exec Creative Dir)*
Brianne Brannan *(VP-Client Svcs)*
Maureen OHare *(VP-Bus Dev)*

Accounts:
Beiersdorf
Beringer

TWIST CREATIVE INC.

2306 W 17th St Ste 3, Cleveland, OH 44113
Tel.: (216) 631-5411
Fax: (216) 631-5413
E-Mail: info@twistcreative.com
Web Site: www.twist-creative.com

Year Founded: 2000

Agency Specializes In: Advertising, Brand Development & Integration, Collateral, Identity Marketing, Print

Connie Ozan *(Founder & Dir-Design)*
Mike Ozan *(Pres & Dir-Creative)*
Christopher Oldham *(VP-Brand Experience)*
Charlene Coughlin *(Acct Svcs Dir)*
Joel Miller *(Dir-Art)*
Todd Sheppard *(Dir-Media Rels)*
Stefanie D'Angelo *(Mgr-Ops)*

Accounts:
Arhaus

TWIST IMAGE

(Acquired by WPP plc)

TWO BY FOUR

10 N Dearborn St Ste 1000, Chicago, IL 60602
Tel.: (312) 382-0100
Fax: (312) 382-8003
Web Site: www.twoxfour.com

Employees: 30
Year Founded: 1997

National Agency Associations: 4A's

Agency Specializes In: Advertising, Advertising Specialties, Broadcast, Electronic Media, Radio, Sponsorship

Approx. Annual Billings: $3,000,000

David W. Stevenson *(Founder, Pres & Exec Dir-Creative)*
Jeff Wood *(CMO)*
Matthew Scholes *(Sr VP & Dir-Strategy & Media)*
Jennifer Nicks *(VP & Dir-Ops)*
Brad Cerwin *(Dir-Brand Mgmt)*
Hamish McDonald *(Dir-Client Leadership)*
Aaron Sanfillippo *(Dir-Art)*
Mike Vithoulkas *(Assoc Dir-Creative)*
Laura Waters *(Acct Supvr)*

Accounts:
Bernina of America
Bradley Corporation
Bridgestone/Firestone Direct Mail
Brookfield Zoo
Chattanooga Metropolitan Airport
Chicago Bears Campaign: "Bear Down", One City One Team
Covenant Transport
Firestone Complete Auto Care
Grossmont Center
The John Buck Company
Labelmaster
Navy Pier
Paslode Creative, Media Buying, Strategy
Red Kap
Ronald McDonald House Charities of Chicagoland & Northwest Indiana (Advertising Agency of Record) Creative
Saint James School of Medicine Search Engine Marketing Strategy
New-SnapOn
VF Imagewear
Wrangler; Greensboro, NC Accessories, Apparel, Jeans; 1999
New-Wrangler Workwear

TWO WEST, INC.

514 W 26th St 2nd Fl, Kansas City, MO 64108
Tel.: (816) 471-3255
Fax: (816) 471-7337
Toll Free: (877) 532-.9378
E-Mail: info@twowest.com
Web Site: my.twowest.com

Employees: 35
Year Founded: 1997

Agency Specializes In: Advertising, Advertising Specialties, Brand Development & Integration, Business-To-Business, Communications, Consulting, Consumer Marketing, Corporate Identity, Digital/Interactive, Direct Response Marketing, Event Planning & Marketing, Logo & Package Design, Media Buying Services, Public Relations, Publicity/Promotions, Radio, Strategic Planning/Research

David Patrick *(Chief Strategy Officer)*
Steve Spencer *(Chief Creative Officer)*
Mark Lopez *(Chief Digital Officer)*
Angela Potts *(Mng Dir-Brand Localization)*
Andrew Mirakian *(Sr Dir-Art)*
Brenda Reagan *(Sr Dir-Art)*
George Bird *(Dir-In-Store Experience)*
Jody Flaherty *(Dir-Studio)*
Blair Vance *(Mgr-Production)*
Barbara Russell *(Acct Supvr)*
Gloria Mavungu *(Acct Coord)*

Accounts:
Sprint; Overland Park, KS Internet, Retail

TWOFIFTEENMCCANN

(Formerly agencytwofifteen)
215 Leidesdorff St, San Francisco, CA 94111
Tel.: (415) 262-3500
Fax: (415) 956-0682
Web Site: www.215mccann.com

Employees: 200
Year Founded: 2006

National Agency Associations: 4A's

Agency Specializes In: Advertising, Sponsorship

Scott Duchon *(Partner & Chief Creative Officer)*
Gabby Gourrier *(Exec VP-Production-Global)*
Mary Beth Barney *(VP-Bus Affairs)*
Alper Kologlu *(Sr Dir-Art)*

Ryan Carver *(Art Dir)*
Julie Sinclair *(Acct Dir)*
Hannah Schaefer *(Mgmt Supvr)*
Sharon Chow-Kaye *(Dir-Art & Assoc Dir-Creative)*
Neil Bruce *(Dir-Creative)*
Steve Couture *(Dir-Art)*
Gabrielle Tenaglia *(Dir-Brand Strategy & New Bus)*
Dana Cui *(Acct Supvr)*
Justin Gonzaga *(Acct Supvr)*
Bryant Marcia *(Acct Supvr)*
Bhumieka Patel *(Acct Supvr)*
Quentin Shuldiner *(Sr Copywriter)*
Anne Cathcart *(Acct Exec)*
Paige Robertson *(Strategist-Social Media)*
Kyle Davis *(Copywriter)*

Accounts:
Gears Of War Campaign: "Dust To Dust"
Help Remedies "Help, I can't sleep"
New-Hulu LLC Campaign: "Director", Campaign: "Fireside", Campaign: "Hello From Hulu", Campaign: "Jingle"
Maglite Campaign: "Morse Code"
Microsoft Corporation "Forza Motorsport 4", "Gears of War 3", "The Un-Filmable Game", Broadcast, Campaign: "All Hail", Campaign: "Awakening", Campaign: "Dust To Dust", Campaign: "Kinect Effect", Campaign: "Leave Your Limits", Campaign: "Rules are Meant to be Exploded", Campaign: "Ryse:Son of Rome", Campaign: "The Cost", Forza Horizon 2, Halo 4, Halo 5: Guardians, Marketing, Online, Sunset Overdrive, Trailer, Xbox, Xbox One
Nestle USA, Inc. Campaign: "Hypnotist", Campaign: "Reminders", Nescafe
Nikiclainos "The Little Blue Letter", HopScout
Pandora (Lead Creative Agency) Campaign: "#ThumbMoments", Campaign: "Now playing. You,", Campaign: "THUMB MOMENTS WITH LINDSEY STIRLING", Campaign: "Thumb Moments With Bush", Online
Under Armour, Inc.

TYSON ASSOCIATES, INC.

109 Federal Rd Ste 308, Danbury, CT 06811
Tel.: (203) 437-4248
Fax: (203) 775-0563
E-Mail: tysonassociates@aol.com
Web Site: www.tysonassociates.com

Employees: 4
Year Founded: 1982

National Agency Associations: ABC-BPA-DMA

Agency Specializes In: Direct Response Marketing

Elaine Tyson *(Owner)*
Karen Tyson *(Partner & VP)*

Accounts:
Alternative Emerging Investor
CRM Magazine
Database Trends & Applications
Design News
Electronic Design News
Electronic Engineering News
Embedded Systems Design
Game Developer
Speech Technology
Streaming Media, Inc.; Medford, NJ

UBM CANON

2901 28th St, Santa Monica, CA 90405
Tel.: (310) 445-4200
Fax: (310) 445-4299
E-Mail: info@ubm.com
Web Site: www.ubmcanon.com

Employees: 150
Year Founded: 1978

Agency Specializes In: Exhibit/Trade Shows, Graphic Design, Medical Products, Publishing, Web (Banner Ads, Pop-ups, etc.)

Pam Moore *(Sr VP-Content & Strategy)*
Laurie Strangia *(Sr VP-Engagement & Insights-Americas)*
Stephen Corrick *(VP & Exec Dir)*
Shana Leonard *(VP-Content)*
Timothy Simone *(VP-Medical Media Sls & Directories)*
Becky Roll *(Reg Dir-Western Sls)*
Steve Everly *(Brand Dir-Pkg)*
Tony Marsh *(Brand Dir)*

UBU ENTERPRISES

405 Loblolly Bay Dr, Santa Rosa Beach, FL 32459
Tel.: (850) 797-1813
Web Site: www.ubuenterprises.com

Agency Specializes In: Advertising, Brand Development & Integration, Collateral, Graphic Design, Internet/Web Design, Public Relations, Social Media

Deborah Esling *(Dir-Creative)*

Accounts:
B-Boy Productions, Inc.
Cummins-Allison Corporation
Flu Shots To Go, LLC
Focusing On You Photography
Jacki Craig
Jill Monaco Ministries
Rickochet Entertainment, LLC.
WeTalkNerdy.tv

UCG MARKETING

566 Commonwealth Ave Mezzanine Level, Boston, MA 02215
Tel.: (617) 713-3900
Fax: (857) 326-7379
E-Mail: info@ucgmarketing.com
Web Site: www.ucgmarketing.com

Employees: 20
Year Founded: 2001

Brendan Guyotte *(Dir-Project Mgmt & Ops)*
Dawn Rose *(Dir-Bus Dev)*
Craig Goldstein *(COO & Client Svcs Dir)*

Accounts:
AOL
CNBC
Disney Communications Croc Hunter Challenge
HBO
Martha Stewart
Midori
Minute Maid Lemonade
NBC
Nestle Waters Aquapod
Neutrogena Fresh Cooling Body Mist Sunblock
Newline Cinema
Nivea
Puma
Skyy Spirits
Smirnoff
Sprint
VH1
Weight Watchers

Branch

Universal Consulting Group

419 Lafayette St 7th Fl, New York, NY 10003
Tel.: (212) 616-6329
Fax: (212) 616-6325
E-Mail: info@ucgmarketing.com
Web Site: www.ucgmarketing.com

Employees: 5

Agency Specializes In: Advertising

Steven Frumin *(Co-Founder & Pres)*
Glenn Morgan *(Principal)*

Accounts:
Acuvue
Animal Planet
Chivas Regal
CNBC
HBO
Johnson & Johnson
Neutrogena
Nivea
Novartis
Trojan
WhiteWave Foods Company

ULTRA 16

15 E 32Nd St, New York, NY 10016
Tel.: (212) 260-6454
Fax: (212) 260-6552
Web Site: www.ultra16.com

E-Mail for Key Personnel:
President: matthew@ultra16.com

Employees: 25
Year Founded: 1999

Agency Specializes In: Digital/Interactive, Electronic Media, Media Buying Services, New Product Development, Strategic Planning/Research

Matthew Chun *(Owner)*

Accounts:
ABC
American Express
Aveda
ESPN
Estee Lauder
Fox
L'Oreal
MTV
My Network
The New York Times
Redken Hair Care
Scholastic
Sony
Time Interactive

UMARKETING

1350 Broadway, New York, NY 10018
Toll Free: (866) 482-0288
Web Site: www.umarketing.com

Year Founded: 2007

Agency Specializes In: Above-the-Line, Advertising, Below-the-Line, Brand Development & Integration, Broadcast, Collateral, Communications, Consumer Goods, Content, Customer Relationship Management, Digital/Interactive, Direct Response Marketing, Electronic Media, Email, Exhibit/Trade Shows, Fashion/Apparel, Financial, Graphic Design, Guerilla Marketing, Health Care Services, In-Store Advertising, Integrated Marketing, Internet/Web Design, Logo & Package Design, Magazines, Market Research, Media Buying Services, Media Planning, Mobile Marketing, New Product Development, Out-of-Home Media, Package Design, Pharmaceutical, Planning & Consultation, Print, Production, Production (Ad, Film, Broadcast), Publicity/Promotions, Regional, Restaurant, Retail, Search Engine Optimization, Social Media, Strategic Planning/Research, T.V., Telemarketing, Trade & Consumer Magazines, Web (Banner Ads,

Pop-ups, etc.)

George Wiedemann *(CEO)*
Ken Lomasney *(COO)*
Chris Wiedemann *(CMO)*
Jackson Barrett *(Pres-Resonant Analytics)*
Meg Goodman *(Sr VP & Dir-Client Svcs)*
Jeff Pajer *(VP & Exec Dir-Creative)*
Alecia Wiedemann *(Acct Supvr)*

Accounts:
PPL Electric

UMLAUT

123 Townsend St Ste 100, San Francisco, CA 94107
Tel.: (415) 777-0123
Fax: (415) 777-4123
E-Mail: edit@umlautfilms.com
Web Site: www.umlautfilms.com

Employees: 12

Agency Specializes In: Production, Production (Ad, Film, Broadcast), T.V.

Gina LoCurcio *(Founder & Exec Producer)*
Rosina Weitekamp *(Head-Production)*

UNANIMOUS

(Formerly Pickering Creative Group)
8600 Executive Woods Dr. Ste. 300, Lincoln, NE 68512
Tel.: (402) 423-5447
Fax: (402) 423-2871
Toll Free: (888) 317-5947
Web Site: www.unanimousagency.com

Employees: 20
Year Founded: 1979

Agency Specializes In: Brand Development & Integration, Communications, Exhibit/Trade Shows, Graphic Design, Local Marketing, Public Relations, Web (Banner Ads, Pop-ups, etc.)

Gary Pickering *(Chm)*
Trenton Wilcox *(Pres)*
Matt O'Gorman *(VP)*
Scott Claypool *(Dir-Art)*
Deb Pickering *(Mgr-Admin Svcs)*
Nina Rohlfs *(Mgr-Acctg)*

Accounts:
Darland Construction
Nebraska Safety Council, Inc.

UNBOUNDARY, INC.

384 Northyards Blvd NW Roundhouse Ste 100, Atlanta, GA 30313
Tel.: (404) 614-4299
Fax: (404) 614-4288
E-Mail: info@unboundary.com
Web Site: www.unboundary.com

Employees: 30
Year Founded: 1988

Agency Specializes In: Brand Development & Integration, Collateral, Consulting, Corporate Communications, Corporate Identity, Graphic Design, Internet/Web Design, Investor Relations, Strategic Planning/Research

Approx. Annual Billings: $4,000,000

Breakdown of Gross Billings by Media: Collateral: $4,000,000

Tod Martin *(Pres & CEO)*
Amanda Young *(Mng Partner)*
Govantez Lowndes *(Exec Dir)*
Shaun Martin *(Exec Dir)*
Laura Gosnell *(Dir-Design)*
Dawn Gahan *(Mgr-Traffic)*

UNDERCURRENT

270 Lafayette St, New York, NY 10012
Tel.: (212) 431-4808
Web Site: www.undercurrent.com

Year Founded: 2007

Agency Specializes In: Advertising, Digital/Interactive, Strategic Planning/Research, T.V.

Clay Parker Jones *(Mng Partner)*
Mike Arauz *(Partner)*
Mark Raheja *(Partner)*
Vladimir Pick *(Head-Strategy Team)*
Jordan Husney *(Dir)*
Jason Spinell *(Dir-Ventures)*
Matthew Daniels *(Assoc Dir-Strategy)*

Accounts:
General Electric Company

UNDERGROUND ADVERTISING

303 Sacramento St, San Francisco, CA 94111
Tel.: (415) 433-9334
Web Site: www.undergroundagency.com

Agency Specializes In: Advertising, Content, Digital/Interactive

Charlie Cardillo *(Pres & Dir-Creative)*
Katie Levine *(VP)*
John Winkleman *(Dir-Strategic Acct Svcs)*

Accounts:
City CarShare
Union of Concerned Scientists

UNDERTONE

340 Madison Ave, New York, NY 10173
Tel.: (212) 685-8000
Fax: (212) 685-8001
E-Mail: info@undertone.com
Web Site: www.undertone.com

Agency Specializes In: Advertising, Digital/Interactive

Michael Cassidy *(Founder & Chm)*
Corey Ferengul *(CEO)*
Mark Attarian *(CFO)*
Greg Glenday *(Chief Revenue Officer)*
George Durden *(Sr VP-Tech)*
Robert Schwartz *(Sr VP-Corp Strategy & Bus Dev)*
Rob Garber *(Mng Dir-EMEA)*
Sal Candela *(VP-Agency Strategy & Partnerships-Global)*
Mark Costa *(VP-Tech & Ops)*
Chris McLoughlin *(VP-Sls-East)*
Michael Nevins *(VP-Mobile)*
Melinda Theo *(VP-Revenue Ops)*
Cameron Hulett *(Exec Dir-EMEA)*
Brian Fife *(Sr Dir-R&D)*
Parker Bohlen *(Dir-Sls)*
Sandy Kelliher *(Dir-Mktg Ops)*
Natalie Pappacoda *(Dir-Advertiser Solutions)*
Marina Lvova *(Assoc Dir-Sls Plng)*
Natalie Breitbach *(Sr Mgr-Mktg Comm)*
Travis Scott *(Sr Mgr-Publr Dev)*
Gregory Thide *(Sr Mgr-Client Svcs)*
Shannon Ingoldsby *(Client Svcs Mgr)*
Cabot Roy *(Client Svcs Mgr)*
Melissa Blazejewski *(Mgr-Mktg & Events)*
Rachel Dushkin *(Mgr-Sls Plng)*
Justin Samuels *(Mgr-Mktg)*
Ron Aviv *(Acct Exec)*
Jason Boche *(Acct Exec)*
Ryan Farrish *(Acct Exec)*
Gena Feldman *(Acct Exec)*
Alyssa Fulchini *(Acct Exec)*
Eliana Goldstein *(Acct Exec)*
Jeff Mendelsohn *(Acct Exec)*
Aliza Rabinowitz *(Acct Exec)*
Henry James *(Planner-Sls)*
Marisa Santillo *(Coord-Mktg Ops)*
Anna Montesano *(Exec Project Dir)*

Accounts:
Blue Cross Blue Shield of Michigan Health Care Services
Bluefly, Inc. Men's & Women's Apparel Store
DirectBuy Furniture Stores
Duncan Hines Bakery Products Mfr
Florida Department of Health Health Care Centers
Hyatt Hotels & Resorts
Virgin America Airline Trasportation Services

THE UNGAR GROUP

2800 Grant, Evanston, IL 60201
Tel.: (312) 541-0000
Fax: (312) 541-0010
E-Mail: tom.ungar@ungargroup.com
Web Site: www.ungargroup.com

Employees: 7
Year Founded: 1987

Agency Specializes In: Advertising, Brand Development & Integration, Broadcast, Business-To-Business, Cable T.V., Co-op Advertising, Consumer Marketing, Food Service, Guerilla Marketing, Integrated Marketing, Internet/Web Design, Media Planning, Newspaper, Outdoor, Print

Tom Ungar *(Pres & Dir-Creative)*
Maria G. Allen *(Dir-Media)*
Lori Teidel *(Office Mgr)*
Mete Moran *(Designer-Interactive)*

Accounts:
Bosch
Chicago Sinfonietta
Helene Curtis
Master Lock
Sharpie

UNION

479 Wellington St W, Toronto, ON M5V 1E7 Canada
Tel.: (416) 598-4944
E-Mail: info@unioncreative.com
Web Site: www.unioncreative.com

Year Founded: 2012

Agency Specializes In: Advertising

Subtej Nijjar *(Pres)*
Lance Martin *(Partner & Exec Dir-Creative)*
Ryan Mcneill *(Sr Dir-Art)*
Vikki Thorpe *(Grp Acct Dir)*
Tyler Brown *(Acct Dir)*
Glen D'Souza *(Dir-Art & Assoc Dir-Creative)*
Mike Takasaki *(Assoc Dir-Creative)*
Adam Thur *(Assoc Dir-Creative)*
Andre Riolo *(Acct Supvr)*
Sean Butler *(Copywriter)*
Michelle Campbell *(Planner)*
Caitlin Keeley *(Copywriter)*
Emmanuel Obayemi *(Designer)*
Matt Stubbings *(Designer)*

Accounts:
Best Buy Creative
Kraft Kraft Dinner, Kraft Singles, Mac n' Cheese
New-Mount Pleasant Group Quitbit
Nissan Advertising, Infiniti (Agency of Record),

Social Media
New-Partnership For a Drug-Free Canada (Agency of Record)
Philadephia Cream Cheese
Unilever United States Axe

UNIT PARTNERS
1416 Larkin St Unit B, San Francisco, CA 94109
Tel.: (415) 409-0000
Fax: (415) 520-6767
E-Mail: info@unitpartners.com
Web Site: www.unitpartners.com

Agency Specializes In: Advertising, Brand Development & Integration, Collateral, Digital/Interactive, Graphic Design, Internet/Web Design, Logo & Package Design, Promotions

Ann Jordan *(Partner & Dir-Creative)*
Shardul Kiri *(Partner & Dir-Creative)*

Accounts:
Stones Throw

UNITED ENTERTAINMENT GROUP
149 5th Ave, New York, NY 10010
Tel.: (212) 445-0100
Web Site: www.uegworldwide.com

Year Founded: 2007

Agency Specializes In: Advertising, Brand Development & Integration, Merchandising, Social Media, T.V.

Jarrod Moses *(Founder, Pres & CEO)*
David F. Caruso *(COO)*
Robby Wells *(Chief Strategy Officer)*
Adam Smith *(Pres-Entertainment)*
Lee Teller *(Exec VP & Head-Rights & Partnerships)*
Dave Santaniello *(Sr VP-Rights & Partnerships)*
Nicole Bradley *(VP-Comm)*
Melanie Washington *(VP-Brand Experiences)*
Nora Graham *(Sr Dir)*
Audra Silverman *(Sr Dir)*

Accounts:
Asics America Corporation (US Public Relations Agency of Record) Media Relations, Strategic Communications Planning, Thought Leadership
AT&T
Clorox
DraftKings Brand Awareness, Public Relations
Frito-Lay
General Mills
HSN Marketing
PGA of America 12 Ryder Cup, 16 PGA Championship (Agency of Record), 2015 PGA Championship (Agency of Record)
The Procter & Gamble Company Covergirl
Speedo USA
Starbucks
Wizard World, Inc. CONtv, Comic Cons, Content Creation, Digital, Experiential, Radio, Social Media, Television

UNITED FUTURE
2105 Colorado Ave Ste 100, Santa Monica, CA 90404
Tel.: (310) 280-7778
E-Mail: info@unitedfuture.com
Web Site: www.unitedfuture.com

Agency Specializes In: Advertising, Digital/Interactive

Eric Neff *(CMO)*
Margarito Mejia *(Designer)*

Accounts:
Audax Health

UNITED LANDMARK ASSOCIATES, INC.
3708 W Swann Ave Ste 201, Tampa, FL 33609
Tel.: (813) 870-9519, ext. 202
Fax: (813) 872-5616
E-Mail: info@unitedlandmark.com
Web Site: www.unitedlandmark.com

Employees: 15
Year Founded: 1985

Agency Specializes In: Advertising, Advertising Specialties, Real Estate

Approx. Annual Billings: $12,000,000 Capitalized

Loran Tripp *(VP-Bus Dev & Strategy)*
Jeremy Moses *(Dir-Creative)*
Heather Baker *(Sr Acct Mgr)*
Tricia Mason *(Sr Acct Mgr)*
Jaimie Frey *(Acct Mgr)*
Allison Rosoff *(Grp Brand Dir)*
Charssi Richichi *(Sr Designer)*

Accounts:
Bob LaFerriere Aircraft, Inc.
Champions Club
Galatl Yacht Sales
Hamilton Harbor Yacht Club
HMY Yacht Sales
Intrepid Powerboats
New-Kolter Urban
New-Mattamy Homes
New-Minto Communities
One thousand ocean
Palm Harbor Marina
The Plaza Harbour Island
The Residences at the Ritz-Carlton; Baltimore, MD
New-Standard Pacific Homes
New-US Ameribank
New-US Assets Group

UNITED MARKETING COMMUNICATIONS
222 W Las Colinas Blvd Ste 1650, Irving, TX 75039
Tel.: (972) 401-4155
Web Site: www.umcconnect.com

Agency Specializes In: Advertising, Digital/Interactive, Media Relations, Sales Promotion

Stuart Myers *(Owner & CEO)*
Shelby Clement *(Acct Dir)*
Georgia Devega Mccullough *(Dir-Media Buying)*

UNLEADED COMMUNICATIONS, INC.
1701 Commerce St 3rd Fl, Houston, TX 77002
Tel.: (713) 874-8200
E-Mail: info@ulcomm.com
Web Site: www.ulcomm.com

Employees: 50

Agency Specializes In: Advertising, Brand Development & Integration, Content, Digital/Interactive, Exhibit/Trade Shows, Internet/Web Design, Investor Relations, Mobile Marketing, Public Relations, Social Media

Revenue: $1,400,000

Ankit Shah *(Grp Dir-Media)*
Dan Galdamez *(Sr Dir-Art)*
Dylan Powell *(Dir-Creative)*
Dominique Shu *(Dir-Market Res)*
Jennifer Valencia *(Dir-Client Rels)*

Accounts:
Champion Fiberglass
Magnum Oil Tools
R360 Environmental Solutions
Rockwater Energy Solutions
Stallion Oilfield Services
Think Energy
Thru Tubing Solutions

THE UNREAL AGENCY
52 Broad St 3rd Fl, Keyport, NJ 07735
Tel.: (732) 888-0055
Fax: (732) 888-0125
E-Mail: askunreal@theunrealagency.com
Web Site: www.theunrealagency.com

Employees: 10
Year Founded: 2001

Agency Specializes In: Advertising, Brand Development & Integration, Business Publications, Business-To-Business, Cable T.V., Co-op Advertising, Commercial Photography, Consulting, Corporate Identity, Digital/Interactive, Direct Response Marketing, Entertainment, Graphic Design, Health Care Services, Identity Marketing, Infomercials, Local Marketing, Logo & Package Design, Multimedia, New Product Development, Newspaper, Newspapers & Magazines, Package Design, Planning & Consultation, Point of Purchase, Print, Production, Production (Ad, Film, Broadcast)

Breakdown of Gross Billings by Media: Cable T.V.: 10%; Graphic Design: 30%; Logo & Package Design: 25%; Newsp. & Mags.: 35%

Christine Bocchiaro *(Partner)*
Cathy Dipierro *(Partner)*

Accounts:
Alure
IEEE
Stonehouse Media

UP AGENCY
7025 E 1st Ave Ste 5, Scottsdale, AZ 85251
Tel.: (480) 945-0028
E-Mail: hi@up-agency.com
Web Site: www.getdownwithup.com

Year Founded: 2010

Agency Specializes In: Advertising, Crisis Communications, Internet/Web Design, Public Relations, Social Media

Stacy Pearson *(Principal)*

Accounts:
Wist Office Products

UPBEAT MARKETING
3409 Executive Ctr Dr Bldg 1 Ste 203, Austin, TX 78731
Tel.: (512) 222-7141
E-Mail: info@upbeatmarketingaustin.com
Web Site: www.upbeatmarketingaustin.com

Year Founded: 2009

Agency Specializes In: Advertising, Event Planning & Marketing, Graphic Design, Internet/Web Design, Logo & Package Design, Public Relations, Social Media

Suzanne Vernau Feezel *(Founder)*

Accounts:
Coco & Duckie
Mothers Milk Bank at Austin
Reel Visuals

UPBRAND COLLABORATIVE
1220 Olive St Ste 220, Saint Louis, MO 63103
Tel.: (314) 615-6574
E-Mail: info@upbrand.com
Web Site: www.upbrand.com

Year Founded: 2010

Agency Specializes In: Advertising, Brand Development & Integration, Digital/Interactive, Internet/Web Design, Social Media

Jeff Insco *(Pres & Exec Creative Dir)*
Lynn Ullman *(VP & Creative Dir)*
Meredith Goette *(Sr Dir-Bus Dev)*
Kerry Crump *(Brand Mgr)*

Accounts:
STL Symphony

UPP ENTERTAINMENT MARKETING
3401 Winona Ave, Burbank, CA 91504
Tel.: (818) 526-0111
Fax: (818) 526-1466
E-Mail: info@upp.net
Web Site: www.upp.net

Employees: 28
Year Founded: 1979

Agency Specializes In: Branded Entertainment, Entertainment, Event Planning & Marketing, Product Placement, Public Relations, Publicity/Promotions

Gary Mezzatesta *(CEO)*
Steve Rasnick *(Sr VP)*

Accounts:
Alba Botanica Alba Sea Salt Scrub
Altadis Cigars
American Heart Association Ancillary Items
Avalon Organics
Avaya
Bally Total Fitness
Barbour Raincoats
BEARPAW
Bee M.D.
CalArts
Carhartt Branded Integration, Celebrity Affinity Program, Product Placement, Public Relations, Rugged Apparel
Coleman Company Coolers
Diesel Jeans
Downy
Dr. Red Nutraceuticals
Finest Call Drink Mixers
Firestarter Vodka
Frederic Fekkai
Gatorade
Godiva Chocolatier
Greyhound Busses Motor Coaches
Hain Celestial Personal Care
Hello Kitty
Helly Hansen
Jack Link's Meat Snacks
Jason
Loud Mouth Golf Apparel
Motorola Solutions, Inc. Cellular & Cordless Phones, Pagers, Wireless Two-Way Radios
Nintendo Gameboy, Nintendo 64, Nintendo DS, Wii
O.N.E. Water
PacSun
Silk Soy Milk
Skype
T2U Green Tea
Tabasco Hot Sauce & Licensed Products
Tetra Pak
UPS
Virtual DJ
Waste Management Recycle America
Wiley X Sunglasses
Zia Skin Care

THE UPPER STOREY
(Acquired by Isobar US & Name Changd to US Isobar)

UPROAR
206 1st Ave S Ste 410, Seattle, WA 98104
Tel.: (206) 447-5574
Fax: (206) 625-0271
E-Mail: info@uproarseattle.com
Web Site: www.uproarseattle.com

Agency Specializes In: Advertising, Brand Development & Integration, Collateral, Communications, Email, Graphic Design, Identity Marketing, Internet/Web Design, Local Marketing, Media Buying Services, Media Planning, Media Relations, Media Training, Newspaper, Outdoor, Planning & Consultation, Print, Promotions, Public Relations, Radio, Strategic Planning/Research, T.V.

Erik Nelson *(Chief Creative Officer)*
Tory Patrick *(VP)*
Karen Denton *(Mgr-Ops)*
Christine Curtin *(Sr Acct Exec)*
Lauren Jaeger *(Acct Exec)*
Anita Lavine *(Specialist-Media Rels)*
Janice Gebhardt *(Asst Acct Exec)*
Mary Dallas Jameson *(Asst Acct Exec)*

Accounts:
abc
AP Associated Press
Business Week
Community Coffee
Fine Living
Hasbro Campaign: "Great Games Trade In", Campaign: "Perfect For You", Jenga, Ratuki
HG TV
InStyle
K2 Women
Paper Delights
Seattle Magazine

UPSHIFT CREATIVE GROUP
333 N Michigan Ave Ste 2225, Chicago, IL 60601
Tel.: (312) 750-6800
Fax: (312) 750-6900
E-Mail: info@upshiftcreative.com
Web Site: www.upshiftcreative.com

Year Founded: 2000

Agency Specializes In: Advertising, Brand Development & Integration, Digital/Interactive, Environmental, Graphic Design, Internet/Web Design, Social Media

Richard Shanks *(Founder & Pres)*
Nick Staal *(Partner & Dir-Design)*
Courtney Reilly *(Acct Dir)*
Dana Albers *(Office Mgr)*

Accounts:
Alliant Credit Union
Chicago Symphony Orchestra
Tartan Realty Group
Thomas E. Wilson Foods
Tyson Foods, Inc.
West Avenue Recording Group

UPSHOT
350 N Orleans St 5th Fl, Chicago, IL 60654
Tel.: (312) 943-0900
Fax: (312) 943-9699
Web Site: upshot.agency

E-Mail for Key Personnel:
President: brian_kristofek@upshotmail.com

Employees: 156
Year Founded: 1994

National Agency Associations: PMA-POPAI-WOMMA

Agency Specializes In: Above-the-Line, Advertising, Below-the-Line, Brand Development & Integration, Consumer Marketing, Environmental, Event Planning & Marketing, In-Store Advertising, Integrated Marketing, Merchandising, Point of Purchase, Point of Sale, Promotions, Regional, Retail, Sales Promotion, Sponsorship, Strategic Planning/Research, Teen Market, Viral/Buzz/Word of Mouth, Women's Market

Kate May *(CFO & Sr VP-Fin & Admin)*
Ellen Slauson *(Exec VP-Acct Mgmt)*
Kristopher Boron *(Sr VP-Acct Mgmt & Strategy)*
Jerry Craven *(Sr VP-Creative Svcs)*
Scott Fujii *(Sr VP-Print Production & Studio Svcs)*
Brian Priest *(Sr VP-Creative)*
Jay Davidson *(VP)*
Bill Fogarty *(VP-Creative)*
Lisa Hurst *(VP-Acct Mgmt)*
Kristie Ritchie *(VP-New Bus & Comm)*
Mary van de Walle *(VP-Strategic Plng)*
Jeff Daniel *(Dir-Media)*
Neil Helsper *(Dir-Creative)*
Lura Meisch *(Dir-Art)*
Whitney Harper *(Sr Acct Mgr)*
Ryan Short *(Supvr-Media)*

Accounts:
ACH Food Companies (Agency of Record) Consumer Promotions, Creative, Mazola, Planning, Shopper Marketing, Spice Islands, Strategy, Weber Spices & Seasonings
Central Garden & Pet
Constellation Wines U.S.
Crown Imports Modelo Collection; 2009
New-Donuts Inc (Agency of Record)
Implementation Engineers
LiftMaster Brand Planning, Brand Strategy, Integrated Marketing, Media Planning & Buying
Metronet (Agency of Record) Advertising, Creative Development, Digital, Marketing, Media Buying, Media Planning, Strategic Development
Procter & Gamble; Cincinnati, OH BJ's Whole Sale Club, CVS/Pharmacy, Corporate Marketing, Cover Girl, Fabric Care, Family Dollar, Folgers, Giant Eagle, Head & Shoulder Old Spice, Health & Beauty Care, In-Store, Loblaws, Meijer, Oral-B, Tampax, Vicks; 1998
Ball Horticultural Company Burpee Home Gardens, Wave
Mondelez International, Inc. Ahold, Corporate Marketing, Customer Marketing, General Dollar, Publix; 2007
New Balance
Nuveen Investments
Omron Healthcare
Physicians Immediate Care
Post Foods
Subway Marketing, Merchandising, Promotions

URI, INC.
3635 Hayden Ave, Culver City, CA 90232
Tel.: (310) 360-9003
Fax: (310) 360-9003
E-Mail: information@uriglobal.com
Web Site: www.uriglobal.com

E-Mail for Key Personnel:
President: xochitl@uriinc.com

Employees: 15
Year Founded: 1996

National Agency Associations: IAA

Agency Specializes In: Advertising, Advertising Specialties, Asian Market, Automotive, Bilingual

Market, Brand Development & Integration, Broadcast, Cable T.V., Consulting, Consumer Publications, Corporate Identity, Digital/Interactive, Entertainment, Event Planning & Marketing, Fashion/Apparel, High Technology, Hispanic Market, Infomercials, Internet/Web Design, Investor Relations, Magazines, Media Buying Services, Merchandising, New Product Development, Newspaper, Newspapers & Magazines, Out-of-Home Media, Outdoor, Over-50 Market, Planning & Consultation, Print, Public Relations, Publicity/Promotions, Radio, Sales Promotion, Sponsorship, Sports Market, Strategic Planning/Research, Syndication, T.V., Trade & Consumer Magazines, Travel & Tourism

Approx. Annual Billings: $10,000,000

Xochitl Hwang *(Founder & CEO)*
Daniel Shin *(Pres)*
KP Moon *(Acct Dir)*
Angela Yun *(Acct Mgr)*

Accounts:
Hyundai Motor Corporation
Hyundai Motors America
Onion Map
Samsung

US +PARTNERS

1674 Broadway, New York, NY 10019
Tel.: (313) 701-9172
Web Site: www.usandpartners.com

Employees: 15
Year Founded: 2002

Agency Specializes In: Advertising, Customer Relationship Management, Digital/Interactive, E-Commerce

Approx. Annual Billings: $4,000,000

Steve Stepanek *(Co-Founder & Mng Dir)*
Jerry Moore *(Mng Partner-West Reg)*
Marcia Stepanek *(Mng Dir-Social & New Media)*

Accounts:
Audi
I-CAR
RebuildingTogether

US INTERACTIVE MEDIA

2603 Main St Ste 850, Irvine, CA 92614
Tel.: (949) 241-8260
Fax: (949) 209-4997
Web Site: www.usinteractivemedia.com

Agency Specializes In: Advertising, Affiliate Marketing, Direct Response Marketing, Search Engine Optimization, Social Media

Eran Goren *(Pres)*
Grae Jones *(Exec VP-Tech)*
Ryan McArthur *(Exec VP)*
Michelle Larsh *(Sr VP-Client Svcs)*
Brad Johnson *(VP-Bus Dev)*

Accounts:
New-OCharleys

USADWEB, LLC

1498-M Reisterstown Rd Ste 330, Baltimore, MD 21208-3835
Tel.: (410) 580-5414
Fax: (410) 580-5417
Toll Free: (866) 872-3932
E-Mail: contact@usadweb.com
Web Site: www.usadweb.com

E-Mail for Key Personnel:
President: elisheva@usaweb.com

Employees: 8
Year Founded: 2001

Agency Specializes In: Legal Services, Media Buying Services, Recruitment

Approx. Annual Billings: $3,000,000

Breakdown of Gross Billings by Media: Newsp. & Mags.: $3,000,000

Russell Rosen *(COO)*

USE ALL FIVE INC.

1800 Abbot Kinney Blvd Unit D & E, Venice, CA 90291
Tel.: (310) 270-5569
Fax: (310) 943-2682
E-Mail: hello@useallfive.com
Web Site: www.useallfive.com

Year Founded: 2006

Agency Specializes In: Advertising, Digital/Interactive, Graphic Design

Levi Brooks *(Founder & CEO)*
Jason Farrell *(Co-Founder & CTO)*
Troy Kreiner *(Dir-Art)*

Accounts:
Ben & Jerry's Homemade, Inc. Chunks for a Change
Prudential Financial, Inc. The Challenge Lab Summit On The Summit

THE UTMOST GROUP

2140 S Hammond Lake Rd W, Bloomfield, MI 48324
Tel.: (248) 496-4142
Fax: (855) 253-5664
Web Site: www.theutmostgroup.com

Year Founded: 2011

Agency Specializes In: Advertising, Brand Development & Integration, Communications, Promotions

Chris Grindem *(Exec Dir)*

Accounts:
Green Living Science

UWG

(Formerly Uniworld Group, Inc.)
1 Metrotech Center N 11th Fl, Brooklyn, NY 11201
Tel.: (212) 219-1600
Fax: (212) 334-2076
E-Mail: newbiz@uwg.is
Web Site: www.uwg.is

Employees: 105
Year Founded: 1969

Agency Specializes In: Advertising, Advertising Specialties, African-American Market, Event Planning & Marketing, Health Care Services, Hispanic Market, Sponsorship, Strategic Planning/Research

Approx. Annual Billings: $90,000,000

Breakdown of Gross Billings by Media: Brdcst.: $25,000,000; Cable T.V.: $40,000; Fees: $22,000,000; Internet Adv.: $3,400,000; Print: $9,200,000; Production: $28,760,000; Sls. Promo.: $100,000; Syndication: $1,500,000

Monique L. Nelson *(CEO)*
Carmon Johnston *(Mng Dir & Sr VP)*
Josie Penzes *(Exec VP & Gen Mgr)*
Belviana TodMann *(Sr VP-Global Brand Licensing & Dir-Branded Entertainment)*
Stella Canlas *(Controller)*
Lynn Pitts *(Grp Dir-Creative & Copywriter)*
Ruth Barnett *(Grp Dir-Media)*
Lorraine DeLeon *(Dir-Digital Production)*
Bruce Kirton *(Dir-Strategic Plng)*
Shirley Lawson *(Dir-Client Svcs & New Bus)*
Lynn Wilson *(Dir-Events Ops & Sponsorships)*
Alicia Guscott *(Sr Mgr-HR)*
Howard Musson *(Mgr-Print Production)*
Ivana Dasaro *(Acct Supvr)*
Rochelle Dorset *(Acct Supvr)*
Christina Adams *(Supvr-Media)*

Accounts:
Colgate-Palmolive Company Colgate Total, Palmolive Ultra
Con Edison
CVS Pharmacy, Inc.; 2010
Ford Motor Company African-American, Fiesta, Lincoln
The Home Depot
Lincoln Mercury
Marriott International, Inc. Campaign: "For You, We're Marriott", Digital Media, Print
Time Warner Cable
United States Marine Corps

Branch

UWG

(Formerly Uniworld Group-Detroit)
500 Town Ctr Dr, Dearborn, MI 48126
Tel.: (313) 615-3337
Fax: (313) 336-9448
E-Mail: newbiz@uwg.is
Web Site: www.uwg.is

Employees: 30

Agency Specializes In: Advertising

Greg Edwards *(Sr VP & Mng Dir)*
Chuck Morrison *(Exec VP, Gen Mgr-Dearborn)*
Cheryl D. Day *(VP-Acct Bus Ops)*
Genifer Stewart *(Acct Dir-Atlanta)*
Doug Evans *(Assoc Dir-Creative)*
Yirayah Garcia *(Assoc Dir-Creative)*
Richole Hall *(Assoc Dir-Media)*
Justin Trapp *(Assoc Dir-Creative)*
Dawnne Amey *(Acct Supvr-Atlanta)*
Chelsea Hood *(Acct Coord-Atlanta)*

Accounts:
Burger King
Colgate-Palmolive Company
Ford
The Home Depot
HSBC
Lincoln Mercury
Time Warner Cable

THE UXB

9701 Wilshire Blvd Ste 1000, Beverly Hills, CA 90212
Tel.: (310) 229-9098
E-Mail: nj@theuxb.com
Web Site: www.theuxb.com

Year Founded: 1999

Agency Specializes In: Advertising, Brand Development & Integration, Collateral, Digital/Interactive, E-Commerce, Email, Environmental, Exhibit/Trade Shows, Graphic Design, Identity Marketing, Local Marketing, Media Buying Services, Multimedia, New Technologies, Package Design, Print, Retail, Search Engine

Optimization

Nancyjane Goldston *(Founder & CEO)*
Daiga Atvara *(Chief Creative Officer-Digital)*
Glenn Sakamoto *(Dir-Creative)*
Bryan Shanaver *(Dir-Tech)*

Accounts:
Arm & Hammer
Cleatskins Web Site
Cleatskins PRO
DRI
Lumeta Web Site
Raul Walters
Revolution Media
Swatfame

V-FLUENCE INTERACTIVE PUBLIC RELATIONS, INC.

7770 Regents Rd Ste 113-576, San Diego, CA 92122-1937
Tel.: (858) 453-9900
Toll Free: (877) 835-8362
E-Mail: info@v-fluence.com
Web Site: www.v-fluence.com

Agency Specializes In: Advertising, Communications, Environmental, Government/Political, Internet/Web Design, Media Relations, Public Relations, Search Engine Optimization

Jay Byrne *(Pres)*
Christopher Phillips *(CFO)*
Nina Shariff *(Sr VP & Dir-Ops)*
Darliene Catron *(VP & Controller)*
Shae Johnson *(VP)*
Jeff Latzke *(VP)*

Accounts:
AstraZeneca

V2 MARKETING COMMUNICATIONS

220 E State St Ste G, Rockford, IL 61104
Tel.: (815) 397-6052
Fax: (815) 397-6799
Web Site: www.marketingv2.com

Agency Specializes In: Advertising, Content, Graphic Design, Internet/Web Design, Media Planning, Public Relations, Social Media, Strategic Planning/Research

Kathy Velasco *(Founder)*
Heather Kelley *(Principal)*
Deb Strout *(Dir-Creative Svcs)*
Chris Kelley *(Acct Exec)*

Accounts:
Applied Ecological Services, Inc.
Goldie B. Floberg Center
Rock Valley College
United Way of Rock River Valley

VALASSIS 1 TO 1 SOLUTIONS

19975 Victor Pkwy, Livonia, MI 48152
Tel.: (800) 437-0479
Fax: (781) 229-0541
E-Mail: info@valassis.com
Web Site: www.valassis.com

Employees: 125
Year Founded: 1993

National Agency Associations: DMA

Agency Specializes In: Advertising, Broadcast, Business-To-Business, Cable T.V., Collateral, Consulting, Consumer Marketing, Direct Response Marketing, E-Commerce, Electronic Media, Fashion/Apparel, Financial, In-Store Advertising, Internet/Web Design, Local Marketing, Magazines, Medical Products, Newspaper, Newspapers & Magazines, Outdoor, Pharmaceutical, Planning & Consultation, Point of Purchase, Point of Sale, Print, Production, Radio, Retail, Strategic Planning/Research, T.V.

Linda Schalek *(Sr VP & Controller)*
Eric Pritchard *(Sr VP-Transformation Leadership Team)*
Frank Kroger *(VP-Shopper Mktg)*
Nelson Rodenmayer *(VP-Client Mktg)*
Jeff Swan *(VP-Client Mktg)*
Dave Cesaro *(Dir-Client Mktg)*
Aimee Englert *(Dir-CPG Client Mktg)*
Greg Godbout *(Dir-Pricing)*
Mary Hesburgh *(Sr Mgr-Client Mktg)*
April Masters *(Mgr-Mktg Comm)*
Frank Moran *(Mgr-Strategic & Natl Accounts)*
Sara Yanchuck *(Mgr-Client Mktg)*

Accounts:
Abbott Laboratories
Bayer Pharmaceuticals
GlaxoSmithKline
Harbor Freight Tools
Pfizer
Stop & Shop
Stride Rite
Talbot's
Toys 'R' Us

VALMARK ASSOCIATES, LLC

4242 Ridge Lea Rd Ste 5, Amherst, NY 14226
Tel.: (716) 893-1494
Fax: (716) 836-3415
E-Mail: joe@valmarkassociates.com
Web Site: www.valmarkassociates.com

Employees: 1

Agency Specializes In: Advertising, Brand Development & Integration, Consumer Goods, Direct Response Marketing, Health Care Services, Leisure, Local Marketing, Media Relations, Print, Public Relations, Retail, Sports Market, Strategic Planning/Research

Joe Lojacono *(Pres & CEO)*

Accounts:
Alliance Advisory Group
Hafner Financial Group Advertising
Kansas Farm Bureau Foundation
Napolis Per La Moda
Rochester Eye & Laser Center (Agency of Record) Broadcast Production, Media Planning & Placement, Mobile Marketing, Print, Social Media, Strategic Marketing
TriSurant
University at Buffalo Athletics
University Emergency Medical Services Occupational & Travel Health (Agency of Record)

VAN SCHOUWEN ASSOCIATES, LLC

175 Dwight Rd Ste 201, Longmeadow, MA 01106
Tel.: (413) 567-8700
Fax: (413) 567-7790
E-Mail: info@vsamarketing.com
Web Site: www.vsamarketing.com

Employees: 10
Year Founded: 1985

Agency Specializes In: Advertising, Bilingual Market, Brand Development & Integration, Broadcast, Business Publications, Business-To-Business, Co-op Advertising, Collateral, Commercial Photography, Communications, Consulting, Consumer Marketing, Consumer Publications, Corporate Communications, Corporate Identity, Digital/Interactive, Direct Response Marketing, E-Commerce, Education, Electronic Media, Engineering, Environmental, Event Planning & Marketing, Exhibit/Trade Shows, Financial, Government/Political, Graphic Design, Health Care Services, High Technology, Hispanic Market, Industrial, Information Technology, Internet/Web Design, Legal Services, Logo & Package Design, Magazines, Marine, Media Buying Services, Medical Products, Multimedia, New Product Development, Newspaper, Newspapers & Magazines, Out-of-Home Media, Outdoor, Over-50 Market, Pharmaceutical, Planning & Consultation, Point of Purchase, Point of Sale, Print, Production, Public Relations, Publicity/Promotions, Radio, Real Estate, Recruitment, Retail, Sales Promotion, Seniors' Market, Strategic Planning/Research, T.V., Technical Advertising, Teen Market, Telemarketing, Trade & Consumer Magazines, Transportation, Travel & Tourism

Breakdown of Gross Billings by Media: Bus. Publs.: 10%; Collateral: 5%; Consulting: 5%; D.M.: 5%; Graphic Design: 10%; Newsp. & Mags.: 10%; Print: 10%; Pub. Rels.: 20%; Spot Radio: 5%; Strategic Planning/Research: 5%; Worldwide Web Sites: 15%

Michelle van Schouwen *(Pres)*
Patrick Rathbun *(Mgr-Strategic Comm)*
Lynne Turner *(Mgr-Production)*

Accounts:
Apex Healthcare Services
InteliCoat Technologies
Kanzaki Specialty Papers
Louis & Clark
The MVA Center
Northeast Treaters, Inc.
Roger Butler Insurance, Inc.
UniTech

VAN WAGNER COMMUNICATIONS, LLC.

800 3rd Ave 28th Fl, New York, NY 10022
Tel.: (212) 699-8400
Fax: (212) 986-0927
E-Mail: jschaps@vanwagner.com
Web Site: www.vanwagner.com

Employees: 250

Agency Specializes In: Outdoor

Approx. Annual Billings: $11,500,000

Richard Schaps *(Chm/CEO-Van Wagner Sports Grp)*
John Massoni *(Pres-Western Div)*
Richard Silverton *(Pres-Real Estate & Dev)*
Brian Broderson *(Sr VP-Ops)*
Gary Grossman *(Sr VP-Sls-Van Wagner Outdoor)*
Jessica Mudry *(VP-Dev & Ops)*
Justin Rinko *(VP-Sls)*
Liza Villafane *(VP-HR)*
Kathleen McDowell *(Acct Exec)*

Accounts:
MetLife, Inc. Event Marketing, Sponsorship
US Figure Skating Association
US Ski & Snowboard
Utimate Fighting Championship

Subsidiary

Van Wagner Sports Group LLC

800 3rd Ave 28th Fl, New York, NY 10022-7604
Tel.: (212) 699-8600
Fax: (212) 986-0927

Employees: 100

Agency Specializes In: Advertising, Sports Market

Hillary Thomas *(COO)*
Scott Epstein *(Pres-Experiential & Activation Mktg & Exec VP-Sls)*
Bob Becker *(Exec VP-Van Wagner BSN Productions)*
Chris Allphin *(Sr VP-Team & Venue Svcs)*
Robert Jordan *(Sr VP)*
Kip Koslow *(Sr VP)*
Peter Honig *(VP-Corp Consulting)*
Jessica Mudry *(VP-Production & Dev)*

Accounts:
Absolut
NBC Universal
Patron
Weather Proof Garment Company

VAN WINKLE & ASSOCIATES

1180 W Peachtree St NW Ste 400, Atlanta, GA 30309
Tel.: (404) 355-0126
Fax: (404) 355-8351
E-Mail: info@vanwinkleassociates.com
Web Site: www.vanwinkleassociates.com

Employees: 12
Year Founded: 1984

Agency Specializes In: Advertising, Broadcast, Internet/Web Design, Logo & Package Design, Media Buying Services, Media Planning, Print, Sales Promotion, Strategic Planning/Research, T.V.

Alex Van Winkle *(Pres)*
Jim Newbury *(Creative Dir)*
Debbie Haber *(Dir-Media)*
Silver Cuellar *(Assoc Dir-Creative)*
Carmin Young *(Media Buyer)*

Accounts:
Ancestry.com Ancestry DNA
Banks Street Partners LLC
Brown & Brown Insurance of Georgia, Inc.
Community Loans of America Inc
EdgeStone Capital Partners Inc.
Great Clips
Home2 by Hilton
Homewood Suites by Hilton
Moda Tequila
North American Mission Board
Piedmont HealthCare
Post Properties, Inc.
New-Toyota Motor Corporation

VANGUARDCOMM

2 Disbrow Court 3rd Fl, East Brunswick, NJ 08816
Tel.: (732) 246-0340
Fax: (732) 243-0502
E-Mail: info@vanguardcomm.com
Web Site: www.vanguardcomm.com

Employees: 10
Year Founded: 1994

Agency Specializes In: African-American Market, Asian Market, Communications, Hispanic Market, Public Relations

Approx. Annual Billings: $2,000,000

Esther Novak *(Founder & CEO)*
William F. Fox *(Mng Partner & COO)*
Joe Kelly *(Exec VP)*
Brenda Foster *(Sr VP)*
Hensley Jemmott *(SR VP-Client Svcs)*
Lillian Ayala *(VP & Acct Dir)*
LeAnne DeFrancesco *(VP)*
Deanna Troust *(VP-Creative Svcs)*
Maria Enie *(Acct Mgr)*
Scott Rieder *(Sr Acct Exec)*

Accounts:
Moen (Global)
Walmart

VANTAGEPOINT, INC

80 Villa Rd, Greenville, SC 29615
Tel.: (864) 331-1240
Fax: (864) 331-1245
E-Mail: info@vantagep.com
Web Site: www.vantagep.com

Employees: 30
Year Founded: 1993

Agency Specializes In: Advertising, Brand Development & Integration, Broadcast, Business Publications, Business-To-Business, Co-op Advertising, Communications, Computers & Software, Consulting, Corporate Communications, Corporate Identity, Digital/Interactive, Direct Response Marketing, E-Commerce, Email, Event Planning & Marketing, Graphic Design, Health Care Services, High Technology, Identity Marketing, Industrial, Information Technology, Integrated Marketing, Internet/Web Design, Investor Relations, Logo & Package Design, Market Research, Media Buying Services, Media Planning, Media Relations, New Product Development, Pharmaceutical, Planning & Consultation, Podcasting, Point of Sale, Production (Print), Sales Promotion, Search Engine Optimization, Strategic Planning/Research, Technical Advertising, Transportation, Web (Banner Ads, Pop-ups, etc.)

Approx. Annual Billings: $15,000,000

Steve Woodington *(Assoc Dir-Creative)*
Angie McEldowney *(Sr Acct Mgr)*
Miller Howard *(Acct Mgr)*
Andrew Smith *(Acct Mgr)*
Virginia Vanvick *(Sr Acct Exec)*
Collin McElhannon *(Acct Exec)*
Nicole Viscome *(Acct Exec)*

Accounts:
A.J. Antunes & Co
Banker Exchange
Capsugel; Greenwood, SC
Cox Industries; Orangeburg, SC
Cryovac
Dodge
Fitesa
Guardian Building Products Distribution; Greer, SC
Henny Penny
Kyrus
LANGUAGE LINE SERVICES HOLDINGS, INC.
Michelin Ag
Nason
Proterra
Rockwell Automation
Saia LTL Freight
ScanSource Inc.; Greenville, SC
Scotsman Ice Systems
T&S Brass, Inc.; Travelers Rest, SC
Wikoff Color Corp

VARGAS & AMIGOS INC.

3055 Waterfront Cir, Marietta, GA 30062-5659
Tel.: (404) 429-5044
E-Mail: dvargas@vargasandamigos.com
Web Site: www.vargasandamigos.com

E-Mail for Key Personnel:
Production Mgr.:
dcaicedo@vargasandamigos.com
Public Relations:
dholzapfel@vargasandamigos.com

Employees: 3
Year Founded: 2001

National Agency Associations: AMA

Agency Specializes In: Advertising, African-American Market, Asian Market, Bilingual Market, Brand Development & Integration, Broadcast, Business-To-Business, Collateral, Consulting, Consumer Marketing, Corporate Identity, Cosmetics, Education, Environmental, Event Planning & Marketing, Exhibit/Trade Shows, Financial, Food Service, Graphic Design, Health Care Services, High Technology, Hispanic Market, In-Store Advertising, Internet/Web Design, Leisure, Media Buying Services, Medical Products, New Product Development, Over-50 Market, Pharmaceutical, Print, Production, Public Relations, Publicity/Promotions, Real Estate, Recruitment, Restaurant, Retail, Sales Promotion, Seniors' Market, Sports Market, Strategic Planning/Research, T.V., Telemarketing, Trade & Consumer Magazines, Transportation, Travel & Tourism

Approx. Annual Billings: $3,847,000

Breakdown of Gross Billings by Media: Collateral: $300,000; Consulting: $300,000; E-Commerce: $250,000; Event Mktg.: $500,000; Exhibits/Trade Shows: $175,000; Graphic Design: $175,000; Local Mktg.: $165,000; Logo & Package Design: $275,000; Mags.: $600,000; Outdoor: $60,000; Pub. Rels.: $375,000; Radio: $180,000; Sports Mktg.: $162,000; T.V.: $60,000; Worldwide Web Sites: $270,000

Daniel Vargas *(Pres & CEO)*

Accounts:
Aqua Blue Waters
The Coca Cola Co.; Atlanta, GA; 1992
State of Georgia Department of Education; 2004
UNUM Provident; 2004

VARIABLE

134 W 26th St Ste 750, New York, NY 10001
Tel.: (212) 462-2870
Web Site: WeAreVariable.com

Year Founded: 2011

Agency Specializes In: Branded Entertainment, Broadcast, Cable T.V., Electronic Media, Experience Design, Guerilla Marketing, Multimedia, Outdoor, Print, Production, Production (Print), Social Media, T.V., Viral/Buzz/Word of Mouth

Jonathan Bregel *(Dir-Creative)*
Kevan Funk *(Dir)*
Salomon Ligthelm *(Dir-Creative)*

Accounts:
ACLU
National Geographic
Tiffany & Co.

THE VARIABLE AGENCY

823 Reynolda Rd, Winston Salem, NC 27104
Tel.: (336) 721-1021
E-Mail: info@thevariable.com
Web Site: www.thevariable.com

Year Founded: 2011

Agency Specializes In: Advertising, Brand Development & Integration, Content, Digital/Interactive, Internet/Web Design

Keith Vest *(Pres)*
Harper Lee *(VP)*
Jennifer Ganshirt *(Dir-Strategy & Insight)*

David Mullen *(Dir-Acct Mgmt)*
Ray Trosan *(Dir-Media & Bus Dev)*
Anna Keller *(Acct Supvr)*
Matt Cook *(Sr Designer)*

Accounts:
Duke University Health System (Agency of Record)
Interface (Agency of Record)
New-Lowes Foods Advertising, In-Store
Primo Water (Agency of Record)
Soffe (Agency of Record)
Spin Master Ltd. (Lead Integrated Marketing Agency of Record) AirHogs, Bunchems, Creative, Strategy, Zoomer

THE VAULT NYC
420 Lexington Ave, New York, NY 10170
Tel.: (212) 913-9499
Web Site: www.thevaultnyc.com

Agency Specializes In: Advertising, Brand Development & Integration, Digital/Interactive, Print, T.V.

Jon Paley *(Exec Dir-Creative)*
Josh Weissglass *(Acct Dir)*

Accounts:
Academy Sports & Outdoors, Ltd.
DIRECTV
ESPN, Inc.
Foot Locker Campaign: "Everything Changes After the Draft"
National Football League
Puma North America, Inc.
Samsung Telecommunications America, LLC
Under Armour, Inc.

VBP ORANGE
201 Post St 4th Fl, San Francisco, CA 94108
Tel.: (415) 962-3000
E-Mail: hello@vbporange.com
Web Site: www.vbporange.com

Agency Specializes In: Advertising, Brand Development & Integration, Graphic Design

Brett Wilson *(Mgmt Supvr)*
Blake Bakken *(Dir-Design)*
Marc Woollard *(Dir-Experience Design)*
Alex Rice *(Assoc Dir-Creative)*
Anne-louise Pettersson *(Office Mgr)*
Ariel Rosen *(Acct Mgr)*
Anna Fields *(Mgr-Post Production)*
Brenda Pyles *(Acct Supvr)*

Accounts:
Audi
Phillips 66

VECTOR MEDIA
708 3rd Ave, New York, NY 10017
Tel.: (212) 557-9405
E-Mail: info@vectormedia.com
Web Site: vectormedia.com

Agency Specializes In: Communications, Digital/Interactive, Out-of-Home Media, Transportation

Rich Liuzzo *(CFO & Controller)*
Chad Silver *(Gen Counsel)*
Gary Greenstein *(Sls Dir-Natl)*
Lynn Mcginness Bilotto *(Dir-HR)*
Matthew Weinreb *(Mgr-Experiential Mktg)*
Meaghan Marrese *(Acct Exec)*
Brett Weinberg *(Acct Exec)*
Arielle Garti *(Sr Coord-Sls)*

Accounts:
JP Morgan Chase

VELA ADVERTISING
127 Pine Island Tpke, Warwick, NY 10990
Tel.: (845) 544-1358
Web Site: www.velaadvertising.com

Agency Specializes In: Advertising, Digital/Interactive, Graphic Design, Internet/Web Design, Logo & Package Design

Tony Vela *(Dir-Creative)*

Accounts:
Axel Plastics Research Laboratories, Inc.
Hillrock Estate Distillery
Valley Mason Supply

VELA AGENCY
315 N Spruce St Ste 215, Winston Salem, NC 27101
Tel.: (336) 245-2436
Fax: (336) 245-2572
E-Mail: info@velaagency.com
Web Site: www.velaagency.com

Agency Specializes In: Advertising, Brand Development & Integration, Digital/Interactive, Media Relations, Media Training, Public Relations, Radio, Social Media, Strategic Planning/Research, T.V.

Ginger Gallagher *(Partner)*
Kevin O'Neill *(VP-Digital Media & Web Solutions)*
Michelle Soyars *(VP-Creative Strategy)*
Miranda Hutchens *(Dir-Creative)*
Kevin Brown *(Mgr-Dealer Database)*
Christina Hussey *(Mgr-Social & Digital Media)*
Cheryl James *(Mgr-Acct & Event)*

Accounts:
Arts for Life
The Law Offices of Timothy D. Welborn
Novant Health, Inc.

VELOCITY AGENCY
710 Papworth Ave, New Orleans, LA 70005
Tel.: (504) 834-8811
Fax: (504) 834-8812
Web Site: www.velocityagency.com

Year Founded: 2012

Agency Specializes In: Advertising, Digital/Interactive, Graphic Design, Media Planning, Outdoor, Print, Promotions, Public Relations, Radio, Social Media

Robert Berning *(Co-Founder & Pres)*
Kevin Patrick Conway *(VP & Sr Acct Exec)*

Accounts:
A1
Lamarque Ford

VELOCITY MEDIA
26 W Dry Creek Cir Ste 600, Littleton, CO 80120
Tel.: (303) 809-0053
Fax: (303) 690-0415
Web Site: www.velocitymediainc.com

Employees: 4
Year Founded: 1998

Agency Specializes In: Advertising, Brand Development & Integration, Cable T.V., Collateral, Commercial Photography, Consulting, Consumer Marketing, Corporate Communications, Corporate Identity, Direct Response Marketing, Electronic Media, Graphic Design, Internet/Web Design, Local Marketing, Logo & Package Design, Media Buying Services, Print, Public Relations, Publicity/Promotions, T.V., Trade & Consumer Magazines

Approx. Annual Billings: $400,000

Breakdown of Gross Billings by Media: Bus. Publs.: $300,000; Cable T.V.: $20,000; Collateral: $50,000; Comml. Photography: $30,000

Derek Fisch *(Pres)*
Andy Kroot *(Principal & Exec VP)*
Darren Pitts *(Exec VP)*
Ron Ault *(Sr VP)*
Judi Butterworth *(Sr VP)*
Brian Gast *(Sr VP)*
Michael Clark *(VP)*
Dean Ingram *(VP)*
Alyssa Beery *(Assoc VP & Office Mgr)*
Larry Miller *(Assoc VP)*
Nancy Hamel *(Coord-Mktg)*
Lea Harper *(Coord-Mktg)*

Accounts:
Custom Window; Englewood, CO Windows

VENABLES, BELL & PARTNERS
201 Post St Ste 200, San Francisco, CA 94108
Tel.: (415) 288-3300
Fax: (415) 421-3683
E-Mail: frontdesk@venablesbell.com
Web Site: www.venablesbell.com

Employees: 180
Year Founded: 2001

Agency Specializes In: Advertising, Advertising Specialties, Automotive, Bilingual Market, Brand Development & Integration, Broadcast, Business Publications, Business-To-Business, Cable T.V., Children's Market, Co-op Advertising, Collateral, Consumer Marketing, Consumer Publications, Corporate Communications, Digital/Interactive, Direct Response Marketing, E-Commerce, Electronic Media, Entertainment, Environmental, Event Planning & Marketing, Exhibit/Trade Shows, Fashion/Apparel, Financial, Food Service, Graphic Design, High Technology, Internet/Web Design, Leisure, Logo & Package Design, Magazines, Media Buying Services, Multimedia, Newspaper, Newspapers & Magazines, Out-of-Home Media, Outdoor, Point of Purchase, Print, Production, Radio, Retail, Sales Promotion, Sponsorship, Sports Market, Strategic Planning/Research, T.V., Teen Market, Trade & Consumer Magazines, Transportation, Travel & Tourism

Approx. Annual Billings: $260,000,000

Paul Venables *(Founder & Chm)*
Kate Jeffers *(Partner & Mng Dir)*
Oliver Fuselier *(Mng Dir)*
Gary Brown *(CFO)*
Lilian Ojeda *(Head-Bus & Grp Acct Dir)*
Michael Davidson *(Head-Strategy)*
Vincenzo LoRusso *(Exec Creative Dir)*
Will McGinness *(Exec Dir-Creative)*
Leander Chapman *(Grp Dir-Strategy)*
Gus Johnston *(Sr Dir-Art)*
Chris Bergen *(Acct Dir)*
Joyce Chen *(Producer-Brdcst)*
Adela Chung *(Producer-Interactive)*
Mike Goldstein *(Creative Dir)*
Vanessa Reid *(Acct Dir)*
Nicole Spinelli *(Acct Dir)*
Robert Woods *(Acct Dir)*
Greg Wyatt *(Art Dir)*
Craig Allen *(Dir-Integrated Production)*
Jeff Burger *(Dir-Analytics)*
Byron Del Rosario *(Dir-Art)*
Lee Einhorn *(Assoc Partner & Dir-Creative)*
Bret Faszholz *(Dir-Retail Mktg)*
Aisha Hakim *(Dir-Art)*

Tyler Hampton *(Dir-Creative)*
Daniel Ieraci *(Dir-Art)*
Eric Pfeifer *(Dir-Creative)*
Tom Scharpf *(Dir-Creative)*
Meredith Vellines *(Dir-PR)*
Eric Boyd *(Assoc Dir-Creative & Writer)*
Oliver Glenn *(Acct Mgr)*
Gillian McBrayer *(Acct Mgr)*
Krista Muir *(Acct Supvr-REI)*
Brenda Pyles *(Acct Supvr)*
Chris Bull *(Copywriter)*
Bryan Karr *(Copywriter)*
Matt Keats *(Copywriter)*
Adam Wolinsky *(Copywriter)*
Faire Davidson *(Asst Acct Mgr)*
Ariel Rosen *(Asst Acct Mgr)*

Accounts:
Adidas Adidas Golf, Creative
Audi of America "Crossover" Q3, "Doberhuahua" Super Bowl 2014, #StayUncompromised, A4, Audi A3, Audi A3 Sedan, Audi A3 TDI Clean Diesel, Audi A6, Audi A7, Audi Quattro, Audi RS7, Audi S6, Broadcast, Campaign: "Ahab Redux", Campaign: "Ahab", Campaign: "Challenge All Givens", Campaign: "Drones", Campaign: "Dues", Campaign: "Estate Sale", Campaign: "Footing", Campaign: "Progress on Powell Street", Campaign: "Release the Hounds", Campaign: "Rewrite", Campaign: "Riot Suppressor", Campaign: "Scripted Life", Campaign: "Something scary", Campaign: "Swim", Campaign: "Teenager", Campaign: "The Forecast", Campaign: "The all-new Audi A3. Designed without compromise" Super Bowl 2014, Creative, Goodnight, Kenny G, Online, Prom, Q7 SUV, R8 Roadster, Season of Audi, TV
Butterball, LLC Campaign: "Slim Jim Baby Shower, Scooter, Sala", Orville Redenbacher, Slim Jim; 2007
Campari America "Holiday Spirits", Campaign: "DoubleTip", Campaign: "West of Expected", Out-of-Home, Skyy Vodka, Social Media
The Coca-Cola Co. Nestea
ConAgra Campaign: "Juice Fast"
ConocoPhillips 76, Conoco, Phillips 66
eBay Inc. Campaign: "Bad Dog", Campaign: "Frenzy", Campaign: "Give-a-Toy Store", Campaign: "Left Out", Campaign: "Mom Jeans", Campaign: "Pony", Campaign: "School Play", Campaign: "Twelve Days", Pest Control
Facebook Campaign: "Ten Year Olds"
Google Broadcast, Campaign: "Bird Watcher", Campaign: "Explore Your World", Campaign: "Why Speed Matters", Google, Google Fiber, Google Maps, Google+
Heavenly
Hebrew National
Lightlife
Massage Envy Limited, LLC Creative, Strategic
McAfee Campaign: "Gregg", Campaign: "Justin", Campaign: "Megan"
New-MillerCoors Blue Moon Craft Beer, Leinenkugel's
P.F. Chang's
PG&E
Phillips 66 Company 76, Billboards, Campaign: "Honk Suppressor", Website
Premier Protein
New-Recreational Equipment, Inc. Campaign: "#OptOutside"
Reebok "#breakyourselfie", "Be More Human Experience", Bacon, Campaign: "Be More Human", Campaign: "Freak Show", Campaign: "Free Range Chicken", Campaign: "Live Free Range", Global Advertising Creative Agency, Online, Out-of-Home, Social, Super Bowl 2015, ZJet
New-Royal Caribbean Cruises Ltd Celebrity Cruises (Agency of Record), Creative
Samsung Online, POWERbot
San Francisco Conservation Corps
New-Sony Network Entertainment PlayStation Vue

VENDI ADVERTISING

125 4th St N Ste 200, La Crosse, WI 54601
Tel.: (608) 788-5020
Fax: (608) 788-5027
E-Mail: contact@vendiadvertising.com
Web Site: www.vendiadvertising.com

Year Founded: 2004

Agency Specializes In: Advertising, Brand Development & Integration, Broadcast, Content, Internet/Web Design

Julie Haas *(Principal-Client Svcs & Strategy)*
Kathy Van Kirk-Przywojski *(Principal-Creative)*
Chris Haas *(Dir-Dev)*
Erik Olson *(Dir-Art)*
Karen Wallander-Bernhardt *(Dir-Art & Creative)*
Josh Schultz *(Acct Mgr & Project Mgr)*
Kate Decook *(Acct Mgr & Mgr-Media)*
Elly Reister *(Sr Writer)*

Accounts:
The Center

VENEZIA DESIGN INC.

1988 L Arbolita Dr, Glendale, CA 91208
Tel.: (323) 965-9700
Fax: (818) 330-9620
Web Site: www.veneziadesign.com

Employees: 2
Year Founded: 1993

Agency Specializes In: Brand Development & Integration, Children's Market, Collateral, Consulting, Graphic Design, Logo & Package Design, Point of Purchase

Jim Venezia *(Principal)*

Accounts:
Alliance; Burbank, CA
Mattel, Inc.; El Segundo, CA (Package Design) Barbie, Uno; 1997

VENTURE

313 Laurel St, San Diego, CA 92101-1630
Tel.: (619) 234-7312
Fax: (619) 234-5159
Web Site: www.venture-sandiego.com/

Employees: 2
Year Founded: 1977

Agency Specializes In: Advertising, Business Publications, Collateral, Consumer Marketing, Consumer Publications, Corporate Identity, Graphic Design, Magazines, New Product Development, Public Relations, Publicity/Promotions

Approx. Annual Billings: $750,000

Thomas E. Ables *(Owner)*

Accounts:
Ambler Tours & Travel Service; San Diego, CA
Paha Que Wilderness; Poway, CA; 1999

VENTURE COMMUNICATIONS LTD.

2540 Kensington Road NW, Calgary, AB T2N 3S3 Canada
Tel.: (403) 237-2388
Fax: (403) 265-4659
E-Mail: president@venturecommunications.ca
Web Site: venturecommunications.ca/

E-Mail for Key Personnel:
Public Relations: mediainquiries@openminds.ca

Employees: 40
Year Founded: 1984

Agency Specializes In: Public Relations, Publicity/Promotions

Revenue: $30,000,000

Paul Hains *(Chief Creative Officer)*
Jordan Campese *(Dir-Client Mktg)*
John Halliday *(Dir-Creative)*
Marie Langille *(Dir-Client Mktg)*
Lindsay Smith *(Mgr-Media)*
Alain Kassangana *(Strategist)*

Accounts:
Alberta's Promise
Canadian Cancer Society
Carma
Lipton Soups & Teas
National Sports
Regus Media Relations, Public Relations, Strategic PR Counsel
Toyota Dealers Association
Unilever Lipton, Sunlight, VIM
Western Canada Lottery Corporation

THE VENTURE DEPT

1222 E 13th Ave EMU Ste 300, Eugene, OR 97403
Tel.: (541) 346-5511
E-Mail: hello@venturedept.com
Web Site: www.venturedept.com

Year Founded: 2013

Agency Specializes In: Advertising, Brand Development & Integration, Digital/Interactive, Internet/Web Design, Social Media

Tyler Rogers *(Creative Dir)*
Grant Lemons *(Dir-Production)*
Monica Sagowitz *(Dir-Project Mgmt)*
Gibson Toombs *(Copywriter)*
Helen Torney *(Designer)*
Sara Novak *(Designer)*
Carolyn Lieberman *(Jr Designer)*

Accounts:
University of Oregon A&AA

VERBFACTORY

1956 Webster St Ste 250, Oakland, CA 94612
Tel.: (415) 359-4906
Fax: (415) 449-6301
E-Mail: info@verbfactory.com
Web Site: www.verbfactory.com

Employees: 15

Agency Specializes In: Advertising, Brand Development & Integration, Logo & Package Design, Media Relations, Media Training

Richard Berman *(CEO)*
Andy Mascola *(Head-Digital Project)*
Peter Kohn *(Dir-Insurance & Fin Practice)*
Lawrence Talbot *(Dir-Environmental Practice)*
Ken Wilan *(Dir-Healthcare, Medicine & Life Sciences Practice)*

Accounts:
Cordys
Cushman & Wakefield
Dome Capital
Fireman's Fund
Masons of California
PeerMe
Rocket
San Francisco Chronicle

Advertising Agencies

Unum
WorkSoft

VERDIN
689 Tank Farm Rd Ste 210, San Luis Obispo, CA 93401
Tel.: (805) 541-9005
Fax: (805) 541-9007
Web Site: www.verdinmarketing.com

Year Founded: 2003

Agency Specializes In: Advertising, Brand Development & Integration, Digital/Interactive, Logo & Package Design, Public Relations

Mary Verdin *(Pres & Chief Strategy Officer)*
Michelle Starnes *(Partner)*
Adam Verdin *(Principal)*
Ashlee Akers *(VP-Client Svcs)*
Stephanie Sawyer *(Acct Mgr & Specialist-Mktg)*
Lisa Campolmi *(Strategist-Media & Res)*
Megan Condict *(Sr Designer)*

Accounts:
Urban Optics

VERMILION INC.
3055 Center Green Dr, Boulder, CO 80301
Tel.: (303) 443-6262
Fax: (303) 443-0131
E-Mail: info@vermilion.com
Web Site: www.vermilion.com

Agency Specializes In: Advertising, Brand Development & Integration, Consumer Marketing, Corporate Identity, Gay & Lesbian Market, Graphic Design, Internet/Web Design, Logo & Package Design

Bob Morehouse *(Founder & CEO)*
Paul Knipe *(Acct Dir)*
Kevin Bonner *(Dir-Art)*
Karen Tan *(Sr Designer)*

Accounts:
Attention Homes
Biodesix
Campbell Law
Colorado Department of Public Health & Environment Campaign: "Beforeplay"
The Colorado Shakespeare Festival
The Colorado Trust
Healthy Eating Research
HW Home
OPower
Roche Colorado
Rudi's Organic Bakery
Tendril

VERSA CREATIVE GROUP
1535 W Loop S Ste 250, Houston, TX 77027
Tel.: (832) 831-7590
Fax: (832) 433-7623
E-Mail: info@versacreativegroup.com
Web Site: www.versacreativegroup.com

Year Founded: 2009

Agency Specializes In: Advertising, Brand Development & Integration, Internet/Web Design, Logo & Package Design, Print, Social Media

Mary Shekari *(Founder & Principal)*
Krista Kesseler *(Acct Mgr)*
Heather Sartin *(Acct Mgr)*
Kelli Krenek *(Copywriter)*

Accounts:
1919 Wine & Mixology
Corner Table
CustomEyes
Shany Cosmetics

VERSANT
11000-A W Park Pl, Milwaukee, WI 53224-3615
Tel.: (414) 410-0500
Fax: (414) 410-0520
E-Mail: mail@versantsolutions.com
Web Site: www.versantsolutions.com

E-Mail for Key Personnel:
President: wruch@versantsolutions.com
Creative Dir.: malbiero@versantsolutions.com

Employees: 35
Year Founded: 1972

Agency Specializes In: Advertising, Advertising Specialties, Automotive, Brand Development & Integration, Broadcast, Business-To-Business, Collateral, Communications, Consulting, Consumer Marketing, Corporate Identity, Digital/Interactive, Direct Response Marketing, E-Commerce, Education, Electronic Media, Financial, Government/Political, Health Care Services, Internet/Web Design, Investor Relations, Legal Services, Logo & Package Design, Magazines, Media Buying Services, Medical Products, Multimedia, New Product Development, Newspaper, Newspapers & Magazines, Out-of-Home Media, Outdoor, Planning & Consultation, Print, Production, Public Relations, Radio, Recruitment, Retail, Strategic Planning/Research, T.V., Technical Advertising, Trade & Consumer Magazines, Transportation

Will Ruch *(CEO & Mng Partner)*
Tod Kinunen *(Controller-Fin)*

Accounts:
Bank Mutual; Milwaukee, WI Financial
Journal Sentinel JS Everywhere
Milwaukee County Transit System; Milwaukee, WI Mass Transit Services
Plunkett Rayfich Architects; Milwaukee, WI; 2002
Thompson-Reuters Corporation; Stamford, CT
Wisconsin DOT; Madison, WI State Agencies

VERSION 2.0 COMMUNICATION
500 Harrison Ave Ste 401R, Boston, MA 2118
Tel.: (617) 426-2222
Fax: (617) 426-1026
E-Mail: info2@v2comms.com
Web Site: www.v2comms.com

Year Founded: 2006

Agency Specializes In: Brand Development & Integration, Media Relations, Public Relations, Social Media

Jean Serra *(Founder & Partner)*
Maura FitzGerald *(Owner)*
Katelyn Holbrook *(VP)*
Libby Botsford *(Acct Mgr)*
Katie Kennedy *(Acct Mgr)*
Jen Kaye *(Sr Acct Exec)*

Accounts:
Acme Packet Communications, Social Media, Thought Leadership
Avid Technology. Inc.
Curata
NaviNet, Inc.
NetProspex Communications, Social Media, Thought Leadership
Smartleaf, Inc
Sonicbids Communications, Social Media, Thought Leadership
Symphony Services

VERSO ADVERTISING, INC.
50 W 17th St 5th Fl, New York, NY 10011-5702
Tel.: (212) 292-2990
Fax: (212) 557-2592
E-Mail: ideas@versoadvertising.com
Web Site: www.versoadvertising.com

E-Mail for Key Personnel:
President: denise@versoadvertising.com
Creative Dir.: joelle@versoadvertising.com

Employees: 25
Year Founded: 1989

Agency Specializes In: Advertising, Publishing, Sponsorship

Breakdown of Gross Billings by Media: Cable T.V.: 5%; Collateral: 1%; Internet Adv.: 4%; Network Radio: 2%; Network T.V.: 2%; Newsp.: 65%; Outdoor: 1%; Spot Radio: 5%; Spot T.V.: 4%; Trade & Consumer Mags.: 10%; Transit: 1%

Denise Berthiaume *(Chm)*
Michael Kazan *(Mng Dir & Exec VP)*
Tom Thompson *(Sr VP-Digital Strategy & Grp Dir)*
Jennifer Pasanen *(VP & Grp Dir)*
Joelle Celestin *(VP & Dir-Creative)*
Wanda Candelario *(Office Mgr)*

Accounts:
Anne Geddes
Basic Books; New York, NY; 1997
Berkley Publishing Group
Books for a Better Life
Crown Publishing Group; NY; 2005
Dutton
Ecco
Egmont USA
Farrar Straus Giroux; New York, NY; 1992
Harper Collins Children's; NY; 2005
Harper Collins; NY Books; 2005
Harper Perennial; NY; 2005
HarperOne
Henry Holt; New York, NY; 1993
Houghton Mifflin/Mariner Books; Boston, MA; 1997
Penguin Academic; 2002
Rodale
Running Press
Tor Books; New York, NY; 1998
W.W. Norton & Co., Inc.; New York, NY; 1989

VERTIC
180 Varick St Ste 1620, New York, NY 10014
Tel.: (866) 951-8660
E-Mail: info@vertic.com
Web Site: www.vertic.com

Year Founded: 2002

Agency Specializes In: Advertising, Brand Development & Integration, Digital/Interactive

Mads Petersen *(Co-Founder & Partner)*
Sebastian Jespersen *(Pres & CEO)*
Camilla Grove Pelle *(Partner & Bus Dev Dir)*
Henrik Ebbesen *(CTO & Head-Production-Vertic)*
Erik Semmelhack *(Sr VP)*
Jonas Kochen *(Grp Dir-Creative)*
Anna Doan *(Exec Program Dir)*

Accounts:
Vestas Wind System A/S

VERTIGO MEDIA GROUP
1593 Locust Ave Bohemia, New York, NY 11716
Tel.: (516) 882-5030
Fax: (516) 882-5077
E-Mail: info@vertigomediagrp.com
Web Site: www.vertigomediagrp.com

Agency Specializes In: Advertising, Brand

Development & Integration, Internet/Web Design, Social Media

Lisa Mirabile *(Founder & COO)*

Accounts:
New-Briscoe Protective Systems Inc.

VERVE MARKETING & DESIGN
36 Derry Dr, Glen Mills, PA 19342-1810
Tel.: (610) 399-1003
Fax: (610) 358-2353
E-Mail: info@vervemarketinganddesign.com
Web Site: www.vervemarketinganddesign.com

Year Founded: 1987

Agency Specializes In: Advertising, Brand Development & Integration, Email, Exhibit/Trade Shows, Identity Marketing, Internet/Web Design, Local Marketing, Newspapers & Magazines, Out-of-Home Media, Package Design, Print, Production, Public Relations, Publishing, Radio, Strategic Planning/Research

Diane Lemonides *(Pres & Strategist-Brand)*
Julie Bernard *(CMO)*

Accounts:
Avante Salon & Spa
Baltic Leisure
Blue Pear Bistro
Brandywine River Museum
Galla Studios
Globus Medical
Heifer International
Temenos

VERY, INC.
PO Box 517, Menlo Park, CA 94026
Tel.: (650) 323-1101
Fax: (650) 323-1102
E-Mail: g.chadwick@very-inc.com
Web Site: www.very-inc.com

Employees: 5
Year Founded: 1997

Agency Specializes In: Brand Development & Integration, Collateral, Consumer Publications, Internet/Web Design, Print, Radio

George Chadwick *(Pres & Dir-Creative)*

Accounts:
Financial Crimes Services
XOJet

VEST ADVERTISING
3007 Sprowl Rd, Louisville, KY 40299-3620
Tel.: (502) 267-5335
Fax: (502) 267-6025
E-Mail: roxie@vestadvertising.com
Web Site: www.vestadvertising.com

Employees: 39
Year Founded: 1991

Agency Specializes In: Advertising, Advertising Specialties, Brand Development & Integration, Broadcast, Collateral, Communications, Consulting, Direct Response Marketing, Event Planning & Marketing, Exhibit/Trade Shows, Logo & Package Design, Outdoor, Print, Publicity/Promotions

Larry Vest *(Chief Creative Officer)*
Mitch Gregory *(Sr Dir-Art)*
Jake Stephenson *(Art Dir)*
Cody Vest *(Dir-Creative)*
Jeremy Williams *(Dir-Art)*
Danielle Fertig *(Acct Mgr)*
Megan Gettelfinger *(Acct Mgr)*
Mary Oxford *(Office Mgr)*
Dana Mason *(Acct Exec)*
Joe Brown *(Designer-Sound)*
Hannah Ulmer *(Media Buyer)*

Accounts:
American Heart Association
Boys & Girls Club of America
Decora
Diamond Cabinets
Grand Ole Opry
Humana
The Lawn Pro

VI MARKETING & BRANDING
(Formerly Visual Image Advertising)
125 Park Ave Ste 200, Oklahoma City, OK 73102
Tel.: (405) 525-0055
Fax: (405) 600-6250
Web Site: www.vimarketingandbranding.com/

Employees: 25
Year Founded: 1989

Agency Specializes In: Advertising, Collateral, Crisis Communications, Event Planning & Marketing, Investor Relations, Media Relations, Multimedia, Outdoor, Public Relations, Radio, T.V.

Revenue: $25,000,000

Steve Sturges *(Owner)*
Tim Berney *(Pres-Brand Strategy)*
Kregg Lee *(VP & Dir-Creative)*
Jacquelyn LaMar *(VP-Brand Dev)*
Greta Anglin *(Grp Acct Dir)*
Renee Harriman *(Dir-Media)*
Larry McAlister *(Dir-PR)*
Hayley Cacioppo *(Strategist-Digital Mktg)*
Rachel Merritt *(Strategist-Social Media)*
Megan Radford *(Strategist-Mktg)*
Trudy Thomason *(Strategist-Social Media)*

Accounts:
Kansas City Research Institute (Agency of Record)
Oklahoma State Department of Health; Oklahoma City, OK (Agency of Record) Advertising, Marketing, Public Relations

THE VIA AGENCY
619 Congress St, Portland, ME 04101
Tel.: (207) 221-3000
Fax: (207) 761-9422
E-Mail: careers@theviaagency.com
Web Site: www.theviaagency.com

Year Founded: 1993

Agency Specializes In: Advertising, Digital/Interactive, Media Planning, Public Relations, Search Engine Optimization, Social Media, Sponsorship, Strategic Planning/Research

Leeann Leahy *(CEO)*
David Burfeind *(Chief Strategy Officer)*
Greg Smith *(Chief Creative Officer)*
Amos Goss *(Exec Creative Dir)*
Teddy Stoecklein *(Exec Dir-Creative)*
Dan Bailin *(Grp Dir-Strategy)*
Meranne Behrends *(Grp Dir-Strategy)*
Jason Wright *(Grp Dir-Strategy)*
Chuck Alexander *(Dir-Media)*
Crista Crews Crum *(Dir-Outreach & Dev)*
Ian Dunn *(Dir-Creative)*
Ken Matsubara *(Dir-Creative)*
Pete Miller *(Dir-Art)*
Lauren Myers *(Dir-Art)*
Steve Street *(Dir-Creative)*
Chris Avantaggio *(Assoc Dir-Creative)*
David Grindon *(Assoc Dir-Creative)*
Chris Jacobs *(Assoc Dir-Creative)*
Judi Cutrone *(Mgr-Social Media)*
Meghan Gildart Nappi *(Mgr-Bus Affairs)*
Benjamin Brazier *(Acct Supvr)*
Lyndsey Fox *(Acct Supvr)*
Mark Hurley *(Acct Supvr)*
Jake Benjamin *(Grp Creative Dir)*
Elizabeth Fagan *(Client Strategist)*

Accounts:
The Chloraseptic Touch Throat & Mouth Pain Relief Centre
Clear Eyes Eye Gel Providers
Comet Soft Cleanser Bathroom Cleaner Mfr & Distr
Discover Bank Banking & Financial Services
DuPont Campaign: "Ant"
New-Elite Airways
New-Facebook, Inc.
Friendly Ice Cream Corporation "Angry Elf"
Golden Corral Corporation (Lead Creative Agency) Campaign: "Golden Bill of Rights"
Greenpeace Campaign: "#ClickClean", Campaign: "Animals", Campaign: "Water", Campaign: "Wind", Internet
Heineken Campaign: "Keep it Legendary"
New-Heinz
JBL Synchros S700 Headphones Campaign: "The Walk"
LoJack Corporation
North American Breweries, Inc. Genesee, Seagram's Escapes, Seagram's Smooth
New-North American Effie Awards
New-Pacific Life Insurance Company
People's United Bank Campaign: "Doors - Business"
Perdue Farms Creative, Social Media, Strategic Communications
Proximo Spirits, Inc. 1800 Tequila, Campaign: "Enough Said", Campaign: "Full Moon", Campaign: "Them Boots", Campaign: "Werewolves of London", Three Olives Vodka
Republic Wireless Campaign: "Just a Fact", Creative, Digital, Integrated Marketing, Media
Romano's Macaroni Grill Campaign: "Menu", Campaign: "The Connoisseur"
Sam's Club
Samsung Campaign: "Slurp", Campaign: "The Wonder of Samsung"
Sharkies
New-Shutterfly
New-TD Ameritrade Holding Corporation
New-Three Olives
Unilever Campaign: "Baby Talk", Campaign: "The Best Ice Cream Bar Ever Conceived", Campaign: "The Good Listener", Kandy Bars, Klondike, Vaseline
Welch's International "Just Hangin", Campaign: "Pass the Glass", Digital, Grapes, Social, TV

VIA MARKETING, INC.
2646 W Lincoln Hwy, Merrillville, IN 46410
Tel.: (219) 769-2299
Fax: (219) 756-9505
Toll Free: (888) 842-6275
E-Mail: friends@viamarketing.net
Web Site: www.viamarketing.net

Employees: 7
Year Founded: 1987

Agency Specializes In: Brand Development & Integration, Business Publications, Business-To-Business, Communications, Consulting, Event Planning & Marketing, Graphic Design, Health Care Services, Local Marketing, Logo & Package Design, Medical Products, Planning & Consultation, Public Relations, Publicity/Promotions, Strategic Planning/Research, Transportation

Julie Olthoff *(Owner & Pres)*
Ryan Thiele *(Dir-Creative)*
Diane Chant *(Mgr-Fin)*

Carlo Labriola *(Sr Graphic Designer)*

Accounts:
LiteracyPro
Powersource Transportation
School Town of Munster
Vanco
Webb Ford

VIA MEDIA

780 Sutter St, San Francisco, CA 94109
Tel.: (415) 552-8040
Fax: (415) 869-3700
Web Site: www.viamedia.net

Agency Specializes In: Advertising, Collateral, Internet/Web Design, Logo & Package Design, Package Design, Public Relations

Kim Norris *(COO)*
Robert Sokol *(Dir-Creative)*
Ron Willis *(Dir-Ops)*

Accounts:
Belo Cipriano
Linda Purl
Sabena Suri

VIAMARK ADVERTISING

233 Middle St Ste 212, New Bern, NC 28560
Tel.: (252) 636-1888
Web Site: www.viamark.com

Agency Specializes In: Advertising, Digital/Interactive, Internet/Web Design, Media Buying Services, Media Planning, Print, Radio, Search Engine Optimization, Social Media, T.V.

Mark Storie *(Pres & Reg Dir-Southeast)*
Glenn Anderson *(VP & Reg Dir-Northeast)*
Jennifer Kingman *(Dir-Digital)*
Lori McIlwain *(Dir-Client Svcs)*
Victoria Pierce *(Dir-Media Svcs)*
Gigi Murphy *(Office Mgr)*

Accounts:
Mill Stores Furniture

VIAS LATINO MARKETING

4322 Stratton Blvd SE, Grand Rapids, MI 49512
Tel.: (616) 920-0878
Web Site: www.vias.us

Year Founded: 2013

Agency Specializes In: Advertising, Bilingual Market, Brand Development & Integration, Broadcast, Consulting, Content, Cosmetics, Education, Financial, Government/Political, Graphic Design, Guerilla Marketing, Health Care Services, Hispanic Market, Local Marketing, Magazines, Market Research, Media Buying Services, Media Planning, Multicultural, Newspaper, Newspapers & Magazines, Out-of-Home Media, Outdoor, Planning & Consultation, Print, Promotions, Radio, Regional, Social Marketing/Nonprofit, Strategic Planning/Research, Travel & Tourism

Gonzalo Ramirez *(Mng Partner)*
Jonathan Barrera-Mikulich *(Dir-Brand Strategies)*

Accounts:
New-YMCA Healthy Eating; 2015

VIBES MEDIA

300 W Adams St 7th Fl, Chicago, IL 60606-5101
Tel.: (312) 753-6330
Fax: (312) 753-6332
E-Mail: contact@vibes.com
Web Site: www.vibes.com

Employees: 75
Year Founded: 1998

Agency Specializes In: Advertising, Children's Market, Electronic Media, Electronics, New Technologies, Teen Market

Revenue: $7,000,000

Jack Philbin *(Co-Founder, Pres & CEO)*
Charley Cassell *(CFO)*
Tania Tawil *(VP-Bus Dev & Client Svc)*
Jeremy Agulnek *(Grp Dir-Sls)*
Mark Hupe *(Grp Dir-Sls)*
Rebecca Grimes *(Sr Dir-Sls Solutions & Strategy)*
Joel Powell *(Acct Dir)*
Mara Miller *(Sr Acct Mgr-East Reg)*

Accounts:
Pittsburgh Penguins

VIBRANT CREATIVE

293 Chestnut St, Oneonta, NY 13820
Tel.: (607) 433-8837
Fax: (607) 433-2384
Web Site: www.vibrantcompany.com

Year Founded: 2002

Agency Specializes In: Advertising, Brand Development & Integration, Collateral, Internet/Web Design, Logo & Package Design, Media Training, Print, Search Engine Optimization, Social Media

Teresa Delaurentiis *(Dir-Client Rels)*
Lucy Bayly *(Copywriter)*
Leah McDonald *(Designer)*

Accounts:
Cooperstown All-Star Village
Unalam

VIBRANT MEDIA

565 5th Ave 15th Fl, New York, NY 10017
Tel.: (646) 312-6100
Fax: (212) 867-4925
Web Site: www.vibrantmedia.com

Employees: 120

Agency Specializes In: Advertising Specialties, Digital/Interactive, E-Commerce, Internet/Web Design, Web (Banner Ads, Pop-ups, etc.)

Ariff Quli *(Pres-Americas)*
Ray Berry *(Sr VP-Fin)*
Donna Estreicher *(VP-HR)*
Alixandra Liner *(VP-US Ad Ops)*
Helen Mussard *(VP-Mktg-Global)*
Chris Davis *(Acct Dir-Direct & Programmatic)*
James Ranson *(Dir-Comml-UK & Intl)*
Mark Whistler *(Dir-Programmatic)*
Colbey Kennedy *(Acct Mgr-Publr Solutions)*
Lindsay Gurciullo *(Mgr-Sls)*
Alana Tabacco *(Mgr-Mktg-US)*
Allison Vatz *(Mgr-Sls)*
Michael Neal *(Specialist-Client Svcs-Post-Sale)*
Sara Stasinos *(Acct Exec)*

Accounts:
Adidas
Coke
Corel
HP
IBM
Intel
Microsoft
Nintendo
Nissan
Sky
Sony
Toyota
Unilever
Universal Pictures

Branches

Vibrant Media Ltd.

7th Floor, 140 Aldersgate Street, London, EC1A 4HY United Kingdom
Tel.: (44) 207 239 0120
Fax: (44) 201 239 9396
E-Mail: bduk@vibrantmedia.com
Web Site: www.vibrantmedia.com

Employees: 50

Frances Day *(Acct Dir-UK)*
Adrian Degutis *(Acct Dir)*
David McConachie *(Dir-UK Publisher Solutions)*
Sebastian Collorafi *(Sr Mgr-Publr Network)*
Krishan Swami *(Sr Acct Mgr-Intl)*
Calum Hopkins *(Acct Mgr)*
Ryan Kelly *(Acct Mgr-Intl)*
James Phillips *(Acct Mgr-Sls)*
Laura Carter *(Sr Acct Exec-Intl)*
Harpreet Kallah *(Sr Acct Exec-Intl)*
Samantha Stennett *(Acct Exec)*
Alex Triggs *(Acct Exec)*

Accounts:
H. J. Heniz

VICTORS & SPOILS

(Acquired by Havas)

VICTORS & SPOILS

1904 Pearl St, Boulder, CO 80302
Tel.: (720) 305-9822
E-Mail: howdy@victorsandspoils.com
Web Site: www.victorsandspoils.com

Employees: 17
Year Founded: 2009

Agency Specializes In: Sponsorship

John Winsor *(CEO)*
Andy Nathan *(CMO)*
Mandy Eckford *(Acct Dir-Consulting)*
Rachel Arther *(Acct Mgr)*
Summer Borowski *(Acct Mgr)*
Jen Miller *(Acct Mgr)*
Michael Dusman *(Acct Supvr)*

Accounts:
Adidas
American Express
Bank Midwest Campaign: "Answering The Phone", Campaign: "Knowing Your Name", Campaign: "Listening"
Coca-Cola Refreshments USA, Inc. Campaign: "Smile Back"
Converse
DISH Network Corporation
Driscoll's
General Mills
Harley Davidson
LivingSocial
Mercedes Benz
Nike
Partnership for a Healthier America Campaign: "FNV", Digital, Outdoor, Print
Unilever
Virgin America

VICTORY HEALTHCARE COMMUNICATIONS

(Formerly Victory Marketing Group)

678 US Hwy 202 Ste 5, Bridgewater, NJ 08807
Tel.: (908) 722-6800
Fax: (908) 252-9042
E-Mail: contact@victorymarketinggroup.com
Web Site: www.victoryhcc.com

Agency Specializes In: Advertising, Corporate Identity, Digital/Interactive, E-Commerce, Email, Internet/Web Design, Logo & Package Design, Point of Sale, Production, Web (Banner Ads, Pop-ups, etc.)

Vincent Mattaliano *(Pres)*
Christopher Foley *(Dir-Bus Dev)*
Aimee Leary *(Dir-Creative)*

Accounts:
Allstate Insurance Services
AT&T Communications Corp.
The Barberi Group
Basking Ridge Country Club
Beacon Medical Real Estate
Canery
Chelsea
Coffee & Roasters
Concrete Works
Equilibrium
Exelon Nuclear Energy Electricity Services
Johnson & Johnson Health Care Products Mfr

VIEO DESIGN, LLC

2575 Willow Point Way Ste 203, Knoxville, TN 37931
Tel.: (865) 381-2231
E-Mail: info@vieodesign.com
Web Site: www.vieodesign.com

Year Founded: 2008

Agency Specializes In: Advertising, Digital/Interactive, Internet/Web Design, Outdoor, Print

Rob Spurlock *(Founder & Principal)*
Mac Bartine *(COO & Principal)*
Holly Yalove *(CMO & Principal)*
John Goethert *(Project Mgr-Inbound Mktg)*
Tim Lott *(Mgr-Sls & Mktg)*
Maria Talley *(Mgr-Internet Mktg)*
Emily Winsauer *(Mgr-Content Mktg)*
Paul Gibson *(Founder Principal & Designer)*

Accounts:
AAF Knoxville
Apple Health & Wellness
Ballantyne Brands LLC
Elle Boutique
Influence At Work
Manning Windows
NEO E-Cigarettes
Rogers Family Dental

VIETTI MARKETING GROUP

1722 S Glenstone St Ste PP, Springfield, MO 65804
Tel.: (417) 368-4646
E-Mail: info@viettimarketing.com
Web Site: www.viettimarketing.com

Year Founded: 2010

Agency Specializes In: Advertising, Content, Digital/Interactive, Graphic Design, Internet/Web Design, Media Buying Services, Media Planning, Print, T.V.

Tammy Vietti *(Pres)*
Kevin Grinder *(COO)*
Andrew Bozarth *(Chief Strategy Officer)*
Jackie Grinder *(Dir-Acctg)*

Accounts:
Discovery Center
Liberty Home Solutions LLC
MSI Constructors
Mothers Brewing Company
Restaurant Creative

VIEWPOINT CREATIVE

55 Chapel St, Newton, MA 02458-1060
Tel.: (617) 597-6667
Fax: (781) 449-7272
E-Mail: info@viewpointcreative.com
Web Site: www.viewpointcreative.com

Employees: 35

Agency Specializes In: Advertising, Brand Development & Integration, Collateral, Consumer Marketing, Entertainment, Event Planning & Marketing, Exhibit/Trade Shows, Identity Marketing, In-Store Advertising, Internet/Web Design, Mobile Marketing, Out-of-Home Media, Package Design, Print, Promotions, Strategic Planning/Research, T.V.

Lisa Dibella *(Controller)*
Jon Anderson *(Editor-Creative)*
Don Days *(Editor-Creative)*
Jonny Ouellette *(Sr Dir-Art)*
Jon Busch *(Dir-Creative)*
Erik Quenzel *(Dir-Engrg)*
Dawn Morton *(Mgr-Ops)*
Michael Barrett *(Sr Designer)*
Matt Barretto *(Designer)*

Accounts:
ABC
Bose
CBS
Cinemax
Discovery Networks
Disney
Duracell
ESPN
Fox Sports
Gillette
Global Post
Hallmark Channel
Hasbro
HBO 'Year-End' Image Spot
HGTV
Mattel
National Geographic Channel
Redbox
Reebok
Staples
Viewpoint Lifestyle

VILLING & COMPANY, INC.

5909 Nimtz Pkwy, South Bend, IN 46628
Tel.: (574) 277-0215
Fax: (574) 277-5513
E-Mail: mailbox@villing.com
Web Site: www.villing.com

E-Mail for Key Personnel:
President: thom@villing.com
Creative Dir.: kelli@villing.com
Media Dir.: sara@villing.com
Production Mgr.: diane@villing.com
Public Relations: jeannine@villing.com

Employees: 14
Year Founded: 1982

National Agency Associations: IAN

Agency Specializes In: Brand Development & Integration, Health Care Services, Public Relations, Sports Market, Transportation

Breakdown of Gross Billings by Media: Bus. Publs.: 5%; Collateral: 15%; Consulting: 5%; Consumer Publs.: 3%; D.M.: 3%; Fees: 10%; Mags.: 2%; Newsp.: 5%; Outdoor: 2%; Production: 10%; Pub. Rels.: 20%; Radio & T.V.: 10%; Worldwide Web Sites: 10%

Thomas A. Villing *(Co-Founder & Pres)*
Brad Rosier *(Dir-Art & Specialist-Motion Design)*
Nathan DeSelm *(Dir-Interactive Comm & Tech)*
Ellen Imbur *(Dir-Art)*
Jeff Middaugh *(Dir-Creative)*
Lori Headley *(Acct Exec)*

Accounts:
AM General; South Bend, IN; 1998
Carleton, Inc.; South Bend, IN
CKF Indiana
Covering Kids & Families of Indiana; South Bend, IN
Insight Business Solutions; Goshen, IN Accountants; 1992
McDonald's Restaurants
Notre Dame Federal Credit Union; 2000
Oaklawn Psychiatric Center, Inc.; Goshen, IN
Order of Malta
Ronald McDonald House Charities; South Bend, IN
South Bend Civic Theatre
South Bend Regional Sports Commission; South Bend, IN
Studebaker National Museum
WNIT-TV

VILOCITY INTERACTIVE, INC.

9927 E Bell Rd Ste 140, Scottsdale, AZ 85260
Tel.: (480) 584-5700
Fax: (480) 584-5701
E-Mail: info@vilocity.com
Web Site: www.vilocity.com

Employees: 16
Year Founded: 1998

Agency Specializes In: Advertising, Affiliate Marketing, Brand Development & Integration, Business-To-Business, Consumer Marketing, Corporate Identity, E-Commerce, Exhibit/Trade Shows, Graphic Design, Internet/Web Design, Media Planning, Public Relations, Publicity/Promotions, Social Marketing/Nonprofit, Social Media, Travel & Tourism, Viral/Buzz/Word of Mouth

Approx. Annual Billings: $2,500,000

Breakdown of Gross Billings by Media: Bus. Publs.: $200,000; Exhibits/Trade Shows: $200,000; Internet Adv.: $600,000; Newsp. & Mags.: $800,000; Pub. Rels.: $300,000; Worldwide Web Sites: $400,000

Jennifer Smith *(Owner)*
Ronald Mileti *(Pres & Dir-Creative)*
Shawn Hardy *(Office Mgr & Acctg Mgr)*
Carissa Sudjono *(Jr Graphic Designer)*

Accounts:
Emergen-C; CA Emergen-C; 2009
Gila River Casinos Hotel & Casinos; 2010
Hoover Dirt Devil; OH Hoover Dirt Devil; 2008
Little Kids Toys; Providence, RI Bubble Toys; 1999
National Coil Coating Association; Cleveland, OH Coil Coated Metal; 2004
ReNew Life Natural Supplements; 2011

THE VIMARC GROUP

1205 E Washington St Ste 120, Louisville, KY 40206
Tel.: (502) 261-9100
Fax: (502) 261-9105
E-Mail: whatworks@vimarc.com
Web Site: www.vimarc.com

Employees: 30

Agency Specializes In: Advertising, Broadcast, Collateral, Crisis Communications, Digital/Interactive, Email, Event Planning & Marketing, Graphic Design, Internet/Web Design, Local Marketing, Media Planning, Media Relations, Print, Product Placement, Production, Public Relations, Sponsorship, Strategic Planning/Research

Richmond Simpson *(Pres)*
Joe Koetter *(CEO)*
Jason Lee *(Exec Dir-Creative)*
Margie Mueller *(Exec Dir-Media)*
Charlotte Browning *(Acct Exec)*
Laura Cates *(Media Planner & Media Buyer)*
Donna Seale *(Sr Media Planner & Media Buyer)*

Accounts:
Collins Ford
Elder Health
McKendree College
Metro United Way
Sprint
The Summit

VIMBY
16333 Raymer St Ste B, Van Nuys, CA 91406
Tel.: (818) 981-1945
Fax: (818) 975-9494
E-Mail: vimby@vimby.com
Web Site: www.vimby.com

Year Founded: 2006

Agency Specializes In: Advertising, Branded Entertainment, Content, T.V.

Dean Waters *(CEO)*
David Goffin *(Partner & Chief Creative Officer)*
Eddie Van Pelt *(CFO & COO)*
Adam Reno *(Head-Production)*
Michelle Willrich *(Dir & Producer)*
Dan Perry *(Copywriter & Producer)*
Allison Drye *(Mgr-Production)*

Accounts:
General Mills
Hyundai
Walmart

VINE COMMUNICATIONS INC
1200 Anastasia Ave Ste 240, Coral Gables, FL 33134
Tel.: (305) 447-8678
Fax: (305) 447-8670
E-Mail: info@vinecommunicationsinc.com
Web Site: www.vinecommunicationsinc.com

Year Founded: 2006

Agency Specializes In: Event Planning & Marketing, Graphic Design, Internet/Web Design, Media Relations, Media Training, New Product Development

Nikki Konefsky Deas *(Founder & Partner)*
Adriana Sol *(Partner)*
Tiffany Townsend *(Partner)*
Andre Sala *(Head-Content Strategy)*
Will Candis *(Dir-Media)*
Christine Siervo *(Sr Acct Exec)*
Alyssa Perez *(Acct Exec)*
Stephanie Romanach *(Acct Exec)*

Accounts:
The Commonwealth Institute
Dominican University of California
GlobalPro Recovery
New-La Cita de las Americas (North America Public Relations Agency of Record) Media
Leica Store Miami
Miami New Construction Show
National Marine Manufacturers Association 75th Progressive Insurance Miami International Boat Show (PR Agency of Record)
Palmcorp Development Group

VIP MARKETING & ADVERTISING
8761 Dorchester Rd Ste 210, North Charleston, SC 29420
Tel.: (843) 760-0707
Fax: (843) 760-0032
E-Mail: info@veryimportantplacement.com
Web Site: www.veryimportantplacement.com

Agency Specializes In: Advertising, Brand Development & Integration, Social Media

Chris Freeman *(Dir-Creative)*

Accounts:
Delta Pharmacy
Seasons of Japan

VIRGEN ADVERTISING, CORP.
(d/b/a Media Mavens)
(Private-Parent-Single Location)
151 E Warm Springs Rd, Las Vegas, NV 89119
Tel.: (702) 616-0624
Fax: (702) 616-0644
E-Mail: info@virgenad.com
Web Site: www.virgenad.com

Employees: 35
Year Founded: 1999

Agency Specializes In: Advertising, Crisis Communications, Media Relations, Media Training, Promotions, Public Relations, Social Media

Revenue: $8,900,000

Merrell Virgen *(Pres)*
Madeleine Weekley *(Exec VP)*
Maurella Bell *(VP-Comm & Analyst-Res)*
Nicole boland *(Creative Dir)*
Nicole Boland *(Dir-Creative)*
Michelle Howell *(Dir-PR & Social Media)*

Accounts:
Fremont Street Experience

VIRILION
(Acquired by & Name Changed to RepEquity)

VIRTUAL FARM CREATIVE INC.
31 A Ridge Rd Ste 1, Phoenixville, PA 19460
Tel.: (610) 917-3131
Fax: (610) 917-3292
Toll Free: (877) GROWART
E-Mail: ideas@virtualfarm.com
Web Site: www.virtualfarm.com

Employees: 22

Agency Specializes In: Advertising, Advertising Specialties, Brand Development & Integration, Business-To-Business, Collateral, Commercial Photography, Communications, Consulting, Consumer Marketing, Corporate Identity, Direct Response Marketing, E-Commerce, Exhibit/Trade Shows, Gay & Lesbian Market, Graphic Design, Internet/Web Design, Logo & Package Design, Multimedia, New Product Development, Outdoor, Point of Purchase, Print, Public Relations, Publicity/Promotions, Strategic Planning/Research, Technical Advertising, Teen Market

Todd Palmer *(Pres & Dir-Creative)*
Darren Price *(Dir-Art)*

Accounts:
Budget Maintenance; Pottstown, PA Commercial Corporate Cleaning; 2002
Catskill Farms; Sullivan County, NY Farm House Restoration & Sales; 2004
Express Data Systems; Pottstown, PA Payroll Processing; 2003
Green Valleys Association; Pottstown, PA Environmental Advocacy Organization; 2000
Raymond C. Rumpf & Son; Sellersville, PA Fly Fishing Products; 2002
Riddell Lacrosse; Newark, NJ Lacrosse Helmets; 2004
Sly Fox Brewery & Restaurant; Phoenixville, PA Microbrewery & Restaurant; 2004

VISION CREATIVE GROUP, INC.
16 Wing Dr, Cedar Knolls, NJ 07927
Tel.: (973) 984-3454
Fax: (973) 984-3314
E-Mail: ab@visioncreativegroup.com
Web Site: www.visioncreativegroup.com

Employees: 45
Year Founded: 1987

Agency Specializes In: Advertising, Automotive, Broadcast, Business-To-Business, Cable T.V., Catalogs, Collateral, Commercial Photography, Consumer Goods, Consumer Marketing, Consumer Publications, Corporate Communications, Corporate Identity, Custom Publishing, Digital/Interactive, Direct Response Marketing, Direct-to-Consumer, E-Commerce, Electronic Media, Electronics, Email, Exhibit/Trade Shows, Financial, Graphic Design, Health Care Services, Household Goods, In-Store Advertising, Internet/Web Design, Logo & Package Design, Market Research, Media Buying Services, Media Planning, New Product Development, Newspapers & Magazines, Out-of-Home Media, Outdoor, Package Design, Pharmaceutical, Point of Purchase, Point of Sale, Print, Production, Production (Ad, Film, Broadcast), Production (Print), Promotions, Radio, Sales Promotion, Sponsorship, Sweepstakes, T.V., Trade & Consumer Magazines, Web (Banner Ads, Pop-ups, etc.)

Approx. Annual Billings: $12,000,000

Breakdown of Gross Billings by Media: Brdcst.: 3%; Exhibits/Trade Shows: 4%; Graphic Design: 20%; In-Store Adv.: 6%; Internet Adv.: 8%; Logo & Package Design: 14%; Newsp. & Mags.: 21%; Out-of-Home Media: 10%; Point of Purchase: 8%; Worldwide Web Sites: 6%

Sharon Petry *(Exec VP)*
Lori Thompson *(VP & Acct Supvr)*
Jennifer Persson *(Acct Dir-Adv)*
Jessica Adler *(Dir-Art)*
James Bonifacio *(Dir-Art)*
Jennifer Greenfield *(Dir-Art & Creative)*
Michael Mazewski *(Dir-Creative)*
Larry Price *(Dir-Creative)*
Heather Tchir *(Dir-Art)*
Angela Horr *(Acct Exec)*
Julie Mott *(Sr Designer)*
Michelle Zuretti *(Sr Graphic Designer)*

VISION MEDIA & MARKETING LLC
2310 Superior Ave E Ste 2501, Cleveland, OH 44114
Tel.: (440) 864-8774
E-Mail: don@visionmediaandmarketing.com
Web Site: www.visionmediaandmarketing.com

Employees: 4
Year Founded: 2008

Agency Specializes In: Advertising, Advertising Specialties, Branded Entertainment, Broadcast,

Cable T.V., Commercial Photography, Graphic Design, Regional, T.V., Teen Market, Web (Banner Ads, Pop-ups, etc.)

Revenue: $200,000

Alex Adzioski *(Acct Exec)*

Accounts:
Antonio's Pizza; Parma, OH Pasta; 2008

VISION7INTERNATIONAL
300 St Paul Street Ste 300, Quebec, QC G1K 7R1 Canada
Tel.: (418) 647-2727
E-Mail: information@v7international.com
Web Site: www.vision7international.com/en/

Employees: 1,200

Brett Marchand *(Pres & CEO)*
Martin Faucher *(CFO & Exec VP)*
Francis Trudeau *(VP-Acq & Treasury)*
Martin Belanger *(Dir-Fin & Admin)*
Claude Lessard *(Exec Chm)*

Branches

Cossette Inc.
300 St Paul Street 3rd Floor, Quebec, QC G1K 7R1 Canada
(See Separate Listing)

Dare
101 New Cavendish St, London, W1W 6XH United Kingdom
(See Separate Listing)

THE VISIONAIRE GROUP
(Name Changed to TVGla)

VISIONMARK COMMUNICATIONS
6115 Falls Rd Ste 100, Baltimore, MD 21209
Tel.: (410) 377-3135
Fax: (410) 377-3138
Web Site: www.visionmarkusa.com

Year Founded: 1995

Agency Specializes In: Advertising, Brand Development & Integration, Content, Exhibit/Trade Shows, Package Design, Print, Social Media, Web (Banner Ads, Pop-ups, etc.)

Mary Ann Bauer *(Partner & Dir-Creative Design)*
Ralph Ringler *(Partner)*
Rick Bowman *(Sr Designer)*

Accounts:
100 Light Street
BlueRidge Bank

VISIONS ADVERTISING MEDIA, LLC
426 Shore Rd Ste B, Atlantic City, NJ 08401
Tel.: (609) 926-6358
Fax: (609) 926-6358
E-Mail: visions@visionsadv.com
Web Site: www.visionsadv.com

Employees: 6
Year Founded: 2002

National Agency Associations: OAAA

Agency Specializes In: Advertising, Alternative Advertising, Collateral, Consulting, Electronic Media, Graphic Design, Media Buying Services, Out-of-Home Media, Outdoor, Production (Print)

Approx. Annual Billings: $1,000,000

Breakdown of Gross Billings by Media: Out-of-Home Media: 50%; Outdoor: 50%

William D. Ade *(Owner & Mng Partner)*

Accounts:
AT&T Mobility LLC; 2006
Beaches/Sandals; Holland, PA Travel; 2007
Bernie Robbins Jewelers; NJ Sales
Borgata Casino & Spa; Atlantic City, NJ Casino Gaming; 2003
Cash for Gold; Cherry Hill, NJ Jeweler; 2009
Charlestown Gaming; West Virginia; 2010
Convention Shows Entertainment; 2004
Coors Light; Monmouth, NJ; 2009
DeSimone Auto; Mount Laurel, NJ Automotive Services; 2008
Dr. Pepper/Snapple; Wildwood, NJ Beverages; 2009
E.I. DuPont; Atlantic City, NJ Health Care; 2005
Harrah's Casinos; Atlantic City, NJ Gaming; 2002
House of Blues; Atlantic City, NJ Entertainment; 2005
PNC Bank; New York, NY; 2010
Showboat Casino; Atlantic City, NJ Gaming; 2004
Six Flags Entertainment Corp.; Monmouth, NJ Theme Park; 2009
Sonic; NJ New Products/Locations
Trump Casinos; Atlantic City, NJ Entertainment, Gaming; 2003
United Way; Atlantic City, NJ Health Care; 2006
University of Sciences; Philadelphia, PA Recruitment; 2007

VISUAL PRINT GROUP & DESIGN
1474 Battlefield Pkwy Ste I-9, Fort Oglethorpe, GA 30742
Tel.: (706) 956-8748
Fax: (706) 956-8759
E-Mail: nathan@visualprintgroup.com
Web Site: www.visualprintgroup.com

Employees: 7

Agency Specializes In: Business-To-Business, E-Commerce, Graphic Design, In-Store Advertising, Industrial, Internet/Web Design, Logo & Package Design, Magazines, Media Buying Services, Media Planning, Out-of-Home Media, Outdoor, Point of Purchase, Point of Sale, Print, Production (Print), Retail

Approx. Annual Billings: $1,500,000

Nathan Smith *(Pres)*
Todd Bradshaw *(Dir-Mktg)*
Michael Maddox *(Dir-Creative)*
Sam Gibson *(Acct Mgr)*

VISUALMAX
630 9th Ave Ste 414, New York, NY 10036
Tel.: (212) 925-2938
E-Mail: feedback@visualmax.com
Web Site: www.visualmax.com

Employees: 10
Year Founded: 2001

Agency Specializes In: Advertising, Alternative Advertising, Co-op Advertising, Communications, Consulting, Digital/Interactive, E-Commerce, Electronic Media, Experience Design, Information Technology, Internet/Web Design, Media Buying Services, Mobile Marketing, Multimedia, Pharmaceutical, Search Engine Optimization, Sweepstakes, Web (Banner Ads, Pop-ups, etc.)

Steve McBride *(Owner & Mng Partner)*
Kate Payne *(Sr Acct Mgr & Producer)*
Allison Brown *(Dir-Client Svcs)*
Peter Sebastian Featherly-Bean *(Acct Mgr)*

Accounts:
New-Allstate
New-Choice Hotels
New-Duracell
New-Fiat500X
New-Grand Marnier
New-Ice Breakers Cool Blasts
Microsoft
New-Panera Bread
New-Toyota
New-Yelp

VITAL & RYZE
(Name Changed to Eisenberg, Vital & Ryze Advertising)

VITALINK
10809 Cokesbury Ln, Raleigh, NC 27614
Tel.: (919) 850-0605
Fax: (919) 850-0678
E-Mail: info@vitalinkweb.com
Web Site: www.vitalinkweb.com

Agency Specializes In: Advertising, Brand Development & Integration, Digital/Interactive, Internet/Web Design, Logo & Package Design, Media Buying Services, Outdoor, Print, Public Relations, Radio

Jeanne Frazer *(Pres)*
Michael Steele *(Creative Dir)*
Mary Ann Grooms *(Dir-Project)*

Accounts:
Brinkley Walser Stoner
Lori Corken & Company

VITAMIN
3237 Eastern Ave, Baltimore, MD 21224
Tel.: (410) 732-6542
Fax: (410) 732-6541
E-Mail: info@vitaminisgood.com
Web Site: vitaminisgood.com

Employees: 5

Agency Specializes In: Advertising, Advertising Specialties, Brand Development & Integration, Business Publications, Business-To-Business, Children's Market, Co-op Advertising, Collateral, Communications, Consulting, Consumer Marketing, Consumer Publications, Corporate Communications, Corporate Identity, Digital/Interactive, Direct Response Marketing, E-Commerce, Education, Electronic Media, Engineering, Entertainment, Environmental, Event Planning & Marketing, Exhibit/Trade Shows, Financial, Food Service, Graphic Design, Health Care Services, High Technology, In-Store Advertising, Information Technology, Internet/Web Design, Leisure, Local Marketing, Logo & Package Design, Magazines, Media Buying Services, Medical Products, New Product Development, Newspaper, Out-of-Home Media, Outdoor, Over-50 Market, Pharmaceutical, Planning & Consultation, Point of Purchase, Point of Sale, Print, Public Relations, Publicity/Promotions, Radio, Real Estate, Recruitment, Restaurant, Retail, Sales Promotion, Seniors' Market, Sports Market, Strategic Planning/Research, Technical Advertising, Teen Market, Trade & Consumer Magazines, Travel & Tourism

Amanda M. Karfakis *(Pres & CEO)*
Michael Karfakis *(COO)*
Doug Hucker *(Dir-Art)*
Nikki Bracy *(Sr Acct Exec)*
Amanda Guagliardo *(Acct Coord)*

Accounts:
1st Mariner Arena
Air Plus International
The Belvedere Restaurant Group 13th Floor, Brand Messaging, Marketing Communications, Media Relations, Print, Website
CBS Radio Network/Infinity Broadcasting
Central Scholarship; Baltimore, MD Brand Messaging, Media Relations, Mission Statement, New Logo, Press, Website
Critical Connection; Gaithersburg, MD Medical, Biomedical & Bioscientific Search Firm; 2006
Discovery Communications
Discovery Education
Discovery International
Ellin & Tucker General Public Relations Counsel, Media, Public Relations Agency of Record, Speakers' Bureau Programming
Garrison & Sisson; Washington, DC Attorney Search Firm; 2006
Gateway School
Gill-Simpson Inc.; Baltimore, MD
Hamilton Bank Brand Messaging, Identity Redesign, Marketing Collateral, Media Relations, Signage, Social Media Strategy, Web Site
Hammond Wilson Architects Brand Messaging, Identity Collateral, Logo, Rebranding, Website
Hardesty & Hanover
The Hearing & Speech Agency
The Hearing & Speech Agency Vibe 07
Heery International
Heffron Company
Hord Coplan Macht
IZI Medical Products (Agency of Record) Brand & Key Product Awareness, Medical Device Accessories, Public Relations
J.E. Harms & Associates
Kids 1, Inc.
King Gimp
KLNB Retail
NAI KLNB Management
NAIOP
NIKA Architects + Engineers
Owl Bar
RMF Engineering (Agency of Record) Communications Strategy, Digital, Marketing, Media Relations, Media Training, Messaging, Public Relations, Website
Saint Agnes Hospital (Agency of Record) Design, Digital Marketing, Media Relations, Public Relations
SmartCEO Magazines
Spartan Surfaces Logo Redesign, Rebranding, Stationery, Website
Strudwick Wealth Strategies
Universal Air Travel Plan
Wall Street Institute

VITAMIN PICTURES

232 E Ohio St 3rd Fl, Chicago, IL 60611
Tel.: (312) 664-6683
Fax: (312) 664-6977
E-Mail: jobs@vitaminpictures.tv
Web Site: www.vitaminpictures.tv

Agency Specializes In: Advertising, Graphic Design, Media Relations, Production (Ad, Film, Broadcast)

Danny DelPurgatorio *(Dir-Creative)*
Tim Sepulveda *(Dir-Technical)*
Sam Gierasimczuk *(Assoc Dir-Creative)*

Accounts:
Nike Footwear Mfr

VITRO

2305 Historic Decatur Rd Ste 205, San Diego, CA 92106
Tel.: (619) 234-0408
Fax: (619) 234-4015
Web Site: www.vitroagency.com

Employees: 75
Year Founded: 1992

National Agency Associations: AMA

Agency Specializes In: Advertising, Affluent Market, Below-the-Line, Brand Development & Integration, Branded Entertainment, Broadcast, Business-To-Business, Children's Market, Collateral, Computers & Software, Consumer Marketing, Consumer Publications, Corporate Identity, Email, Entertainment, Event Planning & Marketing, Exhibit/Trade Shows, Experience Design, Food Service, Graphic Design, Health Care Services, High Technology, In-Store Advertising, Information Technology, Integrated Marketing, Internet/Web Design, Leisure, Local Marketing, Magazines, Marine, Media Planning, Medical Products, Merchandising, New Product Development, Out-of-Home Media, Outdoor, Package Design, Point of Purchase, Point of Sale, Print, Product Placement, Production (Print), Promotions, Publishing, Radio, Real Estate, Restaurant, Retail, Sales Promotion, Social Media, Sponsorship, Sports Market, Strategic Planning/Research, T.V., Viral/Buzz/Word of Mouth

Approx. Annual Billings: $68,000,000

John Vitro *(Partner & Chm-Creative)*
Tom Sullivan *(Principal)*
Glenn Maddocks *(Grp Dir & Dir-Strategy)*
Paul Lambert *(Sr Dir-Art)*
Elliott Allen *(Dir-Creative)*
Michael Berberick *(Dir-Production)*
Ryan Smith *(Dir-Art)*
Jeremy Stabile *(Dir-Creative)*
Jennifer Curless *(Strategist-Comm)*
Dharti Jadav *(Strategist-Comm)*

Accounts:
Alaska Communications Systems Group, Inc. (Agency of Record)
ASICS Campaign: "Nothing but Next", Campaign: "Colors that Run", Campaign: "Levitation Test", Campaign: "The Next Epic Challenge", Campaign: "We Are Marathoners", Campaign: "What's Next?", Creative, GEL-Kayano 19, Performance Athletic Shoes & Apparel; 1996
Budweiser Budweiser.com, Redesign
Bushnell; Overland, KS Eyewear: Bolle, Serengeti; 2006
Elevate Creative
Heineken Campaign: "Goon"
Petco Campaign: "The Power of Together", Creative
P.F.Chang's; Scottsdale, AZ Restaurants; 2007
Red Robin Gourmet Burgers (Agency of Record) Creative, Media Planning
Taylor Guitars Campaign: "Step Forward. Music is Waiting"
Toyo Tire & Rubber Co., Ltd. Creative, Media Planning & Buying
Toyo Tire (U.S.A.) Corporation
Wild Turkey (Agency of Record) Campaign: "#Nevertamed", Creative

Branch

Vitro NY

(Formerly Skinny)
160 Varick St, New York, NY 10013
Tel.: (212) 561-6005
E-Mail: info@vitroagency.com
Web Site: vitroagency.com

Employees: 25
Year Founded: 2008

Agency Specializes In: Above-the-Line, Advertising, Affluent Market, Alternative Advertising, Automotive, Below-the-Line, Brand Development & Integration, Branded Entertainment, Broadcast, Cable T.V., Communications, Consulting, Consumer Goods, Consumer Marketing, Content, Direct-to-Consumer, Entertainment, Environmental, Experience Design, Fashion/Apparel, Graphic Design, Guerilla Marketing, Household Goods, In-Store Advertising, Integrated Marketing, Internet/Web Design, Luxury Products, Men's Market, Mobile Marketing, Multimedia, New Product Development, New Technologies, Newspaper, Out-of-Home Media, Outdoor, Over-50 Market, Planning & Consultation, Point of Purchase, Point of Sale, Product Placement, Social Marketing/Nonprofit, Social Media, Strategic Planning/Research, T.V., Teen Market, Travel & Tourism, Tween Market, Viral/Buzz/Word of Mouth, Web (Banner Ads, Pop-ups, etc.)

Jorge Ramirez *(Sr Dir-Art)*
Jeshua Stevens *(Dir-Art)*
Tegan Smith *(Acct Supvr)*
Jonathan Grayson *(Acct Exec)*
Sialoren Spaulding *(Acct Exec)*

Accounts:
Aldo Shoes Aldo Shoes for Life
ASICS America Corporation
Diageo; United States; 2010
Heineken Campaign: "Goon"
Lexus; United States CT200h; 2009
Nokia; Europe Ovi; 2008
Red Robin Gourmet Burgers, Inc.
Redbox Instant by Verizon
Vodafone; Europe Vodafone360; 2008

VITTLES

141 Santa Rosa Ave, Sausalito, CA 94965
Tel.: (415) 332-0840
Fax: (415) 332-0841
E-Mail: info@vittleinformation.com
Web Site: www.vittleinformation.com

Employees: 10

Tammy Deane *(Partner)*
Tammy Potter *(Sr Dir-Art)*

Accounts:
California Olive Committee
FreeBird Chicken
La Tortilla Factory
Raised Right Chicken
Virginia Seafood

VIVA + IMPULSE CREATIVE CO

1002 Arizona Ste 2, El Paso, TX 79902
Tel.: (915) 996-9947
Fax: (866) 854-8482
Toll Free: (866) 977-8482
E-Mail: inquiries@vivaimpulse.com
Web Site: www.vivaimpulse.com

Agency Specializes In: Advertising, Brand Development & Integration, Collateral, Digital/Interactive, Outdoor, Print, Social Media, T.V.

Armando Alcarez *(Partner & Dir-Creative)*
Brandon Silverstein *(Partner)*
Cassandra Yardeni *(Dir-Mktg)*
Farz Farrokhnia *(Acct Mgr & Mgr-Production)*
Alexander South *(Acct Mgr & Mgr-Production)*
Molly Gunn *(Mgr-Digital Mktg)*
Cam Wilde *(Designer-Visual)*

Accounts:
Plaza Classic

VIVA & CO.

99 Crown's Ln, Toronto, ON M5R 3P4 Canada
Tel.: (416) 923-6355
E-Mail: info@vivaandco.com
Web Site: www.vivaandco.com

Agency Specializes In: Advertising, Graphic Design, Media Buying Services, Package Design, Print

Todd Temporale *(Partner & Dir-Art)*
Frank Viva *(Mng Dir)*
Stuart Brown *(Dir-Art)*
Romina Tina Fontana *(Dir-Bus Affairs)*
Arron Gibson *(Dir-Digital Projects)*
Brett Ramsay *(Sr Designer)*

Accounts:
Butterfield Wines
Earth Inc.
Le Creuset

VIVA PARTNERSHIP
10800 Biscayne Blvd, Miami, FL 33137
Tel.: (305) 576-6007
Fax: (305) 590-5863
E-Mail: jba@vivamia.com
Web Site: www.vivamia.com

Employees: 25

National Agency Associations: AHAA-ICOM

Agency Specializes In: Consumer Marketing, Direct Response Marketing, Graphic Design, Strategic Planning/Research

Approx. Annual Billings: $32,000,000

Linda Lane Gonzalez *(Pres & CEO)*
Deborah Richmond *(Exec VP)*
Romina Lopez *(Acct Dir)*
Ross Vialpando *(Sr Planner/Buyer)*

Accounts:
BJ's Wholesale Club; Natick, MA; 2005
Oil Can Henry's
QVC
Sun Pass
Tire Kingdom

Branch

Viva Media
8207 Callaghan Rd Ste 200, San Antonio, TX 78230-4736
Tel.: (210) 949-1710
Fax: (210) 949-0574
E-Mail: drichmond@vivamia.com
Web Site: www.vivamia.com

Linda Lane Gonzalez *(Pres & CEO)*
Debbie Richmond *(Exec VP)*

VIVAKI
35 W Wacker Dr, Chicago, IL 60601
Tel.: (312) 220-6969
Web Site: www.vivaki.com

Year Founded: 2008

National Agency Associations: 4A's

Agency Specializes In: Advertising

Paul Darling *(CFO)*
Marco Bertozzi *(Pres-Audience On Demand EMEA & North America Client Svcs)*
Cheri Carpenter *(Exec VP & Dir-Mktg Comm)*
Tracey Scheppach *(Exec VP & Dir-Innovations)*
Matt Clemm *(VP-Client Svcs)*
Mary Ellen Debrunner *(VP-Corp Comm)*
Drew Huening *(Product Dir)*
Briana LaGrow *(Dir-Partnerships)*
Ben Lampert *(Dir-Platform Ops)*
Stephanie Mustari *(Dir-Solutions Consulting)*
Andy Debbins *(Acct Mgr-Activation-Mobile)*
Tiana Zhang *(Product Mgr)*
Mehreen Azhar *(Mgr-Platform Ops-Tech)*

Accounts:
BlackBerry
ComScore "SkySkraper Connect"
Kaizers Orchestra
The Procter & Gamble Company Olay

Branch

VivaKi
2001 The Embarcadero, San Francisco, CA 94133
Tel.: (415) 369-6300
Web Site: www.vivaki.com

Year Founded: 2008

Agency Specializes In: Advertising, Digital/Interactive

Luca Montani *(CEO)*
Dave Marsey *(Mng Dir & Exec VP)*
Michael Wiley *(Mng Dir)*
Shirley Xu-Weldon *(Sr VP-Analytics & Strategic Solutions)*
Shelby Farmer *(Client Svcs Mgr)*
Rina Nagashima *(Campaign Mgr-AOD)*

Accounts:
Ebay Inc.
Taco Bell Corp.

VIVID CANDI
22601 Pacific Coast Hwy Ste 230, Malibu, CA 90265
Tel.: (310) 456-1784
Fax: (310) 919-3026
Web Site: www.vividcandi.com

Year Founded: 2001

Agency Specializes In: Advertising, Digital/Interactive, Graphic Design, Internet/Web Design, Logo & Package Design, Media Buying Services, Package Design, Print, Social Media, T.V.

Chris Wizner *(CEO)*

Accounts:
Hosa Technology, Inc.

VIZWERKS
2240 N Interstate Ave Ste 100, Portland, OR 97227
Tel.: (503) 288-7471
Fax: (503) 288-7497
E-Mail: info@vizwerks.com
Web Site: www.vizwerks.com

Year Founded: 2000

Agency Specializes In: Advertising, Arts, Brand Development & Integration, Catalogs, Collateral, Environmental, Package Design, Planning & Consultation, Print, Strategic Planning/Research

Shauna Stinson *(Owner & Principal)*
Marcie Mangers *(Acct Dir)*
Erik Scholtes *(Dir-Creative 2D)*
Alexandria Starr *(Mgr)*
David Abouaf *(Designer)*

Accounts:
ACG
Callaway Golf
Game Crazy Video Game Retailer
Gateway
Mountain Head Wear
Nike
Nikon
Nordstrom
Pharmaca
Relish Home Accessories Furnishings Gifts & Design Services Store
Starbucks Coffee

VLADIMIR JONES
6 N Tejon St 4 Fl, Colorado Springs, CO 80903-1509
Tel.: (719) 473-0704
Fax: (719) 473-0754
E-Mail: vjones@vladimirjones.com
Web Site: www.vladimirjones.com

E-Mail for Key Personnel:
President: nechie@vladimirjones.com
Creative Dir.: george@vladimirjones.com
Media Dir.: kimberly@vladimirjones.com
Public Relations: lisa@vladimirjones.com

Employees: 80
Year Founded: 1970

National Agency Associations: 4A's-PRSA

Agency Specializes In: Above-the-Line, Advertising, Advertising Specialties, Affluent Market, Alternative Advertising, Below-the-Line, Brand Development & Integration, Business Publications, Collateral, Communications, Consulting, Consumer Marketing, Corporate Communications, Corporate Identity, Crisis Communications, Digital/Interactive, Direct Response Marketing, Direct-to-Consumer, Electronic Media, Environmental, Graphic Design, Guerilla Marketing, Health Care Services, High Technology, Hospitality, Identity Marketing, Integrated Marketing, Internet/Web Design, Leisure, Local Marketing, Logo & Package Design, Luxury Products, Magazines, Market Research, Media Buying Services, Media Planning, Media Relations, Media Training, Mobile Marketing, Multimedia, Newspaper, Newspapers & Magazines, Out-of-Home Media, Outdoor, Planning & Consultation, Podcasting, Print, Production, Production (Ad, Film, Broadcast), Promotions, Public Relations, Publicity/Promotions, Radio, Recruitment, Retail, Sales Promotion, Search Engine Optimization, Social Marketing/Nonprofit, Sponsorship, Strategic Planning/Research, Trade & Consumer Magazines, Transportation, Travel & Tourism, Viral/Buzz/Word of Mouth, Web (Banner Ads, Pop-ups, etc.)

Breakdown of Gross Billings by Media: Fees: 18%; Internet Adv.: 5%; Mags.: 15%; Newsp.: 16%; Outdoor: 8%; Pub. Rels.: 6%; Radio: 13%; Strategic Planning/Research: 2%; T.V.: 17%

Debbie Frickey *(Pres)*
Meredith Vaughan *(CEO)*
George Olson *(Chief Creative Officer & Exec VP)*
Mimi Wheeler *(VP-Insight)*
Ashley Maxon *(Acct Dir)*
Jon Bross *(Dir-Media)*
Jennifer Quint *(Supvr-Media Plng)*
Lauren Buonaiuto *(Acct Exec)*
Alexander Clark *(Coord-Digital)*

Accounts:
Bestway Disposal
The Broadmoor Hotel; 2002
Centura Health Centura Health 2020, Penrose-Saint Francis Hospitals; 1988
Cheyenne Mountain Zoo Tourist Attraction; 1995
Colorado Governor's Energy Office
Colorado Restaurant Association

Sandia Resort & Casino
St Julien Hotel & Spa
St. Francis Medical Center
Stockman, Kast & Ryan PC CPA Firm; 1998
Western Union
Xcel Energy; 2006

Branch

Vladimir Jones

677 S Colorado Blvd, Denver, CO 80246
Tel.: (303) 689-0704
Fax: (303) 850-7820
E-Mail: vjones@vladimirjones.com
Web Site: www.vladimirjones.com

Employees: 10
Year Founded: 1997

National Agency Associations: 4A's

Jennifer Hohn *(Partner & Exec Dir-Creative)*
Matt Ingwalson *(Partner & Exec Dir-Creative)*
Chris Powell *(Sr Dir-Interactive Art)*
Rik Patenaude *(Dir-Art)*
Alan Rhatigan *(Dir-Interactive Art)*
Sara Lennon *(Supvr-Media)*
Annie Ratcliffe *(Sr Acct Exec)*
Michelle Scott *(Media Planner)*

VMG CREATIVE

150 5th Ave, New York, NY 10011
Tel.: (917) 887-1074
E-Mail: info@vmg-creative.com
Web Site: www.vmg-creative.com

Employees: 6
Year Founded: 2010

Agency Specializes In: Affluent Market, Arts, Automotive, Brand Development & Integration, Business Publications, Collateral, Consumer Goods, Consumer Marketing, Consumer Publications, Corporate Identity, Cosmetics, Digital/Interactive, Electronics, Exhibit/Trade Shows, Experience Design, Fashion/Apparel, Graphic Design, Guerilla Marketing, Hospitality, Household Goods, Identity Marketing, In-Store Advertising, Industrial, Integrated Marketing, Logo & Package Design, Luxury Products, Market Research, Mobile Marketing, Multimedia, New Product Development, New Technologies, Newspapers & Magazines, Package Design, Planning & Consultation, Point of Sale, Product Placement, Social Marketing/Nonprofit, Social Media, Sports Market, Strategic Planning/Research, Urban Market

Kyle Heller *(Partner)*
Dhani Jones *(Partner)*
Luke Raymond *(Partner)*

Accounts:
Capital One Mascot Challenge; 2011

VML, INC.

250 Richards Rd, Kansas City, MO 64116-4279
Tel.: (816) 283-0700
Fax: (816) 283-0954
Toll Free: (800) 990-2468
Web Site: www.vml.com

E-Mail for Key Personnel:
President: jcook@vml.com
Creative Dir.: ebaumgartner@vml.com

Employees: 750
Year Founded: 1992

National Agency Associations: 4A's

Agency Specializes In: Advertising, Agriculture, Brand Development & Integration, Broadcast, Business-To-Business, Children's Market, Collateral, Communications, Consumer Marketing, Corporate Identity, Digital/Interactive, Direct Response Marketing, E-Commerce, Electronic Media, Event Planning & Marketing, Exhibit/Trade Shows, Financial, Health Care Services, High Technology, Information Technology, Internet/Web Design, Media Buying Services, Newspaper, Outdoor, Planning & Consultation, Point of Purchase, Point of Sale, Print, Production, Radio, Restaurant, Retail, Sales Promotion, Sponsorship, Sports Market, Strategic Planning/Research, T.V., Travel & Tourism, Yellow Pages Advertising

Eric Campbell *(Pres)*
Jon Cook *(Global CEO)*
Chris Haggerty *(Partner & Grp Project Dir)*
Jeremy Schutte *(Mng Dir & Exec Dir-Creative)*
Jim Bellinghausen *(CFO)*
Craig Braasch *(COO)*
Beth Wade *(CMO)*
Jeff Geheb *(CTO)*
Debbie Vandeven *(Chief Creative Officer)*
Amy Winger *(Chief Strategy Officer)*
Mike Yardley *(Chief Integration Officer)*
Paul R. Hauser *(Mng Dir-Plng & Res)*
Jen McDonald *(Mng Dir-Client Engagement)*
Aaron Evanson *(Exec Creative Dir)*
John Godsey *(Dept Head & Exec Dir-Creative)*
Matt Bowne *(Grp Dir-Creative)*
James Holden *(Grp Dir-Creative)*
Christie McFall *(Grp Dir-Client Engagement)*
Adam Seitz *(Grp Dir-Creative)*
Shali Wade *(Grp Dir-Client Engagement)*
Josh Eithun *(Sr Dir-Art)*
Kyle McDowell *(Sr Dir-Art)*
Dylan Smith *(Sr Dir-Art)*
Jaclyn Co *(Art Dir)*
Becky Ervin *(Creative Dir)*
Zac Greason *(Art Dir)*
Libby Hall *(Creative Dir)*
Justin Bell *(Dir-Art)*
James Billinger *(Dir-Client Engagement)*
Abby Fraser *(Dir-Client Engagement)*
Maggie Harn *(Dir-Creative)*
Rebecca Harpole *(Dir-Analytics & Data Insights)*
Chad Martin *(Dir-Social & Emerging Media)*
Stephen Martin *(Dir-Creative)*
John Mulvihill *(Dir-VML Mktg Svcs)*
Bill Patterson *(Dir-Channel-PR)*
Mark Philip *(Dir-Creative)*
Allison Pierce *(Dir-Creative)*
Alison Radke *(Dir-Art)*
Steve Schlegel *(Dir-IT & Network Ops)*
Ben Carmean *(Assoc Dir-Creative)*
Ryan Dillon *(Assoc Dir-Creative)*
Gary Schroer *(Assoc Dir-Creative)*
Angela Shaw *(Assoc Dir-Media)*
Ethan Tedlock *(Assoc Dir-Creative)*
Hannah Kerr *(Sr Acct Mgr)*
Stephanie Maurer *(Sr Acct Mgr)*
Allison Cejka *(Mgr-Channel)*
Belinda Kocen *(Mgr-Media Channel)*
Lynsay Montour *(Mgr-Comm)*
Laura Brand *(Supvr-Social Strategy)*
Ashley Renken *(Supvr-Client Engagement)*
Kristen Sikorski *(Supvr-Channel)*
Kristin Gritt *(Sr Strategist-Social)*
Alyssa Murfey *(Sr Strategist-Social)*
Jessica Wiggins *(Strategist-Social)*
Joey Rath *(Sr Acct Planner)*
James Veinbergs *(Designer)*
Jonathan Vigliaturo *(Copywriter)*

Accounts:
American Century Investments
Assurant Health
Bridgestone
Campbell's
Carlson Hotels
Cobra Puma Golf (Agency of Record) Creative, Digital, Event, Print, Retail Point of Sale
Colgate-Palmolive Afta, Ajax, Ajax Social Wipes, Colgate, Dynamo, Fab, Fabuloso, Irish Spring, Lady Speed Stick, Mennen Speed Stick, Murphy Oil Soap, Palmolive, Skin Bracer, Softsoap, Suavitel; 2000
ConMed
Darden
Dell
Edward Jones
English Premier League
Equinox
Ernst & Young
Folly Theater Campaign: "Plugged-In Live Theater Performance"
Gatorade Campaign: "Be Like Mike", Campaign: "Freaks", Campaign: "We All Want to Still #BeLikeMike", Campaign: G Series "Outfuel", Digital, Everything to Prove, G Series FIT Produc, Gatorade G Force B2B Sales App
H&R Block
Hill's Pet
Hillshire Farms
Honeywell
J.G. Wentworth (Digital Agency of Record) Analytics, Data Infrastructure, Experience Design, Modeling, Reporting, Technology Innovation
Kansas City's Union Station Living History
Kashi Co
Kellogg Co. Digital Strategy, Websites Redesign
Kimberly-Clark
Korean Air
MasterCard
Microsoft; 2004
MillerCoors Coors, Coors Light, Digital
Minddrive Social Fuel Tour
Movember Campaign: "Ribbon, Face, Line, Wind"
Napa Auto Parts (Agency of Record)
Nashville Convention & Visitors Corp. Campaign: "The Story of Nashville"
National Auto Parts Association Digital, Print, Radio, TV
Northland Coalition
PepsiCo
Revlon Inc.
San Diego Zoo
SAP
Sporting Kansas City Marketing, Strategic Consulting, Strategic Planning
Sprint Mass Markets-Consumer, Sprint Brand, Sprint Business, Sprint E-solutions, Sprint International, Sprint Publishing & Advertising, Sprint Wholesale Services Group; 1995
State Street Advisors
Stella Artois (Digital Agency of Record)
Tennessee Department of Tourist Development (Agency Of Record) Brand Development, Made in Tennessee, Marketing Services, Media Buying, Media Planning, Strategic Planning
Tom's of Maine Campaign: "Sheryl Crow Video"
US Bank
US Olympic Committee Brand Communications, Digital, Marketing, Print, Social Media
Virtua Health
Wendy's (Digital Agency of Record) Barbecue, Campaign: "#BBQ4Merica", Campaign: "Love Songs", Campaign: "Pretzel Bacon Cheeseburger Love Songs", Campaign: "Star of Tuscany", Campaign: "Wendy's Romaine Lettuce Journey", Campaign: "You Say "Brioche," We Say "Brioche."", Creative, Marketing, Online, Pretzel Bacon Cheeseburger, Social Media
Xerox Corp. Campaign: "Work Can Work Better", Digital, Website
New-Youth Ambassadors

Branches

VML, Inc.

(Formerly Studiocom)
191 Peachtree St NE Ste 4025, Atlanta, GA 30303
Tel.: (404) 541-9555
Web Site: www.vml.com

Year Founded: 1998

National Agency Associations: 4A's

Agency Specializes In: Brand Development & Integration, Digital/Interactive, Electronic Media, Hispanic Market, Internet/Web Design, Multimedia, Sponsorship

Maurizio Villarreal *(Exec Dir-Creative)*
Jennifer Sims *(Grp Dir-Client Engagement)*
Barbara Mende *(Dir-Channel)*
Leigha Baugham *(Sr Strategist-Social Media)*

Accounts:
Barilla Campaign: "Summer of Italy"
Baskin-Robbins
Coca-Cola Corporate Camp Coke, Coca-Cola USA, Coke 2, CokeMusic, CokeStudios, Vanilla Coke
Dunkin' Donuts
Kleenex Campaign: "Achoo", Campaign: "Kleenex Xperiments.", Media
Mattel
Turner Broadcasting System (TBS)
Turner Network Television (TNT)

VML
Greater London House, Hampstead Road, London, United Kingdom
Tel.: (44) 207 343 3700
Fax: (44) 207 343 3701

Matthew Griffiths *(Mng Dir)*
Chris Wood *(Mng Dir)*
David Sharrod *(Dir-Client Engagement)*

Accounts:
New-Bentley Motors
Virgin Active Website

VML, Inc.
(Formerly Studiocom)
116 Huntington Ave 12th Fl, Boston, MA 02116
Tel.: (617) 426-9555
Web Site: www.vml.com

National Agency Associations: 4A's

Agency Specializes In: Advertising, Brand Development & Integration, Graphic Design, Search Engine Optimization, Social Media

Jim Bellinghausen *(CFO)*
Todd Kirtley *(CIO)*
Beth Wade *(CMO)*
Debbi Vandeven *(Chief Creative Officer)*
Amy Winger *(Chief Strategy Officer)*
Eric Baumgartner *(Chief Innovation Officer)*
Brian Yamada *(Chief Innovation Officer)*
Gard Gibson *(Exec Dir-Insights)*
Mark McClendon *(Exec Dir-Tech)*
Maurizio Villarreal *(Exec Dir-Creative)*

Accounts:
The Coca-Cola Company
Colgate-Palmolive Company
Kimberly-Clark Corporation Campaign: "Softness Worth Sharing"
Nestle USA, Inc. Purina
VisitSavannah VisitSavannah.com

VML-New York
3 Columbus Cir 3rd Fl, New York, NY 10019
Tel.: (212) 210-3653
Fax: (212) 880-7543
Web Site: www.vml.com

Employees: 30

National Agency Associations: 4A's

Agency Specializes In: Advertising, Sponsorship

Michael Wente *(Partner, Mng Dir & Exec Dir-Creative)*
Kim Easley *(Mng Dir-Talent Acq-North America)*
Rosanne Johnson *(Head-Digital & Dir-Global)*
Chris Furse *(Exec Dir)*
Nick Centofante *(Media Dir)*
Dave Quintiliani *(Creative Dir)*
Brett Barash *(Dir-Strategy & Plng-VML West)*
Camellia Tan *(Dir-Network Dev-Asia)*
Alex Ayre *(Mgr-Channel-Media)*
Vanessa Cameron *(Supvr-Strategy)*
Nate Bowers *(Copywriter)*
Harsh Kapadia *(Deputy Dir-Creative)*

Accounts:
Ball Park
Campbell's
Dell B2B, Campaign: "Future Ready", Campaign: "Power to Do More", Mobile, Out-of-Home, Social Media
Hillshire Farms
Kimberly-Clark Digital Creative
Legoland Florida Resort (Agency of Record) Creative, Marketing, Strategy
Microsoft
The Partnership For A Healthier America
Special Olympics
Xerox Campaign: "Thinking"

VML Qais
(Formerly Qais Consulting)
1A Stanley Street, Singapore, 068720 Singapore
Tel.: (65) 6438 5592
Fax: (65) 6532 5954
E-Mail: keith@vmlqais.com
Web Site: www.vmlqais.com/

Employees: 27

Agency Specializes In: Advertising, Below-the-Line, Brand Development & Integration, Consulting, Direct Response Marketing, Direct-to-Consumer, Electronic Media, Internet/Web Design, Local Marketing, Market Research, Sales Promotion, Strategic Planning/Research

Keith Timimi *(Chm)*
Tripti Lochan *(CEO)*
Debbi Vandeven *(Chief Creative Officer)*
Rajeev Lochan *(VP-Res & Fin & Dir)*
Linda Bumgarner *(Exec Dir-Creative)*
Giles Henderson *(Dir-Media & Channels)*
Preethi Sanjeevi *(Dir-Client Solutions)*
Scott Lichtenauer *(Assoc Dir-Creative)*

Accounts:
Banyan Tree Global SEO, Social Media
Civil Aviation Authority of Singapore Changi Airport
Converse Singapore Digital, Social Media
Guide Dogs Association of the Blind
Hilton Worldwide
ICICI Bank
Intercontinental Hotels Group Crowne Plaza, Holiday Inn, Hotel InterContinental
New-Kellogg's Creative, Digital Brand Strategy, Pringles (Digital Agency of Record), Social
Mahindra & Mahindra Brand Positioning, Campaign: "Spark the Rise", Digital, mahindra.com
Nexus CiNE65, Digital Strategy
Remy Martin Digital, Website
RW Genting Digital Media, Social Content
Singapore Ministry of Defense
Sony Electronics
Sony Pictures MIB3
Sun Life Malaysia (Social Marketing Agency of Record) Community Management, Content, Social Strategy
Yahoo!

VML-White Salmon
131B NE Estes Ave, White Salmon, WA 98672-0558
Tel.: (816) 283-0700
Fax: (509) 493-8556
Web Site: www.vml.com

Employees: 4

Agency Specializes In: Advertising

Todd Kirtley *(Partner & CIO)*
Mark McClendon *(Partner & Exec Dir-Tech)*
Rusty Neff *(Partner & Dir-Res)*
Jim Bellinghausen *(CFO)*
Beth Wade *(CMO)*
Debbi Vandeven *(Chief Creative Officer)*
Amy Winger *(Chief Strategy Officer)*
Kris Hiestand *(Mng Dir-Tech)*
David Mitchell *(Mng Dir-Tech)*
Bert Weidt *(Mng Dir-Tech)*
Lore Sampson *(Assoc Dir-Res)*

VML
35 Clarence St, Sydney, New South Wales 2000 Australia
Tel.: (61) 299094411
Fax: (61) 61299094647
Web Site: australia.vml.com

Agency Specializes In: Advertising, Broadcast, Collateral, Corporate Identity, Digital/Interactive, Event Planning & Marketing, Media Buying Services, Media Planning, Outdoor

Aden Hepburn *(Mng Dir-Australia)*
Betsy Ligibel *(Sr Acct Dir)*
Andrew Killey *(Acct Dir)*
Tim Fletcher *(Dir-Tech)*
Mark MacSmith *(Dir-Digital Plng)*
Matt Brown *(Mgr-Social & Planner-Digital)*
Dave Di Veroli *(Sr Strategist-Digital)*
Jessie Jordan *(Copywriter)*
Evan Ross *(Sr Engr-Software)*

Accounts:
Australian Federal Police
Commonwealth Bank of Australia Ltd. Campaign: "CommBank Re-Launch"
McDonald's #FryFlix, Digital, Social, Social Media
New-Microsoft Australia (Lead Creative & Strategic Agency) Above-the-Line, Below-the-Line, Digital, Social
Missing Person Unit
Rip Curl Campaign: "Rip Curl Search GPS"
Transport NSW
Vivid Light Festival

VML
65 E Wacker Pl Ste 2410, Chicago, IL 60601
Tel.: (312) 269-5563
Fax: (312) 332-8277
Web Site: www.vml.com

Year Founded: 2008

National Agency Associations: 4A's

Agency Specializes In: Advertising, Broadcast, Collateral, Corporate Identity, Digital/Interactive, Event Planning & Marketing, Media Buying Services, Media Planning

Julia Hammond *(Mng Dir)*
Mike Gerfen *(Exec Dir)*
Jane Tamraz *(Exec Dir)*
Madeline Nies *(Dir-Content Strategy)*
Emily Lenard *(Acct Supvr-Client Engagement)*

Accounts:
Kellogg Company
Kimberly-Clark Corporation

MillerCoors
Tazo Tea Company

VML
(Formerly Biggs Gilmore Communications)
261 E Kalamazoo Ave Ste 300, Kalamazoo, MI 49007-3841
(See Separate Listing)

VOCO CREATIVE, LLC
8120 Sheridan Blvd Ste A-101, Westminster, CO 80003
Tel.: (720) 381-2460
E-Mail: info@vococreative.com
Web Site: www.vococreative.com

Agency Specializes In: Advertising, Brand Development & Integration, Content, Strategic Planning/Research

Juli Dimos *(Co-Founder & Dir-Creative)*
Jesaka Long *(Sr Writer)*

Accounts:
Colorado Asphalt Services Inc
Cuties
Shoemaker Ghiselli + Schwartz

VOG ADVERTISING
624 Trade Ctr Blvd B, Chesterfield, MO 63005
Tel.: (314) 266-3616
E-Mail: info@vogadvertising.com
Web Site: www.vogadvertising.com

Agency Specializes In: Advertising, Broadcast, Digital/Interactive, Graphic Design, Logo & Package Design, Media Buying Services, Media Planning, Print

Katy Kruze *(COO & VP)*
David Lishman *(Analyst-Media)*
Sienna Ravisa *(Analyst-Media)*
Devory Newsome *(Assoc Producer)*

Accounts:
Dish Network Corporation
VIP TAN Salon

VOGEL MARKETING SOLUTIONS LLC
255 Butler Ave Ste 201-B, Lancaster, PA 17601
Tel.: (717) 368-5143
E-Mail: Mark@VogelMarketing.net
Web Site: www.vogelmarketing.net

National Agency Associations: SMEI

Agency Specializes In: Advertising, Advertising Specialties, Brand Development & Integration, Business Publications, Catalogs, Co-op Advertising, Collateral, Communications, Corporate Identity, Crisis Communications, Digital/Interactive, Direct Response Marketing, Direct-to-Consumer, Electronic Media, Email, Event Planning & Marketing, Exhibit/Trade Shows, Financial, Food Service, Graphic Design, Health Care Services, Hospitality, Identity Marketing, In-Store Advertising, Industrial, Integrated Marketing, Internet/Web Design, Local Marketing, Logo & Package Design, Magazines, Market Research, Media Buying Services, Media Planning, Media Relations, Media Training, Men's Market, Newspaper, Newspapers & Magazines, Out-of-Home Media, Package Design, Paid Searches, Pets , Planning & Consultation, Point of Purchase, Product Placement, Production, Production (Print), Promotions, Publicity/Promotions, Radio, Regional, Sales Promotion, Search Engine Optimization, Social Marketing/Nonprofit, Social Media, Sponsorship, Strategic Planning/Research, T.V., Trade & Consumer Magazines, Web (Banner Ads, Pop-ups, etc.)

Mark Vogel *(Pres)*

Accounts:
Keystruct Construction
Lancaster Community Safety Coalition
Precision Resources Inc.
White Oak Printing

THE VOICE
170 Brookfield Ave, Fairfield, CT 06825
Tel.: (203) 334-0718
Fax: (203) 334-0713
E-Mail: info@the-voice.com
Web Site: www.the-voice.com

Employees: 25
Year Founded: 2001

Agency Specializes In: Advertising, Brand Development & Integration, Collateral, Digital/Interactive, Direct Response Marketing, Identity Marketing, Sports Market

Approx. Annual Billings: $2,000,000

Breakdown of Gross Billings by Media: Print: 50%; Worldwide Web Sites: 50%

Matthew Hallock *(Pres & Dir-Creative)*
Dan Randmer *(Dir-Live Action Video Production & Jr Dir-Art)*
Anthony Russello *(Dir-Art)*
Rachel Olivera *(Sr Acct Mgr)*

Accounts:
Computer Associates
Lifeworx
NFL
Sportscenter of Connecticut

VOICEFLIX INC
227 Bellevue Way NE 670, Bellevue, WA 98004
Tel.: (425) 303-9068
Web Site: www.voiceflix.com

Agency Specializes In: Advertising, Digital/Interactive, Internet/Web Design

Amber Finney *(Founder & CEO)*

Accounts:
Integrated Freight Corp. (Advertising Agency of Record) Branding, Social Media, Website
New-Liberated Energy Inc
New-Seen On Screen TV, Inc. (Advertising Agency of Record)

VOLLRATH & ASSOCIATES
839 N Jefferson St Ste 502, Milwaukee, WI 53202
Tel.: (414) 221-0210
Fax: (414) 221-0220
E-Mail: info@vollrathpr.com
Web Site: www.vollrathpr.com

Employees: 6

Agency Specializes In: Communications, Investor Relations, Public Relations

Phil Vollrath *(Co-Founder & Partner)*
Jessica Vollrath *(VP)*
Sarah McClanahan *(Specialist-Comm)*
Carolyn Guenther *(Acct Coord-PR)*

Accounts:
Marcus Corporation
Tri-Star Tool & Machine, Inc.

VOLTAGE LTD
901 Front St 340, Louisville, CO 80027
Tel.: (303) 664-1687
E-Mail: info@voltagead.com
Web Site: www.voltagead.com

Agency Specializes In: Advertising, Brand Development & Integration, Content, Digital/Interactive, Search Engine Optimization

Eric Fowles *(CEO & Dir-Creative)*
Justin Brunson *(Dir-Video)*
Seth Lofgreen *(Dir-Ops)*
Randy Lybbert *(Dir-Technical)*
Chris Gillmore *(Sr Designer)*
Lindsay Thompson *(Sr Designer)*

Accounts:
Fjallraven
Umpqua

THE VON AGENCY INC
179 Windsor Rd, Staten Island, NY 10314
Tel.: (718) 873-4004
E-Mail: info@thevonagency.com
Web Site: www.thevonagency.com

Agency Specializes In: Advertising, Event Planning & Marketing, Graphic Design, Internet/Web Design, Public Relations, Social Media

Leticia Remauro *(Pres & CEO)*
Lily Zafaranloo *(Dir-Ops)*
Jen Remauro *(Dir-Promotional)*

Accounts:
New-Gotham Motorcycles
New-Staten Island Yankees

VOXUS INC.
117 South 8th St, Tacoma, WA 98402
Tel.: (253) 853-5151
Fax: (253) 853-5110
E-Mail: info@voxuspr.com
Web Site: www.voxuspr.com

Employees: 15

Agency Specializes In: Broadcast, Media Relations, Production, Strategic Planning/Research, Technical Advertising

Paul Forecki *(Pres)*
Beth Parker *(Sr VP)*
Lizanne Sadlier *(Sr VP)*
Tim Heitzman *(Dir-Creative)*
Justin Rouse *(Sr Acct Exec)*

Accounts:
AirMagnet
Internet Identity
WatchGuard Technologies

VOXY MEDIA GROUP
1700 N Monroe St Ste 11, Tallahassee, FL 32303
Tel.: (850) 544-3595
E-Mail: info@voxymediagroup.com
Web Site: www.voxymediagroup.com

Year Founded: 2013

Agency Specializes In: Advertising, Brand Development & Integration, Collateral, Digital/Interactive, Event Planning & Marketing, Internet/Web Design, Logo & Package Design, Media Buying Services, Search Engine Optimization, Social Media

Heather Johnson *(Owner & CMO)*

Accounts:
Tasty Pastry Bakery

VOYAGE LLC
25 Wall St Ste 5, Orlando, FL 32801
Tel.: (407) 489-5944
E-Mail: info@voyage-advertising.com
Web Site: www.voyage-advertising.com

Year Founded: 2013

Agency Specializes In: Advertising, Brand Development & Integration, Internet/Web Design, Outdoor, Print

Jonathan Risteen *(CEO)*
Jim Brothers *(Chief Creative Officer)*

Accounts:
Gilstrap & Associates
Orlando Chiropractic

VREELAND MARKETING & DESIGN
40 Forest Falls Dr, Yarmouth, ME 04096-1938
Tel.: (207) 846-3714
Fax: (207) 846-3899
E-Mail: info@vreeland.com
Web Site: www.vreeland.com

Employees: 15
Year Founded: 1978

National Agency Associations: Second Wind Limited

Agency Specializes In: Business-To-Business, Engineering, Environmental, Retail, Travel & Tourism

Cindy Davies *(Mng Partner)*
Rich Davies *(VP & Dir-Creative)*
Katherine Gallant *(VP-Ops)*
Rebecca Morse *(VP-Creative)*
Kiki O. Connell *(Dir-Content)*
Virginia Archambault *(Sr Acct Exec)*
Jessica Gilman *(Specialist-PR)*

Accounts:
Bath Savings; Bath, ME Finance
Due Fratelli
Skillins Greenhouses; Falmouth, ME

VRTC, INC.
10613 W Sam Houston Pkwy N Ste 150, Houston, TX 77064
Tel.: (281) 664-1190
Fax: (281) 664-1194
Web Site: www.vrtc.us

Year Founded: 2006

Agency Specializes In: Advertising, Communications, Graphic Design, Media Buying Services, Media Planning, Package Design, Print, Production, Public Relations, Social Media

Eduardo Torres *(Pres & CEO)*
Octavio Orozco *(VP & Gen Mgr)*
Jorge Villasenor *(Head-Ops & Project)*
Hugo Rocha *(Sr Dir-Art)*
Luis Mauricio *(Producer-Digital Content)*
Octavio Zarate *(Dir-Art)*
Adriana Moyano *(Acct Exec)*
Melissa Perez *(Specialist-New Bus)*
Cristy Torres *(Jr Graphic Designer)*

Accounts:
Aeromexico Brand Management, Creative Service, Media Buying, Strategic Planning
Gruma
Honda Motor Co., Ltd.
LeaLA
Northgate Supermarket
Puerto Vallarta
Tequila Pueblo Viejo

VSA PARTNERS, INC.
600 W Chicago Ave, Chicago, IL 60654
Tel.: (312) 427-6413
Toll Free: (877) 422-1311
E-Mail: info@vsapartners.com
Web Site: www.vsapartners.com/

Employees: 200

Agency Specializes In: Sponsorship

Dana Arnett *(CEO)*
Jim Toth *(Partner & Exec Dir-Creative)*
Bob Winter *(Partner & Exec Dir-Creative)*
William Rosen *(Partner)*
Jeff Walker *(Partner-Client Engagement)*
Heather Torreggiani *(CMO)*
Curtis Schreiber *(Sr VP & Head-Client Engagement)*
Hugh Allspaugh *(Assoc Partner & Head-Mktg Strategy Practice)*
Patrick Heick *(Head-Digital Practice)*
Jamie Koval *(Head-Client Engagement)*
Karen Semone *(Assoc Partner & Head-Discipline-Content Strategy & Mgmt)*
Adam Reno *(Exec Creative Dir)*
Brock Conrad *(Creative Dir)*
Jesse Rea *(Creative Dir)*
Greg Anderson *(Dir-Creative)*
Sally Beck *(Dir-Admin)*
Kara Bosnic *(Dir-Client Engagement)*
Julie Capalby *(Dir-Creative)*
Nick Cavet *(Assoc Partner & Dir-Strategy)*
Chrystine Doerr *(Dir-Creative)*
Matt Ganser *(Dir-Creative)*
Lisa Gildehaus *(Dir-Integrated Production-Consumer Mktg)*
Tohru Oyasu *(Dir-Creative)*
Tracy Richards *(Dir-Talent Acq)*
Rainer Schmidt *(Dir-Creative)*
Jerry Stiedaman *(Dir-Client Engagement)*
Scott Theisen *(Dir-Creative & Digital)*
Josh Witherspoon *(Dir-Creative)*
Katie Quinn *(Assoc Dir-Creative)*
Emily Vaca *(Assoc Dir-Creative)*
Maureen Curosh *(Sr Designer)*
Anthony Mingo *(Sr Designer)*
Don Peasley *(Assoc Partner)*

Accounts:
American Express
Argo Teas
New-Beam Suntory Inc. 2 Gingers (Advertising & Marketing Agency of Record), Digital, Retail, Social Media
New-Cargill, Inc. Cargill
CME Group Campaign: "Global Reach"
New-Converse
First Data Corporation
New-General Electric
Goose Island Campaign: "To What's Next", Digital, Lolita, Out-Of-Home, Print, Sofie, Video
Harley-Davidson, Inc. Campaign: "Our Night", Campaign: "United by Independents"
IBM Corporation
Kimberly-Clark Corp. Campaign: "Someone Needs One", Campaign: "Time for a Change", Kleenex, TV
New-Mack Trucks
New-Marvin Windows & Doors (Marketing & Advertising Agency of Record) Broadcast, Digital, Marvin & Integrity, Online Advertising, Print, Sales
Mohawk Fine Papers Inc.
Trading Technologies International (Digital Agency of Record) Brand Strategy, Digital Marketing, Web Development & Design
Wilson Sporting Goods Company

Branches

VSA Partners, Inc.
322 First Ave. N., #300, Minneapolis, MN 55401
Tel.: (612) 339-2920
Web Site: www.vsapartners.com

Employees: 10

Jeff Cruz *(Assoc Partner & Exec Dir-Creative)*
Tarek El-Mofty *(Dir-Creative Svcs)*
Shelbi Ladd *(Assoc Dir-Delivery Mgmt)*
Art Corbiere *(Mgr-Office & Facility)*

VSA Partners
42 Greene St Fl 2, New York, NY 10013
Tel.: (212) 966-3535
Web Site: www.tendercreative.com

Adam Berninger *(Partner)*
Cory Clarke *(Partner)*
Andrea Spiegel *(Partner-Client Engagement)*
Ben Sherwood *(Dir-Creative)*
Kendall Flynn *(Sr Strategist-Consumer Mktg)*
Yekaterina Voevodkin *(Sr Designer)*
Lynn Yeom *(Designer)*

Accounts:
Nike

VSA Partners, Inc.
106 7th Ave., 2nd Fl, New York, NY 10011
Tel.: (212) 869-1188
Web Site: www.vsapartners.com

Eric Martinez *(Partner & Head-Strategy Practice)*
Shawn Hoglund *(Dir-Digital Creative)*
Shelbi Ladd *(Assoc Dir-Delivery Mgmt)*
Art Corbiere *(Mgr-Office & Facility)*
Yekaterina Voevodkin *(Sr Designer)*
Lynn Yeom *(Designer)*
Caitlin Smyth *(Sr Program Mgr)*

Accounts:
IBM Corporation

VSBROOKS
255 Alhambra Cir Ste 835, Coral Gables, FL 33134
Tel.: (305) 443-3500
Fax: (305) 443-3381
E-Mail: info@vsbrooks.com
Web Site: www.vsbrooks.com

Employees: 15

National Agency Associations: Second Wind Limited

Diana Brooks *(Mng Partner & Dir-Strategy & Bus Dev)*
Vivian Santos *(Mng Partner & Dir-Creative)*
Junior Jimenez *(Dir-Art & Assoc Dir-Creative)*
Barbara Marchena *(Dir-Admin Svcs & HR & Office Mgr)*
Claudia Varela *(Dir-Consumer Engagement)*
Gabriela Zamorano *(Dir-PR & Event Plng)*
Diana Ocasio *(Assoc Dir-Creative)*
Cristina Gaston *(Acct Mgr)*
Maria Williams *(Mgr-Traffic)*
Danielle Sokoloff *(Acct Exec)*

Accounts:
CarePlus HealthPlans
Coastal Building Maintenance Florida
St. John Vianney College Seminary; Miami, FL

VUP MEDIA
1140 Pk Ave, Cranston, RI 2910

Tel.: (401) 943-2299
E-Mail: info@vupmedia.com
Web Site: www.vupmedia.com

Agency Specializes In: Advertising, Digital/Interactive, Graphic Design, Internet/Web Design, Print

Andrew Fogell *(Owner)*
Sandra DoVale Fogell *(VP-Media Production & Interactive Solutions)*

Accounts:
Delray Beach Downtown Development Authority

W A FISHER, CO.
(d/b/a W A Fisher Printing & Advg Co)
(Private-Parent-Single Location)
123 Chestnut St, Virginia, MN 55792
Tel.: (218) 741-9544
Fax: (218) 741-8216
E-Mail: info@wafishermn.com
Web Site: www.wafishermn.com

Employees: 19
Year Founded: 1999

Agency Specializes In: Advertising, Brand Development & Integration, Broadcast, Collateral, Digital/Interactive, Logo & Package Design, Media Planning, Outdoor, Print, Social Media

Revenue: $1,300,000

Mark Leese *(Pres & Acct Mgr)*
Mark Aulie *(Dir-Adv)*
John Kohlhase *(Dir-Creative)*
Aaron Mehrkens *(Office Mgr)*
Christina Seppanen *(Mgr-Prepress & Graphic Designer)*
Jaimie Niska *(Acct Exec & Specialist-Media)*
Ashley Holm *(Acct Exec)*
Kimberly Holmes *(Designer-Web)*

Accounts:
Leech Lake Tourism Bureau
Minnesota Iron Mining
Pohaki Lumber

W INC.
1215 Hightower Trl Ste B100, Atlanta, GA 30350
Tel.: (770) 993-7204
Fax: (678) 277-9118
E-Mail: lwhelan@wincorporated.com
Web Site: www.wincorporated.com

Employees: 2
Year Founded: 1971

Agency Specializes In: Advertising, Automotive, Brand Development & Integration, Broadcast, Business Publications, Business-To-Business, Cable T.V., Co-op Advertising, Collateral, Communications, Consumer Goods, Consumer Marketing, Consumer Publications, Corporate Identity, Direct Response Marketing, Direct-to-Consumer, Event Planning & Marketing, Exhibit/Trade Shows, Financial, Food Service, Graphic Design, High Technology, In-Store Advertising, Information Technology, Logo & Package Design, Magazines, Media Buying Services, New Product Development, Newspaper, Newspapers & Magazines, Out-of-Home Media, Outdoor, Point of Purchase, Point of Sale, Print, Production, Public Relations, Publicity/Promotions, Radio, Real Estate, Recruitment, Retail, Sales Promotion, Sports Market, Strategic Planning/Research, T.V., Trade & Consumer Magazines

Approx. Annual Billings: $2,000,000

Breakdown of Gross Billings by Media: Cable T.V.: 25%; Internet Adv.: 15%; Newsp. & Mags.: 5%; Outdoor: 5%; Radio: 25%; Spot T.V.: 25%

Libby Whelan *(Pres-Mktg & Adv Comm Firm)*

Accounts:
Day's Chevrolet Automotive Group; Atlanta, GA Automotive Dealership; 2001
eSecuritel; Atlanta, GA Handset Insurance; 2008
Lighthouse Marketing; Atlanta, GA Media Research, Planning & Buying; 2003

W2O GROUP
60 Francisco St, San Francisco, CA 94133
Tel.: (415) 362-5018
E-Mail: info@w2ogroup.com
Web Site: www.w2ogroup.com

Agency Specializes In: Advertising, Brand Development & Integration, Digital/Interactive, Public Relations, Social Media

Jim Weiss *(Chm & CEO)*
Bob Pearson *(Pres & Chief Innovation Officer)*
Paulo Simas *(Mng Partner)*
Tony Esposito *(CFO)*
Mike Hartman *(Chief Creative Officer)*
John Cunningham *(Chief Software Officer)*
Dorinda Marticorena *(Mng Dir-New Entertainment)*
Anita Bose *(Head-Client & Bus Dev)*
Matt Dong *(Dir-Creative)*

Accounts:
Netscout Systems, Inc (Public Relations Agency of Record)

WAGNER DESIGN ASSOCIATES
123 N Ashley Ste 212, Ann Arbor, MI 48104
Tel.: (734) 662-9500
Fax: (734) 662-6590
E-Mail: nancy@wagdesign.com
Web Site: www.wagdesign.com

Employees: 5

Agency Specializes In: Advertising, Collateral, Email, Graphic Design, Logo & Package Design

Kathy Roeser *(Mng Partner & Sr Dir-Art)*
Laura Herold *(Partner)*
Nancy Miller *(Bus Mgr & Copywriter)*

Accounts:
Aztec Publications
BBC Entrepreneurial Training & Consulting LLC; Ann Arbor, MI Coordinate Branding, Email Marketing Campaigns

THE WAGNER JUNKER AGENCY
7317 Santa Monica Blvd, West Hollywood, CA 90046
Tel.: (323) 461-1011
Fax: (323) 461-1150
E-Mail: info@wagnerjunker.com
Web Site: www.wjagency.com

Employees: 15

Agency Specializes In: Advertising, Brand Development & Integration, Event Planning & Marketing, Graphic Design, Local Marketing, Media Buying Services, Promotions, Public Relations, Restaurant, Sponsorship, Strategic Planning/Research, T.V., Web (Banner Ads, Pop-ups, etc.)

Eric Junker *(Partner-Consulting)*

Accounts:
Alliance Residential
Camp Ronald MacDonald
Dakota Restaurant
Gold Class Cinemas
Siegel Group

WAHLSTROM GROUP
800 Connecticut Ave, Norwalk, CT 06854
Tel.: (203) 299-4200
Fax: (203) 299-4299
Toll Free: (800) 348-7347
E-Mail: sales@wahlstrom.com
Web Site: www.wahlstrom.com

Employees: 20
Year Founded: 1954

National Agency Associations: 4A's-ADM-AHAA-ANA-IAB-YPA

Agency Specializes In: Digital/Interactive, Yellow Pages Advertising

Approx. Annual Billings: $225,000,000

Breakdown of Gross Billings by Media: Internet Adv.: $9,000,000; Yellow Page Adv.: $216,000,000

Debora Lance *(Mng Dir & Exec VP)*
Rick Barry *(Mng Dir & VP)*
John Feddern *(Acct Dir)*
Suzanne Spada *(Acct Dir)*
Tim Lathrop *(Dir-Digital)*
Yvette Scaturchio *(Mgr-New Bus Dev)*

Accounts:
General Electric
Sears Home Improvement Products

Branches

Wahlstrom Group
1640 Lyndon Farm Ct, Louisville, KY 40223
Tel.: (502) 423-5520
Fax: (502) 423-5521
Toll Free: (800) 252-4231
E-Mail: sales@wahlstrom.com
Web Site: www.wahlstrom.com

Employees: 40
Year Founded: 1994

National Agency Associations: 4A's

Agency Specializes In: Internet/Web Design, Yellow Pages Advertising

Debora Lance *(Mng Dir & Exec VP)*
Rick Barry *(Mng Dir & VP)*
Suzanne Spada *(Acct Dir)*

Wahlstrom Group
222 S 9th St, Minneapolis, MN 55402
Tel.: (952) 346-6686
Fax: (952) 346-6650
Toll Free: (800) 995-9747
E-Mail: sales@wahlstrom.com
Web Site: www.wahlstrom.com

Employees: 15

National Agency Associations: 4A's

Agency Specializes In: Digital/Interactive, Yellow Pages Advertising

Debbie Lance *(Mng Dir & Exec VP)*
Rick Barry *(Mng Dir & VP)*
Heather Nybo *(Acct Dir)*
Amy Streeter *(Sr Specialist-Ops)*

Wahlstrom Group

200 S Broad St, Philadelphia, PA 19102-3803
Tel.: (215) 790-3100
Toll Free: (800) 447-5005
Web Site: www.wahlstrom.com

Employees: 8

National Agency Associations: 4A's

Rick Barry *(Mng Dir & VP)*

WAKELY ADVERTISING

3420 Pomeroy Rd, Downers Grove, IL 60515
Tel.: (630) 968-2800
Fax: (630) 578-0138
E-Mail: sales@wakelyadvertising.com

E-Mail for Key Personnel:
President: pete@wakelyadvertising.com

Employees: 5
Year Founded: 1999

Agency Specializes In: Automotive, Retail

Approx. Annual Billings: $3,000,000

Pete Wakely *(Owner)*

Accounts:
Chicago Leisure Group; 2002
Classic Oak Design; 2002
Joe Cotton Ford; Carol Stream, IL Dealership; 1998
Northwest Metalcraft
Viking Dodge

WALDINGER CREATIVE

606 Bosley Ave Ste 2B, Towson, MD 21204
Tel.: (410) 321-5522
E-Mail: info@creativew.com
Web Site: www.creativew.com

Agency Specializes In: Advertising, Brand Development & Integration, Digital/Interactive, Exhibit/Trade Shows, Print

Tom Waldinger *(Pres)*
Lopaka Purdy *(Sr Dir-Strategic Comm)*

Accounts:
A&R Companies
JewishCareers.com
Matz Enterprises
Site Resources, Inc.
Turner Troxell, Inc.

WALKER ADVERTISING, INC.

1010 S Cabrillo Ave, San Pedro, CA 90731-4067
Tel.: (310) 519-4050
Fax: (310) 521-0887
Toll Free: (800) 409-0909
E-Mail: info@walkeradvertising.com
Web Site: www.walkeradvertising.com

E-Mail for Key Personnel:
President: maryann@walkeradvertising.com
Media Dir.: nereida@walkeradvertising.com

Employees: 45
Year Founded: 1984

Agency Specializes In: Bilingual Market, Direct Response Marketing, Hispanic Market, Telemarketing

Approx. Annual Billings: $11,500,000

Breakdown of Gross Billings by Media: D.M.: 5%; Newsp.: 5%; Radio: 18%; T.V.: 72%

Mary Ann Walker *(Founder & CEO)*
Nereida Casarez *(VP-Media)*
Alfonso Martinez *(Dir-Creative)*
Connie Romo *(Mgr-Customer Svcs)*
Mary Lou Potter *(Sr Acct Exec)*

Accounts:
Alivio Legal
Legal Rights Defenders 1800 the Law 2; Los Angeles, CA
Los Defensores; Los Angeles, CA Legal Services to the Hispanic Market

WALKER & ASSOCIATES, INC.

5100 Poplar Ave, Memphis, TN 38137
Tel.: (901) 522-1100
Fax: (901) 522-1101
E-Mail: bigideas@walker-assoc.com
Web Site: www.walker-assoc.com

E-Mail for Key Personnel:
President: cwnorris@walker-assoc.com

Employees: 20
Year Founded: 1965

Agency Specializes In: Advertising, Brand Development & Integration, Co-op Advertising, Communications, Consumer Marketing, Corporate Identity, Exhibit/Trade Shows, Financial, Food Service, Government/Political, Graphic Design, Health Care Services, Internet/Web Design, Legal Services, Media Buying Services, Newspaper, Outdoor, Planning & Consultation, Production, Public Relations, Publicity/Promotions, Radio, Recruitment, Restaurant, Retail, Sales Promotion, Sports Market, Strategic Planning/Research, T.V., Technical Advertising, Teen Market, Trade & Consumer Magazines, Travel & Tourism

Ceil T. Walker-Norris *(Pres & CEO)*
Bill Walsh *(VP-Client Svcs)*
Lee Wilson *(Dir-Civil Engrg)*
Deborah Harrison *(Mgr-Bus Dev)*

Accounts:
Thomas & Betts; Memphis, TN Employee Recruitment; 1999

WALKER & COMPANY, INC.

727 Ashland Ave, Santa Monica, CA 90405
Tel.: (323) 309-5450
E-Mail: craig@walkerworldwide.com
Web Site: www.walkerworldwide.com

Employees: 10

Agency Specializes In: Advertising, Brand Development & Integration, Business-To-Business, Consumer Marketing, Direct Response Marketing, Infomercials, Integrated Marketing, Internet/Web Design, T.V.

Approx. Annual Billings: $5,000,000

Breakdown of Gross Billings by Media: Radio & T.V.: 100%

Craig Walker *(Exec Dir-Creative)*
Michael S. Hughes *(Dir-Interactive Mktg & CRM)*
Raquel Lachman *(Dir-Brand Mktg)*

WALKER BRANDS

1810 W Kennedy Blvd, Tampa, FL 33606
Tel.: (813) 875-3322
E-Mail: info@walkerbrands.com
Web Site: www.walkerbrands.com

Employees: 8
Year Founded: 1992

Agency Specializes In: Advertising, Brand Development & Integration, Digital/Interactive, Guerilla Marketing, Identity Marketing, Logo & Package Design, Media Planning, Public Relations, Search Engine Optimization, Strategic Planning/Research

Nancy Walker *(Pres)*
Joy Wynne Galatro *(VP-Brand Strategy)*
Matt McEachern *(Dir-Creative)*
Tara Robinson *(Dir-Brand Svc)*
Whitney Owings *(Office Mgr)*
Shelly Sarbaugh *(Brand Mgr)*

Accounts:
Southwest Properties

WALKER MARKETING, INC.

805 Trade St NW Ste 101, Concord, NC 28027
Tel.: (704) 782-3244
Fax: (704) 262-1100
E-Mail: info@walker-marketing.com
Web Site: www.walker-marketing.com

National Agency Associations: 4A's

Gary Walker *(Pres & CEO)*
Barry Campbell *(Dir-Creative)*
Kristine Goodyear *(Sr Acct Mgr-PR)*
Kristen Cranford *(Acct Mgr)*
Padus Herron *(Mgr)*
Matt Myers *(Mgr-Digital Production)*
Brittany Dagenhart *(Acct Coord)*

Accounts:
Active Day Inc.
The Cascades at Verdae
Ingersoll Rand
Med-Tech Systems
S&D Coffee

WALKING STAR MARKETING & DESIGN

(Formerly Walking Star Marketing, Design & Internet)
921 14th St, Cody, WY 82414
Tel.: (307) 587-5994
Fax: (307) 587-3979
Toll Free: (888) 587-5994
E-Mail: ppotter@walkingstar.com
Web Site: www.walkingstar.com

Employees: 4
Year Founded: 1995

Agency Specializes In: Advertising, Advertising Specialties, Brand Development & Integration, Business Publications, Catalogs, Collateral, Consulting, Consumer Marketing, Corporate Identity, Custom Publishing, Digital/Interactive, Direct Response Marketing, Direct-to-Consumer, Electronic Media, Event Planning & Marketing, Exhibit/Trade Shows, Graphic Design, Identity Marketing, In-Store Advertising, Integrated Marketing, Internet/Web Design, Local Marketing, Logo & Package Design, Multimedia, Newspaper, Package Design, Point of Sale, Print, Production, Promotions, Public Relations, Publishing, Radio, Sales Promotion, Search Engine Optimization, Strategic Planning/Research, Technical Advertising, Web (Banner Ads, Pop-ups, etc.), Yellow Pages Advertising

Approx. Annual Billings: $150,000

Breakdown of Gross Billings by Media: Collateral: 20%; E-Commerce: 20%; Graphic Design: 40%; Internet Adv.: 20%

Peggy Potter *(Owner & Dir-Creative)*
Charity Alexander *(Graphic Designer & Designer-Web)*
Quincy Sondeno *(Graphic Designer & Designer-Web)*

WALKUP ADVERTISING
141 Sullys Trl Ste 4, Pittsford, NY 14534
Tel.: (585) 348-9863
Fax: (585) 264-1177
Web Site: www.walkupadvertising.com

Agency Specializes In: Advertising, Brand Development & Integration, Digital/Interactive

Paul H. Bush *(CEO)*

Accounts:
Allied Financial Partners
Nothnagle Realtors

THE WALLACE AGENCY
1921 Power St SE Bldg 9B1, Roanoke, VA 24013
Tel.: (540) 343-7411
Fax: (540) 685-2920
Web Site: www.bldg9b1.com

E-Mail for Key Personnel:
President: katie@thewallaceagency.com

National Agency Associations: Second Wind Limited

Agency Specializes In: Advertising

Katie Wallace *(Principal)*

Accounts:
Advance Auto Parts
Hayes Seay Mattern & Mattern
Tervita Corporation

WALLACE & COMPANY
(Formerly Fraser Wallace Advertising Ltd)
45195 Business Ct Ste 120, Dulles, VA 20166
Tel.: (703) 264-6400
Fax: (703) 264-1400
Web Site: www.wallaceandcompany.com

Employees: 32

Agency Specializes In: Advertising, Brand Development & Integration, Commercial Photography

Fraser Wallace *(Owner)*
Christine Malloy *(Pres & COO)*
Jaimee Reinertsen *(Chief Creative Officer & VP)*
Meagan Skeel *(Acct Dir)*
Justin Jameyson *(Mgr-Studio)*
Kristin Fox *(Sr Acct Exec)*
Samantha Maslaney *(Sr Acct Exec)*

Accounts:
JBG Companies And Tirzec Properties
Miriada
Park Crest
Van Metre Homes
Velocity

WALLAROO MEDIA
120 W Ctr St, Provo, UT 84601
Tel.: (801) 901-0736
E-Mail: info@wallaroomedia.com
Web Site: www.wallaroomedia.com

Year Founded: 2009

Agency Specializes In: Advertising, Content, Digital/Interactive, Search Engine Optimization, Social Media

Brandon Doyle *(Founder & CEO)*
Kyle Nguyen *(VP-Web Strategy)*
Nathan Roach *(VP-Content Strategy)*
Erik Westesen *(Head-Digital Strategy)*
Nicole Hillstead *(Acct Mgr & Strategist-Content)*

Accounts:
BuildYourJacket.com
Communal Restaurant
Hint Water
Imperial Barber Products
Pizzeria 712
Rising Star Outreach

WALLWORK CURRY MCKENNA
10 City Sq 5th Fl, Charlestown, MA 02129
Tel.: (617) 266-8200
Fax: (617) 266-8270
E-Mail: rmckenna@wcm-partners.com
Web Site: www.wcm-partners.com

E-Mail for Key Personnel:
Production Mgr.: jdelaney@wcm-partners.com

Employees: 30
Year Founded: 1993

Agency Specializes In: Advertising, Corporate Identity, Direct Response Marketing, Financial, Hispanic Market, Internet/Web Design, Logo & Package Design, Newspapers & Magazines, Print, Production, Radio, Retail, T.V.

Rick McKenna *(Pres)*
Jack Wallwork *(CEO & Dir-Creative)*
Alison Costello *(Sr VP & Client Svcs Dir)*
James Rowean *(Sr VP-Acct Svc)*
Emily Weber *(Acct Dir)*

Accounts:
Pannotia
TPG

WALMART LABS
(Formerly Adchemy, Inc.)
850 Cherry Ave, San Bruno, CA 94066
Tel.: (650) 837-5000
Web Site: www.walmartlabs.com

Employees: 32
Year Founded: 1995

Agency Specializes In: Education, Graphic Design, Industrial, Market Research, Web (Banner Ads, Pop-ups, etc.)

Revenue: $8,800,000

Sara Ortloff *(VP-User Experience & Res)*
Nikhil Raj *(VP)*
Bobbie Grafeld *(Dir-HR)*
Pranam Kolari *(Dir-Engrg)*

Accounts:
Amerisave
The Art Institute of Pittsburgh
Capella University
Charter One Bank
Equity Direct
Nationwide Lending
Saint Leo University
Windsor Capital

WALRUS
18 E 17th St Fl 3, New York, NY 10003
Tel.: (212) 645-2646
Fax: (212) 645-2759
Web Site: www.walrusnyc.com

Employees: 20
Year Founded: 2005

National Agency Associations: 4A's

Agency Specializes In: Above-the-Line, Advertising, Affluent Market, Alternative Advertising, Below-the-Line, Brand Development & Integration, Branded Entertainment, Broadcast, Business-To-Business, Cable T.V., Co-op Advertising, Collateral, Communications, Consumer Goods, Consumer Marketing, Consumer Publications, Cosmetics, Digital/Interactive, Direct-to-Consumer, Electronic Media, Electronics, Email, Entertainment, Exhibit/Trade Shows, Fashion/Apparel, Graphic Design, Guerilla Marketing, High Technology, Household Goods, In-Store Advertising, Internet/Web Design, Leisure, Local Marketing, Logo & Package Design, Luxury Products, Magazines, Market Research, Media Buying Services, Media Planning, Men's Market, Mobile Marketing, Multimedia, New Product Development, New Technologies, Newspaper, Newspapers & Magazines, Out-of-Home Media, Outdoor, Over-50 Market, Package Design, Paid Searches, Planning & Consultation, Podcasting, Point of Purchase, Point of Sale, Print, Product Placement, Production, Production (Print), Promotions, Radio, Social Marketing/Nonprofit, Sponsorship, Sports Market, T.V., Trade & Consumer Magazines, Travel & Tourism, Viral/Buzz/Word of Mouth

Approx. Annual Billings: $15,000,000

Breakdown of Gross Billings by Media: Cable T.V.: $3,000,000; Internet Adv.: $2,000,000; Print: $10,000,000

Deacon Webster *(Owner & Chief Creative Officer)*
Frances Webster *(Owner)*
Clementine Barker *(Acct Dir)*
Paula Beer Levine *(Acct Dir)*
Elliott Graham *(Dir-Art)*
Tara B. Lee *(Acct Supvr)*
Aaron Stephenson *(Sr Designer)*

Accounts:
AMC
Bloomberg
Conde Nast
CW-X Conditioning Wear; New York, NY Athletic Performance Wear, Jogging Bras, Running Apparel, Skiing Pants; 2002
The Economist; New York, NY (Trade Advertising); 2005
Emergen-C Say it with Fruit
Food Bank for New York City
Fourth Wall Restaurants, New York (Agency of Record)
Maloney & Porcelli Restaurant
MSG Varsity
Pret A Manger Digital, In-Store, US Marketing
Remy Cointreau USA Botanist Gin, Print Advertising, Single Malt Whiskies
ShiftYourShopping.org Campaign: "Shift Your Shopping", Pro Bono
Smith & Wollensky Campaign: "Your Name Here", Make Smith & Wollensky Yours

WALSH SHEPPARD
111 W 9th Ave, Anchorage, AK 99501
Tel.: (907) 338-3567
Fax: (907) 338-3857
E-Mail: welcome@walshsheppard.com
Web Site: www.walshsheppard.com

Employees: 15

Agency Specializes In: Electronics, Graphic Design, Internet/Web Design, Public Relations

Pat Walsh *(Founder & CEO)*
Jack Sheppard *(Pres & COO)*
Teresa Curran *(Controller & Bus Mgr)*

Accounts:
Denali Alaska Federal Credit Union
K2
Major Marine
Matanuska Electric Association
Matanuska Telephone Association

NANA Regional Corp.
Spenard Builders Supply
United Way

WALT KLEIN ADVERTISING

1873 S. Bellaire St., Ste. 620, Denver, CO 80222-4353
Tel.: (303) 298-8015
Fax: (303) 298-8194
E-Mail: partners@wka.com
Web Site: www.wka.com

E-Mail for Key Personnel:
President: cklein@wka.com

Employees: 3
Year Founded: 1981

Agency Specializes In: Advertising, Aviation & Aerospace, Bilingual Market, Brand Development & Integration, Broadcast, Business-To-Business, Cable T.V., Collateral, Communications, Consulting, Consumer Marketing, Consumer Publications, Corporate Identity, Digital/Interactive, Direct Response Marketing, Environmental, Exhibit/Trade Shows, Financial, Government/Political, Graphic Design, Health Care Services, High Technology, Hispanic Market, Industrial, Infomercials, Information Technology, Internet/Web Design, Investor Relations, Leisure, Logo & Package Design, Magazines, Media Buying Services, Medical Products, Merchandising, New Product Development, Newspaper, Newspapers & Magazines, Out-of-Home Media, Outdoor, Point of Purchase, Point of Sale, Print, Production, Public Relations, Publicity/Promotions, Radio, Real Estate, Retail, Sales Promotion, Strategic Planning/Research, T.V., Travel & Tourism

Approx. Annual Billings: $8,000,000

Cheryl Klein *(Pres)*
Walt Klein *(CEO)*

Accounts:
B/E Aerospace
Breckenridge Lodging & Hospitality
Cimarron Health Plan
Colorado Department of Higher Education
Farm Crest Milk Stores
Fund for Colorado's Future; Denver, CO
Great Outdoors Colorado; Denver, CO
Kavanaugh Homes
Microban
Northeast Denver Housing Center; Denver, CO
Udi's Foods
Yadkin Valley Bank

WALTER F. CAMERON ADVERTISING INC.

350 Motor Pkwy Ste 410, Hauppauge, NY 11788-5125
Tel.: (631) 232-3033
Fax: (631) 232-3111
E-Mail: mpreiser@cameronadv.com
Web Site: www.cameronadv.com

E-Mail for Key Personnel:
President: jcameron@cameronadv.com
Creative Dir.: psussi@cameronadv.com

Employees: 50
Year Founded: 1977

National Agency Associations: 4A's

Agency Specializes In: Advertising, Automotive, Brand Development & Integration, Broadcast, Business-To-Business, Cable T.V., Collateral, Consumer Marketing, Corporate Identity, Digital/Interactive, Direct Response Marketing, Exhibit/Trade Shows, Financial, Graphic Design, Health Care Services, High Technology, Industrial, Internet/Web Design, Legal Services, Local Marketing, Logo & Package Design, Media Buying Services, Newspaper, Newspapers & Magazines, Planning & Consultation, Point of Purchase, Print, Production, Public Relations, Publicity/Promotions, Radio, Real Estate, Recruitment, Retail, Sales Promotion, T.V., Trade & Consumer Magazines

Approx. Annual Billings: $65,000,000

Breakdown of Gross Billings by Media: Adv. Specialities: 1%; Audio/Visual: 2%; Brdcst.: 20%; Bus. Publs.: 5%; Cable T.V.: 10%; Collateral: 10%; Consumer Publs.: 7%; D.M.: 4%; E-Commerce: 2%; Exhibits/Trade Shows: 1%; Graphic Design: 4%; Internet Adv.: 3%; Network Radio: 5%; Newsp.: 19%; Outdoor: 2%; Point of Purchase: 2%; Pub. Rels.: 3%

Joseph J. Cameron, III *(Pres & CEO)*
Andrew Kline *(Partner)*
Mark Preiser *(Principal)*
Benjamin Coggiano *(VP-Client Svcs)*
Sean Beyer *(Dir-Creative)*
Alicia Brauneisen *(Dir-Media)*
Patricia Nelson Zorn *(Sr Acct Exec)*
Betsy Stevens *(Acct Exec)*

Accounts:
Clintrac; Ronkonkoma, NY Clinical Labeling
Flow X-Ray; Hempstead, NY; 2004
Good Samaritan Hospital Medical Center; W. Islip, NY
ITC Trucking; 1985
Karp Buick, Saab & Volvo
Long Island Volvo Association; NY; 1999

WALTON / ISAACSON

3630 Eastham Dr, Culver City, CA 90232
Tel.: (323) 677-5300
Fax: (323) 456-1139
E-Mail: awalton@waltonisaacson.com
Web Site: www.waltonisaacson.com

Employees: 90
Year Founded: 2006

National Agency Associations: 4A's

Agency Specializes In: Advertising, African-American Market, Automotive, Food Service

Revenue: $2,000,000

Cory Isaacson *(Co-Founder & Partner)*
Aaron Walton *(Co-Founder & Partner)*
Juan Bonilla *(Sr VP-Bus Dev)*
Sophia Taylor *(Sr VP-Acct Svcs)*
Alice Rivera *(VP-Hispanic Mktg)*
Martin Cerri *(Grp Dir-Creative-Hispanic Market Div)*
Nick Vitellaro *(Sr Acct Dir)*
John Florek *(Dir-Creative)*
Javier Osorio *(Dir-Creative)*
Mark Westman *(Dir-Creative)*
Nick Kamei *(Assoc Dir-Creative)*
Jose Martinez *(Assoc Dir-Creative)*
Rochelle Newman-Carrasco *(Sr Strategist-Hispanic Mktg)*
Ray Madrigal *(Generalist-HR)*
Miguel Garcia *(Grp Creative Dir)*

Accounts:
American Cinematheque
Avion Tequila
Beam Global Spirits & Wines 2 GINGERS, Basil Hayden's, Campaign: "Booker Said", Courvoisier, Jim Beam, Kilbeggan Irish Whiskey, Knob Creek, Skinnygirl Cocktails
Beam Suntory Campaign: "The Don't Hurry', Cruzan Rum
Caesars Entertainment Company
Caesars Entertainment Corporation US Hispanic Agency of Record
Change.org
Charitybuzz.com
Donuts Media Buying
Forbes, Inc.
General Mills
The Hillshire Brands Company Campaign: "Done (Listo)", State Fair, The Jimmy Dean
Jim Beam
Kilbeggan Whiskey Campaign: "Knitting", Campaign: "The Best-Kept Secret in Whiskey"
Lexus Campaign: "How Far Have We Come?", Campaign: "Make Some Noise", LGBT Marketing, Lexus NX, Super Bowl 2015
Los Angeles Dodgers Marketing
Marriott
McDonald's Corporation
Samsung
New-Spalding (Agency of Record)
Spanish Cinema Festival
Tequila Ocho
Unilever Axe, Clear Hair Care, Degree, Dove, Nexxus, Simple, Suave, TRESemme
Verizon Wireless
The Water Project Foundation
Wells Fargo
Whirlpool
White Memorial Hospital

Branch

Walton Isaacson

729 7th Ave 8th Fl, New York, NY 10019
Tel.: (646) 213-7300
E-Mail: questions@waltonisaacson.com
Web Site: www.waltonisaacson.com

National Agency Associations: 4A's

Agency Specializes In: Advertising, Digital/Interactive, Social Media

Vida Cornelious *(Chief Creative Officer & Exec VP)*
Juan Bonilla *(Sr VP & Head-New Bus Dev)*
Lupe De Los Santos *(Sr Dir & Strategist-Hispanic Mktg)*
Dwayne Crittendon *(Dir-Media)*
David Moreno *(Dir-Strategic Plng)*
Roy Chicas *(Office Mgr)*
Didem Ayturk *(Sr Acct Exec)*
Brielle Defilippis *(Acct Exec)*

Accounts:
Macy's, Inc.

WALZ TETRICK ADVERTISING

6299 Nall Ave Ste 300, Mission, KS 66202-3547
Tel.: (913) 789-8778
Fax: (913) 789-8493
E-Mail: info@wtads.com
Web Site: www.wtads.com

E-Mail for Key Personnel:
President: ctetrick@wtads.com
Creative Dir.: bbellinger@wtads.com
Media Dir.: BOveresch@wtads.com

Employees: 20
Year Founded: 1967

National Agency Associations: 4A's

Agency Specializes In: Advertising, Agriculture, Business-To-Business, Financial, Food Service, Health Care Services, Newspapers & Magazines, Public Relations, Retail, Travel & Tourism

Approx. Annual Billings: $10,000,000

Breakdown of Gross Billings by Media: Mags.: 8%; Newsp.: 6%; Outdoor: 1%; Production: 40%; Radio: 15%; T.V.: 30%

Eric M. Lykins *(CFO)*
Siobhan McLaughlin Lesley *(VP & Client Svcs Dir)*
Kelli Oestreich *(Sr Dir-Art)*
Lesley Hause *(Dir-Adv)*
Blair Overesch *(Dir-Media Svcs)*
Natasha Beaulieu *(Specialist-Media)*
Melba Morris *(Sr Media Buyer)*

Accounts:
Boy Scouts
Dairy Queen; CO; KS; MO; VA; WV; LA; OH Dairy Queen Grill & Chill; 2003
Elanco Animal Health; 2006
GE
GE Transportation Systems Global Signal; Grain Valley, MO Railroad Supplies; 1984
Kansas City Royals Creative, Media Planning
Olathe Health System; Olathe, KS; 2002

WANDERLUST

297 River St, Troy, NY 12180
Tel.: (518) 272-2500
Fax: (518) 272-2500
E-Mail: mshipley@createwanderlust.com
Web Site: www.createwanderlust.com

Employees: 12
Year Founded: 1985

Agency Specializes In: Advertising, Affluent Market, Brand Development & Integration, Cable T.V., Collateral, Communications, Consulting, Consumer Marketing, Corporate Identity, Electronic Media, Experience Design, Guerilla Marketing, Hospitality, Identity Marketing, Internet/Web Design, Leisure, Logo & Package Design, Newspaper, Newspapers & Magazines, Outdoor, Over-50 Market, Planning & Consultation, Point of Purchase, Point of Sale, Print, Production, Production (Print), Radio, Real Estate, Sales Promotion, Strategic Planning/Research, T.V., Trade & Consumer Magazines, Travel & Tourism, Viral/Buzz/Word of Mouth

Approx. Annual Billings: $22,000,000

Mark Shipley *(Pres & Chief Strategic Officer)*
Sara Tack *(Exec VP-Image & Identity)*
Harold Buckland *(Dir-Mktg)*
Sharon Lawless *(Dir-Print)*
Dave Mercier *(Dir-Art)*
Dave Vener *(Dir-Mktg)*
Kate Mcelroy *(Acct Mgr)*
Braden Russom *(Acct Mgr)*
Mo Abele *(Mgr)*

Accounts:
The Chickasaw Nation; Ada, OK Chickasaw Country; 2009
Glimmerglass Opera; Cooperstown, NY Annual Glimmerglass Opera & Music Festival; 2010
Howe Caverns; Howes Cave; NY Cavern Tours; 2008
Mount Snow; Wilmington, VT Mount Snow Resort; 2006
Windham Mountain; Windham, NY Windham Mountain Resort; 2005

WARD ASSOCIATES

(Name Changed to Adtopia Marketing Group)

THE WARD GROUP

15400 Knoll Trl Ste 335, Dallas, TX 75248
Tel.: (972) 818-4050
Fax: (972) 818-4151
Toll Free: (800) 807-3077
E-Mail: rob@mediastewards.com
Web Site: www.mediastewards.com

E-Mail for Key Personnel:
President: rob@mediastewards.com

Employees: 15
Year Founded: 1985

National Agency Associations: AAF

Agency Specializes In: Advertising, African-American Market, Asian Market, Automotive, Bilingual Market, Broadcast, Business-To-Business, Cable T.V., Co-op Advertising, Consulting, Corporate Identity, Digital/Interactive, Direct Response Marketing, Electronic Media, Email, Entertainment, Financial, Health Care Services, Hispanic Market, Magazines, Media Buying Services, Media Planning, Multicultural, Newspaper, Newspapers & Magazines, Out-of-Home Media, Outdoor, Planning & Consultation, Point of Purchase, Point of Sale, Print, Radio, Real Estate, Regional, Restaurant, Retail, Search Engine Optimization, Sponsorship, Strategic Planning/Research, T.V., Trade & Consumer Magazines, Transportation

Rob Enright *(Pres)*
Shirley Ward *(CEO)*
Tom Jago *(Mng Dir)*
Jerry Grady *(VP)*
Lou Nagy *(VP)*
Julie Ried *(VP)*
Pat Zagorski *(Dir-Media)*
Robin Cox *(Media Buyer)*
Chelsea Enright *(Media Buyer)*

Accounts:
DART
Park Place Motorcars; Dallas, TX
The Trinity Trust

WAREHOUSE AGENCY

16 Maiden Ln Ste 1101, New York, NY 10038
Tel.: (212) 608-6320
E-Mail: info@thewarehouseagency.com
Web Site: www.thewarehouseagency.com

Agency Specializes In: Advertising

Lou Stellato *(COO & Dir-Creative)*

Accounts:
16 Handles Frozen Yogurt

WARHAFTIG & LITTMAN ADV/SALES PROMOTION/PR

24 Clonover Rd, West Orange, NJ 07052-4304
Tel.: (973) 731-7963
Fax: (973) 731-4887
E-Mail: wlcreative@comcast.net

E-Mail for Key Personnel:
President: annette@wlcreative.com

Employees: 2
Year Founded: 1983

Agency Specializes In: Business-To-Business, Collateral, Communications, Corporate Identity, E-Commerce, Education, Internet/Web Design, Logo & Package Design, Pharmaceutical, Public Relations

Breakdown of Gross Billings by Media: Bus. Publs.: 20%; Consumer Publs.: 20%; Graphic Design: 35%; Logo & Package Design: 15%; Mags.: 10%

Annette Littman *(Pres)*

Accounts:
New Jersey YMHA-YWHA Camps; Fairfield, NJ

WARHAFTIG ASSOCIATES INC.

740 Broadway, New York, NY 10003
Tel.: (212) 995-1700
Fax: (212) 995-1166
E-Mail: matt@warhaftig.com

Employees: 4
Year Founded: 1982

Agency Specializes In: Health Care Services, Medical Products, Pharmaceutical

Approx. Annual Billings: $1,000,000

Breakdown of Gross Billings by Media: Collateral: $400,000; Consulting: $100,000; Logo & Package Design: $200,000; Other: $300,000

Hande Dogu *(VP-Acct Mgmt)*
Reiner Lubge *(Dir-Art & Designer)*

Accounts:
Abbott
Pfizer

WARK COMMUNICATIONS

1135 Serendipity Way, Napa, CA 94558
Tel.: (707) 266-1445
Web Site: www.warkcommunications.com

Year Founded: 1994

Agency Specializes In: Advertising, Graphic Design, Media Relations, Public Relations, Social Media

Tom Wark *(Owner)*

Accounts:
New-Moraga Estate (Public Relations Agency of Record)

WARNE MARKETING & COMMUNICATIONS

65 Overlea Blvd Ste 112, Toronto, ON Canada
Tel.: (416) 927-0881
Fax: (416) 927-1676
Toll Free: (888) 279-7846
E-Mail: scott@warne.com
Web Site: www.warne.com

Employees: 9
Year Founded: 1979

National Agency Associations: INBA

Agency Specializes In: Advertising, Aviation & Aerospace, Bilingual Market, Brand Development & Integration, Business Publications, Business-To-Business, Catalogs, Collateral, Communications, Consulting, Corporate Communications, Corporate Identity, Digital/Interactive, Direct Response Marketing, E-Commerce, Education, Electronic Media, Email, Engineering, Event Planning & Marketing, Exhibit/Trade Shows, Financial, Graphic Design, Health Care Services, High Technology, Identity Marketing, Industrial, Information Technology, Integrated Marketing, International, Internet/Web Design, Investor Relations, Logo & Package Design, Magazines, Market Research, Media Buying Services, Media Planning, Media Relations, Medical Products, Multimedia, New Product Development, New Technologies, Newspaper, Newspapers & Magazines, Paid Searches, Planning & Consultation, Print, Production, Production (Ad, Film, Broadcast), Production (Print), Public Relations, Publicity/Promotions, Sales Promotion, Search Engine Optimization, Social Marketing/Nonprofit, Stakeholders, Strategic Planning/Research, Technical Advertising, Trade & Consumer Magazines, Transportation, Web (Banner Ads, Pop-ups, etc.), Yellow Pages Advertising

Approx. Annual Billings: $2,500,000

Accounts:
Canadian Business Hall of Fame; Toronto, Canada Business Services; 2007
Datafile; Silverwater, Australia Filing Systems & Services; 2002
G.N. Johnston Equipment Co., Ltd.; Mississauga, Canada Materials Handling; 1981
TAB Canada; Toronto, ON Filing Systems & Services; 2000
TAB USA; Mayville, WI Filing Systems & Services; 2009

WARNE/MCKENNA ADVERTISING
110 S Lowell Ave, Syracuse, NY 13204-2629
Tel.: (315) 478-5781
Fax: (315) 474-2155
Web Site: www.wmck.com

Employees: 4
Year Founded: 1968

Agency Specializes In: Advertising, Automotive, Broadcast, Cable T.V., Communications, Corporate Identity, Financial, Government/Political, Graphic Design, Infomercials, Internet/Web Design, Leisure, Media Buying Services, Newspaper, Out-of-Home Media, Outdoor, Planning & Consultation, Point of Sale, Print, Production, Public Relations, Publicity/Promotions, Radio, Restaurant, Retail, T.V.

Approx. Annual Billings: $1,200,000

Breakdown of Gross Billings by Media: Adv. Specialities: $12,000; Cable T.V.: $120,000; D.M.: $72,000; Graphic Design: $60,000; Internet Adv.: $36,000; Logo & Package Design: $24,000; Newsp.: $180,000; Outdoor: $60,000; Point of Sale: $24,000; Production: $60,000; Pub. Rels.: $96,000; Radio: $216,000; Spot Radio: $180,000; Transit: $60,000

Janice McKenna *(Pres & Dir-Creative)*
Lynn Orlandella *(Media Planner)*

Accounts:
Cashel House Agent of Irish Imports; 1986
Catholic Cemeteries, Diocese of Syracuse; 1999
Diocese of Syracuse; 1976
East Syracuse Chevrolet; East Syracuse, NY; 1977
Geddes Federal Savings & Loan Association; Syracuse, NY; 1980
The Lakehouse Pub
Loretto; Syracuse, NY Elder Care; 2004
Tarson Pools; 1999
Tipperary Hill Shamrock Run

WARP FACTOR 2, LLC
4344 McLaughlin Ave Ste 103, Los Angeles, CA 90066
Tel.: (310) 295-2004
Web Site: www.warpfactor2.com

Employees: 10
Year Founded: 2010

Agency Specializes In: Above-the-Line, Alternative Advertising, Below-the-Line, Branded Entertainment, Broadcast, Cable T.V., Digital/Interactive, Guerilla Marketing, Multimedia, Production, Social Media, T.V.

Approx. Annual Billings: $1,000,000

Michael DeFilippo *(Owner)*
Marshall Sutherin *(Co-Owner)*
Thomas Mikusz *(VP-Ops)*
Grecco Bray *(Coord-PR)*

Accounts:
IGN Entertainment Web Series; 2012
Konami Dance Dance Revolution; 2011
NVISION Commercials; 2010

WASABI RABBIT INC
19 Fulton St Ste 307, New York, NY 10038
Tel.: (646) 366-0000
E-Mail: hello@wasabirabbit.com
Web Site: www.wasabirabbit.com

Employees: 17
Year Founded: 2011

Agency Specializes In: Advertising, Brand Development & Integration, Content, Digital/Interactive, Internet/Web Design, Outdoor, Package Design, Print, Search Engine Optimization, Social Media

Revenue: $3,800,000

John Mustin *(Founder & CEO)*
David Barnum *(Chief Creative Officer)*
Pat Costello *(Exec VP-Brand)*
Tim Lyons *(Mng Dir-Acct Svcs)*
Lena Smart *(Acct Dir)*
Pramod Maharana *(Dir-Design)*
Jonathan McIntosh *(Dir-Art)*
Joe Mihalow *(Dir-Creative)*
Ali Fujii *(Designer)*
Daniel Poena *(Coord-Social Media)*

Accounts:
Blue Star Veterans Network Creative & Marketing Services, Campaign Management; 2013
BlueMetal Creative Services, Marketing Campaign Strategy; 2015
Concordia College Brand, Website Design; 2014
Eli Draws Website, Video Production; 2013
Marketwired Brand, Campaign Management, Event Support, Creative Services; 2012
MAS Website Design, Product Development; 2013
The Olmstead Foundation Brand, Website Design, Social Media Management; 2014
Revelwood Brand, Website Design; 2013
The Steptoe Group Marketing Campaign Management, Website Design; 2013
Sysomos Brand, Campaign Management, Event Support, Creative Services; 2012
USAA Brand Development, Creative Services; 2015

WASHINGTON MEDIA GROUP
525 9th St NW Ste 800, Washington, DC 20004
Tel.: (202) 628-1280
Fax: (202) 628-1218
E-Mail: info@washingtonmedia.com
Web Site: www.washingtonmedia.com

Agency Specializes In: Corporate Communications, Crisis Communications, Digital/Interactive, Media Relations, Public Relations

Gregory L. Vistica *(Pres & CEO)*
Jon Steinman *(Principal)*
Lisa Brasier *(Dir-Creative)*
Ryan Fanning *(Dir-Digital)*
Don McNab *(Dir-West Coast Ops)*
Mavis Baah *(Sr Acct Mgr)*
Jonathan Murphy *(Sr Acct Mgr)*
Laura Hardwick *(Designer-Creative)*

WASSERMAN & PARTNERS ADVERTISING INC.
1020 Mainland St Ste 160, Vancouver, BC V6B 2T4 Canada
Tel.: (604) 684-1111
Fax: (604) 408-7049
E-Mail: info@wasserman-partners.com
Web Site: www.wasserman-partners.com

E-Mail for Key Personnel:
President: awasserman@wasserman-partners.com

Employees: 42
Year Founded: 1995

National Agency Associations: CAB

Agency Specializes In: Advertising, Brand Development & Integration, Broadcast, Collateral, Digital/Interactive, Financial, Food Service, Health Care Services, Media Buying Services, Pharmaceutical, Print, Production, Restaurant, Retail, Strategic Planning/Research

Alvin Wasserman *(Pres & Writer)*
Susan Deans *(CFO & Dir-Admin)*
Pauline Hadley-Beauregard *(VP)*
Karen Nishi *(VP-Strategic Plng)*
Surina Sproul *(Acct Dir)*
Liam Greenlaw *(Dir-Creative)*
Graeme Jack *(Dir-Art)*
Katie Holmes *(Copywriter)*

Accounts:
BC Nurses
Canfisco
Dairyworld Foods
Encorp Pacific (Canada)
Fairmont Hotels & Resorts (B.C.)
Granville Island Brewing; Vancouver, BC (Agency of Record) Point of Sale Merchandise-Sponsorships, Social Media
Homeworks
ICBC
Intrawest ULC
London Drugs
Quigg
Rick Henson
Singapore Airlines
Sonora Resort
Tourism Kelowna
Tourism Whistler
Wesbild
Whistler Blackcomb Mountains
White Spot Restaurants
Worksafe BC

WASSERMAN MEDIA GROUP
10960 Wilshire Blvd Ste 2200, Los Angeles, CA 90024
Tel.: (310) 407-0200
Web Site: www.wmgllc.com

Agency Specializes In: Advertising, Brand Development & Integration, Digital/Interactive, Public Relations, Social Media, Sponsorship

Denise Durante *(Co-Pres-Consulting)*
Steve Astephen *(Mng Dir)*
Mike Watts *(COO)*
Trista Schroeder *(Chief Admin Officer)*
Steve Marshman *(Exec VP)*
John Mascatello *(Exec VP)*
Richard L. Motzkin *(Exec VP)*
Ryan Berenson *(Sr VP-Fin)*
Jennifer Van Dijk *(Sr VP-Digital)*
Circe Wallace *(Sr VP)*
Alexander Chang *(VP-Consulting)*
Michael Spencer *(VP-Olympic & Action Sports)*
Marissa Nilon Kleber *(Client Mgr-Olympic Sports)*

Accounts:
Andrew Farrell
Kekuta Manneh
United States Women's National Soccer Team Abby Wambach, Alex Morgan, Ali Krieger, Ashlyn Harris, Heather O'Reilly, Lauren Holiday, Lori Chalupny, Megan Rapinoe, Sydney Leroux, Tobin Heath

Branch

Laundry Service
(Formerly 247 Laundry Service)
40 W 25th St, New York, NY 10010
(See Separate Listing)

WATAUGA GROUP
(Formerly Watauga Group LLC)
1600 N Orange Ave Ste 13, Orlando, FL 32804
Tel.: (407) 982-2696
Fax: (407) 386-3084
Web Site: www.wataugagroup.com

Employees: 17
Year Founded: 2004

Agency Specializes In: Promotions, Strategic Planning/Research

Charles Osborne *(Mng Partner-Digital Solutions)*
Leslie Osborne *(Partner & Dir-Media)*
Neil Romaine *(Partner-Strategic Mktg)*
Michelle Evans *(Dir-Insights & Media)*
Erin Hartman *(Dir-Media)*
Debra Marrano *(Dir-Search Media)*
Jenny Williams *(Dir-Media)*
Katrina Culberson-Weber *(Supvr-Media)*
Deborah Booker *(Media Planner)*
Nicole Zayas *(Coord-Media)*

Accounts:
The Breakers Palm Beach; 2004
CareSpot; 2013
Dollywood Theme Park and Splash Country; 2015
Smith & Wesson; 2012
University of Miami MBA Programs; 2011

WATERMARK
400 S Colorado Blvd Ste 380, Denver, CO 80246
Tel.: (303) 771-5675
Fax: (303) 771-5656
Web Site: www.watermarkadvertising.net

Agency Specializes In: Advertising, Internet/Web Design, Media Buying Services, Media Relations, Media Training, Public Relations, Social Media

Jason Hanson *(Co-Owner & Pres)*
Heathe Haseltine Cooper *(Dir-Sls & Project Mgmt)*
Gini Queen *(Sr Partner & Sr Acct Exec)*

Accounts:
MWH Global, Inc.

WATERWERKS COMMUNICATIONS
96 LeMarchant Rd, Churchill Square, Saint John's, NL A1C 2H2 Canada
Tel.: (709) 738-5090
Fax: (709) 738-6209
Toll Free: (877) 998-5090
Web Site: www.waterwerkscommunications.com

Agency Specializes In: Corporate Identity, Graphic Design, Internet/Web Design, Logo & Package Design, Media Buying Services, Radio, T.V.

Roxanne Morrissey *(Partner)*
Gail Barnes *(Dir-Creative)*
Dave Sturge *(Dir-Art)*
Pete Newman *(Specialist-Visual Media)*

Accounts:
Caul's
Ice Block
Leon's
Nape
Purity Factories Limited; Saint John's, NL, Canada
Ramada

THE WATSONS
150 W 30 St Ste 905, New York, NY 10001
Tel.: (212) 239-9703
E-Mail: info@itsthewatsons.com
Web Site: www.itsthewatsons.com

Agency Specializes In: Advertising, Collateral, Digital/Interactive, Direct Response Marketing, Graphic Design, Logo & Package Design, Recruitment, Social Media, Sponsorship

Maggie Monteith *(Partner)*
Paul Orefice *(Partner)*
Rachel Leventhal *(Acct Dir)*
Greg Niclas *(Dir-Art)*
Brian Rosenkrans *(Dir-Art)*
Anath Schwarts *(Acct Mgr)*

Accounts:
Cafe Metro Branding, Digital, OOH, Packaging, Social
Hint Inc
New-Montclair State University (Agency of Record)
New York Merger, Acquisition & Collaboration Fund
Physique 57
Whole Foods Market, Inc.

WATT INTERNATIONAL, INC.
300 Bayview Ave, Toronto, ON M5A 3R7 Canada
Tel.: (416) 364-9384
Fax: (416) 364-1098
E-Mail: Contactus@wattisretail.com
Web Site: wattisretail.com

Employees: 50

Agency Specializes In: Brand Development & Integration

Vince Guzzi *(Partner-Strategy)*
Juan Esquijarosa *(VP-Intl Bus)*
Laura Guthrie *(VP-Client Dev)*
Inder Bangari *(Sr Dir-Strategy)*
Brian Bettencourt *(Sr Dir-Creative)*
Sarah Farrand *(Sr Dir-Strategy)*
Bryan Morris *(Sr Dir-Creative)*
Natalie Belda Lake *(Designer-Intermediate)*
Angela Chan *(Sr Designer)*
Maya Czajkowski *(Analyst-Strategy-Watt International)*
Vlad Kushchenko *(Sr Client Mgr)*
Mireille El-boustany Tourangeau *(Sr Client Mgr-Retail Mktg)*
Nadia Valdiosera *(Client Mgr)*

Accounts:
A&P
Alto Los Condes Cencosud S.A.
Canadian Tire
Coco Cola
Cott Corporation
Liquor Control Board of Ontario (LCBO)
Loblaws
Longo's
Longs Drugs
McDonald's
Simons Laval
Simons Montreal

WAVELENGTH
401 Locust St 2nd Fl, Columbia, PA 17512
Tel.: (717) 823-6939
Web Site: www.wavelengthresults.com

Year Founded: 2003

Agency Specializes In: Advertising, Brand Development & Integration, Digital/Interactive, Graphic Design, Internet/Web Design, Logo & Package Design

Jennifer Peterson *(Pres & Strategist)*
Gary Peterson *(VP & Creative Dir)*
C. David Kramer *(Strategist-Brand)*
Kayla Soders *(Specialist-Digital Mktg)*

Accounts:
Our Lady of the Lake

WAVELENGTH MARKETING, LLC
401 Locust St, Columbia, PA 17512
Tel.: (717) 823-6939
Web Site: wavelengthresults.com/

Year Founded: 2003

Agency Specializes In: Business Publications, Collateral, Consumer Publications, Email, Magazines, Newspaper, Newspapers & Magazines, Outdoor, Paid Searches, Print, Radio, Search Engine Optimization, Trade & Consumer Magazines, Web (Banner Ads, Pop-ups, etc.)

Jennifer Peterson *(Pres)*

Accounts:
New-RFK Associates Inc.; 2015

WAX PARTNERSHIP
333 24th Ave Southwest Ste 320, Calgary, AB T2S 3E6 Canada
Tel.: (403) 262-9323
Fax: (403) 262-9399
Web Site: www.wax.ca

Employees: 30

Agency Specializes In: Advertising, Agriculture, Arts, Brand Development & Integration, Cosmetics, Fashion/Apparel, Luxury Products, Medical Products, Men's Market, Multimedia, Technical Advertising

Trent Burton *(Partner & Dir-Creative)*
Monique Gamache *(Partner & Dir-Design)*
James Brown *(Grp Acct Dir)*
Brad Connell *(Art Dir)*
Dan Wright *(Dir-Design)*
Chris Lihou *(Copywriter)*

Accounts:
Anne Paterson's Flowers Campaign: "Free Flower Posters"
Calgary Farmers' Market Campaign: "Fresh Everything", Campaign: "Snow Signs"
Calgary Horror Convention Campaign: "Body Parts"
Calgary International Film Festival Wife
Calgary Society for Persons with Disabilities
Complete Office
energy4everyone
Glenbow Museum
Honda Campaign: "Braking Bad", Campaign: "Xmas Tree"
Mitchell Eye Centre
Mucho Burrito Campaign: "Stamp"
On Hold
Roth & Ramberg Photography
WordFest
WURST

WAXWORDS INCORPORATED
105 Maxess Rd Ste S124, Melville, NY 11747
Tel.: (631) 574-4433
Fax: (631) 574-4434
E-Mail: info@waxwordsinc.com
Web Site: www.waxwordsinc.com

Agency Specializes In: Advertising, Brand Development & Integration, Communications, Local Marketing, Public Relations, Strategic Planning/Research

Alan J. Wax *(Founder & Pres)*

Accounts:
Advantage Title Agency, Inc.
CIBS
Digital Motion Marketing Solutions
Knock Out Pest Control
Ornstein Leyton Company
Paragon Group LLC
Sutton & Edwards Inc.
T. Weiss Realty Corp
Tallgrass Properties
Totus Office Solutions LLC
Vino University
Wachtler Knopf Equities LLC

WC&G AD LOGIC
(Formerly Wolfbone Marketing)
3455 Peachtree Rd NE Ste 600, Atlanta, GA 30326
Tel.: (404) 995-4620
Fax: (404) 995-4625
Web Site: www.wcgadlogic.com

Employees: 6
Year Founded: 2004

Agency Specializes In: Communications

Sadie Lesko *(Dir-Art)*

Accounts:
Kauffman Tires
PGA Tour Superstore
Treadepot.com

WC MEDIA INC.
1824 S MacArthur Blvd, Springfield, IL 62704
Tel.: (217) 241-1224
Fax: (217) 241-3824
E-Mail: info@wcmedia.net
Web Site: www.wcmedia.net

Employees: 6
Year Founded: 1995

Agency Specializes In: Advertising, Advertising Specialties, African-American Market, Agriculture, Asian Market, Automotive, Aviation & Aerospace, Bilingual Market, Brand Development & Integration, Broadcast, Business Publications, Business-To-Business, Cable T.V., Children's Market, Co-op Advertising, Collateral, Commercial Photography, Communications, Consulting, Consumer Publications, Corporate Communications, Corporate Identity, Cosmetics, Digital/Interactive, Direct Response Marketing, E-Commerce, Education, Electronic Media, Engineering, Entertainment, Event Planning & Marketing, Exhibit/Trade Shows, Fashion/Apparel, Financial, Food Service, Gay & Lesbian Market, Government/Political, Graphic Design, Health Care Services, High Technology, Hispanic Market, In-Store Advertising, Industrial, Information Technology, Internet/Web Design, Investor Relations, Legal Services, Leisure, Local Marketing, Logo & Package Design, Magazines, Marine, Media Buying Services, Medical Products, Merchandising, Multimedia, New Product Development, Newspapers & Magazines, Out-of-Home Media, Outdoor, Over-50 Market, Pharmaceutical, Planning & Consultation, Point of Purchase, Point of Sale, Print, Production, Public Relations, Publicity/Promotions, Radio, Real Estate, Recruitment, Restaurant, Retail, Sales Promotion, Seniors' Market, Sports Market, Strategic Planning/Research, Sweepstakes, Syndication, T.V., Technical Advertising, Teen Market, Telemarketing, Trade & Consumer Magazines, Transportation, Travel & Tourism, Yellow Pages Advertising

Revenue: $2,000,000

Nick Giacomini *(Owner, CEO & Gen Mgr)*
Danielle Giacomini *(Co-Owner)*

Accounts:
Cracker Barrel
Travel Centers of America

WDM GROUP
(Formerly White Digital Media)
5901 Priestly Dr Ste 300, Carlsbad, CA 92008
Tel.: (760) 827-7800
Fax: (760) 827-7823
E-Mail: amber.keith@wdmgroup.com
Web Site: www.wdmgroup.com/

Employees: 132
Year Founded: 2007

Agency Specializes In: Advertising, Advertising Specialties, Affiliate Marketing, Agriculture, Alternative Advertising, Asian Market, Automotive, Aviation & Aerospace, Bilingual Market, Brand Development & Integration, Branded Entertainment, Business Publications, Business-To-Business, Catalogs, Co-op Advertising, Communications, Computers & Software, Consulting, Consumer Goods, Consumer Marketing, Consumer Publications, Content, Corporate Communications, Corporate Identity, Crisis Communications, Custom Publishing, Customer Relationship Management, Digital/Interactive, Direct Response Marketing, Direct-to-Consumer, Electronic Media, Electronics, Email, Engineering, Entertainment, Event Planning & Marketing, Exhibit/Trade Shows, Fashion/Apparel, Financial, Food Service, Government/Political, Graphic Design, Health Care Services, High Technology, Hispanic Market, Hospitality, Household Goods, Identity Marketing, Industrial, Information Technology, Integrated Marketing, International, Internet/Web Design, Investor Relations, Legal Services, Leisure, Local Marketing, Logo & Package Design, Luxury Products, Magazines, Market Research, Media Buying Services, Media Relations, Medical Products, Men's Market, Merchandising, Mobile Marketing, Multicultural, Multimedia, New Product Development, New Technologies, Newspaper, Newspapers & Magazines, Out-of-Home Media, Over-50 Market, Package Design, Pharmaceutical, Planning & Consultation, Point of Purchase, Point of Sale, Product Placement, Promotions, Public Relations, RSS (Really Simple Syndication), Regional, Restaurant, Retail, Sales Promotion, Seniors' Market, Social Media, South Asian Market, Sponsorship, Stakeholders, Strategic Planning/Research, Technical Advertising, Telemarketing, Trade & Consumer Magazines, Transportation, Travel & Tourism, Urban Market, Viral/Buzz/Word of Mouth, Web (Banner Ads, Pop-ups, etc.), Women's Market, Yellow Pages Advertising

Approx. Annual Billings: $15,000,000

Breakdown of Gross Billings by Media: Adv. Specialities: $2,000,000; Event Mktg.: $500,000; Exhibits/Trade Shows: $500,000; Internet Adv.: $2,000,000; Newsp.: $2,000,000; Trade & Consumer Mags.: $3,000,000; Worldwide Web Sites: $5,000,000

Sasha Orman *(Editor-Food & Drink Digital)*
James Pepper *(Sls Dir-EME)*
Alex Barron *(Dir-Res)*
Dennis Morales *(Dir-Res)*
Amber Keith *(Office Mgr)*
Holly Bennett *(Asst Designer-Magazine)*
Cellia Harvey *(Interim Mgr-Fin)*

WE ARE SOCIAL INC.
73 Spring St, New York, NY 10012
Tel.: (646) 476-2893
Web Site: www.wearesocial.com

Year Founded: 2008

Agency Specializes In: Advertising, Brand Development & Integration, Media Relations, Public Relations, Social Media, Sponsorship

Rob FitzGerald *(Pres-US)*
Robin Grant *(Mng Dir-Global)*
Robb Henzi *(Sr Dir-Strategy)*
Jenn Bader *(Grp Acct Dir)*
Ben Arnold *(Bus Dir)*
Peter Fontana *(Dir & Sr Analyst)*
Kristie Matfus *(Dir)*
Craig Stauber *(Dir-Res & Insights)*
Rebecca Finn *(Analyst-Social Media)*
Sasha Mariano *(Designer)*

Accounts:
adidas North America
Alliance Boots
AMC Networks Inc.
Banana Republic Campaign: "#ShareHappy", Campaign: "#thenewBR", Community Management, Fall Collection, Social Media Strategy
Beats Electronics LLC
Boots Beauty
Ermenegildo Zegna Global Social Media
Giorgio Armani Corporation
Hotels.com, L.P.
The National Geographic Channel Creative, Social Media Marketing, Strategy
Netflix
The Outnet Global Social Media
PVH Corp IZOD, Van Heusen
Reebok International Ltd.
STA Travel Ltd.

WEB SOLUTIONS INC.
250 Pomeroy Ave Ste 201, Meriden, CT 06450
Tel.: (203) 235-7777
Fax: (203) 639-9327
Toll Free: (866) 415-7777
Web Site: www.websolutions.com

Year Founded: 1996

Agency Specializes In: Advertising, Digital/Interactive, Graphic Design, Integrated Marketing, Outdoor, Print, Public Relations, Strategic Planning/Research, T.V., Technical Advertising

Lori O'Brien *(VP-Accts)*
Diane Lepkowski *(Dir-Art)*
Emily Walker *(Acct Mgr)*
Alan Ashby *(Mgr-Internet Mktg)*
Janaura Bishop *(Mgr-Digital Mktg)*
Michael Rakiec *(Mgr-Internet Mktg)*
Patrick Wampler *(Mgr-Internet Mktg)*
Andrew Smith *(Acct Exec)*
Melissa Tangney *(Acct Specialist)*

WEB STRATEGY PLUS
201 E Fifth St Ste 1900-1008, Cincinnati, OH 45202
Tel.: (513) 399-6025
E-Mail: contactus@webstrategyplus.com
Web Site: www.webstrategyplus.com

Agency Specializes In: Advertising, Graphic Design, Internet/Web Design, Logo & Package Design, Paid Searches, Print, Search Engine Optimization

Michelle Hummel *(Founder & CEO)*

Accounts:
New-Web Media University

WEBB STRATEGIC COMMUNICATIONS
(Formerly Webb PR)
6025 S Quebec St Ste 360, Centennial, CO 80111
Tel.: (303) 796-8888
Web Site: webbstrategic.com

Employees: 10

Agency Specializes In: Brand Development & Integration, Communications, Crisis Communications, Government/Political, Logo & Package Design, Media Relations, Media Training, Sponsorship, Strategic Planning/Research

Peter Webb *(Principal)*
Ginny Williams *(Principal)*
Chris Jenuine *(Dir-Creative & Sr Copywriter)*
Andy Cohen *(Sr Acct Mgr)*
Taunia Hottman *(Acct Mgr)*
Sheryl East *(Mgr-Admin)*
Silvia Solis *(Acct Coord-Bilingual)*

Accounts:
CACI Colorado Association
Colorado Department of Human Services
East Cherry Creek Valley
Pinnacol Assurance

WEBLIFT
18495 S Dixie Hwy Ste 365, Miami, FL 33157-6817
Tel.: (800) 605-4914
Fax: (305) 437-7618
Web Site: www.weblift.com

Agency Specializes In: Advertising, Brand Development & Integration, Digital/Interactive, Internet/Web Design, Social Media

Pedro Sostre *(CEO & Dir-Creative)*
Misty McIntosh *(Dir-Product Mgmt)*
Jia-ying Lin *(Specialist-Social Media)*

Accounts:
1450, Inc.
Blue Ridge Restaurant Group
Energy Upgrade California Windsor Efficiency Pays
Richard Robbins International, Inc.

WEBMETRO
(Name Changed to Revana Digital)

WEBNBEYOND
2280 Grand Ave Ste 314, Baldwin, NY 11510
Tel.: (516) 377-7483
Fax: (516) 377-7999
Toll Free: (888) 880-4313
E-Mail: info@webnbeyond.com
Web Site: www.webnbeyond.com

Employees: 10
Year Founded: 1998

Agency Specializes In: Advertising, Brand Development & Integration, Business-To-Business, Collateral, Communications, Consumer Marketing, Corporate Communications, Corporate Identity, Digital/Interactive, Direct Response Marketing, E-Commerce, Entertainment, Event Planning & Marketing, Gay & Lesbian Market, Graphic Design, Internet/Web Design, Local Marketing, Logo & Package Design, Medical Products, New Product Development, Planning & Consultation, Print, Public Relations, Radio, Restaurant, Sales Promotion, Sports Market, Strategic Planning/Research, Trade & Consumer Magazines

Jason Guida *(Pres)*

Accounts:
Ancona Law
Baldwin Chamber
CCTV Garage
DeMar House
Manhattan Beer Distributors
Red Storm Stable; Oceanside, NY Thoroughbred Horse Ownership; 2004
Sky Athletic

WEBSCOPE
99 W Hawthorne Ave Ste 420, Valley Stream, NY 11580
Tel.: (516) 561-3935
Fax: (516) 561-3935
E-Mail: info@webscope.com
Web Site: www.webscope.com

Employees: 6
Year Founded: 1992

Agency Specializes In: Consulting, Consumer Marketing, Electronic Media, Internet/Web Design, Publicity/Promotions

David Staschover *(Pres)*

Accounts:
Econolodge Hotel
FUBU Clothing; New York, NY Website; 1996
Fubu-The Collection
Norchem Concrete Products
Scientific Industries
Slant/Fin; Greenvale, NY Website; 1996

WEBWORKS ALLIANCE
95 Caterson Ter, Hartsdale, NY 10530
Tel.: (914) 390-0060
Fax: (914) 390-0061
E-Mail: jonparets@webworksalliance.net
Web Site: www.webworksalliance.net

Employees: 5
Year Founded: 2003

Agency Specializes In: Corporate Identity, Digital/Interactive, Health Care Services, Medical Products, Recruitment

jon Parets *(Owner)*
Rob Resnik *(Owner)*

Accounts:
Eastern Connecticut Health Network
Harris Interactive; Rochester, NY; 2004
Oce Document Printing Systems; 2004

WEDGIE CREATIVE
1166 E Warner Rd, Gilbert, AZ 85296
Tel.: (602) 456-2770
E-Mail: info@wedgiecreative.com
Web Site: www.wedgiecreative.com

Agency Specializes In: Advertising, Brand Development & Integration, Internet/Web Design, Radio, Social Media

Ken Moskowitz *(CEO)*

Accounts:
Ryco Plumbing

WEDNESDAY NEW YORK
245 5th Ave 25th Fl, New York, NY 10016
Tel.: (646) 476-3053
E-Mail: newyork@wednesdayagency.com
Web Site: www.wednesdayagency.com

Agency Specializes In: Advertising, Brand Development & Integration, Digital/Interactive, Internet/Web Design, Package Design, Social Media

Justin Edwards *(Dir-Creative)*
Simon Lee *(Dir-Creative)*
Michelle Kordahi *(Acct Mgr)*
Natalee Ranii-Dropcho *(Strategist-Creative)*
Joyce Chen *(Sr Designer)*
Tom Elsey *(Designer)*
Kristen Hoy *(Client Dir)*
Rekishia Jessup *(Client Dir)*

Accounts:
Armani Exchange

WEE BEASTIE
116 Chambers St 5th FL, New York, NY 10007
Tel.: (212) 349-0795
Fax: (866) 317-9430
Toll Free: (866) 317-9430
E-Mail: info@weebeastie.tv
Web Site: www.weebeastie.tv

Employees: 6

Agency Specializes In: Advertising, Brand Development & Integration, Broadcast, Graphic Design, Pets , Production

Travis Blain *(Dir-Art)*
Chris McKenna *(Dir-Creative)*
Alicia Biggs *(Sr Head-Creative)*

Accounts:
Animal Planet
Geico
NatGeo

WEIDERT GROUP INC.
901 Lawe St, Appleton, WI 54915
Tel.: (920) 731-2771
Web Site: www.weidert.com

E-Mail for Key Personnel:
President: gregl@weidert.com
Creative Dir.: megh@weidert.com
Production Mgr.: katen@weidert.com
Public Relations: abbyg@weidert.com

Employees: 12
Year Founded: 1981

Agency Specializes In: Advertising, Automotive, Brand Development & Integration, Broadcast, Business Publications, Business-To-Business, Cable T.V., Catalogs, Collateral, Communications, Consulting, Consumer Goods, Consumer Marketing, Consumer Publications, Corporate Communications, Corporate Identity, Crisis Communications, Digital/Interactive, Direct Response Marketing, Direct-to-Consumer, Education, Electronic Media, Email, Engineering, Event Planning & Marketing, Exhibit/Trade Shows, Financial, Food Service, Graphic Design, Health Care Services, Identity Marketing, Industrial, Integrated Marketing, Internet/Web Design, Legal Services, Local Marketing, Logo & Package Design, Magazines, Market Research, Media Buying Services, Media Planning, Media Relations, Media Training, Medical Products, Merchandising, Multimedia, Newspaper, Newspapers & Magazines, Outdoor, Package Design, Planning & Consultation, Point of Sale, Production (Print), Promotions, Public Relations, Publicity/Promotions, Radio, Regional, Sales Promotion, Search Engine Optimization, Social Marketing/Nonprofit, Strategic Planning/Research, T.V., Technical Advertising, Trade & Consumer Magazines, Viral/Buzz/Word of Mouth, Web (Banner Ads, Pop-ups, etc.), Yellow Pages Advertising

Breakdown of Gross Billings by Media: Brdcst.:

25%; Cable T.V.: 40%; Radio: 35%

Greg Linnemanstons *(Pres & Principal)*
Tami Wessley *(Partner & VP)*
Meg Hoppe *(Principal & Dir-Creative)*
Brent Senske *(Dir-Design & Tech)*
Lawrence Cartwright *(Mgr-Mktg)*

Accounts:
MBM; WI Office Equipment
Solvoyo Content, Marketing, Social Media, Strategy

THE WEINBACH GROUP, INC.
7301 SW 57th Ct Ste 550, South Miami, FL 33143-5334
Tel.: (305) 668-0070
Fax: (305) 668-3029
E-Mail: info@weinbachgroup.com
Web Site: www.weinbachgroup.com

E-Mail for Key Personnel:
President: pweinbach@weinbachgroup.com
Creative Dir.: dweinbach@weinbachgroup.com

Employees: 12
Year Founded: 1987

Agency Specializes In: Advertising, Brand Development & Integration, Broadcast, Business-To-Business, Collateral, Communications, Consulting, Consumer Marketing, Direct Response Marketing, Education, Electronic Media, Fashion/Apparel, Financial, Graphic Design, Health Care Services, Internet/Web Design, Investor Relations, Logo & Package Design, Media Buying Services, Medical Products, Newspapers & Magazines, Outdoor, Over-50 Market, Pharmaceutical, Planning & Consultation, Public Relations, Publicity/Promotions, Recruitment, Seniors' Market, Strategic Planning/Research, T.V., Trade & Consumer Magazines, Travel & Tourism

Approx. Annual Billings: $5,000,000

Breakdown of Gross Billings by Media: Cable T.V.: 10%; Collateral: 15%; Consulting: 20%; D.M.: 15%; Graphic Design: 5%; Logo & Package Design: 2%; Newsp. & Mags.: 25%; Outdoor: 3%; Radio: 5%

N. Phillip Weinbach *(Pres)*
Daniel Weinbach *(Exec VP)*
Elaine Weinbach *(Comptroller)*
Perla Terzian *(Mgr-Client Svcs)*

Accounts:
7-UP Company
Alvey, Inc
HealthFusion Miami Children's Pediatric Electronic Data System
Jackson Health System Campaign: "Miracles Made Daily"
PET, Inc.
Phytrust
The Renfrew Center Women's Mental Health Facility; 1996
Ryder System, Inc.
Susan G. Komen Foundation
Tribeca Medaesthetics
University of Miami

WEINRICH ADVERTISING/COMMUNICATIONS, INC.
915 Clifton Ave Ste 2, Clifton, NJ 07013-2725
Tel.: (973) 473-6643
Fax: (973) 473-0685
E-Mail: info@weinrichadv.com
Web Site: www.weinrichadv.com

Employees: 9
Year Founded: 1968

Agency Specializes In: Advertising, Advertising Specialties, Brand Development & Integration, Business Publications, Business-To-Business, Collateral, Communications, Corporate Communications, Corporate Identity, Digital/Interactive, Direct Response Marketing, E-Commerce, Electronic Media, Event Planning & Marketing, Exhibit/Trade Shows, High Technology, Information Technology, Internet/Web Design, Logo & Package Design, New Product Development, Newspapers & Magazines, Print, Production, Public Relations

Breakdown of Gross Billings by Media: Adv. Specialities: 5%; Collateral: 50%; Exhibits/Trade Shows: 15%; Mags.: 10%; Worldwide Web Sites: 20%

Lori W. Fabisiak *(Pres)*
Lisa Lessner *(Dir-Creative)*

Accounts:
Innovation Data Processing
Tea USA
UNICOR

THE WEINSTEIN ORGANIZATION, INC.
1 S Wacker Dr Ste 1670, Chicago, IL 60606-4670
Tel.: (312) 214-2900
Fax: (312) 214-1120
Web Site: www.twochicago.com

E-Mail for Key Personnel:
President: mweinstein@weinsteinorg.com
Creative Dir.: kherbes@weinsteinorg.com

Employees: 15
Year Founded: 1992

Agency Specializes In: Advertising, Automotive, Bilingual Market, Broadcast, Business Publications, Business-To-Business, Collateral, Consumer Marketing, Customer Relationship Management, Direct Response Marketing, Direct-to-Consumer, E-Commerce, Electronic Media, Email, Financial, Graphic Design, Health Care Services, Hispanic Market, Integrated Marketing, Internet/Web Design, Magazines, Market Research, Newspaper, Newspapers & Magazines, Out-of-Home Media, Package Design, Paid Searches, Print, Production, Production (Ad, Film, Broadcast), Production (Print), Promotions, Retail, Search Engine Optimization, Social Media, Strategic Planning/Research, Sweepstakes, T.V., Telemarketing, Trade & Consumer Magazines, Web (Banner Ads, Pop-ups, etc.)

Approx. Annual Billings: $16,900,000

Breakdown of Gross Billings by Media: D.M.: $9,660,000; E-Commerce: $3,500,000; Internet Adv.: $635,000; Newsp. & Mags.: $2,535,000; T.V.: $210,000; Worldwide Web Sites: $360,000

Bob Weinstein *(Co-Chm)*
Francois Martin *(Exec VP-Mktg & TV Sls)*
Stacy Dautel *(Acct Supvr)*
Julie Determann *(Acct Supvr)*
Kara Monson *(Acct Supvr)*
Janelle Schenher *(Acct Supvr)*
Kim Chapman *(Sr Acct Exec)*

Accounts:
ABC Supply Co.; Beloit, WI Roofing & Building Supplies; 1999
Affinity Group Inc.; Ventura, CA The Good Sam Club; 2006
American Medical Association Insurance Agency; Chicago, IL Insurance; 1995
American Medical Association Publishing Div; Chicago, IL JAMA, Archives, AM News; 2010
Bank of America; Charlotte, NC; Phoenix, AZ Credit Cards; 2001
Credit First National Association; Brook Park OH Consumer Credit; 2011
Firestone Complete Autocare Center; Atlanta, GA; Exton, PA; Laguna Hills, CA; Roanoke, TX Tire & Automotive Services; 1996
Lean & Luscious Ltd.; Charleston, WV Lean & Luscious; 2011
Mercedes Benz Financial; Farmington Hills, MI Credit Products; 2008
Mule-Hide Products Co., Inc.; Beloit, WI Roofing Materials; 2002
RCN Telecom; Chicago, IL Cable TV, Internet & Phone Service; 2010
Weight Watchers Franchise Association; Nashville, TN Weight Loss Program; 2000

WEINTRAUB ADVERTISING
7745 Carondelet Ave Ste 308, Saint Louis, MO 63105-3315
Tel.: (314) 721-5050
Fax: (314) 721-4106
E-Mail: lweintraub@weintraubadv.com
Web Site: www.weintraubadvertising.com

E-Mail for Key Personnel:
Chairman: lweintraub@weintraubadv.com

Employees: 40
Year Founded: 1953

Agency Specializes In: Advertising, Brand Development & Integration, Broadcast, Co-op Advertising, Collateral, Communications, Consumer Marketing, Corporate Identity, Electronic Media, Event Planning & Marketing, Fashion/Apparel, Financial, Media Buying Services, Newspaper, Newspapers & Magazines, Outdoor, Point of Purchase, Point of Sale, Print, Production, Public Relations, Radio, Real Estate, Retail, T.V.

Robert Weintraub *(Pres & Dir-Creative)*
Dwight Stamp *(Sr Dir-Art)*
Susie Penn *(Dir-Creative & Writer)*
Sherri Hensley *(Dir-Fin)*
Danielle Weintraub Block *(Acct Mgr)*
Dawn Walter *(Acct Exec)*

Accounts:
BOMA Saint Louis
Carol House Furniture
CCA Global Partners
The Cedars at the JCA
Floor Trader
Harry's Corner
Jaffe Lighting
Lenders One
Lighting One
Magnus Anderson
Memory Care Home Solutions
Rug Decor
Slumberland Quad Cities
Stone Mountain

WEITZMAN, INC.
3 Church Cir, Annapolis, MD 21401
Tel.: (410) 263-7771
Fax: (410) 263-7834
E-Mail: info@weitzmanagency.com
Web Site: www.weitzmanagency.com

Employees: 11
Year Founded: 1976

Agency Specializes In: Advertising

Approx. Annual Billings: $5,000,000

Breakdown of Gross Billings by Media: Bus. Publs.: $750,000; Collateral: $500,000; Mags.: $1,250,000; Newsp.: $1,250,000; T.V.: $1,250,000

Margriet Mitchell *(Pres)*
Jim Schmidt *(VP & Sr Dir-Creative)*
Jean Contillo *(VP & Dir-Media)*
Alan R. Weitzman *(Exec Dir-Creative)*
Lauren Degeorge *(Mgr-Traffic & Project Coord)*
Heather Haffner *(Sr Acct Exec)*

Accounts:
Advent Funeral & Cremation Service
Bobby Rahal Automotive Group
Crown Automobile
The David Drew Clinic
New-FNB Bank (Agency of Record) Brand Strategy, Creative Messaging, Media Buying, Media Planning, Social Media
Mercedes-Benz of Pittsburgh
Rolls-Royce
Scarborough Capital Management (Agency of Record) Brand Strategy, Creative Messaging, Media Buying, Media Planning
Severn Savings Bank Brand Strategy, Creative Messaging, Media Planning & Buying, Social Media Marketing

WELCH INC.
180 Mitchell's Ln, Portsmouth, RI 02871
Tel.: (401) 846-1370
Fax: (401) 846-1370
E-Mail: welchinc@aol.com

Employees: 1
Year Founded: 1977

Agency Specializes In: Advertising, Affluent Market, Brand Development & Integration, Business-To-Business, Collateral, Corporate Communications, Direct Response Marketing, Electronic Media, Industrial, Integrated Marketing, Internet/Web Design, Media Planning, Media Relations, Public Relations, Publicity/Promotions, Real Estate

Approx. Annual Billings: $500,000

Mark Cavano *(VP-Domestic Sls)*
Karen Mitchell *(Dir-Mktg)*
Phil Drapeau *(Sr Brand Mgr-Shelf-Stable Juice)*
Jackie Lee *(Brand Mgr-Innovation)*
Larry Keenan *(Mgr-Natl Sls-Grocery Area)*

Accounts:
ACBI; Fairfield, CT Insurance; 2005
E.G. Sturveant
Ganom Group; Bridgeport, CT Financial Services; 2004
Precast Building Solutions

WELCOMM, INC.
7975 Raytheon Rd Ste 340, San Diego, CA 92111-1622
Tel.: (858) 279-2100
Fax: (858) 279-5400
Toll Free: (888) WELCOMM
E-Mail: greg@welcomm.com
Web Site: www.welcomm.com

Employees: 12
Year Founded: 1985

Agency Specializes In: High Technology

Gregory W. Evans *(CEO)*
Kathy Naraghi *(CFO)*
Marsha Ryan *(Principal)*
Brad Buckingham *(Mgr-Web Svcs)*
Kevin Burk *(Designer-Multimedia)*
Randy Frank, Sr. *(Writer-Technical)*

Accounts:
Applied Power Electronic Conference
E. Mon L.L.C. Electric Metering; 2007
PowerCET Corporation
Premier Magnetics; Lake Forest CA Magnetic Components, Power Conversion Devices; 1999
ROHM

WELIKESMALL, INC
252 S Edison St, Salt Lake City, UT 84111
Tel.: (801) 467-2207
Web Site: www.welikesmall.com

Employees: 1,000
Year Founded: 2008

Agency Specializes In: Advertising, Consulting, Digital/Interactive, Graphic Design

Michael Kern *(Pres & Exec Dir-Creative)*
Paul Solomon *(Partner, VP & Dir-Tech)*
Tommy Chandler *(Dir-Content)*
Rebecca Clayton *(Designer-Interactive)*

Accounts:
American Express Campaign: "Course Curator"
Toyota Motor Corporation

THE WELL ADVERTISING
435 N LaSalle Dr Ste 201, Chicago, IL 60654
Tel.: (312) 595-0144
Fax: (312) 595-0258
E-Mail: info@thewellinc.com
Web Site: www.thewellinc.com

Employees: 16
Year Founded: 2003

Agency Specializes In: Advertising, Content, Digital/Interactive, Internet/Web Design

Revenue: $5,000,000

Staci Wood *(Mng Partner)*
Julie Petersen *(Dir-Media)*

Accounts:
Camp Wapiyapi
Mitsubishi Electronic Automation
UOP

WELL DONE MARKETING
1043 Virginia Ave, Indianapolis, IN 46203
Tel.: (317) 624-1014
E-Mail: info@welldonemarketing.com
Web Site: www.welldonemarketing.com

Agency Specializes In: Advertising, Brand Development & Integration, Event Planning & Marketing, Graphic Design, Internet/Web Design, Media Relations, Radio, Social Media, Strategic Planning/Research, T.V.

Ken Honeywell *(Pres & Creative Dir)*
Beth Jenkins *(VP-Accts)*
Sarah Stewart *(Art Dir)*
Linda Broadfoot *(Dir-Mktg & Bus Dev)*
Mindy Ford *(Dir-Ops)*
Matt Gonzales *(Assoc Dir-Creative)*
Melissa Yoder *(Acct Supvr)*
Joe Judd *(Sr Acct Exec)*
Abby Reckard *(Strategist-Digital)*

Accounts:
Early Learning Indiana

WELLNESS COMMUNICATIONS
7299 Parkridge Rd, Newburgh, IN 47630
Tel.: (812) 480-8170
Fax: (812) 858-6102
E-Mail: david@wellnesscminc.com
Web Site: wellnesscminc.com/

Employees: 5
Year Founded: 2007

Agency Specializes In: Advertising, Affiliate Marketing, Alternative Advertising, Bilingual Market, Brand Development & Integration, Branded Entertainment, Broadcast, Business Publications, Business-To-Business, Cable T.V., Co-op Advertising, Collateral, Commercial Photography, Communications, Consulting, Consumer Marketing, Consumer Publications, Content, Corporate Communications, Cosmetics, Crisis Communications, Custom Publishing, Direct Response Marketing, Direct-to-Consumer, E-Commerce, Education, Electronic Media, Email, Entertainment, Faith Based, Graphic Design, Guerilla Marketing, Health Care Services, In-Store Advertising, Infomercials, Information Technology, Integrated Marketing, Internet/Web Design, Local Marketing, Logo & Package Design, Magazines, Media Buying Services, Media Planning, Media Relations, Medical Products, Men's Market, Multimedia, New Product Development, Newspaper, Newspapers & Magazines, Out-of-Home Media, Outdoor, Over-50 Market, Paid Searches, Pharmaceutical, Planning & Consultation, Podcasting, Point of Purchase, Point of Sale, Print, Production, Production (Ad, Film, Broadcast), Production (Print), Promotions, Public Relations, Publicity/Promotions, Publishing, RSS (Really Simple Syndication), Radio, Sales Promotion, Search Engine Optimization, Seniors' Market, Social Media, Sponsorship, Strategic Planning/Research, Syndication, T.V., Trade & Consumer Magazines, Viral/Buzz/Word of Mouth, Web (Banner Ads, Pop-ups, etc.), Women's Market

Approx. Annual Billings: $2,000,000

Breakdown of Gross Billings by Media: Corp. Communications: 100%

David K. Wells *(Founder & Pres)*

WELLONS COMMUNICATIONS
195 Wekiva Springs Rd Ste214, Longwood, FL 32779
Tel.: (407) 339-0879
Fax: (407) 339-0879
E-Mail: info@wellonscommunications.com
Web Site: www.wellonscommunications.com

Employees: 5

Agency Specializes In: Communications, Crisis Communications, Media Relations, Newspaper, Public Relations, Strategic Planning/Research, T.V.

Will Wellons *(Owner)*
Tracey Dettmer *(Dir-Mktg)*
Frank Wolff *(Dir-Media Rels)*

WELLS COMMUNICATIONS, INC.
3460 4th St, Boulder, CO 80304
Tel.: (303) 417-0696
Fax: (303) 440-3325
E-Mail: info@wellscommunications.net
Web Site: www.wellscommunications.net

Employees: 5

Agency Specializes In: Advertising, Brand Development & Integration, Business-To-Business, Internet/Web Design, Local Marketing, Media Relations, Media Training, Strategic Planning/Research

Michele Wells *(Pres)*

WELZ & WEISEL COMMUNICATIONS
3950 University Dr Ste 201, Fairfax, VA 22030-2569

Tel.: (703) 218-3555
E-Mail: info@w2comm.com
Web Site: www.w2comm.com

Employees: 12

Tony Welz *(Principal)*
Thomas Resau *(Sr VP-Cybersecurity & Privacy Practice)*
Joyson Cherian *(VP)*
Jayna Kliner *(VP)*
Chris Leach *(Sr Acct Dir)*
Nicole Nolte *(Sr Acct Dir)*
Christy Pittman *(Acct Dir)*
Dex Polizzi *(Acct Dir)*
Dennis McCafferty *(Dir-Content)*

Accounts:
Cyveillance
MegaPath Inc.
Sourcefire Inc.

THE WENDT AGENCY

105 Park Dr S, Great Falls, MT 59401
Tel.: (406) 454-8550
Fax: (406) 771-0603
Web Site: thewendtagency.com

E-Mail for Key Personnel:
Creative Dir.: jstein@iwendt.com
Media Dir.: ckruger@iwendt.com
Production Mgr.: cmoore@iwendt.com
Public Relations: ckruger@iwendt.com

Employees: 17
Year Founded: 1929

Agency Specializes In: Advertising, Brand Development & Integration, Broadcast, Business Publications, Business-To-Business, Cable T.V., Co-op Advertising, Collateral, Communications, Consulting, Consumer Marketing, Consumer Publications, Corporate Identity, Direct Response Marketing, Direct-to-Consumer, E-Commerce, Education, Electronic Media, Entertainment, Event Planning & Marketing, Exhibit/Trade Shows, Financial, Government/Political, Health Care Services, High Technology, Identity Marketing, Internet/Web Design, Logo & Package Design, Magazines, Media Buying Services, Medical Products, Newspaper, Newspapers & Magazines, Out-of-Home Media, Outdoor, Point of Purchase, Point of Sale, Print, Production, Public Relations, Publicity/Promotions, Radio, Sales Promotion, Strategic Planning/Research, T.V., Trade & Consumer Magazines, Transportation, Travel & Tourism, Yellow Pages Advertising

Approx. Annual Billings: $10,000,000

Breakdown of Gross Billings by Media: Collateral: $1,100,000; D.M.: $200,000; Fees: $1,700,000; Internet Adv.: $500,000; Mags.: $1,300,000; Newsp.: $1,000,000; Outdoor: $100,000; Production: $1,800,000; Radio: $200,000; T.V.: $1,700,000; Worldwide Web Sites: $300,000; Yellow Page Adv.: $100,000

Brenda Peterson *(Pres & CEO)*
Lorie Hager *(CFO)*
Carol Kruger *(VP-PR & Media Svcs)*
Joe Stein *(Dir-Creative & Producer-Brdcst)*
Carmen Moore *(Dir-Production)*
Johna Wilcox *(Acct Mgr)*
Pam Bennett *(Sr Media Planner & Media Buyer)*
Merle McLeish *(Media Buyer)*

Accounts:
D.A. Davidson & Co.
Glacier County Tourism
Helena Convention & Visitors Bureau
Montana Department of Transportation
Montana State Parks
Pacific Steel & Recycling
Pizza Hut
Studio Montage

WENDT ROTSINGER KUEHNLE, INC.

3450 W Central Ave Ste 374, Toledo, OH 43606-1416
Tel.: (419) 531-0125
Fax: (419) 531-0128
E-Mail: info@wrk.com
Web Site: www.wrk.com

E-Mail for Key Personnel:
President: gkuehnle@wrk.com

Employees: 8
Year Founded: 1980

Agency Specializes In: Advertising, Advertising Specialties, Automotive, Broadcast, Business-To-Business, Cable T.V., Co-op Advertising, Consumer Marketing, Corporate Identity, Direct Response Marketing, Entertainment, Industrial, Infomercials, Internet/Web Design, Magazines, Newspaper, Newspapers & Magazines, Outdoor, Print, Radio, Retail, T.V., Yellow Pages Advertising

Breakdown of Gross Billings by Media: Bus. Publs.: 12%; Collateral: 10%; Newsp.: 22%; Radio: 28%; T.V.: 28%

Greg F. Kuehnle *(Pres)*
John Guitteau *(VP)*
Sandy Deer *(Comptroller)*
Sue Pruss *(Dir-Art)*

Accounts:
Anderson's General Stores

WESLEY DAY & COMPANY, INC.

(Acquired & Absorbed by Trilix Marketing Group, Inc.)

THE WESSLING GROUP

(See Under Chromium)

WEST ADVERTISING

1410 Park Ave, Alameda, CA 94501
Tel.: (510) 865-9378
Fax: (510) 865-9388
E-Mail: connect@westadvertising.com
Web Site: www.westadvertising.com

Employees: 12
Year Founded: 1988

Agency Specializes In: Advertising, Brand Development & Integration, Email, Internet/Web Design, Logo & Package Design, Print, Radio, Social Media, T.V.

Pete Halbertstadt *(Owner)*
Louise Reed *(Acct Dir)*
Deana Morgan *(Dir-Digital Mktg)*
Laura Giacri *(Office Mgr)*
Tracy Brotze *(Acct Exec)*
John Davis *(Acct Exec)*
Melanie Drewes *(Acct Coord)*
Mei Han *(Coord-Media)*

Accounts:
Alameda County Industries
Alameda Power & Telecom; 2003
CCI Wireless
Cost Plus Nursery
Dublin Honda
Jaguar
King of the Hill
Land Rover
Navlet's Garden Center; Pleasant Hill, CA Home & Garden; 1992
Stead Dealership Group; Walnut Creek, CA Automobiles; 1990
Toyota Walnut Creek; Walnut Creek, CA Automobiles; 1998
The Transplant Pharmacy
Vascular Medical Group
Victory Toyota

WEST & ZAJAC ADVERTISING INC.

7231 W Laraway Rd, Frankfort, IL 60423-7767
Tel.: (815) 464-1400
Fax: (815) 464-0277
E-Mail: info@wza.com
Web Site: www.wza.com

E-Mail for Key Personnel:
President: info@wza.com
Media Dir.: TSmith@wza.com

Employees: 6
Year Founded: 1976

Agency Specializes In: Advertising, Advertising Specialties, Automotive, Broadcast, Business Publications, Business-To-Business, Cable T.V., Co-op Advertising, Collateral, Consumer Marketing, Consumer Publications, Corporate Identity, Direct Response Marketing, E-Commerce, Electronic Media, Exhibit/Trade Shows, Financial, Graphic Design, Health Care Services, High Technology, Information Technology, Internet/Web Design, Logo & Package Design, Magazines, Marine, Media Buying Services, Media Planning, Media Relations, Medical Products, Multimedia, Newspaper, Newspapers & Magazines, Out-of-Home Media, Outdoor, Planning & Consultation, Point of Purchase, Point of Sale, Print, Production, Public Relations, Publicity/Promotions, Radio, Real Estate, Recruitment, Restaurant, Retail, Sales Promotion, Seniors' Market, T.V., Trade & Consumer Magazines, Yellow Pages Advertising

Approx. Annual Billings: $6,600,000

Breakdown of Gross Billings by Media: Cable T.V.: $400,000; Collateral: $850,000; D.M.: $1,500,000; Mags.: $150,000; Newsp.: $2,500,000; Other: $450,000; Outdoor: $100,000; Production: $350,000; Pub. Rels.: $100,000; Radio: $200,000

Teresa Smith *(Office Mgr)*

Accounts:
Alps Development
Brecc Homes
Chesapeake Homes
Crana Homes
Douglass Square
Dunree Homes, Inc.
Keira Construction
PBT
Safety Dig, Inc.

WEST CARY GROUP

5 W Cary St, Richmond, VA 23220
Tel.: (804) 343-2029
Fax: (804) 343-2028
E-Mail: info@westcarygroup.com
Web Site: www.westcarygroup.com

Employees: 5

Agency Specializes In: Brand Development & Integration, Corporate Communications, Direct Response Marketing, Multimedia

Moses Foster *(Pres & CEO)*
Blair Keeley *(Chief Creative Officer & Exec VP)*
Camille Blanchard *(VP & Head-Innovation)*
Rachal Hansen *(Sr Acct Dir)*
Cara Hill *(Acct Dir)*
Alexis Gayle *(Dir-Creative)*

Chris Rayl *(Dir-Media)*
Wendy Thacker *(Dir-Art)*

Accounts:
Capital One
Cephas Industries (Agency of Record)
Ferguson
Henrico Economic Development Authority Henrico.com
Hilton Worldwide
ITAC
MWV
Richmond International Airport Compressed Natural Gas EasyPark Shuttle Fleet, Marketing, Web & Mobile Design, Website Redesign, flyrichmond.com
Suntrust
Union First Market Bank Brand, Broadcast Marketing, Communications, Digital
Virginia Bio-Technology Research Park
Virginia Eye Institute Marketing, Public Relations

WESTBOUND COMMUNICATIONS, INC.
625 The City Dr Ste 360, Orange, CA 92868
Tel.: (714) 663-8188
Fax: (714) 663-8181
E-Mail: staff@westboundcommunications.com
Web Site: www.westboundcommunications.com

Employees: 5

Agency Specializes In: Government/Political, Local Marketing, New Technologies, Public Relations, Strategic Planning/Research

Scott Smith *(Pres)*
Carrie Gilbreth *(Sr VP & Gen Mgr)*
Rick Miltenberger *(Sr VP)*
Robert Chevez *(Acct Dir)*
Gina DePinto *(Acct Dir)*
Angela Meluski *(Acct Supvr)*
Jessica Neuman *(Sr Acct Exec)*

Accounts:
Alaskan Brewing Company
Anaheim Angels
Caltrans
Confederation of Downtown Associations
Coors Brewing Company
Macy's
Meade Instruments
Pioneer
San Bernadino Associated Governments (SANBAG) (Agency of Record)

THE WESTERFELDS, INC.
30B Grove St, Pittsford, NY 14534
Tel.: (585) 385-1690
Fax: (585) 385-1738
E-Mail: thewesterfelds@aol.com

Employees: 4
Year Founded: 1924

Agency Specializes In: Advertising, Advertising Specialties, Automotive, Brand Development & Integration, Broadcast, Business-To-Business, Cable T.V., Communications, Consulting, Consumer Marketing, Consumer Publications, Corporate Identity, Direct Response Marketing, Event Planning & Marketing, Exhibit/Trade Shows, Financial, Food Service, Graphic Design, Leisure, Logo & Package Design, Magazines, Media Buying Services, Newspaper, Newspapers & Magazines, Outdoor, Planning & Consultation, Point of Purchase, Point of Sale, Print, Production, Public Relations, Publicity/Promotions, Radio, Restaurant, Sales Promotion, Seniors' Market, T.V., Trade & Consumer Magazines, Transportation, Travel & Tourism

Breakdown of Gross Billings by Media: Newsp.: 30%; Other: 15%; Radio: 15%; T.V.: 40%

William A. Westerfeld *(Owner)*

Accounts:
Fairport Credit Union
Koerner Ford; Syracuse, NY
Oak Hill Country Club; Rochester, NY
Shepard Bros. Inc.; Canandaigua, NY Specialty Chemicals

WESTON MASON MARKETING
3130 Wilshire Blvd 4th Fl, Santa Monica, CA 90403
Tel.: (310) 207-6507
Fax: (310) 826-8098
E-Mail: info@westonmason.com
Web Site: www.westonmason.com

Employees: 65
Year Founded: 1984

Agency Specializes In: Advertising, Advertising Specialties, Electronic Media, Entertainment, Financial, Real Estate, Travel & Tourism

Beverly Mason *(Pres)*
Thomas Weston *(CEO)*
Ian Simonian *(VP-Client Svcs)*
Julio Cano *(Dir-Art & Mgr-Studio)*
Drusilla De Veer *(Dir-Print Production)*
Rebecca Wilson *(Dir-Creative)*

Accounts:
20th Century Fox; Los Angeles, CA Home Entertainment Products; 1997
Beazer Homes Southern California
Pilates Plus
Universal Home Entertainment; Studio City, CA Home Entertainment Products; 1997

WESTWERK
1621 E Hennepin Ave Ste B26, Minneapolis, MN 55414
Tel.: (612) 353-5349
E-Mail: hello@westwerk.com
Web Site: www.westwerk.com

Year Founded: 2005

Agency Specializes In: Advertising, Brand Development & Integration, Content, Digital/Interactive, Print

Dan West *(Founder & Exec Dir-Creative)*
Dave West *(Partner & Dir)*
Amy Abt *(VP-Mktg & Strategy)*
Todd Asmus *(Head-User Experience & Interactive Design)*
Jackie Menth *(Sr Designer)*

Accounts:
Sandow
Versique Search & Consulting

WEXLEY SCHOOL FOR GIRLS
2218 5th Ave, Seattle, WA 98121
Tel.: (206) 438-8900
E-Mail: headmaster@wexley.com
Web Site: www.wexley.com

Employees: 26
Year Founded: 2003

Agency Specializes In: Advertising, Sponsorship

Ian Cohen *(Owner)*
Gabe Hajiani *(Partner & Dir-Production)*
Christine Wise *(Partner & Dir-Plng & Strategy)*
Tara Cooke *(Assoc Producer)*
Jordan Karr *(Acct Dir)*
Derek Vander Griend *(Dir-Art & Designer)*
Lindell Serrin *(Dir-Art)*
Melissa Wielde *(Sr Acct Mgr)*
Josh Brewer *(Acct Mgr)*
Nicholas Minnott *(Acct Mgr)*
Annie Richards *(Acct Mgr)*
Evan Bross *(Designer)*
Amber Askins *(Client Svc Dir)*

Accounts:
ACLU
AssureStart (Advertising Agency of Record)
Copper Mountain Resort Campaign: "The Copper Mountain Snow Fleet Parade", Ice Melts
Darigold; Seattle, WA
Ford
HomeStreet Bank
Microsoft "The Big Ass Phone", Hey Genius Campaign (College Recruitment), Live Search Maps
Rainier Beer
Seattle Sounders
Sephora
Sony Creative
TACO DEL MAR
Wilson Campaign: "The Tennis Court"

WH2P, INC.
PO Box 22, Yorklyn, DE 19736
Tel.: (302) 530-6555
E-Mail: info@wh2p.com
Web Site: www.wh2p.com

Employees: 4
Year Founded: 1991

Agency Specializes In: Advertising, Automotive, Brand Development & Integration, Business-To-Business, Catalogs, Collateral, College, Consulting, Consumer Marketing, Corporate Communications, Corporate Identity, Digital/Interactive, Email, Environmental, Exhibit/Trade Shows, Government/Political, Graphic Design, Health Care Services, Identity Marketing, In-Store Advertising, Industrial, Integrated Marketing, Internet/Web Design, Logo & Package Design, Medical Products, Newspaper, Outdoor, Package Design, Point of Purchase, Point of Sale, Sales Promotion, Search Engine Optimization, Social Marketing/Nonprofit, Social Media, Technical Advertising, Travel & Tourism, Web (Banner Ads, Pop-ups, etc.)

Brian Havertine *(Partner)*
Roger Poole *(Partner)*
Greg Williamson *(VP & Dir-Creative)*

Accounts:
Life Strategies, LLC
Micropore, Inc.
Microsoft Dynamics
SAP Retail
Siemens Medical Solutions Diagnostics
Silvon Software
Staging Dimensions
Talent Strategy Partners
Wilmington Trust Company

WHAT IF CREATIVE
4301 Regions Pk Dr Ste 12, Fort Smith, AR 72916
Tel.: (479) 434-2488
E-Mail: info@whatifcreative.com
Web Site: www.whatifcreative.com

Agency Specializes In: Advertising, Brand Development & Integration, Event Planning & Marketing, Graphic Design, Internet/Web Design, Logo & Package Design, Print, Search Engine Optimization, Social Media

Lea Taylor *(Pres)*
Kyle Hale *(Sr Designer)*

Accounts:
SSi Incorporated

WHAT'S UP INTERACTIVE
1200 Ashwood Pkwy, Atlanta, GA 30338
Tel.: (770) 407-8918
Web Site: www.whatsupinteractive.com

Employees: 30
Year Founded: 1990

National Agency Associations: AD CLUB-AMA

Agency Specializes In: Advertising, Brand Development & Integration, Broadcast, Business-To-Business, Communications, Consumer Goods, Digital/Interactive, Electronic Media, Information Technology, Integrated Marketing, Internet/Web Design, Mobile Marketing, Multimedia, Podcasting, Production (Ad, Film, Broadcast), Search Engine Optimization, Social Marketing/Nonprofit, Social Media, Strategic Planning/Research, Viral/Buzz/Word of Mouth, Web (Banner Ads, Pop-ups, etc.)

Approx. Annual Billings: $3,000,000

Breakdown of Gross Billings by Media: Internet Adv.: $3,000,000

Richard Warner *(CEO)*
Michael Radney *(Dir-Creative Svcs)*
Ryan Wallace *(Mgr-Bus Dev)*

Accounts:
AmericasMart
Coca-Cola Refreshments USA, Inc.
Ride the Ducks!
United Egg Producers
Women in Technology

WHEELER ADVERTISING
600 Six Flags Dr, Arlington, TX 76011
Tel.: (817) 633-3183
Fax: (817) 633-3186
Toll Free: (800) 678-7822
E-Mail: information@wheeleradvertising.com
Web Site: http://wheeleradvertising.com/

Employees: 28
Year Founded: 1991

Agency Specializes In: Advertising, Automotive, Retail

Ron Wheeler *(Owner)*
Claire Wheeler *(VP & Gen Mgr-Social Motive)*
Bryan Rickelman *(Dir-Creative)*
Tana Burris *(Acct Supvr)*
Andrea Baray *(Acct Exec)*

Accounts:
Bill Plemmons
Burlington RV Superstore
Dub Richardson Toyota
Infiniti of Charlotte
Sansone Automall
Straight Talk
Toms Mechanical
Travel Country RV
Walker Acura

WHEELHOUSE MARKETING ADVISORS
1612 Westgate Cir Ste 120, Brentwood, TN 37027
Tel.: (615) 835-2940
E-Mail: info@wheelhouseworks.com
Web Site: www.wheelhouseworks.com

Year Founded: 2012

Agency Specializes In: Advertising, Brand Development & Integration, Digital/Interactive, Public Relations, Strategic Planning/Research

Joe Harkins *(Co-Founder & Mng Partner)*
Carter Toole *(Mng Partner)*
Leo Blumberg *(Dir-Acct Plng)*
Frank Limpus *(Dir-PR)*
Jason Morgan *(Dir-Web Dev)*

Accounts:
Forty Niners Football Company LLC
National Wholesale Fuels
Seawinds Asset Management

WHIRLED
2127 Linden Ave, Venice, CA 90291
Tel.: (213) 915-8889
E-Mail: info@getwhirled.com
Web Site: www.getwhirled.com

Year Founded: 2009

Agency Specializes In: Advertising

Bobbie Wang *(Mgr-Production & Producer)*
Scott Chan *(Dir-Creative)*
Chris Crutchfield *(Dir)*
Peter Ng *(Dir-Art)*

Accounts:
ASUS ASUS VivoBook
Google Inc. G.Co/Mom, The Big Presentation

WHITE & PARTNERS
13665 Dulles Technology Dr Ste 150, Herndon, VA 20171-4607
Tel.: (703) 793-3000
Fax: (703) 793-1495
Toll Free: (800) 211-0874
E-Mail: mattw@whiteandpartners.com
Web Site: white64.com

E-Mail for Key Personnel:
President: mattw@whiteandpartners.com
Creative Dir.: donaldb@whiteandpartners.com
Media Dir.: missyl@whiteandpartners.com

Employees: 50
Year Founded: 1966

National Agency Associations: 4A's

Agency Specializes In: Advertising, Advertising Specialties, Affluent Market, Brand Development & Integration, Broadcast, Business-To-Business, Co-op Advertising, Collateral, Communications, Consulting, Consumer Marketing, Corporate Communications, Corporate Identity, Direct Response Marketing, Event Planning & Marketing, Exhibit/Trade Shows, Food Service, Government/Political, High Technology, In-Store Advertising, Information Technology, Leisure, Local Marketing, Logo & Package Design, Media Buying Services, Multimedia, New Product Development, Out-of-Home Media, Outdoor, Planning & Consultation, Point of Purchase, Point of Sale, Print, Production, Public Relations, Publicity/Promotions, Radio, Restaurant, Retail, Sales Promotion, Search Engine Optimization, Sponsorship, Sports Market, Strategic Planning/Research, Sweepstakes, T.V., Technical Advertising, Trade & Consumer Magazines, Transportation, Travel & Tourism, Viral/Buzz/Word of Mouth

Approx. Annual Billings: $51,500,000

Breakdown of Gross Billings by Media: Bus. Publs.: 5%; Collateral: 5%; D.M.: 5%; Internet Adv.: 3%; Mags.: 13%; Newsp.: 18%; Other: 3%; Outdoor: 3%; Point of Purchase: 3%; Pub. Rels.: 3%; Radio: 8%; Sls. Promo.: 2%; Sports Mktg.: 2%; Strategic Planning/Research: 3%; T.V.: 24%

Matthew C. White *(Chm & CEO)*
Jim Upson *(CFO, COO, Partner & Sr VP)*
Missy Lieber *(Partner & Chief Media Officer)*
Kipp Monroe *(Partner & Chief Creative Officer)*
Kelly Weismiller *(Sr Acct Supvr)*
Lee O'Neill *(Supvr-Media)*
Nicole Halbach *(Sr Acct Exec)*
Ryan Kasperski *(Sr Acct Exec)*
Erica Eng *(Strategist-Product)*
Tori Hodges *(Acct Exec)*
Becca Marshall *(Acct Exec)*

Accounts:
Acela Express
American Chemistry Council
The American Coalition of Clean Coal Electricity
American Service Center; Arlington, VA
D.C. United Creative Development
Deutsche Bank Championship (Advertising Agency of Record) Digital, Media Buying
Families Against Mandatory Minimums
Hughes Networks; Gaithersburg, MD
The Jack Welch Management Institute
Luray Caverns
MaggieMoos
MagicJack VocalTec Ltd (Agency of Record) Media Planning & Buying
Mandiant
Mercedes
National Fire Protection Association; Quincy, MA
Navy Mutual
Orchestro
Page County
Quicken Loans National (Advertising Agency of Record) Digital, Media Buying, Paid Media
Roy Rogers Restaurants
Strayer University
Touchstone Energy Corporation; Washington, DC
Verizon Wireless
Visit Fairfax
The Washington Auto Show (Agency of Record)
The Washington Metropolitan Area Transit Authority (Agency of Record) Digital Media, Graphic Design, Media Buying
The Washington Nationals
Washington Nationals
Waterways Council Inc
Wolf Trap National Park for the Performing Arts
Wolf Trap

WHITE GOOD & CO. ADVERTISING
226 N Arch St Ste 1, Lancaster, PA 17603
Tel.: (717) 396-0200
E-Mail: squalls@whitegood.com
Web Site: www.whitegood.com

Employees: 10
Year Founded: 1981

National Agency Associations: 4A's-AAF

Agency Specializes In: Advertising, Advertising Specialties, Brand Development & Integration, Broadcast, Collateral, Communications, Consumer Marketing, Consumer Publications, Corporate Identity, Direct Response Marketing, Electronic Media, Event Planning & Marketing, Exhibit/Trade Shows, Graphic Design, In-Store Advertising, Integrated Marketing, Internet/Web Design, Magazines, Market Research, Media Buying Services, Media Planning, Media Relations, Merchandising, Newspapers & Magazines, Out-of-Home Media, Point of Purchase, Point of Sale, Print, Product Placement, Production, Production (Print), Public Relations, Publicity/Promotions, Regional, Sales Promotion, Strategic Planning/Research, T.V., Trade & Consumer Magazines

Breakdown of Gross Billings by Media: Bus. Publs.: 1%; Exhibits/Trade Shows: 1%; Fees: 9%; Internet

Adv.: 1%; Mags.: 10%; Newsp.: 2%; Other: 2%; Print: 10%; Production: 55%; Pub. Rels.: 7%; Trade & Consumer Mags.: 2%

Sherry H. Qualls *(Owner & Pres)*
Rose Lantz *(CFO & Dir-HR)*
Tony Guasco *(Dir-Art)*
Amanda Wolfe *(Dir-Art)*
Vanessa Stahl *(Coord-PR)*

Accounts:
GKD-USA
ICFF (Agency of Record) Public Relations, Social Media
KBIS
Miele, Inc.
National Kitchen & Bath Association (NKBA)
New-Perlick Corporation (North American Agency of Record)
Regupol America
ROHL; Irvine, CA Fixtures; 2005
Thompson Traders (Agency of Record) Brand Strategy, Communications, Media Relations, Public Relations, Social Media
Thos. Moser

WHITE HORSE
3747 NE Sandy Blvd, Portland, OR 97232-1840
Tel.: (503) 471-4200
Fax: (503) 471-4299
Toll Free: (877) 471-4200
E-Mail: sales@whitehorse.com
Web Site: www.whitehorse.com

Employees: 21
Year Founded: 1980

National Agency Associations: AMA-BMA

Agency Specializes In: Business-To-Business, Digital/Interactive, Sponsorship

Jen Modarelli *(Owner & Principal)*
Kim D'Amico *(Dir-Digital Mktg)*
Cheryl Metzger *(Dir-Comm)*
Mike Willey *(Sr Engr-Software)*

Accounts:
Celestial Seasonings
Cisco
Columbia Sportswear Company
Fred Meyer
HSBC
Iberdrola Renewables
Mountain Hardwear
Papa Murphy's

WHITE RHINO PRODUCTIONS, INC.
41 Second Ave, Burlington, MA 01803
Tel.: (781) 270-4545
Fax: (781) 270-5151
E-Mail: info@whiterhino.com
Web Site: www.whiterhino.com

Employees: 10

Agency Specializes In: Digital/Interactive, Direct-to-Consumer, Internet/Web Design, Print, Production (Print)

Dan Greenwald *(Founder & Dir-Creative)*
Teri Sun *(VP-Mktg Transformation)*
Shawn Gross *(Head-Healthcare Practice & Sr Strategist-Digital)*
Pat Elesa *(Controller)*
Irina Muradian *(Acct Dir)*
Tristan Dwyer *(Dir-Digital Experience)*
Kim Parrish *(Dir-Design)*
Jenna Rodrigues *(Designer)*

Accounts:
Gourmet Baking
Ness Technologies

WHITE RICE ADVERTISING & PR
W63 N706 Washington Ave, Cedarburg, WI 53012
Tel.: (262) 474-0104
Web Site: www.whitericeadvertising.com

Year Founded: 2006

Agency Specializes In: Advertising, Digital/Interactive, Internet/Web Design, Logo & Package Design, Media Buying Services, Outdoor, Public Relations, Strategic Planning/Research, T.V.

Terri White *(Partner & CFO)*
Cori Rice *(Partner & Creative Dir)*
Nick Berenz *(Sr Acct Exec)*

Accounts:
Wachtel Tree Science

WHITE/THOMPSON, LLC
(Acquired by & Name Changed to Sullivan Branding)

WHITECOAT STRATEGIES, LLC
718 7th St NW, Washington, DC 20001
Tel.: (202) 422-6999
E-Mail: info@whitecoatstrategies.com
Web Site: www.whitecoatstrategies.com

Agency Specializes In: Advertising, Brand Development & Integration, Communications, Graphic Design, Internet/Web Design, Investor Relations, Media Relations, Publicity/Promotions, Strategic Planning/Research

David Sheon *(Pres)*

Accounts:
Biogas Researchers
Bionor Pharma
BroadAxe Care Coalition
HealthWell Foundation
Singularity University Labs

WHITEMYER ADVERTISING, INC.
254 E 4th St, Zoar, OH 44697
Tel.: (330) 874-2432
Fax: (330) 874-2715
Web Site: www.whitemyer.com

E-Mail for Key Personnel:
Media Dir.: lgeers@whitemyer.com

Employees: 14
Year Founded: 1971

Agency Specializes In: Business Publications, Business-To-Business, Collateral, Communications, Consulting, Corporate Identity, Direct Response Marketing, E-Commerce, Electronic Media, Engineering, Financial, Graphic Design, Industrial, Internet/Web Design, Medical Products, Newspaper, Outdoor, Planning & Consultation, Point of Purchase, Point of Sale, Print, Production, Public Relations, Radio, Retail, Strategic Planning/Research, Technical Advertising, Trade & Consumer Magazines

Breakdown of Gross Billings by Media: Bus. Publs.: 30%; Collateral: 20%; Fees: 20%; Worldwide Web Sites: 30%

Tim Whitemyer *(CEO)*
Lisa Geers *(VP-Interactive Mktg)*
Dan Mehling *(VP-Creative Svcs)*
Ty Simmelink *(VP-Acct Svcs)*
Chris Baio *(Acct Exec)*

Accounts:
Allied Machine Tool; Dover, OH Drill Bits
Architectural Products; Chicago, IL Trade Publication
JLG Industries; Mcconnellsburg, PA Training Department
Kidron, Inc.; Kidron, OH Truck Bodies; 1990
Kimble Companies
Marsh Industries; New Philadelphia, OH Chalkboard Accessories
Penton Media, Inc.
Pro Fab; Canton, OH Fabricated Metal Products
Provon Medical Group
Southeastern Equipment; Cambridge, OH Equipment Distributor
Sure-Foot; Cleveland, OH Stair Treads
Union Hospital; Dover, OH
Vacall Industries
W.W. Cross; Canton, OH Staples

Branch

Zoar Interactive
254 E 4th St, Zoar, OH 44697
Tel.: (330) 874-0313
Fax: (330) 874-2715
E-Mail: info@zoarinteractive.com
Web Site: www.zoarinteractive.com

Employees: 15

Agency Specializes In: Digital/Interactive

Tim Whitemeyer *(Pres)*
Lisa Geers *(VP & Gen Mgr)*

Accounts:
Combi
Cubbison Product Identification
Gradall Company
Kidron, Inc.
Murphy's Classics
Pro-Fab Industries, Inc.
Seaman Corp.
Southeastern Equipment
W.W. Cross, Inc.
Whitemyer Advertising
Zoar Community Association

WHITESPACE CREATIVE
24 N High St Ste 200, Akron, OH 44308
Tel.: (330) 762-9320
Fax: (330) 763-9323
E-Mail: info@whitespace-creative.com
Web Site: www.whitespace-creative.com

Employees: 30
Year Founded: 1994

Agency Specializes In: Advertising, Brand Development & Integration, Business Publications, Business-To-Business, Catalogs, Children's Market, Collateral, Communications, Consulting, Consumer Marketing, Consumer Publications, Corporate Communications, Corporate Identity, Crisis Communications, Custom Publishing, Digital/Interactive, Direct Response Marketing, Direct-to-Consumer, E-Commerce, Email, Environmental, Event Planning & Marketing, Exhibit/Trade Shows, Graphic Design, Guerilla Marketing, Health Care Services, Identity Marketing, In-Store Advertising, Integrated Marketing, Internet/Web Design, Investor Relations, Local Marketing, Logo & Package Design, Magazines, Market Research, Media Buying Services, Media Planning, Media Relations, Merchandising, Multimedia, Newspaper, Outdoor, Package Design, Planning & Consultation, Point of Purchase, Point of Sale, Print, Production, Production (Print), Promotions, Public Relations, Publicity/Promotions, Radio, Restaurant, Sales Promotion, Search Engine Optimization, Social

Marketing/Nonprofit, Strategic Planning/Research, T.V., Trade & Consumer Magazines, Viral/Buzz/Word of Mouth

Approx. Annual Billings: $2,500,000

Breakdown of Gross Billings by Media: Bus. Publs.: 10%; Collateral: 15%; Corp. Communications: 15%; E-Commerce: 20%; Graphic Design: 10%; Logo & Package Design: 10%; Production: 20%

Keeven White *(Pres & CEO)*
Greg Kiskadden *(Exec VP)*
Bob Zajac *(Exec VP)*
Leigh Greenfelder *(VP)*
Craig Satow *(VP)*
Jennifer Snider *(Assoc Dir-Creative & Copywriter)*
Susan Breen *(Assoc Dir-Creative)*
Stephanie Mathias *(Coord-PR)*

Accounts:
Akron-Canton Regional Foodbank; Akron, OH Fundraising; 2001
ALCOA; Cleveland, OH Internal Communications; 2006
FirstMerit Bank; Akron, OH Shareholder Relations, Websites; 2001
John Puglia If These Trees Could Talk Art Show Poster
Movember Imposter Series
Pacific Valley Dairy YoMazing Video
TRC Regional Transportation; Akron, OH Transportation Services; 2006

WHITESPEED

29672 Zuma Bay Way, Malibu, CA 90265
Tel.: (310) 869-9979
Fax: (310) 899-3199
E-Mail: info@whitespeed.com
Web Site: www.whitespeed.com

Employees: 12

Agency Specializes In: Advertising

Susan White *(CEO)*

Accounts:
20th Century Fox
ABC
American Express
Calvin Klein
Charles Schwab
General Motors
HP
J Records
US Postal Service

WHITNEY ADVERTISING & DESIGN, INC.

6410 N Business Park Loop Rd Ste H, Park City, UT 84098
Tel.: (435) 647-2918
Fax: (435) 647-3076
E-Mail: info@whitneyonline.com
Web Site: www.whitneyonline.com

E-Mail for Key Personnel:
Creative Dir.: jim@whitneyonline.com

Employees: 6
Year Founded: 1991

Agency Specializes In: Advertising, Advertising Specialties, Brand Development & Integration, Business-To-Business, Collateral, Consumer Marketing, Corporate Identity, Digital/Interactive, E-Commerce, Email, Graphic Design, Integrated Marketing, Internet/Web Design, Logo & Package Design, Luxury Products, Media Planning, New Product Development, Package Design, Planning & Consultation, Public Relations, Publicity/Promotions, Social Media, Strategic Planning/Research, Travel & Tourism

Robin Whitney *(Partner)*
Pam Prevatt Woll *(Specialist-Promotional Products)*

Accounts:
Aloha Ski & Snowboard Rental; Park City, UT; 2000
Challenger Schools; Salt Lake City, UT; 2007
Connor Sport Court; Salt Lake City, UT; 2009
Consortium for Continuing Legal Education in Europe; London, England; 2000
Empire Luxury Lodging; Park City, UT; 2011
Jess Reid Real Estate; Park City, UT; 2005
KPG Investments; Park City, UT; 2010
LaserTight; Park City, UT LaserTight, SelectScan; 2008
LiteTouch Lighting Control; Salt Lake City, UT; 1999
Luxury Residence Group; Park City, UT; 2011
Marker USA; West Lebanon, NH Ski Bindings; 1996
Moab Brewery; Moab, UT; 2005
Mountain Body Products, Inc.; Park City, UT; 2000
Mountain Body Spa & Herbal Cosmetic Deli; Park City, UT; 2000
Nationwide Drafting & Office Supply, Inc.; Park City, UT; 2003
Park City Clinic; Park City, UT; 2011
Park City Oral Surgery; Park City, UT; 2009
Park City Orthodontics; Park City, UT
Park City Performing Arts Foundation; Park City, UT; 2009
The ResortClubs; Park City, UT; 2005
Revitalized Body; Park City, UT; 2010
The Sky Lodge; Park City, UT; 2004
Snow Logic USA; Park City, UT; 2010
Social Register of Las Vegas; Las Vegas, NV; 2008
Sphere Technologies Inc; Park City, UT; 2011
Vehicle Lighting Solutions; Salt Lake City, UT; 2009
Vertu; Park City, UT Vertu Luxury Properties, Vertu Sport Horses; 2007
Volkl; West Lebanon, NH Skis; 2007

WHITNEY WORLDWIDE INC.

553 Hayward Ave N Ste 250, Saint Paul, MN 55128
Tel.: (651) 748-5000
Fax: (651) 748-4000
Toll Free: (800) 597-0227
Web Site: www.whitneymarketing.com

Employees: 10
Year Founded: 1983

National Agency Associations: DMA

Agency Specializes In: Affluent Market, Agriculture, Business-To-Business, College, Consulting, Direct Response Marketing, Email, Faith Based, Luxury Products, Market Research, Over-50 Market, Pets , Production (Print), Sales Promotion, Seniors' Market, Strategic Planning/Research, Women's Market

Approx. Annual Billings: $3,000,000

Breakdown of Gross Billings by Media: Consulting: 10%; D.M.: 60%; Other: 20%; Sls. Promo.: 10%

Les Layton *(Pres)*

Accounts:
3M; Saint Paul, MN
Calgary Sun
Cargill
Honeywell
IBM
ING
Land O' Lakes, Inc.
Lawson Software; Saint Paul, MN; 1997
Minnesota Twins
Packet Motion
US Bank
Wells Fargo Finance

WHITTEN DESIGN

2894 NE Baroness Pl, Bend, OR 97701
Tel.: (541) 382-9079
Web Site: www.whittendesign.com

Agency Specializes In: Advertising, Graphic Design, Identity Marketing, Internet/Web Design, Package Design, Print, Social Media

Darius Whitten *(Owner & Pres)*

Accounts:
Sunriver Resort Marina McKenzie River

WHOISCARRUS

416 N Fern Creek Ave Ste A, Orlando, FL 32803
Tel.: (407) 477-2528
Fax: (407) 477-2529
E-Mail: e-mail.us@whoiscarrus.com
Web Site: www.whoiscarrus.com

Agency Specializes In: Advertising, Brand Development & Integration, Graphic Design, Internet/Web Design, Media Buying Services, Search Engine Optimization, Social Media

Jeremy A. Carrus *(Partner & Art Dir)*
Shannon S. Carrus *(Partner & Creative Dir)*
Jim Danko *(Dir-Tech)*
Sara Philip *(Sr Designer)*

Accounts:
Mazor Robotics
Toptech Systems

WHOLE WHEAT CREATIVE

1006 W 9th St, Houston, TX 77007
Tel.: (713) 993-9339
Fax: (713) 993-9338
Web Site: wholewheatcreative.net

Employees: 12
Year Founded: 1996

Agency Specializes In: Advertising

Breakdown of Gross Billings by Media: Brdcst.: 30%; Print: 45%; Worldwide Web Sites: 25%

Lee Wheat *(Pres & Exec Dir-Creative)*

Accounts:
Du Pont

WICK MARKETING

3901 S Lamar Blvd Ste 120, Austin, TX 78704
Tel.: (512) 479-9834
Fax: (512) 479-0710
E-Mail: info@wickmarketing.com
Web Site: www.wickmarketing.com

Agency Specializes In: Advertising, Brand Development & Integration, Promotions, Social Media

Amy Wick *(Owner & Principal)*
Joanne Trubitt *(Dir-Art)*
Barbara Wray *(Dir-Social Media)*
Laura Durant *(Mgr-Ops)*
Diana Smith *(Acct Supvr)*
Stephanie Bruno *(Specialist-Social Media)*
Sara Fern *(Coord)*
Wendy Hill *(Coord-Media)*

Accounts:
Universal North America

WIDEGROUP INTERACTIVE

9701 Wilshire Blvd Ste 1000, Beverly Hills, CA 90212
Tel.: (818) 344-9703
E-Mail: info@widegroup.net
Web Site: www.widegroup.net

Agency Specializes In: Communications, Digital/Interactive, Email, Graphic Design, Health Care Services, Internet/Web Design, Local Marketing, Media Relations, Mobile Marketing, Print, Web (Banner Ads, Pop-ups, etc.)

Alexis Posternak *(Pres & Exec Producer)*
Tania Piombetti *(Dir-Creative)*

Accounts:
Bank of America
Dreamworks SKG
Eyeblaster
Greenfield Online
Lotus Cars
Titan Tunes
World Tree Technologies

WIDMEYER COMMUNICATIONS

(Acquired by Finn Partners)

WIEDEN + KENNEDY, INC.

224 NW 13th Ave, Portland, OR 97209
Tel.: (503) 937-7000
Fax: (503) 937-8000
Web Site: www.wk.com

E-Mail for Key Personnel:
President: Dan.Wieden@wk.com

Employees: 327
Year Founded: 1982

Agency Specializes In: Above-the-Line, Advertising, Advertising Specialties, Affiliate Marketing, Affluent Market, African-American Market, Agriculture, Alternative Advertising, Arts, Asian Market, Automotive, Aviation & Aerospace, Below-the-Line, Bilingual Market, Brand Development & Integration, Branded Entertainment, Broadcast, Business Publications, Business-To-Business, Cable T.V., Catalogs, Children's Market, Co-op Advertising, Collateral, College, Commercial Photography, Communications, Computers & Software, Consulting, Consumer Goods, Consumer Marketing, Consumer Publications, Content, Corporate Communications, Corporate Identity, Cosmetics, Crisis Communications, Custom Publishing, Customer Relationship Management, Digital/Interactive, Direct Response Marketing, Direct-to-Consumer, E-Commerce, Education, Electronic Media, Electronics, Email, Engineering, Entertainment, Environmental, Event Planning & Marketing, Exhibit/Trade Shows, Experience Design, Faith Based, Fashion/Apparel, Financial, Food Service, Game Integration, Gay & Lesbian Market, Government/Political, Graphic Design, Guerilla Marketing, Health Care Services, High Technology, Hispanic Market, Hospitality, Household Goods, Identity Marketing, In-Store Advertising, Industrial, Infomercials, Information Technology, Integrated Marketing, International, Internet/Web Design, Investor Relations, Legal Services, Leisure, Local Marketing, Logo & Package Design, Luxury Products, Magazines, Marine, Market Research, Media Buying Services, Media Planning, Media Relations, Media Training, Medical Products, Men's Market, Merchandising, Mobile Marketing, Multicultural, Multimedia, New Product Development, New Technologies, Newspaper, Newspapers & Magazines, Out-of-Home Media, Outdoor, Over-50 Market, Package Design, Paid Searches, Pets , Pharmaceutical, Planning & Consultation, Podcasting, Point of Purchase, Point of Sale, Print, Product Placement, Production, Production (Ad, Film, Broadcast), Production (Print), Promotions, Public Relations, Publicity/Promotions, Publishing, RSS (Really Simple Syndication), Radio, Real Estate, Recruitment, Regional, Restaurant, Retail, Sales Promotion, Search Engine Optimization, Seniors' Market, Shopper Marketing, Social Marketing/Nonprofit, Social Media, South Asian Market, Sponsorship, Sports Market, Stakeholders, Strategic Planning/Research, Sweepstakes, Syndication, T.V., Technical Advertising, Teen Market, Telemarketing, Trade & Consumer Magazines, Transportation, Travel & Tourism, Tween Market, Urban Market, Viral/Buzz/Word of Mouth, Web (Banner Ads, Pop-ups, etc.), Women's Market, Yellow Pages Advertising

Dan Wieden *(Owner)*
Tom Blessington *(Mng Partner)*
Tony Davidson *(Partner-Global & Exec Dir-Creative)*
Antony Goldstein *(VP)*
Mark Bernath *(Exec Dir-Creative)*
Joe Staples *(Exec Creative Dir)*
Alex Barwick *(Grp Dir-Comm)*
Anibal Casso *(Grp Dir-Strategy)*
Alex Dobson *(Grp Dir-Media & Comm Plng)*
Kelly Muller *(Grp Dir-Media)*
John Rowan *(Grp Dir-Media & Comm Plng)*
Britton Taylor *(Grp Dir-Strategy)*
Robert Kendall *(Sr Dir-Art)*
Matt Hunnicutt *(Exec Producer)*
Patrick Marzullo *(Exec Producer-Interactive)*
Erika Madison *(Sr Producer-Brdcst)*
Ollie Watson *(Art Dir & Creative Dir)*
Kirsten Acheson *(Producer-Brdcst)*
Hal Curtis *(Creative Dir)*
Karrelle Dixon *(Acct Dir-Nike-Global)*
Thomas Harvey *(Acct Dir)*
David Hughes *(Acct Dir)*
Evelyn Loomis *(Producer-Interactive)*
Ryan O'Rourke *(Creative Dir)*
Lindsay Reed *(Producer-Brdcst)*
Toliver Roebuck *(Art Dir)*
Jeff Selis *(Producer-Brdcst)*
Max Stinson *(Creative Dir)*
Kelly Quinn *(Acct Supvr & Mgmt Supvr)*
Jesse Johnson *(Mgmt Supvr)*
Vanessa Miller *(Mgmt Supvr)*
Jordan Muse *(Mgmt Supvr)*
Matthew Carroll *(Dir-Art, Copywriter & Sr Designer)*
Craig Allen *(Dir-Creative)*
Justine Armour *(Dir-Creative)*
Kelly Bayett *(Dir-Creative)*
Stuart Brown *(Dir-Creative)*
Jason Campbell *(Dir-Art)*
Reme DeBisschop *(Dir-Media-NA)*
Bertrand Fleuret *(Dir-Art)*
Patty Fogarty *(Dir-Art)*
Mike Giepert *(Dir-Creative)*
Devin Gillespie *(Dir-Art)*
Chris Groom *(Dir-Creative)*
Derrick Ho *(Dir-Art)*
Michael Holz *(Dir-Interactive & Brand Strategy-Old Spice)*
Lee Jennings *(Dir-Art)*
Caleb Jensen *(Dir-Creative)*
Zack Jerome *(Dir-Strategy)*
Jason Kreher *(Dir-Creative)*
Henry Lambert *(Dir-Plng)*
Susan Land *(Dir-Art)*
Jimm Lasser *(Dir-Art)*
Andy Lindblade *(Dir-Grp Strategy -Global)*
James Moslander *(Dir-Art)*
Patrick Nistler *(Dir-Art & Design & Sr Designer)*
Erik Norin *(Dir-Creative)*
Byron Oshiro *(Co-Dir-WK12)*
Sara Philips *(Dir-Art)*
Alberto Ponte *(Dir-Global Creative-Nike)*
Helen Rhodes *(Dir-Art)*
Gianmaria Schonlieb *(Dir-Art)*
Tim Semple *(Dir-Art)*
Dan Sheniak *(Dir-Global Comm Plng-Nike)*
Matt Sorrell *(Dir-Art)*
Bobby Souers *(Dir-Media)*
Michael Tabtabai *(Dir-Integrated Creative)*
Lawrence Teherani-Ami *(Dir-Media)*
Brandon Thornton *(Dir-Brand Strategy)*
Brandon Viney *(Dir-Art)*
Micah Walker *(Dir-Creative)*
Joani Wardwell *(Dir-PR-Global)*
Jeff Williams *(Dir-Art)*
Emily Dalton *(Assoc Dir-Comm Plng-Nike)*
John Furnari *(Assoc Dir-Comm Plng)*
Naoki Ga *(Assoc Dir-Creative)*
Danielle Pak *(Assoc Dir-Comm & Media Strategy)*
Kim Sizemore *(Assoc Dir-Media)*
Danny Sullivan *(Assoc Dir-Media)*
Laura Caldwell *(Sr Mgr-Brdcst Bus Affairs)*
Katie Hull *(Sr Mgr-PR)*
Teresa Lutz *(Sr Mgr-Bus Affairs)*
Dusty Slowik *(Sr Mgr-Bus Affairs)*
Jonas Greene *(Mgr-Adv & Comm)*
Rob Archibald *(Acct Supvr)*
Dana Borenstein *(Acct Supvr)*
Liam Doherty *(Acct Supvr-Global)*
Kelsey Bozanich *(Supvr-Comm)*
Ryan Craven *(Supvr-Media)*
Stephanie Ehui *(Supvr-Media & Comm Plng)*
Lisa Feldhusen *(Supvr-Media)*
Brian Goldstein *(Supvr-Media & Comm Plng)*
Charles Lee *(Supvr-Media & Comm Plng)*
Alyssa Ramsey *(Supvr-Mgmt)*
Sarah Biedak *(Sr Strategist-Interactive)*
Anna Boteva *(Acct Exec)*
Chase Haviland *(Acct Exec)*
Stephanie Montoya *(Acct Exec)*
Heather Morba *(Acct Exec)*
Molly Rugg *(Acct Exec-Nike)*
Irina Tone *(Strategist)*
Brooke Barker *(Copywriter)*
Darcie Burrell *(Copywriter)*
Karl Collins *(Media Planner)*
Sally DeSipio *(Copywriter)*
Jordan Dinwiddie *(Copywriter)*
Shaine Edwards *(Copywriter)*
Mike Egan *(Copywriter)*
Cory Everett *(Designer-Interactive)*
Eric Fensler *(Copywriter)*
Howard Finkelstein *(Copywriter)*
Mario Garza *(Copywriter)*
Jarrod Higgins *(Copywriter)*
Brock Kirby *(Copywriter)*
Andy Laugenour *(Copywriter)*
Nathaniel Lawlor *(Copywriter)*
Dylan Lee *(Copywriter)*
Emily Leonard *(Media Planner)*
Chad Lynch *(Copywriter)*
Ashley Davis Marshall *(Copywriter)*
Alison McClaran *(Media Planner)*
Matt Mulvey *(Copywriter)*
Laddie Peterson *(Copywriter)*
Christina Rhee *(Media Planner-Integrated)*
Alex Romans *(Copywriter)*
Matt Skibiak *(Copywriter)*
Erin Swanson *(Copywriter)*
Derek Szynal *(Copywriter)*
Ansel Wallenfang *(Copywriter)*
Claire Wyckoff *(Copywriter)*
Morrison Conway *(Asst Acct Exec)*
Ramiro Del-Cid *(Asst Acct Exec-Nike)*
Sezay Altinok *(Sr Creative)*
Johan Arlig *(Sr Art Dir)*
Kallie Bullock *(Asst Media Planner)*
Caylen Clark *(Asst Media Planner)*
Matt Hisamoto *(Jr Strategist-Interactive)*
Jocelyn Reist *(Asst Media Planner)*
Ryan Tenzeldam *(Asst Media Planner)*

Accounts:
Andy Award Campaign: "Firefighter", Campaign: "Hurt Locker", Campaign: "Neurosurgeon", Campaign: "Where Only the Bravest Get

Rewarded", Social Media
The Coca-Cola Company Broadcast, Campaign: "Curves", Campaign: "Generous World", Campaign: "Going All the Way" Super Bowl 2014, Campaign: "Happiness Hackathon", Campaign: "ISS" Winter Olympics 2014, Campaign: "It's beautiful" Super Bowl 2014, Campaign: "Just a Kid", Campaign: "Make It Happy", Campaign: "Make Someone Happy", Campaign: "Man & Dog", Campaign: "Mirage", Campaign: "Open Happiness", Campaign: "Polar Bowl", Campaign: "Reactions", Campaign: "Rocket", Campaign: "Roller Coaster", Campaign: "Rose from Concrete", Campaign: "Tale of Contour", Campaign: "The Ahh Effect", Campaign: "This Is AHH", Campaign:"Balloons", Coca-Cola Classic, Diet Coke, Digital, Powerade, Social, Super Bowl 2015, TV, Teen-Focused Campaign; 1994
Cravendale
Danish Dairy Board
Delta Airlines (Agency of Record)
Dodge Durango 2015 Dart, 2015 Dodge Charger Commercial, 2015 Dodge SRT Hellcats, 2015 Dodge SRT Viper, Broadcast, Campaign: "Ballroom - They Dreamed Big", Campaign: "Ballroom Dancers", Campaign: "Do-dge", Campaign: "Downhill Fast", Campaign: "Father", Campaign: "First Dodge", Campaign: "Get The Heck", Campaign: "Gumball Machine", Campaign: "It Comes Standard", Campaign: "It's Not Enough", Campaign: "Lie in Wait", Campaign: "Morse Code", Campaign: "Predators", Campaign: "Ride", Campaign: "Ron Burgundy", Campaign: "Staring Contest", Campaign: "The Spirit Lives On", Digital, Dodge Brothers, Dodge Challenger, DontTouchMyDart.com, Marketing, Online, Print, Social, TV
Electronic Arts Inc. Battlefield 3, Campaign: "Is It Real?", Dante's Inferno, EA Games, Family Play, Hellgate Game, Media Buying, Media Planning, UFC; 2004
ESPN "It's Not Crazy, It's Sports", Campaign: "Team Spirit", Campaign: "This is SportsCenter"
Facebook, Inc. (Agency of Record) "Airplane" (Facebook Home), Campaign: "Couch Skis", Campaign: "Say Love You Better", Campaign: "Tango", Campaign: "Things That Connect", Campaign: "Where will your friends take you?", Campaign: "Why Have One Photographer When You Can Have a Hundred?", TV
Fiat Chrysler 2015 Chrysler 200, 2015 Chrysler 300, Campaign: "America's Import", Campaign: "Beneath the Surface", Campaign: "Drive Proud", Campaign: "Imported from Detroit", Campaign: "Ready To Take On The World", Campaign: "The Kings and Queens of America", Digital, Online, Print, TV
Foot Locker
General Mills Campaign: "World of Yoplait", Yoplait (Lead Agency), Yoplait Original
H. J. Heinz Company
Honda Campaign: "Hands"
Intuit Inc Campaign: "Boston Tea Party", Campaign: "It's Amazing What You're Capable Of" Super Bowl 2014, Campaign: "Love Hurts" Super Bowl 2014, Campaign: "Mardi Gras Loud Noise", Campaign: "Mardi Gras Statues", Campaign: "Mardi Gras", Campaign: "The Year Of You" Super Bowl 2014, Creative, Media Planning, Super Bowl 2015, TurboTax (Agency of Record)
Jeep Cherokee Campaign: "Built Free"
Dodge Campaign: "100 Steps", Campaign: "Defiance", Campaign: "Dodge Charger", Campaign: "Staring Contest", Dart
KFC Corporation Advertising, Broadcast, Campaign: "America's Favorite Music", Campaign: "Baseball", Campaign: "Bucket & Beans", Campaign: "Bucket in My Hand", Campaign: "Hey Look", Campaign: "Merry Go Round", Campaign: "Phillip", Campaign: "Student", Campaign: "The State of Kentucky Fried Chicken Address", Online
Mondelez International, Inc. Campaign: "Friends", Campaign: "Jay", Campaign: "Life Raft", Campaign: "Liquid Gold Diggers Love Liquid Gold", Campaign: "Liquid Gooooold", Campaign: "Sleepover", Lead Creative, Oreo, Trident, Velveeta Cheesy Skillets, Velveeta Shells & Cheese
Nando's Campaign: "Find Yourself", Press, Print & Digital Campaign
National Multiple Sclerosis Society
Nexus Productions Campaign: "Honda Hands"
Nike, Inc. Basketball, Brand Jordan, Broadcast, Campaign: "Better for It", Campaign: "Calvin & Johnson", Campaign: "Cat Flap", Campaign: "Chalkbot", Campaign: "Choose Your Winter", Campaign: "Deceptive by Nature", Campaign: "Fight Winter", Campaign: "Find Your Greatness", Campaign: "Fly Swatter", Campaign: "I Would Run To You", Campaign: "Inner Thoughts", Campaign: "Just Do It", Campaign: "Last", Campaign: "Leave A Message", Campaign: "Made by Kobe", Campaign: "Mirrors", Campaign: "Never Finished", Campaign: "No Cup Is Safe", Campaign: "Possibilities", Campaign: "Ripple", Campaign: "Risk Everything", Campaign: "Running Free/Fly Swatter", Campaign: "Speed Unleashed", Campaign: "Summer Is Serious", Campaign: "TakeonTJ", Campaign: "The Baddest", Campaign: "The Last Game", Campaign: "The Sport of Golf", Campaign: "Toy Claw", Campaign: "Training Day", Campaign: "Why Change?", Campaign: "Winner Stays", Campaign: "Winning in a Winter Wonderland", Campaign: "Write the Future", Digital, Golf, Hyperdunk Basketball Shoes, Hypervenom Phantom Boot, Hyperwarm, Interactive, Kobe System, Nike Brand, Nike Football, Nike Livestrong, Nike Men's Training, Nike Plus, Nike Running, Nike Running Shoes, Nike Sportswear, Nike Tennis, Nike Women's Training, Nike Zoom LeBron VI, Nike+, SPARQ Training, Short A Guy, Some Time Together, TV, The Black Mamba, The Summer Shift, Training Apparel, US & Latin America, Vapor Driver; 1982
Oregon Tourism Commission Campaign: "The 7 Wonders of Oregon", Consumer Engagement Elements, Digital, Public Relations, Search, Social, Travel Oregon; 1987
The Procter & Gamble Company Campaign: "And So It Begins", Campaign: "Baby", Campaign: "Bear Deodorant Protector", Campaign: "Believe in Your Smellf", Campaign: "Best Job", Campaign: "Boardwalk", Campaign: "Checkmate", Campaign: "Dadsong", Campaign: "Devastating Explosions", Campaign: "Drill to Brazil", Campaign: "Get Shaved in the Face", Campaign: "Guy Scents", Campaign: "Hair that gets results", Campaign: "Hardest Job in the World", Campaign: "I Can Do Anything", Campaign: "Interruption", Campaign: "Man Your Man Could Smell Like", Campaign: "Meeting", Campaign: "Meticulous", Campaign: "Momsong", Campaign: "Muscle Music", Campaign: "Muscle Surprise", Campaign: "Nightclub", Campaign: "Nightmare Face", Campaign: "Pick Them Back Up", Campaign: "Shave", Campaign: "Shower", Campaign: "Smell as Great as Nature Is", Campaign: "Smellcome To Manhood", Campaign: "Soccer", Campaign: "Thank you, Mom", Campaign: "That's the Power of Hair", Campaign: "The Man Your Man Could Smell Like", Campaign: "Tough Love" Winter Olympics 2014, Campaign: "Unnecessary Freshness", Campaign: "What I See", Campaign: "When Dirt", Campaign: "Windsurfing", Deodorant & Body Wash, Fiji Bar Soap, Hawkridge, Herbal Essences, Ivory Canada, Old Spice Electric Shavers, Online, Print, Secret (Global Creative), Social, Web, Wolfthorn; 2005
Reckitt Benckiser Creative, Finish
S7 Airlines
Samahope
Samsung Electronics
Sony "Goldie", "Photo Lab", "Plantimal", "Rainy-oke", "Sink Sunk", Campaign: "Be Moved", Campaign: "If a Tree Falls", Campaign: "Join Together", Campaign: "Roof", Campaign: "Script to Screen", Campaign: "Separate Together", Communications Planning, Media Planning, Northlandz, Social Strategy, Strategic Planning, Xperia Z1S
Travel Portland Campaign: "Portland Is Happening Now", Media
Ubisoft Inc. Assassin's Creed
Verizon Brand, Campaign: "Better Matters", Campaign: "Home", Creative, Strategy
Volvo Trucks Campaign: "Smellcome to Manhood"

Branches

Wieden + Kennedy - Amsterdam

Herengracht 258-266, 1016 BV Amsterdam, Netherlands
Tel.: (31) 20 712 6500
Fax: (31) 20 712 6699
Web Site: www.wkams.com/

Employees: 150
Year Founded: 1992

Agency Specializes In: Advertising, Environmental

Blake Harrop *(Mng Dir)*
Joseph Burrin *(Head-Art)*
Joe Togneri *(Head-Brdcst Production)*
Kelsie van Deman *(Head-Interactive Production)*
Mark Bernath *(Exec Creative Dir)*
Mike Farr *(Exec Dir-Creative)*
Eric Quennoy *(Exec Dir-Creative)*
Kathryn Addo *(Grp Acct Dir)*
Clare Pickens *(Grp Acct Dir)*
Jordi Pont *(Grp Acct Dir)*
Katja Dienel *(Acct Dir)*
Jonah Dolan *(Acct Dir)*
Mathieu Garnier *(Art Dir-Interactive)*
Jeffrey Lam *(Art Dir-Interactive)*
Amber Martin *(Acct Dir)*
Sebastien Partika *(Art Dir)*
Szymon Rose *(Creative Dir)*
Paul Skinner *(Creative Dir)*
Alvaro Sotomayor *(Creative Dir)*
Jaime Tan *(Producer-Brdcst)*
Thierry Tudela Albert *(Dir-Creative & Copywriter)*
Riccardo Rachello *(Dir-Creative-Art & Designer)*
Sean Condon *(Dir-Creative)*
Bern Hunter *(Dir-Creative)*
David Smith *(Dir-Creative)*
Erik Verheijen *(Dir-Brdcst Production)*
Vasco Vicente *(Dir-Art & Creative)*
Craig Williams *(Dir-Creative)*
Charlotte Jongejan *(Acct Mgr & Copywriter)*
Max Arlestig *(Copywriter)*
Michelle Arrazcaeta *(Planner)*
Mohammad Diaa *(Copywriter)*
Andrew Dobbie *(Copywriter)*
Thomas Payne *(Designer)*
Evgeny Primachenko *(Copywriter)*
Scott Smith *(Copywriter)*
Emma Wiseman *(Planner-Strategic)*
Stijn Wikkerink *(Asst Producer)*

Accounts:
Anheuser-Busch InBev Corona
Armadillo
Audi Advertising, Broadcast, Campaign: "Leap of Faith", Campaign: "The New Audi TTS Coupe. You Dare or You Don't", TTS Coupe
BASF Campaign: "We create chemistry", Creative
Beeline
Booking.com Booking Now, Broadcast, Campaign: "Booking Hero", Campaign: "Booking Right", Campaign: "Brianless", Campaign: "Dead Bed", Campaign: "Haunted Hotels", Campaign: "Interview", Campaign: "Karate", Campaign:

Advertising Agencies

"Pyscho", Campaign: "Race Car Bed", Campaign: "The Delight of Right", Campaign: "The Shining", Campaign: "Wing Everything", Campaign: "Wing It", Digital, OOH, Online, Print, Social
CARRERA Creative, Online, Teaser Campaign
Child Helpline International Campaign: "Free Our Voices"
Citizen Watch Co. Campaign: "Better Starts Now", Eco-Drive Satellite Wave F100, Identity, Movie, Website
The Coca-Cola Company Campaign: "A pop-up park!", Campaign: "Coca-Cola Sitelets", Campaign: "Falling Dominoes", Campaign: "Pretty Woman", Campaign: "Roll Out Happiness", Campaign: "The Great Happyfication", Happiness Factory The Movie, Music Logo; 1996
Electronic Arts Campaign: "Feel The Game", Campaign: "It Just Got Real", Campaign: "Love Football, Play Football", Campaign: "Messimorphosis", Campaign: "Next-Gen Lionel Messi", Campaign: "Paradise", Campaign: "The Bitter-Sweet Taste of Football", Campaign: "We are Fifa 14", Digital, EA Sports, FIFA 14, FIFA 15, FIFA 16, Fifa Earth, Harry Potter Video Games, Need for Speed, TV
ESPN Campaign: "The Gift"
Foot Locker "The New Baddest", Campaign: "Above Expectations", Campaign: "Baddest", Jordan, Nike's "KD Stratosphere Collection"
General Electric Campaign: "Progress"
Heineken N.V. Broadcast, Campaign: "Crack the Case", Campaign: "Dropped", Campaign: "Dropped: Cambodia", Campaign: "Dropped: Poland", Campaign: "Legendary Making of the Date", Campaign: "Legends", Campaign: "Man of the World", Campaign: "MySunrise", Campaign: "Open Your World", Campaign: "Ride the Wind", Campaign: "Serenade", Campaign: "The Chase", Campaign: "The City", Campaign: "The Insider", Campaign: "The Match", Campaign: "The Odyssey", Campaign: "The One That Played Fire Tennis Against Jimmy Connors", Campaign: "Turn Down the Silence", Campaign: "Way of the Desperados", Desperados, Digital, Heineken, Pantheon, Print, TV, The Entrance
Intel Corporation Campaign: "Go Do Something Wonderful"
Microsoft Gears of War; 2007
Xbox One Campaign: "It Just Got Real"
Mondelez International Milka (Global Advertising Lead Agency)
Nike Europe Campaign: "Better for It", Campaign: "Brazil", Campaign: "Play Russian", Campaign: "Real Girls of Moscow", Nike ACG, Nike France Rugby, Nike Women, Write the Future
P&G
Powerade Campaign: "Nico's Story"
S7 Airlines(Agency of Record) "The Imagination Machine", Broadcast, Campaign: "Fly to Anywhere You can Imagine", Creative, Digital, OOH, Online, Print, Social

W+K Sao Paulo

Rua Natingui 632, Vila Madalena, Sao Paulo, SP CEP 05443-000 Brazil
Tel.: (55) 11 3937 9400
Web Site: wksaopaulo.com.br

Renato Simoes *(Exec Dir-Creative)*
Thiago Andrade *(Art Dir)*
Paula Obata *(Acct Dir)*
Martin Insua *(Dir-Creative)*
Ezequiel Soules *(Dir-Creative)*

Accounts:
Coca-Cola Campaign: "The World's Cup"
Comedy Central Latam Campaign: "Hawks"
New-Mondelez International Lacta
Nike Campaign: "Dare to be Brazilian", Campaign: "Destiny", Campaign: "No one plays like us", Campaign: "Tomorrow Starts Now"

Wieden + Kennedy-New York

150 Varick St, New York, NY 10013
Tel.: (917) 661-5200
Fax: (917) 661-5500
Web Site: www.wk.com

Employees: 105
Year Founded: 1996

Agency Specializes In: Advertising, Sponsorship

Tony Davidson *(Partner-Global & Exec Dir-Creative)*
Nick Setounski *(Head-Content Production & Producer-Brdcst)*
Dan Hill *(Head-Strategy)*
Dan Beckwith *(Exec Creative Dir)*
Mark Bernath *(Exec Dir-Creative)*
Karl Lieberman *(Exec Dir-Creative)*
Eric Quennoy *(Exec Dir-Creative)*
Mathieu Zarbatany *(Sr Dir-Art)*
Patrick Cahill *(Grp Acct Dir)*
Brandon Pracht *(Grp Acct Dir)*
Jonathan Percy *(Exec Producer-Interactive)*
Erik Norin *(Creative Dir)*
Georgina Gooley *(Mgmt Supvr-Global)*
Price Manford *(Mgmt Supvr)*
Brandon Henderson *(Dir-Creative)*
Teressa Iezzi *(Dir-PR & Publ)*
Rick Jacques *(Dir-Art)*
Jimm Lasser *(Dir-Creative)*
Christine Mason *(Dir-Integrated Media Strategy)*
Dan Norris *(Dir-Creative)*
Ray Shaughnessy *(Dir-Creative)*
Matt Sorrell *(Dir-Art)*
Justin Lam *(Assoc Dir-Media)*
Keri Rommel *(Mgr-Traffic)*
Cynthia Valenti *(Mgr-Bus Affairs)*
James Williams *(Mgr-Community)*
Jasmina Almeda *(Acct Supvr)*
Mark Malloy *(Supvr-Integrated Media Strategy)*
Michelle Mandell *(Supvr-Integrated Media)*
Anjali Patel *(Supvr-Comm Plng)*
Wes Young *(Supvr-Media)*
Kemi Adewumi *(Acct Exec)*
Jonathan Chu *(Acct Exec)*
Tom Gibby *(Strategist-Digital)*
Joe Morelli *(Acct Exec)*
Andre Almeida *(Copywriter)*
Dustin Bailey *(Designer)*
Will Binder *(Copywriter)*
Kasey Donnelly *(Media Buyer)*
Trevor Gilley *(Designer)*
Alison Joseph *(Designer)*
Chris Kelsch *(Designer)*
Nathaniel Lawlor *(Copywriter)*
Laddie Peterson *(Copywriter)*
Greg Rutter *(Copywriter)*
Jean Sharkey *(Copywriter)*
Christina Smith *(Media Buyer)*

Accounts:
AICF
Anheuser-Busch InBev Bud Light, Creative
BASF Corporation
Brown-Forman Campaign: "Beach", Campaign: "Shark", Campaign: "Whatever's Comfortable"
The Coca-Cola Company Coca-Cola, Creative, Diet Coke, Powerade, Sprite
Cooper Hewitt, Smithsonian Design Museum Digital, OOH
Delta Air Lines, Inc. "In-Flight Safety", Campaign: "Innovation Class", Campaign: "Keep Climbing", Campaign: "No Bag Left Behind", Campaign: "On the Road", Campaign: "Pay Attention", Campaign: "Reach", Campaign: "Take Off: Why We Go", Campaign: "Your Bag's Journey On Delta", Delta One, Photon Shower
Disney Pictures
Electronic Arts Inc.
Equinox Campaign: "Equinox Made Me Do It", Digital, Out-of-Home, Print, Social
ESPN, Inc. (Agency of Record) "Decaf", "Jersey", Campaign: "This is SportsCenter", Campaign: "A Champion Will Rise", Campaign: "Born Into It", Campaign: "Chicken Curry", Campaign: "DaDaDa DaDaDa", Campaign: "Different Ways In", Campaign: "Empty", Campaign: "Frozen Lunch", Campaign: "Global Issues", Campaign: "Handshakes - English", Campaign: "Human Twitter", Campaign: "In Common", Campaign: "It All Comes Down to Monday Night", Campaign: "Kitchen Warriors", Campaign: "Long Week", Campaign: "No Other Night Is Monday Night", Campaign: "No Other Night Makes Peyton Even Scarier", Campaign: "Nothing Beats First Place", Campaign: "Party Spread", Campaign: "Playoff Ride", Campaign: "Rudy", Campaign: "Satellite", Campaign: "Sensei", Campaign: "Shake on it", Campaign: "Sharks", Campaign: "Swedish Chef", Campaign: "Sweet Serves", Campaign: "Team Spirit", Campaign: "The Message", Campaign: "This is SportsCenter", Campaign: "Tunnel", Campaign: "Universal Remote", Campaign: "Who's In", College Football Playoff, College Football Playoff National Championship, Digital, ESPN Fantasy Football League, ESPN.com, FBS College Football Season, Metallica, Monday Night Football, NASCAR, NBA Games, SportsCenter, TV, This is SportsCenter, Vending Machine; 1993
Gap Inc (Lead Global Agency) Banner Advertising, Campaign: "Black is a Color", Campaign: "Crooner", Campaign: "Dress Like No One's Watching", Campaign: "Dress[ing] Normal", Campaign: "Drive", Campaign: "Gauntlet", Campaign: "Get Caught Wearing the Same Thing", Campaign: "Golf", Campaign: "Kiss", Campaign: "Let Your Actions Speak Louder than Your Clothes", Campaign: "Mistletoe", Campaign: "Pinball", Campaign: "Simple Clothes for you to Complicate", Campaign: "SpringIsWeird", Campaign: "Stairs", Campaign: "The Uniform of Rebellion and Conformity", Campaign: "You Don't Have to Get Them to Give Them Gap", Creative, Digital, Outdoor, Print, Social, Social Media, TV, The Gap
Gilt Groupe
Intuit Media Buying, TurboTax
Lurpak Campaign: "Weave Your Magic"
NIKE, Inc. "BGCP3TV in HD", Air Jordan XXI, Campaign: "Airborne", Campaign: "Blake and Drain", Campaign: "Hockey Is Ours", Campaign: "Jogger", Campaign: "Possibilities", Campaign: "Riquickulous Sideline", Explosive Water Projections, Jordan Brand, Videos; 2006
Old Spice
One Kings Lane Campaign: "Design is Never Done", Campaign: "The Broken Lamp"
Procter & Gamble Company; Cincinnati, OH Graham Webb
Southern Comfort Campaign: "Beach", Campaign: "Dance", Campaign: "Karate", Campaign: "Shampoo", Campaign: "ShottaSoCo", Campaign: "Whatever's Comfortable", Campaign: "Young Gun"
Squarespace Inc. Campaign: "om", Creative, Jeff Bridges Sleeping Tapes, Super Bowl 2015
Walt Disney Pictures/PIXAR
New-Warner Bros Entertainment Inc. Campaign: "The Dunk to End All Dunks.", Looney Tunes, Super.Fly 4

Wieden + Kennedy

16 Hanbury Street, London, E1 6QR United Kingdom
Tel.: (44) 207 194 7000
Fax: (44) 207 194 7100
E-Mail: Bella.laine@wk.com
Web Site: www.wklondon.com

Employees: 150
Year Founded: 1999

Agency Specializes In: Advertising

Tony Davidson *(Partner-Global & Exec Dir-Creative)*
Neil Christie *(Mng Dir)*
Helen Foulder *(Deputy Mng Dir)*
Andrew Kay *(Head-Acct Mgmt)*
James Guy *(Deputy Head-Brdcst)*
Iain Tait *(Exec Creative Dir)*
Kim Papworth *(Sr Dir-Creative)*
David Mannall *(Grp Acct Dir)*
Nick Owen *(Grp Acct Dir)*
Rachel Parker *(Grp Acct Dir)*
Paulo Salomao *(Grp Acct Dir)*
Carlos Alija *(Creative Dir)*
Alex Budenberg *(Acct Dir)*
Eddie Fisher *(Art Dir)*
Hannah Gourevitch *(Acct Dir)*
Hanne Haugen *(Acct Dir)*
Lex Higlett *(Acct Dir)*
Mat Kramer *(Art Dir)*
Sam McCluskey *(Art Dir)*
Laura McGuaran *(Acct Dir)*
James McHoull *(Acct Dir)*
Katherine Napier *(Acct Dir)*
Sanam Petri *(Creative Dir)*
Laura Sampedro *(Creative Dir)*
Kirsteen Scoble-Morton *(Acct Dir)*
Larry Seftel *(Creative Dir)*
Ben Shaffery *(Art Dir)*
Matt Shaw *(Acct Dir)*
Anthony Atkinson *(Dir-Creative)*
Christen Brestrup *(Dir-Art)*
Dave Day *(Dir-Creative)*
Scott Dungate *(Dir-Creative)*
David Goss *(Dir-Art)*
Sam Heath *(Dir-Creative)*
Selena McKenzie *(Dir-Creative)*
Dan Norris *(Dir-Creative)*
Shishir Patel *(Dir-Art)*
Freddie Powell *(Dir-Creative)*
Mark Shanley *(Dir-Art)*
Anders Stake *(Dir-Creative)*
Alex Allcott *(Acct Mgr)*
Alex Blacklock *(Acct Mgr)*
Maria Kofoed *(Acct Mgr)*
Tala Saadeh *(Acct Mgr)*
Holly Baker-Cliff *(Acct Exec)*
Ben Everitt *(Copywriter)*
Rachel Hamburger *(Planner)*
Rob Meldrum *(Planner)*
Sam Oliver *(Copywriter)*
Rebecca Pottinger *(Copywriter)*
Bertie Scrase *(Copywriter)*

Accounts:
Action for Children (Lead Creative Agency)
Amnesty International
Arla Foods Arla Buko, Arla Harmonie, Arla Skyr, Arla Yoggi, Campaign: "A Kitchen Odyssey", Campaign: "Adventure Awaits", Campaign: "Cats with Thumbs", Campaign: "Let in the Goodness", Campaign: "Rainbow", Campaign: "The Messenger", Campaign: "Weave Your Magic", Cravendale PureFiltre Milk, Digital, Global Advertising, LactoFree, Lurpak Butter
Brown-Forman Finlandia, Maximus, Social Media, TV
Cadbury plc
Cravendale Campaign: "Barry the Biscuit Boy", Campaign: "The Milk Drinker's Milk"
D&AD Campaign: "I Wish I'd Done That"
Dodge
ESPN Campaign: "This Is SportsCenter"
New-Finlandia Vodka
The Guardian/The Observer; London, UK
Honda Europe Campaign: "Cog", Campaign: "Decision, Decisions", Campaign: "Feeling", Campaign: "Hands", Campaign: "Ignition", Campaign: "Inner Beauty", Campaign: "Keep Up (Even Faster)", Campaign: "Keep Up (Faster)", Campaign: "Keep Up", Campaign: "Reliability in the Extreme", Campaign: "Spark", Campaign: "Sweetcorn", Campaign: "The Experiment Game", Campaign: "The Other Side", Campaign: "The Power of Dreams", Civic Tourer, Diesel, Honda Civic, Print, TV
Hutchinson 3G
The Kaiser Chiefs Campaign: "The Kaiser Chiefs Bespoke Album Creation Experience"
Lactofree Campaign: "Say Yes to Breakfast", OOH
New-LG LG G4
Lurpak Campaign: "Adventure Awaits", Campaign: "Christmas Makers", Campaign: "Cooking Up a Rainbow", Campaign: "Freestyle", Campaign: "Good Proper Food", Campaign: "Kitchen Odyssey", Campaign: "Lurpak Slow Churned", Creative, Digital, Experiential, In-Store, Lurpak Mighty Meal Timer, Marketing, OOH, Press, Print
Mondelez International "'Gumulon", Bassett's (Lead Creative Agency), Campaign: "Biker", Campaign: "Chewing Hands", Campaign: "Choose Your Trebor", Creative, Digital Media, Halls, Maynards (Lead Creative Agency), Stride Gum, TV, Trebor (Lead Creative Agency), Trident
Nestea
Nike UK Campaign: "Endless Possibilities", Campaign: "My Time is Now", Campaign: "Risk Everything", Campaign: "The Last Game", Nike Football
The Observer
OVO Energy (Lead Creative Agency)
New-Reckitt Benckiser Finish, Nurofen
Richard Hall
New-Rovio Entertainment Angry Birds, Angry Birds 2, Campaign: "Bigger. Badder. Birdier."
Tesco plc Campaign: "#LetsHudl", Campaign: "A Family Christmas", Campaign: "A Turkey Success", Campaign: "Brothers", Campaign: "Decorations", Campaign: "Love Every Mouthful", Campaign: "There's nothing better than Christmas", Creative, Digital, Hudl, OOH Campaign, Press, Price Promise, TV
Three "#SingItKitty", Campaign: "#HolidaySpam", Campaign: "0800 Fun Numbers", Campaign: "CalendarMe", Campaign: "Dance Pony Dance", Campaign: "Pay As You Go - Still Seriously Serious", Campaign: "Prepare Yourself", Campaign: "Silly Stuff. It Matters", Campaign: "pay-as-you go just got serious", Campaign: "we're sorry", Digital, Mobile Phone, Out-of-Home, Outdoor, Press, Radio, Social, TV, The Pony, Video-on-Demand
New-TK Maxx Creative, Strategic
Tyrrells Global Creative
Vagenda
Visit Wales Creative
WWF

Wieden + Kennedy Japan

7-5-6 Roppongi, Minato-ku, Tokyo, 106-0032 Japan
Tel.: (81) 3 5771 2900
Fax: (81) 3 5771 2711
Web Site: www.wk.com

E-Mail for Key Personnel:
Creative Dir.: johnj@wk.com

Employees: 35
Year Founded: 1998

Trish Adams *(Grp Acct Dir)*
Caleb Jensen *(Creative Dir)*
Shingo Ohno *(Art Dir)*
John Rowe *(Acct Dir)*
Kazuhi Yoshikawa *(Art Dir)*
Naoki Ga *(Dir-Art)*
Adam Koppel *(Dir-Creative)*
Kenichiro Shigetomi *(Dir-Art)*
Kohei Adachi *(Acct Supvr)*
Damon Kim *(Copywriter)*

Accounts:
Citizen Watch Co. Campaign: "Better Starts Now", Eco-Drive Satellite Wave F100, Identity, Movie, Website
Facebook Campaign: "You Are Someone's Friend"
Hulu.com Creative
New York City Department of Transportation
Nike Japan Campaign: "Loop", Campaign: "Mercurial Vapor IX", Campaign: "Re:RUN", Campaign: "Shadow Class", Campaign: "The Finish Line", Campaign: "The Run Together", Campaign: "When Fun Wins, You Can't Lose", Digital, Nike Music Shoe, Nike.com, Social, Social Media, Sportswear
New-Nike (Korea) Campaign: "Just do it"
New-Oh My Glasses Inc.
Oronine

Wieden + Kennedy

Floor 5th No1035 ChangLe Road, Shanghai, 200031 China
Tel.: (86) 21 5158 3900
Fax: (86) 21 5158 3988
Web Site: www.wk.com

Year Founded: 2004

Agency Specializes In: Digital/Interactive, Social Media

Yang Yeo *(Exec Dir-Creative)*
Angie Wong *(Sr Producer-Content)*
Dino Xu *(Bus Dir)*
Shaun Sundholm *(Dir-Art & Copywriter)*
Terence Leong *(Dir-Creative)*
Azsa West *(Dir-Creative)*
Chuck Xu *(Acct Mgr)*
Sasa Yang *(Acct Exec)*
Paula Bloodsworth *(Planner)*
Jimmy Chen *(Copywriter)*
Leo Chu *(Reg Head-Digital)*

Accounts:
American Indian College Fund
Chrysler Group Campaign: "Built Free", Jeep Cherokee
Converse Block Party
Dodge
Fiat
IShares
Jeep Campaign: "Built Free"
LAIKA Studios
Levi Strauss "Revel", Campaign: " Let Your Body Do The Talking"
Nestea
Nike International Limited Air Jordan, Campaign: "Free Flyknit", Campaign: "Let the Run Tell You Why", Campaign: "Summer Movement", Campaign: "Use Sport", Campaign: "We Are Jordan", Golf, Your Game Is Your Voice
Old Spice
Procter & Gamble
Shanghai Disneyland Creative
Tiffany & Co
Travel Oregon

Wieden + Kennedy India

314 DLF South Court, Saket, New Delhi, 110017 India
Tel.: (91) 11 4200 9595
Fax: (91) 11 4200 9500
E-Mail: mohit.jayal@wk.com
Web Site: www.wk.com

Employees: 60

Animesh Bhartiya *(Mng Dir)*
Mohit Dhar Jayal *(Mng Dir)*
V. Sunil *(Exec Dir-Creative)*
Sunaina Sainath *(Dir-Strategy)*
Ankit Kumar *(Acct Mgr)*
Aarohi Dhir *(Planner-Strategic Acct)*
Hina Kataria *(Planner-Strategic)*
Vikram Singh *(Assoc Acct Dir-Digital)*

Accounts:
Chevrolet
Clear Trip
Forest Essentials Campaign: "Warrior Princess"
General Motors India Captiva, Chevrolet Cruze
HCL Campaign: "The Employees First Effect"
IndiGo Air
IndiGo Airlines Campaign: "Indigo Food Packaging", Campaign: "Ontime Performance", Campaign: "We're Going International"
Invista Coolmax, Creative, Lycra
Oberoi
P&G Campaign: "Mantastic", Campaign: "Milind Soman, Mantastic Man", Old Spice
The Park Hotels
Royal Enfield Motorcycles Campaign: "Ace Cafe to Madras Cafe", Campaign: "Continental GT", Campaign: "Handmade in Chennai", Thunderbird
Trident
Xylys Creative

WIGWAM CREATIVE
3459 Ringsby Ct Unit 411, Denver, CO 80216
Tel.: (303) 321-5599
E-Mail: info@wigwamcreative.com
Web Site: www.wigwamcreative.com

Year Founded: 2011

Agency Specializes In: Advertising, Brand Development & Integration, Internet/Web Design

Pete Larson *(Dir-Interactive)*
Hollie Schmiedeskamp *(Acct Mgr)*
Charles Carpenter *(Strategist-Visual)*

Accounts:
Denver Pavilions, L P
McGuckin Hardware
National Sport Center for the Disabled
The Navy Reservist
Rogue Performance
TraX N Trails

WIKREATE
145 Vallejo St Ste 6, San Francisco, CA 94111
Tel.: (415) 362-0440
Fax: (415) 362-0430
E-Mail: info@wikreate.com
Web Site: www.wikreate.com

Employees: 8
Year Founded: 2008

National Agency Associations: AHAA-DMA

Agency Specializes In: Advertising, Alternative Advertising, Below-the-Line, Bilingual Market, Business-To-Business, Computers & Software, Customer Relationship Management, Digital/Interactive, Direct Response Marketing, E-Commerce, Environmental, Experience Design, Graphic Design, Guerilla Marketing, Hispanic Market, Information Technology, Integrated Marketing, Internet/Web Design, Multicultural, New Technologies, Planning & Consultation, Social Marketing/Nonprofit, Viral/Buzz/Word of Mouth, Web (Banner Ads, Pop-ups, etc.)

Breakdown of Gross Billings by Media: D.M.: 60%; E-Commerce: 40%

Elena Castanon *(Founder & COO)*
Magdalena Gonzalez *(Partner)*

Accounts:
Anthem Blue Cross Blue Shield/Anthem National Accounts; New York, NY Employee Benefits; 2008
Autodesk; San Francisco, CA; 2008

WILBURN THOMAS
825 Chicago Ave Ste 2D, Evanston, IL 60202
Tel.: (847) 475-1601
Web Site: www.wilburnthomas.com

Year Founded: 2000

Agency Specializes In: Advertising, Brand Development & Integration, Environmental, Exhibit/Trade Shows, Internet/Web Design, Media Planning, Package Design, Print, Social Media

Lawrence Neisler *(Founder & Dir-Creative)*
Mariah Naella *(Dir-Creative)*

Accounts:
Solixir Energy Drinks Working Dead Campaign

WILD CONSORT, INC.
10641 S Hale Ave, Chicago, IL 60643
Tel.: (563) 880-4438
E-Mail: info@wildconsort.com
Web Site: www.wildconsort.com

Year Founded: 2003

Agency Specializes In: Advertising, Collateral, Graphic Design, Internet/Web Design, Logo & Package Design, Print

David Atwood *(Co-Founder)*
Blanca Robledo-Atwood *(Dir-Bilingual Creative)*

Accounts:
Amnesty Youth

WILDBIT LLC
20 N 3rd St 2nd Fl, Philadelphia, PA 19106
Tel.: (267) 200-0835
E-Mail: info@wildbit.com
Web Site: www.wildbit.com

Agency Specializes In: Email, Internet/Web Design

Chris Nagele *(Founder)*
Britt McLaughlin *(Office Mgr)*
Igor Balos *(Mgr-QA)*
Ilya Sabanin *(Mgr-Dev)*
Derek Rushforth *(Designer)*

Accounts:
The Beanstalk Global Brand License Providers
Newsberry Email Campaigns Providers

WILDFIRE LLC
709 N Main St, Winston Salem, NC 27101
Tel.: (336) 777-3473
Fax: (336) 354-0047
E-Mail: bbennett@wildfireideas.com
Web Site: www.wildfireideas.com

Employees: 35
Year Founded: 2004

National Agency Associations: 4A's

Agency Specializes In: Advertising, Advertising Specialties, Affiliate Marketing, Brand Development & Integration, Branded Entertainment, Broadcast, Business Publications, Business-To-Business, Cable T.V., Catalogs, Collateral, Communications, Consulting, Consumer Goods, Consumer Marketing, Content, Corporate Communications, Custom Publishing, Customer Relationship Management, Digital/Interactive, Direct Response Marketing, Direct-to-Consumer, E-Commerce, Electronic Media, Email, Entertainment, Event Planning & Marketing, Exhibit/Trade Shows, Fashion/Apparel, Graphic Design, Guerilla Marketing, In-Store Advertising, Integrated Marketing, Internet/Web Design, Local Marketing, Logo & Package Design, Magazines, Market Research, Media Buying Services, Media Planning, Media Relations, Merchandising, Multimedia, New Product Development, Newspaper, Newspapers & Magazines, Out-of-Home Media, Outdoor, Package Design, Planning & Consultation, Point of Purchase, Point of Sale, Print, Production (Ad, Film, Broadcast), Production (Print), Promotions, Publicity/Promotions, Radio, Retail, Search Engine Optimization, Sponsorship, Sports Market, Strategic Planning/Research, Sweepstakes, Trade & Consumer Magazines, Travel & Tourism, Web (Banner Ads, Pop-ups, etc.)

Approx. Annual Billings: $30,000,000

Brad Bennett *(Owner)*
Jeff Martin *(Dir-IT)*
Crystal Nelson *(Acct Mgr)*
Buddy Parker *(Mgr-Production)*
Christine Hancock *(Sr Graphic Designer)*
Chace Hoglund *(Planner-Strategic)*
Traci Naff *(Sr Graphic Designer)*
Nick Karner *(Acct Coord)*
Jaclyn Petree *(Jr Graphic Designer)*

Accounts:
The Coca-Cola Company
Dewey's Bakery; 2008
Hanes Brands Inc.
Hershey's
Lowes Home Improvement
Mondelez International, Inc.
Nobles Grille
Rubbermaid
Wonderbra

WILDFLOWER ADVERTISING
3317 N Bell Ave, Chicago, IL 60618
Tel.: (773) 698-6516
E-Mail: info@wildflowerchicago.com
Web Site: www.wildflowerchicago.com

Year Founded: 1999

Agency Specializes In: Advertising, Brand Development & Integration, Corporate Identity, Graphic Design, Internet/Web Design, Print

Michelle Jolas *(Owner & Dir-Creative)*

Accounts:
9th & Elm
The Peninsula New York
Protein Bar

WILEN GROUP
5 Wellwood Ave, Farmingdale, NY 11735-1213
Tel.: (631) 439-5000
Fax: (631) 439-4536
Toll Free: (800) 809-4536
E-Mail: info@wilengroup.com
Web Site: www.wilennewyork.com

E-Mail for Key Personnel:
President: dwilen@wilengroup.com

Employees: 135
Year Founded: 1973

National Agency Associations: DMA

Agency Specializes In: Cable T.V., Direct Response Marketing, Media Buying Services, Print, Sponsorship

Richard Wilen *(Owner)*
Darrin Wilen *(Pres)*
Paul Caravello *(Exec VP)*
Corey Wilen *(Exec VP)*
Kevin Wilen *(Exec VP)*
Allison Rekus *(VP & Dir-Client Experience)*

Peter Bryk *(VP-Ops)*
John Dorko *(VP-New Bus Dev)*
Leslee Marin *(VP-Fin)*
Rich Meschi *(VP)*

Accounts:
AAA
Bed, Bath & Beyond
Ben & Jerry
Burger King
Comcast
Comcast Cable
COX
Cox Cable
Dairy Queen
ESPN
HBO HBO Boxing
Hearst Magazines
Herschend Family Entertainment
Macy's
Mazda
Palm Beach Post
Papa John's
ProActiv Solutions
RCN
Ripley's Believe It or Not
Six Flags Entertainment Corp.
Sun Sentinel
Time Warner Cable

Branch

Wilen Direct

3333 SW 15th St, Deerfield Beach, FL 33442
Tel.: (954) 246-5000
Fax: (954) 246-3333
E-Mail: info@wilengroup.com
Web Site: www.wilendirect.com

Employees: 150
Year Founded: 1990

Kevin Wilen *(Exec VP)*
Peter Bryk *(VP-Ops)*
John Dorko *(VP-New Bus Dev)*
Tom Glassman *(Dir-Data Svcs & Postal Affairs)*
Mary Stiles *(Dir-Client Svcs & Production Technologies)*
Steve Lundgren *(Project Mgr-IT)*
Vickie Argento *(Mgr-Acctg)*
Shewa Kidane *(Mgr-Employee Rels)*

Accounts:
Bed Bath & Beyond
Ben & Jerry's
Blockbuster
Comcast
Macys
Mazda
Perry Ellis
Sixflags
Time Warner Cable

WILESMITH ADVERTISING & DESIGN

319 Clematis St Ste 710, West Palm Beach, FL 33401
Tel.: (561) 820-9196
E-Mail: wilesmithadvertising@wadads.com
Web Site: www.wadads.com

Agency Specializes In: Advertising, Brand Development & Integration, Broadcast, Collateral, Internet/Web Design, Outdoor, Package Design, Print

Margaret Wilesmith *(Pres & Dir-Creative)*
Scott Eurich *(VP & Gen Mgr)*
Annmarie Moretti *(VP & Gen Mgr)*

Accounts:
Scripps Research Institute
Temple Terrace

WILL MOKRY DESIGN LLC

3300 Bee Cave Rd Ste 650-182, Austin, TX 78746
Tel.: (512) 305-3599
Fax: (512) 308-3520
Web Site: www.willmokry.com

Agency Specializes In: Advertising, Digital/Interactive, Internet/Web Design, Outdoor, Package Design, Social Media

Will Mokry *(Pres & Dir-Creative)*

Accounts:
Genorite Pharmacy

WILLIAM JOSEPH COMMUNICATIONS

2nd Fl Eau Claire Market, 174 - 200 Barclay Parade SW, Calgary, Alberta T2P 4R5 Canada
Tel.: (403) 770-4900
Fax: (403) 232-8996
E-Mail: info@williamjoseph.com
Web Site: www.williamjoseph.com

Agency Specializes In: Advertising, Brand Development & Integration, Digital/Interactive, Guerilla Marketing, Media Buying Services, Media Planning, Outdoor, Print, Public Relations, T.V.

Ryan Townsend *(CEO)*
Lisa Hryciw *(Acct Dir)*
Terrin Kaminsky *(Dir-Art)*
Jason Miller *(Dir-Creative)*
Adrian Suva *(Dir-Art)*
Joelle Despins *(Mgr-Ops)*

Accounts:
Fabricland (Marketing Agency of Record)
The Jubilee Auditoria of Alberta

WILLIAM MILLS AGENCY

300 W Wieuca Rd Bldg 1 Ste 300, Atlanta, GA 30342
Tel.: (678) 781-7200
Fax: (678) 781-7239
Toll Free: (800) 504-3077
E-Mail: william@williammills.com
Web Site: www.williammills.com

Employees: 30
Year Founded: 1977

Agency Specializes In: Advertising, Communications, Corporate Identity, Internet/Web Design, Media Planning, Media Relations, Public Relations, Sales Promotion, Search Engine Optimization, Strategic Planning/Research

William Mills, III *(CEO)*
Catherine Laws *(Exec VP)*
Kelly Williams *(Sr VP)*
Michael Misoyianis *(VP-Acctg & Fin)*
Mary York Cox *(Acct Dir)*
Bevin Wallace *(Acct Supvr)*
Sarah Wroble *(Acct Supvr)*

Accounts:
ABA Banking Journal
American Banker FinTech Forward 2015 (Agency of Record)
Bank Director
Bank News
Bank Systems
Cardlytics
Community Banker
Credit Union Business
Credit Union Journal
CU Wallet Brand Awareness, Marketing, Strategic Public Relations
Data Select Systems, Inc. PR
Digital Transactions
EFT Source Card@Once, Media
Equifax
Independent Banker
iPay
Jack Henry
Lenders One
Mortgage Originator
OAUG COLLABORATE Conference, Communications, Media Relations, Public Relations
ProfitStars
Questsoft
Symitar
Wipro Galagher

WILLIAM SULLIVAN ADVERTISING, INC.

1600 Us Route 22 E, Union, NJ 07083-3415
Tel.: (908) 302-1220
Fax: (908) 687-9280
E-Mail: bsullivan@jlmedia.com
Web Site: www.williamsullivanadvertising.com

Employees: 10

Agency Specializes In: Broadcast, Media Buying Services, Print, Production, Radio, Trade & Consumer Magazines

William Sullivan *(Founder & Pres)*
Stan Gerber *(Chief Strategy Officer & Exec VP)*

Accounts:
Natural Cures
Proactiv

WILLIAMS AND HOUSE

7 Townpath Ln, Avon, CT 06001
Tel.: (860) 675-4140
Fax: (860) 675-4124
Web Site: www.williamsandhouse.com

Employees: 5
Year Founded: 1990

Agency Specializes In: Advertising, Brand Development & Integration, Business-To-Business, Collateral, Communications, Consumer Marketing, Corporate Communications, Corporate Identity, Direct Response Marketing, Environmental, Event Planning & Marketing, Graphic Design, Health Care Services, Internet/Web Design, Logo & Package Design, Market Research, Media Buying Services, Media Planning, Medical Products, New Technologies, Planning & Consultation, Point of Purchase, Point of Sale, Print, Production, Production (Print), Public Relations, Publicity/Promotions, Seniors' Market, Sponsorship, Strategic Planning/Research, T.V., Viral/Buzz/Word of Mouth

Approx. Annual Billings: $5,000,000

Breakdown of Gross Billings by Media: Newsp.: $750,000; Other: $2,000,000; Pub. Rels.: $2,000,000; Radio: $250,000

Lisa House *(Partner)*
Pamela L. Williams *(Partner)*

Accounts:
Artcraft Engraving
Bristol Hospital; Bristol, CT
Business Lenders
Learning Corridor
Long Island IVF

WILLIAMS/CRAWFORD & ASSOCIATES

415 N 5th St PO Box 789, Fort Smith, AR 72902
Tel.: (479) 782-5230
Fax: (479) 782-6970

E-Mail: chip@williams-crawford.com
Web Site: www.williams-crawford.com

E-Mail for Key Personnel:
President: fred@williams-crawford.com
Creative Dir.: branden@williams-crawford.com
Media Dir.: denisewill@williams-crawford.com

Employees: 21
Year Founded: 1982

National Agency Associations: Second Wind Limited

Agency Specializes In: Consumer Marketing, Financial, Graphic Design, Health Care Services, Media Buying Services, Medical Products, New Product Development, Newspaper, Newspapers & Magazines, Out-of-Home Media, Outdoor, Production, Public Relations, Restaurant, Travel & Tourism

Approx. Annual Billings: $20,000,000

Fred O. Williams *(CEO)*
Denise Williams *(VP-Media)*
Chip Paris *(Client Svcs Dir)*
Brock Girard *(Dir-Creative)*

Accounts:
BHC
Citizens
First Bank Corp; Fort Smith, AR All Products; 2001
Fort Smith Airport; Forth Smith, AR
Golden Corral
Shamrock
Smith
Taco Bell All Products, Kansas City, Forth Smith, Tulsa, Oklahoma City, Fargo, Shreveport, Cedar Rapids, Little Rock, Abilene, Columbia/Jefferson City, Sioux Falls, Sioux City, San Angelo, Sherman/Ada, Springfield & La Crosse/Eauclaire
UA Fort Smith
Wingfoot
Yeagers

WILLIAMS CREATIVE GROUP
330 Marshall St, Shreveport, LA 71101
Tel.: (318) 227-1515
Web Site: www.williamscreativegroup.com

Judy Williams *(Pres)*
Francesca Benten Moreland *(Partner)*
Pat Viser *(Partner)*
Ron Viskozki *(VP)*
Kelly Simpson *(Sr Graphic Designer)*
Aaron Martin *(Asst Acct Exec)*

Accounts:
Shreveport Sizzle, Inc.
SmashBurger

WILLIAMS-HELDE MARKETING COMMUNICATIONS
2929 1st Ave, Seattle, WA 98121
Tel.: (206) 285-1940
E-Mail: slf@williams-helde.com
Web Site: www.williams-helde.com

Employees: 35
Year Founded: 1969

Agency Specializes In: Above-the-Line, Advertising, Affluent Market, Alternative Advertising, Automotive, Aviation & Aerospace, Below-the-Line, Brand Development & Integration, Business-To-Business, Catalogs, Co-op Advertising, Collateral, Commercial Photography, Communications, Consumer Goods, Consumer Marketing, Consumer Publications, Corporate Communications, Custom Publishing, Digital/Interactive, Electronic Media, Electronics, Email, Engineering, Entertainment, Exhibit/Trade Shows, Fashion/Apparel, Food Service, Graphic Design, Health Care Services, High Technology, Hospitality, Household Goods, In-Store Advertising, Industrial, Integrated Marketing, Internet/Web Design, Leisure, Logo & Package Design, Luxury Products, Magazines, Marine, Market Research, Media Buying Services, Medical Products, Men's Market, Mobile Marketing, Multimedia, New Product Development, New Technologies, Out-of-Home Media, Package Design, Paid Searches, Pets , Pharmaceutical, Point of Purchase, Point of Sale, Print, Production, Production (Print), Promotions, Radio, Real Estate, Regional, Restaurant, Retail, Sales Promotion, Sports Market, Strategic Planning/Research, Teen Market, Trade & Consumer Magazines, Travel & Tourism, Tween Market, Web (Banner Ads, Pop-ups, etc.), Women's Market

Approx. Annual Billings: $7,500,000

Marc Williams *(Pres)*
John Young *(Head-Digital & Tech)*
Michael Baldwin *(Dir-Art)*
Sue Boivin *(Dir-Creative)*
Phil Chin *(Dir-Mktg & Partnerships)*
Craig Motlong *(Dir-Creative)*
Brian Piper *(Dir-Creative)*
Amber Hargett *(Sr Graphic Designer)*

Accounts:
Adidas
Alaska Airlines
Darigold
Diadora
Harry's Fresh Food
Insect Shield
Nautilus
Nordic Tugs
Philips
Princess Tours
Taco Del Mar

WILLIAMS MEDIA GROUP
102 W Market St, Lisbon, IA 52253
Tel.: (319) 455-2041
Fax: (319) 455-9863
E-Mail: dwilliams@williamsmediagroup.com
Web Site: www.williamsmediagroup.com

Employees: 8
Year Founded: 1999

Agency Specializes In: Recruitment, Transportation

Approx. Annual Billings: $2,250,000

Breakdown of Gross Billings by Media: Mags.: $900,000; Newsp.: $1,125,000; Radio: $112,500; Trade & Consumer Mags.: $112,500

Darin Williams *(Founder & Pres)*
Kelly Miller *(VP-Sls)*
Clayton Chambers *(Dir-Creative)*

Accounts:
Don Hummer Trucking
GSTC, Inc.; Walford, IA (Employment Recruiting); 1999
Hirschbach Motorlines
McGriff Transportation
McLeod Express
Stevens Transport; Dallas, TX (Employment Recruiting); 1999

WILLIAMS WHITTLE ASSOCIATES, INC.
711 Princess St, Alexandria, VA 22314-2221
Tel.: (703) 836-9222
Fax: (703) 684-3285
E-Mail: rwhittle@williamswhittle.com
Web Site: www.williamswhittle.com

Employees: 28
Year Founded: 1967

National Agency Associations: ICOM

Agency Specializes In: Above-the-Line, Advertising, Affiliate Marketing, Affluent Market, Arts, Automotive, Aviation & Aerospace, Below-the-Line, Brand Development & Integration, Branded Entertainment, Broadcast, Business Publications, Business-To-Business, Cable T.V., Co-op Advertising, Collateral, College, Communications, Computers & Software, Consulting, Consumer Goods, Consumer Marketing, Consumer Publications, Content, Corporate Communications, Corporate Identity, Crisis Communications, Customer Relationship Management, Digital/Interactive, Direct Response Marketing, Direct-to-Consumer, E-Commerce, Education, Electronic Media, Email, Entertainment, Environmental, Experience Design, Financial, Food Service, Graphic Design, Guerilla Marketing, Health Care Services, High Technology, Hospitality, Household Goods, Identity Marketing, Infomercials, Information Technology, Integrated Marketing, Internet/Web Design, Leisure, Logo & Package Design, Luxury Products, Magazines, Market Research, Media Buying Services, Media Planning, Media Relations, Mobile Marketing, Multimedia, Newspaper, Newspapers & Magazines, Outdoor, Over-50 Market, Paid Searches, Planning & Consultation, Podcasting, Point of Purchase, Point of Sale, Print, Production, Production (Ad, Film, Broadcast), Production (Print), Promotions, Public Relations, Publicity/Promotions, RSS (Really Simple Syndication), Radio, Real Estate, Regional, Restaurant, Retail, Search Engine Optimization, Seniors' Market, Social Marketing/Nonprofit, Social Media, Sports Market, Strategic Planning/Research, T.V., Trade & Consumer Magazines, Transportation, Travel & Tourism, Urban Market, Viral/Buzz/Word of Mouth, Web (Banner Ads, Pop-ups, etc.)

Robert L. Whittle *(Pres & CEO)*
Julia McDowell *(VP & Mgmt Supvr)*
Rich Park *(Dir-Creative)*
Wendy Weaver *(Dir-Media Svcs)*
Mike Leimbach *(Assoc Dir-Creative)*

Accounts:
Alex Econ Dev Corp; Alexandria, VA
American Civil War Center
American Red Cross; Washington, DC Non-Profit
The USO; Arlington, VA
Virginia Hospital Center
Virginia Railway Express
Washington Metropolitan Area Transit Authority
The Washington Times

WILLIS DESIGN STUDIOS
1703 Forrest St, Bakersfield, CA 93304
Tel.: (661) 324-2337
Web Site: www.willisdesign.com

Year Founded: 1979

Agency Specializes In: Advertising, Internet/Web Design, Logo & Package Design, Print

Michael Willis *(Owner)*

Accounts:
Bakersfield Symphony Orchestra
San Joaquin Hospital

WILLOW CREATIVE GROUP
(Reformed as Aim Straight Up)

WILLOW MARKETING
3590 N Meridian Ste 200, Indianapolis, IN 46208

Tel.: (317) 257-5225
Fax: (317) 257-0184
Web Site: www.willowmarketing.com

Employees: 17
Year Founded: 1992

Agency Specializes In: Sponsorship

Revenue: $2,200,000

Brad Gillum *(Pres & CEO)*
Kayla Carmichael *(Acct Mgr)*
Taylor Bussick *(Mgr-Video Production)*
Holly Bindley *(Coord-Traffic)*

Accounts:
Toyota

WILLOW ST. AGENCY
3900 Willow St 2nd Fl, Dallas, TX 75226
Tel.: (214) 276-7658
E-Mail: info@willowstagency.com
Web Site: www.willowstagency.com

Agency Specializes In: Advertising, Broadcast, Digital/Interactive, Print

Scott Howell *(Partner)*
Larry Johannes *(Partner)*
Jim Sykora *(Partner)*
Mark Smith *(Sr Dir-Art)*

Accounts:
Uniden America Corporation Digital Direct Marketing, Mobile Apps, Social Media

WILSON CREATIVE GROUP, INC.
6645 Willow Park Dr Ste 100, Naples, FL 34109
Tel.: (239) 597-9480
Fax: (239) 236-1596
E-Mail: info@wcgpros.com
Web Site: www.wcgpros.com

Year Founded: 2007

Agency Specializes In: Advertising, Collateral, Logo & Package Design, Media Planning, Print, Public Relations, Social Media

Peggy Wilson *(Pres & CEO)*
Mike Girard *(Dir-Creative)*
Lydia Wychrij *(Mgr-Production)*
Jake Revak *(Acct Coord)*

Accounts:
Greenscapes Of Southwest Florida, Inc.
Litestream Business-to-Business Communications, Media Relations, Public Relations
Naples Square (Agency of Record) Broadcast Advertising, Digital, Print, Social Media, Strategic & Creative Communications, Website
Seaglass at Bonita Bay (Agency of Record) Digital Advertising, Social Media

WINDSOR PUBLISHING INC.
PO Box 8627, Albany, NY 12077
Tel.: (518) 475-9285

Employees: 1
Year Founded: 2000

Agency Specializes In: Business Publications, Newspaper

Chris Aloisi *(Pres)*

Accounts:
Integra Networks

WINFIELD & ASSOCIATES MARKETING & ADVERTISING
3221 Blue Ridge Rd Ste 105, Raleigh, NC 27612
Tel.: (919) 861-0620
Fax: (919) 861-0625
E-Mail: info@winfieldandassociates.com
Web Site: www.winfieldandassociates.com

Employees: 5
Year Founded: 2002

Agency Specializes In: Automotive, Broadcast, Business-To-Business, Cable T.V., Co-op Advertising, Collateral, Corporate Identity, Digital/Interactive, Direct Response Marketing, Direct-to-Consumer, Education, Email, Government/Political, Graphic Design, Health Care Services, Identity Marketing, Infomercials, Integrated Marketing, Legal Services, Local Marketing, Media Buying Services, Media Planning, Medical Products, Outdoor, Point of Purchase, Radio, Restaurant, Retail, Social Media, T.V., Trade & Consumer Magazines, Web (Banner Ads, Pop-ups, etc.)

Breakdown of Gross Billings by Media: Brdcst.: 20%; Cable T.V.: 5%; Graphic Design: 20%; Newsp. & Mags.: 10%; Outdoor: 5%; Pub. Rels.: 5%; Radio: 35%

Eric Schmidt *(Pres)*
Andrea Schmidt *(VP-Media)*

Accounts:
Pacific West Capital Group; Los Angeles, CA Financial Services; 2001

WING
200 5th Ave 3rd Fl, New York, NY 10010
Tel.: (212) 546-2020
Fax: (212) 500-9483
E-Mail: info@insidewing.com
Web Site: www.insidewing.com

Employees: 80
Year Founded: 1979

National Agency Associations: 4A's-AHAA

Agency Specializes In: Above-the-Line, Advertising, Affluent Market, Arts, Automotive, Below-the-Line, Bilingual Market, Brand Development & Integration, Branded Entertainment, Cable T.V., Communications, Computers & Software, Consulting, Consumer Goods, Consumer Marketing, Cosmetics, Digital/Interactive, Direct-to-Consumer, Education, Electronic Media, Electronics, Entertainment, Event Planning & Marketing, Experience Design, Fashion/Apparel, Graphic Design, Guerilla Marketing, Health Care Services, High Technology, Hispanic Market, Hospitality, Household Goods, Identity Marketing, Integrated Marketing, International, Internet/Web Design, Leisure, Local Marketing, Luxury Products, Magazines, Market Research, Media Buying Services, Media Planning, Men's Market, Mobile Marketing, Multicultural, Multimedia, New Product Development, Newspaper, Newspapers & Magazines, Out-of-Home Media, Outdoor, Pharmaceutical, Planning & Consultation, Point of Sale, Print, Production, Production (Print), Promotions, Radio, Restaurant, Retail, Sales Promotion, Social Marketing/Nonprofit, Sponsorship, Strategic Planning/Research, T.V., Teen Market, Trade & Consumer Magazines, Transportation, Travel & Tourism, Urban Market, Viral/Buzz/Word of Mouth, Women's Market

Approx. Annual Billings: $70,000,000

Sandra Alfaro *(Mng Dir)*
Favio Ucedo *(Chief Creative Officer)*
Veronica Villalpando *(Sr VP & Dir)*
Marc Duran *(Dir-Art & Copywriter)*
Holly Mcgavock *(Dir-Plng)*
Anthoni Rodriguez *(Dir-Art)*
Facundo Paglia *(Assoc Dir-Creative)*
Luz Burgos *(Mgr-Admin Svcs)*
Gabriela Olave *(Acct Exec)*
John Jardine *(Assoc Acct Dir)*

Accounts:
DIRECTV Campaign: "Swim"
Esteban Gergely Campaign: "Our Honeymoon"
Law Offices of Esteban Gergely Campaign: "Josh & Kimberly", Campaign: "Kate & Mike", Campaign: "Tommy & Rachel"
LifeBeat
NFL; 2013
Papa Johns
Partnership for Drug Free America Sheep
Procter & Gamble (USA) Clairol, CoverGirl, Downy, Olay, Pantene; 1979
Red Hot Organization AIDS/STD Awareness, Campaign: "Spreading the word, not the disease", Red Hot Website
The Weather Channel Campaign: "Showers with a Chance of Weather Alerts Subscriptions"
Ximo Abadia

WINGARD CREATIVE
245 Riverside Ave Ste 425, Jacksonville, FL 32202
Tel.: (904) 387-2570
Fax: (904) 329-4488
E-Mail: hello@wingardcreative.com
Web Site: www.wingardcreative.com

Year Founded: 2008

Agency Specializes In: Advertising, Brand Development & Integration, Media Buying Services, Media Planning, Print, Public Relations

David Wingard *(Chief Creative Officer)*
Ben Windsor *(Art Dir)*
Natalie DeYoung *(Dir-Comm & PR)*
Jen Hankey Maki *(Mgr-Production)*
Katie Nail *(Copywriter & Strategist-Media)*
Hannah Cleveland *(Acct Exec)*
Megan O'Steen *(Acct Exec)*

Accounts:
New-Black Sheep Restaurant
New-Burrito Gallery
New-The Candy Apple Cafe & Cocktails

WINGER MARKETING
180 W Washington Ste 700, Chicago, IL 60602
Tel.: (312) 494-0422
Fax: (312) 494-0426
E-Mail: info@wingermarketing.com
Web Site: www.wingermarketing.com

Agency Specializes In: Advertising, Content, Digital/Interactive, Event Planning & Marketing, Media Buying Services, Media Planning, Public Relations, Social Media

Karolyn Raphael *(Pres)*
Leslie Randolph *(VP)*
Alisa Bay *(Dir-PR)*
Nycole Hampton *(Dir-Social Media)*
Stefanie Stein *(Sr Acct Exec)*

Accounts:
Chicago Charity Challenge
Slant

WINGMAN ADVERTISING
4061 Glencoe Ave Ste A, Marina Del Rey, CA 90292
Tel.: (310) 302-9400

Fax: (310) 823-0313
E-Mail: info@wingmanadv.com
Web Site: www.wingmanadv.com

Employees: 28
Year Founded: 2003

Agency Specializes In: Advertising, Affluent Market, Broadcast, Business-To-Business, Cable T.V., Co-op Advertising, Collateral, Consulting, Consumer Goods, Consumer Marketing, Customer Relationship Management, Digital/Interactive, Direct Response Marketing, E-Commerce, Electronic Media, Email, Financial, Household Goods, Integrated Marketing, Investor Relations, Local Marketing, Luxury Products, Magazines, Market Research, Media Buying Services, Media Planning, Media Relations, Men's Market, Newspaper, Newspapers & Magazines, Paid Searches, Planning & Consultation, Point of Purchase, Point of Sale, Print, Product Placement, Production, Production (Ad, Film, Broadcast), Production (Print), Promotions, Radio, Real Estate, Regional, Retail, Sales Promotion, Search Engine Optimization, Shopper Marketing, Social Marketing/Nonprofit, Social Media, Strategic Planning/Research, T.V., Web (Banner Ads, Pop-ups, etc.), Women's Market

Approx. Annual Billings: $50,000,000

Rich Kagan *(Owner)*
Steve Dubane *(Pres)*
Brian Diedrick *(Dir-Digital Mktg)*
Luz Ongkiko *(Dir-Fin)*
Pat Rogge *(Dir-Interactive Mktg)*
Ryan Bowers *(Mgr-Bus Dev)*

WINGNUT ADVERTISING

708 N 1st St Ste 133, Minneapolis, MN 55401
Tel.: (612) 872-4847
Web Site: www.wingnutinc.com

Year Founded: 2004

Agency Specializes In: Advertising, Digital/Interactive

Jim Cousins *(Partner & Pres)*
John Arms *(Partner & CEO)*
Greg Dutton *(Partner & Exec Dir-Creative)*
Chris Stewart *(Sr Dir-Art)*
Ann Elkins *(Acct Dir)*
Colleen Nagel *(Sr Acct Mgr)*
Ashley Tice *(Sr Project Mgr)*
Malarie Holmes *(Assoc Acct Dir)*

Accounts:
Agway, Inc.

WINK, INCORPORATED

126 N 3rd St #100, Minneapolis, MN 55401
Tel.: (612) 455-2642
Fax: (612) 455-2645
E-Mail: info@wink-mpls.com
Web Site: www.wink-mpls.com

Employees: 5
Year Founded: 2000

Agency Specializes In: Advertising, Consumer Goods, Consumer Marketing, Custom Publishing, Fashion/Apparel, Logo & Package Design, Magazines, Multimedia, Package Design, Restaurant, Retail

Scott Thares *(Owner & Dir-Creative)*
Derek Chan *(Designer-Digital Product)*
Tim Cronin *(Jr Designer)*

Accounts:
A.I.G.A.
American Eagle Outfitters
The American Institute of Graphic Artists
Blu Dot
Macys
MTV
Nike
OGI Frames
Target
Works in Progress

WINKREATIVE

776 College Street, Toronto, ON M6G 1C6
Canada
Tel.: (647) 694-2618
Web Site: www.winkreative.com

Agency Specializes In: Advertising, Brand Development & Integration, Broadcast, Corporate Identity, Custom Publishing, Internet/Web Design, Package Design, Publishing

Tyler Brule *(Chm & CEO)*
Rachel Steed *(Acct Dir)*
Maurus Fraser *(Dir-Creative)*

Accounts:
Metrolinx Union Pearson Express

WINSPER

(Formerly J. Winsper & Co.)
115 Broad St 5th Fl, Boston, MA 02110
Tel.: (617) 695-2900
E-Mail: info@winsper.com
Web Site: www.winsper.com

Employees: 14
Year Founded: 2002

Agency Specializes In: Digital/Interactive, Direct Response Marketing, Internet/Web Design, Public Relations, Sponsorship

Jeff Winsper *(Pres)*
Chien-Ming Tu *(CTO)*
Gillian Lynch *(VP & Grp Acct Dir)*
Iuliia Artemenko *(Mgr-Analytics & Mktg Ops)*
Iryna Teixeira *(Specialist-Mktg Ops)*

Accounts:
New-Carpet One Floor & Home (Integrated Brand Agency of Record) Brand Strategy, Broadcast, Digital Marketing, Print
Exeter Hospital
Janome America Analytics, Integrated Creative, Qualitative Research, Social Media, Strategy
Timberland; Stratham, NH Timberland Pro Footwear; 2006
Unica
Young's Brewery; United Kingdom; 2004

WINSTANLEY PARTNERS

114 Main St, Lenox, MA 01240-2353
Tel.: (413) 637-9887
Fax: (413) 637-2045
E-Mail: contact@winstanley.com
Web Site: www.winstanley.com

Employees: 25
Year Founded: 1986

Agency Specializes In: Advertising, Advertising Specialties, Affluent Market, Agriculture, Arts, Bilingual Market, Brand Development & Integration, Branded Entertainment, Broadcast, Business Publications, Business-To-Business, Cable T.V., Catalogs, Children's Market, Co-op Advertising, Collateral, College, Communications, Computers & Software, Consulting, Consumer Marketing, Consumer Publications, Content, Corporate Communications, Corporate Identity, Crisis Communications, Digital/Interactive, Direct Response Marketing, E-Commerce, Education, Electronic Media, Email, Engineering, Entertainment, Environmental, Event Planning & Marketing, Exhibit/Trade Shows, Experience Design, Fashion/Apparel, Financial, Food Service, Gay & Lesbian Market, Government/Political, Graphic Design, Health Care Services, High Technology, Hospitality, Industrial, Information Technology, Integrated Marketing, Internet/Web Design, Investor Relations, Legal Services, Leisure, Local Marketing, Logo & Package Design, Luxury Products, Magazines, Marine, Market Research, Media Buying Services, Media Relations, Media Training, Medical Products, Merchandising, Multimedia, New Product Development, Newspaper, Newspapers & Magazines, Outdoor, Package Design, Pharmaceutical, Planning & Consultation, Point of Purchase, Point of Sale, Print, Production, Production (Ad, Film, Broadcast), Public Relations, Publicity/Promotions, Radio, Real Estate, Recruitment, Restaurant, Retail, Sales Promotion, Search Engine Optimization, Social Marketing/Nonprofit, Social Media, Sports Market, Strategic Planning/Research, Sweepstakes, T.V., Teen Market, Telemarketing, Trade & Consumer Magazines, Transportation, Travel & Tourism, Web (Banner Ads, Pop-ups, etc.)

Approx. Annual Billings: $25,000,000

Nathan B. Winstanley *(Pres)*
Ralph Frisina *(VP & Dir-Creative)*
Michael Coakley *(VP-Acct Svcs)*
David Morrison *(Dir-Art)*
Jaclyn Stevenson *(Dir-PR & Social Media)*
Vanessa Leikvoll *(Coord-Events)*

Accounts:
DuPont
GE
National Association of Home Builders
New York State Energy Research and Development Authority
Spalding; Bowling Green, KY sporting goods & new products; 1990
Suddekor; Agawam, MA laminate flooring; 2002

WINSTAR INTERACTIVE MEDIA

307 7th Ave Ste 2003, New York, NY 10001
Tel.: (212) 916-0713
Web Site: www.winstarinteractive.com

Employees: 20
Year Founded: 1996

Agency Specializes In: Advertising, Digital/Interactive, Graphic Design, Information Technology, Internet/Web Design

David Shamberger *(Pres)*
John Foley *(VP)*
Mark E. Crona *(Dir-Bus Dev-Western Reg)*
Michael A. Palmieri *(Dir-Ops & Bus Dev-Eastern Reg)*
Mila Tokar *(Reg Mgr-Sls)*

Accounts:
Atari United States
Boost Mobile
Fodor's Fodors.com
Fox Searchlight
IFC.com
Interactive Video Network
NASDAQ
ThirdAge
Zagat

WINSTON ADVERTISING

122 E 42nd St, New York, NY 10168
Tel.: (212) 682-1063
Fax: (212) 983-2594

Toll Free: (800) 562-2371
E-Mail: winston@winston.net
Web Site: www.winston.net

E-Mail for Key Personnel:
President: bpapkin@winston.net

Employees: 10
Year Founded: 1984

National Agency Associations: EMA

Agency Specializes In: Magazines, Print, Radio, Real Estate, Recruitment

Sy Kaye *(Chm)*
Bruce Papkin *(Pres)*
Jesse Ulezalka *(CFO)*

WINTR
3621 Stone Way N Ste B, Seattle, WA 98103
Tel.: (206) 783-4570
E-Mail: info@wintr.us
Web Site: www.wintr.us

Agency Specializes In: Advertising, Content, Digital/Interactive

Matt Fordham *(Partner & Dir-Technical)*
Taylor Kieburtz *(Principal & Dir-Strategy)*
Ivan Cruz *(Head-Creative)*
Andy Kribbs *(Head-Creative-Design)*
Christian Cogan *(Mgr-Fin & Ops)*

Accounts:
Lookout

WIRE STONE LLC
920 20th St, Sacramento, CA 95811
Tel.: (916) 446-6550
E-Mail: busdev@wirestone.com
Web Site: www.wirestone.com

Employees: 157
Year Founded: 2000

National Agency Associations: AAF

Agency Specializes In: Advertising, Advertising Specialties, Affluent Market, Brand Development & Integration, Business-To-Business, Collateral, Communications, Computers & Software, Consulting, Consumer Goods, Consumer Marketing, Corporate Identity, Customer Relationship Management, Digital/Interactive, Direct Response Marketing, Direct-to-Consumer, E-Commerce, Electronic Media, Entertainment, Event Planning & Marketing, Exhibit/Trade Shows, Fashion/Apparel, Food Service, Graphic Design, High Technology, Information Technology, Integrated Marketing, Internet/Web Design, Leisure, Logo & Package Design, Luxury Products, Media Planning, Merchandising, Multimedia, Newspapers & Magazines, Paid Searches, Planning & Consultation, Point of Purchase, Print, Production, Public Relations, Publicity/Promotions, Real Estate, Recruitment, Retail, Sales Promotion, Social Marketing/Nonprofit, Sports Market, Strategic Planning/Research, Technical Advertising, Viral/Buzz/Word of Mouth

Approx. Annual Billings: $24,000,000

Dan Lynch *(Pres & CEO)*
Jon Baker *(Mng Dir)*
Tony Schlangen *(Mng Dir)*
Norman Guadagno *(VP-Client Engagement)*
Gary Robinett *(VP-Fin)*
David Smith *(VP-Bus Dev)*
Ryan Schroth *(Assoc-Sls & Strategy)*

Accounts:
Boeing
Carbonite, Inc. (Agency of Record) Digital, Marketing, Media Buying, Media Planning
ConAgra Alexia Frozen Foods, Lamb Weston
HP
Intel
Microsoft
Nike; Beaverton, OR
TAG

Branches

Wirestone, LLC
225 W Illinois Ste 400, Chicago, IL 60654
Tel.: (312) 222-0733
Fax: (312) 222-0744
E-Mail: busdev@wirestone.com
Web Site: www.wirestone.com

Employees: 30

Agency Specializes In: Below-the-Line, Brand Development & Integration, Business-To-Business, Collateral, Computers & Software, Consulting, Consumer Marketing, Content, Corporate Identity, Customer Relationship Management, Digital/Interactive, Direct-to-Consumer, E-Commerce, Electronic Media, Electronics, Event Planning & Marketing, Exhibit/Trade Shows, Fashion/Apparel, Graphic Design, Hospitality, In-Store Advertising, Information Technology, Integrated Marketing, Internet/Web Design, Leisure, Logo & Package Design, Luxury Products, Media Planning, Multimedia, New Technologies, Package Design, Planning & Consultation, Point of Purchase, Point of Sale, Print, Production (Print), Real Estate, Retail, Sales Promotion, Sports Market, Strategic Planning/Research, Travel & Tourism, Viral/Buzz/Word of Mouth, Web (Banner Ads, Pop-ups, etc.)

Ti Bensen *(Mng Dir)*
Gregory Butz *(VP & Mng Dir-Chicago)*
Lianne Morgan *(VP & Mng Dir-Seattle)*
David Smith *(VP-Bus Dev)*
Mike Higgins *(Dir-IT)*
Maria Pontillo *(Dir-Client)*
Eric Ravenstein *(Dir-Creative)*
Kristina Keller *(Sr Acct Mgr)*

Accounts:
CytoSport
Dan Wheldon
Health & Disability Advocates; Chicago, IL (Agency of Record)
Hewlett Packard
Johnson & Johnson
Limelight Networks
The Lyle Anderson Company
Microsoft
Nike
Oakley
Olivet Nazarene University
Shell Energy North America
Skyy Spirits
Strategic Outsourcing
Sun Country Airlines
SunCom Wireless

Wirestone
145 E Mountain Ave, Fort Collins, CO 80525
Tel.: (970) 493-3181
Fax: (970) 484-6497
Web Site: www.wirestone.com

Employees: 40

Agency Specializes In: Advertising

Greg Rattenborg *(Chief Creative Officer)*
Ti Bensen *(VP & Mng Dir-Fort Collins)*
Lisa Tucker *(Acct Dir)*
Jeff Kovacs *(Dir-Technical)*
Nikol Ayers *(Sr Acct Mgr)*
Jackie Abshire *(Acct Mgr)*
Mark Streed *(Mgr-Technical Svcs)*
Cathy Telarico *(Mgr-HR)*
Seth Annis *(Designer)*

Wirestone
913 W River St Ste 200, Boise, ID 83702
Tel.: (208) 343-2868
Fax: (208) 343-1336
Web Site: www.wirestone.com

Agency Specializes In: Advertising, Sponsorship

Dan Lynch *(Pres)*
Lianne Morgan *(VP & Mng Dir-Settle)*
Rob Dalton *(Exec Dir-Creative)*
Riccardo Zane *(Bus Dir-Global)*

Accounts:
HP
Microsoft
Nike

WIRED ISLAND LTD.
PO Box 661, Providenciales, British WI Turks & Caicos Islands
Tel.: (649) 941 4218
Fax: (649) 941 4219
Web Site: www.wiredislandpr.com

Employees: 4

Agency Specializes In: High Technology, Media Planning, Public Relations, Publicity/Promotions

Mike Sottak *(Founder)*
Toni Sottak *(Mng Dir)*

Accounts:
The Athena Group Public Relations
Coventor
GateRocket
GlobalFoundries
SpringSoft
Tela Innovations

WIT MEDIA
1178 Broadway 4th Fl, New York, NY 10001
Tel.: (212) 334-1810
E-Mail: wit@wit-inc.com
Web Site: www.wit-media.com

Year Founded: 2009

Agency Specializes In: Advertising, Brand Development & Integration, Content, Event Planning & Marketing, Internet/Web Design, Logo & Package Design, Media Planning, Public Relations, Social Media, Strategic Planning/Research

Clint White *(Pres & Creative Dir)*
Simona Kilgour *(VP-Ops)*
Kristen Earls *(Acct Dir)*
Sean Keepers *(Creative Dir)*
Zlato Fagundes *(Mgr-Digital Mktg)*
Elyse Familetti *(Acct Exec)*

Accounts:
Los Angeles Chamber Orchestra

WITHERSPOON & ASSOCIATES, INC.
1200 West Fwy, Fort Worth, TX 76102
Tel.: (817) 335-1373
Fax: (817) 332-6044
Toll Free: (877) 267-9133
E-Mail: info@witherspoon.com
Web Site: witherspoon.com

Employees: 10
Year Founded: 1946

Agency Specializes In: Advertising, Automotive, Brand Development & Integration, Business-To-Business, Communications, Consulting, Consumer Marketing, Corporate Identity, Direct Response Marketing, Event Planning & Marketing, Exhibit/Trade Shows, Financial, Graphic Design, Health Care Services, In-Store Advertising, Industrial, Internet/Web Design, Investor Relations, Logo & Package Design, Magazines, Media Buying Services, Medical Products, Newspaper, Newspapers & Magazines, Outdoor, Pharmaceutical, Point of Purchase, Point of Sale, Public Relations, Publicity/Promotions, Radio, Real Estate, Strategic Planning/Research, Trade & Consumer Magazines, Travel & Tourism

Approx. Annual Billings: $4,500,000 Capitalized

Mike Wilie *(Owner)*
Kimberly Wilie *(VP)*
James Cooperware *(Sr Dir-Art)*
Tim Neuman *(Acct Svcs Dir)*
Cathy Coe *(Office Mgr)*
Rhonda Watson *(Mgr-Production)*

Accounts:
Angelos Bar-B-Que
BNSF Railway Company
City of Fort Worth
Dermatology & Laser Center of Fort Worth
Fort Worth Chamber of Commerce
Fort Worth Stock Show Syndicate
Hahnfeld
Hillwood
North Texas Commission
Perrone RX
Power Service Products

WLD COMMUNICATIONS, INC.

24 Eugene Dr, Montville, NJ 07045
Tel.: (973) 809-1695
Web Site: www.wldadvertising.com

Employees: 5
Year Founded: 1980

Agency Specializes In: Brand Development & Integration, Business-To-Business, Cable T.V., Children's Market, Collateral, Consumer Marketing, Consumer Publications, Corporate Identity, Cosmetics, Direct Response Marketing, Entertainment, Event Planning & Marketing, Food Service, Graphic Design, Health Care Services, High Technology, Information Technology, Logo & Package Design, Magazines, Media Buying Services, Medical Products, New Product Development, Pharmaceutical, Print, Radio, Sales Promotion, Seniors' Market, Sports Market, Strategic Planning/Research, T.V.

Breakdown of Gross Billings by Media: Bus. Publs.: 20%; Collateral: 10%; Mags.: 30%; Newsp.: 20%; Radio: 10%; T.V.: 10%

Rob Signorile *(Pres)*

Accounts:
MFV Expositions; Fort Lee, NJ

THE WOLF AGENCY

3900 Willow St Ste 250, Dallas, TX 75226
Tel.: (214) 965-0880
Fax: (214) 760-7518
E-Mail: mark@thewolfagency.com
Web Site: www.thewolfgrp.com

E-Mail for Key Personnel:
President: mark@thewolfagency.com
Creative Dir.: vinny@thewolfagency.com
Media Dir.: Marla@thewolfagency.com

Employees: 15

Agency Specializes In: Advertising, Aviation & Aerospace, Brand Development & Integration, Broadcast, Collateral, Communications, Consulting, Consumer Marketing, Corporate Communications, Corporate Identity, Digital/Interactive, Electronic Media, Fashion/Apparel, Food Service, Government/Political, Graphic Design, Health Care Services, High Technology, Hispanic Market, In-Store Advertising, Infomercials, Internet/Web Design, Logo & Package Design, Media Buying Services, Medical Products, New Product Development, Outdoor, Planning & Consultation, Point of Purchase, Point of Sale, Print, Production, Public Relations, Radio, Retail, Strategic Planning/Research, T.V., Technical Advertising, Trade & Consumer Magazines

Dan Allen *(Principal)*
Jim Sykora *(Dir-Creative)*

Accounts:
American Airlines
Buick
Computer City
Exxon
JCPenney
McDonald's
Neiman Marcus
Pepsi
Shiner Bock
Texas Instruments
Verizon

WOLFBONE MARKETING

(Name Changed to WC&G Ad Logic)

WOLFF ADVERTISING, INC.

896 Westport Rd, Easton, CT 06612-1533
Tel.: (203) 254-9070
E-Mail: wolffadv@mindspring.com

Employees: 3
Year Founded: 1992

Agency Specializes In: Leisure, Marine

Approx. Annual Billings: $3,000,000

Martin J. Wolff *(Owner)*
Chris Cascio *(Sr Dir-Art)*

Accounts:
Empire State Building
Hargrave Custom Yachts; Fort Lauderdale, FL
Kop-Coat Marine Group/Pettit; Rockaway, NJ Marine Paints & Finishes
Pettit Paint Company; Rockaway, NJ

WOLFF OLINS

10 Regents Wharf All Saints Street, London, N1 9RL United Kingdom
Tel.: (44) 20 7713 7733
Fax: (44) 207 713 0217
Web Site: www.wolffolins.com

Employees: 80
Year Founded: 1965

Agency Specializes In: Brand Development & Integration

Brian Boylan *(Chm)*
Caroline Hancock *(Principal-Global)*
Tom Wason *(Principal-Global)*
Rose Bentley *(Head-Bus Dev-Global)*
Camilla Grey *(Head-Content Strategy-Global)*
Estelle Wackermann *(Head-Bus Dev & Mktg)*
Neil Cummings *(Dir-Creative)*
Chris Moody *(Dir-Creative)*

Accounts:
Abbey
Adidas
Airtel
Almeida
AOL New Aol Logo Design
Aviva
Boehringer Ingelheim
BT
GE
Goldfish
Majid Al Futtaim
Oi Mobile Phones
Orange
PepsiCo
Powwow
PwC
Skype Global Branding
Tata Docomo
UNICEF

Branches

Wolff Olins-New York

200 Varick St Ste 1001, New York, NY 10014
Tel.: (212) 505-7337
Fax: (212) 505-8791
E-Mail: peopleny@wolffolins.com
Web Site: www.wolffolins.com

Employees: 45
Year Founded: 1998

Agency Specializes In: Advertising, Sponsorship

Tim Allen *(Pres-North America)*
Sam Wilson *(Principal-Global)*
Angela Kyle *(Head-New Bus-North America)*
Nick O'Flaherty *(Head-Strategy-New York)*
Mike Abbink *(Dir-Design)*
Samuel Liebeskind *(Strategist)*

Accounts:
AOL
Asian Art Museum
Belkin Brand Identity
Current TV Campaign: "Current Tv Logo Design"
i2 institute imagination and ingenuity
NBC Universal Green is Universal
New Museum
Nixon Peabody Digital, Media, Print, Spark

WOMANWISE LLC

PO Box 27008, Minneapolis, MN 55427
Tel.: (952) 797-5000
Fax: (952) 797-5001
E-Mail: dorimolitor@womanwise.com
Web Site: www.womanwise.com

Employees: 15
Year Founded: 1984

National Agency Associations: APMA WORLDWIDE-PMA

Agency Specializes In: Advertising, Brand Development & Integration, Collateral, Communications, Consulting, Consumer Marketing, Corporate Identity, Event Planning & Marketing, Internet/Web Design, Logo & Package Design, Outdoor, Planning & Consultation, Point of Purchase, Point of Sale, Print, Publicity/Promotions, Radio, Restaurant, Retail, Sales Promotion, Sweepstakes, T.V.

Dori Molitor *(CEO)*

Accounts:
Bellisio Foods
Land O'Lakes
Novartis Pharmaceutical
Schwan Food Company
Serta
UnitedHealthcare

WOMENKIND

1441 Broadway Suite 3101, New York, NY 10018
Tel.: (212) 660-0400
Fax: (212) 966-4646
E-Mail: info@womenkind.net
Web Site: womenkind.net/

Employees: 10
Year Founded: 2001

Agency Specializes In: Advertising, Advertising Specialties, Arts, Brand Development & Integration, Branded Entertainment, Broadcast, Cable T.V., Communications, Consulting, Consumer Publications, Content, Cosmetics, Direct Response Marketing, Environmental, Event Planning & Marketing, Experience Design, Fashion/Apparel, Graphic Design, Guerilla Marketing, Health Care Services, High Technology, Identity Marketing, Infomercials, Internet/Web Design, Logo & Package Design, Luxury Products, Magazines, Market Research, Mobile Marketing, Multimedia, New Product Development, Newspapers & Magazines, Package Design, Planning & Consultation, Print, Production, Production (Ad, Film, Broadcast), Promotions, Public Relations, RSS (Really Simple Syndication), Retail, Sports Market, Strategic Planning/Research, T.V., Technical Advertising, Trade & Consumer Magazines, Travel & Tourism, Viral/Buzz/Word of Mouth, Women's Market

Breakdown of Gross Billings by Media: Consulting: $250,000; T.V.: $1,500,000; Trade & Consumer Mags.: $250,000

Kristi Faulkner *(Pres)*
Sandy Sabean *(Chief Creative Officer)*
Kevin Driscoll *(Mng Dir-Client Svcs)*
Belinda Downey *(Dir-Art)*

Accounts:
Citibank Citi, Women & Co; 2008
KFC Strategy; 2014
Mutual of Omaha Mutual of Omaha Insurance; 2014
Post Foods Great Grains Cereal; 2010

WOMEN'S MARKETING INC.

1221 Post Rd E Ste 201, Westport, CT 06880-5430
Tel.: (203) 256-0880
Web Site: www.womensmarketing.com

Employees: 50
Year Founded: 1982

Agency Specializes In: Brand Development & Integration, Broadcast, Cable T.V., Consulting, Consumer Goods, Consumer Marketing, Consumer Publications, Cosmetics, Digital/Interactive, Guerilla Marketing, Infomercials, Media Buying Services, Media Planning, Mobile Marketing, Newspapers & Magazines, Out-of-Home Media, Radio, Search Engine Optimization, Social Media, Sponsorship, T.V., Trade & Consumer Magazines, Viral/Buzz/Word of Mouth, Web (Banner Ads, Pop-ups, etc.)

Andrea Van Dam *(CEO)*
Doug Bivona *(CFO)*
Rich Zeldes *(EVP & Mng Dir-Global Bus Dev)*
Kim Haley *(Exec VP-Acct Strategy)*
Gary Kleinman *(EVP-Bus Dev)*
Marlea Clark *(Sr VP-Mktg)*
Kate Dillon *(Sr VP-HR & Ops)*

Accounts:
New-Moroccanoil Brand Awareness
New-Paige Denim Brand Awareness
New-Similasan Digital, Mobile, Print, Swedish OTC Brand

Branches

Flying Point Digital

35 W 36th St, New York, NY 10018
(See Separate Listing)

WONGDOODY

(Formerly Wong, Doody, Crandall, Wiener)
1011 Western Ave Ste 900, Seattle, WA 98104
Tel.: (206) 624-5325
Fax: (206) 624-2369
Web Site: www.wongdoody.com

Employees: 147
Year Founded: 1993

National Agency Associations: 4A's

Agency Specializes In: Consumer Marketing, Sponsorship

Approx. Annual Billings: $166,000,000

Ben Wiener *(CEO)*
Stacy McCann *(Sr Dir-Integrated Production)*
Erin Billmaier *(Acct Dir)*
Kristie Christensen *(Acct Dir)*
Laura Haithcock *(Producer-Digital)*
Scott Moers *(Acct Dir)*
Adam Nowak *(Creative Dir)*
Mark Watson *(Dir-Creative)*
Jan Clark *(Office Mgr & Mgr-HR)*
Maureen Cronin *(Supvr-Connection Plng)*
Anea Klix *(Sr Acct Exec)*
Damara Dikeou *(Sr Strategist-Digital)*
Tim Koehler *(Copywriter)*
Jason Whitehead *(Copywriter)*
Andrew Willingham *(Copywriter)*

Accounts:
Alaska Airlines, Inc. Campaign: "Announcement", Campaign: "Canoe", Campaign: "Drum Circle", Campaign: "Portland Timbers Territory", Campaign: "Woodcarving"
Amazon Amazon Echo, Amazon Gary Busey: Talking to Things, Campaign: "Do Alines Exist?", Campaign: "Gary Busey Meets Amazon Fire", Kindle Paperwhite, Kindle Voyage
Carnival Corporation Holland America Line
Cedars-Sinai Medical Center
The Coffee Bean & Tea Leaf #PurpleStrawCam, Campaign: "Cool Kew", Outdoor, Pinterest, Radio, Social, Vine
Epson
Holland America Line, Inc.
The National Basketball Association
Phoenix Children's Hospital Campaign: "Notrica - Nurse"
Scion
Seattle International Film Festival; Seattle, WA Campaign: "Showgirl Ingests Fatal Fish"
T-Mobile USA, Inc.
Woodland Park Zoo Campaign: "Alive - Lion Clubs", Campaign: "Family Dog"

Branch

WongDoody

(Formerly Wong, Doody, Crandall, Wiener)
8500 Steller Dr Ste 5, Culver City, CA 90232-2427
Tel.: (310) 280-7800
Fax: (310) 280-7780
Web Site: www.wongdoody.com

Employees: 147
Year Founded: 1997

National Agency Associations: 4A's

Agency Specializes In: Consumer Marketing

Tracy Wong *(Chm)*
Ben Wiener *(CEO)*
Knox Duncan *(Mng Dir)*
Skyler Mattson *(Mng Dir)*
Steven Orenstein *(CFO)*
Pam Fujimoto *(Exec Dir-Creative)*
Kristie Christensen *(Acct Dir)*
Jana Pinkosky *(Acct Dir)*
Elizabeth Lay *(Dir-Art)*
John Schofield *(Dir-Creative)*
Victor Acosta *(Assoc Dir-Plng)*
Dennis Lee *(Assoc Dir-Creative)*
Cosette Chaput *(Acct Exec)*

Accounts:
Alaska Airlines
Alpine Electronics of America, Inc.
Amazon.com
New-American Association of University Women Campaign: "#TheReal10"
Cedars-Sinai Medical Center
New-DoubleDown Casino (Agency of Record) Orange is the New Black
Hitachi
The Methodist Hospital System; Houston, TX
T-Mobile US Retail
Toyota Scion Brand Marketing, Digital, Radio
VIZIO

THE WOO

(Formerly Woo Agency)
9601 Jefferson Blvd, Culver City, CA 90232-3512
Tel.: (310) 558-1188
Fax: (310) 558-0294
E-Mail: info@thewoo.com
Web Site: thewoo.com/

Employees: 36
Year Founded: 1996

Agency Specializes In: Brand Development & Integration, Logo & Package Design, Media Buying Services, Print, Radio, Sponsorship, T.V.

David Abehsera *(Pres & Chief Strategy Officer)*
John Gibson *(VP & Grp Acct Dir)*
Daniel Hill *(Head-Digital Product)*
Caroline Digiulio *(Dir-Creative)*
Scott Hieatt *(Dir-Interactive)*
Mike Rose *(Dir-Consumer Connections & Integrated Media)*
Hope Lee *(Acct Supvr)*

Accounts:
AMD
Beachbody
New-Bosch Home Appliances U.S. (Creative Agency of Record)
Cydcor
New-Intel
The Israel Ministry of Tourism
LA Fitness
Lenovo
Microsoft
Niagara Bottling
New-Office Depot
OOMA
Samsung Home Appliance
Takano Yuri

THE WOOD AGENCY

7550 IH-10 W, San Antonio, TX 78229
Tel.: (210) 474-7400
Fax: (210) 474-7499

Toll Free: (888) 774-7443
E-Mail: twa@thewoodagency.com
Web Site: www.thewoodagency.com

E-Mail for Key Personnel:
President: vtw@thewoodagency.com
Media Dir.: kathy@thewoodagency.com

Employees: 14
Year Founded: 1987

Agency Specializes In: Advertising, Bilingual Market, Brand Development & Integration, Broadcast, Business-To-Business, Cable T.V., Health Care Services, Infomercials, Retail, Strategic Planning/Research

Approx. Annual Billings: $12,000,000

Trevor Wood *(Owner & Pres)*
Elaine Lytle *(Sr Dir-Art)*
Kathy Bellamy *(Dir-Media)*
Christina Medina *(Mgr-Creative Svcs)*
Renee Randolph *(Buyer-Print)*

Accounts:
Methodist Healthcare System

WOODLANDS AD AGENCY
719 Sawdust Rd Ste 115, The Woodlands, TX 77380
Tel.: (281) 651-2220
Web Site: www.woodlandsadagency.com

Agency Specializes In: Advertising, Exhibit/Trade Shows, Graphic Design, Internet/Web Design, Logo & Package Design, Print

Darren Eiswirth *(Exec Dir-Creative)*

Accounts:
Forge USA
Secret Expressions
Service First Automotive Centers
Tangible Difference Learning Center

WOODRUFF SWEITZER, INC.
501 Fay St Ste 110, Columbia, MO 65201
Tel.: (573) 875-7917
Fax: (573) 874-7979
Toll Free: (888) 300-7485
E-Mail: info@woodruffsweitzer.com
Web Site: www.woodruffsweitzer.com

Employees: 30
Year Founded: 1992

National Agency Associations: NAMA

Agency Specializes In: Advertising, Agriculture, Government/Political, Health Care Services, Pharmaceutical

Terry Woodruff *(Pres)*
Shelley Thompson *(COO)*
Scott Kington *(Exec VP-Strategic Plng & Brand Dev)*
Tim McKim *(Exec VP)*
Cheri Johnson *(Dir-PR)*
Gene Petersen *(Sr Mgr-Digital)*
Shannan Baker *(Acct Mgr)*
Sherry Jablonski *(Mgr-Creative Dept)*
Erin Nash *(Mgr-PR)*
Caitlin Christopher *(Acct Coord)*

Accounts:
Abbott Laboratories
Arysta Lifescience; San Francisco, CA Agrochemicals; 2000
Bayer HealthCare
Boone County National Bank; Columbia, MO Financial Services; 1997
City of Columbia
Diamond Pet Foods Nutragold Packaging
IMMVAC, Inc.
Pop's Authentic
Taste the Wild
Ten Pin Management

Branches

Confluence Marketing
1926 Old West Main St, Red Wing, MN 55066
(See Separate Listing)

Woodruff Sweitzer Canada Inc.
1220 Kensington Road NW Ste 303, Calgary, AB T2N 3P5 Canada
Tel.: (403) 291-2922
Fax: (403) 291-2365
E-Mail: info@woodruffsweitzer.com
Web Site: www.woodruffsweitzer.com

Year Founded: 2002

Agency Specializes In: Advertising

Susan Groeneveld *(Partner)*
Shannon Anderson *(Acct Dir)*
Graham Kahl *(Dir-Digital)*

Accounts:
Livestock Identification Services
Morris Industries (Agency of Record)

Woodruff Sweitzer Inc
331 Southwest Blvd, Kansas City, MO 64108
Tel.: (816) 255-1917
Web Site: www.woodruffsweitzer.com

Agency Specializes In: Advertising, Brand Development & Integration, Digital/Interactive, Event Planning & Marketing, Graphic Design, Internet/Web Design, Public Relations, Social Media

Cassie Naes *(Acct Coord)*

Accounts:
New-AMVAC Chemical Corporation

WOODS WITT DEALY & SONS, INC.
110 W 40th St Ste 1902, New York, NY 10018
Tel.: (212) 768-1259
Fax: (212) 768-3520
E-Mail: info@woodswittdealy.com
Web Site: www.woodswittdealy.com

Employees: 10

Agency Specializes In: Experience Design, Internet/Web Design, T.V.

Harry Woods *(Partner & Dir-Creative)*
Phyllis Dealy *(Partner)*
Eric Altbush *(Sr Dir-Art)*
John Sacripanti *(Acct Exec)*

Accounts:
Butternuts Beer & Ale
CNBC
Duracell Campaign: "A Day in the Life"
Hickory Farms
HMDX Audio
Powermat

WOODWARD CREATIVE GROUP LLC
219 Westfield Blvd Ste 100, Temple, TX 76502
Tel.: (254) 773-5588
Fax: (254) 773-9611
Web Site: www.woodwardcreativegroup.com

Employees: 12

Agency Specializes In: Advertising, Graphic Design, Internet/Web Design

Revenue: $1,200,000

Bill Woodward *(Owner)*

Accounts:
KOKE FM
Ralph Wilson Youth Club Capital
University of Mary Hardin-Baylor

WOONTEILER INK
2 Winter St, Waltham, MA 02451
Tel.: (781) 891-1232
Fax: (781) 891-1022
E-Mail: info@woonteilerink.com
Web Site: www.woonteilerink.com

Employees: 10
Year Founded: 1992

Agency Specializes In: Collateral, Communications, Consumer Marketing, Event Planning & Marketing, Graphic Design, Health Care Services, Internet/Web Design, Legal Services, Public Relations, Publicity/Promotions, Real Estate, Restaurant

Gary Woonteiler *(Owner)*

Accounts:
Atrius
The Boston Home; Dorchester, MA
Center for IT Leadership (CITL); Wellesley, MA
Commonwealth Hematology-Oncology; Quincy, MA

WORDS AND PICTURES CREATIVE SERVICE, INC.
1 Maynard Dr Ste 1103, Park Ridge, NJ 07656
Tel.: (201) 573-0228
Fax: (201) 573-8966
Toll Free: (877) 573-0228
E-Mail: info@wordsandpictures.net
Web Site: www.wordsandpictures.net

Employees: 10
Year Founded: 1987

National Agency Associations: BMA-Second Wind Limited

Agency Specializes In: Advertising, Asian Market, Brand Development & Integration, Broadcast, Business Publications, Cable T.V., Collateral, College, Consumer Marketing, Consumer Publications, Corporate Identity, Education, Electronics, Food Service, Graphic Design, Guerilla Marketing, Health Care Services, High Technology, Identity Marketing, Logo & Package Design, Magazines, Media Buying Services, Media Planning, Medical Products, Newspaper, Newspapers & Magazines, Out-of-Home Media, Outdoor, Package Design, Print, Production (Ad, Film, Broadcast), Public Relations, Radio, Seniors' Market, Social Marketing/Nonprofit, Strategic Planning/Research, Syndication, T.V., Trade & Consumer Magazines, Web (Banner Ads, Pop-ups, etc.)

Approx. Annual Billings: $3,000,000

Rhonda Smith *(Pres & Dir-Creative)*
Ryan Huban *(Dir-Engagement)*
Priyanka Shitole *(Dir-Tech)*
Wesley Shaw *(Brand Strategist)*
Laura Ward *(Mgr-Production)*
Emily Shields *(Graphic Designer & Designer-Web)*
James Miller *(Coord-Mktg)*

Accounts:
Kramer
Matisse
Ramapo College
Sans
Sony; Park Ridge, NJ
Source Tech Medical

WORK CLUB
(Acquired by Havas Worldwide & Name Changed to Havas Work Club)

WORK, INC.
2019 Monument Ave, Richmond, VA 23220
Tel.: (804) 358-9372
Fax: (804) 355-2784
E-Mail: info@worklabs.com
Web Site: www.worklabs.com

Employees: 10
Year Founded: 1994

Agency Specializes In: Broadcast, Print

Cabell Harris *(Founder)*
Rahul Sood *(Mng Dir-Google Apps & Search at Work)*

Accounts:
AO/OOC
Budget Saver
Die Happy
Luck Stone Center
Macy's Department Stores (Projects)
Meteor Wines
Richmond Soap Studio
Truth Fishing Reels

WORKER BEES, INC.
500 Aurora Ave N Ste 105, Seattle, WA 98109
Tel.: (206) 930-3417
Fax: (888) 930-3417
E-Mail: hive@workerbees.com
Web Site: www.workerbees.com

Employees: 1
Year Founded: 1992

Agency Specializes In: Advertising, Broadcast, Collateral, Digital/Interactive, Health Care Services, Internet/Web Design, Outdoor, Print, Radio

Revenue: $1,000,000

Larry Asher *(Dir-creative & copywriter)*

Accounts:
Razorfish
Swedish Medical Center
Vulcan Real Estate

WORKTANK ENTERPRISES, LLC
400 E Pine St Ste 301, Seattle, WA 98122-2315
Tel.: (206) 254-0950
Fax: (206) 374-2650
E-Mail: info@worktankseattle.com
Web Site: www.worktankseattle.com

Employees: 30
Year Founded: 2001

Agency Specializes In: Advertising, Broadcast, Digital/Interactive, Event Planning & Marketing, Graphic Design, Identity Marketing, Internet/Web Design, Media Relations, Print, Strategic Planning/Research, T.V.

Leslie Rugaber *(Co-Founder & CEO)*
Theresa Trinidad *(COO)*
Brian Snyder *(VP-Delivery Tech)*

Accounts:
AT&T Communications Corp.
Microsoft

WORLD MARKETING HOLDINGS, LLC
1301 W Canal St, Milwaukee, WI 53233-2667
Tel.: (414) 289-8300
E-Mail: results@worldmarkinc.com
Web Site: www.worldmarkinc.com

Employees: 55

Agency Specializes In: Business-To-Business, Direct Response Marketing, Direct-to-Consumer, Government/Political, Print, Production, Production (Print), Retail

Robert M. Kraft *(CEO)*
Charles Buchanan *(Sr VP-Strategic Accts & Bus Dev)*
Ralph Ford *(Acct Dir)*
Shelby Kirk-Robertson *(Acct Mgr)*

Accounts:
American Airlines
Bloomingdales
Kraft
Omaha Steaks
Universal Music Group

Branches

World Marketing-Atlanta
1961 S Cobb Industrial Blvd, Smyrna, GA 30082
Tel.: (770) 431-2500
Fax: (770) 431-2517
E-Mail: results@worldmarkinc.com
Web Site: www.worldmarkinc.com

Employees: 40

National Agency Associations: DMA-MFSA

Agency Specializes In: Business-To-Business, Direct Response Marketing, Government/Political, Print, Production, Production (Print), Retail

Robert M. Kraft *(CEO)*
Lisa Sanregret *(CFO)*
Tyrone Jeffcoat *(COO)*
Charles Thompson *(Exec VP-Production)*
Steve Addis *(VP-Managed Svcs)*
Wayne Lawson *(VP-Bus Dev)*

World Marketing-Chicago
7950 W Joliet Rd, McCook, IL 60525-3482
Tel.: (708) 871-6000
Fax: (708) 871-6245
E-Mail: results@worldmarkinc.com
Web Site: www.worldmarkinc.com

Employees: 10

Agency Specializes In: Business-To-Business, Direct Response Marketing, Government/Political, Print, Production, Production (Print), Retail

Teresa Frederick *(COO)*
Kurt Hickey *(VP-New Bus Dev)*
Rob Dorre *(Mgr-IT)*

Accounts:
American Airlines
Bristol-Myers Squibb Company
Enterprise Rent-a-Car

World Marketing-Phoenix
2850 S Roosevelt Ste 102, Tempe, AZ 85282-2050
Tel.: (480) 929-8989
Fax: (480) 929-8999
E-Mail: results@worldmarkinc.com
Web Site: www.worldmarkinc.com

Employees: 15

National Agency Associations: DMA-MFSA

Agency Specializes In: Business-To-Business, Direct Response Marketing, Direct-to-Consumer, Government/Political, Print, Production, Production (Print), Retail, Social Marketing/Nonprofit

Steve Addis *(VP-Managed Svcs)*
Mendy Ishibashi *(VP-HR)*
Wayne Lawson *(VP-Bus Dev)*
Wanda Senne *(VP-Postal Affairs)*
Ronnie Thompson *(Mgr-Corp Accts)*

Accounts:
American Airlines
Oakley

World Marketing-St Louis
3466 Bridgeland Dr Ste 105, Bridgeton, MO 63044
Tel.: (314) 739-1864
Fax: (314) 739-8269
E-Mail: results@worldmarkinc.com
Web Site: www.worldmarkinc.com

National Agency Associations: DMA-MFSA

Agency Specializes In: Business-To-Business, Direct Response Marketing, Direct-to-Consumer, Government/Political, Print, Production, Production (Print), Retail

Charlie Pitlyk *(Exec VP-Ops)*
Gezzelle Harris *(Acct Dir)*

WORLD ONE COMMUNICATIONS, LLC
3350 Birney Ave, Moosic, PA 18507
Tel.: (570) 561-1315
Fax: (888) 269-6473
E-Mail: info@worldonecommunications.com
Web Site: www.worldonecommunications.com

Employees: 10
Year Founded: 2005

Agency Specializes In: Catalogs, Collateral, Digital/Interactive, Direct Response Marketing, Direct-to-Consumer, Graphic Design, Health Care Services, Print, Production (Print)

Sales: $200,000

Peter Susko *(Owner)*

Accounts:
AtoZ Vacuum
Nelson Rae + Associates
Old Gunnin Decoys
Reggie Birch Decoys
Summit Realty

WORLDLINK MEDIA
6100 Wilshire Blvd, Los Angeles, CA 90048
Tel.: (323) 866-5900
E-Mail: info@worldlinkmedia.com
Web Site: www.worldlinkmedia.com

Dan Casey *(Exec VP-Sls & Gen Mgr)*
Joey Hastie *(Mgr-Sls)*
Jennifer Coyle *(Acct Exec)*
Lindsay Davis *(Acct Exec)*
Chrissy Doyle *(Acct Exec)*
Jim Kirk *(Acct Exec)*
Rex Janechuti *(Sr Coord-Sls)*

WORLDWALK MEDIA

417A E Washington Blvd, San Francisco, CA 94129-1145
Tel.: (415) 933-8450
E-Mail: brand@worldwalk.net
Web Site: www.worldwalk.net

E-Mail for Key Personnel:
President: brand@worldwalk.net
Media Dir.: media@worldwalk.net

Employees: 15
Year Founded: 1996

National Agency Associations: DMA-IAA

Agency Specializes In: Advertising, Asian Market, Automotive, Brand Development & Integration, Business-To-Business, Cable T.V., Co-op Advertising, Collateral, Commercial Photography, Communications, Consulting, Consumer Marketing, Corporate Identity, Customer Relationship Management, Digital/Interactive, Direct Response Marketing, E-Commerce, Electronic Media, Entertainment, Financial, Game Integration, Graphic Design, Health Care Services, High Technology, Hispanic Market, Identity Marketing, Information Technology, Integrated Marketing, Internet/Web Design, Leisure, Logo & Package Design, Magazines, Market Research, Media Buying Services, Media Planning, Media Relations, Medical Products, Mobile Marketing, Multimedia, New Product Development, Newspaper, Newspapers & Magazines, Out-of-Home Media, Outdoor, Over-50 Market, Pharmaceutical, Planning & Consultation, Point of Purchase, Point of Sale, Print, Production, Production (Ad, Film, Broadcast), Production (Print), RSS (Really Simple Syndication), Radio, Real Estate, Retail, Sports Market, Strategic Planning/Research, T.V., Technical Advertising, Trade & Consumer Magazines, Transportation, Travel & Tourism, Web (Banner Ads, Pop-ups, etc.), Yellow Pages Advertising

Breakdown of Gross Billings by Media: D.M.: 20%; Fees: 5%; Internet Adv.: 15%; Newsp. & Mags.: 30%; Outdoor: 5%; Radio & T.V.: 15%; Strategic Planning/Research: 10%

Paula Storti *(Founder)*

Accounts:
ADM Global; 2010
Google; Mountain View, CA; 2002
Infowave Software; Seattle, WA Wireless Software; 2000
Kaplan Continuing Education
Mediaplex Inc.
San Francisco Department of Health Anti-Crystal Meth; 2004
Wells Fargo; Los Angeles, CA; 2000

WORLDWAYS SOCIAL MARKETING

(Formerly Worldways, Inc.)
240 Thames St, Newport, RI 02840
Tel.: (401) 619-4081
Fax: (303) 779-3010
E-Mail: info@e-worldways.com
Web Site: marketingsocialimpact.com/

Employees: 18

Maureen Cronin *(Co-Founder & CEO)*
Alyssa Smith *(Sr Acct Mgr)*
Melissa Manjarres *(Acct Mgr)*
Chris Parish *(Designer-Digital Media)*
Michael Silvia *(Sr Designer)*
Amanda Brayman *(Coord-Social Media)*

Accounts:
ACLU
Freedom from Hunger

WORTHWHILE

9 Caledon Ct Ste C, Greenville, SC 29615
Tel.: (864) 233-2552
Web Site: www.worthwhile.com

Year Founded: 1994

Agency Specializes In: Advertising, Digital/Interactive, Internet/Web Design, Mobile Marketing, Search Engine Optimization, Social Media

Dan Rundle *(CEO)*
Micah Brandenburg *(VP-New Bus)*
Ruben Hentzschel *(VP-Customer Solutions)*
Dan Dietz *(Dir-Web Dev)*
Greg Warner *(Dir-Art)*
Robert Neely *(Strategist-Content)*
Thomas Sneed *(Acct Exec)*

Accounts:
A Child's Haven
Pharmacy Forward
Tech After Five

WORX BRANDING & ADVERTISING

18 Waterbury Rd, Prospect, CT 06712-1215
Tel.: (203) 758-3311
Fax: (203) 758-6847
Web Site: www.worxbranding.com

Employees: 25
Year Founded: 1986

Agency Specializes In: Advertising, Brand Development & Integration, Broadcast, Business-To-Business, Cable T.V., Consulting, Consumer Marketing, E-Commerce, Electronic Media, Exhibit/Trade Shows, Graphic Design, Health Care Services, Internet/Web Design, Local Marketing, Logo & Package Design, Media Buying Services, Medical Products, Multimedia, Newspaper, Newspapers & Magazines, Outdoor, Print, Production, Trade & Consumer Magazines, Yellow Pages Advertising

Approx. Annual Billings: $4,000,000

Breakdown of Gross Billings by Media: Exhibits/Trade Shows: 10%; Print: 25%; Radio & T.V.: 5%; Worldwide Web Sites: 60%

Grant Copeland *(Pres & Chief Creative Officer)*
Brian Kelley *(Dir-Art)*
Marysia Walker *(Assoc Dir-Creative)*

Accounts:
Advantage
Aetna CCG
Agavue
Arga Printing
AT&T Bobby Choice
AT&T Connecticut Website
AT&T Surf Free
Bironi Coffee
Cool Beans Coffee
ESPN
FedEx Event Marketing
Holiday Inn
Hotel California Tequila Television
IBM
Jaybeam Limited
The Palace Theater
Patriot Outdoors
Special Olympics Connecticut
United Technologies
United Way of Greater Waterbury
UTC Power
Van Staal

THE WOW FACTOR, INC.

11330 Ventura Blvd, Studio City, CA 91604
Tel.: (818) 755-4400
Web Site: www.wowfactor.net

Employees: 12
Year Founded: 1993

Revenue: $1,300,000

Donald Blanton *(Pres & CEO)*
Billy Moran *(VP-Production)*
Felix Castro *(Dir-Creative)*

Accounts:
Coca-Cola Refreshments USA, Inc.

WPP PLC

27 Farm Street, London, W1J 5RJ United Kingdom
Tel.: (44) 20 7408 2204
Fax: (44) 20 7493 6819
E-Mail: enquiries@wpp.com
Web Site: www.wpp.com

Employees: 114,490
Year Founded: 1985

Agency Specializes In: Advertising, Advertising Specialties, Brand Development & Integration, Communications, Corporate Communications, Corporate Identity, Digital/Interactive, Media Buying Services, Publicity/Promotions, Sports Market, Teen Market

Revenue: $15,600,000,000

Martin Sorrell *(CEO)*
Robin Dargue *(CIO-Global)*
Mark Read *(CEO-WPP Digital)*
Danny Josephs *(Mng Dir-Team News UK)*
Belinda Rabano *(Head-Corp Comm-Asia Pacific)*
Efren Gonzalez *(Bus Dir)*
Feona McEwan *(Dir-Corp Comm)*
George Rogers *(Dir-Bus Dev-Global)*

Accounts:
Aston Martin Lagonda Global Marketing
Bayer HealthCare
Diageo
E-Trade Media Buying, Media Planning
Ford Campaign: "Change Is A Wonderful Thing", Figo
Holiday Inn Group
Hotels.com
HSBC
Huawei Global Corporate Branding
Intercontinental Hotels
LVMH
Unilever
Vodafone Global Strategy

Advertising

Addison Group

(Formerly Addison Corporate Marketing Ltd.)
49 Southwark Bridge Road, London, SE1 9HH United Kingdom
Tel.: (44) 20 7815 2000
E-Mail: georgina.herdman@addison-group.net
Web Site: www.addison-group.net/

Employees: 45

Agency Specializes In: Brand Development & Integration, Communications, Corporate Identity, Investor Relations, New Product Development, Outdoor

Tom Robinson *(CEO)*
James Handslip *(Client Svcs Dir)*
Lloyd Nicely *(Acct Dir-Digital)*
Peter Chodel *(Dir-Creative)*

Leif Skogstad *(Dir-Comml)*
Joe Sutton *(Sr Acct Mgr)*

Accounts:
Anglo American
AstraZeneca
BBA
De Beers
ING
JTI
Standard Chartered Bank
TNT
Unilever

AGENDA
03-06 32F, 118 Connaught Road West, Hong Kong, China (Hong Kong)
Tel.: (852) 22983888
Fax: (852) 21446332
Web Site: www.wunderman.com.cn/

Employees: 250

National Agency Associations: ADMA

Agency Specializes In: Advertising, Consumer Goods, Consumer Marketing, Consumer Publications, Education, New Technologies, Production, Production (Print), Publishing, Real Estate

Mike Leung *(Mng Dir)*
Monica Fung *(Acct Dir)*
Yan Hui *(Acct Dir)*
Tracy Chow *(Assoc Dir-Creative)*
Takki Ma *(Assoc Dir-Creative-Social Media)*
Gwyneth Mak *(Assoc Acct Dir)*

Accounts:
Carrefour
Colgate China; 2008
DHL
Disney
GlaxoSmithKline Limited Creative, Print, Social Media, Television
Honda
Johnson & Johnson Acuvue, Bandaid, Clean 'n Clear, Johnson's Baby, OB
New-Kimberly-Clark (Hong Kong) Limited Campaign: "The Story of Softness", Digital, Kotex Softness
Microsoft Campaign: "Simply Play Faster"
Pepsi
Prudential
xBox 360

AKQA, Inc.
360 3rd St 5th Fl, San Francisco, CA 94107
(See Separate Listing)

Bates Chi & Partners
(Formerly Bates Asia Pacific)
3301-09 Tower One Times Square, Causeway Bay, China (Hong Kong)
Tel.: (852) 2283 3333
Fax: (852) 25274086
E-Mail: info@bateschi.com
Web Site: www.bateschi.com

Employees: 110

Conrad Chiu *(CEO-HK & South China)*
Justin Wong *(Dir-Fin & Comml-China)*
Desiree Lim *(Mgr-Corp Comm)*

Accounts:
AP Boots Campaign: "Grasshopper"
Carlsberg
Del Monte Foods S&W
Dell Computers
HSBC Campaign: "Facebook AI Engine", Campaign: "My Spending Decoder"
Li Ning
Mother's Choice
Shell Hong Kong

bcg2
Level 2 1 Cross Street Newton, Auckland, New Zealand
Tel.: (64) 93799007
Web Site: www.bcg2.com/

Year Founded: 2010

Agency Specializes In: Advertising, Brand Development & Integration, Local Marketing

James Blackwood *(CEO & Exec Dir-Creative)*
Stuart Ogden *(Gen Mgr-Healthcare)*
Deborah Cashmore *(Grp Acct Dir)*
Robin Powell *(Creative Dir & Copywriter)*
James Bowman *(Art Dir)*
Marc Chetcuti *(Art Dir)*
Caroline Dunlea *(Acct Dir)*
Michael Evans *(Acct Dir)*
Graeme Cooper *(Designer)*
Mitchell Crowe *(Copywriter)*
Phil Parsonage *(Copywriter)*
Pam McIntyre *(Client Svc Dir)*

Accounts:
1Cover Travel Insurance Creative
Audi New Zealand Campaign: "Orchestra", Car Dealers
Canon New Zealand Cameras, Lenses, Printers & Printing Consumables, Consumer Business
D E Master Blenders1753 Creative, Moccona
European Motor Distributors Parts Limited
Ezetrol
Fletcher Aluminium Commercial
Jesters Pies New Zealand Campaign: "Ridiculously Refined"
Kingdom of Tonga Tourism
Lion Nathan New Zealand Food & Beverages Mfr
Manukau Institute of Technology Campaign: "Put It To Good Use"
Merck Sharpe & Dohme
Nestle NZ Campaign: "Clever Little Minds", Nestle S26 GOLD
Pfizer New Zealand Campaign: "Cigi Maze"
New-Realestate.co.nz Creative
New-Safekids NZ
Sara Lee New Zealand Moccona, TVC
Tongan Government Outdoor Creative, TV, Tonga's Ministry of Commerce, Tourism, Tourism & Labour
Volkswagen Group

BDG architecture+design
(Formerly BDGworkfutures)
33 Saint John Street, London, EC1M 4AA United Kingdom
Tel.: (44) 20 7559 7400
Fax: (44) 20 7559 7401
E-Mail: info@bdg-a-d.com
Web Site: www.bdg-a-d.com

Employees: 20
Year Founded: 1962

Agency Specializes In: Graphic Design, Planning & Consultation, Strategic Planning/Research

Clive Hall *(Dir-Technical)*
Phil Hutchinson *(Dir-Strategy)*
Colin Macgadie *(Dir-Creative)*
Helen Ieronimo *(Mgr-Mktg)*
Lynsey Barr *(Designer)*
Helen Bedford *(Sr Designer)*
Shona Cairns *(Designer)*
Lucy Harrison *(Designer)*
Esther Lockhart *(Jr Designer)*

Accounts:
Barclays
GREY London
Honeywell
HSBC
IBM
Inter Raoles
NHS Direct
Siemens

Blaze Advertising
Level 12 35 Clarence Street, Sydney, NSW 2000 Australia
Mailing Address:
GPO Box 3268, Sydney, NSW 2001 Australia
Tel.: (61) 2 9020 8700
Fax: (61) 2 9020 8766
Web Site: www.blazeadvertising.com.au/

Employees: 50

Agency Specializes In: Advertising, Brand Development & Integration, Corporate Identity, Direct Response Marketing, Internet/Web Design, Media Buying Services

Leanne Krstevski *(CEO)*
Liv Pultar *(Acct Dir)*
Jessica Saethang *(Acct Dir)*
Scott Deakin *(Dir-Creative)*
Ashleigh Cox *(Sr Acct Mgr)*
Simone Gur *(Sr Acct Mgr)*
Danielle Lohse *(Sr Acct Mgr)*
Nathan Salter *(Sr Acct Mgr)*
Christiana Skinner *(Sr Acct Mgr)*
Vicki Cogan *(Acct Mgr)*
Bernice Gibbs *(Client Svc Dir)*

Blaze Advertising
17 Fullarton Road, Kent Town, SA 5067 Australia
Tel.: (61) 8 81301900
Fax: (61) 8 8130 1999
Web Site: www.blazeadvertising.com.au

Leanne Krstevski *(Mng Dir-Natl)*
Casey Aimer *(Head-Digital)*
Peter Grzesch *(Gen Mgr)*
Julie Harding-Aimer *(Acct Dir)*
Liv Pultar *(Acct Dir)*
Jessica Saethang *(Acct Dir)*
Simone Gur *(Sr Acct Mgr)*
Nathan Salter *(Sr Acct Mgr)*
Vicki Cogan *(Acct Mgr)*
Ali Lowe *(Acct Mgr)*
Bernice Gibbs *(Client Svc Dir)*

Blaze Advertising
(Formerly HMA Blaze)
Level 2 162 Collins Street, Melbourne, VIC 3000 Australia
Tel.: (61) 3 8668 8000
Fax: (61) 8668 8001
E-Mail: melbourne@blazeadvertising.com.au
Web Site: www.blazeadvertising.com.au

Employees: 15

Leanne Krstevski *(CEO-Y&R Brands)*
Patrick Rychner *(Exec Dir-Creative)*
Ashleigh Cox *(Sr Acct Mgr)*
Sarah Jacobs *(Sr Acct Mgr)*
Christiana Skinner *(Sr Acct Mgr)*
Tara Hancock *(Acct Mgr)*
Martine Smithies *(Acct Mgr)*

Blue Hive
10 Cabot Square, Canary Wharf, London, E14 4QB United Kingdom
Tel.: (44) 2076748600
E-Mail: hello@thebluehive.com
Web Site: www.thebluehive.com

Year Founded: 2010

Agency Specializes In: Advertising, Communications, Media Relations

Jimmy Evans *(Pres)*
Tony Grigg *(CEO)*
John D'Arcy *(Mng Partner-Analytics)*
Paul Confrey *(Mng Dir)*
Sebastian Castaneda *(Creative Dir)*
Roy Cohen *(Dir-Creative)*
Javier Lourenco *(Dir-Art)*
Joelle Stanford *(Dir-Fin)*
Andrew Douglas *(Acct Mgr)*
Giorgia Spina *(Copywriter)*

Accounts:
Ford Motor Company Limited Campaign: "Go Further", Campaign: "The Road Awaits", Fiestagram, Ford EcoSport, Ford Mustang, Online

Blue State Digital
734 15th St NW Ste 1200, Washington, DC 20005
(See Separate Listing)

Blue State Digital
280 Summer St 7th Fl, Boston, MA 02210
(See Separate Listing)

BPG Group
Level 6 MAF Tower Deira City Center, PO Box 3294, Dubai, United Arab Emirates
Tel.: (971) 4 295 3456
Fax: (971) 4 295 8066
E-Mail: bizdev@batespangulf.com
Web Site: www.batespangulf.com

Agency Specializes In: Advertising

Abdulla Majed Al Ghurair *(Chm)*
Brittany Greer *(Pres)*
Avishesha Bhojani *(Grp CEO)*
Naveed Jamal *(Sr VP & Exec Dir-Design)*
Suneesh Menon *(VP & Gen Mgr)*
Mriganka Kalita *(Grp Head-Creative)*
Yosef Khouwes *(Art Dir & Creative Dir)*
Layla Safwat Fattah *(Acct Dir)*
Sanket Jatar *(Client Svcs Dir)*
Arif Ladhabhoy *(Dir-Client Engagement)*
Siddarth Sivaprakash *(Acct Mgr)*

Accounts:
Eyezone Eyewear
Health Authority Abu Dhabi
Invaders Pest Control
Mahiki Campaign: "Take A Cab"
MBC Group Campaign: "04 - The Transmedia Experience"

The Brand Union
114 Fifth Ave 11th Fl, New York, NY 10011-5604
(See Separate Listing)

cba BE
(Formerly CB'a)
94 Avenue de Villiers, 75017 Paris, France
Tel.: (33) 1 40 54 09 00
Fax: (33) 1 47 64 95 75
E-Mail: info@cba-design.com
Web Site: www.cba-design.com/fr

Employees: 185
Year Founded: 1982

Agency Specializes In: Advertising, Brand Development & Integration, Communications, Consumer Marketing, Cosmetics, Food Service, Graphic Design, Internet/Web Design, Logo & Package Design, Publicity/Promotions

Louis Collinet *(CEO)*
Franck Collin *(Gen Mgr-Activation)*
Anne Malberti *(Gen Mgr-CBA Paris)*

Accounts:
Arteum
Costes
Defi Deco
Minute Maid
Monoprix Bien Vivre
Nestle
Unilever Lipton

Chemistry
1660 Union St 4th Fl, San Diego, CA 92101
(See Separate Listing)

Cole & Weber United
221 Yale Ave N Ste 600, Seattle, WA 98109
(See Separate Listing)

Coley Porter Bell
18 Grosvenor Gardens, London, SW1W 0DH United Kingdom
Tel.: (44) 207 824 7700
Fax: (44) 207 824 7701
E-Mail: beautiful@cpb.co.uk
Web Site: www.coleyporterbell.com/

Employees: 45
Year Founded: 1979

Agency Specializes In: Consulting, Graphic Design

Vicky Bullen *(CEO)*
Sarah Cameron *(Head-Mktg)*
Stephen Bell *(Exec Dir-Creative)*
Cathy Madoc-Jones *(Acct Dir)*
Rachel Fullerton *(Dir-Fin)*
Alex Ririe *(Dir-Bus)*
Helen Westropp *(Dir-Bus)*

Accounts:
New-Chivas Brothers Chivas Regal
Co-operative Food "Loved By Us"
Fresh Pak Chilled Foods Campaign: "Gourmet Street Tucker You Can Enjoy at Home", Packaging, The Hungry Wolf Deli Fillers Branding
Kimberly-Clark Kotex
Lifeplus Campaign: "Lifeplus Range"
Monier
Morrisons Campaign: "Morrisons Savers Foods"
Muller Corner Consumer Awareness, Dessert Inspired, Point Of Sale, Voted By You
Nescafe
Pernod Ricard Beefeater Burrough's Reserve, Olmeca Altos Tequila, Perrier Jouet
Premier Foods Loyd Grossman
TUI Travel Brand Development, Marine Division
Unilever Hellmans
White Knight Laundry Company Campaign: "Laundry your Way", Corporate Identity, Logo, knight's Helmet

Commarco GmbH
Hanseatic Trade Center, Am Sandtorkai 76, 20457 Hamburg, Germany
Tel.: (49) 40 82 21 95 900
Fax: (49) 40 82 21 95 999
E-Mail: info@commarco.com
Web Site: www.commarco.com

Employees: 1,200

Agency Specializes In: Advertising

Frank-Michael Schmidt *(Co-CEO)*
Christian Tiedemann *(CEO)*

crossmedia
Benjamin Franklin 190, Col Condesa CP, 11800 Mexico, Mexico
Tel.: (52) 55 5278 2000
Web Site: www.crossmedia.com.mx

Employees: 120

Agency Specializes In: Digital/Interactive, Sponsorship

Jon Yuson *(Head-Acct & Assoc Dir)*
Toluwalope Okeowo *(Supvr-Media)*

Accounts:
Grupo Bimbo
Premier Exhibitions Media Planning & Buying

Crossmedia
22 W 23rd St, New York, NY 10010
(See Separate Listing)

David
Avenida Pedrosa de Morais 15553, 2 Andar, Sao Paulo, 05477 900 Brazil
(See Separate Listing)

DTDigital
72 Christie Street, St Leonards, Sydney, NSW 2065 Australia
Tel.: (61) 292681550
E-Mail: DT.Sydney@dtdigital.com.au
Web Site: dt.com.au/

Year Founded: 1996

Agency Specializes In: Advertising, Digital/Interactive, Engineering, Graphic Design, Internet/Web Design, Mobile Marketing, Social Media

Brian Vella *(CEO)*
Jerker Fagerstrom *(Partner & Exec Creative Dir)*
Tony Vella *(Dir-Ops)*

Accounts:
Trafalgar Corporate Pty Limited

DTDigital
Lvl 12 Royal Domain Centre, 380 St Kilda Road, Melbourne, Victoria 3004 Australia
Tel.: (61) 396846450
E-Mail: DT.Melbourne@dt.com.au
Web Site: dt.com.au/

Year Founded: 1996

Agency Specializes In: Advertising, Digital/Interactive, Internet/Web Design

Timothy Mark Evans *(Partner)*
Gordon McNenney *(Dir-Content & Comm)*

Accounts:
Officeworks Campaign: "When I Grow Up", Digital

EffectiveUI Inc.
2162 Market St, Denver, CO 80205
(See Separate Listing)

The Farm
611 Broadway, New York, NY 10012
(See Separate Listing)

Fitch
121-141 Westbourne Terrace, London, W2 6JR
United Kingdom
(See Separate Listing)

George Patterson Y&R
Level 15 35 Clarence St, Sydney, NSW 2000
Australia
Tel.: (61) 2 9778 7100
Fax: (61) 2 9778 7599
E-Mail: andrew.dowling@gpyr.com.au
Web Site: www.gpyr.com.au

Year Founded: 1934

Agency Specializes In: Advertising, Agriculture, Automotive, Aviation & Aerospace, Brand Development & Integration, Business-To-Business, Cable T.V., Children's Market, Commercial Photography, Communications, Consulting, Consumer Marketing, Corporate Identity, Direct Response Marketing, E-Commerce, Fashion/Apparel, Financial, Food Service, Government/Political, Graphic Design, Health Care Services, Leisure, Logo & Package Design, Magazines, Media Buying Services, Multimedia, Newspapers & Magazines, Outdoor, Pharmaceutical, Point of Purchase, Point of Sale, Print, Production, Public Relations, Publicity/Promotions, Radio, Recruitment, Retail, Sales Promotion, Sports Market, Strategic Planning/Research, T.V., Telemarketing, Travel & Tourism

Dean Mortensen *(Grp Head-Creative)*
David Joubert *(Exec Dir-Creative-Sydney)*
Miranda Bryce *(Grp Acct Dir)*
Lucy Flower *(Acct Dir)*
Amy Luca *(Bus Dir-GPY&R & VML)*
Liam Seymour *(Dir-Art)*
Brad Stapleton *(Dir-Art)*
Andrew Thompson *(Dir-Creative)*
Waqas Tahir *(Sr Planner-Plng)*
Erin Core *(Planner)*

Accounts:
AFL (Australian Football League)
Alliance Francaise French Film Festival
Amazon Kindle
Animal Logic
Arnott's Biscuits Ltd
Arnott's Wagon Wheels
The Australian Creative, Digital Experience
Avis
Brisbane City Council Campaign: "Shade Cinema"
The Climate Reality Project Campaign: "Why? Why Not?"
Colgate-Palmolive Campaign: "Family Tree", Campaign: "Mouthguard"
Connect Furniture Campaign: "Furniture Separates Us From Animals"
Cougar; Melbourne
Cricket Australia; Melbourne
Cronulla Sharks Football Club
Defence Force Recruiting Campaign: "Impossible Airfield", Campaign: "NAVY SINK'EM"
GenerationOne
Juvenile Diabetes Research Foundation Campaign: "Needle Pricks", Timothy
LG Electronics 4 Out of 5, Campaign: "Fashion Industry Exposed", French Door Fridge
Northern Rivers Writers Centre Campaign: "The Most Beautiful Link"
NSW Department of Health Child Immunisation Campaign
NSW Government Campaign: "Planning to Make a Plan", Digital, Prevention of Sexually Transmitted Infections & HIV Campaign, Rural Fire Service
NSW Rugby; Sydney
Pelikan Artline
Red Cross Campaign: "Embers of Empathy"
Revlon Campaign: "Love is On"
Schweppes Campaign: "Cocktail Mail"
South Pacific Breweries SP Coasters
St Vincent de Paul Society Vinnies Signed Finds
Starlight Children's Foundation Campaign: "Donate By Numbers"
Suncorp Campaign: "Must-have", Insurance
Tatts Lotteries Campaign: "Dentist", Campaign: "Instant Scratch-Its: You-Time"
Tin Billy Budget Hotel, Campaign: "Dining"
Transport for NSW Campaign: "Fishermen"
U&U Executive Recruitment Partners Campaign: "Grape"
V8 Supercars
Wagon Wheels
WaterAid

George Patterson Y&R
Ste 6 The Realm 18 National Circuit, Barton, ACT 2600 Canberra, Australia
Tel.: (61) 2 6122 4200
Fax: (61) 2 6122 4211
Web Site: www.gpyr.com.au

Employees: 5

Andrew Dowling *(Grp Mng Dir-Y&R Group-Sydney)*
Phil Mcdonald *(Grp Mng Dir-Y&R Group)*
Jon Steel *(Chief Strategy Officer & Dir-Global Plng-WPP)*
Ben Coulson *(Chief Creative Officer)*
Rob Hudson *(Chief Digital Officer)*
Richard Boland *(Gen Mgr)*
David Joubert *(Exec Dir-Creative)*
Bart Pawlak *(Exec Dir-Creative-Sydney)*
Brendan Greaney *(Dir-Creative)*
Andrew Thompson *(Dir-Creative)*

Accounts:
AFL
Army
BIFF
Cadbury Promotion
ECQ
Intralot
Smart Energy
Spring Valley
Vodafone
Yellow

George Patterson Y&R
Level 3 162 Collins Street, Melbourne, VIC 3000
Australia
Tel.: (61) 0392871200
Fax: (61) 3 9287 1400
Web Site: www.gpyr.com.au

Employees: 100
Year Founded: 1934

Shane Dawson *(Sr Dir-Art)*
Luke Simkins *(Sr Dir-Art)*
Matthew Hunt *(Sr Acct Dir)*
Romanca Jasinski *(Exec Producer)*
Jake Barrow *(Dir-Creative & Art)*
Isabella Caruso *(Art Dir)*
Matilda Hobba *(Acct Dir)*
Paige Prettyman *(Acct Dir)*
Cathryn Reed *(Acct Dir)*
Michael Hyde *(Dir-Plng)*
Dave Gallow *(Acct Mgr)*
Lachy Lamour *(Acct Supvr)*
Charles Baylis *(Copywriter)*

Accounts:
AFL Campaign: "Australia's Game", Campaign: "Game Signatures", Campaign: "Nothing Like It", Campaign: "World's Most Precious Metal"
Air Force Campaign: "Air Force FM"
Alannah & Madeline Foundation
Army Reserve Campaign: "Inner Pride"
Australia Post (Lead Agency) Campaign: "We Love Delivering", Digital, Outdoor, Print, Social, Social Media, TV
Australian Defence Force Campaign: "Fighter Pilot : Behind the Visor", Campaign: "Mobile Medic", Campaign: "The Paper Baron"
Australian Football League Game Signatures
Australian Rugby Union
BetEasy
Cadbury plc Cottee's, Picnic, There's a Lot to Celebrate When You're a Kid
Clucky Cake
Connect Furniture Campaign: "Furniture separates us from animals"
Cricket Australia A Whole New Ball Game, Campaign: "Not On Our Watch", Campaign: "Play Cricket", Campaign: "United By The Moment"
Danone Campaign: "Bad Brain", Oikos
Defence Force Recruiting Campaign: "Air Force Aviation", Campaign: "Air Force-Anytime Anywhere", Campaign: "Behind the Visor", Campaign: "Impossible Airfield", Campaign: "Lead the way", Campaign: "Mobile Medic", Navy Cooks
Energex
General Mills
George Western Foods
Just Car Insurance
Ladder Campaign: "Homepage For The Homeless"
Lemonex
LG 15x Zoom Camera Phone
The Lost Dogs Home Campaign: "Human Walking Program"
Medibank Campaign: "Circle of Life"
Melbourne Advertising & Design Club
Melbourne Racing Club
MMM
New-Monash University Creative
Mondelez International, Inc.
National Australia Day Council
Navy Campaign: "What it Takes"
NBN
New South Wales Government
Oakley
Odyssey House Victoria Campaign: "The Box"
Public Transport Victoria
Royal Australian Air Force A Typical Day
Royal Australian Navy Navy Sink 'Em
Santos Tour Down Under Campaign: "The Puppet Peloton"
Schweppes Campaign: "Celebrity Cheat Pass", Campaign: "Cocktail Mail", Campaign: "Fancy Food Fight", Campaign: "Pub With No Beer", Campaign: "The Cocktail Revolution", Campaign: "Tumble", Elixir, Mineral Water, Schweppervescence, Spring Valley Juice
Southern Star
Spring Valley
V8X Magazine Campaign: "Burning Rubber Scent"
VB
VicRoads

George Patterson Y&R
Centenary Sq Level 1 108 Wickham St, Fortitude Valley, QLD 4006 Australia
Tel.: (61) 7 3218 1000
Fax: (61) 7 3229 5505
Web Site: www.gpyr.com.au

Employees: 45
Year Founded: 1958

Andrew Leftley *(Sr Dir-Art)*
Fiona Caird *(Grp Acct Dir)*
Brendan Greaney *(Dir-Creative)*
Andrew Thompson *(Dir-Creative)*
Lynsey Murtagh *(Acct Mgr)*

Accounts:
Energex Electricity
Queensland Government
South Pacific Brewery
Suncorp Bank Banking Services, Campaign: "The Genuine Alternative"

Tatts Lotteries Campaign: "Bed"

Green Advertising
7301 N Federal Hwy Studio B, Boca Raton, FL 33487
(See Separate Listing)

Grey Group
200 5th Ave, New York, NY 10010
(See Separate Listing)

Hogarth Worldwide
230 Park Ave S 11th Fl, New York, NY 10003
(See Separate Listing)

Hudson Rouge
257 Park Ave S 20th Fl, New York, NY 10010
(See Separate Listing)

Ireland/Davenport
198 Oxford Rd 2nd Fl, Illovo, Sandton, 2196 South Africa
Tel.: (27) 11 243 1300
Fax: (27) 11 463 2232
E-Mail: Info@ireland-davenport.co.za
Web Site: www.ireland-davenport.com

Employees: 5
Year Founded: 2006

John Davenport *(Owner)*
Sue Napier *(Mng Dir)*
Chad Wright *(Grp Head-Creative & Copywriter)*
Bridget Johnson *(Exec Dir-Creative)*
Wayne Botes *(Acct Dir)*
Matthew Brink *(Creative Dir)*
Julia Rutherford *(Copywriter)*

Accounts:
Adcock Ingram Campaign: "Grannies"
Apple
Avis Campaign: "Optional Gps", GPS, Luxury Car Rental
BankServ
BMW Campaign: "Rear View Camera Cover", M5
Boardmans
Dion Wired
Ditsong National Museum of Military History Campaign: "The Battle of the Somme"
Fight Masters
Fox International Channels Campaign: "Cinema Crime Scene"
Free Zimbabwe Campaign: "Friend Request"
Investec
Johannesburg Wits Planetearium Campaign: "It's a Big Universe"
MTN Group
National Geographic Channel Campaign: "Dogs have issues too", Most Amazing Photos
Nintendo
Panado Campaign: "Baby Headaches", Infant Drops
Plascon
SA Tourism Campaign: "Nothings more fun than a Sho't Left"
Salvation Army
Toys 'R' Us
Vodacom
Vodafone Group plc
The War Museum Campaign: "Deville Wood Dice"

J. Walter Thompson
(Formerly JWT)
466 Lexington Ave, New York, NY 10017-3140
(See Separate Listing)

John St.
172 John Street, Toronto, ON M5T 1X5 Canada
(See Separate Listing)

Jupiter Drawing Room
River Park, 42 Holmstead Rd, Rivonia, 2128 South Africa
Tel.: (27) 11 233 8800
Fax: (27) 11 233 8820
E-Mail: info@thejupiterdrawingroom.com
Web Site: www.thejupiterdrawingroom.com

Employees: 200

Thomas Cullinan *(Partner-Creative)*
Darren Kilfoil *(Grp Head-Creative)*
Kerryn-Lee Maggs *(Art Dir & Designer)*
Dana Cullinan *(Creative Dir)*
Zola Thekiso *(Acct Dir)*
Dana Cohen *(Dir-Creative)*
Cameron Fraser *(Copywriter)*

Accounts:
ABSA Capital
ABSA CAPE EPIC, Campaign: "Team Of Millions"
Arthur Kaplan Jewellers
Children of Fire Campaign: "Candle"
The Coca-Cola Co. Burn Energy Drink
Girls & Boystown
Innscor International Franchising Division
Jet Mart
Jet
Jiffy
Just Juice
Lemon & Nada Campaign: "Spot The Difference"
Luster's Pink
Minute Maid
MTN Campaign: "Facebook", Campaign: "First Day", Magic 8 Ball
Nulaid
PPC Cement Campaign: "Bag Seals"
SA Poultry Association Campaign: "Bush"
Temptations Campaign: "Commitment"
Vida E Caffe Campaign: "Sleeping Pilots"
WeChat South Africa Campaign: "Crazy About WeChat"

JWT
(Formerly Bates Ukraine)
146 Zhilanskaya St 4th Fl, Kiev, 01032 Ukraine
Tel.: (380) 44 461 7916
Fax: (380) 44 461 7917
E-Mail: press@jwt.com.ua
Web Site: www.jwt.com.ua/

Employees: 50
Year Founded: 1998

Olga Lanovyk *(Mng Dir)*
Anna Smirnova *(Mng Dir)*
Vladyslava Denis *(Dir-Creative-JWT Ukraine)*

Accounts:
Microsoft Lumia
Shell Campaign: "Pedestrian Ghost"

Lambie-Nairn
Greencoat House Francis St, London, SW1P 1DH United Kingdom
Tel.: (44) 20 7802 5800
Fax: (44) 20 7802 5801
E-Mail: info@lambie-nairn.com
Web Site: www.lambie-nairn.com

Employees: 40
Year Founded: 1976

Agency Specializes In: Brand Development & Integration

Jim Prior *(CEO)*
Andy Hayes *(Mng Dir-UK, Germany & Middle East)*
Cailie Dimmock *(Head-Production)*
Claire Holmes *(Head-Strategy)*
Adrian Burton *(Exec Dir-Creative)*
Nicky Nicolls *(Exec Dir-Global)*
Elisabeth Pohl *(Reg Dir)*
Tim Beauchamp *(Dir-Fin)*
Sophie Lutman *(Dir-Creative-London)*

Accounts:
BBC
Cognetas
Directgov
Eyes & Ears of Europe Design, Identity, Marketing, Promotion
First Great Western
Friends of the Earth
ITV
Kolkata Knight Riders Campaign: "One Team. One Pledge", Campaign: "We Will Do It, Fight For It, Win It", In Print, Marketing, Online, Outdoor
Leonard Cheshire Disability
Middle East Broadcasting Centre (MBC)
Sainsburys Bank
Telefonica Brand Implementation/Guardianship, Movistar, O2
This Morning

LDV United
Rijnkaai 99, Hangar 26, 2000 Antwerp, Belgium
Tel.: (32) 3229 2929
Fax: (32) 3 229 2930
E-Mail: info@ldv.be
Web Site: www.ldv.be

Employees: 40
Year Founded: 2001

Agency Specializes In: Advertising

Harry Demey *(CEO)*
Petra De Roos *(Mng Dir)*
Dries Debruyn *(Art Dir)*
Thomas Thysens *(Art Dir)*
Han Verschaeren *(Art Dir)*
Bart Gielen *(Dir-Creative)*
Tim Janssens *(Acct Mgr)*
Julie Oostvogels *(Acct Mgr)*
Jean De Moor *(Mgr-Production)*
Frederik Clarysse *(Copywriter)*
Dennis Vandewalle *(Copywriter)*

Accounts:
City of Antwerp Campaign: "Antwerp-Quays Poem", Thank You For Not Speeding
DE Standaard
Essent
Fresh Meals Ready Made Pasta Meals, Ready Meals
Heylen
HUB
KIA
Lampiris Campaign: "The Envelope"
O Cool
Opel Belgium Campaign: "Gabriel", Campaign: "It is Possible Inside the Combo"
Red Bull
Sensoa
Special Olympics Campaign: "Break the Taboos"
Stad Antwerp
Sunweb
Think Media
University of Antwerp
Veritas
Vmmtv TV Media Saleshouse

MetropolitanRepublic
7 Wessel Road Edenburg, Johannesburg, South Africa
Tel.: (27) 112313300
Fax: (27) 112316727
Web Site: www.metropolitanrepublic.com

Agency Specializes In: Advertising

Alison Deeb *(Grp CEO)*
Dale Mullany *(Grp Head-Creative)*
Paul Warner *(Exec Dir-Creative)*
Tim Beckerling *(Creative Dir)*
Sean Harrison *(Creative Dir)*
Sharon Premchund *(Acct Dir)*
Peter Khoury *(Dir-Creative)*
Leon Kotze *(Copywriter)*
Keith Manning *(Copywriter)*
Robert Selmer-Olsen *(Copywriter)*

Accounts:
Hippo
MTN Group Telecommunications Services
Nando's
SA Breweries
Sanlam
Wimpy Campaign: "Braille Burgers"
World Design Capital

Mindshare
1 St Giles High St, London, WC2H 8AR United Kingdom
Tel.: (44) 20 7969 4040
Fax: (44) 20 7969 4000
E-Mail: Nick.Ashley@mindshareworld.com
Web Site: www.mindshareworld.com

Employees: 7,000

Agency Specializes In: Media Buying Services

Nick Emery *(Global CEO)*
Jenny Kirby *(Mng Partner-Performance)*
Enyi Nwosu *(Partner-Strategy-Global)*
Giovanni Romero *(Partner)*
Paul Rowlinson *(COO)*
Helen McRae *(Global Chm-Western Europe & CEO-UK)*
Jed Hallam *(Head-Digital Strategy)*
Sarah Sutton *(Co-Head-Strategy)*
Sharon Dhillon *(Bus Dir)*
Matthew Rouse *(Bus Dir)*
Ben Watson *(Bus Dir-Client Leadership)*
Niall Callan *(Dir-Comml)*
James Chandler *(Dir-Global Mobile)*
Luke Ellis *(Dir-Programmatic & Digital)*
Mark Murray-Jones *(Dir-Client)*
Jeremy Pounder *(Dir-Client-Bus Plng)*
Jane Riley *(Dir-Client Leadership & Comm Plng)*
John Tippins *(Dir-Client & Strategy)*
Robert Thomas *(Acct Mgr-SEO)*
Alison Ashworth *(Planner)*
Chris Cardew *(Joint Head-Strategy)*
Joanna Lyall *(Joint Head-Client Leadership)*

Accounts:
American Express
Anglian Home Improvements Digital Media
Argos Media Buying, Media Planning, Shazam
BlackRock, Inc. Media
BMG Music Entertainment (UK) Ltd. Media Planning & Buying
New-Boehringer Ingelheim
Brewin Dolphin
Capcom
New-Chanel
CISCO
Evans Cycles Media Buying, Media Planning
New-Facebook
Ford Fiesta, Media
Freeview
Garuda Global Media
New-General Mills Global Media
Grohe
Hediard
Holiday Lettings
HSBC Media
IBM
InterContinental Hotels Group CRM, Crowne Plaza, Global Media, Holiday Inn, InterContinental
ITV Media Buying & Planning; 2005
Jaguar Campaign: "Feel Wimbledon", Campaign: "How alive are you?", Campaign: "Life Balanced", Creative, F-Type, Media Buying, Media Planning, XF Sportsbrake
Kimberly Clark Digital, Kleenex, Media Buying
Land Rover Media
Legal & General Creative, Media
Livingsocial
Lufthansa
Mango
Marks & Spencer
Mazda
New-The National Trust Media Buying, Media Planning
Nike
Ocean Spray
Piaggio
Popchips
Post Office Media
Ranstad
River Island
Rolex
New-SAGE
Samaritans
SAP
Slater & Gordon Analytics, Media Buying, Media Planning, Offline Media, Strategy
Sony Music
Specsavers
talkSPORT
Telegraph Media Group
Three Mobile Media Buying
TK Maxx Media
Tommys
Unilever Apollo, Campaign: "Little Big Film Makers", Campaign: "The Summer of Love Not Hate", First Direct, Flora Pro.Activ, Lipton, Lynx, Marmite Love Cafe, Media, Media Planning, PG Tips, Persil, Pot Noodle, Sure Girl
Volvo "100 reasons to love Volvo", Media Planning & Buying, V40 R-Design
Warburtons Media

Ogilvy & Mather
636 11th Ave, New York, NY 10036
(See Separate Listing)

The Partners
Albion Courtyard Greenhill Rents, Smithfield, London, EC1M 6PQ United Kingdom
Tel.: (44) 2076080051
Fax: (44) 2072500473
E-Mail: info@thepartners.co.uk
Web Site: www.the-partners.com

Employees: 200
Year Founded: 1983

Agency Specializes In: Advertising, Brand Development & Integration, Digital/Interactive, Package Design, Social Media

Jim Prior *(CEO)*
Natalie Clark *(CFO)*
Jason Hartley *(Chief Strategy Officer-Global)*
Claire Robinson *(Mng Dir-New York)*
Greg Quinton *(Exec Dir-Creative)*
Robert Ball *(Creative Dir)*
Nick Eagleton *(Dir-Creative-UK)*
Kevin Lan *(Dir-Design)*
Michael Paisley *(Dir-Creative)*
Andrew Webster *(Dir-Client)*

Accounts:
Airasia Campaign: "The Year of the Dragon"
The Connaught
Consortium for Street Children Campaign: "Haunting"
Deloitte Campaign: "Timesaver"
EMCAS Campaign: "Reclaiming your money. Restoring financial justice"
Fia Foundation Campaign: "Un Decade of Action"
Fine Cell Work Campaign: "Fine Cell Work Sewn Guidelines", Campaign: "Sewn Guidelines"
Henry Wood
Made in Britain
Queen's Coronation
Richard House Children's Hospice
Secret Tea Room
New-Silversea Cruises
Tomorrow
New-Tusk Trust
Vodafone Campaign: "Londons Calling"

Possible New York
(Formerly Possible Worldwide)
41 E 11th St 6th Fl, New York, NY 10003
(See Separate Listing)

Possible
(Formerly ZAAZ)
414 Olive Way Ste 500, Seattle, WA 98101
Tel.: (206) 341-9885
Fax: (206) 749-9868
E-Mail: info@possible.com
Web Site: www.possible.com

Employees: 150

Agency Specializes In: Sponsorship

Gareth Jones *(Mng Dir)*
Jon McVey *(Chief Creative Officer-Portland)*
Adam Wolf *(CTO-Americas)*
Brian LeCount *(Exec VP-Strategy & Insights)*
Laurent Burman *(Sr VP & Acct Mgmt Dir)*
Beth Nouguier *(Sr VP-Acct-Portland)*
Josh Schmiesing *(Sr VP)*
Jon Dietrich *(Dir-Creative)*
John Georgopoulos *(Dir-Mktg Sciences)*
Shawn Herron *(Dir-Creative)*
Carrie Ingoglia *(Dir-Creative)*
Jennifer Southwell *(Dir-Bus Dev Ops-North America)*
Sean Weller *(Dir-Strategy)*
Lana Femiak *(Assoc Dir-Media Svcs)*
Erin Kelley *(Assoc Media Dir)*

Accounts:
Converse
Ford
Helio
InterContinental Hotels Group Crowne Plaza, Holiday Inn, Indigo, InterContinental, Social Media Strategy
Lonely Planet
Microsoft Campaign: "The Art of Touch", Surface Website
Morgans Hotel Group Website Development
National Geographic
Nike
PR Newswire
REI
Sony Electronics Web Sites; 2007
Tom's of Maine

Red Cell
Alberto Mario N 19, 20149 Milan, Italy
Tel.: (39) 02772 2981
Fax: (39) 02 782 126
E-Mail: welcome@redcell.com
Web Site: www.redcellgroup.it

Year Founded: 1988

Agency Specializes In: Advertising

Alberto de Martini *(CEO & Planner-Strategic)*
Roberto Giovannini *(Gen Mgr-Rome)*
Roberto Vella *(Exec Dir-Creative)*
Ingrid Altomare *(Acct Dir-Adv & Digital)*

Stefano Longoni *(Dir-Creative)*
Stefano Castagnone *(Copywriter)*

Accounts:
Blockbuster
Boehringer Ingelheim
Bonduelle
Cameo Bakery
De Cecco
Honda
Imetec
Iveco
Mediacom
Yamaha Motorcycles

Rockfish
(Formerly Rockfish Interactive)
3100 Market St Ste 100, Rogers, AR 72758-8261
(See Separate Listing)

Santo Buenos Aires
Darwin 1212, Buenos Aires, C 1414 Argentina
Tel.: (54) 114 777 7757
E-Mail: santo@santo.net
Web Site: www.santobuenosaires.net

Employees: 35

Agency Specializes In: Advertising, Cosmetics, Food Service, New Technologies, Production, Production (Ad, Film, Broadcast), Production (Print)

Maximiliano Anselmo *(Owner)*
Pablo Minces *(Partner & Exec Dir-Creative)*
Fabiana Casal *(CFO)*
Juan Ignacio Etchanique *(Dir-Creative)*
Nicolas Larroquet *(Dir-Creative)*
Sergio Rio *(Copywriter)*

Accounts:
Arnet Broadband
Carlsberg Barclays Premier League
Coca-Cola Co Campaign: "Christmas", Campaign: "Happiness", Campaign: "Parenting", Campaign: "Ser Padres", Campaign: "Transformations", Coke Life
Diesel Campaign: "Constitution"
Telecom Argentina Arnet
TIM Campaign: "Colombo Caravella"

SAY Media, Inc.
(Formerly VideoEgg, Inc.)
180 Townend St 3rd Fl, San Francisco, CA 94107
Tel.: (415) 738-5100
Fax: (415) 979-1586
Web Site: www.saymedia.com/

Employees: 300
Year Founded: 2005

David Lerman *(Co-Founder & CTO)*
Matt Sanchez *(CEO)*
Susan Kravitz *(Head-Sls-Global)*
Joyce Bautista Ferrari *(Exec Dir-Editorial)*
Becky Uden *(Acct Dir)*
Julia Benedict *(Dir-Solutions)*
Justine LoMonaco *(Mgr-Social Media Strategy)*

SCPF
C/Calatrava num 71, Barcelona, 08017 Spain
Tel.: (34) 93 434 3434
Fax: (34) 93 434 3435
E-Mail: scpf@scpf.com
Web Site: www.scpf.com

Dani Garcia Fdez *(Sr Dir-Creative & Art)*
Natalia Cazcarra *(Client Svcs Dir)*
Helena Grau Tarragona *(Client Svcs Dir)*
Jose Izaguirre Liniers *(Dir-Art)*
Miguel Madariaga *(Dir-Creative)*
Eren Saracevic *(Dir-Art)*
Jaime Trapaga *(Dir-Digital Art)*
Meritxell Cots Madueno *(Sr Acct Supvr)*
Javier Diaz-Masa *(Supvr-Creative & Sr Editor)*
Jorge Pezzi *(Supvr-Creative)*

Accounts:
ADC*E
Balearia Campaign: "Paperboys"
Banc Sabadell Campaign: "Conversations on the Future"
BMW X3
Codorniu, S.A. Campaign: "We Are Not Champagne, We Are Codorniu"
Ikea Campaign: "Empieza Algo Nuevo"
Vodafone

SCPF
1688 Meridian Ave Ste 200, Miami Beach, FL 33139
(See Separate Listing)

SCPGrey
(Formerly ScanPartner Goteborg AB)
Ostra Hamngatan 35, 41110 Gothenburg, Sweden
Tel.: (46) 31 726 9800
Fax: (46) 31 7269801
E-Mail: info@scpgrey.se
Web Site: scpgrey.se/

Employees: 51
Year Founded: 1986

Agency Specializes In: Advertising, Affluent Market, Automotive

Jesper Ernholm *(Acct Dir)*
Dragan Pavlovic *(Acct Dir-Global)*
Janne Frankfelt *(Dir-Art)*
Gunnar Hultberg *(Dir-Art)*
Tommy Ostberg *(Dir-Creative)*
Johan Sandton *(Dir-Art)*
Mikael Virtanen *(Sr Copywriter)*

Accounts:
Atlet
Brandon
Classic Vapen AB
The Concert House
Oversea Labs
SOIC
Sca
Specsavers Optik
Stampen
Tibnor
Volvo Exhibition International Car Exhibition
Volvo International
Volvo Sweden Volvo & Renault

SET Creative
12 W 27th St Fl 6, New York, NY 10001
(See Separate Listing)

Soho Square
636 11th Ave, New York, NY 10036
(See Separate Listing)

Sudler & Hennessey Worldwide Headquarters
230 Park Ave S, New York, NY 10003-1566
(See Separate Listing)

Team Detroit
(Formerly TEAM/Y&R Detroit)
550 Town Ctr Dr, Dearborn, MI 48126-2750
Tel.: (313) 615-2000
Fax: (313) 583-8001
Toll Free: (800) 521-8038
Web Site: www.teamdetroit.com

Employees: 1,300
Year Founded: 1932

National Agency Associations: 4A's

Agency Specializes In: Sponsorship

Molly Marchese *(Mng Partner & Exec Dir-Media-US)*
Mary Beth Duffy *(Mng Partner-Digital Customer Experience Team)*
Mike Bentley *(Co-Mng Dir & Chief Strategy Officer)*
Andy Weil *(CFO & Exec VP)*
Kim Brink *(COO)*
Betsy Lazar *(Chief Media Officer & Exec VP)*
Linda Taylor *(Exec VP & Chief Talent Officer-Global)*
Toby Barlow *(Chief Creative Officer)*
David Murphy *(Pres-USA)*
Paul Venn *(Pres-Bus-Global)*
Robert Rosiek *(Exec VP & Dir-Global Client Fin)*
Michele Silvestri *(Exec VP & Dir-Design-Global)*
Susan Mersch *(Sr VP & Grp Dir-Creative)*
Brian New *(Sr VP & Grp Acct Dir)*
Emilie Hamer *(Sr VP-Plng & Dir-Global)*
Ron Harper *(Sr VP & Dir-Creative)*
Vicky Kruslemsky *(Sr VP & Dir-Talent Mgmt)*
Kim LaPlante *(Sr VP & Dir-Global User Experience Res)*
Cathy Tocco *(Sr VP & Dir-Local Brdcst-US)*
Karen Tucker *(Sr VP & Dir-Comm)*
Danielle Dudley *(Sr VP & Reg Mgr-Brdcst)*
Otto Bischoff *(Sr VP & Mgr-Local Integrated Media)*
Brian Curran *(VP & Sr Producer-Print)*
Kelly Trudell *(VP & Sr Producer)*
Timothy W. Galvin *(VP & Acct Dir)*
Stacy Hart Lee *(VP & Acct Dir-Brand Digital Adv)*
Maureen Marnon *(VP & Producer-Integrated Content)*
Ron Kirkman *(VP & Mgr-Brdcst Bus-Integrated Production)*
Philip Shih *(VP-Mktg Platforms)*
Tony Vecchiato *(VP-Strategy & Enablement-Mobile, Digital & Emerging Strategies)*
Stuart O'Neil *(Exec Dir-Creative)*
Christian Colasuonno *(Exec Producer-Digital)*
Michael Johnston *(Sr Producer-Digital)*
Michael Stanford *(Acct Dir-Digital)*
Maria McAvoy *(Mgmt Supvr)*
Kristine Kaligian *(Dir-Strategy Plng-West Reg)*
Stephanie Snell *(Dir-Analytics Implementation)*
Dan Weber *(Dir-Creative)*
Sanja Dardagan *(Assoc Dir-Creative)*
Shannon Dux *(Assoc Dir-Media Plng)*
Rene Tuohy *(Assoc Dir-Media)*
Michael Rykalsky *(Sr Project Mgr-Digital)*
Jaclyn Huffman *(Supvr-Digital Media-Negotiation)*
Sara Dixon *(Strategist-Digital Cross-Channel)*
Andrew Heer *(Strategist-Content)*
Sean Kristl *(Acct Exec-Ford Car & Primary Brand Team)*
Jaimie Mazzola *(Acct Exec)*
Christina Salowich *(Acct Exec)*
Jaime Schram *(Acct Exec-Digital)*
Lana Goodrich *(Copywriter)*
Leslie Siedlak *(Media Planner)*
John Stoll *(Copywriter)*
Dion Spivey *(Coord-Benefits & Compensation)*
Jordan Holmgren *(Asst Media Planner-Digital)*
Jessy Jamison *(Sr Media Planner)*
Jillian Levine *(Sr Media Planner-Digital)*
Susan Watts *(Sr Bus Mgr)*

Accounts:
Bosch
Brine
College For Creative Studies Campaign: "1 in 5 Teens"
Compuware Corporation Strobe
Ford Motor Company 2015 Ford Edge, 2015 Ford Fusion, Campaign: "#OneTankAdventure", Campaign: "Be Unstoppable", Campaign:

"Brainstorm", Campaign: "Built Ford Tough", Campaign: "By Design", Campaign: "Doubly Good" Super Bowl 2014, Campaign: "Doug, the Focus Spokespuppet", Campaign: "Escape My Life", Campaign: "F-150 EcoBoost Torture Test", Campaign: "Frazzled Father", Campaign: "Icy Mad Man", Campaign: "Inner Mustang", Campaign: "It's the Most Distracted Time of the Year", Campaign: "Miss Multi-Task", Campaign: "Poolside", Campaign: "Random Acts of Fusion", Campaign: "Rant", Campaign: "Speed Dating", Campaign: "The New Explorers", Campaign: "We Own Work", Digital, Digital Media, F150, Focus Electric, Ford Escape, Ford Transit, Fusion, Lincoln, Lincoln MKS, Lincoln MKX, Lincoln MKZ, Lincoln Navigator, Media, Mustang, Print, TV, campaign: "9 to 5'ers"
Johnson Controls
Lincoln Motor Company Campaign: "Bull", Campaign: "I Just Liked It", Lincoln MKC, Lincoln MKZ, Lincoln Signed Art Print
New Step
Oakwood
Ohio Art Etch A Sketch, Nanoblocks
Optima Batteries
Ross School of Business
The Scotts Miracle-Gro Company Miracle-Gro, Ortho, Roundup, The Scotts Company, Turf Builder, Turf Builder Plus 2, Turf Builder Plus Halts, Weed-B-Gon
Shell
Sports Authority (Agency of Record) Brand Experience, Consumer Communications, Full Line Sporting Goods Retailer
United Way
Varta
Warrior Lacrosse

VBAT
Pilotenstraat 41 A, 1059 Amsterdam, Netherlands
Tel.: (31) 207503000
Fax: (31) 207503001
E-Mail: info@vbat.com
Web Site: www.vbat.com

Employees: 60

Agency Specializes In: Brand Development & Integration, Corporate Identity, Digital/Interactive, Identity Marketing, Internet/Web Design, Package Design, Product Placement, Retail

Eugene Bay *(Owner)*
Andre Kruger *(CFO)*
Theo Lindemann *(Brand Dir)*
John Comitis *(Dir-Creative)*
Lilian Vos *(Dir-Design)*

Accounts:
BCD Travel
Canei
Cerveza Cristal Beverages Producer
Crystal
Gamma
Heineken Campaign: "Sol Dark Sun"
ING W
Optimal
Royal Club
SNS Bank
Teleac

WPP US
100 Park Ave, New York, NY 10017-5529
Tel.: (212) 632-2200
Fax: (212) 632-2249
E-Mail: enquiries@wpp.com
Web Site: www.wpp.com

Employees: 200

National Agency Associations: 4A's

Agency Specializes In: Sponsorship

Martin Sorrell *(Founder & CEO)*
Kathy Kladopoulos *(Pres)*
Sunder Muturaman *(Mng Partner-Global)*
Alan Couldrey *(CEO-Brand Union AP)*
Bessie Lee *(CEO-China)*
Tom Lobene *(Treas-Americas)*
Anne Newman *(Exec VP-Latin America)*
Lance Maerov *(Sr VP-Corp Dev)*
Vanessa Andrews *(VP-Global Client Ops)*
Erin Miller *(VP-Kantar Retail Americas Consulting)*
Joel Barad *(Head-Knowledge-Global Bus Dev Team)*
David Chapman *(Head-AZ Global Client)*
John McDonald *(Head-Global Client-Team United Airlines)*
Tom O'Connell *(Head-Digital Innovation)*
Christa Felice *(Dir-Integration)*
Elias Goletsas *(Dir-Bus Dev)*
Kevin McCormack *(Dir-Comm-NA)*
Paul Richardson *(Dir-Fin)*
Sean Lynch *(Mgr)*
Joe Natarajan *(Mgr-External Reporting)*
Tae-Ho Cho *(Acct Exec)*

Accounts:
Bank of America Strategic Positioning
Grey Goose Campaign: "Fly Beyond"
Johnson & Johnson Family of Companies Johnson & Johnson
Kimberly-Clark Corporation Kleenex
Mazda North American Operations
Pfizer, Inc.
Samsung Business-to-Business Marketing

Xaxis, LLC
(Formerly 24/7 Media, Inc.)
31 Penn Plaza 132 W 31st St, New York, NY 10001
(See Separate Listing)

Y&R
(Formerly Wunderman)
Level 4 Corner Augustus Terrace & Parnell Rise, Parnell, Auckland, New Zealand
Tel.: (64) 9 308 5444
Fax: (64) 9 308 5359
Web Site: www.yr.com

Employees: 50

Agency Specializes In: Direct Response Marketing, Information Technology, Planning & Consultation, Publicity/Promotions, Sales Promotion

Grant Maxwell *(Gen Mgr)*
Josh Moore *(Exec Dir-Creative)*
Guy Denniston *(Creative Dir)*
Claire Dooney *(Acct Dir)*
Seymour Pope *(Creative Dir)*
Gavin Siakimotu *(Creative Dir)*
Tom Paine *(Assoc Dir-Creative)*
Mel Cutfield *(Acct Mgr)*
Nic Winslade *(Planner-Brand & Content)*
Carlos Savage *(Assoc Creative Dir)*

Accounts:
Animates Campaign: "Doomsday"
Arnott's Campaign: "Distraction"
Avis Budget Left Hand Radio
Beds R Us Campaign: "Flat Cat Lullaby"
Blunt Umbrellas
Brake Campaign: "Living Memories"
New-Burger king
Co-operative Bank Campaign: "Profits", Campaign: "Record Profit", Logo, USP, Visual Identity, Website
The Earthquake Commission Campaign: "Fix. Fasten. Don't Forget", Campaign: "Valuables"
Edgewell Campaign: "The Schibliminizer", Schick, WHAT EMMA SEES
Icebreaker Campaign: "NZ Lucky Dip", Campaign: "Sheep"
New-Jaguar
Land Rover
MetService Campaign: "Weather to Wake"
Red Cross
Resene Campaign: "Colour Dj"
Sea Shepherd Campaign: "For The Ocean"
The Tomorrow Project Standard Drink, Standard Glass
Tuatara Brewery Campaign: "All Blacks DIY Jersey"
York Street Mechanics Campaign: "Dan"

Young & Rubicam
3 Columbus Cir, New York, NY 10019
(See Separate Listing)

Direct, Promotional & Relationship Marketing

Agenda
311 W 43rd St Ste 703, New York, NY 10036
(See Separate Listing)

Catalyst
475 Sansome St Ste 730, San Francisco, CA 94111
(See Separate Listing)

Catalyst
110 Marina Dr, Rochester, NY 14626
(See Separate Listing)

Catalyst
275 Promenade St Ste 275, Warwick, RI 02908
(See Separate Listing)

DesignKitchen
1140 W Fulton Market, Chicago, IL 60607-1219
(See Separate Listing)

F.biz
Rua Tenente Negrao 90/2, Sao Paulo, 4530910 Brazil
Tel.: (55) 1135255336
Fax: (55) 1130786772
Web Site: www.fbiz.com.br

Year Founded: 1999

Agency Specializes In: Advertising, Brand Development & Integration, Digital/Interactive, E-Commerce, Internet/Web Design, Mobile Marketing

Pedro Reiss *(Co-CEO)*
Edivaldo Carvalho *(CFO)*
Marcello Hummel *(COO)*
Guilherme Jahara *(Chief Creative Officer)*
Fabio Astolpho *(Creative Dir)*
Andre Batista *(Art Dir)*
Rafael Magdalena *(Bus Dir-MOBILE)*
Denis Scorsato *(Art Dir)*
Nicholas Almeida *(Dir-Tech)*
Veruska Cicio *(Dir-Media & Bus Intelligence)*
Alexandra Gomes *(Dir-Ops)*
Marcelo Siqueira *(Dir-Creative)*
Anik Strimber *(Dir-Bus)*
Marcus Tomaselli *(Dir-Art)*
Armando Araujo *(Copywriter)*
Rodrigo de Castro *(Copywriter)*
Saulo Filho *(Copywriter)*

Accounts:
Alpha FM
New-Coniacc
New-GRAACC
Itaas Campaign: "The Money Masters"

Minuto Seguros
Netshoes Campaign: "Brandbook"
Pernod Ricard Jameson

Geometry Global
636 11th Ave, New York, NY 10036
(See Separate Listing)

KBM Group
(Formerly KnowledgeBase Marketing, Inc.)
2050 N Greenville Ave, Richardson, TX 75082
Tel.: (972) 664-3600
Fax: (972) 664-3656
E-Mail: sales@kbmg.com
Web Site: www.kbmg.com/

Employees: 100

Gary S. Laben *(CEO)*
Andrew Rutberg *(Pres-Svcs-Global)*
Joe Brehm *(Exec VP-Data Svcs)*
Clark Wooten *(Sr VP & Head-Vertical Practice)*
Raelyn Wade *(Sr VP-Sls)*
Glenn Teitlus *(Sr Dir)*
Jeremy Dowdy *(Dir-Digital Strategy)*
Peggy Garner *(Dir-Mktg Comm)*

Mando Brand Assurance Limited
The Corner Bldg, Aylesbury, Buckinghamshire HP19 8TY United Kingdom
Tel.: (44) 1296 717 900
Fax: (44) 1296 394 273
E-Mail: contact@mando.co.uk
Web Site: www.mando.co.uk

Employees: 35
Year Founded: 1977

Agency Specializes In: Sales Promotion

Ben Brost *(Gen Mgr-Central & Eastern Europe)*
Clare Daly *(Dir-Client Svcs-UK)*
Paul Townsend *(Dir-Fin)*
Nicky Batson *(Mgr-Fin)*
Mark Lewis *(Mgr-Quotes)*
Dan Ward *(Mgr-IT)*
Sam Dodgin *(Acct Exec-Europe)*

Accounts:
Coca-Cola Refreshments USA, Inc.
Danone
Kelloggs
Makro
Mersey Ferries / Merseytravel U-Boat Stories
TomTom
Walkers

Smollan Headcount
(Formerly Headcount Field Marketing)
Kestrel Ct, Pound Rd, Chertsey, Surrey KT16 8ER United Kingdom
Tel.: (44) 1932 560 650
Fax: (44) 1932 560 550
E-Mail: info@smollan.co.uk
Web Site: www.smollan.co.uk/

Employees: 50
Year Founded: 1994

Agency Specializes In: Consumer Marketing, Merchandising

Lynda Edge *(CEO)*
Duncan Miller *(Dir-IT)*
Tim Nicholls *(Mgr-Client IS)*

Accounts:
Defra

TAPSA
Jenner 3, 28010 Madrid, Spain
Tel.: (34) 91 319 0462
Fax: (34) 91 319 2620
E-Mail: tapsa@tapsa.es
Web Site: tapsayr.com

Employees: 189

Agency Specializes In: Communications, Market Research

Susana Albuquerque *(Gen Dir-Creative)*
Maria Jose Alvarez *(VP)*
Luis Manuel Iturbe *(Editor-Creative)*
David Pascual *(Art Dir)*
Fernando Heredia *(Dir-Art)*
Daniel Martin *(Dir-Creative Digital)*
Jaime Rojas *(Sr Copywriter-Digital)*
Juan Cenoz *(Copywriter)*

Accounts:
Angel Camacho
Ausonia
Balay
Carlsberg
CEPSA
DoDot
El Pais
Flex
Fundacion Telefonica
General Motos Opel Campaign: "Tweet Drive"
GOL Television Campaign: "It's not where it takes you. It's what gets you away from.", Campaign: "One Short"
Iberia Airline
Interflora Campaign: "The importance of who you are weighs more than what you have"
Once
Opel AFL Plus
Opel Smartphone Deer, Smartphone Kid, Smartphone Runner
rtve
Telepizza Pizza Delivery Campaign: "If Work Takes Longer Than Expected. We Deliver Until 2 a.m"
University of Malaga Campaign: "Festival Invitation Finger"
Utad-Technological University Of Digital Arts Campaign: "Why not?"
Vodafone

Wunderman World Health
(Formerly RTC Relationship Marketing)
1055 Thomas Jefferson St NW # 200, Washington, DC 20007
(See Separate Listing)

Darwin Healthcare Communications
(Formerly Darwin-Grey Communications)
4th Fl Lynton House 7-12 Tavistock Sq, London, WC1H 9LT United Kingdom
Tel.: (44) 203 037 3624
Fax: (44) 203 037 3610
E-Mail: naturalselection@darwingrey.com
Web Site: www.darwinhc.com

Kate Ashworth *(Client Svcs Dir)*
Emilie Violette *(Acct Dir)*
Frances O'Connor *(Dir-Scientific Svcs)*
Janet Walsh *(Dir-Ops)*
Martinho Coutinho *(Sr Acct Mgr)*
Mona Singh *(Sr Acct Mgr)*
Selina Muthada-Pottayya *(Sr Acct Exec)*

Accounts:
Baxter
Bioenvision
CTI
Genzyme
Mundi Pharma
NAPP
Novartis
Roche
Unipath

GCI Health
200 5th Ave, New York, NY 10010
Tel.: (212) 798-9950
Web Site: www.gcihealth.com

Agency Specializes In: Health Care Services, Public Relations

Wendy Lund *(CEO)*
Kristin Cahill *(Pres-North America)*
Jill Dosik *(Pres-Scientific Comm & Massage Impact)*
Kim Sammons *(Exec VP & Dir-Advocacy & Patient Engagement)*
Craig Heit *(Sr VP)*
Erin Kaiserova *(Sr VP)*
Robyn Leventhal *(Sr VP)*
Elliot Levy *(Sr VP)*
Allison Schneider *(Sr VP)*
Lauren Plate *(VP)*
Sherry Goldberg *(Head-Market-New York)*
Katie Dilyard *(Acct Exec)*
Danielle Kerendian *(Acct Exec)*

Accounts:
Cervilenz Inc.
New-InVivo Therapeutics Communications Strategy
Itamar Medical Campaign: "Don't Ignore Your EndoScore"
New-Neuraltus Pharmaceuticals, Inc
North Shore-LIJ Health System PR
The Parkinson Alliance Parkinson's Disease
YoungStroke, Inc. Branding, Communications Strategies

Ogilvy CommonHealth Worldwide
400 Interpace Pkwy, Parsippany, NJ 07054
(See Separate Listing)

Ogilvy Healthworld
636 11th Ave, New York, NY 10036
(See Separate Listing)

Information & Consultancy

Added Value
6 Lower Teddington Rd, Hampton Wick Surrey, Hampton, KT1 4ER United Kingdom
Tel.: (44) 20 8614 1500
Fax: (44) 20 8614 1600
E-Mail: l.richardson@added-value.com
Web Site: www.added-value.com

Employees: 95
Year Founded: 1989

Agency Specializes In: Brand Development & Integration, Communications, Publicity/Promotions, Strategic Planning/Research

Emily Smith *(Brand Dir)*
Paul Cowper *(Dir)*
Kevin Evans *(Dir-Insight)*
Michelle King *(Dir-Insight)*
Tisha Ubayasiri *(Dir-Talent)*
Matt Woodhams *(Dir-Brand Dev)*
Robin George *(Assoc Dir)*

Accounts:
General Motors
Pepsico
Unilever
Walker's

The Futures Company

11-33 Saint John Street, London, EC1M 4PJ United Kingdom
Tel.: (44) 20 7955 1800
Fax: (44) 20 7955 1900
Web Site: www.thefuturescompany.com

Employees: 50

Agency Specializes In: Planning & Consultation, Strategic Planning/Research

Mark Inskip *(CEO)*
Andre Furstenberg *(CFO)*
Valeria Piaggio *(VP & Head-Multicultural Insights)*
Rob Callender *(Dir-Youth Insights)*
Andrew Curry *(Dir)*
Michelle Trayne *(Dir-Web Applications)*
Karen Kidson *(Mgr-Mktg & Events)*
Kate Turkcan *(Assoc Head-TRU Youth MONITOR)*

Accounts:
Aviva

Ideaworks
Level 10/35 Clarence St, Gpo Pox 3 557, Sydney, NSW 2000 Australia
Tel.: (61) 2 9909 4646
E-Mail: info@ideaworks.com.au
Web Site: www.ideaworks.com.au

E-Mail for Key Personnel:
Chairman: gordona@ideaworks.com.au

Employees: 80
Year Founded: 1980

National Agency Associations: AFA

Agency Specializes In: Communications, Direct Response Marketing, E-Commerce, Graphic Design, Internet/Web Design, Point of Purchase, Point of Sale, Retail, Sales Promotion

Julian Bell *(Mng Partner)*
Andrew Dowling *(Grp Mng Dir-Sydney)*
Steve Kane *(Mng Dir)*
Danny Lattouf *(Mng Dir-Sydney)*
Andy Searles *(Grp Head-Creative)*
Tom Hoskins *(Dir-Creative)*
Mel Spears *(Dir-Creative-Brand Experience)*
Jon Bird *(Exec Chm)*

Accounts:
ASICS Campaign: "Run With Me"
Coates Hire
DealsDirect Creative
Dick Smith Apple Products, Campaign: "Unleash Your Smith", Creative, Digital, Retail Strategy, Store Design, TV
Landcom
Lenards
Muffin Break
NGIA
Onitsuka Tiger Campaign: "The Social Playbook"
Optus
Petbarn
Skins Apparel Campaign: "Quick Fit Station"

The Kantar Group
11 Madison Ave, New York, NY 10010
(See Separate Listing)

Kantar
(Formerly Taylor Nelson Sofres plc)
TNS House Westgate, London, W5 1UA United Kingdom
Tel.: (44) 2089670007
Fax: (44) 2089674060
E-Mail: enquiries@tns-global.com
Web Site: www.tnsglobal.com

Employees: 850

Year Founded: 1997

Wayne Levings *(Pres)*
Richard Ingleton *(CEO-Global)*
Yvonne Pernodd *(CEO-Nordics & Baltics)*
Stefan Stumpp *(CEO-Germany)*
Michelle Harrison *(Head-Political & Social-Global)*
James Brooks *(Dir-Ops-Global)*
Jonathan Chocqueel-Mangan *(Dir-Strategy & Transformation)*
Ishbel Morrison *(Dir-HR-Global)*
Robert A. Wieland *(Chief Res Officer)*

Millward Brown Inc.
3333 Warrenville Rd, Lisle, IL 60532
(See Separate Listing)

Teenage Research Unlimited
222 Merchandise Mart Ste 250, Chicago, IL 60654
(See Separate Listing)

Media Investment Management

GroupM North America & Corporate HQ
498 Seventh Ave, New York, NY 10018
(See Separate Listing)

MEC Interaction
1 Paris Garden, London, SE1 8NU United Kingdom
(See Separate Listing)

Public Relations & Public Affairs

Axon
(Formerly NATIONAL Public Relations)
Parkshot House, 5 Kew Road, Richmond, Surrey TW9 2PO United Kingdom
(See Separate Listing)

Axon
(Formerly NATIONAL Public Relations)
230 Park Ave S 3rd Fl, New York, NY 10003-1566
(See Separate Listing)

Buchanan Communications Ltd.
107 Cheapside, London, EC2V 6DN United Kingdom
Tel.: (44) 20 7466 5000
Fax: (44) 20 7466 5001
E-Mail: contact@buchanan.uk.com
Web Site: www.buchanan.uk.com

Employees: 45
Year Founded: 1980

Agency Specializes In: Communications, Financial, Investor Relations

Richard Oldworth *(Chm)*
Giles Sanderson *(Deputy Chm)*
Mark Court *(Partner)*
Richard Darby *(Partner)*
Mark Edwards *(Partner)*
Henry Harrison-Topham *(Partner)*
Ben Romney *(Partner)*
Charles Ryland *(Partner)*
Gabriella Clinkard *(Acct Dir)*
Sophie Cowles *(Acct Dir)*
Golam Haque *(Dir-Fin)*
Stephanie Watson *(Acct Mgr)*

Accounts:
Abcam
Advanced Medical Solutions Group Healthcare & Woundcare Products
Al Khaliji
Alchem
Alliance Pharma
Andes Energia
Antisoma
Antrim Energy Financial Communications
BACANORA MINERALS LTD AIM, Financial Public Relations, Investor Relations Services
Belvoir Lettings
Cape Corporate PR, Financial PR
CityFibre Financial PR, Investor Relations
Delivered Exactly IPO, Investor Relations, PR
Endeavour Mining Financial & Investor Communications
Euromax Resources Ltd Communications Strategy, Financial PR
Filtrona Financial Communications
Fusionex Plc Financial PR Communications, IPO
Global Energy Development
Gold Oil Plc
Kenmare Resources Public & Investor Relations
London Mining Financial Communications
Minera IRL Limited Financial Public Relations
Plant Impact Financial Public Relations, Investor Relations
Plus500 AIM float, Financial PR
Range Resources Financial & Corporate Public Relations
Rialto Energy Financial Communications
Science in Sport Plc Financial PR
ScS Communications Strategy, Financial
Sinermas Group
Superglass Holdings Plc

Chime Communications Plc
Southside 6th Floor, 105 Victoria St, Victoria, London, SW1E 6QT United Kingdom
Tel.: (44) 20 7096 5888
Fax: (44) 20 7096 5889
Web Site: www.chimeplc.com/

Employees: 1,249

National Agency Associations: IPREX

Agency Specializes In: Advertising, Advertising Specialties, Internet/Web Design, Public Relations, Strategic Planning/Research

Christopher Satterthwaite *(CEO)*
Mark Smith *(COO & Dir-Fin)*
Kevin Murray *(Chm-PR)*
Robert Davison *(Sec)*

Accounts:
Aviva Financial Services
British Sky Broadcasting
Central Office of Information
Cisco
CompareTheMarkets.com
EBLEX
Emirates Airline
Fujitsu
GlaxoSmithKline
Hewlett Packard
Honda
Kelloggs
McDonald's
Muller Yogurt
Pentax of America, Inc. Cameras
Pilsner & Urqell Beer
Sony

Clarion Communications
The Griffin Bldg 83 Clerkenwell Rd, London, EC1R 5AR United Kingdom
Tel.: (44) 20 7479 0910
Fax: (44) 20 7479 0930
E-Mail: mail@clarioncomms.co.uk
Web Site: www.clarioncomms.co.uk

Employees: 42
Year Founded: 1986

National Agency Associations: PRCA

Agency Specializes In: Brand Development & Integration, Communications, Corporate Identity, Event Planning & Marketing, New Product Development, Public Relations, Publicity/Promotions, Sales Promotion, Strategic Planning/Research

Gary Feemantle *(CEO)*
Amanda Meyrick *(Mng Dir)*
Debbie Jackson *(Dir-Bus Dev)*
Flora Neeson *(Assoc Dir)*
Jonathan Smith *(Assoc Dir)*
Matt Stokoe *(Assoc Dir)*
James Watts *(Assoc Dir)*

Accounts:
Aldi Beers, Wines & Spirits, Campaign: "Going Loco For Toro Loco", Consumer PR
Calligaris Cosumer, PR, Social Media
Chessington World of Adventures Resort
Genius Gluten Free Public Relations
Jagermeister Consumer & Trade PR Campaign
Juicy Water Branding, Digital Media, Experiential
New-MOMA Foods Bircher Muesli, Consumer, Oatie Shakes, Porridge, Press, Public Relations
Nestle Purina
Rowse Honey Public Relations
New-Teletext Holidays Digital, Public Relations, Social Media
Unilever "The Summer of Love Not Hate", Marmite, Marmite Love Cafe
The Valspar Corporation Public Relations, Valspar paint
Warburtons Marketing, PR

Essence Communications
Wizo House 107 Gloucester Place, London, W1U 6BY United Kingdom
Tel.: (44) 20 3422 8450
E-Mail: info@essence-communications.com
Web Site: www.essence-communications.com

Agency Specializes In: Advertising, Brand Development & Integration, Communications, Event Planning & Marketing, Public Relations, Social Media, Sponsorship

Nadia Walford *(Acct Mgr)*

Accounts:
EBay
Elite Model London
Google Campaign: "Zeitgeist", Media Planning & Buying
Holiday Taxis
Stunners International

Finsbury
(Formerly RLM Finsbury)
45 Moorfields, London, EC2Y 9AE United Kingdom
Tel.: (44) 20 7251 3801
Fax: (44) 20 7374 4133
E-Mail: enquiries-uk@finsbury.com
Web Site: www.finsbury.com/

Employees: 50
Year Founded: 1994

Agency Specializes In: Communications, Investor Relations, Public Relations

Stephen Labaton *(Pres & Partner)*
Eric Eve *(Partner & Head-Govt Rels & Pub Affairs)*
Faeth Birch *(Partner)*
James Bradley *(Partner)*
Rory Chisholm *(Partner)*
Guy Lamming *(Partner)*
Simon Moyse *(Partner)*
James Murgatroyd *(Partner)*
Roland Rudd *(Sr Partner)*

Accounts:
Alliance Boots
Associated British Ports Holdings PLC
Aviva
Banca Intesa
Blackstone
BNFL
The British Land Company PLC Financial Public Relations
Bunzl plc
C&C Group
Cable and Wireless plc
Centrica plc
Chubb plc
Coral Eurobet
CRH plc
EasyJet
G4S Corporate Communications, Financial Communications, PR
Great Portland Estates P.L.C.
Greene King Financial Public Relations
GUS plc
Home Retail Group
International Power plc
J Sainsbury plc
Kesa Electricals plc
Marks & Spencer Financial PR
Mitchells & Butlers plc
Morgan Crucible plc
Old Mutual plc
Paddy Power Corporate Communications
Pendragon Plc
Permira
Persimmon plc
Pilkington Group Limited
Qatar Holding Global PR
Reed Elsevier Financial PR
RTL Group
Sainsbury
The Shell Transport & Trading Co. plc
SIG plc
Standard Chartered plc
Statoil PR
Worldpay Corporate Communications, Financial Communications

Finsbury
(Formerly RLM Finsbury)
1345 Ave of the Americas, New York, NY 10105
(See Separate Listing)

Hill + Knowlton Strategies
825 3rd Ave 24th Fl, New York, NY 10022
(See Separate Listing)

MQI Brno, spol. s r.o.
Lipova 17, 602 00 Brno, Czech Republic
Tel.: (420) 5 41 420 211
Fax: (420) 5 41 420 220
Web Site: www.mqibrno.cz

Employees: 7

Agency Specializes In: Media Buying Services

Eva Vonavkova *(Mng Dir)*
Tomas Petr *(Acct Dir)*
Eliska Vintrova *(Acct Mgr)*
Johana Janouskova *(Jr Acct Mgr)*

NATIONAL Public Relations
130, Slater St, Ste 400, Ottawa, ON K1P 6L2 Canada
(See Separate Listing)

NATIONAL Public Relations
140 Grande Allee Est Ste 302, Quebec, QC G1R 5M8 Canada
(See Separate Listing)

NATIONAL Public Relations
800 6th Ave SW Ste 1600, Calgary, AB T2P 3G3 Canada
(See Separate Listing)

NATIONAL Public Relations
(Formerly MT&L Public Relations Ltd.)
1701 Hollis St Ste L101, Halifax, NS B3J 3M8 Canada
(See Separate Listing)

NATIONAL Public Relations
310 Front St W 5th Fl, Toronto, ON M5V 3B5 Canada
(See Separate Listing)

NATIONAL Public Relations
2001 McGill College Ave Ste 800, Montreal, QC H3A 1G1 Canada
(See Separate Listing)

NATIONAL Public Relations
931 Fort St 4th Fl, Victoria, BC V8W 2C4 Canada
Tel.: (250) 361-1713
Fax: (250) 384-2102
E-Mail: info-vic@national.ca
Web Site: www.national.ca

Agency Specializes In: Crisis Communications, Public Relations

Zdenka Buric *(Mng Partner)*

Accounts:
Accenture
Allergan
AstraZeneca
BC Lottery Corp. (BCLC)
BHP Billiton
Bayer
Bristol-Myers Squibb
Canadian Centre for Energy Information
Coloplast
Eli Lilly
Enbridge
GlaxoSmithKline
Harlequin Enterprises
Hoffmann-La Roche
Homburg Canada
Home Hardware
Imperial Oil
International Diabetes Federation
Ivanhoe Cambridge
Janssen-Ortho
Johnson & Johnson
McDonald's Restaurants of Canada
Merck Frosst Canada
Molson Coors
Napp Pharmaceuticals
National Bank Financial Group
Novartis
Novo Nordisk
Ontario Power Authority
Pfizer
Sanofi-Aventis
St. Marys CBM
Standard Life
Sun Life Financial
Synenco Energy
TD Bank
TMX Group
Teck
TimberWest Forest Corporation
Toyota Canada
TransTech Pharma
VIA Rail
Wal-Mart

Yellow Pages Group

NATIONAL Public Relations
One Bentall Centre Ste 620 505 Burrard St, Box 34, Vancouver, BC V6C 1M4 Canada
(See Separate Listing)

Ogilvy Public Relations Worldwide
636 11th Ave, New York, NY 10036
(See Separate Listing)

Prime Policy Group
1110 Vermont Ave NW Ste 1200, Washington, DC 20005-3554
Tel.: (202) 530-0500
Fax: (202) 530-4500
E-Mail: primepolicy@was.bm.com
Web Site: www.prime-policy.com

Employees: 30
Year Founded: 1996

Agency Specializes In: Government/Political

John Tanner *(Vice Chm-Prime Policy Grp)*
R. Scott Pastrick *(Pres & CEO)*
Paul Brown *(Mng Dir)*
Gabe Rozsa *(Mng Dir)*
Keith Smith *(Mng Dir)*
Pam Turner *(Mng Dir)*
Becky Weber *(Mng Dir)*
Paul Weiss *(Mng Dir)*
Charles L. Merin *(Exec VP)*
Marty Paone *(Exec VP)*
Theresa Weber *(Dir-Ops)*

Accounts:
Walmart

Proof Integrated Communications
1110 Vermont Ave NW 12th Fl, Washington, DC 20005
(See Separate Listing)

Proof Integrated Communications
(Formerly Proof Interactive Communications)
230 Park Ave S, New York, NY 10003-1502
Tel.: (212) 614-6000
Fax: (212) 598-6966
E-Mail: info@proofic.com
Web Site: www.proofic.com

Employees: 25

National Agency Associations: 4A's

Agency Specializes In: Electronic Media, Graphic Design, Internet/Web Design, Production

Tyler Pennock *(Mng Dir-Digital Health Strategy)*
Ethan Farber *(Sr Dir-Digital Strategy)*
Steve King *(Sr Dir-Digital Strategy)*
Elizabeth Penniman *(Sr Dir-Creative-Production)*
Jody Lange *(Dir-Creative)*
Dan McGiffin *(Dir-Creative)*
Luke Peterson *(Dir-Analytics Products)*
Nick Hartman *(Assoc Dir-Creative)*
Jose Rodriguez *(Assoc Dir-Creative)*

Quinn Gillespie & Associates LLC
1133 Connecticut Ave NW 5th Fl, Washington, DC 20036
(See Separate Listing)

Target McConnells
(Formerly McConnells Advertising Service Ltd.)
20 North Umbeland Road, Ballsbridge, Dublin, 4 Ireland
Tel.: (353) 1 665 1900
Fax: (353) 1 665 1901
E-Mail: info@targetmcconnells.ie
Web Site: www.targetmcconnells.ie

Employees: 110
Year Founded: 1916

National Agency Associations: IAPI

Agency Specializes In: Digital/Interactive, Direct Response Marketing, Production, Public Relations, Publicity/Promotions, Radio, T.V.

Ailbhe Beirne *(Art Dir)*
Andrea Figueroa *(Art Dir)*
Claire McKay *(Acct Dir)*
Andrea Figueira *(Dir-Art)*
Claudio Vieira *(Dir-Creative)*
Stephanie Naughter *(Acct Exec)*
Alan McCafferty *(Copywriter)*
Eamon Quigley *(Designer)*

Accounts:
Arnotts Ltd. Strategic Digital
Mitsubishi Pencils
Vodafone Campaign: "They're Coming, Are You?"

Specialist Communications

Brierley & Partners
Clover House 4th Floor, Farringdon Road, London, United Kingdom
Tel.: (44) 207 239 8880
Fax: (44) 207 153 0599
E-Mail: info@brierly.com
Web Site: www.brierley.com

Employees: 12
Year Founded: 1996

Jim Sturm *(Pres & CEO)*
Chuck Cheatham *(CFO)*
Robert Owen *(CIO & Sr VP)*
Bill Swift *(CTO)*
Jill Goran *(Sr VP & Grp Dir-Creative)*
Jim Huppenthal *(Sr VP-Creative Svcs)*
Billy J. Payton *(Sr VP)*

Accounts:
American Eagle Outfitters
Baylor Health Care Systems
Blockbuster
Bloomingdales
BMI
Borders
eBay
Godiva

Brierley & Partners
15303 Ventura Blvd, Sherman Oaks, CA 91403
Tel.: (323) 965-4000
Fax: (323) 965-4100
Web Site: www.brierley.com

Employees: 20
Year Founded: 1986

Agency Specializes In: Consumer Marketing

David Mellinger *(CFO & Exec VP)*
Bill Swift *(CTO & Exec VP)*
Billy Payton *(Pres-Retail Svcs)*
Jill Goran *(Sr VP & Dir-Creative)*
Jim Huppenthal *(Sr VP-Creative Svcs)*
John Pedini *(Sr VP-Program Mgmt)*
Don Smith *(Sr VP)*

Accounts:
Hertz
Hilton Worldwide
Sony

Brierley & Partners
5465 Legacy Dr Ste 300, Plano, TX 75024
(See Separate Listing)

Etcom
Level 3 72 Christie Street, Saint Leonards, NSW 2065 Australia
Tel.: (61) 295688398
Fax: (61) 292771200
Web Site: www.etcom.com.au

Agency Specializes In: Advertising, Consulting, Event Planning & Marketing, Graphic Design, Market Research, Public Relations

Melissa Chaw *(Gen Mgr)*
Afif Malkoun *(Media Dir)*
Marion Branellec *(Acct Mgr & Specialist)*

Accounts:
New-The NSW Government
St.George Bank Enter the Dragon

The Food Group
589 8th Ave 4th Fl, New York, NY 10018
(See Separate Listing)

Forward
84-86 Regent Street, London, W1B 5DD United Kingdom
Tel.: (44) 20 7734 2303
Fax: (44) 20 7494 2570
Web Site: www.forwardww.com/

Employees: 90

Agency Specializes In: Direct Response Marketing, Graphic Design, Magazines, Print, Trade & Consumer Magazines

Kelli Hunter *(Sr Acct Dir)*
Kirsti Vincent *(Client Svcs Dir)*
Jet Wingham *(Acct Dir)*
Chris Carus *(Dir-Art)*
Paul Hattingh *(Dir-Art)*
Helen Ketchin *(Dir-Mktg & Strategy)*
Jono Owens *(Dir-Digital Art)*
Will Scott *(Dir-Creative)*
Michelle Shepherd *(Dir-Plng)*
Keith Drummond *(Assoc Dir-Creative)*
Jacqui Hoey *(Office Mgr)*

Accounts:
Barclays
Ford
Forward Arts Foundation
Patek Philippe
Standard Life
Transport For London

The Geppetto Group
636 11th Ave, New York, NY 10036
(See Separate Listing)

The Glover Park Group
1025 F St NW 9th Fl, Washington, DC 20004-1409
(See Separate Listing)

HeathWallace Ltd
5-9 Merchants Pl, Reading, RG1 1DT United Kingdom
Tel.: (44) 118 956 1757
Fax: (44) 118 951 1726
E-Mail: info@heathwallace.com
Web Site: www.heathwallace.com

Employees: 55

Will Hunter *(Mng Dir)*
Simon Webb *(Exec Dir-Creative-Global)*
Nick Besseling *(Acct Dir)*
Harriet Holley *(Acct Dir-Global)*
James Leavesley *(Client Svcs Dir)*
Victoria Alexandrovich *(Sr Project Mgr-Digital)*
Samantha-Sophia Felton *(Project Mgr-Digital)*
Melony Lawrance *(Designer-UX)*
Maria Sit *(Reg Mng Dir-Asia Pacific)*
Dave Wallace *(CEO)*

JAN Kelley Marketing
1005 Skyview Dr Ste 322, Burlington, ON L7P 5B1 Canada
(See Separate Listing)

Johannes Leonardo
628 Broadway 6th Fl, New York, NY 10012
(See Separate Listing)

Metro Broadcast Ltd.
53 Great Suffolk Street, London, SE1 0DB United Kingdom
Tel.: (44) 20 7202 2000
Fax: (44) 20 7202 2001
E-Mail: info@metrobroadcast.com
Web Site: www.metrobroadcast.com

Employees: 50
Year Founded: 1980

Agency Specializes In: Event Planning & Marketing, Exhibit/Trade Shows, Multimedia, Production, Publicity/Promotions

Mary Metcalfe *(Mng Dir-London)*
Matt Heirn *(Dir-Fin)*
Liz Rica *(Dir-New Bus & Client Dir)*

PACE Advertising
230 Park Ave S 12th Fl, New York, NY 10003
(See Separate Listing)

Spafax
The Pumphouse 13-16 Jacob's Well Mews, London, W1U 3DY United Kingdom
Tel.: (44) 20 7906 2001
Fax: (44) 20 7906 2003
E-Mail: nmcbain@spafax.com
Web Site: www.spafax.com

Employees: 60
Year Founded: 1985

Agency Specializes In: Aviation & Aerospace, Entertainment, Graphic Design, Media Buying Services, Print, Production

Niall McBain *(CEO)*
Simon Ogden *(CFO)*
Tony Taverner *(CTO & Grp Dir-Technical)*
Ann Willis *(Mng Dir-Specialized Networks & Dev)*
Sam Still *(Dir-New Bus)*
Nick Hopkins *(Sr Mgr-IFM Sls)*

Accounts:
ACE Aviation Holdings Inc. enRoute Magazine
American Airlines
British Airways Campaign: "Highlife Entertainment"
China Airlines Content Management
Emirates Airlines
JetBlue Airways Content, Fly-Fi, IFE, Media Sales, Video
Malaysian Airlines
Qatar Airlines
Royal Jordanian Royal Wings Magazine
SAS
Singapore Airlines Priority Magazine
Swiss Air

WRAY WARD MARKETING COMMUNICATIONS
900 Baxter St, Charlotte, NC 28204
Tel.: (704) 332-9071
Fax: (704) 375-5971
Web Site: www.wrayward.com

E-Mail for Key Personnel:
President: jappleby@wwlcreative.com
Creative Dir.: jappleby@wwlcreative.com
Media Dir.: statge@wwlcreative.com
Public Relations: mbrock@wwlcreative.com

Employees: 60
Year Founded: 1977

National Agency Associations: 4A's

Agency Specializes In: Above-the-Line, Advertising, Arts, Automotive, Below-the-Line, Brand Development & Integration, Broadcast, Business Publications, Business-To-Business, Cable T.V., Collateral, College, Communications, Consulting, Consumer Goods, Consumer Marketing, Consumer Publications, Corporate Communications, Corporate Identity, Crisis Communications, Digital/Interactive, Direct Response Marketing, Education, Electronic Media, Email, Entertainment, Environmental, Event Planning & Marketing, Exhibit/Trade Shows, Fashion/Apparel, Financial, Graphic Design, Health Care Services, High Technology, Household Goods, Identity Marketing, In-Store Advertising, Industrial, Information Technology, Integrated Marketing, Internet/Web Design, Leisure, Local Marketing, Logo & Package Design, Luxury Products, Magazines, Marine, Market Research, Media Buying Services, Media Planning, Media Relations, Media Training, Medical Products, Men's Market, Merchandising, Multimedia, New Technologies, Newspaper, Newspapers & Magazines, Out-of-Home Media, Outdoor, Package Design, Paid Searches, Planning & Consultation, Podcasting, Point of Purchase, Point of Sale, Print, Product Placement, Production, Production (Ad, Film, Broadcast), Production (Print), Promotions, Public Relations, Publicity/Promotions, RSS (Really Simple Syndication), Radio, Real Estate, Regional, Restaurant, Retail, Sales Promotion, Search Engine Optimization, Social Marketing/Nonprofit, Social Media, Sponsorship, Sports Market, Strategic Planning/Research, T.V., Technical Advertising, Trade & Consumer Magazines, Travel & Tourism, Viral/Buzz/Word of Mouth, Web (Banner Ads, Pop-ups, etc.), Women's Market

Approx. Annual Billings: $47,000,000

Breakdown of Gross Billings by Media: Internet Adv.: 16%; Other: 7%; Out-of-Home Media: 10%; Print: 17%; Radio: 13%; T.V.: 37%

Jennifer O. Appleby *(Owner, Pres & Chief Creative Officer)*
Kent Panther *(VP & Dir-Strategic Plng & Bus Dev)*
Bo Hussey *(Head-Acct)*
Jennifer Voorhees *(Head-Acct)*
Scott Ellmaker *(Grp Dir-Creative)*
Rusty Williams *(Grp Dir-Creative)*
David Adams *(Sr Dir-Art & Sr Designer)*
Heather Tamol *(Acct Dir-PR)*
Bill Baker *(Dir-Digital Strategy & Measurement)*
John Mader *(Dir-Content Mktg)*
Dana Haydock *(Sr Acct Mgr-PR)*
Laura King Edwards *(Sr Acct Mgr-PR)*
Candice Michael *(Sr Acct Mgr)*
Meara Lyons *(Acct Mgr-PR)*
Ashley Moran *(Acct Mgr-PR & Content Mktg)*
Jennifer Hight *(Supvr-Media)*
Marlee Murphy *(Acct Coord-PR & Content Mktg)*
Brian Gainey *(Coord-Project Mgmt)*
Ashton Nichols *(Coord-Project Mgmt)*
Molly Nickel *(Coord-Media)*
Michelle Pojasek *(Coord-Project Mgmt)*
MaryJo Scott *(Coord-Project Mgmt)*
Leah Tanner *(Acct Head)*

Accounts:
Belgard Hardscapes
BRITAX USA
Casa Fiora
Crescent Communities
Dal-Tile Corporation
Duke Energy
Eaton Lighting Division
Electrolux
Glen Raven Mills; Glen Raven, NC Sunbrella Fabrics; 1975
GreenFiber
Hale Products, Inc.
Huber Engineered Woods AdvanTech Building Products; 2003
Hunter Douglas; 2005
Hurst Jaws of Life
La-Z-Boy Casegoods Kincaid Furniture
Material Handling Industry of America
Microban Anti-microbials; 2006
Moen Content, Creative, Creative Marketing Communications, Media, Strategic Planning
Mohawk
Nascar Hall of Fame; 2009
NC Education Lottery
Rack Room Shoes, Inc.
Springs Global, Inc. Court of Versailles, Springmaid, Springmaid & Wamsutta Home Furnishings, Springs Home, Springs Industries, Inc., Wamsutta; 2002
Time Warner Cable Inc.
TUUCI
VELUX Skylights Campaign: "VELUX Drama Heights", Skylights, Sun Tunnels; 2001
WIX Filters

WRIGHT EDGE ADVERTISING
2616 Mesilla NE Ste 3, Albuquerque, NM 87110
Tel.: (505) 292-0448
Fax: (505) 332-6390
Toll Free: (800) 334-3187
E-Mail: we@wrightedgeresults.com
Web Site: www.wrightedge.com

Year Founded: 1984

Agency Specializes In: Automotive

Mary Pascale *(Dir-Media)*
Dean Wells *(Sr Acct Exec)*

Accounts:
Ford
Lincoln-Mercury

WRIGHT FEIGLEY COMMUNICATIONS
10000 Perkins Rowe Town Hall W Ste 325, Baton Rouge, LA 70810
Tel.: (225) 769-4844
Fax: (225) 769-3806
E-Mail: connect@wfcommunications.com
Web Site: www.wfcommunications.com

Agency Specializes In: Advertising, Broadcast, Event Planning & Marketing, Media Buying Services, Media Planning, Public Relations, Radio, Social Media, Strategic Planning/Research, T.V.

Stuart Feigley *(Partner & Dir-Creative)*
Jeff Wright *(Partner)*
Mary McFarland *(Controller)*
Ben Benton *(Sr Dir-Art)*
Julie Nusloch Joubert *(Dir-Media)*
Molly Malloy *(Sr Acct Exec-PR)*

Accounts:

Perkins Rowe

WRIGHT ON COMMUNICATIONS
Ste 300 674 Via de la Valle, Solana Beach, CA 92075
Tel.: (858) 755-5411
E-Mail: info@wrightoncomm.com
Web Site: www.wrightoncomm.com

Year Founded: 1998

Agency Specializes In: Communications, Consulting, Market Research, Public Relations, Strategic Planning/Research

Grant Wright *(CEO & Mng Partner)*
Molly Borchers *(Sr Strategist-Comm)*
Erica Schlesinger *(Strategist-Comm)*
Chris Jensen *(Jr Coord-Comm)*

Accounts:
Jet Source Aircraft Management & Maintenance Services

WRIGHTIMC
660 N Central Expressway Ste 450, Plano, TX 75074
Tel.: (866) 628-8467
E-Mail: info@wrightimc.com
Web Site: www.wrightimc.com

Year Founded: 2007

Agency Specializes In: Advertising, Content, Digital/Interactive, Internet/Web Design, Media Buying Services, Paid Searches, Search Engine Optimization, Social Media

Tony Wright *(Founder & CEO)*
Tim Wagner *(VP)*
Jessica Nelson *(Dir-Client Svcs)*

Accounts:
New-Aidmatrix Foundation Inc.

THE WRIJEN COMPANY
225 Green St Ste 1007-C, Fayetteville, NC 28301
Tel.: (910) 480-1800
Fax: (910) 480-2800
E-Mail: admin@wrijencompany.com
Web Site: www.wrijencompany.com

Employees: 8

Agency Specializes In: Advertising, Brand Development & Integration, Branded Entertainment, Broadcast, Electronic Media, Event Planning & Marketing, Fashion/Apparel, Graphic Design, Guerilla Marketing, Identity Marketing, In-Store Advertising, Integrated Marketing, Internet/Web Design, Media Buying Services, Multicultural, Multimedia, Production (Ad, Film, Broadcast), Radio, Retail, T.V., Technical Advertising, Urban Market, Women's Market

Approx. Annual Billings: $2,500,000

Thaddeus Jenkins *(Pres)*

Accounts:
Citi Trends Advertising, Media Buying & Creative; 2004

WRL ADVERTISING, INC.
4470 Dressler Rd NW, Canton, OH 44718-2716
Tel.: (330) 493-8866
Fax: (330) 493-8860
E-Mail: info@wrladv.com
Web Site: www.wrladv.com

E-Mail for Key Personnel:
President: ctlocke@wrladv.com
Creative Dir.: isenberg@wrladv.com

Employees: 23
Year Founded: 1954

Agency Specializes In: Business-To-Business, Communications, Consumer Marketing

Breakdown of Gross Billings by Media: Collateral: 50%; Mags.: 10%; Newsp.: 10%; Point of Purchase: 5%; Radio: 15%; T.V.: 10%

Bob Isenberg *(VP-Creative Svcs)*
Thomas Budinsky *(Sr Dir-Art)*
Norio Saneshige *(Dir-Art & Acct Mgr)*
David Jensen *(Dir-Art)*
Dave Fenn *(Sr Acct Mgr)*
Betty Williams *(Office Mgr)*

Accounts:
Brewster Dairy Inc. All-Natural Cheese; 1989
Canton Chamber of Commerce; 1965
Germantown Systems Food Additives; 1991
Quickdraft Corp. Pneumatic Material Handling Systems; 1972
Rider Dairy, Inc.; Canton, OH Milk/Dairy Products & Ice Cream; 1956
Snyder Manufacturing Tent & Banner Fabrics; 1997
The Timken Company Tapered Roller Bearings & Steel; 1992

WUNDERMAN
3 Columbus Cir, New York, NY 10019
Tel.: (212) 941-3000
Fax: (212) 627-8342
Web Site: www.wunderman.com

Year Founded: 1958

National Agency Associations: 4A's-ABC-APA-BPA-DMA-MCA

Agency Specializes In: Advertising, Alternative Advertising, Automotive, Branded Entertainment, Business-To-Business, Consumer Marketing, Direct Response Marketing, Direct-to-Consumer, E-Commerce, Electronic Media, Email, Event Planning & Marketing, Experience Design, Guerilla Marketing, Household Goods, Integrated Marketing, Internet/Web Design, Media Buying Services, Pharmaceutical, Promotions, Sales Promotion, Sponsorship, Sports Market, Strategic Planning/Research, Sweepstakes, Telemarketing, Viral/Buzz/Word of Mouth, Web (Banner Ads, Pop-ups, etc.)

Approx. Annual Billings: $1,065,000,000

Colby Webb *(CMO)*
Lincoln Bjorkman *(Chief Creative Officer-Global)*
Nelson Freitas *(Chief Strategy Officer)*
Toni Hess *(Chief Creative Officer)*
Seth Solomons *(CEO-North America)*
Brenda Fiala *(Exec VP-Strategy-Global)*
William J. Manfredi *(Exec VP-HR-Global)*
Jill Walker *(Sr VP & Dir-Client Svcs-Global)*
Andrew Sexton *(Sr VP-Press Rels)*
Josh Hilliard *(VP & Dir-Strategy-Team Land Rover)*
Joe McGlynn *(Head-New Bus-North America)*
Jeremy Kinder *(Grp Dir-Creative)*
Brian Madonna *(Dir-Talent Mgmt)*
James Basirico *(Assoc Dir-Creative)*
Josephine Chen *(Assoc Dir-Creative)*
Toni Iacano *(Assoc Dir-HR)*
Cristen Ingram *(Assoc Dir-Creative)*
Michael Loper *(Assoc Dir-Strategy)*
Akram Yacob *(Brand Mgr-Digital)*
Sualidy Cruz *(Mgr-Workflow)*
Olga Platonova *(Mgr-Talent Dev)*
Hayley Clark-Braverman *(Sr Strategist-Digital, Social, CRM & Content)*
Merritt Harper *(Assoc Acct Dir)*
Devon Jordan *(Assoc Acct Dir)*

Accounts:
Best Buy
Burger King Merchandising & Promotions
Citibank
The Coca-Cola Company
Coca-Cola Refreshments USA, Inc.
Colgate
Dell
Diageo Johnny Walker, Whisky
Ford Motor Company
Halo 4
Marriott
Microsoft Direct Marketing, Office 2010, Xbox 360
Nokia
Sabin Vaccine Institute Campaign: "END7"
Shell
United Airlines

New York, NY

Blast Radius
3 Columbus Cir, New York, NY 10019
(See Separate Listing)

Chicago, IL

DesignKitchen
1140 W Fulton Market, Chicago, IL 60607-1219
(See Separate Listing)

Wunderman Interactive
233 N Michigan Ave Ste 1500, Chicago, IL 60601-5519
Tel.: (312) 596-2500
Fax: (312) 596-2600
Web Site: www.wunderman.com

Agency Specializes In: Digital/Interactive

Rick Schreuder *(Pres)*
Peter Townsend *(Mng Dir & CEO-Burrows)*
Peter Law-Gisiko *(CFO)*
Lincoln Bjorkman *(Chief Creative Officer-Global)*
Mel Edwards *(CEO-Europe, Middle East & Africa)*
William J. Manfredi *(Exec VP-Global Talent Mgmt-Young & Rubicam Grp)*

Accounts:
Ford
Jaguar
Microsoft
Nokia
P&G

Wunderman
233 N Michigan Ave Ste 1500, Chicago, IL 60601-5519
Tel.: (312) 596-2500
Fax: (312) 596-2600
E-Mail: info@wunderman.com
Web Site: wunderman.com

Employees: 150

National Agency Associations: 4A's

Agency Specializes In: Direct Response Marketing, Information Technology, Planning & Consultation, Publicity/Promotions, Sales Promotion, Sponsorship

Rick Schreuder *(Pres)*
Keith Kizziah *(Sr VP & Grp Acct Dir)*
Scott Krueger *(Sr VP & Dir-Bus Dev)*
Dan Richlen *(VP & Acct Dir)*
Chris Tull *(VP-Branded Partnerships &*

Entertainment Mktg)
Sam Fitzgerald *(Dir-Art)*
Cassie Burnside *(Sr Acct Exec)*
Jennifer Bochnak *(Asst Acct Exec)*

Accounts:
Abbott
Burger King
COX Communications
Microsoft Computer Game, Motion Controlled Gaming System, Video Game
Mondelez International, Inc.
Nationwide
Novartis
Office Depot
Rogers
TimeWarner

Irvine, CA

Wunderman
2010 Main St Ste 400, Irvine, CA 92614
Tel.: (949) 754-2000
Fax: (949) 754-2001
E-Mail: info@wunderman.com
Web Site: www.wundermanwest.com

Employees: 80

National Agency Associations: 4A's

Agency Specializes In: Direct Response Marketing, Information Technology, Planning & Consultation, Publicity/Promotions, Sales Promotion

Jeff Browe *(COO & Dir-Client Svc-SoCal)*
Daniel Olson *(Mng Dir-Western Reg)*
Susie Lim *(VP & Creative Dir)*
Eaylna Rocha *(Art Buyer & Producer)*
Craig Evans *(Creative Dir)*
Drew Lewis *(Dir-New Media)*
Ben Peters *(Dir-Creative)*
John Turcios *(Dir-Integrated Art)*
Johanna Anderson *(Acct Supvr)*
Kevin Morton *(Acct Exec)*

Accounts:
Diageo
Ford
Microsoft
Mondelez International, Inc.
MSN
Nokia
Public Storage Play House

Miami, FL

Wunderman
Courvoisier Ctr II 601 Brickell Key Dr Ste 1100, Miami, FL 33131
Tel.: (305) 347-1900
Fax: (305) 347-1901
Web Site: wunderman.com

Employees: 30

National Agency Associations: 4A's

Agency Specializes In: Direct Response Marketing, Information Technology, Planning & Consultation, Publicity/Promotions, Sales Promotion

John Lynn *(CEO-Latin America)*

Accounts:
AT&T Communications Corp.
Colgate
Diageo
Microsoft
Natura
Nintendo
Nokia
Rogers
Time Warner

Richardson, TX

KBM Group
(Formerly KnowledgeBase Marketing, Inc.)
2050 N Greenville Ave, Richardson, TX 75082
Tel.: (972) 664-3600
Fax: (972) 664-3656
E-Mail: sales@kbmg.com
Web Site: www.kbmg.com/

Employees: 100

Gary S. Laben *(CEO)*
Andrew Rutberg *(Pres-Svcs-Global)*
Joe Brehm *(Exec VP-Data Svcs)*
Clark Wooten *(Sr VP & Head-Vertical Practice)*
Raelyn Wade *(Sr VP-Sls)*
Glenn Teitlus *(Sr Dir)*
Jeremy Dowdy *(Dir-Digital Strategy)*
Peggy Garner *(Dir-Mktg Comm)*

Seattle, WA

Possible
(Formerly ZAAZ)
414 Olive Way Ste 500, Seattle, WA 98101
Tel.: (206) 341-9885
Fax: (206) 749-9868
E-Mail: info@possible.com
Web Site: www.possible.com

Employees: 150

Agency Specializes In: Sponsorship

Gareth Jones *(Mng Dir)*
Jon McVey *(Chief Creative Officer-Portland)*
Adam Wolf *(CTO-Americas)*
Brian LeCount *(Exec VP-Strategy & Insights)*
Laurent Burman *(Sr VP & Acct Mgmt Dir)*
Beth Nouguier *(Sr VP-Acct-Portland)*
Josh Schmiesing *(Sr VP)*
Jon Dietrich *(Dir-Creative)*
John Georgopoulos *(Dir-Mktg Sciences)*
Shawn Herron *(Dir-Creative)*
Carrie Ingoglia *(Dir-Creative)*
Jennifer Southwell *(Dir-Bus Dev Ops-North America)*
Sean Weller *(Dir-Strategy)*
Lana Femiak *(Assoc Dir-Media Svcs)*
Erin Kelley *(Assoc Media Dir)*

Accounts:
Converse
Ford
Helio
InterContinental Hotels Group Crowne Plaza, Holiday Inn, Indigo, InterContinental, Social Media Strategy
Lonely Planet
Microsoft Campaign: "The Art of Touch", Surface Website
Morgans Hotel Group Website Development
National Geographic
Nike
PR Newswire
REI
Sony Electronics Web Sites; 2007
Tom's of Maine

Wunderman Seattle
221 Yale Ave N Ste 500, Seattle, WA 98109
Tel.: (206) 505-7500
Fax: (206) 505-7672
Web Site: wunderman.com

Employees: 300

Year Founded: 2004

National Agency Associations: 4A's

Michael Joseph *(VP & Client Svcs Dir)*
Krista Hale *(VP & Dir-HR-Global)*
Bonnie Preece *(VP-Global Insights & Optimization)*
Jeffrey Foster *(Head-Global Strategy, Sr Strategist & Planner)*
Dan Miller *(Grp Acct Dir)*
Jason Prew *(Grp Acct Dir)*
Belinda Leworthy *(Dir-Client Svcs-Global)*

Accounts:
Microsoft; Redmond, WA Campaign: "Break Down The Wall", Campaign: "Lync Test Drive", Direct Marketing, Office 2010, XBox 360
T-Mobile US

Washington, DC

Wunderman World Health
(Formerly RTC Relationship Marketing)
1055 Thomas Jefferson St NW # 200, Washington, DC 20007
(See Separate Listing)

Argentina

Wunderman
Pasaje Tupiza 3950 Capital, C1425AFB Buenos Aires, Argentina
Tel.: (54) 11 5777 8500
Fax: (54) 11 5777 8501
E-Mail: reception.buenosaires@wunderman.com
Web Site: wunderman.com

Employees: 190
Year Founded: 1992

Agency Specializes In: Direct Response Marketing, Information Technology, Planning & Consultation, Publicity/Promotions, Sales Promotion

Juan Pablo Jurado *(Pres)*
Jose Azanza Arias *(Exec Dir-Creative)*
Lucas Ortega *(Sr Dir-Creative-Latam Reg)*
Eliana Kaplan *(Grp Acct Dir)*
Matias Lobos Leon *(Dir-Art)*

Accounts:
Coca-Cola Campaign: "Car Incident, Interception, Intruder", Campaign: "Jealousy", Campaign: "Security Cams"
Ford
Nokia Campaign: "Destroy any Web Page!", Fruit Ninja & Angry Birds, Nokia N8

Australia

Wunderman
35 Clarence St, Sydney, NSW 2000 Australia
Mailing Address:
GPO Box 5402, Sydney, NSW 2001 Australia
Tel.: (61) 2 97761700
Fax: (61) 2 9778 7599
Web Site: http://www.wunderman.com/

Employees: 65
Year Founded: 1976

National Agency Associations: ADMA

Agency Specializes In: Direct Response Marketing, Information Technology, Planning & Consultation, Publicity/Promotions, Sales Promotion

Andrew Davie *(Mng Dir-Australia & New Zealand)*
Dom Hickey *(Head-Plng)*
Anna Karena *(Exec Creative Dir)*

Accounts:
Art Gallery Society NSW Campaign: "Portraits"
Coca-Cola
Ford
Microsoft Campaign: "Edge of the Internet", Windows 7
Nokia
Pringles
Schick
Vegemite
Weatherbeeta Campaign: "Dare To Be Dublin"
WWF Australia

Austria

Wunderman
Rotenturnstrasse 16 - 18, A 1010 Vienna, Austria
Tel.: (43) 1 533 58 58 0
Fax: (43) 1 533 58 58 480
Web Site: www.wundermanpxp.at

Employees: 14
Year Founded: 1986

Agency Specializes In: Direct Response Marketing, Information Technology, Planning & Consultation, Publicity/Promotions, Sales Promotion

Tom Krutt *(Chief Creative Officer)*
David Petermann *(Exec Dir-Creative)*
Torsten Michael Riefer *(Dir-Creative)*
Angelika Vater *(Sr Acct Mgr)*
Martina Mina Mekis *(Client Svc Dir)*

Accounts:
Austrian Airlines
Disney
DM-Drogerie Market S-he Stylezone
Euromillionen
FEH
Ford Motor Company Austria Campaign: "Ford G-Force"
Intermarket Bank
Microsoft
S Immobilien AG
SCA

Brazil

Wunderman
Av das Nacoes Unidas 14171-Torre B, CEP 04794-000 Sao Paulo, SP Brazil
Tel.: (55) 11 3026 5500
Fax: (55) 11 3026 5588
Web Site: www.wunderman.com

Employees: 18
Year Founded: 2000

Eduardo Bicudo *(Pres)*
Paulo Sanna *(VP & Exec Dir-Creative)*
Nancy Paez *(VP-Client & Media Svcs-Brazil)*
Bruno Almeida *(Sr Dir-Art)*
Luis Paulo Andrade *(Art Dir)*
Saulo Fusari *(Acct Dir)*
Rodrigo Cassino *(Dir-Production)*
Fabio Matiazzi *(Dir-Creative)*
Daniel Winter *(Dir-Customer Intelligence-Performance)*
Rafael Palermo *(Assoc Dir-Creative)*

Accounts:
BRF - Brasil Foods S.A.
Danone Actimel, Activia, Bottled Water, Campaign: "Augmented Carnaval", Campaign: "The Tweeting Fridge"
Federacao Paulista de Futebol Campaign: "Linesman for Peace"
Ford
Groupe Danone S.A.
Microsoft Campaign: "Chronicles of a PC"
The Procter & Gamble Company
Procto-Glyvenol
Sao Paulo's Football Federation Campaign: "Linesmen For Peace"
TAM Airlines Historic Luggage
Unilever N.V.
Vivo Campaign: "Patriotic Ball"

Canada

Wunderman
60 Bloor Street W Ste 800, Toronto, ON M4W 3Z1 Canada
Tel.: (416) 921-9050
Fax: (416) 961-0971
E-Mail: info@wunderman.ca
Web Site: http://wunderman.com/

Employees: 200

Agency Specializes In: Direct Response Marketing, Sales Promotion

Susan Moore *(COO & Exec VP)*
Kevin Flynn *(Sr VP & Dir-Strategy & Plng)*
Dave Stevenson *(VP & Sr Dir-Creative)*
Janet Mainprize *(VP & Dir-Media)*
Jeremy Marten *(Grp Acct Dir)*
Debra Grelik *(Acct Dir)*
Mitch Steinman *(Dir-Delivery Svcs)*
Trista Vincent *(Assoc Dir-Creative)*
Ken St. Germain *(Project Mgr-Digital)*

Chile

Wunderman
Avenida del Valle 961 Oficina 1707, Huechuraba, Santiago, Chile
Tel.: (56) 2 940 9910
Fax: (56) 2 232 7652
Web Site: www.wunderman.com

Employees: 37

Agency Specializes In: Direct Response Marketing, Information Technology, Media Buying Services, Media Planning, Planning & Consultation, Publicity/Promotions, Sales Promotion

Cristian Garcia *(Gen Mgr)*
Boris Rojas *(Editor-Creative)*
Mauricio Garcia *(Designer-Web)*

Accounts:
Skype

China

AGENDA
03-06 32F, 118 Connaight Road West, Hong Kong, China (Hong Kong)
Tel.: (852) 22983888
Fax: (852) 21446332
Web Site: www.wunderman.com.cn/

Employees: 250

National Agency Associations: ADMA

Agency Specializes In: Advertising, Consumer Goods, Consumer Marketing, Consumer Publications, Education, New Technologies, Production, Production (Print), Publishing, Real Estate

Mike Leung *(Mng Dir)*
Monica Fung *(Acct Dir)*
Yan Hui *(Acct Dir)*
Tracy Chow *(Assoc Dir-Creative)*
Takki Ma *(Assoc Dir-Creative-Social Media)*
Gwyneth Mak *(Assoc Acct Dir)*

Accounts:
Carrefour
Colgate China; 2008
DHL
Disney
GlaxoSmithKline Limited Creative, Print, Social Media, Television
Honda
Johnson & Johnson Acuvue, Bandaid, Clean 'n Clear, Johnson's Baby, OB
New-Kimberly-Clark (Hong Kong) Limited Campaign: "The Story of Softness", Digital, Kotex Softness
Microsoft Campaign: "Simply Play Faster"
Pepsi
Prudential
xBox 360

Wunderman Beijing
#502 Building 17 Jianwal SOHO 39 East 3rd Ring Road, Chao Yang District, Beijing, 100022 China
Tel.: (86) 10 5869 4575
Fax: (86) 10 5869 4670
Web Site: www.wunderman.com.cn

Employees: 120
Year Founded: 1998

Agency Specializes In: Direct Response Marketing, Information Technology, Publicity/Promotions, Sales Promotion

Chung-Tai Kung *(Mng Dir)*
Mike Leung *(Mng Dir)*
Chris Jones *(Exec Dir-Creative-China)*
Weng Justin *(Acct Dir)*
Miranda Kao *(Acct Dir)*
Miley Wang *(Sr Acct Mgr-CRM)*
Huaying Jiang *(Mgr-Data)*
Teresa Zhang *(Mgr-HR)*
Li Meng *(Acct Exec)*
Ellen Hu *(Assoc Acct Dir)*

Wunderman
Room 605-606 Ocean Tower, 550 Yan An Road East, Shanghai, 200001 China
Tel.: (86) 21 6351 8588
Fax: (86) 21 5116 4316
Web Site: www.wunderman.com.cn

Employees: 57
Year Founded: 1998

Bryce Whitwam *(Mng Dir-Shanghai)*
Mark Miller *(Head-Plng)*
Chris Jones *(Exec Dir-Creative China)*
Fiona Wang *(Sr Acct Dir)*
Cecil Chua *(Bus Dir-CRM)*
Weng Justin *(Acct Dir)*
Miranda Kao *(Acct Dir)*
Ashley Ouyang *(Dir-Bus Dev)*
Sindy Shen *(Sr Mgr-HR)*
Vicki Feng *(Acct Mgr)*

Accounts:
Diageo
Entel PCS
Ford
Microsoft
Movistar
MTN
Nike
Nokia
Qoros Digital, Qoros 3 sedan
Schick Campaign: "The Ultimate Battle"
Sunrise
Tao On The Road (Integrated Communications Agency of Record) Creative, Digital, Strategy

Wunderman
Room 04-06 31/f Onelink Center, No. 230-232 Tianhe Road, Guangzhou, 510630 China
Tel.: (86) 20 2863 3338
Fax: (86) 20 2863 3339
E-Mail: k2.kung@wunderman.com
Web Site: www.wunderman.com.cn

Year Founded: 2000

Chung Tai Kung *(Mng Dir)*
Mike Leung *(Mng Dir)*
A. P. Lin *(Mng Dir)*
Laura Cheng *(VP-HR-China)*
Kevin Zhu *(Grp Dir-Creative)*
Stephanie Ji *(Sr Acct Dir)*
Miranda Kao *(Acct Dir)*
Ellen Hu *(Assoc Acct Dir)*

Czech Republic

Wunderman
Nadrazni 32, 150 00 Prague, 5 Czech Republic
Tel.: (420) 2 21 420 130
Fax: (420) 2 21 420 132
E-Mail: info@wunderman.cz
Web Site: www.wunderman.cz

Agency Specializes In: Direct Response Marketing, Information Technology, Publicity/Promotions, Sales Promotion

Eva Basl *(Grp Head-Creative)*
Evzen Drtina *(Gen Mgr)*
Vladimir Rejlek *(Dir-Interactive)*
Richard Stiebitz *(Dir-Creative)*

Accounts:
Citibank
Czech Railways Campaign: "Lets Meet Aliens"
Ford Motor Company, s.r.o. Campaign: "Do it Yourself"
ING
Microsoft
MTC
Nokia
Nutricia
Pedigree
Unilever
Vichy

Denmark

AdPeople Worldwide
Per Henrik Lings Alle 4, DK-2100 Copenhagen, Denmark
Tel.: (45) 33445100
E-Mail: info@adpeople.com
Web Site: www.adpeople.com

Year Founded: 1999

Agency Specializes In: Advertising

Simon Hjorth *(Mng Dir-North America)*
Michel Mommejat *(Mng Dir-Asia Pacific)*
Steve Miller *(Exec Dir-Creative)*
Claus Mollebro *(Dir-Creative)*

Accounts:
Copenhagen Airport
Dell A/S
Jabra
Livslinien Denmark Suicide Helpline
Novozymes A/S
Psychiatric Health Fund Campaign: "Drugs"
Rockwool A/S

Wunderman Helsinki
Koydenpunojankatu 2 a D, 00180 Helsinki, Finland
Tel.: (358) 20 7300 230
Fax: (358) 20 7300 233
E-Mail: helsinki@wunderman.com
Web Site: www.yrbrands.fi

Employees: 24
Year Founded: 1940

Agency Specializes In: Above-the-Line, Advertising, Advertising Specialties, Affiliate Marketing, Affluent Market, African-American Market, Agriculture, Alternative Advertising, Arts, Asian Market, Automotive, Aviation & Aerospace, Below-the-Line, Bilingual Market, Brand Development & Integration, Branded Entertainment, Broadcast, Business Publications, Business-To-Business, Cable T.V., Catalogs, Children's Market, Co-op Advertising, Collateral, College, Commercial Photography, Communications, Computers & Software, Consulting, Consumer Goods, Consumer Marketing, Consumer Publications, Content, Corporate Communications, Corporate Identity, Cosmetics, Crisis Communications, Custom Publishing, Customer Relationship Management, Digital/Interactive, Direct Response Marketing, Direct-to-Consumer, E-Commerce, Education, Electronic Media, Electronics, Email, Engineering, Entertainment, Environmental, Event Planning & Marketing, Exhibit/Trade Shows, Experience Design, Fashion/Apparel, Financial, Food Service, Game Integration, Gay & Lesbian Market, Government/Political, Graphic Design, Guerilla Marketing, Health Care Services, High Technology, Hispanic Market, Hospitality, Household Goods, Identity Marketing, In-Store Advertising, Industrial, Infomercials, Information Technology, Integrated Marketing, International, Internet/Web Design, Investor Relations, Legal Services, Leisure, Local Marketing, Logo & Package Design, Luxury Products, Magazines, Marine, Market Research, Media Buying Services, Media Planning, Media Relations, Media Training, Medical Products, Men's Market, Merchandising, Mobile Marketing, Multicultural, Multimedia, New Product Development, New Technologies, Newspaper, Newspapers & Magazines, Out-of-Home Media, Outdoor, Over-50 Market, Package Design, Paid Searches, Pharmaceutical, Planning & Consultation, Podcasting, Point of Purchase, Point of Sale, Print, Product Placement, Production, Production (Ad, Film, Broadcast), Production (Print), Promotions, Public Relations, Publicity/Promotions, Publishing, RSS (Really Simple Syndication), Radio, Real Estate, Recruitment, Regional, Restaurant, Retail, Sales Promotion, Search Engine Optimization, Seniors' Market, Social Marketing/Nonprofit, Sponsorship, Sports Market, Stakeholders, Strategic Planning/Research, Sweepstakes, Syndication, T.V., Technical Advertising, Teen Market, Telemarketing, Trade & Consumer Magazines, Transportation, Travel & Tourism, Urban Market, Viral/Buzz/Word of Mouth, Web (Banner Ads, Pop-ups, etc.), Women's Market, Yellow Pages Advertising

Henri Kingo *(Mng Dir)*
Jarkko Nieminen *(CFO)*
Aki Ronkainen *(Dir-Sls)*

Wunderman
Strandboulevarden 122 4, DK-2100 Copenhagen, Denmark
Tel.: (45) 3288 7777
Fax: (45) 3288 7788
E-Mail: info@wunderman.dk
Web Site: www.wunderman.dk

Employees: 80
Year Founded: 1976

Agency Specializes In: Direct Response Marketing, Information Technology, Sales Promotion

Beth Larsen *(Acct Dir)*
Immad Shahid *(Client Svc Dir)*
Mads Toft *(Client Svc Dir)*

Accounts:
Ford Scandinavia

France

Wunderman
57 avenue Andre Morizet, 92513 Boulogne-Billancourt, Cedex France
Tel.: (33) 1 46 84 34 22
Fax: (33) 1 46 84 32 72
E-Mail: info@wunderman.com
Web Site: www.wunderman.fr

Employees: 125
Year Founded: 1976

Agency Specializes In: Direct Response Marketing, Information Technology, Planning & Consultation, Publicity/Promotions, Sales Promotion

Brigitte Ralle *(CFO & Sr VP-Fin)*
Philippe Bonnet *(CEO-France)*
Jean-Benoit Bataille *(VP-Data & Analytics)*
Xavier Modin *(Head-Strategy)*
Sandrine Sainson *(Grp Acct Dir)*
Gaia Brunoni *(Acct Dir)*
Lobke Fric *(Acct Dir)*

Accounts:
Danone
Ibis
ITM Enterprises
Nokia Campaign: "Cineday", Campaign: "Les Inshootables"

Germany

facts & fiction GmbH
Anna-Schneider-Steig 2 Rheinauhafen, D-50678 Cologne, Germany
Tel.: (49) 221 95 15 30 0
Fax: (49) 221 95 15 30 22
E-Mail: info@factsfiction.de
Web Site: www.factsfiction.de

Employees: 40
Year Founded: 1992

Agency Specializes In: Consumer Marketing, Information Technology, Planning & Consultation

Kira Brucksch *(Head-New Bus)*
Anke Frei *(Head-HR)*
Andrea Manthey *(Head-PR)*
Philipp Dorendorf *(Dir-Creative)*
Patrizia Widritzki *(Dir-Art)*

Accounts:
ABB
Accenture Services
Bayer
Canon
Ford Bank
German Railway
Goethe-Institut Campaign: "Fairy-Tale"
Intel
Lufthansa
Xerox

Wunderman
Kleyerstrasse 19, 60326 Frankfurt am Main, Germany

Tel.: (49) 69 7502 701
Fax: (49) 69 7506 1430
E-Mail: wunderman-frankfurt.reception@wunderman.com
Web Site: www.wunderman.com

Employees: 143

Agency Specializes In: Consumer Marketing, Direct Response Marketing, Information Technology, Planning & Consultation, Publicity/Promotions, Sales Promotion

Klaus Weigand *(Mng Partner & CTO)*
Wolfgang Haf *(CMO-EMEA)*

Accounts:
Accenture
Airtours Campaign: "The Princess and the Pea", Campaign: "Work Less, Travel More"
Alzheimer Forschung Initiative
Arcor
Citibank
Deutsche Bank Campaign: "2041 Will Be Expensive", Campaign: "When reading is painful"
Deutsche Lufthansa Campaign: "Welcome to the Spray"
Fahrschule Heinze
Fraport
General Electric
Hoerbar Campaign: "Look if you can hear"
Kartell Campaign: "Get pierced for 39", Piercing & Tattoos
Klangkontor Campaign: "We are the music"
KUKA KUKAnizer, Robotics
Lotto Hessen
Lufthansa Campaign: "Molvan an Hairline", Campaign: "Time-Travel to your Birthday", Campaign: "Welcome to the Spray!", Direct Marketing
Microsoft
Monster
Wer Liefert Was?
Xerox

Hungary

Wunderman
Alkotas u 53 C epulet, MOM park, H-1123 Budapest, Hungary
Tel.: (36) 1 801 7500
Fax: (36) 1 801 7501
E-Mail: info@yr.hu
Web Site: wunderman.com

Employees: 23

Agency Specializes In: Direct Response Marketing, Sales Promotion

Philippe Bonnet *(CEO-France)*
Laszlo Forras *(Head-Creative Svcs)*
Attila Banki *(Dir-Digital & Client Svc Dir)*
Orsolya Orban *(Acct Mgr-Digital)*

Accounts:
Colgate
Danette
Danone
Ford
LG
MNV
MVM
Magyar Posta
Palmolive
Pannon
Premier Outlets
Rayfeyssan Bank
Rexona Dusseldorf

India

Rediffusion Wunderman
Building No 9A 4th Floor DLF Cyber City, Phase III, Gurgaon Haryana, New Delhi, 122 002 India
Tel.: (91) 124 4609 000
Fax: (91) 11 614 3241
Web Site: www.wundermanindia.com

Agency Specializes In: Digital/Interactive, Direct Response Marketing, Event Planning & Marketing, Sales Promotion, Strategic Planning/Research

Ajay Gupta *(Partner-Natl Brand)*
Dinanath Rewatkar *(Partner-Strategic Plng)*
Manoj Mansukhani *(Mng Dir-Ops-India)*
Vinay Kumar *(VP)*
Madhumita Mukherjee *(VP & Branch Head)*
Sudhir Thomas Bhengra *(Head-Art & Creative)*
Subhojit Dasgupta *(Head-CRM Strategy)*
Ravindra Pamadi *(Gen Mgr-Fin)*
Smriti Achuthan *(Acct Dir)*
Shyamoli Maniar *(Project Exec)*

Accounts:
Biba Creative, Media, Print

Italy

Wunderman
Via Tortona 37, 20144 Milan, Italy
Tel.: (39) 02 76 05 21 00
Fax: (39) 02 76 00 52 33
E-Mail: info@wunderman.it
Web Site: wunderman.com

Year Founded: 1992

Agency Specializes In: Communications, Consumer Marketing, Direct Response Marketing, Information Technology, Planning & Consultation, Publicity/Promotions, Sales Promotion

Laura Conti *(Gen Mgr)*
Enrico Spinetta *(Dir-Creative)*
Lorenzo Salemme *(Mgr-Interactive)*
Marco Tosti *(Mgr-Digital & Social Media)*
Federico Castelli *(Supvr-Creative)*
Daniele Chieregato *(Strategist-Brand & Engagement)*
Angelo Germano *(Designer-Web)*
Sergio Albanese *(Jr Producer-Digital)*

Accounts:
Citi Group
City of Scaldasole
Ford Mazda
Heineken
New-Jaguar Land Rover Campaign: "WeDefender"
Microsoft
Unilever
Xerox

Japan

Wunderman
San Marino Shiodome 2-4-1 Higashi-shimbashi, Minato-ku, Tokyo, 105-0021 Japan
Tel.: (81) 3 6430 8030
Fax: (81) 3 6430 8002
Web Site: wunderman.com

Agency Specializes In: Direct Response Marketing, Information Technology, Planning & Consultation, Publicity/Promotions, Sales Promotion

Antony Cundy *(Pres)*
Yoskiaki Suzuki *(Grp Acct Dir)*
Hiroyuki Asai *(Acct Dir)*
Saiko Hiraide *(Acct Dir)*
Elina Shima *(Art Dir)*
Kei Yashiro *(Creative Dir)*
Yoshihiro Murata *(Dir-Div)*
Yoshie Toriya *(Dir-Data & CRM Strategy)*
Shinako Tamegai *(Acct Exec)*
Tomohiko Ohmura *(Sr Grp Acct Dir)*

Accounts:
New-Microsoft

Korea

Wunderman Korea
9F Bosung Bldg 891-25, Daechi-dong Gangman-gu, Seoul, 135-840 Korea (South)
Tel.: (82) 2 531 9600
Fax: (82) 2 531 9600
Web Site: wunderman.com/

Employees: 20

Steven Koh *(Mng Dir)*
Seunghee Hahn *(Grp Acct Dir)*
Seo Sonya *(Acct Mgr)*
Minjoo Lee *(Sr Acct Exec)*

Accounts:
Burger King Offline, Online
Diageo
KT
Microsoft Korea
Nokia

Mexico

crossmedia
Benjamin Franklin 190, Col Condesa CP, 11800 Mexico, Mexico
Tel.: (52) 55 5278 2000
Web Site: www.crossmedia.com.mx

Employees: 120

Agency Specializes In: Digital/Interactive, Sponsorship

Jon Yuson *(Head-Acct & Assoc Dir)*
Toluwalope Okeowo *(Supvr-Media)*

Accounts:
Grupo Bimbo
Premier Exhibitions Media Planning & Buying

New Zealand

Y&R
(Formerly Wunderman)
Level 4 Corner Augustus Terrace & Parnell Rise, Parnell, Auckland, New Zealand
Tel.: (64) 9 308 5444
Fax: (64) 9 308 5359
Web Site: www.yr.com

Employees: 50

Agency Specializes In: Direct Response Marketing, Information Technology, Planning & Consultation, Publicity/Promotions, Sales Promotion

Grant Maxwell *(Gen Mgr)*
Josh Moore *(Exec Dir-Creative)*
Guy Denniston *(Creative Dir)*
Claire Dooney *(Acct Dir)*
Seymour Pope *(Creative Dir)*
Gavin Siakimotu *(Creative Dir)*
Tom Paine *(Assoc Dir-Creative)*
Mel Cutfield *(Acct Mgr)*
Nic Winslade *(Planner-Brand & Content)*
Carlos Savage *(Assoc Creative Dir)*

Accounts:

Animates Campaign: "Doomsday"
Arnott's Campaign: "Distraction"
Avis Budget Left Hand Radio
Beds R Us Campaign: "Flat Cat Lullaby"
Blunt Umbrellas
Brake Campaign: "Living Memories"
New-Burger king
Co-operative Bank Campaign: "Profits", Campaign: "Record Profit", Logo, USP, Visual Identity, Website
The Earthquake Commission Campaign: "Fix. Fasten. Don't Forget", Campaign: "Valuables"
Edgewell Campaign: "The Schibliminizer", Schick, WHAT EMMA SEES
Icebreaker Campaign: "NZ Lucky Dip", Campaign: "Sheep"
New-Jaguar
Land Rover
MetService Campaign: "Weather to Wake"
Red Cross
Resene Campaign: "Colour Dj"
Sea Shepherd Campaign: "For The Ocean"
The Tomorrow Project Standard Drink, Standard Glass
Tuatara Brewery Campaign: "All Blacks DIY Jersey"
York Street Mechanics Campaign: "Dan"

Poland

Wunderman

ul Dobra 56/66, 00-312 Warsaw, Poland
Tel.: (48) 22 552 7000
Fax: (48) 22 552 7001
Web Site: wunderman.com

Agency Specializes In: Direct Response Marketing, Information Technology, Planning & Consultation, Publicity/Promotions, Sales Promotion

Piotr Chrobot *(Exec Dir-Creative)*
Bartosz Pinski *(Sr Strategist-Digital)*

Accounts:
Nokia Campaign: "Copter", Campaign: "Finger Battle App", Lumia

Portugal

Wunderman

Avenidas Eng Duarte Pacheco Amoreiras Torre 1 9th Fl, 1070-101 Lisbon, Portugal
Tel.: (351) 21 722 7500
Fax: (351) 21 727 3147
Web Site: wunderman.com

Year Founded: 1992

Agency Specializes In: Direct Response Marketing, Information Technology, Planning & Consultation, Sales Promotion

Jorge Castanheira *(Mng Dir)*
Olga Orfao *(Acct Dir)*
Luis Coelho *(Dir-Creative)*
Miguel Figueiredo *(Dir-Production)*
Raquel Goncalves *(Dir-Strategic Plng)*
Nuno Moreno *(Dir-Tech & Dev)*

Accounts:
Beiersdorf Eucerin, Nivea
Entel PCS
Ford Campaign: "Looking for Champions"
Microsoft
Movistar
MTN
Nike
Nokia
Sunrise

Singapore

Wunderman

50 Scotts Road #03-01, Singapore, 228242 Singapore
Tel.: (65) 6671 3131
Fax: (65) 6671 3135
Web Site: wunderman.com

Employees: 25

Agency Specializes In: Direct Response Marketing, Information Technology, Planning & Consultation, Publicity/Promotions, Sales Promotion

Nimesh Desal *(Mng Dir-Southeast Asia)*
Steven Power *(Gen Mgr)*
Keith Ta *(Exec Dir-Creative-Southeast Asia)*
Bobby Tay *(Dir-Art)*
Allan Zhang *(Dir-Art)*
Nicholas Chia *(Copywriter)*

Accounts:
adidas (Social Media Agency of Record)
Lien Aid
Nokia
Pfizer Consumer Healthcare Caltrate, Centrium

Republic of South Africa

Wunderman Direct

102 Western Service Road, Gallo manor Ext 6, 2052 Johannesburg, South Africa
Tel.: (27) 11 797 9900
Fax: (27) 11 797 9922
Web Site: wunderman.com/

Employees: 43

Agency Specializes In: Direct Response Marketing, Information Technology, Planning & Consultation, Publicity/Promotions, Sales Promotion

Peter Townsend *(Mng Dir & CEO-Burrows)*
Sarita Mans *(Dir-CRM)*

Accounts:
Hollart
Microsoft

Spain

Wunderman

Avenida de Burgos 21, Complejo Triada Torre C 11th Fl, 28036 Madrid, Spain
Tel.: (34) 917 684 400
Fax: (34) 917 668 424
Web Site: www.wunderman.es

Year Founded: 1986

Agency Specializes In: Direct Response Marketing, Internet/Web Design, Planning & Consultation, Point of Purchase, Point of Sale, Print, Production, Telemarketing

Andres Narvaez *(Pres-Southern Europe & Spain)*
Mayte Ruiz De Velasco *(Gen Dir)*
Oscar Ibanez *(Acct Dir)*
Barbara Gras Medina *(Acct Dir)*
Nacho Gallego *(Dir-Art)*
Adrian Rios San Cristobal *(Dir-Art)*
Mercedes Minguez *(Acct Mgr)*
Gonzalo Lopez Serantes *(Mgr-Digital Analytics Strategy & Innovation)*

Switzerland

Wunderman

Hardturmstrasse 133, Postfach, CH-8037 Zurich, Switzerland
Tel.: (41) 1 444 1511
Fax: (41) 1 444 1533
E-Mail: info@wunderman.ch
Web Site: www.wunderman.ch

Employees: 14
Year Founded: 1986

Agency Specializes In: Advertising, Communications

Renato Di Rubbo *(Mng Dir)*
Markus Gut *(Chief Creative Officer)*
Thomas Engeli *(Exec Dir-Creative)*

Accounts:
Basler Versicherungen
DHL
EKZ
Ford Fiesta
IKEA
Maison de la France
Microsoft
Orange
Phonak Campaign: "Hearing is Seeing", Campaign: "Hearing tests"
The Phone House
Reporters Without Borders Campaign: "Mixed up news"
Ringier
Schweizerische Bundesbahn SBB
Siemens
SonntagsZeitung
Sonova
Tele

United Kingdom

Burrows Shenfield

The Burrows Building 5 Rayleigh Road, Shenfield, Brentwood, Essex CM13 1AB United Kingdom
Tel.: (44) 1277 246 666
Fax: (44) 1277 246 777
E-Mail: burrows_uk@burrows.yr.com
Web Site: www.burrows.info

Employees: 150

Agency Specializes In: Direct Response Marketing, Sales Promotion

Peter Townsend *(CEO & Mng Dir)*
Richard Wright *(COO & Head-Ops)*
Daryl Wright *(Head-Bus Strategy-Burrows Mktg Comm)*
Tom Barber *(Producer-Digital)*
Mike Simpson *(Producer-Digital)*
Nigel Hall *(Dir-Tech & VFX-CGI)*
Robin Lowry *(Dir-CGI Creative)*
Claire Batey *(Sr Acct Mgr)*
Jennie Ward *(Project Mgr-Digital)*
Gary West *(Mgr-IT)*

Accounts:
Ford
Mazda
Volvo

Wunderman Interactive

Greater London House Hampstead Road, London, NW1 7QP United Kingdom
Tel.: (44) 20 7611 6333
Fax: (44) 20 7611 6668
E-Mail: info@wunderman.com
Web Site: wunderman.com

Employees: 250

Agency Specializes In: Digital/Interactive

Mel Cruickshank *(CEO)*
Pip Hulbert *(Mng Partner & Head-Shell Global Client)*
Peter Townsend *(Mng Dir & CEO-Burrows)*
Matt Batten *(Chief Creative Officer)*
Josette James *(Sr VP & Acct Mgmt Dir)*
Marc Blaskey *(Bus Dir)*
Caspian Rabone *(Dir-Creative-Global)*
William Rolt *(Dir-New Bus)*
Kevin Mercer *(Strategist)*

Accounts:
Ford
Microsoft
Nike
Nokia

Wunderman

Greater London House, Hampstead Rd 3rd Fl, London, NW1 7QP United Kingdom
Tel.: (44) 207 611 6333
Fax: (44) 20 7611 6668
E-Mail: info@wunderman.com
Web Site: www.wunderman.com

Employees: 250

Agency Specializes In: Direct Response Marketing, Sales Promotion

Matt Batten *(Chief Creative Officer)*
Richard Dunn *(Chief Strategy Officer-UK & EMEA)*
Mel Edwards *(Chm-UK & CEO-Europe, Middle East & Africa)*
Mark Read *(CEO-Global)*
Caspian Rabone *(Grp Head & Creative Dir)*
Kiran Mudhar *(Acct Dir)*
Lauren Pleydell-Pearce *(Creative Dir)*
Annie Gass *(Dir-Strategy)*
Paula Joannou *(Dir-HR)*
Marcus Reynolds *(Dir-Strategy)*
Lezaan Roos *(Dir-Strategy)*
Anna-Maria Teemant *(Acct Exec)*
Kevin Guild *(Designer)*

Accounts:
Childhood Eye Cancer Trust Advertising, Social
Citi
EDF Energy Below-the-Line, Campaign: "Proud to Bring Zingy to the Party", Direct Marketing
Ford Digital, ECOnetic Cars
GlaxoSmithKline (Lead Agency) Global Digital Advertising
New-Ikea
Jaguar
Legal & General Creative, Media
Microsoft Campaign: "At Microsoft, your Privacy is Our Priority", Digital, OOH, Print, TV
Xbox Creative
Nokia Campaign: "Consumer Qwerty", Campaign: "don't flash. Amaze"
Novartis International AG
Shell Global CRM
Sun Bingo Social Media
New-Times Newspapers Ltd.

WUNDERMAN WORLD HEALTH

(Formerly RTC Relationship Marketing)
1055 Thomas Jefferson St NW # 200, Washington, DC 20007
Tel.: (202) 625-2111
Fax: (202) 424-7900
Web Site: wunderman.com/health

Employees: 141
Year Founded: 1967

National Agency Associations: DMA

Agency Specializes In: Advertising, Advertising Specialties, Affluent Market, Automotive, Broadcast, Business-To-Business, Cable T.V., Collateral, Communications, Consumer Marketing, Customer Relationship Management, Digital/Interactive, Direct Response Marketing, Direct-to-Consumer, E-Commerce, Email, Financial, Health Care Services, High Technology, Integrated Marketing, Internet/Web Design, Men's Market, New Technologies, Over-50 Market, Paid Searches, Pharmaceutical, Planning & Consultation, Print, Production (Print), Radio, Search Engine Optimization, Seniors' Market, Social Marketing/Nonprofit, Social Media, Sponsorship, Strategic Planning/Research, T.V., Viral/Buzz/Word of Mouth, Women's Market

Maureen Quattrocki *(CFO & Exec VP)*
John Reid *(Chief Creative Officer & Exec VP)*
Jeffrey Ross *(Pres/CEO-RTC Wunderman)*
Kevin McMonagle *(VP & Creative Dir)*
Sara Collis *(VP & Dir-Insights & Innovation)*
Nathan Gomez *(Sr Dir-Interactive Art)*
Lindsay Lam *(Assoc Dir-Strategy, Insights & Innovation)*
Katherine Piscatelli *(Acct Supvr)*
Hushmath Alam *(Sr Acct Exec)*
Adeline Heymann *(Sr Strategist-Digital-Insights & Innovation)*

Accounts:
AARP AARP Health Care Options
Abbott Diabetes Care
Abbott Laboratories
Biogen Idec
Eli Lilly
Johnson & Johnson
Novo Nordisk
Pfizer Prevnar
Procter & Gamble
Sunovion
Windstream

WWDB INTEGRATED MARKETING

412 SE 13th St, Fort Lauderdale, FL 33316
Tel.: (954) 922-4332
Fax: (954) 923-0126
E-Mail: manny@whatwedobest.com
Web Site: www.whatwedobest.com

Employees: 3
Year Founded: 2010

Agency Specializes In: Above-the-Line, Advertising, Advertising Specialties, Affluent Market, Alternative Advertising, Arts, Automotive, Aviation & Aerospace, Below-the-Line, Bilingual Market, Brand Development & Integration, Branded Entertainment, Broadcast, Business Publications, Business-To-Business, Cable T.V., Catalogs, Children's Market, Co-op Advertising, Collateral, College, Commercial Photography, Communications, Computers & Software, Consulting, Consumer Goods, Consumer Marketing, Consumer Publications, Content, Corporate Communications, Corporate Identity, Cosmetics, Custom Publishing, Customer Relationship Management, Digital/Interactive, Direct Response Marketing, Direct-to-Consumer, E-Commerce, Education, Electronic Media, Electronics, Email, Engineering, Entertainment, Environmental, Event Planning & Marketing, Exhibit/Trade Shows, Experience Design, Faith Based, Fashion/Apparel, Financial, Food Service, Gay & Lesbian Market, Government/Political, Graphic Design, Guerilla Marketing, Health Care Services, High Technology, Hispanic Market, Hospitality, Household Goods, Identity Marketing, In-Store Advertising, Industrial, Infomercials, Information Technology, Integrated Marketing, International, Internet/Web Design, Investor Relations, Legal Services, Leisure, Local Marketing, Logo & Package Design, Luxury Products, Magazines, Marine, Market Research, Media Buying Services, Media Planning, Media Relations, Media Training, Medical Products, Men's Market, Mobile Marketing, Multicultural, Multimedia, New Product Development, New Technologies, Newspaper, Newspapers & Magazines, Out-of-Home Media, Outdoor, Over-50 Market, Package Design, Paid Searches, Pets , Pharmaceutical, Planning & Consultation, Podcasting, Point of Purchase, Point of Sale, Print, Product Placement, Production, Production (Ad, Film, Broadcast), Production (Print), Promotions, Public Relations, Publicity/Promotions, Publishing, RSS (Really Simple Syndication), Radio, Real Estate, Recruitment, Regional, Restaurant, Retail, Sales Promotion, Search Engine Optimization, Seniors' Market, Social Marketing/Nonprofit, Social Media, Sponsorship, Sports Market, Strategic Planning/Research, Sweepstakes, T.V., Technical Advertising, Teen Market, Telemarketing, Trade & Consumer Magazines, Transportation, Travel & Tourism, Tween Market, Urban Market, Viral/Buzz/Word of Mouth, Web (Banner Ads, Pop-ups, etc.), Women's Market, Yellow Pages Advertising

Approx. Annual Billings: $750,000

Breakdown of Gross Billings by Media: Corp. Communications: 5%; Graphic Design: 20%; Internet Adv.: 10%; Local Mktg.: 35%; Logo & Package Design: 10%; Radio & T.V.: 5%; Worldwide Web Sites: 15%

Manny Salomon *(Principal)*

WYSE

668 Euclid Ave, Cleveland, OH 44114
Tel.: (216) 696-2424
Fax: (216) 736-4425
E-Mail: info@wyseadv.com
Web Site: www.wyseadvertising.com

E-Mail for Key Personnel:
President: mmarino@wyseadv.com
Creative Dir.: shinman@wyseadv.com

Employees: 60
Year Founded: 1951

National Agency Associations: 4A's-ABC-BPA-INBA-LIAN

Agency Specializes In: Above-the-Line, Advertising, Automotive, Below-the-Line, Brand Development & Integration, Broadcast, Business Publications, Business-To-Business, Cable T.V., Collateral, Communications, Consumer Goods, Consumer Marketing, Consumer Publications, Corporate Communications, Corporate Identity, Direct Response Marketing, Direct-to-Consumer, Email, Engineering, Environmental, Exhibit/Trade Shows, Graphic Design, Health Care Services, Hospitality, Identity Marketing, In-Store Advertising, Industrial, Integrated Marketing, International, Internet/Web Design, Leisure, Local Marketing, Logo & Package Design, Magazines, Market Research, Media Buying Services, Media Planning, Medical Products, Merchandising, Multimedia, New Product Development, Newspaper, Newspapers & Magazines, Out-of-Home Media, Outdoor, Package Design, Planning & Consultation, Point of Purchase, Point of Sale, Print, Production, Promotions, Public Relations, Radio, Regional, Restaurant, Retail, Sales Promotion, Social Marketing/Nonprofit, Sponsorship, Strategic Planning/Research, T.V., Technical Advertising, Teen Market, Trade & Consumer Magazines, Transportation, Travel & Tourism, Urban Market

Approx. Annual Billings: $144,000,000

Breakdown of Gross Billings by Media: Cable T.V.: 21%; D.M.: 2%; Event Mktg.: 2%; Internet Adv.: 4%; Network T.V.: 4%; Newsp.: 6%; Other: 2%; Outdoor: 1%; Spot Radio: 8%; Spot T.V.: 28%;

Trade & Consumer Mags.: 22%

Michael C. Marino *(CEO)*
Julie Telesz *(VP & Acct Dir)*
Terry Tichy *(VP-Production)*
Cathy Wolf *(Dir-Art)*
Patricia Zivich *(Dir-Integrated Production)*
Lane Strauss *(Assoc Dir-Creative)*
Morgan Schreiber *(Acct Supvr)*
Christian Turner *(Acct Supvr)*
Karen Hudock *(Supvr-Media)*
Laura Fejzoski *(Acct Exec)*
Marie Guzowski *(Acct Exec)*
Jeff Nomina *(Media Planner)*
Tom Okal *(Copywriter)*

Accounts:
ANCO Wiper Blades
Brooklyn Animal Care and Control Campaign: "Lulu"
Champion Spark Plug
Cleveland Clinic Foundation; Cleveland, OH Medical Care
Cleveland State University (Agency of Record) Creative, Direct Marketing, Marketing, Media Planning, Mobile Marketing, Production, Radio, Social Media, Television
Dirt Devil
GOJO Industries Purell
J.M. Smucker Company; Orrville, OH Hungry Jack; 2006
Kelly Services, Inc.; Troy, MI Temporary Employment Firm; 1995
Marathon Petroleum; Findlay, OH; 2004
Mead Westvaco Health Insurance; 2000
Meineke Car Care Centers; Charlotte, NC Lead Creative Agency, Media Planning; 2008
Moen Incorporated; North Olmsted, OH Moen Faucets, ShowHouse by Moen; 2006
National City Bank; Cleveland, OH; 2002
Western Star; Willoughby, OH Premium Heavy-Duty Truck Manufacturer; 2001
Wyndham Vacation Ownership; Orlando, FL
Wyndham Worldwide Corporation

XACTA ADVERTISING

1109 Inverness Dr, Lake Charles, LA 70605
Tel.: (337) 274-7636
Fax: (337) 513-4446
E-Mail: info@xactaadvertising.com
Web Site: www.xactaadvertising.com

Year Founded: 2011

Agency Specializes In: Advertising, Brand Development & Integration, Event Planning & Marketing, Logo & Package Design, Media Buying Services, Media Planning, Outdoor, Print, Promotions, Radio

Lisa D. Sonnier *(Pres & Dir-Creative)*
Justin Lopez *(Media Planner)*

Accounts:
ABA Mavericks
Frontier Shows
Southwest District Livestock Show & Rodeo

XIIK

1801 Century Park E Ste 2400, Los Angeles, CA 90067
Tel.: (310) 746-5684
Fax: (800) 420-2840
E-Mail: la@xiik.com
Web Site: www.xiik.com

Year Founded: 2008

Agency Specializes In: Advertising, Brand Development & Integration, Collateral, Digital/Interactive, Graphic Design, Internet/Web Design, Logo & Package Design, Market Research, Search Engine Optimization, Social Media

Topher Overstreet *(Founder & Pres)*
Barrett Crites *(Client Svcs Dir)*
Leslie Lewis *(Sr Acct Mgr)*
Christopher Maikish *(Acct Mgr)*
Christopher Newgent *(Assoc Creative Dir-Copy)*

Accounts:
National Renewables Cooperative Organization

XL ALLIANCE

122 W 27th St 12th Fl, New York, NY 10001
Tel.: (646) 380-8747
E-Mail: info@xlalliance.com
Web Site: www.xlalliance.com

Year Founded: 2009

Agency Specializes In: Advertising, Branded Entertainment, Digital/Interactive

Liliana Gil Valletta *(Co-Founder & Mng Partner)*
Enrique Arbelaez *(Co-Founder & Chief Innovation Officer)*
Armando L. Martin *(Principal)*
Carlos Macias *(Sr Acct Mgr-Strategic)*
Stephanie Zapata *(Sr Acct Mgr)*

Accounts:
Cesar Camacho
Diageo plc Johnnie Walker
HSN (Multicultural Agency of Record) Content, Hispanic, Strategies
The Kroger Co
Post Foods, LLC
Valeant Pharmaceuticals International Bedoyecta, Caladryl
Wphone Card

XPECTRUM MARKETING GROUP

1953 Ainsley Rd, San Diego, CA 92123
Tel.: (619) 571-7594
Fax: (858) 277-8857
E-Mail: info@xpectrummg.com
Web Site: www.xpectrummg.com

E-Mail for Key Personnel:
President: wlopez@xpectrummg.com

Employees: 3
Year Founded: 1986

National Agency Associations: AAF-AHAA

Agency Specializes In: Advertising, Bilingual Market, Brand Development & Integration, Communications, Consulting, Consumer Marketing, Direct Response Marketing, Event Planning & Marketing, Hispanic Market, Media Buying Services, New Product Development, Planning & Consultation, Publicity/Promotions, Sales Promotion

William G. Lopez *(Pres)*

Accounts:
Alaska Seafoods
Anthem Inc.
Caltrans
Canadian Beef Council
Jessup Auto Plaza

XSTATIC PUBLIC RELATIONS

44 Cook St Ste 100, Denver, CO 80206-5823
Tel.: (303) 928-7144
Fax: (303) 928-7145
E-Mail: info@xstaticpr.com
Web Site: www.xstaticpr.com

Employees: 10

Agency Specializes In: Communications, Crisis Communications, Event Planning & Marketing, Exhibit/Trade Shows, Health Care Services, Local Marketing, Media Relations, Media Training, Newspaper, Product Placement, Public Relations, Publishing, Strategic Planning/Research

Stacey Sepp *(Founder & Principal)*

Y&R AUSTIN

(Formerly SicolaMartin)
206 E 9th St Ste 1800, Austin, TX 78701
Tel.: (512) 343-0264
Fax: (512) 343-0659
Web Site: www.yr-austin.com

Employees: 45
Year Founded: 1985

National Agency Associations: 4A's-AAF

Agency Specializes In: Above-the-Line, Advertising, Below-the-Line, Brand Development & Integration, Business Publications, Business-To-Business, Collateral, Communications, Computers & Software, Consulting, Consumer Marketing, Consumer Publications, Content, Corporate Identity, Digital/Interactive, Direct Response Marketing, Electronics, Email, Event Planning & Marketing, Financial, Graphic Design, Health Care Services, High Technology, Industrial, Information Technology, Integrated Marketing, Internet/Web Design, Logo & Package Design, Magazines, Media Buying Services, Media Planning, Mobile Marketing, New Technologies, Newspaper, Newspapers & Magazines, Out-of-Home Media, Outdoor, Paid Searches, Print, Production (Print), Regional, Sponsorship, Trade & Consumer Magazines, Web (Banner Ads, Pop-ups, etc.)

Cherie Cox *(CEO)*
Nada Saidi Smith *(VP-Acct Ops)*
Alan Vassberg *(VP-Comm Plng)*
Sean-Paul Westfall *(Sr Dir-Art)*
Matt Adamiak *(Jr Dir-Art)*
Jason McQueen *(Dir-Media Svcs)*
Nate Mizelle *(Mgr-HR)*

Accounts:
Avaya; 2012
Breast Cancer Resource Centers of Texas
Dell Campaign: "Beginnings", Dell OEM; 2006
Flamigel Campaign: "Hot or Not"
NetIQ; 2012
SolarBridge Technologies; 2011
St. David's HealthCare; 2008
Texas School for the Deaf; 2011
Xerox; 2012

Y&R, LTD.

60 Bloor Street West, Toronto, ON M4W 1J2 Canada
Tel.: (416) 961-5111
Fax: (416) 961-7890
Web Site: www.yr.com

Employees: 151
Year Founded: 1936

Agency Specializes In: Advertising

Carl McMurray *(CFO & Sr VP)*
Susan Murray *(CMO & Exec VP)*
Kasi Bruno *(Sr VP & Dir-Strategic Plng)*
Gavin Bayley *(Sr VP & Client Head-Global)*
Bharat Puri *(VP-IT)*
Ariel Pagliuso *(Sr Dir-Art)*
Karen Hyman *(Acct Dir)*
Mike Lo Nam *(Art Dir)*
Pearce Cacalda *(Dir-Art & Designer)*
Heidi Prange *(Dir-Production & Art Buyer)*
Diane Graves *(Dir-HR)*

Lisa Mok *(Assoc Dir-Creative)*

Accounts:
Centrum
Colgate-Palmolive Company; 1983
Embur Computers Campaign: "Xporter"
Ford Motor Company of Canada Edge, F-Series Super Duty Pickup, Focus, Ford Escape, Fusion, Interactive Cinema Experience, Mustang Shelby Cobra
Jaguar Campaign: "Devour the road", F-TYPE R Coupe, XFR-S, XJR
PALM
Pfizer Consumer Healthcare Campaign: "Age is Just a Number", Centrum Master, Centrum ProNutrients, Omega 3
Royal Canadian Mint Coin Collection
Scotts Canada
Thomas Hinds Campaign: "Thomas Hinds Success"
Wyeth
Xerox Canada Ltd.; 1990

Branch

Saint-Jacques Vallee Tactik
1600 boul Rene-Levesque W 10th Fl, Montreal, QC H3H 1P9 Canada
(See Separate Listing)

YAAKOV SERLE ADVERTISING
147-25 70th Ave, Flushing, NY 11367
Tel.: (718) 263-2483
Fax: (718) 263-8623
E-Mail: jserle@aol.com

Employees: 3
Year Founded: 1986

Agency Specializes In: Advertising, Brand Development & Integration, Entertainment, Legal Services, Local Marketing, Media Buying Services, Newspaper, Newspapers & Magazines, Public Relations, Publicity/Promotions, Radio, Real Estate, Restaurant, Retail, Transportation, Travel & Tourism, Yellow Pages Advertising

Yaakov Serle *(Pres)*

Accounts:
Leket Leket
S&B Liquidators; Farmingdale, New York Men's Clothing; 1995
Torah Academy For Girls
Yeshivat Shaalvim

YAFFE GROUP
26100 American Dr Ste 401, Southfield, MI 48034
Tel.: (248) 262-1700
Fax: (248) 262-9601
Web Site: www.yaffe.com

Employees: 40
Year Founded: 1959

National Agency Associations: 4A's

Agency Specializes In: Advertising, Brand Development & Integration, Broadcast, Cable T.V., Co-op Advertising, Collateral, College, Communications, Consulting, Consumer Goods, Consumer Marketing, Corporate Communications, Corporate Identity, Crisis Communications, Customer Relationship Management, Direct Response Marketing, Education, Electronic Media, Email, Graphic Design, Health Care Services, Hispanic Market, Household Goods, Integrated Marketing, Internet/Web Design, Local Marketing, Market Research, Media Buying Services, Media Planning, Media Relations, Multimedia, Newspaper, Newspapers & Magazines, Outdoor, Paid Searches, Planning & Consultation, Podcasting, Print, Production, Production (Ad, Film, Broadcast), Production (Print), Promotions, Public Relations, Publicity/Promotions, Radio, Restaurant, Retail, Sales Promotion, Social Marketing/Nonprofit, Social Media, Strategic Planning/Research, T.V., Telemarketing, Web (Banner Ads, Pop-ups, etc.)

Approx. Annual Billings: $40,000,000

Breakdown of Gross Billings by Media: Cable T.V.: 6%; Newsp. & Mags.: 25%; Outdoor: 5%; Production: 11%; Radio: 10%; T.V.: 43%

John Cassidy *(Pres & CEO)*
Mike McClure *(Chief Social Media Officer & Exec Dir-Creative)*
Michael Morin *(Exec VP)*
Buffy O'Connor *(Dir-Media)*
Julie Janks *(Assoc Dir-Media)*

Accounts:
Ameripoint Title; Houston, TX Title Insurance Company
Askar Brands; Bloomfield Hills, MI Papa Romano's, Papa's To Go, Stucci's Ice Cream; 2010
Capuchin Soup Kitchen; Detroit, MI Non-Profit; 2009
Corporate Hands; Houston, TX
Grand Home Furnishings; Roanoke, VA Retail Furniture; 1998
Greenpath Debt Solutions; Farmington Hills, MI
Kane's Furniture; Saint Petersburg, FL Retail Furniture; 1995
Mall Foods, Inc.; Southfield, MI Retail Food Chain
Savon Furniture; St. Petersburg, FL Retail Furniture; 1995
Sentinel Trust; Houston, TX
Star Furniture; Houston, TX Retail Furniture; 2001
The Vallone Group; Houston, TX

Branch

Yaffe Direct
26100 American Dr 4th Fl Ste 401, Southfield, MI 48034
Tel.: (248) 262-1700
Fax: (248) 262-9601
E-Mail: info@yaffe.com
Web Site: www.yaffe.com

Employees: 25

Agency Specializes In: Direct Response Marketing

John Cassidy *(Co-Owner)*
Brad Deutser *(Owner)*
Fred Yaffe *(Chm & CEO)*
Michael Morin *(Pres)*
Buffy O'Connor *(Dir-Media)*

YAMAMOTO MOSS AND MACKENZIE MARKETING
252 First Ave N, Minneapolis, MN 55401
Tel.: (612) 375-0180
Fax: (612) 342-2424
Toll Free: (888) 375-9910
Web Site: www.go-yamamoto.com/

Employees: 35
Year Founded: 1979

National Agency Associations: NAMA

Agency Specializes In: Advertising, Alternative Advertising, Arts, Below-the-Line, Brand Development & Integration, Broadcast, Business-To-Business, Cable T.V., Co-op Advertising, Collateral, Communications, Consulting, Consumer Goods, Consumer Marketing, Content, Corporate Identity, Digital/Interactive, Direct Response Marketing, Email, Environmental, Exhibit/Trade Shows, Experience Design, Faith Based, Financial, Food Service, Graphic Design, Health Care Services, Hospitality, Identity Marketing, In-Store Advertising, Integrated Marketing, Internet/Web Design, Leisure, Logo & Package Design, Medical Products, Mobile Marketing, Outdoor, Over-50 Market, Package Design, Paid Searches, Pharmaceutical, Planning & Consultation, Point of Purchase, Production, Search Engine Optimization, Seniors' Market, Social Marketing/Nonprofit, Social Media, Stakeholders, Travel & Tourism, Viral/Buzz/Word of Mouth, Women's Market

Shelly Regan *(Pres)*
Kathy McCuskey *(CEO)*
Stacey Davies *(CFO)*
Attila Szabo *(Dir-Plng & Digital Solutions)*
Jessica Stanchfield *(Acct Mgr)*

Accounts:
Ameriprise; Minneapolis, MN
New-Animal Humane Society
Blue Belt Technologies Inc
CUNA Mutual Group; Madison, WI
HealthNow; Buffalo, NY
North Memorial Health; Minneapolis, MN
Quali Tech, Inc.; Minneapolis, MN
Russell Brands LLC
UnitedHealth Group; Minneapolis, MN
University Hospitals; Cleveland, OH
Weisman Art Museum; Minneapolis, MN

YANKEE PUBLIC RELATIONS
8 Sunshine Dr, Pittstown, NJ 08867
Tel.: (908) 894-3930
Fax: (908) 238-1450
E-Mail: fred@yankeepr.com
Web Site: www.yankeepr.com

Employees: 2

Agency Specializes In: Collateral, Communications, Crisis Communications, Event Planning & Marketing, Financial, Health Care Services, Local Marketing, Media Relations, Media Training, New Technologies, Pharmaceutical, Public Relations, Real Estate, Strategic Planning/Research, Web (Banner Ads, Pop-ups, etc.)

Fred Feiner *(Pres)*
Anita Feiner *(VP-Client Svcs)*

Accounts:
Octapharma USA; Hoboken, NJ Public Relations
Oncobiologics, Inc.

YARRUM MARKETING, INC.
5761 Ferry Rd, Wakeman, OH 44889
Tel.: (419) 929-0130
Fax: (419) 929-0909
E-Mail: yarrummkt@aol.com

Employees: 2
Year Founded: 1985

Agency Specializes In: Media Buying Services, Retail

Chuck Murray *(Owner)*

YECK BROTHERS COMPANY
2222 Arbor Blvd, Dayton, OH 45439-1522
Mailing Address:
PO Box 225, Dayton, OH 45401-0225
Tel.: (937) 294-4000
Fax: (937) 294-6985
Toll Free: (800) 417-2767
Web Site: www.yeck.com

E-Mail for Key Personnel:
President: byeck@yeck.com

Employees: 40
Year Founded: 1938

National Agency Associations: DMA

Agency Specializes In: Automotive, Business-To-Business, College, Communications, Consumer Marketing, Direct Response Marketing, Direct-to-Consumer, Email, Financial, Graphic Design, Production, Social Marketing/Nonprofit

Breakdown of Gross Billings by Media: D.M.: 100%

Robert A. Yeck *(Pres)*
Sue Hardin *(VP-Database & Info Mktg)*
Sherry Hang *(Dir-Mktg & Creative Svcs)*
Mark Sorah *(Dir-Art)*
Janet Archer *(Acct Mgr)*
Alesia Campbell *(Div Head & Acct Exec)*

Accounts:
GE Capital; Stamford, CT; 1998
GOJO Hand Care Products; 1995
John Deere; Moline, IL Credit, Farm Equipment & Parts; 1986
LexisNexis; Dayton, OH Electronic Information; 1980
Pitney Bowes; Stamford, CT; 1986
Wal-Mart; 2002
WorkFlow One; OH; 2004

YELLO ADVERTISING
489 S Robertson Blvd Ste 104, Los Angeles, CA 90211
Tel.: (310) 844-0828
E-Mail: hello@yelloadvertising.com
Web Site: www.yelloadvertising.com

Year Founded: 2013

Agency Specializes In: Advertising, Brand Development & Integration, Graphic Design, Media Buying Services, Media Planning, Promotions, Social Media

Marvin Green *(Acct Exec & Specialist-Social Media)*

Accounts:
Sofa Designers

YELLOW BUS LLC
312 Lincoln St Ste A, Santa Cruz, CA 95060
Tel.: (831) 457-2877
E-Mail: honk@yellowbusadvertising.com
Web Site: www.yellowbusadvertising.com

Agency Specializes In: Advertising, Brand Development & Integration, Corporate Identity, Graphic Design, Internet/Web Design, Logo & Package Design, Media Buying Services, Print, Radio, Social Media

Austin Sherwood *(Principal)*
George Chalekian *(Dir-Creative)*
Katelyn Gagne *(Acct Exec)*

Accounts:
Erik's Delicafe, Inc.

YELLOW PAGES RESOURCE
999 Oronoque Ln, Stratford, CT 06614
Tel.: (203) 386-0228
Fax: (203) 870-1810
Toll Free: (877) 638-7494
E-Mail: mark@ypresource.com
Web Site: www.ypresource.com

Employees: 8
Year Founded: 2006

National Agency Associations: YPA

Agency Specializes In: Advertising, Advertising Specialties, Consulting, Digital/Interactive, Market Research, Mobile Marketing, Search Engine Optimization, Web (Banner Ads, Pop-ups, etc.), Yellow Pages Advertising

Approx. Annual Billings: $7,000,000

Breakdown of Gross Billings by Media: Digital/Interactive: 25%; Yellow Page Adv.: 75%

Mark O'Halloran *(Pres)*

YELLOW SUBMARINE MARKETING COMMUNICATIONS INC.
220 W Station Sq Dr Ste 200, Pittsburgh, PA 15219
Tel.: (412) 208-6400
Web Site: www.yellowsubmarketing.com

National Agency Associations: 4A's

Agency Specializes In: Advertising

George Garber *(Pres & CEO)*
John Harpur *(Partner, Exec VP & Dir-Media)*
Edward Fine *(Chief Creative Officer)*
Zack Fine *(Chief Creative Officer)*
Holly Humphrey *(Exec VP & Exec Dir-Creative)*
Marianne Shaffer *(Sr VP & Dir-Brdcst)*
Jason Rukas *(Media Buyer)*

Accounts:
Katie On Cars
Orr's Jewelers

YIELD BRANDING
128 Sterling Rd Ste 200, Toronto, ON M6R 2B7 Canada
Tel.: (416) 588-4958
E-Mail: info@yieldbranding.com
Web Site: www.yieldbranding.com/

Employees: 15
Year Founded: 1989

Agency Specializes In: Advertising, Digital/Interactive

Ted Nation *(Pres & Partner)*
Brad Usherwood *(CEO)*
Andrea Tidy *(Dir-Client Bus Dev)*
Chris Torbay *(Dir-Creative)*
Sandra Usherwood *(Dir-Fin)*

Accounts:
407ETR
BLG
Equifax
Fengate Capital
Mud Hero
OMA
Polar Securities

YMARKETING
4000 MacArthur Blvd, Newport Beach, CA 92660
Tel.: (714) 545-2550
Toll Free: (877) SEM-4321
E-Mail: donald.nosek@ymarketing.com
Web Site: www.ymarketing.com

Employees: 12
Year Founded: 2002

Agency Specializes In: Above-the-Line, Advertising, Advertising Specialties, Affiliate Marketing, Affluent Market, African-American Market, Agriculture, Alternative Advertising, Arts, Asian Market, Automotive, Aviation & Aerospace, Below-the-Line, Bilingual Market, Brand Development & Integration, Branded Entertainment, Broadcast, Business Publications, Business-To-Business, Cable T.V., Catalogs, Children's Market, Co-op Advertising, Collateral, College, Commercial Photography, Communications, Computers & Software, Consulting, Consumer Goods, Consumer Marketing, Consumer Publications, Content, Corporate Communications, Corporate Identity, Cosmetics, Crisis Communications, Custom Publishing, Customer Relationship Management, Digital/Interactive, Direct Response Marketing, Direct-to-Consumer, E-Commerce, Education, Electronic Media, Electronics, Email, Engineering, Entertainment, Environmental, Event Planning & Marketing, Exhibit/Trade Shows, Experience Design, Fashion/Apparel, Financial, Food Service, Game Integration, Gay & Lesbian Market, Government/Political, Graphic Design, Guerilla Marketing, Health Care Services, High Technology, Hispanic Market, Hospitality, Household Goods, Identity Marketing, In-Store Advertising, Industrial, Infomercials, Information Technology, Integrated Marketing, International, Internet/Web Design, Investor Relations, Legal Services, Leisure, Local Marketing, Logo & Package Design, Luxury Products, Magazines, Marine, Market Research, Media Buying Services, Media Planning, Media Relations, Media Training, Medical Products, Men's Market, Merchandising, Mobile Marketing, Multicultural, Multimedia, New Product Development, New Technologies, Newspaper, Newspapers & Magazines, Out-of-Home Media, Outdoor, Over-50 Market, Package Design, Paid Searches, Pharmaceutical, Planning & Consultation, Podcasting, Point of Purchase, Point of Sale, Print, Product Placement, Production, Production (Ad, Film, Broadcast), Production (Print), Promotions, Public Relations, Publicity/Promotions, Publishing, RSS (Really Simple Syndication), Radio, Real Estate, Recruitment, Regional, Restaurant, Retail, Sales Promotion, Search Engine Optimization, Seniors' Market, Social Marketing/Nonprofit, Sponsorship, Sports Market, Stakeholders, Strategic Planning/Research, Sweepstakes, Syndication, T.V., Technical Advertising, Teen Market, Telemarketing, Trade & Consumer Magazines, Transportation, Travel & Tourism, Urban Market, Viral/Buzz/Word of Mouth, Web (Banner Ads, Pop-ups, etc.), Women's Market, Yellow Pages Advertising

Approx. Annual Billings: $1,000,000

Ryan Lash *(CEO)*
Jennifer Jee *(VP & Client Svcs Dir)*
Brad Barron *(Producer-Digital)*
Edna Munoz-Lash *(Dir-Corp Social)*
Greg Wilson *(Dir-Database & Tech)*
Manuel Cortez *(Assoc Dir-Digital Content Mktg)*
Jeff Lash *(Mgr-Ops)*
Lonna Dayhoff *(Sr Acct Exec)*
Alex Franks *(Sr Engr-Sys)*

Accounts:
Alcone Marketing
Lerner Entertainment
Natural Health Hoodia
PersonetteWest
ThomsenNull
United Health Group

YODLE, INC.
(Formerly ProfitFuel, Inc.)
50 W 23rd St Ste 401, New York, NY 10010
Tel.: (512) 637-3000
Toll Free: (877) 276-5104
E-Mail: press@yodle.com
Web Site: www.yodle.com

Employees: 65
Year Founded: 2002

Agency Specializes In: Advertising, Web (Banner Ads, Pop-ups, etc.)

Court Cunningham *(CEO)*
Eric Raab *(CIO)*
Danielle Korins *(Chief People Officer)*
Paul Bascobert *(Pres-Local)*
Steven R. Power *(Pres-Brand Networks Bus)*
Fred Voccola *(Gen Mgr-YBN)*
Kristin Covi *(Dir-Paid & Consumer Website Performance)*
Radley Moss *(Dir-Corp Comm)*
Jessica McGinn *(Mgr-PR)*
Charmi Panchal *(Mgr-Digital Mktg)*
Jerry Franklin *(Area Dir-Sls)*

Accounts:
Maaco (Digital Agency of Record)

YOU SQUARED MEDIA
7026 Old Katy Rd Ste 350, Houston, TX 77024
Tel.: (713) 880-3387
Fax: (713) 880-3394
E-Mail: info@yousquaredmedia.com
Web Site: www.yousquaredmedia.com

Year Founded: 2010

Agency Specializes In: Advertising, Internet/Web Design, Media Buying Services, Media Planning, Outdoor, Print, Social Media

Tracey Cleckler *(Pres & CEO)*
Clarence Estes *(VP)*
Kathy Dowling *(Mgr-Acctg)*

Accounts:
BreWingZ Sports Bar & Grill
Frenchy's Chicken (Agency of Record) Advertising, Marketing, Media Buying
Houston Spine Doc
Infinite Optiks
Village Flowery

YOUNG & LARAMORE
407 Fulton St, Indianapolis, IN 46202
Tel.: (317) 264-8000
Web Site: yandl.com

E-Mail for Key Personnel:
Creative Dir.: c.hadlock@yandl.com

Employees: 50
Year Founded: 1983

Agency Specializes In: Advertising, Affluent Market, Alternative Advertising, Aviation & Aerospace, Brand Development & Integration, Broadcast, Business-To-Business, Cable T.V., Catalogs, Co-op Advertising, Collateral, Communications, Consulting, Consumer Goods, Consumer Marketing, Consumer Publications, Content, Corporate Communications, Corporate Identity, Customer Relationship Management, Digital/Interactive, Direct Response Marketing, Direct-to-Consumer, Electronic Media, Electronics, Email, Event Planning & Marketing, Exhibit/Trade Shows, Experience Design, Fashion/Apparel, Financial, Food Service, Graphic Design, Guerilla Marketing, Household Goods, Identity Marketing, In-Store Advertising, Integrated Marketing, Internet/Web Design, Leisure, Logo & Package Design, Luxury Products, Magazines, Market Research, Media Buying Services, Media Planning, Mobile Marketing, New Product Development, Newspaper, Newspapers & Magazines, Out-of-Home Media, Outdoor, Package Design, Planning & Consultation, Point of Purchase, Point of Sale, Print, Production, Promotions, Public Relations, Publicity/Promotions, Radio, Recruitment, Regional, Restaurant, Retail, Search Engine Optimization, Social Media, Sponsorship, Sports Market, Strategic Planning/Research, Syndication, T.V., Trade & Consumer Magazines, Transportation, Web (Banner Ads, Pop-ups, etc.), Women's Market

Approx. Annual Billings: $45,000,000

Jeff Laramore *(Owner)*
Paul J. Knapp *(CEO)*
Carolyn Hadlock *(Exec Creative Dir)*
Dan Shearin *(Art Dir)*
Trevor Williams *(Creative Dir)*
Zac Neulieb *(Dir-Art)*
Sarah Scranton *(Acct Mgr)*
Lynn Kendall *(Mgr-Production)*
Rachel Gershman *(Supvr-Digital-EchoPoint Media)*
Joe Botich *(Strategist-Digital Media)*
Danna Roen *(Media Buyer & Planner-Digital)*
Mitchell Brown *(Designer)*
Marlena Banks *(Asst Acct Mgr)*

Accounts:
Allegion Bricard, Creative, Dexter, Falcon, Fusion Hardware Group, Global Media Planning, Kryptonite, Media Buying, Steelcraft, Von Duprin
Bauducco Foods (Agency of Record) CPG; 2008
Building Tomorrow Campaign: "Uneducate Yourself", Digital, Social, Uneducate.Me
Delta Faucet Company; Indianapolis, IN Brizo, Home; 2003
D.L. Couch; Noblesville, IN Home; 2009
Farm Bureau Insurance
Founders Brewery CPG; 2012
Goodwill Industries; Indianapolis, IN Retail; 1996
Indiana Farm Bureau Insurance Campaign: "Pool", Insurance, Super Bowl 2015; 2010
Kelty
KraftMaid Cabinetry, Inc. Creative Strategy
New Balance Brine, Sporting Goods, Warrior; 2010
Peerless Faucets (Delta Faucet Company) Home; 2004
Procter & Gamble; Cincinnati, OH CPG; 2009
Red Gold, Inc. Red Gold Tomatoes
Schlage Campaign: "Strong Has a Name", Campaign: "The Keyless Era", Home, Keyless Electronic Locks, Social, Social Media; 2011
Scotts Lawn Service (Scotts Miracle Gro) Campaign: "Get The Lawn Your Neighbors Expect", Home; 2010
Ugly Mug Coffee CPG; 2008
Upland Brewing Company
YMCA of Greater Indianapolis; Indianapolis, IN Fitness; 2000

YOUNG & RUBICAM
3 Columbus Cir, New York, NY 10019
Tel.: (212) 210-3000
Fax: (212) 490-9073
Web Site: www.yr.com

Employees: 6,500
Year Founded: 1923

National Agency Associations: 4A's-AAF-ABC-APA-BPA-DMA-TAB

Shelley Diamond *(Chief Client Officer)*
Enrique Yuste *(Pres/CEO-Argentina)*
Matthew Godfrey *(Pres-Asia)*
Magdalena Klimaszewska *(Deputy Mng Dir)*
Jennifer Kohl *(Sr VP & Exec Dir-Integrated Media)*
Michael White *(Sr VP & Grp Acct Dir)*
Fern Cohen *(Sr VP & Dir-Creative)*
Margot Owett *(Sr VP & Dir-Creative)*
Susanne Raymond *(Sr VP & Dir-Brand Plng)*
Laurie Newsome *(VP & Acct Dir)*
Christianna Gorin *(VP & Dir-Brand Plng)*
Dave Pachence *(VP-Creative & Dir)*
Kitty Thorne *(VP & Dir-Creative)*
Shari Sinha *(VP, Asst Dir-Creative & Copywriter)*
Gregory Farley *(Exec Creative Dir)*
Christian Carl *(Exec Dir-Creative-Global)*
Marc Sobier *(Exec Dir-Creative)*
Colleen Briggs *(Grp Dir-Plng)*
Gabriel Jardim *(Sr Dir-Art)*
Troy Palmer *(Sr Dir-Art)*
Chris Wilson *(Acct Mng Dir)*
Lee Abbas *(Acct Dir-Integration-Team BAC)*
Erin Christensen *(Acct Dir)*
Aurora Deidda *(Acct Dir)*
Daisy Delgado *(Acct Dir)*
Shawanda Green *(Acct Dir)*
Justin Kane *(Acct Dir)*
Julie Kwak *(Acct Dir)*
Caleb Lubarsky *(Acct Dir)*
Fernando Urruchua *(Acct Dir)*
Alan Vladusic *(Dir-Creative & Art & Designer)*
Emilio Alvarez-Recio *(Dir-New Bus)*
Lorena Cascino *(Dir-Art)*
Vivian Cunningham *(Dir-Integrated Project Mgmt)*
Miranda Dean *(Dir-Creative)*
Theresa Ferrugio *(Dir-Media)*
Diane Fields *(Dir-Creative Svcs)*
Richard Goldstein *(Dir-Creative)*
Dan Goodman *(Dir-New Bus Ops)*
Simon Hunt *(Dir-Creative)*
Sophie Isherwood *(Dir-Creative)*
Bruce Jacobson *(Dir-Creative)*
Stacy Kallan *(Dir-Bus Affairs Content Production)*
Priya Karnik *(Dir-Brand Plng)*
Sal Lombardo *(Dir-Art)*
Mary Mazza *(Dir-Strategy)*
Anuja Palkar *(Dir-Analytic Insights & Strategy)*
Cynthia Praeg *(Dir-Budgeting & Reporting)*
Rob Rooney *(Dir-Creative)*
Jenna Rounds *(Dir-Strategic Plng)*
Josh Schildkraut *(Dir-Creative)*
Cliff Skeete *(Dir-Creative)*
Yuni Son *(Dir-Art)*
Theresa Tepper *(Dir-PR-North America)*
Camille Ducos *(Assoc Dir-Media)*
Abbey Fortney *(Assoc Dir-Recruiting)*
Maria Ladega *(Assoc Dir-Analytic Insights & Strategy)*
Karl Altenburger *(Sr Mgr-Integrated Media)*
Whitney Goodman *(Acct Mgr)*
John Swan *(Brand Planner-Land Rover & Special Olympics)*
Tasha Gilroy *(Program Mgr-Trng & Diversity)*
Cathy D'Onofrio *(Mgr-Client Fin)*
Mike Dunn *(Mgr-Print Production)*
Alexis Gianoulis *(Mgr-Creative Talent-Global)*
George Liao *(Mgr-Client Fin)*
Roberta Costa *(Acct Supvr)*
Kyunhea Kwon *(Acct Supvr)*
Susan Min *(Acct Supvr)*
Lisa Sannazzaro *(Acct Supvr)*
Geoffrey Sia *(Acct Supvr)*
Jennifer Cheng *(Supvr-Edit Studio Fin)*
Dean Alcott *(Acct Exec)*
Jillian Babcock *(Acct Exec)*
Leanna Criddle *(Acct Exec)*
Shahar Ferber *(Acct Exec)*
Joon Kim *(Acct Exec-Pepperidge Farm)*
Doris Lau *(Acct Exec)*
Hannah Park *(Acct Exec)*
Kim Reyes *(Acct Exec)*
James Cole *(Planner-Brand)*
Anthony DiMichele *(Copywriter)*
Alison Gluck *(Planner-Brand)*
Jacqueline Stabach *(Planner-Brand)*
Charissa Jones *(Asst Acct Exec)*
John Little *(Asst Acct Exec)*
Baird Meem *(Asst Acct Exec)*
Tyrone Boyd *(Coord-Brdcst Traffic)*
Donna Benabib *(Exec Coord-Creative)*
Karolina Galacz *(Deputy Dir-Creative)*
Divya Munjal *(Brand Strategist-Analytic Insights & Strategy)*

Accounts:
AB Electrolux Eureka
Barilla America, Inc.; 1968
Bel Group (Fromageries Bel); 1970

Boehringer Ingelheim; 2002
Campbell Soup Company Campaign: "Copter Caper", Campaign: "Mama's Boy", Chunky Soup, Chunky Soup Fully Loaded, Prego, V8, V8 Soups; 1982
Chevron; 1987
Colgate-Palmolive Campaign: "Shark", Colgate Plax, Octopus; 1983
Danone Oikos; 1971
Dell Computer Campaign: "Beginnings"; 2009
New-The Hillshire Brands Company Ball Park
LG Electronics; Englewood Cliffs, NJ; 1998
Microsoft B-to-B, Creative, Digital
Partnership for a Healthier America
Pfizer; 1977
Shazam
Special Olympics Digital, Global Marketing, Print, Social Media, TV
Telefonica; 1983
Unconventional Partners
U.S. Navy (Agency of Record) Digital Advertising, Media Planning, Mobile Advertising, Public Relations
Valvoline Valvoline Garage
Vodafone; 2009
Xerox; 1964

United States

Berlin Cameron United
100 Ave of the Americas, New York, NY 10013
(See Separate Listing)

The Bravo Group HQ
601 Brickell Key Drive, Suite 1100, Miami, FL 33131
(See Separate Listing)

Burson-Marsteller
230 Park Ave S, New York, NY 10003-1566
(See Separate Listing)

Cohn & Wolfe
200 Fifth Ave, New York, NY 10010
(See Separate Listing)

Landor Associates
1001 Front St, San Francisco, CA 94111
(See Separate Listing)

RTC
1055 Thomas Jefferson Street NW, Washington, DC 20007
Tel.: (202) 625-2111
Fax: (202) 424-7900
E-Mail: info@rtcagency.com
Web Site: www.rtcagency.com/

National Agency Associations: 4A's

Jeff Ross, *(Pres & CEO)*
John Reid *(Chief Creative Officer & Exec VP)*
Aly Hardy *(VP & Acct Dir)*
Ann Wolek *(VP & Dir-Bus Dev)*
Jeff Abelson *(Dir-Art)*

Accounts:
AARP Services Inc.
Abbott Diabetes Care
Audi
Biogen Idec
BlackRock
Dell
Microsoft
Novo Nordisk
Office Depot
Pfizer
Procter & Gamble
Sunovion
Time Warner Cable
Vanguard
Windstream

VML, Inc.
250 Richards Rd, Kansas City, MO 64116-4279
(See Separate Listing)

Wunderman
3 Columbus Cir, New York, NY 10019
(See Separate Listing)

Y&R Austin
(Formerly SicolaMartin)
206 E 9th St Ste 1800, Austin, TX 78701
(See Separate Listing)

Y&R California
303 2nd St 8th Fl S Tower, San Francisco, CA 94107
Tel.: (415) 882-0600
Fax: (415) 882-0601
E-Mail: info@sfo.yr.com
Web Site: www.yr.com

E-Mail for Key Personnel:
President: penny_baldwin@sfo.yr.com

Employees: 70
Year Founded: 1978

National Agency Associations: 4A's

Agency Specializes In: Advertising, Sponsorship

Jennifer Patterson *(Chief Strategy Officer)*
Jacques Borris *(Dir-Creative-Global)*
Marc Sobier *(Dir-Creative-Global)*
James Boyer *(Mgr-IT)*
Elizabeth Chabot *(Mgr-Bus Dev)*
Jason Cohen *(Sr Acct Exec)*

Accounts:
Blue Diamond Growers; Sacramento, CA Almond Breeze, Almonds, Nut Thins; 2012
BMC Software; 2013
Chevron Havoline Motor Oil, Texaco; 1987
Citrix
Crystal Cruises; 2011
Jaguar Campaign: "Rendezvous", Land Rover LR2, Land Rover LR4
SanDisk

Y&R Latin American Headquarters
Courvoisier Ctr II 601 Brickell Key Dr Ste 1100, Miami, FL 33131
Tel.: (305) 347-1950
Fax: (305) 347-1951
Web Site: www.yr.com

Employees: 75
Year Founded: 1992

Agency Specializes In: Advertising, Sponsorship

John Lynn *(CEO)*
Claudio Lima *(Chief Creative Officer)*
Willy Lomana *(Creative Dir)*
Lucy Mejer *(Acct Dir)*
Jesselle Valdes *(Art Dir)*
Noel Artiles *(Dir-Creative)*
Gabriela Laguna *(Sr Acct Mgr)*
Michelle Casey *(Sr Acct Exec)*
Loipa Ramos *(Copywriter)*

Accounts:
AT&T Campaign: "Lifesaver"
Colgate-Palmolive
Dell
FedEx Express
Lan
Microsoft
No More
PopClik Headphones
New-TECHO

Y&R New York
3 Columbus Cir, New York, NY 10019
Tel.: (212) 210-3000
Fax: (212) 210-5169
E-Mail: info@yr.com
Web Site: www.yr.com

Employees: 400
Year Founded: 1923

National Agency Associations: 4A's

Agency Specializes In: Advertising, Sponsorship

Dick deLange *(Chief Strategy Officer)*
Michael Sussman *(Pres-BAV Worldwide)*
Richard Butt *(Exec VP & Exec Dir-Creative)*
Belle Frank *(Exec VP & Dir-Strategy & Res-Global)*
Lynn Fisher *(Exec VP-Global Res & Insights-Cohn & Wolfe)*
Lara Griggs *(Sr VP & Mng Dir-Acct)*
Fern Cohen *(Sr VP & Dir-Creative)*
Richard Goldstein *(Sr VP & Dir-Creative)*
Faye Kleros *(Sr VP & Dir-Creative)*
Margot Owett *(Sr VP & Dir-Creative)*
Jessica Post *(Sr VP & Global Asst Mng Dir-Team Dell)*
Courtney Walker *(Sr VP & Deputy Dir)*
Britta Dahl *(Acct Mng Dir & VP)*
Melanie Cody *(VP & Dir-Talent)*
James Caporimo *(Exec Dir-Creative)*
Christian Carl *(Exec Creative Dir-Global)*
Greg Farley *(Exec Creative Dir)*
Letitia Jacobs *(Exec Dir-Creative)*
Greg Lotus *(Exec Dir-Integrated Production)*
Richard Sinreich *(Grp Dir-Creative)*
Guilherme Racz *(Sr Dir-Art)*
Gonzalo Gallego *(Art Dir)*
Leo Gomez *(Creative Dir)*
Thayer Joyce *(Acct Dir)*
Amber Novosad *(Acct Dir)*
Arun Nemali *(Dir-Creative & Copywriter)*
Alan Vladusic *(Dir-Creative & Art & Designer)*
John Bollinger *(Dir-Creative-Global Deployment)*
Jacques Borris *(Dir-Creative-Global)*
Juan Charvet *(Dir-Experience Strategy)*
Brian Cheung *(Dir-Art)*
Chris Cutone *(Dir-HR-North America)*
Aaron Frisch *(Dir-Creative)*
Eric Glickman *(Dir-Creative)*
Bruce Jacobson *(Dir-Creative)*
Hanso Lee *(Dir-Art)*
Carmelo Rodriguez *(Dir-Creative)*
Rob Rooney *(Dir-Creative)*
Josh Schildkraut *(Dir-Creative)*
Thomas Shim *(Dir-Creative-Dell)*
Sandy Thompson *(Dir-Global Strategic Plng)*
Amanda Wood *(Dir-Client Mktg)*
Kate Lummus *(Assoc Dir-Creative)*
Amanda Neil *(Acct Supvr-Global Digital)*
Alison Geraghty *(Strategist)*
Tre Jordan *(Acct Exec)*
Ethan Scott *(Strategist)*
Arantza Urruchua *(Acct Exec)*
Anthony Dimichele *(Copywriter)*
Lucas Oliveira *(Copywriter)*
Gustavo Quintero *(Planner-Brand)*

Accounts:
Ad Council
Adidas
Arthritis Foundation; 2009
Campbell Soup Co. Campaign: "Knock, Knock", Pace, Pepperidge Farm, Prego, V8; 1996
Chevron; 1987
Colgate-Palmolive Colgate Total, Hill's, Tom's of Maine; 1996

Conrad Metamorphosis; 2010
Consumer Reports; 2011
Dannon Co.; 1998
Dell B2B, Campaign: "5 Second Filmmaker", Campaign: "Future Ready", Campaign: "Power to Do More", Campaign: "Thomas: Creator of an Alternate Universe", Digital, Mobile, Out-of-Home, Social Media; 2009
Footaction; 2012
Green Mountain Coffee; 2001
JC Penney Campaign: "Playground"; 2013
Joyful Heart Foundation Campaign: "No More", Videos
Land Rover Range Rover Discovery Sport, Vanishing Game; 2001
New-Long Live NY
Mattel Inc. American Girl, Fisher-Price; 1994
Merck; 2012
Microsoft Advertising; 2011
Moms Demand Action for Gun Sense in America
MTV Campaign: "Sext Life", Staying Alive Foundation
National Disaster Search for Dog Foundation; 2008
New York Organ Donor Network Campaign: "Keep New York Alive"
Newtown Action Alliance
Partnership For a Healthier America
Pfizer; 2009
The Port Authority of New York and New Jersey; 2011
Protex
New-Signature
Special Olympics
New-Trend On This
Tully's Coffee
Twinings
Tyson Foods Ball Park, Campaign: "Grab Life By The Ball Park", Digital, In-Store, Public Relations
UNCF; 1973
US Olympic Committee Brand Communications, Digital, Marketing, Print, Social Media; 2011
Waldorf Astoria; 2011
Xerox Corp. (Lead Agency) Campaign: "A World Made Simpler", Campaign: "Thinking", Campaign: "Work Can Work Better"; 1964

Young & Rubicam Brands, San Francisco
303 2nd St 8th Fl S Tower, San Francisco, CA 94107
Tel.: (415) 882-0600
Fax: (415) 882-0601

Employees: 80

Shelley Diamond *(Mng Partner-Worldwide)*
Mike Goefft *(Chief Creative Officer & Sr VP)*
Shlomi Avnon *(Chief Dev Officer-Global)*
Tony Granger *(Chief Creative Officer-Global)*
William J. Manfredi *(Exec VP-Talent Mgmt-Global)*
Lee Wilson *(Grp Acct Dir)*
Laura Arm *(Acct Dir)*
Herman Brown *(Dir-Tech)*
Maureen Chan-Lay *(Mgr-Creative Svcs)*

Accounts:
C Spire Wireless
Chevron
Dell
Dr. Pepper Snapple Group 7UP, A&W Brands, Sunkist Soda
LG

Young & Rubicam Midwest
233 N Michigan Ave 16th Fl, Chicago, IL 60601-5519
Tel.: (312) 596-3000
Fax: (312) 596-3130
Web Site: www.yr.com

Employees: 110
Year Founded: 1932

Agency Specializes In: Sponsorship

John Fraser *(Pres)*
Tim Sylvain *(CFO & Exec VP)*
Tricia Russo *(Chief Strategy Officer & Sr VP)*
Juliet Moffat *(Grp Acct Dir)*
Juan Pablo Curioni *(Dir-Creative)*
Greg Getner *(Dir-Strategy)*
Christian Valderrama *(Dir-Art)*

Accounts:
American Red Cross; 2005
Bel Brands Boursin, Campaign: "Reinvent Snacking", Cheese, Creamy Spicy Pepper Jack, Creative, Laughing Cow, Mini Babybel, TV, Website, WisPride
Butterball; 2012
Carfax Campaign: "Mole"
CPG Building Products Azek Building Products, Brand Strategy, Creative, Media Planning & Buying, TimberTech
Danze; 2011
Famous Footwear; 2011
Giant Eagle; 2008
Greater Chicago Food Depository
Hilton Hotels Doubletree, Embassy Suites
National Park Conservation Association; 2006
River North Dance Company; 2008
Sears Holdings Corp. Campaign: "Getaway", Campaign: "His and Hers"

Labstore North America
3 Columbus Circle, New York, NY 10019
Tel.: (646) 808-9201

Agency Specializes In: Shopper Marketing

Tim O'Sullivan *(Mng Dir)*
Jon Bird *(Mng Dir-Global)*
Zachary Kraemer *(Brand Mgr & Mgr-Bus Dev)*

Accounts:
Colgate-Palmolive; Thailand
GE Moneybank; Hungary
Telefonica; Spain

Canada

Saint-Jacques Vallee Tactik
1600 boul Rene-Levesque W 10th Fl, Montreal, QC H3H 1P9 Canada
(See Separate Listing)

TAXI
495 Wellington St W Ste 102, Toronto, ON M5V 1E9 Canada
(See Separate Listing)

Y&R, Ltd.
60 Bloor Street West, Toronto, ON M4W 1J2 Canada
(See Separate Listing)

Headquarters

Dentsu Y&R Japan
2-chome Higashi shinbashi Shiodome KOMODIO No 14 No 1, Minato-ku, Tokyo, 105-8613 Japan
Tel.: (81) 3 5219 9111
Fax: (81) 3 5219 9222
E-Mail: info@dyr.co.jp
Web Site: www.dyr.co.jp

Employees: 230
Year Founded: 1981

Agency Specializes In: Advertising

Yoichi Inose *(Pres & CEO)*
Takafumi Hotta *(Mng Dir)*
Michael Atkins *(Exec Dir)*
Naoko Goto *(Acct Dir)*
George So Sugitomo *(Creative Dir)*
Mai Shibatani *(Dir-Art)*
Shoichi Yamakawa *(Acct Mgr)*
Noriko Osumi *(Copywriter)*

Accounts:
Accenture Campaign: "Broken Tea Bowl"
Dole Japan Campaign: "Tokyo Marathon Lucky Banana"
Fuji Xerox
Tanaka Kikinzoku Kogyo K.K. Campaign: "Tanaka Precious Metals"
Virgin Atlantic Airways Campaign: "30 Sec. Love"

Y&R Hong Kong
32nd Fl 633 Kings Rd, North Point, China (Hong Kong)
Tel.: (852) 2884 6668
Fax: (852) 2886 0989
Web Site: www.yr.com

Employees: 100
Year Founded: 1976

Agency Specializes In: Advertising

Matt Godfrey *(Pres-Asia)*
Beverly Ho *(Gen Mgr)*
Ong Kien Hoe *(Grp Dir-Creative)*
David Thome *(Mgr)*
Craig Love *(Reg Creative Dir)*

Accounts:
ABN Amro; 2008
Accenture
Beijing Xidebao Disinfection Products Toilet
Caltex
Campbell Soup Company
Citibank
Colgate
General Mills
NEC

Australia & New Zealand

Landor Associates
Level 11 15 Blue Street, North Sydney, NSW 2060 Australia
Tel.: (61) 289088700
Fax: (61) 299595639
E-Mail: hello@landor.com
Web Site: www.landor.com

Agency Specializes In: Advertising Specialties, Brand Development & Integration, Digital/Interactive

Marcela Garces *(Mng Dir)*
Christopher Lehmann *(Mng Dir)*
Dominic Walsh *(Mng Dir)*
Monica Au *(Mng Dir-Client-GC)*
Peter Mack *(Exec Dir-Mktg-Greater China)*
Kenzo Makino *(Dir-Mktg)*
Ashley Webster *(Mgr-Mktg)*

Accounts:
Australian Youth Orchestra
Batelco Telecommunication Services
Cafe Coffee Day Coffee Conglomerate Services
Diageo Food & Beverage Products Mfr
FedEx Transportation Services
Jeremie Normandin
Microsoft Campaign: "Microsoft's Extraoridinary Conversations"
PepsiCo Consumer Products Services
Russian Copper Company
Taj Hotels Resorts & Palaces Hotel Services

Young & Rubicam Australia/New Zealand

Level 14, 35 Clarence Street, Sydney, 2000 Australia
Tel.: (61) 2 9778 7100
Web Site: www.yr.com

Employees: 110

Julian Bell *(Mng Partner)*
Phil McDonald *(Grp Mng Dir)*
Ben Coulson *(Chief Creative Officer-Australia & NZ)*
Mathieu Van Hieu *(Bus Dir & Head-French)*
David Joubert *(Exec Dir-Creative)*
Bart Pawlak *(Exec Dir-Creative)*
Blair Burchill *(Grp Acct Dir)*
Matilda Hobba *(Grp Acct Dir)*
Ella Ward *(Grp Acct Dir)*
Rachel Semmens *(Acct Dir)*
Michael Hyde *(Dir-Plng)*
Helen Leech *(Sr Acct Mgr)*
Lynsey Murtagh *(Acct Mgr)*
Erin Core *(Planner)*

Accounts:
Air Force Recruitment

Young & Rubicam NZ Ltd.

Level 4 Corner Augustas Terrace& Parnell Rise, 2A Auckland, New Zealand
Mailing Address:
Private Mail Bag 93-234, Auckland, 2 New Zealand
Tel.: (64) 93085444
Fax: (64) 9308 5405
E-Mail: ian_mcdougall@nz.yr.com
Web Site: www.yr.com

Employees: 60
Year Founded: 1981

Grant Maxwell *(Gen Mgr)*
Josh Moore *(Exec Dir-Creative)*
Victoria Meo *(Acct Dir)*
Jason Wells *(Dir-Ideas-Natl & Planner)*
Lisa Dupre *(Dir-Creative & Art)*
Scott Henderson *(Dir-Creative-Wellington)*
Tom Paine *(Assoc Dir-Creative & Copywriter)*

Accounts:
Accident Compensation Corporation Direct Marketing
Ajax Campaign: "Nothing's quicker"
Arnotts
Budget Rent a Car
Burger King
Celtic
Central Singapore Airlines
Chanel
Cigna Insurance Creative, Media
Co-operative Bank Brand Awareness, Logo, USP, Visual Identity, Website
Colgate
Election
Farmlands
Fuji Film
Hancocks
HRV Creative, Digital, Direct, Media, Strategy
Kirkcaldies
LG Electronics Campaign: "Face-to-Facebook", Creative, Digital, Media, Social, Sponsorship, Strategy
Liquorland
Metservice Campaign: "Dim Outlook", Real Time Weather Browser
Microsoft
Mollers
Novartis
Panasonic Panasonic ECO-max Light 400
Posie+
Quickflix Creative
Schick Razor Campaign: "Would You Kiss You"
SPARC
Tower DM
Westfield

Young & Rubicam Wellington

Level 3 107 Custom House Quay, PO Box 3214, Wellington, 6011 New Zealand
Tel.: (64) 4384 6488
Fax: (64) 4384 6575
E-Mail: info@yr.com
Web Site: www.yr.com

Employees: 12

Tim Ellis *(Mng Dir-Wellington)*
Grant Maxwell *(Gen Mgr)*
Catherine Hamilton *(Dir-Trading)*
Rikki Townsley *(Dir-Strategy)*
James Mason *(Sr Acct Mgr)*
Ruby Dreifuss *(Media Planner)*

Accounts:
Colgate-Palmolive
Sevens Wellington Creative

China

Young & Rubicam Guangzhou

28th Fl 246 ZhongShanSi Road, Guangzhou, 510023 China
Tel.: (86) 20 8363 5990
Fax: (86) 20 8363 5972
E-Mail: hailey.huang@yr.com
Web Site: www.yr.com

Employees: 64
Year Founded: 1992

Michael Xia *(CEO)*
Matthew Godfrey *(Pres-Asia)*
Charles Sampson *(CEO-China)*
Ronnie Wu *(Grp Dir-Creative-Beijing)*
Yvonne Lan *(Acct Exec)*

Accounts:
China Southern Airlines Co. Creative
Ed Hardy
Electrolux Campaign: "Orange"
Gangle Food Campaign: "Cherry"
Guangzhou International Finance Centre (West Tower) Creative
Guangzhou Metro Creative
Midea Home Appliances
PETA Campaign: "Whipped"
Pets Lover Campaign: "The Noose"
Ping An Bank
Shanghai Yichuan Health Science & Technology Co. Campaign: "Peanut Butter"
Tapas Mobile Technology Campaign: "Fire Fighters"
Tencent Creative, OOH, Print, Soso.com, Viral Videos
Wang & Li Asia Resources Campaign: "Bear"

Young & Rubicam Shanghai

Rm 608-606 Ocean Tower 550 Yan An Rd E, Shanghai, 200001 China
Tel.: (86) 21 6351 8588
Fax: (86) 21 6350 1109
Web Site: www.yr.com

Stephen Drummond *(Chm/Chief Strategy Officer-China)*
Annie Boo *(Mng Dir)*
Kaiyu Li *(Chief Strategy Officer)*
Kien Hoe *(Exec Dir-Creative)*
Ong Kien Koe *(Exec Dir-Creative)*
Handsome Wong *(Dir-Creative)*

Accounts:
Burger King China (Agency of Record)
Colgate China (Agency of Record)
CooperVision Avaira, Biofinity, Biomedics, Branding, Proclear
Danone Campaign: "Tilt - Library", Mizone
Disney Store
Funkwerk Security Camera
GAP Campaign: "Let's Gap Together"
Night Safari
Pantone Colors
Renner
Zhang Xiao Quan Knife

India

Everest Brand Solutions

5th Floor Terminal 9 Nehru Road, Vile Parle E, Mumbai, 400099 India
Tel.: (91) 22 61952000
Fax: (91) 22 61952062
Web Site: www.ineverest.com

Employees: 55

Dhunji S. Wadia *(Pres)*
Naveen Saraswat *(COO)*
Aradhana Bhushan *(VP)*
Samir Chonkar *(Head-Creative Function)*
Rajiv Rajadhyaksha *(Head-IT-Natl)*
Manish Thapliyal *(Dir-Bus)*

Accounts:
Aaj Tak
Aditya Birla Group Brand Strategy, Creative, More
Pantaloons Fashion Retail Creative, Strategic
Augere Broadband Wireless Services, Creative, Strategic
Bharat Hotels
B'LUE Water
Borosil Glass Works Brand Strategy, Creative, Microwavable Products
CNN-IBN
Colgate-Palmolive
Danone Blue
Emami
GoAir
JW Marriott Creative
Life Insurance Corporation
Maxx Mobiles Maxx RACE
Onida ACs Creative
Pantaloons Retail India Ltd Campaign: "India in Vogue"
Parle Products Ltd. Campaign: " Perfect Snack", Campaign: "Cafe Mocha", Campaign: "Deliciously Rich", Campaign: "Doon Kya", Campaign: "Milk Shakti Milky Sandwich", Campaign: "Sardar JI", Campaign: "Snakes & Ladders", Campaign: "kacche aam ka xerox", Creative, Gold Star, Golden Arcs, Hide & Seek, Magix Biscuits, Milano, Parle Marie, Parle-G Gold, Poppins, Radio, TV, Wafers
Siemens Home Appliances
Zandu Pancharishta

Everest Brand Solutions

2nd Floor Parsvnath Arcadia, No 1 Mehrauli Gurgaon Road, Gurgaon, 122001 India
Tel.: (91) 124 454 6000
Fax: (91) 124 426 7777
E-Mail: prabhu.kanra@ineverest.com
Web Site: www.ineverest.com

Employees: 35

Agency Specializes In: Communications

Naveen Saraswat *(COO)*
Manish Thapliyal *(Dir-Bus)*
Prabhu Kalra *(Mgr-Studio & Production)*

Accounts:
Ranbaxy Laboratories Creative, Volini

Rediffusion Y&R Pvt. Ltd.
Terminal 9 5th Floor Nehru Road, Vile Parle East, Mumbai, 400 099 India
Tel.: (91) 22 2613 8800
Fax: (91) 22 2612 6422
Web Site: www.rediffusionyr.com

Employees: 500
Year Founded: 1973

Diwan Arun Nanda *(Chm)*
Dhunji S. Wadia *(Pres)*
Dinanath Rewatkar *(Partner-Strategic Plng)*
Shreecharan Nadkarni *(CFO)*
Rahul Jauhari *(Chief Creative Officer)*
Kalyani Srivastava *(VP)*
Roopa Badrinath *(Head-HR)*
Darshan Choudhari *(Head-Creative)*
Uttio Majumdar *(Head-Ops)*
Padmakumar Narasimhamurthy *(Dir-Creative-Natl)*
Sanket Pathare *(Dir-Creative)*

Accounts:
Aashray Adhikar Abhiyan
Abbott India Brand Strategy, Creative, Digene
Anandabazar Patrika Creative
Arvind Clothing Ltd Arrow Readymades
Bank of India
Berger Paints Campaign: "Magician"
Books & Beyond
Bramhacrop Infrastructures
Choco Caramel
DHL Worldwide Express
Economic Times
Emami BoroPlus, Campaign: "Headache", Fast Relief, Mentho Plus, Zandu Balm
Eveready Campaign: "Photo Shoot"
GKB Opticals
New-Hamdard
Heinz Campaign: "Deserted Playground", Campaign: "Kid", Nycil
Hygia India Creative
India Today Creative
Indian Oil Corporation Ltd.
Indian Tobacco Company
ITC Ltd. Campaign: "Be the First One", Campaign: "Signature", Classmate
Kaya Skin Clinic
Kingfisher Airlines
Koolfoam Campaign: "Soft mattresses for sound sleep."
Lafarge India Communication Strategy, Creative
Lotte
McDowell's
Midland Bookshop
Orra
Paras Dairy Creative
Phillips Van Heusen Corporation Arrow
Pioneer Suspension
Rasna
Reliance Industries Limited
Saarc Pharma
Sahara India
SeventyMM
Sistema Shyam TeleServices Limited "Gods on Facebook"
State Bank of India Fund Guru
The Statesman
Sugar Free
The Taj Group of Hotels
Tata Motors Bolt, Campaign: "Celebrate Awesomeness", Communication, Creative, Media, Revotron Petrol Engine, Tata Nano, Zest
Tata Power Creative
Videocon
Zydus Cadila

Rediffusion Y&R Pvt. Ltd.
DLF Cyber City, Building No 9B, Gurgaon, 122 002 India
Tel.: (91) 124 433 8000
Fax: (91) 124 405 0017
Web Site: www.rediffusionyr.com

Employees: 100

Saumya Chattopadhyay *(VP & Head-Delhi Office)*
Madhumita Mukherjee *(VP & Branch Head)*
Jaideep Mahajan *(Head-Creative-Natl)*
Suman Varma *(Head-Ops)*
Bhautik Mithani *(Grp CFO)*

Accounts:
Amway
Everest Building Solutions
New-Experion Creative
Godfrey Philips
New-Hamdard Laboratories Creative, Joshina, Rooh Afza, Safi, Sualin
Hotels.com
IFFCO
JX Nippon
Olympia Gym
Paras Dairy
New-Resurgent Rajasthan Partnership Summit Summit 2015
Sistema Shyam TeleServices Limited MTS
Videocon Flat Panel Television, Telecom
Virgin Atlantic
Xerox

Indonesia

Matari Advertising
Puri Matari Jalan HR Rasuna Said Kav H 1-2, Jakarta, 12920 Indonesia
Tel.: (62) 21 525 5160
Fax: (62) 21 525 6440
E-Mail: contact@matari-ad.com
Web Site: www.matari-ad.com

National Agency Associations: IAA

Agency Specializes In: Consumer Marketing, Corporate Identity

Krishna Handhoko *(CFO)*
Gunawan Solihin *(COO)*
Rusmeini Subronto *(Chief HR Officer)*
Jeffry Katianda *(Sr Dir-Art)*
Agung P. Suhanjaya *(Dir-Creative)*
Pia Ravaie *(Mgr-HR)*

Accounts:
Danone AQUA, Print, TV
Friends Of The National Park Foundation
LG Mobile Indonesia
Lucido-L

Japan

Dentsu Young & Rubicam Inc.
Comodio Shiodome 2-14-1 Higashi Shimbashi, Minato-ku, Tokyo, 105-8613 Japan
Tel.: (81) 3 5219 9111
Fax: (81) 3 5219 9222
E-Mail: mail@dyr.co.jp
Web Site: www.dyr.co.jp

Employees: 296
Year Founded: 1981

Agency Specializes In: Brand Development & Integration, Media Buying Services, Strategic Planning/Research

Accounts:
Accenture
AT&T Communications Corp.
Citi Group
Dole Japan Lakatan Bananas
The North Face

Korea

HS Ad, Inc.
14th Floor LG Mapo Building, Mapo-Gu, 275 Gongdeok-Dong, Seoul, 121-721 Korea (South)
Tel.: (82) 2 705 2600
Fax: (82) 2 786 1988
Web Site: www.hsad.co.kr

Year Founded: 1959

Agency Specializes In: Brand Development & Integration, Media Buying Services, Planning & Consultation, Publicity/Promotions

Yun Mi Lee *(Acct Exec)*

Accounts:
Belif Cosmetic Chok Chok art project Campaign: "Street Artists"
Carito Campaign: "Urinal Ambient"
Chamisul Jinro Whisky
Danone
Jack Wolfskin
Kleannara Campaign: "Land Animals"
Korea Tourism Organization Campaign: "Say Hello, Say Annyeong"
Korean Air Campaign: "Space"
LG Electronics Inc. Campaign: "LTE Metronome"
LG Household & Healthcare Ltd. Campaign: "Isaknox Vibrating Foundation", Campaign: "Ohui Age Recoverytri-Shield"
LG LG 3D TV
Perioe Campaign: "46Cm Cap"
Prospecs Campaign: "Spring Launch"
Skechers Campaign: "Bottom"

Malaysia

Dentsu Young & Rubicam Sdn. Bhd.
6th & 8th Floors Wisma E&C No 2 Lorong Dungan Kiri, Damansara Heights, 50490 Kuala Lumpur, Malaysia
Tel.: (60) 3 2095 2600
Fax: (60) 3 2095 1289
Web Site: www.yr.com

Employees: 60
Year Founded: 1976

National Agency Associations: AAAA (MALAYSIA)

Lisa Hezila *(Mng Dir)*
Matthew Godfrey *(Pres-Asia)*
Gigi Lee *(Exec Creative Dir & Art Dir)*
Law Kok Yew *(Art Dir & Designer)*
Joshua Tay *(Dir-Creative)*
Eliza Wong *(Acct Supvr)*
Nicholas Siew *(Designer)*
Nigel Menezes *(Grp Bus Dir)*

Accounts:
Asia Pacific Breweries Campaign: "Valentine's Day", Tiger Beer
Astro Entertainment
Colgate-Palmolive
Dorling Kindersley Animal Encyclopedias
LG Electronics
LG Health+
New-Malaysian Nature Society
Moonshine Productions
National Cancer Society Malaysia Campaign: "Brain Development"
Naza Premira Campaign: "Spot The Difference"
Penguin Books Malaysia Campaign: "More Than Just The Classics", Cookbook, DK's Animal Encyclopedias, Penguin Audiobooks, Rough Guide Phrasebook

Philippines

Young & Rubicam Philippines
9th Fl Marajo Twr 312 26th St W Corner 1 Ave, Bonifacio Global City, Manila, Philippines
Tel.: (63) 2 403 1800
Fax: (63) 2 885 7392
Web Site: www.yr.com/

Employees: 92
Year Founded: 1948

Agency Specializes In: Communications, Consumer Marketing, Publicity/Promotions

Anna Testa *(CEO)*
Marcus Rebeschini *(Exec Creative Dir-Regional)*
Badong Abesamis *(Chief Creative Officer)*
Herbert Hernandez *(Exec Creative Dir & Dir-Art)*
Gra Benesa *(Art Dir)*
karl Nylander *(Dir-Art)*
Jon Salutal *(Dir-Art)*
Az Talal *(Copywriter)*
Marco Dimaano *(Assoc Creative Dir)*

Accounts:
2GO Group (Agency of Record) 2GO Express, 2GO Freight, 2GO Logistics, 2GO Travel
Aiza Belen
Century Canning Corporation Campaign: "Ultimate Fansign"
CMHI, Land Inc Kangaroo, Kassel Residences
Colgate-Palmolive Phils., Inc.; 1949
Filinvest Creative
Garage Magazine
Maynilad Anti-Dengue Mosquito Trap, Campaign: "Dengue Bottle"
Nokia Campaign: "Taxi Meter App"
New-PRIMER GROUP
Samsonite
The Tinta Awards
United Laboratories Campaign: "Billboard"; 1998

Singapore

Y&R Singapore
50 Scotts Road #03-01, 228242 Singapore, Singapore
Tel.: (65) 6671 3000
Fax: (65) 6296 2016
Web Site: www.yr.com

Employees: 100
Year Founded: 1981

Agency Specializes In: Advertising

Hari Ramanathan *(Chief Strategy Officer)*
Komal Bedi Sohal *(Chief Creative Officer)*
Matthew Godfrey *(Pres-Asia)*
Sanjay Bhasin *(CEO-Thailand & South East Asia)*
Katherine Khor *(Sr Dir-Art)*
Kea Sui Hong *(Grp Acct Dir)*
Wedad Sunny *(Client Svcs Dir)*
Zach Wong *(Acct Dir)*

Accounts:
Al Futtaim Group
Asia Pacific Breweries Campaign: "Kirin Beer Bro-Quet"
Barons Beer Campaign: "Peanut Launcher Coaster"
BMW Asia Creative
Caltex
Cerebos Brand's Essence of Chicken
Chevron
Colgate-Palmolive Campaign: "Glow in the Dark Teen Idol Poster"
Dark Dog Energy Drink
Davis Guitar Music Centre Campaign: "Rock Dm"
Kirin Ichiban Beer
New-Land Rover "52Undiscover", Activation, Digital Engagement, Direct Marketing, Marketing Communications, Print, TV, The Test Drive Billboard
Lend Lease
M1 Campaign: "M1. For Every One", Campaign: "Welcome to the World of M1", Communications, Creative Agency of Record
Marina Bay Sands Creative, The Shoppes
Ministry of Manpower (Creative Agency of Record) Marketing Communications
MINT Museum of Toys Dolls, Sci-Fi, Tin Toys
MobileOne; 2008
Nerf Campaign: "Coin Shooter Business Card"
Operation Smile Singapore Campaign: "Share for Smiles"
Oxford
Popeye's Louisiana Kitchen
Republic of Singapore Navy Battlefleet: Singapore, Campaign: "Go Beyond Horizons", Campaign: "Sea of Support"
Risk
Shiseido
Singapore Sports Hub Communications, Creative Agency of Record, Kallang Wave Mall
Teerath & Co
Tiger Beer
Tripartite Alliance for Fair & Progressive Employment Practices; 2008
Workforce Development Agency; 2008

Thailand

Dentsu Young & Rubicam Ltd.
16-17th & 19th Floors Siam Tower 989 Rama 1 Rd, Pathumwan, Bangkok, 10330 Thailand
Tel.: (66) 2 658 0999
Web Site: www.yr.com

Employees: 115
Year Founded: 1985

National Agency Associations:

Wanvimol Markcayathorn *(COO)*
Marcus Rebeschini *(Chief Creative Officer-Asia)*
Trong Tantivejakul *(Chief Creative Officer)*
Sanjay Bhasin *(CEO-Thailand & South East Asia)*
Jindarat Udomthanapat *(Acct Mgr)*

Accounts:
AB Foods & Beverages Co., Ltd. (Novartis)
Aids Access Foundation
Amway (Thailand) Ltd.
Bacardi Breezer
Bangkok Art & Culture Centre
Caltex Oil (Thailand) Ltd.
Dsg International Campaign: "Teddy Bear"
DTAC Ad, Cellphone
Ford Operations (Thailand) Co., Ltd. (Wunderman Account)
FUJIFILM Holdings Corporation
Harnn
Ichitan Campaign: "Asteroid", Double Drink
Jaguar Cars (Thailand) Co., Ltd.
Katoa Wines Campaign: "Katoa"
LG Electronics Campaign: "Helicopter", LG Solar Dome Microwave
Mai Tan Campaign: "Affair"
Mazda Sales (Thailand) Co. Ltd. (Wunderman Account)
Mondelez International, Inc.
Oishi Black Tea Lemon
Oishi Group
Shiseido Americas Corporation; Thailand
Siam Park City Campaign: "Drown"
Thai Airways International Plc (Wunderman Account)
Thai Health Promotion Foundation Campaign: "Pregnant"
Total Access Communication Public Company Limited

Vietnam

Y&R Vietnam
193 Dinh Tien Hoang St, Dist. 1, 12th Floor, HMC Tower, Ho Chi Minh City, Vietnam
Tel.: (84) 0 8 38 258 351

Vincent Van Dessel *(CEO)*
Kit Ong *(Chief Creative Officer)*

Accounts:
VP Bank (Vietnam Prosperity Bank) Branding, Design

Austria

Y&R GmbH
Rotemturmstrasse 1618 6th Fl, A-1010 Vienna, Austria
Tel.: (43) 1 53 117 0
Fax: (43) 1 53 117 200
Web Site: www.yrvienna.at

E-Mail for Key Personnel:
President: alois_schober@eu.yr.com

Employees: 50
Year Founded: 1982

Agency Specializes In: Advertising

Christian Strassner *(Mng Dir)*
Sebastian Bayer *(CEO-Vienna)*

Accounts:
Alfa Romeo
Barilla
Cyber TV
Danone
DerMann
Hofburg
Integrationshaus
Kotanyi
TUS
Wien Tourismus
Xerox

Belgium

Y&R Belgium S.A.
140a Rue de Streetallestraat, 1180 Brussels, Belgium
Tel.: (32) 2 375 80 12
Fax: (32) 2 375 88 43
Web Site: www.yr.com

Employees: 45
Year Founded: 1964

National Agency Associations: APC

Agency Specializes In: Advertising

Hubert Morent *(CFO)*
Erwin Jansen *(Chm/CEO-Benelux)*

Accounts:
Accenture
Campbell Foods
Colgate-Palmolive
Fromageries Bel
GEOX Campaign: "Bubblegum", Campaign: "The shoe that breathes."
Miele
Otrivin
Philip Morris
Soubry
Xerox

France

Y&R France S.A.
57 Ave Andre Morizet, BP 73, 92105 Boulogne-Billancourt, Cedex France
Tel.: (33) 1 46 84 33 33
Fax: (33) 1 46 84 32 72
Web Site: www.yr.com

Employees: 500
Year Founded: 1964

National Agency Associations: AACC

Agency Specializes In: Advertising

Vanessa Boueyres *(Gen Mgr)*
Montassar Chlaika *(Editor & Designer)*

Accounts:
Barilla Food & Drink
Campbell Soup Company
Colgate-Palmolive Company Body Care, Campaign: "Mime", Cleaning Products, Oral Care
Danacol
Danone Actimel, Bio, Charles Gervais, Coupe du Monde, Creme de Yaourt, Danao, Danette, Danone Nature, Danone Recette Cremeuse, Danone et Fruits, Fjord, Gervita, Institute Danone, Jockey, Kid, Petit Gervais with Fruits, Petit Suisse Gervais, Taillefine, Valoute, Yogurt Natural
Decathlon
Etap Hotel
Fromageries Bel Campaign: "Figs and Nuts"
G6 Hospitality LLC Transportation
GrandOptical
L'Etudiant
Lu
Lysopaine
Obut Campaign: "The Bug"
Opel France Campaign: "The Beach", Lane Departure Warning System
Ricard Transportation
Smallable
Surfrider Foundation Campaign: "Be Proud", Campaign: "Keepers of the Coast T-Shirt", Fish, Seal, Whale
Tiabi Transportation
Trax Magazine

Y&R Paris
67 Avenue Andre Morizet, BP 73, 92105 Boulogne, Cedex 4 France
Tel.: (33) 1 4684 3333
Fax: (33) 1 4684 3272
Web Site: www.yr.com

Employees: 10
Year Founded: 1982

Agency Specializes In: Advertising

Valerie Montiel *(Mng Dir)*
Andrew Dimitriou *(Pres-Europe)*
Neel Majumder *(Exec Dir-Creative)*
Laurent Baghdassarian *(Art Dir)*
Florentine Baron *(Client Svcs Dir)*
Pierre Philippe Sardon *(Art Dir)*
Akim Zerouali *(Art Dir)*
Eric Esculier *(Dir-Art)*
Steven Guyard *(Dir-Art)*
Stephanie Pasteur *(Dir-Art)*
Sophie Cavazza *(Assoc Dir)*
Aure Tessandier *(Assoc Dir)*
Ugo Fossa *(Copywriter)*
Celine Lescure *(Copywriter)*
Laurent Vergnaud *(Copywriter)*
Fanny Renard *(Jr Producer-TV)*

Accounts:
Aoste Group Cochonou
Bel Fromage
Bel Leerdammer Campaign: "The Boss"
Boursin Campaign: "Sensations"
Colgate-Palmolive Ajax Household Cleaner, Bleach, Campaign: "Warning Signs", La Croix Bleach, Max White One, Maxfresh Night, Paic, Paic Excel, Pro Gum Health, Toothpaste
Danone Actimel, Campaign: "The Big Day", Danacol, Gervais, Poster Campaign, Volvic Juiced
Decathlon Artengo
France Galop Campaign: "Backstage"
IFAW - International Fund for Animal Welfare
KelOptic Advertising, Campaign: "Turning Impressionism into Hyperrealism"
L'Etudiant
LG Campaign: "The Chess", Optimus 3D
Meccano Campaign: "Drum Kit", Campaign: "If You Can't Have It, Build It - Dog"
Mini Babybel
Obut Campaign: "Make room for precision"
Opel Campaign: "Always keep an eye on the road", Campaign: "Wir Leben Autos"
Puliamo l'oceano
Satellite
Smallable.com
Surfrider Foundation Europe Campaign: "Everything Must Go", Campaign: "The Shoe", Campaign: "You Buy The Sea Pays", Fish Hunter, Seal Hunter, Whale Hunter
Trax Magazine
New-Volvic Juicy

Germany

Berger Baader Hermes GmbH
(Formerly Baader Hermes/Y&R)
Nymphenburger Strasse 86, 80636 Munich, Germany
Tel.: (49) 89 210227 0
Fax: (49) 89 210227 27
E-Mail: netzwerke@bergerbaaderhermes.de
Web Site: www.bergerbaaderhermes.de

Employees: 28

Agency Specializes In: Advertising

Oliver Hermes *(Co-Founder)*
Matthias Berger *(Owner)*
Sven Nagel *(Head-Creation & Dir-Creative)*

Accounts:
UniCredit

Iconmobile
Wallstrasse 14a, 10179 Berlin, Germany
Tel.: (49) 30 886633 100
Web Site: www.iconmobile.com/start

Year Founded: 2003

Agency Specializes In: Brand Development & Integration, Mobile Marketing

Stephan Linser *(Sr VP-Operational Controlling)*
Jerome Williams *(Head-Production & Dev)*
Tobias Graening *(Sr Dir-User Experience)*
Holger Nosekabel *(Dir-Mobile Consulting)*
Clementine Jinhee Declercq *(Designer-UX)*
Christina Nenke *(Sr Designer-UX)*

Accounts:
Agilsys
Audi
BMW
Deutsche Telekom
Ferrero
Ford
GMX
IBM
Kraft
Land Rover
Mercedes-Benz
Microsoft Windows Phone
Nike
Nivea
Nokia
O2
Orange
Otto
Procter & Gamble
Qype
SchulerVZ
Universal
Vans
Vodafone
Volkswagen
Xbox

Italy

Y&R Italia, srl
Tortona 37, 20144 Milan, Italy
Tel.: (39) 02 77 32 1
Fax: (39) 02 76 00 90 4
E-Mail: reception.yrmilan@it.yr.com
Web Site: www.yr.com

Employees: 300
Year Founded: 1955

Agency Specializes In: Advertising

Marco Bonanni *(CFO-Y & R Italy, Exec VP & Gen Mgr-Young & Rubicam Grp)*
Umberto Mauri *(Art Dir)*
Davide Breghelli *(Art Dir)*
Ruth Arban *(Dir-Client)*
Cinzia Caccia *(Dir-Art)*
Mariano Lombardi *(Dir-Creative)*
Giulia Papetti *(Dir-Art)*
Paolo Pollo *(Copywriter)*
Filippo Testa *(Copywriter)*
Cristian Comand *(Deputy Dir-Creative-Art)*

Accounts:
Allianz SE
Arena Swimwear
Azonzo Travel Campaign: "Australia Map", Campaign: "From tourist to traveller."
Barilla America, Inc. Pasta
Bavaria Air Bag
Bios Line
Bracco
Caf Onlus Charity
Cloetta Italia Galatine
Coop Eco Radio Ad
Cordenons Group Campaign: "Paper Flowers"
Danone Campaign: "Adopt The Salami Village
Distillerie F.LLI Ramazzotti
Elica
Esercito Italiano (Italian Army)
Fondazione Pubblicitae Progresso
Glassing
JT International S.A.
La Repubblica.it Campaign: "The World Changes in Seconds"
Lavazza Growth Strategy, International Advertising
LOfficina Naturale
Parmacotto
Prima Fila Hot Club
Radio 105 Campaign: "Ambulance"
Regione Lombardia
Saila Campaign: "Breath Fish", Campaign: "Breath Garlic", Campaign: "Breath Onion"
TIM
Torggler Chimica
UNHCR
Unione Nazionale Dell'Avicoltura
United International Picture

Y&R Roma srl
Via Giulio Cesare 2, 00192 Rome, Italy
Tel.: (39) 06 326 9811
Fax: (39) 06 32 698154
E-Mail: roma@it.yr.com
Web Site: www.yr.com

Employees: 30
Year Founded: 1989

Agency Specializes In: Advertising

Roberto Bruno *(Exec VP)*
Vicky Gitto *(Exec VP & Grp Exec Dir-Creative)*
Max Di Rubba *(Dir-Art)*
Fabio Dimalio *(Dir-Art)*
Corrado Frontoni *(Dir-Art & Deputy Dir-Creative)*
Andrea Giovannone *(Dir-Art)*
Mariano Lombardi *(Dir-Creative)*
Roberta Lancieri *(Acct Supvr)*

Accounts:
Alluflon Moneta
Amref Italia
Autogrill
La Repubblica
Lottomatica
Moneta
NBC Studio Universal
The Space Cinema
Steel TV

Netherlands

Y&R Amsterdam B.V.
Karperstraat 10, 1075 KZ Amsterdam, Netherlands
Mailing Address:
PO Box 74704, Amsterdam, 1070 BS Netherlands
Tel.: (31) 20 5 795 795
Fax: (31) 20 5 795 799
E-Mail: hello@yr.nl
Web Site: yr.nl/www/

Employees: 54
Year Founded: 1975

Agency Specializes In: Advertising

Thijs de Boer *(Exec Dir-Creative)*
Peter Hamelinck *(Exec Dir-Creative)*
Arjan Hamel *(Dir-Fin-Y&R Netherlands)*

Accounts:
C1000 Campaign: "Groovy Gogos"
Danone
Dutch Stutter Association
LG Smart Thief
Liga
Nederlandse Federatie Stotteren Campaign: "Be Patient With People Who Stutter"
Perfetti van Melle
Surfrider Foundation Europe Surfrider

Portugal

Y&R Portugal
Av Eng Duarte Pacheco, Tower 1 9th Fl, 1070-101 Lisbon, Portugal
Tel.: (351) 21 381 6300
Fax: (351) 21 381 6311
Web Site: www.yr.com

Employees: 42
Year Founded: 1988

National Agency Associations: APAP (Portugal)

Agency Specializes In: Advertising

Pedro Ferreira *(Art Dir & Exec Creative Dir)*
Judite Mota *(Exec Dir-Creative & Copywriter)*
Joao Rocha *(Art Dir)*
Maria Correia *(Dir-Accts)*
Sofia Moutinho *(Copywriter)*
Jose Quintela *(Copywriter)*

Accounts:
AMB3E
AMI Campaign: "Xmas Spirit"
Benfica
BMW Mini
Colgate-Palmolive
Compal
Danone
International Medical Assistance Campaign: "Christmas Spirit Needs Help"
Jornal i Campaign: "Obama", Campaign: "The right words give you the clear picture.Jornal i. Your daily newspaper."
Magnum Photos Campaign: "Flower", Campaign: "History By Capa"
ModaLisboa Campaign: "A Catwalk on the Rooftop"
Paladin
Sacana Hot Sauce Campaign: "Mr.Lava"
Sport Lisboa E Benfica Campaign: "Valentine's Boy"

Spain

Vinizius/Y&R
C/Numancia 164-168 8th Floor, 08029 Barcelona, Spain
Tel.: (34) 93 366 6600
Fax: (34) 93 366 6608
E-Mail: recepcion.vinizius@yr.com
Web Site: www.yr.com

Employees: 130
Year Founded: 1966

Agency Specializes In: Advertising

Gerard Martinez Anguela *(Sr Dir-Creative & Art)*
Nicolas Alberte *(Dir-Creative)*
Joaquim Crespo *(Dir-Creative)*
Nina Fontcuberta *(Dir-Art)*
Pol Mestres *(Dir-Art)*
Alba Ferrer *(Planner-Strategic)*
Salvador Torras *(Copywriter)*

Accounts:
Conservas Isabel
The Dannon Company, Inc. Activia, Campaign: "Dare to Feel Good", Campaign: "The Spill" Super Bowl 2014, Creative, Oikos, Oikos Triple Zero, TV
Gallina Blanca
Industrias Marca
La Piara
Nuprexpa Nocilla, Phoskitos
Pescanova
Swatch

Young & Rubicam, S.L.
Avenida de Burgos 21 Planta 9A, 28036 Madrid, Spain
Tel.: (34) 91 384 2400
Fax: (34) 384 2401
E-Mail: informacion@es.yr.com
Web Site: www.yr.com

Year Founded: 1966

National Agency Associations: AEAP-IAA

Agency Specializes In: Advertising

Jesus Portillo *(CFO)*
Gerard Martinez Anguela *(Sr Dir-Creative & Art)*
Joaquim Crespo *(Dir-Creative)*
Jordi Almuni Font *(Dir-Creative)*
Nina Fontcuberta *(Dir-Art)*
Nacho Diaz Peitx *(Dir-Art)*

Switzerland

Advico Y&R AG
Werbeagentur BSW Hardturmstrasse 133, CH-8037 Zurich, Switzerland
Tel.: (41) 1 801 91 91
Fax: (41) 1 801 9292
E-Mail: info@advico.ch
Web Site: www.advico.ch

Employees: 50
Year Founded: 1981

National Agency Associations: BSW

Agency Specializes In: Advertising

Andreas Widmer *(CEO)*
Markus Gut *(Chief Creative Officer)*
Susan Baumgartner *(Mng Dir-Special Offers Comm)*
Dominik Oberwiler *(Exec Dir-Creative)*
Michael Gallmann *(Art Dir)*
Christoph Schwarz *(Acct Dir)*
Matthias Kadlubsky *(Dir-Art)*

Accounts:
ACAT
AMAG Automobil Campaign: "Night Vision Assist", Cars
Audi Campaign: "Lane Assist Pool"
Bacardi Alcohol
Beads4You Jewellery
BfB Beratungsstelle fur Brandverhutung
Blaues Kreuz Campaign: "Anti alcohol", Diary
Blick Am Abend Newspaper
Brot fur Alle/Fastenopfer
Bucher & Walt Garmin GPS
Cina Bubenberg Campaign: "2D Sucks"
Citterio Campaign: "Finest slices"
Danone Actimel, Activa, Danonino
Farmer Cereal Bars Campaign: "Instant Energy. Put to use by parents since 30 years."
Feldschlosschen AG Arkina, Battery, Rhazunser, Schweppes
Futurecom Iphone App
GE Capital Bank
Giuseppe Citterio Parma Ham
HEKS Campaign: "The Unimportant Person", Campaign: "who is who"
Hotel Montana
Iam Haircare
ILCO, International Labor Organization
Leica
Maestrani Campaign: "Everything seem sweeter", Minor
Migros-Genossenschafts-Bund
Migros Campaign: "Ryffel Running - Forest", Campaign: "Sun Look", Hair Products, SportXX
Psyko Store Campaign: "Welcome To The Dark Side"
Red Cross Campaign: "Switzerland is Running Out of Blood"
Reporters Without Borders Campaign: "Hang Man"
Rhatische Bahn
Roadcross Organisation For Alcohol Prevention
SonntagsZeitung Campaign: "Euro Crisis", Campaign: "Peace talks", Newspaper
SPW Bikes Campaign: "Love Bike", Campaign: "Survival of the Fittest", Campaign: "Tailwind Inclusive", Sportplausch Wider, Tailor-Made Bikes
SRK Campaign: "Blood Donation"
SuddenRush Surf Travel
Sun Look
Supreme Security
Swiss Hemophilia Association Campaign: "The everyday dangers of a hemophiliac brought to life"
Teleclub Campaign: "No Interruptions"
Tierpark Godlau Campaign: "Boy Sitting",

Campaign: "Uncage your kids", Zoo
Total Washing Powder
Zoo Zurich Campaign: "Child"
Zweifel Pomy Chips Campaign: "Ring Ring"

Y&R Business Communications
Rue Lugardon 1, CH-1201 Geneva, Switzerland
Tel.: (41) 22 908 4000
Fax: (41) 22 908 4040
E-Mail: info_yrbc@ch.yr.com
Web Site: www.yrbc.com

Employees: 60
Year Founded: 1961

Agency Specializes In: Advertising

Bob Heron *(Exec Dir-Creative-Young & Rubicam Grp Geneva)*
Alexander Kraev *(Dir-Art)*

Accounts:
Adobe
Caterpillar
DuPont de Nemours International S.A.
UNHCR Campaign: "Dilemmas"

Turkey

C-Section
Istiklal Caddesi Kallavi Sokak No 1 Kat 1, Istanbul, Beyoglu 34430 Turkey
Tel.: (90) 2122510860
E-Mail: reception@c-section.com
Web Site: www.c-section.com/tr

Year Founded: 2004

Agency Specializes In: Advertising, Digital/Interactive, Mobile Marketing, Outdoor, Search Engine Optimization, Social Media

Cicek Kayoglu *(Head-Client Svcs)*
Ceyhun Saracoglu *(Head-Creative)*
Kivanc Kanturk *(Producer-Digital)*
Emre Dinc *(Dir-Art)*
Figen Yuzbasioglu *(Copywriter-Creative)*

Accounts:
Arcelik A.S. We Asked The Public
The Coca-Cola Company Campaign: "Invisible Vending Machine"
TEB JR
Vodafone Group Plc

Y&R Turkey
Bomonti Firin Sokak No: 51, 80260 Istanbul, Turkey
Tel.: (90) 212 224 9070
Fax: (90) 212 241 3561
E-Mail: meslehorn.doggim@yr.com
Web Site: www.yr.com

Employees: 108
Year Founded: 1989

Agency Specializes In: Advertising

Erkan Kaya *(Grp Head-Creative)*
Hilal Birecik *(Gen Mgr)*
Ahmet Sogutluoglu *(Sr Dir-Art)*
Serdar Gungor *(Dir-Art)*
Kadir Ozdemir *(Dir-Art)*
Can Pehlivanli *(Dir-Creative)*
Ugur Say *(Dir-Art)*
Bulent Sengul *(Dir-Art)*
Deniz Atalay *(Acct Supvr)*
Ipek Kardesler *(Acct Exec)*
Can Arabacilar *(Copywriter)*

Accounts:
Arcelik Campaign: "Dishwasher", Self Cleaning Oven, Wide Refrigerator
Barilla
Borusan Automotive
Burger King Campaign: "Hot Sauce Billboard"
Colgate-Palmolive Campaign: "For stronger teeth and healtier gum."
Danone Activia, Campaign: "Lamb, Chicken", Hayet
ING Bank
Mediterranean Traffic Accidents Association Campaign: "Sala"
Opel
Pinar
Uzay Furniture Polish
Vodafone

United Kingdom

Mars Y&R
230 City Road, London, EC1V 2TT United Kingdom
Tel.: (44) 2031193200
E-Mail: hello@marslondon.co.uk
Web Site: www.marslondon.co.uk

Year Founded: 2010

Agency Specializes In: Advertising, Graphic Design

David Driessen *(CFO)*
Matt Page *(CFO)*
Darren Keen *(Mng Dir-Europe)*
Jason Graham *(Head-Copy & Creative Grp-London)*
Erin Duffy *(Dir-Fin)*
Becky Jackson *(Dir-Bus)*
Greg Thorpe *(Dir-Bus)*
Lorna Emery *(Acct Mgr)*
Samuel Guess *(Acct Mgr)*
Taryn Roberts *(Mgr-Comml Fin)*

Rainey Kelly Campbell Roalfe/Y&R
Greater London House Hampstead Rd, London, NW1 7QP United Kingdom
Tel.: (44) 207 611 6568
Fax: (44) 207 611 6011
Web Site: www.rkcryr.com

Employees: 200
Year Founded: 1940

Agency Specializes In: Advertising

Young & Rubicam Ltd.
Greater London House Hampstead Road, London, NW1 7QP United Kingdom
Tel.: (44) 2073879366
Fax: (44) 2076116570

Employees: 180

Saul Betmead *(Chief Strategy Officer)*
Alessandra Cotugno *(Head-Plng & Exploring)*
Simon Milliship *(Exec Dir-Digital EMEA)*
Toby Talbog *(Exec Dir-Creative)*
Henry Gray *(Dir-Strategy)*

Accounts:
BAE Systems plc
Kraft Foods UK Ltd.
Marks & Spencer
Revlon Creative, Global Advertising

Middle East

Team/Y&R Abu Dhabi
3rd Floor AMF Building, Corniche, Abu Dhabi, United Arab Emirates
Tel.: (971) 2 621 5050
Fax: (971) 2 681 6811

Employees: 33
Year Founded: 1973

Agency Specializes In: Advertising

Krishnagopal Kodoth *(Dir-Art)*

Accounts:
Al Yah Satellite Communications Company YahClick

Team/Y&R HQ Dubai
1st Fl Century Plz Jumeirah Beach Rd, Dubai, United Arab Emirates
Tel.: (971) 4 344 5444
Fax: (971) 4 349 6636
E-Mail: dubai@teamyr.com

Employees: 150

Agency Specializes In: Advertising

Nadine Ghossoub *(Mng Dir)*
Emile Atallah *(Exec Dir)*
Kapil Bhimekar *(Sr Dir-Art)*
Shaik Shibli *(Grp Acct Dir)*
Nada Hassan *(Art Dir)*
Uday Desai *(Dir-Bus)*
Dima Malaeb *(Sr Acct Exec)*
Nora Ferneine *(Assoc Acct Dir)*

Accounts:
4Men
Al Noor School Campaign: "See Potential"
Al Noor Training Centre For Children With Special Needs
Al Tayer Group
American Garden Campaign: "Movie Titles", Popcorn
Atul Panase
Audi Audi Quattro
The Coca-Cola Company
Colgate 360, MaxFresh, Palmolive MaxFresh
Domino's Pizza
Emaar
Etisalat
Ford
Gulf News Campaign: "Headline News Cup Sleeve"
Harvey Nichols Airhorn, Altitude Sickness Pills, Campaign: "Pelicans", Campaign: "The Reaction Collection", Defibrillator, Evil Eye Charm, Lipstick Stain Remover, Little Black Book, Personalized Towels
Home & Beyond
Kafa Verbal Abuse Awareness
LG Electronics
LIWA Trading
Mashreq Bank Campaign: "Numbers: Growth", Campaign: "We see more than numbers"
Microsoft Xbox Resident Evil 5, Zombieland
Nandos Campaign: "End of the World Meal"
Neenah Paper Manimal
Paras Pharma Splitting Headache
Quint Campaign: "Dubai's Got Culture"
The Reaction Collection
Red Cross Campaign: "Buried", Campaign: "Flood", Campaign: "Heroes Wanted"
Resident Evil
Rhino's Energy Drink
Saudi Telecom Corporate Advertising
Sony Ericsson
Starco Fashion Group
Stopache Campaign: "Explosive Pain"
Strongbow Gold Hero
Varta Batteries
Visa
Woz Footwear

Czech Republic

Y&R Praha, s.r.o.
Nadrazni 762/32, 150 00 Prague, 5 Czech Republic
Tel.: (420) 221 420 121
Fax: (420) 221 420 132
E-Mail: info.prague@yr.cz
Web Site: www.yr.cz

Employees: 100
Year Founded: 1990

Agency Specializes In: Advertising

Peter Havlicek *(Chm & CEO)*
Tomas Dvorak *(Exec Mng Dir)*
Josef Janousek *(CFO)*
Jaime Mandelbaum *(Chief Creative Officer)*
Atila Martins *(Sr Dir-Art)*
Linda Hennessy *(Client Svcs Dir-Europe)*
Miroslav Pomikal *(Dir-Creative)*
Dora Pruzincova *(Dir-Creative)*

Accounts:
Bel Campaign: "Never Ending Smoothness"
Betadine Campaign: "Running Accident"
Biolit Campaign: "Cockroach, Mosquitos, Spiders", Campaign: "Fear"
Bochemie Campaign: "Stuck Duck"
Campingaz Campaign: "Desert", Campaign: "Fly", Grill Covers, Portable Toilet
Coleman Sleeping Bags
Colgate-Palmolive
Danone
Egis Campaign: "Bike Accident"
Forbes Magazine Campaign: "The Bystander Effect"
Harley Davidson Campaign: "A Piece of Freedom", Campaign: "Feel the road", Campaign: "Stop Reading Start Living"
ING
LG
Museum of Communism Campaign: "Escaping thru Wall, Escaping thru River, Escaping thru Fences", Campaign: "Fidel"
Phd Bikes Campaign: "Sportster Xl1200V"
Philip Morris
Sanoma Campaign: "Iceland"
Sevylor
Two Tales Brewery Campaign: "Beer For Belts"
Unicef
Vodafone Campaign: "Fingers", Campaign: "Invoice without Invoice", Tailor Made Tariffs

Hungary

Y&R Budapest
MOM Park,Alkotasu 53C, 1123 Budapest, Hungary
Tel.: (36) 1 801 7200
Fax: (36) 1 801 7299
E-Mail: info@yr.hu
Web Site: www.yr.hu

Employees: 70
Year Founded: 1989

National Agency Associations: IAA

Agency Specializes In: Advertising

Laszlo Aczel *(Mng Dir)*
Laszlo Falvay *(Dir-Creative)*
Sarolta Gal *(Dir-Strategy)*
Karolina Galacz *(Deputy Dir-Creative)*

Accounts:
Accenture
Actimel
Activia
Amnesty International "Movie Trailer Hijack"
Cherry Queen
Colgate
Danette
Danone Biscuits
ERSTE
Holocaust Memorial Center
Hungarian Bike Club
Katona Jozsef Theatre
Kaucsukprofi Campaign: "Tyre Motel"
Lancia
LG
Magyar Posta
MNV
Opel
Pannon
Pepsi
Premier Outlets
Streamnet Campaign: "Fireplace"
Tibi

Russia

Young & Rubicam FMS
12 Krasnopresnenskaya Nab Office 809, 123610 Moscow, Russia
Tel.: (7) 495 258 2185
Fax: (7) 495 258 1348
E-Mail: yr_moscow@yr.ru
Web Site: www.yr.ru

Employees: 145
Year Founded: 1989

Agency Specializes In: Advertising

Natalia Romanenko *(CEO)*
Yuri Pashin *(Pres-Russia & CIS)*
Luis Tauffer *(Exec Creative Dir)*
Tatiana Tutunnik *(Dir-Creative)*
Maria Zolotareva *(Dir-HR)*
Ruslan Kozlov *(Assoc Dir-Creative)*

Accounts:
Azerfon Blood Donation Campaign: "Life-saving cable"
Beeline (Agency of Record)
Change One Life
Colgate-Palmolive Nutra-Fruit Shower Gel
Dislife Campaign: "More than a Sign"
MTC
Nar mobile
Philip Morris Bond Street, Chesterfield, Muratti, Next, Parliament

Slovakia

Creo/Y&R, spol. s.r.o.
Datelinova 6, 821 01 Bratislava, 2 Slovakia
Tel.: (421) 2 4820 1910
Fax: (421) 2 4820 1911
E-Mail: sekretariat@cyr.sk
Web Site: www.cyr.sk

Employees: 30
Year Founded: 1993

Agency Specializes In: Advertising

Michal Ruttkay *(CEO)*

Accounts:
Danone; 1992
Hubert J.E.
ING
Ispa
Sanofi-Aventis

Latin America

SOJE/Lonsdale Communications Inc./Y&R
Hastings House Balmoral Gap, Hastings, Christ Church, BB1 4034 Barbados
Tel.: (246) 430 2650
Fax: (246) 429 3077
E-Mail: soje@caribsurf.com

Employees: 40

National Agency Associations: PRSA

Agency Specializes In: Advertising

Veoma Ali *(Mng Dir)*
Andrew Corbin *(Dir-Fin)*
Winston Edghill *(Dir-Media & Creative Svcs)*
Margaret Allman Goddard *(Dir-PR)*
Julia Harewood *(Dir-Art)*
Matthew Pilgrim *(Dir-Production)*
Rossann Yearwood *(Dir-Media)*
Michelle Durant *(Office Mgr)*
Kathy-Ann Bynoe *(Specialist-PR)*

Accounts:
Altman Villa Rentals
Apes Hil Club
Bajan Services
Brydens
Cable & Wireless BARTEL, BARTEL Yellow Pages, BET, Caribbean Cellular, Wireless Information Systems
ICBL
Jason Jones Foods
Liat
Port St.Charles
Starcom
Texaco

Y&R Miami
601 Brickell Key Dr Ste 1100, Miami, FL 33131
Tel.: (305) 347-1950
Fax: (305) 347-1951
Web Site: www.yr.com

Employees: 80

National Agency Associations: 4A's

Agency Specializes In: Advertising

Sybil Company *(Mng Dir & VP)*
Claudio Lima *(Chief Creative Officer)*
Victor Amador *(Assoc Dir-Creative)*
Pedro Pinhal *(Assoc Dir-Creative)*
Paola Cedeno *(Acct Mgr)*
Guto Monteiro *(Copywriter)*
Marlon Zanatti *(Copywriter)*

Accounts:
Citibank
Colgate-Palmolive Company
Dell Computer
Microsoft
PopClik Headphones Campaign: "Real World Outside"
We Save Lives

Brazil

Y&R Sao Paulo
Rua General Furtado do Nascimento 9, CEP 05465-070 Sao Paulo, SP Brazil
Tel.: (55) 11 3026 4400
Fax: (55) 11 3022 3090
Web Site: www.yr.com

Employees: 130
Year Founded: 1980

Agency Specializes In: Advertising

Marcos Quintela *(Pres & Partner)*
Paulo Sanna *(Exec Creative Dir)*
Rui Branquinho *(Exec Creative Dir)*
Flavio Casarotti *(Exec Dir-Creative)*
Ideva Batista *(Dir-Art)*
Leandro Camara *(Dir-Art)*
Tiago Marcondes *(Dir-Art)*
Guilherme Racz *(Sr Dir-Art)*
Luiz Villano *(Grp Acct Dir)*
Celso AlfieriA *(Art Dir & Copywriter)*
Daniel Amorim *(Acct Dir)*
Alessandro Cardoni *(Client Svcs Dir)*
Renata El Dib *(Art Dir)*
Diego Passos *(Acct Dir)*
Alexandre Arakawa *(Dir-Creative)*
Fernanda Campos *(Dir-Art)*
Laura Esteves *(Dir-Creative)*
Kleyton Mourao *(Dir-Art)*
Jose Neto *(Dir-Art)*
Felipe Pavani *(Dir-Art & Creative)*
Fernando Takey *(Planner)*
Leandro Brito *(Supvr-Sys)*
Pedro Cavalcanti *(Copywriter)*
Ricardo Dolla *(Copywriter)*
Adriano Eliezer *(Planner)*
Rafael Fagundes *(Copywriter)*
Pedro Guerra *(Copywriter)*
Filipe Leonardos *(Planner)*
Leandro Lourencao *(Copywriter)*
Bruno Souto *(Copywriter)*

Accounts:
18th Festival de cinema Judaico de Sao Paulo
Academia Activa Campaign: "Fat Types"
Accenture
Ajax
ANJ
Annel
Assim Assado Restaurant Campaign: "Like old times", Campaign: "Pork"
BM Empreendimento e Participacoes SPE LTDA
BMW Campaign: "Mini Date"
Boehringer Ingelheim Campaign: "Discomfort T-Shirts"
Brasil Foods Campaign: "Sad Pug"
BRF - Brasil Foods S.A. Boneless Turkey
BRF Brasil Foods Danette, Home Cooking Recipes
Cartoes Elo
New-Casa Hope
Cepera Campaign: "Makes your barbecue deliciously hot. Extra strong pepper sauce.", Campaign: "Springer Spaniel"
Chez Restaurant Campaign: "If You Get Stuck At Home"
Chicken Popcorn
CitiBank
Computer Associates
Danone Bonafont Water, Campaign: "Hippie", Campaign: "Junk Food Patches", Campaign: "The Comics Onomatopeia", Corpus Light, Danette, Densia
Diomedia Campaign: "Illustration Vs Photos Jeep"
Editoria Salvat
Estacao Free Sao Paulo
Estadao Newspaper Campaign: "Media Heroes"
New-Flying Pet
Freddo
Fundaacao Telefonica Campaign: "Beer for Kids"
Goodyear Campaign: "Bubble Wrap Cards", Campaign: "Carball", Campaign: "If it's not Goodyear, good luck.", Campaign: "Knot", Campaign: "More driven", Tyres
Grupo Petropolis Campaign: "Keep Improving", Campaign: "Punchface", Itaipava Beer
Honda
Hopi Hari Theme Park Campaign: "Basketball Team", Campaign: "Cinderella", Campaign: "Rollercoaster. Shows Who You Really Are", Campaign: "Sushi"
Hospital Santa Casa de Sao Paulo
IPE - Instituto de Pesquisas Ecologicas
Ironage Campaign: "Pulse Machine"
Jean-Michel Cousteau's Ocean Futures
Jewish Film Festival Campaign: "Serial Killer"
New-King Star
New-Leaf Sunglasses
LG 3D Smart TV, 84-inch Ultra HD TV, Campaign: "Big Screen", Campaign: "Cyclops", Campaign: "Different Sides", Campaign: "Every side of the sound", Campaign: "You are the lead singer", Fridge, Full Led 3D Borderless TV, Hom-Bot Vacuum Cleaner, Home Theater 3D, Home Theater Blu Ray 3D, Karoke, LG X boom, Mini System With Voice Remover Function, Mobile, Solarium Oven, Washer & Dryer Machine, Washing Machine
Lycra Stretch
Miami Ad School/ESPM "Dumb Ways to Die", Breathalyzer Menu, Campaign: "Brushes", Campaign: "Letraset", Campaign: "Stencil Ruler"
Millward Brown
Mini Cooper
Moto Honda da Amazonia Ltda Campaign: "You're The Voice"
O Estado de S.Paulo Campaign: "Media Heroes", Campaign: "Qr Thanks"
New-Ocean Futures Society
New-Olimpia Flores
Penguin Books
Penguin Companhia das Letras Lollipops
Petra
Petropolis Campaign: "'Marriage Proposal", Campaign: "BBQ GPS", Campaign: "No Sleep No Nightmares", Campaign: "Punchface", TNT Energy Drink
Peugeot Campaign: "Big Mac", Campaign: "Don't Air Guitar & Drive", Peugeot 207
Ponto Frio
Protex Campaign: "Stay Away"
Quinta Da Padrela Quinta da Padrela Grande Reserva
Repetto
Safe Kids Campaign: "Ballerinas"
Santa Casa de Misericordia de Sao Paulo
Santa Casa Hospital Anti-Smoking, Blood Donation, Campaign: "Likes that Help", Campaign: "Tweet a Hospital", Health Checks, Hospital Donation Appeal, Organ Donation
New-Super Cola
TAM Airlines Campaign: "Deliver Like You", Campaign: "Dog", Campaign: "Eagle", Campaign: "Minipastimes", Campaign: "We won't take you to places you don't want to go."
TAM Institutional Campaign: "Catimba"
Telefonica Campaign: "Beer for Kids", Campaign: "Maps", Campaign: "More Than 5000 Different Covers"
TETO Invisigram
Texaco
Tulipan Condoms
Vivo Campaign: "Vivo Stamps", World Cup Online Platform
Weltenburger Kloster Campaign: "Beer-ism"
Whitehall-Robins Inc.

Chile

Prolam Y&R S.A.

Avenida del Parque 5045 Ciudad Empresarial, Huechuraba, Santiago, Chile
Tel.: (56) 2 26408300
Fax: (56) 2 640 8340
E-Mail: contacto-prolam@yr.com
Web Site: www.prolam.cl

Employees: 180
Year Founded: 1980

Agency Specializes In: Advertising, Direct Response Marketing, Direct-to-Consumer, Media Buying Services, Media Planning

Alvaro Becker *(Gen Dir-Creative)*
Cristian Gomez *(Acct Dir)*
Rodrigo Grebe *(Art Dir)*
Fernanda Monett *(Acct Dir)*
Claudio Santis *(Acct Dir)*
Joaquin Toro *(Art Dir)*
Andres Echeverria *(Dir-Art)*
Francisco Cardemil *(Acct Exec)*
Francisco Gonzalez *(Copywriter)*
Patricio Reyes *(Copywriter)*

Accounts:
New-All Nutrition X-Sense
Bacardi Pregnant/Not Pregnant
Banco de Chile
Banco Edwards
Big Time Magnetix
Cachupin
Cartex Campaign: "Bodybuilder"
Colgate-Palmolive Campaign: "Cow", Dental Floss, Fluoride Toothpaste
Colun Light Yoghurt
Danone Campaign: "Neruda"
Dos en Uno Campaign: "Magnetix", Candy
Easy
Fiat
Forus Brooks, Columbia, Environmental Awareness
Fundacion P. Hurtado Campaign: "Beggar"
Fundacion San Jose Campaign: "Abortion"
Gobierno De Chile Campaign: "Ultimate Party"
Hydroaysen
Jano Hot Sauce
Laboratorio Chile Campaign: "Sentence", Heroes Fran, Kitadol, Red Off
Master Dog Light Campaign: "Fat Dogs"
Nutripro Cachupin Dog Food, Nutribalance Light
New-Ozom
Padre Hurtado You Are the Key
PHD Bikes a.s.
Rhein & Stabilo Boss Campaign: "Highlighted", Dulcinea
Rotthammer
Royal & Sun Alliance
Stabilo Boss Campaign: "Highlighted Dulcinea", Campaign: "Highlighted Maria Antonieta"
Telefonica Movil
Un Techo Para Campaign: "Pieces of House"
Unicef
Via'a Botalcura Campaign: "Murderers"
Wasil

Young & Rubicam Bogota

Carrera 11 A #93B-30, 5 Piso Santa Fe De, Bogota, Colombia
Tel.: (57) 1 628 5999
Fax: (57) 1 530 4122
Web Site: www.yr.com

Employees: 90
Year Founded: 1994

Agency Specializes In: Direct Response Marketing, Public Relations, Sales Promotion

German Zuniga *(Gen Dir-Creative)*
Tito Chamorro Fajardo *(VP-Creative)*
Sebastian Sanchez *(Creative Dir)*
Juan Carlos Sosa *(Creative Dir)*
Juan Alvarado *(Dir-Digital Creative)*
Alex Arguello *(Dir-Art)*
Henry Neira- Diego Suarez *(Dir-Art)*
Marcela Zapata *(Dir-Art)*
Sebastian Cuevas *(Copywriter)*
Andres Luque *(Copywriter)*
Sebastian Mojica *(Copywriter)*
Juan Carlos Otalora *(Designer)*
Daniel Piza *(Copywriter)*
Andres Bolivar *(Sr Art Dir)*

Accounts:
A Roof For My Country Campaign: "Tin Roof"
Abaco Food Bank Campaign: "Meal For Share"
Adidas
Assenda
Banco do Bogota
Colombian Alzheimer Foundation Campaign:

"Blackout"
El Corral Hamburgers
Festival De Musica De Cartagena Campaign: "The Sound of the Americas"
Fiat 500 Electronic Brakeforce System
Fundacion Alzheimer de Colombia Campaign: "Blackout"
Fundacion Mi Sangre Campaign: "Guns Can't Teach"
Fundacion Telefonica Campaign: "KIDRESCUE"
Goodyear Campaign: "Farm"
Hamburguesas El Corral
Home Center Campaign: "Beyond The Wall", Campaign: "Lend Your House To El Tino", Glam Kolor Paint, Home Goods Retailer, Klunter Adhesive
Hyundai Campaign: "Dogs", Hyundai i40
La Constancia Campaign: "Mark The Tuna"
La Polar
La Sante
LG Campaign: "Dino"
Mabe Campaign: "Water for Everyone"
Microsoft Campaign: "#TheMagicOfMovement", FIFA 14, Xbox, Xbox Kinect
Movistar Campaign: "Babies"
Ofixpres Books
Tampa Cargo
Telefonica Telecom Campaign: "Glorias=Glory", Campaign: "Kid Rescue"
TUI Antibacterial
Un Techo Para Mi Pais Campaign: "Tin Roof"
UNCHR
Viajes Galeon Campaign: "Twitpoker"

Costa Rica

Asesores/Y&R S.A.

Edificio Asesores Apartado 6947-1000, Iglesia San Francisco de, Guadalupe, 50 Mts Sur San Jose, Costa Rica
Tel.: (506) 257 6727
Fax: (506) 233 5886
Web Site: actividadesasesores.blogspot.com

Employees: 51
Year Founded: 1979

Agency Specializes In: Advertising

Enrique Nieto *(Owner)*

Dominican Republic

Y&R Damaris, C. Por A.

Avenida de los Proceres Corner, Ekman Arroyo Hondo, Santo Domingo, Dominican Republic
Tel.: (809) 562 2441
Fax: (809) 562 4371
Web Site: www.yrdamaris.com

Employees: 120
Year Founded: 1965

Agency Specializes In: Advertising

Franz Garcia *(Gen Dir-Creative)*
Manuel Jose Pena *(VP)*
Henry Ferrer *(Dir-Media)*
Alejandra Marcano *(Dir-Fin)*

Accounts:
Brugal Dominicana
Cerveceria Nacional
claro
Colgate-Palmolive
Listin Diario
Super Mercado Nacional

Ecuador

Rivas & Herrera/Y&R

Edificio La Previsora Av Amazonas Y NNUU Esquina, Torre A Piso 7, Quito, Ecuador
Tel.: (593) 2 243 8993
Fax: (593) 2 226 6127
Web Site: www.rivasherrerayr.com

Employees: 74
Year Founded: 1967

Agency Specializes In: Advertising

Richard Stoyell *(VP)*

Accounts:
Ambev
Budweiser
Chaide Y Chaide
CNT
Telefonica Movistar

Guatemala

ECO Y&R, S.A

8 Calle 2-38 Zona 9, Guatemala City, Guatemala, 01009 Guatemala
Tel.: (502) 2277 7333
Web Site: www.ecoyr.com

Employees: 56
Year Founded: 1987

Agency Specializes In: Advertising, Digital/Interactive, Graphic Design, Radio, T.V.

Gustavo Castaneda de Leon *(Owner)*
Salvador Dominguez *(Dir-Fin)*
Yuliana Dubon *(Acct Exec)*

Accounts:
Campbell Soup Company
Codisa Campaign: "Stop Printing Business Cards"
Colgate-Palmolive Company
Gallo Campaign: "Yo Soy de Aqui"
Revive Microphone
Telefonica

Peru

Y&R Peru

Av Angamos Oeste 915, Miraflores, Lima, Peru
Tel.: (51) 1 447 8282
Fax: (51) 1 444 0436
Web Site: www.yr.com

Employees: 85
Year Founded: 1987

Agency Specializes In: Advertising

Christian Sanchez *(Exec Dir-Creative)*
Gonzalo Arica *(Art Dir)*
Javier Ascue *(Art Dir)*
Percy Chavarry *(Art Dir)*
Romina Fuks *(Acct Dir)*
Jorge Soto *(Art Dir)*
Francisco Suarez *(Acct Dir)*
Charlie Tolmos *(Creative Dir)*
Kevin Contreras *(Dir-Art)*
Edher Espinoza *(Dir-Art)*
Daniel Lobaton *(Dir-Creative)*
Adela Orihuela *(Dir-Fin)*
Gonzalo Paredes *(Dir-Art)*
Jorge Rocca *(Dir-Art)*
Carlos Tapia *(Dir-Art)*
Giuliana Rojas *(Acct Exec)*
Andrea Soria *(Acct Exec)*
Carlos Fernandez *(Copywriter)*
Jim Pino *(Copywriter)*
Luis Alonso Vega *(Copywriter)*

Accounts:
A Roof For My Country Campaign: "Cardiotronic"
ACE Home Center
New-Alicorp
Backus SABMiller Campaign: "Carlos Soto Field", Campaign: "Cristal beer: Pure Cusco"
Britanico English Institute Campaign: "Draword", Campaign: "Say What You Mean to Say ", Campaign: "The Barely Legal Media Space"
British Institute Campaign: "Sacalotepum Maravillezka"
Carsa
New-Cibertec
Citibank
Colgate-Palmolive Company
Cristal Beer Campaign: "Join the call", Campaign: "The Alternate Jerseys"
English Courses
From Peru Campaign: "From Peru For Peru"
Goodyear
Hino Trucks Campaign: "Elephant"
Homecenter Sodimac Campaign: "The Man Who Gave Everything Away"
ING Integra Pension Fund
ING
Instituto Britanico
Instituto San Ignacio de Loyola
LAN Peru Campaign: "Destination Won't Change. But Prices Will", Campaign: "Dreamer"
Land Rover
League Against Cancer Campaign: "Can", Campaign: "Coffins", Campaign: "Hollywood", Campaign: "Jaws", Campaign: "Streets"
Liga Contra El Cancer Peru
Maestro Home Center
Marsh
Movistar Campaign: "Backup Agenda", Campaign: "Cheese", Campaign: "Connected with Peru", Campaign: "Peruvian Goal", Campaign: "Supremacy"
Paladim
Peruvian Government Campaign: "My goal against Argentina"
Repso
Rimac Seguros
Saga Falabella
Toyota Campaign: "Curve", Campaign: "Goodbye", Campaign: "Visible thanks to our lord's procession.", FJ Cruiser 4x4, Guernica, Toyota Concept Vehicles, Zelas
Urban Cruiser

Puerto Rico

Y&R Puerto Rico, Inc.

PO Box 366288, San Juan, PR 00936-6288
Tel.: (787) 622-6500
Fax: (787) 793-3013
Web Site: www.yr.com

Employees: 48

Agency Specializes In: Advertising

Carlos Carbonell *(Pres)*
Sylvia Soler *(Exec VP & Dir-Creative)*
Ivan Santos *(Gen Mgr)*
Arturo Perez *(Art Dir)*
Luis Cosme *(Dir-Sys)*
Luigui Rodriguez *(Dir-Art)*
Vanessa Fernandez *(Assoc Dir-Creative & Copywriter)*
Javier Claudio *(Assoc Dir-Creative)*
Gerardo Vazquez *(Assoc Dir-Creative)*
Aixza Rivera *(Coord-HR)*

Accounts:
Buckler
Campbell Soup Company
Colgate-Palmolive Campaign: "Food Divider"
Danone Campaign: "Ice Cream"
Directv Campaign: "School Play"

Goodyear Campaign: "Trace"
Heineken JAM
Mendez & Compania
Nissan Sentra
T-Mobile US
Texaco

Uruguay

Y&R Uruguay
Bvar Espana 2617, CP 11300 Montevideo, Uruguay
Tel.: (598) 2 708 3097
Fax: (598) 2 708 1742
E-Mail: info.uruguay@yr.com
Web Site: www.yr.com.uy

Employees: 30
Year Founded: 1995

Agency Specializes In: Advertising

Diego Lazcano *(VP-Creative)*
Martin Rumbo *(Editor-Creative)*

Accounts:
930 Montecarlo
Ancel
Bayer
BSE
Diageo Campaign: "Rapvat"
Ministry of Tourism Campaign: "3 Million Tourist", Campaign: "Excel"
Monte Carlo Radio
Seven
Tcc Cable Company Campaign: "Iceberg"
Un Techo Para Mi Paas Campaign: "Ringtones"

Kenya

Young & Rubicam Brands Africa
2nd Fl Panesar Centre Mombasa Road, PO Box 41036, 00-100 Nairobi, Kenya
Tel.: (254) 20 234 8081
Fax: (254) 20 551 336
Web Site: www.yr.com

Employees: 60
Year Founded: 1986

Agency Specializes In: Advertising

Tom Crisp *(Mgr-Production)*

Accounts:
Basco Paints
Caltex
Colgate-Palmolive Company
Del Monte
DHL Express
Housing Finance Company
Kenya Breweries
Mondelez Cadbury
Proctor & Allan
World Health Organization

Namibia

Advantage Y&R
5 Storch Street, Windhoek, Namibia
Mailing Address:
PO Box 21593, Windhoek, Namibia
Tel.: (264) 28 91 600
Fax: (264) 61 220 410
E-Mail: advantageyr@mac.com.na
Web Site: www.advantageyr.com

Employees: 25

Truda Meaden *(Mng Dir)*
Patrick Held *(Creative Dir)*
Annelie Nothnagel *(Art Dir)*
Fortune Kangueehi *(Acct Mgr-Adv)*
Jon Gibson *(Copywriter)*

Accounts:
Colgate
Commodity Exchange
MTC Annual Music Awards, Campaign: "Hugs", Event
Protex
World Health Organization

South Africa

Jupiter Drawing Room
River Park, 42 Holmstead Rd, Rivonia, 2128 South Africa
Tel.: (27) 11 233 8800
Fax: (27) 11 233 8820
E-Mail: info@thejupiterdrawingroom.com
Web Site: www.thejupiterdrawingroom.com

Employees: 200

Thomas Cullinan *(Partner-Creative)*
Darren Kilfoil *(Grp Head-Creative)*
Kerryn-Lee Maggs *(Art Dir & Designer)*
Dana Cullinan *(Creative Dir)*
Zola Thekiso *(Acct Dir)*
Dana Cohen *(Dir-Creative)*
Cameron Fraser *(Copywriter)*

Accounts:
ABSA Capital
ABSA CAPE EPIC, Campaign: "Team Of Millions"
Arthur Kaplan Jewellers
Children of Fire Campaign: "Candle"
The Coca-Cola Co. Burn Energy Drink
Girls & Boystown
Innscor International Franchising Division
Jet Mart
Jet
Jiffy
Just Juice
Lemon & Nada Campaign: "Spot The Difference"
Luster's Pink
Minute Maid
MTN Campaign: "Facebook", Campaign: "First Day", Magic 8 Ball
Nulaid
PPC Cement Campaign: "Bag Seals"
SA Poultry Association Campaign: "Bush"
Temptations Campaign: "Commitment"
Vida E Caffe Campaign: "Sleeping Pilots"
WeChat South Africa Campaign: "Crazy About WeChat"

Y&R Cape Town
Ground & 1st Floor The Warehouse, 24 Alfred St, Cape Town, 8001 South Africa
Tel.: (27) 21 440 3700
Fax: (27) 21 447 5497
E-Mail: yrsa_cape@za.yr.com
Web Site: www.yr.com

Employees: 42
Year Founded: 2000

Agency Specializes In: Advertising

Graham Lang *(Chief Creative Officer)*
Andrew Welch *(CEO-South Africa)*
Alistair Duff *(Head-Strategy)*
Werner Marais *(Grp Head-Creative)*
Rui Alves *(Exec Creative Dir)*
Jacques Shalom *(Grp Dir-Creative)*
Nkanyezi Masango *(Creative Dir)*
Gareth Owen *(Art Dir)*
Ashleigh Hamilton *(Art Buyer & Producer-TV, Radio & Print)*
David Mabotja *(Art Dir)*
Mark Mbugua *(Acct Dir)*
Nobantu Sibeko *(Art Dir)*
Bibi Brink *(Dir-Creative)*
Rowena Fester *(Dir-Bus Unit)*
Jac Sun *(Dir-Art)*
Tyler Botha *(Copywriter)*
Patrick Robertson *(Copywriter)*

Accounts:
Blikkiesdorp4Hope Hope Soap
Caltex Chevron
Colgate-Palmolive Company
New-Edward Snell & Company
Gun Free South Africa
Jaguar Land Rover Land Rover
Pick n Pay
Playboy South Africa
Pulp Books
The Safety Lab
Shimansky Jewellers
New-Surf Shack
Telkom
Travel Counsellors
Western Cape Government
Xtra Space Campaign: "Storage Business Card"

Y&R Johannesburg
Soft Line Technology Park, 56 Lotus Rd, Wendywood, 2148 South Africa
Mailing Address:
Private Bag X9, Wendywood, 2144 South Africa
Tel.: (27) 11 797 6300
Fax: (27) 11 797 6400
Web Site: www.yr.com

Employees: 150
Year Founded: 1984

Agency Specializes In: Advertising

Graham Lang *(Chief Creative Officer)*
Grant Seller *(Grp Head-Creative)*
Bibi Brink *(Dir-Creative)*
Ismaeel Chetty *(Dir-Art)*
Gareth Cohen *(Dir-Art)*
Sampa Diseko *(Dir-Strategy)*
Andrea Ferreira *(Dir-Art)*
Nkanyezi Masango *(Dir-Creative)*
Vusumuzi Khoza *(Copywriter)*
Marijolein Rossouw *(Copywriter)*
Guy Orsmond *(Client Svc Dir)*

Accounts:
Accenture
Airborne Effervescent Tablets
Barnetts
Beechies
British Airways
Caltex
Colgate Plax
Danone
Gulf Drug
Gun Free South Africa
New-Jaguar Land Rover
Johannesburg Zoo Campaign: "Animals can't be recycled. Please don't litter.", Campaign: "Bushveld", Campaign: "Polar Bear", Campaign: "See What Comes Out In The Dark"
Land Rover 360 Faces, Beetle, Campaign: "Cloud Collector", Campaign: "Griqualand", Campaign: "Kalahari", Campaign: "Keep Calm", Campaign: "Okavango Delta", Campaign: "Zimbawe Highlands", Croc, Freelander 2
Lion Matches
MTN
Nintendo
Pick n Pay Campaign: "Sassi Bag"
Playboy South Africa Before & After, Campaign: "Crack Addiction", Campaign: "This wouldn't happen online"
SABC

Safety Lab & Blikkiesdorp 4 Hope
Shimansky International
SKYY Vodka Campaign: "SKYYPAD"
Surf Shack
Tata Motors Limited
Travel Counsellors Campaign: "Amsterdam"
UNICEF Toy Soldiers
Virgin Atlantic Airways Campaign: "Flag"
Xbox 360 Need for Speed?
XtraSpace

Zambia

Armstrong Y&R

Wing F 2nd Floor Comesa Centre Ben bella Rd, Lusaka, Zambia
Tel.: (260) 122 8491
Fax: (260) 122 5173
Web Site: www.yr.com

Employees: 23
Year Founded: 1975

Agency Specializes In: Advertising

Peter Armstrong *(Owner)*
Shelley Diamond *(Chm & Exec Dir-Creative-RKCR/Y&R London)*
Tony Granger *(Chief Creative Officer-Global)*
Jon Cook *(Pres/CEO-VML)*
Stephen Forcione *(CEO-Red Fuse Comm)*
Joseph Ghossoub *(CEO-Red Fuse Comm)*
William J. Manfredi *(Exec VP-Talent Mgmt-Global)*
Sandy Thompson *(Dir-Plng-Global)*

YOUNG COMPANY

361 Forest Ave Ste 105, Laguna Beach, CA 92651
Tel.: (949) 376-8404
Web Site: www.youngcompany.com

Employees: 10

Agency Specializes In: Above-the-Line, Advertising, Advertising Specialties, Affiliate Marketing, Alternative Advertising, Automotive, Aviation & Aerospace, Brand Development & Integration, Branded Entertainment, Broadcast, Business Publications, Business-To-Business, Cable T.V., Catalogs, Co-op Advertising, Collateral, Communications, Consulting, Consumer Goods, Consumer Publications, Content, Corporate Communications, Corporate Identity, Custom Publishing, Digital/Interactive, Direct Response Marketing, E-Commerce, Electronic Media, Electronics, Email, Engineering, Event Planning & Marketing, Exhibit/Trade Shows, Experience Design, Graphic Design, Guerilla Marketing, High Technology, Identity Marketing, In-Store Advertising, Industrial, Infomercials, Information Technology, Integrated Marketing, Internet/Web Design, Local Marketing, Logo & Package Design, Magazines, Market Research, Media Buying Services, Media Planning, Media Relations, Mobile Marketing, Multimedia, New Product Development, Newspaper, Newspapers & Magazines, Out-of-Home Media, Outdoor, Package Design, Paid Searches, Planning & Consultation, Point of Purchase, Point of Sale, Print, Product Placement, Production, Production (Ad, Film, Broadcast), Production (Print), Promotions, Public Relations, Publicity/Promotions, Publishing, RSS (Really Simple Syndication), Radio, Search Engine Optimization, Social Marketing/Nonprofit, Social Media, Sponsorship, Strategic Planning/Research, T.V., Technical Advertising, Trade & Consumer Magazines, Web (Banner Ads, Pop-ups, etc.)

Approx. Annual Billings: $100,000

Bart Young *(CEO & Dir-Creative)*
John Dillon *(VP-PR)*
Rick Jorgenson *(VP)*
Michael Mittelstaedt *(Assoc Dir-Creative)*
Patti Compton *(Acct Mgr)*
Sarah Arbogast *(Mgr-Market Res)*
Lori Robinson *(Mgr-Media)*
Wilbert Cheng *(Acct Exec)*

Accounts:
Abbott; Sun Valley, CA Abbott Technologies; 2011
Casoro; Santa Ana, CA Casoro Jewelry Safes; 2012
New-Imperio Nissan Advertising
Irvine Subaru; Irvine, CA Subaru; 2010
Samsung; Carson, CA Samsung Document Cameras; 2007

YOUNGER ASSOCIATES

97 Directors Row Ste 100, Jackson, TN 38305
Tel.: (731) 668-7367
Fax: (731) 668-0042
Web Site: www.younger-associates.com

Agency Specializes In: Advertising, Brand Development & Integration, Broadcast, Graphic Design, Internet/Web Design, Logo & Package Design, Media Buying Services, Outdoor, Social Media, Strategic Planning/Research

Sharon Younger *(Pres)*
Pam Stanfield *(Partner & Dir-Creative Svcs)*
Leigh Anne Bentley *(Dir-Mktg Strategy)*
Stephanie Riley *(Dir-Creative Svcs)*
Lana Suite *(Dir-Res)*
Billy Worboys *(Dir-Art)*
Kayla Taylor *(Acct Mgr-Mktg)*
Robin Jones *(Coord-Res)*
Alison Kirk *(Coord-Mktg Svcs)*

Accounts:
East Arkansas Planning & Development District
Month Of Miracles

YOUNNEL ADVERTISING, INC.

2502 Beverly Pl, Stockton, CA 95204-4343
Tel.: (209) 948-9339
Fax: (209) 948-4924
E-Mail: craig@younneladv.com
Web Site: www.younneladv.com

E-Mail for Key Personnel:
President: craig@younneladv.com

Employees: 5
Year Founded: 1974

Agency Specializes In: Advertising, Bilingual Market, Brand Development & Integration, Corporate Identity, Event Planning & Marketing, Graphic Design, Hispanic Market, Magazines, Media Buying Services, Newspaper, Newspapers & Magazines, Point of Sale, Radio, T.V.

Approx. Annual Billings: $3,075,000

Breakdown of Gross Billings by Media: Newsp.: $100,000; Newsp. & Mags.: $850,000; Outdoor: $125,000; Radio: $50,000; T.V.: $1,950,000

Creighton Younnel *(Pres)*
Veronica Santiago *(Dir-Creative)*
Bertha Younnel *(Office Mgr)*

Accounts:
Amber Ridge
Catalina
Clairmonto
Delta Bluegrass
Maruchan, Inc. Oriental Dried Soups
Terra Bella
Villa Ticino
The Vineyard
WestBrook

YOUR MAJESTY

29 E 19th St Third Fl, New York, NY 10003
Tel.: (646) 398-8084
E-Mail: info@your-majesty.com
Web Site: yourmajesty.co

Year Founded: 2006

Agency Specializes In: Advertising, Brand Development & Integration, Broadcast, Digital/Interactive, Graphic Design, Logo & Package Design, Print, Production (Ad, Film, Broadcast), Strategic Planning/Research, Technical Advertising

Jens Karlsson *(Co-Founder & Exec Dir-Creative)*
James Widegren *(Co-Founder & Exec Dir-Creative)*
Nina Amjadi *(VP)*
Tore Holmberg *(Dir-Tech)*
Alexander Strand Kristensen *(Dir-Design)*
Rachel Kalagher *(Designer)*
Karoline Engemoen Kristoffersen *(Designer)*
Lotte Peters *(Designer)*
Frida Hellden *(Assoc Producer)*

Accounts:
American Express Company
Apple Inc.
AT&T Communications Corp.
Canon U.S.A., Inc.
Cisco Systems, Inc.
Hyundai Motor America
Lexus Division
Microsoft

YOUTECH & ASSOCIATES

1730 Park St, Naperville, IL 60563
Tel.: (630) 857-9545
E-Mail: info@youtechassociates.com
Web Site: www.youtechassociates.com

Employees: 18
Year Founded: 2012

Agency Specializes In: Advertising, Brand Development & Integration, Digital/Interactive, Email, Exhibit/Trade Shows, Guerilla Marketing, In-Store Advertising, Internet/Web Design, Local Marketing, Mobile Marketing, Paid Searches, Point of Sale, Search Engine Optimization, Social Media, Web (Banner Ads, Pop-ups, etc.)

Wilbur You *(Founder & CEO)*
Trent Anderson *(Dir-Bus Dev)*
Shawn Herrick *(Dir-Digital Media)*
Frank Hilgers *(Dir-Tech)*
Lauren Urban *(Dir-Creative)*
Valente Garza *(Project Mgr & Rep-Sls)*
Carrie Draper *(Mgr-Accts)*

Accounts:
Neebo Business-to-Consumer, College Bookstores, E-Commerce; 2014
Peter Tiberio
Philip Rae & Associates
Teemapping
Weiss Sugar Dvorak & Dusek Ltd

YS AND PARTNERS, INC.

20351 Irvine Ave Ste C9, Newport Beach, CA 92660-0236
Tel.: (949) 263-1600
Fax: (949) 263-1630
E-Mail: contact@ysandpartners.com
Web Site: www.ysandpartners.com

Employees: 15
Year Founded: 2002

Agency Specializes In: Advertising, Collateral, Graphic Design, Internet/Web Design, Local Marketing, Media Buying Services, Media Planning, Outdoor, Print, Radio, Strategic Planning/Research, T.V.

Yoshinabu Yuki *(Pres, CEO & Dir-Creative)*
Nobu Yuki *(Principal & Exec Dir-Creative)*
Ayako Yuki *(VP & Dir-Mktg)*
Larry Feldman *(Specialist-PR)*
Yori Hasumura *(Specialist-Bus Dev & Mktg)*
Yurie Hill *(Acct Exec)*
Yashimi Kazami *(Acct Exec)*
Ryoko Otake *(Acct Exec)*
Ming Lai *(Copywriter)*

Accounts:
Yakult

YUME
1204 Middlefield Rd, Redwood City, CA 94063
Tel.: (650) 591-9400
Fax: (650) 591-9401
Web Site: www.yume.com

Employees: 14

Agency Specializes In: Advertising, Local Marketing, Sales Promotion

Revenue: $1,400,000

Ayyappan Sankaran *(Co-Founder & CTO)*
Scot McLernon *(Chief Revenue Officer)*
Michael Hudes *(Exec VP)*
Frank Barbieri *(Sr VP-Corp Dev & Strategy)*
Joe Farrell *(Sr VP-Natl Sls)*
Venkat Krishnan *(Sr VP-Products)*
Tom Wolfe *(Sr VP-Bus Dev)*
Matt Arkin *(VP-Programmatic)*
Breeze Dake *(VP-Demand Solutions)*
Gary J. Fuges *(VP-IR)*
Alp Pekkocak *(VP-Product Mktg-Programmatic Platform)*
Bryson Smith *(VP-Political, Advocacy & Govt Affairs)*
Vamshi Sriperumbudur *(VP-Platform Mktg)*
Tripp Boyle *(Dir-Mobile & Connected TV Sls-Natl)*
Eric Bozinny *(Dir-Network Quality)*
Felix Gomez *(Dir-West)*
Paul Neto *(Dir-Res)*
Karina Moises *(Sr Mgr-Reg Sls-Latin America)*
Cori Boyce *(Acct Mgr)*
Clay Kilgo *(Mgr-Programmatic Partnerships)*
Emmy Kishida *(Mgr-Pricing & Yield Mgmt)*
Kerry McGuire *(Mgr-Publr Svcs & Bus Dev)*
Andrea Stubbs *(Mgr-Field Mktg)*
Adam Fisher *(Sr Acct Exec-Programmatic Video Sls)*
Katie Flora *(Sr Acct Exec)*
Katina Papas *(Acct Exec)*
John Poor *(Acct Exec)*
Joanne Chen *(Corp Mgr-Mktg)*

Accounts:
BlackBerry
Chase
Clorox
Ford
HBO
Hearst Magazine Digital Media
Jaguar
Kellogg's
Microsoft, Corp.
Sprint
Target

YYES, CO.
2400 Hyperion Ave Ste A, Los Angeles, CA 90027
Tel.: (323) 667-3337
Fax: (323) 297-4397
Web Site: www.yyes.org

Year Founded: 2000

Agency Specializes In: Advertising, Digital/Interactive, Exhibit/Trade Shows, Logo & Package Design, Search Engine Optimization

Ron Fleming *(Owner)*
Alysse Johnson-Strandjord *(Sr Graphic Designer)*

Accounts:
Beta Petrol
Cystic Fibrosis Foundation
Johnson Worldwide Associates
Kia Motors America Inc.
Robertson Properties Group
SCI Real Estate Investments, LLC

Z BRAND
The Gulf Twr Ste 3205 707 Grant St, Pittsburgh, PA 15219
Tel.: (412) 697-2800
Fax: (412) 246-0647
E-Mail: woof@zbrand.com
Web Site: www.zbrand.com

Year Founded: 2009

Agency Specializes In: Advertising, Brand Development & Integration, Digital/Interactive, Graphic Design, Internet/Web Design, Outdoor, Print, Public Relations, Social Media

Goldie Z. Ostrow *(Principal)*
Kimberly Miller *(VP & Dir-Creative Svcs)*
Ben Schmitt *(VP-Written Comm & Social Mktg)*
Brad Hrutkay *(VP & Creative Dir)*
Christopher Bowser *(Dir-Programming Svcs)*

Accounts:
Mario Lemieux Foundation
Peoples Natural Gas
Pittsburgh Action Against Rape

Z COMMUNICATIONS
7830 Old Georgetown Rd Ste 125, Bethesda, MD 20814
Tel.: (240) 395-0225
Fax: (240) 395-0226
E-Mail: info@zpr.com
Web Site: www.zpr.com

Employees: 20
Year Founded: 1989

Agency Specializes In: Email, Internet/Web Design, Media Relations, Media Training, Pets , Podcasting, Production

Rise Birnbaum *(Founder & CEO)*

Accounts:
Abbott
Air Jamaica
Bailey's Irish Cream
Boca Foods
Dove Soap

Z MARKETING PARTNERS
3905 E.Vincennes Rd, Ste 300, Indianapolis, IN 46268
Tel.: (317) 924-6271
Fax: (317) 925-3854
E-Mail: info@zmarketingpartners.com
Web Site: www.zmarketingpartners.com

Employees: 12
Year Founded: 1950

Agency Specializes In: African-American Market, Automotive, Brand Development & Integration, Business-To-Business, Co-op Advertising, Collateral, Communications, Consulting, Consumer Marketing, Consumer Publications, Corporate Identity, Direct Response Marketing, E-Commerce, Electronic Media, Event Planning & Marketing, Exhibit/Trade Shows, Financial, Graphic Design, Health Care Services, Internet/Web Design, Logo & Package Design, Media Buying Services, Multimedia, Newspaper, Newspapers & Magazines, Out-of-Home Media, Outdoor, Point of Purchase, Point of Sale, Print, Production, Public Relations, Publicity/Promotions, Radio, Restaurant, Retail, Seniors' Market, Sports Market, Strategic Planning/Research, T.V., Trade & Consumer Magazines

Approx. Annual Billings: $22,000,000

Allan Zukerman *(Chm & CEO)*
Blair Englehart *(Exec Dir-MZD)*
David Ayers *(Dir-PR & Acct Supvr)*
T.J. Gipson *(Dir-Multicultural)*
Jill Baker *(Mgr-Payroll & Sr Media Buyer)*
Tom Conrad *(Sr Controller)*

Accounts:
Boston Scientific Indiana Division
Cibo Restaurant & Gelo Ultra Lounge
Citizens Health Center
Enthusiasm Foods
GAP Solutions
Hendricks County Convention and Visitors Bureau
IEI Financial Services
Indiana Association of Realtors
Indiana State Fair; Indianapolis, IN; 1990
Indiana Tobacco Prevention & Cessation
Indiana University
Indianapolis City Market
Miller Pipeline Corp.
N.K. Hurst Co.; Indianapolis, IN; 1950
Orange County Convention & Visitors Bureau
Penn Station East Coast Subs
YMCA; Indianapolis, IN
Yosha & Associates

Z11 COMMUNICATIONS LLC
4718 Western Ave, Knoxville, TN 37921
Tel.: (865) 425-7771
Web Site: www.z11communications.com

Year Founded: 2007

Agency Specializes In: Advertising, Brand Development & Integration, Graphic Design, Internet/Web Design, Logo & Package Design, Media Training, Print, Public Relations, Search Engine Optimization, Social Media

Zane Hagy *(CEO)*

Accounts:
Furrow Automotive
Smart Center Knoxville

ZAD COMMUNICATIONS
4446 Saint-Laurent Blvd, Ste 908, Montreal, QC H2W 1Z5 Canada
Tel.: (514) 281-7575
Fax: (514) 281-7595
E-Mail: acloutier@zadcommunications.com
Web Site: www.zadcommunications.com

Agency Specializes In: Brand Development & Integration, Communications, Consulting, Direct Response Marketing, Local Marketing, Promotions, Sponsorship, Strategic Planning/Research

Alain Cloutier *(Pres)*

Accounts:
Uniprix

ZAMBEZI

615 Hampton Dr Ste A311, Venice, CA 90291
Tel.: (310) 450-6800
E-Mail: info@zambezi-la.com
Web Site: www.zambezi-la.com

E-Mail for Key Personnel:
President: chris@zambezi-la.com

Employees: 80
Year Founded: 2006

Agency Specializes In: Above-the-Line, Advertising, Brand Development & Integration, Internet/Web Design, Sponsorship, Sports Market, T.V., Teen Market, Travel & Tourism, Viral/Buzz/Word of Mouth

Approx. Annual Billings: $10,000,000

Breakdown of Gross Billings by Media: Brdcst.: 30%; Internet Adv.: 15%; Newsp. & Mags.: 30%; Out-of-Home Media: 10%; Sports Mktg.: 15%

Chris Raih *(Founder & CEO)*
Pete Brown *(Mng Dir)*
Jean Freeman *(COO)*
Alex Cohn *(Exec Producer)*
Tony Joo *(Sr Producer-Digital)*
Nathan Nowak *(Sr Producer-Brdcst)*
Mark Belot *(Acct Dir)*
Luke Lamson *(Acct Dir)*
Kevin O'Brien *(Acct Dir)*
Nick Rodgers *(Dir-Art & Assoc Dir-Creative)*
Nicole Bush *(Dir-Comm)*
Ricardo Diaz *(Dir-Digital)*
Ben George *(Assoc Dir-Creative & Copywriter)*
Noelle Belling *(Acct Supvr)*
Keely Galgano *(Jr Strategist)*
Iyana Gregory *(Strategist-Social Media)*
Jaysn Kim *(Copywriter)*
Paula Coral *(Jr Art Dir)*

Accounts:
2K Sports
Adams Golf (Lead Creative Agency)
Ashworth Golf (Lead Creative Agency)
New-AutoTrader.com LLC Campaign: "One Search", Campaign: "The Journey"
Caesars Interactive Entertainment Campaign: "whenever, wherever", Creative, Digital, OOH, Online, Radio, TV, World Series of Poker
Coca-Cola Sprite
Comcast; Portland, OR Internet, Phone, Cable; 2007
Eastbay
Emotes; Hong Kong, China Children's Books & Toys; 2008
Energy Brands, Inc. Advertising, Campaign: "Decoy", Campaign: "Jennifer Aniston Goes Viral", Fruitwater, Smartwater
New-Focus Features Suffragette
HEINEKEN USA Strongbow Cider
The Honest Company Creative, TV
Kobe Bryant; Los Angeles, CA Media, Merchandise, Website, Shoes, Membership; 2006
Li-Ning; Portland, OR Campaign: "Make Your Own Way", Campaign: "Way of Wade"
Los Angeles Lakers; Los Angeles, CA Franchise, Tickets, Merchandise; 2006
NESTEA
New Mexico Board of Tourism; USA; 2007
Phiten Campaign: "Still Flexin'"
Popchips Campaign: "popchips.com", Digital
Portland Trail Blazers; Portland, OR Franchise, Tickets; 2007
Sound United (Agency of Record)
TaylorMade Golf Company (Lead Creative Agency) Campaign: "Made of Greatness", Campaign: "Speed Police", Digital, Online, Print, R15 Metalwood, Television
TNT
Upshot; Westlake Village, CA Energy Drink; 2007
VeeV Acai Spirits Campaign: "Cheat on Your Vodka", Marketing, Online Video

ZANDER GUINN MILLAN

831 E Morehead St Ste 660, Charlotte, NC 28202
Tel.: (704) 333-5500
Fax: (704) 333-5588
E-Mail: contact@zgmbrand.com
Web Site: www.zgmbrand.com

Employees: 5

Agency Specializes In: Automotive, Brand Development & Integration, Financial, Restaurant, Technical Advertising

Lynda Folz *(Founder & Dir-Creative)*
Melanie Guinn Buchanan *(CEO & Strategist-Brand)*
Donnie Funderud *(VP-Bus Dev)*

Accounts:
Cefla Finishing
Salice Concealed Hinges Mfr

ZEESMAN COMMUNICATIONS INC.

8383 Wilshire Blvd Ste 310, Beverly Hills, CA 90211
Tel.: (323) 951-9800
Fax: (323) 951-9797
E-Mail: info@zeesman.com
Web Site: www.zeesman.com

Employees: 12
Year Founded: 1990

Bonnie Nijst *(Pres & CEO)*
Michelle Groman *(Acct Dir & Acct Supvr)*
Alison Rice *(Acct Mgr)*
Allison Mercado *(Coord-Mktg)*

Accounts:
AIG SunAmerica
Barco's Nightingales
BelAire Displays
Goodwill Industries
Griffith Observatory
Los Angeles World Airports
Metro Master Chorale
National Association of Women Business Owners
National Council of Jewish Women Los Angeles
Pioneer Electronics
Rock the Vote
Strategic Counsel
Sunrise Telecom Inc.
Toshiba
W.M. Keck Foundation
Walt Disney Company

ZEHNDER COMMUNICATIONS, INC.

650 Poydras St Ste 2450, New Orleans, LA 70130
Tel.: (504) 558-7778
Fax: (504) 558-7779
Toll Free: (877) 558-7778
E-Mail: jzehnder@z-comm.com
Web Site: www.z-comm.com

E-Mail for Key Personnel:
President: jzehnder@z-comm.com
Creative Dir.: mrainey@z-comm.com
Media Dir.: joannh@z-comm.com
Public Relations: aedelman@z-comm.com

Employees: 32
Year Founded: 1996

National Agency Associations: 4A's-ADFED-AMA-PRSA

Agency Specializes In: Advertising, Affluent Market, African-American Market, Alternative Advertising, Automotive, Bilingual Market, Brand Development & Integration, Broadcast, Business Publications, Business-To-Business, Co-op Advertising, Collateral, College, Communications, Consulting, Consumer Goods, Consumer Marketing, Corporate Communications, Corporate Identity, Crisis Communications, Customer Relationship Management, Digital/Interactive, Direct Response Marketing, E-Commerce, Education, Electronic Media, Electronics, Email, Entertainment, Environmental, Event Planning & Marketing, Exhibit/Trade Shows, Financial, Food Service, Government/Political, Graphic Design, Guerilla Marketing, Health Care Services, High Technology, Hispanic Market, Hospitality, In-Store Advertising, Industrial, Information Technology, Integrated Marketing, International, Internet/Web Design, Legal Services, Leisure, Local Marketing, Logo & Package Design, Luxury Products, Magazines, Marine, Market Research, Media Buying Services, Media Planning, Media Relations, Media Training, Medical Products, Men's Market, Merchandising, Mobile Marketing, Multicultural, Multimedia, New Product Development, New Technologies, Newspaper, Newspapers & Magazines, Out-of-Home Media, Outdoor, Package Design, Paid Searches, Planning & Consultation, Podcasting, Point of Purchase, Point of Sale, Print, Production, Promotions, Public Relations, Publicity/Promotions, RSS (Really Simple Syndication), Radio, Real Estate, Recruitment, Regional, Restaurant, Retail, Sales Promotion, Search Engine Optimization, Social Marketing/Nonprofit, Strategic Planning/Research, Sweepstakes, Syndication, T.V., Trade & Consumer Magazines, Transportation, Travel & Tourism, Urban Market, Viral/Buzz/Word of Mouth, Women's Market

Approx. Annual Billings: $25,500,000

Breakdown of Gross Billings by Media: Cable T.V.: 10%; Internet Adv.: 15%; Newsp. & Mags.: 20%; Out-of-Home Media: 10%; Spot Radio: 25%; Spot T.V.: 20%

Craig Schultz *(Owner)*
Joann Habisreitinger *(Partner & Dir-Media)*
Mike Rainey *(Chief Creative Officer & Principal)*
Jennifer Boneno *(Acct Svcs Dir)*
Dave Maher *(Dir-Digital Comm)*
William Gilbert *(Assoc Dir-Creative)*
Tambry Reed *(Sr Mgr-PR)*
Laura Gould *(Supvr-Project Mgmt)*

Accounts:
Alliance Oncology Full Service; 2009
BancorpSouth Insurance Services; Jackson, MS Insurance; 2006
Baton Rouge Area Foundation Creative, Digital, Public Relations, Strategy
Burger King Corporation; Miami, FL Media Planning, Placement; 2006
The Carpenter Health Network Full Service
Cazayoux-Ewing Law PLC Creative, Public Relations
Chila Orchata (Sazerac) Digital, Media, Social Media, Strategy
Community Trust Bank
Dinner Lab Social Media
Dr. McGillicuddy (Sazerac)
DuPage Medical Group Full Service
Edgen Murray Corporation; Baton Rouge, LA Full Service; 2000
Entergy Digital, Social Media
Epic Vodka (Sazerac) Media, Social Media, Strategy
Fireball Cinnamon Whisky (Sazerac) Full Service
Gulf Coast Seafood Coalition Full Service
Jackson Offshore Services Full Service
JD Bank Full Service
Lake Charles CVB Media Planning & Placement
LAMMICO
Louisiana Department of Health & Hospitals Social Media, Strategy

LSU (Flores MBA Program) Creative, Digital, Social Media, Strategy
Lugenbuhl Law PLC Full Service
MMI Culinary
Naked Jay Vodka (Sazerac) Social Media, Strategy
Stevi B's Pizza Buffet Full Service
Stirling Properties Full Service
Terrebonne General Medical Center Creative, Digital, Media, Strategy
Tijuana Sweet Heat Tequila (Sazerac) Full Service
Visit Baton Rouge Full Service
Visit South Walton Creative, Digital, Social Media, Strategy
WAVE Vodka (Sazerac) Media, Social Media, Strategy

ZEITSIGHT

(Formerly 5280 Creative)
100 Fillmore Plz Ste 500, Denver, CO 80206
Tel.: (720) 593-9348
E-Mail: info@wearezeitsight.com
Web Site: www.wearezeitsight.com

Agency Specializes In: Advertising, Brand Development & Integration, Internet/Web Design, Print, Social Media, T.V.

David Skul *(CEO)*

Accounts:
Pollard Friendly Jeep

ZELEN COMMUNICATIONS

1304 DeSoto Ave Ste 200, Tampa, FL 33606
Tel.: (813) 250-1530
E-Mail: info@zelencomm.com
Web Site: www.zelencommunications.com

Agency Specializes In: Advertising, Brand Development & Integration, Event Planning & Marketing, Internet/Web Design, Paid Searches, Print, Public Relations, Search Engine Optimization, Social Media

Terry Zelen *(Owner & Pres)*
Chris McChesney *(Art Dir)*

Accounts:
New-Arthur Rutenberg Homes Inc

ZELLER MARKETING & DESIGN

322 N River St, East Dundee, IL 60118
Tel.: (847) 836-6022
E-Mail: info@zellermail.com
Web Site: www.zellermarketingdesign.com

Agency Specializes In: Advertising, Graphic Design, Print, Radio

Joe Zeller *(Pres)*
LouAnn Zeller *(VP & Dir-Art)*
Bob Fugate *(Assoc Dir-Creative & Copywriter)*
Andy Sauder *(Sr Graphic Designer)*
Jen Walker *(Sr Graphic Designer)*

Accounts:
Protection 1 Security Solutions

ZELLMER MCCONNELL ADVERTISING

3006 Bee Caves Rd Ste C-150, Austin, TX 78746
Tel.: (512) 296-2662
E-Mail: info@zmcadvertising.com
Web Site: www.zmcadvertising.com

Agency Specializes In: Advertising, Internet/Web Design, Outdoor, Print, T.V.

Beth McConnell *(Partner & Dir-Creative)*
Stefani Zellmer *(Partner & Dir-Creative)*
Alvaro Cifuentes *(Dir-Bus & Sr Acct Mgr)*

Accounts:
Central Texas Regional Mobility Authority Advertising, Marketing, MoPac Improvement Project (Agency of Record)
Heart of Texas Midwives

ZEMI COMMUNICATIONS

10 E 40th St Ste 1900, New York, NY 10016
Tel.: (212) 689-9560
Fax: (212) 689-9330
E-Mail: info@zemi.com
Web Site: www.zemi.com

Employees: 10
Year Founded: 1996

Agency Specializes In: Crisis Communications, Media Relations, Public Relations, Strategic Planning/Research

Alan J. Stoga *(Founder & Pres)*
Daniel B. Wilson *(Mng Dir)*

Accounts:
Bancomer
Dataflux
Elektra
Femsa
Gruma
OMA Aeronautical & Ommercial Services

ZENERGY COMMUNICATIONS

1412 Broadway Ste 1200, New York, NY 10018
Tel.: (646) 675-8451
Toll Free: (866) 440-4034
E-Mail: info@zenergycom.com
Web Site: www.zenergycom.com

Agency Specializes In: Advertising, Brand Development & Integration, Digital/Interactive, Event Planning & Marketing, Investor Relations, Public Relations, Social Media

Linda Farha *(Pres)*
Israel Bonequi *(Creative Dir)*
Katie Knopp *(Dir-Ops)*

Accounts:
New-Optimal Payments

ZENMARK VERBAL DESIGN

25 Maiden Ln Ste 300, San Francisco, CA 94108
Tel.: (415) 434-4800
Fax: (415) 434-4850
E-Mail: info@zenmark.com
Web Site: www.zenmark.com

Employees: 10
Year Founded: 1999

Agency Specializes In: Advertising, Arts, Brand Development & Integration, Consumer Goods, Entertainment, Information Technology, Market Research

Rob McDaniel *(Co-Founder)*
Greg Balla *(Pres & Dir-Creative)*
Doug Powell *(Mng Dir-Acct Svcs)*
Jett Drolette *(Dir-Naming & Design)*
Crystal Vann Wallstrom *(Client Dir & Dir-Ops)*

Accounts:
Abbott
AT&T Communications Corp.
GE
GSK
LG
Novartis
Sprint

ZER0 TO 5IVE

28 S Waterloo Rd, Devon, PA 19333
Tel.: (617) 834-2190
Web Site: www.0to5.com

Employees: 20
Year Founded: 1999

Agency Specializes In: Advertising, Brand Development & Integration, Collateral, Communications, Email, Event Planning & Marketing, Graphic Design, Identity Marketing, Local Marketing, Media Relations, Multimedia, Public Relations, Strategic Planning/Research, Web (Banner Ads, Pop-ups, etc.)

Michelle Pujadas *(Founder & Co-CEO)*
Lauren Innella *(Principal & Dir-Creative)*
Kathleen Fusco *(Principal)*
Claire H. Brukman *(Dir-Art)*
Margaret Deiseroth *(Strategist)*
Emily Forgash *(Strategist)*
Sarah Manix *(Strategist)*
Evan Schaeffer *(Assoc Designer)*
Jennifer Moritz *(Mng Principal)*

Accounts:
Air Desk
AuthenTec
ClearCount Medical Solutions
CS Technology
emoney Advisor
iSeatz
Learn now
Mantas
NoBetterDeal.com; Pittsburgh, PA Campaign Name: "Tips for Getting Holiday Deals on Secondary Market"
OraSure Technologies, Inc. Awareness Kit, Campaign: "Make Knowing Your Thing Today", Media
QuadraMed
Vasont

ZERO GRAVITY GROUP, LLC

PO Box 624, New York, NY 10013
Tel.: (914) 579-2301
Fax: (212) 229-0855
E-Mail: larrye@zerogravitygroup.com
Web Site: www.zerogravitygroup.com

Employees: 15
Year Founded: 2001

Agency Specializes In: Brand Development & Integration, Business-To-Business, Communications, Multimedia, Recruitment, Strategic Planning/Research

Approx. Annual Billings: $1,500,000

Breakdown of Gross Billings by Media: Consulting: 25%; E-Commerce: 20%; Production: 20%; Video Brochures: 35%

Larry Eckerle *(Mng Partner)*
Tina B. Rosenblum *(Dir-Res & Assessment)*
Wendie S. Winslow *(Dir-Editorial Svcs)*

Accounts:
Deloitte & Touche; Philadelphia, PA Internal Communication; 2002
JP Morgan Chase; New York, NY PFS; 2001

ZETA INTERACTIVE

25A Abe Vorhees Dr, Manasquan, NJ 08736
Tel.: (732) 612-3500
Fax: (732) 612-3504
Web Site: www.zetainteractive.com

Agency Specializes In: Digital/Interactive, Search

Engine Optimization, Web (Banner Ads, Pop-ups, etc.)

David A. Steinberg *(CEO)*
Chris Spring *(CFO)*
Steven Gerber *(COO)*
Cullen Jowitt *(Exec VP-Actions)*
Anil Unnikrishnan *(Exec VP)*
Laura Saati *(Sr VP-Client Svcs)*

Accounts:
ADP
Avon
Morgans
Sony

ZFACTOR COMMUNICATIONS INC.
160 Frobisher Dr Ste 15, Waterloo, ON N2V 2B1 Canada
Tel.: (519) 884-2000
Fax: (888) 884-7972
Toll Free: (888) 884-7972
E-Mail: info@zfactor.ca
Web Site: www.zfactor.com

Employees: 5
Year Founded: 1998

Agency Specializes In: Advertising, Brand Development & Integration, Internet/Web Design, Package Design, Print, Web (Banner Ads, Pop-ups, etc.)

Massimo Zefferino *(Dir-Creative-Bus Dev-Big Cheese)*

Accounts:
BlackBerry
Brabender Technologies
Easy up Awnings
Essential Image
Janssen-Ortho
KangaROOS
LV Lomas
Royce/Ayr
Sport Nutrition Depot

ZGM
201 322 - 11th Avenue SW, Calgary, AB T2R 0C5 Canada
Tel.: (403) 770-2250
Fax: (403) 770-2255
E-Mail: info@zgm.ca
Web Site: www.zgm.ca

Year Founded: 1999

Agency Specializes In: Advertising, Digital/Interactive, Graphic Design, Internet/Web Design, Mobile Marketing, Social Media, Strategic Planning/Research

Dan King *(Pres & Dir-Creative)*
Mario Amantea *(Partner & Gen Mgr)*
Peter Bishop *(Partner & Dir-Creative)*
Rob Fairhead *(Partner)*
Heleena Webber *(Acct Dir & Dir-Content)*
Scott Irwin *(Dir-Art)*
Lisa Werner *(Office Mgr)*

ZIG MARKETING
(Formerly Zig.marketing)
812 Huron Rd, Cleveland, OH 44115
Tel.: (216) 744-3040
E-Mail: hzoss@zigmarketing.com
Web Site: www.zigmarketing.com

E-Mail for Key Personnel:
President: hzoss@zigmarketing.com
Creative Dir.: msmith@zigmarketing.com
Media Dir.: jsmith@zigmarketing.com

Employees: 15
Year Founded: 2001

Agency Specializes In: Advertising, Brand Development & Integration, Consumer Marketing, Direct Response Marketing, Direct-to-Consumer, Electronic Media, Information Technology, Internet/Web Design, Media Buying Services, New Technologies, Technical Advertising, Travel & Tourism, Web (Banner Ads, Pop-ups, etc.)

Howard Zoss *(Pres & Partner)*
Lorraine Bivin *(Partner & Dir-Art)*
Michael Smith *(Partner & Dir-Creative)*
Jennifer Smith *(CFO)*

Accounts:
Howard's Jewelry Center
PolyOne
Roetzel
Ruby Tuesday
Simonton Windows
Therma-True Doors
UnitedHealthcare

ZILLNER MARKETING COMMUNICATIONS
8725 Rosehill Rd Ste 200, Lenexa, KS 66215
Tel.: (913) 599-3230
Fax: (913) 599-0080
Web Site: www.zillner.com

Employees: 25
Year Founded: 1992

National Agency Associations: 4A's

Agency Specializes In: Advertising, Seniors' Market

Ronda Zillner *(Founder & CEO)*
Kelly Sizemore *(Chief Strategy Officer)*
Andrew Doak *(Exec Dir-Creative)*
Chris Gray *(Exec Dir-Bus Dev)*
Lisa Price *(Exec Dir-Mktg)*
Cristina Mank *(Acct Dir)*
Mark Peterson *(Dir-Art)*
Sally Kinkhorst *(Sr Mgr-Resource)*
Courtney Brennan *(Acct Mgr)*
Jami Felver *(Mgr-Digital Resource)*
Hannah Bower *(Acct Supvr)*
Lori Colhouer *(Acct Supvr)*

ZIMMERMAN ADVERTISING
6600 N Andrews Avenue, Fort Lauderdale, FL 33309-3064
Tel.: (954) 644-4000
Fax: (954) 731-2977
Toll Free: (800) 248-8522
E-Mail: info@zadv.com
Web Site: www.zadv.com

E-Mail for Key Personnel:
President: jzimmerman@zadv.com

Employees: 1,000
Year Founded: 1985

Agency Specializes In: Brand Development & Integration, Media Relations, Planning & Consultation, Sponsorship

Approx. Annual Billings: $2,500,000,000

David Kissell *(Pres)*
Joe Weiner *(CFO)*
Cliff Courtney *(CMO & Exec VP)*
Lori Wiser *(Chief Strategy Officer)*
Ronnie Haligman *(Exec VP & Gen Mgr)*
Rick Friedman *(Exec VP-Picknclick)*
Michael Gelfano *(Exec VP-Retail Technologies)*
Jill Schneider *(Sr VP & Grp Dir-Ops)*
Nichole Robillard *(Sr VP & Grp Acct Dir)*
Jared Koesten *(VP-HR)*
Joe Shook *(VP-IT)*
Richard Gray *(Dir-Creative)*
Shannon Spence *(Assoc Dir-Integrated Media-Digital Activation)*
Julianna Corso *(Mgr-PR)*
Tiant Thompson *(Acct Supvr-Digital)*
Samantha Blanco *(Specialist-Social Mktg)*
Brandy Dalton *(Acct Exec)*
Gabrielle Krugman *(Acct Exec)*
Leonie Massre *(Specialist-Digital)*
Austin Lance Butler *(Media Planner-Integrated Digital)*
Nicole Cramsie *(Media Buyer-Integrated)*
Meagan Ebmeyer *(Planner-Digital Media)*
Xionel Lopez *(Sr Graphic Designer)*
Merritt Milliorn *(Planner-Digital Media)*
John Puleo *(Media Planner-Integrated)*
Zack Roberts *(Jr Copywriter)*
Katherine Terc-Acosta *(Media Planner-Integrated)*
Jennifer Galer *(Sr Media Buyer)*
Adam Herman *(Chief Integrated Media Officer)*
Susie Hinchey *(Asst Media Planner-Integrated)*
Amanda Holmen *(Asst Media Planner-Integrated)*

Accounts:
American Media Inc. Strategic
Atlantis Foods Fresh Soup
Autonation USA All Markets; 2001
Blue Cross & Blue Shield of Florida; Jacksonville, FL Media Planning & Buying, Retail Advertising
Bob's Stores
Boston Market Creative & Media
BPI Sports (Agency of Record) Strategy
Broward Health (Agency of Record) Creative, Digital, Marketing Strategy, Media Buying, Media Planning, Strategy, Traditional
New-CEC Entertainment, Inc. Creative, Media, Promotion, Strategy
Chico's FAS, Inc. Digital, Media
Dell
Dunkin' Donuts
Extended Stay Hotels CRM, Creative, Digital, Media Planning & Buying, Mobile
Firehouse Subs; Jacksonville, FL
New-5 Below (Agency of Record)
The Fresh Market, Inc. (Agency of Record) Creative, Digital Media Planning & Buying, Social Media, Strategic Planning, Traditional Media Planning & Buying
George Foreman Household Appliances (Agency of Record)
Hard Rock Hotel & Casinos Global Public Relations
HHGregg; Indianapolis, IN (Agency of Record) Creative, Media Buying, Media Planning; 2007
Jamba Juice
Lennar Homes
Lucky Brand Jeans (Media Planning & Buying Agency of Record) Digital Advertising, Public Relations, Social Media
Michaels Stores, Inc. (Lead Creative Agency) Analytics, Creative, Digital, Planning, Social Media, Strategy
Nissan USA Altima, Campaign: "Ride of Your Life"
oBand
Party City Corporation (Agency of Record)
The Pep Boys - Manny, Moe & Jack
QVC
The Scooter Store
Smart for Life Weight Loss Program; 2007
Tire Kingdom

Branches

Zimmerman Advertising
5353 Grosvenor Blvd, Los Angeles, CA 90066-6913
Tel.: (310) 305-5000
Fax: (310) 305-6000
Web Site: www.zadv.com

Employees: 8

Agency Specializes In: Automotive, Retail

Kellie Barnett *(Assoc Dir-Media)*
Aaron Gwin *(Assoc Dir-Digital Media)*
Amber Kane *(Assoc Dir-Media)*
Samantha Barnett *(Media Planner)*
Merritt Milliorn *(Media Planner-Digital)*
Rebecca Atkins *(Jr Media Planner)*
Nicole French *(Sr Media Planner)*

Accounts:
Nissan USA

Zimmerman Advertising

2 Mid America Plz Ste 510, Oakbrook Terrace, IL 60181-1937
Tel.: (630) 574-1059
Fax: (630) 472-3148
E-Mail: melaniemamed@zadv.com
Web Site: www.zadv.com

Employees: 8

Agency Specializes In: Retail

Cliff Courtney *(CMO)*
David Nathanson *(Chief Creative Officer)*
David Henry *(Exec VP-Strategic Mktg Intelligence)*
Dan Kissell *(Exec VP-Automotive Retail Div)*
Chris Greene *(Sr VP & Grp Acct Dir)*
Chad Comunale *(Sr VP & Dir-Operational)*
Patrick Sullivan *(VP & Acct Dir)*
Brad Granda *(VP & Dir-Studio)*
Chesney Spivey *(Supvr-Digital Media)*
Ashley Ritter *(Specialist-Social Mktg)*

Accounts:
Nissan USA

Zimmerman Advertising

488 Madison Ave 4th Fl, New York, NY 10022-5702
Tel.: (212) 804-1000
Fax: (212) 804-1485
Web Site: www.zadv.com

Employees: 10

Agency Specializes In: Automotive

David Valdes *(CO-Founder & COO)*
Joe Weiner *(CFO)*
Cliff Courtney *(CMO & Exec VP)*
David Nathanson *(Chief Creative Officer & Exec VP)*
Mike Devine *(Mng Dir-Automotive & Exec VP)*
Richard Nez *(Exec VP, Dir-Brdcst Production & Exec Producer)*
Rick Friedman *(Exec VP-Pick-n-Click)*
Adam Herman *(Exec VP-Integrated Media Svcs)*
Scott Thaler *(Exec VP-Digital Growth & innovation)*
Chad Garcia *(VP & Dir-Creative-Studio)*
Deana Schade *(VP & Dir-Traffic Ops)*
Lauren Wright *(Supvr-Media Plng-Northeastern Nissan)*

Accounts:
Nissan

The Zimmerman Agency LLC

(d/b/a Bright Red LLC)
1821 Miccosukee Commons Dr, Tallahassee, FL 32308-5433
(See Separate Listing)

THE ZIMMERMAN AGENCY LLC

(d/b/a Bright Red LLC)
1821 Miccosukee Commons Dr, Tallahassee, FL 32308-5433
Tel.: (850) 668-2222
Fax: (850) 656-4622
E-Mail: media@zimmerman.com
Web Site: www.zimmerman.com

E-Mail for Key Personnel:
President: curtis@zimmerman.com
Creative Dir.: erich@zimmerman.com
Media Dir.: john@zimmerman.com
Public Relations: carrie@zimmerman.com

Employees: 134
Year Founded: 1987

National Agency Associations: 4A's

Agency Specializes In: Advertising, Sponsorship

Carrie Englert Zimmerman *(Co-Founder & CEO)*
Ryan Linder *(CMO & Exec VP)*
Kerry Anne Watson *(Pres-PR)*
Rusty Howard *(Exec VP & Dir-Digital)*
Tricia Smith *(VP & Acct Dir)*
Ivette Marques Faulkner *(VP-PR)*
Sonia Grunbaum *(VP-Mktg)*
John Nicholas *(VP-Media Activation)*
Sheila Simpson *(VP-HR)*
Danika Kirvin *(Grp Dir-Integrated Media-Zimmerman Adv)*
Steven Waterman *(Grp Dir-Integrated Media)*
Charles DeLong *(Dir-Creative)*
Carol Klopfenstein *(Dir-Production)*
Riccardo Sabioni *(Dir-Creative)*
Jody Sadler *(Assoc Dir-Integrated Media)*
Lauren Harrison *(Sr Acct Mgr)*
Cole Zimmerman *(Sr Acct Mgr)*
Meagan Chestnut *(Acct Mgr)*
Julia Darrenkamp *(Acct Mgr-PR)*
Brittany Gibson *(Acct Mgr-PR)*
Carrie Poole *(Acct Mgr-Adv)*
Bethany Swonson *(Acct Mgr)*
Chris Groom *(Mgr-Acctg)*
Jennifer Jackson *(Acct Supvr)*
Mari Kraljic *(Supvr-Integrated Media)*
Shawn Renshaw *(Supvr-Media)*
Nicole Cramsie *(Media Buyer-Integrated)*
Daniella DelaOsa *(Sr Acct Coord-PR)*
Kathryn Wolter *(Sr Acct Coord-PR)*

Accounts:
Aflac Movie-Tie In - Toy Story 3, Print, Social Media, Sweepstakes
Algonquin Hotel
Aruba Tourism Authority Public Relations
Club Med Americas
Florida Prepaid College Plans Campaign: "Future Diplomas"
Flowers Foods, Inc. Campaign: "Nature's Own BreakFASTer", Nature's Own
La Luce
Mrs Freshleys
Party City
Pilot Pen Campaign: "Power to the Pen Digital"
Tobacco Free Florida
WFRF 1070 AM Faith Radio Poster
Yachts of Seabourn Cruiseline

THE ZIMMERMAN GROUP

21940 Minnetonka Blvd, Excelsior, MN 55331
Tel.: (952) 470-8830
Fax: (952) 470-8807
E-Mail: info@thezimmermangroup.com
Web Site: www.thezimmermangroup.com

E-Mail for Key Personnel:
President: jimz@thezimmermangroup.com
Creative Dir.: gregj@thezimmermangroup.com

Employees: 8
Year Founded: 1984

National Agency Associations: AAF

Agency Specializes In: Advertising, Brand Development & Integration, Broadcast, Business Publications, Business-To-Business, Co-op Advertising, Collateral, Commercial Photography, Communications, Consulting, Consumer Marketing, Consumer Publications, Corporate Identity, Direct Response Marketing, Electronic Media, Food Service, Graphic Design, Internet/Web Design, Logo & Package Design, Magazines, New Product Development, Newspaper, Newspapers & Magazines, Out-of-Home Media, Outdoor, Planning & Consultation, Point of Purchase, Point of Sale, Print, Production, Public Relations, Publicity/Promotions, Radio, Retail, Sales Promotion, Strategic Planning/Research, Sweepstakes, Trade & Consumer Magazines, Yellow Pages Advertising

Approx. Annual Billings: $10,000,000

Jim Zimmerman *(Pres)*
Kathy Ashpole *(VP)*
Brian Doeden *(Dir-Creative)*

Accounts:
Dakota Growers Pasta Co.; 1990
Faribault Foods; Minneapolis, MN; 1984
General Mills; 1991
Nestle Analytical Division; St Louis, MO; 1992
Norwesco; Saint Bonifacius, MN; 1996
Orion Safety Products; 1995
SunButter; 2008

ZION & ZION

432 S Farmer Ave, Tempe, AZ 85281
Tel.: (480) 751-1007
Fax: (480) 753-3177
Web Site: www.zionandzion.com

Employees: 24

Agency Specializes In: Advertising, Digital/Interactive, Public Relations, Social Media, Strategic Planning/Research

Aric Zion *(Partner & CEO)*
Bridgette Foord *(Dir-Media)*
Brandt Bogdanovich *(Sr Mgr-Mktg Automation)*
Teri Morris *(Sr Acct Supvr)*
Sam Fink *(Acct Exec-PR & Social Media)*
Ashley Oakes *(Acct Exec)*
Malory Knutson *(Acct Coord-PR & Social Media)*

Accounts:
AFS Technologies
Alere Inc.
Arizona Blinds (Agency of Record) Content Development, Email Marketing, Online Marketing, SEO, Social Media, Traditional Advertising, Website
Arizona Dermatology Content Strategy, SEO, Social Media, Web Design
Arizona Wild West Beef Jerky (Agency of Record) Branding & Interactive
ARS/Rescue Rooter
AV Homes Inc Marketing, Public Relations, Social Media, Web Development
Aviation Performance Solutions (Agency of Record)
BANK 34 (Agency of Record)
Barro's Pizza (Agency of Record) Branding, Broadcast Media, Email Marketing, Online Presence, PR, Social Media, Web Development
New-Casino Del Sol Resort (Agency of Record) Digital, Media Buying, Media Planning, Public Relations, Social Media
CENTURY 21 Northwest Interactive Campaign Development
Childhelp Digital Strategy, Public Relations, Social Media
Contractor Management Services (Agency of Record) Creative, PR
Digital Tech Frontier; Tempe, AZ
Distinctive Roofing (Agency of Record) Media Strategy, Public Relations, Social Media
DMB Associates

Dutch Bros. Arizona (Agency of Record) Marketing, Public Relations, Social Media
Farm at South Mountain
Fascinations (Agency of Record) Media Buying, Public Relations, Social Media, Web
Fox Restaurant Concepts Community Relations, Farmer Arts District, Public Relations
Garage Floor Coating.com (Agency of Record) Email Marketing, Public Relations, Social Media Strategy, Website Redevelopment
Global Organics Group (Agency of Record) Branding, Marketing, PR, Social Media
Goettl Air Conditioning
Goodwill of Central Arizona (Agency of Record) Branding, Creative, Interactive, Radio, Social Media, Strategy, TV, Traditional & Interactive Media Buying
Great American Merchandise and Events (Agency of Record) Creative
Imperial Wholesale Content Development, Email Marketing, Online Marketing, Social Media, Website
K Couture Branding, Content Development, Design support, E-Commerce Website, Messaging, Social Media
Kevin's Last Walk
MPower Energy Tabs Interactive Development, Social Media
Norterra Family Medicine
Northern Chemical Co.
Paradise Medspa & Wellness
Premier Pools and Spas
Quiessence Email Marketing, Public Relations, Rebranding, Social Media
Rancho Solano Private Schools; Phoenix, AZ Public Relations
Remnant Health Center
Santa Barbara Catering Co.
Shoppers Supply Advertising/Creative, Branding/Positioning, Content Development, Email Marketing, Market Research, Media Planning and Buying, Social Media, Web Development
Sothebys International Realty
Sun City Awning
VanDenBosch
Vinatronic
Weider Global Nutrition (Agency of Record)
World Nutrition Content Development, Product Packaging Design, SEO, Social Media
Zany Zak

ZIP COMMUNICATION INC

388 Saint-Jacques St Ste 500, Montreal, QC H2Y 1F1 Canada
Tel.: (514) 844-6006
Fax: (514) 844-6010
E-Mail: info@zipcom.ca
Web Site: www.zipcom.ca

Employees: 15

Agency Specializes In: Advertising, Brand Development & Integration, Broadcast, Package Design, Print, Strategic Planning/Research, T.V.

Michele Leduc *(Pres & Chief Creative Officer)*
Loic Brignou *(Acct Dir)*
Marie-claude Boulais *(Dir-Artistic)*

ZIZZO GROUP MARKETING + PR + NEW MEDIA, INC.

(Formerly Zizzo Group Advertising + PR)
648 N Plankinton Ave Ste 270, Milwaukee, WI 53203
Tel.: (414) 319-5700
Fax: (414) 319-5717
E-Mail: info@zizzogroup.com
Web Site: www.zizzogroup.com

Year Founded: 1995

Agency Specializes In: Advertising, Brand Development & Integration, Digital/Interactive, Integrated Marketing, Media Buying Services, Media Planning, Public Relations, Social Media, Strategic Planning/Research

Anne Zizzo *(CEO)*
Michelle Sieg *(VP & Dir-Creative)*
Tracey Carson *(VP-Integrated Mktg)*
Dan Augustine *(Assoc Dir-Creative)*
Marko Knezic *(Sr Acct Exec)*
Carly Schroeder *(Sr Acct Exec)*
Jackie Costa *(Acct Exec)*
Josh Paynter *(Sr Designer)*

Accounts:
ActionCOACH Business Coaching Media Relations, Public Relations
Affinity Plus Federal Credit Union Affinity Plus On The Money
BMO Harris Bank
Faith Technologies (Agency of Record)
Helen Bader Foundation, Inc.
Key Technical Solutions Inc
Market Probe Strategic Marketing
Popular Community Bank
Wausau Financial Systems Inc.; Mosinee, WI

Zizzo Group Marketing Services, Inc.

(Name Changed to Zizzo Group Marketing + PR + New Media, Inc.)

ZLRIGNITION

303 Watson Powell Jr Way Ste 100, Des Moines, IA 50309-1724
Tel.: (515) 244-4456
Fax: (515) 244-5749
E-Mail: ceo@zlrignition.com
Web Site: www.zlrignition.com

E-Mail for Key Personnel:
President: llaurent@zlrignition.com
Public Relations: bbrewer@zlrignition.com

Employees: 25
Year Founded: 1987

National Agency Associations: DMA-ICOM-PRSA

Agency Specializes In: Advertising, Brand Development & Integration, Broadcast, Business Publications, Business-To-Business, Cable T.V., Children's Market, Collateral, Communications, Consulting, Consumer Marketing, Consumer Publications, Corporate Identity, Direct Response Marketing, E-Commerce, Education, Electronic Media, Engineering, Entertainment, Event Planning & Marketing, Exhibit/Trade Shows, Financial, Food Service, Government/Political, Graphic Design, Health Care Services, Information Technology, Magazines, Media Buying Services, Medical Products, Merchandising, Newspaper, Newspapers & Magazines, Out-of-Home Media, Outdoor, Planning & Consultation, Point of Purchase, Point of Sale, Print, Production, Public Relations, Publicity/Promotions, Radio, Restaurant, Retail, Strategic Planning/Research, T.V., Trade & Consumer Magazines, Yellow Pages Advertising

Louis Laurent *(Pres)*
James B. Anfinson *(CFO & VP)*
Bill Brewer *(Sr VP)*
Andrea Marinaro *(VP & Dir-Media)*
Bob Delsol *(Exec Dir-Creative)*

Accounts:
Beam Industries; Webster City, IA Central Vacuum Systems
Iowa State University; Ames, IA; 1997

ZOG DIGITAL

18835 N Thompson Peak Pwy, Scottsdale, AZ 85255
Tel.: (480) 426-9954
Web Site: www.zogdigital.com

Employees: 40
Year Founded: 2010

Agency Specializes In: Advertising, Advertising Specialties, Affiliate Marketing, Affluent Market, Automotive, Brand Development & Integration, Business-To-Business, Children's Market, College, Consumer Goods, Consumer Marketing, Content, Cosmetics, Digital/Interactive, Direct-to-Consumer, E-Commerce, Electronics, Fashion/Apparel, Financial, Food Service, Health Care Services, High Technology, Hospitality, Household Goods, Industrial, Integrated Marketing, Internet/Web Design, Leisure, Luxury Products, Media Buying Services, Medical Products, Men's Market, Merchandising, Paid Searches, Pets , Pharmaceutical, Planning & Consultation, Public Relations, Restaurant, Retail, Sales Promotion, Search Engine Optimization, Social Media, Sponsorship, Strategic Planning/Research, Teen Market, Transportation, Travel & Tourism, Tween Market, Web (Banner Ads, Pop-ups, etc.), Women's Market

Austin Lemme *(Co-Founder & Exec Creative Dir)*
Jeff Herzog *(Chm & CEO)*
Jason Squardo *(Mng Dir)*
Kyle Clifford *(Sr VP-Strategic Acct Svcs)*
Thomas Stern *(Sr VP-Client Svcs)*
Kim Giroux *(VP-Paid Media)*
Chris Moreno *(VP-Social Media)*
Rachael Zahn *(VP-Client Svcs)*
Mark Healey *(Dir-SEO)*

Accounts:
KitchenAid Kitchen Appliances; 2012
Pep Boys Car Parts & Service; 2014
Rack Room Shoes Women's, Men's & Children's Footwear; 2013

ZONE 5

25 Monroe St Ste 300, Albany, NY 12210
Tel.: (518) 242-7000
Fax: (518) 242-7092
E-Mail: info@zone5.com
Web Site: www.zone5.com

Employees: 32
Year Founded: 1989

Agency Specializes In: College, Digital/Interactive, Event Planning & Marketing, Financial, Health Care Services, Internet/Web Design, New Technologies, Web (Banner Ads, Pop-ups, etc.)

Todd Mosher *(Pres & CEO)*
Timothy Dunn *(VP)*
Ray Witkowski *(VP)*
Richard Hedges *(Bus Dir)*
Dave Homsey *(Dir-Creative)*
Allison Albrecht *(Acct Exec)*
Victoria Barbeisch *(Acct Exec)*
Brittnay Gilman *(Acct Exec)*
Spencer Raggio *(Strategist-Web)*
Dave Imbarrato *(Designer)*

Accounts:
Finger Lakes Health
Union College
United Memorial Medical Center

ZOOM ADVERTISING

820 W Jackson Blvd, Chicago, IL 60607
Tel.: (312) 279-2900
Fax: (312) 491-0303
E-Mail: info@zoomchicago.com
Web Site: www.zoomchicago.com

E-Mail for Key Personnel:
President: jeff@zoomchicago.com

Employees: 12
Year Founded: 1993

Agency Specializes In: Advertising, Automotive, Publicity/Promotions

Approx. Annual Billings: $7,000,000

Jeffrey J. Halcomb *(Pres & CEO)*
William Moore *(VP-Client Svcs)*
Matthew Robinson *(Dir-Creative)*

Accounts:
Hawkinson Nissan
River Oaks Ford
South Chicago Dodge
South Chicago Nissan
Steve Foley Cadillac
Toyota Scion on Western

ZOOM CREATES

1941 NW Quimby St, Portland, OR 97209
Tel.: (503) 296-1104
E-Mail: info@zoomcreates.com
Web Site: www.zoomcreates.com

Year Founded: 1998

Agency Specializes In: Advertising, Brand Development & Integration, Logo & Package Design, Print, Search Engine Optimization, Social Media, Strategic Planning/Research

Robin Budd *(Dir-Art)*
Lisa Harvey *(Acct Exec)*
June Knightly *(Acct Exec)*

Accounts:
J.R. Johnson Inc.

ZOYES CREATIVE GROUP

1280 Hilton Rd, Ferndale, MI 48220
Tel.: (248) 584-3300
Fax: (248) 584-3303
Web Site: www.zoyescreative.com

Agency Specializes In: Advertising, Brand Development & Integration, Digital/Interactive, Email, Graphic Design, Internet/Web Design, Logo & Package Design, Print, Social Media

Aimee Zoyes *(Principal)*
Meredith Phillips *(Jr Designer)*

Accounts:
8 Degrees Plato
Alidade Capital
Glenda Meads Architects
Linda Jacob Chocolatier
One Detroit Center
The Teich Group

ZUBI ADVERTISING SERVICES, INC.

2990 Ponce De Leon Blvd Ste 600, Coral Gables, FL 33134-5006
Tel.: (305) 448-9824
Fax: (305) 460-6393
E-Mail: jzubi@zubiad.com
Web Site: www.zubiad.com

E-Mail for Key Personnel:
President: tzubi@zubiad.com
Media Dir.: lolmedo@zubiad.com
Production Mgr.: mtriana@zubiad.com

Employees: 130
Year Founded: 1976

National Agency Associations: AHAA

Agency Specializes In: Digital/Interactive, Event Planning & Marketing, Hispanic Market, Media Buying Services, Media Planning, Sponsorship

Approx. Annual Billings: $186,000,000

Breakdown of Gross Billings by Media: Cable T.V.: 15%; Collateral: 3%; Event Mktg.: 1%; Fees: 13%; Network T.V.: 22%; Newsp. & Mags.: 5%; Out-of-Home Media: 4%; Production: 18%; Promos.: 1%; Radio: 10%; Spot T.V.: 8%

Joe Zubizarreta *(COO)*
Michelle Zubizarreta *(Chief Admin Officer)*
Joe Castro *(Exec VP-Integrated Mktg)*
John Arnholt *(Sr VP)*
Julie Figueras *(VP & Comptroller)*
Isabella Sanchez *(VP-Media Integration)*
Troy Valls *(VP-Discovery & Design)*
Ivan Calle *(Exec Dir-Creative)*
Armando Garcia *(Grp Dir-Creative)*
Cristian Duran *(Sr Dir-Art)*
Francisco Losada *(Sr Dir-Art)*
Susan Osorio *(Acct Dir)*
Raul Alfonso *(Dir-Res)*
Claire Zaldivar *(Dir-Brdcst)*
Michael Roca *(Assoc Dir-Media)*
Evie Macias *(Acct Supvr)*
Cristina Rua *(Acct Supvr-Dunkin' Donuts)*
Veronica Socarras *(Acct Supvr)*
Nieves Diaz *(Supvr-Media Billing)*
Damaris Rosales *(Sr Acct Exec)*
Monica Agurto *(Media Buyer)*
Lourdes Banos *(Media Buyer)*
Nour Da Silva *(Copywriter)*
Jorge Jacome *(Copywriter)*
Jennifer Rodriguez *(Media Planner)*
Yanisa Velez *(Copywriter)*
Maria Gutierrez *(Jr Media Planner)*
Lina Roitman *(Sr Media Planner)*

Accounts:
Darden Co. Olive Garden Restaurants; 2000
Dunkin' Brands Donkin' Donuts; 2013
Ford Dealer Associations - California; 2007
Ford Motor Company Campaign: "By Design", Digital Media, Focus Electric, Ford, Ford Warriors in Pink, Fusion, Lincoln, Mustang; 1996
J.M. Smucker Company Packaged Goods; 2005
JP Morgan Chase Bank Retail Banking; 2009
Sunny Delight Beverage Co. SunnyD; 2013
Walgreen Co. Walgreens; 2011

Branches

Zubi Advertising Services, Inc.

10 Pointe Dr Ste 125, Brea, CA 92821
Tel.: (714) 990-1100
E-Mail: jzubi@zubiad.com
Web Site: www.zubiad.com

Employees: 2
Year Founded: 1995

Agency Specializes In: Hispanic Market

Tim Swies *(Exec VP)*
Veronica Zuniga *(Acct Supvr)*
Jose Merino *(Media Planner)*

Zubi Advertising Services, Inc.

3 Parklane Blvd Ste 1050 W, Dearborn, MI 48126
Tel.: (313) 982-9078
Fax: (313) 982-0052
E-Mail: jcastro@zubiad.com
Web Site: www.zubiad.com

Employees: 3
Year Founded: 1996

Agency Specializes In: Hispanic Market

Tim Swies *(Exec VP)*
Isabella Sanchez *(VP-Media Integration)*

ZUCHELLI & JOHNSON HEALTHCARE COMMUNICATIONS

2873 Ocean Ave, Seaford, NY 11783-3455
Tel.: (516) 783-1400
Fax: (516) 783-1805
Toll Free: (800) 562-9031
Web Site: www.adwise.com

E-Mail for Key Personnel:
President: tomj@adwise.com
Creative Dir.: cathy@adwise.com

Employees: 10
Year Founded: 1983

Agency Specializes In: Health Care Services, Medical Products, Pharmaceutical

Breakdown of Gross Billings by Media: Adv. Specialities: 7%; Bus. Publs.: 23%; Collateral: 18%; D.M.: 28%; Event Mktg.: 8%; Exhibits/Trade Shows: 6%; Internet Adv.: 5%; Strategic Planning/Research: 5%

Thomas J. Johnson *(Pres)*
Angela Johnson *(VP-Client Svcs)*

Accounts:
Generamedics
Nalfon
Oceanside Pharmaceuticals
Solco
Suprane

ZUGARA INC.

13101 W Washington Blvd Ste 403, Los Angeles, CA 90066-8128
Tel.: (310) 566-7441
Fax: (310) 566-7443
E-Mail: info@zugara.com
Web Site: www.zugara.com

Agency Specializes In: Advertising, Internet/Web Design, Local Marketing, Mobile Marketing

Matthew Szymczyk *(Owner)*
Alex Goldberg *(CTO)*
Andrey Tkachuk *(Head-R&D)*
Carole Foster *(Dir-HR & Recruitment)*

Accounts:
Activision Blizzard Game Publisher
AT&T Communications Corp. Digital
Deere & Company Farm & Forestry Equipment Mfr
Fletcher Jones Motorcars Automobile Dealer
Nestle
Reebok Sports Products Marketing Services
THQ Sports

ZULLO ASSOCIATES

1 Academy St, Princeton, NJ 08540
Tel.: (609) 683-1800
Fax: (609) 683-4773
E-Mail: rick@zulloagency.com
Web Site: www.zullocreative.com/

Employees: 7
Year Founded: 1983

Agency Specializes In: Advertising, Advertising Specialties, Brand Development & Integration, Broadcast, Co-op Advertising, Consumer Marketing, Consumer Publications, Corporate Identity, Graphic Design, Logo & Package Design, Media Buying Services, New Product Development, Newspaper, Outdoor, Point of

Purchase, Point of Sale, Radio, Retail, Sales Promotion, Strategic Planning/Research, T.V., Trade & Consumer Magazines

Approx. Annual Billings: $8,700,000

Richard C. Zullo *(Pres)*
Teri Lauletti *(Acct Svcs Dir-Zullo Brand Comm & Design)*
Carol Ponzo *(Assoc Dir-Creative)*

Accounts:
The Baker
Briar's Soft Drinks; North Brunswick, NJ
Finlandia Cheese; Parsippany, NJ Cheese Products; 1999
Hale Built
Jana Foods
Mantosantos Foods
Matrix Development Group; Cranbury, NJ Commercial Real Estate; 1994
Neves Jewelers, NJ; 1988
Norseland Inc.
Omega Foods
Rutgers Athletic Department
Tholstrup Cheese USA, Inc.; Warren, NJ SAGA Brand Cheese

ZULU ALPHA KILO
512 King St E, Toronto, ON M5A 1M1 Canada
Tel.: (416) 777-9858
E-Mail: ineedanewagency@zulualphakilo.com
Web Site: www.zulualphakilo.com

Employees: 40
Year Founded: 2008

Agency Specializes In: Advertising, Internet/Web Design, Public Relations

Mike Sutton *(Pres)*
Kate Torrance *(Mng Dir)*
Zak Mroueh *(Chief Creative Officer)*
Heidi Philip *(Chief Strategy Officer)*
Ron Smrczek *(Exec Creative Dir)*
Roy Gruia *(Grp Acct Dir)*
Kerry McKibbin *(Grp Acct Dir)*
Nevena Djordjevic *(Acct Dir)*
Allan Mah *(Art Dir)*
Guilherme Bermejo *(Dir-Art)*
Curtis Denomme *(Dir-Art)*
Rob Feightner *(Dir-Client Svcs)*
Fiorella Martinez *(Dir-Art)*
Jamie Murphy *(Dir-Talent & Culture)*
Sean Atkinson *(Copywriter)*
Catherine Allen *(Assoc Dir-Creative)*
George Ault *(Assoc Dir-Creative)*
Andrew Caie *(Assoc Dir-Creative)*
Noel Fenn *(Assoc Dir-Creative)*
Gail Pak *(Assoc Dir-Creative)*
Ian Simpson *(Assoc Dir-Creative)*
Devina Hardatt *(Acct Supvr)*
Alex Potter *(Acct Supvr)*
Emma Brooks *(Strategist-Digital)*
Winnie Hsiao *(Acct Exec)*
Maegan Thomas *(Acct Exec)*
Samantha Angus *(Copywriter)*

Accounts:
Alterna Savings
Anaphylaxis Campaign: "First Kiss"
Anheuser-Busch InBev N.V./S.A.
Audi Audi Q3, Campaign: "4-Letter Word"
Bell Canada
Canadian Stage Campaign: "Experience Red"
Corona (Agency of Record) Campaign: "Find Your Beach", Campaign: "Live Mas Fina" or "live the good life", Corona Beer
New-Courage Canada Blind Cane
Elvis Presley Enterprises Ads, Collingwood Elvis Festival, Creative, Door Hangers, Elvis Exit Signs, Images, Outdoor, Postings, Social Media
Fangoria Magazine Campaign: "Death By Cheese Greater", Campaign: "Grater", Campaign: "Holiday Horror", Campaign: "Rolling pin", Campaign: "Toaster"
Foresight Features
Grupo Modelo S.A.B. de C.V.
Hershey Canada
Interac (Creative Agency of Record) Campaign: "Have a Merry January", Digital, OOH, Print, Social, TV
Make A Wish Canada Broadcast, Campaign: "FunRaising", Campaign: "Grandma", Campaign: "Lollipop", Campaign: "Snare", Kringl, Online
Mazooma
Modelo Molson Imports L.P. Corona Extra (Creative & Strategy Agency of Record)
National Advertising Benevolent Society Campaign: "Auctioneer", Campaign: "Over Qualified Interns - Direct Mail", Vintage Intern Auction
National Advertising Challenge Online, Video
Nestea Cans
Participaction Campaign: "Make Room For Play"
People for Good Out-of-Home Campaign, Print Campaign
Pleiades Theatre
Puma Athletic Footwear Producer
Simply Orange Campaign: "Juicer", Campaign: "Squeezed"
Tama Art University
Workopolis Campaign: "The Candidate", Campaign: "Vanity", Online Recruitment Services

ZULU CREATIVE
3921 Austin St, Houston, TX 77004
Tel.: (888) 520-1789
Web Site: www.zulucreative.com

Year Founded: 2006

Agency Specializes In: Advertising, Event Planning & Marketing, Graphic Design, Print, Public Relations, Social Media

Tina Zulu *(Founder & Chief Creative Officer)*
W. Ross Wells *(Dir-Film-Zenfilm)*
Danny Cuellar *(Mgr-Global Adv-Continental Airlines)*

Accounts:
Charde Jewelers
Max's Wine Dive
The Tasting Room Wine Cafe

ZUVA MARKETING, INC.
5225 N Wayne Ave, Kansas City, MO 64118
Tel.: (816) 455-9494
Fax: (816) 455-5232
E-Mail: info@zuvamarketing.com
Web Site: www.zuvamarketing.com

Employees: 3
Year Founded: 1996

Agency Specializes In: Advertising, Advertising Specialties, Alternative Advertising, Business-To-Business, Co-op Advertising, Collateral, Commercial Photography, Consulting, Consumer Goods, Consumer Marketing, Consumer Publications, Digital/Interactive, Email, Event Planning & Marketing, Graphic Design, Guerilla Marketing, Hospitality, In-Store Advertising, Leisure, Local Marketing, Magazines, Market Research, Media Buying Services, Media Planning, Media Relations, Multicultural, Multimedia, Newspaper, Newspapers & Magazines, Outdoor, Podcasting, Point of Sale, Production (Ad, Film, Broadcast), Promotions, Public Relations, Publicity/Promotions, RSS (Really Simple Syndication), Real Estate, Regional, Search Engine Optimization, Seniors' Market, T.V., Trade & Consumer Magazines, Travel & Tourism, Urban Market, Viral/Buzz/Word of Mouth, Web (Banner Ads, Pop-ups, etc.), Women's Market

Approx. Annual Billings: $4,000,000

Breakdown of Gross Billings by Media: Cable T.V.: 20%; Mags.: 5%; Outdoor: 5%; Plng. & Consultation: 5%; Pub. Rels.: 5%; Radio & T.V.: 60%

Mary Clark *(Owner & Pres)*

ZUVI CREATIVE LLC
1844 Clacton Dr, Orlando, FL 32837
Tel.: (407) 405-2775
Web Site: www.zuvicreative.com

Agency Specializes In: Advertising, Brand Development & Integration, Corporate Identity, Digital/Interactive, Graphic Design, Internet/Web Design, Logo & Package Design, Print, Social Media

Viviana Castano *(Dir-Creative)*

Accounts:
Camilas Restaurant
Fresh Choice Market
Naneu Bags

ZYNC COMMUNICATIONS INC.
282 Richmond St E Ste 200, Toronto, ON M5A 1P4 Canada
Tel.: (416) 322-2865
E-Mail: info@zync.ca
Web Site: www.zync.ca

Year Founded: 2004

Agency Specializes In: Advertising, Brand Development & Integration, Communications, Social Media, Web (Banner Ads, Pop-ups, etc.)

Colette Morgan *(Mng Dir)*
Marko Zonta *(Principal & Dir-Creative)*
Brad Breinnger *(Principal & Strategist)*
Gabi Gomes *(Acct Dir)*
Jeremy Linskill *(Dir-Design)*
Andrea Charleau *(Project Mgr-Digital)*
Bekki Draper *(Sr Designer)*
Sascha Hass *(Sr Designer)*

Accounts:
Canadian Olympic Committee Digital
Kaypok Inc.

ZYNGA NEW YORK
(Formerly Area/Code)
45 W 21st St Ste 3C, New York, NY 10010
Tel.: (212) 254-5800
Fax: (212) 254-5807
Web Site: www.zynga.com

Agency Specializes In: Entertainment, Game Integration, Internet/Web Design

David Lee *(CFO & Chief Acctg Officer)*
Dani Dudeck *(Chief Comm Officer)*
Devang S. Shah *(Gen Counsel, Sec & VP)*
Tom Casey *(VP-Games)*
Jamie Davies *(VP-Games)*
Maureen Fan *(VP-Games)*
Jonathan Knight *(VP-Games)*
Jonathan Liu *(VP)*
Yousuf Bhaijee *(Sr Dir-Growth)*

Accounts:
A&E Networks
CBS
Discovery Networks

Disney Imagineering
Electrolux Appliances
MTV
Nokia
Qwest Wireless

HOUSE AGENCIES

ABBE LABORATORIES, INC.
1095 Route 110, Farmingdale, NY 11735
Tel.: (631) 756-2223
Fax: (631) 756-0894
Toll Free: (800) 457-0990
Web Site: http://pro.abbelabs.com/

Employees: 10
Year Founded: 1990

Agency Specializes In: Direct Response Marketing

Approx. Annual Billings: $250,000

Robert Posner *(Founder)*
Paul Iannuzzo *(Mng Dir)*

Accounts:
ABBE Laboratories; Farmingdale, NY End-Zit Products, Glycolactic Products, Pro-Med Retinol Products

ALAN GORDON ADVERTISING
5625 Melrose Ave, Los Angeles, CA 90038-3909
Tel.: (323) 466-3561
Fax: (323) 871-2193
E-Mail: ads@alangordon.com
Web Site: www.alangordon.com

E-Mail for Key Personnel:
Creative Dir.: grantl@alangordon.com

Employees: 17
Year Founded: 1970

Agency Specializes In: Above-the-Line, Advertising, Below-the-Line, Business Publications, Business-To-Business, Collateral, College, Corporate Identity, Direct-to-Consumer, Electronic Media, Email, Entertainment, Graphic Design, Internet/Web Design, Magazines, Media Relations, Multimedia, Print, Production, Production (Print), T.V., Trade & Consumer Magazines

Grant Loucks *(Pres)*
Wayne Loucks *(VP)*
Tim Dillard *(Mgr-Rental)*

Accounts:
Alan Gordon Enterprises, Inc.; Hollywood, CA Motion Picture & Video Equipment; 1980

ALIMED INC
(Formerly C&B Associates)
297 High St, Dedham, MA 02026-2852
Tel.: (781) 329-2900
Fax: (781) 326-9218
Toll Free: (800) 225-2610
E-Mail: info@alimed.com
Web Site: www.alimed.com

E-Mail for Key Personnel:
President: jcherubini@alimed.com

Employees: 200
Year Founded: 1970

Agency Specializes In: Brand Development & Integration, Business Publications, Direct Response Marketing, Health Care Services, Medical Products, Pharmaceutical, Publicity/Promotions, Sales Promotion

Approx. Annual Billings: $1,100,000

Julian Cherubini *(Founder & Chm)*
Jane Durkin *(Sec)*
Lisa A. Yarussi *(VP-HR)*
Patricia Keefe *(Sr Dir-Art & Mgr-Production)*
Carol Welch *(Dir-Sls Support & Contracting)*
Karen Orlandi *(Mgr-HR)*
Debbie Kelly Peterson *(Mgr-Customer Care & Inside Sls)*

Accounts:
AliMed, Inc.; Dedham, MA Medical
Medtechna; Dedham, MA Medical

AMERICAN RED BALL MARKETING SERVICES
1335 Sadlier Cir E Dr, Indianapolis, IN 46239-1051
Tel.: (317) 353-8331
Fax: (317) 351-0619
Web Site: www.redball.com

Employees: 40
Year Founded: 1919

Ward B. Hiner *(Founder)*

Accounts:
American Red Ball Transit Co., Inc.; Indianapolis, IN

ANDIS ADVERTISING
1800 Renaissance Blvd, Sturtevant, WI 53177
Tel.: (262) 884-2600
Fax: (262) 884-1100
Toll Free: (800) 558-9441
E-Mail: info@andisco.com
Web Site: www.andis.com

Employees: 5
Year Founded: 1922

Agency Specializes In: African-American Market, Agriculture, Health Care Services, Hospitality, Retail

Breakdown of Gross Billings by Media: Bus. Publs.: 20%; Consumer Publs.: 20%; E-Commerce: 20%; Internet Adv.: 20%; Point of Purchase: 20%

Matthew K. Andis *(Pres)*
Laura Andis *(Sr VP-Fin)*
Marcia Andis *(Sr VP-Market Dev)*
Karen Formico *(VP-Mktg)*
Fred Koeller *(VP-Mktg & Intl Sls)*
Mary L. Kosch *(VP-HR)*
Bruce Bock *(Mgr-Mktg Comm)*
Brian Schalk *(Mgr-Pur)*

ART INSTRUCTION SCHOOLS
3400 Technology Dr, Minneapolis, MN 55418-6000
Tel.: (612) 362-5047
Fax: (612) 362-5260
E-Mail: jstuart@artinstructionschools.edu
Web Site: www.artinstructionschools.edu

Employees: 25
Year Founded: 1914

Agency Specializes In: Direct Response Marketing, Education

Breakdown of Gross Billings by Media: Cable T.V.: 5%; Event Mktg.: 2%; Internet Adv.: 15%; Mags.: 2%; Pub. Rels.: 1%; T.V.: 75%

Patrick Stuart *(COO & Pres-Art Instruction Schools)*
Brad Kroll *(Mgr-Mktg)*

BALL HORTICULTURAL COMPANY
622 Town Rd, West Chicago, IL 60185
Tel.: (630) 231-3600
Fax: (630) 231-3605
Toll Free: (800) 879BALL
Web Site: www.ballhort.com

Employees: 25
Year Founded: 1974

Cees Boonman *(Pres-Ball Seed Co)*
Jan Patranella *(Sr Dir)*
Bill Doeckel *(Dir-Retail & Brands)*
Mark Morris *(Dir-IT)*
Steve Wedemeyer *(Dir-Art)*
Judi Cihock *(Mgr-Adv Production)*
Anderson Doreen *(Mgr-Platforms)*
Jim Nau *(Mgr-The Gardens at Ball)*
Greg Trabka *(Mgr-New Product Dev)*
Claire Watson *(Mgr-Product Mktg)*
Dennis Romito *(Infrastructure Architect)*

Accounts:
Ball Horticulture Co.; West Chicago, IL; 1996
Chrysantis Inc.; West Chicago, IL; 2005
Pan American Seed; West Chicago, IL; 1996

BEECHWOOD CREATIVE, INC.
500 N Broadway, Jericho, NY 11753
Tel.: (516) 935-5555
Fax: (516) 935-3005
Web Site: www.beechwoodhomes.com

Employees: 20
Year Founded: 2001

Agency Specializes In: Financial, Real Estate

Breakdown of Gross Billings by Media: Bus. Publs.: 10%; Collateral: 20%; Mags.: 10%; Newsp.: 60%

Michael Dubb *(Owner)*
Steven Dubb *(Principal)*
Kathy Sheck *(Sr VP)*
Christopher Gonzalez *(VP-Dev & Acq)*
Toni Ann Amico *(Coord-Mktg)*
Lindsay Quackenbush *(Coord-Mktg)*

Accounts:
Richard Rosenberg, Esq.; Dix Hills, NY Legal Services; 2001

BERGHOFF INTERNATIONAL INC.
11063 SR 54, Odessa, FL 33556
Tel.: (727) 853-3350
Fax: (727) 375-5424
Toll Free: (800) 426-2168
E-Mail: info@berghoffusa.com
Web Site: www.berghoffworldwide.com

Employees: 18
Year Founded: 1978

Agency Specializes In: Automotive, Restaurant, Sports Market

Raymond Van Den Langenbergh *(CEO)*
Deborah Van Den Langenbergh *(VP)*

Accounts:
Berghoff USA; New Port Richey, FL Cookware;

1999
Berghoff Worldwide; Belgium Cookware, Cutlery; 1988
Berghoff; Tampa, FL; 1998
Cogels NV; Belgium Autos, Cycles; 1988
Elegant European Kitchenware; Miami, FL
Interio; Odessa; FL
MASforce; New Port Richey; FL Engines, Race Boats; 1988
Vanguard Can Am; Tampa, FL Distributors, Headhunters; 1998

BIG APPLE CIRCUS

One Metrotech Ctr 3rd Fl, Brooklyn, NY 11201-3949
Tel.: (646) 616-6811
Web Site: www.bigapplecircus.org

Employees: 19
Year Founded: 2013

Agency Specializes In: Alternative Advertising, Broadcast, Cable T.V., Collateral, Consumer Publications, Digital/Interactive, Direct Response Marketing, Email, Guerilla Marketing, Local Marketing, Magazines, Mobile Marketing, Multimedia, Newspaper, Newspapers & Magazines, Out-of-Home Media, Outdoor, Print, Promotions, Radio, Search Engine Optimization, Social Media, Sponsorship, Sweepstakes, T.V., Web (Banner Ads, Pop-ups, etc.)

Dina Paul-Parks *(VP-Community Programs)*
Will Maitland Weiss *(VP-Dev)*
Guillaume Dufresnoy *(Dir-Artistic)*
Karen Zornow Leiding *(Dir-Individual Rels)*
Martha Neighbors *(Dir-Institutional Rels)*
Deborah Kaufmann *(Assoc Dir-Creative)*
Sandra Dastagirzada *(Mgr-Ticketing Svcs)*
Byron Johnson *(Mgr-Mktg)*
Dennis Santoyo *(Mgr-Grp Sls)*
Lauren Shoolman *(Mgr-Membership & Special Events)*
Sandra Barron *(Assoc Mgr-Mktg)*
Maria Gooding *(Sr Accountant)*

Accounts:
Big Apple Circus; 2013

BLACK & VEATCH CORPORATE MARKETING & BRANDING

11401 Lamar Ave, Overland Park, KS 66211
Tel.: (913) 458-2000
Fax: (913) 458-2934
E-Mail: corporateinfo@bv.com
Web Site: www.bv.com

Employees: 3,000
Year Founded: 1915

Agency Specializes In: Collateral, Consulting, Direct Response Marketing, Graphic Design, Internet/Web Design, Planning & Consultation, Strategic Planning/Research, Technical Advertising

Karen L. Daniel *(CFO)*
Bill Van Dyke *(Pres-BVSPC)*
Fredrik Winterlind *(VP-Global Mktg & Comm)*
Carl Petz *(Assoc VP-Mktg & Comm-Global)*
George Minter *(Dir-Media Rels & Comm)*
Linda Lea *(Sr Mgr-Mktg & Pursuits-Mgmt Consulting)*
Jennifer Graves *(Rep-Procurement)*

Accounts:
Oklahoma Gas & Electric
PowerSouth

BLOOM ADVERTISING

1443 220th St, Independence, IA 50644-9124
Tel.: (319) 827-1139
Fax: (319) 827-1140
Toll Free: (800) 394-1139
Web Site: www.bloommfg.com

Employees: 20
Year Founded: 1963

Approx. Annual Billings: $500,000

Breakdown of Gross Billings by Media: Mags.: $300,000; Newsp.: $200,000

Michael Walsh *(Creative Dir)*

Accounts:
Bloom Inc.; Independence, IA Winches; 1963

BLUE BELL ADVERTISING ASSOCIATES

1101 S Bluebell Rd, Brenham, TX 77834-1807
Tel.: (979) 836-7977
Fax: (979) 830-2198
Web Site: www.bluebell.com

Employees: 13
Year Founded: 1987

Agency Specializes In: Advertising, Publicity/Promotions

Carl Breed *(Dir-Mktg)*
Karen Krnavek *(Coord-Production)*

BMC ADVERTISING

4025 E 23rd St, Columbus, NE 68601-8501
Tel.: (402) 564-3111
Fax: (402) 563-7405
E-Mail: behlen@behlenmfg.com
Web Site: www.bmcads.com

Employees: 3
Year Founded: 1984

Agency Specializes In: Advertising, Industrial

Mike Krzycki *(Mgr-Adv)*
Kirk Nelson *(Mgr-Mktg-Ag Prods)*

BROOKS ADVERTISING

1016 W 9th Ave Ste 210, King of Prussia, PA 19406
Tel.: (610) 265-8510
Fax: (610) 265-8867
Web Site: www.goddardschool.com

Employees: 14
Year Founded: 2002

National Agency Associations: PAC

Agency Specializes In: Advertising, Broadcast, Cable T.V., Children's Market, Education, Electronic Media, Exhibit/Trade Shows, Graphic Design, Media Buying Services, Media Planning, Media Relations, Media Training, Newspaper, Newspapers & Magazines, Print, Production (Ad, Film, Broadcast), Production (Print), Radio, T.V., Web (Banner Ads, Pop-ups, etc.), Women's Market

Approx. Annual Billings: $9,000,000

Breakdown of Gross Billings by Media: Cable T.V.: $1,000,000; D.M.: $1,000,000; Newsp.: $2,000,000; Radio: $1,500,000; Spot T.V.: $2,000,000; Yellow Page Adv.: $1,500,000

Elana Snyder *(Mgr-Brooks Adv & Digital Strategy)*
Ashley Benzedal *(Coord-Mktg)*

Accounts:
The Goddard School; King of Prussia, PA Child Pre-Care; 2002

BROWN-FORMAN MEDIA SERVICES/B-F ADVERTISING

1600 Division St Ste 540, Nashville, TN 37203
Tel.: (615) 279-4100
Fax: (615) 279-7225
E-Mail: julia_hall@b-f.com
Web Site: www.brown-forman.com/

Employees: 7

Agency Specializes In: Direct Response Marketing, Media Buying Services, Newspapers & Magazines, Out-of-Home Media, Outdoor, Trade & Consumer Magazines

Approx. Annual Billings: $50,000,000

Ann Stickler *(Sr VP & Mng Dir-Tequilas)*
Jason Loehr *(VP & Dir-Global Media & Digital Mktg)*
John Tichenor *(VP & Dir-Consumer & Brand Entrepreneurship)*
John Hudson *(VP-Innovation)*
Tammy Board *(Dir-Digital Compliance)*
Jeff Cole *(Dir-Global Digital Mktg-Jack Daniel's)*
Marjorie Dufek *(Dir-Integrated Comm-North America)*
Julia Hall *(Dir-Media)*
Laura Petry *(Dir-Mktg-Jack Daniel's)*
Alicia Johnson *(Program Mgr-Digital Mktg)*
Lynette Green *(Mgr-Digital Mktg-Vodkas)*
Michelle Laflin *(Mgr-Media)*
Alejandro Solorio *(Mgr-Multicultural Mktg)*
Adam Mcgee *(Supvr-OOH Media)*

Accounts:
Brown-Forman Corp.; Louisville, KY

CALDWELL COMMUNICATIONS

165 Ave Rd, Toronto, ON M5R 3S4 Canada
Tel.: (416) 920-7702
Fax: (416) 922-8646
Web Site: www.caldwellpartners.com/

Employees: 60
Year Founded: 1979

National Agency Associations: CBP

Agency Specializes In: Advertising, Recruitment

Approx. Annual Billings: $2,000,000

Breakdown of Gross Billings by Media: Bus. Publs.: 15%; Newsp.: 75%; Worldwide Web Sites: 10%

John N. Wallace *(CEO)*
Les Gombik *(Co-Mng Partner)*
Sean Mclean *(Co-Mng Partner)*
Harry Parslow *(Mng Partner)*
Elan Pratzer *(Mng Partner)*
Drew Railton *(Mng Partner)*
Denise Tobin *(Mng Partner)*
Jeff Freeborough *(Partner)*
Avo Oudabachian *(Partner)*
Heather Ring *(Partner)*
Kelly Blair *(Sr Partner)*

Accounts:
The Caldwell Partners Executive Search Firm

CAMERON ADWORKS

4646 W Sam Houston Pkwy N, Houston, TX 77041
Tel.: (713) 939-2211
Fax: (713) 939-2753
Web Site: www.c-a-m.com

E-Mail for Key Personnel:
Creative Dir.: sloans@camerondiv.com
Public Relations: sloans@camerondiv.com

Employees: 6
Year Founded: 1970

Breakdown of Gross Billings by Media: Bus. Publs.: 90%; Internet Adv.: 10%

Jack B. Moore *(Chm & CEO)*
Charles M. Sledge *(CFO & Sr VP)*
Owen Serjeant *(Pres-Process & Compression Sys)*
William C. Lemmer *(Gen Counsel & Sr VP)*
John D. Carne *(Exec VP)*
Craig Jones *(VP-Sls & Aftermarket Ops)*
Lee Womble *(VP-Sls & Mktg)*
Mario Diaz *(Project Mgr-V&M Mktg & Tech)*
Lucile Turpin *(Mgr-Mktg Comm)*
Amparo Scott *(Sr Graphic Designer-Corp Mktg Comm)*
Sharon Sloan *(Sr Corp Mgr-Mktg Comm)*

Accounts:
Cameron; Houston, TX

CANALWORKS ADVERTISING
6110 Holabird Ave, Baltimore, MD 21224
Mailing Address:
10 Canal St Ste 336, Bristol, PA 19007
Tel.: (215) 458-6216
Fax: (215) 458-6201

Employees: 4
Year Founded: 2009

Agency Specializes In: Advertising, Alternative Advertising, Cable T.V., Co-op Advertising, Consumer Marketing, Direct-to-Consumer, Email, T.V., Web (Banner Ads, Pop-ups, etc.)

Edith Lever *(Dir-Adv)*

Accounts:
Easy Rest Adjustable Sleep Systems; Baltimore, MD Therapeutic Adjustable Beds

CASEY'S ADVERTISING
1 SE Convenience Blvd, Ankeny, IA 50021
Tel.: (515) 965-6130
Fax: (515) 965-6147
E-Mail: cory.hart@caseys.com
Web Site: www.caseys.com

Employees: 11
Year Founded: 2003

Agency Specializes In: Advertising

Approx. Annual Billings: $5,000,000

James Pistillo *(Treas & VP-Acctg)*
Brian J. Johnson *(Corp Sec & VP-Fin)*
Sam J Billmeyer *(Sr VP-Logistics & Acq)*
Darryl F Bacon *(VP-Food Svcs)*
Hal D Brown *(VP-Support Svcs)*
Rich Schappert *(VP-IT)*
Cindi Summers *(VP-HR)*
Kelli Reinhart *(Mgr-Food Svcs Category)*
Cindy Howe Maly *(Sr Category Mgr)*
Dana Sump *(Sr Category Mgr-Packaged Beverage)*

Accounts:
Casey's General Stores; Ankeny, IA; 2003
Casey's Marketing Company; Ankeny, IA; 2003
Casey's Services; Ankeny, IA; 2003

CASIO, INC.
570 Mount Pleasant Ave, Dover, NJ 07801-1620
Mailing Address:
PO Box 7000, Dover, NJ 07802-7000
Tel.: (973) 361-5400
Fax: (973) 537-8926
Toll Free: (800) 836-8580
Web Site: www.casio.com

Employees: 300
Year Founded: 1970

Approx. Annual Billings: $38,200,000

Shigenori Itoh *(CEO)*
Peter Brinkman *(VP & Gen Mgr)*
Mike Martin *(Gen Mgr-Mktg-Electronic Musical Instruments)*
Larry Sampey *(Gen Mgr-System Products Div)*
Tadashi Shibuya *(Gen Mgr-Timepiece Div)*
Robert Prunk *(Dir-Mktg)*
Susan Vander Schans *(Dir-Mktg & Comm)*
Connie Bearfield *(Mgr-Mktg Svcs)*
Richard Formidoni *(Mgr-Product Mktg)*

CB&S ADVERTISING
3800 SE 22nd Ave, Portland, OR 97202
Tel.: (503) 797-3200

Ross Thomas *(VP)*
Carl Kemp *(Dir-Media)*
Erin Balthazar *(Media Planner)*
Debbie Corlew *(Media Planner)*
Tahra-Lyn Konzen Sibon *(Media Planner)*
Kara McGraw *(Sr Media Buyer)*

CHECKMARK COMMUNICATIONS
1111 Chouteau Ave, Saint Louis, MO 63102-1025
Tel.: (314) 982-3400
Fax: (314) 982-1185
Web Site: www.purina.com

Employees: 100
Year Founded: 1981

Agency Specializes In: Advertising, Advertising Specialties, Brand Development & Integration, Direct Response Marketing, Logo & Package Design, Public Relations, Publicity/Promotions, Sponsorship

Breakdown of Gross Billings by Media: Collateral: 20%; D.M.: 20%; Logo & Package Design: 20%; Mags.: 20%; Point of Purchase: 10%; T.V.: 10%

James K. Lucas *(VP & Gen Mgr)*
Chris S. Krebeck *(Exec Dir-Creative)*
Dalynn S. Spillars *(Grp Dir-Creative)*
Brian Woolbright *(Grp Dir-Creative)*
Sandra A. Zub *(Grp Dir-Creative)*
Nancy Jane Rifkin *(Sr Dir-Art)*
Kim Wagoner *(Sr Dir-Art)*
Mike Bannes *(Dir-Art)*
Emily Puricelli *(Assoc Dir-Creative)*
Stephanie Finch *(Acct Coord)*

Accounts:
Nestle Purina Pet Care Company; Saint Louis, MO Alpo, Beneful, Fancy Feast, Mighty Dog, Pro Plan

CIE DIRECT
1776 E 17th St, Cleveland, OH 44114
Tel.: (216) 781-9400
Fax: (216) 781-0331
Toll Free: (800) CIEOHIO
Web Site: www.cie-wc.edu

Employees: 20
Year Founded: 1989

Agency Specializes In: Education, Engineering

J.R. Drinko *(Pres)*
Paul Valvuda *(Treas)*
Ted Sheroke *(Mgr-Adv)*
Karen Scumacher *(Rep-Student Svc)*

Accounts:
Cleveland Institute of Electronics; Cleveland, OH; Correspondence School

CJP ADVERTISING
4235 Route 9 North, Freehold, NJ 07728
Tel.: (732) 462-5006, ext. 122
E-Mail: cjpadvertising@centraljerseypools.com
Web Site: centraljerseypools.com/cjpadvertising/

Employees: 1

Approx. Annual Billings: $100,000

Steven Metz *(Owner & Pres)*

Accounts:
Central Jersey Pools; Freehold, NJ Furniture, Kitchens, Pools, Spas

COLORADO RARE EARTH
(Name Changed to U.S. Rare Earths, Inc.)

COLUMBIA UNIVERSITY PRESS ADVERTISING GROUP
61 W 62nd St, New York, NY 10023-7015
Tel.: (212) 459-0600
Fax: (212) 459-3678
Toll Free: (800) 944UNIV
E-Mail: info@columbia.edu
Web Site: www.columbia.edu

Employees: 5
Year Founded: 1893

Agency Specializes In: Print, Publicity/Promotions

Revenue: $110,000,000

Doug Levy *(Chief Comm Officer)*
Lee C. Bollinger *(Pres-Columbia University)*
Donna MacPhee *(VP-Alumni Rels)*
Deborah Sack *(VP-Strategic Comm)*
Jaclyn Chu *(Dir-Reg Clubs & Alumni Rels)*
Barri Roberson *(Dir-Mktg)*
David Rogers *(Dir-Faculty-Digital Mktg Strategy Exec Program)*
Jessie Mygatt *(Asst Dir-Alumni Rels)*
Olivier Toubia *(Professor-Mktg-Columbia Business School)*

Accounts:
Columbia University Press; New York, NY
East European Monographs
Edinburgh University Press; Edinburgh, Scotland
Kegan Paul International; United Kingdom
University of Tokyo Press; Tokyo, Japan
Wallflower Press; London, England

COLUMBIAD
2929 Broadway 3rd Fl, New York, NY 10025-7819
Tel.: (212) 854-9511
Fax: (212) 854-9534
Web Site: www.columbia.edu

Employees: 2
Year Founded: 1988

Agency Specializes In: Education

Margery Tippie *(Editor-Production)*
Sandy Kaufman *(Dir-Creative Svcs & Mktg Comm)*
Don Kim *(Mgr-Info Sys)*
Marisol Torres *(Mgr-Adv)*
Jessica Sylla *(Coord-Production)*

Accounts:
Columbia University; New York, NY; 1992

CTB ADVERTISING
611 N Higbee St, Milford, IN 46542
Mailing Address:
PO Box 2000, Milford, IN 46542-2000
Tel.: (574) 658-4191
Fax: (574) 658-3471
E-Mail: ctb@ctbinc.com
Web Site: www.ctbinc.com

Employees: 5
Year Founded: 1952

Agency Specializes In: Agriculture

Victor A. Mancinelli *(Chm & CEO)*
Jeffrey Crawford *(Treas & VP)*
Michael Kissane *(Sec)*
Will Mabee *(VP & Corp Controller)*
Ed Weidenhaft *(Controller-Credit & Risk)*
Susan Hight *(Mgr-Corp Comm)*
Jennifer Leatherman *(Mgr-Corp Bus Systems)*
Bill Roper *(Mgr-Special Projects)*

Accounts:
Agile Manufacturing, Inc.; Anderson, MO
Agro Logic
Brock Grain Systems; Milford, IN
Chore-Time Brock International; Milford, IN
Chore-Time Egg Production Systems; Milford, IN
Chore-Time Hog Production Systems; Milford, IN
Chore-Time Poultry Production Systems; Milford, IN
CTB, Inc.; Milford, IN
Pigtek
Porcon
Roxell
Shenandoah
Uniqfill

DB STUDIOS
(Formerly Display Boys)
17032 Murphy Ave, Irvine, CA 92614
Tel.: (949) 833-0100
Fax: (949) 838-0110
E-Mail: info@dbstudios.com
Web Site: www.dbstudios.com

Employees: 40
Year Founded: 1989

Agency Specializes In: Collateral, Corporate Identity, Exhibit/Trade Shows, Logo & Package Design, Merchandising, Point of Purchase, Point of Sale, Production

Approx. Annual Billings: $5,000,000

John Riley *(Co-Founder & VP)*
Mark Bense *(CFO)*
Mike Mikyska *(VP-Bus Dev)*
Nate Ellis *(Dir-Design)*
Eric Weintraub *(Dir-Ops)*
Franca Del Colle Davis *(Acct Mgr)*
Celeste Maska *(Acct Mgr)*
Scott Parrott *(Acct Mgr)*
Ruben Sanchez *(Mgr-Logistics)*

Accounts:
Adidas
Bacardi
Cobra
Hershey's
Mondelez International, Inc. Kraft Cheese
Pepperidge Farm
Rbk
Vans
Virgin
Whole Foods Market

DIALAMERICA MARKETING, INC.
960 MacArthur Blvd, Mahwah, NJ 07495-0094
Tel.: (201) 327-0200
Fax: (201) 327-4875
Toll Free: (800) 531-3131
E-Mail: rfischer@dialamerica.com
Web Site: www.dialamerica.com

Employees: 400
Year Founded: 1976

Agency Specializes In: Cable T.V., Consumer Marketing, Direct Response Marketing, Information Technology, Magazines, Newspaper, Telemarketing, Trade & Consumer Magazines

Approx. Annual Billings: $3,000,000

Breakdown of Gross Billings by Media: Cable T.V.: 1%; Exhibits/Trade Shows: 2%; Internet Adv.: 10%; Newsp.: 80%; Spot Radio: 4%; Trade & Consumer Mags.: 2%; Yellow Page Adv.: 1%

Arthur W. Conway *(Chm & CEO)*
Christopher W. Conway *(CFO & Sr VP)*
Gerhard Lindenmayer *(Officer-Info Security)*
Mary Conway *(Sr VP)*
Larry Kyse *(Sr VP)*
John Redinger *(Sr VP-Sls & Mktg)*
Tom Gleason *(VP-Bus Dev)*
Jay Hammans *(VP)*
Richelle Litteer *(VP-Bus Dev)*
Frank Conway *(Mgr-Ops)*

DIANE VON FURSTENBERG STUDIO LP
389 W 12th St, New York, NY 10014
Tel.: (212) 741-6607
Fax: (212) 929-3971
E-Mail: studio@dianevonfurstenberg.com
Web Site: www.dvf.com

Employees: 100
Year Founded: 1972

Hamilton South *(Founder & Partner)*
Danielle Abjanich *(Brand Mktg Mgr)*
Irene Barrett *(Dir-Online Mdsg)*
Lisa Parkere *(Asst Mgr-ECommerce-Customer Svc)*
Kristine Laforgia *(Acct Exec-Accessories)*

Accounts:
Diane Von Furstenberg Studio; New York, NY

DISNEY'S YELLOW SHOES CREATIVE GROUP/WALT DISNEY PARKS & RESORTS
PO Box 10000, Lake Buena Vista, FL 32830-1000
Tel.: (407) 566-6700
Fax: (407) 566-5400
Web Site: disneyparks.disney.go.com

Employees: 90
Year Founded: 1975

Tom Aronson *(VP-Digital Mktg-Walt Disney Parks & Resorts)*
Lisa Baldzicki *(VP-Global Retail, Product Design & Dev)*
Tim Klauda *(VP-Digital Creative-Global)*
Joe Rand *(VP-Disney's Yellow Shoes Creative Grp)*
Joe Schneider *(VP-Creative-Global)*
Glen Taylor *(VP)*
Heather Watson *(Acct Dir-Yellow Shoes Creative Grp)*
Will Gay *(Dir-Creative)*
Greg Montz *(Dir-Digital Content)*
Leanne O'Regan *(Dir-Social Media)*
Matt Stewart *(Dir-Art)*
Scott W. White *(Dir-Adv)*
Karen Molessa *(Acct Mgr)*
Stephen Barnes *(Mgr-Digital Media)*
Jennifer Biefel *(Mgr-CRM Mktg)*
Jennifer Brunner *(Mgr-Mktg Strategy)*
Dave Chabot *(Mgr-Mktg Analytics & Optimization)*
Cinthia Douglas *(Mgr-Mktg Strategy-Latin America)*
Valarie Rhodes *(Mgr-Alliance Mgmt-Disney Corp Alliances)*
John Rogers *(Mgr-Digital Mktg)*
Kathleen Winn *(Mgr-Mktg Strategy)*
Michael Sines *(Coord-Disney Grp Ticket Solutions)*

Accounts:
Disney Cruise Line Campaign: "Disney Fantasy Video Journal"
Walt Disney Parks & Resorts; Lake Buena Vista, FL New Fantasyland Desktop Site

DOREL JUVENILE GROUP/COSCO
2525 State St, Columbus, IN 47201-7443
Tel.: (812) 372-0141
Fax: (812) 372-2154
Web Site: www.coscoproducts.com

Employees: 12
Year Founded: 1975

Agency Specializes In: Advertising, Brand Development & Integration, Business-To-Business, Children's Market, Collateral, Commercial Photography, Consumer Marketing, Corporate Communications, Direct Response Marketing, Exhibit/Trade Shows, Graphic Design, Health Care Services, In-Store Advertising, Logo & Package Design, Medical Products, Merchandising, Multimedia, Over-50 Market, Point of Purchase, Point of Sale, Production, Publicity/Promotions, Restaurant, Sales Promotion, Seniors' Market, Trade & Consumer Magazines

Breakdown of Gross Billings by Media: Trade & Consumer Mags.: 100%

Mark Evanko *(Exec VP-Quality Assurance & Product Safety)*
Jason Owens *(VP-Mktg & Product Dev-Cosco Home & Office Products)*

Accounts:
Ameriwood Industries, Inc. Ready-to-Assemble Furniture
Cosco Home & Office Products; Columbus, IN Home Furnishings & Housewares, Juvenile Products & Nursery Furniture
Dorel Industries, Inc. (Canada) Juvenile Group
Dorel UK; United Kingdom Juvenile & Home Furnishings

EDELBROCK ADVERTISING
2700 California St, Torrance, CA 90503
Tel.: (310) 781-2222
Fax: (310) 320-1187
Toll Free: (800) 739-3737
Web Site: www.edelbrock.com

Employees: 6
Year Founded: 1938

Agency Specializes In: Automotive

Vic Edelbrock, Jr. *(Chm)*

Accounts:
Edelbrock Corp.; Torrance, CA Aftermarket Automotive & Motorcycle Mfr.

FELL ADVERTISING
1403 Shoreline Way, Hollywood, FL 33019
Tel.: (954) 925-5242
Fax: (954) 455-4243
E-Mail: fellpub@fellpub.com
Web Site: www.fellpub.com

E-Mail for Key Personnel:

President: dlessne@fellpub.com

Employees: 28
Year Founded: 1943

Agency Specializes In: Magazines

Revenue: $2,000,000

Donald L. Lessne *(Pres & Publr)*

Accounts:
APG Distributing
Frederick Fell Publishers, Inc.; Hollywood, FL

FULTON OUTFITTERS, INC
1292 Fulton St, Brooklyn, NY 11216
Tel.: (718) 622-6278
Fax: (718) 783-8813
Web Site: www.thefultonstores.com

Year Founded: 2008

Agency Specializes In: Co-op Advertising, Consumer Goods, Consumer Marketing, Direct-to-Consumer

Approx. Annual Billings: $125,000

Breakdown of Gross Billings by Media: Cable T.V.: $100,000; D.M.: $25,000

Darren Gordon *(Exec VP)*

Accounts:
The Fulton Stores; Brooklyn, NY Furniture

G&W ELECTRIC CO. ADVERTISING
3500 W 127th St, Blue Island, IL 60406
Tel.: (708) 388-5010
Fax: (708) 388-0755
E-Mail: webmail@gwelec.com
Web Site: www.gwelec.com

Employees: 250
Year Founded: 1905

John H Mueller *(Pres)*
Melissa Amptmann *(VP-HR-Global)*
Scott Ware *(VP-Sls-Intl)*
Ivan Jovanovic *(Gen Mgr)*
Joseph Pellini *(Project Mgr-New Product Dev)*
Katie Cummings *(Product Mgr-Controls & DA)*
Kris Cuthbertson *(Mgr-Trng)*
Nenad Uzelac *(Mgr-Affairs & Tech)*
David R. Erickson *(Specialist-HR)*

Accounts:
G&W Electric Co.; Blue Island, IL

GLOBAL TURNKEY SYSTEMS
2001 Rte 46 Ste 203, Parsippany, NJ 07054
Tel.: (973) 331-1010
Fax: (973) 331-0042
Toll Free: (800) 221-1746
E-Mail: sales@gtsystems.com
Web Site: www.gtsystems.com

Employees: 25
Year Founded: 1969

Agency Specializes In: Business Publications

Approx. Annual Billings: $12,000,000

Accounts:
Aircraft Technical Publishers
Arizona Highways Magazine
Church Publishing
Duke University Press
GreenWood Publishing Group
Grolier
PPC
Springer
Tyndale House Publishers
Walch publishing

GLOUCESTER ENGINEERING-MARKETING DEPARTMENT
11 Dory Rd, Gloucester, MA 01931-0900
Tel.: (978) 281-1800
Fax: (978) 282-9111
Web Site: www.gloucesterengineering.com

Employees: 1
Year Founded: 1969

Agency Specializes In: Advertising Specialties

Approx. Annual Billings: $400,000

Breakdown of Gross Billings by Media: Cable T.V.: $400,000

Carl Johnson *(Pres)*
Per Nylen *(Exec VP-Sigma Plastics Grp)*
Mark Lichtblau *(Corp VP-Haremar Plastic Mfg)*
Paul Brancaleone *(Mgr-Engrg-Software & Controls)*
Jim Ey *(Supvr-Production-Genpak)*

Accounts:
Gloucester Engineering Co.; Gloucester, MA Plastics Extrusion & Converting & Plastics Processing Machinery

GUMP'S MARKETING
135 Post St, San Francisco, CA 94108
Tel.: (415) 984-9297
Fax: (415) 984-9361
Toll Free: (800) 766-7628
E-Mail: info@gumps.com
Web Site: www.gumps.com

Employees: 2
Year Founded: 1861

Agency Specializes In: Advertising

Diana Holland-Cramer *(VP-Store Ops & HR)*
Susan Quintana *(VP-Mktg & ECommerce)*
Tara Voorhis *(VP-Direct Mdsg & Product Dev)*
Nolan Lew *(Dir-Web Mktg)*
Carmen Roberson *(Dir-Retail Mktg)*
Marilou Viray-Mosley *(Dir-IT)*
John Weeth *(Dir-DMM Tabletop & Interiors)*
Hsaio-Hui Yang *(Dir-Mdsg)*
Gina Kwun *(Mgr-Jewelry Ops)*

Accounts:
Gump's; San Francisco, CA Specialty Store

H.A. BRUNO LLC
210 E E Rte 4 Ste 304, Paramus, NJ 07652
Tel.: (201) 543-5060
Fax: (201) 226-1131
E-Mail: mfv@mfvexpo.com
Web Site: www.habruno.com

Employees: 40
Year Founded: 1987

Agency Specializes In: Event Planning & Marketing, Exhibit/Trade Shows, Internet/Web Design

Approx. Annual Billings: $8,000,000

Greg Marco *(VP-FranchiseExpo.com)*
Mark Bosak *(Dir-IT)*
Joel Goldstein *(Dir-Mktg)*
Sonia Perrone *(Dir-Grp Mktg)*
Richard Del Giorno *(Bus Dev Mgr & Mgr-Show-IFE)*
Sheila Fischer *(Asst Grp Dir-Show & Mgr-Show-FES)*
Corali Romero *(Coord-IBP-IFE)*
Erin Layton *(Asst Show Dir-CPP Expo)*

Accounts:
Converting & Package Printing Expo
Florida Franchise Expo
Franchise Expo South
The Franchise Show London
FranchiseExpo.com
FranquiciasHoy.com
International Franchise Expo; 1992
West Coast Franchise Expo

HANDY CUTTER LINE
2968 Randolph Ave, Costa Mesa, CA 92626-4312
Tel.: (714) 662-1033
Fax: (714) 662-7595
Toll Free: (800) 969-3322
E-Mail: promo@pacifichandycutter.com
Web Site: www.handycutterline.com

Employees: 47
Year Founded: 1950

Agency Specializes In: Advertising Specialties

Breakdown of Gross Billings by Media: Mags.: 100%

Joe Garavaglia *(CFO)*
Mark Marinovich *(CEO-Pacific Handy Cutter)*
Dave Puglisi *(Exec VP-Sls & Mktg)*
Julie Punchard *(Mgr-HR-Pacific Handy Cutter, Inc)*

Accounts:
Pacific Handy Cutter, Inc.; Costa Mesa, CA Blades, ProPrep Scrapers, Razor Type Cutting Tools

HARVARD IN-HOUSE AGENCY
1563 Massachusetts Ave, Cambridge, MA 02138-3701
Tel.: (617) 495-2924
Fax: (617) 496-2680
E-Mail: linda_cross@harvard.edu
Web Site: www.harvard.edu

Employees: 12
Year Founded: 1910

Agency Specializes In: Education

Breakdown of Gross Billings by Media: Adv. Specialities: 2%; Bus. Publs.: 5%; Collateral: 35%; D.M.: 5%; Internet Adv.: 5%; Mags.: 2%; Newsp.: 16%; Point of Purchase: 5%; Pub. Rels.: 5%; Radio: 10%; Transit: 5%; Worldwide Web Sites: 5%

David de Haas *(Art Dir)*
Linda Armstrong Cross *(Dir-Ops-Harvard Pro Dev Programs)*

Accounts:
Carlsberg
Harvard Extension School; Cambridge, MA Certificates, Courses, Degrees
Harvard Institute for English Language Programs; Cambridge, MA Courses
Harvard Institute for Learning in Retirement; Cambridge, MA Courses
Harvard Summer School; Cambridge, MA Courses
Vancouver Aquarium Anglerfish
youtube.com

HECKART STUDIOS
9320 Wilshire Blvd, Beverly Hills, CA 90212
Tel.: (310) 247-0079
Fax: (310) 247-4563

House Agencies

E-Mail: info@heckartstudios.com
Web Site: www.heckartstudios.com

Aaron Heck *(Pres)*

Accounts:
Brown Forman Beverages Worldwide Korbel
Heck Estates
Kenwood Vineyards Artist Series
Korbel California Champagne
Lake Sonoma Winery
Resnick Collection
Russian River Brewery
Valley of the Moon
wineexperts.org

INFOGROUP INC.
5711 S 86th Cir, Omaha, NE 68127-4146
Tel.: (402) 593-4500
Fax: (402) 596-0475
Toll Free: (800) 336-8349
E-Mail: marketing@infousa.com
Web Site: www.infogroup.com

Employees: 4,771
Year Founded: 1973

Agency Specializes In: Advertising, Business Publications, Business-To-Business, Consulting, Direct Response Marketing, E-Commerce, Exhibit/Trade Shows, Faith Based, Print, Trade & Consumer Magazines, Yellow Pages Advertising

Breakdown of Gross Billings by Media: Bus. Publs.: 9%; Consumer Publs.: 1%; D.M.: 38%; Internet Adv.: 5%; Mags.: 10%; Newsp.: 1%; Outdoor: 1%; Production: 13%; Radio & T.V.: 4%; Trade Shows: 9%; Yellow Page Adv.: 9%

Jacob Ciesielski *(Pres & Gen Mgr)*
Karen Mayhew *(Exec VP-Consumer Mgmt)*
Jeff Babcook *(VP-Program Mgmt)*
Lynn Bolen *(VP-Mktg Strategy & Insights)*
Steve Borelli *(VP-Enterprise Sls)*
Tom Defloria *(VP-Digital Solutions & Strategic Partnerships)*
Mike Hrin *(VP-Digital Acq Solutions)*
Mary McCabe *(VP-Product & Content Mgmt)*
Sally Westaway *(VP-Ops)*
Shannon Slobotski *(Gen Mgr)*
Matthew Neibert *(Sr Dir-Application Dev)*
Akshay Gandotra *(Sr Mgr-Mktg-B2B List Svcs)*

Accounts:
American Church Lists; Dallas, TX; 2000
American Medical Information
City Directories
Express Copy
InfoGroup
Latino
NWC Opinion Research
OneSource
Opinion Research Corporation
ORC International
ReferenceGROUP
Triplex
Walter Karl; Stamford, CT List Management Company; 1998
YesMail

Branch

Infogroup
(Formerly Edith Roman Associates, Inc.)
2 Blue Hill Plz 3rd Fl, Pearl River, NY 10965
Toll Free: (800) 223-2194
Web Site: www.infogroup.com

Employees: 100
Year Founded: 1956

Agency Specializes In: Advertising, Advertising Specialties, Affiliate Marketing, Affluent Market, African-American Market, Agriculture, Alternative Advertising, Arts, Asian Market, Automotive, Aviation & Aerospace, Bilingual Market, Brand Development & Integration, Broadcast, Business Publications, Business-To-Business, Cable T.V., Catalogs, Children's Market, Co-op Advertising, Collateral, Commercial Photography, Communications, Consulting, Consumer Marketing, Consumer Publications, Corporate Identity, Cosmetics, Custom Publishing, Digital/Interactive, Direct Response Marketing, Direct-to-Consumer, E-Commerce, Education, Electronic Media, Engineering, Entertainment, Environmental, Event Planning & Marketing, Exhibit/Trade Shows, Fashion/Apparel, Financial, Food Service, Government/Political, Graphic Design, Guerilla Marketing, Health Care Services, High Technology, Hispanic Market, Industrial, Infomercials, Information Technology, Internet/Web Design, Investor Relations, Legal Services, Leisure, Logo & Package Design, Luxury Products, Magazines, Marine, Media Buying Services, Medical Products, Men's Market, Merchandising, Mobile Marketing, Multicultural, Multimedia, New Product Development, New Technologies, Newspaper, Newspapers & Magazines, Out-of-Home Media, Outdoor, Over-50 Market, Pharmaceutical, Planning & Consultation, Point of Purchase, Point of Sale, Print, Product Placement, Production, Public Relations, Publicity/Promotions, Radio, Real Estate, Recruitment, Regional, Restaurant, Retail, Sales Promotion, Seniors' Market, Social Marketing/Nonprofit, Sports Market, Strategic Planning/Research, Sweepstakes, Syndication, T.V., Technical Advertising, Teen Market, Telemarketing, Trade & Consumer Magazines, Transportation, Travel & Tourism, Viral/Buzz/Word of Mouth, Web (Banner Ads, Pop-ups, etc.), Women's Market, Yellow Pages Advertising

Mike Iaccarino *(Chm & CEO)*
Kristen Cuddy *(VP-Sls & Mktg)*
Jeff Mungo *(VP-Sls)*
Bart Piccirillo *(Sr Acct Mgr)*

Accounts:
BNP Media; Troy, MI; 2005
CareerTrack; Kansas City, MO Training; 1997
CMP Media; Manhasset, NY Publishing; 1973
McGraw Hill; New York, NY Publishing; 2003
Nielsen Business Media; New York, NY Publishing; 1999
Source Media; New York, NY; 2005
Sys-Con Media; Woodcliff Lake, NJ; 1999

INNOVATIVE COMMUNICATIONS
217 9th St, Pittsburgh, PA 15222-3506
Tel.: (412) 288-1300
Fax: (412) 338-0480
E-Mail: inventinfo@inventhelp.com
Web Site: www.inventhelp.com

Employees: 10
Year Founded: 1984

Agency Specializes In: Advertising

Approx. Annual Billings: $4,000,000

Breakdown of Gross Billings by Media: Cable T.V.: $600,000; Foreign: $50,000; Internet Adv.: $1,535,000; Mags.: $6,000; Radio: $900,000; Spot T.V.: $303,000; Syndication: $600,000; Yellow Page Adv.: $6,000

Liv Dobo *(Mgr-Interactive Adv)*

Accounts:
Copies For Less; Pittsburgh, PA Copy & Printing Services; 1984
INPEX Inventors University; Pittsburgh, PA Seminar Program; 1984
INPEX; Pittsburgh, PA Annual Invention Trade Show; 1984
Intromark; Pittsburgh, PA Invention Licensing; 1984
InventHelp Invention & Patent Referral Services; 1984

JELLYFISH
250 S President St Ste 10, Baltimore, MD 21202
Tel.: (443) 842-5555
Web Site: www.jellyfish.net

Employees: 200

Agency Specializes In: Digital/Interactive, Direct Response Marketing, Mobile Marketing, Search Engine Optimization, Sponsorship, Web (Banner Ads, Pop-ups, etc.)

Approx. Annual Billings: $100,000,000

Jim Hamilton *(Mng Dir & Head-US)*
Carola York *(Mng Dir-Jellyfish Publishing)*
Sean Mulcahy *(Dir-Bus Dev)*
Greg Roberts *(Dir-Bus Dev)*
Jennifer Thorpe *(Dir-US Ops)*
Oliver Bell *(Sr Mgr-Bus Dev)*
Lisa Deeprose *(Mgr-Mktg)*
Louisa Johns *(Mgr-Mktg)*
Stephanie Vander Veen *(Mgr-Mktg)*

Accounts:
ADP
Caesars
Carfax
Fidelity
Fitbit
Pfizer
Walden University
Zipcar

JET ADVERTISING
(Name Changed to YMT Vacations)

JOMIRA ADVERTISING
470 Third St Ste 211, San Francisco, CA 94107
Tel.: (415) 356-7801
Fax: (415) 356-7804
Toll Free: (800) 600-2777
E-Mail: kadeemah@aol.com
Web Site: www.jomira.com

Employees: 5
Year Founded: 1985

Agency Specializes In: Direct Response Marketing

Approx. Annual Billings: $500,000

Gerardo Joffe *(Pres)*
Chris Sanders *(Mgr-Customer Svcs)*

JOSEPH PEDOTT ADVERTISING & MARKETING, INC.
425 California St, San Francisco, CA 94104
Tel.: (415) 397-6992
Fax: (415) 397-0103
Toll Free: (800) 345-6992
E-Mail: newidea@jeiusa.com
Web Site: www.jeiusa.com

Employees: 25
Year Founded: 1958

Agency Specializes In: Consumer Marketing, T.V.

Approx. Annual Billings: $8,000,000

Breakdown of Gross Billings by Media: T.V.: $8,000,000

Joseph Pedott *(Pres)*
Michael P. Hirsch *(VP)*
Alfred Lam *(Office Mgr & Media Buyer)*
Andrew Tam *(Sr Media Buyer)*

Accounts:
CSL LLC
Ignite-O
Joseph Enterprises; San Francisco, CA Scribe-ett Engraving Pen, Chia Pet Mexican Clay Planter & The Clapper Sound-Activated Switch; 1982

KHOURY COMMUNICATIONS
2328 18th Ave, Forest Grove, OR 97116-2414
Tel.: (503) 357-7309

Employees: 1
Year Founded: 1992

Agency Specializes In: Industrial

Breakdown of Gross Billings by Media: D.M.: 25%; Internet Adv.: 25%; Trade & Consumer Mags.: 25%; Trade Shows: 25%

Martha Khoury *(Principal)*

Accounts:
Columbia Weather Systems Inc.; Hillsboro, OR Weather Instruments; 1997

KNIGHT ADV. CO.
2900 MacArthur Blvd, Northbrook, IL 60062-2005
Tel.: (847) 509-2900
Fax: (847) 559-1995
E-Mail: sales@serfilco.com
Web Site: www.serfilco.com

Employees: 9
Year Founded: 1961

Agency Specializes In: Industrial

Jack Berg *(Founder)*

Accounts:
Filterspun; Amarillo, TX Filters
Pacer Pumps; Lancaster, PA
Serfilco, Ltd., a/k/a Service Filtration Corp. Pumps & Filters
Standard Pump; Snellville, GA

KOCH CREATIVE GROUP
4111 E. 37th St North, Wichita, KS 67220
Tel.: (316) 828-5294
E-Mail: kaylan@kochcreativegroup.com
Web Site: www.kochcreativegroup.com

Agency Specializes In: Advertising, Brand Development & Integration, Digital/Interactive, Social Media

Kaylan Gisi *(Sr Acct Dir-Koch Creative Grp)*
Charlie Wells *(Sr Acct Dir)*
Amy Booth *(Dir-Art)*
Deanna Crockett *(Dir-Art)*
Terri McCool *(Dir-Mktg)*
Joe Robertson *(Dir-Creative)*
Joli Sutter *(Mgr-Production)*
Kate Ternes *(Mgr-Office)*
Daniel Brake *(Specialist-Interactive)*
Chad Armstrong *(Copywriter)*
Ryan Schafer *(Copywriter)*
Amber Vogts *(Sr Graphic Designer)*

Accounts:
Koch Industries

KONICA MINOLTA BUSINESS SOLUTIONS
100 Williams Dr, Ramsey, NJ 07446
Tel.: (201) 825-4000
Fax: (201) 825-7567
E-Mail: pr@kmbs.konicaminolta.us
Web Site: www.kmbs.konicaminolta.us

Year Founded: 1977

Richard Taylor *(Pres & COO)*
Chris C. Dewart *(Pres/CEO-Canada)*
Alan Nielsen *(Exec VP-Dealer Sls)*
Jun Haraguchi *(Gen Mgr-Sls & Exec Dir-Sls & Mktg)*
Seiji Hatano *(Sr Exec officer)*
Nobuyasu Ieuji *(Sr Exec officer)*
Kunihiro Koshizuka *(Sr Exec officer)*
Ken Osuga *(Sr Exec officer)*
Yoshitsugu Shiraki *(Sr Exec officer)*
Tsukasa Wakashima *(Sr Exec officer)*

Accounts:
Konica Minolta Business Solutions

KRACO ENTERPRISES
505 E Euclid Ave, Compton, CA 90224
Tel.: (310) 639-0666
Fax: (310) 604-9838
Toll Free: (800) 678-1910
Web Site: www.kraco.com

Employees: 7
Year Founded: 1954

Robert Brocoff *(Pres)*
Dennis Jolicoeur *(CFO)*
John Fiumefreddo *(Sr VP-Ops)*
Kent C. Friend *(Sr VP-Sls & Mktg)*
Steve Lazzara *(Sr VP-Sls & Mktg)*
Michael Villanueva *(Controller)*
Jeff Deleon *(Dir-Mktg)*
Amit Patel *(Dir-Supply Chain & Logistics)*
Katie Cartier *(Sr Product Mgr)*
Dannette Holt *(Product Mgr)*

Accounts:
Kraco Enterprises, Inc.; Compton, CA Supplier of Auto & Marine Sound Products, CB's, Auto Floor Mats & Mobile Security Car Alarms

LANA DUKE CONSULTING
3817 Edenborn Ave, Metairie, LA 70002-1521
Tel.: (504) 888-3985
Fax: (504) 888-3984
E-Mail: lana@lanaduke.com

Employees: 6
Year Founded: 1975

Agency Specializes In: Advertising Specialties, Consulting, Public Relations

Lana Duke *(Owner)*

Accounts:
The Palace Truck Stop; New Orleans, LA Hospitality; 1995
Ruth's Chris Steakhouse; Mississauga, ON; San Antonio, TX & Toronto, ON

LEANIN' TREE, INC.
6055 Longbow Dr, Boulder, CO 80301
Tel.: (303) 530-1442
Fax: (303) 530-7283
Toll Free: (800) 777-8716
Web Site: www.leanintree.com

Employees: 200
Year Founded: 1949

Agency Specializes In: Consumer Marketing

Tom Trumble *(Pres & CEO)*
Duff Bauer *(Controller)*
Dana Pauley *(Dir-Consumer Svcs)*
Susann Powers *(Dir-IT)*
Patrick Wallace *(Dir-Mktg)*
Amy Medhurst *(Sr Mgr-Bus Dev-Key Accounts)*
Kim Diesing *(Mgr-Product Dev)*
Kate Frohlich *(Mgr-Mktg)*
Anne Clark *(Gen Accountant)*

LEGGETT & PLATT INC.
1 Leggett Rd, Carthage, MO 64836
Tel.: (417) 358-8131
Fax: (417) 358-8449
Web Site: www.leggett.com

Employees: 20
Year Founded: 1883

Agency Specializes In: Retail

Approx. Annual Billings: $250,000

Paul Block *(VP-Intl Sls-Asia-Pacific)*
Scott Clark *(Dir-Creative)*
Della Croft *(Dir-Mktg)*
John L. Walsh *(Dir-Creative Svcs)*
Sharon Baird *(Mgr-Exhibit Solutions)*
Jon Gullette *(Mgr-HR & Safety)*
Jessica Glessner *(Coord-Payroll)*

Accounts:
Leggett & Platt; Carthage, MO

THE LESLIE CORPORATION
15110 Mintz Ln, Houston, TX 77014
Tel.: (281) 591-0915
Fax: (281) 591-0921
E-Mail: jleslie@lesliecorp.com
Web Site: www.lesliecorp.com

Employees: 13
Year Founded: 1993

Agency Specializes In: Recruitment

Approx. Annual Billings: $2,000,000

Breakdown of Gross Billings by Media: Bus. Publs.: 20%; Newsp.: 80%

Janice Leslie *(Controller)*

Accounts:
ALCON Laboratories
Amoco Production
AT&T Mobility LLC
BASF Chemicals
DOW Chemical
Kinder Morgan
Service Corporation of America

LIVE NATION
6677 Delmer Ste 320, Saint Louis, MO 63130
Tel.: (314) 657-4900
Fax: (314) 657-4949
Web Site: www.livenation.com

Employees: 5
Year Founded: 1979

Agency Specializes In: Entertainment, Merchandising, Retail, Sales Promotion

Michael Rapino *(Pres & CEO)*
Ryan Okum *(Exec VP-Digital Mktg-US Concerts)*
Jackie Wilgar *(Exec VP-Mktg-North America)*
Jeff Condon *(Sr VP-Mktg Solutions)*
David Fortin *(Sr VP-Mktg)*
Tim Moran *(Sr VP-IT & Fin Sys-Global)*

Dave Clark *(VP-Mktg-North Central Reg)*
Danielle Engel *(VP-Mktg-Live Nation Phoenix, Vegas & Albuquerque)*
Holli Mattison *(VP-Mktg)*
David Niedbalski *(VP-Mktg)*
Jon Reens *(VP-Mktg-Midwest Music)*
Jim Sutcliffe *(VP-Mktg)*
Eric Garland *(Gen Mgr-Live Nation Labs)*
Cori Gadbury *(Sr Dir-Mktg)*
Paul Kuykendal *(Sr Dir-Product Mgmt)*
Laura Rego *(Sr Dir-Mktg-North America Touring)*
Brian Birr *(Mktg Dir-Houston-New Orleans)*
Jill Jacenko *(Dir-Mktg)*
Erica Kilduff *(Dir-Mktg)*
Emily Kopp *(Dir-Mktg)*
Michael Lessner *(Dir-Promo)*
Katie Pederson *(Dir-Sls-Special Events)*
Jeremiah Xenakis *(Dir-Mktg)*
Janette Baxa *(Mgr-Mktg)*
John Canavera *(Mgr-Mktg)*
Andrew Delaney *(Mgr-Digital Mktg)*
Donna Eichmeyer *(Mgr-Mktg-Upstate NY)*
David Gerardi *(Mgr-Market)*
Cori Salinas *(Mgr-Content)*
Todd Flenner *(Specialist-Mktg)*
Sonya Artz *(Coord-Mktg)*
Erica Turer *(Coord-Mktg)*

LOCAL.COM
7555 Irvine Ctr Dr, Irvine, CA 92618
Tel.: (949) 784-0800
Web Site: www.local.com

Agency Specializes In: Advertising

Ken Cragun *(CFO)*
Scott Reinke *(Chief Legal Officer)*
Carlos Caponera *(Sr VP-Consumer Properties)*
Joe Lindsay *(VP-Tech)*
Brian Singleton *(VP-Innovation)*
Xiongwu Xia *(Exec Dir-Engrg)*
Tim Simeonov *(Sr Dir-Tech)*
Mark Sterling *(Sr Dir-Bus Analytics)*
Charles Fuller *(Dir-Sls)*
Tim Williams *(Dir-Sls)*
Sruthi Sunkireddy *(Sr Mgr-Quality Assurance)*

THE MARATHON GROUP
E Gate Corp Ctr 307 Fellowship Rd Ste 315, Mount Laurel, NJ 08054
Tel.: (856) 914-0240
Fax: (856) 642-0047
Web Site: www.barnabashealth.org

Employees: 20
Year Founded: 1990

National Agency Associations: PAC

Agency Specializes In: Advertising, Brand Development & Integration, Business-To-Business, Collateral, College, Communications, Consulting, Consumer Marketing, Corporate Communications, Corporate Identity, Digital/Interactive, Direct Response Marketing, Exhibit/Trade Shows, Experience Design, Graphic Design, Health Care Services, Integrated Marketing, Internet/Web Design, Logo & Package Design, Media Buying Services, Media Relations, Medical Products, Out-of-Home Media, Point of Purchase, Production (Print), Public Relations, Publicity/Promotions, Radio, Recruitment, Strategic Planning/Research

Approx. Annual Billings: $8,800,000

Breakdown of Gross Billings by Media: Cable T.V.: 2%; Collateral: 23%; D.M.: 7%; Internet Adv.: 3%; Newsp. & Mags.: 42%; Outdoor: 3%; Radio: 18%; Transit: 2%

T.A. Hahn *(Sr Dir-Art)*
David McClung *(Reg CFO)*

Accounts:
Atlantic Cape Community College; Mays Landing, NJ Community College; 2008
Capehart Scatchard; Mount Laurel, NJ Legal Services; 2009
Children's Hospital of New Jersey; Newark, NJ Health Care Marketing, Creative Services & Recruitment; 1996
Clara Maass Medical Center; Belleville, NJ Health Care Marketing, Creative Services & Recruitment; 1995
Newark Beth Israel Medical Center; Newark, NJ Health Care Marketing, Creative Services & Recruitment; 1996
Saint Barnabas Ambulatory Care Center; Livingston, NJ Health Care Marketing, Creative Services & Recruitment; 1997
Saint Barnabas Health Care System; West Orange, NJ Health Care Marketing, Creative Services & Recruitment; 1993
Saint Barnabas Medical Center; West Orange, NJ Health Care Marketing, Creative Services & Recruitment; 1993
Saint Barnabas Nursing & Rehabilitation Centers; Union, NJ Health Care Marketing, Creative Services & Recruitment; 1990

MBI INC.
47 Richards Ave, Norwalk, CT 06857
Tel.: (203) 853-2000
Fax: (203) 831-9661
E-Mail: webmail@mbi-inc.com
Web Site: www.mbi-inc.com

Year Founded: 1969

Jim Zulick *(VP & Mgr-Product Dev)*
Jason Brenner *(VP & Sr Program Mgr)*
Jeffrey Kornblum *(VP)*
Mike Rogers *(VP)*
Jay Zibelman *(VP)*
Lynn Zimmermann *(VP)*
Kendall Good *(Asst Product Mgr)*
Michael Scognamiglio *(Asst Product Mgr)*
Tom Reese *(Mgr-HR)*
Rebecca Reicherter *(Assoc Mgr-Product Mktg)*
Rashmi Balasubramanian *(Asst Program Mgr)*

Accounts:
Danbury Mint; Norwalk, CT
The Easton Press
Postal Commemorative Society

MICROFLEX CORPORATION
150 Field Dr Ste 210, Lake Forest, IL 60045
Tel.: (866) 931-3613
Fax: (847) 735-0410
Toll Free: (800) 876-6866
E-Mail: sales@microflex.com
Web Site: www.microflex.com

Employees: 112
Year Founded: 1987

Agency Specializes In: Education

Approx. Annual Billings: $5,000,000

Kathy Zanzucchi *(Dir-Mktg)*

Accounts:
Microflex Corporation; Reno, NV Latex Gloves; 1989

MILLER-STEPHENSON CHEMICAL CO.
George Washington Hwy, Danbury, CT 06810
Tel.: (203) 743-4447
Fax: (203) 791-8702
E-Mail: ct.sales@miller-stephenson.com
Web Site: www.miller-stephenson.com

Employees: 50

Mourad Fahmi *(Pres & CEO)*

MRS. FIELDS'
2855 E Cottonwood Pkwy Ste 400, Salt Lake City, UT 84121
Tel.: (801) 736-5600
Fax: (801) 736-5970
Toll Free: (800) 343-5377
E-Mail: ahogan@mrsfields.com
Web Site: mrsfields.com/

Employees: 12
Year Founded: 1977

Approx. Annual Billings: $1,500,000

Timothy Casey *(Pres & CEO)*
Tim Miller *(VP-Supply Chain)*
Kim Jones *(Dir-ECommerce & Omni Channel Strategy)*
Ryan Thurston *(Dir-Distr)*
Ashley Berland *(Sr Mgr-Supply Chain Program)*
John Brinkerhoff *(Mgr-Online Mktg)*
Bryan Henkelman *(Mgr-Online Mktg)*
Chris Kuhn *(Online Mktg)*
Tyler Molder *(Rep-Corp Sls)*

Accounts:
Mrs. Fields Original Cookies Inc.; Salt Lake City, UT

MUSIC & EVENT MANAGEMENT, INC.
1241 Elm St, Cincinnati, OH 45202
Tel.: (513) 721-3555
Web Site: www.cincinnatisymphony.org

Agency Specializes In: Communications, Event Planning & Marketing

Michael C. Smith *(CEO & Exec VP)*

Accounts:
Cincinnati Symphony Orchestra
Cincy-Cinco Latino Festival
Tall Stacks Music, Arts & Heritage Festival

NABARCO ADVERTISING ASSOCIATES, INC.
2100 Smithtown Ave, Ronkonkoma, NY 11779
Tel.: (631) 200-2000
Web Site: www.nbty.com

Employees: 25
Year Founded: 1960

Dipak Golechha *(CFO)*
Andrea Simone *(CIO-NBTY, Inc.)*
Chris Brennan *(Sr VP, Gen Counsel & Chief Compliance Officer)*
Andrew Archambault *(Chief Comml Officer & Chief Customer Officer)*
Brian Wynne *(Pres-NBTY Americas & CEO-US Nutrition)*
Peter Shapiro *(Pres-Puritan's Pride & Sr VP-Consumer Direct)*
Geir Harstad *(Pres-Intl)*
Jack Krause *(Pres-Vitamin World)*
James P. Flaherty *(Sr VP-Adv & Creative Svcs)*
Vicki Mcguire *(Sr VP-Vitamin World)*
Karla Packer *(Sr VP-HR)*

NATIONAL HOT ROD ASSOCIATION
2035 Financial Way, Glendora, CA 91741
Tel.: (626) 914-4761
Fax: (626) 963-5360
E-Mail: nhra@nhraonline.com
Web Site: www.nhra.com

Employees: 150
Year Founded: 1951

Agency Specializes In: Publicity/Promotions

Linda Louie *(Gen Counsel & VP)*
Gary Darcy *(Sr VP-Sls & Mktg)*
Graham Light *(Sr VP-Racing Ops)*
Glen Gray *(VP-Technical Ops)*
John Siragusa *(Sr Dir-Sls & Bus Dev)*
Phil Burgess *(Dir-Editorial)*
Danny Gracia *(Dir-Natl Technical)*
Marleen Gurrola *(Dir-HR)*
Jared Robison *(Dir-IT)*
Jim Trace *(Dir-Brdcst & Video Comm)*

NEIMAN MARCUS ADVERTISING

1618 Main St, Dallas, TX 75201
Tel.: (214) 743-7600
Fax: (214) 573-5992
Web Site: www.neimanmarcus.com

Employees: 60

Agency Specializes In: Magazines, Newspaper, Newspapers & Magazines, Outdoor, Print, Radio

Michael Kingston *(CIO & Sr VP)*
John Koryl *(Pres-Neiman Marcus Stores & Online)*
Stacie Shirley *(Treas & Sr VP-Fin)*
Liz Allison *(Sr VP-Last Call)*
Craig Campbell *(VP-Mktg & Creative Svcs)*
Jon Gappa *(VP-Real Estate & Spend Mgmt Svcs)*
William Hough *(VP-Credit Svcs)*
Sarah Miller *(VP-Enterprise Applications)*
Rajeev Rai *(VP-Customer Facing Technologies)*
Ginger Reeder *(VP-Corp Comm)*
Mimi Sterling *(VP-Corp Comm & PR)*
Amy Walker *(VP-Last Call Mktg)*
Maggie Lucas *(Mktg Dir)*
Jessica Boland *(Dir-Search & Site Optimization)*
Debbie Butler *(Dir-Web Analytics)*
Kyle Ciborowski *(Dir-Applications Dev)*
Muthukumar Easwaran *(Dir-Engrg & ecommerce-Global)*
Alison Szvoren Magstadt *(Dir-Mktg-Neiman Marcus Stores)*
Cris Brown *(Mgr-Applications Dev)*
Rachel Holt *(Mgr-Web Adv)*
Meghan Lamberth *(Mgr-User Experience)*
Brian McClung *(Mgr-Applications Mgmt)*
April McGlynn *(Mgr-Adv-Intl)*

Accounts:
Neimen Marcus

NELSON ADVERTISING SOLUTIONS

19080 Lomita Ave, Sonoma, CA 95476-1546
Mailing Address:
PO Box 1546, Sonoma, CA 95476-1546
Tel.: (707) 935-6113
Fax: (707) 935-6124
E-Mail: info@nelsonhr.com
Web Site: www.nelsonjobs.com

Employees: 250
Year Founded: 1970

Agency Specializes In: Advertising Specialties, Brand Development & Integration, Business Publications, Business-To-Business, Collateral, Consulting, Consumer Marketing, Corporate Communications, Corporate Identity, Digital/Interactive, Direct Response Marketing, E-Commerce, Event Planning & Marketing, Exhibit/Trade Shows, Graphic Design, High Technology, Information Technology, Internet/Web Design, Local Marketing, Logo & Package Design, Newspaper, Newspapers & Magazines, Planning & Consultation, Print, Production, Public Relations, Publicity/Promotions, Recruitment, Sales Promotion, Strategic Planning/Research, Technical Advertising, Telemarketing, Yellow Pages Advertising

Breakdown of Gross Billings by Media: Bus. Publs.: 5%; Newsp. & Mags.: 95%

Gary D. Nelson *(Founder)*
Brian Gabrielson *(Sr VP)*
Todd Witkin *(Sr VP)*
Lisa Marie Johnson *(Dir-HR)*
Jenifer Martinelli *(Mgr-Field Ops)*
Jenifer Valenzuela *(Supvr-Staffing)*
Lisa De Garmo *(Acct Exec)*
Justin Dugish *(Acct Exec)*
Karen Xiao *(Specialist-Recruitment & Ops)*

Accounts:
HRhome
Nelson & Associates
Nelson Jobs
Nelson Staffing Solutions; Sonoma, CA

NEW ENGLAND MACHINERY ADVERTISING

2820 62nd Ave E, Bradenton, FL 34203
Tel.: (941) 755-5550
Fax: (941) 751-6281
E-Mail: info@neminc.com
Web Site: www.neminc.com

Employees: 35
Year Founded: 1974

Judith Nickse *(Pres & CEO)*
Wes Rule *(Reg Mgr-Sls-Southeast)*
John Hansmann *(Mgr-Engrg)*
Patrick Jones *(Mgr-Customer Svc)*
Michelle Sears *(Mgr-HR)*
Robert Szalay *(Designer-Publ)*

Accounts:
New England Machinery, Inc.; Bradenton, FL

NRC REALTY CAPITAL ADVISORS

(Formerly NRC Media)
363 W Erie St Ste 300E, Chicago, IL 60654
Tel.: (312) 278-6800
Fax: (312) 278-6900
Toll Free: (800) 747-3342
E-Mail: help@nrc.com
Web Site: www.nrc.com

Employees: 15
Year Founded: 1989

Agency Specializes In: Advertising, Business-To-Business, Consulting, Consumer Marketing, Direct Response Marketing, E-Commerce, Electronic Media, Environmental, Graphic Design, Industrial, Internet/Web Design, Media Buying Services, Newspaper, Newspapers & Magazines, Outdoor, Planning & Consultation, Print, Public Relations, Real Estate, Telemarketing, Trade & Consumer Magazines

Approx. Annual Billings: $1,500,000

Breakdown of Gross Billings by Media: Internet Adv.: $100,000; Newsp.: $900,000; Newsp. & Mags.: $200,000; Other: $220,000; Pub. Rels.: $80,000

Thomas H. Wilky *(Mng Dir)*
Ian Walker *(Sr VP)*
Samantha Steiner *(VP & Project Mgr)*
Jonathan Graham *(VP)*
Tracey Suppo *(VP-Mktg)*
Omid Keshtkar *(Mgr-Strategic Support)*
Tisha McClinic *(Mgr-Closing)*

Accounts:
AM/PM Convenience Stores
Arby's Restaurant Group, Inc.
Arco Products Company; La Palma, CA Convenience Stores, Gas Stations; 2000
BP America
BP Amoco; Towson, MD Convenience Stores, Gas Stations; 2001
Giant Industries, Inc.
Spectrum Stores, Inc.
Sunoco, Inc.
White Hen Pantry

OGILVY COMMONHEALTH INSIGHTS & ANALYTICS

440 Interpace Pkwy, Parsippany, NJ 07054
Tel.: (973) 352-3800
Fax: (973) 352-1190
Web Site: www.ogilvychww.com/

Year Founded: 2000

Agency Specializes In: Advertising

Michael Parisi *(Mng Partner)*
Shaun Urban *(Mng Partner)*
Gloria Gibbons *(Pres-EAME)*
Paul O'Neill *(Pres-Wellness Mktg)*
Chris Cullmann *(Sr VP & Dir-Digital Strategy)*
Kristine Dyer *(VP & Acct Dir-Media)*
Skot Kremen *(VP & Dir-User Experience)*
Kerianne Slattery *(Mgr-Comm & PR)*
Rohit Sahgal *(Reg Mng Dir-Asia Pacific-Ogilvy CommonHealth)*

Accounts:
Amagen
AstraZeneca
BMS
Boehringer-Ingelheim
Genentech
GSK
J&J
Janssen Biotech, Inc.
MBS/Vox
Merck
Novartis
Ortho Biotech
Ortho Derm
Ortho-McNeil
Pfizer
Procter & Gamble
Roche
Sanofi-Aventis
Schering-Plough
Shire Pharmaceutical
UCB

OLD FASHION FOODS ADVERTISING

5521 Collins Blvd SW, Austell, GA 30106
Tel.: (770) 948-1177
Fax: (770) 739-3254
E-Mail: info@oldfashsd.com
Web Site: www.oldfashfd.com

Employees: 70
Year Founded: 1984

Terry Coker *(VP-Mktg)*

Accounts:
Old Fashion Foods, Inc.; Austell, GA

OMAHA CREATIVE GROUP

11030 O St, Omaha, NE 68137-2346
Tel.: (402) 597-3000
Fax: (402) 597-8222
Toll Free: (800) 228-2778
E-Mail: custserv@omahasteaks.com
Web Site: www.omahasteaks.com

Employees: 50

Year Founded: 1917

Agency Specializes In: Direct Response Marketing

Approx. Annual Billings: $30,000,000

Breakdown of Gross Billings by Media: D.M.: $29,100,000; Mags.: $300,000; Newsp.: $300,000; T.V.: $300,000

Bruce Simon *(Pres)*
Frederick J. Simon *(Exec VP-Omaha Steaks)*
Todd Simon *(Sr VP)*

Accounts:
Consumer Direct; Omaha, NE Mail Order & Retail; 1999
Incentive Sales Department; Omaha, NE Incentives & Business Gifts; 1999
Omaha Steaks International, Inc.; Omaha, NE Hotel, Restaurant & Institutional Sales; 1999

OMEGA ENGINEERING ADVERTISING
1 Omega Dr, Stamford, CT 06907-0047
Tel.: (203) 359-1660
Fax: (203) 359-7700
Toll Free: (800) 826-6342
E-Mail: info@omega.com
Web Site: www.omega.com

E-Mail for Key Personnel:
Media Dir.: kathy@mbh1.com

Employees: 499
Year Founded: 1980

Agency Specializes In: Brand Development & Integration, Business-To-Business, Direct Response Marketing, Engineering, Industrial, Magazines, Production

Jay Mendelson *(VP-Tech)*
Bill Keating *(Gen Mgr)*
Shahin Baghai *(Dir-Embedded & Software Systems)*
Warren Jones *(Dir-IT)*
Casey Bralla *(Mgr-Operational Excellence)*
Kathy Kwiat *(Mgr-Adv)*
Tom Opalinski *(Mgr-Global Infrastructure)*
Gary Palmer *(Mgr-Engrg)*
George Zisk *(Mgr-Production Engrg)*
Murilo Favari *(Specialist-Mktg)*
Rosita Asnaashari *(Sr Engr-Application)*

Accounts:
Newport Electronics, Inc.; CA
Omega Dyne, Inc.; Sunbury, OH
Omega Engineering, Inc.; Stamford, CT
Omega Vanzetti, Inc.; MA

PEAVEY ELECTRONIC ADVERTISING
5022 Hartley Peavey Dr, Meridian, MS 39305
Tel.: (601) 483-5365
Fax: (601) 486-1278
Web Site: www.peavey.com

Employees: 1,000

Approx. Annual Billings: $200,000

Courtland Gray *(COO)*
Kimberly Smith *(Controller)*
Kevin Ivey *(Gen Mgr-Comml Audio)*
Fred Poole *(Gen Mgr-Product Dev & Sls-North American)*
Keith Varner *(Gen Mgr-Engrg)*
Michael Smith *(Product Mgr)*
John Fields *(Mgr-Engrg)*
John D. Miller *(Mgr-Pur Dept)*
Julie Moscal *(Mgr-Internal Sls)*
Tom Stuckman *(Mgr-Mixer Engrg)*
Tim Benson *(Sr Buyer-Intl)*

Accounts:
Peavey Electronic Corp.; Meridian, MS Electronic Musical Equipment

PETER LI EDUCATION GROUP
2621 Dryden Rd Ste 300, Dayton, OH 45439-1661
Fax: (800) 370-4450
Toll Free: (800) 523-4625
E-Mail: tperkins@peterli.com

E-Mail for Key Personnel:
Creative Dir.: ewright@peterli.com

Employees: 100
Year Founded: 1971

Agency Specializes In: Education

Terry William Perkins *(VP-Mktg-Pflaum Publ Grp)*
Ellen Wright *(Dir-Art & Dir-Creative)*
Kevin Jensen *(Mgr-Production)*

Accounts:
Peter Li, Inc.; Dayton, OH Educational Accounts

POGGENPOHL U.S., INC.
(Formerly Poggenpohl Advertising Group)
350 Passaic Ave, Fairfield, NJ 07004-2007
Tel.: (973) 812-8900
Fax: (973) 812-9320
Toll Free: (800) 987-0553
E-Mail: info@us.poggenpohl.com
Web Site: www.poggenpohl.com

Employees: 75
Year Founded: 1892

Agency Specializes In: Direct-to-Consumer, Event Planning & Marketing, Magazines, Multimedia, T.V., Yellow Pages Advertising

Neil Bailey *(Pres/CEO-US & Canada)*
Jeff Roberts *(VP-Sls)*
Ted Blick *(Mgr-Natl Ops)*
Paul Lennie *(Mgr-Import & Export)*
Murrad Sher *(Mgr-Multi Unit Sls)*
Brandon Cruz *(Designer)*
Beth Priday *(Designer-Natl Projects)*

PUBLISHERS ADVERTISING ASSOCIATES
237 Park Ave 15Fl, New York, NY 10017
Tel.: (212) 364-1100
Web Site: www.hachettebookgroup.com

Employees: 30
Year Founded: 1973

National Agency Associations: MCA

Agency Specializes In: Advertising, African-American Market, Alternative Advertising, Asian Market, Broadcast, Business Publications, Cable T.V., Catalogs, Children's Market, Collateral, Consumer Marketing, Consumer Publications, Email, Gay & Lesbian Market, Guerilla Marketing, Hispanic Market, In-Store Advertising, Magazines, Media Buying Services, Media Planning, Mobile Marketing, Newspaper, Newspapers & Magazines, Out-of-Home Media, Outdoor, Paid Searches, Point of Purchase, Print, Production (Print), Radio, Sponsorship, Strategic Planning/Research, T.V., Teen Market, Trade & Consumer Magazines, Transportation, Tween Market, Urban Market, Viral/Buzz/Word of Mouth, Web (Banner Ads, Pop-ups, etc.), Women's Market

Approx. Annual Billings: $10,000,000

Brad Negbaur *(Dir-Copy)*

Accounts:
Business Plus
Center Street
Faith Words
Grand Central Publishing
Jericho
Little Brown & Company
Little Brown Books for Young Readers
Mulholland Books
Orbit
Poppy
Regan Arthur Books
Twelve
Yen Press

RCG PRODUCTIONS
5944 Coral Ridge Dr Ste 132, Coral Springs, FL 33076
Tel.: (954) 752-5224
Fax: (954) 752-3611
E-Mail: debra4rcgproductions@yahoo.com
Web Site: www.rcgproductions.net

Employees: 2
Year Founded: 2002

Agency Specializes In: Advertising, Brand Development & Integration, Branded Entertainment, Cable T.V., Children's Market, Consumer Marketing, Cosmetics, Direct Response Marketing, Electronic Media, Health Care Services, Household Goods, Infomercials, Local Marketing, Media Buying Services, Multimedia, New Product Development, Outdoor, Seniors' Market, T.V., Teen Market

Robert Greene *(Owner)*
Debra Hall-Greene *(VP)*

Accounts:
Color Cutters; Davie, Florida; 2005
JK Harris; Palm Beach, FL Tax Consultations; 2003
Schwartz Group; Deerfield Beach, FL Mighty Putty, Hercules Hook, Smart Spin; 2004
Water Mirrors; Baltimore, MD; 2006

REPLACEMENTS, LTD.
1089 Knox Rd, McLeansville, NC 27301
Mailing Address:
PO Box 26029, Greensboro, NC 27420-6029
Tel.: (336) 697-3000
Fax: (336) 697-3100
E-Mail: inquire@replacements.com
Web Site: www.replacements.com

E-Mail for Key Personnel:
Media Dir.: mark.donahue@replacements.com

Year Founded: 1981

Agency Specializes In: Consumer Goods, Consumer Marketing, Consumer Publications, Direct Response Marketing, Direct-to-Consumer, Household Goods, Media Planning, Over-50 Market, Print, Retail, Trade & Consumer Magazines

Breakdown of Gross Billings by Media: Network T.V.: 1%; Out-of-Home Media: 43%; Trade & Consumer Mags.: 56%

Blair Friday *(CIO)*
Lisa Conklin *(Mgr-PR)*
Miki Sato *(Mgr-Online Mktg)*
Scott Hovey *(Admin-Web)*

Accounts:
Replacements Ltd.

RONNE BONDER LTD.
117 E 57th St Ste 46 C, New York, NY 10022-

2002
Tel.: (212) 750-9285
Fax: (212) 702-8772
E-Mail: info@hamptonsvodka.com
Web Site: www.hamptonsvodka.com/

E-Mail for Key Personnel:
President: rbonder@hamptonsvodka.com

Employees: 4
Year Founded: 1969

Agency Specializes In: Corporate Identity, Financial, Graphic Design, Logo & Package Design

Approx. Annual Billings: $500,000

Breakdown of Gross Billings by Media: Collateral: $250,000; Other: $250,000

Ronne Bonder *(Pres & Dir-Creative)*

Accounts:
Citicorp; New York, NY; 1982
The Hamptons Spirit Co. Gin, Vodka; 1999
Tasa International; New York, NY; 1992
The Yankelovich Group; Boston, MA; 1986

ROTARY INTERNATIONAL
1560 Sherman Ave, Evanston, IL 60201-4818
Tel.: (847) 866-3000
Fax: (847) 328-8554
E-Mail: pr@rotaryintl.org
Web Site: www.rotary.org

E-Mail for Key Personnel:
Public Relations: kessenik@rotaryintl.org

Employees: 500
Year Founded: 1905

National Agency Associations: ABC

Agency Specializes In: Communications, Direct Response Marketing, Print, Public Relations, Publicity/Promotions, Radio, T.V.

John Rezek *(Editor-in-Chief-The Rotarian & Mgr-Magazines Div)*
Eric Schmelling *(Dir-Fund Dev)*
Vivian Fiore *(Mgr-PR)*
Jane Lawicki *(Mgr-Pub & External Rels)*
Michelle J. Snyder *(Sr Analyst-Fin)*

RUBIK MARKETING
63 Wall St, New York, NY 10005
Tel.: (213) 446-0615
E-Mail: info@rubikmarekting.com
Web Site: www.rubikmarketing.com

Agency Specializes In: Advertising, Advertising Specialties, Alternative Advertising, Brand Development & Integration, Business-To-Business, Communications, Consulting, Event Planning & Marketing, Experience Design, Integrated Marketing, Out-of-Home Media, Product Placement, Promotions, Sponsorship, Strategic Planning/Research

Breakdown of Gross Billings by Media: Consulting: 80%; Event Mktg.: 20%

Diane Nicoletti *(Pres)*

Accounts:
Carmike Cinemas; Atlanta, GA Kids Summer Matinee Program
Educational Networks; New York, NY School Sponorship Program
ZHC Collection; New York, NY Kid-Friendly Handbags

SANTA FE NATURAL TOBACCO ADVERTISING
PO Box 25140, Santa Fe, NM 87504
Tel.: (505) 982-4257
Fax: (505) 982-0156
Toll Free: (800) 332-5595
E-Mail: feedback@sfntc.com
Web Site: www.sfntc.com

Agency Specializes In: Direct Response Marketing, Exhibit/Trade Shows, In-Store Advertising, Trade & Consumer Magazines

Approx. Annual Billings: $7,000,000

Breakdown of Gross Billings by Media: Bus. Publs.: 5%; Collateral: 10%; Event Mktg.: 10%; Mags.: 30%; Network Radio: 30%; Trade Shows: 15%

Keith Grover *(Sr Dir-Corp Sustainability)*
David Lafferty *(Sr Dir-Trade Mktg Ops & Strategy)*
Carrie Carter *(Reg Dir-Southeast)*
John Decuir *(Dir-Natl Accounts)*
Kenny Deloach *(Dir-Product Dev)*
Drew Fairhurst *(Dir-Trade Mktg-West Reg)*
Torsten Gohre *(Dir-Western Sls Area)*
Bernd Michahelles *(Dir)*
Don Pizzolato *(Dir-Analysis & Insights)*
Elise Rodgers *(Sr Mgr-Brand Equity)*
Elizabeth Otto *(Mgr-Market)*
Greg Britner *(Coord-Trade Mktg)*
Sarah Rogoff *(Territory Mgr)*
Danny Thurmond *(Key Acct Mgr)*

Accounts:
Santa Fe Natural Tobacco American Spirit

SAXTON HORNE ADVERTISING
9350 S 150 E, Sandy, UT 84070
Tel.: (801) 304-1000
Fax: (801) 304-1008
E-Mail: contact@saxtonhorne.net
Web Site: www.saxtonhorne.com

Employees: 7

David Blain *(Pres)*
Spencer Beckstead *(Dir-Automotive)*
Kaylan Malm *(Dir-Analytics)*
Jon Menousek *(Dir-Strategic Media)*
Emily Millard *(Dir-Digital)*
Benjamin Bielas *(Mgr-Market)*
Tina Bodrero *(Mgr-Office)*

Accounts:
Larry H. Miller Group
Miller Motorsports Spark
Salt Lake Bees
University of Utah
Utah Jazz Basketball

SCHLUMBERGER LTD.
210 Schlumberger Dr, Sugar Land, TX 77478
Tel.: (281) 285-8500
Fax: (281) 285-8970
Web Site: www.slb.com

Guy Arrington *(Pres-Bits & Advanced Technologies)*
Tony Bowman *(Pres-WesternGeco)*
Aaron Gatt Floridia *(Pres-Reservoir Characterization Grp)*
Steve Kaufmann *(Pres-Drilling & Measurements)*
Patrick Schorn *(Pres-Ops & Integration)*
Hatem Soliman *(Pres-Latin America)*
Ashok Belani *(Exec VP-Tech)*
Kjell-Erik Oestdahl *(Exec VP-Ops)*
J-F Poupeau *(Exec VP-Corp Dev & Comm)*
Stephanie Cox *(VP-HR)*
Dominique Malard *(VP-Cementing)*
Jeff Spath *(VP-Indus & University Rels)*

Accounts:
Schlumberger Limited

SCHNEIDER ELECTRIC'S AGENCY
132 Fairgrounds Rd, West Kingston, RI 02892-1511
Tel.: (401) 398-8450
Fax: (401) 788-2739
E-Mail: advertising@schneider-electric.com
Web Site: www.schneider-electric.com

Employees: 9
Year Founded: 1981

Agency Specializes In: Business Publications, Collateral, Commercial Photography, Consumer Publications, Direct Response Marketing, E-Commerce, High Technology, International, Magazines, Newspaper, Newspapers & Magazines, Trade & Consumer Magazines, Yellow Pages Advertising

Approx. Annual Billings: $4,000,000

Breakdown of Gross Billings by Media: Bus. Publs.: $4,000,000

Laurent Vernery *(Exec VP-Ops-North America)*
Martin Hanna *(VP-Press Rels)*
Cheryl Rapp *(VP-PMO)*
Arthur Silva *(VP-Portfolio Mktg Strategy-Global Solutions Bus)*
Kristen Sisson *(VP-Media Strategy-Global)*
Jennifer Wendt *(Dir-Social Media & Strategist-Social Media ROI)*
Melissa Hertel *(Dir-Mktg)*
Kelly McNair *(Mgr-Customer Experience)*

Accounts:
APC by Schneider Electric; West Kingston, RI High-Tech Manufactured Products; 1992
Availability.com; West Kingston, RI Content Solutions; 2000
BuyUptime.com; Saint Louis, MO E-Commerce; 2000
Data Center University; West Kingston, RI Training Courses; 2006
EnergyOn.com; Silver Spring, MD Utility Savings; 2000
PELCO Video Security; 2012
Schneider Electric; Palatine, IL Electrical Products & Services; 2009

SHOW MANAGEMENT ADVERTISING
1115 NE 9th Ave, Fort Lauderdale, FL 33304-2110
Tel.: (954) 764-7642
Fax: (954) 462-4140
Toll Free: (800) 940-7642
E-Mail: info@showmanagement.com
Web Site: www.showmanagement.com

E-Mail for Key Personnel:
President: kpearson@showmanagement.com
Media Dir.: ssheer@showmanagement.com

Employees: 85
Year Founded: 1976

Agency Specializes In: Entertainment, Event Planning & Marketing, Exhibit/Trade Shows, Graphic Design, Marine, Multimedia, Outdoor, Planning & Consultation, Point of Sale, Production, Public Relations, Publicity/Promotions

Dane Graziano *(COO & Sr VP)*
Andrew Doole *(Sr VP)*
Brett Keating *(VP-Consumer Mktg)*
Steven Sheer *(Dir-Mktg)*

Accounts:
Fort Lauderdale International Boat Show; Fort Lauderdale, FL Trade & Consumer Show

House Agencies

Palm Beach International Boat Show
St. Petersburg Boat Show
Suncoast Boat Show; Sarasota, FL Trade & Consumer
Yachting Promotions, Inc.; Fort Lauderdale, FL Spring Boat Show, Trade & Consumer Show

SIMON & SCHUSTER ADVERTISING
1230 Avenue of the Americas 12th Fl, New York, NY 10020
Tel.: (212) 698-7000
Fax: (212) 698-7174
Toll Free: (800) 223-2348
Web Site:
pages.simonandschuster.com/simonsays

Employees: 25
Year Founded: 1994

Agency Specializes In: Print

Liz Perl *(CMO & Exec VP)*
Louise Burke *(Exec VP & Publr-Gallery Books)*
Sue Fleming *(VP & Exec Dir-Content & Programming)*
Mark Speer *(VP & Dir-Adv & Promo)*
Carolyn Connolly *(Head-HR)*

Accounts:
Alladin
Atheneum
Atria
Folger Shakespeare Library
Howard Books
Paula Wiseman Books
Pimsleur
Simon & Schuster; New York, NY Books
Simon Spotlight Entertainment
Threshold
Toughstone

SKF USA INC.
890 Forty Foot Rd, Lansdale, PA 19446
Tel.: (267) 436-6000
Fax: (267) 436-6001
Toll Free: (800) 440-4753
Web Site: www.skf.com/us/index.html

Employees: 400
Year Founded: 1907

Agency Specializes In: Advertising

Poul Jeppesen *(Pres & CEO)*
Jon Stevens *(Chief Compliance Officer & VP-Corp Sustainability & Compliance)*
Paul Bourgon *(Pres-aeroEngine)*
Randy Bowen *(VP)*
Dan Donnelly *(VP-Sls-USA)*
Jeff Carlisle *(Dir-Forecasting & Res)*
Helena Karlsson *(Coord-Event & Road Shows)*

SMITH GROWTH PARTNERS
3000 Chestnut Ave, Baltimore, MD 21211
Tel.: (410) 235-7004
Fax: (410) 235-7005
E-Mail: info@smithcontent.com
Web Site: www.smithgrowthpartners.com

Year Founded: 1998

John Starling *(Founder & Partner)*

Accounts:
Baltimore City Head Start
Caseworks
Harbor Point Resources
Knott Mechanical
MarinaLife
SmithContent

SOUTHWESTERN INDUSTRIES, INC.
2615 Homestead Pl, Rancho Dominguez, CA 90220
Tel.: (310) 608-4422
Fax: (310) 764-2668
Toll Free: (800) 367-3165
E-Mail: info@southwesternindustries.com
Web Site: www.southwesternindustries.com

Employees: 2
Year Founded: 1952

Stephen F. Pinto *(Pres)*
Michael Mcgarry *(Reg Mgr)*
Christopher Lee *(Mgr-Supply Chain)*
Gianna Williams *(Coord-Info Sys)*
Ericka Dacostta *(Rep-Customer Svc)*

Accounts:
Southwestern Industries, Inc.

STOWE AREA ASSOCIATION AGENCY
51 Main St, Stowe, VT 05672-1320
Tel.: (802) 253-7321
Fax: (802) 253-6628
Toll Free: (800) 24STOWE
E-Mail: askus@gostowe.com
Web Site: www.gostowe.com

E-Mail for Key Personnel:
President: valerier@gostowe.com
Media Dir.: lynne@gostowe.com

Employees: 12
Year Founded: 1972

Agency Specializes In: Co-op Advertising, Collateral, Consumer Marketing, Direct Response Marketing, Entertainment, Event Planning & Marketing, Exhibit/Trade Shows, Internet/Web Design, Local Marketing, Magazines, Media Buying Services, Newspaper, Production, Public Relations, Restaurant, Retail, Sales Promotion, Sports Market, Travel & Tourism

Approx. Annual Billings: $1,000,000

Breakdown of Gross Billings by Media: Co-op Adv.: $80,000; Collateral: $280,000; Comml. Photography: $30,000; Consumer Publs.: $80,000; D.M.: $90,000; Event Mktg.: $10,000; Exhibits/Trade Shows: $40,000; Foreign: $40,000; Graphic Design: $30,000; Internet Adv.: $140,000; Local Mktg.: $10,000; Newsp.: $10,000; Outdoor: $20,000; Pub. Rels.: $50,000; Sports Mktg.: $20,000; Worldwide Web Sites: $70,000

Ed Stahl *(Exec Dir)*
Susan Rousselle *(Dir-Sls)*
Dean Burnell *(Mgr-Fin & HR)*
John Walsh *(Coord-Mktg)*

Accounts:
Stowe Area Association, Inc.; Stowe, VT

STUBS COMMUNICATIONS COMPANY
226 W 47th St, New York, NY 10036-1413
Tel.: (212) 398-8383
Fax: (212) 398-8389
Toll Free: (800) 223-7565
Web Site: www.broadway.com

Employees: 20
Year Founded: 1979

Agency Specializes In: Entertainment, Travel & Tourism

Approx. Annual Billings: $3,700,000

Breakdown of Gross Billings by Media: D.M.: $2,850,000; Mags.: $150,000; Other: $700,000

Stephanie Lee *(Pres)*
Jim Deliman *(Exec Dir-Grp Sls)*
Steven Mann *(Acct Dir-Theatre Parties & Best of Broadway Clubs)*
Heather Jones *(Dir-Broadway Classroom Program)*
Vickie Plummer *(Dir-Broadway Classroom Program)*
Anthony Barone *(Mgr-Grp Sls)*
Kendra Dolton *(Mgr-Special Projects & Sls Event)*
Rebecca Dunkle *(Mgr-Natl Ops)*
Natalie Provenzano *(Specialist-Grp Sls Ticketing)*

Accounts:
Broadway Bucks Discount Theatre Tickets; 2001
Group Sales Box Office; New York, NY Theatre Ticket Sales
The Matinee Club
Stubs Discount Theatre Tickets
Stubs Preview Club
Theatre Party Associates; New York, NY Theatre Ticket Sales

SWIRE
440 E Route 66, Glendora, CA 91740
Tel.: (626) 963-0693
Fax: (626) 963-9432
E-Mail: ca@goswire.com
Web Site: www.goswire.com

Agency Specializes In: Digital/Interactive, Email, Media Buying Services, Media Planning, Mobile Marketing, Print, Radio, Strategic Planning/Research, T.V., Viral/Buzz/Word of Mouth

Kyle Prough *(Dir-Creative)*

Accounts:
eGood

TAYLOR & MARTIN, INC.
1865 N Airport Rd, Fremont, NE 68025
Mailing Address:
PO Box 349, Fremont, NE 68025
Tel.: (402) 721-4500
Fax: (402) 721-4570
E-Mail: info@taylorandmartin.com
Web Site: www.taylorandmartin.com

E-Mail for Key Personnel:
Public Relations: pvogt@taylorandmartin.com

Employees: 40
Year Founded: 1935

Agency Specializes In: Business Publications, Business-To-Business, Consulting, Corporate Identity, Direct Response Marketing, Event Planning & Marketing, Exhibit/Trade Shows, Graphic Design, Logo & Package Design, Magazines, Media Buying Services, Newspaper, Newspapers & Magazines, Outdoor, Public Relations, Publicity/Promotions, Radio, Sales Promotion, Trade & Consumer Magazines

Approx. Annual Billings: $2,000,000

Mark E. Fort *(Owner)*
Paul C. Wachter *(Pres)*
Jessup Wilson *(CFO)*
James M. Conrad *(VP)*
Brad Anderson *(Dir-Online Auction Ops)*
Penny Vogt *(Mgr-Mktg)*

Accounts:
ACT-Acquisitions, Consulting & Turnarounds
All Points Capital Corp.
Allegiance Financial Group, Inc.
Preferred Leasing, Inc.-PLI
Taylor & Martin, Inc.-Appraisals
Taylor & Martin, Inc.-Auctioneers

TECHNICAL ANALYSIS, INC.
4757 California Ave SW, Seattle, WA 98116-4499
Tel.: (206) 938-0570
Fax: (206) 938-1307
Toll Free: (800) 832-4642
E-Mail: mail@traders.com
Web Site: www.traders.com

E-Mail for Key Personnel:
Creative Dir.: cmorrison@traders.com
Production Mgr.: kmoore@traders.com

Employees: 16
Year Founded: 1982

Agency Specializes In: Business Publications, Consumer Publications, Direct Response Marketing, Financial, Investor Relations, Magazines, Newspaper, Newspapers & Magazines, Print, Publishing, Travel & Tourism

Breakdown of Gross Billings by Media: D.M.: 30%; Internet Adv.: 25%; Mags.: 17%; Newsp.: 10%; Point of Sale: 1%; Print: 10%; Pub. Rels.: 1%; Sls. Promo.: 1%; Trade Shows: 5%

Christine Morrison *(Dir-Art)*
Linda Eades Gardner *(Mgr-Credit)*
Edward W. Schramm *(Mgr-Natl Sls-Classified & Web Sls)*

TECHNICAL PROMOTIONS
3003 Breezewood Ln, Neenah, WI 54957-0368
Tel.: (920) 722-2848
Fax: (800) 727-7516
Toll Free: (800) 558-5011
E-Mail: servicesales@jjkeller.com
Web Site: www.jjkeller.com

Employees: 4
Year Founded: 1983

Agency Specializes In: Business-To-Business, Consulting, Direct Response Marketing, Print, Public Relations, Telemarketing

Breakdown of Gross Billings by Media: Bus. Publs.: 10%; D.M.: 90%

Robert L. Keller *(Chm)*
Dana S. Gilman *(CFO)*

Accounts:
Aaron Hoste of Dohrn Transfer Company
Abbyland Foods, Inc.
J.J. Keller & Associates, Inc.
Jerry Smith of Service Electric Co.
Landstar
Photoland, Inc
Rock Road Companies, Inc
Roy Acton of Mission Petroleum Carriers, Inc.
Ryan Transportation
Service Electric Co.

TEXAS FARM PRODUCTS ADVERTISING
915 S Fredonia St, Nacogdoches, TX 75964
Tel.: (936) 564-3711
Fax: (936) 560-8375
Web Site: www.texasfarm.com

Employees: 10
Year Founded: 1970

Agency Specializes In: Agriculture, Pets

M.S. Wright, III *(Pres & CEO)*
Joe-Bob Stewart *(VP-Feed & Fertilizer)*
Marnee White *(Dir-Premium Brands & Mgr-Customer Svc)*
Ramona Keith *(Supvr-Adv)*

Accounts:
Lone Star Feeds; Nacogdoches, TX Feed, Fertilizer & Pet Food
Precise Pet Products; Nacogdoches, TX
Texas Farm Products Co.; Nacogdoches, TX Feed Fertilizer

THINKINGMAN.COM NEW MEDIA
1970 Hanalima St D102, Lihue, HI 96766-8928
Tel.: (808) 652-9243
Fax: (201) 622-9243
E-Mail: adam.prall@thinkingman.com
Web Site: www.thinkingman.com

Employees: 3

Agency Specializes In: Above-the-Line, Advertising, Advertising Specialties, Affiliate Marketing, Affluent Market, African-American Market, Agriculture, Alternative Advertising, Arts, Asian Market, Automotive, Aviation & Aerospace, Below-the-Line, Bilingual Market, Brand Development & Integration, Branded Entertainment, Broadcast, Business Publications, Business-To-Business, Cable T.V., Catalogs, Children's Market, Co-op Advertising, Collateral, College, Commercial Photography, Communications, Computers & Software, Consulting, Consumer Goods, Consumer Marketing, Consumer Publications, Content, Corporate Communications, Corporate Identity, Cosmetics, Crisis Communications, Custom Publishing, Customer Relationship Management, Digital/Interactive, Direct Response Marketing, Direct-to-Consumer, E-Commerce, Education, Electronic Media, Electronics, Email, Engineering, Entertainment, Environmental, Event Planning & Marketing, Exhibit/Trade Shows, Experience Design, Faith Based, Fashion/Apparel, Financial, Food Service, Game Integration, Gay & Lesbian Market, Government/Political, Graphic Design, Guerilla Marketing, Health Care Services, High Technology, Hispanic Market, Hospitality, Household Goods, Identity Marketing, In-Store Advertising, Industrial, Infomercials, Information Technology, Integrated Marketing, International, Internet/Web Design, Investor Relations, Legal Services, Leisure, Local Marketing, Logo & Package Design, Luxury Products, Magazines, Marine, Market Research, Media Buying Services, Media Planning, Media Relations, Media Training, Medical Products, Men's Market, Merchandising, Mobile Marketing, Multicultural, Multimedia, New Product Development, New Technologies, Newspaper, Newspapers & Magazines, Out-of-Home Media, Outdoor, Over-50 Market, Package Design, Paid Searches, Pets, Pharmaceutical, Planning & Consultation, Podcasting, Point of Purchase, Point of Sale, Print, Product Placement, Production, Production (Ad, Film, Broadcast), Production (Print), Promotions, Public Relations, Publicity/Promotions, Publishing, RSS (Really Simple Syndication), Radio, Real Estate, Recruitment, Regional, Restaurant, Retail, Sales Promotion, Search Engine Optimization, Seniors' Market, Social Marketing/Nonprofit, Social Media, South Asian Market, Sponsorship, Sports Market, Stakeholders, Strategic Planning/Research, Sweepstakes, Syndication, T.V., Technical Advertising, Teen Market, Telemarketing, Trade & Consumer Magazines, Transportation, Travel & Tourism, Tween Market, Urban Market, Viral/Buzz/Word of Mouth, Web (Banner Ads, Pop-ups, etc.), Women's Market, Yellow Pages Advertising

Approx. Annual Billings: $400,000

Breakdown of Gross Billings by Media: Consulting: 20%; E-Commerce: 70%; T.V.: 10%

Adam Prall *(Partner)*

Accounts:
Chaminade University; Honolulu, HI Chaminade University; 2000
Fox News; Los Angeles, CA Fox News, Fox Sports; 2006
Open Architecture Network; Sausalito, CA Architecture for Humanity; 2007
Oracle America, Inc.; Sausalito, CA The Open Architecture Network; 2007

TRACK DATA CORPORATION
95 Rockwell Pl, Brooklyn, NY 11217
Tel.: (718) 522-7373
Fax: (718) 260-4375
Web Site: www.trackdata.com

Employees: 4
Year Founded: 1981

Agency Specializes In: Financial

Approx. Annual Billings: $1,500,000

Breakdown of Gross Billings by Media: Cable T.V.: 30%; Collateral: 10%; Consumer Publs.: 20%; Exhibits/Trade Shows: 10%; Mags.: 5%; Newsp. & Mags.: 10%; Newsp.: 15%

Barry Hertz *(Founder & CTO)*
Marty Kaye *(CEO & CFO)*
Roger Karam *(Sr VP)*
Ray Foreman *(Gen Mgr-European Ops)*
Barbara Karol *(Dir-HR)*
Brian O'Reilly *(Dir-IT Ops)*
Sharon Rajmoolie *(Mgr-Billing)*

Accounts:
Track Data NewsWare, TrackTrade, myTrack, myTrack Pro, proTrack

TRACO ADVERTISING, INC.
6355 E Skelly Dr, Tulsa, OK 74135
Mailing Address:
PO Box 3286, Tulsa, OK 74101-3286
Tel.: (918) 591-2113
Fax: (918) 591-2193
Web Site: www.oralroberts.com

E-Mail for Key Personnel:
President: wrichardson@oru.edu

Employees: 160
Year Founded: 1969

Agency Specializes In: Broadcast, Faith Based

Michael Bernard *(Pres)*
Helen Montgomery *(Office Mgr)*

Accounts:
Oral Roberts Evangelistic Association, Inc.; Tulsa, OK Religious Program

TRIBUNE DIRECT MARKETING, INC.
505 NW Ave, Northlake, IL 60164-1662
Tel.: (708) 836-2700
Fax: (708) 836-0605
Toll Free: (800) 545-9657
E-Mail: info@tribunedirect.com
Web Site: www.tribunedirect.com

Employees: 360

Agency Specializes In: Advertising

Lou Tazioli *(Pres & Gen Mgr)*
Jack Curtin *(Gen Mgr)*
Erik Haugen *(Dir-Integrated Mktg)*
Barbara Hepburn *(Sr Acct Mgr)*
Chad Spreen *(Sr Acct Mgr)*
Bob Wetch *(Sr Acct Mgr)*

House Agencies

Larry Gresham *(Mgr-LetterShop Ops)*
Todd Wendling *(Mgr-Sls)*

Accounts:
Tribune Co.

TRILION STUDIOS

659 N 1457 Rd, Lawrence, KS 66049
Tel.: (785) 841-5500
Fax: (419) 851-2293
E-Mail: hello@trilionstudios.com
Web Site: www.trilionstudios.com

Employees: 5
Year Founded: 2000

National Agency Associations: AAF

Agency Specializes In: Advertising, Branded Entertainment, Business-To-Business, Children's Market, Collateral, Corporate Communications, Corporate Identity, Digital/Interactive, Direct Response Marketing, Environmental, Event Planning & Marketing, Exhibit/Trade Shows, Fashion/Apparel, Graphic Design, Identity Marketing, Internet/Web Design, Logo & Package Design, Multimedia, Newspaper, Newspapers & Magazines, Package Design, Print, Retail, Sports Market

Approx. Annual Billings: $300,000

Breakdown of Gross Billings by Media: Graphic Design: 30%; Logo & Package Design: 20%; Worldwide Web Sites: 50%

Brian White *(Dir-Creative)*
Kevin D. Hendricks *(Writer-Creative)*
Amanda Nelson *(Sr Designer)*

TUFFY ADVERTISING

7150 Granite Cir, Toledo, OH 43617
Tel.: (419) 865-6900
Fax: (419) 865-7343
E-Mail: mail@tuffy.com
Web Site: www.tuffy.com

Employees: 35
Year Founded: 1970

Agency Specializes In: Automotive

Breakdown of Gross Billings by Media: Cable T.V.: 25%; D.M.: 30%; Newsp. & Mags.: 15%; Radio: 30%

Roger Hill *(Pres & CEO)*
Karen Vellequette *(CFO)*
Bob Bresler *(VP)*

Accounts:
Tuffy Associates Corp.; Toledo, OH

UNIFIED GROCERS INC.

5200 Sheila St, Commerce, CA 90040
Tel.: (323) 264-5200
Fax: (323) 264-0320
Toll Free: (800) 724-7762
E-Mail: stadheim@unifiedgrocers.com
Web Site: www.unifiedgrocers.com

Employees: 12

Agency Specializes In: Food Service

Joseph L. Falvey *(Pres-Market Centre)*
Steve Diederichs *(VP-Sls-Intl)*
JoAnn Murdock *(Exec Dir-Mktg)*
Terry Stadheim *(Dir-Retail Adv & Mktg)*
Debbie Esparza *(Mgr-Corp Brands)*
Maria Guido *(Mgr-Compensation)*
Kathie Bell *(Div Dir-HR)*

Accounts:
Unified Western Grocers; Los Angeles, CA

UNIVERSAL MUSIC GROUP ADVERTISING & MEDIA SERVICES

825 8th Ave, New York, NY 10019-7416
Tel.: (212) 333-8000
Fax: (877) 804-2230
Web Site: www.universalmusic.com/

Employees: 15
Year Founded: 1912

Approx. Annual Billings: $30,000,000

Lucian Grainge *(Chm & CEO)*
Gustavo Lopez *(Exec VP & Gen Mgr)*
Mike Tunnicliffe *(Exec VP-Bus Dev & Partnerships-USA)*
Chris Monaco *(Sr VP-Strategic Mktg & Brand Dev)*
Alisa Ben *(VP-Insights)*
Chris Horton *(VP-Advanced Tech)*
Kim Gilbert *(Sr Dir-Admin Svcs)*
Christopher Chen *(Sr Mgr-UMG Insights)*
Lauren Bleakney *(Project Mgr-Digital)*
Stephanie Gomez *(Analyst-Social Media, Strategic Insights & Analytics)*

Accounts:
Island/Def Jam
MCA Nashville
Mercury Nashville
The Verve Group/GRP

U.S. RARE EARTHS, INC.

(Formerly Calypso Media Group)
5600 Tennyson Pkwy, Plano, TX 75024
Tel.: (972) 294-7116
Fax: (570) 368-7636
Web Site: www.usrareearths.com/

Employees: 3

Agency Specializes In: Direct-to-Consumer, Internet/Web Design, Outdoor, Print, Production (Ad, Film, Broadcast), Radio, T.V.

Kevin Cassidy *(CEO)*
Scott Chrimes *(CFO)*

Accounts:
Trane

VERMONT SKI AREA ASSOCIATION

26 State St, Montpelier, VT 05601
Tel.: (802) 223-2439
Fax: (802) 229-6917
E-Mail: info@skivermont.com
Web Site: www.skivermont.com

Employees: 5
Year Founded: 1970

Agency Specializes In: Leisure, Travel & Tourism

Parker Riehle *(Pres)*
Kyle Lewis *(Mktg Dir)*
Sarah Wojcik *(Dir-Pub Affairs)*
Hilary Delross *(Mgr-Mktg)*

Accounts:
Long Trail Brewing Co.
Mountain Dew
Rossignol International
Vermont Ski Areas Association, Inc.; Montpelier, VT
Woodchuck Draft Cider

VILLAGE GREEN COMMUNICATIONS, INC.

30833 Northwestern Hwy Ste 300, Farmington Hills, MI 48334-2583
Tel.: (248) 851-9600
Fax: (248) 851-6161
E-Mail: webmaster@villagegreen.com
Web Site: www.villagegreen.com

E-Mail for Key Personnel:
President: JHoltzman@villagegreen.com

Employees: 50
Year Founded: 1984

Agency Specializes In: Advertising, Advertising Specialties, Brand Development & Integration, Collateral, Communications, Corporate Identity, Electronic Media, Graphic Design, Internet/Web Design, Logo & Package Design, Public Relations, Real Estate

Approx. Annual Billings: $3,000,000

Breakdown of Gross Billings by Media: Bus. Publs.: $10,000; Collateral: $605,000; D.M.: $50,000; Mags.: $1,200,000; Newsp.: $1,065,000; Transit: $10,000; Yellow Page Adv.: $60,000

Jonathan Holtzman *(CEO)*

Accounts:
Village Green Communications
Village Green Construction, Inc.
Village Green Management
Village Green Residential Properties, Inc. Residential Properties

VINUM INC.

1111 Cedar Swamp Rd, Glen Head, NY 11545-2109
Tel.: (516) 626-9200
Fax: (516) 626-9218
Web Site: www.vinumcomm.com

Employees: 5
Year Founded: 1980

Agency Specializes In: Advertising, Public Relations

Neill Trimble *(VP-Adv)*
Lars Leicht *(Dir)*
Gerard Hayes *(Acct Exec)*

WE MARKETING GROUP

Tower W1 Oriental Plz, 1 E Change An Ave Ste 1111, Beijing, China
Tel.: (86) 1085150588
Fax: (86) 1585180587
Web Site: www.wemarketinggroup.com

Year Founded: 2005

Agency Specializes In: Advertising, Brand Development & Integration, Communications, Consulting, Market Research, Media Buying Services, Media Planning, Public Relations, Retail

Viveca Chan *(Chm & CEO)*
Kenny Wong *(Partner & Mng Dir)*
Sam Chung *(Chief Creative Officer-China)*
Josh Li *(Mng Dir-Beijing)*
Helen Lo *(Head-Plng)*
Keith Chan *(Dir-Strategic Plng-Hong Kong)*

Accounts:
China Sunergy
Clinique
Dabao Cosmetics Cosmetic Brand
Diageo Alcoholic Beverage
Estee Lauder

Henkel
Infinitus
Lee Kum Kee Creative Campaigns, Digital, Social Media
Mercedes-Benz Automobile Manufacturer
MG
OSM
Panasonic Electronic Equipment
Roewe
The Switch
Syoss Strategic & Creative
TRW
Yanlord Real Estate Services

WESTAR ADVERTISING

2019 W SW Loop 323, Tyler, TX 75701
Tel.: (903) 561-6848
Web Site: www.westaradv.com

Terry Cooper *(Dir-Mktg & Media Planner)*

Accounts:
Cavender's

WHITE'S ADVERTISING AGENCY

1011 Pleasant Valley Rd, Sweet Home, OR 97386
Tel.: (541) 367-6121
Fax: (541) 367-6629
Toll Free: (800) 547-6911
E-Mail: mwise@whiteselectronics.com
Web Site: www.whiteselectronics.com

Employees: 135
Year Founded: 1950

Approx. Annual Billings: $950,000

Breakdown of Gross Billings by Media: Mags.: $237,500; T.V.: $712,500

Kenneth R. White *(Pres)*

THE WONDERFUL AGENCY

(Formerly Roll Global)
11444 W Olympic Blvd Ste 300, Los Angeles, CA 90064
Tel.: (310) 966-8600
Web Site: www.wonderful.com

Agency Specializes In: Advertising, Digital/Interactive, Outdoor, Print, Sponsorship, T.V.

Liz Hendry *(Sr VP & Exec Dir-Creative)*
Brien Grant *(Sr VP-Digital)*
Dave Churchill *(VP-Mdsg)*
Jasmine Hodari *(VP-Mktg-Paramount Farms & Paramount Citrus)*
Jason Fryer *(Dir-Design)*
Chelsea Lee *(Sr Mgr-Social Media Strategy)*
Mara Greensweig *(Mgr-Natl Television Buying)*
Wonji Choi *(Analyst-Digital Mktg)*

Accounts:
Wonderful Pistachios Campaign: "Get Crackin', America" Super Bowl 2014

YMT VACATIONS

(Formerly Jet Advertising)
100 N Sepulveda Blvd Ste 1700, El Segundo, CA 90245
Tel.: (310) 649-3820
Fax: (310) 649-2118
Toll Free: (800) 922-9000
E-Mail: info@ymtvacations.com
Web Site: www.ymtvacations.com

E-Mail for Key Personnel:
President: bprice@goymt.com

Year Founded: 1967

Agency Specializes In: Broadcast, Co-op Advertising, Consumer Publications, Direct-to-Consumer, E-Commerce, Email, Internet/Web Design, Leisure, Magazines, Newspaper, Newspapers & Magazines, Over-50 Market, Print, Radio, Seniors' Market, Travel & Tourism

Jerre Fuqua *(Pres)*
James Frost *(VP-Product, Plng & Dev)*
Marco Jahn *(VP-Ops & Guest Experience)*
Sam Hamedani *(Dir-Sls)*
Melanie Mueller *(Sr Mgr-Mktg)*
Katja Jahn *(Sr Product Mgr)*
Andrea Brzostowski *(Mgr-Mktg)*
Christiane Kano *(Analyst-Bus & Mktg)*
Sandra Lee *(Sr Accountant)*

Accounts:
YMT Vacations; Inglewood, CA Travel

INTERACTIVE AGENCIES

10TH DEGREE
1 Spectrum Pointe Ste 330, Lake Forest, CA 92630
Tel.: (949) 224-5600
E-Mail: contact@10thdegree.com
Web Site: www.10thdegree.com

Employees: 20

Agency Specializes In: Digital/Interactive, Mobile Marketing, Paid Searches, Search Engine Optimization, Social Media, Web (Banner Ads, Pop-ups, etc.)

Breakdown of Gross Billings by Media: D.M.: 25%; Internet Adv.: 30%; Logo & Package Design: 5%; Worldwide Web Sites: 40%

Rodney Ashton *(Dir-Media)*
Mitchell Duarte *(Dir-Creative)*
Kent Solomon *(Dir-Bus Dev)*
Evan Ross *(Media Planner)*
Alexis Pine *(Coord-Media)*

Accounts:
Advantage Rent A Car; 2007
Enterprise Car Sales
loanDepot Display, PPC, SEO; 2014
Mitsubishi Digital Electronics America; 2004
Trident University

2060 DIGITAL
2060 Reading Rd, Cincinnati, OH 45202
Tel.: (866) 344-2060
E-Mail: info@2060digital.com
Web Site: www.2060digital.com

Year Founded: 2012

Agency Specializes In: Digital/Interactive, Internet/Web Design, Search Engine Optimization, Social Media

John Gallagher *(VP)*
Patrick Butler *(Strategist-Digital Mktg)*

Accounts:
New-World Wide Wolf

214 INTERACTIVE
4514 Travis St Ste 240, Dallas, TX 75205
Tel.: (214) 495-1924
Web Site: www.214interactive.com

Year Founded: 2013

Agency Specializes In: Advertising, Content, Digital/Interactive, Internet/Web Design, Search Engine Optimization, Social Media

Terrence Gordon *(Co-Founder & CEO)*
Dave Hanson *(Co-Founder & COO)*
Drew Pickard *(VP-Sls)*

Accounts:
EHI Health Care
State & Allen Kitchen+Bar

24/7 MEDIA, INC.
(Merged with Xaxis to Form Xaxis, LLC)

2N1 MEDIA
PO Box 9214, Naperville, IL 60567
Tel.: (630) 935-0721
E-Mail: info@2n1media.com
Web Site: www.2n1media.com

Agency Specializes In: Collateral, Digital/Interactive, Graphic Design, Internet/Web Design, Logo & Package Design, Social Media

Peter Quinn *(Pres)*
Young Shin *(Mng Partner)*
Paul Devitt *(Mng Partner)*
John Langan *(Mgr-Social Media)*

Accounts:
Change A Life Scholarship Fund
Northwest Suburban Foot & Ankle Clinic
St. Mary Catholic School
StemCutis LLC

312 DIGITAL
1193 Souders Ave, Elburn, IL 60119
Tel.: (312) 448-6400
Web Site: www.312digital.com

Year Founded: 2010

Agency Specializes In: Content, Digital/Interactive, Email, Internet/Web Design, Search Engine Optimization

Sean McGinnis *(Strategist-Digital)*

Accounts:
Haden Law Office

3EIGHTEEN MEDIA
835 Oglethorpe Ave SW 407, Atlanta, GA 30310
Tel.: (404) 425-9890
Web Site: www.3eighteenmedia.com

Year Founded: 2008

Agency Specializes In: Arts, Computers & Software, Consulting, Content, Digital/Interactive, Education, Electronics, Entertainment, Government/Political, Graphic Design, Health Care Services, Identity Marketing, Internet/Web Design, Leisure, Logo & Package Design, New Technologies, Restaurant, Social Marketing/Nonprofit, Strategic Planning/Research, Travel & Tourism, Web (Banner Ads, Pop-ups, etc.)

Maurice Cherry *(Principal-Creative)*

Accounts:
Grady Health Foundation Consulting, Web Design, Web Development; 2010

4HILTON
9115 Judicial Drive #4510, San Diego, CA 92122
Tel.: (858) 356-7658
Web Site: www.4hilton.com/

Employees: 5
Year Founded: 2008

Agency Specializes In: Digital/Interactive

Hilton Sher *(CEO)*

Accounts:
Katlav Winery; 2009

7TH & WIT
530 7th Ave, New York, NY 10005
Tel.: (212) 658-1277
E-Mail: hello@seventhandwit.com
Web Site: www.seventhandwit.com

Agency Specializes In: Content, Digital/Interactive, Social Media

Callan Green *(Dir-Digital Strategy)*

Accounts:
Colorescience Mineral Makeup
Gurneys Montauk Resort & Spa
Triumph Hotels

87AM
42 W 39th St 4th Fl, New York, NY 10018
Tel.: (646) 626-5555
E-Mail: info@87am.com
Web Site: www.87am.com

Year Founded: 2010

Agency Specializes In: Advertising, Brand Development & Integration, Broadcast, Digital/Interactive, Event Planning & Marketing, Outdoor, Print, Public Relations, Radio, Strategic Planning/Research

Adam Cunningham *(CEO)*
Erin Rech *(Sr VP)*
Hetal Patel *(Sr Acct Dir-Accts & Strategy)*
Shai Goller *(Creative Dir)*
Ariana Sverdlik *(Dir-Social Media)*
Trevor Sponseller *(Assoc Dir-Data & Analytics)*
Jake Hirzel *(Acct Mgr)*
Danielle Marcello *(Sr Strategist-Social Media)*

Accounts:
History
N The Queen of Paris

99MEDIALAB
115 Onville Road, Suite 201, Stafford, VA 22556
Tel.: (703) 563-2571
E-Mail: marlenburm@gmail.com
Web Site: www.99medialab.com/

Agency Specializes In: Internet/Web Design, Logo & Package Design, Mobile Marketing, Print, Search Engine Optimization

Piyush Mangukiya *(Mng Partner)*

ACHTUNG
Prins Hendrikkade 20-11, 1012 Amsterdam, Netherlands
Tel.: (31) 206232696
E-Mail: office@achtung.nl
Web Site: www.achtung.nl

Agency Specializes In: Digital/Interactive, Graphic Design, Multimedia

Daniel Sytsma *(Partner & Dir-Creative)*
Dick Buschman *(Partner)*
Mervyn Ten Dam *(Creative Dir)*
Christian Mezofi *(Dir-Design)*
Pascal Rotteveel *(Dir-Creative)*
Elke Ter Bogt *(Acct Mgr)*
Emily Kroes *(Acct Mgr)*
Joost Huver *(Designer)*
Roy Van Dijk *(Sr Designer-Interactive)*

Accounts:
Bavaria Campaign: "Personal Beer Trainer", Tour & Travel Agency Services
Chocomel Chocolate Milk Products
EBay Advertising, Media Buying, Media Planning
Eneco
Komplett.no Campaign: "Revenge of the Nerds"
O'Neill Wetsuits, Drysuits, Sports Clothing Mfr
Sire Social Services
Stop AIDS Now! Campaign: "Staring Is Caring"
Suitsupply Entertainment Services
Suntory Holdings Limited Campaign: "Shake Things Up"
Uncommon
Vodafone Campaign: "FirstConcert", Campaign: "Grand Prix Van Roggel"
Volkswagen Group of America, Inc. Campaign: "Fanwagen", Campaign: "Linkeduit", New Car Dealers, Volkswagen GTI Bannerbahn
Waternet Campaign: "Peeing Contest"

ACQUITY GROUP, LLC
500 W Madison St Ste 2200, Chicago, IL 60661
Tel.: (312) 427-2470
Fax: (312) 427-2471
Web Site: www.acquitygroup.com

Employees: 300
Year Founded: 2001

Agency Specializes In: Brand Development & Integration, Digital/Interactive

Revenue: $106,655,000

Jay Dettling *(Pres-Acquity Group)*
Jim Newman *(Exec VP-HR)*
Karen Jackson *(Sr VP-HR)*
Mark Joseph *(Sr VP)*
Scott Lutzow *(Dir-Front End Dev)*

Accounts:
Allstate Insurance Campaign: "Teen Driver"
Argo Tea, Inc. Digital Marketing, In-Store, Online, SEM
Cycle Gear Digital Marketing, Serach Engine Marketing
M&M's

ADAGIO
555 California St Ste 4925, San Francisco, CA 94104
Tel.: (415) 659-1538
E-Mail: info@adagioagency.com
Web Site: www.adagioagency.com

Employees: 64
Year Founded: 2011

Agency Specializes In: Affiliate Marketing, Digital/Interactive, Mobile Marketing, Social Media, Viral/Buzz/Word of Mouth, Web (Banner Ads, Pop-ups, etc.)

Approx. Annual Billings: $5,000,000

Lucas Decuypere *(Founder & CEO)*

Accounts:
Bayer Aspirin; 2011
Johnson & Johnson Janssen; 2013
Right Brain Bhaalu; 2013

ADPEARANCE INC.
1634 SW Alder, Portland, OR 97205
Tel.: (503) 961-7597
E-Mail: info@adpearance.com
Web Site: www.adpearance.com

Agency Specializes In: Advertising, Brand Development & Integration, Digital/Interactive, Internet/Web Design, Logo & Package Design, Paid Searches, Public Relations, Search Engine Optimization, Social Media

Alison Milleman *(Dir-Client Svcs)*

Accounts:
New-Kia

ADPERIO
2000 S Colorado Blvd Tower 1 Ste 7000, Denver, CO 80222
Tel.: (303) 985-2700
Fax: (303) 985-0328
E-Mail: info@adperio.com
Web Site: www.adperio.com

Employees: 30
Year Founded: 1994

Agency Specializes In: Affiliate Marketing, Digital/Interactive, Direct Response Marketing, Email, Mobile Marketing, Paid Searches, Social Media, Web (Banner Ads, Pop-ups, etc.)

Approx. Annual Billings: $30,000,000

Jill Fletcher *(COO)*
Tracey Mcdonald *(Dir-HR)*
Becky Morang *(Dir-Fin)*
Jennifer Schackel *(Dir-Publr Strategy)*
Chad Helgerson *(Mgr-Affiliate)*
Matt Curtis *(Acct Exec)*
Jason Van Houten *(Acct Exec)*
Alexis Junker *(Media Buyer)*

ADSMART
1666 Ramona St Ste A, Grover Beach, CA 93433
Tel.: (805) 588-2809
E-Mail: sbridge@adsmartnow.com
Web Site: www.adsmartnow.com

Employees: 12
Year Founded: 2013

Agency Specializes In: Digital/Interactive, Mobile Marketing, Paid Searches, Web (Banner Ads, Pop-ups, etc.)

Approx. Annual Billings: $1,500,000

Stephen Bronte *(Specialist-Mktg & Strategy)*

Accounts:
California Fresh Franchise System; 2013

ADSVALUE
16810 E. Ave of the Fountains Ste 240, Fountain Hills, AZ 85268
Tel.: (480) 836-7828
Fax: (480) 733-7828
E-Mail: avinfo@adsvalue.com
Web Site: www.adsvalue.com

Employees: 1
Year Founded: 2007

Approx. Annual Billings: $150,000

Robert Bleau *(Founder & Pres)*

ADVERTISEMINT
604 Arizona Ave, Santa Monica, CA 90401
Tel.: (818) 919-9611
Web Site: www.advertisemint.com

Year Founded: 2014

Agency Specializes In: Advertising, Advertising Specialties, Media Buying Services, Paid Searches, Social Marketing/Nonprofit, Social Media, Viral/Buzz/Word of Mouth

Brian Meert *(CEO)*

Accounts:
Jenson USA; 2014

AKQA, INC.
360 3rd St 5th Fl, San Francisco, CA 94107
Tel.: (415) 645-9400
Fax: (415) 645-9420
E-Mail: info@akqa.com
Web Site: www.akqa.com

E-Mail for Key Personnel:
Media Dir.: media@akqa.com

Employees: 440
Year Founded: 1990

Agency Specializes In: Consumer Marketing, Digital/Interactive, E-Commerce, Internet/Web Design, Sponsorship

Revenue: $140,000,000

Tom Bedecarre *(Co-Founder & Chm)*
Lester Feintuck *(CFO)*
Scott Symonds *(Mng Dir-Media)*
Brian Skahan *(Gen Mgr-Portland)*
Sebastian Gunnewig *(Exec Dir-Strategy & UX)*
Helen Lin *(Grp Dir-Media)*
Miranda Molen *(Grp Dir-Media)*
Allison Gabrys *(Sr Acct Dir)*
Brett Andreson *(Acct Dir)*
Chris Chopek *(Mgmt Supvr)*
Payam Cherchian *(Dir-Analytics & Data Science)*
Brian Kress *(Dir-Strategy)*
Diego Machado *(Dir-Creative-Sao Paulo)*
Meg O'Brien *(Dir-Social Strategy)*
Akira Takahashi *(Dir-Creative)*
Hugo Veiga *(Dir-Creative-Sao Paulo Office)*
Eamonn Dixon *(Assoc Dir-Creative)*
Dan Peters *(Assoc Dir-Creative)*
Rana Cattaneo *(Acct Supvr)*
Christine Elias *(Acct Supvr)*
Priya Vaswani *(Acct Supvr)*
Adam Chinchiolo *(Supvr-Mgmt)*
Lisa Ferragano *(Supvr)*
Vivien Ku *(Supvr-Digital Media)*
Heather Stanley *(Supvr-Media)*
Merima Heric *(Sr Acct Exec)*
Alex Rolfes *(Sr Acct Exec)*
Mal Gretz *(Acct Exec)*
Nik Poon *(Strategist)*
Vanessa Stark *(Acct Exec-Search)*
Emily Bordages *(Media Planner)*
Claire Daugherty *(Media Planner)*
Crystal Yu *(Copywriter)*
Garrett Mitchell *(Assoc Media Planner)*
Allen Stern *(Grp Media Dir)*
Wesley Wu *(Sr Media Planner)*

Accounts:
Air France-KLM
Anheuser-Busch InBev Bud Light, Bud Light Birthday, Bud Light Button, Buds for Buds, Creative, Digital Innovation Agency of Record, Digital Marketing, Stella Artois
Audi of America (US Digital Agency of Record) Audi A6, AudiUSA.com, Campaign: "Autonomous Office Chair", Campaign: "Road Frustration Index", Content Development, Digital, Online Marketing
Bethesda
The Clorox Company Digital Media Buying
Delta Airlines (Global Digital Agency of Record) Dot-Com, Mobile
eBay Inc.
Gap
Hermes

Levi Strauss & Co Digital Content
Nike Campaign: "Make It Count", Campaign: "Music Runs Ellie", Digital, Jordan, Nike+, Running, Shoes, Sister One, Sportswear; 1999
Nissan
NVIDIA Corporation
Old Navy Social
Tommy Hilfiger
Verizon Wireless Campaign: "Inspire Her Mind", Customer Relationship Management, Digital, Ecommerce, Makers, Retail, Social Media
Visa USA; San Francisco, CA Campaign: "The Samba of the World", Credit Cards, Digital, Visa Signature; 2001
Volvo (Lead Digital Agency) Analytics, Content, Social Media, Strategy
World Wildlife Fund WWF Together

Branches

AKQA, Inc.
1 Saint John's Ln, London, EC1M 4BL United Kingdom
Tel.: (44) 207 780 4786
Fax: (44) 207 780 4787
E-Mail: info@akqa.com
Web Site: www.akqa.com

Employees: 300

Agency Specializes In: Brand Development & Integration, Consulting, Consumer Marketing, Electronic Media, Internet/Web Design, Publicity/Promotions

Ben Jones *(CTO)*
Geoff Northcott *(Mng Dir-Intl)*
Ron Peterson *(Gen Mgr)*
Duan Evans *(Exec Dir-Creative-Intl)*
Ross Winterflood *(Sr Acct Dir)*
Toby Barnes *(Dir-Product Strategy)*
Laura Sordi *(Assoc Dir-Creative)*
Nicholas Camacho *(Sr Acct Mgr)*
Tim Smith *(Sr Engr-QA)*
Ian Wharton *(Grp Creative Dir)*

Accounts:
Beiersdorf (Agency of Record) Digital, Elastoplast, Eucerin, Nivea, Nivea Men
EDF Energy Digital Advertising
Levis
NIKE, Inc. "House of Mamba", Campaign: "Makeitcount", Campaign: "Music Runs Ellie", Campaign: "Nike + FuelStation", Nike Run, Nike Training Club, Sports Brand
Oreo Campaign: "Lick for it"
United States Postal Service
Vodafone

AKQA, Inc.
Rm B201-203 Bldg 2 Park 2 Space, 169 Meng Zi Rd, Shanghai, 200023 China
Tel.: (86) 21 6124 8198
Fax: (86) 21 6124 8199
E-Mail: info@akqa.com
Web Site: www.akqa.com

Employees: 30

Agency Specializes In: E-Commerce

Sophia Jiang *(Sr Acct Dir)*
Brenda Mou *(Sr Acct Dir)*
Aijean Cheah *(Grp Acct Dir)*
Leslie Cheng *(Acct Dir)*
Ying Chang *(Assoc Dir-Creative)*
Chloe Yu *(Acct Mgr)*
Michael Donohus *(Client Partner-NIKE)*
Joe Cai *(Mgr-Production)*
Kate Lu *(Assoc Acct Dir)*
Vivian Zhang *(Assoc Program Dir)*

Accounts:
Nike "House of Mamba", LED Basketball Court, Nike Cricket, Nike Rise

AKQA, Inc.
3299 K St NW 5th Fl, Washington, DC 20007
Tel.: (202) 551-9900
Fax: (202) 337-2573
E-Mail: info@akqa.com
Web Site: www.akqa.com

Employees: 55
Year Founded: 1995

Agency Specializes In: Brand Development & Integration, Consulting, Consumer Marketing, Electronic Media, Internet/Web Design, Publicity/Promotions, Sponsorship

Erik Rogstad *(Mng Dir)*
Brendan Dibona *(Exec Dir-Creative)*
Jefferson Liu *(Dir-Creative)*
Sara Thompson *(Acct Mgr)*
Gina Schmidt *(Sr Acct Exec)*
Adam Kauder *(Strategist-Content)*
Amy Shen *(Media Planner)*

Accounts:
Delta

AKQA, Inc.
114 Fifth Ave, New York, NY 10011
Tel.: (212) 989-2572
Fax: (212) 989-2363
Web Site: www.akqa.com

Employees: 91

Agency Specializes In: Advertising, Sponsorship

Scott Symonds *(Mng Dir-Media)*
Giles McCormack *(Gen Mgr)*
Renato Zandona *(Sr Dir-Art)*
Justin Micklish *(Sr Acct Dir)*
Elizabeth Martin *(Grp Acct Dir)*
Georgina Forster *(Client Svcs Dir)*
Charlin Polanco *(Acct Dir)*
Alistair Schoonmaker *(Acct Dir)*
Warren Kinney *(Mgmt Supvr)*
Leandro Bordoni *(Dir-Art)*
Katrina Cabrera *(Dir-PR & Mktg)*
Brian Kress *(Dir-Strategy)*
Kim Laama *(Dir-User Experience)*
Chris Polychronopoulos *(Dir-Creative)*
Felicia Zhang *(Dir-Strategy)*
Kevin DeStefan *(Assoc Dir-Strategy)*
Cesar Munoz *(Sr Mgr-Technical)*
Alexandria Thomas *(Acct Supvr)*
Bridget Schowalter *(Assoc Media Planner)*

Accounts:
Bethesda Softworks
Budweiser
Future Lions
New-Levi's
Time Warner Inc.

AKQA, Inc.
1120 NW Couch St, Portland, OR 97209
Tel.: (503) 820-4300
E-Mail: info@akqa.com
Web Site: www.akqa.com

Jon Reiling *(Grp Dir-Creative)*
Amanda Sims Dwyer *(Acct Dir)*
Ginny Golden *(Dir-Creative)*
Whitney Jenkins *(Dir-Creative)*
Tommy Le Roux *(Dir-Creative)*
Sean Davis *(Designer)*
Docia Nartey-Koram *(Sr Recruiter)*

Accounts:
NIKE, Inc. Campaign: "Your Year"
Volkswagen Group

AMOBEE, INC.
100 Marine Pkwy Ste 575, Redwood City, CA 94065-5172
Tel.: (650) 802-8871
Fax: (650) 802-8951
Web Site: www.amobee.com

Agency Specializes In: Advertising, Digital/Interactive, Mobile Marketing, Social Media

Kim Reed Perell *(Pres)*
Mark Strecker *(CEO)*
Nick Isacke *(Chief People Officer)*
Assaf Henkin *(Sr VP-Brand Intelligence Solutions)*
Raj Gill *(VP-Automotive)*
Greg Castro *(Sr Dir-Bus Dev & Ops)*
Wes Kashiwagi *(Sr Dir-Digital Mktg)*
Patrick Welty *(Sr Dir-Strategic Partnerships)*
Yehonatan Koenig *(Dir-Product-3D)*
Devina Hart *(Sr Mgr-Publr Solutions)*
Tanya NgoAd *(Mgr-Exchange Ops-Mediation & RTB)*
Savannah Westover *(Sr Media Buyer)*

Accounts:
AppsFuel
DSNR Media Group
Globe
Nokia Canada Corporation Lumia 800
Optus
SingTel
Telkomsel

Branches

Amobee
(Formerly Adconion Media Inc.)
1322 3rd St Promenade 2nd Level, Santa Monica, CA 90401
(See Separate Listing)

Branches

Amobee
(Formerly Adconion Media Group)
26 W 17th St 9th Fl, New York, NY 10011
Tel.: (646) 556-7750
Fax: (917) 591-2828
Web Site: amobee.com

Year Founded: 2005

Agency Specializes In: Advertising, Branded Entertainment, Entertainment

T. Tyler Moebius *(Founder & CEO)*
Nathan Jokinen *(VP-Strategic Dev)*
Laura Tormey *(Dir-Sls)*
Alison Leung *(Sr Acct Mgr)*
Samantha Hosler *(Strategist-Sls)*

Accounts:
American Express Credit Card Services
Bank of America Corporation Banking Services
Capital One Banking Services
FRITO-LAY NORTH AMERICA, INC. Snacks Products Distr
Lowe's Companies, Inc. Home Appliances Store
Novartis AG Medical Care
StarCom Telecommunication Services

Amobee
(Formerly Adconion Media Inc.)
20 Maud St., Suite 305, Toronto, ON MV5 2M5 Canada

Tel.: (416) 637-4658
Fax: (416) 981-3951
Web Site: amobee.com

T. Tyler Moebius *(Founder & CEO)*

Amobee
(Formerly Adconion Pty. Ltd.)
Level 9 28 Freshwater Pl, Southbank, VIC 3006 Australia
Tel.: (61) 386212300
Fax: (61) 294754324
Web Site: www.amobee.com

Liam Walsh *(Mng Dir)*

Accounts:
Bluekai

ANNALECT
195 Broadway 19th Fl, New York, NY 10007
Tel.: (212) 590-7667
Web Site: www.annalect.com

National Agency Associations: 4A's

Agency Specializes In: Consulting, Digital/Interactive, Strategic Planning/Research

Scott Hagedorn *(CEO)*
Steve Tobengauz *(CFO)*
Erin Matts *(CMO)*
Charles Butler *(CTO)*
Matt Simpson *(Mng Dir-EMEA)*
Derek Kan *(Dir-Product Mgmt)*
Pamela Marsh *(Dir-Res & Insights)*
Jed Meyer *(Dir-Research & Analytics-Global)*
Jay Rubin *(Dir-Delivery Mgmt)*
Stephanie Fields *(Sr Mgr-Mktg)*
Loren Grossman *(Chief Experience Officer)*
Anna Nicanorova *(Data Scientist)*

APPETIZER MOBILE LLC
115 W 45th St Ste 501, New York, NY 10036
Tel.: (212) 613-1600
E-Mail: contact@appetizermobile.com
Web Site: www.appetizermobile.com

Agency Specializes In: Advertising, Media Buying Services, Search Engine Optimization, Social Media

Jordan Edelson *(Founder & CEO)*
Ian Deschler *(Chief Comm Officer)*

Accounts:
New-Chic Sketch

APPLOVIN CORPORATION
849 High St, Palo Alto, CA 94301
Tel.: (415) 710-5305
E-Mail: info@applovin.com
Web Site: applovin.com

Employees: 70

Agency Specializes In: Digital/Interactive, Media Buying Services, Mobile Marketing

Adam Foroughi *(Co-Founder & CEO)*
John Krystynak *(Co-Founder & CTO)*
Jim Jones *(Sr VP-Sls)*
Katie Jansen *(VP-Mktg)*
Andrew Karam *(VP-Bus Ops)*
Mark Rosner *(Chief Publishing Officer)*

Accounts:
eBay
GREE
Groupon
Hotels.com
OpenTable
Spotify
Zynga

AREA 17
99 Richardson St 2nd Fl, Brooklyn, NY 11211
Tel.: (646) 277-7117
Web Site: www.area17.com

Year Founded: 2003

Agency Specializes In: Content, Corporate Identity, Digital/Interactive, E-Commerce, Experience Design, Publishing, Social Media, Strategic Planning/Research, Technical Advertising

Kemp Attwood *(Partner & Dir-Creative)*
Miguel Buckenmeyer *(Sr Dir-Interactive Art)*
Nikhil Mitter *(Dir-Creative)*
Dina Murphy *(Dir-Production-Global)*
Jeremy Heno *(Designer-User Experience-Info Architecture)*

Accounts:
AdAge.com
Facebook
International Academy of Digital Arts and Sciences Webby Awards People's Voice Application

ATAK INTERACTIVE INC.
1615 Westwood Blvd Ste 206, Los Angeles, CA 90024
Tel.: (855) 472-1892
E-Mail: info@atakinteractive.com
Web Site: www.atakinteractive.com

Year Founded: 2005

Agency Specializes In: Brand Development & Integration, Content, Digital/Interactive, Email, Graphic Design, Internet/Web Design, Print, Search Engine Optimization, Social Media

Josh Goodman *(Co-Founder & CEO)*
David Ephraim *(Co-Founder & Exec VP)*
Austin LaRoche *(CMO & Exec VP)*
Shelly Ulaj *(Strategist-Social Media & Coord-Outreach)*
Milan Vranes *(Designer)*
Madison Guerriero *(Coord-Digital Mktg)*

Accounts:
We Rock the Spectrum Kids Gym

AVINOVA MEDIA GROUP
9088 S Ridgeline Blvd Ste 103, Highlands Ranch, CO 80129
Tel.: (844) 284-6682
E-Mail: info@avinova.com
Web Site: www.avinova.com

Agency Specializes In: Digital/Interactive, Email, Internet/Web Design, Search Engine Optimization, Social Media

Jeff Hunt *(Founder & CEO)*
Nathan Brandt *(Acct Mgr)*

Accounts:
New-Faithful Workouts

AXZM
2940 Commerce St, Dallas, TX 75226
Tel.: (214) 272-9109
E-Mail: info@axzm.com
Web Site: www.axzm.com

Agency Specializes In: Brand Development & Integration, Content, Digital/Interactive, Paid Searches, Print, Search Engine Optimization, Social Media

Ross Edman *(Designer)*

Accounts:
New-American Pregnancy Association

B-REEL
Tjarhovsgatan 4, 116 21 Stockholm, Sweden
Tel.: (46) 850524850
E-Mail: sthlm@b-reel.com
Web Site: www.b-reel.com

Agency Specializes In: Arts, Digital/Interactive, Internet/Web Design, Mobile Marketing, Web (Banner Ads, Pop-ups, etc.)

Jonas Hedegard *(Mng Dir & Exec Producer)*
Lins Karnes *(Mng Dir & Exec Producer)*
Michael McQuhae *(Mng Dir & Producer)*
Bryan Farhy *(Head-Sls & Exec Producer)*
Pelle Nilsson *(Exec Producer)*
Kief Davidson *(Dir-Comml)*
James Jenkins *(Dir-Client Svcs-Europe)*
Josh Miller *(Dir-Comml & Music Video)*

Accounts:
3Live Shop Telecommunication Services
Google Creative Labs Chrome Web Lab
Twentieth Century Fox The Book Thief

BAKERY
507 Calles St Ste 107, Austin, TX 78702
Tel.: (512) 813-0700
Web Site: www.bakery.agency

Employees: 18
Year Founded: 2010

Agency Specializes In: Above-the-Line, Advertising, Alternative Advertising, Automotive, Below-the-Line, Bilingual Market, Brand Development & Integration, College, Communications, Computers & Software, Consumer Publications, Content, Corporate Identity, Custom Publishing, Digital/Interactive, Direct Response Marketing, E-Commerce, Electronic Media, Electronics, Entertainment, Fashion/Apparel, Food Service, Guerilla Marketing, Hispanic Market, In-Store Advertising, Integrated Marketing, Internet/Web Design, Logo & Package Design, Media Planning, Men's Market, Mobile Marketing, Multicultural, Multimedia, New Product Development, Out-of-Home Media, Package Design, Paid Searches, Planning & Consultation, Point of Purchase, Point of Sale, Production, Production (Ad, Film, Broadcast), Restaurant, Retail, Search Engine Optimization, Social Media, Sports Market, Strategic Planning/Research, T.V., Teen Market, Transportation, Travel & Tourism, Viral/Buzz/Word of Mouth, Web (Banner Ads, Pop-ups, etc.)

Juan Carlo Carvajal *(COO)*
Micky Ogando *(Sr Dir-Creative)*

Accounts:
Avid Plate Arcade Midtown Kitchen Restaurants; 2013
Beef Products Incorporated; 2013
BeesFreeze LLC BeesFreeze Ice Cream; 2013
City of Corpus Christi Water CC Conservation App; 2013
Ehco; 2015
Goodwill Industries of Greater New York and Northern New Jersey, Inc.; 2011
HausVac Central Vacuum Systems; 2015
Moonshine Sweet Tea, LLC; 2010
Round Rock Honey LLC Goodbee's Honey, Round Rock Honey; 2010
Texas Department of Transportation (TexDOT) Don't Mess With Texas-Digital; 2014

Tim Doi Food; 2015
Trellistate; 2014
Tugg, Inc; 2012
Union Pacific Railroad; 2014

BEAM
226 Causeway Street, Boston, MA 2114
Tel.: (617) 523-0500
E-Mail: info@beamland.com
Web Site: www.beamland.com

Agency Specializes In: Advertising, Consulting, Customer Relationship Management, High Technology

Birch Norton *(Owner, Partner & Dir-Creative)*
Matt Stanton *(VP-Pub Affairs & Corp Social Responsibility)*
Jim Rich *(Exec Dir-Tech)*
Michelle Cater *(Sr Dir-Activation)*
Cory Brine *(Sr Producer-Digital)*
Jamie Rose *(Sr Brand Mgr)*
Jose Aniceto *(Mgr-Strategy)*
Janu Lakshmanan *(Mgr-Consumer & Market Insights-Global)*

Accounts:
athenahealth Health Care Services
Comcast Telecommunication Services
DWS Asset Management Operation
Living Proof Beauty Experts
Mini New Car Dealers
Puma Footwear Stores
Virgin Telecommunication Services

BEAM INTERACTIVE
24 School St, Boston, MA 02108
Tel.: (617) 523-0500
Fax: (617) 523-0501
E-Mail: info@beamland.com
Web Site: www.beamland.com

Agency Specializes In: Advertising, Brand Development & Integration, Digital/Interactive

Eric Snyder *(Owner, Partner & Pres)*
Birch Norton *(Owner, Partner & Dir-Creative)*
Dave Batista *(Partner & Chief Creative Officer)*
Jim Rich *(Partner & Exec Dir-Tech & Delivery)*
Sebastian Gard *(Sr VP-Data Strategy)*
Cory Brine *(Sr Producer-Digital)*
Hanna Adams *(Assoc Dir-Acct Mgmt)*
Jose Aniceto *(Mgr-Strategy)*

BENDER8
6304 N Monroe Ave, Kansas City, MO 64119
Tel.: (816) 516-8252
Web Site: bender8.com

Employees: 5
Year Founded: 2013

Agency Specializes In: Affluent Market, Alternative Advertising, Consumer Marketing, Electronic Media, Email, Guerilla Marketing, High Technology, International, Luxury Products, Men's Market, Mobile Marketing, Multimedia, Paid Searches, Print, Product Placement, Production, Search Engine Optimization, Teen Market, Viral/Buzz/Word of Mouth, Web (Banner Ads, Pop-ups, etc.), Women's Market

Approx. Annual Billings: $120,000

Brandon Bender *(Dir)*

Accounts:
Mycart E-commerce Platform

BIG DROP INC.
111 John St, New York, NY 10038
Tel.: (212) 858-9580
Web Site: www.bigdropinc.com

Employees: 82
Year Founded: 2012

Agency Specializes In: Branded Entertainment, Digital/Interactive, Print

Approx. Annual Billings: $3,000,000

Garry Kanfer *(Pres)*

Accounts:
Isaac Katz Website

THE BIVINGS GROUP
(Name Changed to The Brick Factory)

BLITZ
1453 3rd St Promenade Ste 420, Santa Monica, CA 90401
Tel.: (310) 551-0200
Fax: (310) 551-0022
Web Site: www.blitzagency.com

Employees: 75
Year Founded: 2001

Agency Specializes In: Digital/Interactive, Game Integration, Sponsorship

Wilson Yin *(VP-Design & Dir-Experience)*
Laura Toneman *(VP-Bus Dev)*
Noah Gedrich *(Grp Dir-Tech)*
Andrea Gedrich *(Sr Dir-Ops & Fin)*
Andy Sullivan *(Grp Acct Dir)*
Sydney D'Oro *(Mgmt Supvr)*
Jonathan Nafarrete *(Dir-Content Mktg)*
Adam Venturella *(Dir-Tech)*
Kevin Wright *(Assoc Dir-Social Media)*
Josh Esguia *(Sr Creative Dir)*

Accounts:
CiCi's Pizza Campaign: "Better. Believe It", Creative
Dell
Disney
Dole
FX Networks
FX
Honda
IZZE Beverage Company Naked Juice
Kaiser Permanente
Mattel
Microsoft Campaign: "Gears of War 3 Website", X-Box
PepsiCo Naked Juice
Pioneer
TaylorMade

BLUE BEAR CREATIVE
1550 Platte St A444, Denver, CO 80202
Tel.: (719) 287-8945
E-Mail: info@bluebearcreative.co
Web Site: www.bluebearcreative.co

Agency Specializes In: Content, Digital/Interactive, Internet/Web Design, Media Relations, Public Relations, Search Engine Optimization, Social Media, Web (Banner Ads, Pop-ups, etc.)

Alex Oesterle *(Co-Founder & Dir-Ideation)*
Nate Amack *(Co-Founder)*
Annie Lake *(Co-Founder)*

Accounts:
Smashburger Social Media

BLUE FOUNTAIN MEDIA
102 Madison Ave, New York, NY 10016
Tel.: (212) 260-1978
E-Mail: brian@bluefountainmedia.com
Web Site: www.bluefountainmedia.com

Employees: 200
Year Founded: 2003

Agency Specializes In: Agriculture, Arts, Aviation & Aerospace, Business-To-Business, Children's Market, College, Computers & Software, Consumer Goods, Consumer Marketing, Content, Cosmetics, Customer Relationship Management, Digital/Interactive, E-Commerce, Education, Electronic Media, Electronics, Email, Engineering, Entertainment, Environmental, Fashion/Apparel, Food Service, Government/Political, Graphic Design, Health Care Services, High Technology, Hospitality, Household Goods, Industrial, Information Technology, International, Internet/Web Design, Investor Relations, Legal Services, Leisure, Luxury Products, Marine, Medical Products, Men's Market, Merchandising, Mobile Marketing, Multicultural, Multimedia, New Technologies, Over-50 Market, Pets , Pharmaceutical, Real Estate, Recruitment, Restaurant, Retail, Search Engine Optimization, Seniors' Market, Sports Market, Teen Market, Transportation, Travel & Tourism, Tween Market, Urban Market, Web (Banner Ads, Pop-ups, etc.), Women's Market

Approx. Annual Billings: $18,000,000

Yoni Ben-Yehuda *(CMO)*
Sara Cotillard *(Controller)*
Ismail Ajakaiye *(Acct Dir & Mgr-Digital Project)*
Vin Decrescenzo *(Acct Dir)*
Jane Durand *(Sr Mgr-Digital Mktg)*
Brian Pitre *(Mgr-Digital Mktg)*
Brittiany Cierra Taylor *(Mgr-Mktg)*
Rishe Groner *(Strategist-Digital Mktg)*
Andrew Haim *(Assoc Acct Dir)*
Austin Paley *(Corp Mgr-Mktg Comm)*
Paige Weiners *(Assoc Specialist-Corp Mktg)*

Accounts:
Allstate Insurance
AOL
Baldor Foods
Bowlmor AMF
Harper Collins
NFL
Procter & Gamble
Sharp
Tishman Speyer

BLUECADET INTERACTIVE
1011 N Hancock St Unit 101, Philadelphia, PA 19123
Tel.: (267) 639-9956
Fax: (267) 639-9958
E-Mail: info@bluecadet.com
Web Site: www.bluecadet.com

Year Founded: 2004

Agency Specializes In: Advertising, Digital/Interactive, Graphic Design, Multimedia

Troy Lachance *(Exec Dir-Creative)*
Liz Russell *(Producer-Interactive)*
Brad Baer *(Dir-Creative-Environments)*
Aaron Richardson *(Dir-Art)*
Rebecca Sherman *(Dir-Studio)*
Wyatt Glennon *(Designer)*
Nate Renninger *(Designer)*

Accounts:
American Revolution Center
Counterspill
The Herb Block Foundation

John P McNulty
National Park Service
University City District

BOOMBOX NETWORK
816 Ouilmette Ln, Wilmette, IL 60091
Tel.: (312) 985-7533
Web Site: www.Boomboxnetwork.com

Year Founded: 2012

Agency Specializes In: College, Consumer Marketing, Digital/Interactive, Direct-to-Consumer, Email, Over-50 Market, Podcasting, Seniors' Market, Social Media, Teen Market, Viral/Buzz/Word of Mouth, Women's Market

Chris Bradshaw *(Principal-Ops & Strategy)*
Anne-Marie Kovacs *(Principal-Mktg & Strategy)*

Accounts:
Alzheimers Prevention Initiative
ASHA.org
VTech

BOOYAH ADVERTISING
(Formerly The Booyah Agency)
11030 Circle Point Rd Ste 350, Westminster, CO 80020
Tel.: (303) 345-6600
Fax: (303) 345-6700
E-Mail: info@thebooyahadvertising.com
Web Site: www.booyahadvertising.com

Employees: 27

Agency Specializes In: Internet/Web Design, Sponsorship

Troy Lerner *(Pres-Booyah Online Adv)*
Dan Gallagher *(Exec VP)*
Kristopher Knight *(VP-Fin)*
Sarah Lockwood *(VP-Client Svcs)*
Jeff Stever *(VP-Bus Dev)*
Katie Holdsworth *(Acct Dir)*
Crystal Stewart *(Acct Dir)*
Chris Kuhn *(Dir-Creative)*
Sara Dorn *(Acct Mgr)*
Kelly Davis *(Supvr-Media)*
Vanessa Pence *(Acct Strategy Dir)*

Accounts:
Archstone
Dish Network
EarthLink
Electrolux
Integer
Lillian Vernon
Little Tikes
Manilla
Pharmaca
Qdoba
Quintess
thoughtequity.com
Vail

BOX CREATIVE
518 Broadway 5th Fl, Manhattan, NY 10012
Tel.: (212) 542-8880
E-Mail: hi@box.biz
Web Site: www.box.biz

Agency Specializes In: Brand Development & Integration, Digital/Interactive, Graphic Design, Internet/Web Design, Package Design, Print

Andrew Weitzel *(Founder & Creative Dir)*

Accounts:
Korilla BBQ

BOXCAR CREATIVE LLC
3720 Canton St, Dallas, TX 75226
Tel.: (469) 227-8537
Fax: (469) 533-0704
Web Site: www.boxcarcreative.com

Year Founded: 2000

Agency Specializes In: Communications, Digital/Interactive, Internet/Web Design, Search Engine Optimization, Social Media

Jim Kuenzer *(Head-Creative)*
Brian Fabian *(Dir-Tech)*
Mollie Milligan *(Dir-Creative Strategy)*
Kalee Heikenfeld *(Designer)*

Accounts:
3Forks

BRANDMOVERS
590 Means St Ste 250, Atlanta, GA 30318
Tel.: (888) 463-4933
Fax: (678) 718-1851
Web Site: www.brandmovers.com

National Agency Associations: 4A's

Agency Specializes In: Advertising, Content, Digital/Interactive, Promotions, Search Engine Optimization, Social Media, Sponsorship

Andrew Mitchell *(CEO)*
Hector Alberto Pages *(VP-Global Strategy)*
Al Skelton *(VP-Client Svcs)*
Eric Stewart *(VP-IT)*
Joe Bechely *(Acct Dir)*
Jeremy Spencer *(Client Svcs Dir)*
Troy Francois *(Dir-Art & Assoc Dir-Creative)*
David Harris *(Dir-Production)*
John Lyons *(Dir-Creative-Global)*
Ricky Reeves *(Dir-Brandmovers Europe Limited)*
Travis May *(Analyst-Bus Intelligence & Strategy)*

Accounts:
Marriott Hotels
Sports Authority
Wonka

BRAVE NEW MARKETS
10811 Red Run Blvd Ste 210, Owings Mills, MD 21117
Tel.: (410) 902-0801
E-Mail: mwaldeck@bravenewmarkets.com
Web Site: www.bravenewmarkets.com

Employees: 14
Year Founded: 1999

National Agency Associations: AMA

Agency Specializes In: Advertising, Agriculture, Aviation & Aerospace, Brand Development & Integration, Business-To-Business, Communications, Consulting, Corporate Communications, Corporate Identity, Digital/Interactive, E-Commerce, Electronic Media, Electronics, Email, Engineering, Graphic Design, High Technology, Industrial, Information Technology, Integrated Marketing, Internet/Web Design, Market Research, Mobile Marketing, New Technologies, Planning & Consultation, Production (Ad, Film, Broadcast), Public Relations, Search Engine Optimization, Social Media, Strategic Planning/Research, Web (Banner Ads, Pop-ups, etc.)

Marc Waldeck *(Founder & Chief Results Officer)*
Randy Mckee *(Sr VP-Client Svcs)*
Molly Merckel *(Assoc Dir-Client Results)*
Kristen Dorn *(Mgr-Creative & Sr Designer-Creative)*

Accounts:
Davis Calibration FastQuote; 2005
Envirobrite Solid-state Lighting; 2014
ezStorage Corporation; 2006
Maryland BuyMaryland Directory; 2014
Radiant Vision Systems Prometric, TrueTest; 2005
Textronix Tektronix Service Solutions; 2010
U.S. Mobile Kitchens; 2011
Zemax Optics Studio; 2010

THE BRICK FACTORY
(Formerly The Bivings Group)
1726 M St NW Ste 201, Washington, DC 20036
Tel.: (202) 499-4200
E-Mail: info@thebrickfactory.com
Web Site: www.thebrickfactory.com

Employees: 30
Year Founded: 1993

Agency Specializes In: Business-To-Business, Communications, Consulting, Digital/Interactive, E-Commerce, Electronic Media, Government/Political, Graphic Design, Health Care Services, High Technology, Industrial, Internet/Web Design, Mobile Marketing, Multimedia, New Technologies, Paid Searches, Search Engine Optimization, Social Media, Sponsorship, Viral/Buzz/Word of Mouth, Web (Banner Ads, Pop-ups, etc.)

Approx. Annual Billings: $2,900,000

Breakdown of Gross Billings by Media: Worldwide Web Sites: $2,900,000

Hannah Del Porto *(Chief Creative Officer)*
John Bafford *(VP-Programming Svcs)*
Chris Roane *(VP-Production)*
Gerry Blackwell *(Controller)*
Chuck Fitzpatrick *(Sr Dir-ImpactWatch Client Svcs)*
Dan Knisley *(Dir-Product Mgmt)*
Mike Lockard *(Sr Mgr-Production)*
Katie Fulton *(Strategist)*
Jei Park *(Sr Designer)*
Teddy Taylor *(Sr Designer)*

Accounts:
Arts+Labs
Critical Exposure
DC Action for Children
Entomological Society of America
Financial Services Roundtable
Mondelez International, Inc.
Forest Stewardship Council
AMD
Hewlett-Packard
American Forest & Paper Association
American Petroleum Institute
Edison Electric Institute

BRIDGE GLOBAL STRATEGIES LLC
(Acquired by Didit)

BROAD STREET CO
2905 San Gabriel St Ste 300, Austin, TX 78705
Tel.: (512) 275-6227
E-Mail: media@broadstreetco.com
Web Site: www.broadstreetco.com

Year Founded: 2007

Agency Specializes In: Advertising, Content, Digital/Interactive, Email, Search Engine Optimization, Social Media

Charlie D. Ray *(Pres)*

Accounts:
CORT Business Services Corporation (Digital Agency of Record)

BROOKLYN UNITED
20 Jay St Ste 402, Brooklyn, NY 11201
Tel.: (718) 254-9048
Web Site: www.brooklynunited.com

Agency Specializes In: Advertising, Brand Development & Integration, Digital/Interactive, Graphic Design, Internet/Web Design, Logo & Package Design, Search Engine Optimization, Social Media

Brian Lemond *(CEO)*

Accounts:
American Folk Art Museum
Feirstein Graduate School of Cinema
Knox College

CAPTURA GROUP
408 Nutmeg St, San Diego, CA 92103
Tel.: (619) 681-1856
Fax: (619) 681-1859
E-Mail: info@capturagroup.com
Web Site: www.capturagroup.com

Year Founded: 2001

Agency Specializes In: Content, Digital/Interactive, Email, Internet/Web Design, Media Buying Services, Media Planning, Social Media

Lee Vann *(Founder & CEO)*
Stacey Abreau *(Mng Dir)*

Accounts:
Knorr

CARNATION GROUP
(Acquired by & Name Changed to Possible)

CENTERLINE DIGITAL
509 W North St, Raleigh, NC 27603
Tel.: (919) 821-2921
Fax: (919) 821-2922
E-Mail: digitalmarketing@centerline.net
Web Site: www.centerline.net

Employees: 30
Year Founded: 1996

Agency Specializes In: Advertising, Brand Development & Integration, Communications, Computers & Software, Internet/Web Design, Local Marketing, Mobile Marketing, T.V., Technical Advertising

Charles Long *(CEO)*
Tami Gaythwaite *(COO)*
John Lane *(Chief Strategy Officer & Sr VP-Creative)*
David Schafermeyer *(Sr Dir-Art)*
Erin Craft *(Grp Acct Dir)*
Kristen Collosso *(Sr Designer-Interactive)*
Jodi Schwartz *(Exec Specialist-Acct)*

Accounts:
IBM
John Deere
Lenovo
Lowe's
Progress Energy Carolinas
Red Hat
Sony Ericsson

CENTRO LLC
222 Hubbard St Ste 400, Chicago, IL 60654
Tel.: (312) 397-3331
Fax: (877) 805-9494
Web Site: www.centro.net

Employees: 130
Year Founded: 2001

Agency Specializes In: Advertising

Scott Neslund *(Exec VP-Media Svcs)*
Emily Barron *(Sr VP-Corp Ops)*
Gunnard Johnson *(Sr VP-Data & Analytics)*
Kristin Haarlow *(Reg VP-Media Strategy & Ops)*
Jill Hamilton *(Reg VP-Media Strategy & Ops)*
Michael Olson *(Reg VP-West)*
Martin Crawford *(VP-South Sls)*
Matt Davis *(VP-Platform Sls-Natl)*
Doug Thomas *(VP-Client Dev)*
Jason Asch *(Head-Digital Acct)*
David Karabag *(Sr Dir-Onboarding Solutions)*
Ryan Manchee *(Sr Dir-Digital Innovations)*
Bob Bernstein *(Reg Dir-Sls)*
Rivka Garver *(Dir-Acct Mgmt-Midwest)*
Rafael Pocasangre *(Dir-Natl Publr Solutions)*
Dan Raffe *(Dir-Programmatic Ops)*
Heather Robertson *(Dir-Video)*
Aubrey Lehrmann *(Assoc Dir-Digital Media Strategy & Ops)*
Jessie Wallin *(Assoc Dir-Media Strategy & Ops)*
Jennifer Debono *(Acct Mgr)*
Terri Han *(Acct Mgr)*
Nicole Mervis *(Acct Mgr)*
Jon Blyth *(Mgr-Client Dev)*
Evan Chadick *(Mgr-Campaign)*
Christine Kim *(Mgr-Platform Education)*
Brad Goldstein *(Supvr-Programmatic Ops)*
Courtney McDanald *(Supvr-Acct Mgmt)*
Ashley O'Dell *(Supvr-Programmatic Ops)*
Lauren Furey *(Sr Specialist-Product Mktg)*
Sarah Aldridge *(Strategist-Media)*
Aundrea Bentley *(Strategist-Media)*
Jackie Brennan *(Strategist-Digital)*
Jodie Dover *(Acct Exec)*
Justin Haber *(Strategist-Media)*
Samantha Kietlinski *(Strategist-Media)*
Ben Morton *(Acct Exec)*
Rhasaan Wilks *(Specialist-RTB-Channel Sls)*
Margaret Lee *(Analyst-Digital Campaign)*
Maria Aintablian *(Campaign Analyst)*
Christopher Theilen *(Acct Head-San Diego)*

Accounts:
Allstate Insurance Brokers
Cleveland.com Entertainment Services
ComCast Telecommunication Services
ESPN Television Networks
Fiat Car Mfr
NBC TV Television Networks
Perkins Diesel & Gas Engines Suppliers
Petco Pet & Pet Products Suppliers
Travel Oregon Tour & Travel Agency Services
Union Bank Banking Services

CHANGO
488 Wellington St W Ste 202, Toronto, ON M5V1E3 Canada
Toll Free: (800) 385-0607
Web Site: rubiconproject.com/buyer-cloud

Julian Mossanen *(Reg VP-Canada)*
Kyle Kargov *(Dir-Art)*
Doris Yip *(Dir-HR-Buyer Cloud)*
Shweta Jacob *(Mgr-Talent Acq)*

Accounts:
New-Pfister, Inc. Media

CIBO
649 Front St, San Francisco, CA 94111
Tel.: (415) 233-6606
E-Mail: hello@cibosf.com
Web Site: cibosf.com/

Employees: 18

Agency Specializes In: Advertising, Affluent Market, Arts, Aviation & Aerospace, Brand Development & Integration, Business-To-Business, Collateral, Communications, Consulting, Corporate Identity, Customer Relationship Management, Digital/Interactive, Direct-to-Consumer, E-Commerce, Electronics, Experience Design, Fashion/Apparel, Financial, Food Service, High Technology, In-Store Advertising, Information Technology, Integrated Marketing, International, Internet/Web Design, Leisure, Logo & Package Design, Luxury Products, Market Research, Mobile Marketing, New Product Development, New Technologies, Package Design, Planning & Consultation, Retail, Search Engine Optimization, Social Media, Sports Market, Strategic Planning/Research, Transportation, Travel & Tourism, Web (Banner Ads, Pop-ups, etc.)

Approx. Annual Billings: $4,000,000

Breakdown of Gross Billings by Media:
Digital/Interactive: $4,000,000

Lu Lacourte *(Co-Founder & CEO)*
Jim Magill *(Co-Founder & CMO)*

Accounts:
Disney
New-Facebook
Gymboree
New-Income& (Brand Experience Agency of Record)
Ken Fulk
Lenovo
New-Motor Image Group (Brand Experience Agency of Record)
New-Salesforce
San Francisco Museum of Modern Art Design, Digital, Website
Seagate Technology; Scotts Valley, CA Storage; 2010
New-Subaru
Tesla
Twitter
Union Bank/MUFG
Volcom

CICERON, INC.
(d/b/a Ciceron Interactive)
(Private-Parent-Single Location)
126 N 3rd St Ste 200, Minneapolis, MN 55401
Tel.: (612) 204-1919
E-Mail: info@ciceron.com
Web Site: www.ciceron.com

Employees: 14
Year Founded: 1995

Agency Specializes In: Advertising, Brand Development & Integration, Content, Digital/Interactive, Internet/Web Design, Search Engine Optimization, Social Media, Strategic Planning/Research

Revenue: $1,100,000

Andrew Eklund *(Co-Founder & CEO)*
Kraig Larson *(Founder, Partner & Chief Creative Officer)*
Matt Beckman *(Dir-Key Accts & Bus Dev)*
Julie Verhulst *(Dir-Strategic Plng)*
Amber Verhulst *(Mgr-Digital Svcs)*
Philip Davis *(Strategist-Social Mktg)*
Ashley Evenson *(Strategist-Digital Media)*

Accounts:
Childrens Hospitals & Clinics of Minnesota (Digital Agency of Record)

CLICKSQUARED INC.

Interactive Agencies

(Acquired by Zeta Interactive)

CLIQUE STUDIOS LLC
410 S Michigan Ave Ste 908, Chicago, IL 60605
Tel.: (312) 379-9329
E-Mail: buildsomething@cliquestudios.com
Web Site: www.cliquestudios.com

Year Founded: 2003

Agency Specializes In: Content, Digital/Interactive, Internet/Web Design, Search Engine Optimization, Social Media

Ted Novak *(Partner & Mng Dir)*
Derek Nelson *(Partner & Dir-Creative)*
Phil Orlandi *(Dir-Change Leadership)*
Francois Bouyer *(Mgr-Integration)*

Accounts:
Marco & Associates, Inc.

CONNECTIONS MEDIA
1428 U St NW 3rd Fl, Washington, DC 20009
Tel.: (202) 387-6377
Fax: (202) 387-6376
Web Site: www.connectionsmedia.com

Year Founded: 2004

Agency Specializes In: Advertising, Content, Digital/Interactive, Search Engine Optimization, Social Media

Jonah Seiger *(Founder & CEO)*
Andy Weishaar *(Chief Creative Officer)*
Phil Lepanto *(CTO)*
Amy Patnovic *(Art Dir)*
Katie Kreider *(Dir-Client Svcs)*
John Parks *(Dir-Digital Media)*
Russ Doubleday *(Sr Mgr-Content Svcs)*
Alison Clark *(Mgr-Fin)*
Rebecca Pomerantz *(Mgr-Content Svcs)*
Sabrina Satchell *(Mgr-Content Svcs)*

Accounts:
NBC News Education Nation Parent Toolkit

CORE DESIGNTEAM
700 W Pete Rose Way Ste 154 B, Cincinnati, OH 45203
Tel.: (513) 564-9112
Fax: (513) 672-0241
Web Site: www.coredesignteam.com

Agency Specializes In: Brand Development & Integration, Digital/Interactive, Internet/Web Design, Print

Craig Herget *(Owner & Designer)*

Accounts:
New-StopTech Ltd.

CRAFTED
205 E 42nd St, New York, NY 10017
Tel.: (646) 765-5596
Web Site: www.craftedny.com

Employees: 8
Year Founded: 2011

Agency Specializes In: Digital/Interactive, Email, Experience Design, Game Integration, Mobile Marketing, Multimedia, Out-of-Home Media, Outdoor, Point of Purchase, Point of Sale, Search Engine Optimization, Web (Banner Ads, Pop-ups, etc.)

Peter Mendez *(Founder & Partner)*
Greg Valvano *(Founder & Partner)*

Accounts:
New-Tishman Speyer Marketing; 2011

CREATE DIGITAL
1015 Technology Pk Dr, Glen Allen, VA 23059
Tel.: (804) 955-4400
Fax: (804) 955-4465
E-Mail: info@createdigital.com
Web Site: www.createdigital.com

Year Founded: 2009

Agency Specializes In: Advertising, Brand Development & Integration, Content, Digital/Interactive, Email, Graphic Design, Internet/Web Design, Media Planning, Social Media

Brett Lewis *(COO)*
Woody Carlisle *(CTO)*
Brad Perry *(Dir-Strategy)*
Sarah-Tyler Moore *(Acct Mgr)*
Emily Jasper *(Mgr-Content)*
Martha Cohen *(Acct Supvr)*
Sarah Lyddan *(Acct Supvr)*
Sarah Keane *(Designer)*
Katlyn Williams *(Copywriter)*

Accounts:
Oberkotter Foundation

CREATIVE MULTIMEDIA SOLUTIONS LLC
1113 Washington Crossing Blvd, Washington Crossing, PA 18977
Tel.: (800) 805-5195
E-Mail: hello@creativemms.com
Web Site: www.creativemms.com

Agency Specializes In: Digital/Interactive, Internet/Web Design, Paid Searches, Search Engine Optimization

Ben LeDonni *(Founder & CEO)*
Ashley Ellsworth Bird *(Dir-Ops)*
Kyle Aikens *(Creative Dir)*

Accounts:
New-Premier Response LLC

DANARI MEDIA
14622 Ventura Blvd. Ste 752, Sherman Oaks, CA 91403
Tel.: (818) 528-8451
Web Site: www.danarimedia.com

Employees: 8

Approx. Annual Billings: $23,000,000

Collin Kay *(VP-Bus Dev)*
Danari Media *(Acct Exec)*
Kyle Moran *(Acct Exec)*

DARE
101 New Cavendish St, London, W1W 6XH United Kingdom
Tel.: (44) 203 451 9101
Fax: (44) 203 451 9100
E-Mail: london@thisisdare.com
Web Site: na.thisisdare.com

Employees: 160

Agency Specializes In: Advertising, Advertising Specialties, Digital/Interactive, Internet/Web Design, Mobile Marketing, Outdoor, Point of Sale

Leigh Thomas *(CEO)*
Vassilios Alexiou *(Partner-Creative)*
Brian Cooper *(Partner-Creative)*
Clinton Schaff *(VP & Gen Mgr-US)*
Bradley Woodus *(Head-Brdcst)*
Anna Kalimbet *(Dir-Creative & Art)*
Gavin Torrance *(Assoc Dir-Creative)*
Summer Cui *(Copywriter)*

Accounts:
Aviva plc Digital, National Social Media
Barclaycard Campaign: "Bespoke Ballad", Campaign: "Win an Easier Christmas", Digital
Barclays #YouAreFootball, Digital, Social Media
BMW BMW 3 Series, Campaign: "Ultimate Track"; 2008
Cancer Research UK Digital
The Coca-Cola Company
EE Digital Proposition, Mobile, Website
Enterprise Rent-A-Car Brand Positioning, Campaign: "Interpreter", Campaign: "Network", Campaign: "Train Plane", Campaign: "We'll Pick You Up", Digital, Print, TV
Heart Transplant UK Campaign: "Give Your Heart This Valentine's Day", Online
Huawei Advertising, Campaign: "School of Pronunciation", Creative
Kingfisher Creative
Mankind
Nike European Football
Post Office Campaign: "Handled with Care", Digital Poster, Integrated Marketing Campaign, Mortgage Offering, Online, Outdoor, Press, TV
Public Health England Campaign: "Car", Campaign: "Mutations", Campaign: "Secondhand Smoke", Campaign: "Stoptober", Digital, Marketing, Outdoor, TV
Ryanair Campaign: "History", Campaign: "Low Fares. Made Simple", Pan-European Creative, TV
Sainsbury's Creative Digital, Online Advertising Strategy
Tetley USA Inc.
Vision Express Campaign: "Not Again", Campaign: "Vision.Taken Seriously", We'll See You Right

Branch

Camp Pacific
(Formerly Dare Vancouver)
1085 Homer Street Ste 500, Vancouver, BC V6B 1J4 Canada
Tel.: (778) 331-8340
Fax: (778) 331-8341
E-Mail: info@camppacific.com
Web Site: camppacific.com

Employees: 45

Agency Specializes In: Brand Development & Integration, Digital/Interactive

Richard J. Hadden *(Pres & Chief Creative Officer)*
Peter Bolt *(Mng Partner & Sr VP)*
Derek Shorkey *(Mng Partner & Sr VP)*
Edith Rosa *(VP & Client Svcs Dir)*
Neal Davies *(Head-Digital)*
Josh Fehr *(Exec Dir-Creative)*
Chris Kleiter *(Grp Acct Dir)*
Addie Gillespie *(Dir-Creative)*
Cindy Son *(Dir-Tech-DARE North America)*
Mathew Stockton *(Dir-Client Svcs)*
Mia Thomsett *(Dir-Creative)*
Julie Nikolic *(Assoc Dir-Creative)*
Todd Takahashi *(Assoc Dir-Creative)*

Accounts:
Amour Campaign: "Dirty Pool", Campaign: "Golf", Campaign: "Make Fantasies Happen"
B2ten Campaign: "Recess", Canadian Sport for Life
BC Children's Hospital Foundation
BC Lottery Corporation
British Columbia Children's Hospital Foundation

Campaign: "Hospital Ward", Campaign: "Operating Room", Optical Illusions
Canadian Breast Cancer Foundation
Canadian Winter Games
Destination British Colombia
Diane's Lingerie
EA SPORTS FIFA Street Campaign: "Street vs Street"
Evergrow Christmas Trees
GAP
GoAuto
Honda Campaign: "CR-V Conveyor Belt", Campaign: "Yahoo! Takeover", Honda Civic
John Frieda Campaign: "Live Ads"
Manitoba Telecom Services
McDonald's Restaurants of Canada Reflective Billboard
MTS
National Money Mart
Ronald McDonald House British Columbia
SAP
Sony Ericsson
Toronto Jewish Film Festival Campaign: "Goat Milk Machine"
Whistler Film Festival Campaign: "Princess"

DBURNS

1431 7th St Ste 305, Santa Monica, CA 90401
Tel.: (310) 882-2167
Web Site: www.dburnsdesign.com

Agency Specializes In: Digital/Interactive, Paid Searches, Search Engine Optimization, Social Media, Strategic Planning/Research

Daniel Burns *(CEO & Dir-Mktg)*
Murilo Ferreira *(Art Dir)*
Avni Agrawal *(Dir-Mktg)*
Erica Zen *(Mgr-Mktg)*

Accounts:
New-Cable News Network LP
New-Los Angeles Dodgers Inc.

DEFYMEDIA

(Formerly Alloy, Inc.)
498 7th Ave, 19th Fl, New York, NY 10018
Tel.: (212) 244-4307
Fax: (212) 244-4311
Toll Free: (877) 360-9688
E-Mail: info@defymedia.com
Web Site: www.defymedia.com/

Employees: 602
Year Founded: 1996

National Agency Associations: WOMMA

Agency Specializes In: Advertising, Advertising Specialties, Brand Development & Integration, Children's Market, Communications, Consumer Marketing, Direct Response Marketing, E-Commerce, Electronic Media, Event Planning & Marketing, Fashion/Apparel, Financial, Hispanic Market, Internet/Web Design, Media Buying Services, Merchandising, New Product Development, Newspapers & Magazines, Out-of-Home Media, Outdoor, Planning & Consultation, Point of Purchase, Publicity/Promotions, Radio, Sales Promotion, Sponsorship, Sports Market, Strategic Planning/Research, Sweepstakes

Geraldine B. Laybourne *(Chm)*
Matt Diamond *(CEO)*
Gina R. DiGioia *(Gen Counsel, Sec & Exec VP)*
Brian Fridell *(Sr VP-East Coast, Midwest & Canadian Sls)*
Alexandria Cox *(Client Svcs Mgr)*
Alison Stewart *(Mgr-Integrated Mktg)*
Sophie Gorson *(Acct Exec)*

Accounts:
New-NBCU Hispanic Enterprises & Content

DELOITTE DIGITAL

837 N 34th St Ste 100, Seattle, WA 98103
Tel.: (206) 633-1167
E-Mail: dd-info@deloitte.com
Web Site: www.deloittedigital.com

Agency Specializes In: Content, Digital/Interactive, Internet/Web Design, Social Media

Daniel Kao *(CTO)*
Alicia Hatch *(Principal)*
Julie Storer *(Grp Acct Dir)*
Andi Rusu *(Dir-Creative)*
Alan Schulman *(Dir-Creative Experience & Content Mktg-Natl)*
Chris Stauch *(Dir-Creative)*
Nancy Martira *(Mgr-Engagement)*

Accounts:
Melissa Etheridge (Digital Agency of Record)

Branch

Mobiento

Savageness 25, 11134 Stockholm, Sweden
Tel.: (46) 8225710
E-Mail: hello@mobiento.se
Web Site: www.mobiento.com

Year Founded: 2001

Agency Specializes In: Advertising, Digital/Interactive, Graphic Design, Mobile Marketing, Strategic Planning/Research

Zelia Sakhi *(Head-Creative)*
Carl Christiansson *(Acct Dir)*
Helena Magnusson *(Acct Mgr)*
Camilla Beltrami *(Sr Designer-Interaction)*
Sofie Karlsson *(Planner-Strategic)*

Accounts:
New-Situation Stockholm SMS is King

DELPHIC DIGITAL

(Formerly Delphic Sage LLC.)
116 Shurs Ln 2nd Fl, Philadelphia, PA 19127
Tel.: (215) 794-0420
Fax: (215) 508-9503
Web Site: www.delphicdigital.com

Employees: 43
Year Founded: 2003

Agency Specializes In: Advertising, Content, Digital/Interactive, Email, Internet/Web Design, Mobile Marketing, Paid Searches, Search Engine Optimization, Social Media, Strategic Planning/Research, Web (Banner Ads, Pop-ups, etc.)

Approx. Annual Billings: $4,449,258

Mark Patten *(Founder & Mng Partner)*
Kate Dalbey *(Acct Dir)*
Joel J. Soucie *(Client Svcs Dir)*
Todd Duchynski *(Dir-User Experience)*
Cristie Setzer *(Sr Mgr-Mktg)*
Andrew Dunlap *(Acct Mgr)*
Priti Patel *(Acct Mgr)*
Julia Russell *(Assoc Acct Mgr)*
Nicole Hess *(Mgr-Mktg & Comm)*

Accounts:
ALL-FILL Inc Powder Filling & Liquid Filling Mechinery Mfr
American Association for Cancer Research Cancer Research Studies Providers
American Executive Centers Office Interior Design Products Mfr
Gale International LLC Real Estate Development Services
Porcelanosa Kitchen & Bath Products Mfr & Distr

DEVELOPMENT NOW

310 SW 4th Ave, Portland, OR 97215
Toll Free: (800) 387-0849
Web Site: www.developmentnow.com

Employees: 15
Year Founded: 2005

Agency Specializes In: Digital/Interactive, Direct Response Marketing, Mobile Marketing, Multimedia, Point of Purchase, Point of Sale, Social Media

Ben Strackany *(CEO)*
Nathan Crawford *(Dir-Accts)*
Mara Connolly *(Mgr-Studio)*
David Strackany *(Designer-UX)*

Accounts:
Alghanim Xcite.com; 2013
Avis Rental Car; 2012
Manheim Automotive; 2010
Time Warner Cable Telecommunications; 2010

DIDIT

330 Old Country Rd Ste 206, Mineola, NY 11501
Tel.: (516) 255-0500
Fax: (516) 255-0509
Toll Free: (800) 932-7761
E-Mail: Marketing@didit.com
Web Site: www.did-it.com

Employees: 90
Year Founded: 1996

Agency Specializes In: Electronic Media, Internet/Web Design, Pets , Web (Banner Ads, Pop-ups, etc.)

Patty Brehm *(CEO-Didit DM)*
Mark Simon *(Exec VP)*
John Virgil *(VP-Tech)*
Heidi Zafran *(VP-HR)*
Eric Wiggins *(Grp Acct Dir)*
Adam Steinberg *(Acct Dir)*
Meridith Afflixio *(Acct Mgr)*
Katie Kiernan *(Acct Mgr)*
Christopher Matuszewski *(Acct Mgr)*
Joseph Rocco, Jr. *(Acct Exec)*
Timothy Fitzgerald *(Assoc Acct Exec)*

Accounts:
DollarDays International
Leading Interactive Reservations LLC; 2008
PetCareRX Search Engine Marketing
Trend Micro Search Engine Marketing

Branches

Bridge Global Strategies LLC

16 W 36th St Ste 1002, New York, NY 10018
(See Separate Listing)

HLD Communications

(Formerly Harrison Leifer DiMarco, Inc.)
330 Old Country Rd Ste 206, Mineola, NY 11501
(See Separate Listing)

JB Cumberland PR

276 Fifth Ave Ste 205, New York, NY 10001
(See Separate Listing)

LVM Group, Inc.

60 E 42nd St Ste 1651, New York, NY 10165-6203

(See Separate Listing)

DIF INC.
1350 Main St Ste 212, Springfield, MA 1103
Tel.: (413) 788-0654
Web Site: www.difdesign.com

Year Founded: 2004

Agency Specializes In: Digital/Interactive, Graphic Design, Internet/Web Design, Search Engine Optimization

Peter Ellis *(Creative Dir)*
John Daley *(Dir-Sls)*

Accounts:
New-Sherman & Frydryk
New-Springfield Water & Sewer LLC

DIGITAL BUNGALOW, INC.
209 Essex St Ste 201, Salem, MA 01970
Tel.: (978) 565-0111
E-Mail: inquiries@digitalbungalow.com
Web Site: www.digitalbungalow.com

Employees: 15

Agency Specializes In: Advertising, Content, Digital/Interactive, Internet/Web Design, Social Media

Revenue: $2,921,000

Nate Wolfson *(Pres & CEO)*
Scott Berkley *(VP-Svc Ops)*
Stacey Forman *(VP-Fin & HR)*
Erin Hegarty *(VP-Sls & Accts)*
Gordon Plutsky *(VP-Mktg)*
Sean Cunningham *(Exec Creative Dir)*
Janelle Casella *(Sr Acct Mgr)*
Jane Tryder *(Office Mgr)*
Alexis Devilling *(Mgr-Mktg)*

Accounts:
Citisoft
CNEDirect
Magnficent Baby
VoIPSupply

DIGITASLBI
(Formerly Digitas Inc.)
33 Arch St, Boston, MA 02110
Tel.: (617) 867-1000
E-Mail: newbusiness@digitas.com
Web Site: www.digitaslbi.com

Employees: 3,000
Year Founded: 1980

National Agency Associations: 4A's-DMA

Agency Specializes In: Automotive, Aviation & Aerospace, Brand Development & Integration, Business Publications, Business-To-Business, Cable T.V., Co-op Advertising, Collateral, Consulting, Consumer Marketing, Consumer Publications, Digital/Interactive, Direct Response Marketing, E-Commerce, Electronic Media, Entertainment, Event Planning & Marketing, Exhibit/Trade Shows, Financial, Graphic Design, High Technology, Internet/Web Design, Leisure, Logo & Package Design, Magazines, Media Buying Services, New Product Development, Newspaper, Newspapers & Magazines, Out-of-Home Media, Outdoor, Pharmaceutical, Planning & Consultation, Point of Purchase, Point of Sale, Print, Production, Public Relations, Publicity/Promotions, Radio, Retail, Sales Promotion, Sponsorship, Sports Market, Strategic Planning/Research, Sweepstakes, Syndication, T.V., Telemarketing, Trade & Consumer Magazines, Transportation, Travel & Tourism

Robert Guay *(Mng Dir & Exec VP)*
Jill Kelly *(Chief Comm Officer)*
Adam Shlachter *(Chief Investment Officer)*
Ewen Sturgeon *(CEO-Intl)*
Robert Rizzo *(Exec VP & Exec Dir-Creative)*
Davin Power *(Exec VP)*
Cathy Butler *(Sr VP, Grp Dir & Head-Acct Mgmt-NY/ATL)*
Jamie Ferreira *(Sr VP & Grp Dir-Creative)*
Greg Stahovec *(Sr VP & Grp Acct Dir)*
Max Fresen *(Sr VP-Creative & Experience Design)*
Megan Jones *(Sr VP & Grp Media Dir)*
Bryan Reilly *(Sr VP-Fin)*
Ellen Gates *(VP & Grp Dir-Strategy & Analysis)*
Brett Leary *(VP & Grp Dir-Mobile)*
Jim Ricciardi *(VP & Grp Dir-Creative)*
Meghan Riley *(VP & Grp Dir-Media)*
Eric Prado *(VP & Acct Dir)*
Mark Book *(VP & Dir-Social Content)*
Sean Costello *(VP & Dir-Media)*
Claire Fanning *(VP & Dir-Strategy & Analysis)*
Emily Hatten *(VP & Dir-Strategy & Analysis)*
Erin Korgie *(VP & Dir-Media)*
Amanda Lynch *(VP & Dir-Strategy & Analysis)*
Tara Reed *(VP & Dir-New Bus)*
John Mataraza *(VP)*
Joe Sharrino *(Head-Creative)*
Greg Coffin *(Sr Dir-Art)*
Joseph Palmer *(Creative Dir)*
Alexandra Rogers *(Acct Dir)*
Ron D'Amico *(Assoc Dir)*
Luiz Freitas *(Assoc Dir-Advanced Analytics)*
Beth McKenna *(Assoc Dir-Media)*
Jennie Scheer *(Assoc Dir)*
Meg Zebroski *(Assoc Dir-Strategy & Analysis)*
Stephanie Repp *(Acct Mgr)*
Jamie Garofano *(Mktg Mgr)*
Steven Bithell *(Mgr)*
Lauren Blute *(Mgr-Strategy & Analysis)*
Tim Chu *(Mgr-Strategy & Analysis)*
Owen Curtis *(Mgr-Strategy & Analysis)*
Leslie Fines *(Mgr-Social & Content Strategy)*
Maysa Jarudi *(Mgr-Strategy & Analysis)*
Ilana Sclar *(Mgr-Strategy & Analysis)*
Benjamin Towne *(Mgr-Strategy & Analysis)*
Oliver Berbecaru *(Supvr-Media)*
Dee Ersu *(Supvr-Media)*
Bridget Scott *(Sr Acct Exec)*
Benjamin Seldin *(Sr Strategist-Creative)*
Tim Cahill *(Sr Analyst-Strategy & Analysis)*
Jonathan deBoer *(Sr Analyst-Media Tech)*
Lina Josephson *(Sr Analyst-Strategy & Analysis)*
John Lagedrost *(Sr Analyst-Strategy & Analysis)*
Kirsten Leshko *(Sr Analyst-Strategy & Analysis)*
Camilla Retecki *(Sr Analyst-Strategy & Analysis)*
KJ Warren *(Sr Analyst-Strategy & Analysis)*
Erin Young *(Sr Analyst-Media System Tech & Advanced Analytics)*
Sam Bernstein *(Analyst-Strategy & Analysis)*
Courtney Blanch *(Analyst-Strategy & Analysis)*
Molly Crawford *(Copywriter)*
Nick Deadrick *(Analyst-Strategy & Analysis)*
Emily Denton *(Analyst-Strategy & Analysis)*
Brian Hasbrouck *(Analyst-Media Tech)*
Kate Hoffman *(Analyst-Strategy & Analysis)*
Elle How *(Media Planner)*
Elizabeth Langer *(Analyst-Strategy & Analysis)*
Michelle Martinelli *(Analyst-Strategy & Analysis)*
Kleida Martiro *(Analyst-Strategy & Analysis)*
Deb Siegel *(Assoc Creative Dir & Copywriter-Digital)*
Dan Stevens *(Analyst-Media Tech)*
Mollie Toomey *(Analyst-Strategy & Analysis)*
Rose Wu *(Analyst-Strategy & Analysis)*
Yohannes Chambers *(Assoc Media Planner)*
Ashley Moran *(Assoc Media Planner)*
Natalia Nicholson *(Assoc Strategist-Creative)*

Accounts:
Aflac Inc. Digital Media Planning & Buying
Ally Bank
American Express Campaign: "Small Business Saturday", Campaign: "Unstaged"
AstraZeneca
AT&T, Inc.
Delta Air Lines Campaign: "An Amazing Year", Campaign: "Keep Climbing", Delta.com
Disneyland Resort
Dunkin' Donuts Loyalty Marketing
Equifax Campaign: "Jewelry Store", Paper Shredder Mailer
General Motors Buick Campaign: "Moment of Truth", Commercial, Corporate Marketing, Digital Marketing, Fleet, GM Vehicle Showroom, OnlyGM.com, Owners Programs, gm.com
Goodyear CRM Activities, Consumer Web Development, Digital Media Planning & Buying, Interactive, Mobile Marketing, NASCAR, Search Advertising, Social Media Marketing
Harley Davidson Campaign: "My Time to Ride"
The Huffington Post Real Time Native Ads
Kao USA Campaign: "Never Pull Back", Digital Creative, Frizz Ease, John Frieda
Lenovo (North American Agency of Record) Analytics, Brand Awareness, Campaign: "Tough Season", Digital Marketing, Media Planning & Buying, YOGA 2 Pro, Yoga Laptop, Yoga Tablet
L'Oreal USA, Inc.
Memorial Sloan Kettering Cancer Center Inc. (Digital Agency of Record)
Pitney Bowes Digital, Website
PUMA "Faster Delivery", Campaign: "Forever Faster", Creative, Digital, Marketing, Online, Social, Social Media
Sprint Campaign: "Jack's Story", Campaign: "Kate's Story", Small Business Solutions Group, Social Media
Travelers
Volvo
Walgreen Company
Whirlpool Jenn-Air

Digitas Health Boston
33 Arch Street, Boston, MA 02110
Tel.: (617) 867-1000
Fax: (617) 867-1111
E-Mail: info@digitashealth.com
Web Site: www.digitashealth.com

Year Founded: 2009

Agency Specializes In: Digital/Interactive, Health Care Services

Jamie Ferreira *(Sr VP & Grp Dir-Creative)*
Kenny Rennard *(Sr VP & Grp Dir-Creative)*
Marc Gottesman *(VP & Grp Dir-Creative)*
Jim Harrington *(VP & Grp Dir-Creative)*

Digitas Health London
23 Howland St, London, W1T 4AY United Kingdom
Tel.: (44) 20 7874 9400
Fax: (44) 20 7874 9510
E-Mail: info@digitashealth.com
Web Site: www.digitashealth.com

Employees: 35
Year Founded: 2009

Agency Specializes In: Digital/Interactive, Health Care Services

Raakhee Thompson *(Mng Dir)*
Vineet Vijayraj Thapar *(Sr VP & Grp Dir-Creative-Europe)*
Gianpaolo Palombella *(Sr Dir-Art)*
Courtney Langhauser *(Acct Dir)*
Amber Friesen *(Dir-Ops)*
Andrea Ruffo *(Dir-Art)*
Danielle Robertson *(Sr Acct Mgr)*
Joyce Higgins *(Strategist-Social Media)*
Claire Ashtekar *(Sr Project Dir)*

Accounts:
AstraZeneca

Digitas Health
355 Park Ave S, New York, NY 10010
Tel.: (212) 610-5000
Fax: (212) 350-7850
Web Site: www.digitashealth.com

National Agency Associations: 4A's

Agency Specializes In: Digital/Interactive, Health Care Services, Sponsorship

Rich Schwartz *(Sr VP-Mktg & Digital Health Innovations)*
Tanya Shepley *(Sr VP-Mktg)*
Shwen Gwee *(VP & Grp Dir-Social Strategy)*
Elisabeth DiCicco *(VP & Dir-Talent Ops)*
Karin Fickes *(VP & Grp Mktg Dir)*
Daniel Dellacona *(Dir-HR)*
Renee Grube *(Assoc Dir-Print Production)*
A.J. Magali *(Sr Mgr-Digital-SEM)*
Marla Mattox *(Mgr-Mktg)*
Rebecca Auerbach *(Acct Supvr)*
Jamie Mulhare *(Media Planner)*
Brandon Swift *(Analyst-Strategy & Analytics)*

Digitas Health
100 Penn Square E 11th Fl, Philadelphia, PA 19107
(See Separate Listing)

DigitasLBi
(Formerly LBi UK)
146 Brick Lane, London, E1 6RU United Kingdom
Tel.: (44) 207063 6465
Fax: (44) 2070636001
E-Mail: enquiries@lbi.com
Web Site: www.digitaslbi.com

Employees: 500

Michael Islip *(CEO)*
Matt Steward *(Mng Dir-UK)*
Fern Miller *(CMO-Intl)*
Chris Clarke *(Chief Creative Officer-Intl)*
Paul Dalton *(Chief Media Officer-Intl)*
Alan Davies *(Chief Strategy Officer)*
Sophie Ling *(Chief People Officer)*
Lorenzo Wood *(Chief Innovation Officer)*
Ewen Sturgeon *(CEO-Intl)*
Marcus Mustafa *(Head-User Experience-Global & Exec Dir-Creative-UK)*
Michele Chang-McGrath *(Head-Res, Strategy & Insight)*
Emma Storer *(Head-New Bus)*
Simon Attwater *(Exec Dir-Creative-MENA)*
Simon Gill *(Exec Dir-Creative)*
Laurent Ezekiel *(Client Svcs Dir-Worldwide)*
Katarina Johnson *(Acct Dir)*
Richard Morgan *(Art Dir)*
Caitlin Blewet *(Dir-Client)*
Tom Burrell *(Dir-Strategy & Insight-Middle East & North Africa)*
Aran Burtenshaw *(Dir-Creative)*
Andrew Girdwood *(Dir-Media Innovations)*
Jonathan Lyon *(Dir-Strategic Insights-Global)*
Mark Sullivan *(Assoc Dir-Integrated Production)*
Jenny Hughes *(Copywriter-Creative)*

Accounts:
Asda Asda Direct, Asda Financial Services, Asda.com, Digital Advertising Strategy, Groceries
Barclays plc Barclay International Banking, Barclay Wealth, Barclaycard, Digital, Strategy
British Gas
Carlsberg Digital
Cunard Line Art-Deco Themed Brand, Digital
Danone Aptaclub, C&G Baby Club, Danone Baby Nutrition
E.ON Best Deal For You, PR, Press, Radio, TV
Etihad Airways Digital
Grolsch Digital
Honda Online
Kuoni Travel Campaign: "Scents of Adventure"
Marks & Spencer
Mr Green Digital Display
Mumsnet Apps In-House, Mobile Development, Partnerships, White-Labelled
National Trust Digital, Mobile
Premier Inn
RBS Content Strategy, Digital Creative, Social Media
Reckitt Benckiser Global Web Revamp, Scholl
SABMiller Digital, Distribution, Grolsch, Mobile App Development, Online Content Creation, Peroni Nastro Azzurro, Social Media
Samsung Europe Digital content, Marketing Strategy, Public Relations, Social Media
Slater & Gordon
Sony Ericsson Mobile Communications AB Campaign: "Tweetsinger", Campaign: "Xperia Studio", Campaign: "Z versus fashion", Sony Xperia Z
Tesco Clubcard Website, Revamp
Virgin Atlantic
WorldPay Global Digital Strategy
Xperia Brand Awareness Campaign, Digital

DigitasLBi
(Formerly LBi Germany AG)
Schafflerstrasse 3, D-80333 Munich, Germany
Tel.: (49) 89 242 167 77
Fax: (49) 89 242 167 66
E-Mail: info-germany@lbi.com
Web Site: www.digitaslbi.com/de

Employees: 40

Agency Specializes In: Digital/Interactive, Electronic Media

Kaan Karaca *(CTO)*
Anke Herbener *(CEO-Germany)*
Simone Mitterer *(Dir-Online Comm)*

Accounts:
BT
Cisco
Ebay
JD
Mtv
Opodo
Shopping 24
Sky
Topman
Topshop

DigitasLBi
(Formerly Digitas India)
90 D Sector 18, Udyog Vihar -IV, Gurgaon, Haryana 122 015 India
Tel.: (91) 12433000600
Fax: (91) 12433000610
Web Site: www.digitaslbi.com/in/

Agency Specializes In: Advertising, Mobile Marketing, Social Media, Strategic Planning/Research

Partho Sinha *(Chief Creative Officer)*
Amaresh Godbole *(Mng Dir-India)*
Upasana Roy *(Head-Strategy)*
Poornima Kamath *(Acct Dir)*
Bhavna Sukhija *(Sr Acct Mgr)*

Accounts:
Eureka Forbes
Real Campaign: "Cheer a Child"
Tata Motors Campaign: "The #Fantastico Hunt", Digital, Zica

DigitasLBi
(Formerly LBi International N.V.)
Joop Geesinkweg 209 1096 AV, PO Box 94829, 1096 AV Amsterdam, Netherlands
Tel.: (31) 20 460 4500
Web Site: www.digitaslbi.com/global

Employees: 1,800

Agency Specializes In: Sponsorship

Luke Taylor *(CEO)*
Thomas Elkan Boisen *(COO/CFO-Intl)*

DigitasLBi
(Formerly LBi Stockholm)
Hamngatan 2, SE-111 47 Stockholm, Sweden
Tel.: (46) 8 4100 1000
Fax: (46) 8 411 65 95
E-Mail: anita.hallgren@lbi.com
Web Site: www.digitaslbi.com/global

Employees: 1,465

Agency Specializes In: Advertising, Digital/Interactive, Internet/Web Design, Strategic Planning/Research

Lotten Holmgren *(CTO)*
Filippos Arvanitakis *(Exec Dir-Creative)*
Paul Collins *(Exec Creative Dir)*
Erik Weidenhielm *(Sr Dir-Art)*
Rebecca Bjarneskog *(Jr Art Dir)*
Rogier 'Chaigneau *(Art Dir)*
Emma Evers *(Acct Dir)*
Oskar Nilsson *(Acct Mgr)*

Accounts:
Audi
Bank Linth
Belgacom TV
General Electric
Husqvarna
Makro
Marks & Spenser
Multiopticas
Nike Football
Orange
Postbank AG
Renault
T-Systems
Trygg-Hansa
Volvo

DigitasLBi
22/F Chinachem Exchange Square 1 Hoi Wan Street, Quarry Bay, Hong Kong
Tel.: () 22360330
E-Mail: hongkong@digitaslbi.com
Web Site: www.digitaslbi.com

Agency Specializes In: Advertising, Digital/Interactive, Event Planning & Marketing, Logo & Package Design, Print, Strategic Planning/Research

Lianne Dixon *(Partner-Client-Global)*
Justin Peyton *(Chief Strategy Officer-APAC & MENA Regions)*
Mark Newton *(Head-Media-Asia Pacific)*
Mike Sutcliffe *(Exec Dir-Creative-Asia Pacific)*
Kaythaya Maw *(Reg CTO-Asia Pacific & Middle East North Africa)*

Accounts:
Cathay Pacific Airways Limited (Global Digital Agency of Record)

DigitasLBi
(Formerly Digitas)
36/40 rue Raspail, Levallois-Perret, 92300 France

Tel.: (33) 149681212
Fax: (33) 149681213
E-Mail: info_france@digitas.com
Web Site: www.digitaslbi.com/fr

Year Founded: 1980

Agency Specializes In: Digital/Interactive, Mobile Marketing, Social Media, Strategic Planning/Research

Leila Bouguerra *(CFO)*
Mathieu Morgensztern *(CEO-France & Europe West)*
Olivier Le Garlantezec *(Gen Mgr-Europe Phonevalley)*
Jean-Baptiste Burdin *(Dir-Creative)*
Emma Hipeau *(Dir-HR)*

Accounts:
Airbus Leading Aircraft Mfr
AOL Inc. Entertainment Services
CIO Magazine Publishers
Disney World Interactive Entertainment Services
Hermes Campaign: "Vive Le Sport"
La Poste Group Mobile, Online
Lancome
Nissan Campaign: "Chase The Thrill", Campaign: "The Big Turn On", Nissan Juke
Renault Campaign: "Megane CC Florida"
Sara Lee Corporation Wonderbra
Studio Baccarat Jewelry Shop

DigitasLBi
2001 The Embarcadero, San Francisco, CA 94133
(See Separate Listing)

DigitasLBi
(Formerly Digitas Inc)
4 Stamford Plaza 107 Elm St Ste 900, Stamford, CT 06902
Tel.: (203) 905-2200
Fax: (203) 905-2399
E-Mail: info@digitas.com
Web Site: www.digitaslbi.com

Amy Murphy Dowd *(CFO)*
Baba Shetty *(Chief Strategy Officer & Chief Media Officer)*
Lorenzo Wood *(Chief Innovation Officer)*
Douglas Ryan *(Pres-Chicago & San Francisco)*
Joanne Zaiac *(Pres-NY Reg)*
Anke Herbener *(CEO-Germany)*

DigitasLBi
(Formerly Digitas Inc)
1447 Peachtree St NE Ste 900, Atlanta, GA 30309
Tel.: (404) 460-1010
Fax: (404) 460-1009
E-Mail: newbusiness@digitas.com
Web Site: www.digitaslbi.com

Employees: 70

National Agency Associations: 4A's

Agency Specializes In: Advertising

Carrie Philpott *(Sr VP & Mng Dir-Atlanta)*
Brian Sherwell *(VP & Grp Dir-Creative Strategy)*
Kama Winters *(VP & Grp Acct Dir)*
Kelly Slothower *(VP & Dir-Creative Strategy)*
Beckie Uhlenberg *(VP & Dir-Media)*
Michael Ashley *(Creative Dir)*
Kelly Jacxsens *(Acct Dir)*
Jamie Krinsky *(Supvr-Media)*
Kori Pensabene *(Supvr-Media)*

Accounts:
Delta AirLines Campaign: "LAX to LUX", Delta One
Equifax Campaign: "Paper Shredder Mailer"
L'Oreal USA, Inc. Digital, Media Planning & Buying

DigitasLBi
(Formerly Digitas, Inc.)
180 N La Salle St, Chicago, IL 60601
Tel.: (312) 729-0100
Fax: (312) 729-0111
E-Mail: contactus@digitas.com
Web Site: www.digitaslbi.com

Employees: 285
Year Founded: 2001

National Agency Associations: 4A's

Agency Specializes In: Digital/Interactive, Sponsorship

Douglas Ryan *(Pres-San Francisco & Chicago)*
Tony Weisman *(CEO-North America)*
Chris Reed *(Exec VP & Head-Acct Mgmt-Chicago & San Francisco)*
Matthew Jacobson *(Exec VP & Dir-Global Executive Design)*
Davin Power *(Exec VP)*
Melissa Pruessing *(Sr VP & Grp Acct Dir)*
Tony Bailey *(Sr VP-Tech)*
Carol Chung *(Sr VP-Media Tech)*
Laura Keeler *(Sr VP-Creative)*
Jason Kodish *(Sr VP)*
Megan McCurry *(Sr VP & Grp Media Dir)*
Casey Hess *(VP & Grp Dir-Bus Dev-Digitas)*
Jenny Pike *(VP & Grp Dir-Creative Strategy)*
Jenna Sheeran *(VP & Grp Dir)*
Andrea Kroll *(VP & Grp Acct Dir)*
Tim Reardon *(VP & Grp Acct Dir)*
Garth Bender *(VP & Dir-Tech)*
Jeanne Bright *(VP & Dir-Paid Social)*
Caitlin Finn *(VP & Dir)*
Kristin Scheve *(VP & Dir-Media)*
Matthew Weiner *(VP & Dir-Creative)*
Brian Zaben *(VP & Dir-Programmatic Strategy & Analysis)*
Katie Schnepf *(VP & Grp Media Dir)*
Ted Gott *(Head-Digital Mktg Analytics-US)*
Keith Soljacich *(Head-Digital Studio-Natl)*
Jerad Koskey *(Sr Dir-Art)*
Jacqueline Hanrahan *(Assoc Dir-Media Tech)*
Jenny Schauer *(Assoc Dir-Media)*
Danny Tica *(Assoc Dir-Creative)*
Lisa Woolf *(Assoc Dir-Search Mktg)*
Melissa Valentino *(Acct Mgr)*
Scott Blessman *(Mgr-Strategy & Analysis)*
Rachael Garcia *(Mgr-Strategy & Analysis)*
Erica Kleinknecht *(Mgr-Media Ops & Tech)*
Michael Dunaway *(Supvr-Media)*
Kris English *(Supvr-Media)*
Kathryn Griffin *(Supvr-Media)*
Mary Claire Kilmer-Lipinski *(Supvr-Media)*
Meaghan MacGuidwin *(Supvr-Media)*
Nicole Nemerovski *(Acct Exec)*
Ghada Soufan *(Acct Exec)*
Molly Steffens *(Acct Exec)*
Gina D'Aveni *(Sr Analyst-Search Mktg)*
Lisa Tencza *(Sr Analyst-Media Tech)*
Jose Aguero *(Analyst-Strategy & Analysis)*
Julian Baker *(Sr Designer)*
Yalin Buyukdora *(Analyst-Strategy & Analysis)*
Kelly Campbell *(Analyst-Strategy & Analysis)*
Janice Kanellis *(Analyst-Search Mktg)*
Jacob Norgren *(Analyst-Media Ops)*
Allie Snyder *(Analyst-Media Tech)*
Elizabeth Thomas *(Analyst-Search Mktg)*
Dolly Vu *(Sr Designer-Visual-UX & UI)*
Allison Wagner *(Media Planner)*
Mel Gray *(Assoc Strategist-Creative)*
Alex Hudson *(Assoc Media Planner)*
Riley Kinsella *(Assoc Media Planner)*
Alexa Millstein *(Assoc Media Planner)*
Hayley Stevens *(Assoc Media Planner)*
Morgan Weiner *(Sr Art Dir)*

Accounts:
eBay (Digital Agency of Record) Media Buying, Media Planning
Foster's
Kaiser Permanente Direct Marketing
Manpower
Mars Petcare Media, Whiskas Temptations
Maytag / Whirlpool Corporation Jenn-Air, Maytag
MillerCoors, LLC Mickey's, Sparks
Mondelez International, Inc. Online Media, Salad Dressings
P&G
Sears Holdings
Sprint Corporation Brand Strategy, Campaign: "I Am Unlimited", Digital, Digital Buying & Analytics, Offline Media
Taco Bell "Waffle Taco", Digital, Digital Media Planning, Dorito Locos Taco Fiery chips, Interactive, Social Media
Walgreen Co.; Deerfield, IL Digital Marketing
Whirlpool Corporation (Agency of Record) "Perceptions of Care", Above-the-Line, Advertising, Amana, Bring Maytag Home, Campaign: "Dad & Andy", Campaign: "Every Day, Care", Campaign: "Finding Time", Campaign: "OK", Content Development, Creative, Digital Media, Interactive, Jenn-Air, KitchenAid, Marketing, Maytag, Media Planning, Online, Social Media, Strategy, TV, Videos

DigitasLBi
(Formerly Digitas, Inc.)
355 Park Ave S, New York, NY 10010-1706
Tel.: (212) 610-5000
Fax: (212) 350-7850
Web Site: www.digitaslbi.com

Employees: 430
Year Founded: 1980

National Agency Associations: 4A's

Agency Specializes In: Digital/Interactive, Sponsorship

Kenneth Parks *(CMO-DigitasLBi North America)*
Alvaro Cabrera *(Chief Strategy Officer-North America)*
Ronald Ng *(Chief Creative Officer-North America)*
Adam Shlachter *(Chief Investment Officer)*
Chia Chen *(Exec VP & Mng Dir-Digital Products & Svcs)*
Mark Kiernan *(Exec VP-Mktg)*
Jorge Urrutia del Pozo *(Head-Ops-North America & Sr VP)*
Jorge Urrutia *(Sr VP & Head-Ops-North America)*
Lewis McVey *(Sr VP & Grp Dir-Creative)*
Lisa Bronson *(Sr VP-Media)*
George Hammer *(Sr VP-Content Strategy & Mktg-Digitas Studios)*
Stewart Pratt *(Sr VP-Strategy & Analysis)*
Doug Speidel *(Sr VP-Creative)*
Jennifer Striegel *(Sr VP-Brand Strategy)*
Matthew Carrow *(VP & Grp Dir)*
Doug Grumet *(VP & Grp Dir-Media)*
Tessa Horehled *(VP & Grp Dir-Social Strategy)*
Will Phipps *(VP & Grp Dir-Connections Plng)*
Aaron Rosenberg *(VP & Grp Dir-Integrated Production)*
Alexa Sanchez *(VP & Grp Dir-Media)*
Chris Senio *(VP & Grp Dir-Media)*
Erica Sklar *(VP & Grp Dir-Media)*
Nigel Storr *(VP & Grp Dir-Fin)*
Emilie Vasu *(VP & Grp Dir-Bus Dev & Mktg)*
Charlie Taylor *(VP & Grp Acct Dir)*
Sam Ciaramitaro *(VP, Dir & Exec Producer)*
Julie Glasser *(VP & Dir-Media Tech)*
Yael Glosser *(VP & Dir-Media)*
Jully Hong *(VP & Dir-Media Ops & Tech)*
Nick Barrios *(VP & Grp Creative Dir)*
Raymonde Green *(VP-Partnerships & Investments)*
Brian Hunn *(VP & Grp Creative Dir)*
Abbie Schultz *(VP-Media)*
Lee Baler *(Grp Dir-Media)*
Debbie Barron *(Sr Dir-Art)*
Forrest Plassmann *(Sr Dir-Art)*
Jennifer Awasano *(Creative Dir)*

Eleanor Solomon *(Mgmt Supvr)*
Whitney Grossman *(Dir-Art)*
Kate Napleton Kysiak *(Dir-Art)*
Rachel Barbarotta *(Assoc Dir-Social Content)*
Stephanie Cunningham-Long *(Assoc Dir-Search Mktg)*
Robert Dibella *(Assoc Dir-Search Mktg)*
Shawn Hardie *(Assoc Dir-Search Mktg)*
Derek Jech *(Assoc Dir-New Bus-Bus Dev & Mktg)*
Cindy Kern *(Assoc Dir-Media)*
Joe Ludwiczak *(Assoc Dir-Media)*
Jennie Scheer *(Assoc Dir)*
Ryan Tobin *(Assoc Dir-Search Mktg)*
Nicole Vanderhurst *(Assoc Dir-Media)*
Julia Lan *(Acct Mgr)*
Jennifer Morgan *(Acct Mgr)*
Erica Ortmann *(Acct Mgr-US)*
Chris Byrne *(Mgr-Strategy & Analysis)*
Meghan Linehan *(Mgr-Mktg)*
Ryanne Donnellon *(Supvr-Media)*
Elizabeth Emery *(Supvr-Media)*
Joseph Kotarski *(Supvr-Media-US)*
Anna-Marieke Stallings *(Supvr-Media)*
Meredith DeHaas *(Acct Exec)*
Samantha Grossman *(Sr Planner-Digital Media)*
Jake Posner *(Acct Exec)*
Michelle Sanchez *(Acct Exec)*
Lauren Victory *(Acct Exec)*
Zoe Bel *(Copywriter)*
Megan Burns *(Media Planner)*
Nicole Callimanis *(Media Planner)*
Allison Grimmel *(Media Planner)*
Kamla Kowalczuk *(Media Planner)*
Jamarr Mills *(Media Planner)*
Sarah Schlein *(Media Planner)*
Kate Sherrill *(Media Planner)*
Mario Aguirre *(Assoc Media Dir)*
Brooke Camarda *(Assoc Media Planner)*
Khemi Cooper *(Sr Media Planner)*
Alexa DiSciullo *(Assoc Media Planner)*
Michael Greene *(Assoc Media Planner)*
Joanne Lee *(Assoc Media Planner)*
Nicole Plunkett *(Assoc Media Planner)*
Kimberly Rimmey *(Assoc Media Planner)*
Margo Rizzi *(Assoc Media Planner)*
Kevin Sami *(Sr Media Planner)*
Lacey Tompkins *(Assoc Media Planner)*

Accounts:
AFLAC, Inc.
American Express Company Small Business Saturday
AOL
AstraZeneca Pharmaceuticals LP Campaign: "Take it from a Fish", Digital, Online, Social
New-Bank of America Corporation Media Planning, Social
BP (US Digital Agency of Record) BP Fuels, Creative, Digital Strategy
Comcast Corporation
Delta Airlines
eBay Inc. Digital, Radio, Video
Goodyear
HSBC
L'Oreal USA, Inc.
Mead Johnson Nutrition Company Campaign: "ExpectingBaby Moabile App", Enfamil
Miller Lite Digital
Mondelez International, Inc. Planters Peanuts
Motorola Solutions, Inc. Campaign: "WIRED", Creative, Moto X, Strategy
NYSE Euronext Campaign: "The Big Stage", Creative, Media
Pitney Bowes Digital Strategy, Media, Website
Renault Campaign: "Plug into the Positive Energy"
New-Rescue Dogs Rock NYC
Samsung
Shell
Taco Bell Breakfast Campaign, Cantina Power Menu, Digital, Mobile Channels, Social
TIAA-CREF Creative

Kitcatt Nohr
(Formerly Kitcatt Nohr Digitas)
91 Brick Lane, London, E1 6QL United Kingdom
Tel.: (44) 207 8749 400
Fax: (44) 20 78749 555
Web Site: www.kitcattnohr.com

Employees: 100

Agency Specializes In: Digital/Interactive, Internet/Web Design

Sue MacLure *(Partner-Grp Data Strategy)*
Ed Beard *(Chief Strategy Officer)*
Nick Burbidge *(Head-Ops)*
Harriet Elsom *(Dir-Bus)*
Suzie Mills *(Dir-Bus)*
Emily Challenor *(Sr Acct Mgr)*
Rosie Kenworthy *(Acct Mgr)*
Nisha Desai *(Sr Partner-HR Bus)*

Accounts:
ASUS Campaign: "In Search Of Incredible"
Axa Digital, Social Media
BSkyB Direct Marketing
Buick Regal
Bupa
Gucci Group Media Planning & Buying UK, France & Asia
Macmillan Cancer Support The World's Biggest Coffee Morning and Night In
Mars Candy Bar, Snickers, World's Longest Football Match
Nissan Campaign: "Behind the Hit"
Puma Social Media, Teamsport
Shell
Weight Watchers Digital, Direct Marketing

DIRECT AGENTS, INC.
740 Broadway Ste 701, New York, NY 10003
Tel.: (212) 925-6558
Fax: (212) 412-9061
E-Mail: marketing@directagents.com
Web Site: www.directagents.com

Employees: 48
Year Founded: 2003

Agency Specializes In: Affiliate Marketing, Digital/Interactive, Email, Search Engine Optimization, Social Media

Dinesh Boaz *(Co-Founder & Mng Dir)*
Josh Boaz *(Co-Founder & Mng Dir)*
Lyle Srebnick *(Exec VP)*
Megan Conahan *(VP-Adv Sls)*
Mark Glauberson *(VP-Media & Bus Dev)*
Rachel Nugent *(VP-Client Svcs)*
Daniel Owen *(VP-Search Mktg & Display)*

Accounts:
AccuQuote Insurance; 2008
bloomspot Daily Deal; 2010
LendingTree Financial; 2011
Scholastic Education; 2009
The SCOOTER Store Health; 2012

DOMANI STUDIOS LLC
32 Avenue of the Americas 19th Fl, New York, NY 10013
Tel.: (646) 744-3501
Fax: (212) 242-4112
Web Site: www.domanistudios.com

Employees: 50
Year Founded: 2001

Agency Specializes In: Brand Development & Integration, Digital/Interactive, Graphic Design, Mobile Marketing, Production (Ad, Film, Broadcast), Search Engine Optimization, Social Media

April Ryde *(Dir-Art)*
Evan Stark *(Dir-Tech)*
Adam Bettencourt *(Interactive Producer)*
Eric Bichan *(Interactive Developer)*
Andres Bonilla *(Sr Interactive Developer)*
Samuel Delesque *(Interactive Developer)*
Fangchi Gato *(Visual Designer)*
Taylor Hills *(Assoc Producer)*
Stephen Matysik *(Interactive Developer)*
Rachel Oliner *(Digital Strategist)*

Accounts:
Aloft Hotels
CODA
Estee Lauder
GC Watches
Nintendo
Scribner Digital, Doctor Sleep, The Shining
Sheraton
Starwood Hotels & Resorts
Stephen King Campaign: "Doctor Sleep"
Umbro
Westin Hotels

DRINKCAFFEINE
(Formerly Caffeine)
897 Boston Post Rd, Madison, CT 06443
Tel.: (203) 468-6396
Fax: (203) 468-7608
E-Mail: info@drinkcaffeine.com
Web Site: drinkcaffeine.com

Employees: 10
Year Founded: 1999

Agency Specializes In: Internet/Web Design

Matt Sawyers *(Partner-Content Strategy)*
Katie Tuttle *(Partner-Mktg Strategy)*
William Mulligan *(CEO-Performance Strategy)*
Sam Tuttle *(VP)*
Bryan Betz *(Dir-Art)*
Eric Webb *(Dir-Creative)*
Michael V. Colianna *(Acct Mgr)*
Janet Kawai *(Mgr-Fin)*
Jenn Church *(Designer-UI)*

Accounts:
Bridges Resort
By Kids for Kids
Connecticut Innovations
Crested Butte Resort Real Estate
Developers Realty
Digital Flannel
Industrial Heater
Jackson Gore Real Estate
Kiosko
Mount Sunapee
Navtec
Okemo Mountain Resort
PGA Championship
Sail America
Shreve, Crump & Low
Solar Connecticut
Tommy Fund
Vanguard Sailboats

DSB CREATIVE
5508 E 38th St, Tulsa, OK 74135
Tel.: (918) 971-8348
E-Mail: contact@dsbcreative.co
Web Site: www.dsbcreative.co

Year Founded: 2010

Agency Specializes In: Advertising, Brand Development & Integration, Digital/Interactive, Internet/Web Design, Search Engine Optimization, Social Media

Daniel Blaho *(Owner)*

Accounts:
Kallay Unbowed

DUKE MORGAN PRODUCTIONS
89 Chateau Whistler Ct, Las Vegas, NV 89148
Tel.: (702) 736-9484
Web Site: www.dukemorgan.com

Employees: 2

Agency Specializes In: Broadcast, Cable T.V., Infomercials

Approx. Annual Billings: $150,000

Candi Cazau *(Mgr-Ops)*

Accounts:
The South Point Hotel & Casino Casino Events, Showrooms, Sporting Events; 2007

DVMAIL FIRST SCREEN MARKETING
623 Judson Ave, Evanston, IL 60202
Tel.: (847) 644-3087
Web Site: www.dvmail.com

Year Founded: 2006

Earl Weingarden *(Pres)*

Accounts:
Tourist Office of Spain; 2012

DW LINKS
1 Pemimpin Dr #09-01, 576151 Singapore, Singapore
Tel.: (65) 0065668411
Web Site: www.dwlinks.com.sg

Year Founded: 2009

Agency Specializes In: Digital/Interactive, Electronic Media, Email, Exhibit/Trade Shows, Experience Design, Mobile Marketing, Multimedia, Paid Searches, Search Engine Optimization, Social Media, Web (Banner Ads, Pop-ups, etc.)

Sam Lai *(Dir-Acct)*
Sebastian Tay *(Dir-Creative)*

Accounts:
BSH Home Appliances Website; 2014
Hilton Worldwide Tablet Application, Website; 2014
NCS Interactive Space; 2014
The Wine Advocate Website; 2013

EASTMONT GROUP
3423 Piedmont Rd NE Ste 485, Atlanta, GA 30305
Tel.: (404) 937-6554
E-Mail: info@eastmontgroup.com
Web Site: www.eastmontgroup.com

Year Founded: 2009

Agency Specializes In: Content, Digital/Interactive, Internet/Web Design, Print, Social Media

Mark Kaufman *(Co-Founder & CTO)*
Michael Gottfried *(Co-Founder & Mgr-Client Rels)*

Accounts:
MessageGears

EBAY ENTERPRISE
(Formerly GSI Commerce, Inc.)
935 1st Ave, King of Prussia, PA 19406
Tel.: (610) 491-7000
Fax: (610) 491-7366
Web Site: www.ebayenterprise.com

Employees: 5,304
Year Founded: 1986

Agency Specializes In: E-Commerce

Revenue: $1,357,994,000

Tom Barone *(VP-Ops-North America)*
Tami Cannizzaro *(Sr Dir-Global Demand Generation)*
Stephen Owens *(Sr Dir-Procurement-Global)*
Rachel Sule *(Sr Product Mgr)*
Juan Alvarado *(Mgr-Display Plng)*
Suresh Bondugula *(Mgr-Delivery Ops)*
Paul Geraghty *(Mgr-Client Svcs)*
Elizabeth Sklaroff *(Mgr-CRM Strategy)*
Laura Guy *(Supvr-ELC Cosmetics)*
Katie Norris *(Specialist-PR)*
Stephen Walz *(Media Planner)*

EFFECTIVEUI INC.
2162 Market St, Denver, CO 80205
Fax: (720) 206-0868
Toll Free: (888) 310-5327
Web Site: www.effectiveui.com

Employees: 82
Year Founded: 2005

Agency Specializes In: Digital/Interactive

Rebecca Flavin *(CEO)*
Scott Esmond *(Mng Dir)*
Ken Guiberson *(Mng Dir)*
Peyton Lindley *(Exec Dir-Experience Design & Customer Insight)*
Amanda Gaube *(Mgr-Engagement)*

Accounts:
Boeing
Navy Federal Credit Union

EIC
10001 Ave of the Americas 4th Fl, New York, NY 10019
Mailing Address:
1674 Broadway Ste 804, New York, NY 10019
Tel.: (212) 315-9522
Web Site: www.eic.net

Employees: 30

Agency Specializes In: Advertising, Brand Development & Integration, Business-To-Business, Corporate Identity, Digital/Interactive, E-Commerce, Electronic Media, Email, Game Integration, Graphic Design, High Technology, Identity Marketing, Information Technology, Internet/Web Design, Local Marketing, Logo & Package Design, Medical Products, New Technologies, Search Engine Optimization, Social Media, Web (Banner Ads, Pop-ups, etc.)

Approx. Annual Billings: $3,000,000

Breakdown of Gross Billings by Media: Digital/Interactive: $2,500,000; Logo & Package Design: $500,000

Sanford Wilk *(CO-Founder & COO)*
Bo Van Kan *(Acct Dir)*

ELLIANCE
600 River Ave Ste 201, Pittsburgh, PA 15212-5994
Tel.: (412) 586-1480
Fax: (412) 586-1481
Toll Free: (888) 926-6262
E-Mail: info@elliance.com
Web Site: www.elliance.com

Employees: 30
Year Founded: 1993

Agency Specializes In: Brand Development & Integration, Business-To-Business, College, E-Commerce, Education, Email, Guerilla Marketing, Internet/Web Design, Mobile Marketing, Paid Searches, RSS (Really Simple Syndication), Search Engine Optimization, Social Marketing/Nonprofit, Web (Banner Ads, Pop-ups, etc.)

Abu Noaman *(CEO)*
Ed Macko *(Dir-Brand Strategy)*
Debbie Wilson *(Mgr-Customer Experience)*
Andrew Ormerod *(Sr Designer-Interactive)*

Accounts:
Duquesne University
Miller Welding
Pepperdine University
Phipps Conservatory
Robert Morris University
Saint Leo University
Search Marketing Expo

EMAIL AGENCY
7999 N Federal Hwy Ste 400, Boca Raton, FL 33487
Toll Free: (877) 674-6366
E-Mail: Info@emailagency.com
Web Site: www.emailagency.com

Employees: 15

Agency Specializes In: Advertising, Business-To-Business, Consumer Goods, Digital/Interactive, Direct Response Marketing, Direct-to-Consumer, E-Commerce, Education, Email, Hospitality, Leisure, Luxury Products, Market Research, Media Buying Services, Media Planning, Pets , Sales Promotion, Shopper Marketing, Sweepstakes, Travel & Tourism, Women's Market

Approx. Annual Billings: $3,200,000

Breakdown of Gross Billings by Media: Digital/Interactive: $3,200,000

Robert Walsh *(Owner & Pres)*
Anthony Loveland *(VP)*
Amie Laventhall *(Dir-Lead Generation)*
John Baker *(Acct Mgr)*

Accounts:
Lead Capsule; Deerfield Beach, FL Lead Management, Lead Generation & Lead Distribution Software
My Digital Pat, LLC; Delray Beach, FL IT Services

EMBARK DIGITAL
38505 Country Club Dr, Farmington Hills, MI 48331
Tel.: (248) 488-7880
Web Site: www.embarkdigital.com

National Agency Associations: 4A's

Agency Specializes In: Digital/Interactive

Beau Hebert *(Exec VP-Ops)*
Russ Hopkinson *(VP & Dir-Strategy)*
Lynette McCombs *(VP & Dir-Delivery Svcs)*
Peter Galio *(VP-Client Engagement)*
Randy Bishop *(Dir-Tech)*
Amy Drill *(Dir-Social Strategy)*
David Kazaryan *(Dir-Digital Art)*

Accounts:
Ally Auto
Ascension Health
Borgess

Braun Ability
Chrysler
Covisint
Detroit Pistons
Falcon Waterfree Technologies
Genesys Health System
Grand Prix
Greektown Casino-Hotel
St. John Providence Health System
St. Joseph Health System
St. Mary's of Michigan
Tim + Clue

ENGINE DIGITAL
260 Lafayette St #860, New York, NY 10012
Tel.: (347) 491-4375
Web Site: www.enginedigital.com

Employees: 25
Year Founded: 2002

Agency Specializes In: Advertising, Brand Development & Integration, Consumer Goods, Content, Digital/Interactive, E-Commerce, Education, Email, Entertainment, Experience Design, Fashion/Apparel, Financial, Food Service, Government/Political, Health Care Services, Hospitality, Internet/Web Design, Market Research, Mobile Marketing, New Product Development, Planning & Consultation, Real Estate, Restaurant, Retail, Search Engine Optimization, Social Marketing/Nonprofit, Social Media, Sports Market, Strategic Planning/Research, Technical Advertising, Travel & Tourism, Web (Banner Ads, Pop-ups, etc.)

Stephen Beck *(Founder & CEO)*
Dean Elissat *(VP-Client Engagement)*
James Richardson *(VP-Ops)*

Accounts:
BC Hydro; 2008
Bravo TV Mobile; 2010
NBA NBA Game Time; 2010
Shea Homes; 2007
Telus; 2006
Western Union; 2013

ENTER:NEWMEDIA
60-62 E 11th St 4th Fl, New York, NY 10003
Tel.: (212) 731-2033
E-Mail: info@enternewmedia.com
Web Site: www.enternewmedia.com

Agency Specializes In: Digital/Interactive, Entertainment, Fashion/Apparel, Retail, Social Media, Sports Market

Mark Curtis *(Founder & CEO)*
Lynn Murray *(Pres)*
Joe Charnitski *(Sr Mgr-Analytics & Acct Mgr)*

Accounts:
Free People

ENVOI DESIGN
1332 Main St, Cincinnati, OH 45202
Tel.: (513) 651-4229
Web Site: www.envoidesign.com

Agency Specializes In: Brand Development & Integration, Digital/Interactive, Graphic Design, Search Engine Optimization, Social Media

Denise Weinstein *(Founder & Pres)*
Steve Weinstein *(VP-Design)*

Accounts:
New-Joe & Carla Tucker

ETHERCYCLE
3 S Prospect Ave Ste 12, Park Ridge, IL 60068
Tel.: (847) 653-0601
Fax: (847) 384-3740
Toll Free: (877) 384-3740
E-Mail: marych@ethercycle.com
Web Site: ethercycle.com

Agency Specializes In: Business-To-Business, Commercial Photography, Digital/Interactive, E-Commerce, Electronic Media, Email, Graphic Design, New Technologies, Search Engine Optimization, Social Media, Web (Banner Ads, Pop-ups, etc.)

Approx. Annual Billings: $100,000

Breakdown of Gross Billings by Media: Worldwide Web Sites: $100,000

Kurt Elster *(Co-Founder)*
David Jakobik *(Co-Founder)*

EXECUTIONISTS
4134 Del Rey Ave, Marina Del Rey, CA 90292
Tel.: (310) 754-3807
E-Mail: info@executionists.com
Web Site: www.executionists.com

Agency Specializes In: Brand Development & Integration, Digital/Interactive, Internet/Web Design, Search Engine Optimization, Social Media

Richard Parr *(CEO & Creative Dir)*
Buya Bat *(Dir-Tech)*
Eric Schoner *(Sr Designer)*

Accounts:
New-Black Ink Communications
New-United Staffing Solutions Inc.

EXTREME GROUP
47 Fraser Avenue North Entrance 2nd Floor, Toronto, Ontario M6K 1Y7 Canada
Tel.: (416) 607-6665
Fax: (416) 588-7401
E-Mail: info@extremegroup.com
Web Site: www.extremegroup.com

Agency Specializes In: Advertising, Consumer Marketing, Investor Relations

Shawn King *(Pres)*
Mike Bevacqua *(Partner & Mng Dir)*
Daniel Tolensky *(Partner & CFO)*
Jeff Simpson *(Art Dir)*
Phil Sylver *(Creative Dir)*
Francheska Galloway-Davis *(Dir-Art)*
Lee Stafford *(Dir-Production)*
Allana MacDonald *(Acct Supvr)*
Jeff Middleton *(Copywriter)*

Accounts:
Bell Aliant Internet Access Provider
Downtown Halifax Business Commission
Grand & Toy Office Products Supplier & Service
Moosehead Breweries Crafted Premium Beers Mfr
Nova Scotia Health Promotion & Protection Svcs
P&G Pharmaceuticals, Cleaning Supplies, Personal Care & Pet Supplies Products Supplier
New-Sante Dental
Shops at Don Mills Fashion, Dining & Entertainment Open Air Centre
Stepping Stone

Branch

Extreme Group
1498 Lower Water Street, Halifax, NS B3J 3R5 Canada
Tel.: (902) 461-2700
Fax: (902) 461-2701
E-Mail: info@extremegroup.com
Web Site: www.extremegroup.com

Agency Specializes In: Advertising, Social Marketing/Nonprofit

Paul LeBlanc *(Founder)*
Shawn King *(Pres & Chief Creative Officer-Extreme Grp)*
Brian Hickling *(Creative Dir-Halifax)*
Phil Sylver *(Creative Dir)*
Lee Stafford *(Dir-Production)*

Accounts:
Diageo Campaign: "Captain Morgan NS Spirit Coasters"
Grand & Toy Home Based Stationery Printing Business Services
Procter & Gamble Consumer Products
Pure Black Sunshine Online Shopping Provider
Quiznos Hotel & Restaurant Services
Red Cross Campaign: "Volunteer Market Website"
RIM Telecommunication Device Providers
New-Stanfield's (Agency of Record) Advertising
Stepping Stone

FANTASY INTERACTIVE, INC.
80 Franklin St, New York, NY 10013
Tel.: (212) 941-5220
Web Site: http://fantasy.co/

Year Founded: 1999

Agency Specializes In: Digital/Interactive, Mobile Marketing, Search Engine Optimization, Social Media, Strategic Planning/Research

David Martin *(CEO)*
Stephen Carpi *(COO)*
Marc Anderson *(Dir-Art)*
Claudio Guglieri *(Dir-Design)*
Peter Smart *(Dir-UX & Strategy)*
Firdosh Tangri *(Dir-Strategic Growth-Global)*
Timmy Chau *(Designer-Intermediate UX)*
Robert Surrency *(Sr Designer-UX)*
Jack Wright *(Sr Designer-UX)*

Accounts:
AOL Inc. Media Network & Interactive Service Providers
BBC Television Network Services
Evite Online Invitation Providers
FOX Online Television Network Providers
Google Inc Campaign: "Cannes Heatmap"
HTC Corporation Mobile Phone & Accessories Mfr & Distr
Porsche Motorsport Car Dealers
Range Rover Car Dealers
Redbull.tv Television Network Services

FATHOM
967 Farmington Ave, West Hartford, CT 6107
Tel.: (860) 677-9737
Web Site: www.fathom.net

Agency Specializes In: Brand Development & Integration, Digital/Interactive, Graphic Design, Social Media

Jonathan Abel *(Designer)*

Accounts:
New-Willington Nameplate

FEAST
852 5th Ave, San Diego, CA 92101
Tel.: (619) 550-2746
E-Mail: hello@wearefeast.com
Web Site: www.wearefeast.com

Interactive Agencies

Employees: 2

Agency Specializes In: Advertising, Brand Development & Integration, Consumer Marketing, Digital/Interactive, Environmental, Game Integration, Identity Marketing, Internet/Web Design, Viral/Buzz/Word of Mouth, Web (Banner Ads, Pop-ups, etc.)

Approx. Annual Billings: $150,000

Paul Larrow *(Partner & Dir-Design & Tech)*

Accounts:
AT Cross; RI Writing Instruments & Accessories
BrewhouseVFX; Boston, MA

FENCE TALK DIGITAL
801 Bluff St, Dubuque, IA 52001
Tel.: (563) 588-5754
Web Site: www.fencetalkdigital.com

Year Founded: 2013

Agency Specializes In: Digital/Interactive, Email, Internet/Web Design, Search Engine Optimization, Social Media

Meredith Flattery *(Coord-Digital Mktg Sls)*

Accounts:
I Hate Heroin

FFW AGENCY
(Formerly Propeople)
467 S 1st St, San Jose, CA 95113
Tel.: (650) 353-7544
Web Site: ffwagency.com

Year Founded: 2000

Agency Specializes In: Advertising, Digital/Interactive, Internet/Web Design, Strategic Planning/Research

Michel Testmann Samucha *(Founder, Partner & Dir-Creative)*
Mihai Moscovici *(COO)*
Troels Feodor Nielsen *(CMO-Global)*
Marc O'Brien *(VP-Bus Dev)*
Michael Drejer *(Global CEO)*
Gus Murray *(Global Chief Digital Strategy Officer)*

Accounts:
New-Divisionsforeningen
New-Lush
New-Randstad
SLAC National Accelerator Laboratory
New-Syngenta
New-Transcom
New-YMCA of the Greater Twin Cities (Digital Agency of Record)

FOCUS ONLINE MARKETING AGENCY
12101 NW MacArthur #A148, Oklahoma City, OK 73162
Tel.: (405) 283-6287
Web Site: allaboutfocus.com

Employees: 5
Year Founded: 1998

Agency Specializes In: Digital/Interactive, Electronic Media, Email, Guerilla Marketing, Local Marketing, Mobile Marketing, Multimedia, Podcasting, RSS (Really Simple Syndication), Search Engine Optimization, Social Media, Viral/Buzz/Word of Mouth, Web (Banner Ads, Pop-ups, etc.)

Approx. Annual Billings: $200,000

Patrick Allmond *(Sr Mgr-Experience)*

Accounts:
TRC Staffing; 2011

FOR OFFICE USE ONLY LLC
212 Forsyth St N Storefront, New York, NY 10002
Tel.: (917) 534-9767
E-Mail: hello@forofficeuseonly.com
Web Site: www.forofficeuseonly.com

Agency Specializes In: Graphic Design, Internet/Web Design, Strategic Planning/Research

Anh Tuan Pham *(Principal & Dir-Creative)*
Filippo Della Casa *(Dir-Interactive)*

Accounts:
DesignMiami Interior Designing Service Providers
Johnson Trading Gallery Home Furniture Mfr & Distr
Public Art Fund Entertainment Event Providers

FORTUNE COOKIE (UK) LIMITED
(Acquired by & Name Changed to Possible Worldwide)

FREQUENCY540
122 S Michigan Ave Ste 900, Chicago, IL 60603
Tel.: (312) 787-8787
E-Mail: info@fq540.com
Web Site: www.fq540.com

Year Founded: 2011

Agency Specializes In: Brand Development & Integration, Content, Corporate Identity, Digital/Interactive, Internet/Web Design

Andrew Swinand *(CEO)*
Dominic Lee *(Exec Dir-Creative)*
Michael Moreland *(Sr Dir-Art & Designer)*
Stephanie Ridley *(Grp Acct Dir)*
Kevin Butler *(Acct Dir)*
Kelsey Kates *(Dir-Analytics)*
Katie Newman *(Dir-Bus Dev)*
Tom Quish *(Dir-Creative)*
Grant Zemont *(Dir-Project Mgmt)*
Liz Nichols *(Acct Supvr)*
Amanda Pietch *(Acct Supvr)*

Accounts:
Bebe Stores Branding, Campaign: "Be More You"
Caterpillar, Inc.
New-Lincoln Park Zoo (Agency of Record) Strategic

FRUITION
201 Fillmore St Ste 200, Denver, CO 80206
Tel.: (303) 395-1880
Web Site: www.fruition.net

Year Founded: 2003

Agency Specializes In: Brand Development & Integration, Content, Digital/Interactive, Email, Internet/Web Design, Public Relations, Search Engine Optimization, Social Media

Melanie Davidson *(Pres)*
Brad Anderson *(CEO)*
David Chapman *(CFO)*
Drew Michael *(VP-Web Ops)*
Chance Carlin *(Dir-E-Commerce)*
Scott Knox *(Dir-SEO)*
Joe Malouff *(Dir-Interactive Design)*
Sara Villegas *(Dir-Social Media & Engagement)*
Todd Atkins *(Sr Mgr-Project)*
Earl Grylls *(Mgr-IT)*
Aaron Scofield *(Designer)*

Accounts:
Ulmer Dermatology

GRASSROOTS MARKETING
(Acquired & Absorbed by Virtual Interactive Center)

GREAT FRIDAYS
Parsonage Chambers 3 The Parsonage, Manchester, M3 2HW United Kingdom
Tel.: (44) 1618349889
E-Mail: manchester@greatfridays.com
Web Site: www.greatfridays.com

Agency Specializes In: Digital/Interactive, E-Commerce, Email, Entertainment, Media Buying Services, Web (Banner Ads, Pop-ups, etc.)

Rob Noble *(Co-Founder & CEO-Americas)*
Stacey Birkett *(Head-Insight & Strategy)*
Chris Hughes *(Dir-Global)*
Ed Valpy *(Dir-Global)*
Nicola Owen *(Mgr-Tech)*
Joe Harrison *(Sr Designer-Visual)*
Mark Sugdon *(Sr Designer-Visual)*

Accounts:
Bowers & Wilkins Loud Speakers Retailer & Services
ITV Entertainment Services
Manchester Council Information Services
Marks & Spencer Retail Institution
Real World Desktop Application Providers
Sainsburys Entertainment Services
Ubisoft Entertainment Services
Vodafone Telecommunication Services

GUILD
110 8th St, Brooklyn, NY 11215
Tel.: (718) 554-7027
E-Mail: info@guildisgood.com
Web Site: www.guildisgood.com

Agency Specializes In: Brand Development & Integration, Digital/Interactive, Graphic Design

Graham Kelman *(Creative Dir)*

Accounts:
New-Microsoft

HAGOPIAN INK
Box 2024, New York, NY 10021
Tel.: (212) 327-1445
Web Site: www.HagopianInk.com

Year Founded: 2002

Agency Specializes In: Affluent Market, Arts, Automotive, Business-To-Business, Computers & Software, Consumer Goods, Consumer Marketing, Cosmetics, Direct-to-Consumer, Electronics, Email, Entertainment, Fashion/Apparel, Financial, Food Service, High Technology, Household Goods, Legal Services, Luxury Products, Production (Print), Promotions, Restaurant, Retail, Social Media, Web (Banner Ads, Pop-ups, etc.), Women's Market

Christina Hagopian *(Pres & Creative Dir)*

Accounts:
Lancome House of Color, Lancome Eye Brightening All-In-One 5 Shadow & Liner Palette, Magic Mirror; 2011
PepsiCo Digital AMP, Diet Pepsi, Mountain Dew, Pepsi, Pepsi MAX, PepsiCo Beverages, PepsiCo Food Services; 2010

Sesame Workshop Sesame Street GO; 2014

HANEKE DESIGN
306 E Tyler St 4th Fl, Tampa, FL 33602
Tel.: (813) 605-3586
Fax: (813) 377-2464
Web Site: www.hanekedesign.com

Agency Specializes In: Brand Development & Integration, Content, Digital/Interactive, Graphic Design, Internet/Web Design

Jody Haneke *(Founder & CEO)*
Bryson Hale *(Dir-Bus Dev)*

Accounts:
New-Apkudo

HAWKEYE
(Acquired by Publicis Groupe & Name Changed to Publicis Hawkeye)

HIVEMIND MARKETING INC.
1724 Alberta Ave, San Jose, CA 95113-1116
Tel.: (408) 266-3162
E-Mail: strategists@hivemindinc.com
Web Site: www.hivemindinc.com

Employees: 8
Year Founded: 1986

National Agency Associations: BMA-DMA-PRSA

Agency Specializes In: Advertising, Brand Development & Integration, Business Publications, Business-To-Business, Collateral, Computers & Software, Consulting, Corporate Communications, Corporate Identity, Digital/Interactive, Direct Response Marketing, E-Commerce, Electronics, Email, Graphic Design, Health Care Services, High Technology, Industrial, Information Technology, Integrated Marketing, Internet/Web Design, Local Marketing, Medical Products, Mobile Marketing, New Technologies, Newspapers & Magazines, Paid Searches, Planning & Consultation, Point of Purchase, Print, Production, Production (Print), Public Relations, Sales Promotion, Search Engine Optimization, Social Marketing/Nonprofit, Social Media, Strategic Planning/Research, Technical Advertising, Trade & Consumer Magazines, Travel & Tourism, Web (Banner Ads, Pop-ups, etc.)

Approx. Annual Billings: $4,500,000

Breakdown of Gross Billings by Media: Digital/Interactive: 20%; Internet Adv.: 10%; Plng. & Consultation: 5%; Trade & Consumer Mags.: 5%; Worldwide Web Sites: 60%

Tom Lauck *(CEO)*

Accounts:
AB Sciex; Foster City, CA Applied Life Sciences Instruments & Reagents, Medical Devices; 2010
Avast Security Software; 2014
Bauer's Transportation; San Francisco, CA Hospitality, Transportation; 2010
Chronicles of Earth Travel Website & App; 2014
Discovia e-Discovery Solution; 2012
Finesse Solutions Bioreactor Systems; 2012
Hector & Lola Luxury Cashmere Sweaters; 2014
LN Curtis & Sons; Oakland, CA Firefighting Equipment; 2008
Molecular Devices, Inc.; Sunnyvale, CA Life Science Research Instruments & Reagents; 2009

HUDSON CREATIVE
132 Prospect St 2L, Midland Park, NJ 7432
Tel.: (201) 785-7564
Web Site: www.hudsoncreative.com

Year Founded: 2011

Agency Specializes In: Advertising, Brand Development & Integration, Digital/Interactive, Graphic Design, Internet/Web Design, Logo & Package Design, Search Engine Optimization, Strategic Planning/Research

James Page *(Owner)*

Accounts:
Rock n Robin Productions

HUEMOR DESIGNS
1855 New Hwy, Farmingdale, NY 11735
Tel.: (631) 393-6116
Toll Free: (888) 399-9050
E-Mail: sayhi@huemor.me
Web Site: https://huemor.rocks/

Employees: 8
Year Founded: 2012

Agency Specializes In: Advertising, Brand Development & Integration, Business-To-Business, Consulting, Consumer Goods, Consumer Marketing, Cosmetics, Digital/Interactive, Direct-to-Consumer, E-Commerce, Education, Email, Entertainment, Experience Design, Fashion/Apparel, Household Goods, Industrial, Internet/Web Design, Medical Products, Package Design, Retail, Search Engine Optimization, Social Media

Jeffrey Gapinski *(Co-Founder & Pres)*
Michael Cleary *(Co-Founder & CEO)*
Lyndsay Kollegger *(Coord-Mktg)*

Accounts:
Club Getaway
Color Club
Lighthouse Films
Live Nation Media & Sponsorship; 2014
Rug & Home Rug & Home Furnishings; 2014

HUSH
68 Jay Street Ste 413, Brooklyn, NY 11201
Tel.: (718) 422-1537
Fax: (718) 422-1539
Web Site: www.heyhush.com

Agency Specializes In: Entertainment, Graphic Design, High Technology, Media Relations

Erik Karasyk *(Partner-Creative)*
David Schwarz *(Partner)*
Rob Cohen *(Head-Strategy)*
Katie Hepp *(Dir-Production)*
Ryan McGrath *(Dir-Ops)*
Dan Rodriguez *(Dir-Engagement)*
Jodi Terwilliger *(Dir-Creative)*
Benjamin Gray *(Designer)*
Ross McCampbell *(Designer)*

Accounts:
Estee Lauder beautyofnight.com
Lyve Campaign: "THE POWER OF MEMORIES", Lyve's Apps, LyveHome
New York Times company
Nike Campaign: "Camp Victory"
Ted Baker Campaign: "Spread the Ted"

ICROSSING NEW YORK
300 W 57th St 20th Fl, New York, NY 10019
Tel.: (212) 649-3900
Fax: (646) 280-1091
Web Site: www.icrossing.com

Employees: 900
Year Founded: 2006

Agency Specializes In: Advertising, Advertising Specialties, Bilingual Market, Broadcast, Business-To-Business, Cable T.V., Consulting, Consumer Marketing, Digital/Interactive, Direct Response Marketing, E-Commerce, Electronic Media, Event Planning & Marketing, Hispanic Market, Information Technology, Internet/Web Design, Media Buying Services, Sponsorship, Sports Market, T.V., Yellow Pages Advertising

Approx. Annual Billings: $250,000

Melissa Brecher *(CMO)*
Mitchell Yoo *(Sr VP & Head-Global Dev)*
Christopher Andrew *(VP-Media)*
Mary Matyas *(VP-Delivery)*
Jake Abraham *(Head-Production-The Studio)*
Bill Connolly *(Assoc Dir-Mktg)*
Chris Moulton *(Assoc Dir)*
Brett Ekblad *(Sr Designer)*
Deyna Jeckell *(Asst Media Planner)*

Accounts:
New-Coca-Cola
Hilton Digital, Hampton
LG Electronics
TD Bank
TXU Energy

Branches

iCrossing Chicago
333 W Wacker Dr Ste 950, Chicago, IL 60606
Tel.: (312) 277-4700
Fax: (312) 277-4740
Web Site: www.icrossing.com

Agency Specializes In: Advertising, Sponsorship

Michael J. Jackson *(CFO & Exec VP)*
Dave Corchado *(Chief Product Officer)*
Stephen Thompson *(Exec VP & Exec Dir-Creative)*
Amanda Moore *(Sr VP-Bus Dev)*
Steve Shay *(VP & Grp Dir-Creative)*
Ellen Corrigan *(VP-Search Strategy)*
Katie Lamkin *(Dir-PR)*
Holly Owiti *(Dir-Media-Digital Media)*
Jack Konys *(Mgr-Media)*
Tom Wierzbinski *(Mgr-Media)*
Grant Rubin *(Sr Media Planner)*

Accounts:
Beam Suntory Inc. Content Strategy, DeKuyper, Digital, Jim Beam Bourbon, Laphroaig, Maker's Mark Bourbon, Marketing, Mobile, Sauza Tequila, Search Media, Skinnygirl Cocktails, Social, Strategy
Belk Analytics, Campaign: "Modern, Southern. Style.", Digital Media Marketing, Display Media, Paid Social, Search Engine Marketing
Charles Schwab
New-Coca-Cola
Kellogg
Pep Boys Digital
PetSmart Search

iCrossing Dallas
2828 Routh St Ste 777, Dallas, TX 75201
Tel.: (214) 210-6800
Fax: (214) 210-6783
Web Site: www.icrossing.com/dallas

Employees: 15

Agency Specializes In: Advertising

Mike Jackson *(CFO & Exec VP)*
Lori Wilson *(Sr VP & Grp Dir-Creative)*
Christine Bensen *(Sr VP-Media Strategy)*

Amanda Moore *(Sr VP-Bus Dev)*
Steven Shay *(VP & Grp Dir-Creative)*
Kent Milton *(Sr Dir-Creative)*
Marc J. Yagoda *(Sr Dir-Bus Dev-North America)*
Adam Lester *(Dir-Bus Dev North America)*
Tim Delaca *(Mgr-Media)*

Accounts:
Hilton Digital, Hampton

iCrossing, Inc.
Moore House 13 Black Lion St, Brighton, BN1 1ND United Kingdom
Tel.: (44) 1 273 827 700
Fax: (44) 1 273 827 701
E-Mail: results@icrossing.co.uk
Web Site: www.icrossing.com

Employees: 100

Agency Specializes In: Advertising

Mark Iremonger *(CEO-UK)*
Malcolm Leach *(CTO)*
Lucy Hancock *(Sr Acct Dir)*
Mat Gardiner *(Acct Dir)*
Sean Philip *(Acct Dir)*
Patti Sweet *(Acct Dir)*
Jay Jadeja *(Sr Acct Mgr)*
Bianca May *(Sr Acct Mgr)*
Joanne South *(Sr Acct Mgr)*
Sam Brakspear *(Acct Mgr)*
Mark Raymond *(Client Partner)*

Accounts:
Ann Summers
ASOS
Evans Cycles
Sainsbury's Bank
Speedo International SEM, SEO
Toyota GB
Unilever
Visit London
Visit Wales Digital Marketing

iCrossing Irvine
15420 Laguna Canyon Rd Ste 210, Irvine, CA 92618
Tel.: (949) 242-1900
Fax: (949) 242-1901
Web Site: www.icrossing.com

Agency Specializes In: Advertising

Michael J. Jackson *(CFO & Exec VP)*
Steven Shay *(VP & Grp Dir-Creative)*
Nicolette Lynch *(Sr Dir-Search Media Ops)*
Kent Milton *(Sr Dir-Creative)*
Juan P. Lesmes *(Dir-Digital Media Strategy)*
Jed Winkler *(Sr Mgr)*
David Shapiro *(Mgr-Search Engrg)*

iCrossing London
22 Chapter St 2nd Fl, London, SW1P 4NP United Kingdom
Tel.: (44) 20 7821 2300
Fax: (44) 20 8433 7055
Web Site: http://www.icrossing.com/uk/

Agency Specializes In: Advertising

Paul Doleman *(CEO-UK)*
Sam Fenton-Elstone *(Head-Media)*
Tim Bax *(Dir-Creative)*
June Robinson *(Dir-Bus Dev)*
Emma Jane Hornsby *(Acct Mgr)*

Accounts:
Alamo
Ann Summers
Argos
Barclays Bank
bmi
Coca-Cola Refreshments USA, Inc.
Comparethemarket.com Marketing Communications Strategy, SEO
Cornhill Direct
Current
Debenhams E-Commerce, Natural Search Strategy
EA Games
eBay
HBOS
Heathrow Digital Marketing, Online Display Advertising
John Lewis
JP Morgan
La Redoute Content Media, SEO, Social Media
Lacoste
LEGO A/S
LG Electronics
M&S Bank
Reed.co.uk Digital Marketing, Online Creative Strategy, PPC, Paid Media
Sainsburys Bank
STA Travel
Superdry Search
Toyota Search Marketing; 2008
Tui
Turner Broadcasting System
Unilever
Villa Plus Paid Search Marketing
Virgin
White Stuff Search Strategy
Woolworths

iCrossing Los Angeles
3000 Ocean Park Blvd, Santa Monica, CA 90405
Tel.: (310) 664-2930
Fax: (310) 302-6001
Web Site: www.icrossing.com

Agency Specializes In: Advertising

Mike Parker *(Pres-West)*
Matt Gross *(VP-Data Science)*
Ty Martin *(Sr Dir-Digital Media Strategy)*
Paul Shin *(Sr Dir-Digital Media Strategy)*
Jeff Campbell *(Dir-Media)*
Holly Owiti *(Dir-Media-Digital Media)*
Tanya Oh *(Sr Acct Mgr)*

Accounts:
Bank of America
Bermuda Department of Tourism
Coca-Cola Refreshments USA, Inc.
Nokia
Unilever

iCrossing Reston
1902 Campus Commons Ste 600, Reston, VA 20191
Tel.: (703) 262-3200
Fax: (703) 262-3201
E-Mail: info@icrossing.com
Web Site: www.icrossing.com

Agency Specializes In: Affiliate Marketing, Brand Development & Integration, Branded Entertainment, Business-To-Business, Consulting, Consumer Goods, Consumer Marketing, Content, Corporate Communications, Customer Relationship Management, Digital/Interactive, Direct Response Marketing, E-Commerce, Email, Information Technology, Internet/Web Design, Mobile Marketing, Multicultural, Pharmaceutical, Podcasting, RSS (Really Simple Syndication), Retail, Search Engine Optimization, Strategic Planning/Research, Viral/Buzz/Word of Mouth, Web (Banner Ads, Pop-ups, etc.)

Michael J. Jackson *(CFO & Exec VP)*
Dave Johnson *(COO)*
Dave Corchado *(Chief Product Officer)*
Stephen Thompson *(Exec VP & Exec Dir-Creative)*
Mitchell Yoo *(Sr VP & Head-Global Dev)*
Christine Bensen *(Sr VP-Media)*
Darren Prock *(Sr VP-Delivery Mgmt)*
Patrick Bertermann *(Mng Dir-iCrossing GmbH)*
Alexander Holden *(Mng Dir-Germany)*

iCrossing Salt Lake City
231 E 400 S Ste 300, Salt Lake City, UT 84111
Tel.: (801) 456-1560
Fax: (801) 415-1380

Agency Specializes In: Advertising

Michael J. Jackson *(CFO & Exec VP)*
Steven Shay *(VP & Grp Dir-Creative)*
Kent Milton *(Sr Dir-Creative)*
Adam Lester *(Dir-Bus Dev North America)*
Maureen O'Malley *(Dir-Talent Acq)*
Tim Delaca *(Mgr-Media)*
David Shapiro *(Mgr-Search Engrg)*

iCrossing San Francisco
550 Kearny St, San Francisco, CA 94108
Tel.: (415) 869-1120
Fax: (415) 869-1211
E-Mail: info@icrossing.com
Web Site: www.icrossing.com

Employees: 850
Year Founded: 1998

Agency Specializes In: Sponsorship

Jonathon Adams *(Sr VP-Global Media)*
Christine Bensen *(Sr VP-Media Strategy)*
Chris Gatewood *(VP & Exec Dir-Creative)*
Andrew Schemeling *(VP & Exec Dir-Creative)*
Michael Dan *(Assoc Dir-Media)*

Accounts:
Adobe
Auto Trader
BMW Group
Charles Schwab Digital Strategy
Coca-Cola Refreshments USA, Inc.
Sunrun Content Marketing, Digital Media, Search Engine Marketing, Search Engine Optimization

iCrossing Santiago
Av President Kennedy 5118 Piso 4, Vitacura, Santiago, Chile
Tel.: (56) 2 432 3220
Web Site: www.icrossing.com/icrossing-santiago

Daniela Callejon *(Mng Dir)*
Gonzaga Valdes *(CEO-Latin America)*
David Oyarzun *(VP-Strategic Plng)*
Fabiola Vasquez Aguilar *(Mgr-Community)*
Nathalia Saavedra *(Supvr-Digital Accts)*
Diego Duarte Cereceda *(Sr Analyst-Social Media)*
Paulina Rodriguez Bascunan *(Analyst-Social Media)*
Nicolas Nunez Perez *(Analyst-Social Media)*

iCrossing Scottsdale
15169 N Scottsdale Rd Ste C400, Scottsdale, AZ 85254
Tel.: (480) 505-5800
Fax: (480) 505-5801
Toll Free: (866) 620-3780
Web Site: www.icrossing.com

Year Founded: 1998

Agency Specializes In: Advertising, Automotive, Digital/Interactive, Direct Response Marketing, E-Commerce, Electronic Media, High Technology, Information Technology, Leisure, Public Relations, Publicity/Promotions, Sponsorship, Travel &

Tourism

Michael J. Jackson *(CFO & Exec VP)*
Stephen Thompson *(Exec VP & Exec Dir-Creative)*
Sudhir Vallamkondu *(VP-Software Engrg)*
Levi Eli *(Dir-Media)*

Accounts:
AAA Digital
Adobe
Ashley Furniture HomeStore (Agency of Record)
Auto Trader
Avery Dennison (Agency of Record)
Cancer Treatment Centers of America Creative & Analytics, Digital, Paid Search, Search Engine Optimization
The Coca-Cola Company
Colgate-Palmolive
Combined Insurance
Comhill Direct
The Company Corporation
DEX Media
DirecTV Digital
ELuxury
Epson America; 2007
Equinox Media
FedEx
GM
Halifax
Harvard Health
Homewood Suites Online
Hyundai Website
Kia
Kiddicare
LEGO
LG Electronics Creative, Global Digital, Media, Mobile, Search, Social
MasterCard
Mazda
Office Depot
Omaha Steaks
Palm Inc.
Pep Boys Community Management, Creative, Display, Email, Marketing Strategy, Mobile, SEM, SEO, Social
Pleasant Holidays
PR Newswire
Toyota Prius
Travelocity.com LP; Southlake, TX
Vegas.com
Williams-Sonoma

IDEA LAB DIGITAL, LLC
(Private-Parent-Single Location)
37 E Main St 2nd Fl, Moorestown, NJ 08057
Tel.: (856) 642-0007
Fax: (856) 642-9967
E-Mail: info@idealabmarketing.com
Web Site: www.idealabdigital.com

Employees: 14
Year Founded: 1999

Agency Specializes In: Advertising, Brand Development & Integration, Corporate Identity, Digital/Interactive, Graphic Design, Internet/Web Design, Logo & Package Design, Media Buying Services, Media Planning, Outdoor, Public Relations, Radio, Social Media

Revenue: $1,200,000

Jay Winkler *(Principal & Creative Dir)*
Diane Pilla *(Sr Acct Exec)*

Accounts:
Camden County College

IE
178 Albert Street, Windsor, VIC Australia
Tel.: (61) 390011700
E-Mail: info@ie.com.au
Web Site: ie.com.au

Agency Specializes In: Advertising, Digital/Interactive, Government/Political, Internet/Web Design, Social Media

Rhys Hayes *(Founder & Chm)*
Berry Driessen *(Mng Partner)*
Jessica Box *(Mgr-Mktg & PR)*
Michelle Milton *(Mgr-Social Media)*
Nathan Smale *(Mgr-Client Engagement)*
Caroline Whitehorn-Parisy *(Mgr-I IR)*

Accounts:
Aurecon
Betts Shoes
Captain's Choice Digital Partner, Sitecore Development
Hoyts Entertainment Service
Maxxia Workplace Benefits Provider
ME Bank
Nike Australia
Pedigree Pets Food Distr
Swinburne Online
Tourism Victoria Digital
TWUSUPER

IFUEL INTERACTIVE
41 E 11th St, New York, NY 10009
Tel.: (212) 994-6694
E-Mail: info@ifuelinteractive.com
Web Site: www.ifuelinteractive.com

Agency Specializes In: Advertising, Brand Development & Integration, Digital/Interactive, Internet/Web Design, Logo & Package Design, Media Buying Services, Media Planning

Tom Didomenico *(Mng Partner)*
Robert Nicklin *(Designer-Interactive)*

Accounts:
Ito En Inc

IGNITE DIGITAL
5579 Quartermain Crst, Mississauga, ON L5M5V2 Canada
Tel.: (905) 399-6626
E-Mail: matt@ignitedigital.ca
Web Site: www.ignitedigital.ca

Employees: 10
Year Founded: 2008

Agency Specializes In: Advertising, Affluent Market, Aviation & Aerospace, Business-To-Business, Consumer Goods, Consumer Marketing, Content, Customer Relationship Management, Digital/Interactive, E-Commerce, Education, Email, Fashion/Apparel, Financial, Food Service, Graphic Design, Health Care Services, Household Goods, Information Technology, Integrated Marketing, International, Internet/Web Design, Luxury Products, Media Buying Services, Media Planning, Men's Market, Mobile Marketing, Paid Searches, Pharmaceutical, Publishing, Retail, Search Engine Optimization, Social Marketing/Nonprofit, Social Media, Sweepstakes, Viral/Buzz/Word of Mouth, Web (Banner Ads, Pop-ups, etc.), Women's Market

Matt Goulart *(Founder)*

Accounts:
Better Homes & Gardens Real Estate Canada; 2010

IGNITE SOCIAL MEDIA
14600 Weston Parkway Suite 100, Cary, NC 27513
Tel.: (919) 653-2590
Web Site: www.ignitesocialmedia.com

Year Founded: 2007

Agency Specializes In: Advertising, Content, Local Marketing, Social Media, Sponsorship

John Andrews *(CMO)*
Gene Smith *(CTO)*
Lisa Braziel *(VP-Strategy & Special Programs)*
Ashlie Lanning *(VP-Community Mgmt)*
Kristina Kelly *(Sr Mgr-Community)*
Emily Spurlock *(Mgr-Promos)*

Accounts:
The Body Shop USA Beauty Care Center
Microsoft
Nature Made Health Care Products Mfr & Distr

IGNITION NETWORK
125 South Wacker Dr, Ste 1750, Chicago, IL 60606
Tel.: (312) 893-5000
E-Mail: inquiries@ignitionnetwork.com
Web Site: www.ignitionnetwork.com

Employees: 25
Year Founded: 2006

Agency Specializes In: Digital/Interactive, Sweepstakes

Approx. Annual Billings: $7,000,000

Mat Kresz *(Gen Mgr)*
Brian Opyd *(Gen Mgr)*
Brent Gross *(Dir-Client Engagement)*
Kelli Thomas *(Mgr-Promos)*

Accounts:
AAA; Los Angeles, CA
MillerCoors; Chicago, IL
US Bank Elan; Milwaukee, WI
US Bank; Minneapolis, MN
VISA; San Francisco, CA

IGNITIONONE
32 Ave of the Americas 5th Fl, New York, NY 10013
Toll Free: (888) 744-6483
E-Mail: press@ignitionone.com
Web Site: www.ignitionone.com

Agency Specializes In: Digital/Interactive

Roger Barnette *(Pres)*
Will Margiloff *(CEO)*
Jonathan Ragals *(COO)*
Craig Pohan *(CTO)*
Eric Bamberger *(Sr VP-Advisor Svcs)*
Katrina Conn *(Sr VP-Strategic Svcs)*
Barry Schnur *(Sr VP-Client Success)*
Mark Ziler *(Sr VP-Implementation-Global)*
Greg Bishop *(Assoc Acct Mgr)*

Accounts:
Ann Taylor
BMW
Fiat
General Motors
Philips
YP

IgnitionOne
120 Charing Cross Road 3rd Fl, London, WC2H 0JR United Kingdom
Tel.: (44) 20 7420 2230
Web Site: www.ignitionone.com

Lauren Wiener *(Pres-Sls & Mktg-Global)*
Florian Gramshammer *(Mng Dir-UK)*
Penry Price *(VP-Mktg Solutions)*

Interactive Agencies

Dominic Gramatte *(Dir-Bus)*
Stephan Van den Bremer *(Dir-European Enterprise Bus Dev)*

IMA INTERACTIVE
2800 3rd St, San Francisco, CA 94107
Tel.: (859) 396-1678
Web Site: www.imainteractive.com

Employees: 11
Year Founded: 2007

Agency Specializes In: Advertising, Affluent Market, Agriculture, Arts, Automotive, Aviation & Aerospace, Brand Development & Integration, Business-To-Business, Computers & Software, Consumer Marketing, Cosmetics, Customer Relationship Management, Digital/Interactive, Direct-to-Consumer, E-Commerce, Education, Electronics, Email, Engineering, Entertainment, Environmental, Food Service, High Technology, Hospitality, Household Goods, Industrial, Information Technology, Integrated Marketing, Internet/Web Design, Investor Relations, Legal Services, Leisure, Luxury Products, Medical Products, Merchandising, Mobile Marketing, Multimedia, New Technologies, Paid Searches, Production, Real Estate, Recruitment, Restaurant, Retail, Search Engine Optimization, Social Marketing/Nonprofit, Social Media, Strategic Planning/Research, Transportation, Travel & Tourism, Web (Banner Ads, Pop-ups, etc.)

Approx. Annual Billings: $1,000,000

Jeff Conlon *(Founder & CEO)*
Stuart Steene Connolly *(Dir-Strategy & Production)*
Taysir El-Abed *(Dir-SEO)*
Amanda Hall *(Dir-Social Media)*
Rob Horsley *(Dir-Conversion Strategy)*

Accounts:
New-Atherton Appliance & Kitchens Content Development, eCommerce; 2008
New-Benjamin Franklin Plumbing Content Development; 2008
New-COIT Cleaning & Restorationa Branding Campaigns; 2007
New-Kanopi Studios Content Development; 2015
New-Mister Sparky Electric Content Development; 2012
New-One Hour Heating & Air Conditioning Content Development; 2012

IMAGINUITY INTERACTIVE, INC.
(Private-Parent-Single Location)
1409 S Lamar Ste 1500, Dallas, TX 75215
Tel.: (214) 572-3900
Fax: (214) 572-3901
Web Site: www.imaginuity.com

Employees: 44
Year Founded: 2003

Agency Specializes In: Brand Development & Integration, Digital/Interactive, Internet/Web Design, Search Engine Optimization, Social Media

Revenue: $6,500,000

Corbett Guest *(Pres & CEO)*
Gary Hooker *(Partner & VP-Bus Dev & Mktg)*
Tony Osterhaus *(VP-Ops)*
Tim Langford *(Exec Dir-Creative)*
Frances Yllana *(Sr Dir-Art)*
Debbie Potaniec *(Sr Mgr-Acct Svcs)*

Accounts:
Dallas Regional Chamber; 2013
E4 Health

INNATE
1320 19th St NW Ste 800, Washington, DC 20036
Tel.: (202) 872-9500
E-Mail: Info@innateagency.com
Web Site: www.innateagency.com

Agency Specializes In: Consulting, Digital/Interactive

Scott Adams *(Pres & CEO)*
Matthew Snyder *(Principal)*
Lisa D'Aromando *(Dir-Client Mktg)*
Casey Hawes *(Dir-Art)*

Accounts:
New-Fairfax County Animal Shelter

INNOVYX
1000 2nd Ave Ste 900, Seattle, WA 98104-1076
Tel.: (206) 674-8720
Fax: (206) 674-8721
Web Site: www.innovyx.com

Employees: 30
Year Founded: 1998

Agency Specializes In: Computers & Software, Email, Entertainment, Health Care Services, High Technology, Hospitality, Mobile Marketing, Pharmaceutical, Restaurant, Social Media

Derek Harding *(Founder & CEO)*
Elizabeth Jacobi *(Acct Dir)*
Caroline Bucciero *(Acct Supvr)*

Accounts:
Amtrak
AOL UK
Chrysler
Citroen
DirecTV
Dodge
Hyatt
Jeep
McDonald's
Mitsubishi
Neutrogena
Norelco
Pfizer
Philips
Rapp Collins Worldwide
Sage Software
Sapphire
Sony Playstation
Virgin Atlantic
Visa

Branch

Innovyx
1660 N Westridge Cir, Irving, TX 75038
Tel.: (972) 582-2229
Web Site: www.innovyx.com

Agency Specializes In: Digital/Interactive, Direct Response Marketing, Electronic Media

Derek Harding *(Founder & CEO)*
Elizabeth Jacobi *(Acct Dir)*
Cathy Lacey *(Mgr-Production)*
Caroline Bucciero *(Acct Supvr)*

Innovyx
711 3rd Ave, New York, NY 10017
Tel.: (212) 801-8370
E-Mail: sales@innovyx.com
Web Site: www.innovyx.com

Employees: 1

Agency Specializes In: Advertising

Derek Harding *(Founder & CEO)*
Diane Lofthus *(Sr Acct Dir)*
Elizabeth Jacobi *(Acct Dir)*
Cathy Lacey *(Mgr-Production)*
Caroline Bucciero *(Acct Supvr)*

Accounts:
Adobe
AOL
Dell
HP
McDonald's
Novartis
Pfizer
VISA

INSEGMENT
313 Washington St #401, Newton, MA 02458
Tel.: (617) 965-0883
Web Site: www.insegment.com

Employees: 50
Year Founded: 2007

Agency Specializes In: Digital/Interactive

Dan Freeman *(Sr VP-Sls)*
Christopher Kennedy *(Sr VP-Bus Dev)*
Dennis Charolle *(VP-Ops)*
Ryan Turner *(VP-Digital Mktg)*
Larysa Domanova *(Dir-Creative & Tech)*
Louis Coates *(Sr Mgr-Digital Mktg)*
Brian McGillicuddy *(Mgr-Campaign)*
Mary Bowering *(Specialist-Media Production)*

Accounts:
Avidia Bank
Cumberland Farms
GlobalSCAPE
Kaspersky
Lesley University
MEDHOST
Proxy Networks
Taurus

INTEGRITY MEDIA GROUP
2900 Bristol St, Costa Mesa, CA 92626
Tel.: (949) 829-3456
Web Site: integritymediacorp.com

Employees: 6
Year Founded: 2011

Agency Specializes In: Brand Development & Integration, Consulting, Corporate Identity, Digital/Interactive, E-Commerce, Electronic Media, Experience Design, Graphic Design, Identity Marketing, Integrated Marketing, Internet/Web Design, Logo & Package Design, Multimedia, Production (Ad, Film, Broadcast), Search Engine Optimization, Social Marketing/Nonprofit, Social Media, Strategic Planning/Research, Web (Banner Ads, Pop-ups, etc.)

Richard Uruchurtu *(Dir-Digital Content)*

Accounts:
Sonic Foamer Beer Accessories; 2015

INTERACTIVEH2O
11 E Hubbard St Ste 701, Chicago, IL 60611
Tel.: (312) 758-7224
Web Site: InteractiveH2O.com

Employees: 10
Year Founded: 2011

Agency Specializes In: Paid Searches

Approx. Annual Billings: $5,000,000

Jason Randolph *(Co-Founder & Pres)*
Richard Bray *(Co-Founder & Dir-Bus Ops)*
Michael Kopp *(Dir-Tech Ops)*
Molly Rod *(Sr Mgr-Digital Optimization)*

INTERACTIVEWEST
1624 Market St Ste 202, Denver, CO 80202
Tel.: (303) 306-8746
E-Mail: info@interactivewest.com
Web Site: www.interactivewest.com

Employees: 1
Year Founded: 2004

Agency Specializes In: Affiliate Marketing, Affluent Market, Arts, Automotive, Aviation & Aerospace, Bilingual Market, Business-To-Business, College, Computers & Software, Consulting, Consumer Marketing, Content, Customer Relationship Management, Digital/Interactive, Direct Response Marketing, Direct-to-Consumer, E-Commerce, Education, Email, Fashion/Apparel, Financial, Government/Political, Graphic Design, Health Care Services, High Technology, Hispanic Market, Industrial, Information Technology, Integrated Marketing, Internet/Web Design, Legal Services, Leisure, Local Marketing, Luxury Products, Medical Products, Men's Market, Mobile Marketing, Multicultural, Multimedia, New Product Development, New Technologies, Over-50 Market, Paid Searches, Pharmaceutical, Podcasting, Publishing, RSS (Really Simple Syndication), Real Estate, Regional, Restaurant, Retail, Search Engine Optimization, Seniors' Market, Social Marketing/Nonprofit, Social Media, Stakeholders, Syndication, Technical Advertising, Transportation, Travel & Tourism, Viral/Buzz/Word of Mouth, Web (Banner Ads, Pop-ups, etc.), Women's Market

Approx. Annual Billings: $250,000

Gene Fourney *(Pres & CEO)*

Accounts:
Alpine Merchant Services; Aspen, CO; 2010
Anton Joseph Productions; Basalt, CO; 2010
Aspen Brownie Works; Aspen, CO; 2009
Brogren Kelley & Associates; Denver, CO; 2010
Carin Christian Church; Lafayette, CO; 2011
Colorado Bioscience Association; Denver, CO; 2005
Colorado Film Commission; Denver, CO; 2006
Colorado Office of Film, TV & Media; Denver, CO; 2007
Colorado Software & Internet Association; Denver, CO; 2005
Concepts Unlimited; Lafayette, CO; 2011
Health Insurance Exchange; Denver, CO; 2011
Jaywalker Lodge; Carbondale, CO; 2010
Junior Achievement - Rocky Mountain Chapter; Denver, CO; 2011
Kasmar Promotions; Thornton, CO; 2007
Linda Roberts Gallery; Aspen, CO; 2009
Mark Mock Design Associates; Denver, CO; 2010
Modern Kitchen Center; Glenwood Springs, CO; 2011
Mountain Medicine Directory; Carbondale, CO; 2007
Panache Events; Pueblo, CO; 2010
Race Across America; Boulder, CO; 2007
The Right Door; Aspen, CO; 2009
Riley Natural Gas; Clarksburg, WV; 2011
Skijunk LLC; Lafayette, LA; 2009
Society of Addiction Counselors of Colorado; Denver, CO; 2009
Sol Energy; Carbondale, CO; 2011
SpoonerSkadron; Aspen, CO; 2009
Stillwater Mining Company; Billings, MT; 2011
Studio Harris; Denver, CO; 2010
Tehama - Nacabi Trading Inc.; Lakewood, CO; 2011
Twist Design Group; Denver, CO; 2009
Walmart Secrets; Lafayette, CO; 2007

INUVO, INC.
(Formerly Vertro, Inc.)
1111 Main St Ste 201, Conway, AR 72032
Tel.: (501) 205-8508
E-Mail: info@inuvo.com
Web Site: www.inuvo.com

Employees: 34
Year Founded: 1998

Agency Specializes In: Affiliate Marketing, Brand Development & Integration, Search Engine Optimization

Revenue: $49,599,000

Richard K. Howe *(Chm & CEO)*
Wally Ruiz *(CFO)*
Trey Barrett *(COO)*
Rick Anderson *(CTO)*
John B. Pisaris *(Gen Counsel)*
Katie Cox *(Mgr-Creative Svcs)*

IQ INTERACTIVE
280 Interstate N Cir SE Ste 300, Atlanta, GA 30339
Tel.: (404) 255-3550
Fax: (770) 956-8014
E-Mail: info@iqinteractive.com
Web Site: www.iqinteractive.com

Employees: 62
Year Founded: 1995

National Agency Associations: SODA

Agency Specializes In: Advertising, Advertising Specialties, Alternative Advertising, Consumer Marketing, Digital/Interactive, Experience Design, Internet/Web Design, Sponsorship

Tony Quin *(Founder & CEO)*
Kevin Smith *(Sr VP & Client Partner)*
Walker Plageman *(Acct Dir)*
Carol Montoto *(Assoc Dir-Creative)*
Seng Lee *(Mgr-IT)*
Sarah Giarratana *(Copywriter)*
Lauren Weir *(Sr Designer)*
Russell Sauve *(Community Mgr-Social Media)*

Accounts:
American Cancer Society
Audi; 2002
Barclays Global Investments
Cardinal health
CIT
Cox Communications; Atlanta, GA; 2003
Ethicon
New-GEICO
Genworth Financial
Georgia Pacific
IBM; 2002
IHG
Microsoft
National Geographic Channel; Washington, DC; 2003
New York Life
Royal Caribbean Cruise Lines; Miami, FL; 2004
SunTrust Bank
Universal Studios Orlando
UPS
Volkswagen Group of America, Inc.
Wachovia
Wells Fargo

ISADORA DESIGN
1600 Rosecrans Ave Bldg 7 4th Flr, Manhattan Beach, CA 90266
Tel.: (310) 560-4675
E-Mail: hello@isadoradesign.com
Web Site: www.isadoradesign.com

Agency Specializes In: Brand Development & Integration, Digital/Interactive, Internet/Web Design, Search Engine Optimization, Social Media

Isadora Marlow-Morgan *(Founder & Pres)*
Alex Mathias *(VP)*

Accounts:
New-Zig Zag Healthcare

JB CUMBERLAND PR
(Acquired by Didit)

JCM MEDIA GROUP
900 Victors Way Ste 340, Ann Arbor, MI 48108
Toll Free: (800) 383-0582
Web Site: jcmmediagroup.com

Employees: 10
Year Founded: 2011

Agency Specializes In: Above-the-Line, Below-the-Line, Cable T.V., Collateral, Digital/Interactive, Electronic Media, Exhibit/Trade Shows, Guerilla Marketing, Local Marketing, Magazines, Mobile Marketing, Multimedia, Newspapers & Magazines, Paid Searches, Print, Production (Print), Search Engine Optimization, Social Media, T.V., Web (Banner Ads, Pop-ups, etc.)

Approx. Annual Billings: $5,000,000

Jeff Travilla *(CEO)*
Mark Landowski *(Dir-Digital)*
Erik Reichenbach *(Dir-Art & Digital)*

Accounts:
Automated Pet Care Products Litter Robot; 2012
Clixie Media Interactive Software; 2012
DT Manufacturing Plastics & Injection Molding; 2012
MedTest Healthcare Supplies; 2013
Pointe Scientific Reagents, Healthcare supplies, Analyzers; 2012
Post Realty Real Estate; 2012
RideFix SaaS Software; 2011
Sharper Image Sharper Image Mobile App; 2012

JOHANNES LEONARDO
628 Broadway 6th Fl, New York, NY 10012
Tel.: (212) 462-8120
Fax: (212) 614-3977
E-Mail: hello@johannesleonardo.com
Web Site: www.johannesleonardo.com

Agency Specializes In: Digital/Interactive, Sponsorship

Jan Jacobs *(Co-Founder & CEO)*
Johannes Leonardo *(Chief Strategy Officer)*
Cedric Gairard *(Head-Production)*
John McCarthy *(Gen Mgr)*
Marc Gellman *(Acct Dir)*
Sam McCallum *(Acct Dir)*
Kelsey Robertson *(Global Brand Dir)*
Andrew Lee *(Dir-Fin)*
Wes Phelan *(Dir-Creative)*
Dave Kerr *(Designer)*
Devin McGillivary *(Copywriter)*

Accounts:
Adidas Adidas Originals (Lead Creative Agency), Campaign: "#OriginalSuperstars", Superstar
New-Airbnb, Inc. Campaign: "Hosted Walks"
Bacardi USA, Inc. Bacardi, Bacardi Flavors, Bacardi Gold
Coca-Cola Refreshments USA, Inc. Campaign: "Choose Love over Like", Campaign: "Obey

Interactive Agencies

You", Campaign: "What Can Your Coca-Cola Become?", Coca-Cola Light, Global Creative, Sprite
Daffy's Inc.; Secaucus, NJ (Agency of Record) Daffy's Underground
Estee Lauder Creative
Google Campaign: "Project Re:Brief", Demo Slam, Google Innovations
Mary Katrantzou Campaign: "Chinese Monologue"
Mondelez International Campaign: "The Chew Life"
Nike
Nomis
Thierry Mugler
TripAdvisor Creative
TTI Floor Care Creative, Dirt Devil (Agency of Record), Hoover (Agency of Record), Oreck (Agency of Record), Planning, Vax
WNYC

JUXT
(Formerly Juxt Interactive, Inc.)
576 Folsom St, San Francisco, CA 94105
Tel.: (415) 671-7840
Fax: (949) 574-5922
E-Mail: info@juxt.com
Web Site: www.juxt.com/

Employees: 30
Year Founded: 1998

National Agency Associations: SODA

Agency Specializes In: Advertising, Brand Development & Integration, Digital/Interactive, Graphic Design, Sponsorship

Revenue: $2,200,000

Michael Polivka *(Pres)*
Bill Fleig *(Principal & VP-Client Svcs)*
Vinicio Vazquez *(Principal & Designer-User Experience)*
John Jakubowski *(Head-Creative)*
Mike Au *(Dir-Production)*
Jesse Fulton *(Dir-Tech)*

Accounts:
BMW
Coca-Cola Refreshments USA, Inc. Cherry Coke, Coke Zero
Toyota Touch Wall at North American International Auto Show
Vanguard University

KDA GROUP INC.
(Formerly Ketchum Directory Advertising/Los Angeles)
4739 Alla Rd Ste 1500, Marina Del Rey, CA 90292
Tel.: (310) 482-6500
Fax: (310) 482-6571

Employees: 116
Year Founded: 1964

National Agency Associations: SEMPO-YPA

Agency Specializes In: Advertising, Advertising Specialties, Affiliate Marketing, Below-the-Line, Consulting, Digital/Interactive, Direct Response Marketing, Electronic Media, Integrated Marketing, Multimedia, Paid Searches, Search Engine Optimization, Social Media, Strategic Planning/Research, Yellow Pages Advertising

Approx. Annual Billings: $105,000,000

Antony Barran *(Pres & CMO)*
Sanceree Ellis *(Acct Dir & Mgr)*

KEPLER GROUP
6 E 32nd St 6th Fl, New York, NY 10016
Tel.: (646) 524-6896
E-Mail: info@keplergrp.com
Web Site: www.keplergrp.com

Year Founded: 2012

Agency Specializes In: Advertising, Digital/Interactive, Email, Search Engine Optimization, Social Media, Sponsorship

Rick Greenberg *(CEO)*
Garrett Dale *(VP)*
Nathaniel Kangpan *(VP-Consulting & Analytics)*
Joshua Lerman *(VP-Client Solutions)*
Vanessa Miceli *(Dir-Client Solutions-Sling TV)*
Allyson Hogan *(Mgr-Optimization & Innovation)*
Noah Kershaw *(Mgr-Client Solutions)*
John Lynch *(Mgr-Optimization & Innovation)*
Rebecca Ryan *(Mgr-Client Solutions)*

Accounts:
Assurant Health
Bed Bath & Beyond Inc. Digital Display Planning , Buying & Optimization
Buy Buy Baby, Inc. Digital Display Planning , Buying & Optimization

KETTLE
180 Varick St Ste 1002, New York, NY 10014
Tel.: (646) 434-1046
Web Site: www.kettlenyc.com

Tyler Peterson *(Co-Founder & Dir-Technical)*
Olivier Peyre *(Co-Founder & Dir-Creative)*
Lauren Diamond Kushner *(Partner & Exec Producer-Digital)*
Ashley Chown *(Sr Project Mgr-Digital & Producer-Digital)*
Amanda Hughes-Watkins *(Dir-Creative)*
Daniel Landsman *(Dir-Ops)*
Shalimar Luis *(Dir-Art)*
Paul Munkholm *(Dir-Strategy)*
Camille Imbert *(Assoc Dir-Creative)*
Jeremy Bloom *(Sr Designer-Visual)*
Michael Winston *(Graphic Designer-Digital)*

Accounts:
American Express
Christie's Auctions House
Google
McGraw-Hill
Sephora
Sesame Street
Youtube

THE LAREDO GROUP
595 Park of Commerce 11860 W State Rd 84 Ste B15, Davie, FL 33325-3815
Tel.: (954) 577-5700
Fax: (954) 577-5720
E-Mail: info@laredogroup.com
Web Site: www.laredogroup.com

Employees: 12

Revenue: $5,000,000

Leslie Laredo *(Pres)*
Jeff Leibowitz *(CEO)*

Accounts:
CBS Interactive
COX Enterprises

LAUNCH DIGITAL MARKETING
22 E Chicago Ave, Naperville, IL 60540
Tel.: (312) 281-5355
E-Mail: info@launchdigitalmarketing.com
Web Site: www.launchdigitalmarketing.com

Year Founded: 2011

Agency Specializes In: Advertising, Digital/Interactive, Email, Internet/Web Design, Search Engine Optimization, Social Media

Joe Chura *(CEO)*
Caitlin Dimare-Oliver *(CTO)*
Allyn Hane *(VP-Digital Strategy)*
Erin Kasch *(Acct Dir)*
Gina Berti *(Acct Mgr)*
Ryan Kwasneski *(Acct Mgr)*
Joel Quest *(Mgr-Content)*

Accounts:
Carnivale Chicago
Esser Air Conditioning & Heating
Howl At The Moon Saloon
Keep It Off
Marcus Leshock
Social Media Beast

LEVELTEN INTERACTIVE
4228 N Central Expressway Ste 210, Dallas, TX 75206
Tel.: (972) 259-7287
E-Mail: contact@getlevelten.com
Web Site: www.getlevelten.com

Agency Specializes In: Digital/Interactive, Internet/Web Design, Paid Searches, Search Engine Optimization, Social Media

Tom McCracken *(CEO)*
John DeRudder *(CFO)*

Accounts:
New-Abila

LEVELWING
260 W 35th St Ste 801, New York, NY 10001
Tel.: (646) 216-8320
E-Mail: info@levelwing.com
Web Site: www.levelwing.com

Year Founded: 2002

Agency Specializes In: Advertising, Digital/Interactive, Email, Search Engine Optimization, Social Media

Jeff Adelson-Yan *(Co-Founder & Pres)*
K. B. Reidenbach *(Mng Dir & Sr VP)*
Andrea Ansley *(VP & Dir-Client Partnerships)*
Jeffrey Breunsbach *(Acct Mgr)*
Christina Hensch *(Acct Mgr)*
Laurie Barber *(Copywriter-Web)*
Hailey Goldstein *(Analyst-Acct)*
Sarah Welch *(Analyst-Digital Media)*
Brittany Pazyniak *(Grp Supvr)*

Accounts:
BMW
Firestone
Novartis
Red Lobster
Wells Fargo

LIFEBLUE
825 Market St Ste 200, Allen, TX 75013
Tel.: (972) 984-1899
E-Mail: marketing@lifeblue.com
Web Site: www.lifeblue.com

Year Founded: 2006

Agency Specializes In: Brand Development & Integration, Digital/Interactive, Graphic Design, Internet/Web Design

Phillip Blackmon *(Owner)*
Shyam Patel *(COO)*

Accounts:
New-Klyde Warren Park
New-Penn State University
New-Southwestern Medical Center
New-University of Texas at Arlington

LIMELIGHT DEPARTMENT
207 E 5th Ave Ste 210, Eugene, OR 97401
Tel.: (503) 321-5019
Toll Free: (800) 550-2049
Web Site: www.limelightdept.com

Year Founded: 2005

Agency Specializes In: Content, Digital/Interactive, Email, Internet/Web Design, Search Engine Optimization, Social Media

Shaylor Murray *(CEO)*
Jonathan Kingsford *(Mgr-IT)*

Accounts:
Eugene Dining
H.G. Schlicker & Associates
Willamalane Park & Recreation District

LINDEN LAB
945 Battery St, San Francisco, CA 94111
Tel.: (415) 243-9000
Fax: (415) 243-9045
Web Site: www.lindenlab.com

Employees: 300
Year Founded: 1999

Agency Specializes In: Electronics, Graphic Design, Internet/Web Design

Ebbe Altberg *(CEO)*
Malcolm Dunne *(CFO)*
Kelly Conway *(Gen Counsel)*
Landon McDowell *(VP-Ops & Platform Engrg)*
Jeff Peterson *(VP-Engrg)*
Pam Beyazit *(Sr Dir-HR)*
Peter Gray *(Sr Dir-Global Comm)*
Don Laabs *(Sr Dir-Product-Virtual Worlds)*
Jackie Abisia *(Mgr-HR Ops)*
Erik Berger *(Mgr-Recruiting)*
Carl Wilson *(Sr Recruiter)*

Accounts:
Second Life

LION DIGITAL MEDIA
(Formerly LION New Media)
(d/b/a LION Digital Media)
6100 219th St SW, Mountlake Terrace, WA 98043
Tel.: (425) 742-6828
Fax: (866) 401-6127
E-Mail: inquiries@lionnewmedia.com
Web Site: www.liondigitalmedia.com

Employees: 18
Year Founded: 2006

Agency Specializes In: Advertising, Digital/Interactive, E-Commerce, Electronic Media, Email, Integrated Marketing, International, Internet/Web Design, Local Marketing, Market Research, Media Buying Services, Media Planning, Mobile Marketing, New Technologies, Promotions, Recruitment, Regional, Strategic Planning/Research, Web (Banner Ads, Pop-ups, etc.)

Revenue: $10,000,000

Breakdown of Gross Billings by Media:
Digital/Interactive: 100%

Conrad Jungmann *(Founder & Partner)*
Mitch Griffin *(Partner & Exec VP)*
Michael Koontz *(Partner & Exec VP)*
Greg Griffin *(Exec Partner & VP-Sls)*
David Englund *(Dir-Digital Sls)*
Marti Lindeman *(Dir-Digital Sls)*
Mark Manion *(Dir-Digital Sls)*
Kelynn Lane *(Acct Mgr & Media Planner)*
Kat Corona *(Acct Mgr)*
Caleigh Chaplin *(Product Mgr)*

LION NEW MEDIA
(Name Changed to LION Digital Media)

LOOK-LISTEN
1495 Northside Dr NW Ste C, Atlanta, GA 30318
Tel.: (404) 861-0530
Fax: (770) 818-5654
E-Mail: hello@look-listen.com
Web Site: www.look-listen.com

Agency Specializes In: Brand Development & Integration, Digital/Interactive, E-Commerce, Strategic Planning/Research

Paul Sternberg *(Co-Founder)*
Kit Hughes *(Mng Dir & Head-Strategy)*
Daniel Crowder *(VP-User Experience & Innovation)*
Andria Freeman *(VP-Performance)*
John Gillett *(VP-Delivery)*
Vincent Mayers *(VP-Bus Dev & Accts)*
Mandy Nesz *(Project Mgr-Digital)*

Accounts:
Beehive

LRXD
(Formerly Xylem CCI)
1480 Humboldt St, Denver, CO 80218
Tel.: (303) 333-2936
Fax: (303) 333-3046
Web Site: lrxd.com

Agency Specializes In: Digital/Interactive, Internet/Web Design, Sponsorship, Web (Banner Ads, Pop-ups, etc.)

Patrick Gill *(Chm)*
Kelly Reedy *(CEO)*
Eric Kiker *(Chief Strategy Officer & Principal)*
John Gilbert *(Chief Digital Officer)*
Mikell Beechinor *(Acct Dir)*
Blakely Strickland *(Client Svcs Dir)*
Jamie Reedy *(Dir-Creative)*
Brett Tesmer *(Dir-Bus Dev)*

Accounts:
Atkins
Bare Snacks Marketing
Chiquita
Davines
First Western Financial, Inc. Campaign: "Turn On The Light"
First Western Trust Creative, Design Websites, Development Websites, Direct Mail, Email, Print
Geek Squad
Jack Links
Jamba Inc.
Jenny Craig, Inc.
Jimmy Johns
Lenny & Larry's Marketing
Red Robin International Digital, Maintenance, Websites
Remax
Which Wich Superior Sandwiches (Lead Agency) Advertising, Digital Strategy, In-Store, Online Marketing, Social Media

MADE BY MANY
Diespeker Wharf 38 Graham Street, N1 8JX London, United Kingdom
Tel.: (44) 2081338510
E-Mail: mailbox@madebymany.co.uk
Web Site: madebymany.com

Agency Specializes In: Digital/Interactive, Entertainment, Game Integration, Graphic Design, High Technology

William Owen *(Founder, Partner & Dir-Strategy)*
Tim Malbon *(Founder & Dir)*
Tom Harding *(Dir-Design)*
Isaac Pinnock *(Dir-Creative)*
Andy Whitlock *(Dir-Strategy)*

Accounts:
British Airways Airline Services
Britvic Soft Drinks Distr
ITV Website
Skype Online Voice Call Provider
Telegraph Telegraph on Fashion - Web Site Design
Vinspired Job Opportunities Provider

MAGIC LOGIX INC.
3234 Commander Dr, Carrollton, TX 75006
Tel.: (214) 694-2162
E-Mail: sales@magiclogix.com
Web Site: www.magiclogix.com

Employees: 9
Year Founded: 2004

Agency Specializes In: Brand Development & Integration, Digital/Interactive, Graphic Design, Internet/Web Design, Search Engine Optimization, Social Media

Revenue: $1,250,000

Hassan Bawab *(Founder & CEO)*
Chris Apaliski *(Mktg Mgr)*
Cristin Padgett *(Mgr-Bus Dev)*

Accounts:
New-24/7
New-Actian
New-CloudShare
New-Doc Response
New-FedEx El Rio Grande
New-Frontrange
New-Gloria's Latin Cuisine
New-InterWest
New-SpringCM
New-Whole Foods Market, Inc
New-WorkForce Solutions

MAKEABLE LLC
11 Harrison St, New York, NY 10013
Tel.: (212) 254-8800
E-Mail: whatup@itsmakeable.com
Web Site: www.itsmakeable.com

Agency Specializes In: Brand Development & Integration, Digital/Interactive, Internet/Web Design, Social Media

Michael Kantrow *(Founder & Owner)*
Todd Lynch *(Dir-Tech)*

Accounts:
New-The Weather Channel

MANIFEST
(Formerly Manifest digital)
4240 Duncan Ave, Saint Louis, MO 63110
Tel.: (314) 881-1900
Web Site: www.manifest.com

Year Founded: 1980

Agency Specializes In: Advertising, Mobile

Marketing, Search Engine Optimization, Sponsorship, Strategic Planning/Research, T.V., Viral/Buzz/Word of Mouth, Web (Banner Ads, Pop-ups, etc.)

Carryn Quibell *(Pres)*
Ryan Brown *(Exec Dir-Creative)*
Alexis Chamberlain *(Acct Dir-Manifesto Agency)*
Andy Angelos *(Dir-Insights)*
Tom Fox *(Dir-Delivery)*
Troy Gross *(Dir-Fin)*
Diana Garbs *(Assoc Dir-Insights & Strategy)*
Shelby Mangum *(Assoc Dir-Recruiting)*
Emily Henderson *(Sr Acct Mgr)*
Spencer Adrian *(Strategist)*

Accounts:
BigWheel Interactive Wellness & Fitness Services
Dymatize Nutrition Creative, Digital Agency of Record, Marketing Communications, Pursuit Rx, Social Media Strategy, Supreme Protein, Websites
NuYu Virtual Gym
Red Burrito
St. Louis Ad Club Advertising Club

Branch

Manifest
(Formerly McMurry)
1010 E Missouri Ave, Phoenix, AZ 85014
Tel.: (602) 395-5850
Fax: (602) 248-2925
Toll Free: (888) 626-8779
Web Site: www.manifest.com

Employees: 200

Agency Specializes In: Advertising, Advertising Specialties, Affluent Market, Automotive, Brand Development & Integration, Broadcast, Business Publications, Business-To-Business, Cable T.V., Collateral, Computers & Software, Consumer Goods, Consumer Marketing, Corporate Communications, Corporate Identity, Crisis Communications, Custom Publishing, Digital/Interactive, Direct Response Marketing, Direct-to-Consumer, E-Commerce, Electronic Media, Environmental, Event Planning & Marketing, Financial, Food Service, Government/Political, Graphic Design, Health Care Services, Hospitality, Identity Marketing, In-Store Advertising, Integrated Marketing, Internet/Web Design, Leisure, Local Marketing, Logo & Package Design, Luxury Products, Magazines, Market Research, Media Buying Services, Media Planning, Media Relations, Media Training, Medical Products, Merchandising, Mobile Marketing, New Product Development, Newspaper, Out-of-Home Media, Outdoor, Package Design, Paid Searches, Planning & Consultation, Podcasting, Point of Purchase, Point of Sale, Print, Production, Production (Ad, Film, Broadcast), Production (Print), Promotions, Public Relations, Publicity/Promotions, Publishing, RSS (Really Simple Syndication), Radio, Real Estate, Restaurant, Retail, Sales Promotion, Search Engine Optimization, Sponsorship, T.V., Technical Advertising, Trade & Consumer Magazines, Travel & Tourism, Urban Market, Viral/Buzz/Word of Mouth, Web (Banner Ads, Pop-ups, etc.), Women's Market

David Barron *(CFO)*
Keith Sedlak *(CMO)*
Jaimie Anderson *(Chief Strategy Officer)*
Matt Chervin *(Sr VP)*
Andrew Hanelly *(Sr VP-Strategy)*
Rachael Cordova *(VP & Dir-Fin)*
Lisa Schwartz *(Acct Dir)*
Gerry Kubek *(Acct Mgr)*
Peter Kornberg *(Chief Experience Officer)*

Accounts:
American Golf Corp; Santa Monica, CA
Amtrak Arrive
ASAE
Billy Casper Golf Management
CBS
The Center for Association Leadership
Cielo Phoenix
Cleveland Clinic
The Ritz-Carlton Hotel Company
San Luis Obispo County Visitors Bureau
Spring Creek Development; Scottsdale, AZ
United Healthcare
UPS
WebMD
Westward Look Resort; Tucson, AZ

MANIFEST DIGITAL
(Merged with McMurry/TMG to form Manifest)

MASSIVE CATALYST
17 Fairfield Ave, Randolph, NJ 7869
Tel.: (862) 324-4100
E-Mail: hello@massivecatalyst.com
Web Site: www.massivecatalyst.com

Agency Specializes In: Advertising, Brand Development & Integration, Content, Digital/Interactive, Internet/Web Design, Print, Search Engine Optimization, Social Media, Strategic Planning/Research

Dan Reinke *(Co-Founder & CEO)*
Cameron Alcorn *(COO)*

Accounts:
Protect Your Pet

MEREDITH XCELERATED MARKETING
(Formerly New Media Strategies)
1100 Wilson Blvd Ste 1400, Arlington, VA 22209
Tel.: (703) 253-0050
Fax: (703) 253-0065
Web Site: meredithxceleratedmarketing.com

Employees: 120
Year Founded: 1999

Agency Specializes In: Advertising, Automotive, Bilingual Market, Branded Entertainment, Communications, Consumer Goods, Consumer Marketing, Consumer Publications, Cosmetics, Crisis Communications, Digital/Interactive, Electronic Media, Electronics, Entertainment, Event Planning & Marketing, Experience Design, Fashion/Apparel, Food Service, Government/Political, Guerilla Marketing, Hispanic Market, Hospitality, Integrated Marketing, Internet/Web Design, Media Relations, Mobile Marketing, Multicultural, Multimedia, Newspapers & Magazines, Paid Searches, Public Relations, Publicity/Promotions, Social Marketing/Nonprofit, Social Media, Sponsorship, Sports Market, Strategic Planning/Research, T.V., Travel & Tourism, Viral/Buzz/Word of Mouth, Women's Market

Approx. Annual Billings: $20,000,000

Doug Stark *(Sr VP & Exec Grp Dir)*
Patti Griffith *(Acct Dir)*
Tracy Fay *(Mgmt Supvr-Social Media)*
Edwin Holmquist *(Dir-Analytics)*
Emmy Scandling *(Dir-Bus Dev)*

Accounts:
ABC
Ann Taylor Loft
BBC America
Chico's
Ford
Intel
NBC Universal; Los Angeles, CA
Sony Pictures; Los Angeles, CA
Syfy

MESS
1500 W Division St Ste 2, Chicago, IL 60642
Tel.: (773) 698-6100
Web Site: www.thisismess.com

Employees: 10
Year Founded: 2005

Agency Specializes In: Advertising, Arts, Children's Market, Consumer Goods, Consumer Marketing, Content, Digital/Interactive, Direct-to-Consumer, E-Commerce, Entertainment, Experience Design, Graphic Design, Internet/Web Design, Multimedia, Teen Market, Tween Market, Viral/Buzz/Word of Mouth

Approx. Annual Billings: $850,000

Rob Robinson *(Partner & Dir-Creative)*
Jack Shedd *(Partner & Dir-Interactive)*
Brian Wolter *(Product Dir)*
Jeff Kelley *(Dir-Creative & Engr)*
Mary Alice Ledoux *(Office Mgr)*
Jemma Hostetler *(Designer)*
Tony Nusret *(Copywriter)*

Accounts:
Hachette Publishing Little, Brown Books for Young Readers
Levy Restaurants
Macmillan Macmillan Teen
Penguin Publishing Young Adult Readers
Random House Random House Teens
Sesame Workshop Sesame Street

METIA
10220 NE Pt Dr, Kirkland, WA 98033
Tel.: (425) 629-5800
Web Site: www.metia.com

Agency Specializes In: Brand Development & Integration, Digital/Interactive, Event Planning & Marketing, Public Relations, Social Media

Liz High *(VP)*

Accounts:
New-Field Day

MINDSTREAM INTERACTIVE
(Formerly Aviatech, LLC)
7220 Trade St, San Diego, CA 92121
Tel.: (858) 777-5000
Fax: (858) 777-5050
Web Site: www.mindstreaminteractive.com

Employees: 40
Year Founded: 2001

National Agency Associations: HSMAI

Agency Specializes In: Advertising, Advertising Specialties, Brand Development & Integration, Broadcast, Cable T.V., Co-op Advertising, Collateral, Consulting, Consumer Marketing, Corporate Identity, Digital/Interactive, Direct Response Marketing, E-Commerce, Electronic Media, Graphic Design, High Technology, Internet/Web Design, Local Marketing, Logo & Package Design, Magazines, Media Buying Services, Newspaper, Newspapers & Magazines, Planning & Consultation, Print, Radio, Real Estate, Sales Promotion, Strategic Planning/Research, T.V., Technical Advertising, Teen Market, Trade & Consumer Magazines, Travel & Tourism, Yellow Pages Advertising

Approx. Annual Billings: $8,000,000

Breakdown of Gross Billings by Media: Cable T.V.: 3%; D.M.: 3%; Internet Adv.: 67%; Newsp. & Mags.: 10%; Radio: 9%; Spot T.V.: 5%; Trade & Consumer Mags.: 3%

Todd Juneau *(Pres)*
Stuart Fish *(CFO)*
James Cholke *(VP-Media)*
Debbie Croft *(VP-Bus Svcs)*
Jason Knill *(VP-Bus Dev)*
Shawn Morrow *(VP-Tech)*
Marti Post *(VP-Strategy)*

Accounts:
The Allen Group
The Little Gym
Mr. Rooter
The Villa Group; 2008
Vistage International

MJD INTERACTIVE AGENCY

4667 Cass St, San Diego, CA 92109
Tel.: (858) 345-8040
Web Site: www.mjdinteractive.com

Year Founded: 2007

Agency Specializes In: Brand Development & Integration, Content, Digital/Interactive, Internet/Web Design, Social Media

Michael Maginnis *(Co-Founder & Pres)*
Jeremy Duimstra *(Co-Founder & CEO)*
Jason Van Peeren *(VP)*
Lindsey Harris *(Dir-Creative)*

Accounts:
Alphatec Spine Inc.
Benefunder
Grammy Awards Mobile
SDG&E
St. Mary's College
The Stride Rite Corporation Advertising, Digital, Rite Feet, Social

MLB ADVANCED MEDIA, L.P.

75 9th Ave 5th Fl, New York, NY 10011
Tel.: (212) 485-3444
Fax: (212) 485-3456
E-Mail: info@mlb.com
Web Site: mlb.mlb.com/home

Employees: 500
Year Founded: 2000

Bob Bowman *(Pres & CEO)*
Edward Weber, Jr. *(CFO & Exec VP)*
Mike Mellis *(Gen Counsel & Sr VP)*
Kenneth Gersh *(Exec VP-Bus)*
Lara Pitaro *(Sr VP-Bus & Legal Affairs)*
Matthew Gould *(VP-Corp Comm)*
Amanda Whichard *(Dir-Mobile Ops)*
Christian Garcy *(Mgr-Adv Ops)*
Kacie Colbert *(Acct Exec)*

Accounts:
Angels Baseball, L.P.
Arizona Diamondbacks
Baltimore Orioles, L.P.
The Baseball Club of Seattle, L.P.
Boston Red Sox Limited Partnership
Chicago National League Ball Club, Inc.
Chicago White Sox Ltd.
Cincinnati Reds
Cleveland Indians Baseball Company, Inc.
Colorado Rockies
Detroit Tigers Baseball Club, Inc.
Florida Marlins, L.P.
Houston Astros Baseball Club
Kansas City Royals
Los Angeles Dodgers Inc.
Milwaukee Brewers Baseball Club, Inc.
Minnesota Twins, LLC
New York Yankees
Oakland Athletics Limited Partnership
The Phillies, L.P.
Pittsburgh Baseball Club
Saint Louis Cardinals, L.P.
San Diego Padres, L.P.
San Francisco Baseball Associates, L.P.
Standard Pacific Homes
Sterling Mets, L.P.
Tampa Bay Rays Baseball, Ltd.
Texas Rangers Baseball Club
Toronto Blue Jays
Washington Nationals

MOBIENTO

(Acquired by Deloitte Digital)

MOBILITY QUOTIENT SOLUTIONS INC.

229 11th Ave SE Ste 130, Calgary, AB Canada
Tel.: (403) 984-3881
E-Mail: inquiries@mobilityquotient.com
Web Site: mobilityquotient.com

Employees: 10

Agency Specializes In: Digital/Interactive

Nikhil Sonpal *(Founder & CEO)*
Dustin Miller *(Dir-Creative)*
Lee Borschowa *(Exec-Sls)*
Paul Frattaroli *(Solution Architect)*

Accounts:
New-GreenThumb
New-Just Wine
New-patch
New-QL2
New-Restaurantbusinessonline.com
New-rivalwatch
New-xtime

MODE MEDIA

(Formerly Glam Media, Inc.)
2000 Sierra Point Parkway Suite 1000 10th Floor, Brisbane, CA 94005
Tel.: (650) 244-4000
Web Site: corp.mode.com

Agency Specializes In: Advertising

Fernando Ruarte *(Co-Founder, CTO-Platform & Products & Exec VP)*
Raj Narayan *(Co-Founder, Sr VP & Chief Architect-Engrg)*
Jack Rotolo *(Pres-Sls & Bus Ops-Global)*
Kari King *(Sr VP-Sls Strategy & VP-Sls)*
John Small *(Sr VP-Corp Dev)*
Colby Mancasola *(VP-Content Products)*
Amy McMahon-Kopp *(VP-Programs & Consumer Products)*
Bianca Posterli *(Dir-Content & Community)*
Katie Schmidt Wallace *(Dir-Mktg Solutions)*
Eric Silverstein *(Dir-Yield Mgmt)*
Rani Schneider *(Program Acct Dir)*

Accounts:
ABC Television Networks
Hearst Corporation Magazine & NewPaper Publishers
MAX Factor Beauty Care Products Distr
Reebok Footwear & Apparel Stores
Victoria's Secret Lingerie Retailer

MONCUR ASSOCIATES MIAMI

801 Brickell Ave Ste 570, Miami, FL 33131
Tel.: (786) 292-2904
Web Site: www.thinkmoncur.com

Agency Specializes In: Advertising, Brand Development & Integration, Crisis Communications, Digital/Interactive, Event Planning & Marketing, Internet/Web Design, Media Relations, Public Relations

David Moncur *(Principal)*

Accounts:
New-Sulzberger Capital Advisors

MOXIE INTERACTIVE INC.

384 Northyards Blvd. NW Ste 290, Atlanta, GA 30313-2440
Tel.: (404) 601-4500
Fax: (404) 601-4505
E-Mail: info@moxieinteractive.com
Web Site: www.moxieusa.com

Employees: 300
Year Founded: 2000

National Agency Associations: 4A's-THINKLA

Agency Specializes In: African-American Market, Bilingual Market, Brand Development & Integration, Business-To-Business, Communications, Consumer Marketing, Corporate Communications, Cosmetics, Digital/Interactive, Direct Response Marketing, Electronic Media, Entertainment, Fashion/Apparel, Financial, Gay & Lesbian Market, Health Care Services, High Technology, Hispanic Market, In-Store Advertising, Information Technology, Internet/Web Design, Local Marketing, Merchandising, New Product Development, Point of Purchase, Point of Sale, Print, Publicity/Promotions, Retail, Sales Promotion, Sponsorship, Strategic Planning/Research, Sweepstakes, Travel & Tourism

Approx. Annual Billings: $38,000,000

Breakdown of Gross Billings by Media: Internet Adv.: 100%

Sean Reardon *(CEO)*
Christopher Walker *(CFO)*
Matthew Fleischman *(CTO)*
Kristina Jonathan *(Exec VP-Strategy)*
Renee Blake *(Sr VP & Exec Dir-Creative)*
Winnifer Cox *(Sr VP & Acct Dir)*
Tina Chadwick *(Sr VP & Dir-Strategic Integration)*
Jane Matthews *(Sr VP-Bus Dev)*
Melanie Santiago *(Sr VP-Media Strategy & Indus Practices)*
Tracy Younglincoln *(Sr VP-Analytics)*
John Rich *(VP & Dir-Digital Strategy)*
Chris Browne *(Sr Dir-Art)*
Barry Delisser *(Dir-Content Strategy)*
Eric Payne *(Dir-Digital Creative & Content Strategy)*
Bridget Szuminsky *(Mgr-Social Media)*
Morgan Harvey *(Acct Supvr)*
Jenn Harchar *(Supvr-Media Platforms & Audience Solutions)*
Katherine Killebrew *(Supvr)*
Whitney Lentz *(Supvr-Media)*
Catherine Morgan *(Supvr-Media)*
Anna Lipmann *(Sr Brand Planner & Strategist)*
Matt Asman *(Analyst-Adv Ops)*
Emily Harbison *(Media Planner)*
Emily Houston *(Media Planner)*
Kenny Ko *(Planner-Digital Media)*
Hailey Logsdon *(Analyst-Digital)*
Samantha Newman *(Media Planner)*
Matthew Newsome *(Media Planner)*
Merelise Rouzer *(Media Planner)*
Jehan Williams *(Media Planner)*
Michael Ann Price *(Coord-Media Ops)*
Sophia Ochoa *(Sr Media Planner)*

Accounts:
20th Century Fox Film Corp.

New-Ainsworth Pet Nutrition
Autotrader.com (Digital Agency of Record)
BB&T Corporation
Bob Evans Farms, Inc.
Cartoon Network
Central Garden & Pet
Amdro Campaign: "No Mercy, No Bugs"
Chick-fil-A, Inc.
New-Cisco Systems
New-Coca-Cola
Food Lion, LLC
Georgia Pacific LLC Brawny, Campaign: "Wounded Warrior", Sparkle
Maybelline; New York
New-Nike
Northside Hospital; Atlanta, GA
Puma
Rachael Ray Nutrish, TV
UPS
Verizon Communications Inc.
Verizon Wireless Campaign: "Breakdown", Campaign: "Reinforcements", Campaign: "Verizon 4G Campaign"

Branches

Moxie Interactive
375 Hudson Street 8th Fl, New York, NY 10014-3658
Tel.: (212) 859-5100
Fax: (212) 658-9740
Web Site: www.moxieusa.com

National Agency Associations: 4A's

Agency Specializes In: Sponsorship

Alan Silverberg *(VP-Media Platforms & Audience Solutions)*
Ben Chua *(Dir-Media)*
Lindsay Howard *(Sr Mgr-Social Engagement)*
Filippia Iboko *(Supvr-Media)*
Jasmine Hughley *(Sr Planner-Digital Media)*
Nicole Carrabus *(Sr Media Planner)*
Deborah Chae *(Sr Media Planner-Digital)*

Accounts:
AIG
Epson
Garnier
L'Oreal
Maybelline
Verizon Wireless Campaign: "4G LTE: Reinforcements"

Moxie Interactive Inc.
(Formerly Engauge Communications)
437 Grant St South Mezzanine, Pittsburgh, PA 15219
Tel.: (412) 471-5300
Fax: (412) 471-3308
Toll Free: (800) 937-3657
Web Site: www.moxieusa.com

Employees: 75
Year Founded: 1966

National Agency Associations: 4A's-DMA

Agency Specializes In: Brand Development & Integration, Business-To-Business, Consumer Marketing, Digital/Interactive, Entertainment, Financial, Food Service, Graphic Design, Health Care Services, High Technology, Internet/Web Design, Leisure, Logo & Package Design, Media Buying Services, Medical Products, Public Relations, Restaurant, Retail, Sales Promotion, Strategic Planning/Research, Travel & Tourism

Steve Swanson *(Exec VP-Sls & Mktg)*
Peter Flink *(Sr VP & Dir-Media)*
Michael Tripodi *(VP & Dir-Media)*
Nisha Contractor *(Dir-Social Media)*
Brandon Hampton *(Assoc Dir-Creative)*
Amanda Maurer *(Sr Mgr-HR)*
Abraham Madampil *(Mgr-Media Technologies & Activation Grp)*

Accounts:
Rachael Ray Promotional
TTI Floor Care North America; 1964

Moxie Interactive Inc.
(Formerly Engauge Digital)
1230 Peachtree St NE Ste 2200, Atlanta, GA 30309
Tel.: (404) 601-4321
Fax: (404) 601-4322
E-Mail: info@moxieusa.com
Web Site: www.moxieusa.com

Employees: 7
Year Founded: 1998

National Agency Associations: 4A's

Agency Specializes In: Advertising

Amy Marinelli *(VP & Acct Dir)*
Neil Schrum *(VP & Acct Dir)*
Mark Unrein *(VP-Project Ops)*
Renee Williams *(Producer-Brdcst)*
Danielle Donnelly *(Dir-Social Engagement)*
Jennifer Leahy *(Dir-Bus Dev)*
Holly Heller *(Assoc Dir-Media)*
Jessica Carruth *(Sr Mgr-Mktg & PR)*

Accounts:
Brawny Campaign: "Tough to the core"
Chick-Fil-A
Cisco Systems
InterContinental Hotels Group
EVEN Hotels Brand Identity
SouthStar Energy Services
Supercuts Social Media

MUDBUG MEDIA INC.
1 Canal Pl 365 Canal St Ste 2325, New Orleans, LA 70130
Tel.: (504) 581-4636
Web Site: www.mudbugmedia.com

Agency Specializes In: Brand Development & Integration, Digital/Interactive, Graphic Design, Internet/Web Design, Print, Promotions

Rachel Haffner *(Mng Dir)*
Michael Roberts *(Dir-Mktg)*
Ashley Hoyuela *(Creative Dir)*
Justin Bantuelle *(Dir-Web Tech)*
Roy Mumaw *(Mgr-Programming)*
Vasu Tummala *(Sr Designer)*

Accounts:
Boh Brothers
Gulf Coast Bank
Teleflex

NDN GROUP
54 W 40th St, New York, NY 10018
Tel.: (646) 726-3553
E-Mail: info@ndndigital.co
Web Site: www.ndndigital.co/

Employees: 50
Year Founded: 2001

Agency Specializes In: Asian Market, Bilingual Market, Content, Customer Relationship Management, Digital/Interactive, E-Commerce, Electronic Media, Experience Design, Internet/Web Design, Social Media

David Kang *(Mng Dir)*

Accounts:
New-Allianz
New-Bailey's Strategic Social Media Planning
New-China Mobile
New-Chivas Facebook Fanpage Management
New-Citi
New-Compass Visa
New-Expedia
New-Four Seasons Hotel
New-HSBC
New-Johnny Walker
New-Microsoft
New-Shu Uemura 30th Anniversary Microsite
New-Tourism Australia

NEA
Espace St-Charles Bat B., 300 rue Auguste Broussonnet, Montpellier, 34090 France
Tel.: (33) 952099113
Web Site: www.nea-design.fr

Employees: 4
Year Founded: 2008

Agency Specializes In: Advertising, Advertising Specialties, Affluent Market, Alternative Advertising, Bilingual Market, Brand Development & Integration, Branded Entertainment, Broadcast, Business Publications, Business-To-Business, Co-op Advertising, Communications, Consulting, Consumer Marketing, Corporate Communications, Corporate Identity, Digital/Interactive, E-Commerce, Graphic Design, High Technology, Identity Marketing, International, Internet/Web Design, Logo & Package Design, Luxury Products, Multimedia, Planning & Consultation, Production, Production (Ad, Film, Broadcast), Promotions, Public Relations, Publicity/Promotions, Radio, Search Engine Optimization, Social Media, T.V., Technical Advertising

Bruno Peres *(Owner)*
Benjamin Mechali *(Co-Mgr)*

Accounts:
ECAM School of Engineering; 2011
Sanofi Aventis Aramon Site Video Production; 2010
SNCF DSI-T Social Club; 2010

NETPRPRO, INC.
6106 Long Prairie Rd #744-114, Flower Mound, TX 75028
Tel.: (214) 600-2683
E-Mail: don@netPRpro.com

Employees: 15
Year Founded: 1978

Agency Specializes In: Advertising, Automotive, Brand Development & Integration, Business Publications, Business-To-Business, Collateral, Communications, Consulting, Corporate Communications, Digital/Interactive, Electronic Media, Graphic Design, Guerilla Marketing, High Technology, Industrial, Internet/Web Design, Logo & Package Design, Market Research, New Product Development, New Technologies, Planning & Consultation, Podcasting, Public Relations, Publicity/Promotions, RSS (Really Simple Syndication), Regional, Restaurant, Sports Market, Strategic Planning/Research, Technical Advertising, Transportation, Viral/Buzz/Word of Mouth

Approx. Annual Billings: $900,000

Breakdown of Gross Billings by Media: Collateral: $20,000; E-Commerce: $50,000; Internet Adv.: $750,000; Print: $80,000

Don Lokke, Jr. *(Founder)*

Ross Jones *(CEO)*

Accounts:
Atcoa Air Tools; Dallas, TX Air Tools & Information Products; 1985
Decorative Concrete Supply; Houston, TX Concrete Supplies; 2010

NEW WAVE INDUSTRIES INC.
135 Day St, Newington, CT 6111
Tel.: (860) 953-9283
Fax: (866) 953-9283
Web Site: www.newwaveindustries.com

Agency Specializes In: Content, Digital/Interactive, Internet/Web Design, Paid Searches, Search Engine Optimization

Jon Rondeau *(Pres & CEO)*

Accounts:
New-Call Before You Dig

NEWQUEST
1818 Market St Ste 3310, Philadelphia, PA 19103
Tel.: (267) 909-9805
E-Mail: contact@newquest.us
Web Site: www.newquest.us

Year Founded: 2007

Agency Specializes In: Advertising, Digital/Interactive, Email, Graphic Design, Internet/Web Design, Print, Social Media

Jerome Cathaud *(Dir-Ops)*

Accounts:
Universal Music

NGAGE LLC
(Name Changed to Manifest)

NIGHT AGENCY
45 Howard St, New York, NY 10003
Tel.: (212) 431-1945
Fax: (917) 677-8327
E-Mail: info@nightagency.com
Web Site: www.nightagency.com

Employees: 40
Year Founded: 2003

Agency Specializes In: Consumer Marketing, Cosmetics, Digital/Interactive, Entertainment, Event Planning & Marketing, Internet/Web Design, Sponsorship, Strategic Planning/Research

Darren Paul *(Mng Partner)*
Evan Slater *(Partner & Exec Dir-Creative)*
Scott Cohn *(Partner)*
Jessica Van Dzura *(Grp Acct Dir)*
Jang Cho *(Dir-Art)*
Justin Steinburg *(Dir-Art)*
Dalyn Francis *(Acct Exec)*
Alex Schwartz *(Copywriter)*

Accounts:
AVON
Christiania
Conde Nast
Dial Corporation
Dial
ESPN
Estee Lauder
Hanes
Keds/Whitney
Kiehl's Campaign: "How To: Put Space on Your Face", Men's Personal Care Products
Live NYC
Lucky Brand
Mark.Blog
markgirl.tv
Mark.reps
Purex
Spotify
Tequila Avion Digital, Social Media
Vines and Voyage

NINA HALE INC.
100 S 5th St Ste 2000, Minneapolis, MN 55402
Tel.: (612) 392-2427
E-Mail: info@ninahale.com
Web Site: www.ninahale.com

Agency Specializes In: Digital/Interactive, Paid Searches, Search Engine Optimization, Social Media

Donna Robinson *(CEO)*
Luke Schlegel *(VP-Ops & Analytics)*
Allison McMenimen *(VP-Client Svcs)*
Tami McBrady *(Dir-Media)*

Accounts:
New-Life Time Fitness Inc

NYC RESTAURANT
7 W 45th St, New York, NY 10036
Tel.: (212) 395-9400
Fax: (917) 591-1020
E-Mail: hello@nycrestaurant.com
Web Site: www.nycrestaurant.com

Year Founded: 2001

Agency Specializes In: Brand Development & Integration, Digital/Interactive, Print, Search Engine Optimization, Social Media, Web (Banner Ads, Pop-ups, etc.)

Alexandra Ow *(Acct Mgr-Digital Mktg)*

Accounts:
New-Bavaria Bier Haus
New-Beckett's Bar & Grill
New-Route 66 Smokehouse

OBSCURA DIGITAL, INC.
729 Tennese, San Francisco, CA 94107
Tel.: (415) 227-9979
Fax: (415) 227-9494
E-Mail: info@obscuradigital.com
Web Site: www.obscuradigital.com

Employees: 40
Year Founded: 2001

Agency Specializes In: Digital/Interactive

Revenue: $16,000,000

Chris Lejeune *(Co-Founder & CEO)*
Travis Threlkel *(Founder & Chief Creative Officer)*
David Shulman *(CFO)*
Peter Sapienza *(VP-Strategy)*
Kimber Sterling *(VP-Client Svcs)*
Sean Holt *(Dir-Sys)*
Marc Melzer *(Dir-Media Arts)*
Barry Threw *(Dir-Software)*
Alex Oropeza *(Sr Exec Producer)*

Accounts:
Coca-Cola Refreshments USA, Inc.

OGILVYINTERACTIVE
636 11th Ave, New York, NY 10036
Tel.: (212) 237-4000
Fax: (212) 237-5123
E-Mail: lauren.crampsie@ogilvy.com
Web Site: www.ogilvy.com

Year Founded: 1983

Agency Specializes In: Digital/Interactive, Sponsorship

Lauren Crampsie *(Sr Partner & CMO-Global)*
Pam Downey *(Dir-Content Strategy)*

Accounts:
IBM Corp
Nestle USA Raisinets

THE OLD STATE LLC
9007 San Benito Way, Dallas, TX 75218
Tel.: (214) 484-4449
Fax: (866) 292-0445
E-Mail: info@theoldstate.com
Web Site: www.theoldstate.com

Year Founded: 2007

Agency Specializes In: Brand Development & Integration, Digital/Interactive, Internet/Web Design, Print

Accounts:
New-William Noble Rare Jewels

OMOBONO
161 N Clark St Ste 4732, Chicago, IL 60601
Tel.: (312) 523-2179
E-Mail: info@omobono.com
Web Site: www.omobono.com

Agency Specializes In: Brand Development & Integration, Content, Digital/Interactive, Email, Internet/Web Design, Search Engine Optimization, Social Media

Tom Kelly *(Mng Dir)*
Jill Kouri *(CMO)*
Philip Black *(Sr Strategist)*

Accounts:
Jones Lang LaSalle

ON ADVERTISING
11022 S 51st St Ste 250, Phoenix, AZ 85044
Tel.: (480) 705-6623
Web Site: www.on-advertising.com

Agency Specializes In: Advertising, Brand Development & Integration, Crisis Communications, Digital/Interactive, Media Buying Services, Media Relations, Print, Public Relations, Social Media, Strategic Planning/Research

Jim Hayden *(Chm)*
Ron Meritt *(Pres)*
John Hernandez *(CEO)*
Noah Dyer *(VP-Mktg Strategies)*
Scott Kasallis *(Creative Dir)*
Jeff Breuer *(Dir-Digital Studio)*
Will Holburn *(Dir-Mktg & Comm)*
Julie Light *(Dir-Media)*
Veronica Hernandez *(Sr Acct Exec-Strategic)*

Accounts:
South Coast Post Acute

ONE SOURCE DIRECT MARKETING, INC.
9900 W. Sample Rd Ste 300, Coral Springs, FL 33065
Fax: (954) 757-6448
Toll Free: (877) 975-0005
E-Mail: info@onesourcedirectmarketing.com
Web Site: www.onesourcedirectmarketing.com

Interactive Agencies

Agency Specializes In: Advertising, Affluent Market, African-American Market, Bilingual Market, Brand Development & Integration, Business-To-Business, Children's Market, College, Consumer Goods, Digital/Interactive, Direct Response Marketing, Direct-to-Consumer, Electronics, Email, Entertainment, Fashion/Apparel, Government/Political, High Technology, Hispanic Market, Household Goods, Leisure, Medical Products, Men's Market, Pets , Pharmaceutical, Retail, Shopper Marketing, Sports Market, Teen Market, Travel & Tourism, Urban Market, Women's Market

Approx. Annual Billings: $1,500,000

Breakdown of Gross Billings by Media: D.M.: 100%

Eric Appel *(Pres)*

ORGANIC, INC.

600 California St, San Francisco, CA 94108
Tel.: (415) 581-5300
Fax: (415) 581-5400
E-Mail: newbiz@organic.com
Web Site: www.organic.com

Employees: 400
Year Founded: 1993

National Agency Associations: ANA-IAB

Agency Specializes In: Above-the-Line, Advertising, Advertising Specialties, Automotive, Below-the-Line, Brand Development & Integration, Branded Entertainment, Business-To-Business, Children's Market, Consumer Goods, Consumer Marketing, Content, Corporate Identity, Cosmetics, Customer Relationship Management, Digital/Interactive, Direct Response Marketing, Direct-to-Consumer, E-Commerce, Electronic Media, Email, Entertainment, Experience Design, Fashion/Apparel, Financial, Game Integration, Graphic Design, Health Care Services, High Technology, Hospitality, Household Goods, Identity Marketing, In-Store Advertising, Integrated Marketing, International, Internet/Web Design, Leisure, Local Marketing, Luxury Products, Market Research, Media Buying Services, Media Planning, Mobile Marketing, Multimedia, New Product Development, New Technologies, Out-of-Home Media, Paid Searches, Pets , Planning & Consultation, Point of Purchase, Point of Sale, Print, Production, Real Estate, Retail, Search Engine Optimization, Shopper Marketing, Social Marketing/Nonprofit, Social Media, Sponsorship, Sports Market, Stakeholders, Strategic Planning/Research, Syndication, Teen Market, Transportation, Travel & Tourism, Tween Market, Urban Market, Viral/Buzz/Word of Mouth, Women's Market

David Shulman *(CEO)*
Monik Sanghvi *(Chief Strategy Officer)*
Sarah Montague *(Sr VP & Gen Mgr)*
Tina Weber *(VP-Fin)*
Lisa Yamamura *(Head-Client Svcs)*
Marney Kerr *(Grp Dir-Creative)*
Kristen Guernsey *(Client Svcs Dir)*
Wynter O-Blanquet *(Acct Dir)*
Amy Rodriguez *(Client Svcs Dir)*
Sunny Lee *(Dir-Strategy)*
Mindy Sears *(Assoc Dir-Creative)*
Kimberly Beale *(Mgr-Resource)*
Angela Vasconcellos *(Mgr-Strategy)*

Accounts:
Foster Farms Campaign: "Take 75", Digital
The Hartford
Hasbro
Hilton Worldwide Campaign: "Bizwords", Campaign: "We Speak Success", Hilton Garden Inn
Intel
Kimberly-Clark Depends, Digital, Goodnites, Kotex, Poise
The Meth Project Campaign: "Ask MethProject.org", Campaign: "Deep End"
The National Park Foundation "I Have a Dream", WeAreStillMarching.com
Nike
PepsiCo Campaign: "Live For Now"
Procter & Gamble
PulteGroup (Agency of Record) Centex, Creative, Del Webb, Digital, Pulte Homes, Pulte Mortgage, Strategy
Visa
Walmart Campaign: "Walmart Ipad"
Wells Fargo Creative, Digital

Branches

Organic, Inc.

1285 Ave of the Americas 7th Fl, New York, NY 10019
Tel.: (212) 827-2200
Fax: (212) 827-2201
E-Mail: newbiz-ny@organic.com
Web Site: www.organic.com

Employees: 135

National Agency Associations: 4A's

Agency Specializes In: Advertising, Sponsorship

David Shulman *(CEO)*
Tracy Richards *(CMO)*
Monik Sanghvi *(Chief Strategy Officer)*
Audrey Melofchik *(Exec VP & Gen Mgr)*
Tricia Hoover *(Dir-Content & Exec Producer)*
Kristen Guernsey Metz *(Client Svcs Dir)*
Tom Heller *(Dir-Delivery Mgmt)*
April Madridejos *(Dir-Tech)*
Keith Pine *(Chief Delivery Officer)*

Accounts:
American Express
Chrysler
Coach
Jeep
Kimberly-Clark Corp. App, Campaign: "Drop Your Pants City", Campaign: "Underwareness", Creative, Depends, Digital, Social Media
Nike
Procter & Gamble
Sprint
Vogue

Organic, Inc.

888 W Big Beaver Rd, Troy, MI 48084
Tel.: (248) 454-4000
Fax: (248) 454-3370
E-Mail: newbiz-det@organic.com
Web Site: www.organic.com

Employees: 5

Agency Specializes In: Advertising

Katie Healey *(Sr VP & Gen Mgr)*
Stephen Timblin *(Grp Dir-Creative)*
Casey Blackwood *(Client Svcs Dir)*
Andrea Steele *(Client Svcs Dir)*

Accounts:
Homewood Suites Digital

ORPHMEDIA LLC

1133 Broadway Ste 1225, New York, NY 10010
Tel.: (646) 688-4000
Fax: (212) 208-4668
E-Mail: info@orphmedia.com
Web Site: www.orphmedia.com

Year Founded: 2000

Agency Specializes In: Digital/Interactive, Graphic Design, Internet/Web Design, Print, Search Engine Optimization, Social Media

Peter Orphanos *(Founder & CEO)*

Accounts:
New-Daniel Churchill
New-Michael White

OVERDRIVE INTERACTIVE

38 Everett St 2nd Fl, Boston, MA 02134
Tel.: (617) 254-5000
Fax: (617) 254-5003
E-Mail: hgold@ovrdrv.com
Web Site: www.ovrdrv.com

Employees: 42
Year Founded: 2001

Agency Specializes In: Advertising, Advertising Specialties, Automotive, Business-To-Business, College, Communications, Computers & Software, Consulting, Consumer Marketing, Corporate Communications, Digital/Interactive, Direct Response Marketing, E-Commerce, Education, Government/Political, Graphic Design, High Technology, Information Technology, Integrated Marketing, International, Internet/Web Design, Logo & Package Design, Luxury Products, Media Buying Services, Medical Products, Multimedia, Newspapers & Magazines, Paid Searches, Podcasting, Production, Production (Ad, Film, Broadcast), RSS (Really Simple Syndication), Retail, Search Engine Optimization, Technical Advertising, Trade & Consumer Magazines, Transportation, Travel & Tourism, Viral/Buzz/Word of Mouth, Web (Banner Ads, Pop-ups, etc.)

Approx. Annual Billings: $25,000,000

Harry Gold *(Founder & CEO)*
Michael Orlinski *(VP & Dir-Search & Media)*
Eric Wholley *(VP & Dir-Bus Dev)*
Shane Kelly *(Acct Dir)*
Andrew Abrahams *(Dir-Interactive Svcs)*
Bob Cargill *(Dir-Social Media)*
Tim Massinger *(Sr Acct Exec)*
Carolyn Berk *(Specialist-Social Media)*
Rachel Cox *(Acct Exec)*
Jessica Kennedy *(Assoc Media Planner)*
Simone C Porter *(Assoc Media Planner & Buyer)*

Accounts:
AAA
Boston.com
Dowjones
Furniture.com
GSN
Harley Davidson
Hasbro
Liberty
Lo Jack
Progress Software
Symmetricom
Zipcar

PACIFIC

2251 San Diego Ave Ste A-218, San Diego, CA 92110
Tel.: (619) 363-5070
E-Mail: wavehello@meetpacific.com
Web Site: www.meetpacific.com

Agency Specializes In: Brand Development & Integration, Digital/Interactive, Internet/Web Design, Search Engine Optimization, Social Media

Norman Brauns *(Founder & CEO)*

Interactive Agencies

Collin Dayley *(VP-Client Svcs)*
George Stein *(Creative Dir)*
Justine McGrath *(Coord-Mktg)*

Accounts:
New-Mint (Agency of Record)

PATRICKORTMAN, INC.
11271 Ventura Blvd Ste 492, Studio City, CA 91604
Tel.: (818) 505-1988
E-Mail: contact@patrickortman.com
Web Site: www.patrickortman.com

Employees: 7
Year Founded: 2007

Agency Specializes In: Advertising, Advertising Specialties, Affluent Market, Alternative Advertising, Arts, Aviation & Aerospace, Brand Development & Integration, Branded Entertainment, Broadcast, Business-To-Business, Commercial Photography, Communications, Consulting, Consumer Goods, Consumer Marketing, Content, Corporate Identity, Cosmetics, Digital/Interactive, Electronic Media, Entertainment, Environmental, Financial, Guerilla Marketing, High Technology, Household Goods, Identity Marketing, Industrial, Infomercials, Internet/Web Design, Investor Relations, Leisure, Local Marketing, Luxury Products, Magazines, Men's Market, Multicultural, Multimedia, New Product Development, Newspapers & Magazines, Out-of-Home Media, Pharmaceutical, Planning & Consultation, Production, Production (Ad, Film, Broadcast), Promotions, Real Estate, Restaurant, Retail, Search Engine Optimization, Social Marketing/Nonprofit, Social Media, Sports Market, T.V., Web (Banner Ads, Pop-ups, etc.)

Approx. Annual Billings: $10,000,000

Breakdown of Gross Billings by Media: Internet Adv.: $3,000,000; T.V.: $7,000,000

Patrick Ortman *(CEO & Dir-Creative)*

POSSIBLE NEW YORK
(Formerly Possible Worldwide)
41 E 11th St 6th Fl, New York, NY 10003
Tel.: (212) 710-2400
E-Mail: newyork@possible.com
Web Site: www.possible.com

Employees: 1,500
Year Founded: 2011

Agency Specializes In: Digital/Interactive, Mobile Marketing, Social Media, Sponsorship, T.V., Web (Banner Ads, Pop-ups, etc.)

Revenue: $100,000,000

Shane Atchison *(CEO)*
Jason Brush *(Exec VP-User Experience Design & Exec Dir-Creative)*
Jason Minyo *(Exec Dir-Creative)*
Mike Rokicki *(Sr Acct Dir)*
Jamie Julian *(Grp Acct Dir)*
Kim Frost *(Acct Dir)*
Ted Ismert *(Acct Dir-Mobile)*
Heather Hay *(Dir-Talent Acq)*
Sean Weller *(Dir-Strategy)*
Lesley Parks *(Mgr-Community)*
Wade Addison *(Acct Supvr)*
Patrick Blauner *(Acct Supvr)*
Sally Hrouda *(Acct Supvr-Digital)*

Accounts:
AMC
AT&T Communications Corp.
Barclays
BBC
Build-A-Bear Workshop, Inc. Digital
Butterball, LLC Orville Redenbacher's (Digital Agency of Record)
Comcast
Dell
Disney
Dow Corning
General Mills
Microsoft
Orange
Procter & Gamble
Samsung
Sony

Branches

Possible Cincinnati
(Formerly Possible Worldwide)
302 W Third St Ste 900, Cincinnati, OH 45202
Tel.: (513) 381-1380
Fax: (513) 381-0248
Web Site: www.possible.com

Employees: 304
Year Founded: 1978

Agency Specializes In: Brand Development & Integration, Consumer Marketing, Corporate Identity, Digital/Interactive, Direct Response Marketing, E-Commerce, Electronic Media, Graphic Design, Health Care Services, High Technology, Information Technology, Internet/Web Design, Medical Products, New Product Development, Pharmaceutical, Planning & Consultation, Print, Sales Promotion, Sponsorship, Strategic Planning/Research

Martha Hiefield *(Pres-Seattle)*
Brian LeCount *(Exec VP-Strategy & Insights)*
Christopher Reintz *(Exec VP-Acct Mgmt)*
Tony Desjardins *(Mng Dir-Cincinnati)*
Dave Maly *(Exec Dir-Creative)*
Tracey Ireland *(Acct Dir)*
Sarah Medley Wingereid *(Bus Dir-P&G)*
Jeff Haun *(Assoc Dir-Strategy & Plng)*
James Robbins *(Assoc Dir-Strategic Plng)*
Lori Kirstein *(Project Mgr-Digital)*
Katie Winkler *(Acct Supvr)*
Brain Murray *(Analyst-Search Mktg)*
Chris Simmons *(Copywriter)*

Accounts:
Abbott Laboratories Diabetes Health Connection, Glucerna
Abbott Nutrition
Artswave Campaign: "Radius"
The Bill & Melinda Gates Foundation
Charmin
ConAgra Foods, Inc.
Conagra Foods Campaign: "Pop Cam Game"
Downtown Cincinnati Inc.; Cincinnati, OH (Agency of Record) Mobile, Outdoor Marketing, Web
Dunkin' Donuts Coffee
Forrester
Frontier Airlines
P&G Everyday Solutions
Pepto-Bismol
Perkins & Marie Callender's Inc.
Pringles
Procter & Gamble Co. Campaign: "Birthday Cake", Campaign: "Vicks Most Dedicated Fan", Cheer & Charmin, Fibersure, Folgers, Health Expressions, Hong Kong Jockey Club, Luvs, Mr. Clean, Noxzema, P&G Brandsaver, Pepto Bismol, Pringles, Puffs, Pur Water Filters, ThermaCare, Vicks Nyquil; 2006
Samsung
Southern Comfort (Agency of Record) Alcohol brand
UNICEF
U.S. Bank

Possible Los Angeles
(Formerly Possible Worldwide)
5780 W Jefferson Blvd, Los Angeles, CA 90016
Tel.: (310) 202-2900
Fax: (310) 202-2910
Web Site: www.possible.com

Employees: 100

National Agency Associations: SODA

Agency Specializes In: Digital/Interactive, Sponsorship

Daniel Chu *(Global Chief Creative Officer)*
Andrew Solmssen *(Mng Dir-Los Angeles)*
Thomas Stelter *(VP-Emerging Solutions)*
Jason Brush *(Exec Dir-Creative)*
Aaron Howe *(Sr Dir-Creative)*

Accounts:
ABC
Accenture
AOL
Cablevision
Clinique
CNN
The Coca-Cola Company
Comcast
Comedy Central
Conde Net
Dell
DirecTV
Disney
Electronic Arts
ESPN
Fox
GE
Google
Intel
Microsoft Corporation
Mitsubishi Digital
Monster
Motorola Solutions, Inc.
MTV
NBC Universal
Nickelodeon
Nissan
Nokia
NRG Energy, Inc.
Sony Pictures
Sony
Starz
Target
THQ
Time Warner Cable
Turner Broadcasting
Warner Bros.

Non US Branches

Possible London
(Formerly Possible Worldwide)
77 Hatton Garden, London, EC1N 8JS United Kingdom
Tel.: (44) 203 349 5800
Web Site: www.possible.com/locations/london

Year Founded: 1997

Agency Specializes In: Advertising, Digital/Interactive, Graphic Design, Mobile Marketing, Social Media

John Cunningham *(CTO-Global)*
Simon Law *(Chief Strategy Officer)*
Darin Brown *(CEO-EMEA)*
Neil Miller *(CEO-UK)*
Jim Chesnutt *(VP & Acct Dir)*
Lucas Peon *(Exec Dir-Creative-London)*
Laura Crofton-Atkins *(Dir-Special Projects UK)*
Mike Watson *(Dir-Creative)*

Interactive Agencies

Accounts:
BP
Canon
GlaxoSmithKline Aquafresh, Sensodyne
Grant Thornton Global Digital
NetJets
Royal Caribbean
Shell (Global Digital Agency)

Possible Singapore
(Formerly Possible Worldwide)
1 Maritime Square Harbour-Front Centre #13-02, Singapore, 099253 Singapore
Tel.: (65) 6333 3336
Fax: (65) 6336 6334
Web Site: www.possible.com

Employees: 1,100
Year Founded: 1999

Agency Specializes In: Digital/Interactive, E-Commerce, Electronic Media, Internet/Web Design

Paul Soon *(CEO-Asia Pacific)*
Ryan Balingit *(Dir-Media)*
Latika Israni *(Dir-Engagement)*
Kelvin Lee *(Dir-Interactive Dev-APAC)*
Desiree Wu *(Dir-Talent & Mktg-Asia Pacific)*
Eugene Hui *(Assoc Dir-Media)*
Tina Gui *(Mgr-eMarketing)*
Jing Hui *(Mgr-Engagement)*
Vincent Ng *(Sr Analyst-Mktg)*
Edwin Kwak *(Sr Exec-Media)*
Colyn Wang *(Assoc Program Dir)*

Accounts:
Barclays
Concraft
Dell
Hewlett-Packard
HP
Johnson & Johnson
Mantha
MasterCard
Microsoft
P&G
Polycom
SAP

Possible
(Formerly Carnation Group)
Bocskai Ut 134-146, Dorottya Udvar, Budapest, 1113 Hungary
Tel.: (36) 18875353
Fax: (36) 18875350
Web Site: cee.possible.com

Year Founded: 1997

Agency Specializes In: Advertising, Communications, Media Relations, Production, Strategic Planning/Research

Krisztian Toth *(CEO & Chief Creative Officer)*
Erik Szabo *(Deputy CEO)*
Gabor Meszaros *(CIO)*
Tamas Varga *(CTO)*
Marton Czebe *(Head-Creative Div)*
Gabor Tamasi *(Client Svc Dir)*

Accounts:
Toyota Motor Hungary Kft.

PROPEOPLE
(See Under FFW Agency)

PTYPE
PO Box 451, San Bruno, CA 94066
Tel.: (650) 260-8984
Web Site: pty.pe

Year Founded: 2010

Agency Specializes In: Experience Design

Debbie Levitt *(Principal)*

Accounts:
Oracle Training
Vindicia

PUBLICIS HAWKEYE
(Formerly hawkeye)
2828 Routh St Ste 300, Dallas, TX 75201
Tel.: (214) 749-0080
Fax: (214) 747-1897
Web Site: www.publicishawkeye.com

Employees: 160
Year Founded: 1999

National Agency Associations: 4A's-AMA-DAL-DMA-PMA-POPAI

Agency Specializes In: Advertising, Advertising Specialties, Affluent Market, Agriculture, Arts, Aviation & Aerospace, Below-the-Line, Bilingual Market, Brand Development & Integration, Business-To-Business, Cable T.V., Co-op Advertising, Collateral, College, Communications, Computers & Software, Consumer Goods, Consumer Marketing, Content, Corporate Communications, Corporate Identity, Customer Relationship Management, Digital/Interactive, Direct Response Marketing, Direct-to-Consumer, E-Commerce, Education, Electronic Media, Electronics, Email, Entertainment, Environmental, Event Planning & Marketing, Exhibit/Trade Shows, Experience Design, Fashion/Apparel, Financial, Game Integration, Graphic Design, Guerilla Marketing, Health Care Services, High Technology, Hispanic Market, Hospitality, Household Goods, Identity Marketing, In-Store Advertising, Infomercials, Information Technology, Integrated Marketing, International, Internet/Web Design, Leisure, Local Marketing, Logo & Package Design, Luxury Products, Magazines, Market Research, Media Planning, Medical Products, Men's Market, Merchandising, Mobile Marketing, Multicultural, Multimedia, New Product Development, New Technologies, Newspaper, Newspapers & Magazines, Out-of-Home Media, Outdoor, Over-50 Market, Package Design, Paid Searches, Planning & Consultation, Podcasting, Point of Purchase, Point of Sale, Print, Product Placement, Production (Ad, Film, Broadcast), Production (Print), Promotions, Public Relations, Publicity/Promotions, RSS (Really Simple Syndication), Radio, Regional, Restaurant, Retail, Sales Promotion, Search Engine Optimization, Seniors' Market, Social Marketing/Nonprofit, Social Media, Sponsorship, Sports Market, Strategic Planning/Research, Sweepstakes, Syndication, T.V., Technical Advertising, Teen Market, Telemarketing, Trade & Consumer Magazines, Transportation, Travel & Tourism, Urban Market, Viral/Buzz/Word of Mouth, Web (Banner Ads, Pop-ups, etc.), Women's Market

Approx. Annual Billings: $68,876,000

Steven G. Dapper *(Chm & CEO)*
Rick Rogers *(CMO & Acct Dir-Worldwide)*
Greg Osenga *(Mng Dir-CRM)*
Wes Wright *(Mng Dir-Digital)*
Helen Prokos *(Grp Dir-Creative)*
Holly Bruinsma *(Sr Dir-Art)*
Amanda Dempsey *(Dir-Sports & Experiential)*
Melinda Gladitsch *(Dir-Insight & Strategy)*

Accounts:
Agilent Technologies; Wilmington, DE; 2006
Ally; 2012
American Airlines; Fort Worth, TX; 2005
AMF; 2010
Anheuser-Busch
BASF; 2008
BestBuy
Bridgestone Americas Campaign: "Birthday", Campaign: "Mess With The World", Digital, DriveGuard, Radio
Cargill; 2011
CiCi's Pizza
Continental Mills
Gortex
Lockheed Martin
Men's Health
Nestea
The North Face; 2006
Peterbilt; 2011
Terminix Digital, Directing Marketing

Branch

Publicis Hawkeye
(Formerly hawkeye)
325 Arlington Ave Ste 700, Charlotte, NC 28203
Tel.: (704) 344-7900
Fax: (704) 344-7920
Web Site: www.publicishawkeye.com

Employees: 40
Year Founded: 1999

Agency Specializes In: Sponsorship

Steven G. Dapper *(Founder & Chm)*
James L. Acuff *(CFO)*
Greg Osenga *(Mng Dir-CRM)*
John Williamson *(VP & Assoc Dir-Creative)*
Scott Gerber *(Sr Dir-Art)*
Michael Hefty *(Sr Dir-Art)*
Jim Williams *(Creative Dir)*
Scott Grissinger *(Dir-Analytics)*
Jeremy McClellan *(Dir-Art)*
Kevin Fenton *(Assoc Dir-Creative)*

Accounts:
Agilent Technologies
Alltel
American Airlines
BASF
Captial One
Magnolia
Siemens

PURE STRATEGIC INC.
6325 Gunpark Dr Ste E, Boulder, CO 80301
Tel.: (720) 336-0530
E-Mail: info@purestrategic.com
Web Site: www.purestrategic.com

Year Founded: 2010

Agency Specializes In: Digital/Interactive, Graphic Design, Internet/Web Design, Search Engine Optimization, Social Media

Christopher Brown *(Pres)*
Laurie Amodeo *(Sr Mgr-Digital Mktg)*
Erin Shimamoto *(Designer)*

Accounts:
Dr Trevor Cates
Walking Tree Travel

RAGE AGENCY
100 S Cass Ave, Westmont, IL 60559
Tel.: (630) 537-0273
Web Site: rageagency.com

Employees: 28
Year Founded: 2014

Agency Specializes In: Advertising, Advertising

Specialties, Affluent Market, Brand Development & Integration, Business-To-Business, Commercial Photography, Communications, Consumer Goods, Consumer Marketing, Content, Cosmetics, Digital/Interactive, Direct-to-Consumer, E-Commerce, Electronic Media, Electronics, Email, Entertainment, Environmental, Fashion/Apparel, Financial, Graphic Design, High Technology, Household Goods, Identity Marketing, Industrial, Information Technology, Integrated Marketing, Internet/Web Design, Legal Services, Logo & Package Design, Luxury Products, Media Training, Medical Products, Merchandising, Mobile Marketing, Multicultural, Multimedia, New Technologies, Package Design, Paid Searches, Pets , Planning & Consultation, Print, Production, Production (Ad, Film, Broadcast), Promotions, Public Relations, Publicity/Promotions, Publishing, Radio, Real Estate, Recruitment, Restaurant, Search Engine Optimization, Social Marketing/Nonprofit, Social Media, Travel & Tourism, Urban Market, Viral/Buzz/Word of Mouth, Web (Banner Ads, Pop-ups, etc.)

David Jackson *(Co-Founder)*
Brian Polacek *(Co-Founder)*

Accounts:
New-Associates in Family Care (Agency of Record) Marketing, Social Media
Managentum Interim Executives; 2014

RAIN
610 W 26th St 9th Fl, New York, NY 10001
Tel.: (212) 206-6850
E-Mail: newbiz@mediarain.com
Web Site: rain.agency

Employees: 90

Agency Specializes In: Advertising, Affluent Market, Brand Development & Integration, Branded Entertainment, Broadcast, Business-To-Business, Cable T.V., Collateral, College, Consumer Marketing, Content, Corporate Communications, Corporate Identity, Cosmetics, Customer Relationship Management, Digital/Interactive, Direct Response Marketing, Direct-to-Consumer, Electronics, Email, Entertainment, Experience Design, Faith Based, Financial, Food Service, Government/Political, Graphic Design, Health Care Services, High Technology, Hispanic Market, Hospitality, Household Goods, Identity Marketing, Information Technology, Integrated Marketing, Internet/Web Design, Investor Relations, Leisure, Logo & Package Design, Luxury Products, Market Research, Media Planning, Men's Market, Multimedia, New Product Development, New Technologies, Newspapers & Magazines, Out-of-Home Media, Outdoor, Paid Searches, Pets , Planning & Consultation, Production (Ad, Film, Broadcast), Search Engine Optimization, Social Marketing/Nonprofit, Social Media, Sports Market, Strategic Planning/Research, T.V., Teen Market, Travel & Tourism, Urban Market, Viral/Buzz/Word of Mouth, Web (Banner Ads, Pop-ups, etc.), Women's Market

Mark Stevenett *(Pres)*
Nick Godfrey *(COO)*
Andrew Howlett *(Chief Digital Officer)*
Mia Azpeitia *(Client Svcs Dir)*
Cassia Brooks *(Designer-Interactive)*

Accounts:
Adobe (Digital Agency of Record) Marketing Cloud Digital Ecosystem & Communication Strategies
Alibaba Reputational Storytelling Initiatives
Campbell's Digital Marketing Strategy
Comcast "Persuasively Informative" Video Development
Douglas Elliman App Development, Social Media Management, Web Development
ESPN 30 For 30 Documentary
Facebook On-going Documentary Film/Video Work
Harmons Social Media Management, Web Development
New-L'Oreal USA
The Mormon Channel App Development, Integrated Marketing Campaign, Web Development
MuseAmi App Development, Campaign Development, Integrated Marketing
National Retail Federation Integrated Marketing Programs
Prego Web Development
Puma Digital, Puma Suede, Social, Video
Spaghettio's Social Media Management
Swanson Content Marketing Initiatives

RAZORFISH NEW YORK
375 Hudson St, New York, NY 10014
Tel.: (212) 798-6600
Fax: (212) 798-6601
Web Site: www.razorfish.com

Employees: 401
Year Founded: 1995

Agency Specializes In: Digital/Interactive, Internet/Web Design, Planning & Consultation, Sponsorship

Patrick Frend *(Pres-US East Reg)*
Kierston Gedeon *(Sr VP-Integrations & Acq)*
Brian Leder *(Sr VP-North America Media)*
Todd Thiessen *(Sr VP-Strategy)*
Christopher McNally *(Mng Dir-New York)*
Stephan Barbier *(VP & Dir-Ops & Fin-Global)*
Tom Cramer *(VP-Strategy)*
Kerri Vickers *(VP-Media)*
Mike Appel *(Gen Mgr-Client Engagement & Bus Dev)*
Andy Jacobs *(Gen Mgr-Web Experience Mgmt Solutions)*
Ryan Clune *(Sr Acct Dir)*
Joe DeVita *(Sr Acct Dir)*
Chad Grospe *(Sr Acct Dir)*
Ivette Pradera *(Acct Dir)*
Michael Keaveny *(Dir-Media)*
Charlotte Lederman *(Dir-Internal Comm-Global)*
April Spicer *(Dir-Experience)*
Elliott Wiener *(Dir-Consumer Insights)*
Jeremy Cross *(Assoc Dir-Creative)*
Hunter Simms *(Assoc Dir-Creative)*
Alison Skodol *(Assoc Dir-Social Media)*
Zach Smalley *(Assoc Dir-Media, Sls Strategy & Support)*
Mike Middleton *(Acct Mgr)*
CRAIG GOLDSTEIN *(Client Partner)*
Cameron Williams *(Mgr-Analytics-Data Sciences)*
Diossy Gonzalez *(Acct Supvr-Client Engagement)*
Colleen Gilbert *(Supvr-Media)*
Christopher Kowall *(Supvr-Media)*
Elizabeth Lawlor *(Sr Planner-Digital Media)*
Michelle Hardy *(Sr Analyst-Strategy)*
Liza Charnack *(Planner-Digital Media)*
Ashley Fox *(Copywriter)*
Taylor Martin *(Planner-Digital Media)*
Giovanni Vocale *(Sr Designer)*
Haley Brown *(Asst Media Planner)*

Accounts:
Adobe Software Development
All
New-Canon Me and my bear
Conde Nast Food Destination Web Sites
EMC Corporation
Ford Motor Company
Forest Labs
H&R Block Digital Display & Web work
L'Oreal
Masco Lead Digital
Mercedes-Benz USA Inc. Campaign: "Build a GLA on Instagram", Campaign: "Tweet Race", Digital
The Patron Spirits Co Digital
Peet's Coffee & Tea Digital
Pershing
Ralph Lauren
Sheraton Hotels & Resorts
New-Spotify
Starwood Hotels & Resorts
T. Rowe Price
New-TE Connectivity Ltd. (Digital Agency of Record)
Unilever AXE Campaign: "The Graphic Novel"
XM Radio

Branches

Razorfish Milan
(Formerly Nurun Italia)
Corso Monforte 36, 20121 Milan, Italy
Tel.: (39) 02 831 37209
Fax: (39) 02 831 37 1
Web Site: www.nurun.com

Employees: 45

Roberto Leonelli *(Pres/CEO-Italy)*
Marco Barbarini *(VP & Dir-Milan)*
Andrea Bracco *(VP-Strategy & Product Design)*
Carlo Maria Fasoli *(Exec Creative Dir)*

Accounts:
Alpitour
Banca della Rete
Dainese
MTV Italia
Pirelli S.p.A.
Telecom Italia

Razorfish Atlanta
730 Peachtree St NE Ste 1100, Atlanta, GA 30303
Tel.: (678) 538-6000
Fax: (678) 538-6001
Web Site: www.razorfish.com

Employees: 60

Agency Specializes In: Digital/Interactive, Sponsorship

Wes Breyfogle *(Sr VP-BD)*
Patricia Camden *(VP-Client Engagement)*
Jim Mason *(Exec Dir-Strategy & Insight)*
Crystal Surrency *(Grp Dir-Strategy)*
Michael Aaron *(Sr Dir-Bus Dev)*
Daniel Israel *(Sr Dir-Client Engagement)*
Brendan Bell *(Acct Dir)*
Dena Martin *(Assoc Dir-Media)*
Bonny Block *(Client Partner)*
Lindsay Wachs *(Mgr-Resource)*
Amy Manus *(Sr Media Dir)*

Accounts:
Mercedes-Benz USA, LLC

Razorfish Australia
(Formerly Amnesia Razorfish)
Bond 3 30 Windmill Street, Millers Point, NSW 2000 Australia
Tel.: (61) 293809317
Fax: (61) 293808312
Web Site: razorfish.com.au

Agency Specializes In: Media Relations, Search Engine Optimization, Social Media, Strategic Planning/Research, Technical Advertising

Doug Chapman *(Mng Dir)*
Ben Hourahine *(Head-Strategy)*
Andy Ford *(Dir-CRM)*
Leslie Nassar *(Dir-Tech)*

Accounts:
Anthony Puharich Ask the Butcher

Aussie Campaign: "Creating Intelligent Sales Channels"
New-Australia Post
BT Financial Service Providers
City of Heidelberg
New-IGA
Levis Jeans & Authentic Cloths Mfr
Lexus Campaign: "LFA Surface Experience"
Mountain Dew Soft Drink Mfr
New-Qantas
New-Samsung
XYZnetworks Television Network Services

Razorfish Chicago
222 Merchandise Mart Plz, Chicago, IL 60654
Tel.: (312) 696-5000
Fax: (312) 876-9866
Web Site: www.razorfish.com

Employees: 250

Agency Specializes In: Digital/Interactive, Sponsorship

Deb Boyda *(Pres-Central Reg)*
Paul do Forno *(Sr VP-Global Commerce & Head-Content)*
Brian Clarey *(Grp VP-Client Engagement)*
Tom Nawara *(VP, Client Partner & Head-Central Commerce)*
Chris Bowler *(VP-Social Media)*
Molly Fuhrer *(VP-HR)*
Jason Goldberg *(VP-Commerce Strategy)*
Sam Cannon *(Exec Dir-Creative-North America)*
Kevin McElroy *(Grp Dir-Creative)*
Matt Horton *(Acct Dir)*
Gibson Patterson *(Sr Strategist-Social Media)*
Samantha Ogborn *(Strategist-Social Media)*
Stefanie Goliszewski *(Asst Media Planner)*

Accounts:
Dell
Kellogg Company Campaign: "My Special K", Campaign: "Top Cheese 2012"
Mondelez International, Inc. E-commerce Strategy
Purina ALPO
Samsung Telecommunications Campaign: "The Emoticon Project"

Razorfish Germany
Stralauer Allee 2b, 10245 Berlin, Germany
Tel.: (49) 3029363880
Fax: (49) 30293638850
Web Site: www.razorfish.com

Agency Specializes In: Advertising

Sascha Martini *(CEO)*
Preethi Mariappan *(Exec Dir-Creative)*
Chris May *(Grp Dir-Creative)*
Luter Filho *(Sr Dir-Art)*
Frank Lazik *(Sr Dir-Art)*
Caren Erhardt *(Acct Dir)*
Nils Hocke *(Acct Dir)*
Eva Langhans *(Acct Dir)*
Daniel Righi *(Sr Art Dir)*
Sonia Lago *(Dir-Strategy)*
Kerstin Angela Murr *(Dir-Art)*
Edward Pelling *(Dir-Client Svc-Intl)*
Thorsten Pfitzke *(Assoc Dir-Creative)*

Accounts:
Audi Audi A3, Audi R8, Audi TT, LED Scoreboard
McDonald's Deutschland GmbH Make Your Own Burger Campaign

Razorfish GmbH
(Formerly Neue Digitale GmbH)
Jakob Latscha Strasse 3, 60314 Frankfurt, Germany
Tel.: (49) 69 70403 0
Fax: (49) 69 70403 500
E-Mail: info@razorfish.de
Web Site: www.razorfish.de

Employees: 150
Year Founded: 1996

Kai Greib *(COO)*
Alina Huckelkamp *(Chief Strategy Officer & Chief Innovation Officer)*
Dirk Songur *(Head-Tech)*
Chris May *(Grp Dir-Creative)*
Nils Hocke *(Acct Dir)*
Matthias Lauten *(Acct Dir)*
Birgit Baier *(Dir-Strategic Alliances-Intl)*
Katharina Boepple *(Dir-Art)*
Felipe Galiano *(Assoc Dir-Creative)*
Sascha Martini *(Exec Partner-Clients)*

Accounts:
20th Century Fox
Adidas
Audi Campaign: "Where is the fuel Tank?"
Chrysler LLC
Coca-Cola Refreshments USA, Inc.
Condenet
Fanta
McDonald's McSundae Melt
Oakley
Olympus
Schirn Kunsthalle Frankfurt
T-Mobile US
Wilkhahn

Razorfish Healthware
100 Penn Sq E 4th Fl, Philadelphia, PA 19107
Tel.: (267) 295-7100
Fax: (267) 295-7101
Web Site: www.razorfishhealthware.com

Year Founded: 2010

National Agency Associations: 4A's

Agency Specializes In: Advertising, Brand Development & Integration, Customer Relationship Management, Digital/Interactive, Email, Media Relations, Search Engine Optimization, Social Media, Strategic Planning/Research

Rocco Albano *(VP & Dir-Web Analytics)*
Robert Harrison *(Head-Client Engagement & Delivery EU)*
Jeff Smith *(Head-Tech-Global)*
Eric Celerier *(Dir-Fin-Global)*
Richard Eden *(Dir-eBusiness Solutions Delivery)*
Eric Morgan *(Dir-Tech)*
Dan mcnally *(Client Partner)*

Accounts:
Aetna Inc. Health Care & Medicare Insurance Providers
Alzheimers Association Health Care & Social Service Providers
The Childrens Hospital of Philadelphia Inpatient & Outpaitent Hospital Services
Genentech Inc. Health Care Products Mfr & Mktg

Razorfish Hong Kong
22/F Chinachem Exchange Square 1, 1 Hoi Wan Street, Quarry Bay, China (Hong Kong)
Tel.: (852) 31024512
Fax: (852) 28657928
Web Site: www.razorfish.com

Agency Specializes In: Advertising

Joanna Kalenska *(Mng Dir)*
Alexander Lee *(COO)*
Vincent Dignonet *(Chief Growth Officer-Intl)*
Anne Davis *(Sr VP & Head-Multi-Natl Clients)*
Alexandre Misseri *(Sr VP & Head-Ecommerce Practice)*
Jonny Stark *(Sr VP-APAC)*
Crystal Chan *(VP-Media-APAC)*
James Chiu *(Exec Dir-Creative-China)*
Kevin Ti *(Grp Acct Dir)*
Nathan Hau *(Assoc Dir-Creative)*

Accounts:
Unilever Bestfoods HK Ltd. Rexona

Razorfish Philadelphia
417 N 8th St Fl 2, Philadelphia, PA 19123-3916
Tel.: (267) 295-7100
Fax: (267) 295-7101
Web Site: www.razorfish.com

Employees: 135
Year Founded: 1996

National Agency Associations: AAF

Agency Specializes In: Digital/Interactive

Antoine Pabst *(Pres-France & Gen Mgr-Europe)*
Jen Friese *(Pres-US West Reg)*
Laure Garboua Tateossian *(Exec VP & Gen Mgr-Paris)*
Anne Davis *(Sr VP & Head-Multi-Natl Clients)*
Erica Schneider *(Sr Acct Dir)*
Amanda Lewin *(Acct Dir)*
Richard Eden *(Dir-eBusiness Solutions Delivery)*
Adair Greene *(Media Planner)*

Accounts:
Alaska Airlines
AstraZeneca; PA; 1998
Brooks Brothers; 2007
Johnson & Johnson
Syracuse University Capital Campaign
Wyeth; PA; 2001

Razorfish San Francisco
303 2nd St 6th Fl Southtower, San Francisco, CA 94107
Tel.: (415) 369-6300
Fax: (415) 284-7090
Web Site: www.razorfish.com

Employees: 100

Agency Specializes In: Digital/Interactive, Planning & Consultation, Sponsorship

Liz Swanson *(Partner-Client)*
Michael Chamberlin *(Mng Dir)*
Brian Berri *(VP-Client Fin-West Reg)*
Joana Micorescu *(Sr Acct Dir)*
Yee-Shing Yang *(Sr Acct Dir)*
Patty Dunlop *(Dir-Creative Svcs)*
Satish Tallapaka *(Dir-Tech)*
Jack Shryne *(Client Partner)*
Erik Troedsson *(Acct Supvr)*
Aaron Brown *(Sr Media Planner)*

Accounts:
Adobe Campaign: "Woo Woo", Twitter Feed, Website
Microsoft Corporation Bing, Consumer Marketing, Digital, Surface, Windows, XBox 360

Razorfish Seattle
424 2nd Ave W, Seattle, WA 98119
Tel.: (206) 816-8800
Fax: (206) 816-8808
Web Site: www.razorfish.com

Employees: 2,200
Year Founded: 1996

Agency Specializes In: Advertising, Brand Development & Integration, Digital/Interactive,

Direct Response Marketing, Electronic Media, High Technology, Internet/Web Design, Planning & Consultation, Sponsorship, Strategic Planning/Research

Rishad Tobaccowala *(Chm)*
Ray Velez *(CTO-Global)*
Samih Fadli *(Chief Intelligence Officer-Global)*
Shannon Denton *(CEO-North America)*
Emily Volpone *(Grp VP & Client Partner)*
Jeremy Lockhorn *(VP & Head-Emerging Media & Mobile-North America)*
Chandra Bornstein *(VP-Adv Svcs)*
Chris Bowler *(VP-Social Media)*
Jon Groebner *(VP-Social Mktg)*
Brandy O'Briant *(Head-West Media)*
Scott Larson *(Exec Dir-Creative)*
Andrea Althauser *(Sr Acct Dir)*
Sandra Ahn *(Dir-Strategy)*
Marc Arbeit *(Dir-Media)*
Nuria Baldello-Sole *(Dir-Social Media)*
Wendi Dunlap *(Dir-Media & Bus Dev)*
Kelsey Daviscourt *(Assoc Dir-Adv Svcs)*
Carly Gray *(Assoc Dir-Media)*
Laura Cook *(Sr Acct Mgr)*
Matthew Cava *(Client Partner-Digital & Mobile)*
Liz Swanson *(Client Partner)*
Sue Gray *(Mgr-Bus Dev)*
Jen Sokol *(Acct Supvr)*
Jay Boynton *(Strategist-Social Media)*
Hannah Rosen *(Media Planner)*
Andrea Stowell *(Media Planner)*
Terry Teigen *(Planner-Digital Media)*
Caitlin Casas *(Sr Media Planner)*
Teresa Hambelton *(Sr Bus Mgr)*
Glenn Pena *(Sr Media Planner)*

Accounts:
Adidas
American Honda Acura, Digital, E-Commerce, Honda, Social Media Marketing, Web Sites
Audi
AXE Campaign: "Anarchy: The Graphic Novel"
Best Buy Co., Inc. Digital Agency or Record
Bmibaby
C&A
Car2Go Creative
Carnival Corporation
Carnival Cruise Lines
Coca-Cola Refreshments USA, Inc.
Conde Nast
DHL
Ford Motor Company
Forest Laboratories
Home Shopping Network Social Advertising
Intel Campaign: "Re-Imagine", Social Media Marketing, Website Development
JCPenney Jewelry
Kraft Foods Group, Inc. Lunchables (Digital Agency)
Levi Strauss & Co. USA
Mattel Barbie, Digital Media Buying
McDonald's
Mercedes Benz
NIKE, Inc.
Red Bull Redbull.com
Samsung Galaxy SIII
SHUTTERFLY, INC
Southwest Airlines Microsite
Starwood Hotels
Target E-Commerce, In-Store Experience, Target.com
Travelocity Digital
Ubisoft Inc.
Unilever Home & Personal Care USA Dove
Unilever North America Lipton
Washington Mutual
Williams-Sonoma

Razorfish UK
23 Howland St, London, W1A 1AQ United Kingdom
Tel.: (44) 207 907 4545
Fax: (44) 207 907 4546
Web Site: www.razorfish.com

Employees: 140

Agency Specializes In: Digital/Interactive, High Technology, Internet/Web Design

David Parry *(Mng Partner & Interim Client Svcs Dir)*
William Lidstone *(CMO)*
Daniel Bonner *(Chief Creative Officer-Global)*
Nick Turner *(Exec Dir-Creative-Intl)*
James Fox *(Sr Acct Dir)*
Cyril Louis *(Dir-Creative)*
Stuart O'Neill *(Dir-Creative)*
Anders Plyhm *(Dir-Creative)*
Paul Stoeter *(Dir-Art)*
Douglas Le Patourel *(Client Partner)*

Accounts:
Argos Digital
New-Aviva plc Customer Insights, Data Analytics, Digital, Mobile Marketing, Social Media
BlackBerry
C&A Digital
New-Canon Campaign: "Me & My Bear", Lifecake
Dell
DHL Digital Strategy, Global Lead Digital
Emirates Group Global Social Media
Kurt Geiger Online Store Redesign
Lindt Creative, Global Digital, Website Redesign
Lloyds Banking Digital
Lynx Campaign: "Epidemic"
McDonald's 1955 burger, Big Mac, Burger Builder, Campaign: "The Big Mac Mind Tests", Campaign: "Discover The Taste Of Summer", Campaign: "Knitmas Greetings", Campaign: "Mixed Up Maps", Campaign: "Moments", Campaign: "Nice Cream Van", Campaign: "The One & Only", Campaign: "Where It All Began", Chicken McBites, Chicken McNuggets, Creative, Digital, Fries, Iced Fruit Smoothie, In Cinema, In Store, Milkshake, Quarter Pounder, Super Spice Dash, TV
NSPCC Media Planning & Buying
Unilever Axe, Dove Hair, Lipton, Rexona, Signal, Surf

REACTIVE MEDIA PTY LTD
374 George Street, Fitzroy, VIC 3065 Australia
Tel.: (61) 394152333
Fax: (61) 394152399
E-Mail: melbourne.enquiries@reactive.com
Web Site: www.reactive.com

Agency Specializes In: Co-op Advertising, Digital/Interactive

Tim Fouhy *(Co-Founder & Joint Mng Dir)*
Tim O'Neill *(Co-Founder & Joint Mng Dir-Reactive)*
Jason Ross *(Gen Mgr)*
Brett Thompson *(Sr Acct Dir)*
Maarten Kleinsma *(Dir-Art)*
Simon Stefanoff *(Dir-Technical)*
Enoch Tan *(Dir-Art)*
Aiya Hassan *(Strategist-Digital)*
Melissa Baillache *(Designer)*
Alex Cameron *(Designer)*
Charmaine Lew *(Sr Designer)*

Accounts:
ANZ bank
Campus Living Villages Student Accomodation Provider
Donate Life Social Network Service Providers
Lee Apparel Manufacturer
Maserati Telecommunication Application Developer
Nissan Australia Campaign: "Your life with a new nissan"

RED CLAY INTERACTIVE
22 Buford Village Way Ste 221, Buford, GA 30518
Tel.: (770) 297-2430
Toll Free: (866) 251-2800
E-Mail: hello@redclayinteractive.com
Web Site: www.redclayinteractive.com

Employees: 18
Year Founded: 2000

Agency Specializes In: Digital/Interactive, Internet/Web Design, Paid Searches, Search Engine Optimization

Revenue: $2,100,000

Lance Compton *(Pres & CEO)*
Brett Compton *(VP & Creative Dir)*
Chris McCoy *(Acct Dir)*
Tim Zack *(Mktg Dir-Interactive)*
Zach Abernathy *(Dir-Dev)*
Heather Jenkins *(Sr Acct Exec)*
Kait Orr *(Acct Exec)*
Phillip Jones *(Copywriter)*
Kristen Lewter *(Designer)*

Accounts:
New-1040.com
New-Cloud Sherpas
New-Merial

RED INTERACTIVE AGENCY
3420 Ocean Park Blvd Ste 3080, Santa Monica, CA 90405
Tel.: (310) 399-4242
Fax: (310) 399-4244
E-Mail: contact@ff0000.com
Web Site: www.ff0000.com

Agency Specializes In: Internet/Web Design, Media Buying Services

Brian Lovell *(Founder & CEO)*
Vance Dubberly *(VP-Tech)*
Nikki Shum-Harden *(VP-Client Dev)*
Derek van den Bosch *(VP-Ops & Delivery)*
Gabe Watkins *(VP-Creative, Brand & Campaigns)*
Noah Roper *(Acct Dir)*
Travis Sterner *(Specialist-Res & Insights-Media & Mktg)*
Phillip Korkis *(Counsel-In-House & Bus Affairs)*

Accounts:
BBC Worldwide Website
BELKIN @TV, Marketing, TV Anywhere
El Rey Network
LucasArts Interactive Entertainment Software Providers
MTV Networks Television Media Entertainment Network Services
Sapporo USA Media Planning & Buying
Wonderful Pistachios Campaign: "The Hunt for the Golden Pistachio"

RED OLIVE
9980 S 300 W Ste 300, Sandy, UT 84070
Tel.: (801) 545-0410
Web Site: www.redolive.com

Employees: 5

Agency Specializes In: Brand Development & Integration, Content, Digital/Interactive, Graphic Design, Internet/Web Design, Logo & Package Design, Print, Search Engine Optimization, Social Media

Revenue: $1,105,000

Matt Moeller *(Founder & CEO)*
Justin Wilde *(Partner & VP-S/s)*
Chris Grayson *(Art Dir)*
Braydn Jones *(Dir-Mktg)*

Garrick Meacham *(Acct Mgr)*
Joshua Luther *(Mgr-Dev)*
Jacque Fairborn *(Strategist-SEO)*

Accounts:
Izon

RELISH INTERACTIVE
156 Augusta Avenue, Toronto, ON M5T 2L5 Canada
Tel.: (647) 477-8192
E-Mail: pickled@relishinteractive.com
Web Site: www.reli.sh

Year Founded: 2007

Agency Specializes In: Digital/Interactive, Internet/Web Design, Mobile Marketing, Multimedia

Sacha Raposo *(Founder & Dir-Creative)*
Paul Pattison *(Principal-Tech)*
Diana Maclean *(Office Mgr)*

Accounts:
Design Edge Canada Graphic Design Industry
FITC Design & Technology Focused Conferences Providers
Motorola Mobility LLC Mobile Phones Mfr & Dealers
Nike Sportswear Mfr & Supplier
RollBots Television Network

RESNICK INTERACTIVE GROUP
3915 W Burbank Blvd, Burbank, CA 91505
Tel.: (818) 763-1988
Fax: (818) 506-9871
E-Mail: toddr@resnickinteractive.com
Web Site: resnickinteractive.com

Employees: 12
Year Founded: 2000

Agency Specializes In: Advertising, Business-To-Business, Children's Market, Computers & Software, Digital/Interactive, Entertainment, Game Integration, Production, Radio, T.V.

Approx. Annual Billings: $1,400,000

Breakdown of Gross Billings by Media: Audio/Visual: $400,000; Digital/Interactive: $400,000; Production: $600,000

Todd Resnick *(Mng Dir)*
Phil Virga *(Specialist-Bus Dev)*

Accounts:
Mattel; Los Angeles, CA Barbie Feature films, TV shows, & web series

RESOLUTE DIGITAL
137 W 25th St 11th Fl, New York, NY 10001
Tel.: (646) 650-3120
E-Mail: info@resolute.com
Web Site: www.resolute.com

Agency Specializes In: Digital/Interactive, Internet/Web Design, Media Buying Services, Media Planning, Search Engine Optimization, Strategic Planning/Research

Benjamin Sanders *(Founder & Mng Partner)*
Daniel Savage *(Mng Partner)*
Jarod Caporino *(Mng Partner)*
Brian McNamee *(Creative Dir)*

Accounts:
The Leukemia & Lymphoma Society (Digital Marketing AOR)

RESULTRIX
The Plz 10800 NE 8th St Ste 220, Bellevue, WA 98004
Tel.: (425) 502-6542
Web Site: www.resultrix.com

Year Founded: 2008

Agency Specializes In: Advertising, Digital/Interactive, Email, Graphic Design, Media Planning, Search Engine Optimization, Social Media

Tanmay Mohanty *(Mng Dir)*
Craig Greenfield *(COO)*
Danielle Gantos *(Grp Dir-Media)*
Brittany Pfund *(Mgr-Media-Affiliates)*
Imani Jackson *(Assoc Mgr-Media)*

Accounts:
Bergman Luggage, Llc.
Bharati AXA Ltd
Corbis Corporation
Edifecs, Inc.
Indiabulls Mutual Funds
L&T Finance Limited
Microsoft Corporation Bing
Puget Sound Energy, Inc.

RETAIL REINVENTED
350 S Beverly Dr Ste 330, Beverly Hills, CA 90212
Tel.: (310) 556-0323
Web Site: www.retailreinvented.com

Employees: 5
Year Founded: 2010

Agency Specializes In: Digital/Interactive, Direct Response Marketing, Experience Design, Mobile Marketing, Search Engine Optimization, Social Media, Web (Banner Ads, Pop-ups, etc.)

Perry Preston *(Pres)*

Accounts:
Beyond Yoga

REVERSED OUT
700 W Pete Rose Way Ste 326, Cincinnati, OH 45203
Tel.: (513) 205-8022
Web Site: www.reversedout.com

Agency Specializes In: Brand Development & Integration, Digital/Interactive, Graphic Design, Internet/Web Design, Logo & Package Design, Print, Public Relations, Search Engine Optimization, Social Media

Adam Koehler *(Owner)*
Stacey Bayes *(Dir-Mktg)*

Accounts:
New-Scott Marketing Solutions

RIDE FOR THE BRAND
221 W Exchange Ave Ste 313, Fort Worth, TX 76164
Tel.: (817) 768-3011
E-Mail: info@rideforthebrand.net
Web Site: www.rideforthebrand.net

Agency Specializes In: Brand Development & Integration, Digital/Interactive, Internet/Web Design, Paid Searches, Search Engine Optimization, Social Media, Web (Banner Ads, Pop-ups, etc.)

Douglas Cox *(Principal)*
David McVey *(Acct Exec)*
Kelly Rahner *(Designer-Digital)*

Accounts:
New-Key School Fort Worth
New-Winchester Safes

ROCK STAR AFFILIATE NETWORK
1830 N. University Blvd. #342, Plantation, FL 33322
Fax: (954) 377-9013
E-Mail: cdeckard@rockstaran.com
Web Site: www.RockStarAN.com

Year Founded: 2010

Eric Dennis *(Dir-Affiliate Mktg)*
Chris Royale *(Dir-Art)*
Chris Blecha *(Mgr-Email Mktg)*

ROCKFISH
(Formerly Rockfish Interactive)
3100 Market St Ste 100, Rogers, AR 72758-8261
Tel.: (479) 464-0622
Web Site: rockfishdigital.com/

Employees: 150
Year Founded: 2006

Agency Specializes In: Advertising, Internet/Web Design, Mobile Marketing, Sponsorship

Approx. Annual Billings: $14,400,000

Dawn Maire *(Chief Strategy Officer)*
Michael Stich *(Chief Growth Officer & Sr VP)*
Melyssa St. Michael *(Sr VP-Anthropology & Search Sciences)*
Lauren Anthony *(VP-Bus Innovations)*
Bryan Radtke *(VP-Bus Innovations)*
Jason Bender *(Exec Dir-Creative)*
Blake Hannan *(Dir-Talent Acq)*
Elmer Boutin *(Assoc Dir-Search Strategy)*
Steven Fulfer *(Assoc Dir)*
Sakinah Sanders *(Sr Analyst-Mktg)*

Accounts:
Arvest
Dave & Buster's Inc. Digital, Digital CRM
Hershey's
Kimberly Clark
Oppenheimer
Procter & Gamble
Sam's Club
SC Johnson
Tyson Foods
Wal-Mart

RUNNER AGENCY
5307 E Mockingbird Ln, Dallas, TX 75206
Tel.: (214) 396-8500
Web Site: www.runneragency.com

Employees: 10
Year Founded: 2004

Agency Specializes In: Advertising, Collateral, Communications, Consulting, Content, Corporate Identity, Digital/Interactive, E-Commerce, Email, Entertainment, Exhibit/Trade Shows, Experience Design, Financial, Graphic Design, Health Care Services, Hospitality, Identity Marketing, Integrated Marketing, Internet/Web Design, Local Marketing, Logo & Package Design, Market Research, Media Buying Services, Media Planning, Medical Products, Mobile Marketing, Multimedia, Outdoor, Paid Searches, Planning & Consultation, Print, Real Estate, Regional, Retail, Social Marketing/Nonprofit, Social Media, Sports Market, Strategic Planning/Research, Technical Advertising, Web (Banner Ads, Pop-ups, etc.)

Approx. Annual Billings: $2,000,000

Reagan Judd *(Co-Founder & Sr Strategist)*
Lacy Judd *(Co-Founder)*
Bryan Daniels *(Project Mgr-Digital)*
Jordan Bundy *(Strategist-Digital)*
Will Hash *(Strategist-Paid Media)*
Jen Nahlik *(Strategist-Digital)*
Scott Adams *(Designer-UX)*
Cody Wagner *(Web Developer)*

Accounts:
Fortress Security Home Security Systems & Cameras; 2013
Galatyn Minerals Oil & Gas; 2013
GiftCard.com Gift Cards; 2012
MediTract Software; 2014
NJ Spine & Orthopedics Orthopedics & Spine Surgery Centers; 2013
Pine Valley Foods Cookie Dough Fundraising; 2014

SABERTOOTH INTERACTIVE
2017 Pacific Ave, Venice, CA 90291
Tel.: (310) 883-8820
Fax: (310) 882-0835
E-Mail: info@sabertooth.tv
Web Site: www.sabertooth.tv

David Cullipher *(Pres & Dir-Creative)*
Richard Epstein *(Partner)*
Jon Epstein *(Head-R&D)*

Accounts:
Comcast
Dell
Doritos
The Ebeling Group Not Possible Labs
Nokia
Subaru

SANDSTORM DESIGN
4619 N Ravenswood Ave Ste 300, Chicago, IL 60640
Tel.: (773) 348-4200
E-Mail: info@sandstormdesign.com
Web Site: www.sandstormdesign.com

Employees: 17
Year Founded: 2001

Agency Specializes In: Digital/Interactive, Experience Design, Mobile Marketing, Search Engine Optimization, Social Media, Sponsorship, Web (Banner Ads, Pop-ups, etc.)

Sandy Marsico *(Founder & Principal)*
Laura Luckman Kelber *(Chief Strategy Officer)*
Janna Fiester *(Exec Dir-Creative)*
Michael Hartman *(Dir-Tech & Usability)*
Emily Kodner *(Sr Strategist-Digital)*
Megan Culligan *(Strategist-Digital)*
Amanda Tacker *(Strategist-Digital)*
Jesse Lankford *(Designer-Interaction)*
Reilly Willson *(Coord-Digital)*

Accounts:
American Medical Association (AMA) Physicians Career Site
Crown Holdings; 2011
National Association of Realtors (AMR)

SANDSTROM PARTNERS
808 SW Third Avenue No 610, Portland, OR 97204
Tel.: (503) 248-9466
E-Mail: jack@sandstrompartners.com
Web Site: www.sandstrompartners.com

Agency Specializes In: Education, Food Service, Identity Marketing, Industrial, Media Relations, Package Design, Print, Sponsorship, Sports Market

Steve Sandstrom *(Partner & Exec Dir-Creative)*
Jon Olsen *(Dir-Creative)*
Chris Gardiner *(Assoc Dir-Creative)*
Lauren French *(Designer)*
Trevor Thrap *(Designer)*

Accounts:
Converse, Inc.
Full Sail Brewing Company
Kobrick Coffee
Kombucha Wonder Drink Tea Beverages Mfr
The One Club
Random House English Language Trade Publisher
Rejuvenation Building Interiors Hardware Mfr
Seeds of Change Food Service Providers
Soloflex Body Building Equipment Distr
Swedish Match Cigar & Pipe Tobacco Mfr
Tenth Caller Tixie Logo
Webtrends Digital Marketing Solution Providers

SHERPA! WEB STUDIOS, INC.
1145 Zonolite Rd Ste 3, Atlanta, GA 30306
Tel.: (404) 492-6281
Toll Free: (800) 590-0188
Web Site: www.sherpaglobal.com

Year Founded: 1999

Agency Specializes In: Digital/Interactive, Information Technology, Internet/Web Design

David Felfoldi *(Founder-SHERPA Global)*
Rusty Parker *(Dir-Data & Analytics)*
Rodrigo Luna *(Sr Designer-Web)*

Accounts:
Imaging Technologies
Lexicon Technologies, Inc.
Maxxis Tires
RaceTrac Petroleum, Inc.

SINGLEY & MACKIE INC
5776D Lindero Cyn Rd Ste 186, Westlake Village, CA 91362
Tel.: (818) 276-1920
Web Site: www.singleymackie.com

Year Founded: 2010

Agency Specializes In: Advertising, Content, Digital/Interactive, Social Media, Strategic Planning/Research

Matt Singley *(CEO)*
Peter Kisich *(Exec Dir-Mktg)*
Mary Renouf *(Brand Dir-Mktg-Global)*
Annika Nagy *(Copywriter-Social Media)*

Accounts:
DogVacay
Realtor.com

SOCIALCODE LLC
1133 15th St NW 9th Fl, Washington, DC 20005
Tel.: (844) 608-4610
E-Mail: info@socialcode.com
Web Site: www.socialcode.com

Agency Specializes In: Advertising, Digital/Interactive, Social Media

Laura O'Shaughnessy *(CEO)*
Dan Federico *(CFO)*
John Alderman *(COO)*
Max Kalehoff *(CMO)*

Accounts:
New-Heineken
New-Visa, Inc. Digital

SOCIALINK MEDIA
1332 N Halsted St Ste 302, Chicago, IL 60642
Tel.: (312) 857-5465
E-Mail: info@socialinkmedia.com
Web Site: www.socialinkmedia.com

Year Founded: 2009

Agency Specializes In: Digital/Interactive, Internet/Web Design, Social Media

Eve Hersh *(Acct Dir)*
Casey Silver *(Dir-Acct Strategy)*
Audrey Hirschl *(Acct Mgr)*

Accounts:
Vienna Beef

SOME CONNECT
180 N Upper Wacker Dr, Chicago, IL 60606
Tel.: (773) 357-6636
E-Mail: info@someconnect.com
Web Site: www.someconnect.com

Year Founded: 2013

Agency Specializes In: Affiliate Marketing, Affluent Market, Business-To-Business, Consulting, Consumer Goods, Consumer Marketing, Cosmetics, Digital/Interactive, E-Commerce, Education, Email, Fashion/Apparel, Financial, Food Service, Graphic Design, Health Care Services, Hispanic Market, Hospitality, Household Goods, Industrial, Integrated Marketing, Internet/Web Design, Legal Services, Media Buying Services, Medical Products, Mobile Marketing, Multicultural, Paid Searches, Podcasting, Production (Ad, Film, Broadcast), Real Estate, Restaurant, Retail, Search Engine Optimization, Social Marketing/Nonprofit, Social Media, South Asian Market, Sweepstakes, Travel & Tourism, Viral/Buzz/Word of Mouth, Web (Banner Ads, Pop-ups, etc.)

Madhavi Rao *(Mng Partner)*
Aalap Shah *(Mng Partner)*

Accounts:
Belgravia Realty Real Estate; 2014
Famous Dave's Food & Beverage; 2014

SOMETHING MASSIVE
6030 Wilshire Blvd Ste 301, Los Angeles, CA 90036
Tel.: (310) 302-8900
Fax: (310) 362-8880
E-Mail: la@somethingmassive.com
Web Site: www.somethingmassive.com

Year Founded: 2008

Agency Specializes In: Advertising, Brand Development & Integration, Content, Internet/Web Design, Mobile Marketing, Search Engine Optimization, Social Media

Rebecca Coleman *(Founder)*
John Moshay *(Founder)*
Chris Gibbin *(Partner)*
Dana Neujahr *(Sr VP-Strategy & Engagement)*
Jen Brian *(VP-Production)*
Vinnie Finn *(Sr Dir-Art)*

Accounts:
Swrve Cycling

SOUTH CENTRAL DIGITAL
214 2nd Ave N Ste 203, Nashville, TN 37201
Tel.: (615) 335-8700
E-Mail: info@southcentraldigital.com

Interactive Agencies

Web Site: www.scdagency.com/

Year Founded: 2008

Agency Specializes In: Content, Digital/Interactive, Email, Internet/Web Design, Search Engine Optimization, Social Media, Strategic Planning/Research

Michael Guess *(Pres)*
Ben Meredith *(Dir-Ops)*
Joshua Milford *(Dir-Production)*
Kristin Sartain *(Dir-Client Svcs)*
Marcus Snyder *(Dir-Media Svcs)*
Shelby George *(Acct Mgr)*
Kaitlyn Kambestad *(Mgr-Social Media)*
Mandy Lauman *(Mgr-Media Svcs)*
Chris Turner *(Mgr-Content & SEO)*
Melissa Grabiel *(Designer)*

Accounts:
National Embryo Donation Center
Perry County Memorial Hospital

SOUTH CENTRAL MEDIA

4751 Trousdale Ave, Nashville, TN 37220
Tel.: (615) 630-6422
Web Site: southcentralmedia.com

Employees: 50
Year Founded: 2009

Approx. Annual Billings: $4,200,000

Joshua Milford *(Dir-Production)*
Marcus Snyder *(Dir-Media Svcs)*
Melissa Grabiel *(Designer-Web)*
Cameron Rachal *(Coord-Media Svcs)*
Leah Sutherland *(Coord-Social Media & Content)*

Accounts:
The Point Church
SmartAuto Repair
SmartWay
SmartWheels

SPACE CHIMP MEDIA

906 E 5th St Ste 500, Austin, TX 78702
Tel.: (512) 485-3016
Fax: (888) 512-9011
E-Mail: info@spacechimpmedia.com
Web Site: https://spacechimp.io/

Year Founded: 2010

Agency Specializes In: Information Technology, Internet/Web Design, Local Marketing, Market Research, Search Engine Optimization

Charles Haggas *(CEO & Strategist)*

Accounts:
ADS Sports Eyewear Marketing, website Redesign
The Associated Press, Inc.
Discount Electronics
Einstein Moving Company Integrated Digital Marketing, Online Ad Management, SEO Services, Website
Fertility Nutraceuticals, LLC Digital Marketing, Nutritional Supplement
The Great Rug Company
Hyper Wear Inc. Marketing, Offline, Online
IAS Direct Marketing
IQ Storage Marketing
The Laundry Alternative Inc. Marketing, Online, SEO
Little Leaves Digital Marketing
Starmap
Timeless Trends Digital, Marketing
Tiny Utopia Marketing

THE SPARK GROUP

30 W 18th St Ste M1, New York, NY 10011
Tel.: (212) 989-3198
E-Mail: info@thesparkgroup.com
Web Site: www.thesparkgroup.com

Year Founded: 2010

Agency Specializes In: Advertising, Brand Development & Integration, Digital/Interactive, Email, Graphic Design, Internet/Web Design, Social Media

Daniela Cuevas *(Partner & Dir-Creative)*
Amy Brightman *(Partner & Strategist-Digital Media)*
Patricia Giehl *(Producer-Social Media)*
Manju Bala *(Designer-Interactive Media)*
Dora Tang *(Designer)*

Accounts:
Huertas

SPEAK CREATIVE

8337 Cordova Rd, Memphis, TN 38016
Tel.: (901) 757-5855
Toll Free: (888) 337-7325
Web Site: www.madebyspeak.com

Agency Specializes In: Content, Digital/Interactive, Email, Internet/Web Design, Search Engine Optimization, Social Media

Jacob Savage *(Pres)*
Matt Ervin *(Dir-Tech Solutions)*
Amanda Evans *(Dir-Mktg)*
Alex Rasmussen *(Dir-Digital Mktg)*
Matt Roberts *(Dir-Bus Dev)*
Tyler Batts *(Acct Mgr)*
Megan Jones *(Acct Mgr)*
Meagan Howard Walley *(Acct Mgr)*
Kindra Svendsen *(Strategist-PR & Digital Mktg)*
Katie Sinclair *(Designer)*
Teresa Hendrix *(Coord-Digital Mktg & PR)*

Accounts:
Christian Brothers University
Wolf River Conservancy

SPECIALISTS MARKETING SERVICES, INC

777 Terrace Ave Ste 401, Hasbrouck Heights, NJ 7604
Tel.: (201) 865-5800
Fax: (201) 288-4295
E-Mail: listinfo@sms-inc.com
Web Site: www.specialistsms.com

Employees: 105
Year Founded: 1987

Agency Specializes In: Digital/Interactive, Media Buying Services, Media Planning

Lon Mandel *(Pres)*
Nora Bush *(CFO)*
Steve Bogner *(Officer)*
Susan Giampietro *(Exec VP)*
Robin B. Neal *(Exec VP-List Mgmt & Insert Media)*
Michael Heaney *(Sr VP-Consumer Targeting Solutions)*
Cyndi Lee *(Sr VP-List Mgmt, Sls & Strategic Dev)*
Anna Feely *(VP-Bus Dev)*
Theresa Horn *(VP-Sls)*
Amy L. Lyons *(VP-Sls & Mktg)*
Mary Ann Montalbano *(VP)*

Accounts:
Adtech Systems Inc.
North American Affinity Group

SPIDERBOOST INTERACTIVE

155 S Miami Ave Penthouse 2B, Miami, FL 33130
Tel.: (305) 712-7992
E-Mail: miami@spiderboost.com
Web Site: www.spiderboost.com

Agency Specializes In: Advertising, Digital/Interactive, Internet/Web Design, Search Engine Optimization, Social Media

Armando Martinez Franco *(Pres)*
Zachary Burton *(CEO)*
Bret Berlin *(CFO & COO)*
Gleisy Jesset *(Dir-Art & Graphic Designer)*
Jorge Montoya *(Acct Mgr-Natl)*
Angelica Martinez *(Mgr-Digital Mktg & Project)*
Jason Dalmau *(Acct Exec)*

Accounts:
3MC Partners
Abs Fuel
Kaufman, Rossin & Co., Professional Association
Key Point Academy
Latite Roofing
Safe-T Nails

SPINX INC.

911 W Washington Blvd, Los Angeles, CA 90015
Tel.: (213) 894-9933
Fax: (818) 660-1981
E-Mail: info@spinxwebdesign.com
Web Site: www.spinxwebdesign.com

Agency Specializes In: Digital/Interactive, Internet/Web Design, Search Engine Optimization, Social Media

Sukesh Jakharia *(Owner)*
Greg Szimonisz *(Acct Dir)*

Accounts:
New-Beats By Dre

SPYDER TRAP

1625 Hennepin Ave, Minneapolis, MN 55403
Tel.: (612) 871-2270
Fax: (612) 871-4199
E-Mail: info@spydertrap.com
Web Site: www.spydertrap.com/

Employees: 35

Agency Specializes In: Communications, Digital/Interactive, Email, Engineering, Graphic Design, Health Care Services, Hospitality, Internet/Web Design, Local Marketing, Mobile Marketing, Paid Searches, Planning & Consultation, Retail, Search Engine Optimization, Social Marketing/Nonprofit, Social Media, Sports Market, Travel & Tourism, Web (Banner Ads, Pop-ups, etc.)

Mike Rynchek *(CEO)*
Aaron Weiche *(COO)*
Knute Sands *(Mgr-Content Mktg)*

Accounts:
American Diabetes Association
Children's Hospital & Clinics of Minnesota
CRAVE Restaurant
The Depot Minneapolis
Gift My Ride
Rye Delicatessen
Shock Doctor
Tucker Hibbert
WA Frost & Company

SS DIGITAL MEDIA

950 Stephenson Hwy, Troy, MI 48083
Tel.: (877) 755-5710
Fax: (248) 268-7670
Web Site: www.ssdigitalmedia.com

Agency Specializes In: Advertising, Brand Development & Integration, Digital/Interactive, Internet/Web Design, Search Engine Optimization

Amanda Friedt *(Dir-Accts & Ops)*

Accounts:
New-Greenhouse Fabrics

ST8 CREATIVE SOLUTIONS INC
1431 7th St Ste 305, Santa Monica, CA 90401
Tel.: (310) 394-7313
E-Mail: info@st8.com
Web Site: www.st8.com

Year Founded: 2007

Agency Specializes In: Digital/Interactive, Internet/Web Design, Paid Searches, Search Engine Optimization, Social Media

Gustavo Morais *(Founder & COO)*
Robert Fox *(VP-Bus Dev)*

Accounts:
New-Fox Sports

STARKMEDIA INC.
219 N Milwaukee St, Milwaukee, WI 53202
Tel.: (414) 226-2710
Fax: (414) 226-2716
E-Mail: info@starkmedia.com
Web Site: www.starkmedia.com

Agency Specializes In: Advertising, Brand Development & Integration, Content, Digital/Interactive, Email, Social Media

Ken Stark *(Pres)*
Jennifer Elias *(Sr Art Dir)*
Benjamin Bernhard *(Dir-Digital Strategy)*
Bruce Krajcir *(Sr Acct Exec)*
Jeff Acton *(Acct Exec)*
Nicholas Dennis *(Sr Designer)*

Accounts:
Apex Tool Group
Putzmeister
TRC Global
Woodway

STIMULANT
180 Capp St Ste 6, San Francisco, CA 94110
Tel.: (415) 255-7081
Fax: (815) 550-1203
E-Mail: hello@stimulant.com
Web Site: stimulant.com/

Agency Specializes In: Integrated Marketing, Mobile Marketing

Darren David *(Founder & CEO)*
Suzanne Hitchcock *(Dir-Fin & Ops)*
Nathan Moody *(Dir-Design)*
Kristi Torgrimson *(Dir-Project Mgmt)*

Accounts:
Hewlett-Packard Computer Products & Services
Intel Corporation Processor Technologies Developers
Kodak Graphic Communications Group Consumer Products Producer & Services
Microsoft Corporation Cloud Computing & Software Developers & Services
Reebok Sporting Goods Providers
SAP Business Management Software Solution Providers

SUM DIGITAL INC
240 2nd St 2nd Fl, San Francisco, CA 94105
Tel.: (415) 673-3220
E-Mail: info@sumdigital.com
Web Site: www.sumdigital.com

Year Founded: 2005

Agency Specializes In: Advertising, Business-To-Business, Digital/Interactive

Terry Whalen *(Pres)*
Joey Muller *(VP)*
Dylan Brannon *(Acct Mgr)*

Accounts:
New-Pura Vida Bracelets

SWARM NYC
16 W 22nd St, New York, NY 10010
Tel.: (646) 709-7407
Web Site: swarmnyc.com

Employees: 18
Year Founded: 2013

Agency Specializes In: Advertising, Affluent Market, African-American Market, Arts, Bilingual Market, Brand Development & Integration, Business Publications, Business-To-Business, Catalogs, Children's Market, College, Communications, Computers & Software, Consulting, Consumer Goods, Consumer Marketing, Consumer Publications, Corporate Identity, Custom Publishing, Customer Relationship Management, Digital/Interactive, Direct-to-Consumer, E-Commerce, Education, Electronic Media, Email, Engineering, Entertainment, Environmental, Experience Design, Faith Based, Fashion/Apparel, Game Integration, Gay & Lesbian Market, Graphic Design, High Technology, Hispanic Market, Hospitality, Household Goods, Identity Marketing, In-Store Advertising, Information Technology, Integrated Marketing, International, Internet/Web Design, Leisure, Local Marketing, Logo & Package Design, Luxury Products, Magazines, Market Research, Men's Market, Mobile Marketing, Multimedia, New Product Development, New Technologies, Over-50 Market, Package Design, Paid Searches, Pets , Pharmaceutical, Planning & Consultation, Print, Product Placement, Production, Production (Print), Promotions, Public Relations, Publishing, Retail, Search Engine Optimization, Seniors' Market, Social Marketing/Nonprofit, Social Media, South Asian Market, Stakeholders, Strategic Planning/Research, Technical Advertising, Teen Market, Transportation, Travel & Tourism, Tween Market, Urban Market, Web (Banner Ads, Pop-ups, etc.), Women's Market

Approx. Annual Billings: $2,200,000

Joel Dietz *(CEO)*
Jacek Grebski *(Partner)*
Somya Jain *(Partner)*
Valerie Lisyansky *(Partner)*
Ed Shapoff *(Head-Bus Dev)*

Accounts:
New-CBSi CBS College Sports, CBS Fantasy Sports, CBS Sports Apple TV; 2013

TRAFFIC DIGITAL AGENCY
412 E 4th St, Royal Oak, MI 48067
Tel.: (877) 772-9223
E-Mail: hello@trafficdigitalagency.com
Web Site: www.trafficdigitalagency.com/

Agency Specializes In: Customer Relationship Management, Digital/Interactive, Internet/Web Design, Logo & Package Design, Paid Searches, Search Engine Optimization, Social Media

Kyle porter *(VP-Client Svcs & Sls)*
Daniel Lee *(Strategist-Digital)*

Accounts:
New-Lumity

TRAPEZE MEDIA
174 Bloor St East, South Tower Ste 900, Toronto, ON M4W 3R8 Canada
Tel.: (416) 601-1999

Agency Specializes In: Advertising, Brand Development & Integration, Digital/Interactive, Strategic Planning/Research

Karen Bennet *(VP-Tech)*
Keefe Lee *(VP-Strategy)*
Victoria Thorpe *(VP-Client Svcs)*
Erin Drew *(Dir-HR)*

Accounts:
Allstate
Kraft Gevalia
Shoppers Drug Mart beautyBOUTIQUE

TREMOR VIDEO
122 W 26th St 8th Fl, New York, NY 10001
Tel.: (646) 723-5300
Fax: (646) 224-8177
Web Site: www.tremorvideo.com/en

Employees: 339
Year Founded: 2006

Agency Specializes In: Advertising, Digital/Interactive, Mobile Marketing, Web (Banner Ads, Pop-ups, etc.)

Approx. Annual Billings: $159,487,000

Bill Day *(CEO)*
Andrew Kornuta *(Mng Dir)*
John Rego *(CFO)*
Adam Lichstein *(COO)*
Melinda McLaughlin *(CMO)*
John Walsh *(CTO)*
Jake Piasecki *(Chief Revenue Officer)*
Manish Jha *(Pres-Publr Platforms)*
Lauren Wiener *(Pres-Sls & Mktg-Global)*
Steven Pearson *(Sr VP-Engrg)*
Alex Macnamara *(Mng Dir-UK)*
Craig Berlingo *(VP-Product-Programmatic)*
Kelly Hollis Brown *(VP-Natl Sls-Automotive)*
Laura Buchman *(VP-Publr Sls)*
Anthony Flaccavento *(VP-Natl CPG Sls)*
Mark Kalus *(VP-Product Mgmt-Buy-Side)*
Hava Kelman *(VP-Bus Dev)*
Billy Kenny *(VP-Corp Comm)*
Katie Seitz *(VP-Product Strategy & Ops)*
Tim Ware *(VP-Advanced TV)*
Kelly Petersen *(Head-Product)*
Greg Smith *(Head-Intl & Programmatic)*
Geordie Holbert *(Sr Dir-Programmatic Partnerships)*
Andrew Posen *(Sr Dir-IR)*
Monica Seebohm *(Sr Dir-Programmatic Sls)*
Ryan Van Fleet *(Sr Dir-Insights & Analytics)*
Janine Cheviot *(Dir-Programmatic Acct Mgmt)*
Kim Dolan *(Dir-Sls-Natl)*
Chris Kiriakatis *(Dir-Bus Dev)*
Clare McCloskey *(Dir-Programmatic Strategy & Optimization)*
Mandy Albers *(Sr Mgr-Comm)*
Samantha Holohan *(Acct Mgr)*
Alicia Bernard *(Mgr-Programmatic Strategy & Optimization)*
Manu Jain *(Mgr-Programmatic Video)*
David Nguyen *(Acct Exec)*
Courtney King *(Campaign Mgr-Programmatic Strategy & Optimization)*

Interactive Agencies

Accounts:
AMC
Dove
Dragonfly Publishing Services
The Enthusiast Network Publishing Services
Gillette
HBO
Honda
IBM
Meredith Corporation
Microsoft
Nestle
Panasonic
Priceline.com Transportation & Tourism
Showtime
Sony
Yahoo

TRIBAL WORLDWIDE
(Formerly Tribal DDB Worldwide)
437 Madison Ave 8th Fl, New York, NY 10022
Tel.: (212) 515-8600
Fax: (212) 515-8660
E-Mail: info@tribalworldwide.com
Web Site: www.tribalworldwide.com

Employees: 1,200
Year Founded: 2000

National Agency Associations: 4A's

Agency Specializes In: Brand Development & Integration, High Technology, Sponsorship

Ryan Mclaughlin *(Chief Strategy Officer)*
Richard Guest *(Pres-US)*
Kyle Snarr *(Head-Client Dev & Mktg)*
Kinney Edwards *(Exec Dir-Creative)*
Jen Stocksmith *(Creative Dir)*
Brent Goldman *(Copywriter)*
Becky Kitlan *(Sr Art Dir)*

Accounts:
AT&T Communications Corp.
BeautyBar.com
Clorox
Diageo
ExxonMobil
George Washington University (Digital Media Agency Of Record) Digital Media Buying, Digital Media Strategy, Display, SEO Management, Social
H&R Block
Hasbro Inc Monopoly
Intel
Johnson & Johnson Medical Device Brands
Jose Cuervo; 2007
KLM
The Lunchbox Fund Feedie
Lutron
McAfee Inc. Technology Security; 2008
McDonald's
Microsoft
Nike
Novartis
PepsiCo
Pfizer, Inc. Advil, Robitussin, Robitussin.com
Pharmavite SoyJoy
Reebok Campaign: "WeRClassic.com", Digital
Sun Power Corporation
UNICEF Campaign: "Safety"
Unilever Lipton Teas
Volkswagen Group of America, Inc.

AMERICAS

Tribal Worldwide Chicago
(Formerly Tribal DDB Chicago)
200 E Randolph St, Chicago, IL 60601
Tel.: (312) 552-6000
Fax: (312) 552-2358
Web Site: www.tribalworldwide.com

Employees: 55

Agency Specializes In: Digital/Interactive, Sponsorship

Richard Guest *(Pres-US Ops)*
Amy Elkins *(Head-Client Svcs)*
Kinney Edwards *(Exec Dir-Creative)*
Cassondra Bazelow *(Dir-Art)*
Jen Stocksmith *(Dir-Creative)*
Matt Wexler *(Dir-Strategy)*

Accounts:
Emerson Electric
H&R Block Creative
Johnson & Johnson
KLM
McAfee
McDonald's
Microsoft
Novartis
OfficeMax
Pepsi
Quaker Oats Digital Marketing, Quaker Life Cereal, Quaker Oatmeal, Quaker Rice Snacks, Quaker Simple Harvest, Quaker Snack Bars
Unilever

Tribal Worldwide San Francisco
(Formerly Tribal DDB San Francisco)
555 Market St Ste 500, San Francisco, CA 94105
Tel.: (415) 732-2200
Fax: (415) 732-2295
E-Mail: richard.guest@tribalworldwide.com
Web Site: www.tribalworldwide.com

Agency Specializes In: Digital/Interactive, Sponsorship

Richard Guest *(Pres-North America)*

Accounts:
McAfee, Inc
Microsoft
Paw Points

Tribal Worldwide Toronto
(Formerly Tribal DDB Toronto)
33 Bloor Street East 12th Floor, Toronto, ON M4W 3T4 Canada
Tel.: (416) 925-9819
Fax: (416) 921-4180
E-Mail: andrewm@tribalddb.ca
Web Site: tribaltoronto.com

Employees: 30

Agency Specializes In: Digital/Interactive

Andrew McCartney *(Sr VP & Mng Dir)*
Stephanie Wall *(VP & Dir-Bus Unit)*
Dino Demopoulos *(VP-Strategy & Innovation)*
Susan Grant *(Acct Dir)*
Ryan O'Hagan *(Acct Dir)*
Jarrod Beaton *(Dir-UX)*
Jake Bundock *(Dir-Art)*
Jeff Vermeersch *(Dir-Creative Tech)*
Diego Bertagni *(Assoc Dir-Creative)*
Zak Usher *(Assoc Dir-Social)*
Monica Bialobrzeski *(Acct Exec)*
Norma Penner *(Designer)*
Jamie Spears *(Copywriter)*

Accounts:
Adidas, Canada
BC Dairy
BMO
Bud Light
Budweiser
Canadian Tire Campaign: "Shovel It Forward", Campaign: "The Canadian Way of Spring", Christmas Spirit Tree, Online, ShovelItForward.ca, Social
Canadian Tourism Commission
Gatorade
General Mills Campaign: "HowToDad", Peanut Butter Cheerios
Glad
Johnson & Johnson Campaign: "Junkface", Neutrogena MEN
KLM
Kol Kid "Simple Play", Campaign: "Toys Should Be Toys"
McDonald's Canada 140 Character Films Contest, Campaign: "From Farm To Fries", Campaign: "Our Food. Your Questions", Campaign: "Welcome to McDonald's", Creative, Design, Digital, Outdoor, Social Media, Strategy, Video
Subaru Campaign: "Car Swap", Campaign: "Subaru Forester Family Rally"

Tribal Worldwide Vancouver
(Formerly Tribal DDB Vancouver)
1600-777 Hornby St, Vancouver, BC V6Z 2T3 Canada
Tel.: (604) 608-4451
Fax: (604) 640-4343
E-Mail: martyy@tribalddb.ca
Web Site: tribalworldwide.com

Employees: 150

Agency Specializes In: Digital/Interactive

Marty Yaskowich *(Mng Dir)*
Stephane Fournier *(Assoc Dir-Creative)*

Accounts:
B.C. Hydro
BC Dairy
Canadian Dental Association Campaign: "Dental Mirror Installation"
Canadian Tourism Commission Campaign: "Keep Exploring", Skiing & Snowboarding

EUROPE

Tribal Worldwide Amsterdam
(Formerly Tribal DDB)
Prof WH Keesomlaan 4, 1183 DJ Amstelveen, Netherlands
Mailing Address:
PO Box 106, 1100 AC Amstelveen, Netherlands
Tel.: (31) 20 406 51 06
Fax: (31) 20 406 5100
E-Mail: info@tribalddb.nl
Web Site: www.tribalworldwide.com

Employees: 50
Year Founded: 1999

Agency Specializes In: Digital/Interactive

Alistair Beattie *(Pres-EMEA)*
Jasper Diks *(Dir-Creative)*
Ralf Hesen *(Dir-Strategy)*
Ed van Bennekom *(Dir-Creative)*

Accounts:
Adidas Campaign: "I am Brazuca"
C&A Creative
Centraal Beheer Achmea Campaign: "Cartoon of the Day", Campaign: "Self Driving Car", Car Insurance, PIM-Personalized Application, TV; 1995
Currence
Elsevier
Eneco
FBTO
Heineken Campaign: "The Candidate"
KLM Royal Dutch Airlines Campaign: "Be My Guest", Campaign: "Tile & Inspire", Campaign: "Travlr", Lost & Found Team, Online, Space

Lotto
Lucky Day
OV-Chipkaart
Mammoet Brand Positioning, Internal Communications, Offline, Online, Visual Language
Novartis
Philips Campaign: "Obsessed With Sound", Campaign: "See What Light Can Do"
Procter & Gamble
Red Bull
TomTom Creative, Smartwatch
Uto Sonnema Berenburg Liquor
Volkswagen Group of America, Inc. Campaign: "Get Happy", Campaign: "Hitchhike With A Like"
Wakf
Zilveren Kruis/Achmea Corporate Site; 2000

Tribal Worldwide Athens
(Formerly Tribal DDB Athens)
4 Kastorias & Messinias Str, Gerakas, GR 153 44 Athens, Greece
Tel.: (30) 210 6175646
Fax: (30) 210 6104775
E-Mail: agathi.plota@tribalddb.gr
Web Site: www.tribalworldwide.com

Agathi Plota *(Mng Dir)*
Christina Stavrinadou *(Acct Dir)*
Dimitris Deligiannis *(Dir-Art)*
Anthony Kyriazis *(Dir-Creative Svcs)*
Maria Hatzoglou *(Mgr-Content)*
Melina Politi *(Mgr-New Bus)*
John Anagnostou *(Sr Designer-UI)*

Accounts:
Unilever

Tribal Worldwide Hamburg
(Formerly Tribal DDB Hamburg)
Willy-Brandt Strasse 1, D-20457 Hamburg, Germany
Tel.: (49) 40 32808 0
Fax: (49) 40 32808 100
E-Mail: hamburg@ddb-tribal.com
Web Site: www.tribalworldwide.com

Employees: 20

Agency Specializes In: Advertising

Toby Pschorr *(Mng Dir)*
Matthias Schmidt *(Mng Dir)*
Nina Rieke *(Chief Strategy Officer)*
Eric Schoeffler *(Chief Creative Officer)*
Jan Diekmann *(Head-Bus Dev)*

Accounts:
BSH Deutschland Campaign: "Icebergs"
Henkel Campaign: "Long Names. Long Lasting."
IKEA Storage Solutions
Pattex Glue

Tribal Worldwide London
(Formerly Tribal DDB Europe/London)
12 Bishops Bridge Rd, Paddington, London, W26 AA United Kingdom
Tel.: (44) 20 7 258 3979
Fax: (44) 20 7258 4253
E-Mail: tom.roberts@tribalddb.co.uk
Web Site: www.tribalworldwide.com

Employees: 200

Agency Specializes In: Digital/Interactive

Tom Roberts *(Mng Dir)*
Simon Poett *(Exec Dir-Creative)*
Victoria Buchanan *(Creative Dir)*
James Hogwood *(Dir-Creative)*

Accounts:
Adidas Originals
Financial Times Campaign: "Graphic World"
Fitness First
GlaxoSmithKline
Government Procurement Service Digital Services Framework
Hasbro
Johnson & Johnson
O2 Digital, o2.co.uk
Star Alliance Campaign: "Star Alliance Picture your Upgrade"
Thomsonfly.com
Unilever Becel, Digital, Flora
Volkswagen Group United Kingdom Ltd. Campaign: "Digital Showrooms", Campaign: "People's Choir", Campaign: "Play The Road", Digital, Online, Volkswagen Golf GTI

Tribal Worldwide Milan
(Formerly Tribal DDB Milan)
via Solari 11, 20144 Milan, Italy
Tel.: (39) 02 83308 451
Fax: (39) 02 83308 490
E-Mail: info@tribalddb.it
Web Site: www.tribalworldwide.com

Employees: 11

Agency Specializes In: Digital/Interactive

Marko Duruzze *(Bus Dir)*

Accounts:
AVIS Rent a Car
Algida
Alitalia
Baby Angel
Berlucchi
Ca'del Bosco
Campari
Cesvi
Citi Financial
E.Capital Partners
Love Therapy
Nescafe
The North Face
Volkswagen Blue Motion

ASIA/PACIFIC

22feet Tribal Worldwide
(Formerly 22feet)
4th Floor Serene 106 4th C Cross 5th Block, Bengaluru, Karnataka India
Tel.: (91) 64560037
Web Site: 22feettribalworldwide.com

Employees: 115

Agency Specializes In: Advertising, Digital/Interactive, Media Planning, Mobile Marketing, Search Engine Optimization, Social Media, Web (Banner Ads, Pop-ups, etc.)

Vineet Gupta *(Mng Dir)*
Deepak Nair *(COO)*
Shirley D'Costa *(Head-Bus Dev)*
Ramraaj Raghunathan *(Head-Bus Dev)*
Mital Dubal *(Mgr-Bus Dev)*
Neha Ladha *(Mgr-Bus Dev)*
Rochelle Noronha *(Mgr-Bus Dev)*
Priyanka Prasad *(Mgr-Bus Dev)*
Brijesh Jacob *(Joint Mng Dir)*

Accounts:
Axe
Cafe Coffee Day
Fastrack
Heineken
Huawei Campaign: "Test of Honor", Honor 4X, Social Media
Kingfisher
Lenovo
Livon
New-McNROE Brand Planning, Digital, Secret Temptation, Strategic Brand Campaign, Wild Stone
Nike
Pantaloons
Parachute
Peter England
Red Bull
Royal Enfield
Titan
Van Heusen

Tribal Worldwide Malaysia
(Formerly Tribal DDB Malaysia)
D601-605 6th Floor Block D Kelana Square 17, Jalan SS7/26 Selangor, 47301 Petaling Jaya, Malaysia
Tel.: (60) 3 7844 7898
Fax: (60) 3 7806 3489
E-Mail: nik.lim@tribalddb.com.my
Web Site: tribalworldwide.com

Lola Chin *(Gen Mgr)*
Benn De Silva *(Acct Dir)*
Aaron Foong *(Acct Dir)*
Diana Chua *(Sr Acct Mgr)*
Shantee Lim *(Acct Mgr)*
Wei Ler Gan *(Community Mgr-Social Media)*

Accounts:
Ciba Vision
Fitness First Asia Campaign: "Let's Get Personal", Digital
Fonterra's Anmum, Anmum Essential, Anmum Lacta, Anmum Materna, Campaign: "The Million Dollar Question", Digital Communications, Online
K & N Kenanga Holdings Berhad Social Media
World Health Organization World Sight Day

Tribal Worldwide Melbourne
(Formerly Tribal DDB Melbourne)
7 Electric St, Richmond, VIC 3121 Australia
Tel.: (61) 3 9254 3509
Web Site: www.tribalworldwide.com

Matt Oxley *(Mng Dir)*
Melinda Parris *(Acct Dir)*
Kristina Frost *(Dir-Ops)*
Carla Hizon *(Dir-Bus)*

Accounts:
AAMI Car Insurance, Christmas Book
Ambulance Victoria
Australian Unity
BF Goodrich
Citysearch
CSL
DDB Shop
Dulux
EA Sports
Jumbuck
McDonald's Campaign: "New Loose Change Menu"
Sensis
Sundance Brewing Campaign: "Cricketers Arms Pitch Maintenance"
Telstra Bigpond OTP

Tribal Worldwide Singapore
(Formerly Tribal DDB Singapore)
Level 10 Pico Creative Centre, 20 Kallang Avenue, Singapore, 339411 Singapore
Tel.: (65) 6671 4488
E-Mail: jeff.cheong@sg.tribalworldwide.com
Web Site: www.tribalworldwide.com

Agency Specializes In: Advertising

Interactive Agencies

Leslie Goh *(Mng Partner & Head-Ops)*
Joshua Lee *(Mng Partner)*
Neil Johnson *(Chief Creative Officer)*
Jeff Cheong *(Pres-Asia)*
Alan Leong *(Head-Art & Assoc Dir-Creative & Digital)*
Jet Aw *(Grp Head-Creative)*
Geraldine Tan *(Dir-Art)*
Chris Lim *(Assoc Dir-Creative)*
Thomas Yang *(Deputy Exec Dir-Creative)*

Accounts:
Civil Aviation Authority of Singapore Singapore Airshow; 2008
DBS Bank Campaign: "Expect The Unexpected", Campaign: "Frozen Car", Campaign: "Halved Car", Campaign: "Magnetised Car"
Fonterra Digital, Website
Health Promotion Board
Unilever Campaign: "Scoops of Happiness", Cornetto, Digital, Walls Ice Cream
Uniqlo; Singapore Creative
Volkswagen Group Singapore Beetle, Digital

Tribal Worldwide Sydney
(Formerly Tribal DDB Sydney)
Wilcox Mofflin Bldg 46-52 Mountain St, Ultimo, Sydney, NSW 2007 Australia
Tel.: (61) 2 8260 2828
Fax: (61) 2 8260 2900
E-Mail: info@tribalddb.com.au
Web Site: www.tribalworldwide.com

Employees: 30

Agency Specializes In: Digital/Interactive

Rich Lloyd *(Mng Dir)*
Ferdinand Haratua *(Dir-Technical)*
Mark Seabridge *(Dir-Digital Art)*
Domenic Bartolo *(Sr Designer)*
Ivan Yip *(Sr Designer-Interactive)*

Accounts:
Cancer Council NSW Campaign: "Hope", Cancer Campaign
Gatorade
ING
Johnson & Johnson
McDonald's
News Limited
Nike
Tourism Australia "Making Tracks"
Westfield
Wrigley

TRIGHTON INTERACTIVE
10125 W Colonial Dr 203, Ocoee, FL 34761
Tel.: (407) 440-2972
Toll Free: (800) 407-2068
E-Mail: info@trighton.com
Web Site: www.trighton.com

Agency Specializes In: Advertising, Digital/Interactive, Integrated Marketing, Internet/Web Design, Search Engine Optimization, Social Media, Strategic Planning/Research

Jody Resnick *(CEO)*
Kenton Smeltzer *(CTO)*
Dave Brinkhus *(Creative Dir)*
Craig Haft *(Creative Dir-Videography)*
Jonathan Anderson *(Dir-Bus Dev)*
Deborah Schwartz *(Dir-Content Strategy & Copywriting)*

Accounts:
Masipack

TRUE NORTH INTERACTIVE
417 Montgomery St Ste 900, San Francisco, CA 94104
Tel.: (415) 732-0301
Web Site: truenorthinc.com/

Employees: 45
Year Founded: 1994

Agency Specializes In: Advertising, Below-the-Line, Digital/Interactive, Direct Response Marketing, Direct-to-Consumer, E-Commerce, Entertainment, Financial, Multimedia, Social Marketing/Nonprofit, Social Media, T.V., Travel & Tourism, Tween Market, Web (Banner Ads, Pop-ups, etc.)

Approx. Annual Billings: $30,000,000

Tom Goosmann *(Chief Creative Officer)*
Matthew Brown *(Acct Dir)*
John Como *(Client Svcs Dir)*
Daniel Brown *(Dir-Creative)*
Dan Levine *(Dir)*
Victoria Wetterer *(Assoc Dir-Creative)*
Emily Chan *(Mgr-Media Ops)*
Meghann Kelley *(Acct Supvr)*
Leah Drewnowski *(Sr Acct Exec)*
Katie Williamson *(Asst Acct Exec)*
Nesara Kishor *(Acct Coord)*
Linsey Sutherland *(Coord-Digital Media)*
Laura Challis *(Asst Media Planner)*
Sherry Moody *(Grp Acct Supvr)*

Accounts:
Walt Disney (ABC & Walt Disney Home Entertainment)

TVA MEDIA GROUP, INC.
3950 Vantage Ave, Studio City, CA 91604
Tel.: (818) 505-8300
Toll Free: (888) 907-5338
E-Mail: info@tvamediagroup.com
Web Site: www.tvamediagroup.com

Agency Specializes In: Digital/Interactive, Direct Response Marketing, Production (Ad, Film, Broadcast), Public Relations, T.V.

Jeffery Goddard *(Founder, CEO & Exec Producer)*
Laura Tu *(CFO, Partner & Exec Producer)*
Bob Levitan *(Sr VP-Strategic Mktg)*
Matthew Kemper *(VP-Production)*
Mark Mannschreck *(Dir-Creative)*

Accounts:
New-Cessna
New-Lexus
New-Marriott
New-MasterCard
New-Oxy
New-Qualcomm
New-Sony
New-Teradata
New-Ubisoft
New-Universal Studios
New-Westinghouse
New-World Vision

TVI DESIGNS
37 W 39th St, New York, NY 10018
Tel.: (212) 213-2740
Fax: (212) 213-2754
E-Mail: support@tvidesigns.com
Web Site: www.tvidesigns.com

Agency Specializes In: Brand Development & Integration, Digital/Interactive, Graphic Design, Internet/Web Design, Search Engine Optimization, Social Media

Mahdad Taheri *(Founder & CEO)*
Gerald Theresin *(VP-Bus Dev & Strategy)*

Accounts:
New-ColorEdge
New-National Aeronautics and Space Administration

UNION
421 Penman St Ste 310, Charlotte, NC 28203
Tel.: (704) 335-5424
Web Site: www.union.co

Employees: 33
Year Founded: 2002

Agency Specializes In: Above-the-Line, Advertising, Advertising Specialties, Affiliate Marketing, Affluent Market, African-American Market, Agriculture, Alternative Advertising, Arts, Asian Market, Automotive, Aviation & Aerospace, Below-the-Line, Bilingual Market, Brand Development & Integration, Branded Entertainment, Broadcast, Business Publications, Business-To-Business, Cable T.V., Catalogs, Children's Market, Co-op Advertising, Collateral, College, Commercial Photography, Communications, Computers & Software, Consulting, Consumer Goods, Consumer Marketing, Consumer Publications, Content, Corporate Communications, Corporate Identity, Cosmetics, Crisis Communications, Custom Publishing, Customer Relationship Management, Digital/Interactive, Direct Response Marketing, Direct-to-Consumer, E-Commerce, Education, Electronic Media, Electronics, Email, Engineering, Entertainment, Environmental, Event Planning & Marketing, Exhibit/Trade Shows, Experience Design, Faith Based, Fashion/Apparel, Financial, Food Service, Game Integration, Gay & Lesbian Market, Government/Political, Graphic Design, Guerilla Marketing, Health Care Services, High Technology, Hispanic Market, Hospitality, Household Goods, Identity Marketing, In-Store Advertising, Industrial, Infomercials, Information Technology, Integrated Marketing, International, Internet/Web Design, Investor Relations, Legal Services, Leisure, Local Marketing, Logo & Package Design, Luxury Products, Magazines, Marine, Market Research, Media Buying Services, Media Planning, Media Relations, Media Training, Medical Products, Men's Market, Merchandising, Mobile Marketing, Multicultural, Multimedia, New Product Development, New Technologies, Newspaper, Newspapers & Magazines, Out-of-Home Media, Outdoor, Over-50 Market, Package Design, Paid Searches, Pets , Pharmaceutical, Planning & Consultation, Podcasting, Point of Purchase, Point of Sale, Print, Product Placement, Production, Production (Ad, Film, Broadcast), Production (Print), Promotions, Public Relations, Publicity/Promotions, Publishing, RSS (Really Simple Syndication), Radio, Real Estate, Recruitment, Regional, Restaurant, Retail, Sales Promotion, Search Engine Optimization, Seniors' Market, Shopper Marketing, Social Marketing/Nonprofit, Social Media, South Asian Market, Sponsorship, Sports Market, Stakeholders, Strategic Planning/Research, Sweepstakes, Syndication, T.V., Technical Advertising, Teen Market, Telemarketing, Trade & Consumer Magazines, Transportation, Travel & Tourism, Tween Market, Urban Market, Viral/Buzz/Word of Mouth, Web (Banner Ads, Pop-ups, etc.), Women's Market, Yellow Pages Advertising

Approx. Annual Billings: $2,000,000

Banks Wilson *(Pres)*
Christy Holland *(Partner & VP-Accts)*
Melanie Jackson *(Acct Mgr)*
Matt Ashbridge *(Mgr-Digital Campaign)*
Lucas Weber *(Strategist-Content)*
Derrick Deese *(Designer)*
Lauren Kerwell *(Sr Designer)*
Emily Ayers *(Acct Coord)*

Accounts:
Bojangles
Comfort Revolution
Duke Energy
Hendrick Motorsports
Kyle Busch
NASCAR Rulebook

UNIONPIXEL
230 Park Ave, New York, NY 10169
Tel.: (844) 369-9500
Web Site: www.unionpixel.com

Employees: 10
Year Founded: 2012

Agency Specializes In: Custom Publishing, Digital/Interactive, Graphic Design, Integrated Marketing, Internet/Web Design, Sweepstakes, Web (Banner Ads, Pop-ups, etc.)

Approx. Annual Billings: $1,000,000

Greg Remillard *(Principal)*

Accounts:
Crain Publications

UNISON PARTNERS LLC
1201 Connecticut Ave NW Ste 850, Washington, DC 20036
Tel.: (202) 337-7887
E-Mail: info@unison.net
Web Site: www.unison.net

Agency Specializes In: Advertising, Brand Development & Integration, Content, Digital/Interactive, Internet/Web Design, Logo & Package Design, Public Relations

Robert Fardi *(Pres)*
Tedi Konda *(Dir-Tech)*

Accounts:
New-Chopt Creative Salad Company
New-Sanitas International

UNIT9
2-4 Hoxton Sq, N16NU London, United Kingdom
Tel.: (44) 207 613 3330
E-Mail: info@unit9.com
Web Site: www.unit9.com

Agency Specializes In: Graphic Design, High Technology

Piero Frescobaldi *(Co-Founder & Chm)*
Tom Sacchi *(Founder & Partner)*
Yates Buckley *(Partner-Technical)*
Valentina Culatti *(Mng Dir)*
Dan Edgar *(Head-Technical)*
Anrick Bregman *(Dir-Creative)*
Henry Cowling *(Dir-Creative)*

Accounts:
Adam&Eve Campaign: "John Lewis Banners"
Best Buy Electronic Accessories Providers
Call + Response Campaign: "Slavery Footprint"
Pernod Ricard Jameson Irish Whiskey
Smolik Campaign: "Forget Me Not"
Stella Artois Black Campaign: "The Black Diamond"

VAYNERMEDIA
315 Park Ave S 16th Fl, New York, NY 10010
Tel.: (212) 228-1365
Web Site: vaynermedia.com/

Employees: 500
Year Founded: 2009

Gary Vaynerchuk *(Co-Founder & CEO)*
AJ Vaynerchuk *(Co-Founder & COO)*
James Orsini *(Chief Integration Officer)*
Tina Cervera *(Sr Vp & Exec Creative Dir)*
Dennis Ossipov-Grodsky *(Sr VP-Digital Strategy)*
Mickey Cloud *(VP)*
Joe Quattrone *(VP)*
Hevan Chan *(Sr Dir-Art)*
Grant Christman *(Sr Dir-Art)*
Alexandra Davis *(Acct Dir)*
Ashley Dolliver *(Acct Dir)*
Lessa Chung *(Dir-Art)*
Deanna Curri *(Dir-Recruitment)*
Pamela Sidran *(Dir-Core Product Strategy)*
Rebecca Wright *(Dir-Comm)*
Adriana Nova *(Assoc Dir-Creative)*
Nik A. Bando *(Mgr-Paid Media)*
Jesse Hutchinson *(Acct Supvr)*
Christopher Gesualdi *(Supvr-Media)*
Jo Beth Stoddard *(Sr Acct Exec)*

Accounts:
Anheuser-Busch Companies, Inc. Bud Light's Bud-E, Budweiser
General Electric Campaign: "#SpringBreakIt", E-Commerce Box, Social Media
Hasbro Furby
Milk-Bone Campaign: "Toothbrush Challenge"
Mondelez Nilla Wafers
Pepsico Baja Blast, Mountain Dew, Social Media
Toyota Motor Sales, U.S.A., Inc. Marketing, Media, Social
Unilever "Self-Esteem Weekend", Dove
Water.org US Social

Branches

VaynerMedia
15000 Ventura Blvd Floor 3, Sherman Oaks, CA 91403
Web Site: vaynermedia.com

Tom McKeever *(Dir-Art)*
Alexandra Wells *(Assoc Dir-Creative)*
Brianna Baxter *(Mgr-Community)*
Matthew Cassinelli *(Mgr-Community)*
Patrick Comeau *(Mgr-Community)*
Claire McGovern *(Acct Supvr)*
Neiki Ullah *(Acct Supvr-Strategy)*
Jessica Druck *(Assoc Copywriter)*
Angela Melero *(Staff Editor-L'Oreal's Makeup com)*

VaynerMedia
144 2nd St 2nd Fl, San Francisco, CA 94105
Web Site: vaynermedia.com

Ciaran Bossom *(Sr VP & Head-SF)*
Aleena Abrahamian *(Head-San Francisco & VP)*
Ben Citron *(Creative Dir)*
Amy Plavner *(Acct Mgr)*
Christina Garcia *(Acct Supvr)*
Zachary McCune *(Supvr-Acct & Strategy)*
Sam Taggart *(Sr Strategist-Core Product)*
Tony Colvin *(Acct Exec)*
Stephanie Bohar *(Designer)*
Geoff Gates *(Copywriter)*
Phillip McInturff *(Designer)*
Han Nguyen *(Designer)*
Raymond Zhuo *(Assoc Acct Exec)*

VIRTUAL INTERACTIVE CENTER
106A W Summit Hill Dr, Knoxville, TN 37902
Tel.: (865) 524-8888
Fax: (865) 524-0740
Toll Free: (888) 811-8681
E-Mail: info@vic.com
Web Site: www.vic.com

Year Founded: 2003

Agency Specializes In: Digital/Interactive, Internet/Web Design, Social Media

Approx. Annual Billings: $2,000,000

Breakdown of Gross Billings by Media: Adv. Specialities: 100%

Steve Siopsis *(Pres)*
John McSpadden *(Dir-Tech)*
Alexis Dean *(Mgr-Product Mktg)*
Greg Kitzmiller *(Mgr-Creative)*
Aaron Marlowe *(Mgr-Dev)*

VIUS
1639 N Hancock St Studio 407, Philadelphia, PA 19122
Tel.: (215) 546-2829
E-Mail: experts@vius.co
Web Site: www.vius.co

Employees: 5
Year Founded: 2011

Agency Specializes In: Digital/Interactive, Electronic Media, Web (Banner Ads, Pop-ups, etc.)

Vinh Chau *(CEO)*
Andrew Croce *(Dir-Creative)*

Accounts:
AIA Pennsylvania Website Design & Development

VML
(Formerly Biggs Gilmore Communications)
261 E Kalamazoo Ave Ste 300, Kalamazoo, MI 49007-3841
Tel.: (269) 349-7711
Fax: (269) 349-3051
E-Mail: DL-VMLcomOther@vml.com
Web Site: www.vml.com

Employees: 120
Year Founded: 1973

National Agency Associations: 4A's-AMIN-APA-DMA-MCA-NAMA-PRSA-WOMMA

Agency Specializes In: Below-the-Line, Brand Development & Integration, Broadcast, Children's Market, Consumer Goods, Consumer Marketing, Content, Corporate Communications, Customer Relationship Management, Digital/Interactive, Direct-to-Consumer, E-Commerce, Email, Entertainment, Fashion/Apparel, Game Integration, Graphic Design, Health Care Services, Household Goods, Integrated Marketing, Internet/Web Design, Investor Relations, Media Buying Services, Media Planning, Medical Products, Mobile Marketing, New Technologies, Pharmaceutical, Planning & Consultation, Print, Production, Publicity/Promotions, RSS (Really Simple Syndication), Sales Promotion, Search Engine Optimization, Sponsorship, Strategic Planning/Research

VML delivers creative solutions at the intersection of marketing and technology. Their specialties include: Interactive marketing, Development, Media, Planning, Social, Creative, Web Analytics, and Multivariate Testing.

Approx. Annual Billings: $19,973,209

Debbi Vandeven *(Chief Creative Officer)*
Bruce Davis *(Mng Dir-Ops)*
Dawn Ridge *(Mng Dir-Client Engagement)*
Dean Suarez-Starfeldt *(Mng Dir-Plng)*
Aaron Evanson *(Exec Dir-Creative)*
Mike Gerfen *(Exec Dir)*
Andy Gould *(Exec Dir-Creative)*

Interactive Agencies

Marino Puhalj *(Exec Dir-Creative)*
Jane Tamraz *(Exec Dir)*
Matt Bowne *(Grp Dir-Creative)*
Michelle Larason *(Grp Dir-Client Engagement)*
Tony Marin *(Dir-Creative)*
Ken Saito *(Dir-Innovation-Global)*
Cathy Staples *(Dir-Mktg)*
Paul Serilla *(Assoc Dir-Plng)*
Charles Gooch *(Sr Mgr-Community)*
Christina Miller *(Sr Mgr-Channel)*
Ali Ellis *(Sr Acct Mgr)*
Maggie Glenski *(Sr Acct Mgr)*
Laura Moran *(Acct Mgr)*
Alex Ayre *(Mgr-Channel-Media)*
Melissa Henriquez *(Mgr-Mktg)*
Melissa Watson *(Mgr-Channel)*
Susan Hansen *(Acct Supvr)*
Morgan Gardner *(Assoc Acct Exec)*
Amanda Janssen *(Asst Acct Mgr)*
Alison Leder *(Asst Acct Mgr)*
Kyle Rogers *(Sr Social Strategist)*

Accounts:
APM
Foster Farms
Heinz Heinz Chili Sauce, Heinz Cocktail Sauce, Heinz Cross-Portfolio CRM, Heinz Foodservice, Heinz Homestyle Beans, Heinz Homestyle Gravy, Heinz Ketchup (Consumer and Foodservice), Heinz Soups, Heinz Vinegar, Heinz57 Sauce
Kalamazoo Literacy Council
Kellogg Company Apple Jacks, Corn Pops, Crunchy Nut, Froot Loops, Frosted Flakes, Gardenburger, Kellogg's Family Rewards (CRM and Loyalty), Krave, Morningstar Farms, Pop-Tarts, Pringles, Rice Krispies
Kimberly Clark Cottonelle, Scott
Stryker Medical

WATSON DESIGN GROUP
7024 Melrose Ave Ste 430, Los Angeles, CA 90038
Tel.: (323) 465-9225
Fax: (323) 465-1915
E-Mail: info@watsondg.com
Web Site: www.watsondg.com

Year Founded: 2005

Agency Specializes In: Advertising, Brand Development & Integration, Content, Digital/Interactive, Internet/Web Design, Print, Social Media

Jordan Cuddy *(VP-Production)*
Greg Meltzer *(Producer-Interactive)*
Hleb Marholin *(Dir-Creative)*
Fernando Ramirez *(Dir-Creative)*

Accounts:
Fox Searchlight Pictures, Inc. Birdman
Lions Gate Entertainment Corp. Hunger Games
Wes Anderson

WEBSITE PROMOTION
916 S Marday Ave, Sioux Falls, SD 57103
Tel.: (605) 332-3799
Web Site: www.web-promotion-specialist.com

Employees: 1
Year Founded: 2001

Agency Specializes In: Advertising, Advertising Specialties, Digital/Interactive, E-Commerce, Internet/Web Design, Promotions, Search Engine Optimization, Social Media, Web (Banner Ads, Pop-ups, etc.)

John Aschoff *(Owner)*

Accounts:
Freebird Custom Motorcycles
Sun Vacations
Two Roads Media

WILLIAM FRASER
611 E 12th Ste 205, Anchorage, AK 99501
Tel.: (907) 677-2950
E-Mail: contact@williamfraser.com
Web Site: www.williamfraser.com

Year Founded: 2008

Agency Specializes In: Advertising, Brand Development & Integration, Broadcast, Digital/Interactive, Graphic Design, Internet/Web Design, Logo & Package Design, Print, Social Media

Julia Vea *(Dir-Creative)*

Accounts:
907life
Alaska Miners Association
Global Block
Manley & Brautigam PC
Marianne B. Miller
Prize Figher Djs

WILMINGTON DESIGN COMPANY
3517 Wrightsville Ave, Wilmington, NC 28403
Tel.: (919) 395-9997
E-Mail: info@wilmingtondesignco.com
Web Site: www.wilmingtondesignco.com

Agency Specializes In: Brand Development & Integration, Digital/Interactive, Graphic Design, Internet/Web Design, Logo & Package Design, Print, Search Engine Optimization, Social Media

Bill Hunter *(Pres & Creative Dir)*
Carolyn Pikoulas *(Art Dir & Designer)*
Eric Jones *(Acct Dir)*
Stephanie Young *(Designer)*

Accounts:
New-Design Workshop

WONDERSAUCE LLC
41 W 25th St 6th Fl, New York, NY 10010
Tel.: (646) 756-5410
E-Mail: hello@wondersauce.com
Web Site: www.wondersauce.com

Year Founded: 2011

Agency Specializes In: Brand Development & Integration, Content, Digital/Interactive, Package Design, Print, Social Media

Eric Mayville *(Co-Founder & Partner)*
John Sampogna *(Co-Founder & Mng Dir)*
Seth Klassen *(Co-Founder & Creative Dir)*
Brett Waszkelewicz *(Partner & Creative Dir)*
Corey Michalek *(Art Dir)*
Megan Blake *(Dir-Product)*
Casey Roeder *(Dir-Product)*
Brandon Bayer *(Assoc Dir-Creative)*
Emily Villany *(Office Mgr)*
Ramon Barcenas *(Designer)*
Dana Mulranen *(Designer)*
Anthony Sampogna *(Designer)*
Valentine Sanders *(Designer)*

Accounts:
Baxter of California
Bill Blass Group Creative, Digital, E-Commerce, Website

XAXIS, LLC
(Formerly 24/7 Media, Inc.)
31 Penn Plaza 132 W 31st St, New York, NY 10001
Tel.: (646) 259-4200
E-Mail: infona@xaxis.com
Web Site: www.xaxis.com

Year Founded: 1995

National Agency Associations: 4A's-IAB

Agency Specializes In: Advertising, Advertising Specialties, African-American Market, Brand Development & Integration, Business-To-Business, Cable T.V., Consumer Marketing, Digital/Interactive, Direct Response Marketing, E-Commerce, Electronic Media, Entertainment, Financial, Gay & Lesbian Market, Health Care Services, High Technology, Hispanic Market, Information Technology, Internet/Web Design, Media Buying Services, Medical Products, Pharmaceutical, Retail, Sales Promotion, Seniors' Market, Sports Market, Strategic Planning/Research, Sweepstakes, Travel & Tourism

Matt Haies *(Gen Counsel, Mng Dir & Sr VP)*
Mark Grether *(Global COO)*
Nicolle Pangis *(Global Chief Revenue Officer)*
Brian Gleason *(CEO-Global)*
Larry Allen *(Sr VP-Bus Dev & Global Platform Sls)*
Sara Hafele *(Sr VP-HR-Global)*
Patrick Bevilacqua *(VP-Ops-Americas)*
Evan Hanlon *(VP-Strategy & Investment-Americas)*
EJ Howard *(VP-Accts)*
Craig Sofer *(VP-Acct Svcs)*
Nicole Cavallaro *(Acct Svcs Dir)*
Curtis Blount *(Dir-IT Security Risk & Compliancy)*
Evan Herman *(Dir-Bus Ops)*
Anthony Martin *(Dir-Ad Ops)*
Mario Vaccari *(Dir-Product Mgmt)*
Deb Bhattacherjee *(Sr Acct Mgr)*
Ilya Vayser *(Acct Mgr & Acct Exec)*
Herry Pierre-Louis *(Product Mgr-Salesforce)*
Alex Block *(Mgr-Client Strategy)*
Alexandra Elkas *(Mgr-Acct Svcs)*
Ewa Maciukiewicz *(Mgr-Global Product Partnerships)*
Kapil Samadhiya *(Mgr-Quality Control)*
Spencer Culbert *(Sr Analyst-Strategy & Investment)*
Amy Anderson *(Sr Recruiter-Acct Svcs)*

Accounts:
Disqus Advertising
GumGum Creative

Branches

Xaxis
(Formerly 24/7 Real Media)
222 Merchandise Mart Plaza Ste 250, Chicago, IL 60654
Tel.: (312) 951-4715
E-Mail: info@xaxis.com
Web Site: www.xaxis.com

Employees: 4

Agency Specializes In: Electronic Media, Media Buying Services

Matthew Haies *(Mng Dir, Gen Counsel & Sr VP)*
John Meringolo *(VP & Dir-Fin-Global)*
Elizabeth Christensen *(VP-Bus Ops-Global)*
Heather Draney *(VP-Client Engagement)*
Mike Evans *(VP-Sls)*
Juan Suarez *(VP-West Coast)*
John Waters *(VP-Mktg)*
Gabrielle Heller *(Dir-User Experience)*
Kenny Lau *(Dir-Product Mgmt-Video)*
Elizabeth Borges *(Acct Mgr)*
Anastasiya Blyukher *(Mgr-Automated Trading)*
Joe Castro *(Mgr-Acct Svcs)*

Interactive Agencies

JR Crosby *(Mgr-Strategy & Investment)*
Jason Grout *(Mgr-Strategic Partner Dev)*
Glenn Jean *(Mgr-Acct Svcs)*
Tricia Shanagan *(Mgr-Audience Campaign)*
Lindsay West *(Mgr-Mktg)*
Anthony Colasacco *(Sr Acct Exec-Digital)*
Craig McAllister *(Sr Analyst-Strategy & Investment)*
John Curaba *(Analyst-Adv Ops)*
Martin Wenerski *(Sr Designer-Global)*
Catherine Agopcan *(Sr Program Mgr)*

Bannerconnect
Poststraat 12, 6135 KR Sittard, Netherlands
Tel.: (31) 46 707 4992
Fax: (31) 46 451 7688
Web Site: www.bannerconnect.net

Sebastiaan Schepers *(CEO)*
Saane van Dooren *(Client Svcs Dir)*
Jeroen Linnemann *(Dir-Ad Ops)*

Xaxis - LATAM Headquarters
601 Brickell Key Dr Ste 800, Miami, FL 33131
Tel.: (305) 341-8152
E-Mail: infolatam@xaxis.com

Lucas Mentasti *(Mng Dir-Latin America)*
Erik Castillo *(Dir-Market-Xaxis Latin America)*
Matthew Jablon *(Analyst-Strategy & Investment)*

Xaxis - APAC Headquarters
18 Cross Street China Square Central, #04-01 & 03, 04823 Singapore, Singapore
Tel.: (65) 6395 3069
E-Mail: infoapac@xaxis.com

Regan Baillie *(Mng Dir)*
Rohan Philips *(VP-Product & Strategy)*
Arshan Saha *(VP-South East Asia)*
Karen Kwan *(Dir-Programmatic Trading-APAC)*
Joe Wilson *(Dir-Client Dev APAC)*
Prathab Kunasakaran *(Assoc Dir-Programmatic Supply Ops-APAC)*
Sebastian Cruz *(Sr Mgr-Programmatic Trading)*
Tasha Kaur *(Sr Mgr-Ops)*
Eugene Woo *(Sr Mgr-Analytics & Ops-APAC)*
Sandeep Agarwala *(Mgr-Programmatic Trading)*
Rupert Chih-Lun Lai *(Mgr-Data Strategy & Product Mktg)*
Shifali Ranawaka *(Mgr-Programmatic Trading)*

Xaxis
(Formerly 24/7 Real Media South Korea)
4F Women Enterprise Supporting Center 733-24 Yeoksam-dong, Gangnam-gu, Seoul, Korea (South)
Tel.: (82) 70 7587 4564
Fax: (82) 2-3459-2381
E-Mail: infokr@xaxis.com

Employees: 60

Agency Specializes In: Electronic Media, Media Buying Services

James Yoon *(Mng Dir)*

Xaxis
(Formerly 24/7 Media Spain S.A.)
C/Norias 92 Majadahonda, Madrid, 28220 Spain
Tel.: (34) 91 405 99 60
E-Mail: infoes@xaxis.com
Web Site: www.xaxis.com/

Employees: 25

Agency Specializes In: Electronic Media, Media Buying Services

Hector Garcia *(Mgr-Data)*

Xaxis - EMEA Headquarters
(Formerly 24/7 Media UK Ltd.)
26 Red Lion Square, Paddington, London, WC1R 4HQ United Kingdom
Tel.: (44) 20 7158 5000
E-Mail: infoemea@xaxis.com

Employees: 25
Year Founded: 1997

Agency Specializes In: Electronic Media, Media Buying Services

Nicolas Bidon *(Mng Dir)*
Richard Lloyd *(VP-Platform-Global)*
Michael Smith *(Head-Sls-EMEA)*
Edward Fanning *(Dir-Product & Tech-Xaxis UK)*
Dean Weaving *(Dir-Programmatic Campaign Mgmt-EMEA)*
Thomas Huttner *(Mgr-Programmatic Campaign)*

Xaxis
(Formerly 24/7 Media Pty Limited)
Level 11 65 Berry Street, Sydney, NSW Australia
Tel.: (61) 2 89131028
E-Mail: infoau@xaxis.com
Web Site: www.xaxis.com

Michel de Rijk *(Mng Dir-APAC)*

Xaxis
(Formerly 24/7 Media)
410 Horsham Rd, Horsham, PA 19044
Tel.: (215) 793-4900
Fax: (215) 591-7500
E-Mail: info@xaxis.com

Employees: 20

Agency Specializes In: Electronic Media, Media Buying Services

Nishant Desai *(Dir-Tech & Partnerships)*

YELLOWHAMMER MEDIA GROUP, LLC
111 W 28th St Ste 2B, New York, NY 10001
Tel.: (646) 490-9841
Web Site: www.yhmg.com

Employees: 15

Agency Specializes In: Digital/Interactive, Social Media

Joe Hirsch *(Founder & CEO)*
Jared Christopherson *(Partner & CIO)*
Rich Lin *(CFO)*
Hagan Major *(COO)*
Jeremy Elbaum *(Chief Revenue Officer)*
Sam Appelbaum *(Sr VP-Bus Dev)*
James Coppens *(Sr Dir-Data Infrastructure)*
Ben Wilson *(Dir-Media Ops)*
Stew Dansby *(Mgr-Ad Ops)*
Andrew Hirsch *(Sr Strategist-Acct)*

Accounts:
LivingSocial, Inc.

YORK & CHAPEL
2 Trap Falls Rd, Shelton, CT 6484
Tel.: (203) 283-5400
E-Mail: info@yorkandchapel.com
Web Site: www.yorkandchapel.com

Year Founded: 2001

Agency Specializes In: Advertising, Digital/Interactive, Internet/Web Design, Print, Promotions, Social Media

Dave Ho *(Pres)*
Felicia Karbo *(Mng Partner)*
Kevin Heslin *(Mng Partner)*
Tom Cook *(Mng Partner)*
Cynthia Kearns *(Dir-HR & Ops)*
Alon Shur *(Dir-Tech)*
Nicole Bonito *(Dir-Client Svc)*
Jason Fountain *(Dir-User Experience)*
Rebecca Sampara *(Acct Mgr)*
Nicole Sorrentino *(Acct Mgr)*
Danielle Levesque *(Strategist-Content)*

Accounts:
Glitter Magazine (Digital Sales Agency of Record)

ZAG INTERACTIVE
148 E Boulevard, Glastonbury, CT 6033
Tel.: (860) 633-4818
E-Mail: socialmedia@zaginteractive.com
Web Site: www.zaginteractive.com

Agency Specializes In: Digital/Interactive, Internet/Web Design, Print, Search Engine Optimization, Social Media

Jennifer Buccini *(Art Dir)*
Michelle Kay Brown *(Dir-Mktg)*

Accounts:
New-Branch Partner Microsite
New-First Financial Credit Union
New-Self-Help Credit Union
New-Thomaston Savings Bank

ZEMOGA
120 Old Ridgefield Rd, Wilton, CT 06897
Tel.: (203) 663-6214
Fax: (917) 591-8174
E-Mail: info@zemoga.com
Web Site: www.zemoga.com

Employees: 70
Year Founded: 2003

Agency Specializes In: Digital/Interactive

Revenue: $4,900,000

D. J. Edgerton *(Founder & CEO)*
Constantine Poulos *(Exec VP-Tech & Delivery)*
Ron Jervis *(Mgr-Client Engagement & Producer-Digital)*
Kristen Link *(Mgr-Client Engagement)*

Accounts:
Paramount Social Media

ZETA INTERACTIVE
185 Madison Ave 5th Fl, New York, NY 10016
Tel.: (212) 660-2500
E-Mail: info@zetainteractive.com
Web Site: www.zetainteractive.com

Employees: 300

Agency Specializes In: Advertising, Communications, Digital/Interactive, Direct Response Marketing, Email, Graphic Design, Market Research, Sales Promotion, Search Engine Optimization, Sponsorship

David A. Steinberg *(CEO)*
Jeffry Nimeroff *(CIO)*
Dan Sommer *(Pres-Global Education)*
Steven Vine *(Gen Counsel & Exec VP-Corp Dev)*
Lauren Laitman *(Exec VP-HR)*
Anil Unnikrishnan *(Exec VP)*
Harrison Davies *(Sr VP & Gen Mgr-Interactive)*

Tom Walsh *(Sr VP & Gen Mgr-ZETAXCHANGE)*
Jeremy A. Klein *(Sr VP-Sls)*
Jess Scott *(SR VP-HR)*
Bharat Goyal *(VP-Engrg)*
John B. Lewis *(VP)*
Eric Osterman *(VP-Sls)*
Nick Zylik *(VP)*
Dex Bindra *(Sr Dir-Strategy & Analytics-ZetaXChange)*
Wendy Hu *(Dir-Product Mgmt)*
Jonathan Jaeger *(Dir-Interactive)*
Alex Gitsis *(Assoc Dir-Interactive Mktg)*
Caitlin Pilkin *(Sr Mgr-Campaign & Interactive)*
Lindsey Buechner *(Acct Mgr)*
Kristen Hessler *(Acct Mgr)*
Kristina Menendez *(Acct Mgr-Digital Mktg)*
Catherine Sutterlin *(Acct Mgr)*
Elizabeth Zator *(Sr Media Planner)*

Accounts:
Century 21; 2008
Foxwoods Resort Casino; 2008
LiveNation
NewsMarket; 2008
Pep Boys; 2008
Sony Electronics Inc.
SourceMedia; 2008
STIHL Inc.; Virginia Beach, VA (Agency of Record)
Time Inc.
United Water; 2008
Universal Studios Theme Parks
Venetian Casino Hotel; Las Vegas, NV
Verizon

Divisions

ClickSquared Inc.
200 W St 3rd Fl E, Waltham, MA 02451
(See Separate Listing)

Zeta Interactive
25A Abe Vorhees Dr, Manasquan, NJ 08736
(See Separate Listing)

ZINK INC
409 King St W Ste 403, M5V 1X1 Toronto, ON Canada
Tel.: (416) 506-8686
Fax: (416) 506-8686
E-Mail: info@zink.ca
Web Site: www.zink.ca

Agency Specializes In: Brand Development & Integration, Commercial Photography, Digital/Interactive, Graphic Design

Raj Dias *(Founder & Partner)*

Accounts:
ALLIANCE FILMS
BOOM 99.7
HGTV cable channel
IndiGo
TSN Communications
UTV

MEDIA BUYING SERVICES

33ACROSS INC

229 W 28th St, New York, NY 10001
Tel.: (646) 606-2174
Web Site: www.33across.com

Agency Specializes In: Advertising, Media Relations

Eric Wheeler *(CEO)*
John Haskin *(CMO)*
Paul Bell *(Chief Revenue Officer)*
Orchid Richardson *(Sr VP-Publr & Media Solutions & Gen Mgr)*
Stephen McDermott *(VP-Sls & Head-Programmatic)*
Adam Alter *(VP-Bus Dev)*
Shyam Kuttikkad *(VP-Engrg)*
Adam Kadet *(Dir-Programmatic Sls)*

Accounts:
Digitas Telecommunication Services

ABSOLUTE MEDIA INC.

1150 Summer St, Stamford, CT 06905
Tel.: (203) 327-9090
Fax: (203) 323-1899
E-Mail: info@absolutemediainc.com
Web Site: www.absolutemediainc.com

Employees: 16
Year Founded: 1994

Agency Specializes In: Automotive, Broadcast, Business Publications, Business-To-Business, Cable T.V., Consulting, Consumer Marketing, Consumer Publications, E-Commerce, Electronic Media, Entertainment, Fashion/Apparel, Financial, Health Care Services, High Technology, Leisure, Magazines, Media Buying Services, Newspaper, Newspapers & Magazines, Out-of-Home Media, Outdoor, Pharmaceutical, Radio, Seniors' Market, Syndication, T.V., Trade & Consumer Magazines, Transportation

Gene Willhoft *(Founder & Pres)*
Barbara Siebert *(Treas)*
Robert Gisler *(Dir-Media Res)*
Mary Ozkan *(Dir-Media Svcs)*
Alison Grice *(Assoc Dir-Media)*
Valerie Calderon *(Media Planner & Buyer)*

Accounts:
Circle One Marketing
Cognito! Communications

ACCESS ADVERTISING LLC

2001 Grand Ave Ste 501, Kansas City, MO 64108
Tel.: (816) 471-1577
Fax: (816) 471-0177
Toll Free: (888) 943-6382
E-Mail: sales@accessadvertising.com
Web Site: www.accessadvertising.com

Employees: 20
Year Founded: 1989

Agency Specializes In: Advertising, African-American Market, Asian Market, Business Publications, Business-To-Business, Cable T.V., Consulting, Hispanic Market, Media Buying Services, Medical Products, Newspaper, Newspapers & Magazines, Print, Radio, Real Estate, Recruitment, Seniors' Market, Sports Market, T.V., Telemarketing, Transportation, Travel & Tourism

Approx. Annual Billings: $6,000,000

Breakdown of Gross Billings by Media: Brdcst.: $10,000; Cable T.V.: $40,000; Newsp.: $5,750,000; Radio: $200,000

Trae Nunnink *(CEO)*
Julia Denniston *(Dir-Fin)*
Brad Furnish *(Chief Economist)*

ACRONYM MEDIA

Empire State Bldg 350 5th Ave Ste 6520, New York, NY 10118
Tel.: (212) 691-7051
Fax: (212) 868-6355
Toll Free: (877) 736-2276
E-Mail: info@acronym.com
Web Site: www.acronym.com

Year Founded: 1995

Agency Specializes In: Affiliate Marketing, Consulting, Internet/Web Design, Market Research, Media Planning, Paid Searches, Search Engine Optimization

Selina Eizik *(CEO)*
Mike Grehan *(CMO & Mng Dir)*
Stephanie Hart *(VP-Client Svcs)*
Daniel Olduck *(VP-Strategy)*
Ploy Tang *(Mgr-Mktg)*
Ellen Moon *(Strategist-PPC)*
Elyse Chu *(Coord-Bus Dev)*

Accounts:
Accenture Software Development Services
BMW Automobiles & Motorcycles Mfr
Four Seasons Hotels and Resorts
HSBC Banking Services
Humana Health Insurance Services
Johnson & Johnson Health Care Products Mfr
SAP Business Management Software Solutions

ACTIVE INTERNATIONAL

1 Blue Hill Plaza 9th Fl, Pearl River, NY 10965-3104
Tel.: (845) 735-1700
Fax: (845) 735-0717
Toll Free: (800) 448-7233
E-Mail: resumes@activeinternational.com
Web Site: www.activeinternational.com

Employees: 600
Year Founded: 1984

National Agency Associations: 4A's

Agency Specializes In: Media Buying Services

Approx. Annual Billings: $855,000,000

Arthur Wagner *(Co-Founder & Pres)*
Jim Porcarelli *(Chief Strategy Officer & Exec VP)*
Elizabeth Topazio *(Exec VP & Chief Legal Officer-Active Travel)*
Jon Arm *(Chief Investment Officer-Brdcst-Natl & Sr VP)*
Alan Izenman *(Chief Digital Officer-US)*
Alan Brown *(Pres-Active International Holdings)*
Bill Georges *(Pres-Sls & Ops)*
Gary Steinbeck *(CFO-Intl Div, Controller & Exec VP-Fin)*
Dayna Frank *(Gen Counsel)*
Lisa Brown *(Exec VP-Strategic Dev)*
Kevin Farkas *(Exec VP-Sls & Bus Dev)*
Karen Gabor *(Exec VP-Media & Strategic Dev Ops)*
Liz Margolis *(Exec VP-Corp Ops & Plng)*
Barbara Martino *(Exec VP-Client Dev)*
Dennis Quinn *(Exec VP)*
Karen Brambani *(Sr VP & Grp Dir)*
Fran Baric *(Sr VP & Dir-Integrated Media)*
Catherine Boera *(Sr VP & Dir-Comm Plng)*
Mark Goldschmidt *(Sr VP & Dir-Media Trade)*
Kathy McGrath *(Sr VP & Dir-Digital Trade)*
Bob O'Neill *(Sr VP & Dir-Local Media)*
John Viserto *(Sr VP & Dir-Brdcst-Natl)*
Darren Riley *(Sr VP)*
Doug Roeder *(Sr VP-New Bus Dev)*
Diahanna Keyes *(VP & Acct Dir-Client Dev)*
Cecilia Barossi *(VP & Dir-Media Rels)*
Joan Kornhaber *(VP & Dir-OOH)*
Steve Goldberg *(VP & Assoc Dir-Plng)*
Denise LoPiccolo *(VP & Acct Mgr-Digital Integration)*
Jon Lumerman *(VP-Integrated Media)*
Ron Malecot *(Dir-Sls Ops)*
Jonathan Wiener *(Dir-New Bus Dev)*
Joanna Gardini *(Media Buyer-Direct Response)*
Rich Vitiello *(Media Buyer-Direct Response)*
Noreen Dambrot *(Sr Media Buyer)*
Melissa Holm *(Sr Media Buyer)*

Accounts:
New-Association of National Advertisers
New-BYB Brands, Inc.
New-Elkay Manufacturing Company
New-IMAN Cosmetics
New-Preferred Hotels & Resorts
New-Premiere Meeting Destinations
New-ServPro Industries, Inc.
New-Sharp Electronics

Branches

Active International Australia Pty Ltd.

Level 3 140 Arthur St, North Sydney, NSW 2060 Australia
Tel.: (61) 2 9466 9166
Fax: (61) 2 9466 9144
Web Site: www.activeinternational.com.au

Employees: 17

Cameron Swan *(Mng Dir)*
Cameron Baxter *(Gen Mgr-Melbourne)*
Nick Draper *(Dir-Media)*
Neesha Coelho *(Mgr-Media)*
Anna Meaclem *(Mgr-Comml)*
Jamie-Lee Harris *(Client Mgr-Travel & Events)*

Active Media Services Canada Inc.

4100 Yonge Street Ste 406 4th Floor, Toronto, ON M2P 2B5 Canada
Tel.: (416) 226-8650
Fax: (416) 225-7375
Web Site: www.activeinternational.com

Employees: 14

Andrew Bulmer *(Mng Dir-Canada & Sr VP)*
Susanne Morello *(Sr VP-Media)*
Mark Spencer *(VP-Strategy & Partner Solutions)*
Karin Macpherson *(Sr Dir-Client Solutions)*
Chris Barr *(Dir-Media)*
Gurjit Bath *(Dir-New Bus Dev)*
Scott Miles *(Dir-Client Solutions)*
Mimi Salviato *(Dir-Media)*
Ameerah Ain *(Mgr-HR)*

Monica So *(Mgr-Fin)*
Jodi Graham *(Supvr-Media)*
Beverly Whyte *(Supvr-Media)*
Victoria Mcminn *(Key Acct Mgr-Tactical)*

Active International (Europe) S.A.R.L.
27 rue Nicolo, 75116 Paris, France
Tel.: (33) 1 45 04 32 90
Fax: (33) 1 40 72 66 16
Web Site: www.activeinternational.com

Employees: 20

Alan S. Elkin *(Owner)*
Franck Boutry *(Dir-Admin & Fin)*
Mayor Francis *(Dir-Media)*
Francis Maire *(Dir-Media)*
Adli Sakka *(Dir-Comml)*
Arnaud Rives *(Mgr-Sls)*
Charlotte Billot *(Coord-Strategic Ops)*
Kahina Bouamour *(Coord-Travel)*
Sandrine Degrave *(Deputy CFO)*

Accounts:
Advertising Strategist
Bel Brands USA
CB Richard Ellis
Codemasters
JELD-WEN
Katz Advantage
Kettle Foods
Leggett & Platt
Rust-Oleum
Transitions Optical Inc

Active International Ltd.
103 New Oxford St, London, WC1A 1DD United Kingdom
Tel.: (44) 207 520 6666
Fax: (44) 207 520 6620
Web Site: www.activeinternational.com

Employees: 25

Mark Chippendale *(Mng Dir-UK)*
Jarrod Gowland-Smith *(Head-Brdcst & Digital)*
Gemma Atkinson *(Dir-Comml)*
Alex Beeden *(Mgr-Comml Partnerships)*
Rob North *(Mgr-Brdcst & Digital Media)*
Michelle Powell *(Mgr-Digital Media)*
Will Singleton *(Mgr-Fin)*
Paul Stubbs *(Mgr-Fin)*
Sarah Younger *(Mgr-Comml)*

AD CLUB
1304 W Roseburg Ave, Modesto, CA 95350-4855
Tel.: (209) 343-1900
Fax: (209) 529-5265
Toll Free: (800) 333-1228
E-Mail: ads@adclub.com
Web Site: www.adclub.com

Employees: 15
Year Founded: 1987

Agency Specializes In: Advertising, Recruitment

Approx. Annual Billings: $20,000,000

Breakdown of Gross Billings by Media: Bus. Publs.: $3,000,000; Internet Adv.: $3,000,000; Newsp.: $14,000,000

Jeremiah Bach *(Dir-Recruitment Adv)*
Toni Galvez *(Acct Exec)*
Jennifer Reddell *(Acct Exec)*
Gary Torkelson *(Rep-Adv)*

Accounts:
AAA (American Automobile Association)
American Heart Association
California State Universities
Caltrans
Dow Pharmaceuticals
E&J Gallo Wine
Evoqua Water Technologies
FedEx
Peterbilt/Kenworth Trucks
Safeway, Inc.
Williams Sonoma/Pottery Barn

ADVERTISING CONNECTION INC.
273 W Point Rd, Ava, IL 62907-2318
Tel.: (618) 426-3384
Fax: (618) 426-3468
Toll Free: (800) 326-3468
E-Mail: customercare@advertisingconnection.com
Web Site: www.advertisingconnection.com

Employees: 4
Year Founded: 1994

Agency Specializes In: Media Buying Services, Newspaper

Approx. Annual Billings: $1,500,000

Larry Dierks *(Owner)*
Pam Dierks *(Owner)*

Accounts:
Benjamin Franklin High School
EMS
National Chemical
Sunset Ranches

AERIAL ADVERTISING SERVICES
333 W Jack London Blvd Hangar 241, Livermore, CA 94551
Tel.: (925) 449-0210
E-Mail: sales@aerialservices.org
Web Site: www.aerialservices.org

Employees: 5
Year Founded: 1992

Agency Specializes In: Advertising, Advertising Specialties, Automotive, Aviation & Aerospace, Brand Development & Integration, Business-To-Business, Co-op Advertising, Corporate Identity, Entertainment, Event Planning & Marketing, Exhibit/Trade Shows, Government/Political, Health Care Services, High Technology, Local Marketing, Out-of-Home Media, Outdoor, Publicity/Promotions, Recruitment, Sales Promotion, Sports Market

Approx. Annual Billings: $2,000,000

Breakdown of Gross Billings by Media: Outdoor: 100%

Robert Franklin *(Pres)*

Accounts:
County of San Mateo
Ford Motor Company
Jelly Belly; Fairfield, CA Food Products; 1992
Oracle America, Inc.
Pizza Orgasmica; San Francisco, CA Restaurant; 1994

AMERICAN CLASSIFIED SERVICES, INC.
1809 W Main Ste 304, Carbondale, IL 62901
Tel.: (618) 351-7570
Fax: (618) 351-7573
E-Mail: email@advertisingresults.com
Web Site: www.advertisingresults.com

Employees: 4
Year Founded: 1997

Agency Specializes In: Advertising, Business-To-Business, Hispanic Market, Media Buying Services, Newspaper, Newspapers & Magazines, Print, Recruitment

Approx. Annual Billings: $2,250,000

Breakdown of Gross Billings by Media: Newsp. & Mags.: $2,250,000

Leigh Ann Kristiansen *(Owner & Pres)*

AMERICAN COMMUNICATIONS GROUP, INC.
21311 Madrona Ave Ste 101, Torrance, CA 90503
Tel.: (310) 530-4100
E-Mail: kcampbell@acgmedia.com
Web Site: www.acgmedia.com

Employees: 100
Year Founded: 1987

Agency Specializes In: Advertising, Local Marketing, Market Research, Media Buying Services, Media Planning, Newspaper, Pets , Print, Retail, Strategic Planning/Research

Approx. Annual Billings: $500,000,000

Breakdown of Gross Billings by Media: Newsp.: $500,000,000

Christopher Cope *(Pres & CEO)*
Jamie Shaw *(CFO & Exec VP)*
Bill Gamble *(VP-Media & Acct Svcs)*
Regina Rospenda *(VP-Admin)*
Christi Ware *(VP-Acctg)*
Ray Young *(VP-Tech & Dev)*
Karli Sikich *(Dir-Corp Comm)*

Accounts:
Aaron Brothers, Inc.
J.C.Penney Company Inc.
Michaels Stores Inc.
PETCO Animal Supplies Inc.

AMERICAN NEWSPAPER REPRESENTATIVES, INC.
2075 W Big Beaver Rd Ste 310, Troy, MI 48084-3439
Tel.: (248) 643-9910
Fax: (248) 643-9914
Toll Free: (800) 550-7557
E-Mail: jjepsen@gotoanr.com
Web Site: www.gotoanr.com

E-Mail for Key Personnel:
President: jjepson@anrinc.net

Employees: 6
Year Founded: 1943

Agency Specializes In: Advertising, Agriculture, Automotive, Co-op Advertising, Financial, Food Service, Health Care Services, High Technology, Hospitality, Leisure, Media Buying Services, Media Planning, Medical Products, Multicultural, Newspaper, Newspapers & Magazines, Planning & Consultation, Print, Restaurant, Retail, Transportation, Travel & Tourism

Breakdown of Gross Billings by Media: Newsp.: 100%

John Jepsen *(Pres)*
Dean Bevacqua *(Mgr-Sls-Natl)*
Paula Stevenson *(Supvr-Plng & Buying)*

AMNET GROUP
150 E 42nd St 14th Fl, New York, NY 10017
Tel.: (212) 591-9122

Web Site: www.amnetgroup.com

John Murray *(Pres-Amplifi Global)*
Benoit Michielsens *(Mng Dir-Belgium)*
Justine Watkins *(Mng Dir-Amnet US)*
Marie Le Guevel *(Gen Mgr-France)*
Stephanie Landrum *(Dir-Client Svcs)*
Jennifer Scheel *(Dir-Client Svcs-General Motors)*
Kelly Schneider *(Dir-Global Client Dev)*
Adam Luther *(Assoc Dir)*
Megan Phelan *(Assoc Dir)*
Lauren Schubeck *(Assoc Dir)*
Leah Feigel *(Sr Acct Mgr)*
David Lee *(Sr Acct Mgr)*
Kyle Brennan *(Acct Mgr)*
Andrew Furst *(Acct Mgr)*
Myles Gamboa *(Acct Mgr-Programmatic Media)*
Devin Elise Jones *(Acct Mgr-Private Marketplaces)*
Michael Lafata *(Acct Mgr-Programmatic Media)*
Ashley McMahan *(Acct Mgr)*
Kristen Peczynski *(Acct Mgr)*
Richard Salazar *(Acct Mgr-Programmatic Media)*
Billy Sessions *(Acct Mgr-General Motors)*
Stacey Shaw *(Acct Mgr)*
Amy Garland *(Mgr-Publr Dev)*
Rachel Boye *(Acct Coord)*
Lauren Brown *(Acct Coord-Programmatic)*
Lauren Command *(Acct Coord-Programmatic Media)*
Matthew Golish *(Acct Coord-Programmatic Media)*
Emily Kennedy *(Acct Coord)*
Maxwell Rivas *(Acct Coord-Programmatic Media)*
Olivia Trocchio *(Acct Coord)*
Robert Wolf *(Acct Coord-Programmatic Media)*
Jacob Lazarowitz *(Sr Campaign Mgr-Programmatic Media & Dev)*

AMOBEE
(Formerly Adconion Media Inc.)
1322 3rd St Promenade 2nd Level, Santa Monica, CA 90401
Tel.: (310) 382-5500
Fax: (310) 382-5501
Web Site: amobee.com

Agency Specializes In: Media Buying Services

Neil V. Sunderland *(Chm)*
Kim Reed Perell *(CEO-Adconion Direct)*
Allen Maximillian *(VP & Controller-Worldwide)*
James Malins *(VP-Cross Channel Solutions)*
Jessie Gardner *(Dir-Culture & Engagement)*
Erin Crapser *(Sr Mgr-Product Mktg)*
Chris Nezu *(Sr Acct Mgr)*
Vincent Pham *(Acct Mgr)*
Lauryn Wells *(Sr Strategist-Sls)*
Laura Milner *(Sr Coord-Mktg)*

ANVIL MEDIA, INC.
310 NE Failing St., Portland, OR 97212
Tel.: (503) 595-6050
Fax: (503) 223-1008
E-Mail: kent@anvilmediainc.com
Web Site: www.anvilmediainc.com

Employees: 12
Year Founded: 2000

National Agency Associations: PAF-SEMPO

Agency Specializes In: Above-the-Line, Advertising, Advertising Specialties, Affiliate Marketing, Affluent Market, African-American Market, Agriculture, Alternative Advertising, Arts, Asian Market, Automotive, Aviation & Aerospace, Below-the-Line, Bilingual Market, Brand Development & Integration, Branded Entertainment, Broadcast, Business Publications, Business-To-Business, Cable T.V., Catalogs, Children's Market, Co-op Advertising, Collateral, College, Commercial Photography, Communications, Computers & Software, Consulting, Consumer Goods, Consumer Marketing, Consumer Publications, Content, Corporate Communications, Corporate Identity, Cosmetics, Crisis Communications, Custom Publishing, Customer Relationship Management, Digital/Interactive, Direct Response Marketing, Direct-to-Consumer, E-Commerce, Education, Electronic Media, Electronics, Email, Engineering, Entertainment, Environmental, Event Planning & Marketing, Exhibit/Trade Shows, Experience Design, Faith Based, Fashion/Apparel, Financial, Food Service, Game Integration, Gay & Lesbian Market, Government/Political, Graphic Design, Guerilla Marketing, Health Care Services, High Technology, Hispanic Market, Hospitality, Household Goods, Identity Marketing, In-Store Advertising, Industrial, Infomercials, Information Technology, Integrated Marketing, International, Internet/Web Design, Investor Relations, Legal Services, Leisure, Local Marketing, Logo & Package Design, Luxury Products, Magazines, Marine, Market Research, Media Buying Services, Media Planning, Media Relations, Media Training, Medical Products, Men's Market, Merchandising, Mobile Marketing, Multicultural, Multimedia, New Product Development, New Technologies, Newspaper, Newspapers & Magazines, Out-of-Home Media, Outdoor, Over-50 Market, Package Design, Paid Searches, Pets , Pharmaceutical, Planning & Consultation, Podcasting, Point of Purchase, Point of Sale, Print, Product Placement, Production, Production (Ad, Film, Broadcast), Production (Print), Promotions, Public Relations, Publicity/Promotions, Publishing, RSS (Really Simple Syndication), Radio, Real Estate, Recruitment, Regional, Restaurant, Retail, Sales Promotion, Search Engine Optimization, Seniors' Market, Shopper Marketing, Social Marketing/Nonprofit, Social Media, South Asian Market, Sponsorship, Sports Market, Stakeholders, Strategic Planning/Research, Sweepstakes, Syndication, T.V., Technical Advertising, Teen Market, Telemarketing, Trade & Consumer Magazines, Transportation, Travel & Tourism, Tween Market, Urban Market, Viral/Buzz/Word of Mouth, Web (Banner Ads, Pop-ups, etc.), Women's Market, Yellow Pages Advertising

Approx. Annual Billings: $2,000,000

Breakdown of Gross Billings by Media: Internet Adv.: $2,000,000

Kent Lewis *(Founder & Pres)*
Mike Terry *(VP)*
Christian Bayley *(Dir-Strategy)*
Joshua Breese *(Dir-Strategy)*
Anna Hutson *(Dir-Acct Svcs)*
Rachel Swaney *(Acct Exec)*
Sarah Shannon *(Coord-Special Projects)*

Accounts:
Advantis Credit Union
American Red Cross, Oregon Trail Chapter
ChefWorks
CreditReport.com
Dr. Martens /AirWair; 2009
Enjoy Life Food
Forum
GolfNow.com; Miami, FL; 2008
Hotel Lucia; OR; 2003
Hotel Max
Icebreaker; New Zealand; 2009
InFocus; OR LCD Projectors; 2003
International Rescue Committee
Kettle Foods
Lucy.com
Moonstruck Chocolatier; Portland, OR; 2009
The Nature Conservancy
Oregon State University
Prana
Provenance Hotels
Real Networks; Seattle, WA RealPlayer, SuperPass; 2009
Right Management
Schering Plough; NJ Foradil, Oncology Products; 2002
SEMA
Seminole Gaming
Sonos
Tahoe Mountain Resorts
TEKsystems
Travel Portland
Trend Micro; Germany; 2010
Yesmail; Portland, OR; 2008

APPLEGATE MEDIA GROUP
405 Lexington Ave 26th Fl, New York, NY 10174
Mailing Address:
PO Box 261, Monroe, CT 06468
Tel.: (203) 223-0107
Fax: (203) 268-4946
Toll Free: (877) 515-5557
E-Mail: info@applegatemediagroup.com
Web Site: www.applegatemediagroup.com

Employees: 17
Year Founded: 1991

Agency Specializes In: Above-the-Line, Advertising, Advertising Specialties, Affiliate Marketing, Affluent Market, African-American Market, Agriculture, Alternative Advertising, Arts, Asian Market, Automotive, Aviation & Aerospace, Below-the-Line, Bilingual Market, Brand Development & Integration, Branded Entertainment, Broadcast, Business Publications, Business-To-Business, Cable T.V., Catalogs, Children's Market, Co-op Advertising, Collateral, College, Commercial Photography, Communications, Computers & Software, Consulting, Consumer Goods, Consumer Marketing, Consumer Publications, Content, Corporate Communications, Corporate Identity, Cosmetics, Crisis Communications, Custom Publishing, Customer Relationship Management, Digital/Interactive, Direct Response Marketing, Direct-to-Consumer, E-Commerce, Education, Electronic Media, Electronics, Email, Engineering, Entertainment, Environmental, Event Planning & Marketing, Exhibit/Trade Shows, Experience Design, Fashion/Apparel, Financial, Food Service, Game Integration, Gay & Lesbian Market, Government/Political, Graphic Design, Guerilla Marketing, Health Care Services, High Technology, Hispanic Market, Hospitality, Household Goods, Identity Marketing, In-Store Advertising, Industrial, Infomercials, Information Technology, Integrated Marketing, International, Internet/Web Design, Investor Relations, Legal Services, Leisure, Local Marketing, Logo & Package Design, Luxury Products, Magazines, Marine, Market Research, Media Buying Services, Media Planning, Media Relations, Media Training, Medical Products, Men's Market, Merchandising, Mobile Marketing, Multicultural, Multimedia, New Product Development, New Technologies, Newspaper, Newspapers & Magazines, Out-of-Home Media, Outdoor, Over-50 Market, Package Design, Paid Searches, Pharmaceutical, Planning & Consultation, Podcasting, Point of Purchase, Point of Sale, Print, Product Placement, Production, Production (Ad, Film, Broadcast), Production (Print), Promotions, Public Relations, Publicity/Promotions, Publishing, RSS (Really Simple Syndication), Radio, Real Estate, Recruitment, Regional, Restaurant, Retail, Sales Promotion, Search Engine Optimization, Seniors' Market, Social Marketing/Nonprofit, Sponsorship, Sports Market, Stakeholders, Strategic Planning/Research, Sweepstakes, Syndication, T.V., Technical Advertising, Teen Market, Telemarketing, Trade & Consumer Magazines, Transportation, Travel & Tourism, Urban Market, Viral/Buzz/Word of Mouth, Web (Banner Ads, Pop-ups, etc.), Women's Market, Yellow Pages Advertising

Breakdown of Gross Billings by Media: Bus. Publs.: 7%; Cable T.V.: 3%; Co-op Adv.: 1%; Internet Adv.: 2%; Local Mktg.: 1%; Newsp. & Mags.: 25%; Out-of-Home Media: 15%; Promos.: 4%; Radio & T.V.: 30%; Sports Mktg.: 4%; Strategic Planning/Research: 5%; Transit: 3%

Susan Y. Applegate *(CEO)*

Accounts:
Clear 4G Media Buying, Wireless Broadband Network
CRN International; Hamden, CT Electronics; 2006

ASHER MEDIA, INC.
15303 Dallas Pkwy Ste 1300, Addison, TX 75001
Tel.: (972) 732-6464
Web Site: www.ashermedia.com

Employees: 22
Year Founded: 1999

Agency Specializes In: Sponsorship

Revenue: $4,700,000

Kalyn Asher *(Owner & Pres)*
Jackie Barrera *(Dir-Brdcst Buying)*
Ami Baxter *(Dir-Media Ops)*
Sarah Lerner *(Dir-Media Plng)*
Libby Lauten *(Assoc Dir-Media)*
Stephanie McCallister *(Supvr-Media)*
Mary Kim *(Assoc Media Dir)*
Meagan Vaughn *(Sr Media Planner & Sr Media Buyer)*

Accounts:
OMNI Corporate OMNI Hotels

ATWELL MEDIA SERVICES, INC.
7238 Murieta Dr Ste A2A #320, Rancho Murieta, CA 95683
Tel.: (916) 354-8585
Fax: (916) 354-1057
E-Mail: info@atwellmediaservices.com
Web Site: www.atwellmediaservices.com

Employees: 3
Year Founded: 2002

National Agency Associations: AAF

Agency Specializes In: Advertising, Advertising Specialties, African-American Market, Brand Development & Integration, Business-To-Business, Education, Hispanic Market, In-Store Advertising, Media Buying Services, Out-of-Home Media, Outdoor, Publicity/Promotions, Sales Promotion

Revenue: $4,000,000

Brian Atwell *(Principal)*
Janelle Atwell *(Client Svcs Dir)*

Accounts:
Consolidated Communications
Healthy Families
State of California
T-Mobile
Wells Fargo

AXIS MEDIA
30495 Canwood St, Agoura Hills, CA 91301
Tel.: (818) 264-1555
Fax: (818) 264-1550
E-Mail: tom@axismedia.org
Web Site: www.axis-media.us

Employees: 2
Year Founded: 2002

Agency Specializes In: Advertising, Advertising Specialties, Automotive, Broadcast, Cable T.V., Co-op Advertising, Consulting, Direct Response Marketing, Food Service, Hispanic Market, Infomercials, Local Marketing, Magazines, Market Research, Media Buying Services, Media Planning, Medical Products, Newspaper, Newspapers & Magazines, Out-of-Home Media, Outdoor, Pharmaceutical, Planning & Consultation, Print, Production, Production (Ad, Film, Broadcast), Production (Print), Promotions, Radio, Recruitment, Regional, Retail, Sponsorship, Sports Market, Strategic Planning/Research, T.V., Web (Banner Ads, Pop-ups, etc.)

Approx. Annual Billings: $5,000,000

Breakdown of Gross Billings by Media: Other: 5%; Radio: 20%; T.V.: 75%

Tony Naish *(Pres)*

BIG KITTY LABS
3900 O Shannon Rd, Dublin, OH 43016
Tel.: (614) 432-1378
E-Mail: info@bigkittylabs.com
Web Site: www.bigkittylabs.com

Year Founded: 2009

Agency Specializes In: Content, Mobile Marketing

Dan Rockwell *(Co-Founder)*

Accounts:
MobileXpeditions LLC. Mobile Phones Retailer
ReserveThat Books Retailer
RightNow Technologies Inc Non-Classified Establishment Providers

BILLBOARD CENTRAL
419 Main St, Huntington Beach, CA 92648
Tel.: (714) 960-5106
E-Mail: dave@billboardcentral.com
Web Site: www.billboardcentral.com

Employees: 2
Year Founded: 1996

Agency Specializes In: Out-of-Home Media, Outdoor

Approx. Annual Billings: $1,000,000

Dave Lindsey *(Owner & Pres)*

Accounts:
AT&T Communications Corp.; 2006
California Pistachio Commission
Jeffrey-Scott Advertising
McDonald's; 1997
Taco Bell; 2007

BILLBOARD CONNECTION
1315 Walnut St, Philadelphia, PA 19107
Tel.: (267) 480-7110
Web Site: www.billboardconnection.com

Year Founded: 2000

Agency Specializes In: Out-of-Home Media, Outdoor

Michael Tolassi *(Mgr-Sls & Mktg)*

Accounts:
Asbury Auto Group Outdoor Media; 2014

BILLBOARD EXPRESS, INC.
23121 Arroyo Vista, Rancho Santa Margarita, CA 92688
Tel.: (949) 589-3500
Fax: (949) 589-4141
Toll Free: (877) 782-7438
E-Mail: rick.zakhar@billboardexpress.com
Web Site: www.billboardexpress.com

Employees: 15
Year Founded: 1994

Agency Specializes In: Advertising, Advertising Specialties, Alternative Advertising, Event Planning & Marketing, Exhibit/Trade Shows, Government/Political, Guerilla Marketing, Media Buying Services, Mobile Marketing, Out-of-Home Media, Outdoor, Promotions, Recruitment

Approx. Annual Billings: $1,500,000

Rick Zakhar *(Pres & CEO)*
Brooke Elson *(Acct Supvr)*
Adam Zakhar *(Acct Exec)*

Accounts:
Barret Jackson
Boost Mobile
Cingular Wireless LLC
Denny's
Disney Films
General Atomics
KB Homes
metroPCS
T-Mobile US
XM Radio

BILLUPS WORLDWIDE
8 N State Ste 121, Lake Oswego, OR 97034
Tel.: (503) 454-0714
Fax: (503) 454-0716
Web Site: billupsww.com/

Employees: 3
Year Founded: 2004

National Agency Associations: OAAA

Agency Specializes In: Advertising, Out-of-Home Media, Outdoor

Approx. Annual Billings: $15,000,000

Breakdown of Gross Billings by Media: Out-of-Home Media: $15,000,000

Benjamin Billups *(CEO)*
Greg Taylor *(Chief Bus Officer & Exec VP)*
Stephanie Calderwood *(Dir-Buying & Vendor Partnerships)*
Ryan Chisholm *(Dir)*
Ross Elder *(Dir-Media)*
Dana Gyllen *(Dir-Studio Svcs)*
Joyce Luna *(Dir-Media Strategy)*
Beth Schissler *(Dir-Media)*
Stacy Repin *(Media Planner)*

BLACK DIAMOND MEDIA
574 Heritage Rd Ste 201A, Southbury, CT 06488
Tel.: (203) 262-0588
Fax: (203) 262-0589
E-Mail: 1blackdiamond@b-d-m.com
Web Site: www.b-d-m.com

Employees: 8

National Agency Associations: DMA

Brian Mahoney *(Pres)*

Accounts:
Cabela's Outfitters
Geico General Insurance Co.
Sony

BLUE DAISY MEDIA
2906 S Douglas Rd Ste 201, Coral Gables, FL 33134
Tel.: (305) 442-4229
Fax: (305) 442-4669
E-Mail: info@bluedaisymedia.com
Web Site: www.bluedaisymedia.com

Employees: 4
Year Founded: 2001

Agency Specializes In: Advertising, Affluent Market, Alternative Advertising, Bilingual Market, Broadcast, Business Publications, Business-To-Business, Cable T.V., Children's Market, Co-op Advertising, Consulting, Consumer Goods, Consumer Publications, Digital/Interactive, Electronic Media, Email, Gay & Lesbian Market, Guerilla Marketing, Health Care Services, Hispanic Market, Infomercials, International, Leisure, Local Marketing, Luxury Products, Magazines, Media Buying Services, Media Planning, Men's Market, Mobile Marketing, Multimedia, Newspaper, Newspapers & Magazines, Out-of-Home Media, Outdoor, Paid Searches, Planning & Consultation, Print, Promotions, Radio, Real Estate, Regional, Restaurant, Retail, Seniors' Market, Strategic Planning/Research, T.V., Teen Market, Trade & Consumer Magazines, Transportation, Travel & Tourism, Urban Market, Web (Banner Ads, Pop-ups, etc.), Women's Market, Yellow Pages Advertising

Diana Fleming *(Partner)*
Jennifer Ford *(Partner)*

Accounts:
IGT Media Holdings Buffets, Inc., Pollo Tropical
Melia Hotels International Gran Melia, Paradisus
Paws 4 You Rescue Non Profit
Related Group of Florida Real Estate Developments
The Ritz-Carlton Residences; Palm Beach, FL Luxury Condos
Senior Resource Group Independent & Assisted Living Facilities

BOSS CREATIVE
18402 US Hway 281 Ste 201, San Antonio, TX 78259
Tel.: (210) 568-9677
Fax: (210) 340-5180
E-Mail: hello@thisisboss.com
Web Site: www.thisisboss.com

Employees: 25
Year Founded: 2005

Agency Specializes In: Advertising, Digital/Interactive, Graphic Design, Publishing, Search Engine Optimization, Web (Banner Ads, Pop-ups, etc.)

Revenue: $30,000,000

Peter Beshay *(Co-Founder, Owner, Pres & CEO)*
Mike Pilkilton *(CFO)*
Robert Littlejohn *(Dir-Internet Mktg)*

Accounts:
CE2
Get NSIDE
Lantrix Liquor
McRanch

BRAIN FARM
525 W Elk Ave Ste 3, Jackson, WY 83001
Tel.: (307) 200-6050
Fax: (307) 200-6052
E-Mail: info@brainfarmcinema.com
Web Site: www.brainfarmcinema.com

Agency Specializes In: Commercial Photography, Digital/Interactive, Entertainment, Production (Ad, Film, Broadcast), T.V., Web (Banner Ads, Pop-ups, etc.)

Curt Morgan *(CEO)*
Shon Tomlin *(Exec VP-Television & Digital)*
Chad Jackson *(Head-Production)*
Ty Evans *(Dir)*
Danny Holland *(Supvr-Post Production)*
Stephanie Buelow *(Coord-Production)*

Accounts:
National Geographic Television Network Services
NBC/Universal Television Network Services
Quiksilver Apparels Mfr
Roxy Clothing & Accessories Distr
Visa Black Card Credit Card Providers

BRAND COOL MARKETING INC
(Acquired by Butler/Till)

BRAVENETMEDIA.COM
100-200 Jensen Ave Ste 101, Parksville, BC V9P 2H5 Canada
Mailing Address:
PO Box 1722, Parksville, BC V9P 2H5 Canada
Tel.: (250) 954-3203
Fax: (250) 954-2164
E-Mail: melanie@bravenetmedia.com
Web Site: www.bravenetmedia.com

Employees: 40
Year Founded: 1997

Agency Specializes In: Advertising, Affiliate Marketing, Business-To-Business, Computers & Software, Consumer Marketing, Digital/Interactive, Internet/Web Design, Media Buying Services, Women's Market

David Shworan *(Owner & CEO)*
Melanie Peake *(Dir-Online Sls & Media Buyer)*

BRAXTON STRATEGIC GROUP
54 Westbrook Rd, Westfield, NJ 07090
Tel.: (908) 209-3331
E-Mail: reatha@braxtonstrategic.com
Web Site: www.braxtonstrategic.com

Employees: 3
Year Founded: 2003

Agency Specializes In: Media Buying Services, Media Planning

Approx. Annual Billings: $2,500,000

Reatha Braxton *(Owner)*

Accounts:
HotJobs.com
Orchard Street Productions

BROADCAST TIME, INC.
91 Blackheath Rd, Lido Beach, NY 11561-4807
Tel.: (516) 431-2215
Fax: (516) 889-8511

Employees: 8
Year Founded: 1981

Agency Specializes In: Advertising, Broadcast, Cable T.V., Consulting, Internet/Web Design, Media Buying Services, Merchandising, Planning & Consultation, Radio, T.V.

Approx. Annual Billings: $24,800,000

Breakdown of Gross Billings by Media: Cable T.V.: $3,472,000; Internet Adv.: $496,000; Network Radio: $1,488,000; Network T.V.: $744,000; Spot Radio: $8,680,000; Spot T.V.: $9,920,000

Bruce Kuperschmid *(Pres)*
Peter Kuperschmid *(Exec VP)*
Caroline Kuperschmid *(VP-Sls)*

BUNTIN OUT-OF-HOME MEDIA
1001 Hawkins St, Nashville, TN 37206
Tel.: (615) 244-5720
Fax: (615) 244-6511
E-Mail: info@buntinoutofhome.com
Web Site: www.buntinoutofhome.com

E-Mail for Key Personnel:
President: hgreiner@buntingroup.com

Employees: 20
Year Founded: 1988

National Agency Associations: OAAA-TAB

Agency Specializes In: Media Planning, Out-of-Home Media, Outdoor, Strategic Planning/Research

Approx. Annual Billings: $50,000,000

Breakdown of Gross Billings by Media: Outdoor: $50,000,000

Howard Greiner *(Pres & COO)*
Jon Carmack *(Exec VP-Ops & Tech)*
David Kelleher *(VP & Mgmt Supvr)*
Bryan Kemp *(VP & Dir-Field Mgmt)*
Don Bailey *(Dir-Art)*
Katie McAfee *(Acct Supvr-Field)*
Laura Nixon *(Acct Supvr)*
Katie Hewson *(Sr Acct Exec)*
Emily Wurz *(Acct Exec)*

Accounts:
Bass Pro Shops
Burger King Corp. Outdoor
La Quinta Inns & Suites
Outback Steakhouse of Florida; Tampa, FL
RBC Capital Markets
Red Lobster
Ruby Tuesday
SERVPRO Industries

BUTLER/TILL
1565 Jefferson Rd Bldg 200 Ste 280, Rochester, NY 14623
Tel.: (855) 472-5100
Fax: (585) 274-5199
E-Mail: info@butlertill.com
Web Site: www.butlertill.com

Employees: 100
Year Founded: 1998

National Agency Associations: 4A's-IAA

Agency Specializes In: Advertising, Affluent Market, Broadcast, Business-To-Business, Cable T.V., College, Communications, Consumer Marketing, Digital/Interactive, Direct Response Marketing, Education, Electronic Media, Email, Environmental, Financial, Food Service, Gay & Lesbian Market, Government/Political, Health Care Services, High Technology, Hispanic Market, Information Technology, International, Local Marketing, Magazines, Market Research, Media Buying Services, Media Planning, Medical Products, Mobile Marketing, Multicultural, Over-50 Market, Pharmaceutical, Planning & Consultation, Regional, Retail, Search Engine Optimization, Seniors' Market, Sponsorship, Strategic Planning/Research, Teen Market, Urban Market, Web (Banner Ads, Pop-ups, etc.), Women's Market

Approx. Annual Billings: $160,000,000

Sue Butler *(Founder & Chm)*
Kimberly Jones *(Pres)*
Melissa Palmer *(Exec VP)*
Amanda DeVito *(VP-Engagement)*
Sue Belias *(Controller)*
Mary Rockefeller *(Grp Acct Dir)*
Michael DiCaprio *(Acct Dir & Strategist-Media)*
Michael Charles Deichmiller *(Acct Dir)*
David Grome *(Acct Dir)*
Kathleen Traver *(Sr Acct Supvr)*
Donna VonDerLinn *(Supvr-Creative)*
Patrick Willome *(Supvr-Data Mgmt)*
Christine Falcipieri *(Sr Acct Exec)*
Nicole Hamlin *(Sr Acct Exec)*
Kerianne Kabureck *(Sr Acct Exec)*
Jennie Jones *(Sr Media Buyer)*
Steve McFarland *(Sr Media Planner & Buyer-Digital)*
Chris Palmeri *(Sr Media Buyer-DR)*

Accounts:
CenturyLink, Inc. Media Buying, Media Planning, Telecommunications
New-Excellus BCBS Healthcare; 1999
Master Lock & Sentry Safe Media
State Farm Insurance
Upstate Niagara Cooperative Milk Farms Cooperative
Valeant Pharmaceutical Jublia, Luzu
New-Valeant Pharmaceuticals; 2013

Branch

Brand Cool Marketing Inc
2300 E Ave, Rochester, NY 14610
(See Separate Listing)

BUY ADS DIRECT
33247 Westwood Dr, Ridge Manor, FL 33523
Tel.: (352) 397-4221
Fax: (352) 797-7745
Toll Free: (877) 510-1007
E-Mail: will@buyadsdirect.com
Web Site: www.buyadsdirect.com

Employees: 3

Agency Specializes In: Advertising, Advertising Specialties, Affiliate Marketing, Affluent Market, African-American Market, Alternative Advertising, Arts, Automotive, Aviation & Aerospace, Below-the-Line, Bilingual Market, Brand Development & Integration, Branded Entertainment, Broadcast, Business Publications, Business-To-Business, Cable T.V., Catalogs, Children's Market, Co-op Advertising, Collateral, College, Commercial Photography, Communications, Computers & Software, Consulting, Consumer Goods, Consumer Marketing, Consumer Publications, Content, Corporate Communications, Corporate Identity, Cosmetics, Crisis Communications, Custom Publishing, Customer Relationship Management, Digital/Interactive, Direct Response Marketing, Direct-to-Consumer, E-Commerce, Education, Electronic Media, Electronics, Email, Engineering, Entertainment, Environmental, Event Planning & Marketing, Exhibit/Trade Shows, Experience Design, Fashion/Apparel, Financial, Food Service, Game Integration, Gay & Lesbian Market, Government/Political, Graphic Design, Health Care Services, High Technology, Hispanic Market, Hospitality, Household Goods, Identity Marketing, In-Store Advertising, Industrial, Infomercials, Information Technology, Integrated Marketing, International, Internet/Web Design, Investor Relations, Legal Services, Leisure, Local Marketing, Logo & Package Design, Luxury Products, Magazines, Marine, Market Research, Media Buying Services, Media Planning, Media Relations, Media Training, Medical Products, Men's Market, Merchandising, Mobile Marketing, Multicultural, Multimedia, New Product Development, New Technologies, Newspaper, Newspapers & Magazines, Out-of-Home Media, Outdoor, Over-50 Market, Package Design, Paid Searches, Pharmaceutical, Planning & Consultation, Podcasting, Point of Purchase, Point of Sale, Print, Product Placement, Production, Production (Ad, Film, Broadcast), Production (Print), Promotions, Public Relations, Publicity/Promotions, Publishing, RSS (Really Simple Syndication), Radio, Real Estate, Recruitment, Regional, Restaurant, Retail, Sales Promotion, Search Engine Optimization, Seniors' Market, Social Marketing/Nonprofit, South Asian Market, Sponsorship, Sports Market, Stakeholders, Strategic Planning/Research, Sweepstakes, Syndication, T.V., Technical Advertising, Teen Market, Telemarketing, Trade & Consumer Magazines, Transportation, Travel & Tourism, Urban Market, Viral/Buzz/Word of Mouth, Web (Banner Ads, Pop-ups, etc.), Women's Market, Yellow Pages Advertising

Approx. Annual Billings: $3,300,000

Breakdown of Gross Billings by Media: Cable T.V.: $2,500,000; Radio: $800,000

Will Crawford *(Owner)*

C2C MEDIA, LLC
353 Lexington Ave Ste 200, New York, NY 10016
Tel.: (212) 209-1519
Web Site: www.c2c-outdoor.com

Employees: 3

Agency Specializes In: Advertising, Out-of-Home Media

Michael Palatnek *(Co-Founder, Pres & CEO)*
Jessica Mallen *(Mng Dir)*
Lee Krackow *(VP)*
Ahmad Sayar *(Grp Dir-Digital Strategy)*
Caroline Todman *(Acct Dir-Out of Home)*
Melissa Ali *(Media Planner-C2C Outdoor)*
Nicole Campana *(Media Planner)*
Alyssa Chianese *(Asst Media Planner)*
Shallamar Marchione *(Jr Media Planner)*

Accounts:
Allure
Fiji Water
Gotham Direct
Hollister Co.
IFC
Oakley
Teleflora
Tiffany & Co.
Ugg Australia

CADREON
100 W 33rd St 9th Fl, New York, NY 10001
Tel.: (212) 883-4751
Web Site: www.cadreon.com

Erica Schmidt *(Mng Dir & Exec VP-North America)*
Arun Kumar *(Pres-Global)*
Ian Johnson *(Exec VP & Mng Dir-Global Product)*
Nick Hippolyte *(Exec VP-Tech Solutions)*
Ryan Bell *(VP-Programmatic)*
Kimber Robbins *(VP-Product Mgmt)*
Darrick Khoa *(Sr Dir-Quality Assurance-Programmatic Infrastructure Sys)*
Robert Anderson *(Dir & Specialist-Programmatic)*
Jennifer Yager *(Dir & Specialist-Programmatic)*
Elina Piskoverov *(Assoc Dir-Reporting & Analytics)*
Michael Horowitz *(Mgr & Specialist-Programmatic)*
Amy Thai *(Mgr-Programmatic Media)*
Brittany Crockett *(Coord-Programmatic)*
Christopher Infanzon *(Coord-Programmatic)*
Conor Marks *(Coord-Programmatic)*
Mark Sly *(Coord-Programmatic)*
Brian You *(Coord-Programmatic)*

CAMELOT COMMUNICATIONS, INC.
8140 Walnut Hill Ln Ste 700, Dallas, TX 75231
Tel.: (214) 373-6999
Fax: (214) 373-6854
Web Site: camelotsmm.com/

Employees: 45
Year Founded: 1983

National Agency Associations: 4A's

Agency Specializes In: Advertising, African-American Market, E-Commerce, Hispanic Market, Media Buying Services, Planning & Consultation, Retail, Sponsorship, Sports Market

Approx. Annual Billings: $421,700,000

Breakdown of Gross Billings by Media: Outdoor: $17,100,000; Print: $16,500,000; Radio: $46,300,000; T.V.: $341,800,000

Brenda Wurst *(Co-Founder)*
Jim Lucero *(Mng Dir)*
Jack McEnaney *(CFO)*
Chris Schembri *(COO)*
Brian Gardenhire *(Chief Integration Officer)*
Alex Richter *(Exec VP-Interactive)*
Roy Brannon *(VP-Mktg)*
Charlie Thomas *(VP)*
Sandra Valdespino *(Acct Mgr)*
Karen Coffey *(Specialist-Market-Camelot Strategic Mktg & Media)*
Jessica Sunderland *(Strategist-Digital)*

Accounts:
The Bombay Co.
Branson
Bugaboo Creek Steak House
Capital Grille
Neiman-Marcus
Payless
Rare Hospitality
Silver Dollar City, Inc.
Stone Mountain

CAMPUS MEDIA GROUP, INC.
2 Appletree Sq 4th Fl, Bloomington, MN 55425
Tel.: (952) 698-7362
Fax: (952) 854-3104
E-Mail: info@campusmediagroup.com
Web Site: www.campusmediagroup.com

E-Mail for Key Personnel:
President: tom@campusmediagroup.com

Employees: 15
Year Founded: 2002

National Agency Associations: AAF

Agency Specializes In: Advertising, Advertising Specialties, Alternative Advertising, Automotive, Brand Development & Integration, College, Direct Response Marketing, Education, Electronic Media, Electronics, Email, Entertainment, Event Planning & Marketing, Experience Design, Financial, Guerilla Marketing, Media Buying Services, Media Planning, Mobile Marketing, Newspaper, Newspapers & Magazines, Out-of-Home Media, Outdoor, Planning & Consultation, Publicity/Promotions, Recruitment, Restaurant, Retail, Social Marketing/Nonprofit, Social Media, Sponsorship, Teen Market, Viral/Buzz/Word of Mouth

Jason Bakker *(COO-Bus Dev)*
Amanda Hudak *(Sr Acct Mgr)*

Brandon Larson *(Sr Acct Dev Mgr)*
Stephanie Murawski *(Acct Dev Mgr)*

Accounts:
Bon Ton Stores Retail; 2006
Deloitte
Pizza Hut Food; 2006

CARAT INSIGHT
150 E 42nd St, New York, NY 10017
Tel.: (212) 591-9100
E-Mail: hello.global@carat.com
Web Site: www.carat.com

National Agency Associations: 4A's

Agency Specializes In: Customer Relationship Management, Digital/Interactive, Market Research, Media Buying Services, Media Planning, Social Media, Sponsorship, Strategic Planning/Research

Gina Banks *(Sr VP & Head-Bus)*
Lauren Dieck *(Assoc Dir-Media)*
Jacqueline Checho *(Supvr-Comm Plng)*
Joseph Baker *(Planner-Digital Media)*

Accounts:
General Motors Co.
The Walt Disney Company Media Planning & Buying

CARAT USA, INC.
(Formerly Carat)
150 E 42nd St, New York, NY 10017
Tel.: (212) 591-9100
Web Site: www.carat.com

Employees: 700
Year Founded: 1968

National Agency Associations: 4A's-AAF-ABC-DMA-IAB

Agency Specializes In: Digital/Interactive, Media Buying Services, Media Planning, Mobile Marketing, Print, Radio, T.V.

Approx. Annual Billings: $6,600,000,000

Jan Weinstein *(Mng Dir & Exec VP)*
Doug Ray *(Pres-Global & CEO-US)*
Sarah Baehr *(Exec VP & Mng Dir-Digital Strategy)*
Robert Hannan *(Exec VP & Mng Dir-Ops-Carat Media Svcs)*
Justine Bloome *(Sr VP & Head-Strategy & Innovation)*
Michael Epstein *(Sr VP & Acct Mgmt Dir)*
Joya Harris *(Sr VP & Dir-Multicultural)*
Ginger Taylor White *(Sr VP-Publ & Dir-Publ Content)*
Tia Shaw *(VP & Grp Dir-Digital)*
Robert Nishiyama *(VP & Dir-Comm Plng)*
Deanna Buggy *(Dir-Comm Plng)*
Daniel Maree *(Dir-Strategy)*
Frank Balice *(Assoc Dir-Media & Comm Plng)*
Ivy Cheung *(Assoc Dir-Media & Digital)*
Gerard DePersio *(Assoc Dir-Integrated Plng)*
Elyse Nitzberg *(Assoc Dir)*
Aryn Richards *(Assoc Dir-Plng-Smucker's)*
Chris Wilson *(Assoc Dir-Media)*
Jonathan Roman *(Mgr-Ad Ops)*
Stephanie Anderson *(Supvr-Comm Plng)*
Janelle Cababa *(Supvr-Comm Plng)*
Jayme Cangelosi *(Supvr-Natl Video Activation)*
Alexander Colcord *(Supvr-Digital Media)*
Kendall Dolbec *(Supvr-Digital)*
Jeff Fang *(Supvr-Comm Plng)*
Emily Kaufman *(Supvr-Comm Plng)*
Jaclyn McGuire *(Supvr-Integrated Comm Plng)*
Elizabeth McKeen *(Supvr-Media)*
Rory Morrin *(Supvr-Plng-Adidas)*
Dana Russo *(Supvr-Media Plng)*
Joshua Schirle *(Supvr-Digital Plng)*
Maris Cohen *(Planner-Comm)*
Mina Hirsch *(Media Planner)*
Dylan Mullen *(Planner-Digital Plng & Activation)*
Estee Jaffe *(Assoc Planner-Comm)*
Kyle Campbell *(Assoc Media Planner-Integrated)*
Paul Dorset *(Assoc Media Planner)*
Shayne Minick *(Assoc Media Dir-Plng)*
Juliana Monzon *(Assoc-Natl Audio Activation)*
Sejal Patel *(Asst Media Planner)*
Andrea Walters *(Sr Media Buyer-Local Brdcst)*

Accounts:
Adidas Group Reebok, Rockport, TaylorMade, adidas; 2002
ARS Rescue Rooter; 2010
Black & Decker
Blue Shield of California; 2006
British Airways
Burberry Global Media
Danone Activia, Evian Water, Stonyfield
Darden Restaurants LongHorn Steakhouse, Media
Daytona Tourism; 2000
Diageo Baileys, Captain Morgan, Guinness, J&B, Johnnie Walker, Media Planning, Smirnoff, US Media
Discover Financial Services (Media Agency of Record)
Draeger; 2010
Drivetime Auto; 2010
General Motors Company Media Planning & Buying, Spark, Volt; 2012
The Home Depot, Inc. (Media Buying & Media Planning); 2010
The J.M. Smucker Company Cafe Bustelo, Cafe Pilon, Crisco, Digital Media Planning & Buying, Dunkin at Home, Eagle, Folgers, Jif, MDO, Martha White Natural Peanut Butters, Pillsbury Baking, Smucker's, Traditional Media Planning & Buying; 2008
Kohler Media; 2008
L'Oreal Softsheen-Carson; 1994
Macy's, Inc. Broadcast & Digital, Media Planning & Buying
MasterCard Inc. Global Media
Microsoft Corporation
New-Mondelez International Media Buying, Media Planning
MTV
Nokia; 2009
O'Reilly Auto Parts; 2000
Pfizer Inc. Consumer Healthcare, Media Buying, Pharma; 2010
Philips Healthcare, Lighting; 2001
The Procter & Gamble Company Bounty, Campaign: "The World's Scariest Shave", Charmin, Eukanuba, Gillette Men's Grooming Products, Gillette ProGlide, Iams, Luvs, Nutura, P&G Corporate & Scale, Pampers, Puffs
RE/MAX; 1999
Relativity Media Media Buying, Media Planning
Skype; 2009
Sony Computer Entertainment America LLC GoPro, Media Planning & Buying, PlayStation, Red Bull
Staples, Inc. Media
Swiss Re Group; 2006
Western Digital

CHEROKEE COMMUNICATIONS INC.
11 River Rise Rd, New City, NY 10956-5601
Tel.: (845) 638-6700
Fax: (845) 638-3347
E-Mail: cherokeecomm@optonline.net
Web Site: www.millercherokee.com

Employees: 2
Year Founded: 1986

Agency Specializes In: Advertising, Broadcast, Business Publications, Business-To-Business, Cable T.V., Collateral, Consumer Publications, Education, Financial, Food Service, Graphic Design, Health Care Services, Internet/Web Design, Leisure, Logo & Package Design, Magazines, Market Research, Media Buying Services, Media Planning, Newspaper, Newspapers & Magazines, Out-of-Home Media, Outdoor, Planning & Consultation, Production, Radio, Recruitment, Retail, T.V.

Approx. Annual Billings: $351,500

Breakdown of Gross Billings by Media: Cable T.V.: $225,000; Collateral: $8,500; Outdoor: $35,000; Print: $10,000; Production: $8,500; Radio: $45,000; Spot T.V.: $7,500; Worldwide Web Sites: $12,000

Kent Murphy *(Pres)*
Jenny Sanchez *(VP)*

CHESS COMMUNICATIONS GROUP
901 E Fayette St, Baltimore, MD 21202-4731
Tel.: (410) 732-7400
Fax: (410) 563-0045
Toll Free: (800) 551-0158
E-Mail: info@chesscg.com
Web Site: www.chesscg.com

Employees: 11
Year Founded: 1988

Agency Specializes In: Broadcast, Financial, Media Buying Services, Newspapers & Magazines, Retail

Bruce Lannatuono *(Chm)*
Michael Powers *(Mgr-Production)*

Accounts:
Baltimore Dog Magazine
Cassidy & Pinkard Colliers International
Charles Town R&S
Coors Brewing Co.
Cruzan Rum
Digex
Discovery Channel
Expression Magazine
Trump Plaza Casino & Hotel

CLASSIFIED ADVERTISING PLUS, LLC
(d/b/a myclassifiedads.net)
6535 Gunn Hwy, Tampa, FL 33625
Tel.: (813) 920-0197
Fax: (813) 792-2630
E-Mail: blaire@myclassifiedads.net
Web Site: www.myclassifiedads.net

E-Mail for Key Personnel:
President: steve@myclassifiedads.net
Creative Dir.: ella@myclassifiedads.net
Media Dir.: blaire@myclassifiedads.net
Public Relations: blaire@myclassifiedads.net

Employees: 12
Year Founded: 2004

Agency Specializes In: Advertising, Advertising Specialties, Affiliate Marketing, Alternative Advertising, Branded Entertainment, Broadcast, Business-To-Business, Co-op Advertising, Commercial Photography, Consulting, Consumer Marketing, Consumer Publications, Corporate Identity, Custom Publishing, Direct Response Marketing, Direct-to-Consumer, Education, Electronic Media, Email, Entertainment, Environmental, Exhibit/Trade Shows, Graphic Design, Health Care Services, Hispanic Market, Infomercials, Information Technology, Integrated Marketing, International, Internet/Web Design, Legal Services, Local Marketing, Logo & Package Design, Magazines, Marine, Market Research, Media Buying Services, Media Planning, Media Relations, Media Training, Medical Products, Merchandising, Mobile Marketing, Multimedia, New Product Development, Newspaper, Newspapers & Magazines, Out-of-Home Media, Outdoor, Over-50 Market, Package Design, Paid Searches, Planning

Media Buying Services

& Consultation, Podcasting, Point of Purchase, Point of Sale, Print, Product Placement, Production, Production (Print), Promotions, Public Relations, Publicity/Promotions, Publishing, RSS (Really Simple Syndication), Radio, Real Estate, Recruitment, Regional, Retail, Sales Promotion, Search Engine Optimization, Seniors' Market, Sports Market, T.V., Technical Advertising, Teen Market, Telemarketing, Trade & Consumer Magazines, Transportation, Travel & Tourism, Viral/Buzz/Word of Mouth, Women's Market, Yellow Pages Advertising

Approx. Annual Billings: $5,000,000

Breakdown of Gross Billings by Media: Newsp.: $4,000,000; Other: $1,000,000

Rusty Rich *(CIO)*
Cathi Helm *(Dir-Immigration Media)*
Tamara E Huber *(Dir-Natl Media)*
Steve Juanette *(Dir-Fin Ops)*
Raeanne Meyer *(Dir-Media Strategy)*
Alex Clevenger *(Sr Specialist-Natl Brdcst Media)*
Becca Fagnano *(Specialist-Labor Certification Media)*
Kelsey Schepmann *(Coord-Media & Support)*
Raenelle Turnbull *(Coord-Press Release & Newspaper Support)*

CLICKBOOTH

5901 N Honore Ave, Sarasota, FL 34243
Tel.: (941) 483-4188
Toll Free: (866) 867-6333
Web Site: www.clickbooth.com

Year Founded: 2002

Agency Specializes In: Advertising, Graphic Design, High Technology, Publishing

Sarah Chase *(VP-Ops)*
Cara Redding *(VP-Res)*
Laura Miller *(Acct Dir-Adv)*
Katie Rose Cianfaglione *(Dir-Affiliates)*
Julie Martin *(Dir-Ops)*
Mike Storey *(Dir-Affiliates)*
Joe Lendrum *(Mgr-Talent Acq)*
Maddie Ross *(Strategist-Affiliate)*
Aaron Wiseman *(Strategist-Affiliate)*

COLLECTIVE MEDIA

99 Park Ave, New York, NY 10016
Tel.: (888) 460-9513
Fax: (646) 422-6529
Toll Free: (888) 460-9513
E-Mail: contactus@collective.com
Web Site: www.collective.com

Employees: 11
Year Founded: 2005

Agency Specializes In: Advertising, Digital/Interactive, Search Engine Optimization, Social Media, Web (Banner Ads, Pop-ups, etc.)

Revenue: $1,400,000

Jill Botway *(Pres & Chief Revenue Officer)*
Joe Apprendi *(CEO)*
Mike Facendola *(CFO)*
Eoin Townsend *(Chief Product Officer)*
John Vandermay *(CTO)*
Todd Taplin *(Chief Revenue Officer)*
Jerome FitzGibbons *(Exec VP)*
Joe Gallagher *(Sr VP-Channel Sls)*
Lee Levitan *(Sr VP-Fin)*
Ken Nelson *(Sr VP-Advertiser Svcs)*
Shana Pergament *(Sr VP-People)*
Lance Wolder *(Sr VP-Integrated Mktg)*
Phil Frank *(VP)*
Barry Garbarino *(VP-Mktg Strategy & Events)*
Julie Kurtz *(VP-Media Sls-East)*
Jon Barracca *(Sr Dir-Bus Dev)*
Benjamin Bring *(Sr Dir-Performance)*
Matt Durkin *(Sr Dir-Reg Sls-Central)*
Adam Goldsmith *(Sr Acct Dir)*
Chase Altenbern *(Acct Dir)*
Jordan Kohun *(Acct Dir)*
Annie Merriman *(Acct Dir)*
Scott Winkler *(Acct Dir)*
Allyse Slocum *(Dir-Product Mktg)*
Nikki Solomon *(Dir-Product Solutions & Strategy)*
Kristy Woolbright *(Acct Mgr)*
Amanda Marsh *(Planner-Integrated)*

Accounts:
Accel Partners
DggiFinogi
Eye Wonder
Jivox
Linkstorm
LiveRail

COLSKY MEDIA

2740 Van Ness Ave Ste 220, San Francisco, CA 94109-0216
Tel.: (415) 673-5400
Fax: (415) 673-1820
E-Mail: info@colskymedia.com
Web Site: www.colskymedia.com

E-Mail for Key Personnel:
President: rickc@colskymedia.com

Employees: 9
Year Founded: 1973

Agency Specializes In: Advertising, Automotive, Broadcast, Business-To-Business, Cable T.V., Co-op Advertising, Communications, Computers & Software, Digital/Interactive, Electronic Media, Entertainment, Financial, Food Service, Government/Political, High Technology, Local Marketing, Magazines, Media Buying Services, Media Planning, Mobile Marketing, Newspaper, Newspapers & Magazines, Out-of-Home Media, Outdoor, Paid Searches, Planning & Consultation, Print, Radio, Retail, Search Engine Optimization, Social Marketing/Nonprofit, Social Media, Sports Market, Strategic Planning/Research, T.V., Web (Banner Ads, Pop-ups, etc.)

Approx. Annual Billings: $46,000,000

Breakdown of Gross Billings by Media: Newsp.: $15,000,000; Other: $1,000,000; Radio: $3,000,000; T.V.: $27,000,000

Richard A. Colsky *(Pres & CEO)*
Helen Katz *(Dir-Brdcst Media)*
Susana Sanchez *(Assoc Dir-Brdcst Media)*

COMPAS, INC.

4300 Haddonfield Rd, Pennsauken, NJ 08109
Tel.: (856) 667-8577
Web Site: www.compasonline.com

Employees: 75

Agency Specializes In: Digital/Interactive, Health Care Services, Media Buying Services, Strategic Planning/Research

Stan Woodland *(CEO)*
John Donovan *(CFO)*
James Woodland *(COO)*
Susan Dorfman *(CMO & Chief Innovations Officer)*
Nicole Woodland-DeVan *(Sr VP-Buying Svcs & Deliverables)*
Mary Padula *(VP & Dir-Media)*
Carly Kuper *(VP-Strategic Mktg & Comm)*
Nancy Logue *(VP-HR)*
Alena Minarovicova *(Sr Media Planner)*

Accounts:
Alcon
AstraZeneca
Bayer
Johnson & Johnson

COMPASS POINT MEDIA

510 Marquette Ave, Minneapolis, MN 55402
Tel.: (612) 347-1000
Fax: (612) 347-6969
Web Site: everythingtalks.com/compasspointmedia

Employees: 40
Year Founded: 1976

National Agency Associations: 4A's

Agency Specializes In: Direct Response Marketing, Media Buying Services, Sponsorship, Strategic Planning/Research

Approx. Annual Billings: $445,000,000

Breakdown of Gross Billings by Media: Brdcst.: $290,000,000; D.M.: $140,000,000; Mags.: $15,000,000

Richard A. Hurrelbrink *(Pres)*
Melissa Schoenke *(Mng Dir)*
Tom McCarthy *(Sr VP & Grp Dir-Content Strategy & Media Ops-General Mills)*
Melanie Skoglund *(Sr VP & Dir-Media Strategy & Investments)*
Lisa Blevins *(Assoc Dir-Media)*
Stephani Estes *(Assoc Dir-Media)*
Sarah Prunty *(Supvr-Media Strategy)*
Melissa Winnig *(Supvr-Media Strategy)*
Connor Johnson *(Analyst-Media-Campbell Mithun)*

Accounts:
Airborne Health; Minneapolis, MN
Ashley Furniture Industries, Inc.
BizFilings, Inc; Madison, WI
General Mills, Inc.; Minneapolis, MN Cereals, Snacks
Great Clips; Minneapolis, MN Nationwide Hair Cutting Franchise
The Hartford; Hartford, CT
Johnsonville Sausage, LLC Media Buying, Media Planning
KeyBank Digital, Print, Radio, Television
Pandora Media Inc.
Schwans Consumer Brands; Minneapolis, MN Freschetta, Red Baron, Tony's, Mrs Smith's, Edwards
SuperValu Inc. Acme, Albertson's, Biggs, Bristol Farms, Cub Foods, Farm Fresh & Pharmacy, Hornbacher's Jewel/Osco, Shaws/Star Market, Shop 'n Save, Shoppers Food & Pharmacy
Syngenta; Minneapolis, MN
The Toro Company Lawn-Boy, The Toro Company Toro Lawn & Snow Products
Wellmark, Inc

CONVERSANT, INC.

(Formerly ValueClick, Inc.)
30699 Russell Ranch Rd Ste 250, Westlake Village, CA 91362-7319
Tel.: (818) 575-4500
Fax: (818) 575-4501
Toll Free: (877) 361-3316
Web Site: www.conversantmedia.com

Employees: 2,857
Year Founded: 1997

Agency Specializes In: Electronic Media

Revenue: $573,121,000

Peter J. Wolfert *(CTO)*

Jim Rund *(Chief Revenue Officer-Media)*
Oded Benyo *(Pres-Conversant Europe)*
John Ardis *(Sr VP-Sls-CRM Solutions Grp)*
Matthew Boyd *(Sr VP-Western Sls)*
Raju Malhotra *(Sr VP-Products)*
Richard Sharp *(Mng Dir-Media & Mobile UK, DE & MENA)*
Matt Fitzsimons *(VP-Media Delivery)*
Liane Gonzalez *(Dir-Client Dev)*
Eric Lemberger *(Sr Acct Mgr)*
Sarah Barger Ranney *(Mgr-Acct Mgmt)*
Lee Feldmann *(Sr Acct Exec)*
Megan Shvets *(Strategist-Client)*

CORINTHIAN MEDIA, INC.
500 8th Ave 5th Fl, New York, NY 10018
Tel.: (212) 279-5700
Fax: (212) 239-1772
E-Mail: lmiller@mediabuying.com
Web Site: www.mediabuying.com

Employees: 55
Year Founded: 1974

Agency Specializes In: Advertising, Affluent Market, African-American Market, Alternative Advertising, Asian Market, Automotive, Bilingual Market, Brand Development & Integration, Branded Entertainment, Broadcast, Business Publications, Business-To-Business, Cable T.V., Children's Market, Co-op Advertising, Collateral, College, Consulting, Consumer Goods, Consumer Marketing, Consumer Publications, Content, Cosmetics, Digital/Interactive, Direct Response Marketing, Direct-to-Consumer, E-Commerce, Education, Electronic Media, Email, Entertainment, Event Planning & Marketing, Fashion/Apparel, Financial, Food Service, Guerilla Marketing, Health Care Services, High Technology, Hispanic Market, Hospitality, Household Goods, In-Store Advertising, Industrial, Infomercials, Integrated Marketing, International, Internet/Web Design, Legal Services, Leisure, Local Marketing, Luxury Products, Magazines, Market Research, Media Buying Services, Media Planning, Media Training, Medical Products, Men's Market, Merchandising, Mobile Marketing, Multicultural, Multimedia, New Product Development, New Technologies, Newspaper, Newspapers & Magazines, Out-of-Home Media, Outdoor, Over-50 Market, Package Design, Paid Searches, Pharmaceutical, Planning & Consultation, Point of Purchase, Point of Sale, Print, Product Placement, Production, Promotions, Publicity/Promotions, Publishing, Radio, Real Estate, Regional, Restaurant, Retail, Sales Promotion, Search Engine Optimization, Seniors' Market, Social Marketing/Nonprofit, Sponsorship, Sports Market, Strategic Planning/Research, Syndication, T.V., Teen Market, Trade & Consumer Magazines, Transportation, Urban Market, Women's Market

Approx. Annual Billings: $305,000,000

Larry Miller *(Owner & Pres)*
Ellen Carry *(Exec VP)*
Bob Klein *(Exec VP-New Bus & Trade)*
Larry Schneiderman *(Exec VP-Direct Response)*
Tina Snitzer *(Exec VP-Buying)*
Mary Cannon *(Sr VP-Buying)*
Maggie Good *(Sr VP-Print & Out of Home)*
Ann Mazzini *(Sr VP)*
Jessica Penney *(Acct Mgr)*

CPC STRATEGY
2820 Camino Del Rio S, San Diego, CA 92108
Tel.: (619) 501-3093
Web Site: www.cpcstrategy.com

Employees: 40
Year Founded: 2007

Agency Specializes In: Paid Searches, Shopper Marketing, Social Media

Rick Backus *(CEO)*
Nii Ahene *(COO)*

Accounts:
Omaha Steaks Digital Marketing, Retail Search Channels; 2011
Payless Shoes Comparison Shopping, Digital & Retail Stores; 2011
Teespring Retail Search Channels; 2015

CPMEDIA SERVICES, INC.
6047 Frantz Rd Ste 105, Dublin, OH 43017
Tel.: (614) 717-4910
Fax: (614) 717-4915
E-Mail: infodesk@cpmedia.com
Web Site: www.cpmedia.com

E-Mail for Key Personnel:
President: bclark@cpmedia.com

Employees: 5
Year Founded: 1993

Agency Specializes In: Advertising, Broadcast, Business Publications, Business-To-Business, Cable T.V., Co-op Advertising, Consulting, Electronic Media, Food Service, Health Care Services, Magazines, Media Buying Services, Medical Products, Newspaper, Newspapers & Magazines, Out-of-Home Media, Outdoor, Print, Radio, Recruitment, Restaurant, Retail, Trade & Consumer Magazines

Approx. Annual Billings: $22,000,000

Breakdown of Gross Billings by Media: Cable T.V.: 5%; Out-of-Home Media: 1%; Outdoor: 5%; Print: 36%; Spot Radio: 20%; Spot T.V.: 28%; Transit: 5%

Charli King *(Principal)*

CROSSMEDIA
22 W 23rd St, New York, NY 10010
Tel.: (212) 206-0888
Fax: (212) 206-0938
Web Site: xmedia.com

Employees: 230

Agency Specializes In: Communications, Content, Digital/Interactive, International, Media Buying Services, Media Planning, Search Engine Optimization, Social Media, Strategic Planning/Research

Jim Tricarico *(Chief Revenue Officer)*
Jon Yuson *(Head-Acct & Assoc Dir)*
Lauren Gray *(Head-Acct)*
David Bauer *(Dir-Programmatic Buying & Digital Ad Ops)*
Laura Deurrschmid *(Supvr-Media)*
Hayley Fox *(Media Planner & Media Buyer)*
Christopher McCann *(Media Planner & Media Buyer)*
Daniel Gore *(Planner & Buyer-Performance Media)*
Brittany Resnick *(Media Planner)*
Fareeha Khan *(Asst Media Planner)*

Accounts:
CBR
Crown Castle
delivery.com
Dover
Gannett
GNC Holdings, Inc. Advertising, Brand Management, Creative, Media Buying, Media Planning
Go Veggie
Happy Family
Julliard
KIND Snacks
Madison Square Garden
Merz
MSG Entertainment
National Basketball Association Media Buying, Media Planning, Phoenix Suns (Agency of Record)
New Era
New York Knicks
New York Rangers
NYU Langone
Pacsun
People Magazine
Premier
Sesame Place
ShopKeep Communications Planning, Media
Sidney Frank Importing Co., Inc. Jagermeister
Skyn
Tribe
University of Michigan
University of Texas
Ventura Foods
Visit Scotland
Vita Coco
White Castle System, Inc. Media Buying, Media Planning
Whole Foods
New-Women's National Basketball Association Media Buying, Media Planning, Phoenix Mercury (Agency of Record)
WP

DATAXU, INC.
281 Summer St 4th Fl, Boston, MA 02210
Tel.: (857) 244-6200
Fax: (617) 426-5971
Web Site: www.dataxu.com

Willard Simmons *(Co-Founder & CTO)*
Bruce Journey *(Co-Founder & Chief Customer Officer)*
Sandro Katanzaro *(Founder & Sr VP-Analytics & Innovation)*
Michael Baker *(Pres & CEO)*
Gerard Keating *(COO)*
Brian Atwood *(Sr VP-Sls-North American)*
Brennan Beyer *(VP-Sls-West)*
Mike Sclabassi *(VP-Sls-Central)*
Maria Martinez-Diaz *(Sr Mgr-Bus Dev)*
Katherine Bugbee *(Acct Exec)*
David Moss *(Acct Exec)*
Allyson Zeitz *(Acct Exec-Programmatic Sls)*

DENTSU AEGIS NETWORK AMERICAS
(Formerly Aegis Media North America)
150 E 42nd St, New York, NY 10017
Tel.: (212) 591-9100
Fax: (212) 252-1250
E-Mail: contact@dentsuaegis.com
Web Site: www.dentsuaegisnetwork.com

Employees: 2,000
Year Founded: 1966

National Agency Associations: 4A's

Agency Specializes In: Advertising, Branded Entertainment, Broadcast, Business-To-Business, Cable T.V., Communications, Consulting, Consumer Marketing, Digital/Interactive, Direct Response Marketing, Entertainment, Event Planning & Marketing, Experience Design, Game Integration, Guerilla Marketing, Integrated Marketing, Internet/Web Design, Local Marketing, Magazines, Market Research, Media Buying Services, Media Planning, Mobile Marketing, Multicultural, Multimedia, Newspaper, Newspapers & Magazines, Out-of-Home Media, Outdoor, Paid Searches, Planning & Consultation, Print, Promotions, Publicity/Promotions, Radio, Search Engine Optimization, Sponsorship, Sports Market,

T.V., Trade & Consumer Magazines, Viral/Buzz/Word of Mouth

Michelle Lynn *(Mng Dir & Exec VP)*
Jeffrey Maloy *(CMO)*
Ray White *(CMO)*
Nigel Morris *(CEO-Dentsu Aegis Network Americas & EMEA)*
Jennifer Hungerbuhler *(Exec VP & Mng Dir-Local Video & Audio Investment)*
Michael Law *(Exec VP & Mng Dir-Video Investments)*
David Fasola *(Exec VP & Dir-Chevrolet-Global)*
Tecla Palli-Sandler *(Exec VP & Dir-HR)*
Therese Jreige *(Sr VP & Head-Media Strategy & Innovation-Global)*
Jason Newport *(Sr VP & Head-Mobile Strategy)*
Jeremy Cornfeldt *(Sr VP & Dir-Integrated Bus)*
Mike Mchale *(VP & Acct Dir-Global)*
Corrina Miller *(VP & Dir-Traffic Ops-Amplifi US)*
Mark Hodor *(VP-Direct Response)*
Travis Freeman *(Head-Social)*
Dennis Nierra *(Sr Dir-Art)*
Kevin Broomes *(Dir-Comm Plng)*
Michael Kotick *(Dir-Comm Plng)*
Belle Lenz *(Dir-Comm-Americas)*
Patrick Rubin *(Dir-Advanced TV Strategy & Investment)*
Josh Berkley *(Assoc Dir-Media)*
Crystal Bert *(Assoc Dir-Comm Plng)*
Bradley Craven *(Assoc Dir)*
Joseph Gatdula *(Assoc Dir-Comm Plng)*
Jason Gore *(Assoc Dir-Global Ops)*
Rita Gutkovich *(Assoc Dir-Digital)*
Kathleen Kim *(Assoc Dir-Comm Plng)*
Catherine Leung *(Assoc Dir-Digital)*
David Vogt *(Assoc Dir-Digital Strategy & Media Partnerships)*
Rachel Weinstein *(Assoc Dir-Digital Strategy)*
Allie Feinstein *(Supvr-Comm Plng-Xbox Global)*
Ashley Klett *(Supvr-Comm Plng)*
Bona Park *(Supvr-Comm Plng)*
Dominique Salinas *(Supvr-Digital)*
Alex Velasco *(Supvr-Comm Plng)*
Jenni Aaker *(Assoc Planner-Comm)*
Diptoroop Mukherjee *(Assoc Planner-Comm)*

Accounts:
Alberto TRESemme
Credit Agricole
Eircom
Guinness
Kelloggs Special K
Meteor
Microsoft Corporation Xbox
Reckitt Benckiser Media Planning & Buying

DICOM, INC.
1650 Des Peres Rd Ste 100, Saint Louis, MO 63131-1851
Tel.: (314) 909-0900
Fax: (314) 909-1015
E-Mail: jsteward@dicominc.net
Web Site: dicominc.com/

E-Mail for Key Personnel:
Media Dir.: ahowell@dicominc.net

Employees: 20
Year Founded: 1989

National Agency Associations: YPA

Agency Specializes In: Broadcast, Business-To-Business, Co-op Advertising, Consulting, Consumer Marketing, Consumer Publications, Direct Response Marketing, Magazines, Media Buying Services, Media Planning, Newspaper, Newspapers & Magazines, Out-of-Home Media, Outdoor, Planning & Consultation, Radio, Real Estate, Restaurant, Strategic Planning/Research, T.V., Yellow Pages Advertising

Approx. Annual Billings: $5,775,000

Breakdown of Gross Billings by Media: D.M.: $400,000; E-Commerce: $25,000; Mags.: $100,000; Newsp.: $750,000; Out-of-Home Media: $250,000; Radio: $1,250,000; T.V.: $1,900,000; Trade & Consumer Mags.: $500,000; Yellow Page Adv.: $600,000

Jim Steward *(Pres)*
Athalia P. Howell *(Partner)*
David B. Travers *(Partner-Digital Media, Database Mktg & Yellow Pages)*
Chuck Stillwell *(Exec VP)*
Charmaine Cook *(Controller)*
Kathy Hoffmann *(Acct Dir)*
Lisa Pavia *(Mgr-Media)*

Accounts:
American Equity Mortgage
AT&T Communications Corp.; Atlanta, GA
CEFCU; Peoria, IL
Central Bank
CitiMortgage
Dobbs Tire & Auto; Saint Louis, MO Tire & Auto Service
First Colonial Eye Center
Jensen Tire & Auto; Omaha, NE
MS Society; Saint Louis, MO
Ranken Technical College; Saint Louis
Saint Louis Zoo; Saint Louis, MO
Schnucks Grocery
Shelter Insurance; MO, NV, IL, IN
SIUE; Edwardsville, IL University

DIRECT EFFECT MEDIA SERVICES
1042-B N El Camino Real Ste 329, Encinitas, CA 92024
Tel.: (760) 943-9400
E-Mail: info@directeffectmedia.com
Web Site: www.directeffectmedia.com

Employees: 3
Year Founded: 1990

Agency Specializes In: Business-To-Business, Direct Response Marketing, Email, High Technology, Information Technology, Media Buying Services, Media Planning, Planning & Consultation, Technical Advertising, Telemarketing, Web (Banner Ads, Pop-ups, etc.)

Approx. Annual Billings: $2,500,000

Breakdown of Gross Billings by Media: D.M.: $500,000; Internet Adv.: $2,000,000

Bernard Ryan *(Pres & CEO)*

THE DIRECT RESPONSE GROUP, LLC
(d/b/a DRG)
445 Broadhollow Rd Ste CL 42, Melville, NY 11747
Tel.: (631) 752-3590
Toll Free: (888) 420-0063
Web Site: www.directresponsegroup.com

Employees: 10
Year Founded: 2002

Agency Specializes In: Direct Response Marketing, Internet/Web Design, Market Research, Media Buying Services, Search Engine Optimization

Revenue: $2,000,000

Christopher Ulrich *(CEO-New York SEO)*

DOM CAMERA & COMPANY, LLC
52 Vanderbilt Ave, New York, NY 10017-6705
Tel.: (212) 370-1130
Fax: (212) 370-1201
E-Mail: info@domcameracompany.com
Web Site: www.domcameracompany.com

Employees: 12
Year Founded: 1985

Agency Specializes In: Media Buying Services, Outdoor, Print, Radio, T.V.

Approx. Annual Billings: $80,000,000

Breakdown of Gross Billings by Media: Network T.V.: $20,000,000; Out-of-Home Media: $8,000,000; Print: $800,000; Radio: $11,200,000; Spot T.V.: $40,000,000

Chris Camera *(Principal)*
Jeanine Domich *(Principal)*
Jacqueline Pegno *(Media Buyer)*
Natalie Cadillo *(Sr Media Buyer)*
Sue Prial *(Sr Media Buyer)*

Accounts:
MonsterMedia

DRAKE ADVERTISING LTD
320 Bay St Ste 1400, Toronto, ON M5H 4A6 Canada
Tel.: (416) 216-1000
Fax: (416) 216-1064
Toll Free: (800) GODRAKE
E-Mail: info@drakeintl.com
Web Site: ca.drakeintl.com/

Employees: 40
Year Founded: 1952

National Agency Associations: CBP

Agency Specializes In: Recruitment

R. W. Pollock *(Chm)*

DRM PARTNERS, INC.
50 Harrison Street Ste 208, Hoboken, NJ 07030
Tel.: (201) 418-0050
Fax: (201) 418-0030
E-Mail: info@drm-partners.com
Web Site: www.drm-partners.com

Employees: 10
Year Founded: 2004

Agency Specializes In: Advertising, Advertising Specialties, Broadcast, Cable T.V., Consumer Marketing, Direct Response Marketing, Direct-to-Consumer, Hispanic Market, Infomercials, International, Media Buying Services, Media Planning, Over-50 Market, Pharmaceutical, Print, Radio, Seniors' Market, Syndication, T.V.

Approx. Annual Billings: $30,000,000

Breakdown of Gross Billings by Media: Cable T.V.: 60%; Spot T.V.: 30%; Syndication: 10%

Susan Pensabene *(Pres)*
Katie McNamara *(VP & Acct Supvr)*
Nicola Brathwaite *(Acct Supvr)*
Amanda LaConte *(Acct Exec)*
Sara Landries *(Media Buyer)*
Amy Tannenbaum *(Media Buyer-Direct Response)*
Simone Burns *(Sr Media Buyer)*

DWA
1160 Battery St W, San Francisco, CA 94111
Tel.: (415) 296-8050
Fax: (415) 296-5170
E-Mail: info-us@dwamedia.com
Web Site: www.dwamedia.com

Employees: 50
Year Founded: 1996

National Agency Associations: PPA

Agency Specializes In: Above-the-Line, Advertising, Advertising Specialties, Asian Market, Bilingual Market, Broadcast, Business Publications, Business-To-Business, Computers & Software, Consulting, Digital/Interactive, Electronic Media, Electronics, High Technology, Information Technology, Integrated Marketing, International, Magazines, Media Buying Services, Media Planning, New Technologies, Newspaper, Out-of-Home Media, Outdoor, Paid Searches, Planning & Consultation, Podcasting, Print, RSS (Really Simple Syndication), Radio, Regional, Search Engine Optimization, Social Marketing/Nonprofit, Social Media, Sponsorship, Sports Market, Strategic Planning/Research, T.V., Technical Advertising, Trade & Consumer Magazines, Viral/Buzz/Word of Mouth, Web (Banner Ads, Pop-ups, etc.)

Approx. Annual Billings: $25,000,000

Breakdown of Gross Billings by Media: Brdcst.: 5%; Internet Adv.: 65%; Out-of-Home Media: 5%; Print: 25%

David Wood *(CEO)*
Phil Talbot *(Mng Partner)*
Robert Ray *(Pres-Americas)*
James Miller *(Sr VP-Bus Dev)*
Isabelle Kane *(VP-Client Svcs & Head-Content & Inbound Practice)*
Ben Barenholtz *(Dir-Mktg & Comm)*
Catherine Reilley *(Assoc Dir-Media)*
Jessica Stark *(Media Planner)*
Thatcher Hoyt *(Asst Media Planner)*
Dominique Salinas *(Sr Media Planner)*
Michelle Stewart *(Sr Media Planner)*

Accounts:
Acer Aspire s7 Campaign, EMEA Media Planning & Buying
Akamai Technologies, Inc.
ESET; San Diego, CA NOD 32, Smart Security
TriNet Campaign: "Faux Startups"

EFX MEDIA

2300 S 9th St Ste 136, Arlington, VA 22204
Tel.: (703) 486-2303
Fax: (703) 553-9813
E-Mail: info@efxmedia.com
Web Site: www.efxmedia.com

Employees: 20
Year Founded: 1983

Agency Specializes In: Media Buying Services, Sponsorship

Jim Franco *(Pres & CEO)*
Joseph Gross *(COO & Exec Producer)*
Bruce Dixon *(CTO & VP)*
Robin Evans *(VP-Bus Dev)*
Victor Van Rees *(VP-Federal Sls & Mktg)*
Julianne Otto *(Producer-Video & Interactive)*
Kevin Schmitt *(Dir-Interactive Svcs & Art)*
Tracy Fitzpatrick *(Office Mgr)*
Kyle Brant *(Mgr-Bus Dev)*

Accounts:
AOL
ExxonMobil
National Science Foundation

ELITE MEDIA, INC.

145 Brightmoor Ct, Henderson, NV 89074
Tel.: (702) 492-0654
Fax: (702) 269-0761
Toll Free: (866) 823-5483
E-Mail: info@elitemediainc.com
Web Site: www.elitemediainc.com

Employees: 5
Year Founded: 2002

National Agency Associations: AAF

Agency Specializes In: Electronic Media, Exhibit/Trade Shows, Out-of-Home Media, Outdoor

Chad McCullough *(Pres)*

Accounts:
French Connection; New York, NY Clothing
LG Electronics
Samsung
Sony
T-Mobile US

ELITE SEM

142 W 36th St, New York, NY 10018
Tel.: (646) 350-2789
Fax: (413) 294-5557
Web Site: www.elitesem.com

Employees: 102
Year Founded: 2004

Agency Specializes In: Advertising, Direct Response Marketing, International, Media Planning, Mobile Marketing, Paid Searches, Search Engine Optimization, Social Media

Ben Kirshner *(CEO)*
Abby Stone *(Dir-Paid Media)*
Marc Weisinger *(Dir-Mktg)*
Tony Edward *(Sr Mgr-SEO)*
Robert Galinsky *(Sr Mgr-SEO)*
Jane Serra *(Sr Mgr-Mktg)*
Anthony De Pascale *(Sr Acct Mgr)*
Alan Hernandez *(Sr Acct Mgr)*
Elise Del Rio *(Acct Mgr-Search Engine Mktg SEM)*
Daniel Eng *(Acct Mgr-SEO)*
Craig Hammitt *(Acct Mgr)*
Adrienne Gaines *(Mgr-Client Strategy)*
Kendall Giglio *(Mgr-Conversion Rate Optimization)*
Lucas Hardison *(Mgr-Creative)*
Kristin Wanek *(Mgr-Client Strategy)*
Robert Di Zillo, Jr. *(Analyst-Fin)*
Danielle Copeland *(Jr Media Planner-Digital)*

Accounts:
Anytime Fitness
ASSOULINE Books Publishing & Printing
New-Audible, Inc. Search Engine Marketing
C & J Clark America Inc. Men & Women Footwear & Dress Mfr & Retailers
Chrome Industries Shoes & Bags Mfr & Retailers
eCornell
New-Etsy
Gilt City
Hugo Boss; 2011
Ideeli
Kaplan
Lily Pulitzer
Pandora
Rockport
ServiceMaster
Solstice
Terminix
Tommy Bahama; 2009
TruGreen; 2008
USA Today
USTA

EMC OUTDOOR

5074 W Chester Pike, Newtown Square, PA 19073-4279
Tel.: (610) 353-9300
Fax: (610) 353-9301
E-Mail: info@emcoutdoor.com
Web Site: www.emcoutdoor.com

Employees: 25
Year Founded: 1991

National Agency Associations: AHAA-OAAA

Agency Specializes In: Alternative Advertising, Event Planning & Marketing, Exhibit/Trade Shows, Experience Design, Guerilla Marketing, Health Care Services, Media Buying Services, Mobile Marketing, Out-of-Home Media, Outdoor, Pharmaceutical, Planning & Consultation, Recruitment, Sports Market, Transportation

Approx. Annual Billings: $10,000,000

Breakdown of Gross Billings by Media: Outdoor: $10,000,000

Edward J. Japhe *(Pres)*
Betsy McLarney *(CEO)*
Song C. Heo *(COO)*
S. Thomas Japhe *(Exec VP-OOH Media Strategy & Specialist-Outdoor Adv Branding)*
Maryann Ingham *(Exec VP-OOH & Outdoor Adv Media Strategy)*
Mary Jo Pittera *(Exec VP-OOH Media & Strategic Partnership)*
Jerry Buckley *(Dir-Mktg & New Bus & Strategist-OOH Media)*
Jennifer Stuart *(Dir-Events)*

Accounts:
Alcon Laboratories

EMPOWER MEDIAMARKETING

1111 Saint Gregory St, Cincinnati, OH 45202
Tel.: (513) 871-9454
Fax: (513) 871-1804
Web Site: www.empowermm.com

Employees: 142
Year Founded: 1985

National Agency Associations: 4A's

Agency Specializes In: Advertising, African-American Market, Alternative Advertising, Automotive, Broadcast, Cable T.V., Co-op Advertising, Communications, Consulting, Consumer Goods, Consumer Marketing, Consumer Publications, Content, Cosmetics, Digital/Interactive, Direct Response Marketing, Direct-to-Consumer, Education, Electronic Media, Email, Entertainment, Fashion/Apparel, Financial, Food Service, Health Care Services, Hispanic Market, Household Goods, In-Store Advertising, Integrated Marketing, Leisure, Local Marketing, Luxury Products, Magazines, Market Research, Media Buying Services, Media Planning, Media Training, Medical Products, Men's Market, Mobile Marketing, Multicultural, New Technologies, Newspaper, Newspapers & Magazines, Out-of-Home Media, Outdoor, Paid Searches, Pharmaceutical, Print, Product Placement, Radio, Regional, Restaurant, Retail, Search Engine Optimization, Sponsorship, Strategic Planning/Research, Syndication, T.V., Teen Market, Trade & Consumer Magazines, Travel & Tourism, Tween Market, Urban Market, Web (Banner Ads, Pop-ups, etc.), Women's Market

Approx. Annual Billings: $250,000,000

Breakdown of Gross Billings by Media: Cable T.V.: 9%; Digital/Interactive: 18%; Network T.V.: 13%; Other: 1%; Out-of-Home Media: 4%; Print: 11%; Spot Radio: 13%; Spot T.V.: 29%; Syndication: 2%

Jim Price *(Pres & CEO)*
Lynne Veil *(COO)*
Mark Sancrant *(Sr VP-Corp Strategy)*

Michele Toller *(VP & Head-Practice-Offline Investment & Activation)*
Stacy Anderson *(VP-Client Leadership)*
Tim Glover *(VP-Client Leadership)*
Alison Lang *(VP-Client Strategy)*
Mareka Miller *(Head-Adv Ops Team)*
Chris Blum *(Acct Dir-Online Mktg)*
Christy Bidwell *(Dir-Comm Plng)*
Amber Bondick *(Dir-Online Mktg)*
Kate Rechtsteiner *(Dir-Client Leadership)*
Ben Schmidt *(Dir-Growth)*
Katy Batchler *(Assoc Dir-Client Leadership)*
Bethany Mercer *(Assoc Dir-Client Leadership)*
Trisha Tolly *(Assoc Dir-Digital Media)*
Jennifer Schneller *(Mgr-Campaign-Client Leadership)*
Amanda Birck *(Sr Specialist-Brdcst)*
Katie Burkhart *(Sr Specialist-Digital)*
Jamie Campbell *(Strategist-Digital Media)*
Sarah Ungar *(Coord-Mktg)*

Accounts:
Axcess Financial (Check 'n Go); Mason, OH Stores; 2005
Brown Shoe Media Planning & Buying; 2012
Bush Brothers & Company; Knoxville, TN Bakes, Grillin' & Variety Beans; 1995
New-Champion Windows
Christ Hospital; Cincinnati, OH; 1996
Cincinnati USA; Cincinnati, OH Regional Tourism; 2006
Clopay Corporation Avante, Clopay Plastic Products, Gallery, Grand Harbor, LifeSafety, Reserve Collection, WINDCODE
Famous Footwear
New-Formica Corporation (Agency of Record) Media
Gorilla Glue Company Display, Gorilla, Media, O'Keeffe's, Online, Search Engine Marketing
Herschend Family Entertainment Multiple Parks; 2008
HGTV Home; 2012
HRM Pfizer; 2009
Inventiv EpiPen; 2011
Inventive Stryker; 2012
J.D. Byrider; 2012
Land O'Frost Content Strategy, Media Planning & Buying, Social Media Marketing
LCA Vision LasikPlus; 2010
Lebanon Seaboard Preen; 2007
Merz Pharmaceuticals Mederma; 2006
Pacific Gas & Electric; 2012
Papa John's Atlanta & Macon Markets; 2010
Paycor; 2012
Rust-Oleum; 2009
Shaw Flooring; Dalton, GA Shaw Floors; 2006
Stonyfield Organic Content Marketing, Media, Paid Media Efforts, SEO; 2012
Totes/Isotoner; 2002
TTI Floorcare, Hoover; Glenwillow, OH Hoover; 2009
U.S. Bank; 1992
Wendy's Select Markets; 2011

ENVISION CREATIVE GROUP
3400 Northland Dr, Austin, TX 78731-4927
Tel.: (512) 292-1049
Web Site: www.envision-creative.com

Year Founded: 2001

Agency Specializes In: Advertising, Digital/Interactive, Exhibit/Trade Shows, Graphic Design, Internet/Web Design, Logo & Package Design, Print

David Smith *(Pres & CEO)*
Stephanie Silver *(VP)*
Rhonda Smith *(Office Mgr)*
Michael Gabriel *(Mgr-Mktg)*
Rachael Hellman *(Copywriter & Strategist-Content)*
Sarah Beattie *(Sr Graphic Designer)*

Accounts:
Acumen Inc Health & Wellness Tools Mfr

EPICENTER NETWORK, INC
3400 188th St SW, Lynnwood, WA 98037
Tel.: (425) 744-1474
Fax: (801) 858-6059
Web Site: www.epicenter.net

Employees: 30
Year Founded: 2005

Agency Specializes In: Advertising, Affiliate Marketing, Consumer Marketing, Direct Response Marketing, Direct-to-Consumer, Email, Internet/Web Design, Media Buying Services, Paid Searches, Search Engine Optimization, Social Media

Approx. Annual Billings: $15,000,000

Breakdown of Gross Billings by Media: Internet Adv.: 100%

Dylan McDanniel *(CO-Founder & COO)*
Smokey Burns *(CEO)*
Andy Kahn *(Sr Exec VP)*
Jane Moreton *(Mgr-Acctg)*
John Trotter *(Mgr-Bus Dev)*

Accounts:
Epicenter In House; Lynnwood, WA Auto Loan, Auto Warranty, Cash Advance, Debt Consolidation, Education Lead, Generation, Lasik Lead Generation, Mortgage Lead, Student Load Consolidation, Tax Relief

EXPLORE COMMUNICATIONS
3213 Zuni St, Denver, CO 80211
Tel.: (303) 393-0567
Fax: (303) 393-0568
E-Mail: info@explorehq.com
Web Site: www.explorehq.com

Employees: 12
Year Founded: 1996

National Agency Associations: AMA-BMA-Second Wind Limited

Agency Specializes In: Advertising, Advertising Specialties, African-American Market, Brand Development & Integration, Broadcast, Business Publications, Business-To-Business, Cable T.V., Children's Market, Co-op Advertising, Communications, Consulting, Consumer Marketing, Consumer Publications, Corporate Communications, Digital/Interactive, Direct Response Marketing, Electronic Media, Entertainment, Event Planning & Marketing, Exhibit/Trade Shows, Fashion/Apparel, Gay & Lesbian Market, Health Care Services, High Technology, Hispanic Market, Industrial, Information Technology, Leisure, Local Marketing, Magazines, Media Buying Services, Medical Products, Merchandising, Newspaper, Newspapers & Magazines, Out-of-Home Media, Outdoor, Over-50 Market, Planning & Consultation, Print, Radio, Real Estate, Recruitment, Restaurant, Retail, Seniors' Market, Sports Market, Strategic Planning/Research, T.V., Teen Market, Trade & Consumer Magazines, Travel & Tourism

Approx. Annual Billings: $10,000,000

Breakdown of Gross Billings by Media: Brdcst.: $3,000,000; Bus. Publs.: $1,000,000; Cable T.V.: $1,000,000; Consumer Publs.: $1,100,000; D.M.: $100,000; Event Mktg.: $300,000; Internet Adv.: $1,000,000; Newsp. & Mags.: $1,500,000; Out-of-Home Media: $1,000,000

Mindy Gantner *(VP & Dir-Media)*
Sarah Chapin *(Media Planner & Media Buyer)*
Cassie Wysel *(Media Planner & Media Buyer)*
Kathleen Pittman *(Planner)*
Pierson Bridges *(Coord-Media)*

Accounts:
CollegeInvest Media
HealthONE Marketing Division, Recruitment Division
Weber-Stephen Products Co.

FERRYADS.COM
83 Cromwell Ave, Staten Island, NY 10304
Tel.: (718) 351-2557
Fax: (718) 979-1874
E-Mail: djr@comm-associates.com
Web Site: www.comm-associates.com/ferryads/index.htm

Employees: 10
Year Founded: 1987

Agency Specializes In: Electronic Media, Out-of-Home Media, Outdoor, Transportation

Approx. Annual Billings: $4,000,000

Breakdown of Gross Billings by Media: Out-of-Home Media: $2,000,000; Outdoor: $2,000,000

David J. Rampulla *(Pres)*
Teresa Rampulla *(Dir-Mktg)*

Accounts:
Allstate
Berkeley College
Energetic
Gray Line NY Sightseeing
Solstice
Time Warner
Verizon

FINGERPRINT COMMUNICATIONS
1179 King St W Ste 011, Toronto, ON M6K 3C5 Canada
Tel.: (416) 535-9441
Fax: (416) 588-7950
E-Mail: info@fingerprintcommunications.com
Web Site: www.fingerprintcommunications.com

Year Founded: 2002

Agency Specializes In: Digital/Interactive, Internet/Web Design, Media Buying Services, Media Planning, Mobile Marketing, Production, Social Media

Jessica Meisels *(Pres & CEO)*
Tim Keenleyside *(Partner & Co-Dir-Creative)*
Denzil Wadds *(Partner & Dir-Creative)*
Danielle Taylor *(Dir-Art & Sr Designer)*
Michelle Sabourin *(Acct Mgr)*

Accounts:
Peace Bridge Duty Free

FIRST CLASS, INC.
5410 W Roosevelt Rd Unit 222, Chicago, IL 60644-1570
Tel.: (773) 378-1009
Fax: (773) 378-1018
E-Mail: info@firstclassinc.com
Web Site: www.firstclassinc.com

E-Mail for Key Personnel:
President: lonna.schulz@firstclassinc.com
Public Relations: mike.caines@firstclassinc.com

Employees: 10
Year Founded: 1992

Agency Specializes In: Advertising, Business-To-Business, Direct Response Marketing, Legal Services, Newspaper, Print

Approx. Annual Billings: $1,000,000

Breakdown of Gross Billings by Media: D.M.: $900,000; Newsp.: $100,000

Lonna Schulz *(Co-Pres)*
Michael Caines *(CEO)*
Bailey Hughes *(Project Mgr & Mgr-Case)*

Accounts:
Arrow Financial Services; 2001
Consumer Advocacy Center; Chicago, IL Legal; 2000
EC&L; Chicago, IL Legal
Hinshaw & Culbertson; Chicago, IL Legal; 1998
Northern Trust Bank; Chicago, IL Banking; 1994
Quantum Color Graphics; 2001

FITZGERALD MEDIA

(Formerly The Media Investment Group)
3333 Piedmont Rd NE Ste 100, Atlanta, GA 30305
Tel.: (404) 504-6900
Fax: (404) 262-8930
Web Site: www.fitzco.com

E-Mail for Key Personnel:
Media Dir.: liz.daney@fitzco.com

Employees: 16

National Agency Associations: 4A's

Agency Specializes In: Broadcast, Business-To-Business, Consumer Publications, Financial, Food Service, Magazines, Media Buying Services, Newspapers & Magazines, Out-of-Home Media

Approx. Annual Billings: $83,000,000

Keri Palmer *(CFO & Exec VP)*
Liz Daney *(Chief Media Officer & Exec VP)*
Evan Levy *(Chief Digital Officer)*
Rob Baskin *(Pres-WEBER SHANDWICK)*
Pam Piligian *(Sr VP & Grp Acct Dir)*
Joyce Faulkner *(Sr VP & Acct Dir-New Bus)*

Accounts:
Amway
Coca-Cola Refreshments USA, Inc.
Delta
IHG
InterContinental
UPS
Wendy's

FLYING A

35 N Arroyo Pkwy, Pasadena, CA 91103
Tel.: (626) 376-4770
Web Site: www.flyingamedia.com

E-Mail for Key Personnel:
President: flyinga@att.net
Media Dir.: kc@flyingamedia.com
Public Relations: liz@flyingamedia.com

Employees: 7
Year Founded: 1978

National Agency Associations: AAF

Agency Specializes In: Advertising, African-American Market, Bilingual Market, Brand Development & Integration, Broadcast, Business-To-Business, Cable T.V., Consumer Marketing, Direct Response Marketing, Education, Electronic Media, Entertainment, Hispanic Market, Hospitality, Local Marketing, Magazines, Media Buying Services, Newspaper, Newspapers & Magazines, Out-of-Home Media, Outdoor, Planning & Consultation, Promotions, Publicity/Promotions, Radio, Restaurant, Seniors' Market, Strategic Planning/Research, T.V., Trade & Consumer Magazines, Transportation, Travel & Tourism

Approx. Annual Billings: $13,000,000

Sharon Reid *(Dir-Media)*
Shanel Stephens *(Acct Mgr)*

Accounts:
Oakland International Airport
Pechanga Resort & Casino
Peralta Community College District
Quilceda Casino
See's Candies
Tulalip Casino

FOSINA MARKETING

51-53 Kenosia Ave, Danbury, CT 6810
Tel.: (203) 790-0030
Web Site: www.fosinamarketinggroup.com

Year Founded: 2003

Agency Specializes In: Customer Relationship Management, Email, Internet/Web Design, Media Planning, Print, Radio, Search Engine Optimization, Social Media, Strategic Planning/Research

Jim Fosina *(Founder & CEO)*
Ron Lichwalla *(COO)*
Diane Petruzzelli *(Exec VP-Bus Dev)*
Gary Krasnow *(Sr VP-Bus Plng & Analysis)*
Barbara Nicotera *(Sr VP-Fin & HR)*
Kenneth Sciuto *(Sr VP-Tech)*
Jason Sommerville *(VP-Media)*
Kelly Mariano *(Acct Dir)*
Stephanie Olivieri *(Acct Mgr)*

Accounts:
Holsted Jewelers Jewelry Shop
Mondelez International, Inc. Food & Beverage Products Mfr
NPD Group Data Collection Service Providers
Smithsonian Museum

GOODWAY GROUP

The Pavilion 261 Old York Rd Ste 930, Jenkintown, PA 19046
Tel.: (215) 887-5700
Fax: (215) 881-2239
Web Site: www.goodwaygroup.com

E-Mail for Key Personnel:
President: david@goodwaygroup.com

Employees: 350
Year Founded: 1979

Agency Specializes In: Advertising, Automotive, Co-op Advertising, Communications, Digital/Interactive, Direct Response Marketing, Direct-to-Consumer, Electronic Media, Internet/Web Design, Local Marketing, Media Buying Services, Media Planning, Print, Sales Promotion, Sweepstakes

Breakdown of Gross Billings by Media: D.M.: 10%; Internet Adv.: 85%; Newsp.: 5%

David Wolk *(Pres)*
Jay Friedman *(Mng Dir & COO)*
Dan Mauch *(Exec VP-Sls)*
David Kertesz *(VP-Digital Media)*
Jeff Hastedt *(Acct Dir-North Central Reg)*
Ami Sirlin *(Acct Dir-Natl)*
John Estalilla *(Dir-Sls & Western Reg)*
Zoe Matthews *(Acct Planner)*
Leanne Price *(Media Buyer-Digital)*
Jen Douthit *(Coord-Digital Media)*

Accounts:
American Cancer Society
BMW
Emory College
Ford
Friendly's
Honda
Lexus
Poland Springs
Porsche
Subaru
Toyota
White Castle System, Inc.

GREENSTRIPE MEDIA, INC.

424 N Newport Blvd, Newport Beach, CA 92663-4211
Tel.: (949) 650-5081
Fax: (949) 752-0207
E-Mail: gsm@greenstripe.com

Employees: 8
Year Founded: 1977

Agency Specializes In: Asian Market, Automotive, Bilingual Market, Broadcast, Cable T.V., Co-op Advertising, Consumer Marketing, Consumer Publications, Education, Electronic Media, Event Planning & Marketing, Food Service, Gay & Lesbian Market, Magazines, Media Buying Services, Newspaper, Newspapers & Magazines, Outdoor, Print, Radio, Real Estate, T.V., Yellow Pages Advertising

Joe Winkelmann *(Pres & CEO)*
Tony De Dios *(Media Buyer)*
David Takara *(Media Buyer)*
Mike De Dios *(Acct Coord)*

Accounts:
Fletcher Jones Motorcars

GROUPM NORTH AMERICA & CORPORATE HQ

498 Seventh Ave, New York, NY 10018
Tel.: (212) 297-8181
Fax: (212) 297-7001
Web Site: www.groupm.com

National Agency Associations: 4A's

Agency Specializes In: Brand Development & Integration, Branded Entertainment, Content, Digital/Interactive, Entertainment, Media Buying Services, Search Engine Optimization, Sponsorship

Approx. Annual Billings: $90,700,000,000

Dominic Proctor *(Pres)*
Louis-Philippe Cavallo *(Mng Partner & Controller)*
Scott Kruse *(Mng Partner & Dir-Print)*
Jeanne Clark *(Mng Partner)*
George Janson *(Mng Partner)*
Mebrulin Francisco *(Partner & Dir-Mktg Analytics-Multicultural)*
Pratush Gupta *(Partner & Dir-GroupM Data & Analytics Svcs)*
Julie Kandel *(Partner & Dir-Digital Campaign Mgmt)*
Colin Barlow *(COO)*
Harvey Goldhersz *(CEO-Analytics & Chief Data Officer)*
Rob Norman *(Chief Digital Officer-Global)*
Michael Bologna *(Pres-MODI Media)*
Chris Copeland *(CEO-GroupM Next)*
Anton Kopytov *(CEO-Ukraine, Belarus & Moldova)*
Brian Lesser *(CEO-North America)*
Girish Menon *(CEO-Malaysia)*
Koji Watanabe *(CEO-Japan)*
Jad Nehme *(Sr VP-Engrg)*
Gibbs Haljun *(Mng Dir-Media Investment)*

Media Buying Services

Elizabeth McCune *(Global Head-Mktg, Comm & Bus Dev)*
Dan Cristo *(Dir-SEO Innovation)*
Abby Free *(Sr Partner & Dir-Digital Ad Ops)*
David Grabert *(Global Dir-Corp Comm)*
Ricky Joyce *(Dir-Ad Tech)*
Oksana Krynsky-Kiefer *(Sr Partner & Dir-Digital Vendor Policies & Rels)*
Shekhar Sharma *(Dir-GroupM Interaction-Natl)*
Silke Vollman *(Dir-OOH Product Dev)*
Kathleen Ehresman *(Sr Partner & Assoc Dir)*
John Duffy *(Mgr-Paid Social)*
Aileen Kirby *(Mgr-Print)*
Grace Park *(Mgr-Plng-MetaVision Media)*
Jacquelin Johnson *(Supvr-Direct Branding)*
Ari Bluman *(Chief Digital Investment Officer-North America)*
Shannon Hopkins *(Print Analyst-Kimberly Clark)*
Jordan Verrilli *(Asst Analyst-Print)*

Accounts:
Accenture, Ltd.
American Express
AT&T Communications Corp.
Barclays Capital
Cablevision Systems
Colgate-Palmolive Company Colgate-Palmolive Company, Speed Stick Stainguard, Speedstick
IKEA IKEA North America Services, LLC
Mars, Incorporated Media
Nestle USA, Inc. Digital, Media Planning & Buying, Nespresso USA, Nestle Health Sciences, Nestle Nutrition, Nestle Purina PetCare, Nestle USA, Nestle Waters North America
Unilever

Subsidiaries

Catalyst Online
320 Nevada St 1st Fl, Newton, MA 02460
Tel.: (617) 663-4100
Fax: (617) 663-4104
E-Mail: catalyst.info@catalystsearchmarketing.com
Web Site: www.catalystsearchmarketing.com

Employees: 60

Agency Specializes In: Advertising, Integrated Marketing, Internet/Web Design, Market Research, Media Planning, Paid Searches, Search Engine Optimization, Web (Banner Ads, Pop-ups, etc.)

Andrew Ruegger *(Partner & Dir-Strategy & Insights-GroupM)*
Patrick Bonomo *(COO)*
Stephen Hall *(Sr Partner & Grp Acct Dir)*
Dan Cristo *(Dir-SEO Innovation)*
Katelyn Delaney *(Dir-Organic Search)*
Scott Julewitz *(Dir-Search)*
Nicole Kapopoulos *(Dir-Paid Search)*
Paul Shapiro *(Dir-SEO)*
Patricia Caltabiano *(Assoc Dir-Paid Search)*
Joe Voshchin *(Assoc Dir-Paid Search)*

Accounts:
American Family Insurance
Novartis
P&G
Pfizer
Royal Caribbean

DataXu, Inc.
281 Summer St 4th Fl, Boston, MA 02210
(See Separate Listing)

GroupM Search
(Formerly Outrider)
111 W Port Plz Ste 350, Saint Louis, MO 63146
Tel.: (212) 474-0000
Fax: (314) 682-2037
Web Site: www.groupm.com

Employees: 80

National Agency Associations: 4A's

Brandon Fischer *(Partner & Dir-Predictive Insights)*
Jesse Wolfersberger *(Dir-Consumer Insights)*
Ridhi Malhotra *(Sr Mgr)*
Andy Leindecker *(Mgr-Tech & Insights)*

Accounts:
AstraZeneca
AT&T Communications Corp.
Chevron
Coach
Dell
Diageo
Hallmark
Microsoft
Sears
Showtime
Texas Instruments

Kinetic
230 Park Ave, New York, NY 10003
(See Separate Listing)

M80 Services, Inc.
3400 Cahuenga Blvd, Los Angeles, CA 90068
(See Separate Listing)

Maxus Global
498 Seventh Ave, New York, NY 10018
(See Separate Listing)

MEC, Global HQ, New York
825 7th Ave, New York, NY 10019-6014
(See Separate Listing)

MediaCom
498 7th Ave, New York, NY 10018
(See Separate Listing)

Mindshare
498 7th Ave, New York, NY 10018
Tel.: (212) 297-7000
Fax: (212) 297-7001
E-Mail: david.pullan@mindshareworld.com
Web Site: www.mindshareworld.com

Year Founded: 1997

National Agency Associations: 4A's

Agency Specializes In: Media Buying Services, Sponsorship

Ted Ellet *(Mng Partner & Mng Dir)*
Michael Souza *(Mng Partner & Mng Dir)*
Jonathan Hsia *(Mng Partner & Head-Digital Investment)*
George Musi *(Mng Partner-Analytics, Insights & Attribution)*
Stacey Abreu *(Partner & Grp Dir-Plng)*
James Cooley *(Partner & Grp Dir-Search & Social)*
Rebecca Dishner *(Partner & Dir-Strategy & Partnerships)*
Nicole Hladko *(Partner & Dir-Media)*
Sabrina Nelson *(Partner & Dir)*
Lindsey Phillips *(Partner & Dir-Media)*
Emma Witkowski *(Dir & Partner-Digital Investment)*
Patricia Wolfe *(Partner & Dir-Client Leadership)*
Erica Lee *(Partner & Assoc Dir-Search & Social)*
Mohamad Munruddin *(Partner & Assoc Dir)*
Amy Wing *(Partner & Assoc Dir-Unilever)*
Daniel Bueckman *(Mng Dir & Head-Client-Volvo Cars Acct)*
Ed Hughes *(Mng Dir & Head-Client-Worldwide)*
Joe Migliozzi *(Mng Dir & Head-Digital-NY)*
Smita Allex *(Sr Partner & Mng Dir)*
Karen Bennett *(Mng Dir)*
Melissa Coffas *(Mng Dir)*
Andrew Davidson *(Sr Partner & Mng Dir)*
Robert Genovese *(Sr Partner & Mng Dir)*
Mariya Kemper *(Sr Partner & Mng Dir)*
Joe Maceda *(Mng Dir)*
Rolf Olsen *(Chief Data Officer-North America)*
David Lang *(Pres-Mindshare Entertainment)*
David Pullan *(Pres-New York)*
Colin Kinsella *(CEO-North America)*
Greg Manago *(Mng Dir-North America & Sr Producer-Mindshare Entertainment)*
Lisa DiBenedetto *(Mng Dir-Digital Investment-Unilever)*
Christine Lamson *(Mng Dir-Unilever)*
Wendi Smith *(Mng Dir-Agency Comm & Content-NA)*
Rich Vietri *(Mng Dir-Client Leadership)*
David Adelman *(Head-Mindshare Chicago & Exec Dir)*
Jennifer Peterson *(Sr Partner, Head-Client & Dir)*
Craig Sanders *(Head-Adaptive Mktg & Project Mgr)*
Tobias Wolf *(Exec Dir-Client Svcs)*
Laura Powers *(Sr Partner & Grp Dir-Plng)*
Jessica Lenehan *(Acct Dir-Digital)*
Greg Brooks *(Dir-Mktg-Global)*
Tom Cugini *(Dir-Strategic Plng)*
Robert Daitch *(Dir-Plng)*
Brady Dollard *(Dir-Client Leadership)*
Mindi Ikeda *(Sr Partner & Dir-Digital Investment)*
Alexandra Jones *(Dir-Digital Strategy)*
Jason Maltby *(Dir-Brdcst TV-Natl)*
Kristine Munsen *(Sr Partner & Dir-Digital)*
Russell Nathan *(Sr Partner & Dir)*
Derek Topel *(Sr Partner & Dir-Digital)*
Suzanne Barsi Weis *(Sr Partner & Dir-Strategic)*
Angela Boyce *(Assoc Dir-Global Strategy & Ops Team IBM)*
Michael Cardini *(Assoc Dir-Media)*
Kim Cooney *(Assoc Dir-Media)*
Noam Dorros *(Assoc Dir-Search)*
Anne Dupuis *(Assoc Dir-Media)*
Keith Evans *(Assoc Dir-Strategic Plng)*
Josh Forney *(Assoc Dir)*
Andrew Grabel *(Assoc Dir)*
Mark Gurwitz *(Sr Partner & Assoc Dir)*
Ruth Hilton *(Assoc Dir-Plng)*
Jamie Jones *(Assoc Dir-Search & Social)*
Paul Komutanon *(Assoc Dir-Search)*
Janet Levine *(Assoc Dir)*
Jesse Math *(Assoc Dir)*
Tracy McMullen *(Sr Partner & Assoc Dir)*
Kathy Meier *(Assoc Dir-Media)*
Yael Muhlrad *(Assoc Dir-Digital)*
Dominick Pace *(Assoc Dir-Digital Investment)*
Lauren Seigel *(Assoc Dir)*
Marisa Skolnick *(Assoc Dir-Media)*
Brian Tuchalski *(Assoc Dir-Media)*
Lance Whitehead *(Assoc Dir-Digital)*
Jessica Wurm *(Assoc Dir)*
Daniela Sayegh *(Acct Mgr-Digital)*
Ashley Casiano *(Mgr-Bus Dev & Mktg)*
Angela Dahir *(Mgr-Integrated Media)*
Tara Ezer *(Mgr-Search)*
Hilary Fried *(Mgr)*
Benjamin Howard *(Mgr-Search)*
Julie Kandel *(Mgr-Digital Metrics)*
Devin Keogh *(Mgr-Media Plng)*
Casey Kilkenny *(Mgr-Search & Social)*
Jeff Klein *(Mgr-Digital Investment)*
Shanyna Lascano *(Mgr-Strategic Plng)*
Daniel Lee *(Mgr-Digital Plng)*
Vin Masullo *(Mgr-Client Fin)*
Francia Miller *(Mgr-Digital)*
Kaitlyn Rich *(Mgr-Digital Investment)*
Jackie Sedotto *(Mgr-Brdcst-Natl)*
Alka Shah *(Mgr-Digital Investment)*
Thomas Simpson *(Mgr-Digital Investment)*
Grace Smith *(Mgr)*
Deione Sydnor *(Mgr-Trade Desk)*
Ferris Van Raalte *(Mgr)*
Jerry Yip *(Mgr-Digital Investments)*
Lisa Feng *(Supvr-Digital Media Investment)*
Alexandra Spaseff *(Supvr-Media)*

Emily Highet *(Sr Planner-Digital Investment)*
Mark Manglicmot *(Sr Analyst-Digital)*
Stephanie Aurora Morton *(Planner-Integrated Media)*
Danielle Clark *(Planner-Integrated Strategic)*
Marina Golden *(Media Planner-Integrated)*
Liz Goslin *(Assoc Media Buyer)*
Arel Greif *(Media Buyer)*
Greg Harris *(Media Planner-Integrated)*
Lee Anne LaRue *(Media Buyer-Brdcst-Natl)*
Mina Owliaei *(Assoc Media Buyer-Natl Brdcst)*
Tom Rosatelli *(Media Buyer)*
Simone Thomas *(Planner-Digital Media)*
Brianne Shannon *(Asst Buyer-Brdcst-Natl)*
John Boisi *(Assoc Media Planner)*
Kevin Camacho *(Assoc-Digital Investment)*
Sean Cantwell *(Asst Media Buyer)*
Christina Catalano *(Buyer-Brdcst-Natl)*
Nicole Cerone *(Asst Media Buyer)*
Jackie Fontaine *(Assoc Media Planner)*
Lucia Garofalo *(Assoc Media Planner-American Express)*
Sarah Kaduc *(Asst Media Buyer)*
Ashley Long *(Sr Assoc-Plng & Strategy)*
Amanda McCloskey *(Sr Assoc)*
Gina Morrone *(Asst Media Buyer)*
Josh Olsen *(Assoc Media Dir)*
Katherine Pippitt *(Asst Media Buyer)*
Brandon Plutner *(Assoc Media Planner)*
Ryann Quinn *(Asst Media Buyer)*
Christina Reinemann *(Asst Media Buyer)*
Paola Sucno Quiroz *(Sr Assoc Planner)*
Julie Tahan *(Assoc Media Planner)*

Accounts:
21st Century Insurance Corp. Media Planning & Buying
Abbott Labs
American Express Media, OPEN
American Family Insurance; 2008
AMPM
Bayer
Boehringer-Ingelheim
New-Booking.Com Media Buying, Media Planning, Media Strategy
Boost Mobile; Irvine, CA Media
Castrol GTX
Domino's Pizza, Inc.
Dyson Ltd.
Ford Fiesta
New-General Mills US Media
HSBC
IBM
Intercontinental Hotels Group Candlewood Suites, Crowne Hotels, Crowne Plaza, Global Strategic Planning, Holiday Inn, Holiday Inn Express, Holiday Inn Hotels & Resorts, Hotel Indigo, Intercontinental Hotels & Resorts, Media Buying & Planning, Staybridge Suites
Jaguar Land Rover North America Campaign: "#GoodToBeBad", Campaign: "British Intelligence", Campaign: "The Loop", Jaguar Cars, Jaguar Land Rover North America, Jaguar R, Jaguar X-TYPE, Jaguar XF, Jaguar XJ, Jaguar XK, Land Rover Discovery, Land Rover LR2, Land Rover LR4, Land Rover Range Rover, Media, Print Advertising
Kimberly Clark Campaign: "Achoo", Campaign: "Poise 1 In 3 Like Me", Depends, Display, In-App Gaming, Kleenex, Media Buying, Media Planning, Pull-Ups, Search Ads, Viva Paper Towels
LG Electronics U.S.A., Inc. LG Chocolate
LG Mobile Media
Lionsgate
Mattel
Mazda North American Operations CX-7, CX-9, MX-5 Miata, Mazda 2, Mazda 3 4-Door, Mazda 3 5-Door, Mazda 5, Mazda North American Operations, MazdaSpeed3
Museum of Modern Art
Rent-A-Center; Plano, TX Media Buying, Media Planning, Radio, TV
Skyy Spirits Media Planning & Buying
Sprint Corporation
Takeda Pharmaceuticals
Unilever United States, Inc. #kissforpeace, Axe, Breyers, Campaign: "Calls for Dad", Campaign: "Magnum Ice Cream", Dove, I Can't Believe It's Not Butter, Lynx, Men+Care, Suave, Sunsilk
Upworthy Sunlight
Volvo Global Creative, Media Buying & Planning
Zurich Financial Services Group

Branches

GroupM APAC HQ
Level 14, 65 Berry Street, Sydney, NSW 2060 Australia
Tel.: (61) 2 8913 1000
Fax: (61) 2 9463 7270
E-Mail: info@groupm.com
Web Site: www.groupm.com

Agency Specializes In: Brand Development & Integration, Branded Entertainment, Content, Digital/Interactive, Entertainment, Media Buying Services, Search Engine Optimization, Sponsorship

Mark Patterson *(CEO)*
Jeff Hunt *(CFO)*
Jonathan Thurlow *(COO)*
Sebastian Rennie *(Chief Investment Officer)*
Mike Rich *(CEO-Entertainment Sports & Partnerships-APAC)*
Matt Nunney *(Dir-Tech & Ops)*

GroupM China
31th Fl 1038 Nanjing Xi Rd, Westgate, Shanghai, 200041 China
Tel.: (86) 21 2307 7700
Fax: (86) 21 2307 7706
Web Site: www.groupmchina.com

Mark Patterson *(CEO-GroupM Asia Pacific & Chm)*
Stephen Chan *(CFO)*
Albert Hsieh *(CIO)*
Andrew Carter *(Pres-GroupM Trading)*
Christian Guinot *(Pres-MEC China)*
Annie Zhu *(Gen Mgr)*
Jennifer Ba *(Dir-Fin)*
Ravin Chan *(Dir-IT-Bus Intelligence & Collaboration)*
Eric Jin *(Dir-Fin)*
Wellington Song *(Dir-IT-Apps)*
Wendy Yeh *(Dir-Fin-Natl)*

Accounts:
Aflac Media Planning
Amway China
Chengdu Municipal Government Chengdu City Image Campaign, Consultancy, Evaluation, Global Media Buying & Planning
Kinetic
Maxus
MEC
Mediacom
Mindshare
Yili Media

GroupM EMEA HQ
101 St Martins Lane, London, WC2N 4DB United Kingdom
Tel.: (44) 207 896 4700
Fax: (44) 207 896 4701
Web Site: www.groupm.com

Agency Specializes In: Brand Development & Integration, Branded Entertainment, Digital/Interactive, Entertainment, Media Buying Services, Search Engine Optimization, Sponsorship

Dominic Proctor *(Pres)*
Dominic Grainger *(CEO-EMEA)*
Ruud Wanck *(COO-Digital-Global)*
Jakob Nielsen *(Mng Dir-Interaction UK)*
Istvan Kozari *(Head-Digital-Greenhouse)*
Adam Smith *(Dir-Futures)*
Simon Willis *(Dir-Trading)*
Harvey Zalud *(Dir-Content-EMEA & LATAM)*

Accounts:
Bayer HealthCare; Europe, Asia & Latin America Media Planning & Buying
Everything Everywhere Media Buying

GroupM Entertainment
2425 Olympic Blvd, Santa Monica, CA 90404-4030
(See Separate Listing)

ESP Brands
(Formerly GroupM ESP)
825 7th Ave, New York, NY 10019
(See Separate Listing)

GroupM LATAM HQ
Avenida Ejercito Nacional, No. 216, piso 2 col. Veronica Anzures, Mexico, 11590 Mexico
Tel.: (52) 55 8503 8390
Fax: (52) 1 55 5250 2365
Web Site: www.groupm.com

Agency Specializes In: Brand Development & Integration, Branded Entertainment, Digital/Interactive, Entertainment, Media Buying Services, Search Engine Optimization, Sponsorship

Lilia Barroso *(Head-MindShare & CEO-GroupM)*
Gerardo Morales *(CFO & COO)*

GroupM Singapore
700 Beach Rd 07-01, Singapore, 199598 Singapore
Tel.: (65) 6225 1262
Web Site: www.groupm.com

Puneet Arora *(CEO)*
Angela Ryan *(Chief HR Officer & Chief Talent Officer-China & APAC)*
Diana Higgs *(Reg Dir-Fin)*
Sanjay Maheshwari *(Reg Dir-Comml-Trading APAC)*
William Chan *(Dir-Data & Analytics Svcs)*
Jason Woolley *(Dir-Search Ops-Asia Pacific)*
Christine Liau *(Sr Mgr-Fin)*
Adam Cooke *(Mgr-Talent Acq-Asia Pacific)*
Raja Kanniappan *(Reg CFO-APAC)*

Accounts:
Jollibee Foods Corporation
Ministry of Manpower Marketing Communications

GroupM Thailand
Ploanchit Center 23rd Floor, 2 Sukhumvit Road Khlong Toey, Bangkok, Thailand
Tel.: (66) 2629 6256
Web Site: www.groupm.com

Puneet Arora *(Chm)*
Kevin Clarke *(CEO)*
Jitirath Supornjirapat *(Dir-Digital-Minteraction)*
Thitikarn Krisanaviparkporn *(Mgr-HR)*

PLAY Communication
Level 1 91 Campbell Street, Surry Hills, NSW 2010 Australia
Tel.: (61) 281999900
Fax: (61) 292818125

Web Site: playcomms.com

Year Founded: 2003

Agency Specializes In: Brand Development & Integration, Event Planning & Marketing, Media Relations, Sponsorship

Johannes Weissenbaeck *(Founder)*
Shani Langi-Latukefu *(CEO)*
Jarryd Zankovic *(Sr Dir-Art)*
Jenn Forrest *(Acct Dir)*
Simon Horauf *(Dir-Creative & Production)*

Accounts:
Fairfax Media Newspaper & Magazine Distr
Free Hills Legal Services
iinet Computers & Electronic Products Mfr
Lion Co. Food & Beverage Products Mfr
Samsung Computers & Electronics Products Mfr
Vodafone Telecommunication services

GRP MEDIA, INC.

401 N Michigan Ave, Chicago, IL 60611
Tel.: (312) 970-7551
Fax: (312) 836-1221
E-Mail: grp@grpmedia.com
Web Site: www.grpmedia.com

E-Mail for Key Personnel:
President: guylay@grpmedia.com
Media Dir.: jenniferlay@grpmedia.com

Employees: 26
Year Founded: 1996

Agency Specializes In: Broadcast, Business Publications, Cable T.V., Consumer Marketing, Consumer Publications, Digital/Interactive, Electronic Media, Financial, Health Care Services, Hispanic Market, Internet/Web Design, Local Marketing, Magazines, Media Buying Services, Media Planning, Newspaper, Newspapers & Magazines, Out-of-Home Media, Outdoor, Planning & Consultation, Print, Radio, Restaurant, Retail, Sponsorship, Sports Market, Strategic Planning/Research, T.V., Teen Market, Trade & Consumer Magazines, Transportation, Web (Banner Ads, Pop-ups, etc.)

Approx. Annual Billings: $150,000,000

John Reebel *(Owner)*
Guy Lay *(Pres & CEO)*
Bob Porcaro *(Mng Dir & Exec VP)*
Wendy Smith *(Exec VP & Dir-Strategy)*
Jennifer Lay *(Sr VP & Dir-Media)*
Krista Schmitt *(Supvr-Media)*

Accounts:
Jockey Media Buying & Planning

GT MEDIA

(Acquired by Havas Media to Form Havas Media Ireland)

HARMELIN MEDIA

525 Righters Ferry Rd, Bala Cynwyd, PA 19004-1315
Tel.: (610) 668-7900
Fax: (610) 668-9548
E-Mail: harmelinmedia@harmelin.com
Web Site: www.harmelin.com

E-Mail for Key Personnel:
Public Relations: ddizio@harmelin.com

Employees: 137
Year Founded: 1983

Agency Specializes In: Advertising, Affluent Market, African-American Market, Alternative Advertising, Arts, Automotive, Bilingual Market, Broadcast, Business Publications, Business-To-Business, Cable T.V., Co-op Advertising, College, Computers & Software, Consumer Goods, Consumer Marketing, Consumer Publications, Cosmetics, Direct Response Marketing, Direct-to-Consumer, Electronic Media, Entertainment, Financial, Food Service, Gay & Lesbian Market, Government/Political, Guerilla Marketing, Health Care Services, High Technology, Hispanic Market, Hospitality, In-Store Advertising, Leisure, Luxury Products, Magazines, Media Buying Services, Media Planning, Men's Market, Mobile Marketing, Multicultural, Newspaper, Newspapers & Magazines, Out-of-Home Media, Over-50 Market, Paid Searches, Pharmaceutical, Planning & Consultation, Print, Product Placement, Promotions, Publishing, Radio, Real Estate, Regional, Restaurant, Retail, Search Engine Optimization, Seniors' Market, Social Media, Sponsorship, Sports Market, Strategic Planning/Research, T.V., Trade & Consumer Magazines, Travel & Tourism, Tween Market, Urban Market, Viral/Buzz/Word of Mouth, Women's Market

Approx. Annual Billings: $350,000,000

Mary Meder *(Pres)*
Lyn Pierce Strickler *(Mng Dir & Exec VP)*
John Camilleri *(Sr VP)*
Cheryl Klear *(Sr VP)*
Brad Bernard *(VP-Online Media & Analytics)*
Irene Neveil *(VP)*
Betsy Ostroff *(VP)*
Joyclyn Faust *(Sr Dir-Buying & Mgr-Brdcst & Convergence)*
Janine Cross *(Sr Dir-Media)*
David Moore *(Sr Dir-Media)*
Nicole Pearse *(Sr Dir-Media Plng)*
Wendy Rumer *(Sr Dir-Brdcst)*
Gina Yeakel *(Mgr-Print & Convergence & Dir-Media)*
Alison Bolognese *(Dir-Media)*
Greg Ebbecke *(Dir-Bus Intelligence)*
Cheryl Goldberg *(Dir-Media)*
Jennifer McFarlane *(Assoc Dir-Media)*
Lisa Reynolds *(Assoc Dir-Media)*
Dan DeLozier *(Mgr-Digital Media)*
Melissa Rutz *(Mgr-Media)*
Christina Smith *(Mgr-Media)*
Rick Wiener *(Mgr-Media)*
Kelly O'Neill *(Sr Strategist-Media)*
Caitlin Walsh *(Sr Strategist-Media)*
Noelle Allen *(Strategist-Media)*
Sam DiTomasso *(Strategist-Digital)*
Kaiti English *(Strategist-Media)*
Jeff Salkowski *(Strategist-Online Media)*
Corey Buller *(Media Buyer-Online Display)*
Olivia Klein *(Analyst-Digital Media)*

Accounts:
Belk Broadcast Media Buying
Beneficial Bank Media Planning & Buying
BET
Blue Diamond Growers Media Planning & Buying
Boscov's; Reading, PA Department Store; 2001
Commonwealth of Pennsylvania; Harrisburg, PA State Agencies; 2003
Cumberland Packing Corp. Digital Advertising, In The Raw Products, Media, Online, Print, Sweet'N Low, TV
Dex Mobile
Dex One Corporation; Denver, CO Yellow Page Directories; 2007
Ford Dealers Association; Fort Washington, PA Cars & Trucks; 1986
Ford Fiesta
New-GreenWorks Tools Campaign: "80 Volt", Display, Media Buying, Media Planning, Print, Search
Herr Foods; Nottingham, PA Snack Foods; 1996
New-New York Racing Association Media Buying, Media Planning, Media Research
Panzano & Partners Malls, Media
Pennsylvania Department of Health; 2005
Pennsylvania Department of Insurance; 2005
Pennsylvania Department of Welfare; 2005
Philadelphia Inquirer; Philadelphia, PA Newspaper; 1998
New-Ricoh US Digital, Media Buying, Media Planning, Outdoor, Print
Royal Purple Media Planning & Buying
Sheetz; Altoona, PA Convenience Stores, Media Buying, Sheetz Brothers Coffeez; 2000
Sinclair Broadcast Group, Inc.
New-SugarHouse Casino (Media Planning & Media Buying Agency of Record) Brand Awareness
SunGard Availability Services; Wayne, PA; 2000
Tasty Baking Co.; Philadelphia, PA Tastykake Baked Goods; 2003
Turkey Hill Dairy, Inc.; Conestoga, PA Yellow Page Directories; 1998
The Vitamin Shoppe; North Bergen, NJ Retail Locations; 2005
Weight Watchers; Fort Washington, PA Weight Loss; 1993

HAVAS MEDIA

(Formerly MPG)
200 Hudson St, New York, NY 10013
Tel.: (646) 587-5000
Fax: (646) 587-5005
Web Site: www.havasmedia.com

Employees: 472
Year Founded: 1978

National Agency Associations: 4A's

Agency Specializes In: Advertising, African-American Market, Automotive, Bilingual Market, Brand Development & Integration, Branded Entertainment, Broadcast, Business Publications, Business-To-Business, Cable T.V., Communications, Consulting, Consumer Goods, Consumer Marketing, Consumer Publications, Direct Response Marketing, Entertainment, Event Planning & Marketing, Financial, Food Service, Gay & Lesbian Market, Health Care Services, Hispanic Market, Hospitality, Internet/Web Design, Magazines, Media Buying Services, Media Planning, Multicultural, Newspaper, Out-of-Home Media, Outdoor, Pharmaceutical, Planning & Consultation, Print, Radio, Restaurant, Retail, Sponsorship, Strategic Planning/Research, Syndication, T.V., Transportation, Travel & Tourism, Yellow Pages Advertising

Approx. Annual Billings: $2,770,000,000

Breakdown of Gross Billings by Media: Cable T.V.: 20%; Internet Adv.: 12%; Network T.V.: 33%; Newsp.: 6%; Other: 4%; Outdoor: 3%; Radio: 8%; Spot T.V.: 7%; Trade & Consumer Mags.: 7%

Greg James *(Chief Strategy Officer & Chief Dev Officer)*
Michael Kaushansky *(Exec VP)*
Amy Ballis *(Sr VP & Grp Acct Dir)*
David Buklarewicz *(Sr VP & Grp Acct Dir)*
Amy Maguire *(Sr VP & Grp Acct Dir)*
Laura Woodson *(Sr VP & Grp Acct Dir)*
James Brickley *(Sr VP & Dir-Talent Acq-NA)*
Kevin Hung *(Sr VP & Dir-Digital Innovations)*
Tom Goodwin *(Sr VP-Strategy & Innovation)*
Jenna Gino *(VP & Gen Mgr-Affiperf & AdCity North America)*
Lisa Anderson *(VP & Acct Dir-MPG)*
Jennifer Carroll *(VP & Acct Dir)*
Kristin Hammill *(VP & Acct Dir)*
Nakesha Holley *(VP & Acct Dir)*
Femaris Pena *(VP & Acct Dir)*
Pattie Reid *(VP & Acct Dir)*
Tim Simko *(VP & Acct Dir)*
Kallana Warner *(VP & Acct Dir)*
Clayton Mclaughlin *(VP & Dir-Search)*
Janna Moskin Greenberg *(VP-Strategy)*

Kim Goldstein *(Acct Dir)*
Kellie Holt *(Acct Dir)*
Rebecca Rivera *(Acct Dir)*
Emily Silvera *(Acct Dir)*
Lauren Grant *(Dir-Programmatic Engagement)*
Nelson Ariowitsch *(Acct Mgr)*
Wendy Roberts *(Mgr-Mktg & Comm)*
Jennifer Bjorklund *(Supvr-Media)*
Jessica Doolittle *(Supvr-Media)*
Steve Fagioli *(Supvr-Media)*
Katie Kozlowski *(Supvr-Media)*
Ana Maria Moreno *(Supvr-Integrated Media)*
Ian Mullin *(Supvr-Natl Video Investments)*
Sarah E Russell *(Supvr-Media)*
Caitlin Wendell *(Supvr-Media Plng & Buying)*
Shannon Green *(Specialist-Search Mktg)*
Michelle Carpenter *(Media Planner & Media Buyer)*
Brittany Moten *(Media Planner & Media Buyer)*
Joanne Cheung *(Media Planner-Integrated)*
Catherine Jeanbart *(Media Planner-Integrated)*
Mia Stenger *(Planner)*
Molly Dickinson *(Buyer-Video Investments)*
Natalia Hall *(Asst Media Planner & Buyer)*
Wendy Luong *(Jr Producer)*
Jennifer Terranella *(Buyer-Print)*
Joshua Wohlstadter *(Asst Media Planner)*

Accounts:
Air France-KLM Group
Atlantic City Alliance
Australian Tourism Board
AutoZone; 2005
AXA Equitable Life Insurance Company
Brewin Dolphin
Certified Financial Planner Board of Standards
Choice Hotels International Media; 1999
Credit Suisse Securities (USA) LLC
Deutsch Family Wine & Spirits Yellow Tail
EDF Energy
Emirates Media Planning & Buying
Esurance; San Francisco, CA Direct Response Marketing, Planning & Buying, Print, Radio, TV; 2006
Goodyear Tire & Rubber Company; 2004
Hugo Boss Media Planning & Buying; 2008
Huntington Bank
Inter Rhone
Jones Apparel; 2008
KLM Royal Dutch Airlines
Kmart Corp. (Agency of Record) Media Buying
La Francaise des Jeux
LAN
Moet Hennessy
Mucinex
National Railroad Passenger Corporation Amtrak Acela; 2003
New-NBTY, Inc. Media Buying, Media Planning
NewsX (Agency of Record)
NYSE Euronext
OppenheimerFunds Media Relations
Panasonic Corporation of America Panasonic, Panasonic Viera
PayPal Inc.
Philips Consumer Lifestyle, Media
Reckitt Benckiser Clearasil, Dettol, Lemsip, Lysol, Media Buying, Nurofen, Vanish, Woolite; 2000
Sears Holdings Co. Media Buying
Spanish Tourism Board
Swarovski North America & Southeast Asia
Turespana
Virgin Mobile USA, Inc. Media Planning & Buying
VistaPrint
YP Event Marketing, Media Planning & Buying

Branches

Havas Media Ireland
(Formerly GT Media)
Park View House Beech Hill Office Campus, Clonskeagh, Dublin, 4 Ireland
Tel.: (353) 1 218 7145
Fax: (353) 1 218 7110
E-Mail: media@gtmedia.ie
Web Site: www.havasmedia.com/

Employees: 11
Year Founded: 1983

Agency Specializes In: Media Buying Services

Graham Taylor *(CEO)*
Adam Taylor *(Head-Digital)*
Valerie O'Toole *(Client Svcs Dir)*
Leigh Cunningham *(Acct Mgr)*
Ryan Glynn *(Acct Mgr)*

Accounts:
Allianz Allianz Direct, Allianz Insurance
Bord na Mona/Shamrock Peat Moss
Colortrend Paints
De Care
Dyson Ireland Vacuum Cleaners
Febvre Wines Caliterra, Two Oceans
Greenstar
Honda
KAL AGA, Elica, Falcon, Franke, Indesit, Insinkerator, Neff
LG Electronics LG
Lifes 2 Good
Low Cost Holidays
Merchamp Optical Marco Sunglasses
Monsanto Round Up Weedkiller
National Craft Fair
NTR/Easy Pass
One Life Mortgages
Oxfam
Pepe Pepe Jeans
Peugeot Cars Partner
Remington
Rockwell
Snap Printing
Snickers Workwear
Stephens Green Shopping Center
Universal Honda Accord, CRV, Civic, FR-V, Jazz
Wavin

Havas Media
(Formerly MPG (Media Planning Group))
60 St Martin's Lane, London, WC2N 4JS United Kingdom
Tel.: (44) 2073939000
Fax: (44) 2073932525
Web Site: www.havasmedia.com

Employees: 276
Year Founded: 1996

Agency Specializes In: Media Buying Services

Paul Frampton *(CEO)*
Peter Bennett *(Mng Partner)*
David Goodall *(Mng Partner-Intl-London)*
Natasha Murray *(Mng Dir)*
Dominique Delport *(Chm-France & Mng Dir-Global)*
Nick Wright *(Grp Dir-Creative)*
Ashley Bolt *(Acct Dir-Digital Global & Strategist)*

Accounts:
Air France-KLM Group
Ask.com UK
AXA UK Media Buying
BBC BBC Orchestras, BBC Worldwide, World Service & Global News, Media
Bell Direct
Broadbandchoices Media Buying, Media Planning
Brother
Burberry
Burt's Bees
Cheshire Building Society
Clarks
Conservatives
Credit Suisse
Derbyshire
Diamond
East Coast Mainline Planning
EBLEX
EDF Energy
elephant.co.uk
Espana
Expedia.com.uk
Fairtrade Foundation
Freesat Digital Satellite Service; 2008
G6 Hospitality LLC
GOLA
Gossard
Guylian
Harrison's Fund Campaign: "I Wish My Son Had Cancer"
Hermes
Hotels.com
Hugo Boss
Hyundai Kia Automotive Group; 2009
Ibis Hotels Media
IG Group
Illva Saronno Disaronno, Media Planning & Buying, Tia Maria
Isklar
Israel
Jones Apparel
Kenneth Green Associates
KLM
LaTasca
lowcostholidays.com
Mega Brands Media Planning & Buying
National Express
Nationwide Planning & Buying; 2008
New-O2
P&O Ferries
PayPal Media
Penguin Books DK UK, Media, Penguin Random House
Pernod Ricard Media Planning & Buying
Peroni
Pioneer
Playtex
PUIG
Rightmove.co.uk
New-Source International Media Planning & Buying
Spanish Tourism Board-Turespana
Telefonica O2 UK Limited Media Buying, Media Planning
Tilda
Your Move Media Planning & Buying

Havas Media
(Formerly Media Contacts)
Avda General Peron No 38 Planta 14, Madrid, 28002 Spain
Tel.: (34) 91 456 90 50
Fax: (34) 91 770 15 86
E-Mail: javier.navarro@havasdigital.com
Web Site: www.havasmedia.com

Employees: 80

Agency Specializes In: Media Buying Services

Alfonso Rodes Vila *(CEO)*
Luca Boer *(Chief HR Officer)*
Laurent Cayet *(Officer-Global Client)*
Niko Munoz *(Sr VP-Digital Bus Transformation & Head-Corp Dev)*
Maria Delaguardia *(VP-Corp Dev-Global)*
Marie Viszkei *(VP-Global Client Svcs)*
Bhavna Karani *(Dir-Talent Mgmt)*
Carlos Pacheco *(Dir-Strategy Projects)*
Enrique Escalante Sierra *(Dir-Global Talent Mgmt)*
Janet Wong *(Dir-Strategy-Global)*

Accounts:
Antena 3
Caja Madrid
Carrefour
El Corte Ingles
Goodyear Dunlop
Stage Holding
Tour Espana
Whiskers

Havas Media
(Formerly MPG Canada)
473 Adelaide Street West Ste 300, Toronto, ON M5V 1T1 Canada
Tel.: (416) 487-1393
Web Site: www.havasmedia.com

Employees: 35

Hannah Savage *(VP & Head-Strategy)*
Azadeh Mahinpou Dindayal *(VP)*
Nicole Viger-Collins *(Dir-Brdcst)*
Lina Kim *(Sr Acct Mgr)*
Stephanie Harrison *(Supvr-Media)*
Patsy Porras *(Supvr-Media-Agilent Technologies)*
Bryan Banka *(Media Planner)*
Sarah-Emily Collette *(Media Buyer)*
Julie Forbes *(Sr Media Planner)*
Cassandra Piazza *(Sr Media Planner)*

Havas Media
(Formerly MPG Los Angeles)
12100 Wilshire Blvd 8th Fl, Los Angeles, CA 90025
Tel.: (310) 806-9266
Web Site: www.havasmedia.com/

Employees: 6

Agency Specializes In: Media Buying Services

Marc Schader *(Chief Comml Officer-Havas Media Group)*
Rob Griffin *(Exec VP-Media Futures & Innovation)*
Dominique Delport *(Mng Dir-Global)*
Taylor Wynne *(VP & Acct Dir)*
Michel Sibony *(Head-Middle Office Global-Havas Media Grp)*
Jordi Ustrell *(Head-Back Office-Havas Media Group-Global)*
Jacqueline Cordova *(Supvr-Search)*
Kathryn Meehan *(Supvr-Media)*

Havas Media
(Formerly MPG Miami)
5301 Blue Lagoon Dr Ste 850, Miami, FL 33126
Tel.: (305) 377-1907
Fax: (305) 337-1906
Web Site: www.havasmedia.com

Employees: 60

National Agency Associations: 4A's

Agency Specializes In: Media Buying Services, Sponsorship

Lori Hiltz *(CEO-North America)*
Anabela Bonuccelli *(Sr VP & Head-Ops)*
Jose Cabanillas *(Client Svcs Dir)*
Angela Berrio *(Media Planner)*
Sophia Del Zoppo *(Media Planner)*
Luisa Foulques *(Media Planner)*
Juliana Munoz *(Reg Jr Media Planner)*

Havas Media
(Formerly MPG Chicago)
36 E Grand Ave 5th Fl, Chicago, IL 60611
Tel.: (312) 640-4700
Fax: (312) 337-3898
Web Site: www.havasmedia.com

Employees: 33

National Agency Associations: 4A's

Agency Specializes In: Media Buying Services, Sponsorship

Paul Traeger *(VP-Strategy)*
Heather Maguire *(Acct Dir)*
Shawn Mulroney *(Acct Dir)*
Bethany Whipple *(Acct Dir)*
Lindsay Todd Maumus *(Mgr-Programmatic Engagement)*
Randi Born *(Supvr-Local Brdcst)*
Liz Gaydos *(Supvr-Media Plng)*
Amanda Smidt *(Supvr-Media)*
Taryn Stewart *(Supvr-Mktg Analytics & Data Consulting)*
Ana Maria Gutierrez *(Planner-Digital)*
Keenan O'Shea *(Media Planner)*
Natalie Arroyo *(Asst Media Buyer)*

Accounts:
Hefty & Reynolds Media Planning & Buying
Reynolds Consumer Products
Safelite AutoGlass (US Agency of Record) Buying, Digital, Planning, Social Media
Sears Holdings Corp. Media

Havas Media
(Formerly Media Contacts)
10 Summer St, Boston, MA 02110
Tel.: (617) 425-4100
Fax: (617) 425-4101
Web Site: www.havasmedia.com

Employees: 70

National Agency Associations: 4A's

Agency Specializes In: Media Buying Services, Sponsorship

Adam Kasper *(Chief Media Officer-North America)*
Leon Barsoumian *(Sr VP-Analytics & Res)*
Victor Davidson *(VP & Grp Acct Dir)*
Ashley Locke Anderson *(VP & Acct Dir)*
Karen Graf *(VP & Acct Dir)*
Jacob Davis *(VP & Dir-Search Mktg)*
Elizabeth Hannigan *(Acct Dir)*
Tracy Kochan *(Acct Dir)*
Alexander Lock *(Acct Dir)*
Bobby Metcalfe *(Acct Dir)*
Andy Beatman *(Dir-SEO)*
Rebecca Arnold *(Project Mgr-Media)*
Ashley Blais *(Supvr-Media Plng)*
Ryan Patti *(Supvr-Media)*
Anya Slavin *(Supvr-Digital Media)*
Kelsee Wadas *(Supvr-Media)*
Taylor Wishman *(Supvr-Search Mktg)*
Nicole Goldstein *(Acct Exec)*
Ware Cady *(Media Planner & Buyer-Digital)*
Justin Chere *(Media Planner)*
Alexandra Glazer *(Media Planner & Buyer-Digital)*
Shoshana Levine *(Media Planner & Buyer-Digital)*
Alexa Simons *(Media Planner & Buyer-Digital)*
Andrew Suskin *(Media Planner & Buyer-Digital)*
Allyson Dilsworth *(Asst Media Planner & Buyer)*

Accounts:
Boss
New-National Association of Realtors (Media Agency of Record) Analytics, Digital, Media Buying, Media Planning, Strategy
Amtrak
Auto Zone Duralast
Choice Hotels
Colonial Williamsburg
Fidelity Investments
Goodyear
Tyson Foods

Havas Media
(Formerly MPG Minneapolis)
8500 Normandale Lk Blvd Ste 1960, Minneapolis, MN 55437
Tel.: (952) 832-9510
Fax: (952) 832-9505
Web Site: www.havasmedia.com

Employees: 7

Agency Specializes In: Media Buying Services

Dominique Delport *(Mng Dir-Global)*
Michel Sibony *(Head-Middle Office Global-Havas Media Grp)*
Jordi Ustrell *(Head-Back Office-Havas Media Group-Global)*
Joe Abruzzo *(Dir-Res)*

Accounts:
Agilent Technologies
BAE Systems
Carnival
Kmart
McDonald's
Pinnacle

Havas Media
(Formerly MPG Washington D.C.)
1310 N Court House Rd, Arlington, VA 22201
Tel.: (703) 288-7300
Fax: (703) 399-3601
Web Site: www.havasmedia.com

Employees: 20
Year Founded: 1978

Anthony Esponda *(Supvr-Media)*
Stephanie Garcia *(Supvr-Media)*

HAWORTH MARKETING & MEDIA COMPANY
45 S 7 St, Minneapolis, MN 55402
Tel.: (612) 677-8900
Fax: (612) 677-8901
E-Mail: haworth@haworthmedia.com
Web Site: www.haworthmedia.com

E-Mail for Key Personnel:
President: aluhtanen@haworthmedia.com

Employees: 100
Year Founded: 1970

Agency Specializes In: Brand Development & Integration, Entertainment, Event Planning & Marketing, Hispanic Market, Media Buying Services, Newspaper, Out-of-Home Media, Radio, Retail, Sponsorship, Sports Market, Strategic Planning/Research, T.V., Trade & Consumer Magazines

Approx. Annual Billings: $630,000,000

Breakdown of Gross Billings by Media: Cable T.V.: $39,000,000; Internet Adv.: $41,000,000; Mags.: $61,000,000; Network T.V.: $296,000,000; Newsp.: $35,000,000; Out-of-Home Media: $20,000,000; Spot Radio: $27,000,000; Spot T.V.: $111,000,000

Andrea Luhtanen *(Pres)*
Heather Kruse *(Sr VP & Media Dir)*
Chris Dennehy *(Sr VP-Partnership Dev)*
Scott Slater *(VP & Grp Dir-Media)*
Marcie Durkot *(Grp Dir-Media)*
Claudia Eggan *(Dir-Brdcst)*
Maggie Lunetta *(Dir-Media)*
Marie Rodman *(Dir-Brdcst)*
Shari Schraber *(Dir-Media)*
Ashley Hartley *(Assoc Dir-Media)*
Colleen Moe *(Assoc Dir-Media)*
Brittney Rogowski *(Assoc Dir-Media)*
Kristin Atherton *(Mgr-Media)*
Tom Donovan *(Mgr-Digital)*
Jennifer Karni *(Mgr-Digital)*
Chris Pope *(Mgr-Digital Media)*
Jennifer Rokke *(Mgr-Digital)*
Jamie Wacholz *(Mgr-Media)*
Abigail Hawthorne *(Supvr-Media)*
Julia Lodge *(Supvr-Out-of-Home)*
Allison Marshall *(Supvr-Digital Media)*
Meredith Zander *(Supvr-Media)*
Caitlin Zellmann *(Sr Buyer-Brdcst)*

Amie Eller *(Media Planner & Media Buyer)*
Amie Jaroscak *(Media Buyer & Planner)*
Melanie Blevins *(Media Planner)*
Julia Brock *(Planner-Digital Media)*
Jenny Jurek *(Media Planner)*
Maren Kalland *(Planner-Audio & Video)*
Carlyn Steffen *(Media Planner-Strategy)*
Ali Vitek *(Media Planner)*
Bailey Moomaw *(Asst Media Buyer)*
Marnie Wirth *(Assoc Media Dir)*

Accounts:
Ameristar Casinos; 2008
Beats Electronics LLC
Ben & Jerry's Homemade, Inc.
Caribou Coffee Company, Inc. National Media Planning & Buying
DreamWorks Animation SKG, Inc.
General Growth Properties; 1997
Honeywell International Inc.
Mrs. Meyers/Caldrea; 2008
Oscars
Target Corporation Media Buying, Retail; 1971

Branch

Haworth Marketing & Media Company
10940 Wilshire Blvd Ste 2050, Los Angeles, CA 90024
Tel.: (310) 824-7777
Fax: (310) 824-7778
E-Mail: haworth@haworthmedia.com
Web Site: www.haworthmedia.com

Employees: 6
Year Founded: 1970

Agency Specializes In: Media Buying Services, Sponsorship

Gary Tobey *(Chm & CEO)*
Ashley Hartley *(Assoc Dir-Media)*

HELEN THOMPSON MEDIA
8035 Broadway St, San Antonio, TX 78209-2628
Tel.: (210) 822-2158
Fax: (210) 822-9001
E-Mail: info@helentmedia.com
Web Site: www.helentmedia.com

Employees: 5
Year Founded: 1989

Agency Specializes In: Media Buying Services, Sponsorship

Approx. Annual Billings: $13,000,000

Helen Thompson *(Chm)*
Brandon Thompson *(Pres & CEO)*
Stacey Schneider *(VP-Media)*
Dustin Goskeson *(Media Planner & Media Buyer)*
Gaby Arredondo *(Media Buyer)*
Guille Hernandez *(Media Buyer)*

Accounts:
Advantage Rent-A-Car
Auto Valve
Blue Clover
La Mansion Watermark
Security Service

HOCKING MEDIA GROUP INC.
1700 W Big Beaver Rd Ste 360, Troy, MI 48084
Tel.: (248) 731-7820
Web Site: www.hockingmedia.com

Kara Hocking *(CEO)*
Lori Richard *(Partner)*
Jessica Larose *(Dir-Fin)*
Dayna Henninger *(Mgr-Traffic & Production)*
Alyssa Alexandra Lowe *(Acct Exec)*
Erin Forbes *(Media Buyer)*
Amy Muskovitz *(Asst Acct Exec & Acct Coord)*
Whitney Weaver *(Acct Coord)*
Jane Favret *(Sr Media Planner)*

Accounts:
Belle Tire Inc.
Comerica Media Buying, Outdoor

HOME RUN MEDIA
344 N Ogden Ave 3rd Fl E, Chicago, IL 60607
Tel.: (773) 244-1882
Web Site: hrmedia.com

Employees: 10
Year Founded: 1999

Agency Specializes In: Alternative Advertising, Cable T.V., Direct Response Marketing, Game Integration, Outdoor, Print, Product Placement, Radio, T.V., Telemarketing

Approx. Annual Billings: $15,000,000

Andrew Blickstein *(Founder)*
Haley Skisak *(Sr Media Buyer)*

Accounts:
Fanduel.com
Mailine Sensationail
Mobile Help
Oliso
Right Size Nutrition
Teeter Hang Ups
TheBidcactus.com

HORIZON MEDIA, INC.
75 Varick St, New York, NY 10013
Tel.: (212) 220-5000
Web Site: www.horizonmedia.com

E-Mail for Key Personnel:
President: shall@horizonmedia.com

Employees: 800
Year Founded: 1989

National Agency Associations: 4A's

Agency Specializes In: Advertising, Advertising Specialties, African-American Market, Asian Market, Bilingual Market, Brand Development & Integration, Broadcast, Business Publications, Business-To-Business, Cable T.V., Communications, Consumer Marketing, Consumer Publications, Corporate Communications, Digital/Interactive, Direct Response Marketing, E-Commerce, Education, Electronic Media, Entertainment, Event Planning & Marketing, Financial, Government/Political, Health Care Services, High Technology, Hispanic Market, In-Store Advertising, Local Marketing, Media Buying Services, Newspaper, Newspapers & Magazines, Out-of-Home Media, Outdoor, Pharmaceutical, Planning & Consultation, Point of Purchase, Print, Publicity/Promotions, Radio, Restaurant, Retail, Sales Promotion, Sports Market, Strategic Planning/Research, Syndication, T.V., Teen Market, Telemarketing, Trade & Consumer Magazines, Travel & Tourism

Approx. Annual Billings: $4,300,000,000

Bill Koenigsberg *(Founder, Pres & CEO)*
Katy Ferguson *(Mng Partner & Exec VP)*
Stan Fields *(Mng Partner & Exec VP)*
Charlie Rutman *(Mng Partner & Exec VP)*
Gene Turner *(Mng Partner & Exec VP)*
David Besegai *(Mng Dir & Sr VP)*
Jeff Francisco *(Mng Dir & Sr VP)*
Jake Phillips *(Mng Dir & Sr VP)*
Megan Riley *(Mng Dir & VP)*
Dan Parise *(Mng Dir)*
Vinnie O'Toole *(CFO, COO & Exec VP)*
Cliff Cree *(CIO & Sr VP)*
Charlotte Cochrane *(Sr VP & Mng Dir-Digital)*
Mia Cosgrove *(Sr VP & Mng Dir-Direct Mktg Div)*
Maria Freda *(Sr VP & Controller)*
David Campanelli *(Sr VP & Dir-Nat Television)*
Chris Fitzgerald *(Sr VP & Dir-Activation)*
Brad Adgate *(Sr VP-Res)*
Steve Faske *(Sr VP-Bus Affairs)*
Michael O'Connor *(Sr VP-Direct Mktg Activation)*
Tim McCarthy *(Mng Dir-Brand Strategy & VP)*
Lauren Russo *(Mng Dir-Local Audio & Promos & VP)*
Niki DeCou *(VP & Grp Dir-Brand)*
Alison Sidrane *(VP & Grp Dir-Brand)*
Marc Fenty *(VP & Dir-OOH)*
Michelle Gordon *(VP & Dir-Consumer Insights-WHY Grp)*
Steven Indich *(VP & Dir-Digital Activation)*
Chris Varian *(VP & Dir-Creative)*
Sarah Bachman *(VP-Mobile Strategy)*
Nancy Starring Blucher *(Assoc Mng Dir & VP)*
Lizzie Diller *(Assoc Mng Dir & VP)*
Michele Donati *(VP & Assoc Mng Dir-WHERE)*
Moffat Frazier *(VP-Consumer Insights-WHY Group)*
Kyung Kim *(VP-Digital Activation)*
LJ Kobe *(VP-Digital Strategy)*
Shana Kohen *(VP-Digital Media Activation)*
Kaya Lobaczewski *(VP-Comm)*
Cristina Marrus *(Assoc Mng Dir & VP)*
Maikel O'Hanlon *(VP-Social Media Strategy)*
Kirk Olson *(VP-TrendSights)*
Anthony Salerno *(Assoc Mng Dir & VP)*
Ericka Santos *(VP & Assoc Mng Dir)*
Jason Smith *(VP-Digital Media Activation)*
Tim Surowiecki *(VP-Digital Media, Search & Analytics)*
Katie Comerford *(Dir-Digital)*
Skylar Kim *(Dir-Data Strategy, Digital Brand Strategy & Entertainment)*
Devin McGrath *(Dir-Invention)*
Sam O'Brien Rose *(Dir-Natl TV)*
Jeremy Shure *(Dir-Invention)*
Emilee Stansell *(Dir-Digital Media)*
Alex Stone *(Dir-Digital)*
Amanda Taubman *(Dir-Mobile Strategy)*
Dale Tzeng *(Dir-Analytics)*
Michael Cha *(Assoc Dir-Performance Mktg & Digital)*
Karen Chan *(Assoc Dir-Mobile Strategy)*
Louise Chu *(Assoc Dir-Digital Search & Analytics)*
Jane Eun *(Assoc Dir-Media)*
Britney Greenhouse *(Assoc Dir-Media)*
Alexandra Haack *(Assoc Dir-Mobile Strategy)*
Brittany Hennessy *(Assoc Dir-Social Strategy & Influence)*
Kristin Lagreca *(Assoc Dir-Strategy & Analytics)*
Jerly Marquez *(Assoc Dir-Multicultural Brand Strategy)*
Kaitlyn McInnis *(Assoc Dir-Digital Media)*
Morgan Merrifield *(Assoc Dir-Digital)*
Rachel Schlesinger *(Assoc Dir-Digital-Turner)*
Eric Silvera *(Assoc Dir-Media)*
Rose Carollo *(Sr Brand Strategist-Entertainment Television)*
Alyse Zabalgoitia *(Sr Brand Strategist)*
Alyssa Augenstein *(Supvr-Digital Media)*
Sarah Capodice *(Supvr-Natl TV)*
Carly Chan *(Supvr-Brand Strategy)*
Andrew Cotlov *(Supvr-Brand Strategy)*
Garrett Dargan *(Supvr-Strategy)*
Lindsey DeLeo *(Supvr-Digital)*
Aita Djigo *(Supvr-OOH)*
Joseph Doran *(Supvr-Strategy)*
Melissa Flynn *(Supvr-Brand Strategy)*
Clare Frattarola *(Supvr-Brand Strategy)*
Heather Gentle *(Supvr-Brand Strategy)*
Justin Jarmus *(Supvr-Digital Media)*
Richard Kelly *(Supvr-Digital Media)*
Emily Klarfeld *(Supvr-Brand Strategy)*
Rebecca Levi *(Supvr-Digital Media)*

Media Buying Services

Stephanie Macarounas *(Supvr-Media)*
Jami Macklin *(Supvr-Brand Strategy)*
Melissa Marascia *(Supvr-Brand Strategy)*
Jackie Newman *(Supvr-Digital)*
Graham Pearson *(Supvr-Digital Strategy)*
Dwayne Thompson *(Supvr-Out of Home)*
Anita Walsh *(Supvr-Brand Strategy)*
Rebecca Winston *(Supvr-Brand Strategy)*
Michael Wolf *(Supvr-Brand Strategy)*
Shukmei Wong *(Supvr-Brdcst)*
Mark Yeager *(Supvr-Brand Strategy)*
Catherine Pinkham *(Sr Strategist-Mobile Strategy)*
Nicole Trimble *(Sr Strategist-Social Media Mktg)*
Elena Carroll *(Strategist-Integrated Brand)*
Kelly Donnelly *(Strategist-Brand)*
Jena Fanelli *(Strategist-Brand)*
Elise Fisher *(Strategist-Brand)*
Dominic Forte *(Sr Planner-Digital Media)*
Dani Haskin *(Strategist-Brand)*
Melissa Hui *(Strategist-Brand)*
Alexandra Ingenito *(Sr Planner-Media & Digital)*
Ariana Malushi *(Strategist-Brand)*
Jordan McDaniel *(Sr Planner-Digital Media)*
Kristin Parris *(Strategist-Brand)*
Brianne Sullivan *(Strategist-Brand-Lifetime Brand Team)*
Alex Willig *(Sr Planner-Digital Media)*
Francois Anderson *(Media Buyer)*
Alexa Bieber *(Assoc Media Buyer)*
Devin Edge *(Assoc Media Buyer)*
Zoe Efrus *(Planner-Digital Media)*
Courtney Fischer *(Planner-Digital Media)*
Lauren Futterman *(Media Buyer-Natl TV & HorizonAdvanced)*
Devin George *(Media Planner)*
Sana Ghias *(Planner-Digital Media)*
Kourtney Lavin *(Media Buyer-Local Audio)*
Lindsay O'Brien *(Planner-Digital Media)*
Michael Oppito *(Assoc Media Buyer)*
Gillian Ramos *(Media Buyer-Natl TV)*
Natalie Ryan *(Assoc Media Buyer)*
Ben Wheeler *(Media Buyer)*
Carly Wilden *(Media Buyer-Direct Mktg)*
Brian Altman *(Asst Media Buyer-Natl TV)*
Alana Cohen *(Sr Media Buyer)*
Vanessa Curcuru *(Assoc Mng Dir)*
Katie Dye *(Sr Media Buyer)*
Katie Herman *(Asst Media Buyer-Natl TV)*
Maggie Landon *(Jr Media Planner-Digital)*
Maria Micchelli *(Sr Media Buyer)*
Monica Oliveira *(Jr Media Planner-Digital)*
Lisa Tarulli *(Sr Media Buyer)*
Taylor Valentine *(Chief Invention Officer)*

Accounts:
1&1
A&E Television Networks
Amerifit Nutrition, Inc. AZO, Culturelle, Estroven
Buddy Media Media
Buffalo Wild Wings; Minneapolis, MN Media Buying
Burger King Holdings Inc. Media
Capital One Financial Corporation Media
CarMax, Inc. Media Buying, Media Planning
Clearwire Corporation Clear
Crown Imports
David's Bridal
Dish Network Corporation Media Planning & Buying
Drive Time
Edible Arrangements Media
Fruit of the Loom
Geico Media
Golden Corral Corporation Media Buying, Media Planning
Google, Inc. Google, Google +, Google Adwords, Google Earth, Google TV
Green Dot Corporation; 2010
J. Crew
Jack in the Box, Inc. Digital Media Planning & Buying, OOH Media, Radio, Television
Kraft Cadbury, Macaroni & Cheese, Media Planning
Lifetime Digital Out-of-Home
Lindt USA (Media Agency of Record)
Little Caesars Media
Mike's Hard Lemonade
NBC Universo Media
One Billion Rising
New-Partnership for Drug Free Kids
Qdoba Mexican Grill Media
Readly (Agency of Record) Activation, Communications Planning, Digital Creative, Social Outreach
Ruby Tuesday Restaurant Media Planning & Buying
New-Scripps Networks
Sleepy's Media Planning & Buying
Snyder's-Lance, Inc Cape Cod (Media Agency of Record), Communications Planning, Lance (Media Agency of Record), Snack Factory Pretzel Crisps (Media Agency of Record), Snyder's of Hanover (Media Agency of Record)
Sobieski Campaign: "Truth in Vodka", Media
Stanley Steemer; Dublin, OH Media Planning & Buying
Stoli Group USA (Agency of Record) Consumer Awareness, Media, Stolichnaya Vodka
Telemundo Network Media
Turner Broadcasting CNN, Cartoon Network, Media Buying, Media Planning, TBS, TNT, Turner Sports
United Continental Holdings Creative, Digital, Media
Vonage Holdings Corp. Media Planning & Buying
VTech Electronics (Media Agency of Record) Communications, Media Buying, Media Planning
Weight Watchers International, Inc.
Wildlife Conservation Society "96 Elephants", Digital Signage, Media Activation, Media Planning

Branches

Scout Sports Marketing & Entertainment
75 Varick, New York, NY 10013
Tel.: (212) 220-1744

Year Founded: 2010

Michael A. Neuman, *(Mng Partner)*

Accounts:
FanDuel Brand Awareness, Marketing
Schneider Electric (Global Sports Marketing Agency of Record) Strategy

Horizon Media, Inc.
1888 Century Park E, Los Angeles, CA 90067-1700
Tel.: (310) 282-0909
Fax: (310) 229-8104
Toll Free: (800) 282-0901
E-Mail: zrosenberg@horizonmedia.com
Web Site: www.horizonmedia.com

Employees: 95
Year Founded: 1989

National Agency Associations: 4A's

Agency Specializes In: Advertising, Advertising Specialties, African-American Market, Asian Market, Bilingual Market, Brand Development & Integration, Broadcast, Business Publications, Business-To-Business, Cable T.V., Communications, Consulting, Consumer Goods, Consumer Marketing, Consumer Publications, Corporate Communications, Digital/Interactive, Direct Response Marketing, E-Commerce, Education, Electronic Media, Entertainment, Event Planning & Marketing, Financial, Government/Political, Health Care Services, High Technology, Hispanic Market, In-Store Advertising, Local Marketing, Media Buying Services, Multimedia, Newspaper, Newspapers & Magazines, Out-of-Home Media, Outdoor, Pharmaceutical, Planning & Consultation, Point of Purchase, Print, Publicity/Promotions, Publishing, Radio, Restaurant, Retail, Sales Promotion, Sponsorship, Sports Market, Strategic Planning/Research, Syndication, T.V., Teen Market, Telemarketing, Trade & Consumer Magazines, Travel & Tourism

Ricki Goldhamer *(Partner-HR Bus & VP)*
Eric Geiger *(Mng Dir & Sr VP)*
Sarah Robertson *(Mng Dir & Sr VP)*
Serena Duff *(Exec VP & Gen Mgr-Los Angeles)*
Erin FoxworthySr *(Sr VP & Mng Dir-Innovation & Partnerships)*
Jared Gruner *(Mng Dir/VP-Why Grp)*
Tiffany Kirk *(VP & Mng Dir-Local Brdcst & Promos)*
Mina Kamarasheva *(Mng Dir-Audio & Promos)*
Concetta Lombardi *(VP & Dir-Local Brdcst-Eden Road Trading)*
Angela Mailloux *(Assoc Mng Dir & VP)*
Brandon Birkmeyer *(Dir-Media, Mktg & Bus Dev)*
Brandis DeZon *(Assoc Dir-Media-Digital)*
Sunny Nguyen *(Assoc Dir-Media)*
Jill Shiffman *(Assoc Dir-Media)*
Oury Tamboura *(Sr Mgr-Media)*
Daniella Horta *(Brand Strategist)*
Traci Brown *(Acct Supvr)*
Tara Campomenosi *(Supvr-OOH)*
Mark Italia *(Supvr)*
Cristin McGrath *(Supvr-Social Strategy & Community)*
Marsha Torres *(Supvr-Brand Strategy)*
Erin Driscoll *(Sr Strategist-Digital)*
Allison Grabell *(Strategist-Media-Out of Home)*
Yousuf Lakanwal *(Strategist-Brand)*
Julia Nayerman *(Strategist-New Bus)*
Mackenzie Patterson *(Strategist-Brand)*
Eric Adamus *(Analyst-Media)*
Alyson Winemberg *(Planner-Digital Media)*
Sabrina Zubieta *(Media Buyer)*
Veronica Brown-Robinson *(Sr Media Buyer-TV)*
Andrew Choi *(Asst Media Planner-Digital)*
Robin Curtis *(Sr Media Buyer)*
Caitlin Dudley *(Assoc Media Dir)*
Matt Steinbach *(Sr Media Planner-Digital)*
Dakota Williams *(Asst Media Planner)*

Accounts:
New-ABC Entertainment Digital Buying, Digital Media, Social
Constellation Wines Arbor Mist, Black Box, Clos Du Bois, Constellation Wines, Kim Crawford, Robert Mondavi Private Selection
Crown Imports LLC Corona, Corona Light, Crown Imports LLC, Modelo Especial, Negra Modelo, Pacifico, St. Pauli Girl, Tsingtao, Victoria
FilmDistrict Media Planning & Buying
Focus Features
GEICO Corporation
Health Net, Inc.
Jack in the Box, Inc.
NBC Universo (Agency of Record) Analytics, Strategic Planning
Southern California Honda Dealers Association Media Planning & Buying
STX Entertainment (Agency of Record) Analytics, Broadcast, Digital, Media Buying, Media Planning, Mobile, Out-of-Home, Print, Radio, Social Media, Strategic, Video-on-Demand
Telemundo (Agency of Record) Analytics, Strategic Planning, Telenovela
Tillamook Cheese Media Planning & Buying
Valley Honda Dealer Association Media Planning & Buying

HORIZON PRINT SERVICES GROUP
75 Varick St, New York, NY 10017
Tel.: (212) 220-5000
Fax: (212) 916-8653
Web Site: www.horizonmedia.com/contact

Employees: 7
Year Founded: 2006

Agency Specializes In: Newspapers & Magazines, Production (Print)

Bill Koenigsberg *(Founder, Pres & CEO)*
Paul Santello *(Exec VP & Mng Partner-LA Office)*
Donald Williams *(Chief Digital Officer)*
Serena Duff *(Exec VP & Gen Mgr-Los Angeles)*
Sarah Bachman *(VP-Mobile Strategy)*
Lizzie Diller *(VP & Assoc Mng Dir)*
Kaya Lobaczewski *(VP-Comm)*
Maikel O'Hanlon *(VP-Social Media Strategy)*
Scott Flynn *(Brand Dir-Plng)*
Tugce Caglayan *(Assoc Dir-Intl Brand Strategy)*

Accounts:
ING Direct
NBC Universal
Sobieski Vodka

HUDSON MEDIA SERVICES LLC

3 Stone Dr, West Orange, NJ 07052
Tel.: (973) 951-9930
E-Mail: info@hudson-media.com
Web Site: www.hudson-media.com

Employees: 2
Year Founded: 2009

Agency Specializes In: Advertising, Affluent Market, African-American Market, Alternative Advertising, Arts, Automotive, Broadcast, Business Publications, Business-To-Business, Cable T.V., Co-op Advertising, Consulting, Consumer Goods, Consumer Marketing, Consumer Publications, Cosmetics, Crisis Communications, Direct-to-Consumer, Education, Electronic Media, Electronics, Entertainment, Experience Design, Fashion/Apparel, Financial, Food Service, Gay & Lesbian Market, High Technology, Hispanic Market, Hospitality, Household Goods, In-Store Advertising, Industrial, Infomercials, Legal Services, Leisure, Local Marketing, Luxury Products, Magazines, Media Buying Services, Media Planning, Media Training, Medical Products, Men's Market, Multicultural, Multimedia, New Product Development, Newspaper, Newspapers & Magazines, Out-of-Home Media, Outdoor, Over-50 Market, Pets , Pharmaceutical, Planning & Consultation, Print, Product Placement, Promotions, Radio, Real Estate, Regional, Restaurant, Retail, Seniors' Market, Sports Market, Strategic Planning/Research, Syndication, T.V., Trade & Consumer Magazines, Transportation, Travel & Tourism, Women's Market

Approx. Annual Billings: $10,000,000

Breakdown of Gross Billings by Media: Bus. Publs.: $500,000; Cable T.V.: $1,700,000; Internet Adv.: $1,000,000; Network T.V.: $1,300,000; Newsp.: $1,200,000; Out-of-Home Media: $800,000; Spot Radio: $800,000; Spot T.V.: $2,700,000

Ed Weiner *(CEO)*
Jeremy Weiner *(VP)*

Accounts:
Amazon New York
AMC TV; 2012
Apollo Theatre; New York, NY Musical Performances; 2010
IFC TV; New York, NY Tune-in; 2009
Outdoor Channel TV Tune In; 2012
Planetshoes.com Online Footwear Retailer; 2012
PlaSmart, Inc. TV Tune In; 2012
Wall & Associates; Fairfax, VA Legal Services; 2009

ICON INTERNATIONAL INC.

107 Elm St 4 Stamford Plz, Stamford, CT 06902
Tel.: (203) 328-2300
Fax: (203) 328-2333
E-Mail: info@icon-intl.com
Web Site: www.icon-intl.com

E-Mail for Key Personnel:
President: jkramer@icon-intl.com

Employees: 200
Year Founded: 1986

Agency Specializes In: Advertising Specialties, Automotive, Broadcast, Cable T.V., Consumer Marketing, Consumer Publications, Digital/Interactive, Electronic Media, Financial, Media Buying Services, Merchandising, Newspapers & Magazines, Out-of-Home Media, Print, Radio, Real Estate, T.V., Travel & Tourism

John P. Kramer *(CEO)*
Clarence V. Lee *(CFO & Exec VP)*
Tom Bartholomew *(Exec VP & Dir-Media & Fulfillment)*
Dan Carroll *(Sr VP & Dir-Digital)*
Ed Gentner *(Sr VP & Dir-Brdcst-Natl)*
Reid Steinberg *(Sr VP & Dir-Media)*
Ken Miller *(VP & Grp Dir-Natl Broadcast)*
Joanne Cancro *(VP & Dir-Trade Dev)*

ICON MEDIA DIRECT

5910 Lemona Ave, Van Nuys, CA 91411
Tel.: (818) 995-6400
Fax: (818) 995-6405
E-Mail: nancyl@iconmediadirect.com
Web Site: www.iconmediadirect.com

Employees: 65
Year Founded: 2000

Agency Specializes In: Children's Market, Consumer Goods, Cosmetics, Direct Response Marketing, Electronic Media, Entertainment, Financial, Hispanic Market, Infomercials, Integrated Marketing, Magazines, Media Buying Services, Media Planning, Pharmaceutical, Planning & Consultation, Print, Sponsorship, T.V.

Breakdown of Gross Billings by Media: Print: 20%; T.V.: 80%

Nancy Lazkani *(Founder & CEO)*
Jefferey Bailes *(Exec VP-Client Svcs)*
Carrie Bernards *(VP-Fin)*
Cindy Borges *(Dir-Strategy & Plng)*
Daryll Aguinaldo *(Media Buyer)*
Benjamin Purcell *(Media Buyer-Long Form)*
Claudia Machuca *(Sr Media Buyer)*

Accounts:
Church & Dwight Co., Inc. Kaboom, Orange Glo Wood, Oxi Clean, Toss N GO Detergent; 2000
Guthy Renker; Santa Monica, CA Pro Activ; 2001
ITW; San Diego, CA Space Bag; 2000
Jarden Consumer Solutions
Ontel Products; NJ Deli Pro, Glass Wizard, Gopher, Shed Ender, Stick N Click, Swivel Sweeper; 2001

ID MEDIA

100 W 33rd St, New York, NY 10001
Tel.: (212) 907-7011
Fax: (212) 907-7290
E-Mail: cshaw@idmediaww.com
Web Site: www.idmediaww.com

E-Mail for Key Personnel:
Public Relations: eburns@idmediaww.com

Employees: 200
Year Founded: 2002

National Agency Associations: 4A's-AWNY-BPA-DMA

Agency Specializes In: Broadcast, Cable T.V., Digital/Interactive, Direct Response Marketing, Direct-to-Consumer, E-Commerce, Electronic Media, Electronics, Financial, Food Service, Health Care Services, Household Goods, Infomercials, Local Marketing, Media Buying Services, Media Planning, Mobile Marketing, New Technologies, Paid Searches, Search Engine Optimization, Sponsorship, T.V., Web (Banner Ads, Pop-ups, etc.)

Breakdown of Gross Billings by Media: Cable T.V.: 70%; D.M.: 10%; Internet Adv.: 10%; Mags.: 2%; Newsp. & Mags.: 2%; Other: 5%; Outdoor: 1%; Radio: 1%

Amy Armstrong *(Pres)*
Thor Peterson *(CFO & Exec VP)*
Michael Baliber *(Sr VP & Dir-Media Strategy)*
Danielle Dorter *(Sr VP & Dir-HR)*
Kirk Pratt *(Sr VP & Dir-Media Strategy)*
Morgan Rosin *(Sr VP & Dir-Mktg & New Bus Dev)*
Becky Burdick *(VP & Dir-Media Strategy)*
Felicia Thomas *(VP & Dir-Media Investment)*
Ben Chua *(VP-Digital Investment)*
Carla Edmunds *(Assoc Dir-Media-Strategy)*
Jessica Voci *(Assoc Dir-Media Strategy)*
Jordan Corvallis *(Sr Strategist-Media)*
Alex White *(Sr Strategist-Media)*
Zinmin Zhang *(Sr Strategist-Media)*
Tien Phan *(Strategist-Digital Media)*
Jocelyn Hahn *(Asst Strategist-Media)*
Dan Bier *(Media Buyer-Investment)*
Jenna Stanton *(Media Buyer-Investment)*
Lesley Carpenter *(Media Supvr-Investment)*
Izzy Manaloto *(Asst Media Buyer-Investment)*
Nicole Miqueli *(Asst Media Buyer-Investment)*

Accounts:
American Express
Bristol Myers Squibb
CA
Cayman Islands Department of Tourism
CME Group, Inc.
Intuit
Jamaica Tourism
Johnson & Johnson
Kaiser Permanente
Lindblad Expeditions Digital, Media, Multimedia Campaign, Print
LivingSocial Media Planning & Buying
Match.com
Meineke Car Care Centers Lead Agency (Print)
Merck
Microsoft
Nationwide
Neutrogena Corporation Deep Clean, Healthy Skin
Nikon Americas Inc.
Real Mex
Sandals & Beaches Resorts
SC Johnson
Universal Technical Institute
Verizon

Branches

ID Media-Los Angeles

8687 Melrose Ave 8th Fl, West Hollywood, CA 90069
Tel.: (310) 360-5700
Fax: (310) 360-5711
Web Site: www.idmediaww.com

Employees: 75

National Agency Associations: 4A's

Agency Specializes In: Media Buying Services, Sponsorship

Maggie Chin *(VP & Dir-Media Strategy)*
Lysa Stone *(Dir-Media Strategy)*
Dana Hamdan *(Assoc Dir-Media-Strategy)*

Aesha Ohelo *(Assoc Dir-Media-Strategy)*
Lisa Martin *(Acct Supvr)*
Christine Chen *(Supvr-Media Strategy)*
Stephanie Loud *(Sr Strategist-Media)*
Karen Acevedo *(Sr Planner-Digital Media)*
Marine Galstyan *(Strategist-Media)*
Sarah Loeb *(Strategist-Media)*
Alexander White *(Strategist-Media)*

Accounts:
New-Capital Brands (Media Agency of Record) Digital, Magic Bullet, NutriBlast Smoothie, NutriBullet
HBO
Microsoft
Verizon

ID Media-Chicago

633 N Saint Clair 18th Fl, Chicago, IL 60611
Tel.: (312) 799-6900
Fax: (312) 799-6950
E-Mail: mcomins@idmediaww.com
Web Site: www.idmediaww.com

Employees: 20

National Agency Associations: 4A's

Agency Specializes In: Media Buying Services, Sponsorship

Angie Given-Cook *(Mng Dir & Sr VP)*
Cindi Grant *(VP & Dir-Brdcst)*
Erica Corso *(Assoc Dir-Media & Strategy)*
Megan Majchrowicz *(Assoc Dir-Media Investment)*
Alycia Moller *(Assoc Dir-Media)*
Becky Tristano *(Supvr-Media Strategy)*
Jordan Corvallis *(Sr Strategist-Media)*
Adam Wylie *(Media Buyer-Investment)*

Accounts:
Cox Communications Acquisition Campaigns, Cox Business (Media Agency of Record), Digital Media, Multimedia Branding, Print, Television
Sandals & Beaches Resorts Online Media Buying/Planning; 2008

INITIATIVE

100 W 33rd St, New York, NY 10001
Tel.: (212) 605-7000
Fax: (917) 305-4003
Web Site: www.initiative.com

Year Founded: 1975

Agency Specializes In: Agriculture, Automotive, Broadcast, Consumer Goods, Cosmetics, Digital/Interactive, Direct-to-Consumer, Education, Electronic Media, Entertainment, Fashion/Apparel, Financial, Food Service, Government/Political, Hospitality, Household Goods, Media Buying Services, Media Planning, Mobile Marketing, Pharmaceutical, Restaurant, Retail, Sponsorship, T.V., Travel & Tourism

Leah Meranus *(Mng Partner-Bus Dev-Global)*
Kris Magel *(Chief Investment Officer)*
Cynthia Machata *(Exec VP & Mng Dir-Strategy)*
Steve Turner *(Sr VP & Grp Acct Dir)*
Tracy Kalfas *(Sr VP & Dir-Local Brdcst)*
John Mossawir *(Sr VP & Dir-Res)*
Jaclyn Goer *(VP & Dir-Natl Broadcast)*
Rachel Schlanger *(VP & Dir)*
Tracy-Ann Goodwin *(VP-Strategy-Global)*
Jeff Johnson *(VP-Client Svcs)*
Gracie McCrary *(Dir-Holiday Morale & Sr Specialist-Digital Media)*
Lisa Benadi *(Dir-TV Investment)*
Rima Chodha *(Dir-Search)*
Melissa Handley *(Dir-Client & Strategy)*
Jason Hehman *(Dir-Client & Digital Strategy)*
Natalie Kritzler *(Dir-Client-Strategy)*
Rachael Moin *(Dir-Strategy)*
Shayland Moise *(Dir-TV Investment)*
Jen Iarossi *(Assoc Dir-Investment & Supvr-Natl Brdcst)*
Roland Brenner *(Assoc Dir-Media Strategy)*
Anisha Vora *(Assoc Dir-Strategy)*
Bernice Bareng *(Supvr)*
Livan Grijalva *(Supvr-Bus Dev)*
Winsome Kirton *(Supvr-Digital Investment)*
Shannon Moffitt *(Supvr-Multicultural Strategy)*
Mariel Moscatello *(Supvr-Brdcst-Natl)*
Tiffany Pohle *(Supvr-Media Strategy)*
David Yuan *(Supvr-Social Media)*
Jamie Berkovitz *(Sr Strategist)*
Joshua Posner *(Sr Strategist-Media)*
Victoria Shaul *(Sr Strategist-Digital Investment)*
Ashley Bernot *(Sr Planner-Strategy)*
Daniel Blinn *(Specialist-Digital Investment)*
Lance Cvarak *(Strategist-Media)*
Christie Ewing *(Strategist-Media)*
Dana Howard *(Strategist)*
Aaron Nahas *(Specialist-Digital Investment)*
Chloe Shaouli *(Strategist)*
Mark Stephens *(Strategist-Digital)*
Lupita Tena *(Specialist-Digital Media)*
Alix Hoberman *(Media Planner-Digital)*
Andrew Rome *(Asst Buyer & Coord-Local Brdcst)*
Michael Knott *(Client Dir-Strategy)*
Raven Miller *(Assoc Strategist-Media)*
Andra Passen *(Sr Media Planner)*
Christy Walshe *(Assoc Strategist-Consumer)*

Accounts:
American Standard & Trane
Ameriprise Financial Media Buying, Media Planning
Arby Media
AT&T Communications Corp. Southern Region
Big Lots!; 2007
Blistex Inc Media
Boeing
CKE Restaurants; 1973
Computer Associates
Dr Pepper Snapple Group; 2008
Hitachi
Hyundai Motor America Campaign: "Mix Lab"; 2008
Merck Human Health, Media Planning & Buying; 1991
MillerCoors LLC Media Buying; 2002
Nikon
OSI Restaurant Partners Bonefish Grill
Papa John's International, Inc. Digital, Media Buying, Media Planning, Social
PetCo Media
Red Robin Gourmet Burgers Media Buying
S.C. Johnson; 2002

INITIATIVE WORLDWIDE

100 W 33rd St, New York, NY 10001
Tel.: (212) 605-7000
Fax: (212) 605-7200
Web Site: www.initiative.com

Employees: 3,500
Year Founded: 1975

National Agency Associations: 4A's

Agency Specializes In: Advertising, Consumer Marketing, Content, Digital/Interactive, Media Buying Services

Approx. Annual Billings: $13,500,000,000

Jim Elms *(CEO)*
Randy Bixler *(Mng Dir & Exec VP)*
Kris Magel *(Chief Investment Officer)*
Peter Mears *(CEO-North America)*
Sarah Ivey *(Exec VP & Dir-Comm Plng-Worldwide)*
Shannon Von Hassel *(Sr VP & Grp Acct Dir)*
Andy Von Kennel *(Sr VP & Acct Mgmt Dir)*
Carolyn Dubi *(Sr VP & Dir-Print)*
Phillip McDonnell *(Dir-Client-Strategy)*
Tanya Meyers *(Assoc Dir-Print Investment)*

Accounts:
Amazon Global Media
Ameriprise
Big Lots!
Bose Corporation Direct Response, Media
Burger King (Media Buying & Planning)
Burlington Coat Factory Media
Carl's Jr.
Computer Associates
Dr Pepper Snapple Group Americas Beverages; 2008
Food & Drug Administration Media Buying
Grupo Bimbo Media Strategy, Planning & Buying in China
Hitachi
Hooters Marketing
Hyundai Motor America; 2007
Ingersoll-Rand/Trane
Kia Motors America Media Buying; 2007
Korean Airlines
Merck
MillerCoors
Nikon
PETCO
Rabobank
Samsonite
SeaWorld Parks & Entertainment Media
Serta
Sony
Telekom Malaysia
Trulia Planning & Buying
Unilever Global Communication Planning, Household Care
USAA Financial Services
Viacom Europe
Vizio

Regional Offices

Initiative Atlanta

5909 Peachtree-Dunwoody Rd Ste 600, Atlanta, GA 30328
Tel.: (678) 441-7100
Fax: (678) 441-7263
Web Site: www.initiative.com

Year Founded: 1975

Agency Specializes In: Media Buying Services, Sponsorship

Alicia Cartisano *(Supvr-Local Investment)*
Brenda Labbee *(Supvr-Investment)*
Brigida Savine *(Sr Specialist-Local Investment)*
Mandy Bubel *(Sr Buyer-Brdcst)*
Lindsey Fast *(Strategist-Media)*
Jaimie Goss *(Asst Media Buyer & Coord)*
Hillary Patton *(Coord-Client)*

Accounts:
AT&T Communications Corp.
Best Western
Brasil
Hertz
Iberia
Microsoft

Initiative Los Angeles

5700 Wilshire Blvd Ste 400, Los Angeles, CA 90036-3648
Tel.: (323) 370-8000
Fax: (323) 370-8950
Web Site: www.initiative.com

Employees: 250
Year Founded: 1975

National Agency Associations: 4A's

Agency Specializes In: Media Buying Services, Sponsorship

Wendy Aldrich *(Mng Partner-Global & Exec VP)*
Jennifer Nyhan *(Mng Dir & Grp Head-Bus)*
Anne Marie Yanez *(Mng Dir & Head-Bus)*
Sue Johenning *(Exec VP & Grp Dir-Local Brdcst)*
Greg Johns *(Sr VP & Sr Dir-Digital Strategy)*
Tom Williams *(Sr VP & Grp Acct Dir)*
Caleb Wines *(Sr VP & Grp Acct Dir-Plng)*
Elvin Kawasaki *(VP & Acct Dir-Digital Grp)*
Charles Kim *(VP & Dir)*
Christiana Messina *(VP & Dir-Strategy)*
Caroline Wilson *(Sr Dir-Branded Content Strategy)*
Kat Chung *(Dir-Digital Strategy)*
Robert Han *(Dir-Client-Strategy)*
Collin Middleton *(Dir-Digital Strategy)*
Madhavi Tadikonda *(Dir-Client-Investment)*
Scott Cooper *(Assoc Dir-Media Strategy)*
Erin Dahl *(Assoc Dir)*
Ali Dusenbery *(Assoc Dir-Digital Investment)*
Brad May *(Assoc Dir-Branded Content)*
Ben Uy *(Assoc Dir-Analytics)*
Gavin Carr *(Supvr-Strategy)*
Whitney Champion *(Supvr-Strategy)*
Kirsten Cole *(Supvr-TV Investment)*
Alison Cutting *(Supvr-Strategy)*
Victor Faria *(Supvr-Digital)*
Jan Gonzales *(Supvr-Digital Investment)*
Stephanie Kim *(Supvr-Strategy)*
Anthony Oliveira *(Supvr-Strategy)*
David Pinto-Carpenter *(Supvr-Brand Strategy)*
Kelly Wetmore *(Supvr-Strategy)*
Tim Chough *(Specialist-Digital Investment & Media Planner)*
Christian Aguillon *(Strategist-Media-Strategy & Brand)*
John Cheek *(Strategist-Consumer)*
Roy Cho *(Specialist-Digital Investment)*
Terrence Glover *(Specialist-Digital Investment)*
Marc Jones *(Acct Exec)*
Filisha Kapadia *(Strategist-Media)*
Cory Massiet *(Specialist-Digital Investment)*
Matt Penner *(Strategist-Hyundai Brand)*
Albert Rios *(Specialist-Digital-Investment)*
Eugene Yi *(Media Planner-Digital)*
Trisha Atkinson *(Acct Media Dir)*
Eric Fader *(Client Dir-Analytics)*

Accounts:
Ameriprise
Best Western International, Inc.; Phoenix, AZ
California Lottery Media Assignment
Carl's Jr.
CBS
Dr. Pepper Snapple Group
Go Daddy Inc. Analytics, Brand Media Strategy, Media Buying Agency of Record, Video
Hardee's
HBO
Hyundai Motor America
Kaiser Permanente
Kia Motors America Inc.
LucasArts
Merck
Roadside Attractions Digital Marketing, Media
Sonos Digital Marketing, Media Planning & Buying

Initiative
100 W 33rd St, New York, NY 10001
(See Separate Listing)

Satellite Offices

Initiative Miami
4500 Biscayne Blvd, Miami, FL 33137
Tel.: (305) 572-2150
Web Site: www.initiative.com

Employees: 10

Agency Specializes In: Media Buying Services

Andrea Suarez *(Pres-World Markets-IPG Mediabrands)*

Accounts:
Lions Gate
Paramount
Rabo Bank

Initiative Philadelphia
200 S Broad St 10th Fl, Philadelphia, PA 19102
Tel.: (215) 790-4200
Fax: (215) 790-4373
Web Site: www.initiative.com

Agency Specializes In: Media Buying Services

Pamela Davis *(Sr Media Buyer)*

Initiative Toronto
10 Bay St Ste 1605, Toronto, ON M5J 2R8 Canada
Tel.: (416) 933-5800
Fax: (416) 933-5864
Web Site: www.initiative.com

Employees: 45
Year Founded: 1988

Agency Specializes In: Media Buying Services

Adam Luck *(Pres-Canada)*
Sarah Ivey *(Exec VP & Dir-Comm Plng-Worldwide)*
Madeleine Dube *(Media Planner)*
Nicole Pinelli *(Media Planner)*

Accounts:
Hotwire, Inc. Digital Buying, Media Planning
Hyundai Auto Canada

Other Initiative Companies

Media Partnership Corporation
800 Connecticut Ave 3rd Fl N Wing, Norwalk, CT 06854
(See Separate Listing)

Newspaper Services of America, Inc.
3025 Highland Pkwy Ste 700, Downers Grove, IL 60515-5506
Tel.: (630) 729-7500
Fax: (630) 241-7223
Web Site: www.nsamedia.com

Employees: 350
Year Founded: 1991

Agency Specializes In: Media Buying Services, Newspaper

Shannon Wagner *(Pres-SPM)*
Cathy Petritz *(VP & Acct Dir)*
Kerry Smith *(VP & Acct Dir)*
Katie Kiss *(VP & Dir-Acct Svcs)*
Karin Kasper *(VP-Activation Svcs)*
Randy Novak *(VP-Bus Dev)*
Susan Saarnio *(VP & Dir HR)*
Beth Zeitner *(VP-Media Plng & Analysis)*
Allison Patz *(Dir-Digital Strategy)*
Janie Hartwig-Smith *(Sr Media Buyer)*
Shelley Zurek *(Sr Media Buyer)*

Accounts:
American Electric & Power
BMW of North America
Coldwell Banker
Gander Mountain
Golfsmith International Holdings, Inc.
The Home Depot Expo Design Center, Villager's Hardware
Kmart Big K, Super Kmart
National City Bank
Office Depot North American Print
Qwest
Safeway Inc.
Sears Roebuck & Co. Dealer Stores, Full Line Stores, Hardware Stores, Home Services, Outlet Stores, The Great Indoors
The Sports Authority
Target
Toys 'R' Us
United States Navy
United States Postal Service

Wahlstrom Group
800 Connecticut Ave, Norwalk, CT 06854
(See Separate Listing)

Latin America

Initiative Buenos Aires
Leandro N Alem 1110 4th Fl, Buenos Aires, 1119 Argentina
Tel.: (54) 114 318 6500
Fax: (54) 114 318 6532
Web Site: www.initiative.com

E-Mail for Key Personnel:
President: fernando.colombres@ar.initiative.com

Employees: 70
Year Founded: 1998

Agency Specializes In: Media Buying Services

Matias Artigue *(Mgr-Media)*
Gustavo Cosentino *(Mgr-Media)*
Daniel Irueta *(Sr Planner-Integrator Digital)*
Natalia Ratto *(Planner)*
Florencia Cossoy *(Jr Planner)*
Lucia Yanes *(Jr Planner)*

Accounts:
Akzo Nobel
Alpargatas SA
Bayer
BMW
CCU
CIE
Daihatsu
Honda
KIA
Kimberly Clark
Omint
Smash BTL
Sony
Unilever
United Continental Holdings

Initiative Caracas
Av Principal de La Castelina, Edf Multinvest Piso 4, Caracas, 1060 Venezuela
Tel.: (58) 212 816 6996
Fax: (58) 212 263 2785
E-Mail: carmen.gonzalez@draftfcb.com
Web Site: www.initiative.com

Employees: 20
Year Founded: 1998

Agency Specializes In: Media Buying Services

Carmen Maria Diaz *(VP-Media)*

Initiative Budapest
Vajdahhunyad U. 33-43, H-11082 Budapest, Hungary
Tel.: (36) 802 5100
Fax: (36) 8025101
E-Mail: bela.nemeth@hu.initiative.com

Media Buying Services

Year Founded: 1996

Agency Specializes In: Media Buying Services

Bela Nemeth *(Mng Dir-Initiative Budapest & Reg Dir-Central & Eastern Europe)*

Initiative Hamburg

Schloss-Strasse 8e, Hamburg, 22041 Germany
Tel.: (49) 40 431 96 0
Fax: (49) 40 431 96 720
Web Site: www.initiative.com

Employees: 13
Year Founded: 1996

Agency Specializes In: Media Buying Services

Dirk Schroeder *(CFO)*
Mathias Glatter *(COO)*
Christa Pfennigschmidt *(Dir-HR)*
Lisa Marie Kaven *(Acct Mgr-Media)*
Maike Becker *(Planner-Digital Media)*

Accounts:
Pandora Campaign: "The Perfect Placement"
Reckitt Benckiser Veet
Unilever Campaign: "Wow-Like"
United Continental Holdings
Vattenfall Campaign: "The Spirit of Winter Sports"

Initiative London

42 St Johns Sq, London, EC1M4EA United Kingdom
Tel.: (44) 20 7663 7000
Fax: (44) 20 7663 7002
E-Mail: claire.gardner@uk.initiative.com
Web Site: initiative.com

Year Founded: 1990

Agency Specializes In: Media Buying Services

Gary Birtles *(Mng Partner)*
Sally Weavers *(Mng Dir)*
Ben Walton *(Head-Digital)*
Deborah Mackay *(Sr Acct Dir)*
Sarah De Martin *(Grp Acct Dir-Intl)*
Simon Smith *(Acct Dir)*
Rick Coombs *(Dir-Digital Acct)*
Tania Harwood *(Dir-Bus)*
Meliz Kannur *(Sr Acct Exec-Intl)*
Jack Winter *(Sr Acct Exec)*
Rhian Withers *(Sr Acct Exec)*

Accounts:
ACE Aviation Holdings Inc.
Amazon
Austrian National Tourist Office
Body Shop
Chantelle
Computer Associates
Four Seasons Hotels
Intersnack
Omega Pharma Media
Ricoh
Rugby Football Union
SAAB
Timberland
Unipath Ltd.

Initiative Moscow

Office 407-408 Bldg 1, 18 Malaya Pirogovskaya str, Moscow, 119435 Russia
Tel.: (7) 095 77 53 602
Fax: (7) 095 77 53 603
E-Mail: info@initiativemedia.ru
Web Site: www.initiativemedia.ru

Employees: 25
Year Founded: 1995

Agency Specializes In: Media Buying Services

Egor Bormusov *(Grp Head-Media)*
Kseniya Bormusova *(Grp Head-Media)*
Bednyakov Petr *(Head-Digital Dept)*
Elmira Sabitova *(Dir-Media)*
Artyom Khokhlov *(Media Planner)*
Daria Makeshina *(Media Planner)*
Yana Krasavina *(Sr Media Planner)*

Accounts:
Unilever

Initiative Prague

Palac Karlin Thamova 11, Prague, 8 Czech Republic
Tel.: (420) 225 341 160
Fax: (420) 225 341 180
Web Site: initiative.com

Year Founded: 2000

Agency Specializes In: Media Buying Services

Petr Cech *(Sr Mgr-Media)*
Mariana Theiszova *(Specialist-Digital Media)*
Iva Mickova *(Media Buyer-OOH)*
Vit Zubek *(Sr Media Planner)*

Initiative Universal Media Norway

(Formerly Initiative Universal Oslo)
Sandakerveien 24C, Bygning C1, 0473 Oslo, Norway
Mailing Address:
Postboks 4229, Nydalen, 0401 Oslo, Norway
Tel.: (47) 22 54 38 80
Fax: (47) 22 54 38 81
E-Mail: braathen@iumas.no
Web Site: www.ium.no

Employees: 30
Year Founded: 1996

Agency Specializes In: Media Buying Services

Borre Sunde *(CEO & Mng Dir)*

Initiative Universal Stockholm

Grevturegatan 11A, SE-114 97 Stockholm, Sweden
Tel.: (46) 8 5630 1400
Fax: (46) 8 5630 1490
Web Site: www.ium.se

Employees: 47
Year Founded: 1987

Agency Specializes In: Media Buying Services

Matts Westerblom *(CFO)*
Jochum Forsell *(COO)*
Jonas Malm *(Head-Brdcst)*
Maria Gustafsson *(Acct Dir)*
Christian Hess *(Acct Dir)*
Birgitta Von Heijne *(Acct Dir)*
Maria Carlsson *(Dir-Analysis & Insight)*
Cecilia Jonson *(Dir-Digital)*
Peter Cederholm *(Specialist-Online Video & Brdcst)*

Accounts:
Burger King
ICA
Statoil
Vattenfall Media

Initiative Universal Warsaw

6 Altowa St, 02-386 Warsaw, Poland
Tel.: (48) 22 572 33 00
Fax: (48) 22 572 33 01
E-Mail: dariusz.dulnik@pl.initiative.com
Web Site: initiative.com

Employees: 50
Year Founded: 1998

Agency Specializes In: Media Buying Services

Michal Strzalkowski *(Acct Dir)*
Monika Dukaczewska *(Dir-Digital)*
Pawel Orkwiszewski *(Dir-Plng)*
Aleksandra Osinska *(Mgr-Traffic)*
Justyna Trzaska *(Mgr-Digital Media)*
Magda Borys *(Media Planner & Media Buyer)*
Robert Franckowski *(Coord-Online Plng)*
Katarzyna Glowacka *(Sr Media Planner & Buyer)*
Katarzyna Smarczewska *(Sr Media Planner)*
Malgorzata Zaorska *(Sr Media Planner)*

Initiative Vienna

Operngasse 21/9, A-1040 Vienna, Austria
Tel.: (43) 1 588 96 0
Fax: (43) 1 588 96 200
E-Mail: vienna.reception@at.initiative.at
Web Site: initiative.com

Employees: 90
Year Founded: 1987

Agency Specializes In: Media Buying Services

Sascha Berndl *(Dir-Media)*
Romana Gungl *(Client Svc Dir & Strategist-Digital)*

Accounts:
BMW Digital
Patek Philippe
Red Bull
UPC Telekabel
Velux

Initiative

Atlas ArenA Amsterdam Asia Building, Hoogoorddreef 5, 1101 BA Amsterdam, Netherlands
Tel.: (31) 20 799 3000
Fax: (31) 20 799 3099
E-Mail: leonie.kining@nl.initiative.com

Employees: 60
Year Founded: 1987

Agency Specializes In: Media Buying Services, Sponsorship

Leonie Koning *(Mng Dir)*
Irene Duivestein *(Head-Digital)*
Menno Van Der Steen *(Head-Media Brands Mktg Sciences)*
Dennis Huijsman *(Dir-Comm)*
Linda Van Dijk *(Dir-Comm)*
Bart Vijlbrief *(Dir-Strategy)*
Esther Van Hemert *(Sr Acct Mgr)*
Iris Van Den Berg *(Acct Mgr)*
Dean Koekebakker *(Planner-Multimedia)*
Dick Heerkens *(Jr Planner-Digital)*
Diana Vaarkamp *(Sr Media Planner)*

Middle East & Africa

Initiative Beirut

Badaro Trade Center Suite 801 Sami El Solh Avenue, PO Box 16-6070, Beirut, Lebanon
Tel.: (961) 1 39 39 50
Fax: (961) 1 38 31 19
E-Mail: philip.issa@lb.initiative.com
Web Site: www.initiative.com

Employees: 5
Year Founded: 2003

National Agency Associations: 4A's

Agency Specializes In: Media Buying Services

Philip Issa *(Mng Dir)*
Rana Chaaya *(Mgr-Media)*

Accounts:
Brasil
ca
Fujitsu Siemens

Initiative Dubai

Office 214-215 Bldg No 4, PO Box 502149, Dubai Media City, Dubai, United Arab Emirates
Tel.: (971) 4 3903001
Fax: (971) 4 3904858
E-Mail: info@ae.initi
Web Site: www.initiative.com

Employees: 30
Year Founded: 2003

Agency Specializes In: Media Buying Services

Mona Osman *(Mng Dir)*
Mazher Abidi *(Head-Social Media-Middle East)*
Raffoul Mattar *(Gen Mgr-Abu Dhabi)*
Spencer Moody *(Reg Dir-Strategy-MENA)*
Seema Radhakrishnan *(Reg Dir-Plng)*
Abdallah Zeid Safieddine *(Acct Dir)*
Mahdi Jaber *(Dir-Media-Acct Leadership)*
Ali Berjawi *(Assoc Dir)*
Alistair Burton *(Assoc Dir-Digital)*
Racha Semaan *(Supvr-Media)*
Mohammed Wehbi *(Supvr-Digital Media)*
Ramzy Abouchacra *(Reg Mng Dir-GCC)*

Accounts:
Americana
Etisalat Media Buying, Media Services, Strategic Planning
Johnson & Johnson Media

Initiative South Africa

PO Box 67716, 2021 Bryanston, South Africa
Tel.: (27) 11 78 06 117
Fax: (27) 11 70 61 066
E-Mail: marc.taback@sa.initiativemedia.com
Web Site: www.initiative.com

Employees: 40
Year Founded: 2002

Agency Specializes In: Media Buying Services

Marc Taback *(CEO)*
Elsa Carpenter Frank *(Mng Partner)*
Hilary Lindsay *(Mng Partner)*
Cindy Beyer *(Planner-Implementation)*

Accounts:
Adcock Ingram OTC
SouthAfrican Breweries

Initiative Melbourne

Level 2 468 St Kilda Road, Melbourne, VIC 3004 Australia
Tel.: (61) 3 8888 2900
Fax: (61) 3 9445 2130
E-Mail: info@au.initiative.com
Web Site: initiative.com/locations/australia-melbourne

Employees: 19
Year Founded: 1975

Agency Specializes In: Media Buying Services

Andrew Mudgway *(Mng Dir-Melbourne)*
Stephen Fisher *(Gen Mgr)*
David Lee *(Dir-Digital Strategy)*
Melissa Mullins *(Dir-Strategy-Natl)*
Emily Capsis *(Media Buyer)*
Elecia Lay *(Media Buyer)*
Marli Tapsall *(Media Buyer)*
Eleanor Batchelor *(Coord-Media)*
Tom Newton *(Coord-Media)*
Samantha Zagin *(Coord-Media)*

Accounts:
CPA Australia Digital, Media strategy, Planning & Buying, SEM, Traditional Media
Madmen Entertainment Media Buying, Media Communications, Media Planning, Media Strategy
Manheim Automotive Auctions Online, Outdoor, Print Media, Radio
ME Bank Media
Officeworks Media
Swinburne Online Media
Swinburne University Media
Tourism Tasmania Media

Initiative Sydney

LEVEL 3, 100 CHALMERS STREET, Surry Hills, NSW 2010 Australia
Tel.: (61) 2 8586 2000
Fax: (61) 2 8586 2984
E-Mail: Andrew.Livingston@au.initiative.com
Web Site: www.initiative.com

Year Founded: 1975

Agency Specializes In: Media Buying Services

Lee Leggett *(CEO)*
Joe Perkins *(Dir-Digital Client)*
Julie Schougaard *(Dir-Client)*

Accounts:
The Athlete's Foot Media Strategy, Planning & Buying
The Iconic Retail

INLINE MEDIA, INC.

1600 Stout St Ste 700, Denver, CO 80202-3160
Tel.: (303) 893-4040
Fax: (303) 893-6718
E-Mail: markh@inlinemedia.com
Web Site: www.inlinemedia.com

Employees: 12
Year Founded: 1994

National Agency Associations: AAF

Agency Specializes In: Advertising, Advertising Specialties, Broadcast, Co-op Advertising, Media Buying Services, Newspapers & Magazines, Out-of-Home Media, Outdoor, Planning & Consultation, Print, Radio, Strategic Planning/Research, T.V., Trade & Consumer Magazines

Approx. Annual Billings: $20,000,000

Nancy Haven *(Mng Partner)*
Susan Penta *(Acct Dir)*
Ilene Nathanson *(Dir-Media)*
Deborah Platt *(Assoc Dir-Media)*
Victoria Lindsay *(Mgr-Direct Response Media)*
Mike Stoumbaugh *(Specialist-IT)*
Joella Monroe *(Media Planner & Media Buyer)*

Accounts:
Adventure Golf & Raceway
Cochlear America
Colorado Quitline
Craftwerks
Goodwill
K-12
Mile High Flea Market
Papa Murphy's
Viasat
Water World
Wendy's

INTEGRAL AD SCIENCE

37 E 18th St FL 7, New York, NY 10003
Tel.: (646) 278-4871
E-Mail: info@integralads.com
Web Site: integralads.com

Year Founded: 2009

Agency Specializes In: Advertising, Brand Development & Integration, Content, Media Planning, Strategic Planning/Research

Scott Knoll *(CEO)*
Bryan St. John *(Sr VP-Intl)*
Kiril Tsemekhman *(Sr VP)*
Harmon Lyons *(VP-Bus Dev)*
Ian Wallin *(VP-Sls)*
Kevin Lenane *(Gen Mgr-Video)*
Cori Plotnick *(Sr Dir-Platform Solutions)*
Joseph Quaglia *(Sr Dir-Bus Dev)*
Dave Marquard *(Dir-Product Mgmt)*

Accounts:
AudienceScience Internet Software & Services

INTEGRAL MEDIA INC.

350 Hwy 7 #140, Excelsior, MN 55331-3160
Tel.: (952) 470-5254
Fax: (952) 546-0849
E-Mail: eric@integralprintmedia.com
Web Site: www.integralprintmedia.com

Employees: 7
Year Founded: 1989

Agency Specializes In: Advertising, Advertising Specialties, Affluent Market, Catalogs, Children's Market, College, Consumer Goods, Consumer Marketing, Consumer Publications, Direct Response Marketing, Direct-to-Consumer, High Technology, Household Goods, Identity Marketing, Magazines, Media Buying Services, Media Planning, Pharmaceutical, Planning & Consultation, Print, Seniors' Market, Teen Market, Trade & Consumer Magazines, Women's Market

Approx. Annual Billings: $14,000,000

Breakdown of Gross Billings by Media: Consumer Publs.: 100%

Eric Sims *(Founder-Integral Media)*
Kayla Byrd *(Acct Mgr & Media Buyer)*

Accounts:
First Street

INTER/MEDIA ADVERTISING

22120 Clarendon St, Woodland Hills, CA 91367
Tel.: (818) 995-1455
Fax: (818) 995-7115
Toll Free: (800) 846-3289
E-Mail: ryallen@intermedia-advertising.com
Web Site: www.intermedia-advertising.com

Employees: 75
Year Founded: 1974

Agency Specializes In: Advertising, Brand Development & Integration, Consumer Goods, Consumer Marketing, Cosmetics, Direct Response Marketing, Direct-to-Consumer, Education, Financial, Health Care Services, Household Goods, Infomercials, Internet/Web Design, Legal Services, Local Marketing, Market Research,

Media Buying Services, Media Planning, Merchandising, New Product Development, Pharmaceutical, Point of Purchase, Production, Publicity/Promotions, Radio, Retail, Sales Promotion, Search Engine Optimization, Strategic Planning/Research, Syndication, T.V., Telemarketing, Web (Banner Ads, Pop-ups, etc.)

Approx. Annual Billings: $400,000,000

Breakdown of Gross Billings by Media: Cable T.V.: 50%; D.M.: 1%; Internet Adv.: 8%; Network Radio: 7%; Network T.V.: 7%; Print: 2%; Spot Radio: 10%; Spot T.V.: 10%; Strategic Planning/Research: 5%

Robert B. Yallen *(Pres & CEO)*
Lucy St. George *(Exec VP-Client Svc)*
Richard Pike *(Sr VP)*
Kevin Szymanski *(Sr VP)*
Oscar Bassinson *(Dir-Creative)*
Adam Seigel *(Dir-Mktg)*
Laura Harp *(Sr Media Buyer & Supvr)*
Tricia Lynch *(Planner-Digital Media)*
Geri Taylor *(Media Buyer)*

Accounts:
1-800-NO-CUFFS "Your Get Out of Jail Card", Radio, TV
1928 Jewelry
Axial Rx (Agency of Record) Creative, Media Buying, Media Planning
Brita
Budget Blinds
Cal Direct
Chicago Tribune
Clorox
Corinthian Colleges
Dish Network
Ditech
GMAC Insurance
Marinello Schools of Beauty
Public Storage
New-Rosland Capital
The Storage Barn
Time Life
Truecredit
United States Army

THE INTERCONNECT GROUP
4470 Chamblee Dunwoody Rd Ste 324, Atlanta, GA 30338
Tel.: (678) 990-0919
Fax: (678) 990-0921
E-Mail: joe@addate.com
Web Site: www.addate.com

E-Mail for Key Personnel:
President: narayan@ticg-usa.com

Employees: 8
Year Founded: 2001

Agency Specializes In: Advertising, Advertising Specialties, Asian Market, Aviation & Aerospace, Broadcast, Cable T.V., Consumer Marketing, Digital/Interactive, E-Commerce, Entertainment, Financial, Health Care Services, High Technology, Infomercials, Information Technology, Media Buying Services, Medical Products, Planning & Consultation, Recruitment, Sports Market, Syndication, T.V., Teen Market, Telemarketing, Transportation, Travel & Tourism

Narayan Swamy *(CEO)*

Accounts:
Georgia Highway Safety

INTERNATIONAL MEDIA PARTNERS, INC.
103 118th Ave SE Ste 100, Bellevue, WA 98005-3753
Tel.: (425) 455-5900
Fax: (425) 454-1092
E-Mail: contactimp@intlmediapartners.com
Web Site: www.intlmediapartners.com

E-Mail for Key Personnel:
President: gbryson@intlmediapartners.com

Employees: 10
Year Founded: 1985

Agency Specializes In: Direct Response Marketing, Media Buying Services, Media Planning, Planning & Consultation

Gordon D. Bryson *(Pres)*
Betsy J. Moseley *(Exec VP)*
Shirley Eclipse *(Client Svcs Dir)*

Accounts:
Lifewise of Oregon

INTERNETWEBBUILDERS.COM
6520 Lonetree Blvd, Rocklin, CA 95765-5874
Tel.: (417) 278-6737
E-Mail: sales@internetwebbuilders.com
Web Site: www.internetwebbuilders.com

Employees: 10
Year Founded: 1999

Agency Specializes In: Advertising, Advertising Specialties, Affiliate Marketing, Alternative Advertising, Broadcast, Business Publications, Business-To-Business, Computers & Software, Direct Response Marketing, Direct-to-Consumer, E-Commerce, Electronic Media, Email, Exhibit/Trade Shows, Guerilla Marketing, High Technology, Infomercials, Information Technology, Internet/Web Design, Logo & Package Design, Market Research, Media Buying Services, Media Planning, Mobile Marketing, Multimedia, New Product Development, New Technologies, Podcasting, Production (Ad, Film, Broadcast), Promotions, Publicity/Promotions, Publishing, Radio, Search Engine Optimization, Trade & Consumer Magazines, Viral/Buzz/Word of Mouth, Web (Banner Ads, Pop-ups, etc.)

Approx. Annual Billings: $150,000

Kurt Willmon *(Owner)*

Accounts:
MasterCard
Visa

INTERSECT MEDIA SOLUTIONS
766 N Sun Dr Ste 2000, Lake Mary, FL 32746-2553
Tel.: (866) 404-5913
Fax: (850) 577-3646
E-Mail: info@intersectmediasolutions.com
Web Site: www.intersectmediasolutions.com

Employees: 30
Year Founded: 1959

Agency Specializes In: Advertising, Media Buying Services, Newspaper

Approx. Annual Billings: $51,000,000

Breakdown of Gross Billings by Media: Newsp.: 100%

Dean Ridings *(Pres & CEO)*
Melanie Mathewson *(VP-Sls)*
Jessica Pitts *(Mgr-Media)*
Sheila Ellison *(Specialist-Mktg)*
Kathy Tracy *(Specialist-Media)*
Robyn Robison *(Clients Svcs Mgr)*

Accounts:
AARP
Communication Workers of America
Florida Division of Forestry
Gatorland
Homegoods
Publix Supermarkets
Sierra Club
TJX Companies Inc. Marshalls, TJ Maxx

IPROSPECT
(Formerly Range Online Media)
1021 Foch St, Fort Worth, TX 76107
Tel.: (817) 625-4157
Fax: (817) 625-4167
Web Site: www.iprospect.com

Employees: 135

National Agency Associations: 4A's-IAB

Agency Specializes In: Brand Development & Integration, Internet/Web Design, Media Buying Services, Sales Promotion, Sponsorship

Revenue: $8,000,000

Misty Locke *(CMO-Global)*
Sam Huston *(Chief Strategy Officer)*
Kim Sivillo *(Sr VP & Mng Dir-East)*
Parks Blackwell *(VP-New Bus & Mktg)*
Nathan Ice *(VP-Tech)*
Jordan McManama *(Head-Acct)*
Ellen Fokas *(Sr Acct Dir)*
Joshua Bledsoe *(Reg Dir-Performance & Search)*
Danielle Smith *(Grp Acct Dir)*
Jeremy Hull *(Dir-Bought Media)*
Sarah Strauss *(Dir-Mktg)*
Brittany Richter *(Assoc Dir-Paid Social)*
Aaron Mullens *(Acct Supvr)*

Accounts:
Accor Hotels
Bass Pro Shops
Bergdorf Goodman Web Site
COMPUSA Search Engine Marketing
Converse
Darphin
Godiva Chocolatier; 2008
Johnston & Murphy
Journey's
Kaspersky Lab
L'Occitane; Provence, France Search Campaign; 2007
Macys.Com
Michael Kors
Motel 6
Neiman Marcus Web Site
NRG Energy, Inc.
Samsung
Timberland
Toshiba Search Engine Marketing
TSIC, Inc.
Wyndham Worldwide Corporation Search Engine Marketing

JL MEDIA, INC.
1600 Rte 22 E, Union, NJ 07083-3415
Tel.: (908) 302-1285
Fax: (908) 687-9280
E-Mail: jlevy@jlmedia.com
Web Site: www.jlmedia.com

Employees: 60
Year Founded: 1981

Agency Specializes In: Media Buying Services, Sponsorship

Approx. Annual Billings: $560,000,000

Glenn Dennis *(Mng Dir)*

Laurel Welch *(Exec VP & Dir-Media)*
Susan Ringel *(VP-Client Svcs)*
Paula Brooks *(Client Svcs Dir)*
Marc Gross *(Acct Svcs Dir)*
Alexandra Hinz *(Dir-Digital Media)*
Rich Russo *(Dir)*
Meryl Young *(Dir-Ops)*
Jon Katz *(Assoc Dir-Media-Direct Response)*
Katrina Marshall *(Assoc Dir-Digital)*
David Bahniuk *(Acct Mgr)*
William Ryden *(Media Buyer-Broadcast)*
Maureen Whyte *(Media Buyer)*

Accounts:
DeLonghi
Home Depot
JC Penney
JSSI Lugz Footwear
Macy's
NORA
Office Depot
Ricola, USA
Stacker 2
STS Tire
Subaru Distributors Corp.
TOPPS
uPromise

Branch

JL Media, Inc.
1400 NW 107th Ave Ste 306, Miami, FL 33172
Tel.: (305) 591-0242
Fax: (305) 591-9819
Web Site: www.jlmedia.com

Agency Specializes In: Media Buying Services

Laurel Welch *(Exec VP & Dir-Media)*
Chris Robbie *(Exec VP)*
Karin Suttmann *(Exec Dir)*

Accounts:
International House of Pancakes
JCPenney
JSSI Lugz Footwear
Macy's
The Mall at Millenia
Ricola
The Sun Sentinel

JSML MEDIA, LLC
11200 86th Ave N, Minneapolis, MN 55369
Tel.: (763) 657-2263
Fax: (763) 657-2261
Toll Free: (800) 657-3100
E-Mail: jsakin@jsml.com
Web Site: www.jsml.com

Employees: 5
Year Founded: 2006

Agency Specializes In: Brand Development & Integration, Broadcast, Business Publications, Business-To-Business, Cable T.V., Co-op Advertising, Consulting, Consumer Marketing, Consumer Publications, Corporate Communications, Digital/Interactive, Entertainment, Financial, Food Service, Health Care Services, Household Goods, Investor Relations, Luxury Products, Media Buying Services, Media Planning, Men's Market, Newspapers & Magazines, Out-of-Home Media, Outdoor, Print, Radio, Regional, Retail, Social Media, Strategic Planning/Research, Syndication, T.V., Trade & Consumer Magazines

Approx. Annual Billings: $20,000,000

Michelle Leatherman *(Partner & Exec VP)*
Jill Sakin *(Pres-JSML Media)*
Tim Olsen *(Assoc Dir-Media)*

Accounts:
Boston Scientific Corporation; Boston, MA; Minneapolis, MN
Cummins Power Generation
Nonin Medical
Ultimate Fighting Championship; Las Vegas, NV
Von Maur

JUST MEDIA, INC.
6475 Christie Ave Ste 100, Emeryville, CA 94608-1056
Tel.: (510) 740-2300
Fax: (510) 740-2301
Web Site: www.justmedia.com

Employees: 13
Year Founded: 1997

Agency Specializes In: High Technology, Media Buying Services, Planning & Consultation, Sponsorship

Approx. Annual Billings: $30,000,000

Breakdown of Gross Billings by Media: Bus. Publs.: 40%; Internet Adv.: 45%; Newsp.: 5%; Outdoor: 5%; Radio: 5%

Brandon Friesen *(Pres)*
Dick Reed *(CEO)*
Sabrina Galati *(Sr VP & Grp Dir-Media)*
Deborah Lauzardo *(Sr VP-Fin & Ops)*
Patrick Fenton *(Dir-Media)*
Katie Hauff *(Assoc Dir-Media)*
Cindy Nguy *(Assoc Dir-Media & Sr Media Mgr)*
Dale Viger *(Acct Mgr-Media)*

Accounts:
Fujitsu
Motorola Solutions, Inc.

KELLY SCOTT MADISON
303 E Wacker Dr 8th Fl, Chicago, IL 60601
Tel.: (312) 977-0772
Fax: (312) 977-0874
E-Mail: info@ksmmedia.com
Web Site: www.ksmmedia.com

E-Mail for Key Personnel:
President: jwilliams@ksmmedia.com

Employees: 150
Year Founded: 1966

National Agency Associations: 4A's

Agency Specializes In: Advertising, African-American Market, Broadcast, Business Publications, Business-To-Business, Cable T.V., Co-op Advertising, Consulting, Consumer Publications, Digital/Interactive, Direct Response Marketing, Electronic Media, Event Planning & Marketing, Financial, Gay & Lesbian Market, Government/Political, Guerilla Marketing, Health Care Services, Hispanic Market, Local Marketing, Magazines, Market Research, Media Buying Services, Media Planning, Medical Products, Multicultural, New Product Development, Newspaper, Newspapers & Magazines, Out-of-Home Media, Outdoor, Over-50 Market, Pharmaceutical, Planning & Consultation, Print, Product Placement, Promotions, Publicity/Promotions, Radio, Real Estate, Restaurant, Retail, Seniors' Market, Social Media, Sponsorship, Sports Market, Strategic Planning/Research, T.V., Teen Market, Trade & Consumer Magazines, Transportation, Travel & Tourism, Web (Banner Ads, Pop-ups, etc.)

Kelly Scott Madison is a leading independent media agency that delivers results through original media solutions. As one of the original architects of the media industry, our media specialists have the diverse experience, powerful buying alliances and unconventional intuition necessary to address the most ambitious multi-platform marketing objectives. Additionally, we stay attuned to the latest industry trends, eager to provide clients with the next business-transforming insight. From experienced professionals to fresh minds, everyone at KSM shares the distinct desire to deliver innovative solutions that go beyond the expected. To find out how KSM helps solve the toughest brand challenges, visit www.ksmmedia.com

Approx. Annual Billings: $440,000,000

Breakdown of Gross Billings by Media: Bus. Publs.: 5%; Mags.: 7%; Network Radio: 6%; Network T.V.: 15%; Newsp.: 5%; Outdoor: 8%; Spot Radio: 19%; Spot T.V.: 35%

Joni Williams *(Pres & Partner)*
Jonathan Lichter *(Partner & Chief Strategy Officer)*
Sy Chaba *(Exec VP & Dir-Strategic Plng & Acct Svc)*
David Warso *(Exec VP)*
Mel Greve *(Sr VP & Dir-Brdcst)*
Mark Willson *(Sr VP)*
Patty Brick *(VP & Grp Dir-Media)*
Jon Christens *(Dir-Comm)*

Branches

KSM South
300 W 6th St Ste 1500, Austin, TX 78701
Tel.: (512) 579-4660
E-Mail: info@ksmsouth.com
Web Site: ksmmedia.com/

Employees: 30

National Agency Associations: 4A's

Agency Specializes In: Media Buying Services, Sponsorship

Jonathan Lichter *(Partner & Chief Strategy Officer)*
David Warso *(Treas & Partner)*
Sy Chaba *(Exec VP & Dir-Strategic Plng & Acct Svcs)*
Elizabeth Amstutz *(Sr VP & Grp Dir-Media)*
Elizabeth Kalmbach *(VP & Grp Dir-Media)*
Donna Kleinman *(VP & Dir-Media Rels)*
Kay Wesolowski *(VP & Dir-Digital Media)*
Katie Stewart *(Dir-Acct Svc)*
Trevor Monteiro *(Assoc Dir-Strategy)*
Rachael Muhlenbeck *(Mgr-Promos)*

KINETIC
230 Park Ave, New York, NY 10003
Tel.: (212) 204-8252
E-Mail: info@kineticww.com
Web Site: www.kineticww.com

Employees: 130
Year Founded: 2005

National Agency Associations: 4A's

Agency Specializes In: Advertising, Advertising Specialties, Aviation & Aerospace, College, Experience Design, Guerilla Marketing, Health

Care Services, Hispanic Market, In-Store Advertising, Integrated Marketing, Media Buying Services, Media Planning, Mobile Marketing, Multicultural, Out-of-Home Media, Outdoor, Point of Purchase, Production, Retail, Sponsorship

Mauricio Sabogal *(CEO)*
Tanza Bove *(Pres-US)*
David Krupp *(CEO-US)*
David Payne *(CEO-World Markets)*
Erik Bottema *(Mng Dir-Aviator North America)*
Maureen McCloskey *(Mng Dir-Acct Svcs)*
Jennifer Greufe *(Dir-Target: Health)*
Justin Symons *(Dir-Acct Svcs)*
Wendy Yang *(Dir)*
Harry Burton *(Acct Mgr)*
Angelica Del Villar *(Mgr-Aviator North America)*

Accounts:
Allergan
AMD
American Express
AMPM
ANA
Bacardi Martini
BBC World
British Airways Club World
CITI Campaign: "Say Hello to Your Credit Card"
Cleawire
Coca-Cola Refreshments USA, Inc.
Con Agra
Coors
Dell
Delonghi
Elle MacPherson
Escada
The Estee Lauder Companies Inc.
Ford
H&M
HSBC Bank
Kaplan
Kimberly Clark
Magnum; Spain
Mars North America
Mars Media Buying
Michelin
Morrisons
Nordstrom
Novartis AG
Olive Garden
Pepsi
PG&E
Red Bull Red Bull Air Race
Red Cross of Greater New York
Rolex
Royal Caribbean
SAP
Snickers
Tommy Hilfiger
Unilever; UK Axe, Flora, Percil, Wall's Ice Cream
Unilever; US
Virgin Atlantic
VP Corp
Warner Bros.
Weight Watchers
Welch's
Western Union
Westfield Shopping Centre
Wrigley
Wyndham Hotels
Yahoo!

Branches

Kinetic
12180 Millennium Dr Ste 360, Playa Vista, CA 90094
Tel.: (310) 309-8150
Web Site: kineticww.com/us/

Agency Specializes In: Sponsorship

Cherie Johnson *(Mng Dir)*
Tanza Bove *(COO)*
Erika Altman *(Dir-Acct Svcs)*
Melanie Garber *(Dir-Comm Ops)*
Piper Wirth *(Dir-Acct Svcs)*
Stacy Enderle *(Acct Mgr)*
Jeffrey Vance *(Specialist-Plng)*
Melanie Zajac *(Specialist-Media)*
Rebekah Zabarsky *(Assoc Planner-Media)*

Joule
10 E 40th St 37th Fl, New York, NY 10016
Tel.: (212) 796-8382
E-Mail: info@jouleww.com
Web Site: www.jouleww.com

Year Founded: 2007

National Agency Associations: 4A's

Agency Specializes In: Media Buying Services, Mobile Marketing, Sponsorship

Melinda Toscano *(Acct Dir)*
Jessica Sanfratello *(Acct Planner)*

Accounts:
American Family Insurance Group Digital
Colgate-Palmolive Company
Paramount Pictures Creative, Mobile Media

Kinetic Design & Advertising Pvt. Ltd.
2 Leng Kee Rd #04-03A, Thye Hong Ctr, Singapore, 048543 Singapore
Tel.: (65) 6475 9377
Fax: (65) 6472 5440
E-Mail: info@kineticww.com
Web Site: www.kineticww.com

Year Founded: 1997

Agency Specializes In: Outdoor

King Lai *(CEO-Asia Pacific)*
Irene Revilla *(Reg Dir-APAC)*
Sherry Chan *(Mgr-Fin)*
Franck Vidal *(Reg Acct Dir)*

Accounts:
Bayerische Motoren Werke Aktiengesellschaft Campaign: "We Tow You Drive", Mini Cooper
Church of Saints Peter & Paul
Digi Telecom
Fox International Channels Campaign: "A-Z of Endangered & Extinct Wildlife"
Holycrap.sg Campaign: "Rennlim by Rennlim"
Maki-San
Mentholatum Singapore
Mini Asia Campaign: "Screensavers"
National Council on Problem Gambling Campaign: "Pick Up the Dice & Your World Collapses - Childhood"
National Geographic
Neon Sound Pte Ltd
Urgent Rubber Stamp Makers Urgent

Kinetic
Piazza della Conciliazione n 1, 20123 Milan, Italy
Tel.: (39) 02 433595 1
Fax: (39) 02 433595595
Web Site: www.kineticww.com/it-IT

Employees: 40

Carlo Grillo *(CFO)*
Michaela Zanardi *(COO)*
Fabio Nobili *(Dir-Comml)*
Rossana Rugginenti *(Mgr-Mktg & Comm)*
Francesca Bregonzio *(Media Planner)*
Laura Ferraresi *(Media Planner)*
Alice Rombolotti *(Media Planner)*
Eleonora Nani *(Client Dir)*

Accounts:
Alfa Romeo
Alitatia
Dahlia
Ford
Mercedes
Moto Guzzi
OVS
Piaggio
Sky
Smart

Kinetic
31 Ballsbridge Terr, Dublin, Ireland
Tel.: (353) 1668 1822
Fax: (353) 16681340
E-Mail: simon.durham@kineticww.com
Web Site: www.kinetic.com

Employees: 20

Simon Durham *(Mng Dir-Ireland)*
JoJo Cox *(Client Svcs Dir)*
Carol Hogan *(Dir)*

Accounts:
The Economist
Jockey
Molson Coors Carling, Cobra, Coors Light, Media Buying, Media Planning
Nokia
Sony Ericsson
Vodafone

Kinetic
121-141 Westbourne Terrace, London, W2 6JR United Kingdom
Tel.: (44) 207 544 4600
E-Mail: info@kineticww.com
Web Site: www.kinetic.com

Year Founded: 2005

Agency Specializes In: Experience Design, Media Buying Services, Mobile Marketing, Out-of-Home Media, Outdoor, Pharmaceutical, Production, Promotions

Stuart Taylor *(CEO)*
Nick Parker *(Chief Investment Officer-Global)*
Martyn Stokes *(Chief Strategy Officer)*
Richard Jacobs *(Mng Dir-UK)*
Roshan Singh *(Mng Dir-Kinetic Active)*
Lucy Catchpole *(Bus Dir)*
Oliver Ford *(Bus Dir)*
Colin Bundock *(Dir-Trading)*
Nicole Lonsdale *(Client Svc Dir)*

Accounts:
British Airways
CBS Outdoor UK Lynx Apollo campaign
EE
Jaguar Campaign: "Life Balanced", Digital, Press, TV, XF Sportsbrake
Lloyds Interactive Outdoor Campaign
Molson Coors Carling, Cobra, Coors Light, Media Buying, Media Planning
Tesco Outdoor Planning & Buying
Unilever
Vodafone
Warner Bros. Distributors

Kinetic
11-B Country Space 1 Building HV dela Costa St, Salcedo Village, Makati, Philippines
Tel.: (63) 894 3365
Web Site: www.kinetic.com

Carlo Mostoles *(Chief Creative Officer & VP)*

Roland Dallarte *(Mng Dir-Philippines)*
Rey Inobaya *(Mng Dir-Philippines)*
Julian Paul Narag *(Dir-Media)*

Kinetic

Commerz 9th Floor International Business Park Oberoi Garden City, Off Western Expres Highway, Goregaon East, Mumbai, 400063 India
Tel.: (91) 22 4239 9309
E-Mail: madhuri.sapru@kineticww.com
Web Site: www.kineticww.com

Employees: 40

Suresh Balakrishna *(CEO-South Asia & Middle East)*
Mick Ridley *(Mng Dir-Meta)*
Shermann Colaco *(Gen Mgr-West)*
Pallavi Patil Raina *(Sr Dir-Plng & Strategy)*
Pranay Khatu *(Bus Dir)*
Udayan Banerjee *(Dir-Fin)*
Trupti Arnalkar *(Sr Mgr)*

Accounts:
New-Senco Gold Creative, Media, OOH

Kinetic

2 Ploenchit Ctr 18th Fl Sukhumvit Rd, Klongtoey, Bangkok, 10110 Thailand
Tel.: (66) 2 656 8611
Web Site: www.kinetic.com

Kasinee Amattayakul *(Dir-In-Store)*

Accounts:
ASCOA
Awarix
Bayer Properties
BBVA Compass
Birmingham Childrens Theatre
Grede Foundries
HECA
Hinman Dental Society
Impression Solutions
Lakeshore Foundations

Kinetic

Rue de Stallestraat 65 6th Fl, Uccle, 1180 Brussels, Belgium
Tel.: (32) 2 333 81 77
Fax: (32) 23323665
E-Mail: Arnaud.Vandenberghen@kineticww.com
Web Site: www.kinetic.com

Employees: 5

Thomas De Greef *(Dir-Comml-Belgium)*
Dominique De Bast *(Mgr-OOH)*
Myriam Romain *(Mgr-OOH)*

Kinetic

Karperstraat 8, Amsterdam, Netherlands
Tel.: (31) 6 10 67 02 81
Fax: (31) 255757790
E-Mail: dennis.kuperus@kineticww.com
Web Site: www.kinetic.com

Employees: 12

Carolyn Nugent *(Head-Digital-UK)*
Arno Buskop *(Dir-Res)*
Robert van der Starre *(Dir-Benelux-Investment)*
Marja Gorter *(Mgr-Insights)*
Judith Klein *(Mgr-OOH Media)*
Monique Scherks *(Mgr-Investment)*
Maarten Smulders *(Mgr-Fin & Ops-Benelux)*
Yvette Van Den Berg *(Mgr-Insights)*
Marjan Leeuwenkuijl *(Bus Dev Dir-Kinetic Zone)*

Accounts:
KPN
Nike Campaign: "Hologram"
T-Mobile US
Unilever

Kinetic

Darmstadter Landstrasse 110, 60598 Frankfurt, Germany
Tel.: (49) 69 66 777 61 0
Fax: (49) 69667776166
E-Mail: germany@kineticww.com
Web Site: www.kinetic.com

Employees: 20

Ralf Stoffel *(Mng Dir)*

Accounts:
The Economist
Grolsch
Nokia
Sony Ericsson

Kinetic

222 Merchandise Mart Plz Ste 250, Chicago, IL 60654
Tel.: (312) 205-0054
Web Site: www.kinetic.com

Employees: 22

Agency Specializes In: Sponsorship

Joe Hoh *(Owner)*

Accounts:
BP
ConAgra
IKEA
Kimberly
MillerCoors LLC
Motorola Solutions, Inc.
Unilever
Wrigley

Mediacom Dusseldorf

Derendorfer Alle 10, 40476 Dusseldorf, Germany
Tel.: (49) 211171620
Fax: (49) 211171623200
E-Mail: freshness@mediacom.de
Web Site: www.mediacom.de

Employees: 552
Year Founded: 1986

Agency Specializes In: Media Buying Services

Jake Vander Linden *(Mng Partner & Head-Acct)*
Daniela Tollert *(Mng Dir)*
Claus Brockers *(Chief Investment Officer)*
Susanne Grundmann *(Mng Dir-Client Svcs)*
Christopher Kaiser *(Mng Dir-Hamburg)*
Inke Rausch *(Mng Dir-Munich)*
Reiner Schmitt *(Mng Dir-Plng & Client Svcs)*
Manuela Speckamp-Schmitt *(Mng Dir-Human Capital)*
Matthias Hellmann *(Dir-Mobile)*

Accounts:
Audi Online
Coca-Cola Refreshments USA, Inc.
Hasbro Campaign: "Office War: Helping Germany Have Fun At Work", Nerf Blasters
Volkswagen Group of America, Inc.

Branch:

Kinetic

(Formerly Magic Poster)
Derendorf Allee 10, 40476 Dusseldorf, Germany
Tel.: (49) 211 87 67 05 886
Fax: (49) 211 87 67 05 557
Web Site: www.kineticww.de

Employees: 60
Year Founded: 2000

Agency Specializes In: Out-of-Home Media, Outdoor

Stefan Engels *(Mng Partner)*
Stefan-peter Radner *(Mng Partner)*
Andreas Voss *(Mng Partner)*
Dietmar Birkner *(Mng Dir)*
Thorsten Ebbing *(Mng Dir)*
Nina Merz *(Head-Production)*
David Rusch *(Head-Intl & Aviation Media)*
Alexander Gock *(Dir)*
Andreas Michelbrink *(Dir)*
Sonja Nestingen *(Dir)*

Accounts:
Coca-Cola Refreshments USA, Inc.
Deutsche Telekom T-Mobile
Eon Energy
Ikea
Volkswagen Group of America, Inc. Audi, Seat Cars, Skoda

Target:Health

261 Madison Ave, New York, NY 10016
Tel.: (212) 681-2100
Fax: (212) 681-2105
Web Site: www.targethealth.com

Employees: 75
Year Founded: 2007

Jennifer Greufe *(Mng Dir)*
Dean Gittleman *(Head-Ops)*
Glen Park *(Sr Dir-Clinical & Regulatory Affairs)*

KREIGER & ASSOCIATES

1800 E Lancaster Ave, Paoli, PA 19301
Tel.: (610) 640-1255
Fax: (610) 640-4258
E-Mail: info@kriegerassociates.com
Web Site: www.kriegerassociates.com

Year Founded: 1997

Agency Specializes In: Advertising

Gail Krieger *(Pres)*
Ken Krieger *(CFO & VP)*
June Mento *(Mgr-Media)*
Kathy Rowan *(Mgr-Ops)*

Accounts:
American Steel Span
Aztec Steel Buildings
Liberty Guardian Angel
Mini-Dish DirecTV
National Review Magazine
Patent Lean Dietary Supplement
Quarter Coin Collection
Ronald Reagan Videos

LINCOLN MEDIA SERVICES, INC.

51 Sherwood Ter Ste Y, Lake Bluff, IL 60044
Tel.: (224) 880-5501
Fax: (224) 880-5505
E-Mail: info@lincolnmedia.com
Web Site: lincolnmedia.com

Employees: 8
Year Founded: 1999

Agency Specializes In: Advertising, Brand Development & Integration, Broadcast, Cable T.V.,

Co-op Advertising, Consulting, Consumer Marketing, Email, Faith Based, Financial, Health Care Services, Hospitality, Household Goods, Leisure, Media Buying Services, Media Planning, Men's Market, New Product Development, Newspaper, Over-50 Market, Planning & Consultation, Print, Production, Production (Ad, Film, Broadcast), Radio, Seniors' Market, T.V.

Approx. Annual Billings: $2,000,000

Breakdown of Gross Billings by Media: Cable T.V.: 40%; Fees: 5%; Internet Adv.: 5%; Newsp.: 3%; Production: 7%; Spot T.V.: 40%

Gary A. Jones *(Pres & CEO)*
Amanda Jones *(Exec VP)*
Shelby Schmidt *(Dir-Mktg)*
Sally Shoemaker *(Mgr-Traffic)*

M&K MEDIA

(Formerly McIlroy & King Communications Inc.)
688 Richmond St W Ste 401, Toronto, ON M6J 1C5 Canada
Tel.: (416) 516-5969
Fax: (416) 203-6494
E-Mail: juliem@mkmedia.biz
Web Site: www.mkmedia.biz/

Employees: 7
Year Founded: 2001

Agency Specializes In: Media Buying Services, Media Planning

Julie King *(Partner)*
Julie McIlroy *(Partner)*
Laura Templin *(Acct Dir-Media)*
Marnie Shainhouse *(Supvr-Media & Planning)*
Niamh Barry *(Media Planner & Media Buyer)*
Breanne Scott *(Asst Media Planner & Buyer)*

Accounts:
407 ETR
ACH Foods-Mazola
Chattem Canada
Credit Canada
Franklin Templeton Investments
Hain Celestial Canada
Harry Rosen
Hydropool Canada
La-Z-Boy
Little Caesars Pizza
Raising The Roof Media, Social Media
The Royal Agricultural Winter Fair
Shaw Festival
Triumph Lingerie Canada

MACDONALD MEDIA

185 Madison Ave 4th Fl, New York, NY 10016
Tel.: (212) 578-8735
Fax: (212) 481-1030
E-Mail: amacdonald@macdonaldmedia.com
Web Site: www.macdonaldmedia.com

E-Mail for Key Personnel:
President: amacdonald@macdonaldmedia.com

Employees: 20
Year Founded: 1997

National Agency Associations: 4A's-OAAA-TAB

Agency Specializes In: Advertising, Advertising Specialties, Event Planning & Marketing, Media Buying Services, Out-of-Home Media, Outdoor, Planning & Consultation, Point of Purchase, Print, Production, Publicity/Promotions, Sports Market, Strategic Planning/Research

Breakdown of Gross Billings by Media: Out-of-Home Media: 100%

Andrea Macdonald *(CEO)*
Stephen Faso *(Dir-Media)*
Peter MacDonald *(Dir-Ops)*
Kathie Wright Montague *(Dir-Media)*
Simone Davis *(Acct Supvr)*
Kevin McCabe *(Supvr-Media)*
Tressa Adams *(Media Planner)*
Rosemary McDermott *(Media Buyer-OOH)*
Kristy Nichols *(Media Planner)*
Donovan Zink *(Coord-Media)*

Accounts:
AIG
Bacardi USA B&B, Bacardi Light, Bacardi Limon, Bacardi O, Bombay Sapphire Gin, Dewars, Drambuie, M&R Asti
ESPN
Kohl's Department Stores
L'Oreal
McCann-Erickson
Toyota

Branches

MacDonald Media/Los Angeles

701 E 3rd St Ste 320, Los Angeles, CA 90013
Tel.: (213) 680-3094
Fax: (213) 680-3000
E-Mail: rrobinson@macdonaldmedia.com
Web Site: www.macdonaldmedia.com

Employees: 5

National Agency Associations: 4A's

Agency Specializes In: Media Buying Services

Andrea MacDonald *(Pres & CEO)*
David Koppelman *(Mng Dir)*
Kathie Wright Montague *(Dir-Media)*

Accounts:
Brandman University
Citrix
ConocoPhillips
Ebay
Guitar Center
Insomniac
Microsoft
Monterey Bay Aquarium
Petsmart
Shakey's
UCLA
Ugg

MacDonald Media

1306 NW Hoyt St 204, Portland, OR 97209
(See Separate Listing)

MANSI MEDIA

3899 N Front St, Harrisburg, PA 17110-1535
Tel.: (717) 703-3043
Fax: (717) 703-3033
E-Mail: lisak@mansimedia.com
Web Site: www.mansimedia.com

E-Mail for Key Personnel:
President: timw@mansimedia.com

Employees: 32
Year Founded: 1954

Agency Specializes In: Media Buying Services, Media Planning, Newspaper, Web (Banner Ads, Pop-ups, etc.)

Breakdown of Gross Billings by Media: Production: 90%; Worldwide Web Sites: 10%

Brad Simpson *(CFO)*
Lisa Knight *(VP-Adv)*
Chris Kazlauskas *(Dir-Media Placement)*
Wes Snider *(Dir-Client Solutions)*
Kevin Wert *(Dir-Client Solutions)*
Carin Hoover *(Mgr-Major Accts)*
Ken Sanford *(Mgr-Major Accounts-Placement)*

MARKETING MIDWEST, INC.

4969 Olson Memorial Hwy, Golden Valley, MN 55422
Tel.: (763) 225-8600
Fax: (763) 225-8601
E-Mail: michelle@mmimediapros.com
Web Site: mb25media.com/

E-Mail for Key Personnel:
President: barb@marketingmidwest.com

Employees: 15
Year Founded: 1988

Agency Specializes In: Alternative Advertising, Broadcast, Business Publications, Business-To-Business, Cable T.V., Co-op Advertising, Direct Response Marketing, Education, Electronic Media, Government/Political, Media Buying Services, Media Planning, Newspapers & Magazines, Promotions, Strategic Planning/Research

Breakdown of Gross Billings by Media: Adv. Specialities: 1%; Cable T.V.: 6%; Newsp. & Mags.: 3%; Outdoor: 4%; Radio: 48%; Spot T.V.: 38%

Steve Karolewski *(Co-Owner)*
Barbara Allen *(Mgr-Traditional Media, Sr Media Buyer & Planner)*
Roshanda Jenkins *(Mgr-Traffic)*
Melissa Pickert *(Coord-Continuity)*

Accounts:
Health Partners; Minneapolis, MN; 1998
Regions Hospital

MARKETING PERFORMANCE GROUP

4755 Technology Way Ste 103, Boca Raton, FL 33431-3331
Tel.: (561) 988-2181
Fax: (561) 988-2182
E-Mail: info@mpgmarketing.com
Web Site: www.marketingperformancegroup.com

Employees: 10
Year Founded: 1986

Agency Specializes In: Broadcast, Business-To-Business, Cable T.V., Consulting, Consumer Marketing, Direct Response Marketing, Entertainment, Game Integration, Health Care Services, Hospitality, Legal Services, Magazines, Media Buying Services, Newspaper, Out-of-Home Media, Outdoor, Planning & Consultation, Print, Radio, Retail, T.V., Web (Banner Ads, Pop-ups, etc.)

Approx. Annual Billings: $20,000,000

Brad Kurtz *(CEO)*
Cindy Kurtz *(Principal)*
Kristen Carpenter *(Acct Supvr)*
Blanca Granja *(Supvr-Media)*
David Aviles *(Asst Media Buyer)*
Marge Pistulka *(Sr Media Buyer)*

Accounts:
Compass Furniture; New Orleans, LA Retail Furniture; 1986
DG; FL; 2011
Gila River Gaming Enterprises; Chandler, AZ Casino Gaming; 2011
Mardi Gras Casino Casino Gaming; 2012
Tech Results BI & CRM Software for Casinos; 2012

MARLIN OUTDOOR ADVERTISING LTD.

PO Drawer 6567, Hilton Head Island, SC 29938
Tel.: (843) 785-5769
Fax: (843) 785-8139

E-Mail for Key Personnel:
President: brucewelden@islc.com

Employees: 6
Year Founded: 1981

Agency Specializes In: Out-of-Home Media, Outdoor

Breakdown of Gross Billings by Media: Outdoor: 95%; Radio: 5%

Walter M. Czura *(Pres)*
Will Settle *(VP-Sls & Ops)*
Bruce Welden *(Mgr-Sls)*

Accounts:
Comfort Inn Hotels
Cracker Barrel
Days Inn Hotels
Hampton Inn Hotels
Holiday Inn Express

MATOMY MEDIA GROUP

(Formerly MediaWhiz Holdings, LLC)
77 Water St, New York, NY 10005
Tel.: (212) 717-1578
Fax: (646) 638-4889
Toll Free: (888) 866-9449
Web Site: www.matomy.com

Employees: 140
Year Founded: 2001

Agency Specializes In: Media Buying Services, Media Planning, Search Engine Optimization, Sweepstakes, Web (Banner Ads, Pop-ups, etc.)

Ido Pollack *(CTO)*
Ido Barash *(Gen Counsel)*
Assaf Suprasky *(Exec VP-Media)*
Daryl Colwell *(Sr VP-Sls & Bus Dev)*
Menachem Salinas *(Sr VP-Social)*
David Zerah *(Sr VP-Corp Dev-Global)*
Lauren Gumport *(Mgr-PR & Content Mktg)*

Accounts:
American Laser Centers
American Singles
CCA Global
CTU/AIU
The Frisky
MyPoints
NPD Group
Primus
SC Johnson

MATRIX MEDIA SERVICES, INC.

463 E Town St, Columbus, OH 43215-4757
Tel.: (614) 228-2200
Fax: (614) 228-8404
Toll Free: (800) 589-6674
E-Mail: info@matrixmediaservices.com
Web Site: www.matrixmediaservices.com

Employees: 25
Year Founded: 1988

National Agency Associations: OAAA

Agency Specializes In: Advertising, Advertising Specialties, Affluent Market, African-American Market, Alternative Advertising, Arts, Automotive, Brand Development & Integration, Broadcast, Cable T.V., Co-op Advertising, Collateral, College, Communications, Consulting, Consumer Goods, Corporate Communications, Corporate Identity, Custom Publishing, Education, Entertainment, Event Planning & Marketing, Experience Design, Faith Based, Financial, Food Service, Gay & Lesbian Market, Government/Political, Guerilla Marketing, Health Care Services, Hispanic Market, Hospitality, In-Store Advertising, Internet/Web Design, Local Marketing, Market Research, Media Buying Services, Media Planning, Media Relations, Men's Market, Mobile Marketing, Multicultural, New Product Development, Newspaper, Out-of-Home Media, Outdoor, Planning & Consultation, Podcasting, Point of Purchase, Point of Sale, Print, Production, Production (Print), Promotions, Radio, Restaurant, Search Engine Optimization, Seniors' Market, Social Marketing/Nonprofit, Social Media, Sports Market, Strategic Planning/Research, Syndication, Transportation, Urban Market, Web (Banner Ads, Pop-ups, etc.)

Approx. Annual Billings: $27,000,000

Breakdown of Gross Billings by Media: Out-of-Home Media: 100%

Terri Kraft *(Sr VP-Media Sls)*
Jeremy Mitchell *(Sr VP)*
Marty Blanton *(VP-OOH Sls)*
Ann Garcia *(VP-Ops & Production)*
Ashley Shipley *(Dir-Social Media & Online Mktg)*
Emily Beringer *(Acct Mgr)*
Jennifer Hoffmannbeck *(Acct Supvr)*
Michelle Gaines *(Media Buyer)*
Ashley Griffith-Roach *(Media Buyer)*
Krista Lyons *(Asst Media Buyer)*

MAXUS GLOBAL

498 Seventh Ave, New York, NY 10018
Tel.: (212) 297-8300
Web Site: www.maxusglobal.com

Employees: 2,000

National Agency Associations: 4A's

Agency Specializes In: Customer Relationship Management, Media Buying Services, Media Planning, Media Relations, Sponsorship

Lindsay Pattison *(CEO)*
David Gaines *(Mng Partner)*
Cassandra Tryon *(Mng Partner)*
Ryan Cassidy *(Partner & Grp Dir-Plng)*
Robyn Edwards *(Partner & Grp Dir-Plng)*
Sarah Giannantonio *(Partner & Grp Dir-Plng-NBC Ent)*
Nadia Harrison *(Partner & Grp Dir-Plng)*
Leah Levison *(Partner & Grp Dir-Plng)*
Elizabeth Papadakos *(Partner & Dir-Client Fin)*
David Kaganovsky *(CIO)*
Jonathan Adams *(Chief Digital Officer-North America)*
Bijan White *(Chief Digital Officer-EMEA)*
Federico de Nardis *(CEO-EMEA)*
Steve Williams *(CEO-Americas)*
Brian Gearhart *(Sr Partner & Grp Dir-Plng-Global)*
Nancy Ramos *(Grp Dir-Media)*
Kathy Richter *(Sr Partner & Bus Dir)*
Trixie Ferguson Gray *(Sr Partner & Dir-Comm Plng)*
Lori Greene *(Sr Partner & Dir-Content)*
Karen Kaufman *(Dir-Product Dev-Global)*
Doug Ng *(Sr Partner & Dir-Strategic Plng)*
Nicole Nowakowski *(Sr Partner & Dir-Strategic Plng)*
Rosemarie Paragham *(Dir-Res)*
Juan Pablo Silva Oliveira *(Dir-Digital)*
Sara Bailer *(Assoc Dir-Plng)*
Carly Anne Catalano *(Assoc Dir)*
Jennifer Dixon *(Assoc Dir-Plng)*
Dana Friedman *(Assoc Dir-Plng)*
Joe Pellicano *(Assoc Dir-Digital Media)*
Cory Schmidt *(Assoc Dir-Plng)*
Tara Schuster *(Assoc Dir-Plng)*
Tiffany Wang *(Assoc Dir-Media)*
Lauren Menno *(Mgr-Creative)*
Daniel Landers *(Supvr-Digital Media & Media Planner)*
Chris Athens *(Supvr-Digital Media)*
Samantha Effman *(Supvr-Media)*
Erin English *(Supvr-Integrated Media)*
Jamie Finstein *(Supvr-Media)*
Kim Heller *(Supvr-Media)*
Greg Hyde *(Supvr-Integrated Media-NBC Universal)*
Kristina Klaffenboeck *(Supvr-Strategic Media Plng-Global)*
Adam Parz *(Supvr-Digital-GroupM)*
Eddie Yniguez *(Supvr-Media)*
Julie Chen *(Sr Planner-Digital)*
Prerana Katti *(Strategist-Integrated Comm)*
Jyothi Ajithkumar *(Media Planner)*
Emily Declusin *(Planner-Media)*
Mollie Doherty *(Planner-Digital Media)*
Kelly Geer *(Media Planner-Integrated)*
Jennifer Havard *(Planner-Digital Media)*
Jana Heath *(Media Planner-Integrated)*
Melissa Helm *(Planner-Digital Media)*
Anna Kalachyan *(Planner-Digital Media)*
Amber Latorre *(Media Planner-Digital-NBCU Digital)*
Lily Levine *(Planner-Integrated Media-NBC Sports Grp & NBC Owned)*
Patrick Link *(Media Planner-Strategic)*
Mario Mercado *(Media Planner)*
Melanie Nelson *(Media Planner)*
Ankita Nigam *(Media Planner-Integrated)*
Christina Ream *(Planner-Digital Media)*
Kari Shepard *(Media Planner)*
Charlotte Skinner *(Media Planner)*
Matt Stein *(Planner-Digital Media)*
Brian Sullivan *(Media Buyer)*
Amy Gong *(Asst Media Planner)*
Kayla Gonzalez *(Asst Media Planner-Digital)*
Lily Hansen *(Asst Media Planner-Digital)*
Mollie Levy *(Asst Media Planner)*
Alex Malin *(Asst Media Planner)*
Alishia Natiello *(Asst Media Planner-Digital)*
Aaron Panther *(Asst Media Planner)*
Natalie Stehr *(Asst Media Planner)*
Lauren Weisberg *(Asst Media Planner)*
Miriam Yong *(Asst Media Planner-Digital)*

Accounts:
Barclay Bank
Bausch & Lomb
Church & Dwight
Fiat
L'Oreal Media Buying, Media Planning, Nordics Account
NBC Universal Television Networks Group Digital, Entertainment, Media, Universal Studios
PANDORA A/S (Media Planning & Buying Agency of Record)
Panera Bread Media Buying, Media Planning
S.C. Johnson Hispanic
United Parcel Service Media Planning & Buying; 2009
Welches

Branches

Maxus

2 Ploenchit Center 14th Floor, Sukhumvit Rd Klongtoey, Bangkok, 10110 Thailand
Tel.: (66) 2 629 6200
Fax: (66) 2 629 6291
Web Site: maxusglobal.com

Year Founded: 1999

Agency Specializes In: Media Buying Services

Tapanee Kaewprasith *(Dir-Plng)*
Warin Tinprapa *(Dir-Bus)*
Nunthida Wasanakamol *(Dir-Media Plng)*
Fiezt Malice *(Planner)*

Songchaiwattana Pavaya *(Sr Media Planner)*

Accounts:
Fiat Punto Evo
Kalyan Jewellers Media Buying
L'Oreal

Maxus
Rm 503 5/F Jin Bao Building 89 Jin Bao St, Dong Cheng District, Beijing, 100005 China
Tel.: (86) 10 8523 3569
Fax: (86) 10 6512 2393
E-Mail: cathy.kuang@maxusglobal.com
Web Site: maxusglobal.com

Year Founded: 2004

Agency Specializes In: Media Buying Services

Vicky Hsueh *(Mng Dir)*
Stephanie Li *(Mng Dir-Guangzhou)*
Milton Liao *(VP-South China)*
Li Meng *(Gen Mgr)*
Avon Hsu *(Dir-Talent)*
Corin Somerville *(Dir-Comm Plng-North Asia)*
Matilda Wei *(Dir-Digital-Beijing)*

Accounts:
DFS
Haier Casarte, Digital
Lee
Lenovo
Luxgen Auto
Renhe Pharmaceuticals

Maxus
36/F PCCW Tower Taikoo Pl 979 Kings Rd, Quarry Bay, China (Hong Kong)
Tel.: (852) 2280 3488
Fax: (852) 2866 2630
E-Mail: hkinfo@maxusglobal.com
Web Site: www.maxusglobal.com

Employees: 70
Year Founded: 1998

Agency Specializes In: Media Buying Services

Stanley Ngai *(Mng Dir)*
Martin Shaw *(Head-Digital-APAC)*
Yvonne Lau *(Gen Mgr)*
Chris Chong *(Dir-Bus)*

Accounts:
HTC
Mars Group Campaign: "You are Not Yourself When You are Hungry", Snickers
Maxim's Arome Mooncakes, Media
PepsiCo

Maxus
Ground Fl Orbit Plz, New Prabhadevi Rd, Mumbai, 400025 India
Tel.: (91) 22 566 3888
Fax: (91) 22 566 38500
E-Mail: ajit.varghese@maxusglobal.com
Web Site: www.maxusglobal.com

Year Founded: 2001

Agency Specializes In: Media Buying Services

Ajit Varghese *(CEO-Asia Pacific)*
Kartik Sharma *(Mng Dir-South Asia)*
Vishal Jacob *(Head-Digital Strategy & Partnerships)*
Jigar Rambhia *(Head-Client)*
Anil Sathiraju *(Gen Mgr-South)*
Aarti Bhat *(Dir-Bus)*
Rrahul Deo Manerao *(Dir-Bus)*
Yogesh Pawar *(Dir-Bus)*
Sheena Huria *(Assoc Dir-Bus)*
Asma Quadri *(Assoc Dir)*
Rohit Kuruvilla *(Media Planner)*
Bhakti Nago *(Media Planner)*
Saif Shaikh *(Client Head-Insights)*

Accounts:
Aristocrat
Colors
Dabur Oral Care
Fiat
Google
New-Greenlam Industries Limited Media
Hero Honda
International Cricket Council ICC Cricket World 2015, Media
Kotak Mahindra Media
L'Oreal Media
Musafir.com
Nestle India Digital, Maggi, Milkmaid, Mobile Marketing, Nescafe, Social
Nokia
Perfetti Van Melle
Red Bull; 2009
redBus
Ruchi Soya Mahakosh, Media, Ruchi Gold, Sunrich
Tata Global Beverages Tata Tea
TataSky
Titan
Viacom18
VIP Luggage Ladies Handbags, Media
Vodafone Campaign: "Responsible Mobility"
Xylys Media

Maxus
Menara Jamsostek Gedung Utara 12A Floor, Jln Gatot Subroto No 38, Jakarta, Selatan 12710 Indonesia
Tel.: (62) 21 5291 6360
Fax: (62) 21 5291 6361
Web Site: www.maxusglobal.com

Employees: 24
Year Founded: 1997

Agency Specializes In: Media Buying Services

Partha Kabi *(Mng Dir)*
Vina Yustiana *(Gen Mgr)*
Nurina Setiawati *(Dir-Bus)*

Accounts:
Fiat Punto Evo

Maxus
25 F Philamlife Tower, 8767 Paseo de Roxas St, Makati City, Manila, 1200 Philippines
Tel.: (63) 2 368 7510
Web Site: maxusglobal.com

Employees: 15
Year Founded: 2000

Agency Specializes In: Above-the-Line, Consumer Marketing, Corporate Communications, Media Buying Services

Joselle Custodia *(Mgr-Digital)*
Kimberly Cena *(Media Planner & Media Buyer)*

Accounts:
Boehringer Ingelheim Bisolvon, Pharmaton; 2004
Fiat Punto Evo
Red Bull Media

Maxus
Level 3 Pelaco Bldg 21-31 Goodwood St, Richmond, VIC 3121 Australia
Tel.: (61) 3 9916 5350
Fax: (61) 3 9916 5351
Web Site: www.maxusglobal.com

Employees: 5
Year Founded: 2000

Agency Specializes In: Media Buying Services

Karly Leach *(Mng Dir)*
Sam Tedesco *(Client Svcs Dir)*
Leah Dickenson *(Dir-Digital)*
Andrew Pascoe *(Dir-Plng-Natl)*
Dale Putt *(Dir-Client Svc)*
Alison Chong *(Client Svc Dir)*
Shaun Harmor *(Client Svc Dir)*
Julie Saunders *(Client Svc Dir)*

Accounts:
Aldi
Chrysler Fiat
Domino's Pizza Media Buying, Out of Home, Print, Television
Forty Winks
GlaxoSmithKline Media
Greens
Hungry Jack's
Spirit of Tasmania
Suzuki

Maxus
PB 454 Sentrum, Stortovet 10, N-0104 Oslo, Norway
Tel.: (47) 22338410
Web Site: www.maxusglobal.no

Employees: 22
Year Founded: 2004

Agency Specializes In: Media Buying Services

Cecilie Faye *(Chief Creative Officer & Mng Dir)*
Nathalie Eyde Warembourg *(CEO-Norway)*
Tanja Westhagen *(Sr Mgr-Media Acct)*
Marte Aagesen Trondsen *(Mgr-Brdcst)*
Astrid Mattson *(Planner)*
Cathrine Sundin *(Planner)*

Accounts:
Aker Solutions Industry
Aleris Helse Health
DFDS Seaways Travel
Hansa Borg Bryggerier Beverage
Jysk Retail
Sektor Shopping Mall
Toyota Norway Automotive
Unilever FMCG
Visma Services IT & Finance

Maxus
35 F Westgate 1038, Nanjing Road, Shanghai, 200041 China
Tel.: (86) 21 2307 7777
Fax: (86) 21 2307 7737
Web Site: www.maxusglobal.com

Year Founded: 2000

Agency Specializes In: Media Buying Services

Annie Hsiao *(Pres-China)*
Nico Abbruzzese *(Head-Digital APAC)*
James Gee Ng Fey *(Dir-Digital Bus)*
Wei-Wei Pan *(Dir-Comml)*
Jessy Ji *(Assoc Dir-Digital)*

Accounts:
ECCO
Falcon
Fiat
JetStar
Karcher
Lee
Pfizer Caltrate, Centrum, Media Planning, Robitussin

UPS
Victoria Tourism

Maxus
Level 11 65 Berry St, Sydney, NSW 2060 Australia
Tel.: (61) 2 9287 8400
Fax: (61) 2 9947 2411
E-Mail: david.gaines@maxusglobal.com
Web Site: www.maxusglobal.com

Employees: 10

Agency Specializes In: Media Buying Services

Gaye Jackson *(Partner & Assoc Dir)*
Katy Websdell *(Mng Dir)*
Mark McCraith *(CEO-Australia)*
Lakun Agrawal *(Dir-Comml)*
Ricky Chanana *(Dir-Natl Digital & Trading)*
Ros Hamilton *(Dir-Strategic Intelligence)*
Kristin Muter *(Dir-Sydney Trading)*
Chris Koenig *(Assoc Dir-Plng)*
Matthew Wing *(Supvr-Digital Trading)*
Megan Koval *(Strategist-Comm)*

Accounts:
Disney.com
Jetstar Media Planning & Buying
Mortgage Choice Media

Maxus
6th Fl Bldg No 9A Cyber City DLF Phase III, Gurgaon, Haryana 122002 India
Tel.: (91) 124 419 8663
Fax: (91) 124 409 2404
E-Mail: mausumi.kar@maxusglobal.com
Web Site: www.maxusglobal.com

Employees: 300
Year Founded: 2001

Agency Specializes In: Media Buying Services

Priti Murthy *(Chief Strategy Officer)*
Shibu George *(Head-Client)*
Sandeep Pandey *(Head-Mktg Effectiveness-Asia Pacific)*
Mimi Deb *(Gen Mgr)*
Ashutosh Samal *(Bus Dir)*
Chidirala Anil Shankar *(Dir-Bus)*
Harish Shankaran *(Dir-Creative Tech)*
Traptika Chauhan *(Assoc Bus Dir)*
Kiran Lata *(Assoc Bus Dir)*

Accounts:
Getit Infomedia Media, askme.com, askmebazaar.co
Indian Premier League
McCain Foods India Media
Nokia
PolicyBazaar.com Media
Reebok
ShopClues.com (Media Agency of Record) Media Planning
TataSky Live
Titan Fastrack, Sonata, Tanishq
Vodafone

Maxus
24-28 Bloomsbury Way, London, WC1A 2PX United Kingdom
Tel.: (44) 207 025 3900
E-Mail: mail@maxusglobal.com
Web Site: www.maxusglobal.co.uk

Employees: 60

Nick Baughan *(CEO)*
Clare Chapman *(Mng Partner)*
Gill Hunter *(Mng Partner-Europe)*
Kirsten Miller *(Mng Partner)*
Tim Irwin *(COO)*
Damian Blackden *(Chief Strategy Officer-Global)*
Richard Stokes *(Chief Dev Officer-Global)*
Bijan White *(Chief Digital Officer-EMEA)*
Stephanie Marks *(Head-Client Svcs)*
Ruth Cartwright *(Dir-Brdcst)*
Tom Dunn *(Dir-Digital Strategy)*
Martin Lawson *(Dir-Data & Insights-Global)*
Nick Vale *(Dir-Plng-Global)*
Oliver Wood *(Dir-Search & Biddable)*
Jo Cronk *(Assoc Dir-Comm)*
Vince Amato *(Acct Mgr)*
John Maloney *(Office Mgr)*
Nick Thirsk *(Acct Mgr)*
Nicky Bradley *(Mgr-Mktg)*

Accounts:
Alfa Romeo
Arcadia Media Planning & Buying
Associated British Foods Kingsmill Bread, Media Planning & Buying, Ovaltine, Patak's, Ryvita, Twinings Tea
Avis Budget
Barclays plc Media Buying, Media Planning
Bench Above the Line, Online Media
Betfair
BT BT Sport, Media, TV
DMGT DMG Media, Daily Mail, DailyMailTV, MailOnline, Media Buying, Media Planning, The Mail on Sunday'
Fiat UK Media Planning & Buying
Karcher Media Planning & Buying
L'Oreal Media Planning & Buying
Mercedes-Benz Digital Strategy, Media Planning, Programming
National Book Tokens Campaign: "Choosing a Book is An Adventure in Itself", Media Buying & Planning
Npower Digital, Media Planning & Buying, Offline, Online, Social & Content Creation
ODL Markets
Powermat Media
Seiko
Tabasco Campaign: "Brunch", Media
Triumph/Sloggi
Twinings Media
Ubisoft Media Buying, Media Planning

Maxus
700 Beach Rd 07 01, Singapore, 199598 Singapore
Tel.: (65) 6395 0755
Fax: (65) 6324 5046
E-Mail: audrey.kuah@maxusglobal.com
Web Site: www.maxusglobal.com

Year Founded: 1998

Agency Specializes In: Media Buying Services

Barbara Delfyett Hester *(Mng Partner & Dir-Strategic Plng-Global)*
Desh Balakrishnan *(Mng Dir)*
Ajit Verghese *(CEO-Asia Pacific)*
Nico Abbruzzese *(Head-Digital APAC)*
Rose Huskey *(Head-Client Leadership-Asia Pacific)*
Lena Goh *(Gen Mgr-Singapore)*
Rachna Julka *(Reg Dir-Digital-APAC)*
Jia Hui Lim *(Sr Media Planner)*

Accounts:
Fitness First Media, Media Buying, Media Planning
Fraser Property Media Buying, Media Planning
Frasers Centrepoint Malls Media
GuocoLand Limited Media Buying, Media Planning
Jetstar Media Planning & Buying
Line Digital, Outdoor, Print, Social Media, TV
Ministry of Education Media; 2007
Shangri-la
Shell
New-Temasek Holdings Campaign: "Growing with the Nation", Jubilee Celebrations
UPS

MAYOSEITZ MEDIA
751 Arbor Way Ste 130, Blue Bell, PA 19422
Tel.: (215) 641-8700
Fax: (215) 641-8712
E-Mail: info@mayoseitzmedia.com
Web Site: www.mayoseitzmedia.com

Employees: 27
Year Founded: 1997

National Agency Associations: 4A's

Agency Specializes In: Broadcast, Business-To-Business, Cable T.V., Communications, Digital/Interactive, Electronic Media, Entertainment, Financial, Media Buying Services, Newspaper, Newspapers & Magazines, Out-of-Home Media, Outdoor, Print, Radio, Social Media, Sponsorship, Sports Market, T.V., Trade & Consumer Magazines, Travel & Tourism

Ray Mayo *(Co-Founder & Mng Dir)*
Mary Tyrrell *(Sr VP & Dir-Media Strategy)*
Andy DelQuadro *(Dir-Digital Strategy)*
Jessica Rosenthal *(Dir-Brdcst)*
Jared Orth *(Assoc Dir-Media Strategy)*
Krista Coonelly-Becker *(Supvr-Digital Strategy)*
Megan Lawless *(Supvr-Media Strategy)*
Katie Thompson *(Supvr-Brdcst Negotiations)*
Katie Dalhoff *(Sr Strategist-Media)*
Kate Gomulka *(Sr Specialist-Media-Insights & Analytics)*
Samantha Gundlach *(Sr Specialist-Brdcst)*
Kimberlee Courtney *(Specialist-Digital)*
Kelly Dent *(Specialist-Digital)*
Michael Brisgone *(Asst Media Planner)*

Accounts:
Automobile Dealers Association of Greater Philadelphia; 2007
Comcast SportsNet; Philadelphia, PA Sports Cable Network; 1998
Dietz & Watson
Greater Philadelphia Tourism; Philadelphia, PA Tourism; 2000
Hershey Entertainment & Resorts; Hershey, PA Tourism; 2002
Penn Medicine Health System; 2002
Philadelphia Phillies; 1999
Sea Research Foundation Media
Subway QSR; 2002
Trex Company, Inc. Home Products; 2007
Virtua Health System
Visit Philadelphia
Wharton Executive Education Media Agency of Record, Media Strategy

MCILROY & KING COMMUNICATIONS INC.
(Name Changed to M&K Media)

MDDC PRESS ASSOCIATION & PRESS SERVICE
(Formerly MD-DE-DC Ad Placement Service)
2000 Capital Dr The Capital Gazette Bldg, Annapolis, MD 21401
Toll Free: (855) 721-6332
Web Site: www.mddcpress.com

Employees: 8
Year Founded: 1996

Agency Specializes In: Advertising, Media Buying Services, Media Planning, Newspaper, Newspapers & Magazines, Publicity/Promotions

Approx. Annual Billings: $10,800,000

Breakdown of Gross Billings by Media: Newsp.: 100%

Stacey Riley *(Controller & Coord-HR)*
Rebecca Snyder *(Exec Dir)*
Wanda Smith *(Coord-Ad Network)*
Jen Thornberry *(Coord-Member Svcs)*

Accounts:
AETNA
Carroll County Times
Delaware State News
FEMA
Garrett County Weekende
Hershey Park
Milford Beacon
Salvation Army
Tuesday Morning
Washington Times

MEC, GLOBAL HQ, NEW YORK

825 7th Ave, New York, NY 10019-6014
Tel.: (212) 474-0000
Fax: (212) 474-0003
E-Mail: info.na@mecglobal.com
Web Site: www.mecglobal.com

Year Founded: 2001

National Agency Associations: ANA

Agency Specializes In: Above-the-Line, Affiliate Marketing, Affluent Market, Asian Market, Automotive, Aviation & Aerospace, Below-the-Line, Bilingual Market, Branded Entertainment, Broadcast, Business Publications, Business-To-Business, Cable T.V., Children's Market, Co-op Advertising, Communications, Computers & Software, Consulting, Consumer Marketing, Consumer Publications, Content, Cosmetics, Customer Relationship Management, Digital/Interactive, Direct Response Marketing, Direct-to-Consumer, Electronics, Engineering, Event Planning & Marketing, Experience Design, Fashion/Apparel, Financial, Food Service, Game Integration, Gay & Lesbian Market, Guerilla Marketing, Health Care Services, High Technology, Hispanic Market, Hospitality, Household Goods, In-Store Advertising, Information Technology, Integrated Marketing, International, Internet/Web Design, Investor Relations, Leisure, Luxury Products, Magazines, Market Research, Media Buying Services, Media Planning, Men's Market, Mobile Marketing, Multicultural, Multimedia, New Technologies, Newspapers & Magazines, Out-of-Home Media, Outdoor, Over-50 Market, Paid Searches, Pharmaceutical, Planning & Consultation, Podcasting, Point of Purchase, Point of Sale, Print, Product Placement, Public Relations, RSS (Really Simple Syndication), Radio, Recruitment, Regional, Restaurant, Retail, Sales Promotion, Search Engine Optimization, Seniors' Market, Social Marketing/Nonprofit, Sponsorship, Sports Market, Strategic Planning/Research, Sweepstakes, Syndication, T.V., Teen Market, Trade & Consumer Magazines, Transportation, Travel & Tourism, Viral/Buzz/Word of Mouth, Women's Market, Yellow Pages Advertising

Mason Franklin *(Mng Partner & Head-Integrated Plng Practice-North America)*
Kristen Metzger *(Mng Partner-People & Culture)*
Kat So *(Mng Partner)*
Ravi Pahilajani *(Partner & Sr Dir-Digital)*
Natalie Lee *(Partner & Dir-Digital Analytics)*
Carl Fremont *(Chief Digital Officer-Global)*
Rick Acampora *(Pres-Client Svcs-North America)*
Alison Coley *(Pres-Client)*
Gibbs Haljun *(Mng Dir-Media Investment)*
Matthew Bell *(Head-Digital Strategy)*
Sharona Sankar-King *(Head-Practice-Digital Advanced Analytics-North America)*
Pele Cortizo-Burgess *(Dir-Integrated Plng-Global)*
Lindsey Schiffman Yoselevitz *(Sr Partner & Dir-Mktg Comm)*
Kim Vasey *(Sr Partner & Dir-Radio)*
Kinjal Parikh *(Assoc Dir)*
Alyssa Byron *(Mgr)*

Accounts:
Amazon Digital Media
AT&T Communications Corp. (Media Agency of Record) Campaign: "Around the World for Free"
Chanel
Citi; 2007
Citigroup Inc.
Colgate-Palmolive
DHL
Edgewell Personal Care EverReady, Media, Schick
New-Energizer Media
Evian Media
General Electric Media Buying & Planning
IKEA
Innocent Campaign: "Big Knit"
LegalZoom
Macy's
Mercedes-Benz India (Agency of Record)
Michelin
Paramount Pictures; 2004
Shearings Media Strategy
Sony Electronics Media Buying & Planning-Asia; 2007
Texaco
Tiffany & Co Media

United States (Regional Offices)

MEC - NA HQ, New York

825 7th Ave, New York, NY 10019-5818
(See Separate Listing)

Atlanta

MEC

3340 Peachtree Rd NE Ste 100, Atlanta, GA 30326
Tel.: (404) 806-1950
Fax: (404) 806-1951
E-Mail: info.northam@mecglobal.com
Web Site: www.mecglobal.com

Employees: 200

Agency Specializes In: Media Buying Services, Sponsorship

Nelson Pinero *(Partner & Sr Dir)*
Sarah Minton *(Partner & Dir-Local Plng)*
Bryan Jackson *(Sr Partner & Acct Dir)*
Matt Martin *(Mgr-Digital)*
Kipp Mullis *(Mgr & Reg Supvr-Media-Southeast & South Central Reg-AT&T)*
Amy Porter *(Supvr-Digital Media)*

Accounts:
AT&T Communications Corp.

Irvine

MEC

7525 Irvine Center Dr, Irvine, CA 92618
Tel.: (949) 623-6500
Fax: (310) 309-4802
E-Mail: info.northam@mecglobal.com
Web Site: www.mecglobal.com

Employees: 25

National Agency Associations: 4A's

Agency Specializes In: Media Buying Services, Sponsorship

Andrea Hartman *(Mng Partner & Client Svc Dir)*
Brian Ko *(Mng Partner-Digital)*
Katie Brown *(Partner & Sr Dir-Plng & Strategy)*
Sharon Pardee *(Partner & Sr Dir-Plng)*
Kristin Hunt *(Mgr)*

Accounts:
Chanel
Chevron
LegalZoom; Glendale, CA Data Analytics, Media Planning & Buying
Mitsubishi
Wrigley's

Los Angeles

MEC

6300 Wilshire Blvd, Los Angeles, CA 90048
Tel.: (323) 761-1400
Fax: (323) 817-1870
Web Site: www.mecglobal.com

Employees: 50

National Agency Associations: 4A's

Agency Specializes In: Media Buying Services, Sponsorship

Mark Miller *(Mng Partner & Sr Dir)*
Catherine Johnson *(Partner & Sr Dir)*
Carol Lansen *(Mng Dir)*
Michael Jones *(CEO-Latin America)*
Cynthia Evans *(Head-Strategy-Latin America)*
Marci Sovitsky *(Sr Partner & Sr Dir)*
Laura Bonetti *(Reg Dir-Trading-LATAM)*
Jorge Canton *(Acct Dir)*
Kristi Cox *(Dir)*
Raquel Puchol *(Dir-Interaction)*
Lauren Currence *(Mgr-Intl Plng)*
Melissa Gonzalez *(Mgr-SEO)*
Davide Grossi *(Mgr-Interaction Search)*
James Vance *(Mgr-Interaction & Digital)*
Amisha Govan *(Supvr-Media)*
Aileen Markarian *(Supvr-Media-Digital)*
Reni Pernova *(Supvr-Digital Media)*
Lauren Blake *(Assoc Planner-Digital)*
Lawson Marian *(Assoc Planner-Digital Media)*
Katherine Siu *(Coord-Adv Ops & Jr Planner)*
Jennifer Chan *(Sr Grp Dir)*
Jennifer Lee *(Sr Assoc-Digital)*
Virginia To *(Assoc Media Planner)*

Accounts:
Paramount Theatrical

Miami

MEC

601 Brickell Key Dr Ste 804, Miami, FL 33131
Tel.: (786) 264-7600
Fax: (786) 264-7620
E-Mail: info.northam@mecglobal.com
Web Site: www.mecglobal.com

Employees: 35
Year Founded: 2001

Agency Specializes In: Media Buying Services, Sponsorship

Carl Fremont *(Chief Digital Officer-Global)*
Shenan Reed *(Pres-Digital-North America)*
Renato de Paula *(CEO-Latin America)*
Marla Kaplowitz *(CEO-North America)*
Jose Miranda *(Reg Dir-Analytics & Insights-Latin America)*
Veronica Amsler *(Acct Dir)*

Accounts:
Bayer
Monster
Telecom Italia

Wrigley's

San Francisco

MEC

303 2nd St North Tower 3rd Fl, San Francisco, CA 94107
Tel.: (415) 764-1300
Fax: (415) 764-1333
E-Mail: info.na@mecglobal.com
Web Site: www.mecglobal.com

Employees: 20

National Agency Associations: 4A's

Agency Specializes In: Media Buying Services, Sponsorship

Kristine Segrist *(Mng Partner & Head-Client)*
Brian Ko *(Mng Partner-Digital)*
Hans Logie *(Mng Partner)*
Bruce Kiernan *(Partner & Sr Dir)*
Molly Berger *(Mgr-Media Strategy)*
Chelsea Donlin *(Planner-Integrated)*

Accounts:
AT&T Communications Corp.
Bon Bon Bum Lollipop
Chanel
Chevron Corporation
Netflix Media

Canada

MEC

160 Bloor St E Ste 500, Toronto, ON M4W 3S7 Canada
Tel.: (416) 987-9100
Fax: (416) 987-9150
E-Mail: info.northam@mecglobal.com
Web Site: www.mecglobal.com

Agency Specializes In: Media Buying Services

Nick Williams *(CFO)*
Alastair Taylor *(Sr VP & Acct Mgmt Dir)*
Wes Wolch *(Grp Dir-Strategy)*
Claus Burmeister *(Dir-Comm Strategy)*
Nicole Lambe *(Dir-Digital)*
Michael So *(Dir-Comm Strategy)*
Suzanne Thibeault *(Dir-Media)*
Chris Stewart *(Assoc Dir)*
Alicia Mavreas *(Sr Mgr)*
Dorothy Zarska *(Sr Mgr-Plng)*
Katelynn Breukelman *(Mgr-Trading)*
Aileen Cruikshank *(Mgr-Trading)*
Breanne Morrison *(Mgr-Digital)*
Lyndsey Rebelo *(Mgr-Digital)*
Reza Alibhai *(Strategist-Digital)*
Meryl Fernandes *(Strategist-Digital)*
Mike Laidman *(Media Planner & Media Buyer)*
Christine Fukumoto *(Media Buyer)*
William Hart *(Media Planner)*
Srdjana Ilic *(Media Planner)*
Marijana Mitolinski *(Media Buyer)*
Charlotte Peters *(Media Buyer)*
Michelle Ho *(Sr Media Planner)*
Caitlin Neve *(Asst Media Planner)*
Sammy Rifai *(Sr Media Planner)*
Laura Ritchie *(Sr Media Planner)*

Accounts:
Cara Operations Campaign: "Milestones - Top Chef Canada Activation"
Dare Foods Media
Molson Coors Campaign: "Coors Light Silver Bullet Express", Campaign: "The Action's On The Ice", Coors Light

Europe, Middle East, Africa

MEC Global HQ, London

1 Paris Garden, London, SE1 8NU United Kingdom
Tel.: (44) 20 7803 2000
Fax: (44) 20 7803 2001
E-Mail: info.emea@mecglobal.com
Web Site: www.mecglobal.co.uk

Year Founded: 2001

Agency Specializes In: Above-the-Line, Affiliate Marketing, Affluent Market, Asian Market, Automotive, Aviation & Aerospace, Below-the-Line, Bilingual Market, Branded Entertainment, Broadcast, Business Publications, Business-To-Business, Cable T.V., Children's Market, Communications, Computers & Software, Consulting, Consumer Goods, Consumer Marketing, Consumer Publications, Cosmetics, Customer Relationship Management, Digital/Interactive, Direct Response Marketing, Direct-to-Consumer, Electronics, Entertainment, Event Planning & Marketing, Experience Design, Fashion/Apparel, Financial, Food Service, Game Integration, Gay & Lesbian Market, Guerilla Marketing, Health Care Services, High Technology, Hispanic Market, Hospitality, Household Goods, In-Store Advertising, Information Technology, Integrated Marketing, International, Internet/Web Design, Investor Relations, Leisure, Luxury Products, Magazines, Market Research, Media Buying Services, Media Planning, Men's Market, Mobile Marketing, Multicultural, Multimedia, New Technologies, Newspapers & Magazines, Out-of-Home Media, Outdoor, Over-50 Market, Paid Searches, Pharmaceutical, Planning & Consultation, Podcasting, Point of Purchase, Point of Sale, Print, Product Placement, Public Relations, RSS (Really Simple Syndication), Radio, Recruitment, Regional, Restaurant, Retail, Sales Promotion, Search Engine Optimization, Seniors' Market, Social Marketing/Nonprofit, Sponsorship, Sports Market, Strategic Planning/Research, Sweepstakes, Syndication, T.V., Teen Market, Trade & Consumer Magazines, Transportation, Travel & Tourism, Viral/Buzz/Word of Mouth, Women's Market, Yellow Pages Advertising

Tom George *(CEO)*
Dermott Mullan *(Mng Partner & Head-Programmatic Global Solutions & EMEA)*
Duncan Smith *(Mng Partner)*
Greg Shickle *(Partner-Performance)*
Shula Sinclair *(Partner-Strategy-Global)*
Steve Ball *(Mng Dir)*
Sarah Hennessy *(Mng Dir)*
Paul Hutchison *(COO)*
David Fletcher *(Chief Data Officer)*
Ben Poole *(Chief Digital Officer)*
Alex Altman *(Mng Dir-Global Solutions)*
Justin Taylor *(Mng Dir-MEC Digital)*
Vicki Ferris *(Head-Affiliate Mktg)*
Chien-Wen Tong *(Head-Digital Strategy-Global Solutions)*
Ian Edwards *(Grp Dir-Bus, Client & Comm)*
Jonathan Edwards *(Reg Dir-Analytics, Data & Tech-APAC)*
Claire Billings *(Dir-Mktg-UK)*
Scott Brenman *(Dir-Strategy)*
Dan Plant *(Dir-Grp Strategy & Real Time Plng)*
Lucie Radford *(Dir-New Bus)*

Accounts:
Accenture
Activision Blizzard, Inc Media
B&Q Media
BBC Worldwide
BGL Group Beagle Street, Bennetts, Media Buying, Media Planning, lesfurets.com, verzekeringsite
Bupa
Campbell's Soup
Central Office of Information Elections, Media Communications & Planning
Chanel
Chevron
Citi
Colgate-Palmolive
Danone Danio, Evian, Media Planning & Buying, Outdoor
Department for Work & Pensions Jobcentre Plus
Department of Health Media Planning
DHL
Energizer Wilkinson Sword
Everything Everywhere Media Planning & Buying
Ferrero
Freeview Media
GoDaddy Media Planning
The Gym Group Below-the-Line, Digital Marketing, Media Buying, Media Strategy Planning
Heinz Complan
Henkel
Morrisons Media
Mulberry Media Planning & Buying
Nintendo
Orange plc Offline Media Planning/Buying, Online Brand Advertising Planning/Buying
Paramount
The Saucy Fish Co. Integrated Marketing Campaign, Media Planning & Buying
Singapore Airlines
Tic Tac
Transport for London Media Planning & Buying
Vodafone Media
Xerox

EMEA (Regional Offices)

MEC - EMEA HQ

1 Paris Garden, London, SE1 8NU United Kingdom
Tel.: (44) 20 7803 2000
Fax: (44) 20 7803 2001
E-Mail: info.emea@mecglobal.com
Web Site: www.mecglobal.com

Employees: 300
Year Founded: 1976

Agency Specializes In: Above-the-Line, Affiliate Marketing, Affluent Market, Asian Market, Automotive, Aviation & Aerospace, Below-the-Line, Bilingual Market, Branded Entertainment, Broadcast, Business Publications, Business-To-Business, Cable T.V., Children's Market, Communications, Computers & Software, Consulting, Consumer Goods, Consumer Marketing, Consumer Publications, Content, Cosmetics, Customer Relationship Management, Digital/Interactive, Direct Response Marketing, Direct-to-Consumer, Electronics, Entertainment, Event Planning & Marketing, Experience Design, Fashion/Apparel, Financial, Food Service, Game Integration, Gay & Lesbian Market, Guerilla Marketing, Health Care Services, High Technology, Hispanic Market, Hospitality, Household Goods, In-Store Advertising, Information Technology, Integrated Marketing, International, Internet/Web Design, Investor Relations, Leisure, Luxury Products, Magazines, Market Research, Media Buying Services, Media Planning, Men's Market, Mobile Marketing, Multicultural, Multimedia, New Technologies, Newspapers & Magazines, Out-of-Home Media, Outdoor, Over-50 Market, Paid Searches, Pharmaceutical, Planning & Consultation, Podcasting, Point of Purchase, Point of Sale, Print, Product Placement, Public Relations, RSS (Really Simple Syndication), Radio, Recruitment, Regional, Restaurant, Retail, Sales Promotion, Search Engine Optimization, Seniors' Market, Social Marketing/Nonprofit, Sponsorship, Sports Market, Strategic Planning/Research, Sweepstakes, Syndication, T.V., Teen Market, Trade & Consumer Magazines, Transportation, Travel & Tourism, Viral/Buzz/Word of Mouth,

Women's Market, Yellow Pages Advertising

Keith Tiley *(Chief Investment Officer-Global)*
Rogier Croes *(Chief Digital Officer)*
Alex Altman *(Mng Dir-Solutions-Global)*
Kevin Ayadassen *(Grp Acct Dir)*
Sarah Homer *(Dir-People &Culture-EMEA)*
Ryan Murdoch *(Dir-Analytics)*
Ian Redman *(Dir-Bus Dev-Europe, Middle East & Africa)*
Amy Chamberlain *(Acct Mgr-Activation)*
Hamish Davies *(Reg Client Svc Dir-Europe, Middle East & Africa)*

Accounts:
Absolute Radio
Accenture
Accenture
Blockbuster UK Media Planning & Buying
Colgate-Palmolive UK Ltd. Colgate Oral Range, Colgate-Palmolive Body Care
Department of Health
Energizer
Lloyds Banking Group plc Lloyds TSB, Media Buying, Media Planning
Michelin Media Planning & Media Buying
Nintendo
Orange
Paramount
Star Alliance
Tiffany & Co. Global Media
United Biscuits (Holdings) Limited Media Buying, Media Planning
Visa Campaign: "Flow Faster", Media, Media Buying, Media Planning
Wm Morrison Supermarkets
Wrigley
Xerox

Belgium

MEC
Rue de Stallestraat 65, 1180 Brussels, Belgium
Tel.: (32) 2 333 0900
Fax: (32) 2 332 2002
E-Mail: alain.hendrickx@mecglobal.com
Web Site: www.mecglobal.com/

Employees: 40

Agency Specializes In: Media Buying Services

Alain Hendrickx *(CEO)*
Veronique Bulens *(Grp Acct Dir)*
Nathalie Dubois *(Grp Acct Dir)*
Laurence Hellinckx *(Dir-Television)*
Gaelle Daoust *(Sr Mgr-Digital)*
Florence Glibert *(Mgr-Print & Buyer-Digital)*

Accounts:
Bpost Communications, Strategic Experience
Chanel
Chrysler
Citibank
Colgate
Deutsche Bank
Flen Pharm
Mercedes Benz
NBCU
Toyota
Twinings

Denmark

MEC
St Kongengade 59, DK 1264 Copenhagen, Denmark
Tel.: (45) 33 38 1800
Fax: (45) 33 38 1900
E-Mail: infodk@mecglobal.com
Web Site: www.mecglobal.com

Employees: 80

Agency Specializes In: Media Buying Services

Uffe Henriksen *(CEO)*
Christina Jessen *(Sr VP & Acct Mgmt Dir)*
Cecilia Boll *(Dir-Social Media)*
Jesper Mikkelsen *(Dir-Creative Strategy)*
Sandra Moe Nissen *(Dir-Client)*
Camilla Palmy *(Dir-Strategic Plng)*
Claus Enggaard *(Client Svc Dir)*
Mia Lunau Nielsen *(Client Dir-Nordic)*

Accounts:
Beiersdorf Elastoplast, Eucerin, Media, Nivea
Colgate Campaign: "Student Club"
Nescafe
Sony Ericsson
Urban Ears

Finland

MEC
Unioninkatue 24, 00180 Helsinki, Finland
Tel.: (358) 207 199 211
Fax: (358) 209 199 219
Web Site: www.mecglobal.com

Employees: 12

Agency Specializes In: Media Buying Services

Maarika Virtanen *(Acct Dir)*
Reija Niiranen *(Acct Mgr)*

Accounts:
Beiersdorf Elastoplast, Eucerin, Media, Nivea
Gina Tricot

France

MEC
32 Rue Guersant TSA 70022, CEDEX, 75837 Paris, 17 France
Tel.: (33) 1 53 57 6464
Fax: (33) 1 53 57 6465
E-Mail: info.emea@mecglobal.com
Web Site: www.mecglobal.com

Agency Specializes In: Media Buying Services

Angelique Provost-Chargelegue *(Mng Partner & Head-Interaction)*
Delcoustal Matthieu *(Mng Partner)*
Christophe Brossard *(CEO-France)*
Coline Bevilacqua *(Grp Acct Dir)*
Juliette Marcadet *(Grp Acct Dir-Intl)*
Emmanuelle Vazquez *(Acct Dir)*
Olivier Carluy *(Dir-Strategy)*
Marie Giraud *(Acct Mgr-Intl)*
Anastasia Poux *(Acct Mgr-Plurimedia)*
Luc Buhot *(Mgr)*

Accounts:
Fiat Digital
Michelin

Germany

MEC GmbH
Oberbaumbruecke 1, 20457 Hamburg, Germany
Tel.: (49) 40 3255000
Fax: (49) 69 15302 500
E-Mail: mecgermany.contact@mecglobal.com
Web Site: www.mecglobal.de

Employees: 100

Agency Specializes In: Media Buying Services

Lars Magnus Kirschke *(CEO)*
Jochen Franke *(Mng Dir)*
Marc Lehmann *(Mng Dir)*
Frank Lenssen *(Mng Dir)*
Martin Rose *(Mng Dir)*
Neeso Tammena *(CFO)*
Arvid Bostrom *(Chief Strategy Officer)*
Stefan Ege *(Chief Investment Officer)*
Karin Immenroth *(Mng Dir-Analytics & Insights)*

Accounts:
Boston Consulting Group
Griesson De Beukelaer
Hachette
International Copper Association
Smart Vertriebs Park King Campaign
Wander Ovomaltine

MEC
Theresienhohe 13a, 81737 Munich, Germany
Tel.: (49) 89 638 8900
Fax: (49) 89 638 89310
E-Mail: mecgermany.contact@mecglobal.com
Web Site: www.mecglobal.com

Employees: 20

Agency Specializes In: Media Buying Services

Marc Lehmann *(Mng Dir)*
Frank Lenssen *(Mng Dir)*
Neeso Tammena *(CFO)*
Tino Krause *(COO)*
Arvid Bostrom *(Chief Strategy Officer)*
Karin Immenroth *(Mng Dir-Analytics & Insight)*
Marin Curkovic *(Head-Strategy & Bus Dev)*
Elke Sudholt *(Acct Dir)*
Jan Konig *(Dir-Digital Strategy)*
Jens Kleine *(Sr Mgr-Digital Plng)*

MEC
Rosstrasse 92, 40476 Dusseldorf, Germany
Tel.: (49) 211 55880
Fax: (49) 211 5588160
E-Mail: info.emea@mecglobal.com
Web Site: www.mecglobal.com

Agency Specializes In: Media Buying Services

Arvid Bostrom *(Mng Dir)*
Matthias Bruell *(CEO-Germany & Switzerland)*
Karin Immenroth *(Mng Dir-Analytics & Insight)*
Marc Lehmann *(Mng Dir-Client Svc)*
Anett Jasmann *(Acct Grp Head)*
Marin Curkovic *(Head-Strategy & Bus Dev)*
Jens Kleine *(Grp Head-Digital Plng)*
Tina De Le Roi *(Dir-Digital Plng)*
Thomas Oesterling *(Dir-Data Tech &Svcs)*

Accounts:
AT&T Communications Corp.
Bang & Olufsen
Barclays
New-DHL Global Media

Hungary

MEC
Lajos utca 80, H-1037 Budapest, Hungary
Tel.: (36) 1 801 8111
Fax: (36) 1 801 8112
Web Site: www.mecglobal.com

Agency Specializes In: Media Buying Services

Janos Gulyas *(CEO)*
Ingrid Ihasz *(Head-Digital)*

Media Buying Services

Accounts:
Cora

Slovak Republic

MEC
Karadzicova 8, 821 08 Bratislava, 1 Slovakia
Tel.: (421) 2 5788 0410
Fax: (421) 2 5788 0413
E-Mail: daniel.zivica@mecglobal.com
Web Site: www.mecglobal.com

Agency Specializes In: Media Buying Services

Branislav Marko *(Media Dir-CEE)*
Dusan Horvath *(Dir-Bus Unit)*
Pavol Zahradnik *(Dir-Analytics & Insight)*

Ireland

MEC
6 Ely Pl, Dublin, 2 Ireland
Tel.: (353) 1 669 0090
Fax: (353) 1 669 0099
E-Mail: david.hayes@mecglobal.com
Web Site: www.mecglobal.com

Employees: 10

Agency Specializes In: Media Buying Services

David Hayes *(Mng Dir)*
Kevin Gordon *(Acct Dir)*
Eimear Hughes *(Acct Dir)*
Mark James *(Bus Dir)*
Gavin Collins *(Sr Acct Mgr)*
Paul McPartlin *(Sr Acct Mgr)*
Phoebe Laing *(Acct Mgr)*
Kieran Lynch *(Acct Exec)*
Justin Ronan *(Planner-Digital)*

Accounts:
Beiersdorf Elastoplast, Eucerin, Media, Nivea
H.J.heinz Company Ireland Tomato Ketchup
Nintendo
Specsavers
Xtra-vision

Italy

MEC
Via Carducci 14, 20123 Milan, Italy
Tel.: (39) 02 467 671
Fax: (39) 02 467 67344
E-Mail: info.emea@mecglobal.com
Web Site: www.mecglobal.com

Employees: 250

Agency Specializes In: Media Buying Services

Luca Vergani *(CEO)*
Silvio Corbi *(Head-Digital Plng & Dir-Media)*
Valeria Mares *(Dir-Strategy)*
Raffaele Natale *(Mgr-Digital Media)*
Sara Carminati *(Supvr-Media)*
Walter Ferrari *(Supvr-Digital Media)*
Giulia Ambrosi *(Media Planner)*
Barbara Bolognesi *(Media Planner-Online)*
Francesca D'Adda *(Planner-Digital Media)*
Giorgia Yasmine Rocca *(Planner-Digital Media)*

Accounts:
Amita
Camomilla
Cisalfa
Dahlia TV
Finmeccanica
Gioco del Lotto
Google
Grimaldi
Italy Monte dei Paschi di Siena
Lucky Red
Molinari
Nuvaring
Olympus
Pedrini
Q8
Recordati
Stage Entertainment
Star
Yakult

MEC
Via Cristofo Colombo 163, 00196 Rome, Italy
Tel.: (39) 06322 9661
Fax: (39) 06320 1693
E-Mail: roberto.parodi@mecglobal.com
Web Site: www.mecglobal.com

Agency Specializes In: Media Buying Services

Roberto Parodi *(Dir)*
Maddalena Marino *(Mgr-Digital)*
Giulia Ambrosi *(Media Planner)*
Michela Confalonieri *(Planner-Digital)*
Chiara Spezie *(Media Planner)*
Mario Vedetta *(Planner-Digital Media)*

MEC
Via Leoncino 16, 37121 Verona, Italy
Tel.: (39) 045 805 3911
Fax: (39) 045 8036 488
E-Mail: domiziana.pandolfi@mecglobal.com
Web Site: www.mecglobal.com

Agency Specializes In: Media Buying Services

Alessandro Villoresi *(Chm)*
Luca Vergani *(CEO)*
Domiziana Pandolfi *(Dir-Client)*
Maddalena Marino *(Mgr-Digital)*
Giulia Ambrosi *(Media Planner)*
Michela Confalonieri *(Planner-Digital)*
Chiara Spezie *(Media Planner)*
Mario Vedetta *(Planner-Digital Media)*

The Netherlands

MEC
Karperstraat 10, PO Box 8804, 1075 KZ Amsterdam, Netherlands
Tel.: (31) 20 355 0000
Fax: (31) 20 355 0001
E-Mail: info-nld@mecglobal.com
Web Site: www.mecglobal.com

Employees: 80

Agency Specializes In: Media Buying Services

Eric Kramer *(CEO)*
Niels Langeries *(Head-Strategy)*
Marco Ruivenkamp *(Head-Digital)*
Rianne Met *(Dir-Comm)*
Simone Van Der Graaf *(Dir-Comm)*
Hidde Zwaagstra *(Dir-Bus Dev)*

Accounts:
Biersdorf Elastoplast, Eucerin, Media, Nivea
Henkel

Norway

MEC
Stortorvet 10, 0155 Oslo, Norway
Tel.: (47) 22 472 600
Fax: (47) 22 472 601
E-Mail: info.emea@mecglobal.com
Web Site: www.mecglobal.com

Employees: 60

Agency Specializes In: Media Buying Services

Stig Jossund *(Head-Paid Digital Media)*
Inger K. Halvorsen *(Dir)*
Anette Solli *(Dir-Strategic)*
Hanne Brauten *(Acct Mgr)*
Line Gronberg Evensen *(Planner-Media & Project Coord-Direct Mktg)*
Henning Braathen *(Client Svc Dir)*
Glenn Engebretsen *(Client Svc Dir)*

Accounts:
Beiersdorf Elastoplast, Eucerin, Media, Nivea
Mercedes
Piso

Poland

MEC
ul Dobra 56/66, 00312 Warsaw, Poland
Tel.: (48) 22 552 7777
Fax: (48) 22 552 7770
E-Mail: anna.lubowska@mecglobal.com
Web Site: www.mecglobal.com

Agency Specializes In: Media Buying Services

Izabela Albrychiewicz *(CEO)*
Tomasz Fochtman *(Mng Partner-Strategy & Innovation)*
Pawel Gala *(Mng Partner)*

Accounts:
H&M Media Strategic & Buying
IKEA
Lisner
Sarantis Kolastyna

Portugal

MEC
Av Fontess Pereira de Melo 6 2nd Fl 2 Andar Dir, Lisbon, Portugal
Tel.: (351) 21 359 2200
Fax: (351) 21 351 2267
E-Mail: jose.cardoso@mecglobal.com
Web Site: www.mecglobal.com

Employees: 50

Agency Specializes In: Media Buying Services

Jose Manuel Cardoso *(Mng Dir)*
Maria Joao Oliveira *(Chief Client Officer)*
Karine Santos *(Head-Strategy)*
Frederico Correia *(Acct Dir)*
Diogo Marnoto *(Dir-Interaction)*
Andre Tavares *(Acct Supvr-Digital)*
Cristina Braga *(Supvr-Media)*
Madalena Magalhaes *(Specialist-Digital)*

Accounts:
Cerealis Milaneza
EDP
Media Markt
New-Ubisoft

Russia

MEC
23 Osenniy Blvd Krylatsky Business Centre, Moscow, 121609 Russia
Tel.: (7) 495 641 23 14
Fax: (7) 495 641 23 15

E-Mail: info.emea@ru.mecglobal.com
Web Site: www.mecglobal.com

Agency Specializes In: Media Buying Services

Victoria Prostyakova *(Mng partner & Dir-MEC Access)*
Anastasia Donchenko *(Mng Partner-Bus Dev)*
Vlad Ivanov *(Mng Partner)*
Maria Kolosova *(Exec Dir)*
Olga Selezneva *(Sr Mgr-Internet)*
Philipp Nemtsev *(Sr Media Planner)*
Lena Yarulina *(Sr Media Planner)*

Accounts:
ECCO BIOM

Spain

MEC
Calle Las Norias 92, 2 planta, 28027 Madrid, Spain
Tel.: (34) 91 709 25 00
Fax: (34) 91 405 34 99
E-Mail: info.emea@mecglobal.com
Web Site: www.mecglobal.com

Agency Specializes In: Media Buying Services

Roberto Lopez Garcia *(Head-Digital)*
Lara Bilbao Melcon *(Head-Plng)*
Alicia Pena Rada *(Head-Strategy & New Bus)*
Sonia Fernandez *(Acct Dir)*
Maite Gonzalez Gutierrez *(Acct Dir)*
Cristina Gordo Sardon *(Dir-Digital Trading & Ops)*
Victoria Caceres *(Acct Exec-Digital)*
Marta Gonzalez Fernandez *(Acct Exec)*
Neus Martinez Albero *(Planner-Digital)*
Laura Liz *(Sr Media Planner)*

Accounts:
Henkel
Loterias y Apuestas del Estado Media

MEC
Calle Las Norias 92, 28221 Madrid, Spain
Tel.: (34) 91 709 25 00
Fax: (34) 652 924738
Web Site: www.mecglobal.com

Agency Specializes In: Media Buying Services

Roberto Lopez Garcia *(Head-Digital)*
Penelope Garcia Jimenez *(Head-Comm & Mktg)*
Lara Bilbao Melcon *(Head-Plng)*
Alicia Pena Rada *(Head-Strategy & New Bus)*
Ruth De La Torre Vega *(Acct Dir)*
Emiliano Chedrese Luciani *(Client Svcs Dir)*
Maite Gonzalez Gutierrez *(Dir-Accts)*
Victoria Caceres *(Acct Exec-Digital)*
Marta Gonzalez Fernandez *(Acct Exec)*
Jorge Pesquero Henche *(Acct Exec-Digital)*
Laura Liz *(Sr Media Planner)*

Accounts:
Ubisoft Campaign: "The Biggest Cyber Party Ever"

MEC Mediterranea
C/Naturalista Charles Robert Darwin, 5 Parque Tecnologico, 46980 Valencia, Spain
Tel.: (34) 96 382 65 25
Fax: (34) 96 382 65 29
E-Mail: info.mecspain@mecglobal.com
Web Site: www.mecglobal.com

Agency Specializes In: Media Buying Services

Roberto Lopez Garcia *(Head-Digital)*
Penelope Garcia Jimenez *(Head-Comm & Mktg)*
Lara Bilbao Melcon *(Head-Plng)*
Alicia Pena Rada *(Head-Strategy & New Bus)*
Cristina Rodriguez *(Head-Client Project)*
Ruth De La Torre Vega *(Acct Dir)*
Emiliano Chedrese Luciani *(Client Svcs Dir)*
Maite Gonzalez Gutierrez *(Dir-Accts)*
Yemina Banks *(Acct Mgr)*
Victoria Caceres *(Acct Exec-Digital)*
Marta Gonzalez Fernandez *(Acct Exec)*
Jorge Pesquero Henche *(Acct Exec-Digital)*
Neus Martinez Albero *(Planner-Digital)*

Switzerland

MEC
Rue Bellefontaine 2, 1003 Lausanne, Switzerland
Tel.: (41) 21 632 82 40
Fax: (41) 21 632 82 41
E-Mail: info.emea@mecglobal.com
Web Site: www.mecglobal.com

Employees: 12

Agency Specializes In: Media Buying Services

Stephane Anken *(Dir-Client Svcs)*
Laurence Acerbis *(Sr Acct Mgr)*

MEC
Seestrasse 315, 8038 Zurich, Switzerland
Tel.: (41) 44 2883840
Fax: (41) 44 2883841
E-Mail: info.emea@mecglobal.com
Web Site: www.mecglobal.com

Employees: 15

Agency Specializes In: Media Buying Services

Ulrich Tacke *(Mng Dir)*

Accounts:
Bolton Group
Colgate Palmolive
IKEA
The New Americans

Turkey

MEC
Dereboyu Caddesi No 78/1-4 Ortakoy, 4347 Istanbul, Turkey
Tel.: (90) 212 227 17 00
Fax: (90) 212 227 67 56
E-Mail: info.emea@mecglobal.com
Web Site: www.mecglobal.com

Employees: 40

Agency Specializes In: Media Buying Services

Gizem Tekin *(Dir-Interaction)*
Seda Cataltas *(Supvr-Interaction)*
Merve Gurayca *(Supvr-Plng)*
Hasan Polat *(Supvr-Media Plng)*
Melike Yilmazel *(Specialist-Ops & Asst Media Planner)*
Cankiz Akkaya *(Media Planner)*
Aylin Aykut *(Media Planner)*
Sina Karaca *(Planner-Interaction Digital)*
Nihan Candan *(Sr Media Planner)*

Accounts:
Citi
Dogus Publishing Group
Mitsubishi
Tamek

United Kingdom

MEC
Bass Warehouse 4 Castle Street, Castlefield, Manchester, M3 4LZ United Kingdom
Tel.: (44) 161 930 9000
Fax: (44) 161 930 9030
E-Mail: info.emea@mecglobal.com
Web Site: www.mecglobal.com

Agency Specializes In: Media Buying Services

Chris Murphy *(Mng Dir)*
Mick Style *(Mng Dir-Manchester)*
Nick Dobson *(Head-Digital Engagement)*
Chris Garner *(Head-Performance Mktg)*
Richard Stanton *(Head-Digital Plng)*
Lyndsay Broughton *(Dir-Digital Plng)*
Oliver Levy *(Dir-Digital Plng)*
Ben Plastow *(Dir-Data Integration)*
Steven Richards *(Mgr-Digital Tech)*
Alice Roughton *(Mgr-Digital Engagement)*

Accounts:
Beiersdorf Campaign: "The Moment Before the Moment", Elastoplast, Eucerin, Media, Nivea
Birmingham City University
First4lawyers DRTV, Media Planning & Buying
Jet2.com Digital, Media
Jet2holidays Digital, Media
Paramount SEO
Polish Tourist Board
POM Wonderful
Seven Seas
SIBA
Transform Cosmetic Surgery
Vimto
Wacky Warehouse Media
Webuyanycar.com Media

Kuwait

MEC
Fahed Al Salem Street Rakan Tower, 6th Floor, Kuwait, 13011 Kuwait
Tel.: (965) 22901571345
Fax: (965) 22901570
E-Mail: w.kanafani@mec-me.com
Web Site: www.mecglobal.com

Agency Specializes In: Media Buying Services

Morocco

MEC
157 Boulevard d'Anfa Immeuble Racine d'Anfa 4eme Etage, PO Box 20000, Quartier Racine, Casablanca, Morocco
Tel.: (212) 522 361339
Fax: (212) 522 360309
E-Mail: n.rhaleb@mec-me.com
Web Site: www.mecglobal.com

Agency Specializes In: Media Buying Services

Asmaa Fahmi *(Mng Dir)*
Mehdi Slaoui *(Sr Acct Mgr)*

MEC Saudi Arabia
Al Khairiya Tower 2nd Floor King Fahad Road, PO Box 19462, Riyadh, 11435 Saudi Arabia
Tel.: (966) 1 466 0750
Fax: (966) 1 462 8219
E-Mail: info@mecglobal.com
Web Site: www.mecglobal.com

Agency Specializes In: Media Buying Services

Omar Koleilat *(Gen Mgr-KSA)*

Egypt

MEC
8 Gazirat El Arab St 2 Fl, Al Mohandessin, Cairo, Egypt
Tel.: (20) 2 333 74073
Fax: (20) 2 337 4563
E-Mail: info.emea@mecglobal.com
Web Site: www.mecglobal.com

Employees: 30

Agency Specializes In: Media Buying Services

Emad Mahmoud *(Head-MEC Interaction & Dir-Digital)*
Wassim Hmaidan *(Gen Mgr)*
Mona Raouf *(Assoc Dir-Media)*
Ayman Al-Banhawi *(Mgr-Media Plng)*
Nael Fadel *(Sr Exec-Media)*

Kenya

MEC
CVS Plaza 3rd Floor, Lenana Road, Nairobi, Kenya
Tel.: (254) 20 271 0600
Fax: (254) 20 551 335
Web Site: www.mecglobal.com

Agency Specializes In: Media Buying Services

Monica Kambo Achola *(Mng Dir)*

MEC South Africa
Merton Place The Avenues Office Park, 45 Homestead Rd,, 2128 Rivonia, 2128 South Africa
Tel.: (27) 11 582 6000
Fax: (27) 86 504 8786
E-Mail: michelle.meyjes@mecglobal.com
Web Site: www.mecglobal.com

Employees: 40

Agency Specializes In: Media Buying Services

Michelle Meyjes *(CEO)*
Lwandile Qokweni *(Chief Strategy Officer)*
Erica Gunning *(Mng Dir-MEC GROUP)*
Eric Van Rookhuyzen *(Head-Digital Media)*
Paul Buys *(Mgr-Production & Producer)*
Alistair Aitken *(Dir-Comml & Ops-South Africa)*
Jacqui Grigg *(Dir-Buying)*
Michele Smuts *(Mgr-Ops)*
Nadine Van Der Merwe *(Strategist-Digital)*
Asher Vorster *(Strategist-Media)*

Accounts:
Blackberry
Brandhouse
Chevron
Hollard Insurance Media Planning & Buying
KFC Journey of Hope

Argentina

MEC
Juramento 1775 piso 11, C1428DNA Buenos Aires, Argentina
Tel.: (54) 11 4896 1700
Fax: (54) 11 4896 4525
E-Mail: info.latam@mecglobal.com
Web Site: www.mecglobal.com

Employees: 35

Agency Specializes In: Media Buying Services

Santiago Arieu *(Dir-MEC Access)*
Patricio Busso *(Dir-Interaction)*
Leopoldo Frederic *(Dir-Analytics & Insights)*
Facundo Gonzalez Moreno *(Acct Exec)*
Catalina Borrelli *(Media Planner)*
Ignacio Figueredo *(Media Planner)*
Maria Laura Fuente Portela *(Acct Coord)*
Florencia Di Pietro *(Coord-Digital)*
Marina Ines Waldman Amaya *(Coord-Digital)*
Eric Caamano *(Client Svc Dir)*

Accounts:
Citibank
Toyota

Chile

MEC
Av del Condor N 844 OF 103 1er PISO Ciudad Empresarial, Huechuraba, Santiago, Chile
Tel.: (56) 2 941 6400
Fax: (56) 2 274 9915
E-Mail: info.latam@mecglobal.com
Web Site: www.mecglobal.com

Employees: 25

Agency Specializes In: Media Buying Services

Roberto Vargas Alvarez *(Dir-Customer Svc & MEC Sport)*
Claudia Guzman *(Dir-Analytics & Insights)*
Maria Eugenia Lemaitre *(Dir-Customer Svcs)*
Solange Ortiz Mateluna *(Dir-Customer Svcs)*
Rodrigo Moyano *(Dir-Digital)*
Sebastian Cortes *(Supvr-Media)*
Marco Garcia Araneda *(Media Planner)*
Patricio Alvear Nunez *(Planner)*

Colombia

MEC
Cra14 No 94-65 Piso 3 Edificio Plazuela 94, Bogota, DC Colombia
Tel.: (57) 1 638 2593
Fax: (57) 1 638 2595
E-Mail: info.latam@mecglobal.com
Web Site: www.mecglobal.com

Agency Specializes In: Media Buying Services

Hector Alvarez *(Dir-Interaction-Colombia)*
Leonardo Gonzalez Ceballos *(Dir-Access)*
Carlos Alberto Pacheco Rivera *(Dir-Unidad Out of Home)*
Giovanna Rosero *(Dir-Pur)*
Diana Corredor *(Acct Mgr)*
Luisa Echeverri Garcia *(Acct Mgr-Interaction)*
Jessica Gutierrez Avila *(Media Buyer)*

Accounts:
AT&T Communications Corp.
Bang & Olufsen
Bayer(YAZ)
Bon Bon Bum
Delisoda
Juan Valdez
Mandal-Guaymaral
Marca Pais
Presidencia De La Republica
Suppla

MEC
Carrera 43A No9 Sur-91 Oficina 1304 Centro de Negocios Las Villas, Torre Norte, Medellin, Colombia
Tel.: (57) 4 313 1076
Fax: (57) 4 313 1042
E-Mail: info.latam@mecglobal.com
Web Site: www.mecglobal.com

Agency Specializes In: Media Buying Services

Hector Alvarez *(Dir-Interaction-Colombia)*
Leonardo Gonzalez Ceballos *(Dir-Access)*
Carlos Rivera *(Dir-Unidad Out of Home MEC)*
Giovanna Rosero *(Dir-Pur)*
Diana Corredor *(Acct Mgr)*
Luisa Echeverri Garcia *(Acct Mgr-Interaction)*
Angelica Maria Jerez Mayorga *(Acct Mgr)*
Mario Lopez Moscoso *(Acct Mgr-Plng)*

Costa Rica

Y&R Media
Iglesia San Francisco Guadalupe, 50 Mts Sur Edificio Asesores, Apartado 6947-1000, San Jose, Costa Rica
Tel.: (506) 2257 6727
Fax: (506) 2256 1959
E-Mail: info.latam@mecglobal.com
Web Site: www.mecglobal.com

Agency Specializes In: Media Buying Services

Fernando Retana *(Dir-Media)*

Dominican Republic

Y&R Media
Avenida de los Proceres, Esquina Eric Leonard Ekman #25,, Arroya Hondo, Santo Domingo, Dominican Republic
Tel.: (809) 562 2441
Fax: (809) 562 4371
E-Mail: info.latam@mecglobal.com
Web Site: www.mecglobal.com

Employees: 100

Agency Specializes In: Media Buying Services

Henry Ferrer *(Dir-Media)*
Wilson Chiang *(Copywriter)*

Ecuador

MEC/Y&R Media
Avenida Amazonas y Naciones Unidas, Edificio La Previsora,, Torre A, Piso 8, Quito, Ecuador
Tel.: (593) 2 2555410
Fax: (593) 2 2509895
E-Mail: info.latam@mecglobal.com
Web Site: www.mecglobal.com

Employees: 10

Agency Specializes In: Media Buying Services

Soledad Hermosa *(Gen Mgr)*

Guatemala

MEC
14 calle 3-51 zona 10 Edificio Murano Center, Oficina 402, Guatemala, Guatemala
Mailing Address:
PO Box 2-5289. Section 363, Miami, FL 22102-5289
Tel.: (502) 22798666
Fax: (502) 22798676
E-Mail: alejandra.toriello@mecglobal.com
Web Site: www.mecglobal.com

Employees: 19
Year Founded: 2004

Agency Specializes In: Media Buying Services

Alejandra Toriello *(Gen Mgr)*
Ana Estela Alvarez *(Media Planner)*

Accounts:
Boquitas Diana
Camiones Jac
Cementos Progreso
Cerveza Gallo
Chevron Texaco
Colgate-Palmolive
Construred
Distribuidora Maravilla
Michelin
Sony Electronics

Mexico

MEC
Avenida Ejercito Nacional 216-20 Piso, Colonia, Veronica Anzures, 11590 Mexico, DF Mexico
Tel.: (52) 55 8503 8423
Fax: (52) 55 5250 2429
E-Mail: mec.mexico@mecglobal.com
Web Site: www.mecglobal.com

Agency Specializes In: Media Buying Services

Veronica Isunza *(Mng Partner)*
Fanny Garcia *(Mng Dir)*
Renato De Paula *(CEO-Latin America)*
Irving De La Torre *(Acct Dir)*
Salvador Lopez *(Acct Dir)*
Alfredo Marcilio *(Acct Dir)*
Juan Carlos Martinez Lopez *(Acct Mgr)*
Eugenio Teran Roura *(Acct Mgr)*
Daniela Chavarria *(Acct Supvr)*
Jose Miguel Herrera Rangel *(Acct Exec)*
Emilie De Oteyza *(Client Svc Dir)*

Accounts:
RIU

Puerto Rico

MEC
270 Ave. Munoz Rivera, 3rd Fl, San Juan, PR 00918
Tel.: (787) 474-8800
Fax: (787) 474-8815
E-Mail: info.latam@mecglobal.com
Web Site: www.mecglobal.com

National Agency Associations: 4A's

Agency Specializes In: Media Buying Services

Jose Antonio Martinez *(Gen Dir-Comml)*

United Arab Emirates

MEC
Thuraya Tower 1, 3rd Floor, Office |P5304, Dubai Internet City, PO Box 25998, Dubai, United Arab Emirates
Tel.: (971) 4 367 8666
Fax: (971) 4 390 8025
E-Mail: dubai@mec-me.com
Web Site: www.mecglobal.com

Agency Specializes In: Media Buying Services

Mohan Nambiar *(CEO)*
Chris Brookes *(Gen Mgr)*
Pradeep Menon *(Gen Mgr-Qatar & Bahrain)*
Peter Considine *(Bus Dir-Integrated)*
Rolando Canlas *(Mgr-Comml)*
John Ekambi *(Mgr-Digital Media)*
Yves-Michel Gabay *(Reg Grp Mgr)*
Bhaskar Khaund *(Reg Head-TV & Multiscreen)*

Accounts:
Dubai International Film Festival Media Buying
Global Export
Kansai Paints Media Buying, Media Planning
Land Rover

Asia Pacific

MEC APAC HQ
700 Beach Road #04-01, Singapore, 068811 Singapore
Tel.: (65) 6225 1262
Fax: (65) 6227 9827
E-Mail: info.apac@mecglobal.com
Web Site: www.mecglobal.com

Agency Specializes In: Above-the-Line, Affiliate Marketing, Affluent Market, Aviation & Aerospace, Below-the-Line, Bilingual Market, Branded Entertainment, Broadcast, Business Publications, Business-To-Business, Cable T.V., Children's Market, Communications, Computers & Software, Consulting, Consumer Goods, Consumer Marketing, Consumer Publications, Content, Cosmetics, Customer Relationship Management, Digital/Interactive, Direct Response Marketing, Direct-to-Consumer, Electronics, Entertainment, Event Planning & Marketing, Experience Design, Fashion/Apparel, Financial, Food Service, Game Integration, Gay & Lesbian Market, Guerilla Marketing, Health Care Services, High Technology, Hispanic Market, Hospitality, Household Goods, In-Store Advertising, Information Technology, Integrated Marketing, International, Internet/Web Design, Investor Relations, Leisure, Luxury Products, Magazines, Market Research, Media Buying Services, Media Planning, Men's Market, Mobile Marketing, Multicultural, Multimedia, New Technologies, Newspapers & Magazines, Out-of-Home Media, Outdoor, Over-50 Market, Paid Searches, Pharmaceutical, Planning & Consultation, Podcasting, Point of Purchase, Point of Sale, Print, Product Placement, Public Relations, RSS (Really Simple Syndication), Radio, Recruitment, Regional, Restaurant, Retail, Sales Promotion, Search Engine Optimization, Seniors' Market, Social Marketing/Nonprofit, Sponsorship, Sports Market, Strategic Planning/Research, Sweepstakes, Syndication, T.V., Teen Market, Trade & Consumer Magazines, Transportation, Travel & Tourism, Viral/Buzz/Word of Mouth, Women's Market, Yellow Pages Advertising

Peter Vogel *(CEO)*
Raj Gupta *(Chief Strategy Officer)*
Connie Chan *(Mng Dir-Global Solutions-APAC)*
Amy Dabbs *(Head-Digital)*
Kunal Robert *(Dir-Digital)*
Joshua Campanella *(Assoc Dir-Digital)*

Accounts:
Accenture
Chanel
Chevron
Citi
Colgate-Palmolive
Daimler
DHL
Dorsett Hospitality International
Energizer
Ikea
Microsoft Xbox 360
MSIG
Paramount
New-Park Hotel Group Digital Media Buying, Digital Media Planning, Search Engine Marketing
New-Sentosa Development Corporation Media
Singapore Airlines
Singapore Tourism Board "Singapore: Inside Out", Media
SingTel
Sony Electronics (Agency of Record) Media, Strategic Media
Star Alliance
Xerox
Zuji Search Engine Marketing

Australia

MEC
Level 14 65 Berry Street, Sydney, NSW 2060 Australia
Tel.: (61) 2 8356 0600
Fax: (61) 2 8356 0604
E-Mail: amy.choi@mecglobal.com
Web Site: www.mecglobal.com

Employees: 60

Agency Specializes In: Media Buying Services

Tim Flattery *(Head-Bus Dev & Diversified Svcs)*
James Graver *(Head-Digital-Natl)*
James Boardman *(Dir-Client & Comm)*
Marcus Layman *(Dir-Digital)*
Grant Lequesne *(Dir-Strategy)*
Natalie Monds *(Dir-Client & Comm)*
Philippa Noilea-Taniq *(Dir-Investment & Activation)*
Steven Bale *(Mgr-Investment & Activation)*
Anna-marcella Colnan *(Mgr-Digital)*
Sarah Ganiatsos *(Mgr-Investment & Activation)*
Gregory Cattelain *(Assoc Mgr-Digital)*
Jan Aguilar *(Reg Assoc Category Head-P&G Skincare-MediaCom)*

Accounts:
Arnott's Agency of Record, Media, Roadies
Blackmores Media Buying
Colgate Dynamo
Mitsubishi Motors
Nestle Media
Paramount Pictures Anchorman 2
Schwarzkopf Media

MEC
Level 1 46 Fullarton Rd Norwood, Adelaide, SA 5067 Australia
Tel.: (61) 8 8366 4744
Fax: (61) 8 8331 8586
Web Site: www.mecglobal.com

Employees: 23

Agency Specializes In: Media Buying Services

Royce Zygarlicki *(Mng Dir)*
Matt Hofmeyer *(Gen Mgr)*
Andrew Zanker *(Sr Acct Mgr)*

Accounts:
Mitsubishi Motors Media Buying
SA Lotteries
The South Australian Government Advertising, Media Buying

China

MEC
1206 12/F The Huali Building No 58 Jinbao Street, Dongcheng District, Beijing, 100005 China
Tel.: (86) 10 852 33758
Fax: (86) 10 651 21916
E-Mail: info@mecglobal.com
Web Site: www.mecglobal.com

Employees: 30

Agency Specializes In: Media Buying Services

Michelle Yang *(Mng Dir)*
Michelle Sario *(Gen Mgr-China)*

Marty Wang *(Dir-Plng)*
Vincent Zheng *(Dir-Bus)*
Kittie Fan *(Assoc Dir-Digital)*
Abel Tang *(Assoc Dir-Digital)*
Katy Sun *(Mgr-Plng)*

Accounts:
Amway
Florentia Village On & Offline Media Planning & Buying
Mercedes-Benz China

MEC

37th Floor PCCW Tower Taikoo Place 979 King's Road, Quarry Bay, China (Hong Kong)
Tel.: (852) 2280 3928
Fax: (852) 2280 3945
E-Mail: maggie.law@mecglobal.com
Web Site: www.mecglobal.com

Employees: 25

Agency Specializes In: Media Buying Services

David Primmer *(Mng Partner)*
Doris Kuok *(Mng Dir)*
Herbert Lam *(Head-Digital)*

Accounts:
China Light & Power; 2007
Colgate Palmolive
Regal Hotels International Holdings Ltd Global Search Engine Marketing
Zuji Media Buying, Media Planning, Performance Marketing, Search

India

MEC

8th Floor Commerz International Business Park, Oberoi Garden City, Mumbai, 400063 India
Tel.: (91) 22 4239 8888
Fax: (91) 22 67403800
E-Mail: info.asia@mecglobal.com
Web Site: www.mecglobal.com

Agency Specializes In: Media Buying Services

Gangs T. Gangadhar *(Mng Dir)*
Roopam Garg *(Gen Mgr-North)*
Sidhraj Shah *(Dir-Brand Activations-Natl)*

Accounts:
ANZ New Zealand
The Ask Group
Cavinkare Media
CIGNA
Citi
Colgate Palmolive
DHL
General Electric Media Planning & Buying
HDFC Standard Life Insurance
Helix
Honda Motors & Scooters
Jaypee Cements
Kraft Foods
Loyalty NZ
McDonald's
Mercedes-Benz
Nationalist Congress Party
Nivea India
NZ Lotteries
Oberoi Construction
Pidilite
Radikal Rice
Reliance Communications Media
Singapore Airlines
Tata AIG Insurance Creative, Direct to Consumer
Tikona Digital Networks
Wattie's
Yellow
Zee Network
Zee New Media Ditto, Media

MEC

Mahalaxmi Chambers 5th Floor, 29 M G Road, Bengaluru, 560 001 India
Tel.: (91) 80 4119 3197
Fax: (91) 80 4113 3030
E-Mail: info.asia@mecglobal.com
Web Site: www.mecglobal.com

Employees: 6

Agency Specializes In: Media Buying Services

Geetha Shiv *(Dir-MEC MediaLab-Natl)*
Sakshi Kohli-Mehta *(Mgr-Access)*
Bhoomi Vyas *(Planner-Digital Media)*
Premnath Unnikrishnan *(Reg Head-Digital)*

Accounts:
BlueStone Media
Brittania Media
Dixcy Scott Media
Flipkart Media
Global Consumer Products Media, Online

MEC

New No. 13, Old No. 7, 5th Street, Nandanam Extension, Chennai, 600 035 India
Tel.: (91) 44 4289 1000
Fax: (91) 44 4289 1040
Web Site: www.mecglobal.com

Agency Specializes In: Media Buying Services

T. Gangadhar *(Mng Dir)*
Rajendra Prasad *(Gen Mgr)*

Accounts:
New-ParentCircle Media

Indonesia

MEC

Menara Jamsostek Gedung Utara Lantai 12A, Jalan Jend Gatot Subroto No 38, Jakarta, Selatan 12710 Indonesia
Tel.: (62) 21 5219 6300
Fax: (62) 21 5219 6300
E-Mail: info.asia@mecglobal.com
Web Site: www.mecglobal.com

Agency Specializes In: Media Buying Services

Accounts:
Belfoods
Bentoel Cigarettes
Hawley & Hazel
Henkel Media Buying, Planning
Manulife
Media World
Pizza Hut
Surya Citra Television
Telkomsel
TVS Motor

New Zealand

MEC

2nd Fl Corner, Augustus Terr & Parnell Rise, Priv Bag 93234, Parnell, Auckland, New Zealand
Tel.: (64) 9 308 5335
Fax: (64) 9 308 5405
E-Mail: sean.mccready@nz.mediaedgecia.com
Web Site: www.mecglobal.com

Employees: 15

Agency Specializes In: Media Buying Services

Catherine Hamilton *(Dir-Trading)*

Accounts:
Schwarzkopf Media

MEC

81 Abel Smith ST, TE ARO, Wellington, 6011 New Zealand
Mailing Address:
PO Box 295, Auckland, New Zealand
Tel.: (64) 4 801 1097
Fax: (64) 4 384 6575
E-Mail: grant.maxwell@mecglobal.com
Web Site: www.mecglobal.com

Employees: 8

Agency Specializes In: Media Buying Services

Catherine Hamilton *(Dir)*

Accounts:
Calce
Colgate Palmolive

Singapore

MEC

700 Beach Road #04-01, Singapore, 199598 Singapore
Tel.: (65) 6225 1262
Fax: (65) 6227 9827
E-Mail: info.asia@mecglobal.com
Web Site: www.mecglobal.com

Employees: 70

Agency Specializes In: Media Buying Services

Sharon Soh *(Mng Dir)*
Stephen Li *(CEO-Asia Pacific)*
Mike Jackson *(Mng Dir-MEC Access APAC)*
Alex Meaden *(Reg Dir-Mktg-Asia Pacific)*
Michael Wong *(Dir-Search)*
Zoe Madden *(Assoc Dir-Trading-APAC)*

Accounts:
Caltex Singapore Campaign: "The Fuel Democracy"
Sentosa Development Corporation Media Buying
Singapore Airlines Media Planning & Buying

Taiwan

MEC

4F No 31-2 Lane 11 GuangFu N Road, Taipei, 10560 Taiwan
Tel.: (886) 2 7710 6288
Fax: (886) 2 7710 6289
E-Mail: info.asia@mecglobal.com
Web Site: www.mecglobal.com

E-Mail for Key Personnel:
President: vince.cheng@mecglobal.com

Agency Specializes In: Media Buying Services

Kelly Huang *(Mng Dir)*
Janet Liu *(Bus Dir)*
Charlotte Tang *(Dir-Bus)*

Accounts:
Brother International
E.Sun Bank
LINE Naver Korea
Mercuries Life Insurance
United International Pictures; 2008
Yu Long Food

MEC - NA HQ, NEW YORK

825 7th Ave, New York, NY 10019-5818
Tel.: (212) 474-0000
Fax: (212) 474-0003
E-Mail: info.na@mecglobal.com
Web Site: www.mecglobal.com

National Agency Associations: 4A's

Agency Specializes In: Above-the-Line, Affiliate Marketing, Affluent Market, Asian Market, Automotive, Aviation & Aerospace, Below-the-Line, Bilingual Market, Branded Entertainment, Broadcast, Business Publications, Business-To-Business, Cable T.V., Children's Market, Communications, Computers & Software, Consulting, Consumer Goods, Consumer Marketing, Consumer Publications, Content, Cosmetics, Customer Relationship Management, Digital/Interactive, Direct Response Marketing, Direct-to-Consumer, Electronics, Entertainment, Event Planning & Marketing, Experience Design, Fashion/Apparel, Financial, Food Service, Game Integration, Gay & Lesbian Market, In-Store Advertising, Information Technology, Integrated Marketing, International, Internet/Web Design, Investor Relations, Leisure, Luxury Products, Magazines, Market Research, Media Buying Services, Media Planning, Merchandising, Multicultural, Multimedia, New Product Development, New Technologies, Newspapers & Magazines, Out-of-Home Media, Outdoor, Over-50 Market, Paid Searches, Pharmaceutical, Planning & Consultation, Podcasting, Point of Purchase, Point of Sale, Print, Product Placement, Public Relations, RSS (Really Simple Syndication), Radio, Real Estate, Recruitment, Regional, Restaurant, Retail, Sales Promotion, Search Engine Optimization, Seniors' Market, Social Marketing/Nonprofit, Sponsorship, Sports Market, Strategic Planning/Research, Sweepstakes, Syndication, T.V., Teen Market, Trade & Consumer Magazines, Transportation, Travel & Tourism, Viral/Buzz/Word of Mouth, Women's Market, Yellow Pages Advertising

Tej Desai *(Mng Partner & Head-Global Client)*
Kristine Segrist *(Mng Partner & Head-Client)*
Erik Neubart *(Mng Partner & Acct Dir-Consumer)*
Dorian Roth *(Partner & Sr Dir)*
Jessica Sberlati *(Partner & Sr Dir-Social Media)*
Mike Valentin *(Partner & Sr Dir-Digital)*
Brad Backenstose *(Partner & Dir-Dev)*
Jen Civitano *(Partner & Dir)*
Sara D'Alto *(Partner & Dir)*
Dennis Donlin *(Pres-Team AT&T)*
Mark Jones *(Pres-Global Solutions)*
Marla Kaplowitz *(CEO-North America)*
Josh Berman *(Sr Partner & Head-Practice-Digital Product Dev)*
Noah Mallin *(Sr Partner & Head-Social-North America)*
Jennifer Byrnes *(Sr Partner & Sr Dir)*
Jake Chun *(Sr Dir-Plng)*
Jessica Gagliardi *(Sr Partner & Sr Dir)*
Hilary Kolman *(Sr Partner & Sr Dir-Analytics & Insight)*
Jason Lee *(Sr Partner & Sr Dir-Digital)*
Kathryn Smolen *(Sr Partner & Sr Dir-Engagement Planning)*
Ken Solano *(Sr Dir-Digital Strategy)*
Kariina Rand *(Acct Dir-J&J EMEA & Tiffany Europe)*
Rachel Andreus *(Dir-Digital)*
Chris Elliott *(Dir-Plng)*
Rebecca Hallac *(Dir-Search)*
Melissa Lee *(Dir-Social Media)*
Meghann Longo *(Dir-Plng)*
Rob Pecci *(Dir-Digital Media)*
Ian Chin *(Assoc Dir)*
Jennifer Longobardi *(Assoc Dir)*
Caroline Smith *(Assoc Dir-Analytics & Insights)*
Erica Atkins *(Mgr-Digital Media)*
Ashley Blenman *(Mgr)*
Alyssa Byron *(Mgr)*
Patrick Foglia *(Mgr-Integrated Media)*
Kimberly Frechette *(Mgr)*
Maureen Krol *(Mgr-Digital Media)*
Shivani Kulkarni *(Mgr-Plng)*
Camille Lightell *(Mgr-Comm Plng-IKEA)*
Breanne Loso *(Mgr-Plng & Strategy)*
Matt Martin *(Mgr-Digital)*
Kipp Mullis *(Mgr & Reg Supvr-Media-Southeast & South Central Reg)*
Frank O'Connor *(Mgr-Brdcst-Natl)*
Amy Videtto *(Mgr-Social Media)*
Kimberly Laier *(Supvr-Digital)*
Kimberly McCormack *(Supvr-Digital)*
Sean Kingston Clark *(Community Mgr)*
Meredith Gibson *(Sr Assoc Media Planner)*
Alexandra Watson *(Sr Assoc-Social Strategy)*

Accounts:
ABB
Accenture
Advanced Micro Devices
Alcon Precision
American Institute of CPA
Amgen
AT&T Communications Corp. Media Planning & Buying, Wireless; 2007
Bacardi USA, Inc. Bombay Sapphire
Barclays
Biogen Analytics, Buying, Media, Planning
Campbell's Soup Co
Chanel
Chevron Corporation
Coach Leatherware
Colgate-Palmolive
DHL
E&J Gallo Winery
Energizer
Genworth
Harman International Industries; Stamford, CT Media
IKEA Campaign: "Fix This Kitchen", IKEA North America Services, LLC
The Kaplan University
KFC Corporation
L'Oreal USA, Inc. Communications, Giorgio Armani, Lancome, Planning, Viktor & Rolf, Yves Saint Laurent
Marriott International, Inc. Courtyard by Marriott, Fairfield Inn by Marriott, JW Marriott Hotels & Resorts, Marriott Hotels & Resorts, Marriott International, Inc., Media, Renaissance Hotels & Resorts, Residence Inn by Marriott, Spring Hills Suites
Mars
Mattel (Media Agency)
MetLife, Inc. Media Buying, Media Planning
Michelin
National Football League
Otsuka Pharmaceutical Analytics, Brexpiprazole, Media Buying, Media Planning
Paramount Campaign: "Paranormal Activity 3"
Pepperidge Farm
Playtex Products Banana Boat Sunscreen, Infant & Feminine Care Products; 2008
Polycom
SAP
Singapore Airlines
Star Alliance
TomTom
Toshiba
Verisign
Xerox
YUM!

MEDIA BROKERS INTERNATIONAL, INC.

11720 Amberpark Drive Ste 600, Alpharetta, GA 30009
Tel.: (678) 514-6200
Fax: (678) 514-6299
E-Mail: info@media-brokers.com
Web Site: www.media-brokers.com

Employees: 46

Agency Specializes In: Event Planning & Marketing, Outdoor, Print

Bill Mathews *(Exec VP)*
Marina Stacy *(Exec VP-Media)*
Jane Prescott *(Sr VP & Dir-HR)*
Joe Cohen *(VP)*
Shawn Gant *(Mktg Dir)*
Irene Feigin *(Dir-Media-Brdcst)*
Jim Sullivan *(Dir-Media)*
Joy Cantilo *(Media Planner & Media Buyer)*

Accounts:
Diet Product
Intrepid Travel Media Buying, Print
Luxury Condominiums

MEDIA BUYING DECISIONS

18959 N Dallas Pkwy Ste 1913, Dallas, TX 75287-3185
Tel.: (214) 485-2494
E-Mail: todd@mediabuyingdecisions.com
Web Site: www.mediabuyingdecisions.com

Employees: 1
Year Founded: 1986

Agency Specializes In: African-American Market, Automotive, Broadcast, Direct Response Marketing, Hispanic Market, Media Buying Services, Medical Products, Outdoor, Strategic Planning/Research

Approx. Annual Billings: $400,000

Todd Brewster *(Dir-Media)*

Accounts:
Buy-Tel Communications
Chandler Park Dental
Color Tyme Rentals; Plano, TX Rent-to-Own
Eternity Forever Evangelizing
Fibonacci Dental
McKinney Regional Cancer Center; TX Medical
The String Bean; Dallas, TX Restaurant

MEDIA BUYING SERVICES, INC.

4545 E Shea Blvd Ste 162, Phoenix, AZ 85028-6008
Tel.: (602) 996-2232
Fax: (602) 996-5658
Toll Free: (888) 996-2232
E-Mail: chuck@mediabuyingservices.com
Web Site: www.mediabuyingservices.com

E-Mail for Key Personnel:
President: kmunson@mediabuyingservices.com

Employees: 11
Year Founded: 1986

Agency Specializes In: Advertising, Business-To-Business, Consumer Marketing, Digital/Interactive, Media Buying Services

Approx. Annual Billings: $19,000,000

Breakdown of Gross Billings by Media: Cable T.V.: $1,900,000; Network Radio: $380,000; Newsp.: $1,500,000; Outdoor: $1,800,000; Spot Radio: $6,220,000; Spot T.V.: $7,000,000; Trade & Consumer Mags.: $200,000

Kathy Munson *(Founder & CEO)*
Chuck Munson *(CFO & COO)*
Cheri Moreno *(Sr Buyer & Planner)*
Heather Papp *(Sr Media Planner & Media Buyer)*
Laura Gastelum *(Sr Media Planner & Buyer)*

Accounts:
Apache Gold Casino
Arizona Department of Transportation Government; 1997
Desert Botanical Garden
John C. Lincoln Health Network

MEDIA DIRECTIONS ADVERTISING, INC.

9724 Kingston Pike Ste 301, Knoxville, TN 37922-6910
Tel.: (865) 691-9482
Fax: (865) 531-7585
E-Mail: mediadirections@mdadv.com
Web Site: www.mdadv.com

E-Mail for Key Personnel:
President: maureen@mdadv.com

Employees: 5
Year Founded: 1982

Agency Specializes In: Advertising, Arts, Automotive, Broadcast, Business Publications, Cable T.V., Co-op Advertising, Consulting, Consumer Marketing, Electronic Media, Entertainment, Event Planning & Marketing, Government/Political, Health Care Services, Leisure, Local Marketing, Magazines, Media Buying Services, Media Planning, Medical Products, Newspaper, Outdoor, Paid Searches, Planning & Consultation, Print, Production, Promotions, Public Relations, Publicity/Promotions, Radio, Recruitment, Restaurant, Retail, Seniors' Market, Sports Market, Strategic Planning/Research, T.V., Trade & Consumer Magazines, Transportation

Approx. Annual Billings: $5,000,000

Breakdown of Gross Billings by Media: Digital/Interactive: $100,000; Mags.: $50,000; Newsp.: $750,000; Outdoor: $750,000; Radio: $750,000; T.V.: $2,600,000

Maureen Patteson *(Owner)*
Carey Merz *(COO & Exec VP)*

Accounts:
Airport Cadillac; Knoxville, TN Automotive; 2003
Airport Motor Mile; Alcoa, TN Dealer Group; 1995
Airport Toyota; Knoxville, TN Automotive; 1994
Covenant Health Care; Knoxville, TN Corporate Brand, Hospitals, Specialty Medical Centers; 2005
Covenant Health Credit Union; Knoxville, TN Credit Union; 2007
Dogwood Arts Festival; Knoxville, TN Arts Festival; 2007
Knoxville Area Transit Authority; Knoxville, TN Public Transit; 1993
Mercy Health Partners; Knoxville, TN Hospitals
Michael Brady Inc.; Knoxville, TN Architectural & Engineering; 2010

MEDIA EDGE, INC.

531 Hadley Dr, Palm Harbor, FL 34683
Tel.: (727) 641-6800
Fax: (727) 784-9579
E-Mail: gchism@mediaedgeinc.com
Web Site: www.mediaedgeinc.com

Employees: 6
Year Founded: 1986

Agency Specializes In: Media Buying Services, Outdoor, Publicity/Promotions

James Kelley *(Pres)*

Accounts:
ChoicePoint, Inc.
Queen Realty
WMOR - TV

MEDIA EXPERTS

495 Wellington St W Ste 250, Toronto, ON M5V 1E9 Canada
Tel.: (416) 597-0707
Fax: (416) 597-9927
E-Mail: info@mediaexperts.com
Web Site: www.mediaexperts.com

Employees: 130
Year Founded: 1981

Agency Specializes In: Media Buying Services

Mark Sherman *(Founder, Owner & Exec Chm)*
Penny Stevens *(Pres)*
Kris Davis *(Sr VP-Customer Svc)*
Phil Borisenko *(Acct Plng Dir)*
Carol Cummings *(Dir-Brdcst Solutions)*
Daniel Mak *(Sr Acct Planner)*
Johari Williams *(Sr Acct Planner)*
Mike Burton *(Coord-Digital Media)*

Accounts:
ALDO Group Fashion Accessories, Footwear, Retail; 1984
BC Hydro Media Buying, Media Planning
Bell Canada Telecommunications; 2005
Best Buy Canada Consumer Electronics, Media Buying; 2006
BMW Canada Automotive; 2000
Casino Rama Media Buying, Media Planning
Corby Spirit and Wine (Media Agency of Record)
Future Shop Restaurants; 2006
New-Interac
MINI Canada Automotive; 2005
Workopolis Career Search; 2010

Branch

Media Experts

7236 ru Marconi, Montreal, QC H2R 2Z5 Canada
Tel.: (514) 844-5050
Fax: (514) 844-1739
E-Mail: marks@mediaexperts.com
Web Site: www.mediaexperts.com

Employees: 80

Mark Sherman *(CEO)*
Joaquin Murillo *(Mng Dir-Search Mktg)*
Jonathan Levitt *(VP & Head-R&D)*
Kalliope Efstathiou *(Supvr-Digital Solutions)*
Lauren Rosenblum *(Supvr-Digital Solutions)*
Carla Museitef *(Sr Buyer-Digital Solutions)*
Lindsay Garfinkle *(Acct Planner)*
Shawn LeBelle *(Analyst-Search Mktg-SEO & SEM)*
Dylan Duvall *(Coord-Brdcst)*
Melissa Ottoni *(Coord-Search Mktg)*
Kathleen McCallan *(Jr Buyer-Brdcst)*

Accounts:
Bell Canada
Best Buy
BMW Group Canada
MINI Canada
TD Bank Group
WestJet

THE MEDIA KITCHEN

160 Varick St, New York, NY 10013
Tel.: (646) 336-9400
E-Mail: info@mediakitchen.tv
Web Site: www.mediakitchen.tv

Employees: 65
Year Founded: 2001

National Agency Associations: 4A's

Agency Specializes In: Affluent Market, Business-To-Business, Children's Market, College, Consumer Goods, Consumer Marketing, Cosmetics, Entertainment, Fashion/Apparel, Financial, Food Service, Health Care Services, Media Buying Services, Media Planning, Pharmaceutical, Retail, Social Marketing/Nonprofit, Sponsorship, Strategic Planning/Research, Women's Market

Josh Engroff *(Chief Digital Media Officer)*
Brian Nadres *(Dir-Programmatic Media)*
Bruce Harwood *(Assoc Dir)*
Victoria Gugilev *(Supvr-Strategy)*
Marykate Byrnes *(Strategist)*
Alex Cohen *(Strategist)*
Anna Fertel *(Strategist)*
Carly Bennett *(Assoc Strategist)*
Mahlon Henderson *(Assoc Strategist)*

Accounts:
ableBanking; 2012
AD Council
Aerin; 2013
Ban
The Bank of New York Mellon Corporation; 2005
BMW
Church's Chicken Eastern Region Media
CIT Group, Inc.; 2007
Dreyfus; 2007
Elizabeth Arden (Give Back Brands) Justin Bieber Girlfriend, Justin Bieber Someday, Nicki Minaj Pink; 2011
FTSE; 2012
Giorgio Armani Armani Exchange; 2010
Home Goods
LEO Pharma; 2011
Limited Brands Victoria's Secret
Panasonic Media Buying
PBS/PBS Kids; 2003
Sesame Workshop; 2009
The Vanguard Group, Inc.; 2009
William Grant & Sons Glenfiddich, Balvenie, Grant's, Rekya, Sailor Jerry, Hendrik's, Tullamore Dew and Milagro; 2008
Windstream Communication; 2008
Wyndham Hotels & Resorts; Dallas, TX

MEDIA PARTNERSHIP CORPORATION

800 Connecticut Ave 3rd Fl N Wing, Norwalk, CT 06854
Tel.: (203) 855-6711
Fax: (203) 855-6705
E-Mail: info@mediapartnership.com
Web Site: www.mediapartnership.com

E-Mail for Key Personnel:
President: matt.thornbrough@mediapartnership.com
Media Dir.: jsc@mediapartnership.com

Employees: 14
Year Founded: 1996

National Agency Associations: 4A's-LIAN

Agency Specializes In: Media Buying Services, Planning & Consultation, Sponsorship

Approx. Annual Billings: $176,000,000

Alex Chik *(Sr VP & Dir-Brdcst Svcs)*
Jim Jarboe *(Sr VP & Dir-Brdcst Svcs)*
Gregory Young *(Assoc Dir-Media Strategy)*
Diego Lopez-Vega *(Sr Strategist-Media)*
Andrea Reinhardt *(Strategist-Media)*
Ben Spiegel *(Strategist-Media)*
Julian Choi *(Asst Strategist-Media)*
Cassandra Nizolek *(Asst Strategist-Media)*
Brittany Sims *(Media Buyer-Investment)*

Accounts:
Children's Place; 2005
Fujifilm

Lucille Roberts; New York, NY; 1996
Netzero
Papa Murphy's
Royal Doulton
United Online; CA; 1999
Waterford Crystal
Wedgwood

MEDIA PERIOD

7115 Orchard Lake Rd Ste 220, West Bloomfield, MI 48322
Tel.: (248) 539-9119
Fax: (248) 539-3703
Web Site: www.mediaperiod.com

Employees: 6

Harvey Rabinowitz *(Mng Partner)*
Vikki Stoddart *(Acct Exec)*

Accounts:
Carl's Golfland

THE MEDIA PLACE, INC.

2326 N 64th St, Seattle, WA 98103
Tel.: (206) 524-2919
Fax: (206) 524-1016
E-Mail: mediaplace@aol.com

Employees: 3
Year Founded: 1982

Agency Specializes In: Media Buying Services, Strategic Planning/Research

Approx. Annual Billings: $5,000,000

Breakdown of Gross Billings by Media: Radio: $2,500,000; T.V.: $2,500,000

Carol Ann DeCoster *(Pres & Dir-Media)*

Accounts:
Seattle Boat Show

MEDIA POWER ADVERTISING

5009 Monroe Rd Ste 101, Charlotte, NC 28205-7847
Tel.: (704) 567-1000
Fax: (704) 567-8193
E-Mail: media@mediapoweradvertising.com
Web Site: www.mediapoweradvertising.com

Employees: 12
Year Founded: 1985

Agency Specializes In: Advertising, Automotive, Broadcast, Cable T.V., Co-op Advertising, Consulting, Consumer Marketing, Direct Response Marketing, Education, Electronic Media, Entertainment, Fashion/Apparel, Health Care Services, Infomercials, Legal Services, Magazines, Media Buying Services, Newspaper, Newspapers & Magazines, Out-of-Home Media, Outdoor, Planning & Consultation, Print, Radio, Retail, Strategic Planning/Research, T.V.

Barbara Goldstein *(Pres)*
Don Irons, Jr. *(Acct Exec)*

Accounts:
Piedmont Natural Gas
SpeeDee Oil Change & Tune-Up

MEDIA RESOURCES, LTD.

4450 Belden Vlg Ave NW Ste 502, Canton, OH 44718
Tel.: (330) 492-1111
Fax: (330) 492-8472
Toll Free: (888) 492-5053
E-Mail: gloria.cuerbo@mediaresourcesonline.com
Web Site: www.mediaresourcesonline.com

Employees: 40
Year Founded: 1996

National Agency Associations: DMA

Agency Specializes In: Advertising, Advertising Specialties, African-American Market, Automotive, Bilingual Market, Brand Development & Integration, Business Publications, Co-op Advertising, Collateral, Communications, Consumer Marketing, Consumer Publications, Corporate Communications, Digital/Interactive, Direct Response Marketing, E-Commerce, Electronic Media, Email, Event Planning & Marketing, Graphic Design, Hispanic Market, In-Store Advertising, Integrated Marketing, Local Marketing, Magazines, Market Research, Media Buying Services, Media Planning, Media Relations, Multicultural, Newspaper, Newspapers & Magazines, Planning & Consultation, Podcasting, Point of Purchase, Point of Sale, Print, Production, Production (Print), Promotions, Publicity/Promotions, Retail, Sales Promotion, Strategic Planning/Research, Sweepstakes, Travel & Tourism, Web (Banner Ads, Pop-ups, etc.)

Approx. Annual Billings: $40,000,000

Gloria Cuerbo-Caley *(Pres & CEO)*
Augustine Cuerbo *(COO & Exec VP)*
Dick Dunster *(Reg Mgr-Sls)*
Tracey Laclair *(Acct Mgr)*

Accounts:
AT&T Communications Corp.
BBDO Chrysler, Dodge & Jeep
Chemistri
Daimler Chrysler
Ford Motor Company
General Motors
J. Walter Thompson
Ogilvy & Mather
PHD

Branches

Media Resources/Boston

6 Parkview Rd, Reading, MA 01867
Tel.: (330) 492-1111
Fax: (330) 492-8472
E-Mail: ddunster@mediaresourcesonline.com
Web Site: www.mediaresourcesonline.com

Employees: 1

Agency Specializes In: Advertising, Advertising Specialties, African-American Market, Automotive, Digital/Interactive, E-Commerce, Email, Hispanic Market, Magazines, Market Research, Media Buying Services, Media Planning, Media Relations, Multicultural, Newspaper, Newspapers & Magazines, Podcasting, Print, Production (Ad, Film, Broadcast), Production (Print), Sweepstakes, Travel & Tourism, Web (Banner Ads, Pop-ups, etc.)

Augustine Cuerbo *(Chief Creative Officer & Exec VP)*
Dick Dunster *(Reg Mgr-Sls)*
Tracey Laclair *(Acct Mgr)*
Derek Domer *(Acct Exec-eDirect)*

Accounts:
AT&T Communications Corp.
Daimler Chrysler
Ford
General Mills
Ogilvy & Mather
Unicel

MEDIA SOLUTIONS

707 Commons Dr #201, Sacramento, CA 95825
Tel.: (916) 648-9999
Fax: (916) 648-9990
Web Site: www.mediasol.com

Employees: 10
Year Founded: 1991

National Agency Associations: AAF

Agency Specializes In: Advertising, Advertising Specialties, Affluent Market, African-American Market, Agriculture, Alternative Advertising, Asian Market, Automotive, Bilingual Market, Broadcast, Business Publications, Business-To-Business, Cable T.V., Co-op Advertising, Communications, Consulting, Consumer Goods, Consumer Marketing, Consumer Publications, Crisis Communications, Digital/Interactive, Direct Response Marketing, Direct-to-Consumer, Electronic Media, Email, Environmental, Event Planning & Marketing, Experience Design, Food Service, Government/Political, Guerilla Marketing, Health Care Services, Hispanic Market, Household Goods, In-Store Advertising, Integrated Marketing, Local Marketing, Magazines, Marine, Market Research, Media Buying Services, Media Planning, Medical Products, Men's Market, Mobile Marketing, Multicultural, Multimedia, New Technologies, Newspaper, Newspapers & Magazines, Out-of-Home Media, Outdoor, Over-50 Market, Paid Searches, Planning & Consultation, Print, Promotions, Publicity/Promotions, Radio, Regional, Restaurant, Retail, Search Engine Optimization, Seniors' Market, Social Marketing/Nonprofit, Social Media, South Asian Market, Sponsorship, Sports Market, Strategic Planning/Research, T.V., Teen Market, Trade & Consumer Magazines, Transportation, Urban Market, Web (Banner Ads, Pop-ups, etc.)

Approx. Annual Billings: $14,000,000

Breakdown of Gross Billings by Media: Cable T.V.: 10%; Internet Adv.: 9%; Mags.: 3%; Newsp.: 2%; Other: 5%; Outdoor: 10%; Radio: 30%; T.V.: 30%; Trade & Consumer Mags.: 1%

Cynthia Metler *(Founder & Partner)*
Carol Michael *(Pres)*
Debi Giorchino *(Dir-Media Svcs)*
Jennifer Franz *(Acct Exec)*
Anna Schweissinger *(Acct Exec)*
Aaron Samson *(Acct Coord)*
Katrina Fruhmann *(Coord-Media)*

Accounts:
California Department of Insurance
California Department of Public Health; CA H1N1, Pertussis; 2010
California Franchise Board
Department of Boating & Waterways; CA Clean Vessel; 2008
Future Ford Clovis; 2004
Future Ford of Concord; 2005
Future Ford, Lincoln; Roseville, CA Auto Dealer; 1999
Future Nissan; Roseville, CA Auto Dealer; 1999
Papa Murphy's; Sacramento, San Francisco, Fresno & Monterey, CA; Reno, NV; 2001
Public Utilities Commission; 2009

MEDIA STORM LLC

99 Washington St, South Norwalk, CT 06854
Tel.: (203) 852-8001
Fax: (203) 852-5592
E-Mail: info@mediastorm.biz
Web Site: www.mediastorm.biz

Employees: 65
Year Founded: 2001

National Agency Associations: 4A's

Agency Specializes In: Above-the-Line, Advertising, Affiliate Marketing, Affluent Market, Alternative Advertising, Below-the-Line, Bilingual Market, Branded Entertainment, Broadcast, Business Publications, Business-To-Business, Cable T.V., Co-op Advertising, Consumer Goods, Consumer Marketing, Consumer Publications, Content, Digital/Interactive, Direct Response Marketing, Direct-to-Consumer, Electronic Media, Electronics, Email, Entertainment, Experience Design, Graphic Design, Guerilla Marketing, Hispanic Market, In-Store Advertising, Infomercials, Integrated Marketing, Internet/Web Design, Leisure, Local Marketing, Luxury Products, Magazines, Market Research, Media Buying Services, Media Planning, Media Relations, Men's Market, Mobile Marketing, Multicultural, Multimedia, New Technologies, Newspaper, Newspapers & Magazines, Out-of-Home Media, Outdoor, Paid Searches, Planning & Consultation, Podcasting, Print, Product Placement, Production, Production (Ad, Film, Broadcast), Promotions, Publicity/Promotions, Radio, Regional, Retail, Search Engine Optimization, Sponsorship, Sports Market, Strategic Planning/Research, Syndication, T.V., Teen Market, Trade & Consumer Magazines, Transportation, Travel & Tourism, Urban Market, Viral/Buzz/Word of Mouth, Web (Banner Ads, Pop-ups, etc.), Women's Market

Approx. Annual Billings: $160,000,000

Breakdown of Gross Billings by Media: Brdcst.: 10%; Cable T.V.: 25%; Consulting: 3%; D.M.: 5%; Event Mktg.: 5%; Internet Adv.: 22%; Out-of-Home Media: 10%; Print: 10%; Radio: 5%; Strategic Planning/Research: 5%

Craig C. Woerz *(Co-Founder, Co-Owner & Mng Partner)*
Tim Williams *(Co-Founder & Co-Owner)*
Heather Gregg *(Mng Dir)*
Charlie Fiordalis *(Chief Digital Officer)*
Erin Richards *(Mng Dir-Ninety9X)*
Jill Grant *(Dir-Fin)*
Lisa Moriwaki *(Dir-Digital)*
Jorge Paz *(Dir-Plng)*
John Thomas *(Dir-Digital Media)*
Evgeny Turkin *(Dir-Creative & Art)*
Brenda Zambrello *(Dir-Media)*
Kim Daigle *(Assoc Dir-Media & Supvr-Strategic Plng)*
Lindsey Corbetta *(Assoc Dir-Media)*
Elisa Dao *(Assoc Dir-Media & Digital)*
Nicole DeMarzo *(Assoc Dir-Media-Strategic Plng)*
Jose Diaz *(Assoc Dir-Media & Strategic Plng)*
Jennifer Jankowski *(Assoc Dir-Media)*
Michael Lux *(Supvr-Strategic Plng)*
Danielle Pugliese *(Supvr-Plng)*
Jennifer Sacks *(Supvr-Digital Media)*
Jason Wolf *(Supvr-Strategic Plng)*
Amy Clark *(Sr Planner-Digital)*
Kayla Demers *(Sr Planner-Digital)*
Laura Domenech *(Sr Planner-Media & Digital)*
Nicole Blaker *(Planner-Strategic)*
Genevieve Chong *(Media Buyer-Brdcst-Natl)*
Jackie Mahoney *(Planner-Search & Social)*
Lorraine Schwartz *(Planner-Digital Media)*
Noah Suchoff *(Media Planner-Digital)*
Rachel Todd *(Planner-Digital Media)*
Geng Wang *(Planner-Digital)*
Ravi Jayanath *(Assoc Media Planner-Digital)*
Nicholas Longo *(Assoc Media Planner)*
Kate Nissen *(Grp Mgr-Brdcst)*
Marcy Sackett *(Grp Mgr-Brdcst)*

Accounts:
New-CBS Sports
New-Celebrity Cruises Media
CMT(Country Music Television); New York, NY Media Buying & Planning
CT Tourism
Food Network
Fox Broadcasting; Los Angeles, CA FX Network, Fox Sports, Fox VOD; 2001
FX Networks, LLC Digital Media, FX, FXM, FXNOW, FXX
New-Glory Kickboxing
iNDemand; New York, NY PPV & VOD Programming; 2002
lafrivole.ru
Logo (Agency of Record)
Memorial Sloan-Kettering Cancer Center Inc. (Media Agency of Record)
Military Mortgage Campaign: "Battleship"
Miramax; 2008
MLB Network Media Buying
Mohegan Sun (Agency of Record) Media Buying, Media Planning, Strategy
Morton Campaign: "Wedding"
MTV Networks Company
My Network TV; Los Angeles, CA; 2006
The N Television Network for Teens; 2008
NFL Network; Los Angeles, CA; 2006
Open Road Films
Popcorn Entertainment; Los Angeles, CA Filmed Entertainment; 2005
POPSUGAR Inc Campaign: "We Search, We Find, We ShopStyle", Media Planning, ShopStyle
Savelovsky
Scripps Networks DIY, Scripps Networks
Shopzilla; Los Angeles, CA Consumer Website; 2006
Showtime Network; New York, NY; 2003
Speed Network; Charlotte, NC; 2003
Tribune Entertainment; Los Angeles, CA Syndicated Programming; 2002
Turner Broadcasting Media Buying, TruTV; 2005
UFC
Viggle Campaign: "Rewards", TV
WE: Women's Entertainment Network; Bethpage, NY Bridezillas; 2003

MEDIA WORKS, LTD.
1425 Clarkview Rd Ste 500, Baltimore, MD 21209
Tel.: (443) 470-4400
E-Mail: mselby@medialtd.com
Web Site: www.medialtd.com

E-Mail for Key Personnel:
President: jberg@medialtd.com

Employees: 14
Year Founded: 1988

National Agency Associations: 4A's

Agency Specializes In: Automotive, Business-To-Business, Health Care Services, Real Estate, Retail

Michele Selby *(Pres)*
Amy Wisner *(Exec VP)*
Beth Jenkins *(Head-Acct, Media Planner & Media Buyer)*
Mandy Remeto *(Supvr-Media)*
Ashlea Wolcott *(Sr Strategist-Digital)*
Jennifer Pupshis *(Sr Planner)*
Monica Lazarus *(Media Planner & Media Buyer)*
Jamie Feagans *(Planner-Digital & Buyer)*
Ryan Trott *(Media Buyer)*
Marissa DeMilio *(Coord-Media)*
Paige Connor *(Asst-Media)*
Casey Schmiegel *(Asst-Media)*
Amy White *(Asst Media Buyer)*

Accounts:
Advance Business Systems; Baltimore, MD; 1993
Berkshire Hathaway Automotive Group
The Big Screen Store
BUBBLES Salons (Agency of Record) Digital Media Planning & Buying, Traditional Media Planning & Buying
Chase Brexton Health Services, (Agency of Record) Media Buying, Media Planning
Citifinancial Nascar
Dyslexia Tutoring; Baltimore, MD; 2003
Erickson Retirement Communities
ExpressCare (Agency of Record) Branding, Broadcast TV, Digital, Direct Mail, Outdoor, Radio, Social Media
Feld Entertainment; Vienna, VA; 1998
Hood College; Frederick, MD; 2004
Maryland Tourism & Travel
Mile One Automotive
National Aquarium Media Buying, Media Planning
Offenbacher's (Agency of Record) Digital, Media Buying, Media Planning, Print, Radio, TV
Sears Hometown and Outlet Stores (Agency of Record) Out-of-Home, Radio, TV
Sinclair Broadcasting; Baltimore, MD; 1999
St. Agnes Hospital; Baltimore, MD; 2000
Sylvan Learning Centers
United Way of Central; MD
Villanova University
Walters Art Gallery
The White House Historical Association (Agency of Record) Digital Media, Print

Branch

Media Works Charlotte
9401 Standerwick Ln, Huntersville, NC 28078
Tel.: (704) 947-2000
E-Mail: tfrey@medialtd.com
Web Site: www.medialtd.com

Employees: 20
Year Founded: 2007

Amy Wisner *(Sr Exec VP)*
Tami Frey *(VP)*
Cheryl Rogers, III *(VP)*
Anu Jain *(Mgr-Mktg Analytics)*
Ashlea Wolcott *(Sr Strategist-Digital)*
Kate Forbes *(Media Planner & Media Buyer)*
Beth Jenkins *(Media Planner & Media Buyer)*
Allison Shields *(Media Planner & Media Buyer)*
Halley Weinstein *(Media Planner & Media Buyer)*
Colleen Winterling *(Media Planner & Media Buyer)*

MEDIACOM
498 7th Ave, New York, NY 10018
Tel.: (212) 912-4200
Fax: (212) 912-4719
E-Mail: usa@mediacom.com
Web Site: www.mediacomusa.com/en/home.aspx

National Agency Associations: 4A's

Agency Specializes In: Advertising, Sponsorship

Approx. Annual Billings: $23,000,000,000

Stephen Allan *(Chm & CEO)*
Mark Fortner *(Mng Partner & Head-Innovation)*
Jake Vander Linden *(Mng Partner & Head-Acct)*
Tamara Alesi *(Mng Partner-Product & Strategy)*
Andrea McAteer *(Mng Partner)*
Mick Mernagh *(Mng Partner)*
Andrew Pappalardo *(Mng Partner-Natl Brdcst Implementation)*
Seow Leng Porter *(Mng Partner)*
Thomas Rocco *(Mng Partner)*
Larry Swyer *(Mng Partner)*
Marc Wallen *(Mng Partner)*
Stephanie Gay *(Partner, VP & Grp Dir-Digital Media-Global)*
Karen Silverstein *(Partner & Grp Dir)*
Sean Williamson *(Partner & Reg Dir)*
Priscilla Baez *(Partner & Dir-Digital Media)*
Fernando Cadena *(Partner & Dir-Comm Plng)*
Angelina Chung *(Partner & Dir-Digital Media)*
Rachel Lippman *(Partner & Dir-Digital Media)*
Rachel Nowick *(Partner & Dir-Comm Plng)*
Leslie Rasimas *(Partner & Dir-Mktg)*
Diana Shin *(Partner & Mgr)*
Trixie Ferguson Gray *(Sr Partner-Branded Content*

& Experiences-Innovation Grp)
Simon Tray *(CFO)*
Phil Cowdell *(CEO-Mediacom Nam)*
Toby Jenner *(COO-Worldwide)*
Tom Cijffers *(Chief Client Officer)*
Deirdre McGlashan *(Chief Digital Officer-Global)*
Fraser Riddell *(Chief Bus Dev Officer)*
Jeremy Griffiths *(Officer-Bus Science-Global)*
Andrew Chernick *(VP-Customer Retention)*
Kyong Coleman *(Sr Partner & Head-Strategy)*
Tom Kuhn *(Sr Partner & Reg Dir)*
Michelle Leonardo *(Sr Partner & Grp Acct Dir)*
Neal Lucey *(Sr Partner & Grp Acct Dir)*
Denis Philipps *(Sr Partner & Grp Acct Dir)*
Delia O'Grady *(Media Dir-Digital Investment)*
Kim Abend *(Sr Partner & Dir-Comm Plng)*
Louis Ambrose *(Dir-Digital Media)*
Jasmine Belassie-Page *(Dir-Digital Media & Strategy)*
Caitlin Bergmann *(Dir-Content & Creative)*
Joerg Bursee *(Dir-Buying-Global)*
Ilana Casser *(Dir-Media Plng)*
Dean Challis *(Dir-Strategy-Global)*
Beth Crane *(Sr Partner & Dir-Comm Plng)*
Nicoletta D'Elia-Napoli *(Sr Partner & Dir-Media Ops)*
Paul Greenhalgh *(Dir-Comml-Global)*
Ida Hemmingsson-Holl *(Dir-Mktg-Global)*
Marcela Hinojosa *(Dir-Multicultural)*
Ken O'Donnell *(Dir-Digital Media)*
Elisabeth Riedl *(Dir-Bus Insights)*
Justin Sorrentino *(Dir-Search & Social Media)*
Rebecca Wenstrup *(Dir-Digital Media)*
Denysha Davis *(Assoc Dir-Media & Digital Investment)*
Julia Nizinski *(Assoc Dir-Media-Digital Investment)*
Max Sinelnikov *(Assoc Dir-Media)*
Steve Wolf *(Assoc Dir-AB InBev)*
Connie Cassiday *(Reg Mgr-Media-Audi)*
Kenneth Grosso *(Reg Mgr-Media)*
Rosemarie Sanchez *(Reg Mgr-Media)*
Litsa Theodorakis *(Sr Mgr-Search & Social)*
Courtney Barker *(Acct Mgr)*
Carlos Cervantes *(Mgr)*
Alyssa Hurley *(Mgr-Adv & Promos)*
Rayan Jamshidi *(Mgr-Paid Search)*
Magnor Maxi *(Mgr-Search)*
Jillian Moss *(Mgr-Media Ops)*
Courtney Berg *(Supvr-Digital Media)*
Johanna Branagan *(Supvr-Digital Media)*
Joanna Corn *(Supvr-Comm Plng)*
Brian Damon *(Supvr-Comm Plng)*
Ally Day *(Supvr-Digital Media)*
Laura Debello *(Supvr-Comm Plng)*
Lance Demonteiro *(Supvr-Digital Investment)*
Rob Dickens *(Supvr-Media Plng)*
Julie Fein *(Supvr-Comm Plng)*
Nicole Francesco *(Supvr-Comm Plng-Canon)*
Lisa Garcia *(Supvr-Comm Plng)*
Allison Goodman *(Supvr-Comm Plng)*
Gladys Hall *(Supvr-Comm)*
Derek Hartman *(Supvr-Digital Media)*
Juliana Herring *(Supvr-Digital, Investment & Strategic Partnerships)*
Tommy Huthansel *(Supvr-Integrated Media)*
Jacqueline King *(Supvr-Digital Media)*
Daniel Mendez *(Supvr-Digital Media)*
Nick Rane *(Supvr-Digital Investment)*
Kendra Richardson *(Supvr)*
Lynn Sandford *(Supvr-Digital Media)*
Jennifer Santos *(Supvr-Media Plng)*
Amisha Shah *(Supvr-Digital)*
Vera Su *(Supvr-Digital Media)*
Trish Wang *(Supvr-Comm Plng)*
Rebecca Wingfield *(Supvr-Digital Media)*
Ted Lowenfels *(Sr Buyer-Digital Investment)*
Kasey Carpenter *(Planner-Comm)*
Meagan Haas *(Planner-Comm)*
Alex Kim *(Analyst-Digital)*
Maryann Kuriakose *(Planner-Digital Media)*
Stephanie Litsas *(Planner-Comm)*
Britani Luckman *(Planner-Digital Media)*
Alyssa Maneri *(Media Planner-Integrated)*
Stephen Marzocca *(Planner-Digital Media)*
Colin Mauro *(Planner-Digital Media)*
Erica Miles *(Media Planner-Integrated-eBay)*
Matthew Mittlemann *(Analyst-Digital)*
Allison Newman *(Planner-Digital Media)*
Joshua Poolat *(Planner-Digital Media)*
Samantha Ruiz *(Planner-Digital Media)*
Jessica Sardo *(Planner-Comm)*
Blaine Schoen *(Planner-Digital Media)*
Alyssa Vilinsky *(Planner-Digital Media)*
Danielle Ciappara *(Asst Media Planner)*
Jackie Elliot *(Assoc Media Dir)*
Rachel Gropper *(Asst Media Planner)*
Daniel Han *(Assoc Media Dir)*
Stephen Ingber *(Asst Media Planner-Digital)*
David Kyffin *(Chief ROI & Direct Mktg Officer-Global)*
Andrew Montemarano *(Asst Media Planner-Digital)*
Kristin Reilly *(Assoc Media Dir)*
Marissa Yoss *(Assoc Media Dir-Anheuser-Busch InBev)*

Accounts:
AARP
ADT Media Planning & Buying
Allergan, Inc. Allergan, Inc., Botox, Juvederm, Lap-Band, Latisse, Restasis
Allianz Life Insurance Company of North America
New-American Airlines Global Media Agency
American Eagle Outfitters Media
Anheuser-Busch InBev Media Buying, Media Planning
Audi of America, Inc. Audi A6, Campaign: "Return to Snake River Canyon", Campaign: "Untitled Jersey City Project", Digital, Media, Social Content
Bayer Consumer Care Division Aleve, Alka-Seltzer, Alka-Seltzer Plus, Bayer Aspirin, Bayer Consumer Care Division, Citracal, Flintstones Vitamins, Midol, One-A-Day 50 Plus Advantage Vitamins, One-A-Day Men's Formula Vitamins, One-A-Day Vitamins, Phillips
Bayer HealthCare Pharmaceuticals
Bayer HealthCare (Lead Media Agency) Bain de Soleil, Claritin, Coppertone, Dr. Scholl's, Media Buying, Media Planning, Merck
Bose Corporation
Canon USA, Inc. Canon USA, Inc., Eos, PowerShot
Citizens Banking Corporation Citizens Banking Corporation, F&M Bank, Perfect Fit Checking
Coldwell Banker Campaign: "Blue Carpet", Media Buying
Comcast NBCUniversal Overseas
ConAgra Campaign: "Healthy Choice Top Chef Showdown", Frozen Dinners, Grocery Food, Refrigerated Food, Snack Food
Crystal Cruises
Dave & Buster's National Media Planning & Buying
Dell Inc. Alienware, Dell, Inc., Inspiron, dell.com
Direct General Media
Discover Card Media Buying & Planning; 2008
Doctor's Associates, Inc. Subway
DSW Media Buying, Media Planning, Media Strategy
EBay Creative, Media
Edible Arrangements Media
GlaxoSmithKline plc Abreva, AquaFresh, Beano, Citrucel, Contac, FiberChoice, Flex, Geritol, Levitra, Massengill, Nicoderm, Nicorette, Novartis, Oscal, PoliGrip, Polident, Remifemin, Sensodyne, Sominex, Tums, Vivarin
Hasbro
Indeed.com Media
Legacy Media Planning & Buying
Lindt & Sprungli USA, Inc. Ghirardelli Chocolate Company, Lindor, Lindt & Sprungli USA, Inc.
LVMH BeneFit Cosmetics
Mars, Incorporated Media Planning
Planet Fitness Media
Procter & Gamble Latin American & Caribbean Digital Agency
Revlon Media Planning & Buying
Sargento Foods, Inc. Media
Shell Lubricants Black Magic, Gumout, Jiffy Lube, Pennzoil, Pennzoil Platinum Motor Oil, Pennzoil Ultra, Quaker State, Rain-X, Shell Lubricants, Slick 50
Shell Oil Campaign: "Earth 2050: The Future Of Energy"
Siemens AG Global Media
Sony Corporation of America
Spin Master Ltd. Media Buying, Media Planning
Subway Restaurants Media
The United Nations Campaign: "My World"
Universal Music Group Geffen Records, Island Def Jam Music Group
Volkswagen Group of America, Inc. (Media Agency of Record) Golf TDI, Media Buying, Media Planning, Seat, The Beetle Shark Cage
Wrigley 5 Gum
Wyndham Worldwide Super 8, Wyndham Worldwide

U.S. Offices

MediaCom US
498 Seventh Ave, New York, NY 10018
Tel.: (212) 912-4200
Fax: (212) 912-4719
E-Mail: usa@mediacom.com
Web Site: www.mediacomusa.com

Employees: 516

Alan Rush *(Mng Partner & Grp Acct Dir)*
Michael Farasciano *(Mng Partner)*
Stephanie Gay *(Partner, VP & Grp Dir-Digital Media-Global)*
Andrew Friedman *(Partner & Dir-Digital Media)*
Rachel Lippman *(Partner & Dir-Digital Media)*
Lowell Simpson *(CIO)*
Archana Kumar *(Chief Strategy Officer)*
Laetitia Kieffer *(Grp Dir-Search & Social)*
Giuseppe De Angelis *(Producer-Video & Designer)*
Brenna Kolomer *(Sr Partner & Acct Dir)*
Jamie Umans *(Dir-Comm Plng)*
Leisha Bereson *(Assoc Dir-Media-Digital)*
Jessica Drake *(Assoc Dir-Digital)*
Hani Khatib *(Assoc Dir-Media)*
Natalia Rocha *(Assoc Dir-Multicultural Plng)*
Lisa Merola *(Sr Mgr-Paid Search & Social)*
Carlos Cervantes *(Mgr)*
Fion Su *(Mgr-Search)*
Johanna Branagan *(Supvr-Digital Media)*
Robert Jackson *(Supvr-Comm Plng)*
Britani Luckman *(Planner-Digital Media)*
Kerry Mowbray *(Media Planner-Digital)*
Zachary Sorscher *(Planner-Digital Media)*
Marissa Yoss *(Assoc Media Dir-Anheuser-Busch InBev)*

Accounts:
CIMZIA
Mars
Revlon
Sargento Cheese; 2009
Subway Restaurants Digital Media, Media Planning & Buying, Mobile, Search; 2004

MediaCom USA
1601 Cloverfield Blvd Ste 3000 North, Santa Monica, CA 90404
Tel.: (310) 309-8210
E-Mail: gnathan@mediacommail.com
Web Site: www.mediacom.com/en/contact/north-america/santa-monica

Employees: 27

National Agency Associations: 4A's

Agency Specializes In: Sponsorship

Tamara Alesi *(Mng Partner & Head-Digital Strategy)*
Andy Littlewood *(Mng Partner & Head-Knowledge)*

Jose Bello *(Mng Partner)*
Ryan Johnson *(Partner & Head-Interaction)*
Steven Abraham *(Mng Dir & Exec VP)*
Steve Carbone *(Mng Dir-Digital & Analytics)*
Stephanie Starr *(Grp Acct Dir-Audi of America)*
Shelby Craig *(Creative Dir)*
Tiffany Cheng *(Media Planner-Integrated)*
Dain Kang *(Asst Media Planner)*

Accounts:
BMW of North America, LLC
Crystal Cruises
New-Europa Corp
New-J.G. Wentworth Broadcast, Digital Media
Spin Master Media Planning & Buying
Symantec Global Media Strategy, Norton, Planning & Buying
Tempur Sealy International Media
Universal Music Group
Volkswagen

Canada

MediaCom Vancouver
850 West Hastings St Ste 700, Vancouver, BC V6C 1E1 Canada
Tel.: (604) 687-1611
Fax: (604) 687-1441
E-Mail: canada@mediacom.com
Web Site: www.mediacom.com

Employees: 5

Agency Specializes In: Media Buying Services

Jamie Edwards *(CEO)*
Michael Neale *(Chief Investment Officer)*
Kelly Young *(Grp Acct Dir)*
Veronica Gonzales *(Acct Dir)*
Erin Rahn *(Dir-Investment Digital)*
Bruno Severinski *(Dir-Investment)*
Niri Panaram *(Mgr-Investment)*
Nancy Kye *(Supvr-Digital)*
Jessica Senders *(Supvr-Acct Plng)*
Rachel Garbutt *(Coord-New Bus & Mktg)*

Accounts:
ADT (Agency of Record) Media Planning & Buying
BC Used Oil
BestBuy Future Shop
Canon Canada Campaign: "Timeplay - Interactive Cinema"
Coca-Cola Refreshments USA, Inc.
Dell; India
Downy; Philippines
New-Fisherman's Friend
Gillette; India
H&M; USA Campaign: "H & M Styles"
Mars & Wrigley Traditional & Digital Media
Mars Canada Ben's Beginners, Media Buying, Uncle Ben's
Mini
Oral B; Israel
PMC Sierra
Roger's Broadcasting
Starbucks
T-Mobile US
TransLink
Wrigley Campaign: "Return Of Electric Circus"

Austria

MediaCom Vienna
Vordere, Zollamtsstrasse 13/5. OG, 1030 Vienna, Austria
Tel.: (43) 1605550
Fax: (43) 160555500
E-Mail: vienna.office@mediacom.com
Web Site: www.mediacom.at

Employees: 130

Joachim Feher *(CEO)*
Mick Mernagh *(Mng Partner)*
Andreas Vretscha *(COO)*
Omid Novidi *(Head-Creative Unit & Client Svc Dir)*
Edgar Castellanos *(Dir-Art)*
Bianca Stumpf *(Dir-Investment)*
Thomas Urban *(Dir-Digital Media)*

Accounts:
Allianz
Findmyhome.at
T-Mobile US
UniCredit Bank Austria AG

Belgium

MediaCom
Rue Jules Cockxstraat 8-10, 1160 Brussels, Belgium
Tel.: (32) 27731714
Fax: (32) 27711104
E-Mail: info@mediacom.be
Web Site: www.mediacom.com

Employees: 13

Christian Kevers *(Mng Dir)*
Patricia Raye *(Acct Mgr-Media)*
Kris Schelck *(Acct Mgr-Media)*
Anja Schotsaert *(Acct Mgr-Media)*
Dorothee Six *(Acct Mgr-Media)*
Chloe Bilbault *(Media Planner)*
Anne-Laure De Bernis *(Media Planner)*
Tom Lemaitre *(Client Svc Dir)*

Accounts:
Nokia

Czech Republic

MediaCom Praha
Nadrazni 32, 515000 Prague, Czech Republic
Tel.: (420) 234299400
Fax: (420) 234299401
E-Mail: mediacom@mcpraha.cz
Web Site: www.mcpraha.cz

Employees: 58

Petra Pipkova *(CEO)*
Lucie Steflova *(Acct Mgr)*
Michaela Jirouchova *(Mgr-Digital Dev)*
Hana Kopecka *(Mgr-Interaction)*
Martina Lestinova *(Acct Supvr)*
Petr Lobl *(Supvr-Interaction)*

Denmark

MediaCom Denmark
Europaplads 2 3.sal, 8000 Aarhus, 1106 Copenhagen, Denmark
Tel.: (45) 33760000
Fax: (45) 33760001
E-Mail: info@mediacom.dk
Web Site: www.mediacom.dk

Employees: 152

Rasmus Fisker *(Dir-Content & Strategy)*
Henriette Lillholm *(Mgr-Insight)*
Henriette Bruun Lillhom *(Mgr-Insight Team)*

Accounts:
Fitness World
Ikea
Procter & Gamble
SAS
TDC
TV2

France

MediaCom Paris
32 Rue Guersant, Paris, 75837 France
Tel.: (33) 173002100
Fax: (33) 173002199
E-Mail: france@mediacom.com
Web Site: www.mediacom.com

Employees: 152
Year Founded: 1993

Agency Specializes In: Media Buying Services

Jean-Pierre Levieux *(COO & CMO-Content & Connections)*
Elodie Callegari *(Acct Dir-Plurimedia)*
Stephanie Cantau *(Acct Dir)*
Olivia Deschamps *(Acct Dir-Global)*
Sarah Formosa *(Acct Dir-Global)*
Emmanuel Jacquet *(Acct Dir-Global)*
Matthieu Viot *(Acct Dir)*
Anthony Loret *(Dir-Customer)*
Aurelie Marragou *(Acct Mgr)*
Laurent Chatoux *(Mgr-Media)*

Accounts:
3M Europe
Bahlsen
GlaxoSmithKline
GSK
Levi Strauss
Nokia
P&G (Non TV)
Volkswagen Group

Germany

Mediacom Dusseldorf
Derendorfer Alle 10, 40476 Dusseldorf, Germany
Tel.: (49) 211171620
Fax: (49) 211171623200
E-Mail: freshness@mediacom.de
Web Site: www.mediacom.de

Employees: 552
Year Founded: 1986

Agency Specializes In: Media Buying Services

Jake Vander Linden *(Mng Partner & Head-Acct)*
Daniela Tollert *(Mng Dir)*
Claus Brockers *(Chief Investment Officer)*
Susanne Grundmann *(Mng Dir-Client Svcs)*
Christopher Kaiser *(Mng Dir-Hamburg)*
Inke Rausch *(Mng Dir-Munich)*
Reiner Schmitt *(Mng Dir-Plng & Client Svcs)*
Manuela Speckamp-Schmitt *(Mng Dir-Human Capital)*
Matthias Hellmann *(Dir-Mobile)*

Accounts:
Audi Online
Coca-Cola Refreshments USA, Inc.
Hasbro Campaign: "Office War: Helping Germany Have Fun At Work", Nerf Blasters
Volkswagen Group of America, Inc.

Greece

MediaCom Athens
350 Kifisias Avenue & 2 Christou Lada, 15233 Chalandri, Athens, Greece
Tel.: (30) 2108114620
Fax: (30) 2108114649
E-Mail: info@mediacomathens.gr
Web Site: www.mediacom.se

Employees: 11

Petros Belesakos *(Gen Mgr)*

Ireland

MediaCom Ireland
Marconi House, Lower Ground Floor, 2 Dublin, Ireland
Tel.: (353) 12321800
Fax: (353) 2321890
E-Mail: ireland@mediacom.com
Web Site: www.mediacomdublin.com

Employees: 36

Andrew Dunn *(Mng Dir)*
Emma Marley *(Head-Plng)*
Martin Pugh *(Head-Digital)*
Dave Hendrick *(Acct Dir)*
Garrett Tallon *(Acct Dir)*
Aisling Baker *(Acct Mgr)*
Egle Jankeviciene *(Mgr-Investment)*

Accounts:
Brita
Dell
Dulux
First Active
Muller
Nokia
Sky Media Buying, Media Planning
Universal
Wrigley

Italy

MediaCom Italy
Corso Sempione 2, Milan, 20154 Italy
Tel.: (39) 02336441
Fax: (39) 0234537770
E-Mail: italy@mediacom.com
Web Site: www.mediacom.com/en/home

Employees: 90

Agency Specializes In: Advertising

Barbara Robecchi *(Mng Dir)*

Accounts:
Autogerma
Eagle
Nokia
Procter & Gamble
Sky

Netherlands

MediaCom Amsterdam
Karperstraat 8, Amsterdam, 1075 DE Netherlands
Mailing Address:
PO Box 75516, 1070 AM Amsterdam, Netherlands
Tel.: (31) 205757700
Fax: (31) 205757701
E-Mail: info@medicacom.nl
Web Site: www.mediacom.nl

Employees: 69

Frank Bitter *(CEO)*
Dorien De Jong *(Head-Media Investment)*
Suzanne Bertus *(Dir-Comm-P&G)*
Tessa Van Der Starre-Rawie *(Dir-Client & Dev)*
Eva Bertus *(Sr Planner-Comm)*
Hanneke Van Rozendaal *(Client Head-Mgmt Team)*

Nigeria

All Seasons Mediacom
(Formerly Insight Communications)
No 50 Adekunle Fajuyi Way, GRA Ikeja, Lagos, Nigeria
Tel.: (234) 17745021
Fax: (234) 14932697
Web Site: www.mediacom.com

Employees: 41

Agency Specializes In: Media Buying Services

Jimi Awosika *(Mng Dir)*
Kayode Situ *(Exec Dir-Sys & Fin)*
Mowunmi Fatodu *(Dir-Bus Process-Insight Grey)*
Ayo Owoeye *(Office Mgr)*

Accounts:
Amstel
BankPHB
Cobranet
Dublin City Council Sponsorship, Tourism
Dunlop
Emirates
eTranzact
Jagal Pharma
Nestle
Nigeria Breweries
PepsiCo
Samsung
Stallion Motors
Sterling Bank
Suzuki
Yudoo

Norway

MediaCom AS
Torggata 5 PB 8904, Youngstorget, Oslo, N-0028 Norway
Tel.: (47) 22911000
Fax: (47) 22911010
E-Mail: mediacom@mediacom.no
Web Site: www.mediacom.no

Employees: 83

Stale Gjerset *(Deputy Mng Dir)*
Kjersti Nesbakk *(Acct Dir)*
Olav Pedersen *(Acct Dir)*
Sten Brathen *(Dir-Strategy)*

Accounts:
Danske Bank; 2009
H&M
IKEA
Kid Interior

Poland

MediaCom Warszawa
u Postepu 6, 02-676 Warsaw, Poland
Tel.: (48) 223100000
Fax: (48) 223100010
E-Mail: mcw@mcw.com.pl
Web Site: www.mcw.com.pl

Employees: 224

Agency Specializes In: Outdoor, Planning & Consultation

Anna Dzierzedzka *(Mng Partner-Comm Plng)*
Stanislaw Kejler *(Mng Partner)*
Daria Sacha *(Mng Partner)*
Marcin Boglowski *(Mng Dir)*
James Kossut *(Mng Dir)*
Marzena German *(Specialist-Special Project)*

Accounts:
Deloitte
Fulltime Tauron
Ministry of Environment
Ministry of Health
Oferty.net

Portugal

MediaCom Portugal
(Formerly MediaCom Iberia)
Edificio 5C 4o Lagoas Park, 2470-298 Porto Salvo, 2770 Portugal
Tel.: (351) 211208750
Fax: (351) 211209090
E-Mail: portugal@mediacom.com
Web Site: www.mediacom.se

Employees: 35

Ricardo Clemente *(CEO-Portugal)*
Andre Folque *(Head-Digital)*

Accounts:
Biocol
Fitness Hut
Fiva
GSK
IG Markets
Ikea
Procter & Gamble
Seat
SSL

South Africa

MediaCom South Africa
GroupM House, 7 Naivasha Rd, Johannesburg, 2191 South Africa
Tel.: (27) 11 582 6600
Fax: (27) 112341475
Web Site: www.mediacom.co.za

Employees: 49

Britta Reid *(Mng Dir)*
Tish Farrell *(Dir-Media Ops)*
Bulumko Nomoyi *(Dir-Fin)*

Accounts:
MTN
PPC Digital, Media
Revlon

Sweden

MediaCom Sverige AB
Birger Jarlsgatan 52, S-103 77 Stockholm, Sweden
Tel.: (46) 850757200
Fax: (46) 850757202
E-Mail: info@mediacom.se
Web Site: www.mediacom.se

Employees: 90

Anna Winblad *(Grp Acct Dir-Nordics-P&G)*
Caroline Bauer *(Acct Dir)*
Hanna Bergius *(Acct Dir)*
Malena Bjalkdahl *(Acct Dir)*
Jonas Blomqvist *(Acct Dir)*
Anna Broden *(Acct Dir)*
Jenny Ferngren *(Acct Dir)*
Maria Nordstrom *(Client Svcs Dir)*
Christina Kopp Ovren *(Acct Dir-Nordic)*
Patrick Wallin *(Dir-Television)*
Marie Brander-Hestreus *(Client Svc Dir)*

Accounts:
Comviq

Findus
GlaxoSmithKline
Procter & Gamble Campaign: "Head & Shoulders For Men"
SIF
Tele2

Switzerland

MediaCom Switzerland
Manessestrasse 85, Zurich, CH-8005 Switzerland
Tel.: (41) 445674747
Fax: (41) 445674700
E-Mail: switzerland@mediacom.com

Employees: 80

Agency Specializes In: Event Planning & Marketing, Radio, T.V.

Axel Beckmann *(CEO)*
Anastasios Antonopoulos *(CFO)*
Lennart Hintz *(COO)*
Lukas Basista *(Dir-Insight)*
Bjorn Hagenheide *(Dir-Trading)*
Jessica Galler *(Client Svc Dir)*
Benjamin Moser *(Client Svc Dir)*

Accounts:
Bayer; 2008
Navyboot

United Kingdom

MediaCom Edinburgh
6 Dock Pl, Edinburgh, EH6 6LU United Kingdom
Tel.: (44) 1315551500
Fax: (44) 1315552343
Web Site: www.mediacomedinburgh.com

Employees: 43

David Shearer *(Mng Dir)*
Murray Calder *(Dir-Strategy)*
Charlie Crawford *(Dir)*
Tony Jervis *(Dir-Comml)*
Jane Stewart *(Acct Mgr)*

Accounts:
AFG Media Ltd Media Buying, Media Planning, Morphsuits
Allianz Group Media
Baxters Media Buying
Blipfoto Campaign: "Save Your Life", Media
Camping & Caravanning Club Media Buying
Cancer Research UK
Coca-Cola Coke Zero, Diet Coke, Fanta, Media Buying, Media Planning, Sprite
DF Concerts Media Planning & Buying
Edinburgh Fringe Festival Media Buying, Media Planning
Erskine Media Planning & Buying
Golden Charter Media Buying, Media Planning
Innovation Norway Tourism Media Planning & Buying
Kwik-Fit Direct Mail, In-Centre POS, Media Buying, Radio
Nuffield Health Media Planning & Buying
Quality Solicitors Media
Royal Bank of Scotland
Scottish Ballet Autumn Season, Dance GB, Media Planning & Buying, The Nutcracker
Scottish Rugby Union Media Planning & Buying
New-Suntory Holdings Ltd Media, Ribena
Teesside University Media Planning & Buying
Tyne & Wear Metro Media
Velux Media Planning & Buying

Mediacom London
124 Theobalds Road, London, WC1X 8RX United Kingdom
Tel.: (44) 207 158 5500
Fax: (44) 207 158 5999
E-Mail: info@mediacomuk.com
Web Site: www.mediacomuk.com

Employees: 888

Jane Ratcliffe *(Chm)*
Nick Jefferies *(Mng Partner & Head-Brand Response Client Strategy)*
Sarah Treliving *(Mng Partner & Head-Digital Direct)*
Claire Ferguson *(Mng Partner & Joint Head-Client Svcs)*
Steve Gladdis *(Mng Partner & Joint Head-Challenge & Inspiration)*
Josh Krichefski *(COO)*
Dominic Guba *(Chief Investment Officer-Global)*
Matthew Mee *(Chief Strategy Officer-Global)*
Sue Unerman *(Chief Strategy Officer)*
Karen Blackett *(CEO-UK)*
Nick Lawson *(CEO-EMEA)*
Ian Rotherham *(CEO-Team VWG & WPP)*
David Beale *(Mng Dir-Mediacom Response, Data & Analytics)*
Claudine Collins *(Mng Dir-UK)*
Costin Mihaila *(Mng Dir-EMEA)*
Kate Rowlinson *(Mng Dir-EMEA)*
Susie Dabbs *(Head-Client Content & Assoc Dir)*
Max-Philipp Deitmer *(Head-Digital Analytics-Europe, Middle East & Africa)*
Tim Lawrence *(Head-Digital Media Dev)*
Natalia Lopez *(Head-Digital)*
Jody Aird *(Bus Dir)*
Charlotte Simpson *(Bus Dir)*
Tom Curtis *(Dir-Creative-MediaCom Beyond Adv)*
Martin Galvin *(Dir-Digital Trading)*
Renee Mellow *(Dir-Paid Social)*
Matt Semple *(Dir-Global)*
Peter Wade *(Dir-Fin-EMEA Reg)*
Catherine Chater *(Acct Mgr)*
Fran Darvill *(Mgr)*
Mac Stephenson *(Mgr-Media-Intl)*

Accounts:
AkzoNobel Cuprinol, Media Buying, Media Planning
Appliances Online Rebrand
Arriva UK Bus Media Buying & Planning, Online & Offline
Audi
BeatBullying Media Buying, Media Planning
BetVictor Media Planning
Bose Corporation Media Planning & Buying
British Army Media Planning
Britta Water Filters
BSkyB Campaign: "The Finale", Media Planning & Buying, Now TV
Cancer Research UK Campaign: "Oi Cancer", Media Buying, Media Planning, Website
Centrepoint Media
Churchill Insurance Media Buying, Media Planning
Clarins Eau Dynamisante
COI Communications
Dell
DFS Furniture Press Buying
Digital UK
Direct Line Insurance Media Buying, Media Planning
Dolmio
Dry Like Me Media
eBay (Lead Media Planning & Buying Agency)
EFD
E.ON UK plc Media Buying, Media Planning
Etihad Airways Media
Everest Media Planning & Buying
Express Newspapers
FIA Formula E Championship Agency of Record
GlaxoSmithKline Horlicks, UK Media Planning & Buying
GMG Radio
Goodyear & Dunlop brands Media
Great Ormond
Greene King Pubs
The Guardian Campaign: "Think Of England", Media Planning & Buying
Harper Collins Media Planning & Buying
Hillarys Blinds
HomeForm
Ikea Campaign: "Ikea Sofa Invasion"
Internet Advertising Bureau Campaign: "Unzipped", Online, Pan-European Campaign
IPC Media Paid Search
Kepak Campaign: "Hunger Monkey", Rustlers
Kwik Fit
Lexmark
LVMH
Majestic Wine Warehouse Media
Mars Campaign: "Kitten Kollege", Confectionery, Digital, Galaxy, Media Planning, Snickers, Whiskas
McCain
Merlin Entertainment
Metropolitan Police Authority Media Planning & Buying
Moneysupermarket.com Media
Muller
Neff UK
NetWest
Nikon
Northern & Shell
The Health Lottery Media Planning & Buying
Northern Foods Goodfella's, Media Buying
Old Speckled Hen
Procter & Gamble Pampers, Press Buying
Provident Financial Group Media Buying, Media Planning, Satsuma Loans
QualitySolicitors Media
RBS Insurance
Revlon Media Planning & Buying
Royal Dutch Shell
RSPCA Media Planning & Buying, Mobile, Search, Social, Traditional & Digital Channels
Ryanair Media Buying, Media Planning
Scope Social Media, TV
Scottish Association for Mental Health Media Buying, Online, Press, TV
Siemens Home Appliances Media
Sky Sports Media Planning & Buying
New-Sky Media Buying, Media Planning, Sky Movies
Sony Global Media Planning, Media Buying, Sony Electronics, Sony Mobile
Stage Entertainment
T-Mobile US
Tea Time Centre Anti-Racisme
New-The Telegraph Media Buying, Media Planning
Tesco Media Buying
Tomy
TUI
Universal Music Group Media Planning & Buying
Universal Pictures
Volkswagen Group of America, Inc. Media Buying, Media Planning
Wrigley Digital, In-Store, Media Planning, Press, Print
Young's Seafood Media

Costa Rica

jotabequ Advertising
(Affiliate of Grey Worldwide)
Avenue 1 & 3, San Jose, Costa Rica
Mailing Address:
PO Box 60-2050, San Jose, Costa Rica
Tel.: (506) 284 9800
Fax: (506) 225 5512
E-Mail: jotabequ@jotabequ.com
Web Site: www.jotabequ.com

Employees: 150

Jaime Jimenez *(Owner)*
Alberto Quiros *(Partner)*
Wagner Cornejo *(Gen Mgr)*

Accounts:
Belmont
Dos Pinos
Gold's Gym
Grupo Nacion Perfil, Revistas
La Florida
Purdy Motor
Roche
World Wildlife Foundation

Puerto Rico

MediaCom Puerto Rico
270 Ave Munoz Rivera, San Juan, PR 00918
Mailing Address:
PO Box 366518, San Juan, PR 00936-6518
Tel.: (787) 522-8820
Fax: (787) 522-8825
E-Mail: puertorico@mediacom.com
Web Site: www.mediacom.com

Employees: 18

National Agency Associations: 4A's

Jose Bello *(Mng Partner)*
Jasmine Belassie-Page *(Dir-Digital Media & Strategy)*
Selin Cebeci *(Dir-Global Digital Media)*
Lauren Wormser *(Dir-Comm Plng)*
Colleen Canty *(Assoc Dir-Media)*
Rebecca Wingfield *(Assoc Dir-Media)*
Courtney Berg *(Supvr-Digital Media)*
Derek Hartman *(Supvr-Digital Media)*
Blaine Schoen *(Planner-Digital Media)*

Australia

MediaCom Australia Pty. Ltd.
Level 1 195 Little Collins Street, Melbourne, VIC 3000 Australia
Tel.: (61) 399407000
Fax: (61) 399407113
E-Mail: australia@mediacom.com
Web Site: www.mediacom.com

Employees: 72
Year Founded: 1996

Agency Specializes In: Media Buying Services

Sean Seamer *(CEO)*
Anny Havercroft *(Mng Dir)*
Helen Black *(Chief Strategy Officer)*
Nicole Turley *(Chief Investment Officer)*
Willie Pang *(Chief Digital Officer)*
Mark Heap *(CEO-Asia Pacific)*
Paul Walker *(Grp Dir-Client Comm Plng)*
Youmna Borghol *(Dir-Data & ROI)*
Stephen Meares *(Dir-Comml)*
Dean Rawnsley *(Mgr-Comml)*

Accounts:
Bank of Melbourne
Beyond Blue
Bonds
Carsguide.com.au Media
Chemist Warehouse Media Planning & Buying
Competitive Foods Hungry Jack's
Cricket Australia
Deakin University Media
EA Games
Forty Winks
GlaxoSmithKline Pharmaceuticals
Holden
Indeed.com Media
LVMH; Australia Media Buying & Planning; 2007
Mitre 10
Morris Johnston Walpole
News Corp Australia Media
NRMA Media Buying, Paid Search Marketing
Pizza Hut
Queensland Government
Queensland Health Campaign: "Sun Mum", Media
REA Group Buying, Communications Strategy, Planning
Rinnai
Specsavers
Suzuki Australia
TT Lines
Universal Film
Universal Music
WorldVision
Yum! Restaurants

MediaCom Sydney
Level 17, 65 Berry St North, 2060 Sydney, NSW Australia
Tel.: (61) 294637000
Fax: (61) 294637333
E-Mail: australia@mediacom.com
Web Site: www.mediacom.com

Employees: 257

Agency Specializes In: South Asian Market

James Sneddon *(Mng Dir)*
Gemma Newlands *(Head-Mediacom Beyond Adv)*
Brittany Crowley *(Dir-Implementation Plng & Investment)*
Bakari Blouin *(Mgr-Plng)*

Accounts:
Alienware
DealsDirect Media
DeLonghi Icona Vintage
New-KFC Media
NBC Universal
Volkswagen Campaign: "The Rok Adventure"

China & Hong Kong

MediaCom Beijing
Room 1205B Jin Bao Tower 89 Jino Bao St, Dong Cheng District, Beijing, 100005 China
Tel.: (86) 1085131399
Fax: (86) 1085131366
E-Mail: china@mediacom.com

Employees: 218

Agency Specializes In: Media Buying Services

Dominic Yuen-Tong *(Mng Partner-China)*
Rain Dong *(Head-MediaCom Response Beijing & Gen Mgr)*
Leon Zhang *(Head-Social Media-Natl)*
Nicole Lam *(Gen Mgr-MediaCom China)*
Cindy Li *(Dir-Talent)*
Liang Liang *(Dir-Plng)*
Helen Qiao *(Dir-Plng)*
Christine Yi *(Dir-Bus)*

Accounts:
China National Cereals, Oils & Foodstuffs (COFCO) Fortune Oil, Great Wall Wine, Lohas Fruit Juice, Media Planning & Buying
China Unicom; 2007
Dassault Systemes
Jamba

MediaCom Hong Kong
36 Floor PCCW Tower 979 Kings Road Taikoo Place, Quarry Bay, China (Hong Kong)
Tel.: (852) 22803480
Fax: (852) 25675534
E-Mail: hongkong@mediacom.com
Web Site: www.mediacom.com

Employees: 41
Year Founded: 1995

Agency Specializes In: Media Buying Services

Dominic Ng *(Mng Partner-China)*
Alice Chow *(Mng Dir)*
Natalie Chan *(Dir-Bus)*
Danny Chung *(Dir-Bus)*
Eva Lam *(Dir-Bus)*
Elaine Kwan *(Assoc Dir-Plng)*
Jamie Ng *(Sr Planner-Digital)*
Cecilia Chow *(Sr Media Planner)*

Accounts:
Anmum
New-Audi Hong Kong Media
Bandai
Cafe de Coral Campaign: "Everyday's Value Menu Offers", Microdocumentary, OOH, Print, TV
General Mills

MediaCom Shanghai
989 Changle Rd, The Centre 26th Fl, Shanghai, 200031 China
Tel.: (86) 2123077788
Fax: (86) 2123077753
E-Mail: china@mediacom.com

Employees: 133

Agency Specializes In: Media Buying Services

Dominic Ng *(Mng Partner-China)*
Jason Theodore *(Mng Dir)*
Karl Wu *(COO)*
Michelle Fu *(Dir-Natl Insight)*
Titan Chen *(Assoc Dir)*
Rex Tang *(Mgr-Media Plng)*
Yolanda Tian *(Planner)*
Prasanna Kumar Bhavsar *(Category Head-Asia-Team P&G)*

Accounts:
Akzo Nobel Swire Paints Digital, Media

India

MediaCom India
201 2nd Fl Kamla Executive Park Opp Vazir Glass Factory, Andheri East, Mumbai, 400059 India
Tel.: (91) 2242448888
Fax: (91) 2242448700
E-Mail: india@mediacom.com
Web Site: www.mediacom.com

Employees: 295

Agency Specializes In: Advertising

Avinash Pillai *(Mng Partner-Team P&G)*
Debraj Tripathy *(Mng Dir)*
Sriram Sharma *(Head-Client Leadership-South India)*
Jasmine Sachdeva *(Bus Dir-Client servicing & Insights)*
Junaid Hakim *(Planner-Media)*

Accounts:
New-Future Group Media
New-Koovs.com Media Buying
Makemytrip.com
Qyuki.com
Tata Docomo Media
Urban Ladder (Media Agency of Record)

MediaCom Bangalore
(Formerly MediaCom)
3rd Fl Mahalakshmi Chambers, No 29 M G Road, Bengaluru, 560001 India
Tel.: (91) 8042593200
Fax: (91) 8041133031

E-Mail: india@mediacom.com

Employees: 295

Agency Specializes In: Media Buying Services

Prem Anand *(Bus Dir-Media Buying)*
Tushar Deshmukh *(Dir-Fin)*
Sahil Gala *(Sr Bus Mgr-Media)*
Husain Kapadia *(Sr Bus Mgr)*
Vandana Mehra *(Sr Bus Dir)*
John Xavier *(Bus Grp Head-Digital Plng)*

Accounts:
Aegon Religare Life Insurance
Dell India Media
Miayas Beverages and Foods Media
Procter & Gamble Gillette
Revlon
Roche Diagnostics Accu-Chek, Digital, Media Agency of Record
Universal
Volkswagen Group of America, Inc. Skoda Yeti; 2007

Japan

MediaCom Japan
Yebisu Garden Place Tower 30F, 4-20-3 Ebisu Shibuya-ku, Tokyo, 150-0013 Japan
Tel.: (81) 357914660
Fax: (81) 357914742
E-Mail: japan@mediacom.com
Web Site: www.mediacom.com/en/contact/asia-pacific/tokyo

Employees: 65

Agency Specializes In: Media Buying Services

Satoshi Ishii *(Mng Partner)*
Tetsuya Ikeda *(Dir)*
Shota Nagayoshi *(Media Planner)*
Xin Zheng Tracy *(Media Planner-Digital-Team P&G)*
Shinji Hirai *(Rep Dir)*

Accounts:
AXA
Clarion
Dell
De'Longhi Japan
Manpower
McAfee
Nihon Unisys
Stratus Computer
Taiki
Universal Pictures Japan
Wrigley

Korea

MediaCom Korea
7F SB Tower 318, Doan Daero Gangnam-gu, 135-819 Seoul, Korea (South)
Tel.: (82) 262001500
Fax: (82) 262001598
E-Mail: korea@mediacom.com

Employees: 36
Year Founded: 2000

Agency Specializes In: Media Buying Services

Accounts:
Audi

Singapore

MediaCom Singapore
China Square Central, 18 Cross Street, Singapore, 048423 Singapore
Tel.: (65) 62325460
Fax: (65) 62238523
E-Mail: singapore@mediacom.com

Employees: 166
Year Founded: 2000

Agency Specializes In: Media Buying Services

Matthew Wigham *(Chief Investment Officer-APAC)*
Darragh Hardy *(Chief Client Officer-Asia Pacific)*
Mark Heap *(CEO-Asia Pacific)*
Vivian Yeung *(Gen Mgr)*

Accounts:
Carrefour
Dell South Asia
Fonterra Media Planning & Buying
Network Associates Software
Nokia

MEDIACOMP, INC.
13810 Champion Forest Dr Ste 210, Houston, TX 77069
Tel.: (713) 621-1071
Fax: (281) 640-8288
Web Site: www.mediacomp.com

Employees: 7
Year Founded: 1973

National Agency Associations: AAF

Agency Specializes In: Affluent Market, African-American Market, Asian Market, Automotive, Bilingual Market, Broadcast, Business Publications, Cable T.V., Co-op Advertising, College, Communications, Consulting, Consumer Goods, Consumer Marketing, Consumer Publications, Digital/Interactive, Direct-to-Consumer, Education, Electronic Media, Entertainment, Food Service, Government/Political, Health Care Services, Hispanic Market, Household Goods, Legal Services, Leisure, Local Marketing, Magazines, Media Buying Services, Media Planning, Medical Products, Multicultural, Newspaper, Newspapers & Magazines, Out-of-Home Media, Outdoor, Over-50 Market, Paid Searches, Pets , Planning & Consultation, Print, Radio, Real Estate, Recruitment, Restaurant, Retail, Sponsorship, T.V., Teen Market, Tween Market, Web (Banner Ads, Pop-ups, etc.), Women's Market

Approx. Annual Billings: $1,000,000

Tami Weitkunat *(Pres/CEO-MediaComp)*
Linda Gilbert *(Controller)*
Jordan Miller *(Media Planner & Media Buyer)*
Debbie Kelley *(Media Buyer)*

Accounts:
Dialyspa Medical - Dialysis; 2010
Fiesta Mart Grocery; 1988

MEDIASMITH
115 Sansome St, San Francisco, CA 94114-9991
Tel.: (415) 252-9339
Fax: (415) 252-9854
E-Mail: jcate@mediasmith.com
Web Site: www.mediasmith.com

E-Mail for Key Personnel:
President: smith@mediasmithinc.com

Employees: 45
Year Founded: 1989

National Agency Associations: 4A's-ICOM

Agency Specializes In: Above-the-Line, Advertising, Affluent Market, Automotive, Brand Development & Integration, Broadcast, Business Publications, Business-To-Business, Cable T.V., Children's Market, Co-op Advertising, Communications, Computers & Software, Consulting, Consumer Goods, Consumer Marketing, Consumer Publications, Corporate Communications, Digital/Interactive, Direct Response Marketing, Direct-to-Consumer, E-Commerce, Electronic Media, Email, Entertainment, Environmental, Financial, Guerilla Marketing, High Technology, Information Technology, Integrated Marketing, International, Leisure, Local Marketing, Luxury Products, Magazines, Market Research, Media Buying Services, Media Planning, Media Training, Mobile Marketing, Multimedia, New Product Development, New Technologies, Newspaper, Newspapers & Magazines, Out-of-Home Media, Outdoor, Paid Searches, Pets , Planning & Consultation, Podcasting, Print, RSS (Really Simple Syndication), Radio, Real Estate, Recruitment, Regional, Search Engine Optimization, Social Marketing/Nonprofit, Social Media, Sponsorship, Sports Market, Strategic Planning/Research, T.V., Technical Advertising, Teen Market, Trade & Consumer Magazines, Travel & Tourism, Viral/Buzz/Word of Mouth

Approx. Annual Billings: $49,850,000

David L. Smith *(Founder & CEO)*
Karen T. McFee *(Co-Founder & Dir-Media Ops)*
John Cate *(Pres & COO)*
Rachel Miller-Garcia *(VP-Client Svcs)*
Marcus Pratt *(VP-Insights & Tech)*
Susan Engle *(Dir-HR)*
Abraham Alegria *(Assoc Dir-Media)*
Adriana Oliveira *(Assoc Dir-Media)*
Jamie Rice *(Specialist-Mktg Communications)*
Stuart Siebold *(Strategist-Digital)*
Amy McTaggart *(Asst Media Planner)*

Accounts:
Alouette Cheese
Analytics Consulting
Blurb; San Francisco, CA Personal Books & Photobooks Online; 2012
Blurb
Breastcancer.org; Ardmore, PA (Agency of Record); 2011
Children's International; Kansas City, MO International Children Support Fund; 2012
Citrix Online; Santa Barbara, CA GoToAssist, GoToManage, GoToMeeting, GoToMyPC, GoToTraining, GoToWebinar, Interactive/Digital, Print; 2009
Everyday Hero
lynda.com
Meyer Corporation
Mulesoft
Salesforce
The San Jose Sharks
Stanford Children's Health
Teradata
TRX (Fitness Anytime)

MEDIASPACE SOLUTIONS
101 Merritt 7 Corp Park 3rd Fl, Norwalk, CT 06851
Tel.: (203) 849-8855
Fax: (203) 849-5946
Toll Free: (888) 672-2100
E-Mail: info@mediaspacesolutions.com
Web Site: www.mediaspacesolutions.com

Employees: 60
Year Founded: 1999

Agency Specializes In: Co-op Advertising, Digital/Interactive, Financial, Gay & Lesbian Market, Hispanic Market, Information Technology, Local Marketing, Media Buying Services, Media Planning, Newspaper, Newspapers & Magazines,

Over-50 Market, Planning & Consultation, Print, Travel & Tourism

Approx. Annual Billings: $100,000,000

Breakdown of Gross Billings by Media: Newsp.: 100%

Randy Grunow *(CEO)*
Brian St. Cyr *(VP-Bus Dev & Mktg)*
Richard Benson *(Dir-Fin)*
Colin May *(Dir-Media Dev)*
Peter Krohse *(Mgr-Buying-Eastern Reg)*
Carol Wagner *(Mgr-Media Dev & Buying)*
Katy Rogalski *(Acct Supvr-Dev)*
Jessica Rave *(Coord-Adv Ops & Productions)*

MEDIASPOT, INC.

1550 Bayside Dr, Corona Del Mar, CA 92625-1711
Tel.: (949) 721-0500
Fax: (949) 721-0555
E-Mail: info@mediaspot.com
Web Site: www.mediaspot.com

E-Mail for Key Personnel:
President: ayelsey@mediaspot.com

Employees: 25
Year Founded: 1991

Agency Specializes In: Media Buying Services, Sponsorship

Approx. Annual Billings: $200,000,000

Breakdown of Gross Billings by Media: Internet Adv.: 5%; Mags.: 5%; Newsp.: 5%; Other: 5%; Outdoor: 5%; Radio: 35%; T.V.: 40%

Arthur R. Yelsey *(Pres)*
Tamiko Fujimoto *(Sr VP)*
Quinn Truong *(Controller)*
Erin Hopkins *(Dir-Local Brdcst & Acct Supvr)*
Miko Hoshino *(Mgr-Digital Media)*
Jennifer Connell *(Acct Supvr)*
Daisy Lok *(Acct Supvr)*
Deborah Hohman *(Sr Media Buyer)*

Accounts:
3-Day Blinds
Aquarium of the Pacific
Bank of the West, Inc.
BlueAnt Wireless
Catalina Express
Medieval Times
Mercedes Benz of Foothill Ranch
Mercedes Benz of Laguna Niguel
Orchard Supply Hardware
Pacific Life Insurance Company
Paramount Pictures Television Group
Paramount Pictures Video-On-Demand
PIMCO
Quiksilver
Rubio's Fresh Mexican Grill
Sterling BMW

MEDIASSOCIATES, INC.

75 Glen Rd, Sandy Hook, CT 06482
Tel.: (203) 797-9500
Fax: (203) 797-1400
Toll Free: (800) 522-1660
E-Mail: information@mediassociates.com
Web Site: www.mediassociates.com

Employees: 12
Year Founded: 1994

Agency Specializes In: Advertising, Broadcast, Business-To-Business, Cable T.V., Consumer Marketing, Consumer Publications, Direct Response Marketing, Education, Electronic Media, Financial, Magazines, Media Buying Services, Media Planning, New Technologies, Newspaper, Out-of-Home Media, Outdoor, Print, Radio, Social Marketing/Nonprofit, Sponsorship, Strategic Planning/Research, T.V., Trade & Consumer Magazines, Yellow Pages Advertising

Approx. Annual Billings: $24,000,000

Scott Brunjes *(Pres & CEO)*
Ben Kunz *(VP-Strategic Plng)*
Charlie Menduni *(VP-Client Svcs)*
Erin McCollam *(Dir-Acctg & Assoc Dir-Media)*
Glenn Bourque *(Dir-Ops)*
Evan Nichols *(Dir-Online Adv)*
Justin Anderson *(Mgr-Bus Dev)*
Erica Stadnyk *(Mgr-Plng)*
Chris Coladarci *(Sr Acct Planner)*
Nicole Moreland *(Acct Planner)*
Brian Poe *(Media Buyer-Online)*

MERCURY COMMUNICATIONS

520 Broadway Ste 400, Santa Monica, CA 90401-2462
Tel.: (310) 451-2900
Fax: (310) 451-9494
E-Mail: info@mercurymedia.com
Web Site: www.mercurymedia.com

Employees: 88
Year Founded: 1989

Agency Specializes In: Advertising, Direct Response Marketing, E-Commerce, Infomercials, Media Buying Services, Strategic Planning/Research

Approx. Annual Billings: $152,000,000

Breakdown of Gross Billings by Media: Cable T.V.: $59,000,000; Network T.V.: $80,000,000; Radio: $1,000,000; Spot T.V.: $9,000,000; Syndication: $3,000,000

Ruben Hernandez *(Pres-Long Form & Espanol)*
Keith Kochberg *(Pres-Digital)*
Beth Vendice *(Pres-Performance Div)*
Cheryl Green *(Sr VP-Media)*
Itai Sutker *(Sr VP)*
Gina Pomponi *(VP & Mng Dir-Short Form)*
John Golden *(VP-Client Svcs)*
Justin Henderson *(VP-Digital Svcs)*

Accounts:
ICan
In Style
Liberty
Magic Bullet
Neutrogena

THE MGS GROUP

3639 N Harding Ave, Chicago, IL 60618-4024
Tel.: (773) 583-5383
Fax: (773) 583-2632
E-Mail: mgs.consulting@comcast.com

Employees: 3
Year Founded: 1993

Agency Specializes In: Automotive, Broadcast, Business-To-Business, Cable T.V., Consulting, Consumer Marketing, Consumer Publications, Electronic Media, Health Care Services, Magazines, Media Buying Services, Newspaper, Newspapers & Magazines, Planning & Consultation, Print, Radio, Strategic Planning/Research, Syndication, T.V., Trade & Consumer Magazines

Maureen Gorman *(Owner)*

Accounts:
Pappas Toyota

MIDWEST COMMUNICATIONS & MEDIA

2015 Roundwyck Lane, Powell, OH 43065
Tel.: (614) 440-4449
E-Mail: bobclegg@ameritech.net
Web Site: www.midwestcommunicationsandmedia.com

E-Mail for Key Personnel:
President: prussell@ameritech.net

Employees: 10
Year Founded: 1994

Agency Specializes In: Government/Political, Media Buying Services

Approx. Annual Billings: $10,000,000

Patty Russell *(Pres)*
Neil Clark *(Exec VP)*
Robert Clegg *(Sr VP)*
John Feldhouse *(Dir-Corp Mktg Art)*
Terry Eyears *(Media Buyer)*
Nicholas Ver Duin *(Sr Designer-Web)*

Accounts:
American Lung Association
AT&T Communications Corp.
Columbus Zoo
Drug Free Action Alliance Underage Drinking; 1994
Franklin County Republican Party; Columbus, OH Political Campaigns; 1982
Glimcher Realty
Initiative Consulting
Ohio Grape Industries

MILNER BUTCHER MEDIA GROUP

(d/b/a MBMG)
2056 Cotner Ave, Los Angeles, CA 90025
Tel.: (310) 478-0555
Fax: (310) 478-2482
E-Mail: jwilson@mbmg-media.com
Web Site: www.mbmg-media.com

Employees: 25
Year Founded: 2003

Agency Specializes In: Advertising, Automotive, Broadcast, Cable T.V., Consumer Marketing, Digital/Interactive, Direct Response Marketing, E-Commerce, Education, Electronic Media, Entertainment, Event Planning & Marketing, Fashion/Apparel, Financial, Government/Political, Health Care Services, Hispanic Market, Media Buying Services, Medical Products, Newspapers & Magazines, Out-of-Home Media, Package Design, Planning & Consultation, Publishing, Radio, Restaurant, Retail, Sports Market, Strategic Planning/Research, Syndication, T.V., Technical Advertising, Teen Market, Trade & Consumer Magazines, Travel & Tourism

Andrew Butcher *(Chm)*
Bruce Milner *(Pres)*
Pam Bentz *(Partner & Exec VP)*
Greg Davis *(Exec VP-Digital)*
John Wilson *(Exec VP)*
Robert Chusid *(Acct Dir)*
Teresa Kees *(Sr Buyer-Brdcst)*
Lindsay Joseph *(Sr Media Buyer)*
Darrah Rachman *(Assoc Strategist-Media)*
Jason Scribner *(Sr Media Buyer)*

MINDSHARE

3630 Peachtree Rd NE, Atlanta, GA 30326
Tel.: (404) 832-3400
Fax: (404) 832-3430
E-Mail: cindy.giller@mindshareworld.com
Web Site: www.mindshareworld.com

Employees: 50

National Agency Associations: 4A's

Agency Specializes In: Media Buying Services, Sponsorship

Cindy Giller *(Mng Partner)*
Allison Fillman *(Partner & Assoc Dir)*
Matt Chamberlin *(Assoc Dir)*
Lauren Jopling *(Assoc Dir-Media)*
Candii Woodson *(Assoc Dir)*
Bunrort Em *(Mgr-Digital)*
Stacy Staranowicz *(Supvr-Global Comm)*
Mike Rey *(Specialist-Product Info)*
Nicole Guba *(Coord-Media Ops)*

Accounts:
Armed Forces Insurance
BBVA
Jiffy Lube Media
John Deere
Orkin
Scana Energy
Transamerica
U.S. Marine Corps
U.S. Virgin Islands

MISSISSIPPI PRESS SERVICES
371 Edgewood Ter, Jackson, MS 39206
Tel.: (601) 981-3060
Fax: (601) 981-3676
E-Mail: mspress@mspress.org
Web Site: www.mspress.org

Employees: 12
Year Founded: 1978

Agency Specializes In: Newspaper

Breakdown of Gross Billings by Media: Newsp.: 100%

Layne Bruce *(Exec Dir)*
David Gillis *(Dir-Sls)*
Monica Gilmer *(Mgr-Member Svcs)*
Sue Hicks *(Mgr-Bus Dev)*
Andrea Ross *(Media Buyer)*
Beth Boone *(Coord-Foundation)*

MNI TARGETED MEDIA INC.
(Formerly Media Networks Inc.)
225 High Ridge Rd, Stamford, CT 06905
Tel.: (203) 967-3100
Fax: (203) 967-6472
Toll Free: (800) 225-3457
E-Mail: info@nmi.com
Web Site: www.mni.com

Employees: 180
Year Founded: 1980

Agency Specializes In: Digital/Interactive, Media Buying Services, Media Planning

Approx. Annual Billings: $30,000,000

Robert Reif *(Pres)*
John Kenyon *(Mng Dir & VP)*
Matthew Fanelli *(Sr VP-Digital)*
Mark Glatzhofer *(VP & Gen Mgr)*
Laura West *(VP-Adv)*
Vicki Brakl *(Dir-Mktg)*
Heather Hein *(Dir-Sls)*
Jen Hendry *(Dir-Client Svcs)*
Lisa Ouyang *(Dir-Fin)*

Accounts:
New-AAA
New-Arizona Office of Tourism
New-Barber Foods
New-Benjamim Moore Paints
New-Best Buy
New-BMW
New-Boston University
New-Caribou Coffee
New-Carnival
New-Cedars-Sinai
New-Celebrity Cruises
New-Charles Schwab
New-Chase
New-The Children's Hospital of Philadelphia
New-Connecticut Department of Social Services
New-Country Financial
New-CVS
New-Del Monte
New-Disney
New-Downtown Cleveland Alliance
New-Duquesne Light
New-Emirates
New-Farmland
New-Fifth Third Bank
New-First Niagara
New-Foxwoods
New-General Mills
New-Giant Eagle
New-Hartford Healthcare
New-Hershey
New-Hood
New-Liberty Mutual
New-McDonald's
New-Mount Snow
New-Nevada State Bank
New-Perdue
New-PNC
New-Premium Outlets
New-Publix
New-Qatar
New-Rolex
New-Stressless
New-Target
New-Thomson Reuters
New-Walmart

MULTI MEDIA SERVICES CORP.
915 King St 2nd Fl, Alexandria, VA 22314
Tel.: (703) 739-2160
Fax: (703) 836-9517
E-Mail: info@multi-media-services.com
Web Site: www.multi-media-services.com

Employees: 4
Year Founded: 1984

Agency Specializes In: Media Buying Services, Planning & Consultation

Approx. Annual Billings: $8,000,000

Anthony M. Fabrizio *(Chm & Treas)*
Dwight Sterling *(Pres)*
Neal McDonald *(Sr Media Buyer)*

Accounts:
Advantage Human Resourcing
Air Life Line
Cavalier Telephone
Cleveland Saves
Jamestown Associates
National Restaurant Association
Norwalk Community College
Sabre Radio Group
St. Lawrence Cement
U.S. Chamber of Commerce

MULTI-NET MARKETING, INC.
224 E Monument St, Colorado Springs, CO 80903
Tel.: (719) 444-0371
Fax: (719) 444-0374
Toll Free: (800) 776-8289
Web Site: www.multinetmarketing.com

Employees: 8
Year Founded: 1995

Agency Specializes In: Advertising, Broadcast, Communications, Electronic Media, Internet/Web Design, Media Buying Services, Media Relations, Radio

Approx. Annual Billings: $15,000,000

Howard F. Price *(Pres & CEO)*
Jane E. Price *(COO)*
Alana King *(Dir-Traffic)*
Kerstin Poole *(Dir-Traffic)*

NAILMEDIA GROUP
260 Madison Ave 8th Fl, New York, NY 10016
Tel.: (212) 686-9710
Fax: (212) 686-9713
E-Mail: info@nailmarketing360.com
Web Site: nailmarketing360.com

Employees: 10

Agency Specializes In: Advertising, Broadcast, Cable T.V., Consulting, Consumer Goods, Consumer Marketing, Consumer Publications, Digital/Interactive, Direct Response Marketing, Electronic Media, Electronics, Entertainment, Health Care Services, Magazines, Media Buying Services, Media Planning, Newspaper, Newspapers & Magazines, Out-of-Home Media, Outdoor, Planning & Consultation, Print, Radio, Sponsorship, Strategic Planning/Research, Syndication, T.V., Trade & Consumer Magazines, Transportation, Web (Banner Ads, Pop-ups, etc.)

Approx. Annual Billings: $40,000,000

Jack Nail *(CEO)*
Anne Distassio *(Acct Dir)*
Jennifer Creegan *(Dir-Media)*
Chhaya Dagli *(Dir-Brand Strategy & Mktg)*
John Fletcher *(Dir-Creative)*

Accounts:
Bose
Cold-EEZE
HoMedics

NATIONWIDE COURT SERVICES, INC.
4250 Veterans Memorial Hwy Ste 4000, Holbrook, NY 11741-4018
Tel.: (631) 981-4400
Fax: (631) 981-2417
Toll Free: (888) 941-1234
E-Mail: info@nationwidecourtservices.com
Web Site: nationwidecourtservice.com

Employees: 30
Year Founded: 1993

Agency Specializes In: Legal Services

Approx. Annual Billings: $6,000,000

Breakdown of Gross Billings by Media: Newsp.: 100%

Arlene Nelson *(Pres & CEO)*
George V. Nelson, Jr. *(VP)*
Paula Parrino Altiere *(Dir-Ops & HR)*
Olivia Charpentier *(Office Mgr)*

Accounts:
Berkman, Henoch, Peterson; Garden City, NY (NY Legal Ads)
Jon B. Felice & Associates, PC; New York, NY (NY Legal Ads)
Relin, Goldstein & Crane; Rochester, NY (NY Legal Ads)
Shapiro & DiCaro; Commack, NY (NY Legal Ads)
Upton, Cohen, & Siamowitz; Syosset, NY (NY Legal Ads)
Weinreb & Weinreb; West Babylon, NY (NY Legal

Ads)

NEW & IMPROVED MEDIA

1222 E Grand Ave, El Segundo, CA 90245
Tel.: (310) 321-3606
Fax: (310) 578-9548
E-Mail: info@newandimprovedmedia.com
Web Site: www.newandimprovedmedia.com

E-Mail for Key Personnel:
President: terrell@newandimprovedmedia.com
Media Dir.:
yokogawa@newandimprovedmedia.com

Employees: 15
Year Founded: 1988

Agency Specializes In: Advertising, Broadcast, Business-To-Business, Cable T.V., Electronic Media, Entertainment, Fashion/Apparel, High Technology, Magazines, Media Buying Services, Newspaper, Newspapers & Magazines, Out-of-Home Media, Outdoor, Planning & Consultation, Radio, Restaurant, Retail, T.V., Travel & Tourism

Approx. Annual Billings: $50,000,000

Don Terrell *(Pres)*
Tori Davis *(VP-Media)*
Danna Prosser *(Dir-Fin & Ops)*
Casey Baker *(Supvr-Media)*
Courtney Burke *(Supvr-Brdcst)*
Kristin Sellens *(Supvr-Digital Media)*
Uzair Moon *(Media Planner & Media Buyer)*

Accounts:
Fox Broadcasting Company
Lellikelly
My Network TV
Resources
Tarantula
Tequila Rose
Valley Presbyterian Hospital

NEW DAY MARKETING, LTD.

923 Olive St, Santa Barbara, CA 93101
Tel.: (805) 965-7833
Fax: (805) 965-1284
E-Mail: robert@ndm.tv
Web Site: www.newdaymarketing.com

Employees: 20
Year Founded: 1987

Agency Specializes In: Infomercials

Approx. Annual Billings: $70,000,000

Robert Hunt *(Pres)*
Frank Kelly *(VP)*
Jeff Thomson *(VP-Media)*
Elisabeth Wenzl *(Media Buyer)*

Accounts:
AAA Automobile Club
Amazing Goods
Beachbody, LLC
Black & Decker
Boardroom, Inc
Incredible Discoveries
KB Home
L'oreal
MDR Vital Factors
Medicus Golf
Midwest Center for Stress & Anxiety
NGC Sports
Pfizer
Proactiv Solution
Sonicare
Sylmark, Inc
Thane International

NEW ENGLAND PRESS SERVICE

370 Common St, Dedham, MA 02026
Tel.: (781) 320-8050
Fax: (781) 320-8055
E-Mail: info@nenpa.com
Web Site: www.nenpa.com

Employees: 4
Year Founded: 1950

Agency Specializes In: Newspaper

Breakdown of Gross Billings by Media: Newsp.: 100%

Robert A. Bertsche *(Gen Counsel)*
Linda Conway *(Exec Dir)*
Megan Sherman *(Mgr-PR & Events)*
Erica Siciliano *(Media Buyer)*

NEWTON MEDIA

824 Greenbrier Pkwy Ste 200, Chesapeake, VA 23320
Tel.: (757) 547-5400
Fax: (757) 547-7383
Toll Free: (866) 656-1929
E-Mail: info@newtonmedia.com
Web Site: www.newtonmedia.com

E-Mail for Key Personnel:
Media Dir.: jburke@newtonmedia.com

Employees: 10
Year Founded: 1995

Agency Specializes In: Advertising, Brand Development & Integration, Broadcast, Business-To-Business, Cable T.V., Consulting, Cosmetics, Direct Response Marketing, Electronic Media, Event Planning & Marketing, Hispanic Market, Infomercials, Internet/Web Design, Media Buying Services, Medical Products, Over-50 Market, Planning & Consultation, Production, Radio, Strategic Planning/Research, T.V., Telemarketing

Approx. Annual Billings: $12,000,000

Breakdown of Gross Billings by Media: Brdcst.: 50%; Cable T.V.: 35%; Radio: 15%

Janet Burke *(Dir-Media)*
Steve Warnecke *(Dir-New Bus Dev)*
Aubry Winfrey *(Acct Exec & Media Buyer)*
Aimee James *(Media Buyer)*

Accounts:
American Marketing Systems; IL Real Estate Products; 1995

NEXGEN MEDIA WORLDWIDE

1120 Ave of the Americas 4th Fl, New York, NY 10036
Tel.: (212) 957-7660
Fax: (212) 626-6697
Web Site: www.drmedia.com/

E-Mail for Key Personnel:
President: neil.faber@nexgenmedia.com

Employees: 10
Year Founded: 1979

Agency Specializes In: Advertising, Advertising Specialties, Brand Development & Integration, Broadcast, Business Publications, Business-To-Business, Cable T.V., Co-op Advertising, Consulting, Consumer Marketing, Consumer Publications, Direct Response Marketing, Direct-to-Consumer, Education, Electronic Media, Entertainment, Event Planning & Marketing, Health Care Services, Magazines, Media Buying Services, Merchandising, New Product Development, Newspaper, Newspapers & Magazines, Out-of-Home Media, Outdoor, Pharmaceutical, Planning & Consultation, Print, Radio, Retail, Strategic Planning/Research, Syndication, T.V., Trade & Consumer Magazines, Travel & Tourism, Web (Banner Ads, Pop-ups, etc.), Yellow Pages Advertising

Approx. Annual Billings: $51,725,000

Breakdown of Gross Billings by Media: Bus. Publs.: $300,000; Cable T.V.: $7,000,000; D.M.: $350,000; Internet Adv.: $3,500,000; Mags.: $6,000,000; Network Radio: $500,000; Network T.V.: $3,500,000; Newsp.: $9,000,000; Out-of-Home Media: $2,000,000; Spot Radio: $7,000,000; Spot T.V.: $12,000,000; Syndication: $500,000; Yellow Page Adv.: $75,000

Amy Hochberg *(Pres)*
Neil Faber *(CEO)*
Allan Tepper *(Dir-Corp Media)*

Accounts:
Perillo Tours; Woodcliff Lake, NJ; 1992

NEXTMEDIA INC.

3625 N Hall St Ste 1100, Dallas, TX 75219
Tel.: (214) 252-1782
Fax: (214) 525-4852
E-Mail: michaell@nextm.com
Web Site: www.nextm.com

Employees: 8
Year Founded: 1997

National Agency Associations: 4A's

Agency Specializes In: Advertising, Affluent Market, Automotive, Brand Development & Integration, Broadcast, Business Publications, Business-To-Business, Cable T.V., Co-op Advertising, Consumer Goods, Consumer Marketing, Consumer Publications, Digital/Interactive, Direct-to-Consumer, Financial, Food Service, Health Care Services, High Technology, Magazines, Media Buying Services, Media Planning, Newspaper, Out-of-Home Media, Outdoor, Over-50 Market, Pharmaceutical, Planning & Consultation, Print, Restaurant, Retail, Search Engine Optimization, Strategic Planning/Research, T.V., Trade & Consumer Magazines, Travel & Tourism, Women's Market

Breakdown of Gross Billings by Media: Bus. Publs.: 2%; Cable T.V.: 35%; Consumer Publs.: 2%; Internet Adv.: 5%; Network Radio: 15%; Network T.V.: 15%; Out-of-Home Media: 4%; Spot Radio: 10%; Spot T.V.: 10%; Strategic Planning/Research: 2%

Karon Klein *(Grp Dir-Plng)*

Accounts:
AARP Services, Inc.
Citracal Calcium Supplement
FASTSIGNS International; Carrollton, TX; 2005
Genie Garage Door Openers
Midas International
Overhead Door Corp.; Lewisville, TX; 1997

NIKITA MEDIA, INC.

6243 136th Ave, Saugatuck, MI 49453
Tel.: (248) 514-4449
Web Site: NikitaMediaInc.com

Agency Specializes In: Broadcast, Cable T.V., Digital/Interactive, Game Integration, Guerilla Marketing, In-Store Advertising, Local Marketing, Magazines, Mobile Marketing, Multimedia, Newspaper, Newspapers & Magazines, Out-of-Home Media, Outdoor, Paid Searches, Print,

Radio, Search Engine Optimization, Syndication, T.V., Trade & Consumer Magazines, Web (Banner Ads, Pop-ups, etc.)

Diane Pastor *(CEO)*

Accounts:
Anchor Bay Entertainment

NORBELLA INC.

46 Plympton St #5, Boston, MA 02118
Tel.: (617) 542-1040
Web Site: www.norbella.com

Employees: 20

Agency Specializes In: Broadcast, Business Publications, Business-To-Business, Cable T.V., Co-op Advertising, Direct Response Marketing, Direct-to-Consumer, Email, Local Marketing, Magazines, Media Buying Services, Newspaper, Out-of-Home Media, Outdoor, Print, Radio, Strategic Planning/Research, T.V.

Approx. Annual Billings: $40,000,000

Stephanie Noris *(Pres)*
Greg Angland *(Dir-Media)*
Jessica Carmona *(Dir-Media)*
Davi Harte *(Dir-Media)*
Pam Caputo *(Assoc Dir-Media)*
Phil Decoteau *(Assoc Dir-Digital)*
Teresa Conant *(Supvr-Brdcst)*
Alison Weitzner *(Supvr-Media)*
Andrea Lancione *(Media Buyer-Coravin, Lahey Health, Sea Cuisine & WGBH)*
Nate Leach *(Sr Digital Buyer-Boyne, BSO, Exact Sciences, Moo com & Summit Gas)*

Accounts:
AAASNE
Arbella Insurance
BrainLab
High Liner Foods (USA) Incorporated
Lahey Clinic
Tetley Tea
Uno Chicago Grill Media Planning & Buying

NOVUS MEDIA INC

2 Carlson Pkwy Ste 400, Plymouth, MN 55447
Tel.: (612) 758-8600
Fax: (612) 336-8600
Toll Free: (888) 229-4656
E-Mail: info@novusprintmedia.com
Web Site: www.novusmediainc.com

Employees: 160
Year Founded: 1986

National Agency Associations: 4A's-DMA

Agency Specializes In: Advertising Specialties, Business Publications, Consumer Publications, Direct Response Marketing, Magazines, Media Buying Services, Newspaper, Newspapers & Magazines, Planning & Consultation, Print, Strategic Planning/Research

Approx. Annual Billings: $500,000,000

Jay Deverell *(CFO)*
Gwen Maass *(CMO)*
Margy Campion *(Sr VP-Bus Ops)*
Dan Briley *(Grp Acct Dir)*
Amanda Geistfeld *(Dir-Local Media Investment)*
Jennifer Grimm *(Dir-Media Investment)*
Renae Hermen *(Dir-Digital Plng & Buying)*
Marsha Lawrence *(Dir-Media Investment)*
Scott Wyffels *(Dir-Digital Strategy & Innovation)*
Lisa Brooks *(Assoc Dir-Local Media Investment)*
Ashley Smith *(Assoc Dir-Local Media Investment)*

Accounts:
Dell
Discovery Channel
FedEx
Intercure
Life Lock

NYM WORLDGROUP, INC.

1333 Broadway Ste 514, New York, NY 10018
Tel.: (212) 564-9550
Fax: (212) 564-9551
E-Mail: info@nymworldgroup.com
Web Site: www.nymworldgroup.com

Employees: 6
Year Founded: 1992

Agency Specializes In: Advertising, Advertising Specialties, Arts, Broadcast, Cable T.V., Co-op Advertising, Communications, Consulting, Consumer Publications, Digital/Interactive, Direct Response Marketing, Education, Electronic Media, Entertainment, Event Planning & Marketing, Fashion/Apparel, Financial, Food Service, Game Integration, Gay & Lesbian Market, Guerilla Marketing, Health Care Services, High Technology, In-Store Advertising, Integrated Marketing, Local Marketing, Magazines, Market Research, Media Buying Services, Media Planning, Mobile Marketing, Newspaper, Newspapers & Magazines, Out-of-Home Media, Outdoor, Over-50 Market, Planning & Consultation, Point of Purchase, Point of Sale, Print, Production, Promotions, Publicity/Promotions, Radio, Real Estate, Regional, Retail, Strategic Planning/Research, T.V., Trade & Consumer Magazines, Transportation, Travel & Tourism, Urban Market, Viral/Buzz/Word of Mouth

Approx. Annual Billings: $55,000,000

James E. Parker *(Pres)*
Thomas Deluca *(Comptroller)*
Mary Marengo *(Acct Dir)*

Accounts:
Blur Communications
Direct Advantage
Eclipse Advertising
FIT
The Gate Worldwide
Integrated Media Solutions
Lasik Vision
NY State Bar Association
NYC Ballet
O&R Utility
Plus Media, Inc.
Renegade Media
Serino Coyne, Inc.
SSGA
Station Digital

OCEAN MEDIA INC.

17011 Beach Blvd, Huntington Beach, CA 92647
Tel.: (714) 969-5244
Fax: (714) 969-6589
E-Mail: info@oceanmediainc.com
Web Site: www.oceanmediainc.com

Employees: 60
Year Founded: 1996

Agency Specializes In: Advertising, Brand Development & Integration, Broadcast, Cable T.V., Digital/Interactive, Direct Response Marketing, E-Commerce, Magazines, Media Buying Services, Media Planning, Newspaper, Planning & Consultation, Radio, Sponsorship, Strategic Planning/Research, T.V.

Approx. Annual Billings: $210,000,000

Breakdown of Gross Billings by Media: Brdcst.: 10%; Cable T.V.: 60%; Out-of-Home Media: 5%; Print: 5%; Radio: 20%

Ron Louis Luebbert *(COO)*
Gregg Bender *(VP & Client Svcs Dir)*
Dave Coleman *(VP-Strategy & Dev)*
Staci Larkin *(VP-Media)*
Katie Gallagher *(Acct Dir)*
Samantha Stecker *(Acct Dir)*
Jared Lake *(Dir-Digital Strategy)*
Jessica Groot *(Coord-Media)*
Taylor Johns *(Coord-Media)*
Jackie Ginsbarg *(Jr Media Buyer)*
Lidia Hernandez *(Asst Media Buyer)*
Laura Houtkooper *(Sr Media Buyer)*
Krystel Rheaume *(Sr Media Buyer)*
Diana Sosa *(Jr Media Buyer)*
Tara Starnes *(Jr Media Buyer)*
Kimberly Webster *(Sr Media Buyer)*
Cindy Zacarias *(Asst Media Buyer)*

Accounts:
Ancestry.com (Agency of Record)
Angie's List Inc
Care.com (Agency of Record)
eBates
eHarmony.com, Inc. (Agency of Record) Online Dating; 2002
Freecreditreport.com; CA Credit Services; 1999
Gazelle, Inc. Media Planning & Buying
Gilt Media
Innogames
JustFab.com (Agency of Record) Advertising Planning & Buying
LendingTree, LLC Analytics, Buying, Media Efficiency, Media Planning
New-LifeLock Inc. (Agency of Record)
Lumosity
lynda.com Media Planning & Buying, TV
Mini Cooper
MyLife
Newtek Business Services Media Planning & Buying
Overstock.com, Inc. (Agency of Record) Online Retail Outlet; 2003
The Priceline Group Inc. Media Buying, Media Planning, Travel and Hotels; 1997
New-Realtor.com (Agency of Record)
Sensa
New-SharperImage.com (Media Planning & Media Buying Agency of Record)
Vitacost.com
New-Weebly (Media Planning & Buying Agency of Record) Television

OCEANOS MARKETING, INC.

892 Plain St, Marshfield, MA 02050
Tel.: (781) 804-1010
Fax: (617) 687-8008
Web Site: www.oceanosinc.com/

Employees: 10
Year Founded: 2001

National Agency Associations: AMA

Agency Specializes In: Business-To-Business, Consulting, Consumer Marketing, Direct Response Marketing, E-Commerce, Education, Exhibit/Trade Shows, Health Care Services, High Technology, Industrial, Media Buying Services, Medical Products, Over-50 Market, Pharmaceutical, Planning & Consultation, Strategic Planning/Research, Teen Market

Brian P. Hession *(Founder & Pres)*
Lindsay Fraser *(Dir-Strategy & Ops)*
John Lutts *(Dir-Cloud Tech)*
Kristopher Matney *(Dir-Software Engrg)*
Stacey Elliot *(Sr Mgr-Customer Acq & Brand Mgmt)*
Chrissie Dahlstrom *(Coord-Mktg)*
Tim Dupuis *(Sr Program Mgr)*

OLANDER GROUP

(Formerly Olander Media Group)
1224 Ottawa Ave, Ottawa, IL 61350
Tel.: (815) 680-6500
Fax: (815) 434-3069
E-Mail: molander@olandergroup.com
Web Site: www.olandergroup.com

Employees: 4
Year Founded: 2001

Agency Specializes In: Above-the-Line, Advertising, Advertising Specialties, Affluent Market, Alternative Advertising, Below-the-Line, Branded Entertainment, Broadcast, Business-To-Business, Cable T.V., Children's Market, Co-op Advertising, College, Communications, Computers & Software, Consulting, Consumer Marketing, Corporate Communications, Customer Relationship Management, Digital/Interactive, Direct Response Marketing, Direct-to-Consumer, Education, Electronic Media, Email, Entertainment, Environmental, Experience Design, Financial, Food Service, Government/Political, Health Care Services, High Technology, Hospitality, In-Store Advertising, Industrial, Infomercials, Information Technology, Integrated Marketing, Leisure, Local Marketing, Magazines, Media Buying Services, Media Planning, Medical Products, Men's Market, Mobile Marketing, Multimedia, New Technologies, Newspaper, Newspapers & Magazines, Out-of-Home Media, Outdoor, Over-50 Market, Paid Searches, Pharmaceutical, Planning & Consultation, Podcasting, Point of Purchase, Point of Sale, Print, Product Placement, Publicity/Promotions, RSS (Really Simple Syndication), Radio, Real Estate, Regional, Search Engine Optimization, Social Marketing/Nonprofit, Social Media, Sports Market, Strategic Planning/Research, T.V., Teen Market, Trade & Consumer Magazines, Transportation, Travel & Tourism, Viral/Buzz/Word of Mouth, Web (Banner Ads, Pop-ups, etc.), Yellow Pages Advertising

Approx. Annual Billings: $4,500,000

Breakdown of Gross Billings by Media: Adv. Specialities: 75%; Plng. & Consultation: 25%

Mike Olander *(Founder & Pres)*
Ruth Perry *(Acct Mgr)*
Mary Ann Neuman *(Coord-Mktg)*

Accounts:
CMK Companies; Chicago, IL; 2005
Edward Hospital & Health Services; Naperville, IL Edward Hospital; Edward Medical Group; Edward Health & Fitness Centers; Linden Oaks Hospital2008; 2008
Elysian Hotels; Chicago, IL; 2011
Gateway Foundation; Chicago, IL; 2010
TargetCom; Chicago, IL; 2011
XSport Fitness; Chicago, IL; 2011

OMD NORTH AMERICA

195 Broadway, New York, NY 10007
Tel.: (212) 590-7100
E-Mail: info@omd.com
Web Site: www.omd.com

Employees: 500
Year Founded: 2002

Agency Specializes In: Consulting, Media Buying Services, Sponsorship, Strategic Planning/Research

Monica Karo *(CEO)*
Mark Mirsky *(Mng Dir)*
Kathleen Brookbanks *(COO)*
Jonathan Schaaf *(Pres-Digital Investment)*
Adam Vernick *(Sr VP-Digital)*
Albert Samuelian *(Mng Dir-West & Strategy)*
Alison Zarecki *(Head-US & Grp Acct Dir)*
Jon Kaiser *(Head-Global Digital Strategy-PepsiCo)*
Laura Correnti *(Grp Dir-Digital)*
Nicole Ferera *(Grp Dir-Digital Investment)*
Mark Freibott *(Grp Dir-Omnicom Media Grp)*
Nicole Moscardini *(Grp Dir-Digital Investment)*
Brian Moynihan *(Grp Dir-Strategy)*
Catherine Nassa *(Grp Dir-Strategy)*
Tom O'Brien *(Grp Dir-Strategy)*
Sharon Cullen *(Reg Dir-East Coast)*
Jan Gerits *(Reg Dir-Bus Dev & Intelligence)*
Whitney Arnold *(Grp Acct Dir)*
Stacy Gatto *(Grp Acct Dir-Strategy)*
Regina Gitelman *(Grp Acct Dir-Digital Investment)*
Jenny Lang *(Grp Acct Dir)*
Chris Leins *(Grp Acct Dir)*
Katherine Orozco *(Grp Acct Dir)*
Elena Pavloff *(Grp Acct Dir)*
Joel Redmount *(Grp Acct Dir)*
Brian Sypniewski *(Grp Acct Dir)*
Lindsay Belisle *(Acct Dir-Intl)*
Lisa Condran *(Acct Dir-Global)*
James Armstrong *(Dir-Global Media-Center of Excellence)*
Adam Chang *(Dir-Digital)*
Rob D'Asaro *(Dir-Stream-US)*
Rayna Elliott *(Dir-Digital)*
Amanda Jason *(Dir-Content)*
Kelly Leach *(Dir-Global Strategy-Hasbro)*
Julie Levin *(Dir-Print-J&J)*
Jeff Minsky *(Dir-Emerging Media Investment & Publr Relationship Mgmt)*
Andre Moraes *(Dir-Performance Analytics)*
Jennifer Napolitano *(Dir-Bus Dev)*
Tracy Quitasol *(Dir-Ignition Factory)*
Evan Rosenblum *(Dir-Performance Analytics)*
Natalie Swed Stone *(Dir-Natl Radio-US)*
Veronika Ward *(Dir-Digital-East Coast)*
Lisa Benigno *(Assoc Dir)*
Odalice Brito *(Assoc Dir)*
Jeff Chung *(Assoc Dir-Global)*
Liza Davidian *(Assoc Dir)*
Denise Donovan *(Assoc Dir-Media)*
Michelle Falco *(Assoc Dir-Media)*
Michael Foley *(Assoc Dir)*
Amber Hansinger *(Assoc Dir-Digital Investment & Content Partnerships)*
Nick Kapetanakis *(Assoc Dir-Strategy)*
Mallory Kopel *(Assoc Dir-Media)*
Alli Krisel *(Assoc Dir-Strategy)*
John LaGrosse *(Assoc Dir-Media)*
Jackie LaLetta *(Assoc Dir)*
Raymond Lee *(Assoc Dir-Media)*
Cassandre Lubin *(Assoc Dir-Digital)*
Ashley Malone *(Assoc Dir-Media)*
Brian McCloskey *(Assoc Dir-Media)*
Stephen McNaughton *(Assoc Dir)*
Zoe Meeran *(Assoc Dir-Digital Investment)*
Carl Miller *(Assoc Dir-Digital Media)*
Kayla Miller *(Assoc Dir-Media-Strategy)*
Jocelyn Monroe *(Assoc Dir-Integrated Programs)*
Morgan Petti *(Assoc Dir-Mobile)*
Jacqueline Robin *(Assoc Dir-Media)*
Whitney Shopis *(Assoc Dir-Strategy)*
Alexis Sotsky *(Assoc Dir)*
David Stone *(Assoc Dir-Digital)*
Courtenay Swasey *(Assoc Dir-Brdcst-Natl)*
Simone Totaram *(Assoc Dir-Media)*
Jessica Vassallo *(Assoc Dir)*
Danielle Vigue *(Assoc Dir)*
Dan Vincent *(Assoc Dir-Media)*
Tracy Wereb *(Assoc Dir-Media)*
Ryan Wojcik *(Assoc Dir-Digital)*
Carla Giorgio *(Sr Mgr-Integrated)*
Elaine Steinbok *(Sr Mgr-Johnson & Johnson)*
Laura Mullen *(Mgr-Mobile)*
Wa Phung *(Mgr-Fin)*
Lisa Bernstein *(Supvr)*
Nicole Bonita *(Supvr-Natl Audio Investment)*
Amanda Boyce *(Supvr-Social)*
Blair Brzeski *(Supvr-Digital)*
Natalie Duckor *(Supvr-Strategy)*
Jayce Favero *(Supvr)*
Dan Fogarty *(Supvr-Digital Investment)*
Cory Gordon *(Supvr)*
Morgan Leathers *(Supvr-Strategy)*
John Monti *(Supvr-Media)*
Eve Rabin *(Supvr-Digital)*
Viviana Rodriguez *(Supvr-Multicultural)*
Liz Russo *(Supvr-Local Brdcst)*
Abigail Staples *(Supvr-Content)*
Fatima Teke *(Supvr-Digital-Omnicom Grp)*
Rebeca Wanderman *(Supvr-Natl Television Investment)*
Gunther Barberena *(Acct Exec)*
Matthew Buckholz *(Strategist-Digital)*
Samantha Coghan *(Strategist-Digital)*
Eric Esposito *(Strategist-Digital)*
Paul Fields *(Strategist-Mobile)*
Zachary Freeman *(Strategist)*
Christina Gallo *(Strategist)*
Swati Govil *(Strategist-Digital)*
Eric Klappholz *(Strategist-Digital Media)*
Connor Mara *(Strategist-Media)*
Anne McCarty *(Strategist)*
Sami Metovic *(Strategist)*
Christopher Panaro *(Strategist-Digital)*
Julia Weiss *(Strategist)*
Lauren McNamara *(Asst Strategist-Digital)*
Alexandra Dennett *(Analyst-Digital)*
Karolina Gaide *(Analyst-Media-Digital Investment)*
Emily Graham *(Media Planner)*
Javier Hernandez *(Planner-Digital)*
Allison McManus *(Analyst-Media)*
Nicholas Mejia *(Analyst-Media & Digital Investment)*
Brock Moxon *(Analyst-Media & Digital Investment)*
Lisa Longhitano *(Coord-Media)*
Laura Reyes *(Coord-Mktg & Bus Dev)*
Lauren Bass *(Sr Assoc Dir-Integrated)*
Alexandra Colbert *(Asst Analyst-Digital Investment)*
Dana Kasdin *(Negotiator-Media Investment)*
Brooke Lewis *(Digital Supvr-Estee Lauder Acct)*
Jennifer Liddle *(Assoc Media Dir)*
Gladimar Llorens *(Reg Supvr-Digital Media)*
Rosemary Ramirez *(Reg Acct Dir)*

Accounts:
Absolut
American Century Investments
Apple
Armstrong Floors
AskJeeves
Cars.com Media Buying
CBS Corp.
CIGNA Media Buying, Media Planning
Clorox Network TV Buying, Scoop Away
The CW Television Network
Disney Studio Media Buying, Movies
Eli Lilly & Co.
FedEx Campaign: "Shazam Super Bowl Sponsorship"
Frito-Lay, Inc. Media Buying
GE Global Media
H&R Block, Inc. Campaign: "Get Your Billion Back America", Media
H. Stern Jewelers, Inc.
Hasbro Media Planning & Buying
Henkel Media Buying & Planning
Hershey
Hertz; Park Ridge, NJ
Hilton Worldwide Embassy Suites, Media Planning & Buying
JCPenney Corporation, Inc. American Living, JCPenney Corporation, Inc., JCPenney Portrait Studios
Levi Strauss Docker's, Levi's, Media Buying & Planning
McDonald's Corporation Media
Nissan Infiniti, Media, Rogue
NY Lottery Media
PepsiCo Inc. Aquafina, Campaign: "Pepsi's Game Changing X Factor Partnership", Diet Mountain Dew, Diet Pepsi, Gatorade, Lipton Brisk, Media, Mountain Dew, Mountain Dew MDX, Pepsi, Sierra Mist
Sobe Campaign: "Try Everything Challenge"
State Farm Network TV Buying

Toys R Us, Inc. Digital, Media
Wells Fargo Media Planning & Buying

Branches

OMD Atlanta
3500 Lenox Rd Ste 1800, Atlanta, GA 30326
Tel.: (404) 443-6800
Fax: (404) 443-6882
E-Mail: info@omd.com
Web Site: www.omd.com

National Agency Associations: 4A's

Agency Specializes In: Media Buying Services

Daryl Simm *(CEO)*
Nikki Mendonca *(Pres-EMEA)*
Colin Gottlieb *(CEO-EMEA)*
Page Thompson *(CEO-Omnicom Media Grp-North America)*
Ludwig Haderer *(Mng Dir-LATAM)*
Johnathan Fisher *(Dir-Strategy)*
Eunice Kim *(Assoc Dir-Strategy)*
Jessica Claus *(Supvr-Global)*

OMD Chicago
225 N Michigan Ave 19th Fl, Chicago, IL 60601-7757
Tel.: (312) 324-7000
Fax: (312) 324-8201
Web Site: www.omd.com

Employees: 250
Year Founded: 1999

National Agency Associations: 4A's

Agency Specializes In: Media Buying Services, Sponsorship

Scott Downs *(Mng Dir)*
Michael Solomon *(Mng Dir)*
Trish Chuipek *(Pres-Midwest Reg)*
Sumeet Kanwar *(Mng Dir-Midwest & Strategy)*
Mariel Cummins *(Grp Dir-Strategy)*
Brian Lipman *(Grp Dir-Digital)*
Amanda Plotkin *(Grp Dir-Digital Marketplace)*
Allison Saegebrecht *(Grp Dir-Strategy)*
Sarah Wittosch *(Grp Dir-Digital & Print Investment-CPG)*
David Blake *(Grp Acct Dir)*
Susanna Earnest *(Grp Acct Dir)*
Montrew Newman *(Grp Acct Dir)*
Ashley Bahlmann *(Acct Dir-Global)*
Latha Sundaram *(Acct Dir-Global)*
Karen Goulet *(Dir-Intelligence)*
Danny Huynh *(Dir-Digital-Midwest Reg)*
Iris Chang *(Assoc Dir-Print Investment)*
Lavina Karnani *(Assoc Dir-Global Strategy-McDonald's)*
Brian McCloskey *(Assoc Dir-Media)*
Jasmine Perez *(Assoc Dir)*
Elizabeth Peterman *(Assoc Dir-Media)*
Allison Povse *(Assoc Dir)*
Jenna Salm *(Assoc Dir-Media)*
Dawn Sumoski *(Assoc Dir-Media)*
Sara Mirarefi *(Acct Supvr-SCJ Global Media)*
William Roman *(Acct Supvr)*
Allison Cipolla *(Supvr-Media)*
Andoni Dieguez *(Supvr-Strategy)*
Elizabeth Frakes *(Supvr-Strategy-Worldwide)*
Amy Frumkin *(Supvr-Strategy)*
Tracie Gibson *(Supvr)*
Whitney Graves *(Supvr)*
Christie Kiesel *(Supvr-Digital Media)*
Lisa Koziol *(Supvr-Strategy & Digital)*
Erin Madden *(Supvr-Strategy)*
Angelica Maneykowski *(Supvr-Media)*
Andrew McNees *(Supvr)*
Patrick Mixdorf *(Supvr)*
Elizabeth Pedersen *(Supvr-Local Investment)*
Matt Pickerel *(Supvr-Digital Media)*
Brandon Saranik *(Supvr-Digital Strategy)*
Jennifer Schmidt *(Supvr-Digital Media)*
Kelly Cappelletti *(Strategist)*
Anthony Gaba *(Strategist)*
Kevin Gaughan *(Strategist)*
Nathan Joslin *(Strategist)*
Mallory Kyle *(Strategist-Media)*
MiRon Leveston *(Strategist)*
Molly Loeffler *(Strategist)*
Caitlin O'Brien *(Strategist)*
Alicia Wolff *(Strategist)*
Lizzy Wingels *(Analyst-Digital)*
Amy Adelbush *(Assoc Media Dir)*
Mary Mills *(Assoc Grp Dir-Local Brdcst)*

Accounts:
Barilla America, Inc. Media Buying & Planning; 2007
Bel Brands USA
Busch Gardens; Tampa, FL
The Field Museum
Frito-Lay, Inc. Baked!, Cheetos, Doritos, Frito-Lay, Inc., Lay's, Ruffles, Stacy's Pita Chips, SunChips, Tostitos
H&R Block, Inc.
Hewlett-Packard Company Envy, HP TouchPad, HP Veer, HP.com, Hewlett-Packard Company, Pavilion, Technology Solutions Group Division
Intel Corporation
J.C. Penney Company, Inc. Media
McDonald's Corporation Happy Meals, McCafe, McDonald's Corporation, Ronald McDonald House Charities
Norwegian Cruise Line Media Buying, Media Planning
New-Pep Boys
PepsiCo, Inc. Amp, Aquafina, Aunt Jemima, Cap'n Crunch, Diet Mountain Dew, Diet Pepsi, Gatorade / Gatorade G, Gatorade G Series Perform, Gatorade G Series Prime, Gatorade G Series Pro, Gatorade G Series Recover, Gatorade G2, Life Cereal, Lipton Brisk, Lipton Green Tea, Mountain Dew, Near East, Pasta Roni, Pepsi, Pepsi Throwback, PepsiCo, Inc., Quaker Chewy Granola Bars, Quaker Instant Grits, Quaker Instant Oatmeal, Quaker Oats, Quaker Oh's! Cereal, Quaker Rice Cakes, Quaker True Delights, Rice-A-Roni, Sierra Mist Natural, SoBe, Spudz, Tropicana, Tropicana Pure Premium
PetSmart, Inc. Media Buying, Media Planning
Pier 1 Imports, Inc.
State Farm Insurance Companies Media, State Farm Auto Insurance, State Farm Home Insurance, State Farm Insurance Companies, State Farm Life Insurance
Walgreens Digital, Media, Media Planning & Buying, Mobile, Multicultural

OMD Los Angeles
5353 Grosvenor Blvd, Los Angeles, CA 90066
Tel.: (310) 301-3600
Fax: (646) 278-8000
E-Mail: info@omd.com
Web Site: www.omd.com

Employees: 300

National Agency Associations: 4A's

Agency Specializes In: Media Buying Services, Sponsorship

Wanda Kato *(Mng Dir)*
Anthony Viccars *(Head-Digital)*
Kevin Boyle *(Grp Acct Dir-Strategy)*
Jennifer Reece *(Grp Acct Dir)*
Daniel Block *(Dir-Strategy-Global)*
Natalie Holbrook *(Dir-Media)*
Chris Inners *(Dir-West Coast-OMD Word)*
Katie Ioffe *(Dir-Digital Investment)*
Dario Raciti *(Dir-Zero Code)*
Tony Shan *(Dir-Strategy-US)*
Natalie Gengaro *(Assoc Dir)*
Candace Hollar *(Assoc Dir-Digital)*
Lindsay Arnold *(Supvr-Strategy)*
Taryn Benner *(Supvr)*
Anna Chau *(Supvr-Strategy)*
Crystal Chou *(Supvr-Strategy)*
Lauren Crotzer *(Supvr-Strategy)*
Syuzi Gorgoyan *(Supvr-Integrated)*
Lisa La *(Supvr-Strategy)*
Abigail Lee *(Supvr-Fin)*
Kristen Masino *(Supvr-Digital)*
Desiree Mondello *(Supvr-Strategy)*
Richard Murphy *(Supvr-Digital Analytics)*
Natassia Trinh *(Supvr-Digital)*
Jamie Cohen *(Sr Strategist-Digital-Nissan North America)*
Ashley Jackson *(Sr Strategist-Digital)*
Genevieve Jordan *(Strategist-Infiniti)*
Kevyn Kurata *(Strategist)*
Leah Rotti *(Strategist)*
Carolina Uribe *(Strategist)*
Eric Barbato *(Asst Strategist-Digital Media)*
Shari Mills *(Sr Analyst-Digital Investment)*
Justin Bitensky *(Planner-Digital Media)*
Angela Chang *(Analyst-Digital Analytics)*
Josie Garcia *(Media Planner-Digital-Walt Disney Studios)*
Stephanie Schafer *(Analyst-Media & Digital Investment)*
Walker Smith *(Analyst-Media-Digital Investment)*
Emily Graham *(Sr Media Planner)*
Robyn Shapiro *(Sr Media Buyer-Local Brdcst)*

Accounts:
Apple
Conservation International Media
CW Network
The CW Television Network Campaign: "Do You Have the Power?"
Disney Studios Media Buying, Movies
Dockers
Experian Media Planning & Buying
Henkel Media Planning & Buying
Hilton Hampton, Media
Homewood Suites Media Buying
Nissan Infiniti
Principal Financial Group Media Planning & Buying
The Walt Disney Company
Warner Bros Campaign: "Do You Have The Power"
Wells Fargo Digital, Lead Media Buying & Planning Agency, Search

OMD San Francisco
555 Market St Ste 750, San Francisco, CA 94105
Tel.: (415) 229-8500
Fax: (415) 315-4250
Web Site: www.omd.com

Employees: 100

National Agency Associations: 4A's

Agency Specializes In: Media Buying Services, Sponsorship

Page Thompson *(CEO)*
Kristi Lind *(Mng Dir)*
Greg Castronuovo *(Pres-West)*
Christopher Murphy *(Mng Dir-Programmatic)*
Andrea Barberi *(Grp Dir-Strategy)*
Jet Wharton *(Reg Dir-Digital-West Coast)*
Carrie Davis *(Acct Dir-Global)*
Katie Ioffe *(Dir-Digital Investment)*
Owen Jones *(Dir-Digital-Global)*
Jamie Costa *(Assoc Dir-Media)*
Annie Ma *(Assoc Dir-Media)*
Cheryl Nguyen *(Assoc Dir)*
Kara Rozek *(Assoc Dir-Media)*
Julia Shapira *(Assoc Dir-Media)*
Leigh Anna Trelenberg *(Assoc Dir-Media)*
Brittany Strametz *(Supvr-Strategy)*
Rebecca Ting *(Supvr-Strategy)*

Yuko Wada *(Supvr-OMD USA)*
Samuel Chin *(Sr Strategist-Digital)*
Kena Flynn *(Sr Strategist-Digital)*
Ashley Jackson *(Sr Strategist-Digital)*
Avery Anderson *(Strategist)*
Samantha Benson *(Strategist-Media)*
Chasen Fong *(Strategist-Media)*
Simonne Kennedy-Moore *(Strategist-Digital)*
Laura McNulty *(Strategist)*
Faviola Vega *(Strategist)*
Khanh Nguyen *(Asst Strategist-Digital)*
Cory Wagner *(Asst Analyst-Media)*

Accounts:
Apple, Inc. Apple, Inc., iPad, iPhone, iPod, iTunes
Brooks Sports Inc. Media Planning & Buying
Clorox Media Planning

Prometheus

225 N Michigan Ave, Chicago, IL 60601
Tel.: (312) 324-7000
Fax: (312) 324-8204
E-Mail: info@prometheus.com

Employees: 200
Year Founded: 2005

Agency Specializes In: Media Buying Services, Sponsorship

Nicole Purcell *(Pres-CLIO)*
Kathleen Dailey *(Grp Acct Dir)*
Dan Lynch *(Assoc Dir-Media)*

Accounts:
BMO Capital Markets
BMO Financial Group BMO Bankcorp, Bank of Montreal
Cars.com Media Buying
Harris Bank

OMD Cross Cultural

(Formerly OMD Latino)
6205 Blue Lagoon Dr Ste 650, Miami, FL 33126
Tel.: (305) 341-2530
Fax: (305) 446-7707

National Agency Associations: 4A's

Agency Specializes In: Sponsorship

Cathy Collier *(CEO-OMD CANADA)*
John Swift *(CEO-North America Investment Omnicom Media Group)*
Amy Adelbush *(Assoc Dir-Media)*
Allison Povse *(Assoc Dir)*
Anna Sawicki *(Assoc Dir-Media)*
Nidia Ramirez Troche *(Acct Mgr)*
Erin Madden *(Supvr-Strategy)*
Jasmine Perez *(Supvr-Strategy)*
Claire Eisenhuth *(Strategist)*

Accounts:
The Clorox Company
H&R Block, Inc.
JCPenney Corporation, Inc.
Visa, Inc.

OMD WORLDWIDE

195 Broadway, New York, NY 10007
Tel.: (212) 590-7100
Web Site: www.omd.com

Employees: 700

Agency Specializes In: Advertising

Mainardo DeNardis *(CEO)*
Angela Malone *(Mng Dir)*
Mark Mirsky *(Mng Dir)*
Kate Stephenson *(Pres-Global Acct Mgmt)*
Daryl Simm *(CEO-Omnicom Media Grp)*
Shaina Boone *(Mng Dir-Mktg Decision Sciences)*
Kari Seitz *(Mng Dir-San Francisco)*
Brett Covell *(Grp Dir-Strategy)*
Veronika Ward *(Reg Dir-Digital Investment-East)*
Steve DiRado *(Grp Acct Dir)*
Clara Flikstein *(Grp Acct Dir-Comm Plng & Strategy)*
Scott Minor *(Grp Acct Dir)*
Scott Schwartz *(Grp Acct Dir)*
Angie Ahn *(Dir-Comm Plng-Global)*
Natalie Holbrook *(Dir-Media)*
Carolyn Kim *(Dir-Bus Intelligence)*
Natalie Swed Stone *(Dir-Natl Radio-US)*
Denise Donovan *(Assoc Dir-Media)*
Dana Grinkevich *(Assoc Dir-Media & Digital)*
Jennifer Liddle *(Assoc Dir-Media)*
Shannon Urce *(Assoc Dir-Media)*
Millie Zhao *(Assoc Dir)*
Michelle Higgins *(Mgr-Actability)*
Laura Mullen *(Mgr-Mobile)*
Dan Fogarty *(Supvr-Digital Investment)*
Nick Grainger *(Supvr-Strategy)*
Kristen Masino *(Supvr-Digital)*
Patrick Mixdorf *(Supvr)*
Andrew Moore *(Supvr)*
Christina Gallo *(Strategist)*
Brittany Latney *(Strategist-Digital)*
James Markowitz *(Strategist-Digital Media)*
Kristen Nicolai *(Strategist)*
Danielle Quiat *(Strategist)*
Ilana Videlefsky *(Strategist-Digital)*
Julia Weiss *(Strategist)*
Meghan Barron *(Analyst-Digital Investment)*
Josie Garcia *(Media Planner-Digital-Walt Disney Studios)*
Blaire Johns *(Analyst-Digital)*

Accounts:
Acer Global Intel Media
Activision Blizzard Media, Traditional Digital Planning & Buying
Apple
Bacardi Limited Buying, Digital, Global Media, Planning, Social
Barclays
Bel Brands USA Boursin, Laughing Cow, Media, Mini Babybel
Carlsberg Malaysia; 2008
CBS
Chobani LLC
New-Coca-Cola
The Estee Lauder Companies Inc.; New York, NY Global Media
FedEx Corporation Campaign: "Shazam"
Frito-Lay Campaign: "All Natural Farmville", Lay's, Media Buying
GE Consumer & Industrial; Louisville, KY
HBO
Intel Campaign: "IdeaJam", Media Buying, Media Planning, Shazam; 2008
J.C. Penney Company, Inc.; Plano, TX Media Buying
Levi's
Lowe's
McDonald's Campaign: "McDonald's CityVille"
Monster.com
PepsiCo AMP Energy Drink, X Factor
PSA Peugeot Citroen S.A
Renault Nissan EMEA, Media Buying & Planning
Sabra Dipping Co. Media Buying, Media Planning
Sony PlayStation
Time Warner Cable Analytics, Digital Marketing, Digital Media Planning & Buying, Mobile, Social Media
Virgin Atlantic
Vodafone Group Media Buying, Media Planning

Branches

OMD Australia

32 Pyrmont Bridge Road, Pyrmont, Sydney, NSW 2009 Australia
Tel.: (61) 2 9692 2000
Fax: (61) 2 9692 2222

Employees: 300

Peter Horgan *(CEO)*
Aimee Buchanan *(Mng Dir)*
Mark Jarrett *(Mng Dir)*
Stuart Bailey *(Chief Digital Officer)*
Leigh Terry *(CEO-Australia & New Zealand)*
Russ Mitchinson *(Head-Strategy-McDonald's)*
Dan Robins *(Head-Interactive)*
Daniel Clark *(Dir-Bus)*
Nathan Young *(Dir-Bus Dev & Mktg)*
Nick Barbour *(Mgr-People & Dev)*
Nathan Fischer *(Mgr-Programmatic Trading-Telstra)*

Accounts:
Ancestry.com.au Media Planning & Buying
Beiersdorf
Chivas Regal Media
Clinique Campaign: "StartBetter", Social Media
EHarmony.com.au Media Planning & Buying
New-Estee Lauder Group
ExxonMobil
Fantastic
FedEx
Fonterra
GE
Helloworld
H.J. Heinz Company Media
Intel
Luxottica
McDonald's Campaign: "It's a Knockout", National Media
New-Pacific Brands
Qantas Media Buying
Sara Lee Harris, Media Planning & Buying, Moccona, Piazza D'Oro, Pickwick Tea
Schwarzkopf Campaign: "Under the Cover"
Selleys
New-Sony PlayStation
Tabcorp Holdings Online, Social Media
Telstra Campaign: "Let Your Business Flow", Media Buying
Tourism Australia Media
Weight Watchers Campaign: "Awaken Your Incredible", Media
The Wrigley Company Campaign: "5X Mutant Gum"

OMD Canada

67 Richmond St W 2nd Fl, Toronto, ON M5H 1Z5 Canada
Tel.: (416) 681-5600
Fax: (416) 681-5620
Web Site: www.omd.com

Employees: 130

Cathy Collier *(CEO)*
Bruce Baumann *(Mng Dir)*
Lori Gibb *(Mng Dir)*
John Killam *(Mng Dir)*
Nancy Surphlis *(Mng Dir)*
Shane Cameron *(Mng Dir-Digital)*
Elaine Lindsay *(Grp Dir-Strategy)*
Sean Dixon *(Dir-Emerging Media-Ignition Factory-Toronto)*
Jeremy Simpson *(Dir-Digital Solutions)*
Nisha Kumar *(Supvr-Digital Strategy)*
Samantha Redshaw *(Supvr-Digital)*
Jennifer Santos-Abella *(Supvr-Strategy)*
Alana Hamilton *(Strategist-Media)*
Megan Henry *(Specialist-Digital)*
Sabrina Sandhu *(Strategist-OMD Toronto)*
Stephanie Stewart *(Strategist)*
Michelle Arksey *(Media Buyer)*
Sarah Pease *(Sr Media Buyer)*

Accounts:
Apple

British Columbia Automobile Association (Media Agency of Record) Media Buying
Campbell Company of Canada
Canadian Olympic Committee Media
Clorox Company Brita, Media Buying
Crime Stoppers Media
GE Canada
McDonald's Canada Media Buying, Media Planning
Nissan
PepsiCo Canada
Rogers Communications Media Planning & Buying
SickKids Foundation (Media Agency of Record) Media Planning
SIRIUS Canada Inc. Media Buying
Subaru Media Buying
Visa Inc. Media Buying
Warner Bros.

OMD Finland Oy

Fredrikinkatu 42, 00100 Helsinki, Finland
Tel.: (358) 9 693 661
Fax: (358) 9 694 1005
E-Mail: omdfinland@omd.com
Web Site: http://www.omd.com/finland/global-media-agency

Employees: 50
Year Founded: 1976

Agency Specializes In: Advertising, Brand Development & Integration, Business-To-Business, E-Commerce, Electronic Media, Magazines, Media Buying Services, Newspapers & Magazines, Planning & Consultation, Radio, Strategic Planning/Research, T.V.

Niina Pankko *(Deputy Mng Dir)*
Laura Hartikainen *(Grp Dir-Plng)*
Vilja Grotenfelt *(Acct Dir)*
Minna Lindqvist *(Dir-Media)*
Kristiina Railo *(Dir-Digital)*
Taru Karlsson *(Mgr-Media)*

Accounts:
PepsiCo. Mountain Dew

OMD Guangzhou

Rm 3707 Tower B Ctr Plz, 161 Linhe Rd W Tianhe District, Guangzhou, 510610 China
Tel.: (86) 20 3825 1088
Fax: (86) 20 3825 1603

Employees: 85

Denise Lim *(Mng Partner)*
Eric Nygard *(Mng Partner)*
Alex Tan *(Mng Partner)*
Elaine Ip *(Mng Dir)*
Arlene Ang *(CEO-OMD China)*
Doug Pearce *(CEO-Omnicom Media Grp Greater China)*
Dickie Cheng *(Gen Mgr)*
Alex Wang *(Bus Dir)*
Alessandro Pang *(Dir-Bus Intelligence)*
Anthony Tang *(Dir-Plng-OMD Media Direction)*
Jenny Hsu *(Asst Dir-Plng)*
Kimi Shi *(Assoc Dir-Comm Insights & Res)*

Accounts:
Amway Digital Buying, Media Planning, Outdoor, Print, TV Buying
Axa Financial Services, Media Account
Fonterra
Guangzhou Pharmaceutical
Intel
Zhenai.com Media Planning & Buying

OMD Hong Kong

Unit 808 Core E Cyberport 3, 100 Cyberport Rd, Hong Kong, China (Hong Kong)
Tel.: (852) 2911 1668
Fax: (852) 2827 1200
E-Mail: omdhk.enquiry@omd.com
Web Site: www.omd.com

Employees: 100

Rold Sin *(CEO)*
Ivan Chui *(Sr Dir-Digital Plng)*
Juliane Bumke *(Acct Dir-Global)*
Vienna Tsang *(Acct Mgr)*
Yau Him Alex Fong *(Mgr-Plng)*
Selina Fung *(Media Planner)*
Kevin Luk *(Planner)*
Kammy Wong *(Media Buyer)*

Accounts:
Axa Financial Services, Media Account
Carlsberg Group Kronenbourg 1664, Media
Compass Visa
CSL; Hong Kong Mobile Phones; 2005
Henkel Media Planning & Buying, Schwarzkopf
Hilton Worldwide
Hong Kong Buddhist Association Marketing, Strategic Communications
Hong Kong Jockey Club
Hong Kong University
New-Infiniti Motor Company
Johnson & Johnson Carefree, Clean & Clear
Levi Strauss Hong Kong 501 Jeans, Media Buying
McDonald's Media
Pfizer Corporation Campaign: "Truth & Dare"
Wyeth Nutrition

OMD Malaysia

Level 3 Tower C Uptown 5, No 5 Jalan SS21/39, Petaling Jaya, Selangor 47400 Malaysia
Tel.: (60) 376519999
Fax: (60) 376606130
Web Site: www.omd.com

Agency Specializes In: Advertising

Andreas Vogiatzakis *(CEO)*
Anil Jayachandran *(Head-Comm Plng)*
Shyam Ravishankar *(Head-Digital)*
Agnes Yee *(Gen Mgr)*
Kelvin Lim *(Dir-Digital)*

Accounts:
Audemars Piguet Media, Strategic Media Buying & Planning
Resorts World Genting

OMD Nederland

Amsterdams sawag 204, 1182 HL Amstelveen, Netherlands
Mailing Address:
P.O. Box 682, Amstelveen, 1180 AR Netherlands
Tel.: (31) 20 712 0000
Fax: (31) 20 712 0001
E-Mail: info@omdnl.nl
Web Site: www.omd.com

E-Mail for Key Personnel:
President: esther.hendriks@omdnl.nl

Employees: 100
Year Founded: 1999

Agency Specializes In: Media Buying Services

Remko De Jong *(Dir-RTV)*
Amancio Frankel *(Dir-Trading & Accountability)*
Pravin Bhagwandin *(Planner-RTV)*

OMD New Zealand/Auckland

Level 1 33 College Hill, Posonby, Auckland, 1010 New Zealand
Tel.: (64) 3 353 7440
Fax: (64) 9 306 2888
E-Mail: info@omdnz.com
Web Site: www.omd.com

Employees: 70
Year Founded: 2004

Matt McNeil *(Mng Partner)*
Zac Stephenson *(Gen Mgr)*
Penelope Burns *(Client Svcs Dir)*
Nick Ascough *(Dir-Strategy)*
Adriana Botha *(Dir-People & Dev)*
Chloe Hardy *(Assoc Dir)*
Ains Kislev Baguion *(Acct Mgr-Digital)*
Liam Dunne *(Acct Mgr)*
Rory Graham *(Acct Mgr)*
Lauren Hagan *(Acct Mgr)*
Simon Pearce *(Acct Mgr)*
Lee Underwood *(Acct Mgr)*
Charlotte White *(Acct Exec)*

Accounts:
Air New Zealand
Audi New Zealand
BDM Grange - TRESemme' Campaign: "TRESemme Stylist Search"
Beiersdorf
Dulux Campaign: "Whats Dulux Colour of New Zealand"
Fonterra Brands
Frucor Beverages Ltd Campaign: "Mountain Dew Skatepark"
Heart of the City Campaign: "#loveyourcityblc"
Heinz Wattie's Campaign: "Spaghetti vs Baked Bean"
Inland Revenue Campaign: "I'll be your friend if you pay your fees"
Loyalty New Zealand Campaign: "Dream Machine", Campaign: "Flats Extreme Trolley Challenge"
McDonald's
New Zealand Transport Agency
Roadshow Film Distributors Campaign: "Contagion", Campaign: "The Green Lantern"
Soho
Sony PlayStation Campaign: "Little Big Planet"
Tourism Australia
The Wellington International Ukulele Orchestra

OMD Philippines

11th Floor Bankmer Building 6756 Ayala Ave, Makati City, Manila, 1226 Philippines
Tel.: (63) 2 889 8663
Fax: (63) 2 889 7774

Carla J. Cifra *(Gen Mgr)*
Bernie Nepomuceno *(Dir-Bus Unit)*
Rowena Munsayac *(Mgr-Investment)*
Stephanie Ching *(Client Svc Mgr)*

OMD Singapore

3 Anson Road #30-03 Springleaf Tower, Singapore, 079909 Singapore
Tel.: (65) 6876 6800
Fax: (65) 6876 6868
Web Site: www.omd.com

Scott Kimberley *(Mng Partner)*
Chloe Neo *(Mng Partner)*
Torie Henderson *(Pres-Global Accts-APAC)*
Cheuk Chiang *(CEO-Omnicom Media Group, APAC)*
Stephen Li *(CEO-Asia Pacific)*
Jodie Collins *(Reg Dir-Digital Strategy)*
Pankaj Nayak *(Dir-Bus Dev-Asia Pacific)*
Jian Yang *(Dir-Global Strategy-Transformers)*

Accounts:
Audemars Piguet Media, Strategic Media Buying & Planning
Axa Financial Services, Media Account
The Building and Construction Authority
CapitaLand Limited Media
Carlsberg
The Changi Airport Group

Clear Channel Singapore
Exxonmobil
Fedex
Fonterra
General Mills Haagen-Dazs, Media, Nature Valley
H&M Media
Hasbro Transformers
Intel
Johnson & Johnson Clean & Clear
McDonald's
National Library Board Media Buying, Media Planning, S.U.R.E. (Source, Understand, Research & Evaluate)
Pepsico
SilkAir Media Buying
Visa
Watsons Singapore Campaign: "At Watsons, There's Always More", Campaign: "Wow", Logo Design, Packaging

OMD UK

1-4 North Crescent Chenies Street, London, WC1E 7ER United Kingdom
Tel.: (44) 203 023 4500
Web Site: www.omd.com/uk/global-media-agency

Employees: 450

Hamid Habib *(Mng Partner-Strategy)*
Dan Clays *(Mng Dir)*
Jess Roberts *(Chief Client Officer)*
Suzanna Balchin *(Bus Dir)*
Matthew Merrett *(Bus Dir-Manning Gottlieb)*
Dan Bowers *(Dir-Strategy)*
Jenny Williams *(Assoc Dir)*
Laura Fenton *(Client Partner)*
Kelly Parker *(Client Partner)*

Accounts:
118 118
Airbnb Gottlieb, Media
Bel
Boots Media Buying, Media Planning
Bosch
Camelot Media
Carlsberg Global Media
Channel 4 Online Media Buying & Planning
Citroen UK Citroen Seekers
Disney Media Buying, Media Planning
EasyJet Campaign: "generation easyJet", Media Planning & Buying
Emap Limited
Ernst & Young
Garmin Media Planning & Buying
Go-Ahead Media Buying, Media Planning
Google Campaign: "Zeitgeist", Media Planning & Buying
Hasbro
Huawei Media, Mobile, Planning & Buying, Strategy
Levi's Campaign: "#MakeOurMark", Campaign: "#Moves", Planning
McDonald's Big Mac, Campaign: "Good to Know", Campaign: "McDonald's Extended Hours", Chicken McNuggets, Fries, Media Planning & Buying, Milkshake, Outdoor
Onken
Oxbow
PepsiCo 7Up Free, Campaign: "Pepsico 10", Media, Pepsi Max, Planning, Quaker, Soft Drinks, Tropicana, Walkers
Peugeot Print
Premier Inn Media
RCL Cruises Azamara Club Cruises, Celebrity Cruises, Royal Caribbean, Search Engine Optimisation, Social Media
Reckitt Benckiser
Red Sky Snacks
The Renault-Nissan Purchasing Organisation
Renault Media Planning & Buying, Twizy
Ronald McDonald House Charities
The Royal National Lifeboat Institution Above-the-Line, Data Analytics, Media Planning & Buying, Media Strategy, Paid Search, SEO
Sara Lee Media Planning & Buying
Sequel Gc Watches, Guess Jewellery, Guess Watches, Media Planning & Buying
Sing Up
Specsavers Media
SSE Media Planning & Buying
Starbucks
Tanfield Food Company Media
Tetra Pak
Tigi
Very.co.uk Planning
Visit London
Waterstone's Booksellers Media Buying
Weight Watchers Analytics, Digital Buying, Offline Media
YouView Media Planning & Buying

OMD North America

195 Broadway, New York, NY 10007
(See Separate Listing)

OMD Vancouver

777 Hornby Street Suite 1600, Vancouver, BC V6Z 2T3 Canada
Tel.: (604) 640-4336
Fax: (604) 640-4337
Web Site: www.omd.com

Jason Snider *(Gen Mgr)*
Erin Mcwhinnie *(Grp Dir-Strategy)*
Angela Dong *(Assoc Dir-Strategy)*
Diana Walter *(Assoc Dir-Digital Strategy)*

Accounts:
British Columbia Automobile Association Creative, Media Buying & Planning, Strategy
New-Rocky Mountaineer
Strategic Milk Alliance

OMD

Friedrichstrasse 61, Berlin, 10117 Germany
Tel.: (49) 30 340003 0
Fax: (49) 30 340003 770
E-Mail: presse@omd.com
Web Site: www.omdgermany.de

Employees: 13

National Agency Associations: 4A's

Thomas Hinkel *(Mng Dir)*
Sascha Dermanowicz *(Mng Dir-Bus Dev)*
Ann Sophie Altmeier *(Dir-PR)*

Accounts:
Innovatives Niedersachsen
Sixt Media
Sony

OPTIMEDIA INTERNATIONAL US INC.

375 Hudson St 7th Fl, New York, NY 10014
Tel.: (212) 820-3200
Fax: (212) 820-3300
E-Mail: mina.choe@optimedia-us.com
Web Site: www.optimedia-us.com

Employees: 200
Year Founded: 2000

National Agency Associations: 4A's

Agency Specializes In: Cable T.V., Electronic Media, Magazines, Newspaper, Out-of-Home Media, Radio, Sponsorship, Syndication, T.V., Trade & Consumer Magazines

Breakdown of Gross Billings by Media: D.M.: 5%; Internet Adv.: 2%; Out-of-Home Media: 3%; Print: 17%; Radio & T.V.: 73%

Dave Ehlers *(CEO)*
Keith Mackay *(Pres-Strategy)*
Maureen Bosetti *(Exec VP & Grp Dir-Brdcst-Natl)*
Randy Novick *(Sr VP)*
Michael Wyllie *(Sr VP)*
Justine Dolan *(VP & Grp Dir-Activation Standards & Ops)*
Valarie McCubbins *(VP & Grp Dir)*
Nicholas Caputo *(VP & Dir-Strategic Comm)*
Shannon Taylor *(VP & Dir-Strategic Comm)*
Jeffrey Vider *(VP & Dir-Strategic Comm)*
Jessie Schwartzfarb *(VP & Assoc Dir)*
David Fineman *(VP-Digital)*
Patrick Jurasic *(VP & Grp Media Dir)*
Greta Matiash *(VP-Brdcst-Natl)*
Karen Zelenka *(Dir-Strategic Comm)*
Kimberly Regenstreich *(Assoc Dir-Media & Digital)*
Chris Simon *(Assoc Dir-Media)*
Erin Heffernan *(Sr Acct Mgr)*
Antonette Maysonet *(Office Mgr)*
Lauren Casey *(Supvr-Comm Plng)*
Stephanie Chiu *(Supvr-Digital Media)*
Gerry Lanzilotti *(Supvr-Comm Plng)*
Jessica Mark *(Supvr)*
Robert Mooney *(Supvr-Digital Media)*
Carlos Rodriguez *(Supvr-Digital)*
Alanna Battaglia *(Sr Planner-Comm)*
Heather Bleiberg *(Sr Planner-Comm)*
Melissa Carazo *(Sr Planner-Comm)*
Carrie Woods *(Acct Exec & Asst Media Planner & Buyer)*
Cassandra Armstrong *(Planner-Digital)*
Jacquelyn DeFeo *(Media Planner)*
Jessica Farley *(Planner-Comm-Maybelline New York)*
Christiana Lam *(Planner-Social Media-Interactive)*
James Monderine *(Media Planner)*
Edwina Morales *(Media Planner)*
Sarah Straub *(Planner-Comm)*

Accounts:
Boiron
New-Bridgestone Golf (Media Strategy, Planning & Buying Agency of Record) Broadcast, Digital Buying
Dairy Queen
Denny's
Garnier
Hewlett-Packard Company
Liberty Mutual Campaign: "See Car Insurance In A Whole New Light", Media Buying, Media Planning
L'Oreal USA Lancome, Maybelline Cosmetics, Rhapsody America (U.S. Media Planning for Digital Music Service); 1981
OpenSkies Broadcast, Media, Out Of Home, Print; 2008
Payless Media Planning & Buying
Pinnacle Foods Group Inc. Birds Eye, Birds Eye Steamfresh, Birds Eye Voila, Pinnacle Foods Corporation
Pizza Hut Media Planning & Buying
Purina
Sanofi Pasteur Offline Media; 2002
Sanofi SA Ambien, Ambien CR, Lantus, Sanofi SA
ServiceMaster Corporation; 1996
Simon Property Group, Inc.
T-Mobile US
Whirlpool Canada, Inc. Inglis
Whirlpool

Branches

Optimedia-Dallas

7300 Lone Star Dr Ste 200, Plano, TX 75024
Tel.: (469) 366-2550
Fax: (972) 628-7890
E-Mail: info@optimedia-us.com
Web Site: www.optimedia-us.com

Employees: 20
Year Founded: 2000

National Agency Associations: 4A's

Agency Specializes In: Media Buying Services, Sponsorship

Susan Eberhart *(Mng Dir & Exec VP)*
Keith Mackay *(Pres-Strategy)*
Andy Rowe *(Sr VP & Grp Dir-Comm)*
Patrick English *(VP & Grp Dir)*
Liza Mandell *(VP & Assoc Dir)*
Kyle Russ *(Assoc Dir-Media)*
Jessica Whitfield-Glassman *(Assoc Dir-Media)*
Jessica Deeken *(Supvr-Strategic Insights)*
Molly Kennedy *(Supvr-Media Plng & Comm)*
Jamin Svendsen *(Supvr-Comm)*
Jessica Cullinan *(Media Planner)*

Accounts:
New-Bridgestone Golf (Media Strategy, Planning & Buying Agency of Record)

Optimedia-Indianapolis

200 S Meridian St Ste 500, Indianapolis, IN 46225-1076
Tel.: (317) 639-5135
Fax: (317) 639-5132
Web Site: www.optimedia-us.com

Employees: 11
Year Founded: 2000

National Agency Associations: 4A's

Agency Specializes In: Media Buying Services

Susan Eberhart *(Mng Dir & Exec VP)*
Jay Schemanske *(VP & Dir-Strategic Comm)*
Tyler Riordan *(Media Planner & Media Buyer)*
Morgan Greer *(Media Planner)*
Porscha Kirkwood *(Media Planner)*
Kelley McClain *(Planner-Comm)*
Rebecca Peters *(Asst Media Planner & Media Buyer)*
Lana Wombolt *(Jr Media Buyer & Planner)*

Accounts:
Asheville Savings Bank; NC "The Best Checking" Checking Account Product; 2008
BBC America
British Airways
L'OReal
Mont Blanc
Nestle
T-Mobile US

Optimedia-San Francisco

2001 The Embarcadero, San Francisco, CA 94133
Tel.: (415) 398-2669
Fax: (415) 293-2199
E-Mail: info@optimedia-us.com
Web Site: www.optimedia-us.com

Employees: 10
Year Founded: 2000

National Agency Associations: 4A's

Agency Specializes In: Media Buying Services, Sponsorship

Kim Tanimoto *(Dir-Media)*
Elizabeth Mann *(Assoc Dir-Media)*
Chris Simon *(Assoc Dir-Media)*
Rachel Bell *(Supvr-Digital)*
Jasmine Hum *(Supvr-Media)*
Robert Mooney *(Sr Planner-Digital)*
Shirley Lope *(Planner-Digital)*
Jenna Millan *(Media Planner)*
Lauren Clark *(Sr Media Planner)*
Alexa Pandika *(Asst Media Planner-Digital)*

Accounts:
Denny's Corporation
Princess Cruises

Optimedia-Seattle

424 2nd Ave W, Seattle, WA 98119-4013
Tel.: (206) 272-2300
Fax: (206) 272-2499
Web Site: www.optimedia-us.com

Employees: 26
Year Founded: 2000

National Agency Associations: 4A's

Agency Specializes In: Media Buying Services, Sponsorship

David Ehlers *(Pres)*
Tom McElroy *(CFO)*
Jason Harrington *(Sr VP & Mng Dir-T-Mobile)*
Tom Scott *(Sr VP & Grp Dir-Strategic Comm)*
Jay Schemanske *(VP & Dir-Strategic Comm)*
Kate Renz *(Media Dir)*
Nicole Whitesel *(Dir-Media)*
Dan Bartos *(Assoc Dir-Programmatic)*
Molly Kennedy *(Supvr-Media Plng & Comm)*
Trinidy Yinger *(Supvr-Comm Plng)*
Jessica Cullinan *(Media Planner)*
Cameron Oriard *(Media Planner)*

Accounts:
Ben Bridge Jewelers
T-Mobile USA, Inc.

OREGON NEWSPAPER ADVERTISING CO.

4000 Kruse Way Pl Bldg 2 Ste 160, Lake Oswego, OR 97035
Tel.: (503) 624-6397
Fax: (503) 624-9811
E-Mail: onpa@orenews.com
Web Site: www.orenews.com

E-Mail for Key Personnel:
Media Dir.: linda@orenews.com

Employees: 8
Year Founded: 1935

National Agency Associations: AAF-ABC

Agency Specializes In: Newspaper

Approx. Annual Billings: $10,000,000

Breakdown of Gross Billings by Media: Newsp.: 100%

Laurie Hieb *(Exec Dir)*
Linda Hutcheson *(Mgr-Adv Svcs)*

ORION TRADING

622 3rd Ave, New York, NY 10017
Tel.: (646) 534-9400
Fax: (212) 605-7448
E-Mail: brian.mcmahon@oriontradingww.com
Web Site: oriontradingww.com

Employees: 35

National Agency Associations: 4A's

Agency Specializes In: Media Buying Services

Tom Telesco *(Pres)*
Michael Hooper *(Partner-Client Svcs)*
Abbi Palmer *(Partner-Client Svcs)*
Brian McMahon *(Pres/CEO-Orion Holdings Worldwide)*
Laura Ryan *(Pres-US)*
Barbara Di Maria *(Sr VP & Media Dir-Natl)*
Rich Wakeford *(Sr VP-Local Brdcst)*
Regina Philip Gatdula *(Assoc Partner-Client Svcs)*

Accounts:
American Express
Bank of America
Honda
Johnson & Johnson
Lowe's Home Improvement
Pfizer
Quidco Campaign: "Brands you know. Rewards you'll love", Media Planning & Buying
S.C. Johnson

OUTDOOR FIRST, INC.

W175 N 111117 Stonewoor Dr Ste 206, Germantown, WI 53022
Tel.: (262) 253-4900
Fax: (262) 253-4919
Web Site: www.outdoorfirst.com

E-Mail for Key Personnel:
President: linda@outdoorfirst.com

Employees: 6
Year Founded: 1994

National Agency Associations: OAAA-TAB

Agency Specializes In: Advertising Specialties, African-American Market, Agriculture, Alternative Advertising, Automotive, Business-To-Business, Communications, Consumer Goods, Consumer Marketing, Financial, Health Care Services, Legal Services, Market Research, Media Buying Services, Media Planning, Out-of-Home Media, Outdoor, Planning & Consultation, Production, Real Estate, Recruitment, Restaurant, Strategic Planning/Research, Transportation, Travel & Tourism

Approx. Annual Billings: $18,000,000

Breakdown of Gross Billings by Media: Out-of-Home Media: 100%

Lee Ann Smith *(Office Mgr)*
Sarah Grob *(Specialist-Out-of-Home Media)*

PALISADES MEDIA GROUP, INC.

1620 26th St Ste 200 S, Santa Monica, CA 90404-4013
Tel.: (310) 564-5400
Fax: (310) 828-9117
E-Mail: contact@palisadesmedia.com
Web Site: www.palisadesmedia.com

E-Mail for Key Personnel:
President: rschaffner@palisadesmedia.com

Employees: 92
Year Founded: 1996

National Agency Associations: 4A's

Agency Specializes In: Advertising, African-American Market, Brand Development & Integration, Broadcast, Cable T.V., Children's Market, Consumer Marketing, Consumer Publications, Cosmetics, Digital/Interactive, Direct Response Marketing, E-Commerce, Electronic Media, Entertainment, Event Planning & Marketing, Fashion/Apparel, Financial, Government/Political, Hispanic Market, Internet/Web Design, Leisure, Magazines, Media Buying Services, Newspaper, Newspapers & Magazines, Out-of-Home Media, Outdoor, Planning & Consultation, Print, Radio, Restaurant, Retail, Sponsorship, Sports Market, Strategic Planning/Research, Syndication, T.V., Technical Advertising, Teen Market, Trade & Consumer Magazines, Travel & Tourism

Approx. Annual Billings: $500,000,000

Breakdown of Gross Billings by Media: Cable T.V.: $165,000,000; D.M.: $7,500,000; Internet Adv.: $10,125,000; Mags.: $8,300,000; Network Radio:

$4,150,000; Network T.V.: $145,750,000; Newsp.: $4,150,000; Out-of-Home Media: $8,300,000; Plng. & Consultation: $1,000,000; Radio: $24,900,000; Spot T.V.: $95,000,000; Syndication: $20,750,000; Trade & Consumer Mags.: $3,000,000; Transit: $2,075,000

Roger A. Schaffner *(Owner & CEO)*
Laura Jean Bracken *(Pres & COO)*
Jean Brooks *(Exec VP)*
Erin Morgan *(Sr VP-Audio & Local Video)*
Pamela McCarthy *(VP & Dir-HR)*
Matt Lundstrom *(Dir-Digital Creative)*
Summer Slater *(Dir-Digital Mktg)*
Jen-jen Tsang *(Dir-Natl Video)*
Rachel Moore *(Assoc Dir-Media)*
Brian O'Donnell *(Assoc Dir-Bus Intelligence)*
Mia Duncan *(Supvr-Strategy)*
Anna Galatsky *(Supvr-Digital Media)*
Eddie Ong *(Supvr-Natl Brdcst)*
Elizabeth Thrash *(Sr Planner-Digital Media)*
Leslie Beightler *(Planner-Digital Media)*
Carly Cunha *(Planner-Digital Media)*
Daniella Lavi *(Media Buyer-Natl Television)*
Matthew Glaeser *(Assoc Media Dir)*
Joshua Jacobs *(Asst Media Planner-Digital)*
Melissa Rooney *(Asst Media Buyer)*

Accounts:
Barclays Global Investing; San Francisco, CA Financial
Behr Paint, Los Angeles, CA Paints & Stains
Belkin International, Inc.
Del Taco LLC; Lake Forest, CA Media Planning & Buying, Mexican Restaurant; 2006
Dropbox
Genius
Los Angeles Philharmonic Association; Los Angeles, CA
Virgin Megastores; Los Angeles, CA
The Weinstein Co.

PARR MOTO
(Formerly Parr Media)
13120 W Link Terr Blvd #4, Fort Myers, FL 33913
Fax: (239) 561-8091
Toll Free: (866) 722-1381
E-Mail: info@parrmoto.com
Web Site: www.parrmoto.com

Employees: 13

Agency Specializes In: Media Buying Services

David Grant *(Pres & CEO)*
Bill Taylor *(Mng Partner & VP)*
Dana Parr *(VP-Ops)*
Erik Vilnius *(Sr Designer)*
Adam Glick *(Acct Coord)*
Lindsey Childs *(Coord-Mktg)*

Accounts:
Harley Davidson; Fort Myers & Naples, FL & Huntsville, AL
Henricks Jewelers
Pinchers

PERKINS NICHOLS MEDIA
11691 Fall Creek Rd Ste 214-216, Indianapolis, IN 46256
Tel.: (317) 585-0000
Fax: (317) 585-0010
E-Mail: info@perkins-nichols.com

E-Mail for Key Personnel:
President: bperkins@pnmedia.com

Employees: 4
Year Founded: 1980

Agency Specializes In: Advertising, Market Research, Media Buying Services, Media Planning, Outdoor, Print, Radio, T.V.

Approx. Annual Billings: $6,000,000

Breakdown of Gross Billings by Media: Brdcst.: 80%; Cable T.V.: 5%; Newsp. & Mags.: 2%; Outdoor: 1%; Radio: 12%

Diane Nichols *(Owner)*

Accounts:
The Estridge Group; Indianapolis, IN
Financial Center Federal Credit Union; Indianapolis, IN
Indiana University; Bloomington, IN
IUPY
The Promotion Company
WGE Credit Union; Muncie, IN

PHD
220 E 42nd 7th Fl, New York, NY 10017
Tel.: (212) 894-6600
Fax: (212) 894-4100
Web Site: www.phdmedia.com/United-States/home.aspx

Employees: 530
Year Founded: 2001

National Agency Associations: 4A's-AD CLUB-AWNY-IAB-PAMA-TAB-THINKLA

Agency Specializes In: Advertising Specialties, African-American Market, Automotive, Broadcast, Business Publications, Business-To-Business, Cable T.V., Communications, Consulting, Consumer Marketing, Consumer Publications, Direct Response Marketing, Electronic Media, Entertainment, Fashion/Apparel, Financial, Health Care Services, Hispanic Market, Magazines, Media Buying Services, Newspaper, Newspapers & Magazines, Out-of-Home Media, Pharmaceutical, Planning & Consultation, Print, Radio, Retail, Sports Market, Strategic Planning/Research, Syndication, T.V., Trade & Consumer Magazines, Viral/Buzz/Word of Mouth, Yellow Pages Advertising

Breakdown of Gross Billings by Media: Cable T.V.: 17%; Internet Adv.: 7%; Network T.V.: 17%; Newsp.: 3%; Other: 1%; Outdoor: 4%; Print: 8%; Radio: 11%; Spot T.V.: 32%

Mike Cooper *(CEO)*
Loretta Lurie *(Mng Dir & Sr VP)*
Will Wiseman *(Pres-Strategy & Plng)*
Corina Constantin *(VP & Dir-Digital Analytics-US)*
Chantell Haskins *(VP & Assoc Dir-Brdcst)*
Bhaya Nabis *(Grp Acct Dir)*
Lorraine Jones *(Dir-Plng)*
Jesse Missad *(Dir)*
Patrick Ryan *(Dir-Bus Dev-Worldwide)*
Liz Armstrong *(Assoc Dir-Strategy)*
Kelly Fahner *(Assoc Dir-Strategy)*
Sabrina Malen *(Assoc Dir-Strategy)*
Ieva Matulaitis-Kunca *(Assoc Dir-Mktg Sciences)*
Melissa Sutton *(Assoc Dir-Strategy)*
Justin Williams *(Assoc Dir)*
Kaitlyn Burrows *(Supvr-Paid Search & Social Media)*
Dan Jablon *(Supvr-Integrated Strategy)*
Lydia McMillan *(Supvr-Strategy)*
Stephen Selsor *(Supvr-Strategy)*
Jaimee Benach *(Strategist-Integrated Media)*
Silvia Garcia *(Strategist-Integrated)*
Carolyn Harpster *(Strategist-Performance Mktg)*
Shannon O'Connor *(Strategist-Digital)*
Sarah Platt *(Strategist-Integrated)*
Jessica Palmer *(Asst Strategist-Published Media)*
Julia Ruxin *(Analyst-Digital Investment)*
Mason Burril *(Asst Analyst-Digital Investment)*
Julie Greico *(Assoc Media Dir)*

Accounts:
Alzheimer's Association; 2003
American Legacy Foundation Campaign: "Night of the Gummies", Truth; 2007
Animal Planet Campaign: "River Monsters Season 3"
Bentley Motors Media Planning & Buying
Cablevision Systems Corporation
Carnival Cruises Media
Charles Schwab & Co.; 2002
Converse Inc. North America Media Buying, North America Media Planning, Traditional & Digital Media
Cricket Communications; 2004
Discovery Channels Campaign: "Storm Chasers Season 4", Media Planning & Buying
The Economist; 2004
Elizabeth Arden Fragrances Curious; 2004
Enterprise Rent-A-Car Alamo Rent A Car, National Car Rental System; 2004
Expedia Media Planning & Buying
Ferrero USA Ferrero Rocher, Media, Tic Tac
Gap Inc Campaign: "Back to Blue", Media Buying; 1994
Glaxosmithkline PLC Global Media, Novartis; 2010
Havaianas; 2006
HBO Campaign: "Boardwalk Empire"; 2006
Hewlett-Packard
Hiscox plc Media
Humana Digital, Health Insurance, Media
Hyatt Hotels Corporation Global Digital Media, Media Buying, Media Planning, SEM, SEO, Social; 2008
Kayak Software Corporation Media Planning and Buying
Kohler Media Buying, Media Planning
Lord & Taylor
Mercedes Benz USA; 2002
New-MGM Resorts International (Media Agency of Record)
Mitsubishi Motors North America; 2004
Newell Rubbermaid Global Media Buying, Strategic Communication Planning
Porsche Global Media Planning & Buying
Roche Diagnostics; 2003
SAP Media
Schiff Nutrition; 2006
Timex Corporation; 2006
Unilever Foods & Homecare, Global Communications, Global Search, Personal Care, Refreshment, Search Engine Marketing, Search Engine Optimization

Branches

PHD New York
220 E 42nd St 7th Fl, New York, NY 10017-5806
Tel.: (212) 894-6600
Fax: (212) 894-4100
E-Mail: info@phdus.com
Web Site: www.phdmedia.com

Year Founded: 1984

National Agency Associations: 4A's-AD CLUB-AWNY-IAB-OAAA-TAB

Agency Specializes In: Media Buying Services, Sponsorship, Strategic Planning/Research

Nathan Brown *(CEO)*
Loretta Lurie *(Mng Dir & Sr VP)*
Harry Keeshan *(Exec VP)*
Andrea Cardamone *(Sr VP & Grp Acct Dir)*
Asli Hamamci *(Sr VP & Acct Dir-Global)*
Coreen Gelber *(Sr VP & Dir-Local Media)*
Dave Kornett *(Sr VP & Dir-Brdcst-Natl)*
Andrea Montano *(VP & Grp Acct Dir)*
Aileen Larsen *(VP & Assoc Dir-Brdcst)*
John Wagner *(Grp Dir-Published Media)*
Melissa Gordon-Ring *(Grp Acct Dir)*
Bill Bradley *(Dir-Strategy)*
Tara Nolan *(Dir-Mktg & Comm)*
Christina Polk *(Dir-Innovation-Google)*

Media Buying Services

Kannan Selvaratnam *(Dir-Strategy)*
Lane Sorkin *(Dir-Strategy)*
Robyn Athans *(Assoc Dir-Media)*
Rachel Baumann *(Assoc Dir-Media)*
Nathan Brendal *(Assoc Dir-Digital Investment)*
Janet Campuzano *(Assoc Dir-American Red Cross, Omega & Vanda)*
Michael Finegan *(Assoc Dir-Print Investment)*
George Gerritsen *(Assoc Dir-Strategy)*
John Shannon *(Assoc Dir-Digital)*
Phillip Vicario *(Assoc Dir-Strategy)*
Kathrina Fernandez *(Mgr-HR)*
Robin Carter *(Supvr-Brdcst-Natl)*
Jenna Scorsese *(Supvr)*
Samantha Seidler *(Supvr-Strategy)*
Stephen Selsor *(Supvr-Strategy)*
Sam Valle *(Supvr-Digital Investment)*
Annmarie Cartolano *(Strategist-Integrated)*
Seema Harryginsingh *(Strategist)*
Teal Kratky *(Strategist-Channel)*
Maria Pendergast *(Coord-Mktg & Bus Dev)*
Melissa Getlen *(Assoc Media Dir-Natl Television Brdcst)*

Accounts:
Elizabeth Arden Fragrances; 2004
Gap Inc.; 1984
GlaxoSmithKline
Havaianas; 2006
HBO; 2006
Janus
OfficeMax
Serino Coyne
Siemens; 2004
Transamerica

PHD Chicago
225 N Michigan Ave Ste 800, Chicago, IL 60601
Tel.: (312) 595-2800
Fax: (312) 467-0977
E-Mail: infous@phdnetwork.com
Web Site: www.phdmedia.com/United-States/home.aspx

Employees: 32

National Agency Associations: 4A's

Agency Specializes In: Media Buying Services, Sponsorship

Allison Howald *(Mng Dir & Sr VP)*
Phila Broich *(Chief People Officer-US)*
Tom Bell *(Grp Acct Dir)*
Abigail Luther *(Dir-Digital-Midwest Reg)*
Garrett Self *(Dir-Strategy-Global)*
Abigail Berek *(Assoc Dir)*
Ellen Griffin *(Assoc Dir)*
Molly Moore *(Assoc Dir-Digital Investment)*
Allyson Schnitzer *(Assoc Dir-Media)*
Toni Baysinger *(Supvr-Strategy)*
Mario DiMercurio *(Supvr-Digital Project)*
Sarah Barbieri *(Strategist)*
Elizabeth Betsanes *(Strategist)*
Hannah Hammer *(Strategist)*
Kate Mills *(Strategist)*
Erin Pohlman *(Strategist-Media)*
Nicholas Voutiritsas *(Strategist-Hybrid)*
Christopher Sweet *(Asst Strategist-Media)*
Kaitlyn Main *(Sr Analyst-Digital Mktg)*
Yates Webb *(Coord-Integrated)*

Accounts:
Enterprise Rent-A-Car
Erickson Retirement Communities; 2008
Hormel Foods
HP
Kohler
S.C. Johnson & Son, Inc. Campaign: "Great Expectations", Digital, Global Media Buying, Global Media Planning, Public Relations, Shopper Marketing, Social Media

PHD Los Angeles
10960 Wilshire Blvd, Los Angeles, CA 90024
Tel.: (310) 405-8700
Fax: (310) 405-8797
E-Mail: infous@phdnetwork.com
Web Site: www.phdmedia.com

Employees: 50

National Agency Associations: 4A's

Agency Specializes In: Media Planning, Sponsorship

Anne-Marie Schaffer *(Pres-PHD West)*
Churita Boston *(VP & Dir-Brdcst Traffic)*
Chantell Haskins *(VP & Assoc Dir-Brdcst)*
Jennifer Park *(Dir-Comm Plng)*
Celeste Bazan *(Assoc Dir-HR-West Coast)*
James Mason *(Assoc Dir-Brdcst Traffic)*
Aja Wall *(Mgr-Brdcst Traffic)*
Jayson Mckeon *(Supvr)*
Lauren Turner *(Supvr-Strategy)*
Iheanyi Anyaso *(Media Buyer)*

Accounts:
Air New Zealand; 2006
Caesars Entertainment Corporation; 2008
California Lottery; 2004
Financial Freedom
Mitsubishi Motors North America; 2004

Canada

PHD Toronto
s: 96 Spadina Avenue Suite 600, Toronto, ON M5V 2J6 Canada
Tel.: (416) 922-0217
E-Mail: info@phdca.com
Web Site: www.phdmedia.com

Fred Auchterlonie *(Exec VP & Dir-Client Ops)*
Matt Devlin *(Mng Dir-Comm Plng)*
Zoryana Loboyko *(VP & Dir-Client Svcs)*
Stephen Wendt *(VP & Client Svc Dir)*
Scott Henderson *(Grp Acct Dir)*
Ellie Longhin *(Acct Dir)*
Michelle Mitchell *(Acct Dir)*
Jim Orr *(Acct Dir)*
Paul Paterson *(Acct Supvr-Traditional & Digital Strategy)*
Stacy Pringle *(Acct Supvr)*

Accounts:
Honda
Moen Media
Scotia Bank

Asia Pacific

PHD Philippines
10F Bankmer Bldg, 6756 Ayala Avenue, Makati, 1226 Philippines
Tel.: (63) 2 813 7797
Fax: (63) 2 817 7791
Web Site: www.phdmedia.com

Mean Bernardo *(Gen Mgr)*
Fen Marquez *(Dir-Mktg Comm & Bus Dev)*
Sherwin Bautista *(Mgr-Media)*
Ivy Fajardo *(Mgr-Media)*

Accounts:
Champion Detergents
Hewlett Packard
SC Johnson

PHD China
Rm 1101 Tower 2, No 3 Hongqiao Rd, Shanghai, 200030 China
Tel.: (86) 21 6407 8080
Fax: (86) 21 6447 1059
Web Site: www.phdmedia.com

Employees: 150

Aaron Wild *(CEO)*
Anna Chitty *(Mng Dir)*
Lars Bjorge *(Chief Digital Officer-Greater China)*
Kel Hook *(Head-Strategy & Creative Comm Plng)*

Accounts:
Elizabeth Arden Digital Media Planning & Buying, Fragrance, Makeup, Skincare, Traditional Media Planning & Buying
HGP
Porsche
Siemens
Standard Chartered Bank
Unilever Campaign: "Unbeatable Season 2", Cornetto, Media Buying & Planning
Zhonghua Campaign: "Find Your Reason To Smile"

PHD New Zealand
Level 7 University of Otago Bldg, 385 Queen St, Auckland, New Zealand
Tel.: (64) 9 3377000
Fax: (64) 9 337 7007
Web Site: www.phdmedia.com

Employees: 70

Jane Stanley *(Mng Dir)*
Nikki Grafton *(Mng Dir-Spark PHD & PHDiQ)*
Stuart Rutherford *(Mng Dir-Spark PHD)*
Robin Wilson *(Gen Mgr-PR, Social & Experiences-Park PHD)*
Amanda Cater *(Dir-Media-Spark PHD)*
Angela Forward *(Dir-Media-Spark PHD)*
Fou Brown *(Mgr-Media)*
Jamie Graham *(Media Buyer-Spark PHD)*
Chloe Parker *(Media Buyer-Spark PHD)*

Accounts:
Air New Zealand
Daikin Media
DB Breweries
Sanitarium Health Foods
Unilever Media Buying

PHD Thailand
10 Floor Amarin Plaza, 500 Ploenchit Road, Bangkok, 10330 Thailand
Tel.: (66) 2 256 9360
Fax: (66) 22569366
Web Site: www.phdmedia.com

Employees: 17

Nuvee Pongsathidporn *(Mng Dir)*
Tasanai Ranusawad *(Assoc Dir-Plng)*
Chavut Tianpaasook *(Media Planner)*

Accounts:
Elizabeth Arden Digital Media Planning & Buying, Fragrance, Makeup, Skincare, Traditional Media Planning & Buying
Hershey's
Hotels.com
HTC Mobile
SC Johnson

PHD Singapore
3 Anson Rd 31-02 Springleaf Tower, Singapore, 0799090 Singapore
Tel.: (65) 6877 8770
Web Site: www.phdmedia.com

Employees: 20

Agency Specializes In: Advertising, Asian Market

Susana Tsui *(CEO)*
Sony Wong *(Mng Dir)*
Natalie Ng *(Head-Performance Mktg & Assoc Dir)*
Chris Stephenson *(Head-Strategy & Plng-APAC)*
Jessica Lok *(Dir-Media)*
Catherine Ganapathy *(Reg Acct Dir)*
Cheri Lim *(Assoc Bus Dir)*

Accounts:
Airbnb, Inc. Media
BS Groups Asian Skin Solutions, Brazilian Experts, Media
Elizabeth Arden Alberta Ferrari, Badgley Mishka, Britney Spears, Danielle Steel, Digital Media Planning & Buying, Elizabeth Taylor, Fragrance, Geoffrey Beene, Giorgio Beverly Hills, Halston, Hilary Duff, Makeup, Mariah Carey, Skincare, Traditional Media Planning & Buying
Esplanade Media
Far East Organization Media Buying, Media Planning
Singapore National Environment Agency; 2008
Singapore Sports Council Media
Spring Singapore Media Planning & Buying
Times Publishing Media Planning & Buying
Transitions Optical Media

Europe, Middle East & Africa (EMEA)

Drum OMG
(Formerly Drum PHD Limited)
11 Chenief St, London, WC1E 7EY United Kingdom
Tel.: (44) 207 446 7200
Web Site: www.drum.co.uk/

Employees: 35

Ella d'Amato *(Mng Dir)*
Luke Southern *(Deputy Mng Dir)*
James Larman *(Head-Plng)*
Gemma Folkard *(Acct Dir)*
Ruth Griffin *(Client Svcs Dir)*
Natasha Taylor *(Dir-New Bus & Mktg)*
Siobhan Woodrow *(Dir-Bus)*

Accounts:
HP
Kraft Foods
Mondelez International Oreo, Print
O2
Sony Computer Entertainment America LLC Campaign: "#playstationmemories", Content Creation & Partnership Marketing, PlayStation

PHD MEDIA UK
The Telephone Exchange 5 N Crescent, Chenies St, London, WC1E 7PH United Kingdom
Tel.: (44) 20 7446 0555
Fax: (44) 20 7446 7100
E-Mail: phduk@phdmedia.com
Web Site: www.phdmedia.com/United-Kingdom/home.aspx

Employees: 200

Agency Specializes In: Media Buying Services

Mike Cooper *(CEO)*
Verica Djurdjevic *(Mng Dir)*
Robert Ray *(Mng Dir)*
Daren Rubins *(CEO-UK)*
Nathalie Coulibeuf *(Head-Social)*
Toby Roberts *(Head-Strategy-Unilever-Global)*
Steve Taylor *(Head-Digital Strategy)*
Rebecca Stafford *(Media Dir)*
Avril Canavan *(Dir-Mktg & Comm-Worldwide)*
Reema Mitra *(Dir-Strategy)*
Louise Rowcliffe *(Dir-Media)*
Becky Smithson *(Dir-Brdcst Plng)*

Accounts:
ACT ON CO2
Admiral Media Planning & Buying
AEGON UK plc Media
British Heart Foundation Media Buying & Planning
New-C&C Group Plc Magners, UK Media
Cadbury Cadbury Dairy Milk, Campaign: "Unwrap Joy", Creme Egg, Media Planning & Buying, TV
Canon Media Buying, Media Planning
Confused.com Media Planning & Buying, Rebrand
Department for Work & Pensions Benefit Fraud
eBay Media
Edge
EHarmony Offline Media Planning & Buying
Elizabeth Arden Digital Media Planning & Buying, Fragrance, Makeup, Skincare, Traditional Media Planning & Buying
European Aeronautic Defence & Space Co. EAD N.V.
Expedia.co.uk
Experian Media Planning & Buying
Fairfx.com Digital, Media, Social, TV
The Guardian
Harrods Media
J. Sainsbury plc Media, Sainsbury's Perfect Christmas
McCain Foods Campaign: "Mccain Ready Baked Jackets", Media Buying
Otto
Smart Energy GB Media Buying, Media Planning
Twitter UK Media
UNICEF
Vestas Wind Systems; 2008
New-Virgin Atlantic Media Buying, Media Planning
Volkswagen Media Buying, Media Planning, Seat UK
Warner Bros Lego
Whitbread Beefeater, Costa Coffee
Zuto Advertising, Digital, Media, Social Media

Branch

PHD Canada
96 Spadina Ave Ste 600, Toronto, ON M5V 2J6 Canada
Tel.: (416) 922-0217
Fax: (416) 922-8469
E-Mail: info@phdnetwork.com
Web Site: www.phdmedia.com

E-Mail for Key Personnel:
President: fforster@phdca.com

Employees: 125
Year Founded: 1979

Agency Specializes In: Media Buying Services, Planning & Consultation

Matt Devlin *(Mng Dir-Comm Plng)*
Caroline Moul *(VP-Digital & Emerging Media)*
Michelle Mitchell *(Acct Dir)*
Joel Koepfler *(Acct Mgr)*
Christine Macphee *(Acct Mgr)*
Andrew Young *(Acct Mgr)*
Paul Paterson *(Acct Supvr-Traditional & Digital Strategy)*
Liz Jewett *(Supvr-Digital)*
Aviva Attis *(Specialist-Digital Media)*
Carlos Lemus *(Analyst-Digital)*

Accounts:
Boston Pizza International
Glaxosmithkline Media
Honda Canada Inc.
New-Ontario Honda Dealers Media Buying, Media Planning
New-Rexall Media Buying
SABMiller Media Buying, Media Planning, Miller Lite
Scotiabank Media Buying
Tangerine Media Buying, Media Planning

PLANITRETAIL, LLC
360 Bloomfield Ave Ste 406, Windsor, CT 06095
Tel.: (860) 687-9900
Web Site: www.planitretail.net

Employees: 13
Year Founded: 2007

Agency Specializes In: Digital/Interactive, Local Marketing, Newspaper, Newspapers & Magazines, Print, Web (Banner Ads, Pop-ups, etc.)

Approx. Annual Billings: $100,000,000

Matthew Spahn *(Founder & CEO)*
John Miarecki *(Acct Dir)*
Kathryn Marchitto *(Dir-Media Buying)*
Christine Arens *(Media Buyer)*

PLAY COMMUNICATION
(Acquired by GroupM North America & Corporate HQ)

POWER MEDIA INC.
500 N Broadway Ste 102, Jericho, NY 11753
Tel.: (516) 390-8004
Fax: (516) 931-1320
E-Mail: info@powermedia.net
Web Site: www.powermedia.net

Employees: 35
Year Founded: 1975

Agency Specializes In: Business-To-Business, Direct Response Marketing, Health Care Services, Media Buying Services, Retail

Approx. Annual Billings: $30,000,000

Michael Feldman *(Pres)*
Brian Feldman *(CEO & Partner)*
Meredith Woods *(Mng Supvr-Media)*

Accounts:
AB Underwear
Costamar Travel Intl
Creativa Interiors-Primor
NYX Cosmetics
Selman Chevrolet
Universal Music Latin

PRIMEDIA INC.
1775 Bald Hill Rd, Warwick, RI 02886-4210
Tel.: (401) 826-3600
Fax: (401) 826-3644
Toll Free: (800) 397-5804
E-Mail: jcooney@primediahq.com
Web Site: www.primediahq.com

E-Mail for Key Personnel:
President: jcooney@primediahq.com

Employees: 16
Year Founded: 1990

Agency Specializes In: Advertising, Alternative Advertising, Automotive, Broadcast, Business Publications, Business-To-Business, Cable T.V., Children's Market, Co-op Advertising, Communications, Consulting, Consumer Goods, Consumer Marketing, Consumer Publications, Direct Response Marketing, Education, Electronic Media, Entertainment, Environmental, Financial, Food Service, Government/Political, Health Care Services, Infomercials, Legal Services, Leisure, Magazines, Media Buying Services, Media Planning, Multimedia, New Product Development, Newspaper, Newspapers & Magazines, Out-of-Home Media, Outdoor, Over-50 Market, Paid Searches, Pharmaceutical, Planning &

Consultation, Print, Radio, Real Estate, Restaurant, Retail, Sales Promotion, Seniors' Market, Social Media, Sports Market, Strategic Planning/Research, Syndication, T.V., Teen Market, Trade & Consumer Magazines, Transportation, Travel & Tourism, Web (Banner Ads, Pop-ups, etc.), Yellow Pages Advertising

Approx. Annual Billings: $40,000,000

Breakdown of Gross Billings by Media: Brdcst.: 30%; D.M.: 20%; Mags.: 5%; Network T.V.: 3%; Newsp.: 20%; Outdoor: 10%; Point of Purchase: 1%; Syndication: 3%; Transit: 5%; Yellow Page Adv.: 3%

Edward Valenti *(Founder & COO)*
James J. Cooney, Jr. *(Pres, CEO & Dir-Creative)*
Rick Boles *(VP-Media & Ops)*
Stephen Romanello *(VP-Acct Svcs)*
Frank Jones *(Dir-Creative Svcs)*
Katelyn Thompson *(Dir-Digital, Print & Outdoor Media)*
Greg Stewart *(Mgr-Acctg)*
Elizabeth O'Sullivan *(Media Buyer)*

Accounts:
Town Fair Tire

PROFESSIONAL MEDIA MANAGEMENT
528 Bridge St NW Ste 7, Grand Rapids, MI 49504
Tel.: (616) 456-5555
Fax: (616) 456-8244
Web Site: professionalmediamanagement.com

Employees: 7
Year Founded: 1977

Agency Specializes In: Advertising, Direct-to-Consumer, Electronic Media, Faith Based, Media Buying Services, Media Planning, Media Training, Newspaper, Newspapers & Magazines, Planning & Consultation, Promotions, Publicity/Promotions, Retail, Social Media, Sponsorship, Web (Banner Ads, Pop-ups, etc.)

Approx. Annual Billings: $15,000,000

Breakdown of Gross Billings by Media: Newsp.: $15,000,000

Jack Ponstine *(Pres)*
Julie Kiel *(VP-S/s)*
Lee Amundson *(Sr Mgr-Database)*
Leigh Engelbrecht *(Mgr-Ops & Customer Svc)*

PROVING GROUND MEDIA, INC.
2218 Commerce Rd Ste 5A, Forest Hill, MD 21050
Tel.: (410) 420-6343
Fax: (410) 420-6358
Toll Free: (800) 509-1425
E-Mail: info@pgmedia.tv
Web Site: www.pgmedia.tv

E-Mail for Key Personnel:
President: debra.payne@pgmedia.tv

Employees: 6
Year Founded: 2003

Agency Specializes In: Broadcast, Cable T.V., Direct Response Marketing, Infomercials, Media Buying Services, Syndication, T.V.

Approx. Annual Billings: $15,000,000

Breakdown of Gross Billings by Media: Brdcst.: 40%; Cable T.V.: 50%; Syndication: 10%

Debra Payne *(Pres)*
Michelle Mason *(Acct Supvr)*

RECIPROCAL RESULTS
193 A Rice Av, Staten Island, NY 10314
Tel.: (718) 370-3977
Fax: (718) 761-7103
E-Mail: info@reciprocalresults.com
Web Site: www.reciprocalresults.com

Year Founded: 1997

National Agency Associations: AD CLUB-AMA

Agency Specializes In: Advertising, Broadcast, Business Publications, Cable T.V., Consulting, Consumer Publications, Cosmetics, Entertainment, Fashion/Apparel, Local Marketing, Magazines, Media Buying Services, Newspaper, Out-of-Home Media, Outdoor, Planning & Consultation, Print, Public Relations, Publicity/Promotions, Radio, Sports Market, Syndication, T.V., Teen Market, Trade & Consumer Magazines

Breakdown of Gross Billings by Media: Cable T.V.: 8%; Consulting: 8%; D.M.: 4%; Newsp.: 8%; Other: 8%; Out-of-Home Media: 8%; Pub. Rels.: 8%; Radio: 8%; T.V.: 8%; Trade & Consumer Mags.: 32%

Roy Moskowitz *(Chm, Pres & CEO)*

Accounts:
Andrew Rasiej for Public Advocate Ad Industry PR
Artisan News Service Copywriting
Asmara Channel Marketing
Assemblyman Matt Titone PR & Polling
Concord Fragrances Media Buying
Congregation B'nai Jeshurun Media Buying, PR, Print Creative
Cuba the Fragrance Media Buying
Debi Rose 4 City Council Media Buying, PR, Web Design
Delkin Media Buying
Duane Reade Barter
Dweck Media Planning
Esports PR
Estroven Media Buying
Flycast Media Buying
The Fortune Society Branding
ISO Real Estate Media Buying & PR
Lea & Perrins Barter
National Foundation for Teaching Entrepreneurship Branding
New Way Home PR
Payless Barter
Scoops Barter
Site 59 Media Planning
Steve Harrison for Congress Copywriting, Media Buying, PR, Research, Speechwriting, Web Design
TCCD Barter
Ugo.com Sales Promotion
Virgin Channel Marketing
Zeborg Consulting
Zilo Media Planning

RECRUITMENT AD PLACEMENT LLC
6660 Delmonico Ste 333, Colorado Springs, CO 80949
Tel.: (719) 535-2915
Fax: (719) 535-2358
Toll Free: (800) 655-3146
E-Mail: vjmaione@hotmail.com
Web Site: www.recruitadplacement.com

Employees: 3
Year Founded: 2009

Agency Specializes In: Advertising, Legal Services, Media Buying Services, Newspaper, Print

Approx. Annual Billings: $600,000

Breakdown of Gross Billings by Media: Internet Adv.: $50,000; Newsp. & Mags.: $550,000

Vincent J. Maione *(Owner & Pres)*
Brigitte Maione *(Owner)*

RED COMMA MEDIA, INC.
133 S Butler St, Madison, WI 53703-3543
Tel.: (608) 661-3781
Fax: (608) 237-2404
E-Mail: info@redcommamedia.com
Web Site: www.redcommamedia.com

Employees: 5
Year Founded: 2003

Agency Specializes In: Advertising, Broadcast, Business-To-Business, Cable T.V., Consumer Marketing, Consumer Publications, Electronic Media, Industrial, Local Marketing, Magazines, Market Research, Media Buying Services, Media Planning, Newspaper, Newspapers & Magazines, Out-of-Home Media, Outdoor, Print, Production (Print), Radio, Strategic Planning/Research, T.V., Web (Banner Ads, Pop-ups, etc.)

Carrie Dellinger *(Pres)*
Jena Rortvedt *(Supvr-Media)*
Ben Caulfield *(Media Planner & Media Buyer)*
Alyssa Smith *(Media Planner & Media Buyer)*

Accounts:
Anderson Pest Solutions
Generac Power Systems
Mission Investment Fund
Pacific Cycle
Rasmussen College

RIVENDELL MEDIA INC.
1248 US Hwy 22 W, Mountainside, NJ 07092
Tel.: (212) 242-6863
Fax: (908) 232-0521
E-Mail: info@rivendellmedia.com
Web Site: www.rivendellmedia.com

E-Mail for Key Personnel:
President: todd@rivendellmedia.com

Employees: 8
Year Founded: 1979

Agency Specializes In: Gay & Lesbian Market, Media Buying Services

Approx. Annual Billings: $12,000,000

Todd L. Evans *(Pres & CEO)*

Accounts:
Pernod Ricard USA Absolut, Media

RJW MEDIA
12827 Frankstown Rd Ste B, Pittsburgh, PA 15235
Tel.: (412) 361-6833
Fax: (412) 361-8005
E-Mail: julie@rjwmedia.com

E-Mail for Key Personnel:
President: julie@rjwmedia.com

Employees: 12
Year Founded: 1985

Agency Specializes In: Advertising, Automotive, Broadcast, Cable T.V., Consumer Publications, Education, Electronic Media, Entertainment, Financial, Health Care Services, Legal Services, Leisure, Magazines, Media Buying Services, Media Planning, Media Relations, Medical Products, Mobile Marketing, Newspaper, Newspapers & Magazines, Out-of-Home Media, Outdoor, Print, Radio, Real Estate, Restaurant, Retail, Sponsorship, T.V., Travel & Tourism

Approx. Annual Billings: $42,000,000

Julie Smith *(Owner & Pres)*

Accounts:
CCAC (Community College of Allegheny County) College/Academia; 2007
Children's Hospital of Pittsburgh; Pittsburgh, PA Pediatric Care; 2005
Clarion University College/Academia; 2012
Comcast/Adelphia; PA Broadband, Cable; 2005
Dollar Bank; Pittsburgh, PA;Cleveland, OH Financial; 2009
Fort Pitt Capital Group; Pittsburgh, PA Investment Management; 2009
Geneva College; PA College/Academia; 2008
Giant Eagle, Inc.; Pittsburgh, PA Grocery Store Chain; 1993
Harry S. Cohen & Associates; Pittsburgh, PA Attorney; 1999
Howard Hanna Real Estate; Pittsburgh, PA Real Estate Services; 1988
Kennywood Entertainment Co.; Pittsburgh, PA Idlewild Park, Kennywood Park, Sand Castle; 1998
Kings Family Restaurants; Pittsburgh, PA Food Service; 2003
SBCG; New York, NY Retail Liquidation; 1986
Sinclair Broadcasting; Pittsburgh, PA; Charleston-Huntington, WV; West Palm Beach, FL Television Stations; 2010
Today's Home; Pittsburgh, PA Home Furnishings; 1989
West Penn Allegheny Health System; Pittsburgh, PA Healthcare; 1998

ROCKETT INTERACTIVE
(Acquired by Dentsu Aegis Network Americas)

ROI MEDIA
5801 E 41st St Ste 600, Tulsa, OK 74135-5628
Tel.: (918) 582-9777
Fax: (918) 592-6635

Employees: 15
Year Founded: 1985

Agency Specializes In: Advertising, Media Buying Services, Media Planning, Media Relations, Outdoor

Sales: $8,000,000

Lester J. Boyle *(Owner)*
Truman O. Criss *(Pres)*
Mike Hay *(Sr Dir-Strategic Mktg Intelligence & Analytics)*
Deanna McClure *(Office Mgr & Acct Coord)*
Maggie Wade *(Mgr-Bus)*
Kim Conner *(Acct Coord)*
Stacie Maddox *(Acct Coord)*

Accounts:
Drysdales
KOTV; Tulsa, OK
KWTV; Oklahoma City, OK
Shelter Insurance
Tulsa Chamber
Tulsa Zoo

RPM-RIGHT PLACE MEDIA
437 Lewis Hargett Cir Ste 130, Lexington, KY 40503
Tel.: (859) 685-3800
Fax: (859) 685-3801
E-Mail: info@rightplacemedia.com
Web Site: www.rightplacemedia.com

E-Mail for Key Personnel:
Media Dir.: cbrough@rightplacemedia.com

Employees: 20
Year Founded: 2000

Agency Specializes In: Advertising, Automotive, Broadcast, Business Publications, Business-To-Business, Cable T.V., Co-op Advertising, Consulting, Consumer Publications, Digital/Interactive, Direct Response Marketing, Education, Electronic Media, Email, Financial, Health Care Services, Information Technology, Integrated Marketing, Internet/Web Design, Magazines, Media Buying Services, Media Planning, Medical Products, Newspaper, Newspapers & Magazines, Out-of-Home Media, Outdoor, Paid Searches, Planning & Consultation, Print, Radio, Recruitment, Restaurant, Retail, Social Marketing/Nonprofit, Sponsorship, Strategic Planning/Research, T.V., Trade & Consumer Magazines, Travel & Tourism

Approx. Annual Billings: $40,000,000

Breakdown of Gross Billings by Media: Bus. Publs.: 4%; D.M.: 7%; Internet Adv.: 12%; Newsp. & Mags.: 21%; Out-of-Home Media: 9%; Radio & T.V.: 47%

Joel Rapp *(Pres & CEO)*
W.C. Corbin *(CFO)*
Stephanie Dowdy *(VP & Dir-Media)*
Devin Johnson *(VP & Dir-Media)*
Joey Banks *(Dir-Media)*
Amy Lynne Dickinson *(Dir-Media)*
Karl Hauser *(Dir-Interactive Media)*
Liz Fenner *(Mgr-Interactive Mktg)*
Tara Williams *(Sr Acct Exec)*
Kate Mudd *(Coord-Interactive Media)*

Accounts:
Austin Grill; 2009
Back Yard Burgers; 2012
Bella Notte Italian Trattoria; 2001
Captain D's (Media) Seafood Restaurant Chain; 2006
Donan Engineering; 2007
Fazoli's Digital Marketing, Media Buying; 2000
Lexington Clinic; 2009
Mississippi Credit Union League; 2009
Norton Healthcare; 2010
Papa Murphy's; 2005
Smashing Tomato; 2007
Stoney River; 2011
Thompson Hospitality; 2009
United Methodist Communications; 2011

SALESFORCE MARKETING CLOUD
(Formerly Buddy Media, Inc.)
155 6th Ave 12th Fl, New York, NY 10013
Tel.: (646) 380-7300
Web Site: www.salesforce.com/marketing-cloud

Agency Specializes In: Digital/Interactive, Internet/Web Design, Media Buying Services, Social Media

Scott McCorkle *(CEO)*
Susan St. Ledger *(Chief Revenue Officer-Mktg Cloud)*
Patrick Stokes *(VP-Product Mgmt)*
Blake Miller *(Dir-Product Mktg)*
Rick Buie *(Mgr-West Reg Svcs)*
Kristen Aicholtz *(Strategist-Social)*
Derek Pigott *(Sr Program Mgr)*

Accounts:
ABC
American Express
Anheuser Busch Busch Entertainment
Carnival
Charles Schwab
The Dallas Cowboys
The Gym Group Marketing Automation
InStyle.com
J. Crew
Mattel
Mitsubishi Motors
NHL
Parents Magazine
Samsung
Sprint Nextel Corporation Virgin Mobile USA
Wonka Candy

SELF OPPORTUNITY, INC.
808 Ofc Park Cir, Lewisville, TX 75057
Tel.: (214) 222-1500
Fax: (214) 222-8884
Toll Free: (800) 594-7036
Web Site: www.selfopportunity.com

Employees: 33
Year Founded: 2001

Agency Specializes In: Advertising, Food Service, Hispanic Market, Recruitment, Restaurant, Retail

Approx. Annual Billings: $5,000,000

Breakdown of Gross Billings by Media: Network Radio: $50,000; Network T.V.: $4,950,000

Kim Self *(VP & Mgr-Talent Acq)*
Amy Cuilla *(VP-HR)*
Brad Holley *(VP)*

Accounts:
Brinker; Dallas, TX
Chuck E. Cheese's
Rent-A-Center; Dallas, TX

SIDECAR MEDIA
1844 W Superior St Ste 200, Chicago, IL 60622
Tel.: (312) 829-6789
Fax: (312) 829-6020
E-Mail: susan.babin@sidecarmedia.com
Web Site: www.sidecarmedia.com

Employees: 5
Year Founded: 2005

National Agency Associations: OAAA

Agency Specializes In: Advertising, Hispanic Market, Mobile Marketing, Out-of-Home Media, Outdoor

Approx. Annual Billings: $5,500,000

Breakdown of Gross Billings by Media: Out-of-Home Media: 100%

Mike Farrell *(Sr Dir-Client Success)*
Cesar Torres *(Dir-Design)*
Tian Hao Luo *(Product Mgr)*
Jathaniel Spengler *(Product Mgr)*
Jeremy O'Briant *(Mgr-Growth & Ops)*
Jenna Richard *(Mgr-Comm)*
Bobby Battista *(Analyst-Innovation Strategy)*
Matthew Sheaffer *(Sr Program Mgr)*

SILVERLIGHT DIGITAL
265 W 37th St, New York, NY 10018
Tel.: (646) 650-5330
Web Site: www.silverlightdigital.com

Employees: 23

Agency Specializes In: Digital/Interactive, Mobile Marketing, Paid Searches, Social Media, Sponsorship, Web (Banner Ads, Pop-ups, etc.)

Approx. Annual Billings: $35,000,000

Lori Goldberg *(CEO)*
Michael Ackerman *(VP-Bus Dev)*
David Sapinski *(Acct Dir)*

Media Buying Services

Matthew Granish *(Dir-Media)*
Sandra Leung *(Sr Mgr-Search & Acct)*
Brooks Welsh *(Assoc-Bus Dev)*

Accounts:
New-Aetrex; 2014
New-Curacao Tourism Board; 2014
New-Jiffy Lube; 2013
New-Meda Aerospan, Dymista; 2014

SKYACHT AIRCRAFT INC.

(d/b/a Personal Blimp)
110 Pulpit Hill Rd, Amherst, MA 01002
Tel.: (413) 549-1321
E-Mail: info@personalblimp.com
Web Site: www.personalblimp.com

Employees: 3

Agency Specializes In: Media Buying Services, Outdoor

Mike Kuehlmuss *(Dir-Mechanical Design)*

SLADE CREATIVE MARKETING

209 W Anapamu St, Santa Barbara, CA 93101
Tel.: (805) 568-1801
Fax: (805) 568-1804
Toll Free: (800) 549-1833
E-Mail: slade@silcom.com
Web Site: www.sladecreative.com

Employees: 2
Year Founded: 1978

National Agency Associations: AAF

Agency Specializes In: Media Buying Services, Publicity/Promotions, Restaurant

Approx. Annual Billings: $600,000

Breakdown of Gross Billings by Media: D.M.: $270,000; Other: $90,000; Radio: $80,000; T.V.: $160,000

S. Richard Slade *(Pres & Dir-Creative)*

Accounts:
Santa Barbara Airport; Santa Barbara, CA; 1996

SMY MEDIA, INC.

211 E Ontario St Ste 900, Chicago, IL 60611
Tel.: (312) 621-9600
Fax: (312) 621-0924
E-Mail: info@smymedia.com
Web Site: www.smymedia.com

Employees: 15
Year Founded: 1969

Agency Specializes In: Advertising, African-American Market, Broadcast, Business-To-Business, Cable T.V., Co-op Advertising, Consumer Marketing, Consumer Publications, Food Service, Hispanic Market, Media Buying Services, Medical Products, Newspaper, Outdoor, Over-50 Market, Pharmaceutical, Print, Radio, Real Estate, Restaurant, Retail, Strategic Planning/Research, T.V., Trade & Consumer Magazines

Approx. Annual Billings: $36,000,000

Breakdown of Gross Billings by Media: Cable T.V.: $3,600,000; Internet Adv.: $1,800,000; Mags.: $5,400,000; Network T.V.: $1,800,000; Newsp. & Mags.: $10,800,000; Radio & T.V.: $10,800,000; Strategic Planning/Research: $1,800,000

Gerry Grant *(Owner)*
Karen Sheridan *(Pres & Dir-Media Svcs)*
Gia Nguyen *(VP-Acctg & Mgr-MIS)*
Sheila Hollins *(Assoc Dir-Media)*

SOUND COMMUNICATIONS, INC.

149 W 36th St, New York, NY 10018
Tel.: (212) 489-1122
Fax: (212) 489-5214
E-Mail: steve@scommunications.com
Web Site: www.scommunications.com

E-Mail for Key Personnel:
President: steve@scommunications.com
Media Dir.: jill@scommunications.com

Employees: 15
Year Founded: 1987

Agency Specializes In: Bilingual Market, Broadcast, Business-To-Business, Cable T.V., Co-op Advertising, Communications, Consumer Marketing, Direct Response Marketing, Entertainment, Government/Political, Infomercials, New Product Development, Newspapers & Magazines, Out-of-Home Media, Outdoor, Print, Production, Publicity/Promotions, Radio, T.V.

Approx. Annual Billings: $25,000,000

Steven Sackler *(Pres)*
Chris Elser *(VP)*
Aj Jordan *(VP-Digital Media)*
John Sadowski *(Dir-Bus Dev)*
Jennifer Holmes *(Acct Exec)*
Kristen Aleo *(Media Buyer & Planner)*

SOUTHWEST MEDIA GROUP

2100 Ross Ave Ste 3000, Dallas, TX 75201
Tel.: (214) 561-5678
Fax: (214) 561-5640
E-Mail: info@swmediagroup.com
Web Site: www.swmediagroup.com

Employees: 62
Year Founded: 1995

National Agency Associations: 4A's

Agency Specializes In: Alternative Advertising, Branded Entertainment, Broadcast, Business-To-Business, Cable T.V., Co-op Advertising, Communications, Consumer Publications, Direct Response Marketing, Electronic Media, Entertainment, Experience Design, Fashion/Apparel, Guerilla Marketing, Hispanic Market, In-Store Advertising, Internet/Web Design, Magazines, Media Buying Services, Media Planning, Mobile Marketing, Newspaper, Newspapers & Magazines, Out-of-Home Media, Outdoor, Over-50 Market, Paid Searches, Planning & Consultation, Podcasting, Print, Radio, Restaurant, Retail, Sales Promotion, Search Engine Optimization, Sponsorship, Strategic Planning/Research, T.V., Teen Market, Trade & Consumer Magazines, Transportation, Travel & Tourism, Viral/Buzz/Word of Mouth, Web (Banner Ads, Pop-ups, etc.), Women's Market, Yellow Pages Advertising

Approx. Annual Billings: $195,000,000

Heather Tatarsky *(Grp Dir-Plng)*
Francisco Milian *(Dir-Plng)*
Kurt Schweitzer *(Dir-Media)*
Danielle Peters *(Mgr-Agency Mktg)*
Jill Cain *(Sr Strategist-Media Plng)*
Kimberly Long *(Media Buyer-Brdcst)*
Kim Kohler *(Chief Relationship Officer)*

Accounts:
At Home Digital, Media Planning & Buying, Strategy
Bank of Oklahoma Digital, Media Planning & Buying, Strategy
Dave & Buster's Inc.
Dillard's Media Planning & Buying, Strategy
Fiesta Restaurant Group, Inc. Media Buying, Media Planning, Pollo Tropical, Programmatic, Taco Cabana
Half Price Books, Records, Magazines, Inc. (Media Agency of Record) Buying, Media Strategy, Planning
The Parking Spot Digital, Media Planning & Buying, Strategy
Regis Corp. Digital, Magicuts, Media Planning & Buying, Pro-Cuts, SmartStyle, Strategy
Texas Health Resources Digital, Media Planning & Buying, Programmatic, Strategy
Texas Tourism Media Planning & Buying, Strategy

SPACETIME, INC.

35 E Wacker Dr Ste 3100, Chicago, IL 60601-2307
Tel.: (312) 425-0800
Fax: (312) 425-0808
E-Mail: rlampert@spacetimemedia.com
Web Site: www.spacetimemedia.com

E-Mail for Key Personnel:
President: rlampert@spacetimemedia.com

Employees: 14
Year Founded: 1994

Agency Specializes In: Broadcast, Business Publications, Business-To-Business, Cable T.V., Co-op Advertising, Consumer Marketing, Consumer Publications, Digital/Interactive, Education, Electronic Media, Event Planning & Marketing, Fashion/Apparel, Financial, Health Care Services, Hispanic Market, Magazines, Media Buying Services, Newspaper, Newspapers & Magazines, Out-of-Home Media, Outdoor, Planning & Consultation, Print, Radio, Retail, Sports Market, Strategic Planning/Research, Syndication, T.V., Trade & Consumer Magazines, Travel & Tourism

Approx. Annual Billings: $76,500,000

Breakdown of Gross Billings by Media: Bus. Publs.: $1,500,000; Internet Adv.: $45,000,000; Mags.: $3,000,000; Newsp.: $2,000,000; Outdoor: $4,000,000; Radio: $8,000,000; T.V.: $13,000,000

Robin Lampert *(Pres)*
Dick McCullough *(Exec VP)*
Lauren Lampert *(VP & Grp Dir-Media)*
Melissa Johnston *(Assoc Dir-Media)*
Melanie Ivanov *(Sr Mgr-Media)*
Bev Berni-Bernardo *(Office Mgr)*
Susanna Avila *(Mgr-Acctg)*

Accounts:
CNA
Optima
People's Gas
Roosevelt University
Ulta-Lit

SPARK COMMUNICATIONS

222 Merchandise Mart Plz Ste 550, Chicago, IL 60654-1032
Tel.: (312) 970-8400
Fax: (312) 970-8409
Web Site: www.sparksmg.com

Employees: 70

National Agency Associations: 4A's

Agency Specializes In: Digital/Interactive, Media Buying Services, Sponsorship, Strategic Planning/Research

Harold Dawson *(Mng Dir & Exec VP)*
Brent Lux *(Mng Dir & Exec VP)*
Marie Myszkowski *(Mng Dir & Exec VP)*

Shelby Saville *(Mng Dir & Exec VP)*
Scott Hess *(Exec VP & Dir-Human Intelligence)*
Eric Levin *(Sr VP & Grp Dir-Brand Content)*
Amy Engel *(Sr VP & Dir)*
Shaun Killeen *(Sr VP & Dir-Fin)*
Kelly Stetler *(VP & Media Dir)*
Laura Kleyweg *(VP & Dir-Media)*
Sean Ryan *(VP & Dir)*
Allison Shaffron *(VP & Dir)*
Jaclyn Sinclair *(VP & Dir)*
Kyle Jackson *(VP-Biddable Media)*
Steve Carlson *(Dir-Media)*
Donna Cimino *(Dir-Brdcst Buying)*
Nobelle de la Rosa *(Dir-Media)*
Abby DeMong *(Dir-Media)*
Lori Thompson *(Dir-Digital Strategy)*
Colette Trudeau *(Dir)*
Rachel Abbott *(Assoc Dir-Media)*
Brian Elrod *(Assoc Dir-Media)*
Allison Fennell *(Assoc Dir)*
Cody Gundrum *(Assoc Dir-Media)*
Haley Hayman *(Assoc Dir-Search)*
Kristina Holz *(Assoc Dir-Media)*
Rebecca Jones *(Assoc Dir-Media-Spark SMG)*
Stephanie Kelch *(Assoc Dir-Natl Brdcst Investment)*
Amanda Mollet *(Assoc Dir-Media)*
Blair Nugent *(Assoc Dir)*
Lindsay Poulton *(Assoc Dir-Res & Human Experience-Spark SMG)*
Michelle Silverblatt *(Assoc Dir-Media-LiquidThread)*
Ryan Stoer *(Assoc Dir-Media)*
David Turman *(Assoc Dir)*
Jessica Venard *(Assoc Dir-Media & Strategy)*
Elise Henry *(Office Mgr)*
Elizabeth Magnuson *(Mgr-Programmatic)*
Emily Beatty *(Supvr)*
Rachel Domeyer *(Supvr-Media)*
Jessica Faber *(Supvr-Strategy)*
Christine Griesmaier *(Supvr-Brand Reputation & Comm)*
Amanda Hinrichs *(Supvr-Out of Home Media)*
Diana Hoskins *(Supvr-Media)*
Brian Kim *(Supvr-Media)*
Julia Leddy *(Supvr-Media)*
Annette Liput *(Supvr)*
Michelle Maman *(Supvr-Media)*
Kate Moen *(Supvr-Media)*
Jackie Muench *(Supvr-Media Strategy)*
Erika Odioso *(Supvr-Media)*
Jacquie Pelusi *(Supvr-Media)*
Kristen Schneider *(Supvr-Video Investment)*
Gina Szafarczyk *(Supvr-Media)*
Erica Weaver *(Supvr-Media)*
Lindsey Dulla *(Assoc Media Buyer)*
Kevin Byrne *(Assoc Media Dir-Data & Analytics)*
Tracie Jasper *(Assoc Media Dir)*
Nate Knaeble *(Assoc Media Dir)*
Shannon Lowery *(Assoc Media Dir)*
Catie Pechiney *(Assoc Media Dir)*
Stacy Scheets *(Assoc Media Dir-Digital)*

Accounts:
AbbVie; Chicago, IL Media, Online & Offline Media Planning & Buying
Ace Hardware Corporation Digital, Media Planning & Buying
Aon Hewitt
Avis Budget Group Avis Car Rental, Media Planning & Buying
Conagra Digital, Media Planning & Buying
Dairy Queen Media Buying, Media Planning
Fifth Third Bancorp
Hanes
Hanon McKendry
Haribo of America, Inc. Brand Awareness, Digital Buying, Gold-Bears, Happy-Cola, Peaches, Raspberries, Smurfs, Sour Gold-Bears, Sour S'Ghetti, Twin Cherries
Heidelberg
Hyatt Hotels
iRobot Corp. Braava Floor Mopping Robot, Digital, Looj Gutter Cleaning Robot, Mira Pool Cleaning Robot, Roomba (Media Agency of Record), Scooba Floor Scrubbing Robot, Strategy, Traditional
Kao Brands Co. Inc. Biore, Curel, Digital, Jergens, Traditional Media Planning & Buying
Montana Office of Tourism Big Sky Country, Montana Department of Tourism, Pat Yourself in Montana, Simply Better Skiing, Travel Montana
New-Morgan Stanley Global Media
National Auto Parts Association Media
NBC Universal; 2005
Nickelodeon Direct Inc. Digital Media, Media Buying, Media Planning, Traditional Media
Northwestern Mutual (Media Agency)
Orbitz Worldwide, Inc. Media
Peugeot Peugeot 207CC
New-Providence Health & Services (Media Agency of Record)
Purina
Recreational Equipment Inc Media Buying & Planning
Red Lobster Media Buying
Sara Lee
Shure Microphones
Suzuki
Taco Bell Corp. Digital Media Buying, Digital Media Planning, Media Buying, Strategy
TGC, Inc
New-Valspar (Media Agency of Record) Media Buying, Media Planning, Media Strategy
Warby Parker
YETI Coolers (Agency of Record) Media Buying, Media Planning

SPECIALIZED MEDIA SERVICES, INC.

741 Kenilworth Ave Ste 204, Charlotte, NC 28204
Tel.: (704) 333-3111
Fax: (704) 332-7466
E-Mail: info@specializedmedia.net
Web Site: www.specializedmedia.net

E-Mail for Key Personnel:
President: darlene@specializedmedia.net

Employees: 9
Year Founded: 1982

Agency Specializes In: Broadcast, Cable T.V., Consumer Publications, Digital/Interactive, Electronic Media, Electronics, Entertainment, Government/Political, Media Buying Services, Media Planning, Newspaper, Out-of-Home Media, Outdoor, Planning & Consultation, Radio, Restaurant, Retail, Sales Promotion, Social Media, T.V.

Approx. Annual Billings: $15,000,000

Breakdown of Gross Billings by Media: Cable T.V.: 20%; Internet Adv.: 7%; Newsp.: 1%; Out-of-Home Media: 5%; Radio: 20%; T.V.: 47%

Rick Apfel *(Co-Owner)*
Darlene S. Jones *(Pres)*

Accounts:
Autobell; North & South Carolina, Norfolk, VA, Atlanta, GA. Car Washes; 2011
Greenman Eye Associates; Charlotte, NC Eye Care, Lasik Surgery; 2006
Hensley Fontana; Charlotte, NC Charlotte Restaurant Week; 2009
ICars; Charlotte, NC Used Cars; 2010
Ski & Tennis; Charlotte & Greensboro, NC; 1995
Wendy's Co-Ops 12 DMAs; 1982

SPOKE AGENCY

(Acquired by Dentsu Aegis Network Americas)

SPURRIER MEDIA GROUP

101 South 15th Ste 106, Richmond, VA 23219
Tel.: (804) 698-6333
Fax: (804) 698-6336
E-Mail: info@spurriermediagroup.com
Web Site: www.spurriermediagroup.com

Employees: 10
Year Founded: 1997

Agency Specializes In: Automotive, Broadcast, Business Publications, Business-To-Business, Cable T.V., Consumer Marketing, Consumer Publications, Digital/Interactive, Direct-to-Consumer, Education, Electronic Media, Financial, Government/Political, Health Care Services, Local Marketing, Magazines, Media Buying Services, Media Planning, Mobile Marketing, Multimedia, Newspaper, Newspapers & Magazines, Out-of-Home Media, Outdoor, Over-50 Market, Paid Searches, Print, Promotions, Radio, Recruitment, Search Engine Optimization, Seniors' Market, Social Media, Sponsorship, Strategic Planning/Research, T.V., Teen Market, Trade & Consumer Magazines, Transportation, Travel & Tourism, Web (Banner Ads, Pop-ups, etc.)

Approx. Annual Billings: $50,000,000

Breakdown of Gross Billings by Media: Co-op Adv.: 5%; Consulting: 5%; Event Mktg.: 10%; Network Radio: 10%; Network T.V.: 10%; Newsp.: 5%; Out-of-Home Media: 5%; Radio & T.V.: 30%; Strategic Planning/Research: 10%; Trade & Consumer Mags.: 10%

Ingrid Vax *(Pres & Dir-Bus Dev)*
Donna Spurrier *(CEO & Exec Strategist)*
Emily Baldridge *(Dir-Fin)*
Carol Davis *(Sr Mgr-Media)*
Aleece Hurt *(Office Mgr)*
Pemberton Carter *(Mgr-Fin)*
Debra Brame *(Media Planner & Media Buyer)*
Jennifer Walker *(Media Planner & Media Buyer)*
Angie Aleksa *(Buyer-Digital & Planner)*

Accounts:
Advanced Orthopedic Health Care; 2012
Brain Injury Association Nonprofit; 2012
C&F Bank Financial Services; 2014
CarFax Automotive; 2013
Federal Emergency Management Agency Flood Insurance; 2011
Identity Guard Identity Theft Services; 2007
JenCare Neighborhood Medical Centers Health Care; 2012
Melwood Nonprofit; 2010
n1 Health
Ortho On-Call Health Care; 2012
Petersburg Transit Authority State Government/Transportation Services; 2014
RMA Fertility Specialists
TowneBank
University of Richmond Education/Recruitment; 2004
US Department of Veterans Affairs Veterans Services; 2012
Virginia Department of Rail and Public Transportation Transportation Services; 2008
Virginia Department of Transportation Transportation Services; 2013
Virginia Housing Development Authority; Richmond, VA State Government /Housing; 2005
Virginia Museum of Fine Arts Tourism; 2010

STANDARD OUT-OF-HOME MEDIA NETWORK, INC.

27 W 731 Garys Mill Rd, Winfield, IL 60190
Tel.: (630) 668-9773
Fax: (630) 668-9859
E-Mail: richardblossfield@comcast.net

Employees: 5
Year Founded: 1981

Agency Specializes In: Out-of-Home Media

Media Buying Services

Approx. Annual Billings: $10,000,000

Breakdown of Gross Billings by Media: Out-of-Home Media: $10,000,000

Richard J. Blossfield *(Owner & Pres)*

THE STRATACT MEDIA GROUP LLC
PO Box 2573, Rockwall, TX 75087
Tel.: (214) 697-1482
Fax: (888) 805-5664
Web Site: www.stratactmedia.com

Agency Specializes In: Advertising, Aviation & Aerospace, Business-To-Business, Financial, Hispanic Market, Media Buying Services, Media Planning, Media Relations, Medical Products

Jana Doll *(Principal)*
Kenneth Hougaard *(Principal)*
Paul Solomons *(Principal)*

Accounts:
Black Lab Creative Advertising Services
Dallas Kids Expo Entertainment Services
Samsung Electronic Products Mfr & Distr
T-Mobile US Telecommunication Services

SWEENEY MEDIA MARKETING
3525 Del Mar Heights Rd Ste 665, San Diego, CA 92130
Tel.: (858) 756-3000
Fax: (858) 756-3230
E-Mail: maureen@sweeneymedia.com
Web Site: www.sweeneymedia.com

Employees: 4

Agency Specializes In: Media Buying Services

Maureen Sweeney *(Founder & Pres)*

Accounts:
Coles Carpets
Planned Parenthood

SWING MEDIA INC.
(Formerly Swing Media)
7421 Beverly Blvd Ste 13, Los Angeles, CA 90036
Tel.: (323) 936-3000
Fax: (323) 549-0008
E-Mail: info@swingmedia.com
Web Site: swingmediaoutdoor.com

Employees: 11
Year Founded: 1998

Agency Specializes In: Advertising, Advertising Specialties, Brand Development & Integration, Cable T.V., Entertainment, Exhibit/Trade Shows, Magazines, Media Buying Services, Mobile Marketing, Newspaper, Newspapers & Magazines, Outdoor, Print, Radio, T.V., Trade & Consumer Magazines, Web (Banner Ads, Pop-ups, etc.)

Jason Swing *(Founder & CEO)*
Majd Elias *(Pres)*
Mekela Swing *(Acct Grp Dir-OOH & Specialist-Fashion)*

Accounts:
Diesel
Guess
Hudson Jeans
Joe Jeans

TANGIBLE MEDIA, INC.
12 W 37th St Fl 2, New York, NY 10018-7391
Tel.: (212) 359-1440
Fax: (212) 649-1555
E-Mail: info@tangiblemedia.com
Web Site: www.tangiblemedia.com

E-Mail for Key Personnel:
President: mitchboden@tangiblemedia.com

Employees: 27
Year Founded: 1972

Agency Specializes In: Broadcast, Cable T.V., Children's Market, Digital/Interactive, Media Buying Services, Media Planning, Men's Market, Newspapers & Magazines, Outdoor, Print, Radio, Syndication, T.V., Teen Market, Tween Market, Women's Market

Approx. Annual Billings: $100,000,000

Breakdown of Gross Billings by Media: Cable T.V.: $40,000,000; Internet Adv.: $10,000,000; Network Radio: $2,000,000; Network T.V.: $13,000,000; Out-of-Home Media: $5,000,000; Print: $10,000,000; Spot Radio: $5,000,000; Spot T.V.: $10,000,000; Syndication: $5,000,000

Mitchell Boden *(Pres)*
Nadine Berg *(Exec VP)*
Phyllis Starsia *(Exec VP)*
Miriam Ko *(Controller)*
Kevin Christian *(Dir-Media)*
Zach Smith *(Assoc Dir-Media & Digital)*
Louis Guerrero *(Mgr-Social Media)*
Jenny Liu *(Sr Planner-Digital)*

TARGET ENTERPRISES, INC.
15260 Ventura Blvd Ste 1240, Sherman Oaks, CA 91403
Tel.: (818) 905-0005
Fax: (818) 905-1444
E-Mail: info@targetla.com
Web Site: www.targetla.com

E-Mail for Key Personnel:
President: dbienstock@targetla.com

Employees: 10
Year Founded: 1975

Agency Specializes In: Cable T.V., Government/Political, Media Buying Services, Outdoor, Planning & Consultation, Print, Radio, T.V.

David L. Bienstock *(Founder & CEO)*
Julie Iadanza *(Dir-Media)*
Shelia Lavin *(Mgr-Acctg)*

TARGETING GROUP
1800 W Loop S, Houston, TX 77027
Tel.: (713) 867-3242
Fax: (713) 869-6560
E-Mail: lkelley@targetinggroup.com
Web Site: www.targetinggroup.com

Employees: 35
Year Founded: 1995

National Agency Associations: AAF

Agency Specializes In: Bilingual Market, Broadcast, Business Publications, Business-To-Business, Cable T.V., Co-op Advertising, Communications, Consulting, Consumer Marketing, Consumer Publications, Digital/Interactive, Direct Response Marketing, Education, Electronic Media, Entertainment, Event Planning & Marketing, Exhibit/Trade Shows, Financial, Food Service, Health Care Services, High Technology, In-Store Advertising, Industrial, Infomercials, Information Technology, Internet/Web Design, Leisure, Local Marketing, Magazines, Media Buying Services, Newspaper, Newspapers & Magazines, Out-of-Home Media, Outdoor, Planning & Consultation, Point of Purchase, Print, Publicity/Promotions, Radio, Real Estate, Recruitment, Restaurant, Retail, Sports Market, Strategic Planning/Research, Syndication, T.V., Trade & Consumer Magazines, Travel & Tourism, Yellow Pages Advertising

Approx. Annual Billings: $200,000,000

Larry Kelley *(Pres)*
Kyle Allen *(Mng Dir)*

Accounts:
DriveTime Automotive Group; Phoenix, AZ Automotive Dealerships; 2005

TEC DIRECT MEDIA, INC.
134 N LaSalle St Ste 840, Chicago, IL 60602
Tel.: (312) 551-0832
Fax: (312) 551-0835
E-Mail: info@tec-direct.com
Web Site: www.tec-direct.com

Employees: 10
Year Founded: 2001

Agency Specializes In: Advertising, Advertising Specialties, African-American Market, Alternative Advertising, Broadcast, Cable T.V., Children's Market, College, Consulting, Consumer Marketing, Consumer Publications, Direct Response Marketing, Direct-to-Consumer, Electronic Media, Email, Entertainment, Gay & Lesbian Market, Guerilla Marketing, Infomercials, Internet/Web Design, Local Marketing, Logo & Package Design, Magazines, Media Buying Services, Media Planning, Mobile Marketing, New Product Development, Newspaper, Newspapers & Magazines, Out-of-Home Media, Outdoor, Over-50 Market, Pets , Planning & Consultation, Print, Production, Production (Ad, Film, Broadcast), Seniors' Market, Social Media, Syndication, T.V., Teen Market, Trade & Consumer Magazines, Tween Market, Urban Market, Web (Banner Ads, Pop-ups, etc.), Women's Market

Approx. Annual Billings: $10,000,000

Charles Fetterly *(Founder)*
Larisa Fetterly *(Sr VP)*
Cassandra Erdmier *(Media Planner & Media Buyer)*
Michael Michetti *(Planner)*

Accounts:
Anchor Bay Entertainment; 2010
AOLon; 2014
Big Machine; 2013
InGrooves; 2011
Magnolia Pictures; 2013
Rhino Entertainment; 2007
Sony Music; 2003
Universal Music Group; 2007
Warner Bros Records; 2008

TELEVISION AD GROUP
20436 Rte 19 Ste 360, Cranberry Township, PA 16066
Tel.: (212) 844-9057
Toll Free: (800) 588-2347
E-Mail: contact@televisionadgroup.com
Web Site: www.televisionadgroup.com

Agency Specializes In: Advertising, Internet/Web Design, Media Planning, Radio, T.V.

Bruce Koehler *(Pres)*
Tom Stoviak *(Acct Mgr-Natl)*

Accounts:
RX Recovery

Revlabs
Sqeeqee Inc
SurviveALL Expo
Thrifty Vac

TENNESSEE PRESS SERVICE, INC

435 Montbrook Ln, Knoxville, TN 37919
Tel.: (865) 584-5761
Fax: (865) 558-8687
E-Mail: bjarrell@tnpress.com
Web Site: www.tnpress.com

Employees: 15
Year Founded: 1947

National Agency Associations: AMA-NAMA

Agency Specializes In: Media Buying Services, Newspaper, Print

Approx. Annual Billings: $6,500,000

Breakdown of Gross Billings by Media: Newsp.: 93%; Worldwide Web Sites: 7%

Laurie Alford *(Controller-Bus)*
Greg Sherrill *(Exec Dir)*
David Wells *(Dir-Adv)*
Beth Elliott *(Mgr-Network Adv)*
Robyn Gentile *(Mgr-Member Svcs)*
Tessa Wildsmith *(Media Buyer)*
Earl Goodman *(Sr Media Buyer)*

Accounts:
Subway
U.S. Bank

TEXAS PRESS ASSOCIATION

718 W 5th St Ste 100, Austin, TX 78701-2799
Tel.: (512) 477-6755
Fax: (512) 477-6759
Toll Free: (800) 749-4793
Web Site: www.texaspress.com

Employees: 13
Year Founded: 1880

National Agency Associations: NAMA

Agency Specializes In: Media Buying Services, Newspaper, Planning & Consultation

Approx. Annual Billings: $4,000,000

Breakdown of Gross Billings by Media: Newsp.: $4,000,000

Donnis Baggett *(Exec VP)*
Stephanie Hearne *(Controller)*
Michael Hodges *(Exec Dir)*
Fred Anders *(Dir-IT)*
Ed Sterling *(Dir-Member Svcs)*
Diane Byram *(Mgr-Adv)*
Priscilla Loebenberg *(Mgr-Publ)*
Katie Butler *(Coord-Statewide Adv Network)*

Accounts:
Association of Electric Companies of Texas Advocacy Issues
Embarq
Mr. W. Fireworks
Texas Land Bank; 2000
Texas Secretary of State
Texas Utilities (TXU) Southwestern Public Services, Xcel Energy
TU Electric; TX Advocacy Issues
TXU/Lone Star Pipeline
Xcel Energy

THAYER MEDIA, INC.

9000 E Nichols Ave Ste 202, Centennial, CO 80112
Tel.: (303) 221-2221
Fax: (303) 221-3559
E-Mail: info@thayermedia.com
Web Site: www.thayermedia.com

E-Mail for Key Personnel:
Chairman: april.thayer@thayermedia.com

Employees: 7
Year Founded: 1993

Agency Specializes In: Advertising, Advertising Specialties, Alternative Advertising, Broadcast, Cable T.V., College, Consumer Goods, Consumer Marketing, Consumer Publications, Digital/Interactive, Electronic Media, Health Care Services, Hispanic Market, Local Marketing, Magazines, Media Buying Services, Media Planning, Medical Products, Multicultural, Newspaper, Newspapers & Magazines, Out-of-Home Media, Outdoor, Over-50 Market, Paid Searches, Planning & Consultation, Print, Radio, Real Estate, Regional, Restaurant, Retail, Seniors' Market, Strategic Planning/Research, T.V., Trade & Consumer Magazines, Travel & Tourism, Web (Banner Ads, Pop-ups, etc.)

Approx. Annual Billings: $16,943,000

April Thayer *(Founder & Pres)*
Chessie Little *(Dir-Acct & Media)*
Nicole Martinez *(Supvr-Vendor Billing & Planner)*
Penny Kirk *(Supvr-Vendor Billing)*
Michelle Watson *(Supvr-Media)*
Ali Jenkins *(Media Planner & Media Buyer)*

Accounts:
Cardel Homes; Denver, CO Homebuilder; 2011
Denver Cyberknife; Denver, CO Cancer Treatment; 2009
Forest City Stapleton; Denver, CO Residential Development; 2006
MoneyGram; Dallas, TX Money Transfer Services; 2002
Solterra; Denver, CO Residential Development; 2009
Trilipiderm; Jackson, WY Personal Care Products; 2011
Wayne Homes; Ohio Home Builder; 2009

THESEUS COMMUNICATIONS

67 West St, Brooklyn, NY 11222
Tel.: (646) 527-1727
Web Site: www.theseuscomms.com

Employees: 6
Year Founded: 2014

Agency Specializes In: Above-the-Line, Branded Entertainment, Broadcast, Cable T.V., Co-op Advertising, Consumer Publications, Custom Publishing, Digital/Interactive, Electronic Media, Game Integration, Guerilla Marketing, In-Store Advertising, Local Marketing, Magazines, Mobile Marketing, Multimedia, Newspaper, Newspapers & Magazines, Out-of-Home Media, Outdoor, Paid Searches, Print, RSS (Really Simple Syndication), Radio, Search Engine Optimization, Social Media, Sponsorship, Syndication, T.V., Trade & Consumer Magazines, Viral/Buzz/Word of Mouth, Web (Banner Ads, Pop-ups, etc.)

Approx. Annual Billings: $13,000,000

Charles Pinkerton *(Founder & Partner)*
Imir Leveque *(Dir-Strategy)*

Accounts:
Beau & Ro Sue's Hot Dogs
Prophet Consulting

TRADE MEDIA INTERNATIONAL CORP.

421 7th Ave, New York, NY 10001-2002
Tel.: (212) 564-3380
Fax: (212) 594-3841

Employees: 5
Year Founded: 1963

Agency Specializes In: Automotive, Aviation & Aerospace, Business Publications, Engineering, Food Service, High Technology, Industrial, Information Technology, International, Marine, Media Buying Services, Trade & Consumer Magazines

Approx. Annual Billings: $2,500,000

Breakdown of Gross Billings by Media: Foreign: $2,500,000

Corrie de Groot *(Owner)*

TRAFFICBUYER DIGITAL

215 Park Ave S Ste 1303, New York, NY 10003
Tel.: (212) 642-8460
E-Mail: info@trafficbuyer.com
Web Site: www.trafficbuyer.com

Agency Specializes In: Media Buying Services, Media Planning, Media Training

Andrew Wagner *(Founder & CEO)*
Emily Granger *(VP)*
Jason Dellaripa *(Dir-Search & Programmatic Media)*
Dan Horowitz *(Dir-Media Plng & Buying)*
Anna Rachminov *(Dir-Ops & Corp Strategy)*

Accounts:
Athena Health
Britain
Getsmart
ING Direct
NYC & Co.
Totally London

TRANSIT MEDIA GROUP

14067 Hoppe Dr, Rancho Cucamonga, CA 91739
Tel.: (909) 581-0887
Fax: (909) 581-1811
Toll Free: (866) 4-TMGROUP
E-Mail: info@tm-g.com
Web Site: www.tm-g.com

Employees: 10
Year Founded: 2003

Agency Specializes In: Advertising, Affiliate Marketing, Alternative Advertising, Arts, Automotive, Brand Development & Integration, Branded Entertainment, Co-op Advertising, Consumer Publications, Cosmetics, Direct-to-Consumer, Electronics, Entertainment, Experience Design, Food Service, Gay & Lesbian Market, Graphic Design, Guerilla Marketing, Health Care Services, Hispanic Market, Hospitality, Leisure, Local Marketing, Luxury Products, Men's Market, Mobile Marketing, Multicultural, New Product Development, New Technologies, Out-of-Home Media, Outdoor, Pharmaceutical, Point of Purchase, Production, Promotions, Publicity/Promotions, Radio, Regional, Sales Promotion, Social Marketing/Nonprofit, Sports Market, T.V., Transportation, Urban Market, Women's Market

Approx. Annual Billings: $2,700,000

Breakdown of Gross Billings by Media: Outdoor: 100%

Michael Scafuto *(CEO)*

Accounts:
Boot Barn Shoes; 2005
Budweiser; 2006
CMT Katrina Awareness; 2007
Ford Motors; 2005
Harley Davidson; 2006
KING OF THE CAGE / UFC Fighting; 2007
Redken Haircare Products; 2005
Standard Pacific Homes Homes; 2008
Symbolic Motors; San Diego, CA High End Automobiles; 2005
Vail Sky Resort Ski Resort; 2008

TRIBAL FUSION, INC.

2200 Powell St Ste 600, Emeryville, CA 94608
Tel.: (510) 250-5500
Fax: (510) 250-5700
Web Site: exponential.com/marketing-services/audience-engagement-solutions/tribal-fusion/

Employees: 175
Year Founded: 2000

Agency Specializes In: Digital/Interactive, Internet/Web Design

Randy Rains *(Reg VP-Sls)*
Mario Schiappacasse *(Gen Mgr-Tribal Fusion)*
Diane Johnson *(Dir-Sls-Southwest)*
John Pullen *(Dir-Tribal Fusion-West)*
Brandon Carrington *(Mgr-Sls)*

Accounts:
Microsoft MSN

TRILOGIC OUTDOOR, LLC

801 Brickell Ave 9th Fl, Miami, FL 33131
Tel.: (305) 347-5156
E-Mail: sales@trilogicoutdoor.com
Web Site: www.trilogicoutdoor.com

Employees: 13
Year Founded: 1992

Agency Specializes In: International, Out-of-Home Media, Outdoor

Breakdown of Gross Billings by Media: Out-of-Home Media: 50%; Outdoor: 50%

Alberto Garcia *(VP)*
Irene Fernandez *(Mgr-Mktg)*

Accounts:
Absolut Vodka
Anheuser Busch Bud Light, Stella Artois, Beck's, Presidente
Bacardi
BMW
Brown-Forman Tequila Herradura
BVK Media Dominican Republic
Chase Bank
Dewar's
Dominican Republic
FIAT
Geico
GNC
Heineken
Hennessy
Jackson Health System; Miami, FL Jackson Health Plan
Jaguar
Level Vodka
Miami Dolphins
Microsoft
Mini Cooper
NBC
ONE Coconut Water
Posterscope USA; Los Angeles, CA Honda
Red Bull
Remy
Stolichnaya
Sunglass Hut
T-Mobile
Tag Heuer
Tequila Desperados
Tequila El Capo
Tropicana
Verizon Wireless
Vitamin Water
Volkswagen
Wells Fargo

TRUE MEDIA

500 Business Loop 70 W, Columbia, MO 65203
Tel.: (573) 443-8783
Fax: (573) 443-8784
E-Mail: jmiller@truemediaservices.com
Web Site: www.truemediaservices.com

Employees: 40
Year Founded: 2005

Agency Specializes In: Agriculture, Broadcast, Business Publications, Business-To-Business, Cable T.V., College, Consumer Marketing, Digital/Interactive, Education, Electronic Media, Financial, Government/Political, Guerilla Marketing, International, Local Marketing, Magazines, Market Research, Media Buying Services, Media Planning, Media Relations, Mobile Marketing, Newspaper, Newspapers & Magazines, Out-of-Home Media, Outdoor, Paid Searches, Pets , Planning & Consultation, Print, Public Relations, Radio, Regional, Sports Market, Syndication, T.V., Teen Market, Transportation

Approx. Annual Billings: $30,000,000

Breakdown of Gross Billings by Media: Internet Adv.: $4,500,000; Mags.: $3,000,000; Newsp.: $4,500,000; Out-of-Home Media: $1,500,000; Radio & T.V.: $16,500,000

Jack Miller *(Pres-USA & Canada)*
Travis Ballenger *(VP-Client Dev)*
DW Cole *(VP-Client Dev)*
Jim Miles *(Controller-USA & Canada)*
Caroline Andriano *(Dir-HR-USA & Canada)*
Leon Halbert *(Assoc Dir-Media)*
Kelly Roberts *(Assoc Dir-Media & Digital)*
Chris Turnbull *(Assoc Dir-Media)*
Allison Freeman *(Acct Supvr)*
Eric Noll *(Specialist-Digital)*
Adam Ansoff *(Media Buyer)*
Annette Bruch *(Acct Planner)*
Gary Cianciosi *(Media Buyer)*
Jim Hall *(Media Buyer)*
Amy Nethero *(Acct Planner)*
Mike Stone *(Media Buyer-USA)*
Barb Throm *(Media Buyer-USA)*
Nadine Wessling *(Media Buyer)*
Nan Brown *(Sr Media Buyer-USA)*

Accounts:
Burger's Smokehouse; 2007
Landrum Company; 2007
MFA Oil Company; 2005
Nature's Variety (Media Agency of Record) Digital, Media Buying, Media Planning, Social Media, TV
Orscheln Farm & Home; 2008
Runnings Buying, Digital Media, Media Communication Strategy, Planning, Social Media
University of Missouri; 2005
Western Financial Group; 2007

TWO NIL

5501 Lincoln Blvd, Los Angeles, CA 90094
E-Mail: careers@twonil.com
Web Site: www.twonil.com/

Employees: 50
Year Founded: 2011

Agency Specializes In: Consumer Goods, Cosmetics, Digital/Interactive, Entertainment, Media Buying Services, Media Planning, Men's Market, Mobile Marketing, New Technologies, Outdoor, Planning & Consultation, Radio, Strategic Planning/Research, T.V., Transportation, Travel & Tourism, Women's Market

Mark Zamuner *(Founder & CEO)*
Shannon Adams *(VP & Assoc Dir-Broadcast)*
Vin Yam *(VP-Engrg)*
Heather Sullivan *(Sr Dir-Video Investment)*
Yvonne Lacey *(Dir-Media)*
Isaac Ortiz *(Dir-Strategy)*
Mike Rodriguez *(Dir-Strategy)*
Enrique Westrup *(Dir-Business Insights)*
Richard Case *(Assoc Dir-Media)*
Grace Dewson *(Strategist-Uber, Zillow, Acorns)*
Candace Callahan *(Media Buyer)*
Nick Steinauer *(Media Buyer)*

Accounts:
New-Dollar Shave Club
New-HauteLook
New-The Honest Company
New-NatureBox
New-PlayKids
New-Trip Advisor
New-Uber
New-Zillow

UM NY

(Formerly Universal McCann)
100 W 33rd St, New York, NY 10001
Tel.: (212) 883-4700
Web Site: www.umww.com

National Agency Associations: 4A's

Agency Specializes In: Sponsorship

Jon Stimmel *(Exec VP & Mng Partner-Integrated Investment)*
Colleen Campbell *(Mng Partner)*
Jason Gole *(Sr VP & Partner-Integrated Investment)*
Chris Portella *(Partner-Portfolio Mgmt & Sr VP)*
Chandon Jones *(Partner-Ad Ops & VP)*
Josh Mallalieu *(VP & Partner-Portfolio Mgmt)*
Tim Mosback *(Partner-Integrated Investment & VP)*
Justine Lyn *(Partner-Integrated Investment)*
David Mihalek *(Partner-Search & Social)*
Lara Miller *(Partner-Integrated Plng)*
Matt Smith *(Partner-Integrated Plng Team)*
Lauren Williams *(Partner-Portfolio Mgmt)*
Kasha Cacy *(Pres-US)*
Dani Benowitz *(Exec VP & Mng Dir-Integrated Investment)*
Sean Young *(Exec VP & Head-New Bus-Global)*
Stacey Stewart *(Sr VP & Grp Dir)*
Tim Hill *(Grp Partner-Integrated Investment & Sr VP)*
Rebecca Mills *(Grp Partner-Integrated Plng & Sr VP)*
Nicole Romanik *(Sr VP & Grp Partner-Integrated Investment)*
Kimberly Conon *(VP & Grp Dir-Media Res)*
Christine Potter *(VP & Dir-Global IMC-J3)*
Robert Allaire *(VP & Supvr)*
Steve Sanvicente *(VP & Supvr-Natl Brdcst Dept)*
David Tucker *(VP-Tech)*
Mindy Mizrahi *(Assoc Dir-Media)*
Sarah Brasell *(Sr Mgr-Integrated Investment)*
Chandra Jawalaprasad *(Sr Mgr)*
Rich Lee *(Sr Mgr-Integrated Investment)*
Marissa Ryder *(Sr Mgr-Portfolio Mgmt)*
Chris Clarke *(Mgr-Integrated Investment)*
Alysha DeNichilo *(Mgr-Integrated Investment)*
Lindsey Lehmann *(Mgr-Activation)*
Michael Lovisa *(Mgr-Decision Sciences)*
Matthew Merrill *(Mgr-Strategy)*
Brendan Murphy *(Mgr-Portfolio Mgmt)*
Bianca DeLeon Passaro *(Mgr-Investment)*

Carolina Portela *(Mgr-Integrated Investment)*
Ellen Shnayder *(Mgr-Investment-Natl Brdcst)*
Nicole Torres *(Mgr-Integrated Investment)*
Valerie Tovar *(Mgr-Portfolio Mgmt)*
Ann Kim *(Supvr-Media)*
Travis Kushner *(Supvr-Media)*
Andrea Valdes *(Supvr-Brdcst-Natl)*
Josh Bareno *(Planner-Digital Media)*
Thomas Perretta *(Coord-Production & Assoc Producer)*
Norman Greenfield *(Sr Assoc-Portfolio Mgmt)*
Bryan Vargas *(Sr Assoc-Integrated Investment)*

Accounts:
ABInBev
Aetna Consumer, Medicare & Individual Plan Divisions, Media
American Airlines
Applebee's Media
BASF Corporation
BMW Media Buying, Media Planning, Medium, Re:form
Branston Pickle Media Planning & Buying
Build-A-Bear Workshop, Inc. (Media Agency of Record) Analytics, Digital, Media Buying, Media Planning, Strategy
Cathay Pacific
Charles Schwab Media Planning & Buying
Chrysler Media Buying, Media Planning
Coca-Cola (Lead Media Agency - North America)
New-CVS Health Media
Edmunds.com Media Buying
Facebook Media Buying, Online, TV
General Motors Chevrolet
Hershey Co Global Media Buying, Global Media Planning
Hotwire, Inc. Digital Buying, Media Planning
Joe's Crab Shack Media Buying & Planning
Johnson & Johnson Band-Aids, Media Planning
Lockheed Martin Media
L'Oreal USA, Inc.(Agency of Record) Media Planning & Buying, Print, TV
MasterCard (U.S. Media) Media
New-McCormick (Media Agency of Record) Grill Mates, Integrated Planning, Lawry's, McCormick Gourmet, Media Buying, Old Bay, Stubb's, Zatarain's; 2015
Microsoft XBOX 360
Mini
Nationwide Insurance Digital, Media Buying, Planning & Buying, Traditional Media
New York State Lottery (Media Agency of Record)
Office Depot Media Buying, Media planning
S.C. Johnson
Six Flags Entertainment Corp.
Sony Corporation of America; New York, NY Bravia HDTV, Media Planning & Buying; 2002
Sony Entertainment
Subaru of America, Inc. Impreza WRX
United States Army
U.S. Postal Service Campaign: "Amazing Delivery", Media
Zurich Insurance

Branches

J3 New York
1400 Broadway, New York, NY 10018
(See Separate Listing)

UM LA
(Formerly Universal McCann)
5700 Wilshire Blvd Ste 450, Los Angeles, CA 90036
Tel.: (323) 900-7400
Web Site: www.umww.com

Year Founded: 2005

National Agency Associations: 4A's

Agency Specializes In: Advertising, Alternative Advertising, Brand Development & Integration, Broadcast, Business-To-Business, Cable T.V., Children's Market, Communications, Consumer Marketing, Consumer Publications, Direct-to-Consumer, Entertainment, Household Goods, In-Store Advertising, Integrated Marketing, Magazines, Media Buying Services, Media Planning, Mobile Marketing, Newspaper, Newspapers & Magazines, Out-of-Home Media, Outdoor, Planning & Consultation, Podcasting, Print, Production, Production (Print), RSS (Really Simple Syndication), Sponsorship, Strategic Planning/Research, Syndication, T.V., Technical Advertising, Transportation

Karen Hunt *(Exec VP & Mng Partner-Global)*
John-Paul Aguirre *(Mng Partner, Sr VP & Head-Strategy-SF)*
Kristin Jones *(Sr VP & Mng Partner-Global)*
Andrea Ebert *(Partner-Portfolio & Sr VP)*
Peter Lofaro *(Partner, VP & Portfolio Mgr-BMW)*
Daniel DiGiuseppe *(Partner-Integrated Plng)*
Jacob Gole *(Partner-Decision Sciences)*
Karen Stutenroth *(Exec VP & Dir-Fin)*
Jodi Schwartzmann *(Sr VP & Grp Dir-Brdcst)*
Monica Aguilar *(Dir-Media)*
Ronnie Landez *(Assoc Dir-Portfolio Mgmt)*
Erica Lee *(Assoc Dir-Media & Digital)*
Alicia Ostarello *(Assoc Dir-Media)*
Ryan Young *(Assoc Dir)*
Alexa Lefton *(Portfolio Mgr-Sony Pictures Entertainment & Supvr-Media)*
Kelly Johnson *(Mgr-Mktg & Consumer Comm)*
Lauren Miele *(Mgr-Media-Portfolio Mgmt)*
Leslie Toltzman *(Mgr-Portfolio Mgmt)*
Sarah Wong *(Mgr-Portfolio Mgmt)*
Samantha Yeung *(Mgr)*
Carolyn Loo *(Supvr-Digital Media)*
Tiffany Marsolek *(Supvr-Media & Digital Comm)*
Kendra Rousselet *(Supvr-Media-Digital)*
Stephanie Case *(Media Planner-Sony Pictures)*
Tony Chanes *(Sr Assoc-Portfolio Mgmt)*
Patrick Jurga *(Assoc-Portfolio Mgmt-Integrated Media Plng)*

Accounts:
Bumble Bee
California Science Center
ExxonMobil Media
The Fulfillment Fund
Northrop Grumman
Sony Pictures Entertainment Inc. Columbia/TriStar Home Video, Columbia/TriStar Pictures, GSN, Home Video Interactive, Sony Pictures TV
Sony Pictures Home Entertainment
Zicam

UM
(Formerly Universal McCann)
360 W Maple Rd, Birmingham, MI 48009
Tel.: (248) 203-8352
Web Site: www.umww.com/global

Year Founded: 2003

Agency Specializes In: Advertising, Sponsorship

Lora Mashione *(Partner-Investment & Sr VP)*
Jeff Alderman *(VP & Partner-Performance Digital-Search)*
Greg Bloom *(VP & Partner-Analytics)*
Jackie Popelier *(Partner-Portfolio Mgmt & VP)*
Shalise Tempest *(Partner-Acct Svcs & VP)*
Dan Fried *(Partner-UM Studios)*
Charlie van Becelaere *(Partner-Res)*
Kathy Doyle *(Sr VP & Dir-Local Brdcst)*
Gary Holme *(Sr VP & Dir-Creative)*
David Queamante *(Sr VP & Dir-Media)*
Jessica Ross *(Sr VP & Client Partner-Bus)*
Adria Ross *(VP & Assoc Dir-Media)*
Heidi Parmann *(VP-Partner Acct Svc)*
Tim Kennedy *(Sr Dir-Art)*
Stephen Crosbie *(Sr Mgr-Analytics)*
Lori Kenny *(Sr Mgr-Integrated Investment)*
Dave Metcalfe *(Sr Mgr-Ad Ops)*
Ritsa Papakonstantinou *(Sr Mgr)*
Lisa Ulrich *(Sr Mgr-Client Fin)*
Kathryn Caruso *(Acct Mgr)*
Ponti Ang *(Mgr-Paid Search & Social)*
Nancy Barber *(Mgr-Integrated Investment)*
Madeline Coyne *(Mgr-Decision Sciences)*
Margareta Farca *(Mgr-Client Fin)*
Cindy Gemmete *(Mgr-Portfolio Mgmt)*
Steve Germain *(Mgr-Portfolio Mgmt-Alfa Romeo & Maserati)*
Christina Haupt *(Mgr-Portfolio Mgmt)*
Megan Hebert *(Mgr-Portfolio Mgmt)*
Ingrid Hughes *(Mgr-Investment)*
Lindsay Krcaj *(Mgr-Decision Sciences)*
Nathan Lewalski *(Mgr)*
Ben Rice *(Mgr-Decision Sciences)*
Nancy Snider *(Mgr-Integrated Investment)*
Roma Varyani *(Mgr-Portfolio Mgmt)*
Shelby Veldman *(Mgr-Search Mktg)*
Nicole Ventimiglia *(Mgr-Integrated Investments)*
Andrew Copenhaver *(Supvr-Media Plng)*
Teresa Voss *(Supvr-Client Svcs)*
Jordan Biel *(Acct Exec)*
Kelsey Weidman *(Sr Planner-Digital Media)*
A.J. Fearn *(Sr Analyst-Performance Digital)*
Amanda Bitonti *(Media Planner)*
Michelle Burke *(Media Planner)*
Matt Craig *(Media Buyer)*
Cristina Jamo *(Analyst-Client Svcs)*
Kayla Rice *(Media Buyer)*
Anthony Borgia *(Assoc-Adv Ops)*
Blair Colson *(Assoc Media Planner)*
Kimberly Dolengowski *(Assoc-Strategy)*
Kelly Eldred *(Sr Portfolio Mgr)*
Brianna Fitzsimons *(Asst Media Planner)*
Lauren Forshee *(Sr Assoc-Portfolio Mgmt)*
Josh Kinney *(Sr Assoc-Portfolio Mgmt-Search)*
Kayla Knitter *(Assoc Portfolio Mgr)*
Meghan Lafferty *(Assoc-Portfolio Management)*
Kristen Maloney *(Sr Assoc-Portfolio Mgmt)*
Katherine Palmer *(Assoc-Acct Svcs)*
Brittany Ponius *(Sr Assoc)*
Brooke Sickmiller *(Sr Assoc-Fin)*
Nicole Smithson *(Assoc-Portfolio)*
Kate Tesch *(Asst Media Buyer)*
Andrea Zoia *(Assoc-Ad Ops)*
Jill Zoltowski *(Sr Media Buyer)*

Accounts:
Build-A-Bear Workshop, Inc. (Media Agency of Record) Analytics, Digital, Media Buying, Media Planning, Strategy
The Coca-Cola Company
Exxon Mobil Corporation
Johnson & Johnson
L'Oreal USA, Inc.
Microsoft Corporation
Sony Corporation of America
True Value Company US Media Buying
Yorkshire Building Society Media Buying, Media Planning

UNDERSCORE MARKETING LLC
920 Broadway, New York, NY 10010
Tel.: (212) 647-8436
Fax: (917) 591-8557
E-Mail: contactus@underscoremarketing.com
Web Site: www.underscoremarketing.com

Employees: 30
Year Founded: 2002

Agency Specializes In: Customer Relationship Management, Electronic Media, Integrated Marketing, Media Buying Services, Media Planning, Paid Searches, Podcasting, Search Engine Optimization, Sponsorship, Web (Banner Ads, Pop-ups, etc.)

Approx. Annual Billings: $11,700,000

Breakdown of Gross Billings by Media: Consumer Publs.: 85%; Newsp. & Mags.: 10%; Other: 5%

Tom Hespos *(Founder & Chief Media Officer)*
Lauren Boyer *(CEO & Partner)*
Chris Tuleya *(VP-eDR)*
Cindy Seebeck *(Sr Dir-Brand Adv)*
Rachel Garfield *(Dir-Brand Adv)*
Hemali Lakhani *(Assoc Dir)*
Susan Brock *(Supvr-Brand Adv)*
Robert Kolis *(Supvr-Media)*

UNIVERSAL MCCANN
(Name Changed to UM NY)

UNIVERSAL MEDIA INC.
4999 Louise Dr, Mechanicsburg, PA 17055
Tel.: (717) 795-7990
Fax: (717) 795-7998
E-Mail: info@umiusa.com
Web Site: www.umiusa.com

Employees: 35
Year Founded: 1986

Agency Specializes In: Media Buying Services, Sponsorship

Paul Michelle *(Sr VP-Mktg)*
Randall Young *(VP-Bus Dev, Media Buying & Buyer-TV)*
Shaun Baker *(Dir-Analytic Svcs)*
Cristi Casey *(Media Buyer)*
Danny Dierdorff *(Analyst-Digital Medial)*
Eileen Jessick *(Coord-Print)*
Patricia Piro *(Coord-Media)*
Rick Jones *(Founding Partner)*

Accounts:
Purchasing Management Association of South Bend

URBAN COMMUNICATIONS
275 Madison Ave 40th Fl, New York, NY 10016
Tel.: (212) 471-3200
Fax: (212) 471-3199
E-Mail: radiospecialist@urbancommunications.com
Web Site: www.urban-communications.com

Employees: 11
Year Founded: 1987

Agency Specializes In: Media Buying Services, Publicity/Promotions, Radio

Jay Levinson *(Founder & Co-CEO)*
Tracey Bowden *(VP-Media Svcs)*

Accounts:
HBO

U.S. INTERNATIONAL MEDIA
1201 Alta Loma Rd, Los Angeles, CA 90069-2403
Tel.: (310) 482-6700
Fax: (310) 482-6701
E-Mail: info@usintlmedia.com
Web Site: www.usintlmedia.com

Employees: 230
Year Founded: 2004

Agency Specializes In: African-American Market, Asian Market, Bilingual Market, Broadcast, Business-To-Business, Cable T.V., Consulting, Consumer Goods, Consumer Marketing, Consumer Publications, Digital/Interactive, Direct Response Marketing, Education, Electronic Media, Email, Entertainment, Financial, Food Service, Gay & Lesbian Market, Health Care Services, Hispanic Market, Household Goods, In-Store Advertising, Integrated Marketing, Internet/Web Design, Leisure, Local Marketing, Luxury Products, Magazines, Media Buying Services, Media Planning, Media Training, Mobile Marketing, Multicultural, Newspaper, Newspapers & Magazines, Out-of-Home Media, Outdoor, Paid Searches, Pharmaceutical, Planning & Consultation, Print, Promotions, RSS (Really Simple Syndication), Radio, Real Estate, Regional, Restaurant, Retail, Search Engine Optimization, Seniors' Market, Social Marketing/Nonprofit, Sports Market, Strategic Planning/Research, Sweepstakes, Syndication, T.V., Teen Market, Telemarketing, Trade & Consumer Magazines, Transportation, Travel & Tourism, Urban Market

Russell Zingale *(Pres)*
Dot DiLorenzo *(Exec VP & Dir-Plng)*
Alicia Nelson *(Exec VP-Brdcst Media)*
Jack Silver *(Exec VP)*
Kelly Wong *(Sr VP & Dir-Media)*
John Black *(Sr VP-Institutional Bus Dev Officer)*
Marguerite Brophy *(Sr VP-Natl Broadcast Activation)*
Mark Everly *(VP-Client Svcs)*
Sean Eldred *(Dir-Client Svc)*
Joyce Fairman *(Assoc Dir-Media)*
Elizabeth Kelly *(Assoc Dir-Media)*

Accounts:
New-Aruba
Century 21 Department Stores Media Planning & Buying
Empire State Building Media Planning & Buying
New-New American Funding (Media Agency) Media Buying, Media Planning
North Shore-LIJ Health System Media Planning & Buying
O'Charley's Inc. Media Planning & Buying
Palace Entertainment Media Planning & Buying

Branch

US International Media
52 Vanderbilt Ave Ste 501, New York, NY 10017
Tel.: (212) 986-0711
Web Site: www.usintlmedia.com

Agency Specializes In: Broadcast, Cable T.V., Digital/Interactive, Media Planning, Multicultural, Out-of-Home Media, Print, Sponsorship

Russell W. Zingale *(Pres)*
Steve Berger *(Pres-Patriot Media Grp)*
Dot Dilorenzo *(Exec VP & Dir-Plng)*
Alicia Nelson *(Exec VP & Dir-Media)*
Sixto Castillo *(Exec VP-Fin & Acctg)*
Sherry Catchpole *(Exec VP-Ops)*
Jack Silver *(Exec VP-Client Svcs)*
Leila Winick *(Exec VP-US Multicultural Grp)*
Janet Bescoby *(Sr VP & Dir-West Coast)*
Kelly Wong *(Sr VP & Dir-Media)*
Kristen Tucciarone *(Media Planner)*

Accounts:
Aruba Tourism Authority
Bethpage Federal Credit Union
Century 21 Department Stores
Empire State Building Observatory
North Shore-LIJ Health System Agency of Record, Marketing, Media, Media Planning & Buying, Strategic Development
Perdue Pharmaceuticals
WellPet Market Research, Marketing, Media Planning & Buying, Strategic Development

VALPO MEDIOS, INC.
3362 Baden Ct, Riverside, CA 92503
Tel.: (949) 525-3840
Fax: (949) 544-0416
E-Mail: info@valpomedios.com
Web Site: www.valpomedios.com

Employees: 1
Year Founded: 2007

Agency Specializes In: Advertising, Consulting, Hispanic Market, Media Buying Services, Media Planning, Multicultural

Approx. Annual Billings: $3,200,000

Breakdown of Gross Billings by Media: Brdcst.: 80%; Print: 20%

Patty Homo *(Owner)*

Accounts:
US Army Army Advantage Fund, National Awareness Media; 2010
US Census National 2010 Census; 2009

VALUECLICK, INC.
(Name Changed to Conversant, Inc.)

VARICK MEDIA MANAGEMENT
160 Varick St, New York, NY 10013
Tel.: (347) 709-8323
E-Mail: info@varickmm.com
Web Site: varickmm.com

National Agency Associations: 4A's

Paul Rostkowski *(Pres)*
Sandie Milberg *(Sr VP-Platform Sls)*
Jim Caruso *(VP-Product Strategy)*
Erik Thorson *(VP-Data & Engrg)*
Stephen Renz *(Dir-Product Mgmt)*
Tara Blackman *(Sr Acct Exec)*

WALSH ADVERTISING INC.
3823 Beech Ave, Baltimore, MD 21211-2223
Tel.: (410) 235-3035
Fax: (410) 235-7635
E-Mail: walsh.advertising@juno.com

Employees: 1
Year Founded: 1988

Agency Specializes In: Education, Media Buying Services, Newspaper, Newspapers & Magazines, Recruitment, Trade & Consumer Magazines

Revenue: $300,000

Nancy Walsh *(Principal-Walsh Designs)*

WENSTROM COMMUNICATIONS
2431 Estancia Blvd Bldg C, Clearwater, FL 33761
Tel.: (727) 791-1188
Fax: (727) 791-4976
E-Mail: steve@wenstrom.net
Web Site: www.wenstrom.net

Employees: 9
Year Founded: 1991

Agency Specializes In: Advertising, Advertising Specialties, Affiliate Marketing, Affluent Market, Alternative Advertising, Automotive, Broadcast, Cable T.V., Co-op Advertising, College, Consulting, Consumer Goods, Consumer Marketing, Consumer Publications, Cosmetics, Direct Response Marketing, Direct-to-Consumer, Electronic Media, Entertainment, Food Service, Government/Political, Health Care Services, Hispanic Market, In-Store Advertising, Legal Services, Leisure, Local Marketing, Luxury Products, Magazines, Market Research, Media Buying Services, Media Planning, Media Relations, Medical Products, Mobile Marketing, Multimedia,

Newspaper, Newspapers & Magazines, Out-of-Home Media, Outdoor, Over-50 Market, Paid Searches, Planning & Consultation, Print, Promotions, Radio, Recruitment, Regional, Restaurant, Search Engine Optimization, Social Media, Sponsorship, Sports Market, Strategic Planning/Research, Syndication, T.V., Trade & Consumer Magazines, Transportation, Urban Market, Web (Banner Ads, Pop-ups, etc.), Women's Market, Yellow Pages Advertising

Steve Wenstrom *(Pres)*
Lisa Ennis *(VP & Dir-Media)*
Judy A. Wendzel *(Office Mgr)*
Heidi Slayton *(Sr Specialist-Media)*

Accounts:
Applebee's
The Tampa Bay Rays

WF OF R, INC.

804 Moorefield Park Dr Ste 200, Richmond, VA 23236
Tel.: (804) 272-9810
Fax: (804) 379-0961
E-Mail: info@wfofr.com
Web Site: www.wfofr.com

Employees: 25
Year Founded: 1980

Agency Specializes In: Brand Development & Integration, Broadcast, Cable T.V., Consulting, Consumer Marketing, Consumer Publications, Electronic Media, Health Care Services, Local Marketing, Magazines, Media Buying Services, Outdoor, Print, Radio, Sponsorship, Strategic Planning/Research, Syndication, T.V., Trade & Consumer Magazines

Approx. Annual Billings: $160,000,000

Breakdown of Gross Billings by Media: Cable T.V.: 5%; Spot Radio: 5%; Spot T.V.: 90%

Jeff Jones *(Chm & CEO)*
Jinx Mancini *(VP-Media Svcs)*
Harry Moore *(VP-Acct Svcs)*
Stacey Beville *(Supvr-Media Buying)*
Audrey Bondurant *(Sr Media Buyer)*
Margaret Wilson *(Sr Media Buyer)*

Accounts:
Dunkin' Brands Group, Inc. Baskin-Robbins
Flex-All
McCain Foods
Nature Sweet
Visionworks of America, Inc.

YELLIN/MCCARRON, INC.

326 A St, Boston, MA 02210
Tel.: (617) 426-9211
Fax: (617) 426-7443
E-Mail: info@yellinmccarron.com
Web Site: www.yellinmccarron.com

Employees: 6
Year Founded: 1978

Agency Specializes In: Advertising, Alternative Advertising, Broadcast, Business-To-Business, Cable T.V., Co-op Advertising, Education, Electronic Media, Entertainment, Environmental, Financial, Gay & Lesbian Market, Government/Political, Guerilla Marketing, Health Care Services, Hispanic Market, International, Leisure, Local Marketing, Magazines, Media Buying Services, Media Planning, Men's Market, Mobile Marketing, Multicultural, Multimedia, Newspaper, Newspapers & Magazines, Out-of-Home Media, Outdoor, Paid Searches, Pets, Planning & Consultation, Podcasting, Print, Radio, Regional, Seniors' Market, Social Media, Sponsorship, Strategic Planning/Research, T.V., Trade & Consumer Magazines, Transportation, Travel & Tourism, Urban Market, Viral/Buzz/Word of Mouth, Women's Market

Approx. Annual Billings: $10,000,000

Breakdown of Gross Billings by Media: Out-of-Home Media: 15%; Print: 20%; Radio & T.V.: 50%; Worldwide Web Sites: 15%

Patricia E. Mccarron *(Pres)*
Melissa Noyes *(VP & Dir-Media)*
Terence Morrissey *(Controller)*
Adrienne Palen *(Specialist-Media)*
Hannah Roberts *(Asst Media Planner)*

Accounts:
Island Alliance; Boston, MA Tourism
Miltons Media Planning & Buying

ZENITH MEDIA SERVICES

299 W Houston St 10th Fl, New York, NY 10014-4806
Tel.: (212) 859-5100
Fax: (212) 727-9495
E-Mail: info@zenithoptimedia.com
Web Site: www.zenithoptimedia.com

Employees: 400
Year Founded: 1995

National Agency Associations: 4A's-ARF

Agency Specializes In: Communications, Digital/Interactive, Media Buying Services, Pets , Planning & Consultation

Breakdown of Gross Billings by Media: Internet Adv.: 9%; Mags.: 6%; Newsp.: 7%; Out-of-Home Media: 5%; Radio: 7%; T.V.: 66%

Suzy Herrell *(CTO)*
John Nitti *(Chief Investment Officer-Worldwide ZenithOptimedia)*
Elizabeth Fox *(Exec VP & Mng Dir-Local Activation)*
Helen Lin *(Exec VP & Mng Dir-Digital & Magazine Activation)*
Mac Hagel *(Exec VP & Acct Dir)*
Shelley Gayford *(Exec VP & Dir-Integrated Plng)*
Gary Feldman *(Sr VP-Strategy)*
Liam O'Neill *(Sr VP-Bus Dev-North America)*
Nina Blaustein *(VP & Dir-Brdcst Traffic Svcs)*
Andrea Duray *(VP & Assoc Dir-Media)*
Dana Kazerman *(VP & Assoc Dir-Brdcst)*
Christine Noto *(VP & Assoc Dir)*
Sofia Colantropo *(VP-Bus Dev)*
Ryan Davidson *(VP-Strategy)*
Jaclyn Goldhawk *(VP-Strategy)*
Katie Klein *(VP-Natl Video Activation)*
Joseph Pilla *(VP-Social Insights)*
Autumn Retzke *(VP-Strategy)*
Sandy Shahinian *(VP-Strategy)*
Vanessa Sherman *(VP-Strategy)*
Michael Siewert *(Dir-Brand Activation)*
Arupa Chandradath *(Assoc Dir-Media)*
Gwen Coursen *(Assoc Dir-Strategy)*
Christian Farrell *(Assoc Dir-Media)*
Jillian Marcella *(Assoc Dir-Plng)*
Marcela Maryniak *(Assoc Dir)*
Amanda Ritondo *(Assoc Dir)*
Lauren Seifert *(Assoc Dir-Media)*
Caroline Stenback *(Assoc Dir-Digital & Magazine Activation)*
Stephen Wraspir *(Assoc Dir-Media)*
Kari Brickowski *(Supvr)*
Tiffany Cheng *(Supvr-Strategy)*
Danielle Ciarlante *(Supvr-Integrated Media)*
Cynthia Goldman *(Supvr-Digital & Magazine)*
Tara Gottlieb *(Supvr-Media)*
Angelique Hernandez *(Supvr)*
Evan Hirschhorn *(Supvr-Digital & Print Activation)*
Robin Mackechnie *(Supvr-Comm Plng-Zenith GPE)*
Alexandra Rozzi *(Supvr-Digital & Magazine Activation)*
Derek Schaub *(Supvr-Local Activation-Print, Out-of-Home, Local Broadcast)*
Matt Ubriaco *(Supvr-Local Activation)*
Scott Walker *(Supvr)*
Sarah Josephs *(Strategist-Brand)*
Stamatina Demetis *(Media Planner-Digital)*
Kevin Levin *(Planner-Strategy)*
Carrie Lyden *(Planner-Comm)*
Daniel Pineda *(Media Planner-Strategy)*
Joanna Sapienza *(Media Buyer)*
Stephanie Singer *(Planner-Strategic, Media Ops & Res)*
Danielle Dookie *(Asst Media Planner)*
Ben Hui *(Reg Media Dir-Digital-APAC)*
Zachary Santucci *(Sr Media Planner)*

Accounts:
AstraZeneca Pharmaceuticals Pharmaceuticals; 2002
Aviva
The Boston Beer Company, Inc.; 2003
Caesars Entertainment Corporation Bally's Las Vegas, Caesars Palace Las Vegas, Campaign: "How to Poker", Flamingo Las Vegas, Harrah's Caesars Hotel & Casino, Harrah's Entertainment, Inc., Horseshoe Casino Hammond, Imperial Palace, Media Planning & Buying, Paris Las Vegas, Showboat Casino (Atlantic City)
Chase Media Buying
Dreyer's/Edy's/Haagen Dazs; 2005
Electrolux Major Appliances Media Buying, Media Planning, Media Strategy
Garnier; 2005
Georgia-Pacific Corporation Angel Soft, Brawny, Content, Dixie, Dixie Ultra, Georgia-Pacific Building Products, Media, Quilted Northern Bathroom Tissue, Sparkle; 2002
Gucci America, Inc. Alexander McQueen, Balenciaga, Beaute, Bedat & Co., Bottega Veneta, Boucheron, Gucci America, Inc., Gucci Apparel & Footwear, Gucci Eyewear, Gucci Fragrance, Gucci Handbags, Gucci Jewelry, Gucci Luggage, Gucci Watches, Sergio Rossi, Stella McCartney, Yves Saint Laurent
Gulf States Toyota; Houston, TX Media Planning & Buying
Harrah's Casino & Hotel
Jenny Craig; 2007
JPMorgan Chase Media; 2005
Kohl's Media Buying & Planning
Lexus; 1988
Maybelline NY; 2005
Merial; 2000
Nespresso USA, Inc.
Nestle Prepared Foods Company Buitoni, HOT POCKETS, Lean Pockets, Stouffer's, Stouffer's Corner Bistro
Nestle Purina PetCare Billboards, Cat Chow, Media; 2005
Nestle USA, Inc. Nestle Tidy Cats; 1984
Nestle Waters North America; 2004
Nintendo of America, Inc.
Ocean Spray; 2005
Puma; 2000
Reckitt Benckiser Inc. Air Fresh, Air Wick, Air Wick Freshmatic, Air Wick Lumin'Air, Air Wick Scented Oil, Brasso, Cattlemen's Barbeque Sauce, Clearasil, Clearasil Overnight Lotion, Cling Free, Delsym, Dettol, Disprin, Easy-Off, Easy-Off BAM, Electrasol, Finish, Finish Quantum, Frank's RedHot Cayenne Pepper Sauce, French's Classic Yellow Mustard, French's French Fried Onions, Glass Mate, Glass Plus, Jet-Dry, Lemsip, Lime-A-Way, Lysol, Lysol All Purpose, Lysol Disinfectants Wipes, Lysol Healthy Touch, Lysol Neutra Air, Lysol Toilet Bowl, Media, Mop & Glo, Mucinex, Mucinex Cold, Mucinex DM, Neutra Air, Old

Media Buying Services

English, Resolve, Resolve Bright & White, Resolve Max, Resolve Multi-Fabric Cleaner, Resolve Spray'n Wash, Rid-x, Sagrotan, Steradent, Vanish, Veet, Woolite, Woolite Rug Stick, d-Con
Richemont; 2005
Scion; 2003
SONIC Corporation Media; 2010
Toyota Broadcast, Media Buying, Out-Of-Home; 1979
Twentieth Century Fox Film Corporation American Horror Story: Freak Show, FX, FX Networks, FXM, FXNOW, FXX, Media Buying
Ubisoft
Verizon Communications Inc.
Verizon Wireless Media Buying; 1997
Zurich Financial; 2004

Branches

Zenith Media

1777 S Harrison St Ste 303, Denver, CO 80210
Tel.: (303) 758-4730
Fax: (303) 721-1788
E-Mail: linda.vorenkamp@zenithmedia-na.com
Web Site: www.zenithoptimedia.com

Employees: 4

National Agency Associations: 4A's

Agency Specializes In: Media Buying Services, Out-of-Home Media, Outdoor

Sebastien Danet *(CEO-France, Mng Partner-Belgium & Chm-Vivaki France)*
Gerry Boyle *(Chm-Asia Pacific & Mng Partner-Worldwide)*
Cindy Han *(Supvr-Local Brdcst)*
Kevin Ripp *(Supvr)*
Brenda Vyles *(Media Buyer)*
Nathan Weaver *(Media Buyer)*

Accounts:
Chase Bank
Lexus
Sonic Drive-In
Toyota

Zenith Media

2049 Century Park E Ste 1300, Los Angeles, CA 90067
Tel.: (310) 551-3500
Fax: (310) 551-4119
Web Site: www.zenithoptimedia.com

Employees: 35

National Agency Associations: 4A's

Agency Specializes In: Media Buying Services

Brian Dailey *(Exec VP-Strategy)*
Allen Singer *(Sr VP & Dir-Digital Ops)*
Michele Fukumoto *(Sr VP-Strategy)*
Marti Grimsley *(Sr VP-Local Activation)*
Dave Bosch *(VP-Strategy)*
Desiree Redding *(Supvr-Local Activation)*
Laura Zapakin *(Supvr-Media Plng & Strategy)*
Christopher McMahon *(Planner-Strategy)*
Megan Woram *(Media Buyer)*
Ashley Wall *(Asst Planner-Strategy)*

Accounts:
20th Century Fox Home Entertainment, Inc.
FX Networks American Horror Story: Freak Show, FX, FXM, FXNOW, FXX, Media Planning
The Hallmark Channel Media Buying
Jenny Craig Media Planning & Buying
Lexus
Toyota
Ubisoft Inc. Media Buying & Planning; 2008

Zenith Media

Ste 4 - 160A 222 Merchandise Mart Plz, Chicago, IL 60654
Tel.: (312) 980-7140
Fax: (312) 592-8404
Web Site: www.zenithoptimedia.com

Employees: 34
Year Founded: 1995

National Agency Associations: 4A's

Agency Specializes In: Advertising, Sponsorship

Patricia Kennedy *(Assoc Dir-Media)*
Rachel Coburn *(Media Buyer)*
Teresa Keeney *(Asst Media Planner-Strategy)*

Zenith Media

384 Northyards Blvd NW Ste 480, Atlanta, GA 30318
Tel.: (404) 601-4500
Fax: (404) 586-9465
E-Mail: info@zenithoptimedia.com
Web Site: www.zenithoptimedia.com

Employees: 8
Year Founded: 1995

National Agency Associations: 4A's

Mark Howley *(Grp Mng Dir-UK)*
Stefan Bardega *(Chief Digital Officer)*
Oliver Harwood-Matthews *(Chief Bus Dev Officer-UK & Worldwide)*
Stephen Farquhar *(Pres-VM1)*
Mark Waugh *(Mng Dir-Newcast-Global)*
John Nuding *(VP & Dir-Res)*
Lucy Divall *(Dir-Client Plng)*
Keith Gawla *(Supvr-Local Activation)*

Accounts:
L'Oreal
Nestle
Puma
Toyota

Moxie Interactive Inc.

384 Northyards Blvd. NW Ste 290, Atlanta, GA 30313-2440
(See Separate Listing)

ZenithOptimedia

2001 The Embarcadero, San Francisco, CA 94133
Tel.: (415) 293-2440
Fax: (415) 293-2613
Web Site: www.zenithoptimedia.com

Employees: 40

National Agency Associations: 4A's

Agency Specializes In: Sponsorship

Sharon Boddie *(Sr VP-Digital & Magazine Activation)*
Marti Wishengrad Grimsley *(Sr VP-Local Activation)*
Mike Salvo *(Sr VP-Strategy)*
Janet Langer *(VP & Assoc Dir-Local Brdcst-Zenith Media SRL)*
Ivan Tafur *(Assoc Dir-Strategy)*
Joella Duncan *(Supvr-Digital & Magazine Activation)*
India Lott *(Supvr-Strategy)*
Anna Leung *(Media Planner)*
Kelly O'Neill *(Planner-Strategy)*
Ashley Zwoyer *(Media Planner)*

Accounts:
Toyota Motor Corporation Scion

ZENITHOPTIMEDIA

24 Percy Street, London, W1T 2BS United Kingdom
Tel.: (44) 207 961 1000
Fax: (44) 207 961 1113
E-Mail: info@zenithoptimedia.com
Web Site: www.zenithoptimedia.com

Employees: 3,900
Year Founded: 1988

Agency Specializes In: Digital/Interactive, Direct Response Marketing, Media Buying Services, Planning & Consultation, Sports Market

Approx. Annual Billings: $15,500,000,000

Steve King *(CEO)*
Natalie Cummins *(Grp Mng Dir-UK)*
Mark Howley *(Grp Mng Dir)*
Ian Liddicoat *(CIO)*
Stefan Bardega *(Chief Digital Officer)*
Nico Guiridlian *(Mng Dir-Intl Clients APAC)*
Karl Guard *(Head-Strategy)*
Pedro Mona *(Head-Digital Tech & Data)*
David Norris *(Head-Strategy-Optimedia UK)*
Lucy Ogilvie *(Head-Strategy-Zenith Media)*
Tamina Plum *(Client Svcs Dir-Global)*
Elizabeth Brennan *(Dir-Plng)*
Tim Collison *(Dir-Comm-Global)*
Simon Fuller *(Client Partner)*

Accounts:
Asus Campaign: "Guitar", Campaign: "In Search of Incredible", Campaign: "Laptop", Campaign: "Micro", Campaign: "Peacocks", Campaign: "Piano", Campaign: "Record-Player"
Aviva Digital, Global Media
BBC Worldwide
Bel Group Media
BMW
Carling British Cider Media Planning & Buying
Comparethemarket.com Campaign: "Agent Maiya", Media Planning & Buying
Costa Coffee Campaign: "Little Moments of Fun", Costa Ice, Marketing, Media Planning & Buying, Multimedia
Creative Content UK "Education Programme", Media Buying, Media Planning
eOne Media planning & Buying
Gucci Group Media Planning & Buying UK, France & Asia
Harvey Nichols Group Limited Media
Hewlett Packard
HomeAway, Inc. Media Buying, Media Planning
Kayak Digital, Offline Media Planning & Buying
Lexus Media Buying, Media Planning
Mars Media Planning & Buying, Pedigree Dog Food, Pedigree Pet Accessories, Sheba Cat Food, Whiskas Cat Food
Maxxium UK Courvoisier, Famous Grouse, Jim Beam, Media, PR, Promotions, Sampling, Sourz, Stand-Out In-Store
Mirror Group Newspapers Daily Mirror, Media Planning & Buying, Sunday Mirror, The People
Molson Coors Above-The-Line, Carling Zest lager, Cobra, Coors Light, Digital, Media Buying, Media Planning
NatWest Media Planning & Buying
Nestle Buying, Planning
New Look
NSPCC Above-the-Line
Omega Pharma Media
Puma
Reckitt Benckiser Clearasil Ultra Blemish + Marks, Dettol, Durex, Lemsip, Lysol, Media Planning & Buying, Nurofen, Vanish, Woolite
The Royal Bank of Scotland Pay-Per-Click, Retail Digital Media Planning & Buying, SEO
Sanofi-Aventis
Superdrug Media Planning & Buying, The Perfume Shop

Svenska Cellulosa Aktiebolaget Media Buying, Media Communications, Media Planning
Swarovski
Totaljobs Group Media Planning & Buying, Offline
Toyota
Uniqlo
Unitech

United States

Zenith Media Services

299 W Houston St 10th Fl, New York, NY 10014-4806
(See Separate Listing)

ZenithOptimedia

299 W Houston St 11th Fl, New York, NY 10014
Tel.: (212) 859-5100
Fax: (212) 727-9495
E-Mail: tim.jones@zenithoptimedia.com
Web Site: www.zenithoptimedia.com

National Agency Associations: 4A's

Agency Specializes In: Digital/Interactive, Direct Response Marketing

Tim Jones *(Chm-North America)*
Barry Sands *(Mng Partner & Sr VP)*
Lisa Torres *(Pres-Multicultural)*
Helen Lin *(Exec VP & Mng Dir-Digital & Magazine Activation)*
Brian Dailey *(Exec VP-Strategy)*
Josh Martin *(Exec VP)*
Neil Vendetti *(Sr VP & Mng Dir-Natl Video Activation)*
Nakia Clements *(Sr VP & Dir-Strategy)*
Diego Fernandez-Martin *(Sr VP-Reg Client Svcs)*
Karen Finelli *(Sr VP-Digital & Magazine Activation)*
Jacky Flood *(Sr VP-Strategy)*
Larry Hunt *(Sr VP-Mktg & Sls)*
Michael Pierre *(Sr VP-Digital & Magazine Activation)*
Kim Iadevaia *(VP & Grp Dir-Branded Entertainment-Newcast)*
Jenna Goldstein *(VP & Acct Dir)*
Minyi Shih *(VP & Dir-Media)*
Krista Macchione *(VP & Acct Mgr)*
Anjan Haalder *(VP-Analytics)*
Robert Inferri *(VP-Strategy)*
Timothy Rafferty *(VP-Strategy)*
David Sandoval *(VP-Strategy)*
Kimberly Chau *(Head-Mobile Strategy & Analyst-Digital-Social Media)*
Anita Arcentales *(Dir-Media)*
Jacqueline Fernandez *(Dir-Branded Entertainment-Newcast)*
Samantha Andryc *(Assoc Dir-Strategy)*
Lauren Bryan *(Assoc Dir-Strategy)*
Samantha Burke *(Assoc Dir-Media & Strategy)*
Jeff Cohen *(Assoc Dir-Buying)*
Molly Enbysk *(Assoc Dir-Kering & Swarovski)*
Erin Flynn *(Assoc Dir-Strategy)*
Jason Fuchs *(Assoc Dir-Awareness-Global)*
Aleksandra Lacka *(Assoc Dir-Strategic Insights)*
Scott Lingor *(Assoc Dir-Strategy)*
Rachel Spiro Pierce *(Assoc Dir-Media-Digital)*
Carly Silverman *(Assoc Dir-Media-Strategy)*
Sheila Wiegand *(Assoc Dir-Natl Video)*
Andrea Wong *(Assoc Dir-Digital Strategy)*
Daniel Wittenberg *(Mgr-Branded Entertainment)*
Martha Calcutt *(Supvr-Strategy)*
Danielle Ciarlante *(Supvr-Integrated Media)*
Rose Fung *(Supvr-Digital Media)*
Cynthia Goldman *(Supvr-Digital & Magazine)*
Amanda Hellrung *(Supvr-Strategy)*
Joniece Hinds *(Supvr-Digital & Magazine Activation)*
Tiffany Ku *(Supvr-Integrated Plng)*
Racine Levy *(Supvr-Natl Video Activation)*
Kristin Misdom *(Supvr-Comm)*
Derek Schaub *(Supvr-Local Activation-Print, Out-of-Home & Local Brdcst)*
Jose Uruena *(Supvr-Digital Media)*
Luis Vazquez *(Supvr)*
Mackie Reilly *(Sr Planner-Comm)*
Eli Heath *(Sr Analyst-Digital)*
Beth Anderson *(Planner-Digital & Magazine Activation)*
Jackie Carey *(Media Planner)*
Jacqueline Kimball *(Media Buyer-Local Activation)*
Joseph Kiwanuka *(Media Planner)*
Alexandra Kushel *(Media Planner)*
Mabel Leung *(Planner-Digital Media)*
Ashley Mohr *(Media Planner)*
Nathan Rhule *(Media Planner)*
Jacqueline Smith *(Media Planner)*
Cindy Zheng *(Media Planner-Strategy)*
Christina Chen *(Asst Media Buyer)*

Accounts:
Coty (Global Media Agency of Record) Advertising, Digital Media, Print, Strategy, TV
Jenny Craig
L'Oreal USA, Inc. Garnier, Maybelline New York, Media Planning
Ocean Spray
Puma Media
Scion
Travelocity
Verizon Communications Inc.

Canada

ZenithOptimedia Canada Inc.

111 Queen St E Ste 200, Toronto, ON M5C 1S2 Canada
Tel.: (416) 925-7277
Fax: (416) 975-8208
Web Site: www.zenithoptimedia.com

Employees: 90
Year Founded: 1998

Agency Specializes In: Media Buying Services

Kristine Lyrette *(Pres)*
Veronica Holmes *(Pres-Digital)*
Dominik Majka *(VP & Head-Programmatic & Digital Ops)*
Michael Fielding *(VP & Grp Acct Dir)*
Sandra Hayes *(Grp Acct Dir)*
Jennifer Crosby *(Acct Dir-Integrated Plng)*
Janet Cheong *(Coord-Accts Receivable)*

Accounts:
Hyundai Auto Canada Corp. Media Buying
Purina

ZenithOptimedia Canada Inc.

3530 St-Laurent Boulevard Ste 400, Montreal, QC H2X 2V1 Canada
Tel.: (514) 288-8442
Fax: (514) 288-9886
E-Mail: info@publicis.ca
Web Site: www.zenithoptimedia.com

Employees: 20

Agency Specializes In: Media Buying Services

Adam Mills *(VP & Grp Acct Dir)*

Latin America

Optimedia

Armenia 1528, C1414 DKH Buenos Aires, Argentina
Tel.: (54) 11 5556 3500
Fax: (54) 11 5556 3500
Web Site: www.zenithoptimedia.com

Employees: 5

Agency Specializes In: Media Buying Services

Fernando Alvarez Colombres *(CEO)*
Ariel Sangiorgio *(Mng Dir)*
Philippe Seignol *(Head-Digital-Latin America)*

Balkans

ZenithOptimedia

Abacus Business Building, fl.5, 118, Bulgaria Blvd., Sofia, 1680 Bulgaria
Tel.: (359) 2 43 40 710
Fax: (359) 2 43 40 879
Web Site: www.zenithoptimedia.com

Employees: 12

Agency Specializes In: Media Buying Services

Dessislava Stoyanova *(Mng Dir)*
Dobrinka Stoykova *(Mng Dir)*
Vessela Apostolova *(Deputy Mng Dir)*
Lilyana Boneva *(Head-Digital)*
Ana Georgieva *(Dir-Media)*
Alexander Kochev *(Media Planner)*
Mina Zafirova *(Media Planner)*
Kinchi Gizdova *(Sr Media Planner)*
Maria Shtereva *(Sr Media Planner)*

ZenithOptimedia

Heinzelova 33, Zagreb, 10000 Croatia
Tel.: (385) 1 23 09 300
Fax: (385) 1 23 09 301
Web Site: www.zenithoptimedia.com

Employees: 15

Agency Specializes In: Media Buying Services

Marin Latkovic *(Mng Dir)*
Kresimir Djakovic *(Acct Dir)*
Morana Maric *(Mgr-Media)*

ZenithOptimedia

Dunajska 22, Ljubljana, 1000 Slovenia
Tel.: (386) 1 23 43 500
Fax: (386) 1 23 43 540
E-Mail: info@publicis.si
Web Site: www.zenithoptimedia.com

Employees: 12

Agency Specializes In: Media Buying Services

Natasa Smirnov *(Mng Dir)*
Jasna Spelko Smerajc *(COO)*

Belgium

ZenithOptimedia

Clos Lucien Outers 11-21, B-1160 Brussels, Belgium
Tel.: (32) 2 716 01 20
Fax: (32) 2 725 85 89
E-Mail: rik.provoost@zenithoptimedia.be
Web Site: www.zenithoptimedia.com

Employees: 45

Agency Specializes In: Media Buying Services

Rik Provoost *(Mng Dir)*
Karine Ysebrant de Lendonck *(COO)*
Davy Caluwaerts *(Deputy Mng Dir)*
Joke De Block *(Acct Dir)*
Fabienne Planche *(Dir-R&D, Productivity)*
Julie Wijns *(Dir-Audiovisual)*

Morgane Carly *(Acct Mgr)*
Claudia Charlier *(Media Planner-Strategic)*
Lahbib Meriem *(Buyer-Print)*

Accounts:
Nestle

France

ZenithOptimedia
68 bis rue Marjolin, CEDEX, 92685 Levallois-Perret, France
Tel.: (33) 1 58 74 86 00
Fax: (33) 1 58 74 88 88
E-Mail: daniel.saada@zenithoptimediafrance.com
Web Site: www.zenithoptimedia.com

Employees: 350

Agency Specializes In: Media Buying Services

Sebastien Danet *(CEO)*
Agnes Hautbois *(Deputy Dir Gen)*
Gautier Picquet *(COO & Dir-France Grp)*
Marie Delahays *(Acct Dir)*
Roberto Passariello *(Bus Dir-Luxe-Intl)*
Christelle Gimat *(Dir-Comml)*
Olivier Lagoutte *(Dir-Consulting & Strategies)*
Nicolas Schmitz *(Dir-Gen Trading)*

Accounts:
Anheuser-Busch InBev Media
L'Oreal Paris Campaign: "The Run Ny Season 1"

Greece

ZenithOptimedia
(Formerly Optimedia)
17B Kokkinaki Street, 145 61 Kifissia, Athens Greece
Tel.: (30) 21 0 623 5000
Fax: (30) 21 0 623 5009
E-Mail: andonis.passas@zenithoptimedia.gr
Web Site: www.zenithoptimedia.com

Employees: 20
Year Founded: 1996

Agency Specializes In: Media Buying Services

Andonis Passas *(CEO)*

Ireland

ZenithOptimedia
3rd Fl Molyneax House Bride St, Dublin, 8 Ireland
Tel.: (353) 1 4804444
Fax: (353) 1 480 4455
E-Mail: shay.keany@zenithoptimedia.ie
Web Site: www.zenithoptimedia.com

Employees: 18

Agency Specializes In: Media Buying Services

Shay Keany *(CEO)*
Claire Nardone *(Client Svcs Dir)*
Larry Neary *(Dir)*

Accounts:
Molson Coors Carling, Cobra, Coors Light, Media Buying, Media Planning

Italy

ZenithOptimedia Interactive Direct
5 via Cavriana, 20134 Milan, Italy
Tel.: (39) 02 75299 1
Fax: (39) 02 70121 957
Web Site: www.zenithoptimedia.com

Employees: 5

Agency Specializes In: Digital/Interactive, Media Buying Services

Vittorio Bonori *(CEO)*
Stefania De Stefani *(Dir-Natl & Intl Media)*
Simona Maiocchi *(Dir-Media)*
Terpsi Tsopanoglou *(Dir-Comm Plng)*
Benedetta Barbieri *(Mgr-Media)*
Antonio D. Casillo *(Mgr-Digital Media)*
Alberto Chiari *(Mgr-Media)*
Francesco Lucini *(Mgr-Digital Media)*
Giorgia Vanacore *(Mgr-Media)*
Valentina Vimercati *(Mgr-Media)*
Laura Strocchia *(Media Planner & Coord-Intl Media)*
Manuela Rufolo *(Planner-Digital Media)*

ZenithOptimedia
Piazza G Marconi 15, 00144 Rome, Italy
Tel.: (39) 06 32803730
Fax: (39) 06 324 2605
E-Mail: cvilla@zenithoptimedia.it
Web Site: www.zenithoptimedia.com/

Employees: 11

Agency Specializes In: Media Buying Services

Stefania De Stefani *(Dir-Natl & Intl Media)*
Benedetta Barbieri *(Mgr-Media)*
Paola Ingenito *(Mgr-Media)*
Giorgia Vanacore *(Mgr-Media)*
Giuliana Massari *(Sr Planner-Media)*

ZenithOptimedia
5 via Cavriana, 20134 Milan, Italy
Tel.: (39) 02 75299 1
Fax: (39) 02 701219 57
Web Site: www.zenithoptimedia.com

Employees: 90

Agency Specializes In: Media Buying Services

Vittorio Bonori *(Reg Chm-SE & MENA & CEO-ZenithOptimedia Italia)*
Sabrina Buono *(Head-Intl)*
Stefania De Stefani *(Dir-Natl & Intl Media)*
Simona Maiocchi *(Dir-Media)*
Silvia Presi *(Mgr & planner-Strategic)*
Benedetta Barbieri *(Mgr-Media)*
Antonio D. Casillo *(Mgr-Digital Media)*
Laura Giovenzana *(Mgr-Media)*
Roberto Galli *(Media Planner-Intl)*
Elena Zappi *(Media Planner)*

Middle East

Optimedia
Omar Saab Building Verdun Rachid Karame Street, 2nd Fl, Beirut, Lebanon
Mailing Address:
PO Box 6716, Beirut, Lebanon
Tel.: (961) 1 738 644
Fax: (961) 1 7475 75
Web Site: www.zenithoptimedia.com

Employees: 9

Agency Specializes In: Media Buying Services

Hala Badran *(Mgr-Ops)*
Rola Younes *(Mgr-Fin)*

Accounts:
Banque Libano-Francaise
Ferrero
TSC

Zenith Media
3 Chilason St, Ramat Gan, 52522 Israel
Tel.: (972) 3 755 2655
Fax: (972) 3 755 2655
E-Mail: a_hochdorf@zenithmedia.co.il
Web Site: www.zenithmedia.com

Employees: 20
Year Founded: 1995

Agency Specializes In: Media Buying Services

Alon Hochdorf *(CEO)*

Netherlands

ZenithOptimedia
Prof WH Keesomlaan 12, 1183 DG Amstelveen, Netherlands
Mailing Address:
PO Box 1860, 1000 BW Amsterdam, Netherlands
Tel.: (31) 20 46 22 760
Fax: (31) 20 46 22 761
E-Mail: info@zenithoptimedia.nl
Web Site: www.zenithoptimedia.nl

Employees: 78
Year Founded: 1990

Agency Specializes In: Media Buying Services

Linda Boks *(CEO)*
Jos Wolsing *(Chief Strategy Officer & Chief Innovation Officer)*
Kees De Groot *(Dir-Bus & Comm)*
Gerben Keizer *(Media Planner)*
Debbie Van Rhijn *(Media Planner)*
Jelke Overzet *(Sr Media Planner-ZenithOptimedia)*

Accounts:
All Secur
Audax Media
Garnier
Hasbro
Hyundai
Nestle USA
Puma

Poland

ZenithOptimedia
ul Domaniewska 42, 02-672 Warsaw, Poland
Tel.: (48) 22 345 21 40
Fax: (48) 22 345 21 41
Web Site: www.zenithoptimedia.pl

Employees: 136
Year Founded: 1994

Agency Specializes In: Media Buying Services

Krzysztof Sobieszek *(Chief Strategy Officer)*
Agnieszka Szysz *(Mng Dir-Optimedia)*
Katarzyna Pawlowska *(Grp Acct Dir)*
Norbert Kaluzny *(Acct Dir)*
Michal Siniarski *(Acct Dir)*
Maria Majka Kierzkowska *(Dir-Digital Solutions)*
Anna Marszalik-Kraszewska *(Dir-Res Dev)*
Karolina Perkowska *(Acct Mgr-Interactive)*
Lukasz Zalesny *(Mgr-Strategy)*

Accounts:
BANK PEKAO S.A.
British Airways
De Agostini
OBI

Sanofi-Synthelabo

Portugal

Optimedia
Rua Goncalves Zarco 14 R C, 1449-013 Lisbon, Portugal
Tel.: (351) 21 391 3400
Fax: (351) 21 391 3499
E-Mail: zo@zenithoptimedia.com.pt
Web Site: www.zenithoptimedia.com

Employees: 28

Agency Specializes In: Media Buying Services

Jose Ignacio Garcia *(CEO)*

Slovakia

Optimedia
Panonska cesta 7, 851 04 Bratislava, Slovakia
Tel.: (421) 2 32 15 35 01
Fax: (421) 2 32 15 35 04
E-Mail: zenithoptimedia@zenithoptimedia.sk
Web Site: www.zenithoptimedia.sk

Employees: 20
Year Founded: 2002

Agency Specializes In: Media Buying Services

Slavomir Herman *(Head-Acct Team)*
Alexander Matus *(Exec Dir)*
Romana Barcikova *(Acct Mgr-Media)*
Zdena Pethoova *(Acct Mgr)*
Sona Pollakova *(Acct Mgr)*
Peter Rac *(Acct Mgr)*
Silvia Takacova *(Mgr-Buying)*
Simona Mihalkova *(Acct Exec)*
Zuzana Secova *(Media Buyer-Print & Radio)*

Accounts:
Toyota

Scandinavia

Zenith Media
Solbjergvej 3 3 sal, 2000 Frederiksberg, N Denmark
Tel.: (45) 33 33 00 67
Fax: (45) 33 33 00 68
Web Site: www.zenithoptimedia.com

Employees: 15
Year Founded: 1998

Agency Specializes In: Media Buying Services

Stine Halberg *(Mng Dir-Scandinavia)*

ZenithOptimedia
Munkedamsveien 35, P.O. Box 1769, Vika, 0122 Oslo, Norway
Tel.: (47) 90 53 60 01
Fax: (47) 22 83 27 02
Web Site: www.zenithoptimedia.com

Employees: 10
Year Founded: 2002

Agency Specializes In: Media Buying Services, Sponsorship

Thomas Magnusen *(Bus Dir)*
Ingrid Holstad *(Dir-Fin-VivaKi Norway)*
Beate Nybakken *(Dir-Ops-VivaKi Norway)*
Linn Renate Brekke *(Planner-AdOps)*
Martin Grondahl *(Planner-Brdcst)*
Caroline Jansson *(Media Planner)*
Sandra Markovic *(Media Planner)*
Anne Lise Olsen *(Planner-Social Media)*
Gaelle David *(Client Svc Dir)*

Spain

Optimedia
Paseo de la Castellana 95 20th Floor, Torre Europa, 28046 Madrid, Spain
Tel.: (34) 91 308 0540
Fax: (34) 91 319 3567
E-Mail: fernando.rodriguez@optimedia.es
Web Site: www.optimedia.es

Employees: 160

Agency Specializes In: Media Buying Services

Miguel Esteban *(Chief Digital Officer)*
Cristina Rey Alvarez *(Gen Dir)*
Ana Arias *(Dir-Talent & Digital Transformation)*
Aurea Gomez *(Dir-Barcelona)*

Accounts:
Polo Ralph Lauren
Yoigo

Zenith Media
Puerta de Europa Paseo de la Castellana 216 Floor 16, 28046 Madrid, Spain
Tel.: (34) 91 567 4600
Fax: (34) 91 567 4611
Web Site: blogginzenith.zenithmedia.es/

Employees: 75
Year Founded: 1981

Agency Specializes In: Media Buying Services, Sponsorship

Jesus Gonzalez Parra *(Head-Plng)*
Candi Rodriguez *(Dir)*
Carmen Caballero *(Acct Mgr)*
Patricia Sierra Lopez *(Strategist-Multimedia & Planner)*
Patricia Carceller Garcia *(Media Planner-Online & Planner-Strategic)*
Maria Del Mar Nieto Sanchez *(Campaign Controller)*
Maria Jesus Lara Luque *(Sr Media Planner)*

Accounts:
Dia
Heineken
ING Direct
Indas
Jazztel
MAN
Osborne
Sanitas
Varma
Ya.com

Ukraine

ZenithOptimedia
Vorovskogo 24, Kiev, 01054 Ukraine
Tel.: (380) 44 492 9980
Fax: (380) 44 492 9981
Web Site: www.zenithoptimedia.com

Employees: 30

Agency Specializes In: Media Buying Services

Denis Storozhuk *(Mng Dir)*
Elena Grechenkova *(Grp Head-Plng)*
Vyacheslav Levchenko *(Dir-Media)*
Natalia Ostrovskaya *(Sr Media Planner)*

Accounts:
Raiffeisen Bank Aval Strategic Planning

United Kingdom

Blue 449
(Formerly Walker Media)
Middlesex House 34-42 Cleveland St, London, W1T 4JE United Kingdom
Tel.: (44) 20 7447 7500
Fax: (44) 20 7447 7501
E-Mail: info@blue449.com
Web Site: www.blue449.com

Employees: 100
Year Founded: 1998

Agency Specializes In: Media Buying Services

Phil Georgiadis *(Chm)*
Nicki Hare *(Vice Chm)*
Jon Horrocks *(Mng Partner, Head-Investment & Dir-Screen)*
Malcolm Boxall *(Mng Partner & Head-Screen)*
Samantha Hale *(Mng Partner)*
Chris Smith *(Mng Partner)*
Andras Vigh *(CEO-Global)*
James Shoreland *(Mng Dir-Global)*
Anthony Swede *(Head-Plng)*

Accounts:
New-BASF Campaign: "We Create Chemistry", Media Communications
Blue Cross
Boots Media Planning & Buying, Search
Butcher's Pet Care
Center Parcs Media Planning & Buying
Currys PC Media
David Lloyd Leisure Media Buying, Media Planning
Dixons Carphone Carphone Warehouse, Currys PC World, Dixons Travel, Geek Squad, Knowhow, Media
DSG International plc Currys, PC World
Dyson
Evening Standard Media Planning & Buying
FitFlop Media Planning & Buying
Fox TV
Freedrinks Above-the-Line, Digital, Media Planning & Buying, PPC, Paid Social, Press, SEO, Zeo
Halfords Group plc Digital, Media, Media Buying, Planning
Harveys Media Planning & Buying
The Independent Media Buying
Kayak Media, Media Buying, Media Planning
KFC
Ladbrokes
Multiyork
National Geographic Channel Media Planning & Buying
NFU Mutual Media
Njoy Media Planning & Buying
One & Only Resorts
PC World
Sony Entertainment Television Media Planning & Buying, Sony Movie Channel
Taco Bell
Tapi Media Buying, Media Planning
Travelex
Viking River Cruises
Vision Express

Meridian Outdoor Advertising
24 Percey Street, London, W1T 2BS United Kingdom
Tel.: (44) 207 961 1000
Fax: (44) 207 961 1001
E-Mail: info@meridianoutdoor.com
Web Site: www.zenithoptimedia.com

Employees: 25

Year Founded: 1990

Agency Specializes In: Media Buying Services, Out-of-Home Media, Outdoor

Tim Sapsford *(Mng Dir)*
Pannie Hopper *(Bus Dir)*

Accounts:
Audi
Hewlett Packard
Intercontinental Hotels
Lexus
Nokia
Procter & Gamble
Toyota

Australia

ZenithOptimedia
Bond Store 3 30 Windmill St, Walsh Bay, Sydney, NSW 2000 Australia
Tel.: (61) 2 9258 9100
Fax: (61) 2 9258 9101
Web Site: www.zenithoptimedia.com

Employees: 145
Year Founded: 1964

Agency Specializes In: Communications, Media Buying Services

Matt James *(CEO)*
Andrew Sherman *(COO)*
Aaron Michie *(Chief Innovation Officer)*
Ebru Barlak *(Supvr-Digital Media)*
Amzie Nash *(Supvr-Strategy)*

Accounts:
The Australian Media Strategy
Clarins Media Business
Heineken
Henkel Dry Idea, Media, Persil, Pritt, Schwarzkopf Haircare, Sellotape
Lion
5 Seeds Campaign: "The 5 Seeds Orchard", Media
NSW Government
Tooheys Extra Dry Campaign: "Repay Your Mouth"
Twentieth Century Fox Consumer Insights, Strategic Planning

China

ZenithOptimedia
1-4/F900 Huai Hai Zhong Road, Shanghai, China
Tel.: (86) 21 6133 8399
Fax: (86) 21 6133 8398
Web Site: www.zenithoptimedia.com.cn

Agency Specializes In: Media Buying Services

Mathias Chaillou *(Mng Dir)*
Mykim Chikli *(CEO-Greater China)*
SiewPing Lim *(CEO-China)*
Shann Biglione *(Head-Strategy-China)*
Krys Piotrowski *(Head-Bus Dev)*
Nancy Lan *(Gen Mgr-Newcast)*
Ruey Ku *(Grp Dir-Content Mktg)*

Accounts:
Bank of China Media Planning & Buying
Bausch & Lomb Digital, Media
Beijing Tourism Bureau
Burger King; China Media Buying & Planning; 2008
Carlsberg Media
Champagne Taittinger
China Citic Bank Corp
China Mobile
Coach Interactive Media
Daphne Group Aee, Daphne, Shoebox
HTC
Hyundai
Labatt USA LLC Sedrin Beer
Lee Kam Kee
Lexus
LVMH
Mengniu Media
Petronas
PPTV Media
PUMA
QQ.com
Reckitt Benckiser
Red Bull
Siemens
Swarovski
Toyota
Whirlpool
Wyeth
Zurich

Hong Kong

ZenithOptimedia
Room 1403-05 14/F 1063 Kings Road, Quarry Bay, China (Hong Kong)
Tel.: (852) 2236 9000
Fax: (852) 2250 9333
E-Mail: adanm.wong@zenithoptimedia.com.hk
Web Site: www.zenithoptimedia.com

Agency Specializes In: Media Buying Services

Philip Talbot *(CEO-Intl)*
Ada Wong *(Gen Mgr)*
Susan Chung *(Reg Dir-Digital)*
Russell Lai *(Chief Dir-Plng)*
Jackie Lau *(Reg Dir)*
Guy Abrahams *(Dir-Strategic Mktg-Worldwide)*
Fendi Tong *(Reg Acct Dir)*

Accounts:
Abbott Nutrition Ensure, Gain, Glucerna, Media Buying, PediaSure, Prenatal, Similac
China Mobile
Global Beauty International Management
SHK Finance Below the Line, Media

India

ZenithOptimedia India
90 D Sector 18 Udyog Vihar, Phase 4, Gurgaon, Haryana 122015 India
Tel.: (91) 124 389 3607
Fax: (91) 124 389 3185
Web Site: www.zenithoptimedia.com

Employees: 150

Agency Specializes In: Media Buying Services

Anupriya Acharya *(Grp CEO)*
Hari Krishnan *(Mng Dir)*
Tanushree Radhakrishnan *(Sr VP)*

Accounts:
AMD India Media
Aviva
Best Foods Media Planning & Buying
Bharti Walmart Media
New-Fitbit Campaign: "#Findyourfit", Media
Foodpanda.in Digital, Media Buying, Media Planning
Haier
Honda Siel Cars India Ltd Media
IDBI Bank
IFB Media
IMX
Incredible India
Indiahomes.com Digital, Media Buying, Media Planning
IPG
Jabong.com Media
Junglee Games Buying, Digital, Media, Media Planning, OOH, Print, TV
Micromax
Nestle
OLX Media
Paras Pharmaceuticals Media
Reckitt Benckiser Media, Strategy
Siemens Media
Thomas Cook
Toshiba Corporation Branding, Laptops, LCD TV & Home Appliances, Media
Uninor Media
Unitech Group
Viber Media Planning & Buying
Yatra.com Marketing, Media

New Zealand

ZenithOptimedia
The Textile Centre 4th Fl Kenwyn St, Parnell, Auckland, 1071 New Zealand
Tel.: (64) 9 914 6784
Fax: (64) 9 914 6785
Web Site: www.zenithoptimedia.com

Employees: 40

Agency Specializes In: Media Buying Services

Sophia Quilian *(Gen Mgr-New Zealand)*

Accounts:
Lion Co. Campaign: "Steinlager We Believe"
Merial Ancare Animal Health Products, Media
Nescafe
Nestle Purina
Panasonic Campaign: "Life Through a Lens Panasonic Lumix"
PUMA New Zealand

South East Asia

Optimedia Malaysia
Level 16, Menara Olympia, 8 Jalan Raja Chulan, 50200 Kuala Lumpur, Malaysia
Tel.: (60) 3 2059 2600
Fax: (60) 3 2032 3166

Wong Pi Yee *(Mng Dir)*
Ali Memon *(Gen Mgr)*
Yanyee Soon *(Media Planner)*

Accounts:
Inbisco Content Creation, Event Coverage, Social Activation, Social Media
IPC International Group Content Creation, Event Coverage, Social Activation, Social Media
OpenRice Media Agency of Record, Media Buying, Media Planning

Zenith Malaysia
9th Fl, Menara BRDB,, 285 Jalan Maarof, Bangsar, 59000 Kuala Lumpur, Malaysia
Tel.: (60) 3 2299 1222
Fax: (60) 3 2299 1223
E-Mail: geraldm@zenithmedia-asia.com
Web Site: www.zenithoptimedia.com

Agency Specializes In: Media Buying Services

Gerald Miranda *(CEO)*
Chan Yuet Wah *(Gen Mgr)*
Adeline Lester *(Sr Dir-Plng)*
Soo Ken *(Dir-Media Ops)*
T. Y. Lee *(Dir-Digital)*
Ann Ann Ng *(Dir-Plng)*
Firdaus Shah *(Dir-Plng)*

Accounts:
The Axiata Group Campaign: "Axiata Crew Takes

Media Buying Services

Off!"
Mango Campaign: "Mango Storms the Streets to Stores"

ZenithOptimedia

137 Telok Ayer Street #07-01, Singapore, 068602 Singapore
Tel.: (65) 6438 2722
Fax: (65) 6438 5955
Web Site: www.zenithoptimedia.com

Employees: 65

Agency Specializes In: Media Buying Services

Adam Hemming *(CEO)*
Helen Lee *(Mng Dir)*
Chris Harrison *(Chief Strategy Officer-Asia Pacific)*
Ernita Ariestanty *(CEO-Indonesia)*
Gareth Mulryan *(CEO-Southeast Asia)*
Jason Tan *(Gen Mgr)*
Felix Cartoux *(Dir-Corp Dev-Asia Pacific)*

Accounts:
Clarins Media
CozyCot.com
Datacraft
Frisco Digital Out-of-Home Campaign, Social Media; 2007
JobsDB Media
New-Nikon Singapore Media, Media Buying, Media Planning
New-Singapore Airlines Ltd. Global Media
Singapore Management University Media
Singapore Media Fusion
URA Marina Bay Series
Wildlife Reserves Singapore

Taiwan

ZenithOptimedia

8th Floor 6 Xinyi Road, Taipei, Taiwan
Tel.: (886) 2 2700 3151
Fax: (886) 2 2700 3171
Web Site: www.zenithoptimedia.com

Agency Specializes In: Media Buying Services

Robert Hsieh *(CEO-Taiwan)*
Sidney Lin *(Assoc Acct Mgr)*
Sampson Chen *(Acct Exec)*

Accounts:
Disney Movies Media; 2010
TC Bank

SALES PROMOTION AGENCIES

4INFO
177 Bovet Rd Ste 400, San Mateo, CA 94402-3120
Tel.: (650) 350-4800
E-Mail: contact@4info.net
Web Site: www.4info.com

Agency Specializes In: Advertising, Mobile Marketing

Tim Jenkins *(CEO)*
Chuck Moxley *(CMO)*
Ken Mallon *(Chief Product Officer)*
Brian Slitt *(VP-Sls & Bus Dev)*
Dennis Shresta *(Sr Dir-Bus Dev)*
Grafton Connor *(Acct Exec)*

Accounts:
Coors Brewing Company Brewery
Keystone Light Beer

THE A TEAM, LLC
1441 Broadway, New York, NY 10018
Tel.: (212) 239-0499
Fax: (212) 239-0575
E-Mail: acohen@ateampromo.com
Web Site: www.theateamagency.com/

E-Mail for Key Personnel:
President: acohen@ateampromo.com
Creative Dir.: dkonopka@ateampromo.com

Employees: 15
Year Founded: 1999

Agency Specializes In: Automotive, Brand Development & Integration, Business-To-Business, Collateral, Consumer Marketing, Corporate Identity, Direct Response Marketing, Event Planning & Marketing, Graphic Design, Logo & Package Design, Merchandising, Pets , Planning & Consultation, Point of Purchase, Point of Sale, Public Relations, Publicity/Promotions, Restaurant, Retail, Sales Promotion, Sports Market, Sweepstakes

Approx. Annual Billings: $5,500,000

Andy Cohen *(Pres & CEO)*
Dana Gross *(VP-Entertainment & Partnership Mktg)*
James Groom *(Creative Dir)*
Ilyssa Bernstein *(Acct Exec)*

Accounts:
American Express; New York, NY; 2003
Frederick Wildman; New York, NY Folonari Wines, Melini Wines
Glaceau; Queens, NY; 2006
Grand Marnier
Hill's Pet Products; Topeka, KS; 2007
Jaguar Cars; Irvine, CA; 1999
New York & Company
Ricola; Morris Plains, NJ; 2004
SCA; Philadelphia, PA Tena Serenity; 2006
SKYY Spirits; New York, NY Carolans, Cutty Sark, Midori; 1999
Tesoro
Vitamin Water

Branch

The A Team Promotional
8001 Irvine Ctr Dr 4th Fl, Irvine, CA 92618
Tel.: (949) 754-3022
Fax: (949) 754-4001
E-Mail: acohen@ateampromo.com
Web Site: www.theateamagency.com

Employees: 3
Year Founded: 2001

Agency Specializes In: Promotions

Dana Gross *(VP-Entertainment & Partnership Mktg)*
Bernard Lee *(VP)*
James Groom *(Dir-Creative)*
Ilyssa Bernstein *(Acct Exec)*

Accounts:
American Express
Duanereade
Grand Marnier
H-E-B
Hills
Jaguar
Ricola
Tesoro
Weight Watchers

A2G
(Formerly A Squared Group)
8000 Sunset Blvd Ste A301, Los Angeles, CA 90046
Tel.: (310) 432-2650
Fax: (310) 432-2655
E-Mail: info@a2g.la
Web Site: a2g.la/

Employees: 14
Year Founded: 2004

National Agency Associations: MAA-PMA-WOMMA

Agency Specializes In: Affluent Market, Brand Development & Integration, Branded Entertainment, Business-To-Business, Communications, Consumer Goods, Consumer Marketing, Corporate Identity, Cosmetics, Direct-to-Consumer, Entertainment, Event Planning & Marketing, Experience Design, Fashion/Apparel, Game Integration, Guerilla Marketing, Hospitality, Integrated Marketing, Luxury Products, Merchandising, Mobile Marketing, Planning & Consultation, Product Placement, Production, Promotions, Publicity/Promotions, Retail, Social Marketing/Nonprofit, Social Media, Sponsorship, Strategic Planning/Research, Viral/Buzz/Word of Mouth

Approx. Annual Billings: $14,000,000

Amy Cotteleer *(Pres & Chief Creative Officer)*
Rulivia Wong *(VP-Ops & Acct Svcs)*
Jennifer Truc *(Acct Mgr)*

Accounts:
Cosmopolitan Magazine Fun Fearless Male Awards
Gap; San Francisco, CA BabyGap, Co-branded Partnerships, Gap, Gap 1969 Denim, GapKids, Mobile Tours, Pop-up Retail, Product (RED)
Levi's Levi's Curve ID Campaign, PowerSlide Event, Size Does Matter Campaign
Motorola Solutions, Inc. Moto 6, Moto 7, Moto 8, Moto 9, Razr2 Launch
Nintendo 3DS, DS, Girlfriend's Guide to Gaming Program, Nintendo Wii
Old Navy Super Modelquin Search

ADEXCITE
(Acquired & Absorbed by Q1Media, Inc.)

ADKINS DESIGN VISUAL COMMUNICATIONS LLC
35 Corporate Drive Suite 1090, Trumbull, CT 06614
Tel.: (203) 375-2887
Fax: (203) 386-1203
E-Mail: tom@adkins-design.com
Web Site: www.sabinc.com

E-Mail for Key Personnel:
Creative Dir.: tom@sabinc.com

Employees: 2
Year Founded: 1985

Agency Specializes In: Advertising, Brand Development & Integration, Business Publications, Business-To-Business, Communications, Consulting, Consumer Marketing, Corporate Communications, Corporate Identity, Cosmetics, Digital/Interactive, Direct Response Marketing, Education, Event Planning & Marketing, Exhibit/Trade Shows, Financial, Graphic Design, In-Store Advertising, Industrial, Internet/Web Design, Investor Relations, Local Marketing, Logo & Package Design, Merchandising, Multimedia, Newspaper, Pharmaceutical, Point of Purchase, Point of Sale, Print, Production, Public Relations, Sales Promotion, Strategic Planning/Research, Technical Advertising, Trade & Consumer Magazines, Travel & Tourism, Yellow Pages Advertising

Approx. Annual Billings: $35,000,000

Thomas C. Adkins *(Dir-Art & Graphic Designer)*

Accounts:
Black & Decker
Dual-Lite; Cheshire, CT Emergency Lighting
Emhart Teknologies
Honeywell
IBM Corporation
Mondelez International, Inc.
Nestle Waters,NA
Panasonic
Pitney Bowes
Praxair, Inc.; Danbury, CT
Project Wet

AGIO BRAND SOLUTIONS
1315 Walnut St, Philadelphia, PA 19107
Tel.: (267) 480-7110
Web Site: www.agiobrandsolutions.com

Employees: 5
Year Founded: 2007

Agency Specializes In: Alternative Advertising, Exhibit/Trade Shows, Print, Production (Print), Promotions

Michael Tolassi *(Principal)*

Accounts:
Drexel University Promotional Products; 2011

ALCONE MARKETING GROUP
4 Studebaker, Irvine, CA 92618-2012
Tel.: (949) 770-4400
Fax: (949) 770-2957

Web Site: https://alcone.com/

Employees: 200
Year Founded: 1976

National Agency Associations: ISMI-PMA

Agency Specializes In: Consumer Marketing, Digital/Interactive, Email, Experience Design, Guerilla Marketing, Hispanic Market, Integrated Marketing, Internet/Web Design, Local Marketing, Mobile Marketing, Point of Purchase, Point of Sale, Promotions, Publicity/Promotions, Regional, Sales Promotion, Sponsorship, Sweepstakes, Viral/Buzz/Word of Mouth, Web (Banner Ads, Pop-ups, etc.)

Bill Hahn *(Pres & CEO)*
Teal Williams *(Mng Dir)*
Mike Leber *(CFO & COO)*
Monica Simoneaux *(VP & Acct Dir)*
Kevin Kleber *(VP-Ideas)*
Kevin Knight *(VP-Web Design & Dev)*
Claire Markovsky *(Acct Dir)*
Chad LaSota *(Assoc Dir-Creative)*
Maddy Bell *(Mgr-Bus Dev)*
Melissa Hickey *(Acct Supvr)*
Rachel Bartholomew *(Assoc Planner-Digital & Social Activation)*

Accounts:
Ateeco
Bel Brands USA, Inc.
Cadbury Adams
CalHFA
California State Lottery Commission
Chicken of the Sea
Dogswell Campaign: "Unleash the Happy"
Dreyer's Ice Cream
Ghiradelli Chocolate
Hasbro
Intuit
JM Smucker
Lg Mobile Phones
Nestle
Paramount Farms
Pernod Ricard USA
Safeway
Sun Products
Unilever HPC
The UPS Store
Visa, Inc.

Branches

Alcone Marketing Group
320 Post Rd, Darien, CT 06820-3605
Tel.: (203) 656-3555
Fax: (203) 656-4111
E-Mail: jim.zembruski@alconemarketing.com
Web Site: https://alcone.com/

Employees: 100
Year Founded: 1976

National Agency Associations: PMA

Agency Specializes In: Collateral, Consumer Marketing, Digital/Interactive, E-Commerce, Email, Event Planning & Marketing, Experience Design, Integrated Marketing, Internet/Web Design, Local Marketing, Mobile Marketing, Point of Purchase, Point of Sale, Promotions, Publicity/Promotions, Regional, Retail, Sales Promotion, Sponsorship, Viral/Buzz/Word of Mouth, Web (Banner Ads, Pop-ups, etc.)

Bill Hahn *(Pres & CEO)*
Mike Leber *(CFO & COO)*
Jim Zembruski *(Exec VP-Insights, Ideas & Analytics)*
Julianna Maston *(Sr Dir-Art)*
Andrea Kelly *(Acct Dir)*
Michael Alcutt *(Assoc Dir-Creative)*
Chad Lasota *(Assoc Dir-Creative)*
Annie Choe *(Mgr-Creative Svcs)*
Christen Spencer *(Acct Supvr)*
Alla Arutcheva *(Copywriter)*
Alyssa Mantilla *(Acct Coord)*

Accounts:
Hasbro
The Laughing Cow
Mondelez International, Inc.
Pernod Ricard USA Wyndham Estate
Treasury Wine Estates

Alcone Marketing Group
1596 Howard St, San Francisco, CA 94103
Tel.: (415) 856-8120
Web Site: https://alcone.com/

Agency Specializes In: Sales Promotion

Corey Saenz *(Sr VP-Client Engagement)*
Chris Gilman *(VP & Dir-Creative)*
Andrea Kelly *(Acct Dir)*
Claire Markovsky *(Acct Dir)*
Cory Deweese *(Dir-Client Engagement)*
Chad Lasota *(Assoc Dir-Creative)*
Carol Boyer *(Mgr-HR)*
Christen Spencer *(Acct Supvr)*
Chelsea Doyle *(Acct Exec)*

Accounts:
Ghiradelli
Intuit
Safeway
Visa

THE ALISON GROUP
2090 NE 163rd St, North Miami Beach, FL 33162
Tel.: (305) 893-6255
Fax: (305) 895-6271
E-Mail: info@alisongroup.com
Web Site: www.alisongroup.com

E-Mail for Key Personnel:
President: larry@alisongroup.com

Employees: 25
Year Founded: 1959

Agency Specializes In: Advertising Specialties, Automotive, Corporate Identity, Graphic Design, Internet/Web Design, Logo & Package Design, Package Design, Point of Purchase, Point of Sale, Print, Sales Promotion

Approx. Annual Billings: $12,000,000

Jeff Schweiger *(Owner)*
Larry J. Schweiger *(Pres)*
Tony Azar *(Reg VP)*
Ron Castro *(Dir-Intl & Reg Sls)*
Edwin Nunez *(Dir-Art)*
Charles Cerami *(Acct Exec)*
Lina Duque *(Acct Exec-LATAM & Caribbean Markets)*

Accounts:
Alaskan Amber
Carnival
Heineken
NCL
Nicklaus Golf
Pollo Tropical
Ryder
SKYY
Sony
Spyder
Toshiba
Toyota; 1996
Toyota
VIGO

ALL STAR INCENTIVE MARKETING, INC.
660 Main St, Fiskdale, MA 01518
Tel.: (508) 347-7672
Fax: (508) 347-5404
Toll Free: (800) 526-8629
E-Mail: info@incentiveusa.com
Web Site: www.incentiveusa.com

E-Mail for Key Personnel:
President: brian@incentiveusa.com

Employees: 50
Year Founded: 1970

Agency Specializes In: Advertising Specialties, Automotive, Brand Development & Integration, Business-To-Business, Communications, Consulting, Consumer Marketing, Corporate Communications, Corporate Identity, Direct Response Marketing, E-Commerce, Financial, Internet/Web Design, Logo & Package Design, Medical Products, Merchandising, Pharmaceutical, Planning & Consultation, Point of Purchase, Publicity/Promotions, Retail, Sales Promotion, Sweepstakes, Transportation

Approx. Annual Billings: $20,000,000

Brian Galonek *(CEO & VP-Sls)*
Ann Galonek *(CFO)*
Mike Balcom *(VP-Corp Identity Div)*
Heidi Chatfield *(VP-Mktg & New Bus Dev)*
Jeff Becotte *(Dir-IT)*
Edward Galonek, Jr. *(Exec Mgr-Bus Dev)*
Ryan Chase *(Mgr-Warehouse)*
Gary Galonek *(Mgr-Natl Sls-Gaming)*
Geri Labonte *(Mgr-HR)*

Accounts:
CertainTeed
Crown Imports
Foxwoods Resort Casino
Mohegan Sun
Serta
Simmons
Trump Plaza
Unum

ALL-WAYS ADVERTISING COMPANY
1442 Broad St, Bloomfield, NJ 07003
Tel.: (973) 338-0700
Fax: (973) 338-1410
Toll Free: (800) 255-9291
E-Mail: awa@awadv.com
Web Site: www.awadv.com

Employees: 210
Year Founded: 1969

Agency Specializes In: Advertising, Advertising Specialties, Brand Development & Integration, Catalogs, Consulting, Corporate Identity, Cosmetics, Direct Response Marketing, Event Planning & Marketing, Exhibit/Trade Shows, Financial, Graphic Design, Health Care Services, Hospitality, In-Store Advertising, Leisure, Logo & Package Design, Medical Products, Merchandising, New Product Development, Planning & Consultation, Point of Sale, Production, Promotions, Publicity/Promotions, Real Estate, Retail, Sales Promotion, Sweepstakes

Approx. Annual Billings: $25,000,000

Breakdown of Gross Billings by Media: Adv. Specialties: $21,000,000; In-Store Adv.: $2,000,000; Promos.: $2,000,000

Robert J. Lieberman *(Pres)*
Diane Dellefave *(VP)*
Ron Selling *(Dir-Creative)*
Susan Singer *(Mgr-Sls)*

David Cohen *(Sr Acct Exec)*
Jay Weinberg *(Acct Exec)*

AMP AGENCY (ALLOY MARKETING & PROMOTION)

77 N Washington St, Boston, MA 02114
Tel.: (617) 837-8100
Fax: (617) 723-2188
E-Mail: info@ampagency.com
Web Site: www.ampagency.com

Employees: 100
Year Founded: 1984

Agency Specializes In: Brand Development & Integration, Communications, Consumer Marketing, Event Planning & Marketing, Internet/Web Design, New Product Development, Publicity/Promotions, Sales Promotion, Sponsorship, Strategic Planning/Research

Gary Colen *(CEO)*
Matt Jacobs *(Mng Dir & VP)*
Joel Breen *(Sr VP-ECommerce)*
Robyne Tanner *(VP-Fin & Controller)*
Rich Grogan *(VP-Measurement & Analytics)*
Michael Mish *(VP-Bus Dev)*
Nicole Peterson *(VP-Production)*
Elaine Tocci *(VP-Media Svcs)*
Liz Dorrance *(Acct Dir)*
Sarah Wickman *(Acct Supvr)*
Marykate Desimone *(Sr Acct Exec)*
Shannon Murphy *(Sr Acct Exec)*
Nicole Merritt *(Acct Exec)*
Devon Wescott *(Assoc Acct Exec)*
Jaclyn Gaughan *(Sr Media Planner)*

Accounts:
360 Vodka
Ansell; Red Bank, NJ LifeStyles; 2007
ARAMARK
AXE
Bad Martha Brewing Company Go-to-Market Strategy, Labels, Package Design, Website
Burt's Bees
Elsevier (Agency of Record) Netter Anatomy
Food Bank For New York City
Hasbro Analytics, Creative, Digital Strategy, Monopoly, My Little Pony, Paid Search, Playskool, Search, Search Engine Optimization, Transformers
Heineken
HTC
IHP
John Hancock
LexisNexis U.S. Legal Markets Business Unit (Media Agency of Record)
LifeStyles Condoms SKYN
L'Oreal USA, Inc. Maybelline
Marriott Resorts
New Balance
NFL Players Association
Rally Labs Blowfish, Integrated Marketing, Offline, Online
Rock Coast Media
Samsung
Simon Property Group
Squaw Valley USA
UNO's Pizzeria & Grill (Agency of Record)
U.S. Cellular
Verizon Wireless
The Wall Street Journal

Branch

AMP Agency

317 Madison Ave Ste 1700, New York, NY 10010
Tel.: (617) 723-8929
Web Site: www.ampagency.com

Year Founded: 2013

Agency Specializes In: Advertising, Brand Development & Integration, Digital/Interactive, Internet/Web Design, Print, Public Relations, Social Media

Erica Melia *(Sr VP-Acct Mgmt)*
Graham Nelson *(Sr VP-Strategy)*
Matt Jacobs *(Mng Dir-New York & VP)*
Elaine Tocci *(VP-Media)*
Colin Booth *(Dir-Creative)*

Accounts:
Rally Labs

ANSIRA

(Formerly NSI Marketing Services/CoAMS)
35 East Wacker Dr Ste 1100, Chicago, IL 60601
Tel.: (312) 243-2667
Fax: (312) 235-0565
Web Site: www.ansira.com

Employees: 75
Year Founded: 1982

Agency Specializes In: Advertising Specialties, Agriculture, Automotive, Co-op Advertising, Collateral, Consulting, High Technology, Information Technology, Merchandising, Multimedia, Point of Purchase, Point of Sale, Publicity/Promotions, Retail, Sales Promotion

Sammy Mynes *(VP-Client Svcs)*
T. J. North *(VP-Client Partnership)*
Karlyn Bentley *(Asst VP-Client Partnership)*
Rob Newinski *(Sr Acct Dir)*
Katie Costello *(Supvr-Digital Media)*
Laura Cooling *(Acct Exec)*
Anne Rakowiecki *(Acct Rep)*
Chloe Olson *(Sr Acct Rep)*
Jessica Small *(Sr Acct Rep)*

Accounts:
Bass Pro Shops
Benjamin Moore Paints
BMW
GE Lighting
HP
IBM
Microsoft
Rolex

APPLE ROCK

7602 Business Park Dr, Greensboro, NC 27409
Tel.: (336) 232-4800
Fax: (336) 217-2750
Toll Free: (800) 478-2324
E-Mail: salesconsultants@applerock.com
Web Site: www.applerock.com

E-Mail for Key Personnel:
President: eric.burg@applerock.com

Employees: 50
Year Founded: 1988

Agency Specializes In: Exhibit/Trade Shows

Approx. Annual Billings: $8,000,000

Breakdown of Gross Billings by Media: D.M.: $400,000; Other: $7,600,000

Eric Burg *(Owner)*
Randy Neese *(VP-Fin)*
John Ognosky *(VP-Acct Svcs)*
Diane Rowell *(VP-Ops)*
Patricia Garner *(Dir-Ops & Mgr-Safety)*
Jonathan Hackler *(Dir-Creative)*
Andrea Harris *(Dir-Bus Dev)*
Denise Lineberry *(Dir-Mktg)*
Kathryn Mittelstadt *(Dir-New Bus Dev)*
Lori Chester *(Acct Exec)*

Accounts:
Advanced L&E
Healthy Living
HSBC
MDI

ARC WORLDWIDE

35 W Wacker Dr 15th Fl, Chicago, IL 60601
Tel.: (312) 220-3200
Fax: (312) 220-1995
Web Site: www.arcww.com

E-Mail for Key Personnel:
President: Rich.Stoddart@arcww.com

Employees: 1,100
Year Founded: 2004

National Agency Associations: 4A's-CSPA-DMA

Agency Specializes In: Digital/Interactive, Direct Response Marketing, Event Planning & Marketing, In-Store Advertising, Internet/Web Design, Logo & Package Design, Point of Purchase, Point of Sale, Retail, Sales Promotion, Sponsorship, Sports Market, Strategic Planning/Research, Sweepstakes, Telemarketing

Bob Raidt *(Pres)*
Ian Thomas *(Mng Partner)*
Jim Carlton *(Exec VP & Mng Dir-Creative)*
Nick Jones *(Exec VP & Head-Retail Practice)*
Karuna Rawal *(Exec VP & Bus Dir)*
Lisa Gillis *(Exec VP & Dir-Digital Practice)*
Brad Black *(Sr VP & Acct Dir-Global)*
Brendan Nash *(Sr VP & Creative Dir)*
April Carlisle *(Sr VP-Global Shopper Mktg)*
Marie Roche *(VP)*
Laura Dauley *(Dir-Creative)*
Molly Garris *(Dir-Digital Strategy)*
Chad Ingram *(Dir-Creative)*
Alma Klein *(Dir-Creative-Concepting)*
Jacqueline Lane *(Dir-Strategy)*
Michael McMillen *(Dir-Creative)*
John Menefee *(Dir-Creative)*
Daron Mitchell *(Dir-Art)*
Casey Diehl *(Assoc Dir-Creative)*
Kaila Dunn *(Assoc Dir-Creative)*
Maria Jose Guirados *(Assoc Dir-Creative)*
Anna Rudy *(Assoc Dir-Creative)*
Amy Gunderson *(Acct Supvr)*
Megan Hague *(Acct Supvr-P&G Fabric Care & Household Care)*
Lani Chevlin *(Sr Acct Exec)*
Alyce Iwanaga *(Sr Acct Exec-Alcon Labs)*
Ian C. Forrester *(Acct Exec)*
Connor McShane *(Sr Art Dir)*

Accounts:
Chicago Shakespeare Theater Campaign: "Will and George Come to Life"
Coca-Cola North America
Comcast
Intel Campaign: "Get in the Mix with NE-YO"
Mcdonald's Campaign: "You Want Mcdonald's Fries With That"
Millercoors Campaign: "Call of the Cup", Campaign: "Can Hunt", Campaign: "Canhole", Campaign: "I Am Rich", Creative, Digital, Foster's, Keystone Light, Miller High Life, Molson Canadian, Print Advertising, Social Media, Sparks, Television
Nestle Purina Campaign: "Great", Inside Every Good Dog Is A Great Dog
The Procter & Gamble Company Campaign: "Beautiful Hair Whatever the Weather", E-Commerce, Marketing
United Airlines
Walgreen Co.; Deerfield, IL Campaign: "Walk With Walgreens", Cause Marketing, Way to Well
Whirlpool Campaign: "Faces of Dependability", Maytag

North America

Arc Worldwide, North America
35 W Wacker 15th Fl, Chicago, IL 60601
Tel.: (312) 220-3200
Fax: (312) 220-6212
Web Site: www.arcww.com

National Agency Associations: PMA

Karuna Rawal *(Exec VP, Head-Plng-Global & Bus Dir)*
Brad Black *(Sr VP & Acct Dir-Global)*
Andrew Browning *(Sr VP-Dir Database Mktg & CRM)*
April Carlisle *(Sr VP-Global Shopper Mktg)*
Nora McGillicuddy *(VP & Acct Dir)*
Julie Rothweiler *(VP & Acct Dir)*
Patrick McDowell *(VP & Dir-Mktg Ops)*
Maria Rentzelos *(VP & Dir-Digital Solutions)*
Kim Sharon *(Acct Dir)*
Jeff Falcon *(Dir-Bus Analysis)*
Kathleen Finn Bell *(Mgr-Database Mktg)*
Laura Kidney Burns *(Mgr-Mktg Ops)*
Stephanie Kierzek *(Mgr-Mktg Ops)*
Kristin Schwallie *(Mgr-Mktg Optimization & Analytics)*

Accounts:
Kellogg
McDonald's
MillerCoors; Milwaukee, WI Miller Genuine Draft
Procter & Gamble Marketing
Samsung
Whirlpool Corporation

Latin America

Arc Worldwide
Carrera 13 No 90-21, Oficina 406, Bogota, Colombia
Tel.: (57) 1 628 5959
Fax: (57) 1 218 9073
Web Site: www.arcww.com

Luis Prieto *(Dir)*

Arc Worldwide
25/F Tower 2 The Enterprise Ctr, 6766 Ayala Ave, Corner Paseo de Roxas, Makati, 12 Philippines
Tel.: (63) 2 884 8413
Fax: (63) 2 884 8415
E-Mail: ichay.bulaong@ph.arcww.com
Web Site: www.arcww.com

Employees: 120

Maristel Angeles *(Gen Mgr)*
Krisha Armaine Dula *(Writer-Social Media Content-McDonald's Philippines)*

Accounts:
Shell Philippines

Arc Worldwide
162 Blues Point Road, McMahons Point, Sydney, NSW 2060 Australia
Tel.: (61) 2 9931 6900
Fax: (61) 2 9957 2152
Web Site: www.arcww.com

Mark Renshaw *(Chief Innovation Officer)*

Arc Worldwide, Asia Pacific
Level 5 Menara Olympia, 8 Jalan Raja Chulan, 50200 Kuala Lumpur, Malaysia
Tel.: (60) 3 2031 0998
Fax: (60) 3 2031 0995
E-Mail: charles.cadell@leoburnett.com.my
Web Site: www.leoburnett.com.my

Employees: 150

Tan Kieng Eng *(CEO)*
Eswari Kalugasalam Lawson *(Dir-PR)*

Accounts:
Alpha 245
BMW 7 Signs
Breast Cancer Welfare Assocation
Dewan Filharmonik Petronas Campaign: "Mpo Campaigns"
Dignity For Children's Foundation Campaign: "Jamilah & Punita"
Dutch Lady Milk Industries
ING Campaign: "Meet Your Future Self"
Kinokuniya Book Stores Campaign: "Interior Book Sale"
McDonald's
Paws Animal Welfare Society Malaysia
Petronas Campaign: "Coming Home", Campaign: "Raya Treasures", Creative, Digital, Media, Public Relations
Proton
Samsung Malaysia Electronics Campaign: "Musicopolis", Campaign: "Turtle Rock"
Women's Aid Organization

EMEA

Publicis
62 Quai des Charbonnages, Brussels, 1080 Belgium
Tel.: (32) 2645 3511
E-Mail: info@publicis.be
Web Site: publicis-brussels.tumblr.com

Employees: 60

Louis Haffreingue *(Art Dir)*
Tom Berth *(Dir-Creative)*
Laurence Van De Putte *(Dir-Art)*
Daniel Van den Broucke *(Dir-Art)*
Jean-Marc Wachsmann *(Dir-Art)*
Jonas De Wit *(Acct Mgr)*
Sabrina Schuller-Rysman *(Acct Mgr)*
Maarten de Maayer *(Copywriter)*

Accounts:
3M Scotch Brite Post-It Super Sticky
ALS League
belgian league of alhzeimer
BNP Paribas Fortis Campaign: "RSCA Hymn"
Carrefour Itunes Music Card
Centre du prevention Suicide Campaign: " Don't Skip A Suicidal Person"
Handicap Car Campaign: "Pee", Campaign: "Very different cars for not-that-different drivers."
International Guide Dog Federation
Kooaba Campaign: "The End Of Qr"
Maggi
Nescafe
Oral-B
Quirit
Renault Belgique Luxembourg Campaign: "Courtesy Day", Campaign: "The Ultimate Speed Date", Panoramic Glass Roof, Renault Clio RS, Renault Espace
Reporters Without Borders Campaign: "Blood", Campaign: "Talking Poster", Campaign: "Vroooar Bahrain"
Responsible Young Drivers Campaign: "The Impossible Text & Drive Test", Campaign: "The alcohol barrier"
Stagg
Stihl Campaign: "All the muscles you need"
Wonderbra
Yarrah Organic Pet Food

ASPEN MARKETING SERVICES
1 Gatehall Dr Ste 309, Parsippany, NJ 07054
Tel.: (973) 775-6700
Fax: (973) 775-6732
Toll Free: (800) 526-8712
E-Mail: jdraper@aspenms.com
Web Site: www.aspenms.com

Employees: 100
Year Founded: 1985

National Agency Associations: APMA WORLDWIDE-PMA

Agency Specializes In: Advertising, Brand Development & Integration, Co-op Advertising, Collateral, Communications, Consumer Marketing, Corporate Identity, Digital/Interactive, Direct Response Marketing, E-Commerce, Event Planning & Marketing, Graphic Design, Health Care Services, Internet/Web Design, Logo & Package Design, Merchandising, Newspapers & Magazines, Out-of-Home Media, Pharmaceutical, Point of Sale, Production, Public Relations, Radio, Sales Promotion, Sponsorship, Strategic Planning/Research, Sweepstakes, T.V.

William Donlin *(Mng Dir, CFO & Exec VP)*
Lauren Jacobus Ardolino *(Acct Supvr)*

Accounts:
Absolut
Citi
Ford
Georgia-Pacific
JVC U.S.A.
Kraft Crystal Light
Motorola Solutions, Inc.
Omaha Steaks
Outback
Qwest Communications
Us bank
Verizon

ATS MOBILE
(Formerly Advanced Telecom Services)
1150 First Ave, King of Prussia, PA 19046
Tel.: (610) 688-6000
E-Mail: sales@atsmobile.com
Web Site: www.atsmobile.com

Employees: 65
Year Founded: 1989

Agency Specializes In: Advertising, Affiliate Marketing, Crisis Communications, Digital/Interactive, Direct Response Marketing, Mobile Marketing, Multimedia, Retail, Search Engine Optimization, Social Media, Sweepstakes, Teen Market, Telemarketing, Viral/Buzz/Word of Mouth, Web (Banner Ads, Pop-ups, etc.)

Michael Candelori *(Dir-Creative)*
Margie Varallo *(Mgr-Client Svcs)*
Brad Bierman *(Strategist-Digital & Mobile Mktg)*

Accounts:
Advanced Mobile Solutions; Wayne, PA; 2005
Advanced Telecom Services
MatchLink.com; Des Plaines, IL; 1993
PromoTXT.com; Wayne, PA; 2003
Spark Network Services; Des Plaines, IL; 1993
WebFriends.com; Wayne, PA; 1998

AVID MARKETING GROUP
1344 Silas Deane Hwy Ste 510, Rocky Hill, CT 06067
Tel.: (860) 436-3004
Web Site: www.avidinc.com

E-Mail for Key Personnel:
President: jgross@avidinc.com

Employees: 18

Year Founded: 1986

Agency Specializes In: Advertising, Brand Development & Integration, Broadcast, Business Publications, Business-To-Business, Catalogs, Collateral, Consumer Marketing, Corporate Communications, Corporate Identity, Direct-to-Consumer, Exhibit/Trade Shows, Graphic Design, Integrated Marketing, Logo & Package Design, Multimedia, Point of Purchase, Point of Sale, Print, Production, Production (Print), Promotions, Public Relations, Sales Promotion, Shopper Marketing, Sweepstakes

DeAnna Drapeau *(Mng Partner)*
Ken Krupa *(Dir-Analytics & Info Sys)*
Chris Moran *(Dir-Design)*
Annee Newton *(Dir-Art)*
Laura Greim *(Acct Mgr)*
Kristin Brady *(Acct Coord-Digital)*
Lauren Lisitano *(Acct Coord)*
Jenna Bell *(Asst Acct Coord)*
Meredith Johnson *(Asst Project Mgr)*

Accounts:
Amgraph; CT
Comcast
Diageo
Fetzer
Pentax Medical; Montvale, NJ
SBLI
VantisLife
Walter; Canada

B-LINE APPAREL, INC.
4671 E 11th Ave, Hialeah, FL 33013
Tel.: (305) 953-8300
Fax: (305) 953-7909
Toll Free: (888) 425-4630
E-Mail: info@blineapparel.com
Web Site: www.blineapparel.com

Employees: 20
Year Founded: 1997

Agency Specializes In: Advertising Specialties, Corporate Identity, Fashion/Apparel, Point of Sale, Print, Publicity/Promotions, Sweepstakes, Travel & Tourism

Approx. Annual Billings: $4,000,000

Breakdown of Gross Billings by Media: Adv. Specialities: $4,000,000

Joe Beguiristain *(CEO)*

B2B MEDIA
34 Ellwood Ct Ste C, Greenville, SC 29607
Tel.: (864) 627-1992
Fax: (864) 627-1019
E-Mail: info@b2bmedia.com
Web Site: www.b2bmedia.com

Employees: 20
Year Founded: 2001

Agency Specializes In: Brand Development & Integration

Daniel Jones *(Dir-Art)*
Jan Clippard *(Mgr-Ops)*
Chris Grubbs *(Mgr-Customer Care)*
Lauren Knight *(Acct Exec)*

Accounts:
AT&T West; San Antonio, TX DSL, Long Distance; 2002
Comporium; Rock Hill, SC Cellular; 2003
Goodwill; Atlanta, GA; Greenville, SC Donation Services; 2002
Time Warner Cable
Verizon; Atlanta, GA Cellular

BADGEVILLE
1400-B Seaport Blvd, Redwood City, CA 94063
Tel.: (650) 492-5618
E-Mail: marketing@badgeville.com
Web Site: www.badgeville.com

Year Founded: 2010

Agency Specializes In: Communications, E-Commerce, Education, Entertainment, Health Care Services, Media Relations, Publishing, Retail

Jon Shalowitz *(Pres & CEO)*
Steve Sims *(VP-Solutions & Design)*
Roel Stalman *(VP-Product Dev)*
Christine Lynch *(Mgr-Mktg Comm)*
Marisa Duggan *(Corp Attorney)*

Accounts:
The Active Network Inc. Software Service Providers
allkpop Online News Providers
Barnes & Noble
Bell Media
EMC
Microsoft
Online Shopping Providers
Oracle
Rogers Communications Inc. Electronics Products Mfr & Distr
SAMSUNG Computers & Electronics Mfr
Universal Music
Volkswagen Turkey

BENCHMARK DISPLAYS
44311 Monterey Ave, Palm Desert, CA 92260
Tel.: (760) 775-2424
Fax: (760) 600-2810
Toll Free: (800) 600-2810
E-Mail: info@benchmarkdisplays.com
Web Site: www.benchmarkdisplays.com

Employees: 45
Year Founded: 1985

Agency Specializes In: Advertising, Advertising Specialties, Agriculture, Automotive, Branded Entertainment, Business-To-Business, Cable T.V., Children's Market, College, Corporate Identity, Cosmetics, Education, Electronics, Event Planning & Marketing, Exhibit/Trade Shows, Fashion/Apparel, Financial, Food Service, Health Care Services, Hospitality, Household Goods, Identity Marketing, In-Store Advertising, Leisure, Luxury Products, Package Design, Pharmaceutical, Point of Purchase, Point of Sale, Promotions, Restaurant, Retail, Sales Promotion, Travel & Tourism

Approx. Annual Billings: $3,200,000

Breakdown of Gross Billings by Media: Adv. Specialities: 30%; Mdsg./POP: 50%; Point of Purchase: 10%; Point of Sale: 10%

Joanne Frohman *(Pres)*
Richard Frohman *(VP-Mktg)*
Bonnie Miller *(VP-Sls)*

BENCHMARK USA
25 Skycrest, Mission Viejo, CA 92692
Tel.: (949) 380-9400
Fax: (949) 475-1212
E-Mail: benchmark@benchmarkadv.com

E-Mail for Key Personnel:
President: adepauw@benchmarkadv.com

Employees: 4
Year Founded: 1987

Agency Specializes In: African-American Market, Bilingual Market, Children's Market, Consumer Marketing, Event Planning & Marketing, Exhibit/Trade Shows, Graphic Design, Hispanic Market, Pharmaceutical, Point of Purchase, Point of Sale, Restaurant, Seniors' Market, Sports Market, Sweepstakes, Trade & Consumer Magazines

Approx. Annual Billings: $2,500,000

Breakdown of Gross Billings by Media: Event Mktg.: 10%; Exhibits/Trade Shows: 15%; Graphic Design: 25%; Mdsg./POP: 20%; Promos.: 30%

Anita Depauw *(Pres)*
John J. Borer, III *(Sr Mng Dir & Head-Investment Banking)*
Ronnie Kell *(Exec VP-Creative)*
Christine Mueller *(VP-Integrated Direct Mktg & CRM)*
Cory Atkinson *(Sr Mgr-Marketplaces & Pricing)*

Accounts:
Colgate Palmolive
Kimberly Clark; 2004
Pathway School; Laguna Hills, CA; 2005
Windsor Frozen Foods

BOUNCE MARKETING AND EVENTS, LLC
1101 E 6th St, Austin, TX 78702
Tel.: (512) 524-2953
Web Site: www.bounceaustin.com

Employees: 10
Year Founded: 2008

Agency Specializes In: Advertising, Event Planning & Marketing, Public Relations

Michelle Graham *(Founder & CEO)*
Drex Earle *(COO & Dir-Creative)*
Lindsay Smith *(Sr Acct Mgr)*
Aracely Gonzalez *(Acct Exec)*

BRANDLINK COMMUNICATIONS LLC
28 W 25th St, New York, NY 10010
Tel.: (212) 338-0070
Fax: (212) 338-0131
Web Site: www.brandlinkcommunications.com

Agency Specializes In: Event Planning & Marketing, Media Relations, Social Marketing/Nonprofit, Social Media, Sponsorship

Carol Bell *(Partner)*
Greg Link *(Partner)*
Selmin Arat *(Mng Dir)*
Jose Martinez *(VP-Media)*
Sasa Nikolic *(VP)*

Accounts:
Acqualina Resort & Spa on the Beach Beach Resort & Spa
Gallaghers Steakhouse Creative Event Marketing, Media
Hint Water Celebrity Relations, Event Marketing, Strategic Partnerships
Ingenious Designs, LLC Media Awareness
Jay Strongwater (Public Relations Agency of Record)
Supergoop! (Public Relations Agency of Record)

Branch

BrandLinkDC
3109 M Street NW, Washington, DC 20007
Tel.: (202) 733-5223

Annie Perezchica *(VP-Events)*
Brooke Henderson *(Mgr-PR)*
Misty Holbert *(Mgr-PR)*

Accounts:
&pizza; Washington, DC (Public Relations Agency of Record)

BRANDSPARX
406 Broadway Ste 225, Santa Monica, CA 90401
Tel.: (310) 740-9992
Web Site: www.brandsparx.com

Employees: 17
Year Founded: 1999

Agency Specializes In: Alternative Advertising, Branded Entertainment, Event Planning & Marketing, Exhibit/Trade Shows, Game Integration, Guerilla Marketing, Mobile Marketing, Outdoor, Production, Promotions, Social Media, Viral/Buzz/Word of Mouth

Approx. Annual Billings: $4,578,000

Rosy Chavez *(Dir-Ops)*

Accounts:
Arizona Iced Tea Cherry Lime Rickey; 2012
Burger King; 2011
Coffee Bean; 2013
Google
HTC
Microsoft
Poppin New Educational Supplies; 2012

BRIGANDI & ASSOCIATES, INC. MARKETING COMMUNICATIONS
1918 N Mendell Ste 200, Chicago, IL 60642
Tel.: (773) 278-9911
Fax: (773) 278-2535
E-Mail: brigandi@brigandi.com
Web Site: www.brigandi.com

Employees: 22
Year Founded: 1991

National Agency Associations: APMA WORLDWIDE

Agency Specializes In: African-American Market, Collateral, Communications, Digital/Interactive, E-Commerce, Electronic Media, Entertainment, Event Planning & Marketing, Graphic Design, Hispanic Market, Internet/Web Design, Merchandising, Package Design, Point of Purchase, Point of Sale, Print, Sales Promotion, Sponsorship, Sports Market, Strategic Planning/Research, Trade & Consumer Magazines

Approx. Annual Billings: $7,000,000

Karen Kolodzey *(Exec VP)*
Bill Forsberg *(VP-Production & IT Svcs)*
Lori Brayer *(Dir-Special Projects)*

Accounts:
Corona
Kellogg's; Battle Creek, MI Cereal; 1999

BROADSTREET
242 W 30th St, New York, NY 10001
Tel.: (212) 780-5700
Fax: (212) 780-5710
E-Mail: info@broadstreet.com
Web Site: www.broadstreet.com

Employees: 25
Year Founded: 1981

Agency Specializes In: Advertising Specialties, Affiliate Marketing, Affluent Market, Automotive, Brand Development & Integration, Broadcast, Business-To-Business, Collateral, Communications, Consulting, Consumer Goods, Consumer Marketing, Content, Corporate Communications, Corporate Identity, Cosmetics, Digital/Interactive, Direct Response Marketing, Education, Electronic Media, Electronics, Email, Entertainment, Event Planning & Marketing, Exhibit/Trade Shows, Experience Design, Fashion/Apparel, Financial, Game Integration, Graphic Design, Health Care Services, High Technology, Hospitality, Household Goods, Industrial, Integrated Marketing, International, Internet/Web Design, Investor Relations, Leisure, Local Marketing, Logo & Package Design, Luxury Products, Medical Products, Mobile Marketing, Multimedia, New Product Development, New Technologies, Outdoor, Package Design, Paid Searches, Pharmaceutical, Print, Production, Production (Ad, Film, Broadcast), Production (Print), Promotions, Real Estate, Retail, Sales Promotion, Search Engine Optimization, Technical Advertising, Travel & Tourism, Web (Banner Ads, Pop-ups, etc.)

Approx. Annual Billings: $20,000,000

Breakdown of Gross Billings by Media: Adv. Specialities: $20,000,000

Mark Baltazar *(CEO & Mng Partner)*
Ed Gibbons *(Partner & CFO)*
Claudia Rodriguez Tressler *(Partner & COO)*

Accounts:
Comcast
Diageo; New York, NY; 2005
ESPN
Nickelodeon
Reebok; Canton, MA; 2006
Roche Pharmaceuticals
Royal Caribbean Cruise Lines; Miami, FL; 2005
Scripps
W Hotels; New York, NY; 2003

BRYDAN CORPORATION
1643 Bell Hill Rd, Delhi, NY 13753
Tel.: (607) 821-4350
Fax: (866) 394-1377
Toll Free: (866) 538-8906
E-Mail: jb@brydan.com
Web Site: www.brydan.com

E-Mail for Key Personnel:
President: jb@brydan.com

Employees: 5
Year Founded: 2002

Agency Specializes In: Advertising, Brand Development & Integration, Communications, Digital/Interactive, Electronic Media, Information Technology, Internet/Web Design, Media Buying Services, Multimedia, Publicity/Promotions, Travel & Tourism

Approx. Annual Billings: $500,000

Breakdown of Gross Billings by Media: Adv. Specialities: $500,000

Bryan Hickman *(Pres & CEO)*

Accounts:
Hull-O Farm; Durham, NY Farm Vacations, Hunting Vacations
Sunny Hill Resort & Golf Course; Greenville, NY Golf, Vacations

CAPRICORN
29 Northcote Dr, Melville, NY 11747
Tel.: (917) 534-0402
Fax: (212) 214-0685
E-Mail: contact@netcapricorn.com
Web Site: www.netcapricorn.com

E-Mail for Key Personnel:
President: toullier@netcapricorn.com

Employees: 3
Year Founded: 1999

Agency Specializes In: Advertising, Advertising Specialties, African-American Market, Bilingual Market, Consulting, Consumer Publications, Direct Response Marketing, E-Commerce, Education, Entertainment, Fashion/Apparel, Food Service, Government/Political, Internet/Web Design, Legal Services, Leisure, Magazines, Media Buying Services, Newspaper, Newspapers & Magazines, Print, Real Estate, Restaurant, Travel & Tourism

Approx. Annual Billings: $250,000

Breakdown of Gross Billings by Media: Consulting: $11,500; D.M.: $10,000; Event Mktg.: $6,900; Graphic Design: $11,500; Internet Adv.: $57,500; Mags.: $34,500; Network Radio: $23,000; Network T.V.: $11,500; Newsp.: $11,500; Newsp. & Mags.: $23,000; Other: $26,100; Radio: $11,500; Syndication: $11,500

Herbert S. Winokur Jr. *(Chm & CEO)*
Cyril Toullier *(Principal)*

CENTRA360
(Formerly Centra Marketing & Communications, LLC)
1400 Old Country Rd Ste 420, Westbury, NY 11590-5119
Tel.: (516) 997-3147
Fax: (516) 334-7798
E-Mail: bbell@centra360.com
Web Site: www.centra360.com

Employees: 10
Year Founded: 1996
National Agency Associations: PMA

Agency Specializes In: Automotive, Brand Development & Integration, Consulting, Consumer Marketing, Customer Relationship Management, Digital/Interactive, Direct Response Marketing, Entertainment, Event Planning & Marketing, Experience Design, Fashion/Apparel, Game Integration, Integrated Marketing, Internet/Web Design, Planning & Consultation, Point of Purchase, Point of Sale, Promotions, Publicity/Promotions, Sales Promotion, Social Media, Strategic Planning/Research, Sweepstakes, Web (Banner Ads, Pop-ups, etc.)

Approx. Annual Billings: $5,000,000

Breakdown of Gross Billings by Media: Collateral: $700,000; Event Mktg.: $400,000; Fees: $1,750,000; Radio: $400,000; Sls. Promo.: $1,750,000

Robert A. Bell *(COO)*
Randi Berger *(Exec VP)*
Mark Biggin *(VP-Strategic Mktg)*
Chariot Crespo *(VP-Mktg Partnerships)*
John Northrop *(VP-Digital Solutions)*
Karen Romanelli *(VP-Acct Mgmt)*
Linda Suraci *(Sr Brand Dir-Activation)*
Susan Mysel *(Sr Dir-Brand Activation)*

Accounts:
American Express; 2012
Dr. Bronner's Magic Soaps; 2012
E&J Gallo Winery; Modesto, CA Wines; 1997
Fair World Project, Inc.; 2012
JetBlue Airways; New York, NY; 2004

Lion Brand Yarn; 2012
Lorillard, Inc.; Greensboro, NC; 2001
Martha Stewart Living Omnimedia, Inc.; New York, NY; 2001
Meguiar's Inc.; Irvine, CA Surface Care Products; 2008
New York Post; New York, NY; 2005
News America Marketing; New York, NY Special Events; 1997
Popchips Snack Foods; 2010
Robert Bosch Corporation; Broadview, IL; 1999
Sears Holdings Corporation; Hoffman Estates, IL; 2008
Subaru of America; 2012
Upromise, Inc.; Newton Center, MA Financial; 2008

CINETRANSFORMER INTERNATIONAL INC.

4770 Biscayne Blvd Ste 1450, Miami, FL 33137
Tel.: (305) 576-5970
Fax: (305) 576-5970
E-Mail: sales@cinetransformer.com
Web Site: www.cinetransformer.com

Employees: 50

Agency Specializes In: Agriculture, Arts, Automotive, Aviation & Aerospace, Below-the-Line, Business-To-Business, College, Computers & Software, Consumer Goods, Consumer Marketing, Electronics, Entertainment, Event Planning & Marketing, Exhibit/Trade Shows, Experience Design, Financial, Government/Political, Health Care Services, Hispanic Market, Hospitality, Household Goods, Information Technology, International, Investor Relations, Leisure, Local Marketing, Marine, Medical Products, Mobile Marketing, Multicultural, Pharmaceutical, Promotions, Real Estate, Sales Promotion, Sports Market, Travel & Tourism

Approx. Annual Billings: $50,000,000

Breakdown of Gross Billings by Media: Event Mktg.: $12,500,000; Sls. Promo.: $2,000,000

Raul Fernandez *(COO)*
Michael Pine *(VP-Bus Dev)*

Accounts:
Amazon Kindle Fire HDX; 2013
AMC TV Breaking Bad National Tour
American Express Blue Card; 2003
Amway
AOL Latino; Chicago, IL; Miami, FL AOL Latino; 2004
Buena Vista International
Citibank
Coca-Cola Refreshments USA, Inc.
Disney XD
Fox Sports en Espanol
GlaxoSmithKline
Mattel; Mexico City, Mexico Barbie Fairytopia; 2005
McDonald's
MTV
Nokia
Paramount Pictures; 2004
Pepsi
Sobe Beverages; 2003
Subaru
Universal Studios
US Army National Guard
VIZ Media
Walt Disney Co.
Warner Brothers; 2013

CLARUS PUBLIC RELATIONS

1099 18th St 500, Denver, CO 80202-1950
Tel.: (303) 296-0343
Web Site: www.teamclarus.com

Year Founded: 1998

Agency Specializes In: Crisis Communications, Public Relations, Social Media, Strategic Planning/Research

Mara Conklin *(Founder & Pres)*

Accounts:
Aprimo, Incorporated
CPS Innovations
CTI Group Holdings Inc.
NorthWestern Corporation
Pitney Bowes Software Systems
Proforma Corporation
Remedy Corporation

CLICKMAIL MARKETING, INC.

155 Bovet Rd Ste 310, San Mateo, CA 94402
Tel.: (650) 653-8102
Fax: (650) 288-3449
E-Mail: marco@clickmail.com
Web Site: clickmail.com/

Employees: 16
Year Founded: 2001

Agency Specializes In: Business-To-Business, Consumer Marketing, Corporate Communications, Corporate Identity, Crisis Communications, Customer Relationship Management, Email, High Technology, Integrated Marketing

Michael Kelly *(Co-Founder-Bus Dev)*
Marco Marini *(CEO)*
Russ Cerminaro *(CFO & COO)*
Cameron Kane *(CTO)*
Grant Johnson *(VP-Strategic Svcs)*

Accounts:
Arnold Worldwide
Assist2Sell
Audatex
Branded Solutions
Butler Till Media
City/County of San Francisco
Classic Industries
Clontech, Inc.
CMP
ConsumerLab
CSI Global Education
Dataprint
Footage Firm, Inc.
Footwear Etc
Funny or Die
Funnyordie.com
Genesys
Go Industry- Dovebid
Health Grades,CO
Hilco Industrial
Jigsaw
Laplink Software
Martin Agency
NComputing
TE Connectivity Ltd.
TravelMuse
WYSE
YAPTA

CLICKSQUARED INC.

200 W St 3rd Fl E, Waltham, MA 02451
Tel.: (857) 246-7800
Fax: (857) 246-7645
Toll Free: (866) 402-5425
Web Site: www.clicksquared.com

Agency Specializes In: Communications, Market Research, Strategic Planning/Research

Brad Woloson *(Gen Partner)*
Michaela Goodwin *(CFO)*
Robert King *(Sr VP & Gen Mgr-Client Svcs)*
Scott Philips *(VP-IT)*

Accounts:
Aramark
Atlantis
Bank Of America
Capital one
Comcast
HomeAway
Hyatt
March Second
Verizon
Virgin Money USA Banking Services

CO-COMMUNICATIONS INC.

332 E Main St, Mount Kisco, NY 10549
Tel.: (914) 666-0066
Web Site: www.cocommunications.com

Year Founded: 1997

Agency Specializes In: Advertising, Corporate Identity, Direct Response Marketing, Logo & Package Design, Market Research, Media Buying Services, Media Planning, Media Training, Public Relations, Search Engine Optimization

Stacey Cohen *(Pres & CEO)*
Jessica Lyon *(Partner)*
Danielle Cyr *(VP-Integrated Mktg)*
Katie Lechase *(Assoc Dir-Bus Dev)*
Lyndsay Bouchal *(Sr Acct Mgr)*
Kelly Lee *(Sr Acct Mgr)*
Andrew Saginor *(Mgr-Creative Svcs)*

Accounts:
Hudson Valley Tourism Online Marketing, PR
Robert Martin Company LLC Investment Services
Westchester Dental Group Dental Services

CO-OP PROMOTIONS

2301 S Ocean Dr Ste 2504, Hollywood, FL 33019
Tel.: (954) 922-2323
Fax: (954) 922-2071
E-Mail: art@co-oppromotions.com
Web Site: www.co-oppromotions.com

E-Mail for Key Personnel:
President: art@co-oppromotions.com

Employees: 10
Year Founded: 1987

Agency Specializes In: Alternative Advertising, Consumer Goods, E-Commerce, Pharmaceutical, Point of Purchase, Point of Sale, Promotions, Sales Promotion, Travel & Tourism

Approx. Annual Billings: $4,000,000

Breakdown of Gross Billings by Media: Other: 33%; Sls. Promo.: 67%

Arthur S. Averbook *(Founder & Pres)*
Duncan Gray *(Sr Partner)*

Accounts:
College Bookstore
Foster's Wines
National Motorcoach Networks
Ninja Kitchen System
Seagram Escape Coolers

COOPTIONS SHOPPER MARKETING

120 A North Salem St, Apex, NC 27502
Tel.: (919) 303-3223
Fax: (919) 654-6810
E-Mail: sales@cooptions.com
Web Site: www.cooptions.com

Employees: 14
Year Founded: 1994

Agency Specializes In: Alternative Advertising, Broadcast, Children's Market, College, Consumer Goods, Consumer Marketing, Consumer Publications, Digital/Interactive, Experience Design, Market Research, Promotions, Publicity/Promotions, Retail, Sponsorship, Sports Market, Strategic Planning/Research, Teen Market, Travel & Tourism, Viral/Buzz/Word of Mouth, Women's Market

Approx. Annual Billings: $2,100,000

Breakdown of Gross Billings by Media: Promos.: 85%; Radio: 15%

Brian Scott Sockin *(Pres & CEO)*
Darlene Genander *(Sr VP-Sls & Bus Dev & Gen Mgr-Co-Options Health & Wellness)*
John Richard Branca *(Reg VP-Sls & Bus Dev-Bentonville)*
Kristen Kelley Cianni *(Dir-Program Mgmt)*
Patricia Gonzalez De Mitter *(Dir-Creative)*
Maria Bunn *(Mgr-Partnership Dev & Platform)*
Jamie Hendrick *(Coord-Sls & Mktg)*

CRC MARKETING SOLUTIONS

6321 Bury Dr Ste 10, Eden Prairie, MN 55346-1739
Tel.: (952) 937-6000
Fax: (952) 937-5155
E-Mail: newclient@crc-inc.com
Web Site: www.crc-inc.com

E-Mail for Key Personnel:
President: lundeby@crc-inc.com

Employees: 15
Year Founded: 1979

Agency Specializes In: Corporate Identity, Internet/Web Design, Logo & Package Design, Sales Promotion

Approx. Annual Billings: $2,000,000

Breakdown of Gross Billings by Media: Collateral: 13%; D.M.: 2%; Internet Adv.: 56%; Logo & Package Design: 4%; Mags.: 2%; Newsp.: 1%; Promos.: 21%; Radio: 1%

Elizabeth Petrangelo *(Owner & Exec VP)*
Michael Lundeby *(Owner)*
Kriscel Estrella *(Mgr-Ops)*
Brianna Miller *(Mgr-Design)*
Sacha Orozco *(Mgr-Production)*
Lindsay Campbell *(Acct Exec)*
Ruben Gonzalez *(Strategist-Interactive & Technical)*
Shannon Burgess *(Asst Acct Exec)*
Amy Semelhack *(Asst Acct Exec)*

Accounts:
Ecolab; Saint Paul, MN Industrial Products
European Roasterie; Minneapolis, MN Specialty Coffees
Gopher Resource
Thomson West; Saint Paul, MN
United Healthcare

CREATIVE PRODUCTIONS

4510 Pacific Coast Hwy Ste 500, Long Beach, CA 90804
Tel.: (562) 985-1363
Fax: (562) 985-1365
E-Mail: info@creativeproductions.com
Web Site: www.creativeproductions.com

Employees: 30
Year Founded: 1981

Agency Specializes In: Digital/Interactive, Print, Production (Ad, Film, Broadcast), Promotions

Deborah Golian Castro *(Pres & CEO)*
Erin Suarez *(Acct Dir)*

Accounts:
Goodwill Industries
Lexus
Toyota

CRN INTERNATIONAL, INC.

1 Circular Ave, Hamden, CT 06514-4002
Tel.: (203) 288-2002
Fax: (203) 281-3291
Toll Free: (800) 688-CRN1
E-Mail: info@crnradio.com
Web Site: www.crnradio.com

E-Mail for Key Personnel:
President: barryb@crnradio.com

Employees: 75
Year Founded: 1973

National Agency Associations: PMA-RAB

Agency Specializes In: Advertising, Automotive, Brand Development & Integration, Broadcast, Business Publications, Co-op Advertising, Communications, Computers & Software, Consumer Goods, Consumer Marketing, Cosmetics, Direct Response Marketing, Electronics, Entertainment, Fashion/Apparel, Food Service, Health Care Services, Hispanic Market, Household Goods, Integrated Marketing, Local Marketing, Media Buying Services, Merchandising, Multicultural, Pharmaceutical, Point of Sale, Promotions, Publicity/Promotions, Radio, Retail, Sales Promotion, Sponsorship, Sports Market, Strategic Planning/Research, Sweepstakes, T.V., Teen Market, Trade & Consumer Magazines, Viral/Buzz/Word of Mouth

Approx. Annual Billings: $40,000,000

Barry H. Berman *(Pres)*
S. Richard Kalt *(Partner & Exec VP)*
John Prinner *(CFO)*
Rob O'Mara *(Mng Dir-Strategy & Dev)*
Jennifer A. Anderson *(VP-HR)*
Patrick Leeney *(VP-Bus Dev)*
Jim Alkon *(Dir-Mktg)*
Katie Geddes *(Dir-Media Rels)*
Ron Pell *(Dir-Media Rels)*
Kelly Travers *(Dir-Trade Mktg)*
Amy McLaughlin *(Analyst-Media)*

Accounts:
Absolut Spirits Company
Allstate
Applegate Media Group
Arc Marketing
B&G Foods
Bayer Corporation
BBDO
Cadillac
Campbell-Ewald
Campbell Soup Company; Camden, NJ; 1982
Chrysler
Citibank
ConAgra
Diageo
Disney
Dole Food Company, Inc.
ExxonMobil; Washington, DC Superflow Oil; 1995
General Motors
Georgia Pacific
GSD&M
Hallmark
The Hershey Company
Hewlett-Packard
HIP Advertising
The History Channel
Hormel Foods
Initiative
Johnson & Johnson
JWT
Kellogg's; Battle Creek, MI
Kmart
Kraft
Major League Baseball; New York, NY
Mars North America
MEC
Mediavest
Microsoft Corp.
MillerCoors
Mindshare
Nestle USA
Novartis
Pepsi Bottling Group
Playtex
Prestige Brands, Inc.
Procter & Gamble
Samsung
Sandoz Pharmaceuticals
Sara Lee Corporation
Sargento Foods, Inc.
S.C. Johnson & Son
Sears
SPARK
Sprint
Starcom
T-Mobile US
Target
TBWA
UM
Unilever; Englewood Cliffs, NJ Lipton, Ragu
United Distillers & Vintners
U.S. Navy
Verizon
Wal-Mart
Wm. Wrigley Jr. Company
Xinc

THE DATA FACTORY

888 Biscayne Blvd, Miami, FL 33132
Tel.: (786) 609-6596
E-Mail: affiliation@thedata-factory.com
Web Site: www.thedata-factory.com

Employees: 12
Year Founded: 2013

Agency Specializes In: Affiliate Marketing, Digital/Interactive, Email, Local Marketing, Social Media, Sweepstakes, Web (Banner Ads, Pop-ups, etc.)

Alexandre Ameline Juffroy *(Co-Founder & Mng Partner-US)*

Accounts:
Hackett Website; 2014

DEALER IGNITION

PO Box 35, Greenville, SC 29602
Mailing Address:
PO BOX 35, Greenville, SC 29602-0035
Fax: (801) 922-6090
Toll Free: (888) 344-6483
E-Mail: info@dealerignition.com

Employees: 9
Year Founded: 2007

National Agency Associations: AMA-SEMPO-WSAA

Agency Specializes In: Advertising, Affiliate Marketing, Affluent Market, Automotive, Brand Development & Integration, Consumer Marketing, Customer Relationship Management, Digital/Interactive, E-Commerce, High Technology, Internet/Web Design, Local Marketing, Luxury Products, Planning & Consultation, Retail, Sales Promotion, Search Engine Optimization, Social Media, Sponsorship, Sports Market, Sweepstakes,

Syndication, Web (Banner Ads, Pop-ups, etc.)

Approx. Annual Billings: $1,000,000

Breakdown of Gross Billings by Media: Co-op Adv.: 30%; Consulting: 20%; Internet Adv.: 40%; Local Mktg.: 10%

Steven Wagner *(CEO)*
Cristina Fumagalli *(Controller)*

Accounts:
All State; Chicago, IL Insurance; 2009
Karastan; Dalton, GA Home Furnishings; 2007
Mountain Hard Wear; Mountain View, CA Outdoor Clothing; 2009
Synnex; Greenville, SC; 2009
Toyota Motor Company (South East); Miami, FL Automobiles; 2007

DESIGN NORTH, INC.

8007 Douglas Ave, Racine, WI 53402
Tel.: (262) 898-1090
Fax: (262) 639-5230
Toll Free: (800) 247-8494
E-Mail: leeiii@designnorth.com
Web Site: www.designnorth.com

E-Mail for Key Personnel:
President: leeiii@designnorth.com
Creative Dir.: gwen@designnorth.com

Employees: 13
Year Founded: 1962

Agency Specializes In: Brand Development & Integration, Collateral, Commercial Photography, Communications, Consulting, Consumer Goods, Consumer Marketing, Corporate Identity, Graphic Design, Logo & Package Design, Merchandising, Package Design, Planning & Consultation, Point of Purchase, Point of Sale, Print, Production, Retail, Strategic Planning/Research

Approx. Annual Billings: $1,000,000

Breakdown of Gross Billings by Media: Collateral: $10,000; Comml. Photography: $100,000; Logo & Package Design: $840,000; Point of Sale: $50,000

Gwen Granzow *(VP, Principal & Dir-Creative)*
Paul Walker *(VP-Brand Initiatives)*
Jane Marcussen *(Dir-Design)*
Zeynep Tangun-Kaplan *(Dir-Design)*

Accounts:
Esselte Americas; NY; 2007
Gehl's Guernsey Dairy; WI; 2007
Glue Dots; WI Adhesive; 2010
Heartland; WI Produce
InSinkErater; Racine, WI; 1997
Johnsonville
Lactalis Retail Dairy Cheese
Lavelle; WI; 2007
Omron; IL; 2007
Schroeder; IL Dairy; 2010
Snikiddy Natural Snack Foods; 2008

D.L. BLAIR INC.

400 Post Ave, Westbury, NY 11590
Tel.: (516) 746-3700
Fax: (516) 746-3889
E-Mail: tconlon@dlblair.com
Web Site: www.dlblair.com

E-Mail for Key Personnel:
President: sreichard@dlblair.com

Employees: 150
Year Founded: 1959

National Agency Associations: MAAW-PMA

Agency Specializes In: Brand Development & Integration, Business-To-Business, Collateral, Consulting, Consumer Marketing, Direct Response Marketing, E-Commerce, Entertainment, Event Planning & Marketing, Financial, Food Service, Game Integration, Hispanic Market, Internet/Web Design, Magazines, Newspaper, Newspapers & Magazines, Planning & Consultation, Point of Purchase, Point of Sale, Publicity/Promotions, Sales Promotion, Sponsorship, Strategic Planning/Research, Sweepstakes, Telemarketing, Transportation, Travel & Tourism

Thomas J. Conlon *(Chm)*
Brian T. Conlon *(Vice Chm & CEO)*
Sandy M. Reichard *(Pres & COO)*
Terry Brechbill *(Exec VP)*
Richard P. Isham *(Exec VP)*
Michael Malinowitz *(Sr VP)*
Barbara Trobiano *(VP)*

Accounts:
Abbott Laboratories
Art Institute of Chicago
Crown Imports LLC
Discover Financial Services
Farmers Insurance Exchange
Ferrero USA
HBO
Interactive Communications International
Intercontinental Hotels Group
LEGO
LEGOLAND Florida
Mars Chocolate North America
Mars Food US Uncle Ben's
Philip Morris
Playboy Enterprises
Procter & Gamble
S. C. Johnson & Son
Verizon
Webster Bank
Xcel Energy

Branch

D.L. Blair Inc.

1548 Front St, Blair, NE 68008-1641
Tel.: (402) 426-4701
Fax: (402) 426-4706
Web Site: www.dlblair.com

Employees: 60
Year Founded: 1959

Terry Brechbill *(Exec VP)*
Richard P. Isham *(Exec VP)*

DON JAGODA ASSOCIATES, INC.

100 Marcus Dr, Melville, NY 11747-4229
Tel.: (631) 454-1800
Fax: (631) 454-1834
E-Mail: info@dja.com
Web Site: www.dja.com

Employees: 70
Year Founded: 1962

National Agency Associations: PMA

Agency Specializes In: Hispanic Market, Promotions, Sales Promotion, Sweepstakes

Approx. Annual Billings: $15,000,000

Don Jagoda *(Pres)*
Andrew Gusman *(CFO)*
Larry Berney *(COO)*
Bruce Hollander *(CMO & Exec VP)*
Suzanne Gulbransen *(Sr VP)*
Jacqueline Lamberti *(Sr VP-Promos)*
Steve Greco *(VP-Creative Svcs)*

Accounts:
AARP
Apple & Eve
Bank of America
FedEx
GE Capital
Ghirardelli
Johnson & Johnson
Marriott
Newport News
Pepsi Cola
Pillsbury
Six Flags Theme Parks
Spiegel
Sterling Jewelers
Time Warner Cable
Tupperware Brands Corporation

DOVETAIL PARTNER PROMOTIONS

17011 Beach Blvd, Huntington Beach, CA 92647
Tel.: (877) 709-5755
Fax: (913) 660-7437
E-Mail: dovetailoffice@att.net
Web Site: www.dovetailpp.com

Employees: 1
Year Founded: 1984

Agency Specializes In: Sales Promotion

Vicky Carlew *(Owner & Pres)*

ECOMMERCE PARTNERS

59 Franklin St Ste 6B, New York, NY 10013
Tel.: (212) 334-3390
Fax: (503) 218-5585
Toll Free: (866) 431-6669
E-Mail: info@ecommercepartners.net
Web Site: www.ecommercepartners.net

Employees: 70
Year Founded: 1995

Agency Specializes In: Advertising, Affluent Market, Brand Development & Integration, Business-To-Business, Communications, Consulting, Consumer Goods, Consumer Marketing, Content, Customer Relationship Management, Digital/Interactive, Direct-to-Consumer, E-Commerce, Electronics, Email, Entertainment, Fashion/Apparel, Integrated Marketing, Internet/Web Design, Leisure, Logo & Package Design, Luxury Products, Magazines, New Product Development, Newspaper, RSS (Really Simple Syndication), Real Estate, Restaurant, Retail, Sales Promotion, Search Engine Optimization, Sports Market, Strategic Planning/Research, Travel & Tourism, Viral/Buzz/Word of Mouth, Web (Banner Ads, Pop-ups, etc.)

Breakdown of Gross Billings by Media: E-Commerce: 60%; Internet Adv.: 40%

Gil Levy *(Founder & Mng Partner)*
Vincent Corbo *(Mgr-Sls)*
Nicole Panzica *(Mgr-Mktg)*
George Sprouse *(Sr Acct Exec-Digital Mktg)*

Accounts:
David's Cookies; NY; 2005
L'Oreal; New York, NY; 2005
Pery; NY; 2006

ELEVENTH DAY ENTERTAINMENT INC.

29229 Canwood St Ste 202, Agoura Hills, CA 91301
Tel.: (805) 435-1701
E-Mail: mail@eleventhday.com
Web Site: www.eleventhday.com

Employees: 2
Year Founded: 1994

Agency Specializes In: Broadcast, Business-To-Business, Corporate Identity, Production

Frank Martin *(Pres)*

Accounts:
Love of Liberty

ELITE MARKETING GROUP
900 3rd Ave, New Hyde Park, NY 11040
Tel.: (516) 437-1500
Fax: (516) 437-7404
E-Mail: info@elitemg.com
Web Site: www.elitemg.com

Employees: 50

Mardi Galdamez *(CTO)*
Gary Marcus *(Sr VP-Bus Dev)*
Risa Price *(Dir-Client Svcs & New Bus Dev)*
Brandon C. Day-Anderson *(Acct Exec)*
Bonnie Pampinella *(Acct Exec)*
Toni Luciano *(Acct Coord)*

Accounts:
AllState
American Express
Bank of America
Barclays
Best Buy
Boars Head
Cablevision
Circuit City
Citibank
CMT
Country Music Television
Cure
ESPN
HBO
Lindt
US Bank

EMI STRATEGIC MARKETING, INC.
15 Broad St, Boston, MA 02109
Tel.: (617) 224-1101
Fax: (617) 224-1190
Web Site: www.emiboston.com

E-Mail for Key Personnel:
President: cedlund@emiboston.com

Employees: 40
Year Founded: 1989

Agency Specializes In: Brand Development & Integration, Business-To-Business, Communications, Consulting, Corporate Communications, Customer Relationship Management, Digital/Interactive, Direct Response Marketing, Direct-to-Consumer, E-Commerce, Electronic Media, Email, Financial, Guerilla Marketing, High Technology, Identity Marketing, Information Technology, Integrated Marketing, Internet/Web Design, Market Research, New Product Development, Pharmaceutical, Point of Sale, Sales Promotion, Social Marketing/Nonprofit, Sponsorship, Strategic Planning/Research

Campbell Edlund *(Pres)*
Charlene Paradise *(Mng Dir-Payments Practice)*
Paul O'Brien *(VP-Fin & Ops)*
Mark Malloy *(Exec Dir-Creative)*
Christina Nagler *(Sr Acct Dir)*
Christy O'Neil *(Sr Acct Dir)*
Nathan Hepp *(Dir-Interactive Art)*
Ken Lubar *(Dir-Mgmt)*

Accounts:
FedEx
The Hartford
Pioneer Mutual Funds
State Street
Verizon
Webster Bank

ENGLANDER KNABE & ALLEN
801 S Figueroa St Ste 1050, Los Angeles, CA 90017
Tel.: (213) 741-1500
Fax: (213) 747-4900
Web Site: www.englanderpr.com

Year Founded: 2005

Agency Specializes In: Media Relations, Media Training, Public Relations, Strategic Planning/Research

Harvey A. Englander *(Founder & Mng Partner)*
Marcus Allen *(Partner)*
Paul A. Haney *(Partner)*
Matt Knabe *(Partner)*
Jeff McConnell *(Partner)*
Gary Townsend *(Partner)*
Adam Englander *(Gen Counsel & VP)*
Tyrone Bland *(Sr VP)*

Accounts:
AT&T Communications Corp. Telecommunication Services
Downey Hospital Healthcare Services
The Los Angeles Police Protective League Security Services
Motorola Solutions, Inc. Communication Devices Mfr

EXCALIBUR EXHIBITS
7120 Brittmoore Rd Ste 430, Houston, TX 77041
Tel.: (713) 856-8853
Fax: (713) 856-8854
Web Site: www.excaliburexhibits.com

Employees: 24
Year Founded: 1997

Peggy Swords *(Pres)*
Jeff Wellings *(Dir-Ops)*
David Chappell *(Acct Mgr)*
Carla Coy *(Acct Mgr)*
Thomas P. Martinez *(Acct Mgr)*
Stacy Meeks *(Acct Mgr)*
Philip B. Moore *(Acct Mgr)*
Keith Berg *(Acct Exec)*
Tom Short *(Acct Exec)*
Matt Hitt *(Sr Designer)*
Jeremy Hahn *(Estimator)*

Accounts:
Arkex
C Mex
Cameron
Insights
Nexans
ODI

FAMOUS MARKS, INC.
4105 Ridgebrook Bluffs, Raleigh, NC 27603
Tel.: (919) 779-5968
Fax: (919) 779-3866
E-Mail: customerservice@famousmarks.com
Web Site: www.famousmarks.com

Employees: 3
Year Founded: 1994

National Agency Associations: PMA

Agency Specializes In: Consumer Marketing, Sales Promotion

Approx. Annual Billings: $1,000,000

Breakdown of Gross Billings by Media: D.M.: $500,000; Newsp.: $500,000

Joyce A. Shevelev-Putzer *(Pres)*

Accounts:
Coty; New York, NY Preferred Stock Men's Fragrance
Redstorm Entertainment; Morrisville, NC

FHC MARKETING
4711 N Lamon Ave, Chicago, IL 60630
Tel.: (773) 777-6100
Fax: (773) 777-6118
E-Mail: info@fhcmarketing.com
Web Site: www.fhcmarketing.com

Employees: 60
Year Founded: 1920

National Agency Associations: POPAI

Agency Specializes In: Brand Development & Integration, Communications, Consumer Marketing, Digital/Interactive, Education, Graphic Design, In-Store Advertising, Logo & Package Design, Merchandising, Point of Purchase, Point of Sale, Retail, Sales Promotion

Approx. Annual Billings: $15,000,000

Breakdown of Gross Billings by Media: Graphic Design: $500,000; In-Store Adv.: $4,000,000; Logo & Package Design: $500,000; Mdsg./POP: $9,000,000; Sls. Promo.: $1,000,000

Roger Wolf *(Owner & Pres)*
Baris Taser *(VP-Design)*
Denise Pulido *(Dir-Bus Dev)*
Manuel Zapien *(Mgr-Warehouse-FHC Mktg)*
Sandy Nguyen *(Designer)*

Accounts:
CVS Health
K-Mart
Krogers
Publix
Regis Corp.
Safeway
Sears
Tires Plus
Zales

FIREHOUSE, INC.
14860 Landmark Blvd No 247, Dallas, TX 75254
Tel.: (972) 692-0911
Fax: (972) 692-0912
E-Mail: info@firehouseagency.com
Web Site: www.firehouseagency.com

E-Mail for Key Personnel:
President: mhall@fhdallas.com
Creative Dir.: gregn@fhdallas.com
Public Relations: mhall@fhdallas.com

Employees: 29
Year Founded: 1997

Agency Specializes In: Advertising, Brand Development & Integration, Consumer Marketing, Corporate Identity, Direct Response Marketing, Exhibit/Trade Shows, Graphic Design, Health Care Services, Internet/Web Design, Logo & Package Design, Point of Purchase, Point of Sale, Production, Publicity/Promotions, Sales Promotion, Sponsorship, Strategic Planning/Research, Sweepstakes

Mark Hall *(Founder & Pres)*
Everett Wilder *(Principal & Grp Dir-Creative)*
Tripp Westbrook *(Exec Dir-Creative)*

Amanda Driggers *(Acct Dir)*
Evan Henderson *(Acct Dir)*
Blair Torres *(Acct Dir)*
Megan Brueggemann *(Dir-Project Mgmt)*
Nichole Kirsch *(Dir-Media)*
Elizabeth Dale *(Acct Supvr)*
Leigh Quicksall *(Supvr-Media)*
Joshua Lee *(Strategist-Digital-Search)*
Ashley Shadowens *(Strategist-Social Media)*
Mark Shonka *(Acct Exec)*
Zack Ward *(Sr Art Dir)*

Accounts:
1 Million 4 Anna Foundation
Arena Brands; Garland, TX Lucchese, Resistol, Stetson; 2008
Baylor Healthcare System; Dallas, TX Hospital Network; 2001
Blackmon Mooring Brand Development, Creative Development, Media Planning, Social Media, Strategic Planning
Blockbuster; Dallas, TX; 2005
Brooklyn's Pizzeria; 2006
Dallas Farmers Market Campaign: "Fries", SNAP Program
IntelliCentrics
La Madeleine Country French Cafe (Agency of Record) Creative Development, Media Planning, Strategic Planning
National Cheerleaders Association (Agency of Record) Brand & Creative Development, Stage, Strategic Planning
Nothing Bundt Cakes; Las Vegas, NV
Service King Collision Repair Centers Brand Strategy, Creative Development, Digital marketing, Media Planning, Outdoor Advertising, PR, Radio, Searching Marketing, Social Media, TV
The St. Lucia Project
Taco Cabana Brand Strategy, Creative
Taylor's Gift Foundation
Thomson Reuters
ThyssenKrupp; Dallas, TX Elevators; 2005
TXU Energy Services Energy Services; 2003
UDR, Inc; Highlands Ranch, CO; 2006
VertsKebap (Agency of Record) Advertising, Brand Planning, Creative, Media Planning
Winstar Casinos; 2006

FIRELIGHT GROUP
PO Box 2407, Madison, WI 53701
Tel.: (608) 441-3473
Fax: (914) 397-0815
E-Mail: info@firelightgroup.com
Web Site: firelightgroup.com/

Employees: 10
Year Founded: 1981

Agency Specializes In: Advertising Specialties, Business-To-Business, Collateral, Consulting, Digital/Interactive, E-Commerce, Event Planning & Marketing, Exhibit/Trade Shows, High Technology, Internet/Web Design, Sales Promotion, Travel & Tourism

Breakdown of Gross Billings by Media: Collateral: 20%; Mags.: 20%; Newsp.: 10%; Other: 50%

Anjee M. Sorge *(Dir-Ops)*
Dustin Sorge *(Dir-Natl Accounts)*
Ashley Himebaugh *(Acct Mgr)*

Accounts:
Banco Popular
Citibank
Coca-Cola Refreshments USA, Inc.
Heineken
Manpower
Panasonic
Tire Guru

FISHBOWL MARKETING
44 Canal Ctr Plz Ste 500, Alexandria, VA 22314
Tel.: (703) 836-3421
Fax: (703) 836-3422
Toll Free: (800) 836-2818
E-Mail: info@fishbowl.com
Web Site: www.fishbowl.com

Employees: 107

Agency Specializes In: Email

Dev Ganesan *(Pres & CEO)*
Aaron Levine *(CFO)*
Joel Pulliam *(CMO)*
Andrew McCasker *(CTO)*
Scott Shaw *(Chief Innovation Officer)*
Karen Willison *(VP-Strategic Accounts & Partnerships)*
Tama Looney *(Acct Dir)*
Heather Cote *(Generalist-HR)*
Kate Frantz *(Specialist-Online Mktg)*

Accounts:
Bennigan's
Denny's
Famous Dave's
Fox & Hound
Gordon Biersch
Houlihan's
Maggiano's
Palm Restaurant

FLAIR COMMUNICATIONS AGENCY, INC.
214 W Erie St, Chicago, IL 60654
Tel.: (312) 943-5959
Toll Free: (800) 621-8317
Web Site: flairagency.com/

E-Mail for Key Personnel:
President: amiller@flairagency.com

Employees: 55
Year Founded: 1964

Agency Specializes In: Business-To-Business, Consumer Goods, Consumer Marketing, Financial, Food Service, Strategic Planning/Research

Lee F. Flaherty *(Founder & CEO)*
Kevin Kennedy *(VP-Client Svcs)*

Accounts:
Action for Healthy Kids
Dairy Farmers of America
Dairy Management Inc.
Saputo Cheese U.S.A.

FOCUS MEDIA INC
10 Matthews St, Goshen, NY 10924
Tel.: (845) 294-3342
Fax: (845) 294-1118
Web Site: www.focusmediausa.com

Year Founded: 2002

Agency Specializes In: Advertising, Broadcast, Collateral, Digital/Interactive, Media Planning, Outdoor, Print, Public Relations, Radio, Social Media

Josh Sommers *(Pres & CEO)*
William J. Bratton, Jr. *(CFO)*
Tony Morino *(Sr VP-Client Svcs)*
Lisa Kelly *(VP-Client Svcs)*
Jp McGuirk *(VP)*
Victor Coreas *(Dir-Art)*
Mike Bieger *(Mgr-PR)*
Nancy Kriz *(Mgr-PR)*
Ryann Hannigan *(Sr Acct Exec)*
Mary Ann Ellsworth *(Sr Graphic Designer)*

Accounts:
Catskill Regional Medical Center Medical Services
Gentle Dentistry Dental Practice Services
Grey's Woodworks Inc Construction Services
Hudson Valley Economic Development Corporation Relocation Services
Metropolitan Vacuum Cleaner Company Inc
Orange County Business Accelerator Technology Services
Orange Regional Medical Center Medical Services
Shawangunk Wine Trail Marketing
Walden Savings Bank Banking Services

FORGE SPONSORSHIP CONSULTING, LLC
25 Terrace Ave Ste 104, San Anselmo, CA 94960
Tel.: (415) 456-8588
E-Mail: jlaurent@forgesponsorship.com
Web Site: www.forgesponsorship.com

Employees: 3
Year Founded: 2004

Agency Specializes In: Advertising, Automotive, Brand Development & Integration, Business-To-Business, Co-op Advertising, Communications, Consulting, Consumer Marketing, Corporate Identity, Entertainment, Event Planning & Marketing, Leisure, Local Marketing, Planning & Consultation, Publicity/Promotions, Sales Promotion, Sports Market, Strategic Planning/Research, Sweepstakes, T.V.

Approx. Annual Billings: $1,000,000

Breakdown of Gross Billings by Media: Event Mktg.: 30%; Sports Mktg.: 70%

Marla Murphy *(Owner & Partner)*

Accounts:
AARP
CARAC; 2004
Clorox
Memorial Herman Healthcare
Super 8
Texas Health Resources
Wyndham Hotels

GAGE
10000 Hwy 55, Minneapolis, MN 55441-6300
Tel.: (763) 595-3800
Fax: (763) 595-3871
Toll Free: (877) TRY-GAGE
E-Mail: info@gage.com
Web Site: www.gage.com

Employees: 125
Year Founded: 1992

National Agency Associations: DMA-MIMA-PMA

Agency Specializes In: Advertising, Below-the-Line, Brand Development & Integration, Business-To-Business, Children's Market, Collateral, Communications, Computers & Software, Consumer Goods, Consumer Marketing, Customer Relationship Management, Digital/Interactive, Direct Response Marketing, E-Commerce, Electronic Media, Email, Financial, Graphic Design, Health Care Services, High Technology, Household Goods, Integrated Marketing, Internet/Web Design, Investor Relations, Legal Services, Planning & Consultation, Print, Production, Promotions, Sales Promotion, Social Media, Sponsorship, Strategic Planning/Research, Sweepstakes

Approx. Annual Billings: $80,000,000

Breakdown of Gross Billings by Media: Collateral: $10,000,000; Plng. & Consultation: $70,000,000

Sales Promotion Agencies

Thomas Belle *(Pres & CEO)*
Jeff Schutt *(VP-Fin & Ops)*
Michael Sichmeller *(VP-Customer Experience Design)*
Lee Allan *(Dir-Creative)*
Sara N. Blood *(Dir-PR & Agency Outreach)*
Jennifer Lorenz *(Acct Mgr)*
Jeffery Cannata *(Mgr-Emerging Mktg)*
Becky Fetzich *(Mgr-Production)*
A J Jahnig *(Mgr-Engagement)*
Michelle Hoffman *(Sr Specialist-PR)*

Accounts:
3M
Best Buy
BMW
Coca-Cola Refreshments USA, Inc.
Microsoft Microsoft ExpertZone
PreciouStatus Marketing & Communications
Truven Health Analytics
WalMart

GEM GROUP

7090 Shady Oak Rd, Eden Prairie, MN 55344
Tel.: (952) 831-6313
Fax: (952) 653-5900
E-Mail: info@gemmpls.com
Web Site: www.gemmpls.com

E-Mail for Key Personnel:
President: dkuettel@gemgroup.com

Employees: 44
Year Founded: 1971

National Agency Associations: APMA WORLDWIDE-MAA-PMA

Agency Specializes In: Advertising Specialties, Brand Development & Integration, Business-To-Business, Collateral, Communications, Consulting, Consumer Marketing, Corporate Identity, Digital/Interactive, Direct Response Marketing, E-Commerce, Electronic Media, Engineering, Entertainment, Event Planning & Marketing, Exhibit/Trade Shows, Graphic Design, Internet/Web Design, Logo & Package Design, Merchandising, Planning & Consultation, Point of Purchase, Point of Sale, Production, Public Relations, Publicity/Promotions, Sales Promotion, Sports Market, Strategic Planning/Research, Sweepstakes

David Kuettel *(Pres)*
Mike Brunner *(Dir-Strategic Brand Plng)*

Accounts:
3M; Saint Paul, MN; 1988
Bob Barker
JCB
Land O'Lakes
Polaris
Quantum Labs
Schwan's
SLK Development Group
Smead Manufacturing
UnitedHealth Group

GFA MARKETING

(d/b/a George Fencik)
1006 Arnold Ave, Point Pleasant, NJ 08742-2309
Tel.: (732) 295-8092
Fax: (732) 295-1729
Toll Free: (800) 443-6743
E-Mail: gfencik@aol.com

E-Mail for Key Personnel:
President: gfencik@aol.com

Employees: 4
Year Founded: 1979

Agency Specializes In: Advertising Specialties, Brand Development & Integration, Consulting, Consumer Marketing, Direct Response Marketing, Event Planning & Marketing, Exhibit/Trade Shows, Health Care Services, Infomercials, Medical Products, Merchandising, New Product Development, Over-50 Market, Pharmaceutical, Retail, Sales Promotion, Seniors' Market, Strategic Planning/Research

Approx. Annual Billings: $875,000

Breakdown of Gross Billings by Media: Cable T.V.: 15%; Consulting: 20%; Mags.: 15%; Sls. Promo.: 15%; Strategic Planning/Research: 15%; Trade & Consumer Mags.: 10%; Trade Shows: 10%

George Fencik *(Owner & Pres)*
Paul Danforth *(Reg VP)*
Dave Arthur *(VP-Sls & Mktg)*
Travis Merrick *(Branch Mgr)*
Steven Snyder *(Mgr-Environmental Dept)*

Accounts:
Continental Quest; Carmel, IN Pain Buster R III; 1981
Forecare
Gibson Auer
Jersey Shore Super Coups; 1984
Numark Laboratories
Prevent Care Products; 1981
Smartcover

GMR MARKETING LLC

5000 S Towne Dr, New Berlin, WI 53151-7956
Tel.: (262) 786-5600
Fax: (262) 786-0697
E-Mail: events@gmrlive.com
Web Site: gmrmarketing.com

E-Mail for Key Personnel:
President: cconnelly@gmrlive.com

Employees: 355
Year Founded: 1979

Agency Specializes In: Automotive, Brand Development & Integration, Business-To-Business, Consumer Marketing, Entertainment, Event Planning & Marketing, Exhibit/Trade Shows, Financial, Health Care Services, Hispanic Market, Medical Products, Pharmaceutical, Planning & Consultation, Publicity/Promotions, Radio, Retail, Sales Promotion, Sponsorship, Sports Market, Strategic Planning/Research, Sweepstakes, Teen Market

Gary M. Reynolds *(Chm)*
Craig Connelly *(Pres)*
Lisa Cieslak *(CFO)*
Joe Sutter *(Chief Creative Officer)*
Steve Dupee *(Exec VP-Bus Dev)*
Ann Janikowsky *(Exec VP)*
Alex Beer *(Sr VP-Client Mgmt)*
Tony Fowler *(Sr VP-Program Solutions)*
Jon Steltenpohl *(VP & Grp Acct Dir)*
Dave Bohnsack *(VP-Insights & Analytics)*
Heather Gaecke *(VP-HR)*
Steve Heisdorf *(VP-Fin)*
Allison Kelly *(VP-Client Mgmt)*
Chris Lierman *(VP-Strategy)*
Andy Martin *(VP-Procurement)*
Mike Thompson *(VP-Client Mgmt)*
Andy Hayman *(Head-Content Dev & Production)*
Jeff Bayson *(Exec Dir-Creative)*
Joni Vasos *(Grp Dir-Events-Mall Mktg)*
Jeff Magnuson *(Acct Dir)*
Aubrey Walker *(Creative Dir-Ideation)*
Anne Casey *(Dir-Promos)*
JoAnne Lynch *(Dir-Bus Ops)*
Dave Perry *(Dir-Social Media)*
Tim Witmer *(Dir-Digital Project Mgmt)*
LeAnn Hoksch *(Project Mgr-Digital & Mobile)*
Megan Gavin *(Mgr-Bus Dev)*
Terri Neitzel *(Mgr-Financial Analysis)*
Michael Schinabeck *(Mgr-Financial Analysis)*
Emily Morrison *(Acct Supvr)*
Jason Bolz *(Supvr-Ops)*
Dana Aschaker *(Acct Exec-Client Svcs)*
Leah Thomas *(Acct Exec-Comcast, Sports Strategy)*
Andy Hoban *(Asst Controller)*
Craig Miller *(Acct Coord)*
Dave Rosenberg *(Chief Strategic Officer)*

Accounts:
Best Buy; 2001
Comcast Corporation
FX Network Campaign: "House Calls"
New-Johnsonville
Lowes Home Improvement; 2002
Major League Baseball; 1998
McDonald's; 2004
MillerCoors
National Football League Campaign: "Official NFL Gameday Music"
Orbitz Travel
Pepsi Co; Purchase, NY; 1999
New-Polaris
New-TuneIn TuneIn Premium
New-Weber

Branches

GMR Marketing

220 E 42nd St 15th Fl, New York, NY 10017
Tel.: (212) 505-3636
Fax: (212) 505-0455
E-Mail: rarnstein@gmrlive.com
Web Site: gmrmarketing.com

Employees: 20
Year Founded: 1981

Agency Specializes In: Entertainment, Event Planning & Marketing

Steve Knill *(Exec VP-Music & Entertainment)*
Matt Hill *(Sr VP-Global Sports & Entertainment Consulting)*
Philip Kirsch *(Acct Dir)*
Kelsey Philpott *(Acct Dir)*
Kailee Crawford *(Mgr-Mktg & Comm)*
Andrew Kihn *(Mgr-Bus Dev)*
Bobby Isom *(Acct Supvr-Comcast-Freedom Region)*
David Miller *(Acct Coord)*

GMR Marketing

200 E Randolph St Ste 3400 34th Fl, Chicago, IL 60601-6533
Tel.: (312) 324-8950
Fax: (312) 324-8960
E-Mail: sjarvis@gmrmarketing.com
Web Site: www.gmrmarketing.com

Employees: 40
Year Founded: 1983

Agency Specializes In: Entertainment, Event Planning & Marketing, Sponsorship

Brad Bergren *(Exec VP)*
Steve Dupee *(Exec VP-Bus Dev)*
Steve Jarvis *(Exec VP-Client Dev)*
Vince O'Brien *(Sr VP-Global Sports & Entertainment Consultancy)*
Lesley Pinckney *(Sr VP-Digital Strategy)*
Todd Fischer *(VP-Client Mgmt)*
Dave Mullins *(VP-Client Dev)*
Shanley Giglio *(Asst Controller)*

Accounts:
Audi of America, Inc.
Comcast

Humana, Inc.
Nissan North America, Inc.
PepsiCo Inc.
Volvo Trucks North America, Inc.

GMR Marketing
1435 W Morehead St Ste 190, Charlotte, NC 28208
Tel.: (704) 342-4450
Fax: (704) 342-4452
E-Mail: mboykin@gmrlive.com
Web Site: gmrmarketing.com

Employees: 67

Agency Specializes In: Event Planning & Marketing, Sponsorship

Brad Bergren *(Exec VP)*
Jeff Handler *(VP-Sports Mktg)*
Julie Yenichek *(VP-Client Mgmt)*
Jeremy Gomez *(Sr Acct Dir)*
Thomas Pierce *(Acct Dir)*
Kristine Curley *(Dir-Media Rels)*
Farnoush Ansari *(Sr Acct Mgr-SAP)*
David Mueller *(Acct Supvr)*

Accounts:
Baby Ruth
Chobani LLC
Gillette
Hilton Worldwide
ING
Jeep
Levis
Lowe's
Microsoft
Procter & Gamble
RBitz

GMR Marketing
14931 72nd Pl NE Ste A, Kenmore, WA 98028
Tel.: (206) 529-4891
Web Site: www.gmrmarketing.com

Employees: 600

Bryan Rasch *(Chief Digital Officer)*
Cameron Barratt *(Acct Mgr-MillerCoors & Pacific Reg)*
Dave Rosenberg *(Chief Strategic Officer)*

Accounts:
MillerCoors

GMR Marketing Spain
Calle Aviador Lindbergh 3, 28002 Madrid, Spain
Tel.: (34) 91 570 5475
Fax: (34) 91 570 6578
Web Site: gmrmarketing.com/es-es

E-Mail for Key Personnel:
President: raulsanchez@delfingroup.com

Employees: 45
Year Founded: 1994

Agency Specializes In: Below-the-Line

Oscar Coto *(CEO)*
Luis Gonzalez-Aller Vazquez *(Exec Dir-Creative)*
Almudena Gallego Garcia *(Client Svcs Dir)*
Heidi Portillo Navarro *(Client Svcs Dir)*
Inma Martin *(Acct Mgr)*
Teddy Anderson *(Mgr-Bus Dev)*
Oscar Cano *(Acct Supvr)*
Raquel Novoa Martinez *(Acct Supvr)*

Accounts:
Movistar Campaign: "The Room"

GRAPEVINE DESIGNS
8406 Melrose, Lenexa, KS 66214
Tel.: (913) 307-0225
E-Mail: info@grapevinedesigns.com
Web Site: www.grapevinedesigns.com/

Agency Specializes In: Medical Products, Merchandising, Promotions, Publicity/Promotions

Janie Gaunce *(Pres & CEO)*
Victoria Brashears *(Acct Dir)*
Holly Robertson *(Acct Dir)*
Meredith Wallace *(Sr Acct Mgr)*
Laurie Mazon *(Acct Mgr)*
Kristin Wood *(Acct Mgr)*

G.W. HOFFMAN MARKETING & COMMUNICATIONS
757-767 Post Rd, Darien, CT 06820-4720
Tel.: (203) 655-8321
Fax: (203) 656-2641
E-Mail: info@gwhoffman.com
Web Site: www.gwhoffman.com

E-Mail for Key Personnel:
President: ghoffman@gwhoffman.com

Employees: 27
Year Founded: 1981

National Agency Associations: PMA

Agency Specializes In: Communications, Consumer Marketing, Digital/Interactive, Event Planning & Marketing, Graphic Design, Health Care Services, In-Store Advertising, Internet/Web Design, Pharmaceutical, Planning & Consultation, Point of Purchase, Print, Sales Promotion, Sponsorship

Approx. Annual Billings: $6,000,000

Breakdown of Gross Billings by Media: Plng. & Consultation: $1,500,000; Sls. Promo.: $4,500,000

Karen Goyette *(Owner, Pres & Mng Dir)*
Kathy Gouin *(Sr VP & Acct Dir)*
Liz Cahill *(Sr VP)*
Dan Walker *(VP & Dir-Ops)*
Jim Buzak *(VP & Assoc Dir-Creative)*
Richard Keith *(VP & Assoc Dir-Creative)*

Accounts:
Activia
Banquet
Barilla Pasta & Sauce
Coca Cola USA Fountain
ConAgra Healthy Choice, Marie Callenders
Dannon New Products
High Liner Captain's Cut, Fisher Boy
Johnson & Johnson
Lipton
Nestle
Ortho Biotech Ortho Visc, Procrit
Snack Pack
Unilever Hellman's, Knorr

HALEY MIRANDA GROUP
8654 Washington Blvd, Culver City, CA 90232
Tel.: (310) 842-7369
Fax: (310) 842-8932
E-Mail: jvonk@haleymiranda.com
Web Site: www.haleymiranda.com

E-Mail for Key Personnel:
President: jwest@haleymiranda.com

Employees: 18
Year Founded: 1993

Agency Specializes In: Advertising

Approx. Annual Billings: $5,000,000

Jed West *(Pres)*
Tina Hopkins *(Exec VP)*
Rob Buscher *(VP & Dir-Creative)*
Donna Landau *(VP-Bus Dev & Client Svcs)*
Ashton Spatz *(Dir-Social Media & PR)*
Maggie Waters *(Sr Mgr-PR)*
Lindsay Hilton *(Sr Acct Mgr)*
Rick Chan *(Mgr-Acctg)*
Sarah Ledesma *(Mgr-Social Media)*

Accounts:
Cable News Network
Comcast
TNT
Universal Home Studio Entertainment
Viacom Marketing Council
Warner Bros. Entertainment Inc.

HURRAH MARKETING
1110 S Robertson Blvd Ste 5, Los Angeles, CA 90035
Tel.: (310) 285-0252
Fax: (310) 285-0253
Web Site: www.hurrahproductions.com

Year Founded: 2008

Agency Specializes In: Sales Promotion

Carol Eisenrauch *(Pres-Bus Dev-Global)*
Grace Lau *(Designer-UX)*

Accounts:
Brave Dog
Holographics.com Holographic Creative Services
King & Country Miniature Figures
Lucalizod Print & Web Design Designing Services
METAphrenie
Newspeak
Stun Media Social Media Marketing

ICE FACTOR
11 W Main St Ste 304, Carpentersville, IL 60110-1706
Tel.: (847) 844-0814
Fax: (630) 206-1036
E-Mail: rkellogg@icefactor.com
Web Site: www.icefactor.com

Employees: 10

Agency Specializes In: Advertising, African-American Market, Alternative Advertising, Brand Development & Integration, Branded Entertainment, Business-To-Business, Communications, Consumer Goods, Consumer Marketing, Direct-to-Consumer, Entertainment, Event Planning & Marketing, Exhibit/Trade Shows, Guerilla Marketing, Integrated Marketing, Local Marketing, Mobile Marketing, Out-of-Home Media, Outdoor, Promotions, Retail, Sales Promotion, Social Media, Travel & Tourism, Viral/Buzz/Word of Mouth

Russ Kellogg *(Co-Founder, COO & VP)*

Accounts:
American Airlines
American Express
AT&T Communications Corp.
Citibank
Cricket
Heineken
Novartis Pharmaceuticals
Pepsi
Radio Disney
RCN Cable
Sears-Kenmore Brand
Southwest Airlines
T-Mobile US
Verizon Wireless

IGM CREATIVE GROUP
166 Main St Ste 202, Lincoln Park, NJ 07035
Tel.: (973) 709-1126
Web Site: www.igmcreativegroup.com

Employees: 12

Agency Specializes In: Above-the-Line, Advertising, Advertising Specialties, Affiliate Marketing, Arts, Brand Development & Integration, Branded Entertainment, Business Publications, Business-To-Business, Catalogs, Co-op Advertising, Collateral, College, Commercial Photography, Communications, Consulting, Consumer Goods, Consumer Marketing, Consumer Publications, Content, Corporate Communications, Corporate Identity, Custom Publishing, Digital/Interactive, Direct Response Marketing, Direct-to-Consumer, E-Commerce, Email, Environmental, Event Planning & Marketing, Exhibit/Trade Shows, Game Integration, Graphic Design, Guerilla Marketing, High Technology, Identity Marketing, In-Store Advertising, Industrial, Information Technology, Integrated Marketing, Internet/Web Design, Investor Relations, Legal Services, Local Marketing, Logo & Package Design, Magazines, Media Buying Services, Media Planning, Media Training, Medical Products, Merchandising, Mobile Marketing, Multimedia, New Product Development, New Technologies, Newspaper, Newspapers & Magazines, Outdoor, Over-50 Market, Package Design, Pharmaceutical, Planning & Consultation, Podcasting, Point of Sale, Print, Product Placement, Promotions, Publishing, Real Estate, Restaurant, Sales Promotion, Social Marketing/Nonprofit, Sports Market, Technical Advertising, Trade & Consumer Magazines, Travel & Tourism, Web (Banner Ads, Pop-ups, etc.)

Jay Stack *(Pres)*

Accounts:
Avaya
ERT

IMC
960 Holmdel Rd, Holmdel, NJ 07733-2138
Tel.: (732) 332-0515
Fax: (732) 332-0520
Web Site: www.imc-nj.com

E-Mail for Key Personnel:
President: rzick@imc-nj.com

Employees: 15
Year Founded: 1983

Agency Specializes In: Co-op Advertising, Collateral, Consumer Marketing, Corporate Identity, Cosmetics, E-Commerce, Electronic Media, Graphic Design, Health Care Services, Internet/Web Design, Logo & Package Design, Merchandising, Pharmaceutical, Point of Purchase, Point of Sale, Publicity/Promotions, Sales Promotion, Strategic Planning/Research, Sweepstakes

Robert Zick *(Owner)*
Steven Aronson *(Partner-Integrated Mktg Comm & Strategy)*
Stephen Norton *(VP-Digital Mktg Svcs & CRM Strategy)*
Julie Evans *(Dir-Production)*
Danielle Miles *(Dir-Creative)*
Regina Sherman *(Dir-Creative)*

Accounts:
Aveeno
B. Manischewitz Company
Clean&Clear
Colgate-Palmolive
Johnson & Johnson Consumer Products
Johnson & Johnson Personal Products
Johnson's Baby Products
National Safe Kids Campaign
ROC

IN MOTION PROMOTION MOBILE EVENT MARKETING
2100 Cloverleaf St E, Columbus, OH 43232
Tel.: (614) 866-9111
Fax: (614) 866-6182
Toll Free: (888) 801-0078
E-Mail: rhunt@inmotionpromotion.com
Web Site: www.inmotionpromotion.com

Employees: 20
Year Founded: 1999

Agency Specializes In: Event Planning & Marketing, Exhibit/Trade Shows, New Product Development, Transportation

Robert Hunt *(Pres)*
Charles Hunt *(CEO)*

Accounts:
Allison Transmission Holdings, Inc.
Alstrom
Aurora Exhibits
CMI
Exxon Mobil
Fahlgren Advertising
Lenova/IBM
McDonald's
Microsoft
Mobile Exxon
Morrison Communications
Ohio State University Medical Center
Rogers Athletics
SBC
Sea Change International
Simmons Bedding Company
Sunny D
UPS NHRA Racing

INNERWORKINGS INC.
600 W Chicago Ave Ste 850, Chicago, IL 60610
Tel.: (312) 642-3700
Fax: (312) 642-3704
E-Mail: info@inwk.com
Web Site: www.inwk.com

Employees: 1,600
Year Founded: 2001

Agency Specializes In: Advertising Specialties, Collateral, Print, Production (Print)

Revenue: $1,000,133,000

Eric D. Belcher *(CEO)*
Leigh Segall *(CMO)*
Ron Provenzano *(Gen Counsel)*
Jennifer Krebs *(Sr VP-HR)*
Brad M. Moore *(VP-Dev-Global)*
Lisa Watkins *(Dir-Talent Acq)*
Ryan Spohn *(Interim CFO)*

Accounts:
Graphic Resource Group, Inc.
IHG
Inkchasers
InterContinental Hotels Group
Samsung
Scotts
Spectrum Printing Services

Subsidiaries

InnerWorkings, Inc.
3557 Butterfield Rd Ste 105, Aurora, IL 60502-2400
Tel.: (312) 642-3700
Fax: (630) 820-1930
Toll Free: (800) 929-5415
Web Site: www.inwk.com

Employees: 25
Year Founded: 1965

Eric Belcher *(Pres & CEO)*
Alex Castroneves *(Pres-LATAM)*
Seth Kessler *(Pres-Global Solutions)*

Accounts:
Service Masters

InnerWorkings Inc.
(Formerly Corporate Edge Inc.)
1140 Broadway 22nd Fl, New York, NY 10018
(See Separate Listing)

THE INTEGER GROUP-DALLAS
1999 Bryan St Ste 1700, Dallas, TX 75201
Tel.: (214) 758-6800
Fax: (214) 758-6901
E-Mail: ldeatherage@integer.com
Web Site: www.integer.com

Employees: 75
Year Founded: 1994

Agency Specializes In: Advertising, Below-the-Line, Brand Development & Integration, Collateral, Communications, Computers & Software, Consumer Marketing, Electronics, Entertainment, Exhibit/Trade Shows, Graphic Design, High Technology, In-Store Advertising, Integrated Marketing, Planning & Consultation, Point of Purchase, Point of Sale, Print, Promotions, Publicity/Promotions, Restaurant, Retail, Sales Promotion, Sponsorship, Strategic Planning/Research

Jeremy Pagden *(Chm)*
Mike Sweeney *(CEO)*
Jan Gittemeier *(COO)*
Ellen Cook *(Pres-Dallas)*
Will Clarke *(Sr VP & Exec Dir-Creative)*
Nick Hoadley *(Sr VP & Dir-Insight & Strategy)*
Michael Farmer *(Sr VP-Ops)*
In Lee *(VP-Creative Tech)*
Courtney Jones *(Grp Acct Dir)*
Samer Salfiti *(Acct Dir-FedEx)*
Jamie Foster *(Dir-HR)*
Lana Saylor *(Dir-Process Dev & Implementation)*
Barbara Barry *(Mgr-Print Production)*
Tara Thompson *(Acct Supvr)*
Charlotte Moss *(Supvr-Digital Media)*
Brian Hambrick *(Sr Acct Planner)*
Courtney King *(Reg Acct Exec)*

Accounts:
7-Eleven Campaign: "Dip-A-Drip"
AT&T Communications Corp.; 2001
Bimbo Bakeries, USA
Deoleo North America (Agency of Record) Bertolli, Carapelli, Carbonell, Media Planning, Shopper Marketing Strategy
Dr. Oetker
FedEx Office; 2007
Illinois Lottery
Intrepid Potash
Slurpee BrainFreeze Laboratory

THE INTEGER GROUP - DENVER
7245 W Alaska Dr, Lakewood, CO 80226
Tel.: (303) 393-3000
E-Mail: ldeatherage@integer.com
Web Site: www.integer.com

Employees: 638

Agency Specializes In: Advertising, Advertising Specialties, Asian Market, Bilingual Market, Brand Development & Integration, Broadcast, Business-To-Business, Catalogs, Collateral, Communications, Consumer Goods, Consumer Marketing, Customer Relationship Management, Digital/Interactive, Direct Response Marketing, Direct-to-Consumer, E-Commerce, Entertainment, Event Planning & Marketing, Exhibit/Trade Shows, Experience Design, Financial, Graphic Design, Hispanic Market, Household Goods, In-Store Advertising, Integrated Marketing, International, Internet/Web Design, Logo & Package Design, Market Research, Media Buying Services, Media Planning, Men's Market, Merchandising, Mobile Marketing, Multicultural, Multimedia, Newspapers & Magazines, Out-of-Home Media, Outdoor, Package Design, Pharmaceutical, Planning & Consultation, Point of Purchase, Point of Sale, Print, Production, Production (Print), Promotions, Publicity/Promotions, Radio, Regional, Sponsorship

Craig Elston *(Exec VP-Insight & Strategy)*
Scott Meyer *(Exec VP-Creative)*
Tisha Kirkpatrick *(Sr VP-Acct Leadership)*
Todd Hossfeld *(VP)*
Mike Manion *(VP)*
Bob Strausser *(VP-Acct Svc)*
Fred Gardner *(Exec Dir-Art)*
Michelle Tremblay *(Grp Dir-Insight & Strategy)*
Ralph Alvarez *(Grp Acct Dir)*
Jessica Garretson *(Grp Acct Dir)*
Chava Ziff *(Grp Acct Dir)*
Sarah Plotnik *(Acct Dir & Dir-Digital)*
Jenny Dahl *(Acct Dir)*
Kyle Ingram *(Acct Dir-Kellogg's)*
Stacie Keiter *(Acct Dir)*
Dillon Snyder *(Creative Dir)*
Kelly Spehar *(Acct Dir)*
Nate Craner *(Dir-Creative)*
Jennine Friess *(Dir-Network Comm)*
Tera Gill *(Dir-Engagement & Collaboration)*
Michael Glunk *(Dir-Insight & Strategy)*
Caryn Golden *(Dir-Production Ops)*
Mandy French Grosh *(Dir-Project Mgmt)*
Kang Ha *(Dir-Digital)*
Ryan Karlstrom *(Dir-Brand & Promos-Miller Lite)*
Balind Sieber *(Dir-Digital Creative)*
Brad Vermeer *(Dir-Art)*
Shannan Garrison *(Assoc Dir-Creative)*
Tom Goodrich *(Assoc Dir-Creative)*
Kelley McClellan *(Assoc Dir)*
Kerney Daniel *(Sr Mgr-Print Production)*
Dana Taylor *(Sr Mgr-Production)*
Kathryn Bacon Cvancara *(Acct Supvr)*
Laurie Dolan *(Acct Supvr)*
Sara Dwiggins *(Acct Supvr)*
Josh Jacobsen *(Acct Supvr)*
Trent Killian *(Acct Supvr)*
Brian McCarthy *(Acct Supvr-Naked Juice Emerging Brands)*
Emily McMahon *(Acct Supvr)*
Amy Neujahr *(Acct Supvr)*
Natalie Bosler *(Supvr)*
Max Blum *(Sr Acct Exec)*
Kristen Brelig *(Sr Acct Exec-Procter & Gamble)*
Amanda Leavelle *(Sr Acct Exec-Digital)*
Wendy Nakajima *(Sr Acct Exec-Digital)*
Kira Torgersen *(Sr Acct Planner)*
Rob Soltan *(Copywriter)*
Michael Tully *(Copywriter)*
Donna Keffeler *(Coord-Event)*

Accounts:
Glaxo Smith Kline
Grocery Manufacturers Association
New-Izze
Johnson & Johnson Acuvue, LifeScan
Kellogg Company Cheez-It, Frosted Flakes, Mini Wheats, Rice Krispies
LifeScan Inc
Marisco Funds
Mars
MillerCoors Blue Moon, Coors Banquet, Coors Light, Miller Light
The Procter & Gamble Company

THE INTEGER GROUP-MIDWEST

2633 Fleur Dr, Des Moines, IA 50321-1753
Tel.: (515) 288-7910
Fax: (515) 288-8439
Toll Free: (800) 752-2633
E-Mail: Ideatherage@integer.com
Web Site: www.integer.com

Employees: 125
Year Founded: 1977

Agency Specializes In: Advertising, Agriculture, Below-the-Line, Brand Development & Integration, Broadcast, Business Publications, Business-To-Business, Co-op Advertising, Collateral, Communications, Consumer Marketing, Consumer Publications, Corporate Identity, Digital/Interactive, Direct Response Marketing, Education, Electronic Media, Environmental, Exhibit/Trade Shows, Financial, Government/Political, Graphic Design, Household Goods, In-Store Advertising, Industrial, Integrated Marketing, Internet/Web Design, Local Marketing, Logo & Package Design, Magazines, Media Buying Services, Media Planning, Media Relations, Media Training, Multimedia, Newspaper, Newspapers & Magazines, Out-of-Home Media, Outdoor, Planning & Consultation, Point of Purchase, Point of Sale, Print, Production, Public Relations, Publicity/Promotions, Radio, Recruitment, Retail, Sales Promotion, Sponsorship, Sports Market, Strategic Planning/Research, T.V., Trade & Consumer Magazines, Travel & Tourism

Jeremy Pagden *(Chm)*
Mike Sweeney *(CEO)*
Frank Maher *(Grp Pres & COO)*
Xan McNelly *(Chief Strategy Officer, Chief Integration Officer & Exec VP)*
Robin Casmirri *(VP & Dir-Media Svcs)*
Michael Rivera *(Exec Dir-Creative)*
Chris Beard *(Grp Acct Dir)*
Danielle Fengel *(Acct Dir)*
Kelsey Meyer *(Dir-Art)*
Jami Milne *(Sr Acct Planner)*
Brenna Musfeldt *(Designer-Production)*

Accounts:
Allsteel Office Furniture; 2008
Electrolux Frigidaire; 2007
Michelin BFGoodrich, Michelin; 2006
Mohawk Industries Columbia Flooring Quick-Step, Daltile
Pella Corporation Doors, Windows; 1997
Shell Pennzoil, Quaker State, Rotella Lubricants

INTEGRATED MARKETING WORKS

260 Newport Ctr Dr Ste 425, Newport Beach, CA 92660
Tel.: (949) 833-3822
Fax: (949) 833-3810
E-Mail: info@imwagency.com
Web Site: www.imwagency.com

Employees: 14
Year Founded: 1990

Agency Specializes In: Advertising, Agriculture, Automotive, Consulting, Food Service, Health Care Services, Hispanic Market, Logo & Package Design, Planning & Consultation, Public Relations, Publicity/Promotions, Radio, Strategic Planning/Research

Approx. Annual Billings: $5,500,000

Breakdown of Gross Billings by Media: Consulting: 10%; Game Shows: 10%; Print: 30%; Radio: 50%

Kari Bretschger *(Pres & CEO)*
Peter Bretschger *(Co-Pres & CMO)*
Christopher Bretschger *(Dir-Digital Strategy)*
Marcie Gonzalez *(Assoc Dir-Creative)*
Mairim Martinez *(Sr Acct Supvr)*

Accounts:
American Management Association; New York, NY; 1996
APEAM - Avocados from Mexico
The Balboa Bay Club & Resort
Crime Produce Inc.
DENSO Heavy Duty
Denso Sales California
Fit-LINE, Inc.
The Flower Fields; Carlsbad, CA; 1998
Newport Ocean Sailing Association; 2003
Orbis Education University of Oklahoma College of Nursing Program
Original Los Angeles Flower Market
Policy Options
Roche Diagnostics; Indianapolis, IN MyDoc
Sonora Spring Grapes
Sunkist Foods
UMe Federal Credit Union

INTEGRITY SPORTS MARKETING, MEDIA & MANAGEMENT

228 Roundway Down, Davidson, NC 28036
Tel.: (704) 896-8181
Fax: (704) 896-8441
Web Site: www.is3m.com

Employees: 5
Year Founded: 1993

Agency Specializes In: Brand Development & Integration, Catalogs, Consulting, E-Commerce, Email, Integrated Marketing, Mobile Marketing, Podcasting, Sponsorship, Sports Market, Web (Banner Ads, Pop-ups, etc.)

Approx. Annual Billings: $3,000,000

Breakdown of Gross Billings by Media: Consulting: $3,000,000

Pat Millen *(Pres & CEO)*

J. BRENLIN DESIGN, INC.

2054 Tandem Way, Norco, CA 92860
Tel.: (951) 549-1515
Fax: (951) 549-1453
Web Site: www.jbrenlindesign.com

E-Mail for Key Personnel:
Creative Dir.: jbrenlin@jbrenlin.com

Employees: 9
Year Founded: 1985

Agency Specializes In: Collateral, Graphic Design, Logo & Package Design, Media Buying Services, New Product Development, Point of Purchase, Print, Trade & Consumer Magazines

Approx. Annual Billings: $1,200,000

Jane Brenlin *(Pres & Partner)*
Rick Haan *(Partner & VP)*
Vicki James *(Dir-Sls)*
Andrew Phipps *(Dir-Internet Mktg)*
Susana Djuanda *(Mgr-Media & Acct Exec)*

Accounts:
Lam Weston

J PUBLIC RELATIONS

1620 5th Ave, San Diego, CA 92101

Tel.: (619) 255-7069
Fax: (619) 255-1364
Web Site: www.jpublicrelations.com

Agency Specializes In: Crisis Communications, Event Planning & Marketing, Media Relations, Social Media

Jamie Lynn Sigler *(Founder & Partner)*
Sarah Evans *(Partner)*
Lauren Clifford Knudsen *(VP)*
Amy Ogden *(VP-Brand Dev)*
Callan Green *(Dir-Digital Strategy)*
Heidi Baldwin *(Sr Acct Supvr)*
Emma Hartland-Mahon *(Sr Acct Supvr)*
Tanya Scalisi *(Sr Acct Supvr)*
Jillian Hunter *(Acct Supvr)*
Marrissa Mallory *(Acct Supvr)*

Accounts:
New-89 Agave
ART Hotel
Autograph Collection
Block16 Hospitality; Las Vegas, NV PR
New-The Camby Hotel
The Cannery
Cheeca Lodge & Spa
Colorescience
El Cholo
Elli Quark Brand Positioning, PR
The Embassy Row Hotel
F3 Foods
Fairmont Mayakoba
New-Flour & Barley Brick Oven Pizza
Four Seasons Resort Lana'i
Gaijin Noodle + Sake Hour
Good Time Design
The Goring Hotel
Grand Hotel Tremezzo
Gurney's Montauk Resort & Seawater Spa
Hard Rock Hotel Las Vegas Restaurant Services
Hilton San Diego Bayfront Restaurant Services
Hotel Belleclaire; New York, NY
The Ivy Hotel; Baltimore, MD
Jumeirah Group PR
Katsuya; San Diego, CA
La Valencia Hotel; La Jolla, CA
Lantern's Keep & Triomphe in Iroquois; New York, NY
L'Auberge de Sedona; Sedona, AZ
Le Diner a San Diego
The Lodge at Glendorn
The Lodge at Ventana Canyon
New-The Lot
New-LumaRx
New-Madison Restaurant & Bar
Marquee Restaurant Restaurant Services
Marqui Los Cabos
ME! bath
MetWest Terra Hospitality; San Francisco, CA Casa Madrona, Hotel Abri, Hotel Terra Jackson Hole, Lodge at Tiburon, Teton Mountain Lodge & Spa, Toll House
Mountain Trek
NOIR; Manhattan, NY
OPUS Montreal
OPUS Vancouver
New-our & Barley Brick Oven Pizza
New-Paleta
Phoenix CVB
New-The Restoration
The Ritz-Carlton, Amelia Island
The Ritz-Carlton, Bal Harbour
New-The Ritz-Carlton, Chicago
The Ritz-Carlton, Fort Lauderdale
The Ritz-Carlton Golf Resort, Naples
The Ritz-Carlton Key Biscayne, Miami
The Ritz-Carlton, Naples
The Ritz-Carlton, New Orleans
The Ritz-Carlton New York, Battery Park
The Ritz-Carlton New York, Central Park
The Ritz-Carlton New York, Westchester
The Ritz-Carlton, Pentagon City
The Ritz-Carlton, Philadelphia
The Ritz-Carlton, Rancho Mirage
The Ritz-Carlton, Sarasota
The Ritz-Carlton, South Beach
New-The Ritz-Carlton, Washington, DC
Royal Palms Resort & Spa
Salamander Resort & Spa; Middleburg, VA
Scottsdale Magazine Marketing, Media Relations, Social Media, Strategy
Searsucker; Scottsdale, AZ
Side Bar; San Diego Night Clubs
SmartFlyer
Sotto 13
New-Sparkle Bar
The Surrey; New York, NY
Tanque Verde Ranch; Tucson, AZ
Tessemae's
Topnotch Resort; Stowe, VT
True Food Kitchen; San Diego, CA
The W Hotels; San Diego Hotels Management Services
Westfield UTC
The Westin Lake, Las Vegas
The Wigwam
Zen Monkey Breakfast

JACK NADEL, INC.

8701 Bellanca Ave, Los Angeles, CA 90045
Tel.: (310) 815-2600
Fax: (310) 815-2660
E-Mail: info@nadel.com
Web Site: www.nadel.com

Employees: 325
Year Founded: 1953

Agency Specializes In: Advertising Specialties, Direct Response Marketing, Direct-to-Consumer, Recruitment

Revenue: $50,000,000

Bob Kritzler *(Mng Partner & CFO)*
David Falato *(Partner, VP & Dir)*
Josh Ebrahemi *(Partner & VP)*
Mike Powell *(Partner & VP)*
Bruce Pettinari *(Partner)*
Debbie Abergel *(Sr VP-Mktg)*
Carol Stevens *(Office Mgr & Acct Coord)*
Ben Block *(Acct Mgr-Natl)*
Melissa Choi *(Acct Mgr)*
Laurie Dowell *(Specialist-Creative Mktg)*
Barbara Schwab *(Acct Exec)*

Accounts:
NASDAQ

Branch

Jack Nadel International

25 Surf Rd, Westport, CT 06880
(See Separate Listing)

JACK NADEL INTERNATIONAL

25 Surf Rd, Westport, CT 06880
Tel.: (203) 226-7733
Fax: (203) 226-4470
E-Mail: lynne.duvivier@nadel.com
Web Site: www.nadel.com

Employees: 4
Year Founded: 1954

Agency Specializes In: Advertising Specialties, Business-To-Business, Catalogs, Co-op Advertising, Collateral, E-Commerce, Event Planning & Marketing, Exhibit/Trade Shows, Internet/Web Design, Logo & Package Design, Merchandising, Package Design, Point of Purchase, Point of Sale, Promotions, Sales Promotion, Sports Market

Lynne DuVivier *(Acct Mgr)*
Kym Chartash *(Sr Acct Exec)*
David Frank *(Sr Acct Exec)*
Judy Taitz *(Sr Acct Exec)*
Jayme Fiumara *(Acct Exec)*
Justin Henry *(Acct Exec)*
Bill Oliver *(Acct Exec)*
Kris Podber *(Acct Exec)*
Barbara Schwab *(Acct Exec)*
Toniann Cocca *(Acct Coord)*

KAHN MEDIA INC

6900 Canby Ave Ste 102, Reseda, CA 91335
Tel.: (818) 881-5246
Web Site: www.kahnmedia.com

Year Founded: 2008

Agency Specializes In: Advertising, Magazines, Media Relations, Newspaper, Public Relations, Radio, Social Marketing/Nonprofit, Social Media, T.V., Viral/Buzz/Word of Mouth

Dan Kahn *(Pres)*
Jonathan Barrett *(VP)*
Cory Burns *(Acct Mgr)*
Kyle Hyatt *(Mgr-Content)*
Caroline Yun *(Mgr-Digital Mktg)*
Tom Morr *(Acct Supvr)*
Summer Rogers *(Acct Exec)*
Jason Thompson *(Acct Exec)*

Accounts:
Auctions America
B&M Automotive Group B&M Racing & Performance, Consumer Awareness, Event Support, Flowmaster Exhaust, Hurst Driveline Conversions, Hurst Shifters, PR, Product Visibility, Sales, Social Media
Bodie Stroud Industries, Inc (Public Relations Agency of Record) Media, Strategic Communications
New-Centerforce Clutches
Classic Recreations
New-Coker Group (Agency of Record)
Dinan Engineering Media Outreach, Public Relations, Social Media Marketing, Strategic Communications
First Place Auto Products
Flowmaster
Hedman Hedders
Hedman Performance Event & Trade Show, Traditional & Digital Media
Hotchkis
HRE Performance Wheels Inc Sports Vehicle Wheels Mfr
International AERO Products Aircraft Dealing & Engineering Services
L.A. Prep, Inc B2B Communications, Media Outreach, PR, Social Media Marketing, Strategic Communications
MagnaFlow (Public Relations Agency of Record) B2B Communications, Marketing
Midway Industries (Agency of Record) Centerforce, Drivetrain Products, Media, Media Relations, Public Relations, Social Media Marketing, Strategic Communications
MotoAmerica (Communications Agency of Record) Branding, Creative, Public Relations, Social Media Marketing
Nitto Tire U.S.A Event Promotions, Media, Public Relations
Parts Unlimited Interiors
Petersen Automotive Museum Media Outreach, Public Relations, Strategic Communications
Red Line Oil
Ringbrothers Media, PR, Social Marketing, Strategic Communications
Spectre Performance
Surf City Garage (Agency of Record) Enthusiast Grade, Media Relations, Public Relations, Social Media Marketing, Strategic Communications
Trim Parts, Inc.

The Ultimate Street Car Association
Venchurs Vehicle Systems
New-Weistec Engineering (Public Relations Agency of Record) Brand Strategy
XPLORE Vehicles

KEENE PROMOTIONS, INC.

450 Lexington St Ste 102, Newton, MA 02466
Tel.: (617) 426-1200
Fax: (617) 243-0202
Toll Free: (800) 533-6324
E-Mail: info@keenepromotions.com
Web Site: www.keenepromostore.com

Employees: 12
Year Founded: 1949

Agency Specializes In: Event Planning & Marketing, Promotions

Breakdown of Gross Billings by Media: Adv. Specialities: 100%

Michael Keene *(Pres & CEO)*
Matt Reynolds *(Acct Mgr)*

THE KIRBY GROUP

Regents Place, 33 Euston Road, London, NW1 3BT United Kingdom
Tel.: (44) 20 7834 6714
E-Mail: enquiries@thekirbygroup.co.uk
Web Site: www.thekirbygroup.co.uk

Employees: 45
Year Founded: 1972

Agency Specializes In: Agriculture, Automotive, Education, Engineering, Entertainment, Food Service, Health Care Services, Hospitality, Industrial, Information Technology, Internet/Web Design, Legal Services, Leisure, Media Buying Services, Media Planning, Media Relations, New Technologies, Pharmaceutical, Real Estate, Restaurant, Retail, Search Engine Optimization, Technical Advertising, Transportation, Travel & Tourism, Web (Banner Ads, Pop-ups, etc.)

Steve Budge *(Mgr-M&E)*
John Holdridge *(Mgr-Procurement)*
Steve Marshall *(Mgr-T & D Contracts-UK)*
Kevin McCartney *(Mgr-Comml-UK)*
Garry Smith *(Mgr-Site)*

Accounts:
Honeywell; 2010

LATITUDE

8750 N Central Expwy Ste 1200, Dallas, TX 75231
Tel.: (214) 696-7900
Fax: (214) 696-7999
E-Mail: shayashi@latitude-trg.com
Web Site: www.latitude-trg.com

E-Mail for Key Personnel:
President: shayashi@latitude-trg.com
Creative Dir.: pvonheeder@latitude-trg.com
Production Mgr.: gpeterman@latitude-trg.com

Employees: 14
Year Founded: 1988

Agency Specializes In: Brand Development & Integration, Business-To-Business, Collateral, Communications, Consumer Goods, Consumer Marketing, Corporate Identity, Direct Response Marketing, Entertainment, Event Planning & Marketing, Exhibit/Trade Shows, Experience Design, Guerilla Marketing, Health Care Services, High Technology, In-Store Advertising, Integrated Marketing, Local Marketing, Logo & Package Design, Medical Products, Merchandising, New Product Development, Point of Purchase, Promotions, Restaurant, Retail, Sales Promotion, Sponsorship, Sports Market, Strategic Planning/Research, Sweepstakes, Teen Market

Terry Baughman *(Grp Head-Creative)*
Jason Strong *(Exec Dir-Creative)*
Tammy Lucas *(Sr Dir-Art)*
Anna Olah *(Product Mgr-Studio)*
Pat Hartman *(Mgr-Production & Experiential Mktg)*

Accounts:
Brampton Retail Products Group; Dallas, TX; 2008
Dr. Pepper Snapple Group; Plano, TX; 1988
Frito-Lay, Inc.; Plano, TX; 1999
Hansen Pressure Pipe; 2007
Highland Homes; Dallas, TX; 2005
INGUAT Marketing, Public Relations
Red Lobster; Orlando, FL; 2004
VF Outlet; Reading, PA; 2009
Weight Watcher's International; Woodbury, NY; 2004

LEGEND CREATIVE GROUP

815-B Oakwood Rd, Lake Zurich, IL 60047-6704
Tel.: (847) 438-3528
Fax: (847) 438-3526
Toll Free: (800) 408-3528
E-Mail: info@legendcreative.com
Web Site: www.legendcreative.com

Employees: 12
Year Founded: 1989

Agency Specializes In: Advertising Specialties, Sales Promotion

Approx. Annual Billings: $1,200,000

David Voitik *(Pres)*

Accounts:
Precision
Sears
Sunbeam
Walgreens

LOOK MEDIA USA, LLC

330 W 38th St Ste 1500, New York, NY 10018
Tel.: (305) 940-4949
E-Mail: info@lookmediausa.com
Web Site: www.lookmediausa.com

Employees: 5
Year Founded: 2006

Agency Specializes In: Alternative Advertising, Consumer Marketing, Event Planning & Marketing, Experience Design, Guerilla Marketing, In-Store Advertising, Media Planning, Mobile Marketing, Out-of-Home Media, Outdoor, Point of Purchase, Point of Sale, Promotions, Shopper Marketing, Urban Market, Viral/Buzz/Word of Mouth

Mike Alladina *(Dir)*
Michael Baker *(Dir)*
Elisabeth Wilson *(Mgr-Natl Campaign)*

MADETOORDER

1244-A Quarry Ln, Pleasanton, CA 94566-4756
Tel.: (925) 484-0600
Fax: (925) 215-2228
E-Mail: accounting@madetoorder.com
Web Site: www.madetoorder.com

Employees: 20
Year Founded: 2002

Agency Specializes In: Advertising Specialties, Business-To-Business, E-Commerce, Event Planning & Marketing, Exhibit/Trade Shows, Fashion/Apparel, Food Service, High Technology, Merchandising, Sales Promotion

Approx. Annual Billings: $10,000,000

Breakdown of Gross Billings by Media: Adv. Specialities: $10,000,000

Barbara Brown *(CEO)*
Cris Aldridge *(Partner-Sls)*
Kevin Spawn *(Partner-Sls)*
Rick Ventimiglia *(Partner-Sls)*
Rod Brown *(Mng Dir & CFO)*
Tony Brennan *(Exec VP)*
Rex Shoemake *(VP-Sls)*
Sandy Gonzalez *(Sr Partner-Sls)*

MANGO PR LTD.

2nd Fl Commonwealth House, 1-19, New Oxford Street, London, WC1A 1NU United Kingdom
Tel.: (44) 20 7 421 2500
E-Mail: info@mangopr.com
Web Site: www.mangopr.com

Year Founded: 2004

Agency Specializes In: Crisis Communications, Event Planning & Marketing, Media Relations, Public Relations, Social Media, Strategic Planning/Research

Lucinda Buxton *(Founder, Partner & Dir)*
Sarah Curra *(CEO)*
Clare Corry *(Mng Dir)*
Olivia Graham *(Grp Acct Dir)*
Victoria Coombes *(Acct Dir)*
Emma Gates *(Acct Mgr)*

Accounts:
&Beyond PR
Cap Rocat; Mallorca Hotel Management Services
Dormy House PR
Fashion Foie Gras Hotels Management Services
The Grove; Hertfordshire Hotels Management Services
The James Online, PR, Print
Le Pavillon des Lettres; Paris Hotels Management Services
The Merrion Hotels Management Services
Pure France Hotels Management Services
The Surrey PR
WEXAS Media, PR

MARDEN-KANE, INC.

195 Froehlich Farm Blvd, Woodbury, NY 11797
Tel.: (516) 365-3999
Fax: (516) 365-5250
E-Mail: expert@mardenkane.com
Web Site: www.mardenkane.com

Employees: 22
Year Founded: 1957

National Agency Associations: PMA

Agency Specializes In: Advertising Specialties, Broadcast, Business-To-Business, Cable T.V., Co-op Advertising, Consulting, Consumer Marketing, Digital/Interactive, Direct Response Marketing, Event Planning & Marketing, Internet/Web Design, Over-50 Market, Planning & Consultation, Print, Production, Publicity/Promotions, Sales Promotion, Strategic Planning/Research, Sweepstakes, Telemarketing

Approx. Annual Billings: $6,000,000

Leonard Bierman *(Partner & Exec VP)*
Paul Goldman *(Partner & Exec VP)*
Alan Richter *(CFO & Gen Mgr)*
Martin Glovin *(Chief Product Officer)*
Jennifer Hibbs *(VP & Acct Dir-Interactive)*

Josephine Angiuli *(VP & Acct Mgr)*
Peggy Seeloff *(VP)*
Katie Blaney *(Acct Supvr)*
Barbara Chien *(Asst Controller)*

Accounts:
AMGEN
BarclayCard
Bayer HealthCare LLC
Ben & Jerry's
Broder Bros., Inc.
Build A Bear Workshop
Colonial Penn
Digitas
Energizer
First Data Corp.
Gerber Childrenswear LLC
Google
Microsoft
Starbucks
TJMAXX
VISA
We-Care
Western Union

Subsidiary

Marden-Kane, Inc.
611 Rockland Rd Ste 204, Lake Bluff, IL 60044-2000
Tel.: (847) 283-0441
Fax: (847) 283-0442
E-Mail: mkchicago@mardenkane.com
Web Site: www.mardenkane.com

Employees: 5

Agency Specializes In: Digital/Interactive, Sales Promotion, Sweepstakes

Alan Richter *(CFO & Gen Mgr)*
Rosemary Stein *(VP & Gen Mgr)*

Accounts:
ACCO Brands
Brooks
Constellation
Illy
Ingersoll Rand
Insight Express
Kikkoman International Inc
Liberty Richter
Major League Baseball Players Association
MapMyFitness
Marketing Werks
The National Arbor Day Foundation
Palm Inc
PSCU
Purina
rEvolution
Showtime Networks Inc
Sony Electronics Inc
Verizon Communications
Vibes Media, LLC

MARKETING DRIVE
800 Connecticut Ave 3rd Fl E, Norwalk, CT 06854
Tel.: (203) 857-6100
Fax: (203) 857-6171
E-Mail: info@marketingdrive.com
Web Site: www.matchmg.com

Employees: 150
Year Founded: 1989

National Agency Associations: PMA

Agency Specializes In: Automotive, Below-the-Line, Brand Development & Integration, Broadcast, Cable T.V., Children's Market, Co-op Advertising, Collateral, Communications, Consulting, Consumer Goods, Consumer Marketing, Corporate Identity, Direct Response Marketing, Direct-to-Consumer, Environmental, Event Planning & Marketing, Experience Design, Financial, Government/Political, Guerilla Marketing, Health Care Services, Household Goods, In-Store Advertising, Integrated Marketing, Medical Products, Men's Market, Mobile Marketing, Package Design, Pharmaceutical, Planning & Consultation, Point of Purchase, Point of Sale, Promotions, Publicity/Promotions, Radio, Retail, Sales Promotion, Social Marketing/Nonprofit, Sponsorship, Strategic Planning/Research, Sweepstakes, Viral/Buzz/Word of Mouth, Women's Market

Jeff Henkes *(Acct Dir)*
Angie McDermott *(Acct Dir)*

Accounts:
The Art Institute
EPA
ExxonMobil Mobil Delvac
Kellogg
Mondelez International, Inc.
New Balance
Novartis Consumer Health
Pernod Ricard Aberlour, Ballantine's, Don Pedro, Glenlivet, Jameson, Kahlua, Malibu, Presidente, Wild Turkey
Pernod Ricard USA G.H. Mumm, Jacob's Creek, Jameson Irish Whiskey, Perrier-Jouet, Sandeman, Wyndham Estate; 2007
Procter & Gamble
Select Comfort

Branch

Marketing Drive - Boston
116 Huntington Ave 12th Fl, Boston, MA 02116-4308
Tel.: (617) 368-6700
Fax: (617) 368-6799
E-Mail: info@marketingdrive.com
Web Site: www.matchmg.com

Employees: 40
Year Founded: 2001

Agency Specializes In: Sales Promotion

Michael Dill *(Mng Partner-Match Mktg Grp)*
Chris Miller *(Mng Partner)*
Howard Rubin *(Mng Partner)*
Cal Manfreda *(Sr VP-Fin & Ops)*
Kristen Clough *(VP)*
Alison Swift *(Assoc Dir-Media)*

Accounts:
CVS Health
Novartis Multibrand Wellness
Welch's

Promotion Services Group
6001 Shady Oak Rd Ste 280, Minnetonka, MN 55343
Tel.: (952) 933-0105
E-Mail: gparker@promotionservicesgroup.com
Web Site: www.promotionservicesgroup.com

Agency Specializes In: Sales Promotion, Sweepstakes

Gretchen Parker *(Mng Dir & VP)*
Bridget Neigebauer *(Acct Mgr)*
Jennifer Allen *(Acct Supvr)*

Accounts:
The Allstate Foundation
Bourbon
Dannon
Gillette
Kahlua
Krispy Kreme Doughnuts
Malibu
Mobil Delvac

MARKETING RESOURCES, INC.
945 Oaklawn Ave, Elmhurst, IL 60126
Tel.: (630) 530-0100
Fax: (630) 530-0134
Toll Free: (888) 220-4238
E-Mail: info@mrichi.com
Web Site: www.marketingresources.com

Employees: 30
Year Founded: 1995

National Agency Associations: PMA

Agency Specializes In: Brand Development & Integration, Collateral, Consumer Marketing, Digital/Interactive, Direct Response Marketing, Entertainment, Food Service, Graphic Design, Internet/Web Design, Legal Services, New Product Development, Point of Purchase, Print, Production, Production (Print), Promotions, Publicity/Promotions, Restaurant, Sales Promotion, Sweepstakes

Aaron Burger *(Dir-Fulfillment)*
Tasha Hook *(Sr Mgr-Fulfillment)*
Mike Kida *(Sr Mgr-Bus Dev)*
Matt Early *(Acct Mgr)*
Tarah Kraft *(Acct Mgr)*
Melissa Najera *(Acct Mgr)*
Pam Diesness *(Mgr-Warehouse)*
Laurie Kucera *(Mgr-Fulfillment)*
Rick Sack *(Mgr-Bus Dev)*
Shannon Stallone *(Mgr-Bus Dev)*
Daria Barranco *(Acct Supvr)*
Tim Hobbs *(Acct Supvr)*

Accounts:
The Chicago Tribune
Comcast Spotlight
Dodge
Frito-Lay, Inc.
Pepsi Cola Co.

THE MARKETING STORE
55 W Monroe Ste 1400, Chicago, IL 60603
Tel.: (312) 614-4600
Fax: (630) 932-5200
E-Mail: hello.chicago@themarketingstore.com
Web Site: chi.tmsw.com/

Employees: 145
Year Founded: 1987

National Agency Associations: DMA-PMA

Agency Specializes In: Brand Development & Integration, Consumer Marketing, Corporate Identity, Electronic Media, Event Planning & Marketing, Retail, Sales Promotion, Sponsorship

Doug Johnson *(Mng Partner)*
Christine Schipke *(Sr VP & Dir-Creative)*
Kurk Karlenzig *(Sr VP-Digital Strategy-Global)*
Rob Morgan *(Sr VP-Global Consumer Data Analytics Practice)*
Rob Pieper *(Sr VP-Strategy & Plng)*
Jim Higgins *(VP-Digital)*
Liz Robinson *(VP-Plng & Strategy)*
Jawan Sheppard *(Grp Acct Dir)*
Nichole Kmiec *(Acct Dir-Digital & Mobile)*
Jeff Rahman *(Dir-Digital Creative)*
Carie Pflug *(Mgr-Bus Dev)*
Kelly O'Neill *(Acct Supvr)*

Accounts:
Coca-Cola Refreshments USA, Inc.
General Mills Inc.
L'Oreal Paris

McDonald's Creative, Digital, Fry Boxes, Strategy
MetLife
Redbox

Branches

The Marketing Store
16 Hatfields, Southwark, London, SE1 8DJ United Kingdom
Tel.: (44) 20 7981 9300
Fax: (44) 207 745 2112
Web Site: chi.tmsw.com

Employees: 150

Lisa Bonney *(Mng Dir)*
Jonathan Allen *(Sr Acct Dir)*
Sam Eddy *(Acct Dir)*
Emma Kelly *(Bus Dir-FMCG & Bus Dev)*
Katie Metz *(Acct Dir-Retail Strategy)*
Ross Sewley *(Acct Dir)*
Peter Gamble *(Dir-Bus)*
Geraldine Kenway *(Dir-Bus)*
Kate Randolph *(Acct Mgr)*
Helen Wesley *(Acct Mgr)*
Luke Perry *(Acct Exec)*
Rachel Smith *(Acct Exec)*

Accounts:
Britvic Soft Drinks Gatorade, Robinsons
Canon
Carlsberg Campaign: "Time To Take Your Seats", San Miguel, Somersby, Staropramen, Tetley's
Cheestrings
CPW SA
GSK
Heineken Below the Line, Campaign: "Lose the Tie, Gain Some Espiritu Libre", Sol
Mars
McDonald's
Nissan
Shell
Unilever
Vodafone
Weetabix

Boxer Creative
Fort Pkwy, Birmingham, B24 9FD United Kingdom
Tel.: (44) 121 384 9000
Fax: (44) 1675 430 416
Web Site: chi.tmsw.com

Employees: 15

Agency Specializes In: Communications, Consulting, Publicity/Promotions, Retail, Sales Promotion

Paul Castledine *(Chief Creative Officer & Partner-Creative)*
Mark Watson *(Partner-Bus)*
Tracy Mardell *(VP & Client Svcs Dir)*
Wendy Lanchin *(Dir-Plng & Strategy)*
Kevin Thomas *(Dir-Art)*
Jo Taylor *(Sr Acct Mgr)*
Catherine Cudd *(Acct Mgr)*
Jolly Hanspal *(Sr Designer)*

Accounts:
McDonald's

The Marketing Store
105 rue Anatole France, Levallois-Perret, 92300 France
Tel.: (33) 1 46 17 02 21
Fax: (33) 1 46 17 02 23
E-Mail: hello.paris@themarketingstore.com
Web Site: www.tmsw.com/paris/contact

Employees: 13

Agency Specializes In: Food Service, Publicity/Promotions, Sales Promotion

Delphine Duchene *(Acct Dir)*
Caroline Radat *(Dir-Location)*
Guillaume Saez *(Sr Acct Mgr)*
Pauline Giannini *(Acct Mgr)*
Marie Dumas *(Mgr-Acct & Licensing-McDonald's)*

The Marketing Store
1209 King Street W Suite 100, Toronto, ON M6K 1G2 Canada
Tel.: (416) 533-8679
Fax: (416) 583-3979
Web Site: chi.tmsw.com

Employees: 130

Michael Oliver *(Mng Partner)*
Carlos Garavito *(VP & Dir-Creative)*
Jeremy Ages *(Dir-Strategy)*
Katie Clarke *(Dir-People & Practices)*
Jillian Jacobs *(Mgr-HR)*

Accounts:
Canadian Tire
Diageo Campaign: "The True Brew of Halloween", Guinness
The Home Depot
Infiniti
McDonald's
McGregor
Nissan
Ontario Lottery
PetSmart
Unilever

The Marketing Store
18 Westlands Rd, Quarry Bay, China (Hong Kong)
Tel.: (852) 2880 8100
Fax: (852) 2102 0617
E-Mail: hello.hongkong@themarketingstore.com
Web Site: www.tmsw.com/hong-kong

Employees: 9

Agency Specializes In: Brand Development & Integration, Publicity/Promotions, Sales Promotion

Tony Judge *(Sr VP-Global Quality & Safety-Global Sourcing & Supply Chain)*
Andrew Kingham *(Mng Dir-Hong Kong, Shanghai & Tokyo)*
Taylor Host *(VP-Global & Head-Digital & Mobile Platforms)*
Alice Lui *(VP-HR-Asia Pacific)*
Stephan Schwaabe *(VP-Seating & Decor)*
Addy Ho *(Sr Dir-Bus Dev)*
Alice Fong *(Grp Acct Dir)*
Scott Edwards *(Creative Dir-Asia)*
Vienna Cheung *(Dir-Strategic & Demand Plng)*

Accounts:
Coca-Cola Refreshments USA, Inc.
Diageo
McDonald's

The Marketing Store-Promotional Products
18 Westlands Road, Quarry Bay, China (Hong Kong)
Tel.: (852) 2880 8125
Fax: (852) 2800 5990
E-Mail: hello.hongkong@tmsw.com
Web Site: www.tmsw.com/hong-kong

Employees: 150

Andrew Kingham *(Mng Dir-Hong Kong, Shanghai & Tokyo)*

Accounts:
Coca-Cola Refreshments USA, Inc.
GMI
McDonald's
Shell

Boxer
Fort Dunlop Unit 201 Fort Parkway, Birmingham, B24 9FD United Kingdom
Tel.: (44) 121 384 9001
Fax: (44) 121 384 9009
E-Mail: sayhello@boxercreative.co.uk
Web Site: www.boxerbranddesign.com

Employees: 16
Year Founded: 1996

Mark Watson *(Mng Partner)*
Paul Castledine *(Partner-Creative & Chief Creative Officer)*
Tracy Mardell *(VP & Client Svcs Dir)*
Wendy Lanchin *(Dir-Plng & Strategy)*
Matt Rogers *(Dir-Art)*
Jo Taylor *(Sr Acct Mgr)*
Catherine Cudd *(Acct Mgr)*
Jolly Hanspal *(Sr Designer)*

Accounts:
Brahma
McDonald's
Tesco
Urban Splash

MARKETING VISIONS, INC.
520 White Plains Rd Ste 500, Tarrytown, NY 10591-5118
Tel.: (914) 631-3900
Fax: (914) 693-8338
E-Mail: jsloofman@marketing-visions.com
Web Site: www.marketing-visions.com

Employees: 10
Year Founded: 1986

National Agency Associations: PMA

Agency Specializes In: Advertising Specialties, Business-To-Business, Consulting, Consumer Marketing, Direct Response Marketing, Entertainment, Event Planning & Marketing, Financial, Food Service, Government/Political, Graphic Design, Health Care Services, High Technology, Industrial, Internet/Web Design, Leisure, Logo & Package Design, Medical Products, Merchandising, New Product Development, Pharmaceutical, Planning & Consultation, Point of Purchase, Point of Sale, Print, Production, Public Relations, Publicity/Promotions, Restaurant, Retail, Sales Promotion, Seniors' Market, Sports Market, Strategic Planning/Research, Sweepstakes

H. Jay Sloofman *(Pres)*
Paul Fuller *(Dir-Art)*

Accounts:
Pep Boys; Philadelphia, PA; 2001
Pepsi; 1986
The Topps Company; 1994

MARKETING WERKS, INC.
130 E Randolph St Ste 2400, Chicago, IL 60601
Tel.: (312) 228-0800
Fax: (312) 228-0801
Toll Free: (800) 694WERK
Web Site: www.marketingwerks.com

Employees: 150
Year Founded: 1987

Agency Specializes In: African-American Market,

Alternative Advertising, Automotive, Below-the-Line, Bilingual Market, Brand Development & Integration, Branded Entertainment, Business-To-Business, Children's Market, College, Consulting, Consumer Marketing, Corporate Identity, Direct-to-Consumer, Electronics, Entertainment, Event Planning & Marketing, Experience Design, Food Service, Game Integration, Guerilla Marketing, Health Care Services, Hispanic Market, Hospitality, Integrated Marketing, Local Marketing, Media Relations, Media Training, Men's Market, Mobile Marketing, Multicultural, Out-of-Home Media, Over-50 Market, Pharmaceutical, Promotions, Public Relations, Publicity/Promotions, Recruitment, Regional, Retail, Sales Promotion, Seniors' Market, Sponsorship, Sports Market, Strategic Planning/Research, Sweepstakes, Teen Market, Urban Market, Viral/Buzz/Word of Mouth, Women's Market

Approx. Annual Billings: $61,000,000

Holly Meloy *(Sr VP-Acct Mgmt)*
Julie Schweigert *(Sr VP-Client Svc)*
Cyndi Dunn *(VP-Platform Mktg)*
Emily Berg *(Dir-Trends & Insights)*
Kevin Conners *(Dir-Client Fin)*
Marieli Ronda *(Acct Mgr)*

Accounts:
BlackBerry
Charbroil
Choco Milk
Citibank
Gore-Tex
La Costena
La Costena Por Sabor Tour
Live Like a Champion
The National Pork Board
Sony Computer Entertainment America LLC
Verizon Telecom
Verizon Wireless
Walgreens

MARKETLOGIC
3785 NW 82nd Ave Ste 415, Miami, FL 33166-6632
Tel.: (305) 513-8980
Fax: (305) 513-4199
E-Mail: info@mymarketlogic.com
Web Site: www.mymarketlogic.com

Employees: 18

Agency Specializes In: E-Commerce, Event Planning & Marketing, Exhibit/Trade Shows, Graphic Design, Package Design, Point of Purchase, Print, Production (Print), Promotions, Publicity/Promotions, Sales Promotion

Eduardo Sarmiento *(Dir-Creative)*
Randy Summerford *(Dir-Sls)*
Jorge Ferret Vincench *(Dir-Art)*
Nancy Anguiano *(Sr Acct Exec)*
Yasi Mendoza *(Acct Exec)*
Xiomara Zavarce *(Acct Exec)*
Adrian Fernandez *(Graphic Designer & Designer-Web)*
Margot Doejo *(Planner-Strategic)*

Accounts:
Palm
Samsung
Sony Ericsson
Toshiba
Toyota

MASTERMIND MARKETING
1450 W Peachtree St NW, Atlanta, GA 30309-2955
Tel.: (678) 420-4000
Fax: (678) 420-4090
E-Mail: info@mastermindmarketing.com
Web Site: www.mastermindmarketing.com

E-Mail for Key Personnel:
President:
dan.dodson@mastermindmarketing.com

Employees: 48
Year Founded: 1985

National Agency Associations: PMA

Agency Specializes In: Advertising, Below-the-Line, Brand Development & Integration, Broadcast, Business-To-Business, Collateral, Communications, Consulting, Consumer Marketing, Custom Publishing, Customer Relationship Management, Direct Response Marketing, Entertainment, Event Planning & Marketing, Guerilla Marketing, In-Store Advertising, Integrated Marketing, Internet/Web Design, Mobile Marketing, Planning & Consultation, Point of Purchase, Point of Sale, Print, Production, Promotions, Radio, Restaurant, Sports Market, Strategic Planning/Research, Viral/Buzz/Word of Mouth

Approx. Annual Billings: $140,000,000

Daniel Dodson, Jr. *(CEO)*
Mike Gelfond *(Partner & Exec VP)*
Maria Akridge *(VP)*

Accounts:
Bayer
Citi
Coca-Cola
Harley-Davidson
Harman

MATCHCRAFT, INC.
3205 Ocean Park Blvd Ste 140, Santa Monica, CA 90405
Tel.: (310) 314-3320
E-Mail: bizdev@matchcraft.com
Web Site: www.matchcraft.com

Agency Specializes In: Advertising, Advertising Specialties, Engineering, New Technologies, Yellow Pages Advertising

Approx. Annual Billings: $1,000,000

Dorab Patel *(Co-Founder)*
Uzi Eliahou *(Chm)*
Alex Dionysian *(CTO)*
Marianne Faas *(Head-Partner Experience-EMEA & Acct Mgr)*
Jennifer Coats *(Dir-Trng & Dev)*
Austin Luther *(Dir-Mktg)*
Amie Slott *(Sr Acct Mgr)*
Leah Levy *(Acct Coord)*
Jade Mayberry *(Acct Coord)*
Michael A. Sadler *(Acct Coord-SEM)*

Accounts:
GoldenPages.ie
Google
Herold.at
Lokaldelen.se
Paginas Amarelas
ThomasNet
Truvo
Yahoo

MAXIMUM IMPACT INC.
1410 Broadway Ste 1001, New York, NY 10018-9357
Tel.: (212) 447-7857
Fax: (212) 447-7674
E-Mail: info@maximumimpact.net
Web Site: maximumimpact.net

Employees: 8
Year Founded: 1994

Agency Specializes In: In-Store Advertising, Logo & Package Design, Publicity/Promotions, Sales Promotion

Valerie Haskell *(Pres & CEO)*
Paul Haskell *(CFO & COO)*
Ryan Goldstein *(Dir-Bus)*
James Watson *(Area Mgr-Midwest)*
David Herman *(Mgr-Production)*
Wendi Lowenstein *(Mgr-Acctg)*
Alex Melville *(Mgr-Field Ops)*
Mike Jones *(Coord-Shipping)*

Accounts:
Diageo
J Group

MCCABE PROMOTIONAL ADVERTISING
384 Sovereign Rd, London, ON N6M 1A5 Canada
Tel.: (519) 455-7009
Fax: (519) 455-7963
Toll Free: (800) 387-0360
E-Mail: info@mccabepromo.com
Web Site: www.mccabepro.com

Employees: 40
Year Founded: 1981

Sandi McCabe *(Owner)*
Michelle Merrifield *(VP-Ops)*
Colin Rous *(VP)*
Adrienne Wilson *(Acct Mgr)*
Rebecca Korhonen *(Mgr-Inside Sls)*
Jenni Zeineddine *(Acct Exec)*

Accounts:
Certified Pre-Owned Trucks; 2006
Cummins
General Dynamics
Heins
International
Tigercat
YMCA

MERYL D. PEARLSTEIN PUBLICITY
21 E 87th St Ste 5A, New York, NY 10128
Tel.: (917) 359-3512
Fax: (212) 534-3227
E-Mail: pr@mdppublicity.com
Web Site: www.mdppublicity.com

Year Founded: 2003

Agency Specializes In: Market Research, Media Relations, Media Training, Strategic Planning/Research

Meryl Pearlstein *(Pres)*

Accounts:
Adventure Center Travel Agency
Cactus Language Training & Language Vacations Language & Business Training Provider
iExplore Travel Agency
Italiaoutdoors Public Relations Campaign
Jackson Hole;Wyoming Hotel Management Services
Munich Airport Public Relations Campaign
Sierra Realty Corp Real Estate Services
Spring Creek Ranch Hotel Management Services
St. Augustine/Ponte Vedra & The Beaches; FL Hotel Management Services
Tabacon Grand Spa Thermal Resort Hotel Management Services
The Wayfarers Travel Agency

MKTG, INC.
75 9th Ave 3rd Fl, New York, NY 10011

Tel.: (212) 660-3800
Fax: (212) 660-3878
E-Mail: info@mktg.com
Web Site: www.mktg.com/

Employees: 300
Year Founded: 1972

National Agency Associations: 4A's

Agency Specializes In: Automotive, Below-the-Line, Bilingual Market, Brand Development & Integration, Broadcast, Business-To-Business, Collateral, College, Communications, Consumer Goods, Consumer Marketing, Corporate Communications, Corporate Identity, Customer Relationship Management, Digital/Interactive, Electronic Media, Entertainment, Event Planning & Marketing, Exhibit/Trade Shows, Experience Design, Fashion/Apparel, Graphic Design, Guerilla Marketing, Health Care Services, Hispanic Market, Hospitality, Household Goods, In-Store Advertising, Integrated Marketing, Internet/Web Design, Local Marketing, Luxury Products, Merchandising, Mobile Marketing, Multicultural, Multimedia, Planning & Consultation, Point of Purchase, Point of Sale, Production, Promotions, Publicity/Promotions, Radio, Recruitment, Regional, Retail, Sales Promotion, Social Media, Sponsorship, Sports Market, Strategic Planning/Research, T.V., Teen Market, Tween Market, Urban Market, Viral/Buzz/Word of Mouth, Women's Market

Sales: $139,028,963

Charles W. Horsey *(Chm & CEO)*
Peter Office *(COO)*
Ben Roth *(Chief Creative Officer)*
James Ferguson *(Exec VP-Corp Dev)*
James R. Haughton *(Sr VP-Fin Reporting)*
Marlena Edwards *(VP-HR)*
Tim Owens *(VP-Production)*
Richard Tubman *(Dir-Digital)*

Accounts:
Bayer
CBS Interactive
Clinique
Coca-Cola Refreshments USA, Inc.
CVS Health
Diageo North America, Inc.
EA Sports
Electronic Arts
Fas Mart
FedEx Corporation
Fresh Express, Inc.
Gatorade
Google
Johnnie Walker Whisky
Jose Cuervo Alcoholic Drink
Kikkoman International, Inc.
Kroger
Levi Strauss & Co.
Lexus
Moet Hennessy
Nike Sports Apparel
Nintendo of America
The Procter & Gamble Company Vocalpoint
T-Mobile US
Tiffany & Co.
Toyota

MOTIVATORS INC.
123 Frost St Ste 201, Westbury, NY 11590
Tel.: (516) 735-9600
Fax: (516) 735-9698
Web Site: www.motivators.com

Employees: 40
Year Founded: 1979

Ken Laffer *(Pres & CEO)*
Rachel Levin *(Dir-Sls & Mktg)*
Tony McNally *(Dir-Ops & Customer Care)*
Kimberly Nick *(Dir-Strategic Dev)*
Bill O'Shea *(Mgr-ECommerce)*
Sarah Salooja *(Mgr-Mdsg & Vendor Rels)*
Alison Derkatch Strauss *(Mgr-Sls)*
Kristen Siegel *(Supvr-Mdsg & Vendor Rels)*

MP DISPLAYS LLC
704 Executive Blvd Ste I, Valley Cottage, NY 10989
Tel.: (845) 268-4113
Fax: (845) 268-4154
E-Mail: mparkes@mpdisplays.com
Web Site: www.mpdisplays.com

Employees: 25

Agency Specializes In: In-Store Advertising, Point of Purchase, Point of Sale

Breakdown of Gross Billings by Media: Point of Purchase: 100%

Michael Parkes *(Pres)*
Vincent Esposito *(Gen Mgr)*
Chip Chisena *(Mgr-Production)*
Nate Binger *(Acct Exec)*

MVS MEDIA GROUP
(Formerly MVS Media)
1800 S Ocean Dr, Hallandale, FL 33009
Tel.: (305) 428-3888
E-Mail: alex@mobilevideosigns.com
Web Site: www.mvsmediagroup.com

Employees: 6
Year Founded: 2004

Agency Specializes In: Advertising, Advertising Specialties, Affiliate Marketing, Brand Development & Integration, Branded Entertainment, Consumer Marketing, Digital/Interactive, Electronic Media, Electronics, Entertainment, Event Planning & Marketing, Exhibit/Trade Shows, Game Integration, Guerilla Marketing, Local Marketing, Media Planning, Mobile Marketing, New Product Development, Out-of-Home Media, Outdoor, Promotions, Sales Promotion, South Asian Market, Sponsorship, Sports Market, Urban Market

Alex Bushtaber *(Pres)*

Accounts:
Adidas Adidas Shoe Launch
Atlantic Records; NY Music Artists
Bad Boy Entertainment; NY Artists
BET Network BET Awards
Ciroc Vodka; NY
Clinique Clinique Makeup
Florida Marlins
Fuji Film Fuji Finepix
Lionsgate Films; Canada Movie Trailers
Sean John Sean John Clothing
Sony Pictures; Canada Movie Trailers
Sony/BMG Music Artists
Universal Music; CA Artists
Universal Pictures; CA Movie Trailers

NEW MOVERS MAIL
605 Territorial Dr, Bolingbrook, IL 60440
Tel.: (866) 828-0446
Web Site: newmoversmail.com/

Agency Specializes In: Direct Response Marketing, Promotions

Courtney Tobe *(Mgr-Mktg)*

Accounts:
PETCO

NEWDAY COMMUNICATIONS
50 Water St, Norwalk, CT 06854
Tel.: (203) 851-5700
Fax: (203) 831-5622
E-Mail: pvarco@newdaycom.com
Web Site: www.newdaycom.com

Employees: 4
Year Founded: 1995

Agency Specializes In: Sales Promotion

Peter S. Varco *(Owner)*
George Blystone *(VP-Acct Svcs)*
Greg Jontos *(Sr Dir-Art)*

Accounts:
Avis Rent-A-Car; Parsippany, NJ; 1999
Baileys
Canon
CellularOne
Classic Malts of Scotland
Dewar's
Diageo
Diet Coke
Hennessy
Jefferies
Johnnie Walker
Pepsi; New York, NY Lipton Tea, Pepsi; 1998
Smirnoff
Tanqueray

NORTHEAST PROMOTIONS
700 Perry Hill Rd, Coventry, RI 02816
Tel.: (401) 392-8400
Fax: (401) 392-1154
Toll Free: (800) 486-6690
E-Mail: info@neastgroup.com
Web Site: www.neastgroup.com

Employees: 11
Year Founded: 1978

Agency Specializes In: Advertising Specialties, Business-To-Business, Collateral, Consulting, Corporate Identity, Direct Response Marketing, Event Planning & Marketing, Exhibit/Trade Shows, Graphic Design, Industrial, Integrated Marketing, Pharmaceutical, Planning & Consultation, Print, Production, Sales Promotion

Approx. Annual Billings: $9,050,000

Breakdown of Gross Billings by Media: Adv. Specialities: $2,000,000; Bus. Publs.: $70,000; Collateral: $5,000; D.M.: $166,000; Fees: $250,000; Mags.: $65,000; Newsp.: $69,000; Plng. & Consultation: $1,000,000; Point of Purchase: $100,000; Production: $300,000; Pub. Rels.: $25,000; Sls. Promo.: $5,000,000

W.C.S. Mays, III *(Pres)*
Fran Mays *(Exec VP & Acct Exec)*
Barbara Gerstenblatt *(Acct Exec)*

NORTHEASTERN MEDIA
12321 Hollow Ridge Rd, Doylestown, OH 44230
Tel.: (330) 861-3684
Fax: (330) 247-4121
E-Mail: northeasternmedia@gmail.com
Web Site: www.northeasternmedia.com

Employees: 25

Agency Specializes In: Advertising, African-American Market, Alternative Advertising, Automotive, Business-To-Business, Co-op Advertising, College, Consumer Marketing, Direct-to-Consumer, Event Planning & Marketing, Graphic Design, Guerilla Marketing, Identity Marketing, Local Marketing, Men's Market, Mobile Marketing,

Multicultural, Out-of-Home Media, Outdoor, Over-50 Market, Recruitment, Regional, Retail, Seniors' Market, Sports Market, Transportation, Urban Market, Viral/Buzz/Word of Mouth

James Schooling *(Mgr)*

Accounts:
American Cancer Society; Akron, OH
Camping World
CenturyLink, Inc. Telephone Service
Lincoln-Mercury
National City Bank Banking
Sprint; Detroit, MI Cellular Phones
Summa Health Systems
The United Way

O'MALLEY HANSEN COMMUNICATIONS
180 N Wacker Dr Ste 400, Chicago, IL 60606
Tel.: (312) 377-0630
Fax: (708) 406-1537
Web Site: www.omalleyhansen.com

Employees: 10
Year Founded: 2006

National Agency Associations: COPF

Agency Specializes In: Consumer Marketing, Corporate Communications, Crisis Communications, Event Planning & Marketing, Financial, Media Relations, Public Relations, Publicity/Promotions, Sponsorship

Kelly O'Malley *(Owner)*
Todd Hansen *(Principal)*
Noah Messel *(Acct Supvr)*
Jennifer DeBerge *(Mng Supvr)*

Accounts:
Barclaycard US Digital, Marketing, Media Relations, Public Relations, Social Media, Strategic Communications
Lane Furniture Home Entertainment Solutions Provider
Sara Lee Consumer Products Mfr

OMNICO PROMOTIONS, LTD.
PO Box 713, Mount Kisco, NY 10549
Tel.: (914) 241-1648
Fax: (914) 241-1649
E-Mail: omnico@omnicopromotions.com
Web Site: www.omnicopromotions.com

Employees: 2
Year Founded: 1975

Agency Specializes In: Automotive, Financial, Food Service, Sales Promotion

Approx. Annual Billings: $230,000

Robin Halperin *(Owner & Pres)*

Accounts:
ADP
Finnair
Janney Montgomery; Philadelphia, PA
Turner Broadcasting

ON BOARD ENTERTAINMENT, INC.
(Name Changed to On Board Experiential Marketing)

ON BOARD EXPERIENTIAL MARKETING
(Formerly On Board Entertainment, Inc.)
85 Liberty Ship Way Ste 114, Sausalito, CA 94965-3314
Tel.: (415) 331-4789
Fax: (415) 331-4790
E-Mail: nickolai@obexp.com
Web Site: www.obexp.com/

Employees: 15
Year Founded: 1996

Dan Hirsch *(Founder & CEO)*
Debra Murray *(Pres & Partner)*
John Sullivan *(VP-Ops)*
Kelsey Han *(Dir-Accts)*

ONECOMMAND, LLC
(d/b/a Call Command)
4680 Parkway Dr Ste 202, Mason, OH 45040-8173
Tel.: (800) 464-8500
Fax: (513) 792-9218
E-Mail: support_online@onecommand.com
Web Site: www.onecommand.com

Employees: 60
Year Founded: 2002

Agency Specializes In: Advertising, Automotive

Revenue: $27,500,000

Jeff Hart *(Pres & CEO)*
James R. Hendricks *(CFO)*
Mary Braunstein *(CIO)*
Andrew Smith *(CTO-HIGHGEAR CRM)*
Robert C. Gruen *(Pres-HIGHERGEAR CRM)*
Marvin Grimm *(Exec VP-Bus Dev)*
Jill Whitehead *(Exec VP-Sls)*
Tonia Ruppert *(VP-HR)*
Leonard Traficanti *(VP-Ops)*

Accounts:
Acura
Audi
BMW
Chrysler
Ford
GM
Honda
Jaguar
Lexus
Nissan

OOH PITCH INC.
375 Hudson St Fl 7, New York, NY 10014
Tel.: (212) 820-3177
Web Site: www.oohpitch.com

Year Founded: 2001

Agency Specializes In: Strategic Planning/Research

Dave Matera *(Co-Founder & CEO)*
Jessica Traviglia *(Co-Founder & COO)*
Jennifer Seickel *(Grp Dir-Media)*
Glynnis Reilly *(Supvr-Media)*
Emily Scopinich *(Supvr-Media)*
Alexandra Wilkins *(Supvr-Media)*
Alyssa Doane *(Sr Media Planner)*
Marisa Spagnolo *(Asst Media Planner)*

Accounts:
BMW
Bombay
ISE
Pepsi Co.
Simon
T-Mobile US Wireless Voice, Messaging, & Data Services
TXU

PARASOL MARKETING
350 5th Ave 59th Fl, New York, NY 10118
Tel.: (212) 372-7633
E-Mail: info@parasolmarketing.com
Web Site: www.parasolmarketing.com

Agency Specializes In: Brand Development & Integration, Media Relations, Over-50 Market, Strategic Planning/Research

Andrea Werbel *(Founder & Mng Dir)*
Dinah Saglio *(Acct Mgr)*
Nicole Difasi *(Specialist-PR & Brand Mktg)*

Accounts:
Fairmont Miramar Hotel & Bungalows Hotels Management Services
Hotel Arts;Barcelona Luxury Hotel Rooms & Suites
Miramar Hotels & Bungalows Luxury Hotel Rooms & Suites
Ojai Valley Inn & Spa Golf Club & Spa
The Ritz-Carlton;Palm Beach Hotels & Resorts
The Surrey Hotel Luxury Hotel Rooms & Suites

PARTNERS FOR INCENTIVES
6545 Carnegie Ave, Cleveland, OH 44103
Tel.: (216) 881-3000
Fax: (216) 881-7413
Toll Free: (800) 292-7371
E-Mail: sales@spihq.com
Web Site: www.pfi-awards.com

E-Mail for Key Personnel:
President: mac@spihq.com

Employees: 75
Year Founded: 1963

Agency Specializes In: Business-To-Business, Catalogs, Communications, Consumer Goods, Electronic Media, Merchandising, Sales Promotion, Sweepstakes

Approx. Annual Billings: $28,000,000

Breakdown of Gross Billings by Media: Sls. Promo.: 100%

Mary Anne Comotto *(Owner)*
Susan Mayrant *(VP-Bus Dev)*
Joy Smith *(VP-Sls & Mktg)*
Gregory Losh *(Mgr-C/S)*

PHOENIX CREATIVE CO.
611 N 10th St Ste 700, Saint Louis, MO 63101
Tel.: (314) 421-5646
Fax: (314) 421-5647
Web Site: www.phoenixcreative.com

Employees: 30
Year Founded: 1989

Agency Specializes In: Advertising, Print, Sales Promotion

Approx. Annual Billings: $7,000,000

Matt O'Neill *(Owner)*
David Dolak *(Partner & Chief Creative Officer)*
Steve Wienke *(Dir-Creative)*
Tiffany Hubbell *(Acct Mgr)*

Accounts:
Anheuser-Busch, Inc.
Borders Group
Brown-Foreman
Dobbs Tires & Auto Centers
Edison Brothers Stores/J. Riggings Apparel
Heartland Bank
Jensen Tire & Auto
Kaldi's Coffee Roasting
Kelty Pack Inc.
The Midnight Company
National Association of Recording Merchandisers
Pearl Izumi
Robert G. Grimm Photography

St. Louis Music/Crate Amplifiers

PICTURE MARKETING, INC.

20 Miwok Dr, Novato, CA 94947
Tel.: (949) 429-3052
E-Mail: sales@picturemarketing.com
Web Site: www.picturemarketing.com

Employees: 30
Year Founded: 2002

Agency Specializes In: Advertising, Entertainment, Event Planning & Marketing, Guerilla Marketing, Internet/Web Design, Viral/Buzz/Word of Mouth

Terry Tonini *(Co-Founder & Mng Partner)*
Ron Tonini *(CEO)*
Louis Zuckerman *(CTO)*
Cortney Mills *(Dir-Ops)*

Accounts:
Anheuser Busch
California State Lottery
Chrysler

PIERCE PROMOTIONS

511 Congress St 5th Fl, Portland, ME 04101
Tel.: (207) 523-1700
Fax: (207) 761-4570
Toll Free: (800) 298-8582
E-Mail: info@piercepromotions.com
Web Site: piercepromotions.com

Employees: 200

Agency Specializes In: Event Planning & Marketing, Publicity/Promotions

Matthew Carle *(Exec VP)*
Ned Flint *(VP)*
Hilary Dupuis Mitchell *(Sr Dir)*
Jennifer Ortwein *(Sr Dir-Client Svcs)*
Lindsey Kimball *(Client Svcs Dir)*
Jill Peterson *(Acct Dir)*
Lisa Beeler *(Dir-Ops)*
John Muir *(Dir-Production)*
Matt Therrien *(Dir-Creative)*
Andrea Hernandez *(Mgr-Client Svcs)*
Brian C. Tupper *(Mgr-Production)*

Accounts:
Procter & Gamble
Sam's Club
Verizon Communications

PILOT PMR

250 The Esplanade, Courtyard Ste 107, Toronto, M5A 1J2 Canada
Tel.: (416) 462-0199
Fax: (416) 462-1281
E-Mail: team@pilotpmr.com
Web Site: www.pilotpmr.com

Year Founded: 2004

Agency Specializes In: Brand Development & Integration, Digital/Interactive, Public Relations

David Doze *(Pres & CEO)*
Alex Mangiola *(VP)*
Laura Creedon *(Acct Dir)*
Robert Furtado *(Acct Dir)*
Sarah Lazarovic *(Creative Dir)*
Wendy Bairos *(Dir-Media Rels)*
James Beardmore *(Dir-User Experience)*
Natalie Bomberry *(Dir-Client Experience)*
Stuart Inglis *(Dir-Art)*

Accounts:
BBC Canada
Clover Leaf Seafoods
Electrolux Home Care Products North America
TerraChoice

PRO MOTION, INC.

18221 Edison, Saint Louis, MO 63005
Tel.: (314) 997-0101
Fax: (314) 997-6831
E-Mail: marketing@promotion1.com
Web Site: www.promotion1.com

Year Founded: 1995

Agency Specializes In: Cable T.V., Consumer Marketing, Publicity/Promotions, Sales Promotion

Steve Randazzo *(Pres)*
Cathi Kennedy *(Acct Dir-Experiential Mktg)*
Brian Dooley *(Sr Mgr-Mktg)*

Accounts:
Anheuser-Busch
Disney
Dr Pepper Snapple Group
Duck Tape
Energizer
HP
Sony Pictures

PROMARK DIRECT INC.

300 N Midland Ave Ste 2, Saddle Brook, NJ 07663-5723
Tel.: (201) 398-9000
Fax: (201) 398-9212
Toll Free: (800) 404-1900
E-Mail: solutions@promarkdirect.com
Web Site: www.promarkdirect.com

Employees: 4
Year Founded: 1977

Agency Specializes In: Advertising, Business-To-Business, Consulting, Direct Response Marketing, Direct-to-Consumer, Regional, Sales Promotion

Breakdown of Gross Billings by Media: D.M.: 100%

Donna Johns *(Pres)*

Accounts:
ADP; 2001
Humanitees
Konica Business Machines; Windsor, CT Office Equipment; 1985
The Magna Group; Glen Rock, NJ; 2000
North Jersey Media; 1997
Photogenic Inc.
QualCare Preference Providers; Piscataway, NJ Healthcare Insurance; 1994
The Record Newspaper Publisher; 1998
Saddle River Valley Day Camp
Spirit Cruises, LLC

PROMO PARTNERS INC.

30 Ridgeborne Ln, Melville, NY 11747
Tel.: (631) 253-3339
Fax: (866) 356-2232
E-Mail: info@promopartnersinc.com
Web Site: www.promopartnersinc.com

Employees: 5
Year Founded: 2002

National Agency Associations: PMA

Rhonda Kugelman *(VP)*

Accounts:
Alberto Culver
Bayer
Chatham
Goody Products
Hershey's
Kraft

PROMOGROUP

444 N Orleans St Ste 300, Chicago, IL 60610-4494
Tel.: (312) 467-1300
Fax: (312) 467-1311
E-Mail: pgc@promogroup.com
Web Site: www.promogroup.com

E-Mail for Key Personnel:
President: kld@promogroup.com

Employees: 23
Year Founded: 1970

Agency Specializes In: Brand Development & Integration, Collateral, Consumer Marketing, Digital/Interactive, Direct Response Marketing, Internet/Web Design, Merchandising, Point of Purchase, Point of Sale, Production, Retail, Sales Promotion, Sweepstakes

Approx. Annual Billings: $16,000,000

Breakdown of Gross Billings by Media: Collateral: $2,400,000; Point of Purchase: $2,400,000; Promos.: $11,200,000

Kelly L. Drumm *(Co-Founder & CEO)*
Dan Desmond *(VP-Ops)*

Accounts:
Allstate
Apple Inc.; Cupertino, CA
Best Western
Capital One
Cell Star
Chuck E. Cheese's
Coca-Cola Refreshments USA, Inc.
CompUSA
Daimler Chrysler
Delphi
Discover Card; Bannockburn, IL Financial Services; 2000
Dockers
Domino's Pizza
Edy's
Frigidaire
fye
GE
H&R Block
Harley Davidson
Hertz
Hilton Worldwide
Holiday Inn
XM Satellite Radio

PROSPECT MEDIA GROUP LTD.

129 Spadina Ave Ste 300, Toronto, ON M5V 2L3 Canada
Tel.: (416) 348-7386
Fax: (416) 351-9606
E-Mail: info@prospectmedia.com
Web Site: www.prospectmedia.com

Employees: 35
Year Founded: 1999

Agency Specializes In: Advertising, Advertising Specialties, Automotive, Bilingual Market, Business-To-Business, Consumer Goods, Consumer Marketing, Consumer Publications, Direct Response Marketing, Direct-to-Consumer, Entertainment, Event Planning & Marketing, Experience Design, Media Buying Services, Multimedia, Newspapers & Magazines, Over-50 Market, Planning & Consultation, Print, Retail, Sales Promotion, Women's Market

Approx. Annual Billings: $32,000,000

David G. Maples *(Pres)*
David Mathews *(Partner & Mng Dir)*
Allison Madigan *(Partner & VP)*
Pam Fallow *(Dir-HR & Event Mktg)*
Nicole Hegedus *(Dir-New Bus Dev)*
Emily Bosomworth *(Sr Acct Exec)*
Maria Paguirigan *(Sr Acct Exec)*
Cindy Guzman *(Acct Exec)*

PROXY SPONSORSHIPS
(Formerly Proxy Partners LLC)
7900 E Union Ave Ste 1100, Denver, CO 80237
Tel.: (720) 284-8845
Fax: (303) 296-3410
Web Site: www.proxy-sponsorships.com

Employees: 25
Year Founded: 1999

Agency Specializes In: Advertising, Affiliate Marketing, Branded Entertainment, Co-op Advertising, Consulting, Custom Publishing, Customer Relationship Management, Digital/Interactive, Email, Event Planning & Marketing, Financial, Guerilla Marketing, In-Store Advertising, Integrated Marketing, Local Marketing, Media Buying Services, Mobile Marketing, Multimedia, New Product Development, Out-of-Home Media, Outdoor, Planning & Consultation, Product Placement, Publicity/Promotions, Sales Promotion, Sponsorship, Sports Market, Strategic Planning/Research, T.V., Trade & Consumer Magazines, Travel & Tourism, Viral/Buzz/Word of Mouth

Approx. Annual Billings: $5,000,000

Breakdown of Gross Billings by Media: Consulting: 34%; Other: 33%; Out-of-Home Media: 33%

Mala Alvey *(Principal)*

Accounts:
Frontier Airlines' Wild Blue Yonder Inflight Entertainment Inflight Media
HealthONE; 2008
MillerCoors; 2006
Subaru

PUBLIGROUPE LTD.
Avenue Mon-Repos 22, CH-1002 Lausanne, Switzerland
Tel.: (41) 21 317 7111
Fax: (41) 21 317 7555
E-Mail: info@publigroupe.com
Web Site: www.publigroupe.com

Employees: 2,349
Year Founded: 1890

Agency Specializes In: Advertising

Revenue: $1,602,912,402

Hans-Peter Rohner *(Chm)*
Arndt C. Groth *(CEO)*
Brigitte Schleipen *(Chief HR Officer)*
Andreas Schmidt *(CFO-Fin & Controlling)*
Beat Werder *(head-Corp Comm)*
Jean-Denis Briod *(Gen Sec)*

Branches

Adnative Switzerland
7 Chemin Maisonneuve, Chatelaine, CH 1219 Geneva, Switzerland
Tel.: (41) 227964626
Fax: (41) 227970270
E-Mail: geneva@adnative.net
Web Site: www.adnative.net

Philippe Girardot *(Mng Dir)*

Adnative
26 Ave Victor Hugo, F-75116 Paris, France
Tel.: (33) 1 53 64 88 90
Fax: (33) 1 45 00 25 81
E-Mail: gilles.vaillon@publicitas.com
Web Site: www.adnative.net/fr

Agency Specializes In: Magazines, Media Buying Services, Media Relations, Sales Promotion

Claire Goueythieu *(Mng Dir)*
Florence De Moussac *(Dir-Sls)*
Hildegard Addari *(Mgr-Adv)*

M & M International Media AB
Vasterlanggatan 67, 111 29 Stockholm, Sweden
Tel.: (46) 8 24 54 01
Fax: (46) 8 25 54 02
E-Mail: markus@mmim.se
Web Site: www.mmim.se/

Year Founded: 1972

Agency Specializes In: Media Buying Services, Public Relations

Markus Saving *(Owner & Founder)*
Mathias Saving *(Owner & Founder)*

Accounts:
Ericksen
H&M
Nokia

McGown/Intermac/Publicitas North America
1281 W Georgia Street 502,, Vancouver, BC V6E 3G7 Canada
Tel.: (778) 34-0 1324
Fax: (604) 689-0703
E-Mail: bfinn@mcgown.com
Web Site: www.publicitas.com

Agency Specializes In: Sales Promotion

Rosalind Genge *(Dir-Sls)*

Permedia Athens Ltd.
4 Kastorias St, Gerakas, GR 153 44 Athens, Greece
Tel.: (30) 210 685 15 25
Fax: (30) 210 685 33 57
E-Mail: info@publicitas.gr
Web Site: www.publicitas.com

Year Founded: 1992

Hara Koutelou *(Dir)*

Publicitas Charney/Palacios & Co., Inc.
5201 Blue Lagoon Dr Ste 200, Miami, FL 33126
Tel.: (786) 388-6340
Fax: (786) 388-9113
E-Mail: ppn-miami@publicitas.com
Web Site: www.publicitas.com

E-Mail for Key Personnel:
President: aferro@publicitas.com
Media Dir.: tgarcia@publicitas.com

Year Founded: 1980

National Agency Associations: IAA

Agency Specializes In: Hispanic Market, Media Buying Services

Lucio Grimaldi *(Mng Dir-AMERICAS & VP)*
Myriam Milgrom *(Sr Acct Dir)*
Gina Tinoco *(Acct Dir-Digital-US Hispanic & Latin America)*
Roberto Lago *(Dir-Digital-LATAM & US Hispanic)*
Tammy Garcia *(Mgr-Media Rels)*

Publicitas Eastern Europe Ltd.
Novy Arbat str 21 Bldg 1 6th Fl Office 611, Moscow, 119019 Russia
Tel.: (7) 095 258 38 56
Fax: (7) 095 258 38 57
E-Mail: moscow@publicitas.com
Web Site: www.publicitas.com/russia

Year Founded: 1995

Agency Specializes In: Sales Promotion

Vladimir Barkov *(Mng Dir)*
Tatyana Smirnova *(Mgr-Adv)*

Accounts:
Aeroflot
Aquatoria of Luxury Life
Bereg
Delovoy Peterburg
Karavan Istoriy
Kommersant
Modny Magazine
The Moscow Times
Playboy
RBC-Daily
Robb Report
Russkiy Reporter
Sekret Firmy
Vokrug Sveta
Voyage

Publicitas Germany GmbH
Oederweg 52-54, D-60318 Frankfurt am Main, Germany
Tel.: (49) 69 7191 490
Fax: (49) 69 7191 4930
E-Mail: germany@publicitas.com
Web Site: www.publicitas.com/germany

Employees: 15
Year Founded: 1968

Agency Specializes In: Magazines, Newspaper, Newspapers & Magazines, Sales Promotion

Christian Nemere *(Mng Dir)*
Petra Becker *(Dir-Sls)*
Irina Kaiser *(Mgr-Sls Support)*
Samir Van Lith *(Key Acct Mgr)*

Accounts:
Air Berlin PLC & Co. Luftverkehrs KG
COR Sitzmobel Helmut Lubke GmbH & Co. KG
Hugo Boss AG

Publicitas Hellas Ltd.
4 Kastorias & Messinias Street, Gerakas, GR-153 44 Athens, Greece
Tel.: (30) 211 1060 300
Fax: (30) 210 6618 477
E-Mail: info@publicitas.gr
Web Site: www.publicitas.com

Employees: 7
Year Founded: 1979

Agency Specializes In: Advertising

Fani Koilakou *(Dir-Fin)*
Hara Koutelou *(Dir-Greece)*
Nikos Dimos *(Mgr-Sls & Media)*

Publicitas Hong Kong
25/F & 26/F Two Chinachem Exchange Square, 338 Kings Road, North Point, China (Hong Kong)
Tel.: (852) 2516 1001
Fax: (852) 2561 3260
E-Mail: ppn-hongkong@publicitas.com
Web Site: www.publicitas.com/hongkong

Employees: 10

Agency Specializes In: Media Buying Services, Sales Promotion

Mariam Wang *(Mng Dir)*
Pauline Wong *(Mng Dir)*
Jorg Nurnberg *(CEO-Global)*
Jason Kwong *(Mng Dir-East Asia & Australia)*
Michele Li *(Gen Mgr-Sls)*
Emily Chan *(Mgr-Adv)*

Emilio Zerboni *(Mng Dir)*
Simon Taylor *(Mng Dir-EMEA)*
Marta Cerniglia *(Mgr-Admin & Internal Sls)*

Accounts:
CU Alumni
IDN
Longyin Review

Accounts:
Acer
Alitalia
Casa Damiani
Fiere di Verona
Giorgio Armani
Regione Veneto

Publicitas Internacional S.A.
Goya 21 1D, 28001 Madrid, Spain
Tel.: (34) 91 323 79 11
Fax: (34) 91 733 59 58
E-Mail: madrid@publicitas.com
Web Site: www.publicitas.com

Employees: 14
Year Founded: 1972

Agency Specializes In: Event Planning & Marketing, International, Media Relations, Publicity/Promotions

Maria Navarro *(Sls Mgr-Europe & Latam)*
Pedro Lourido *(Mgr-Sls)*

Accounts:
Spanish Tourist Board

Publicitas International AG
Kornhausgasse 5/7, PO Box 3843, 4002 Basel, Switzerland
Tel.: (41) 61 275 43 00
Fax: (41) 61 275 47 47
E-Mail: basel-international@publicitas.com
Web Site: www.publicitas.com

Employees: 4

Johannes Braun *(Mng Dir)*
Silvana Imperiali *(Mng Dir)*
Alain Lamy *(Mng Dir)*
Laetitia Foeller *(Head-Digital Media)*
Cordula Nebiker *(Dir-Sls)*
Heinrich Jung *(Mgr-Sls)*
Tudisco Fabrizio *(Client Svc Dir)*

Publicitas International Switzerland
Hochbergerstrasse 15, Post Box 3868, 4002 Basel, Switzerland
Tel.: (41) 61 275 46 46
Fax: (41) 61 275 47 77
E-Mail: ppn-basel@publicitas.com
Web Site: www.publicitas.com

Employees: 10

Alain Lamy *(Mng Dir)*
Suter Christian *(Head-Customer Svc)*
Frank Forrer *(Head-IT-Switzerland)*
Ines Conley *(Controller & Bus Analyst)*

Publicitas International
Via Besana 9 - 2 piano, I-20122 Milan, Italy
Tel.: (39) 02 5519 4385
Fax: (39) 02 5519 9019
E-Mail: ppn-milan@publicitas.com
Web Site: www.publicitas.com/it/italy/homepage/

Publicitas AG
Muertschenstrasse 39, CH - 8010 Zurich, Switzerland
Tel.: (41) 21 213 6311
Fax: (41) 21 213 6312
E-Mail: zurich-international@publicitas.com
Web Site: www.publicitas.com/switzerland

Employees: 2
Year Founded: 1979

Agency Specializes In: Newspapers & Magazines, Sales Promotion

Christoph Marty *(CEO & Dir-Sls)*
Fabio Balmelli *(Mng Dir)*
Silvana Imperiali *(Mng Dir)*
Stephan Bauerle *(COO)*
Cordula Nebiker *(Dir-Sls)*
Heinrich Jung *(Mgr-Sls-Publicitas International)*
Francesco Peroni *(Mgr-Digital Sls & Admin)*

Publicitas Leman
Rue de la Synagogue 35, CH-1204 Geneva, Switzerland
Tel.: (41) 22 807 3400
Fax: (41) 22 320 0162
E-Mail: geneve@publicitas.ch
Web Site: www.publicitas.ch

Employees: 65

Agency Specializes In: Advertising, Sales Promotion

Fabio Balmelli *(Mng Dir)*
Silvana Imperiali *(Mng Dir)*
Alain Lamy *(Mng Dir)*
Laetitia Foeller *(Head-Digital Media)*
Patrick Cuenoud *(Reg Dir-Western Switzerland)*
Cordula Nebiker *(Dir-Sls)*
Heinrich Jung *(Sls Mgr)*
Francesco Peroni *(Mgr-Digital Sls & Admin)*
Tudisco Fabrizio *(Client Svc Dir)*
Rose-marie Rey *(Area Dir-Sls)*

Publicitas Ltd.
Comercialstrasse 20, PO Box 238, CH-7007 Chur, Switzerland
Tel.: (41) 81 255 58 58
Fax: (41) 81 255 58 59
E-Mail: chur@so-publicitas.ch
Web Site: www.publicitas.com

Employees: 62

Agency Specializes In: Advertising

Fabio Balmelli *(Mng Dir)*
Heinrich Jung *(Sls Mgr)*
Francesco Peroni *(Mgr-Digital Sls & Admin)*
Tudisco Fabrizio *(Client Svc Dir)*

Publicitas Ltd.
Neumattstrasse 1, PO Box 3501, CH-5001 Aarau, Switzerland
Tel.: (41) 62 838 0808
Fax: (41) 62 838 0800
E-Mail: aarau@publicitas.ch
Web Site: www.publicitas.ch

Employees: 9

Agency Specializes In: Publicity/Promotions

Fabio Balmelli *(Mng Dir)*
Heinrich Jung *(Sls Mgr)*
Francesco Peroni *(Mgr-Digital Sls & Admin)*
Tudisco Fabrizio *(Client Svc Dir)*
Franz Stutz *(Key Acct Mgr)*

Publicitas Ltd.
Kornhausgasse 5/7, Postfach 3843, CH-4002 Basel, Switzerland
Tel.: (41) 61 275 46 46
Fax: (41) 61 275 47 77
E-Mail: basel-international@publicitas.com
Web Site: www.Publicitas.com/Switzerland

Employees: 60

Agency Specializes In: Publicity/Promotions

Fabio Balmelli *(Mng Dir)*
Silvana Imperiali *(Mng Dir)*
Alain Lamy *(Mng Dir)*
Cordula Nebiker *(Dir-Sls)*
Heinrich Jung *(Sls Mgr)*
Bryndis Bjornsdottir *(Mgr-Sls)*
Laetitia Foeller *(Mgr-Sls-Digital Media)*
Francesco Peroni *(Mgr-Digital Sls & Admin)*
Tudisco Fabrizio *(Client Svc Dir)*

Accounts:
Swiss International Airlines

Publicitas Ltd.
Gordon House, 10 Green Coat Pl, London, SW1P 1PH United Kingdom
Tel.: (44) 207 592 8300
Fax: (44) 207 592 8301
E-Mail: london@publicitas.com
Web Site: www.publicitas.com/uk

Employees: 30

Agency Specializes In: Sales Promotion

Oliver Eills *(Mng Dir)*
Jeremy Butchers *(Head-Sls)*
Thomas Meixner *(Dir-Sls-LATAM)*
Agata Zukowska *(Dir-Sls)*
Adam J. Bell *(Acct Mgr-Intl)*
Silvia Torner *(Mgr-Mktg-Europe)*

Publicitas Ltd.
Avenue Mon-Repos 22, PO Box 7082, 1001 Lausanne, Switzerland
Tel.: (41) 21 317 7121
Fax: (41) 21 317 7899
E-Mail: dg@publicitas.ch
Web Site: www.publicitas.ch

Employees: 50

Agency Specializes In: Publicity/Promotions

Martina Basler *(Mgr-Sls)*
Oliver Michler *(Mgr-Sls)*
Olivia Spiess *(Mgr-Sls Support)*
Rose-Marie Rey *(Area Dir-Sls)*
Fabrizio Tudisco *(Client Svc Dir)*

Publicitas Ltd.
Rue St Maurice 4, 2001 Neuchatel, Switzerland
Tel.: (41) 32 729 4242
Fax: (41) 32 729 4243
E-Mail: neuchatel@publicitas.ch
Web Site: www.publicitas.com

Employees: 22

Agency Specializes In: Publicity/Promotions

Fabio Balmelli *(Mng Dir)*
Patrick Cuenoud *(Reg Dir)*
Heinrich Jung *(Sls Mgr)*
Francesco Peroni *(Mgr-Digital Sls & Admin)*
Tudisco Fabrizio *(Client Svc Dir)*

Publicitas Ltd.
Vadianstrasse 45, Postfach 1642, 9001 Saint Gallen, Switzerland
Tel.: (41) 71 221 0021
Fax: (41) 75 221 0221
E-Mail: stgallen@publicitas.ch
Web Site: www.publicitas.com

Employees: 100

Agency Specializes In: Publicity/Promotions

Alain Lamy *(Mng Dir)*
Laetitia Foeller *(Head-Digital Media)*
Belinda Fassler Marti *(Dir-Admin)*
Cordula Nebiker *(Dir-Sls)*
Martina Basler *(Mgr-Sls)*
Silvia Gschwind *(Mgr-Sls Admin)*
Markus Merkli *(Mgr-Sls)*
Alessandra Esposito Romeo *(Mgr-Sls)*
Olivia Spiess *(Mgr-Sls Admin)*
Rose Marie Rey *(Area Dir-Sls)*
Fabrizio Tudisco *(Client Svc Dir)*

Publicitas Malaysia
S105 2nd Floor Centrepoint, Lebuh Bandar Utama, 47800 Petaling Jaya, Selangor Malaysia
Tel.: (60) 3 7729 6923
Fax: (60) 3 719 7115
E-Mail: kualalumpur@publicitas.com
Web Site: www.publicitas.com

Employees: 5

Siew-Sai Hoo *(Mng Dir-Southeast Asia)*

Accounts:
Malaysia Airlines
Tourism Malaysia

Publicitas McGown
(Formerly McGown/Intermac/Publicitas North America)
468 Queen Street E Ste 300, Toronto, ON M5A 1T7 Canada
Tel.: (416) 966-1622
Fax: (416) 966-1434
E-Mail: cynthia.jollymore@publicitas.com
Web Site: www.publicitas.com

Employees: 10

Agency Specializes In: Print, Sales Promotion

Rosalind Genge *(Mng Dir)*
Wayne St. John *(CEO-Publicitas Canada)*
Francoise Chalifour *(VP-Sls)*
Cynthia Jollymore *(VP-Sls)*

Publicitas Media S.A.
Lozenberg 23, B-1932 Zaventem, Belgium
Tel.: (32) 2 639 8420
Fax: (32) 2 639 8430
E-Mail: brussels@publicitas.com
Web Site: www.publicitas.com/belgium

Employees: 11
Year Founded: 1976

Agency Specializes In: Magazines, Newspaper, Newspapers & Magazines

Peter Landsheere *(Mng Dir)*
Ingrid Bellis *(Client Svcs Dir)*
Martine De Groodt *(Dir-Sls)*
Britt Caremans *(Mgr-Sls)*
Anne Costermans *(Mgr-Sls)*

Accounts:
Trend; Vienna, Austria Lifestyle Magazine

Publicitas North America
14211 Dickens St, Sherman Oaks, CA 91423
Tel.: (310) 601-7618
Fax: (818) 647-0139
E-Mail: losangeles@publicitas.com
Web Site: www.publicitas.com

Bruce Brandfon *(VP & Mng Dir-North America)*
Francisca Hoogeveen *(Sr Acct Dir-Intl)*
Shireen Stangl *(Sr Acct Dir-West Coast)*

Publicitas North America
50 California St Ste 1547, San Francisco, CA 94111
Tel.: (415) 439-5278
Fax: (415) 439-5299
E-Mail: Hsanfrancisco@publicitas.com
Web Site: www.publicitas.com

Employees: 1

Agency Specializes In: Advertising, International, Magazines, Newspaper, Newspapers & Magazines

Bruce Brandfon *(Mng Dir & VP)*
Moreno Cavaliere *(Mng Dir-Adv & Client Bus)*
Chris Morgan *(Head-Media & Product Mgmt)*
Francisca Hoogeveen *(Sr Acct Dir-Intl)*
Katrin Barbarello *(Acct Dir-Digital)*
Carolyn Wagner *(Acct Dir-Fashion & Luxury)*

Publicitas USA
(Formerly Publicitas North America)
330 7th Ave, New York, NY 10001
Tel.: (212) 330-0720
Fax: (212) 599-8298
E-Mail: jill.gutekunst@publicitas.com
Web Site: www.publicitas.com

Employees: 15

Agency Specializes In: Media Buying Services, Newspapers & Magazines

Bruce Brandfon *(Mng Dir & VP)*
Kent Edens *(Controller-Fin)*
Francisca Hoogeveen *(Sr Acct Dir-Intl)*
Katrin Barbarello *(Acct Dir-Digital)*
Delci Lopez *(Acct Dir-Intl)*
Carolyn Wagner *(Acct Dir-Fashion & Luxury)*
Dina Moriguchi *(Office Mgr)*
Jill Gutekunst *(Mgr-Mktg & Sls Dev)*
Christopher Pasqual-Kwan *(Mgr-Digital Campaign)*
Brooke Simmons *(Sr Acct Coord)*

Accounts:
ELLE International Titles
The Globe and Mail
Guardian UK
Suddeutsche Zeitung
Le Monde
The Nikkei
South China Morning Post
The Straits Times
The Times of India

Publicitas S.A.
26 Avenue Victor Hugo, F-75116 Paris, France
Tel.: (33) 145 00 66 08
Fax: (33) 145 00 94 81
E-Mail: paris@publicitas.com
Web Site: www.publicitas.com/en/france

Employees: 13
Year Founded: 1947

Agency Specializes In: Media Buying Services, Sales Promotion

Claire Goueythieu *(Mng Dir)*
Geraldine Roger *(Acct Dir)*
Valerie Bellamy *(Dir-Digital Svcs)*
Alexandra Ignatieff *(Dir-Luxury Goods Div)*
Caroline Merdy *(Dir-Digital Media Buying)*
Julie Bentolila *(Acct Mgr)*
Sofia Neiada *(Acct Mgr-Digital)*
Ginette Matusiak *(Mgr-Admin)*
Marisol Babe Lopez *(Key Acct Mgr)*

Accounts:
Air France-KLM Group
Arcelor Mittal
Areva
BNP Paribas
Capgemini
Packad Bell
Sodexo

Publicitas Singapore
72 Bendemeer Road #02-20 The Luzerne Bldg, Singapore, 339941 Singapore
Tel.: (65) 6836 2272
Fax: (65) 6735 9653
E-Mail: singapore@publicitas.com
Web Site: www.publicitas.com

Employees: 8

Siew-Sai Hoo *(Mng Dir-Southeast Asia)*
Lee Walsh *(Mng Dir-Southeast Asia & India)*
Joel Choo *(Dir-Programmatic Sls-Asia Pacific)*
Jessica Goh *(Dir-Sls-Digital & TV-Southeast Asia)*
Peggy Thay *(Dir-Media Sls)*
Lee Ann-Kee *(Sr Mgr)*
Francis Tay *(Mgr-Accounts-Fin)*

Publicitas Thailand
5th Fl Lumpini I Bldg, 239/2 Soi Sarasin Rajdamri Rd, Lumpini Bangkok, 10330 Thailand
Tel.: (66) 2 651 9273-7
Fax: (66) 2 651 9278
E-Mail: ppn-thailand@publicitas.com
Web Site: www.publicitas.com

Employees: 6

Steven Fong *(Mng Dir)*
Supavadee Vaivanitckij *(Sec-Traffic & Admin)*
Siew-Sai Hoo *(Mng Dir-South East Asia Reg)*
Janya Limmanee *(Mgr)*

Accounts:
Tourism Authority of Thailand

Xentive
(Formerly Pixedia)
Avenue des Mousquines 4, 1005 Lausanne, Switzerland
Tel.: (41) 21 213 61 11
Fax: (41) 21 312 44 09
E-Mail: info@xentive.ch
Web Site: www.xentive.ch

Employees: 200

Agency Specializes In: Information Technology

Matthias Stocklin *(Product Mgr)*
Giuseppe Catanese *(Mgr-Infrastructure)*
Magali David-Cruz *(Mgr-Architect & Ops Team)*
Pascal Bridel *(Sr Engr-Software)*

Q1MEDIA, INC.

11401 Century Oaks Ter Ste 470, Austin, TX 78758
Tel.: (512) 388-2300
Fax: (509) 275-6366
E-Mail: bill@q1media.com
Web Site: next.q1media.com

Employees: 10
Year Founded: 2004

Agency Specializes In: Advertising, Brand Development & Integration, College, Consulting, Consumer Goods, Digital/Interactive, Education, Entertainment, Men's Market, Planning & Consultation, Regional, Teen Market, Women's Market

Approx. Annual Billings: $10,000,000

Breakdown of Gross Billings by Media: Internet Adv.: $10,000,000

Bill Wiemann *(Founder & Pres)*
Alex Esquilin *(Acct Mgr & Publr)*
Suzanne Tobias *(VP-Product)*
Jason Appelbaum *(Dir-Mktg)*
Lene Lay *(Dir-Sls)*
Jesse Rogowsky *(Dir-Bus Dev)*
Fabio Bartolai *(Mgr-Sls-Natl)*
Kilty Brendan Cleary *(Mgr-Bus Dev)*
Kevin Schwed *(Mgr-Bus Dev)*
Hunter Temperton *(Mgr-Ad Ops)*
Megan Mayo *(Sr Acct Exec)*
Taylor Waltmon *(Sr Acct Exec)*
Reid Howell *(Specialist-Digital Adv Ops)*
Brian Rusk *(Analyst-Bus-Product Mgmt Team)*
Emmy Palos *(Coord-HR)*

R.A. DINKEL & ASSOCIATES, INC.

(d/b/a The Idea People)
4641 Willoughby Rd, Holt, MI 48842
Tel.: (517) 699-7000
Fax: (517) 699-7700
E-Mail: sales@ideasideas.com
Web Site: www.ideasideas.com

Employees: 15
Year Founded: 1965

Agency Specializes In: Consumer Marketing, Publicity/Promotions

Approx. Annual Billings: $2,000,000

Liz Dinkel *(Pres)*
Julie Welch *(Mgr)*
Kim Pipekow *(Specialist-Mktg)*
Vickie Swindall *(Specialist-Mktg)*
Katie Taszreak *(Specialist-Mktg)*

RPM MARKETING & PROMOTIONS

138 Mulberry St 3rd Fl, New York, NY 10013
Tel.: (212) 375-6211
Fax: (212) 375-6205
E-Mail: info@therpmgrp.com

Employees: 10
Year Founded: 1997

Agency Specializes In: Brand Development & Integration, Consumer Marketing, Event Planning & Marketing, Publicity/Promotions, Sales Promotion

Rene McLean *(Founder & Partner)*
Lylette Pizarro *(Partner)*

Accounts:
Pepsi

RPMC, INC.

23975 Park Sorrento Ste 410, Calabasas, CA 91302
Tel.: (818) 222-7762
Fax: (818) 222-0048
E-Mail: info@rpmc.com
Web Site: www.rpmc.com

Employees: 30
Year Founded: 1986

Agency Specializes In: Business-To-Business, Consumer Marketing, Entertainment, Event Planning & Marketing, Experience Design, Guerilla Marketing, Hospitality, International, Local Marketing, Pharmaceutical, Point of Sale, Promotions, Publicity/Promotions, Sports Market, Sweepstakes, Travel & Tourism, Viral/Buzz/Word of Mouth

Approx. Annual Billings: $30,000,000

Simon Temperley *(CEO)*
Tami Rittberg *(Sr VP)*
Von Parish *(VP-Acct Svcs)*
Brad Mulholland *(Controller-Fin)*
Karen Bell *(Sr Dir)*
Lisa Moran *(Sr Dir-Individual Incentives)*
Pat Bilodeau *(Dir-Air Ops)*
Heather Edmondson *(Dir-Meetings & Incentives)*
Allison Leo *(Mgr-Dev)*

Accounts:
CBS
DIRECTV
Discover Financial Services
Discovery Networks
Mattel
Valeant Pharmaceuticals

SCA PROMOTIONS, INC.

3030 LBJ Freeway Ste 300, Dallas, TX 75234
Tel.: (214) 860-3700
Fax: (214) 860-3723
Toll Free: (888) 860-3700
E-Mail: info@scapromo.com
Web Site: www.scapromotions.com

Employees: 75
Year Founded: 1986

National Agency Associations: DMA-PMA

Agency Specializes In: Sales Promotion, Sponsorship, Sweepstakes

Breakdown of Gross Billings by Media: Mags.: 4%; Newsp.: 3%; Other: 73%; Radio: 15%; T.V.: 5%

Robert D. Hamman *(Founder & Pres)*
Christine Bennett *(Dir-Sls-Worldwide)*
Wendy Collins *(Dir-Risk Mgmt)*
Janell James *(Dir-Ops)*
Tanya Mathis *(Dir-Mktg)*
Max Rhodes *(Dir-Fishing)*
Jackie Walker *(Sr Acct Mgr)*
Todd Overton *(Acct Mgr)*
Becky R. Young *(Mgr-Client Dev)*
Ray French *(Sr Acct Exec)*
Paul Panzera *(Sr Acct Exec)*

Accounts:
ESPN Regional
General Mills
Harley Davidson
Mazda Motors of America, Inc
MGM Grand Detroit Casino
Motorola Solutions, Inc.
Ohio University
Pepsi-Cola
Sony
Taco Bell
Venetian Resort Hotel
Ventura Associates, Inc.

SELLING SOLUTIONS, INC.

3525 Piedmont Rd Bldg 5 Ste 515, Atlanta, GA 30305
Tel.: (404) 261-4966
Fax: (404) 264-1767
Toll Free: (800) 638-9728
E-Mail: information@selsol.com
Web Site: www.selsol.com

Employees: 10
Year Founded: 1983

Agency Specializes In: Food Service

Approx. Annual Billings: $7,500,000

Breakdown of Gross Billings by Media: D.M.: $7,500,000

James Paulin *(VP-Comm & Sls Motivation)*
Lauren Paulin *(Asst Project Mgr)*

Accounts:
Coca-Cola Refreshments USA, Inc.; Atlanta, GA
MillerCoors
Minute Maid
Real Facts
Shell; Houston, TX

SIITE INTERACTIVE

132 E 43rd St, New York, NY 10017-4019
Tel.: (212) 481-9070
Fax: (212) 481-9074
Web Site: http://lightningjar.agency/

Agency Specializes In: Affluent Market, Consumer Goods, Cosmetics, Digital/Interactive, E-Commerce, Email, Environmental, Game Integration, Graphic Design, Health Care Services, Hospitality, Identity Marketing, Information Technology, Internet/Web Design, Medical Products, Mobile Marketing, Multicultural, Multimedia, Pharmaceutical, Podcasting, Point of Sale, Production (Ad, Film, Broadcast), RSS (Really Simple Syndication), Retail, Search Engine Optimization, Sweepstakes, Teen Market, Web (Banner Ads, Pop-ups, etc.)

Approx. Annual Billings: $9,000,000

Breakdown of Gross Billings by Media: Consulting: 20%; Internet Adv.: 80%

Alan Ruthazer *(Founder)*
Ashley Laing *(Chief Digital Officer & Partner)*
Kevin Peckham *(Principal & Sr Brand Strategist)*

Accounts:
Aetna; London, England aetna-uk.co.uk
American Express; New York, NY
Broan-NuTone; OH Re-Branding Campaign Support
GE Financial; Stamford, CT
Hearst Business Media; New York, NY
Hearst; New York, NY
Intel; New York, NY
Kawasaki; New York, NY
Time magazine; New York, NY
Toyota; New York, NY
Turner Construction; New York, NY
United Rentals; New York, NY URData Account

Sales Promotion Agencies

Tracking Software

SJI, INC.

1918 Innerbelt Business Center Dr, Saint Louis, MO 63114
Tel.: (314) 336-1331
Fax: (314) 336-1332
E-Mail: webmaster@sji-inc.com
Web Site: www.sji-inc.com

E-Mail for Key Personnel:
President: mshevitz@sji-inc.com

Employees: 10
Year Founded: 1988

National Agency Associations: MAA

Agency Specializes In: Brand Development & Integration, Business-To-Business, College, Communications, Consulting, Consumer Marketing, Corporate Identity, E-Commerce, Event Planning & Marketing, Point of Purchase, Point of Sale, Production, Promotions, Publicity/Promotions, Sales Promotion, Sports Market, Sweepstakes

Mark H. Shevitz *(Pres)*

Accounts:
Hilex Poly, Inc.; Hartsville, SC; 2008
House Party, Inc.; Irvington, NY; 2007
Reser's Fine Foods; Beaverton, OR; 2009
Wachovia Bank, A Division of Wells Fargo; Charlotte, NC; 2005

Branch

SJI Fulfillment

1918 Inner Belt Business Ctr Dr, Saint Louis, MO 63114-5760
Tel.: (314) 336-1331
Fax: (314) 336-1332
Web Site: www.sji-inc.com

E-Mail for Key Personnel:
President: mshevitz@sjicompanies.com

Employees: 7

Agency Specializes In: Advertising

Mark Shevitz *(Pres)*
Janice Schmitt *(VP-Fulfillment)*

Accounts:
Porsche

SKYTYPERS, INC.

10650 San Sicily St, Las Vegas, NV 89141
Toll Free: (888) SKYTYPE
E-Mail: sales@skytypers.com
Web Site: www.skytypers.com

Year Founded: 2004

Agency Specializes In: Advertising, Asian Market, Aviation & Aerospace, Bilingual Market, Brand Development & Integration, Communications, Corporate Identity, Direct-to-Consumer, E-Commerce, Entertainment, Event Planning & Marketing, Game Integration, Guerilla Marketing, High Technology, Hispanic Market, Integrated Marketing, Media Relations, Mobile Marketing, Multicultural, New Product Development, Out-of-Home Media, Outdoor, Over-50 Market, Promotions, Publicity/Promotions, Sales Promotion, Social Marketing/Nonprofit, Sponsorship, Sports Market

Approx. Annual Billings: $2,500,000

Breakdown of Gross Billings by Media: Outdoor: 100%

Greg Stinis *(Owner)*
Stephen Stinis *(Pres)*

Accounts:
HBO

SMITH & MARGOL, INC.

11777 Water Tank Rd Ste A1, Burlington, WA 98233
Tel.: (360) 707-2244
Fax: (360) 707-2266
E-Mail: information@smith-margol.com
Web Site: www.smith-margol.com

E-Mail for Key Personnel:
President: sam@smith-margol.com

Employees: 3
Year Founded: 1984

Agency Specializes In: Sales Promotion

Susanne Margol Holmes *(Pres)*
Sarah Diamond *(VP)*

Accounts:
C&H Cookie Cutter
The Gap
Intel Wood Massager
Swiss Miss Hot Chocolate
Taco Time Face Paints

SOURCE MARKETING LLC

761 Main Ave, Norwalk, CT 06851
Tel.: (203) 291-4000
Fax: (203) 291-4010
E-Mail: info@source-marketing.com
Web Site: http://www.sourcecxm.com/

E-Mail for Key Personnel:
President: Correia@source-marketing.com

Employees: 115
Year Founded: 1989

National Agency Associations: DMA-PMA

Agency Specializes In: Brand Development & Integration, Business-To-Business, Co-op Advertising, Collateral, Consulting, Consumer Marketing, Direct Response Marketing, Electronic Media, Entertainment, Event Planning & Marketing, Infomercials, Pharmaceutical, Planning & Consultation, Point of Purchase, Point of Sale, Print, Production, Publicity/Promotions, Radio, Sales Promotion, Sponsorship, Sweepstakes

Approx. Annual Billings: $600,000,000

Breakdown of Gross Billings by Media: Event Mktg.: 10%; Fees: 20%; Graphic Design: 15%; Out-of-Home Media: 10%; Promos.: 15%; Radio: 30%

Kersten Mitton Rivas *(Pres)*
Derek Correia *(CEO)*
Richard Feldman *(Mng Partner)*
Neil Cameron *(VP-Digital & Interactive)*
Lindsay Maloney *(Dir-Experiential & Entertainment Partnerships)*
Maureen Jones *(Mgr-Accounts)*
Will Mentz *(Sr Acct Exec)*

Accounts:
AARP
Alcon
BIC; Milford, CT Campaign: "Make Your Own Sun"
Chase
Dick's Sporting Goods
Erie Insurance
Mylan
Philips
Purina Mills
Sheetz
Sonos
Tata Global Beverages
Unilever
Verizon

SPECIALTY TRUCK RENTALS

406 Broadway Ste 225, Santa Monica, CA 90401
Tel.: (310) 740-9992
Web Site: www.specialtytruckrental.com

Employees: 27
Year Founded: 1999

Agency Specializes In: Advertising, Advertising Specialties, Affluent Market, African-American Market, Alternative Advertising, Asian Market, Automotive, Bilingual Market, Brand Development & Integration, Branded Entertainment, Business-To-Business, Children's Market, College, Consumer Goods, Consumer Marketing, Cosmetics, Direct-to-Consumer, Education, Electronics, Entertainment, Event Planning & Marketing, Exhibit/Trade Shows, Experience Design, Faith Based, Fashion/Apparel, Financial, Food Service, Gay & Lesbian Market, Government/Political, Guerilla Marketing, Health Care Services, High Technology, Hispanic Market, Household Goods, Identity Marketing, Integrated Marketing, International, Luxury Products, Men's Market, Merchandising, Mobile Marketing, Multicultural, New Product Development, New Technologies, Outdoor, Over-50 Market, Pets , Pharmaceutical, Promotions, Real Estate, Recruitment, Restaurant, Retail, Sales Promotion, Seniors' Market, South Asian Market, Sports Market, Teen Market, Transportation, Travel & Tourism, Tween Market, Urban Market, Viral/Buzz/Word of Mouth, Women's Market

Approx. Annual Billings: $2,500,000

Matt Miller *(Acct Mgr)*

Accounts:
Converse; 2013
Metro PCS; 2013

SPONSORSHIPU

25 Broadway, New York, NY 10004
Tel.: (319) 594-0149
Web Site: www.sponsorshipu.com

Employees: 4
Year Founded: 2015

Agency Specializes In: Sponsorship

Patrick Diamitani *(Founder & CEO)*
Benjamin Clack *(CFO & Gen Counsel)*
Jared Dickman *(CTO)*
Elaine Kanuk *(VP-Sls & Mktg)*

Accounts:
New-Fooze Fooze Mobile App; 2015
New-Ocho.Co Panama; 2015

THE SUNFLOWER GROUP

14001 Marshall Dr, Lenexa, KS 66215
Tel.: (913) 890-0900
Fax: (913) 307-8339
E-Mail: jim.fitterer@sunflowergroup.com
Web Site: www.sunflowergroup.com

Employees: 185
Year Founded: 1978

Agency Specializes In: Advertising Specialties,

College, Consumer Marketing, Event Planning & Marketing, Experience Design, Guerilla Marketing, Hispanic Market, In-Store Advertising, Merchandising, Mobile Marketing, Newspaper, Newspapers & Magazines, Out-of-Home Media, Point of Sale, Print, Promotions, Publicity/Promotions, Retail, Sales Promotion, Shopper Marketing, Sponsorship, Sports Market, Viral/Buzz/Word of Mouth

Approx. Annual Billings: $80,000,000

Dennis Garberg *(Chm)*
Robert Turley *(CIO)*
Pete Reininga *(Sr VP-Mktg)*
Eric Douglas *(VP-Bus Dev)*
Tom Roberts *(VP)*
John Sandwick *(VP-Bus Dev)*

Accounts:
Ahold USA
Coca-Cola Refreshments USA, Inc.
The Dannon Company
Frito-Lay
General Mills
Kraft
Nestle USA
PepsiCo, Inc.
Serta Mattress Company
Target Corporation

TARGET MARKETING

120 Tillson Ave Ste 205, Rockland, ME 04841-3424
Tel.: (207) 596-6203
E-Mail: info@targetmaine.com
Web Site: www.targetmaine.com

Employees: 20
Year Founded: 1991

Agency Specializes In: Automotive, Print

Carolyn Goodman *(Pres & Dir-Creative)*
Keith Klein *(Gen Mgr)*
Thorin McGee *(Editor-in-Chief & Dir-Content-Target Mktg)*
Jen Brooks *(Mgr-Production Control)*

Accounts:
America's Mattress and Furniture
Domino's Pizza Portland
Dunn Furniture
Dutch Chevrolet Buick Pontiac
Haley's Tire
Syfy

TIPTON & MAGLIONE INC.

1010 Northern Blvd Ste 208, Great Neck, NY 11021-1471
Tel.: (516) 466-0093
Fax: (516) 482-3871
E-Mail: martin@tiptonandmaglione.com
Web Site: www.tiptonandmaglione.com

E-Mail for Key Personnel:
Chairman: martin@tiptonandmaglione.com
President: jtipton@tiptonandmaglione.com
Creative Dir.: jtipton@tiptonandmaglione.com
Production Mgr.: sbonifiglio@tiptonandmaglione.com

Employees: 10
Year Founded: 1982

National Agency Associations: PMA

Agency Specializes In: Above-the-Line, Brand Development & Integration, Business-To-Business, Cable T.V., Catalogs, Collateral, Communications, Consulting, Consumer Marketing, Consumer Publications, Corporate Communications, Corporate Identity, Direct Response Marketing, Email, Exhibit/Trade Shows, Game Integration, Graphic Design, Guerilla Marketing, Hispanic Market, In-Store Advertising, Local Marketing, Logo & Package Design, Magazines, Mobile Marketing, Newspaper, Newspapers & Magazines, Outdoor, Package Design, Pharmaceutical, Planning & Consultation, Point of Purchase, Point of Sale, Print, Production, Production (Print), Promotions, Publicity/Promotions, Radio, Retail, Sales Promotion, Social Media, Strategic Planning/Research, Sweepstakes, Trade & Consumer Magazines, Web (Banner Ads, Pop-ups, etc.)

Approx. Annual Billings: $14,200,000

Breakdown of Gross Billings by Media: Adv. Specialities: $2,000,000; Collateral: $1,600,000; D.M.: $200,000; Fees: $1,500,000; Graphic Design: $1,200,000; Logo & Package Design: $300,000; Sls. Promo.: $6,900,000; Strategic Planning/Research: $500,000

Martin Maglione *(Owner)*

Accounts:
AC Delco
Advantage Communications Telecom Services; 2011
Aiwa
Banfi Vintners Concha & Toro Wines; 2007
Citre Shine
Coca-Cola Refreshments USA, Inc.
Cointreau
Dunlop Sport
Elsevier; New York, NY Biofuel Software; 2008
Energy Independence Partners Water Processing; 2011
Gillette
Idaho Potato Commission Idaho Potatoes
Kirin
MIAC Analytics Financial Software; 2010
Pfizer
Snapple
Snickers
Sony
Sports Illustrated
White Rain

TOTAL PROMOTIONS

1340 Old Skokie Rd, Highland Park, IL 60035
Tel.: (847) 831-9500
Fax: (847) 831-2645
Toll Free: (800) 277-6668
E-Mail: info@totalpromote.com
Web Site: www.totalpromote.com

Employees: 25
Year Founded: 1976

Agency Specializes In: Advertising, Advertising Specialties, Graphic Design, Production, Sales Promotion

Approx. Annual Billings: $2,500,000

Howard Wolff *(Pres)*
Art Lurie *(Exec VP)*
Tim Schwab *(VP)*
Mark Warren Wolff *(VP)*
Stefanie Lenzi *(Office Mgr)*
Laura Levine *(Acct Mgr)*
Felice Gertz *(Mgr-Sls-Natl)*
Stephanie Milnarik *(Sr Acct Exec)*
Ellie Kalish *(Acct Exec)*
Scott Kinzelberg *(Acct Exec)*
David Strzepek *(Acct Exec)*

TPN INC.

9400 N Central Expwy Ste 1500, Dallas, TX 75231-5044
Tel.: (214) 692-1522
Fax: (214) 692-8316
E-Mail: liz_schwab@tpnretail.com
Web Site: www.tpnretail.com/

Employees: 200

Agency Specializes In: Publicity/Promotions, Sales Promotion, Sponsorship

Richard Feitler *(Pres & COO)*
Sharon Love *(CEO)*
Mike Pate *(CFO)*
Tim Austin *(Chief Creative Officer)*
Tracy Faloon *(Sr VP & Strategist-Retail)*
Manolo Almagro *(Sr VP-Digital)*
Sarah Cunningham *(Sr VP-Client Svc)*
Christy O'Pella *(Sr Mng Dir-Client Svc & Dev)*
Nancy Shamberg *(Mng Dir-Shopper Mktg)*
Cynthia Thayer *(VP-Strategic Plng)*
Wesley Porter *(Grp Dir-Creative)*
Tina Kolovchevich *(Grp Acct Dir)*
Helen Chan *(Dir-Strategic Plng)*
Kristin Strayhan *(Dir-Culture)*
Devin Christopher *(Acct Exec)*
Catherine Davis *(Acct Exec)*
Kevin Romesser *(Acct Exec)*
Kate Weber *(Acct Exec)*
Kennan Wood *(Acct Exec)*

Accounts:
7 Eleven
Arch
Bank of America
Bimbo Bakeries USA Thomas'
Cricket Wireless Campaign: "Gift Wrap", Campaign: "Half is More"
Disney & ESPN Media Networks
Gatorade
The Hershey Co.
HTC
Jockey International, Inc.; Kenosha, WI Brand Strategy, Digital, Marketing
Lowe's
Propel
Reese's
Safeway
Tropicana
Wal-Mart

TREPOINT BARC

(Formerly B.A.R.C. Communications, Inc.)
170 Columbus Ave, San Francisco, CA 94133
Tel.: (415) 689-7781
Fax: (415) 772-8964
E-Mail: challengeus@trepoint.com
Web Site: www.trepoint.com/

E-Mail for Key Personnel:
President: jrandazzo@barccom.com
Creative Dir.: ablavins@barccom.com

Employees: 25
Year Founded: 1989

National Agency Associations: PMA

Agency Specializes In: Advertising, Brand Development & Integration, Business-To-Business, Co-op Advertising, Collateral, Communications, Consulting, Consumer Marketing, Corporate Identity, Direct Response Marketing, Event Planning & Marketing, Exhibit/Trade Shows, Financial, Food Service, Graphic Design, Logo & Package Design, Magazines, Merchandising, Newspapers & Magazines, Point of Purchase, Point of Sale, Print, Radio, Retail, Sales Promotion, Sponsorship, Strategic Planning/Research, Sweepstakes, T.V., Trade & Consumer Magazines

Approx. Annual Billings: $28,600,000

Breakdown of Gross Billings by Media: Collateral: $2,860,000; Consulting: $3,718,000; Graphic Design: $4,891,000; Internet Adv.: $1,087,000;

Point of Purchase: $2,431,000; Print: $2,860,000; Promos.: $3,718,000; Radio & T.V.: $1,201,000; Strategic Planning/Research: $5,834,000

John Anthony Randazzo *(Vice Chm)*
John Randazzo, Sr. *(Vice Chm)*
Bill Carmody *(CEO)*
Felix Lam *(CFO & VP)*
Eric Salas *(Exec VP)*

Accounts:
Abbott Diabetes Care Trade Marketing Division (Agency of Record)
C&H Sugar
The Clorox Co., Professional Products Div.; Oakland, CA; 1999
Diageo Wine & Estates; Napa, CA
Dole Package Foods; Westlake Village, CA
Hewlett Packard; Vancouver, WA Printing Supplies; 1998
JM Smuckers Co.
Kikkoman International (Agency of Record)
Menage a Trois
Rinnai America Corp.; Atlanta, GA
Smuckers
Sutter Home
Tree Top
Warner Bros

TRIGGER AGENCY

3539 Clipper Mill Rd, Baltimore, MD 21211
Tel.: (410) 878-9900
Fax: (410) 878-9911
Toll Free: (800) 830-3976
E-Mail: info@triggeragency.com
Web Site: www.triggeragency.com/

Employees: 10
Year Founded: 1995

Agency Specializes In: Advertising, Brand Development & Integration, Event Planning & Marketing, Graphic Design, Guerilla Marketing, Media Relations, Public Relations, Sponsorship, Strategic Planning/Research

Kat Arnold *(Sr Mgr-Event)*
Nick Johnson *(Ops Mgr & Mgr-Logistics)*
Emily Connell *(Mgr-Event)*
Anne Fitzgerald *(Mgr-Event Sls)*
Sarah Linzey *(Mgr-Event Sls)*
Lisa Masterhouse *(Mgr-Acctg)*

TRUTH BE TOLD PR

9350 Wilshire Blvd Ste 324, Beverly Hills, CA 90210
Tel.: (310) 550-7200
E-Mail: amanda@tbtpr.com
Web Site: tbtpr.wordpress.com

Agency Specializes In: Event Planning & Marketing, Public Relations

Amanda Schuon *(Owner)*
Gary Damiano *(Dir-Fin)*
Alexandra Cook *(Sr Acct Exec)*
Erica Kletzky *(Sr Acct Exec)*

Accounts:
Basq Skincare Skin Care Products Mfr
Canada Goose Apparels
Grand Marnier Orange Flavored Liqueur
Jennifer Meyer Jewelry Jewelry Mfr
Martin Miller's Gin Gin Mfr
Tullamore Dew Irish Whiskey Blended Irish Whisky
Van Gogh Imports Vodka Importer
Yamazaki Single Malt Japanese Whisky Single Malt Whisky Mfr

VECTOR 5

175 Kimball St, Fitchburg, MA 01420
Tel.: (978) 348-2997
E-Mail: vectorfive@yahoo.com
Web Site: www.vectorfive.com

Agency Specializes In: Business-To-Business, Exhibit/Trade Shows, Point of Purchase

Breakdown of Gross Billings by Media: Exhibits/Trade Shows: 100%

Dawn Perkins *(Owner & Principal)*
William Miller *(Partner & Gen Mgr)*
Kathy Carney *(Sr Acct Exec)*
Martha Jalbert *(Acct Exec)*
John Davis *(Designer-Indus)*

Accounts:
Abiomed
TomTom

VENTURA ASSOCIATES INTERNATIONAL LLC

(Formerly Ventura Associates, Inc.)
60 E. 42nd St, Ste 650, New York, NY 10165
Tel.: (212) 302-8277, ext. 3015
Fax: (212) 302-2587
E-Mail: info@sweepspros.com
Web Site: www.sweepspros.com

E-Mail for Key Personnel:
President: maltberg@sweepspros.com

Employees: 17
Year Founded: 1971

National Agency Associations: DMA-PMA

Agency Specializes In: Advertising Specialties, Children's Market, Collateral, Direct Response Marketing, Promotions, Publicity/Promotions, Sales Promotion, Sponsorship, Sweepstakes

Approx. Annual Billings: $2,645,100

Al Wester *(Pres)*
Marla Altberg *(CEO)*
Nigel Morgan *(CFO)*
Lisa Manhart *(CMO & Exec VP)*
Orlando Santiago *(Sr VP & Acct Dir)*
Mary Saini *(Dir-Social Mktg)*
Betty Woods *(Sr Acct Mgr)*
Virginia Puliafito *(Coord-Accts)*

Accounts:
Bonnier Corp.
Comcast
Saks Fifth Ave
Time Inc.
TV Guide
Victoria's Secret

VERTICAL MARKETING NETWORK LLC

15147 Woodlawn Ave, Tustin, CA 92780
Tel.: (714) 258-2400
Fax: (714) 258-2409
E-Mail: contact@verticalmarketing.net
Web Site: www.verticalmarketing.net

E-Mail for Key Personnel:
President: phil@verticalmarketing.net

Employees: 24
Year Founded: 1996

Agency Specializes In: Advertising, Bilingual Market, Collateral, Communications, Consumer Marketing, Direct-to-Consumer, Entertainment, Event Planning & Marketing, Experience Design, Graphic Design, Hispanic Market, Integrated Marketing, Internet/Web Design, Logo & Package Design, Merchandising, Multicultural, New Product Development, Out-of-Home Media, Outdoor, Point of Purchase, Point of Sale, Promotions, Publicity/Promotions, Radio, Sales Promotion, Sports Market, Strategic Planning/Research, Sweepstakes, T.V.

Breakdown of Gross Billings by Media: Consulting: 100%

Philip B. Saifer *(Pres)*
Meryl Kotin *(CFO)*
Nicco Mouleart *(VP & Grp Acct Dir)*
Diane Solem *(VP & Rep-Mgmt)*
Valerie Isozaki *(Acct Dir)*
Tonja Hughes *(Dir-Media)*
Noelle Frey *(Acct Supvr)*
Karen Linderman *(Acct Supvr-Promos & Partnerships)*

Accounts:
Abbott Medical Optics; Santa Ana, CA; 2005
Bandai America Incorporated; Cypress, CA Toys; 2008
Warner Home Video; Burbank, CA Home Entertainment; 1997

WESTOVER MEDIA

11578 SW Riverwood Rd, Portland, OR 97219
Tel.: (503) 675-2580
Fax: (503) 675-2581
Web Site: www.westovermedia.com

E-Mail for Key Personnel:
President: kathio@europa.com

Employees: 3
Year Founded: 1994

Agency Specializes In: Brand Development & Integration, Children's Market, Co-op Advertising, Collateral, Consumer Marketing, Consumer Publications, Cosmetics, Education, Entertainment, Event Planning & Marketing, Fashion/Apparel, Hispanic Market, Leisure, Magazines, Merchandising, New Product Development, Newspapers & Magazines, Over-50 Market, Pharmaceutical, Point of Purchase, Point of Sale, Publicity/Promotions, Retail, Seniors' Market, Teen Market, Trade & Consumer Magazines

Approx. Annual Billings: $600,000

Breakdown of Gross Billings by Media: Promos.: $600,000

Kathi O'Neil *(Founder, Pres & Publr)*

Accounts:
Barney Butter
Clingy Thingy
Conde Nast Magazines
Guideposts
Hearst Magazines
Meredith Magazines

WORKPLACE IMPACT

(Formerly WorkPlace Media)
9325 Progress Pkwy, Mentor, OH 44060-1855
Tel.: (440) 639-9100
Fax: (440) 639-9190
Toll Free: (800) 435-7576
E-Mail: info@workplaceimpact.com
Web Site: www.workplaceimpact.com

Employees: 60
Year Founded: 1988

National Agency Associations: DMA

Agency Specializes In: Direct Response Marketing, Food Service, Print, Publicity/Promotions, Retail, Sales Promotion

Approx. Annual Billings: $10,000,000

Breakdown of Gross Billings by Media: Collateral:

$2,000,000; D.M.: $8,000,000

Shelly Sekki *(Pres)*
Terry Goins *(Exec VP-Sls & Mktg)*
Mary Beth Agase *(VP-Sls-CPG)*
Pete Aranavage *(VP-Ops)*
Dan Llewellyn *(VP-CPG & Shopper Mktg Bus Dev)*
Dori Wile *(VP-Sls)*
Dani Kenady *(Dir-Sls & Natl Accts)*
Molly Church *(Acct Mgr)*
Kristina Artiste *(Mgr-Bus Dev)*

Accounts:
Baja Fresh
Coca-Cola Refreshments USA, Inc.
Denny's
Godfather's Pizza
Hardee's; Rocky Mount, NC
Kmart
Lenscrafters
McDonald's
Pizzeria Uno
Quizno's
Sheetz
Sprint PCS Stores
Subway

WPROMOTE, INC.
1700 E Walnut Ave Fl 5, El Segundo, CA 90245-2610
Tel.: (310) 421-4844
Fax: (310) 335-0488
Toll Free: (866) 977-6668
E-Mail: contact@wpromote.com
Web Site: www.wpromote.com

Employees: 70

Agency Specializes In: Advertising, Search Engine Optimization

Revenue: $4,000,000

Michael Mothner *(Founder & CEO)*
Alison Quinn-Angel *(CFO)*
Michael Block *(COO)*
Michael Stone *(Chief Revenue Officer)*
Jamie Lane *(VP-Mktg)*
Michael Wilde *(VP-Bus Dev)*
Andrew Mclellan *(Sr Dir-SEO)*
Marcy Stelle *(Mktg Dir)*
Joanne Coghill *(Dir-HR)*
Adria Holtzinger *(Dir-Social Media Optimization)*
Jeff Pickett *(Dir-Search Strategy)*
Aimee Abad *(Sr Mgr-Social Media)*
Aubrie Richey *(Sr Mgr-Social Media)*
Christina Weir *(Sr Mgr-Social Media)*

Accounts:
Adobe
Case Load
Hewlett Packard
Verizon
New-Zenni Optical

X! PROMOS
15375 Barranca Pkwy Ste I-103, Irvine, CA 92618
Tel.: (949) 450-8190
Fax: (949) 753-0050
E-Mail: info@xpromos.com
Web Site: http://www.xpromos.com/

E-Mail for Key Personnel:
President: snomady@xpromos.com
Creative Dir.: ybrown@xpromos.com

Employees: 5
Year Founded: 1989

National Agency Associations: PMA

Agency Specializes In: Sales Promotion, Sweepstakes

Approx. Annual Billings: $2,500,000

Breakdown of Gross Billings by Media: Event Mktg.: 15%; Mdsg./POP: 10%; Promos.: 25%; Sls. Promo.: 20%; Strategic Planning/Research: 30%

Yvette Brown *(Owner)*
Shari Nomady *(Pres)*

Accounts:
Bandai America
Bank of America
BW Container Systems
Canon
Coca-Cola Refreshments USA, Inc.
Dep Corporation
Dubble Bubble
Major League Soccer
Makita USA
Mattel
Nestle
Sony
Tecate

PUBLIC RELATIONS FIRMS

10 SQUARED PR
(Formerly Aw Media Group)
2115 Monroe Drive Ste 110, Atlanta, GA 30324
Tel.: (678) 637-0982
E-Mail: pr@10SquaredPR.com
Web Site: www.10squaredpr.com

Year Founded: 2006

Agency Specializes In: Digital/Interactive, Event Planning & Marketing, Internet/Web Design, Media Training, Public Relations, Social Media

Angela Watts *(Pres)*
Maire Mcmahon *(Sr Acct Exec)*

Accounts:
Bronzelens Film Festival

104 DEGREES WEST PARTNERS
1925 Blake St Ste 200, Denver, CO 80202
Tel.: (720) 407-6060
Fax: (720) 407-6061
E-Mail: info@104degreeswest.com
Web Site: www.104west.com

Employees: 8
Year Founded: 2003

Agency Specializes In: Media Relations, Public Relations

Patrick Ward *(CEO)*
Alissa Bushnell *(Mng Dir-Media Rels)*
Joanie Kindblade *(Mng Dir-Content Svcs)*
Kelli Flores *(Acct Mgr)*

Accounts:
3 Crowd
Advisen
Agencyport
Evolv; San Francisco; CA
EWise Public Relations, Traditional & Social Media
Homesnap
Info Now
Intermap
North Plains Public Relations, Traditional & Social Media
Smartling Public Relations, Traditional & Social Media

10FOLD COMMUNICATIONS
(Formerly Trainer Communications)
6130 Stoneridge Mall Rd, Pleasanton, CA 94588
Tel.: (925) 271-8200
Web Site: 10fold.com

Employees: 15

Agency Specializes In: Brand Development & Integration, Consulting, Event Planning & Marketing, Exhibit/Trade Shows, High Technology, Information Technology, Investor Relations, New Product Development, Public Relations, Publicity/Promotions

Revenue: $2,000,000

Ross Perich *(VP & Gen Mgr-Video Practice)*
Angela Griffo *(VP)*
Fran Lowe *(VP)*
Travis Anderson *(Acct Mgr)*
Renae Cazet *(Sr Acct Exec)*
Kristina Richmann *(Sr Acct Exec)*
Kristen Sheeran Evans *(Acct Exec)*
Angel Rodriguez *(Acct Exec)*
Maria Venegas *(Acct Exec)*

Accounts:
AppDynamics
Autonomic Network
Axcient
Bear Valley Mountain Resort
Brocade
Dyyno
Glimmerglass
Lumenetix
Nanostellar
NextG Networks
Onstor
Panasas
Permabit
Presidio Networked Solutions
Presidio
Rohati
SanFrancisco Baykeeper
Vantos
WhereNet
Xyratex
YMCA

19 IDEAS INC.
32C Essex St, Buffalo, NY 14213
Tel.: (716) 218-0585
Web Site: www.19ideas.com

Agency Specializes In: Advertising, Brand Development & Integration, Digital/Interactive, Event Planning & Marketing, Internet/Web Design, Media Relations, Public Relations, Search Engine Optimization, Social Media, Strategic Planning/Research

Katie Krawczyk *(Pres)*
Amber Rampino *(Creative Dir)*
Jon Tashijan *(Sr Mgr-PR & Comm)*
Kevin Heffernan *(Mgr-Mktg)*

Accounts:
Hydraulic Hearth
SelectOne

1CCU PR
(Formerly 1 Creative Concept Unlimited, Inc)
PO Box 524, Liberty, NY 12754
Tel.: (800) 825-2975
Fax: (866) 643-6773
E-Mail: info@1creativeconcepttpr.com
Web Site: www.1creativeconceptpr.com

Agency Specializes In: Advertising, Digital/Interactive, Event Planning & Marketing, Market Research, Public Relations, Social Media

Cynthia Sutherland *(Pres & CEO)*

Accounts:
Loud'e Cosmetics (Public Relations Agency of Record) Branding, Marketing

THE 2050 GROUP
1177 Ave of the Americas 5th Fl, New York, NY 10036
Tel.: (646) 202-1612
Web Site: www.the2050group.com

Agency Specializes In: Crisis Communications, Media Relations, Media Training, Public Relations, Social Media

Adam J. Segal *(Pres)*

Accounts:
New-Home Box Office

20K GROUP
1210 W Clay St Ste 18, Houston, TX 77019
Tel.: (713) 224-1877
Fax: (713) 583-5549
E-Mail: brand@20kgroup.com
Web Site: www.20kgroup.com

Agency Specializes In: Content, Crisis Communications, Digital/Interactive, Email, Event Planning & Marketing, Media Relations, Media Training, Public Relations, Social Media

Debbie Fiorito *(Pres)*
Courtenay Siegfried *(VP)*

Accounts:
Ann Richards School Foundation

30 MILES NORTH
1640 5th St Ste 222, Santa Monica, CA 90401
Tel.: (310) 933-6416
Web Site: www.30milesnorth.com

Year Founded: 2008

Agency Specializes In: Content, Crisis Communications, Event Planning & Marketing, Print, Promotions, Public Relations, Social Media, T.V.

Priscilla Vento *(Founder & CEO)*
Joe Sloan *(Dir-Accts)*

Accounts:
FameBit
TripScope

360 MEDIA INC
PO Box 725188, Atlanta, GA 31139
Tel.: (404) 577-8686
Fax: (404) 577-8644
E-Mail: info@360media.net
Web Site: www.360media.net

Agency Specializes In: Event Planning & Marketing, Hospitality, Public Relations

Laura Cubbage *(Dir-Ops)*

Accounts:
New-521 Kitchen & Que
New-Atlanta Food & Wine Festival
New-Murphy's Restaurant

360 PUBLIC RELATIONS
1 Little W 12th, New York, NY 10014
Tel.: (212) 729-5833
Web Site: www.360publicrelations.com

Year Founded: 2001

National Agency Associations: COPF

Agency Specializes In: Crisis Communications, Internet/Web Design, Public Relations, Social Media

Rob Bratskeir *(Exec VP, Dir-Creative & Gen Mgr-*

NYC)
Carol Garrity *(VP-HR & Ops)*
Caitlin Melnick *(VP)*
Caroline Pierce *(VP)*
Caitlin Chalke *(Dir-Washington, DC)*
Meredith Gandy *(Mgr-Media Rels)*
Dana Moody *(Asst Acct Exec)*

Accounts:
Alberto VO5
Blue Chair Bay Public Relations
Charles River Apparel Public Relations, Social Media
ComiXology PR
Harvest Hill Beverage Company Content, Earned Media, Event Marketing, Influencer Relations
Kensington & Sons, LLC.

360 PUBLIC RELATIONS LLC
140 Clareedon St Ste 401, Boston, MA 02116
Tel.: (617) 585-5770
Fax: (617) 585-5789
E-Mail: info@360publicrelaions.com
Web Site: www.360publicrelations.com

Employees: 20

National Agency Associations: COPF

Agency Specializes In: Broadcast, Co-op Advertising, Consulting, Event Planning & Marketing, Exhibit/Trade Shows, In-Store Advertising, Integrated Marketing, Internet/Web Design, Media Planning, Media Relations, Production, Promotions, Public Relations, Radio, Sponsorship

Laura Tomasetti *(Founder & CEO)*
Stacey Clement *(Sr VP)*
Carol Garrity *(VP-HR & Ops)*
Lindsay Durr *(Acct Dir)*
Carolyn Evert *(Dir-Media Rels)*
Morgan Salmon *(Dir-Fin)*
Mike Ruta *(Mgr-Digital Media)*
Lana Tkachenko *(Mgr-Digital Media)*
Talia Pinzari *(Sr Acct Exec-Consumer, Healthy Living, Beauty & Fashion)*
Kelsey Revens *(Sr Acct Exec)*
Sheila Tayebi *(Sr Acct Exec-Consumer PR)*
Kristen Thompson *(Sr Acct Exec)*

Accounts:
Allstar Products Group Public Relations, Snuggie Blanket Fashion Show
Balance Bar PR
Ball Jars
Charles River Apparel (Public Relations & Social Media Agency of Record)
Disney Interactive Media Group
Erba Vita
GN Netcom
High Ridge Brands; Stamford, CT Alberto VO5, Events, Media, Social Media
Jarden Corporation Ball
Marcal Manufacturing LLC
Meredith Corporation FamilyFun Magazine
Nasoya
Public Broadcasting Service PBS Kids
Sir Kensington's Ketchups
Snuggie
Stonyfield Farm YoBaby, YoKids
Walkers Shortbread Public Relations, Social Media
WellPet Eagle Pack, Holistic Select, Old Mother Hubbard, Wellness
Wizards of the Coast, Inc.
Yasso Public Relations

3A/WORLDWIDE
900 SW 8th St Ste C-1 & C-2, Miami, FL 33130
Tel.: (786) 362-6500
E-Mail: info@3aworlwide.com
Web Site: www.3aworldwide.com

Agency Specializes In: Brand Development & Integration, Digital/Interactive, Event Planning & Marketing, Media Buying Services, Media Planning, Public Relations, Strategic Planning/Research

Edward De Valle *(Founder & CEO)*
Adam Horowitz *(CFO)*
Mauricio Acuna *(Pres-Americas)*
Brenda Sandoval *(VP-Global Media & Dir-Agency Alliances)*
Rosa Soto *(VP-PR)*
Omar DeWindt *(Assoc Dir-PR)*
Bronson Soares *(Sr Acct Mgr)*
Tiffany Doll *(Mgr-Events & Logistics)*
Laura Bries *(Acct Exec)*
Betsy Pujols *(Acct Exec)*

Accounts:
Casa de Campo
Emerge
Park Central Hotel (International Public Relations Agency of Record)

3RD COAST PUBLIC RELATIONS
541 N Fairbanks Ct Ste 2730, Chicago, IL 60611
Tel.: (312) 257-3030
E-Mail: info@3rdcoastpr.com
Web Site: www.3rdcoastpr.com

Year Founded: 2011

Agency Specializes In: Consumer Goods, Public Relations, Sponsorship

Rich Timmons *(Pres & Chief Strategy Officer)*
Kerri Erb Byler *(Sr VP)*
Betsi Schumacher *(Client Svcs Dir)*
Krista Cortese *(Dir-Media Svcs)*
Mary Clare Middleton *(Dir-Strategic Dev)*
Meredith Payette *(Acct Supvr)*
Dana Trebella *(Sr Acct Exec)*

Accounts:
Blue by Blueair
International Floriculture Expo Media
Kuros!
New-Lifes2Good North America (Agency of Record) Pettura, Public Relations
MAT Holdings Kennel, Pet Crates, Sales
The Saucy Fish Co
Sleep Innovations Inc
Socius Ingredients

451 MARKETING
100 N Washington St, Boston, MA 02114
Tel.: (617) 259-1605
Web Site: www.451marketing.com

Year Founded: 2004

Agency Specializes In: Event Planning & Marketing, Graphic Design, Public Relations, Social Media

A. J. Gerritson *(Co-Founder & Partner)*
Karyn Martin *(Exec VP)*
Nicole Russo *(Exec VP)*
Francis Skipper *(Exec VP)*
Jessica Alario *(VP-Hospitality PR)*
Susan Anderson *(VP-Social Media)*
Lisa Bell *(VP-PR)*
Kristina Lupo *(VP-Digital Ops)*
Heather Smith *(Sr Acct Dir-PR)*
Alice Dubois *(Acct Dir)*
Nathalie Nourian *(Acct Dir)*
Melissa Sciorra *(Acct Dir-SEO)*
Tyrone Pardue *(Dir-Branding)*
Grace Galloway *(Acct Mgr-Social Media)*
Jessica Lavoie *(Acct Mgr)*
Kathy Abreu *(Mgr-Billing)*
Samantha Gorin *(Mgr-Social Media Strategy)*
Laura Christo *(Sr Acct Exec)*
Jillian Watts *(Sr Acct Exec-Hospitality PR)*
Laura Lynn *(Asst Acct Exec-PR)*
Kristin Foley *(Acct Coord)*
Aleena Virani *(Acct Coord-PR)*
Hilary Bokoff *(Coord-Content-Social Media)*
Samantha Cohen *(Coord-Social Media Content)*
Megan Fahey *(Coord-Internal Mktg)*
Zachary Sousa *(Coord-Social Media Content)*
Thomas Lee *(Sr Partner)*

Accounts:
New-Boston Harbor Hotel Marketing, Public Relations
Foxwoods Resort Casino

48 COMMUNICATIONS INC.
8648 Holloway Plaza Dr, Los Angeles, CA 90069
Tel.: (310) 902-5777
Web Site: www.48communications.com

Agency Specializes In: Brand Development & Integration, Event Planning & Marketing, Public Relations

Jeff Respress *(Pres & CEO)*
Vijay Lalwani *(Sr VP)*

Accounts:
New-The Nerd Machine
New-Skyn Iceland
New-Zumba fitness

5W PUBLIC RELATIONS
1166 Ave of the Americas 4th Fl, New York, NY 10036
Tel.: (212) 999-5585
Fax: (646) 328-1711
E-Mail: info@5wpr.com
Web Site: www.5wpr.com

E-Mail for Key Personnel:
President: ronn@5wpr.com

Employees: 70
Year Founded: 2002

National Agency Associations: PRSA

Agency Specializes In: Advertising, African-American Market, Asian Market, Brand Development & Integration, Broadcast, Business-To-Business, Cable T.V., Children's Market, Collateral, Communications, Consulting, Consumer Marketing, Consumer Publications, Corporate Identity, E-Commerce, Entertainment, Event Planning & Marketing, Faith Based, Fashion/Apparel, Financial, Gay & Lesbian Market, Government/Political, Graphic Design, Health Care Services, High Technology, Hispanic Market, Internet/Web Design, Investor Relations, Legal Services, Leisure, Magazines, Media Buying Services, New Product Development, Newspaper, Newspapers & Magazines, Over-50 Market, Pets , Pharmaceutical, Planning & Consultation, Print, Production, Public Relations, Publicity/Promotions, Radio, Real Estate, Recruitment, Restaurant, Retail, Sales Promotion, Seniors' Market, Sponsorship, Sports Market, Strategic Planning/Research, T.V., Transportation, Travel & Tourism

Approx. Annual Billings: $11,000,000

Erika Kauffman *(Exec VP & Gen Mgr)*
Dara Busch *(Exec VP-Consumer Practice)*
Susan Mallory *(Exec VP)*
Juda Engelmayer *(Sr VP & Grp Dir)*
Matthew Caiola *(Sr VP)*
Nicole Milazzo *(Sr Acct Supvr)*
Michael Paffmann *(Acct Supvr)*
Maria Carfagno *(Sr Acct Exec)*

Jenna Hreshko *(Sr Acct Exec)*
Megan Kopf *(Sr Acct Exec)*
Jessica Moschella *(Sr Acct Exec)*
Allison Stephens *(Acct Exec-Beauty Div)*
Kayla Kaplan *(Asst Acct Exec)*

Accounts:
Absorption Pharmaceuticals Media Relations Campaign
Aerosoles (Agency of Record) Consumer Awareness, Public Relations
Affinia Hotels
AHAVA Skincare; 2007
All-Clad Metalcrafters Public Relations
New-All-Clad
Allergy & Asthma Network Mothers of Asthmatics Public Relations
AltogetherHome.com Celebrity Seeding, Co-Branded partnerships, Event Management, Media Relations, Product Integrations, Spokesperson Procurement
Aluminyze
Amy Matto (Agency of Record) Co-branding Partnerships, Communications Program, Events, Media Relations
Anheuser-Busch InBev
Ansell Limited Lifestyles; 2007
Appwiz (Agency of Record)
Appy Pie
Ashkenazy Acquisition Corporation; New York, NY Public Relations
Astor Group Brand Awareness, Expert Positioning, Media Relations
New-Avant (Public Relations Agency of Record) Media Relations
Baby Gooroo Public Relations Program
Badichi Belt Boutique (Agency of Record)
Beezid.com (Agency of Record) Public Relations Program
Benny Hinn Ministries & Christians
Beyond Verbal
BioElixia Public Relations
BioHarvest Public Relations
BLP Commerce, Inc. Brand Awareness, Marketing, OrganicBouquet.com, PR, Web
Caffebene USA Coffeehouse Brand
CAG Beauty Public Relations Program
New-Camp Bow Wow
Caribbean Shopping Channel Media Relations
Celsius
Cernium Corporation Public Relations
Cheaopoair.com
Christians United for Israel; 2007
Citibabes (Agency of Record); New York, NY Branding, Preschool, Publicity
Cluck 'n Moo (Agency of Record) Communication Development, Public Relations
Coastal Contacts Inc. Co-Branded Partnerships, Event Management, Media Relations, Product Integrations
Cold-EEZE Celebrity Integrations, Co-branded Partnerships, Media Relations, Public Relations, Special Events
Courtroom Connect Media Relations, PR Campaign, Thought Leadership
Coyuchi Co-Branded Partnerships, Event Management, Media Relations, Product Integrations
Creative Edge Nutrition, Inc. Public Relations
CEN Biotech, Inc Public Relations
Creflo Dollar Ministries (Public Relations Agency Of Record) Media Relations, Thought Leadership
D'Angelico Guitars Public Relations
Danilo Gabrielli Public Relations
Deeyoon.com Digital, Media Relations, PR Campaign, Thought-Leadership Positioning
DigitalOcean Media Relations, Strategic Communications Counsel
Diono USA (Agency of Record) Brand Awareness, Media Relations, RadianRXT
Do You Remember PR
Donald J. Pliner (Agency of Record)
Dotmenu.com Company Award Recognition, Media Relations, Product Integration Initiatives, Public Relations
Dr. Michael Fiorillo
Dr. Mitchell Chasin Reflections, Center for Skin and Body
Dr. Robert Dorin Media Relations
Duane Reade; New York, NY PR
New-Eligo Energy (Public Relations Agency of Record) Media Relations
EQuala Media Relations, PR Campaign, Strategic Partnerships
EShakti Co-Branded Partnerships, Media, Public Relations
Evian
Exadel; San Francisco, CA PR
Excel Corp. Public Relations
Fairy Tales Hair Care (Public Relations Agency of Record) Strategic Media Relations
Faithlife Corporation (Agency of Record)
Fareportal
Fashion Forward Maternity Co-Branded Partnerships, Media Relations, Online Events, Public Relations
Feedvisor (Agency of Record)
Fitness IQ Celebrity Seeding, Co-branded Partnerships, Media Relations, Product Integrations, Shake Weight
New-Fitz & Floyd (Agency of Record)
FiveCurrents Media Relations, Outreach Campaign, PR, Thought Leadership Positioning
Footzyrolls Public Relations
FragranceNet.com Beauty PR
Frames (Agency of Record) Public Relations Program
Fresh Harvest Products, Inc. Public Relations
Friendthem Public Relations Campaign
Giutzy.com Co-Branded Partnerships, Media Relations, Online Events, PR, Social Media
GlassesUSA.com Celebrity Seeding, Co-Branded Partnerships, Event Support, Media Relations, Product Integrations
GoBites Pr
Grandparents.com
GreatApps.com (Agency of Record) Public Relations
Gripevine.com CRM, Media Relations, Public Relations Program, Thought Leadership
Guillemot Corporation Hercules, Thrustmaster
Gummybear International, Inc. Gummibar Christmas DVD, Media
Halo/Air Salt Rooms
Harris Law Legal PR
Hint, Inc. Hint Water; 2007
HOLMES Company Award Recognition, Media Relations, Product Integration Initiatives, Public Relations
Iberia PR
IDenta Corp Brand Awareness
IMMUNE Pharmaceuticals Media Relations, Messaging, Public Relations, Speaker Engagement, Web Strategies
IMUSA USA, LLC PR
Interacting Technology Ltd (Agency of Record) Moovz, Public Relations
Iredale Mineral Cosmetics, Ltd. Brand Awareness, PR
IWave Consumer Electronics, Personal Technology Products, Public Relations
Jetbay (Public Relations Agency of Record) Strategic Media Relations
New-JetSmarter
JetSmarter (Agency of Record)
John Rowley
JuveRest Public Relations Agency of Record, Sleep Wrinkle Pillow
Kabrita Public Relations
KeKu Event Management, Media Relations, PR Campaign, Strategic Partnerships, Thought Leadership Positioning
New-KidsTrade (Public Relations Agency of Record)
New-Kora Rae (Public Relations Agency of Record)
Lagostina (Agency of Record) Public Relations
Latitude 360 (Public Relations Agency of Record) Media Relations, Public Affairs
Le Marais
Life Quality Improvement Center (Agency of Record)
New-L'Oreal
Luna Park Celebrity Seeding, Co-Branded partnerships, Event Management, Media Relations, Product Integrations, Spokesperson Procurement
Majesco Entertainment NBA Baller Beats
Marriott Hotels
Mass Appeal PR
New-MD Insider (Public Relations Agency of Record)
New-Medifast
Merle Norman Cosmetics; Los Angeles, CA PR
MitoQ PR
Muse Apparel Co-Branded Partnerships, Media Relations, Online Events, Public Relations
My Love Affair (Agency of Record) Brand Awareness, Creative
MyRegistry.com Co-branded Partnerships, Event Management, Media Relations, Product Integrations
Nanoosh Mediterranean Hummus Bar; New York, NY (Agency of Record)
National Law Enforcement & Firefighters Children's Foundation (Agency of Record) PR
Natural Child World PR
NeoCell Broadcast, Print, Public Relations, Strategic Media Relations, Websites
New York Bariatric Group PR
NORDEN Laser Eye Associates Media Awareness, PR
Norton, LLC
One Stop Plus
New-OneJet (Public Relations Agency of Record)
Organic Beverage Company
New-PCS Edventures!, Inc (Agency of Record) Public Relations
Perky Jerky (Agency of Record) Public Relations
Philip Stein (Agency of Record)
Philippe Restaurant; 2007
Phoenix Marketing International Brand Awareness, Public Relations
Pomegranate PR
Private Stock Denim (Agency of Record)
Promises Treatment Center Public Relations
Promotion in Motion, Inc. Celebrity Seeding, Co-Branded Partnerships, Event Management, Media Relations, PR, Product Integrations, Spokesperson Procurement
Pulse Laser & Skincare Center; New York, NY PR
RealBeanz Public Relations
Regent University; 2007
Rent2Buy.com (Agency of Record)
Repechage PR
RetinaX Studios (Agency of Record) Media Relations, Strategic Communications
Rewarding Student Commitment Brand-building
Rokkan (Agency of Record)
Roomer
Ryan Partnership Co-Branded Partnerships, Media Relations, Product Integrations
Safe Drive Systems (Agency Of Record) Public Relations
Salon Bar PR
Scheckter's Organic Energy Public Relations
Senada Adzem
Sense of Fashion Co-Branded Partnerships, Media Relations, Public Relations
Skirt Sports (Public Relations Agency of Record)
SNAP Infusion Public Relations
Socialbuy.com
SOHH.com
Solo Restaurant
New-Sparkling ICE
SpeedMedia (Agency of Record) PR
Star Farm Ventures Creative Messaging, Media Outreach, Strategy
Sticky
Strike Ten Entertainment (Public Relations Agency of Record) Media
SuperJeweler.com Brand Awareness, Celebrity &

Spokesperson Integrations, Co-Branded Partnerships, Media Relations, Online Events, Social Media
T-fal ActiFry
New-T-Fal Krups
Ten Thousand Villages PR
TikTakTo Media Relations, PR Campaign, Thought Leadership
Tracy Pfeifer
Travel Alberta
Travelong, Inc.
Trinity Broadcasting Network
TuneCore
New-Ultra Mobile (Agency of Record)
New-Unilever
ValueMyStuff.com PR
Vanderbloemen Search Group (Agency of Record)
New-Videoblocks (Agency of Record)
Vinod Gupta
Vividas Group Videos; 2007
VOGA Italia Wines PR
Voices Against Brain Cancer Event Support, Media Relations
New-Walgreens
New-Welch Foods, Inc. Welch's
Western Kentucky University Instruments of American Excellence
Westminster Kennel Club Celebrity Seeding, Event Support, Media Relations, Product Integrations
Westside Market NYC Celebrity Seeding, Co-Branded partnerships, Event Management, Media Relations, Product Integrations, Spokesperson Procurement
Work Rest Karma; New York, NY (Agency of Record) CSR, Celebrity Integration, Co-branding Partnerships, Digital, Media Relations, Social Media, Special Events, Trade Marketing
XIPWIRE PR
YouBeauty.com (Public Relations Agency of Record) Strategic Media Relations
YouContent Media (Public Relations Agency of Record) Strategic Media Relations
Zenith Technologies Consumer Awareness, Public Relations, Retailer Awareness, Soniclean
New-Zeta Interactive
New-Zeta Interactive (Agency of Record)

Branch

5W Public Relations
11111 Santa Monica Blvd 16th Fl, Los Angeles, CA 90025
Tel.: (424) 270-2347
Fax: (310) 492-4314
E-Mail: info@5wpr.com
Web Site: www.5wpr.com

Employees: 5

Agency Specializes In: Food Service, Public Relations

Ronn Torossian *(Pres & CEO)*
Erika Kauffman *(Exec VP & Gen Mgr)*
Annette Banca *(VP)*
Melanie Gordon-Felsman *(VP)*
Jocelyn Kahn *(VP-Consumer Products & Brands)*
Randy Mayer *(VP-Mktg)*
Amy Lash *(Acct Supvr)*
Jacolyn Gleason *(Sr Acct Exec)*
Kayci Powell *(Asst Acct Exec)*

Accounts:
Evian
Hint
Kate Farms Komplete Ultimate Shake, PR
Loews Hotels
The Original SoupMan
Petina Restaurant Group
Prime Grill
Shiseido Americas Corporation
Three Olives Vodka
Tzell Travel
Wellspring
Willow Stream at Fairmont

9SPR
116 S Catalina Ave Ste 117, Redondo Beach, CA 90277
Tel.: (310) 928-6446
Fax: (310) 626-4437
E-Mail: info@9spr.com
Web Site: www.9spr.com

Year Founded: 2011

Agency Specializes In: Brand Development & Integration, Event Planning & Marketing, Media Relations, Public Relations, Social Media

Katie Hammond *(Pres)*
Kimberly Babcock *(Dir-New York Office)*

Accounts:
7AM Enfant
Appaman
Apple Park
Crawlings
Earth Mama Angel Baby
Hiho Batik
Nununu
Skylar Luna
Stokke, LLC.
Umi Shoes

A&C AGENCY
119 Spadina Ave Ste 900, Toronto, Ontario M5V 2L1 Canada
Tel.: (416) 966-3421
Fax: (416) 966-3088
E-Mail: info@artscom.ca
Web Site: www.artscom.ca

Employees: 10

Agency Specializes In: Digital/Interactive, Media Relations, Public Relations, Social Media, Strategic Planning/Research

Deborah Belcourt *(Mng Dir)*
Lisa Huie *(Acct Dir)*
Adam Dermer *(Acct Coord)*

Accounts:
Carter's/OshKosh Canada Digital Strategy, Experiential Marketing, Media, Public Relations
Diageo Johnnie Walker
Metro Ontario Inc. (Public Relations Agency of Record)
Nestle Perrier
Shaw Festival

A&O PR
29 Powers Ave, San Francisco, CA 94110
Tel.: (415) 577-1275
E-Mail: info@aopublic.com
Web Site: www.aopublic.com

Agency Specializes In: Brand Development & Integration, Digital/Interactive, Event Planning & Marketing, Internet/Web Design, Public Relations

Lainya Magana *(Founder & Principal)*
Kathryn McKinney *(Acct Mgr-West Coast)*

Accounts:
Tappan Collective
Wallplay
Wishbone Woodworking

A. BRIGHT IDEA
210 Archer St, Bel Air, MD 21014
Tel.: (410) 836-7180
Fax: (410) 836-0186
E-Mail: info@abrightideaonline.com
Web Site: www.abrightideaonline.com

Employees: 17
Year Founded: 1996

Anita Brightman *(Founder & Pres)*
Chad Mitchell *(CFO)*
T. J. Brightman *(VP-Client Rels)*
Brian Lobsinger *(Mgr-Multimedia & Sr Designer)*
Luz Esmeralda Mahecha Martinez *(Specialist-Bilingual Comm)*
Crystal Maynard *(Specialist-Comm)*

Accounts:
Bel Air Centre for Addiction
GIS Inventory
Hillside Lawn Service
The John Carroll School
Jordan Thomas Salon & Spa
Kenwood Kitchens

AAM BRAND MANAGEMENT GROUP
2 W 45th St Ste 1702, New York, NY 10036
Tel.: (212) 661-1336
Fax: (212) 661-1332
E-Mail: info@aammanagement.com
Web Site: www.aammanagement.com

Agency Specializes In: Advertising, Brand Development & Integration, Collateral, Event Planning & Marketing, Internet/Web Design, Media Training, Public Relations, Social Media, Sponsorship, Strategic Planning/Research

Cathy OBrien Yaffa *(Pres)*
Sarah Perskie Bell *(Dir-Mktg)*

Accounts:
New-Juice press

THE ABBI AGENCY
275 Hill St Ste 250, Reno, NV 89501
Tel.: (775) 323-2977
E-Mail: info@theabbiagency.com
Web Site: www.theabbiagency.com

Year Founded: 2008

Agency Specializes In: Crisis Communications, Event Planning & Marketing, Media Relations, Media Training, Public Relations, Social Media

Liz Bowling *(Acct Dir)*
Tiana Campagna *(Dir-Events & Acct Coord)*
David Bunker *(Dir-Content)*
Matt Lush *(Acct Exec)*
Stephanie Myers *(Acct Exec)*
Brooke Rose *(Acct Exec)*

Accounts:
Holland & Hart LLP (Marketing Agency of Record) Public Relations, Strategic Marketing
Home Advisor
Post Planner
Q&D Construction Public Relations

ABEL COMMUNICATIONS, INC.
2031 Clipper Park Rd Ste 105, Baltimore, MD 21211
Tel.: (410) 843-3808
E-Mail: info@abelcommunications.com
Web Site: www.abelcommunications.com

Agency Specializes In: Media Relations, Media Training, Production, Public Relations, Social Media

Greg Abel *(Founder & Pres)*

Adrienne Peres *(VP)*
Gina Zuk Gerber *(Dir-Client Svcs)*
Courtney Benhoff *(Acct Mgr)*
Adam Curtis *(Acct Mgr)*
Jessica Fast *(Acct Mgr)*
Amanda Ratner *(Acct Exec)*

Accounts:
1st Mariner Bank (Public Relations Agency of Record) Media Relations, Strategic Communications
ALK Technologies Inc. CoPilot Live
Civic Works Marketing, Public Relations
CohnReznick PR, Strategic Communications
Hipcricket Content Development, Media Relations, Strategic Communications
Medifast
Metropolitan Regional Information Systems, Inc; Rockville, MD PR, Strategic Communications Campaign
STX, LLC

ABELOW PR
23 Washington Ave, Westport, CT 06880
Tel.: (203) 226-9247
E-Mail: info@abelowpr.com
Web Site: www.abelowpr.com

Agency Specializes In: Brand Development & Integration, Media Relations, Media Training, Public Relations, Social Media

Lorraine Abelow *(Founder & Pres)*

Accounts:
Martin Millers Gin

ABELOW PUBLIC RELATIONS
330 W 38th St Ste 1100, New York, NY 10018
Tel.: (212) 941-9247
Web Site: www.abelowpr.com

Agency Specializes In: Brand Development & Integration, Media Relations, Public Relations, Social Media

Lorraine Abelow *(Founder & Pres)*
Katrina Leo *(Acct Exec)*

Accounts:
New-Gogobot

ABERNATHY MACGREGOR GROUP-NEW YORK
(Formerly Abernathy MacGregor Group, Inc.)
501 Madison Ave 13th Fl, New York, NY 10022-5617
Tel.: (212) 371-5999
Fax: (212) 371-7097
Web Site: www.abmac.com/

Employees: 65
Year Founded: 1984

Agency Specializes In: Crisis Communications, Financial, Investor Relations, Public Relations, Sponsorship

James L. Abernathy *(Chm & CEO)*
Tom Johnson *(Pres & Head-Mergers & Acq)*
Charles L. Burgess *(Pres)*
Rhonda Barnat *(Mng Dir)*
Chuck Dohrenwend *(Mng Dir)*
Michael M. Pascale *(Mng Dir)*
Shawn H. Pattison *(Mng Dir)*

Accounts:
Aspen Insurance Holdings Limited
Evercore Partners Inc.
Hershey Co. Communications, Social
Ticketmaster Entertainment, Inc.

Branch

Abernathy MacGregor Group-Los Angeles
(Formerly Abernathy MacGregor Group, Inc.)
707 Wilshire Blvd Ste 3950, Los Angeles, CA 90017-3110
Tel.: (213) 630-6550
Fax: (213) 489-3443
E-Mail: idc@abmac.com
Web Site: www.abmac.com

Employees: 15
Year Founded: 1998

Agency Specializes In: Financial, Public Relations

Ian D. Campbell *(Vice Chm)*
David Schneiderman *(Mng Dir & Head-San Francisco Office)*
Chuck Dohrenwend *(Mng Dir)*
James B. Lucas *(Mng Dir)*
Shawn H. Pattison *(Mng Dir)*
Sydney Isaacs *(Exec VP)*
Glen L. Orr *(Exec VP)*
Alan Oshiki *(Exec VP)*
Allyson Vento *(Exec VP)*
Heather Wilson *(Exec VP)*
Amy Feng *(Sr VP)*

ABI MARKETING PUBLIC RELATIONS
29 Broadway Ste 1300, New York, NY 10006
Tel.: (212) 529-4500
Fax: (212) 529-4442
Web Site: www.abipr.com

Employees: 23
Year Founded: 1980

Agency Specializes In: Brand Development & Integration, Media Buying Services, Media Relations, New Technologies, Package Design, Print, Public Relations, Search Engine Optimization, Sponsorship

Revenue: $2,000,000

Alan B. Isacson *(CEO)*
Bernard Guly *(Mng Dir-EMEA)*
Nicole Zampino *(Exec Dir)*
Coli Anand *(Dir-Fin)*
Christina Wilcox *(Dir)*
Sharon Corrigan *(Deputy Mng Dir EMEA)*

Accounts:
Bosch
Crown Holdings
Eastman Chemical Company
Yupo
Zip-Pak

ABRAHAM PAISS & ASSOCIATES, INC.
1460 Quince Ave Ste 102, Boulder, CO 80304
Tel.: (303) 413-8066
Web Site: www.abrahampaiss.com

Agency Specializes In: Internet/Web Design, Public Relations

Neshama Abraham *(CEO)*
Zev Paiss *(COO)*

Accounts:
New-Cool Energy, Inc.

ABSOLUTELY PUBLIC RELATIONS
3343 S Nelson Ct, Lakewood, CO 80227
Tel.: (303) 984-9801
Fax: (303) 986-4630
E-Mail: maggie@absolutelypr.com
Web Site: www.absolutelypr.com

Employees: 1
Year Founded: 1999

National Agency Associations: AMA-BMA-PRSA

Agency Specializes In: Agriculture, Business-To-Business, Consulting, Consumer Publications, Corporate Communications, Education, Entertainment, Environmental, Health Care Services, Internet/Web Design, Medical Products, Pets , Pharmaceutical, Public Relations, Publicity/Promotions, Restaurant, Retail

Maggie Chamberlin Holben *(Owner)*

Accounts:
CID4; Aurora, CO Biotech, Medical Device & AgBio Business Support; 2010
Medivance; Louisville, CO Medical Devices; 2011

ACCENT MEDIA PRODUCTIONS, INC.
1657 Strine Dr, McLean, VA 22101
Tel.: (703) 356-9427
Fax: (703) 506-0643
Toll Free: (888) 895-1035
E-Mail: jackjorgens@accentmediainc.com
Web Site: www.accentmediainc.com

Employees: 10
Year Founded: 1988

Agency Specializes In: Bilingual Market, Communications, Graphic Design, Health Care Services, Hispanic Market, Logo & Package Design, Production, Public Relations, Publicity/Promotions, Radio, Seniors' Market, T.V., Telemarketing

Approx. Annual Billings: $1,000,000

Breakdown of Gross Billings by Media: Collateral: $250,000; Radio: $500,000; T.V.: $250,000

Cecilia Domeyko *(Pres, Dir & Exec Producer)*

Accounts:
American Association of Retired Persons
American Nurses Association
Fleishman-Hillard
Maslow Media Group, Inc.
Merck Pharmaceuticals
Ministry of Culture Government of Chile
National Eye Institute
National Heart, Lung, and Blood Institute
National Institute of Mental Health
National Library of Medicine
Organization of American States
The Sugar Association, Inc
Univision
U.S. Department of Education
US Department of Veterans Affairs
The World Bank

ACCENTUATE PR
3114 Carrington Dr, Crystal Lake, IL 60014
Tel.: (815) 479-1833
Fax: (866) 721-1834
E-Mail: info@accentuatepr.com
Web Site: www.accentuatepr.com

Agency Specializes In: Content, Crisis Communications, Event Planning & Marketing, Internet/Web Design, Media Relations, Public Relations, Search Engine Optimization, Social Media, Strategic Planning/Research

Julie Shepherd *(Pres)*

Accounts:

Intercept Energy Services

ACHIEVE PR
1409 S Lamar Loft 812, Dallas, TX 75215
Tel.: (972) 850-8527
E-Mail: info@achievepr.net
Web Site: www.achievepr.net

Agency Specializes In: Digital/Interactive, Event Planning & Marketing, Public Relations, Social Media, Strategic Planning/Research

Denita Lacking-Quinn *(Pres)*

Accounts:
GlamourWeave Inc

ACKERMANN PR
1111 Northshore Dr Ste N-400, Knoxville, TN 37919
Tel.: (865) 584-0550
Fax: (865) 588-3009
Toll Free: (888) 414-7787
E-Mail: info@ackermannpr.com
Web Site: www.ackermannpr.com

E-Mail for Key Personnel:
President: cackermann@ackermannpr.com

Employees: 15
Year Founded: 1981

National Agency Associations: COPF

Agency Specializes In: Advertising, Advertising Specialties, Brand Development & Integration, Business Publications, Business-To-Business, Collateral, Communications, Consulting, Consumer Marketing, Consumer Publications, Corporate Communications, Corporate Identity, Event Planning & Marketing, Exhibit/Trade Shows, Investor Relations, Local Marketing, Logo & Package Design, Public Relations, Publicity/Promotions

Cathy Ackermann *(Pres & CEO)*
Jeff Hooper *(Chief Strategy Officer)*
Crystal Cardwell *(VP-Fin)*
Tommy Smith *(VP-Mktg Strategy)*
Chris Goodrich *(Sr Acct Exec)*
Ryan Willis *(Sr Acct Exec)*

Accounts:
Clayton Homes / Vanderbilt Mortgage
East TN Medical Center; Alcoa, TN; 2002
Invisible Fence Inc. Electronic Containment Devices; 2007
Mountain Commerce Bank; Johnson City, TN; 2007
Natural Resources Recovery; Baton Rouge, LA; 2007
Power Equipment Co.; Knoxville, TN
Ruby Tuesday; Maryville, TN; 2007
Saddlebrook, Inc.; Knoxville, TN; 2007
Siemens
Tennessee National; Loudon, TN
United States Enrichment Corporation
USEC Inc.
Vaughn & Melton; Knoxville, TN; 2005
Vulcan Materials; Birmingham, AL
Well Mate
The White Stone Group; Knoxville, TN; 2001

A.D. ADAMS ADVERTISING, INC.
560 Sylvan Ave, Englewood Cliffs, NJ 07632
Tel.: (201) 541-3111
Fax: (201) 266-0086
E-Mail: info@ad-adams.com
Web Site: www.ad-adams.com

Employees: 9
Year Founded: 1949

Agency Specializes In: Advertising, Business Publications, Business-To-Business, Commercial Photography, Engineering, High Technology, Magazines, Public Relations, Publicity/Promotions, Technical Advertising

Connie Adams *(Owner)*

Accounts:
Acotion Power Supplies
Barta Microbattery
Bel Fuse, Inc.; Jersey City, NJ Delay Lines, Fuses, Magnetics, Thick Film Hybrids; 1996
Bomar Interconnect Products, Inc.; Ledgewood, NJ Connectors for Voice & Data Transmission; 1994
Signal Transformer
Signio Transformer
Stewart Connectors
Sullins Electronic Corp.; San Marcos, CA Backplanes, Connectors; 2001

ADAM FRIEDMAN ASSOCIATES
11 E 44 St 5th Fl, New York, NY 10017
Tel.: (212) 981-2529
Fax: (212) 981-8174
E-Mail: info@adam-friedman.com
Web Site: www.adam-friedman.com

Employees: 11

Agency Specializes In: Public Relations

Adam I. Friedman *(Owner)*
Elizabeth Howard *(Mng Dir)*
George Mcgrath *(Mng Dir)*

Accounts:
Alseres Pharmaceuticals
Brendan Wood International; Toronto, Canada
Cabot Corporation
Cadence Design Systems
COGO Group, Inc.
Dollar Tree Stores, Inc
Federal Realty Investment Trust
Federal Realty Investment Trust
Free Scale Semiconductor
Tesoro Corporation
Tower General Contractors
Turner Construction

ADAMS UNLIMITED
80 Broad St Ste 3202, New York, NY 10004
Tel.: (212) 956-5900
Fax: (212) 956-5913
E-Mail: marie@adams-pr.com
Web Site: www.adams-pr.com

Employees: 5
Year Founded: 1985

Agency Specializes In: Leisure, Public Relations, Travel & Tourism

Candice Adams Kimmel *(Owner & Pres)*
Marie Rosa *(VP)*

Accounts:
Bonaire Tourist Office
The DEMA Show
Divi Aruba Beach Resort; Aruba, NA; 1992
Diving Equipment & Marketing Association (DEMA)
St. Kitts Tourism Authority
Tamarijn Aruba Beach Resort; Aruba, NA; 1992
The Wings Club

AGENCY 33
455 Sherman St Ste 205, Denver, CO 80203-4404
Tel.: (303) 894-3130
Fax: (303) 322-6105
Web Site: www.agency33.com

Employees: 3

Agency Specializes In: Public Relations

Revenue: $500,000

James Wall *(Pres & CEO)*
Vincent Dipas *(Partner)*
Andrew Laing *(Partner)*
Gwen Kawashima *(Office Mgr)*

Accounts:
Moye White

AGENDA GLOBAL
(Formerly DW Turner, Inc.)
400 Gold Ave SW 12th Fl, Albuquerque, NM 87102
Tel.: (505) 888-5877
Fax: (505) 888-6166
E-Mail: info@agenda-global.com
Web Site: www.agenda-global.com

Employees: 20

Agency Specializes In: Advertising, Broadcast, Corporate Communications, Crisis Communications, Email, Government/Political, Graphic Design, Media Relations, Outdoor, Podcasting, Print, Production, Public Relations, Radio, Strategic Planning/Research, T.V., Viral/Buzz/Word of Mouth

Revenue: $10,000,000

Max Hamel *(Partner)*
Gerges Scott *(VP-Energy Unit)*
Adam Turner *(Product Dir)*
Janice Arroyo *(Dir-Art)*
Alicia Patterson *(Dir-Comm)*
Alicia Pompa *(Dir)*
Leslie Wood *(Specialist-PR & Strategic Comm)*

Accounts:
URI
Walmart

AGILECAT: COMMUNICATIONS CATALYSTS
1818 Market St Ste 220, Philadelphia, PA 19103
Tel.: (215) 508-2082
Fax: (215) 241-1193
E-Mail: 411@agilecat.com
Web Site: www.agilecat.com

Employees: 15
Year Founded: 2000

Agency Specializes In: Brand Development & Integration, Corporate Identity, Graphic Design, Public Relations, Sponsorship

Peter Madden *(Pres & CEO)*
David Doyle *(Strategist-Digital)*

Accounts:
CFI
Valley Forge Convention & Visitors Bureau Advertising, Brand Development

AGNES HUFF COMMUNICATIONS GROUP, LLC.
Howard Hughes Ctr 6601 Ctr Dr W Ste 100, Los Angeles, CA 90045
Tel.: (310) 641-2525
Fax: (310) 641-2544
Web Site: www.ahuffgroup.com

Employees: 12
Year Founded: 1995

Agency Specializes In: Affluent Market, Brand Development & Integration, Communications, Consumer Marketing, Email, Environmental, Event Planning & Marketing, Exhibit/Trade Shows, Market Research, Media Relations, Package Design, Pets , Planning & Consultation, Promotions, Public Relations, Publicity/Promotions, Social Marketing/Nonprofit, Strategic Planning/Research, Travel & Tourism

Approx. Annual Billings: $1,000,000

Breakdown of Gross Billings by Media: Pub. Rels.: 100%

Agnes Huff *(Pres & CEO)*

Accounts:
Animal Defenders International; UK Animal Welfare
British Airways
Hotel Shangri Brand Awareness, PR
Orthopaedic Hospital; Los Angeles, CA Healthcare
PhaseOne Communications; Los Angeles, CA Marketing Research
Tower Wound Care of Santa Monica; Santa Monica, CA Healthcare
VCA-Antech; Los Angeles, CA Veterinary Care

AGUILAR PUBLIC RELATIONS
8387 Winter Berry Dr, Castle Rock, CO 80108
Tel.: (303) 488-9469
Fax: (303) 496-0009
Web Site: www.aguilarpr.com

Agency Specializes In: Brand Development & Integration, Event Planning & Marketing, Media Planning, Media Relations, Public Relations, Social Media, Strategic Planning/Research

Timi Aguilar *(Pres & CEO)*

Accounts:
AT&T Corporate Affairs
AT&T Public Affairs
Alvarado Construction, Inc.
Colorado Contractors Association
Colorado Latino Forum
Corporex Companies, Inc.
Move Colorado

AHA CREATIVE STRATEGIES INC.
1423 Sunrise Pl, Gibsons, BC V0N 1V5 Canada
Tel.: (604) 303-1052
Toll Free: (877) 303-1052
E-Mail: info@ahacreative.com
Web Site: www.ahacreative.com

Employees: 3
Year Founded: 2003

Agency Specializes In: Consulting, Crisis Communications, Event Planning & Marketing, Media Training, Newspapers & Magazines, Public Relations, RSS (Really Simple Syndication)

Paul Holman *(Principal)*
Barbara Wickens *(Sr Acct Exec)*
Nala Henkel *(Strategist-Creative & Writer)*
Lori Simeunovic *(Acct Exec & Writer)*
Ruth Atherley *(Strategist-Comm)*
Tzaddi Gordon *(Designer-Online)*
Laurie Hanley *(Coord-PR)*

Accounts:
Tourism New Zealand

AIELLO PUBLIC RELATIONS & MARKETING
600 Grant St Ste 610, Denver, CO 80203
Tel.: (303) 355-3838
Fax: (303) 318-6367
E-Mail: admin@aiellopr.com
Web Site: www.aiellopr.com

Agency Specializes In: Brand Development & Integration, Corporate Communications, Electronic Media, Media Relations, Public Relations

Wendy Aiello *(Pres)*
Anne Pearson *(COO)*

Accounts:
Aurora Economic Development Council
Blowdry Lounge
BMC Investments
Boomers Leading Change in Health
Boys & Girls Clubs
Cantor Group
Childrens Diabetes Foundation
Franklin D Azar
Metro Taxi Co., Inc.
Oakwood Homes LLC
Sterling Ranch
Urban Peak

AIGNER ASSOCIATES PR/EVENTS
(Name Changed to Aigner/Prensky Marketing Group)

AIGNER/PRENSKY MARKETING GROUP
(Formerly Aigner Associates PR/Events)
214 Lincoln St Ste 300, Allston, MA 02134
Tel.: (617) 254-9500
Fax: (617) 254-3700
Web Site: www.aignerprenskymarketing.com

Employees: 10
Year Founded: 1984

Agency Specializes In: Event Planning & Marketing, Public Relations

Janet Prensky *(Partner)*

Accounts:
Acme Supermarkets
Electric Library
The Hanover Mall
iParty
Mount Auburn Hospital; 1999
Peapod Online Grocery Shopping
The Pinehills
Serendipity Restaurant
Simon Property Group

AINSWORTH MAGUIRE
Unit 28 Peel Indus Estate, Chamberhall Street, Bury, Lancashire BL9 0LU United Kingdom
Tel.: (44) 161 447 8550
Fax: (44) 161 447 8556
E-Mail: pr@ainsmag.co.uk
Web Site: www.ainsmag.co.uk

Employees: 3
Year Founded: 1987

National Agency Associations: CIPR

Agency Specializes In: Business-To-Business, Environmental, Industrial, New Technologies, Public Relations, Publicity/Promotions, Technical Advertising

Kevin Ainsworth *(Owner & Partner)*
Adrian Maguire *(Partner)*
Amy McCandlish *(Acct Mgr)*

Accounts:
Crown Energy; Manchester, UK Energy, Telecom & Utility Service; 2009
Cudis; Manchester, UK Circuit Protection; 2003
Fueltek; Lancashire, UK Fuel Management; 2009
Hawke International; Manchester, UK Ex compliant electrical connectors, and terminations; 2002
Hy-ten; Liverpool, UK Concrete reinforcement; 2009
Rowe Hankins; Manchester, UK Components and systems for rail applications; 1987
Street Crane Company; Derbyshire, UK Factory Cranes & Hoists; 1993

AIRFOIL
(Formerly Airfoil Public Relations)
336 N Main St, Royal Oak, MI 48067
Tel.: (248) 304-1400
Fax: (248) 304-1401
Toll Free: (866) AIRFOIL
E-Mail: detroit@airfoilgroup.com
Web Site: airfoilgroup.com

Employees: 50
Year Founded: 2000

National Agency Associations: PRSA

Agency Specializes In: High Technology, Public Relations, Publicity/Promotions, Sponsorship

Lisa Vallee Smith *(Founder & CEO)*
Tracey Parry *(Partner-Airfoil Silicon Valley & Sr VP)*
Sharon Neumann *(Sr VP-Fin & Admin)*
Amy Bryson *(VP)*
Tim Wieland *(VP)*
Liz Pandzich *(Acct Dir)*
Jon Gunnells *(Mgr-Social & Digital Media)*
Jim Korona *(Supvr-Acctg)*
Harmony Cook *(Coord-Sls & Mktg Admin)*

Accounts:
New-Ambassador
AppConext Auto Marketing Communications, PR
Armaly
New-Automation Alley
Brookstone
CiRBA Inc. (Agency of Record)
Comcast Cable, Heartland Region Social Media Advertising, XFINITY
Ebay
FRY
FuzeBox
Gas Station TV
New-Glance Networks
GoAnimate Lead PR
ilumysis
LinkedIn
MetroMile
Microsoft Worldwide OEM
Microsoft
New-NH Learning Solutions
Nvidia
SME Rapid Conference
solidThinking
SurveyMonkey PR
New-WorkWave

AJGPR
124 S Mansfield Ave, Los Angeles, CA 90036
Tel.: (310) 494-1554
Web Site: www.ajgpr.com

Agency Specializes In: Brand Development & Integration, Media Training, Public Relations, Social Media

Alison Graham *(Owner & Pres)*

Accounts:
New-Dr. Rita Eichenstein
New-Evolve Treatment Centers
New-Mari Winsor Pilates Expert

AKINSCRISP PUBLIC STRATEGIES
173 Mitchell Rd, Oak Ridge, TN 37830

Public Relations Firms

Tel.: (865) 483-8850
Fax: (865) 483-8851
E-Mail: dakins@akinscrisp.com
Web Site: www.akinsps.com

Employees: 4

Agency Specializes In: Public Relations

Darrell Akins *(Founder & CEO)*
Jennifer Wiggins *(VP-Client Svcs)*

Accounts:
Baker Concrete
EnergySolutions
Infographics
Whitson Construction Company
WSI, Inc.

Branches

AkinsCrisp Public Strategies
301 Sparkman Dr Technology Hall Ste 101 S, Huntsville, AL 35899
Tel.: (256) 722-5557
Fax: (256) 722-5501
E-Mail: ekoshut@akinscrisp.com
Web Site: www.akinsps.com

Employees: 2

Agency Specializes In: Communications, Consulting, Media Relations, Public Relations

Jennifer Wiggins *(VP-Client Svcs)*

Accounts:
Aldis Group
Arnold Engineering Development Center
Business Tennessee Magazine
Comcast Corporation

ALAN MILLER PR
1 Main St, Roosevelt Island, NY 10044
Tel.: (718) 317-8745
Web Site: www.alanmillerpr.com

Year Founded: 2001

Agency Specializes In: Crisis Communications, Event Planning & Marketing, Media Relations, Public Relations, Social Media

Alan Miller *(Pres)*

Accounts:
Professional Bull Riders

ALAN WEINKRANTZ AND COMPANY
3737 Broadway St Ste 280, San Antonio, TX 78209-6553
Tel.: (210) 820-3070
Fax: (210) 820-3080
E-Mail: alan@weinkrantz.com
Web Site: alanweinkrantz.com/

E-Mail for Key Personnel:
President: alan@weinkrantz.com

Employees: 12
Year Founded: 1980

Agency Specializes In: Business-To-Business, Digital/Interactive, E-Commerce, Electronic Media, Event Planning & Marketing, Exhibit/Trade Shows, High Technology, Information Technology, Internet/Web Design, Public Relations, Trade & Consumer Magazines

Alan L. Weinkrantz *(Pres)*

Accounts:
Emoze; 2006
N-trig
Surf Communication Solutions; 2006
Waves

ALBERS COMMUNICATIONS GROUP
PO Box 285, Bellevue, NE 68005
Tel.: (888) 296-2411
Fax: (402) 292-5488
E-Mail: info@alberscommunications.com
Web Site: www.alberscommunications.com

Year Founded: 2000

Agency Specializes In: Broadcast, Crisis Communications, Internet/Web Design, Media Relations, Print, Public Relations, Social Media

Debbie Hilt *(VP & Dir-PR)*
Julie Swartz *(Acct Dir-Mgmt)*
Gina Pappas *(Dir-New Media & Sr Specialist-PR)*
Kristin Danley-Greiner *(Sr Acct Mgr)*
Judy Daniel *(Acct Mgr)*
Stacy Ford-Bingham *(Acct Mgr)*
Dani Hatfield *(Acct Mgr)*
Ann McIntire-Hadfield *(Specialist-PR)*

Accounts:
Home Instead Senior Care

ALEXANDERG PUBLIC RELATIONS LLC
751 E 63rd St Ste 213, Kansas City, MO 64110
Tel.: (816) 416-8002
Web Site: www.alexgpr.com

Year Founded: 2010

Agency Specializes In: Content, Crisis Communications, Media Relations, Media Training, Public Relations, Social Media

Stephanie Greenwood *(Principal & VP-Client Svcs)*
Alexander Greenwood *(Principal)*

Accounts:
Premier Grounds Maintenance

ALICE MARSHALL PUBLIC RELATIONS
126 5th Ave Ste 801, New York, NY 10011
Tel.: (212) 861-4031
E-Mail: info@alicemarshall.com
Web Site: www.alicemarshall.com

Agency Specializes In: Communications, Public Relations, Social Media, Strategic Planning/Research

Alice Marshall *(Owner)*
Danielle Pagano McGunagle *(Mng Dir)*
Ulku Erucar *(Acct Dir)*
Jordanna Gualtieri *(Acct Mgr)*
Lauren Wintemberg *(Acct Mgr)*
Sybil Bunn Pool *(Sr Acct Exec)*
Bethany Christie *(Acct Exec)*

Accounts:
UXUA Casa Hotel & Spa

ALISON BROD PUBLIC RELATIONS
440 Park Ave S, New York, NY 10016
Tel.: (212) 230-1800
Fax: (212) 230-1161
E-Mail: info@alisonbrodpr.com
Web Site: www.alisonbrodpr.com

Employees: 50

Agency Specializes In: Public Relations, Sponsorship

Alison Brod *(Owner)*
Rayna Greenberg *(VP)*
Carey Burgess *(Acct Supvr)*
Joanna Cella *(Acct Supvr-Home Decor & Lifestyle)*
Erica Warren *(Jr Acct Exec)*

Accounts:
Ahava
Beauty.com
Burger King Female Consumers, Marketing, PR
Kmart
L'Oreal Paris
Mercedes Benz
Parlux Fragrances, Inc. Jessica Simpson Fragrance
Piperlime
Sears Holdings Fashion Business
Skyy Spirits (Agency of Record) Event Support, Midori Melon, Online Awareness, Public Relations, Skyy Vodka, X-Rated Fusion
Stila Cosmetics
Victoria's Secret Stores, Inc. Pink

ALL POINTS PUBLIC RELATIONS, LLC
500 Lake Cook Rd Ste 350, Deerfield, IL 60015
Tel.: (847) 580-4233
E-Mail: contact@allpointspr.com
Web Site: www.allpointspr.com

Agency Specializes In: Brand Development & Integration, Crisis Communications, Media Training, Public Relations, Social Media

Jamie Izaks *(Pres)*
Lauren Izaks *(COO & Exec VP)*
Rosie Gillam *(Sr Acct Head)*
Katharine Nichols *(Sr Head-Acct)*
Whitney Sirard *(Acct Head-Creative & Digital)*

Accounts:
A Buyer's Choice Media
Bottle & Bottega, Inc.
CMIT Solutions Trade Placements
Vom Fass AG

ALLEN & CARON
(Acquired by Dresner Corporate Services & Name Changed to Dresner Allen Caron)

ALLEN/COOPER ENTERPRISES
109 Norfolk St Ground Fl, New York, NY 10002
Tel.: (212) 260-8100
E-Mail: info@allencooperenterprises.com
Web Site: www.allencooper.com

Agency Specializes In: Crisis Communications, Event Planning & Marketing, Media Relations, Public Relations, Social Media

Helen Allen *(Co-Founder & Principal)*
Meryl Weinsaft Cooper *(Co-Founder & Principal)*

Accounts:
Appleton Rum
Belvedere Vodka
Champagne Charles Heidsieck
Champagnes Piper-Heidsieck
Hop City Brewery
Purity Vodka
Veuve Clicquot

ALLEN NELSON & CO.
1906 California Ave SW, Seattle, WA 98116-1905
Tel.: (206) 938-5783
Fax: (206) 938-2072

E-Mail for Key Personnel:
President: anelson@worldproxy.com

Employees: 8

Year Founded: 1977

Agency Specializes In: Corporate Communications, Financial, Investor Relations

Breakdown of Gross Billings by Media: Newsp. & Mags.: 100%

Allen Nelson *(Pres)*
Johanna Nelson *(Treas & Sec)*
Peggy Flett *(Controller)*

ALLISON & PARTNERS
505 Sansome St 7th Fl, San Francisco, CA 94111-3310
Tel.: (415) 277-4907
Fax: (415) 217-7503
E-Mail: info@allisonpr.com
Web Site: www.allisonpr.com

Employees: 106
Year Founded: 2001

Agency Specializes In: Brand Development & Integration, Communications, Consumer Marketing, Corporate Identity, High Technology, Media Planning, Media Training, Travel & Tourism

Scott Pansky *(Founder & Sr Partner)*
Kent Schwartz *(Partner & Sr VP-Fin)*
Zach Colvin *(Partner & Gen Mgr)*
Karyn Barr Amin *(Sr VP-Client Svc & Ops)*
Tania Condon *(Sr VP)*
Paul Sears *(VP-Integrated Mktg)*
Phil Carpenter *(Sr Partner-West Coast)*

Accounts:
Boost Mobile
Giants Community Fund Pro-Bono
Pioneer Electronics PR
Progressive Boat & Personal Watercraft, Commercial Auto, Motorcycle, Private Passenger Auto, Public Relations, RV
Toyota PR
New-Viber Public Relations
The Vitamin Shoppe (Agency of Record)
WhaleShark Media Public Relations, RetailMeNot

Branches

Allison & Partners
7135 E Camelback Rd, Scottsdale, AZ 85251
Tel.: (623) 201-5555
Fax: (480) 966-0111
E-Mail: sappel@allisonpr.com
Web Site: www.allisonpr.com

Employees: 12

Cathy Planchard *(Partner & Pres)*
Karyn Barr Amin *(Sr VP-Client Svc)*
Alan Weatherbee *(Sr VP-Talent Search)*
David Wolf *(Mng Dir-Global China Practice-Los Angeles)*
Cortney Read *(Acct Mgr)*
Laura Zilververg *(Acct Mgr)*
Amy Ohara *(Sr Acct Exec)*

Accounts:
Best Western International; Phoenix, AZ
Boost
GE Healthcare
Hasbro
International Game Technology; Las Vegas, NV Campaign: "Ghostbusters Slots Launch"
L'Oreal USA
Progressive
Samsung
Sony
YouTube

Allison & Partners
8880 Rio San Diego Dr Ste 1090, San Diego, CA 92108
Tel.: (619) 533-7978
Fax: (619) 543-0030
E-Mail: timw@allisonpr.com
Web Site: www.allisonpr.com

Brian Brokowski *(Gen Mgr)*
Jeannie Horner *(Acct Mgr)*
Jessica Fix *(Sr Acct Exec)*
Julia Yuryev *(Sr Acct Exec)*
Rebecca Buddingh *(Acct Exec)*
Erin Flemming *(Acct Coord)*

Accounts:
ARAMARK Parks & Destinations
Envision Solar International, Inc. (Agency of Record)
Healthcare Leadership Council
KPMG Corporate Finance
SONY
The Vitamin Shoppe

Allison & Partners
11611 San Vicente Blvd Ste 910, Los Angeles, CA 90049-6510
Tel.: (310) 452-7540
Fax: (310) 452-9005
E-Mail: dawn@allisonpr.com
Web Site: www.allisonpr.com

Employees: 15

Agency Specializes In: Public Relations, Sponsorship

Paul Breton *(Sr VP-Corp Comm Practice)*
David Wolf *(Mng Dir-Global China Practice)*
Emily Wilson *(VP-Consumer)*
Carline Jorgensen *(Gen Mgr)*
Dana Block *(Grp Acct Dir-Technology & Consumer Tech)*
Ashley Wallace *(Dir-Consumer)*
Marilyn Finegold *(Office Mgr)*
Elizabeth Villafan *(Asst Acct Exec)*
Nicole Walker *(Asst Acct Exec)*

Accounts:
ASICS America Corporation ASICS America Corporation

Allison & Partners
71 5th Ave, New York, NY 10003
Tel.: (646) 428-0612
Fax: (212) 302-5464
E-Mail: info@allisonpr.com
Web Site: www.allisonpr.com

Employees: 15

Agency Specializes In: Advertising, Sponsorship

Thomas Smith *(Mng Dir)*
Lisa Rosenberg *(Chief Creative Officer)*
Matthew Della Croce *(Pres-Global Corp & Europe)*
Jonathan Heit *(Sr Partner & Pres-Americas)*
Linda Burns *(Sr VP-Media Rels)*
Kevin Nabipour *(Sr VP-Content Strategies)*
Alan Weatherbee *(Sr VP-Talent Search)*
Jenny Braga *(VP)*
Carolina Guana *(VP-Multicultural & Hispanic Practice)*
Jeremy Rosenberg *(Head-Digital)*
Anne Colaiacovo *(Sr Partner & Gen Mgr-New York)*
Cynthia Patnode *(Acct Mgr)*
Amanda Roark *(Sr Acct Exec)*
Cat Forgione *(Asst Acct Exec)*

Accounts:
Affinity
Airbnb Media
Apple
Aramark
Asics
B&G Foods, Inc. Consumer Public Relations, Marketing, Publicity Initiatives, Social Media
Best Western
Boost
Bulova Corporation Digital, Marketing Strategy
Dignity Health
Equity Residential
ForSaleByOwner.com Brand Awareness, Digital, Media, Social, Thought Leadership
GE Health Care
Gowalla
Hasbro
Intermedia Brand Awareness
Johnny Rockets
Joico; New York, NY (Agency of Record) Consumer Activations, Consumer PR, Digital Campaigns, Events, Media Relations, Partnerships, Product Launches, Social Media, Sponsorships
Kimpton Hotel Group
Loreal USA
PhRMA
PKWARE
Progressive
RetailMeNot (Public Relations Agency of Record)
Seventh Generation Public Relations, Social Media
TiVo, Inc.

Allison & Partners
(Formerly Frause)
1411 4th Ave Ste 1210, Seattle, WA 98101
(See Separate Listing)

ALLYSON CONKLIN PUBLIC RELATIONS
P.O. Box 272703, Fort Collins, CO 80527
Tel.: (303) 895-0495
E-Mail: info@allysonconklinpr.com
Web Site: www.allysonconklinpr.com

Employees: 3
Year Founded: 2010

Agency Specializes In: Brand Development & Integration, Broadcast, Logo & Package Design, Media Relations, Print, Public Relations, Social Media

Allyson Conklin *(Founder & Principal)*

Accounts:
Cecilia Wong Skincare
Claria Renee Beauty
Coveted Home
Esoteric Events
HollyBeth Organics
J. Wheeler Designs
Ladies & Gents
Nerd Skincare
Pyar&Co.
Shop Ten 25
Studio Ten 25
Times Two Design
Waiting On Martha

ALM PUBLIC RELATIONS
7083 Hollywood Blvd, Hollywood, CA 90028
Tel.: (323) 962-0204
Web Site: www.alinemedia.com

Year Founded: 2001

Agency Specializes In: Brand Development & Integration, Event Planning & Marketing, Public Relations, Social Media

Jennifer Mitzkus *(Partner)*

Jana Khamo *(Dir-Social Media)*

Accounts:
Shinymix
True Lipz

ALPAYTAC INC.
888 16th St Ste 800, Washington, DC 20006
Tel.: (202) 650-5500
E-Mail: info@alpaytac.com
Web Site: www.alpaytac.com

Agency Specializes In: Brand Development & Integration, Crisis Communications, Media Training, Public Relations, Social Media, Strategic Planning/Research

Rory Davenport *(Gen Mgr & Dir-Pub Affairs)*

Accounts:
Turkish Airlines

ALTA COMMUNICATIONS INC.
(Name Changed to The Karma Agency)

AMDUR SPITZ & ASSOCIATES INC.
135 S LaSalle St Ste 2900, Chicago, IL 60604
Tel.: (312) 784-7986
Fax: (312) 377-1804
Web Site: www.amdurspitz.com

Year Founded: 1992

Agency Specializes In: Advertising, Brand Development & Integration, Graphic Design, Internet/Web Design, Public Relations, Social Media, Strategic Planning/Research

Jennifer Amdur Spitz *(Principal)*

Accounts:
One Hope United

AMP3 PUBLIC RELATIONS
349 5th Ave Ste 535, New York, NY 10016-5021
Tel.: (646) 827-9594
Fax: (212) 677-2929
E-Mail: info@amp3pr.com
Web Site: www.amp3pr.com

Employees: 8

Agency Specializes In: Event Planning & Marketing, Internet/Web Design, Public Relations, Publicity/Promotions

Alyson Roy *(Co-Founder & Partner)*

AMW PR INC.
1 Little W 12th St, New York, NY 10014
Tel.: (212) 542-3146
E-Mail: info@amwpr.com
Web Site: www.amwpr.com

Year Founded: 2008

Agency Specializes In: Crisis Communications, Event Planning & Marketing, Graphic Design, Media Training, Public Relations

Adam Weiss *(Pres & CEO)*
Angela Trostle *(Partner & VP)*

Accounts:
Uri Tours

AMY LEVY PUBLIC RELATIONS
11022 Santa Monica Blvd Ste 350, Los Angeles, CA 90025
Tel.: (310) 444-5250
Fax: (310) 444-5259
E-Mail: info@amylevypr.com
Web Site: www.amylevypr.com

Employees: 2

Agency Specializes In: Brand Development & Integration, Business-To-Business, Consulting, Corporate Identity, Food Service, Internet/Web Design, Media Training, Newspaper, Restaurant, Social Marketing/Nonprofit, Strategic Planning/Research

Amy Levy *(Pres)*
Jennifer Harris *(Specialist-Product)*
Kendall Legan *(Acct Exec)*

Accounts:
Anaitte Vaccaro
LA Beerathon
Paula Jerome Designs
Sherman Infinity Rings Product Photography, Public Relations, Trade & Consumer Advertising, Website Updates
The Survivor Mitzvah Project
Wrinkle Prevention Pillow

ANDOVER COMMUNICATIONS, INC.
1 Bridge Plz N Ste 325, Fort Lee, NJ 07024-7586
Tel.: (201) 947-4133
Fax: (201) 947-5580
Toll Free: (800) 866-5580
E-Mail: andovercomm@aol.com
Web Site: www.andovercommunications.com

E-Mail for Key Personnel:
President: sclark@andovercommunications.com

Employees: 5
Year Founded: 1989

Agency Specializes In: Communications, Consumer Marketing, Health Care Services, Public Relations, Publicity/Promotions

Approx. Annual Billings: $1,905,000

Breakdown of Gross Billings by Media: Print: 30%; Pub. Rels.: 70%

Steven Clark *(Pres)*

Accounts:
Accenture; 2000
Brand Keys
CARE
Exodon
Gentle Dentistry; 1991
IBM
Kosherfest
MasterCard International
Medical Nutrition USA
The Power Practice
Prio Corp.; Portland, OR Optometric Eyewear; 1997
Stollow Consulting Group; 1998
Vital Basics; Portland, ME Nutritional Supplements; 2006

ANDREW E. FREEDMAN PUBLIC RELATIONS
9127 Thrasher Ave, Los Angeles, CA 90069
Tel.: (310) 271-0011
Fax: (310) 271-0033
E-Mail: info@aefpr.com
Web Site: www.aefpr.com

Agency Specializes In: Brand Development & Integration, Event Planning & Marketing, Public Relations

Andrew E. Freedman *(Founder & Pres)*
Patty Freedman *(Partner)*
Paul Reader *(Chief Strategy Officer & VP)*

Accounts:
Book Soup, Inc.
Ginny Gardner
Simply Eartha

ANDREW EDSON & ASSOCIATES, INC.
89 Bounty Ln, Jericho, NY 11753-2209
Tel.: (516) 931-0873
Fax: (516) 644-5588
E-Mail: andrew@edsonpr.com
Web Site: www.edsonpr.com

Employees: 4
Year Founded: 1996

Agency Specializes In: Communications, Investor Relations, Media Relations, Media Training, New Technologies, Public Relations, Publicity/Promotions, Strategic Planning/Research, Travel & Tourism

Andrew S. Edson *(Pres & CEO)*
Tom Donoghue *(Mng Dir)*
Martin Skala *(VP)*

Accounts:
CTW Consulting
DataTreasury Corporation
GrooveCar, Inc.
The Silver Institute
Welsh, Carson, Anderson & Stowe

ANDREW JOSEPH PR
229 W 116th St Ste 5B, New York, NY 10026
Tel.: (212) 724-6728
Web Site: www.andrewjosephpr.com

Agency Specializes In: Collateral, Event Planning & Marketing, Media Relations, Public Relations, Social Media

Jenny Melendez *(Sr Acct Exec)*

Accounts:
New-Alan Tanksley Inc
New-Sandra Espinet

ANGLIN PUBLIC RELATIONS, INC.
720 NW 50th St Ste 200a, Oklahoma City, OK 73118
Tel.: (405) 840-4222
Fax: (405) 840-4333
Web Site: www.anglinpr.com

Year Founded: 1999

Agency Specializes In: Brand Development & Integration, Crisis Communications, Logo & Package Design, Media Relations, Public Relations, Social Media

Debbie Anglin *(CEO & Principal)*
Karen Holmes *(Office Mgr)*
Lori Johnson *(Sr Acct Exec)*
Becky Cavnar *(Acct Coord)*

Accounts:
Dale Rogers Training Center, Inc.

ANNE KLEIN COMMUNICATIONS GROUP, LLC
1000 Atrium Way Ste 102, Mount Laurel, NJ 08054
Tel.: (856) 866-0411
Fax: (856) 866-0401

E-Mail: akcg@annekleincg.com
Web Site: www.annekleincg.com

Employees: 8
Year Founded: 1982

National Agency Associations: COPF-PRSA

Agency Specializes In: Business-To-Business, Environmental, Financial, Health Care Services, Pharmaceutical, Public Relations, Strategic Planning/Research

Approx. Annual Billings: $900,000

Breakdown of Gross Billings by Media: Pub. Rels.: $900,000

Christopher Lukach *(Co-Owner, COO & Sr VP)*
Anne Sceia Klein *(Pres)*
Gerhart L. Klein *(Exec VP)*
Elizabeth Archer *(VP)*
Jenna Poor *(Dir-Mktg)*
Darrah Foster *(Sr Acct Exec)*
Kathryn M. Conda *(Acct Exec)*

Accounts:
Catholic Health East
Exelon Generation
Mercy Health System
New Jersey American Water
Truven Health Analytics

ANREDER & CO.

286 Madison Ave Ste 907, New York, NY 10017
Tel.: (212) 532-3232
Fax: (212) 679-7999
E-Mail: information@anreder.com
Web Site: www.anreder.com

Employees: 12
Year Founded: 1990

Revenue: $1,300,000

Steven Anreder *(CEO)*
Michael Wichman *(VP)*
Andrew Ginsberg *(Dir-Admin)*

Accounts:
Calyon Americas
Morgan Joseph TriArtisan LLC
Penson Worldwide, Inc.

ANTENNA GROUP, INC.

135 Main St Ste 800, San Francisco, CA 94105-8110
Tel.: (415) 896-1800
Fax: (415) 896-1094
E-Mail: info@antennagroup.com
Web Site: www.antennagroup.com

Employees: 22

Agency Specializes In: E-Commerce, Electronic Media, Event Planning & Marketing, Exhibit/Trade Shows, Financial, Health Care Services, High Technology, Information Technology, Legal Services, Public Relations, Publicity/Promotions, Real Estate, Strategic Planning/Research

Keith Zakheim *(CEO)*
Denyse Dabrowski *(Exec VP)*
Albino Matesic *(Dir-Web Dev & Creative Svcs)*
Brigit Carlson *(Sr Acct Exec)*
Carlie Guilfoile *(Sr Acct Exec)*
Megan Decker *(Acct Exec)*
Audrey Neuman *(Acct Exec)*

Accounts:
3M Corp. Renewable Energy Group
3M Renewable Energy
Bidgely
BlueFire Ethanol
CEIVA Energy
Cogenra
The Eye Tribe
HelioVolt
illumitex
ISI Technology
KoolSpan
NanoH2O
National Semiconductor
New Energy Technologies
NextAxiom
OriginOil
Uskape

ANTHOLOGY MARKETING GROUP

(Formerly StarrTech Interactive)
1003 Bishop St Pauahi Tower 9th Fl, Honolulu, HI 96813
Tel.: (808) 544-3000
Web Site: http://www.anthologygroup.com/

Employees: 4
Year Founded: 1987

Agency Specializes In: Asian Market, Bilingual Market, Communications, Entertainment, Event Planning & Marketing, Investor Relations, Leisure, Multimedia, Public Relations, Publicity/Promotions, Travel & Tourism

Andrew Jackson *(COO & Exec VP)*
Mary Fastenau *(Pres-Interactive Grp & Principal-Anthology Mktg Grp)*
Mei Jeanne Wagner *(Sr VP)*
Dennis Mahaffay *(VP-Brdcst)*
Rebecca Pang *(Sr Acct Supvr-PR)*
Shannon Fujimoto *(Media Planner & Buyer-Adv)*
Jacie Matsukawa *(Acct Coord)*

Accounts:
Bank of Hawaii
Group 70 Foundation
Group 70 International
Hawaiian Telcom

ANTHONYBARNUM

515 S Capital of Texas Hwy Sie 240, Austin, TX 78746
Tel.: (512) 329-5670
E-Mail: info@anthonybarnum.com
Web Site: www.anthonybarnum.com

Agency Specializes In: Crisis Communications, Media Training, Public Relations, Social Media

Melissa Anthony Sinn *(Founder & CEO)*
Amanda Abbott *(VP)*
Leslie Silver *(Acct Dir)*
Matt Maurel *(Sr Acct Exec)*
Mikala Wright *(Acct Exec)*

Accounts:
New-Charlie Bravo Aviation
New-Theme Park frog
New-Under Cover Tourist

APEX PUBLIC RELATIONS

600-1075 Bay St, Toronto, ON M5S 2B1 Canada
Tel.: (416) 924-4442
Fax: (416) 924-2778
E-Mail: info@apexpr.com
Web Site: www.apexpr.com

Employees: 30

Agency Specializes In: Event Planning & Marketing, Media Relations, Media Training, Promotions, Public Relations, Strategic Planning/Research

Pat McNamara *(CEO)*
Kenneth Evans *(Sr VP)*
Jennifer Stein *(VP)*
Cole Douglas *(Acct Coord)*
Jessica Spremo *(Acct Coord)*

Accounts:
Atkins Nutritionals (Public Relations Agency of Record)
Biore
BMO Bank of Montreal, Harris Private Banking, Investor Line, Mutual Funds, Nesbitt Burns, Private Client Group
Brooks Brothers
Curel
Energizer
Ferrero
Google
Husqvarna Canada Consumer Engagement, Media Relations
Jergens
John Frieda Collections
Kellogg's
Levi's
Mastercard
Nestle Canada Black Magic
New-New Balance Canada (Agency of Record) Digital Marketing, Public Relations, Social Media, Strategic Planning
Nike
Nintendo
NPD Group
Orthomolecular Health
Polysporin
RSA Insurance Consumer Communications, Copywriting, Corporate Reputation, Media Relations, PR
SABMiller Communications, Miller Lite, Public Relations
Second Cup
Taste of Nature Consumer Communications
Tech Data
Tetra Park
UPS
Visit Orlando Corporate Communications, Media Relations, Public Relations, Social Media, Strategic Planning
Walmart Canada Public Relations
Yoplait

ARGYLE COMMUNICATIONS INC.

Ste 1007 S Tower 175 Bloor Street E, Toronto, ON M4W 3R8 Canada
Tel.: (416) 968-7311
Fax: (416) 968-6281
E-Mail: pr@argylepr.com
Web Site: argylepr.com

Employees: 29
Year Founded: 1979

Agency Specializes In: Communications, Pets , Public Relations

Ray Argyle *(Founder)*
Daniel Tisch *(Pres & CEO)*
Roanne Argyle *(Sr VP)*
Alison George *(Sr VP)*
Ashley O'Connor *(Dir-Digital Comm-Argyle Comm)*
Kelly Robinson *(Office Mgr)*

Accounts:
American Peanut Council Peanut Bureau of Canada
Durham College
Ethoca
Government of Ontario
Heritage Financial
Kronos
MasonryWorx
Nestle Canada
Nestle Purina PetCare

NOVX Systems
Ontario Association of Children's Aid Societies (OACAS)
Periodical Marketers of Canada
Princess Margaret Hospital Foundation
Rembrandt Oral Health & Beauty
RSM Richter
Saxon Financial
SEI
Sleep Country Canada
Soya World Inc.
Telesat

ARLENE HOWARD PUBLIC RELATIONS

2701 Ocean Pk Blvd Ste 210, Santa Monica, CA 90405
Tel.: (310) 399-3483
Web Site: www.arlenehowardpr.com

Agency Specializes In: Brand Development & Integration, Content, Event Planning & Marketing, Media Relations, Public Relations, Social Media

Arlene Howard *(Owner & Pres)*

Accounts:
Counting Sheep Coffee
The Discovery House

ARMANASCO PUBLIC RELATIONS, INC.

787 Munras Ave, Monterey, CA 93940
Tel.: (831) 372-2259
Fax: (831) 372-4142
E-Mail: pr@armanasco.com
Web Site: www.armanasco.com

Employees: 6

David Armanasco *(Pres)*
Elizabeth Diaz *(VP)*

Accounts:
AirTrails

ARPR

3423 Piedmont Rd NE 4th Fl, Atlanta, GA 30305
Tel.: (855) 300-8209
Web Site: www.arpr.co

Year Founded: 2012

Agency Specializes In: Brand Development & Integration, Event Planning & Marketing, Media Relations, Media Training, Public Relations, Social Media

Anna Ruth Williams *(Founder & CEO)*
Blair Broussard *(VP)*
Jennifer Blackburn *(Acct Mgr)*
Colleen Pinto *(Acct Mgr)*

Accounts:
Azuga
Bastille Networks
New-Canara
Country Club Prep
Fitnet
New-Hired
New-ICCN + Palladium Press, Social Media, Thought Leadership
MessageGears
Nuance Communications
One Ring Networks, Inc.
New-Prevedere
ShopVisible
New-Siege Technologies
New-StarMobile
Total Founder
New-Ventiv Technology
WeCare Card

ARPR INC./KNOWLEDGE IN A NUTSHELL

1420 Centre Ave Ste 2213, Pittsburgh, PA 15219-3536
Tel.: (412) 765-2020
Fax: (412) 765-3672
Toll Free: (800) NUTSHELL
E-Mail: audrey@knowledgeinanutshell.com
Web Site: www.knowledgeinanutshell.com

E-Mail for Key Personnel:
President: audrey@knowledgeinanutshell.com

Employees: 3
Year Founded: 1980

National Agency Associations: PRSA

Agency Specializes In: Advertising Specialties, Business Publications, Business-To-Business, Children's Market, Communications, Consumer Marketing, Consumer Publications, Infomercials, Medical Products, New Product Development, Over-50 Market, Public Relations, Publicity/Promotions, Radio, Seniors' Market

Approx. Annual Billings: $200,000

Breakdown of Gross Billings by Media: Pub. Rels.: $200,000

Audrey Reichblum *(Pres)*

Accounts:
Campos Market Research; 1994
The Dr. Knowledge Show; 2004
The Edible Game A Smart Cookie; 2000
Knowledge in a Nutshell Publishing, Inc.
Pittsburgh Family Foot Care; 1996

ARTICULATE COMMUNICATIONS INC.

40 Fulton St, New York, NY 10038
Tel.: (212) 255-0080
Fax: (212) 255-0090
E-Mail: info@articulatecomms.com
Web Site: www.articulatecomms.com

Employees: 16
Year Founded: 2002

Agency Specializes In: Broadcast, Business Publications, Business-To-Business, Communications, Computers & Software, Corporate Communications, Corporate Identity, Crisis Communications, High Technology, Information Technology, Magazines, Media Relations, Media Training, Mobile Marketing, New Technologies, Newspaper, Newspapers & Magazines, Public Relations, Strategic Planning/Research

Audra Tiner *(CEO)*
Clare Rhodes *(Mng Dir)*
Adrienne Robbins *(Dir-Ops)*
Emily Pan *(Acct Mgr)*
Diana Kearns-Manolatos *(Assoc Acct Supvr)*

Accounts:
Antenna Software
Ci&T (Agency of Record)
CT (Agency of Record)
EDM Council (Agency of Record)

ARTICULON

(Merged with mckeeman to form articlon mckeeman)

ARTICULON MCKEEMAN

(Formerly Articulon)
8480 Honeycutt Rd, Raleigh, NC 27615
Tel.: (919) 232-5008
Fax: (919) 232-5388
Web Site: www.articulonmckeeman.com

Employees: 6

Agency Specializes In: Communications, Crisis Communications, Event Planning & Marketing, Media Relations

Cindy Stranad *(Owner & CMO)*
Kathy Erp Howell *(Dir-Creative)*
Mike Gauss *(Mgr-Media Rels & Acct Supvr)*
Lisa Schaut *(Mgr-Fin)*
Mary Karabatsos *(Copywriter-IT)*
Anna Roesler *(Acct Coord)*
Ashley Spruill *(Acct Coord)*

Accounts:
Banyon Rock & Talent
Boulevard Animal Hospital
New-CAI Media Relations
Catering By Design
Citizens for Sig Hutchinson
Defense Nutrition
Defond North America
Holiday Express
HumanCentric Technologies
Interim Connexions
International Focus, Inc.
John Rex Endowment
LA Weight Loss Centers
The Leadership Trust
The Magnificent Mile
Massey Preserve
McDonald's Corporation
Nagoya University NU Tech Regenerative Medicine Roundtable (Agency of Record)
National Kidney Foundation of NC
Network South Business Telephone Systems
North Carolina Conservation Council
North Carolina State University
New-North Raleigh Law Group Website
One Source
Panera Bread
Pelnik Insurance & Financial Services
Regency Office Products
Residences at Quorum Center
SAFE Haven For Cats
SAKS Fifth Avenue
Second Empire 5K Classic
Sphere Technical Resources
Sustainable North Carolina
TOURtech
Universal Construction
Villas at Millbrook
White Dahlia Massage & Wellness Center

THE ARTIGUE AGENCY

2400 E Arizona Biltmore Cir Bldg 2 Ste 1290, Phoenix, AZ 85016
Tel.: (602) 633-2122
Web Site: www.artigueagency.com

Agency Specializes In: Brand Development & Integration, Event Planning & Marketing, Media Relations, Media Training, Promotions, Public Relations, Social Media, Strategic Planning/Research

Ray Artigue *(Pres)*
Megan Dean *(Acct Supvr-Mktg & PR)*
Ian La Cava *(Sr Acct Exec)*
Morgan O'Crotty *(Acct Exec)*
Cathy Herman *(Coord-Admin)*

Accounts:
Taste of the NFL

ASGK PUBLIC STRATEGIES

(Merged with M Public Affairs to form Kivvit)

ASPECTUS PR

117 E 24th St Ste 2A, New York, NY 10010
Tel.: (646) 202-9845
Web Site: www.aspectuspr.com

Agency Specializes In: Brand Development & Integration, Content, Media Relations, Public Relations, Search Engine Optimization, Social Media

Jed Hamilton *(Mng Dir)*

Accounts:
New-ITG

ATOMIC PUBLIC RELATIONS
(Acquired by Grayling Global & Name Changed to Grayling)

ATREBOR GROUP
580 Broadway, New York, NY 10012
Tel.: (212) 764-0340
Web Site: www.atreborgroup.com

Year Founded: 2004

Agency Specializes In: Advertising, Event Planning & Marketing, Media Relations, Promotions, Public Relations

Roberta Garzaroli *(Pres)*
Mary Brennan *(Acct Dir)*

Accounts:
Blue Sky Luxury

AUDRA CLEMONS MEDIA SERVICES
320 W 20th St, New York, NY 10011
Tel.: (213) 457-3205
Web Site: www.audraclemons.com

Agency Specializes In: Brand Development & Integration, Internet/Web Design, Media Buying Services, Public Relations, Social Media

Audra Clemons *(Pres)*

Accounts:
Andean Discovery
Casa Oniri
Columbus Travel

AVALON COMMUNICATIONS
9050 N Capital of Texas, Austin, TX 78759
Tel.: (512) 382-6229
Web Site: www.avalonprgroup.com

Year Founded: 2005

Agency Specializes In: Brand Development & Integration, Collateral, Corporate Identity, Internet/Web Design, Logo & Package Design, Public Relations, Social Media, Strategic Planning/Research

Kristyn Moll *(Mng Dir)*
Kaitlin Dilworth *(Sr Acct Exec)*
Taylor Coen *(Acct Exec)*
Rachel Hoffman *(Acct Exec)*

Accounts:
Harry & David
KMN Home
Swiss Diamond

AWE COLLECTIVE
7120 E Indian School Rd Ste K 2nd Fl, Scottsdale, AZ 85251
Tel.: (480) 275-8888
E-Mail: sayhi@awecollective.com
Web Site: www.awecollective.com

Agency Specializes In: Advertising, Crisis Communications, Digital/Interactive, Event Planning & Marketing, Graphic Design, Logo & Package Design, Media Training, Public Relations, Social Media, Strategic Planning/Research

Ty Largo *(Principal & Creative Dir)*
Justin Lee *(Acct Mgr)*
Chianne Nass *(Office Mgr)*
Stefanie Gastelum *(Mgr-Mktg)*
Courtney Markgraf *(Designer)*

Accounts:
Downtown Tempe

A.WORDSMITH
420 SW Washington Ste 205, Portland, OR 97204
Tel.: (503) 227-0833
E-Mail: info@awordsmithcomm.com
Web Site: www.awordsmithcomm.com

Year Founded: 2009

Agency Specializes In: Brand Development & Integration, Corporate Identity, Crisis Communications, Event Planning & Marketing, Media Relations, Public Relations, Social Media

Ann Smith *(Founder & Pres)*
Molly Benito *(Mgr-PR)*

Accounts:
New-ACME Business Consulting LLC

AXON
(Formerly NATIONAL Public Relations)
230 Park Ave S 3rd Fl, New York, NY 10003-1566
Tel.: (212) 614-4124
Fax: (212) 598-5523
E-Mail: info-nyc@national.ca
Web Site: www.national.ca

Year Founded: 1976

Agency Specializes In: Communications, Corporate Communications, Crisis Communications, Digital/Interactive, Graphic Design, Investor Relations, Media Relations, Media Training, Public Relations, Social Media

Mario Nacinovich *(Mng Partner)*
Krista Middleton *(Mgr-Ops)*
Tracy Rands *(Mgr)*
Nathalie Rheaume *(Coord-HR)*

Accounts:
Accenture
Allergan
Amgen Canada
Bayer
BC Lottery Corp. (BCLC)
BHP Billiton
Canadian Centre for Energy Information
Coloplast
Eli Lilly
EnCana
GlaxoSmithKline
Harlequin Enterprises
Homburg Canada
Home Hardware
Imperial Oil
International Diabetes Federation
Ivanhoe Cambridge
Johnson & Johnson
McDonald's Restaurants of Canada
Merck Frosst Canada
Napp Pharmaceuticals
National Bank Financial Group
Nestle Waters Canada
Novartis
Novo Nordisk
Perdue Pharma
Pfizer
Sanofi-Aventis
Spectra Energy
Standard Life
Sun Life Financial
Synenco Energy
TD Bank
TimberWest Forest Corporation
TMX Group
Toyota Canada
University of Montreal
VIA Rail
Walmart
Yellow Pages Group

AZIONE PR
6605 Hollywood Blvd Ste 210, Hollywood, CA 90028
Tel.: (323) 462-6600
Fax: (323) 462-6606
Web Site: www.azionepr.com

Year Founded: 2010

Agency Specializes In: Event Planning & Marketing, Market Research, Public Relations, Social Media

Leland Drummond *(Co-Founder & Co-Pres)*
Michele Thomas *(Co-Founder & Pres)*
Ashleigh Hults *(VP & Head-Brand Strategy)*
Ashley Dillahunty *(VP-Entertainment Mktg)*
Mary Florino *(Sr Acct Exec)*
Claudia Garcia *(Sr Acct Exec)*
Rachel Koggan *(Acct Exec)*

Accounts:
Hoodie Buddie

B PUBLIC RELATIONS LLC
2500 Larimer St Ste 204, Denver, CO 80205
Tel.: (303) 658-0605
E-Mail: hello@wearebpr.com
Web Site: www.wearebpr.com/

Year Founded: 2011

Agency Specializes In: Broadcast, Crisis Communications, Media Training, Print, Public Relations, Social Media

Jordan Blakesley *(Principal & Partner)*
BrieAnn Fast *(Partner & Principal)*
Merideth Milliner *(Mgr-Social Media & Digital)*
Catie Mayer *(Acct Coord)*

Accounts:
C Lazy U Guest Ranch
Denver Botanic Gardens
Kevin Taylor Restaurant Group
The Outlook Lodge
Renaissance Denver Downtown City Center
Solaris Vail
St Julien Hotel & Spa

B2 COMMUNICATIONS
333 3rd Ave N Ste 530, Saint Petersburg, FL 33701
Tel.: (727) 895-5030
E-Mail: info@b2communications.com
Web Site: www.b2communications.com

Year Founded: 2010

Agency Specializes In: Crisis Communications, Media Relations, Public Relations, Social Media, Strategic Planning/Research

Missy Hurley MacFarlane *(Principal)*

Kyle Parks *(Principal)*
Laura Fontanills *(Sr Acct Exec)*
Leah Saunders *(Sr Acct Exec)*

Accounts:
Aliant Bank (Public Relations Agency of Record)
Arnstein & Lehr LLP (Public Relations Agency of Record)
Buildings Alive Ybor City Architecture Hop (Public Relations Agency of Record)
Colliers International (Public Relations Agency of Record)
Environmental Pest Service (Public Relations Agency of Record)
Fisher & Phillips LLP (Public Relations Agency of Record)
Gulf To Bay Charters (Public Relations Agency of Record)
Halpern Enterprises (Public Relations Agency of Record)
Paramedics Plus (Public Relations Agency of Record)
Premier Eye Care (Public Relations Agency of Record)

BABEL PUBLIC RELATIONS LTD
1 Hallidie Plz 2nd Fl, San Francisco, CA 94102
Tel.: (415) 255-5974
Web Site: www.babelpr.com

Agency Specializes In: Content, Event Planning & Marketing, Media Relations, Public Relations, Search Engine Optimization, Social Media

Caroline Kawashima *(Exec VP & Head-Ops-US)*

Accounts:
Axell Wireless
BICS
Devicescape
Fastback Networks
Infobip
Intercede
MailChannels
Ruckus Wireless
Tektronix Communications

BACKBONE MEDIA LLC
65 N 4th St Ste 1, Carbondale, CO 81623
Tel.: (970) 963-4873
Fax: (303) 265-9854
Toll Free: (866) 963-4873
Web Site: www.backbonemedia.net

Employees: 17
Year Founded: 1997

Agency Specializes In: Communications, Consulting, Exhibit/Trade Shows, Media Buying Services, New Product Development, Planning & Consultation, Print, Public Relations, Publicity/Promotions, Sponsorship

Stephen Turcotte *(Pres & CEO)*
Greg Williams *(Partner & Dir-Media)*
Penn Newhard *(Partner)*
Paul Salvaggio *(VP-Ops)*
Ian Anderson *(Dir-PR)*
Charlie Lozner *(Dir-Integrated Svcs)*
Brian Holcombe *(Assoc Dir-PR)*
Cory Lowe *(Acct Mgr)*
David DeMartini *(Mgr-Digital Media)*
Holly Potter *(Mgr-Mktg & New Bus)*
Laura Merino *(Supvr-Media)*
Alex Aufmann *(Media Planner)*
Maggie Edmunds *(Acct Coord)*

Accounts:
Big Agnes
Black Diamond, Inc.
Chaco PR
The Clymb Communications Strategy, PR
Eddie Bauer, Inc. First Ascent, Media, PR
New-EnerPlex (Communications Agency of Record) Public Relations
The Feed Public Relations
New-Field Trip Jerky (Public Relations Agency of Record)
Fishpond
High Sierra (Agency of Record) Public Relations
Honey Stinger Energy Gels & Bars
Hydrapak
Jett MTB
Kastle
Klean Kanteen
Polygiene Public Relations
Rogers Corporation Brand Awareness, PORON, Public Relations
Serotta
Sperry Top-Sider Performance Line PR
Stower (Public Relations Agency of Record) Strategic Communications
Thermacell Repellents, Inc (Media Agency of Record) Media Buying, Media Planning, Public Relations, Social Media
Velogear
YETI Coolers, LLC Brand Awareness, Communications Strategy, PR

THE BADDISH GROUP
28 W 39th St Ste 302, New York, NY 10018
Tel.: (212) 221-7611
E-Mail: info@thebaddishgroup.com
Web Site: www.thebaddishgroup.com

Agency Specializes In: Event Planning & Marketing, Media Relations, Public Relations, Social Media, Sponsorship

Laura Baddish *(Founder & CEO)*

Accounts:
New-Baron Cooper Wine
New-Four Roses Bourbon
New-Teeling Whiskey Company

THE BAILIWICK COMPANY
4 Sanford Rd, Stockton, NJ 08559
Tel.: (609) 397-4880
Fax: (609) 397-4879
E-Mail: info@bailiwickpr.com
Web Site: www.bailiwickpr.com

Employees: 7
Year Founded: 1992

Agency Specializes In: Business-To-Business, Collateral, Communications, Corporate Communications, Corporate Identity, Crisis Communications, Customer Relationship Management, High Technology, Information Technology, Media Relations, Public Relations

Janis Burenga *(Founder & CEO)*
Bobbie Cummins *(Dir-Mktg & Comms)*

Accounts:
AT&T Communications Corp.
Avaya
CIT
Empire Technologies
Eureka
Global Crossing
Intergis
Juniper
Lucent
Telx
United Stations Radio Networks
USA.NET
Veramark

BAISE COMMUNICATIONS
520 Dorman St, Indianapolis, IN 46202
Tel.: (317) 753-3258
Fax: (317) 263-3806
Web Site: www.baisecommunications.com

Year Founded: 2006

Agency Specializes In: Event Planning & Marketing, Graphic Design, Internet/Web Design, Media Buying Services, Media Planning, Media Relations, Public Relations, Social Media, Strategic Planning/Research

Kelly Young *(Pres)*

Accounts:
Gen Con LLC
Thomas Catering

BAKER PUBLIC RELATIONS
104 Everett Rd 1st Fl Ste C, Albany, NY 12205
Tel.: (518) 426-4099
Fax: (518) 426-0040
Web Site: www.bakerpublicrelations.com

Year Founded: 2007

Agency Specializes In: Crisis Communications, Event Planning & Marketing, Logo & Package Design, Media Relations, Public Relations, Social Media, Strategic Planning/Research

Megan Baker *(Pres & CEO)*
Melissa Luke *(Dir-Bus Dev & Strategy)*
Andrea Colby *(Sr Acct Mgr)*
Jason Politi *(Specialist-PR & Mktg)*

Accounts:
Phinney Design Group

BALLANTINES PR
561 Paseo Miramar, Pacific Palisades, CA 90272
Tel.: (310) 454-3080
Fax: (310) 388-6027
E-Mail: info@ballantinespr.com
Web Site: www.ballantinespr.com

Employees: 10

Agency Specializes In: Brand Development & Integration, Direct Response Marketing, E-Commerce, Public Relations, Search Engine Optimization, Strategic Planning/Research, Web (Banner Ads, Pop-ups, etc.)

Sarah Robarts *(Founder & Pres)*
Virginia Lawrence *(Sr VP-Tech)*
Kendal Hurley *(Acct Dir)*
Austin Ruth *(Acct Dir)*
Arraya Moss *(Office Mgr & Intern Mgr)*
Jasmine Prodonovich *(Mgr-Acctg)*
Dara Toulch *(Sr Acct Exec)*
Lyn Winter *(Sr Strategist-West Coast & Intl)*

Accounts:
AKA Beverly Hills Events, Press
Albuquerque Studios
American Airlines
Ballantines Movie Colony Hotel
Caesarstone
City of West Hollywood
Culver Studios
Delta Airlines
Disney
Double Tree
Four Seasons Resorts
Fox
Hilton Worldwide
Lionsgate
The Little Door
Mandarin Oriental Hotel Group
Marriott International, Inc. AC Hotels by Marriott (International Public Relations Agency of

Record), Autograph Collection Hotels (International Public Relations Agency of Record), Moxy Hotels (International Public Relations Agency of Record), Renaissance Hotels (International Public Relations Agency of Record)
Marvel
Motorola
New Mexico State Tourism Department
Raleigh Studios
Sony
Starbucks Coffee
State of South Carolina Film Office
Sun Center Studios
Sunset Marquis Brand Awareness, Media, PR Strategy
Trib
UK Trade & Investment
Universal Music Group
Virgin Atlantic
Warner Brothers
West Hollywood Design District

BALSERA COMMUNICATIONS

2020 Ponce de Leon Ste 1003, Coral Gables, FL 33134
Tel.: (305) 441-1272
Fax: (305) 441-2487
E-Mail: news@balseracommunications.com
Web Site: www.balseracommunications.com

Year Founded: 1999

Agency Specializes In: Media Relations, Public Relations, Social Media

Alfredo J. Balsera *(Founder & Mng Partner)*
Freddy Balsera *(CEO)*
Carlos Gimenez *(Gen Counsel & VP)*
Sonia V. Diaz *(Dir-PR & Digital Strategies)*

Accounts:
Our Kids of Miami-Dade and Monroe Digital Communications, Public Relations
VME Television

BALTZ & COMPANY

49 W 23rd St, New York, NY 10010
Tel.: (212) 982-8300
Fax: (212) 982-8302
E-Mail: info@baltzco.com
Web Site: www.baltzco.com

Employees: 15

Agency Specializes In: Advertising, Consulting, Crisis Communications, Event Planning & Marketing, Media Relations, Media Training, Public Relations, Restaurant, Retail, Social Marketing/Nonprofit, Travel & Tourism

Revenue: $1,500,000

Phillip Baltz *(Pres)*
Ilana Alperstein *(VP)*
Chloe Mata Crane *(VP)*
Amanda Schinder *(Acct Dir)*
Diana Tsuchida *(Mgr-Digital Comm)*
Cristina Krumsick *(Acct Supvr)*
Emmie Kunhardt *(Acct Supvr)*
Madeline Block *(Sr Acct Exec)*
Meredith Sidman *(Sr Acct Exec)*
Beth Hengeveld *(Acct Exec)*
Emma Rowland *(Acct Exec)*

Accounts:
American Express
Kimpton Hotels
Morimoto
Rosa Mexicano Kitchen

BARBOUR GRIFFITH & ROGERS, LLC

(Name Changed to BGR Group)

BAREFOOT PR

190 E 9th Ave Ste 370, Denver, CO 80203
Tel.: (720) 515-4282
E-Mail: info@barefootpublicrelations.com
Web Site: www.barefootpublicrelations.com

Agency Specializes In: Media Relations, Media Training, Public Relations

Cori Streetman *(Principal)*
Sarah Hogan *(Principal)*

Accounts:
New-The Kempe Foundation

BARKLEY PUBLIC RELATIONS

1740 Main St, Kansas City, MO 64108
Tel.: (816) 842-1500
E-Mail: mswenson@barkleyus.com
Web Site: www.barkleyus.com

Employees: 300
Year Founded: 1987

National Agency Associations: IAAA-IPREX-PRSA

Agency Specializes In: Advertising, Affluent Market, Brand Development & Integration, Branded Entertainment, Broadcast, Business-To-Business, Cable T.V., Children's Market, Co-op Advertising, Communications, Consulting, Consumer Goods, Consumer Marketing, Consumer Publications, Corporate Communications, Corporate Identity, Cosmetics, Crisis Communications, Direct Response Marketing, Education, Email, Entertainment, Environmental, Event Planning & Marketing, Exhibit/Trade Shows, Experience Design, Fashion/Apparel, Financial, Government/Political, Guerilla Marketing, Identity Marketing, Investor Relations, Logo & Package Design, Media Planning, Mobile Marketing, Planning & Consultation, Point of Sale, Print, Production (Ad, Film, Broadcast), Promotions, Public Relations, Publicity/Promotions, Recruitment, Regional, Restaurant, Retail, Social Marketing/Nonprofit, Social Media, Sponsorship, Sports Market, Sweepstakes, T.V., Teen Market, Trade & Consumer Magazines, Viral/Buzz/Word of Mouth, Web (Banner Ads, Pop-ups, etc.), Women's Market

Approx. Annual Billings: $4,600,000

Breakdown of Gross Billings by Media: Pub. Rels.: 100%

Bill Fromm *(Founder)*
Jason Parks *(Mng Dir & Exec VP)*
Brad Hanna *(Exec VP & Grp Acct Head)*
Mark Logan *(Sr VP-Innovation)*
Berk Wasserman *(VP & Dir-Creative)*
Paul Corrigan *(Dir-Design)*
Jennifer Karns *(Mgr-HR-Recruiting)*

Accounts:
ITC Holdings; 2007
Lee Jeans Company; Merriam, KS; 1996
The March of Dimes; 2007
March of Dimes Birth Defects Foundation
UMB Bank

BAROKAS PUBLIC RELATIONS

71 Columbia St, Seattle, WA 98104
Tel.: (206) 264-8220
Fax: (206) 264-8221
E-Mail: howard@barokas.com
Web Site: www.barokas.com

Employees: 20
Year Founded: 1998

Agency Specializes In: Information Technology, Public Relations

Frances Bigley *(VP)*
Johanna Erickson *(VP)*
Karli Overmier *(VP)*
Morgan Bradley *(Sr Acct Mgr)*
Kristin Scheidegger *(Acct Mgr)*
Bailey Fox *(Sr Acct Exec)*
Nick McDonald *(Sr Acct Exec)*
Constance McBarron *(Acct Exec)*
Bri Rios *(Acct Exec)*

Accounts:
Apptio
BDA
Clearwell Systems
Daptiv
Jager
Kitchen Monki
Medify, Inc.
Pokemon, USA
Shiftboard
Skytap
Technology Business Management Council

BARRY R. EPSTEIN ASSOCIATES, INC.

11922 Waterwood Dr, Boca Raton, FL 33428-1026
Tel.: (561) 852-0000
Fax: (561) 451-0000
Web Site: www.publicrelations.nu

Employees: 3
Year Founded: 1979

National Agency Associations: PRSA

Agency Specializes In: Brand Development & Integration, Business-To-Business, Communications, Consulting, Corporate Identity, Direct Response Marketing, E-Commerce, Entertainment, Event Planning & Marketing, Financial, Government/Political, High Technology, Legal Services, Leisure, Medical Products, New Product Development, Newspaper, Newspapers & Magazines, Over-50 Market, Planning & Consultation, Public Relations, Publicity/Promotions, Real Estate, Restaurant, Retail, Sales Promotion, Seniors' Market, Strategic Planning/Research, T.V., Telemarketing, Transportation, Travel & Tourism

Approx. Annual Billings: $500,000

Breakdown of Gross Billings by Media: Fees: $500,000

Barry R. Epstein *(Pres & CEO)*

THE BATEMAN GROUP

1550 Bryant St Ste 770, San Francisco, CA 94103
Tel.: (415) 503-1818
Fax: (415) 503-1880
E-Mail: fbateman@bateman-group.com
Web Site: www.bateman-group.com

Employees: 14
Year Founded: 2004

Agency Specializes In: Media Relations, Media Training, Public Relations

Revenue: $1,400,000

Frederick Bateman *(Founder & CEO)*
Bill Bourdon *(Partner & Gen Mgr)*
Tyler L. Perry *(Partner & Gen Mgr)*
Paula Cavagnaro *(Sr VP)*
Steph Johnson *(Sr VP)*

Public Relations Firms

Syreeta Mussante *(Sr VP)*
Matt Coolidge *(Dir)*
Elinor Mills *(Dir-Content & Media Strategy)*

Accounts:
Animoto Blogger Outreach, Content Marketing, Corporate & Product Messaging, Media, Social Media Marketing, Thought Leadership
Apprenda
Aspect; Westford, MA
Braintree
Bunchball
Digimind
EchoUser
edo; Nashville, TN Content Marketing, PR, Social Media
Greenstart Content Development, Media, Messaging, Strategic Communications
LifeStreet Media; San Carlos, CA Content Marketing, PR, Social Media
LightSpeed
Netskope
Nutanix
Platform Computing
PublicStuff PR
Qualys; Redwood Shores, CA PR, Social Media
RecycleBank Corporate, Partnership & Consumer Communications, Public Relations
Sitecore
Sociable Labs; San Mateo, CA PR, Social Media
Solace Systems
Tidemark
Virtustream
Xamarin
Xeround

BAWDEN & LAREAU PUBLIC RELATIONS
5012 State St, Bettendorf, IA 52722
Tel.: (563) 359-8423
Fax: (309) 764-0975
Web Site: www.bawdenlareaupr.com

Agency Specializes In: Brand Development & Integration, Public Relations

Mike Bawden *(Partner)*
Liz Lareau *(Partner)*

Accounts:
American Food Styles LLC Mama Bosso
Mrs. Wages

THE BAWMANN GROUP
1755 High St, Denver, CO 80218-1305
Tel.: (303) 320-7790
Fax: (303) 320-7661
Toll Free: (888) 320-7790
E-Mail: info@morethanpr.com
Web Site: www.morethanpr.com

Employees: 7
Year Founded: 1995

National Agency Associations: PRSA

Agency Specializes In: Consulting, Corporate Identity, Public Relations

Brad Bawmann *(Owner)*
Jennifer Nuhfer *(VP-Comm)*
Maggie Spain *(VP)*
Tammy Stratton *(VP-Client Svcs)*
Alyssa Strazza *(Acct Mgr)*
Sara Buettmann *(Designer)*
Richelle Moulin *(Acct Coord)*

BAY BIRD INC PR
433 G St Ste 204, San Diego, CA 92101
Tel.: (858) 382-4922
Web Site: www.baybirdinc.com

Year Founded: 2008

Agency Specializes In: Event Planning & Marketing, Media Relations, Public Relations, Social Media, Strategic Planning/Research

Peyton Robertson *(Founder & Pres)*

Accounts:
Magnifico Giornata
Westfield North County

BAZINI HOPP LLC
163 Amsterdam Ave Ste 318, New York, NY 10023
Tel.: (917) 574-5490
E-Mail: liz@bazinihopp.com
Web Site: www.bazinihopp.com

Year Founded: 2009

Agency Specializes In: Crisis Communications, Event Planning & Marketing, Market Research, Media Relations, Media Training, Public Relations, Social Media

Karen Hopp *(Co-Founder & Partner)*
Liz Bazini *(Partner)*

Accounts:
Catalyst Investors
Goodmail Systems, Inc.
Pacing Technologies, LLC
Say Media, Inc

BE INSPIRED PUBLIC RELATIONS
820 Manhattan Ave 204, Manhattan Beach, CA 90266
Tel.: (323) 375-7763
E-Mail: sayhello@beinspiredpr.com
Web Site: www.beinspiredpr.com

Agency Specializes In: Brand Development & Integration, Public Relations, Social Media

Leila Lewis *(CEO & Mgr-Brand)*
Alex Meyers *(Mgr-Comm)*

Accounts:
New-The Hidden Garden
New-Joanna August
New-WedPics

BE SOCIAL PUBLIC RELATIONS LLC
143 S Cedros Ave Ste V105-A, Solana Beach, CA 92075
Tel.: (858) 764-0566
E-Mail: contact@besocialpr.com
Web Site: www.besocialpr.com

Year Founded: 2011

Agency Specializes In: Event Planning & Marketing, Media Relations, Public Relations, Social Media

Ali Grant *(Dir-PR & Talent)*
London Glendenning *(Mgr-Digital & Influencer)*
Kirsten Weinberg *(Mgr-PR)*
Monica Chang *(Coord-PR)*

Accounts:
Cyndi Allcott

BEAUTIFUL PLANNING MARKETING & PR
1375 Broadway Ste 1100, New York, NY 10018
Tel.: (877) 841-7244
Fax: (866) 694-3505
E-Mail: info@beautifulplanning.com
Web Site: beautifulplanning.com

Year Founded: 2005

Agency Specializes In: Brand Development & Integration, Event Planning & Marketing, Public Relations, Social Media

Monique Tatum *(Pres & CEO)*
Wendy Vazquez *(Jr Acct Exec)*
Janita Mercado *(Coord-Sls)*

Accounts:
New-7 Charming Sisters Public Relations
New-Aurelia Garza
Dr. Joshua Perlman
New-Mane Choice
New-Model Launcher
New-Moulin Rouge "Best of France", Public Relations
Out-Fit Challenge
Silvia Bours
Texas de Brazil Public Relations
Troy Mass
Vivian Billings
Y-Clad
New-Your Hollywood Pro
Z Skin Cosmetics

BECCA PR
270 Lafayette, New York, NY 10012
Tel.: (212) 633-2129
E-Mail: bpr@beccapr.com
Web Site: www.beccapr.com

Agency Specializes In: Brand Development & Integration, Crisis Communications, Digital/Interactive, Event Planning & Marketing, Media Relations, Public Relations, Social Media

Becca Parrish *(Owner)*
Jamie Siskin *(VP)*
Casey Kahn *(Acct Dir)*

Accounts:
New-La Pecora Bianca

BECK ELLMAN HEALD
4275 Executive Sq Ste 325, La Jolla, CA 92037
Tel.: (858) 453-9600
Web Site: www.beckellmanheald.com

Year Founded: 1986

Agency Specializes In: Brand Development & Integration, Crisis Communications, Event Planning & Marketing, Media Relations, Media Training, Public Relations, Social Media

Alyssa Enwright *(Sr Acct Exec)*

Accounts:
New-Salk Institute

BECKER COMMUNICATIONS
119 Merchant St Ste 300, Honolulu, HI 96813
Tel.: (808) 533-4165
Web Site: www.beckercommunications.com

Year Founded: 1986

Agency Specializes In: Advertising, Promotions, Public Relations, Strategic Planning/Research

Ruth Ann Becker *(Chm & CEO)*
Caroline Witherspoon *(Pres)*
Chris Parsons *(VP)*
Marc Witter *(Dir-Mktg)*
Lisa Gaitan *(Office Mgr)*
Wilbur Wong *(Mgr-Online Comm)*

Meaghan Blackburn *(Specialist-Online Comm)*
Randy Soriano *(Specialist-Online Comm)*
Samantha Tsui *(Acct Exec)*

Accounts:
The Cookie Corner

BECKERMAN PUBLIC RELATIONS
One University Plz Ste 507, Hackensack, NJ 07601
Tel.: (201) 465-8000
Fax: (201) 465-8040
E-Mail: contact@beckermanpr.com
Web Site: www.beckermanpr.com

Employees: 50
Year Founded: 1990

Agency Specializes In: Consulting, Digital/Interactive, Print, Public Relations, Real Estate, Social Media

Approx. Annual Billings: $10,000,000

Denyse Dabrowski *(Exec VP)*
Stefanie Matteson *(VP)*
Christa Segalini *(VP-Real Estate)*
Timothy White *(VP-Pub Affairs & Pro Svcs)*
Jerry Schranz *(Dir-Media Strategy)*
Daniel Bryan *(Sr Acct Supvr)*
Kyle Kirkpatrick *(Acct Supvr)*
Caroline Bligh *(Acct Exec)*
Shlomo Morgulis *(Acct Exec)*
Bayan Abbasi *(Coord-Social Media)*

Accounts:
ARCWheeler
Avidan Management
Centaur Properties
Claremont Companies
Coalco New York
Direct Invest
First Potomac Realty Trust
Hollister Construction Services
HyperSolar, Inc.
Ivy Realty
KOR Companies
Matrix Development Group
New Jersey Travel Industry Association; 2008
Solar3D, Inc.

Subsidiary

Antenna Group, Inc.
135 Main St Ste 800, San Francisco, CA 94105-8110
(See Separate Listing)

THE BECKET AGENCY
49 Elizabeth St, Charleston, SC 29403
Tel.: (843) 606-0896
E-Mail: inquiries@thebecketagency.com
Web Site: www.thebecketagency.com

Year Founded: 2008

Agency Specializes In: Event Planning & Marketing, Graphic Design, Media Relations, Promotions, Public Relations, Social Media

Jonah Jeter *(Mng Partner)*
John Treadaway *(Head-Future Creative)*
Scott West *(Head-Future Creative)*
Adam Hart *(Dir-Creative & Sr Brand Mgr)*
Jenna Palatiello *(Brand Mgr)*
Heather Pruitt *(Brand Mgr)*

Accounts:
Mellow Mushroom Florence
Mellow Mushroom Myrtle Beach

BEEHIVE PR
1021 Bandana Blvd E Ste 226, Saint Paul, MN 55108-5112
Tel.: (651) 789-2232
Fax: (651) 789-2230
E-Mail: info@beehivepr.biz
Web Site: www.beehivepr.biz

Agency Specializes In: Brand Development & Integration, Corporate Communications, Crisis Communications, Digital/Interactive, Media Relations, Public Relations, Social Media, Strategic Planning/Research

Lisa Hannum *(Pres & CEO)*
Nicki Gibbs *(Sr VP-Strategy)*
Ayme Zemke *(VP-Client Svc)*
Rebecca Martin *(Exec Dir-Talent & OPS)*
Abigail Greenheck *(Acct Dir)*
Brian Israel *(Acct Dir)*
Tiffany Jackson *(Strategist-Acct)*
Amy Clark *(Sr Graphic Designer)*
Maggie Pendleton *(Acct Coord)*

Accounts:
3M Infection Prevention
6PM.COM
Anser Innovation
BMS Group Brand Awareness, Global Media Relations
Coloplast Corp
Deluxe Corporation
Friends of the Boundary Waters Wilderness
HLT, Inc.
JB Hudson Jewelers Welcome Back To The Diamond
Murphy Warehouse Company
PreferredOne Brand Awareness, Communication strategy
Women's Foundation of Minnesota MN Girls are Not for Sale Campaign

BEELER MARKETING
16400 Westview Rd, Lake Oswego, OR 97034
Tel.: (503) 908-0808
E-Mail: kim@beelermarketing.com
Web Site: www.beelermarketing.com

Employees: 1
Year Founded: 2002

Agency Specializes In: Advertising, Direct Response Marketing, Public Relations

Kim Beeler *(Owner)*

Accounts:
Bainbridge Organic Distillers
Convergence Networks
Kaady Car Washes
Oswego Lake House
Slick's Big Time Sauces
Willamette Valley Vineyards

BEHAN COMMUNICATIONS, INC.
86 Glen St, Glens Falls, NY 12801
Tel.: (518) 792-3856
Fax: (518) 745-7365
E-Mail: info@behancom.com
Web Site: www.behancommunications.com

Employees: 15
Year Founded: 1988

National Agency Associations: COPF

Agency Specializes In: Internet/Web Design, Print, Public Relations, T.V.

Revenue: $2,000,000

Mark L. Behan *(Pres)*
John H. Brodt, Jr. *(Partner & VP)*
Kathy Messina *(CFO)*
Jonathan Cohen *(COO)*
Troy Burns *(VP-Tech & Design)*
Joan Gerhardt *(VP)*
Bill Richmond *(Dir-Res & Sr Project Mgr)*

Accounts:
Atlas Holdings LLC
BASF
Boston Scientific
Bulova
Catholic Conference of New York State
Crandall Public Library
Ellis Hospital
The Evangelist
Finch Paper LLC
General Electric
Juvenile Diabetes Research Foundation
Lancaster Development
Moncure Plywood LLC
Original Works Art Institute
Regeneron Pharmaceuticals
Roman Catholic Diocese of Albany
TRC

BELLA PR
226 W 37th St 15th Fl, New York, NY 10018
Tel.: (212) 868-8183
Fax: (212) 868-8187
E-Mail: info@bellapr.com
Web Site: www.bellapr.com

Agency Specializes In: Brand Development & Integration, Public Relations

Sue Small *(VP)*
Lauren Verini *(Acct Mgr)*

Accounts:
New-ProfilePRO

BELLE COMMUNICATIONS
1620 E Broad St, Columbus, OH 43203
Tel.: (614) 304-1463
Web Site: www.thinkbelle.com

Year Founded: 2013

Agency Specializes In: Content, Media Relations, Public Relations, Search Engine Optimization, Social Media

Kate Finley *(Pres & CEO)*
Heather Allen *(Community Mgr & Mgr-Content)*
Ryan Baker *(Mgr-Ops)*
Tara Parsell *(Specialist-PR)*
Taylor Redick *(Coord-PR)*

Accounts:
Kahiki Foods Inc (Public Relations Agency of Record)

BELLEVUE COMMUNICATIONS GROUP
200 S Broad St Ste 850, Philadelphia, PA 19102
Tel.: (215) 735-5960
E-Mail: info@bellevuepr.com
Web Site: www.bellevuepr.com

Agency Specializes In: Crisis Communications, Event Planning & Marketing, Internet/Web Design, Media Relations, Media Training, Public Relations, Search Engine Optimization, Social Media, Strategic Planning/Research

Kevin Feeley *(Pres)*
Susan Buehler *(Exec VP)*
Pete Peterson *(VP)*
Jeff Jubelirer *(VP)*
Diana Torralvo *(Sr Acct Exec)*

Alex Styer *(Acct Exec)*

Accounts:
Free to Breathe

BENDER GROUP PUBLIC RELATIONS
546 Valley Rd, Montclair, NJ 07043
Tel.: (973) 744-0707
Fax: (973) 746-2199
E-Mail: info@bhgpr.com
Web Site: www.bhgpr.com

Employees: 15

Agency Specializes In: Public Relations

Stacey Bender *(CEO)*
Haley Hammerling *(Mng Supvr)*

Accounts:
Finlandia Cheese
Logan & Company INC
The Manischewitz Company
Prestige Brands
R.A.B. Foods Guiltless Gourmet, Manischewitz
Reckitt Benckiser Cattlemen's Barbecue Sauce, Frank's RedHot Cayenne Pepper Sauce, French's French Fried Onions, French's Mustard

BENDER/HELPER IMPACT, INC.
11500 W Olympic Blvd Ste 655, Los Angeles, CA 90064-1530
Tel.: (310) 473-4147
Fax: (310) 478-4727
E-Mail: info@bhimpact.com
Web Site: www.bhimpact.com

E-Mail for Key Personnel:
President: lee_helper@bhimpact.com

Employees: 62
Year Founded: 1986

Agency Specializes In: Consumer Marketing, Entertainment, Event Planning & Marketing, Public Relations

Approx. Annual Billings: $6,000,000

Lee Helper *(Co-Founder, Pres, Partner & Principal)*
Dean Bender *(Principal)*
Shawna Lynch *(Exec VP)*
Eric Wein *(VP-Interactive Entertainment)*
Michelle Sawatka-Fernandez *(Dir-Bus Dev & Mktg)*
Nicole Yavasile *(Acct Mgr)*
Morgan Tongish *(Sr Acct Exec-Entertainment Content)*
Zac Gunnell *(Acct Exec)*
Steven Kunz *(Acct Exec)*
Marissa Cohnen *(Assoc Acct Exec)*

Accounts:
Genius Products
Konami Digital Entertainment Inc.
Lionsgate
Nerjyzed Entertainment, Inc.; 2007
Sony Online Entertainment
Square Enix Media, PR
Universal Studios Home Entertainment

Branch

Bender/Helper Impact, Inc.
470 7th ave 5th Fl, New York, NY 10001
Tel.: (212) 689-6360
Fax: (212) 689-6601
E-Mail: info@bhimpact.com
Web Site: www.bhimpact.com

Employees: 25
Year Founded: 1988

Agency Specializes In: Communications, Entertainment, Information Technology, Public Relations

Roger Resnicoff *(VP)*
Jerry Griffin *(Gen Mgr-New York)*
Mark Karges *(Acct Supvr)*
Steve Solomon *(Acct Supvr)*
Crystal McCoy *(Acct Exec)*
Samantha Valletta *(Acct Coord)*

Accounts:
Guinness World Records
Lionsgate Family

BENDURE COMMUNICATIONS INC
1101 Penn Ave NW, Washington, DC 20004
Tel.: (202) 756-7729
Fax: (540) 687-3470
Web Site: www.bendurepr.com

Agency Specializes In: Advertising, Brand Development & Integration, Crisis Communications, Logo & Package Design, Public Relations, Social Media

Vicki Bendure *(Pres)*
Scott Stephens *(Exec VP)*
Marcia Massenberg *(Acct Exec)*

Accounts:
Virginia Gold Cup Association

BENNET GROUP
735 Bishop St Ste 401, Honolulu, HI 96813
Tel.: (808) 531-6087
Fax: (808) 531-4290
E-Mail: info@bennetgroup.com
Web Site: www.bennetgroup.com

Agency Specializes In: Advertising, Crisis Communications, Integrated Marketing, Media Relations, Media Training, Public Relations, Social Media

Joan Bennet *(Pres & CEO)*
Monica Salter *(Sr VP)*
Tayte Brock *(Creative Dir)*
Megan Tsuchida *(Sr Acct Exec)*
Emma Wo *(Sr Acct Exec)*
Meg Fingert *(Acct Exec)*
Breana Grosz *(Acct Exec)*

Accounts:
Hana Ranch
Ward Village

BENVENUTI PUBLIC RELATIONS
303 5th Ave Ste 1806, New York, NY 10016
Tel.: (212) 696-9883
E-Mail: info@benvenutipr.com
Web Site: www.benvenutipr.com

Year Founded: 1993

Agency Specializes In: Crisis Communications, Event Planning & Marketing, Internet/Web Design, Logo & Package Design, Media Planning, Public Relations, Social Media

Maria Benvenuti *(Pres)*
Telmiza Benvenuti *(VP)*
Christian Leue *(Acct Exec-New Bus)*

Accounts:
Andanada
Bar d'Eau
BEA
Benares Indian Restaurant
By The Hudson
Calvisius Cavia
Carlota Restaurant
Commerce
Desi Galli
Gradisca Ristorante
La Piscina
Malai Marke
Mo Gelato
Moti Mahal Deluxe
Oro Restaurante
Pennsylvania 6
Pizzetteria Brunetti
SoHi
Tavola

BERK COMM & MARKETING GROUP
350 7th Ave Ste 2204, New York, NY 10001
Tel.: (212) 889-0440
E-Mail: info@berkcommunications.com
Web Site: www.berkcommunications.com

Agency Specializes In: Event Planning & Marketing, Public Relations

Ron Berkowitz *(Founder & Pres)*
Alexandra Spang *(VP)*
Jennifer Mendelsohn *(Acct Exec)*

Accounts:
New-Jay Z

BERLINROSEN
15 Maiden Ln Ste 1600, New York, NY 10038
Tel.: (646) 452-5637
Fax: (646) 200-5333
Web Site: www.berlinrosen.com

Agency Specializes In: Brand Development & Integration, Digital/Interactive, Media Relations, Media Training, Print, Public Relations, Social Media

Jonathan Rosen *(Principal)*
Alex Navarro-McKay *(Mng Dir)*
Ben Wyskida *(Sr VP)*
Lynsey Kryzwick *(Sr VP)*
Jaclyn Kessel *(VP)*
Moira Herbst *(VP)*

Accounts:
New-Two Trees Management
New-United Auto Workers

BERNIE DIMEO COMMUNICATIONS
5901 N Cicero Ave, Chicago, IL 60646
Tel.: (773) 647-1220
Fax: (773) 647-1706
E-Mail: info@berniedimeo.com
Web Site: www.berniedimeo.com

Agency Specializes In: Brand Development & Integration, Collateral, Crisis Communications, Event Planning & Marketing, Internet/Web Design, Logo & Package Design, Media Relations, Media Training, Public Relations, Social Media

Robin Boesen *(VP)*
Maggie McKeon *(Dir-Art)*

Accounts:
Rocco Shirts

BERNS COMMUNICATIONS GROUP, LLC
475 Park Ave S 29th Fl, New York, NY 10016
Tel.: (212) 994-4660
Fax: (212) 994-4688
E-Mail: sberns@bcg-pr.com
Web Site: www.bernscommunications.com/

Employees: 8

Agency Specializes In: Communications, Corporate Communications, Corporate Identity, Financial, Public Relations, Publicity/Promotions

Stacy R. Berns *(Owner)*
Michael J. McMullan *(Mng Dir)*
Melissa H. Jaffin *(Sr VP)*
Joy Murphy *(VP)*
Danielle Poggi *(Acct Supvr)*
Laura Di Fabio *(Asst Acct Exec)*

Accounts:
Andrew Marc
Bluefly
Born Sportswear
Converse Inc.
Donna Karan
Le Sportsac
Smoothmed
Talbots
World Retail Congress

BERRY ECKE ASSOCIATES
93 Spring St Ste 6, Newton, NJ 07860
Tel.: (973) 984-3100
Fax: (973) 984-5559
Web Site: www.berryassociates.com

Year Founded: 1972

National Agency Associations: PRSA

Agency Specializes In: Business-To-Business, Communications, Consulting, Corporate Communications, Media Relations, Public Relations

Approx. Annual Billings: $1,000,000

Breakdown of Gross Billings by Media: Consulting: $150,000; Corp. Communications: $500,000; Newsp. & Mags.: $100,000; Pub. Rels.: $150,000; Strategic Planning/Research: $100,000

Richard Ecke *(Pres)*
Laura Squier *(VP-Fin)*
Scott Olson *(Dir-Design)*
Tom Rice *(Dir-Design)*
Susan Scutti *(Acct Exec)*

Accounts:
C.R. Bard, Inc.
Novartis Pharmaceuticals Corp.

BETH DICKSTEIN ENTERPRISES
665 Broadway Ste 704, New York, NY 10012
Tel.: (212) 353-1383
Web Site: www.bdeonline.biz

Agency Specializes In: Digital/Interactive, Media Buying Services, Print, Public Relations, Social Media

Beth Dickstein *(Owner)*
Beth Hurtubise *(Sr Acct Mgr)*

Accounts:
ACME Studios Inc
Alessi
Artek
Be Original Americas
Coalesse
Designtex Group Inc.
Flavor Paper
Flos
Fritz Hansen
Haworth, Inc.

BEUTLER INK
1316 3rd St Promenade Ste 301, Santa Monica, CA 90401
Tel.: (424) 238-8000
E-Mail: hello@beutlerink.com
Web Site: www.beutlerink.com

Year Founded: 2010

Agency Specializes In: Content, Digital/Interactive, Public Relations

William Beutler *(Pres)*
Robyn Baker *(Dir-Art)*
Sheri Cook *(Dir-Accts)*
Jehoaddan Kulakoff *(Dir-Art)*
Saige Z. Hooker *(Strategist-Social Media)*
Pete Hunt *(Strategist-Creative)*
Heather Robertson *(Strategist-Content)*

Accounts:
Northwood Hospitality Social Media Agency of Record

BEWLEY COMMUNICATIONS
10310 Majestic Perch Ct, Indianapolis, IN 46234
Tel.: (317) 777-2031
Web Site: www.bewleycomm.com

Year Founded: 2013

Agency Specializes In: Crisis Communications, Internet/Web Design, Media Relations, Print, Public Relations, Social Media

Timothy Bewley *(Dir-Digital)*
Mary Louise Bewley *(Strategist)*

Accounts:
ProAct Community Partnership

BEYOND FIFTEEN COMMUNICATIONS, INC.
5319 University Dr Ste 257, Irvine, CA 92612
Tel.: (949) 733-8679
Fax: (949) 271-4595
Web Site: www.beyondfifteen.com

Year Founded: 2009

Agency Specializes In: Media Relations, Public Relations, Social Media, Strategic Planning/Research

Lauren Ellermeyer *(Pres)*
Leslie Licano *(Pres)*
Rosemarie Cosio *(Acct Exec)*
Adriana Cone *(Acct Coord)*

Accounts:
AgreeYa Solutions LLC

BGR GROUP
(Formerly Barbour Griffith & Rogers, LLC)
The Homer Building Eleventh Floor South, Washington, DC 20005
Tel.: (202) 333-4936
Fax: (202) 833-9392
E-Mail: information@bgrdc.com
Web Site: www.bgrdc.com

Employees: 60
Year Founded: 1991

Agency Specializes In: Government/Political, Legal Services, Public Relations

Ed Rogers *(Chm)*
Lanny Griffith *(CEO)*
Todd Eardensohn *(CFO)*
Loren Monroe *(COO)*
Jeffrey H. Birnbaum *(Pres-BGR PR)*
Robert D. Wood *(Pres-BGR Govt Affairs)*
Bill Viney *(Principal)*
Daniel R. Murphy *(Gen Counsel)*
Frank Ahrens *(VP)*
Maya Seiden *(VP)*

Accounts:
ACS State & Federal Solutions
Alfa Bank
Caesars Entertainment Strategic Counsel
Clarian Health Partners
Competitor Group
Donald Jordan
DTN Investments

BIANCHI PUBLIC RELATIONS INC.
888 W Big Beaver Rd Ste 777, Troy, MI 48084
Tel.: (248) 269-1122
Fax: (248) 269-8202
E-Mail: bianchipr@bianchipr.com
Web Site: www.bianchipr.com

Employees: 8
Year Founded: 1992

Agency Specializes In: Automotive, Brand Development & Integration, Business-To-Business, Consulting, Corporate Communications, Corporate Identity, E-Commerce, Education, Engineering, Event Planning & Marketing, Financial, High Technology, Industrial, Legal Services, Media Relations, Media Training, Planning & Consultation, Public Relations, Publicity/Promotions, Real Estate, Retail, Strategic Planning/Research, Transportation

Approx. Annual Billings: $1,000,000

Breakdown of Gross Billings by Media: Pub. Rels.: 100%

James A. Bianchi *(Pres & CEO)*
Jessica Killenberg Muzik *(VP-Acct Svc)*
Leslie Dagg *(Acct Supvr)*
Adriana Van Duyn *(Acct Supvr)*
Jaclyn L. Bussert *(Sr Acct Exec)*

Accounts:
3M Automotive; St. Paul, MN Automotive Innovations, Enabling Technologies; 2008
BASF; Southfield & Wyandotte, MI Auto Coatings, Plastics, Polyurethanes
Cooper-Standard Automotive; Novi, MI Auto Body Sealing, Fluid Handling, NVH Products; 2008
Eisele Connectors, Inc North American Public Relations
Freudenberg-NOK Sealing Technologies Automotive Seals, Corporate & Brand communications, Simrit
FRIMO North America
Johnson Controls, Inc.: Plymouth, MI Auto Interiors, Electronics, Seating; 1997
Schaeffler Group Automotive; Troy, MI Powetrain Components; 2007
TRW Automotive Inc.: Livinia, MI Auto Safety Systems; 1994

BIG INK PR & MARKETING
1409 S Lamar Ste 214, Dallas, TX 75214
Tel.: (214) 485-7300
Fax: (214) 485-7304
E-Mail: jeffrey@biginkpr.com
Web Site: www.biginkpr.com

Employees: 12

Agency Specializes In: Crisis Communications, Event Planning & Marketing

Jeffrey Yarbrough *(CEO)*
Todd Eckardt *(CFO)*
Mallory Jensen *(Acct Coord)*

Public Relations Firms

BIG PICTURE MEDIA INC.
1133 Broadway, New York, NY 10010
Tel.: (212) 675-3103
Web Site: www.bigpicturemediaonline.com

Employees: 7
Year Founded: 2007

Agency Specializes In: Digital/Interactive, Email, Public Relations, Social Media, Strategic Planning/Research, T.V.

Revenue: $2,500,000

Dayna Ghiraldi *(Owner & Pres)*

Accounts:
My Body Sings Electric
Sleeping With Sirens
The Wonder Years

BIG PICTURE PR
391 Sutter St Ste 208, San Francisco, CA 94108
Tel.: (415) 362-2085
E-Mail: info@bigpicpr.com
Web Site: www.bigpicpr.com

Agency Specializes In: Brand Development & Integration, Collateral, Content, Event Planning & Marketing, Media Relations, Public Relations, Social Media

Amy Cunha *(Principal)*

Accounts:
New-Diamondere
New-Vionic

BIGFISH COMMUNICATIONS
7 Kent St, Brookline, MA 02445
Tel.: (617) 713-3800
Web Site: bigfishpr.com

Year Founded: 1999

Agency Specializes In: Brand Development & Integration, Event Planning & Marketing, Internet/Web Design, Public Relations, Social Media

David Gerzof Richard *(Founder & Pres)*
Jessica Crispo *(Partner & VP)*
Meredith Frazier *(Partner & Acct Dir)*
Brigid Gorham *(Acct Mgr)*
Jack Cooper *(Mgr-Resource)*
Bristol Whitcher *(Asst Acct Mgr)*

Accounts:
TYLT

BIRNBACH COMMUNICATIONS, INC.
20 Devereux St Ste 3A, Marblehead, MA 01945
Tel.: (781) 639-6701
Fax: (781) 639-6702
E-Mail: birnbach@birnbachcom.com
Web Site: www.birnbachcom.com

Employees: 10
Year Founded: 2001

National Agency Associations: PRSA

Agency Specializes In: Business Publications, Business-To-Business, Communications, Content, Corporate Communications, Health Care Services, Information Technology, Media Relations, Medical Products, New Technologies, Newspapers & Magazines, Podcasting, Promotions, Public Relations, Publicity/Promotions, Social Marketing/Nonprofit

Approx. Annual Billings: $500,000

Breakdown of Gross Billings by Media: Bus. Publs.: 33%; Consumer Publs.: 34%; Newsp. & Mags.: 33%

Norman Birnbach *(Pres)*
Margaret Bonilla *(Client Svcs Dir)*
Steven Webster *(Acct Dir)*

Accounts:
Couplets.com; Greenwich, CT; 2006
UNIT4 Business Software PR, Social Media, Thought Leadership

BITNER GOODMAN
2101 NE 26th St, Fort Lauderdale, FL 33305
Tel.: (954) 730-7730
Fax: (954) 730-7130
E-Mail: info@bitnergoodman.com
Web Site: www.bitnergoodman.com

E-Mail for Key Personnel:
President: gary@bitner.com

Employees: 17
Year Founded: 1980

National Agency Associations: PRSA

Agency Specializes In: African-American Market, Automotive, Bilingual Market, Business-To-Business, Collateral, Communications, Consulting, Consumer Marketing, Financial, Graphic Design, Health Care Services, High Technology, Hispanic Market, Medical Products, Public Relations, Publicity/Promotions, Real Estate, Restaurant, Retail, Strategic Planning/Research, Transportation, Travel & Tourism

Gary E. Bitner *(Partner)*
Elizabeth Senk-Moss *(Acct Supvr)*

Accounts:
American Express Company
Granite Transformations PR, Social Media
Seminole Casino Coconut Creek
Seminole Hard Rock Hotel & Casino Seminole Gaming Administration
Seminole Tribe of Florida; 2000
Simon Property Group; FL Malls, Outlets & Lifestyle Centers; 2008

Branch

Bitner/Hennessy PR
3707 Edgewater Dr, Orlando, FL 32804
Tel.: (407) 290-1060
Fax: (407) 290-1052
E-Mail: kimbra@bitner.com
Web Site: www.bitner.com

Employees: 7
Year Founded: 1986

Kimbra Hennessy *(Owner & Partner)*
Nancy Glasgow *(VP)*
Minnie Escudero Morris *(Acct Supvr & Coord-Hispanic Mktg)*

BJC PUBLIC RELATIONS
(Private Single Location)
650 N 6th Ave, Phoenix, AZ 85003
Tel.: (602) 277-9530
Fax: (602) 234-3397
E-Mail: info@bjc.com
Web Site: www.bjc.com

Employees: 11
Year Founded: 1983

Agency Specializes In: Crisis Communications, Event Planning & Marketing, Media Relations, Media Training, Public Relations, Social Media

Revenue: $1,800,000

Sara Fleury *(Pres)*

Accounts:
Arizona Leafy Greens
Arizona Office of Tourism
BHP Copper
Curis Resources Ltd
Foundation for Senior Living
Kitchell
Neighborhood Housing Services
Ogletree Deakins
Sheraton Phoenix Downtown Hotel

BKWLD
808 R St Ste 202 Suite 202, Sacramento, CA 95814
Tel.: (916) 922-9200
E-Mail: info@bkwld.com
Web Site: www.bkwld.com

Year Founded: 2001

Agency Specializes In: Advertising, Media Relations, Sponsorship

Ryan Vanni *(Founder & CEO)*
Justin Jewett *(VP & Dir-Tech)*
Isis Keigwin *(Acct Dir & Dir-Strategy)*
Ethan Martin *(Dir-User Strategy)*
Jeremy McCain *(Dir-Interactive Art)*
Dan Otis *(Dir-Art)*
Jeff Toll *(Dir-Creative)*

Accounts:
The Beach Boys Music Albums Provider
Clif Bar (Digital Agency of Record) Content, Creative, Website
Hard Hat City Construction Community Services
McDonald's Campaign: "Unexpected Moments", McDonald's Breakfast

BLACK BENAK
2805 2nd Ave S Ste 200, Birmingham, AL 35233
Tel.: (205) 202-5759
E-Mail: hello@blackbenak.com
Web Site: www.blackbenak.com

Year Founded: 2013

Agency Specializes In: Brand Development & Integration, Content, Event Planning & Marketing, Promotions, Public Relations, Social Media, Strategic Planning/Research

Hannah Benak *(Pres)*
Laurel McQuinn *(Dir-Brand Mgmt)*
Catherine Perez *(Dir-Digital Comm)*

Accounts:
Whitlee Mullis Graphic Design

THE BLACK SHEEP AGENCY
1824 Spring St Studio 105, Houston, TX 77007
Tel.: (832) 971-7725
E-Mail: info@theblacksheepagency.com
Web Site: www.theblacksheepagency.com

Year Founded: 2009

Agency Specializes In: Advertising, Brand Development & Integration, Event Planning & Marketing, Graphic Design, Media Relations, Public Relations, Social Media

Monica Danna *(Chief Strategy Officer)*
Jessica Craft *(Dir-Client Svcs & Ops)*
Sarah Gabbart *(Dir-Content)*
Jo Skillman Gray *(Dir-Art)*
Emily Van Keppel *(Dir-PR)*
Katie Thomson *(Acct Exec-PR)*

Accounts:
Ragin Cajun Restaurant

BLACKBIRD PR
261 5th Ave Fl 22, New York, NY 10016
Tel.: (212) 683-2442
Fax: (212) 683-2022
Web Site: www.blackbird-pr.com

Year Founded: 2009

Agency Specializes In: Broadcast, Print, Public Relations, Social Media

Melanie Brandman *(Founder & CEO)*
Kirsten Magen *(VP)*
Holly Schnabel *(Acct Mgr)*

Accounts:
Black Tomato (Public Relations Agency of Record)
New-Blue Waters Resort Public Relations
Mondrian London Public Relations
Morgans Hotel Group
NYLO
The Ritz-Carlton, Bali
XpresSpa Media Relations

THE BLAINE GROUP
8665 Wilshire Blvd Ste 301, Beverly Hills, CA 90211-2932
Tel.: (310) 360-1499
Fax: (310) 360-1498
E-Mail: devon@blainegroupinc.com
Web Site: blainegroupinc.com

Employees: 10
Year Founded: 1975

Agency Specializes In: Advertising, African-American Market, Brand Development & Integration, Business Publications, Business-To-Business, Collateral, College, Communications, Computers & Software, Consulting, Consumer Goods, Consumer Marketing, Consumer Publications, Corporate Communications, Corporate Identity, Cosmetics, Crisis Communications, Education, Electronic Media, Entertainment, Environmental, Event Planning & Marketing, Exhibit/Trade Shows, Fashion/Apparel, Financial, Food Service, Health Care Services, High Technology, Household Goods, Information Technology, Investor Relations, Legal Services, Local Marketing, Magazines, Market Research, Media Relations, Media Training, Medical Products, Multicultural, New Product Development, New Technologies, Newspaper, Newspapers & Magazines, Pharmaceutical, Print, Promotions, Public Relations, Publicity/Promotions, Publishing, Radio, Regional, Restaurant, Retail, Sales Promotion, Seniors' Market, Social Marketing/Nonprofit, Trade & Consumer Magazines, Women's Market

Approx. Annual Billings: $1,000,000

Breakdown of Gross Billings by Media: D.M.: 1%; Newsp. & Mags.: 1%; Production: 1%; Pub. Rels.: 97%

Gene Siciliano *(CFO)*

Accounts:
Lawfund Management Group

BLAKE ZIDELL & ASSOCIATES
321 Dean St 5, Brooklyn, NY 11217
Tel.: (718) 643-9052
E-Mail: info@blakezidell.com
Web Site: www.blakezidell.com

Agency Specializes In: Public Relations

John Wyszniewski *(Mng Dir)*
Ronald Gaskill *(VP)*

Accounts:
New-Soho Rep

BLANC & OTUS PUBLIC RELATIONS
1001 Front St, San Francisco, CA 94111
Tel.: (415) 856-5100
Fax: (415) 856-5193
Web Site: www.blancandotus.com

Year Founded: 1985

Agency Specializes In: High Technology, New Technologies, Public Relations, Sponsorship

Simon Jones *(Sr VP)*
Suzi Owens *(Sr VP)*
Kristin Reeves *(VP)*
Danielle Tarp *(VP)*
Annemiek Hamelinck *(Gen Mgr)*
Jennifer Smith *(Acct Supvr)*
Neil Desai *(Sr Acct Exec)*
Natalie Pridham *(Sr Acct Exec)*
Megan Gregorio *(Acct Exec)*
Christine Pai *(Acct Exec)*
Sophie Sieck *(Acct Exec)*

Accounts:
CalCEF
Lyris, Inc; Wilmington, DE
NETQOS
Oracle
Passenger
Proactive Communications
SanDisk
Universal Electronics
Video Egg
Visible Technologies (Agency of Record)
Xactly Corporation

Blanc & Otus Public Relations
206 E 9th St Ste 1850, Austin, TX 78701
Tel.: (512) 691-0650
E-Mail: rweber@blancandotus.com
Web Site: www.blancandotus.com

Employees: 10

Agency Specializes In: Public Relations

Simon Jones *(Sr VP)*
Suzi Owens *(Sr VP)*
Kristin Reeves *(VP)*
Danielle Tarp *(Acct Dir)*
Drew Smith *(Sr Acct Exec)*

BLAST! PR
123 A El Paseo, Santa Barbara, CA 93101
Tel.: (919) 833-9975
Fax: (919) 833-9976
Toll Free: (855) 526-1216
E-Mail: information@blastpr.com
Web Site: www.blastpr.com

Employees: 10
Year Founded: 2000

Agency Specializes In: Communications, Digital/Interactive, E-Commerce, Entertainment, Event Planning & Marketing, Financial, Government/Political, Information Technology, Integrated Marketing, Media Buying Services, Media Planning, Media Relations, Mobile Marketing, Promotions, Public Relations, Publicity/Promotions, Retail, Social Media, Strategic Planning/Research

Kathleen Bagley Formidoni *(Founder & Principal)*
Bryan Formidoni *(Founder & Principal)*
Lana McGilvray *(Principal)*
Hollis Guerra *(Sr Dir-PR)*
Alexis Roberts *(Dir-PR)*
Brook Marlowe *(Specialist-PR)*

Accounts:
Adara Media
AdBidCentral
Anchor Intelligence
Apogee Search
AudienceScience
Authentication and Online Trust Alliance
BlueLithium
Bronto Software
Buysight
Buzz Corps
Centro
Cicero
Compass Labs Media
Context Optional
Datran Media
eMetrics Marketing Optimization Summit
ESPC
HookLogic
Krishna
Krux Digital
LifeStreet Digital
Magnetic
MailChimp
Moxie Kids
NetPlus Marketing
Network Advertising Initiative
Permuto
Poptent
Port25
Potrero Media
Preference Central
Questus
SocialMedia Networks
Swap Negotiators
The Trade Desk, Inc.
TRUSTe
UnsubCentral, Inc.
Web Analytics Association
XLNTads
Zenbe
Zoove

BLASTMEDIA
11313 USA Pkwy Ste B 302, Fishers, IN 46037
Tel.: (317) 806-1900
E-Mail: info@blastmedia.com
Web Site: www.blastmedia.com

Agency Specializes In: Media Relations, Public Relations, Social Media

Kelly Hendricks *(CEO)*
Mendy Werne *(COO)*
Jacqueline Simard Ireton *(Dir-Accts)*
Kimberly Jefferson *(Dir-Accts)*
Meghan Matheny *(Sr Acct Exec)*
Kiersten Von Grimmenstein *(Sr Acct Exec-PR)*
Rachael McKenney *(Acct Exec)*
Kathleen Shurtz *(Acct Exec)*
Grace Williams *(Acct Exec)*

Accounts:
Adaptive Computing
Kenra Professional
New-Long John Silver's, LLC (Social Media Agency of Record)
MokaFive
Solavei LLC
TinderBox

BLH CONSULTING
502 Pryor St Ste 301, Atlanta, GA 30312-2767
Tel.: (404) 688-0415
Fax: (404) 688-1425
Web Site: www.blhconsulting.net

E-Mail for Key Personnel:
President: betsy@blhconsulting.net

Year Founded: 2002

National Agency Associations: PRSA

Agency Specializes In: African-American Market, Bilingual Market, Business-To-Business, Communications, Event Planning & Marketing, Exhibit/Trade Shows, Graphic Design, Hispanic Market, Multimedia, Public Relations, Publicity/Promotions, Strategic Planning/Research

Approx. Annual Billings: $500,000

Betsy L. Helgager Hughes *(Pres & CEO)*
Ashish Mistry *(Mng Partner)*
George M. Hughes, Jr. *(COO)*
Kathy Cahill *(Dir-Creative)*

Accounts:
Concessions International, LLC
GlaxoSmithKline
ING Financial Services
National CASA Association
National Foster Care Month

BLICK & STAFF COMMUNICATIONS
130 S Bemiston Ste 501, Saint Louis, MO 63105
Tel.: (314) 727-5700
Web Site: www.blickandstaff.com

Agency Specializes In: Event Planning & Marketing, Public Relations, Social Media

Harriet Blickenstaff *(Pres)*

Accounts:
Better Life
Brado Creative Insight
ZeaVision

BLINK PR
1150e E Hallandale Beach Blvd, Hallandale, FL 33009
Tel.: (305) 490-5911
Web Site: www.blinkpr.com

Agency Specializes In: Event Planning & Marketing, Media Training, Public Relations, Social Media

Katherine Fleischman *(Pres & CEO)*
Toni Taha *(Office Mgr)*

Accounts:
Callet
Cameo Nouveau
Dr. L, A Happy You
Femme Coiffure
Flipme
Jeffrey James Botanicals
Marissa Del Rosario PR
Out of Print
RUBR Watches
Swell Bottle

Branch

Blink PR
580 Broadway, New York, NY 10012
Tel.: (212) 966-8797
Web Site: www.blinkpr.com

Agency Specializes In: Event Planning & Marketing, Media Training, Public Relations, Social Media

Toni Taha *(Office Mgr)*

Accounts:
Ta-ta-toos

BLUE HERON COMMUNICATIONS
3260 Marshall Ave, Norman, OK 73072
Tel.: (405) 364-3433
Fax: (405) 364-5447
Toll Free: (800) 654-3766
E-Mail: info@blueheroncomm.com
Web Site: www.blueheroncomm.com

Year Founded: 1987

Agency Specializes In: Advertising, Corporate Communications, Outdoor, Public Relations, Social Media

Gary Giudice *(Pres)*
Ron Giudice *(VP)*
Josh Ward *(Mgr-Creative & Acct Exec)*
Trisha Dodson *(Mgr-Traffic)*
Matt Rice *(Sr Acct Supvr)*
Greg Duncan *(Acct Exec)*
Jeff Puckett *(Acct Exec)*
Steve Wagner *(Acct Exec)*
Matt Pangrac *(Coord-Pro Staff Svcs)*

Accounts:
New-Abu Garcia
New-Benelli USA (Public Relations Agency of Record) A.Uberti, Benelli, Content, Events, Franchi, Media Relations, News, Promotions, Stoeger, Stoeger Airguns
New-Berkley
New-BLACKHAWK!
New-Boone and Crockett Club
New-DSC
New-National Hunting and Fishing Day
New-Ranger Boats
New-Smith & Wesson
New-Thompson/Center
Winchester Safes

BLUE WATER COMMUNICATIONS
435 12th St W, Bradenton, FL 34205
Tel.: (800) 975-3212
Fax: (941) 746-3731
E-Mail: info@bluewatercommunications.biz
Web Site: www.bluewatercommunications.biz

Agency Specializes In: Graphic Design, Internet/Web Design, Media Buying Services, Media Relations, Media Training, Public Relations, Social Media

Lynnette Werning *(Owner)*

Accounts:
The Perlman Music Program Suncoast

BLUEIVY COMMUNICATIONS
290 NE 5th Ave, Delray Beach, FL 33483
Tel.: (561) 310-9921
E-Mail: info@blueivycommunications.com
Web Site: www.blueivycommunications.com

Year Founded: 2011

Agency Specializes In: Communications, Content, Media Relations, Media Training, Public Relations, Social Media

Melissa Perlman *(Founder & Pres)*

Accounts:
Fit Food Express
PC Professor Computer Training & Repairs
Signature Veterinary Care

BLUEPOINT VENTURE MARKETING
17 Draper Rd, Wayland, MA 01778
Tel.: (508) 358-6371
Fax: (781) 861-7810
E-Mail: info@bluepointmktg.com
Web Site: www.bluepointmktg.com

Agency Specializes In: Advertising, Public Relations, Strategic Planning/Research

Alison Moore *(Owner)*
Rob Moore *(Principal)*

Accounts:
Dmailer
HCL Technologies
Ruckus
Sitecore

THE BLUESHIRT GROUP
456 Montgomery St 11th Fl, San Francisco, CA 94104
Tel.: (415) 217-7722
Fax: (415) 217-7721
Web Site: www.blueshirtgroup.com

Agency Specializes In: Crisis Communications, Investor Relations, Media Relations, Public Relations

Alex Wellins *(Co-Founder & Mng Dir)*
Chris Danne *(Mng Dir)*
Gary Dvorchak *(Mng Dir)*
Cynthia Hiponia *(Mng Dir)*
Peter Salkowski *(Mng Dir)*
Suzanne Schmidt *(Mng Dir)*
Shawn Severson *(Mng Dir-Energy, Environmental & Indus Technologies)*
Jeff Fox *(Dir)*
Kim Hughes *(Dir)*
Jennifer Jarman *(Dir)*
Melanie Solomon *(Dir-IR)*

Accounts:
Actions
Analogic Tech
Aruba Networks
Bigband Networks
BMC Select
Broadsoft
CafePress
Cogent Systems
DTS, Inc.
Fitbit Financial Communications, Investor Relations
Keek Inc Communications Strategy
Liquid Holdings Group, Inc. Investor Relations, Media Relations
Mitel
Move
Openwave Systems Inc. Investor Relations
Points International
ReachLocal, Inc. Investor Relations
Scientific Learning Corporation
ServiceSource International, Inc.
SMART Modular Technologies, Inc.
TeleNav, Inc.

Branch

The Blueshirt Group
230 Park Ave 10th Fl, New York, NY 10169
Tel.: (212) 551-1452
Web Site: www.blueshirtgroup.com

Monica Gould *(Mng Dir)*
Christine Greany *(Mng Dir)*
Brinlea Johnson *(Mng Dir)*
David Niederman *(Mng Dir)*
Jonathan Schaffer *(Mng Dir)*
Bob Jones *(Mng Dir-Health Care IR Practice)*

BLUETONE MARKETING & PUBLIC RELATIONS
999 Corporate Dr Ste 100, Ladera Ranch, CA 92694
Tel.: (619) 807-6349
E-Mail: info@bluetonemarketing.com
Web Site: www.bluetonemarketing.com

Agency Specializes In: Broadcast, Collateral, Logo & Package Design, Media Relations, Print, Public Relations, Radio, Social Media, Strategic Planning/Research

Jonathan Abramson *(Pres)*
Susy Sellers *(Dir-Bus Dev)*
Ken Coleman *(Copywriter)*

Accounts:
Beforeplay.org
Free Wheelchair Mission
MSHIPCO
Petite My Sweets
Rebecca's House
SprinkleBit

BML PUBLIC RELATIONS
356 Bloomfield Ave Ste 2, Montclair, NJ 7042
Tel.: (973) 337-6395
E-Mail: info@bmlpr.com
Web Site: www.bmlpr.com

Agency Specializes In: Brand Development & Integration, Crisis Communications, Exhibit/Trade Shows, Media Relations, Public Relations, Social Media

Brian M. Lowe *(Pres & CEO)*
Katherine Baldasarre *(Acct Exec)*

Accounts:
New-Wayback Burgers

BOARDROOM COMMUNICATIONS INC.
1776 N Pine Island Rd Ste 320, Fort Lauderdale, FL 33322
Tel.: (954) 370-8999
Fax: (954) 370-8892
E-Mail: bci@boardroompr.com
Web Site: www.boardroompr.com

Employees: 20

Agency Specializes In: Public Relations

Julie Silver Talenfeld *(Pres)*
Don Silver *(COO)*
Todd Templin *(Exec VP)*
Caren Berg *(VP)*
Jennifer Clarin *(VP)*
Michelle Friedman *(Acct Dir)*
Yarden Cohen *(Dir-Social Media)*
Sandy Gans *(Dir-Creative Svcs)*
Laura Burns *(Specialist-PR & Crisis Comm)*

Accounts:
New-Bijou Bay Harbor (Public Relations Agency of Record) Media Relations, Social Media
Florida Medical Center
New-Minto Communities (Public Relations Agency of Record) Media Relations
New-SRF Ventures (Public Relations Agency of Record) Media Relations

Branch

Boardroom Communication Inc.
601 Brickell Key Dr Ste 700, Miami, FL 33131
Tel.: (786) 453-8061
Web Site: www.boardroompr.com

Agency Specializes In: Advertising, Brand Development & Integration, Crisis Communications, Media Relations, Media Training, Public Relations, Social Media

Julie Silver Talenfeld *(Founder & Pres)*

Accounts:
New-Marina Palms Yacht Club & Residences

BOB GOLD & ASSOCIATES
(d/b/a B G & A)
1640 S Pacific Coast Hwy, Redondo Beach, CA 90277
Tel.: (310) 320-2010
E-Mail: admin@bobgoldpr.com
Web Site: www.bobgoldpr.com

Employees: 15

Agency Specializes In: Brand Development & Integration, Corporate Communications, Crisis Communications, Direct Response Marketing, Exhibit/Trade Shows, Industrial, Local Marketing, Market Research, Media Relations, Media Training, New Product Development, Promotions, Public Relations, Sponsorship, Strategic Planning/Research

Bob Gold *(Founder, Pres & CEO)*
Chris Huppertz *(Acct Exec)*
Christina Doan *(Assoc Acct Exec)*

Accounts:
beIN SPORT
Channel Master
Clearleap Communication Strategies
Envivio Global Communications
Long Beach Grand Cru Public Relations
Penthera
Residents Medical Communications
SEMrush Communications
New-Skypicker Public Relations
New-South Coast Botanic Garden Nature Connects, Publicity
Telit Wireless Solutions, Inc. Global PR, Marketing, Media Relations, Social Media
Toberman Neighborhood Center Kobe and Vanessa Bryant, Publicity
New-TVGear Public Relations
Viamedia (Agency Of Record) Public Relations
New-ZeeVee, Inc. (Global Agency of Record) Public Relations

BODENPR
7791 NW 46th St Ste 304, Miami, FL 33166
Tel.: (305) 639-6770
Fax: (866) 334-0145
Web Site: www.bodenpr.com

Year Founded: 2005

Agency Specializes In: Digital/Interactive, Event Planning & Marketing, Graphic Design, Media Relations, Media Training, Public Relations, Social Media

Natalie Boden *(Founder & Mng Dir)*
Valerie Barbosa *(Acct Dir)*
Natalie Asorey *(Dir-Millennial Content & Res)*
Mariam Melul *(Sr Mgr-Social Media)*
Megh McArthur *(Mgr-Digital Mktg)*
Lauren Gongora *(Acct Supvr)*
Alejandra Serna *(Sr Acct Exec)*
Frances Ramos *(Acct Exec)*

Accounts:
New-Delta Dental
New-Jarden Consumer Solutions (Latin America Agency of Record) Bionaire, Content Marketing, Influencer Relations, Oster, Oster Beauty, Public Relations
New-McDonald's
New-PepsiCo
Target

BOETTCHER COMMUNICATIONS
242 Michigan St Ste 301, Sturgeon Bay, WI 54235
Tel.: (920) 818-0377
Fax: (920) 818-0378
E-Mail: info@boettchercommunications.com
Web Site: www.boettchercommunications.com

Agency Specializes In: Graphic Design, Internet/Web Design, Logo & Package Design, Media Relations, Print, Public Relations, Radio, Social Media, T.V.

Mark Summerfield *(Pres)*
Ashley Richmond *(Dir-Social Media)*

Accounts:
Tea Thyme

THE BOHLE COMPANY
2030 N Beverly Glen, Los Angeles, CA 90077
Tel.: (424) 248-0512
Fax: (310) 277-2066
Web Site: www.bohle.com/

E-Mail for Key Personnel:
President: sue@bohle.com

Employees: 12
Year Founded: 1987

National Agency Associations: PRSA

Agency Specializes In: Children's Market, Consumer Goods, Consumer Marketing, Crisis Communications, E-Commerce, Electronics, Guerilla Marketing, High Technology, Media Relations, Media Training

Approx. Annual Billings: $1,000,000

Breakdown of Gross Billings by Media: Pub. Rels.: 100%

Sue Bohle *(CEO)*
Derek Asato *(VP)*

Accounts:
Caesar Golf; Beverly Hills, CA Golf Class and Equipment; 2006
East Coast Game Conference
First5 Games
Gen Audio Audio Technology; 2011
Grand Metropolitan; Beverly Hills, CA Luxury Products; 2006
IndieCADE
Indiecade Festival
LB Games Christian Based Games; 2005
Penny Arcade; Seattle WA PAX Expos
Resolution Economics; Beverly Hills, CA Research; 2011
Snuff Mill
Spacetime Studios; Austin, Texas Mobile Games; 2009
Stelulu Technologies
Stompy Bot Productions
Zing Games

BOHLSENPR INC.
201 S Capitol Ave Ste 800, Indianapolis, IN 46225-1092

Tel.: (317) 602-7137
Fax: (317) 536-3775
E-Mail: info@bohlsengroup.com
Web Site: bohlsengroup.com/

Agency Specializes In: Public Relations

Vicki Bohlsen *(Owner & CEO)*
Andrew Hayenga *(VP-Nonprofit & Corp)*
Andy Wilson *(VP-Events & Entertainment Div)*
Mandy Bray *(Dir-Copywriting)*
Terry Million *(Dir-Creative & Art)*
Kerry Barmann *(Acct Supvr)*
Lauren Cascio *(Acct Exec & Strategist-Ops)*
Marc Backofen *(Assoc Media Buyer)*
Courtney Alvey *(Acct Coord)*
Muriel Cross *(Acct Coord)*
Heidi Harmon *(Acct Coord)*

Accounts:
Author Solutions Inc.
Authorhive
Center on Philanthropy at Indiana University
Christiana Care
The Hoosier Environmental Council
Indianapolis Opera Media Relations, Public Relations, Publicity
iUniverse
Rainbow's End
Rib America Festival
SAVI
Spirit & Place Festival
The Timmy Foundation
The Vogue

BOLLARE
8935 Beverly Blvd, Los Angeles, CA 90048
Tel.: (310) 246-0983
E-Mail: info@bollare.com
Web Site: www.bollare.com

Agency Specializes In: Brand Development & Integration, Digital/Interactive, Public Relations

Sara Flores *(VP)*
Kassidy Babcock *(Dir-Brand Strategy)*
Niki Bonjoukian *(Acct Mgr)*

Accounts:
New-Smythe Inc

BOLT PUBLIC RELATIONS
9731 Irvine Ctr Dr, Irvine, CA 92618
Tel.: (949) 218-5454
Web Site: www.boltpr.com

Agency Specializes In: Advertising, Collateral, Crisis Communications, Digital/Interactive, Email, Event Planning & Marketing, Public Relations, Social Media

Brent Callaway *(Owner)*
Jo-anne Chase *(VP)*
Jennifer Staats *(Office Mgr)*
Nicole Kypraios *(Acct Exec)*
Lindsay Miller *(Acct Exec)*
Danielle Solich *(Acct Exec)*
Elizabeth Titchener *(Acct Exec)*
Shannon White *(Acct Exec)*
Anakaren Cardenas *(Asst Acct Exec)*
Alexa Steevens *(Asst Acct Exec)*
Rachael Morrison *(Acct Coord)*

Accounts:
Spicy City
Tamarind
TriDerma

Branch

Bolt Public Relations
115 S St Marys St Ste C, Raleigh, NC 27603
(See Separate Listing)

BOND PUBLIC RELATIONS & BRAND STRATEGY
1104 6th St, New Orleans, LA 70115
Tel.: (504) 897-0462
Fax: (504) 897-0748
Web Site: www.bondpublicrelations.com

Year Founded: 2004

Agency Specializes In: Advertising, Brand Development & Integration, Content, Crisis Communications, Event Planning & Marketing, Media Relations, Public Relations, Social Media, Strategic Planning/Research

Jennifer Bond *(Partner)*
Skipper Bond *(Partner)*
Jordan Friedman *(Partner)*
Suzette Lake *(Mgr-Social Media)*
Ryan Evans *(Acct Supvr)*
Emily Reimsnyder *(Sr Acct Exec)*
Hannah Topping *(Sr Acct Exec)*
Andrew Freeman *(Acct Exec)*
Abhi Bhansali *(Mng Supvr)*

Accounts:
Arana Taqueria y Cantina
Cafe Hope
Hard Rock Cafe Foundation, Inc.
The Hotel Modern
Imoto Real Estate Photography
LiveAnswer
Paradigm Investment Group
Saddles Blazin
West Elm

BONEAU/BRYAN-BROWN
1501 Broadway Ste 1314, New York, NY 10036
Tel.: (212) 575-3030
Web Site: www.boneaubryanbrown.com

Agency Specializes In: Media Training, Public Relations

Jim Byk *(VP)*
Michelle Farabaugh *(Acct Exec)*

Accounts:
New-Amazing Grace Musical

BOOK PUBLICITY SERVICES
24772 Largo Dr, Laguna Hills, CA 92653
Tel.: (805) 807-9027
Web Site: bookpublicityservices.com

Year Founded: 2013

Agency Specializes In: Broadcast, Magazines, Newspaper, Newspapers & Magazines, Print, Promotions, Radio, Social Media, T.V.

Kelsey McBride *(Publicist)*

Accounts:
Bennett Jacobstein "The Joy of Ballpark Food"
Iain Reading "Kitty Hawk and the Curse of the Yukon Gold"
Lola Smirnova "Twisted"

BOTTOM LINE MARKETING & PUBLIC RELATIONS
600 W Virginia St Ste 100, Milwaukee, WI 53204
Tel.: (414) 270-3000
Web Site: www.blmpr.com

Agency Specializes In: Brand Development & Integration, Crisis Communications, Government/Political, Media Relations, Media Training, Public Relations, Social Media

Jeffrey Remsik *(Pres & CEO)*

Accounts:
New-Health Payment Systems Inc.

BOXCAR PR
2906 Eastpoint Pkwy, Louisville, KY 40223
Tel.: (502) 805-2006
E-Mail: contact@boxcarpr.com
Web Site: www.boxcarpr.com

Agency Specializes In: Advertising, Crisis Communications, Event Planning & Marketing, Graphic Design, Internet/Web Design, Media Buying Services, Public Relations, Social Media

Bob Gunnell *(Owner)*

Accounts:
New-Bionic Gloves (Public Relations Agency of Record) Corporate Communications, Media Relations
Blue Equity, LLC
Churchill Downs, Inc.
Dr. Mark Lynn & Associates
J Wagner Group
Louisville Marriott Downtown
Miller Transportation
The Salvation Army
The Voice Tribune
Wehr Constructors Inc
Whiskey Row

BR PUBLIC RELATIONS
144 E 84th St Ste 7G, New York, NY 10028
Tel.: (212) 249-5125
Web Site: www.brpublicrelations.com

Agency Specializes In: Brand Development & Integration, Consumer Goods, Corporate Communications, Crisis Communications, Media Training, Public Relations, Social Media

Diane Blackman *(Principal)*

Accounts:
Diner en Blanc - New York
Igudesman & Joo
Revolution Movie

BRACY TUCKER BROWN & VALANZANO
1615 L St NW Ste 520, Washington, DC 20036-5608
Tel.: (202) 429-8855
Fax: (202) 429-8857
E-Mail: mbracy@btbv.com
Web Site: www.btbv.com

Employees: 15
Year Founded: 1982

Agency Specializes In: Aviation & Aerospace, Consulting, Environmental, Government/Political, Transportation

Approx. Annual Billings: $2,500,000

Michael M. Bracy *(Owner)*
Anthony Valanzano *(Partner)*
Tracy P. Tucker *(VP)*
Terrence L. Bracy *(Sr Partner)*

Accounts:
Chrysler Corp.
City of Saint Louis; MO
City of Tucson; AZ
Colorado River Regional Sewer Coalition

Fort Worth Transportation Authority
Future of Music Coalition
Mental Health Connection of Tarrant County
Webster University

THE BRADFORD GROUP

2115 Yeaman Pl Ste 210, Nashville, TN 37206
Tel.: (615) 515-4888
Fax: (615) 515-4889
E-Mail: info@bradfordgroup.com
Web Site: www.bradfordgroup.com

Agency Specializes In: Brand Development & Integration, Event Planning & Marketing, Media Relations, Media Training, Public Relations, Social Media, Strategic Planning/Research

Jeff Bradford *(Pres & CEO)*
Gina Gallup *(COO & VP)*
Brooke Berger *(Dir-Strategy & Sr Acct Exec)*
Melinda Dale *(Sr Acct Exec)*
Molly Garvey *(Sr Acct Exec)*
Samantha Prichard *(Sr Acct Exec)*
Meredith Yates *(Sr Acct Exec)*
Sarah Castille *(Acct Exec)*
Caitlin Davis *(Davis)*
Avery Driggers *(Acct Exec)*
Paula Jones *(Acct Exec)*

Accounts:
New-Medalogix

BRAFF COMMUNICATIONS LLC

PO Box 500, Fair Lawn, NJ 07410
Tel.: (201) 612-0707
Fax: (201) 612-0760
E-Mail: mbraff@braffcommunications.com
Web Site: www.braffcommunications.com

Employees: 2
Year Founded: 1993

Agency Specializes In: Business-To-Business, Media Relations, Public Relations, Publicity/Promotions

Mark Braff *(Founder)*

Accounts:
ABC Family
Balihoo
Cason Nightingale
Channel One News
College Television Network
Enversa
Hallmark Channel
Interep
Mondo Media
Regional News Network
Sheridan Broadcasting
Turner Broadcasting
Wizzard Media

BRAITHWAITE COMMUNICATIONS

1500 Walnut St 18th Fl, Philadelphia, PA 19102-3509
Tel.: (215) 564-3200
Fax: (215) 564-3455
E-Mail: info@gobraithwaite.com
Web Site: www.gobraithwaite.com

Employees: 18
Year Founded: 1996

Agency Specializes In: Advertising, Brand Development & Integration, Crisis Communications, Digital/Interactive, Market Research, Media Planning, Media Training

Hugh Braithwaite *(Founder & Pres)*
Jason Rocker *(Principal)*
Alex Dalgliesh *(Assoc VP)*
Sarah Promisloff *(Assoc VP)*
Shelly Orlacchio *(Acct Supvr)*
Steve Wanczyk *(Acct Supvr)*
Lee Procida *(Sr Acct Exec)*
Andrew Africk *(Acct Exec)*
Heather Robertson *(Coord-Office Svcs)*
Lisa Suszek *(Jr Designer)*

Accounts:
Glenmede Trust Company
SEI

BRANDRENEW PR

121 Monument Cir Ste 523, Indianapolis, IN 46204
Tel.: (317) 440-1898
E-Mail: info@brandrenewpr.com
Web Site: www.brandrenewpr.com

Agency Specializes In: Brand Development & Integration, Event Planning & Marketing, Graphic Design, Media Relations, Print, Public Relations

Cris Dorman *(Founder & Principal)*

Accounts:
New-The Columbia Club
New-Hotel Tango Artisan Distillery

BRANDSTYLE COMMUNICATIONS

14 E 60th St Ste 407, New York, NY 10022
Tel.: (212) 794-0060
E-Mail: info@brandstylecommunications.com
Web Site: www.brandstyle.com

Agency Specializes In: Event Planning & Marketing, Media Relations, Public Relations, Sponsorship

Zoe Weisberg Coady *(Founder & CEO)*
Victoria Hood *(Sr Acct Exec)*
Sarah Markowitz *(Acct Exec)*

Accounts:
New-CEP
New-Cobram Estate Olive Oil
New-Dr. Armando Hernandez-Rey
New-Eloquii
New-Fashion to Figure
New-Handsome Brook Farm
Magnises
Quad Jobs
New-Quiet Logistics

BRANDWARE PUBLIC RELATIONS

8399 Dunwoody Place Bldg 6 Ste 200, Atlanta, GA 30350-3302
Tel.: (707) 649-0880
Fax: (707) 649-0820
Web Site: www.brandwarepr.com

Year Founded: 2000

Agency Specializes In: Communications, Content, Digital/Interactive, Event Planning & Marketing, Media Relations, Public Relations, Social Media

Elke Martin *(Pres)*
Tom Crumlish *(VP-Ops)*
Keith Osbon *(VP)*
Kristie Schutz *(Dir-Ops)*
Bill Soule *(Dir-Bus Dev)*

Accounts:
AAP3 Public Relations
New-Bandago Van Rentals (Public Relations Agency of Record) Media Communications
Cantor, Dolce and Panepinto Law; Buffalo, NY Content Development, Digital Asset, Marketing Communications, Measurement/Analytics, PR, Social & Digital Media Campaign
DealerRater.com
Elco Motor Yachts Public & Media Relations
Falken Tire Corp. (Public Relations Agency of Record) Business-to-Business Communications, Content, Media Relations, Strategic, Thought Leadership
G2G Collection Public Relations
Johnny Pag Motorcycles
Lexol Leather Care Communication, Media Relations, Product Introductions, Public Relations Agency of Record, Social Content
Mighty Auto Parts PR
Morris Yachts Media, PR
MyAssist
Okabashi Public Relations
New-Pellisari LLC (Public Relations Agency of Record) Consumer Marketing, Media Strategy, Public Relations, ZEMI Aria
RKM Collector Car Auctions
Sonic Tools USA (Public Relations Agency of Record) B2B Content Marketing, Consumer, Media Strategy

BRAVE PUBLIC RELATIONS

1718 Peachtree St Ste 999, Atlanta, GA 30309
Tel.: (404) 233-3993
Fax: (404) 260-4318
E-Mail: info@bravepublicrelations.com
Web Site: www.bravepublicrelations.com

Year Founded: 1999

Agency Specializes In: Crisis Communications, Media Relations, Public Relations, Social Media

Kristin Cowart *(Founder & CEO)*
Jennifer Walker *(Mng Dir)*
Lara Bronstein *(Office Mgr & Acct Coord)*
Ann Bates *(Acct Exec)*
Shannon King *(Acct Exec)*
Kellie Rehn *(Jr Acct Exec)*

Accounts:
Aurora Theater (Agency of Record)
Calhoun Premium Outlets
Center for Puppetry Arts (Agency of Record)
The Children's Museum of Atlanta (Agency of Record)
The Fresh Market
LEGOLAND Discovery Center Atlanta (Agency of Record)
MedZed (Agency of Record) At-Home Pediatric Care
North Georgia Premium Outlets
Orangetheory Fitness
Room & Board
Taste of Atlanta

BRAVO GROUP INC.

20 N Market Sq Ste 800, Harrisburg, PA 17101
Tel.: (717) 214-2200
Web Site: www.bravogroup.us

Agency Specializes In: Brand Development & Integration, Crisis Communications, Digital/Interactive, Media Buying Services, Media Relations, Outdoor, Print, Public Relations, Strategic Planning/Research

Chris Bravacos *(Pres & CEO)*
Dennis Walsh *(Pres-Govt Rels)*
Megan Madsen *(Mng Dir)*
Rhett Hintze *(COO)*
Sean Connolly *(Sr Dir)*
Megan Dapp *(Sr Dir)*
Jerry King Musser *(Creative Dir)*
Steven Kratz *(Sr Acct Exec)*
Megan Earley *(Acct Exec)*

Accounts:
DOW Chemical
Sunoco Inc

BREAD AND BUTTER PUBLIC RELATIONS
2404 Wilshire Blvd Ste 6A, Los Angeles, CA 90057
Tel.: (213) 739-7985
Web Site: www.breadandbutterpr.com

Agency Specializes In: Media Relations, Media Training, Promotions, Public Relations

Rachel Mays Ayotte *(Pres)*

Accounts:
New-Gelato Messina
New-Hopdoddy

BREAKAWAY COMMUNICATIONS LLC
381 Park Ave S Ste 1216, New York, NY 10016-8806
Tel.: (212) 616-6010
Fax: (212) 457-1144
E-Mail: info@breakawaycom.com
Web Site: www.breakawaycom.com

Employees: 5
Year Founded: 2002

Agency Specializes In: Business-To-Business, Consumer Marketing, Corporate Communications, High Technology, Information Technology, Public Relations

Kelly Fitzgerald *(Co-Founder & Mng Partner)*
Barbara Hagin *(Mng Partner-San Francisco)*
Pamela F. Preston *(Mng Partner-New York)*
Jim Katz *(Principal)*
Tracey Sheehy *(VP)*
Cait Hagaman *(Mgr-PR)*
Constance Rose-Edwards *(Sr Acct Exec)*
Stacey Paris-Bechtel *(Specialist-Media Rels)*
Amanda Scaccianoce *(Acct Exec)*
Cameron Deordio *(Acct Coord)*
Jenna Finkelstein *(Acct Coord)*

Accounts:
Alcatel-Lucent
Aruba Networks
Gartner
Info Print Solutions Company
Intel
Paglo

Branch

Breakaway Communications LLC
300 Broadway, San Francisco, CA 94133
Tel.: (415) 358-2480
Fax: (415) 357-9887
E-Mail: info@breakawaycom.com
Web Site: www.breakawaycom.com

Employees: 16

Agency Specializes In: Public Relations

Barbara Hagin *(Mng Partner)*
Patty Oien *(VP)*
Stephannie Depa *(Sr Acct Exec)*
Ariana Kalff *(Assoc Acct Exec)*

Accounts:
Aruba Networks
NDS Group

BRENDY BARR COMMUNICATIONS LLC
144 Knorrwood Ct, Oakland Township, MI 48306
Tel.: (248) 651-4858
Fax: (248) 651-4868
E-Mail: brendy@barrcommunications.com
Web Site: www.barrcommunications.com

Year Founded: 1999

Agency Specializes In: Arts, Broadcast, Business Publications, Business-To-Business, Cable T.V., Communications, Consulting, Consumer Goods, Consumer Marketing, Consumer Publications, Corporate Communications, Corporate Identity, Crisis Communications, E-Commerce, Electronic Media, Electronics, Entertainment, Event Planning & Marketing, Exhibit/Trade Shows, Experience Design, Health Care Services, Hospitality, Internet/Web Design, Legal Services, Leisure, Local Marketing, Magazines, Media Relations, Media Training, Newspaper, Newspapers & Magazines, Planning & Consultation, Podcasting, Print, Promotions, Public Relations, Publicity/Promotions, Radio, Restaurant, Retail, Sales Promotion, Social Marketing/Nonprofit, Social Media, Strategic Planning/Research, T.V., Trade & Consumer Magazines, Travel & Tourism, Web (Banner Ads, Pop-ups, etc.), Women's Market

Brendy Barr *(Pres)*

Accounts:
7-Eleven, Inc.; Dallas, TX
Best Buy
Chevrolet
Cold Stone Creamery
The Fisher Theatre; Detroit, MI
Iams Pet Food
Krispy Kreme Doughnuts
Laura's Bridal Collection
Luvs Diapers
Marriott International Inc.; Washington, DC
MJR Digital Cinemas; Oak Park, MI
SolidSignal.com; Novi, MI
Wal-Mart

BRENER, ZWIKEL & ASSOCIATES, INC.
(Private-Parent-Single Location)
6901 Canby Ave Ste 105, Reseda, CA 91335
Tel.: (818) 344-6195
Fax: (818) 344-1714
Web Site: www.bzapr.com

Employees: 19
Year Founded: 1991

Agency Specializes In: Media Relations, Media Training, Promotions, Public Relations, Social Media, Strategic Planning/Research

Revenue: $2,000,000

Steve Brener *(Pres)*
Toby Zwikel *(VP)*
Susie Levine *(Office Mgr)*
Dana Gordon *(Sr Acct Exec)*
Brian Robin *(Sr Acct Exec)*
Greg Ball *(Acct Exec)*
John Beyrooty *(Acct Exec)*
Matt Donovan *(Acct Exec)*
Liz McCollum *(Acct Exec)*
Steve Pratt *(Acct Exec)*
Damian Secore *(Acct Exec)*

Accounts:
Auto Club Speedway
The Barclays
Beau Rivage
College Football Awards Show
Deutsche Bank Championship
FX Network
Humana Challenge
IndyCar
Kia Classic
Longines
Los Angeles Dodgers
LPGA
Mackie Shilstone
MGM Resorts International
MLB Urban Youth Academy
NFL
NHL
Ojai Valley Tennis Tournament
Omega
Professional Baseball Scouts Foundation
Ricoh Women's British Open
Rose Bowl
Santa Anita Race Track
SCP Auctions
Showtime Sports
Speedo
Time Inc.
United States Tennis Association

BRG COMMUNICATIONS
110 S Union St Ste 300, Alexandria, VA 22314
Tel.: (703) 739-8350
Fax: (703) 739-8340
E-Mail: info@brgcommunications.com
Web Site: www.brgcommunications.com

Year Founded: 2001

Agency Specializes In: Brand Development & Integration, Media Relations, Public Relations, Social Media, Strategic Planning/Research

Jane Barwis *(Pres & CEO)*
Shannon McDaniel *(Sr VP)*
Laurie Mobley *(Sr VP)*
Jennifer Mitchell *(Dir-Social Media)*
Allison Kassel *(Sr Acct Mgr)*
Maureen Salazar *(Acct Mgr)*
Chrissy Sparrow *(Acct Coord)*
Meghan Amoroso *(Assoc Acct Dir)*

Accounts:
Heart Rhythm Society

BRIAN COMMUNICATIONS
40 Morris Ave Ste 300, Bryn Mawr, PA 19010
Tel.: (484) 385-2900
Fax: (484) 385-2901
E-Mail: info@briantierney.com
Web Site: www.briancom.com

Agency Specializes In: Crisis Communications, Event Planning & Marketing, Media Relations, Public Relations, Social Media, Strategic Planning/Research

Matt Broscious *(Exec VP)*
Ed Mahlman *(Exec VP)*
Scott Hoeflich *(Sr VP)*
Michelle Hunt *(VP)*
Meg Kane *(VP)*
Deborah Massa *(VP)*
Frank Neil *(VP-Content Mktg)*
Aimee Tysarczyk *(VP)*
Tom Lazaunikas *(Exec Creative Dir)*
Jennifer Zandier *(Sr Acct Supvr-Integrated Comm)*
Rachael Harleman *(Acct Supvr)*
John K. Strain *(Acct Supvr)*
Carly Buggy *(Acct Exec)*
Anthony Mallamaci *(Acct Exec-PR)*

Accounts:
Archdiocese of Philadelphia

BRICKELL & PARTNERS PUBLIC RELATIONS
484 Viking Dr Ste 151, Virginia Beach, VA 23452
Tel.: (757) 463-4500
Fax: (757) 498-5948
E-Mail: sean@brickellpr.com
Web Site: www.brickellpr.com

E-Mail for Key Personnel:

President: sean@brickellpr.com

Employees: 3
Year Founded: 1985

Agency Specializes In: Public Relations

Sean Brickell *(Owner)*

Accounts:
Cellar Door
Hampton Roads Automobile Dealers Association
Norfolk Tides
The Worldcom Group

BRICKHOUSE PUBLIC RELATIONS
PO Box 2042, Palm Beach, FL 33480
Tel.: (561) 320-2030
E-Mail: info@brickhousepr.com
Web Site: www.brickhousepr.com

Year Founded: 2011

Agency Specializes In: Brand Development & Integration, Event Planning & Marketing, Media Relations, Public Relations, Social Media, Strategic Planning/Research

David Sabin *(Pres)*
Carli Brinkman *(Mng Dir)*

Accounts:
Del Friscos Restaurant Group Inc

BRIDGE GLOBAL STRATEGIES LLC
16 W 36th St Ste 1002, New York, NY 10018
Tel.: (212) 583-1043
Fax: (212) 967-1311
E-Mail: lsiegel@bridgeny.com
Web Site: www.bridgeny.com

Employees: 4

National Agency Associations: PRSA

Agency Specializes In: Affluent Market, Below-the-Line, Broadcast, Business Publications, Business-To-Business, Cable T.V., Children's Market, Collateral, College, Communications, Computers & Software, Consulting, Consumer Goods, Consumer Marketing, Consumer Publications, Content, Corporate Communications, Crisis Communications, E-Commerce, Education, Electronics, Environmental, Event Planning & Marketing, Exhibit/Trade Shows, Financial, Food Service, Government/Political, Health Care Services, High Technology, Hospitality, Household Goods, Information Technology, Integrated Marketing, International, Legal Services, Leisure, Local Marketing, Luxury Products, Magazines, Media Relations, Media Training, Medical Products, Multicultural, New Technologies, Newspaper, Newspapers & Magazines, Pharmaceutical, Planning & Consultation, Promotions, Public Relations, Publicity/Promotions, Radio, Sales Promotion, Social Marketing/Nonprofit, Social Media, Travel & Tourism, Urban Market, Viral/Buzz/Word of Mouth, Women's Market

Approx. Annual Billings: $650,000

Breakdown of Gross Billings by Media: Pub. Rels.: $650,000

Lucy B. Siegel *(Pres & CEO)*
Keiko Okano *(VP)*
Carinna Gano *(Acct Coord)*

Accounts:
AnGes MG; Tokyo, Japan Life Sciences; 2011
Guberman Garson; Toronto, Canada Legal Services; 2011
New York Pharma Forum
Nikko Hotels International; Tokyo, Japan Hospitality; 1997

BRIDGEMAN COMMUNICATIONS, INC.
85 Devonshire St 9th Fl, Boston, MA 02109
Tel.: (617) 742-7270
Fax: (617) 742-7548
E-Mail: info@bridgeman.com
Web Site: www.bridgeman.com

E-Mail for Key Personnel:
President: roger@bridgeman.com

Employees: 6
Year Founded: 1986

National Agency Associations: IPREX-PRSA

Agency Specializes In: Advertising, Business-To-Business, Computers & Software, Consumer Marketing, Corporate Communications, Crisis Communications, Direct Response Marketing, E-Commerce, Electronics, Engineering, Health Care Services, High Technology, Industrial, Information Technology, Integrated Marketing, Media Relations, Media Training, New Technologies, Pharmaceutical, Public Relations, Publicity/Promotions, Stakeholders, Technical Advertising, Viral/Buzz/Word of Mouth

Roger Bridgeman *(Pres)*

Accounts:
170 Systems
Agfa Compugraphic
Arthur Blank & Company; Boston, MA Retail & Loyalty Cards; 1996
Ecora
Galorath Technology
Global Grid Forum; Chicago, IL Grid Computing; 2005
HP Data Storage
KellySearch/Reed Business Info; Waltham, MA B2B Online Search Engine; 2003
Kodak Imaging Systems
Raytheon Defense Systems
Texas Instruments; Attleboro, MA; Dallas, TX Sensors & Controls, TI-RFid; 1987
Vasco Data Security
Xionics

BRIMMCOMM, INC.
1301 N Waukegan Rd Ste 103, Deerfield, IL 60015
Tel.: (847) 444-1198
Fax: (847) 444-1197
E-Mail: info@brimmcomm.com
Web Site: www.brimmcomm.com

Employees: 2
Year Founded: 1998

Agency Specializes In: Business-To-Business, Consumer Marketing, Corporate Communications, Direct-to-Consumer, Food Service, Health Care Services, Industrial, Local Marketing, Media Relations, Pharmaceutical, Public Relations, Publicity/Promotions, Retail, Women's Market

Approx. Annual Billings: $500,000

David Brimm *(Founder & Pres)*

Accounts:
Assisting Hands; Naperville, IL Home Care for Seniors; 2011
Charism; Westmont, IL Eldercare Services; 2011
Market Day; IL Food; 2007

BRISTOL PUBLIC RELATIONS, INC.
364 Sevilla Ave, Coral Gables, FL 33134
Tel.: (305) 447-6300
Fax: (888) 401-8878
E-Mail: info@bristolpr.com
Web Site: www.bristolpr.com

Agency Specializes In: Event Planning & Marketing, Media Relations, Promotions, Public Relations, Social Media

Eloise E. Rodriguez *(Pres)*
Rafael L. Rodriguez *(VP)*
Magali R. Abad *(Mgr-Internal Comm)*
Carol Crisafi *(Acct Exec)*
Juliana Cucalon *(Specialist-Mktg)*
Kimi Hurtado *(Acct Coord)*

Accounts:
CBT College
The Children's Trust Family Expo
The Children's Trust
Florida Center for Allergy & Asthma Care
Los Ranchos Steakhouse
Miami-Dade County Fair & Exposition, Inc.
Rasco Klock Perez Nieto

BRITT BANTER
40 Fulton St, New York, NY 10038
Tel.: (212) 797-0224
Web Site: www.brittbanter.com

Year Founded: 2007

Agency Specializes In: Content, Media Relations, Media Training, Public Relations, Social Media

Amy Britt *(Mng Partner)*

Accounts:
MOVIEQU (Agency of Record)
New York Independent Film Festival (Public Relations Agency of Record)

THE BRITTO AGENCY
234 W 56th St Penthouse, New York, NY 10019
Tel.: (212) 977-6772
Fax: (212) 977-4350
E-Mail: tba@thebrittoagency.com
Web Site: www.thebrittoagency.com

Employees: 10
Year Founded: 1995

Marvet Britto *(Pres)*

Accounts:
Ananda Lewis
Eve
Foxy Brown
Kim Cattrall
Mariah Carey

BROADREACH PUBLIC RELATIONS
19 Commercial St, Portland, ME 04101
Tel.: (207) 619-7350
Fax: (888) 251-4930
E-Mail: info@broadreachpr.com
Web Site: www.broadreachpr.com

Year Founded: 2006

Agency Specializes In: Advertising, Crisis Communications, Event Planning & Marketing, Media Relations, Media Training, Public Relations, Social Media, Strategic Planning/Research

Linda Varrell *(Pres)*
Dan DIppolito *(Mgr-Production)*
Jillian Kanter *(Acct Exec & Coord-Client Ops)*
Michael Geneseo *(Acct Exec)*
Nick Cormier *(Coord-Ops)*

Accounts:
Maine Savings (Agency of Record)

BRODEUR PARTNERS
399 Boylston St, Boston, MA 02116-2622
Tel.: (617) 587-2800
Fax: (617) 587-2828
E-Mail: info@brodeur.com
Web Site: www.brodeur.com

Year Founded: 1985

National Agency Associations: PRSA

Agency Specializes In: Brand Development & Integration, Business-To-Business, Communications, Consulting, Consumer Marketing, Corporate Communications, Corporate Identity, Digital/Interactive, E-Commerce, Electronic Media, Entertainment, Event Planning & Marketing, Government/Political, Health Care Services, High Technology, Information Technology, Internet/Web Design, Investor Relations, Local Marketing, Planning & Consultation, Public Relations, Publicity/Promotions, Sponsorship, Strategic Planning/Research, Trade & Consumer Magazines

John Brodeur *(Chm)*
Andrea Coville *(CEO)*
Andrew P. Beaupre *(Partner-Brodeur Strategies)*
Mike Brewer *(Partner)*
Renzo Bardetti *(CFO & COO)*
Judy Feder *(Exec VP & Gen Mgr)*
Jerry Johnson *(Exec VP-Strategic Plng)*
Steve Marchant *(Exec VP)*
Heather Shea *(Sr Acct Dir)*
Caroline Beers *(Acct Supvr)*
Cleve Langton *(Chief Partnership Officer)*

Accounts:
American Cancer Society
Avnet
Corning Incorporated
Dartmouth College
Dignity Health
Discovery Education
FM Global Public Relations
GE Digital Cameras
Hankook Tire
Harvard University
Hologic
Hughes
IBM
LSI Corp.; Milpitas, CA
Primarion, Inc.
Ricoh
Robert Wood Johnson Foundation
Sage
Thermo Fisher
United Nations Foundation

US Offices

Beaupre & Co. Public Relations Inc.
1 Harbour Pl Ste 230, Portsmouth, NH 03801-3837
Tel.: (603) 436-6690
Fax: (603) 436-8054
E-Mail: info@beaupre.com
Web Site: www.beaupre.com

E-Mail for Key Personnel:
President: abeaupre@beaupre.com

Employees: 20
Year Founded: 1983

Agency Specializes In: Public Relations

Andrew P. Beaupre *(Partner-Brodeur Strategies)*
Karen Beaupre *(Partner-Ops)*
Stephen Hodgdon *(Exec VP)*
Jeff Aubin *(VP)*
Kim Orso *(Dir-Speakers Bureau)*

Accounts:
AptSoft; Burlington, MA
Arrow Point Communications
Captivate Network
Cosmos; Los Angeles, CA
Ember; Boston, MA
Identrus
Ingram Micro
KANA
Navic
Oce Business Services
Oracle America, Inc.
Parlano
SolidWorks; Concord, MA
Stratus; Maynard, MA
WebCT
Z Corporation

Brodeur Partners
2201 E Camelback Rd Ste 515, Phoenix, AZ 85016-4771
Tel.: (480) 308-0300
Fax: (480) 308-0310
Web Site: www.brodeur.com

Employees: 4
Year Founded: 1985

Agency Specializes In: Public Relations

Sarah Marshall *(Sr VP-Southwest Reg)*
Jamie Cohen Ernst *(Sr Acct Dir)*
Michelle Dillon *(Acct Dir)*
Sara Errickson *(Acct Dir)*
Carrie Norton O'Neil *(Acct Dir)*
Kali Pickens *(Acct Exec)*
Mark Pozin *(Acct Exec)*
H. Beecher Dinapoli *(Acct Coord)*
Billy Moody *(Acct Coord)*
Molly O'Connor *(Acct Coord)*

Accounts:
Avenet, Inc. Avnet Electronics Marketing
Azzurri Technology Ltd
OnScreen; OR; 2007

Brodeur Partners
2101 L St NW, Washington, DC 20037
Tel.: (202) 350-3220
Fax: (202) 775-1801
Web Site: www.brodeur.com

Employees: 15
Year Founded: 1985

Agency Specializes In: Public Relations

Keith Lindenburg *(Exec VP & Gen Mgr-NY)*
Jim Larkin *(Head-Natl Media Rels)*
Jerry Johnson *(Grp Dir-Strategy)*
Michelle Dillon *(Acct Dir)*
Carrie Norton O'Neil *(Acct Dir)*
Billy Moody *(Acct Coord)*
Molly O'Connor *(Acct Coord)*

International Offices

Compass Porter Novelli
Diagonal 97 #17-60 Piso 3, Bogota, Colombia
Tel.: (57) 1 635 6074
Fax: (57) 1 255 0498
E-Mail: fernando.gastelbondo@compass.net.co
Web Site: www.porternovelli.com

Employees: 12
Year Founded: 1993

Agency Specializes In: Advertising, Brand Development & Integration, Business-To-Business, Communications, Crisis Communications, Digital/Interactive, Event Planning & Marketing, Financial, Food Service, Government/Political, Graphic Design, High Technology, Investor Relations, Media Relations, Media Training, New Product Development, Planning & Consultation, Public Relations, Publicity/Promotions, Sports Market, Teen Market

Fernando Gastelbondo *(Pres)*

EASTWEST Public Relations
77B Amoy Street, Singapore, 069896 Singapore
Tel.: (65) 6222 0306
Fax: (65) 6222 0124
E-Mail: pr@eastwestpr.com
Web Site: www.eastwestpr.com

Employees: 15

Melinda Ilagan *(Assoc Dir)*
Jim James *(Founder & Chm)*

Accounts:
Avnet Technology Solutions
East West
Hao2.eu Brand Positioning, Communications Strategies, Media Relations, Message Development, Social Media Communications
Lehman Brown
New-Sansan (Southeast Asia Public Relations Agency of Record) Communications Strategy

EBA Communications - Beijing
Room 909 SCITECH Tower No 22 Jian Guo Men, Wai Da Jie, Beijing, 100004 China
Tel.: (86) 10 6522 8081
Fax: (86) 10 6515 7201
Web Site: www.ebacomms.com/Markets/China

Employees: 20
Year Founded: 1995

Agency Specializes In: Public Relations

Qiong Ao *(Grp Acct Dir)*
Leona Liu *(Grp Acct Dir)*
Brian Paterson *(Dir)*
Lynn Hong *(Acct Mgr)*
Hellen Tan *(Mgr)*

Accounts:
Air Products
AMD
AUO
Avnet
CITRIX
Dow Corning
DYnet
Fujitsu
Gartner
Honeywell

EBA Communications Ltd
Unit B 19/F On Hing Bldg 1 On Hing Terrace, Central, China (Hong Kong)
Tel.: (852) 2537 8022
Fax: (852) 2537 3012
E-Mail: info@ebacomms.com
Web Site: www.ebacomms.com

Employees: 16
Year Founded: 1987

Agency Specializes In: Public Relations

Claudia Choi *(Mng Dir)*

Qiong Ao *(Grp Acct Dir)*
Leona Liu *(Grp Acct Dir)*
Lynn Hong *(Acct Mgr)*

Accounts:
Air Products
Avnet
Behr
Citrix Systems
CLP
Compuware
Datacraft Asia
ECA
Fuji Xerox
Gartner
HK Computer Society
Infor
Invista
Johnson Controls
Johnson Matthey
Microchip
NetApp
Oracle
Premiere Global Services
Radica
SAP
T9
Teradata
Tourism Australia
Tourism New South Wales
Tourism Victoria
Walton
Zetex

EBA Communications - Shanghai
Rm 1608 Shanghai CITS Bldg 1277 Beijing Rd W, Shanghai, 200040 China
Tel.: (86) 21 6289 3488
Fax: (86) 21 6289 5891
E-Mail: hellen.tan@ebacomms.com
Web Site: www.ebacomms.com

Year Founded: 1998

Agency Specializes In: Public Relations

Claudia Choi *(Mng Dir)*
Hellen Tan *(Gen Mgr)*
Angela Ao *(Grp Acct Dir)*
Qiong Ao *(Grp Acct Dir)*
Leona Liu *(Grp Acct Dir)*
Lynn Hong *(Acct Mgr)*

Accounts:
Air Products
Alexandermann Solutions
Austria Micro Systems
Behr
Jaybeam Limited
Cirrus Logic
Citrix
Datacraft
ECA International
Fujitsu

Lynx Porter Novelli AS
Bryggegata 5, 0250 Oslo, Norway
Tel.: (47) 23 13 14 80
Fax: (47) 23 13 14 81
E-Mail: lynx@lynx.no
Web Site: www.lynx.no

Employees: 9
Year Founded: 1985

Agency Specializes In: Consumer Marketing, Corporate Identity, Health Care Services, High Technology, Public Relations

Turid Viker Brathen *(Owner)*
Anne Finstadsveen *(Acct Mgr)*
Ragnhild Dohlen *(Client Dir)*
Lucie Meyer-Landrut *(Client Dir)*

Prisma Public Relations
Jl Padang No 18, Jakarta, 12970 Indonesia
Tel.: (62) 21 829 5454
Fax: (62) 829 3770
E-Mail: prismapr@prismapr.co.id
Web Site: www.prismapr.co.id

Employees: 30

Agency Specializes In: Public Relations

Rulita Anggraini *(Founder, Pres & Dir)*
Liza Marsin *(Sr Acct Mgr)*
Leyana Riesca *(Acct Supvr)*
Lintang Indah Juwita *(Acct Exec)*

Accounts:
Hitachi
WorldCom

Spark Communications
11/F One Pacific Pl, 140 Sukhumvit Road Klong Toey, Bangkok, 10110 Thailand
Tel.: (66) 2 653 2717
Fax: (66) 2 653 2725
E-Mail: tom@spark.co.th
Web Site: www.spark.co.th

Employees: 15

Tom Athey *(Owner)*

Accounts:
Emirates Airlines

Spot On Public Relations
PO Box 71578, Dubai, United Arab Emirates
Tel.: (971) 4 3491 686
Fax: (971) 4 3493 245
E-Mail: info@spotonpr.com
Web Site: www.spotonpr.com

Employees: 6

Agency Specializes In: Public Relations

Carrington Malin *(Mng Dir)*
Alexander McNabb *(Dir)*

Accounts:
IBM
Sony Corporation

Affiliate

Recognition Public Relations
Level 2 51 Pitt Street, Sydney, NSW 2000 Australia
Tel.: (61) 2 9252 2266
Fax: (61) 2 9252 7388
E-Mail: inforec@recognition.com.au
Web Site: www.recognition.com.au

Employees: 14

Agency Specializes In: Public Relations

Aye Verckens *(Gen Mgr)*
Adam Benson *(Dir)*
Elizabeth Marchant *(Dir)*

Accounts:
BEA Systems
BSA
BTAS
CommuniCorp Public Relations
Computer Associates
Eclipse
Fuji Xerox Australia
Mincom
UXC Eclipse PR

THE BROOKS GROUP
10 W 37th St 5th Fl, New York, NY 10018
Tel.: (212) 768-0860
Web Site: www.brookspr.com

Agency Specializes In: Event Planning & Marketing, Media Relations, Media Training, Promotions, Public Relations, Social Media

Rebecca Brooks *(Founder & Pres)*
Brianne Perea *(Sr VP)*

Accounts:
Cholula Hot Sauce
Dwell Studio
Willie Degel

BROTMAN WINTER FRIED COMMUNICATIONS
1651 Old Meadow Rd Ste 500, McLean, VA 22102
Tel.: (703) 748-0300
Fax: (703) 564-0101
E-Mail: wint@bwfcom.com
Web Site: bwfcom.com/

E-Mail for Key Personnel:
President: wint@bwfcom.com

Employees: 12
Year Founded: 1969

National Agency Associations: AD CLUB-PRSA

Agency Specializes In: Consumer Marketing, Entertainment, Sports Market

Approx. Annual Billings: $3,000,000

Breakdown of Gross Billings by Media: Event Mktg.: 10%; Print: 10%; Promos.: 20%; Pub. Rels.: 50%; Radio & T.V.: 10%

Charles J. Brotman *(Chm & CEO)*
Steve Winter *(Pres)*
Kenny Fried *(Partner)*
Brian Bishop *(VP)*
Kerry Lynn Bohen *(VP)*

Accounts:
Casa Noble Tequila
Crime & Punishment Museum
DC United Soccer; Herndon, VA Pro Soccer
Foremost Appliances
Mervis Diamond Importers
Montgomery County Department of Public Works; Rockville, MD
Mr. Wash Brushless Car Wash; Kensington, MD
Octagon
Potbelly Sandwich Works
U.S. Department of Agriculture
Virginia Athletic Trainer's Association
The Washington Design Center

BROWER MILLER & COLE
4199 Campus Dr Ste 550, Irvine, CA 92612
Tel.: (949) 509-6551
Fax: (949) 509-6574
E-Mail: jbrower@browermillercole.com
Web Site: www.browermillercole.com

E-Mail for Key Personnel:
President: jbrower@browermiller.com

Employees: 10
Year Founded: 1994

Agency Specializes In: Advertising, Brand

Development & Integration, Business-To-Business, Collateral, Commercial Photography, Communications, Consulting, Consumer Marketing, Corporate Communications, Corporate Identity, Direct Response Marketing, Electronic Media, Engineering, Entertainment, Environmental, Event Planning & Marketing, Exhibit/Trade Shows, Fashion/Apparel, Financial, Graphic Design, Local Marketing, Logo & Package Design, Media Buying Services, Out-of-Home Media, Print, Public Relations, Publicity/Promotions, Radio, Real Estate, Restaurant, Retail, Strategic Planning/Research, Travel & Tourism

Approx. Annual Billings: $1,000,000

Breakdown of Gross Billings by Media: Bus. Publs.: $100,000; Cable T.V.: $20,000; Corp. Communications: $100,000; Event Mktg.: $50,000; Exhibits/Trade Shows: $20,000; Graphic Design: $50,000; Newsp. & Mags.: $50,000; Pub. Rels.: $550,000; Radio: $20,000; Worldwide Web Sites: $40,000

Judith Brower Fancher *(Founder & CEO)*
Jenn Quader *(Mng Dir)*
Corynne Randel *(Sr Acct Exec)*
Alexis Astfalk *(Acct Exec)*

Accounts:
Blackband Design Marketing, Public Relations
Muldoon's Irish Pub; Newport Beach, CA Marketing Strategy, PR
Passco Companies Marketing, Public Relations, Website

BROWN PUBLIC RELATIONS LLC
PO Box 740448, New Orleans, LA 70174
Tel.: (769) 218-8577
Web Site: www.brown-pr.com

Year Founded: 2010

Agency Specializes In: Advertising, Collateral, Crisis Communications, Media Buying Services, Media Relations, Media Training, Public Relations, Radio, Social Media, Strategic Planning/Research

Eddie Brown *(Founder & CEO)*

Accounts:
Church of Christ Holiness USA
Dathan Thigpen
Families & Friends of Louisianas Incarcerated Children
State Education Agency

BROWN+DUTCH PUBLIC RELATIONS, INC.
PO Box 1193, Malibu, CA 90265
Tel.: (310) 456-7151
E-Mail: info@bdpr.com
Web Site: www.bdpr.com

Agency Specializes In: Crisis Communications, Event Planning & Marketing, Media Training, Promotions, Public Relations

Alyson Dutch *(Founder)*

Accounts:
MacroLife Naturals

BROWNSTONE PR
1315 Walnut St Ste 320, Philadelphia, PA 19107
Tel.: (215) 410-9879
Web Site: www.brownstonepr.com

Agency Specializes In: Media Relations, Media Training, Public Relations, Social Media

Megan R. Smith *(Founder & CEO)*
Elysse Ciccone *(Asst Acct Exec)*

Accounts:
National Urban League
PECO Energy Company
ResilienC

THE BRPR GROUP
4141 NE 2nd Ave Ste 203E, Miami, FL 33137
Tel.: (305) 573-1439
Web Site: www.brprgroup.com

Year Founded: 2008

Agency Specializes In: Brand Development & Integration, Digital/Interactive, Public Relations, Sponsorship

Christopher Renz *(Co-Founder)*

Accounts:
AdvancED
The Dream Defenders Bulletproof Vests, Campaign: "Vest or Vote"
Juvia Miami
Moet & Chandon USA
Vogue

BRUSTMAN CARRINO PUBLIC RELATIONS
4500 Biscayne Blvd Ste 204, Miami, FL 33137
Tel.: (305) 573-0658
Fax: (305) 573-7077
E-Mail: bcpr@brustmancarrinopr.com
Web Site: www.brustmancarrinopr.com

Employees: 12
Year Founded: 1985

Agency Specializes In: Arts, Entertainment, Event Planning & Marketing, Fashion/Apparel, Graphic Design, Hospitality, Public Relations, Publicity/Promotions, Real Estate, Retail, Travel & Tourism

Susan Brustman *(Founder)*
Larry Carrino *(Pres)*
Lauren Busch *(VP-Ops)*
Liz Hanes *(Dir-HR & Office Mgr)*
Kyrsten Cazas *(Acct Exec)*
Kristine McGlinchey *(Acct Exec)*
Carolina Navarro *(Acct Exec)*
Liz Rincon *(Acct Exec)*
Teresa Shum *(Acct Exec)*

Accounts:
BLT Steak
Blue Star Foods
Goldman Properties
The Hotel
Joey's Italian Cafe
Michael's Genuine Food & Drink
Whole Foods Market

BRYNN BAGOT PUBLIC RELATIONS, LLC
703 McKinney Ave Ste 412, Dallas, TX 75202
Tel.: (214) 528-5600
Fax: (214) 528-5616
Web Site: www.brynnbagot.com

Year Founded: 2001

Agency Specializes In: Advertising, Event Planning & Marketing, Media Planning, Media Relations, Media Training, Public Relations

Brynn Bagot Allday *(Pres)*
Mills Davis *(Acct Exec)*
Shelby Sabin *(Acct Exec)*
Elyse Scott *(Acct Exec)*

Accounts:
Adriana Hoyos
Chi Omega Christmas Market
The Dallas Zoological Society
The Family Place Partners Card
Fashionomics
Intellidex Solutions
Junior League of Dallas
MyForce Texas
Nest
The PilatesBarre
Rhonda Sargent Chambers RSC Show Productions
Scardello Artisan Cheese
Thanks-Giving Foundation

BUBBLEFISH MEDIA
118 Spring St 3rd Fl, New York, NY 10012
Tel.: (212) 941-6244
E-Mail: info@thebubblefish.com
Web Site: www.bubblefishmedia.com

Year Founded: 2008

Agency Specializes In: Brand Development & Integration, Event Planning & Marketing, Promotions, Public Relations, Social Media

Accounts:
Control Sector

BUCHANAN PUBLIC RELATIONS
700 Pont Reading Rd Ste 200, Ardmore, PA 19003
Tel.: (610) 649-9292
Fax: (610) 649-0457
E-Mail: info@buchananpr.com
Web Site: www.buchananpr.com

Employees: 8
Year Founded: 1998

Agency Specializes In: Advertising, Business-To-Business, Crisis Communications, Event Planning & Marketing, Graphic Design, Market Research, Media Relations, Public Relations, Strategic Planning/Research

Anne A. Buchanan *(Pres)*
Nancy Page *(Exec VP)*
Rachel Neppes *(VP & Co-Mgr-Digital Strategy)*
Nicole Lasorda *(Asst VP & Co-Mgr-Digital Strategy)*
Megan Keohane *(Acct Exec)*
Jennifer Tedeschi *(Acct Coord)*

Accounts:
Pepper Hamilton LLP
World Affairs Council of Philadelphia

BUCKLEY & KALDENBACH
3810 N Upland St, Arlington, VA 22207
Tel.: (703) 533-9805
Fax: (703) 533-9887
E-Mail: info@buckleykaldenbach.com
Web Site: www.buckleykaldenbach.com

Employees: 2

Robin Buckley *(Co-Founder)*

Accounts:
Intertrust Technologies

BUFFALO BRAND INVIGORATION GROUP
(Formerly Buffalo Communications)
8300 Boone Blvd Ste 350, Vienna, VA 22182

Tel.: (703) 761-1444
Fax: (703) 893-3504
Web Site: www.buffalobig.com/

Year Founded: 2001

Agency Specializes In: Brand Development & Integration, Media Relations, Public Relations, Social Media

Rich Katz *(Mng Dir)*
Tom Williams *(Sr VP)*
Shane Sharp *(VP)*
Dan Shepherd *(VP)*
Glenn Gray *(Dir-PR)*

Accounts:
BOYNE Golf Broadcast, Digital, Media Relations, Print, Public Relations
Branson/Lakes Area Convention and Visitors Bureau Branson/Lakes Area Golf, Public Relations
Canadian Rockies Golf Integrated Communications, PR, Social Media
Castle & Cooke Highgate at Seven Oaks, Media, Public Relations
CHAMP/MacNeill Engineering Worldwide Global Golf PR, Marketing
Cordillera Ranch PR, Real Estate
ECCO Brand Awareness, ECCO Sport, Lead Global PR, Marketing Communications, Strategic PR
Foresome Inc.
Galvin Green Public Relations
Gary Player "A Game For Life", Public Relations
Golf Membership Consultants Business Strategy, Marketing, Public Relations
GolfBoard Brand Communications, Brand Development, Media, Promotions, Public Relations
The Gulf Shores Golf Association Media Relations
New-Hydrapak Public Relations
Keswick Hall Pete Dye Golf, Public Relations
Lizzie Driver Public Relations
Myrtle Beach Seaside Resorts Media Relations
Mystical Golf Public Relations
PHIT America Broadcast Outlets, Digital, Media Relations, Print, Publicity
Rio Verde Community Public Relations
Sports Turf Managers Association Public Relations, Social Media
Team Express BaseballExpress.com, External Communications, FootballAmerica.com, Media Planning & Buying, Softball.com, TeamExpress.com
Telluride Ski & Golf Resort Public Relations

BUIE & CO
2815 Exposition Blvd Bldg 200, Austin, TX 78703
Tel.: (512) 482-8691
Web Site: www.buieco.com

Year Founded: 2013

Agency Specializes In: Communications, Crisis Communications, Media Relations, Public Relations, Social Media

Jed Buie *(Pres)*
Ashley Kegley Whitehead *(VP)*
Laurie Walker *(Acct Exec)*
Austin Stewart *(Coord-Creative Svcs)*

Accounts:
Williamson County

BURSON-MARSTELLER
230 Park Ave S, New York, NY 10003-1566
Tel.: (212) 614-4000
Fax: (212) 598-5320
E-Mail: ContactUS@BM.com
Web Site: www.burson-marsteller.com

Employees: 2,000
Year Founded: 1953

National Agency Associations: 4A's-COPF-WOMMA

Agency Specializes In: Advertising, Advertising Specialties, Aviation & Aerospace, Brand Development & Integration, Business Publications, Business-To-Business, Communications, Consulting, Consumer Marketing, Consumer Publications, Corporate Identity, Digital/Interactive, Direct Response Marketing, E-Commerce, Electronic Media, Environmental, Event Planning & Marketing, Financial, Government/Political, Health Care Services, High Technology, Hispanic Market, Internet/Web Design, Investor Relations, Logo & Package Design, Media Buying Services, Medical Products, Multimedia, New Product Development, Pharmaceutical, Public Relations, Publicity/Promotions, Real Estate, Recruitment, Sponsorship, Strategic Planning/Research, Transportation, Travel & Tourism

Donald A. Baer *(Chm & CEO)*
Katherine Lipsitz *(Mng Dir & Head-Ops-Corp & Fin Practice-US)*
Stephen Naru *(Mng Dir & Head-US Media Rels)*
David Coronna *(Mng Dir)*
Mary Crawford *(Mng Dir)*
Christine Gerstle *(Mng Dir)*
Debra Kieke *(Mng Dir)*
Scott Sykes *(Mng Dir)*
Patrick Przybyski *(CFO)*
Thomas Gensemer *(Chief Strategy Officer)*
Jason Teitler *(Chm-Fan Experience & Mng Dir-Consumer & Brand Mktg)*
Gary R. Koops *(Chm-Global Media Practice)*
Ramiro Prudencio *(Pres/CEO-Latin America)*
Daisy King *(Pres-China)*
Maury Lane *(Pres-Burson Campaigns)*
Michael Law *(CEO-US)*
Erica Swerdlow *(Exec VP-US & Head-Midwest Market)*
Deborah Nelson *(Sr VP-Strategic Media Practice)*
Jodi Brooks *(Mng Dir-Tech Practice)*
Yesenia Chambers *(Mng Dir-Reg HR-Latin America)*
Laura Feinberg *(Mng Dir-Healthcare Practice)*
Maya Kalkay *(Mng Dir-HR)*
Eric Kuhn *(Mng Dir-Consumer & Brand Mktg)*
Tyler Pennock *(Mng Dir-Digital Health)*
Sarah Tyre *(Mng Dir-Pub Affairs & Crisis Practice)*
Kimberly Axelrod *(Head-Global Client Ops & Dir)*
Angelena Abate *(Sr Dir)*
Ryan Barr *(Sr Dir)*
Steve Christensen *(Sr Dir)*
Ashley DiLeo *(Sr Dir)*
Peter Dixon *(Sr Dir)*
Michael Egbert *(Sr Dir)*
Ethan Farber *(Sr Dir)*
Lisa Gordon-Miller *(Sr Dir)*
Mary Heather *(Sr Dir-Healthcare)*
Allison Hudson *(Sr Dir)*
Steve King *(Sr Dir-Digital Strategy)*
Diana Levine *(Sr Dir)*
Jennifer McClellan *(Sr Dir)*
Tom Olson *(Sr Dir)*
Anna Sekaran *(Sr Dir)*
Sion Rogers *(Acct Dir)*
Andrew Bard *(Dir-Fan Experience, Consumer & Brand Mktg)*
Kevin Bennett *(Dir-Knowledge Sharing Worldwide)*
Kevin Bubel *(Dir)*
Jan Doesselmann *(Dir-Analytics Dev)*
Lora Grassilli *(Dir-Healthcare)*
Sarah Lackritz *(Dir-Digital Strategy)*
David Passantino *(Dir-IT Comm)*
Emily Wilson *(Dir-Brand Mktg)*
Carly Yanco *(Dir-Strategic Plng)*
Vinti Bhatnagar *(Mgr)*
Ella Burton *(Mgr-Bus Dev)*
Alexandra Churcher *(Mgr)*
Maria Davies *(Mgr-Events & Video Production)*
Paul Wegerson *(Mgr)*
Irene De Sousa *(Reg CFO-Latin America)*

Accounts:
Accenture
AstraZeneca Pharmaceuticals LP
Bank of America PR, Wealth-Management Business
Carlson Rezidor Hotel Group
Century 21 Real Estate Corporation
Cheung Kong Graduate School
FedEx Corporate Communications, Public Relations
Ford Motor Company
GAP, Inc. / Banana Republic / Old Navy Old Navy
Gibbs Sports Amphibians
Hawaiian Airlines
Hormel Foods Corporation; Austin, MN
HotelPlanner (Communications Agency of Record) Public Relations
HP
Intel
LG Electronics U.S.A., Inc. LG Appliances
Marriott Hotels & Resorts Corporate PR
Meltwater (Agency of Record) Content, Media Relations
Merrill Lynch Finance, Global Wealth Management, PR
Monster Worldwide, Inc.
Nestle Purina PetCare PR
New-NextVR (Agency of Record) Media Relations
Pfizer, Inc. Pregabalin
Pitney Bowes Global Public Relations, Media Relations, Social Media
Saban Brands Business Publications, Consumer, Event Management, Trade
San Diego Zoo
SAP Public Relations
Shell Oil Co.
Sony Electronics, Inc. Bravia
Sony Mobile Public Relations
Special Olympics International (Agency of Record) Communications, Media Relations, Unified Sports
New-Zebra Technologies (North America Agency of Record)

Austin

Burson-Marsteller Austin
98 San Jacinto Blvd, Austin, TX 78701
Tel.: (512) 879-0990
Fax: (512) 373-6360
E-Mail: info@burson-marsteller.com
Web Site: www.burson-marsteller.com

Employees: 5
Year Founded: 2000

National Agency Associations: COPF

Agency Specializes In: Public Relations

Ramiro Prudencio *(Pres/CEO-Latin America)*
Michael Law *(CEO-US Reg)*
Michele Chase *(Mng Dir-HR-Worldwide)*
Rachel Rodin Wolman *(Mng Dir-HR Worldwide)*
Dena Gellmann *(Dir-US Recruitment)*
Michael L. Dorff *(Mgr-Pub Affairs)*
Caitlin McCusker *(Mgr-HR)*

Accounts:
Blue Bell Creameries

Chicago

Burson-Marsteller
222 Merchandise Mart Plz Ste 250, Chicago, IL 60654-1022
Tel.: (312) 596-3400

Public Relations Firms

Fax: (312) 596-3600
Web Site: www.burson-marsteller.com

Employees: 90
Year Founded: 1961

National Agency Associations: 4A's-COPF

Agency Specializes In: Public Relations, Sponsorship

Jane Madden *(Mng Dir & Head-Corp Responsibility)*
David M. Coronna *(Mng Dir)*
Tim Frey *(Head-Pub Affairs)*
Pam Montagno *(Sr Dir-Healthcare Practice)*
Susan Carney *(Dir-Consumer & Brand Mktg)*
Melita Gaupp *(Strategist-Digital)*

Accounts:
Celestial Seasonings
Discover Financial Services Global Public Relations
Hormel Foods Corporation Hormel
Lloyds Barbeque Company; Saint Paul, MN

Dallas

Burson-Marsteller
1845 Woodall Rodgers Hwy, Dallas, TX 75201-2287
Tel.: (214) 224-8400
Fax: (214) 224-8450
E-Mail: mike.lake@bm.com
Web Site: www.burson-marsteller.com

Employees: 20
Year Founded: 1999

National Agency Associations: COPF

Agency Specializes In: Hispanic Market, Public Relations

Karen Hughes *(Vice Chm-Worldwide)*
Jeremy Galbraith *(CEO-EMEA)*
Jeff Donaldson *(Dir-Consumer & Brand Mktg)*

Accounts:
The City of Dallas Grease Abatement, Water Conservation
Susan G. Komen for the Cure Susan G. Komen Breast Cancer Foundation, Inc.

Los Angeles

B/W/R
9100 Wilshire Blvd West Tower 5th Fl, Beverly Hills, CA 90212
Tel.: (310) 550-7776
Fax: (310) 550-1701
E-Mail: info@bwr-la.com
Web Site: www.bwr-pr.com/

Employees: 80

Agency Specializes In: Public Relations

Nancy Ryder *(Founder & Partner)*
Paul Baker *(Co-CEO)*
Larry Winokur *(Co-CEO)*
Ron Hofmann *(Mng Dir)*
Paulette Kam *(Mng Dir)*
Hayley Scheck Antonian *(VP)*
Molly O'Gara *(Sr Acct Exec)*
Robin Weitz *(Sr Writer)*

Accounts:
New-TOMS Editorial, Entertainment Marketing, Social Media, Special Events

Burson-Marsteller
2425 Olympic Blvd Ste 200E, Santa Monica, CA 90404-4047
Tel.: (310) 309-6600
Fax: (310) 309-6630
Web Site: www.burson-marsteller.com

Employees: 34
Year Founded: 1966

National Agency Associations: 4A's

Agency Specializes In: Hispanic Market, Public Relations, Sponsorship

Lynda Herrera *(Mng Dir)*
Stephen Burns *(Mng Dir-West-Public Affairs & Crisis Practice)*
Fiona Jing *(Dir-Brand Mktg)*
Julie Strack *(Mgr-Healthcare Practice)*
Mary Hedge *(Sr Acct Exec)*

Accounts:
Konami
Saban Brands
San Diego Zoo
Tommy Bahama

New York

B/W/R
292 Madison Ave, New York, NY 10017
Tel.: (212) 901-3920
Fax: (212) 901-3995
E-Mail: leslie.sloane@bwr-ny.com
Web Site: www.bwr-pr.com

Employees: 20

Larry Winokour *(Co-Founder & CEO)*
Nanci Ryder *(Co-Founder)*
Sheryl Dennis *(Exec VP)*
Jeffrey Chassen *(Sr Acct Exec)*
Kevin McLaughlin *(Sr Acct Exec)*
Lauren Peteroy *(Sr Acct Exec)*
Jamie Reisman *(Acct Exec-Fashion & Beauty)*

Pittsburgh

Burson-Marsteller
1 Gateway Ctr 444 Liberty Ave Ste 310, Pittsburgh, PA 15222-1220
Tel.: (412) 471-9600
Fax: (412) 394-6610
Web Site: www.burson-marsteller.com

Employees: 20
Year Founded: 1957

National Agency Associations: 4A's-COPF

Agency Specializes In: Public Relations

Tom Dowling *(Mng Dir-Chair Consumer & Brand Mktg)*

Accounts:
Bayer Corporation

San Diego

Burson-Marsteller
4025 Camino Del Rio S Ste 300, San Diego, CA 92108-4107
Tel.: (619) 542-7812
Fax: (619) 542-7813
E-Mail: rhonda.brauer@bm.com
Web Site: www.burson-marsteller.com

Employees: 11
Year Founded: 1997

National Agency Associations: COPF

Agency Specializes In: Public Relations

Ryan Barr *(Mng Dir)*

Accounts:
Sony Electronics Consumer Electronics, PR

San Francisco

Burson-Marsteller
303 Second St Ste 350 N Twr, San Francisco, CA 94107
Tel.: (415) 591-4000
Fax: (415) 591-4030
Web Site: www.burson-marsteller.com

Employees: 50
Year Founded: 1981

National Agency Associations: 4A's-COPF

Agency Specializes In: Public Relations

Susan Pasarow *(Mng Dir)*
Gary R. Koops *(Chm-Global Media Practice)*
Michael Law *(CEO-US)*

Washington, DC

Burson-Marsteller
1110 Vermont Ave NW Ste 1200, Washington, DC 20005-3554
Tel.: (202) 530-0400
Fax: (202) 530-4500
E-Mail: contactus@bm.com
Web Site: www.burson-marsteller.com

Employees: 225
Year Founded: 1968

National Agency Associations: 4A's-COPF

Agency Specializes In: Public Relations

Dag Vega *(Mng Dir)*
Mike Heimowitz *(Mng Dir-Issues & Crisis Grp)*
Kathryn Stack *(Mng Dir-US Public Affairs-Crisis Grp)*
Patrick Kerley *(Sr Dir)*
Michael Sessums *(Sr Dir)*
Leigh Strope *(Sr Dir-Public Affairs & Crisis)*
Chad Cowan *(Dir)*
Luke Dickinson *(Dir)*
Luke Peterson *(Dir-Analytics Products)*
Shannon David *(Mgr-Pub Affairs)*
Catharine Montgomery *(Mgr)*

The Direct Impact Company
1110 Vermont Ave NW Ste 450, Washington, DC 20005
Tel.: (202) 530-0400
E-Mail: info@directimpact.com
Web Site: www.directimpact.com

Employees: 50
Year Founded: 1988

Agency Specializes In: Government/Political

Connie Partoyan *(Pres)*
Ralph Posner *(Exec VP)*
Amy Cloessner *(Sr VP)*
Ray Glendening *(Sr VP)*
Steven Soper *(Sr VP)*
Katie Feldman *(VP)*
Courtney Sieloff *(VP)*
Jeff Copeland *(Dir-Creative)*

Molly Douglas *(Dir-Content Dev)*

Accounts:
OfficeMax
TiVo

Prime Policy Group
1110 Vermont Ave NW Ste 1200, Washington, DC 20005-3554
Tel.: (202) 530-0500
Fax: (202) 530-4500
E-Mail: primepolicy@was.bm.com
Web Site: www.prime-policy.com

Employees: 30
Year Founded: 1996

Agency Specializes In: Government/Political

John Tanner *(Vice Chm-Prime Policy Grp)*
R. Scott Pastrick *(Pres & CEO)*
Paul Brown *(Mng Dir)*
Gabe Rozsa *(Mng Dir)*
Keith Smith *(Mng Dir)*
Pam Turner *(Mng Dir)*
Becky Weber *(Mng Dir)*
Paul Weiss *(Mng Dir)*
Charles L. Merin *(Exec VP)*
Marty Paone *(Exec VP)*
Theresa Weber *(Dir-Ops)*

Accounts:
Walmart

Latin America

Burson-Marsteller
Courvoisier Ctr II 601 Brickell Key Dr Ste 900, Miami, FL 33131
Tel.: (305) 347-4300
Fax: (305) 347-4301
E-Mail: santiago_hinojosa@mia.bm.com
Web Site: www.burson-marsteller.com

Employees: 50
Year Founded: 1988

National Agency Associations: 4A's

Agency Specializes In: Bilingual Market, Hispanic Market, Public Relations, Sponsorship

Jorge Ortega *(Mng Dir & Exec VP)*
David Coronna *(Mng Dir)*
Joseph Ramirez *(Mng Dir)*
Ramiro Prudencio *(Pres/CEO-Latin America)*
Sharron Silvers *(Sr Dir-Corp & Fin Practice)*
Gabriel Andriollo *(Mgr-Digital)*
Heather Sieberg *(Mgr-Pub Affairs & Crisis Practice)*

Accounts:
New-Zebra Technologies (Latin America Agency of Record)

Argentina

Burson-Marsteller
Rivadavia 620 4to piso, C1002AAR Buenos Aires, Argentina
Tel.: (54) 11-4338-1000
Fax: (54) 11-4338-1025
E-Mail: latam@bm.com
Web Site: www.burson-marsteller.com

Employees: 45
Year Founded: 1994

Agency Specializes In: Public Relations

Diego Segura *(Gen Mgr)*

Accounts:
AstraZeneca
CAPROVE
CELSAM
Cerveceria y Malteria Quilmes
Equant Orange Business Services
Ford
GEPSA
GlaxoSmithKline
SAP Region Sur

Brazil

Burson-Marsteller, Ltda.
Chedid Jafet 222 5th Fl, 04551-065 Sao Paulo, SP Brazil
Tel.: (55) 11 3094 2240
Fax: (55) 11 3094 2241
E-Mail: francisco.carvalho@bm.com
Web Site: www.burson-marsteller.com

Employees: 70
Year Founded: 1976

Agency Specializes In: Public Relations

Francisco Carvalho *(Pres, CEO & Mng Dir)*
Patricia Avila *(COO)*
Paula Goes Bakaj Cavagnari *(Dir-Pub Affairs)*
Eliana Paschoalin *(Dir-Consumer & Brand Mktg Practice)*
Elaine Rodrigues *(Dir-Corp & Fin Comm)*
Danilo Valeta *(Mgr-Innovation & Tech Grp)*
Cely Carmo Giraldes *(Sr Strategist-Digital-Latin America)*
Vitor Pavarini *(Strategist-Digital Media)*
Felipe Reviglio *(Generalist-HR)*

Chile

Burson-Marsteller
Edificio Millenium Av Vitacura 2939 piso 3ro Oficina 301, Las Condes, Santiago, 6760235 Chile
Tel.: (56) 2 751 7100
Fax: (56) 2 751 7180
Web Site: www.burson-marsteller.com

Employees: 25
Year Founded: 1994

Agency Specializes In: Public Relations

Barbara Rochefort *(Gen Mgr)*

Colombia

Burson-Marsteller
Carrera 11 A # 93 B - 30 Piso 3, Bogota, Colombia
Tel.: (57) 1 745 6060
Fax: (57) 1 530 0832
Web Site: www.burson-marsteller.com

Employees: 18
Year Founded: 1997

Agency Specializes In: Public Relations

Liliana Fernandez *(Mgr-Consumer Practice)*

Mexico

Burson-Marsteller Mexico, S.A. de C.V.
Boulevard Manuel Avila Camacho No 176 5to Piso, Col. Reforma Social, Miguel Hidalgo, 11650 Mexico, DF Mexico
Tel.: (52) 555 351 6500
Fax: (52) 555 351 6520
Web Site: latam.bm.com

Employees: 50
Year Founded: 1991

Agency Specializes In: Communications, Public Relations

Adriana Valladares *(Pres/CEO-Mexico)*

Venezuela

Burson-Marsteller
Avenida La Estancia, Centro Benaven (Cubo Negro) Torre C, Piso 2, Oficina C-23, Chuao, 1064 Caracas, Venezuela
Tel.: (58) 2129023360
Fax: (58) 2129599050
E-Mail: alexander_barrios@ve.bm.com
Web Site: latam.bm.com

Employees: 10
Year Founded: 1994

Agency Specializes In: Public Relations

Belgium

Burson-Marsteller S.A./N.V.
37 Square de Meeus, 1000 Brussels, Belgium
Tel.: (32) 2 743 6611
Fax: (32) 2 733 6611
Web Site: www.burson-marsteller.com/offices/brussels-burson-marsteller-brussels/

Employees: 45
Year Founded: 1965

Agency Specializes In: Government/Political, Public Relations

David Earnshaw *(Pres)*
Karen Massin *(CEO)*
Jeremy Galbraith *(Global Chief Strategy Officer & CEO-EMEA)*

Accounts:
New-Zebra Technologies (EMEA Agency of Record)

Denmark

Burson-Marsteller
Oestergade 26B, DK-1100 Copenhagen, K Denmark
Tel.: (45) 33 32 7878
Fax: (45) 33 32 7879
E-Mail: info@burson-marsteller.dk
Web Site: www.burson-marsteller.dk

Employees: 20
Year Founded: 1985

Agency Specializes In: Financial, Government/Political, Health Care Services, Public Relations, Publicity/Promotions

Nikolaj Buchardt *(CEO)*
Niels Aabye Madsen *(Dir-Fin-Denmark & Sweden)*
Anne Koster *(Mgr)*

Finland

Pohjoisranta - Helsinki
Kalevankatu 20, PO Box 1062, 00101 Helsinki, Finland

Tel.: (358) 10 4245 900
Fax: (358) 10 4245 910
Web Site: www.burson-marsteller.fi/

Employees: 44
Year Founded: 1995

Agency Specializes In: Public Relations

Heinonen Jouni *(CEO & Partner)*
Laine Riitta *(Partner)*
Tuomas Valimaa *(COO & Head-Digital Practice & Nordic Digital Expertise Team)*
Reetta Merinen *(Dir-Fin & HR)*
Veli-Matti Peltola *(Mgr & Strategist-Digital)*
Hanna Ikonen *(Mgr-Fin)*
Kyosti Knuuttila *(Mgr)*
Maija Laakso *(Mgr)*
Minna Lofstrom *(Mgr-Admin)*
Paula Niemisto *(Mgr)*
Jenni Peteja *(Strategist-Digital)*

France

Burson-Marsteller
6 rue Escudier, CEDEX, 92772 Boulogne-Billancourt, France
Tel.: (33) 1 41 86 76 76
Fax: (33) 1 41 86 76 00
E-Mail: philippe.pailliart@bm.com
Web Site: www.burson-marsteller.fr

Employees: 50
Year Founded: 1977

Agency Specializes In: Public Relations

Philippe Pailliart *(Pres)*
Matthias Lufkens *(Chm-EMEA Digital Practice)*
Michelle Boivin *(Dir-Integration & Internal Comm Dept)*
Tea Lucas de Peslouan *(Co-Dir-Crisis & Pub Affairs Dept)*
Marc Eskenazi *(Co-Dir-Crisis & Pub Affairs Dept)*
Frederic Guidoux *(Dir-Admin & Fin)*
Lorie Lichtlen *(Dir-Corp & Fin Comm Practice)*
Karine Meniri *(Dir-Innovation Practice)*
Benedicte Pouilly *(Dir-Dept-Corp & Brand)*

Accounts:
APEC
Accenture
Sanofi-Aventis Research & Development
Bosch
Bristol Myers Squibb
Cegos
Danone
Decathlon
Ford
France Telecom
GTIE/Vinci
HSBC/CCF
Heineken
Hotel Ritz
Johnson & Johnson
Kraft Foods France
Lufthansa
McCain
Merrill Lynch
Nestle Waters
ONERA
S.A.P.
SPB
Bayer Schering Pharma AG
Sony Ericsson
UK Trade & Investment
Unilever The Lipton
Valeo
Visa

Germany

Burson-Marsteller GmbH
Hanauer Landstrabe 126 - 128, 60314 Frankfurt am Main, Germany
Tel.: (49) 69 23 80 90
Fax: (49) 69 23 80 9 44
E-Mail: info@burson-marsteller.de
Web Site: www.burson-marsteller.de

Employees: 63
Year Founded: 1973

Agency Specializes In: Public Relations

Anita Walz *(Mng Dir & Head-Practice)*
Marco Hardt *(Mng Dir)*
Alexander Fink *(CEO-Germany)*
Karl-Heinz Heuser *(CEO-Germany)*
Julian Worner *(Mgr-Corp Comm)*

Burson-Marsteller
Lennestrasse 1, D-10785 Berlin, Germany
Tel.: (49) 30 40 81 94 5-50
Fax: (49) 30 40 81 94 5-51
E-Mail: info@burson-marsteller.de
Web Site: www.burson-marsteller.de

Employees: 20
Year Founded: 1999

Agency Specializes In: Public Relations

Anita Walz *(Mng Dir & Head-Practice)*
Christian Thams *(COO)*
Alexander Fink *(CEO-Germany)*
Hardy Herlt *(Dir-Pub Affairs)*
Tarja Muller *(Mgr)*
Julian Worner *(Mgr-Corp Comm)*

Accounts:
Lufthansa

Ireland

Heneghan PR
54 Pembroke Road, Dublin, 4 Ireland
Tel.: (353) 1 660 7395
Fax: (353) 1 660 7588
E-Mail: info@hpr.ie
Web Site: www.hpr.ie

Employees: 9

Agency Specializes In: Public Relations

Nigel Heneghan *(Mng Dir)*
Victoria Keogh *(Acct Dir)*
Gareth O'Connor *(Dir-Digital)*
Eoghan O'Neachtain *(Dir-Pub Affairs)*
Eve Noone *(Sr Acct Mgr)*
Catherine Carey *(Mgr-Fin)*
Emma Gallagher *(Sr Acct Exec)*
Fiona Sherlock *(Sr Acct Exec)*
Aislinn Hughes *(Acct Exec)*

Italy

Burson-Marsteller S.r.l.
Via Gregoriana 54, 00187 Rome, Italy
Tel.: (39) 06 688 9631
Fax: (39) 06 688 96368
Web Site: www.burson-marsteller.it

Employees: 12
Year Founded: 1989

Agency Specializes In: Public Relations

Fabio Caporizzi *(CEO)*
Riccardo Corsini *(Mng Dir & Head-Rome)*
Vito Basile *(Mng Dir)*
Irma Cordella *(Sr Dir-Govt & Pub Affairs-Italy)*
Valeria Redaelli *(Mgr)*

Accounts:
Accenture
Adobe
Aeroporto di Firenze
Billa
Brita
Cembre
Global Refund
Johnson & Johnson
Roche
Sony Ericsson

Burson-Marsteller S.r.l.
Via tortona 37, I-20144 Milan, Italy
Tel.: (39) 02 721 431
Fax: (39) 02 878 960
Web Site: www.burson-marsteller.it

Employees: 50
Year Founded: 1982

Agency Specializes In: Public Relations

Daniele Cazzaniga *(Mng Dir)*
Caporizzi Fabio *(CEO-Italy)*
Rossella Carrara *(Head-Crisis Comm & Healthcare Practices & Sr Dir)*
Giuliana Gentile *(Mgr-Tech practice)*
Poggio Laura *(Mgr-PR & Comm)*
Francesca Osella *(Mgr)*
Raffaella Tosi *(Mgr)*
Maja Minino *(Sr Specialist-PR & Comm)*

Accounts:
AESVI Campaign: "Video Games Take over Milan"

Marsteller
Via Tortona 37, 20144 Milan, Italy
Tel.: (39) 02 7214 3577
Fax: (39) 02 878 960
E-Mail: burson.italia@bm.com
Web Site: www.burson-marsteller.it

Employees: 60
Year Founded: 2000

Agency Specializes In: Event Planning & Marketing, Public Relations

Daniele Cazzaniga *(Mng Dir)*
Riccardo Corsini *(Mng Dir)*
Gianfranco Mazzone *(Mng Dir)*
Rossella Carrara *(Head-Crisis Comm & Healthcare Practices & Sr Dir)*
Giuliana Gentile *(Mgr-Burson-Marsteller Tech)*
Poggio Laura *(Mgr-PR & Comm)*
Francesca Osella *(Mgr)*
Valeria Redaelli *(Mgr)*
Maja Minino *(Sr Specialist-PR & Comm)*

Norway

Burson-Marsteller A/S
Sjolyst Plass 4, 0278 Oslo, Norway
Tel.: (47) 23 16 45 00
Fax: (47) 23 16 45 01
E-Mail: oslo@no.bm.com
Web Site: www.burson-marsteller.no

Employees: 40
Year Founded: 1982

Agency Specializes In: Public Relations

Per Anders Muri *(Mng Dir)*
Morten Pettersen *(CEO-Norway)*

Peter Skovholt Gitmark *(Sr Dir)*
Jonas Jolle *(Sr Dir)*
Ann Elin Hvidsten *(Dir-Creative)*

Spain

Burson-Marsteller, S.A.
Avenida Diagonal 545 4th Fl 1st Door, 08029 Barcelona, Spain
Tel.: (34) 93 201 1028
Fax: (34) 93 414 3390
E-Mail: info@bursonmarsteller.es
Web Site: www.burson-marsteller.com/offices/barcelona-burson-marsteller/

Employees: 60
Year Founded: 1985

Agency Specializes In: Public Relations

Francisco Lopez Dominguez *(Mng Dir)*
Juan Astorqui Portera *(Sr VP)*
Sara Blazquez *(Mng Dir-Madrid)*
Paul Herrick *(Mng Dir-HR-EMEA)*
Beatriz Garcia Cabanas *(Mgr)*
Santiago Esteban *(Mgr)*
Celia Garcia Llorente *(Coord-HR)*
Alberto Cois *(Mgr Talent Acq-EMEA)*
Carmen Valera *(Exec Pres-Spain)*

Accounts:
CB Richard Ellis
Carburos Metallicos

Sweden

Burson-Marsteller AB
Master Samuelsgatan 56 6th floor, 10120 Stockholm, Sweden
Tel.: (46) 8 440 12 00
Fax: (46) 8 440 12 01
E-Mail: mail.stockholm@se.bm.com
Web Site: www.burson-marsteller.se

Employees: 12
Year Founded: 1981

Agency Specializes In: Public Relations

Helena Olsson *(CEO & Mng Dir)*
Bo Lieden *(Controller)*
Carina Nildalen *(Dir-Health Care)*
Bergetta Belaiaff *(Office Mgr)*

Switzerland

Burson-Marsteller
Konsunstrasse 20, CH-3000 Bern, 14 Switzerland
Mailing Address:
PO Box 264, Bern, 15 Switzerland
Tel.: (41) 31 356 7300
Fax: (41) 31 356 7301
E-Mail: info.bm@ch.bm.com
Web Site: www.burson-marsteller.ch/

E-Mail for Key Personnel:
President: Roman_Geiser@ch.bm.com

Employees: 15
Year Founded: 1999

National Agency Associations: BSW

Agency Specializes In: Public Relations

Roland Oberhauser *(CFO & Head-HR)*
Matthias Lufkens *(Chm-Digital Practice-EMEA)*
Christian Fisch *(Head-IT)*
Corina Haselmann *(Mgr-HR)*

Accounts:
Association of Swiss Pharmaceutical Industry

Burson-Marsteller
18 bd des Philosophes, CH-1205 Geneva, Switzerland
Tel.: (41) 22 593 69 20
Fax: (41) 22 593 69 39
E-Mail: info_bm@ch.bm.com
Web Site: www.burson-marsteller.ch/index.php

Employees: 7

Chris Cartwright *(Mng Dir-Geneva)*
Annabel Watson *(Head-Practice & Dir)*
Heidi Salon *(Dir-Comm)*
Andrew Wigram *(Dir-Fin & Head HR)*
Daniela Gugliotta Bagaian *(Mgr)*

Burson-Marsteller
Grubenstrasse 40, PO Box 5010, CH-8045 Zurich, Switzerland
Tel.: (41) 1 455 84 00
Fax: (41) 1 455 84 01
E-Mail: info.bm@ch.bm.com
Web Site: www.burson-marsteller.ch/

Year Founded: 1999

Agency Specializes In: Public Relations

Marie-Louise Baumann-Bruckner *(Chm)*
Matthias Graf *(CEO)*
Roland Oberhauser *(CFO & Head-HR)*
Andrew Wigram *(Dir-Fin & Head-HR)*
Louise Everett *(Head-Practice-Health & Science & Bus Dev Dir)*
Christian Fisch *(Head-IT)*
Tim Frey *(Head-Practice-Pub Affairs)*
Peter Kiessling *(Controller-Fin)*
Sabine Tuerk *(Dir-Art)*

Accounts:
Abb
Accenture
Geberit
Kimberly-Clark
Miele
Migros
Nestle
Pfizer
SAP
Volvo

United Arab Emirates

ASDA'A Burson - Marsteller
212 Spectrum Bldg, PO Box 28063, Oud Metha, Dubai, United Arab Emirates
Tel.: (971) 43344550
Fax: (971) 43344556
Web Site: www.asdaabm.com/

Employees: 40

Agency Specializes In: Public Relations

Sunil John *(Founder & CEO)*
Margaret Flanagan *(Mng Dir)*
Bashar Alkadhi *(Chief Creative Officer)*
Amr Diab *(Acct Dir)*
Rasha Ghanem *(Acct Dir-Middle East & North Africa)*
Tricia Rego *(Acct Dir-Fin Practice)*
Nedal Alasaad *(Assoc Dir)*
Ragini Shah *(Sr Mgr-HR)*
Medhat Juma *(Sr Acct Mgr)*
Daniela Gorini *(Acct Mgr)*
Khalid Yahya *(Sr Acct Exec)*
Tameem Alkintar *(Assoc Acct Dir-Fin Practice)*

Accounts:
Daman
DHL
Dubai Islamic Bank
Microsoft Gulf
Muscat City Centre
Sony Ericsson

United Kingdom

Burson-Marsteller Ltd.
24-28 Bloomsbury Way, London, WC1A 2PX United Kingdom
Tel.: (44) 20 7831 6262
Fax: (44) 20 7430 1033
E-Mail: paul.haugen@bm.com
Web Site: www.burson-marsteller.co.uk

Employees: 140
Year Founded: 1967

Agency Specializes In: Public Relations

Mike Love *(Chm)*
Amanda Pierce *(CEO)*
Stephen Day *(Mng Dir & Chm-Pub Affairs & Political Comm)*
Clarence Mitchell *(Mng Dir & Head-Media-EMEA)*
Kate Hawker *(Chm-EMEA Healthcare Practice & Mng Dir-Healthcare)*
Matt Owen *(Head-Integrated Strategy)*
Michael Hartt *(Sr Dir-Corp Comm & Intl Affairs)*
Ruci Fixter *(Assoc Dir)*

Accounts:
New-Addison Lee Public Affairs
Beiersdorf PR
Cheung Kong Graduate School of Business
Findus UK
Gates Cambridge Trust
The Government of Iceland
Heineken UK
Jamaica Tourist Board Public Relations
The Royal British Legion The 2010 Poppy Appeal
SportAccord Global Communications

China

Burson-Marsteller
Suite 602 Tower W1 Oriental Plaza 1 East Chang An Avenue, Dong Cheng District, Beijing, 100738 China
Tel.: (86) 10 5816 2525
Fax: (86) 10 5816 2560
E-Mail: cindy_china@bm.com
Web Site: www.bmchina.com.cn

Year Founded: 1992

Agency Specializes In: Public Relations, Sponsorship

Douglas Dew *(Mng Dir & Head-Pub Affairs-China)*
Helen Huan *(Mng Dir)*
Ryan Fenwick *(Assoc Dir)*
Ada Song *(Assoc Dir)*
Tong Xie *(Mgr)*
Hunter Zhang *(Mgr)*

Accounts:
Cathay Pacific Airways Cathay Pacific, Crisis PR, Dragonair, Media Relations
Cheung Kong Graduate School of Business
HNA Property Branding
Swire Properties Corporate Communications, Media Communication, Media Strategies
Vipshop Holdings Limited Media Relations
Yuexiu Property Company Limited Branding, Creative Campaign

Hong Kong

Burson-Marsteller

23/F Chinachem Exchange Square, 1 Hoi Wan Street, Quarry Bay, China (Hong Kong)
Tel.: (852) 2880 0229
Fax: (852) 2856 1101
Web Site: www.burson-marsteller.com

Year Founded: 1953

Agency Specializes In: Brand Development & Integration, Communications, Corporate Identity, Financial, Government/Political, Investor Relations

Margaret Key *(CEO-Asia Pacific)*
Elaine Chan *(Mng Dir-Fin Comm)*
Ian R. McCabe *(Mng Dir-Pub Affairs & Govt Comm-Asia Pacific)*
Shrey Khetarpal *(Reg Dir)*
Lynn He *(Assoc Dir-Corp Comm & Pub Affairs)*
Hunter Zhang *(Mgr)*
Lena Zheng *(Mgr)*
Mariko Sanchanta *(Reg Mng Dir-Media-Asia Pacific)*

Accounts:
Fujitsu
Huawei Global PR

Indonesia

Burson-Marsteller

Wisma BNI 46 Kota BNI Suite 16-07, Jln Jend Sudirman Kav 1, Jakarta, 10220 Indonesia
Tel.: (62) 21 251 5060
Fax: (62) 21 251 5061
E-Mail: sahala.sianipar@bm.com
Web Site: www.burson-marsteller.com

Mayang Schreiber *(CEO & Head-Market)*
Dody Rochadi *(Head-Corp PR & Pub Affairs Practices & Dir)*
Harry Deje *(Head-Digital-Singapore & Indonesia)*
Helmy Anam *(Assoc Dir)*
Santi Dharmawan *(Mgr)*
Dian Pertiwi *(Mgr)*
Lucas Suryanata *(Mgr)*

Accounts:
HP

India

Genesis Burson-Marsteller

807-B Signature Towers South City, Gurgaon, Haryana 122 001 India
Tel.: (91) 124 441 7600
Fax: (91) 124 408 6663
Web Site: www.genesisbm.in

Employees: 250
Year Founded: 1992

Agency Specializes In: Public Relations

Prema Sagar *(Founder, Vice Chm-Asia Pacific & Principal)*
Vidisha Chatterjee *(Mng Partner)*
Vishal Gaba *(Partner)*
Deepshikha Dharmaraj *(CMO & Chief Growth Officer)*
Atul Sharma *(Chm-India Practice-Telecom & Tech & Head-India-Step Up)*
Vandana Sandhir *(Chm-India Practice-Corp & Fin Svcs)*
Nikhil Dey *(Pres-PR)*
Abhishank Babbar *(Specialist-Digital)*
Nikhil Kharoo *(Assoc Partner)*
Radhika Sharda *(Assoc Partner)*
Malvika Sinha *(Assoc Partner)*

Accounts:
Apollo Hospitals Consumer & Brand Marketing, Healthcare
Ashoka University Consumer & Brand Marketing, Healthcare
BBC World
Benetton
Biocon
BITS (Pilani) PR
Flipkart
Ford India
GAS
Get it PR
Google Consumer & Enterprise, PR
Hindustan National Glass
JK Group PR
Loyalty One
Medium Healthcare Consulting
Michelin Tires
Micromax Consumer & Brand Marketing, Healthcare
Pepsico
Prime Focus Consumer & Brand Marketing, Healthcare
Sumbun
Times of India Film Awards Consumer & Brand Marketing, Healthcare
UFO Moviez PR
Visa Indian Communications

Korea

Burson-Marsteller

9F East Tower Signature Towers, 99 Supyo-dong Jung-gu, Seoul, 100-230 Korea (South)
Tel.: (82) 2 3782 6400
Fax: (82) 2 3782 6480
E-Mail: sunyoung.lee@bm.com
Web Site: www.burson-marsteller.com

Year Founded: 1989

Agency Specializes In: Public Relations

Accounts:
Abbott Laboratories
Amway
BAE Systems
De Beers
Diageo
Emirates
FedEx Express
JP Morgan
Levi's
LG Display Corporate & Product Communications, Global PR
Philip Morris
QUALCOMM
SAP
UBS
Unilever
VISA

Singapore

Burson-Marsteller (SEA) Pte. Ltd.

8 Temasek Boulevard, 40-02 Suntec Tower Three, 038988 Singapore, Singapore
Tel.: (65) 6336 6266
Fax: (65) 6829 9301
Web Site: www.burson-marsteller.com

Employees: 40
Year Founded: 1973

Agency Specializes In: Public Relations

Mabel Ng *(Sec)*
John Mullins *(Mng Dir-HR-Asia Pacific)*
Ayesha Khan *(Assoc Dir-Corp & Brand Mktg)*
Aaron Yeo *(Assoc Dir)*

Accounts:
Ministry of Manpower Marketing Communications

Thailand

Aziam Burson-Marsteller

16th Fl Alma Link Bldg 25 Soi Chidlom, Ploenchit Rd, Bangkok, 10330 Thailand
Tel.: (66) 2 252 9871
Fax: (66) 2 254 8353
E-Mail: steve.vincent@abm.co.th
Web Site: www.burson-marsteller.com

Employees: 34
Year Founded: 1986

Agency Specializes In: Public Relations

Steve Vincent *(Mng Dir)*
James Best *(Dir-Comm)*
Wilasinee Chayabejara *(Dir-Comm)*
Tom Poldre *(Dir-Trng & Dev)*
Hongsinunt Somboonwanna *(Dir-Comm)*
Nattaporn Boonprapa *(Mgr-Knowledge)*
Haruehun Airry *(Specialist-Social Media)*

Compass Public Relations

10th Fl C 167 Tun Hwa N Rd, 105 Taipei, Taiwan
Tel.: (886) 2 2546 6086
Fax: (886) 2 2546 6087
E-Mail: center@compasspr.com.tw
Web Site: www.compasspr.com.tw

Employees: 30

Agency Specializes In: Communications, Consumer Marketing, Food Service, Health Care Services, Public Relations, Travel & Tourism

Beatrice Lin *(Pres)*
Pauline Leung *(CEO)*
Karen Chou *(Sr Acct Mgr)*
Yi Chen Chen *(Strategist-Digital)*
Eleven K.H Liu *(Acct Exec-PR)*

Accounts:
Airbus Industries
Dodge
Dunhill
Foxconn
Guam Visitors Bureau
Jeep
Kelloggs
LG
Lockheed Martin
Mercedes Benz
P&G
Zespri

Australia

Burson-Marsteller

65 Berry Street Level 16, Sydney, NSW 2060 Australia
Tel.: (61) 2 9928 1500
Fax: (61) 2 9928 1557
Web Site: www.burson-marsteller.com

Employees: 35
Year Founded: 1980

Agency Specializes In: Public Relations

Christine Jones *(CEO-Australia)*
Carrie Cousins *(Head-Corp, Pub Affairs & Tech)*

Accounts:

Accenture
CSL Biotherapies
Hewlett-Packard
Jetstar
LG Electronics
Novartis
ResMed
SAP
Shell
V8 Supercars

Burson-Marsteller Affiliate

NATIONAL Public Relations
2001 McGill College Ave Ste 800, Montreal, QC H3A 1G1 Canada
(See Separate Listing)

BUSINESS STRATEGIES & BEYOND
1512 Fox Trl Ste B1, Mountainside, NJ 07092
Tel.: (908) 232-5977
Fax: (908) 232-6868
E-Mail: info@bizstratbeyond.com
Web Site: www.bizstratbeyond.com

E-Mail for Key Personnel:
President: gsteckler@bizstratbeyond.com

Employees: 3
Year Founded: 1985

Agency Specializes In: Brand Development & Integration, Business-To-Business, Collateral, Consulting, Corporate Identity, Event Planning & Marketing, Exhibit/Trade Shows, Industrial, Internet/Web Design, New Product Development, Pharmaceutical, Planning & Consultation, Print, Public Relations, Publicity/Promotions, Strategic Planning/Research, Technical Advertising

Gail Steckler *(Chief Strategy Officer)*

BUTLER ASSOCIATES
204 E 23rd St, New York, NY 10010-4628
Tel.: (212) 685-4600
Fax: (212) 481-2605
E-Mail: info@butlerassociates.com
Web Site: www.butlerassociates.com

Year Founded: 1996

Thomas P. Butler *(Owner)*
Denis J. Butler *(Partner)*
Lisa Chernak *(Partner)*
Stuart Miller *(Sr VP)*

Accounts:
BellTel Retirees Inc
Hostelworld Group Communications
Institute for Workplace Studies
NY Area Alliance
NYSCOPBA
ProtectSeniors.Org
Windham Mountain

THE BUZZ AGENCY
104 W Atlantic Ave, Delray Beach, FL 33444
Tel.: (855) 525-2899
Fax: (561) 526-8440
E-Mail: info@thebuzzagency.net
Web Site: www.thebuzzagency.net

Agency Specializes In: Brand Development & Integration, Corporate Communications, Email, Event Planning & Marketing, Media Relations, Public Relations, Social Media

Elizabeth Kelley Grace *(Co-Founder & Partner)*
Julie Mullen *(Co-Founder & Partner)*
Debbie Abrams *(VP-PR)*
Alex Bimonte *(Dir-Social Media)*
Jill Pavlov *(Acct Exec-PR & Social Media)*
Danielle Quintero *(Acct Exec-PR)*

Accounts:
Amaize Arepas
Aviation Week Events
Boca Bacchanal The 11th Annual Boca Bacchanal
Boca West Country Club
BoConcept Furniture
Burger Bar
BYL Network
Chamber Music Series
Citrus Distillers
Clive Daniel Interiors
Congregation B'nai Israel
Digital Media Arts College, Llc.
Elements Therapeutic Massage
Engel & Volkers
Fresh Meal Plan
Gift of Life
Habit Burger
Hospital Albert Schweitzer Haiti
Nick's New Haven Style Pizzeria & Bar
Palm Beach County Film & Television Commission
Seminole Coconut Creek Casino Sweet Dreams Event
Snow Lizard Products
Sunflower Creative Arts
US Immigration Fund

BYRNE PR, LLC
3451 Halliday Ave, Saint Louis, MO 63118
Tel.: (314) 737-1847
Web Site: www.byrnepr.net

Agency Specializes In: Media Relations, Public Relations, Social Media

Paul Byrne *(Principal)*

Accounts:
Shawnee Bluffs Canopy Tour

C&M MEDIA
307 7th Ave Ste 1801, New York, NY 10001
Tel.: (646) 336-1398
Fax: (646) 336-1401
E-Mail: info@cmmediapr.com
Web Site: www.cmmediapr.com

Agency Specializes In: Brand Development & Integration, Digital/Interactive, Fashion/Apparel, Public Relations, Social Media

Angela Mariani *(CEO)*

Accounts:
New-Missoni

C BLOHM & ASSOCIATES INC
5999 Monona Dr, Monona, WI 53716
Tel.: (608) 216-7300
E-Mail: info@cblohm.com
Web Site: www.cblohm.com

Agency Specializes In: Content, Media Relations, Public Relations, Social Media, Strategic Planning/Research

Charlene Blohm *(Founder & Pres)*
Emily Embury *(Acct Dir)*
Saul Hafenbredl *(Acct Mgr)*
Chris Swietlik *(Acct Exec)*
Kristina Rozenbergs *(Acct Exec)*
Dusten Carlson *(Acct Exec)*

Accounts:
New-Consortium for School Networking

C. MILAN COMMUNICATIONS
916 Kearny St Zoetrope Bldg, San Francisco, CA 94133
Tel.: (415) 392-6600
E-Mail: info@cmilancomm.com
Web Site: www.cmilancomm.com

Year Founded: 2005

Agency Specializes In: Media Relations, Public Relations

Charlotte Milan *(Founder & Pres)*
Keely Garibaldi *(VP)*

Accounts:
Atelier Melka
Dana Estates
Domaine Carneros
E-cep
Flowers Vineyard & Winery
Grace Family Vineyards
Ladera Vineyards
Melka Wines
Merryvale Vineyards
Napa Valley Vine Trail
Rams Gate Winery
Vineyard 29

C-SQUARED PR, INC.
8071 Slater Ave Ste 255, Huntington Beach, CA 92647
Tel.: (714) 841-6777
Web Site: www.c-squaredpr.com

Agency Specializes In: Brand Development & Integration, Crisis Communications, Media Relations, Public Relations, Social Media

Barbara Caruso *(Principal)*

Accounts:
New-Del Taco LLC

C2 COMMUNICATIONS
4660 Slater Rd Ste 130, Eagan, MN 55122
Tel.: (612) 770-0026
Web Site: www.c2comms.com

Year Founded: 2012

Agency Specializes In: Corporate Communications, Media Relations, Public Relations

Chuck Grothaus *(Founder & Pres)*

Accounts:
Asure Software, Inc.

C3 COMMUNICATIONS INC
11211 Carmel Creek Rd Ste 3, San Diego, CA 92130
Tel.: (858) 794-6974
E-Mail: info@c3publicrelations.com
Web Site: www.c3publicrelations.com

Agency Specializes In: Crisis Communications, Event Planning & Marketing, Media Relations, Public Relations, Social Media

Sean Curry *(Owner)*

Accounts:
New-University of San Diego

C3PR
1269 Oak Creek Way, Sunnyvale, CA 94089
Tel.: (408) 730-8506
Fax: (408) 730-8516
Web Site: www.c3pr.com

Year Founded: 2002

Agency Specializes In: Advertising, Communications, Media Relations, Public Relations

Mar Junge *(Principal)*
Lisa Bianchi *(Dir-Art)*
Vanessa Bradford *(Acct Mgr-PR)*

Accounts:
Contoural, Inc.
Floor Seal Technology, Inc.
Taos

CALYSTO COMMUNICATIONS
861 Sapphire Ln Sugar Hill, Atlanta, GA 30518
Tel.: (404) 266-2060
Fax: (404) 266-2041
E-Mail: awhittaker@calysto.com
Web Site: www.calysto.com

Employees: 40
Year Founded: 2000

Agency Specializes In: Communications, High Technology, Investor Relations, Public Relations, Strategic Planning/Research

Laura Borgstede *(Founder & CEO)*
Sue O'Keefe *(Chief Content Officer & Exec VP)*
Kristine Bennett *(Exec VP-Client Svcs)*
Jason Meyers *(Exec VP)*
Rhonda Harris *(Dir-Ops)*

Accounts:
3e Technologies International Analyst & Blogger Relations, Branding, Marketing, Messaging, Public Relations, Social Media
Aquantia
BeQuick Software Brand Awareness, Content Development & Delivery, Media & Analyst Relations, Messaging, Social & Traditional Public Relations, Social Media, Strategic Planning
Certes Networks Communications Strategy, Content Strategy, Public Relations, Social Media
Ceterus Networks
Clearfield Content Development, Media & Analyst Relations, Public Relations, Social Media, Strategic Planning
Compass Intelligence Content Marketing, PR, Social Media
Encoding.com
Global Wireless Solutions
iBasis Content Marketing, Social Media, Iteroaming.info
JMango
One Source Networks
RACO Wireless Marketing Communications, Public Relations, Social Media
SOLiD Technologies Content Media, PR, Social Media
Syntonic Wireless Communications Strategy, Marketing, Public Relations, Social Media
Wolfe
Zipwhip

CAMEO PUBLIC RELATIONS
10 W 33rd St Ste 1118, New York, NY 10001
Tel.: (646) 360-3488
E-Mail: info@cameopr.com
Web Site: www.cameopr.com

Agency Specializes In: Brand Development & Integration, Fashion/Apparel, Public Relations, Social Media

Malorie Kaye *(Founder & Pres)*
Ariel Kaye *(VP)*

Accounts:
New-IYLIA

CAMPAIGN CONNECTIONS
3141 John Humphries Wynd Ste 136, Raleigh, NC 27612
Tel.: (919) 834-8994
Fax: (919) 869-2992
E-Mail: info@campaignconnections.com
Web Site: www.campaignconnections.com

Agency Specializes In: Crisis Communications, Media Training, Public Relations

Brad Crone *(Pres)*
Clark Coggin *(Creative Dir)*

Accounts:
New-Gene McLaurin

CANDOR
729 W Sheridan Ave #100, Oklahoma City, OK 73102
Tel.: (405) 972-9090
E-Mail: info@candorpr.com
Web Site: www.candorpr.com

Year Founded: 2012

Agency Specializes In: Crisis Communications, Digital/Interactive, Media Relations, Public Relations, Social Media

Karen Wicker *(Founder & Pres)*
Jim Kessler *(Principal)*
Jacqueline Sit *(Acct Exec)*
Larisha Hunter *(Acct Exec)*
Ally Glavas *(Acct Exec)*

Accounts:
New-Greater Oklahoma City Chamber of Commerce

CAPITAL CITY PUBLIC RELATIONS
Cheesman Park, Denver, CO 80206
Tel.: (303) 241-0805
Web Site: www.capitalcitypr.com

Year Founded: 2013

Agency Specializes In: Collateral, Content, Media Relations, Public Relations, Radio, Social Media, T.V.

Cathie Beck *(Pres)*

Accounts:
Anthonys Pizza & Pasta
Clayton Early Learning (Agency of Record)
Moonbeam Harvest
Rupert's at the Edge

CAPLAN COMMUNICATIONS
1700 Rockville Pike Ste 400, Rockville, MD 20852
Tel.: (301) 998-6592
E-Mail: ccinfo@caplancommunications.com
Web Site: www.caplancommunications.com

Agency Specializes In: Environmental, Graphic Design, Media Relations, Public Relations, T.V., Travel & Tourism

Aric Caplan *(Founder & Pres)*

Accounts:
Mobile Bay Keeper

CAPONIGRO PUBLIC RELATIONS, INC.
4000 Town Ctr Ste 1750, Southfield, MI 48034
Tel.: (248) 355-3270
Fax: (248) 353-6759
E-Mail: jcap@caponigro.com
Web Site: www.caponigro.com

Employees: 15
Year Founded: 1995

Agency Specializes In: Public Relations

Approx. Annual Billings: $2,500,000

Jeff Caponigro *(Founder)*
Chuck Ragains *(Sr VP)*
Maribeth Farkas *(Acct Supvr)*

THE CAPSTONE GROUP LLC
1576 Sherman St Ste 300, Denver, CO 80203
Tel.: (303) 860-0555
Web Site: www.capstonegroupllc.com

Agency Specializes In: Event Planning & Marketing, Public Relations

Moira Cullen *(Principal)*

Accounts:
New-Colorado Contractors Association

CAPSTRAT
(Acquired by Ketchum)

CAPSTRAT
1201 Edwards Mill Rd 1st Fl, Raleigh, NC 27607-3625
Tel.: (919) 828-0806
Fax: (919) 834-7959
E-Mail: webmaster@capstrat.com
Web Site: www.capstrat.com

E-Mail for Key Personnel:
Creative Dir.: tcoats@capstrat.com

Employees: 110
Year Founded: 1994

National Agency Associations: AMA-COPF-PRSA

Agency Specializes In: Advertising, Advertising Specialties, Brand Development & Integration, Business-To-Business, Collateral, Communications, Consulting, Corporate Communications, Corporate Identity, Digital/Interactive, Education, Electronic Media, Event Planning & Marketing, Government/Political, Graphic Design, Health Care Services, Information Technology, Internet/Web Design, Media Buying Services, New Product Development, Newspaper, Newspapers & Magazines, Pharmaceutical, Print, Production, Public Relations, Publicity/Promotions, Radio, Strategic Planning/Research, T.V., Teen Market

Approx. Annual Billings: $14,200,000

Ken Eudy *(Founder & Chm)*
Karen Albritton *(Pres & CEO)*
Debbie Reed *(CFO)*
Todd Coats *(Chief Creative Officer)*
Leslie Coman *(Exec VP-Govt Rels)*
John Barlow *(Sr VP & Grp Dir-Digital)*
Angela Connor *(Sr VP & Grp Dir)*
Elizabeth Hamner *(Sr VP & Grp Dir)*
Shane Johnston *(Sr VP & Grp Dir)*
Scott Ballew *(Sr VP & Dir-Creative)*
Adam Cohen *(Sr VP & Dir-Creative)*
Brad Bennett *(VP & Acct Dir)*
John Romano *(VP & Dir-Digital & Creative Tech)*
Kyle Sutton *(VP & Dir-Digital Strategy)*
Jonathan Wisely *(VP & Assoc Dir-Creative)*
Ryan Cuthriell *(Sr Dir-Art)*
Brandon Goldsworthy *(Sr Dir-Art)*

Jennifer Carey *(Acct Dir)*
Christina Martin *(Dir-Promo)*
Stephanie Dunford *(Sr Mgr-Resource)*
Jeanette Castle *(Sr Project Mgr-Creative)*
Alison Whisenant *(Acct Mgr-Social & Digital Media)*
Terry Beal *(Mgr-Production)*
Katie Cocker *(Mgr-Mktg)*
Kimberly Eller *(Mgr-Social Media)*
Lera Germaine *(Acct Supvr)*
Jay Dolan *(Sr Strategist-Social Media)*
Jessica Guiton *(Acct Exec)*
Heather Harder *(Acct Exec-Pub Affairs)*
Jessie Jenkins *(Acct Exec)*
Mallory Pickard *(Acct Exec)*
Lauren Stafford *(Acct Exec)*
Mandy Steinhardt *(Strategist-Customer Relationship Mgmt)*
Jessica Swanner *(Acct Exec)*
Sydni Collins *(Media Planner & Media Buyer)*
Matt Rostetter *(Designer)*
Megan Van Patten *(Copywriter)*

Accounts:
AICPA Campaign: "Book of Wisdom"
BASF
Blue Cross & Blue Shield of NC
Cotton Incorporated Consumer Marketing Headquarters
Deloitte
GlaxoSmithKline
North Carolina Economic Development Association

CARABINER COMMUNICATIONS

4372 Misty Morning Ln, Lilburn, GA 30047
Tel.: (770) 923-8332
Fax: (888) 686-7688
E-Mail: info@carabinerpr.com
Web Site: http://www.carabinercomms.com/

Employees: 15
Year Founded: 2004

Agency Specializes In: Automotive, Business Publications, Business-To-Business, Collateral, Computers & Software, Consulting, Corporate Communications, Corporate Identity, Customer Relationship Management, E-Commerce, Electronic Media, Electronics, Email, Event Planning & Marketing, Health Care Services, High Technology, Information Technology, Integrated Marketing, Internet/Web Design, Investor Relations, Local Marketing, Market Research, Media Relations, Media Training, New Technologies, Newspaper, Newspapers & Magazines, Planning & Consultation, Podcasting, Product Placement, Public Relations, Publicity/Promotions, Search Engine Optimization, Sponsorship, Strategic Planning/Research, Trade & Consumer Magazines

Peter Baron *(Owner)*
Dana Cogan *(VP)*
Suzanne Moccia *(VP)*
Marcy Theobald *(Acct Dir & Strategist)*
Leslie Tentler *(Dir-Editorial & Sr Writer)*
Sara Wakefield *(Acct Mgr)*
Angela Manzella *(Asst Acct Mgr-Social Media & Strategist-Digital Content)*

Accounts:
Applied Software Autodesk Resale; 2008
Blancco Data Erasure & End-of-Life Cycle Solutions; 2008
CardioMEMS
Digital Element
Excel4apps
Five x Five
Fulcrum Ventures
InterSOC Enterprise Security Management Solutions; 2008
JouleX
Oversight Systems, Inc.

CAREN WEST PR, LLC

130 Blvd NE Studio 5, Atlanta, GA 30312
Tel.: (404) 614-0006
Fax: (404) 522-5115
Web Site: www.carenwestpr.com

Year Founded: 2005

Agency Specializes In: Brand Development & Integration, Event Planning & Marketing, Graphic Design, Public Relations

Caren West *(Pres)*
Chad David Shearer *(COO & Dir-Creative)*
Elizabeth White *(Strategist-Publicity)*
Lauren Klopfenstein *(Coord-PR)*

Accounts:
The Albert
The Atlanta Dog Wizard
Camp Bisco Music + Art Festival 12
CHC International
Cucina Asellina
Cypress Street Pint & Plate
D.B.A. Barbecue
Diesel Filling Station
The Drafting Table
Eddies Attic
Edgewood Speakeasy
Euphoria Music Festival
Frozen Pints
Genki Noodle & Sushi
The Georgia Theatre
Gucci America Inc.
Magnetic Music Festival
Ocean Catering Company
P'cheen International Bistro & Pub
Park Bar
Pizzeria Vesuvius
Pure Melon
The Real Chow Baby
Sidebar
Soccer in the Streets
STK Atlanta
Sunny's Hair & Wigs
Where's Waldo Bar Crawl
Wild Heaven Craft Beers

CARMA PR

404 Washington Ave Ste 730, Miami Beach, FL 33139
Tel.: (305) 438-9200
Web Site: www.carmapr.com

Agency Specializes In: Entertainment, Event Planning & Marketing, Fashion/Apparel, Hospitality, Public Relations

Chad Fabrikant *(Partner)*
Lyndsey Cooper *(Principal)*

Accounts:
New-The Color Run Miami (Public Relations Agency of Record)
New-Funkshion Fashion Week Miami Beach (Public Relations Agency of Record)
New-Peace Love World

CARNEY COMMUNICATIONS

100 Merrimack St Ste 205 E, Lowell, MA 01852
Tel.: (617) 340-9337
E-Mail: info@carneycommunications.com
Web Site: www.carneycommunications.com

Year Founded: 2013

Agency Specializes In: Content, Corporate Communications, Crisis Communications, Digital/Interactive, Internet/Web Design, Media Training, Public Relations, Social Media

Brent R. Carney *(CEO)*
Chris Carney *(VP & Dir-California)*
Sherry Hao *(Dir-Nonprofit Strategy)*

Accounts:
Orangetheory Fitness
Society for Free Radical Biology & Medicine

CARO MARKETING

719 S Los Angeles St Studio 1106, Los Angeles, CA 90014
Tel.: (323) 781-2276
E-Mail: showroom@caromarketing.com
Web Site: www.caromarketing.com

Year Founded: 2004

Agency Specializes In: Brand Development & Integration, Digital/Interactive, Event Planning & Marketing, Public Relations, Social Media

Caroline Rothwell Gerstein *(Founder, Pres & Creative Dir)*
Cathleen Mari Madrona *(Mgr-PR & Event)*

Accounts:
New-Coye Nokes

CAROLINA PUBLIC RELATIONS/MARKETING, INC.

1017 E Morehead St Ste 150, Charlotte, NC 28204
Tel.: (704) 374-9300
Fax: (704) 374-9330
Toll Free: (866) 526-6382
E-Mail: info@carolinapr.com
Web Site: www.carolinapr.com

Employees: 10
Year Founded: 1983

National Agency Associations: PRSA

Agency Specializes In: Public Relations

Sig Huitt *(Pres & Mng Principal)*
Louise Dixon *(Principal & VP)*
Adam Bernstein *(Principal)*
Amanda DeWeese *(Acct Supvr)*

Accounts:
Philip Morris

Branch

Carolina Public Relations/Marketing, Inc.

1634 Main St Ste 200, Columbia, SC 29201-2818
Tel.: (803) 799-1115
Fax: (803) 799-3766
Toll Free: (866) 526-6381
E-Mail: info@carolinapr.com
Web Site: www.carolinapr.com

Employees: 20
Year Founded: 1983

Agency Specializes In: Public Relations

Sig Huitt *(Pres & Mng Principal)*

Accounts:
Bon Secours Health System
Capstone Advancement Partners
Charlotte Housing Authority

CAROLYN GRISKO & ASSOCIATES INC.

400 W Erie St Ste 400, Chicago, IL 60654
Tel.: (312) 335-0100
Fax: (312) 335-0103
E-Mail: info@grisko.com

Web Site: www.grisko.com

Employees: 20
Year Founded: 1995

Agency Specializes In: Public Relations

Carolyn Grisko *(Pres & CEO)*
Ambar Mentor-Truppa *(VP)*
Terri Cornelius *(Acct Dir)*
Holly Dotterer *(Acct Supvr)*

Accounts:
Chicago & Illinois Bar Foundations
The Chicago Housing Authority (CHA) Affordable Senior Housing Units
Chicago Transit Authority Brand Development, Community Outreach, Marketing, Media, Public Relations
Equal Justice Illinois Campaign
Mayor's Hemispheric Forum
PhRMA Pharmaceutical Trade Association

CAROLYN IZZO INTEGRATED COMMUNICATIONS

37 N Broadway Ste 1, Nyack, NY 10960
Tel.: (845) 358-3920
Fax: (845) 358-3927
E-Mail: info@ciicnews.com
Web Site: www.ciicnews.com

Employees: 10

Agency Specializes In: Brand Development & Integration, Broadcast, Business-To-Business, Direct Response Marketing, Logo & Package Design, Print, Product Placement, Promotions, Public Relations, Trade & Consumer Magazines

Carolyn Izzo-Feldman *(Pres & Sr Strategist)*
Jennifer Barry *(Partner)*
Audrey Doherty *(Partner)*
Kate Johnston Wark *(Sr VP)*
Rosemarie Capasso *(Acct Mgr)*
Alyssa DiPalma *(Sr Acct Exec)*
Amy Sedeno *(Sr Acct Exec)*

Accounts:
BreaDr PR, Social Media
El Ganzo Hotel Social Media
Epoque Hotels Resorts & Hotels
Los Cabos Convention & Visitors Bureau
Los Cabos Tourism Board Public Relations
RealBeanz Media Outreach, PR, Social Media, Trade Shows & Events
Youareonthelist.com Media Relations, Social Media Counseling, Strategic Brand Partnerships

CAROLYN LEBER PUBLIC RELATIONS

70 Arnold Dr, Novato, CA 94949
Tel.: (323) 924-9137
E-Mail: info@carrieleberpr.com
Web Site: leberpr.com/intro/

Year Founded: 1996

Carolyn Leber *(Owner)*

Accounts:
Erbaviva
Orbit Design

CARTER WEST PUBLIC RELATIONS

411 Cleveland St Ste 239, Clearwater, FL 33755
Tel.: (727) 288-2159
Fax: (727) 475-8390
Web Site: www.carterwestpr.com

Agency Specializes In: Event Planning & Marketing, Media Relations, Media Training, Public Relations, Social Media

Sara West Callahan *(Founder & Pres)*

Accounts:
Auto USA
Auto/Mate, Inc.
Car Research, Inc.
DealerRater
MPi
The Media Trac
NCM Associates
Redbumper

CARTERTODD & ASSOCIATES, INC.

1233 Washington St Ste 101, Columbia, SC 29201-3221
Tel.: (803) 779-4005
Fax: (803) 978-7543
E-Mail: info@cartertodd.com
Web Site: www.cartertodd.com

Employees: 6
Year Founded: 1998

Agency Specializes In: Collateral, Communications, Consumer Marketing, Event Planning & Marketing, Internet/Web Design, Media Buying Services, Public Relations, Publicity/Promotions

Lorri-Ann Carter *(Pres & CEO)*
Grant Hughes *(Sr Graphic Designer)*

Accounts:
AcroSoft Corporation Creative, Industry Analyst Relations, Marketing, Media, Product Branding, Public Relations Agency of Record
AIG Technology
Carolina Carillion Parade
City Center Partnership
DP Professionals
Impact Technologies Group
Integrated Business Systems & Services
National Association of Home Builders
Palmetto Center for Women
USC Columbia Technology Incubator
VC3
World Beer Festival-Columbia

CASEY & SAYRE

(Formerly Casey Sayre & Williams)
12517 Venice Blvd, Los Angeles, CA 90066
Tel.: (310) 636-1888
Fax: (310) 636-4888
E-Mail: info@caseysayre.com
Web Site: www.caseysayre.com/

Employees: 15

Agency Specializes In: Public Relations

Barbara Sayre Casey *(CEO)*
Jo Ellen Ashton *(Controller)*
Ashley Greer *(Dir-Media Rels)*
Anne Sage *(Dir-Legal Svcs)*
Meredith Red *(Mgr-PR-Los Angeles)*
Jordan Kuker *(Coord-Talent Rels & Social Media)*

Accounts:
Arent Fox
AT&T Communications Corp.
Conrad N. Hilton Foundation
Lowe Enterprises

CASHMAN & ASSOCIATES

1000 N Hancock St, Philadelphia, PA 19123
Tel.: (215) 627-1060
Fax: (215) 627-1059
E-Mail: info@cashmanandassociates.com
Web Site: www.cashmanandassociates.com

Employees: 18
Year Founded: 2001

Agency Specializes In: Arts, Consumer Marketing, Entertainment, Event Planning & Marketing, Fashion/Apparel, Food Service, Graphic Design, Health Care Services, Media Relations, Pets , Product Placement, Promotions, Public Relations, Real Estate, Retail, Social Marketing/Nonprofit, Sports Market

Nicole A. Cashman *(Pres & CEO)*
Laura Krebs Miller *(VP)*
Rob Nonemacker *(Mgr-Special Events)*
Rachel Petery *(Exec Asst Mgr & Mgr-Ops)*

Accounts:
AP Bags USA Handbags & Accessories
Atlantic City Alliance
Bernie Robbins Fine Jewelers
Boathouse Row Bar
Boyds
Brandow Clinic
Eventions Productions Event Production
Fresh Salon
GiGi
Glow Salon
The Harnels Foundation Inner-City School Assistance
Hotel Sofitel Philadelphia
Innove Events & Paper Event Design & Stationery
New-The Kimmel Center for the Performing Arts (Public Agency of Record) 2016 Philadelphia International Festival of the Arts
Niche Media
Omega Optical Eyewear
Philadelphia Park Casino & Racetrack
Philly.com News & Information
The Piazza at Schmidts
Rescue Rittenhouse Spa Day Spa
Select Greater Philadelphia
Tower Investments Urban Development
Trump Marina
Trump Plaza
Trump Tower Philadelphia

CASTER COMMUNICATIONS, INC.

155 Main St, Wakefield, RI 02879
Tel.: (401) 792-7080
Fax: (401) 792-7040
E-Mail: info@castercomm.com
Web Site: www.castercomm.com

Employees: 4

Agency Specializes In: Brand Development & Integration, Communications, Consumer Marketing, Corporate Communications, Crisis Communications, Event Planning & Marketing, Exhibit/Trade Shows, Internet/Web Design, Investor Relations, Local Marketing, Media Relations, Media Training, Public Relations, Social Media

Revenue: $1,000,000

Kimberly Lancaster *(Founder & Pres)*
Alex Crabb *(VP-Acct Svcs)*
Rebecca Pelton *(Dir-Caster Resources)*
Dennis Burger *(Writer-Technical)*
Peter Girard *(Sr Acct Coord)*
Kalyn Schieffer *(Sr Acct Coord)*

Accounts:
Control4
SurgeX
Vutec Corporation (Agency of Record) Branding, Content Development, Digital Marketing, Public Relations, Social Media

THE CASTLE GROUP

38 Third Ave Charlestown Navy Yard, Boston, MA

02129
Tel.: (617) 337-9500
Fax: (617) 337-9539
E-Mail: info@thecastlegrp.com
Web Site: www.thecastlegrp.com

Employees: 30

Agency Specializes In: Advertising, Advertising Specialties, Brand Development & Integration, Business Publications, Collateral, Corporate Communications, Event Planning & Marketing, Exhibit/Trade Shows, Internet/Web Design, Media Buying Services, Multimedia, Print, Publicity/Promotions, Radio, T.V.

Sandy Lish *(Founder & Principal)*
Hilary Allard *(Sr VP)*
Keri Mcintosh *(Sr VP)*
Sheila Green *(VP-PR)*
Andrea Teixeira *(Dir-Bus Dev & Event Mgmt)*
Callie Cleary *(Mgr-Event)*
Nicole Solera *(Acct Supvr)*
Shayna Chapel *(Sr Acct Exec)*

Accounts:
Deloitte & Touche; 2007
FutureM Public Relations
Pete and Gerry's Organics; Monroe, NH Public Relations

CATAPULT PR-IR, L.L.C.
6560 Gunpark Dr Ste C, Boulder, CO 80301
Tel.: (303) 581-7760
Fax: (303) 581-7762
Toll Free: (866) 700-7760
E-Mail: contact@catapultpr-ir.com
Web Site: www.catapultpr-ir.com

Employees: 7

Agency Specializes In: Business-To-Business, Financial, High Technology, Investor Relations, New Technologies, Public Relations, RSS (Really Simple Syndication)

Terri Douglas *(Co-Founder & Principal)*
Guy Murrel *(Co-Founder & Principal)*
Jeremy Douglas *(Sr Acct Exec)*
Charles Trowbridge *(Jr Acct Exec)*
Halie Noble *(Acct Coord)*

Accounts:
Agile Alliance Media; 2007
BlogFrog Public Relations
CollabNet; Brisbane, CA; 2011
FreeWave Technologies; Boulder, CO; 2006
Inovonics
JNBridge; Boulder, CO; 2007
Room 214; Boulder, CO; 2007
Thought Works

CAUGHERTY HAHN COMMUNICATIONS, INC.
233 Rock Rd Ste 248, Glen Rock, NJ 07452
Tel.: (201) 251-7778
Fax: (201) 251-7776
E-Mail: president@chcomm.com
Web Site: www.chcomm.com

Employees: 2
Year Founded: 1993

National Agency Associations: PRSA

Agency Specializes In: Arts, Business-To-Business, Catalogs, Children's Market, Collateral, Communications, Consulting, Consumer Goods, Consumer Marketing, Corporate Communications, Crisis Communications, Customer Relationship Management, Direct Response Marketing, Direct-to-Consumer, E-Commerce, Event Planning & Marketing, Exhibit/Trade Shows, Faith Based, Fashion/Apparel, Health Care Services, Household Goods, Integrated Marketing, Local Marketing, Magazines, Media Relations, Medical Products, New Product Development, Newspaper, Planning & Consultation, Public Relations, Publicity/Promotions, Publishing, Restaurant, Retail, Search Engine Optimization, Seniors' Market, Social Marketing/Nonprofit, Social Media, Stakeholders, Strategic Planning/Research, Teen Market, Trade & Consumer Magazines, Travel & Tourism, Women's Market

Approx. Annual Billings: $1,000,000

Breakdown of Gross Billings by Media: Corp. Communications: 50%; Pub. Rels.: 25%; Strategic Planning/Research: 25%

John N. Hahn *(Owner)*
Lisa C. Hahn *(Pres & CEO)*

Accounts:
Highlights for Children; Columbus, OH
Highlights High Five; Honesdale, PA
Johnson Smith Co.; Bradenton, FL
Millard Group, Inc.; Peterborough, NH
NEMOA; Portland, ME
Trainers Warehouse; Natick, MA

CAVER PUBLIC RELATIONS
(Name Changed to Reputation Lighthouse)

CAWOOD
1200 High St Ste 200, Eugene, OR 97401-3222
Tel.: (541) 484-7052
Fax: (541) 345-1474
E-Mail: info@cawood.com
Web Site: www.cawood.com

E-Mail for Key Personnel:
President: liz@cawood.com
Media Dir.: melindad@cawood.com

Employees: 11
Year Founded: 1979

National Agency Associations: PRSA

Agency Specializes In: Advertising, Advertising Specialties, Brand Development & Integration, Communications, Consulting, Corporate Identity, Education, Government/Political, Graphic Design, Health Care Services, High Technology, Internet/Web Design, Logo & Package Design, Media Buying Services, Media Planning, Medical Products, Multimedia, Planning & Consultation, Public Relations, Publicity/Promotions, Radio, Strategic Planning/Research, T.V.

Liz Cawood *(Pres)*
Melinda Dille *(Dir-Media)*
Lindsey Ferguson *(Dir-Bus Dev)*
Cari Ingrassia *(Dir-Art)*
Paul Adkins *(Mgr-Internet & Sr Designer)*

Accounts:
Cascade Health Solutions
Mercedes-Benz of Eugene
Oregon Imaging Centers; Eugene, OR Imaging Service
Sure Crop Farm Services

CAYENNE COMMUNICATION
1250 Oakmead Pkwy Ste 210, Sunnyvale, CA 94085
Tel.: (408) 501-8829
Fax: (252) 940-4681
Web Site: www.cayennecom.com

Agency Specializes In: Advertising, Event Planning & Marketing, Media Relations, Public Relations, Strategic Planning/Research

Michelle Clancy *(Pres)*
Linda Marchant *(VP)*

Accounts:
Ansys, Inc.
Apache Corporation
Atoptech
AWR Corporation
Berkeley Design Automation, Inc.
Cliosoft
Concept Engineering, Inc.
Gradient, Corp.
Satin Technologies
Tanner EDA
Tuscany Design Automation

CBR PUBLIC RELATIONS
1495 N Maitland Ave, Maitland, FL 32751
Tel.: (407) 834-7777
Fax: (407) 834-7746
E-Mail: info@cbrpr.com
Web Site: www.cbrpr.com

Employees: 15
Year Founded: 1984

Agency Specializes In: Business-To-Business, Corporate Communications, Corporate Identity, Financial, Government/Political, Public Relations

Lori C. Booker *(Founder & CEO)*
Robert Perez *(Sr Acct Exec)*
Brittany Hobbs *(Acct Exec)*

Accounts:
Insperity

CCH MARKETING & PUBLIC RELATIONS
227 S Orlando Ave Ste 2B, Winter Park, FL 32789
Tel.: (407) 228-1901
E-Mail: info@cchmarketing.com
Web Site: www.cchmarketing.com

Agency Specializes In: Brand Development & Integration, Content, Email, Media Relations, Public Relations, Search Engine Optimization, Social Media

Cristina Calvet Harrold *(Founder & Pres)*
Bryan Harrold *(CFO & VP)*
April Stagl *(Art Dir)*
Kate Greenberg *(Acct Mgr)*
Cathrina Dionisio *(Mgr-Creative Svcs)*

Accounts:
New-Armando Soto
New-Orlando Health

CECE FEINBERG PUBLIC RELATIONS
336 W 37th St Ste 840, New York, NY 10018
Tel.: (212) 939-7265
Fax: (646) 224-2271
E-Mail: cece@feinbergpr.com
Web Site: www.feinbergpr.com

Employees: 6

Agency Specializes In: Entertainment, Fashion/Apparel, Local Marketing, Public Relations

Cece Feinberg *(Owner)*
Priscilla Burgos *(Acct Exec)*
Michelle Marcos *(Sr Acct Coord)*

Accounts:
Crystal Jin Swimwear
Shapeez
The Swimwear Association of Florida
Tees By Tina

Public Relations Firms

V Del Sol
Voga Italia Wines
Vonderbitch Public Relations

CEL PUBLIC RELATIONS INC

15600 36th Ave N Ste 120, Minneapolis, MN 55446
Tel.: (763) 559-6058
Toll Free: (888) 235-2780
E-Mail: info@celpr.com
Web Site: www.celpr.com

Agency Specializes In: Advertising, Brand Development & Integration, Content, Digital/Interactive, Graphic Design, Internet/Web Design, Media Relations, Package Design, Public Relations, Social Media

Cindy Leines *(Founder & Strategist)*
Kari Logan *(VP-PR)*
Chelsea Janke *(Client Svcs Mgr)*
Scott Rogers *(Specialist-Brand & Designer)*
Carol Scheer *(Specialist-Media Rels)*

Accounts:
Prosperwell Financial

CERRELL ASSOCIATES, INC.

320 N Larchmont Blvd, Los Angeles, CA 90004
Tel.: (323) 466-3445
Fax: (323) 466-8653
Web Site: www.cerrell.com

Employees: 30

National Agency Associations: PRSA

Agency Specializes In: Government/Political, Public Relations, Sponsorship

Approx. Annual Billings: $3,000,000

Breakdown of Gross Billings by Media: Pub. Rels.: $3,000,000

Lee Cerrell *(Owner)*
Mark Wittenberg *(Owner)*
Hal Dash *(Chm & CEO)*
Lisa Gritzner *(Pres)*
Steve Bullock *(CFO)*
Alisa Karlan *(VP-Land Use & Plng)*
Sean Rossall *(VP)*
Brandon Stephenson *(VP)*
Alex Comisar *(Mgr-Pub Affairs)*

Accounts:
Alameda Corridor Transportation Authority (ACTA)
Aquatic Foundation of Metropolitan Los Angeles
BP
California Association of Health Underwriters
California Climate Action Registry
GC Services
Law Enforcement Systems
Qantas Airways
University of Southern California
Watt Commercial Properties

CFM STRATEGIC COMMUNICATIONS, INC.

(Formerly Conkling Fiskum & McCormick, Inc.)
1100 SW 6th Ave Ste 1425, Portland, OR 97204
Tel.: (503) 294-9120
Fax: (503) 294-9152
Web Site: www.cfm-online.com

E-Mail for Key Personnel:
President: garyc@cfm-online.com

Employees: 50

National Agency Associations: WOMMA

Agency Specializes In: Communications, Consulting, Consumer Marketing, Corporate Identity, Event Planning & Marketing, Government/Political, Public Relations

Dan Jarman *(Co-Owner & Partner)*
Gary Conkling *(Pres)*
Tom Eiland *(Partner)*
Dave Fiskum *(Partner)*
J.E. Isaac *(Principal)*
Cindy Brown *(Office Mgr)*
Hannah Smith *(Strategist-Digital)*

Accounts:
Columbia River Pilots
EDS
M/A-COM Private Radio Systems, Inc.
Marion County
Oregon Public Broadcasting
T-Mobile US

Branches

CFM Strategic Communications, Inc.

(Formerly Conkling Fiskum & McCormick, Inc.)
3621 Augusta National Dr S, Salem, OR 97302
Tel.: (503) 362-8025
Fax: (503) 362-5096
E-Mail: davef@cfmsalem.com
Web Site: www.cfm-online.com

Employees: 1

Agency Specializes In: Public Relations

Dave Fiskum *(Partner)*

Accounts:
Providence

CFM Strategic Communications, Inc.

(Formerly Conkling Fiskum & McCormick, Inc.)
750 1St St NE, Washington, DC 20002
Tel.: (202) 347-9170
Fax: (503) 544-5321
E-Mail: danj@cfmdc.com
Web Site: www.cfm-online.com

Employees: 3

Agency Specializes In: Digital/Interactive, Government/Political, Public Relations, Viral/Buzz/Word of Mouth

Dan Jarman *(Co-Owner & Partner)*
Gary Conkling *(Pres)*
Dave Fiskum *(Partner)*
Joe Rubin *(VP-Federal Affairs)*
Alison Santore *(VP-Federal Affairs)*
Julie Crockett *(Mgr-Federal Affairs)*

Accounts:
City of Lacey
Clackamas County
Columbia River Pilots
Darden Restaurants
Hewlett-Packard
Oregon Public Broadcasting
Transcanada

CHAMBERLAIN HEALTHCARE PUBLIC RELATIONS

450 W 15th St Ste 405, New York, NY 10011
Tel.: (212) 884-0650
Fax: (212) 884-0628
E-Mail: info@chamberlainpr.com
Web Site: www.chamberlainpr.com

Employees: 35
Year Founded: 1993

Agency Specializes In: Health Care Services, Public Relations

Bob Josefsberg *(Exec VP)*
Leslie Casey *(VP-HR)*

Accounts:
Abbott Laboratories
American Association of Cancer Research
American Society of Hypertension
Boehringer Ingelheim Pradaxa
Eisai
National Lipid Association
Novartis Prexige Pain Reliever
Novavax
Pamlab
Pharmacopeia, Inc.

CHAMPION MANAGEMENT

15455 Dallas Pkwy, Addison, TX 75002
Tel.: (972) 930-9933
Fax: (972) 930-9903
E-Mail: info@championmgt.com
Web Site: www.championmgt.com

Agency Specializes In: Communications, Event Planning & Marketing, Public Relations

Ladd Biro *(Founder & Principal)*
Eric Spiritas *(Principal)*
Russell Ford *(Sr VP-Mktg)*
Courtney Hale *(Sr Mgr-Mktg)*

Accounts:
Bennigan's
CiCi's Pizza (Public Relations Agency of Record)
El Fenix
Genghis Grill
Lone Star Steakhouse
Nestle Toll House Cafe
Raising Cane's Chicken Fingers
Romano's Macaroni Grill
Snuffer's
Texas Land & Cattle

CHANGE COMMUNICATIONS

350 Townsend St Ste 720, San Francisco, CA 94107
Tel.: (415) 375-0663
E-Mail: info@bethechangepr.com
Web Site: www.bethechangepr.com

Year Founded: 2010

Agency Specializes In: Crisis Communications, Digital/Interactive, Public Relations, Social Media

Katy Lim *(Mng Dir)*

Accounts:
Drift Innovation

CHARLES ZUKOW ASSOCIATES LLC

1 Hallidie Plz Ste 501, San Francisco, CA 94102
Tel.: (415) 296-0677
Fax: (415) 296-0663
E-Mail: info@charleszukow.com
Web Site: www.charleszukow.com

Year Founded: 2002

Agency Specializes In: Advertising, Media Buying Services, Media Planning, Promotions, Public Relations, Sponsorship

Charles Zukow *(Owner)*
Kevin Kopjak *(Dir-PR)*
John Ferrara *(Mgr-Fin)*
Julie Richter *(Sr Acct Exec)*
James Smith *(Acct Exec)*
Viviana Uribe *(Asst Acct Exec-PR)*

Accounts:
American Conservatory Theater
Beach Blanket Babylon
Cirque du Soleil
Na Lei Hulu I Ka Wekiu
Pooch Hotels
Safeway Holiday Ice Rink
San Francisco Arts Education Project
San Francisco General Hospital Foundation
Tout Sweet

CHARTWELL AGENCY
(Formerly PR Etc.)
120 W State St Ste 305, Rockford, IL 61101
Tel.: (815) 282-9976
Fax: (815) 282-9986
E-Mail: info@chartwell-agency.com
Web Site: www.chartwell-agency.com/

Employees: 3

Agency Specializes In: Advertising, Event Planning & Marketing, Media Buying Services, Media Training, Public Relations, Strategic Planning/Research

Rebecca Kopf *(Pres & CEO)*
Emily Hartzog *(Dir)*
Michelle Polivka *(Dir)*
Deanna Jensen-Valliere *(Mgr-Relationship)*
Karli Smith *(Sr Acct Exec)*
Nancee Long *(Acct Exec)*
Cassi Steurer *(Strategist-Content Mktg)*

Accounts:
A Latino Community Resource Center
Bart Bike For The Arts
Chicago Rockford International Airport
Doculabs
First Congregational Church
Fitme Wellness
Gordon Food Service
Impact Advisors
In Home Medical Group Brand Identities, Produce Marketing, Rebranding Initiative
J. Kyle Braid Leadership Foundation
Larson & Darby Group
Medithin Weight Loss Clinics
Monmouth College
Reno & Zahm LLP
River District Association
Rockford Area Convention & Visitors Bureau
Rockford Area Economic Development Council
Rockford Area Venues & Entertainment
Rockford Art Museum; 2004
Rockford Bank & Trust
Rockford Chamber of Commerce
Rockford Mutual Insurance Company
Rockford Rescue Mission
Rockford Spine Center
Rockford YMCA
Rockford Youth Initiative, Inc.
Savant Capital Management
Southern Imperial Inc
XL Academics (Agency of Record) Content Marketing Strategy, Public Relations

Branch

Chartwell Agency
(Formerly PR Etc.)
4230 E Towne Blvd Ste 292, Madison, WI 53704
Tel.: (608) 239-0745
Fax: (815) 282-9986
E-Mail: info@chartwell-agency.com
Web Site: www.chartwell-agency.com

Agency Specializes In: Above-the-Line, Affiliate Marketing, Affluent Market, Agriculture, Arts, Automotive, Brand Development & Integration, Broadcast, Business Publications, Business-To-Business, Cable T.V., Catalogs, Children's Market, Collateral, College, Communications, Computers & Software, Consulting, Consumer Goods, Consumer Marketing, Consumer Publications, Content, Corporate Communications, Cosmetics, Crisis Communications, Customer Relationship Management, Digital/Interactive, Direct Response Marketing, Direct-to-Consumer, E-Commerce, Education, Electronic Media, Electronics, Email, Engineering, Entertainment, Environmental, Event Planning & Marketing, Exhibit/Trade Shows, Experience Design, Fashion/Apparel, Financial, Food Service, Government/Political, Guerilla Marketing, Health Care Services, High Technology, Hospitality, Household Goods, In-Store Advertising, Industrial, Infomercials, Information Technology, Integrated Marketing, International, Legal Services, Leisure, Local Marketing, Luxury Products, Magazines, Market Research, Media Buying Services, Media Planning, Media Relations, Media Training, Medical Products, Men's Market, Multicultural, Multimedia, New Product Development, New Technologies, Newspaper, Over-50 Market, Pharmaceutical, Planning & Consultation, Point of Sale, Print, Production, Production (Print), Promotions, Public Relations, Publicity/Promotions, Publishing, RSS (Really Simple Syndication), Radio, Real Estate, Recruitment, Regional, Restaurant, Retail, Sales Promotion, Seniors' Market, Social Marketing/Nonprofit, Sponsorship, Sports Market, Stakeholders, Strategic Planning/Research, Syndication, T.V., Teen Market, Trade & Consumer Magazines, Transportation, Travel & Tourism, Urban Market, Viral/Buzz/Word of Mouth, Women's Market

Rebecca Epperson *(Pres)*
Elizabeth Lazdins *(Office Mgr)*
Deanna jensen-Valliere *(Mgr-Relationship)*
Cassi Steurer *(Strategist-Content Mktg)*

Accounts:
Applied Ecological Services
Bacchus Wine Bar & Restaurant
Carlyle Brewing Company
InstallShield Software
LifeStream International
Milwaukee Public Schools
Riviana Foods
Westin Hotels

CHATTERBOX PR INK
14141 Covello St Ste 4A, Van Nuys, CA 91405
Tel.: (818) 203-6060
E-Mail: inkme@chatterboxink.com
Web Site: www.chatterboxink.com

Year Founded: 2001

Agency Specializes In: Corporate Communications, Event Planning & Marketing, Media Relations, Media Training, Print, Public Relations, Radio, Social Media, Strategic Planning/Research, T.V.

Gretchen Hydo *(Pres)*
Ray Young *(Sr VP)*
John Hydo *(VP-Mktg & Events)*

Accounts:
CleanCierge
Heretick Theatre Lab
The Israel Conference

CHEMISTRY
1660 Union St 4th Fl, San Diego, CA 92101
Tel.: (619) 236-8397
Fax: (619) 236-8497
E-Mail: mixitup@prchemistry.com
Web Site: www.prchemistry.com

Employees: 5
Year Founded: 1999

Agency Specializes In: Business-To-Business, Consumer Goods, Consumer Marketing, Corporate Communications, Entertainment, Event Planning & Marketing, Fashion/Apparel, Food Service, Government/Political, Health Care Services, Hospitality, Local Marketing, Luxury Products, Media Relations, Media Training, Public Relations, Real Estate, Restaurant, Retail, Sponsorship, Strategic Planning/Research, Travel & Tourism, Viral/Buzz/Word of Mouth, Women's Market

Audrey Doherty *(Owner)*
Mike Garner *(Dir-Creative)*
Paloma Colon *(Sr Acct Exec)*
Rob Maguire *(Copywriter)*
Katie Barton *(Asst Acct Exec)*
Kerrianne Key *(Acct Coord)*
Chelsea Lashua *(Acct Coord)*

Accounts:
Andaz; San Diego
Barona Resort & Casino; San Diego, CA Casino Resort; 2001
Britvic Ireland Campaign: "The Ultimate Wingman"
Evolve Saloon
The Glass Door
Hyatt Regency Mission Bay; San Diego, CA Hotel; 2007
Ivy Hotel; San Diego, CA Luxury Hotel; 2006
Kelly Capital
Kerry Foods Campaign: "Adland Gal "
KMA Architecture & Engineering
San Diego Building Owners & Managers Association (BOMA)

CHERYL ANDREWS MARKETING COMMUNICATIONS
331 Almeria Ave, Coral Gables, FL 33134-5814
Tel.: (305) 444-4033
Fax: (305) 447-0415
E-Mail: info@cam-pr.com
Web Site: www.cam-pr.com

Employees: 18
Year Founded: 1984

Agency Specializes In: Communications, Public Relations, Travel & Tourism

Cheryl Andrews *(Pres & CEO)*
Claire Kunzman *(VP-Client Svcs)*
Ileana Perez *(VP-Fin)*
Jim Stephens *(VP-Creative)*
Jennifer Johnson *(Sr Acct Supvr)*
Melissa Benhaim *(Acct Exec)*
Manuel Cedeno *(Acct Exec)*

Accounts:
Bucuti Beach Resort & Tera Suite; Aruba
Costa Rica Tourism Board Campaign: "Save the Americans", PR
Four Seasons Resort Nevis (North American Public Relations Agency of Record)
Grand Residences Riviera Cancun
Hyatt Regency Trinidad
The Marker Resort (North American Public Relations Agency of Record)
Montserrat Development Corporation Economic Growth, Investment Opportunities, Public Relations
Ocean Club Resorts
Provident Luxury Suites Fisher Island
Sirenis Hotels & Resorts Public Relations
Unikgo.com
New-Viceroy Anguilla (Public Relations Agency of Record) Digital, Print, Social Media

CHILD'S PLAY COMMUNICATIONS
12 W 31 St 6th Fl, New York, NY 10001
Tel.: (212) 488-2060, ext. 11
Fax: (212) 488-2059

E-Mail: sa@childsplaypr.com
Web Site: www.childsplaypr.com

Employees: 10
Year Founded: 1988

Agency Specializes In: Children's Market, Collateral, Entertainment, Exhibit/Trade Shows, Guerilla Marketing, Promotions, Public Relations, Publicity/Promotions, Retail, Sales Promotion, Strategic Planning/Research, Teen Market, Viral/Buzz/Word of Mouth, Women's Market

Stephanie Azzarone *(Founder & Pres)*
Debbie Bookstaber *(Acting Dir-Media Social)*
Selena Rodriguez *(Sr Acct Exec)*
Nancy Johnson Horn *(Community Mgr)*

Accounts:
Aurora World Bogger Outreach, Media Relations
Bundoo
New-Captain McFinn & Friends Media Relations, Public Relations
Creata Blogger, Communication, Marketing, Media Relations, Monster 500
Disney
DK Media Relations
Entertainment One Public Relations, Social Media
Filip Technologies FiLIP2 Wearable Phone
Ganz; Ontario, Canada Public Relations, Tail Towns Friends facebook Game & Gift Collection, Traditional Media
Gund Media
Hasbro
Heinz
Hewlett Packard
iDeaUSA Media Relations, Q Whoo, THE Q
Kiwi Crate
Legacy Games Crayola DJ, Media Relations
littleBits
MAM USA (Agency of Record) Bottles, Oral Care Products, Pacifiers, Teethers, Traditional & Social Media Relations
Mibblio Blogger Outreach, Traditional Media
Parents Magazine
Produce for Kids Media, Public Relations
RoomMates Blogger Outreach, Line of Peel & Stick Wall Decal, Magic Hooks, Mirrors, PR, Room Decor
RRKidz; Los Angeles, CA Reading Rainbow
SoCozy Hair Care Social Media
Sylvan Learning Center
Time Inc
Toy State
Warner Bros
Wildlife Conservation Society
Wunderkind Media & Technology Corp. Marketing, Media Relations, Preggie

CHRISTIE & CO
(Formerly Christie Communications, Inc.)
800 Garden St Ste B, Santa Barbara, CA 93101
Tel.: (805) 969-3744
Fax: (805) 969-3697
Web Site: www.christieand.co/

Employees: 15
Year Founded: 1992

Agency Specializes In: Crisis Communications, Event Planning & Marketing, Exhibit/Trade Shows, Internet/Web Design, Investor Relations, Market Research, Package Design, Print, Production, Public Relations

Revenue: $1,600,000

Gillian Christie *(Founder & CEO)*
Marty Brown *(COO)*
Alissa Sears *(Dir-Betterment-Global & Sr Strategist)*
Ava Ames *(Dir-Comm)*
Tony de Moraes *(Co-Dir-Creative)*
Lisa Lashaway *(Dir-Market Res)*
Arthur Rumaya *(Co-Dir-Creative)*
Chelsea Locatelli *(Mgr-Comm)*
Rajan De Los Santos *(Sr Acct Exec-PR)*
Lauren Haines *(Acct Exec)*

Accounts:
Agro Innova Suavva
Icebox Water In a Box Marketing, Public Relations, Social Media
PRO-LAB Allergen Test Kits, Marketing
New-Rebbl (Agency of Record)

CHRISTIE COMMUNICATIONS, INC.
(Name Changed to Christie & Co)

C.I. VISIONS INC.
281 Ave C Ste 9A, New York, NY 10009
Tel.: (212) 477-4755
Fax: (212) 253-1556
E-Mail: info@civisions.com

Employees: 20

Agency Specializes In: Above-the-Line, Advertising, Advertising Specialties, Affiliate Marketing, Affluent Market, African-American Market, Agriculture, Alternative Advertising, Arts, Asian Market, Automotive, Aviation & Aerospace, Below-the-Line, Bilingual Market, Brand Development & Integration, Branded Entertainment, Broadcast, Business Publications, Business-To-Business, Cable T.V., Catalogs, Children's Market, Co-op Advertising, Collateral, College, Commercial Photography, Communications, Computers & Software, Consulting, Consumer Goods, Consumer Marketing, Consumer Publications, Content, Corporate Communications, Corporate Identity, Cosmetics, Crisis Communications, Custom Publishing, Customer Relationship Management, Digital/Interactive, Direct Response Marketing, Direct-to-Consumer, E-Commerce, Education, Electronic Media, Electronics, Email, Engineering, Entertainment, Environmental, Event Planning & Marketing, Exhibit/Trade Shows, Experience Design, Fashion/Apparel, Financial, Food Service, Game Integration, Gay & Lesbian Market, Government/Political, Graphic Design, Guerilla Marketing, Health Care Services, High Technology, Hispanic Market, Hospitality, Household Goods, Identity Marketing, In-Store Advertising, Industrial, Infomercials, Information Technology, Integrated Marketing, International, Internet/Web Design, Investor Relations, Legal Services, Leisure, Local Marketing, Logo & Package Design, Luxury Products, Magazines, Marine, Market Research, Media Buying Services, Media Planning, Media Relations, Media Training, Medical Products, Men's Market, Merchandising, Mobile Marketing, Multicultural, Multimedia, New Product Development, New Technologies, Newspaper, Newspapers & Magazines, Out-of-Home Media, Outdoor, Over-50 Market, Package Design, Paid Searches, Pharmaceutical, Planning & Consultation, Podcasting, Point of Purchase, Point of Sale, Print, Product Placement, Production, Production (Ad, Film, Broadcast), Production (Print), Promotions, Public Relations, Publicity/Promotions, Publishing, RSS (Really Simple Syndication), Radio, Real Estate, Recruitment, Regional, Restaurant, Retail, Sales Promotion, Search Engine Optimization, Seniors' Market, Social Marketing/Nonprofit, South Asian Market, Sponsorship, Sports Market, Stakeholders, Strategic Planning/Research, Sweepstakes, Syndication, T.V., Technical Advertising, Teen Market, Telemarketing, Trade & Consumer Magazines, Transportation, Travel & Tourism, Urban Market, Viral/Buzz/Word of Mouth, Web (Banner Ads, Pop-ups, etc.), Women's Market, Yellow Pages Advertising

Revenue: $2,000,000

Carol A. Ientile *(Owner)*

Accounts:
Sea Change New York

CIER B. PUBLIC RELATIONS
PO Box 1295, Fairburn, GA 30213
Tel.: (770) 558-7582
E-Mail: info@cierpr.com
Web Site: www.cierpr.com

Year Founded: 2013

Agency Specializes In: Corporate Identity, Media Relations, Public Relations

Accounts:
Parents Against Distracted Driving

CINCH PR & BRANDING GROUP
632 Commercial St 2nd Fl, San Francisco, CA 94111
Tel.: (415) 392-2230
E-Mail: info@cinchpr.com
Web Site: www.cinchpr.com

Agency Specializes In: Event Planning & Marketing, Media Relations, Media Training, Public Relations, Social Media, Strategic Planning/Research

Alli Goldstein *(Founder & Pres)*
Tegan Kopilenko *(Sr Acct Mgr)*
Emily Beaven *(Acct Mgr)*
Alexandra Ludmer *(Acct Mgr)*
Amanda Beck *(Acct Exec)*
Michael Radlick *(Acct Exec)*
Erin Carpenter *(Acct Coord)*

Accounts:
Visit Mendocino County

CINDY RICCIO COMMUNICATIONS, INC.
1133 Broadway Ste 1021, New York, NY 10010
Tel.: (646) 205-3573
E-Mail: info@cricciocomm.com
Web Site: www.cricciocomm.com

Year Founded: 2007

Agency Specializes In: Corporate Communications, Event Planning & Marketing, Media Relations, Public Relations, Social Media

Cindy Riccio *(Founder & Pres)*
John Mooney *(Dir-Corp Comm, Sports Mktg & Media)*
Anna Dutkowsky *(Acct Exec)*

Accounts:
Charles & Colvard Ltd
Dr. Rosemarie Ingleton Communications, Marketing
New-Nicole Andrews Collection (Agency of Record) Public Relations
Perfect Corp. (Agency of Record) Consumer, Marketing Communications, Media, Public Relations Strategy, Social

CITIZEN OPTIMUM
500 King St W, Toronto, ON M5V 1L9 Canada
Tel.: (416) 934-8011
Web Site: ca.citizenrelations.com/

Agency Specializes In: Communications, Corporate Communications, Crisis Communications, Media Relations, Media Training, Public Relations, Social

Media

David Brodie *(Sr VP-Rels Intl)*
Nick Cowling *(VP & Gen Mgr)*
Sherry Boisvert *(VP-Citizen Rels)*
Christine Scott *(VP-Experiential Events)*
Amanda Shuchat *(VP-Citizen Rels Intl)*
Andrea Anders *(Sr Dir-Citizen Rels)*
Ive Balins *(Assoc Dir)*
Megan Vieira *(Sr Mgr-Ops-Citizen Rels)*
Nicole Brightling *(Acct Mgr)*
Kathleen Edmondson *(Acct Mgr)*

Accounts:
Canadian Carpet Recovery Effort
Hyundai Auto Canada
Sleeman Breweries National PR
Solar Power Network

CITIZEN RELATIONS
(Formerly Citizen Paine)
19000 MacArthur Blvd, Irvine, CA 92612
Tel.: (949) 809-6700
Web Site: us.citizenrelations.com

National Agency Associations: COPF

Agency Specializes In: Brand Development & Integration, Communications, Public Relations, Sponsorship

Laura Bremer *(Mng Dir)*
Cynthia Rude *(COO)*
Megan Van Vleet *(Mgr-Mktg)*
Vanessa Barbieri *(Client Svc Mgr)*

Accounts:
Avery Office Products Supply Services
Cadbury Dentyne Dental Mint
Duracell Battery Mfr, PR, Social Media
General Motors Automobile Mfr
Green & Black's Organic Chocolate Mfr
L.A. Care Health Plan Health Insurance Services
Mondelez International, Inc. Food Products Mfr
Procter & Gamble Pampers
New-Rocky Mountaineer

Branches:

Citizen Paine
(Formerly PainePR)
415 Madison Ave 2nd Fl, New York, NY 10017
Tel.: (212) 613-4900
Fax: (212) 868-7206
Web Site: us.citizenrelations.com

Employees: 20

Agency Specializes In: Public Relations

Jon Cronin *(Mng Dir-Social Engagement)*
Amanda Teitler *(Dir-Citizen Rels Intl)*
Megan Van Vleet *(Mgr-Mktg)*
Katelyn Driscoll *(Client Svc Mgr)*
Chelsea Levy *(Client Svc Mgr)*
Alix Parkinson *(Client Svc Mgr)*
Susan Rotante *(Client Svc Mgr)*

Accounts:
Dreft
Duracell Campaign: "Power those Who Protect us"
GM
Luvs
Pampers
Procter & Gamble Co Old Spice, Public Relations
Sony
Suzuki
Toshiba

Citizen Paine
(Formerly PainePR)
660 S Figueroa St 20th Fl, Los Angeles, CA 90017-3442
Tel.: (213) 430-0480
Fax: (213) 430-0494
Web Site: us.citizenrelations.com

Employees: 25
Year Founded: 1992

National Agency Associations: COPF

Agency Specializes In: Business-To-Business, Public Relations

Angela Alvarez *(Mng Dir)*
Laura Bremer *(Mng Dir)*
Erin Georgieff *(Mng Dir)*
Megan Van Vleet *(Mgr-Mktg)*
Vanessa Barbieri *(Client Svc Mgr)*

CJ PUBLIC RELATIONS
(Formerly The Kotchen Group)
50 Center St, Southington, CT 06489
Tel.: (860) 676-2266
Fax: (860) 676-2267
Web Site: cjpr.com

Employees: 5
Year Founded: 1991

Agency Specializes In: Automotive, Consumer Marketing, Entertainment, Fashion/Apparel, Food Service, Public Relations, Retail

Approx. Annual Billings: $287,606

Elizabeth Cowles Johnston *(Pres)*
Michele Brysgel *(Office Mgr)*

Accounts:
Cognate Nutritionals
Energize Connecticut
Hartford Marathon Foundation
NU Hartford Marathon
School Nutrition Association of Georgia
School Nutrition Association of Minnesota
United Illuminating

CKC AGENCY
28580 Orchard Lake Rd Ste 210, Farmington Hills, MI 48334
Tel.: (248) 788-1744
Fax: (248) 788-1742
E-Mail: info@ckcagency.com
Web Site: www.ckcagency.com

Agency Specializes In: Event Planning & Marketing, Internet/Web Design, Media Planning, Media Relations, Public Relations, Social Media

Pat Baskin *(Mng Dir)*
Alison Schwartz *(VP-PR)*
Vickie Sullen-Winn *(VP-Media & Community Rels)*
Alanna Cohen *(Mgr-Social Media)*

Accounts:
Annette J. Benson & Associates
Motor City Comic Con
Shanbom Eye Specialist
Trenton Summer Festival
Von Maur Inc.

CLAIREMONT COMMUNICATIONS
101 S Bloodworth St, Raleigh, NC 27601
Tel.: (615) 294-1886
Web Site: www.clairemontcommunications.com

Agency Specializes In: Communications, Crisis Communications, Event Planning & Marketing, Media Relations, Public Relations, Social Media

Dana Hughens *(CEO)*
Sarah Hattman *(Acct Exec)*
Cherith Mangum *(Acct Exec)*

Accounts:
Il Palio Ristorante (Agency of Record)
The Siena Hotel (Agency of Record) Communications, Public Relations
New-Triangle Dairy Queen

CLARK COMMUNICATIONS
131 Division Ave S Ste 100, Grand Rapids, MI 49503-4282
Tel.: (616) 550-4396
Fax: (616) 458-9600
E-Mail: info@clarkcommunication.com
Web Site: www.clarkcommunication.com

Employees: 2

Craig Clark *(Owner)*

CLARUS COMMUNICATIONS
620 Mullady Pkwy, Libertyville, IL 60048
Tel.: (847) 816-9411
E-Mail: mconklin@teamclarus.com
Web Site: www.teamclarus.com

Year Founded: 1998

Agency Specializes In: Business-To-Business, Crisis Communications, Media Relations, Media Training, Public Relations, Social Media, Strategic Planning/Research

Mara Conklin *(Founder & Pres)*
Linda Muskin *(Partner)*

Accounts:
Clifton Gunderson Public Accounting & Consulting Services
Compendium Brand Awareness
YourEncore

CLARY COMMUNICATIONS
(Name Changed to FrazierHeiby, Inc.)

CLEARPOINT AGENCY
511 Saxony Pl Ste 102A, Encinitas, CA 92024-2871
Tel.: (760) 230-2424
Fax: (858) 724-0614
E-Mail: info@clearpointagency.com
Web Site: www.clearpointagency.com

Employees: 7
Year Founded: 2002

Agency Specializes In: High Technology, Information Technology, Public Relations, Publicity/Promotions, Retail

Bonnie Shaw *(Pres)*
Beth Walsh *(VP)*
Samantha Peterson *(Acct Exec)*
Amanda Whitlock *(Acct Exec)*
Julie Willis *(Specialist-PR)*

Accounts:
5D Robotics PR
Across Systems GmbH
BluFi Direct Mortgage (Agency of Record)
BrandMaker, Inc
Connequity Digital, Marketing Communications, Public Relations
CUSO Financial Services
Drug Information Association Public Relations
HERAE
New-San Diego County Vintners Association Digital Strategy, Public Relations
Synteract HCR Content Development, Graphic

Design, Media Relations, Messaging
Zodiac Pool Systems, Inc. Digital & Social Media, Jandy Pro Series, Media Relations, Polaris, Public Relations, Social Media Consumer Campaigns, Zodiac

CLIVE HOFFMAN ASSOCIATES

9107 Wilshire Blvd Ste 500, Beverly Hills, CA 90210
Tel.: (310) 205-9930
Fax: (310) 205-9932
E-Mail: info@clivehoffmanassociates.com
Web Site: www.clivehoffmanassociates.com

Employees: 2

Agency Specializes In: Corporate Communications, Financial, Real Estate

Clive Hoffman *(Pres & CEO)*
Jill Hoffman *(VP)*

Accounts:
American National Bank
Arden Realty, Inc.
Deloitte & Touche, LLP
Los Angeles Neighborhood Land Trust
Mortgage Association of California
The RREEF Funds
Southern California Bank
Tishman Realty & Construction
Walker & Associates

CLY COMMUNICATION

80 Pine ST 24th Fl, New York, NY 10005
Tel.: (212) 256-1153
E-Mail: office@c-l-y.com
Web Site: www.c-l-y.com

Agency Specializes In: Brand Development & Integration, Event Planning & Marketing, Public Relations, Social Media

Castelli Raffaele *(Owner)*
Carmen Schoeller *(Dir-Ops)*

Accounts:
New-American Tourister
New-Michalsky StyleNite
New-Photowall

CMPR LLC

1600 Rosecrans Ave Bldg 2B 3rd Fl, Manhattan Beach, CA 90266
Tel.: (310) 426-9900
Web Site: www.cmpr.net

Year Founded: 2004

Agency Specializes In: Event Planning & Marketing, Media Training, Public Relations, Social Media

Steve Webster *(Pres & CEO)*
Mike Semanoff *(VP-CMPR Outdoors)*
Daniel Almond *(Dir-Publicity & Events)*
Sean Bell *(Dir-Social Media)*
Audrey Capin *(Dir-Bus Ops)*
Candice Rosenkranz *(Dir-Events & Publicity)*
John Swidzinski *(Mgr-Publicity)*

Accounts:
The Apprentice
The Celebrity Apprentice
One Three TV
Shine America
The Voice

COBURN COMMUNICATIONS

130 W 42nd St Ste 950, New York, NY 10036
Tel.: (212) 730-7277
Fax: (212) 730-4738
E-Mail: winston.beigel@coburnww.com
Web Site: www.coburnww.com

Employees: 30

Agency Specializes In: Entertainment, Food Service, Health Care Services, Luxury Products, Media Planning, Media Relations, Pets, Promotions, Public Relations, Sponsorship, Strategic Planning/Research

Shirine Coburn *(Owner)*
Winston Beigel *(CMO)*
Quinn Daly *(Exec VP)*
Melissa Montgomery *(VP-Ops)*
Katie Waters *(Assoc VP)*
Caroline Brayson *(Acct Dir)*
Dan Perlowitz *(Acct Supvr)*
Michael Butler *(Specialist-Mktg)*
Laura Finkelstein *(Assoc Acct Exec)*
Chelsea Simmons *(Assoc Acct Supvr)*

Accounts:
The CLIO Awards
New-CustomInk
Discovery/Animal Planet
Every Day with Rachael Ray
MTV
Rodale

COHN & WOLFE

200 Fifth Ave, New York, NY 10010
Tel.: (212) 798-9700
Fax: (212) 329-9900
E-Mail: donna_imperato@cohnwolfe.com
Web Site: www.cohnwolfe.com

Year Founded: 1984

National Agency Associations: COPF

Agency Specializes In: Public Relations, Sponsorship

Donna Imperato *(CEO)*
Tiffany Bai *(Mng Dir)*
Marta Karlqvist *(Pres-Nordics)*
Chad Latz *(Pres-Digital Innovation Grp-Global)*
Olga Fleming *(Exec VP & Mng Dir-NY Healthcare Practice)*
Jillian Janaczek *(Exec VP & Mng Dir-NY Healthcare)*
Lisa Talbot *(Exec VP & Mng Dir-NY Healthcare Practice)*
Maura Bergen *(Exec VP)*
Vicky Lewko *(Sr VP & Head-Digital Health)*
Kim Erlichson *(Sr VP)*
Stephanie Howley *(Sr VP-HR)*
Belinda Martin *(Sr VP)*
Jacelyn Seng *(Sr VP)*
Laura Ryan *(Mng Dir-US Corp Practice)*
Kerri Allen *(VP-Multicultural Practice-US)*
Jessica Donnelly *(VP-Healthcare Media Rels)*
Dana Gulick *(VP)*
Blake Sweat Overby *(VP)*
Anne Draddy *(Acct Dir)*
Krystina Fisher *(Acct Dir)*
James Walker *(Acct Dir-Digital)*
Helen Cheuck *(Mgr-HR)*
Christianna Giordano *(Acct Supvr & Strategist-Digital)*
Bailey Pescatore *(Acct Supvr)*
Tara Horan *(Sr Acct Exec)*
Lesley Stanley *(Sr Acct Exec)*
Gwen Baer *(Acct Exec-Digital)*
Sarah El-Qunni *(Acct Exec)*
Lauren Minella *(Acct Exec)*
Dana Simone *(Acct Exec)*
Shayda Teymourpour *(Acct Exec)*

Accounts:
3M
AeroDesigns, Inc
ASISA
Aventis Pharmaceuticals
Bang & Olufsen
Berkeley Point Capital Rebranding
Buick Brand Promotion
Chattem, Inc.
Children's Health Fund Creative, Digital
Choice Hotels International Public Relations
Colgate Irish Spring Body Wash
Eli Lilly
Hilton Worldwide
Hipmunk Brand Awareness
Homeward Residential, Inc.; Dallas, TX Rebranding
IBM Internet Security Systems, Inc.
Interwoven
Invesco PowerShares Media Relations, PR
Iroko Pharmaceuticals
The J.M. Smucker Company
Kaspersky Lab Americas
Lego
LexisNexis Content Development, Media & Analyst Relations, PR, Risk Solutions, Thought Leadership
LG Electronics
MasterCard Digital, Social
The Medicines Company
Merck
Moet Hennessy USA Hennessy, Media, Public Relations
Monument Wealth Management Content Development, Positioning, Strategic Marketing
Nike
Nissan North America (Agency of Record) Hispanic Public Relations, Media
Nokia Global PR
Panasonic HC-V10
PANDORA A/S (Public Relations Agency of Record) Consumer Public Relations, Content Marketing, Event Marketing, Media Relations
Pete & Gerry's Heirloom Eggs, Media, Organic Eggs, PR
Rock in Rio US Agency of Record
Rolex
Samsung
Scuderi Group; Springfield, MA
Tom's of Maine, Inc.

Branches

AxiCom Cohn & Wolfe

AxiCom Court 67 Barnes High Street, London, SW13 9LE United Kingdom
Tel.: (44) 20 8392 4050
Fax: (44) 20 8392 4055
E-Mail: jtanner@axicom.com
Web Site: www.axicom.com

Employees: 40
Year Founded: 1994

Agency Specializes In: High Technology, Information Technology, Public Relations

Julian Tanner *(Founder & Chm)*
Helen Ridgway *(CEO)*
Henry Brake *(Mng Dir)*
Lyle Closs *(Mng Dir-Europe)*
Sabine Mannhardt *(Dir-Fin-Europe)*
Stephen Orr *(Dir-Media Tech)*
Kate Stevens *(Dir-Consumer Tech)*
Richard White *(Dir-Telecoms)*

Accounts:
Blurb Publishing Services
Cirrus Logic
Dell
edge IPK
Fujitsu Analyst Relations
Harmonic Inc.

Imprivata
Ingres Corporation Software
Intelligent Energy Hydrogen Fuel Cells
LaCie Computer Peripherals
Neato Robotics
The Neverfail Group Software
Nokia
OpenText GXS
Pace
Panasonic AVC Systems Europe
Qualcomm Electric Vehicles, Media, PR
RealNetworks, Inc. Digital Entertainment Services
Red Hat
ShoreTel, Inc.
Sling Media; 2006
Stratus Technologies
Vizioncore Inc.

Cohn & Wolfe XPR Indonesia
Equity Tower Building 35th Fl JL Jend, Sudirman Kav 52-53, Jakarta, 12190 Indonesia
Tel.: (62) 21 2927 7912
E-Mail: info@cohnwolfexpr.com
Web Site: www.cohnwolfexpr.com

Andrew Goldman *(Mng Dir-Indonesia)*
Maria Tobing *(Sr Acct Dir)*

Accounts:
Bayer
Channel News Asia
Dell
Fox Sports
Google
Grant Thornton
Living Social
Skyscanner
SPC

Blackie McDonald
(Formerly Blackie McDonald - Melbourne)
Level 8 65 Berry St, North Sydney, NSW 2060 Australia
Tel.: (61) 2 8907 4900
Fax: (61) 2 8907 4988
E-Mail: info@bmcd.com.au
Web Site: www.bmcd.com.au

Employees: 25

Agency Specializes In: Communications, Event Planning & Marketing, Exhibit/Trade Shows, Investor Relations, Planning & Consultation, Publicity/Promotions, Strategic Planning/Research

Mark Lenyszyn *(Gen Mgr)*
Derek Evans *(Sr Acct Dir)*
Rachel Love *(Sr Acct Mgr)*

Accounts:
EMC
Lexmark
Panasonic Australia Campaign: "Lostproof"
Qantas
RSA

Cohn & Wolfe Austin
(Formerly Cohn & Wolfe Read-Poland)
327 Congress Ave Ste 500, Austin, TX 78701-3656
Tel.: (512) 472-4122
Fax: (512) 472-5970
Toll Free: (800) 472-4122
Web Site: www.cohnwolfe.com/

Employees: 20
Year Founded: 1952

National Agency Associations: COPF

Agency Specializes In: Government/Political, Public Relations

Matt McGinnis *(Exec VP & Mng Dir-Austin)*
Brooke Hovey *(Exec VP-Strategy & Dev-Global)*
Emily Poe *(Exec VP)*
Nicole Hubik Pampe *(VP)*
Madison Laroche *(Acct Dir)*
Matthew Young *(Sr Acct Exec)*
Paola Reyes *(Asst Acct Exec)*

Accounts:
Bazaarvoice
Dell
Pervasive
Sonic Corp. Cause Marketing, External Communications, Issues Management, Local Store Marketing, PR, Social Media Strategy

Cohn & Wolfe Benelux
Danzigerkade 53, Amsterdam, 1013AP Amsterdam, Netherlands
Tel.: (31) 20 676 86 66
Fax: (31) 20 6735 431
E-Mail: erik@cohnwolfe.nl
Web Site: www.cohnwolfe.com/nl

Employees: 14
Year Founded: 1984

Agency Specializes In: Communications, Government/Political, Public Relations

Erik Graadt Van Roggen *(Mng Dir)*

Accounts:
The Bolton Group
Colgate-Palmolive Colgate, Elmex, Public Relations, Sanex
The Elephant Parade
Jysk
Medtronic
Navigon
Royal Club Campaign: "Royal Club Shandy"
Stichting Nederland Schoon
War Trauma Foundation

Cohn & Wolfe
via Benedetto Marcello 63, 20124 Milan, Italy
Tel.: (39) 02 202 391
Fax: (39) 02 201 584
E-Mail: franco_guzzi@cohnwolfe.com
Web Site: www.cohnwolfe.com

Employees: 30
Year Founded: 1995

Agency Specializes In: Public Relations

Franco Guzzi *(Pres-Milan)*
Lorenzo Petracco *(Head-Digital Innovation Grp-Italy)*
Alessandra Bettelli *(Sr Acct Mgr)*
Stefania Biagini *(Sr Acct Mgr)*
Silvia Colleoni *(Sr Acct Mgr)*
Roberto Peraboni *(Sr Acct Mgr-Digital Innovation Grp)*
Giulia Perani *(Acct Mgr)*
Valentina Sargenti *(Acct Mgr)*

Accounts:
Skyscanner

Cohn & Wolfe
1 Rue Lugardon, CH-1201 Geneva, Switzerland
Mailing Address:
PO Box 2344, 1211 Geneva, 1 Switzerland
Tel.: (41) 22 908 40 70
Fax: (41) 22 908 40 40
E-Mail: victoria.dix@cohnwolfe.com
Web Site: www.cohnwolfe.com

Employees: 10

Agency Specializes In: Public Relations

Cohn & Wolfe
30 Orange Street, London, WC2H 7LZ United Kingdom
Tel.: (44) 207 331 5300
Fax: (44) 207 331 9083
E-Mail: jonathan_shore@uk.cohnwolfe.com
Web Site: www.cohnwolfe.com

Employees: 70
Year Founded: 1987

Agency Specializes In: Electronic Media, Health Care Services, Public Relations, Publicity/Promotions, Sports Market

Jeremy Baka *(Chief Creative Officer & Exec VP)*
Scott Wilson *(CEO-UK & Mng Dir-EMEA)*
Andrew Escott *(Mng Dir-Corp Affairs)*
Rebecca Grant *(Mng Dir-Consumer Mktg-UK & EMEA)*
Helen Searle *(Mng Dir-Corp Affairs)*
Kate Joynes-Burgess *(Head-Digital & Integrated Mktg-UK & EMEA)*
Gabrielle Lovering *(Head-Digital)*
Christine Chapman *(Sr Dir)*

Accounts:
Barclaycard UK Corporate Public Relations
BazaarVoice Social & E-Commerce Software; 2013
Burger King Public Affairs
Caran d'Ache PR
Consorzio Grana Padano PR
New-Crop Protection Association Issues Management, Media Relations
New-Global Blue Global Public Relations
Twinings Public Relations
GlaxoSmithKline

Cohn & Wolfe
C/ Fuencarral 6, 28006 Madrid, Spain
Tel.: (34) 91 531 42 67
Fax: (34) 91 531 39 88
E-Mail: almudena.alonso@cohnwolfe.com
Web Site: www.cohnwolfe.com

Employees: 15
Year Founded: 2000

Agency Specializes In: Brand Development & Integration, Health Care Services, New Technologies, Public Relations

Almudena Alonso *(CEO)*
Ignacio Casas *(Sr Acct Exec)*

Accounts:
Dell
Kelisto.es
Skyscanner

Cohn & Wolfe
175 Bloor St E Ste 705, Toronto, ON M4W 3R8 Canada
Tel.: (416) 924-5700
Fax: (416) 924-6606
E-Mail: peter.block@cohnwolfe.ca
Web Site: www.cohnwolfe.ca

Employees: 35

Agency Specializes In: Public Relations

Tim Moro *(Mng Partner-Calgary)*
Larry Clausen *(Exec VP-Western Canada)*
Jennifer Meehan *(Sr VP-Consumer Mktg & Digital)*
Lindsay Peterson-Chisholm *(VP)*
Gal Wilder *(Acct Grp Dir)*
Christine Boivin *(Dir-Mktg Comm)*

Craig Ritchie *(Dir-Creative)*
Genevieve Benoit *(Acct Coord)*
Olivier Gagnon *(Acct Coord)*
Laetitia Dubois-Poggi *(Coord)*

Cohn & Wolfe
2001 Ave McGill College Bureau 760, Montreal, QC H3A 1G1 Canada
Tel.: (514) 845-2257
Fax: (514) 845-4075
E-Mail: melanie.joly@cohnwolfe.ca
Web Site: www.cohnwolfe.ca

Employees: 15

Agency Specializes In: Public Relations

Andre Bouthillier *(Mng Partner-Montreal)*
Tim Moro *(Mng Partner-Calgary)*
Larry Clausen *(Exec VP-Western Canada)*
Francois Crete *(VP)*
Joanne Koskie *(VP)*
Christine Boivin *(Dir-Mktg Comm)*
Pierre Langlois *(Dir-Pub Affairs & Govt Rels)*
Jamie Leong-Huxley *(Exec Counsel-Comm & Strategy)*

Hering Schuppener Consulting
Kreuzstrasse 60, 40210 Dusseldorf, Germany
Tel.: (49) 211 430 79 0
Fax: (49) 211 430 79 33
Web Site: www.heringschuppener.com

Employees: 65
Year Founded: 1995

Agency Specializes In: Public Relations

Tina Mentner *(Mng Partner)*
Phoebe Kebbel *(Partner)*
Dirk Von Manikowsky *(Mng Dir)*
Marlies Peine *(Sr Dir)*
Ali Yeganeh Azimi *(Assoc Dir)*
Matthis Kaiser *(Assoc Dir)*
Sebastian Merkle *(Assoc Dir)*
Marc Christian Theurer *(Assoc Dir)*

Accounts:
Cotton Council International
Hoesch Design

Hering Schuppener-Frankfort AmMain
Mainzer Land Street 41, 60329 Frankfurt, AmMain Germany
Tel.: (49) 69 921 874 0
Fax: (49) 69 921 874 13
E-Mail: info@heringschuppener.com
Web Site: www.heringschuppener.com

Employees: 50

Agency Specializes In: Communications, Public Relations

Alexander Geiser *(Mng Partner)*
Ralf Hering *(Principal & Partner)*
Kristin Jakobs *(Partner)*
Phoebe Kebbel *(Partner)*
Dirk Von Manikowsky *(Mng Dir)*
Claudia Orth *(Dir)*
Ali Yeganeh Azimi *(Assoc Dir)*
Matthis Kaiser *(Assoc Dir)*

Cohn & Wolfe
Hanseatic Trade Center, Am Sandtorkai 76, Hamburg, D-20457 Germany
Tel.: (49) 40 808016 110
Fax: (49) 40 808016 199

Wolfgang Lunenburger-Reidenbach, *(Mng Dir-Germany)*

Accounts:
New-Elbphilharmonie Hamburg Global Public Relations
New-HRA Pharma Public Relations, ellaOne

Cohn & Wolfe
6300 Wilshire Blvd, Los Angeles, CA 90048
Tel.: (323) 602-1100
Fax: (310) 967-2910
E-Mail: annette.johnson@cohnwolfe.com
Web Site: www.cohnwolfe.com

Employees: 26

National Agency Associations: COPF

Agency Specializes In: Public Relations, Sponsorship

Lisa Fern-Talbot *(Exec VP & Mng Dir-NY Healthcare Practice)*
Marcy Carmena *(Acct Supvr)*
Colleen Hanrahan *(Sr Acct Exec)*
Lindsay Mason *(Sr Acct Exec)*
Eva Marie Wasko *(Acct Exec)*
Ana Vila *(Asst Acct Exec)*

Accounts:
Hennessy
Hub TV
Nissan North America Hispanic Public Relations, Media
Nokia
Sam's Club
SENSA
Sony
Ubisoft
ZillionTV

Cohn & Wolfe
1001 Front St, San Francisco, CA 94111-1424
Tel.: (415) 365-8520
Fax: (415) 365-8530
E-Mail: annie_longsworth@cohnwolfe.com
Web Site: www.cohnwolfe.com

National Agency Associations: COPF

Agency Specializes In: Public Relations

Cory Stewart *(Sr VP-Crisis & Issues Mgmt)*
Mischa Dunton *(Mng Dir-Western Reg)*
Megan Atiyeh *(VP)*
Chip Dehnert *(VP)*
Chris Lalli *(VP)*
Gwendolyn Poor *(Acct Dir)*
Connor Murphy *(Sr Acct Exec)*
Laura Wagstaff *(Asst Acct Exec)*

Accounts:
LG Electronics U.S.A., Inc. LG Digital Display Monitors
Neato Robotics
Wellcore

Cohn & Wolfe
233 N Michigan Ave 16th Fl Two Illinois Ctr, Chicago, IL 60610
Tel.: (312) 596-3330
Fax: (312) 596-3331
Web Site: www.cohnwolfe.com

National Agency Associations: COPF

Agency Specializes In: Public Relations

Donna Imperato *(CEO)*
Tom Petrosini *(CFO)*
Robert Walsh *(CIO-Global)*
Jill Tannenbaum *(CMO)*
Lisa Fern-Talbot *(Exec VP & Mng Dir-NY Healthcare Practice)*
Stephanie Howley *(Sr VP-HR)*

Accounts:
Solta Medical Inc.

Consultores del Plata S.A.
Santa Fe 911 1st Fl Office A, CP 1059ABD Buenos Aires, Capital Federal Argentina
Tel.: (54) 11 43 27 76 00
Fax: (54) 11 43 27 76 00
E-Mail: consultores@cdelplata.com
Web Site: www.cdelplata.com

Employees: 13
Year Founded: 1992

Agency Specializes In: Communications, Public Relations

Nestor Marcelo Landoni *(Exec Dir)*
Maria Amelia Jauregui *(Acct Exec)*
Agustina Monti *(Acct Exec)*

Accounts:
ACTA
Banco Comafi
Bayer Argentina
Camara De La Industria Aceitera De La Republica Argentina (CIARA)
Centro De Exportadores De Cereales (CEC)
Compass Group Management LLC
Dell Computer Argentina
Deutsche Bank
HASAR
LAN Argentina
Repsol
Universidad Argentina De La Empresa (UADE)

Grey Worldwide Warsaw
Ul Jasna 24, 00-054 Warsaw, Poland
Tel.: (48) 22 332 93 00
Fax: (48) 22 332 93 02
E-Mail: grey@grey.pl
Web Site: www.grey.pl

Agency Specializes In: Communications, Public Relations

Gosia Skorwider *(Mng Dir)*
Ireneusz Turski *(Acct Dir)*
Marcin Ejsmont *(Dir-Plng)*
Agnieszka Gozdek *(Dir-Strategy & Brand Plng)*
Krzysztof Kosz *(Dir-Digital Creative)*
Marcin Zaborowski *(Dir-IT)*
Krzysztof Bogdalik *(Planner-Strategic)*

Accounts:
3M
BAT
Chevrolet
Coca Cola Warsaw
DWS
ESKA
GSK
P&G
Pfizer
Totalizator Sportowy
Widex

Cohn & Wolfe impactasia
Ste 801 Chinachem Hollywood Ctr 1 Hollywood Rd, Central, China (Hong Kong)
Tel.: (852) 25211498
Fax: (852) 28046786
E-Mail: Susan.Field@cohnwolfe.com
Web Site: www.cohnwolfe.com/zh-en

Year Founded: 1990

Agency Specializes In: Consumer Marketing, Digital/Interactive, Event Planning & Marketing, Exhibit/Trade Shows, Graphic Design, Media Training, Newspapers & Magazines, Production (Print), Public Relations, Publicity/Promotions

Tiffany Bai *(Mng Dir)*
Diana Pong *(Mng Dir)*
Louise Oram *(Acct Dir)*
Chris Wong *(Dir-Creative)*
Jessica Man *(Acct Mgr)*
Frankie Lau *(Acct Coord)*

Accounts:
New-AliCloud
Bonhams
Carlsberg Hong Kong Campaign: "Made of More", Creative, Guinness, Guinness Draught, Media, Perfect Pint Challenge, TV
New-Dell Dell Enterprise Forum, Media Relations
Fairmont Hotels & Resorts Hotel Management Services
FitFlop Sandals
New-Hong Kong Internet Registration Corporation Media, Public Relations
Jack Wills Public Relations, Social Media
Mandarin Oriental Hotel Group Hotel Management Services
MGM Hospitality
MSC Cruises Transportation Services
Pernod Ricard
Robert Half International
Rolls Royce
Sheraton Hotel Management Services
Singapore Tourism Board Tourism Services
Sofitel Luxury Hotels Hotel Management Services
TW Steel
W Hotels Hotel Management Services

COLANGELO & PARTNERS PUBLIC RELATIONS
1010 Ave of the Americas Ste 300, New York, NY 10018
Tel.: (646) 624-2885
Fax: (646) 624-2893
E-Mail: info@colangelopr.com
Web Site: www.colangelopr.com

Employees: 20

Agency Specializes In: Communications, Food Service, Luxury Products, Promotions, Public Relations, Publicity/Promotions, Strategic Planning/Research

Gino Colangelo *(Pres)*
Michael Colangelo *(Partner & COO)*
Sara Gorelick *(Acct Dir)*
Alessandro Boga *(Acct Supvr)*
Paul Yanon *(Sr Acct Exec)*
Pola Avrasin *(Acct Exec & Specialist-Digital Media)*
Juliana Colangelo *(Asst Acct Exec)*
Jennifer Ziplow *(Asst Acct Exec)*

Accounts:
Amarone Families
Arnaldo Caprai
Atalanta
Averna
Avignonesi
Ballymaloe
Berlucchi
Cultivate Wines
Damilano
Garofalo Pasta
Golden Blossom Honey
Harlem Spirituals
Il Gattopardo
Kusmi Tea
Movimento Turismo Vini Puglia
Mozzarella & Vino
Mulderbosch Vineyards
Nocciolata Rigoni Di Asiago Social Media
Partida Tequila
Sapporo USA Public Relations
St. Michael's Food & Wine Festival
Victor Rallo
Vinitaly
Winery Exchange Media Relations, Ogio, Social Media
Wines of South Africa
Wines of the Veneto

COLETTE PHILLIPS COMMUNICATIONS
One Mckinley Square 46, Boston, MA 02109
Tel.: (617) 357-5777
Fax: (617) 357-7114
Web Site: www.cpcglobal.com

Employees: 7
Year Founded: 1986

Agency Specializes In: Public Relations

Colette A.M. Phillips *(Pres & CEO)*
Adra Darling *(Sr Acct Dir)*
Mike English *(Dir-Fin)*

Accounts:
American Red Cross
Blue Cross & Blue Shield of Massachusetts
Chase Manhattan Bank
Foxwoods Resort & Casino
Mass Bay Community College
Nike
Reebok
YWCA Boston

COMBLU INC.
(Formerly HLB Communications, Inc.)
875 N Michigan Ave, Chicago, IL 60611-1896
Tel.: (312) 649-1687
Fax: (312) 649-1119
Web Site: comblu.com

Employees: 25
Year Founded: 1978

Agency Specializes In: Brand Development & Integration, Business-To-Business, Consulting, Health Care Services, High Technology, Information Technology, Public Relations, Real Estate, Strategic Planning/Research

Approx. Annual Billings: $2,500,000

Breakdown of Gross Billings by Media: Corp. Communications: 30%; Pub. Rels.: 50%; Strategic Planning/Research: 20%

Maureen Zufan *(Controller)*

Accounts:
American Hospital Association-Financial Solutions, Inc.
CapitalSource
GE Capital Real Estate
Wight + Co.

COMMON GROUND PUBLIC RELATIONS
16690 Swingley Ridge Rd Ste 220, Chesterfield, MO 63017
Tel.: (636) 530-1235
Fax: (636) 530-5995
Web Site: www.commongroundpr.com

Employees: 12

Agency Specializes In: Public Relations

Denise Bentele *(Owner)*
Lynese Hoffman *(CFO)*
Jenna Todoroff *(Mgr-Digital Comm & Acct Exec)*
Nina Kult *(Acct Supvr)*
Cheri Winchester *(Acct Supvr)*
Pia Reinhold *(Sr Acct Exec)*
Maria Lemakis *(Acct Coord)*

Accounts:
Bethesda Health Group
Brown Smith Wallace, L.L.C.
United Healthcare

COMMONWEALTH PUBLIC RELATIONS INC.
2001 E Franklin St Ste 101, Richmond, VA 23223
Tel.: (804) 510-0039
Fax: (804) 557-3654
E-Mail: mail@commonwealth-pr.com
Web Site: www.commonwealth-pr.com

Year Founded: 2009

Agency Specializes In: Brand Development & Integration, Business-To-Business, Crisis Communications, Digital/Interactive, Graphic Design, Media Relations, Public Relations, Social Media

Brian Chandler *(Pres)*
Caroline Browell *(Acct Mgr)*

Accounts:
New-PWIA

COMMUNICATIONS 21
834 Inman Vlg Pky Ste 150, Atlanta, GA 30307
Tel.: (404) 814-1330
Fax: (404) 814-1332
E-Mail: info@c21pr.com
Web Site: www.c21pr.com

Employees: 8
Year Founded: 1992

National Agency Associations: AMA-PRSA

Agency Specializes In: Agriculture, Brand Development & Integration, Business-To-Business, Consumer Goods, Consumer Marketing, Corporate Communications, Direct Response Marketing, Email, Environmental, Event Planning & Marketing, Food Service, Health Care Services, High Technology, Internet/Web Design, Legal Services, New Product Development, Public Relations, Publicity/Promotions, Real Estate, Social Marketing/Nonprofit, Transportation

Approx. Annual Billings: $925,000

Breakdown of Gross Billings by Media: Collateral: $127,500; Event Mktg.: $127,500; Promos.: $52,500; Pub. Rels.: $490,000; Worldwide Web Sites: $127,500

Sharon L. Goldmacher *(Pres)*
Marlena Reed *(VP-Interactive Svcs)*
Amy Patterson *(Dir-Ops & Atlanta Local Organizing Committee)*
Lauren Vocelle *(Sr Acct Mgr)*
Jamie Donaldson *(Acct Mgr)*
Jordan Garofalo *(Acct Mgr)*
Natalie Simone *(Acct Mgr)*
Diana Trujillo *(Coord-Special Projects-Atlanta Local Organizing Committee)*

Accounts:
Atlanta Botanical Garden; Atlanta, GA Botanical Garden; 2009
Braden Fellman Group; Atlanta, GA Real Estate; 2009
Cousins Properties, Inc.; Atlanta, GA Real Estate Development, Property Management & Sales
Fit Foodz
Georgia's Clean Air Force; Atlanta, GA Emissions

Testing; 2005
NCAA Football; Lexington, KY; 2008
Ogletree, Deakins, Nash, Smoak & Stewart, PC
Oldcastle Architectural Products; Atlanta, GA
Xytex Cryo International Ltd.

THE COMMUNICATIONS AGENCY

450 Massachusetts Ave NW, Washington, DC 20001
Tel.: (202) 742-5923
E-Mail: info@tcapublicrelations.com
Web Site: www.tcapublicrelations.com

Agency Specializes In: Advertising, Event Planning & Marketing, Graphic Design, Media Relations, Public Relations, Social Media

Ivy K. Pendleton *(Principal)*
Liza Rodriguez *(Art Dir)*

Accounts:
New-World Bank Group

COMMUNICATIONS & RESEARCH INC.

509 N Harrison Ave, East Lansing, MI 48823
Tel.: (517) 333-3133
Web Site: www.prcr.biz

Agency Specializes In: Graphic Design, Media Relations, Public Relations, Social Media

Accounts:
New-ACD.net

COMMUNICATIONS PACIFIC

700 Bishop St Ste 600, Honolulu, HI 96813
Tel.: (808) 521-5391
Fax: (808) 690-9172
Web Site: www.commpac.com

Agency Specializes In: Brand Development & Integration, Digital/Interactive, Event Planning & Marketing, Graphic Design, Media Relations, Media Training, Public Relations

Kitty Lagareta *(CEO)*
Russell Pang *(Exec VP)*
Nalani Choy *(Sr VP)*
Nicole Fuertes *(VP)*
Jean Dickinson *(VP)*
Charley Memminger *(Dir-Editorial Svcs)*
Chase Conching *(Dir-Design)*
Sheree Young *(Sr Acct Exec)*
Courtney Matsuki *(Acct Exec)*

Accounts:
New-Crackin Kitchen

COMMUNIQUE PR

314 W Galer Ste 100, Seattle, WA 98119
Tel.: (206) 282-4923
Fax: (206) 284-2777
E-Mail: info@communiquepr.com
Web Site: www.communiquepr.com

Year Founded: 2004

National Agency Associations: COPF

Agency Specializes In: Media Relations, Media Training, Public Relations, Social Media, Strategic Planning/Research

Jennifer Gehrt *(Partner)*
Colleen Moffitt *(Partner)*
Richard L. Tso *(VP)*
Danielle Zarrella *(Acct Mgr)*
Ann Kwong *(Sr Strategist-PR)*
Sarah Elson *(Acct Exec)*
Christie Melby *(Acct Exec)*
Maddie Beck *(Asst Acct Exec)*

Accounts:
Lively LLC
New-Ya Joe (Agency of Record) Public Relations

COMMUNITECH

80 Emerson Ln Ste 1303, Bridgeville, PA 15017-3472
Tel.: (412) 221-4550
Fax: (412) 221-5125
E-Mail: info@ctechrocks.com
Web Site: www.ctechrocks.com

Employees: 10

Agency Specializes In: Digital/Interactive, Exhibit/Trade Shows, Print, Public Relations, Strategic Planning/Research

Pam Selker Rak *(Founder & Pres)*

CONCEPT PR

75 Broadway Ste 202, San Francisco, CA 94111
Tel.: (415) 342-3435
Web Site: www.conceptagency.com

Agency Specializes In: Event Planning & Marketing, Media Planning, Media Training, Public Relations, Social Media, Strategic Planning/Research

Veronica Skelton *(Mng Partner)*
Samantha Steinwinder *(Mng Partner)*

Accounts:
UpTake

CONCEPTS INC.

2 Wisconsin Cir Ste 700, Chevy Chase, MD 20815
Tel.: (301) 570-0115
Fax: (301) 570-3124
Web Site: www.conceptspr.com

Year Founded: 1996

Agency Specializes In: Exhibit/Trade Shows, Graphic Design, Internet/Web Design, Market Research, Media Relations, Public Relations

Karen H. Vaughn *(Pres)*
Caitlin Hochul *(Dir-Comm & Client Rels)*
Diana Zeitzer *(Dir-Comm)*
Hope Adler *(Acct Exec)*
Carolyn Vanbrocklin *(Specialist-Comm)*

CONE COMMUNICATIONS

855 Boylston St, Boston, MA 02116
Tel.: (617) 227-2111
Fax: (617) 523-3955
E-Mail: jbang@coneinc.com
Web Site: www.conecomm.com

E-Mail for Key Personnel:
President: jbang@coneinc.com

Employees: 100
Year Founded: 1980

National Agency Associations: COPF

Agency Specializes In: Brand Development & Integration, Communications, Consumer Goods, Consumer Marketing, Crisis Communications, Digital/Interactive, Fashion/Apparel, Integrated Marketing, Media Relations, Media Training, Pets , Public Relations, Publicity/Promotions, Retail, Social Marketing/Nonprofit, Social Media, Sponsorship, Teen Market, Viral/Buzz/Word of Mouth, Women's Market

Jens Bang *(Chm)*
Bill Fleishman *(CEO)*
Lucia Ferrante *(CFO)*
Marie O'Neill *(CFO)*
Mike Lawrence *(Exec VP)*
Lisa Manley *(Exec VP-CSR Strategy)*
Marc Berliner *(VP)*
Heather Breslau *(VP)*
Cheryl Herbert *(VP-Client Partnerships & Bus Dev)*
Alexandra Nicholson *(VP-New & Social Media)*
Sarah Faith *(Acct Dir)*
Jessica Hesselschwerdt *(Acct Dir)*
Tara Olivier *(Acct Dir-Social Impact)*
Chrissy Redmond *(Acct Dir)*
Simon Bowers *(Sr Acct Supvr-Corp Social Responsibility)*
Hailey Broderick *(Sr Acct Supvr)*
Ashley Aruda *(Acct Supvr-PR & Brand Comm)*
Nicholle Connolly *(Acct Supvr)*
Molly Owen *(Acct Supvr)*
Lindsey Shumway *(Acct Supvr)*
Andrea List *(Supvr-Acct Plng)*
Jamie Berman *(Sr Acct Exec)*
Molly Odre *(Sr Acct Exec)*
Aashna Moitra *(Acct Exec)*
Caroline Regan *(Acct Exec)*
Katie Rie *(Acct Exec)*
Jason Feldman *(Asst Acct Exec)*
Liza Lanphier *(Asst Acct Exec)*
Alison Moriarty *(Asst Acct Exec)*

Accounts:
AARP
American Heart Association Nonprofit Marketing
Autism Speaks Nonprofie Marketing
Avon
Ben & Jerry's
Bosch Inspection Technology Inc.
Cheerios
Chicco Juvenile Products
Ecolab Inc.
FIRST
General Mills
Green Mountain Coffee Roasters
HAI Group PR
Hilton Worldwide
ITT/Xylem
Jiffy Lube
Jockey International
Keurig
Lindt Chocolates; 2006
Nature Valley Packaged GoodsF&B
Pan-Mass Challenge (Agency of Record) Media Relations
Purina Tidy Cats
Reebok
Snuggle
Starbucks
Sun Trust
Timberland
Time Warner Cable Inc.
USO Nonprofit Marketing
Wisk
Yoplait USA, Inc.

Branch

Cone Communications LLC

711 Third Ave 11th Fl, New York, NY 10017
Tel.: (617) 227-2111
Web Site: www.conecomm.com

Year Founded: 1980

National Agency Associations: COPF

Agency Specializes In: Brand Development & Integration, Corporate Communications, Media Relations, Public Relations, Social Media

Byron Calamese *(Exec VP & Mng Dir-New York)*
Alison Dasilva *(Exec VP)*

Mike Lawrence *(Exec VP)*
Marc Berliner *(VP)*
Rebecca Dickson *(VP-Brand Comm)*
Molly Finnegan *(Sr Acct Supvr)*
Jamie Kaseta *(Sr Acct Supvr)*
Jessica Benjamin *(Acct Supvr)*
Katie Goudey *(Acct Supvr)*
Molly Owen *(Acct Supvr)*

Accounts:
Alcoa Foundation Public Relations
Josh Cellars
Saffron Road Food Media Relations

CONKLING FISKUM & MCCORMICK, INC.
(Name Changed to CFM Strategic Communications, Inc.)

CONNECT MARKETING, INC.
One Market St 36th Fl, San Francisco, CA 94105
Tel.: (415) 222-9691
Fax: (800) 455-8855
E-Mail: info@connectmarketing.com
Web Site: www.connectmarketing.com

Year Founded: 1989

Agency Specializes In: Communications, Public Relations

Neil Myers *(Founder & Pres)*
Janeen Bullock *(Mng Partner)*
Mike Bradshaw *(Partner)*
Chris Walker *(Partner)*
Benjamin Jolley *(Acct Dir)*
Holly Hagerman *(Sr Partner)*
Sherri Walkenhorst *(Sr Partner)*

Accounts:
New-AtHoc
New-The CA Security Council
New-CoreMedia
New-Corsa
New-Elekta
New-FireFox Group
New-Forum Systems
New-goBaito
New-Igneous
NKK Switches
New-Nokia Networks
Oversight
New-Primary Data
New-Riverbed Technology
New-Sage
New-ServiceNow
New-Sivantos
New-SmartDraw
New-Sophos
Tail-F
New-Tempered Networks
New-Verisign
New-Wedge Networks

CONNECT PUBLIC RELATIONS
80 E 100 N, Provo, UT 84606
Tel.: (801) 373-7888
Fax: (801) 373-8680
E-Mail: info@connectmarketing.com
Web Site: www.connectmarketing.com/

Employees: 31
Year Founded: 1989

Agency Specializes In: Business-To-Business, Computers & Software, High Technology, Information Technology, Media Relations, Public Relations

Neil Myers *(Pres)*
Janeen Bullock *(Mng Partner)*
Mike Bradshaw *(Partner)*
Chris Walker *(Partner)*
Benjamin Jolley *(Acct Dir)*
Sherri Walkenhorst *(Sr Partner)*

Accounts:
DreamFactory
F5 Networks
Network Instruments
NKK Switches
RadioTime
Siemens
SunDisk
Symantec

CONNELLYWORKS, INC.
2200 Wilson Blvd, Arlington, VA 22201
Tel.: (571) 323-2585
Fax: (866) 545-0353
E-Mail: info@connellyworks.com
Web Site: www.connellyworks.com

Employees: 10

Agency Specializes In: Advertising, Collateral, Event Planning & Marketing, Exhibit/Trade Shows, Internet/Web Design, Media Planning, Public Relations

Joanne Connelly *(Owner)*
James Hanson *(Mng Dir)*
Margo Dunn *(Dir-Mktg)*
Kristin Graybill *(Dir-Digital Strategy)*
A. J. Guenther *(Dir-PR)*
Mary Alice Johnson *(Dir-Strategic Accts)*
Melissa King *(Dir-Events)*
Amanda Hall *(Sr Acct Mgr)*
Kay Logan *(Acct Mgr)*
Brittany Infante *(Jr Acct Mgr)*

Accounts:
1105 Government Information Group
AFCEA DC Chapter Bethesda Operations
Centuria
Dev
Federra
Fortress Technologies
FOSE Marketing, PR
Guident
LexisNexis

CONNORS COMMUNICATIONS
7 W 22nd St, New York, NY 10010
Tel.: (212) 798-1411
Fax: (212) 807-7503

Employees: 25

Agency Specializes In: Business-To-Business, Communications, Consulting, Entertainment, Health Care Services, High Technology, Internet/Web Design, Public Relations

Maarti Defonce *(Principal & Bus Strategist)*
Matt Mack *(Acct Exec)*

Accounts:
Citizenbay
Goodmail Systems
nextSource, Inc.
RedRoller
Videoegg; 2006

CONRANPR
629 5th Ave Ste 212, Pelham, NY 10803
Tel.: (212) 447-1010
E-Mail: info@conranpr.com
Web Site: www.conranpr.com

Year Founded: 1999

Agency Specializes In: Digital/Interactive, Media Planning, Public Relations, Social Media

Gayle Conran *(Pres)*
Everett Potter *(Dir-Editorial)*

Accounts:
The Alfond Inn

CONSENSUS COMMUNICATIONS, INC.
201 S Orange Ave Ste 950, Orlando, FL 32801-3472
Tel.: (407) 608-5900
Fax: (407) 835-0656
Web Site: www.onmessage.com

Employees: 9

Agency Specializes In: Advertising, Communications, Crisis Communications, Government/Political, Graphic Design, Local Marketing, Media Relations, Public Relations, Strategic Planning/Research

John Sowinski *(Founder & Partner)*
Dan Cunningham *(Producer-Media)*
Christina Morton *(Sr Acct Exec)*
Andrew Abdel-Malik *(Strategist-Digital)*
Ryan Houck *(Strategist-Comm)*

CONSENSUS INC
1933 S Broadway Ste 1100, Los Angeles, CA 90007
Tel.: (213) 438-1755
Fax: (213) 438-1764
E-Mail: info@consensusinc.com
Web Site: www.consensusinc.com

Agency Specializes In: Media Relations, Public Relations, Social Media

Julie Gertler *(Founder & CEO)*
Josh Gertler *(Pres)*
Nazan Armenian *(Sr VP)*
Andrea Campbell *(VP)*
Lexi Wiley *(Acct Mgr)*

Accounts:
New-LAX

CONVENTURES, INC.
1 Design Ctr Pl Ste 718, Boston, MA 02210-2335
Tel.: (617) 439-7700
Fax: (617) 439-7701
E-Mail: info@conventures.com
Web Site: www.conventures.com

E-Mail for Key Personnel:
President: drhodes@conventures.com

Employees: 17
Year Founded: 1977

Agency Specializes In: Event Planning & Marketing, Government/Political, Public Relations, Publicity/Promotions

Ted R. Breslin, Jr. *(CFO & VP)*
Lynne Vendetti *(Controller)*
Joy Bannon *(Acct Dir)*
Melissa Giese *(Acct Dir)*
Sydney Marshall Turner *(Dir-Bus Dev)*
Dick Dray *(Sr Mgr-Res)*
Samantha Croteau *(Acct Coord)*
Alicia Morse *(Acct Coord)*

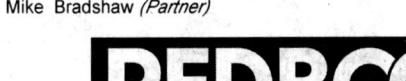

Accounts:
Adopt-A-Student Foundation
Au Bon Pain
Mt. Auburn Hospital
New England Council
Perkins School for the Blind

Suffolk University
The Susan G. Komen Breast Cancer Foundation
Tuft's Health Plan
Tufts Associated Health Plans

CONVERSA
707 N Franklin St Fl 6, Tampa, FL 33602
Tel.: (813) 579-2157
E-Mail: info@conversaco.com
Web Site: www.conversaco.com

Agency Specializes In: Crisis Communications, Graphic Design, Public Relations, Social Media

Arlene Dibenigno *(Mng Partner)*
Kelsey Lehtomaa Frouge *(Mng Partner)*
Carmela Zabala *(Creative Dir)*
Jennifer Dunn *(Dir-PR)*
Sarah Schwirian *(Sr Acct Exec)*

Accounts:
New-Bloomberg
New-Women's Conference of Florida

COOK & SCHMID
3033 5th Ave, San Diego, CA 92103
Tel.: (619) 814-2370
Fax: (619) 814-2375
Toll Free: (866) 615-9181
E-Mail: info@cookandschmid.com
Web Site: www.cookandschmid.com

Employees: 10
Year Founded: 2001

National Agency Associations: PRSA

Agency Specializes In: Brand Development & Integration, Business-To-Business, Consumer Marketing, Corporate Communications, Entertainment, Environmental, Financial, Health Care Services, High Technology, Investor Relations, Pharmaceutical, Public Relations, Publicity/Promotions, Real Estate, Strategic Planning/Research, Transportation, Travel & Tourism

Revenue: $1,200,000

John Schmid *(Pres & CEO)*
Genevieve Deperio Fong *(Sr Acct Exec)*
Celeste Sotomayor Schmid *(Strategist-Pub Affairs)*
JoAn Tamares *(Sr Graphic Designer)*
Katie Schaa *(Acct Coord)*

Accounts:
Illumina
Ocean Discovery Institute
San Bernardino County
San Diego Minority Supplier Development Council
San Diego Port District
SCS Engineers; San Diego & Long Beach, CA Public Relations

COOKERLY PUBLIC RELATIONS
3500 Lenox Rd 1 Alliance Ctr Ste 510, Atlanta, GA 30326
Tel.: (404) 816-2037
Fax: (404) 816-3037
E-Mail: contactus@cookerly.com
Web Site: www.cookerly.com

Employees: 18

Agency Specializes In: Communications, Consumer Goods, Consumer Marketing, Environmental, Experience Design, Government/Political, Health Care Services, Hospitality, Internet/Web Design, Media Relations, New Technologies, Public Relations, Social Marketing/Nonprofit

Stephen M. Brown *(Chief Innovation Officer & Sr VP)*
Jane Stout *(Sr VP)*
Keith Bowermaster *(VP)*
Beth McKenna *(VP)*
Lydia Caffery Wilbanks *(VP-Mktg & New Bus)*
Tim Pengelly *(Dir-Design)*
Michael Rieman *(Acct Supvr)*
Chris Glazier *(Sr Acct Exec)*
Cortney Johnston *(Asst Acct Exec)*

Accounts:
American Trade Products
Chateau Elan Winery & Resort
Client Profiles
Club Ride Commuter Services Commute Alternatives
Georgia Solar Energy Association
HCA Holdings Inc.
Priority Payment Systems Payment Processing
PT Power
Secure POS Vendor Alliance
Stonebranch
Sun Trust Banks Inc.
U.S. Micro Corporation Collateral & Business Development Support, Media Relations, Message Development
Warbird Consulting Partners
Waste Management Electronics Recycling Awareness

COOKSEY COMMUNICATIONS, INC.
5525 N MacArthur Blvd Ste 530, Irving, TX 75038
Tel.: (972) 580-0662
Fax: (972) 580-0852
E-Mail: info@cookseypr.com
Web Site: www.cookseypr.com

Employees: 10
Year Founded: 1994

National Agency Associations: PRSA

Agency Specializes In: Communications, Legal Services, Public Relations

Approx. Annual Billings: $1,700,000

Gail Cooksey *(Pres)*
Karen Cooperstein *(Sr VP)*
Jason Meyer *(Sr VP)*
Colby Walton *(Sr VP)*
Michael Landon *(Dir-Creative)*
Michelle Hargis *(Acct Mgr)*
Alan Phillips *(Acct Supvr)*
Tyler Bailey *(Acct Exec)*
Loren Bolton *(Acct Exec)*
Matt Johns *(Acct Exec)*

Accounts:
35W Coalition
City of Irving
Dallas Regional Mobility Coalition
Devon Energy
Fort Worth Chamber of Commerce
Gotshal & Manges LLP
Hillwood Properties
Holland Services
Jackson-Shaw
National Math + Science Initiative
OmniAmerican Bank
Richardson Chamber of Commerce
Sheraton Dallas Hotel
SPCA of Texas
Tarrant Regional Transportation Coalition
United Way of Metropolitan Dallas
United Way Worldwide
Weil Gotshal & Manges, LLP
Whitley Penn, LLP Strategic Communications

COOKSON STEPHENS CORPORATION
36 Lowell St Ste 202, Manchester, NH 03101
Tel.: (603) 782-8192
E-Mail: reachus@cooksonstephens.com
Web Site: www.cooksonstephens.com

Year Founded: 2010

Agency Specializes In: Collateral, Corporate Identity, Crisis Communications, Digital/Interactive, Internet/Web Design, Media Relations, Media Training, Public Relations, Search Engine Optimization, Social Media

Matthew Cookson *(Founder & Pres)*
Michelline Dufort *(VP-Pub Affairs & Dir-Bus Rels-NHHTC)*
Dia Kalakonas *(Dir-Strategic Comm)*
Marian Caisse *(Project Mgr-Mktg-Cookson Strategies Corp)*
Jen Nickulas *(Coord-Strategic Comm)*

Accounts:
CustomScoop
FreePriceAlerts
NH Housing I'm Finding my Financial Freedom Campaign

COOPER HONG INC.
2560 Foxfield Rd Ste 320, Saint Charles, IL 60174
Tel.: (630) 377-2555
Fax: (630) 377-2554
E-Mail: info@cooperhong.com
Web Site: www.cooperhong.com

Agency Specializes In: Advertising, Brand Development & Integration, Collateral, Corporate Communications, Graphic Design, Internet/Web Design, Media Buying Services, Media Training, Public Relations, Social Media

Jane Cooper *(Pres)*
Timothy Montgomery *(VP)*
Mark Smith *(Acct Mgr)*

Accounts:
Jetstream of Houston

COOPER SMITH AGENCY
416 W 8th St, Dallas, TX 75208
Tel.: (214) 329-9191
E-Mail: info@coopersmithagency.com
Web Site: www.coopersmithagency.com

Agency Specializes In: Communications, Content, Media Relations, Public Relations, Social Media

Cooper Smith Koch *(Principal)*
Mina Vu *(Mgr-Community)*

Accounts:
Demilec USA Inc

CORBIN-HILLMAN COMMUNICATIONS
1776 Broadway Ste 1610, New York, NY 10019
Tel.: (212) 246-6515
Fax: (212) 246-6516
E-Mail: info@corbinpr.com
Web Site: www.corbinpr.com

Employees: 12
Year Founded: 1978

Agency Specializes In: Integrated Marketing, Public Relations

Revenue: $1,200,000

Michelle Corbin Hillman *(Founder & CEO)*
Sean-Patrick M. Hillman *(Principal & Exec VP)*
Kelly Doyle *(Acct Supvr-PR)*
Karina Welch *(Asst Acct Exec)*

Accounts:
Ascentium Corporation
Bacardi B-Live
Clayspray
European Wax Center
New-GoViral, Inc. (Agency of Record) Diply.com
Harvest Snaps
iCube
K-10+
Peter Max Studios
Planned Parenthood Federation of America
PROPER ATTIRE (Condoms)
POP International Galleries PR, Social Media
Potter & Moore Lee Stafford, Public Relations Program
Scent of Wealth
Shecky's Media Media
Stoddard + Partners
The Tanee
New-Tommy John (Agency of Record) Event Marketing, Public Relations
Valery Joseph
New-Zazen Bear (Agency of Record) Experiential, Public Relations

CORKTREE CREATIVE
60 S State Rte 157 Box 3, Edwardsville, IL 62025
Tel.: (618) 656-7333
Web Site: www.corktreecreative.com

Year Founded: 2009

Agency Specializes In: Advertising, Crisis Communications, Graphic Design, Internet/Web Design, Logo & Package Design, Media Training, Print, Public Relations, Radio, Social Media

Jan Carpenter *(Principal & Dir-Creative)*
Laura Reed *(Principal & Dir-PR)*
Nicole Dicks *(Dir-Bus Dev)*
Alyssa Eason *(Strategist-Social Media)*

Accounts:
Butler Home Improvement Print Advertising, Public Relations, Social Media
Fodder Harvest Inc
WA Schickedanz Inc

CORNERSTONE AGENCY, INC.
71 W 23rd St Fl 13, New York, NY 10010
Tel.: (212) 741-7100
Fax: (212) 741-4747
E-Mail: info@cornerstonepromotion.com
Web Site: www.cornerstonepromotion.com

Employees: 30
Year Founded: 1997

Agency Specializes In: Public Relations, Publicity/Promotions

Rob Stone *(Owner)*
Anthony Holland *(COO & CTO)*
Jeff Tammes *(Chief Creative Officer)*
Winifred Chance *(Dir-Events)*
Adam Cohen *(Acct Mgr-Cornerstone Agency)*
Erica Mapa *(Acct Mgr-PR)*
Caitlin Stevens *(Coord-Mktg)*

Accounts:
Babelgum
The Battle for Manhattan
Born Ready Lance Stephenson; 2008
Bushmills
New-Converse
John Lennon Educational Tour Bus
Microsoft Corporation
PepsiCo Inc. NFL Pepsi Anthems Campaign
SportsNet New York SNY Invitational; 2008
Vowch Commonwealth PR
ZUUS Media

CORNERSTONE COMMUNICATIONS
575 Madison Ave Ste 1006, New York, NY 10022
Tel.: (212) 605-0370
E-Mail: cornerstonepr@gmail.com
Web Site: www.cornerstonepr.com

Agency Specializes In: Communications, Crisis Communications, Event Planning & Marketing, Internet/Web Design, Media Relations, Public Relations, Sales Promotion, Social Media, Sponsorship

Marsha Palanci *(Founder & CEO)*
John Christensen *(Principal)*
Beth Cotenoff *(Sr VP)*
Elyse Genderson *(Sr Acct Exec)*
Chelsea Thompson *(Acct Exec)*
Casey Galasso *(Acct Coord)*
Lesley Hennen *(Acct Coord)*

Accounts:
The Esporao Group
Lieb Cellars Bridge Lane Wines, Digital Media, Marketing, Online, Out-of-Home, Print, Public Relations
New-The Napa Valley Vintners (East Coast Agency of Record) Digital Media

CORPORATE INK
90 Washington St, Newton, MA 02458
Tel.: (617) 969-9192
Fax: (617) 969-1124
E-Mail: abermar@corporateink.com
Web Site: www.corporateink.com

Employees: 16
Year Founded: 1989

Agency Specializes In: High Technology, Information Technology, Public Relations

Revenue: $2,000,000

Amy Bermar *(Founder & Pres)*
Corinne Federici *(Sr VP)*
Susan Bassett *(VP)*
Jill McGrath *(Office Mgr)*
Kristen Carlson *(Sr Acct Exec)*
Gil Haylon *(Acct Exec)*
Abigail E. Holmes *(Asst Acct Exec)*

Accounts:
Axeda Corp.; 2007
CertiPath TSCP; 2007
MCA Solutions; 2004

COUNTRY ROAD COMMUNICATIONS
62 Taylor Rd, Mount Kisco, NY 10549
Tel.: (914) 584-7952
E-Mail: countryroadcomm@aim.com
Web Site:
www.countryroadcommunications.squarespace.com

Agency Specializes In: Advertising, Brand Development & Integration

Elise Cooper *(Pres)*

Accounts:
The James Brown Family Foundation

COUNTZ PUBLIC RELATIONS
4 Indigo Run Dr, Hilton Head Island, SC 29926
Tel.: (816) 585-2164
Web Site: www.countzprfirm.com

Agency Specializes In: Public Relations, Social Media

Carmela Watson-Countz *(CEO)*

Accounts:
Dininglicious

COWAN & COMPANY COMMUNICATIONS, INC.
20 Bay Street 11th Floor, Toronto, ON M5J 2N8 Canada
Tel.: (416) 462-8773
Fax: (416) 461-9486
Web Site: cowanandcompany.ca/

Agency Specializes In: Brand Development & Integration, Collateral, Crisis Communications, Digital/Interactive, Event Planning & Marketing, Internet/Web Design, Media Relations, Public Relations, Publicity/Promotions, Strategic Planning/Research

Cathy Cowan *(Owner)*
Margaret Batuszkin *(Dir-Comm)*

Accounts:
Bier Markt
CAA
Canoe.ca
Casey's Grill Bar
Change Lingerie
Costco
East Side Marios
ECO Car
Food Banks Canada
Kraft Canada
L'Oreal Paris
Philips
Pokemon
Prime Pubs
Shopbot.ca Digital, Marketing, Media Relations, Strategic PR

COYNE PUBLIC RELATIONS
5 Wood Hollow Rd, Parsippany, NJ 07054
Tel.: (973) 588-2000
Fax: (973) 588-2361
E-Mail: tcoyne@coynepr.com
Web Site: www.coynepr.com

Employees: 78

National Agency Associations: COPF

Agency Specializes In: Public Relations, Sponsorship

Approx. Annual Billings: $7,000,000

Rich Lukis *(Pres)*
Thomas F. Coyne *(CEO)*
Mike Sloan *(CFO)*
Luis Hernandez *(Chief Digital Officer & Sr VP)*
Brad Buyce *(Exec VP-Client Strategy)*
John Gogarty *(Exec VP)*
Chris Brienza *(Sr VP & Head- New York City)*
Kelly Dencker *(Sr VP & Dir-HC & Academics)*
David Carter *(Sr VP-Bus Dev)*
Joe Gargiulo *(Sr VP)*
Jennifer Kamienski *(Sr VP)*
Kevin Lamb *(Sr VP)*
Tim Schramm *(Sr VP)*
Deborah Kelco Sierchio *(Sr VP)*
Lisa Wolleon *(Sr VP)*
Matt Leung *(VP & Dir-Adv)*
Norman Booth *(VP)*
David Cooper *(VP)*
Kim Duffy *(VP-HR)*
Janet Schiller *(VP)*
Ann Smith *(VP-Healthcare Practice)*
Chris Vancheri *(VP-Healthcare Practice)*
Amanda Early *(Sr Acct Supvr)*
Lela Cloutier *(Acct Supvr)*
Christine Denham *(Acct Supvr)*

Public Relations Firms

Kelly Kasper *(Acct Supvr)*
Amanda Iodice *(Sr Acct Exec)*
Cristin Johnson *(Sr Acct Exec)*
Jamie Maralla *(Sr Acct Exec)*
Brian Farley *(Acct Exec)*
Angelina Franco *(Acct Exec)*
Chris Gebhard *(Acct Exec-Social)*
Stacey Palmieri *(Acct Exec)*
Kimberly Riccardi *(Acct Exec-Travel)*
Heather Scott *(Acct Exec-Consumer & Lifestyle Div)*
Alaina Blekicki *(Asst Acct Exec)*
Beau Hayhoe *(Asst Acct Exec)*
Alissa Mandanici *(Asst Acct Exec-Fashion & Beauty)*
Tehani Manochio *(Asst Acct Exec)*

Accounts:
BabyBjorn Messaging, Traditional & Social Media
Beam Suntory Inc. (Public Relations Agency of Record) Campaign: "Make It With a Cowboy", Hornitos Black Barrel, Sauza 901, Sauza Sparkling Margarita Watermelon, Strategic Media Relations, Tequila
Bimbo Bakeries USA
Casio Computer Co., Ltd.
Casio, Inc.
Cayman Islands Department of Tourism (Agency of Record) Crisis Communications, Public Relations, Social Media, US Tourism Public Relations
Chrysler
Columbia Business School (Agency of Record) Public Relations
Crystal Light
David's Bridal Media Relations, Program Development & Planning, Public Relations Campaign
Daytona International Speedway
Eggland's Best, Inc.
New-Emerald Expositions NY Now (Agency of Record), Public Relations
ESPN, Inc.
Express Scripts
General Mills
Good Year
The Goodyear Tire & Rubber Company
Hard Rock International Global Public Relations, Hard Rock Cafes
Harlem Globetrotters International, Inc.
Hong Kong Tourism Board (Agency of Record) Brand Positioning, Crisis Management
Imax Corporation
Ironman
Jockey Campaign: "Get real", Social Outreach
LA MARATHON LLC Marketing, PR
Mondelez International, Inc. Capri Sun, Cote-d'Or, Jacobs and Carte Noire, Kraft Cheeses, LU Biscuits, Lacta & Toblerone Chocolates, Maxwell House, Milka, Oreo, Oscar Mayer Meats, Philadelphia Cream Cheese, Ritz, Tang
Motel 6 (PR, Crisis Communications & Social Media Agency of Record)
Nabisco
National Canine Research Council Campaign: "Police and Dog Encounters Video Training Series: Tactical Strategies and Effective Tools to Keep Our Communities Safe and Humane", Influencer Campaigns, Media Relations, Public Relations Agency of Record
National Senior Games Association Development, Public Relations, Strategy
Old Bay
Pennzoil Motor Sports
Pepsi
Pfizer Consumer Healthcare
Playmates Toys Hearts for Hearts Girls Brands, Teenage Mutant Ninja Turtles
Quaker State
rain X
Red Robin Gourmet Burgers
Shell Rotella
Solstice Sunglasses
South African Tourism
Stratosphere Corporation
Tazo
Timberland (North America Agency of Record) Digital, Media Relations, Press, Strategic Public Relations
The United States Golf Association
UPS Media Relations, PR
VTech Program Development
Walt Disney World Parks & Resorts Walt Disney World

CREATETWO
824 E Glenn Ave, Auburn, AL 36830
Tel.: (334) 246-1535
E-Mail: hello@createtwo.com
Web Site: www.createtwo.com

Agency Specializes In: Collateral, Email, Graphic Design, Internet/Web Design, Media Relations, Print, Promotions, Public Relations, Search Engine Optimization, Social Media

Jessie King *(Dir-Comm)*
Charissa Jones *(Mgr-Traffic)*
Katy Harper Doss *(Sr Acct Exec)*

Accounts:
Auburn Downtown Association
Findleys Eatery
Solar Expressions

CREATIVE COMMUNICATIONS CONSULTANTS, INC.
1277 N Morningside Dr, Atlanta, GA 30306
Fax: (404) 898-0424
E-Mail: info@creativecomminc.com
Web Site: www.creativecomminc.com

Employees: 2
Year Founded: 1998

Agency Specializes In: Advertising, Communications, Crisis Communications, Event Planning & Marketing, Internet/Web Design, Local Marketing, Media Relations, Print, Promotions, Social Marketing/Nonprofit, Strategic Planning/Research, Web (Banner Ads, Pop-ups, etc.)

Claudia Brooks D'Avanzo *(Founder & Pres)*
Arielle D'Avanzo *(Acct Mgr)*

Accounts:
Bahamas Ministry of Tourism
Coldwell Banker
Georgia Child Care Council
Hill PHOENIX
Kroger
MasterCard International
Morrison Management Specialists
National Marine Manufacturers Association
Physicians Formula Cosmetics

CREATIVE MEDIA MARKETING
594 Broadway Ste 500, New York, NY 10012
Tel.: (212) 979-8884
Fax: (212) 979-8577
Toll Free: (888) 826-6477
E-Mail: cmmstacey@aol.com
Web Site: www.cmmpr.com

Employees: 19

Agency Specializes In: Public Relations

Revenue: $2,000,000

Corinne Pipitone *(VP)*
Danielle Hale *(Acct Dir)*
James Campbell *(Dir-Media)*
Erika Wochna *(Mgr-Community)*
Casey Endo *(Sr Acct Exec)*
Kylie Daniels-Diehl *(Acct Exec)*
Nya-Gabriella Peets *(Community Mgr)*

Accounts:
Goody
Lamas Beauty Hair & Skin Care; 2008
Valeant Pharmaceuticals International, Inc.

CREATIVE RESPONSE CONCEPTS
2760 Eisenhower Ave 4th Fl, Alexandria, VA 22314
Tel.: (703) 683-5004
Fax: (703) 683-1703
E-Mail: crc@crcpublicrelations.com
Web Site: www.crcpublicrelations.com/

Employees: 23
Year Founded: 1989

Agency Specializes In: Brand Development & Integration, Communications, Corporate Communications, Corporate Identity, Government/Political, Legal Services, Public Relations, Strategic Planning/Research

Approx. Annual Billings: $6,000,000

Leif Noren *(Chm)*
Greg Mueller *(Pres-CRC PR)*
Mike Thompson, Jr. *(Sr VP)*
Maria E. Hatzikonstantinou *(VP-Accts)*
Erica Hawksworth *(Sr Acct Mgr)*
Travis Burk *(Sr Acct Exec)*
Katie Hughes *(Sr Acct Exec)*
Hugh Norton *(Sr Acct Exec)*

Accounts:
AT&T Communications Corp.
Chevron
Golden Rule Insurance
Microsoft Corporation
Parents Television Council

CRENSHAW COMMUNICATIONS
36 W 20th St, New York, NY 10011
Tel.: (212) 367-9700
Fax: (212) 367-9701
Web Site: www.crenshawcomm.com

E-Mail for Key Personnel:
President: dorothy@stantoncrenshaw.com

Employees: 15
Year Founded: 1996

National Agency Associations: COPF

Agency Specializes In: Business-To-Business, Communications, Consumer Goods, Corporate Communications, Crisis Communications, Electronic Media, Financial, Health Care Services, High Technology, Public Relations, Publicity/Promotions, Social Marketing/Nonprofit, Social Media, Viral/Buzz/Word of Mouth

Approx. Annual Billings: $2,000,000

Breakdown of Gross Billings by Media: Pub. Rels.: 100%

Dorothy Crenshaw *(CEO & Dir-Creative)*
George David Drucker *(Partner & Pres-West Coast)*
Michelle S. Han *(Sr Acct Supvr)*
Richard Krueger *(Acct Supvr)*
Cliff Maroney *(Acct Exec)*
Nicholas Theccanat *(Acct Exec)*

Accounts:
20x200 Public Relations
Alwil Software Avast!
Five Elements Robotics Digital Content, Media

Relations, Public Relations
McGraw-Hill Federal Credit Union Media Relations, PR
Mitch-Stuart, Inc Digital, Media Relations, PR
Mosquito 86
Quiznos
Sharp Electronics Corporation
TechMediaNetwork Executive Visibility, Marketing Communications, PR, Traditional & Digital Media Relations
UGallery Digital, Media Relations, PR
Verizon Wireless; Morristown, NJ New York Metropolitan Region Public Relations
Xplenty
ZetrOZ, Inc Digital, Media Relations, PR

CRISTOFOLI-KEELING, INC.
310 Culvert St The Edge 4th Fl, Cincinnati, OH 45202
Tel.: (513) 381-3248
Fax: (513) 381-3249
E-Mail: info@cristofolikeeling.com
Web Site: www.cristofolikeeling.com

Employees: 4

National Agency Associations: PRSA

Agency Specializes In: Public Relations

Approx. Annual Billings: $500,000

Ann M. Keeling *(Pres)*

Accounts:
Coppertree Ltd.
dunnhumbyUSA Retail Loyalty Programs
KSS Retail
Larosa's
LPK Brand Design Agency
Marsh, Inc.

CRITICAL PR
27 Stony Hill Rd, Burlington, CT 06013-2601
Tel.: (860) 255-7524
E-Mail: joncrane@criticalpr.com

Employees: 5
Year Founded: 1997

Agency Specializes In: Public Relations

Jon Crane *(Principal)*

Accounts:
Amalgamated Industries
Campaign for Science-Based Healthcare
Dematteo Fine Arts
NSI
Studio North
VNA Healthcare

CROCKER & CROCKER
1614 19th St, Sacramento, CA 95811
Tel.: (916) 491-3161
E-Mail: info@crockercrocker.com
Web Site: www.crockercrocker.com

Agency Specializes In: Advertising, Brand Development & Integration, Public Relations, Social Marketing/Nonprofit

Lucy Eidam Crocker *(Pres)*
Lindsay Pangburn *(Dir-Pub Outreach)*

Accounts:
New-WEAVEWorks Recycled Fashion
New-West Sac Flood Protect

CROSS MARKETING
210 Post St Ste 1113, San Francisco, CA 94108
Tel.: (415) 986-0342
Fax: (415) 986-0367
Web Site: www.crossmarketingpr.com

Year Founded: 2005

Agency Specializes In: Advertising, Collateral, Event Planning & Marketing, Media Planning, Promotions, Public Relations, Social Media

Claudia Ross *(CEO & Principal)*
Tiffany Cummins *(Partner)*
Vicky Morel *(CFO)*
David McDonald *(CMO)*
Mark Olson *(Acct Mgr)*

Accounts:
Drybar

CROSSROADS PUBLIC RELATIONS
136 E Morgan St Ste 100, Raleigh, NC 27601
Tel.: (919) 821-2822
Fax: (919) 834-0448
E-Mail: info@crossroadspr.com
Web Site: www.crossroadsprm.com

Agency Specializes In: Public Relations

Kristi Lee-John *(Co-Founder & Principal)*
Shawn Ramsey *(Founder & Principal)*
Molly Thompson *(Sr Acct Exec)*
Laurel Melton *(Asst Acct Coord)*

Accounts:
Bivarus
Clinipace
Inlet Technologies
Overture Networks
Papa Mojos

CROSSWIND COMMUNICATIONS, LLC.
701 Brazos St Ste 550, Austin, TX 78701
Tel.: (855) 277-7963
Fax: (855) 204-6620
E-Mail: info@crosswindpr.com
Web Site: www.crosswindcommunications.com

Agency Specializes In: Corporate Communications, Crisis Communications, Digital/Interactive, Internet/Web Design, Investor Relations, Media Relations, Public Relations

Thomas Graham *(Pres & CEO)*
Mostafa Razzak *(Partner-Corp Affairs & Tech-Washington)*
James Bernsen *(VP-Corp Affairs)*
Angela Dejene *(VP-Crosswind Media & PR)*

Accounts:
New-GreyCastle Security (Agency of Record)
The Texas A&M University System

CROSSWIND MEDIA AND PUBLIC RELATIONS
701 Brazos St Ste 1100, Austin, TX 78767
Tel.: (512) 354-2772
Fax: (855) 204-6620
E-Mail: info@crosswindpr.com
Web Site: www.crosswindpr.com

Agency Specializes In: Brand Development & Integration, Crisis Communications, Digital/Interactive, Event Planning & Marketing, Investor Relations, Media Relations, Public Relations

Thomas Graham *(Pres)*
Angela Dejene *(VP)*

Accounts:
New-Central Texas Mobility Authority

CULTIVATE PUBLIC RELATIONS
1308 Rosewood Ave, Austin, TX 78702
Tel.: (512) 213-0212
Web Site: www.cultivatepr.com

Year Founded: 2008

Agency Specializes In: Communications, Content, Crisis Communications, Event Planning & Marketing, Media Planning, Public Relations, Social Media

Samantha Davidson *(Partner)*
Amanda Sprague *(Acct Dir)*
Lindsey LeRoy *(Sr Acct Exec)*
Caroline Pinkston *(Sr Acct Exec)*

Accounts:
Apis Restaurant
New-Ozinga Bros Inc. Campaign: "Born to Build", Online, Out-of-Home, Print, Radio, TV

CURATOR
419 Occidental Ave Ste 606, Seattle, WA 98104
Tel.: (206) 973-5570
Web Site: www.curatorpr.com

Agency Specializes In: Communications, Media Relations, Public Relations, Social Media

Scott Battishill *(Founder & Principal)*
Ann Marie Ricard *(VP & Grp Acct Dir)*
Jennifer Carroll *(Acct Supvr)*
Chelsey Allodi *(Sr Acct Exec)*
Annie Zanin *(Sr Acct Exec)*
Paul Balcerak *(Strategist-Social Media)*

Accounts:
Allrecipes.com
The Food & Wine Festival in Ixtapa Zihuatanejo
Macy's, Inc.
Root Metrics
Safeco Insurance Company of America
Seattle's Best Coffee
Starwood Hotels & Resorts Worldwide, Inc.
Washingtons Lottery
West Elm
Whole Foods Market, Inc.

CURLEY & PYNN
258 Southhall Ln Ste 130, Maitland, FL 32751
Tel.: (407) 423-8006
Fax: (407) 648-5869
Web Site: www.thestrategicfirm.com

Year Founded: 1984

Agency Specializes In: Advertising, Collateral, Identity Marketing, Public Relations

Roger Pynn *(Pres & CEO)*
Dan Ward *(Partner & VP)*
Heather Keroes *(Sr Strategist-Comm)*
Kacie Boniberger *(Specialist-Comm)*
Vianka McConville *(Assoc Strategist-Comm)*

Accounts:
Walton County Tourist Development Council

CURLEY COMPANY INC
919 18th St NW Ste 925, Washington, DC 20006
Tel.: (202) 263-2574
E-Mail: info@curleycompany.com
Web Site: www.curleycompany.com

Year Founded: 2002

Agency Specializes In: Content, Crisis

Communications, Event Planning & Marketing, Media Relations, Media Training, Public Relations, Social Media

Jennifer Curley *(Pres & CEO)*
Victoria Lion Monroe *(Partner-Strategic)*
Greg Wilson *(Sr VP & Dir-Creative)*
Elizabeth Shaffer *(Acct Supvr)*
Riley Smith *(Acct Supvr)*
Maria Treacy *(Acct Supvr)*
Emma Jekowsky *(Sr Acct Assoc)*

Accounts:
Aspen Dental Management, Inc Public Relations
Counsels Center for Organizational Excellence
New-L'Oreal USA, Inc. For Women in Science
New-The McClatchy Company How Does the Road to the White House Lead Through the South, Strategic
New-National Defense University Foundation 2015 American Patriot Award Gala
New-New Markets Tax Credit Coalition Media Relations
New-Rapoza Associates Media Relations

CURRENT LIFESTYLE MARKETING
875 N Michigan Ave Ste 2700, Chicago, IL 60611
Tel.: (312) 929-0500
Web Site: www.talktocurrent.com

Year Founded: 2006

National Agency Associations: 4A's

Agency Specializes In: Digital/Interactive, Public Relations, Social Media, Strategic Planning/Research

Lisa Dini *(Exec VP)*
Sara Joseph *(Sr VP & Head-Travel & Lifestyle Grp)*
Jonathan Kreissman *(VP)*
Kari Streiber *(VP)*
Christine Bridger *(Exec Dir-Creative)*
Kenny Roa *(Art Dir)*
Jennifer Dingman *(Mgr-Social Strategy)*
Emily Sheehan *(Mgr-Community)*
Leigh Lehman *(Acct Supvr)*
Sarah Prejean *(Acct Supvr)*
Marin Seifert *(Acct Exec)*

Accounts:
Azamara Club Cruises North America Agency of Record
The Clorox Company Brita, Content Strategy, Public Relations
New-Coca-Cola
General Mills, Inc.
Hanesbrands Inc.
Renaissance Hotels
Samsung America, Inc.
The Setai

CURVE COMMUNICATIONS
122-1020 Mainland St, Vancouver, BC V6B 2T5 Canada
Tel.: (604) 684-3170
Fax: (604) 684-3171
E-Mail: info@curvecommunications.com
Web Site: www.curvecommunications.com

Employees: 11
Year Founded: 2000

Agency Specializes In: Event Planning & Marketing, Exhibit/Trade Shows, Government/Political, T.V.

George Affleck *(Founder & Pres)*
Amanda Bates *(Mng Partner)*
Gina Robinson *(Mgr-Client Svcs)*
Kerry Slater *(Mgr-Special Projects)*

Accounts:
B.C. & Yukon Community Newspapers Association
Inimex
Sinu Cleanse
Sun Peaks Resort
Whistler

CUTLER PR
9415 Culver Boulevard, Culver City, CA 90232
Tel.: (212) 220-2534
E-Mail: info@cutlerpr.co
Web Site: www.cutlerpr.co

Year Founded: 2009

Agency Specializes In: Brand Development & Integration, Digital/Interactive, Media Relations, Print, Public Relations, Search Engine Optimization, Social Media

Zach Cutler *(Founder & CEO)*
Molly Cutler *(CMO)*
Scott Rosenblum *(VP)*

Accounts:
New-Duda (Public Relations Agency of Record)
New-Oomph (Public Relations Agency of Record)

CWR & PARTNERS LLP
21 Sheridan Cir, Attleboro, MA 02703
Tel.: (508) 222-4802
Fax: (508) 699-0094
Web Site: www.cwrpartners.com.

Year Founded: 2001

Agency Specializes In: Crisis Communications, Media Relations, Media Training, Newspaper, Public Relations, Trade & Consumer Magazines

Kelly Cinelli *(Founder & Principal)*
Veronica Welch *(Founder & Principal)*
Michelle Thompson *(Sr Acct Exec)*
Melissa Mitchell *(Acct Exec)*

Accounts:
NuView Systems Inc
SpectraScience Inc Medical Devices Mfr

CYPRESS MEDIA GROUP
PO Box 53198, Atlanta, GA 30355-1198
Tel.: (770) 640-9918
Fax: (770) 640-9819
E-Mail: info@cypressmedia.net
Web Site: www.cypressmedia.net

Employees: 5
Year Founded: 1978

Agency Specializes In: Exhibit/Trade Shows, Radio, T.V.

Randall P. Whatley *(Pres)*

Accounts:
Atlanta Dog Trainer
City Councilman Rich Dippolito
Gray's Furniture Galleries
Lee, Eadon, Isgett, Popwell & Reardon
Rinck Advertising

D. WILLIAMS PUBLIC RELATIONS & EVENT MANAGEMENT GROUP
700 N Green St 303, Chicago, IL 60642
Tel.: (312) 225-8705
Fax: (708) 590-0764
Web Site: www.dwilliamspr.com

Agency Specializes In: Brand Development & Integration, Event Planning & Marketing, Media Relations, Multicultural, Public Relations

Dionne Williams *(Founder & CEO)*

Accounts:
New-The History Makers
New-Yana German

DABO & CO
(Acquired by & Name Changed to Edelman DABO)

DADA GOLDBERG
195 Chrystie St 603F, New York, NY 10002
Tel.: (212) 673-3232
E-Mail: info@dadagoldberg.com
Web Site: www.dadagoldberg.com

Agency Specializes In: Brand Development & Integration, Content, Event Planning & Marketing, Media Buying Services, Media Planning, Public Relations, Social Media

Rebecca Goldberg *(Owner)*

Accounts:
New-Arper
New-Azure

DAHLIA PUBLIC RELATIONS
4678 Lee Hill Dr, Boulder, CO 80302
Tel.: (303) 898-3390
E-Mail: ckemp@dahliapr.com
Web Site: www.dahliapr.com

Year Founded: 2003

Agency Specializes In: Communications, Internet/Web Design, Media Relations, Media Training, Newspapers & Magazines, Public Relations, Strategic Planning/Research

Christy Kemp *(Pres)*

Accounts:
Cavalier Telecommunication Services
Contactual Communication Services
Intellifiber Networks Telecommunication Services
Specops Software Software Inventory & Management Services

DALGAR COMMUNICATIONS GROUP LLC
2800 S Syracuse Way, Denver, CO 80231
Tel.: (303) 695-8180
E-Mail: info@dalgarcommunications.com
Web Site: www.dalgarcommunications.com

Agency Specializes In: Brand Development & Integration, Collateral, Communications, Crisis Communications, Event Planning & Marketing, Media Relations, Media Training, Public Relations, Social Media, Strategic Planning/Research

Stefanie Dalgar *(Mng Dir)*

Accounts:
A Private Guide
American Mountain Holidays
Clear Creek County
Colorado Dude & Guest Ranch Association
Denver Botanic Gardens
Doxys
Oster Jewelers
SBDC
South Metro Denver Chamber

DALY-SWARTZ PUBLIC RELATIONS
23591 El Toro Rd Ste 215, Lake Forest, CA 92630
Tel.: (949) 470-0075

Web Site: www.dsprel.com

Year Founded: 1986

Agency Specializes In: Brand Development & Integration, Media Relations, Public Relations

Jeffrey Swartz *(Pres)*
Alan Graner *(Chief Creative Officer)*
Suzie Swartz *(VP)*

Accounts:
New-TechBiz Connection

DANA AGENCY
7251 NE 2nd Ave Ste 106, Miami, FL 33138
Tel.: (305) 758-1110
E-Mail: info@thedanaagency.com
Web Site: www.thedanaagency.com

Agency Specializes In: Event Planning & Marketing, Graphic Design, Internet/Web Design, Logo & Package Design, Media Relations, Print, Public Relations, Social Media

Dana Rhoden *(Pres)*
Cynthia Demos *(Mng Partner)*
Rachael Bobman *(Acct Coord)*

Accounts:
American Social
Charriol
Duracell Quantum Battery
MS Turanor PlanetSolar
Novecento Brickell
Pure Barre Miami

DANCIE PERUGINI WARE PUBLIC RELATIONS
808 Travis Ste 1100, Houston, TX 77002
Tel.: (713) 224-9115
Fax: (713) 224-3248
E-Mail: info@dpwpr.com
Web Site: www.dpwpr.com

Agency Specializes In: Broadcast, Collateral, Media Relations, Media Training, Print, Promotions, Public Relations

Dancie Perugini Ware *(Owner)*
Marta Fredricks *(Sr VP)*
Jamie Sava *(Acct Dir)*
Annie Weglicki *(Sr Acct Exec & Strategist-Digital)*
Katy Ellis *(Sr Acct Exec)*
Brooke Grisebaum *(Sr Acct Exec)*
Katelyn Roche *(Sr Acct Exec)*
Hayden Rome *(Sr Acct Exec)*
Michaela Williams *(Sr Acct Exec)*

Accounts:
Barbara Bush Houston Literacy Foundation

DANIELLE ASHLEY GROUP, INC.
8 S Michigan Ave Ste 1600, Chicago, IL 60603
Tel.: (312) 640-9550
Fax: (312) 470-0267
Web Site: www.danielleashley.com

Agency Specializes In: Event Planning & Marketing, Media Buying Services, Media Planning, Public Relations, Sponsorship, Strategic Planning/Research

Peggy Austinq *(VP)*

Accounts:
The Illinois Lottery

DANIKA COMMUNICATIONS, LLC
15 East Putnam Ave PBM 386, Greenwich, CT 06830
Tel.: (203) 661-3663
E-Mail: info@danikapr.com
Web Site: www.danikapr.com

Agency Specializes In: Event Planning & Marketing, Public Relations, Social Media, Strategic Planning/Research

Anne Ryan *(Pres)*

Accounts:
Park Hotel Kenmare
Samas Spa

DARBY COMMUNICATIONS
8 Magnolia Ave Ste G1, Asheville, NC 28801
Tel.: (828) 254-0914
Web Site: www.darbycommunications.com

Agency Specializes In: Outdoor, Public Relations

Coral Darby *(Founder)*
Mandy Giles *(Dir & Sr Acct Exec)*
Anna Elliott *(Dir-Digital & Media)*
Angie Houck *(Dir-Sponsorship)*
Mandy Gresham *(Mgr)*
Shelly Smith *(Acct Exec)*
Julie Hansell *(Coord-Sponsorship)*

Accounts:
Astral Buoyancy Company
Aventura Clothing
Backpacker Media Relations, National Parks Centennial Tour (Public Relations Agency of Record)
Eagle's Nest Outfitters
Ecoths
Feetures!
FloydFest
Granite Gear
Headsweats
Hyland's
New-IceMule Coolers (Public Relations Agency of Record)
Industrial Revolution
The Mann Group GEAR, Profitability Project, Rep Training, Strategic Planning
OverLand Equipment
Sierra Designs
Suspension Experts; Asheville, NC
Vasque

DARCY COMMUNICATIONS, INC.
11055 W Center Ave, Lakewood, CO 80226
Tel.: (303) 980-0123
Fax: (303) 987-2382
E-Mail: hq@darcycom.com
Web Site: www.darcycom.com

E-Mail for Key Personnel:
President: jcollins@darcycom.com

Employees: 6
Year Founded: 1971

Agency Specializes In: Consulting, Corporate Communications, Corporate Identity, Crisis Communications, Media Relations, Public Relations

James Collins *(Pres)*

Accounts:
Arte Universal; 1991
Catholic Health Initiatives; Denver, CO; 1996
Geovic Ltd.
Grund + Nelson
OpSec Security, PLC; London, UK; 1998

DARNELL WORKS INC
367 Pk St, Boone, NC 28607
Tel.: (828) 264-8898
Web Site: www.darnellworks.com

Year Founded: 2000

Agency Specializes In: Media Relations, Public Relations, Social Media, Strategic Planning/Research

Roger Darnell *(Principal & Chief Comm Officer)*

Accounts:
Authors & Artists
Brewster Parsons
Cap Gun Collective LLC
Cutters Studios
Envoy
Leviathan Corp.

DASH MEDIA PR
423 W 127th St Ste 7, New York, NY 10027
Tel.: (212) 939-7544
Web Site: www.dashmediapr.com

Year Founded: 2006

Agency Specializes In: Event Planning & Marketing, Public Relations, Social Media

Donnette Dunbar *(CEO)*

Accounts:
Vince Morgan

DAVID & GARCIA PR
(Name Changed to David PR Group)

DAVID PEARSON ASSOCIATES
1000 Hardee Rd, Coral Gables, FL 33146
Tel.: (305) 798-8446
Fax: (305) 662-2360
E-Mail: david@davidpearsonassociates.com
Web Site: www.davidpearsonassociates.com

Employees: 5
Year Founded: 1966

Agency Specializes In: Bilingual Market, Business Publications, Collateral, Consulting, Consumer Publications, Direct Response Marketing, Environmental, Government/Political, Hispanic Market, Leisure, Magazines, Newspaper, Newspapers & Magazines, Outdoor, Planning & Consultation, Public Relations, Publicity/Promotions, Real Estate, Sales Promotion, Seniors' Market, Trade & Consumer Magazines, Travel & Tourism

Approx. Annual Billings: $1,000,000

Breakdown of Gross Billings by Media: Bus. Publs.: $250,000; Mags.: $250,000; Newsp.: $250,000; Radio: $250,000

David Pearson *(Mng Dir)*

Accounts:
La Reserva; Trujillo Bay, Honduras
The Landings; St. Lucia, BWI
Luxury Resorts; Boca Raton, FL
Rose Hall; Montego Bay, Jamaica; 1999
Santa Barbara Plantation

DAVID PR GROUP
(Formerly David & Garcia PR)
9990 SW 77th Ave Ste 304, Miami, FL 33156
Tel.: (305) 255-0035
Fax: (866) 214-6612
E-Mail: john@davidpr.com

Web Site: www.davidpr.com

Employees: 5
Year Founded: 2005

National Agency Associations: PRSA

Agency Specializes In: Business Publications, Business-To-Business, Corporate Communications, Hispanic Market, Over-50 Market, Public Relations, Publicity/Promotions, Seniors' Market

Breakdown of Gross Billings by Media: Pub. Rels.: 100%

John P. David *(Pres)*

Accounts:
IRA Financial Group
Spotify Campaign: "#thatsongwhen", Marketing, Online, Social Media

DBC PR & SOCIAL MEDIA
28 W 27th St Ste 705, New York, NY 10001
Tel.: (888) 294-5008
Web Site: www.dbcpr.com

Agency Specializes In: Digital/Interactive, Event Planning & Marketing, Media Relations, Public Relations, Social Media

Jon Cunningham *(Sr VP)*
Briana Haas *(VP)*
Kara Pinato *(Acct Dir)*
Ben Brodette *(Sr Acct Exec)*

Accounts:
Q Drinks (Agency of Record)

DBC PR+NEW MEDIA
1027 33rd St Ste 250, Washington, DC 20007
Tel.: (202) 298-8044
E-Mail: info@dbcpr.com
Web Site: www.dbcpr.com

Year Founded: 2000

Agency Specializes In: Digital/Interactive, Event Planning & Marketing, Media Relations, Public Relations, Social Media, Sponsorship

Jessica Phlipot *(Pres)*
Dan Baum *(CEO & Dir-Creative)*
Jaclyn C. Gower *(VP)*
Briana Haas-Zak *(VP)*
Molly Kinsella Lynch *(Acct Dir)*
Christopher Ryan Vaughan *(Acct Dir)*
Tiffany Mathis *(Mgr-Ops)*
Callie Burrows *(Sr Acct Exec)*
Ruben Marinbach *(Acct Exec)*
Rebecca Winship *(Assoc Acct Exec)*

Accounts:
Ace Hardware Consumer PR
Kilbeggan
Q Drinks (Public Relations Agency of Record)

DBRAY MEDIA
95 Morton St Ground Fl, New York, NY 10014
Tel.: (973) 739-9152
Web Site: www.dbraymedia.com

Year Founded: 2012

Agency Specializes In: Communications, Crisis Communications, Event Planning & Marketing, Internet/Web Design, Media Relations, Production, Public Relations, Search Engine Optimization, Social Media

David Bray *(Founder)*
Carly Fink *(Head-Strategy & Res)*
Meg Berberich *(Dir-Content Mktg)*
Melody Wolff *(Dir-Accts)*
Laci Texter *(Strategist-Social Media)*

Accounts:
Amazing Kreskin
Becker Brothers
BlueLink Marketing
Cinchcast
MyEchain

DCI GROUP
1828 L St NW Ste 400, Washington, DC 20036
Tel.: (202) 546-4242
Fax: (202) 546-4243
Web Site: www.dcigroup.com

Agency Specializes In: Government/Political, Public Relations

Thomas J. Synhorst *(Chm & Mng Partner)*
Douglas M. Goodyear *(CEO & Mng Partner)*
Brian McCabe *(Mng Partner)*
Justin Peterson *(Mng Partner)*
Dan Combs *(Partner)*
Ed Patru *(VP)*
Karin Peterson *(VP-Strategic Dev & Mktg Svcs)*
Craig Stevens *(VP)*
Mark Szalay *(VP-Tech)*
Suzanne Zurn *(VP-Digital Strategy)*
Caitlin Fisher *(Dir)*

Accounts:
Applied Digital
Aquasciences
AT&T Communications Corp.
Blount County Memorial Hospital
Blount County, TN
City of Alcoa, TN
City of Cheyenne
City of Maryville, TN
EchoStar Communications
ExxonMobil Corp.
Federal Home Loan Bank of San Francisco
GTECH Corp.

DDR PUBLIC RELATIONS
444 Bedford Rd Ste 201, Pleasantville, NY 10570-3055
Tel.: (914) 747-2500
Fax: (914) 747-2592
E-Mail: ddr@ddrpr.com
Web Site: www.ddrpr.com

Employees: 3
Year Founded: 1989

National Agency Associations: PRSA

Agency Specializes In: Brand Development & Integration, Commercial Photography, Graphic Design, New Product Development, Public Relations, Retail, Strategic Planning/Research

Dawn Dankner-Rosen *(Pres)*
Jennifer Topiel *(Acct Supvr)*
Ilana Arazie *(Strategist-Social Media)*

Accounts:
Compass Learning
Coyaba Beach Resort & Spa
JP McHale Pest Control
WeeZee World of Yes I Can Media Relations, Social Media, Strategic Communications
Westchester Italian Cultural Center

DE LA GARZA PUBLIC RELATIONS, INC.
5773 Woodway Dr Ste 296, Houston, TX 77057
Tel.: (713) 622-8818
Fax: (713) 683-8090
E-Mail: info@delagarza-pr.com
Web Site: www.delagarza-pr.com

Employees: 5

National Agency Associations: PRSA

Agency Specializes In: Business-To-Business, Communications, Consumer Marketing, Direct Response Marketing, Event Planning & Marketing, Government/Political, Hispanic Market, Internet/Web Design, Investor Relations, Legal Services, Public Relations, Publicity/Promotions, Sports Market, T.V., Telemarketing

Henry A. de La Garza *(Sec-Press & Dir-Comm)*

DEANE/SMITH
(Formerly Deane Smith & Partners)
209 10th Ave S, Nashville, TN 37203
Tel.: (615) 454-5745
Web Site: www.deanesmith.agency

Year Founded: 1999

Agency Specializes In: Advertising, Graphic Design, Print, Public Relations, Strategic Planning/Research

Todd Smith *(Co-Founder, Pres & CEO)*
Silas Deane *(Co-Founder & Sr Partner)*
David Catterton *(Mgr-Creative Svcs)*
Allison Carter *(Acct Exec)*
Laura Hunt *(Acct Exec)*
Laura McClellan *(Acct Exec)*

Accounts:
Cybera, Inc.

DEBRA SEIFERT COMMUNICATIONS
11930 NW Dumar Ln, Portland, OR 97229
Tel.: (503) 626-7539
Web Site: www.debraseifert.com

Agency Specializes In: Advertising, Collateral, Communications, Promotions, Public Relations

Debra L. Seifert *(Principal)*

Accounts:
Signal Hound

THE DECKER/ROYAL AGENCY
54 W 40th St Fl 7, New York, NY 10018
Tel.: (646) 650-2180
Fax: (646) 650-2190
Web Site: www.deckerroyal.com

Agency Specializes In: Crisis Communications, Digital/Interactive, Media Relations, Promotions, Public Relations, Social Media, Strategic Planning/Research

Cathleen Decker *(Pres)*
Stacy Royal *(Mng Dir)*

Accounts:
New-City Wonders Ltd
New-Stylist Julie Sabatino

DELAUNAY COMMUNICATIONS, INC.
2430 Boyer Ave E Ste B, Seattle, WA 98112-2119
Tel.: (206) 682-3699
Fax: (206) 682-3899
E-Mail: info@delaunay.com
Web Site: www.delaunay.com

Employees: 7

Agency Specializes In: Agriculture, Entertainment,

Health Care Services, Public Relations, Trade & Consumer Magazines, Travel & Tourism

Pete DeLaunay *(Pres)*

Accounts:
Master Builders Associates
PWC Safety,WA
WestPort

DELICIOUS BUZZ COMMUNICATIONS
315 S Coast Hwy 101, Encinitas, CA 92024
Tel.: (858) 224-2460
Web Site: www.deliciousbuzz.com

Year Founded: 2009

Agency Specializes In: Brand Development & Integration, Event Planning & Marketing, Media Relations, Promotions, Public Relations, Social Media

Tiffany Melone *(Owner)*

Accounts:
Vixen Pop Up Boutique & Fashion Show

DELIGHTFUL COMMUNICATIONS LLC
1118 33rd Ave, Seattle, WA 98122
Tel.: (970) 325-5007
Web Site: www.delightfulcommunications.com

Year Founded: 2012

Agency Specializes In: Content, Digital/Interactive, Event Planning & Marketing, Public Relations, Social Media

Mel Carson *(Founder)*

Accounts:
Efesse Business Solutions
Majestic SEO

DELTA MEDIA
350 Sparks St Ste 405, Ottawa, ON K1R 7S8 Canada
Tel.: (613) 233-9191
Fax: (613) 233-5880
E-Mail: info@deltamedia.ca
Web Site: www.deltamedia.ca

Employees: 15
Year Founded: 1991

Agency Specializes In: Bilingual Market, Engineering, Environmental, Government/Political, Health Care Services, Internet/Web Design, Public Relations, Strategic Planning/Research, Transportation

Timothy M. Kane *(Chm)*
Sheena Pennie *(Pres)*
Ken Anderson *(VP)*
Karen Bennett *(VP-Client Svcs)*
Kelly Mccormick *(Coord-Trng)*

Accounts:
Association of Universities & Colleges of Canada
Canada Mortgage & Housing Corporation
Canadian Hard of Hearing Association
Independent Living Canada
Perleay Rideau Veterans Health Center
Service Canada
University of Ottawa

DEMOSS
3343 Peachtree Rd NE Twr Ste 1000 E, Atlanta, GA 30326
Tel.: (770) 813-0000
E-Mail: inquiry@demoss.com
Web Site: www.demoss.com

Year Founded: 1991

Agency Specializes In: Advertising, Brand Development & Integration, Crisis Communications, Digital/Interactive, Media Relations, Public Relations

Rob Forrester *(COO)*
Karen Dye *(Dir-PR)*
Drew Hawkins *(Dir-Digital & Social Media)*

Accounts:
Passages Exhibit

DENNIS PR GROUP
41 Crossroads Ste 228, West Hartford, CT 06117
Tel.: (860) 523-7500
Fax: (720) 533-7501
Toll Free: (800) 990-6685
E-Mail: info@dennispr.com
Web Site: www.dennispr.com

Employees: 6
Year Founded: 2000

Agency Specializes In: Business-To-Business, Corporate Communications, Crisis Communications, Faith Based, Government/Political, Media Relations, Public Relations, Publicity/Promotions, Travel & Tourism

Approx. Annual Billings: $1,600,000

Breakdown of Gross Billings by Media: Brdcst.: 15%; Newsp. & Mags.: 10%; Pub. Rels.: 75%

Ron Dresner *(Pres)*

Accounts:
Bob's Discount Furniture; Manchester, CT
Connecticut Business Hall of Fame; New Haven, CT
Dutch Iris Resorts
FMAMRadio.com; New York, NY
Jewish Ledger Publications; West Hartford, CT
Sam Gejdenson International
Whistling Bird Resort; Negril, Jamaica
Zer01 Mobile; Las Vegas, NV

DENNY INK
155 W Gill Ave, Jackson, WY 83001
Tel.: (307) 200-6001
Web Site: www.dennyink.com

Agency Specializes In: Brand Development & Integration, Public Relations

Chris Denny *(Owner)*
Sally Francklyn *(Acct Exec)*
Sam Petri *(Acct Exec)*

Accounts:
Kill Cliff Recovery Drink

DENOR BRANDS & PUBLIC RELATIONS
700 Craighead St Ste 107, Nashville, TN 37204
Tel.: (855) 809-6697
E-Mail: info@denorbrands.com
Web Site: www.denorbrands.com

Year Founded: 2010

Agency Specializes In: Brand Development & Integration, Content, Event Planning & Marketing, Internet/Web Design, Promotions, Public Relations, Social Media

Ashley Norr *(Pres)*

Accounts:
Arekah the Goddess Photography

DEPTH PUBLIC RELATIONS
798 N Parkwood Rd, Atlanta, GA 30030
Tel.: (404) 378-0850
Web Site: www.depthpr.com

Agency Specializes In: Internet/Web Design, Market Research, Public Relations, Search Engine Optimization, Strategic Planning/Research

Kerri S. Milam *(Pres, Principal & Strategist)*

Accounts:
Del Mar DataTrac Mortgage Software Development Services
International Document Services Inc Brokerage Services

DEREK FARLEY PUBLIC RELATIONS, LLC
15720 John J. Delaney Dr Ste 300, Charlotte, NC 28277
Tel.: (704) 941-7353
E-Mail: derek@dfpr.com
Web Site: www.dfpr.com

Year Founded: 2006

Agency Specializes In: Crisis Communications, Media Relations, Public Relations, Publicity/Promotions, Strategic Planning/Research

Derek Farley *(Pres)*
Tom Beyer *(Exec VP)*
Linsey Beford *(Sr Specialist-Bus Dev)*

Accounts:
Allstate
Applebee's
New-Arooga's
Carlson Restaurant Worldwide
Carolina Investment Property
New-Champps
Country Roads of the Carolinas, LLC
New-CUPS Frozen Yogurt
New-Fox & Hound
New-JJ's Red Hots
New-On The Border Mexican Grill & Cantina
New-Paciugo
Pick Up Stix
Safe Step Walk-In Tub Co. (Public Relations Agency of Record)
Shoney's
T.G.I. Friday's
New-UFC GYM (Public Relations Agency of Record)
New-Zinburger Wine & Burger Bar

DEVENEY COMMUNICATIONS
2406 Chartres St, New Orleans, LA 70117
Tel.: (504) 949-3999
Fax: (504) 949-3974
E-Mail: pr@deveney.com
Web Site: www.deveney.com

Employees: 10

Rachel Wilson *(Creative Dir)*
Carrie Devries *(Sr Acct Exec)*
Cory Cart *(Acct Exec)*
Andy Cole *(Acct Exec)*
Mary Petikas *(Acct Exec)*
Savannah Urban *(Acct Exec)*
Brittany Cruickshank *(Sr Acct Coord)*

Accounts:
Audubon Nature Institute
Cox Communications

Louisiana Office of Tourism
Louisiana State University Museum of Art
New Orleans Convention & Visitors Bureau
New Orleans Museum of Art
New Orleans Police Foundation
NFL Youth Education Town
Prospect New Orleans Prospect.3
Ralph Brennan Restaurant Group
Starbucks
Windsor Court Hotel Marketing Campaign, Public Relations, Social Media

DEVINE + PARTNERS
(Formerly Devine + Powers)
2300 Chesnut St, Philadelphia, PA 19103
Tel.: (215) 568-2525
Fax: (215) 568-3909
Web Site: devinepartners.com

Year Founded: 2003

Agency Specializes In: Advertising, Communications, Education, Email, Graphic Design, Media Relations, Public Relations, Real Estate, Restaurant, Social Marketing/Nonprofit, Social Media, Sponsorship, Travel & Tourism

Jay Devine *(Pres & CEO)*
Don Galletly *(Sr VP & Dir-IR & Fin Comm Div)*
Christine Reimert *(Sr VP)*
Susan Hamilton *(VP)*
Brianna Taylor *(Acct Supvr)*
Molly Early *(Acct Exec)*
John Latchaw *(Acct Exec)*
Molly Stieber *(Acct Exec)*
Cassandra McAllister *(Acct Coord)*

Accounts:
AMC Institute
Blank Rome
Brown Hill Development
Cabrini College
Computers for Youth
Maaco
Moore College of Art
PECO Economic Development
PGW
The Philadelphia Zoo Faris Family Education Center, KidZooU
Valley Forge Convention & Visitors Bureau PR, Social Media

DEVINE MULVEY LONGABAUGH
(Formerly Devine Mulvey)
2141 Wisconsin Ave NW Suite H, Washington, DC 20007
Tel.: (202) 337-9600
Fax: (202) 337-9620
Web Site: dmlmessage.com/

Employees: 8
Year Founded: 2000

Agency Specializes In: Advertising, Government/Political, Public Relations, Publicity/Promotions

Tad Devine *(Pres)*
Mark Longabaugh *(Partner)*
Julian Mulvey *(Partner)*
Scott Turner *(Dir-Production & Sr Producer)*
Anne Tully *(Mgr)*

THE DEVON GROUP
1715 Hwy 35 N Ste 106, Middletown, NJ 07748
Tel.: (732) 706-0123
Fax: (732) 706-0199
E-Mail: jeanne@devonpr.com
Web Site: www.devonpr.com

Employees: 10

Year Founded: 1994

Agency Specializes In: Business-To-Business, Collateral, Communications, Corporate Communications, High Technology, Information Technology, Public Relations, Publicity/Promotions, Trade & Consumer Magazines

Jeanne Achille *(CEO)*
Adam Mandelbaum *(VP-Content)*

Accounts:
Applied Research Corporation
CyberShift
Cynergy Systems
The Human Capital Institute Media
iCIMS
Jobs2Web Public Relations
Kenexa
NelsonHall Business Processing Outsourcing; 2005
Talent Board; Middletown, NJ Candidate Experience Awards

DEVRIES GLOBAL
(Formerly DeVries Public Relations)
909 Third Ave, New York, NY 10022
Tel.: (212) 546-8500
Fax: (212) 644-0291
Web Site: www.devriesglobal.com

Employees: 110
Year Founded: 1978

National Agency Associations: 4A's-COPF

Agency Specializes In: Brand Development & Integration, Branded Entertainment, Consumer Goods, Consumer Marketing, Exhibit/Trade Shows, Fashion/Apparel, Household Goods, Integrated Marketing, Public Relations, Social Marketing/Nonprofit, Social Media, Sponsorship, Women's Market

Approx. Annual Billings: $25,000,000 Capitalized

Breakdown of Gross Billings by Media: Pub. Rels.: 100%

Laura Springer *(Mng Dir)*
Jessica O'Callaghan *(Exec VP)*
Janess Messner *(Sr VP-Fin)*
Daniel Maree *(VP-Creative Intelligence)*
Yvonne Shaw *(VP-HR)*
Megan VanBlarcom *(Sr Dir-Art)*
Ann Marie Almariei *(Dir-Content & Strategy)*
Tasia Hurt *(Sr Acct Supvr)*
Lindsay Talley *(Sr Acct Supvr-Pantene)*
Douglas Ruchefsky *(Acct Supvr)*

Accounts:
Accolade Wines
Hardys Digital Content Creation, Events, Led Publicity, PR, Press Office, Social Media Community Management
Boston Beer Co. Samuel Adams Beer
E&J Gallo Winery; Modesto, CA Black Swan, Ecco Domani; 2001
GlaxoSmithKline, Inc.
Markwins Beauty Products Brand Awareness, Creating Strategic, Wet n Wild (Public Relations Agency of Record)
Procter & Gamble; Cincinnati, OH Bounce, DDF, Downy, Olay, PR, Pantene, Sebastian, Secret (Public Relations), ThermaCare, Tide, Vicks, Wella; 1983
Tupperware Brands Corporation Tupperware Corporation

DI MODA PUBLIC RELATIONS
124 Lasky Dr 2nd Fl, Beverly Hills, CA 90212
Tel.: (310) 288-0077
Fax: (310) 288-0092
E-Mail: info@dimodapr.com
Web Site: www.dimodapr.com

Agency Specializes In: Brand Development & Integration, Media Training, Public Relations, Social Media

Diana Bianchini *(Founder & Creative Dir)*

Accounts:
New-Project Angel Food

DIALOGO PUBLIC RELATIONS
477 Madison Ave 6th Fl, New York, NY 10022
Tel.: (646) 455-3551
Web Site: www.dialogo.us

Year Founded: 2007

Agency Specializes In: Content, Event Planning & Marketing, Media Relations, Public Relations, Social Media

Richie Matthews *(Pres)*

Accounts:
Coco Jack Hispanic Public Relations Agency of Record

DIAMOND PUBLIC RELATIONS
4770 Biscayne Blvd, Miami, FL 33129
Tel.: (305) 854-3544
Web Site: www.diamondpr.com

Agency Specializes In: Brand Development & Integration, Digital/Interactive, Media Relations, Media Training, Promotions, Public Relations, Social Media, Strategic Planning/Research

Jody Diamond *(Pres)*
Kara Rosner *(COO & VP)*
Lisa Schwartz *(Dir-Lifestyle, Leisure & Resorts)*
Luisana Suegart *(Dir-Hotels & Leisure-Latin America)*
Cheryl Azar *(Mgr-Fin & Office Mgr)*
Alyson Marks *(Sr Acct Exec)*
Taylor Cinalli *(Assoc Acct Exec)*

Accounts:
Casa Palopo
CasaMagna Marriott Puerto Vallarta Resort & Spa (Agency of Record) Public Relations, Social Media
Circa 39
Curacao Tourist Board PR
Ecoventura Galapagos Network
Grand Cayman Marriott Beach Resort
New-Le Meridien Chambers Minneapolis (Agency of Record) Public Relations
Lord Balfour PR, Strategy
Ocean Properties, Ltd. PR Campaign
The Palms Hotel & Spa Miami
New-Renaissance Tuscany Il Ciocco Resort & Spa (Agency of Record) North American Public Relations
Santa Barbara Beach & Golf Resort
South Beach Marriott
Southbridge Hotel & Conference Center North American Public Relations, Social Media
Sun International
New-W Minneapolis ? The Foshay (Agency of Record) Public Relations

DIAN GRIESEL INC.
396 W Bdwy, New York, NY 10012
Tel.: (212) 825-3210
Web Site: www.dgicomm.com

Agency Specializes In: Content, Crisis Communications, Public Relations, Radio, Social Media, T.V.

Dian Griesel *(Founder & Pres)*
Susan Fay Forman *(Sr VP)*
Cheryl Schneider *(Sr VP)*
Tom Caden *(Dir-Team Mktg)*
Laura Radocaj *(Acct Exec)*
Brenna Goodsitt *(Assoc Acct Exec)*

Accounts:
Chanticleer Holdings, Inc.

DIANE TERMAN PUBLIC RELATIONS
47 E 77th St, New York, NY 10075
Tel.: (212) 744-6055
E-Mail: info@dianetermanpr.com
Web Site: www.dianetermanpr.com

Agency Specializes In: Digital/Interactive, Public Relations, Social Media

Diane Terman *(Founder)*
Deborah Kerner *(Pres)*
Derek Grover *(Exec Dir)*

Accounts:
Maddyloo

DIAZ COMMUNICATIONS
781 Natalie Dr, Windsor, CA 95492
Tel.: (707) 620-0788
Fax: (707) 838-9159
E-Mail: info@diaz-communications.com
Web Site: www.diaz-communications.com

Employees: 2
Year Founded: 2001

Agency Specializes In: Consumer Marketing, Leisure, Public Relations

Revenue: $250,000

Jo Diaz *(Co-Owner)*
Jose Diaz *(Co-Owner)*
Melanie Diaz *(Office Mgr)*
Lyla Diaz *(Copywriter & Graphic Designer)*

Accounts:
Affairs of the Vine
Charles Creek Vineyard
Concannon Vineyard
Happy Camper Wines
Oak Knoll Winery
Wine-Blog.org

DIETCH PR
1923 S Santa Fe Ave, Los Angeles, CA 90021
Tel.: (323) 661-4225
Web Site: www.dietchpr.net

Agency Specializes In: Brand Development & Integration, Public Relations, Social Media

David Dietch *(Owner)*

Accounts:
New-Kahlo

DIFFUSION INC
415 Madison Ave 15th Fl, New York, NY 10017
Tel.: (646) 673-8685
Web Site: www.diffusionpr.com

Agency Specializes In: Advertising, Brand Development & Integration, Communications, Digital/Interactive, Public Relations, Social Media

Ivan Ristic *(Pres-Diffusion US)*
Daljit Bhurji *(Mng Dir-Global)*
Kate Ryan *(VP)*

Accounts:
CyberLink Public Relations Agency of Record
HiringSolved Brand Awareness
Luta Bloggers, Brand Ambassador Engagement, Media
Moven (Public Relations Agency of Record) Consumer, Social Media
Skulpt (Agency of Record) National Media, Skulpt Aim
Tresorit Public Relations Agency of Record
Tsu (Public Relations Agency of Record) Communications

DIGITAL INFLUENCE GROUP
(Acquired & Absorbed by Racepoint Global)

THE DINGES GANG, LTD.
421 Chapel Hill Ln, Northfield, IL 60093
Tel.: (847) 386-6953
E-Mail: info@dingesgang.com
Web Site: www.dingesgang.com

Agency Specializes In: Communications, Public Relations

Barnaby Dinges *(Pres)*

Accounts:
Jim Beam Brands Co.

DITTOE PUBLIC RELATIONS, INC.
2815 E 62nd St Ste 300, Indianapolis, IN 46220-2983
Tel.: (317) 202-2280
Fax: (317) 202-2290
Web Site: www.dittoepr.com

Employees: 7

Revenue: $1,000,000

Chris Dittoe *(Co-Founder & Pres)*
Christy Chen *(Partner & VP-Sls & Mktg)*
Megan Custodio *(Partner & VP)*
Lauren Sanders *(Partner & VP-Acct Svcs)*
Eric Kokonas *(VP)*
Michelle Bower *(Sr Acct Mgr & Coord-Internship)*
Ashley Eggert *(Sr Acct Mgr)*
Britny Kalule *(Acct Exec)*
Kalyn Long *(Acct Exec)*
Mallory Sturgeon *(Acct Exec)*
Kasie Sturm *(Acct Exec)*

Accounts:
Atlas Van Lines; Evansville, IN Public Relations
Bella Sara
CareerScribe
ExactTarget
Klipsch
Rev Trax
Scott Jones
Senario
Zotec Partners

DIXON JAMES COMMUNICATIONS
109 N Marion St #200, Oak Park, IL 60301
Tel.: (708) 848-8058
E-Mail: info@dixon-james.com
Web Site: www.dixon-james.com

Employees: 10
Year Founded: 2009

Agency Specializes In: Below-the-Line, Business Publications, Collateral, Consumer Publications, Email, Local Marketing, Newspaper, Promotions, Search Engine Optimization, Social Media, Sponsorship, Sweepstakes, Web (Banner Ads, Pop-ups, etc.)

Jim Heininger *(Founder & Principal)*

Accounts:
BurtchWorks; 2014
Cantata Adult Life Services; 2008
Enova; 2008
McDonald's Corporation; 2003

DKC NEW YORK
261 5th Ave, 2nd Fl, New York, NY 10016
Tel.: (212) 685-4300
Fax: (212) 685-9024
E-Mail: ny@dkcnews.com
Web Site: www.dkcnews.com

Employees: 150
Year Founded: 1991

Agency Specializes In: Corporate Communications, Crisis Communications, Integrated Marketing, Public Relations, Publicity/Promotions

John Marino *(Mng Partner & Dir)*
William Cunningham *(Mng Dir)*
Joe DePlasco *(Mng Dir)*
Jeffrey Klein *(Mng Dir)*
Liz Anklow *(Exec VP)*
Bruce Bobbins *(Exec VP)*
Phil Crimaldi *(Exec VP)*
Diana Kashan *(Exec VP)*
Robert Leonard *(Exec VP)*
Adam Schiff *(Exec VP)*
Ed Tagliaferri *(Exec VP)*
Marie Ternes *(Exec VP)*
Brian Moriarty *(Sr VP)*
Brian Reiner *(Sr VP)*
Stephanie Tuck *(Sr VP)*
Gary Baronofsky *(VP-Media)*
Sebastian Moreira *(Dir-Digital Content)*
Chelsey Lutz *(Acct Supvr)*

Accounts:
AOL
Citigroup Inc.
Continuum Health Partners
Esquire Magazine
Gannett
The Jefferson (Agency of Record) Public Relations, Strategies
The London West Hollywood Public Relation
Meetinghouse Production
Mondelez International, Inc. TASSIMO
National Football League PR
Sports Illustrated
Ulta Consumer Publicity
New-Visit West Hollywood (Public Relations Agency of Record) Communications Strategy
X Factor

Branch

DKC Los Angeles
9911 W Pico Blvd Ste 1495, Los Angeles, CA 90035
Tel.: (310) 280-2013
Fax: (310) 280-2014
E-Mail: la@dkcnews.com
Web Site: www.dkcnews.com

Agency Specializes In: Digital/Interactive, Public Relations, Social Media

Joe Quenqua *(Exec VP & Dir-Entertainment)*
Molly Currey *(Exec VP)*
Jenn DeMartino Callister *(Sr VP)*
Brooke Hudis *(Sr VP)*
Karen Silberg *(Sr VP)*
Stephanie Tuck *(Sr VP)*
Malisa Meresman *(VP)*
Meredith Obendorfer *(VP)*
John Singh *(VP-Entertainment Practice)*

Christina Stejskal *(VP)*
Greta Vanhersecke *(VP)*
Courtney Greenberg *(Acct Supvr)*
Brandon Sansone *(Acct Supvr)*
Abbie Strichman *(Acct Supvr)*
Audrey Chen *(Sr Acct Exec)*

Accounts:
Syco Productions

DNA CREATIVE COMMUNICATIONS
103 E Park Ave, Greenville, SC 29601
Tel.: (864) 235-0959
Fax: (864) 235-1304
Web Site: www.dnacc.com

Year Founded: 1997

Agency Specializes In: Integrated Marketing, Logo & Package Design, Media Training, Outdoor, Print, Public Relations, T.V.

Debbie Nelson *(Founder & CEO)*
Sonya Brown *(Dir-Creative)*
Janice Baddley *(Sr Acct Mgr)*

Accounts:
CommunityWorks Carolina
Institute for Child Success
Mobile Meals of Spartanburg
Public Education Partners of Greenville County
Renewable Water Resources
University Center of Greenville

DODGE COMMUNICATIONS, INC.
11675 Rainwater Dr Ste 300, Alpharetta, GA 30009-8685
Tel.: (770) 998-0500
Fax: (770) 998-0208
E-Mail: info@dodgecommunications.com
Web Site: www.dodgecommunications.com

Employees: 18
Year Founded: 2001

National Agency Associations: COPF-PRSA

Agency Specializes In: Public Relations

Brad Dodge *(Founder & Pres)*
Brian Parrish *(Principal & Exec VP)*
Elisabeth Deckon *(VP)*
Jenny Orr *(Dir-Creative)*
Nicole Wojno *(Dir-Mktg)*
Alexandra Singerman *(Acct Mgr)*

Accounts:
Advanced ICU Care Public Relations
Clinithink LLC Public Relations
Kareo Public Relations
Liaison Technologies
NexTech Systems Marketing, Public Relations
NextGen
Pate Rehabilitation New Logo, PR, Rebranding Program, Website
Patientco Media, Public Relations
Predilytics, Inc. Brand Awareness, Strategic PR, Website Development
Rubbermaid Medical Solutions
SigmaCare Marketing, Messaging, Public Relations, Website
Telcare, Inc. B2B, Messaging, Strategic PR
Wright Direct Strategic PR

DOERR ASSOCIATES
31 Church St, Winchester, MA 01890
Tel.: (781) 729-9020
Fax: (781) 729-9060
Web Site: www.mdoerr.com

Employees: 4

Agency Specializes In: Public Relations, Real Estate

Revenue: $1,200,000

Maureen Doerr *(Owner & Pres)*
Alexandra Fiore *(Dir-Art)*
Joan Wilking *(Dir-Creative)*
Janet Carvalho *(Mgr-Acctg)*
Tom Doerr *(Copywriter)*

Accounts:
Berkley Investments
Tyco International

DONLEY COMMUNICATIONS
30 Vesey St Ste 1705, New York, NY 10007
Tel.: (212) 751-6126
Fax: (212) 935-6715
Web Site: www.donleycomm.com

Agency Specializes In: Crisis Communications, Event Planning & Marketing, Media Relations, Media Training, Public Relations

Newton W. Lamson *(Pres & CEO)*
Anna Ray-Jones *(VP)*
Tamara Zupancic *(Mgr-Creative Mktg)*
Kristie Gee *(Coord-Preconstruction Dept)*
Cathy Wolfe *(Coord-Mktg)*
Jessica Donley *(Sr Coord-Mktg)*
Shane Stack *(Sr Coord-Mktg)*

Accounts:
Abacus Finance
Amalgamated Bank
Brookings Management Group
Care to Care
Dash Financial
Direct Foreign Exchange
FBR Capital Markets Corporation
Fuel Cell Today
Johnson Matthey Ceramics Inc.
Milliman Inc

THE DOOR
37 W 17th St 5th Fl, New York, NY 10011
Tel.: (646) 340-1760
E-Mail: info@thedooronline.com
Web Site: www.thedooronline.com

Year Founded: 2008

Agency Specializes In: Brand Development & Integration, Event Planning & Marketing, Graphic Design, Media Relations, Media Training, Public Relations, Social Media

Eric Wielander *(Exec VP-Ops)*
Gia Vecchio *(Assoc VP)*
Alexandra Reichek *(Sr Dir)*

Accounts:
New-Shake Shack

DOTTED LINE COMMUNICATIONS
206 W 96th Ste 2C, New York, NY 10025
Tel.: (646) 596-7502
E-Mail: info@dottedlinecomm.com
Web Site: www.dottedlinecomm.com

Employees: 6

Agency Specializes In: Event Planning & Marketing, Media Training, Promotions, Public Relations

Darcy Cobb *(Co-Founder)*
Aimee Yoon *(Mng Partner)*
Jennifer Conway *(Acct Supvr)*
Nikki Neumann *(Acct Exec)*
Denise Welch *(Assoc Partner)*

Accounts:
Buzz Logic
Captivate Network
Citysearch
Coupons.com
Demandbase
Doxo Campaign: "Connect with Businesses like you Connect with Friends"
FlipKey
Harris Interactive
Jumio
nrelate
Partech International
The Search Agency
Smartertravel.com
Sprig.com (A Division of WRNI)
United Way
Urbanspoon

Branch

Dotted Line Communications
227 N Bowling Green, Los Angeles, CA 90049
Tel.: (310) 472-8600
E-Mail: info@dottedlinecomm.com
Web Site: www.dottedlinecomm.com

Employees: 7

Darcy Cobb *(Co-Founder)*
Jennifer Conway *(Acct Supvr)*
Stephanie Cooley *(Acct Supvr)*
Nikki Neumann *(Acct Exec)*

Accounts:
CrownPeak

DOUBLE FORTE
49 Stevenson St Ste 575, San Francisco, CA 94105
Tel.: (415) 863-4900
Fax: (415) 863-4994
Web Site: www.double-forte.com

Agency Specializes In: Corporate Communications, Crisis Communications, Event Planning & Marketing, Media Relations, Public Relations, Social Media, Sponsorship

Lee McEnany Caraher *(Pres)*
Bill Orr *(Chief Strategy Officer & Exec VP)*
Liz ODonnell *(Sr VP)*
Maggie Zeman *(Sr VP)*
Michelle Curran *(VP)*
Heather Hawkins *(VP)*
Jonathan Poretz *(VP)*
Brian Stevens *(VP)*
Loretta Stevens *(VP)*
Savannah McBride *(Acct Exec)*

Accounts:
New-Dryne
New-Entertainment Software Association
New-Saison Beauty

DOVETAIL PUBLIC RELATIONS
15951 Los Gatos Blvd Ste 16, Los Gatos, CA 95032
Tel.: (408) 395-3600
Fax: (408) 395-8232
Web Site: www.dovetailpr.com

Employees: 5
Year Founded: 1993

Agency Specializes In: Communications, Consulting, Event Planning & Marketing, Financial,

Health Care Services, Newspaper, Publicity/Promotions, Strategic Planning/Research, Trade & Consumer Magazines

Keri McKie *(Mgr-Fin & HR)*
Corey Oiesen *(Sr Partner)*

Accounts:
Avast!
CyberPatrol
Knowledge Genie
Smashwords

DOVETAIL SOLUTIONS
1407 Larimer St Ste 200, Denver, CO 80202
Tel.: (720) 226-9595
Fax: (720) 221-9213
Web Site: www.dovetailsolutions.com

Agency Specializes In: Brand Development & Integration, Crisis Communications, Public Relations, Social Media

Andy Boian *(Founder & CEO)*
James Cullen *(Partner-Client Svcs)*
Emily Holleran *(COO)*

Accounts:
New-Daniels College of Business
New-University of Denver

DPR GROUP, INC.
12850 Middlebrook Rd Ste 107, Germantown, MD 20874
Tel.: (240) 686-1000
Fax: (240) 686-0600
E-Mail: info@dprgroup.com
Web Site: www.dprgroup.com

Employees: 10
Year Founded: 1998

Agency Specializes In: Brand Development & Integration, Business-To-Business, Communications, Consulting, Corporate Identity, Direct Response Marketing, Education, Exhibit/Trade Shows, Financial, High Technology, Industrial, Information Technology, Internet/Web Design, Investor Relations, Logo & Package Design, New Product Development, Newspapers & Magazines, Planning & Consultation, Public Relations, Publicity/Promotions, Strategic Planning/Research, Trade & Consumer Magazines, Transportation

Dan Demaree *(Owner)*
Liz Palm *(Dir-Mktg)*
Jeanne Zepp *(Dir-PR)*
Laura Asendio *(Acct Exec)*
Alan Fleming *(Acct Exec)*
Kristina Negas *(Acct Exec)*

Accounts:
4Sight Technologies Inc Marketing, Media Relations, PR
CRG Medical Marketing, Media Relations, Strategic Public Relations
DHA Group Marketing, Strategic Public Relations
Engage Marketing, Public Relations
Merkle

Branch

DPR Group, Inc.
200 Cascade Point Ln Ste 104, Cary, NC 27513
Tel.: (919) 678-9200
Fax: (919) 678-9255
E-Mail: mperkins@dprgroup.com
Web Site: www.dprgroup.com

Employees: 3

Agency Specializes In: Public Relations

Dan Demaree *(Owner)*

Accounts:
Oncology Partners LLC

DQMPR
25 E 21 St 11 Fl, New York, NY 10010
Tel.: (212) 598-1160
E-Mail: info@dqmpr.com
Web Site: www.dqmpr.com

Agency Specializes In: Event Planning & Marketing, Media Relations, Promotions, Public Relations, Strategic Planning/Research

Yves Gentil *(Pres)*
Katie Papadopoulos *(Acct Dir)*
Mia Salazar *(Acct Dir)*
Julia Levi *(Sr Acct Mgr)*
Stephanie DAdamo *(Acct Coord)*

Accounts:
St. Barth Properties, Inc. (Public Relations Agency of Record)

DREAMSTYLE MEDIA
4424 N Pasadena St, Indianapolis, IN 46226
Tel.: (317) 643-2304
E-Mail: info@dreamstylemedia.com
Web Site: www.dreamstylemedia.com

Agency Specializes In: Brand Development & Integration, Public Relations

Samantha Pounds *(Founder & Strategist-PR)*

Accounts:
Arif Assaf (Agency of Record)

DREAMWEAVER BRAND COMMUNICATIONS
3470 W Hillsboro Blvd 102, Pompano Beach, FL 33073
Tel.: (954) 857-4059
E-Mail: hello@dreamweaverbrand.com
Web Site: www.dreamweaverbrandcommunications.com

Agency Specializes In: Advertising, Brand Development & Integration, Crisis Communications, Event Planning & Marketing, Market Research, Media Planning, Media Training, Public Relations, Social Media, Strategic Planning/Research

Gerard T. Rogan *(Founder & Mng Dir)*
Cynthia Srednicki *(CMO)*

Accounts:
SproutLoud Media Networks

DRESNER ALLEN CARON
(Formerly Allen & Caron)
276 Fifth Ave, New York, NY 10001
Tel.: (212) 691-8087
Fax: (212) 691-8116
E-Mail: info@allencaron.com
Web Site: www.allencaron.com

E-Mail for Key Personnel:
President: rene@allencaron.com

Employees: 15
Year Founded: 1981

Agency Specializes In: Corporate Communications, Investor Relations, Public Relations

Rene Caron *(Pres & COO)*
Steven D. Carr *(CEO)*
Joseph Allen *(Exec VP)*
Mike Mason *(VP)*
Rudy Barrio *(Acct Mgr)*
Nathan Abler *(Sr Acct Exec)*
Mark Reilly *(Acct Exec)*

Accounts:
Axion Power International
BIOLASE, Inc.
Box Ships, Inc
Caragenia
CleanEquity Monaco
DecisionPoint Systems, Inc.
Digirad Corp.
Emrise Corp
Fusion
Gentherm
HeartWave International Inc
Innovative Biodefense Inc.
Leatt Corp.
MDxHealth
National Technical Systems
Omagine, Inc.
Paragon Shipping Inc.
Rheonix, Inc.
Sonendo, Inc.

DRESNER CORPORATE SERVICES
20 N Clark St Ste 3550, Chicago, IL 60602
Tel.: (312) 780-7211
Fax: (312) 726-7448
Toll Free: (800) 373-7637
E-Mail: scarr@dresnerco.com
Web Site: www.dresnerco.biz

Employees: 30
Year Founded: 1992

Agency Specializes In: Investor Relations

Charles N. Funk *(Pres & CEO)*
Steven D. Carr *(Mng Dir)*
Gary J. Ortale *(CFO & Exec VP)*
David E. Gutierrez *(Sr VP & Head-PR Practice)*
Kristine Walczak *(Sr VP-IR)*
Philip A. Kranz *(VP-IR)*
Tim Golomb *(Exec Dir)*
Stephen Mullin *(Dir-Mktg & Bus Dev)*

Accounts:
Bunge Global Markets, Inc
Charter Financial Bank; Atlanta, GA Financial Services; 2011
Coleman Cable
Corrections Corporation of America; Nashville, TN Government Services; 1995
DeVry Inc.
Emprimus
Enviro-log; Atlanta, GA Environmentally Friendly Logs; 2010
Four Winds Casino Resort
Group 1; Dallas, TX Automobile Brands; 2010
Grupo TMM; Mexico Infrastructure Services; 1992
IMAP Public Relations
Lone Star Gold Gold & Silver
MidwestOne Financial Group; Iowa City, IA Financial Services; 2011
North Park University
Pernix Group, Inc
QCR Holdings; Moline, IL Financial Services; 2011
Red Hawk Casino
Schawk Inc.; Chicago, IL Branding & Advertising-related Services; 1992
TZ Ltd.

Branch

Dresner Allen Caron
(Formerly Allen & Caron)

276 Fifth Ave, New York, NY 10001
(See Separate Listing)

DRIVEN PUBLIC RELATIONS
41593 Winchester Rd Ste 110, Temecula, CA 92590
Tel.: (951) 719-1040
Fax: (951) 587-9243
E-Mail: info@drivenpublicrelations.com
Web Site: www.drivenpublicrelations.com

Employees: 5

Agency Specializes In: Event Planning & Marketing, Media Planning, Media Relations, Public Relations

Flora Caudill *(CFO & VP)*
Natasha Nelson *(Sr Partner & VP)*
Andrew De Lara *(Dir-Mktg Comm & Social Media)*
Maggie Underwood *(Mgr-HR)*
Tiffany Egner *(Sr Acct Exec)*
Gabby Batto *(Acct Exec)*
Jessica Ernstberger *(Acct Exec)*
Robert Knoll *(Acct Exec)*

Accounts:
Borla Performance (Agency of Record) Branding, Marketing, Media, Social Media, Strategic Public Relations
The Creative Bar
Decked
Inland Empire Auto Show
Maisberger
Mosi Bicycles
NADAguides.com
Renovo Motors, Inc. Renovo Coupe
New-Weego Media Plan, Strategic Public Relation

DROESE PUBLIC RELATIONS
2001 Irving Blvd Ste 141, Dallas, TX 75207
Tel.: (214) 752-4444
E-Mail: info@droesepr.com
Web Site: www.droesepr.com

Agency Specializes In: Brand Development & Integration, Event Planning & Marketing, Media Relations, Public Relations

Kelle Knight *(Acct Dir)*

DROHLICH ASSOCIATES, INC.
22 Balcon, Saint Louis, MO 63141
Tel.: (314) 434-0002
Fax: (314) 567-0703
E-Mail: mdrohlich@drohlich.com
Web Site: www.drohlich.com

E-Mail for Key Personnel:
President: mdrohlich@drohlich.com

Employees: 11
Year Founded: 1958

National Agency Associations: PRSA

Agency Specializes In: Government/Political, Public Relations, Strategic Planning/Research

Michael L. Drohlich *(Pres)*

Accounts:
Armstrong Teasdale
Eagle Back
Grey Eagle Distributors
Heidman Associates
Hepler Broom
TricorBraun

DROTMAN COMMUNICATIONS
368 Veterans Memorial Hwy Ste 8, Commack, NY 11725
Tel.: (631) 462-1198
Fax: (631) 462-2257
E-Mail: info@drotmanpr.com
Web Site: www.drotmanpr.com

Employees: 2

Agency Specializes In: Consulting, Public Relations, Sports Market

Doug Drotman *(Pres)*

Accounts:
Strat-O-Matic Game Co., Inc.

DSTREET
1400 16th St 16 Market Sq Ste 400, Denver, CO 80202
Tel.: (303) 722-9552
E-Mail: info@dstreetpr.com
Web Site: www.dstreetpr.com

Year Founded: 2004

Agency Specializes In: Brand Development & Integration, Crisis Communications, Media Relations, Media Training, Public Relations, Search Engine Optimization, Social Media

Jennifer Dulles *(Pres)*

Accounts:
Fenix Lighting
LSR

DUBLIN & ASSOCIATES, INC.
3015 San Pedro, San Antonio, TX 78212-4721
Tel.: (210) 227-0221
Fax: (210) 227-6634
E-Mail: jdublin@dublinandassociates.com
Web Site: www.dublinandassociates.com

Employees: 11
Year Founded: 1982

Agency Specializes In: Automotive, Event Planning & Marketing, Financial, Food Service, Public Relations, Publicity/Promotions, Strategic Planning/Research, Travel & Tourism

James R. Dublin *(Chm & CEO)*
Mary Rohmer Uhlig *(Pres)*
Edna Strey *(Controller)*
Rose Marie Eash *(Sr Acct Mgr)*

Accounts:
Southwest Foundation for Biomedical Research

DUE NORTH MARKETING COMMUNICATIONS INC
7180 NW Bay Shore Dr, Northport, MI 49670
Tel.: (231) 386-9206
Web Site: www.duenorthmarketing.net

Year Founded: 2004

Agency Specializes In: Internet/Web Design, Print, Public Relations, Radio, Social Media, T.V.

Ruth Steele Walker *(Pres)*
Scott Walker *(VP)*

Accounts:
Dan Brady Painting Tricks of the Trade

DUFFEY COMMUNICATIONS, INC.
3379 Peachtree Rd NE Ste 300, Atlanta, GA 30326
Tel.: (404) 266-2600
Fax: (404) 262-3198
E-Mail: info@duffey.com
Web Site: www.duffey.com

Employees: 35
Year Founded: 1984

Agency Specializes In: Business-To-Business, Consumer Marketing, Government/Political, High Technology, Public Relations, Sponsorship

Approx. Annual Billings: $7,200,000

Sherri Fallin *(Pres & CEO)*
Arlene Large *(COO)*
Jessica DuBois *(Dir-Gov Affairs)*
Allen Haynes *(Acct Exec)*

DUGARD ELLIS PUBLIC RELATIONS
1506 Church St Ste 230, Nashville, TN 37203
Tel.: (615) 763-3433
E-Mail: info@dugardellis.com
Web Site: www.dugardellis.com

Year Founded: 2012

Agency Specializes In: Brand Development & Integration, Public Relations, Social Media, Strategic Planning/Research

Perri duGard Owens *(Partner)*
Aerial Ellis *(Partner)*
Kim Johnson *(Dir-Admin)*

Accounts:
Metropolitan Nashville Airport Authority
Music City Dental

DUKAS PUBLIC RELATIONS, INC.
100 W 26th St 2nd Fl, New York, NY 10001
Tel.: (212) 704-7385
Fax: (212) 242-3646
E-Mail: info@dukaspr.com
Web Site: www.dukaspr.com

Employees: 20
Year Founded: 2003

Agency Specializes In: Communications, Corporate Communications, Public Relations

Approx. Annual Billings: $800,000

Breakdown of Gross Billings by Media: Pub. Rels.: $800,000

Richard Dukas *(Founder, Chm & CEO)*
Seth Linden *(Pres)*
Stephanie Dressler *(VP-PR & Digital Strategy)*
Doug Hesney *(VP)*
Zach Leibowitz *(VP)*
Zach Kouwe *(Dir)*

Accounts:
JMP Group (Agency of Record) Brand Awareness
PublicRoutes
Raymond James (Agency of Record)
Venture for America PR Counsel

DUO PR
3609 1st Ave NW, Seattle, WA 98107
Tel.: (206) 706-0508
Fax: (206) 706-0668
E-Mail: info@duopr.com
Web Site: www.duopr.com

Employees: 8
Year Founded: 2004

Agency Specializes In: Brand Development & Integration, Broadcast, Consumer Goods, Event

Planning & Marketing, Exhibit/Trade Shows, Local Marketing, Media Relations, Media Training, Product Placement, Viral/Buzz/Word of Mouth

Amanda Foley *(Founder & Partner)*
Rebecca Mosley *(Co-Founder & Partner)*
Kelsey Richards *(Sr Acct Exec)*

Accounts:
Claudio Corallo Chocolate
Dream Dinners, Inc. (Agency of Record)
Expedia.com
Flip Flop Shops "Live Work Play with their Toes Exposed", Celebrity Work, Grand Openings, In-Shop & Cross Marketing Promotions, Large-Scale Special Events, Marketing, PR
Full Circle Studios
Hasbro
Holiday Golightly
Hyatt at Olive 8
Kimpton Hotels Seattle
Maryhill Winery
Oiselle Running
Savers/Value Village
SousVide Supreme
Two Mountain Winery
Zavida Gemstones
Zwaggle.com

DUREE & COMPANY
10620 Griffin Rd Ste 208, Fort Lauderdale, FL 33328
Tel.: (954) 723-9350
Fax: (954) 723-9535
E-Mail: info@dureeandcompany.com
Web Site: www.dureeandcompany.com

Year Founded: 1999

Agency Specializes In: Advertising, Collateral, Media Relations, Promotions, Public Relations, Radio, Search Engine Optimization, Social Media

Duree Ross *(Pres)*
Jenna Matthews *(VP)*
Ana Maria Colmenares *(Acct Mgr)*
Vinessa Cirrito *(Acct Exec)*
Louise Hendry *(Acct Exec)*
Brittany Holtz *(Acct Exec)*
Jennifer Martinez *(Acct Exec)*
Christina Rodriguez *(Acct Exec)*
Jennifer Davis *(Copywriter)*

Accounts:
The Crockett Foundation
Gimme A Burger
Optiwow
Riva Condominiums Fort Lauderdale
Tsukuro

DUX PUBLIC RELATIONS
PO Box 1329, Canton, TX 75103
Tel.: (903) 865-1078
E-Mail: info@duxpr.com
Web Site: www.duxpr.com

E-Mail for Key Personnel:
Public Relations: kevin@duxpr.com

Employees: 2
Year Founded: 2001

National Agency Associations: PRSA

Agency Specializes In: Business Publications, Business-To-Business, Communications, Consulting, Consumer Publications, Corporate Identity, Education, Event Planning & Marketing, Exhibit/Trade Shows, Food Service, High Technology, Information Technology, Magazines, Newspaper, Newspapers & Magazines, Pets , Planning & Consultation, Public Relations, Publicity/Promotions, Radio, Restaurant, Retail, Strategic Planning/Research, T.V., Trade & Consumer Magazines

Kristine Ryan Tanzillo *(Founder & Pres)*
Kevin Tanzillo *(Owner)*

Accounts:
Sprint Nextel

DVA MEDIA & MARKETING
4515 Van Nuys Blvd Ste 402, Sherman Oaks, CA 91403
Tel.: (818) 995-0050
Fax: (818) 995-0250
E-Mail: info@dvahq.com
Web Site: www.dvahq.com

Agency Specializes In: African-American Market, Cable T.V., Communications, Direct Response Marketing, Entertainment, Hispanic Market, Leisure, Magazines, Media Buying Services, T.V.

Ava DuVernay *(Founder)*

Accounts:
America Magazine
AOL, LLC
Blockbuster Video
CBS
Dimension/Miramax Films
Disney Channel
Disney Theatricals
Dreamworks
Focus Features
Fox Home Video
FX Networks
HBO
MGM
The Music Center
Paramount Television
PBS
Sony/Screen Gems
Trimark Pictures
UA/Intermedia
Warner Home Video

DVL SEIGENTHALER
(Formerly DVL Public Relations & Advertising)
700 12th Ave S Ste 400, Nashville, TN 37203
Tel.: (615) 244-1818
Fax: (615) 780-3301
Web Site: www.dvl.com

Employees: 80
Year Founded: 1980

Agency Specializes In: Advertising, Public Relations

Approx. Annual Billings: $11,000,000

Beth Seigenthaler Courtney *(Pres)*
Ronald Roberts *(CEO)*
Jimmy Chaffin *(Mng Partner)*
Nelson Eddy *(Mng Partner)*
Amy Seigenthaler Pierce *(Mng Partner)*
Katie Seigenthaler *(Mng Partner)*
Sarah Brawner *(Acct Supvr)*
Karen Orne *(Acct Exec)*
Rachel Lane *(Copywriter)*

Accounts:
Airbus DS Communications
AMSURG
Bridgestone Americas, Inc.
Brown-Forman
Electronic Recyclers International
Goodwill Industries of Middle Tennessee
The J.M. Smucker Company
LifePoint Hospitals, Inc.
Metropolitan Nashville Airport Authority
Nashville Electric Service
Natural Resources Defense Council
Regions Financial Corp.
Singer Sewing Company

E. BOINEAU & COMPANY
128 Beaufain St, Charleston, SC 29401
Tel.: (843) 723-1462
Fax: (843) 723-9332
Web Site: www.eboineauandco.com

E-Mail for Key Personnel:
President: eboineau@eboineauandco.com
Creative Dir.: tjones@eboineauandco.com

Employees: 3
Year Founded: 1990

Agency Specializes In: Advertising, Brand Development & Integration, Business Publications, Collateral, Communications, Consulting, Consumer Marketing, Consumer Publications, Corporate Identity, Crisis Communications, Direct-to-Consumer, Education, Electronic Media, Engineering, Environmental, Event Planning & Marketing, Financial, Health Care Services, Integrated Marketing, Internet/Web Design, Legal Services, Local Marketing, Media Relations, Newspaper, Newspapers & Magazines, Planning & Consultation, Promotions, Public Relations, Publicity/Promotions, Real Estate, Retail, Search Engine Optimization, Social Marketing/Nonprofit, Strategic Planning/Research, Travel & Tourism, Viral/Buzz/Word of Mouth, Web (Banner Ads, Pop-ups, etc.)

Approx. Annual Billings: $425,000

Breakdown of Gross Billings by Media: Graphic Design: $50,000; Pub. Rels.: $375,000

Elizabeth Boineau *(Owner)*
Melissa Pluta Parker *(Sr Acct Exec)*
Sarah Reed *(Graphic Designer & Designer-Web)*
Haley M. Metcalfe *(Asst Acct Exec)*

Accounts:
Bessinger's Barbeque (Agency of Record)
Buist, Byars & Taylor; 2004
Byers Design Group; 2004
Clore Law Group
New-Dennis O'Neill Attorney at Law (Agency of Record)
New-Diamonds Direct
East Cooper Habitat for Humanity
Edisto Chamber of Commerce (Agency of Record)
Frampton Construction (Agency of Record)
Jarrard, Nowell & Russell, LLC (Agency of Record) CPA's; 2005
John Tecklenburg for Mayor of Charleston
New-Law Offices of Robertson Wendt (Agency of Record)
Leath, Bouch & Crawford LLP; Charleston, SC; 2007
Palmetto Behavioral Health; Charleston, SC Healthcare System; 2007
New-Palmetto Carriage Works
Palmetto Detitling; Charleston, SC; 2007
Peters Paint & Wallcovering; Charleston, SC; 2008
Sewee Preserve/Avery Development, Inc.; 2003
South Carolina Federal Credit Union
Thurmond Kirchner Timbes & Yelverton, LLC
New-Timberlane, Inc (Agency of Record)
Trident Habitat for Humanity

E3 COMMUNICATIONS
551 Franklin St, Buffalo, NY 14202
Tel.: (716) 854-8182
Fax: (716) 816-0900
E-Mail: info@e3communications.com
Web Site: www.e3communications.com

Year Founded: 2001

Agency Specializes In: Communications, Crisis Communications, Event Planning & Marketing, Media Relations, Media Training, Public Relations, Social Media

Earl V. Wells,III *(Pres)*
Brian A. Gould *(VP)*
Kevin G. Banes *(Dir-Govt Affairs)*
Laura E. Jacobs *(Sr Acct Exec)*
Danielle DelMonte *(Acct Exec)*

Accounts:
Absolut Facilities, Inc.
Ahold USA
Beech-Nut Nutrition Corporation
Buffalo Philharmonic Orchestra
Cohen & Lombardo
Community Health Foundation of Western & Central New York
CUBRC
Erie County Water Authority
Giant Food Stores/Martin's Food Markets
Healthcare Information Xchange of New York
HEALTHeLINK
Honeywell
Interboro Insurance
Kleinhan's Music Hall
Lawley Insurance
Malcolm Pirnie
Mount St. Mary's Hospital & Health Center
National Grid
Neighborhood Health Center
New Directions Youth and Family Services
New York State Public High School Athletic Association
Niagara County Industrial Development Agency
Niagara Falls Water Board
NOCO Energy Corporation
NOCO Express Shops
Olin Corporation
People, Inc.
Praxis
Pyramid Companies
Pyrotek
School Administrators Association of New York State
The Vinyl Institute

EAG SPORTS MANAGEMENT
909 N Sepulveda Blvd, El Segundo, CA 90245
Tel.: (310) 301-4274
Fax: (310) 301-4275
Web Site: www.eagsportsmanagement.com

Agency Specializes In: Crisis Communications, Event Planning & Marketing, Public Relations, Social Media

Denise L. White *(Founder & CEO)*
Lindsey Deierling *(VP)*

Accounts:
New-Anthony Pettis
New-Christen Press
New-Patrick Peterson
New-Tyrann Mathieu

EASTWICK COMMUNICATIONS
111 W Evelyn Ave Ste 210, Sunnyvale, CA 94086
Tel.: (408) 470-4850
Fax: (650) 396-4430
Toll Free: (877) 314-0873
E-Mail: info@eastwick.com
Web Site: www.eastwick.com

Employees: 30

Agency Specializes In: High Technology

Revenue: $5,800,000

Barbara Bates *(Founder & CEO)*
Heather Kernahan *(Pres)*
Douglas A. Liddie *(COO & Exec VP)*
Dave De Jear *(Sr VP-Client Svcs)*
Erin McCabe *(Sr VP-Client Svcs)*
Karen Clyne *(VP)*
Jun Quintana *(VP-Res & Analytics)*
Jason Brown *(Dir-Cleantech)*
Stephanie Kays *(Dir)*

Accounts:
Bridgelux Inc.
Fujitsu
Fujitsu Computer Systems
Lucid Imagination
Seagate Technology, Inc.

Branch

Eastwick Communications
201 Post St 8th Fl, San Francisco, CA 94108
Tel.: (650) 480-4040
Fax: (650) 480-4035
E-Mail: info@eastwick.com
Web Site: www.eastwick.com

Employees: 5

Barbara Bates *(Founder & CEO)*
Heather Kernahan *(Exec VP & Gen Mgr)*
Gwen Murphy *(Exec VP-Client Svcs)*
Karen Clyne *(Sr VP-Client Svcs)*
Sahana Jayaraman *(VP & Head-Social & Digital Practice)*
Jun Quintana *(VP-Res & Analytics Grp)*

Accounts:
Adobe
Antea Group (Agency of Record)
Fujitsu
Kaleidescape
PowWow (Public Relations Agency of Record)
Sonic Solutions
Untangle
VantagePoint Venture Partners

EBERLY & COLLARD PUBLIC RELATIONS
455 Glen Iris Dr NE Loft U, Atlanta, GA 30308
Tel.: (404) 574-2900
Fax: (404) 574-2905
E-Mail: info@eberlycollardpr.com
Web Site: www.eberlycollardpr.com

Agency Specializes In: Advertising, Brand Development & Integration, Graphic Design, Integrated Marketing, Media Relations, Public Relations, Social Media

Don Eberly *(Owner)*
Kristen Pappaterra *(Coord-PR)*

Accounts:
New-Big River Industries
New-Stevens & Wilkinson

ED LEWI AND ASSOCIATES
6 Chelsea Pl, Clifton Park, NY 12065
Tel.: (518) 383-6183
Fax: (518) 383-6755
E-Mail: info@edlewi.com
Web Site: www.edlewi.com

Agency Specializes In: Advertising, Crisis Communications, Event Planning & Marketing, Media Relations, Media Training, Promotions, Public Relations, Social Media

Mark Bardack *(Pres)*
Eleanor Antonacci *(Specialist-Social Media)*
David Filkins *(Specialist-PR)*
Caitlin Merrill *(Specialist-PR)*
Juliann Goronkin *(Coord-Office, Events & Mktg)*

Accounts:
Alpin Haus
Hannaford Brothers Co.
New York Racing Association

EDELMAN
(Formerly Daniel J. Edelman, Inc.)
200 E Randolph St Fl 63, Chicago, IL 60601-6705
Tel.: (312) 240-3000
Fax: (312) 240-2900
E-Mail: chicago@edelman.com
Web Site: www.edelman.com

Employees: 5,500
Year Founded: 1952

National Agency Associations: COPF-PRSA

Agency Specializes In: Public Relations, Sponsorship

Approx. Annual Billings: $445,000,000

Jay Porter *(Pres)*
Victor Malanga *(CFO & Exec VP)*
Kevin Cook *(COO)*
Kevin King *(Chm-Global Practice-Edelman Digital)*
David Brain *(Pres/CEO-Edelman Asia Pacific)*
Russell Dubner *(CEO-US)*
Bob Grove *(CEO-North Asia)*
Matt Vander Laan *(Exec VP & Gen Mgr-Corp Affairs Practice)*
Dan Cornell *(Exec VP & Grp Dir-Strategy)*
Cheryl Cook *(Exec VP & Dir-Media Rels)*
Rita Glaze *(Exec VP & Dir-US Market Access)*
Jahna Lindsay-Jones *(Exec VP & Mgr-Global Client Relationship)*
Heather Oldani *(Exec VP)*
Whitney Browne *(SVP & Head-User Experience)*
J. T. Anderson *(Sr VP & Grp Dir-Creative)*
Jani Westcott *(Sr VP & Dir-Plng-Consumer)*
Ofelia Casillas *(Sr VP-Crisis & Risk Mgmt)*
AJ Goodman *(Sr VP-Media, Corp & Pub Affairs)*
Kristena Lucky *(Sr VP-Consumer Mktg)*
Laura Pietraszek *(Sr VP-Benefits-US)*
Elizabeth Pigg *(Sr VP)*
Una Pipic *(Sr VP)*
Simi Ranajee *(Sr VP)*
David Greenbaum *(Mng Dir-Digital)*
Gina Hayes *(Mng Dir-Client Programming)*
Laura Kowalski *(VP & Dir-Strategic Plng)*
April Umminger *(VP & Dir-Chicago Newsroom & Media Svcs)*
Nissy Atassi *(VP)*
Carrie Becker *(VP)*
Rebecca Camhi *(VP-United Entertainment Grp)*
Jenny Heinrich *(VP-Digital Strategy)*
Rich Ketter *(VP-Global Server Infrastructure-Global IT)*
Isabel Long *(VP)*
Mindi Wood *(VP)*
Kathy Krenger *(Gen Mgr-Edible)*
Julie Biber *(Dir-Recruitment-Global)*
Liz Meyers *(Dir-New Bus)*
Brent Fagerburg *(Assoc Dir-Creative)*
Jillian Collins *(Sr Acct Supvr)*
Michelle Prieb *(Sr Acct Supvr)*
Eric Tatro *(Sr Acct Supvr)*
Erin Fitzgerald *(Acct Supvr)*
Marianne Geiger *(Acct Supvr)*
Maggie May Graham *(Acct Supvr)*
Jonathan Hecht *(Acct Supvr-Bus & Social Purpose)*
Molly McFerran *(Acct Supvr)*
Saramaya Weissman *(Acct Supvr)*
Corey DiGiovanni *(Sr Acct Exec)*
Kayla Jaroch *(Sr Acct Exec)*
Megumi Kato *(Sr Acct Exec)*
Becca Lakin *(Sr Acct Exec-Crisis & Risk Mgmt)*
Kathryn Manofsky *(Sr Acct Exec)*
Lynn Hanessian *(Sr Strategist-Science)*

Rachel Drakulich *(Acct Exec)*
Matthew Kochis *(Acct Exec)*
Eileen Meyer *(Acct Exec)*
Andra Pintiliuc *(Acct Exec)*
Ellina Stein *(Acct Exec & Asst Producer)*
Katie Keidan *(Asst Acct Exec)*
Emily McNitt *(Asst Acct Exec-New Bus & Mktg)*
Deirdre Walsh *(Asst Acct Exec)*
Angela Salerno-Robin *(Sr Supvr-Media)*

Accounts:
Adobe Systems Incorporated
New-American Marketing Association Marketing
Barilla
Butterball, LLC
California Walnut Board Communications, Public Relations Agency of Record, Social Agency of Record, Social Media
California Walnut Commission Communications, Public Relations Agency of Record, Social Agency of Record, Social Media
The Clorox Company Brita
The Coca-Cola Company Fairlife, Public Relations
Darden Restaurants Longhorn Steakhouse, Olive Garden
eBay
ExteNet Systems, Inc. Communications, Content Creation, Media, Public Relations Agency of Record
New-Florida Department of Citrus Florida Citrus, Marketing, Public Relations
General Electric
Greyhound (Agency of Record); 2007
Heineken USA Amstel, Brand PR, Cider, Consume & Corporate PR, Corporate Communications, Dos Equis, Heineken, Media Relations, Public Relations, Reputation Management, Strongbow
Johnson & Johnson Family of Companies Johnson & Johnson
Kimberly-Clark Corporation GoodNites, Huggies Pure & Natural, Pull-Ups
New-LEGO
Mondelez International, Inc. Campaign: "Do What You Do", Kraft Singles
National Dairy Council
Navigant Thought Leadership
Nestle USA PR
Papa John's International, Inc (Public Relations Agency of Record) Public Relations
New-PayPal
PepsiCo, Inc. Quaker Oats
Rug Doctor Public Relations Strategies
Samsung
New-S.C. Johnson & Son, Inc. Campaign: "Great Expectations", Digital, Public relations, Shopper Marketing, Social Media
The Scotts Miracle-Gro Company The Scotts Company
Smiths Detection Asia Pacific PR Agency of Record
Southwest Airlines Community Outreach Programs
Symantec (Agency of Record) Norton, PR
New-U.S. Dairy

North America Branches:

Assembly
2301 5th Avenue Ste 500, Seattle, WA 98121
Tel.: (206) 223-1606
Web Site: www.edelman.com/specialty/assembly/

Agency Specializes In: High Technology

Ken Birge *(Mng Dir & Exec VP)*
Cindy Davidson *(VP & Grp Dir)*
Eric Kwan *(VP & Grp Dir)*
Jamey Chown Starkey *(VP)*
Dane Estes *(VP)*
Ken Beasley *(Dir-Mktg & Bus Strategy)*
Jessica Khoshnood *(Asst Acct Exec)*
Taos Boudjemai *(Asst Media Planner)*

Accounts:
Microsoft Xbox

Blue Worldwide
1875 Eye St NW Ste 900, Washington, DC 20006
Tel.: (202) 371-0200
Fax: (202) 371-2858
Web Site: blueadvertising.com

Agency Specializes In: Public Relations

Robert McKernan *(Pres)*
Diane Bancroft *(Exec VP-SMS)*
Nancy Wright *(Sr VP)*
Chad McGinnis *(Exec Dir-Creative)*
John Verzemnieks *(Sr Dir-Art)*
Kathy Coffey *(Dir-Art)*
Stephen Szostak *(Sr Buyer & Planner-SMS)*
Jessica Murray *(Specialist-Digital Media & SMS)*

Edelman Public Relations
(Formerly Vollmer Public Relations)
1201 Louisiana St Ste 830, Houston, TX 77002
(See Separate Listing)

Edelman
214 King Street W Suite 600, Toronto, ON M5H 3S6 Canada
Tel.: (416) 979-1120
Fax: (416) 979-0176
E-Mail: toronto@edelman.com
Web Site: www.edelman.com

Employees: 100
Year Founded: 1972

Agency Specializes In: Public Relations

John Clinton *(Chm/CEO-Canada & Head-Creative & Content-North American)*
Jason Kinnear *(Head-Natl Sector & Tech & Sr VP)*
Lisa Bednarski *(Sr VP-Plng)*
Dave Fleet *(Sr VP-Digital-Canada East)*
Michael Murphy *(Sr VP-Natl Sector Lead & Health)*
David Ryan *(Sr VP-Fin Comm)*
Catherine Yuile *(Sr VP-Insights & Analytics)*
Tristan Roy *(Mng Dir-Edelman Digital Canada)*
Rob Manne *(VP-Digital & Creative Strategy)*
Paul Ortchanian *(VP-Ops & Tech)*
Scott Evans *(Gen Mgr)*
Bianca Freedman *(Acct Dir-Digital-Corp Practice)*
Melissa Turlej *(Acct Dir-Digital)*
Camielle Clark *(Dir-Creative Production)*
Hira Gomes *(Dir-Art)*
Leilah Ambrose *(Assoc Dir-Creative)*
Matt Smith *(Assoc Dir-Creative)*
Hilary Bassett *(Sr Acct Mgr)*
Devon Burke *(Sr Acct Mgr-Digital-Search)*
Meghan Sharp *(Acct Mgr-Health & Digital)*
Rosie Shipton *(Acct Mgr)*
Erika Strong *(Acct Supvr-Tech)*
Alexandra Fahmey *(Sr Acct Exec-Health)*
Victoria Neufeld *(Acct Exec-Consumer Mktg)*

Accounts:
AstraZeneca
Cancer Care Ontario
Cara Foods
Expedia.ca
Ford of Canada
Government of Ontario
Mondelez International, Inc.
Pfizer Canada
Red Bull
Sirius Canada
Teacher's Private Capital

Edelman
1000 Sherbrooke West Suite 1900, Montreal, QC H3A 3G4 Canada
Tel.: (514) 844-6665
Fax: (514) 844-2588
E-Mail: montreal@edelman.com
Web Site: www.edelman.com

Employees: 30
Year Founded: 1972

Agency Specializes In: Public Relations

Louise Dion *(VP-Ops-Montreal)*
Andrean Gagne *(Sr Acct Dir)*
Catherine Pouliot *(Acct Dir)*
Tracy Cuixiao Jiang *(Mgr)*
Samantha Wannemacher *(Sr Acct Supvr)*
Challin Meink *(Acct Supvr)*
Ben Brodette *(Sr Acct Exec)*

Accounts:
Pfizer

Edelman
1035 Cambie St 2nd Fl, Vancouver, BC V6B 5L7 Canada
(See Separate Listing)

Edelman
201 Baldwin Ave, San Mateo, CA 94401-3914
Tel.: (650) 762-2800
Fax: (650) 762-2801
E-Mail: silicon.valley@edelman.com
Web Site: www.edelman.com

Employees: 170
Year Founded: 1992

Agency Specializes In: High Technology, Public Relations

Michael Casey *(Sr VP-Plng)*
Stacy Sommer *(Sr VP-Digital)*
Elliott Burr *(Acct Supvr)*
Jaclyn Percy *(Acct Supvr)*
Marissa Hopkins *(Sr Acct Exec)*
Sera Michael *(Sr Acct Exec)*
Jorie Westley *(Acct Exec)*
Maria Amundson *(Global Chm-Tech)*

Accounts:
Adobe PR, Software
Churchill Club Public Relations
Energous Corporation (Communications Marketing Agency of Record) Communications, Content, Media
GE
Motorola E-W Lan
Palm Inc.
Pantone
Samsung Semiconductor
Serena
Synaptics

Edelman
921 11th St Ste 250, Sacramento, CA 95814
Tel.: (916) 442-2331
Fax: (916) 447-8509
E-Mail: sacramento@edelman.com
Web Site: www.edelman.com

Employees: 13
Year Founded: 1994

National Agency Associations: COPF

Agency Specializes In: Government/Political, Public Relations

Steve Telliano *(Gen Mgr)*
Christi W. Black *(Exec VP)*
Kish Rajan *(Sr VP-Pub Affairs)*
Tom Knox *(VP)*
Matt Notley *(Sr Acct Supvr)*

Alicia Eagan *(Acct Supvr)*
Gina Jacobs *(Acct Supvr)*
Candace Koehler *(Acct Supvr)*
Breana Landman *(Sr Acct Exec)*

Accounts:
Adobe Systems Incorporated
Kaiser Permanente

Edelman
5900 Wilshire Blvd 24th & 25th Floors, Los Angeles, CA 90036
Tel.: (323) 857-9100
Fax: (323) 857-9117
E-Mail: los.angeles@edelman.com
Web Site: www.edelman.com

Employees: 125
Year Founded: 1965

Agency Specializes In: Entertainment, Public Relations, Sponsorship

Gail Becker *(Pres-Strategic Partnerships & Global Integration)*
Deb Kazenelson Deane *(Exec VP & Grp Head-Corp-Los Angeles)*
James Williams *(Gen Mgr & Exec VP)*
Kathryn Kranhold *(Exec VP)*
Jordan Atlas *(Sr VP & Dir-Creative)*
Robb Hittner *(Sr VP-Digital)*
Victoria Rangel *(Sr Acct Supvr)*
Daniel Brackins *(Acct Supvr)*
Brittney Sochowski *(Sr Acct Exec)*
Jocelyn Swift *(Sr Acct Exec-Measurement & Insights)*

Accounts:
Microsoft Corporation; Redmond, WA Zune
New Mexico Department of Tourism
Skype
Starbucks Public Relations
Symantec Corporation
Volkswagen AG

Edelman
525 Market St Ste 1400, San Francisco, CA 94105
Tel.: (415) 222-9944
Fax: (415) 222-9924
E-Mail: san.francisco@edelman.com
Web Site: www.edelman.com

Employees: 80
Year Founded: 1984

National Agency Associations: COPF

Agency Specializes In: Public Relations

T.J. Kelly *(Mng Dir & Exec VP)*
Kristine Boyden *(COO-Western Reg)*
Jessica Clifton-Czarny *(Exec VP & Grp Head-Digital)*
Liz Foster *(Sr VP)*
Ellie Hardy *(Sr VP-Production)*
Steve Kerns *(Sr VP)*
Kate Shay *(VP & Assoc Dir-Creative)*
Jennifer Tomaro Evans *(VP-Consumer PR, Food & Beverage)*
Nam Nguyen *(VP-Creative Content)*
Brooke Kaplan Turner *(VP-Digital)*
Wayne Hickey *(Gen Mgr)*
Cybil Wallace *(Dir-Editorial & Exec Producer-Creative Newsroom)*

Accounts:
New-Adobe Systems Inc. Adobe Photoshop, Campaign: "Photoshop Murder Mystery"
Advanced Micro Devices, Inc Campaign: "AMD Steals Intel's Spotlight", Public Relations
Charles Schwab
The Clorox Company Brita, Environmental
eBay, Inc.
Hawaiian Airlines PR
Hewlett-Packard Company
HootSuite Digital Marketing, Media Relations, PR
Microsoft Campaign: "A Year in the Like"
The North Face, Inc. Public Relations
Starbucks
Trilliant (Agency of Record)

Edelman
International Sq 1875 Eye St NW Ste 900, Washington, DC 20006-5422
Tel.: (202) 371-0200
Fax: (202) 371-2858
E-Mail: washington.dc@edelman.com
Web Site: www.edelman.com

Employees: 160
Year Founded: 1969

National Agency Associations: COPF

Agency Specializes In: Public Relations, Sponsorship

Sean Neary *(Exec VP & Grp Head-Corp Affairs & Fin Comm)*
Mory Fontanez *(Exec VP & Mgr-Global Client Relationship-Hewlett Packard)*
Emma Gilding *(Exec VP-Strategy)*
Esther Lee *(Sr VP & Acct Mgmt Dir)*
David Almacy *(Sr VP)*
Jeremy Gosbee *(Sr VP)*
Lynette Johnson Williams *(Sr VP)*
Jackie Kahn *(Sr VP)*
Lynnette Williams *(Sr VP)*
Craig Brownstein *(VP)*
Dina Cappiello *(VP-Energy)*
Tatiana Posada *(Head-Digital Creative Content Strategy & Sr Acct Supvr)*
Laura Gordon *(Gen Mgr)*
Tish Van Dyke *(Gen Mgr)*
Matt Wagner *(Gen Mgr)*
Zachary Giglio *(Acct Mgr)*
Chelsea Bodow *(Mgr-New Bus-US)*
Pheniece Jones *(Sr Acct Supvr)*
Shelby Lichliter *(Acct Supvr)*
Chase Noyes *(Acct Supvr)*
Hilary Teeter *(Acct Supvr)*
Kimberly Wingert *(Acct Supvr)*
Katie Bertram *(Sr Acct Exec-Digital Strategy)*
Charlotte Gruen *(Sr Acct Exec)*
Polly Mingledorff *(Sr Acct Exec)*
Christine Shen *(Media Planner & Strategist-SEO)*
Danika Felt *(Strategist-Media)*
Laura Sandberg *(Acct Exec)*
Molly Keyes *(Planner-Strategic)*
Jade Thomas *(Asst Acct Exec)*

Accounts:
100 Lives Foundation National Commemoration of the Armenian Genocide Centennial, Public Relations
The Dannon Company Public Relations
Home Matters
Microsoft Corporation Microsoft Office, Windows Vista
The Nature Conservancy
The Red Cross

Edelman
1221 Brickell Ave Ste 1140, Miami, FL 33131
Tel.: (305) 358-3767
Fax: (305) 358-1270
E-Mail: miami@edelman.com
Web Site: www.edelman.com

Employees: 30
Year Founded: 2009

Agency Specializes In: Public Relations

Tim Peters *(Exec VP-Corp Affairs)*
Allison Hannon Cirullo *(Sr VP-Consumer Mktg)*
Carlos Correcha-Price *(Gen Mgr)*
Kelsey Marineau *(Sr Acct Exec)*

Accounts:
Bayer
Disney
HBO
Johnson & Johnson
Microsoft
Novartis
Roche
Starbucks
Symantec
Unilever

Edelman
1075 Peachtree St NE Ste 3100, Atlanta, GA 30309
Tel.: (404) 262-3000
Fax: (404) 264-1431
E-Mail: atlanta@edelman.com
Web Site: www.edelman.com

Employees: 72
Year Founded: 1994

National Agency Associations: COPF

Agency Specializes In: Public Relations, Sponsorship

Steven Behm *(Pres-Southeast)*
Marilynn Mobley *(Exec VP-Talent Mgmt)*
Patty Tucker *(Exec VP-US Corp Practice & B-to-B Center of Excellence)*
Holly Richmond *(VP)*
Amy Salloum *(VP-Corp Comm)*
Alicia Thompson *(Gen Mgr)*
Anne Mitchell *(Acct Supvr-Digital)*
Kristin Wooten *(Acct Supvr)*
Telleen Anderson Lozano *(Sr Acct Exec)*
Max Davis *(Sr Acct Exec)*
Sara Dever *(Sr Acct Exec)*
Telleen Gegner *(Sr Acct Exec)*
Megan Beavers *(Acct Exec)*

Accounts:
Char-Broil
Tiffany & Co.

Edelman
250 Hudson St, New York, NY 10013
Tel.: (212) 768-0550
Fax: (212) 704-0128
E-Mail: new.york@edelman.com
Web Site: www.edelman.com

Employees: 700
Year Founded: 1960

National Agency Associations: COPF

Agency Specializes In: Public Relations, Sponsorship

Susan Isenberg *(Vice Chm-Health-Global)*
Jennifer Cohan *(Pres)*
Carol O'Hehier *(Mng Dir)*
Kevin King *(Chm-Global Practice-Edelman Digital)*
Ben Boyd *(Pres-Practices, Sectors & Offerings)*
Lisa Sepulveda *(Pres-Client Mgmt-Global)*
Michael Berland *(CEO-Edelman Berland)*
Melanie Wine Tolan *(Exec VP, Grp Head & Dir-Ops-NY Consumer)*
Steven Slivka *(Exec VP & Exec Creative Dir)*
Drew Vogelman *(Exec VP & Dir-Creative Production)*
Paul Leys *(Exec VP-Digital)*
Aaron Noffsinger *(Exec VP & Grp Creative Dir)*
Tom Potts *(Exec VP-Paid Media)*
Debra A. Wasser *(Exec VP-Fin Comm & Special*

Situations)
James Todd Anderson *(Sr VP & Grp Dir-Creative)*
Lee Alman *(Sr VP-Corp & Pub Affairs)*
Nadia Damouni *(Sr VP-Fin Comm & Special Situations)*
Joe DeSalazar *(Sr VP-Consumer Mktg)*
Kristin Dwyer *(Sr VP)*
Renee Edelman *(Sr VP)*
Elizabeth Pigg *(Sr VP)*
Ellie Polack *(Sr VP-Wellness 360)*
David Rosen *(Sr VP-Digital Corp & Pub Affairs)*
Yocasta Shames *(Sr VP)*
Jennifer Simon *(Sr VP-Bus & Social Purpose)*
Trisch Smith *(Sr VP)*
Todd Ringler *(Mng Dir-Media Rels)*
Lex Suvanto *(Mng Dir-Fin Comm & Special Situations Offering)*
Cassel Kroll *(VP-Paid Media Strategy & Head-Reg Paid Media Practice)*
John Battistini *(VP & Dir-User Experience-Digital)*
Dave Brown *(VP & Dir-Creative-Experience Design)*
Brooke Murphy *(VP & Assoc Dir-Creative)*
Kate Burke *(VP-Bus Dev)*
Julia Entwistle *(VP)*
Aman Singh *(VP-Bus & Social Purpose)*
Neil Steinberg *(VP-Tech Practice)*
Richard Myers *(Grp Head-Fin-New York)*
David Armano *(Dir-Strategy-Global)*
Jennifer Garcia *(Mgr-Fin)*
Ashley Zak *(Mgr-Special Projects)*
Marissa Florindi *(Sr Acct Supvr)*
Nancy McCarthy *(Sr Acct Supvr)*
Janet Yoo *(Sr Acct Supvr)*
Diana Beard *(Acct Supvr)*
Valerie Ferreyra *(Acct Supvr-Digital)*
Lauren Walsh *(Acct Supvr)*
Jennifer Borland *(Sr Acct Exec)*
Sarah McCarthy *(Sr Acct Exec)*
Grace Naugle *(Sr Acct Exec)*
Nicholas Sampogna *(Sr Acct Exec-Consumer Mktg)*
Bobby Hammelman *(Acct Exec)*
Amanda Hodge *(Acct Exec-Consumer Health Practice)*
Alexander Jacobs *(Acct Exec-Consumer Mktg)*
Meredith Lowe *(Acct Exec)*
Ari Okonofua *(Acct Exec-Natl Health Media Team)*
Nick Dover *(Asst Acct Exec)*

Accounts:
American Health Association
American Heart Association
AstraZeneca Pharmaceuticals LP Crestor
CA Technologies
Church & Dwight Arm & Hammer Essentials, Trojan
Cincinnati Children's Hospital "Buckle Up for Life"
GE Healthcare
Girl Scouts of the USA
Heineken
Humana
ITT Industries
Jim Beam Campaign: "Sue The Bears"
Microsoft Games Console, Kinect For Xbox 360
Motorola Enterprise Mobility; Holtsville, NY; 2005
Ocean Power Technologies, Inc; Pennington, NJ
Office Depot, Inc.
Pfizer, Inc. Chantix
Samsung Electronics Global Public Relations
Samsung Telecommunications America, LLC
Staples PR
Toyota "Buckle Up for Life"
Unilever "Self-Esteem Weekend", Axe Brand Promotion, Ben & Jerry's, Campaign: "Dove Go Sleeveless", Campaign: "Parading with You with More Style", Campaign: "Real Moments", Dove, Dove Men+Care, Global Digital, Public Relations

Edelman
14241 Dallas Pkwy Ste 450, Dallas, TX 75254
Tel.: (214) 520-3555
Fax: (214) 520-3458
Web Site: www.edelman.com

Employees: 20
Year Founded: 1983

National Agency Associations: COPF

Agency Specializes In: Public Relations, Sponsorship

Spike Jones *(Mng Dir & Sr VP-Digital)*
Helen Vollmer *(Pres-Southwest Reg)*
David Chamberlin *(Exec VP, Head-Data Security & Privacy & Gen Mgr)*
Jackie Hopkins *(Exec VP & Gen Mgr)*
Denisha Stevens *(Exec VP-Consumer Mktg)*
Chris Hershberger *(VP-Digital SW)*
Chris Manzini *(Gen Mgr)*
Danielle Veneski *(Gen Mgr)*
Rupa Patel *(Sr Acct Supvr-Corp Practice)*

Accounts:
Access Pharmaceuticals MuGard
ACU
Advanced Micro Devices, Inc.
Freeman
Heelys Inc.
Hilton Anatole
The International Association of Exhibitions & Events (Agency of Record) Media Relations
Project Management Institute
Texas Oncology
T-Mobile US
Viva Wyndham

Edelman
2301 5th Ave Ste 500, Seattle, WA 98121-1678
Tel.: (206) 223-1606
Fax: (206) 467-7978
E-Mail: seattle@edelman.com
Web Site: www.edelman.com

Employees: 100
Year Founded: 1992

National Agency Associations: COPF

Agency Specializes In: Public Relations, Sponsorship

Will Ludlam *(Gen Mgr & Exec VP)*
Paige Young *(Exec VP & Mgr-Global Client Relationship)*
Josh Chaitin *(Sr VP)*
Mary Horvat *(Sr VP-Digital)*
Steve Sack *(VP & Grp Dir)*
Jaclyn Anderson *(VP-Corp & Pub Affairs)*
Michael Thomas *(VP)*
David Buckley *(Grp Dir-Creative-Pacific Northwest)*
Katie Carter *(Dir-Global Specialist Talent)*
Chelsea Bodow *(Mgr-US New Bus)*
Kate McEwan *(Sr Acct Supvr)*
Nadine Bedford *(Acct Supvr-Digital Consumer Mktg)*
Liz Freeman *(Acct Supvr)*
Jon Ramsey *(Acct Supvr)*
Grace Wahlbrink *(Acct Supvr)*
Christine Weiss *(Acct Supvr)*
Kimberly Wingert *(Acct Supvr)*
Anna Anderson *(Acct Exec-Edelman for Xbox One)*
Alexandria Hall *(Asst Acct Exec)*
Courtney L'Ecuyer *(Asst Acct Exec)*

Accounts:
Allen Institute for Brain Science
Brooks Sports
Fred Hutchinson Cancer Research Center
Microsoft
Seattle Seahawks
Spring Wireless
Starbucks Corporation Starbucks Corporation, Via
Washington Wine Commission

ZENO Group
44 E 30th St, New York, NY 10016
(See Separate Listing)

Branch

ZENO Group
Hammersley House, 5-8 Warwick St, London, W1B 5LX United Kingdom
Tel.: (44) 20 3047 2380
Web Site: www.zenogroup.com

Year Founded: 1998

Agency Specializes In: Brand Development & Integration, Communications, Digital/Interactive, Public Relations

Steve Earl *(Mng Dir-Europe)*
Claire Gurr *(Acct Dir)*
Dominique King *(Acct Dir)*
Linda Sciancalepore *(Acct Dir-Health)*
Katie Taylor *(Dir-Consumer UK)*
Rachel Vrettos *(Dir-Healthcare UK)*
Claire Pay *(Assoc Dir)*
Gurjit Hothi *(Sr Acct Mgr)*
Olga Fraczek *(Acct Mgr)*
Liz Hebditch *(Acct Exec)*
Emily Morrison *(Acct Exec)*

Accounts:
ASUS Tablets
Blue Diamond Almonds Almond Breeze, Almond Milk, Iced Coffee, Media, Public Relations, Snack Almonds
New-LPK Public Relations
Six Physio Physio Services
Stork Home Conception Aid
Taj Hotels Public Relations
Tidal Music Streaming

International Branches:

Deportivo
Kornhamnstorg 49, Stockholm, 11127 Sweden
Tel.: (46) 841027553
E-Mail: hello@deportivo.se
Web Site: www.deportivo.se

Year Founded: 2010

Agency Specializes In: Advertising, Internet/Web Design, Media Relations, Public Relations, Social Media

Stefan Ronge *(Chief Creative Officer)*
Anders Hallen *(Chief Innovation Officer)*
Jennie Knutsson *(Dir)*

Accounts:
Bilpriser
Christian-Wagner-Gesellschaft
Crossing Borders Twee-Q
Foersakringskassan
ICA Vanadis
iZettle
Mynewsdesk.com
Philips
Samtrafiken
Stockholms Stadsmission Campaign: "Paywall for the Homeless"
Unicef Campaign: "Escape Ends Her"

Edelman Brussels
Avenue Marnix 28, B-1000 Brussels, Belgium
Tel.: (32) 2 227 6170
Fax: (32) 2 227 6189
E-Mail: brussels@edelman.com

Web Site: www.edelman.be

Employees: 25
Year Founded: 1995

Agency Specializes In: Government/Political, Public Relations

Jere Sullivan *(Vice Chm-Global PA)*
Kajsa Wilhelmsson *(Exec VP & Head-Health Policy & Market Access)*
Esther Busscher *(Gen Mgr-Bus)*
Xavier aerts *(Dir-IT-Europe)*
Miguel Fernandes da Silva *(Dir-European Food Policy)*
Valeria Botta *(Acct Mgr)*
Nicolas Boulart *(Sr Acct Exec)*
Adam Almirall *(Acct Exec)*
Davide Carrino *(Acct Exec)*
Sunniva D'Aloya *(Acct Exec)*
Bernard D'Heygere *(Acct Exec)*
Anais Willain *(Acct Exec)*

Accounts:
Bose
BT
Bunge
Business Software Alliance
Chevron
Danone
European Justice Forum (EJF)
Eurostar
Fediol
GE
Johnson & Johnson
The Nielsen Company
Novartis
Shell
VF

Edelman Frankfurt

(Formerly Edelman)
Niddastrasse 91, D-60329 Frankfurt am Main, Germany
Tel.: (49) 69 75 61 990
Fax: (49) 69 75 61 9910
E-Mail: martin.floerkemeier@edelman.com
Web Site: www.edelman.de/standorte/frankfurt

Employees: 50
Year Founded: 1970

Agency Specializes In: Public Relations

Martin Floerkemeier *(Mng Dir & Sec Head-Health)*
Nadine Dusberger *(Exec Dir)*
Sophia Gorges *(Acct Dir)*
Gabriele Stoewe *(Dir-Fin-Germany & Mgr-Sys-Europe)*
Katrin Weisbach *(Dir-Health)*
Bjoern Christian Hasse *(Mgr-Global Client Relationship)*
Daya Houdayer *(Sr Acct Exec)*
Miriam Chiara Theilacker *(Sr Acct Exec)*
Nadine Hoffmann *(Asst Acct Exec)*
Uta Behnke *(Mgr Dir)*

Accounts:
Novartis
Pfizer

Edelman

Via Varese 11, 20121 Milan, Italy
(See Separate Listing)

Edelman

54 Rue de Monceau, 75008 Paris, France
Tel.: (33) 1 56 69 75 00
Fax: (33) 1 56 69 75 75
E-Mail: paris.reception@edelman.com
Web Site: www.edelman.com

Employees: 40
Year Founded: 1989

Agency Specializes In: Corporate Identity, Crisis Communications, Direct-to-Consumer, Government/Political, Media Relations, Medical Products, Promotions, Public Relations, Sponsorship

Jeremy Cohen *(Chm-Bus & Social Purpose-EMEA & Deputy Gen Mgr-Edelman France)*

Accounts:
AstraZeneca
Bouygues Telecom
BT Group
Discovery Networks France
Dualstar
Infocus
Maharahstra Tourism
Pfizer
Unilever
Veolia Environnement

Edelman

18th Fl Ferrum Tower, Suha Dong Jungu, Seoul, Korea (South)
Tel.: (82) 2 725 2001
Fax: (82) 2 725 2007
E-Mail: seoul@edelman.com
Web Site: www.edelman.kr

Employees: 45
Year Founded: 1996

Agency Specializes In: Brand Development & Integration, Corporate Communications, New Product Development, Public Relations

Sung Bin Jang *(Mng Dir)*
Kay Lee *(Mgr-Edelman Korea)*
Kylie Yoon *(Mgr)*
Romy Shin *(Sr Acct Exec)*
Alicia Youngshin Kim *(Sr Supvr)*
Rachel Um *(Sr Supvr-Corp & Consumer Practice)*

Edelman

3rd Floor Toranomon 45 MT Bldg, 5-1-5 Toranomon Minato-ku, Tokyo, 105-001 Japan
Tel.: (81) 3 6403 5200
Fax: (81) 3 6403 5201
E-Mail: japan@edelman.com
Web Site: www.edelman.jp

Agency Specializes In: Brand Development & Integration, Consumer Marketing, Crisis Communications, Event Planning & Marketing, Financial, Government/Political, International, Media Planning, Media Relations, Media Training, Product Placement, Public Relations, Publicity/Promotions, Strategic Planning/Research

Ian Messer *(Dir-Comm Trng Grp)*
Saori Adachi *(Acct Supvr)*
Akiko Asami *(Sr Acct Exec)*
Yu Matsuzaki *(Acct Exec)*
Ry Sullivan *(Acct Exec)*
Yuko Yamahira *(Acct Exec)*
Mio Coxon *(Asst Acct Exec)*

Accounts:
APRIL (Asia Pacific Resources International Holdings Ltd.)
AstraZeneca Crestor
Avaya
Banque AIG
Boston Scientific Corporation
Bunge Ltd
Cable & Wireless Plc
Chipworks
Elcoteq SE
United Continental Holdings

Edelman

Huguenot House 37 Saint Stephens Green, Dublin, 2 Ireland
Tel.: (353) 1 678 9333
Fax: (353) 1 661 4408
E-Mail: dublin@edelman.com
Web Site: www.edelman.ie

Employees: 25
Year Founded: 1981

Agency Specializes In: Public Relations

Jim Glennon *(Chm)*
Alex Bigg *(Gen Mgr)*
Olwyn Enright *(Dir-Pub Affairs)*

Accounts:
Abbott
British Midland
Diageo
Discover Science & Engineering
Eircom Phonewatch
Enterprise Ireland
EU Jet Airlines
Glanbia Consumer Foods
Hosting365
Mars North America
Mars Petcare
PepsiCo
Pfizer
Rabobank Ireland
Reckitt Benckiser
Sky Ireland
SMA Nutrition
Sustainable Energy Ireland
Visa Europe
Vodafone
Zamano

Edelman

Southside 105 Victoria Street, London, SW1E 6QT United Kingdom
Tel.: (44) 20 3047 2000
Fax: (44) 20 3047 2507
Web Site: www.edelman.com

Employees: 349
Year Founded: 1967

Agency Specializes In: Public Relations

Paul Myners *(Chm)*
Mel Hinds *(Mng Dir)*
Carolyn Paul *(Mng Dir-Global Health & Chm-European Health Practice)*
Jackie Cooper *(Chm-Creative Strategy-Global)*
Stephanie Lvovich *(Chm-Pub Affairs-Global)*
Ed Williams *(CEO-UK & Ireland)*
Gurpreet Brar *(Mng Dir-UK Pub Affairs)*
Justin Westcott *(Mng Dir-Tech-London)*
Nick Howard *(Dir & Head-EMEA Practice-Employee Engagement)*
Alex Bigg *(Gen Mgr)*
Ben Lock *(Dir)*
Andrew Robinson *(Dir)*
Elizabeth Tagge *(Dir-Property)*
Saratha Rajeswaran *(Assoc Dir-Pub Affairs)*
Eleanor Wilcox *(Assoc Dir-Corp & Fin)*

Accounts:
Advanced Micro Devices, Inc (EMEA Communications Agency of Record) Global Public Relations
Airbnb PR
Atos Media, Technology
Autonomy Systems Ltd. PR
Balfour Beatty
Candarel
Capco

Capital Shopping Centres
Care.com PR
Climate-KIC Public Relations
Diageo Campaign: "The Captain's Island"
The Economist Group Corporate Relations
Facebook PR
GE
Hometrack Messaging, Public Relations, Strategy
Lithium Technologies Bespoke Solutions, Go-to-Market, Partner Strategy
Microsoft B2b Comms
Motorola Solutions, Inc.
PayPal Consumer & Tech PR
Sainsbury's
SAP Corporate Communications, Media Relations, PR
Shell Campaign: "The Network of Champions"
Starbucks
TD Waterhouse
TripAdvisor Corporate B2B, Digital, Public Affairs
Unilever Campaign: "Every Child Has The Right To Play", Omo
UPS
New-Vue Cinemas Communications
Young's

Edelman
Paseo de la Castellana 91-5A Pta, Edificio Centro 23, Madrid, 28046 Spain
Tel.: (34) 915560154
Fax: (34) 915560557
E-Mail: madrid@edelman.com
Web Site: www.edelman.com

Employees: 52
Year Founded: 1995

Agency Specializes In: Public Relations

Miguel Angel Aguirre *(Dir Gen-Edelman Spain)*
Jordi Ballera *(Deputy Mgr & Dir)*
David Moran *(Dir-Digital-Spain)*
Pelayo Alonso *(Sr Acct Mgr)*
Beatriz Clavero *(Sr Acct Mgr-Tourism & Lifestyle)*
Enrique Gonzalez Martinez *(Sr Acct Mgr)*
Tamara Garcia-Noblejas Sandigo *(Acct Mgr)*
Mar Lazaro Borrell *(Sr Acct Exec-Healthcare)*
Irene Cervera *(Sr Acct Exec)*
Yrene Cuadrado *(Sr Acct Exec)*
Raquel Alonso Hernandez *(Sr Acct Exec)*
Juan Salgueiro Montero *(Sr Acct Exec-Tourism & Lifestyle Dept)*
Angela Prieto Lopez *(Acct Exec)*

Accounts:
Abbvie
Air Liquide
Astra Zeneca
Avis
eBay
Hewlett Packard
Johnson & Johnson
Mahou San Miguel
Mylan
Ryanair
Shire
Volkswagen

Edelman
Santa Margarita #108 Piso 1, Col Del Valle, Mexico, DF 03100 Mexico
Tel.: (52) 55 5350 1500
Fax: (52) 55 5350 1555
E-Mail: mexico.df@edelman.com
Web Site: www.edelman.com/office/mexico-city

Employees: 60
Year Founded: 1994

Agency Specializes In: Public Relations

Eduardo Cisneros *(VP-Creative)*
Sergio Sanchez *(VP-Strategic Plng)*

Accounts:
Abbott
AMD
Aspel Mexico
Church & Dwight
Compania de Turismo de Puerto Rico (CTPR)
E.J. Krause de Mexico
La Negrita
LEGO Group
Merck Sharp & Dohme
Samsung Electronics Mexico
Schering-Plough
Sunbeam
Unilever
UPS
Wal-Mart de Mexico

Edelman
Landshuter Allee 10, 80637 Munich, Germany
Tel.: (49) 89 41 30 16
Fax: (49) 89 41 30 1700
Web Site: www.edelman.com/office/munich

Employees: 20

Agency Specializes In: Public Relations

Susanne Marell *(CEO-Germany)*
Martina Pennekamp *(Mng Dir-Munich)*
Tanja Schuermann *(Exec Dir)*
Bjorn Sievers *(Exec Dir)*
Gabriele Stoewe *(Dir-Fin-Germany & Mgr-System-Europe)*
Anica Thalmeier *(Sr Mgr-PR & Acct Mgr)*
Jessica Moser *(Sr Acct Mgr)*
Susanne Richardsen *(Acct Mgr)*
Danny Schwarze *(Acct Exec)*

Accounts:
C&A Corporate Account, Strategic Planning
Microsoft

Edelman
Level 7 1 York Street, Sydney, NSW 2000 Australia
Tel.: (61) 2 9241 3131
Fax: (61) 2 9221 2676
E-Mail: australia@edelman.com
Web Site: www.edelman.com

Employees: 35
Year Founded: 1987

Agency Specializes In: Public Relations

Michelle Hutton *(CEO-Australia)*
Jamal Hamidi *(Exec Dir-Creative)*
Kate Ferguson *(Client Svc Dir-Australia)*
Brian Shrowder *(Sr Counsel)*

Accounts:
ABN AMRO
Audi Australia (Public Relations Agency of Record) Brand Awareness, Creative, Media Strategy
CSL
Gumtree.com.au PR
iiNet
KFC Public Relations
Nikkei Asian Review Campaign: "Tea"
Nissan
Origin
Pfizer
QT Hotels & Resorts Below-the-Line Marketing, Online, Public Relations
Samsung
Shell Retail
Unilever

Edelman
10F No 36 Pateh Road Sec 3, Taipei, 105 Taiwan
Tel.: (886) 2 2570 7588
Fax: (886) 2 2570 7379
E-Mail: taipei@edelman.com
Web Site: www.edelman.com

Employees: 20
Year Founded: 1997

Agency Specializes In: Public Relations

Kuang-kai Peter Tou *(Gen Mgr)*
David Kuan *(Acct Exec)*

Accounts:
Aviva
Fiji Water
Johnson & Johnson
Merck Sharp & Dohme Gardasil, Januvia; 2008
Microsoft

Edelman
Rm 3301 Office Tower A Beijing Fortune Plaza, No 7 Dongsanhaun Zhonglu, Chaoyang District, Beijing, 100020 China
Tel.: (86) 10 5828 6588
Fax: (86) 10 5828 6566
E-Mail: beijing@edelman.com
Web Site: www.edelman.com

Employees: 100
Year Founded: 1985

Agency Specializes In: Public Relations

Cindy Tian *(Vice Chm-A-P Reg)*
Janet Dai *(Mng Dir)*
Tony Tao *(Mng Dir)*
Bob Grove *(CEO-North Asia)*
Delicia Tan-Seet *(Sr Dir & Head-Corp)*
Ashley Hegland *(Dir-Sustainability Practice)*

Accounts:
Cotton Incorporated PR

Edelman
6th Floor, Vatika Triangle, Sushant Lok-1, Block - A, Gurgaon, Haryana India
Tel.: (91) 124 413 1400

Rakesh Thukral *(Mng Dir)*
Kunal Arora *(Dir-Natl)*
Aman Singh *(Mgr-Pub Affairs)*

Accounts:
New-Energy Efficient Services Limited Communication Strategy, Creative
Microsoft Public Relations

Edelman
Medienpark Kampnagel Barmbeker Str 4, 22303 Hamburg, Germany
Tel.: (49) 40 37 47 980
Fax: (49) 40 37 28 80
E-Mail: hamburg@edelman.com
Web Site: www.edelman.com

Employees: 35
Year Founded: 1995

Agency Specializes In: Public Relations

Susanne Marell *(CEO)*
Martin Florkemeier *(Mng Dir)*
Glenn Engler *(Chief Strategy Officer-Global)*
Anja Guckenberger *(Deputy Mng Dir-Hamburg & Head-Strategy & Creative-Germany)*
Andreas Kloevekorn *(Mng Dir-Digital)*
Sandy Laliberte *(Sr Acct Supvr-Digital)*
M. Alba Castro Torruella *(Sr Acct Exec)*

Accounts:
Mars
Unilever

Edelman

3F Want Want Plaza, 211 Shi Men Yi Lu, Shanghai, Shanghai 200041 China
Tel.: (86) 21 6193 7588
Fax: (86) 21 6193 7566
E-Mail: shanghai@edelman.com
Web Site: www.edelman.com

Employees: 42
Year Founded: 1992

Agency Specializes In: Public Relations

Anita Cai *(Sr Dir & Head-Natl Health Practice)*
Liru Chan *(Sr Dir)*
Kok Kuan Tan *(Sr Dir)*
Natalie Xu *(Dir-HR)*
Kailun Ma *(Sr Mgr-Corp Comm Practice)*
Qian Ouyang *(Sr Mgr)*
Devin Du *(Mgr-Digital)*
Elly Hao *(Mgr-Tech Practice)*

Accounts:
3M
Anheuser-Busch
GlaxoSmithKline
IDA Singapore
IMAX

Edelman

Gustaz Mahlerplein 66a, 1082 MA Amsterdam, Netherlands
Mailing Address:
PO Box 7913, 1008 AC Amsterdam, Netherlands
Tel.: (31) 20 30 10 980
Fax: (31) 20 30 10 981
E-Mail: nl@edelman.com
Web Site: www.edelman.com

Employees: 70
Year Founded: 1993

Agency Specializes In: Public Relations, Sponsorship

Annemieke Kievit *(Gen Mgr)*
Marc Hinfelaar *(Dir-Health, Food & Consumer Unit-Amsterdam)*
Patricia Stuivenberg *(Sr Acct Mgr)*
Gijs Toxopeus *(Sr Acct Mgr & Sr Media Supvr)*
Britt Van De Voort *(Acct Mgr)*
Marije Dippel-Nieuwenhuis *(Mgr-Mktg)*
Sabina Ernst *(Mgr-HR)*
Estelle Muys *(Asst Acct Exec)*
Wieteke Beerepoot *(Corp Dir)*
Thomas McNeill *(Corp Dir)*

Accounts:
BT
Exact Software
Fort Dodge
General Electric
GlaxoSmithKline Consumer Healthcare
Labatt USA LLC
Microsoft Xbox
Nissan
PepsiCo
Shell
Starbucks

Edelman

Passeig De Gracia 86, 3A planta, 08008 Barcelona, Spain
Tel.: (34) 93 488 1290
Fax: (34) 93 215 0767
E-Mail: barcelona@edelman.com
Web Site: www.edelman.com

Employees: 20
Year Founded: 1995

Agency Specializes In: Health Care Services, Pharmaceutical, Public Relations

Edu Villanua Aranda *(Acct Mgr & Mgr-Knowledge)*
Carla Humet Mir *(Acct Mgr)*
Anna Casals *(Sr Acct Exec-Digital)*
Laura Toha Planisoles *(Sr Acct Exec)*
Anna Lopez Bermudez *(Acct Exec)*
David Pastor Ussetti *(Designer-Digital)*

Accounts:
Bayer
Gilead

Edelman

Room 707 Dongshan Plaza 69 Xianlie Zhong Road, Guangzhou, 510095 China
Tel.: (86) 20 8732 2111
Fax: (86) 20 8732 2119
E-Mail: guangzhou@edelman.com
Web Site: www.edelman.com

Employees: 11
Year Founded: 1992

Agency Specializes In: Public Relations

Tony Tao *(Mng Dir)*
Helena Wang *(Head-Practice & Dir)*
Delicia Tan-Seet *(Sr Dir & Strategist-Client)*
Vivian Chin *(Dir)*
Grace Fu *(Dir-Reg Talent Recruitment-Asia Pacific, Middle East & Africa)*
Wang Crystal *(Sr Mgr)*
Amanda Mooney *(Sr Mgr-Plng-India, South Asia, Middle East & Africa)*
Elly Hao *(Mgr-Tech Practice)*
Ricco Wang *(Mgr)*

Accounts:
OTIS Elevator
San Miguel
Watsons Personal Care Stores

Edelman

701 Central Plaza 18 Harbour Rd, Hong Kong, China (Hong Kong)
Tel.: (852) 2804 1338
Fax: (852) 2804 1303
E-Mail: hongkong@edelman.com
Web Site: www.edelman.com

Employees: 65
Year Founded: 1986

Agency Specializes In: Public Relations

Ben Boyd *(Pres-Practices, Sectors & Offerings)*
Chadd McLisky *(Mng Dir-Asia Pacific Corp Practice)*
Andres Vejarano *(Sr Dir-Consumer Mktg)*
Pierre Desfretier *(Creative Dir-Digital)*
Yeelim Lee *(Dir)*
Ian Messer *(Dir-Comm Trng Grp)*
Jane Morgan *(Dir-Consumer Mktg)*

Accounts:
New-Alvarez & Marsal (Public Relations Agency of Record) Awareness, Public Relations
AXA An Shing Investment, Protection & Retirement Solutions, Strategic Communications
British Airways
Dairy Farm Jasons Food & Living, Market Place by Jasons, Media, Oliver's the Delicatessen, ThreeSixty
Ikea Hong Kong Brand Marketing, PR
ING Investment
OKAY.com Media Relations, Public Relations
Agency of Record, Strategy
Qantas Airways
Savannah College of Art & Design Media, Public Relations
Sony Pictures Television Public Relations
UPS

Edelman

Rua Joaquim Floriano N 820 20 andar, Sao Paulo, SP 04534-003 Brazil
Tel.: (55) 11 3017 5300
Fax: (55) 11 3078 5230
E-Mail: sao.paulo@edelman.com
Web Site: www.edelman.com.br

Employees: 50
Year Founded: 1997

Agency Specializes In: Public Relations

Richard Edelman *(Pres & CEO)*
Natalia Martinez *(Exec VP-Strategic Projects & Mktg-Latin America)*
Cristina Schachtitz *(Exec VP)*
Daniel Rimoli *(Head-Edelman Digital-Brazil & Sr Dir)*
Ligia Cavalcanti *(Office Mgr)*
Raquel Vitorino *(Mgr)*
Paula Nadal *(Sr Acct Supvr-Digital)*
Marcio Martins Coimbra *(Sr Acct Exec)*
Raquel Ticianelli *(Acct Exec)*
Paula Dourado *(Analyst-Comm & Mktg-LATAM)*

Edelman

111 Somerset Unit 14-03, Singapore, 238164 Singapore
Tel.: (65) 6733 1110
Fax: (65) 6733 5550
E-Mail: singapore@edelman.com
Web Site: www.edelman.com

Employees: 50
Year Founded: 1989

Agency Specializes In: Public Relations

Amanda Goh *(CEO)*
Gavin Coombes *(Pres-Edelman Digital-Asia-Pacific)*
Iain Twine *(CEO-South East Asia & Australasia)*
Jamie Read *(Reg Dir-South East Asia-Health Sector)*
Derek Ng *(Dir-Reg CRM-Starbucks-Global Client Mgmt-APACMEA)*
Juliette Van der Burgt *(Dir-Consumer Mktg Bus)*
Rachel Lee Puah *(Mgr)*

Accounts:
BlackBerry Campaign: "How Love Built a Social Media Megabrand", Social Media
EA Mobile Communications, Public Relations
Marina Bay Sands
Microsoft
Ministry of Manpower Marketing Communications
Ministry of National Development
Samsung
SHELL
Singapore Sports Hub Pte Ltd Digital Engagement, Events Management, Media Relations, PR
Singapore Tourism Board (Agency of Record) "Singapore: Inside Out", PR, Strategy
Starbucks Corporation
Zespri

Edelman

Brunnsgatan 21B, 111 38 Stockholm, Sweden
Tel.: (46) 8 54 54 55 70
Fax: (46) 8 54 54 55 71
E-Mail: stockholm@edelman.com
Web Site: www.edelman.com

Employees: 15
Year Founded: 2000

Agency Specializes In: Public Relations

Mattias Ronge *(CEO)*
Stefan Ronge *(Chief Creative Officer)*
Sandra Andersson *(Media Dir)*
Amanda Lindgren *(Dir-Consumer)*
Cecilia Reimann *(Dir-Corp)*
Jasper Hein Nordling *(Assoc Dir-Plng)*
Jonas Axblom *(Mgr-Community)*

Accounts:
Taxi Stockholm Campaign: "Taxi charter"

Edelman
Paraguay 610 Piso 29, C1057AAH Buenos Aires, Argentina
Tel.: (54) 11 4315 4020
Fax: (54) 11 4311 7161
E-Mail: buenosaires@edelman.com
Web Site: www.edelman.com.ar

Employees: 35
Year Founded: 1997

Agency Specializes In: Public Relations

Natalia Quintana *(Sr Dir-Consumer Products & Entertainment)*
Natalia Martinez *(Reg Dir-Insights & Tech Practices-Latin America)*
Jimena Guffanti *(Acct Dir-Tech)*
Paula Herreros *(Acct Dir-Digital)*
Natalia Soler *(Acct Dir)*
Mariano Vila *(Acct Dir-Pub Affairs)*
Sabrina Valls *(Sr Acct Exec)*

Accounts:
Amadeus
AstraZeneca
Bain & Company
Bridgestone
CESSI
Citrix
Lenovo
Manpower Group
Mastercard
Metlife
MetLife
Norton Symantec
Oracle
Orange
S.C. Johnson
Tyco
Universal

Edelman
45-9 The Boulevard Mid Valley City, Lingkaran Syed Putra, 59200 Kuala Lumpur, Malaysia
Tel.: (60) 3 2287 8689
Fax: (60) 3 2287 0234
E-Mail: edelman.kl@edelman.com
Web Site: www.edelman.com

Employees: 28
Year Founded: 1984

Agency Specializes In: Public Relations

Robert Kay *(CEO)*
Christine Chang *(Dir-Integrated Brand & Digital)*

Accounts:
AstraZeneca PLC
Microsoft Corporation
P.T. Unilever Indonesia Tbk
Samsung Group
Unilever N.V.
Uniqlo Marketing, Media, Online Community Management, PR

Europe:

AMI Communications
Tyn 4/641, 110 00 Prague, 1 Czech Republic
Tel.: (420) 234 124 112
Fax: (420) 234 124 120
E-Mail: management@amic.cz
Web Site: www.amic.cz

Employees: 70
Year Founded: 1995

National Agency Associations: APRA-ICCO

Agency Specializes In: Consulting, Crisis Communications, Investor Relations, Media Relations, Media Training, Public Relations

Milan Hejl *(Co-Founder & Mng Dir)*
Marek Stransky *(Mng Partner)*
Eva Sroka *(Mng Dir-Healthcare & Tech)*
Miroslav Novak *(Sr Acct Dir)*

Accounts:
L'Oreal

Communique
Ryvangs Alle 50, DK-2900 Hellerup, Denmark
Tel.: (45) 3698 3400
E-Mail: info@communique.dk
Web Site: communique.dk

Employees: 16
Year Founded: 1972

Agency Specializes In: Public Relations

Christian Bentsen *(Partner)*
Michael Buksti *(Mng Dir)*
Frans Grandjean *(Dir)*

Accounts:
Shell
United Parcel Services

Edelman Imageland
Kozhevnichesky Proezd 4 Bldg 2, Moscow, 115114 Russia
Tel.: (7) 495 785 22 55
Fax: (7) 495 787 10 62
E-Mail: moscow@edelman.com
Web Site: www.edelman.com

Employees: 45
Year Founded: 1990

Agency Specializes In: Public Relations

Accounts:
Israel Government Tourist Office
Rusavtoprom
Samsung
Skyscanner

Africa:

Edelman South Africa
(Formerly Baird's Renaissance (Pty) Ltd.)
11 Ralda Rd, Blairgowrie, 2194 Randburg, 2125 South Africa
Mailing Address:
PO Box 3674, Randburg, 2125 South Africa
Tel.: (27) 11 504 4000
Fax: (27) 11 886 2474
Web Site: www.edelman.com/office/johannesburg

Employees: 25
Year Founded: 1987

Agency Specializes In: Communications, Public Relations

Tod Donhauser *(Mng Dir-South Africa)*
Kate Guerin *(Acct Dir)*
Deeran Moodley *(Dir-Fin & HR)*
Jocelyn Newmarch *(Acct Mgr)*
Kieron Stevenson *(Acct Mgr)*
Joseph J. Akhidenor *(Asst Acct Exec)*

Accounts:
Dewswana
Edward Nathan Friedland
HSRC
IAVI
IDION
KFC
Levi Strauss
North-West Parks
Novartis Consumer Health
Southern Sun
Statistics SA
Total SA
Tsogo Sun/Montecasino
Visa International
Woolworths

Middle East:

Edelman DABO
(Formerly Dabo & Co)
Villa 162a 2d Street, Al Wasl Road, Dubai, United Arab Emirates
Tel.: (971) 43444901
Fax: (971) 43444898
E-Mail: pr@daboandco.com
Web Site: www.daboandco.com

Year Founded: 2004

Agency Specializes In: Digital/Interactive, Event Planning & Marketing, Public Relations

Camilla d'Abo *(Mng Partner)*
Lucy d'Abo *(Mng Partner)*
Jason Leavy *(Mng Dir)*
Clare Curran *(Sr Acct Mgr)*
Ashfana Abdul Hameed *(Acct Mgr)*
Natalie Walsh *(Office Mgr)*
Flavia Fernandes *(Mgr-Ops)*
Rijosh Joseph *(Assoc Acct Dir)*

Accounts:
New-Art Dubai
New-Bayerische Motoren Werke Aktiengesellschaft Stay Alert Stay Alive Campaign
Canon (U.K.) Ltd.
Equinix, Inc.
New-HSBC Bank Middle East Limited
New-Jumeirah Restaurants LLC
New-JW Marriott Marquis
Nokia Corporation
Qantas Airways Limited

Wolf Press & Public Relations
65 Yigal Alon St, Tel Aviv, 67443 Israel
Tel.: (972) 3 561 0808
Fax: (972) 3 561 1666
E-Mail: info@wolfppr.com
Web Site: www.wolfppr.com

E-Mail for Key Personnel:
President: roni@wolfppr.com

Employees: 10
Year Founded: 1992

Agency Specializes In: Public Relations

Roni Wolf *(Founder & CEO)*
Erez Banks *(Deputy CEO & Exec Mgr-Client)*
Keren Shamir *(Sr Acct Mgr)*

Galit Zahavi *(Sr Acct Mgr-Global)*
Ori Shtuden *(Mgr-Social Media & Acct Mgr)*

Accounts:
Alcatel Lucent
Bose
cVidya
DBSI
Energtek Inc PR Campaign
Henkel-Soad
Henkel
ITL Optronics
ITL
Mercedes-Benz
Mitsubishi Motors
Modu
Taavura Group
UBank
United Parcel Service
The ZOE Group

Pacific:

IndoPacific Edelman
Recapital Bldg 3rd Fl Jl Adityawarman Kav 55, Kebayoran Baru, Jakarta, 12160 Indonesia
Tel.: (62) 21 721 59000
Fax: (62) 21 727 81919
E-Mail: ipe@indopacedelman.com
Web Site: www.edelman.id

Employees: 90
Year Founded: 1993

Agency Specializes In: Public Relations

Bambang Chriswanto *(Vice Chm & Head-Consulting)*
Raymond Siva *(CEO)*
Julien Courant *(Mng Dir-Integrated Brand Comm)*
Rachna Sharma *(VP-Integrated Brand & Digital Comm)*
Dian Wulan Suling *(Mgr)*
Alfredo Ferdireza *(Sr Acct Exec-Consumer Lifestyle Div)*
Inge Soeroso *(Acct Exec)*
Fannie Waldhani *(Coord-Media)*

Accounts:
New-Asus Indonesia Communications Strategy
Australian Government
Coca-Cola Refreshments USA, Inc.
Computer Associates
Deutsch Bank
European Commission
Hitachi
Jakarta City Council
Thames Pam Jaya
World Vision

Pegasus Communications
Room No 801 MapleTree Tower No 108, Chaoyang District, Beijing, 100022 China
Tel.: (86) 10 5869 3376
Fax: (86) 10 5869 3375
Web Site: www.realpegasus.com

Employees: 25

Agency Specializes In: Advertising, Automotive, Consumer Marketing, Electronics, Event Planning & Marketing, Financial, Industrial, Public Relations, Real Estate

Accounts:
Abbott Labs
Adobe
BMW
CCTV
CITI Bank
IMAX
Keyline Brand Bio-Oil, Creative, Cuticura, PR, Press, Soft & Gentle
Motorola Solutions, Inc.
NetEase
Panasonic
Papa Johns Pizza
Pepsico
Radio Netherland Worldwide
Red Bull
Siemens
World Economic Forum

EDELMAN PUBLIC RELATIONS
(Formerly Vollmer Public Relations)
1201 Louisiana St Ste 830, Houston, TX 77002
Tel.: (713) 970-2100
Fax: (713) 970-2140
Web Site: www.edelman.com

Employees: 45
Year Founded: 1981

Agency Specializes In: Business-To-Business, Health Care Services, Internet/Web Design, Public Relations

Helen Vollmer *(Pres-Edelman Southwest)*
Danielle Allen *(Sr VP)*
Jamie Kaplan *(Sr VP-Heath & Wellness-Southwest Reg)*
Amber Jaynes Casanave *(VP-Consumer Mktg)*
Juan Labaqui *(VP)*
Maureen Burke *(Acct Exec-Digital)*
Sanah Sadaruddin *(Acct Exec)*
Kelli Mcbee *(Asst Acct Exec)*

Accounts:
Tyco Flow Control
Whole Foods Market

EDGE COMMUNICATIONS, INC.
5419 Hollywood Blvd Ste 727, Los Angeles, CA 90027
Tel.: (323) 469-3397
Fax: (323) 645-7054
E-Mail: info@edgecommunicationsinc.com
Web Site: www.edgecommunicationsinc.com

Employees: 20
Year Founded: 1996

National Agency Associations: PRSA

Agency Specializes In: Advertising, Advertising Specialties, Alternative Advertising, Brand Development & Integration, Business Publications, Business-To-Business, Communications, Consulting, Consumer Marketing, Digital/Interactive, E-Commerce, Electronic Media, Electronics, Entertainment, Event Planning & Marketing, Exhibit/Trade Shows, Health Care Services, High Technology, Information Technology, Integrated Marketing, Internet/Web Design, Local Marketing, Market Research, Media Relations, Media Training, New Technologies, Public Relations, Publicity/Promotions, Search Engine Optimization, Social Marketing/Nonprofit, Social Media

Approx. Annual Billings: $1,200,000

Sara Flint *(Owner)*

Accounts:
Green Plug; San Ramon, CA Green electronics;Gadgets;Power;Energy;Environment; Consumer electronics;Smart power;Smart grid; 2009
Ocean Media; Huntington Beach, CA Advertising;Advertising agency;Media planning;Media buying;TV advertising;Radio advertising;Direct response;DRIV ;ROI; 2011
SteelHouse; Los Angeles, CA Online advertising;Behavioral targeting;Retargeting;Remarketing;Online shopping trends;Online retail;Ecommerce; 2011
uSamp; Encino, CA Online surveys;Market research;Surveys;Online research; 2009
Velodyne Acoustics, Inc
WebVisible; Irvine, CA SEO;Web marketing;Online marketing;Web search;Search engine;SEM;Small business marketing; 2010

EDIBLE INK, INC.
168 N Clinton St Ste 618413, Chicago, IL 60661
Tel.: (847) 462-8489
E-Mail: info@edibleinkpr.com
Web Site: www.edibleinkpr.com

Year Founded: 2008

Agency Specializes In: Advertising, Event Planning & Marketing, Promotions, Public Relations

Lauri DeGiacomo *(Co-Founder)*
Britt Roehm *(Owner)*

Accounts:
Bakersfield
Taco Joint
ZED451
Zocalo Restaurant & Tequila Bar

EFFECTIVE IMMEDIATELY PR
325 Broadway Ste 303, New York, NY 10007
Tel.: (212) 777-6727
E-Mail: info@ei-pr.com
Web Site: www.effectiveimmediatelypr.com

Agency Specializes In: Event Planning & Marketing, Media Training, Print, Public Relations, Social Media

Eshy Gazit *(CEO)*
Patrick Ermlich *(CMO)*

Accounts:
New-Terry Manning

E.H. ANDERSON PUBLIC RELATIONS
801 Wooded Acres Dr, Waco, TX 76710
Tel.: (254) 772-5909
E-Mail: info@ehandersonpr.com
Web Site: www.ehandersonpr.com

Year Founded: 2002

Agency Specializes In: Advertising, Broadcast, Media Relations, Print, Public Relations, T.V.

Liz Anderson *(Owner)*
Bage Anderson *(Dir-Video)*
Megan Fleetwood *(Acct Mgr)*

Accounts:
Care Net Pregnancy Center of Central Texas

THE EHRHARDT GROUP
365 Canal St Ste 1750, New Orleans, LA 70130
Tel.: (504) 558-0311
Fax: (504) 558-0344
E-Mail: malcolm@theehrhardtgroup.com
Web Site: www.theehrhardtgroup.com

Year Founded: 1996

Agency Specializes In: Business-To-Business, Corporate Communications, Crisis Communications, Market Research, Media Relations, Media Training, Public Relations, Social Marketing/Nonprofit, Strategic Planning/Research

Marc Ehrhardt *(Sr VP)*

Terri Terri Argieard *(VP-Fin & Admin)*
Erin Doucette *(Acct Mgr)*
Caitlin Switzer *(Acct Mgr)*
Haley Olver *(Acct Exec)*
Morgan Wampold *(Acct Exec)*
Emily Good *(Asst Acct Exec)*
Rona Hoang *(Asst Acct Exec)*
Amy Rakestraw *(Asst Acct Exec)*
Rachael Stanton *(Asst Acct Exec)*
Jim Lestelle *(Sr Counsel)*

Accounts:
Capital One Bank
Gordon Biersch Restaurant
Harmony Oaks Apartments
Louisiana Credit Union League
The Roosevelt Hotel
Waste Management

EILEEN KOCH & COMPANY, INC.
1627 Pontius Ave, Los Angeles, CA 90025
Tel.: (310) 441-1000
Fax: (310) 441-3030
E-Mail: eileen@eileenkoch.com
Web Site: www.eileenkoch.com

Agency Specializes In: Advertising, Brand Development & Integration, Entertainment, Event Planning & Marketing, Fashion/Apparel, Local Marketing, Magazines, Media Relations, Product Placement, Production (Ad, Film, Broadcast), Public Relations, Publishing, Sports Market, T.V.

Eileen Koch *(Founder & CEO)*

Accounts:
Brian Wright
Deanna Shapiro
Dennis Logan Band
DJ Mix Master Miguel
Kourosh Zolani
Linette Beaumont
Mother-in-Law Hell
Starbrite Music Supervision
WritingRoom.com, LLC.

EILER COMMUNICATIONS
900 Victors Way Ste 180, Ann Arbor, MI 48108-5208
Tel.: (734) 761-3399
Fax: (734) 761-3724
Web Site: www.eilerpr.com

Employees: 6
Year Founded: 1987

Agency Specializes In: Public Relations

Larry T. Eiler *(Co-Founder, Chm & CEO)*

Accounts:
Association for Vascular Access; Herriman, UT
CFI Group; Ann Arbor, MI Consulting
Ditech; Costa Mesa, California
Eastern Michigan University; Ypsilanti, MI College of Business
Ford Field; Detroit, MI Playing Field of the Detroit Lions
GDI Info Tech; Ann Arbor, MI
Gene Codes; Ann Arbor, Michigan

EIN COMMUNICATIONS
1712 N St NW Ste 101, Washington, DC 20036
Tel.: (202) 775-0200
Web Site: www.eincomm.com

Year Founded: 1980

Agency Specializes In: Brand Development & Integration, Corporate Communications, Crisis Communications, Event Planning & Marketing, Media Relations, Public Relations, Social Media

Marina Ein *(Founder & Pres)*

Accounts:
Sprinkles

EISBRENNER PUBLIC RELATIONS
301 W 4th St Ste 301, Royal Oak, MI 48067
Tel.: (248) 554-3500
E-Mail: info@eisbrenner.com
Web Site: www.eisbrenner.com

Employees: 28

Agency Specializes In: Advertising, Brand Development & Integration, Communications, Digital/Interactive, Event Planning & Marketing, Media Relations, Public Relations, Social Media, Sponsorship

Ray Eisbrenner *(Chm)*
Tom Eisbrenner *(Pres)*
Steve Blow *(VP)*
Lisa Litinas *(Office Mgr)*
Jared Bryan *(Acct Supvr)*
Tom Rippinger *(Acct Supvr)*
Katelyn Crain *(Acct Exec)*
Patricia Marion *(Acct Exec)*
Jennifer Biter *(Acct Coord)*

Accounts:
FABTECH
Lightning Hybrids
New-Linamar
Magna International
Michigan Science Center
MSX International
PwC
Robert Bosch LLC
Square One Education Network

ELASTICITY
1101 Lucas Ave Ste 202, Saint Louis, MO 63101
Tel.: (314) 561-8253
E-Mail: hello@goelastic.com
Web Site: www.goelastic.com

Year Founded: 2009

Agency Specializes In: Brand Development & Integration, Content, Crisis Communications, Digital/Interactive, Media Relations, Media Training, Public Relations, Social Media

Andrew Barnett *(Mng Partner & Dir-Digital)*
Mark Sutherland *(Chief Comm Officer)*
Jason Falls *(Sr VP-Digital Strategy)*
Ann Balsamo *(VP-Accts)*
Sam Weigley *(Coord-PR-Elasticity & Head-Global Tribal Councils)*
Emily Ann Brown *(Dir-Media & Analytics)*
Mallory Nezam *(Mgr-Social Media)*

Accounts:
Ballpark Village
CafePress.com, Inc.
Charter Communications
H&R Block
Soft Surroundings
St. Louis County Economic Development Partnership
St. Louis Regional Chamber
Suddenlink
Turtle Beach

ELEMENT-R PARTNERS LLC
28955 W Midway St, Cary, IL 60013
Tel.: (847) 639-8300
Fax: (847) 639-8333
E-Mail: info@rurelevant.com
Web Site: www.rurelevant.com

Agency Specializes In: Advertising, Digital/Interactive, Event Planning & Marketing, Graphic Design, Internet/Web Design, Media Relations, Media Training, Public Relations, Social Media, Strategic Planning/Research

Susan Duensing *(Co-Founder & Partner)*
Bob Reed *(Co-Founder & Partner)*

Accounts:
Capsys Technologies
Covance Laboratories
Innocorp
Integrated Document Technologies Inc
Integrated Project Management Company, Inc.
Nortek Security & Control LLC

ELEVATE INC.
4115 W Spruce St, Tampa, FL 33607
Tel.: (813) 364-4769
E-Mail: info@elevate-inc.com
Web Site: www.elevate-inc.com

Year Founded: 2011

Agency Specializes In: Public Relations, Social Media

Aakash M. Patel *(Founder & Pres)*
Lauren Albert *(Sr Acct Exec)*

Accounts:
New-Trinity Graphic Inc.

ELIZABETH CHRISTIAN PUBLIC RELATIONS
823 Congress Ave Ste 1505, Austin, TX 78701
Tel.: (512) 472-9599
Fax: (512) 472-9699
Web Site: www.echristianpr.com

Agency Specializes In: Brand Development & Integration, Crisis Communications, Event Planning & Marketing, Graphic Design, Media Planning, Media Relations, Public Relations, Social Media, Strategic Planning/Research

Elizabeth Christian *(Pres & CEO)*
Kristin Marcum *(COO)*
Meg Meo *(Sr VP-Acct Mgmt)*
Kathleen Smith *(Sr VP-Bus Affairs)*
Levente McCrary *(VP-Acct Mgmt)*
Erin Ochoa *(VP-Acct Mgmt)*
Katherine Harris *(Sr Acct Exec)*
Lia Pette *(Sr Acct Exec)*
Misty Whited *(Sr Acct Exec)*
Whitney Herrick *(Acct Exec)*
Hannah White *(Acct Exec)*

Accounts:
New-Concordia University
New-Trinity University
New-United Way for Greater Austin

ELLE COMMUNICATIONS
1300 Factory Pl #306, Los Angeles, CA 90013
Tel.: (855) 438-3553
Fax: (858) 876-1992
E-Mail: info@ellecomm.com
Web Site: www.ellecomm.com

Employees: 15
Year Founded: 2008

Agency Specializes In: Crisis Communications, Event Planning & Marketing, Media Relations, Public Relations, Social Media, Strategic Planning/Research

Danielle Gano *(Founder & CEO)*
Emily Aschbrenner *(Mng Partner)*
Jessica McAlister *(Mgr-VIP Rels)*

Accounts:
ESPEROS
MiiR
Parcel & Journey
Raven + Lily
Soko
Sseko Designs

ELLIPSES PUBLIC RELATIONS INC
405 14th St Ste 900, Oakland, CA 94612
Tel.: (510) 735-9667
Web Site: www.ellipsespr.com

Year Founded: 2007

Agency Specializes In: Brand Development & Integration, Event Planning & Marketing, Media Relations, Public Relations, Social Media

Diana G. Haven *(Pres)*
Caitlin Sandberg *(Acct Exec)*

Accounts:
Fog City
Half Moon Bay Brewing Company
La Condesa Napa Valley
Nicks Cove Restaurant
Parallel 37
Urban Putt

EMERGING INSIDER
222 W Merchandise Mart Plz, Chicago, IL 60654
Tel.: (312) 933-5205
Web Site: www.emerginginsider.com

Year Founded: 2013

Agency Specializes In: Brand Development & Integration, Crisis Communications, Public Relations, Social Media, Strategic Planning/Research

Zach Weiner *(CEO)*

Accounts:
iPowow
Iris.TV Public Relations

EMERGING MEDIA PR
(Formerly Lotus Public Relations Inc.)
305 Madison Ave Ste 1050, New York, NY 10165
Tel.: (212) 922-5885
Fax: (212) 656-1206
Web Site: www.emergingmediapr.com

Employees: 6
Year Founded: 2002

Agency Specializes In: Public Relations

Susan Lindner *(Founder & CEO)*
Kayla Lloyd *(Mgr-Internal Mktg & Acct Exec)*

Accounts:
New-Advantages (Agency of Record) Public Relations, Strategic, Thought Leadership
Babbler (Agency of Record) Corporate Communications, Marketing, Media, Public Relations, Strategic Messaging
CatalystWeb
Equitrac Corp. (Agency of Record)
New-iOffice (Agency of Record) Public Relations, Strategic, Thought Leadership
Microgaming
National City
Notegraphy (Agency of Record) Marketing, Media, Public Relations, Strategic, Thought Leadership
Prime Poker
TargetSpot
Xcel Brands, Inc. Communications Agency of Record, Media, Public Relations, Strategic Messaging

EMERSON GERARD ASSOCIATES
5600 N Flagler Dr Ste 601, West Palm Beach, FL 33407
Tel.: (561) 881-7318
Fax: (603) 806-8508
E-Mail: consultation@emersongerard.com
Web Site: www.emersongerard.com

Employees: 6
Year Founded: 1992

Agency Specializes In: Media Buying Services, Media Relations

Gerard M. Jennings *(Founder & Pres)*

Accounts:
Club Entrepreneur
Marine Exploration Inc.

ENC MARKETING & COMMUNICATIONS
1430 Spring Hill Rd Ste 575, McLean, VA 22102
Tel.: (703) 288-1620
Fax: (703) 288-1637
E-Mail: info@encmarketing.com
Web Site: www.encstrategy.com

Employees: 15
Year Founded: 1992

Agency Specializes In: Advertising, Brand Development & Integration, Collateral, Communications, Consulting, Digital/Interactive, Direct Response Marketing, Electronic Media, Event Planning & Marketing, Government/Political, Internet/Web Design, Logo & Package Design, Public Relations, Strategic Planning/Research, Telemarketing

Eva Neumann *(Pres/CEO-ENC Strategy)*
Matthew Arozian *(VP-Strategy & Creative Svcs)*
Julie Craven Brown *(VP)*
Nancy Steelberg *(Acct Dir)*
Sarah Field *(Sr Acct Mgr)*
Beth Johnson *(Mgr-Production)*

Accounts:
AAC
Booz Allen Hamilton
Kforce
Oracle
RedHat
SAIC
Tower Software
Unisys

ENCHANTED PR
2195 Defoors Hill Rd Ste F, Atlanta, GA 30318
Tel.: (678) 499-0297
Web Site: www.enchantedpr.net

Year Founded: 2012

Agency Specializes In: Brand Development & Integration, Event Planning & Marketing, Media Training, Public Relations, Social Media

Christal D. Jordan *(Pres)*
Shantez Evans *(Sr Acct Exec)*
Kassia Ishmael *(Jr Acct Exec)*

Accounts:
Scarzeo

ENGAGE PR
1321 Harbor Bay Pkwy Ste 201, Alameda, CA 94502
Tel.: (510) 748-8200
Fax: (510) 748-8201
E-Mail: info@engagepr.com
Web Site: www.engagepr.com

Employees: 13
Year Founded: 1996

Agency Specializes In: Public Relations

Jeannette Bitz *(Owner & Principal)*
Leslie Johnson *(VP-Accts)*
Marc Davies *(Exec Dir)*
Anna Singman-Aste *(Office Mgr)*
Mike Tomlinson *(Acct Mgr)*
Reno Ybarra *(Acct Mgr)*
Bob Eastwood *(Sr Acct Exec)*
Michael O. Cooper *(Strategist)*

Accounts:
Metaswitch Networks
Open Networking Lab
Open Networking Summit
Opera Software B2B Public Relations
Wichorus

ENGSTROM PUBLIC RELATIONS
14722 102nd Ave NE, Bothell, WA 98011
Tel.: (425) 487-0682
Fax: (425) 939-5286
Web Site: www.engstrompr.com

Employees: 2
Year Founded: 1998

Agency Specializes In: Brand Development & Integration, Media Training, Public Relations, Social Media, Strategic Planning/Research

Cheryl Engstrom *(Pres & Principal)*

Accounts:
Bellevue Square
Dolan Designs
Pendleton Woolen Mills
Washington State Housing Finance Commission

ENROOT PR
3011 Ave N 2nd Fl, Brooklyn, NY 11210
Tel.: (646) 270-6177
Web Site: www.enrootpr.com

Agency Specializes In: Email, Podcasting, Public Relations, Radio, Social Media

Richard Saxe Coulson *(Founder & Pres)*
Aziz Libourki *(Acct Mgr)*

Accounts:
New-The Cube Guys

ENTERTAINMENT FUSION GROUP
6363 Wilshire Blvd Ste 206, Los Angeles, CA 90048
Tel.: (310) 432-0020
Fax: (310) 432-0029
Web Site: www.efgpr.com

Year Founded: 2001

Agency Specializes In: Advertising, Entertainment, Event Planning & Marketing, Guerilla Marketing, Integrated Marketing, Market Research, Media Relations, Mobile Marketing, Product Placement, Public Relations, Publicity/Promotions, Strategic Planning/Research

Peter Philip Wingsoe *(Founder)*

Rembrandt Flores *(Mng Partner)*
Taryn Owens *(Dir-Fashion & Bus Dev)*
Danielle Thur *(Dir-New York Ops)*

Accounts:
Ad.ly (Agency of Record)
Vital Action Water (Agency of Record)

ENVIRONICS COMMUNICATIONS INC.
2000 L St NW Ste 520, Washington, DC 20036
Tel.: (202) 296-2002
Fax: (202) 296-4944
E-Mail: communicate@ecius.net
Web Site: www.environicspr.com

Employees: 68
Year Founded: 1994

Agency Specializes In: Communications, Consumer Marketing, Digital/Interactive, Government/Political, Public Relations

Josh Cobden *(Sr VP-Corp & Fin Svcs)*
Vanessa Eaton *(Sr VP-Health Sciences)*
Mimi Carter *(VP)*
Vanessa Cohen *(VP-Tech)*
Jake Lynn *(VP)*
Greg Maceachern *(VP-Govt Rels)*
Kelly Mack *(VP)*
Robin Shimkovitz *(VP-Consumer)*
Kristen D. Wesley *(VP-Digital Mktg)*
David Groobert *(Gen Mgr-US)*
Jennifer Sherman *(Asst Acct Exec)*

Accounts:
American Chemical Society Green Chemistry Institute Chemical Manufacturer, Formulator's Industry Segment, National PR, Pharmaceutical Awareness
America's Promise Alliance
EBay
Fusion Social, Traditional Marketing
Natural Products Association Media Strategy, Messaging, PR
Northern Virginia Technology Council Public Relations
WE ACT for Environmental Justice PR

EPIC COMMUNICATIONS (PTY) LTD
(Acquired by MSL Group & Name Changed to Epic MSLGROUP)

EPIC PR GROUP
218 N Lee St Ste 206 A, Alexandria, VA 22314
Tel.: (703) 299-3404
E-Mail: info@epicprgroup.com
Web Site: www.epicprgroup.com

Agency Specializes In: Brand Development & Integration, Crisis Communications, Media Training, Public Relations

Adele Gambardella-Cehrs *(CEO)*
Dara Beaulieu *(VP)*
Korenna Cline-Wilson *(VP)*
Giselle-Marie Roig *(Sr Acct Exec)*

Accounts:
New-American Society of Association Executives

EPOCH 5 PUBLIC RELATIONS
755 New York Ave, Huntington, NY 11743
Tel.: (631) 427-1713
Fax: (631) 427-1740
E-Mail: lsinger@epoch5.com
Web Site: www.epoch5.com

Employees: 16

Agency Specializes In: Public Relations

Katherine Heaviside *(Pres)*
Andrew Kraus *(Sr VP-Strategy)*
Lloyd Singer *(Sr VP-Accounts)*
Kathleen Caputi *(VP)*
Audrey Cohen *(Dir)*
Peggy Kalia *(Acct Supvr)*

Accounts:
Bethpage Federal Credit Union
Cablevision Systems Corp.
Island Harvest Branding, Marketing, Public Relations
Salenger, Sack, Schwartz & Kimmel; Woodbury, NY Law Firm; 2007

ERICHO PUBLIC RELATIONS
333 Mamaroneck Ave Ste 222, White Plains, NY 10605
Tel.: (914) 834-2199
Fax: (914) 834-2203
Web Site: erichopr.com

Agency Specializes In: Communications, Crisis Communications, Direct Response Marketing, Event Planning & Marketing, Graphic Design, Media Relations, Promotions, Public Relations

Eric Yaverbaum *(Pres)*
Danielle Nacco *(Acct Dir)*

Accounts:
American Express Gift Cheques
Bell Atlantic
General Cigar
HarperCollins
IKEA Home Furnishings
Juice Energy
Motto Magazine
National Hockey League
Tappening
Trillium Health Products
Zeigler's Apple Cider

ESTES PUBLIC RELATIONS
1938 Frankfort Ave, Louisville, KY 40206
Tel.: (502) 721-0335
Web Site: www.estespr.com

Employees: 9

Agency Specializes In: Crisis Communications, Email, Event Planning & Marketing, Media Relations, Media Training, Promotions, Public Relations

Jamie Estes *(Pres)*
Rachel Goldenberg *(Editor, Mgr-Social Media & Acct Exec)*
Jesse Hendrix-Inman *(Editor & Sr Acct Exec)*
Julie Brooks *(Office Mgr)*
Tammie Franck *(Sr Acct Exec)*
Jaimie Schapker *(Acct Exec-PR)*
Blair Shelby *(Acct Exec)*

EUCALYPT MEDIA
PO Box 6773, Scarborough, ME 04070
Tel.: (207) 749-6814
Web Site: eucalyptmedia.com

Employees: 2
Year Founded: 2007

Agency Specializes In: Business Publications, Collateral, Consumer Publications, Custom Publishing, Digital/Interactive, Direct Response Marketing, Email, Magazines, Newspapers & Magazines, Print, Publishing, Search Engine Optimization, Trade & Consumer Magazines, Viral/Buzz/Word of Mouth

Approx. Annual Billings: $130,000

Jeff Hawkins *(Partner)*
Kathryn Hawkins *(Principal)*

Accounts:
The Atlantic Porsche; 2012
Bizo Targeted Display Marketing Solution; 2011
Goldfarb Center, Colby College; 2013
Husson University; 2010
Instore iPad Point of Sale Solution; 2013
YarcData; 2013

EVANS COMMUNICATIONS
345 E Orange Dr, Phoenix, AZ 85012
Tel.: (602) 448-5483
Fax: (602) 200-9053
Web Site: www.evanscommunications.com

Year Founded: 2003

Agency Specializes In: Communications, Event Planning & Marketing, Graphic Design, Media Buying Services, Media Planning, Media Training, Print, Public Relations

Andrea Tyler Evans *(Principal)*
Mike Saucier *(Specialist-PR)*

Accounts:
American Red Cross-Grand Canyon Chapter
Arizona Latino Research Enterprise
Association for Corporate Growth
ASU Lodestar Center
Avana Capital
Barrett-Jackson Classic Car Auction
Biltmore Preparatory Academy
BioAccel
Childrens Angel Foundation
Desert Island Restaurants
Devereux Arizona
Dr. Andrew Nava
Healthcare Trust of America Inc
Kitchen Sink Studios
Ling & Louies Asian Bar & Grill
Mario E Diaz & Associates
Native American Connections
The Nature Conservancy
OMR Builders & OMR Services
Paradise Valley Unified School District
Paul Dembow for Paradise Valley Town Council
Pearson Digital Education
Phoenix Indian Center
Phoenix Union High School District
Plaza Companies
Scott LeMarr
SkySong The ASU Scottsdale Innovation Center
Tony Rivero for Peoria City Council
Tryst Cafe
Valley Leadership
Valley of the Sun United Way
The Wolff Companies
Your Source Financial

EVERGREEN PR
51 Mount Bethel Rd, Warren, NJ 07059
Tel.: (908) 322-1100
E-Mail: info@evergreenpr.com
Web Site: www.evergreenpr.com

Agency Specializes In: Public Relations

Karen Kessler *(Pres)*
Bob Wilson *(Sr VP-Mdse Sls)*
Andria Lykogiannis *(Office Mgr)*

Accounts:
NJPAC
Paper Mill Playhouse

THE EVIL GENIUS GROUP INC

205 E 42nd St, New York, NY 10017
Tel.: (844) 438-3845
E-Mail: info@evilgenius.nyc
Web Site: www.eggnyc.com

Agency Specializes In: Brand Development & Integration, Event Planning & Marketing, Internet/Web Design, Public Relations, Social Media

Sabatini Toro *(Creative Dir)*

Accounts:
New-Francesco Coli
New-Joseph Wooten

EVINS COMMUNICATIONS, LTD.
635 Madison Ave, New York, NY 10022-1009
Tel.: (212) 688-8200
Fax: (212) 935-6730
E-Mail: info@evins.com
Web Site: www.evins.com

E-Mail for Key Personnel:
President: louise.evins@evins.com

Employees: 45
Year Founded: 1988

Agency Specializes In: Brand Development & Integration, Broadcast, Business Publications, Business-To-Business, Cable T.V., Children's Market, Communications, Consulting, Consumer Marketing, Consumer Publications, Corporate Identity, Cosmetics, Direct Response Marketing, Entertainment, Event Planning & Marketing, Fashion/Apparel, Health Care Services, High Technology, Information Technology, Leisure, Magazines, Merchandising, New Product Development, Newspapers & Magazines, Pharmaceutical, Public Relations, Publicity/Promotions, Restaurant, Retail, Strategic Planning/Research, T.V., Teen Market, Trade & Consumer Magazines, Travel & Tourism

Mathew L. Evins *(Chm)*
Louise Evins *(Vice Chm & COO)*
Elyse Heckman *(VP & Dir-Travel & Hospitality)*
Jaimie Chew *(VP-Lifestyle & Travel)*
Jacqueline Long *(VP)*
Drew Tybus *(VP)*
Mathew Berritt *(Dir-Lifestyle Div)*

Accounts:
Leica Camera
Maker's Mark Bourbon

EVOLUTIONARY MEDIA GROUP
1111 N Las Palmas Ave, Los Angeles, CA 90038
Tel.: (323) 658-8700
Fax: (323) 658-8750
Web Site: www.emgpr.com

Agency Specializes In: Brand Development & Integration, Public Relations

Tiffany Caronia *(VP)*
Alanna Navitski *(Acct Exec)*

Accounts:
New-Studio Collective

EVOLVE COMMUNICATIONS
712 Westover Rd, Baltimore, MD 21208
Tel.: (443) 326-3444
Web Site: www.simplyevolve.com

Year Founded: 2009

Agency Specializes In: Advertising, Content, Media Buying Services, Media Planning, Media Relations, Public Relations, Social Media

Daniel Waldman *(Pres)*

Accounts:
NeedRegistry

EXPEDITION PR
147 Prince St Ste 10, Brooklyn, NY 11201
Tel.: (718) 312-8209
Web Site: www.expeditionpr.com

Year Founded: 2009

Agency Specializes In: Business-To-Business, Corporate Communications, Media Training, Public Relations, Social Media

Katja Schroeder *(Pres)*

Accounts:
Seed & Spark

EXPONENT PR
400 First Ave N Ste 700, Minneapolis, MN 55401
Tel.: (612) 305-6003
Fax: (612) 305-6501
E-Mail: info@exponentpr.com
Web Site: www.exponentpr.com

Employees: 25
Year Founded: 2005

Agency Specializes In: Brand Development & Integration, Digital/Interactive, Media Relations, Public Relations, Social Media

Tom Lindell *(Mng Dir)*
Mike Caguin *(Chief Creative Officer)*
Annie Dubsky *(Acct Dir)*
Rebecca Lunna *(Acct Dir)*
Ed Bennett *(Dir-Design)*
Steve Bailey *(Acct Supvr)*
Caroline Geiser *(Acct Supvr)*
Allison Heilman *(Acct Supvr)*
Seth Hendricks *(Acct Supvr)*
John Poferl *(Acct Supvr)*
Lia Sherman *(Acct Supvr-PR)*
Eliza Casper *(Acct Exec)*

Accounts:
Aveda
Caribou Coffee Event Marketing, Media Relations, PR
Cenex
CHS
Duluth Trading Company Brand Communications, Media Relations, Special Events
KINKY Liqueur Brand Awareness, Media Relations, Social Media
Medtronic Foundation
Nestle Purina
The North American Olive Oil Association
Novartis
Novartis Animal Health
Terra Delyssa Olive Oil
The University of Nebraska Robert B. Daugherty Water for Food Institute
Winfield Solutions
Wolfgang Puck

EXPOSED PR & EVENTS LLC
901 Progresso Dr, Fort Lauderdale, FL 33304
Tel.: (954) 900-3691
Web Site: www.exposedprandevents.com

Year Founded: 2010

Agency Specializes In: Advertising, Event Planning & Marketing, Media Relations, Public Relations

Sara Shake *(Principal)*
Kori Sumner *(Dir-Ops)*

Accounts:
Culinary Related Entertainment & Marketing
Rok:Brgr Burger Bar + Gastropub

FAISS FOLEY WARREN
100 N City Pkwy Ste 750, Las Vegas, NV 89106
Tel.: (702) 933-7777
Fax: (702) 933-1261
Web Site: www.ffwpr.vegas

Employees: 11
Year Founded: 1990

National Agency Associations: PRSA

Agency Specializes In: Government/Political, Public Relations

Linda Faiss *(Pres)*
Karen Griffin *(VP-Pub Affairs)*
Daniella Cortez Alvarez *(Mgr-PR & Social Media)*
Mckinzie A. Cogswell *(Sr Acct Exec-PR)*
Amy Spanbauer Maier *(Sr Acct Exec-PR)*
Lisa Robinson *(Sr Acct Exec)*
Susan Black-Manriquez *(Acct Exec)*

Accounts:
Cox Communications
International Academy of Design and Technology
Pardee Homes
Southern Nevada Water Authority

FALK ASSOCIATES
1120 W Belmont, Chicago, IL 60657
Tel.: (773) 883-2580
Fax: (773) 975-1999
E-Mail: contact@falkpr.com
Web Site: www.falkpr.com

Agency Specializes In: Event Planning & Marketing, Media Relations, Promotions, Public Relations, Social Media

Amy Falk *(Pres)*
Rochelle Falk *(Dir-Mktg & Client Rels)*

Accounts:
New Moms Inc

FALLON THATCHER
424 Findlay St, Cincinnati, OH 45202
Tel.: (513) 621-7676
E-Mail: hello@fallonthatcher.com
Web Site: www.fallonthatcher.com

Agency Specializes In: Brand Development & Integration, Digital/Interactive, Event Planning & Marketing, Print, Public Relations

Micah Paldino *(CEO)*

Accounts:
New-FRCH Design Worldwide
New-Sundry & Vice

FALLS COMMUNICATIONS
50 Public Sq 25th Fl, Cleveland, OH 44113
Tel.: (216) 696-0229
Fax: (216) 696-0269
Web Site: www.fallscommunications.com

E-Mail for Key Personnel:
President: rfalls@robertfalls.com
Creative Dir.: slesko@robertfalls.com

Employees: 30
Year Founded: 1989

National Agency Associations: PRSA

Agency Specializes In: Collateral, Communications, Consumer Marketing, Corporate Identity, Exhibit/Trade Shows, Financial, Government/Political, Graphic Design, Investor Relations, Logo & Package Design, Media Relations, Multimedia, New Product Development, Planning & Consultation, Public Relations, Sports Market, Strategic Planning/Research

Robert F. Falls *(Pres & CEO)*
Robert G. Berick *(Mng Dir & Sr VP)*
Brian Bloom *(Sr VP & Dir-New Bus Dev)*
Jennifer Allanson *(Sr VP)*
Julie Brosien *(Sr VP)*
Chris Lynch *(Sr VP)*
Eileen J. Petridis *(Sr VP)*
Jordan Testerman *(Sr Acct Supvr)*
Jamie Dalton *(Acct Supvr)*
Keith Mabee *(Grp Pres-Corp Comm & IR)*

Accounts:
Arthritis Foundation
Ave Maria University
The Bingham
Calfee
Carl Marks Advisory Group, LLC
Community Care Network
Creative Specialties International
Dutch Boy
Easy 2 Technologies
Emerald Performance Materials LLC
Fabri-Form Inc.
FSM Capital Management
Garfield-Traub Development LLC
The Gates Group
GE Consumer Appliance
The Gunlocke Co.
H & C Stains
Hartland & Co.
The HON Company
Hylant Group; Toledo, OH
Kipling Jones & Co.
L'Albatros
The Lincoln Electric Co.
Lubrizol
New-Mace Security International, Inc. (Communications Agency of Record) Investor Relations
Mark-My-Time
Moen Incorporated
MTD Products
National City; Cleveland, OH
Northwood University
Parafllax
Renewal Biodiesel Fuels Inc.
Revol Wireless
Sherwin-Williams Automotive Finishes Corp.
Sisters of Charity of St. Augustine Health System
St. John West Shore Hospital
Table 45
Tarkett Residential
Templar Tactical
Vocon Inc.

FAMA PR, INC.

Liberty Wharf 250 Northern Ave Ste 300, Boston, MA 02110
Toll Free: (866) 326-2552
E-Mail: info@famapr.com
Web Site: www.famapr.com

Year Founded: 2002

Agency Specializes In: Public Relations

Approx. Annual Billings: $4,000,000

Breakdown of Gross Billings by Media: Pub. Rels.: 100%

Matt Flanagan *(Co-Founder & Partner)*
Keith Watson *(Co-Founder & Partner)*
Ed Harrison *(Mng Partner)*
Gail Scibelli *(Sr VP)*
Ted Weismann *(Sr VP)*
Whitney Parker *(VP)*
Kate Thermansen *(VP)*
Alex Howe *(Acct Dir)*
Erik Milster *(Acct Dir)*
Chrissy Kinch *(Acct Mgr)*
Caitlin Mattingly *(Acct Mgr)*

Accounts:
Allurent
BluePort
boSox Club
Cashstar
Courion
Covergence
CyberArk
Dining In
Imprivata, Inc
ITA Software
matchmine
New England Clear Energy Council
Organic
Ping Identity Corporation
QuickPlay Media
Sedo
ShopAdvisor
Symphony Metreo
Triad Retail Media; Tampa, FL
Trialpay
Veracode
VidSys

FARRAR PUBLIC RELATIONS, INC.

5924 Forrest Ln, Fort Worth, TX 76112-1043
Tel.: (817) 937-1557
E-Mail: nancyfarrar@att.net

Employees: 1
Year Founded: 1999

Nancy Farrar *(Owner)*

FAULHABER COMMUNICATIONS

666 Greenwich St Ste 821, New York, NY 10014
Tel.: (917) 434-6576
E-Mail: usa@faulhabercommunications.com
Web Site: www.faulhabercommunications.com

Agency Specializes In: Digital/Interactive, Event Planning & Marketing, Public Relations, Social Media

Christine Faulhaber *(Pres & CEO)*
Patricia Amato *(Acct Mgr)*
Sarah Leone *(Sr Acct Exec)*
Megan Taylor *(Acct Exec)*

Accounts:
New-Bacardi
New-Dermalogica
New-National Bank
New-Ted Baker

FAYE CLACK COMMUNICATIONS INC.

108a Royal York Road, Toronto, ON M8V 2V1 Canada
Tel.: (416) 255-6879
E-Mail: info@fayeclack.com
Web Site: www.fayeclack.com

Employees: 20
Year Founded: 1978

Agency Specializes In: Agriculture, Bilingual Market, Brand Development & Integration, Business-To-Business, Co-op Advertising, Communications, Consulting, Consumer Marketing, Event Planning & Marketing, Exhibit/Trade Shows, Food Service, In-Store Advertising, Merchandising, Point of Purchase, Point of Sale, Public Relations, Publicity/Promotions, Restaurant, Retail, Strategic Planning/Research

Approx. Annual Billings: $2,500,000

Virginia Zimm *(Pres)*
Pereina Choudhury *(Acct Dir)*
Susan Sansom *(Office Mgr)*

Accounts:
California Department of Agriculture
California Walnut Commission
Canola Council
Foreign Agricultural Service; Canada Agri-Food Products; 1999
National Watermelon Promotional Board; Canada; 2004
Ontario Apple Growers
Ontario Red Tart Cherries
Ontario Tender Fruit Producers' Marketing Board Grapes, Peaches, Pears, Plums, Sweet/Sour Cherries; 1978
Stonemill Bakehouse
Trade Commission of Spain
USA Rice Federation; Canada; 1997

THE FEAREY GROUP

1809 7th Ave Ste 1111, Seattle, WA 98101
Tel.: (206) 343-1543
Fax: (206) 622-5694
E-Mail: tfg@feareygroup.com
Web Site: www.feareygroup.com

Employees: 15
Year Founded: 1981

National Agency Associations: PRSA

Agency Specializes In: Government/Political, Industrial, Public Relations

Aaron Blank *(Pres & CEO)*
Chris Nettles *(Chief Admin Officer)*
Laura Ray *(Sr VP)*
Nandi Thorn *(Dir-Health & Life Sciences)*
Heather Fernandez *(Acct Supvr)*
Amy Snow Landa *(Acct Supvr)*

Accounts:
Allen Institute for Brain Science
Arthritis Foundation
The Landing
Safeway
Sleep Medicine Associates
Swedish Medical Center
TalkingRain Sparkling Ice
Teragren
Thornton Place
UnitedHealthcare
Urban Land Institute
Virginia Mason
Vulcan Inc.

FEED MEDIA PUBLIC RELATIONS

7807 E 24th Ave, Denver, CO 80238
Tel.: (303) 388-8460
E-Mail: contact@feedmedia.com
Web Site: www.feedmedia.com

Year Founded: 2002

Agency Specializes In: Crisis Communications, Guerilla Marketing, Media Relations, Media Training, Public Relations, Social Media

Stefanie Jones *(Founder & Pres)*
Derek Jones *(Founder & COO)*

Accounts:

New-OZ Architecture

FEINTUCH COMMUNICATIONS

245 Park Ave 39th Fl, New York, NY 10167
Tel.: (212) 808-4900
Fax: (212) 808-4915
E-Mail: info@feintuchpr.com
Web Site: www.feintuchcommunications.com

Year Founded: 2009

Agency Specializes In: Corporate Identity, Event Planning & Marketing, Exhibit/Trade Shows, Graphic Design, Investor Relations, Media Relations, Media Training, Product Placement, Public Relations, Strategic Planning/Research

Henry Feintuch *(Founder & Pres)*
Scott Gordon *(Mng Dir)*
Bennie Sham *(Acct Dir)*
Emily Simmons *(Acct Dir)*
Darby Fledderjohn *(Acct Exec)*
Alex Feintuch *(Asst Acct Exec)*

Accounts:
Antel Communications (Agency of Record) Public Relations
New-Blue Fountain Media Public Relations
New-ChargeItSpot Consumer Public Relations
Convene
Dobleas PR
Glebar Company (Public Relations Agency of Record)
Global Systems Integration Marketing, PR
GSI, Inc. Marketing, PR
Hanger Network Green Marketing Services
Internet Advertising Institute (Agency of Record) Web Based Education & Training Portal
Kenaz Translations (Agency of Record) Corporate Website, Media Relations
LDR PR
LifeThreads LLC (Agency of Record) Communications
Maxine Morgan Eyewear (Agency of Record)
MIIAtech Marketing & Public Relations Campaign
Optimal Payments Public Relations
Provide Support, LLC; New York, NY PR & Marketing
Smartclip LLC.
SmrtGuard (Agency of Record) Strategic Communications Campaign
Synthesis Energy Systems, Inc. Public Relations
TheMediaDash.com, Inc.; Westport, CT Media, Strategic Communications

THE FERRARO GROUP

9516 W Flamingo Rd Ste 310, Las Vegas, NV 89147
Tel.: (702) 367-7771
Fax: (702) 367-7773
Web Site: www.theferrarogroup.com/

Employees: 10

Agency Specializes In: Public Relations

Greg Ferraro *(Founder & Pres)*
Barbara Smith Campbell *(Principal)*
Robert Ostrovsky *(Principal)*
Jared Austin *(Mgr-Social Media)*
Nicole Willis-Grimes *(Mgr-Pub Policy)*
Laura Carroll *(Acct Exec & Writer)*
Amanda Llewellyn *(Acct Exec-PR)*
Raquel Sanchez *(Acct Exec-PR & Social Media)*

Accounts:
Crazy Pita Rotisserie & Grill (Agency of Record) Marketing, Media Communications, Public Relations, Social Media
Grand Canyon Development Partners
JPMorgan Chase
New-Western Governors University (Agency of Record)

FETCH PR

1250 W Augusta Blvd 1st Fl, Chicago, IL 60642
Tel.: (312) 554-5023
Web Site: www.fetch-pr.com

Agency Specializes In: Brand Development & Integration, Event Planning & Marketing, Media Training, Public Relations, Social Media

Lina Khalil *(CEO)*
Veronica Feldmeier *(Acct Exec)*

Accounts:
New-Academy for Urban School Leadership

FETCHING COMMUNICATIONS

PO Box 222, Tarpon Springs, FL 34688
Tel.: (877) 703-3824
Fax: (888) 537-3564
E-Mail: hello@fetchingcommunications.com
Web Site: www.fetchingcommunications.com

Year Founded: 2003

Agency Specializes In: Brand Development & Integration, Business-To-Business, Exhibit/Trade Shows, Internet/Web Design, Promotions, Public Relations, Search Engine Optimization, Social Media, Strategic Planning/Research

Kristen Levine *(Founder & Pres)*
Liz Bard Lindley *(CEO)*
Lisa Thomas *(Dir-Ops)*
Shannon Stevens *(Acct Mgr)*
Meredith Schneider *(Assoc Client Svc Dir & Mgr)*

Accounts:
Amazing Pet Expos
Applebrook Animal Hospital
Bark Busters Home Dog Training
Calico Group
Charleston Veterinary Referral Center
CheapPetDrugs.com PR, Social Media, Website design
Day by Day Pet Caregiver Support Public Relations, Social Media, Strategic Positioning
DOGTV
Emergency Animal Clinic of Arizona Public Relations, Social Media, Strategic Positioning
Farewell Products Farewell Pet Kit, Press Kit
John Paul Pet Media Relations
K9 Fit Club
The Language of Dogs Media, Social Media
NutralifePet Blogger Outreach, SAMe, Social Media
Pet Dental Services
Pet Sitters International Media Relations
PetHub, Inc
PetSafe Public Relations, Social Media, Website Design
PETSYNC Education Services Public Relations, Social Media, Website Design
Reach-in Technologies iPet Companion
New-Veterinary Practice Partners
New-VetSpecialists.com
New-Voyce Pro
Waggers, Inc. Waggers' TenderMoist Cat Food
Washington Laight Business Solutions, LLC Brochure Design, Consulting, Public Relations, Writing
Women in the Pet Industry Network
New-Yabozi Products, LLC

FINEMAN PR

150 Post St Ste 620, San Francisco, CA 94108
Tel.: (415) 392-1000
Fax: (415) 392-1099
E-Mail: mfineman@finemanpr.com
Web Site: www.finemanpr.com

E-Mail for Key Personnel:
President: mfineman@finemanpr.com
Creative Dir.: mfineman@finemanpr.com

Employees: 15
Year Founded: 1988

Agency Specializes In: Agriculture, Bilingual Market, Communications, Consumer Goods, Consumer Marketing, Corporate Communications, Crisis Communications, Education, Engineering, Hispanic Market, Local Marketing, Media Relations, Media Training, Multicultural, Public Relations, Publicity/Promotions, Sponsorship, Strategic Planning/Research

Breakdown of Gross Billings by Media: Pub. Rels.: 100%

Michael B. Fineman *(Pres & Dir-Creative)*
Lorna Bush *(Sr VP)*
Travis Taylor *(VP)*
Heidi White *(VP)*
Karmina Zafiro *(VP)*
Serene Buckley *(Sr Dir-Content Strategy)*
Juan Lezama *(Dir-Latino & Multicultural Div)*

Accounts:
American Humane Association
Athletic Heart of San Francisco Sports Cardiology Practice
Autism Research Institute Autism is Treatable, Media Outreach
Fabric Restoration Service Team
Faust Winery
Foster Farms Events Support, Public Relations
Guckenheimer; Redwood City, CA Brand Awareness, Media Relations
New-HealthRIGHT 360 Public Awareness
HNTB Corporation B2B
KonaRed
Lynmar Estate Culinary Offerings, Estate, Wine
Mission Economic Development Agency
National Marine Manufacturers Association 2015 Progressive Insurance San Francisco Boat Show
Olympus Calistoga LLC Issues Management
The Pacific Companies Marketing, Messaging
New-Pro Ecuador Media
Quintessa wines Brand Awareness, Media Relations
New-Renteria Wines Brand Message
Roadhouse Winery Brand Development, Traffic-Building
The San Francisco Marathon
Spelletich Family Winery Brand Awareness, Media Relations
Truchard Vineyards Brand Awareness, Media Relations
UC Hastings College of Law Issues Management
New-Zaca Mesa

FINGERPRINT

1925 Century Pk E, Los Angeles, CA 90067
Tel.: (310) 276-7500
Fax: (310) 276-7965
E-Mail: info@fingerprintcommunications.net
Web Site: www.fingerprintcom.net

Agency Specializes In: Event Planning & Marketing, Public Relations, Social Media

Jessica Meisels *(Pres & CEO)*
Rica Hermosura *(Sr Acct Exec)*
Alexandra Sclavos *(Acct Exec)*

Accounts:
New-Ryka
New-Sears

FINSBURY

(Formerly RLM Finsbury)

1345 Ave of the Americas, New York, NY 10105
Tel.: (646) 805-2000
E-Mail: enquiries@finsbury.com
Web Site: www.finsbury.com/

Agency Specializes In: Crisis Communications, Investor Relations, Public Relations

Roland Rudd *(Chm)*
Stephen Labaton *(Pres & Partner)*
Michael Gross *(CEO & Partner)*
Paul Holmes *(Partner & Mng Partner-New York)*
Kal Goldberg *(Partner)*
Peter Land *(Partner)*
Walter Montgomery *(Partner)*
Deborah Solomon *(Principal)*
Ned Potter *(Sr VP)*

Accounts:
AppNexus
Independence Bancshares, Inc. Media
International Enterprise Singapore Marketing Communications, Online, Public Relations, Social Media

THE FIRM PUBLIC RELATIONS & MARKETING
6157 S Rainbow Blvd, Las Vegas, NV 89118
Tel.: (702) 739-9933
Fax: (702) 739-9779
E-Mail: thefirm@thefirmpr.com
Web Site: www.thefirmpr.com

Employees: 10
Year Founded: 1993

National Agency Associations: PRSA

Agency Specializes In: Event Planning & Marketing, Health Care Services, Luxury Products, Media Relations, Media Training, Public Relations, Retail, Social Media, Sponsorship, Travel & Tourism

Jasen Woehrle *(Sr VP)*
Jesse Scott *(Sr Specialist-PR)*
Annie Waggoner *(Asst Specialist-PR)*

Accounts:
Bally Technologies PR
Comprehensive Cancer Centers of Nevada
Global Gaming Expo (G2E)
NVPR Nevada Public Radio Corp.; Las Vegas, NV
Southern Nevada Health & Immunization Coalition
Treasure Island

FIRST COMMUNICATION GROUP INC.
1995 Tiffin Ave Ste 307, Findlay, OH 45839-0866
Mailing Address:
PO Box 866, Findlay, OH 45839-0866
Tel.: (419) 422-3646
Fax: (419) 422-3869
E-Mail: frstgroup@aol.com
Web Site: www.firstgrp.com

E-Mail for Key Personnel:
President: jlittlfcg@aol.com

Employees: 8
Year Founded: 1995

Agency Specializes In: Aviation & Aerospace, Brand Development & Integration, Business Publications, Business-To-Business, Commercial Photography, Communications, Consulting, Consumer Marketing, Consumer Publications, Corporate Identity, Direct Response Marketing, E-Commerce, Event Planning & Marketing, Financial, Graphic Design, Health Care Services, Industrial, Internet/Web Design, Investor Relations, Logo & Package Design, Media Buying Services, Medical Products, New Product Development, Planning & Consultation, Print, Public Relations, Publicity/Promotions, Sales Promotion, Strategic Planning/Research

Approx. Annual Billings: $600,000

Breakdown of Gross Billings by Media: Bus. Publs.: 2%; Comml. Photography: 5%; Consulting: 10%; Fees: 5%; Graphic Design: 15%; Logo & Package Design: 5%; Newsp. & Mags.: 10%; Print: 10%; Pub. Rels.: 15%; Worldwide Web Sites: 23%

James A. Little *(Pres-First Grp)*
Carol Little *(VP)*

Accounts:
Light Sport America
National Lime & Stone Co.; Findlay, OH Quarrying
Ohio Logistics; Findlay, OH Warehousing; 2002

FISCHTANK
125 Maiden Ln Ste 210, New York, NY 10038
Tel.: (646) 699-1414
E-Mail: info@fischtankpr.com
Web Site: www.fischtankpr.com

Agency Specializes In: Advertising, Graphic Design, Public Relations, Search Engine Optimization

Matt Bretzius *(VP)*

Accounts:
New-3DIcon
New-SITO Mobile
New-Zoomph

FISHMAN PUBLIC RELATIONS
3400 Dundee Rd.Ste. 300, Northbrook, IL 60062
Tel.: (847) 945-1300
Fax: (847) 945-3755
E-Mail: sfish@fishmanpr.com
Web Site: www.fishmanpr.com

Employees: 19

Agency Specializes In: Public Relations, Sponsorship

Brad Fishman *(CEO)*
Debra Vilchis *(COO)*
Sara Faiwell *(VP)*
Kelly McNamara *(Acct Mgr)*
Lindsey Warriner *(Acct Mgr)*
Rebecca Daniel *(Sr Acct Exec)*
Doris Obranovic *(Acct Exec)*

Accounts:
New-Complete Nutrition
New-Corner Bakery Cafe Public Relations

FITZ & CO
423 W 14th St 429-2F, New York, NY 10014
Tel.: (212) 627-1455
Fax: (212) 627-0654
E-Mail: artpr@fitzandco.com
Web Site: www.fitzandco.com

Year Founded: 1995

Agency Specializes In: Brand Development & Integration, Event Planning & Marketing, Media Relations, Public Relations, Social Media

Sara Fitzmaurice *(Pres)*
Rebecca Taylor *(Exec VP)*
Jennifer Isakowitz *(Sr Acct Exec)*
Liza Eliano *(Acct Exec)*

Accounts:
New-Storm King Art Center

FLACKABLE LLC
100 N Pk Rd Ste 1235, Wyomissing, PA 19610
Tel.: (215) 429-8569
Web Site: www.flackable.com

Agency Specializes In: Brand Development & Integration, Content, Media Relations, Media Training, Public Relations, Search Engine Optimization, Social Media, Strategic Planning/Research

Brian Hart *(Founder & Pres)*
Hailey Lanier *(Acct Exec)*
Alexa Miller *(Acct Exec)*

Accounts:
New-Chapman Associates
New-Chris Markowski
New-Equity Concepts (Integrated Communications Agency of Record) Content Strategy, Media Relations
New-Local Life Agents (Integrated Communications Agency of Record) Content Strategy, Media Relations
Vesticor Advisors (Integrated Communications Agency of Record) Brand Marketing, Digital Strategy, Media Relations, Public Relations

FLASHPOINT PUBLIC RELATIONS, LLC
2475 3rd St Ste 253, San Francisco, CA 94107
Tel.: (415) 551-9620
E-Mail: info@flashpointpr.com
Web Site: www.flashpointpr.com

Year Founded: 2005

Agency Specializes In: Media Relations, Public Relations, Social Media, Sponsorship

Christopher Downing *(Owner & Principal)*
Jennifer Colton *(Principal)*
Clint Bagley *(VP)*
Karen Nolan *(Acct Dir)*
Leah Barash *(Acct Supvr)*
Kelly Hickman *(Acct Supvr)*
Ashley Edwards *(Sr Strategist-Media)*
Kelsey Johnson *(Acct Exec)*
Sasha Litvakov *(Acct Exec)*
Shelby Quickstad *(Acct Coord)*

Accounts:
Looxcie
Shutterfly, Inc.
Solar Components Corp.

FLAVOR PUBLIC RELATIONS
PO Box 10789, Chicago, IL 60610
Tel.: (312) 833-7947
Web Site: www.flavorpublicrelations.com

Year Founded: 2011

Agency Specializes In: Event Planning & Marketing, Media Relations, Print, Public Relations, Radio, Social Media

Andrea Rodriguez *(Owner)*

Accounts:
Film Festival Flix
Sara Chana
Sure Couture

FLEISHMAN-HILLARD INC.
200 N Broadway, Saint Louis, MO 63102-2730
Tel.: (314) 982-1700
Fax: (314) 982-0586
Web Site: fleishmanhillard.com/

Year Founded: 1946

Public Relations Firms

National Agency Associations: COPF

Agency Specializes In: Above-the-Line, Advertising, Advertising Specialties, African-American Market, Agriculture, Alternative Advertising, Arts, Asian Market, Bilingual Market, Brand Development & Integration, Branded Entertainment, Business-To-Business, Communications, Consumer Marketing, Content, Corporate Communications, Corporate Identity, Crisis Communications, Customer Relationship Management, Digital/Interactive, Direct-to-Consumer, Education, Electronic Media, Entertainment, Environmental, Event Planning & Marketing, Experience Design, Fashion/Apparel, Financial, Food Service, Gay & Lesbian Market, Government/Political, Graphic Design, Health Care Services, High Technology, Hispanic Market, Identity Marketing, Infomercials, Information Technology, Integrated Marketing, International, Internet/Web Design, Investor Relations, Legal Services, Leisure, Logo & Package Design, Marine, Market Research, Media Planning, Media Relations, Media Training, Medical Products, Mobile Marketing, Multicultural, Multimedia, New Product Development, Newspaper, Newspapers & Magazines, Over-50 Market, Pharmaceutical, Planning & Consultation, Point of Purchase, Product Placement, Production (Ad, Film, Broadcast), Production (Print), Public Relations, Publicity/Promotions, Radio, Regional, Sales Promotion, Seniors' Market, Social Marketing/Nonprofit, South Asian Market, Sponsorship, Sports Market, Strategic Planning/Research, Sweepstakes, T.V., Teen Market, Telemarketing, Trade & Consumer Magazines, Transportation, Travel & Tourism, Viral/Buzz/Word of Mouth, Women's Market, Yellow Pages Advertising

John D. Graham *(Chm)*
John Saunders *(Pres & CEO)*
Danielle Hurtt *(Partner, Sr VP & Dir-Mktg)*
Kristen Whipple *(Sr VP & Partner)*
Marianna Deal *(Mng Dir)*
Fred Rohlfing *(CFO, Sr Partner & Exec VP)*
Jonella Donius *(CIO & Exec VP)*
Shawn Amos *(Chief Content Innovation Officer-Americas)*
Janise Murphy *(Pres-US South & Sr Partner)*
Jim Mayfield *(Sr VP & Grp Dir-Creative)*
Tim Beecher *(Sr Partner & Sr VP)*
Jeff Davis *(Sr Partner & Sr VP)*
Marla Dicandia *(Sr Partner & Sr VP)*
Cara Elsas *(Sr Partner & Sr VP)*
Terry Hoffmann *(Sr VP)*
Lynn Oppelt *(Sr Partner & Sr VP)*
Mark Polzin *(Sr Partner & Sr VP)*
Marty Richter *(Sr VP)*
Jenny Vatterott *(VP & Dir-Production)*
Lisa Hanly *(VP)*
Chris Ward *(VP)*
Bill Power *(Head-Global Practice-Brand Mktg)*
Tom Hudder *(Sr Partner & Exec Creative Dir)*
Joyce Fogerty *(Dir & Mgr-Facilities)*
Amanda Abukhader *(Sr Acct Exec)*
Ana-Maria Echenique *(Sr Acct Exec)*
Molly Hulsey *(Sr Acct Exec)*
Amanda Rast *(Sr Acct Exec)*
Nichole Hamilton *(Acct Exec)*

Accounts:
3M
Abbott Laboratories Hepatitis C, PR
Admongo
The Allstate Foundation Campaign: "Purple Purse"
American Cruise Lines
American Petroleum Institute
AT&T Communications Corp. Campaign: "Journey to Better Health"
Avaya Content
Blue Cross & Blue Shield of Minnesota Campaign: "The Human Do.Ing"
BMW of North America
Boy Scouts of America (Agency of Record) Campaign: "Build an Adventure", Campaign: "Rocketman", Digital, Hispanic Youth, Marketing, PSA, Print, Social Media
Buffalo Wild Wings; Minneapolis, MN Public Relations
Butterball, LLC Child Hunger In America
Chobani PR
Citi Campaign: "Private Pass"
New-Crocs, Inc. (Global Public Relations Agency of Record)
The Emma L. Bowen Foundation (Agency of Record) Content, Digital Media Strategy, Public Relations, Social Media Strategy
Energizer Campaign: "The Battery Controlled"
Enterprise
Federal Trade Commission
Gander Mountain Public Relations, Social Media
Gatorade Campaign: "Inside Endurance"
General Motors Cadillac, Chevrolet, Public Relations, Strategic Communications
Great Wolf Resorts
Hallmark
Lenovo Group Limited
Papa John's International National Pizza Chain
Pepsico
Procter & Gamble Tide
Response Genetics, Inc.
Russell Hobbs, Inc.
Select Comfort Corporation Sleep Number (PR Agency of Record)
Three Forks Ranch
Tyson Foods Crisis Communications
UN Foundation Rio+Social

United States

Fleishman-Hillard Inc.

4 Studebaker, Irvine, CA 92618
Tel.: (949) 855-5997
Web Site: fleishmanhillard.com/

Geoff Mordock *(Partner & Sr VP)*
Ryan Peal *(Sr Partner, Sr VP & Gen Mgr)*
David Goldman *(Sr VP-Brand Mktg)*
Chris Ward *(VP)*
Anne Leverdier *(Acct Supvr)*

Paul Wilmot Communications

581 Sixth Ave, New York, NY 10011
Tel.: (212) 206-7447
Fax: (212) 206-7557
E-Mail: pwc@paulwilmot.com
Web Site: www.paulwilmot.com

Agency Specializes In: Public Relations

Accounts:
Alexandra Clancy
Anastasia
Bionda Castana
Cache
Cacique
David Stark
Elie Saab
Estee Lauder
eva mendes
Galet
H&M
Hublot
Iman
Jack Spade
Jane
Kate Spade
Ken Paves
Kilian
Lane Bryant
Liebeskind
L.K.Bennett
MAC
Natori
Parmigiani
Perricone MD
Pitbull
SarastoryDesign
SeanJohn
Sequence
Timo Weiland
True Religion
Vanidades
Vans
yummie
Yves Delorme

Fleishman-Hillard Inc.

525 B St Ste 700, San Diego, CA 92101-4477
Tel.: (619) 237-7700
Fax: (619) 235-9994
E-Mail: della.sweetman@fleishman.com
Web Site: fleishmanhillard.com/

Employees: 20

National Agency Associations: COPF

Agency Specializes In: Communications

Susan Veidt *(Pres-US Central Reg & Gen Mgr-St. Louis Office)*
Janise Murphy *(Pres-US South & Sr Partner)*
Shin Tanaka *(Pres-Japan & Sr Partner)*
Rachel Catanach *(Sr VP & Mng Dir-Hong Kong)*
Della Sweetman *(Sr Partner & Sr VP-Bus Dev-Americas)*
Stephanie Twining *(Acct Supvr)*
Mark Larson *(Sr Acct Exec)*
Julie Rizio *(Sr Acct Exec)*
Yusuf Hatia *(Reg Head)*
Brittany Rawlings *(Mng Supvr)*
Joanne Wong *(Reg Head)*

Fleishman-Hillard Inc.

500 Capitol Mall, Sacramento, CA 95814
Tel.: (916) 441-7606
Fax: (916) 441-7622
E-Mail: dan.barber@fleishman.com
Web Site: fleishmanhillard.com/

Employees: 18

National Agency Associations: COPF

Agency Specializes In: Communications, Public Relations

Yusuf Hatia *(Mng Dir)*
Yvonne Park *(Mng Dir)*
Joanne Wong *(Mng Dir)*
Shin Tanaka *(Pres-Japan & Sr Partner)*
Rachel Catanach *(Sr VP & Mng Dir-Hong Kong)*
Dan Barber *(Sr Partner, Sr VP & Gen Mgr)*
Kim Bedwell *(Sr VP)*

Fleishman-Hillard Inc.

555 Market St 20th Fl, San Francisco, CA 94105
Tel.: (415) 318-4000
Fax: (415) 318-4010
E-Mail: larry.kamer@fleishman.com
Web Site: fleishmanhillard.com

Employees: 50

National Agency Associations: COPF

Agency Specializes In: Communications, Public Relations, Sponsorship

J.J. Carter *(Pres & Sr Partner-US West, Canada & Mexico)*
Pete Hillan *(Sr Partner & Sr VP)*
Catherine Topping *(VP)*
Caitlin Garlow *(Acct Supvr)*

Joshua Luebke *(Acct Supvr)*
Tala Esguerra Chmiel *(Sr Acct Exec)*
Genna Young *(Sr Acct Exec)*
Casey Brennan *(Mng Supvr-Corp Responsibility & Global Impact)*
Tim O'Keeffe *(Mng Supvr)*

Accounts:
AT&T, Inc.
EA Sports Campaign: "Support Madden NFL 12"
Hispanic Scholarship Fund
Visa

Fleishman-Hillard Inc.
4745 Alla Rd, Marina Del Rey, CA 90292-6311
Tel.: (310) 482-4270
Fax: (310) 482-4271
E-Mail: mary.yousef@fleishman.com
Web Site: fleishmanhillard.com/

Employees: 15

National Agency Associations: COPF

Agency Specializes In: Communications, Sponsorship

Yusuf Hatia *(Mng Dir)*
Yvonne Park *(Mng Dir)*
Joanne Wong *(Mng Dir)*
Shin Tanaka *(Pres-Japan & Sr Partner)*
Rachel Catanach *(Sr VP & Mng Dir-Hong Kong)*
Marc Enger *(Sr VP-Integrated Comm)*
Della Sweetman *(Sr Partner & Sr VP-Bus Dev Americas)*
Jamie Douglas *(Acct Exec)*

Accounts:
YWCA of the USA

Fleishman-Hillard Inc.
2800 Ponce de Leon Blvd Ste 1400, Coral Gables, FL 33134-5202
Tel.: (305) 520-2000
Fax: (305) 520-2001
Web Site: fleishmanhillard.com/

Employees: 20

Agency Specializes In: Communications, Public Relations

Dario Cutin *(Partner, Sr VP & Mng Dir-Client Svcs Latin America)*
Susan Veidt *(Pres-US Central Reg & Gen Mgr-St. Louis Office)*
Janise Murphy *(Pres-US South & Sr Partner)*
Shin Tanaka *(Pres-Japan & Sr Partner)*
Rachel Catanach *(Sr VP & Mng Dir-Hong Kong)*
Isabel Abislaiman *(Sr VP)*
Patricia Alvarado *(Sr VP)*
Jorge Diaz de Villegas *(Sr Partner & Sr VP)*
Adriana Sinta-Huerta *(Sr VP)*
Nathalie Alberto *(Mng Supvr)*
Carla Santiago *(Mng Supvr)*

Fleishman-Hillard Inc.
229 Peachtree St NE International Twr Ste 1600, Atlanta, GA 30303
Tel.: (404) 659-4446
Fax: (404) 659-4452
E-Mail: kaplank@fleishman.com
Web Site: fleishmanhillard.com/

Employees: 20

National Agency Associations: COPF

Agency Specializes In: Communications, Sponsorship

Jerry Tolk *(Partner & Gen Mgr)*
Paul Dusseault *(Sr Partner & Sr VP)*
Caitlin Crowley *(Acct Supvr)*
Amelie Smith *(Acct Supvr)*
Nancy Bauer *(Sr Partner)*
Paul Donsky *(Mng Supvr)*
Maria Jewett *(Mng Supvr)*

Accounts:
Aflac
AT&T Communications Corp.
Gas South Crisis Management, Media Relations, Public Relations, Thought Leadership
Newell Rubbermaid, Inc.
Zep, Inc. Media

Fleishman-Hillard Inc.
200 E Randolph St 37th Fl, Chicago, IL 60601
Tel.: (312) 729-3700
Web Site: fleishmanhillard.com/

Employees: 76

National Agency Associations: COPF

Agency Specializes In: Communications, Public Relations, Sponsorship

Brett McCall *(Partner, Sr VP & Exec Dir-Creative)*
Darrell Jursa *(Partner-Global Emerging Media & Tech & Sr VP)*
Laura Shulman *(Sr VP & Head-Food & Nutrition Practice Grp)*
Jack Yeo *(Sr VP & Head-Corp Grp Practice)*
Marjorie Benzkofer *(Sr Partner & Sr VP)*
Jason Miller *(VP-Emerging Media)*
Maxine Winer *(Sr Partner & Gen Mgr)*
Brian Carr *(Sr Mgr-Social Media Analytics)*
Caroline Baumgartner *(Sr Acct Exec)*
Rachel Coleman *(Acct Exec)*

Accounts:
The Allstate Foundation Campaign: "Power of the Purple Purse"
Gatorade Campaign: "Beat the Heat", Campaign: "Gatorade Goes Inside Endurance", Campaign: "Workout Water", G Series, Propel, Public Relation
General Motors Company Chevrolet
Get Covered Illinois Affordable Care Act, PR
Illinois Office of Tourism PR

Fleishman-Hillard Inc.
855 Boylston St 5th Fl, Boston, MA 02116
(See Separate Listing)

Fleishman-Hillard Inc.
150 S 5th St Ste 320, Minneapolis, MN 55402-1241
Tel.: (612) 337-0354
Fax: (612) 337-0355
Web Site: fleishmanhillard.com/

Employees: 37

National Agency Associations: COPF

Agency Specializes In: Communications

Dave Schad *(Sr VP, Partner & Gen Mgr)*
David Hakensen *(Sr VP-Minneapolis & St. Paul)*
Lisa Hanly *(VP)*
Sarah Young *(Mng Supvr-Internal Comm)*

Fleishman-Hillard Inc.
2405 Grand Blvd Ste 700, Kansas City, MO 64108-2522
Tel.: (816) 474-9407
Fax: (816) 474-7783
E-Mail: warren.dudley@fleishman.com
Web Site: fleishmanhillard.com/

Employees: 100

National Agency Associations: COPF

Agency Specializes In: Communications, Public Relations, Sponsorship

Angie Read *(Partner & Sr VP)*
Li Hong *(Pres-China & Sr Partner)*
Rachel Catanach *(Sr VP & Mng Dir-Hong Kong)*
Nick Andrews *(Sr Partner & Sr VP)*
Mary Bosco Heinrich *(Sr VP)*
Harald Simons *(Mng Dir-Bus Dev-EMEA)*
Andrea Margolin *(VP)*
Kevin Koestner *(Assoc Dir-Creative)*
Kara Hendon *(Sr Partner)*
Mandy Levings *(Sr Partner)*

Accounts:
Agro-Farma, Inc. Chobani Greek Yogurt
Applebee's Services, Inc. Applebee's International, Inc.
Bayer Corporation
CCW
FHX
GMMB
Hallmark Cards
High Road Communication
Louis Paul & Partners
Procter & Gamble Pet Care Iams
Stratacomm
Togo Run
VOX Global

Fleishman-Hillard Inc.
4350 Lassiter at North Hills Ave Ste 260, Raleigh, NC 27609
Tel.: (919) 457-0744
Fax: (919) 457-0741
E-Mail: britt.carter@fleishman.com
Web Site: fleishmanhillard.com/

Employees: 25

National Agency Associations: COPF

Yvonne Park *(Mng Dir)*
Joanne Wong *(Mng Dir)*
Caroline Wunnerlich *(Mng Dir)*
Britt Carter *(Sr VP & Gen Mgr)*
Elizabeth Romero *(Sr VP)*
Yusuf Hatia *(Mng Dir-Client Svc)*
Jayme Owen *(VP)*
Vanessa Fusco *(Sr Acct Exec-Healthcare)*
Lexi Rudolph *(Sr Acct Exec)*

Fleishman-Hillard Inc.
6000 Fairview Rd Ste 315 SouthPark Towers, Charlotte, NC 28210-2225
Tel.: (704) 556-2626
Fax: (704) 556-2621
Web Site: fleishmanhillard.com/

Employees: 57
Year Founded: 2003

National Agency Associations: COPF

Jake Rosen *(Partner & Sr VP)*
Britt Carter *(Sr Partner, Sr VP & Gen Mgr)*
Winn Maddrey *(Sr VP)*
Jaclynne Vettorino *(VP-Digital)*
Matthew Garner *(Acct Supvr)*
Richie Goodman *(Acct Supvr)*
Amber Forrest *(Asst Acct Exec)*
Dani Burns *(Mng Supvr-Digital)*
Cameron Reed *(Mng Supvr-PR)*

Fleishman-Hillard Inc.
220 E 42nd St 12th Fl, New York, NY 10017-5806
Tel.: (212) 453-2000
Fax: (212) 453-2020

Web Site: fleishmanhillard.com/

Employees: 100

National Agency Associations: COPF

Agency Specializes In: Communications, Public Relations, Sponsorship

Mary Curtin *(Partner & Sr VP)*
Suzanne Klotz *(Partner & Sr VP)*
Carolyn Chiang Rosebrough *(Partner & Sr VP)*
Sarah Vellozzi *(Sr VP & Partner-Reputation Mgmt)*
Chris Nelson *(Partner & Head-Crisis-Americas)*
Stephanie Marchesi *(Sr Partner & CMO)*
Erin Roche *(Sr Partner, Sr VP & Dir-Tech)*
Ephraim Cohen *(Sr VP & Sr Partner-Social & Digital)*
Joann DiVito *(Sr Partner & Sr VP)*
Della Sweetman *(Sr Partner & Sr VP-Bus Dev-Americas)*
Hollie Pantano *(VP)*
Steven Schwadron *(VP)*
Emily Shapoff *(VP-Brand Mktg)*
Bill Power *(Head-Global Practice-Brand Mktg)*
Steven Boersma *(Dir-Strategy)*
Laura Elliott *(Dir-Engagement)*
Lauren Price *(Acct Supvr-Digital)*
Eric Traver *(Acct Supvr-Engagement)*
Elizabeth Bushelow *(Acct Exec)*
Christopher McElwain *(Acct Exec)*

Accounts:
Agro-Farma, Inc. Chobani Greek Yogurt
American Dental Association Global Strategic Communications
Barnes & Noble Nook Color
Bayer AG
Boar's Head Provisions Co., Inc.
Carnival Corporation
Caron Treatment Centers (Agency of Record) Public Relations, Social Engagement, Strategic Communications
CIGNA Corporation
The Dannon Company, Inc.
Food & Drug Administration PR
Johnson & Johnson
LivingSocial
The Procter & Gamble Company Tide
Pure TalkUSA Campaign: "Jeremy"
Samsung Global Mobile
The Singapore Tourism Board

Fleishman-Hillard Inc.
1999 Bryan St Ste 3400, Dallas, TX 75201
Tel.: (214) 665-1300
Fax: (214) 953-3944
E-Mail: mullinar@fleishman.com
Web Site: fleishmanhillard.com/

National Agency Associations: COPF

Agency Specializes In: Public Relations, Sponsorship

Janise Murphy *(Pres-US South & Sr Partner)*
Lauren Walters *(Sr Partner, Sr VP & Gen Mgr)*
Andy Shaw *(Sr VP)*
Devon Alter *(Acct Supvr)*
Jillian Emens *(Acct Supvr)*
Claire Jameson *(Sr Acct Exec)*
Meredith Adams *(Mng Supvr)*

Fleishman-Hillard Inc.
Williams Tower 2800 Post Oak Blvd Ste 6060, Houston, TX 77056-6111
Tel.: (713) 513-9500
Fax: (713) 961-3316
E-Mail: jamie.greenheck@fleishman.com
Web Site: fleishmanhillard.com/

Employees: 20

National Agency Associations: COPF

Agency Specializes In: Communications, Public Relations

Yusuf Hatia *(Mng Dir)*
Yvonne Park *(Mng Dir)*
Joanne Wong *(Mng Dir)*
Shin Tanaka *(Pres-Japan & Sr Partner)*
Rachel Catanach *(Sr VP & Mng Dir-Hong Kong)*
Jamie Greenheck *(Gen Mgr)*
Catherine Mitchell *(Sr Acct Exec)*
Alison Perehoduk *(Mng Supvr)*

Greer, Margolis, Mitchell, Burns & Associates (GMMB)
3050 K St NW, Washington, DC 20007
Tel.: (202) 338-8700
Fax: (202) 338-2334
E-Mail: gmmb_dc@gmmb.com
Web Site: www.gmmb.com

National Agency Associations: 4A's

Agency Specializes In: Communications, Government/Political, Media Buying Services, Public Relations, Publicity/Promotions, Sponsorship

Raelynn Olson *(Partner)*
John Gundlach *(Sr VP & Grp Dir-Creative)*
Adam Ferrari *(Sr VP & Sr Producer)*
Trudi Benford *(Sr VP & Dir-Creative Svcs)*
Daniel Jester *(Sr VP & Dir-Media)*
Julie Bataille *(Sr VP)*
Don Corrigan *(Dir-Creative)*
Sarah Whitworth *(Acct Supvr)*
Meghan Kemp *(Rep-Mktg)*

Accounts:
Corporation for National & Community Service Digital Strategy, FEMA Corps, National Media Outreach Campaign
Dave Thomas Foundation for Adoption Campaign: "Unadoptable is Unacceptable"
Save Darfur Coalition
VISA Corporate Identity
Washington State Department of Health

Lois Paul & Partners
828 W 6th St, Austin, TX 78703
Tel.: (512) 638-5300
Fax: (512) 638-5310
E-Mail: info@lpp.com
Web Site: www.lpp.com

Employees: 10
Year Founded: 1986

Agency Specializes In: Communications, Public Relations, Sponsorship

Lois Paul *(Founder & Pres)*
Bill McLaughlin *(Exec VP)*
Christine Simeone *(Exec VP)*
Jackson Connell *(Acct Rep)*

Accounts:
Aspen Technology
Blabbelon
Bomgar
CleanFUEL
Freescale Semiconductor
Kronos Inc.
LANDesk Software
National Instruments
RADVISION (Agency of Record)
Scuderi Group
Skyonic Corporation

Stratacomm, Inc.
28175 Haggerty Rd, Novi, MI 48377
Tel.: (248) 975-2800
Fax: (248) 975-2820
E-Mail: info@stratacomm.net
Web Site: www.stratacomm.net

Employees: 10

Agency Specializes In: Communications, Sponsorship

Bill Buff *(Mng Partner)*
John Fitzpatrick *(Mng Partner)*
Charlotte Seigler *(Partner & Sr VP)*
Kristin Tyll *(Partner & Sr VP)*
Shannon Blair *(Partner)*
Karah Davenport *(VP)*
Maggie Easterlin *(Acct Supvr)*
Nicole Burdiss *(Sr Acct Exec)*
Kenneth L. Gayles, Jr. *(Sr Acct Exec)*
Kevin Raftery *(Sr Acct Exec)*
Travis Austin *(Sr Partner)*

Accounts:
Tognum America Inc. MTU, MTU Onsite Energy, Media Relations, Positioning, Trade Show Support

TogoRun
220 E 42nd St 12th Fl, New York, NY 10017
Tel.: (212) 883-9080
Fax: (212) 453-2070
Web Site: www.togorun.com

Year Founded: 1993

Agency Specializes In: Communications, Health Care Services, Public Relations, Sponsorship

Gloria M. Janata *(Pres & Sr Partner)*
Liliana Coletti Da Costa *(Mng Dir-NY, Sr Partner & Sr VP)*
Jon Tilton *(Sr VP-Digital)*
Monica McAteer *(VP)*
Jesse Tarlton *(Acct Supvr)*
Lizzy Belz *(Asst Acct Exec)*
Diana Haugen *(Mng Supvr)*
Allison Mead *(Mng Supvr)*

Accounts:
GlaxoSmithKline, Inc.
L'Oreal
Rx Response (Agency of Record) Marketing, Strategic Communications Planning, Website

Canada

Fleishman-Hillard
100 Queen Street 13th Floor, Ottawa, ON K1P 1J9 Canada
Tel.: (613) 238-2090
Fax: (613) 238-9380
E-Mail: michael.vonherff@fleishman.ca
Web Site: fleishmanhillard.com

Employees: 12

Agency Specializes In: Communications, Government/Political, Public Relations

Kevin Macintosh *(Partner & Sr VP)*
Gordon Taylor Lee *(Sr VP)*
Nicolas Ruszkowski *(Gen Mgr)*

Accounts:
Enercare Communications
Mars Canada Ben's Beginners, Contest Facilitation, Public Relations, Social Media, Uncle Ben's

Fleishman-Hillard
540 5th Ave SW,Suite 1410, T2R 1M1 Calgary, AB Canada
Tel.: (403) 266-4710
Fax: (403) 269-5346
E-Mail: morten.paulsen@fleishman.ca
Web Site: fleishmanhillard.com

Agency Specializes In: Communications, Government/Political, Public Relations

Bryan Thomas *(Sr VP)*
Nic Ruszkowski *(Gen Mgr)*

Fleishman-Hillard
33 Bloor Street E Ste 1500, Toronto, ON M4W 3H1 Canada
Tel.: (416) 214-0701
Fax: (416) 214-0720
Web Site: fleishmanhillard.com

Employees: 40
Year Founded: 1993

Agency Specializes In: Communications, Public Relations

Angela Carmichael *(Partner, Sr VP & Gen Mgr)*
Anne Marie Quinn *(Partner & Sr VP)*
Jennifer Shah *(Sr VP & Partner-Digital & Mktg Comm)*
Leslie Walsh *(Partner & Sr VP-Reputation Mgmt)*
Nick Drew *(Sr VP-Res & Analytics)*
Ojas Naik *(Sr VP)*
Caroline Bretsen *(VP)*
Andrew Addison *(Assoc VP-Reputation Practice)*
Jay Armitage *(Assoc VP)*
Shauna Kelleher *(Sr Acct Exec)*

Accounts:
Foraco (Agency of Record) Communications Strategy

Fleishman-Hillard
777 Hornby St Ste 1920, Vancouver, BC V6Z 1S4 Canada
Tel.: (604) 688-2505
Fax: (604) 688-2519
E-Mail: ellen.bird@fleishman.ca
Web Site: fleishmanhillard.com

Employees: 20

Agency Specializes In: Communications, Government/Political, Public Relations

Mark Reder *(Sr Partner, Sr VP & Gen Mgr)*
Jennifer Torney *(Sr VP)*
Jackie Asante *(VP)*
Elisha McCallum *(VP)*
Jeffrey Ferrier *(Assoc VP)*
Gabe Garfinkel *(Assoc VP)*
Nic Ruszkowski *(Gen Mgr)*
Katie Robb *(Acct Dir)*
Jeremy Twigg *(Acct Dir)*
Anna Lilly *(Dir)*

High Road Communications
100 Queen St ste 1300, Ottawa, ON K1Y 4S1 Canada
Tel.: (613) 236-0909
Fax: (613) 236-2117
Web Site: www.highroad.com

Employees: 23
Year Founded: 1996

Agency Specializes In: Communications, Public Relations

Katherine Fletcher *(Sr Partner, Mng Dir & Sr VP)*
Adrienne Connell *(VP-Digital & Social)*
Lesley Sturla *(VP)*

Accounts:
Enercare Communications
Solace Systems
Virgin Mobile (Agency of Record) Public Relations Strategy

High Road Communications
360 Adelaide St W 4th Fl, Toronto, ON M5V 1R7 Canada
Tel.: (416) 368-8348
Fax: (416) 368-6253
E-Mail: jcreally@highroad.com
Web Site: www.highroad.com

Employees: 100

Agency Specializes In: Communications, High Technology, Public Relations

Neil Johnson *(Sr VP-Creative Strategy)*
Kristy Pryma *(Sr VP)*
Adrienne Connell *(VP-Digital Comm)*
Michael Sax *(Dir-Fin)*
Becky Brescacin *(Acct Supvr)*
Allison Colalillo *(Acct Supvr)*
Shelly Verzosa *(Acct Exec-Digital)*

Accounts:
American Express Campaign: "Building Brand With Big Ideas"
Canadian Internet Registry Authority
Canon
Canpages
New-Clarks Canada Content Creation, Public Relations, Social
Ferrero Canada Nutella
First Asset
Insertech
Nike Influencer Programs, Media Relations
New-Pavilion Financial
Sobeys Campaign: "Better Food For All", Digital, PR, Social
New-Women's College Hospital Foundation (Agency of Record) Advertising, Digital Strategy, Media Buying, Media Relations

High Road Communications
3575 Blvd St-Laurent Ste 200, Montreal, QC H2X 2T7 Canada
Tel.: (514) 908-0110
Fax: (514) 86-6 8981
Web Site: www.highroad.com

Agency Specializes In: Communications, Government/Political, Public Relations

Nathalie Bergeron *(Sr VP)*
Neil Johnson *(Sr VP-Creative Strategy)*
Michael Macmillan *(Sr VP)*
Adrienne Connell *(VP)*
Danna Barak *(Acct Dir)*
Stacie Bumbacco *(Acct Dir)*
Allison Macdonald *(Acct Supvr)*

Accounts:
Ludia (Agency of Record) PR

Europe

Fleishman-Hillard Czech Republic
Lomnickeho 1705/9, 14 000 Prague, Czech Republic
Tel.: (420) 2 2423 2650
Fax: (420) 2 2423 2653
E-Mail: radek.marsik@fleishmaneurope.com
Web Site: www.fleishman-hillard.eu

Employees: 20
Year Founded: 1998

National Agency Associations: APRA-ICCO

Agency Specializes In: Communications, Public Relations

Radek Marsik *(Mng Dir)*
Marcel Bodnar *(Acct Dir)*
Ondrej Peterka *(Acct Dir-Digital & Social Media)*
Andrea Frydlova *(Assoc Dir)*
Roman Pavlik *(Assoc Dir)*
Michaela Bartosova *(Sr Acct Mgr)*
Eliska Bajtova *(Acct Mgr)*
Lenka Aliapuliu *(Sr Acct Exec)*
Libena Kubikova *(Acct Exec)*
Viktorie Dvorakova *(Exec Acct Mgr)*

Accounts:
Lenovo
Philips
Tesco

Fleishman-Hillard France
37 Rue Delabiensaisance, 75008 Paris, France
Tel.: (33) 1 47 42 19 56
Fax: (33) 1 42 66 39 59
Web Site: www.fleishman.fr

Employees: 40
Year Founded: 1987

Agency Specializes In: Communications, Public Relations

Mario Cocherel *(Sr VP, Head-Healthcare & Dir)*
Mathilde Bordron *(Sr VP-Corp Comm & Dir)*
Sandrine Cormary *(Gen Mgr)*
Kenza Remaoun *(Acct Dir & Sr Acct Mgr)*
Antoine Mery *(Acct Dir)*

Accounts:
Autodesk Ltd.
Expedia, Inc.

Fleishman-Hillard Germany
Herzog-Wilhelm-Strasse 26, D-80331 Munich, Germany
Tel.: (49) 89 230 31 60
Fax: (49) 89 230 31 631
E-Mail: tamara.reigberger@fleishmaneurope.com
Web Site: www.fleishman-hillard.eu

Employees: 20
Year Founded: 1994

Agency Specializes In: Communications, Public Relations

Dirk Krieger *(Mng Dir & CFO)*
Ronny Winkler *(Sr VP & Head-Tech Practice-Germany)*
Hanning Kempe *(Gen Mng Dir)*

Accounts:
Fujitsu Technologies

Fleishman-Hillard Group Ltd.
40 Long Acre, Covent Garden, London, WC2E 9LG United Kingdom
Tel.: (44) 20 7306 9000
Fax: (44) 20 7497 0096
E-Mail: lucien.vallun@fleishmaneurope.com
Web Site: www.fleishman-hillard.eu/

Employees: 140
Year Founded: 1988

Agency Specializes In: Communications, Public Relations

Dave Bennett *(Partner, Head-Brand Mktg & Dir)*
Paul Haugen *(Partner & Dir-Plng-EMEA)*
Sophie Scott *(Partner & Dir)*
Charlotte Shyllon *(Partner)*
Anne de Schweinitz *(Sr Partner, Sr VP & Mng Dir-Global Healthcare)*
Brandy Fleming *(Head-Digital, Social & Content-EMEA)*
Sophie Nicholas *(Acct Dir)*
Robin Hamman *(Dir-Social Bus & Coord-EMEA Digital Network)*
James Dowling *(Dir)*
Cheryl Pitcher *(Assoc Dir)*
Tania Chuppe *(Sr Acct Exec-PR)*

Accounts:
AT&T
Autodesk
Avaya Intel
Aviva Insurance
Barnes & Noble Nook E-Reader, Nook HD, Nook HD+
Bernard Hodes Corporate Reputation
British Insurance Brokers Association Public Affairs
The Carlyle Group Public Affairs
Chobani Greek Yogurt PR, Social Media Campaign
Crosscare Limited Communications, Content Development, Online, Social Strategy
CytoSport, Inc. Consumer Public Relations, Content, MUSCLE MILK PROTEIN
Freeview
Hallmark Cards Communications, Forever Friends, Online Media
Illinois Office of Tourism Blogger Relations, Consumer & Trade Media, PR
Lebara
MGA Entertainment Little Tikes, PR, Social Media Campaign
Mimecast Analyst Relations, PR
National Funding Scheme Consumer Brand, Digital Donation Box
Nike Campaign: "Designed to Move", Public Affairs
P&G Pampers
Santander UK Public Affairs
Seagate Technology plc (Public Relations Agency of Record)
Sorenson Communications Campaign: "VRS Today!"
Starwood Hotels
Symington's Ainsley Harriott, Digital, PR, Social Media
TCS
Velcro Consumer & Trade Media Relations

Fleishman-Hillard Italy
Via Solari 11, 20144 Milan, Italy
Tel.: (39) 02 31804 1
Fax: (39) 02 3361 4827
Web Site: www.fleishman-hillard.eu/

Employees: 20
Year Founded: 1996

Agency Specializes In: Communications, Public Relations

Laura Meroni *(VP)*
Martina Della Morte *(Controller-Fin)*
Massimo Moriconi *(Gen Mgr)*
Barbara Papini *(Acct Dir)*
Carlo Patassi *(Sr Acct Exec)*
Grazia Coppola *(Acct Exec)*
Chiara Laudicina *(Acct Exec)*
Ilaria Carfi *(Asst Acct Exec)*

Accounts:
New-Expedia

Fleishman-Hillard Limited
15 Fitzwilliam Quay, Dublin, 4 Ireland
Tel.: (353) 1 618 8444
Fax: (353) 1 660 2244
E-Mail: rhona.blake@fleishmaneurope.com
Web Site: www.fleishman-hillard.eu/

Employees: 30

Agency Specializes In: Communications, Public Relations

James Dunny *(Head-Issues Mgmt & Assoc Dir)*
Kevin Moore *(Head-Sports Mktg)*
Rhona Blake *(Gen Mgr)*
Ann Coyne *(Dir-Fin-EMEA)*
Julian Davis *(Dir-Consumer & Brands)*
Astrid Brennan *(Client Dir)*

Accounts:
AS Roma Stadio Della Roma
Chevrolet Campaign: "Sponsorship of Manchester United", Public Relation
New-Expedia
Philips
New-WhatClinic.com Global Communications

Fleishman-Hillard Poland
ul Burakowska 5/7, 01-066 Warsaw, Poland
Tel.: (48) 22 532 95 40
Fax: (48) 22 434 24 90
E-Mail: julia.kozak@fleishmaneurope.com
Web Site: www.fleishman-hillard.eu/

Employees: 20

Agency Specializes In: Communications, Public Relations

Julia Kozak *(Mng Dir)*
Magda Staniszewska *(Acct Dir)*

Accounts:
GSK
Philips
Toshiba

Fleishman-Hillard
35 Square de Meeus, B-1000 Brussels, Belgium
Tel.: (32) 2230 0545
Fax: (32) 2230 5706
E-Mail: caroline.wunnerlich@fleishmaneurope.com
Web Site: www.fleishman-hillard.eu/

Employees: 70

Agency Specializes In: Communications, Government/Political, Public Relations

Donald Ricketts *(Partner & Head-Fin Svcs, Sr VP)*
Michelle Gibbons *(Sr Partner, Deputy Mng Dir & Sr VP)*
Teresa Calvano *(Sr VP & Dir)*
David Turier *(Acct Dir)*
Stephan Thalen *(Acct Mgr)*
Annette Simson *(Mgr-Creative)*
Ewa Abramiuk *(Specialist-Pub Affairs)*
Arnaud Eard *(Specialist-Pub Affairs)*
Aaron McLoughlin *(Specialist-Pub Affairs)*
Cillian O'Donoghue *(Specialist-Pub Affairs)*
Lucia Pecchini *(Acct Exec)*

Accounts:
MasterCard
Nestle
SHV Energy Campaign: "Future of Rural Energy"

South Africa

Fleishman-Hillard/South Africa
15 Georgian Crescent Ground Floor, PO Box 71181, Bryanston, 2021 Johannesburg, South Africa
Tel.: (27) 1 1 548 2000
Fax: (27) 1 1 706 7320
E-Mail: kevin.welman@fleishman.co.za
Web Site: fleishmanhillard.com/

Employees: 50
Year Founded: 1985

Agency Specializes In: Communications, Public Relations

Vanessa Baard *(Partner & Dir)*
Kevin Welman *(Mng Dir)*
Joan Theodorides *(Dir-Fin)*
Jared Carneson *(Assoc Dir)*

Accounts:
Nike
Nokia

Asia & Australia

BlueCurrent Hong Kong
Suite 1501, Cityplaza 4, 12 Taikoo Wan Road, Taikoo Shing, China (Hong Kong)
Tel.: (852) 2513 0279
Web Site: bluecurrentgroup.com/

Agency Specializes In: Advertising

Chris Plowman *(Sr VP)*
James Hacking *(VP)*
Cheryl Pan *(Sr Acct Exec)*

Accounts:
Brand Hong Kong Campaign: "Our Hong Kong", Creative
Urban Land Institute Asia Pacific Content Creation, Digital, Event Management, PR, Social

BlueCurrent Japan
Nichirei Higashi-Ginza Bldg 7F, 6-19-20 Tsukiji Chuo-Ku, Tokyo, 104-0045 Japan
Tel.: (81) 3 352 44600
Fax: (81) 62785781
E-Mail: smi.onuki@bluecurrentpr.com
Web Site: www.bluecurrentprjapan.com

Tetsuya Honda *(CEO)*
Hara Hideto *(Sr VP)*
Megumi Hayakawa *(VP)*
Shimo Tetsutaro *(Sr Mgr-Media Solution Mktg Solution Grp)*
Nakasato Shinobu *(Sr Acct Mgr)*
Kazuya Hirai *(Sr Acct Exec)*
Saki Yoshimura *(Sr Acct Exec)*
Tatsuya Hirosawa *(Acct Exec)*

Accounts:
Adidas Running Shoes
GoPro Marketing, Social Media

Fleishman-Hillard Guangzhou
3707 F Center Plz No 161 Linhe Road W, Tianhe District, Guangzhou, China
Tel.: (86) 20 3825 1368
Fax: (86) 20 3825 1585
Web Site: www.fleishman.cn

Employees: 4

Agency Specializes In: Communications, Public Relations

Ada Gu *(Acct Dir)*
Ricky Wu *(Acct Dir)*
Jessie Song *(Sr Acct Mgr)*
Bridget Hong *(Acct Mgr)*
Roxy Li *(Sr Acct Exec)*
Yalin Luo *(Acct Exec)*

Accounts:
Li Ning PR

Fleishman-Hillard Hong Kong Ltd.
Suite 1501 Cityplaza 4 12 Taikoo Wan Road, Taikoo Shing, China (Hong Kong)
Tel.: (852) 2530 0228
Fax: (852) 2845 0363
E-Mail: rachel.catanach@fleishman.com
Web Site: www.fleishmanhillard.com/

Year Founded: 1997

Agency Specializes In: Communications, Public Relations

Raj Seth *(Partner, Sr VP & Head-Corp Tech-Asia Pacific)*
Patrick Yu *(Sr VP, Partner-Fin & Pro Svcs Sector & Head-Asia Pacific)*
Sally Woo *(Partner, Sr VP & Reg Head-HR-Asia Pacific)*
Rachel Catanach *(Sr Partner, Mng Dir & Sr VP)*
Joanne Wong *(Mng Dir)*
Kitty Lee *(VP & Dir-Mktg)*

Accounts:
City of Dreams
Comvita
Dassault Falcon Corporate Communications, Media Relations, Public Relations
GoHome Media Relations, Public Relations
Gome Campaign: "Lights on Gome"
Hitachi Data Systems Public Relations
Ista Brand Image
LJ International Financial Communications, Investor Relations, Strategic Counsel
Nike
Standard & Poor's Media Relations, S&P 500, S&P GSCI, S&P Indices, Strategic Consulting
Walt Disney Company China; 2007

Fleishman-Hillard/Japan
Nichirei Higashi-Ginza Building 7F 6-19-20, Tsukiji Chuo-Ku, Tokyo, 104-0045 Japan
Tel.: (81) 3 3524 4600
Fax: (81) 3 3524 4602
E-Mail: tanakas@fleishman.com
Web Site: www.fleishman.co.jp

Employees: 45
Year Founded: 1997

Agency Specializes In: Communications, Public Relations

Shin Tanaka *(Pres-Japan & Sr Partner)*
Yoko Sumida *(VP)*
Daisuke Nakahara *(Sr Acct Mgr)*
Yufuko Toyoda *(Sr Acct Mgr)*
Saemaro Ishihara *(Acct Mgr & Strategist-Digital)*
Akihiro Nojiri *(Specialist-Pub Affairs)*
Rie Sugiyama *(Acct Exec)*
Atsuo Ishida *(Designer-Comm)*

Accounts:
Fukushima Conference Organisers

Fleishman-Hillard Korea
24th Fl City Air Tower 159-9 Samsung-Dong, Kangnam-Ku, Seoul, 135-973 Korea (South)
Tel.: (82) 251 869 02
Fax: (82) 225 186 904
E-Mail: yvonne.park@fleishman.com
Web Site: fleishmanhillard.com/

Year Founded: 1998

Agency Specializes In: Communications, Public Relations

Sarah Ha *(Sr VP)*
Eunah Emma Kim *(Acct Dir)*
Jackelyn Yeseul Ahn *(Acct Mgr)*
Saemi Chung *(Sr Acct Exec)*
Sam Kim *(Sr Acct Exec)*
Annie Lee *(Asst Acct Exec)*

Accounts:
Korean Communications Consortium
Korean Ministry of Health & Welfare , Childcare & Child-Rearing Facilities Awareness; 2008
The Korean Society Of Obstetrics & Gynecology
Seoul Metropolitan Government; 2008

Fleishman-Hillard Link Ltd.
Room 3006 Jianwai SOHO Office Tower B 39 East Third Ring Road, Chaoyang District, Beijing, 100022 China
Tel.: (86) 10 5869 1666
Fax: (86) 10 5869 5088
Web Site: www.fleishman.cn

Employees: 100
Year Founded: 1994

Agency Specializes In: Communications, Public Relations

Fang Laura Qiu *(VP)*
Teresa Song *(VP)*
Caroline Fu *(Acct Dir)*
Luo Vivian *(Acct Dir)*
Josephine Wang *(Acct Dir)*
Echo Yang *(Acct Dir-Corp Comm & Pub Affairs)*
Jing Kuai *(Sr Acct Exec)*
Linna Wang *(Acct Exec)*

Accounts:
TCL Brand Reputation Management, Campaign: "Turn a Corporate Celebration into a Public Event"
Tiffany

Fleishman-Hillard Link, Ltd.
1 Grand Gateway 1 Hongqiao Rd, Xu Hui District, Shanghai, 200003 China
Tel.: (86) 21 6407 0066
Fax: (86) 21 6407 1155
E-Mail: lih@fleishman.com
Web Site: www.fleishman.cn

Employees: 15
Year Founded: 1997

Agency Specializes In: Communications, Public Relations

Miranda Cai *(Partner, Sr VP & Gen Mgr-Fleishman Hillard Shanghai)*
Ada Gu *(Acct Dir)*
Jessie Song *(Sr Acct Mgr)*
Bridget Hong *(Acct Mgr)*
Roxy Li *(Sr Acct Exec)*
Yalin Luo *(Acct Exec)*

Accounts:
Philips
Tiffany

Fleishman-Hillard Malaysia
Suite 1702 Level 17 Centrepoint South The Boulevard, Mid Valley city Lingkaran Sye, 59200 Kuala Lumpur, Malaysia
Tel.: (60) 3 2283 2730
Fax: (60) 3 2283 2750
E-Mail: kuk@fleishman.com
Web Site: fleishmanhillard.com/

Employees: 13
Year Founded: 1997

Agency Specializes In: Communications, Public Relations

Eswari Kalugasalam Lawson *(VP)*
Magdalene Lee *(Gen Mgr)*

Fleishman-Hillard Manila
4/F Zeta Building 191 Salcedo Street, Legaspi Village Makati City, Manila, Philippines
Tel.: (63) 2 813 0559
Fax: (63) 2 813 0634
E-Mail: cosette.romero@fleishman.com
Web Site: fleishmanhillard.com/

Employees: 4
Year Founded: 1998

Agency Specializes In: Communications, Public Relations

Cosette Romero *(Partner, Sr VP & Gen Mgr)*
Ferdinand Bondoy *(VP-Consumer Mktg & Digital Practice Grp)*

Fleishman-Hillard Pte. Ltd.
20 Kallang Avenue, Level 8, PICO Creative Centre, Singapore, 339411 Singapore
Tel.: (65) 6339 1066
Fax: (65) 6424 6355
Web Site: fleishmanhillard.com/

Employees: 30
Year Founded: 1996

Agency Specializes In: Communications, Public Relations

Michel Mommejat *(Partner, Sr VP & Mng Dir-Digital Engagement Asia Pacific)*
Shafaat Hussain *(Partner & Sr VP-Tech)*
Brian West *(Chm-Crisis Mgmt-Global & Mng Dir-Reputation Mgmt-Asia Pacific)*
Don Anderson *(Sr VP-Reg Strategic Digital Integration)*
Khoo Yin *(Gen Mgr)*

Accounts:
Genzyme Corporation Synvisc
Philips Consumer Lifestyle Campaign: "Transforming Fried Cooking in Southeast Asia"
Scoot Corporate Communications, Media Relations

Fleishman-Hilliard Inc.
Hero Building II, 7/F J1 Jend Gatot, Jakarta, 12870 Indonesia
Tel.: (62) 21 8296768
Fax: (62) 21 8317786
Web Site: indonesia.fleishmanhillard.com/

Louisa Tuhatu *(Partner, Sr VP & Gen Mgr)*

Branches

Fleishman-Hillard Inc.
1615 L St NW Ste 1000, Washington, DC 20036
Tel.: (202) 659-0330
Fax: (202) 296-6119
Web Site: fleishmanhillard.com

Employees: 10

Agency Specializes In: Government/Political, Sponsorship

Gwen Foutz *(Partner, Sr VP & Head-Social-Americas)*
Michael Adolph *(Partner, Sr VP & Sr Dir-Creative)*
Elizabeth Cook *(Sr VP & Partner)*
Maria Gallagher *(Partner & Sr VP)*

Peter Klaus *(Partner & Sr VP)*
David Wickenden *(Exec VP & Mng Dir-Global Strategic Plng & Dev)*
Dan Horowitz *(Sr Partner & Exec VP)*
Kris Balderston *(Sr Partner, Sr VP & Gen Mgr)*
John Estafanous *(Sr Partner, Sr VP & Dir-Digital Integration-Global)*
Emilie Moghadam Dworkin *(Sr VP)*
Nathan Naylor *(Sr VP-Pub Affairs)*
Julia Kilberg *(Acct Supvr)*
Piper Evans *(Mng Supvr)*

Accounts:
Approva
Bloomberg Government Campaign: "Capital Meets Capitol"
The Department of Homeland Security Cybersecurity & Communications, Strategic Outreach
The Procter & Gamble Company Tide
Vocera Communications; 2007
White House Office Of National Drug Control Policy Teen Anti-Drug Campaign

FLOCK & RALLY
701 Whaley St Loft 202, Columbia, SC 29201
Tel.: (803) 348-8861
E-Mail: info@flockandrally.com
Web Site: www.flockandrally.com

Year Founded: 2010

Agency Specializes In: Advertising, Event Planning & Marketing, Print, Public Relations, Social Media, Strategic Planning/Research

Tracie Broom *(Partner)*
Debi Schadel *(Partner)*
Chloe Rodgers *(Acct Mgr)*

Accounts:
Brian Maynor

FLS MARKETING
405 Madison Ave Ste 1550, Toledo, OH 43604-1226
Tel.: (419) 241-1244
Fax: (419) 241-5210
E-Mail: email@flsmarketing.com
Web Site: www.flsmarketing.com

E-Mail for Key Personnel:
President: mluetke@flsmarketing.com

Employees: 25
Year Founded: 1984

Agency Specializes In: Collateral, Consumer Marketing, Environmental, Event Planning & Marketing, Government/Political, Graphic Design, Health Care Services, Multimedia, Planning & Consultation, Print, Production, Promotions, Public Relations, Publicity/Promotions, Radio, Sponsorship, Strategic Planning/Research, T.V., Travel & Tourism

Approx. Annual Billings: $2,750,000

Breakdown of Gross Billings by Media: Graphic Design: $225,000; Production: $325,000; Pub. Rels.: $1,390,000; Radio & T.V.: $810,000

Mark D. Luetke *(Pres)*
B.J. Fischer *(Dir-Strategic Svcs)*

Accounts:
Lucas County Auditor
Lucas County Childrens Services Board
Lucas County Commissioners
Mercy Health Partners; Toledo, OH; 1999
Toledo Zoo; Toledo, OH; 1999
YMCA

FOLSOM & ASSOCIATES
44 Montgomery St Ste 3710, San Francisco, CA 94104
Tel.: (415) 978-9909
Web Site: www.folsomandassociates.com

Year Founded: 1993

Agency Specializes In: Crisis Communications, Event Planning & Marketing, Media Relations, Media Training, Public Relations, Social Media, Strategic Planning/Research

Sam Folsom *(Pres)*
Lisa Klinck-Shea *(VP)*
Peggy Murphy *(Office Mgr)*
Brooke Buringrud *(Acct Exec)*

Accounts:
B R Cohn Winery Inc.
Biltmore Wines
Gary Farrell Winery
Geyser Peak Winery
Helfrich
La Follette
Lobels
Mandolin
Mumm Napa
Quivira Vineyards, Llc.
Robert Mondavi Winery
Steelhead Vineyards
Stinson Vineyards
Waterstone Winery

THE FONTAYNE GROUP
PO Box 751, Marysville, CA 95901
Fax: (310) 496-2937
Toll Free: (800) 841-0850
E-Mail: wired@fontayne.com
Web Site: www.fontayne.com

E-Mail for Key Personnel:
President: cynthia@fontayne.com

Employees: 7
Year Founded: 1982

Agency Specializes In: Advertising, Aviation & Aerospace, Consulting, Consumer Marketing, E-Commerce, Electronic Media, Event Planning & Marketing, Information Technology, Internet/Web Design, Leisure, Print, Public Relations, Publicity/Promotions, Travel & Tourism

Cynthia L. Fontayne *(CEO & Dir-Creative)*
Nina Laramore *(Dir-Media Rels-Western US)*
Nonette Puno *(Office Mgr)*

Accounts:
Austrian National Tourist Office; 1982

FORMULATIN
580 Broadway, New York, NY 10012
Tel.: (212) 219-0321
Fax: (212) 219-8846
E-Mail: info@formulatin.com
Web Site: havasformulatin.com

Agency Specializes In: Brand Development & Integration, Consumer Marketing, Entertainment, Sponsorship, Travel & Tourism

Michael A. Olguin *(Pres)*
Alexis McCance *(Sr VP-Ops)*
Maria Amor *(VP)*
Andy Checo *(Dir-HavasFormulatin Hispanic)*

Accounts:
Copa Tecate Entertainment Services
Tequila Herradura Alcoholic Drinks Mfr

FORTE PR
511 S 7th St, Las Vegas, NV 89101
Tel.: (702) 898-2547
Web Site: www.forteprlv.com

Year Founded: 2005

Agency Specializes In: Brand Development & Integration, Crisis Communications, Media Relations, Public Relations, Social Media, Strategic Planning/Research

Aimee Wenske *(Mgr-Social Media)*
Veronica Kawka *(Acct Exec)*

Accounts:
CLIF Bar CrossVegas (Public Relations Agency of Record) Strategic Planning, Traditional Media Strategy
Essentia Water
Fitmoo Inc (Public Relations Agency of Record)
Las Vegas Ski & Snowboard Resort
The Meadows School
Skye Canyon (Public Relations Agency of Record) Social Media

FORTUNE PUBLIC RELATIONS
2319 California St, Berkeley, CA 94703
Tel.: (510) 548-1097
Fax: (510) 841-7006
Web Site: fortunepublicrelations.com

Agency Specializes In: Food Service, Media Relations, Public Relations

Deborah Fortune *(Co-owner)*
Thomas Walton *(Owner)*

Accounts:
Boncora Biscotti
Cybele's Free to Eat
GimMe Health Organic Roasted Seaweed
Musco Family Olive Co.

FOUR LEAF PUBLIC RELATIONS LLC
2989 Stony Point Rd, Charlottesville, VA 22911
Tel.: (434) 972-7278
Web Site: www.fourleafpr.com

Agency Specializes In: Event Planning & Marketing, Media Relations, Public Relations, Social Media, Strategic Planning/Research

Suzanne E. Henry *(Pres & CEO)*

Accounts:
The Outdoor Power Equipment Institute Look Before You Pump

FOX GREENBERG PUBLIC RELATIONS
48 W 21st St Ste 1000, New York, NY 10010
Tel.: (212) 334-1212
Fax: (212) 334-5924
E-Mail: info@foxgreenberg.com
Web Site: www.foxgreenberg.com

Employees: 6
Year Founded: 2003

Agency Specializes In: Broadcast, Entertainment, Event Planning & Marketing, Fashion/Apparel, Food Service, Hospitality, Media Relations, Product Placement, Public Relations, Real Estate, Social Marketing/Nonprofit, Sponsorship, Strategic Planning/Research, Web (Banner Ads, Pop-ups, etc.)

Michelle Fox *(Co-Owner)*
Sarah Greenberg *(Co-Owner)*
Kacy Shaw *(Acct Dir-Natl)*

Lauren Hedstrom *(Acct Exec)*
Gina Lengeling *(Acct Exec)*

Accounts:
BizBash Marketing, Public Relations
Niche Media Group, LLC
Prive Salon

FRANCHISE ELEVATOR
3400 Dundee Rd Ste 300, Northbrook, IL 60062
Tel.: (847) 945-1300
Fax: (847) 945-3755
Web Site: www.franchiseelevator.com

Agency Specializes In: Crisis Communications, Media Training, Public Relations

Michael Misetic *(Mng Partner)*
Seamus Riley *(Acct Coord)*

Accounts:
Persona Neapolitan Pizzeria

FRANCO PUBLIC RELATIONS GROUP
400 Renaissance Ctr Ste 1000, Detroit, MI 48243
Tel.: (313) 567-2300
Fax: (313) 567-4486
E-Mail: info@franco.com
Web Site: www.franco.com

Employees: 16
Year Founded: 1964

Agency Specializes In: Public Relations

Approx. Annual Billings: $3,000,000

Tina Kozak *(Pres)*
Dan F. Ponder *(CEO)*
Tina Benvenuti Sullivan *(Sr VP)*
Stephanie Angelyn Casola *(Mgr-Social Media & Acct Mgr-Consumer)*
Ann Marie Fortunate *(Acct Supvr)*
Daniel Horn *(Sr Acct Exec)*
Erica Swoish *(Acct Exec)*
Sarah Kornacki *(Asst Acct Exec)*
Sasha Reeves *(Asst Acct Exec)*

Accounts:
Allied Printing Company
Applebee's Neighborhood Grill & Bar; Detroit, MI
Arbor Hospice
The Bird and the Bread
Blue Tractor BBQ & Brewery Mash
Brooks Kushman P.C.
Buddy's Pizza; Detroit, MI
Chevrolet Detroit Belle Isle Grand Prix Social Media
Feld Entertainment Family Entertainment
Grow Michigan
Henry Ford Estate-Fairlane
Hines Management Co. (Reniassance Center)
Inergy
International Transmission Co.
ITC Holdings Corp
Michigan International Speedway
Milford Downtown Development Authority Commercial District Revitalization
The Oakland: Art Novelty Company
Powers Distributing
RTT USA, Inc
The Salvation Army Eastern Michigan Div. (Pro Bono)
The Salvation Army of Southeast Michigan Adult Rehabilitation Center
Santorini Estiatorio
Security Credit Union
Tera Networks
Vinology
YWCA of Metropolitan Detroit

FRANK PR
15 Maiden Ln Ste 608, New York, NY 10038
Tel.: (646) 861-0843
Web Site: www.frankpublicity.com

Year Founded: 2008

Agency Specializes In: Advertising, Event Planning & Marketing, Public Relations, Social Media

Clare Anne Darragh *(Partner)*
Lina Plath *(Partner)*
Stephanie Davidson *(VP-Publicity)*
Nastasya Morauw *(Dir-PR)*

Accounts:
Hamptons Film Festival
NY Comedy Festival
SnagFilms

FRAZIERHEIBY, INC.
(Formerly Clary Communications)
1500 Lake Shore Dr Ste 300, Columbus, OH 43204
Tel.: (614) 481-7534
Fax: (614) 481-8261
E-Mail: info@frazierheiby.com
Web Site: www.frazierheiby.com

Employees: 10
Year Founded: 1983

Agency Specializes In: Brand Development & Integration, Crisis Communications, Graphic Design, Internet/Web Design, Local Marketing, Logo & Package Design, Public Relations, Strategic Planning/Research

Bryan Haviland *(Pres)*
Tom Heiby *(CEO)*
Doug Frazier *(Chief Strategy Officer)*
Kathleen Anthony *(VP)*
Lara Kretler *(VP-Client Strategy & Product Dev)*
Denise Clark *(Client Svcs Dir)*
Ann Mulvany *(Acct Exec)*
Jillian Cameron *(Asst Acct Exec)*
Chelsea Hagan *(Asst Acct Exec)*

Accounts:
Ohio Corn Growers
Ohio Soybean Council; OH Direct Marketing, Media Kit, Media Relations, Soy Oil Ohio, Website
Sport Imports; Columbus, OH
Steptoe & Johnson

FREEBAIRN & COMPANY PUBLIC RELATIONS
3475 Lenox Rd Ste 900, Atlanta, GA 30326
Tel.: (404) 237-9945
Fax: (404) 231-2214
Toll Free: (800) 715-9435
E-Mail: cgriffith@freebairn.com
Web Site: www.freebairn.com

E-Mail for Key Personnel:
President: jfreebairn@freebairn.com
Public Relations: jtillinghast@freebairn.com

Employees: 20
Year Founded: 1980

National Agency Associations: PRSA

Agency Specializes In: Brand Development & Integration, Business Publications, Business-To-Business, Communications, Consulting, Consumer Marketing, Consumer Publications, Corporate Communications, Corporate Identity, Digital/Interactive, Electronic Media, Event Planning & Marketing, Exhibit/Trade Shows, Financial, Health Care Services, High Technology, Industrial, Information Technology, Internet/Web Design, Logo & Package Design, Magazines, New Product Development, Planning & Consultation, Point of Sale, Public Relations, Publicity/Promotions, Sports Market, Strategic Planning/Research

Approx. Annual Billings: $4,000,000

John C. Freebairn *(Pres)*
Sandy Chapman *(Sr VP & Dir-Media)*
Don Patton *(Sr Dir-Art)*
Jean G. Cobb *(Mgmt Supvr)*
Mack Kirkpatrick *(Dir-Creative)*
Jay Tillinghast *(Acct Exec-PR)*

Accounts:
AG First
The Baddour Center
Chamberlin Edmonds; Atlanta, GA Healthcare Revenue Recovery Services
Mana
Terry College of Business
Walker
YKK AP

FREESTYLE MEDIA INC
2611 40th St, Des Moines, IA 50310
Tel.: (703) 798-2395
E-Mail: info@freestylepr.com
Web Site: www.freestylepr.com

Agency Specializes In: Brand Development & Integration, Corporate Communications, Media Relations, Media Training, Public Relations

David Splivalo *(Pres & Chief Strategy Officer)*

Accounts:
Alliance Technologies
Caleris, Inc.
Cellcontrol
Farrells Extreme Bodyshaping
Iowa State
The ISU Research Park
Smashwords
Stickley on Security
Tikly
Vivisimo

THE FRESH IDEAS GROUP
2400 Spruce St Ste 100, Boulder, CO 80302
Tel.: (303) 449-2108
Fax: (303) 247-0058
E-Mail: info@freshideasgroup.com
Web Site: www.freshideasgroup.com

Agency Specializes In: Public Relations, Social Media

Flavia Florezell *(Gen Mgr)*
Glenda Catron *(Acct Mgr)*

Accounts:
New-Burpee Gardens
New-Conscious Alliance

FRONTIER STRATEGIES LLC
529 Pear Orchard Rd Ste C, Ridgeland, MS 39157
Tel.: (601) 856-1544
Fax: (601) 856-1625
Web Site: www.frontier.ms

Employees: 6

Agency Specializes In: Public Relations

Josh Gregory *(Co-Owner)*
Renee Ebner *(Head-Community & Acct Exec)*
Mary Lee *(Dir-Creative)*
Drew Hardin *(Acct Coord)*

Accounts:
College Savings Mississippi
Community Bank
Florence Gardens
Gregg Harper
Michael Guest
Mike Randolph
Mississippi Development Authority; Jackson, MS
Mississippi Republican Party
Neopolis Development
Phil Bryant
Randy Bubba Pierce

FSB CORE STRATEGIES
(Formerly Schubert Flint Public Affairs)
1415 L St Ste 1250, Sacramento, CA 95814
Tel.: (916) 448-4234
Fax: (916) 448-5933
E-Mail: kristy@fsbcorestrategies.com
Web Site: www.fsbcorestrategies.com

Employees: 13
Year Founded: 2003

Agency Specializes In: Advertising, Consumer Marketing, Government/Political, Health Care Services, High Technology, Planning & Consultation, Public Relations

Jeff Flint *(Pres)*
Kristy Babb *(Partner)*
Jerry Amante *(Gen Counsel & Sr VP)*
Sarah Pollo *(Acct Supvr & Dir-Social Media)*
Alex Burrola *(Sr Acct Exec)*
Will Hixson *(Asst Acct Exec)*
Alejandra Lauer *(Acct Coord)*

Accounts:
Allstate
Association of California Life & Health Insurance Companies
Coalition for California Jobs
PhRMA

FTI CONSULTING
(Formerly FD U.S. Communications, Inc.)
Wall St Plz 88 Pine St 32nd Fl, New York, NY 10005
Tel.: (212) 850-5600
Fax: (212) 850-5790
Web Site: www.fticonsulting.com/

Employees: 75
Year Founded: 1982

Agency Specializes In: Brand Development & Integration, Communications, Consumer Marketing, Corporate Identity, Financial, Graphic Design, Health Care Services, High Technology, Investor Relations, Logo & Package Design, New Product Development, Public Relations, Real Estate

David Roady *(Sr Mng Dir & Head-M&A Practice-Americas Strategic Comm)*
Lou Colasuonno *(Sr Mng Dir)*
David Grant *(Sr Mng Dir)*
Christa Hart *(Sr Mng Dir)*
Cara O'Brien *(Sr Mng Dir)*
Kevin Condron *(Mng Dir)*
Peter Decaro *(Mng Dir)*
Allan Kaufman *(Mng Dir)*
Hansol Kim *(Mng Dir)*
Kevin O'hare *(Mng Dir)*
Liz Park *(Mng Dir)*
Sudhi Rao *(Mng Dir)*
Jeff Turbedsky *(Mng Dir)*
Patricia Woodbury *(Mng Dir)*
John Yozzo *(Mng Dir)*
Ed Reilly *(CEO-Strategic Comm-Global)*
Shauna Wreschner *(Sr VP-Strategic Comm)*
Jeffrey Amling *(Sr Mng Dir-Bus Dev & Mktg)*
Doug Donsky *(Sr Mng Dir-Strategic Comm)*
Brian Maddox *(Sr Mng Dir-Strategic Comm)*
Bryan Armstrong *(Mng Dir-Strategic Comm)*
William Berkowitz *(Mng Dir-Forensic & Litigation Consulting)*
Stephen Calk *(Mng Dir-Strategic Comm)*
Russell Craig *(Sr Dir-Mktg)*
Alicia Jones *(Mktg Dir-Digital)*
Raina Gajjar *(Dir)*
Tom Papas *(Dir-Design)*
Heather Spence *(Coord-Learning & Dev Event)*

Accounts:
The Tractor Supply Company

Branches

FTI Consulting
(Formerly FD Third Person)
The Courtyard 33 Broadway, Nedlands, WA 6009 Australia
Tel.: (61) 8 9386 1233
Fax: (61) 8 9386 1715
Web Site: www.fticonsulting.com/

Employees: 7
Year Founded: 1993

Agency Specializes In: Public Relations

Stefan Dopking *(Sr Mng Dir-Corp Fin & Restructuring)*
Lachlan McIntosh *(Sr Mng Dir-Corp Fin & Restructuring)*
Kelly-Anne Trenfield *(Sr Mng Dir-Corp Fin & Restructuring)*
James Taplin *(Mng Dir-Corp Fin & Restructuring)*
Cameron Morse *(Sr Dir-Corp & Pub Affairs)*
Matthew Glennon *(Dir-Corp Fin & Restructuring)*
Shane Murphy *(Dir-Strategic Comm)*
Andrew Weatherley *(Dir-Corp Fin & Restructuring)*
Erin Graham *(Bus Dev Mgr)*

FTI Consulting
(Formerly FD U.S. - Boston)
200 State St 2nd Fl, Boston, MA 02109
Tel.: (617) 897-1500
Fax: (617) 747-3636
Web Site: www.fticonsulting.com

Employees: 10

Agency Specializes In: Public Relations, Sponsorship

Stephen J. Burlone *(Sr Mng Dir)*
Chris George *(Sr Mng Dir)*
Mark Grover *(Sr Mng Dir)*
Peter J. Lawson *(Sr Mng Dir)*
Ellen Smith *(Sr Mng Dir)*
John Sullivan *(Sr Mng Dir)*
Melanie Finn *(Mng Dir)*
Stephen L. Coulombe *(Sr Mng Dir-Corp Fin)*
Keith Jelinek *(Sr Mng Dir-Corp Fin)*
Mark Renzi *(Sr Mng Dir-Corp Fin)*
Jeffrey Bessette *(Mng Dir-Health Solutions)*
Brian M. Cashman *(Mng Dir-Corp Fin)*
Abby Healy *(Mgr-IR & Comm)*

Accounts:
Kratos Defense & Security Solutions, Inc

FTI Consulting Inc.
(Formerly FD U.S. - Chicago)
227 W Monroe St Ste 900, Chicago, IL 60602
Tel.: (312) 553-6700
Fax: (312) 553-6740
Web Site: www.fticonsulting.com/

Employees: 48

Agency Specializes In: Corporate Communications, Investor Relations

Bryan Armstrong *(Mng Dir)*
Angie Gorman *(Mng Dir)*
Edward Reilly *(CEO-Strategic Comm-Global)*
Tilden Katz *(Mng Dir-Crisis Comm & Issues Mgmt Practice)*
Katie Fitzgerald *(Sr Dir)*
Jocelyn Landau *(Sr Dir-Comm, Strategy & Res Practice)*
Shannon Marciano *(Dir-Integrated Mktg)*
Geoff Serednesky *(Dir)*
Shannon Sullivan *(Dir-Mktg-Tech Practice)*
Jessica Wagner *(Dir-Strategic Comm)*

Accounts:
Ace Hardware Media Relations

FTI Consulting
(Formerly FD U.S. - San Francisco)
1 Front St Ste 1600, San Francisco, CA 94111
Tel.: (415) 293-4410
Fax: (415) 293-4411
Web Site: www.fticonsulting.com

Employees: 10

Agency Specializes In: Investor Relations, Public Relations

Brian W. Napper *(Sr Mng Dir & Head-Dispute Advisory Svcs)*
Christine Beliveau *(Sr Mng Dir)*
Shelly D. Irvine *(Sr Mng Dir)*
Adam S. Bendell *(Chief Innovation Officer)*
Gregory R. Attiyeh *(Mng Dir-Corp Fin)*
Brandon Beal *(Mng Dir-Corp Fin)*
Jennifer Byrne *(Mng Dir-Corp Fin & Restructuring)*
Ann Hall *(Specialist-Mktg)*

Accounts:
FEMA
FTI Consulting

FUESSLER GROUP INC.
73 Louder's Ln, Jamaica Plain, MA 02130
Tel.: (617) 522-0550
Fax: (617) 522-0955
Toll Free: (888) FUESSLER
E-Mail: fuessler@fuessler.com
Web Site: www.fuessler.com

Employees: 2
Year Founded: 1984

Agency Specializes In: Advertising, Business-To-Business, Collateral, Communications, Consulting, Corporate Identity, Engineering, Environmental, Exhibit/Trade Shows, Gay & Lesbian Market, Graphic Design, Health Care Services, Industrial, Internet/Web Design, Logo & Package Design, Media Relations, Planning & Consultation, Public Relations, Publicity/Promotions, Real Estate, Strategic Planning/Research, Technical Advertising, Trade & Consumer Magazines

Approx. Annual Billings: $500,000

Breakdown of Gross Billings by Media: Collateral: 10%; Consulting: 20%; E-Commerce: 5%; Logo & Package Design: 5%; Pub. Rels.: 60%

Rolf A. Fuessler *(Founder)*

Accounts:
Erdman Anthony; Rochester, NY Engineering Services; 2008
Harriman Associates; Auburn, ME Architectural & Engineering Services; 1989
Hyman Hayes; Albany, NY Architects; 1998
Lombardo Associates; Newton, MA Engineering;

1986
Nantucket Architecture Group; Nantucket, MA; 1999
Ratio Architects; Indianapolis, IN Architects; 2008

FUJITA & MIURA PUBLIC RELATIONS INC
PO Box 3996, Lihue, HI 96766
Tel.: (808) 245-3677
Fax: (808) 245-3602
E-Mail: info@fmpr.net
Web Site: www.fmpr.net

Year Founded: 2000

Agency Specializes In: Advertising, Brand Development & Integration, Collateral, Crisis Communications, Event Planning & Marketing, Media Relations, Print, Promotions, Public Relations, Social Media

Jenny Fujita *(Partner)*
Joy Miura Koerte *(Partner)*

Accounts:
Kauai Community College

FULL CIRCLE PUBLIC RELATIONS
1 Independence Point Ste 115, Greenville, SC 29615
Tel.: (864) 672-9614
Fax: (864) 672-9619
E-Mail: info@fullcirclepr.com
Web Site: www.fullcirclepr.com

Year Founded: 2009

Agency Specializes In: Communications, Event Planning & Marketing, Media Relations, Public Relations, Social Media, Strategic Planning/Research

Liza Jones *(Partner)*
Kim Banks *(Client Svcs Dir)*
Carolyn Canington *(Acct Mgr)*
Heather Miller *(Acct Mgr)*
Hannah Trotter *(Acct Mgr)*

Accounts:
Milliken & Company

FULL SCALE MEDIA
276 5th Ave Ste 704, New York, NY 10001
Tel.: (212) 537-9236
Fax: (866) 297-6067
E-Mail: info@fullscalemedia.com
Web Site: www.fullscalemedia.com

Agency Specializes In: Advertising, Content, Promotions, Public Relations, Search Engine Optimization, Social Media, Strategic Planning/Research

Allison Kugel *(Creative Dir)*

Accounts:
New-The Grand Healthcare System
New-M Boutique International
New-Project Overlord

FURIA RUBEL COMMUNICATIONS
2 Hidden Ln Bldg 2, Doylestown, PA 18901
Tel.: (215) 340-0480
Fax: (215) 340-0580
E-Mail: gina@furiarubel.com
Web Site: www.furiarubel.com

Employees: 7
Year Founded: 2002

National Agency Associations: PRSA

Agency Specializes In: Business-To-Business, Cable T.V., Communications, Health Care Services, Hispanic Market, Legal Services, Pharmaceutical, Planning & Consultation, Public Relations, Publicity/Promotions, Strategic Planning/Research, Yellow Pages Advertising

Gina Furia Rubel *(Pres & CEO)*
Laura Powers *(CMO)*
Sarah Larson *(VP-PR)*
Kim Tarasiewicz *(Mgr-Acct & Production)*
Heather Truitt *(Sr Graphic Designer)*
Megan Quinn *(Acct Coord)*
Rose Strong *(Office Administrator)*

Accounts:
20nine Design
Broadband Consumer Services
Bucks County Bar Association
Bucks County Covered Bridges Festival
Chamberlain Hrdlicka Legal Marketing, Public Relations, Strategic Planning
Citrin Cooperman
Corodemus & Corodemus
Curtin & Heefner LLP (Agency of Record)
Elephant's Eye Bucks County Artist Studio Tour; 2008
Feldman Shepherd
First Federal of Bucks County (Agency of Record)
First Savings Bank of Perkasie (Agency of Record)
Furia & Turner; Philadelphia, PA
The Grain Exchange
Harmony Clean
Hepatitis B Foundation
Hope C. Lefeber LLC Legal Marketing, Public Relations, Strategic Planning
iQ Media Corp.
The James A. Michener Art Museum
Newman ADR Legal Marketing, Public Relations, Strategic Planning
Panitch Schwarze Belisario & Nadel Legal Marketing, Public Relations, Strategic Planning
Peacock Keller
Putney Food Co-op
Roland & Schlegel, LLC (Agency of Record)
Stampone D'Angelo Renzi DiPiero
Twilight Wish Foundation; Doylestown, PA; 2003
Veritext Legal Solutions Public Relations
White & Williams LLP
Willig, Williams & Davidson; Philadelphia, PA
Women's Business Forum; Doylestown, PA; 2003
Womens Resource Center

FUSION PUBLIC RELATIONS
570 7th Ave 9th Fl, New York, NY 10018
Tel.: (212) 651-4200
Fax: (212) 840-0505
E-Mail: info@fusionpr.com
Web Site: www.fusionpr.com

Employees: 35

Agency Specializes In: Advertising, Brand Development & Integration, Corporate Communications, Crisis Communications, Local Marketing, Media Relations, Media Training, Newspaper, Public Relations, Search Engine Optimization, Strategic Planning/Research, Viral/Buzz/Word of Mouth, Web (Banner Ads, Pop-ups, etc.)

Revenue: $2,000,000

Jordan R. Chanofsky *(Founder)*
Robert Geller *(Pres)*

Accounts:
Nationwide Building Society
Sierra Atlantic

Branches

Fusion Public Relations, Inc.
12121 Wilshire Blvd Ste 303, Los Angeles, CA 90025
Tel.: (310) 481-1431
Fax: (310) 481-1432
Web Site: www.fusionpr.com/

Employees: 10

Jorge Lajara *(Controller)*
Lauren Hillman *(Acct Supvr)*
Mark Prindle *(Acct Supvr)*
Fehmida Bholat *(Sr Acct Exec)*
Sara Preto *(Sr Acct Exec)*
Nicole Santos *(Asst Acct Exec)*

FYN PUBLIC RELATIONS
239 E 4th St Ste A-103, Loveland, CO 80537
Tel.: (970) 682-2420
Web Site: www.fynpr.com

Agency Specializes In: Digital/Interactive, Event Planning & Marketing, Media Planning, Media Relations, Media Training, Public Relations, Strategic Planning/Research

Nicole Yost *(Founder & Pres)*

Accounts:
Tutor Doctor Front Range

GABLE PR
(Acquired & Absorbed by Nuffer Smith Tucker Public Relations)

GAFFNEY BENNETT PUBLIC RELATIONS
1 Liberty Square Ste 201, New Britain, CT 6051
Tel.: (860) 229-0301
Fax: (860) 225-4627
Web Site: www.gbpr.com

Agency Specializes In: Brand Development & Integration, Crisis Communications, Media Relations, Media Training, Public Relations, Social Media, Strategic Planning/Research

Patrick Kinney *(Partner)*
Hank Spring *(Principal)*
Christina Griffin *(Acct Mgr)*

Accounts:
NBCUniversal

GALLAGHER PR
4115 Blackhawk Plz Cir Ste 100, Danville, CA 94506
Tel.: (925) 648-2014
Web Site: www.gallagherpr.com

Agency Specializes In: Content, Media Relations, Public Relations, Social Media, Strategic Planning/Research

Kevin Gallagher *(Mng Partner)*
Kimberly Hathaway *(Acct Dir)*

Accounts:
WibiData

GAME DAY COMMUNICATIONS
700 W Pete Rose Way, Cincinnati, OH 45203
Tel.: (513) 929-4263
Fax: (513) 929-0245
Web Site: www.gamedaypr.com

Agency Specializes In: Event Planning &

Marketing, Media Relations, Public Relations, Social Media, Strategic Planning/Research

Betsy Ross *(Founder & Pres)*
Jackie Reau *(CEO)*
Dayna De Leon *(Dir-Client Svcs)*
Pam McFarland *(Dir-Event Mktg)*
Rebecca Potzner *(Strategist-Social Media)*

Accounts:
Major League Baseball All-Star Game

THE GARNER CIRCLE LLC
303 Peachtree St Ste 1660, Atlanta, GA 30308
Tel.: (888) 560-6660
E-Mail: pr@thegarnercircle.com
Web Site: www.thegarnercircle.com

Year Founded: 2005

Agency Specializes In: Brand Development & Integration, Event Planning & Marketing, Media Buying Services, Media Relations, Public Relations, Social Media

Nicole Garner *(Founder & CEO)*
Carolyn Hilliard *(Dir-PR)*
Eugenia Johnson *(Dir-PR)*

Accounts:
Oxygen Media

GARRITY GROUP PUBLIC RELATIONS LLC
4110 Wolcott Ave NE Ste B, Albuquerque, NM 87109
Tel.: (505) 898-8689
Fax: (505) 294-5919
E-Mail: info@garritypr.com
Web Site: www.garritypr.com

Agency Specializes In: Collateral, Crisis Communications, Event Planning & Marketing, Graphic Design, Internet/Web Design, Media Relations, Public Relations, Social Media

Tom Garrity *(Pres & CEO)*
Amanda Molina *(VP)*
Tammy Luksich *(Acct Exec)*
Lily Quezada *(Acct Exec)*

Accounts:
BeWellNM Advertising, Communications, Digital Design, Public Relations, Research, Website
Fiery Foods Show

GBG & ASSOCIATES
500 W Harbor Dr, San Diego, CA 92101
Tel.: (619) 255-1661
Fax: (619) 255-8597
Web Site: www.gbgandassociates.com

Year Founded: 1978

Agency Specializes In: Advertising, Event Planning & Marketing, Media Relations, Public Relations, Social Media, Strategic Planning/Research

Georgi Bohrod *(Pres)*

Accounts:
Travel To Go

GBK PRODUCTIONS
7815 Beverly Blvd 3rd Fl, Los Angeles, LA 90036
Tel.: (323) 933-9989
Fax: (323) 933-9199
E-Mail: info@gbkkr.com
Web Site: www.gbkproductions.com

Agency Specializes In: Event Planning & Marketing, Public Relations

Gavin Keilly *(Founder & CEO)*
Carla Domen *(Exec VP)*
Ana Martins *(VP)*

Accounts:
New-M TV

GBRITT P.R. & MARKETING
505 Ocean St, South Portland, ME 04106
Tel.: (207) 775-2126
Fax: (207) 774-1653
E-Mail: jim@gbritt.com
Web Site: www.gbritt.com

Employees: 5

Agency Specializes In: Faith Based, Public Relations

Gillian Britt *(Owner)*
James Britt *(Principal)*
Emily Broadbent *(Acct Coord)*

Accounts:
Back Bay Grill
McTeague Higbee
Portland Ballet
Portland Harbor Hotel
Portland Symphony Orchestra

GCK PARTNERS
307 Seventh Ave Ste 2403, New York, NY 10001
Tel.: (212) 488-1080
Fax: (212) 488-1082
E-Mail: info@gckpartners.com
Web Site: gckpartners.com/

Year Founded: 2010

Agency Specializes In: Brand Development & Integration, Communications, Media Relations, Public Relations, Social Media

Scott Cooke *(Partner)*
Lionel Geneste *(Partner)*
Jim Kloiber *(Partner)*
Britta Towle *(Sr Acct Exec)*
Jeffrey Trosch *(Sr Acct Exec)*

Accounts:
Car2go North America LLC
New-Rodeo Drive Committee (Agency of Record) Beverly Hills Holiday Lighting Ceremony, Events, Marketing, Public Relations, Rodeo Drive Concours d'Elegance, Rodeo Drive Walk of Style

GEAR COMMUNICATIONS
39 Pleasant St, Stoneham, MA 2180
Tel.: (781) 279-3200
Fax: (781) 279-3201
Web Site: www.gearcommunications.com

Year Founded: 2009

Agency Specializes In: Crisis Communications, Email, Event Planning & Marketing, Media Relations, Media Training, Public Relations, Social Media

Jennifer Gear *(Owner)*
Connie Swaebe *(VP)*
Carla DAgostino *(Office Mgr)*
Kerry Keohane *(Mgr-Special Project)*
Megan Cunningham *(Acct Exec)*
Audrey Genest *(Asst Acct Exec)*

Accounts:
The Arc of MA
Coppermill Kitchen
CyndiBands
Magic Chef
Michelle Stacy
Orlando Pita
Reliable Corporation
T3 Hair Styling Products

GEBEN COMMUNICATION
539 S 5th St, Columbus, OH 43206
Tel.: (614) 364-2888
Web Site: www.gebencommunication.com

Year Founded: 2009

Agency Specializes In: Communications, Crisis Communications, Email, Media Relations, Public Relations, Social Media

Heather Whaling *(Founder & Pres)*
Megan Severs *(VP-Client Strategy)*
Tyler Durbin *(Dir-Bus Strategy)*
Rose Finnerty *(Acct Mgr)*
Taylor Ray Orsbon *(Acct Mgr)*
Jeana Harrington *(Mgr-Content & Community)*
Miranda Scott *(Mgr-Social Media)*
Lexi Messenger *(Acct Exec)*
Beth Shaheen *(Acct Exec)*
Heather Phillips *(Acct Coord)*

Accounts:
Columbus Marathon
Sysomos

GEIGER & ASSOCIATES PUBLIC RELATIONS INC
1846 Junwin Ct, Tallahassee, FL 32308
Tel.: (850) 942-6685
Fax: (850) 942-1057
E-Mail: info@geigerpr.com
Web Site: www.geigerpr.com

Year Founded: 1985

Agency Specializes In: Public Relations

Debbie Geiger *(Pres)*
George Percy *(Sr VP)*
Sharon Mathews *(VP)*

Accounts:
New-The Roanoke Valley Convention & Visitors Bureau

GEOFFREY WEILL ASSOCIATES
27 W 24 St, New York, NY 10010
Tel.: (212) 288-1144
Fax: (212) 288-5855
E-Mail: info@geoffreyweill.com
Web Site: www.geoffreyweill.com

Employees: 11

Agency Specializes In: Advertising, Collateral, Consulting, Crisis Communications, Direct-to-Consumer, Event Planning & Marketing, Exhibit/Trade Shows, International, Internet/Web Design, Media Buying Services, Media Planning, Media Relations, Print, Production (Print), Public Relations, Radio, Sponsorship, T.V., Telemarketing, Web (Banner Ads, Pop-ups, etc.)

Geoffrey Weill *(Pres)*
Ann-Rebecca Laschever *(Exec VP)*
Tania Philip *(Sr VP)*
Mark Liebermann *(VP)*
Suzanne Flores *(Acct Supvr)*

Accounts:
Algodon Mansion

Aman Resorts
Aqua Expeditions; Peru
Ashford Castle; Ireland
Beau-Rivage Palace
Cape Grace Hotel; Cape Town, South Africa
DouroAzul PR
Eleven Experience International Public Relations
Hotel Hassler Roma
Israel Ministry Of Tourism
IsramWorld
Jet Airways
New-Monastero Santa Rosa Public Relations
Nandana Private Resort
New-Paris Made Perfect Public Relations
QT Sydney Public Relations
The Set Public Relations
SHA Wellness Clinic Public Relations

GEORGE COHEN COMMUNICATIONS
1895 Ctr St Ste 9, Boston, MA 02132
Tel.: (617) 325-0011
Web Site: www.gccpr.com

Year Founded: 1993

Agency Specializes In: Communications, Event Planning & Marketing, Media Training, Public Relations, Social Media

George Cohen *(Pres)*
Tamara Gruber *(Partner)*
Amelie Gardella Johnson *(Dir-PR)*

Accounts:
Checkpoint Systems, Inc.
FitLinxx
Lumesse
Neotys
OATSystems
VaultLogix

GEORGE H. SIMPSON COMMUNICATIONS
280 Madison Ave, New York, NY 10006
Tel.: (203) 521-0352
E-Mail: george@georgesimpson.com
Web Site: georgesimpson.com/

Agency Specializes In: High Technology, Media Relations, Media Training, New Technologies, Public Relations

George H. Simpson *(Pres)*

Accounts:
New-Adaptly
New-Connexity, Inc.
New-PushSpring

GERMINDER & ASSOCIATES INC.
747 3rd Ave 2nd Fl, New York, NY 10017
Tel.: (212) 367-2170
Web Site: www.germinder.com

Agency Specializes In: Advertising, Content, Digital/Interactive, Media Relations, Promotions, Public Relations, Social Media, Strategic Planning/Research

Lea-Ann Germinder *(Pres)*

Accounts:
Assisi Animal Health Public Relations
Cat Writers Association (Agency of Record)

GETO & DEMILLY, INC.
276 5th Ave Ste 806, New York, NY 10001
Tel.: (212) 686-4551
Fax: (212) 213-6850
E-Mail: pr@getodemilly.com
Web Site: www.getodemilly.com

Employees: 15
Year Founded: 1980

Agency Specializes In: Arts, Communications, Crisis Communications, Event Planning & Marketing, Gay & Lesbian Market, Government/Political, Health Care Services, Media Relations, Public Relations, Real Estate

Michele de Milly *(Principal)*
Ethan Geto *(Principal)*
Joyce Baumgarten *(Sr VP)*
Kelly Ferraro *(VP & Acct Exec)*
Michael Gough *(Controller)*
Julie Hendricks *(Acct Exec)*
Daniel White *(Acct Exec)*

Accounts:
Common Ground
Fisher Brothers Real Estate
Jewish Home Lifecare; New York; 2007
Local 802, American Federation of Musicians
Sportime Tennis Center at Randall's Island
Zeckendorf Realty

GG BENITEZ & ASSOCIATES PUBLIC RELATIONS INC.
10755F Scripps Poway Pkwy Ste 537, San Jose, CA 92131
Tel.: (858) 621-0691
Web Site: www.ggbenitezpr.com

Year Founded: 2008

Agency Specializes In: Brand Development & Integration, Crisis Communications, Event Planning & Marketing, Public Relations, Social Media

G. G. Benitez *(Founder & CEO)*

Accounts:
Carousel Designs
Fun Kins
Mabels Labels
Net Nanny Software International Inc.
Open Me
Pleygo
Posh Mommy
Shaidee

GHIDOTTI COMMUNICATIONS
509 President Clinton Ave, Little Rock, AR 72201
Tel.: (501) 837-0206
Web Site: www.ghidotticommunications.com

Agency Specializes In: Crisis Communications, Event Planning & Marketing, Media Planning, Media Relations, Public Relations, Social Media, Strategic Planning/Research

Natalie Ghidotti *(Pres & CEO)*
Caroline Puddephatt *(Acct Exec-PR)*
April Fatula *(Acct Exec-PR)*

Accounts:
Outlets at Little Rock

GHOST COMMUNICATIONS
2836 Lyndale Ave S Ste 180, Minneapolis, MN 55408
Tel.: (612) 886-2806
E-Mail: info@ghost-pr.com
Web Site: www.ghost-pr.com

Agency Specializes In: Brand Development & Integration, Public Relations, Social Media, Strategic Planning/Research

Steve Gill *(Pres)*
Jo Watson *(Strategist-Brand)*

Accounts:
Lifetrack Resources

GIANT NOISE
1208 E 7th St 1st Fl, Austin, TX 78702
Tel.: (512) 382-9017
E-Mail: hello@giantnoise.com
Web Site: www.giantnoise.com

Agency Specializes In: Media Relations, Media Training, Public Relations, Social Media, Strategic Planning/Research

Elaine Garza *(Principal)*
Courtney Knittel *(VP-PR)*

Accounts:
New-Austin Food & Wine Alliance
New-The Hightower
New-Olamaie

GIBSON COMMUNICATIONS, INC.
2145 W Charleston St, Chicago, IL 60647
Tel.: (773) 278-7700
Fax: (773) 278-7750
E-Mail: information@gibsoncommunications.com

Glynis Gibson *(Pres)*
Chere Gibson *(Partner)*

Accounts:
Airis Computer Corporation
Cat Hospital of Chicago
Companion Worlds
JELCO, Inc
Jelco, Inc.
Mondo
Norvax
Palindrome
Progio
Video Furnace
Zenith Data Systems

GILES COMMUNICATIONS, LLC
2975 Westchester Ave Ste 402, Purchase, NY 10577
Tel.: (914) 644-3500
Fax: (914) 696-4120
E-Mail: info@giles.com
Web Site: www.giles.com

Employees: 15
Year Founded: 1986

Agency Specializes In: Communications, Event Planning & Marketing, Exhibit/Trade Shows, High Technology, Internet/Web Design, Investor Relations, Multimedia, Public Relations

Peter Giles *(Pres)*
Marc Ferris *(Acct Mgr)*

Accounts:
Carlson and Carlson Inc.
Michael Colina
NAMM (the National Association of Music Merchants)
NewTek
Yamaha Corporation of America
Yamaha Electronics Corp.

GINNY RICHARDSON PUBLIC RELATIONS
15 Salt Creek Ln Ste 122, Hinsdale, IL 60521
Tel.: (630) 789-8555
Fax: (630) 789-9911
E-Mail: info@gr-pr.com
Web Site: www.gr-pr.com

Year Founded: 1979

Agency Specializes In: Media Relations, Public Relations, Social Media

Ginny Richardson *(Founder & Pres)*
Andy Richardson *(VP)*

GIOMBETTI PUBLIC RELATIONS

30060 Rancho California Rd Ste 240, Temecula, CA 92591
Tel.: (612) 355-0512
Web Site: www.giombettipr.com

Year Founded: 2001

Agency Specializes In: Brand Development & Integration, Corporate Communications, Crisis Communications, Public Relations, Social Media, Strategic Planning/Research

Anthony Giombetti *(Mng Dir & Principal)*

Accounts:
Cherry Blooms

GLOBAL-5, INC.

(d/b/a Global-5 Communications)
2180 W State Rd 434 Ste 1150, Longwood, FL 32779
Tel.: (407) 571-6789
Fax: (407) 571-6777
Toll Free: (800) 570-5743
E-Mail: info@global-5.com
Web Site: www.global-5.com

Employees: 12
Year Founded: 1995

Agency Specializes In: Advertising, Affiliate Marketing, Automotive, Aviation & Aerospace, Brand Development & Integration, Broadcast, Business Publications, Business-To-Business, Collateral, Commercial Photography, Communications, Consulting, Corporate Communications, Crisis Communications, Custom Publishing, Customer Relationship Management, Electronic Media, Event Planning & Marketing, Government/Political, Graphic Design, High Technology, Identity Marketing, In-Store Advertising, Information Technology, Integrated Marketing, Internet/Web Design, Logo & Package Design, Market Research, Media Buying Services, Media Planning, Media Relations, Media Training, Multimedia, New Technologies, Out-of-Home Media, Planning & Consultation, Point of Purchase, Point of Sale, Promotions, Publishing, Regional, Sales Promotion, Social Marketing/Nonprofit, Sponsorship, Strategic Planning/Research, T.V., Transportation

Jenni Luke *(CFO)*
Matt Hamill *(COO & Exec VP)*
C. J. Stankiewicz *(Dir-Creative)*
Chris Patton *(Sr Mgr-Media & Outreach)*
Tracie Kendziora *(Project Mgr-Pub Info & Mktg)*
Jerame Rief *(Mgr-IT & Specialist-Security)*
Jane O'Dowd *(Supvr-Comm & Outreach)*
Kathy Yarosh *(Supvr-Video Production)*
Caitlin Vaiskauskas *(Specialist-Outreach & Media)*

Accounts:
AAA
BMW
Federal Highway Administration
Florida Department of Transportation District 5
Honda
LYNX
Mercedes-Benz
Transportation Security Administration
U.S Air Force

GLOBAL RESULTS COMMUNICATIONS

2405 Mccabe Way # 210, Irvine, CA 92614-6244
Tel.: (949) 608-0276
Fax: (949) 955-3616
E-Mail: bruelas@globalresultspr.com
Web Site: www.globalresultspr.com

Employees: 10

Agency Specializes In: Communications, Public Relations

Valerie Christopherson *(Mng Dir)*
Lora Friedrichsen *(Exec VP)*
Charlotte Rubin *(Sr VP)*
Barbara Ruelas *(Sr Mgr-Ops)*
Evan Sneider *(Sr Acct Exec)*
Lauren Bruschi *(Acct Exec)*

Accounts:
151 Advisors PR, Social Media Campaign
CellTrust Brand Awareness, Public Relations, Strategic Media
Epson America Epson Moverio, Strategic PR
INSTEON Analyst Relations, Strategic Media
LSN Mobile Brand Awareness, Media Relations
mGage Brand Awareness, Public Relations, Strategic Media
The Mobile Marketing Association
Myriad Analyst Relations, Event Coordination, Media Relations, Social Media Strategy, Trade Show
Nuance Inc.
Numerex Brand Awareness, Public Relations, Strategic Media
Somo Case Studies, Events, Marketing, PR, Strategic Media Relation
New-View Technologies Media Relations, Social Media, Strategic Communication
Voxox Analyst Relations, Cloud Phone, Consumer Solutions, Media, SMB, Telecoms
WDS PR

GLOBAL STRATEGY GROUP

215 Park Ave S 15th Fl, New York, NY 10003
Tel.: (212) 260-8813
E-Mail: info@globalstrategygroup.com
Web Site: www.globalstrategygroup.com

Agency Specializes In: Corporate Communications, Crisis Communications, Digital/Interactive, Media Relations, Public Relations, Strategic Planning/Research

Jefrey Pollock *(Pres)*
Jon Silvan *(CEO)*
Scott Elder *(Partner)*
Britt Power *(Partner)*
Tanya Meck *(Mng Dir & Exec VP)*
Jim Papa *(Exec VP)*
Robert Bibel *(Sr VP-Fin)*
Glen Caplin *(Sr VP)*
Dana Yeganian *(Sr VP)*
Marjorie McCarthy *(VP-Mktg & Bus Dev)*

Accounts:
Airbnb
Congressional Special Elections
ESPN
PhRMA
Utilidata (Communications & Public Relations Agency of Record) Press
Valeant Pharmaceuticals

GLOBALFLUENCY

4151 Middlefield Rd, Palo Alto, CA 94303
Tel.: (650) 328-5555
Fax: (650) 328-5016
E-Mail: donovan@globalfluency.com
Web Site: www.globalfluency.com

Employees: 55
Year Founded: 1987

Agency Specializes In: Consulting, Consumer Marketing, Public Relations, Publicity/Promotions

Approx. Annual Billings: $8,500,000

Donovan Neale-May *(Pres)*
David Murray *(Exec VP)*
Bryan DeRose *(VP-Bus Dev)*
Liz Miller *(VP-Ops)*
Monica Noriega *(Controller-Fin)*
Mary Anne Hensley *(Dir-Content & Mktg Programs)*
Alex Holt *(Dir-Web & Interactive)*

Accounts:
Customer Experience Board; Palo Alto, CA
MarketClik; Palo Alto, CA
Wilocity; Sunnyvale, CA

GMG PUBLIC RELATIONS INC

23 Blauvelt St, Nanuet, NY 10954
Tel.: (845) 627-3000
Web Site: www.gmgpr.com

Year Founded: 1991

Agency Specializes In: Advertising, Collateral, Internet/Web Design, Media Relations, Public Relations, Social Media

Risa B. Hoag *(Pres)*

Accounts:
Monster Mini Golf

GOFF PUBLIC

(Private-Parent-Single Location)
255 E Kellogg Blvd Ste 102, Saint Paul, MN 55101
Tel.: (651) 292-8062
Fax: (651) 292-8091
Web Site: www.goffpublic.com

Employees: 16
Year Founded: 1978

Agency Specializes In: Crisis Communications, Event Planning & Marketing, Media Relations, Media Training, Public Relations, Social Media, Strategic Planning/Research

Revenue: $1,500,000

Chris Georgacas *(Pres & CEO)*
Heidi Larson *(CFO & Principal)*
Jennifer Hellman *(COO & Principal)*
Lynda Chilstrom *(Acct Dir)*
Chris Duffy *(Dir-Media Rels)*
Elizabeth Emerson *(Dir-Govt Rels)*
Tricia Nissen *(Sr Acct Exec & Sr Writer)*
Sara Thatcher *(Sr Acct Exec)*
Jonathan Bohn *(Acct Exec)*
Kelly Sam *(Acct Exec)*

Accounts:
Minnesota Innocence Project

GOGERTY MARRIOTT

(Formerly Gogerty Stark Marriott)
2900 Century Sq 1501 4th Ave Ste 2900, Seattle, WA 98101
Tel.: (206) 292-3000
E-Mail: info@gogertymarriott.com
Web Site: www.gogertymarriott.com

Employees: 15
Year Founded: 1978

Agency Specializes In: Business-To-Business, Communications, Corporate Identity, Electronic

Media, Entertainment, Food Service, Health Care Services, Industrial, Investor Relations, Logo & Package Design

Revenue: $25,000,000

Robert E. Gogerty *(Founder, Chm & Partner)*
Joel VanEtta *(Sr Principal)*

Accounts:
AT&T Communications Corp.
The Boeing Company
Davis Wright Tremaine
Regional Transit Authority (RTA)
Swedish Medical Center

GOLDBERG MCDUFFIE COMMUNICATIONS, INC.
250 Park Ave Fl 7, New York, NY 10177-0799
Tel.: (212) 705-4211
Fax: (212) 980-5228
E-Mail: bookpr@goldbergmcduffie.com
Web Site: www.goldbergmcduffie.com

Lynn Goldberg *(Owner)*
Angela Baggetta Baggetta *(VP & Dir-Publicity)*
Kathleen Carter Zrelak *(VP & Dir-Publicity)*
Jeff Umbro *(Mgr-Digital Mktg)*

Accounts:
Library of America

GOLDIN SOLUTIONS
928 Broadway Ste 900, New York, NY 10010
Tel.: (212) 319-3451
E-Mail: info@goldinsolutions.com
Web Site: www.goldinsolutions.com

Agency Specializes In: Brand Development & Integration, Crisis Communications, Media Relations, Public Relations, Social Media

John Eddy *(VP)*

Accounts:
New-iboss Inc.

GOLDMAN & ASSOCIATES
2428 Almeda Ave Ste 170, Norfolk, VA 23513
Tel.: (757) 625-2518
Fax: (757) 625-4336
E-Mail: info@goldmanandassociates.com
Web Site: www.goldmanandassociates.com

Employees: 11
Year Founded: 1967

Agency Specializes In: Public Relations

Dean S. Goldman *(Owner & Pres)*
Audrey Knoth *(Exec VP)*
Scott McCaskey *(Acct Dir)*

Accounts:
Government
Information Technology Industries

GOLIN
(Formerly GolinHarris)
875 N. Michigan Ave 26th Fl, Chicago, IL 60611
Tel.: (312) 729-4000
Fax: (312) 729-4010
E-Mail: ptrocks@golin.com
Web Site: www.golin.com

Employees: 150
Year Founded: 1956

National Agency Associations: 4A's-AAF-COPF

Agency Specializes In: Brand Development & Integration, Business-To-Business, Communications, Consumer Marketing, Corporate Communications, Environmental, Event Planning & Marketing, Financial, Food Service, Government/Political, Health Care Services, Pets , Pharmaceutical, Public Relations, Publicity/Promotions, Sponsorship, Sports Market, Strategic Planning/Research, Travel & Tourism

Ellen Ryan Mardiks *(Vice Chm & Pres-Consumer Mktg Practice)*
Fred Cook *(CEO)*
Brian Beck *(CFO & Exec VP)*
Ron D'Innocenzo *(Chief Creative Officer)*
Gary Rudnick *(Pres-Americas)*
Zandra Zuno *(Exec VP & Head-Natl Practice-Multicultural Mktg)*
Brian Snyder *(Exec VP & Exec Dir-Digital)*
Greg Sendi *(Exec VP)*
Farah Bulsara Speer *(Exec VP)*
Carrie Von Der Sitt *(Exec VP)*
Amy Kennedy *(Sr VP)*
Samantha Schwarz *(Sr VP)*
Elizabeth DeLuca *(VP & Dir-Media Rels)*
Natalie Sundquist *(VP & Dir-HR & US Talent Mgmt)*
Jesse Dienstag *(Head-Plng & Exec Dir)*
Hertha A. Meyer *(Exec Dir-Res & Analytics)*
Mitch Delaplane *(Dir-Creative)*
Sarah Spearing *(Dir-HR)*
Brittany Rouse *(Sr Mgr-Media)*
Stephanie Scott *(Sr Mgr-Digital)*
Erica Fischer *(Sr Acct Mgr)*
Daniel Hernandez *(Mgr-Media Rels)*
Kristen Lueck *(Mgr)*
Pepe Maldonado *(Mgr-Media-Multicultural)*
Traci Thurmond *(Mgr-Digital)*
Scott Farrell *(Co-Reg Mng Dir)*

Accounts:
American Frozen Food Institute PR
Astellas Pharma US, Inc. Immunology, Organ Donation, Public Relations; 2008
BP Consumer PR, US Fuels; 2008
Catalist LLC
Crayola LLC Public Relations
Discover Financial Services Global Agency of Record
Dow Chemical Dow Building & Construction, Dow Building Solutions, Dow Construction Chemicals, PR
General Mills; Minneapolis, MN Fiber One
Harmonix Guerrilla Marketing, Social Media, Special Events
Humana Inc (Public Relations Agency of Record)
IndyCar Series
Las Vegas Sands Corporation Sands Eco 360 Global Sustainable Program
Matrixx Initiatives, Inc.; Scottsdale, AZ
MATTEL, INC. Barbie, Hot Wheels, Media Relations, Public Relations
McDonald's Corporation Campaign: "National Hiring Day: I Love My McJob", Public Relations, Sirloin Burger, Social, Videos
McDonald's USA
National Peanut Board (Public Relations Agency of Record) Advertising, Client Engagements, Consumer, Content Creation, Digital, Marketing, Social Media, Traditional Advertising
NBTY, Inc (Agency of Record) Brand Awareness, Consumer Marketing, Media Relations, Social Media
Nintendo of America 3DS, Campaign: "How PR Proved That Seeing Is Believing", PR, Wii
Owens Corning
PepsiCo Inc.
Ronald McDonald House Charities
Sargento Foods (Agency of Record)
Schwan's Bakery Inc.
Society of Actuaries PR
Sprint (US Strategic Communications & Creative Services Agency of Record) Media Relations
State of Florida Department of Citrus; Lakeland, FL
Symmetricom
Tier 3
Toyota Motor Sales Campaign: "Real Camry/Virtual Reveal"
Tyson Foods, Inc.; Springdale, AR
Unilever; Englewood Cliffs, NJ Bertolli, Breyers, Campaign: "Selling Pleasure, Not Ice Cream", Klondike, Magnum Ice Cream, Public Relations, Social Media
Wal-Mart Stores, Inc.; Bentonville, AR Brand PR
The Waters Corp
The Wrigley Company

Golin
(Formerly GolinHarris)
3200 Park Center Dr Ste 750, Costa Mesa, CA 92626
Tel.: (714) 662-5100
Fax: (714) 662-5198
Web Site: www.golin.com

Employees: 6

National Agency Associations: 4A's

Agency Specializes In: Public Relations

Traci Renner *(Exec Dir)*
Joshua Levitt *(Sr Mgr)*
Kimberly Osborne *(Mgr-Digital)*

Accounts:
Bling Nation Analyst Relations, Consumer Education, Consumer Public Relations, Influencer Relations, Mobile Tap Services, Multi-Market Launches, National Media Relations, Pay Point-of-Sale Services
Mitsubishi Digital Electronics America LDD & DLP HDTVs, LaserVue HDTV; 2008

Golin
(Formerly GolinHarris)
601 W 5th St 4th Fl, Los Angeles, CA 90071-2004
Tel.: (213) 623-4200
Fax: (213) 895-4746
Web Site: www.golin.com

Employees: 80
Year Founded: 1973

National Agency Associations: 4A's-COPF

Agency Specializes In: Communications, Public Relations, Sponsorship

Timothy Bruns *(Head-Creator Community & Dir-Creative)*
Negin Kamali *(Exec Dir)*
Corey Langworthy *(Exec Dir)*
Kelly Carkeek Striewski *(Exec Dir)*
Kristen Berry-Owen *(Dir-Res & Analytics)*
Shannon Nelson *(Dir-HR-Western Reg & New York)*
Chad Nishimura *(Sr Mgr)*
Angela Seits *(Sr Mgr-Digital)*
Joshua Weisz *(Sr Mgr)*
Alison Holt Brummelkamp *(Exec Media Dir)*
Samantha Sackin *(Assoc Mng Dir)*

Accounts:
B3 Fit, Inc 'R.I.P.P.E.D', PR
Cunard Campaign: "Media Manager"
Kaiser Permanente Public Relations; 2008
Nestle USA Butterfinger, Campaign: "Concession Stands to the Big Screen!"
Nintendo of America, Inc.
Toyota Motor Sales, U.S.A., Inc.
VTech Communications, Inc.

Golin
(Formerly GolinHarris)
600 Battery St, 3rd Fl, San Francisco, CA 94111
Tel.: (415) 318-4360

E-Mail: ssimkrause@golin.com
Web Site: www.golin.com

Employees: 10
Year Founded: 1982

National Agency Associations: 4A's-COPF

Agency Specializes In: Communications, High Technology, Public Relations, Sponsorship

Keith Martin *(Mng Dir)*
Deanne Yamamoto *(Mng Dir)*
Scott Farrell *(Pres-Global Corp Comm)*
Matt Neale *(Pres-Intl)*
Stephen Jones *(Exec VP & Head-Catalyst Community)*
Brian Snyder *(Exec VP & Exec Dir-Digital)*
Jennifer Baker-Asiddao *(Exec Dir)*
Alison Holt Brummelkamp *(Exec Dir-Media)*
Leah Kissel Talbot *(Dir-Recruiting)*
Corianda Dimes *(Sr Mgr-Digital)*
Audrey Luk *(Sr Writer)*
Samantha Sackin *(Assoc Mng Dir)*

Accounts:
New-Clif Bar Inc. Company & Brand Initiatives, Public Relations

Golin
(Formerly GolinHarris)
4500 Biscayne Blvd Ph, Miami, FL 33137
Tel.: (305) 573-9955
Fax: (305) 573-1649
E-Mail: iabrams@golin.com
Web Site: www.golin.com

Employees: 11

National Agency Associations: 4A's-COPF

Agency Specializes In: Communications, Public Relations

Julie Dixon *(Deputy Mng Dir)*
Ian Abrams *(Exec VP & Exec Dir)*
Kimberley Collins *(Sr VP)*
Shannon Varroney *(VP & Acct Dir)*
Amgad Naguib *(VP-Pub Affairs & Dir)*
Katie Castillo *(Dir-Media)*
Zach Schmitz *(Dir-Creative)*
Naylet Aguayo *(Sr Mgr)*
Andrea Nank *(Sr Mgr)*
Darlene Smiley *(Office Mgr)*

Accounts:
Alberta Cancer Board Tobacco Control & Cessation; 2008
American Cancer Society, Florida Division; 2008
The American Legacy Foundation
Auxilium Pharmaceuticals
BBC Mundo; 2008
Enterprise Florida
Florida Dept. of Citrus PR
International Kids Foundation; 2008
Jackson Memorial Foundation Philanthropic Program; 2008
Staples

Golin
(Formerly GolinHarris)
1575 Northside Dr NW Bldg 200 Ste 200, Atlanta, GA 30318
Tel.: (404) 880-4600
Fax: (404) 523-3483
E-Mail: kcosgrove@golin.com
Web Site: www.golin.com

Employees: 25
Year Founded: 1956

National Agency Associations: 4A's-COPF

Agency Specializes In: Communications, Public Relations

Kathy Cosgrove *(Mng Dir)*
Lillian Ansley *(Exec Dir)*
Susan Chana *(Exec Dir-Media)*
Mark Dvorak *(Exec Dir)*
Matthew Henson *(Exec Dir)*

Accounts:
American Peanut Council
Flowers Foods
Georgia Department of Economic Development; 2008
Grand Ole Opry PR
Morehouse School of Medicine; Atlanta, GA (Agency of Record) Branding, Communication, Direct Marketing, Media Relations, Message Development, Strategic Counsel, Support, Website Content Redevelopment
National Peanut Board (Public Agency of Record) Advertising, Client Engagements, Consumer, Content Creation, Digital, Marketing, Social Media, Special Events, Trade Engagement, Traditional Advertising
United Egg Producers

Golin
(Formerly GolinHarris)
2809 Boston St Ste 8, Baltimore, MD 21224
Tel.: (410) 558-2103
Fax: (410) 558-2188
E-Mail: jdixon@golin.com
Web Site: www.golin.com

Employees: 4

National Agency Associations: COPF

Agency Specializes In: Public Relations

Neal Flieger *(Mng Dir)*
Ginger Porter *(Mng Dir)*
Deanne Yamamoto *(Mng Dir)*
Julie Dixon *(Deputy Mng Dir)*
Shannon Varroney *(VP & Acct Dir)*
Andrea Nank *(Sr Mgr)*

Golin
(Formerly GolinHarris)
919 3rd Ave 15th Fl, New York, NY 10022
Tel.: (212) 373-6000
Fax: (212) 373-6001
E-Mail: ttelloni@golin.com
Web Site: www.golin.com

Employees: 25
Year Founded: 1985

National Agency Associations: 4A's-COPF

Agency Specializes In: Communications, Public Relations

Matt Neale *(Co-Pres)*
Mark Rozeen *(Exec VP-Insights & Innovations)*
Jennifer Dobrzelecki *(Sr VP & Exec Dir)*
Ashley Hurst *(Sr VP & Dir-Digital)*
Gaston Terrones Dimant *(Exec Dir & Head-Corp Practice)*
David Catlett *(Exec Dir-Healthcare Practice)*
Adam Pawluk *(Exec Dir-Creative)*
Mary Cunney *(Dir-Media Rels)*
Joy Lee-Calio *(Dir-Consumer & Bus Dev)*
Jon Silver *(Dir-Digital)*
Andrea Nank *(Sr Mgr)*
Shae Sneed *(Sr Mgr)*
Barbara Vaccaro *(Office Mgr)*
Leah-Michelle Nebbia *(Mgr)*

Accounts:
AccuWeather, Inc Digital Media, Public Relations, Social Media
Blythedale Children's Hospital Public Relations Strategy, Strategic Communications
GlaxoSmithKline Consumer Healthcare Alli, Aquafresh, NicoDerm, Nicorette, Sensodyne, TUMS
Kayak
NYX Cosmetics
Olympus America Inc.; 2007
Stoli Group USA PR Strategy, Stolichnaya Vodka
Unilever Lipton

Golin
(Formerly GolinHarris)
Three Galleria Tower 13155 Noel Rd Ste 750, Dallas, TX 75240
Tel.: (972) 341-2500
Fax: (972) 341-2501
E-Mail: gporter@golin.com
Web Site: www.golin.com

Employees: 25

National Agency Associations: 4A's-COPF

Agency Specializes In: Public Relations, Sponsorship

Ginger Porter *(Mng Dir & Exec Dir)*
Jacqi Richardson *(VP & Dir)*
Alex Tan *(Exec Dir-Digital & Social Media)*
Lisa Zlotnick *(Exec Dir-Media Rels-Nintendo of America)*
Jason Wright *(Creative Dir)*
Victoria Cardenas *(Sr Mgr-Digital)*
Mariam Shahab *(Sr Mgr-Digital)*
Kimberly Kulesh *(Mgr)*
Meredith Lockhart *(Mgr-Media)*
Austin Reed *(Mgr-Content)*

Golin
(Formerly GolinHarris)
2200 Clarendon Blvd Ste 1100, Arlington, VA 22201
Tel.: (703) 741-7500
Fax: (703) 741-7501
E-Mail: lbailey@golin.com
Web Site: www.golin.com

Employees: 30

Agency Specializes In: Public Relations

Robert Philips *(Exec Dir-Digital)*

Accounts:
First Candle
McDonald's
Rosetta Stone Language-Learning Software; 2008
United Postal Service

Golin
(Formerly GolinHarris)
1809 7th Ave Ste 600, Seattle, WA 98101
Tel.: (425) 895-8527
Fax: (206) 505-8265
Web Site: www.golin.com

Year Founded: 1982

Don Varyu *(Exec Dir)*
Eileen Tanner *(Dir-Media)*

Accounts:
HTC America (Agency of Record)

Publicom
Torre De Rio Sul, Rau Lauro Muller 116, CJ 1206 Botafogo, CEP 22290-160 Brazil
Tel.: (55) 21 2543 3388
Fax: (55) 21 2543 6565
Web Site: www.s2publicom.com.br

Employees: 150

Agency Specializes In: Public Relations

Luciana Gurgel *(Mng Partner)*
Roberto Tucci *(CFO)*
Lorena Ribeiro *(Dir-Rio de Janeiro)*

Accounts:
General Shopping Brasil
Grupo Santillana
Honeywell
McDonald's
OSI Restaurant Partners, Inc.
Petrobras
UCI Cinemas
Warner Home Entertainment

Publicom
Ed Sudameris Av Eng Luiz Carlos Berrini, 1297 - 3 andar, Sao Paulo, CEP 04571-010 Brazil
Tel.: (55) 11 5505 1628
Fax: (55) 11 5505 7426
Web Site: www.s2publicom.com.br

Employees: 40

Agency Specializes In: Public Relations

Luciana Gurgel *(Mng Partner)*
Alessandra Ritondaro *(Exec Dir)*
Ian Castello Branco *(Dir-Digital)*
Marcia Cirino *(Dir-New Bus)*
Thiago Massari *(Dir-IT & Entertainment)*
Claudia Pires *(Dir-Agribusiness & Fin)*
Priscila Rocha *(Dir-Education & Tourism)*
Everton Schultz *(Dir-Digital & Creation)*
Gabriel Maturino Dos Anjos *(Analyst-Social Media)*

Accounts:
Club Med
Honeywell
Kraft Foods Brasil
McDonald's Ronald McDonald House Charities
Petrobras
SC Johnson

Europe, Middle East & Africa

Action Global Communications
6 Kondilaki Street, 1090, Nicosia, Cyprus
Mailing Address:
PO Box 24676, 1302 Nicosia, Cyprus
Tel.: (357) 22 818884
Fax: (357) 22 873632
E-Mail: george.k@actionprgroup.com
Web Site: www.actionprgroup.com

Agency Specializes In: Public Relations

Rebecca Theodorou *(Head-Intl Client Hub)*
Dimitris Ioannides *(Gen Mgr)*
Natalie Christophidou *(Acct Dir)*
Kathy Christodoulou *(Dir & Bus Dev Mgr)*
Ria Argyrides *(Acct Mgr)*
Demetra Eleftheriou *(Acct Mgr-PR)*
Panayiotis Othonos *(Acct Mgr)*
Leslie Savva *(Acct Exec-PR)*
Amanda Chick *(Client Mgr-Intl)*

Accounts:
Amadeus
Boehringer Ingelheim
British Airways
Handy's Security Systems Digital Communications Strategy, Email Marketing, Public Relations, Social Media
Microsoft Windows 7
OMV
Oxford Business Group
Voestalpine

Golin
(Formerly GolinHarris)
Capricorn Tower 7th Fl, PO Box 116462, Sheikh Zayed Rd, Dubai, United Arab Emirates
Tel.: (971) 4 332 3308
Fax: (971) 4 331 6733
E-Mail: yvafeas@golin.com
Web Site: www.golin.com

Employees: 22
Year Founded: 2004

Agency Specializes In: Event Planning & Marketing, Media Relations, Public Relations

Yiannis Vafeas *(Mng Dir)*
Gregory Tikhanoff *(Reg Mng Dir)*

Accounts:
3M
MasterCard Worldwide

Golin
(Formerly GolinHarris)
Via Pietrasanta 14, 20141 Milan, Italy
Tel.: (39) 02 57 61 0155
Fax: (39) 02 57 37 8300
E-Mail: gmentore@golin.com
Web Site: www.golin.com

Agency Specializes In: Public Relations

Franco Ricchiuti *(Mng Dir)*
Nicola Rovetta *(Dir-Creative)*

Golin
(Formerly GolinHarris)
Square d"Orleans, 80 rue Taitbout, 75439 Paris, France
Tel.: (33) 140415600
Fax: (33) 140415656
Web Site: www.golin.com

Agency Specializes In: Advertising

Pierre-Hubert Meilhac *(Mng Dir)*
Alois Nuffer *(Corp Head)*

Accounts:
The Biomedecine Agency
Foods International OVOmaltine, Twinings, La Tisaniere, & Jordans
The French Ministry for Agriculture
State of Florida Department of Citrus

Golin
(Formerly GolinHarris)
Fox Court, 14 Gray's Inn Road, London, WC1X 8WS United Kingdom
Tel.: (44) 20 7067 0600
Fax: (44) 870 990 5447
E-Mail: mneale@golin.com
Web Site: www.golin.com

Employees: 200

Bibi Hilton *(Mng Dir)*
Matthew Neale *(Pres-Intl)*
Nick Bishop *(Head-Corp Comm)*
Charlie Coney *(Head-Creative-EMEA)*
Neil Kleiner *(Head-Social Media)*
Elizabeth Littlewood *(Head-Tech)*
Kate Miller *(Head-Media)*
Martin Frizell *(Exec Dir-Media)*
Zac Schwarz *(Exec Dir-Creative)*
Gemma Vardon *(Exec Dir-Creative)*
Tom Parker *(Corp Dir)*

Accounts:
AB InBev UK Leffe, Stella Artois
Baringa Partners Corporate Communications, Media
Danone Campaign: "World's Tastiest Spoon", Digital, Oykos, Press, Public Relations, Social Media
Diageo Consumer PR, Smirnoff
Dow Chemical
Dr Schar Consumer PR, DS-gluten-free, Glutafin
EMC PR
Expedia
Globalaw International PR
Lastminute.com Campaign: "Love Living Last Minute", Consumer PR, Media
Mondelez International Cadbury, Cadbury Crispello, Campaign: "Joyville", Consumer PR, Digital, Experiential, In-Store, OOH, Outdoor, Public Relations, Sampling, Social, Social Media, TV, VOD
Nokia
Omega Pharma Consumer & Trade Media, Jungle Formula, Nytol, Over-the-Counter, Solpadeine
Orange
Reckitt Benckiser MegaRed Omega-3 Krill Oil, PR
Rosetta Stone Language-Learning Software; 2008
Sainsbury's Consumer Communications
TotallyMoney.com PR
Unilever Lipton, PR, Social Media
William Hill Consumer PR
Worldpay Corporate Public Relations
Wrigleys

Golin
(Formerly GolinHarris)
Box 6518, Birger Jarlsgatan 57c, SE-11383 Stockholm, Sweden
Tel.: (46) 8 506 353 00
Fax: (46) 8 506 353 33
E-Mail: sara.wretblad-carreras@golinharris.se
Web Site: www.golin.com

Jesper Kling *(Mng Dir)*
Kristina Oldfeldt *(Exec Dir)*
Anna Hansson *(Dir-Media)*

Accounts:
Blomdahl Medical
Cefar
Finnair
Getty Images
LANDesk
Merck Sharp & Dohme, MSD
Philips
Samsung
Scandinavian Copper Development Association
Wrigley Scandinavia

Asia Pacific

Golin
(Formerly GolinHarris)
17th Floor China Life Tower 16 Chao Yang Men Wai Street, Beijing, 100020 China
Tel.: (86) 10 8569 9898
Fax: (86) 10 8569 9988
E-Mail: eddie.yang@golin.com
Web Site: www.golin.com

Jeremy Walker *(Mng Dir)*
Eddie Yang *(VP & Gen Mgr)*
Duoduo Xu *(Sr Mgr-Corp Comm & Pub Affairs)*

Accounts:
Florentina Village Consumer & Corporate Communication

Golin
8/F Oxford House, Taikoo Place, 979 King's Road, Quarry Bay, China (Hong Kong)
Tel.: (852) 2522 6475

Marc Sparrow, *(Exec Dir)*

Accounts:
The Economist (Public Relations Agency of Record) Communications, Marketing

Golin
(Formerly GolinHarris)
18/F HuaiHai Plz, 1045 HuaiHai Zhong Rd, Shanghai, 200031 China
Tel.: (86) 21 2411 0088
Fax: (86) 21 2411 0066
E-Mail: schin@golin.com
Web Site: www.golin.com

Sarah Chin *(VP & Gen Mgr)*
Eddi Yang *(VP & Gen Mgr)*
Adrian Looi *(Dir-Digital Comm)*
Winnie Yang *(Mgr)*
Danielle Yu *(Mgr)*

Accounts:
Bel Group Lezhiniu, Public Relations
Cimarron Jeans; 2007
Delta Airlines
Florentia Village Digital, Public Relations
Forterra Trust Communication, Digital, Marketing, Media, Public Relations, Strategic, The Place
Hansgrohe AXOR Brands, Digital Services, Media Communications
New Balance
Nippon Paint
Unilever Dove, Lux

Golin
(Formerly GolinHarris)
Unit 2408-09 Guangdong Telecom Plaza, No 18 Zhongshan Er Road, Guangzhou, 510080 China
Tel.: (86) 20 8888 8098
Fax: (86) 20 8888 8099
E-Mail: lylee@golinharris.com
Web Site: golin.com

Sarah Chin *(VP & Gen Mgr)*
Erica Liang *(Acct Mgr)*

Golin
(Formerly GolinHarris)
40A Orchard Rd #07-01, The MacDonald House, Singapore, 238838 Singapore
Tel.: (65) 6235 3121
Fax: (65) 6836 3121
Web Site: www.golin.com

Employees: 20

Agency Specializes In: Public Relations

Tarun Deo *(Mng Dir-Singapore & Southeast Asia)*
Simon Ruparelia *(Head-Digital-Asia)*
Geraldine Kan *(Exec Dir)*
Lim Le-Anne *(Exec Dir)*
Phillip Raskin *(Dir-Learning & Dev-Asia)*
Charlene Ho *(Mgr)*
Chew Laura *(Mgr)*

Accounts:
Ben & Jerry's
Carlsberg Singapore Brand Marketing, Carlsberg, Carlsberg Special Brew, Connor's, Corona, Jolly Shandy, Kronenbourg, PR, SKOL, Somersby, Tetley's
DesignSingapore Council
The Health Promotion Board PR
IMCD
McDonald's Singapore; 2008
Nippon Paint Social Media

GOODMAN PUBLIC RELATIONS
1995 E Oakland Pk Blvd Ste 100, Fort Lauderdale, FL 33306
Tel.: (954) 446-0800
Fax: (954) 446-0801
Web Site: www.goodmanpr.com

Agency Specializes In: Advertising, Brand Development & Integration, Corporate Identity, Crisis Communications, Media Buying Services, Media Relations, Media Training, Public Relations, Search Engine Optimization, Social Media

Michael Goodman *(Owner)*
Fran Folic *(VP-Lifestyle)*
Beth Zuckerkorn *(VP-Creative Svcs)*
Melissa Conowal *(Art Dir)*
Lauren Fyke *(Sr Acct Mgr)*
Kellee Santiago *(Acct Mgr)*
Christina Agront *(Mgr-Media)*
Robert Wagenseil *(Mgr-Social Media)*
Rachel Leshinsky *(Acct Exec)*
Tasha Yohan *(Acct Exec)*
Sarah Martinez *(Acct Coord)*

Accounts:
New-The Galleria
New-South Florida Regional Transportation Authority

GORDON C JAMES PUBLIC RELATIONS
4715 N 32nd St Ste 104, Phoenix, AZ 85018
Tel.: (602) 274-1988
Fax: (602) 274-2088
E-Mail: info@gcjpr.com
Web Site: www.gcjpr.com

Agency Specializes In: Event Planning & Marketing, Media Relations, Media Training, Public Relations, Social Media

Gordon James *(Owner)*
Brian OMalley *(Dir-Events)*

Accounts:
New-Florence Crittenton of Arizona
New-Maricopa Health Foundation

GORGEOUS MEDIA GROUP
7551 Melrose Ave Ste 7, Los Angeles, CA 90046
Tel.: (323) 782-9000
Fax: (323) 658-6189
E-Mail: info@gorgeousmediagroup.com
Web Site: www.gorgeousmediagroup.com

Agency Specializes In: Crisis Communications, Media Training, Public Relations, Strategic Planning/Research

Versa Manos *(Pres)*
Alexander Salewicz *(VP-Bus)*

Accounts:
Galvanized Souls

GRAHAM & ASSOCIATES INC.
111 Maiden Lane Ste 650, San Francisco, CA 94108
Tel.: (415) 986-7212
Fax: (415) 986-7216
Web Site: www.graham-associates.com

Agency Specializes In: Brand Development & Integration, Media Relations, Public Relations

Masha Rumer *(Acct Exec)*

Accounts:
New-Hulk Energy Technology

GRAMERCY COMMUNICATIONS
225 River St, Troy, NY 12180
Tel.: (518) 326-6400
Fax: (518) 514-1551
Web Site: www.gramercycommunications.com

Agency Specializes In: Advertising, Crisis Communications, Media Training, Public Relations

Tom Nardacci *(Founder & Principal)*
Jake Dumesnil *(Mng Partner)*
Mia Ertas *(Dir-Creative)*
Jill Montag *(Dir-Media Strategy)*
Charles Wiff *(Dir-Content & Media Strategy)*
Kevin Dugan *(Mgr-Pub Affairs)*
Andrew Mangini *(Mgr-PR)*
Wallace Altes *(Exec Counsel)*

GRAPEVINE PR
8033 Sunset Blvd Ste 831, West Hollywood, CA 90046
Tel.: (323) 386-2300
Fax: (323) 872-5187
E-Mail: info@theprgrapevine.com
Web Site: www.theprgrapevine.com

Agency Specializes In: Advertising, Event Planning & Marketing, Media Relations, Media Training, Public Relations, Social Media

Steven Le Vine *(Pres & CEO)*

Accounts:
Mara Marini
Nicole Russin
Universal Broadcasting Network

GRAY PUBLIC RELATIONS
616 Overview Ln, Franklin, TN 37064
Tel.: (615) 497-1799
Web Site: www.graypr.com

Agency Specializes In: Advertising, Graphic Design, Media Relations, Print, Public Relations, Social Media

Amy Gray Kovar *(Principal)*

Accounts:
Banded

GRAYLING
8455 Beverly Blvd Ste 300, Los Angeles, CA 90048
Tel.: (323) 648-5420
Web Site: www.grayling.com

Agency Specializes In: Brand Development & Integration, Communications, Corporate Communications, Digital/Interactive, Investor Relations, Public Relations, Social Media

Andrew Reynolds *(Mng Dir)*
Ashley Colette *(Acct Mgr)*
Rebekah Nicodemus *(Sr Acct Supvr)*
Monica Caires *(Acct Supvr)*
Brian Chui *(Sr Acct Exec)*
Katie Chalmers *(Assoc Acct Exec)*

Accounts:
Sun Edison, LLC (US Agency of Record)
New-Transcosmos America Inc.
New-VAIO Corp.

GRAYLING CONNECTING POINT
(Formerly Connecting Point Communications)
665 3rd St Ste 100, San Francisco, CA 94107
Tel.: (415) 442-4018
Fax: (415) 442-0288
Web Site: us.grayling.com

Year Founded: 1985

Agency Specializes In: Communications, Consulting, Public Relations, Strategic Planning/Research

Peter Harris *(CEO-United States)*
Steve Gilmore *(VP)*
Katherine Madariaga *(VP)*
Chris Brown *(Dir)*
Ashley Colette *(Acct Mgr)*
Jessie Adams-Shore *(Acct Supvr)*
Alexandra Nguy *(Sr Acct Exec-Digital)*
Danielle Bruckman *(Strategist-Digital)*
Nancy Ly *(Acct Exec-Digital)*

Accounts:
ACD Systems
Affinova
AvantGo
Craiglist Foundation
Nexaweb Technologies, Inc.
Rambus
Virtual Iris

GRAYLING GLOBAL

405 Lexington Ave, New York, NY 10174
Tel.: (646) 284-9400
Fax: (646) 284-9494
E-Mail: jacinta.gauda@us.grayling.com
Web Site: www.grayling.com

Employees: 35

Agency Specializes In: Investor Relations, Public Relations

Dixon Chen *(Mng Dir)*
Peter Harris *(CEO-US)*
Ivette Almeida *(Mng Dir-Corp & Fin Comm)*
Steve Gilmore *(VP)*
Lisette Paras *(VP)*
Kate Chesnut *(Acct Mgr)*
Heedrin Bustamante *(Analyst-Ops)*

Accounts:
Bioniche Life Sciences Inc.
Brasil Telecom S.A.
Codice Software Corporate Communications
North American Insulation Manufacturers
Satyam Computer Services Limited
Third Millennium Russia Fund

Branch

Grayling

(Formerly Atomic Public Relations)
735 Market St 4th Fl, San Francisco, CA 94103
Tel.: (415) 593-1400
Fax: (415) 402-0237
Web Site: us.grayling.com

Employees: 50
Year Founded: 1999

Martha Shaughnessy *(Mng Dir)*
Dong Chen *(Mng Dir-China)*
Julia Konstantinovsky *(VP)*
Katherine Madariaga *(VP)*
Amity Gay *(Acct Dir)*
William Hanlon *(Mgr-Community)*
Faith Markham *(Acct Supvr)*

Accounts:
Acendi
Actian Corporation
Animoto
Anti-Phishing Working Group
ArcSight
Baker Avenue Asset Management
Bebo
BeenVerified Public Relations
Betterment.com (PR Agency of Record) Media Relations, Public Relations
BrightScope
Coupons, Inc; Mountain View, CA
Credit Karma
CyberSource
DG FastChannel Executive Positioning, Media Strategy, Public Relations, Search, Social Media, Video
Echelon Corporation
Edeems
Electronic Frontier Foundation
GreenStar Hub Media Relations, Social, Strategic Communications
Guidance Software
The Hotlist
Hotwire, Inc; San Francisco, CA
Ingres
Intuit
Knewton
Lending Club
LivingSocial
MarkLogic Corporation
Message Systems
MI5 Networks
Mint.com; 2007
NETGEAR, Inc.
Polaroid
Ratheon Oakley Systems
RealtyTrac
RingCentral Public Relations
Shopkick, Inc. (Agency of Record)
Sidecar Media Relations, Social, Strategic Communications
Simplifi
Smule (Public Relations Agency of Record) Interactive Sonic Applications for iPhone
Sony Electronics Audio Products, Camcorders, Cameras, Digital, Home Theater, PCs, Public Relations, Retail Stores, Social Media, Tablets
The Technology Council of Southern California (Agency of Record)
Teros
Trusted ID
Verizon; 2007
Vontu

GREEN OLIVE MEDIA LLC

361 17th St Ste 1, Atlanta, GA 30363
Tel.: (404) 815-9327
Fax: (404) 815-9328
E-Mail: info@greenolivemedia.com
Web Site: www.greenolivemedia.com

Year Founded: 1998

Agency Specializes In: Consumer Marketing, Email, Event Planning & Marketing, Promotions, Public Relations, Social Media

Jeffrey Moore *(Partner)*
Meggan Talley *(Dir-Design & Branding)*

Accounts:
New-Taqueria del Sol

GREENLEAF MARKETING COMMUNICATIONS

43 Wood Ln, Beverly, MA 01915
Tel.: (978) 922-2585

Agency Specializes In: Communications, Public Relations

Suzanne Jack Ewer *(Owner)*

Accounts:
BTS Partners
Columbia Construction Company
Farm Fresh Delivery
IMA Associates
K&G Entrances
Margulies Perruzzi Architects
Sullivan & McLaughlin Companies
Trident Building and Properties Group

GREENOUGH COMMUNICATIONS

9 Harcourt St, Boston, MA 02116
Tel.: (617) 275-6500
Fax: (617) 275-6501
E-Mail: greenough@greenoughcom.com
Web Site: www.greenough.biz

Employees: 30
Year Founded: 1999

Jamie Parker *(Pres)*
Phil Greenough *(CEO)*
Scott Bauman *(Exec VP)*
Ed Coletti *(Exec VP-Ops)*
Paul Greenough *(VP-IT)*
Jennifer Hrycyszyn *(VP)*
Andrea LePain *(VP-Media Rels)*
Amy McHugh *(VP-Acct Svcs)*
Amy Legere *(Acct Dir)*
Rachel Vaccari *(Acct Dir)*
Brad Puffer *(Dir-Media Rels & Mktg)*

Accounts:
Advanced Pharmacy Concepts
Aprimo (Agency of Record) Business and Marketing Strategies, Influencer Relations, Social Media and Marketing
Artists For Humanity Media Relations
New-Bridgewell (Agency of Record)
CareWell Urgent Care Brand Awareness, PR
CoalTek (Agency of Record) Marketing, Traditional & Social Media Relations
ConnectWise; Tampa, FL Integrated Marketing, Media Relations
Conservation Services Group Clean Energy Programs, Content Development, Media Relations, Social Media Strategy
Day Pitney LLP
Dayton Home Traditional & Social Media
EcoCAR: The NeXt Challenge (Agency of Record)
Edge Dynamics; Redwood City, CA; Newtown, PA Channel Commerce Management Solutions; 2006
Exact Online Analyst Relations, Awards, Social Marketing, Trade, Vertical Media Relations
Fazenda Coffee Roasters Social Media, Traditional Media
Harvest Power (Agency of Record)
Hydroid, LLC
Inovalon (Agency of Record)
LabTech; Tampa, FL Integrated Marketing, Media Relations
New-Lovin' Spoonfuls (Agency of Record)
New-The Lowell Institute (Agency of Record)
New-The Museum of World War II (Agency of Record)
Myriant Marketing, PR, Social Media
New England Clean Energy Council (Agency of Record)
Quest Software Inc.
Right90
Shure
Smartleaf
Speechworks
Texas Instruments
Tribridge Media, Public Relations
UC4 Software (Agency of Record); 2008
Unica Corp. Enterprise Marketing Management; 2004
Velocity Technology Solutions (Agency of Record) Social CRM, Social Media, Traditional Media Relations
Verizon
New-WBUR (Agency of Record)
Worldwide TechServices; Tewksbury, MA (Agency of Record)
WorldWinner Online Casual Game Competitions; 2008

GREENSMITH PUBLIC RELATIONS LLC
1818 Library St Ste 500, Reston, VA 20190
Tel.: (703) 623-3834
Web Site: www.greensmithpr.com

Year Founded: 2000

Agency Specializes In: Event Planning & Marketing, Media Training, Public Relations, Social Media

Mike Smith *(Founder & CEO)*
Cheryl Vosburg *(VP)*
Leah Nadeau *(Sr Acct Exec)*

Accounts:
Mobility Lab
National Fish & Wildlife Foundation
Nextility

GREGORY FCA
27 W Athens Ave Ste 200, Ardmore, PA 19003
Tel.: (610) 642-8253
Fax: (610) 649-9029
Toll Free: (800) 499-4734
E-Mail: doug@gregoryfca.com
Web Site: www.gregoryfca.com

Employees: 40
Year Founded: 1991

National Agency Associations: COPF

Agency Specializes In: Business-To-Business, Corporate Communications, Financial, Investor Relations, Public Relations, Publicity/Promotions, Real Estate, Transportation

Approx. Annual Billings: $4,000,000

Breakdown of Gross Billings by Media: Pub. Rels.: $4,000,000

Gregory Matusky *(Founder & Pres)*
Doug Rose *(COO)*
Mike Lizun *(Sr VP)*
Matthew McLoughlin *(Assoc VP)*
Katie Nicolai *(Assoc VP)*
Leigh Sperun *(Assoc VP)*
Jessica Emery *(Asst Acct Exec)*

Accounts:
Dranoff
Evolve IP
LA Weight Loss
MeetMe, Inc IR, PR
MetroStar Systems, Inc. Brand Awareness, PR, Zoomph
Mitsubishi
Moxy Vote
Nutrisystem, Inc.; Fort Washington, PA (Investor Relations Agency of Record)
Pilot Freight Services
Safeguard
SAP
ScripsAmerica, Inc. (Investor Relations Agency of Record)
Unisys
Universal Display; Princeton, NJ
USA Technologies, Inc.
Willow Financial
YOH

GRIFFIN & COMPANY
3050 K St NW Ste 210, Washington, DC 20007
Tel.: (202) 625-2515
E-Mail: info@griffinco.com
Web Site: www.griffinco.com

Agency Specializes In: Brand Development & Integration, Crisis Communications, Media Relations, Public Relations, Social Media

Cary B. Griffin *(Founder & Pres)*

Accounts:
New-Mitsubishi Electric Cooling & Heating

GRIFFIN INTEGRATED COMMUNICATIONS
260 5th Ave 6th Fl, New York, NY 10001
Tel.: (212) 481-3456
Fax: (212) 684-0606
E-Mail: bgriffin@griffinpr.com
Web Site: www.griffin-pr.com

Employees: 15
Year Founded: 1982

Agency Specializes In: Consumer Marketing, Electronic Media, Entertainment, Government/Political, High Technology, Public Relations, Retail

Approx. Annual Billings: $5,000,000

Robert E. Griffin *(Pres)*
Liza McIntosh *(Acct Exec)*
Jessica Passananti *(Acct Exec)*

Accounts:
Advanced Micro Devices
AKG Acoustics Professional & Consumer Microphones & Headphones
Arriflex
Crown Audio
Eventide Music Recording Equipment
Fairlight Digital Audio Workstation Manufacturer
Fostex
Hitachi Interactive Software Interactive White Boards & Tablets
JBL Professional Professional Loudspeaker Systems
Periscope Book Lights
The Response Network
Studer-Soundcraft

GROUNDFLOOR MEDIA, INC.
1923 Market St, Denver, CO 80202
Tel.: (303) 865-8110
Fax: (303) 253-9763
E-Mail: pr@groundfloormedia.com
Web Site: www.groundfloormedia.com

Year Founded: 2001

Agency Specializes In: Crisis Communications, Event Planning & Marketing, Industrial, Internet/Web Design, Media Relations, Media Training, Public Relations, Sponsorship, Strategic Planning/Research

Brian Dally *(Co-Founder & CEO)*
Ramonna Robinson *(Pres)*
Jim Licko *(VP)*
Carissa McCabe *(VP)*
Gil Rudawsky *(VP)*
Jeremy Story *(VP)*
Wendy Artman *(Sr Dir-Comm)*
Rich Miller *(Sr Dir-Comm)*
Amy Moynihan *(Sr Dir-Comm)*
Carolann Samuels *(Sr Dir-Comm)*
Kristina Reilly *(Dir-Bus Ops)*
Tricia Bennett *(Sr Mgr-PR)*

Accounts:
34 Degrees; Denver, CO Online Content Development, Optimization, PR, Strategic Planning
Alliance for Early Success Digital, Logo, Strategic Counsel, Website Development
Alta Colleges
America On the Move
American Blue Ribbon Holdings, LLC; Denver, CO
Bakers Square
Bellco Credit Union
BNSF Railway
Boulder Community Hospital
CH2M HILL
The Children's Hospital; Aurora, CO
ClickBank; Broomfield, CO Communications Program, Media Relations, Message Development, Public Relations, Social Media
Colorado Department of Public Health & Environment; Denver, CO Blogs, Internet, TV, What If? Colorado, Youtube
The Colorado Health Foundation (Agency of Record) Social Media, Strategic Council on Communications Initiatives, Traditional Media
Coors Brewing Company
Coors Light
Door to Door Organics Media Relations
Earth Balance Media Relations
Fuser; Boulder, CO
LiveWell Colorado
Molson
National Indian Gaming Association; Washington, DC
Orange Leaf Frozen Yogurt; Oklahoma City, OK Public Relations, Strategic Planning, Traditional & Social Media Strategy
Oskar Blues; Longmont, CO Communications Planning, Event Promotions, Media Relations, Social Media Strategy
The Peloton Boulder
Phoenix Multisport; Boulder, CO (Agency of Record)
Qdoba Mexican Grill; Wheat Ridge, CO
Qdoba
Similasan USA; Highlands Ranch, CO Media, PR, Strategic Communications Program
SlimGenics; Centennial, CO Brand Awareness, PR
SmartyPig; Des Moines, LA
St. Anthony Central Hospital (Agency of Record)
Starbucks Coffee Company; Gulch Helena, MT
The Tennyson Center for Children
USA Swimming
Village Inn

GRUMAN & NICOLL PR
10641 SE 25th St, Bellevue, WA 98004
Tel.: (425) 451-4387
E-Mail: getresults@gruman-nicoll.com
Web Site: www.gruman-nicoll.com

Agency Specializes In: Communications, Public Relations, Social Media

Lissa Gruman *(Owner)*
Margaret Nicoll *(Partner)*

Accounts:
Parfait Ice Cream

GS STRATEGY GROUP
350 N 9th St Ste 550, Boise, ID 83702
Tel.: (208) 342-1545
Fax: (208) 336-2007
Web Site: www.gsstrategygroup.com

Agency Specializes In: Brand Development & Integration, Crisis Communications, Internet/Web Design, Print, Public Relations, Social Media, Strategic Planning/Research

Greg Strimple *(Pres)*
Brooks Kochvar *(Sr VP)*

Accounts:
Idaho Health Insurance

GUTENBERG COMMUNICATIONS
555 8th Ave Ste 1509, New York, NY 10018-4631
Tel.: (212) 239-8475
Fax: (212) 239-8476

E-Mail: info@gutenbergpr.com
Web Site: www.gutenbergpr.com

Employees: 40

Agency Specializes In: Public Relations

Harjiv Singh *(Co-Founder & Co-CEO)*
Hugh Burnham *(CEO)*
Michael Gallo *(Mng Dir)*
Jeff Platon *(CMO & Exec VP-Mktg Svcs Practice)*
Liana Hawes *(VP-Media Strategy)*
DJ Lavanya *(VP)*

Accounts:
BeyondTrust
Group FMG
Total Defense, Inc.

Branch

Gutenberg Communications
A-85 East oif Kailash, New Delhi, 110065 India
Tel.: (91) 11 4132 4969
Fax: (91) 1141324968
E-Mail: harjiv@gutenbergpr.com
Web Site: www.gutenbergpr.com

Harjiv Singh *(Co-Founder & Co-CEO)*
Sonali Madbhavi *(VP & Country Head)*
Amardeep Singh *(Dir-Fin & Ops)*
Ritika S. Mishra *(Assoc Dir)*
Elita Sequeira *(Sr Mgr)*
Varun Bhagath *(Acct Mgr)*
Priyanka Bhattacharya *(Acct Mgr)*
Richa Chauhan *(Acct Mgr)*
Priyanka Pandit *(Acct Mgr)*
Pallavi Jha *(Sr Acct Exec)*
Sanchita Choudhary Mukherjee *(Sr Acct Exec)*

GUTHRIE/MAYES
545 S 3rd St, Louisville, KY 40202
Tel.: (502) 584-0371
Fax: (502) 584-0207
E-Mail: pr@guthriemayes.com
Web Site: www.guthriemayes.com

Employees: 12
Year Founded: 1977

Agency Specializes In: Education, Government/Political, Health Care Services, Medical Products, Pharmaceutical, Public Relations, Publicity/Promotions

Jack Guthrie *(Founder)*
Andy Eggers *(Owner & Principal)*
Clair Nichols *(Owner)*
Dan Hartlage *(Principal)*
Ashley Brauer *(Acct Mgr)*
Mckenzi Loid *(Assoc Acct Mgr)*
Danielle Waller *(Acct Mgr)*

Accounts:
Louisville Regional Airport Authority; 1977
National Center for Family Literacy
Toyota Motor Manufacturing; 1996

GYMR PUBLIC RELATIONS
1825 Connecticut Ave NW Ste 300, Washington, DC 20009
Tel.: (202) 745-5100
Fax: (202) 234-6159
E-Mail: contact@gymr.com
Web Site: www.gymr.com

Employees: 28
Year Founded: 1998

Agency Specializes In: Public Relations

Patrick McCabe *(Partner)*
Sharon Reis *(Partner)*
Becky Watt Knight *(Sr VP)*
Sarah Beth Cloar *(Acct Supvr)*
Brianna Gavio *(Acct Supvr)*
Frank Walsh *(Acct Supvr)*
Jessica Easter *(Sr Acct Exec)*
Stephanie Wight *(Acct Exec)*
Haydn Bush *(Mng Supvr)*

Accounts:
Academy of Psychosomatic Medicine; Washington, DC Messaging, Strategic Communications
New-The Advisory Board Company Communications
The American Academy of Family Physicians
American Board of Internal Medicine; Pennsylvania, PA Media Relations, Strategy
Banner Alzheimer's Institute
Bristol-Myers Squibb Company
New-Child Life Council
Genentech & Roche Diagnostics; San Francisco, CA Media Relations
Gordon & Betty Moore Foundation; Palo Alto, CA Messaging
Health Affairs; Washington, DC
HealthPocket.com; Sunnyvale, CA Consumer Website
Institute for Health Technology Studies
New-Kate B. Reynolds Charitable Trust Communications, Media Relations, Strategic Counsel
The Markle Foundation
National Association of Social Workers Assurance Services Marketing Communications
New-Physician Advocacy Institute Communications, Planning
The SCAN Foundation; Long Beach, CA
New-Society to Improve Diagnosis in Medicine

H & R PUBLIC RELATIONS
200 N Larchmont Blvd, Los Angeles, CA 90004
Tel.: (323) 389-7900
Web Site: www.h-rpr.com

Agency Specializes In: Brand Development & Integration, Business-To-Business, Graphic Design, Internet/Web Design, Media Relations, Media Training, Public Relations, Social Media, Strategic Planning/Research

Heather Duffy Boylston *(Pres & CEO)*
Rebecca Hutchinson *(Principal)*

Accounts:
New-Larchmont Charter School
New-Salt & Straw

H2 PUBLIC RELATIONS
3106 W Lyndale Ste 4B, Chicago, IL 60647
Tel.: (858) 232-1874
Web Site: www.h2publicrelations.com

Year Founded: 2007

Agency Specializes In: Event Planning & Marketing, Media Relations, Promotions, Public Relations, Social Media

Heidi Hageman *(Founder & Pres)*

Accounts:
Cohn Restaurant Group

HAGER SHARP INC.
1030 15th St NW Ste 600E, Washington, DC 20005
Tel.: (202) 842-3600
Fax: (202) 842-4032
E-Mail: kcassida@hagersharp.com
Web Site: www.hagersharp.com

Employees: 25
Year Founded: 1973

Agency Specializes In: Communications, Government/Political

Approx. Annual Billings: $3,800,000

Barbara Davis Blum *(Chm)*
Jennifer Wayman *(CEO)*
Walter Watts *(CFO)*
Debra Silimeo *(Exec VP)*
Christina Nicols *(Sr VP & Dir-Strategic Plng & Res)*
David J. Hoff *(Sr VP)*
Aaron Murphy *(VP & Dir-Digital Design)*
Lisa Matthews *(VP)*
Shelly Spoeth *(VP)*
Mike Gallagher *(Dir-Creative)*
Elizabeth Osborn *(Sr Acct Supvr)*

Accounts:
Educational Testing Service Communication
National Cancer Institute
National Center for Education Statistics National Assessment of Educational Progress
National Diabetes Education Program
National Institute of Diabetes & Digestive & Kidney Diseases
Safe & Sound Schools
U.S. Department of Health & Human Services Marketing, Media, Office on Women's Health

HALL COMPANY
161 W 23rd St 3rd Fl, New York, NY 10011
Tel.: (212) 684-1955
E-Mail: info@hallpr.com
Web Site: www.hallpr.com

Year Founded: 1996

Agency Specializes In: Media Relations, Public Relations, Social Media

Steven Hall *(Pres)*
Sam Firer *(VP)*
Karen Carzo *(Acct Dir)*

Accounts:
New-Tasca Chino

HALL STRATEGIES
217 5th Ave N Ste 200, Nashville, TN 37219
Tel.: (615) 242-8856
Fax: (615) 242-8857
Web Site: www.hallstrategies.com

Agency Specializes In: Media Relations, Public Relations, Social Media, Strategic Planning/Research

Joe Hall *(Owner)*
Abby Trotter *(Partner)*

Accounts:
New-Anderson Benson Insurance & Risk Management
New-Live Nation

HAMILTON PUBLIC RELATIONS
102 Madison Ave 7th Fl, New York, NY 10016
Tel.: (212) 328-5200
Fax: (212) 328-1100
E-Mail: jfrew@getpr.com
Web Site: www.getpr.com

Employees: 5
Year Founded: 2000

Agency Specializes In: Automotive, Business-To-

Business, Communications, Event Planning & Marketing, Financial, Leisure, Media Relations, Public Relations, Sports Market, Travel & Tourism

John H. Frew *(Pres-Hamilton PR)*

HANDCRAFTED PR

53 Monroe St, Brooklyn, NY 11238
Tel.: (347) 689-2111
Web Site: www.handcraftedpr.com

Agency Specializes In: Brand Development & Integration, Collateral, Event Planning & Marketing, Media Training, Public Relations, Social Media

Ana Jovancicevic *(Founder & Pres)*

Accounts:
Becherovka Herbal Liqueuer
Foragers City Grocer
Foragers City Table
Greenhook Ginsmiths
Innis Gunn
The Pitch & Fork
Rhum Clement
Silk Rd Tavern
Simon Ford

THE HANNON GROUP

137 National Plaza Ste 300, Fort Washington, MD 20745
Tel.: (301) 839-2744
E-Mail: info@thehannongroup.com
Web Site: www.thehannongroup.com

Agency Specializes In: Government/Political, Public Relations, Strategic Planning/Research

Sandra Wills Hannon *(Owner)*
Jillian Fisher *(VP)*

Accounts:
New-Centers for Disease Control & Prevention

HANSER & ASSOCIATES PUBLIC RELATIONS

Neptune Bldg Ste 212, West Des Moines, IA 50266
Mailing Address:
4401 Westown Pkwy Ste 212, West Des Moines, IA 50266-1037
Tel.: (515) 224-1086
Fax: (515) 224-0991
Toll Free: (800) 340-6434
E-Mail: hanser@hanser.com
Web Site: www.hanser.com

E-Mail for Key Personnel:
President: rhanser@hanser.com

Employees: 8
Year Founded: 1996

National Agency Associations: COPF

Agency Specializes In: Business-To-Business, Communications, Consumer Goods, Consumer Marketing, Crisis Communications, Event Planning & Marketing, Exhibit/Trade Shows, Financial, Health Care Services, Integrated Marketing, Media Buying Services, Media Planning, Media Relations, Media Training, Pharmaceutical, Planning & Consultation, Promotions, Public Relations, Strategic Planning/Research, Travel & Tourism, Viral/Buzz/Word of Mouth

Ronald Hanser *(Chm & Principal)*
Ryan C. Hanser *(Pres & Principal)*
Bonnie K. Hanser *(COO & Principal)*
Katelin Schwarck *(Acct Mgr)*
Kelly Van De Walle *(Acct Mgr)*
Lindsey Schwarck *(Acct Exec)*

Accounts:
Catholic Health System
City of West Des Moines
Coach USA Megabus.com
College Savings Iowa
EMCO Enterprises
Hawkins Construction Company
HOK
Hubbell Realty Company
Iowa Health System
Iowa Pharmacy Association
MidAmerican Energy Company
RegenaCorp
Roche Pharmaceuticals
Upper Iowa University
West Bancorporation
World Technologies

HANSON & SCHWAM PUBLIC RELATIONS

9350 Wilshire Boulevard Ste 315, Beverly Hills, CA 90212
Tel.: (310) 248-4488
Web Site: www.hspr.biz

Agency Specializes In: Brand Development & Integration, Public Relations

Gene Schwam *(Owner & Pres)*

Accounts:
New-Barbara Eden

HARDEN COMMUNICATIONS PARTNERS

32 Cathy Ln, Oakland, CA 94619
Tel.: (510) 635-4150
Fax: (510) 969-4980
Web Site: www.hardenpartners.com

Agency Specializes In: Brand Development & Integration, Communications, Crisis Communications, Digital/Interactive, Event Planning & Marketing, Media Relations, Media Training, Public Relations

Patricia L. Harden *(Mng Partner)*
Liam Collopy *(Exec VP)*
Christine Burkhart *(Office Mgr)*
Ross Coyle *(Sr Acct Supvr)*
Asia Camagong *(Acct Exec)*
Nina Newhouse *(Acct Exec)*
Lexi Kantz *(Acct Coord)*

Accounts:
Fireman's Fund Insurance Company
John Muir Health (Agency of Record) Medical Services
RS Investments

HARRISON & SHRIFTMAN LLC

141 W 36th St 12th Fl, New York, NY 10018
Tel.: (917) 351-8600
Fax: (917) 351-8601
E-Mail: contact@hs-pr.com
Web Site: www.hs-pr.com

Employees: 40
Year Founded: 1995

Agency Specializes In: Fashion/Apparel, Public Relations, Publicity/Promotions, Sponsorship, Travel & Tourism

Elizabeth Harrison *(CEO & Principal)*
Anu Rao *(VP)*
Nikole Flores *(Sr Acct Supvr)*
Jennifer Valdes *(Acct Supvr)*
Tara Dillon *(Acct Exec)*
Amanda Anderson *(Asst Acct Exec-Lifestyle & Spirits)*
Virgil Cebrian *(Asst Acct Exec-Studio HS)*
Alyssa Dupre *(Asst Acct Exec)*

Accounts:
BlackBerry
BooHoo
Chic Outlet Shopping
China Center
Christie's Events Strategy, Hispanic
Dylans Candy Bar
Eleven by Venus Williams Events, Media Relations, Social Media, Website
Ferrari
Great American Cookies
Grey Goose Vodka
Harbor Footwear
Kairo Society
Lane Bryant
Marble Slab Creamery
Playstation
Prada
Pretzel Maker
Saint Regis Hotels
Sebago
SLS Hotels
Tone
Traub
W Hotels
Waterford
Wolfgang Puck

Branches

Harrison & Shriftman

8523 Sunset Blvd, Los Angeles, CA 90069
Tel.: (310) 855-1600
Fax: (310) 855-7510
E-Mail: contact@hs-pr.com
Web Site: www.hs-pr.com

Employees: 12
Year Founded: 1998

Agency Specializes In: Advertising

Elizabeth Harrison *(CEO & Principal)*
Rebecca Chu *(Asst Acct Exec)*

Accounts:
W Hotels

Harrison & Shriftman

1680 Meridian Ave Ste 300, Miami, FL 33139
Tel.: (305) 534-0008
Fax: (305) 534-0158
Web Site: www.hs-pr.com/

Employees: 12
Year Founded: 2001

Agency Specializes In: Public Relations, Real Estate, Retail

Elizabeth Harrison *(CEO & Principal)*
Celia De La Llama *(Dir)*
Jennifer Valdes *(Acct Supvr)*
Jennifer Gillespie *(Sr Acct Exec-PR)*
Annelisa Sichel *(Sr Acct Exec)*

Accounts:
Bal Harbour Shops
Black Berry
Lacoste
Palms
W South Beach
William Rast

HARRON & ASSOCIATES

229 Berkeley St, Boston, MA 02116

Tel.: (617) 267-7366
Fax: (617) 267-7612
E-Mail: harron@harronandassociates.com
Web Site: www.harronandassociates.com

Employees: 5
Year Founded: 1979

Agency Specializes In: Faith Based, Public Relations

Harron Ellenson *(Pres)*

Accounts:
Boston Landmarks Orchestra
British Telecom
Fidelity Investments
Hebrew College; Newton, MA; 2004
Homart
Massport
NEWIRE (New England Women in Real Estate)
Nova Scotia Tourism
Prudential Financial
Riverdeep Interactive Learning
Seagrams
Sorrento Cheese

HARVEST PUBLIC RELATIONS
715 SW Morrison St Ste 602, Portland, OR 97205
Tel.: (503) 274-0086
Fax: (503) 961-7055
Web Site: www.harvest-pr.com

Agency Specializes In: Crisis Communications, Event Planning & Marketing, Public Relations, Social Media, Strategic Planning/Research

Heidi Nelson *(Owner & Principal)*
Amy Wood *(Mng Dir & Partner)*
Eric Davis *(VP & Grp Acct Dir)*
Amy Brown *(Acct Dir)*
Adriane Marten *(Sr Acct Exec-Digital & Social)*
Trista Cady *(Acct Exec)*
Kyle Donovan *(Acct Exec)*
Holly Sturdivan *(Acct Exec)*
Amanda Schlesner *(Acct Coord-PR)*

Accounts:
New-The Mushroom Council (Agency of Record) Consumer Public Relations
Willamette Egg Farms LLC

THE HATCH AGENCY
25 Maiden Ln 6th Fl, San Francisco, CA 94108
Tel.: (415) 655-3015
E-Mail: info@thehatchagency.com
Web Site: www.thehatchagency.com

Year Founded: 2012

Agency Specializes In: Crisis Communications, Media Training, Public Relations, Social Media, Strategic Planning/Research, Viral/Buzz/Word of Mouth

Kiersten Hollars *(Sr VP)*
Christina Goethe *(Dir-PR)*

Accounts:
New-Ammunition Group
New-Dropbox

HAVAS FORMULA
(Formerly Formula PR)
810 Parkview Dr N, El Segundo, CA 90245
Tel.: (310) 578-7050
Fax: (310) 578-7077
E-Mail: lainfo@formulapr.com
Web Site: havasformula.com

Employees: 15

Agency Specializes In: Brand Development & Integration, Branded Entertainment, Communications, Multicultural, Public Relations, Sports Market

Revenue: $15,000,000

Michael A. Olguin *(Pres)*
Emily Porter *(Sr VP-Bus & Tech)*
Katie Lippman *(Assoc VP)*
Melody Demel *(Dir)*
Stephanie Proos *(Assoc Dir)*
Christina Gregor *(Acct Supvr)*
Linda Battaglia *(Sr Acct Exec)*

Accounts:
76 Lubricants
Abandon Interactive Entertainment Freaky Creatures; 2007
AirDrives Earphones; 2007
Aqua Lung Aqua Sphere, Brand Awareness, PR
Bioserie (Agency of Record)
Boostcase Brand Awareness, Media, Strategic Public Relations
Bulldog Gin
CJ Foods (North American Agency of Record) Social Media, Traditional PR
Cost Plus World Market
Delicato Family Vineyards Noble Vines, Public Relations
Dunkin' Donuts Media
Ingersoll Rand Nexia, Schlage
Kashi
Kendall Oil
Liquid Nutrition National PR Strategy
MobiTV
Monoprice (Public Relations Agency of Record) Ecommerce Site (Generic Brand Consumer Electronics)
mophie, Inc.
Music Television
Neuro Drinks Bliss Drink
Ormco Corporation
Pert Plus (Agency of Record) Rebranding
Popchips
Prairie Organic Spirits
Puma Cobra Golf, Media Outreach
Shure (Agency of Record)
Snap Infusion North American Advertising
Sport Chalet
Taco Bell Corporate Reputation, Influencer Engagement, Public Relations
UV Vodka

Branch

Formulatin
580 Broadway, New York, NY 10012
(See Separate Listing)

HAVAS PR
(Formerly Euro RSCG Worldwide PR)
200 Madison Ave, New York, NY 10016
Tel.: (212) 367-6800
Fax: (212) 367-7154
E-Mail: marian.salzman@havasww.com
Web Site: www.havaspr.com

Employees: 110
Year Founded: 1935

National Agency Associations: 4A's-COPF

Agency Specializes In: Agriculture, Automotive, Brand Development & Integration, Business-To-Business, Children's Market, Collateral, Communications, Consulting, Consumer Goods, Consumer Marketing, Corporate Communications, Corporate Identity, Cosmetics, Crisis Communications, Electronics, Event Planning & Marketing, Fashion/Apparel, Guerilla Marketing, Health Care Services, High Technology, Hispanic Market, Household Goods, Industrial, Integrated Marketing, Leisure, Media Relations, Medical Products, Men's Market, Multicultural, New Technologies, Over-50 Market, Pharmaceutical, Planning & Consultation, Public Relations, Publicity/Promotions, Retail, Seniors' Market, Sponsorship, Strategic Planning/Research, Teen Market, Transportation, Travel & Tourism, Viral/Buzz/Word of Mouth, Women's Market

Matt Weiss *(Mng Partner-Havas Worldwide New York & CMO)*
Andrew Benett *(CEO-Havas Worldwide & Havas Creative Grp)*
Jody Sunna *(Exec VP & Dir-Consumer & Lifestyle)*
John Casey *(Exec VP)*
Samantha Wolf *(VP)*
Meghan Burek *(Acct Supvr)*
Maricela Rios *(Acct Exec)*

Accounts:
Au Bon Pain Gluten-Free Products
B&G Foods Gluten-Free CLVR Bars
Bayer MaterialScience; 1994
Cabot Creamery
Colliers International
Coty (Corporate Communications Agency of Record) Strategic Messaging
The Economist Group
Epic Hearing Healthcare
Lymphoma & Leukemia Society
National Lipid Association
#Giving Tuesday
Pirate Brands Pirate's Booty Gluten-Free Products
Ruby Rocket's Fruit & Vegetable Frozen Snacks
United Nations Foundation

Branches

Havas PR
1027 E Washington St, Phoenix, AZ 85034
Tel.: (541) 261-8189
Web Site: havaspr.com

Year Founded: 2015

Stephanie Clarke *(Acct Supvr)*
Angela Carrasco *(Supvr-Havas Conexiones)*
Katie Snyder *(Sr Acct Exec)*

Accounts:
Big Lots
Fox Restaurant Concepts (Agency of Record)
Indigenous Peoples Law and Policy Program
SocialWhirled

Havas PR
(Formerly Euro RSCG Chicago)
36 E Grand Ave, Chicago, IL 60611
Tel.: (312) 640-6800
Fax: (312) 640-6801
E-Mail: ana.nennig@havasww.com
Web Site: www.havaspr.com

Employees: 250

National Agency Associations: COPF

Agency Specializes In: Advertising, Advertising Specialties, Alternative Advertising, Brand Development & Integration, Communications, Corporate Communications, Digital/Interactive, Direct Response Marketing, Email, In-Store Advertising, Internet/Web Design, Mobile Marketing, Publicity/Promotions, Radio, Retail, Sales Promotion, Shopper Marketing, Social Marketing/Nonprofit, Sponsorship, Strategic Planning/Research, T.V.

Laura Maness *(Chief Growth Officer-US)*
Miguel Gonzalez *(Grp Dir-Strategy)*
Anna Newburn *(Grp Dir-Strategy)*

Accounts:
Beam Campaign: "Inspired by design", Campaign: "Make It With A Fireman", Campaign: "Particle Cherry", Effen, Pucker, Sauza
Citibank Direct Mail
Claire's
Cracker Barrel Campaign: "Home"
Groupon
Hefty
Hornitos Campaign: "Cable"
Reynolds
Sears
Sonic
Sony Computer Entertainment America LLC CRM, Digital, E-mail, Mobile, PlayStation, Social

Havas PR
(Formerly Euro RSCG Worldwide PR)
4 PPG Pl 2nd Fl, Pittsburgh, PA 15222
Tel.: (412) 456-4305
Fax: (412) 456-4310
E-Mail: katie.mcsorley@havasww.com
Web Site: www.havaspr.com

Employees: 16

National Agency Associations: COPF

Agency Specializes In: Brand Development & Integration, Business-To-Business, Communications, Consulting, Industrial, Public Relations

Susan English *(Sr VP)*
Lesley Sillaman *(VP)*
Melissa Rieger *(Assoc VP)*
Christina Misch *(Sr Acct Exec)*

One Green Bean
Level 1 276 Devonshire Street, Surry Hills, Sydney, NSW 2010 Australia
Tel.: (61) 280201800
Fax: (61) 296991036
Web Site: onegreenbean.com

Agency Specializes In: Digital/Interactive, Public Relations

Kat Thomas *(Co-Founder & Exec Creative Dir)*
Anthony Freedman *(Co-Founder)*
Carl Ratcliff *(CEO)*
Claire Salvetti *(Mng Partner)*
Louise Pogmore *(Bus Dir)*
Pia Chaudhuri *(Assoc Dir-Creative)*
Joy Leaper *(Assoc Bus Dir)*

Accounts:
Coca-Cola Refreshments USA, Inc.
CommBank
The Commonwealth Bank
IKEA Campaign: "Hundstol", Campaign: "Matresses"
Jetstar (Lead Public Relations Agency) Brand Marketing, Content Strategy
Kimberley Clark
Lego Toys Mfr
New-Meat & Livestock Australia Public Relations
New-nbn network
New-Nike Public Relations
Pacific Brands Campaign: "Search for Australia's Well Worn Volleys"
Pfizer Campaign: "The Tarmy"
Sony Computer Entertainment PlayStation (Lead Public Relations Agency)
Toyota
Unilever
Virgin Mobile A Fair Ride For All, Campaign: "Covers For A Cause", Campaign: "Fair Go Bro", Social Media
Warner Brothers Interactive Entertainment Gaming Entertainment Services
Weight Watchers Australia Public Relations, Publicity, Social Media
Westfield
Woolworths Limited Public Relations

HAWKINS INTERNATIONAL PUBLIC RELATIONS
(Private-Parent-Single Location)
119 W 23rd St Ste 401, New York, NY 10011
Tel.: (212) 255-6541
Fax: (212) 255-6716
Web Site: www.hawkpr.com

Employees: 15

Agency Specializes In: Digital/Interactive, Internet/Web Design, Media Relations, Public Relations, Social Media

Revenue: $1,500,000

Jennifer Hawkins *(Pres)*
Jennifer A. Oberstein *(Mng Dir)*
Corey Finjer *(Sr VP)*
Michelle Kelly *(VP-Client Svcs)*
Amy Newcomb *(VP)*
Martha Carrera *(Dir)*

Accounts:
Accor Hotels
Digital Air Strike
New-Dream Downtown
New-Dream Midtown
Happier
Hotel Guanahani & Spa
New-John Hall's
New-JW Marriott Venice
Kaptivating
La Compagnie
Lake Arrowhead Resort & Spa
Montage Hotels & Resorts
Mountain Lodges of Peru
Novotel New York Times Square
Sofitel
New-Tradewind Aviation
New-The Tryall Club
Wilderness Safaris

HAYSLETT GROUP
50 Glenlake Pkwy Ste 430, Atlanta, GA 30328
Tel.: (770) 522-8855
Fax: (770) 522-8898
E-Mail: chayslett@hayslettgroup.com
Web Site: www.hayslettgroup.com

Employees: 15
Year Founded: 1994

Agency Specializes In: Public Relations, Sponsorship, Web (Banner Ads, Pop-ups, etc.)

Charles N. Hayslett *(Owner)*
Judy Hayslett *(Chief Admin Officer)*
Jessica Hayslett Moseley *(Sr Acct Mgr)*
Mike King *(Sr Counsel)*
Teri Lynn Reed *(Sr Counsel)*

Accounts:
Arnall Golden Gregory LLP Legal Services
Chamberlain Hrdlicka Legal Services
Georgia Association of REALTORS Real Estate Services
McCarthy Building Companies Commercial Construction Services
Sumter Regional Hospital Healthcare Services

HAYTER COMMUNICATIONS
7805 Broadstone Pl SW, Port Orchard, WA 98367
Tel.: (360) 313-7070
E-Mail: media@hayterpr.com
Web Site: www.hayterpr.com

Agency Specializes In: Crisis Communications, Event Planning & Marketing, Market Research, Media Training, Public Relations, Social Media

Ryan Hayter *(Pres & CEO)*
Tara Yant *(Sr Acct Dir)*
Christina Erb LoVullo *(Sr Mgr-PR)*
Elana Rabin *(Mgr-PR)*

Accounts:
Outdoor Tech

HEMSWORTH COMMUNICATIONS
12505 Orange Dr Ste 907, Davie, FL 33330
Tel.: (954) 716-7614
Web Site: www.hemsworthcommunications.com

Agency Specializes In: Brand Development & Integration, Crisis Communications, Event Planning & Marketing, Media Relations, Media Training, Print, Promotions, Public Relations, Strategic Planning/Research

Samantha Jacobs *(Founder & Pres)*
Gillian Love *(Sr Acct Exec)*
Kristin Soto *(Sr Acct Exec)*
Kara Freedman *(Acct Exec)*
Alyssa Wickham *(Acct Coord)*

Accounts:
Margaritaville Hollywood Beach Resort
Sonesta Bayfront Hotel Coconut Grove
Sonesta Fort Lauderdale
WorldCruise.cn

THE HENDRA AGENCY INC.
142 Sterling Pl, Brooklyn, NY 11217
Tel.: (718) 622-3232

Employees: 6
Year Founded: 1979

Agency Specializes In: Broadcast, Business Publications, Business-To-Business, Cable T.V., Consulting, Consumer Marketing, Entertainment, Event Planning & Marketing, Financial, Food Service, High Technology, Leisure, Magazines, Newspapers & Magazines, Print, Public Relations, Publicity/Promotions, Radio, T.V.

Barbara J. Hendra *(Pres)*
Jan Andrew *(Acct Exec)*

Accounts:
Avenus Global Strategy & Operational Change Firm
Charles Green, Trusted Advisors Associates
Craig Nova Novelist
Dr. David Katz Nutritionist & Author
Frank Armstrong Investor Solutions Investment Company
James Champy, Chairman of Consulting, Perot Systems Management Consultant; 1992
NeuroFocus; CA
The New York Review of Books
Omar Khan-Sensei International Management Consultant
Peter Navarro Economist/Professor/Author
Robert Galford Managing Director of The Center for Executive Development
Stephen T. McClellan Author/Security Analyst
W.Y. Boyd Author

HENRY & GERMANN PUBLIC AFFAIRS LLC
(Formerly Holt & Germann Public Affairs LLC)
Edgewood Grange Hall 1669 Edgewood Rd Ste 207, Yardley, PA 19067
Tel.: (215) 493-1426
Fax: (215) 493-1427
Web Site: www.hgpa.com

Employees: 5
Year Founded: 1980

National Agency Associations: PRSA

Agency Specializes In: Business-To-Business, Consulting, Corporate Identity, Environmental, Government/Political, Health Care Services, Planning & Consultation, Public Relations, Restaurant, Strategic Planning/Research, Transportation

Approx. Annual Billings: $1,000,000

Ray Germann *(Owner)*
Kelly Henry *(Principal)*
Tony Bianchini *(VP)*
John McKeegan *(VP)*
Allison Kuronya *(Acct Exec)*

Accounts:
Johnson & Johnson
McDonald's Corporation
PECO Energy
PPG
Wine Institute

HENSON CONSULTING, INC.
205 W Wacker Ste 1100, Chicago, IL 60606
Tel.: (312) 374-8534
E-Mail: jack@hensonconsulting.com
Web Site: www.hensonconsulting.com

Agency Specializes In: Communications, Consulting, Crisis Communications, Media Relations, Public Relations, Strategic Planning/Research

Michelle Mekky *(Sr Strategist & Dir-New Bus Dev)*
Jerica Lancaster *(Dir-Acctg)*
Steve Singerman *(Dir-Client Engagement)*
Julia Baker *(Acct Mgr)*
Abby Baric *(Acct Mgr)*
Joanna Meagher *(Acct Mgr)*
Stephanie Poquette *(Acct Mgr)*
Kendra Smith *(Acct Mgr)*
Amanda Urban *(Acct Mgr)*
Anna Treiber *(Mgr-Hospitality Div)*
Lauren Kerr *(Acct Exec)*
Erin Chambers *(Copywriter)*

Accounts:
Allstate Foundation
Biggs
C Chicago
Catherine Cook School
Celeste
Chef Art Smith
Chicago Cut Steakhouse
Coldwell Banker Residential Brokerage
Destination Kohler Local Media, National Media
The Food Network Magazine Campaign: "No Kid Hungry"
Frank Lloyd Wright Unity Temple Restoration Foundation
Hard Rock Hotel Hotels
Joes
Land O'Frost Lunch Meats, PR
Life Sources
LISA
The Local Chicago
Lovie & MaryAnne Smith Foundation
Metro Mix
Mondelez International, Inc. PR, Philadelphia Cream Cheese
New-Navy Pier (Public Relations Agency of Record)
Pork & Mindy's
R J Grunts
Ronald McDonald House Charities of Chicagoland & Northwest Indiana
Smokey Bones
Sprig
Starwood Retail
Ticor Title Insurance Company
Tillman Carson Snyder
Waldorf Astoria Chicago
Walter E. Smithe Furniture Store
Western Pistachio Association Pistachio Growers

HERMAN & ALMONTE PUBLIC RELATIONS, LLC
(Formerly Herman Associates Public Relations)
275 Madison Ave Ste 800, New York, NY 10016
Tel.: (212) 616-1190
Fax: (212) 725-0172
E-Mail: info@herman-almontePR.com
Web Site: www.herman-almontepr.com/

E-Mail for Key Personnel:
Chairman: pherman@hermanassociatesnewyork.com
President: sherman@hermanassociatesnewyork.com
Public Relations: pherman@hermanassociatesnewyork.com

Employees: 5
Year Founded: 1986

Agency Specializes In: Advertising, Advertising Specialties, Affluent Market, Alternative Advertising, Arts, Below-the-Line, Business Publications, Business-To-Business, Cable T.V., Catalogs, Co-op Advertising, Collateral, College, Commercial Photography, Communications, Consulting, Consumer Publications, Corporate Communications, Corporate Identity, Crisis Communications, Custom Publishing, Direct Response Marketing, Electronic Media, Event Planning & Marketing, Financial, Government/Political, Guerilla Marketing, High Technology, Information Technology, Integrated Marketing, Internet/Web Design, Investor Relations, Leisure, Logo & Package Design, Media Buying Services, Media Planning, Media Relations, Media Training, Multimedia, New Product Development, Newspaper, Planning & Consultation, Production (Print), Promotions, Public Relations, Publicity/Promotions, Recruitment, Regional, Retail, Sales Promotion, Search Engine Optimization, Seniors' Market, Strategic Planning/Research, Syndication, T.V., Teen Market, Trade & Consumer Magazines, Transportation, Travel & Tourism, Viral/Buzz/Word of Mouth, Web (Banner Ads, Pop-ups, etc.), Women's Market

Mario Almonte *(Mng Partner)*
Paula Herman *(Partner)*
Sophie Latish *(Asst Acct Exec)*

Accounts:
Air India; New York, NY; 2004
Amelia International
American Roll-On Roll-Off Carrier
Atlantic Bank of New York
Austrian Airlines
Christie, Inc.; Cyprus, CA
Clearwater Festival; Poughkeepsie, NY
Club ABC Tours
DriverLoans.com
EgyptAir
European Waterways; UK Barge Cruising; 2005
GermanRail
Hirshorn Insurance Agency
Insight International
JAT Yugoslav Airlines
Senior Health Partners
Spanish Heritage Tours
Trafalgar Tours
United Bus Owners Association
Wallenius Wilhelmsen

HERMANOFF PUBLIC RELATIONS
(Formerly Hermanoff & Associates)
31500 W 13 Mile Rd Ste 110, Farmington Hills, MI 48334-2122
Tel.: (248) 851-3993
Fax: (248) 851-0706
E-Mail: sandyh@hermanoff.net
Web Site: www.hermanoff.net

E-Mail for Key Personnel:
President: sandyh@hermanoff.net

Employees: 7
Year Founded: 1985

National Agency Associations: PRSA

Agency Specializes In: African-American Market, Automotive, Brand Development & Integration, Business-To-Business, Communications, Consulting, Consumer Marketing, Corporate Communications, Education, Entertainment, Environmental, Event Planning & Marketing, Food Service, Government/Political, Health Care Services, Information Technology, Local Marketing, Medical Products, New Product Development, Pharmaceutical, Public Relations, Publicity/Promotions, Real Estate, Restaurant, Retail, Sports Market, Strategic Planning/Research, Transportation, Travel & Tourism

Marc Pasco *(Mgr-Client Svcs)*

HIGH RISE PR
59 Kent St Ste 2B, Brooklyn, NY 11222
Tel.: (347) 689-2461
E-Mail: info@highrisepr.com
Web Site: www.highrisepr.com

Year Founded: 2009

Agency Specializes In: Print, Public Relations, T.V.

Alexandra Baker *(Founder & CEO)*

Accounts:
New-Absolut Vodka
New-Dr. Martens

HIGH VIEW COMMUNICATIONS INC.
422 Richards St 3rd Fl, Vancouver, BC V6B 2Z3 Canada
Tel.: (416) 322-5897
E-Mail: info@highviewcommunications.com
Web Site: www.highviewcommunications.com

Year Founded: 2002

Agency Specializes In: Crisis Communications, Media Relations, Media Training, Public Relations

Ann Gallery *(Founder & Pres)*

Accounts:
Ford Motor Company of Canada, Limited
Xylitol Canada Inc Xyla Sweetener

HIGHWIRE PUBLIC RELATIONS
(Formerly Borders + Gratehouse)
727 Sansome St, San Francisco, CA 94111
Tel.: (415) 963-4174
E-Mail: connect@highwirepr.com
Web Site: www.highwirepr.com/

Agency Specializes In: Media Relations, Media Training, Public Relations

Carol Carrubba *(Principal)*
Kathleen Gratehouse *(Principal)*
Carolyn Adams *(VP)*
Christine McKeown *(VP)*
Elliott Suthers *(VP)*
Lindsey Coyle *(Acct Dir)*

Bill Rundle *(Acct Mgr)*

Accounts:
AppDirect
Polaris Wireless Software Services
SoftLayer Technologies
Sustainable Energy Technologies Ltd Solar Inverter Mfr & Distr
Xero

HILL + KNOWLTON STRATEGIES
825 3rd Ave 24th Fl, New York, NY 10022
Tel.: (212) 885-0300
Fax: (212) 885-0570
Web Site: www.hkstrategies.com

Employees: 120
Year Founded: 1927

National Agency Associations: COPF

Agency Specializes In: Public Relations, Sponsorship

Richard Millar *(Chm-Creative Strategy-Global & CEO-UK)*
Mike Coates *(Pres/CEO-Americas Reg)*
Chris Winans *(Exec VP & Gen Mgr-NY Office)*
Amy Rosenberg *(Exec VP & Dir-Media Rels-US)*
James Anstey *(Sr VP-Digital & Head-East Coast Practice)*
Drew Levinson *(Sr VP-Media Rels)*
Jim Meredith *(Controller-US)*
Karen Butcher *(Assoc Dir)*
Brandon Skop *(Sr Acct Supvr)*

Accounts:
20th Century Fox Home Entertainment (Agency of Record) Campaign: "The Sandlot"
Aflac Public Relations
AmericaSpeaks; 2007
Best Buy
Del Monte Nature's Recipe
Deloitte
Dillard University; 2008
Emirates (Agency of Record) Consumer, Travel Trade and Corporate Communications
Ford Motor Company
GEROVA Financial Group, Ltd (Communications Agency of Record) Communications Strategy, Investor Relations
Harold Hamm Diabetes Center
Informatica Digital Media, Global PR, Media Relations, Social
InterContinental Hotels Corporate & Brand PR
International Monetary Fund Global Reach; 2008
Mazda North American Operations (Agency of Record)
Miami Beach Visitor & Convention Authority (Agency of Record) Brand Awareness, Strategic Media
Motorola Solutions, Inc.
NES Group
North American Working Group Brand Positioning, Messaging Strategy
PeaceJam Foundation Campaign: "One Billion Acts of Peace"
Procter & Gamble
Rio Tinto plc; London, UK; 2007
SanDisk
The Snoring Center (Agency of Record) Public Relations, Traditional & Social Media Programs
Tata Communications
TomTom, Inc.
Unilever UK Foods Hellmann's Mayonnaise, Ragu Express
Western Red Cedar Lumber Association; Vancouver; 2007

Offices

Blanc & Otus Public Relations
1001 Front St, San Francisco, CA 94111
(See Separate Listing)

Group SJR
22 W 21st St 9th Fl, New York, NY 10010
Tel.: (917) 267-2930
Web Site: groupsjr.com

Agency Specializes In: Content, Digital/Interactive, Sponsorship

Alexander Jutkowitz *(Mng Partner)*
Tom Blim *(Partner)*
Margaret Sullivan *(Partner)*
Gary Goldhammer *(Mng Dir)*
Gillian Melrose *(Mng Dir)*
Shai Almagor *(Exec Dir-Accts & Project Mgmt)*
Matt Higgins *(Sr Dir-Digital Strategy & Media)*
Anthony Sheehan *(Sr Dir)*
Jessica Barraco *(Dir-New Bus Strategy & Audience Dev)*
Damien Cortese *(Dir-Strategy & Accts)*

Accounts:
CBRE Group "Blueprint", Digital
Dell
GE
The Motion Picture Association of America
TED
Xerox

H+K Strategies
255 Alhambra Cir Ste 330, Miami, FL 33134
Tel.: (305) 443-5454
Web Site: www.hkstrategies.com

Agency Specializes In: Communications, Corporate Identity, Public Relations, Social Media

Mark Thorne *(Vice Chm & COO-Global)*
Jack Martin *(Chm-Global & CEO)*
Michael Coates *(Pres/CEO-America)*
Michael Kehs *(Exec VP, Head-Global Energy Practice & Gen Mgr-Houston)*
David Bowen *(Exec VP)*
Cori Rice *(Gen Mgr)*

Accounts:
Miami Beach Visitor & Convention Authority Public Relations Agency of Record

Hill + Knowlton Strategies
(Formerly Hill & Knowlton, Inc.)
3200 Bristol St Ste 300, Irvine, CA 92626
Tel.: (949) 223-2300
Fax: (949) 752-2130
E-Mail: erica.amestoy@hkstrategies.com
Web Site: www.hkstrategies.com

Employees: 20

National Agency Associations: COPF

Agency Specializes In: Public Relations

Ted Donath *(Sr VP-Mktg Comm)*
Nurha Hindi *(Sr VP)*
Larry Krutchik *(Sr VP)*
Monica Bouldin *(Gen Mgr)*

Hill + Knowlton Strategies
(Formerly Hill & Knowlton, Inc.)
60 Green St, San Francisco, CA 94111
Tel.: (415) 281-7120
Fax: (415) 281-7121
E-Mail: kevin.elliot@hillandknowlton.com
Web Site: www.hkstrategies.com

Employees: 35

National Agency Associations: COPF

Agency Specializes In: Public Relations, Sponsorship

Kevin Elliott *(Sr VP & Dir-Risk & Crisis Comm Practice-US)*
Barbara Edler *(Sr VP)*
Rick Foote *(Sr VP-Digital)*
Nora Feeley *(VP)*
Barbara Melchin *(VP-HR-Western Reg)*
Monica Bouldin *(Gen Mgr)*

Accounts:
Dolby Laboratories (Agency of Record)
Informatica Digital, Global PR, Media Relations, Social
VMware

Hill + Knowlton Strategies
(Formerly Hill & Knowlton, Inc.)
607 14th St NW Ste 300, Washington, DC 20005-2000
Tel.: (202) 333-7400
Fax: (202) 333-1638
Web Site: www.hkstrategies.com

Employees: 60

National Agency Associations: COPF

Agency Specializes In: Public Relations

Vivian Lines *(Vice Chm-Global, Chm-Asia Pacific & Co-Head-Client Svcs)*
Ellen Moran *(Exec VP & Gen Mgr)*
David Bowen *(Exec VP)*
Howard Opinsky *(Exec VP-US Eastern Reg)*
Kathie Boettrich *(Sr VP & Head-Practice-Change & Employee Comm)*
David Bloomgren *(Sr VP)*
Soren Dayton *(Sr VP)*
Rebecca Fannin *(Sr VP)*
Stacie Paxton *(Sr VP)*
Lauren Olsen Herchert *(VP)*
Rebecca Francis Ballard *(Head-External Comm)*
Jennifer Capps *(Sr Acct Supvr & Sr Writer)*
Patrick Ryan *(Sr Acct Supvr)*

Accounts:
Adidas
American Natural Gas Alliance
American Red Cross
BBMG Corporation
eBay; 2007
HP China
Johnson & Johnson
Nestle
Prince William Health System
Robinsons
Virgin

Hill + Knowlton Strategies
(Formerly Hill + Knowlton, Inc.)
201 E Kennedy Blvd Ste 1611, Tampa, FL 33602-5117
Tel.: (813) 221-0030
Fax: (813) 229-2926
E-Mail: harry.costello@hkstrategies.com
Web Site: www.hkstrategies.com

Employees: 20

National Agency Associations: COPF

Agency Specializes In: Public Relations

James Fuller *(Pres, CEO & Exec VP)*
Harry Costello *(Exec VP & Gen Mgr)*
Lu Anne Stewart *(Sr VP)*
Christine Duffy *(VP)*
Lena Davie *(Head-Internal Comm)*
Martin Forbes *(Mgr-Fin & HR)*
Jennifer Hamilton *(Acct Supvr)*
Berit Mansour *(Acct Supvr)*

Susan Thurston *(Sr Acct Exec)*

Accounts:
Adidas
BBMG Corporation
Florida Healthcare
Johnson & Johnson
Novartis
Virgin

Hill + Knowlton Strategies
(Formerly Hill & Knowlton, Inc.)
222 Merchandise Mart Plz Ste 275, Chicago, IL 60654
Tel.: (312) 255-1200
Fax: (312) 255-3030
Web Site: www.hkstrategies.com

Employees: 45

National Agency Associations: COPF

Agency Specializes In: Public Relations

Vivian Lines *(Vice Chm-Global, Chm-Asia Pacific & Co-Head-Client Svcs)*
Jennifer Eidson *(Sr VP-Chicago Corp Practice)*
Cathleen Bleers *(VP)*
Brent Curry *(VP)*
Renae Godish *(VP)*
Jessi Langsen *(VP-Digital)*
Madonna Duncan *(Sr Acct Supvr)*
Meghan Hodgdon *(Acct Supvr)*
Amy Dalkoff *(Sr Acct Exec)*
Mackenzie Smith *(Sr Acct Exec)*

Accounts:
Underwriters Laboratories Global PR

Hill + Knowlton Strategies
(Formerly Hill & Knowlton, Inc.)
1001 Fannin St Ste 500, Houston, TX 77002
Tel.: (713) 752-1900
Fax: (713) 752-1930
Web Site: www.hkstrategies.com

Employees: 12

National Agency Associations: COPF

Agency Specializes In: Public Relations

Sam Lythgoe *(Mng Dir & Sr VP-New Bus & Mktg-UK & EMEA)*
Mark Bunker *(CFO)*
Ragan Altizer *(CFO-US & Controller-Global)*
Marvin Singleton *(Exec VP & Gen Mgr-Dallas)*
Merrill Davis *(Sr VP)*
Amy Mcmichael Paddock *(Sr VP)*
Elisabeth Rutledge *(Sr VP)*
Melanie Laurence Martin *(VP-Digital & Creative)*
Allison Knaupe *(Gen Mgr)*
Katie Boshart *(Sr Acct Supvr)*

Hill + Knowlton Strategies
(Formerly Hill & Knowlton)
221 Yale Ave N, Seattle, WA 98109
Tel.: (415) 281-7146
Fax: (509) 744-3355
E-Mail: jennifer.west@hillandknowlton.com
Web Site: www.hkstrategies.com

Employees: 3
Year Founded: 1986

Agency Specializes In: Government/Political, Public Relations

Mark Thorne *(Vice Chm & COO-Global)*
Alexander Jutkowitz *(Vice Chm & Sr Strategist-Global)*
Thomas Hoog *(Vice Chm-Trng & New Bus)*
Norman Mineta *(Vice Chm-Pub Policy)*
Peter Zandan *(Vice Chm-Global)*
Erin Gentry *(Exec VP & Co-Head-Client Svcs-Global)*
Alison Eyles-Owen *(Exec VP-Mktg Comm Worldwide)*
Andy Sutherden *(Head-Sports Marketing & Sponsorship-Global)*
Ruth Clark *(Dir-Talent-Global)*

Hill + Knowlton Strategies
1601 Cloverfield Blvd Ste 3000N, Santa Monica, CA 90404
Tel.: (310) 633-9400
Fax: (310) 633-9401
Web Site: www.hkstrategies.com

Employees: 40

Agency Specializes In: Public Relations, Sponsorship

Larry Krutchik *(Sr VP-Public Affairs)*
Monica Bouldin *(Gen Mgr)*

Accounts:
Avery Dennison

PBN Hill + Knowlton Strategies
(Formerly The PBN Company)
1150 18th St NW Ste 325, Washington, DC 20036
(See Separate Listing)

Branches

PBN Hill + Knowlton Strategies
(Formerly The PBN Company)
3 Uspensky Pereulok Bldg 4, Moscow, Russia
Tel.: (7) 495 775 0077
Fax: (7) 495 775 0075
Web Site: www.pbn-hkstrategies.com/en/Home

Employees: 30

Maria Kuzkina *(VP-Client Svcs & Head-Moscow)*
Anton Gubnitsyn *(VP-Govt Rels)*
Victoria Khinevich *(Dir-Media Monitoring & Analysis)*
Igor Tolkachev *(Dir-Tech & Digital)*
Dominic Fean *(Sr Acct Mgr)*
Arina Khodyreva *(Sr Acct Mgr)*
Timur Shishkin *(Sr Acct Mgr)*
Maria Grigorieva *(Assoc Acct Mgr)*
Lyubov Reshetilo *(Acct Mgr)*
Uliana Isakova *(Sr Analyst-Media)*

Accounts:
Abbott International
Alibaba Alibaba.com, Aliexpress.com, Public Relations
Bank of New York Mellon
Dell
Deutsche Bank
Dixy Group
Dyckerhoff AG
Gazprom Neft
LG Electronics
Nord Stream
Renaissance Group

Wexler & Walker Public Policy Associates
1317 F St NW Ste 600, Washington, DC 20004-1105
Tel.: (202) 638-2121
Fax: (202) 638-7045
E-Mail: melberg@wexlerwalker.com
Web Site: www.wexlerwalker.com

Employees: 53
Year Founded: 1986

Agency Specializes In: Government/Political, Public Relations

Dale W. Snape *(Vice Chm)*
Jody Hoffman *(Mng Dir & Sr VP)*
Timothy F. Hannegan *(Mng Dir)*
R. D. Folsom *(Sr VP)*
Robert L. Healy *(Sr VP)*
Tom Carpenter *(VP)*
James K. Melberg *(Dir-Coalitions & Grassroots)*

Accounts:
Analogic Corporation
Ball Aerospace & Technologies
DigitalGlobe Inc
General Motors Corporation
Hughes Communications
RC2 Corporation
Skyterra

Canada

H+K Strategies
(Formerly HKDP Communications & Public Affairs)
1100 Rene Levesque Blvd W Ste 600, Montreal, QC H3B 4N4 Canada
Tel.: (514) 395-0375
Fax: (514) 395-1999
Web Site: www.hkstrategies.com

E-Mail for Key Personnel:
President: dmatte@hkdp.qc.ca

Employees: 15

Agency Specializes In: Public Relations

Dimitri Gourdin *(Sr VP & Gen Mgr-Montreal)*
Simon Poitras *(Sr VP & Gen Mgr)*
Chris Davies *(VP & Dir-Natl Creative)*
Stephane Michaud *(VP)*
Julie Perrier *(Sr Dir)*
Alain Blanchette *(Sr Mgr-PR)*

Accounts:
3M Canada (Public Relations Agency of Record) B2B Communications, Campaign: "Tweet Machine", Media Relations

Hill + Knowlton Strategies
(Formerly Hill & Knowlton (Canada) Limited)
55 Metcalfe St Ste 1100, Ottawa, ON K1P 6L5 Canada
Tel.: (613) 238-4371
Fax: (613) 238-8642
E-Mail: brian.mersereau@hillandknowlton.ca
Web Site: hkstrategies.ca/

Employees: 45

Agency Specializes In: Public Relations

Goldy Hyder *(Pres & CEO)*
Joseph Peters *(Chief Strategy Officer)*
Boyd Neil *(Sr VP & Sr Strategist-Digital)*
Craig Rowsell *(VP & Grp Head-Procurement & Trade)*
Jane Billings *(VP & Dir-Procurement Svcs)*
Jason MacDonald *(VP-Corp Comm)*
Michelle Mclean *(VP)*
Steven MacKinnon *(Head-Natl Practice-Fin Comm & Transactions)*
Ruth Clark *(Sr Dir-Talent-Global)*

Accounts:
New-Cineplex Entertainment (Public Relations Agency of Record)
Motorola Mobility Canada Public Relations & Digital
Thomas Cook Canada

Hill + Knowlton Strategies
(Formerly Hill & Knowlton, Inc.)
Ste 300 Watermark Tower 530 8th Ave SW, Calgary, AB T2P 3S8 Canada
Tel.: (403) 299-9380
Fax: (403) 299-9389
E-Mail: info@hillandknowlton.ca
Web Site: www.hkstrategies.com/canada

Agency Specializes In: Public Relations

Jane Shapiro *(Sr VP & Head-Natl Practice)*
Dimitri Gourdin *(Sr VP & Gen Mgr)*
Joy Jennissen *(Sr VP & Gen Mgr)*
Simon Poitras *(Sr VP & Gen Mgr)*
Ilyse Smith *(Sr VP & Gen Mgr)*
Chrystal Boudreau *(Sr Dir-HR)*
Stephen Carter *(Dir-Campaign Strategy-Natl)*

Accounts:
Allied Bakeries
Debswana; UK
HP Photo Big Bang; Europe
Lock & Lock; China
Pfizer Detrol; Puerto Rico
Sega Sonic
Smithsonian; US

HKDP Communications & Public Affairs
580 Grand Allee E Ste 240, Quebec, QC G1R 2K2 Canada
Tel.: (418) 523-3352
Fax: (418) 521-1548
Web Site: fr.hkstrategies.ca

Employees: 30

Agency Specializes In: Public Relations

Simon Poitras *(Sr VP & Gen Mgr-Quebec)*
Julie Perrier *(Sr Dir)*

Argentina

Hill & Knowlton de Argentina
Lavalle 1675, Piso 7, Oficina 8, Ciudad Autonoma de, 1654 Buenos Aires, Argentina
Tel.: (54) 11 4737 2300
Fax: (54) 11 4737 2300
Web Site: www.hkstrategies.com

Employees: 10

Agency Specializes In: Public Relations

Paola Rodriguez *(Acct Dir)*
Federico Spitznagel *(Client Svcs Dir)*
Maria Dolores Frias *(Acct Exec)*
Marcelo Benavides *(Acting Gen Mgr)*

Brazil

Hill & Knowlton Brazil
Rua Andre Ampere 34 8 andar, Sao Paulo, SP 04562-080 Brazil
Tel.: (55) 11 5503 2860
Fax: (55) 11 5505 9487
E-Mail: smagri@hillandknowlton.com

Employees: 25

Agency Specializes In: Public Relations

Daniel Medina *(Pres & Mng Dir-Brazil)*
Cassia Schittini *(VP)*
Livia Hormigo *(Acct Dir)*
Ive Cristina De Andrade *(Acct Supvr)*

Accounts:
Hitachi Data Systems
Lenovo Group Limited
Novo Nordisk
Yahoo! Inc.

Chile

Hill & Knowlton Captiva
Alcantara 271 Piso 4th Fl, Las Condes, Santiago, Chile
Tel.: (56) 2 372 0420
Fax: (56) 2 372 0427

Employees: 30

Agency Specializes In: Communications, Corporate Communications, Crisis Communications, Financial, Market Research, Media Relations, Public Relations, Publicity/Promotions

Pamela Leonard *(Dir-Gen Accounts)*

Accounts:
Delta Air Lines
Procter & Gamble

Mexico

Hill + Knowlton Strategies Mexico
Prol Paseo de la Reforma No 490 1st Fl, 01210 Mexico, DF Mexico
Tel.: (52) 55 9177 1860
Web Site: www.hkstrategies.com

Employees: 25

Agency Specializes In: Public Relations

Daniel Karam *(Pres & Mng Dir)*
Haide Garcia *(CFO)*
Claudia Gioia *(Pres/CEO-Latin America)*
Iliana Perez *(VP-Consumer & ITC-Digital)*
Mariana Tuis *(Dir-Strategic Plng)*

Puerto Rico

Hill & Knowlton
PO Box 2126, San Juan, PR 00922-2126
Tel.: (787) 474-2525
Fax: (787) 474-2552
E-Mail: jennifer.wolff@hillandknowlton.com
Web Site: www.hkstrategies.com

Employees: 10

Agency Specializes In: Public Relations

Marvin Singleton *(Exec VP & Gen Mgr-Dallas)*
Howard Opinsky *(Exec VP-US Eastern Reg)*
Kathie Boettrich *(Sr VP & Head-Practice-Change & Employee Comm)*
David Bloomgren *(Sr VP)*
Rebecca Fannin *(Sr VP)*
Cathleen Bleers *(VP)*
Holly Fisher Skillin *(VP)*
Amanda White *(VP)*
Gina Ribaudo *(Acct Supvr-Corp & Pub Affairs)*

Belgium

Hill + Knowlton Strategies
(Formerly Hill & Knowlton International Belgium S.A./N.V.)
Neo Building, Rue Montoyer 51 Box 7, B-1000 Brussels, Belgium
Tel.: (32) 2 737 95 00
Fax: (32) 2 737 95 01
E-Mail: brussels-info@hkstrategies.com
Web Site: www.hkstrategies.be

Employees: 50

Agency Specializes In: Public Relations

Julie Santens *(CFO)*
Jeroen van Seeters *(Dir-Strategy-Europe)*
Katia Delvaille *(Assoc Dir)*
David Carroll *(Acct Mgr-EU Pub Affairs)*
Joanna Hasson Dwek *(Acct Mgr)*
Ellen Hof *(Acct Mgr)*
Olivia Schwarz *(Acct Mgr)*
Jessica Faure *(Acct Exec-Pub Affairs)*

Accounts:
Abbott
Adidas
Aquiris
Boeing
Bolton Group
Deloitte
Fujitsu
Intel
Pfizer
Visa (Public Relations Agency) Communications, Strategy

France

Hill & Knowlton/Thompson Corp.
88 Avenue Charles de Gaulle, CEDEX, 922522 Neuilly-sur-Seine, France
Tel.: (33) 1 41 05 44 00
Fax: (33) 1 41 05 44 02
E-Mail: contact@hillandknowlton.com
Web Site: www.hkstrategies.com

Employees: 40

Agency Specializes In: Financial, Government/Political, Investor Relations, Media Relations, Public Relations

Anne Le Brouster *(Deputy Dir Gen)*
Marina Quesnel *(CFO)*
Agnes Gicquel *(Head-Tech & Sr Acct Dir)*
Corinne Got *(Gen Mgr)*
Olivier Casabielhe *(Acct Supvr-PR)*

Accounts:
Bayer
Bel
CODA
Canderel
Cisco
Ocean Spray
Segafredo
Solar Century
TomTom

Germany

Hill + Knowlton Strategies
(Formerly Hill & Knowlton Frankfurt)
Schwedlerstrasse 6, 60314 Frankfurt, Germany
Tel.: (49) 69 97 362 0
Fax: (49) 69 73 086 6
Web Site: www.hkstrategies.de/en

Year Founded: 1963

Agency Specializes In: Public Relations

Thomas Wimmer *(Mng Dir)*
Catherine Dachert-Tessier *(CFO)*
Miriam Holbe-Finkelnburg *(Head-Mktg Comm & Brand PR)*
Patrick Racky *(Head-Fin & Pro Svcs)*
Ute Richter *(Head-Tech)*
Yasmin Akbal *(Acct Mgr)*
Insa Vanessa Rath *(Acct Mgr)*
Gesa Seibel *(Acct Exec)*

Accounts:
New-eToro Integrated Communications

Greece

PubliCom/Hill + Knowlton Strategies
Charilaou Trikoupi & Xenias 5 Street, Amarousiou, 145 62 Athens, Greece
Tel.: (30) 21 0 628 1800
Fax: (30) 21 0 628 1820
Web Site: www.hkstrategies.gr

Employees: 15

Agency Specializes In: Public Relations

Petros Constantinidis *(Pres & Partner)*
Eleni Constantinidi *(CEO)*

Accounts:
Sotheby's

Italy

Hill & Knowlton Gaia
Via Nomentana 257, 00161 Rome, Italy
Tel.: (39) 06 440 4627
Fax: (39) 06 440 4604
E-Mail: hkgaia@hkgaia.com

Employees: 10

Agency Specializes In: Communications, Public Relations

Ilaria Catastini *(Pres)*
Annalisa Nunziata *(Sr Acct Mgr)*
Federica Petra Colombo *(Acct Mgr)*
Monica Marsiglia *(Acct Supvr)*
Alessia Calvanese *(Sr Acct Exec-PR)*
Maria Luisa De Petris *(Sr Acct Exec-PR)*
Mauro Pedruzzi *(Sr Acct Exec-Pub Affairs)*
Michele Bon *(Acct Exec)*
Elena Visentini *(Acct Exec)*
Federica D'Amato *(Jr Acct Exec-PR)*

Accounts:
API
Ariel P&G
Cobat
E.on
Ecodeco
GlaxoSmithKline Singapore
HP
Mengozzi
Microsoft
Motorola Solutions, Inc.
Procter & Gamble
Saras
Ser
Trenitalia
Vectrix
Watsons
Ziggs
Zoomarine

Hill & Knowlton Italy
Via Paolo Lomazzo 19, 20154 Milan, Italy
Tel.: (39) 02 31914 1
Fax: (39) 02 3453 7197
E-Mail: cesare.valli@hillandknowlton.com
Web Site: www.hkstrategies.com

Employees: 40

Agency Specializes In: Public Relations

Angelo Pacillo *(CFO)*
Nicolo Michetti *(CEO-Digital PR)*
Sandro Pello *(VP)*
Gianpaolo Bertocchi *(Sr Controller)*
Alessandra Favilli *(Gen Mgr)*

Latvia

Hill & Knowlton Latvia
Brivibas iela 40 36, Riga, LV 1050 Latvia
Tel.: (371) 67 24 0571
Fax: (371) 67 24 0572
E-Mail: ralfs.vilands@hillknowlton.com
Web Site: http://www.hkstrategies.com/global-presence/riga

Employees: 14

Agency Specializes In: Public Relations

Marika Gruniceva *(Office Mgr)*

Accounts:
Airbotic
Coca-Cola Refreshments USA, Inc.
Neste
Swed Bank

Netherlands

Hill+Knowlton Strategies B.V.
Weerdestein 20, 1083 GA Amsterdam, Netherlands
Mailing Address:
Postbus Box 87360, 1080 JJ Amsterdam, Netherlands
Tel.: (31) 204044707
Fax: (31) 206449736
E-Mail: Ingo.Heijnen@hkstrategies.com
Web Site: www.hkstrategies.nl

Employees: 40
Year Founded: 1972

Agency Specializes In: Public Relations

Ingo Heijnen *(Pres-EMEA)*
Robin Den Hoed *(Dir-Corp Mktg Comm)*
Anthony Hellegers *(Dir-Comm-Pub Affairs)*
Paul Kok *(Dir-Strategy)*
Monique Landman *(Dir-Project Mgmt)*
Tanno Massar *(Dir-Strategy)*
Sabine Post-de Jong *(Dir-Fin & Corp Comm)*
Jeroen van Seeters *(Dir-Strategy-Europe)*
Kareth Weaver *(Assoc Dir-Lifestyle & Mktg PR)*
Marika Horikx *(Mgr-Bus Intelligence & Dev)*

Accounts:
BlackBerry
BlackRock
KPN
McDonald's
NetApp
Nutricia

Poland

Hill+Knowlton Strategies Poland
(Formerly Feedback/Hill & Knowlton)
Ul Adama Branickiego 17, 02-972 Warsaw, Poland
Tel.: (48) 22 536 38 00
Fax: (48) 22 536 38 01
E-Mail: public.warsaw@hkstrategies.com
Web Site: hkstrategies.pl/pl/H-K-Strategies

Employees: 39

Agency Specializes In: Pets , Public Relations

Agnieszka Dziedzic *(CEO)*
Katarzyna Lutkiewicz *(Gen Dir)*
Maciej Szaroleta *(Brand Dir & Sr Strategist)*
Tomasz Relewicz *(Acct Dir)*
Jan Sciegienny *(Acct Dir)*
Agata Janczak *(Project Mgr-Digital)*
Sandra Kaczmarek *(Sr Acct Exec)*
Joanna Manarczyk *(Sr Acct Exec)*
Aleksandra Daniszewska *(Acct Exec)*

Accounts:
Antonio Berardi
Celgene
Deloitte
Gedeon Richter Marketing Polska
Kompania Piwowarska
Michelin
Nokia
Novartis
Peroni
SABMiller
Samsung
yoox.com

Spain

Hill+Knowlton Strategies
Nunez de Balboa 83 bajo dcha Oquendo 23 4 planta, 28006 Madrid, Spain
Tel.: (34) 91 435 11 22
Fax: (34) 91 576 38 97
Web Site: www.hkstrategies.com/Madrid

E-Mail for Key Personnel:
President: cuadrado@hillandknowlton.com

Employees: 20

Agency Specializes In: Public Relations

Nidardo Cuadrado *(Pres)*
Joan Ramon Vilamitjana *(Gen Mgr)*
Monica Navas Grane *(Dir-Health Division-H + K Spain)*
Xavier Mortes *(Dir-Consumer Div)*
Adriana Diaz Covaleda *(Sr Acct Exec)*
Arnau Vidal *(Acct Exec-Mktg Comm & Social Media)*

Accounts:
New-eToro Integrated Communications

Hill & Knowlton Espana, S.A.
Corsega Street 329 6th Floor, 08037 Barcelona, Spain
Tel.: (34) 93 410 82 63
Fax: (34) 93 439 55 27
E-Mail: recepcion.bcn@hkstrategies.com
Web Site: hkstrategies.es

Employees: 15

Agency Specializes In: Public Relations

Eloisa Alonso *(CEO & Gen Mgr)*
Joan Ramon Vilamitjana *(Gen Mgr)*

United Kingdom

Hill + Knowlton Strategies
(Formerly Hill & Knowlton (UK) Ltd.)
The Buckley Building 49, Clerkenwell Green, London, EC1R 0EB United Kingdom
Tel.: (44) 20 7413 3000
Fax: (44) 20 7413 3111
E-Mail: info@hillandknowlton.com
Web Site: www.hkstrategies.com

Employees: 300
Year Founded: 1952

Agency Specializes In: Communications, Corporate Identity, Financial, Government/Political, Health

Care Services, High Technology, Pharmaceutical, Public Relations, Social Media

Tim Luckett *(Co-Chm-Crisis Comm & Risk Mgmt-Global)*
Richard Millar *(Pres/CEO-Strategies-UK & Europe)*
Lalu Dasgupta *(Sr VP-Corp Advisory Practice-Global)*
Caroline Samuel *(Mng Dir-HR)*
Andy Sutherden *(Mng Dir-Sports Mktg & Sponsorship)*
Will Dunn *(VP)*
Sam Lythgoe *(Head-Bus Dev)*
Charlie Morgan *(Head-Tech)*
Suzannah Greenwood *(Sr Acct Dir-Energy & Industrials)*
Alex Bishop *(Acct Dir)*
Remy Le Fevre *(Acct Dir)*
Clare Murphy-McGreevey *(Acct Dir)*
Daisy Thomas *(Acct Dir-Healthcare & Wellbeing)*
Matt Bright *(Dir)*
Vikki Chowney *(Dir-Content & Publ Strategies)*
Verity Dephoff *(Assoc Dir)*
Chris Gibbs *(Assoc Dir)*
Henry Groundes-Peace *(Assoc Dir-Fin Svcs)*
Joanna Hoare *(Assoc Dir)*
Robert Roessler *(Assoc Dir)*
Joe McNamara *(Acct Mgr)*
Neil Thomas *(Acct Mgr)*
Charlotte Pearson *(Jr Acct Exec)*

Accounts:
Abu Dhabi Food Control Authority
Adidas
Aeroflot
Ariel
Autoglass B2B Comm, Brand Awareness, Digital
Aviva UKA Academy
Belvita Breakfast
Blue Square Consumer Communications
BMW Oracle Racing
Brand South Africa
Casio UK
Centre for Skills Development Training for Rural Development
Comet
Crowne Plaza
Dong Energy Corporate PR, Public Affairs
Eidos Interactive Championship Manager
England Rugby 2015
New-E.ON UK plc Public Relations
New-eToro Integrated Communications
Fairy Non Bio Gel
Ford of Europe
GE Capital
Gillette Shavercare
Global Peace Index
GSK Consumer, Human Performance Lab, Public Relations
Hermes Fund Managers
Holiday Inn
HSBC
Hymans Robertson
McDonald's Campaign: "Green Education"
Mondelez International, Inc. Advertising, Chips Ahoy, Digital, In-Store, Out-of-Home, Public Relations, Ritz Crisp & Thin, Sampling, TV, Video
NOT JUST A LABEL PR, Website
Pringles
Procter & Gamble Campaign: "Febreze Man in a Box"
RenewableUK Digital Communications, Media Relations, Research
Stora Enso
Visa Europe (Public Relations Agency) Communications, Strategy

Bahrain

Gulf Hill & Knowlton
1 Government Ave Bldg 4th Fl Ofc 402, PO Box 1596, Manama, Bahrain
Tel.: (973) 17 533532
Fax: (973) 17 533370
Web Site: www.hkstrategies.com

Employees: 10

Agency Specializes In: Public Relations

Chris Pratt *(Dir)*

United Arab Emirates

Gulf Hill & Knowlton
PO Box 50653, Dubai, United Arab Emirates
Tel.: (971) 4 33 44 930
Fax: (971) 4 33 44 923
Web Site: www.hkstrategies.com

Employees: 50

Agency Specializes In: Public Relations

Sconaid McGeachin *(Pres/CEO-India, Middle East, Africa & Turkey)*
Iman Issa *(Head-Tech & Corp & Grp Acct Dir)*
James Bishop *(Head-Practice-Fin & Pro Svcs)*
Lisa Welsh *(Gen Mgr)*
Marwan Abu-Ghanem *(Reg Dir-Media)*
Andrew Bone *(Reg Dir-Middle East & Africa)*
Katy Branson *(Reg Mgr-HR)*
Jo Agnew *(Sr Acct Mgr)*
Nora Layous *(Sr Acct Mgr)*
Lama El-Ali *(Acct Mgr)*

Accounts:
Dubai World Trade Centre
ITIDA

Hong Kong

Hill & Knowlton Hong Kong Ltd.
36/F PCCW Tower Taikoo Place 979 Kings Road, Quarry Bay, China (Hong Kong)
Tel.: (852) 2894 6321
Fax: (852) 2576 3551
E-Mail: dmaguire@hkstrategies.com
Web Site: www.hkstrategies.com

Employees: 100

Agency Specializes In: Public Relations

Ye Yu *(Chm & Exec VP-APAC)*
KW Lam *(Mng Dir)*
Kristy Chan *(Deputy Mng Dir)*
Judy Guo *(Sr VP)*
Zhao Nancy *(Acct Dir)*
Michelle You *(Acct Dir)*
Cathy Zhang *(Acct Dir)*
M. Lilian *(Mgr-HR & Office Admin)*

Accounts:
Finnair PR
Microsoft Hong Kong Public Relations

Japan

Hill + Knowlton Strategies
(Formerly Hill & Knowlton Japan, Ltd.)
3-5-27 Roppongi Minato-Ku, Yamada Roppongi Building 8F, Tokyo, 106-0032 Japan
Tel.: (81) 3 4520 5800
Fax: (81) 3 4520 5801
Web Site: www.hkstrategies.com/

Employees: 30
Year Founded: 1958

Agency Specializes In: Communications, Public Relations

Shoko Nangu *(Acct Mgr)*
Michiyo Hongu *(Acct Exec)*

Accounts:
Merck Serono

Malaysia

Hill & Knowlton (SEA) Sdn. Bhd.
7th floor Wisma Genting, Jalan Sultan Ismail, Kuala Lumpur, 50250 Malaysia
Tel.: (60) 3 2026 0899
Fax: (60) 3 2026 0699
E-Mail: jahmad@hillandknowlton.com.my
Web Site: www.hkstrategies.com

Agency Specializes In: Public Relations

Julia Ahmad *(Mng Dir)*
Justin Then *(Mng Dir)*
Kharis Idris *(Head-Tech & Digital Practice & Acct Dir)*

Singapore

Hill & Knowlton (SEA) Pvt. Ltd.
50 Scotts Road, #04-01, 228242 Singapore, Singapore
Tel.: (65) 6338 2881
Fax: (65) 6339 2738
E-Mail: jimtay@hillandknowlton.com.sg
Web Site: www.hkstrategies.com

Employees: 50

Agency Specializes In: Public Relations

Vivian Lines *(Vice Chm-Global, Chm-Asia Pacific & Co-Head-Client Svc)*
Michelle Tham *(Mng Dir)*
Chip Ng *(Deputy Mng Dir & Reg Dir-Fin Comm-Southeast Asia)*
Pamela Teo *(Dir-HR-Asia Pacific)*
Raoul Le Blond *(Assoc Dir)*

Accounts:
Experia Events IMDEX Asia, Integrated Communications, Singapore Airshow
New-Nikon Singapore Content Strategy, Public Relations
PropertyGuru Public Relations
Singapore Learning Festival

Thailand

H+K Strategies Thailand
Unit 14C 14th Fl Q House Ploenjit Bldg 598 Ploenchit Rd, Lumpini Pathumwan, Bangkok, 10330 Thailand
Tel.: (66) 2 627 3501
Fax: (66) 2 627 3510
E-Mail: kungpakorn@hkstrategies.com
Web Site: www.hkstrategies.com/global-presence/bangkok

Employees: 40

Agency Specializes In: Public Relations

Kanpirom Ungpakorn *(Mng Dir)*
Jennifer Poulson *(Acct Dir)*
Suthatip Boonsaeng *(Assoc Dir)*
Pornravee Suramool *(Assoc Dir)*

Accounts:
DHL

Intel
Microsoft
Starbucks

Australia & New Zealand

Hill & Knowlton Australia Pty. Ltd.
Level 13 338 Pitt Street, Sydney, NSW 2000 Australia
Tel.: (61) 2 9268 0242
Fax: (61) 2 9268 0243
E-Mail: info@hillandknowlton.com.au
Web Site: www.hkstrategies.com.au

Employees: 45
Year Founded: 1946

Agency Specializes In: Communications, Government/Political, Investor Relations, Public Relations

Penelope Holloway *(Mng Dir-Australia)*
Sian Jenkins *(Client Svcs Dir)*
Helen Reiher *(Acct Dir)*
Michael Woods *(Acct Dir)*
Marcha Van Den Heuvel *(Sr Acct Mgr)*
Georgina Hardy *(Sr Acct Exec)*
Lucinda Bell *(Acct Exec)*

Accounts:
Air New Zealand PR
New-Coca-Cola
New-goCatch Consumer Communications
Krispy Kreme
LG
National Indigenous Development Centre
Roche
TomTom
New-Wrigley's

HILLSTROMPR INC
253 N 1st Ave, Sturgeon Bay, WI 54235
Tel.: (920) 818-0153
Fax: (920) 839-2688
Web Site: www.hillstrompr.com

Agency Specializes In: Crisis Communications, Event Planning & Marketing, Media Planning, Public Relations, Social Media

Jane Hillstrom *(CEO)*
Samantha Baudhuin *(Specialist-Social Community)*

Accounts:
United Dairy Industry of Michigan

HILSINGER MENDELSON PUBLIC RELATIONS
8916 Ashcroft Ave, Los Angeles, CA 90048
Tel.: (323) 931-5335
Fax: (323) 938-5335
E-Mail: hmiwest@aol.com
Web Site: hilsingermendelson.com

Employees: 2

Agency Specializes In: Promotions, Public Relations, Publicity/Promotions, Publishing

Judy Hilsinger *(CEO)*

Accounts:
Anne Geddes
Dr. Jeffry Life
Joan Lunden
National Geographic Books
National Geographic Traveler
Nigella Lawson
Parade Magazine
Peter Matthiessen
Stephen J. Cannell
Susan Miller

Branch

Hilsinger Mendelson Public Relations
245 5th Ave Ste 1401, New York, NY 10016
Tel.: (212) 725-7707
Fax: (212) 725-7708
E-Mail: hmi@hmieast.com
Web Site: hilsingermendelson.com

Agency Specializes In: Advertising, Print, Public Relations, Publicity/Promotions

Sandi Mendelson *(CEO)*
Deborah Jensen *(Dir-Coordinating Comm)*
David Kass *(Dir-Publicity)*
Renee Gulotta *(Office Mgr)*

Accounts:
Anne Geddes

HISPANIA PUBLIC RELATIONS, INC.
8306 Mills Dr Ste 310, Miami, FL 33183
Tel.: (305) 271-5680
Fax: (305) 273-0663
Web Site: www.hispaniapublicrelations.com

Year Founded: 2000

Agency Specializes In: Communications, Crisis Communications, Graphic Design, Hispanic Market, Public Relations, Sponsorship, Strategic Planning/Research

Sergio Lopez-Miro *(Founder & Pres)*
Marta Pelaez *(VP-Media Rels)*

Accounts:
Beech-Nut Nutrition Corporation

HKA INC MARKETING COMMUNICATIONS
150 Yorba St, Tustin, CA 92780
Tel.: (714) 426-0444
E-Mail: info@hkamarcom.com
Web Site: www.hkamarcom.com

Agency Specializes In: Content, Media Relations, Public Relations, Social Media, Strategic Planning/Research

Hilary Kaye *(Founder & Pres)*
Kevin Twer *(Sr VP)*
Kristina Sarenas *(Acct Mgr)*
Andrew King *(Acct Mgr)*
Annie Chambers *(Mgr-Mktg)*

Accounts:
New-Fish & Tsang LLP
New-Laura's House

HLB COMMUNICATIONS, INC.
(Merged with ComBlu to form ComBlu Inc.)

HMA PUBLIC RELATIONS
3610 N 44th St Ste 110, Phoenix, AZ 85018
Tel.: (602) 957-8881
Fax: (602) 957-0131
E-Mail: shanson@hmapr.com
Web Site: www.hmapr.com

Employees: 6
Year Founded: 1991

National Agency Associations: PRGN-PRSA

Agency Specializes In: Public Relations

Scott Hanson *(Pres)*
Abbie Fink *(VP & Gen Mgr)*
Alison Bailin Batz *(Sr Acct Exec)*
Rachel Brockway *(Sr Acct Exec)*
Shelby Ray *(Acct Coord)*

Accounts:
Arizona Fall League
Boys & Girls Clubs of Greater Scottsdale
Harrah's Ak-Chin Casino Resort
Partnership for Drug Free America
SMACNA Arizona
Subway Restaurants
W.J. Maloney Plumbing Co., Inc.

HODGES PARTNERSHIP
1805 E Broad St, Richmond, VA 23223
Tel.: (804) 788-1414
Fax: (804) 788-0085
Web Site: www.hodgespart.com

Year Founded: 2002

Agency Specializes In: Business-To-Business, Media Relations, Public Relations, Social Media

Jon Newman *(Owner)*
Josh Dare *(Principal)*
Paulyn Roman *(Acct Mgr)*
Megan Irvin *(Acct Exec)*
Emily Shane *(Strategist-Social Media)*

Accounts:
New-Collared Greens

THE HOFFMAN AGENCY
70 N 2nd St, San Jose, CA 95113-1204
Tel.: (408) 286-2611
Fax: (408) 286-0133
E-Mail: llau@hoffman.com
Web Site: www.hoffman.com

E-Mail for Key Personnel:
President: lhoffman@hoffman.com

Employees: 100
Year Founded: 1987

National Agency Associations: COPF-PRSA

Agency Specializes In: Asian Market, Brand Development & Integration, Broadcast, Business Publications, Business-To-Business, Communications, Computers & Software, Consulting, Consumer Marketing, Content, Corporate Communications, Corporate Identity, Crisis Communications, Digital/Interactive, E-Commerce, Electronic Media, Electronics, Environmental, Exhibit/Trade Shows, Financial, High Technology, Information Technology, International, Internet/Web Design, Legal Services, Magazines, Market Research, Media Relations, Media Training, Medical Products, New Technologies, Out-of-Home Media, Planning & Consultation, Podcasting, Public Relations, Publicity/Promotions, Radio, Search Engine Optimization, Social Media, Sponsorship, Stakeholders, Strategic Planning/Research, T.V., Trade & Consumer Magazines, Viral/Buzz/Word of Mouth

Approx. Annual Billings: $9,500,000

Breakdown of Gross Billings by Media: Pub. Rels.: 100%

Lou Hoffman *(Pres & CEO)*
Kymra Knuth *(VP)*
Steve Burkhart *(Gen Mgr-North America)*
Kali Bean *(Acct Dir)*
Jane Wang *(Acct Dir)*
Erin Hartwig *(Sr Acct Exec)*

Public Relations Firms

Lauren Ho *(Sr Acct Exec)*

Accounts:
IDT
Intelepeer
Loring Ward
PayPal
RAE Systems
SuVolta
Virtual PBX
Xilinx

Branches

The Hoffman Agency
The Workstation 16th Fl 43 Lyndhurst Terrace, Central, China (Hong Kong)
Tel.: (852) 2581 9380
Fax: (852) 2581 9389
E-Mail: ctang@hoffman.com
Web Site: www.hoffman.com

Agency Specializes In: Asian Market, Brand Development & Integration, Business-To-Business, Communications, Computers & Software, Consulting, Consumer Marketing, Corporate Identity, Crisis Communications, E-Commerce, Electronic Media, Electronics, High Technology, Information Technology, International, Media Relations, Media Training, New Technologies, Planning & Consultation, Public Relations, Viral/Buzz/Word of Mouth

Jenny Chan *(VP-Bus Dev & Mktg-APAC)*
Lydia Lau *(VP-Ops-Global)*
Elma Wan *(Sr Acct Exec)*
Aaron Kreuscher *(Assoc Acct Dir)*
Terence Nip *(Assoc Acct Dir)*

Accounts:
Alexander Mann Solutions
AppsFlyer (Agency of Record) Brand Positioning, Communications
Bosch Public Relations
FiftyThree (Agency of Record)
New-Fuji Xerox (Public Relations Agency of Record) Media Outreach
Kellett School
LiquaVista
Net One Systems
New-Nutanix Marketing Communications, Public Relations
OKI
Solarwinds
Sony
TeamQuest Public Relations, Strategic

The Hoffman Agency
CITIC Bldg 19 Jianguomenwai St Ste 2104, Beijing, 100004 China
Tel.: (86) 10 6507 0985
Fax: (86) 10 6586 8950
Web Site: www.hoffman.com

Employees: 9
Year Founded: 1999

Agency Specializes In: Asian Market, Brand Development & Integration, Business-To-Business, Communications, Computers & Software, Consulting, Consumer Marketing, Corporate Communications, Corporate Identity, Crisis Communications, E-Commerce, Electronic Media, Electronics, High Technology, Information Technology, International, Media Relations, Media Training, New Technologies, Public Relations, Viral/Buzz/Word of Mouth

Kevin Chen *(Gen Mgr-China)*
Lucia Liu *(Gen Mgr-Beijing)*
Linda Li *(Acct Mgr)*
Agnes Tang *(Acct Mgr)*
Toby Yu *(Acct Mgr)*
Wen Mao *(Office Supvr)*
Deborah Wang *(Assoc Acct Dir)*

Accounts:
Aptare
Axis Communications
Backbase
Black & Veatch
Continuum Media Relations, Public Relations
Datacraft
Electrocomponents Plc
Epicor
Fenwick & West
Fujitsu
Google

The Hoffman Agency
Burex Kyobashi Suite 515 2-7-14 Kyobashi, Chuo-ku, Tokyo, 104-0031 Japan
Tel.: (81) 3 5159 2145
Fax: (81) 3 5159 2166
E-Mail: snomura@hoffman.com
Web Site: www.hoffman.com

Year Founded: 1998

Agency Specializes In: Asian Market, Brand Development & Integration, Broadcast, Business-To-Business, Communications, Computers & Software, Consulting, Consumer Marketing, Corporate Communications, Electronic Media, Electronics, High Technology, Information Technology, International, Media Training, New Technologies, Public Relations

Shingo Nomura *(VP-North Asia)*
Masayuki Ando *(Acct Dir)*
Hiromi Matsuda *(Acct Exec)*

Accounts:
BackBase
Epicor
Fenwick & West
Fotoglif
Fujitsu

The Hoffman Agency
175A Bencoolen St, 08-01/02 Burlington Sq, Singapore, 189650 Singapore
Tel.: (65) 6252 2866
Fax: (65) 6252 2811
E-Mail: mjutahkiti@hoffman.com
Web Site: www.hoffman.com

Employees: 7
Year Founded: 1987

Agency Specializes In: Asian Market, Broadcast, Computers & Software, Consulting, Consumer Marketing, Corporate Communications, Corporate Identity, Electronic Media, Electronics, High Technology, Information Technology, International, Media Relations, Media Training, New Technologies, Public Relations

Cassandra Cheong *(Mng Dir-Asia Pacific)*
Shawn Balakrishnan *(Gen Mgr)*
Idran Junadi *(Acct Dir)*
Rasheed Abu Bakar *(Acct Mgr)*
Czarina Mae Cabuyadao *(Acct Mgr)*
Jacintha Ng *(Acct Mgr)*
Neritta Low *(Acct Exec)*
Adele Soh *(Acct Exec)*

Accounts:
The Association of Chartered Certified Accountants (PR & Social Media Agency of Record) Content Development, Corporate Communications, Strategic Counsel
Brother International Singapore (Agency of Record) Media Relations, Product Awareness, Strategic Counsel
comGateway PR
New-Lazada (Singapore Public Relations Agency of Record) Strategic
LEGOLAND Malaysia Resort (Agency of Record) Public Relations, Strategic Counsel
Lien AID Brand Positioning, Media Relations, Media Strategies, Message Development, PR, Social Media Outreach
OANDA Brand Awareness, Media Strategy, PR
Piaggio Asia Pacific (Public Relations Agency of Record) Communications Strategy
Red Hat Media Strategy, Public Relations

The Hoffman Agency
The Horton Mix Third Floor 86-90 Paul Street, London, EC2A 4NE United Kingdom
Tel.: (44) 20 3137 9480
Web Site: www.hoffman.com

E-Mail for Key Personnel:
President: lhoffman@hoffman.com

Year Founded: 2000

Agency Specializes In: Asian Market, Broadcast, Business-To-Business, Communications, Computers & Software, Consulting, Consumer Marketing, Corporate Communications, Crisis Communications, Electronic Media, High Technology, Media Relations, Media Training, New Technologies, Public Relations

Lou Hoffman *(Pres & CEO)*
Mike Sottak *(Mng Dir-Europe & ME)*

HOLLYWOOD PUBLIC RELATIONS
50 Cole Pkwy Ste 33, Scituate, MA 02066
Tel.: (781) 378-1731
Fax: (781) 846-0571
Web Site: www.hollywoodpr.net

Year Founded: 2005

Agency Specializes In: Corporate Identity, Crisis Communications, Event Planning & Marketing, Media Relations, Media Training, Public Relations, Social Media

Darlene Hollywood *(Principal)*
Courtney Curzi *(VP)*
Jeff Dillow *(Acct Dir)*
Meg Parker *(Acct Dir)*
Brooks Wallace *(Acct Mgr & Specialist-Media)*
Monica Higgins *(Acct Supvr)*
Melissa Parrelli *(Acct Exec)*

Accounts:
American Blanket Company
Born Free
Guidant Financial Group, Inc. Strategy
JMATEK North America, LLC Dehumidifiers, Evaporative Air Coolers, Portable Air Conditioners
Ovuline (Agency of Record); Boston, MA Media Relations, Ovia Fertility, Ovia Pregnancy
Parfums de Coeur
PlanetShoes.com
Runkeeper Media Relations
Summer Infant, Inc

HOME FRONT COMMUNICATIONS
1121 14th St NW 5th Fl, Washington, DC 20005
Tel.: (202) 544-8400
E-Mail: info@homefrontdc.com
Web Site: www.homefrontdc.com

Year Founded: 1998

Agency Specializes In: Advertising,

Digital/Interactive, Public Relations, Strategic Planning/Research

Paul Frick *(Co-Founder & Partner)*
Dan Sallick *(Partner)*
Carlos Roig *(Exec VP-Media & Content Strategy)*
Kevin Richards *(Sr VP & Creative Dir)*
Steve Jost *(Sr VP-Content Strategy)*
Wyatt Queener *(VP & Dir-Interactive)*
Joy Cameron *(VP-Media)*
Carly Vendemia *(Acct Dir)*
Patrick Everson *(Sr Art Dir)*

Accounts:
Association of American Railroads
Robert Wood Johnson Foundation
Tedmed
U.S. Census Bureau

THE HONIG COMPANY
3500 W Olive Ave Ste 300, Burbank, CA 91505
Tel.: (818) 986-4300
Fax: (818) 981-3141
E-Mail: info@honigcompany.com
Web Site: www.honigcompany.com

Employees: 6
Year Founded: 2002

Accounts:
Ernst & Young
Fiore Films
Inception Media Group
Marty Ingels
Shirley Jones
Victoria Gotti
Zowie Bowie

HOPKINS PR
2017 Young St Ste 101, Dallas, TX 75201
Tel.: (214) 828-0066
Web Site: www.hopkinspr.com

Agency Specializes In: Crisis Communications, Digital/Interactive, Event Planning & Marketing, Media Relations, Media Training, Public Relations

Marilyn Pippin *(Pres & Principal)*
Meagan Guidry *(Mng Dir)*
Barbara Hyman *(COO)*
Lisa Alves *(Chief Admin Officer)*

Accounts:
Universal Technical Institute, Inc.

HOT SCHATZ PR
701 Harpeth Trace Dr, Nashville, TN 37221
Tel.: (615) 782-0078
E-Mail: info@hotschatzpr.com
Web Site: www.hotschatzpr.com

Agency Specializes In: Event Planning & Marketing, Media Buying Services, Promotions, Public Relations

Schatzi Hageman *(Owner)*

Accounts:
The Alabama Band
Jamie ONeal
Jimbeau Hinson
Momentum Label Group
Rachele Lynae
Robert Mirabal
Steve Azar

HOTWIRE
16 W 22nd St 12th Fl, New York, NY 10010
Tel.: (646) 738-8960
Web Site: www.hotwirepr.us

Agency Specializes In: Brand Development & Integration, Digital/Interactive, Media Planning, Media Relations, Public Relations

Rebecca Honeyman *(Sr VP & Gen Mgr)*
Christa Conte *(Assoc Dir)*

Accounts:
New-Indeed

HOWARD COMMUNICATIONS INC
289 Hwy Cc, Elsberry, MO 63343
Tel.: (573) 898-3422
Fax: (573) 898-3407
Web Site: www.howardcommunications.com

Agency Specializes In: Communications, Public Relations, Social Media

Kevin Howard *(Pres)*
Elaine Howard *(Principal)*
Mike Capps *(Acct Exec)*
Andrew Howard *(Acct Exec)*
Laura Robinson *(Acct Coord)*
Sydney Beauchamp *(Coord-Database & Media Coverage)*

Accounts:
Signature Products Group Public Relations
STI International, Inc. (Public Relations Agency of Record)
United States Concealed Carry Association

HOWARD RUBEN PR
12522 Moorpark St, Studio City, CA 91604
Tel.: (818) 823-1971
Fax: (818) 445-4543
Web Site: www.howardrubenpr.com

Year Founded: 1991

Agency Specializes In: Brand Development & Integration, Collateral, Communications, Event Planning & Marketing, Media Relations, Public Relations, Social Media, Strategic Planning/Research

Jeffrey Graubard *(Strategist-Mktg)*

Accounts:
Goldwin America

THE HOYT ORGANIZATION
23001 Hawthorne Blvd Ste 200, Torrance, CA 90505
Tel.: (310) 373-0103
Fax: (310) 378-9805
E-Mail: helpdesk@hoytorg.com
Web Site: www.hoytorg.com

Agency Specializes In: Brand Development & Integration, Crisis Communications, Logo & Package Design, Media Planning, Media Relations, Media Training, Public Relations, Social Media

Leeza Hoyt *(Pres)*

Accounts:
New-HGA Architects & Engineers

HP PR
16 W 23rd St, New York, NY 10010
Tel.: (631) 553-1370
Web Site: www.hp-pr.com

Agency Specializes In: Event Planning & Marketing, Media Relations, Media Training, Public Relations, Social Media

Helen Patrikis *(Founder & Pres)*

Accounts:
New-Manoir Hovey
New-The Wickaninnish Inn

HPR, INC.
3771 Rio Rd, Carmel, CA 93923
Tel.: (831) 375-1747
Fax: (831) 655-8749
E-Mail: khunter@hunter-pr.com
Web Site: www.hunter-pr.com

Employees: 7
Year Founded: 1990

Agency Specializes In: Event Planning & Marketing, Public Relations, Real Estate, Sports Market, Travel & Tourism

Karen Moraghan *(Pres)*
Kristen Hunter *(VP)*
Kerry Maveus *(Mgr-Asset)*
Corrin Sullivan *(Mgr-Media Database)*
Ed Vyeda *(Sr Acct Exec)*
Doug Thompson *(Sr Writer)*

Accounts:
The Art of Living Well
AT&T Pebble Beach National Pro-Am Media Center; Pebble Beach, CA
Bayonet & Black Horse Golf Courses
Bedford Springs Resort
California Golf Writers Association Annual Awards Dinner; Pebble Beach, CA
Camp Reveille; Maine
The First Tee Open Media Center; Pebble Beach, CA
The Golf Courses at Hershey Resorts; Hershey, PA
Hershey Country Club & Spring Creek Golf Course
John Fought Golf Course Architecture; Scottsdale, AZ
Pebble Beach Resorts; Pebble Beach, CA Golf Courses
Rancho San Carlos Education Foundation
Reynolds Plantation; Greensboro, GA
The Ritz-Carlton Dove Mountain
Santa Lucia Preserve; Carmel, CA
The Shawnee Inn and Golf Resort
The Spa at The Ritz-Carlton Resort; Dove Mountain
Spa Shawnee and Salon
United States Golf Association; Far Hills, NJ
Villas of Grand Cypress
Wintergarden Spa
Wintergreen Resort
Women's Wellness; PA

Branch

HPR, Inc.
11 W Fox Hill Rd, Long Valley, NJ 07853-3025
Tel.: (908) 876-5100
Fax: (908) 876-4845
E-Mail: kmoraghan@hunter-pr.com
Web Site: www.hunter-pr.com

E-Mail for Key Personnel:
President: kmoraghan@hunter-pr.com

Year Founded: 1990

Agency Specializes In: Event Planning & Marketing, Public Relations, Sports Market, Travel & Tourism

Karen Moraghan *(Pres)*
Kristen Hunter *(VP)*

Accounts:
Grand Cypress

La Costa Resort and Spa
Reynolds Plantation
Wellness Lifestyles
Wintergarden Spa
Wintergreen Resort

HUNTER PUBLIC RELATIONS

41 Madison Ave Fl 5, New York, NY 10010-2202
Tel.: (212) 679-6600
Fax: (212) 679-6607
E-Mail: info@hunterpr.com
Web Site: www.hunterpr.com

E-Mail for Key Personnel:
President: gleong@hunterpr.com

Employees: 55
Year Founded: 1989

Agency Specializes In: Public Relations, Sponsorship

Donetta Allen *(Partner)*
Erin Brennan Hanson *(Partner)*
Jonathan Lyon *(Partner)*
John Ferrari *(CFO)*
Alex Conway *(Sr VP)*
Elizabeth Mitolo *(Sr Acct Supvr)*
McKenzie Mahoney *(Acct Supvr)*
Melody Snellgrove *(Acct Supvr)*
Kim Ciocon *(Sr Acct Exec)*
Kristin Archambeau *(Asst Acct Exec)*

Accounts:
3M; 1997
Bloomberg BusinessWeek
Church & Dwight Co.
Diageo
Dole Foods
Energy Kitchen
Hasbro Games; 2005
McIlhenny Company Tabasco; 1989
Melvita
Mondelez International, Inc. Cheddar Explosion; 1990
New Zealand King Salmon
Pompeian, Inc.
Post Cereal Company; 1998
Post Foods, LLC
Signature Brands
Smithfield Packing Company

HUTCHENS PR

1005 Rosecrans St Ste 201, San Diego, CA 92106
Tel.: (619) 236-0200
Fax: (619) 236-0230
E-Mail: info@hutchenspr.com
Web Site: www.hutchenspr.com

Agency Specializes In: Crisis Communications, Media Relations, Public Relations, Social Media

Karen Hutchens *(Pres)*
Lucia Stone *(VP)*

Accounts:
The John Corcoran Foundation

HVM COMMUNICATIONS

1133 Broadway Ste 332, New York, NY 10010
Tel.: (866) 472-5510
Web Site: www.h-vm.com

Agency Specializes In: Brand Development & Integration, Content, Event Planning & Marketing, Media Relations, Media Training, Public Relations, Social Marketing/Nonprofit, Social Media

Laura Henson *(Founder & Pres)*

Accounts:
New-Jill Heller Jewelry
New-Pirch

HWH PUBLIC RELATIONS

1173A 2nd Ave #397, New York, NY 10065
Tel.: (212) 355-5049
Fax: (212) 593-0065
E-Mail: info@hwhpr.com
Web Site: www.hwhpr.com

Employees: 30
Year Founded: 1977

Agency Specializes In: Corporate Identity, Event Planning & Marketing, New Product Development, Public Relations, Sponsorship

Approx. Annual Billings: $4,000,000

Lois Whitman-Hess *(Founder & Pres)*
Eliot Hess *(Co-Owner)*
Jason Henriques *(VP-Social Media & Client Svcs)*

Accounts:
Aanvex
Classical Archives
Helen of Troy; El Paso, TX
Hot Tools
IRiver; 2008
Royal Consumer Business Products
Samsung Information Systems of America

I-ADVIZE CORPORATE COMMUNICATIONS, INC.

20 Broad St 25th Fl, New York, NY 10005-2605
Tel.: (212) 406-3690
Fax: (212) 509-7711
E-Mail: info@i-advize.com
Web Site: www.i-advize.com

Employees: 5

Agency Specializes In: Investor Relations, Public Relations

Maria Barona *(Co-Founder & Mng Partner)*
Melanie Carpenter *(Mng Dir)*
Rafael Borja *(Sr VP)*
Juan Carlos Gomez Stolk *(VP)*

Accounts:
BBVA Bancomer
Compania de Minas Buenaventura S.A.A.
Credicorp
Cristalerias de Chile
LAN Airways SA

I DO PR

902 Broadway 6th Fl, New York, NY 10010
Tel.: (212) 603-9197
E-Mail: info@idopr.com
Web Site: www.idopr.com

Agency Specializes In: Brand Development & Integration, Content, Event Planning & Marketing, Exhibit/Trade Shows, Media Relations, Public Relations, Social Media

Sasha Vasilyuk *(Founder & CEO)*

Accounts:
New-Yael Designs

ID CREATIVE

6406 N Interstate 35 Ste 2520 A, Austin, TX 78752
Tel.: (512) 750-5852
E-Mail: general@idcreative.com
Web Site: www.idcreative.com

Year Founded: 2012

Agency Specializes In: Content, Crisis Communications, Digital/Interactive, Event Planning & Marketing, Internet/Web Design, Media Buying Services, Media Relations, Public Relations, Social Media

Jill Wedel *(Coord-Media Rels)*

Accounts:
Hopfields
Vivo

ID PUBLIC RELATIONS

7060 Hollywood Blvd 8th Fl, Los Angeles, CA 90028
Tel.: (323) 822-4800
Fax: (323) 822-4880
E-Mail: info@id-pr.com
Web Site: www.id-pr.com

Agency Specializes In: Brand Development & Integration, Communications, Digital/Interactive, Event Planning & Marketing, Public Relations

Kelly Bush Novak *(Founder & CEO)*
Mara Buxbaum *(Pres)*
Carrie Byalick *(Sr VP)*
Heather Greenfield *(Sr VP-Brand Strategies)*
Natalie Bruss *(VP-Digital Strategy)*
Allison Elbl *(VP-Music & Brand)*
Harlan Gulko *(VP-Film)*
Michael Braun *(Dir-Brands)*
Sheri Goldberg *(Dir-Film)*

Accounts:
New-UNICEF USA

IDENTITY MARKETING & PUBLIC RELATIONS, LLC

30700 Telegraph Rd Ste 1475, Bingham Farms, MI 48025-4590
Tel.: (248) 258-2333
Fax: (248) 258-1942
Web Site: www.identitypr.com

Employees: 22
Year Founded: 1998

Mark Winter *(Mng Partner)*
Andrea Trapani *(Partner)*
Nikki Little *(Acct Dir-Social Media)*
Jennifer Carey *(Dir-Creative Dept)*
Oliver Higgs *(Dir-Editorial)*
Michele Dickens *(Assoc Dir-Art)*
Whitney Mcgoram *(Sr Acct Exec)*
Chris Austin *(Acct Exec)*
Amanda Braniecki *(Acct Exec)*
Stephanie Cosby *(Acct Exec)*
Katie Land *(Acct Exec)*
Sarah Ambrose *(Asst Strategist-Social Media)*

Accounts:
Baker Katz
Dialogue Marketing
Hunt Leibert
iGroup
Midway Companies; Houston, TX International Real Estate, Investment; 2008
Powerlink Facilities Management Services; Detroit, MI
RCS Real Estate Advisors; New York, NY
S3 Entertainment Group; Ferndale, MI Film Production Services; 2008
Tax Appeal Team
Tri-Land Properties, Inc. Property Management, Retail Development; 2008

IDENTITY MEDIA CO

253 NE 2nd St Ste 1601, Miami, FL 33132
Tel.: (786) 281-3259

E-Mail: info@identitymediaco.com
Web Site: www.identitymediaco.com

Agency Specializes In: Event Planning & Marketing, Graphic Design, Integrated Marketing, Internet/Web Design, Promotions, Public Relations, Search Engine Optimization, Social Media, Strategic Planning/Research

Ana C. Rivera *(Pres)*

Accounts:
New-Steak Brasil
New-Well Groomed Gentleman

IGNITE PUBLIC RELATIONS, LLC
333 Gellert Blvd Ste 218, Daly City, CA 94015
Tel.: (650) 227-3280
Fax: (650) 227-3283
E-Mail: info@ignitepr.com
Web Site: www.ignitepr.com

Agency Specializes In: Event Planning & Marketing, Media Relations, Media Training, Public Relations, Social Media, Strategic Planning/Research

Carmen Hughes *(Principal)*
Kimberly Weber *(Sr Acct Dir)*
Galina Shmeleva *(Sr Acct Exec)*

Accounts:
Fortumo
FortyCloud
Telerik

IMAGE ONE PUBLIC RELATIONS
1 Research Ct Ste 450, Rockville, MD 20850
Tel.: (301) 519-8040
Fax: (301) 519-8001
E-Mail: mail@imageonepr.com
Web Site: www.imageonepr.com

Employees: 3
Year Founded: 2003

Bill Weger *(Founder & Sr Partner)*

Accounts:
Circle Solutions
Collective Protection Inc.
Lockheed Martin
Lockheed Martin Aspen Systems
Lockheed Martin Aspen Systems Corp
Midway Alarms
Rampf Molds
Washington Times

IMAGEWORKS STUDIO
3859 Centerview Dr Ste 400, Chantilly, VA 20151
Tel.: (703) 378-0000
Fax: (703) 968-5560
E-Mail: sales@imageworksstudio.com
Web Site: www.imageworkscreative.com

Agency Specializes In: Public Relations

Scott Margenau *(CEO)*
Aimee Aryal *(Office Mgr & Copywriter)*
Jessica DelBalzo *(Mgr-SEO & Online Mktg)*
Cynthia Lee *(Graphic Designer & Designer-Web)*
Sabrina Bourne *(Sr Graphic Designer)*
Amber White *(Designer-Web)*

Accounts:
Adiva
Allstate Insurance Company
Bean Tree Learning
Concept Solutions
Eden Technologies
FlexRN
The Loyalton Group
Sheaterra Organics
Vorsight

IMILLER PUBLIC RELATIONS
221 Harbor Hill Mamaroneck, New York, NY 10543
Tel.: (866) 307-2510
E-Mail: info@imillerpr.com
Web Site: www.imillerpr.com

Agency Specializes In: Crisis Communications, Digital/Interactive, Event Planning & Marketing, Media Relations, Public Relations, Social Media

Ilissa Miller *(Founder & CEO)*
Daniel Freedman *(VP-Ops)*

Accounts:
New-AquaComms

IMJ COMMUNICATIONS LLC
205 Baker St, Royal Oak, MI 48067
Tel.: (248) 547-5576
Web Site: www.imjcommunications.com

Agency Specializes In: Advertising, Graphic Design, Internet/Web Design, Media Relations, Public Relations, Social Media

Jeanne Micallef *(Owner)*

Accounts:
Chrome Bumper Films
Cloverleaf Bar & Restaurant
Royal Oak Music Theatre

IMMEDIACY PUBLIC RELATIONS INC
1208 US 1, North Palm Beach, FL 33408
Tel.: (561) 776-7659
E-Mail: info@immediacypr.com
Web Site: www.immediacypublicrelations.com

Agency Specializes In: Collateral, Event Planning & Marketing, Graphic Design, Internet/Web Design, Media Buying Services, Media Relations, Media Training, Public Relations

Cheryl K. Crowley *(Owner)*

Accounts:
Adelphia, Inc.
American Red Cross
Arthritis Foundation
Ballet Florida, Inc.
Bamboo Clothiers
Bankrate, Inc.
Burman Critton Luttier & Coleman Law Firm
Chuck Shaw
Dillard's Inc.
Easter Seals Florida
Everglades Foundation
Family Zone
Florida Atlantic University
Forum Club of the Palm Beaches
Genesis Partners, Lp.
Grassy Waters
Great Deals in My City
Haile Shaw & Pfaffenberger Law Firm
Hanley Center
Hospice of Palm Beach County
Jacek Gancarz
La Z Boy Furniture Galleries
Levenger Company
Literacy Coalition of Palm Beach County
The Lords Place
Michael Brown
The Northern Trust Company
NPC Improvement District
Palm Beach Casino Line
Palm Beach County Aquarium Corp
Palm Beach Fine Craft Show
Palm Beach Zoo
Park Avenue BBQ & Grille Inc.
PGA Commons
Poinciana Day School
RosettaStone Fine Arts
Woodrow Wilson International Center for Scholars
WPBF News 25

IMPACT COMMUNICATIONS
2007 W 91st St Ste 201, Leawood, KS 66206
Tel.: (913) 649-5009
Fax: (866) 565-2935
Toll Free: (800) 974-7753
E-Mail: info@impactcommunications.org
Web Site: www.impactcommunications.org

Agency Specializes In: Event Planning & Marketing, Graphic Design, Internet/Web Design, Logo & Package Design, Public Relations

Marie Swift *(Pres & CEO)*

Accounts:
AllBackoffice Consulting LLC

IMPACTASIA
(Aquired by Cohn & Wolfe & Name Changed to Cohn & Wolfe impactasia)

THE IMPETUS AGENCY
661 Sierra Rose Dr, Reno, NV 89511
Tel.: (775) 322-4022
Web Site: www.theimpetusagency.com

Year Founded: 2010

Agency Specializes In: Advertising, Crisis Communications, Event Planning & Marketing, Graphic Design, Media Training, Public Relations, Social Media

Tierra Bonaldi *(Principal)*
Julie Rowe *(Principal)*
Kim Kimbriel *(Controller)*
Jamie Baxter *(Mgr-PET Div)*
Stacie Eliopulos *(Mgr-Social Media Community)*
Katie Hippert *(Mgr-Social Media)*
Brooke Gersich *(Acct Exec)*
Ashlee Verba *(Acct Coord)*

Accounts:
Bionic Pet Products
Pets Add Life

INDRA PUBLIC RELATIONS
295 Madison Ave 12th Fl, New York, NY 10017
Tel.: (646) 593-7211
Fax: (646) 430-8411
Web Site: www.indrapr.com

Agency Specializes In: Crisis Communications, Digital/Interactive, Event Planning & Marketing, Public Relations, Social Media, Sponsorship

M. J. Pedone *(Founder & CEO)*
Michael Stone *(CFO)*
Mark Berryhill *(Dir-Media & Brand Production)*
Lori Perry *(Dir-PR & Special Events)*
Gina Mason *(Coord-PR & Event & Strategist-Social Media)*
Michael Kelley *(Strategist-Entertainment Branding & Mktg)*
Dallas J. Short *(Strategist-Digital)*

Accounts:
Aquacai USA (Public Relations Agency of Record)
Berenice Electrolysis & Personal Beauty Center
Deron Williams
Jala Bars Greek Yogurt, Public Relations Agency

of Record
James Valenti
MAXILLOFACIAL Surgery Services Public Relations Agency of Record
The THRIVE Network (Agency of Record)
Trent Tucker

INFUSED PR & EVENTS

33228 W 12 Mile Rd Ste 102, Farmington Hills, MI 48334
Tel.: (248) 914-4578
E-Mail: info@infusedpr.com
Web Site: www.infusedpr.com

Agency Specializes In: Brand Development & Integration, Event Planning & Marketing, Media Relations, Public Relations, Social Media

Tatiana Grant *(Pres)*

Accounts:
New-Trainers Total Fitness

INGEAR PUBLIC RELATIONS INC

1299 E 4500 S, Salt Lake City, UT 84117
Tel.: (954) 392-6990
Fax: (801) 266-0778
Web Site: www.ingearpr.com

Agency Specializes In: Advertising, Brand Development & Integration, Collateral, Communications, Email, Internet/Web Design, Media Relations, Multimedia, Public Relations, Social Media

Veronica Esbona *(Pres)*
Dave Netz *(COO)*
Pat Brown *(Dir-Admin)*
Rachel Dwyer *(Acct Mgr)*

Accounts:
Atlona Technologies Electronics Products Mfr & Distr
BenQ Corporation
BTX Technologies Inc Surgical & Medical Instrument Mfr
Core Brands Aton, BlueBOLT, Furman Sound, NIles, Panamax, Sunfire, Xantech
Guifx LLC Touch Screen Products Mfr
PLUS Corporation of America Public Relations
Pro Control Public Relations, Social Media, Trade Press
Remote Technologies Inc House Hold Products Mfr
Revolabs Inc Wireless Audio Products Mfr & Distr
Women In CE
X2O Media Inc

INGENEUS PR

1303 Briarlake Ct NE, Atlanta, GA 30345
Tel.: (404) 548-1390
E-Mail: info@ingeneuspr.com
Web Site: www.ingeneuspr.com

Year Founded: 2012

Agency Specializes In: Brand Development & Integration, Event Planning & Marketing, Media Buying Services, Media Relations, Media Training, Public Relations, Social Media

Ronnika Ann Joyner *(Pres & Head-Publicist)*
Danasha Wise *(Mgr-Campaign)*
Tristan Lee *(Coord-Social Media)*
Dede Payton *(Coord-Outreach & Events)*

Accounts:
Miles D Mealing & Nu Movement
Sleeper Recruit
We Train Atlanta

INITIATEPR

11901 Santa Monica Blvd Ste 494, Los Angeles, CA 90025
Tel.: (310) 710-1903
E-Mail: contact@initiatepr.com
Web Site: www.initiatepr.com

Year Founded: 2012

Agency Specializes In: Corporate Communications, Public Relations, Social Media, Strategic Planning/Research

Stephen Gendel *(Mng Partner)*
Adolpho Ayala *(VP & Gen Mgr)*
Steven Gibson *(Dir-Client-Search)*

Accounts:
Neurovance

INK, INC.

511 Delaware St Ste 200, Kansas City, MO 64105
Tel.: (816) 753-6222
Fax: (816) 753-8188
Toll Free: (866) 753-6222
E-Mail: newbiz@inkincpr.com
Web Site: www.inkincpr.com

Employees: 8
Year Founded: 1997

Agency Specializes In: Communications, Crisis Communications, Event Planning & Marketing, Exhibit/Trade Shows, Investor Relations, Media Relations, Media Training, Public Relations

Approx. Annual Billings: $1,500,000

Breakdown of Gross Billings by Media: Promos.: 100%

Richard Grove *(CEO)*
Ryan Gerding *(VP-Client Svcs)*
Cindy West *(VP)*
Sean Mahoney *(Acct Dir)*
Teresa Grove *(Dir-Event Svcs & Specialist-Media)*

Accounts:
Digital Map; Santa Clara, CA
Enigma Software Group; Stamford, CT
Entertainment Properties Trust; Kansas City, MO
IQ4bis; Irvine, CA
Kevin B Sands; Hollywood, CA
Leakey Collection; Newport Beach, CA
McFeedia; Burbank, CA
Mercent; Seattle, WA
Merix Pharmaceutical; Barrington Hills, IL
Nationwide Tax Relief; Los Angeles, CA
Peregrine Pharmaceuticals Inc.
Project Insight; Irvine, CA
T Bones; Kansas City, MO
Wells Art; San Diego, CA
Wizzard Media; Pittsburgh, PA

INK PUBLIC RELATIONS

202 S Lowell Ln, Austin, TX 78733
Tel.: (512) 382-8980
E-Mail: hello@ink-pr.com
Web Site: www.ink-pr.com

Agency Specializes In: Brand Development & Integration, Media Relations, Public Relations, Social Media

Kari Hernandez *(Pres)*
Starr Million Baker *(CEO)*
Blair Poloskey *(VP)*
Candice Eng *(Acct Mgr)*
Kris Johnston *(Acct Mgr)*
Nikol Moen *(Acct Mgr)*
Kim Mackley *(Mgr-Ops)*

Accounts:
New-Austin Technology Council
New-Run for the Water

INKHOUSE MEDIA + MARKETING

221 Crescent St, Waltham, MA 02453
Tel.: (781) 966-4100
Fax: (781) 642-7742
E-Mail: info@inkhouse.net
Web Site: inkhouse.com

Year Founded: 2007

Agency Specializes In: Collateral, Communications, Crisis Communications, Media Training, Podcasting, Public Relations, Search Engine Optimization, Social Media, Strategic Planning/Research

Beth Monaghan *(Co-Founder & Principal)*
Meg O'Leary *(Co-Founder & Principal)*
Tina Cassidy *(Chief Content Officer & Sr VP)*
Jason Morris *(Exec VP & Gen Mgr)*
Susan Elsbree *(VP)*
John McElhenny *(VP)*
Kelly Mcfalls *(VP)*
Alison Morra *(VP)*
Stephanie Olesen *(Sr Acct Exec)*

Accounts:
Fiksu, Inc.

INKLINK MARKETING

7900 NW 155th St, Miami Lakes, FL 33016
Tel.: (305) 631-2283
Fax: (954) 793-4973
E-Mail: kmiller@inklinkmarketing.com
Web Site: www.inklinkmarketing.com

Employees: 10
Year Founded: 2012

Agency Specializes In: Brand Development & Integration, Crisis Communications, Event Planning & Marketing, Media Relations, Media Training, Public Relations, Social Media

Kim Miller *(Pres & Dir-Creative)*
Kampi Chaleunsouk *(Sr VP-Client Svcs)*
Lexi Rich *(Client Svcs Dir)*
Catherine Diaz *(Acct Exec)*
Carlos Martinez *(Acct Coord)*
Jessica Chacoff *(Coord-Mktg)*

Accounts:
Church's Chicken (Public Relations Agency of Record) Marketing; 2014
The Krystal Company (Public Relations & Promotions Agency of Record) Local Store Marketing, PR, Promotions; 2014
MIC Food PR; 2012
Ovation Brands PR & Promotions; 2012

INSIDE OUT PR

PO Box 775772, Steamboat Springs, CO 80477
Tel.: (970) 291-4155
E-Mail: info@insideout-pr.com
Web Site: www.insideout-pr.com

Agency Specializes In: Communications, Content, Event Planning & Marketing, Graphic Design, Media Relations, Promotions, Public Relations, Social Media

Paige Boucher *(Founder & Partner)*

Accounts:
Mystery Ranch (Communications Agency of Record)

INSIDER MEDIA MANAGEMENT
621 NW 53rd St Ste 330, Boca Raton, FL 33487
Tel.: (561) 995-6560
E-Mail: inquiry@insidermediamgmt.com
Web Site: www.insidermediamanagement.com

Year Founded: 2010

Agency Specializes In: Advertising, Brand Development & Integration, Crisis Communications, Guerilla Marketing, Media Relations, Media Training, Print, Public Relations, Radio, Social Media

J. P. Hervis *(Pres)*
Chris Cheng *(Acct Exec & Specialist-Media Rels)*
Robin Cross *(Specialist-Acct Exec & Social Media)*
Richard Lemus *(Strategist-Media)*
Garrett Appleton *(Graphic Designer & Designer-Web-VFX)*
Nickelson Louis *(Graphic Designer & Designer-Web)*

Accounts:
The American Stamp Dealers Association Campaign: "The Stamp Love", PR
Anne Rodgers Kiss and Tell, PR
Everglades Holiday Park Public Relations Agency of Record
The Heart Health Foundation
Hodas Law (Public Relations Agency of Record)
Lauri Valjakka
New-LifeSafety Management (Public Relations Agency of Record)
Lighthouse Recovery Institute Media, Public Relations Agency of Record
Maureen Whelihan Kiss and Tell, PR
The Tax Defense Network PR, Social Media
University Research and Review (Public Relations Agency of Record)
ZOE Sports Public Relations

INTEGRATE
(Formerly IntegratePR)
3801 Kirby Dr, #740, Houston, TX 77098
Tel.: (713) 225-0880
E-Mail: info@integrateagency.com
Web Site: integrateagency.com/

Agency Specializes In: Corporate Communications, Public Relations, Social Media

Allie Herzog Danziger *(Founder & Pres)*
Mary Paolantonio *(Acct Mgr & Media Buyer)*
Alyssa Austin *(Office Mgr)*
Jenny Gustafson *(Acct Mgr)*
Ashley Tucker *(Acct Supvr)*
Ahna Gavrelos *(Sr Acct Exec-PR)*
Allison Huseman *(Sr Acct Exec-PR)*
Julianne Agno *(Acct Exec-PR & Social Media)*
Ryan Cantrell *(Jr Acct Exec-PR)*

Accounts:
Houston Humane Society
Penner Houston

INTEGRATED CORPORATE RELATIONS, INC.
761 Main Ave, Norwalk, CT 06851
Tel.: (203) 682-8200
Fax: (203) 682-8201
Web Site: www.icrinc.com

Year Founded: 1998

Agency Specializes In: Communications, Corporate Communications, Financial, Investor Relations, Sponsorship

Thomas M. Ryan *(Co-Founder & CEO)*
Don Duffy *(Pres)*
Timothy Dolan *(Mng Partner)*
Anton Nicholas *(Mng Dir)*
John Rouleau *(Mng Dir)*
Michael Fox *(Pres-Corp Comm Grp)*
Alecia Pulman *(Sr VP & Sr Dir-Media Rels)*
Christine Beggan *(Asst Acct Exec)*

Accounts:
American Eagle Outfitters
Blackbaud
Chipotle
Circuit City
Fushi Copperweld
ICU Medical
Kellwood
Metabolix
Open Energy
Quiksilver
Sealy
Synchronoss
Town Sports International

Branches

Integrated Corporate Relations - Boston
20 Custom House St Ste 930, Boston, MA 02110
Tel.: (617) 956-6725
Fax: (617) 956-6726
E-Mail: info@icrinc.com
Web Site: icrinc.com

Employees: 4

David Galper *(Mng Dir & Head-Fin Sponsor Coverage & Capital Markets Advisory)*
Brendon Frey *(Mng Dir)*
Denise Garcia *(Mng Dir)*
Raphael Gross *(Mng Dir)*
Staci Mortenson *(Mng Dir)*
Anton Nicholas *(Mng Dir)*
Bo Park *(Mng Dir)*
Seth Potter *(Mng Dir)*
John Sorensen *(COO)*
Thomas M. Ryan *(CEO-Leisure, Entertainment & Restaurants)*

Accounts:
American Eagle Outfitters
American Oriental Bioengineering Inc
Chipotle
Crocs, Inc.
Jefferies
Raymond James
Restaurant Partners, LLC
Visa U.S.A
Warnaco Group
Wedbush

Integrated Corporate Relations - New York
350 Park Ave 5th Fl, New York, NY 10022
Tel.: (212) 753-2138
Fax: (212) 753-2114
Web Site: icrinc.com/en

Don Duffy *(Pres)*
Thomas M. Ryan *(CEO)*
Michael Fox *(Mng Partner)*
Joseph Teklits *(Mng Partner-Retail & Consumer)*
Phil Denning *(Mng Dir)*
Raphael Gross *(Mng Dir)*
John Jannarone *(Sr VP)*
Brad Cohen *(Sr Mng Dir-Fin Svcs & Real Estate)*
Jean Fontana *(Mng Dir-Retail, Apparel & Footwear)*
Brendon Frey *(Mng Dir-Retail, Apparel & Footwear)*

Integrated Corporate Relations - Beijing
Unit 805 Tower 1 Prosper Center No 5 Guanghua Road, Chao Yang District, Beijing, 100020 China
Tel.: (86) 10 6583 7500
Fax: (86) 10 8523 3001
Web Site: icrinc.com

Edmond Lococo *(Sr VP)*

INTERFACEPR.COM
7926 Talladega Spring Ln, Richmond, TX 77469
Tel.: (713) 454-9995
Fax: (832) 550-2705
E-Mail: contact@interfacepr.com
Web Site: interfacepr.com

Employees: 10

Mark Brimm *(Founder, Owner & Dir)*

Accounts:
Heller Networks

INTERMARKET COMMUNICATIONS
425 Madison Ave Ste 600, New York, NY 10017-1110
Tel.: (212) 888-6115
Fax: (212) 888-6157
E-Mail: information@intermarket.com
Web Site: www.intermarket.com

Employees: 20
Year Founded: 1986

Agency Specializes In: Financial, Public Relations

Breakdown of Gross Billings by Media: Pub. Rels.: 100%

Matt Zachowski *(Chm & Mng Partner)*
Martin B. Mosbacher *(CEO & Mng Partner)*
Neil Shapiro *(COO & Mng Partner)*
William Ferri *(Exec VP & Mng Dir-Intermarket Comm)*
Stephanie Diiorio *(VP)*
Corey Jefferson *(Mgr-Admin)*
Jade Faugno *(Sr Acct Supvr)*
Erica Fidel *(Sr Acct Supvr)*
Nick Lawler *(Sr Acct Supvr)*
Mike Gelormino *(Acct Supvr)*
Casey Sheets *(Sr Acct Exec)*

Accounts:
BondDesk Group LLC
ICap
Keefe, Bruyette & Woods, Inc.

INTERPROSE INC.
2635 Steeplechase Dr, Reston, VA 20191
Tel.: (703) 860-0577
Fax: (703) 860-1623
E-Mail: info@interprosepr.com
Web Site: www.interprosepr.com

Employees: 20

Agency Specializes In: Public Relations

Revenue: $50,000,000

Vivian Kelly *(Founder & CEO)*
John Wengler *(VP-Mktg)*
Melissa Power *(Acct Dir)*
Renee Ayer *(Acct Mgr)*
Melissa Drozdowski *(Acct Mgr)*
Amy Foschetti *(Acct Mgr)*
Lisa Mccausland *(Acct Mgr)*
Brian Walker *(Acct Mgr)*
Ryan Alford *(Mgr-Mktg)*
Carrie Owens *(Mgr-Mktg)*
Laurie Davis *(Coord-PR)*

Accounts:
Amedia Networks

Atreaus Systems
Cambrian
Cisco Systems; Herndon, VA; 2002
Clarabridge; Reston, VA; 2006
Ethernet Alliance
Hatteras Networks
Pair Gain
Polaris Wireless; Mountain View, CA
Strangeloop Networks; Vancouver, BC; 2007
Tera Burst
Viewgate

INTERSTAR MARKETING & PUBLIC RELATIONS

610 Grove St, Fort Worth, TX 76102-5555
Tel.: (817) 332-6522
Fax: (817) 334-0125
E-Mail: cw@interstargroup.com
Web Site: www.interstargroup.com

E-Mail for Key Personnel:
President: js@interstargroup.com

Employees: 10
Year Founded: 1975

National Agency Associations: AAF-PRSA

Agency Specializes In: Automotive, Aviation & Aerospace, Broadcast, Business Publications, Collateral, Communications, Consulting, Consumer Marketing, Consumer Publications, Education, Event Planning & Marketing, Exhibit/Trade Shows, Financial, Health Care Services, High Technology, Leisure, Public Relations, Publicity/Promotions, Restaurant, Retail, Trade & Consumer Magazines, Transportation, Travel & Tourism

Approx. Annual Billings: $6,000,000

Jane E. Schlansker *(Pres & CEO)*

Accounts:
Child Care Associates
Renfro Foods, Inc.; Fort Worth, TX Salsa, Specialty Food Products
Trail Care Associates

INTRAPROMOTE LLC

591 Boston Mills Rd Ste 550, Hudson, OH 44236
Tel.: (866) 570-1785
Fax: (630) 604-7656
E-Mail: information@intrapromote.com
Web Site: www.intrapromote.com

Agency Specializes In: Advertising, Multimedia, Search Engine Optimization

Doug Ausbury *(Co-Founder)*
John Lustina *(Co-Founder)*
Erik Daffron *(Pres & Dir-Search)*
Angela Moore *(VP-Client Ops)*
Evelyn Hepner *(Dir-Bus Dev)*
Kyle Misencik *(Dir-Campaign)*
Dylan Price *(Dir-Social Media Mktg)*
Mary Lee Sutter *(Mgr-Social Media)*
Kristel Klank *(Sr Strategist-Social Media)*

Accounts:
American Honda Motor Co.
ASCO
Blue Cross Blue Shield
The Cleveland Clinic
GENCO
Microsoft
Road & Travel Magazine
Schumacher Homes Article Optimization, Link Development, Online Press, Organic Search Campaign, Paid Search Campaign, Real Estate Services, Search, Social Media
Virtua Health

INTREPID

375 W 200 S Ste 275, Salt Lake City, UT 84101
Tel.: (801) 481-9482
Fax: (801) 481-9483
E-Mail: intrepid@intrepidagency.com
Web Site: www.intrepidagency.com

Year Founded: 1996

Agency Specializes In: Advertising, Crisis Communications, Digital/Interactive, Media Buying Services, Media Relations, Public Relations

Mike Grass *(Owner)*
Chris Thomas *(Pres)*
Leigh Gibson *(Acct Dir)*
Anne Williams *(Acct Dir)*
Beau Hunter *(Dir-Pub Involvement)*

Accounts:
The Art Institute of Salt Lake City
Daniels Summit Lodge
Hotel Park City
Levi Strauss & Co.
Resorts West, G P

INVESTORCOM INC.

65 Locust Ave, New Canaan, CT 06840
Tel.: (203) 972-9300
E-Mail: jgrau@investor-com.com
Web Site: www.investor-com.com

Employees: 10
Year Founded: 2000

Agency Specializes In: Corporate Communications, Financial, Investor Relations, Media Relations, Public Relations

Approx. Annual Billings: $2,500,000

Breakdown of Gross Billings by Media: Corp. Communications: 25%; Other: 75%

John Glenn Grau *(Pres)*
Douglas Jaffe *(VP-Capital Markets Grp)*

INVIEW COMMUNICATIONS

(Formerly SSA Public Relations)
8400 E Crescent Pkwy Ste 600, Greenwood Village, CO 80111
Tel.: (303) 707-1776
Fax: (303) 734-8831
E-Mail: denver@inviewcommunications.com
Web Site: www.inviewcommunications.com/

Employees: 7

Agency Specializes In: Business-To-Business, Communications, Education, Entertainment, Event Planning & Marketing, Exhibit/Trade Shows, Financial, Hospitality, Local Marketing, Media Relations, Media Training, New Technologies, Newspaper, Product Placement, Public Relations, Search Engine Optimization, Social Marketing/Nonprofit, Telemarketing, Web (Banner Ads, Pop-ups, etc.)

Susan Sears Ludwick *(Pres)*
Scott Huscher *(Acct Exec)*

Accounts:
TeleTech (Agency of Record)

IRIS PR SOFTWARE

(Formerly Ubiquity Public Relations)
4105 N 20th St, Phoenix, AZ 85016
Tel.: (866) 869-6645
E-Mail: info@myirispr.com
Web Site: www.irispr.com/

Agency Specializes In: Crisis Communications, Event Planning & Marketing, Media Relations, Public Relations, Social Media

Aly Saxe *(Founder & CEO)*
Jennifer Jewett *(Dir)*
Valerie Fenyn *(Mgr-Content)*
Sarah Broome *(Sr Acct Exec)*
Rebecca Hasulak *(Sr Acct Exec)*

Accounts:
Firehost
Flypaper
Infusionsoft

ISABELLI MEDIA RELATIONS

PO Box 221325, Chicago, IL 60622
Tel.: (312) 878-1222
Web Site: imrchicago.com

Year Founded: 2011

Agency Specializes In: Graphic Design, Media Relations, Media Training, Public Relations, Social Media

Janet Isabelli Wilkerson *(CEO & Partner)*
John Wilkerson *(COO & Partner)*
Brenna OLeary *(Sr Acct Exec)*
Courtney Kenny *(Acct Exec)*
Sarah Sackett *(Acct Exec)*

Accounts:
Mk Restaurant

ISSA PR

611 Broadway Rm 838, New York, NY 10012
Tel.: (646) 369-9221
E-Mail: info@issa-pr.com
Web Site: www.issa-pr.com

Agency Specializes In: Brand Development & Integration, Event Planning & Marketing, Public Relations

Viet Nguyen *(Founder & CEO)*
Josh Rasiel *(Art Dir)*

Accounts:
Pernod Ricard Absolut Elyx (Agency of Record)
START
New-Try The World Spain & Holiday Gourmet Boxes

IT GIRL PUBLIC RELATIONS

255 Howland Canal, Venice, CA 90291
Tel.: (310) 577-1122
Fax: (310) 821-6227
E-Mail: juliette@itgirlpublicrelations.com
Web Site: www.itgirlpublicrelations.com

Employees: 5
Year Founded: 1998

Agency Specializes In: Event Planning & Marketing, Public Relations, Publicity/Promotions

Juliette Harris *(CEO)*

Accounts:
Kelly Rowland
Los Angeles Lightning
Mark Harwell

IVY PUBLIC RELATIONS

216 E Simpson Ave, Fresno, CA 93704
Tel.: (559) 917-4476
E-Mail: info@ivypublicrelations.com
Web Site: www.ivypublicrelations.com

Agency Specializes In: Collateral, Graphic Design, Public Relations, Social Media

Natasha Biasell *(Owner)*

Accounts:
Adventure Cat Sailing Charters
Bright Power Inc
Kquinn Designs
Lemi Shine
Music in the Vineyards

J LAUREN PR LLC
502 S College Ave 3rd Fl, Tempe, AZ 85281
Tel.: (480) 626-8290
Web Site: www.jlaurenpr.com

Agency Specializes In: Broadcast, Print, Public Relations, Radio, Social Media

Jan Bracamonte *(Owner & Pres)*
Anthony Bracamonte *(Sr Mgr-Bus Intelligence & Analytics)*

Accounts:
Amara Resort & Spa
Royal Palms Resort
T Cooks
Thirty Five Dolores

J SHARPE AGENCY PUBLIC RELATIONS
304 Park Ave S 11th Fl, New York, NY 10010
Tel.: (347) 221-0532
E-Mail: info@jsharpeagency.com
Web Site: www.jsharpeagency.com

Agency Specializes In: Corporate Communications, Crisis Communications, Event Planning & Marketing, Media Relations, Media Training, Public Relations

Jennifer A. Williams *(CEO)*

Accounts:
Demetria Entertainment Services
Incoming Inc Brand Acceleration Services

JACKSON SPALDING
750 N Saint Paul St Ste 1700, Dallas, TX 75201
Tel.: (214) 269-4400
E-Mail: dallas@jacksonspalding.com
Web Site: www.jacksonspalding.com

Agency Specializes In: Advertising, Brand Development & Integration, Broadcast, Digital/Interactive, Graphic Design, Logo & Package Design, Media Buying Services, Print, Public Relations, Social Media, Sponsorship

Kim Hardcastle *(Partner)*
Traci Buch Messier *(Partner)*
Joanna Singleton *(Partner)*
Rita Izaguirre *(Dir-HR)*
Kara Myrick *(Dir-Art)*
Kathryn Brand *(Office Mgr)*
Suzanne Rutledge *(Acct Exec)*

Accounts:
The Mattress Firm, Inc. (Public Relations & Social Media Agency of Record)

JAM MEDIA COLLECTIVE
220 Halleck St Ste 120A, San Francisco, CA 94129
Tel.: (415) 839-7546
E-Mail: culprits@jamcollective.net
Web Site: www.jamcollective.net

Agency Specializes In: Brand Development & Integration, Public Relations, Social Media, Strategic Planning/Research

Julie Atherton *(Principal)*
Deborah Tomecek Pleva *(Acct Dir)*
Julie Campagnoli *(Dir-PR)*
Sara Murphy *(Strategist-Comm & Social Media)*

Accounts:
Icebreaker
Mountain Hardwear
Moving Comfort
Oru Kayak (Public Relations Agency of Record)
Osmo (Public Relations Agency of Record)
Osprey Packs
Seavees (Agency of Record)
Snow Peak
Sunski
Yakima Products Inc

JAMES HOGGAN & ASSOCIATES, INC.
#510-1125 Howe St, Vancouver, BC V6Z 2K8 Canada
Tel.: (604) 739-7500
Fax: (604) 736-9902
E-Mail: info@hoggan.com
Web Site: www.hoggan.com

Employees: 8
Year Founded: 1984

Agency Specializes In: Brand Development & Integration, Communications, Consulting, Corporate Communications, Corporate Identity, Environmental, Event Planning & Marketing, Financial, Food Service, Government/Political, High Technology, Investor Relations, Planning & Consultation, Public Relations, Publicity/Promotions, Strategic Planning/Research

James Hoggan *(Pres)*
Nancy McHarg *(VP & Counsel-Strategic)*

Accounts:
A&W Food Services of Canada Inc.
Dalai Lama Center For Peace & Education
Outdoor Adventures Vizsla
Vancouver Aquarium

JANE OWEN PR
408 N Doheny Ste 6, Los Angeles, CA 90048
Tel.: (424) 279-9424
Web Site: www.janeowenpr.net

Year Founded: 2011

Agency Specializes In: Event Planning & Marketing, Public Relations

Jane Owen *(CEO)*

Accounts:
Exofab
Jase Whitaker

JASCULCA/TERMAN AND ASSOCIATES
730 N Franklin St Ste 510, Chicago, IL 60654
Tel.: (312) 337-7400
Fax: (312) 337-8189
E-Mail: info@jtpr.com
Web Site: www.jtpr.com

Employees: 50
Year Founded: 1981

Agency Specializes In: Event Planning & Marketing, Government/Political, Sponsorship

Jim Terman *(Co-Owner & Pres)*
Richard J. Jasculca *(Owner)*
Mary Kelley Patrick *(Mng Partner)*
Holly Bartecki *(Sr VP-Creative & Strategic Dev)*
Dan Regan *(Sr VP)*
Jennifer Hutchison *(VP)*
Marci May *(VP)*
Carly Olsman *(VP-Events & Intl Advance)*

JAYMIE SCOTTO & ASSOCIATES LLC (JSA)
(Formerly Jaymie Scotto & Associates LLC)
PO Box 20, Middlebrook, VA 24459
Mailing Address:
PO BOX 20, Middlebrook, VA 24459-0020
Tel.: (866) 695-3629
Fax: (201) 624-7316
Toll Free: (866) 695-3629
E-Mail: pr@jaymiescotto.com
Web Site: www.jaymiescotto.com

Employees: 25
Year Founded: 2005

Agency Specializes In: Event Planning & Marketing, Internet/Web Design, Media Planning, Media Training, Mobile Marketing, Public Relations

Lisa Garrison *(Exec VP-Fin & Bus Ops)*
Ashley Emmons *(Acct Dir)*
Matthew Pera *(Acct Dir)*
Dean Perrine *(Acct Dir)*
Katherine Spitler *(Dir-Art)*
Vincent Ascolese *(Acct Mgr)*
Terri Goggins *(Mgr-Event Logistics)*
Krista Puleri *(Mgr-JSA's Event Sls)*
Jaclyn Riback *(Acct Coord)*
Matthew Sabio *(Acct Coord)*
Jl Williams *(Acct Coord)*
Shannon Ashe-Law *(Coord-Mktg & Events)*

Accounts:
451 Research Telecom Analyst Firm; 2014
ColoAtl Meet Me Room Operator; 2010
DECIX Global IX Peering Fabric; 2012
Faction IAAS Cloud Service Provider; 2014
FirstLight Lit Fiber Provider; 2013
GlobeNet Subsea Connectivity Between Americas; 2007
Hibernia Networks High Bandwidth Connectivity; 2005
Lightower Lit Services; 2008
NYI Internet Service Provider; 2013
PEG Bandwidth Network Infrastructure Solutions; 2013
RCN Data, Voice & Video Services; 2013
Telehouse America Data Center & Meet Me Room Services; 2008
ViaWest Data Center Services; 2011

JB CUMBERLAND PR
276 Fifth Ave Ste 205, New York, NY 10001
Tel.: (646) 230-6940
Fax: (646) 230-6935
E-Mail: info@jbcumberland.com
Web Site: www.jbcumberlandpr.com

Employees: 10
Year Founded: 1985

National Agency Associations: PRSA

Agency Specializes In: Brand Development & Integration, Broadcast, Business Publications, Cable T.V., Children's Market, Collateral, Communications, Consulting, Consumer Marketing, Consumer Publications, Cosmetics, Direct Response Marketing, E-Commerce, Entertainment, Event Planning & Marketing, Exhibit/Trade Shows, Fashion/Apparel, Food Service, Health Care Services, Internet/Web Design, Leisure, Magazines, New Product Development, Newspaper, Newspapers & Magazines, Outdoor, Over-50 Market, Public Relations, Publicity/Promotions, Retail, Sales Promotion, Seniors' Market, Sports Market,

Strategic Planning/Research, Teen Market, Trade & Consumer Magazines, Travel & Tourism

Joanna Cumberland *(Owner, Pres & CEO)*
Marie Cacciato *(VP)*

Accounts:
Architec Consumer, Digital Public Relations, Media, Retail, Totally Sweet Products
JAWS (Just Add Water System) Public Relations, Social Media

JC MARKETING ASSOCIATES INC.

467 Main St PO Box 289, Wakefield, MA 01880-0589
Tel.: (781) 245-7070
Fax: (781) 245-1086
E-Mail: annhadley@jcmarketingassociates.com
Web Site: www.jcmarketingassociates.com

Employees: 7
Year Founded: 1964

Agency Specializes In: Advertising, Consulting, Event Planning & Marketing, Exhibit/Trade Shows, Financial, Graphic Design, Internet/Web Design, Pets , Public Relations, Real Estate, Restaurant

Approx. Annual Billings: $650,000

Breakdown of Gross Billings by Media: Bus. Publs.: $15,000; Collateral: $55,000; D.M.: $20,000; Newsp.: $50,000; Pub. Rels.: $300,000; Yellow Page Adv.: $10,000

Ann Hadley *(Pres)*
Jayne D'Onofrio *(VP)*
Carolyn Dydzulis *(Mgr-Office)*

Accounts:
Best Western Lord Wakefield
IT Works
Massachusetts Highway Association
Municipal Light Departments
Quashnet Valley Condominiums; Mashpee, MA
Reading Municipal Light Department; Reading, MA
Saugus Federal Credit Union
The Savings Bank
Wakefield Department of Public Works

Branch

JCM Events

PO Box 289, Wakefield, MA 01880-0589
Tel.: (781) 245-7070
Fax: (781) 245-1086
E-Mail: lhadley00@aol.com
Web Site: www.jcmarketingassociates.com

Employees: 4
Year Founded: 2001

Agency Specializes In: Event Planning & Marketing

Ann Hadley *(Pres)*

JC PUBLIC RELATIONS, INC.

1 Gatehall Dr Ste 107, Parsippany, NJ 07054-4514
Tel.: (973) 850-7300
Fax: (973) 732-3523
E-Mail: info@jcprinc.com
Web Site: jcprinc.com

Employees: 12

Agency Specializes In: Brand Development & Integration, Collateral, Crisis Communications, Event Planning & Marketing, Media Relations, Media Training, Product Placement, Public Relations, Strategic Planning/Research, Trade & Consumer Magazines

Jennifer Connelly *(CEO)*
Greg Jawski *(Mng Dir & Gen Mgr-NY Office)*
Robert Keane *(Mng Dir)*
Andrea Trachtenberg *(Mng Dir)*
Carol Anne Harves *(CFO)*
Karen Pellicone *(COO)*
Steven Stoke *(Mng Dir-Video Content)*

Accounts:
Hightower Advisors

JCIR

(Formerly Jaffoni & Collins)
116 E 16th St 11th Fl, New York, NY 10003-2112
Tel.: (212) 835-8500
Fax: (212) 835-8525
E-Mail: info@jcir.com
Web Site: www.jcir.com

Joseph N. Jaffoni *(Founder & Pres)*
Richard Land *(Sr Mng Dir)*
Norberto Aja *(VP)*
James Leahy *(VP)*
Jennifer Neuman *(VP)*

Accounts:
Agilysys, Inc.
Ballantyne Strong, Inc.
Beasley Broadcast Group, Inc.
BJ's Restaurants, Inc
Carmike Cinemas, Inc.
Cinemark Holdings, Inc.
Mad Catz Interactive, Inc. Investor Relations
Multimedia Games, Inc.
Nexstar Broadcasting Group, Inc.
Penn National Gaming, Inc.
Revel Entertainment, LLC
REX American Resources Corporation
Scientific Games Corporation
SFX Entertainment, Inc
TransAct Technologies Incorporated

JCPR, INC.

1 Gatehall Dr Ste 107, Parsippany, NJ 07054
Tel.: (973) 850-7300
Fax: (973) 850-7399
E-Mail: contact@jcprinc.com
Web Site: www.jcprinc.com

Year Founded: 2003

Agency Specializes In: Event Planning & Marketing, Media Relations, Public Relations, Social Media

Carol Graumann *(Pres)*
Jennifer Connelly *(CEO)*
Greg Jawski *(Mng Dir & Gen Mgr)*
Andrea Trachtenberg *(Mng Dir)*
Michelle Pittman *(Chief Strategy Officer)*
Evelyn Cashen *(Asst VP)*
Jessica Torchia *(Asst VP)*
Phil Sievers *(Dir-Mktg)*
Megan Snyder *(Mgr-Mktg)*

Accounts:
Altegris
Evestnet
Gemini Fund Services
Hightower
Hollister Construction Services
iBillionaire
Nationwide Funds
RBC Wealth Management
Reality Shares

JEFF DEZEN PUBLIC RELATIONS

13 E Coffee St, Greenville, SC 29601
Tel.: (864) 233-3776
Fax: (864) 370-3368
Web Site: www.jdpr.com

Agency Specializes In: Collateral, Content, Crisis Communications, Media Relations, Public Relations, Social Media

Jeff Dezen *(Pres)*
Matt Lochel *(Dir-Media & Content Strategies)*
Terry Pearson *(Office Mgr)*
Wendy Huston *(Sr Acct Exec)*
Jared Kelowitz *(Sr Acct Exec)*
Drew Dezen *(Acct Exec)*

Accounts:
Kentwool (Public Relations Agency of Record) Content Development, KentWool Performance, Marketing Communications, Media Relations, Strategic Planning
Serola Biomechanics, Inc Brand Development, Communications, Public Relations, Social Media, Strategic Planning
Vom Fass USA

THE JEFFREY GROUP

1111 Lincoln Rd 8th Fl, Miami Beach, FL 33139
Tel.: (305) 860-1000
Fax: (305) 532-2590
E-Mail: miami@jeffreygroup.com
Web Site: www.jeffreygroup.com

Employees: 32
Year Founded: 1993

National Agency Associations: COPF

Agency Specializes In: Communications, Event Planning & Marketing, Hispanic Market, Public Relations, Sponsorship

Approx. Annual Billings: $5,500,000 Fees Only

Jeffrey R. Sharlach *(Chm)*
Brian Burlingame *(CEO)*
Gerson Penha *(Gen Dir-Brazil)*
Theresa Rice *(Mng Dir-Latin America)*
Martin Bidegaray *(Mgr-Insights & Analytics)*

Accounts:
Cengage Learning Communications, Content Development, Media Relations, Online
Facebook
Johnnie Walker
Kaspersky Lab
Miami Marlins Corporate Communications
TD Bank Hispanic PR
Victaulic B2B Public Relations, Social Media, Trade Show

Branches

Jeffrey Group Mexico

(Formerly The Jeffrey Group Mexico)
Homero 1343 No 402, Col Los Morales Polanco, Mexico, CP 11540 Mexico
Tel.: (52) 55 5281 1121
Fax: (52) 55 5281 1448
E-Mail: echacon@jeffreygroup.com
Web Site: www.jeffreygroup.com

Employees: 18

Agency Specializes In: Public Relations

Mariana Villarreal *(Mng Dir)*
Maria Eugenia Caamano *(Acct Mgr)*
Alejandro Viquez *(Sr Acct Exec)*
Camila Garcia *(Specialist-Comm)*
Georgina Vazquez Riosvelasco *(Acct Exec)*

Accounts:

Air Bus
Ryder

The Jeffrey Group Brazil
Joaquim Floriano 466 5 cj 508 Itaim Bibi, 04534-002 Sao Paulo, SP Brazil
Tel.: (55) 11 2165 1655
Fax: (55) 11 2165 1642
E-Mail: info@tjgmail.com
Web Site: www.jeffreygroup.com

Employees: 30

Agency Specializes In: Public Relations

Cristina Iglecio *(Mng Dir)*
Gerson Penha *(Gen Dir)*
Ana Bueno *(Acct Dir)*
Suzeli Damaceno *(Acct Dir)*
Amanda Sanchez *(Dir-Creative)*
Claudia Cardoso *(Sr Acct Mgr)*
Leticia Suzuki *(Sr Acct Mgr)*
Wilson Barros *(Acct Mgr)*
Erica Rizzi *(Acct Mgr)*
Cyntia Okanishi *(Mgr-Digital Comm)*
Priscila Marques *(Sr Acct Exec)*
Licia Soares *(Acct Exec)*
Rafael Ryuiti Akao *(Acct Coord)*

Accounts:
Abbott
Bayer Bayer CropScience, Customer Relations Program, HealthCare Groups
Cisco
Diageo
FedEx PyMEx Program
Fox Sports
Johnnie Walker
Johnson & Johnson Corporate Communications, OTC, Oral Care, Women's Health
Kodak Graphic Communications Group
Microsoft
Nintendo
Ryder
Sony Ericsson
Western Union

The Jeffrey Group Argentina
Talcahuano 833 Piso 8 G, C1013AAP Buenos Aires, Argentina
Tel.: (54) 11 4813 1130
Fax: (54) 11 4814 5480
E-Mail: info@tjgmail.com
Web Site: www.jeffreygroup.com

Employees: 8
Year Founded: 1993

Agency Specializes In: Hispanic Market, Promotions, Public Relations, Publicity/Promotions

Maria Eugenia Vargas *(Mng Dir)*
Maria Martin *(Sr Acct Exec-The Jeffrey Group)*

Accounts:
Abbott
American Express
BRP
Ciena
Cisco
Coca-Cola Refreshments USA, Inc.
Diageo
Discovery Channel
Fox Sports
Johnnie Walker
Jose Cuervo
Jumex
Kaspersky
Kodak Graphic Communications Group
Microsoft
Nintendo
Regus
Sony Ericsson
T-Mobile US
Western Union

The Jeffrey Group New York
60 E 42Nd St, New York, NY 10165
Tel.: (212) 620-4100
Fax: (212) 918-9038
E-Mail: mvaldesfauli@tjgmail.com
Web Site: www.jeffreygroup.com

Employees: 6
Year Founded: 2006

National Agency Associations: COPF

Agency Specializes In: Below-the-Line, Business-To-Business, Hispanic Market, Multicultural, Public Relations, Publicity/Promotions, Viral/Buzz/Word of Mouth

Jeffrey Sharlach *(Chm & CEO)*

Accounts:
Abbott
AirBus
American Airlines
Clorox
Diageo Jose Cuervo
Fox Hispanic Media Campaign: "Latino Entertainment. American Attitude."
T-Mobile US
Volkswagen Group of America, Inc.

JENERATION PR
4335 Van Nuys Blvd Ste 108, Sherman Oaks, CA 91423
Tel.: (818) 501-1205
E-Mail: buzz@jenerationpr.com
Web Site: www.jenerationpr.com

Year Founded: 2005

Agency Specializes In: Event Planning & Marketing, Public Relations, Social Media

Jennifer Berson *(Founder)*

Accounts:
Olivine
Twistband Inc

JENNA COMMUNICATIONS LLC
1835 Market St Ste 1000, Philadelphia, PA 19103
Tel.: (484) 238-0355
Web Site: www.jennacommunications.com

Year Founded: 2007

Agency Specializes In: Crisis Communications, Email, Event Planning & Marketing, Media Relations, Media Training, Public Relations, Search Engine Optimization, Social Media, Strategic Planning/Research

Jennifer Sherlock *(Pres)*

Accounts:
Casey Cares Foundation
Doreen Taylor
NetCost Market

JERRY THOMAS PUBLIC RELATIONS
200 E Randolph St Ste 5100, Chicago, IL 60601
Tel.: (312) 275-5801
Fax: (312) 967-5883
E-Mail: info@jerrythomaspr.com
Web Site: www.jerrythomaspr.com

Agency Specializes In: Crisis Communications, Event Planning & Marketing, Media Relations, Media Training, Public Relations

Jerry Thomas *(Founder & Pres)*

Accounts:
New-Diversity MBA Magazine

JESSICA AUFIERO COMMUNICATIONS
1350 Ave of the Americas Fl 2, New York, NY 10019
Tel.: (212) 832-7000
E-Mail: info@ja-pr.com
Web Site: www.ja-pr.com

Year Founded: 2011

Agency Specializes In: Brand Development & Integration, Event Planning & Marketing, Media Relations, Public Relations, Social Media, Strategic Planning/Research

Jessica Aufiero *(Principal)*
Kimberly Deangelo *(Acct Mgr)*
Alexis Weisman *(Acct Coord)*

Accounts:
Airstream 2 Go
Artisan
Borgo Egnazia
Eli Zabar
Kittichai
Masseria Cimino
Masseria San Domenico
Obika Mozzarella Bar
San Domenico House
San Domenico a Mare

JESSON + COMPANY COMMUNICATIONS INC.
77 Bloor St W, Toronto, M5S 1M2 Canada
Tel.: (416) 323-7828
Fax: (416) 923-0226
Toll Free: (855) 811-7828
E-Mail: info@jessonco.com
Web Site: www.jessonco.com

Year Founded: 2002

Agency Specializes In: Event Planning & Marketing, Media Relations, Public Relations, Strategic Planning/Research

Barbara Jesson *(Pres)*
Nicola Blazier *(VP)*
Sharyn Thomas-Counce *(VP)*
Kim Banjac *(Acct Dir)*
Shauna Frampton *(Acct Dir)*
Sarah Jesson *(Acct Dir)*
Ronica Sajnani *(Dir-Meetings & Travel Trade)*

Accounts:
Arbonne International LLC Marketing, PR
CAVIRTEX BitAccess Bitcoin Teller Machines, Bitcoin Currency, Canadian Agency of Record, Contest, Marketing, Merchant Solutions, Online Trading, Pre-Paid MasterCards, Trade Shows
Mill Street Brewery

J.F. MILLS & WORLDWIDE
6106 E Yale Ave, Denver, CO 80222
Tel.: (303) 639-6186
Fax: (303) 639-1125
E-Mail: jfmills@jfmillsworldwide.com
Web Site: www.jfmillsworldwide.com

Employees: 7
Year Founded: 1995

Agency Specializes In: Business-To-Business, Corporate Communications, Digital/Interactive, E-

Commerce, Exhibit/Trade Shows, Financial, Health Care Services, High Technology, Information Technology, International, Media Planning, Media Relations, Media Training, New Product Development, Newspapers & Magazines, Product Placement, Public Relations, Publicity/Promotions, Real Estate, Sales Promotion, Travel & Tourism

Approx. Annual Billings: $750,000

Breakdown of Gross Billings by Media: Corp. Communications: $750,000

James F. Mills *(Principal)*

Accounts:
Skins Global

JFK COMMUNICATIONS INC.
Princeton Corp Ctr 5 Independence Way Ste 300, Princeton, NJ 08540
Tel.: (609) 514-5117
Fax: (609) 514-5234
Web Site: www.jfkhealth.com

John F. Kouten *(CEO)*
David Patti *(Sr VP)*
Peter Steinberg *(Dir-Editorial Svcs)*
Jamie Hipple *(Sr Acct Exec)*
Jessica Stanek *(Acct Coord)*

Accounts:
Aerocrine
American Cancer Society
Eisai, Inc.
Eusa Pharma (USA) Inc.; 2007
EUSA Pharma, Inc
Fujirebio Diagnostics Inc.; Malvern, PA; 2008
GE Healthcare Medical Diagnostics
Ligand Pharmaceuticals
MDS Pharma Services
Novartis Oncology
PharmaNet Development Group
Terumo Medical Corporation
Theravance

JG BLACK BOOK OF TRAVEL
594 Broadway Ste 1001, New York, NY 10012
Tel.: (212) 967-5895
Fax: (212) 967-9723
Toll Free: (888) 241-9763
E-Mail: info@jgblackbook.com
Web Site: jgblackbook.com

Employees: 18
Year Founded: 2002

Agency Specializes In: Brand Development & Integration, Collateral, Promotions, Public Relations, Social Media

Revenue: $2,100,000

Jena Gardner *(Pres & CEO)*
Cathy Courtney *(VP-Branding & Comm)*
Dolores Simonds *(VP-Indus Rels)*
Jide Iruka *(Brand Mktg Mgr)*
Tyler LaMont *(Dir-Indus Rels)*
Malcolm MacFarlane *(Mgr-Sls-UK)*

Accounts:
British Virgin Islands Media Relations, Public Relations, Trade
New-Le Quartier Francais Leeu Estates (North American Agency of Record), Leeu House (North American Agency of Record), Public Relations, Strategic Marketing

J.GRIFFITH PUBLIC RELATIONS
5535 Memorial Dr Ste F, Houston, TX 77007
Tel.: (713) 568-5376
Fax: (713) 449-2931
Web Site: www.jgriffithpr.com

Year Founded: 2006

Agency Specializes In: Brand Development & Integration, Digital/Interactive, Event Planning & Marketing, Public Relations, Social Media

Julie O. Griffith *(Founder & Principal-Creative)*

Accounts:
Naturally Happy Hair

JITSU PUBLIC RELATIONS, INC.
(Formerly The Storch-Murphy Group)
299 Stoughton Ave, Cranford, NJ 07016
Tel.: (908) 276-0777
Fax: (908) 276-0888
Web Site: www.jitsupr.com

Employees: 8
Year Founded: 1980

Agency Specializes In: Communications, Consulting, Consumer Marketing, Corporate Identity, Event Planning & Marketing, Exhibit/Trade Shows, Health Care Services, Medical Products, Newspaper, Newspapers & Magazines, Pharmaceutical, Public Relations

Accounts:
Cordis Cardiology
Matrixx Initiatives; Phoenix, AZ
McNeil Consumer & Specialty Pharmaceuticals
Songbird Hearing, Inc.
Vistakon

JMPR, INC.
5850 Canoga Ave Ste 300, Woodland Hills, CA 91367
Tel.: (818) 992-4353
Fax: (818) 992-0543
E-Mail: reception@jmprpublicrelations.com
Web Site: www.jmprpublicrelations.com

Employees: 12
Year Founded: 1977

Agency Specializes In: Automotive, Brand Development & Integration, E-Commerce, Electronic Media, Entertainment, Event Planning & Marketing, Public Relations, Publicity/Promotions, Sponsorship

Joseph Molina *(Founder & Pres)*
Breanna Buhr *(VP)*
Alexia Bunce *(Acct Supvr)*
Ashley Anderson *(Sr Acct Exec)*
Natalie Hamlin *(Acct Exec)*

Accounts:
The ACCEL Performance Group
Airstream Trailers
AMA Pro Flat Track (Agency of Record) Communications, Marketing, Media
AutoWeb (Public Relations Agency of Record) Brand Strategies, Creative, Media Relations
Barrett-Jackson Auction Company Media Relations, Public Relations
Bel-Ray
Bentley Motors
Beverly Hills Motoring Accessories (Agency of Record) Media Relations, Public Relations, Strategic
Boyd Gaming Public Relations
Bugatti Automobiles S.A.S.
Bugatti
Calumet Packaging Media Relations, Trade Media, TruFuel
Classic Industries
Coker Group Media
Driven Performance Brands Classic Industries (Agency of Record), Hurst Performance Vehicles (Agency of Record), Media Relations, Meguiar's (Agency of Record), Pep Boys (Agency of Record), Public Relations, Royal Purple (Agency of Record), SEMA Show (Agency of Record)
Fast Toys Club Media
Funrise Customer, Media Relations, Strategy, TONKA
Galpin Motors
IDQ, Inc. AC Pro, Media Relations, do-it-yourself
Infiniti JX, Lifestyle Communications, Media Relations, Sedan
Larte Design Media Relations, North America Agency of Record
Live Media Group (Agency of Record) Media
Los Angeles Auto Show Strategic Communications
McLaren Automotive (North American Agency of Record) Public Relations
Meguiar's, Inc.
Mullin Automotive Museum Automotive Television Program
NanoHiFi Brand Awareness, Media Outreach
Omix-ADA, Inc. Brand Awareness, Consumer Tradeshows, Events, Media Outreach, Media Relations
Orchex
The Pep Boys-Manny, Moe & Jack (Agency of Record) Media, PR
Pep Boys
Petersen Automotive Museum
Piaggio Aero
Prestolite Performance ACCEL, Brand Awareness, Consumer Media Relations, Mr. Gasket, Trade
Red Bull Global Rallycross
Royal Purple Brand Development, Events & Consumer Tradeshows, Media Outreach
SlamStop
Stack's Bowers Galleries Media Outreach
Strider Sports International (Agency of Record) Media Outreach, Outdoor

JOELE FRANK, WILKINSON BRIMMER KATCHER
140 E 45th St 37th Fl, New York, NY 10017
Tel.: (212) 355-4449
Fax: (212) 355-4554
E-Mail: info@joelefrank.com
Web Site: www.joelefrank.com

Employees: 65
Year Founded: 2000

Agency Specializes In: Corporate Communications, Crisis Communications, Investor Relations, Public Relations, Sponsorship

Joele Frank *(Founder & Mng Partner)*
Eric Brielmann *(Partner)*
Andrew Brimmer *(Partner)*
Steve Frankel *(Partner)*
Michael Freitag *(Partner)*
Tim Lynch *(Partner)*
Jamie Moser *(Partner)*
Meaghan Repko *(Partner)*
Andrew Siegel *(Partner)*
Sharon Stern *(Partner)*
Kelly Sullivan *(Partner)*
Adam Pollack *(Sr Acct Exec)*

Accounts:
BioScrip
Gleacher & Company, Inc. Media
Tenet Healthcare Corporation

JOHNSTONWELLS
1600 Wynkoop St, Denver, CO 80202
Tel.: (303) 623-3366
Fax: (303) 623-7915
E-Mail: gwin@johnstonwells.com
Web Site: www.johnstonwells.com

E-Mail for Key Personnel:
President: gg@johnstonwells.com

Employees: 25
Year Founded: 1971

Agency Specializes In: Public Relations

Approx. Annual Billings: $1,800,000

Breakdown of Gross Billings by Media: Pub. Rels.: $1,800,000

Mark Hernandez *(Controller)*

Accounts:
Allonhill Public Relations
Lerch Bates PR

JONESWORKS INC.
211 E 43rd St Ste 1501, New York, NY 10017
Tel.: (212) 839-0111
E-Mail: info@jonesworksinc.com
Web Site: www.jonesworks.com

Year Founded: 2011

Agency Specializes In: Brand Development & Integration, Digital/Interactive, Public Relations

David Nurnberg *(Exec VP)*

Accounts:
New-Hilarity for Charity
nugg Beauty
Pencils of Promise
New-Trust Fund Beauty
New-Wtrmln Wtr

JOTO PR
411 Cleveland St Ste 204, Clearwater, FL 33755
Tel.: (888) 202-4614
Web Site: www.jotopr.com

Year Founded: 2009

Agency Specializes In: Crisis Communications, Email, Internet/Web Design, Market Research, Public Relations, Social Media, Strategic Planning/Research

Karla Jo Helms *(CEO)*
Ashley Richardson *(Sr Project Mgr-PR)*
Alexa Gedigian *(Specialist-Media Rels)*

Accounts:
Actionable Intelligence Technologies
New-BodyHealth
Centers of Integrative Medicine and Healing
Clearstream, LLC Antimicrobial, Media, Public Relations
Consumer Energy Solutions, Inc.
D-Mar General Contracting and Development
eConsumerServices
Elements Fitness
Handymen for All
Payscout, Inc
SCI Distribution, LLC Campaign: "Every Drop Counts"
Skinspirations
Sports Facilities Advisory PR
Sterling
Stratus Video Interpreting
Sunstate Labs Dazz
New-Tampa Bay Accounting and Associates

JPR COMMUNICATIONS
5950 Canoga Ave Ste 430, Woodland Hills, CA 91367-5008
Tel.: (818) 884-8282
Fax: (818) 884-8868
E-Mail: info@jprcom.com
Web Site: www.jprcom.com

Employees: 15
Year Founded: 1991

Agency Specializes In: High Technology, Public Relations

Judy Smith *(Owner)*
Mark Smith *(Partner & Exec VP)*
Dan Miller *(Sr Acct Dir)*
Matt Walker *(Dir-Writing)*
Gary Smith *(Acct Mgr)*

Accounts:
C2C; Springfield, MA
Caringo; Austin, TX
NetEx
Ocarina Networks; San Jose, CA

JSH&A PUBLIC RELATIONS
2 TransAm Plz Dr Ste 450, Oakbrook Terrace, IL 60181
Tel.: (630) 932-4242
Fax: (630) 932-1418
E-Mail: jim@jsha.com
Web Site: www.jsha.com

Employees: 20

Agency Specializes In: Crisis Communications, Media Relations, Sponsorship

Jonni Hegenderfer *(Owner)*
Jim Kokoris *(Pres & Gen Mgr)*
Cheryl Georgas *(Sr VP & Deputy Gen Mgr)*
Deanna Killackey *(Sr VP)*
Monica Bhandarkar *(VP-Social Media & Mktg)*
Jennifer Nau *(Sr Acct Supvr)*
Hannah Pomatto *(Sr Acct Supvr)*
Amanda Bothen Nagele *(Acct Supvr)*

Accounts:
Beam Global Spirits & Wine Inc
Dremel
Hershey Company; Hershey, PA Campaign: "Hershey's Air Delight Chocolate Launch"
Master Lock
Redbox
Renkitt Benkiser
Robert Bosch Tool Corporation Brand Awareness, Dremel, Media Relations, Power Tools, Accessories & Measuring Tools, Public Relations, ROTOZIP, Social Media, Trade Show & Event Support
SKIL Power Tools Public Relations; 2010

JTS COMMUNICATIONS, INC.
2525 Ponce de Leon Blvd Ste 300, Coral Gables, FL 33134
Tel.: (305) 740-8191
Fax: (212) 419-3894
Toll Free: (866) 740-8191
Web Site: www.jtscom.com

Year Founded: 2003

Agency Specializes In: Brand Development & Integration, Communications, Content, Digital/Interactive, Graphic Design, Media Training, Public Relations

Juan Thomas Sanchez *(Pres & CEO)*
Andrew Dixon *(Mng Dir)*
Carolina Copello *(Acct Mgr)*
Elizabeth Haag *(Acct Mgr)*
Christine Herrera *(Acct Mgr)*

Accounts:
Entic LLC

JUDGE PUBLIC RELATIONS
960A Harbor Lk Ct, Safety Harbor, FL 34695
Tel.: (727) 463-1295
E-Mail: contact@judgepr.com
Web Site: www.judgepr.com

Year Founded: 2013

Agency Specializes In: Crisis Communications, Media Relations, Media Training, Public Relations, Social Media, Strategic Planning/Research

James Judge *(Founder & Pres)*
Thanos Genos *(VP)*

Accounts:
Carlson, Meissner, Hart & Hayslett
Clegg Insurance Group

JZPR
105 E De La Guerra St Ste 5, Santa Barbara, CA 93101
Tel.: (805) 845-4068
Web Site: www.jzpr.com

Agency Specializes In: Broadcast, Print, Public Relations

Jennifer Zacharias *(Principal)*
Sydney Gardner *(Acct Dir)*

Accounts:
Granada Books
Reed Floors & Interiors
Urban Wine Trail

K PUBLIC RELATIONS LLC
99 Hudson, New York, NY 10013
Tel.: (646) 756-4217
Fax: (646) 688-3017
E-Mail: contact@kpr-nyc.com
Web Site: www.kpr-nyc.com

Agency Specializes In: Brand Development & Integration, Public Relations, Social Marketing/Nonprofit, Social Media

Kira Kohrherr *(Founder & Pres)*

Accounts:
New-LookBooker
New-Neocutis

K. SUTHERLAND PR
14988 Sand Canyon Ave Studio 8, Irvine, CA 92618
Tel.: (949) 328-4895
Web Site: www.ksutherlandpr.com

Agency Specializes In: Collateral, Content, Corporate Communications, Crisis Communications, Logo & Package Design, Media Relations, Media Training, Public Relations, Social Media

Kerry Sutherland *(Founder & Principal)*
Jill O'Driscoll *(Dir-PR)*

Accounts:
imoova.com
Nutram
Paw Pods
Pawalla
Wondercide

Branch

K. Sutherland PR

201 W Liberty St Ste 207, Reno, NV 89501
Tel.: (775) 391-0118
Web Site: www.ksutherlandpr.com

Agency Specializes In: Brand Development & Integration, Crisis Communications, Digital/Interactive, Internet/Web Design, Media Relations, Media Training, Public Relations, Social Media

Jillian Johnson *(Dir-PR)*

Accounts:
New-Carson Tahoe Health

K2 KRUPP KOMMUNICATIONS, INC
(Formerly Krupp Kommunications, Inc)
636 Ave of the Americas 4th Fl, New York, NY 10011
Tel.: (212) 886-6700
Fax: (212) 265-4708
E-Mail: jgarbowski@kruppnyc.com
Web Site: www.kruppkommunications.com

Employees: 16
Year Founded: 1996

Agency Specializes In: Affluent Market, African-American Market, Brand Development & Integration, Branded Entertainment, Broadcast, Business Publications, Business-To-Business, Cable T.V., Children's Market, Collateral, College, Communications, Consulting, Consumer Goods, Consumer Marketing, Consumer Publications, Content, Corporate Communications, Corporate Identity, Cosmetics, Customer Relationship Management, Digital/Interactive, Entertainment, Event Planning & Marketing, Experience Design, Faith Based, Fashion/Apparel, Financial, Game Integration, Guerilla Marketing, Health Care Services, Hospitality, Household Goods, Identity Marketing, Integrated Marketing, Internet/Web Design, Leisure, Local Marketing, Luxury Products, Magazines, Media Relations, Media Training, Medical Products, Men's Market, Multicultural, Multimedia, New Product Development, Over-50 Market, Pharmaceutical, Print, Product Placement, Promotions, Public Relations, Publicity/Promotions, Publishing, Radio, Real Estate, Regional, Restaurant, Retail, Sales Promotion, Seniors' Market, Social Marketing/Nonprofit, Social Media, Sponsorship, Strategic Planning/Research, T.V., Teen Market, Trade & Consumer Magazines, Travel & Tourism, Tween Market, Urban Market, Viral/Buzz/Word of Mouth, Women's Market

Approx. Annual Billings: $5,000,000

Breakdown of Gross Billings by Media: Pub. Rels.: 100%

Heidi Krupp-Lisiten *(CEO)*
Steve Schonberg *(Mng Dir)*
Darren Lisiten *(COO)*
Eric Engram *(Dir-Acctg & Controller)*
Jennifer Garbowski *(Dir-New Bus)*
Li Wang *(Dir-Digital)*
Jo Migano *(Acct Mgr-K2 Entertainment)*

Accounts:
Armondo Montelongo
Big City Moms, Inc
Bret Michaels
Farnoosh Torabi Brand Management, National Media Relations
Glimmer Body Art, LLC
Karla Dennis Brand Management, National Media Relations
Nerium International Brand Management, Communications Strategy, Media outreach, Public Relations
Taste of Home
Weight Watchers Weight Watchers Online for Men

KAHN TRAVEL COMMUNICATIONS
77 N Centre Ave Ste 215, Rockville Centre, NY 11570
Tel.: (516) 594-4100
Fax: (516) 594-4104
E-Mail: info@ktcpr.com
Web Site: www.kahn-travel.com

Employees: 8
Year Founded: 1988

Agency Specializes In: Travel & Tourism

Richard S. Kahn *(Pres)*
Theresa Oakes *(Sr Acct Supvr)*
Josh Kahn *(Sr Acct Exec)*
Leigh-Mary Kearney *(Sr Acct Exec)*
Nicole Hellmers *(Acct Exec)*
Kayla Lynskey *(Jr Acct Exec)*

Accounts:
Blue Horizons Garden Resort; Grenada
Caribbean Hotel & Tourism Association
Club Getaway; Connecticut
Interval International; Miami, Florida
La Cabana All Suite Beach Resort & Casino; Aruba
Mango Bay Barbados
Pink Beach Club; Bermuda
Spice Island Beach Resort; Grenada
St. Maarten Tourism Bureau
Travel Impressions
Victoria Cruises

KANATSIZ COMMUNICATIONS INC
10 Mar del Rey, San Clemente, CA 92673
Tel.: (949) 443-9300
Fax: (949) 443-2215
E-Mail: info@kcomm.com
Web Site: www.kcomm.com

Agency Specializes In: Event Planning & Marketing, Government/Political, Public Relations, Search Engine Optimization, Social Marketing/Nonprofit, Social Media

Jeff Montejano *(Pres)*
Sinan Kanatsiz *(CEO)*
Heather Reeves *(VP-Pub Rels)*
Rachel Reenders *(VP-Pub Rels)*
Dave Holscher *(VP-Pub Rels)*
Lei Lani Fera *(Creative Dir)*

Accounts:
New-Evite

KAPLOW
19 W 44th St 6th Fl, New York, NY 10036
Tel.: (212) 221-1713
Fax: (212) 768-1960
E-Mail: email-liz@kaplowpr.com
Web Site: www.kaplow.com

Employees: 60

National Agency Associations: COPF

Agency Specializes In: Brand Development & Integration, Digital/Interactive, Public Relations, Publicity/Promotions, Publishing, Sponsorship

Evan B. Jacobs *(Owner)*
Liz Kaplow *(Pres & CEO)*
Dana Glaser *(Sr VP & Exec Producer-Kstudio)*
Chris Livingston *(VP-Tech)*
Gloria Quinn-Doyle *(VP)*
Jee Nah Walker *(Acct Dir-Fashion)*
Brian Fanelli *(Mgr-Analytics)*
Adrienne Klein *(Mgr-Content)*
Jacqueline Agosta *(Sr Acct Supvr)*
Danielle Ratner *(Sr Acct Supvr)*
Emily Hendricks *(Acct Supvr)*

Accounts:
Conair Product Launch
Mark
Skype Campaign: "Skype Brings You Closer to Home"
Target

KAPOR HAMILTON PUBLIC RELATIONS
11847 Gorham Ave Ste 116, Los Angeles, CA 90049
Tel.: (310) 295-1189
Web Site: www.khpublicrelations.com

Dawn Hamilton *(Co-Owner)*
Rachel Kapor *(Owner)*

Accounts:
Asics

KARBO COMMUNICATIONS
(Formerly K/F Communications, Inc.)
601 Fourth St Ste 204, San Francisco, CA 94107
Tel.: (415) 255-6510
E-Mail: info@karbocom.com
Web Site: www.karbocom.com

Agency Specializes In: Brand Development & Integration, Content, Event Planning & Marketing, Guerilla Marketing, Media Relations, Media Training, Social Media

Julie A. Karbo *(Founder & CEO)*
Margaret Pereira *(VP)*
Cameron Smead *(Sr Acct Dir)*

Accounts:
New-Townsquared

KAREN CANAVAN PR
3522 Ashford Dunwoody Rd Ste 253, Atlanta, GA 30319
Tel.: (404) 803-2563
Web Site: www.karencanavanpr.com

Year Founded: 2010

Agency Specializes In: Crisis Communications, Event Planning & Marketing, Public Relations, Social Media

Karen Canavan *(Founder & Owner)*

Accounts:
Amura

KARLA OTTO
545 W 25th St, New York, NY 10001
Tel.: (212) 255-8588
E-Mail: info.newyork@karlaotto.com
Web Site: www.karlaotto.com

Agency Specializes In: Brand Development & Integration, Digital/Interactive, Event Planning & Marketing, Public Relations

Aleta Spitaleri *(VP)*
Marlene Cimicato Capron *(Dir-PR)*
Jessica Stanley *(Sr Mgr-VIP)*

Accounts:
New-Stuart Weitzman

THE KARMA AGENCY
(Formerly Alta Communications Inc.)
230 S Broad St, Philadelphia, PA 19102
Tel.: (215) 790-7800
Fax: (215) 790-9751
E-Mail: hello@karmaverse.com

Web Site: karmaagency.com

Employees: 20

Agency Specializes In: Advertising, Education, Government/Political, Legal Services

Revenue: $2,000,000

Caroline Kennedy *(Pres)*
Kate Allison *(CEO)*
Natalie Kay *(Grp Acct Dir)*
Heather Dougherty *(Acct Dir)*
Sarah Ann Walters *(Acct Dir)*
Robin Atkinson *(Dir-Fin Mgmt)*
Ford Haegele *(Dir-Creative)*
Tracy Thompson *(Dir-Creative)*
Bruce Boyle *(Exec Strategist-Comm)*

Accounts:
American Lung Association
ElephantLibrary.org
TWC Group

KATALYST PUBLIC RELATIONS
663 Valley Ave Ste 202, Solana Beach, CA 92075
Tel.: (858) 481-5107
Fax: (858) 481-5107
E-Mail: info@katalyst-pr.com
Web Site: www.katalyst-pr.com

Year Founded: 2009

Agency Specializes In: Digital/Interactive, Event Planning & Marketing, Public Relations, Social Media

Katherine Randall *(Owner)*

Accounts:
The Cat Eye Club
I Love Poke Festival
Souplantation & Sweet Tomatoes
Yoga Six

KATHY DAY PUBLIC RELATIONS
2440 Maylen Cir, Anchorage, AK 99516
Tel.: (907) 868-4884
Web Site: www.kdprvirtual.com

Agency Specializes In: Crisis Communications, Event Planning & Marketing, Media Relations, Print, Public Relations, Radio

Kathy Day *(Pres)*
Elizabeth Odom *(Partner)*

Accounts:
Kenai River Sportfishing Association
The Salvation Army

KATHY HERNANDEZ & ASSOCIATES
2567 Porterview Way, Orlando, FL 32812
Tel.: (407) 381-0428
E-Mail: kathy@khapr.com
Web Site: www.khapr.com

Employees: 3
Year Founded: 2006

Agency Specializes In: Crisis Communications, Media Relations, Public Relations, Strategic Planning/Research

Kathy A. Hernandez *(Pres)*

Accounts:
American Resort Development Association
Dominican Republic National Hotel
The Family of Orange Lake Resorts
Lifestyle Holidays Vacation Resort
Pak UrDerm Travel Kit

KATHY SCHAEFFER AND ASSOCIATES, INC.
17 N State St Ste 1690, Chicago, IL 60602
Tel.: (312) 251-5100
Fax: (312) 251-0081
E-Mail: smart@ksapr.com
Web Site: www.ksapr.com

Agency Specializes In: Crisis Communications, Event Planning & Marketing, Media Relations, Media Training, Public Relations, Search Engine Optimization, Social Media

Kathy Schaeffer *(Pres)*

Accounts:
New-American Veterinary Medical Foundation

KAYE COMMUNICATIONS INC.
1515 S Federal Hwy Ste 103, Boca Raton, FL 33432-7404
Tel.: (561) 392-5166
Fax: (561) 392-5842
E-Mail: greatideasbegin@kcompr.com
Web Site: www.kcompr.com

Employees: 8

Agency Specializes In: Public Relations

Bonnie S. Kaye *(Founder, Pres & Sr Strategist)*
Jon Kaye *(COO & Sr Strategist-Mktg)*

Accounts:
Boca Raton Bridge Hotel
Boca Raton Resort & Club
Boston Market
California Pizza Kitchen
Cartier
Downtown Boca
Federal Realty Investment Trust Marketing, Public Relations
The Grand Estate Collection
Lifestyle Vacation Incentives
Loews Hotels
Muvico Theaters
Promise Healthcare
Radisson Aruba Resort & Casino
Royal Palm Place
Town Center at Boca Raton

KB NETWORK NEWS
(Formerly KBHall Creative Group)
156 5th Ave Penthouse 2, New York, NY 10010
Tel.: (212) 777-3455
Fax: (212) 352-2195
Web Site: www.kbnetworknews.com

Employees: 7

Agency Specializes In: Brand Development & Integration, Hospitality, Public Relations, Strategic Planning/Research

Karime Bakhoum *(Founder & Pres)*
Elana Levin *(Acct Exec)*
Samantha Meister *(Acct Exec)*

KB WOODS PUBLIC RELATIONS
2633 E Indian School Rd Ste 410, Phoenix, AZ 85016
Tel.: (602) 606-7047
Web Site: www.kbwoodspublicrelations.com

Agency Specializes In: Crisis Communications, Event Planning & Marketing, Market Research, Media Buying Services, Promotions, Public Relations, Social Media

Keith Woods *(Pres)*
Polly Palmer *(Dir-Media)*

Accounts:
Pat Moran
Private Client Group LLC
Start Fresh Executive Recovery

THE KBD GROUP LLC
500 E Plume St Ste 219, Norfolk, VA 23510
Tel.: (757) 333-6901
Web Site: www.thekbdgroup.com

Agency Specializes In: Brand Development & Integration, Media Planning, Public Relations, Social Media

Kelli B. Davis *(Founder & Principal)*

Accounts:
New-Kam Chancellor

KBHALL CREATIVE GROUP
(Name Changed to KB Network News)

KCD, INC.
450 W 15th St Ste 604, New York, NY 10011
Tel.: (212) 590-5100
Fax: (212) 590-5101
Web Site: www.kcdworldwide.com

Employees: 25
Year Founded: 1985

Agency Specializes In: Cosmetics, Event Planning & Marketing, Fashion/Apparel, Food Service, Public Relations, Travel & Tourism

Ed Filipowski *(Pres)*
Nan Richards *(Mng Dir)*
Julie Mannion *(Pres-Creative Svcs)*
Rachna Shah *(Exec VP-PR & Mng Dir-KCD Digital)*
Marty Griffeth *(Sr VP-Fin)*
Hallie Chrisman *(VP-PR)*
Matthew Bires *(Sr Dir-KCD LA)*
Souri Kim *(Sr Dir-Publicity)*
Adam McCollum *(Sr Dir)*
Danielle Mcgrory *(Dir-Digital PR)*
Michelle Viau *(Sr Mgr-Fashion)*

Accounts:
3.1 Phillip Lim
Anna Sui
Banana Republic
Givenchy
Gucci
Marc Jacobs
McQueen
Puma
Rag & Bone
Victoria's Secret
Zac Posen

KCD PUBLIC RELATIONS
2760 5th Ave Ste 215, San Diego, CA 92103
Tel.: (619) 955-7759
E-Mail: info@kcdpr.com
Web Site: www.kcdpr.com

Year Founded: 2009

Agency Specializes In: Content, Media Relations, Print, Public Relations, Social Media

Kevin Dinino *(Founder & Pres)*
Jarrad Clark *(Sr VP-Production)*
Matthew Bires *(Sr Dir-KCD LA)*
Souri Kim *(Sr Dir-Publicity)*
Danielle McGrory *(Dir-Digital PR)*
Michelle Viau *(Sr Mgr-Fashion)*

Public Relations Firms

Aaron Clayton *(Mgr-Production)*
Max Hill *(Mgr-Production)*
Ryan Hall *(Sr Acct Exec)*
Amanda Powers *(Acct Exec)*
Becky Parker *(Acct Coord)*

Accounts:
1st Global
The Advisor Center Media Relations
AIG Advisor Group (Agency of Record) Communications, Strategic
Pavia Systems, Inc.
New-San Diego Cyber Center of Excellence (Public Relations Agency of Record) Communications
Toppan Vite New York

KCSA STRATEGIC COMMUNICATIONS

880 3rd Ave 6th Fl, New York, NY 10022
Tel.: (212) 682-6300
Fax: (212) 697-0910
E-Mail: info@kcsa.com
Web Site: www.kcsa.com

Employees: 35
Year Founded: 1969

Agency Specializes In: Communications, Investor Relations, Public Relations

Breakdown of Gross Billings by Media: Pub. Rels.: 100%

Jeff Corbin *(CEO & Mng Partner)*
Herbert L. Corbin *(Mng Partner)*
Todd Fromer *(Mng Partner-IR)*
Lewis Goldberg *(Mng Partner)*
Jeffrey Goldberger *(Mng Partner)*
Danielle DeVoren *(Mng Dir)*
Garth Russell *(Mng Dir-IR)*

Accounts:
3Power Energy Group
4Kids Entertainment, Inc.; New York, NY
ACG New York (Public Relations Agency of Record) Media Relations
ACORN
ADDvantage Technologies Group
Adspace Networks; Burlingame, CA
Attitude Drinks (Agency of Record)
Attunity Ltd.
BioRestorative Therapies
Bixby Energy Systems
Canadian Oil Recovery & Remediation Enterprises Ltd. Communication, Investor Relations Programs
Cascal N.V.
Cellufun
ChyronHego
Dewey Electronics Corp.; Oakland, NJ
East Coast Diversified Corporation Communication Strategy, Investor Relations, Public Relations
Electronic Motors Corporation
GAIN Capital Group (Agency of Record)
Generation Mortgage
Genesis Lease Limited; Shannon, Ireland
Global Traffic Network; New York, NY
New-ICM Registry Public Relations
IDX Capital
IEEE (Institute of Electrical & Electronics Engineers, Inc.)
IncrediMail, Ltd.; Tel Aviv, Israel
Index Oil and Gas Inc.
Insite Security Inc.; New York, NY
Jet Support Services, Inc.; Chicago, IL
KYP Systems, Inc. Public Relations, iKYP; 2008
LaBranche & Co Inc.; New York, NY
Lighting Science Group Corp.
Linkstorm; New York, NY Online Advertising System; 2007
Marchon Eyewear, Inc. Communications Campaign, Marchon3D, Public Relations
MedLink International, Inc. Investor Relations, Strategic Counsel
MG Concepts; Central Islip, NY
MGT Capital Investments, Inc.
Midland Oil & Gas, Ltd.
MobileBits Investor Relations, PR, Pringo Connect
NeuLion Inc.
Ophthalmic Imaging Systems; Sacramento, CA
Optibase Ltd.; Herzliyah, Israel
Pala Interactive LLC (Public Relations Agency of Record) Communications, Digital, Media, PalaCasino.com, PalaPoker.com, Social Media
Pennsylvania Real Estate Investment Trust; Philadelphia, PA
PFSweb, Inc
PolyMet Mining Corp.; Hoyt Lakes, MN
Radiant Oil & Gas Investor Relations
Rand Worldwide
RM Santilli Foundation MagneGas, MagneHydrogen, Media Outreach
New-RR Media Investor Relations
New-SDKA International Public Relations
SIGA Technologies Inc.; New York, NY
Silver Touch Investor Relations Program, Strategic Counsel
Skywire Software
SMTP, Inc Strategic Investor Relations
SpectrumDNA, Inc.; Park City, UT Investor Relations, Public Relations
Tanenbaum-Harber
Ubiquity
VSP Global
Wendy's/Arby's Group, Inc.
WisdomTree Investments; New York, NY
YTB International, Inc.; Wood River, IL

KEATING & CO.

285 West Broadway Ste 460, Florham Park, NJ 10013
Tel.: (212) 925-6900
E-Mail: rkeating@keatingco.com
Web Site: www.keatingco.com

Employees: 13
Year Founded: 1969

National Agency Associations: PRSA

Agency Specializes In: Brand Development & Integration, Business Publications, Business-To-Business, Collateral, Communications, Corporate Communications, Corporate Identity, Exhibit/Trade Shows, Financial, Government/Political, Health Care Services, High Technology, Information Technology, Leisure, Magazines, Newspapers & Magazines, Pharmaceutical, Public Relations, Strategic Planning/Research, T.V., Travel & Tourism

Rick Keating *(Partner)*

Accounts:
Allergan, Inc.
Bass
British Airways
Emirates
Nice
Nikon
Skanska
Wealth Touch

KEITH SHERMAN & ASSOCIATES, INC.

234 W 44th St Ste 1004, New York, NY 10036
Tel.: (212) 764-7900
Fax: (212) 764-0344
Web Site: www.ksa-pr.com

E-Mail for Key Personnel:
President: keith@ksa-pr.com

Employees: 7
Year Founded: 1989

National Agency Associations: PRSA

Agency Specializes In: Cable T.V., Communications, Corporate Communications, Entertainment, Event Planning & Marketing, Gay & Lesbian Market, Newspapers & Magazines, Public Relations, Publicity/Promotions, Travel & Tourism

Keith Sherman *(Owner)*
Scott Klein *(VP)*
Brett Oberman *(Acct Exec)*

Accounts:
54 BELOW Media Relations

KELLEY CHUNN & ASSOC.

Hibernian Hall 184 Dudley St Ste 106, Boston, MA 02119
Tel.: (617) 427-0997
Fax: (617) 427-3997
Toll Free: (866) 427-0997
E-Mail: kc4info@aol.com
Web Site: www.kelleychunn.com

Employees: 3
Year Founded: 1991

National Agency Associations: PRSA

Agency Specializes In: African-American Market, Asian Market, Bilingual Market, Brand Development & Integration, Collateral, Communications, Consulting, Corporate Identity, Entertainment, Event Planning & Marketing, Financial, Government/Political, Health Care Services, Hispanic Market, Media Buying Services, Planning & Consultation, Public Relations, Strategic Planning/Research

Kelley Chunn *(Owner)*

Accounts:
Black Ministerial Alliance of Greater Boston
Boston Public Health Commission
Central Boston Elder Services
Dana Farber Cancer Institute
Emerson College
Gillette
Harvard School of Public Health
The MA Department of Public Health
MassHousing
Nellie Mae Education Foundation
The New England Conservatory
Third Sector of New England

KELLOGG & CAVIAR LLC

25 Broadway 5th Fl Ste 5129, New York, NY 10004
Tel.: (646) 389-5235
E-Mail: info@kelloggandcaviar.com
Web Site: www.kelloggandcaviar.com

Agency Specializes In: Content, Digital/Interactive, Public Relations, Search Engine Optimization

Elizabeth Kellogg *(Founder & Pres)*
Michaela Rollings *(Acct Exec)*

Accounts:
New-Pizza Beach
New-Untamed Sandwiches

KELLY OLIVER PR INC

859 N Madison St Ste 101, Arlington, VA 22205
Tel.: (703) 307-9404
E-Mail: info@kellyoliverpr.com
Web Site: www.kellyoliverpr.com

Year Founded: 2013

Agency Specializes In: Content, Media Relations, Media Training, Public Relations

Kelly Oliver *(Owner & Principal)*

Accounts:
Parents Television Council

KELSEY MCBRIDE PR
PO Box 1541, Hermosa Beach, CA 90254
Tel.: (805) 807-9027
E-Mail: info@kelseymcbridepr.com
Web Site: www.kelseymcbridepr.com

Agency Specializes In: Print, Public Relations, Radio, Social Media

Accounts:
Author Nicholas Maze
Daniel Michael Salon

KELTON RESEARCH
9724 W Washington Blvd, Culver City, CA 90232
Tel.: (310) 479-4040
Fax: (310) 815-8109
Toll Free: (888) 853-5866
E-Mail: contact@keltonresearch.com
Web Site: keltonglobal.com

Employees: 30
Year Founded: 2003

Agency Specializes In: Advertising, Market Research, Public Relations, Strategic Planning/Research

Martin Eichholz *(Partner-Quantitative Res)*
Jen Pevar *(Sr Dir)*
Rachel Bonsignore *(Dir-Brand & Media Comm)*
John Phillips *(Assoc Dir-Design & Innovation Res)*
Allison Slotnick *(Assoc Dir-Quantitative Res)*
Esther Thomas *(Assoc Dir)*
Jenna Bellini *(Mgr-Quantitative Res)*

Accounts:
Bank of America
Hilton Worldwide
Logitech
McDonald's
Microsoft Corporation
NASA
P&G
Samsung

KEMPERLESNIK
500 Skokie Blvd 4th Fl, Northbrook, IL 60062
Tel.: (847) 850-1818
Fax: (847) 559-0406
E-Mail: info@kemperlesnik.com
Web Site: www.kemperlesnik.com

Employees: 30
Year Founded: 1979

National Agency Associations: BMA-PRSA

Agency Specializes In: Advertising, Event Planning & Marketing, Government/Political, Investor Relations, Public Relations, Sports Market

Steven Skinner *(CEO)*
Tom Valdiserri *(Exec VP)*
Amy Littleton *(Sr VP-PR)*
Steve Knipstein *(VP)*
Cybil Rose *(VP-PR)*
Megan Godfrey *(Acct Supvr-PR)*

Accounts:
AON Corporation
Aon eSolutions
Brunswick Billiards Brand Awareness, PR, Social Media
Chicago Elite Classic Ticket
Forsythe Solutions Group
Jackman Reinvention Events, Media Relations, Social Media
Maui Visitors Bureau
Prescient Solutions; Chicago, IL (Agency of Record) Brand Awareness, Media Relations Programs, Social Media Program
Sea Island Company Public Relations
Streamsong Resort Golf Operations, Media Relations
Vistage International Media Relations, Public Relations, Social Media Strategies
Wilson Golf Wilson Golf; 2007

KENWERKS
320 W 37th St 3rd Fl Ste 302, New York, NY 10018
Tel.: (646) 450-6536
E-Mail: ny@kenwerks.com
Web Site: www.kenwerks.com

Agency Specializes In: Brand Development & Integration, Public Relations, Social Media

Kenneth Loo *(Founder & CEO)*
Jennifer Gomez *(VP-Womens Div)*
John Jones *(VP)*
Michael Shane Stephens *(Sr Acct Mgr)*

Accounts:
New-Australia Luxe
New-Triton (Marketing & Public Relations Agency of Record) Brand Marketing

KEO MARKETING INC
4809 E Thistle Landing Dr Ste 100, Phoenix, AZ 85044
Tel.: (480) 413-2090
Fax: (480) 413-1267
E-Mail: info@keomarketing.com
Web Site: www.keomarketing.com

E-Mail for Key Personnel:
President: shelia@keomarketing.com
Creative Dir.: dave@keomarketing.com
Media Dir.: sue@keomarketing.com
Production Mgr.: dave@keomarketing.com
Public Relations: shelia@keomarketing.com

Employees: 10
Year Founded: 2000

National Agency Associations: AMA-BMA

Agency Specializes In: Affiliate Marketing, Brand Development & Integration, Business-To-Business, Collateral, Consulting, Content, Corporate Communications, Digital/Interactive, Direct Response Marketing, Direct-to-Consumer, E-Commerce, Electronic Media, Gay & Lesbian Market, Graphic Design, Information Technology, Integrated Marketing, Internet/Web Design, Logo & Package Design, Media Buying Services, Media Planning, Mobile Marketing, Multimedia, Paid Searches, Pharmaceutical, Planning & Consultation, Podcasting, Print, Production (Print), Public Relations, Publicity/Promotions, RSS (Really Simple Syndication), Regional, Retail, Sales Promotion, Search Engine Optimization, Social Marketing/Nonprofit, Strategic Planning/Research, Syndication, Technical Advertising, Teen Market, Viral/Buzz/Word of Mouth, Web (Banner Ads, Pop-ups, etc.), Women's Market, Yellow Pages Advertising

Approx. Annual Billings: $2,000,000

Sheila Kloefkorn *(Pres & CEO)*
Linda Capcara *(Dir-PR)*
Dave Fish *(Dir-Mktg & Creative)*
Ryan Grimes *(Dir-Bus Intelligence & Adv)*
Jenn McQuester *(Dir-Inbound Mktg & Project Mgmt)*
Chase Hunt *(Coord-Mktg)*

Accounts:
Avnet Electronics Distributor; 2009
CyrusOne Inc; 2011
Honeywell Industrial Automation & Control Solutions; 2010
OneNeck IT Services Managed Hosting & Application Development; 2009
Regions Financial Banking; 2009

KERMISH-GEYLIN PUBLIC RELATIONS
4 Park St, Harrington Park, NJ 07640
Tel.: (201) 750-3533
Fax: (201) 750-2010
E-Mail: info@kgpr.com
Web Site: www.kgpr.com

Employees: 10

Michael Geylin *(Pres)*
David Ferroni *(Gen Mgr-Midwest)*
Andrew Schupack *(Gen Mgr-New England)*
Rachel Geylin *(Supvr-Social Media)*

Accounts:
BMW Group Financial Services Communications, Media Relations
Don Schumacher Racing U.S. Army NHRA Top Fuel Team
Porsche Cars North America

KETCHUM
1285 Ave of the Americas, New York, NY 10019
Tel.: (646) 935-3900
Fax: (646) 935-4482
Web Site: www.ketchum.com

Employees: 280
Year Founded: 1923

National Agency Associations: COPF

Agency Specializes In: Affiliate Marketing, Asian Market, Brand Development & Integration, Business Publications, Business-To-Business, Cable T.V., Children's Market, Communications, Consulting, Consumer Goods, Consumer Marketing, Corporate Identity, Cosmetics, Crisis Communications, Customer Relationship Management, Direct-to-Consumer, E-Commerce, Electronic Media, Entertainment, Event Planning & Marketing, Exhibit/Trade Shows, Fashion/Apparel, Financial, Food Service, Government/Political, Graphic Design, Health Care Services, High Technology, Hispanic Market, Household Goods, Industrial, Information Technology, Integrated Marketing, International, Internet/Web Design, Investor Relations, Legal Services, Leisure, Market Research, Media Planning, Media Relations, Media Training, Medical Products, Multicultural, Multimedia, Pharmaceutical, Podcasting, Product Placement, Public Relations, Publicity/Promotions, RSS (Really Simple Syndication), Retail, Search Engine Optimization, Sponsorship, Sports Market, Strategic Planning/Research, Transportation, Travel & Tourism, Women's Market

Rob Flaherty *(Pres & CEO)*
Debra Forman *(Partner & Pres-Digital)*
Craig Mersky *(Partner, Gen Counsel & Sec)*
Marc Drechsler *(Partner, Sr VP & Head-Fin Comm)*
Roy Edmondson *(Partner & Mng Dir-Integrated Svcs)*
Mike Doyle *(Partner & Dir)*
James Kelly *(Partner & Dir-Strategic & Creative Plng-Global)*
Amanda Kowal Kenyon *(Partner & Dir-Strategy & Organizational Effectiveness)*
Kelley Skoloda *(Partner & Dir-Global Brand Mktg Practice)*
Scott Proper *(Partner)*

Esty Pujadas *(Partner)*
Karen Strauss *(Partner)*
John Weckenmann *(Partner)*
Kiersten Zweibaum *(Partner)*
Ann Wool *(Mng Dir)*
Bill Visone *(CFO)*
Jerry Olszewski *(Chief Client Officer)*
David Gallagher *(CEO-Europe)*
Jon Higgins *(CEO-Intl)*
Barri Friedman Rafferty *(CEO-North America)*
Paul Wood *(Exec VP & Dir-New York Corp Practice)*
Marcus Peterzell *(Exec VP-Ketchum Sports & Entertainment)*
Bob Osmond *(Sr VP & Acct Dir-Brand Practice)*
Joe Becker *(Sr VP & Dir-Digital Client Strategy)*
Sara Garibaldi *(Sr VP & Dir-Brand Practice)*
Amy McCarthy *(Sr VP & Dir-NY Healthcare Practice)*
Katherine Yustak *(Sr VP & Dir-HR-North America)*
Don Bartholomew *(Sr VP-Digital & Social Media Res)*
Patrick Wixted *(VP & Client Svcs Dir)*
Catherine Douglas *(VP)*
Anne Marie Kearns *(VP)*
Amy Podurgiel *(VP)*
Julie Ferriot *(Dir-Ketchum Social Responsibility-Global)*
Ryan Shell *(Sr Mgr-Online Comm)*
Alicia Stetzer *(Sr Mgr-Corp Comm)*
Dorothy Carter *(Mgr-CTN Production)*
Laura Alito *(Acct Supvr-Brand)*
Sara Bosco *(Acct Supvr)*
Alexandra Demetriades *(Acct Exec)*
Kate Malenczak *(Acct Exec)*
Kara Grossman *(Asst Acct Exec)*

Accounts:
7-Eleven
Altana Pharma
American Iron & Steel Institute
Avocados from Mexico Public Relations
Beam Global/Casa Sauza
Beam Global Wine & Spirits
Best Buy Co. Geek Squad
Boehringer-Ingelheim
California Dried Plum Board
California Strawberry Commission
Centers for Medicare & Medicaid Services International Classification of Diseases Diagnosis & Procedure Codes
Chase Card Services
Cleveland Clinic PR
The Clorox Company B-to-B, Clorox 2, Professional Products
ConAgra Foods
Daisy Brand Cottage Cheese; Dallas, TX Digital, Message Development, PR, Research & Analytics
DoubleTree
Dr Pepper Snapple Group
Eastman Kodak Company
FedEx Corporation
Frito-Lay Campaign: "Crash The Super Bowl", Doritos, Lay's, Public Relations, Tostitos
Fruit of the Loom; Bowling Green, KY Campaign: "Start Happy", Lucky Looms, Media, Public Relations
Genentech, Inc.
Gillette External Relations, PR
H&R Block, Inc.
Health Information Technology for Economic and Clinical Health (HITECH) Act
Hershey Co. Communications, Reese's, Social
Hertz Consumer PR, Press, Product Communications, Special Projects
Hyundai Motor America
IBM Corp.
Ikea IKEA North America Services, LLC
International Trucks Navistar
Kimberly-Clark Campaign: "Achoo", Public Relations, Travelling Promotions
Kohler Co. (Public Relations Agency of Record) Corporate & Consumer Brand Communication, Social Media, Strategic Counsel
Koninklijke Philips Electronics N.V.
MasterCard Consumer PR
Mattel
National Honey Board
National Pork Board
Nestle Dreyer's, Drumstick, Haagen-Dazs
Old World Industries PR, Strategic Positioning
Penn State Crisis Communications
Pernod Ricard USA (Entertainment Marketing Agency of Record) Digital, Malibu Island Spiced, Music Marketing, Strategy, Television
Pfizer Campaign: "Take The Right Steps To A Healthier You with Centrum"
Phonak PR
Procter & Gamble Global Olympic PR, Wella Koleston
Sharp Electronics Corporation
Sony Computer Entertainment America LLC Campaign: "The Nathan Drake Half-Tuck"
Takeda Pharmaceuticals
Toshiba
Toshiba America Medical Systems Inc.
Tourism Australia
U.S. Cellular; Chicago, IL Public Relations
U.S. Farmers & Ranchers Alliance
Visit Florida PR
Wal-Mart
Wendy's Campaign: "Pretzel Cheeseburger", Public Relations
World Triathlon Corporation

U.S. Branches:

Capstrat
1201 Edwards Mill Rd 1st Fl, Raleigh, NC 27607-3625
(See Separate Listing)

Ketchum
12555 W Jefferson Blvd Ste 250, Los Angeles, CA 90066
Tel.: (310) 437-2600
Fax: (310) 437-2599
Web Site: www.ketchum.com

Agency Specializes In: Sponsorship

Ann Wool *(Pres-Ketchum Sports & Entertainment)*
Dave Chapman *(Dir-Ketchum West)*
Christy Salcido *(Sr VP & Dir-Brand)*
Kevin Oates *(VP)*

Emanate
711 3rd Ave 12th Fl, New York, NY 10017
Tel.: (212) 805-8000
Fax: (212) 805-8098
E-Mail: kim.sample@emanatepr.com
Web Site: www.emanatepr.com

Employees: 50
Year Founded: 2006
National Agency Associations: COPF

Agency Specializes In: Brand Development & Integration, Public Relations, Sponsorship

Marissa Mastellone *(VP-Consumer Mktg)*
Lisa Rigney *(VP)*
Talley Summerlin *(VP)*
Barrett Tripp *(VP-Play Anywhere Content)*
Scott Cocchiere *(Dir-Creative Relevance)*
Katherine Ducker *(Dir)*
Blair Meisels *(Dir-Plng & Insights)*
Evelyn Sprigg *(Dir-Healthcare Mktg)*

Accounts:
AkzoNobel Glidden (PR Agency of Record)
Bank of America Corporation
Beiersdorf Public Relations, Social Media
Embassy Suites Hotels; McLean, VA (Agency of Record) Embassy Suites Hotels Awkward Family Vacation Photo Contest
Hilton Worldwide Embassy Suites, Hampton, Public Relations
House of Mandela Digital, Media Relations, Royal Reserve, Thembu
KFC (Consumer & Corporate Public Relations Agency of Record) Social Media
LYSOL
Materne North America GoGo squeeZ, Integrated Marketing Campaign, Social Media
Nissan PR
Philips Electronics North America Corporation Norelco
Royal Caribbean Cruises, Ltd. Celebrity Cruises

Ketchum
1050 Battery St, San Francisco, CA 94111-1209
Tel.: (415) 984-6100
Fax: (415) 984-6102
E-Mail: dave.chapman@ketchum.com
Web Site: www.ketchum.com

Employees: 100

National Agency Associations: COPF

Agency Specializes In: Brand Development & Integration, Consumer Marketing, Electronic Media, Event Planning & Marketing, Exhibit/Trade Shows, New Product Development, Point of Purchase, Point of Sale, Public Relations, Sponsorship, Strategic Planning/Research

Suzanne Maloney *(Partner, Sr VP & Dir-Strategic & Creative Plng)*
Dave Chapman *(Partner & Dir)*
Cheryl Damian *(Sr VP-Sustainability)*
Angela Fernandez *(VP & Acct Dir)*
Chris Jones *(VP & Dir-Creative)*
Alicia Balkrishna *(VP & Acct Supvr)*
Erin Jundef *(Sr Specialist-Media)*
Shannon Carroll *(Mng Supvr-Digital Strategist)*

Accounts:
California Dried Plum Board
California Milk Advisory Board; 2008
Chase Card Services
The Clorox Company
Haagen Dazs
Kikkoman International Inc.
Liberty Mutual Group; Boston, MA
Mattel, Inc.

Ketchum
2000 L St NW Ste 300, Washington, DC 20036-4923
Tel.: (202) 835-8800
Fax: (202) 835-8879
Web Site: www.ketchum.com

National Agency Associations: COPF

Agency Specializes In: Corporate Identity, Government/Political, Health Care Services, High Technology, Legal Services

Kathy Jeavons *(Partner & Assoc Dir)*
Katie Conover *(Sr VP & Dir-Media Rels-Pub & Corp Affairs)*
Kim Essex *(Sr VP & Dir-North American Food Practice)*
Christopher Handler *(Sr VP & Dir-Social Mktg Practice)*
Matthew Simmons *(VP & Acct Supvr)*
Erica Saviano Tsioutas *(VP & Sr Specialist-Media)*
Bill Mashek *(VP)*
Jeremy Pelofsky *(VP-Media Strategy)*
Noam Gelfond *(Dir-Bus Dev)*
Ward Cole *(Assoc Dir-Creative-Ketchum Digital)*
Casey Myburgh *(Acct Supvr)*
Maggie Travis *(Sr Acct Exec)*

Rachel Winer *(Sr Strategist-Digital-Paid Media)*
Rebecca Miller *(Acct Exec)*
Jayshri Patel *(Acct Exec)*
Sean Fitzpatrick *(Mng Acct Supvr)*

Accounts:
American Legacy Foundation Campaign: "Truth", Public Relations
Aspen Dental Management, Inc. Public Relations
Centers for Medicare & Medicaid Services
Clorox
Department of Health & Human Services IT Promo
The Embassy of Ecuador Economic Development, Tourism, Trade
Geek Squad
Gillette
The Hertz Corporation
Kodak Graphic Communications Group
Legacy Campaign: "Ugly Truth", Digital, Public Relations Agency of Record, Social Media
New-Library of Congress 2015 National Book Festival, Media Relations
Penn State University
Pfizer
Vladimir V. Putin Public Relations

Ketchum
3500 Lenox Rd Ste 1250, Atlanta, GA 30326
Tel.: (404) 879-9000
Fax: (404) 879-9001
E-Mail: info@ketchum.com
Web Site: www.ketchum.com

National Agency Associations: COPF

Agency Specializes In: Brand Development & Integration, Consumer Marketing, Corporate Identity, Electronic Media, Hispanic Market, Investor Relations, Public Relations, Sponsorship, Sports Market

Hilary Hanson McKean *(Partner & Mng Dir-Global Practices)*
Sharon Jones *(Sr VP & Dir-HR, Diversity & Inclusion-North America)*
Lauren Butler *(Sr VP-Brand Mktg)*
Diana Garza Ciarlante *(Dir-Atlanta)*
Kristin Kelley *(Acct Supvr)*
Stephanie Glessner *(Sr Acct Exec)*
Randy Spoon *(Acct Exec)*
Lauren Fincher *(Asst Acct Exec)*

Accounts:
New-Build-A-Bear (Public Relations Agency of Record); 2015
The Clorox Company
Cox Communications
Eastman Kodak Company
FedEx Corporation
Georgia-Pacific
The Home Depot
Husqvarna Chainsaws, Garden Tractors, Lawn Mowers, Public Relations, Trimmers
IBM
Manheim
Medtronic Inc.
St. Jude's Children's Research Hospital

Ketchum
E Randolph Ste 3600, Chicago, IL 60601-5925
Tel.: (312) 228-6800
Fax: (312) 228-6868
Web Site: www.ketchum.com

Employees: 50

National Agency Associations: COPF

Agency Specializes In: Brand Development & Integration, Communications, Public Relations, Strategic Planning/Research

Peter Fleischer *(Partner)*
Rand Carpenter *(Sr VP & Acct Dir)*
Kim Essex *(Sr VP & Dir-North American Food Practice)*
Corinne Gudovic *(Sr VP & Dir-Brand Practice-Home & Family)*
Ben Foster *(Sr VP-Digital Strategy)*
Laura Bernhardt *(VP-Bus Dev)*
Ilana Shenitzer *(VP)*
Linda Eatherton *(Dir-Global Food & Nutrition)*
Bill Zucker *(Dir-Midwest)*
Kristen Neuckranz *(Sr Acct Supvr)*
Rachel Provenzano *(Acct Supvr)*
Jill Howard *(Mng Acct Supvr)*

Accounts:
Ardent Mills
Beam Global Wine & Spirits
Friskies
Frito-Lay, Inc. Doritos
Horizon Organic
Kimberly-Clark Cottonelle Bath Tissue, Kleenex Brand Facial Tissue, Public Relations, Scott Brand Bath Tissue & Paper Towels, Viva Brand Paper Towels
PureCircle Public Relations, Stevia Sweetner
Welch's (Agency of Record)
Wendy's Campaign: "Pretzel Cheeseburger"
Whirlpool Affresh, Amana Brands, Maytag, PR, Whirlpool, Whirlpool Water Filtration
WhiteWave, Inc.

Ketchum
6 PPG Pl, Pittsburgh, PA 15222-5425
Tel.: (412) 456-3500
Fax: (412) 456-3834
E-Mail: info@ketchum.com
Web Site: www.ketchum.com

Employees: 20

National Agency Associations: COPF

Agency Specializes In: Business-To-Business, Communications, Consumer Marketing, High Technology, Public Relations, Sponsorship

Debbie Brannan *(Partner & Controller)*
Kelley Skoloda *(Partner & Dir-Global Brand Mktg Practice)*
Bill Visone *(CFO)*
David Gallagher *(CEO-Europe & Chm-London)*
Pete Donina *(Exec VP-IT)*
Stacey Neighbour *(Assoc Dir-Talent Acq)*

Accounts:
American Iron & Steel Institute (AISI)
Best Buy
Canned Manufacturer's Institute

Ketchum
Harwood Ctr 1999 Bryan St Ste 2500, Dallas, TX 75201
Tel.: (214) 259-3400
Fax: (214) 259-3450
Web Site: www.ketchum.com

Employees: 12

National Agency Associations: COPF

Agency Specializes In: Brand Development & Integration, Corporate Identity, High Technology, Hispanic Market, Sports Market

Lorraine Thelian *(Vice Chm)*
Sean Fitzgerald *(Partner & Dir-Corp & Pub Affairs Practice-North America)*
Bill Visone *(CFO)*
Jon Higgins *(Sr Partner & CEO- EMEA)*
Barri Friedman Rafferty *(CEO-North America)*
Jamey Peters *(Dir-South)*

Accounts:
New-Build-A-Bear
Nokia

Zocalo Group
200 E Randolph St Ste 4200, Chicago, IL 60601-6517
Tel.: (312) 596-6300
Fax: (312) 596-6310
E-Mail: info@zocalogroup.com
Web Site: www.zocalogroup.com

Employees: 38
Year Founded: 2007

National Agency Associations: WOMMA

Agency Specializes In: Advertising, Business-To-Business, Sponsorship, Viral/Buzz/Word of Mouth

Emily Bader *(Partner)*
Andrea Wood *(Mng Dir)*
Paul M. Rand *(Pres/CEO-Zocalo Grp)*
Allison Branen *(VP & Acct Dir)*
Agatha Kubalski *(VP & Acct Dir)*
Jeffrey Woelker *(VP & Dir-Digital)*

Foreign Branches:

Gricorp Ketchum
Bosque de Ciruelos 186-301, Col Bosques de las Lomas, Mexico, DF 11700 Mexico
Tel.: (52) 55 5245 8855
Fax: (52) 55 5245 8851
Web Site: www.ketchum.com

E-Mail for Key Personnel:
President: alejandro.rodriguez@ketchum.com

Year Founded: 2000

Agency Specializes In: Brand Development & Integration, Communications, Government/Political, High Technology, Investor Relations, Public Relations, Strategic Planning/Research

Alejandro Rodriguez *(Pres & Gen Mgr)*

Accounts:
Fashion TV
ISACA

Ketchum ICON Singapore
(Formerly ICON International Communications)
28 Maxwell Rd, #03-03 RedDot Traffic Bldg, Singapore, 069120 Singapore
Tel.: (65) 6220 2623
Fax: (65) 6220 0610
E-Mail: enquiries@ketchum.com.sg
Web Site: www.ketchum.com/singapore

Employees: 50

John Bailey *(Mng Dir)*
Bill Visone *(CFO)*
Judith Knight *(Sr VP)*
Serada Chellam *(Acct Dir)*
Joyce Peh *(Acct Mgr)*
Ling Hui Seah *(Sr Acct Exec)*
Jen Stewart *(Acct Exec)*
Liz Yip *(Acct Exec)*

Accounts:
adidas; Singapore Public Relations
Applied Materials
Arup
Barclays Singapore Open PR
Baskin-Robbins Marketing, Public Relations
The Boeing Company
Boeing
Bridgestone
Carlson Hotels Worldwide Park Plaza Sukhumvit
Garuda Indonesia

Public Relations Firms

GlaxoSmithKline
Hilton Worldwide
Kodak Graphic Communications Group
Lufthansa
Nippon Paint Corporate Branding, Media Relations, Public Relations
Overseas Union Enterprise Ltd.
Siemens Pte Ltd
Westpac
Wildlife Reserves Singapore

Ketchum Canada
33 Bloor St E Ste 1607, Toronto, ON M4W 3H1 Canada
Tel.: (416) 355-7400
Fax: (416) 355-7420
E-Mail: Geoffrey.rowan@ketchum.com
Web Site: www.ketchum.com

Employees: 40

Agency Specializes In: Brand Development & Integration, Communications, Consumer Marketing, Health Care Services, High Technology, Public Relations

Emma Capombassis *(Sr VP)*
Erin Manning *(VP-Brand Mktg)*
Jennifer Beck *(Acct Supvr)*
Leslie Jackson *(Acct Supvr)*
Nicole McKnight *(Acct Supvr)*
Miriam Sherkey *(Sr Acct Exec)*
Samantha Campana *(Acct Exec)*
Hayley Findlay *(Acct Exec)*
Giovana Chichito *(Assoc Acct Exec)*
Tricia Weagant *(Mng Acct Supvr)*

Accounts:
Avokia Inc.
Beiersdorf Canada Inc.
Borden Ladner Gervais
Ceridian
ConAgra
IBM
Kodak Graphic Communications Group
Lenovo Inc.
Nokia
White Wave Foods

Ketchum Pleon Public Affairs
Avenue des Arts 44, 1040 Brussels, Belgium
Tel.: (32) 2 213 40 40
Fax: (32) 2 213 40 49
E-Mail: hermann.drummer@pleon.com
Web Site: www.ketchum.com

Employees: 15

Agency Specializes In: Government/Political, Public Relations

Peter Otten *(Partner & Mng Dir)*
Auke Haagsma *(Head-Pub Affairs)*
Alessandra Teston *(Acct Dir)*
Bram Smets *(Dir-Bus Unit)*
Amandine Servotte *(Acct Exec)*
Jordy Van Overmeire *(Acct Exec)*

Ketchum Pleon Roma
Via Cassia 1081, 00189 Rome, Italy
Tel.: (39) 06 3026 0341
Fax: (39) 06 3026 0344
Web Site: www.ketchum.com

Employees: 3

Agency Specializes In: Public Relations

Marcello Laugelli *(Bus Dir)*

Accounts:
Ai-Software
CeBit
Datamat
GME

Ketchum Pleon
35-41 Folgate Street, London, E1 6BX United Kingdom
Tel.: (44) 207 611 3500
Fax: (44) 207 479 5657
Web Site: www.ketchum.com

Employees: 150
Year Founded: 1981

Agency Specializes In: Public Relations

Deirdre Murphy *(Partner & Sr Mng Dir)*
Jo-Ann Robertson *(Partner & Mng Dir-Corp & Pub Affairs-UK)*
Harry King *(Mng Dir)*
David Gallagher *(CEO-Europe)*
David Vindel *(Mng Dir-European Tech)*
Patrick Blewer *(Dir-Practice)*
Mike Copland *(Dir-Intl Partner Rels)*
Rupert Lewis *(Dir-Practice-Corp & Pub Affairs)*
Kate Matlock *(Assoc Dir-Digital)*

Accounts:
New-Dwell Public Relations, Social Media
FedEx
Geek Squad
IBM
IMEDEEN PR
Roche
World Economic Forum

Ketchum Pleon
Amsterdamseweg 206, 1182 HL Amstelveen, NL-1070 Netherlands
Tel.: (31) 20 487 4000
Fax: (31) 20 669 7265
E-Mail: tim.deboer@pleon.com
Web Site: www.ketchum.com

Employees: 45

Agency Specializes In: Public Relations

Tim De Boer *(CEO)*
Annelies De Boer *(CEO-Netherlands)*

Accounts:
G6 Hospitality LLC
IBM
Ministry of Economic Affairs

Ketchum Pleon
Bahnstrasse 2, 40212 Dusseldorf, Germany
Tel.: (49) 211 9541 0
Fax: (49) 211 5516 51
E-Mail: timo.sieg@pleon.com
Web Site: www.ketchum.com

Employees: 100
Year Founded: 1996

Agency Specializes In: Public Relations

Dirk Popp *(CEO)*
Kristina Schepers *(Project Mgr-Intl Mktg)*
Eliza Steingassner *(Project Mgr-Mktg, PR & Events)*
Tasso Enzweiler *(Mgr)*
Isabel Estor *(Key Acct Mgr)*

Accounts:
Arcor
Avnet
Deutschland GmbH
Heidelberger Druckmaschinen AG
Lucent
Netscalibur
Oracle
Software AG
SuSE Linux AG
WRQ

Ketchum-Public Relations Ltd.
10/F Tower A, Vantone Center, No 6, Chaowal Street, Chaoyang District, Beijing, 100020 China
Tel.: (86) 10 5907 0055
Fax: (86) 10 5907 0188
E-Mail: info@knprbj.com
Web Site: www.ketchum.com

Employees: 30

Agency Specializes In: Brand Development & Integration, Corporate Identity, Health Care Services, High Technology, Public Relations

Bruce Shu *(Mng Dir-China)*
Tiffany Hu *(VP & Deputy Gen Mgr of Shanghai)*

Accounts:
FedEx
Voith

Ketchum-Public Relations
Rm 2707-2710 Tower One Kerry Everbright City, No 218 Tian Mu Rd W, Shanghai, 200070 China
Tel.: (86) 21 5289 5838
Fax: (86) 21 5289 5363
E-Mail: info@knprsh.com
Web Site: www.ketchum.com

Agency Specializes In: Brand Development & Integration, Corporate Identity, Crisis Communications, Health Care Services, High Technology, Public Relations

Tiffany Hu *(VP & Deputy Gen Mgr)*
George Gu *(VP)*
Corrie Wollet *(VP-Consumer Practice-Shanghai)*
Emma Chen *(Sr Acct Mgr)*
Mandy Mao *(Sr Acct Mgr)*
Gavin Kwan *(Acct Supvr)*

Accounts:
Almond Board of California
FedEx
McDonald's
P&G Vidal Sassoon
TAG Heuer

Ketchum-Public Relations
Room 2003 Peace World Plaza 362-366 Huanshi Dong Lu, Guangzhou, 510060 China
Tel.: (86) 20 8387 0810
Fax: (86) 20 8385 2476
E-Mail: eddi.yang@knprgz.com
Web Site: www.ketchum.com

Employees: 15

Agency Specializes In: Brand Development & Integration, Communications, Corporate Identity, Health Care Services, High Technology, Public Relations

Joe Tong *(Gen Mgr)*

Accounts:
FedEx
Grand View Plaza
Mead Johnson
Skechers

Ketchum-Public Relations

33rd Floor Two Chinachem Exchange Square, 338 King's Road, North Point, China (Hong Kong)
Tel.: (852) 2566 1311
Fax: (852) 2510 8199
E-Mail: info@knprhk.com
Web Site: www.ketchum.com

Agency Specializes In: Brand Development & Integration, Communications, Corporate Identity, Event Planning & Marketing, Health Care Services, High Technology, Investor Relations, Public Relations, Strategic Planning/Research

Kenneth Chu *(Partner & CEO)*
Simeon Mellalieu *(Partner & Gen Mgr)*
Bruce Shu *(Mng Dir-China)*
Kent Lau *(Sr Acct Mgr)*
Yvonna Law *(Acct Mgr)*
Gladys Kwok *(Acct Exec-Corp, Tech Practice & Tech Focus)*

Accounts:
FedEX
GP Batteries
ISACA
Kodak Graphic Communications Group

Ketchum Publico

(Formerly Pleon Publico)
Neulinggasse 37, A-1030 Vienna, Austria
Tel.: (43) 1 717 860
Fax: (43) 1 717 86 60
E-Mail: office@ketchum-publico.at
Web Site: www.ketchum.com

Employees: 40

Agency Specializes In: Public Relations

Saskia Wallner *(CEO)*

Accounts:
AGES
British American Tobacco
Constantia Packaging
McDonald's
Nestle
Novartis Austria
T-Mobile US

Ketchum Seoul

(Formerly InComm Brodeur)
24th Fl City Air Tower, 159-9 Samsung-Dong Kangnam Ku, Seoul, Korea (South)
Tel.: (82) 2 2016 7114
Fax: (82) 2 516 4938
Web Site: www.ketchum.com

Employees: 70
Year Founded: 1993

Jon Higgins *(Sr Partner & CEO-Intl)*
Jay Gieun Kim *(VP)*
Yonnie Woo *(Gen Mgr)*
Jamie Yaewon Oh *(Sr Acct Exec)*

Accounts:
ADT
Corning
Interbrand
Lilly
Morgan Stanley
Polycom
Rambus
Sony Ericsson

Ketchum Spain

Luchana 23 4, 28010 Madrid, Spain
Tel.: (34) 91 788 3200
Fax: (34) 91 788 3299
E-Mail: ketchum.spain@ketchumpleon.com
Web Site: www.ketchum.com

Agency Specializes In: Communications, Consumer Marketing, Corporate Identity, Environmental, Financial, Health Care Services, High Technology, Public Relations

Tony Noel *(Chm & CEO)*
Ludi Garcia *(Dir-Digital)*
Rosa Fernandez Conde *(Assoc Dir)*
Ana Gonzalez *(Assoc Dir)*

Accounts:
Abello
AECC
Ariel
Avaya
The Boston Consulting Group
BP Solar
Braun
Dunhill Pursuit
Eroski
Kodak Graphic Communications Group
LINE Corporation
Medion
Microsoft
MTV
Procter & Gamble
Roche
Samsonite

Ketchum Taipei

3F-2 No 51 Sec 2 Keelung Rd, 110 Hsinyi District, Taipei, Taiwan
Tel.: (886) 2 27383038
Fax: (886) 2 27383035
E-Mail: marian.ma@knprtw.com.tw
Web Site: www.ketchum.com

Employees: 8

Agency Specializes In: Bilingual Market, Communications, Corporate Identity, Event Planning & Marketing, Health Care Services, High Technology, Public Relations, Strategic Planning/Research

Ketchum

Via Fatebenefratelli 19, 20121 Milan, Italy
Tel.: (39) 02 6241 1911
Fax: (39) 02 2901 1411
E-Mail: info@ketchum.it
Web Site: www.ketchum.com/milan

Employees: 32

Agency Specializes In: Brand Development & Integration, Communications, Corporate Identity, Financial, Health Care Services, High Technology, Publicity/Promotions

Andrea Cornelli *(CEO & VP)*
Cristina Risciotti *(Partner & Bus Dir)*
Silvia Cattaneo *(Sr Acct Dir)*
Elena Faccio *(Bus Dir)*
Lucia Ricchetti *(Dir-Bus)*

Accounts:
Baxter
Cesvi
Dymo
Edison
Emirates
Fimap
Intel
Kodak Graphic Communications Group
Lilly
Marionnaud
Mars
NFI
Samsonite
Scotwork
Shire
Takeda
Terumo
Titan
Valentino
viamichelin.com
Volkswagen Group of America, Inc.
Whirlpool

Ketchum

54 Rue de Clichy, CEDEX, 75009 Paris, 08 France
Tel.: (33) 1 53 32 56 01
Fax: (33) 1 53 32 56 28
Web Site: ketchumfrance.wordpress.com/

Employees: 65
Year Founded: 1994

Agency Specializes In: Public Relations

Philippe Beteille *(Pres)*
Jean Martial-Ribes *(Partner)*
Christophe Gerault *(CFO)*
Christelle Lepietre *(Acct Dir)*
Claire Mariat *(Acct Dir)*
Elise Mourocq *(Acct Dir)*
Laurie Pierrin *(Acct Dir)*
Alain Rousseau *(Dir-Corp Affairs)*
Bastien Rousseau *(Acct Mgr)*

Accounts:
Adobe
FedEx
Jaeger-Le Coultre La Squadra
Kodak Graphic Communications Group Campaign: "Kodak Frees Your Facebook Photos", Kodak EasyShare Gallery
Suntory
Symantec
Whirlpool; 2005

Ketchum

35-41 Folgate St, London, E1 6BX United Kingdom
Tel.: (44) 20 7611 3500
Fax: (44) 20 7611 3501
Web Site: www.ketchum.com

Agency Specializes In: Brand Development & Integration, Communications, Consumer Marketing, Corporate Identity, Electronic Media, Graphic Design, Health Care Services, High Technology, Public Relations

Denise Kaufmann *(Partner & CEO)*
Clare Pring *(Partner & Mng Dir-Brand)*
Patricia Dessert *(Mng Dir)*
Deirdre Murphy *(COO)*
David Vindel *(Mng Dir-European Tech)*
Tara Munday *(Dir-European Food & Beverage Practice)*
Ben Saft *(Dir-Practice-Corp & Public Affairs)*
Darren Young *(Dir-Practice-Corp & Pub Affairs)*

Accounts:
AstraZeneca Atacand
Britvic/Pepsi
Cambridge Consultants Media Relations
New-Dwell Public Relations, Social Media
FedEx
Gillette for Women
HBO
Hertz Consumer PR, Press, Product Communications, Special Projects
LINE Corporation
MasterCard Europe Campaign: "Dirty Cash", Multimedia, Press, Public Relations, Social Media, Video
The Movember Foundation Communications, Public Relations
Nissan UEFA Super Cup, Union of European

Football Associations Champions League
Orange
Perfect World Ice Cream PR, Social Media
Pfizer Lipitor
RingCentral PR
Roche HIV Pharmaceuticals
Saxony
Sony
UCB

Ketchum
R Alvaro Rodrigues 182-2 andar, Brooklin, Sao Paulo, SP 04582-000 Brazil
Tel.: (55) 11 5096 4334
Fax: (55) 11 5096 4335
E-Mail: rp@ketchum.com.br
Web Site: www.ketchum.com

Employees: 130
Year Founded: 1987

Agency Specializes In: Brand Development & Integration, Communications, Electronic Media, Health Care Services, High Technology, Public Relations

Valeria Perito *(CEO & Partner)*
Gabriel Araujo *(Exec Creative Dir)*
Anderson Borges *(Art Dir)*
Rosana Monteiro *(Dir)*
Rosana Rossi *(Mgr-Fin)*
Sergio Avila *(Planner)*
Daniel Kfouri *(Copywriter)*
Jerry Olszewski *(Sr Partner)*

Accounts:
Burger King
Caloi
Cielo
FedEx
Friboi
Oracle
SBCBM Campaign: "Obesity Without Marks"
Visa Credit Card

KETNER GROUP
8911 Capital of Texas Hwy Ste 4220, Austin, TX 78759
Tel.: (512) 794-8876
E-Mail: info@ketnergroup.com
Web Site: www.ketnergroup.com

Agency Specializes In: Collateral, Media Training, Public Relations, Retail, Social Media

Jeff Ketner *(Pres)*
Catherine Reeds *(VP)*
Sara Lasseter *(Acct Mgr)*
Kirsty Hughan *(Acct Mgr)*
Kathleen See *(Acct Exec)*

Accounts:
New-360pi
New-Order Dynamics

KEYBRIDGE COMMUNICATIONS
1722 A Wisconsin Ave NW Ste 21, Washington, DC 20007
Tel.: (202) 471-4228
E-Mail: info@keybridge.biz
Web Site: www.keybridgecommunications.com

Year Founded: 2003

Agency Specializes In: Graphic Design, Media Training, Public Relations, Radio, Social Media

Sam Ryan *(Pres & CEO)*
David White *(COO)*
Robby Schrum *(VP)*
Kali Edwards *(Dir-Art)*
Mike McElhaney *(Dir-Web Dev Tech)*
Laura Scharfeld *(Dir-Bus Dev)*
Maria Sliwa *(Dir-Brdcst)*
Kristen Thomaselli *(Dir-Earned Media)*
Rich Zeoli *(Dir-Media Trng)*
Cynthia Shultz Cusick *(Mgr-Ops)*

Accounts:
Fitdeck, Inc.

KIDSTUFF PUBLIC RELATIONS
9504 Union Valley Rd, Black Earth, WI 53515
Tel.: (608) 767-1102
Fax: (608) 767-1103
E-Mail: info@kidstuffpr.com
Web Site: www.kidstuffpr.com

Year Founded: 1994

Agency Specializes In: Event Planning & Marketing, Media Relations, Media Training, Public Relations

Lisa Orman *(Founder & Pres)*

Accounts:
Brixy Marketing, Public Relations
Famosa Group
Sugar Lulu

KILROY COMMUNICATIONS
9630 W Linebaugh Ave, Tampa, FL 33626
Tel.: (813) 610-3211
Web Site: www.kilroycommunications.com

Year Founded: 2013

Agency Specializes In: Brand Development & Integration, Content, Crisis Communications, Digital/Interactive, Event Planning & Marketing, Internet/Web Design, Logo & Package Design, Media Relations, Public Relations, Strategic Planning/Research

Lynn Kilroy *(Founder & Mng Dir)*
Michelle Sulzer *(Creative Dir)*
Cloe Cabrera *(Dir-Social Media Content)*
Scott Eggert *(Dir-Digital)*
Kasey Waterman *(Mgr-Comm)*

Accounts:
Locale Market

KIMBALL COMMUNICATIONS LLC
417 Cattell St, Easton, PA 18042
Tel.: (610) 559-7585
Fax: (610) 559-7796
E-Mail: info@kimballpr.com
Web Site: www.kimballpr.com

Year Founded: 1995

Agency Specializes In: Communications, Crisis Communications, Media Relations, Public Relations, Publicity/Promotions

Gary Kimball *(Pres)*
Rod Hughes *(VP)*
Samantha Kimball *(Mgr-Content)*
Mark Ladley *(Mgr-PR)*
Lisa Kimball *(Strategist & Writer)*
Elizabeth Rubino *(Coord-Media Rels)*

Accounts:
Brownyard Group
Ecopax PR, Strategy
Health Care Council Of Lehigh Valley Strategic Communications
Invision
Napco
PMA Companies
Russell Program Managers; Westminster, MD
Sorilito Foods LLC In-House Social Media, PR
Vera Track

KING + COMPANY
(Formerly The Morris + King Company)
101 5th Ave, New York, NY 10003
Tel.: (212) 561-7450
Fax: (212) 561-7461
E-Mail: info@kingcompr.com
Web Site: www.kingcompr.com/

Employees: 20

Agency Specializes In: Public Relations

Revenue: $2,000,000

Judith R. King *(Founder & Owner)*
Micheal Richards *(Partner & COO)*
Caren Browning *(Partner & Exec VP)*
Chelsey Tolerico *(Sr VP)*
Elizabeth Hanske *(Sr Dir-Media)*
Lindsey Steinseifer *(Acct Supvr)*
Juyoung Lee *(Sr Acct Exec)*
Victoria Shannon *(Sr Acct Exec)*

Accounts:
ABC Carpet & Home; New York, NY PR Campaign
Akimbo PR
Alaris Health Public Relations
Aperture Foundation; New York, NY Public Relations Campaign
Arby's Foundation; Atlanta, GA Brand Strategy
Beliefnet
Biomarkers Consortium
BlueCava (Agency of Record)
BUZZMEDIA
Cafe Metro PR Campaign
City Parks Foundation; New York, NY Central Park Summer Stage Programming
CNBC
The Cult of Individuality
Dachis Group
Davenport Theatrical Enterprises
Dirtball Fashion PR
Dolphin Entertainment (Agency of Record) Children's Entertainment; 2008
emortal.com (Agency of Record) Software Applications
Engage121 (Agency of Record)
Flu Near You PR
fluid; 2007
Friends of Hudson River Park/Hudson River Park Trust Media, Public Relations
Fullstack Academy (Agency of Record) Media, Public Relations
GOOD Integrated Media; 2008
Heifer International Public Relations
Helen Diller Family Foundation
Jeffrey Scheuer The Big Picture; 2007
Juice from the Raw (Agency of Record) Public Relations
Kidz Bop (Agency of Record)
LBi IconNicholson US (Agency of Record)
Leveraging Investment in Creativity Branding, Messaging
Luxury Retreats Public Relations
Lymphoma Research Foundation Media, Public Relations
New York Code + Design Academy Public Relations
Qtrax; 2007
Remy Martin USA
Rensselaer Polytechnic Institute (Agency of Record) Molecules to the Max!
The Resolution Project PR
The Ritz-Carlton Hotel Company, LLC
Rodale's E-Commerce Site, PR
Scarpasa (Agency of Record) Lifestyle, Luxury & Consumer Sectors, Online Shoe Store, Public Relations Campaign
Sonar (Agency of Record)

Tapad PR Campaign
Taste of the NFL Party with a Purpose
Tourette Syndrome Association Media, Public Relations
Tracx PR
True Fit (Agency of Record) Consumer, Digital, Fashion, Lifestyle
University of California; San Francisco, CA Helen Diller Family Comprehensive Cancer Center Research Building
Worldwide Orphans Foundation Messaging

KIP MORRISON & ASSOCIATES
101 S Robertson Blvd 213, Los Angeles, CA 90048
Tel.: (310) 274-6726
Web Site: www.kipmorrison.com

Agency Specializes In: Brand Development & Integration, Media Relations, Public Relations

Kip Morrison *(Pres)*
Brooke Cockrell *(VP)*

Accounts:
New-The Ecology Center

KIP-PR INC
154 Grand St Sixth fl, New York, NY 10013
Tel.: (646) 568-3177
E-Mail: info@kip-pr.com
Web Site: www.kip-pr.com

Agency Specializes In: Brand Development & Integration, Event Planning & Marketing, Public Relations, Social Media

Christine Galasso *(Founder & Pres)*

Accounts:
New-Hamptons Glow
New-Lashes on 5th

KIRVIN DOAK COMMUNICATIONS
(Private-Parent-Single Location)
7935 W Sahara Ave Ste 201, Las Vegas, NV 89117
Tel.: (702) 737-3100
Fax: (702) 737-1222
E-Mail: info@kirvindoak.com
Web Site: www.kirvindoak.com/

Employees: 24
Year Founded: 1989

Agency Specializes In: Digital/Interactive, Event Planning & Marketing, Media Relations, Promotions, Public Relations, Social Media

Revenue: $2,200,000

Bill Doak *(Partner)*
Dave Kirvin *(Partner)*
Terri L. Maruca *(Sr VP)*
Debbi Medsker *(Sr VP-Mktg Div)*
Natalie Mounier *(VP)*
Kate Turner Whiteley *(VP-PR)*

Accounts:
MGM Grand Detroit

KITE HILL PR LLC
115E 23rd St, New York, NY 10010
Tel.: (347) 421-2507
Web Site: www.kitehillpr.com

Agency Specializes In: Advertising, Communications, Content, Crisis Communications, Media Relations, Media Training, Public Relations, Social Media

Tiffany Guarnaccia *(Founder & CEO)*
Stephanie Tackach *(Dir-PR)*

Accounts:
Crowdtap

KIVVIT
(Formerly ASGK Public Strategies)
730 N Franklin St Ste 404, Chicago, IL 60654
Tel.: (312) 664-0153
E-Mail: info@kivvit.com
Web Site: www.kivvit.com

Year Founded: 2002

Maggie Moran *(Mng Partner)*
Judy Erwin *(Mng Dir)*
Sarah Hamilton *(Mng Dir)*
Eric Herman *(Mng Dir)*
Kent Holland *(Mng Dir)*
Sophie McCarthy *(Mng Dir)*
Michael Organ *(Mng Dir)*
Tracy Schmaler *(Mng Dir)*
Grace Turiano *(Principal & Supvr)*

Accounts:
Aluminum Association

Branches

Kivvit
608-612 Cookman Ave Unit 5, Asbury Park, NJ 7712
Tel.: (732) 280-9600
E-Mail: info@kivvit.com
Web Site: www.kivvit.com

Agency Specializes In: Advertising, Brand Development & Integration, Crisis Communications, Digital/Interactive, Media Training, Paid Searches, Public Relations, Social Media

Chris Donnelly *(Principal)*

Accounts:
New-Water Infrastructure Protection Act

KLICK COMMUNICATIONS
36 N Hotel St Ste B, Honolulu, HI 96817
Tel.: (808) 333-1887
Web Site: http://klick.com.au/

Agency Specializes In: Crisis Communications, Digital/Interactive, Public Relations, Social Media, Strategic Planning/Research

Bree Dallwitz *(VP)*

Accounts:
New-Black Sand Publishing
New-The Modern Honolulu
New-OluKai

KOCH COMMUNICATIONS
330 NW 10th St, Oklahoma City, OK 73103
Tel.: (405) 815-4027
Web Site: www.kochcomm.com

Agency Specializes In: Crisis Communications, Market Research, Media Relations, Public Relations, Social Media

Shaundra Blundell *(VP-Media Rels)*
Jenny Herzberger *(VP-Digital Media)*
Brooke Wigington *(VP-Digital Media)*
Krista Bruce *(Mgr-Media Rels)*
Gina Campbell *(Mgr-Bus Dev & Traffic)*
Caroline Cotton *(Mgr-eCommunity)*
Lindsey Fry *(Mgr-eCommunity)*
Dusky Hamm *(Mgr-Creative)*
Thomas Larson *(Mgr-Media Rels)*
Kaci Eckel *(Strategist-Digital Media)*

Accounts:
Oklahoma 529 College Savings Plan

KOENIG ADVERTISING PUBLIC RELATIONS
309 S Franklin St, Syracuse, NY 13202
Tel.: (315) 475-1603
Fax: (315) 475-1613
Web Site: www.koenig-adpr.com

Agency Specializes In: Event Planning & Marketing, Exhibit/Trade Shows, Graphic Design, Media Buying Services, Media Planning, Print, Public Relations, Radio, Sales Promotion, T.V.

Stewart Koenig *(Founder & Pres)*
Judy Schmid *(CFO, Office Mgr & Project Mgr)*

Accounts:
The Syracuse Diocese Catholic Schools

KOLT COMMUNICATIONS, INC.
2104 Jolly Rd Ste 200, Okemos, MI 48864
Tel.: (517) 706-0001
Web Site: www.koltcommunications.com

Robert Kolt *(Pres & CEO)*
Narine Manukova *(Dir-Adv & Mktg)*

Accounts:
CMS Energy

KONNECT PUBLIC RELATIONS
888 S Figueroa St Ste 630, Los Angeles, CA 90017
Tel.: (213) 988-8344
Fax: (213) 988-8345
E-Mail: info@konnect-pr.com
Web Site: www.konnect-pr.com

Year Founded: 2009

Agency Specializes In: Event Planning & Marketing, Promotions, Public Relations, Social Media

Sabina Gault *(Pres)*
Monica Guzman *(COO)*
Amanda Bialek *(Mgr)*
Tara Blank-Lopez *(Mgr-Benefits)*
Jessica Lieu *(Mgr)*
Kim Le *(Acct Supvr)*
Shelby Lopaty *(Acct Supvr)*
Brandy Stone *(Supvr)*
Caitlin Armstrong *(Acct Exec-PR)*
Kylie Banks *(Acct Exec)*
Nancy Cheng *(Acct Exec)*
Madison Jones *(Acct Exec)*

Accounts:
New-Capriotti's Sandwich Shop
Goddard Systems, Inc Brand Positioning, Consumer Media Relations
Kapital K
Menchie's (Agency of Record) Media Relations, PR

KOROBERI
1506 E Franklin St Ste 300, Chapel Hill, NC 27514
Tel.: (919) 960-9794
Fax: (919) 960-8570
E-Mail: info@koroberi.com
Web Site: www.koroberi.com

Employees: 10

Agency Specializes In: Advertising, Brand Development & Integration, Business-To-Business, Market Research, Public Relations

Bruce Olive *(Co-Founder & CEO)*
Glen Fellman *(Chief Creative Officer & Exec VP)*
Mirko Mueller-Goolsbey *(Exec VP & Grp Acct Dir)*
Cindy Joung *(Project Mgr-Technical)*
Natalie Fioto *(Acct Supvr)*
Carly Diette *(Acct Exec-PR & Writer-Technical)*
Carrie Cappiello *(Acct Exec)*
Dan Gauss *(Acct Exec-PR)*

KORTENHAUS COMMUNICATIONS, INC.

75 Newbury St, Boston, MA 02116
Tel.: (617) 536-5352
Fax: (617) 536-8883
E-Mail: info@kortenhaus.com
Web Site: www.kortenhaus.com

Employees: 12
Year Founded: 1984

Agency Specializes In: Advertising, Direct Response Marketing, Electronic Media, Email, Event Planning & Marketing, Hospitality, Internet/Web Design, Local Marketing, Media Planning, Merchandising, Promotions, Public Relations, Retail, Strategic Planning/Research

Lynne M. Kortenhaus *(Pres & CEO)*
Steven Pellegrino *(Principal)*
Alex Szafranski *(Sr Acct Exec)*
Maria Elaina Albini *(Acct Exec)*

Accounts:
Bambara
The Catered Affair
Commonwealth Worldwide Chauffeured Transportation
Kimpton Hotels & Restaurants
Loews Boston Hotel
Onyx Hotel
Simon Property Group
Starwood Hotels & Resorts Worldwide, Inc. aloft

KOVAK LIKLY COMMUNICATIONS

23 Hubbard Rd, Wilton, CT 06897
Tel.: (203) 762-8833
Fax: (203) 762-9195
E-Mail: info@klcpr.com
Web Site: www.klcpr.com

Employees: 15
Year Founded: 1985

Agency Specializes In: Brand Development & Integration, Communications, Corporate Communications, Crisis Communications, Event Planning & Marketing, Local Marketing, Media Training, Public Relations, Publicity/Promotions, Strategic Planning/Research

Bruce Likly *(Principal)*
Elizabeth Likly *(Principal)*
Kelsey Robinette *(Specialist-Media Rels)*

Accounts:
CD PHP
Celltech
Cochlear
Ferring Pharmaceuticals
Sanofi-Aventis Research & Development
Sheffield

KP PUBLIC RELATIONS

1201 K St Ste 800, Sacramento, CA 95814
Tel.: (916) 448-2162
Fax: (916) 448-4923
E-Mail: mburns@ka-pow.com
Web Site: www.ka-pow.com

Employees: 30
Year Founded: 1996

Agency Specializes In: Public Relations

Michael Burns *(Partner)*
Eloy Z. Garcia *(Partner)*
Ed Manning *(Partner)*
Eric Newman *(Partner)*
Jonathan Ross *(Partner)*
Brian White *(VP-Legislative Affairs)*
Patrick George *(Dir-Media Rels)*
Emily Lynn Smith *(Specialist-PR)*

Accounts:
Afton Chemical Corporation
California Correctional Peace Officers Association
California Restaurant Association
Citi
Gencorp
Google, Inc.

KRAKOWER POLING PR CORP

(Formerly White Bear PR Corp)
6404 Hollywood Blvd Ste 408, Los Angeles, CA 90028
Tel.: (323) 800-2570
E-Mail: office@krakowerpolingpr.com
Web Site: www.krakowerpolingpr.com

Year Founded: 2011

Agency Specializes In: Event Planning & Marketing, Media Training, Promotions, Public Relations, Social Media

Chandler Poling *(Pres)*
Thomas Mikusz *(CFO & VP-Ops)*
Grecco Bray *(Coord-PR)*

Accounts:
Andy Gowan
Gabe Hilfer & Season Kent
Noah Sorota
Pedro Bromfman
Rahman Altin

KRAUSE TAYLOR ASSOCIATES, LLC

111 W Evelyn Ave Ste 210, Sunnyvale, CA 94086-6129
Tel.: (408) 981-2429
Fax: (408) 918-9090
Web Site: www.krause-taylor.com

Year Founded: 1996

Agency Specializes In: Communications, Media Relations, Public Relations

Barbara Krause *(Co-Founder)*
Betty Taylor *(Owner)*

Accounts:
Aggregate Knowledge
Blue Planet Run
Garage Technology Ventures
Numenta

KREAB

(Formerly Kreab Gavin Anderson Worldwide)
Scandinavian House 2-6 Cannon Street, London, EC4M 6XJ United Kingdom
Tel.: (44) 207 074 1800
Fax: (44) 207 554 1499
Web Site: www.kreab.com

Employees: 45
Year Founded: 1991

Agency Specializes In: Corporate Communications, Financial, Government/Political, Public Relations

Gunilla Baner *(Mng Partner)*
Chris Philipsborn *(Partner & Head-Energy Practice)*
Chris Pond *(Partner & Head-Pub Affairs-UK)*
Robert Speed *(Partner)*
Renfeng Zhao *(Partner)*
Matthew Jervois *(Head-Fin Svcs)*
Tom Poston *(Dir-Pub Affairs)*
Jeremy Walker *(Dir-Fin-Global)*

Accounts:
Brintons Corporate Communications
The Camco Group
Cellnex Telecom Communications Strategy, Media Relations
Ernst & Young Media Communications
EuroTunnel
Ffrees Communications Strategy, Public Affairs
Institutional Limited Partners Association Communications, Media Relations, Public Affairs

Branches

Kreab Barcelona

(Formerly Kreab Gavin Anderson Barcelona)
C Mandri 36 bajos, 08022 Barcelona, Spain
Tel.: (34) 93 418 5387
Fax: (34) 93 212 6533

Employees: 3

Agency Specializes In: Media Relations, Public Relations

Teresa Lloret *(Partner & Head-Barcelona)*
Carmen Basagoiti *(Partner)*
Gonzalo Torres Martin *(Dir-Fin Comm)*
Alfredo Gazpio Irujo *(Assoc Dir-Pub Affairs)*
Isabel Pardinas *(Assoc Dir)*
Astrid Regojo *(Assoc Dir)*

Accounts:
Aguirre Newman
Avertis Foundation
BDO
Banesta Foundation
Berkelsmann Foundation
Laborsalus
Lantero
Manpower
Memora
Sagardoy Abogados
Singapore Airlines

Kreab Brussels

(Formerly Kreab Gavin Anderson Brussels)
Av de Tervueren 2, B-1040 Brussels, Belgium
Tel.: (32) 2 737 6900
Fax: (32) 2 737 6940
Web Site: www.kreab.com

Employees: 40

Agency Specializes In: Public Relations

Karl Isaksson *(Mng Partner-Brussels)*
Hannalena Ivarsson *(Mng Partner)*
Mark Foster *(Partner)*
Simona Amati *(Dir & Sr Mgr-Fin Svcs)*
Petra Arts *(Assoc Dir)*
Jason Besga *(Assoc Dir)*
Clara Bruck *(Assoc Dir)*
Stephanie Gayant *(Assoc Dir)*
Veerle Abeel *(Office Mgr)*
John Houston *(Sr Partner)*

Kreab Canberra

(Formerly Kreab Gavin Anderson Canberra)

Minter Ellison Building 25 National Circuit, Forrest, Canberra, ACT 2603 Australia
Tel.: (61) 2 9552 8935
Fax: (61) 2 6239 6622
Web Site: www.kreab.com

Employees: 12

Agency Specializes In: Communications

Sandra Eccles *(Partner & Head-Melbourne)*
Peter Sekuless *(Dir)*
Zackary McLennan *(Assoc Dir)*
Jessica McIntyre *(Office Mgr)*

Kreab Helsinki
(Formerly Kreab Gavin Anderson Helsinki)
Etelaesplanadi 18, 00130 Helsinki, Finland
Tel.: (358) 9 228 441
Fax: (358) 9 228 4240
Web Site: www.kreab.com

Employees: 28

Kreab Hong Kong
(Formerly Kreab Gavin Anderson & Company Hong Kong)
19/F Kinwick Centre 32 Hollywood Road, Suite 1902-04, Central, China (Hong Kong)
Tel.: (852) 2 2523 7189
Fax: (852) 2 2810 1239
E-Mail: hongkong@kreab.com
Web Site: www.kreab.com/hong-kong

Employees: 9

Agency Specializes In: Financial, Government/Political, Public Relations

Walter Jennings *(Mng Partner-Hong Kong & China)*
Natalie Biasin *(Dir)*
Tommy Patterson *(Assoc Dir-Govt & Pub Affairs Consulting & Res)*
Sophie Sophaon *(Assoc Dir)*
Vianna Yau *(Assoc Dir)*
Phyllis Tam Suk Ling *(Mgr-Fin)*

Kreab Madrid
(Formerly Kreab Gavin Anderson Madrid)
Capitan Haya 38, Edificio Cuzco II-8, Madrid, 28020 Spain
Tel.: (34) 91 702 71 70
Fax: (34) 91 308 24 67
Web Site: www.kreab.com/madrid

Employees: 10

Agency Specializes In: Financial, Government/Political

Eugenio Martinez Bravo *(Mng Partner)*
Carmen Basagoiti Pastor *(Partner)*
Jaime Olmos *(Dir-Pub Affairs)*
Susana Sanjuan *(Dir-Corp Comm)*
Francisco Calderon Silva *(Dir-Corp Comm)*
Manuel Garcia Vila *(Dir)*
Jose Luis Gonzalez *(Assoc Dir)*
Astrid Regojo *(Assoc Dir)*

Kreab Melbourne
(Formerly Kreab Gavin Anderson Melbourne)
Level 6, 2 Russell Street, Melbourne, VIC 3000 Australia
Tel.: (61) 396593000
Fax: (61) 3 9659 3030
Web Site: www.kreab.com

Employees: 12

Agency Specializes In: Financial, Government/Political, Public Relations

Casey Cahill *(Mng Partner-Western Australia)*
Michael Morgan *(Mng Partner)*
Pete Wilson *(Mng Dir)*
Carmel Bordignon *(Dir)*
Lucy Chamberlain *(Assoc Dir)*
Michelle Kirszner *(Assoc Dir)*
Zack Mclennan *(Assoc Dir)*
Emily Minson *(Assoc Dir)*

Kreab Singapore
(Formerly Kreab Gavin Anderson Singapore)
24 Raffles Place #21-05 Clifford Centre, Singapore, 048621 Singapore
Tel.: (65) 6339 9110
Fax: (65) 6339 9578
Web Site: www.kreab.com/singapore

Employees: 8

Agency Specializes In: Financial, Government/Political, Public Relations

Martin Alintuck *(Mng Partner)*
May Nah Chin *(Mng Partner)*
David Ibison *(Partner)*
Shane Fitzgerald *(Dir-Pub Affairs)*
Vanessa Ho *(Assoc Dir)*
Evangelina Wee *(Assoc Dir)*

Kreab Sydney
(Formerly Kreab Gavin Anderson Sydney)
137 Pyrmont Street Level 2, Sydney, NSW 2009 Australia
Tel.: (61) 2 9552 4499
Fax: (61) 2 9552 4899
Web Site: www.kreab.com/sydney

Employees: 25

Agency Specializes In: Communications

Michael Morgan *(Mng Partner)*
Pete Wilson *(Partner & Mng Dir)*
Shane Evans *(Partner)*
Paula Hannaford *(Partner)*
Suzanne Mercer *(Dir)*
Michelle Kirszner *(Assoc Dir)*
Lars Madsen *(Assoc Dir)*
Jeff Sorrell *(Assoc Dir)*

Accounts:
Foxtel

Kreab Tokyo
(Formerly Kreab Gavin Anderson Tokyo)
Shibakoen Ridge Bldg 1-8-21 Shibakoen, Tokyo, Minato-ku 105-0011 Japan
Tel.: (81) 35 404 0640
Fax: (81) 3 5408 3225
Web Site: www.kreab.com

Employees: 36
Year Founded: 1985

Agency Specializes In: Communications, Financial, Public Relations

Jonathan Kushner *(Mng Partner)*
Masami Doi *(Partner)*
Kayoko Harada *(Dir & Acctg Mgr)*
Masako Okura *(Dir)*
Nanami Watanabe *(Assoc Dir)*
Kaori Iwasaki *(Office Administrator)*

KREAB GAVIN ANDERSON WORLDWIDE
(Name Changed to Kreab)

KREPS DEMARIA, INC.
(Private-Parent-Single Location)
1501 Venera Ave, Coral Gables, FL 33146
Tel.: (305) 663-3543
Fax: (305) 663-9802
E-Mail: info@krepspr.com
Web Site: www.krepspr.com

Employees: 12
Year Founded: 1987

Agency Specializes In: Crisis Communications, Event Planning & Marketing, Media Relations, Public Relations

Revenue: $1,100,000

Sissy DeMaria *(Pres)*
Israel Kreps *(CEO)*
Cindi Perantoni Rodgers *(Sr VP)*
Veronica Villegas *(Dir-Accts)*
Michele Reese *(Sr Acct Exec)*

Accounts:
Bellini Williams Island

KULESA FAUL INC.
107 S B St Ste 330, San Mateo, CA 94401
Tel.: (650) 340-1979
Fax: (650) 340-1849
E-Mail: angelique@kulesafaul.com
Web Site: www.kulesafaul.com

Employees: 14
Year Founded: 2003

Agency Specializes In: Communications, Public Relations, Social Media

Revenue: $1,300,000

Angelique Faul *(Principal)*
Joanna Kulesa *(Principal)*
Robin Bulanti *(VP)*
Kristina Molfino *(Dir)*
Julie Tangen *(Dir)*
Cathy Wright *(Dir)*
Scott Lechner *(Acct Mgr)*

Accounts:
cloudshare
Dell Kace
Jitterbit
Modelmetrics
up time software

KUNDELL COMMUNICATIONS
210 W 89 St, New York, NY 10024
Tel.: (212) 877-2798
Fax: (212) 877-3387
E-Mail: kundellcom@nyc.rr.com
Web Site: www.kundellcommunications.com

Employees: 6

Agency Specializes In: Advertising, Broadcast, Business-To-Business, Collateral, Communications, Consulting, Corporate Communications, Email, Internet/Web Design, Media Relations, Multimedia, Newspaper, Print, Production, Public Relations, Radio, Strategic Planning/Research, T.V.

Linda Kundell *(Owner)*
Edwina Arnold *(Specialist-PR)*
Roberta Chopp Rothschild *(Specialist-PR)*
Patty Tobin *(Specialist-Media Placement)*

Accounts:
Homeric Tours Social Media
US Travel Insurance Association

KURMAN COMMUNICATIONS, INC.
345 N Canal St Ste 1404, Chicago, IL 60606-1366
Tel.: (312) 651-9000
Fax: (312) 651-9006
E-Mail: kurmanstaff@kurman.com
Web Site: www.kurman.com

Employees: 8
Year Founded: 1983

National Agency Associations: PRSA

Agency Specializes In: Automotive, Bilingual Market, Brand Development & Integration, Business Publications, Business-To-Business, Cable T.V., Children's Market, Collateral, Communications, Consulting, Consumer Marketing, Consumer Publications, Corporate Identity, Cosmetics, Digital/Interactive, Direct Response Marketing, Electronic Media, Email, Entertainment, Event Planning & Marketing, Experience Design, Fashion/Apparel, Food Service, Gay & Lesbian Market, Guerilla Marketing, Health Care Services, High Technology, Hispanic Market, Hospitality, Leisure, Magazines, Newspaper, Newspapers & Magazines, Over-50 Market, Planning & Consultation, Podcasting, Print, Public Relations, Publicity/Promotions, RSS (Really Simple Syndication), Radio, Real Estate, Restaurant, Retail, Seniors' Market, Sports Market, Strategic Planning/Research, T.V., Teen Market, Trade & Consumer Magazines, Travel & Tourism, Urban Market, Women's Market

Breakdown of Gross Billings by Media: Collateral: 10%; Event Mktg.: 15%; Local Mktg.: 25%; Pub. Rels.: 50%

Cindy Kurman Barrie *(Pres & CEO)*
Lee A. Barrie *(VP)*

Accounts:
Chicago French Market
Crowne Plaza, Chicago Metro
Dine, Chicago, IL Restaurant; 2008
Doubletree Arlington Heights; Chicago, IL Hotel; 2006
Karma; 2005

KUSZMAUL DESIGN & PR INC
1637 Savannah Hwy, Charleston, SC 29407
Tel.: (864) 706-9612
Web Site: www.kuszmauldesignpr.com

Year Founded: 2012

Agency Specializes In: Advertising, Collateral, Corporate Identity, Graphic Design, Internet/Web Design, Logo & Package Design, Print, Promotions, Public Relations, Social Media

Katherine Kuszmaul *(Owner & Designer)*

Accounts:
Converse Deli & Converse Deli West
Moonshadow Kennel

KWE PARTNERS, INC.
75 SW 15th Rd, Miami, FL 33129
Tel.: (305) 476-5424
Fax: (305) 577-8686
E-Mail: pr@kwepr.com
Web Site: www.kwegroup.com

E-Mail for Key Personnel:
President: escalera@kwegroup.com

Employees: 4
Year Founded: 1979

National Agency Associations: HSMAI-PRSA

Agency Specializes In: Affluent Market, Business-To-Business, Communications, Consulting, Consumer Marketing, Hispanic Market, Hospitality, Internet/Web Design, Leisure, Media Relations, Public Relations, Publicity/Promotions, Restaurant, Retail, Travel & Tourism, Women's Market

Karen Weiner Escalera *(Pres & Sr Strategist)*

Accounts:
Adriana Hoyos Social Media Marketing
Aloft Miami Doral Public Relations
Bertram Yachts & Ferretti Group Social Media Marketing
Cindy Christensen Home Design Marketing, Public Relations, Web Site
Velas Resorts; Mexico Marketing, Public Relations, Social Media

KYNE
360 W 31st St Ste 1501, New York, NY 10001
Tel.: (212) 594-5500
E-Mail: info@kyne.com
Web Site: www.kyne.com

Agency Specializes In: Health Care Services, Media Relations, Public Relations, Social Marketing/Nonprofit

David Kyne *(Founder & CEO)*
Maureen Byrne *(Exec VP & Gen Mgr)*
Tegwyn Collins *(Exec VP)*
Wendy Woods Williams *(Exec VP)*
Orla Barnewell *(VP)*
Mindy A.G. Huber *(VP)*
Michael Grela *(VP)*
Amanda Mulally *(VP)*
Kelli Raymor *(VP)*
Michele Malter Kleinmann *(VP)*
Susan McGowan *(Mgr-Fin)*

Accounts:
New-CDC Foundation
New-We Are Africa United

LA TORRE COMMUNICATIONS
509 N 2nd St, Harrisburg, PA 17101
Tel.: (717) 234-1333
Fax: (717) 635-9816
Web Site: www.latorrecommunications.com

Agency Specializes In: Collateral, Consulting, Crisis Communications, Media Relations, Media Training, Print, Public Relations

David La Torre *(Founder)*
Kara Luzik *(Dir-Acct Strategy)*

Accounts:
Agora Cyber Charter School
American Eagle Paper Mills
Bion Environmental Technologies, Inc.
Dunkin' Brands Group, Inc. Dunkin' Donuts
P3 Power Group
Penn State University
Pennsylvania State Troopers Association
Worth & Co., Inc.

LAFAMOS PR & BRANDING
4657 Hollywood Blvd, Hollywood, CA 90027
Tel.: (323) 668-9383
E-Mail: contact@lafamos.com
Web Site: www.lafamos.com

Agency Specializes In: Brand Development & Integration, Public Relations, Social Media

Amanda Blide *(Dir-Publicity)*

Accounts:
New-Ben Mauro

LAFORCE & STEVENS
41 E 11th St 6th Fl, New York, NY 10003
Tel.: (212) 242-9353
Fax: (212) 242-9565
Web Site: www.laforce-stevens.com

Year Founded: 1995

Agency Specializes In: Brand Development & Integration, Consumer Marketing, Fashion/Apparel, Public Relations, Sponsorship, Strategic Planning/Research, Travel & Tourism

Leslie Stevens *(Co-Owner)*
Rebecca Gordon *(Exec VP-Ops)*
Jennifer Hinchey *(VP)*
Lauren McGinnis *(VP)*
Ernest J. Bannister, Jr. *(Acct Supvr)*
Becky Katz *(Acct Supvr)*
Lindsay Porter *(Acct Supvr)*
Rebecca Greenhalgh *(Sr Acct Exec)*
Brianne Mulligan *(Sr Acct Exec)*
Allison Strassberg *(Sr Acct Exec)*
Megan Freiler *(Acct Exec)*
Rebekah Margulis *(Acct Exec)*
Mary Kate Richardson *(Acct Exec)*
Elizabeth Blumenthal *(Jr Acct Exec)*

Accounts:
B.R. Guest Restaurants
Belvedere Vodka
Dream Bangkok
Keds
Lalique
Perry Ellis
The President Hotel
Viceroy Miami
WET

LAGES & ASSOCIATES INC.
15635 Alton Parkway Ste 125, Irvine, CA 92618
Tel.: (949) 453-8080
Fax: (949) 453-8242
Web Site: www.lages.com

Agency Specializes In: Brand Development & Integration, Event Planning & Marketing, Media Training, Public Relations, Social Media

Beverly J. Lages *(Pres)*
Dena Jacobson *(Sr Acct Exec)*

Accounts:
New-Toshiba America Electronic Components

LAK PR
(Formerly Linden Alschuler & Kaplan, Inc.)
1251 Ave of the Americas, New York, NY 10020
Tel.: (212) 575-4545
Fax: (212) 575-0519
E-Mail: llinden@lakpr.com
Web Site: www.lakpr.com

E-Mail for Key Personnel:
Chairman: lkaplan@lakpr.com
President: salschuler@lakpr.com

Employees: 40

Agency Specializes In: Corporate Communications, Financial, Government/Political, Public Relations

Lloyd A. Kaplan *(Chm)*
Lisa Linden *(Pres & CEO)*
Colleen Roche *(Mng Dir & Principal)*
Hannah K. Arnold *(Principal & Sr Exec VP)*
Suzanne Dawson *(Principal & Gen Mgr)*
Richard Edmonds *(Sr VP & Dir-Real Estate Grp)*
Alix Friedman *(Sr VP)*
Angel Strickland Fahy *(VP)*
Sharon Horowitz *(VP)*
David Simpson *(VP)*

Samuel Eisele *(Acct Mgr)*
Lauren Whisenant *(Acct Mgr)*
Giselle Blanco *(Acct Exec)*

Accounts:
Aberdeen Group, Inc.; Boston, MA
Hostess Brands

LAMBERT, EDWARDS & ASSOCIATES, INC.
47 Commerce Ave SW, Grand Rapids, MI 49503
Tel.: (616) 233-0500
Fax: (616) 233-0600
E-Mail: mail@lambert-edwards.com
Web Site: www.lambert-edwards.com

Employees: 25

Jeffrey T. Lambert *(Pres & Mng Partner)*
Tara Powers *(Partner & Mng Dir)*
Steve Groenink *(Mng Dir & COO)*
Christi Cowdin *(Mng Dir)*
Robert Burton *(Mng Dir-Fin Comm practice)*
Matt Jackson *(Sr Dir-Consumer PR)*
Heather Wietzel *(Sr Dir)*
Brenda Brissette-Mata *(Dir-Pub Affairs)*
Chelsea Dubey *(Dir-Bus Dev)*
Abby Timmer *(Specialist-Digital)*

Accounts:
Entertainment Strategic Communication Planning
Great Expressions Dental Centers Expert Positioning, Media Relations, Strategic Counsel
Greatland Corp.
HBO Branding, Crisis Communications, Media Relations, Social Media, Strategic Counsel
Huron Capital Public Relations
Michigan's University Research Corridor Marketing Communications, Public Affairs, Social Media Development
Peak Resorts, Inc. Investor Relations
Recaro Automotive Seating Digital, Social Media, Strategy, Traditional Media
Wright & Filippis Designed Brochures, Internal & External Communications, Marketing, Media, Newsletters, Radio Spots, Research, Signage, Videos, Website

Subsidiaries

Lambert Edwards & Associates
1420 Broadway 1st Fl, Detroit, MI 48226
Tel.: (313) 309-9500
Web Site: www.lambert-edwards.com

Agency Specializes In: Communications, Corporate Communications, Investor Relations, Media Relations, Public Relations, Social Media, Strategic Planning/Research

Andy Heller *(Sr Dir)*
Tiffany Jones *(Sr Dir)*
Brad Warner *(Sr Dir)*
Renee Ketels *(Dir-IR Practice Grp)*

Accounts:
Downtown Detroit Partnership (Public Relations & Social Media Agency of Record)

Lambert Edwards & Associates
101 S Washington Sq Ste 800, Lansing, MI 48933
Tel.: (517) 316-0210
Fax: (517) 316-7590
E-Mail: mail@lambert-edwards.com
Web Site: www.lambert-edwards.com

Employees: 30

Agency Specializes In: Collateral, Communications, Exhibit/Trade Shows, Public Relations

Bob Burton *(Mng Partner)*
Christi Cowdin *(Mng Partner)*
Don Hunt *(Partner & Mng Dir)*
Tara Powers *(Partner & Mng Dir-Consumer Practice)*
Steve Groenink *(Mng Dir & COO)*
Joe Dibenedetto *(Sr Dir)*
Matthew Jackson *(Sr Dir)*
Heather Wietzel *(Sr Dir)*
Brenda Brissette-Mata *(Dir)*
Chelsea Dubey *(Dir-Bus Dev)*
Clare Liening *(Sr Assoc)*

Accounts:
Axios Mobile Assets Corporation External Public Relations, Internal Communications
Cascade Engineering
DuPont Automotive
HEAT (Help Eliminate Auto Theft)
Iserv
Rubbermaid
Saleen
Smokefree Air
Tecumseh

LANDIS COMMUNICATIONS INC.
1388 Sutter St Ste 901, San Francisco, CA 94109
Tel.: (415) 561-0888
Fax: (415) 561-0778
E-Mail: david@landispr.com
Web Site: www.landispr.com

Employees: 15
Year Founded: 1990

Agency Specializes In: Advertising, Arts, Business-To-Business, Communications, Consumer Goods, Corporate Communications, Corporate Identity, Crisis Communications, E-Commerce, Education, Entertainment, Environmental, Event Planning & Marketing, Fashion/Apparel, Financial, Food Service, Gay & Lesbian Market, Guerilla Marketing, Health Care Services, Hospitality, Household Goods, Leisure, Local Marketing, Luxury Products, Marine, Media Relations, Media Training, Multicultural, Podcasting, Public Relations, Publicity/Promotions, Retail, Social Marketing/Nonprofit, Strategic Planning/Research, Transportation, Travel & Tourism, Viral/Buzz/Word of Mouth

Approx. Annual Billings: $1,200,000

David Landis *(Pres & CEO)*
Sean Dowdall *(CMO & Gen Mgr)*
David Cumpston *(Client Svcs Dir)*
Ashley Boarman *(Sr Acct Exec)*
Brigitta Shouppe *(Sr Acct Exec)*
Tyler Arnold *(Strategist-Digital & Acct Exec)*
Kristin Schellinger Cockerham *(Acct Exec)*
Eric Steckel *(Strategist-Digital Media)*
Zach Spirer *(Acct Coord)*

Accounts:
Abe's Market Public Relations
The Academy of California Sciences
New-Art Miami LLC Art Silicon Valley San Francisco, Media Relations, Promotions
California Bank & Trust Multi-Cultural Campaign
California Society of Anesthesiologists
Fairmont Heritage Place
French American International School; San Francisco, CA
Jack London Square; Oakland, CA
Jack London Square
Kitebridge
Merlin Entertainments Group
MetLife
Museum of Craft and Design
Museum of the African Diaspora "MoAD in the Neighborhood"
NorthStar Memorial Group
New-On Lok, Inc. Brand Awareness
Out & Equal Public Relations
Port of San Francisco Public Relations
Save The Redwoods League
New-The Shanti Project Communications
Tower Two At One Rincon Hill
Troon Pacific Inc
UC San Francisco Public Relations, UCSF Mission Bay Hospitals
New-UDR, Inc. 399 Fremont Street, Communications Strategy
Vino Volo

LANE PR
905 SW 16th Ave, Portland, OR 97205
Tel.: (503) 221-0480
Fax: (503) 221-9765
E-Mail: info.portland@lanepr.com
Web Site: www.lanepr.com

Employees: 28
Year Founded: 1990

Agency Specializes In: Advertising, Hospitality

Revenue: $3,000,000

Wendy Lane Stevens *(Pres)*
Dominga Ramirez *(Mng Dir)*
Lisa Heathman *(VP)*
Vicki Ruse *(Controller)*
Claire Castellanos *(Acct Dir)*
Erin Tassey Krug *(Acct Dir)*
Jeff Segvich *(Acct Dir)*
Rob Bitter *(Sr Acct Exec)*
Rachael Kaapu *(Sr Acct Exec)*
Ted Lane *(Sr Acct Exec)*
Samantha Chulick *(Acct Exec)*
Heather McLendon *(Strategist-Digital)*

Accounts:
Agri Beef
Balanced Body (Public Relations Agency of Record) Blogger, Digital Marketing, Media, Social Media
Brasada Ranch
Charles & Colvard Investor Relations
Consumer Cellular
Craft Brewers Alliance, Inc.
DA Davidson
Digital Domain Media Group Public Relations
EFI Recycling
Heathman Hotel; Portland, OR
Heathman Restaurant; Portland, OR Cuisine
InFocus; Portland, OR
Miller Nash LLP
Network Redux; Portland, OR
One Degree Organics
Orchard Supply Hardware Stores
Oregon Ryegrass, Tall Fescue & Fine Fescue Commissions Branding, Consumer PR Campaign, Integrated Communications, Media Relations, Natural Turf, Online Marketing
Paulson Investment Company; Portland, OR Financial Services
New-Portland Roasting Coffee
New-Regal Springs Tilapia
Respect Your Universe
Roundarch
New-Steaz
Sterling Bank Creative Campaigns, Digital, Traditional PR
Travel Oregon Media Relations, Public Relations, Strategy
Travel Portland Public Relations
Widmer Brothers Brewing
ZAGG iFrogz
Zupan's Markets Events & Promotions, Media, PR

Branch

Lane Marketing

415 Madison Ave 15th Fl, New York, NY 10017
Tel.: (646) 673-8559
Fax: (646) 673-8401
E-Mail: info.newyork@lanepr.com
Web Site: www.lanepr.com

Agency Specializes In: Public Relations

Lisa Heathman *(Mng Dir & VP)*
Shannon Brewer Riggs *(Mng Dir & VP)*
Paula Ordway *(COO & Dir-HR)*
Amber Robert *(Sr VP)*
Vicki Ruse *(Controller)*
Kelly Rasmussen *(Editor-Copy & Acct Supvr)*
Claire Castellanos *(Acct Dir)*
Rob Bitter *(Sr Acct Exec)*
Sonal Haladay *(Sr Acct Exec)*
Rachael Kaapu *(Sr Acct Exec)*

Accounts:
The Heathman Hotel
Integra Telecom
Redhook Brewery
Thoma Bravo, LLC
Umpqua Bank
Wines from Spain

LANGDON FLYNN COMMUNICATIONS

2760 Lake Sahara Rd Ste 100, Las Vegas, NV 89117
Tel.: (702) 889-2705
E-Mail: info@langdonflynn.com
Web Site: www.langdonflynn.com

Agency Specializes In: Crisis Communications, Digital/Interactive, Media Relations, Media Training, Public Relations, Social Media

Michelle St. Angelo *(VP)*
Rosalind Congleton *(Acct Dir)*
Kristin Weddingfeld *(Acct Exec)*

Accounts:
New-Rick Moonen's Seafood

LARGEMOUTH COMMUNICATIONS, INC.

1007 Slater Rd, Ste 150, Durham, NC 27703
Tel.: (919) 459-6450
Fax: (919) 573-9139
Web Site: www.largemouthpr.com/

Employees: 12
Year Founded: 2005

Agency Specializes In: Public Relations

Brandon Bryce *(Pres)*
Kelly Propst *(Dir-Strategic Accts)*
Sarah Haas *(Acct Supvr)*
Alex Huffman *(Acct Supvr)*
Chantal O'Connell *(Sr Acct Exec)*
Bernadette Chepega *(Acct Exec)*
Julie Cooper *(Acct Exec)*
Jessica Highsmith *(Acct Exec)*
Sam Rinderman *(Acct Exec)*
Ginny Talley *(Acct Exec)*
Greyson Feurer *(Acct Coord)*

Accounts:
CORT
Eye Care Associates Digital, Media Relations, Public Relations, Social Media, Strategy
Hooters
Kangaroo Express
North Carolina Restaurant & Lodging Association Media Relations, Media Strategy, Public Relations, Strategic
Old Chicago
The Pantry Inc.; Cary, NC Salute Our Troops
Rho Media Relations, Public Relations
Sensus Water, Gas & Electric Business Units

LATITUDE

134 W 29th St Ste 904, New York, NY 10001
Tel.: (212) 633-2047
Fax: (212) 633-2086
Web Site: www.latitude-intl.com

Agency Specializes In: Crisis Communications, Exhibit/Trade Shows, Internet/Web Design, Media Training, Public Relations

Jeremy Carroll *(Co-Founder)*

Accounts:
Quito Tourism

LAUNCHIT PUBLIC RELATIONS

1804 Garnet Ave Ste 416, San Diego, CA 92109
Tel.: (858) 490-1050
E-Mail: info@launchitpr.com
Web Site: www.launchitpr.com

Year Founded: 2000

Agency Specializes In: Advertising, Email, Internet/Web Design, Print, Promotions, Public Relations

Susan Fall *(Owner)*

Accounts:
MacroPoint
TrakLok Inc

LAURA BURGESS MARKETING

PO Box 13978, New Bern, NC 28561
Tel.: (252) 288-5805
Fax: (252) 288-5806
E-Mail: info@lauraburgess.com
Web Site: www.lauraburgess.com

Agency Specializes In: Advertising, Corporate Communications, Event Planning & Marketing, Market Research, Media Buying Services, Public Relations, Social Media

Eric Burgess *(Owner & Partner)*

Accounts:
Eagle Imports Inc (Agency of Record) Bersa Firearms, Comanche Pistols, Metro Arms Corporation
Maryland Firearms Training Academy, LLC (Agency of Record) Advertising Strategy, Marketing, Public Relations, Social Media

LAVOIE STRATEGIC COMMUNICATIONS GROUP, INC.

One Thompson Sq, Boston, MA 02109
Tel.: (617) 347-8800
E-Mail: info@lavoiegroup.com
Web Site: www.lavoiehealthscience.com

Employees: 9
Year Founded: 2001

Agency Specializes In: Corporate Communications, Crisis Communications, Health Care Services, Medical Products, Public Relations

Donna L. LaVoie *(Pres & CEO)*
David Connolly *(VP)*
Richard Hantke *(Asst VP-IR & Capital Markets)*
Ron Aldridge *(Acct Dir-IR)*
Nancy Biddle *(Dir-Creative Design & Interactive)*
Lisa Descenza *(Dir-HR & Talent)*
Kristina Coppola *(Acct Supvr)*
Lindsay LeCain *(Acct Supvr-PR)*
Kathy Vigneault *(Acct Supvr-LaVoieHealthScience)*
Cole Bunn *(Asst Acct Exec)*

Accounts:
BIO; 2014
Commonwealth of Massachusetts Event Planning, Marketing, Public Relations
Cortendo AB Metabolic Orphan; 2014
Cydan Development Orphan Drug Accelerator; 2014
DARA BioScience Oncology Supportive Care Products; 2011
Depexium Pharmaceuticals Diabetic Foot Ulcer; 2015
NewLink Genetics Immunotherapy, Infectious Disease; 2015
NewLink Pharmaceutials S.p.A. Central Nervous System; 2015
Novadaq Technologies Imaging Technology; 2011
Xcovery Oncology; 2009

LAVOIEHEALTHSCIENCE

One Thompson Sq, Boston, MA 2129
Tel.: (617) 374-8800
E-Mail: info@lavoiehealthscience.com
Web Site: www.lavoiehealthscience.com

Agency Specializes In: Advertising, Brand Development & Integration, Content, Crisis Communications, Event Planning & Marketing, Investor Relations, Media Relations, Public Relations

Donna L. LaVoie *(Pres & CEO)*
David Connolly *(Sr VP)*
Ella Deych *(Dir-Finance & Ops)*

Accounts:
New-Xcovery

LAWRENCE RAGAN COMMUNICATIONS, INC.

316 N Michigan Ave Ste 400, Chicago, IL 60601-3774
Tel.: (312) 960-4100
Fax: (312) 861-3592
Toll Free: (800) 878-5331
E-Mail: cservice@ragan.com
Web Site: www.ragan.com

Employees: 20
Year Founded: 1970

Agency Specializes In: Public Relations

Revenue: $2,000,000

Mark Ragan *(CEO & Dir)*
Yolanda Maggi *(VP-Conferences & Events)*
Matt Wilson *(Co-Editor-PR Daily)*

Accounts:
Shel Holtz Webinars; 2007

L.C. WILLIAMS & ASSOCIATES, LLC

150 N Michigan Ave 38th Fl, Chicago, IL 60601-7558
Tel.: (312) 565-3900
Fax: (312) 565-1770
Toll Free: (800) 837-7123
E-Mail: info@lcwa.com
Web Site: www.lcwa.com

E-Mail for Key Personnel:
President: kdahlborn@lcwa.com

Employees: 25
Year Founded: 1985

National Agency Associations: COPF

Agency Specializes In: Business-To-Business, Communications, Consulting, Consumer

Marketing, Corporate Communications, Corporate Identity, Financial, Graphic Design, Industrial, Investor Relations, Local Marketing, New Product Development, Newspapers & Magazines, Public Relations, Publicity/Promotions, Retail, Sponsorship, Strategic Planning/Research, Trade & Consumer Magazines

Approx. Annual Billings: $4,000,000

Breakdown of Gross Billings by Media: Pub. Rels.: $4,000,000

Kim Blazek Dahlborn *(Pres & CEO)*
Barbara Thul *(CFO)*
Gary Goodfriend *(Exec VP)*
Allison Kurtz *(Exec VP)*
Shannon Quinn *(Exec VP)*
Mary Moster *(Sr VP)*
Jay Kelly *(VP)*
Debra Baum *(Sr Dir-Client Svcs)*
Laura Bohacz *(Client Svcs Dir)*
Tim Young *(Client Svcs Dir)*

Accounts:
Admiral at the Lake
American Nurses Association
Electrolux Floor Care
Eureka
First Alert
Jarden Safety & Security
Monessen
Pergo, Inc.; 2002
Snow Joe
Stepan Co.; 1985
Theater Wit
Thodos Dance Chicago
Timeline Theatre Co.
Trex
UnitedHealthcare of Illinois

LCH COMMUNICATIONS
18 Crestwood Rd, Port Washington, NY 11050
Tel.: (516) 767-8390
Fax: (516) 944-7369
E-Mail: lisa@lchcommunications.com
Web Site: www.lchcommunications.com

Employees: 5
Year Founded: 1998

Agency Specializes In: Asian Market, Computers & Software, Consumer Goods, High Technology, Luxury Products, Media Relations, Public Relations, Publicity/Promotions

Lisa Hendrickson *(Principal)*
Jenna Kern-Rugile *(Sr Writer)*

Accounts:
Excel Aire
Oxbridge Communications, Inc.
Stacy Blackman Consulting
Symbio Group; Beijing, China Software Product Development Software

LEAP PUBLIC RELATIONS
1755 High St, Denver, CO 80206
Tel.: (720) 295-3271
E-Mail: info@leappr.com
Web Site: www.leappr.com

Year Founded: 2010

Agency Specializes In: Crisis Communications, Media Relations, Public Relations, Social Media, Strategic Planning/Research

Merredith Branscombe *(Founder)*
Stacey E. Fields *(Sr Dir)*
Jennifer Shanks *(Dir)*
Kimberly Moran *(Mgr-Bus & Ops)*

Accounts:
Fon

THE LEDLIE GROUP
2970 Peachtree Rd Ste 805, Atlanta, GA 30305
Tel.: (404) 266-8833
Fax: (404) 266-9620
E-Mail: info@theledliegroup.com
Web Site: www.theledliegroup.com

E-Mail for Key Personnel:
President: joe.ledlie@theledliegroup.com

Employees: 11
Year Founded: 1998

Agency Specializes In: Aviation & Aerospace, Brand Development & Integration, Business-To-Business, Communications, Corporate Communications, Corporate Identity, Crisis Communications, Environmental, Event Planning & Marketing, Legal Services, Media Relations, Media Training, Medical Products, Planning & Consultation, Public Relations, Sponsorship, Trade & Consumer Magazines, Transportation, Women's Market

Joseph M.A. Ledlie *(Pres)*
Phillip Hauserman *(VP-Ops)*

Accounts:
A. Montag & Associates
Amedisys
Archdiocese of Atlanta
ASTI
AT&T Communications Corp.
DAL Global Services
Delta Air Lines
Digital Insight
Earth University Foundation
EnergySouth
Ethikos
Firethorn Holdings, LLC
Hotel Chocolat
InComm
Karcher
King & Spalding
Manheim
Northern Leasing Systems
Popeyes Chicken & Biscuits

LEE & ASSOCIATES, INC.
145 S Fairfax Ave Ste 301, Los Angeles, CA 90036-2166
Tel.: (323) 938-3300
Fax: (323) 938-3305
E-Mail: pr@leeassociates.com
Web Site: www.leeassociates.com

Employees: 9
Year Founded: 1950

National Agency Associations: PRSA

Agency Specializes In: Advertising, Advertising Specialties, Agriculture, Bilingual Market, Brand Development & Integration, Broadcast, Business Publications, Business-To-Business, Cable T.V., Co-op Advertising, Collateral, Communications, Computers & Software, Consulting, Consumer Goods, Consumer Marketing, Consumer Publications, Corporate Communications, Cosmetics, Crisis Communications, Direct Response Marketing, Direct-to-Consumer, E-Commerce, Education, Electronic Media, Email, Event Planning & Marketing, Exhibit/Trade Shows, Fashion/Apparel, Financial, Food Service, Guerilla Marketing, Health Care Services, High Technology, Hispanic Market, Hospitality, Household Goods, In-Store Advertising, Industrial, Infomercials, Integrated Marketing, Leisure, Local Marketing, Logo & Package Design, Luxury Products, Magazines, Market Research, Media Buying Services, Media Planning, Media Relations, Media Training, Medical Products, Men's Market, Merchandising, Multimedia, New Product Development, New Technologies, Newspaper, Newspapers & Magazines, Out-of-Home Media, Over-50 Market, Package Design, Pharmaceutical, Planning & Consultation, Point of Purchase, Point of Sale, Print, Product Placement, Production, Production (Ad, Film, Broadcast), Production (Print), Promotions, Public Relations, Publicity/Promotions, Radio, Restaurant, Retail, Sales Promotion, Search Engine Optimization, Seniors' Market, Strategic Planning/Research, Sweepstakes, T.V., Trade & Consumer Magazines, Travel & Tourism

Approx. Annual Billings: $4,000,000

Breakdown of Gross Billings by Media: E-Commerce: 10%; Pub. Rels.: 70%; Radio & T.V.: 10%; Trade & Consumer Mags.: 10%

Leo Pearlstein *(Founder & Pres)*
Howard Pearlstein *(Co-Owner & Principal)*
Frank Pearlstein *(Principal & VP)*

Accounts:
California Salmon Council
Morehouse Foods; Los Angeles, CA Mustard
Mrs. Cubbison's Foods, Inc.; Los Angeles, CA Croutons, Poultry Dressing Mixes

LEESBURG PR
3904 N Druid Hills Rd Ste 311, Decatur, GA 30033
Tel.: (404) 687-0400
E-Mail: info@leesburgpr.com
Web Site: www.leesburgpr.com

Year Founded: 2002

Agency Specializes In: Brand Development & Integration, Media Relations, Public Relations, Strategic Planning/Research

Amanda Leesburg *(Pres)*

Accounts:
Get a Job Skateboards
Healthy Green Schools
Mind-FX
Sky Zone Trampoline
Tin Laser Aesthetic & Wellness Spa
UnCorked Glass
Wagging Green

LEFF & ASSOCIATES
2646 Danforth Ln, Decatur, GA 30033
Tel.: (404) 861-4769
Web Site: www.leffassociates.com

Agency Specializes In: Crisis Communications, Event Planning & Marketing, Media Relations, Media Training, Public Relations, Strategic Planning/Research

Mitch Leff *(Pres)*

Accounts:
All About Developmental Disabilities
Boys & Girls Clubs of America
Boys & Girls Clubs of Metro Atlanta
Cardlytics
Hedgepeth Heredia Crumrine & Morrison
Radiance Solar
Sterling Risk Advisors
UHY Advisors
The Walker School

LER PUBLIC RELATIONS
22 E 21st St Ste 6F, New York, NY 10011

Tel.: (212) 242-2069
E-Mail: info@lerpr.com
Web Site: www.lerpr.com

Agency Specializes In: Brand Development & Integration, Event Planning & Marketing, Public Relations, Strategic Planning/Research

Tracie Heffernan *(Acct Mgr)*
Lauren Pelosi *(Acct Exec)*
Kaylee Conley *(Acct Coord)*

Accounts:
Phoenix Keating
Resort West
Thaddeus O'Neil

LESIC & CAMPER COMMUNICATIONS

172 E State St Ste 410, Columbus, OH 43215
Tel.: (614) 224-0658
Fax: (614) 232-8328
E-Mail: prteam@lesiccamper.com
Web Site: www.lesiccamper.com

Employees: 6
Year Founded: 2002

Agency Specializes In: Public Relations

Nancy Lesic *(Owner)*
Jenny Camper *(Pres)*
Mark Rickel *(VP)*
Angela Snyder *(Acct Exec)*

Accounts:
Credit Suisse
Dots
Fairmount
First Interstate
Flats East Bank
Gateway Economic Development Corp.
International Trucks
NOPEC
Ohio Dental Association
Ohio Department of Taxation
OhioHealth
Pfizer
PhRMA

Branch

Lesic & Camper Communications

812 Huron Rd Ste 460, Cleveland, OH 44115-1123
Tel.: (216) 696-7686
Fax: (216) 696-7687
E-Mail: prteam@lesiccamper.com
Web Site: www.lesiccamper.com

Employees: 10

Agency Specializes In: Public Relations

Steve Luttner *(VP)*
Meagan Meyer Mulloy *(Sr Acct Exec)*

Accounts:
Cleveland-Cuyahoga County Port Authority
Credit Suisse
Dots
Fairmount
Firepanel
Flats
Greater Cleveland Partnership
Nopec
Pfizer
PPA
Vorys

LESLEY FRANCIS PR

33 Park of Commerce Blvd, Savannah, GA 31405
Tel.: (912) 429-3950
Web Site: www.lesleyfrancispr.com

Agency Specializes In: Event Planning & Marketing, Internet/Web Design, Media Relations, Public Relations, Strategic Planning/Research

Ashley Roberts *(Acct Mgr)*
Chelsea Bremer *(Acct Exec)*

Accounts:
Asbury Memorial Theatre
Maritime Bethel

LESTELLE COMMUNICATIONS, LLC

1 Canal Pl 365 Canal St Ste 1750, New Orleans, LA 70130
Tel.: (504) 552-2727
Fax: (504) 558-0344
E-Mail: jim@lestellecommunications.com
Web Site: www.lestellecommunications.com

Employees: 1

Agency Specializes In: Communications, Consulting, Corporate Communications, Crisis Communications, Media Relations, Public Relations, Social Marketing/Nonprofit

Jim Lestelle *(Pres)*

LEVENSON & BRINKER PUBLIC RELATIONS

717 Harwood 20th Fl, Dallas, TX 75201
Tel.: (214) 932-6000
Fax: (214) 880-0628
E-Mail: s.levenson@levensonbrinkerpr.com
Web Site: www.levensongroup.com

Employees: 20

Agency Specializes In: Public Relations

Stanley R. Levenson *(CEO)*

Accounts:
The Austonian
The Beck Group Marketing, Public Relations
Bostons Gourmet Pizza
Hope Cottage
Pollo Campero
Trammell Crow Company

LEVERAGE PR

111 Congress Ave Ste 400, Austin, TX 78701
Tel.: (855) 505-7360
E-Mail: info@leverage-pr.com
Web Site: www.leverage-pr.com

Agency Specializes In: Internet/Web Design, Public Relations, Social Media

Joy Schoffler *(Founder & Principal)*
Emily Thomson *(Sr VP)*
Kimberley Brown *(Sr Acct Mgr)*
April Wareham *(Acct Mgr)*
Michelle Yandre *(Acct Mgr)*
Traci Sepp *(Mgr-Bus Dev)*
Erin Goulding *(Acct Exec)*

Accounts:
Alliance of Merger Acquisition Advisors Media Relations, Public Relations, Social Media
BBC Easy Marketing, Media, PR, Thought Leadership
EarlyShares Media, National, PR, Social Media, Thought Leadership
GATE Global Impact Inc Marketing, Media Relations, Public Relations
Givelocity
Invested.In
The South by Southwest Interactive Festival Communication, Media Relations Outreach, SXSW Accelerator (Agency of Record)

LEVICK

(Formerly Levick Strategic Communications, LLC)
1900 M St NW Ste 400, Washington, DC 20036
Tel.: (202) 973-1300
Fax: (202) 973-1301
E-Mail: info@levick.com
Web Site: www.levick.com

Employees: 75
Year Founded: 1998

Richard Levick *(Chm & CEO)*
Mark Irion *(Pres)*
Patricia Ramsay *(COO & Exec VP)*
Jason Maloni *(Chm-Litigation Practice & Sr VP)*
Connie Mack, IV *(Exec VP)*
Melissa Arnoff *(Sr VP)*
Ian McCaleb *(Sr VP)*
Larry Smith *(Sr VP)*
Jack Deschauer *(VP)*
Jennifer Tong *(Acct Supvr)*
Coniah Adams *(Acct Exec)*

Accounts:
Advertising Age
AshleyMadison.com Crisis Communications, Public Relations
Bloomberg BusinessWeek
Bloomberg
CBS News
CoreBrand; New York, NY
ESPN
Eversheds LLP
National Volunteer Firefighters Council
The New York Times
The Nigerian Government Campaign: "#BringBackOurGirls", Public Relations
Politico
PRWeek
Roger Clemens
Special Olympics
Stew Leonard's
The Wall Street Journal
Washington Business Journal

THE LEVITT GROUP

2573 Eagle Run Ln, Weston, FL 33327-1527
Tel.: (954) 349-2596
Fax: (954) 349-2597
E-Mail: info@levittgroup.com

E-Mail for Key Personnel:
President: ron@levittgroup.com
Creative Dir.: howard@levittgroup.com

Employees: 9
Year Founded: 1961

National Agency Associations: PRSA

Agency Specializes In: Asian Market, Business-To-Business, Collateral, Communications, Consulting, E-Commerce, Entertainment, Event Planning & Marketing, Exhibit/Trade Shows, Graphic Design, Internet/Web Design, Magazines, Newspaper, Newspapers & Magazines, Over-50 Market, Planning & Consultation, Print, Publicity/Promotions, Real Estate, Sports Market, Travel & Tourism

Approx. Annual Billings: $1,250,000

Breakdown of Gross Billings by Media: Bus. Publs.: $225,000; Collateral: $150,000; Mags.: $225,000; Newsp.: $75,000; Pub. Rels.: $500,000; T.V.: $75,000

Ronald Levitt *(Owner)*

Accounts:
Canadian Tourism
City of Coral Gables, FL
Curacao Caribbean Hotel Casino; Curacao, NA
European-American Chamber of Commerce
The Mackenzie Companies
Outdoor Garden, Inc.
Performance Enhancement Professionals Inc.
Precision Trading
Royal Services Inc.
Saniglaze Inc.
Vinisud Wine Expo; France

LEWIS PR
535 Boylston St Ste 603, Boston, MA 02116
Tel.: (617) 226-8840
Fax: (617) 421-8619
E-Mail: info@lewispr.com
Web Site: www.lewispr.com

Employees: 50
Year Founded: 1995

Agency Specializes In: Event Planning & Marketing, Government/Political, Media Relations

Chris Lewis *(Founder & CEO)*
Noah Dye *(Partner & VP)*
Kim Karelis *(Mng Dir)*
Lucy Allen *(Chief Strategy Officer & Exec VP)*
Morgan McLintic *(Exec VP-US)*
Claire Rowberry *(Sr VP)*
Stephen Corsi *(VP-Digital Mktg-US)*
Ian Lipner *(VP-Washington)*
Lillian Dunlap *(Acct Dir)*
Evan Burkhart *(Sr Acct Exec)*
Lindsay Schwimer *(Sr Acct Exec)*

Accounts:
Apama
ARIN
Dreamstime (Agency of Record) Media Relations
Fiba
Le Bristol
Panasonic
Quantenna Communications, Inc
Samsung
Sanyo
Symantec

Branches

Davies Murphy Group
200 Wheeler Rd N Tower, Burlington, MA 01803
(See Separate Listing)

LEWIS PUBLIC RELATIONS
7616 Lyndon B Johnson Fwy, Dallas, TX 75251
Tel.: (214) 635-3050
Fax: (214) 635-3030
Toll Free: (866) 398-4516
Web Site: www.lewispublicrelations.com

Employees: 3

Agency Specializes In: Public Relations

Blake Lewis *(Principal)*
Amanda Lewis Hill *(Dir-Strategic Dev)*
Christi Chesner *(Acct Svc Dir)*

Accounts:
Infomart Data Centers (Agency of Record) Media Relations, Strategic Messaging

LEWIS PULSE
(Formerly Page One PR, LLC)
575 Market St, San Francisco, CA 94105
Tel.: (415) 432-2400
Fax: (650) 565-9801
E-Mail: info@lewispulse.com
Web Site: www.lewispr.com

Employees: 20
Year Founded: 2004

Revenue: $3,100,000

Noah Dye *(Partner & VP)*
Jade Wilkinson *(Mng Dir)*
Lucy Allen *(Chief Strategy Officer & Exec VP)*
Morgan Mclintic *(Exec VP)*
Haley Hebert *(VP-Digital Mktg & Head-LEWIS Pulse US)*
Katherine Nellums *(VP)*
Katie Pierini *(VP-San Diego)*
Kristine De Guzman *(Dir-Digital Mktg)*
Lillian Smith *(Mgr-Digital Mktg)*
Chris Ulbrich *(Sr Acct Exec)*
Shelly Gregory *(Sr Specialist-Digital Mktg)*

Accounts:
Cisco
CloudBees, Inc.
Cloudera
Couchio
McAfee
Revolution Analytics
SAP
SolarWorld AG
WildPackets, Inc

LEXICON COMMUNICATIONS CORP.
520 Bellmore Way, Pasadena, CA 91103
Tel.: (626) 683-9200
Fax: (622) 628-1960
E-Mail: information@lexiconcorp.com
Web Site: www.crisismanagement.com

E-Mail for Key Personnel:
President: sfink@lexiconcorp.com

Employees: 15
Year Founded: 1983

Agency Specializes In: Brand Development & Integration, Business Publications, Business-To-Business, Communications, Consulting, Consumer Goods, Consumer Marketing, Consumer Publications, Corporate Communications, Corporate Identity, Crisis Communications, Customer Relationship Management, Direct-to-Consumer, Education, Environmental, Event Planning & Marketing, Food Service, Government/Political, Health Care Services, Industrial, Legal Services, Media Relations, Media Training, Multimedia, Newspaper, Newspapers & Magazines, Pharmaceutical, Planning & Consultation, Promotions, Public Relations, Publicity/Promotions, Real Estate, Restaurant, Sales Promotion, Sports Market, Strategic Planning/Research, Transportation, Travel & Tourism

Approx. Annual Billings: $1,000,000

Harriet Braiker *(Chm)*
Steven B. Fink *(Pres & CEO)*

Accounts:
Heublein-Jose Cuervo Black Velvet Canadian Whisky

LFB MEDIA GROUP
210 W 29th St 2nd Fl, New York, NY 10001
Tel.: (646) 455-0042
E-Mail: info@lfbmediagroup.com
Web Site: www.lfbmediagroup.com

Year Founded: 2009

Agency Specializes In: Brand Development & Integration, Event Planning & Marketing, Public Relations

Ashley Berg *(Owner)*
Sarah Uibel *(Dir-Lifestyle)*
Brittany Blake *(Acct Mgr)*
Andrew Borello *(Mgr)*
Alexandra Taylor *(Acct Supvr)*
Denise Finnegan *(Sr Acct Exec)*
Crystal Ramirez *(Sr Acct Exec)*
Helen Zhang *(Sr Strategist-Media)*

Accounts:
Viceroy Hotel Group Brand Strategy, Public Relations

LFPR LLC
8935 Research Dr, Irvine, CA 92618
Tel.: (949) 502-6200
E-Mail: irvine@lfpr.com
Web Site: www.lfpr.com

Agency Specializes In: Content, Corporate Communications, Crisis Communications, Event Planning & Marketing, Media Relations, Public Relations, Social Media

Shana Starr *(Mng Partner)*
Tiffany Allegretti *(VP)*
Fern Altobelli *(Mgr-Social Media)*
Jamie Andersen *(Acct Supvr-PR)*
David Feistel *(Mng Acct Exec)*

Accounts:
derma e Public Relations Agency of Record, Strategic Communication
Sage Software, Inc.

LG-PR PUBLIC RELATIONS
14007 S Bell Rd Ste 110, Homer, IL 60491
Tel.: (312) 473-5477
E-Mail: info@lg-pr.com
Web Site: www.lg-pr.com

Agency Specializes In: Brand Development & Integration, Crisis Communications, Media Relations, Media Training, Public Relations, Social Media

Lisa Gunggoll *(Principal)*

Accounts:
Casa of Will County
Catholic Extension
Teski

LIBERTY COMMUNICATIONS
156 2nd St, San Francisco, CA 94105
Tel.: (415) 852-6930
E-Mail: info@libertycomms.com
Web Site: www.libertycomms.com

Agency Specializes In: Corporate Communications, Digital/Interactive, Event Planning & Marketing, Public Relations, Search Engine Optimization, Social Media

Dee Gibbs *(CEO-Global)*
Elena Davidson *(Client Svcs Dir)*
Jen Hibberd *(Assoc Dir)*
Suzanne Hirsh *(Sr Acct Exec)*

Accounts:
InReality Public Relations

LIGHT YEARS AHEAD
8812 Hollywood Hills Rd, Los Angeles, CA 90046
Tel.: (323) 650-2201
Web Site: www.lightyearsahead.com

Agency Specializes In: Advertising, Broadcast, Media Planning, Print, Public Relations

Bette Light *(Pres)*
Megan Brown Bennett *(VP-Media Rels)*
Jan Sheehan *(Dir-Creative)*
Chloe Licht *(Acct Coord)*

Accounts:
Binaca Breath Fresheners
CapriClear
Clear Poreformance Hair Care
Dr. Fresh Personal Care Products
Dr. Kens Natural Oral Care
Eyedoll Chatter
Fincher Dermatology & Cosmetic Surgery
Kelo-cote
Orazyme Mouthwash
Out of Africa Shea Butter Skin Care

LIGHTSPEED PUBLIC RELATIONS
422 Atlantic Ave, Brooklyn, NY 11217
Tel.: (917) 770-9435
E-Mail: info@lightspeedpr.com
Web Site: www.lightspeedpr.com

Agency Specializes In: Content, Event Planning & Marketing, Media Relations, Media Training, Public Relations, Social Media

Ethan Rasiel *(CEO)*
Amanda Proscia *(Mng Dir)*
Martin Levy *(VP-Media & Analyst Rels)*
Josh Rasiel *(Creative Dir)*

Accounts:
New-4C Insights Inc
New-VSN Mobil

THE LILIAN RAJI AGENCY
55 Pharr Rd NW Ste A304, Atlanta, GA 30305
Tel.: (646) 789-4427, ext. 701
E-Mail: lilianraji@lmrpr.com
Web Site: www.lmrpr.com

Employees: 6
Year Founded: 2003

Agency Specializes In: Affluent Market, Arts, Automotive, Aviation & Aerospace, Brand Development & Integration, Branded Entertainment, Collateral, Communications, Consulting, Consumer Goods, Consumer Marketing, Consumer Publications, Corporate Communications, Cosmetics, Customer Relationship Management, Direct-to-Consumer, Electronics, Entertainment, Event Planning & Marketing, Exhibit/Trade Shows, Experience Design, Fashion/Apparel, Guerilla Marketing, Hospitality, Household Goods, Identity Marketing, International, Leisure, Local Marketing, Luxury Products, Magazines, Media Buying Services, Media Planning, Media Relations, Men's Market, Merchandising, New Product Development, Newspaper, Newspapers & Magazines, Planning & Consultation, Product Placement, Promotions, Public Relations, Publicity/Promotions, Real Estate, Regional, Restaurant, Retail, Social Marketing/Nonprofit, Social Media, Sponsorship, Strategic Planning/Research, T.V., Trade & Consumer Magazines, Transportation, Travel & Tourism, Viral/Buzz/Word of Mouth, Women's Market

Approx. Annual Billings: $250,000

Breakdown of Gross Billings by Media: Consulting: $50,000; Event Mktg.: $50,000; Pub. Rels.: $125,000; Strategic Planning/Research: $25,000

Lilian M. Raji *(Pres)*

Accounts:
Aaron Faber Gallery Jewelry & Watch Retailer; 2012
Claudio Pino Fine Jewelry; 2012
CREA Gallery Interior Design, Jewelry, Gallery, Art; 2012
French Trade Commission; New York, NY Fine Jewelry; 2009
Mathon Paris; Paris, France Fine Jewelry; 2008
OYOBox Luxury Eyewear Organizer Fine Accessories; 2014
Prestige Promenade Fine Jewelry; 2012
Quebec Trade Delegation Fine Jewelry; 2012
S.T. Dupont; Paris, France Leather Goods, Lighters, Men's Accessories, Pens; 2009

LINDA GAUNT COMMUNICATIONS
72 Madison Ave 9th Fl, New York, NY 10016
Tel.: (212) 810-2894
E-Mail: info@lindagaunt.com
Web Site: www.lindagaunt.com

Agency Specializes In: Digital/Interactive, Event Planning & Marketing, Media Relations, Public Relations, Social Media

Linda Gaunt *(Owner)*
Amy Keller *(Dir-Digital Strategy)*
Jessica Gioia *(Dir-PR)*
Margaret Reder Lynch *(Acct Mgr)*
Maggie Long *(Mgr-PR)*

Accounts:
New-Hunter Boots
New-Kendra Scott

LINHART PUBLIC RELATIONS
1514 Curtis St Ste 200, Denver, CO 80202
Tel.: (303) 620-9044
Fax: (303) 620-9043
E-Mail: info@linhartpr.com
Web Site: www.linhartpr.com

Employees: 15

National Agency Associations: COPF-ICOM

Agency Specializes In: Public Relations, Sponsorship

Approx. Annual Billings: $2,111,000

Sharon Haley Linhart *(Mng Partner)*
Carri Clemens *(Partner & CFO)*
Kelly Womer *(Partner & VP)*
Tim Streeb *(Partner & Sr Acct Dir)*
Ashley Campbell *(Acct Dir)*
Geoff Renstrom *(Sr Acct Exec)*
Robin Zimmerman *(Sr Acct Exec)*
Courtney Brunkow *(Acct Exec)*
Noel Runkle *(Specialist-Digital Media)*
Kaitlyn Viater *(Strategist-Digital Media)*
Courtney Hilow *(Designer-Visual Comm)*

Accounts:
Alagasco
Aurora Organic Dairy
Celestial Seasonings (Agency of Record) Brand Awareness, Digital Strategy & Engagement, Events, Kombucha, Media & Blogger Relations
Chipolte Quick-Gourmet Restaurant
Comcast
CoreSite Realty Corporation Media Relations
Crocs
DSM Nutritional Products Strategic Communications
Ganeden Biotech
GTC Nutrition
Making Colorado Media Relations, Social Media Engagement
New-Meyer Natural Foods (Public Relations Agency of Record) Media Relations
MWH Global Global Engineering & Consulting Firm
New West Physicians Medical Practice Management
Panera Bread Bakery-Cafes
Rudi's Organic Bakery Campaign: "Let's Doodle Lunch", PR
Southwest Airlines
United Healthcare
WhiteWave Foods Horizon Organic Milk, Silk Soymilk

LIPPE TAYLOR
215 Park Ave S 16th Fl, New York, NY 10003
Tel.: (212) 598-4400
Fax: (212) 598-0620
E-Mail: lippetaylor@lippetaylor.com
Web Site: www.lippetaylor.com

Employees: 60
Year Founded: 1988

National Agency Associations: COPF

Agency Specializes In: Public Relations, Sponsorship

Sheryl Kornfeld *(Exec VP)*
Elise Titan *(Exec VP)*
Nicholas Pattakos *(Sr VP-Fin)*
Kristin Pehush *(VP)*
Michelle Ponto *(VP-Consumer)*
Gerald Taylor *(Gen Mgr)*
Emmy Lou Kelly *(Dir-Creative)*
Nick Taylor *(Assoc Mgr-Mktg)*
Alexis Fabricant *(Acct Supvr)*
Alli Good *(Acct Supvr)*
Jamie Ress *(Acct Supvr)*
Yun Yu *(Supvr-Media)*
Cami Clarkson *(Sr Acct Exec-Digital Mktg)*
Jenna Rotner *(Sr Acct Exec)*
Noelle Cantarano *(Sr Strategist-Digital)*
Allison Kublin *(Acct Coord)*
Lori Rubinson *(Chief Strategic Officer)*

Accounts:
Built PR, Social Media Strategy & Content, Strategic Alliances
Chrysler
FaceCake Marketing Technologies Brand Awareness; 2008
Freeman Beauty Direct-to-Consumer Sampling, Influencer Outreach, PR
IKEA
Jenny Craig
Medicis Restylane Cosmetic Dermal Filler, Ziana; 2006
Procter & Gamble
Shaklee
Shionogi Osphena
Tampax
Taylor Precision Products, Inc Public Relations

LIPPERT/HEILSHORN & ASSOCIATES, INC.
800 Third Ave 17th Fl, New York, NY 10022
Tel.: (212) 838-3777
Fax: (212) 838-4568
E-Mail: klippert@lhai.com
Web Site: www.lhai.com

Employees: 25

Agency Specializes In: Corporate Communications, Investor Relations, Media Relations

Keith L. Lippert *(Founder, Partner & CEO)*
John W. Heilshorn *(Partner)*
Jody Burfening *(Mng Dir & Principal)*
Peter Mirabella *(CFO, Principal & VP)*
Kim Golodetz *(Principal & Sr VP)*
Anne Marie Fields *(Sr VP-NY Healthcare Team)*

Don Markley *(Sr VP)*
Jake Hindelong *(Dir-Market Intelligence)*

Accounts:
General Electric Co. Job Opportunities, Media Relations
International Stem Cell Corporation
Schiff Nutrition International, Inc. Invester Relations

THE LIPPIN GROUP

6100 Wilshire Blvd Ste 400, Los Angeles, CA 90048-5109
Tel.: (323) 965-1990
Fax: (323) 965-1993
E-Mail: losangeles@lippingroup.com
Web Site: www.lippingroup.com

Employees: 50
Year Founded: 1986

Agency Specializes In: Consulting, Entertainment, Public Relations

Pamela Golum *(Pres-Entertainment & West Coast)*
Alexandra Lippin *(Sr VP)*
Lindsay Lopez *(Sr Acct Exec)*
Mario Gonzalez *(Acct Exec)*
Allison Ivers *(Acct Exec-Publicity)*
Ronda Kalaji *(Acct Exec)*
John Solowiej *(Asst-PR)*

Accounts:
BBC Technology
Brian Wilson
Compact Disc Group
Futurist
Jennifer Fisher Jewelry
Kenny Wayne Shepherd
loudENERGY.com
Microsoft WebTV
Picture Pipeline
PricewaterhouseCoopers Global Entertainment
Sony DVD
Wyler Designs
Yowza

Branches

The Lippin Group

369 Lexington Ave 22 Fl, New York, NY 10017-6518
Tel.: (212) 986-7080
Fax: (212) 986-2354
E-Mail: newyork@lippingroup.com
Web Site: www.lippingroup.com

Employees: 7
Year Founded: 1987

Agency Specializes In: Consulting, Entertainment, Public Relations

Don Ciaramella *(Pres-Corp Comm)*
Matt Biscuiti *(Sr VP)*
Sara Stern Levin *(VP)*
Lisa Lugassy *(VP)*
Ashley Bond *(Acct Supvr)*
Katie Fuchs *(Sr Acct Exec)*
Dana Gaiser *(Acct Exec)*

Accounts:
NYTVF Media Relations, Red Carpet PR, Thought Leadership

The Lippin Group

31 Southampton Row, London, WC1B 5HJ United Kingdom
Tel.: (44) 203 008 5405
Fax: (44) 203 008 6011
E-Mail: london@lippingroup.com
Web Site: www.lippingroup.com

Employees: 5
Year Founded: 1993

Agency Specializes In: Consulting, Entertainment, Public Relations

Debbie Lawrence *(Mng Dir)*

LITZKY PUBLIC RELATIONS

320 Sinatra Dr, Hoboken, NJ 07030
Tel.: (201) 222-9118
Fax: (201) 222-9418
E-Mail: mlitzky@litzkypr.com
Web Site: www.litzkypr.com

Employees: 30

Michele Litzky *(Pres)*
Josslynne Lingard Welch *(VP)*
Melissa Fogarty Winston *(VP)*
Monique Febbraio *(Acct Exec)*
Kelsey Tarczanin *(Acct Exec)*
Christie Damato *(Jr Acct Exec)*
Elise Leonard *(Jr Acct Exec)*
Erica Paton *(Jr Acct Exec)*
Leah Schwint *(Jr Acct Exec)*
Sara Mcgovern *(Acct Coord)*
Kelsey Wojdyla *(Acct Coord)*

Accounts:
Baby Alive
Easy Bake
Funrise Toy Corporation Media Relations, PR
FurReal
Hasbro, Inc.
Kamik PR
Mamas & Papas Brand Awareness, Media Outreach, Social Media
My Little Pony
Playskool
SwimWays Corporation (Agency of Record) Leisure & Recreational Water Products
Time to Play

LIVE WIRE MEDIA RELATIONS, LLC

2800 S Shirlington Rd, Arlington, VA 22206
Tel.: (703) 519-1600
Web Site: www.livewiredc.com

Agency Specializes In: Media Relations, Media Training, Print, Public Relations

Chryssa I. Zizos *(Founder & Pres)*
Nicole Davidow *(Acct Mgr)*

Accounts:
New-Briana Scurry

LIZ LAPIDUS PUBLIC RELATIONS

The Bradley Bldg 772 Edgewood Ave NE, Atlanta, GA 30307
Tel.: (404) 688-1466
Fax: (404) 681-5204
E-Mail: info@lizlapiduspr.com
Web Site: www.lizlapiduspr.com

Agency Specializes In: Brand Development & Integration, Event Planning & Marketing, Media Relations, Media Training, Public Relations, Social Media

Liz Lapidus *(Owner)*
Andi Hill *(Acct Dir)*

Accounts:
New-Antico Pizza
New-Watershed on Peachtree

LOIS PAUL & PARTNERS

1 Beacon St, 2nd Fl, Boston, MA 02108
Tel.: (617) 986-5700
Fax: (781) 782-5999
E-Mail: info@lpp.com
Web Site: www.lpp.com

Year Founded: 1986

Agency Specializes In: Business Publications, Business-To-Business, Communications, Electronic Media, High Technology, Information Technology, Magazines, Media Training, Newspaper, Newspapers & Magazines, Print, Product Placement, Public Relations, Strategic Planning/Research

Lois Paul *(Founder, Pres & CEO)*
Christine Simeone *(Exec VP)*
Don Jennings *(Sr VP)*
Melissa Zipin *(Sr VP-Healthcare)*

Accounts:
Arbor Networks
CleanFUEL
Medidata Solutions

Branch

Lois Paul & Partners

828 W 6th St, Austin, TX 78703
Tel.: (512) 638-5300
Fax: (512) 638-5310
E-Mail: info@lpp.com
Web Site: www.lpp.com

Employees: 10
Year Founded: 1986

Agency Specializes In: Communications, Public Relations, Sponsorship

Lois Paul *(Founder & Pres)*
Bill McLaughlin *(Exec VP)*
Christine Simeone *(Exec VP)*
Jackson Connell *(Acct Rep)*

Accounts:
Aspen Technology
Blabbelon
Bomgar
CleanFUEL
Freescale Semiconductor
Kronos Inc.
LANDesk Software
National Instruments
RADVISION (Agency of Record)
Scuderi Group
Skyonic Corporation

LOLA RED PR

107 N Washington Ave Ste 200, Minneapolis, MN 55401
Tel.: (612) 333-1723
Web Site: www.lolaredpr.com

Year Founded: 2000

Agency Specializes In: Communications, Media Relations, Media Training, Public Relations, Social Media, Strategic Planning/Research

Alexis Walsko *(Founder & CEO)*

Accounts:
Best Cheese Corporation Parrano Cheese; 2013
Creative Kidstuff Toys; 2009
Home Franchise Concepts Budget Blinds, Inc., Premier Garage, Tailored Living, LLC; 2014
Sunny Delight Beverages Co. Sparking Fruit 2O, Sparkling Fruit2O Lime Twists; 2014

YOXO Toys Toys; 2015

LORRIE WALKER PUBLIC RELATIONS

1633 E Elm Rd, Lakeland, FL 33801
Tel.: (863) 614-0555
Web Site: www.lorriewalkerpr.com

Agency Specializes In: Media Relations, Public Relations, Social Media

Lorrie Delk Walker *(Pres)*

Accounts:
New-FITniche

LOTUS823

55 Gilbert St N Ste 3104, Tinton Falls, NJ 07701
Tel.: (732) 212-0823
Web Site: www.lotus823.com

Year Founded: 2009

Agency Specializes In: Communications, Internet/Web Design, Public Relations, Social Media

David Hernandez *(Mng Partner)*
Brian Herlihy *(VP-Bus Dev)*
Christine Rochelle *(Dir-Digital Mktg & Ops)*
Beth Gard *(Acct Supvr)*
Nicole Cobuzio *(Sr Acct Exec)*
Cristina Trecate *(Acct Coord)*
Craig Capron *(Assoc Strategist-Digital Mktg)*

Accounts:
Biscotti Inc.
New-Gumdrop Cases Media Relations
Healbe Brand Awareness, Public Relations
Knomo Public Relations, Social Media
Life n Soul Content Marketing, Public Relations, Social Media
New-Maverick Industries Social Media, Traditional Public Relations
RCA Online Brand Visibility, Social Media

LOU HAMMOND & ASSOCIATES, INC.

39 E 51st St, New York, NY 10022-5916
Tel.: (212) 308-8880
Fax: (212) 891-0200
E-Mail: lha@lhammond.com
Web Site: www.louhammond.com

E-Mail for Key Personnel:
President: louh@lhammond.com

Employees: 40
Year Founded: 1984

Agency Specializes In: Event Planning & Marketing, Food Service, Public Relations, Restaurant, Retail, Travel & Tourism

Approx. Annual Billings: $6,300,000

Lou Rena Hammond *(Founder & Chm)*
Stephen Hammond *(Pres)*
Terry Gallagher *(Pres-Lou Hammond & Associates New York)*
Michael Hicks *(VP)*
Mary Messias *(Controller)*
Alyssa Schmid *(Acct Supvr)*
Heyward Brockinton *(Sr Acct Exec)*
Sean Layton *(Sr Acct Exec)*
Gillian Love *(Sr Acct Exec)*
Gina McNamee *(Acct Exec)*
Kerstin Hjelm *(Acct Coord)*

Accounts:
3RD HOME Digital Marketing, Positioning, Public Relations
Avocet Hospitality Group Digital Marketing, Public Relations
Beach Company
Certified Angus Beef Meat Brand; 2008
Charleston Hospitality Group Digital Marketing, Positioning, Public Relations
City of Lexington Digital Marketing, Public Relations
New-CompareCards Digital Marketing, Positioning, Public Relations
Crawford High Performance Composites PR, Positioning, Social Marketing
Deep Water Cay PR, Positioning, Social Marketing
Domestic Estate Management Association
Elbow Beach, Bermuda Digital Marketing, Positioning, Public Relations
Emerson Resorts
Five Gables Inn & Spa
Foxwoods Resorts Casino
Gaillard Center
GROHE America Digital Marketing, Positioning, Public Relations
Groupe Lucien Barriere
Guayas Province; Ecuador; 2008
Guayas Tourism
Gurney's Inn
Halls Hospitality
Haunted Attraction Association Digital Marketing, Positioning, Public Relations
The High Concepts of the High Lonesome Ranch Digital Marketing, Positioning, Public Relations
High Country Rugs
Hilton Orlando Bonnet Creek; 2008
Holiday Isle Beach Resort & Marina Positioning, Public Relations, Social Marketing
Hotel Ella; Austin, TX
Hotel Le Bristol
Housing Solutions
Howard Miller; Zeeland, MI Clocks; 1995
Hunter Douglas Inc. Carole Fabrics, Duette Window Fashions, Horizontal Blinds Div., Pleated Shades Div., Silhouette Window Shadings, Vertical Blinds Div.; 1989
The Inn at Dos Brisas
JW Marriott Guanacaste Resort & Spa, Costa Rica Digital Marketing, Positioning, Public Relations
L'Apogee Courchevel
Le Massif de Charlevoix
Le Meridien Cancun Resort & Spa; 2008
Lulan Artisans Textiles; 2008
Mandarin Oriental Hotel Group; Causeway Bay, Hong Kong; 1987
Mansion at Peachtree; Atlanta, GA Residence/Hotel Tower; 2008
Market New Haven Historic Destination; 2008
New-McCall Farms Digital Marketing, Positioning, Public Relations
MGM Grand at Foxwoods
Montreal Highlights & Jazz Festivals
Mount Washington Resort at Bretton Woods
New-Nantahala Outdoor Center Digital Marketing, Positioning, Public Relations
Naples Bay Resort; 2008
Nassau Paradise Island Promotion Board
New Hampshire Division of Travel & Tourism Development Media
Norfolk Convention & Visitors Bureau
Oceania Cruises (Agency of Record) Cruise Line, Marketing Communications
Oheka Castle Hotel & Estate Positioning, Public Relations, Social Marketing
Omni La Mansion Del Rio
Paradise Coast Positioning, Public Relations, Social Marketing
Paradise Island Tourism Development Association
Patton Hospitality Management PR, Positioning, Social Marketing
Pink Sands Resort Digital Marketing, Positioning, Public Relations
New-PlanSource Digital Marketing, Positioning, Public Relations
The Polar Express Digital Marketing & Positioning, PR
Premier Rail Collection Digital Marketing & Positioning, PR
Providence Tourism Council
Rail Europe, Inc. (Agency of Record)
Regent Seven Seas Cruises
Sandals Resorts International Beach Resorts
Sir Cliff Richard
SnapCap Digital Marketing, Public Relations
Sonoma County Tourism Bureau, Vintners, Winegrape Commission
St. Regis Deer Valley
St. Regis Resort & Residences; Miami, FL Condo & Hotel Development; 2008
Tivoli Properties
Tourism Saint Barths Digital Marketing, Public Relations
Tourism Santa Fe Public Relations, Strategic Planning
The Umstead Hotel & Spa
Uncommon Journeys PR, Positioning, Social Marketing
UNITERS North America Digital Marketing, Positioning, Public Relations
Urbangreen Digital Marketing & Positioning, PR
New-Visit Natchez Digital Marketing, Positioning, Public Relations
VisitNorfolk
The Waldorf-Astoria; New York, NY The Waldorf Towers; 1990
Waldorf-Astoria Orlando; 2008
Wall Pops
Wild Dunes Resort; Charleston, SC
Wilson Associates Architectural Design; 2008

LOUDMAC CREATIVE

11632 SW 127 Terr, Miami, FL 33176
Tel.: (786) 693-2886
Fax: (305) 407-1221
E-Mail: loudmac@gmail.com
Web Site: www.loudmac.com

Employees: 5

Agency Specializes In: Advertising, Affiliate Marketing, Alternative Advertising, Brand Development & Integration, Business Publications, Business-To-Business, Cable T.V., Catalogs, Collateral, Communications, Consulting, Consumer Goods, Consumer Marketing, Consumer Publications, Content, Corporate Communications, Corporate Identity, Crisis Communications, Custom Publishing, Direct Response Marketing, Direct-to-Consumer, E-Commerce, Email, Exhibit/Trade Shows, Graphic Design, Guerilla Marketing, Identity Marketing, Infomercials, Integrated Marketing, Internet/Web Design, Local Marketing, Logo & Package Design, Media Buying Services, Media Planning, Media Relations, Media Training, New Product Development, Newspaper, Newspapers & Magazines, Package Design, Paid Searches, Planning & Consultation, Podcasting, Print, Promotions, Public Relations, Publicity/Promotions, RSS (Really Simple Syndication), Retail, Sales Promotion, Strategic Planning/Research, T.V., Technical Advertising, Telemarketing, Viral/Buzz/Word of Mouth, Web (Banner Ads, Pop-ups, etc.)

Brian McLeod *(Owner)*

Accounts:
42nd Street Studios
International Technology Transfer, Inc. (ITT)
Invent-Tech, Invention Technologies, Inc.
LandMark Productions

LOVIO GEORGE INC.

681 W Forest Ave, Detroit, MI 48201-1113
Tel.: (313) 832-2210
Fax: (313) 831-0240
E-Mail: ideas@loviogeorgeinc.com
Web Site: www.loviogeorge.com/index.htm

Employees: 15

Year Founded: 1979

Agency Specializes In: Advertising, Communications, Direct Response Marketing, Graphic Design, Public Relations

Christina Lovio-George *(Pres & CEO)*
Marlene Bruder *(CFO)*
John George *(VP & Dir-Creative)*
Heather George *(Dir-Integrated Mktg)*
Sara Gouin *(Dir-Art & Sr Designer)*
Michelle Caldwel *(Sr Acct Mgr)*
Megan Ewend *(Acct Exec)*

Accounts:
Cadillac Coffee
Detroit Festival of the Arts
Detroit Riverfront Conservancy
Detroit Symphony Orchestra
EWI Worldwide
Exhibit Works; Livonia, MI Exhibit & Museum Design
Ilitch Holdings
The Parade Company
Wayne State University; Detroit, MI School of Business; 2000

LT PUBLIC RELATIONS
917 SW Oak St Ste 303, Portland, OR 97205
Tel.: (503) 477-9215
Web Site: www.ltpublicrelations.com

Agency Specializes In: Content, Crisis Communications, Media Relations, Media Training, Public Relations, Social Media, Strategic Planning/Research

Casey Boggs *(Pres)*
Eric Miller *(Mng Dir)*
Kurt Heath *(Acct Dir)*
Kevin Hartman *(Acct Mgr)*

Accounts:
Cabelas Tualatin
Luke-Dorf

LUKAS PARTNERS
11915 P St Ste 100, Omaha, NE 68137
Tel.: (402) 895-2552
E-Mail: info@lukaspartners.com
Web Site: www.lukaspartners.com

Year Founded: 1973

Agency Specializes In: Event Planning & Marketing, Public Relations, Social Media

Joan Lukas *(Owner & Pres)*
Tom McLaughlin *(VP)*
Kevin Schuster *(Sr Acct Exec)*
Laura Mitchell *(Sr Acct Exec)*
Karl Bieber *(Sr Acct Exec)*
Diane Knicky *(Sr Acct Exec)*
Caroline Gran *(Sr Acct Exec)*
Trenton Albers *(Acct Exec)*
Sean Robinson *(Acct Exec)*

Accounts:
Outlook Nebraska Inc
U.S. Cellular

LUX COMMUNICATIONS
1127 S Genevieve Ln, San Jose, CA 95128
Tel.: (408) 244-1880
E-Mail: info@luxpr.com

Employees: 1

Agency Specializes In: Corporate Communications, Corporate Identity, Engineering, Industrial, Information Technology, Public Relations

Lori Lux *(Owner)*
Lynn Miller *(Specialist-Marcom & PR)*

Accounts:
Ample Communications
Apdex Alliance
Extreme Networks; Santa Clara, CA Networking Solutions
Finisar
ForeScout Technology
ServGate
Shomiti Systems
Tasman Networks
Trapeze Networks

LUXURIA PUBLIC RELATIONS
1761 Hotel Cir S Ste 226, San Diego, CA 92108
Tel.: (619) 487-0363
E-Mail: contact@luxuriapr.com
Web Site: www.luxuriapr.com

Agency Specializes In: Collateral, Event Planning & Marketing, Media Relations, Media Training, Public Relations, Social Media

Claudia Huizar *(Partner)*
Jamie Reyes *(Partner)*

Accounts:
New-Blo
Blow Hookah
New-Lupita Morales
New-Togally

LVM GROUP, INC.
60 E 42nd St Ste 1651, New York, NY 10165-6203
Tel.: (212) 499-6500
Fax: (212) 751-2862
E-Mail: david@lvmgroup.com
Web Site: www.lvmgroup.com

Employees: 8
Year Founded: 1974

National Agency Associations: COPF-PRSA

Agency Specializes In: Communications, Education, Event Planning & Marketing, Financial, Government/Political, Health Care Services, High Technology, Industrial, Public Relations, Publicity/Promotions, Real Estate, Travel & Tourism

David M. Grant *(Pres)*
Jeannette Boccini *(Principal & Exec VP)*
Rachel Antman *(VP)*
Mary Rauso *(Office Mgr)*

Accounts:
Blesso Properties; New York, NY Public Relations
BOCA Group; New York, NY Public Relations
CoreNet Global; New York, NY Public Relations
CRESAPartners
Dewey Pegno & Kramarsky LLP PR
Donnelly Mechanical Corp
Eastchester Heights
Gateway Center; Newark, N.J. PR
Goddard Group; North Hollywood, CA PR
Levien & Co.
Interior Demolition Contractors Association; New York, NY Public Relations
Kevin Roche John Dinkeloo and Associates LLC
Lymphatic Education & Research Network PR
Malkin Properties
The Mufson Partnership; New York, NY Public Relations
New World Home
Real-Time Computer Services, Inc. Public Relations
Rose Associates Residential Marketing
Sherwood Equities; New York, NY Public Relations; 2007
WSP Flack + Kurtz (Agency of Record)

LYNN ARONBERG PUBLIC RELATIONS
(Formerly Lynn Lewis Public Relations)
503 E Jackson St Ste 155, Tampa, FL 33602
Tel.: (305) 509-9958
Web Site: http://lynnaronberg.com/

Agency Specializes In: Event Planning & Marketing, Internet/Web Design, Media Relations, Public Relations, Social Media

Lynn Aronberg *(Founder & CEO)*
Ashton Landgraf *(VP-Ops)*
Neil Reynolds *(Dir-European Ops)*

Accounts:
Beth Bentley

LYNOTT & ASSOCIATES
10773 Alcott Way, Westminster, CO 80234
Tel.: (303) 460-8080
Fax: (303) 460-7272
E-Mail: info@lynottpr.com
Web Site: www.lynottpr.com

Year Founded: 1986

Agency Specializes In: Advertising, Corporate Communications, Crisis Communications, Media Relations, Public Relations, Strategic Planning/Research

Greg Lynott *(Co-Founder)*
Yvonne Lynott *(Partner)*

Accounts:
Conduant Digital Recording Services
Core logic SafeRent

LYONS PUBLIC RELATIONS, LLC
10410 N Kensington Pkwy Ste 305, Kensington, MD 20895
Tel.: (301) 942-1306
Fax: (301) 942-1361
E-Mail: info@lyonspr.com
Web Site: www.lyonspr.com

Agency Specializes In: Broadcast, Media Buying Services, Media Relations, Public Relations, Radio, T.V.

Dan Lyons *(Pres)*
Mercedes Marx *(Mng Dir)*
Cherise Adkins *(Sr Acct Exec)*
Kelsey Stone *(Jr Acct Exec)*

Accounts:
Kaiser Permanente

M&C SAATCHI PR
250 Park Ave S 10th Fl, New York, NY 10003
Tel.: (646) 619-2797
Fax: (917) 208-6325
Web Site: www.mcsaatchi.com/new-york/

Employees: 40
Year Founded: 1995

Agency Specializes In: Communications, Public Relations

Sandra Carreon-John *(Sr VP)*
Eric Mugnier *(Sr VP-North America)*
Laura Hall *(Mng Dir-US)*
Richard Barker *(VP)*
Gabriel Cheng *(VP-Mobile Strategy & Solutions)*
Steve Deangelis *(VP-North America)*
Jessie Carney *(Acct Dir)*

Public Relations Firms

Chelsea Whitaker *(Mgr-Paid Social-US)*
Mike Sim *(Strategist-Bus)*
Michael Raysor *(Media Planner & Media Buyer)*
Emily Scoggin *(Media Planner & Media Buyer)*
Elliot Alston *(Media Planner & Buyer)*
Alexandra Wolynski *(Sr Media Planner & Media Buyer)*

Accounts:
Alzheimer's Association Public Relations Strategy, Rita Hayworth Gala
Association of Volleyball Professionals Media Outreach
General Electric
MegaRed Campaign: "Whose Heart Do You Love"
The National Center for Entrepreneurship & Innovation
New York Cosmos Gala, Media Outreach, Strategy
NYC Pride Campaign: "Virtual Pride Day"
Pernod Ricard
PROFOOT Marketing
Reckitt Benckiser
Schiff Nutrition
Ubersense Media, PR, Strategic Development
Ugg PR
United States Olympic Committee

M&G/ERIC MOWER + ASSOCIATES
(Formerly Middleton & Gendron, Inc.)
845 3rd Ave, New York, NY 10022
Tel.: (212) 980-9060
Fax: (212) 759-6521
Web Site: www.mower.com

Employees: 15

Mary Gendron *(Partner)*
Yvonne Middleton *(Partner)*
Todd Middleton *(Mng Dir)*
Jay Austin *(Sr VP)*
Patricia Nugent *(Sr VP)*
Annette Russo *(Sr VP-Acctg & Admin)*
Lucy Vlahakis *(Dir-Content)*
Shara Seigel *(Acct Supvr)*

Accounts:
Pelcor PR
Trump Hotel Las Vegas
Trump International Hotel & Tower Chicago
Trump SoHo New York

M&P FOOD COMMUNICATIONS, INC.
151 N Michigan Ave Ste 804, Chicago, IL 60601
Tel.: (312) 201-9101
Fax: (312) 201-9161
E-Mail: foodexperts@mpfood.com
Web Site: www.mpfood.com

Employees: 10
Year Founded: 1987

Agency Specializes In: Collateral, Communications, Event Planning & Marketing, Exhibit/Trade Shows, Health Care Services, Local Marketing, Media Relations, Product Placement, Public Relations, Radio, Sponsorship, Strategic Planning/Research

Brenda McDowell *(Owner)*
Rebecca Galloway *(Office Mgr)*
Jessie Vicha *(Mgr)*

Accounts:
Dreamfields Foods Pasta
Seneca Foods Corporation
United Dairy Industry Association
Wilton Enterprises, Inc

M. SILVER/A DIVISION OF FINN PARTNERS
(Formerly M. Silver Associates Inc. - Public Relations)
747 3rd Ave Fl 23, New York, NY 10017-2803
Tel.: (212) 754-6500
Fax: (212) 754-6711
E-Mail: info@msilver-pr.com
Web Site: www.finnpartners.com/about/brands/m-silver.html

E-Mail for Key Personnel:
President: virginia@msilver-pr.com

Employees: 40
Year Founded: 1970

Agency Specializes In: Business-To-Business, Communications, Consumer Marketing, Corporate Communications, Crisis Communications, Event Planning & Marketing, Guerilla Marketing, Hospitality, Integrated Marketing, Luxury Products, Media Relations, Media Training, Pets , Podcasting, Promotions, Public Relations, Publicity/Promotions, Social Marketing/Nonprofit, Strategic Planning/Research, Trade & Consumer Magazines, Travel & Tourism, Viral/Buzz/Word of Mouth

Approx. Annual Billings: $4,500,000

Morris Silver *(Chm & CEO)*
Virginia Sheridan *(Pres)*
Maria Brewer *(VP)*
Linda Ayares *(Sr Partner)*

Accounts:
Aviva Hotels
Capella Washington, D.C Events, Media Development, Promotions, Strategic Partnerships
Epic
Hotel Sierra
Interjet Events, Media Development, Promotions, Strategic Partnerships
Jumeirah International
Lodge Works
One Atlantic
The Polo Club of Boca Raton Events, Media Development, Promotions, Strategic Partnerships
Pure Solutions LLC
The Residences at the Ritz-Carlton; Grand Cayman
Sheraton Nassau
Singapore Tourism Board
St. Giles Hotel New York Brand Strategy, Media Relations, Promotions & Business Partnerships, Public Relations, Social Media Communications, Special Events
St. Regis Resort Events, Media Development, Promotions, Strategic Partnerships
Turkey
Westin Rocoki; Dominican Republic

Branch

M. Silver Associates Inc.
110 E Broward Blvd Ste 1610, Fort Lauderdale, FL 33301-3532
Tel.: (954) 765-3636
Fax: (954) 765-3441
E-Mail: rosalie@msilver-pr.com
Web Site: www.finnpartners.com/about/brands/m-silver.html

Employees: 7

Agency Specializes In: Public Relations

Morris Silver *(Chm & CEO)*
Maria Brewer *(VP)*
Linda Ayares *(Sr Partner)*
Rosalie M. Hagel *(Sr Partner)*

Accounts:
Aruba
Epic Hotel
Hotel Sierra
Lodge Works
The Palmyra
The Plaza
Singapore Tourism Board
Turkey
Weastin

M-SQUARED PUBLIC RELATIONS
241 W Wieuca Rd Ste 260, Atlanta, GA 30342
Tel.: (404) 303-7797
E-Mail: hello@msquaredpr.com
Web Site: www.msquaredpr.com

Agency Specializes In: Brand Development & Integration, Crisis Communications, Event Planning & Marketing, Media Relations, Public Relations

Marsha Middleton *(Founder & Pres)*
Stephanie Fisher *(Acct Dir)*

Accounts:
New-Chef Linkie Marais
New-Four Seasons Hotel Atlanta

M18 PUBLIC RELATIONS
119 W 23rd St Ste 500, New York, NY 10011
Tel.: (212) 604-0318
E-Mail: info@m18pr.com
Web Site: www.m18pr.com

Year Founded: 2010

Agency Specializes In: Hospitality, Public Relations, Real Estate

Michael Tavani *(Co-Founder)*
Joey Arak *(Sr VP)*
Philip Ramirez *(VP)*
Nicola Amos *(Assoc Dir)*
Brittany Wechsler *(Acct Exec)*

Accounts:
Chelsea Improvement Company
The Line Hotel; Los Angeles
Macklowe Properties 432 Park Avenue Luxury Apartments
The NoMad Hotel; New York

MACCABEE GROUP, INC.
211 N 1st St Ste 425, Minneapolis, MN 55401
Tel.: (612) 337-0087
Fax: (612) 337-0054
E-Mail: paul@maccabee.com
Web Site: maccabee.com

Year Founded: 1996

Agency Specializes In: Communications, Crisis Communications, Direct Response Marketing, Event Planning & Marketing, Government/Political, Identity Marketing, Internet/Web Design, Local Marketing, Magazines, Media Relations, Media Training, Newspaper, Pets , Public Relations, Publicity/Promotions, Radio, Social Marketing/Nonprofit, Sponsorship, T.V.

Paul Maccabee *(Owner & Pres)*
Gwen Chynoweth *(Chief Talent Officer & Exec VP)*
Jean Hill *(Sr VP)*
Christina Milanowski *(Dir-Social Media & Acct Supvr)*

Accounts:
Start Fresh Recovery Program Communications, Media Relations, Public Relations, Social Media Marketing

MACIAS MEDIA GROUP LLC
(Acquired & Absorbed by MWWPR)

MACIAS PR
349 5th Ave, New York, NY 10016
Tel.: (646) 770-0541
Web Site: www.maciaspr.com

Agency Specializes In: Crisis Communications, Internet/Web Design, Newspaper, Public Relations, Social Media

Mark Macias *(Founder & CEO)*

Accounts:
New-Provident Loan

MAHOGANY BLUE PR
2729 Merrillee Dr Ste 413, Fairfax, VA 22031
Tel.: (312) 375-2752
Web Site: www.mahoganybluepr.com

Agency Specializes In: Media Relations, Public Relations, Social Media

Angel West *(Strategist-Media)*

Accounts:
Blush Wedding & Event Planning

MAIER & WARNER PUBLIC RELATIONS
90 Church St, Rockville, MD 20850
Tel.: (301) 424-4141
Web Site: www.maierwarnerpr.com

Agency Specializes In: Advertising, Brand Development & Integration, Collateral, Communications, Crisis Communications, Graphic Design, Logo & Package Design, Media Relations, Media Training, Public Relations

Charlie Maier *(Partner)*
Jennifer Shepherd *(CFO)*
Theresa Dipeppe *(Mgr-Mktg)*
Kristine Warner *(Specialist-Corp Comm)*

Accounts:
JBG Companies

MAJESTIC RELATIONS
13-15 W 28th St 8th Fl, New York, NY 10001
Tel.: (917) 993-0001
Web Site: www.majesticrelations.com

Year Founded: 2006

Agency Specializes In: Corporate Communications, Media Relations, Public Relations, Social Media

Vanessa Cabezas *(Owner)*
Ana Juarez *(Dir-Admin)*

Accounts:
Resort Martino
Telemundo Network Inc.
Univision Communications Inc.

MAKOVSKY & COMPANY, INC.
16 E 34th St 15th Fl, New York, NY 10016
Tel.: (212) 508-9600
Fax: (212) 751-9710
E-Mail: info@makovsky.com
Web Site: www.makovsky.com

Employees: 50
Year Founded: 1979

National Agency Associations: CIPR

Agency Specializes In: Business-To-Business, Electronic Media, Financial, Health Care Services, High Technology, Investor Relations, Sponsorship

Kenneth D. Makovsky *(Pres)*
Denise Vitola *(Mng Dir)*
Stacey Wachtfogel *(Chief HR Officer & Exec VP)*
Andrew Beck *(Exec VP & Gen Mgr-DC)*
Scott Tangney *(Exec VP)*
Michael Goodwin *(Sr VP-Fin & Pro Svcs)*
Tom Jones *(Sr VP-Health)*
Kona Luseni Barrasso *(Grp VP-Tech)*
Gaby Hui *(Asst Acct Exec-Fin & Pro Svcs)*
Michael Francoeur *(Acct Associate)*

Accounts:
Alexion Pharmaceuticals
New-Amarin Corporation
Aspex Eyewear (Agency of Record) EasyClip, EasyTwist, Greg Norman, Messaging, Strategy, Takumi
ATM Corporation
Bausch & Lomb, Inc.
Charles Schwab & Co., Inc.
Corporate Resource Services, Inc. Communications, Media Relations Strategy, Public & Investor Relations Agency of Record
Dataram Corporation Communications Campaign
Docent, Inc.
Equities First Holdings Branding, Corporate Identity, Interactive, Public Relations, Reputation Management, Social Media, Website
Frank Crystal & Company Branding, Corporate Identity, Interactive, Marketing, Public Relations, Social Media, Website
The Future In Focus Press, Public Relations
General Motors Asset Management
Johnson & Johnson
LC Connect
National Financial Partners
Neoprobe Corp.
Publicis Healthcare
Rocket Racing League Public Relations
Russell Reynolds Associates (Agency of Record); 2008
Touchstone Funds
TradeWeb
Weiss, Peck & Greer
Yasheng Group

MALEN YANTIS PUBLIC RELATIONS
PO Box 4868, Vail, CO 81658
Tel.: (970) 949-7919
E-Mail: info@myprco.com
Web Site: www.myprco.com

Year Founded: 2007

Agency Specializes In: Brand Development & Integration, Crisis Communications, Media Training, Public Relations, Social Media

Kristin Yantis *(Principal)*
Taylor Prather *(Asst Acct Exec)*

Accounts:
Black Tie Ski Rentals
Resort at Squaw Creek

MANA MEANS ADVERTISING & PUBLIC RELATIONS
1088 Bishop St Ste 1209, Honolulu, HI 96813
Tel.: (808) 521-1160
Fax: (808) 521-1104
E-Mail: info@manameansadvertising.com
Web Site: www.manameansadvertising.com

Employees: 10

Agency Specializes In: Public Relations

Janet M. Scheffer *(Pres & CEO)*

Accounts:
Century 21
G P Roadway Solutions
Hawaii Yacht Club
Hawaiian Eye Center
Security One
SMEI

MANIFEST
79 Madison Ave, New York, NY 10016
Tel.: (646) 893-3009
E-Mail: hello@manifest.nyc
Web Site: www.manifest.rocks

Agency Specializes In: Brand Development & Integration, Content, Digital/Interactive, Graphic Design, Media Relations, Public Relations, Social Media

Alex Myers *(CEO)*
John Conmy *(Mng Dir & Exec VP)*
Beth Tomkiw *(Exec VP & Gen Mgr-Manifest Life)*
Eric Goodstadt *(Exec VP-Client Svcs)*
Neil Hallmark *(Head-Digital)*
Stacy Newcomb *(Dir-Art)*
Camilla Jones *(Acct Exec)*

Accounts:
Closed on Mondays
Glug
Hot Octopuss
La Tasca
Morph Costumes
New-Sugru
Viber
William Reed International Wine Challenge

MANN BITES DOG
230 Park Ave 10th Fl Ste 1000, New York, NY 10169
Tel.: (949) 529-5110
Fax: (949) 612-0082
E-Mail: info@mannbitesdog.com

Agency Specializes In: Event Planning & Marketing, Public Relations

Lori Mann *(Pres & CEO)*

Accounts:
New-Burton Gray

MANNFOLK PR
606 N Larchmont Blvd Ste 206, Los Angeles, CA 90004
Tel.: (323) 460-2633
Web Site: www.mannfolkpr.com

Year Founded: 2000

Agency Specializes In: Advertising, Brand Development & Integration, Event Planning & Marketing, Media Relations, Public Relations, Social Media, Strategic Planning/Research

Dorothy Mannfolk *(Owner)*
Honor Hamilton *(Mgr-Showroom)*
Joseph Pastrana *(Mgr-Accounts)*

Accounts:
Pink Basis

MANNING SELVAGE & LEE, INC.
(Name Changed to MSLGROUP)

MANTRA PUBLIC RELATIONS, INC.
110 W 26th St 3rd Fl, New York, NY 10001
Tel.: (212) 645-1600
Fax: (212) 989-6459

Public Relations Firms

Toll Free: (800) 556-9495
E-Mail: info@mantrapublicrelations.com
Web Site: www.mantrapublicrelations.com

Employees: 3
Year Founded: 1987

Agency Specializes In: Affluent Market, Arts, Automotive, Aviation & Aerospace, Broadcast, Business-To-Business, Cable T.V., Children's Market, Communications, Computers & Software, Consulting, Consumer Goods, Consumer Publications, Corporate Communications, Corporate Identity, Cosmetics, Crisis Communications, Digital/Interactive, Education, Electronic Media, Electronics, Engineering, Entertainment, Environmental, Event Planning & Marketing, Faith Based, Fashion/Apparel, Financial, Food Service, Gay & Lesbian Market, Government/Political, Health Care Services, High Technology, Hospitality, Household Goods, Industrial, Information Technology, International, Leisure, Luxury Products, Magazines, Media Relations, Media Training, Medical Products, Men's Market, Multicultural, New Product Development, New Technologies, Newspaper, Newspapers & Magazines, Over-50 Market, Pets , Pharmaceutical, Planning & Consultation, Print, Product Placement, Public Relations, Publicity/Promotions, Radio, Real Estate, Restaurant, Retail, Seniors' Market, Social Media, Strategic Planning/Research, T.V., Teen Market, Trade & Consumer Magazines, Transportation, Travel & Tourism, Tween Market, Urban Market, Women's Market

Approx. Annual Billings: $1,000,000

Breakdown of Gross Billings by Media: Fees: $1,000,000

Gaye Carleton *(Founder & Pres)*

Accounts:
Cascade Coil Drapery Architectural Products
inFormed Space; Sonoma, CA Non Functional Furniture for the Staging Industry; 2011
Portico West; San Francisco, CA Real Estate Development; 2001

MAPLES COMMUNICATIONS, INC.

2591 Acero, Mission Viejo, CA 92691-2784
Tel.: (949) 276-7119
Fax: (949) 855-3566
E-Mail: info@maples.com
Web Site: www.maples.com

Employees: 13
Year Founded: 1993

National Agency Associations: PRSA

Agency Specializes In: High Technology

Robert E. Maples *(Pres)*

Accounts:
(ISC)2
Atlantic
Cisco Consumer Business Group (Agency of Record)
Fujitsu Microelectronics
Networks-in-Motion

MARCH COMMUNICATIONS

226 Causeway St 4th Fl, Boston, MA 02114
Tel.: (617) 960-9875
Fax: (617) 960-9876
E-Mail: info@marchpr.com
Web Site: www.marchpr.com

Agency Specializes In: Communications, Content, Digital/Interactive, Public Relations, Search Engine Optimization, Social Media, Sponsorship

Courtney Allen *(Acct Mgr-PR)*
Marina Askari *(Asst Acct Exec)*
Samantha Bell *(Sr Acct Exec)*
Beth Brenner *(VP)*
Christian Chrysogiannis *(Assoc Media Planner)*
Meredith L. Eaton *(Acct Dir)*
Erica Frank *(Acct Dir)*
Cheryl Gale *(Mng Partner)*
James Gerber *(Acct Mgr)*
Jordan Ingram *(Acct Exec)*
Stephanie Jackman *(Sr Acct Exec)*
Martin Jones *(CEO)*
Hailey Melamut *(Acct Coord)*
Lisa Pastor *(Acct Coord)*

Accounts:
3Q Digital Content Marketing, Email Marketing
ArcTouch Content Marketing, Email Marketing
ASG Software Solutions
Brand Protect
Cambridge Consultants
Canonical
CloudSigma
CSR
Deep Information Sciences Content Marketing, Email Marketing
Fasetto Content Marketing, Email Marketing
FitNatic Content Marketing, Email Marketing
Mimecast Public Relations
Mobally
Open-Xchange
OriginGPS Content Marketing, Email Marketing
The Rey3 Design Collaborative Brand Messaging, Marketing Communications, Public Relations, Social Media
Scredible Content Marketing, Email Marketing
Taykey Public Relations
Trapit

MARGIE KORSHAK INC.

875 N Michigan Ave Ste 1535, Chicago, IL 60611
Tel.: (312) 751-2121
Fax: (312) 751-1422
E-Mail: ledwards@korshak.com
Web Site: www.korshak.com

E-Mail for Key Personnel:
President: mkorshak@korshak.com
Media Dir.: lplumbtree@korshak.com

Employees: 30
Year Founded: 1969

Agency Specializes In: Advertising, Brand Development & Integration, Business Publications, Children's Market, Communications, Consulting, Consumer Marketing, Consumer Publications, Electronic Media, Entertainment, Event Planning & Marketing, Fashion/Apparel, Graphic Design, Magazines, Media Buying Services, Newspaper, Newspapers & Magazines, Print, Public Relations, Publicity/Promotions, Radio, Restaurant, Retail, Sports Market, T.V., Trade & Consumer Magazines, Travel & Tourism

Approx. Annual Billings: $2,500,000

Breakdown of Gross Billings by Media: Radio: $1,250,000; T.V.: $1,250,000

Margie Korshak *(Chm)*
Janie Goldberg-Dicks *(Pres)*
Lada Plumtree *(VP-Adv & Promos)*
Tori Bryan *(Asst Acct Exec)*

Accounts:
Elizabeth Arden Salon
Encyclopedia Britannica, Inc.
Exhale Spa
Gap
Illinois Lottery
Illinois Office of Tourism
J. Brach Corporation
Lettuce Entertain You Enterprises Restaurants; Chicago, IL; 1997
McDonald Owners of Chicagoland & N.W. Indiana; Chicago,IL; 1997
McDonald's Corporation
Piper Sonoma Wines
Pump Room
Sofitel
Spago
The Upjohn Company

MARIA CHRISSOVERGIS PUBLIC RELATIONS

567 St Claude Pl, Jacksonville, FL 32259
Tel.: (904) 762-4573
E-Mail: info@mcpragency.com
Web Site: www.mcpragency.com

Year Founded: 2012

Agency Specializes In: Advertising, Content, Event Planning & Marketing, Internet/Web Design, Media Planning, Media Relations, Media Training, Public Relations, Social Media, Strategic Planning/Research

Maria Chrissovergis *(Owner & Pres)*
Dana Jiles *(Dir-PR)*
Anastasia Mann *(Mgr-Digital Mktg)*

Accounts:
Cote Renard Architecture
Dunes Properties
Kiawah & Seabrook Real Estate & Rentals
Orangetheory Fitness
Paradise Key
Point Pleasant Resort
Youth Crisis Center

MARINA MAHER COMMUNICATIONS

830 3rd Ave, New York, NY 10022
Tel.: (212) 485-6800
Fax: (212) 355-6318
E-Mail: mmaher@mahercomm.com
Web Site: www.mahercomm.com

E-Mail for Key Personnel:
President: mmaher@mahercomm.com

Employees: 150
Year Founded: 1983

National Agency Associations: COPF

Agency Specializes In: African-American Market, Communications, Consumer Marketing, Cosmetics, Entertainment, Event Planning & Marketing, Exhibit/Trade Shows, Fashion/Apparel, Food Service, Health Care Services, Hispanic Market, Medical Products, Over-50 Market, Pharmaceutical, Public Relations, Publicity/Promotions, Retail, Sponsorship, T.V., Teen Market

Marina Maher *(CEO)*
Suzanne Haber *(Mng Dir)*
Aimee Leonido *(Mng Dir)*
David Richeson *(Mng Dir)*
Susan Bean *(Exec VP-Media Connections)*
Nancy Lowman LaBadie *(Exec VP)*
Diana Paige *(Exec VP)*
Matthew Rotker *(Dir-Fin & Sr VP)*
Edwin Endlich *(Sr VP-Digital Consumer)*
Samara Finn *(Sr VP-Online Media & influencer Rels)*
Mary Beth Murphy *(Sr VP-HR)*
Kimberly Stokes *(Mng Dir-Digital & Social Media)*
Matt Duralek *(VP-Talent Acq)*
Annie Fileta *(VP-Mktg)*
Veronica Rodriguez *(VP-Digital Strategy)*

Lucia Jimenez *(Acct Supvr)*
Alexandra Papazis *(Acct Supvr)*
Jenna Glynn *(Sr Acct Exec)*
Alexandra Kahrer *(Sr Acct Exec)*
Lauren Lonson *(Sr Acct Exec)*
Stacey Levine *(Asst Acct Exec & Specialist-Consumer Media)*
Janelle Cracco *(Acct Exec)*
Ronna Waldman *(Specialist-Media)*
Caitlin Schumacher *(Asst Acct Exec)*

Accounts:
Bayer HealthCare Aleve, Aspirin, Flintstones Vitamins, One-A-Day
Celgene Abraxane, Otezla
Eisai Epilepsy Franchise
Henkel Dial
Invista Stainmaster
Kimberly-Clark Corporation Depends, Kotex, Poise
Merck Merck Manuals, Merck for Mothers, Women's Health
Merz Mederma
Novo Nordisk Insulin Franchise, Victoza
Procter & Gamble Aussie, Clairol, Covergirl, Downy, Global Olympic PR, Head & Shoulders, Herbal Essences, Secret, Tide, Venus
RB Durex, K-Y

MARIPOSA COMMUNICATIONS
167 Madison Ave Ste 204, New York, NY 10016
Tel.: (212) 534-7939
E-Mail: info@mariposa-communications.com
Web Site: www.mariposa-communications.com

Agency Specializes In: Digital/Interactive, Public Relations, Social Media

Liz Anthony *(Founder & Pres)*
Mallory Goldstein *(Acct Exec)*

Accounts:
New-Kiel James Patrick
New-Rosena Sammi Jewelry

THE MARKET CONNECTION
20051 SW Birch St, Newport Beach, CA 92660
Tel.: (949) 851-6313
Fax: (949) 833-0253
E-Mail: tmc@tmcauto.com
Web Site: www.tmcauto.com

Employees: 2
Year Founded: 1986

Agency Specializes In: Advertising, Automotive, Collateral, Consulting, Consumer Publications, Corporate Communications, Event Planning & Marketing, Graphic Design, Media Relations, Public Relations, Publicity/Promotions, Publishing, Trade & Consumer Magazines

Jay Jones *(Pres & CEO)*

Accounts:
Toyo Tire USA Corp.; Cypress, CA Toyo Tires

MARKETCOM PUBLIC RELATIONS, LLC
36 E 23rd St 3rd Fl, New York, NY 10010
Tel.: (212) 537-5177
E-Mail: lbrophy@marketcompr.com
Web Site: www.marketcompr.com

Employees: 8

Greg Miller *(Founder & Pres)*
Rosalia Scampoli *(Sr Dir-Media)*
Laura Brophy *(Dir-Client Svcs & New Bus Dev)*
Tracy Van Buskirk *(Sr Acct Mgr)*
Sue Mattison *(Mgr-Client Support)*
Joan Motyka *(Sr Writer)*

Accounts:
Altus Capital Partners
Association Junior League International
Canon Communications LLC; 2006
DMi Partners
GNC Financial Communications
J.G. Wentworth; 2007
Summit Business Media

MARKETING MAVEN PUBLIC RELATIONS, INC.
2390 C Las Posas Rd Ste 479, Camarillo, CA 93010
Tel.: (310) 994-7380
Fax: (310) 868-0222
E-Mail: info@marketingmavenpr.com
Web Site: www.marketingmavenpr.com

Year Founded: 2009

Agency Specializes In: Direct Response Marketing, Event Planning & Marketing, Hispanic Market, Internet/Web Design, Public Relations, Search Engine Optimization, Social Media

Lindsey Carnett *(Pres & CEO)*
Phil Rarick *(COO)*
Natalie Rucker *(VP-Bus Dev)*
John Carnett *(Exec Dir-Bus Dev)*
Aljolynn Sperber *(Mgr-Social Media)*
Mari Escamilla *(Sr Acct Exec)*
Valeria Velasco *(Acct Exec)*

Accounts:
American Beverage Consortium
Bulu Box

MARKETING RESOURCE MANAGEMENT
PO Box 58, Aldie, VA 20105
Tel.: (703) 304-3852
E-Mail: info@stevehines.com
Web Site: www.stevehines.com

Steve Hines *(Owner)*

Accounts:
American Society of Association Executives
Building Owners and Managers Association
Conservation & Research Center Foundation
Estwing Manufacturing

MARLO MARKETING COMMUNICATIONS
667 Boylston St 3rd Fl, Boston, MA 02116
Tel.: (617) 375-9700
Fax: (617) 375-9797
E-Mail: info@marlomc.com
Web Site: marlomarketing.com

Employees: 20

Agency Specializes In: Public Relations

Lisa LaMontagne MacGillivray *(Mng Dir)*
Marlo Fogelman *(Principal)*
Brian Charron *(Dir-Creative)*
Meghan McCarrick *(Acct Mgr)*
Robbin Watson *(Acct Mgr)*
Emma Wilson *(Acct Exec)*
Matt Willett *(Designer)*

Accounts:
New-Ames Street Deli
Andegavia Cask Wines National Media Communications
New-Backbar (Agency of Record)
New-Cameron Mitchell Restaurant Group
Canti Prosecco
New-The Envoy Hotel Marketing Campaign, Media Relations, Social Media
New-Grand Amore Hotel and Spa Marketing, Public Relations
New-Journeyman (Agency of Record)
New-Latitude Beverage Company 90+ Cellars, Mija Sangria, Trade Outreach
LimoLiner LLC Advertising, Marketing, Public Relations, Social Media
New-Locke-Ober Yvonne's
The Mary Jane Group CannaCamp, Media
Motto Sparkling Matcha Tea Social Media
New-Northbridge Companies
Privateer Rum Consumer & Trade Events, National & Regional Media Communications
New-Simply7 Snacks (Agency of Record) National & Regional Marketing Public Relations
New-South Hollow Spirits
New-StarChefs International Chefs Congress 10th Annual Congress, Media Relations
New-Study
New-WeWork Boston
Zoo New England

MAROON PUBLIC RELATIONS
Columbia Corporate Park 8825 Stanford Blvd Ste 145, Columbia, MD 21045
Tel.: (443) 864-4246
Fax: (443) 864-4266
E-Mail: info@maroonpr.com
Web Site: www.maroonpr.com

Employees: 13
Year Founded: 2006

Agency Specializes In: Sports Market

John Maroon *(Founder & CEO)*
Mitchell Schmale *(VP-Client Svcs)*
Chris Daley *(Dir-Brand & Bus Dev)*
Megan Pringle *(Dir-News & Multimedia)*
Carolyn Maroon *(Office Mgr)*
Breana Fischer *(Mgr-Social Media & Digital)*
Eleanor Arlook *(Sr Acct Exec)*
Eve Hemsley *(Sr Acct Exec)*
Alex Jackson *(Sr Acct Exec)*
Marlene Cummingham *(Assoc Acct Exec)*

Accounts:
Anacostia Watershed Society
Atlantic League of Professional Baseball Clubs, Inc. Brand Development, Media Relations, Social Media, Strategic Communications
Authobahn Indoor Speedway
Babe Ruth Museum
Big Cork Vineyards Digital Media Marketing, Media Relations, Social Marketing
Carluccio's Event Support, Media Buying, Media Relations, Social Media
Catholic Charities of the Archdiocese of Washington Brand Development, Media Relations
The Colonial Athletic Association Media Relations, Social Media, Strategic Partnerships
Decisive Communications Marketing Communications
Famous Dave's Event Support, Marketing, Media Buying, Media Relations, Public Relations, Social Media
New-Feherty's Troops First Foundation (Agency of Record) Media Relations, Program Development, Social Media Marketing
The First Tee of Baltimore Marketing Communications
Ford Gum & Machine Co. Big League Chew (Agency of Record), Media, Public Relations, Social Media
Geier Financial Group
Hard Rock Cafe
Hero Rush Market-to-Market, National Media Relations, Social Media, Strategic Partnership
House of Ruth Maryland Marketing Communications
Jamie Moyer Baseball Pitcher, Media Relations
Legacy Direct
LPGA International Crown
Madd Gear

Maryland Live! Casino
MBRT
MDMEP
Mid-Atlantic Nursery Trade Show Media Relations, Social Media
Mission BBQ
MNS Group
New Day USA
The Oregon Grille
Players' Philanthropy Fund PR
POWERHANDZ Marketing Communications
Ripken Baseball Social Media
Sagamore Racing
ShakeUp Marketing Communications
Share Our Strength Digital Media Marketing, Media Relations, Social Marketing
Towson University Athletics
Under Armour All-America Baseball Game
U.S. Soccer Foundation Digital Media Marketing, Media Relations, Social Marketing
Walmart Public Relations

MARQUET MEDIA, LLC

353 E 83rd St, New York, NY 10028
Tel.: (917) 355-2225
E-Mail: info@marquet-media.com
Web Site: www.marquet-media.com

Year Founded: 2009

Agency Specializes In: Content, Crisis Communications, Public Relations, Social Media, Strategic Planning/Research

Accounts:
Mixed Digital LLC

MARSHALL FENN COMMUNICATIONS LTD.

890 Yonge St Ste 300, Toronto, ON M4W 3P4 Canada
Tel.: (416) 962-3366
Fax: (416) 962-3375
E-Mail: info@marshall-fenn.com
Web Site: www.marshall-fenn.com

Employees: 20
Year Founded: 1955

Agency Specializes In: Advertising, Digital/Interactive, Direct Response Marketing, Entertainment, Event Planning & Marketing, Market Research, Media Planning, Promotions, Public Relations

Approx. Annual Billings: $23,000,000

Paul Chater *(Owner)*
Andrew Gage *(Partner & Exec VP)*
David Zbar *(Partner & Sr VP)*
Tom Batho *(VP-Media Strategy)*
Rizwan Siddiqui *(Comptroller)*
Monika Capriotti *(Sr Dir-Interactive Art)*
Steve Markham *(Sr Acct Dir)*
Jennifer Lynch *(Dir-Digital & Social Media Strategy)*
Lorie Spencer *(Sr Acct Mgr)*
Janet Brooks *(Office Mgr)*
Dan Zinman *(Acct Mgr)*
Ryan Franklin *(Sr Graphic Designer)*

Accounts:
24 Hours
BOOST for KIDS Campaign: "Make the Call"
The Brick
Caesars
Canadian Tour
Engineers Canada
Green Shield
Jamaica Tourist Board
Mount Sinai Hospital
Nisim
Novajet
Ontario Lottery Corp.; ON
Panasonic Canada; Mississauga, ON
Sun Media
Volvo

MARTIN DAVISON PUBLIC RELATIONS

477 Main St, Buffalo, NY 14203
Tel.: (716) 604-7772
Web Site: www.mdavison.com

National Agency Associations: 4A's

Agency Specializes In: Crisis Communications, Media Training, Public Relations

Matt Davison *(Mng Partner)*

Accounts:
New-43North
New-Niagara Falls Bridge Commission

MARTIN FLORY GROUP

PO Box 360, Gurnee, IL 60031
Tel.: (847) 662-9070
Fax: (847) 336-7126
E-Mail: info@martinflory.com
Web Site: www.martinflory.com

Agency Specializes In: Outdoor, Public Relations

Laura Martin *(Pres)*

Accounts:
TideSlide

MARTIN THOMAS INTERNATIONAL, PUBLIC RELATIONS DIVISION

42 Riverside Dr, Barrington, RI 02806
Tel.: (401) 245-8500
Fax: (866) 899-2710
E-Mail: contact@martinthomas.com
Web Site: www.martinthomas.com

E-Mail for Key Personnel:
President: mpottle@martinthomas.com

Employees: 7
Year Founded: 1987

National Agency Associations: Second Wind Limited

Agency Specializes In: Advertising, Brand Development & Integration, Business-To-Business, Collateral, Consulting, Corporate Identity, Direct Response Marketing, Graphic Design, Industrial, Internet/Web Design, Logo & Package Design, Medical Products, New Product Development, Pharmaceutical, Public Relations, Publicity/Promotions, Strategic Planning/Research, Technical Advertising, Trade & Consumer Magazines

Approx. Annual Billings: $2,000,000

Martin K. Pottle *(Founder)*

Accounts:
Beaumont Technologies, Inc.; Erie, PA Processing Software; 2001
Gros Plastic Recruiters
Inoex, Inc.
National Plastics Center & Museum; Leominster, MA
Polyzen, Inc.; Cary, NC Medical Products; 1998
PVC Container Corporation

MARY BETH WEST COMMUNICATIONS

3401 Russ Cir St C, Alcoa, TN 37701
Tel.: (865) 982-6626
E-Mail: info@marybethwest.com
Web Site: www.marybethwest.com

Year Founded: 2003

Agency Specializes In: Advertising, Digital/Interactive, Print, Public Relations, Social Media

Randy McGinnis *(COO)*
Mary Beth West *(Principal)*
Tori Rose *(Dir-Creative-Digital Media)*
Taylor Hathorn *(Mgr-Comm)*
Marijo Soto *(Designer)*
April Timko *(Client Svc Dir)*

Accounts:
Sugarlands Distilling Company

MAS BRANDING

2431 Bartlett St, Houston, TX 77098
Tel.: (619) 254-1962
Web Site: www.masbranding.com

Year Founded: 2009

Agency Specializes In: Brand Development & Integration, Content, Event Planning & Marketing, Public Relations, Social Media

Alejandra Gomez *(Mgr-Multicultural Outreach)*

Accounts:
La Casa Del Caballo Houston

MASTO PUBLIC RELATIONS

1811 Western Ave, Albany, NY 12203
Tel.: (518) 786-6488
Fax: (518) 786-6497
E-Mail: mastopr@mastopr.com
Web Site: www.mastopr.com

Employees: 8
Year Founded: 1986

Agency Specializes In: High Technology, Industrial, Public Relations

Howard T. Masto *(Pres)*
Ken Darling *(VP)*

Accounts:
GE Energy
GE Oil & Gas
GE Water

MATTHEW VLAHOS PUBLIC RELATIONS, LLC.

1 Penn Sq W 30 S 15th St 14th Fl, Philadelphia, PA 19102
Tel.: (267) 687-0222
E-Mail: hello@vlahospr.com
Web Site: www.vlahospr.com

Agency Specializes In: Public Relations, Social Media

Matthew Vlahos *(Founder & Principal)*

Accounts:
Bar AIDS
Daisy Martinez
Philadelphia Science Festival

MAVERICK PUBLIC RELATIONS

37 Madison Ave, Toronto, ON M5R 2S2 Canada
Tel.: (416) 640-5525
Fax: (416) 640-5524
Web Site: www.wearemaverick.com

Employees: 14

Agency Specializes In: Communications, Corporate Communications, Crisis Communications, Entertainment, Exhibit/Trade Shows, Financial, Food Service, Government/Political, Health Care Services, Investor Relations, Leisure, Media Relations, Media Training, Promotions, Public Relations, Real Estate, Sponsorship, Travel & Tourism

Julie Rusciolelli *(Founder & Pres)*
Gerry Riddell *(Owner)*
Rick Byun *(VP-Strategy & Bus Dev)*
Colin Nekolaichuk *(Acct Dir)*
Micha Goddard *(Dir-Integrated Consumer Mktg)*
Melanie Filipp *(Acct Mgr)*
Anne Mullen *(Office Mgr)*
Magda Jarota *(Acct Supvr-Consumer Mktg)*

Accounts:
Evian
Moneris
Richtree Natural Market Restaurants PR
Royal Winter Agricultural Fair (Agency of Record) PR

MAX BORGES AGENCY

3050 Biscayne Blvd Ste 701, Miami, FL 33137
Tel.: (305) 374-4404
Fax: (305) 402-6373
E-Mail: info@maxborgesagency.com
Web Site: www.maxborgesagency.com

Employees: 25

National Agency Associations: COPF

Agency Specializes In: Computers & Software, Electronics, High Technology, Public Relations

Max Borges *(Pres)*
Michael Young *(Exec VP)*
Greg Mondshein *(VP-Bus Dev)*
Matt Shumate *(VP)*
Kristen Mondshein *(Sr Acct Exec)*
Lissette Calveiro *(Acct Exec)*
Nichole Teixeira *(Acct Coord)*

Accounts:
Ambient
AOC (Agency of Record)
Archos (Agency of Record)
AT&T Mobility (National Social Agency of Record)
AT&T Cricket (National Social Agency of Record)
Bracketron (Agency of Record)
Clarion
New-Custom Electronic Design & Installation Association (Agency of Record)
Goal Zero Public Relations
Jaybird (Agency of Record)
Jorno (Agency of Record) Pocket-Sized, Folding, Bluetooth Keyboard
Kanex (Agency of Record)
Keyport Inc. (Agency of Record)
Monster Arts, Inc Communications, Marketing, Media Relations, Public Relations Agency of Record
Moshi (Agency of Record)
Motrr
MSI (Agency of Record)
Music Wizard Group; Boulder, CO Blackline GPS
Musubo
MyPix2Canvas
NetSecure (Agency of Record)
NuForce (Agency of Record)
Numark Industries (Agency of Record)
OGIO International, Inc. Marketing, Marketing Campaign, Silencer Golf Bag, Social Media, TV
Palo Alto Audio
Pandora
Party Poker (National Social Agency of Record)
PLX Devices (Agency of Record) Consumer Electronics
Polar (Agency of Record) Experiential
Portable Sound Laboratories (Agency of Record) Portable Speaker Systems
PowerSkin Public Relations
PowerSkin (Agency of Record)
RageGage (Agency of Record)
Root Four Imagination (Agency of Record) Automotive Consumer Electronics
Safe Skies (Agency of Record)
Samson
ScheduALL Public Relations
Sculpteo (Agency of Record) 3D Custom Printing Service
SmartShopper (Agency of Record) Marketing Communications, PR
SpareOne Public Relations
Stem Innovation (Agency of Record) Marketing Communications, PR
SuperTooth (Agency of Record) Marketing Communications, PR
Swissvoice Public Relations
Urbanears
V-MODA (Agency of Record)
Verbatim Americas, LLC; Charlotte, NC (Agency of Record) Marketing Communications, Media Relations, Public Relations
VeriFone Systems, Inc.
Vogel's (Agency of Record)
Wattbike (Agency of Record)
Zepp Labs (National Social Agency of Record)
Zero1 (Agency of Record)
Zibra
Zound Industries Urban Ears

MAXIMUM EXPOSURE PUBLIC RELATIONS & MEDIA

(Formerly Maximum Exposure P.R. & Media)
50 Tice Blvd, Woodcliff Lake, NJ 07677-7654
Tel.: (201) 573-0300
Fax: (201) 573-0376
E-Mail: info@maximumexposurepr.com
Web Site: www.maximumexposurepr.com

E-Mail for Key Personnel:
President: renee@maximumexposurepr.com

Employees: 5
Year Founded: 1986

Agency Specializes In: Advertising Specialties, African-American Market, Brand Development & Integration, Business Publications, Business-To-Business, Collateral, Communications, Consumer Marketing, Consumer Publications, Corporate Identity, Cosmetics, Direct Response Marketing, E-Commerce, Education, Electronic Media, Entertainment, Event Planning & Marketing, Exhibit/Trade Shows, Fashion/Apparel, Food Service, Gay & Lesbian Market, Graphic Design, Hispanic Market, Infomercials, Internet/Web Design, Logo & Package Design, Magazines, Media Buying Services, Medical Products, New Product Development, Newspaper, Newspapers & Magazines, Over-50 Market, Print, Public Relations, Publicity/Promotions, Real Estate, Retail, Seniors' Market, Sweepstakes, T.V., Teen Market, Trade & Consumer Magazines, Transportation, Travel & Tourism

Renee Sall *(Owner & Pres)*

Accounts:
Calko Medical Center
Confections of a Rock Star Bakery
Gramercy Pain Management
The Marcal Group
Modiani Kitchens
New Image Camps
Ron White Memory Training
The Style Duo
USA Memory Championship

MAXWELL PR

3934 Sw Corbett Ave, Portland, OR 97239
Tel.: (503) 231-3086
Fax: (503) 231-3089
E-Mail: info@maxwellpr.com
Web Site: www.maxwellpr.com

Employees: 7
Year Founded: 1997

National Agency Associations: PRSA-WOMMA

Agency Specializes In: Public Relations

Jennifer Maxwell-Muir *(Founder & Principal)*
Amber Lindsey *(Owner)*
Vicky Hastings *(Mng Dir)*
Erika Simms *(Acct Dir)*
Kevin Lee *(Acct Supvr)*
Marta Drevniak *(Sr Acct Exec)*
Jessica Lyness *(Specialist-Social Media)*
Sara Stewart *(Acct Exec)*
Nicole Dionisopoulos *(Acct Coord)*
Niki Inouye *(Coord-Digital)*

Accounts:
Alima Pure
Argyle Winery
Astoria-Warrenton Chamber of Commerce
Columbus Foods Public Relations
Dave's Killer Bread Media, National Brand Building, Social Advertising
Diamond Foods Diamond of California, National Brand Building
Kettle Brands
Kettle Foods (Agency of Record)
La Terra Fina
McMenamins Pubs Breweries & Historic Hotels Media, Tourism Communications
Oregon Cherry Growers
Pacific Natural Foods
Pamela's Products Company Profile, Product Awareness
Traditional Medicinals Company Profile, Product Awareness
Travel Oregon
USA Dry Pea & Lentil Council Consumer Awareness, Media Engagement, Social Media
Willamette Valley Visitors Association

THE MAYFIELD GROUP

1401 Oven Pk Dr Ste 101, Tallahassee, FL 32308
Tel.: (850) 421-9007
E-Mail: info@mayfieldpr.com
Web Site: www.mayfieldpr.com

Agency Specializes In: Event Planning & Marketing, Media Relations, Media Training, Public Relations, Social Marketing/Nonprofit, Strategic Planning/Research

Autumn Mayfield *(Founder & Principal)*
Nancy Click *(Acct Dir)*

Accounts:
New-Cotoncolors

MAYO COMMUNICATIONS

7248 Bernandine Ave 2nd Fl, Los Angeles, CA 91307
Tel.: (818) 340-5300
Fax: (818) 340-2550
E-Mail: Publicity@MayoCommunications.com
Web Site: www.mayocommunications.com

Employees: 14

Agency Specializes In: Public Relations, Publicity/Promotions

Aida Mayo *(Pres & Owner-PR & Entertainment Publicity)*
George McQuade *(Owner)*

Accounts:
Book Author Tom Rock
California Green Collar Jobs
Children of the Caribbean, Inc. (Agency of Record) National Public Relations
Community Distribution Center
Kristen Faulconer
The Los Angeles County Economic Development Corporation (LAEDC) (Agency of Record)
Silver To Rust Productions
Sol Romoero
Sun Born Natural Products Co.; Grass Valley, CA (Agency of Record) National Education Campaign, National Publicity, The California Combat Sports Triple-Challenge
World Trade Center Los Angeles-Long Beach (WTCA LA-LB) (Agency of Record)
WW2 Reflections
WW2-Reflections
WYATT Films, LLC

MCCLENAHAN BRUER COMMUNICATIONS
5331 SW Macadam Ave Ste 220, Portland, OR 97239
Tel.: (503) 546-1000
Fax: (503) 546-1001
E-Mail: info@mcbru.com
Web Site: www.mcbru.com

Employees: 20
Year Founded: 1993

National Agency Associations: PRSA

Agency Specializes In: High Technology

Kerry McClenahan *(Founder & CEO)*
James McIntyre *(Partner & VP-Client Svcs)*
Jonathan Adams *(Dir-Creative)*
Erica Harbison *(Strategist-Client)*
Sarah Mackenzie *(Acct Coord)*
Anna Reinhard *(Acct Coord)*

Accounts:
Altium
Itanium Solutions Alliance (Agency of Record)
ON Semiconductor Public Relations
Reaction Design
SMSC

MCCLOUD & ASSOCIATES PR
4834 26th Ave N, Saint Petersburg, FL 33713
Tel.: (727) 385-0691
Web Site: www.mccloudpra.com

Year Founded: 1995

Agency Specializes In: Crisis Communications, Media Relations, Media Training, Promotions, Public Relations, Strategic Planning/Research

Hubert McCloud *(Founder & Chief Comm Officer)*

Accounts:
Hot City Records LLC

MCCULLOUGH PUBLIC RELATIONS, INC.
3570 Executive Dr Ste 104, Uniontown, OH 44685
Tel.: (330) 244-9980
Fax: (330) 244-9981
Web Site: www.mcculloughpr.com

Employees: 8

Agency Specializes In: Automotive, Public Relations

Shari McCullough-Arfons *(Pres)*
Becky Shephard *(Dir-Ops)*

Accounts:
American Force Wheels Aftermarket Light Truck Wheels
ARE Fiberglass Truck Caps and Tonneau Covers
Corsa Performance Exhausts Automotive, Truck Performance Exhaust Systems
Lingenfelter Performance Engineering; Decatur, IN Experts in Performance Engine Design, Building and Installation
Maradyne High Performance Cooling Fans, Blowers, AC/DC Motors & Heaters
Prolong Super Lubricants Advanced Automotive Engine & Fuel Treatments
Standards Testing Labs; Massillon, OH Independent Testing Facility for Tires, Wheels & Automotive Components

THE MCDONNELL GROUP INC.
2010 Stonegrove Pl, Roswell, GA 30075-3582
Tel.: (404) 583-0003
Fax: (770) 565-1218
E-Mail: inquiry@themcdonnellgroup.com
Web Site: www.themcdonnellgroup.com

Agency Specializes In: Public Relations, Strategic Planning/Research

Charlotte McDonnell *(Chm)*
Don McDonnell *(CEO)*
Paige Besson *(Mng Dir & Exec VP)*
Nancy Broe *(Dir-PR)*
Alisa Ellison *(Mgr-Ops)*
Whitney McDonnell *(Mgr-PR)*
Jason Farhadi *(Acct Exec-PR)*

Accounts:
ABB
Advanced Control Systems Inc. Grid Automation & System Solutions
GridMaven Utility Solutions GridMaven Network Manager, Media Relations, Public Relations
KEMA Business-to-Business Communications, Public Relations, Strategic Media Relations
Line Imaging
MEDecision
OSLsoft
Powel
Signum Group Enterprise Asset Management Services
Utility Associates
Utility Integration Solutions Inc. Utility Industry Business Integration Services

MCDOUGALL COMMUNICATIONS LLC
2423 Monroe Ave 2nd Fl, Rochester, NY 14618
Tel.: (585) 441-0202
E-Mail: info@mcdougallpr.com
Web Site: www.mcdougallpr.com

Year Founded: 2011

Agency Specializes In: Crisis Communications, Media Training, Public Relations, Social Media

Mike Mcdougall *(Pres)*
Brandonne Rankin *(Acct Mgr)*
Julie Rudd *(Coord)*

Accounts:
3Pound Health
Bergmann Associates
Boylan Code
CooperVision, Inc
International Association of Contact Lens Educators
The New York Golf Trail
Pura Naturals
Transcat, Inc.

MCGOVERN COMMUNICATIONS
27 Elmore St, Arlington, MA 02476
Tel.: (781) 315-3400

Employees: 5
Year Founded: 1995

Agency Specializes In: Advertising

Approx. Annual Billings: $1,000,000

Sue McGovern *(Founder & Dir-PR)*

Accounts:
The Full Yield
JUST LABEL IT; Washington, DC; 2011
Organic Trade Association
Red Tomato
StonyField

MCGRATH/POWER
333 W San Carlos St Ste 900, San Jose, CA 95110
Tel.: (408) 727-0351
Fax: (408) 885-9317
Web Site: www.mcgrathpower.com

Employees: 20

Agency Specializes In: E-Commerce, Electronic Media, High Technology, Information Technology, Public Relations, Publicity/Promotions

Jonathan Bloom *(Founder & CEO)*
Kathryn Walker *(Partner & Sr VP)*
Derek James *(Partner & VP)*
Patti Adams-Murphy *(Dir-Ops & Fin)*
Andi Bean *(Sr Acct Exec)*
Lisette Rauwendaal *(Sr Acct Exec)*
Marta Weissenborn *(Sr Acct Exec)*

Accounts:
Abode Systems Communications
Apriva Social Media
Clearswift Communications, Social Media, Traditional Media
Cognitive Networks
DayMen Brand Awareness, Communications, Consumer, Strategy
Fusion Garage (Agency of Record) Grid-10 Tablet
GuardianEdge
IDA Ireland
INXPO
LeanKit
LiveOps Corporate & Product Communications, Social & Traditional Media, Strategy Development
Mellanox Technologies (Agency of Record) Analyst Relations Strategy, Awards, Communications, Tradeshow, Traditional Media
Monkeybars PR
Moovweb PR
Open Networking Foundation (Agency of Record) Media Relations, Messaging, PR, Social Media, Strategy
Rainmaker Systems
SST/ShotSpotter
Ubiquity, Inc Branding, Communications, U.S. Agency of Record
Velocify

MCKENDALL COMMUNICATIONS
7519 Dunfield Ave, Los Angeles, CA 90045
Tel.: (310) 641-1556
Web Site: www.mckendall.com

Agency Specializes In: Event Planning & Marketing, Media Relations, Media Training, Public Relations, Social Media, Strategic Planning/Research

Lisa McKendall *(Pres & Partner)*
Lauren Yacker *(Sr VP)*
Shannon Kalvig *(VP)*

Mara Parker *(VP)*
Paul June *(Specialist-Strategic Socially Digital Mktg)*
Lydia Smith *(Acct Exec)*

Accounts:
Idea Health & Fitness Association Idea World Fitness Convention

MCNEELY, PIGOTT & FOX

611 Commerce St Ste 2800, Nashville, TN 37203
Tel.: (615) 259-4000
Fax: (615) 259-4040
Toll Free: (800) 818-6953
E-Mail: info@mpf.com
Web Site: www.mpf.com

Employees: 70
Year Founded: 1987

Agency Specializes In: Public Relations, Sponsorship

Mark McNeely *(Owner)*
Alice Pearson Chapman *(Partner)*
David Fox *(Partner)*
Andrew Maraniss *(Partner)*
Keith Miles *(Partner)*
Katy Varney *(Partner)*
Jennifer Brantley *(Sr VP)*
Mandy Cawood *(VP)*
Mary Ruth Raphael *(VP)*
Lynn Vincent *(Sr Dir-Art)*
Brooks Harper *(Dir-Art)*
Roger Shirley *(Dir-Editorial)*
Dan Schlacter *(Sr Acct Supvr)*
Matt Griffin *(Acct Supvr)*
Tom Hayden *(Acct Supvr)*
Leigh Kelley Lindsey *(Acct Supvr)*
Pam Veach Schmidt *(Acct Supvr)*
Colby Sledge *(Acct Supvr)*
Eric Tieles *(Acct Supvr)*
Lauren Ward *(Acct Supvr)*
Jessica Darden *(Sr Acct Exec)*
Erin Clements *(Acct Exec)*
Eric Dorman *(Acct Exec)*
Danielle Hall *(Acct Exec)*
Mara Naylor *(Acct Exec)*
Sarah de Jong *(Asst Acct Exec)*
Morey Hill *(Asst Acct Exec)*
Maddie Taylor *(Asst Acct Exec)*

Accounts:
AT&T Communications Corp.
CSX Transportation
Hennessy Industries
Lilly USA
Nashville Area Chamber of Commerce
United States Department of Labor Job Corps

MCNEIL, GRAY & RICE

1 Washington Mall, Boston, MA 02108-2603
Tel.: (617) 367-0100
Fax: (617) 367-0160
E-Mail: info@gr2000.com
Web Site: www.mcneilgrayandrice.com/index.php

Employees: 35
Year Founded: 1989

Agency Specializes In: Business-To-Business, High Technology, Public Relations

Robert Mcneil *(Principal)*
Susan Rice McNeil *(Principal)*
Judi Handel *(Dir-HR)*

Accounts:
3M
Acrilex
Adchem
Ames Rubbers
Anderson Power Products
APEM Components, Inc.
Beta Max Inc.
Carl Zeiss
Carlo Gavazzi
Cintec
Cognex
Cole Hersee; Boston, MA Vehicle, Off-Highway, Industrial & Marine Electrical & Electronic Switches, Connectors & Related Products
Extech Data
FCI-BURNDY
Goss
Hawe Hydraulics
Hendrix
Honeywell Notifier, Silent Knight
Hypertherm
ICM Controls
Kerk Motion Products
Koch Knight
Koch Membrane
Koch Unifin
Krohne
Lista International Corporation; Holliston, MA Distributor of Industrial Storage Products, Office & Lab Furniture
Metcar
Microfluidics
Millipore Corporation
Neopost
Notifier
Schroeder
Standard Knapp
Sultzer Mixpac
Symmons
Telequip
Watson Marlow/Bredel Pumps, Inc.; Wilmington, MA Peristaltic & Hose Pumps

MCNEIL WILSON COMMUNICATIONS, INC.

1003 Bishop St 9th Fl, Honolulu, HI 96813
Tel.: (808) 531-0244
Fax: (808) 531-0089
E-Mail: info@mcneilwilson.com
Web Site: www.mcneilwilson.com

Employees: 80
Year Founded: 1982

Agency Specializes In: Brand Development & Integration, Broadcast, Collateral, Education, Government/Political, Media Training, Travel & Tourism

Nathan Kam *(Pres-PR Grp-Anthology Mktg Grp)*
Bernie Caalim *(Sr VP)*
Patrick Dugan *(Sr VP)*

Accounts:
American Savings Bank
Atlantis Adventures
Hawaii Hotel & Lodging Association
Hawaii Visitors & Convention Bureau Public Relations
Hawaiian Airlines Local PR
Kaua'i Visitors Bureau
Leeward Land LLC
Polynesian Cultural Center
Prince Resorts Hawaii
USS Missouri Memorial Association
Waikoloa Beach Marriott Resort & Spa
Wilson Homecare

MCNEILL COMMUNICATIONS GROUP INC.

202 Neal Pl, High Point, NC 27262
Tel.: (336) 884-8700
Fax: (336) 884-4141
E-Mail: brosso@mcneillcommunications.com
Web Site: www.mcneillcommunications.com

E-Mail for Key Personnel:
President: kmh@mcneillcommunications.com

Employees: 15

National Agency Associations: PRSA

Agency Specializes In: Business Publications, Children's Market, Consumer Publications, Event Planning & Marketing, Exhibit/Trade Shows, Graphic Design, Magazines, Newspaper, Newspapers & Magazines, Public Relations, Publicity/Promotions, Trade & Consumer Magazines

Breakdown of Gross Billings by Media: Graphic Design: 20%; Pub. Rels.: 80%

Lauren Estep *(VP-Media Rels)*
Kristin Hawkins *(VP)*
Brenda Rosso *(VP-Integrated Media)*
Anne Wear *(VP-Media Rels)*
Colleen Sellers *(Dir-Allergy & Eye Care)*

THE MCRAE AGENCY

2130 Walecitos Ste 348, La Jolla, CA 92037
Tel.: (480) 990-0282
Fax: (858) 459-1227
Web Site: www.mcraeagency.com

Employees: 2
Year Founded: 1995

National Agency Associations: PRSA

Agency Specializes In: Public Relations

Beth McRae *(Pres)*

Accounts:
Solatube International Inc. Tubular Skylights

Branch

The McRae Agency

5685 N Scottsdale Rd Ste E100, Scottsdale, AZ 85250-5901
Tel.: (480) 990-0282
Fax: (480) 990-0048
Web Site: www.mcraeagency.com

Employees: 10

Agency Specializes In: Public Relations

Elizabeth Mcrae *(Pres)*
Jessica Pate *(Specialist-Social Media)*

MCS HEALTHCARE PUBLIC RELATIONS

(Formerly MCS)
1420 US Hwy 206 N Ste 100, Bedminster, NJ 07921-2652
Tel.: (908) 234-9900
Fax: (908) 470-4490
E-Mail: jeffh@mcspr.com
Web Site: www.mcspr.com

Employees: 30
Year Founded: 1985

Agency Specializes In: Communications, Health Care Services, Public Relations

Jeff Hoyak *(Pres)*
Joe Boyd *(CEO)*
Cindy Romano *(Sr VP & Gen Mgr)*
Laura de Zutter *(VP)*
Karen Dombek *(VP)*
Eliot Harrison *(VP)*

Accounts:
BD

Genentech; South San Francisco, CA Activase, Cathflo, TNKase
Horizon Blue Cross Blue Shield of New Jersey Public Relations
MannKind Corporation
Merck
Reckitt Benckiser

MEDIA & COMMUNICATIONS STRATEGIES INC.
1500 Massachusetts Ave NW Ste 836, Washington, DC 20005
Tel.: (301) 793-1480
Web Site: www.macstrategies.com

Agency Specializes In: Content, Corporate Communications, Crisis Communications, Event Planning & Marketing, Internet/Web Design, Media Relations, Media Training, Public Relations, Search Engine Optimization

Scott Sobel *(Pres)*
Cindi Flahive-Sobel *(VP & Comptroller)*
Kate Connors *(Sr Acct Mgr & Strategist-Social Media)*
Kipp Lanham *(Acct Exec)*

Accounts:
Indian National Bar Association (Public Relations Agency of Record)

MEDIA FRENZY GLOBAL
2300 Lakeview Pkwy Ste 700, Alpharetta, GA 30009
Tel.: (678) 916-3973
E-Mail: info@mediafrenzyglobal.com
Web Site: www.mediafrenzyglobal.com

Agency Specializes In: Brand Development & Integration, Communications, Content, Public Relations, Social Media

Sarah Tourville *(Founder & CEO)*
Katie Kern *(Dir-PR & Mktg)*
Dan OBrien *(Dir-Res & Content)*
Kiera Stein *(Dir-Social Media)*
Jessica Newland *(Mgr-Mktg)*
Daniella Gutierrez *(Coord-Mktg & PR)*

Accounts:
New-LNL Systems (Agency of Record) Branding, Content Creation, Digital, Public Relations, Social Advertising, Social Media
New-Pyramid Solutions
New-Velociti Facility Services (Communications Agency of Record)

MEDIA PLAYGROUND PR
845 S Los Angeles St, Los Angeles, CA 90014
Tel.: (213) 250-6200
E-Mail: info@mediaplaygroundpr.com
Web Site: www.mediaplaygroundpr.com

Year Founded: 2003

Agency Specializes In: Event Planning & Marketing, Exhibit/Trade Shows, Media Relations, Public Relations, Social Media, Strategic Planning/Research

Kimberly Goodnight *(Owner)*

Accounts:
New-The Autry Odd Market

THE MEDIA PUSH
3039 W Peoria Ave Ste C 102-149, Phoenix, AZ 85029
Tel.: (602) 418-8534
Web Site: www.themediapush.com

Agency Specializes In: Print, Public Relations, Radio, Social Media, T.V.

Charlotte Shaff *(Owner)*

Accounts:
J Philipp Centers for Family & Cosmetic Dentistry

MEDIA SOLSTICE MARKETING & PUBLIC RELATIONS
158 Pke St Ste 5, Port Jervis, NY 12771
Tel.: (845) 430-1396
E-Mail: info@mediasolstice.com
Web Site: www.mediasolstice.com

Year Founded: 2011

Agency Specializes In: Advertising, Collateral, Digital/Interactive, Event Planning & Marketing, Internet/Web Design, Media Planning, Media Relations, Public Relations, Social Media, Strategic Planning/Research

Jessica Gardner *(Pres)*
Matthew OSullivan *(Dir-Digital Mktg)*
Johanna Seidel *(Strategist-Mktg)*

Accounts:
Amazein Cabo Race

MEDIALINE PR
2030 Main St 3rd Fl, Dallas, TX 75201
Tel.: (218) 379-7000
Web Site: www.medialinepr.com/

Suzanne Miller *(Founder)*
Rebecca Wilkins *(Pres)*
Christelle Dupont *(Acct Supvr)*
Alvin Jordan *(Sr Acct Exec)*

Accounts:
New-Cheddar's Scratch Kitchen

MEDIASOURCE
1800 W Fifth Ave, Columbus, OH 43212
Tel.: (614) 932-9950
Fax: (614) 932-9920
E-Mail: info@mediasourcetv.com
Web Site: www.mediasourcetv.com

Agency Specializes In: Brand Development & Integration, Media Relations, Public Relations

Lisa Arledge Powell *(Pres)*
Kaitlynn Grady *(Acct Exec)*

Accounts:
New-The Ohio State University Wexner Medical Center

MELISSA LIBBY & ASSOCIATES
1425 Ellsworth Industrial Blvd Ste 10, Atlanta, GA 30318
Tel.: (404) 816-3068
Web Site: www.melissalibbypr.com

Agency Specializes In: Event Planning & Marketing, Media Relations, Public Relations, Social Media

Melissa Libby *(Pres)*
Tuan Huynh *(VP)*
Emily Robinson *(Dir-Client Svcs)*
Mandy Betts *(Dir-Social Media)*
Brandon Amato *(Mgr-Client Svcs)*

Accounts:
New-Masti
New-Rays Restaurants

MELROSE PR
710 Wilshire Blvd Ste 320, Santa Monica, CA 90401
Tel.: (310) 260-7901
E-Mail: info@melrosepr.com
Web Site: www.melrosepr.com

Year Founded: 2012

Agency Specializes In: Broadcast, Event Planning & Marketing, Print, Public Relations, Social Media

Kelley Coughlan *(Owner)*
Lexie Olson *(Acct Dir-Melrose PR)*

Accounts:
Zipit Bedding

THE MEPR AGENCY
230 4th Ave N 3rd Fl, Nashville, TN 37219
Tel.: (615) 592-6377
E-Mail: info@mepragency.com
Web Site: www.mepragency.com

Year Founded: 2006

Agency Specializes In: Advertising, Brand Development & Integration, Collateral, Corporate Communications, Event Planning & Marketing, Graphic Design, Internet/Web Design, Media Buying Services, Public Relations, Social Media

Kia Jarmon *(Dir-Creative)*
Carrie Wingfield *(Acct Mgr & Project Mgr)*

Accounts:
Jarmon Transportation

MERCURY LABS
3118 Locust St, Saint Louis, MO 63103
Tel.: (800) 652-6014
Web Site: www.mercury-inc.com

Agency Specializes In: Media Relations, Media Training, Public Relations, Social Media, Strategic Planning/Research

Chris Lawing *(Pres)*
Angie Lawing *(CEO)*
Marla Kertzman *(VP)*
Mark Giles *(Sr Art Dir)*
Carrie Trent *(Acct Dir)*
Derek Weikle *(Art Dir)*
Ollie Clerc *(Mgr-Bus)*
Dewayne Nickerson *(Mgr-Client Comm)*

Accounts:
New-Employers Council on Flexible Compensation Marketing Communications
New-The Saint Louis Art Museum

MERCURY PUBLIC AFFAIRS
250 Greenwich St, New York, NY 10007
Tel.: (212) 681-1380
Fax: (212) 681-1381
E-Mail: info@mercurypublicaffairs.com
Web Site: www.mercuryllc.com

Agency Specializes In: Government/Political, Public Relations

Michael Duhaime *(Partner)*
Michael McKeon *(Partner)*
Tracy Arnold *(Mng Dir)*
Ben Feller *(Mng Dir)*
Jan Feuerstadt *(Mng Dir)*
John Gallagher *(Mng Dir)*
John Lonergan *(Mng Dir)*
Patrick Mccarthy *(Mng Dir)*

Rachel Noerdlinger *(Mng Dir)*
Erin Pelton *(Mng Dir)*
Violet Moss *(Sr VP)*
Nicole Flotteron *(VP-Digital)*

Accounts:
AT&T Communications Corp.
Distilled Spirits Council
Government of Nigeria Bilateral Diplomatic, Economic Relations, Security Relations
Keyspan Energy
Vanguard Health Systems

Branches

Mercury Public Affairs
1414 k St 6 Fl, Sacramento, CA 95814
Tel.: (916) 444-1380
Fax: (916) 265-1869
E-Mail: info@mercuryllc.com
Web Site: mercuryllc.com/

Employees: 15

Fernando Ferrer *(Co-Chm)*
Adam Ereli *(Vice Chm)*
Fabian Nunez *(Partner)*
Tracy Arnold *(Mng Dir)*
Paul Bauer *(Mng Dir)*
Ben Feller *(Mng Dir)*
Duncan McFetridge *(Mng Dir)*
Conor Fennessy *(Sr VP)*
Austin Finan *(Sr VP)*
Vince Galko *(Sr VP)*
Adam Keigwin *(Sr VP)*

Mercury Public Affairs
444 S Flower St Ste 3675, Los Angeles, CA 90071
Tel.: (213) 624-1380
Fax: (213) 624-1387
Web Site: www.mercuryllc.com

Agency Specializes In: Advertising, Broadcast, Crisis Communications, Digital/Interactive, Media Relations, Print, Public Relations, Social Media

Stefan Friedman *(Partner)*
Shayna Englin *(Mng Dir)*
Glenn Gritzner *(Mng Dir)*

Accounts:
Golden Boy Promotions (Agency of Record)

Mercury Public Affairs
(Formerly International Government Relations)
701 8th St NW, Washington, DC 20001
Tel.: (202) 551-1440
Fax: (202) 551-9966
Web Site: www.mercuryllc.com

Employees: 3

Agency Specializes In: Communications, Government/Political, Public Relations

Adam Ereli *(Vice Chm)*
Kieran Mahoney *(CEO)*
Vincent Frillici *(Mng Dir)*
Dan Gonzalez *(Mng Dir)*
Max Sandlin *(Gen Counsel)*
Kevin Allen *(Sr VP)*
Conor Fennessy *(Sr VP)*
Vince Galko *(Sr VP)*
Mike McSherry *(Sr VP)*

Mercury Public Affairs
701 8th St NW Ste 650, Washington, DC 20001-3854
Tel.: (202) 551-1440
Fax: (202) 551-9966
Web Site: www.mercuryllc.com

Employees: 15

Kirill Goncharenko *(Founder & Partner)*
Michael DuHaime *(Partner)*
Vince Frillici *(Mng Dir)*
John Lonergan *(Mng Dir)*
Morris L. Reid *(Mng Dir)*
Alan Rubin *(Mng Dir)*
Becky Warren *(Mng Dir)*
Vince Galko *(Sr VP)*
Vicky Vadlamani *(VP)*

MERITUS MEDIA
2400 Lincoln Ave, Altadena, CA 91001
Tel.: (626) 296-6218
Fax: (626) 296-6301
Web Site: www.meritusmedia.com

Year Founded: 2008

Agency Specializes In: Content, Digital/Interactive, Media Relations, Public Relations, Social Media

Sally Falkow *(CEO)*
Mike Falkow *(Dir-Creative)*
Joe Kutchera *(Strategist-Content)*

Accounts:
Cafe Mango Six
Lucy's
Mizuno USA, Inc. The Mizuno Running Mezamashii

MERRITT GROUP
11600 Sunrise Valley Dr Ste 320, Reston, VA 20191-1416
Tel.: (703) 390-1500
Fax: (703) 860-2080
E-Mail: hr@merrittgrp.com
Web Site: www.merrittgrp.com

Employees: 30
Year Founded: 1996

Agency Specializes In: High Technology, Public Relations

Thomas Rice *(Partner & Exec VP)*
John Conrad *(Partner & Sr VP)*
Jayson Schkloven *(Partner & Sr VP)*
Alisa Valudes *(Sr Partner & COO)*
Patty Groce *(VP-Organizational Dev)*
Paul Miller *(VP-Fin & Acctg)*
Michelle Schafer *(VP-Security)*

Accounts:
Apptix
ARTEL
Blue Coat Systems, Inc.
Elluminate
Fortify Software Inc.
MANDIANT
MedAssurant, Inc.
Metastrom
Microsoft Federal
Microsoft PS
NIPTE
PGP
ServiceBench
Software AG
Vangent
Varent
Verint
Verizon

MESEREAU PUBLIC RELATIONS
7912 Windwood Way, Parker, CO 80134
Tel.: (720) 842-5271
Fax: (720) 842-5273
Web Site: www.mesereaupr.com

Year Founded: 1996

Agency Specializes In: Crisis Communications, Event Planning & Marketing, Media Relations, Public Relations

Mona Mesereau *(Principal)*
Tom Mesereau *(Principal)*

Accounts:
Buffalo Bills Cody / Yellowstone Country
Far & Away Adventures
Furnace Creek Resort
Grand Canyon National Park Lodges
Idaho Rocky Mountain Ranch
Ohio State Park Lodges
Xanterra Parks & Resorts
Yellowstone Association Institute
Yellowstone National Park Lodges

METHOD COMMUNICATIONS
47 W 200 S Ste 402, Salt Lake City, UT 84101
Tel.: (801) 461-9790
Fax: (801) 461-9791
Web Site: www.methodcommunications.com

Year Founded: 2010

Agency Specializes In: Crisis Communications, Media Relations, Media Training, Public Relations, Social Media

David Parkinson *(Co-Founder & CEO)*
Alex Koritz *(Partner & Exec VP)*
Brad Plothow *(Exec VP-Strategy)*
Amanda Butterfield *(VP)*
Spencer Parkinson *(VP)*
Clayton Blackham *(Dir)*
Adam Denison *(Acct Supvr)*

Accounts:
Bitglass
Cylance
Goal Zero
Jetpac
Mastery Connect
MokiMobility
New-Tongal

Branch

Method Communications
214 Grant Ave Ste 301, San Francisco, CA 94108
(See Separate Listing)

METIS COMMUNICATIONS INC.
121 E Berkeley St 4th Fl, Boston, MA 2118
Tel.: (617) 236-0500
E-Mail: info@metiscomm.com
Web Site: www.metiscomm.com

Year Founded: 2005

Agency Specializes In: Content, Media Relations, Public Relations, Social Media

Melissa Cohen *(Sr VP-Acct Svcs)*
Erin Rohr *(Acct Dir)*
Rebecca Joyner *(Dir-Content Svcs)*
Erin Caldwell *(Acct Mgr)*
Crystal Monahan *(Acct Mgr)*
Christina Andrade *(Mgr-Ops)*
Justine Boucher *(Sr Acct Exec)*
Sylvie Tse *(Sr Acct Exec)*
Ali Keppler *(Acct Exec)*

Accounts:
Clearsky Data
Crimson Hexagon

KeyInfo
Water Defense

METZGER ALBEE PUBLIC RELATIONS
(Formerly Metzger Associates)
2503 Walnut St Ste 301, Boulder, CO 80302
Tel.: (303) 786-7000
Fax: (303) 786-7456
E-Mail: info@metzgeralbee.com
Web Site: metzgeralbee.com

Employees: 12
Year Founded: 1991

Agency Specializes In: High Technology, Public Relations

Doyle Albee *(Pres)*
Sarah Engle *(CFO)*
Amy Sigrest *(Dir-Digital Mktg)*

Accounts:
New-Acroname
AllSource Analysis
Clip Interactive
CTEK
New-Email on Acid
New-Frontline Aerospace
Goldsystems
Green Garage PR, Social Media
Hythane Co.
Komen for the Cure
Massively Parallel Technologies
New-Morphis
Silver Creek Systems
SQFT
New-Techtonic Group

MGA COMMUNICATIONS, INC.
1999 Broadway Ste 1450, Denver, CO 80202-5728
Tel.: (303) 298-1818
Fax: (303) 297-3526
E-Mail: info@mgacommunications.com
Web Site: www.mgacommunications.com

Employees: 20

Agency Specializes In: Business-To-Business, Consumer Marketing, Corporate Communications, Financial, Government/Political, Graphic Design, Health Care Services, Industrial, Logo & Package Design, Public Relations

Jeffrey P. Julin *(Owner & Pres)*
Michael Gaughan *(Chm)*
Cricket Smith *(Exec VP)*
Doug Magee *(VP-Res)*
Kevin Frisbie *(Acct Exec)*
Matt Rodriguez *(Acct Exec)*

Accounts:
HealthONE
JPMorgan Chase
Pfizer

MICHAEL A. BURNS & ASSOCIATES, INC.
7557 Rambler Rd, Dallas, TX 75231
Tel.: (214) 521-8596
Fax: (214) 521-8599
E-Mail: info@mbapr.com
Web Site: www.mbapr.com

Employees: 20
Year Founded: 1987

Agency Specializes In: Public Relations

Revenue: $1,500,000

Michael A. Burns *(Owner)*
Lois Weaver *(Sr VP & Dir-Creative)*
Jeff Green *(VP & Acct Supvr)*
Natalie Coca *(Asst Acct Exec)*

Accounts:
American Leather LP
Faulkner Design Group; Dallas, TX Brand Awareness, PR
Wick, Phillips, Gould & Martin, LLP

MICHAEL J. LONDON & ASSOCIATES
4 Daniels Farm Rd Ste 330, Trumbull, CT 06611
Tel.: (203) 261-1549
Fax: (203) 459-1032
E-Mail: mjlondon@aol.com
Web Site: www.mjlondon.com

Employees: 3
Year Founded: 1990

Agency Specializes In: Advertising, Brand Development & Integration, Business-To-Business, Consulting, Consumer Marketing, Corporate Communications, Corporate Identity, Event Planning & Marketing, Investor Relations, Public Relations, Publicity/Promotions

Michael J. London *(Chm)*
Diane Casaretti *(Acct Exec)*
Emmanuel S. Forde *(Sr Partner)*

Accounts:
The Auto Body Association of Connecticut
Consumers for Dental Choice; Washington, DC Consumer Advocates
Kostoff, Kostoff & Bieder
Tremont & Sheldon, PC

MICHAEL MEYERS PUBLIC RELATIONS
11875 Dublin Blvd Ste 247C, Dublin, CA 94568
Tel.: (925) 551-8080
Fax: (925) 551-8282
E-Mail: michael@mmpr.com
Web Site: www.mmpr.com

Agency Specializes In: Digital/Interactive, Entertainment, Public Relations

Michael Meyers *(Owner)*

MICHELE MARIE PR
1261 Broadway Ste 405, New York, NY 10001
Tel.: (646) 863-3923
Fax: (646) 863-3937
Web Site: www.michelemariepr.com

Agency Specializes In: Brand Development & Integration, Event Planning & Marketing, Media Planning, Public Relations, Social Media

Jill Cooper *(Owner)*
Gabrielle Perez *(Acct Exec)*

Accounts:
New-Julie Brown Designs

MILLDAM PUBLIC RELATIONS
45 Walden St Ste 1, Concord, MA 1742
Tel.: (978) 369-0406
Web Site: www.milldampr.com

Agency Specializes In: Event Planning & Marketing, Newspapers & Magazines, Public Relations, Social Marketing/Nonprofit, Social Media

Adam Waitkunas *(Pres)*
Brendon Stellman *(Assoc VP)*
Loraine Lamsa *(Dir-Content)*
Caroline Haley *(Mgr-Client Rels)*

Accounts:
New-Bluestone Energy Services
New-The Critical Facilities Summit
New-Future Facilities
New-Hurricane Electric
New-Upsite Technologies

MILLER MAXFIELD INC
133 Mission St Ste 101, Santa Cruz, CA 95060
Tel.: (831) 227-6469
Web Site: www.millermaxfield.com

Year Founded: 2002

Agency Specializes In: Advertising, Collateral, Graphic Design, Internet/Web Design, Logo & Package Design, Media Relations, Media Training, Public Relations, Social Media, Strategic Planning/Research

Bill Maxfield *(Principal)*
Paula Maxfield *(Principal)*
Eva Zeno *(Dir-Art)*
Jennifer Squires *(Sr Acct Mgr)*
J. M. Brown *(Strategist-Comm)*

Accounts:
Coastal Watershed Council
San Lorenzo River Alliance
Santa Cruz Womens Health Center

MILLER PR
8455 Beverly Blvd Ste 400, Los Angeles, CA 90048
Tel.: (323) 761-7220
Fax: (323) 761-7230
E-Mail: info@miller-pr.com
Web Site: www.miller-pr.com

Agency Specializes In: Brand Development & Integration, Crisis Communications, Event Planning & Marketing, Public Relations, Social Media

Dawn Miller *(Founder & CEO)*
Jennifer Reiss *(Acct Supvr)*

Accounts:
Funny or Die Inc

MILLER PUBLIC RELATIONS
1209 Hall Johnson Rd, Colleyville, TX 76034
Tel.: (817) 281-3440
Fax: (817) 281-3442
Web Site: www.millerpublicrelations.com

Agency Specializes In: Advertising, Internet/Web Design, Logo & Package Design, Media Training, Public Relations, Social Media

Cyndi Miller *(Founder & CEO)*
Doug Miller *(COO)*

Accounts:
Balin Eye & Laser Center
ClearNailz
Destination Beauty of Texas
Destination Health
Foundation i4
Heart Test Laboratories
Hoopes Vision
Kleiman Evangelista Eye Center
Mann Eye Institute & Laser Center
The Medical Record Group
Omaha Eye & Laser Institute
R. Chris Kuhne
RPM xConstruction LLC
Southwest Age Intervention Institute
Surgical Specialists of Charlotte
USMD Prostate Cancer Center
Virginia Eye Consultants

Webb-Barton & Associates

THE MILLERSCHIN GROUP
3250 University Dr Ste 115, Auburn Hills, MI 48326
Tel.: (248) 276-1970
E-Mail: jmillerschin@millerschingroup.com
Web Site: www.millerschingroup.com

Employees: 8
Year Founded: 1998

Agency Specializes In: Advertising, Consumer Goods, Crisis Communications, Email, Event Planning & Marketing, Exhibit/Trade Shows, Graphic Design, Information Technology, Investor Relations, Local Marketing, Media Relations, Newspaper, Public Relations, Publishing, Social Marketing/Nonprofit, Strategic Planning/Research, Web (Banner Ads, Pop-ups, etc.)

Erin Millerschin *(Pres & CEO)*
John Millerschin *(COO)*
Dick Pacini *(Sr VP)*
Steve Plumb *(VP & Dir-Editorial)*
Dena Meldrum *(Mgr-Graphic Design)*
Glenn McDaniel *(Specialist-Comm)*
Sarah Moore *(Acct Exec)*
David Smith *(Sr Counsel)*

Accounts:
Mitsubishi Electric Automotive America
RheTech
SKF
Witzenmann USA

THE MILLS AGENCY
16107 Kensington Dr 370, Sugar Land, TX 77479
Tel.: (281) 491-2369
Fax: (281) 491-1389
E-Mail: nmills@tmagency.com
Web Site: tmagency.com

Employees: 3
Year Founded: 1998

National Agency Associations: PRSA

Agency Specializes In: Education

Approx. Annual Billings: $250,000

Nancy V. Mills *(Pres)*

MILLS PUBLIC RELATIONS
142 Berkeley St 4th Fl, Boston, MA 02116
Tel.: (617) 350-6200
Web Site: www.millspr.com

Year Founded: 2004

Agency Specializes In: Crisis Communications, Digital/Interactive, Internet/Web Design, Media Relations, Media Training, Public Relations, Social Media

Scott Farmelant *(Pres & CEO)*

Accounts:
Boys & Girls Clubs of Boston
Cambridge Bank Savings

MIRAMAR EVENTS
1327 Livingston Ave, Pacifica, CA 94044
Tel.: (650) 726-3491
Fax: (650) 726-5181
E-Mail: tim@miramarevents.com
Web Site: www.miramarevents.com

Employees: 6
Year Founded: 1986

Agency Specializes In: Event Planning & Marketing, Publicity/Promotions

Approx. Annual Billings: $10,000,000

Breakdown of Gross Billings by Media: Mags.: $1,000,000; Newsp.: $2,000,000; Other: $5,000,000; Radio: $1,000,000; T.V.: $1,000,000

Timothy R. Beeman *(Chm & CEO)*

Accounts:
A La Carte & Art; Mountain View, CA Festival; 1995
Half Moon Bay Pumpkin Festival; Half Moon Bay, CA Festival; 1971
Millbrae Art & Wine Festival; Millbrae, CA Festival; 1971
Mountain View Art & Wine Festival Festival; 1972
Pacific Coast Dream Machines Show; Half Moon Bay, CA Classic Car & Air Show; 1990
The Safeway World Championship Pumpkin Weigh-off Festival; 1974

MISSY FARREN & ASSOCIATES LTD
33 E 33rd St, New York, NY 10016
Tel.: (212) 528-1691
E-Mail: info@mfaltd.com
Web Site: www.mfaltd.com

Agency Specializes In: Corporate Communications, Event Planning & Marketing, Media Relations, Media Training, Public Relations, Social Media, Strategic Planning/Research

Missy Farren *(Founder & CEO)*
Greg Kincheloe *(CFO)*
Karen Clough *(COO)*
Caroline Andrew *(Sr VP)*
Agatha Capacchione *(Sr VP)*
Adele McConnell *(Acct Mgr)*
Cynthia Patnode *(Acct Supvr)*
Joseph Giumarra *(Sr Acct Exec)*
Theresa Bischof *(Acct Exec)*

Accounts:
Care2
Charles & Colvard
No Kid Hungry Chefs Cycle and Cook
Skins Inc
Stance

MJ LILLY ASSOCIATES LLC
30 Schermerhorn St Ste 1, Brooklyn Heights, NY 11201
Tel.: (718) 855-1853
Fax: (718) 855-1843
Web Site: www.mjlilly.com

Agency Specializes In: Brand Development & Integration, Graphic Design, Media Planning, Media Training, Print, Public Relations, Social Media

Maria Lilly *(Principal)*

Accounts:
New-Experian Capital Markets

MK COMMUNICATIONS INC
350 W Hubbard St Ste 200, Chicago, IL 60654
Tel.: (312) 822-0505
Fax: (312) 822-0568
Web Site: www.mkcpr.com

Year Founded: 1983

Agency Specializes In: Advertising, Corporate Communications, Crisis Communications, Internet/Web Design, Media Relations, Print, Public Relations, Strategic Planning/Research

Marilyn Katz *(Founder & Pres)*
Lindsey Lerner *(Dir-Creative)*
Natasha Norris *(Strategist-Comm, Mktg & Social Media)*

Accounts:
The Chicago Conservation Center Fine Art Care Services
Chicago Housing Authority Public Housing Services
Chicagoans Against War & Injustice Anti Terrorism Services
City of Chicago Department of Housing Housing Services
Hispanic Housing Development Corporation Housing Programs Administration Services
O2Diesel Additive Fuel Developers
Perspectives Charter School Educational Services
Residential Land Fund Equity Capital Fund Suppliers

MMI PUBLIC RELATIONS
223 E Chatham St Ste 102, Cary, NC 27511-3475
Tel.: (919) 233-6600
Fax: (919) 233-0300
E-Mail: mmi@mmipublicrelations.com
Web Site: www.mmipublicrelations.com/

Employees: 25
Year Founded: 1994

Agency Specializes In: Content, Local Marketing, Public Relations

Robert Buhler *(Chm)*
Al Leach *(Pres & Chief Strategy Officer)*
Michelle Fowler *(Exec VP)*
Katharine Buhler *(Mgr-Fin)*
Erin Smith *(Sr Acct Supvr)*
Amanda Marinelli *(Sr Acct Exec)*
Amanda Romano *(Acct Exec)*
Michelle Wingate *(Acct Exec)*
Jeffrey Turner *(Asst Acct Exec)*

Accounts:
A Cultivated Mindset Creative, Mobile Applications, Web Applications
New-BioMarine
CFO Enterprise Community Relations, Media Relations, Strategic Planning
The Chefs Academy Public Relations
Click Culture
DocuTAP
Douglas Carroll Salon Community Relations, Media Relations, Public Relations Campaign, Social Media, Strategic Planning
ESP/SurgeX PR
Esteem Me Montessori & Creative Play Community Relations, Local Brand Awareness, Media Relations, PR, Strategic Planning
Gupta Psychiatry Community Relations, Media Relations, PR Campaign, Social Media, Strategic Planning
Harrison College ICD-10 Training Curriculum, IT Development Program
Hatteras Group PR
Healing Waters Spa & Cosmetic Clinic PR Campaign
New-KDI Capital Partners
Kroger Community Relations, Media Outreach, Strategy Development
Lenovo
NAMPAC
New-Nurse Care of North Carolina
Park West Barber School (Agency of Record) Digital Advertising, Public Relations, Social Media, Video Services
New-Raleigh Orthopaedic Clinic
The Red Room Tapas Lounge
New-Riley Contracting Group

The Spectacle; Raleigh, NC Community Relations, Media Relations, Public Relations, Strategic Planning
Taxi Taxi Brand Awareness, Community Relations, Media Relations, PR, Strategic Planning
Terramor Homes
VMZINC
World of Art Showcase Community Relations, Media Relations, Public Relations, Strategic Planning

MML INC.

137 Bay St Bungalow #4 and #5, Santa Monica, CA 90405
Tel.: (310) 664-0600
Fax: (310) 664-0500
Web Site: www.mmlpr.com

Employees: 7
Year Founded: 2001

Agency Specializes In: Cosmetics, Fashion/Apparel, Public Relations

Merritt Meade Loughran *(Pres)*
Claire Nilsson *(VP)*
Kelly Kupper *(Dir-Fashion & Lifestyle)*
Mimi Levine *(Acct Mgr-Fashion Div)*
Jenna Smith *(Mgr-NYC Showroom)*
Kim Perry *(Acct Supvr)*

Accounts:
Arcona; 2007
Blackbird Backery
Chobani
ESPN
Jane Magazine
Mix 1
Patio Culture
The Tea Spot
Xgames

MO DESIGN

3025 Hilton Rd, Ferndale, MI 48220
Tel.: (248) 556-5799
E-Mail: info@lessismo.com
Web Site: www.lessismo.com

Year Founded: 2007

Agency Specializes In: Advertising, Collateral, Digital/Interactive, Internet/Web Design, Media Relations, Media Training, Outdoor, Print, Public Relations, Social Media

Julia Gillespie *(Principal)*
Blake Moore *(Principal)*
Evan Mikalonis *(Coord-PPC)*

Accounts:
WellnessMats

MOBILITY PUBLIC RELATIONS, LLC.

5285 Meadows Rd Ste 430, Lake Oswego, OR 97035
Tel.: (503) 946-3310
Fax: (503) 210-8882
Toll Free: (800) 660-6677
Web Site: www.mobilitypr.com

Year Founded: 2006

Agency Specializes In: Corporate Communications, Mobile Marketing, Public Relations, Social Media

John Sidline *(CEO)*
Melissa Burns *(Exec VP)*
John Giddings *(Exec VP)*
Paula Larson *(VP-Client Svcs)*
Stacy Sidline *(VP-Fin & Admin)*

Accounts:
Redline Communications Group Inc.
RGB Networks, Inc.
Tektronix, Inc.

MOGUL MEDIA GROUP

171 17th St Ste 1550, Atlanta, GA 30363
Toll Free: (800) 664-8577
E-Mail: info@mogulpr.com
Web Site: www.mogulentertainment.com

Agency Specializes In: Media Planning, Media Relations, Public Relations, Social Media, Strategic Planning/Research

Ryan Hattaway *(Pres)*

Accounts:
McLaren Auto

MOLISE PR

120 N Green St Ste 2E, Chicago, IL 60601
Tel.: (313) 549-3137
E-Mail: info@molisepr.com
Web Site: www.molisepr.com

Agency Specializes In: Brand Development & Integration, Graphic Design, Media Relations, Public Relations, Social Media

Michelle Molise *(Principal)*
Brittany Johnson *(Acct Exec)*

Accounts:
Amfar Aids Research
Balani Custom Clothiers
The Dobbins Group
First Look for Charity
Garrett Popcorn
Gene & Georgetti
Home Scout Realty
Imerman Angels
Lawry's Restaurants, Inc.
Real Urban Barbeque

MOMENTUM MEDIA PR

299 Pearl St Ste 402, Boulder, CO 80302
Tel.: (617) 875-5553
E-Mail: info@momentummediapr.com
Web Site: www.momentummediapr.com

Year Founded: 2000

Agency Specializes In: Advertising, Digital/Interactive, Event Planning & Marketing, Media Planning, Media Training, Public Relations, Social Media, Strategic Planning/Research

Alycia Cavadi *(Founder & Principal)*
Bethany Mousseau *(Dir-PR)*
Anya Frans *(Sr Acct Exec)*

Accounts:
Bogs Footwear Brand Awareness, Public Relations
New-Darn Tough Vermont (Public Relations Agency of Record) Digital Media
Niche Snowboards
SealSkinz Brand Awareness, Digital, Public Relations, Social Media
Teva

MONTAGNE COMMUNICATIONS

814 Elm St Ste 205, Manchester, NH 03101
Tel.: (603) 644-3200
Fax: (603) 644-3216
Web Site: www.montagnecom.com

Year Founded: 2007

Agency Specializes In: Advertising, Event Planning & Marketing, Internet/Web Design, Media Planning, Media Relations, Public Relations, Social Media, Strategic Planning/Research

Scott Tranchemontagne *(Pres)*
E. J. Powers *(Exec VP)*
Jeff Mucciarone *(Asst Acct Exec)*
Kayleigh Robertson *(Asst Acct Exec)*

Accounts:
WWPass Corp

MORGAN MARKETING & PUBLIC RELATIONS LLC

78 Discovery, Irvine, CA 92618
Tel.: (949) 261-2216
Fax: (949) 261-2272
Web Site: www.mmpr.biz

Employees: 5
Year Founded: 1991

National Agency Associations: PRSA

Agency Specializes In: Affluent Market, Business Publications, Communications, Consumer Publications, Corporate Communications, Crisis Communications, Direct Response Marketing, Event Planning & Marketing, Food Service, Hispanic Market, Luxury Products, Media Relations, Media Training, Public Relations, Publicity/Promotions, Real Estate, Restaurant, Social Media

Approx. Annual Billings: $900,000

Melinda Morgan Kartsonis *(Principal)*
Bryn Mohr *(Acct Dir)*
Kristin Daher *(Dir)*
Brian Devenny *(Sr Acct Supvr)*
Samantha Tyson *(Asst Acct Exec)*

Accounts:
Arizona Canning Company Branding, Recipe Development
BRAVO BRIO Restaurant Group BRIO Tuscan Grille, Marketing, Public Relations
Daphne's Greek Cafe; San Diego, CA
Del Taco
Embarcadero California Bistro; Rancho Santa Margarita, CA Marketing, Media Relations
Hawaiian Host AlohaMacs, Media Relations, Public Relations
Juice It Up! In-store, Marketing, Public Relations
Lugano Diamonds; Newport Beach, CA
Maro Wood Grill
Panda Restaurant Group Panda Express, Panda Inn Mandarin Cuisine
Pieology (Public Relations Agency of Record) Communications Strategy, Media Relations
Ramirez International; Newport Beach, CA
Tamarind of London Marketing, Media Relations, PR
Tastee Freez
True Food Kitchen
Wienerschnitzel (Public Relations Agency of Record) Marketing, Public Relations, Social Media
Wildfish Seafood Grille

MOTION PR

221 N LaSalle St, Chicago, IL 60601
Tel.: (312) 670-8949
Fax: (773) 409-7171
E-Mail: contact@motionpr.net
Web Site: www.motionpr.net

Year Founded: 2006

Agency Specializes In: Collateral, Event Planning & Marketing, Media Relations, Media Training, Public Relations, Strategic Planning/Research

Kimberly Eberl *(Principal)*
Bonni Pear *(Exec VP & Dir-Entertainment & Lifestyle Brands)*
Kevin Lints *(Acct Mgr)*
Derek Serafin *(Acct Supvr)*
Erin McGraw *(Sr Acct Exec)*
Ashley Moses *(Sr Acct Exec)*
Valerie Galassini *(Acct Exec)*
Blair Hickey *(Acct Exec)*
Bruce Kennedy *(Acct Exec)*

Accounts:
Alpina and Advocate Construction
Eyeneer TV
Food Genius
Michael Best & Friedrich
Red Bull
Shoreline Sightseeing
Trattoria Gianni Chicago

MOUNT & NADLER, INC.
425 Madison Ave, New York, NY 10017
Tel.: (212) 759-4440
Fax: (212) 371-0787
E-Mail: mountnadler@aol.com
Web Site: www.mountandnadler.com

Employees: 5
Year Founded: 1980

Agency Specializes In: Financial, Public Relations

Hedda C. Nadler *(Owner)*
Burt Hurvich *(VP)*
Tom Pinto *(VP)*
Janice Aman *(Acct Exec)*
Lynn Cocchiola *(Acct Exec)*

Accounts:
Ballon, Stoll, Bader & Nadler, PC; 1982
LJ Oldfest & Co
Wintergreen

MOVEMENT MEDIA
3166 Mt Pleasant St NW, Washington, DC 20010
Tel.: (202) 641-0277
E-Mail: info@wearemovementmedia.com
Web Site: www.wearemovementmedia.com

Agency Specializes In: Event Planning & Marketing, Media Training, Promotions, Public Relations, Social Media

Lauren Stansbury *(Mgr-Comm)*

Accounts:
Organic Consumers Association Fair World Project

MPRM PUBLIC RELATIONS
5670 Wilshire Blvd Ste 2500, Los Angeles, CA 90036
Tel.: (323) 933-3399
Fax: (323) 939-7211
E-Mail: info@mprm.com
Web Site: www.mprm.com

Employees: 31

Agency Specializes In: Business Publications, Business-To-Business, Cable T.V., Children's Market, Communications, Consulting, Corporate Identity, Digital/Interactive, E-Commerce, Entertainment, Event Planning & Marketing, Exhibit/Trade Shows, Financial, Public Relations, Publicity/Promotions, Sponsorship, Teen Market, Trade & Consumer Magazines

Rachel McCallister *(Co-Founder & Chm)*
Mark Pogachefsky *(Co-Founder & Pres)*
Alan Amman *(COO & Exec VP)*
Rene Ridinger *(VP-Entertainment)*
Betty Lourie *(Dir-Admin)*
Clay Dollarhide *(Sr Mgr-Digital Mktg & PR)*
Courtney Dolliver *(Acct Supvr)*
Shelby Kimlick *(Acct Supvr)*
Caitlin McGee *(Acct Supvr)*
Melissa Mills *(Acct Supvr)*

Accounts:
ABC Family
Apparition
Outfest
RMG Networks; San Francisco, CA (Agency of Record)
Strand Releasing

MRB PUBLIC RELATIONS
2 E Main St Fl 3, Freehold, NJ 07728-2289
Tel.: (732) 758-1100
Fax: (732) 933-0993
E-Mail: info@mrb-pr.com
Web Site: www.mrb-pr.com

Employees: 10

Agency Specializes In: Above-the-Line, Advertising, Advertising Specialties, Affiliate Marketing, Affluent Market, African-American Market, Agriculture, Alternative Advertising, Arts, Asian Market, Automotive, Aviation & Aerospace, Below-the-Line, Bilingual Market, Brand Development & Integration, Branded Entertainment, Broadcast, Business Publications, Business-To-Business, Cable T.V., Catalogs, Children's Market, Co-op Advertising, Collateral, College, Commercial Photography, Communications, Computers & Software, Consulting, Consumer Goods, Consumer Marketing, Consumer Publications, Content, Corporate Communications, Corporate Identity, Cosmetics, Crisis Communications, Custom Publishing, Customer Relationship Management, Digital/Interactive, Direct Response Marketing, Direct-to-Consumer, E-Commerce, Education, Electronic Media, Electronics, Email, Engineering, Entertainment, Environmental, Event Planning & Marketing, Exhibit/Trade Shows, Experience Design, Fashion/Apparel, Financial, Food Service, Game Integration, Gay & Lesbian Market, Government/Political, Graphic Design, Guerilla Marketing, Health Care Services, High Technology, Hispanic Market, Hospitality, Household Goods, Identity Marketing, In-Store Advertising, Industrial, Infomercials, Information Technology, Integrated Marketing, International, Internet/Web Design, Investor Relations, Legal Services, Leisure, Local Marketing, Logo & Package Design, Luxury Products, Magazines, Marine, Market Research, Media Buying Services, Media Planning, Media Relations, Media Training, Medical Products, Men's Market, Merchandising, Mobile Marketing, Multicultural, Multimedia, New Product Development, New Technologies, Newspaper, Newspapers & Magazines, Out-of-Home Media, Outdoor, Over-50 Market, Package Design, Paid Searches, Pharmaceutical, Planning & Consultation, Podcasting, Point of Purchase, Point of Sale, Print, Product Placement, Production, Production (Ad, Film, Broadcast), Production (Print), Promotions, Public Relations, Publicity/Promotions, Publishing, RSS (Really Simple Syndication), Radio, Real Estate, Recruitment, Regional, Restaurant, Retail, Sales Promotion, Search Engine Optimization, Seniors' Market, Social Marketing/Nonprofit, South Asian Market, Sponsorship, Sports Market, Stakeholders, Strategic Planning/Research, Sweepstakes, Syndication, T.V., Technical Advertising, Teen Market, Telemarketing, Trade & Consumer Magazines, Transportation, Travel & Tourism, Urban Market, Viral/Buzz/Word of Mouth, Web (Banner Ads, Pop-ups, etc.), Women's Market, Yellow Pages Advertising

Breakdown of Gross Billings by Media: Audio/Visual: 10%; Collateral: 5%; Event Mktg.: 5%; Pub. Rels.: 80%

Michael Becce *(Pres & CEO)*

Accounts:
Alteva PR

MSI COMMUNICATIONS
3501 Denali St Ste 202, Anchorage, AK 99503-4039
Tel.: (907) 569-7070
Fax: (907) 569-7090
E-Mail: info@msialaska.com
Web Site: www.msialaska.com/

E-Mail for Key Personnel:
President: laurie@msialaska.com
Media Dir.: geri@msialaska.com

Employees: 22

Agency Specializes In: Brand Development & Integration, Communications, Corporate Identity, Crisis Communications, Integrated Marketing, Media Planning, Media Relations, Package Design, Public Relations, Strategic Planning/Research, Web (Banner Ads, Pop-ups, etc.)

Laurie Fagnani *(Pres)*
Lana Johnson *(Sr VP)*
Jim Coe *(VP)*
Bryan Meshke *(Dir-Web)*
Amy Guse *(Acct Mgr & Strategist)*
Geri Groeneweg *(Strategist-Media)*

Accounts:
Anchorage Convention & Visitor's Bureau
BP Exploration (Alaska)
Carlile Transportation Systems
Department of Commerce, Community, & Economic Development
Koniag, Inc.
Nana Development Corporation
Teck Resources Limited

MSLGROUP
(Formerly Manning Selvage & Lee, Inc.)
375 Hudson St, New York, NY 10014
Tel.: (646) 500-7600
Web Site: www.mslgroup.com

E-Mail for Key Personnel:
President: mark.hass@mslpr.com

Employees: 1,300
Year Founded: 1938

National Agency Associations: COPF

Agency Specializes In: Public Relations, Sponsorship

Guillaume Herbette *(CEO)*
Andrew Silver *(Mng Dir)*
Peter Miller *(CFO)*
Shellie Winkler *(Chief Strategy Officer)*
Ron Guirguis *(CEO-US)*
Julie Jack *(Sr VP-Corp Practice)*
Erin Lanuti *(Sr VP-Paid Media & Cross Channel Strategy-North America)*
Mark McClennan *(Sr VP-Digital Svcs)*
Jeff Melton *(Sr VP-Global Tech & Platforms)*
Margarita Miranda-Abate *(Sr VP-Consumer)*
Andrea Morgan *(Sr VP)*
Katie Stevens *(Sr VP)*
Keith Strubhar *(Sr VP)*
Andy Tannen *(Sr VP)*
Curt Kundred *(Mng Dir-Western Reg & Head-Strategic Partnerships & Acq-Global)*
Steve Bryant *(Mng Dir-Seattle & Dir-Food & Beverage)*

Erin Dorr *(VP-Digital & Social Strategy & Head-Digital-Chicago)*
Taylor Lehman *(VP & Sr Acct Supvr)*
Gina Kelly *(VP-HR)*
Kevin Tressler *(VP)*
Stephanie Walter *(VP)*
Gailanne Grosso *(Exec Creative Dir)*
Brian Burgess *(Dir-Employee Practice-Global)*
Davida Dinerman *(Dir)*
Michael Echter *(Dir-Corp Comm-Global)*
Krista Kuhn *(Dir-Creative)*
Stephanie Smith *(Dir-Global Client Engagement)*
Bria Bryant *(Sr Acct Supvr)*
Rebecca Price *(Acct Supvr)*
Paula Bryant *(Sr Acct Exec)*
Matt MacPherson *(Sr Acct Exec)*
Katie Pearson *(Sr Acct Exec)*
Danielle Sullivan *(Sr Acct Exec)*
Laura Underwood *(Sr Acct Exec-P&G Consumer Team & Integrated Mktg Team)*
Melanie Garvey *(Acct Exec)*

Accounts:
3M
Abbott Laboratories Campaign: "Mother 'Hood", Digital, Similac
Adecco
Adidas
Air France-KLM Group
Allergen
Ann Inc. Ann Taylor, Ann Taylor Loft
AstraZeneca
AVG Technologies (Agency of Record)
Bayer AG
Berlex
Best Buy
BLACK GIRLS ROCK
Braeburn Pharmaceuticals Probuphine
Citigroup Inc.
Clinique; 2008
Cloudmark
Coca-Cola Refreshments USA, Inc.
Dow Chemical
The Emirates Group Arabian Adventures, Dnata, Emirates Skywards, SkyCargo
Encore Capital Group, Inc. Global Public Relations, Government Affairs, Investor Relations Efforts, Media Relations, Reputation Management Program
Ferrero
General Motors Chevrolet Campaign: "Steering Influencers into the Sonic Driver's Seat", Information Systems & Services, Parts & Operations, Regional PR Services
GlaxoSmithKline
GMAC Commercial Mortgage
Home Depot
John Morrell Food Group
Johnson & Johnson
JP Morgan Fleming Asset Management
JP Morgan Private Bank
Kellogg's Toaster Pastries
Labatt USA LLC
LaSalle Investment Management PR, Profile & Brand Awareness
March of Dimes Foundation Creative, Imbornto Cause Marketing Campaign, Out-of-Home, PR, PSAs, Social Media, Strategy
The Mexico Tourism Board PR
Nestle
Nike
Nokia
Novartis Pharmaceuticals Corporation
PayPal North American PR
Pepsico
Pfizer
Philips Electronics North America Corporation Philips Consumer Lifestyle
Procter & Gamble Align, Always, Beauty Care, Campaign: "Like a Girl", Dawn, Fabric & Home Care, Feminine Care, Health & Oral Care, Oral Care, Oral-B, PR, Pet Food, Prilosec, Vicks
The Public Relations Society of America Mobile App for Ethics
Puma
Rogers
Sanofi-Aventis Rimonabant, Uroxatral
Solvay
Sunkist Growers Sunkist Lemons
TruGreen (Public Relations Agency of Record) Community Relations, Government Relations, Marketing, Media Relations
Western Union
World Gold Council

North America

Manning Selvage & Lee
175 Bloor Street E Suite 801, North Tower, Toronto, ON M4W 3R8 Canada
Tel.: (416) 967-3702
Fax: (416) 967-6414
E-Mail: francine.raymond@mslworldwide.com
Web Site: northamerica.mslgroup.com

Employees: 36
Year Founded: 1989

Agency Specializes In: Public Relations

Gayla Brock-Woodland *(Pres)*
Catherine Heroux *(Sr VP-Consumer)*
Katie Marie MacKay *(Acct Exec)*
Marni Zaretsky *(Acct Exec)*

Accounts:
Emirates PR
Enbridge Gas Distribution
Fujifilm Canada
Janssen-Ortho/Ortho Biotech
Loblaw Companies Joe Fresh Style, President's Choice
Philips
Procter & Gamble
Rogers Cable
Rogers Wireless
Sanofi Aventis

Manning Selvage & Lee
2029 Century Park East Ste 1750, Los Angeles, CA 90067
Tel.: (310) 461-0383
Web Site: northamerica.mslgroup.com

Employees: 28

National Agency Associations: COPF

Agency Specializes In: Public Relations

David Close *(Mng Dir)*
Mark McClennan *(Sr VP-Digital Svcs)*
Helen Shik *(Sr VP-Health & Content Mktg)*
Mercedes Carrasco *(VP)*
Erin Dorr *(VP-Digital & Social)*
Brianne Killinger *(VP)*
Vickie Fite *(Dir-Multicultural Practice)*
Patty Tazalla *(Acct Supvr)*
Tessa Weber *(Sr Acct Exec)*
Tyler King *(Asst Acct Exec)*

Accounts:
Best Buy
Del Monte Foods Kibbles & Bits
DineEquity, Inc.
Nestle Nutrition Division
OpenTV
Procter & Gamble
Red Bull
Sunkist Growers

Manning Selvage & Lee
1170 Peachtree St NE Ste 400, Atlanta, GA 30309-7677
Tel.: (404) 875-1444
Fax: (404) 892-1274
E-Mail: kyle.farnham@mslworldwide.com
Web Site: northamerica.mslgroup.com

Employees: 50
Year Founded: 1965

National Agency Associations: COPF

Agency Specializes In: Public Relations

Kyle Farnham *(Mng Dir)*
Sophie Merven *(VP & Dir-Consumer Practice)*
Taylor Lehman Gray *(VP)*
Lindsay Ash *(Acct Supvr)*
Jennifer Barabas *(Sr Acct Exec)*
Marissa Moss *(Sr Acct Exec)*
Lauren Camdzic *(Asst Acct Exec)*
Karlenne Trimble *(Chief Client Engagement Officer)*

Accounts:
ADP
ARC
Artlite
AT&T Southeast
BB&T
Best Buy
GDEcD
Heidelberg USA, Inc.
The Home Depot
Roche
UPS Capital
UPS Supply Chain Solutions

Manning Selvage & Lee
222 Merchandise Mart Plz Ste 4-150, Chicago, IL 60654
Tel.: (312) 861-5200
Fax: (312) 861-5252
E-Mail: joel.curram@mslpr.com
Web Site: northamerica.mslgroup.com

Employees: 26

National Agency Associations: COPF

Agency Specializes In: Public Relations

David Close *(Mng Dir)*
Greg Eppich *(Sr VP)*
Jayme Maniatis *(Sr VP)*
Helen Shik *(Sr VP-Health & Content Mktg)*
Mercedes Carrasco *(VP)*
Erin Dorr *(VP-Digital & Social)*
Dane Goldbloom *(Sr Mgr-Production)*
Jolyn Koehl *(Acct Supvr)*
Tessa Weber *(Sr Acct Exec)*
Tyler King *(Asst Acct Exec)*

Accounts:
American Society of Home Inspectors
General Mills
Kellogg School of Management
Masco Corporation
Reynolds Packaging Group; 2006
Ronald McDonald House Charities of Chicagoland and Northwest Indiana Public Relations, Social Media Marketing

MSL Seattle
(Formerly Publicis Consultants)
424 2nd Ave W, Seattle, WA 98119-4013
Tel.: (206) 285-5522
Fax: (206) 272-2497
Web Site: northamerica.mslgroup.com

E-Mail for Key Personnel:
President: steve.bryant@publicis-pr.com

Employees: 239

National Agency Associations: COPF

Agency Specializes In: Business-To-Business, Children's Market, Event Planning & Marketing, Exhibit/Trade Shows, Food Service, Health Care Services, Pharmaceutical, Public Relations, Publicity/Promotions, Restaurant, Teen Market

Lisa Kelly *(Sr VP & Grp Dir-Mgmt)*
Greg Eppich *(Sr VP)*
Vicki Nesper *(Sr VP)*
Patty Tazalla *(Acct Supvr)*
Tessa Weber *(Sr Acct Exec)*
Jennifer Egurrola Leggett *(Acct Exec)*

Accounts:
DuPont Crop Protection
Mori Building Company
T-Mobile US Campaign: "Alter Ego"

Qorvis MSLGROUP
(Formerly Qorvis Communications)
1201 Connecticut Ave NW Ste 500, Washington, DC 20036
(See Separate Listing)

International

20:20 MSL
A/12 1st Floor Vikas Center, S V Road, Santa Cruz West, Mumbai, 400054 India
Tel.: (91) 22 3965 1700
Fax: (91) 22 3965 1777
E-Mail: chetan@2020india.com
Web Site: www.2020india.com

Employees: 300
Year Founded: 1989

Amit Misra *(Co-Mng Dir-India)*
Rekha Rao *(Gen Mgr)*
Ketan Pote *(Acct Dir)*
Ruby Sinha *(Acct Dir)*
Monica Srivastava *(Acct Dir)*
Amrit Ahuja *(Dir-Client Svcs-Tech & B2B lead Asia)*
Monica Miglani *(Acct Mgr)*
Mriga Arora *(Sr Acct Exec)*
Preeti Nair *(Sr Acct Exec)*
Rinu Jha *(Assoc Acct Dir)*

Accounts:
Canon
Chhattisgarh Tourism Board Engagement Campaign, Strategic Communications
Cognizant
Ferns N Petals Brand Awareness
Hay Group Brand Awareness, Strategic Communications
Intel Corporation

Andreoli/MS&L
Av Ibirapuera, 2332 Torre 1 - 14 andar, Moema, 04028-002 Sao Paulo, SP Brazil
Tel.: (55) 11 3169 9300
Fax: (55) 11 3169 9317
E-Mail: andreoli@andreolimsl.com.br
Web Site: www.andreolimsl.com.br

Employees: 70
Year Founded: 1993

Agency Specializes In: Event Planning & Marketing, Public Relations

Josh Shapiro *(Dir-Client Engagement-Global)*
Felipe Endrigo *(Analyst-Social Networks)*

Accounts:
3G Americas
Abrabe
Adidas Brazuca, Campaign: "All Day and All of the Night"
Albert Einstein
ANIP
Arycom
Banco Espirito Santo
Bimbo
BlackRock
Brenco
Bridgewater Systems
Coca-Cola Refreshments USA, Inc.
COMERC
Danone
Engevix
Ericsson
FDC
GS1
Inmarsat
InPar
iShares
KLM
LDC SEV
Louis Dreyfus
Medicina dos Olhos
OHL Brasil
Oral B
PacificHydro
ProCobre
Rolex
SBM Offshore
Sebrae SP
Sinditabaco
Sodexho do Brasil
Souza, Cescon, Barrieu & Flesch
Starwood
SulAmerica
World Economic Forum

CNC - Communications & Network Consulting AG
(Formerly Capital MS&L)
55 Whitfield Street, London, W1T 4AH United Kingdom
Tel.: (44) 20 32 19 88 00
Fax: (44) 20 7 307 5331
E-Mail: london@cnc-communications.com
Web Site: www.cnc-communications.com

Employees: 19
Year Founded: 2001

Agency Specializes In: Public Relations

Roland Klein *(Mng Partner)*
Steffan Williams *(Mng Partner)*
Kevin Soady *(Partner)*
Nick Bastin *(Mng Dir)*
Richard Campbell *(Mng Dir)*
Ben Curson *(Mng Dir)*
Claire Maloney *(Mng Dir)*
Oliver Mann *(Mng Dir)*
Campbell Hood *(Head-Fin Svcs-MENA & Dir)*
Anna Davies *(Assoc Dir)*
Simon Evans *(Assoc Dir)*

Accounts:
Bavarian Nordic
BLME
Cantor Index
DEXIA
Emirates NBD
Englefield
Ezz Steel
Greene King PLC Corporate & Financial Communications, Financial PR
Halbank
Hochtief
Huawei
Hunter Fleming
Intelligent Environments
Investcom
Manchester Independent Economic Review
MCB Finance
Morgan Stanley
NAEEM
NXT
Oakwood
T-Online

Epic MSLGROUP
(Formerly Epic Communications (Pty) Ltd)
10th Floor Fredman Towers, 13 Fredman Drive, Johannesburg, South Africa
Tel.: (27) 117844790
Web Site: www.epicmslgroup.com

Year Founded: 2007

Agency Specializes In: Brand Development & Integration, Corporate Communications, Digital/Interactive, Email, Event Planning & Marketing, Internet/Web Design, Investor Relations, Media Relations, Media Training, Public Relations

Elian Wiener *(CEO)*
Sergio Dos Santos *(Acct Dir)*
Candice Hellriegel *(Acct Dir-PR)*
Cara Louw *(Acct Dir-PR)*
Pearl Ndlazi *(Acct Dir)*
Gavin Etheridge *(Dir)*
Roline Bosch *(Sr Acct Mgr-PR)*
Caitlin Robertson *(Sr Acct Mgr)*
Rene Engelbrech *(Acct Exec)*

Accounts:
Cipla Medpro South Africa Limited
Cipla
DHL Express
DHL
Nedbank
Old Mutual
Samsung

Genedigi Group
6-7F Easy Home Tower No 3 Dongzhimen South Ave, Dongcheng District, Beijing, 100007 China
Tel.: (86) 10 57691166
Fax: (86) 10 57691088
E-Mail: sales@genedigi.com
Web Site: www.genedigi.com

Employees: 400

Agency Specializes In: Public Relations

Xiao Jun *(Pres)*
Ji Miki *(Sr Acct Mgr)*
Cathy Wang *(Sr Acct Exec)*
Yan Cao *(Acct Exec)*
Charlie Ling Yat Wai *(Assoc Acct Dir)*

Accounts:
Tsingtao

Hollander en Van der Mey/MS&L
Villa Vronesteijn Oosteinde 237, 2271 EG Voorburg, The Hague Netherlands
Tel.: (31) 70 354 90 00
Fax: (31) 70 350 31 45
E-Mail: info@hvdm.nl
Web Site: www.hvdm.nl

Employees: 10
Year Founded: 1951

Agency Specializes In: Government/Political, Public Relations

Robbert Vreeburg *(Acct Dir)*
Natascha Derogee *(Acct Exec)*
Thijs Ros *(Acct Exec)*
Dick Boot *(Assoc Designer-New Media)*

Accounts:
Blue Ray Disk Association

Koninklijk Verbond van Nederlandse Baksteenfabrikanten
Samsung Group
Superunie

JKL Copenhagen
Amaliegade 41 A, DK-1256 Copenhagen, Denmark
Tel.: (45) 33 38 56 80
Fax: (45) 33 38 56 99
E-Mail: peter.steere@jklgroup.com
Web Site: www.jklgroup.com

Employees: 11

Agency Specializes In: Public Relations

Peter Steere *(Partner & CEO-JKL Grp)*
Soren Berg *(Mng Dir-Copenhagen)*

JKL Stockholm
Sveavagen 24-26, PO Box 1405, 111 84 Stockholm, Sweden
Tel.: (46) 8 696 12 00
Fax: (46) 8 696 00 15
E-Mail: info@jklgroup.com
Web Site: www.jklgroup.com

Employees: 57
Year Founded: 1985

Agency Specializes In: Public Relations

Peter Steere *(Partner & CEO-JKL Grp)*
Jan Lindow *(Partner & Mng Dir-MSLGROUP Sweden)*
Per Ola Bosson *(Partner)*
David Ingnas *(Partner)*
Anders Kempe *(Partner)*
Anna Gronlund Krantz *(Partner-JKL Grp)*
Gabriel Francke Rodau *(Partner)*
Henrik Nilsson *(Mng Dir-Gothenburg)*
Kjersti Oppen *(Mng Dir-Oslo)*
Leonardo Sforza *(Mng Dir-MSLGroup Brussels)*
Pontus Bostrom *(Mgr-IT)*

Manning, Selvage & Lee Frankfurt
Otto Messmer St 1, 60431 Frankfurt, Germany
Tel.: (49) 69 6612 456 0
Fax: (49) 69 6612 456 8399
E-Mail: info@mslpr.de
Web Site: northamerica.mslgroup.com

Employees: 15
Year Founded: 1988

Agency Specializes In: Public Relations

Wigan Salazar *(CEO-MSL-Germany & Berlin)*
Philip Maravilla *(Mng Dir-Bus Dev & Head-EMEA Tech Practice)*

Accounts:
Bayer Vital GmbH
Bosch (Global Agency of Record)
Dow Automotive
Procter & Gamble
Schott AG Global PR

Manning Selvage & Lee London
55 Whitfield Street, London, W1T 4AH United Kingdom
Tel.: (44) 02032198700
Fax: (44) 2078783030
E-Mail: info@mslgroup.com
Web Site: www.mslgroup.co.uk

Employees: 50
Year Founded: 1987

National Agency Associations: PRCA

Agency Specializes In: Consumer Marketing, Corporate Communications, Crisis Communications, Health Care Services, Public Relations

Kelly Walsh *(CEO)*
Mallika Basu *(Acting Mng Dir-Corp Practice)*
Avril Lee *(Mng Dir-Health Practices-UK & EMEA)*
Alexandra Sananes *(Acct Dir)*
Kinda Jackson *(Dir-Consumer PR Practice)*
Matthew Shannon *(Dir-Creative)*
Jonathan Williams *(Sr Acct Mgr)*

Accounts:
Atos
AVG
Coca-Cola
Danone
General Mills
GsK
Lily Gabriella PR, Trade Press
Michelin
Nestle Cereal Partners
Novartis
Procter & Gamble
Retina Implant
RichRelevance
Siemens
Slendertone

Maruri
(Formerly De Maruri Publicidad DMP)
Avenida Raul Gomez Lince Av 32 N-O #640, Edificio MCG, Bajo el Mirador de Urdenor, Guayaquil, Ecuador
Tel.: (593) 4 2888 120
Fax: (593) 4 28881 40
E-Mail: aseminario@mcg.com.ec
Web Site: www.maruri.ec

Employees: 120
Year Founded: 1993

Santiago Crespo *(VP-Customer Svc)*
Andres Maruri *(VP-Consumer Relationship)*
Santiago Maruri *(VP-Consumer Relationship)*
Luis Campoverde *(Dir-Creative)*
Sime Grzunov *(Dir-Art)*
Carlos Haz *(Dir-Fin)*
Adrian Morano *(Dir-Creative)*
Carlos Vascones *(Dir-Media)*
Gabriela Vaca De Guzman *(Mgr-Relationship)*
Diego Gangotena *(Copywriter-Creative)*
Viviana Holguin *(Coord)*

Accounts:
3M
Alzheimer Foundation
Artefacta
Asociacion de Radios de Ecuador
Club Emelec Campaign: "90 Minute Card"
Don Cafa Campaign: "Wake Up World"
Ecuador Government Campaign: "Yasuni Itt"
Ecuadorian Football Association
Extra Newspaper
Glue It
Industrias Lacteas Toni Campaign: "Garden", Campaign: "Parent Detector"
Kids-Tab Campaign: "Bambi in the Woods", Campaign: "Flowers in April", Campaign: "Ice fox"
La Fabril Campaign: "Delfina Mission"
The National Football Association Safety Committee
Nature's Garden Campaign: "Large Url", Campaign: "Spa"
Olimpia
Umbro Campaign: "1 Million Dollar T-Shirt"
Vicente Sarmiento Foundation Campaign: "Jail"

MS&L China
12F 01-03 Prospect Center West, 5 Guanghua Road, Beijing, 100020 China
Tel.: (86) 10 8573 0688
Fax: (86) 10 6588 0668
E-Mail: john.hong@sh.mslpr.com
Web Site: northamerica.mslgroup.com/

Agency Specializes In: Public Relations

Benjamin Tan *(Reg Dir-Client Engagement & Dev-Asia)*
Leslie Lin *(Reg Assoc Dir-Asia China P&G SPOC)*

Accounts:
Allergan Botox, Communications, Natrelle
Cola-Cao Consumer
Keppel Land China Corporate Communications
New Balance
Nu Skin Digital, Social
Perfetti Van Melle Campaign: "Sweeten China with Small Acts of Kindness"
Ping An Financial Technology Brand Awareness

MS&L France
15 rue Bleue, CEDEX, 75341 Paris, 09 France
Tel.: (33) 1 55 33 4300
Fax: (33) 155 33 42 44
Web Site: mslgroup.com

Employees: 25
Year Founded: 1997

Agency Specializes In: Public Relations

Aurelie De Labarriere *(Mng Dir)*
Pascal Beucler *(Chief Strategy Officer & Sr VP)*

MS&L Italia
Viale Vittorio Veneto 22, 20124 Milan, Italy
Tel.: (39) 02 773 3661
Fax: (39) 02 773 36360
Web Site: www.mslgroup.it/

Employees: 50
Year Founded: 1961

Agency Specializes In: Public Relations

Adriana Mavellia *(Pres)*
Daniela Canegallo *(CEO)*
Germano Calvi *(Head-Strategy)*
Marco Fornaro *(Head-Digital)*
Giusi Viani *(Dir-Bus Unit)*
Elena Zaco *(Dir-Bus Unit Mktg)*
Kim Piquet *(Exec Planner-Strategic)*

Accounts:
Arca SGR
The Carlyle Group
Cheres Beer
Dompe Public Relations
EDS
Fiditalia
Gillette Group Italy Braun, Duracell, G. Grooming, Oral B
Mitsubishi
Procter & Gamble Ace, Febreze, Pantene e Infasil, Swiffer
Rotary
San Pellegrino Acqua Panna
Sanofi-Aventis

MS&L Japan
14F JR Tokyu Meguro Blg, 3-1-1 Kami-Osaki Shinagawa-ku, Tokyo, 141-0021 Japan
Tel.: (81) 3 5719 8901
Fax: (81) 357198919
Web Site: mslgroup.com

Employees: 30

Agency Specializes In: Asian Market

Eric Hess *(Mng Dir)*
Kiminori Takeuchi *(Deputy Mng Dir)*
Sei Naganuma *(Head-Digital)*
Koichi Nishida *(Acct Supvr)*

Accounts:
Merck

MS&L Shanghai
Room F 15/F No755 Huai Hai Zhong Road, Shanghai, 200020 China
Tel.: (86) 21 5465 8488
Fax: (86) 21 5465 8440
Web Site: northamerica.mslgroup.com/

Par Uhlin *(Mng Dir)*
Glenn Osaki *(Pres-Asia)*
Laura Lee *(Mng Dir-King Harvests)*
Daisy Zhu *(Mng Dir-China)*
Benjamin Tan *(Reg Dir-Client Engagement & Dev-Asia)*
Charlotta Lagerdahl-Gandolfo *(Reg Bus Dir-Asia)*

MS&L Stockholm
(Formerly MS&L Sweden)
Sveavagen 24-26, SE-111 84 Stockholm, Sweden
Tel.: (46) 8 550 511 00
Fax: (46) 8 550 511 99
E-Mail: jan.lindow@se.mslworldwide.com
Web Site: mslnordic.com/

Employees: 20
Year Founded: 2006

Jan Lindow *(CEO)*
Martin Gleissner *(Grp Head-Tech Practice & Sr Acct Mgr)*
Kristina Ebenius *(Dir-Healthcare-JKL)*
Pernilla Ivarsson *(Dir-HR)*

Accounts:
Nikon
Philips
Royal Caribbean
TDC

MS&L
6/F Cityplaza 3, 14 Taikoo Wan Rd, Hong Kong, China (Hong Kong)
Tel.: (852) 2886 5523
Fax: (852) 2904 0340
Web Site: northamerica.mslgroup.com/

Employees: 7

Agency Specializes In: Public Relations

Accounts:
Atos Origin
Bombardier Skyjet International
Business Software Alliance
Coca-Cola Refreshments USA, Inc.
Corel
Diamond Trading Company (DTC)
Huawei
ICICI Bank
Nestle
Oregon Scientific
P&G
Philips Electronics
Sony
State of California Governor's Office
Sunkist Growers

MSL Warsaw
(Formerly 180 Degrees)
Platinum Business Park Woloska 9, 02-583 Warsaw, Poland
Tel.: (48) 22 444 48 30
Fax: (48) 22 444 48 31
Web Site: www.mslwarsaw.pl

Employees: 15
Year Founded: 1999

Agency Specializes In: Consumer Marketing, Event Planning & Marketing, Public Relations

Jerzy Ciszewski *(Chm)*
Sebastian Hejnowski *(CEO)*
Zofia Bugajna *(Mng Dir)*
Pawel Tomczuk *(CEO-Financial Comm)*
Malgorzata Pietrucha *(Sr Acct Mgr)*
Martyna W grzyn *(Sr Acct Mgr)*
Magdalena Marzec *(Sr Acct Exec)*

Accounts:
Adidas Poland
Baker & McKenzie
Corel Corporation
Diageo Polska
DLA Piper
ECE Project Management
Ericsson
FIAT Polska
Lockheed Martin
Nestle Waters
Novartis
Philip Morris
Sony
Thomson Multimedia

MSL
(Formerly Publicis Van Sluis Consultants)
Jan van Goyenkade 10, 1075 HP Amsterdam, Netherlands
Tel.: (31) 20 305 59 00
Fax: (31) 20 305 59 46
Web Site: mslgroup.nl

Employees: 40
Year Founded: 1973

Agency Specializes In: Communications, Financial, Government/Political, Industrial, Investor Relations, Public Relations

Henjo Guitjens *(CEO)*
Carin Kleiweg *(CFO)*
Alex De Vries *(Dir-Media Rels)*
Erik Martens *(Dir-Pub Affairs-Netherlands)*
Bart Van Wanrooij *(Dir-Creative)*
Fieke Kalkman *(Office Mgr)*

Accounts:
Boeing
FedEx
Interpolis
Rabobank Group; Utrecht, Netherlands

MSLGroup
(Formerly Ciszewski MSL)
ul Domaniewska 42, Warsaw, 02-672 Poland
Tel.: (48) 22 278 38 00
E-Mail: kontakt@mslgroup.com
Web Site: www.mslgroup.pl

Employees: 80

Zofia Bugajna *(Mng Dir)*
Anna Borowiec-Gora *(Deputy Mng Dir)*
Maja Grocholska *(Acct Exec)*
Patrycja Banczyk *(Jr Acct Exec)*
Jakub Zajdel *(Team Head-Capital Market & M&A)*

Accounts:
Carrefour Polska
CitiBank
Credit Suisse
Diverse
Dom Maklerski BZ WBK
EuroTax
Finnair
Gold Finance
Hilti
Legg Mason
New World Alternative Investments
Pocztylion OFE
Riverside
Ryanair
Rynki Kapitalowe BZ WBK S.A
Saski Partners
Stanley
TNT
Warta

Muchnik, Alurralde, Jasper & Assoc./MS&L
Callao 1046 Piso 4, Buenos Aires, C1023AAQ Argentina
Tel.: (54) 11 5031 1300
Fax: (54) 11 5031 1301
E-Mail: laura.muchnik@mslpr.com
Web Site: northamerica.mslgroup.com

Employees: 50

Agency Specializes In: Public Relations

Laura Muchnik *(Founder)*
Karina Riera *(Owner)*
Pascal Beucler *(Chief Strategy Officer)*
Belen Nunez Ferreira *(Acct Dir-Consumer)*
Dolores Lezama *(Acct Dir)*
Jose Ignacio De Carli *(Dir-Pub Affairs)*
Malena Gimenez *(Acct Exec-Consumer Products)*
Florencia Racana *(Acct Exec-Media & Crisis Trng)*
Evelyn Botti *(Acct Coord)*
Barbara Regina Rant *(Acct Coord)*
Agustin Gutierrez *(Coord-Accts)*

Accounts:
3G Americas
AC Nielsen
Andromaco - Dermaglos
BASF Argentina SA
Beam Global Spirits & Wine
Coca-Cola Refreshments USA, Inc.
Philips
Procter & Gamble
Shell Capsa

MSR COMMUNICATIONS
832 Sansome St 2nd Fl, San Francisco, CA 94111-1558
Tel.: (415) 989-9000
Fax: (415) 989-9002
Toll Free: (866) 247-6172
E-Mail: info@msrcommunications.com
Web Site: www.msrcommunications.com

Employees: 10
Year Founded: 1999

Agency Specializes In: Business-To-Business, Corporate Communications, Corporate Identity, Information Technology, Internet/Web Design, Public Relations

Mary Shank-Rockman *(Owner)*
Chris Blake *(Acct Dir)*
Crisel Ortiz *(Acct Mgr)*
Michael Burke *(Acct Supvr)*

Accounts:
Aback
AirBed & Breakfast (Agency of Record)
Arbia
Autonomy Pleasanton
Bluxome Street Winery
Face Time
Financial Navigator
Infochimps

JangoMail (Agency of Record)
Kentico Software
Kinek PR
Kinek PR
LIM
Meta TV
mybotto
Sendmail PR
Ubiquiti Networks

MT&L PUBLIC RELATIONS LTD.
(Acquired by & Name Changed to NATIONAL Public Relations)

MUCH & HOUSE PUBLIC RELATIONS
8075 W 3rd St Ste 500, Los Angeles, CA 90048
Tel.: (323) 965-0852
Fax: (323) 965-0390
Web Site: www.muchandhousepr.com

Agency Specializes In: Event Planning & Marketing, Print, Public Relations, Radio, Social Media

Sharon W. House *(Owner)*
Elizabeth Much *(Owner)*
Bryan Decastro *(Principal)*
Heather Weiss *(VP)*
Kelly Shryock *(Acct Exec)*

Accounts:
W3 The Future

MUELLER COMMUNICATIONS INC
1749 N Prospect Ave, Milwaukee, WI 53202
Tel.: (414) 390-5500
Fax: (414) 390-5515
Web Site: www.muellercommunications.com

Agency Specializes In: Corporate Communications, Crisis Communications, Media Relations, Public Relations, Social Media

H. Carl Mueller *(Founder, Chm & CEO)*
Lori Richards *(Pres)*
James Madlom *(COO)*
Elizabeth A. Hummitzsch *(Client Svcs Dir)*
Phill Trewyn *(Sr Acct Exec)*
Natalie Verette *(Acct Exec)*
Amelia Venegas *(Coord-Admin Svcs)*
Tim McMurtry II *(Of Counsel)*

Accounts:
Local Initiatives Support Corporation

MURPHY O'BRIEN, INC.
(d/b/a Murphy O'Brien Public Relations)
11444 Olympic Blvd Ste 600, Los Angeles, CA 90064
Tel.: (310) 453-2539
Fax: (310) 264-0083
E-Mail: info@murphyobrien.com
Web Site: www.murphyobrien.com

Employees: 35
Year Founded: 1989

National Agency Associations: PRSA

Agency Specializes In: Leisure, Public Relations, Real Estate, Travel & Tourism

Brett O'Brien *(Co-Founder)*
Karen Murphy O'Brien *(Chm & CEO)*
Allyson Rener *(Pres)*
Stacy Lewis *(Sr VP)*
Kimi Ozawa *(Sr VP)*
Emily Warner *(Sr VP)*
Rachel Esserman *(VP)*
Laura Millet *(VP)*
Lisa Pieczko *(VP)*
Brooke Badger *(Acct Supvr)*
Marissa Girolamo *(Acct Exec)*

Accounts:
Abano Grand Hotel
Andaz Maui Strategic PR Campaigns
New-Arizona Biltmore A Waldorf Astoria Resort
Auberge du Soleil Resorts
Bruxie Gourmet Waffle Sandwiches
Casey's Cupcakes
The Cheesecake Factory, Inc.
Cinepolis Luxury Cinemas
Coeur d'Alene Resort; Coeur d'Alene, ID
Eau Palm Beach Resort & Spa
Esperanza Resort & Villas
Farmhouse Inn
Flor de Cana
Four Seasons Resort Punta Mita
The Grafton on Sunset
Hilton Palacio del Rio
Hilton Worldwide Hilton Worldwide, Media Relations, Public Relations; 2010
Hirsch Bedner Associates Design Consultants
New-HKS Hospitality Group
Honua Kai Resort & Spa
Hotel Jackson
Hotel Jerome
Hotel Wailea
Hotel ZaZa Dallas, Houston
New-Hotel Zephyr
Hunt Valley Inn
Hyatt Regency Huntington Beach Resort & Spa
Ice Cream Lab
New-Laurus Corporation
Les Clefs d'Or
Mayacama
Montelucia Resort & Spa
Napa Valley Festival del Sole
Ocean Avenue South
Ojai Valley Inn & Spa; Ojai, CA
The Palazzo, Las Vegas
The Peninsula Hotels
The Pizza Studio; Los Angeles, CA
PizzaRev (Strategic Communications Agency of Record)
Preferred Hotel Group
New-Pullman Miami Airport
Quail Lodge & Gold Club
New-QUIGG
New-The St. Regis Monarch Beach
Union Station Hotel
The Venetian, Las Vegas
New-Ventana Big Sur

MUTO COMMUNICATIONS, LLC
PO Box 537, Port Jefferson, NY 11777
Tel.: (631) 849-4301
Fax: (631) 849-4301
E-Mail: info@mutocomm.com
Web Site: www.mutocomm.com

Employees: 5
Year Founded: 2000

Agency Specializes In: Consumer Goods, Entertainment, High Technology, Luxury Products

Approx. Annual Billings: $1,500,000

Breakdown of Gross Billings by Media:
Audio/Visual: $1,500,000

Paul Muto *(Pres & COO)*

Accounts:
3D Mediacast; Fairfield, NJ
Oasis Home Theatre Seating; Toronto, CA
Seymour-Screen Excellence; Ames, IA
Triad Speakers, Inc.; Portland, OR

MWWPR
(Formerly MWW)
1 Meadowlands Plz, East Rutherford, NJ 07073
Tel.: (201) 507-9500
Fax: (201) 507-0092
Toll Free: (800) 724-7602
E-Mail: mattermore@mww.com
Web Site: www.mww.com

E-Mail for Key Personnel:
President: mkempner@mww.com

Employees: 200
Year Founded: 1986

Agency Specializes In: Communications, Consumer Marketing, Government/Political, Public Relations, Sponsorship

Douglas Smith *(Exec VP & Gen Mgr)*
Alissa Blate *(Exec VP & Dir-Global Practice-Consumer Lifestyle Mktg)*
Tara Naughton *(Exec VP)*
Leslie Linton *(Sr VP-MWW Grp)*
Kimberly Youngstrom *(Grp VP)*
Robyn Schweitzer *(VP)*
Loren Waldron *(VP-Bus Dev Svcs)*
Mark Umbach *(Acct Dir)*
Gina Ormand *(Chief of Staff)*

Accounts:
1800 Flowers
Aetrex Worldwide Inc. Communications Program
Aldi
ANCILE Solutions Media
Atkins Nutritionals (Agency of Record) Low Carbohydrate Food Program
Ball Park Franks
Blackhawk Network
Blurb
Bowling Proprietors' Association of America (Agency of Record)
Bowlmor AMF (Public Relations Agency of Record)
Caesars Entertainment Public Relations, Waterfront Conference Center
Coinstar CSR, Corporate Communications, Crisis, Financial Media Outreach
ConnectOne Bank
Danhov
D'Artagnan
De'Longhi (Public Relations Agency of Record)
Discovery Bay Games (Agency of Record) Branding, Communications Programs, Media Relations, Positioning, Product Launch Strategy, Special Events, Tradeshow Marketing
Dubai Aerospace Enterprise
Eckerd College
The Ethisphere Institute Public Relations
Fan Freedom Project, inc.
Federated Investors
Financial Service Centers of America
Florida A&M University
Frontier Airlines Brand Positioning, Leadership Positioning, Media Relations, Public Relations, Strategy
Garden State Wine Growers Association Campaign: "Stronger then the Storm"
Gold's Gym Consumer Awareness
Golfsmith Gifting, Retail, Sports
Google
H5 Public Relations
Healthcare Trust of America, Inc.
The Hillshire Brands Company
Honeywell
iGPS
ING Direct
Jackson Family Wines, Inc.
JetBlue Airways Issues Management Counseling; 2008
JFK Health System
Johnson & Johnson
Kapstone Paper
Kendall-Jackson
Kinkisharyo International
Leggett & Platt
Lighting Science Group Corporation

Luxury Retreats International
Mack-Cali
McDonald's
Medscape LLC
Morehouse College (Agency of Record)
National Parkinson Foundation Awareness Campaign
Network for Teaching Entrepreneurship (Agency of Record)
Nextag, Inc.; San Mateo, CA (Agency of Record) Brand Positioning, Consumer Lifestyle Marketing, Corporate Communications, Corporate Reputation, Executive Eminence, Social Media
Nikon, Inc.
Nimbuzz BV
Nutrisystem
Office Max Incorporated
Pegasus Capital Advisors
Reckitt Benckiser
Red Lobster
Related Companies
Samsung Telecommunications of America
Sbarro
Scruff Public Relations Agency of Record
Strike Ten Entertainment Bowling Centers; 2007
Subaru of America
Universal Music Enterprises Social Media, Zumba Fitness Dance Party
U.S. Bank Corporate Communications, Lead Public Relations Agency, Research & Insight, Social Media; 2015
Vimeo (Agency of Record) Media Relations
Virgin America Inc.
Walgreen Co
Westwood One
Xango LLC
Zumba Fitness, LLC. Public Relations, Strategy

Offices

MWWPR
(Formerly The MWW Group)
660 S Figueroa St Ste 1400, Los Angeles, CA 90017
Tel.: (213) 486-6560
Fax: (213) 486-6501
E-Mail: cking@mww.com
Web Site: www.mww.com

Employees: 22

Agency Specializes In: Communications, Consumer Marketing, Public Relations

J. P. Schuerman *(Pres-Western Reg)*
Stephen Macias *(Sr VP)*
Peter A. Brown *(VP-Pub Affairs & PR)*
Joe Keenan *(VP-LGBT Practice)*
Sheena Stephens *(VP)*
Mikaela Liboro *(Sr Acct Exec)*

Accounts:
Agent Ace Brand Awareness
Asolva; Los Angeles, CA Business Process Management Solutions; 2007
New-Digiboo Brand Awareness, Public Relations
Edmunds.com Public Relations
Gay Men's Chorus Of Los Angeles (Public Relations Agency of Record) "Alive Music Project", "Outside Voices", "the it gets better Tour", Marketing, Strategic Media Relations
Here Media OUT Magazine, The Advocate
Jack in the Box Public Relations
Kendall-Jackson Wine Estates Campaign: "Goes Well with Friends", Creative, K-J Recommends
Los Angeles Department of Public Health
Mercury Insurance Group Home & Auto Insurance; 2008
Paul Katami & Jeff Zarrillo Public Relations
Runtastic Social Media Outreach
Sanuk National Brand Communications, PR

MWWPR
(Formerly The MWW Group)
99 Osgood Pl Ste 100, San Francisco, CA 94133
Tel.: (415) 464-6422
Web Site: www.mww.com

Employees: 10
Year Founded: 2007

Alison Schwartz *(Sr VP & Gen Mgr)*
Jesica Church *(VP)*

Accounts:
Azumio
BACtrack Product Awareness
Blurb
DHgate Media Relations
Eventbrite; San Francisco, CA Eventbrite Mobile App, Public Relations
Nimbuzz Brand Messaging/Positioning
NQ Mobile Inc. Brand Awareness, Digital, Marketing Public Relations, Technology
Opera Software Communications, Public Relations
Synqera
Twist
Wize Commerce

MWWPR
(Formerly The MWW Group)
901 New York Ave NW Ste 310 W, Washington, DC 20001
Tel.: (202) 600-4570
E-Mail: dsmith@mww.com
Web Site: www.mww.com

Employees: 14

Agency Specializes In: Communications, Consumer Marketing, Government/Political, Public Relations

Douglas A. Smith *(Exec VP & Gen Mgr-Washington)*
Paul Tencher *(Sr VP & Dir-Pub Affairs-Natl)*
Ryan Haaker *(Sr VP)*
Elizabeth Lowery *(Sr VP)*
Erin Bzymek *(Acct Supvr)*
Mitzi Emrich *(Sr Strategist-Social Media)*

Accounts:
Alpha Natural Resources
The American Museum of Natural History
Atlantic Health Systems
BMW of North America
Barry University
City of Albany; GA
City of Chino Hills; CA
City of Gainesville; FL
City of Miami Beach; FL
Cooper University Hospital
Deloitte
Dubai Aerospace Enterprises
Eckerd College
Johnson & Johnson
Morehouse College
North Jersey Community Bank
RF Micro Devices
Strike Ten Entertainment
United Natural Foods
Xactware Solutions

MWWPR
(Formerly The MWW Group)
205 N Michigan Ave, Chicago, IL 60601
Tel.: (312) 981-8540
Fax: (312) 853-0955
Web Site: www.mww.com

Employees: 15

Agency Specializes In: Communications, Consumer Marketing, Public Relations, Sponsorship

John Digles *(Exec VP & Gen Mgr-Chicago)*
Alissa J. Blate *(Exec VP-Global Brand Mktg & Comm)*
Steven E. Some *(Sr VP & Gen Mgr-Trenton)*
Lori Price Abrams *(VP-Govt Rels)*

Accounts:
Affiliated Managers Group, Inc
American Water Works Company
AutoReturn
Emnos B2B, Media Relations, Public Relations
The Hershey Company
Hoopla Digital Digital Counsel, Influencer Outreach, Marketing, Media, Public Relations, Trade relations
National Parkinson Foundation Media, Social Media
NBTY, Inc. Osteo Bi-Flex
Samsung Mobile
Sleep Innovations, Inc
United Nurses Associations of California
Walgreen

MWWPR
(Formerly The MWW Group)
222 W State St Ste 306, Trenton, NJ 08608
Tel.: (609) 396-0067
Fax: (609) 396-2272
E-Mail: kfrechette@mww.com
Web Site: www.mww.com

Employees: 10

Agency Specializes In: Communications, Consumer Marketing, Government/Political, Public Relations

John Digles *(Exec VP & Gen Mgr-CHICAGO)*
Alissa J. Blate *(Exec VP-Global Brand Mktg & Comm)*
Lori Price Abrams *(VP-Govt Rels)*
Rich Levesque *(VP-Pub Affairs)*
Tom Cosentino *(Acct Dir-Pub Affairs)*

Accounts:
Health Promotion Council of Southeastern Pennsylvania; Philadelphia, PA; 2008

MWWPR
(Formerly The MWW Group)
304 Park Ave S, New York, NY 10010
Tel.: (212) 704-9727
Fax: (212) 704-0917
Toll Free: (866) 304-7035
E-Mail: mattermore@mww.com
Web Site: www.mww.com

Employees: 248
Year Founded: 1986

Agency Specializes In: Communications, Consumer Marketing, Public Relations

Arthur Schwartz *(Mng Dir)*
JP Schuerman *(Pres-Western Reg)*
Bill Murray *(Exec VP & Dir-Pub Affairs-Natl)*
Carreen Winters *(Exec VP-Corp Comm)*
Kristen Sharkey *(Sr VP & Head-East Coast Tech)*
Carl Sorvino *(Sr VP & Exec Dir-Creative)*
Nicole Schoenberg *(Sr VP & Dir-Fin Comm)*
Cecilia Coakley *(Sr VP)*
Leslie Linton *(Sr VP-MWW Grp)*
Stephen Macias *(Sr VP)*
Dave Arnold *(VP)*
Nicole Bott *(VP)*
Jackie Glick *(VP)*
Susan Goodell *(VP)*
Lauren Karasek *(VP-Social Media Strategy, Corp Reputation & Pub Affairs)*

Kevin McCauley *(VP-Editorial Svcs)*
Ryan Smith *(VP-Media)*
Laura Hansen *(Mktg Mgr)*
Mary Kate Leahy *(Mgr-Pub Affairs Dept)*
Sarah Lewis *(Mgr-Nutrition Comm)*
Karen Vega *(Sr Strategist-Digital & Acct Supvr)*

Accounts:
1-800-Flowers.com
21st Century Fox
AdRoll
Air New Zealand
Atkins
BBC
Booking.com Brand Awareness, PR
Brown-Forman Corporation
Discovery Networks
Gay Men's Chorus of Los Angeles
Golfsmith International
Haier America
Harry & David (Public Relations Agency of Record) Social Media Strategy
Here Media Inc.
JCP&L (First Energy)
Men's Wearhouse
Microsoft Corporation
Monster Energy
News UK
Nikon, Inc.
Opera Media Works
Red Lobster
Samsung
SKETCHERS USA
Subaru of America, Inc. Lifestyle Marketing
Thomas Jefferson University
Tyson Foods
US Bank National Association
US Bank (Public Relations Agency of Record) Brand Awareness, Communications, Media
The Weather Channel

MWWPR
(Formerly MWW Group)
One McKinney Plz 3232 McKinney Ave, Dallas, TX 75204
Tel.: (972) 231-2990
Fax: (972) 231-9442
E-Mail: info@mww.com
Web Site: www.mww.com

Employees: 10

Michael W. Kempner *(Founder, Pres & CEO)*
Douglas Smith *(Exec VP & Gen Mgr)*
Jennifer Little *(Sr VP & Gen Mgr-Southwest Reg)*
Alison Cox *(VP)*
Ashley Gregory *(Sr Acct Exec)*
Alexandra Rosenzweig *(Sr Acct Exec)*
Quincy Zhai *(Sr Acct Exec-Tech)*

Accounts:
Johnson & Johnson
McDonald's
Nikon, Inc.
RAVE Restaurant Group (Public Relations Agency of Record) Brand Awareness, Media Relations Strategy, Strategic Communications, Thought Leadership
Samsung
Volkswagen Group of America, Inc.

MWWGroup@Deutsch
111 8th Ave, New York, NY 10011-5201
Tel.: (212) 981-7600
Fax: (212) 981-7525
Web Site: www.deutschinc.com

Agency Specializes In: Event Planning & Marketing, Government/Political, Public Relations, Publicity/Promotions

Val Difebo *(CEO-Deutsch NY)*
Vonda LePage *(Exec VP & Dir-Corp Comm)*

Subsidiaries

Carlton Fields Jorden Burt
(Formerly Jorden Burt, Llp.)
1 State St Ste 1500, Hartford, CT 06103
Tel.: (860) 392-5000
Fax: (860) 392-5058
Web Site: www.cfjblaw.com

Employees: 22

James F. Jorden *(Mng Partner)*
Kate Barth *(Mgr-PR)*

MWW UK
(Formerly Parys Communications)
56A Poland St, 2nd Fl, London, W1F 7NN United Kingdom
Tel.: (44) 207 046 6080
Web Site: www.mww.com/uk

Agency Specializes In: Advertising

Rebecca Blinston-Jones *(Deputy Mng Dir-London)*
Matt Bourn *(Sr VP & Head-European Media Practice)*
Patrick Herridge *(Mng Dir-UK)*
Pippa Ellis *(Sr Acct Dir)*
Rachel Channing *(Dir)*
Eleanor Crossman *(Sr Acct Mgr)*
Caroline Horwich *(Assoc Acct Exec)*

Accounts:
AdRoll
Archant Advertising, Creative, Media, Public Relations, Strategic
Brand Licensing Europe National & International Awareness
New-Glaad
Licensing Industry Merchandisers Association
Magnetic Public Relations, Social Media
New-Mindshare UK Public Relations
News International Marketing, Media Relations
Opera Mediaworks Communications, Trade
Outdoor Media Centre
Sky Media Sky AdSmart

NADEL PHELAN, INC.
269 Mt Hermon Rd Ste 107, Scotts Valley, CA 95066
Tel.: (831) 439-5570
Fax: (831) 439-5575
E-Mail: info@nadelphelan.com
Web Site: www.nadelphelan.com

Employees: 20
Year Founded: 1993

Agency Specializes In: Public Relations

Paula Phelan *(CEO)*
Fred Nadel *(COO & VP-Market Res)*
Cara Sloman *(VP)*
Michael Salmassian *(Sr Acct Mgr)*
Sean Wood *(Sr Acct Mgr)*
Shannon Tierney *(Acct Mgr)*
Lisa Christensen *(Mgr-Ops)*

Accounts:
ATEME PR
Enova Technology Public Relations
Microsoft
SOTI Inc. Media, Public Relations

Branch

Nadel Phelan, Inc.
535 5th Ave 14th Fl, New York, NY 10017
Tel.: (831) 234-4334
Fax: (831) 439-5575
E-Mail: info@nadelphelan.com
Web Site: nadelphelan.com

Agency Specializes In: Public Relations

Paula Phelan *(Pres & CEO)*

NANCY MARSHALL COMMUNICATIONS
20 Western Ave, Augusta, ME 04332
Tel.: (207) 623-4177
Fax: (207) 623-4178
E-Mail: info@marshallpr.com
Web Site: www.marshallpr.com

Employees: 17
Year Founded: 1991

Agency Specializes In: Public Relations

Approx. Annual Billings: $1,000,000

Charlene Williams *(Pres)*
Nancy Marshall *(CEO)*
Dianne Chamberlain *(Mgr-Internet Traffic & Acct Coord)*
John Van Pelt *(Mgr-Digital Mktg)*
Jennifer Boes *(Strategist-Integrated Mktg Comm)*
Jessica Donahue *(Acct Exec)*
Greg Glynn *(Acct Exec)*
Whitney Moreau *(Acct Exec)*

Accounts:
Maine Beer & Wine Distributors Association; 2010
Maine Children's Home; 2010
Maine Office of Tourism; 1993
Summit Natural Gas of Maine; 2012

NATIONAL PUBLIC RELATIONS
2001 McGill College Ave Ste 800, Montreal, QC H3A 1G1 Canada
Tel.: (514) 843-7171
Fax: (514) 843-6976
E-Mail: info-mtl@national.ca
Web Site: www.national.ca

Employees: 275
Year Founded: 1976

Agency Specializes In: Communications, Corporate Communications, Crisis Communications, Digital/Interactive, Graphic Design, Investor Relations, Media Relations, Media Training, Public Relations, Social Media

Andrew T. Molson *(Chm)*
Jean-Pierre Vasseur *(Pres & CEO)*
Zdenka Buric *(Mng Partner)*
Luc Ouellet *(Mng Partner)*
Serge Paquette *(Mng Partner)*
Ralph Sutton *(Mng Partner-Intl)*
Janet MacMillan *(Partner)*
Joanna Wilson *(VP & Head-Practice & Healthcare)*

Accounts:
Amazon.com
AstraZeneca
BC Hydro
Boehringer Ingelheim
Bristol-Myers Squibb
Canadian Energy Pipeline Association
Chevron
Danone Canada (Agency of Record) Public Relations, Social Media
Enbridge
Fiera Capital
Ford
GlaxoSmithKline
Global Salmon Initiative
GMCR Canada

Hewlett-Packard
Home Hardware
Ivanhoe Cambridge
Janssen
Juvenile Diabetes Research Foundation
Kohler Canada
McDonald's Restaurants of Canada
Merck Serono
Microsoft
National Bank of Canada
Nestle Waters Canada

Branches:

NATIONAL Public Relations
(Formerly MT&L Public Relations Ltd.)
1701 Hollis St Ste L101, Halifax, NS B3J 3M8 Canada
(See Separate Listing)

NATIONAL Public Relations
130, Slater St, Ste 400, Ottawa, ON K1P 6L2 Canada
(See Separate Listing)

NATIONAL Public Relations
140 Grande Allee Est Ste 302, Quebec, QC G1R 5M8 Canada
(See Separate Listing)

NATIONAL Public Relations
800 6th Ave SW Ste 1600, Calgary, AB T2P 3G3 Canada
(See Separate Listing)

NATIONAL Public Relations
310 Front St W 5th Fl, Toronto, ON M5V 3B5 Canada
(See Separate Listing)

Axon
(Formerly NATIONAL Public Relations)
Parkshot House, 5 Kew Road, Richmond, Surrey TW9 2PO United Kingdom
(See Separate Listing)

NATIONAL Public Relations
931 Fort St 4th Fl, Victoria, BC V8W 2C4 Canada
Tel.: (250) 361-1713
Fax: (250) 384-2102
E-Mail: info-vic@national.ca
Web Site: www.national.ca

Agency Specializes In: Crisis Communications, Public Relations

Zdenka Buric *(Mng Partner)*

Accounts:
Accenture
Allergan
AstraZeneca
BC Lottery Corp. (BCLC)
BHP Billiton
Bayer
Bristol-Myers Squibb
Canadian Centre for Energy Information
Coloplast
Eli Lilly
Enbridge
GlaxoSmithKline
Harlequin Enterprises
Hoffmann-La Roche
Homburg Canada
Home Hardware
Imperial Oil
International Diabetes Federation
Ivanhoe Cambridge
Janssen-Ortho
Johnson & Johnson
McDonald's Restaurants of Canada
Merck Frosst Canada
Molson Coors
Napp Pharmaceuticals
National Bank Financial Group
Novartis
Novo Nordisk
Ontario Power Authority
Pfizer
Sanofi-Aventis
St. Marys CBM
Standard Life
Sun Life Financial
Synenco Energy
TD Bank
TMX Group
Teck
TimberWest Forest Corporation
Toyota Canada
TransTech Pharma
VIA Rail
Wal-Mart
Yellow Pages Group

NATIONAL Public Relations
One Bentall Centre Ste 620 505 Burrard St, Box 34, Vancouver, BC V6C 1M4 Canada
(See Separate Listing)

Axon
(Formerly NATIONAL Public Relations)
230 Park Ave S 3rd Fl, New York, NY 10003-1566
(See Separate Listing)

Branch

madano partnership
76 Great Suffolk Street, Southwalk, London, SE1 0BL United Kingdom
Tel.: (44) 20 7593 4000
Fax: (44) 20 7928 7102
E-Mail: info@madano.com
Web Site: www.madano.com

Agency Specializes In: Communications, Market Research

Andy Eymond *(Founder)*
Michael Evans *(Mng Partner)*
Nick Turton *(Head-Energy Practice & Dir)*
Oliver Buckley *(Acct Dir-Energy & Natural Resources)*
Rory Edwards *(Acct Dir)*
Kimberley Richardson *(Acct Dir)*
Samantha Dawe *(Dir)*
Jonathan Oldershaw *(Mgr-Res)*
Tom Reynolds *(Acct Exec)*
Gareth Turner *(Acct Exec-Energy Practice)*

Accounts:
Tees Valley Unlimited Carbon Capture Storage, Communications Services
Urenco

NAUTILUS COMMUNICATIONS , INC.
PO Box 1600, Vienna, VA 22183
Tel.: (703) 938-4540
Fax: (703) 938-8524
E-Mail: info@nautiluscommunications.com
Web Site: www.nautiluscommunications.com

Agency Specializes In: Public Relations

Connie Kotke *(Principal)*
Andi Harris *(Dir-Art)*
Laurel Thomas *(Dir-Online Res)*

Accounts:
Americans Charities
Ashoka: Innovators for the Public
Council of Better Business Bureaus
Generations of Hope Development Corp.
Humane Farm Animal Care

NECTAR COMMUNICATIONS
20 California St Ste 250, San Francisco, CA 94111
Tel.: (415) 399-0181
E-Mail: info@nectarpr.com
Web Site: www.nectarpr.com

Year Founded: 2008

Agency Specializes In: Communications, Content, Media Training, Public Relations, Social Media

Rachel Petersen *(Partner)*
Tracy Sjogreen *(Partner)*
Sarah McGeary *(VP-Strategy & Ops)*
Nora Murray *(VP)*
Ashley Carlson *(Acct Supvr)*
Freya Waldern *(Acct Supvr)*
Rachel Ousley *(Sr Acct Exec)*
Shannon Reed *(Acct Exec)*
Shannon Smith *(Acct Exec)*
Kent Bravo *(Asst Acct Exec)*

Accounts:
New-Autodesk Public Relations
Biba
ClearSlide
LinkedIn Corporation
Platfora
Quip
VMware, Inc.
Workday, Inc.

THE NEELY AGENCY INC
5670 Wilshire Blvd, Los Angeles, CA 90036
Tel.: (323) 252-9173
Web Site: www.theneelyagency.com

Agency Specializes In: Advertising, Brand Development & Integration, Event Planning & Marketing, Public Relations, Social Media

Sheri D. Neely *(CEO)*

Accounts:
The Bar Kays
Marcus L. Matthews
Personal Praise

NEHLSEN COMMUNICATIONS
3000 16th St, Moline, IL 61265
Tel.: (309) 736-1071
Web Site: www.ncpr.com

Agency Specializes In: Brand Development & Integration, Collateral, Content, Digital/Interactive, Graphic Design, Internet/Web Design, Print, Public Relations, Social Media, Strategic Planning/Research

Nancy Nehlsen *(Pres)*
Woody Perkins *(CFO)*

Accounts:
MCA Chicago
Quad City Electrical Training Center

NEOTROPE
4332 W 230th St, Torrance, CA 90505-3411
Tel.: (310) 373-4856
Fax: (509) 355-3090
Toll Free: (866) 473-5924
E-Mail: info@neotrope.com
Web Site: www.neotrope.com

Employees: 4
Year Founded: 1983

National Agency Associations: PRSA

Agency Specializes In: Digital/Interactive, Electronic Media, Fashion/Apparel, High Technology, Internet/Web Design, Multimedia, Public Relations, Trade & Consumer Magazines, Travel & Tourism

Revenue: $1,000,000

Chris Simmons *(Founder & CEO)*
Ann M. Audette *(Specialist-PR)*

Accounts:
ACSIA Partners
Bash Foo
Depth Public Relations
EPIC Insurance Brokers
Insight Research Corp.
Profundity Communications
Voices.com

NETPR, INC.
132 Emerald Rdg, Santa Rosa Beach, FL 32459
Tel.: (850) 267-2231
Fax: (850) 267-4971
E-Mail: info@netpr.net
Web Site: www.netpr.net

Employees: 2

Agency Specializes In: Exhibit/Trade Shows, Game Integration, Internet/Web Design, Magazines, Public Relations, Publicity/Promotions, Publishing, Real Estate

Kimberly Maxwell *(Pres & CEO)*

Accounts:
Babies-n-town
Jolly Bay Inc
SoftLetter
SoWalbikes.com

NEVINS & ASSOCIATES
32 West Rd, Towson, MD 21204
Tel.: (410) 568-8800
Fax: (410) 568-8804
E-Mail: info@nevinspr.com
Web Site: www.nevinspr.com

Employees: 12
Year Founded: 1983

Agency Specializes In: Advertising, Collateral, Communications, Crisis Communications, Event Planning & Marketing, Financial, Government/Political, Investor Relations, Market Research, Media Relations, Point of Purchase, Print, Radio, Sales Promotion, T.V.

Kirstie Durr *(Sr VP)*
Matthew R. Hombach *(Sr VP)*
Mary Miles *(Acct Exec)*
Beth Wanamaker *(Acct Exec)*

Accounts:
AT&T Communications Corp.
Babar & Celeste Cosmetics
Comcast Cablevision, Inc.
Comcast Online Communications
Morton's The Steak House; Chicago, IL Community Relations, Event Planning, Media Relations
PrimeStar Satellite
Teleport Communications Group
The Travel Channel

NEW HARBOR GROUP
1 Davol Sq Ste 300, Providence, RI 2903
Tel.: (401) 831-1200
E-Mail: info@nharbor.com
Web Site: www.nharbor.com

Agency Specializes In: Brand Development & Integration, Crisis Communications, Integrated Marketing, Media Relations, Public Relations

David Preston *(Founder & Pres)*

Accounts:
New-Rhode Island Housing

NEW LIFE COMMUNICATIONS
167 Poplar Creek Dr, Wilkesboro, NC 28697
Tel.: (336) 880-7066

Year Founded: 2010

Agency Specializes In: Brand Development & Integration, Collateral, Event Planning & Marketing, Internet/Web Design, Logo & Package Design, Media Planning, Media Training, Public Relations, Social Media, Strategic Planning/Research

Claire Garstka *(Pres & CEO)*

Accounts:
AdvantageWest
Bridlewood Executive Suites
Hip Chics
Hope Mental Health
Wrights Care Services
YWCA of High Point

NEWBERRY PUBLIC RELATIONS & MARKETING INC
1445 Wampanoag Trl Ste 104, East Providence, RI 02915
Tel.: (401) 433-5965
Fax: (401) 431-5965
Web Site: www.newberrypr.com

Agency Specializes In: Advertising, Collateral, Crisis Communications, Logo & Package Design, Media Relations, Media Training, Public Relations, Social Media, Strategic Planning/Research

Elisabeth N. Galligan *(Founder & Pres)*
Jane Haynes *(Mgr-Creative Production)*
Judy Downey *(Acct Exec)*

Accounts:
Ocean State Job Lot

NEWGROUND PR & MARKETING
4712 Admiralty Way Ste 271, Marina Del Rey, CA 90292
Tel.: (310) 437-0045
E-Mail: info@newgroundco.com
Web Site: www.newgroundco.com

Year Founded: 2011

Agency Specializes In: Broadcast, Event Planning & Marketing, Print, Public Relations, Social Media

Shelley Miller *(Pres)*
Robert O'Shaughnessy *(Pres-Online Mktg)*
Carol Ruiz *(Principal)*
Jamie Latta *(Dir-Social Media)*
Katy Biggerstaff *(Mgr-PR)*

Accounts:
Forrest Performance Group

NEWMAN COMMUNICATIONS
125 Walnut St Ste 205, Watertown, MA 02472-4050
Tel.: (617) 254-4500
Fax: (617) 254-9088
E-Mail: sales@newmancom.com
Web Site: www.newmancom.com

E-Mail for Key Personnel:
President: david.ratner@newmancom.com

Employees: 20
Year Founded: 1989

National Agency Associations: PRSA

Agency Specializes In: Consulting, Corporate Communications, Media Relations, Public Relations, Publicity/Promotions

Robert Newman *(CEO)*
Elise Bogdan *(VP)*

Accounts:
City Capital Corporation
Grand Central Publishing
Harper Collins
Houghton Mifflin Harcourt Publishing Company
John Wiley
The Penguin Group

NEWSMARK PUBLIC RELATIONS INC.
20423 State Rd 7 Ste F6-289, Boca Raton, FL 33498
Tel.: (561) 852-5767
Fax: (561) 852-8733
E-Mail: pr@newsmarkpr.com
Web Site: www.newsmarkpublicrelations.com

Year Founded: 2003

National Agency Associations: PRSA

Agency Specializes In: Advertising, Affluent Market, African-American Market, Brand Development & Integration, Business Publications, Business-To-Business, Collateral, Communications, Consulting, Corporate Communications, Corporate Identity, Crisis Communications, Education, Environmental, Faith Based, Fashion/Apparel, Financial, Government/Political, Graphic Design, Health Care Services, Hospitality, Internet/Web Design, Investor Relations, Legal Services, Local Marketing, Logo & Package Design, Luxury Products, Media Buying Services, Media Relations, New Product Development, New Technologies, Over-50 Market, Planning & Consultation, Promotions, Public Relations, Publicity/Promotions, Real Estate, Retail, Search Engine Optimization, Social Marketing/Nonprofit, Social Media, Sports Market, Strategic Planning/Research

Approx. Annual Billings: $500,000

Breakdown of Gross Billings by Media: Bus. Publs.: 20%; Cable T.V.: 30%; Internet Adv.: 15%; Pub. Rels.: 30%; Radio: 5%

Mark Hopkinson *(Founder)*

Accounts:
BallenIsles Country Club; Palm Beach Gardens, FL Golf, Lifestyle, Spa, Tennis; 2009
Community Foundation; West Palm Beach, FL Non-Profit Services; 2008
Mark A. Tepper, P.A; Fort Lauderdale, FL Legal Services; 2007
Stephen Burrows; New York, NY Designer Fashion; 2004
The Technological University of America; Broward, Miami Dade, Palm Beach, FL Education Services; 2010

NEWTON O'NEILL COMMUNICATIONS

5508 Fort Benton Dr, Austin, TX 78735
Tel.: (512) 494-6178
Web Site: www.newtononeill.com

Year Founded: 2009

Agency Specializes In: Event Planning & Marketing, Graphic Design, Media Relations, Public Relations, Social Media

Lisa O'Neill *(Principal)*
Jenna Williams *(Dir-PR)*

Accounts:
Benolds Jewelers
Casa Brasil Coffees
Finn & Porter
H4M
Jardin De Ninos Interlingua
The Leukemia & Lymphoma Society
Liberty Tavern
Motostalgia
Rallyhood
Whislers

NICKERSON PR
1000 Winter St Ste 3100, Waltham, MA 2451
Tel.: (617) 848-4225
Web Site: www.nickersonpr.com

Year Founded: 2003

Agency Specializes In: Brand Development & Integration, Email, Event Planning & Marketing, Internet/Web Design, Media Relations, Public Relations, Search Engine Optimization, Social Media, Strategic Planning/Research

Kathleen Coffey *(Chief Strategy Officer)*
Lisa A. Nickerson *(Principal & Mng Dir-PR)*
Matthew M. King *(Mng Dir-Creative Svcs)*
Carrie E. Richards *(Mng Dir-Event Mgmt)*
Bridget Kelly *(Dir-Client Engagement)*
Tim Kirwan *(Dir-Hospitality Div)*
Kevin McMahon *(Dir-Social Media & Digital Content)*

Accounts:
Tocci Building Corporation

NICOLAZZO & ASSOCIATES
101 Federal St Ste 710, Boston, MA 02110
Tel.: (617) 951-0000
Fax: (617) 439-9980
E-Mail: rnicolazzo@nicolazzo.com
Web Site: www.nicolazzo.com

Employees: 4
Year Founded: 1975

Agency Specializes In: Brand Development & Integration, Communications, Consulting, Corporate Communications, Investor Relations, Media Planning, Media Training, Planning & Consultation, Public Relations, Strategic Planning/Research

Richard E. Nicolazzo *(Mng Partner)*
Joseph M. Grillo *(Partner)*

Accounts:
Donoghue Barrett & Singal, P.C.
Foley Hoag LLP
Frederick Memorial Hospital
Jordan Hospital
LibbyHoopes, P.C.
Lincare, Inc.; Clearwater, FL
Nortek Holdings, Inc.; Providence, RI
Ropes & Gray; Boston, MA
Saints Medical Center; Lowell, MA
UniFirst Corporation
Weil, Gotshal & Manges
Weil, Gotshal & Manges

NICOLL PUBLIC RELATIONS
1502 Providence Hwy Ste 2, Norwood, MA 02062
Tel.: (781) 762-9300
Fax: (781) 255-7777
E-Mail: lucette@nicollpr.com
Web Site: www.nicollpr.com

Employees: 6

Agency Specializes In: Public Relations

Lucette Nicoll *(Pres)*
John Nicoll *(Exec VP)*
Sue Toscano *(VP)*

Accounts:
Bowers & Wilkins
JL Audio
Meridian
Pure Music
Rotel
Total Mobile Audio
Tributaries

NIKE COMMUNICATIONS, INC.
75 Broad St Ste 510, New York, NY 10004
Tel.: (212) 529-3400
Fax: (212) 353-0175
E-Mail: info@nikecomm.com
Web Site: www.nikecomm.com

E-Mail for Key Personnel:
President: ninak@nikecomm.com
Creative Dir.: peterm@nikecomm.com

Employees: 30
Year Founded: 1984

National Agency Associations: PRSA

Agency Specializes In: Automotive, Brand Development & Integration, Consumer Marketing, Event Planning & Marketing, Fashion/Apparel, Hospitality, Leisure, Luxury Products, Promotions, Public Relations, Publicity/Promotions, Real Estate, Strategic Planning/Research, Trade & Consumer Magazines, Travel & Tourism, Women's Market

Breakdown of Gross Billings by Media: Pub. Rels.: 100%

Nina Kaminer *(Pres)*
Callie Shumaker *(VP)*
Pieter Van Vorstenbosch *(VP)*
Erin Jaffe *(Acct Supvr)*
Amber Appelbaum *(Sr Acct Exec)*
Kimberly Hanson *(Sr Acct Exec-Luxury Travel)*
Felicia Kwong *(Sr Acct Exec-Spirits Div)*
Amelia Lovaglio *(Sr Acct Exec)*
Jaclyn York *(Sr Acct Exec)*
Morgan Roth *(Acct Exec)*
Chelsea Slavin *(Acct Exec)*

Accounts:
Geox
Miraval Resort & Spa
Moet Hennessy Wines
Robert Mondavi Wines
Vertu

NINICO COMMUNICATIONS
PO Box 759, San Jose, CA 95106
Tel.: (408) 594-0758
Web Site: www.ninicocommunications.com

Year Founded: 2011

Agency Specializes In: Advertising, Brand Development & Integration, Collateral, Crisis Communications, Media Planning, Print, Public Relations, Radio, Social Media, T.V.

Nicholas Adams *(Pres)*
Tess Mooney *(Creative Dir)*

Accounts:
Crew Silicon Valley

NKPR
87 Walker St Ste 6B, New York, NY 10013
Tel.: (917) 691-7262
E-Mail: info@nkpr.net
Web Site: www.nkpr.net

Year Founded: 2002

Agency Specializes In: Advertising, Content, Crisis Communications, Digital/Interactive, Promotions, Public Relations, Social Media, Strategic Planning/Research

Natasha Koifman *(Pres)*
Bunmi Adeoye *(VP)*
Lauren Cohan *(Acct Mgr)*
Nicole Manes *(Acct Mgr)*
Rebecca Kogon *(Mgr-Bus Dev & Strategic Partnerships)*
Erin Poetschke *(Mgr-Ops)*
Kristin Newbigging *(Acct Exec)*

Accounts:
Natural Balance Foods Eat Nakd, Media Relations, Public Relations, Strategic Communications
New-Patrick Assaraf (North American Public Relations Agency of Record) Brand Strategy, Event Management, Media Relations, Outreach, Strategic Counsel
New-Sympli (Public Relations Agency of Record) Digital, Media Relations, Strategic Planning
YourTea.com

NOBLES GLOBAL COMMUNICATIONS LLC
820 Howard St, Marina Del Rey, CA 90292
Tel.: (310) 795-0497
Fax: (323) 443-1283
E-Mail: info@noblesgc.com
Web Site: www.noblesgc.com

Year Founded: 2006

Agency Specializes In: Corporate Communications, Digital/Interactive, Internet/Web Design, Print, Public Relations

Laura Nobles *(Founder & CEO)*
Julie A. Johnson *(Chief Strategy Officer)*

Accounts:
Calhoun Vision

NOLAN/LEHR GROUP
214 W 29th St Fl 10, New York, NY 10001
Tel.: (212) 967-8200
Fax: (212) 967-7292
E-Mail: dblehr@cs.com

Employees: 4
Year Founded: 1972

Agency Specializes In: Education, Engineering, Environmental, Event Planning & Marketing, Public Relations

Approx. Annual Billings: $900,000

Breakdown of Gross Billings by Media: Pub. Rels.: $900,000

Donald Lehr *(Owner & Pres)*
Nolan Haims *(Principal)*

Accounts:
The American Friends of Australian Koala Foundation Publishing; Australia; 1988
Forum on Religion & Ecology; 1998
National Engineers' Week; Washington, DC; 1996
Templeton Prize ; PA; 1991

NOREEN HERON & ASSOCIATES
1528 W Fullerton Ave, Chicago, IL 60614
Tel.: (773) 477-7666
Fax: (773) 477-7388
E-Mail: nheron@heronpr.com
Web Site: http://heronagency.com/

E-Mail for Key Personnel:
President: nheron@heronpr.com

Employees: 7
Year Founded: 2000

Agency Specializes In: Public Relations

Noreen Heron Heron *(Pres)*
Lianne Wiker *(VP)*
Katharine Hughes *(Sr Acct Exec)*
Jodi Emery *(Media Buyer)*
Jessica Carns *(Coord-Grp Sls)*
Ellen Molina *(Sr Publicist)*

Accounts:
Baileys
Final Fantasy
Geja's Cafe
The Hunt Club
Hyatt Hotels
Marriott Theatre
SPACE
Theatre at the Center

NORTH STRATEGIC
380 Wellington St W, Toronto, ON M5V 1E7 Canada
Tel.: (416) 895-9269
E-Mail: info@northstrategic.com
Web Site: www.northstrategic.com

Year Founded: 2011

Agency Specializes In: Communications, Media Relations, Public Relations, Social Media

Justin Crealy *(Co-Founder & Strategist-Creative)*
Mia Pearson *(Co-Founder & Strategist-Corp)*
Victoria Freeman *(Sr Acct Dir)*
Wendie Godbout *(Sr Acct Dir)*
Alice Choe *(Dir-Digital & Social Media)*

Accounts:
New-Sport Chek Public Relations, Social
New-Tim Hortons #WarmWishes, Social
Twitter Canada (Public Relations Agency of Record)

NORTHEAST MEDIA ASSOCIATES
141 Brigham St, South Portland, ME 04106
Tel.: (207) 653-0365
Web Site: www.nemediaassociates.com

Agency Specializes In: Logo & Package Design, Multimedia, Public Relations, T.V.

Angie Helton *(Pres)*

Accounts:
Downeast Energy
Mad Girl world
Wright Express

NORTHSTAR
(Formerly NorthStar Entertainment)
501-I S Reino Rd Ste 380, Thousand Oaks, CA 91320
Tel.: (805) 498-5880
Fax: (805) 498-5246
E-Mail: sheryl@northstar-ccm.com
Web Site: www.northstar-ccm.com/

Year Founded: 2005

Agency Specializes In: Public Relations, Publicity/Promotions

Sheryl Northrop *(Pres)*

Accounts:
Lisa Loeb

NORTHWEST STRATEGIES
441 W 5th Ave, Anchorage, AK 99501
Tel.: (907) 563-4881
Fax: (907) 562-2570
E-Mail: info@nwstrat.com
Web Site: www.nwstrat.com

Employees: 18
Year Founded: 1987

Agency Specializes In: Advertising, Advertising Specialties, Internet/Web Design, Public Relations, Strategic Planning/Research

Tim Woolston *(Pres)*
Christian Behr *(Sr Dir-Art)*
Saba Adley *(Dir-Media)*
Charles Fedullo *(Dir-PR)*
Kristi Kordewick *(Office Mgr)*
Shawn McCalip *(Mgr-Interactive & Video Production)*
Raquel Ranger *(Acct Supvr)*
Amanda Combs *(Acct Exec)*
Megan Moore *(Acct Exec)*
Hillary Walker *(Specialist-PR)*

Accounts:
Alaska Regional Hospital
Cook Inlet Region Inc.; Anchorage, AK; 1989

NOW + ZEN PUBLIC RELATIONS
589 8th Ave 9th Fl, New York, NY 10018
Tel.: (212) 564-2122
E-Mail: info@nowandzenpr.com
Web Site: www.nowandzengroup.com

Agency Specializes In: Brand Development & Integration, Public Relations

Christine Caravana *(Sr Acct Exec)*

Accounts:
New-iHome

NOYD COMMUNICATIONS INC
232 Manhattan Bch Blvd Unit D, Manhattan Beach, CA 90266
Tel.: (310) 374-8100
Fax: (310) 347-4209
E-Mail: info@noydcom.com
Web Site: www.noydcom.com

Agency Specializes In: Advertising, Brand Development & Integration, Event Planning & Marketing, Internet/Web Design, Package Design, Public Relations, Social Media, Strategic Planning/Research

Jim Noyd *(Pres)*
Michael Wood *(VP)*
Eva Lopez *(Acct Exec)*

Accounts:
New-Questyle Audio
New-RIVA Audio
New-Vizio

NUFFER SMITH TUCKER PUBLIC RELATIONS
4045 Third Ave Ste 200, San Diego, CA 92103
Tel.: (619) 296-0605
Fax: (619) 296-8530
E-Mail: results@nstpr.com
Web Site: www.nstpr.com

Employees: 26
Year Founded: 1974

Agency Specializes In: Agriculture, Brand Development & Integration, Consumer Marketing, Crisis Communications, E-Commerce, Electronics, Event Planning & Marketing, Exhibit/Trade Shows, Graphic Design, Internet/Web Design, Media Relations, Media Training, New Product Development, Planning & Consultation, Public Relations, Social Marketing/Nonprofit, Strategic Planning/Research, Web (Banner Ads, Pop-ups, etc.)

Approx. Annual Billings: $3,500,000

Bill Trumpfheller *(Pres)*
Kerry Tucker *(CEO)*
Teresa Siles *(VP & Dir-Social Media)*
Price Adams *(VP)*
Derek Danziger *(VP)*
Emily Forgeron *(VP)*
Jessica Northrup *(Acct Supvr)*
Natalie Haack *(Sr Acct Exec)*
Paige Nordeen *(Acct Exec)*
Paul Worlie *(Specialist-Govt Rels & Pub Affairs)*
Melissa Rubbelke *(Acct Coord)*

Accounts:
Chicken of the Sea International
Dairy Council of California
San Diego Foundation Public Service, Video
San Diego Public Library Foundation Campaign: "Buy-A-Brick", PR
Sony Electronics
WD-40 Company

NUNEZ PR GROUP
(Name Changed to True Point Communications)

NYHUS COMMUNICATIONS LLC
720 3rd Ave Fl 12, Seattle, WA 98104
Tel.: (206) 323-3733
Fax: (206) 323-7004
E-Mail: info@nyhus.com
Web Site: www.nyhus.com

Employees: 20
Year Founded: 2004

National Agency Associations: COPF

Agency Specializes In: Communications, Public Relations, Social Media

Revenue: $2,500,000

Roger Nyhus *(Pres & CEO)*
Beth Hester *(VP-Client Svcs)*
Mike Wiegand *(VP-Exec Comm)*
Gary Fuller *(Dir-Acctg & Fin)*
Heidi Happonen *(Dir-Integrated Comm)*
Charles McCray, III *(Dir-Pub Affairs)*
Steve Smith *(Mgr-Ops)*
Stephany Rochon *(Acct Supvr)*

Accounts:
IPREX

O2 SPORTS MEDIA

1755 Van Ness Ave Ste 502, San Francisco, CA 94109
Tel.: (415) 359-0730
Fax: (509) 351-0730
E-Mail: pskilbeck@o2sm.com
Web Site: www.o2sm.com

Employees: 1
Year Founded: 2003

Agency Specializes In: Event Planning & Marketing, Leisure, Outdoor, Public Relations, Publicity/Promotions, Sports Market

Matt Butterman *(Acct Coord-East USA)*

OCG PR

101 Summit Ave Ste 208, Fort Worth, TX 76102
Tel.: (817) 332-0404
Fax: (817) 531-1520
E-Mail: info@ocgpr.com
Web Site: www.ocgpr.com

Year Founded: 2009

Agency Specializes In: Content, Graphic Design, Internet/Web Design, Public Relations, Social Media, Strategic Planning/Research

Tonya Veasey *(CEO)*
Raquel Daniels *(Chief Strategy Officer)*
Cynthia Northrop White *(Sr VP-Pub Engagement)*
Kimberly Sims *(VP-Pub Engagement & Dir)*
Justin Adu *(Head-The Creative Dept)*
Tamesha Walker *(Dir-Employee Rels)*

Accounts:
Dr. Cherie LeFevre

O'CONNELL & GOLDBERG

450 N Park Rd Ste 600, Hollywood, FL 33021
Tel.: (954) 964-9098
Fax: (954) 964-9099
E-Mail: info@oandgpr.com
Web Site: oandgpr.com

Employees: 14
Year Founded: 1993

Agency Specializes In: Event Planning & Marketing, Media Relations, Media Training, Newspaper, Promotions, Public Relations, Publicity/Promotions

Revenue: $1,300,000

Barbara W. Goldberg *(Founder, CEO & Partner)*
Jeff Bray *(Sr Editor & Acct Supvr)*
Sarah Hendricks *(Acct Supvr)*
Jamie Russell *(Acct Supvr)*

Accounts:
Anthony's Coal Fired Pizza
Aventura Mall
Bricks & Mayors, Inc.
The Continental Group
Da Vinci on the Ocean
Destin Commons Public Relations, Social Media
Goldstein Law Group PR, Social Media
Macys
Noble House
The Orange Bowl Committee
Paradise Island
Tiffany & Co
Toll Brothers, Florida East Division PR
Turnberry Associates
Turnberry Retail Division
Viceroy Miami PR
W Fort Lauderdale
Zyscovich Architects

OGAN/DALLAL ASSOCIATES, INC.

530 7th Ave Ste 606, New York, NY 10018
Tel.: (212) 840-0888
Fax: (212) 840-8849
E-Mail: info@odapr.com
Web Site: www.odapr.com

Employees: 8
Year Founded: 1986

Agency Specializes In: Consumer Marketing, Public Relations

Evelyn Dallal *(Pres)*
Charlotte Hohorst *(Mgr-PR)*

Accounts:
Agraria Home
Badgley Mischka; New York, NY; 1991
Marsia Holzer Studio

OGILVY PUBLIC RELATIONS WORLDWIDE

636 11th Ave, New York, NY 10036
Tel.: (212) 880-5200
Fax: (212) 370-4636
E-Mail: rachel.foltz@ogilvypr.com
Web Site: www.ogilvypr.com

Year Founded: 1980

National Agency Associations: 4A's-COPF-PRSA

Agency Specializes In: Brand Development & Integration, Communications, Public Relations

Stuart Smith *(CEO)*
Kate Cronin *(Mng Dir)*
Jennifer Scott *(Mng Dir)*
Michael Briggs *(Exec VP & Head-Insight & Strategy)*
April Scott *(Exec VP & Head-Social@Ogilvy New York)*
Nicky McHugh *(Exec VP & Exec Dir-The New York Corp Practice)*
Christopher Myles *(Exec VP & Grp Dir-Consumer Mktg)*
Kerry Sette *(Exec VP & Dir-Res-Res Grp)*
Sandra Saias *(Exec VP)*
Bruce McConnel *(Sr VP & Head-Global Acct-Digital Comm)*
Brooke Blashill *(Sr VP & Dir-The Boutique)*
David Brooks *(Sr VP-Digital & Social Strategy)*
Lindsay Garrison *(Sr VP)*
Christine Hanson *(Sr VP-Healthcare)*
Jennifer Risi *(Mng Dir-Media Influence & Head-Media Rels-North America)*
Betsy Stark *(Mng Dir-Content & Media Strategy)*
Jeannine Feyen *(VP-Consumer Mktg Grp)*
Nancy Goldstein *(VP-Corp Practice)*
Stacey Johnes *(VP-Brand Mktg Grp)*
Robert Murphy *(VP)*
Christie Shein *(VP)*
Janet Sousa *(Mgr-Bus Dev)*
Alberto Gestri *(Sr Acct Exec)*
Rebecca Yi *(Asst Acct Exec)*

Accounts:
ADP Automatic Data Processing, Inc.
The American Society for Quality Campaign: "A World of Quality - Building a New Brand Positioning"
Bayer Healthcare
Bitdefender (Agency of Record)
Brand USA (Global Media Relations Agency of Record) Content, Social Media, Strategic
Castrol Castrol Index, EDGE, GTX, Media Relations
Centers for Disease Control & Prevention (CDC)
Consejo De Promocion Turistica De Mexico Campaign: "The Place You Thought You Knew"
Core Technologies Campaign: "Built for the Assembly Line"
DECA
DocuSign Inc.
Dow Jones & Company
Dupont
EarthLink, Inc.
Endo Health Solutions, Inc PR
FEMA
FM Global
Ford Motor Company
Great American Cookies
Hitachi Data Systems; 2007
J & J
Kimberly-Clark Huggies
Lance Armstrong Foundation LiveStrong Cancer Awareness Campaign
LensCrafters
LG LG Text Ed Campaign
Lipton
Mattel Campaign: "It's Your Word Against Ours!"
Mazatlan Public Relations
Merck
The Mexican State of Sinaloa
National Institute of Health
Navis, LLC
Nestle Campaign: "Share the Joy of Reading"
Novartis
Pfizer, Inc. Celebrex
SAVVIS, Inc.
Shutterstock Images LLC; New York, NY
Silicon Image
Standard Innovation Corporation Media Relations, PR, Thought Leadership
Sunglass Hut
SunPower Corporation
Themis Media
Unilever Campaign: "Singin' In The Rain"
United States Department of Health & Human Services
United States Department of Justice
Virgin America
VTech
YieldBuild
Zebra Technologies Corporation

Headquarters

Ogilvy PR/New York

636 11th Ave, New York, NY 10036
Tel.: (212) 880-5200
Fax: (212) 884-1997
Web Site: www.ogilvypr.com

Agency Specializes In: Sponsorship

Robyn Massey *(Global Chief Comm Officer)*
Kim Slicklein *(Pres-Ogilvy Earth)*
Judy Brennan *(Exec VP-Reputation Mgmt)*
Christine Gennaro Meberg *(Sr VP)*
Larissa Severenko *(Sr VP)*
Jennifer Risi *(Mng Dir-Media Influence & Head-Media Rels-North America)*
Suresh Raj *(Mng Dir-Bus Dev-Global)*
Robert Mathias *(Reg CEO-North America)*

Accounts:
American Express
Cricket Communications, Inc
Ford
Novartis
Pfizer, Inc.
Rakuten (Corporate & Enterprise Public Relations Agency of Record) E-Commerce Site
Themis Media
ZTE Corporation US Advertising

United States

Feinstein Kean Healthcare

245 1st St 14th Fl, Cambridge, MA 02142-1292
Tel.: (617) 577-8110
Fax: (617) 577-8985

E-Mail: marcia.kean@fkhealth.com
Web Site: www.fkhealth.com

Employees: 50

Agency Specializes In: Sponsorship

Craig Martin *(CEO)*
Marcia A. Kean *(Chm-Strategic Initiatives)*
Colleen Beauregard *(Exec VP)*
Prescott Taylor *(Sr VP & Dir-Fin)*
Patrick O'Grady *(Sr VP-Creative Svcs)*
Jamie Yacco *(Acct Supvr)*

Ogilvy PR/Atlanta

3340 Peachtree Rd NE Ste 300, Atlanta, GA 30326
Tel.: (404) 881-2300
Fax: (404) 881-2349
E-Mail: mickey.nall@ogilvypr.com
Web Site: www.ogilvypr.com

Employees: 20

National Agency Associations: COPF

Agency Specializes In: Public Relations, Sponsorship

Mickey Nall *(Mng Dir)*
Victoria Barksdale McGhee *(VP)*
Brian Smith *(VP)*
Derek Walls *(Sr Acct Exec)*

Accounts:
Boy Scouts Campaign: "Glasses", Campaign: "Knife", Campaign: "Smirk", Flashlight
Frozen Pints Campaign: "Regifting", Campaign: "Snow Day", Campaign: "Virginia"
NexCen Brands Public Relations, Zoosk

Ogilvy PR Worldwide

1414 K St Ste 300, Sacramento, CA 95814
Tel.: (415) 677-2744
Fax: (916) 418-1515
E-Mail: christi.black@ogilvypr.com
Web Site: www.ogilvypr.com

Employees: 25

National Agency Associations: COPF

Agency Specializes In: Public Relations

Valerie Vento *(Exec VP)*
Kevin Slagle *(Sr VP)*
Carol Lyn Colon *(VP-Corp & Pub Affairs)*
Vicky Waters *(VP-Pub Affairs Grp)*
Jordan Saletan *(Dir-Tech Mgmt)*
Jonathan Rigby *(Assoc Dir-Engagement Plng)*
Gabriela Ruano *(Acct Supvr)*
Kiersten Popke *(Acct Exec)*
Nathan Friedman *(Reg Mng Dir)*

Accounts:
Covered California (Agency of Record) Communications, Content Creation, Media Relations, Public Relations, Social Media
Energy Upgrade California Public Relations

Ogilvy PR Worldwide

555 17th St 3rd Fl, Denver, CO 80202
Tel.: (303) 615-5070
Fax: (303) 615-5075
E-Mail: amy.messenger@ogilvypr.com
Web Site: www.ogilvypr.com

Employees: 13

National Agency Associations: COPF

Amy Messenger *(Mng Dir & Head-US Tech Practice)*
Jennifer Banovetz *(Sr VP & Grp Dir)*
Kabira Cher Ferrell *(Sr VP)*
Ashley Kleinstein *(Acct Supvr)*

Accounts:
EVOL Foods Brand Marketing, Media Relations, Social Media
IBM

Ogilvy PR

3530 Hayden Ave, Culver City, CA 90232
Tel.: (310) 280-2200
Web Site: www.ogilvypr.com

Employees: 18

National Agency Associations: 4A's

Agency Specializes In: Public Relations

Patricia Galea *(Exec VP & Head-Office-LA)*
Jennifer Banovetz *(Sr VP & Grp Dir)*
Nathan Friedman *(Reg Mng Dir-Ogilvy PR West)*

Accounts:
Lunera Lighting; Redwood City, CA Communications Strategy, Influencer Outreach, Message Development, Thought Leadership
Ostara Nutrient Recovery Technologies Inc Communications Strategy, Influencer Outreach, Message Development, Thought Leadership
Project Frog Communications Strategy, Influencer Outreach, Message Development, Thought Leadership
Search Optics (Agency of Record) Strategic Marketing
Tourism Fiji PR
ZeaChem Inc Communications Strategy, Influencer Outreach, Message Development, Thought Leadership

Ogilvy PR

111 Sutter St 11th Fl, San Francisco, CA 94104-4541
Tel.: (415) 677-2700
Fax: (415) 677-2770
Web Site: www.ogilvypr.com

Employees: 40

Agency Specializes In: Public Relations

Dan La Russo *(Exec VP & Grp Dir-Tech)*
Kate Brooks *(Sr VP)*
Adrian Eyre *(Sr VP)*
Ola Beilock *(Acct Dir)*
Taylor VanAllen *(Acct Supvr & Strategist-Social Media)*
Lin Shen *(Sr Acct Exec)*
Kelly Xie *(Sr Acct Exec)*
Kiersten Popke *(Acct Exec)*

Accounts:
Autonomy Systems Ltd.
Avigilon Corporate Communications, Media Relations, Product PR, Thought Leadership
BMC Software Analyst Relations, Corporate Communications, Digital, Global Public Relations, Media Relations, Social Media
Lithium Technologies (Agency of Record)
SAVVIS, Inc.
Silicon Graphics International (Agency of Record) Brand Awareness
Silicon Image
Storage Networking Industry Association
SunPower Corporation
The Tech Museum of Innovation
Virgin America
YieldBuild

Ogilvy PR

350 W Mart Ctr Dr 11th Fl, Chicago, IL 60654
Tel.: (312) 397-6000
Fax: (312) 397-8841
E-Mail: betsy.neville@ogilvypr.com
Web Site: www.ogilvypr.com

Employees: 35

National Agency Associations: 4A's-COPF

Agency Specializes In: Public Relations, Sponsorship

Michele Anderson *(Mng Dir)*
Sandra Saias *(Exec VP)*
Drew Ferguson *(Sr VP)*
Kathy Cummings *(VP)*
Bradley Silber *(Acct Dir)*
Maury Postal *(Dir-Creative-Social@Ogilvy)*
Jen Tatro *(Dir-Bus Dev)*

Accounts:
American Express
CDW Corporation Campaign: "North Pole"
Ethicon
GlaxoSmithKline
Hitachi Data Systems
LG Electronics
McGraw-Hill Education (Public Relations Agency of Record) ALEKS, Media Relations, Mobile, Online, SmartBook, Social, Social Media, Traditional Media
Sam's Club
Unilever
University of Chicago
Zebra Technologies (Agency of Record)

Ogilvy Public Relations Worldwide

1111 19th St NW 10th Fl, Washington, DC 20036
Tel.: (202) 729-4000
Fax: (202) 729-4001
E-Mail: robert.mathias@ogilvypr.com
Web Site: www.ogilvypr.com

Employees: 200

National Agency Associations: 4A's-COPF

Kate Hays *(COO & VP)*
Rachel Caggiano *(Exec VP & Head-Content-North America)*
Rebecca Davis *(Exec VP-Digital & Social)*
Irfan Kamal *(Sr VP-Social@Ogilvy & Head-Social Data, Products & Partners)*
Natalie Adler *(Sr VP)*
Nick Ludlum *(Sr VP-Corp & Pub Affairs, Insight & Strategy)*
Dan Scandling *(Sr VP-Corp & Pub Affairs)*
Linda Weinberg *(Sr VP)*
Jamie Moeller *(Mng Dir-Global Pub Affairs Practice)*
Carol Colon *(VP-Corp & Pub Affairs)*
Madeline McCaul *(VP-Content)*
Kai Fang *(Exec Dir-Creative)*
Jose Martinez Salmeron *(Exec Dir-Creative)*
Valerie Vardaro *(Acct Dir & Sr Producer-Digital-Social@Ogilvy)*
Nadia Bashir *(Acct Dir & Strategist-Digital)*

Accounts:
American Chemistry Council
BP Public Affairs
Bristol-Myers Squibb
Centers for Disease Control and Prevention Choose Respect Initiative, Dating Matters; 2007
Centers for Medicare & Medicaid Services
CSC Holdings, LLC; Falls Church, VA
Dupont
E.I. du Pont de Nemours & Company
Family Online Safety Institute
FEMA
Hitachi Data Systems
Lance Armstrong Foundation

LG Electronics
Luxottica
Medtronic
National Cancer Institute
National Crop Insurance Services
National Institutes of Health
Recreational Boating and Fishing Foundation Campaign: "Take Me Fishing", Media Outreach, PR
Savvis, Inc. (Agency of Record)
The Storage Networking Industry Association (SNIA)
Tandberg
United Service Organizations (Agency of Record)
United States Department of Homeland Security
United Way of the National Capital Area
Virgin America (Agency of Record) Corporate Communications, Crisis Communications, Digital, Public Relations
YMCA of Metropolitan Washington (Agency of Record) Mission-Focused Branding; 2010

Austria

Ogilvy PR
Bachosengasse 8, A-1190 Vienna, Austria
Tel.: (43) 190 100
Fax: (43) 1 90 100 300
E-Mail: office@ogilvypr.com
Web Site: www.ogilvypr.com

Employees: 70

Florian Krenkel *(CEO)*
Elisabeth Pechmann *(Dir-PR)*

Accounts:
Bpier
Ford
IBM
Volvo

Belgium

Ogilvy Public Relations Worldwide
Boulevard de l'Imperatrice 13 Keizerinlaan, 1000 Brussels, Belgium
Tel.: (32) 2 545 6600
Fax: (32) 2 545 6610
Web Site: www.ogilvy.be/

Employees: 70

Agency Specializes In: Health Care Services, Technical Advertising

Ann Maes *(Mng Dir)*
Koen Van Impe *(CEO-Ogilvy Belgium)*
An Vande Velde *(Mng Dir-OgilvyOne)*
Jeff Chertack *(Reg Dir-Corp & Pub Affairs-MENA)*
Sam De Win *(Dir-Creative)*
Tomas Sweertvaegher *(Dir-Strategy)*
Barbara Malengreaux *(Assoc Dir-Consumer & Health)*

Accounts:
Electrabel
European Commission
European Space Agency
Jones, Day, Bain & Company
Lessius Hogeschool Mechelen Campaign: "KloutBattle"
NATO
Toyota

Czech Republic

Ogilvy PR
Privozni 2a, Prague, 7 1 7000 Czech Republic
Tel.: (420) 2 199 8111
Fax: (420) 2 199 8333
Web Site: www.ogilvypr.com

Employees: 33

National Agency Associations: APRA-ICCO

Agency Specializes In: Public Relations

Dita Stejskalova *(Owner)*
Ondrej Obluk *(Exec Mng Dir)*
Radek Vitek *(Mng Dir)*

France

Ogilvy Public Relations
40 Avenue Georges V, 75008 Paris, France
Tel.: (33) 1 53 67 1250
Fax: (33) 53 67 1251
E-Mail: eric.maillard@ogilvy.com
Web Site: www.ogilvypr.com

E-Mail for Key Personnel:
President: Eric.Maillard@ogilvy.com

Employees: 24

Agency Specializes In: Consumer Goods, Electronics, Financial, Public Relations

Eric Maillard *(Mng Dir-France)*
Elodie Doan Van *(Sr Acct Dir-Brand Content & PR)*
Myriam Nouicer *(Grp Acct Dir)*
Amrita Bourdon *(Acct Dir)*
Laurent Chauffeteau *(Bus Dir-Intl)*
Antoine Petit *(Acct Dir)*
Laetitia Attali *(Dir-Social@Ogilvy)*
Anne-sophie Carbo *(Dir-Bus)*
Eloise Haye *(Acct Supvr)*
Marc-antoine Lecocq *(Acct Supvr-Global)*
Jane Crobeddu *(Acct Exec)*
Lucie Le Squeren Caulfield *(Acct Exec)*
Helene Quevreux *(Acct Exec)*

Accounts:
Amcor
Ford
The Grenelle Environment
Invest in France
Jones Day
Louis Vuitton
Medtronic
Motorola Solutions, Inc.
NIDDK
Sony

Germany

Ogilvy Healthworld GmbH
Am Handelshafen 2-4, 40221 Dusseldorf, Germany
Mailing Address:
Postfach 190024, 40110 Dusseldorf, Germany
Tel.: (49) 211-49700-0
Fax: (49) 211-49700505
Web Site: www.ogilvy.de

Employees: 20
Year Founded: 1986

Agency Specializes In: Advertising, Advertising Specialties, Alternative Advertising, Below-the-Line, Brand Development & Integration, Branded Entertainment, Broadcast, Business Publications, Business-To-Business, Catalogs, Co-op Advertising, Communications, Consulting, Consumer Goods, Consumer Publications, Content, Corporate Communications, Corporate Identity, Cosmetics, Crisis Communications, Custom Publishing, Customer Relationship Management, Direct Response Marketing, Direct-to-Consumer, E-Commerce, Education, Email, Entertainment, Environmental, Event Planning & Marketing, Exhibit/Trade Shows, Food Service, Gay & Lesbian Market, Graphic Design, Guerilla Marketing, Health Care Services, Hospitality, Identity Marketing, In-Store Advertising, Integrated Marketing, International, Internet/Web Design, Local Marketing, Logo & Package Design, Market Research, Media Relations, Medical Products, Men's Market, Merchandising, Mobile Marketing, New Product Development, Outdoor, Over-50 Market, Package Design, Pets , Pharmaceutical, Planning & Consultation, Podcasting, Point of Purchase, Point of Sale, Print, Product Placement, Production (Ad, Film, Broadcast), Promotions, Public Relations, Publicity/Promotions, Radio, Sales Promotion, Seniors' Market, Social Marketing/Nonprofit, Social Media, Sponsorship, Technical Advertising, Teen Market, Telemarketing, Web (Banner Ads, Pop-ups, etc.), Women's Market, Yellow Pages Advertising

Ulrich Tillmann *(Chm)*
Ulrike Aretz *(Mng Dir)*
Helmut Hechler *(CFO)*
Dirk Lapaz *(CFO)*
Michael Kutschinski *(Chief Creative Officer)*
Stephan Vogel *(Chief Creative Officer)*
Mona Tillinger *(Head-HR)*
Tim Stubane *(Exec Creative Dir)*

Greece

Ogilvy PR Worldwide
7 Granikou Street, Maroussi, 15125 Athens, Greece
Tel.: (30) 210 6199 286
Fax: (30) 210 6199 281
Web Site: www.ogilvypr.com

Agency Specializes In: Advertising, Public Relations

Kostas Bakoulas *(CFO)*
Daphni Lokoviti *(Chief Digital Officer)*
Vassilios Dascalopoulos *(Mng Dir-Asset Ogilvy PR)*
Christos Latos *(Gen Mgr-OgilvyOne Worldwide Athens)*
Panos Sambrakos *(Exec Dir-Creative)*
Maria Dimopoulou *(Sr Acct Dir)*
Despina Stathopoulou *(Grp Acct Dir-Digital)*
Alcibiades Siaravas *(Acct Dir)*
Dimitris Savvakos *(Dir-Creative)*
Stella Sfakaki *(Dir-Talent & Trng-HR)*
Vicky Fili *(Acct Mgr)*
Nicole Panagiotou *(Acct Mgr)*
Eleni Anastasiou *(Acct Exec)*

Accounts:
American Express
Bayer
Citizen's Bank
EarthLink
Ford
Grant Thornton
LG Electronics
Merck
Novartis
Unilever

Ireland

Wilson Hartnell (WH)
6 Ely Pl, Dublin, 2 Ireland
Tel.: (353) 1 669 0030
Fax: (353) 1 669 0039
E-Mail: info@wilsonhartnell.ie
Web Site: www.wilsonhartnell.ie

Employees: 40
Year Founded: 1971

Agency Specializes In: Public Relations

Roddy Guiney *(Chm)*
Brian Bell *(Mng Dir)*
Lorraine Dwyer *(Head-Lifestyle PR & Dir)*
Sheila Gahan *(Head-Corp & Dir)*
Alistair Hodgett *(Head-Pub Affairs & Dir)*
Sharon Murphy *(Head-Consumer PR & Dir)*
Ciara Kennedy *(Acct Dir)*

Accounts:
Diageo Ireland
Marks & Spencer
National Lottery
Safefood

Italy

Ogilvy & Mather S.p.A.
Via Lancetti 29, 20158 Milan, Italy
Tel.: (39) 02 607 891
Fax: (39) 02 607 8954
Web Site: www.ogilvypr.com

Employees: 250

Agency Specializes In: Advertising, Public Relations

Guerino Delfino *(Chm & CEO)*
Michael Berger *(Head-Digital)*
Ethiopia Abiye *(Acct Dir)*
Elena Angaroni *(Acct Dir)*
Alexandre Gabriel Levy *(Dir-New Bus)*
Emmanuele Rossi *(Acct Mgr-Ogilvy Interactive)*
Federica De Paoli *(Acct Supvr)*
Vincenza Mattana *(Acct Supvr)*
Barbara Falanga *(Strategist-Digital)*
Arianna Moscardini *(Acct Exec)*
Carlotta Piccaluga *(Acct Exec)*

Spain

Ogilvy & Mather Comunicacion
(Formerly Bassat, Ogilvy & Mather Comunicacion)
Enrique Larreta 2, 28036 Madrid, Spain
Tel.: (34) 91 398 4710
Fax: (34) 91 398 4727
Web Site: www.ogilvypr.com

E-Mail for Key Personnel:
President: borja.puig@ogilvy.com

Employees: 100

Borja Puig de la Bellacasa *(CEO)*
Javier Oliete *(Mng Dir-Neo@Ogilvy Spain)*
Eva Snijders *(Gen Mgr)*
Carlos Perez-Sauquillo *(Copywriter)*

Accounts:
Ford Bi-xenon Lights, Campaign: "It won't last long.6200 discount only till the end of the month.", Campaign: "Olor a nuevo", Corporate Event, Ford Coupe Cabriolet, Ford Focus Rs, Ford Ka, Ford Mondeo, Powershift
Mitsubishi

Bassat, Ogilvy & Mather Comunicacion
Josep Tarradellas 123-2nd Fl, 08029 Barcelona, Spain
Tel.: (34) 93 495 9444
Fax: (34) 93 495 9445
E-Mail: salvador.aumedes@ogilvy.com
Web Site: www.grupobassatogilvy.es/

Year Founded: 1991

Agency Specializes In: Advertising, Communications, Digital/Interactive, Health Care Services, Publicity/Promotions, Sales Promotion

Nuria Padrosinto *(Gen Mgr)*
Camil Roca *(Exec Dir-Creative-Ogilvy Barcelona)*
Nacho Magro *(Dir-Creative)*
Francesc Talamino *(Dir-Creative)*
Manuel Cardenas *(Copywriter)*

Accounts:
Barcelona Music Palace
Beneo
Borges Campaign: "Popitas Zero"
Cardiplus
Caritas Campaign: "A No for Anyone"
Channel 3 Telethon Campaign: "Death should be the end of life. Not cancer"
Chile
Cruzcampo Beer
FCC
Florette Salad Gourmet
Ford Campaign: "Ford's Global CEO Visit to Spain"
Grauvell Campaign: "Punk"
IWC
Josep Carreras Foundation Leukemia Foundation Appeal
La Marata De Tv3 Campaign: "One Life Ends, Six Begin"
Mindshare Campaign: "Accurate Radio Commercial"
Motorola Solutions, Inc.
Panasonic Campaign: "Eiffel", Lumix, Wide-Angle Lenses
Procter & Gamble
Realia
Sony
TMB Campaign: "Christmas Carol", Campaign: "Subtravelling"
TV3 Telethon Campaign: "Regeneration, organs anf tissue transplant", Campaign: "Team Hoyt"

Sweden

Ogilvy Public Relations
Kaknasvagen 80, 11527 Stockholm, Sweden
Tel.: (46) 733 440049
Fax: (46) 856 258 201
Web Site: www.ogilvypr.com

Employees: 10

Helena McShane *(Mng Dir)*

European Headquarters

Ogilvy PR Worldwide
10 Cabot Square, Canary Wharf, London, E14 4QB United Kingdom
Tel.: (44) 20 7309 1000
Fax: (44) 20 7309 1001
Web Site: www.ogilvypr.com

Employees: 80

Agency Specializes In: Public Relations

Michael Frohlich *(CEO & COO-EMEA)*
Robyn Massey *(Chief Comm Officer-Global)*
Lara Leventhal *(Deputy Mng Dir-Ogilvy PR London)*
Serge Vaezi *(Mng Dir-Strategy & Plng-EMEA)*
Adam Powell *(Sr Dir & Head-Corp & Pub Affairs)*
Alice Cadwgan *(Head-Mktg-EMEA)*
Blair Metcalfe *(Head-Media & Entertainment)*
Iain Bundred *(Dir-Corp-EAME)*
Alex Wood *(Dir-Creative)*

Accounts:
Addison Lee Media
Captain Morgan for Western Europe
Confused.com Consumer, Content, Integrated Communications, PR, Social Media
Google
Guinness
InterContinental Hotels Group Global Marketing
Maastricht University Campaign: "The Burger That Will Change the World", Cultured Beef, Media, TV
National Social Marketing Centre Global Strategy
Reed Smith Thought Leadership
United Nations Campaign: "Momentum for Change"
WGSN (Global Public Relations Agency of Record)
New-YouTube, LLC Brand Marketing

Headquarters

Ogilvy Public Relations Worldwide
23rd Floor The Center 99 Queens Road, Central, China (Hong Kong)
Tel.: (852) 2567 4461
Fax: (852) 2885 3227
E-Mail: clara.shek@ogilvy.com
Web Site: www.ogilvypr.com

E-Mail for Key Personnel:
President: christopher.graves@ogilvy.com

Employees: 40

Agency Specializes In: Business-To-Business, Communications, Consumer Marketing, Government/Political

Clara Shek *(Mng Dir)*
Debby Cheung *(Pres-Shanghai Grp)*
Marion McDonald *(Dir-Myanmar Integration)*
Amy Tam *(Mgr-Corp Comm)*

Accounts:
Logitech
Real Estate Developers Association

Australia

Ogilvy PR Worldwide
Level 2 72 Christie Street, Saint Leonards, NSW 2065 Australia
Tel.: (61) 2 8281 3292
Fax: (61) 2 8281 3829
Web Site: www.ogilvypr.com

Employees: 20

Kieran Moore *(CEO)*
Leon Beswick *(Mng Dir)*
Susan Redden Makatoa *(Grp Mng Dir-Corp)*
Alexandra Kelly *(Mng Dir-Ogilvy PR Melbourne)*
Sam North *(Dir-Media)*
Nino Tesoriero *(Dir)*

Accounts:
Canon PR
Citrix
DuPon
EarthLink
Ford
Hitachi Data Systems
LG Electronics
Microsoft (Consumer Agency of Record) Communications, Social
MYOB Limited (Agency of Record) Brand Communications, Business-to-Business, Communications Strategies
Novell
Telstra International Global Public Relations
Uniden
Veda PR Campaign

China

H-Line Ogilvy Communications Co Ltd
17D Boai Tower, 758 Nanjing Xilu, Shanghai,

200041 China
Tel.: (86) 21 6272 8896
Fax: (86) 21 6272 8834
Web Site: www.h-line.com

Employees: 20
Year Founded: 2002

Agency Specializes In: Public Relations

Jimmy Lam *(Vice Chm & Chief Creative Officer)*
James Chen *(VP & Mng Dir)*
Neil Holt *(Mng Dir)*
Denise Tang *(Chief Strategy Officer)*
Edward Zhang *(VP)*
Emen Chong *(Gen Mgr)*
Philip Romans *(Gen Mgr)*
Steven Cheng *(Exec Dir-Creative)*
Jason Wu *(Dir-Bus)*
Wendy Xue *(Country Mgr-Ogilvy CommonHealth Worldwide)*

Ogilvy PR Worldwide
Room 1901-1904 19th Floor Jinbao Tower, No 89 Jinbao Street, Beijing, 10005 China
Tel.: (86) 10 8520 6688
Fax: (86) 10 8520 6600
E-Mail: scott.kronick@ogilvy.com
Web Site: www.ogilvypr.com

Scott Kronick *(Pres/CEO-Asia Pacific)*
Colleen Cheng *(Sr VP & Bus Dir-Natl)*
Kevin Lee *(VP)*
Rick Zhao *(VP)*
Wei Wang *(Assoc Dir)*
Robbie Yang *(Assoc Dir)*
Haowei Zhang *(Assoc Dir)*
Chen Zhou *(Assoc Dir)*

Accounts:
361 Degrees International Limited Campaign: "Run With Love", Campaign: "What is Speed"
Air China; 2008
Beijing Nokia Mobile Telecommunications; 2008
The Boao Forum For Asia
Caterpillar China (Agency of Record) Corporate Brand Campaign, Digital, Print, Public Relations
Dolby
GSK
IBM Campaign: "Mr Bao Knows It All"
Tencent
VisionChina Media Inc.
Volkswagen Group of America, Inc. Campaign: "Scirocco Cup"
The World Economic Forum "Summer Davos", Media Outreach, Media Relations, Public Relations, Social Media Strategy

Ogilvy PR Worldwide
26th Floor The Center, 989 Changle Road, Shanghai, 200031 China
Tel.: (86) 21 2405 1888
Fax: (86) 21 2405 1880
E-Mail: debby.cheung@ogilvy.com
Web Site: www.ogilvypr.com

Employees: 250

Debby Cheung *(Pres-Shanghai Grp)*
Colleen Cheng *(Sr VP & Bus Dir-Natl)*
Fiona Kao *(Assoc Dir)*
Gillian Li *(Assoc Dir)*
Roy Lu *(Assoc Dir)*

Accounts:
The Coca-Cola Company Campaign: "Cokehands"
Diageo Campaign: "Johnnie Walker Walks the Talk"
ECCO
Eu Yan Sang
Goodyear Campaign: "A Lifetime Commitment to Safety"
Grand Optical Campaign: "Shopping"
VF Campaign: "Finding True North"

Ogilvy PR Worldwide
Bldg 12 No 1 Xia Shi Zhi Street, Fangcun Ave Liwan District, Guangzhou, 510613 China
Tel.: (86) 20 8113 6288
Fax: (86) 20 8113 6055
E-Mail: frangelica.liang@ogilvy.com
Web Site: www.ogilvypr.com

Agency Specializes In: Public Relations

Selina Teng *(Co-Mng Dir-Ogilvy PR, Beijing)*
Frangelica Liang *(VP)*
Wei Wang *(Assoc Dir)*

India

Ogilvy PR Worldwide, Mumbai
11th Floor Oberoi Commerz International Business Park Oberoi Garden, City Off Western Express Hwy, Gurgaon (East), Mumbai, 400 063 India
Tel.: (91) 22 4434 4700
Fax: (91) 22 4434 4710
E-Mail: deepali.girdhar@ogilvy.com
Web Site: www.ogilvypr.com

Agency Specializes In: Public Relations

Arijit Sengupta *(Pres)*

Ogilvy PR Worldwide
11th Floor Oberoi Commerz International Business Park, Off Western Express Highway, Mumbai, 400 063 India
Tel.: (91) 22 4434 4700
E-Mail: arijit.sengupta@ogilvy.com
Web Site: www.ogilvypr.com

Sanyukta Dutta *(Partner)*
Shivani Sharma *(Partner)*
Navin Talreja *(Pres-Mumbai & Kolkata)*
Kunal Jeswani *(CEO-India)*
Ashwath Ganesan *(VP & Head-Plng)*
Ramesh Keshavan *(VP)*
Garima Misra *(Assoc Partner)*
Hitesh Motwani *(Assoc Partner)*

Ogilvy PR Worldwide
Level - 06 Fifth Floor Bagmane Laurel 65/2 Bagmane Teck Park, CV Raman Nagar Byrasandra, Bengaluru, 560 093 India
Tel.: (91) 44 4434 4700
Fax: (91) 44 4434 4710
Web Site: www.ogilvypr.com

Agency Specializes In: Public Relations

Arijit Sengupta *(Pres)*
Nalini Guhesh *(Mng Dir-Network Analytics Team)*
Ganga Ganapathi Poovaiah *(VP)*
Garima Misra *(Assoc Partner)*

Malaysia

Ogilvy PR Worldwide
Level 11 Menara Milenium 8 Jalan Damanlela, Bukit Damansara, Kuala Lumpur, 50490 Malaysia
Tel.: (60) 3 2718 8288
Fax: (60) 3 2710 6966
E-Mail: rajan.moses@ogilvy.com
Web Site: www.ogilvypr.com

Agency Specializes In: Public Relations

Steve Dahllof *(Reg CEO-Asia Pacific)*

Accounts:
Eu Yan Sang

Philippines

Ogilvy PR Worldwide
15th Floor Philamlife Tower 8767 Paseo de Roxas, Makati, Metro Manila 1200 Philippines
Tel.: (63) 2 885 0001
Fax: (63) 885 0030
E-Mail: leah.huang@ogilvy.com
Web Site: www.ogilvypr.com

Employees: 16

Agency Specializes In: Public Relations

Leah M. Huang *(Mng Dir)*
Carla Laus *(Grp Acct Dir)*
Lu-ann Fuentes *(Bus Dir & Dir-Editorial & Comm Svcs)*
Mervin Teo Wenke *(Acct Dir)*
Lhen Hasal *(Mgr-Media Rels)*
Hannah Tejuco *(Mgr-Media Rels)*

Accounts:
Ford
Johnson & Johnson BONAMINE, PR & Digital Campaign
Nike

Sri Lanka

Ogilvy PR Worldwide
No 16 Barnes Pl, Colombo, Sri Lanka
Tel.: (94) 11 2675 016
Fax: (94) 11 2697 635
E-Mail: manilka.philips@ogilvy.com
Web Site: www.ogilvypr.com

Agency Specializes In: Public Relations

Manilka Philips *(Gen Mgr)*

Ogilvy Public Relations Taiwan
3F No 89 Song Ren Road, Taipei, 110 Taiwan
Tel.: (886) 277451688
Fax: (886) 277451598
Web Site: www.ogilvy.com.tw

Employees: 80

Agency Specializes In: Public Relations

Joseph Pai *(Chm)*
Abby Hsieh *(Mng Dir)*
Adonis Chang *(VP)*
Kate Lee *(Grp Acct Dir)*
Janette Sung-En Huang *(Acct Dir)*
Teresahl Liu *(Assoc Dir-Plng)*
Kelly Chen *(Acct Mgr)*
Maggie Chien *(Acct Mgr)*
Yi-Yun Liu Esther *(Acct Mgr-Digital)*
William Hsu *(Acct Mgr)*
Bernice Chen *(Sr Acct Exec)*
Chan Yun Yeh *(Acct Exec)*

Accounts:
UPS

Kenya

Ogilvy PR Worldwide
CVS Plaza 3rd Floor Lenara Rd, PO Box 30280, 00100 Nairobi, Kenya
Tel.: (254) 20 271 7750
Fax: (254) 20 271 7610

Public Relations Firms

E-Mail: info@ogilvy.co.ke
Web Site: www.ogilvy.com

Alfred Nganga *(Acct Mgr)*

United Arab Emirates

Memac Ogilvy PR

Al Attar Bus Tower 24th Fl, PO Box 74170, Shiekh Zayed Rd, Dubai, United Arab Emirates
Tel.: (971) 43320002
Fax: (971) 43050306
Web Site: www.memacogilvy.com

Ronald Howes *(COO)*
Ali Youssef Soudah *(Sr Dir-Mktg Comm)*
Rendala Majdalani *(Acct Dir-Consumer & Healthcare Practice)*
Sami Moutran *(Bus Dir-PR)*
Atul Shenoy *(Client Svcs Dir)*
Lavanya Mandal *(Sr Acct Mgr-Healthcare Practice)*
Mani DuPlessis *(Acct Mgr)*
Hayan Shadaydeh *(Mgr-Media Rels)*
Joaquin Lajud *(Account Executive)*

Accounts:
Ad Of Da Month.Com
Arqaam Capital
Aujan Industries
Barclays
Chili's
Coco Collection (Agency of Record)
DuPont
Google Mena
Huawei Technologies Co. Ltd
Jam Jar
MAX
Samsung Electronics
Volkswagen

OKEEFFE

1118 Pendleton St Ste 400, Cincinnati, OH 45202
Tel.: (513) 221-1526
E-Mail: info@okeeffepr.com
Web Site: www.okeeffepr.com

Agency Specializes In: Content, Public Relations, Social Media

Dan OKeeffe *(Pres & CEO)*
Dale Justice *(VP-Client Svcs)*
Drew Boehmker *(Strategist-Content)*

Accounts:
New-Greater Cincinnati & Northern Kentucky Film Commission

O'KEEFFE & CO.

921 King St, Alexandria, VA 22314
Tel.: (703) 883-9000
Fax: (703) 883-9007
E-Mail: info@okco.com
Web Site: www.okco.com/

Employees: 65
Year Founded: 1997

Agency Specializes In: Collateral, Communications, Event Planning & Marketing, Government/Political, Graphic Design, High Technology, Internet/Web Design, Public Relations, Publicity/Promotions

Approx. Annual Billings: $10,000,000

Janice Clayton *(Acct Dir)*
Martin Nott *(Acct Dir)*
Kirk Brown *(Dir)*
Lacy Cooper *(Sr Acct Exec)*
Lisa Fisher *(Sr Acct Exec)*
Katie Sheridan *(Sr Acct Exec)*
Kate Denardi *(Acct Coord)*

Accounts:
Adobe
Brocade
CDW Corporation
Citrix
Commuter Choice
Curam Software, Ltd.
Data Path
Federal Open Source Alliance Hewlett-Packard, Intel, Red Hat
Google
GovMark Council
Guidance Software
Intel
Intelligent Decisions
Lexmark
Mechanical Protection Plan
Meri Talk
Merlin International
Oracle
Rim
Riverbed
Symantec
Telework Exchange
Transurban; 2008
Unisys; 2008

Branches

O'Keeffe & Co.

1430 Dresden Dr #335, Atlanta, GA 30319
Tel.: (404) 254-5881
Web Site: www.okco.com

Agency Specializes In: Public Relations

Janice Clayton *(Acct Dir)*
Gail Repsher Emery *(Acct Dir)*
Erin Leahy *(Acct Dir)*
Lacy Cooper *(Sr Acct Exec)*

O'Keeffe & Co.

15783 Summit Rock Way, Clackamas, OR 97015
Tel.: (503) 658-7396
Web Site: www.okco.com

Agency Specializes In: Public Relations

Gail Emery *(Acct Dir)*
Martin Nott *(Acct Dir)*

Accounts:
CDW Corporation

O'Keeffe & Co.

837 Parkridge Dr, Media, PA 19063
Tel.: (610) 566-2909
E-Mail: info@okco.com
Web Site: www.okco.com

Agency Specializes In: Public Relations

Maureen O'Keeffe *(Dir)*

Accounts:
Adobe
Akamai
Axway
Brocade
Citrix
HP
Intel
Lenovo
Oracle

O'Keeffe & Co.

99 San Gabriel Drive, Rochester, NY 14610
Tel.: (585) 271-1141
Fax: (703) 883-9007
E-Mail: info@okco.com
Web Site: www.okco.com

Employees: 1

Agency Specializes In: Public Relations

Steve O'Keeffe *(Owner)*

Accounts:
CDW Corporation

OLMSTEAD WILLIAMS COMMUNICATIONS, INC.

10940 Wilshire Blvd Ste 1210, Los Angeles, CA 90024
Tel.: (310) 824-9000
Fax: (310) 824-9007
E-Mail: info@olmsteadwilliams.com
Web Site: www.olmsteadwilliams.com

Year Founded: 2008

Agency Specializes In: Crisis Communications, Media Relations, Media Training, Public Relations, Social Media

Tracy Williams *(Pres & CEO)*
Trent Freeman *(VP)*

Accounts:
New-BankWorks (Agency of Record)
Bruin Biometrics
Creative Care
Cynvenio Biosystems
DreamHammer, Inc.
Geneva Healthcare
The Great Courses
Ice Energy
SmartMetric
T+ink
New-TaskUs (Agency of Record)
University of California-Los Angeles Sustainable Technology & Policy Program
USC Marshall School of Business

OLSON

(Formerly Dig Communications)
564 W Randolph St, Chicago, IL 60661
Tel.: (312) 577-1750
Fax: (312) 577-1760
Web Site: www.olson.com

Year Founded: 2004

Agency Specializes In: Brand Development & Integration, Corporate Communications, Crisis Communications, Public Relations, Sponsorship, Technical Advertising

Bryan Specht *(Pres-Olson Engage)*
Brian Flad *(Sr VP & Gen Mgr)*
Matt Hargarten *(Sr VP-Corp Dev)*
Russin Royal *(Sr VP-Corp Affairs)*
Jen Boyles *(Dir-Social Strategy)*
Katie Cosgrove *(Sr Acct Exec)*
Kylie Burness *(Acct Exec-PR)*
Hillary Churchill *(Copywriter)*

Accounts:
EcoMedia Public Space Recycling Company
The Elations Company Food Products Producer
Fitbit Inc Body Fitness Products Mfr, Public Relations
General Mills
Glu Mobile Mobile Entertainment Services
Johnson Controls
Kraft Foods
Mars

MillerCoors Crispin Cider, Leinenkugel, Miller High Life, Redd's Apple Ale
Mondelez International, Inc. "#Tweet2Lease.", Campaign: "Bacon Barter", Communications Strategy, Media Relations, Oscar Mayer, PR, Wienermobile
OfficeMax
PepsiCo
Sharp Electronics (Social Media Agency of Record) Creative, Design, Digital
Trulia
Wrigley

ON 3 PUBLIC RELATIONS
200 W College Ave Ste 210, Tallahassee, FL 32301
Tel.: (850) 391-5040
Fax: (850) 224-5040
Web Site: www.on3pr.com

Agency Specializes In: Advertising, Collateral, Corporate Communications, Media Training, Public Relations

Christina Johnson *(Pres)*
Courtney Heidelberg *(Dir-Accounts)*
Anna Alexopoulos *(Acct Mgr)*
Sara Sowerby *(Acct Coord)*

Accounts:
Central Florida Partnership

ONE7 COMMUNICATIONS
375 N Stephanie St Ste 1213, Henderson, NV 89014
Tel.: (702) 472-7692
Fax: (702) 472-7694
E-Mail: info@one7communications.com
Web Site: www.one7communications.com

Agency Specializes In: Event Planning & Marketing, Graphic Design, Media Buying Services, Media Planning, Media Relations, Print, Promotions, Public Relations, Social Media, Strategic Planning/Research

Dawn Britt *(Founder & Pres)*
Carrie Giverson *(Acct Dir)*

Accounts:
Double Helix Wine
Spoon Bar & Kitchen

ONPR
PO Box 50428, Bellevue, WA 98015
Tel.: (425) 454-6840
Fax: (503) 802-4401
E-Mail: email@onpr.com

Employees: 10

Agency Specializes In: Communications, Event Planning & Marketing, Exhibit/Trade Shows, High Technology, Investor Relations, New Product Development, Public Relations, Strategic Planning/Research

Jody Peake *(CEO)*
Dave Wilson *(CFO, COO & Principal)*

Accounts:
Fujitsu

OnPR GmbH
Grasserstrasse 10, 80339 Munich, Germany
Tel.: (49) 89 3090 51610
Fax: (49) 89 3090 51617
Web Site: www.onpr.de

Employees: 10

Agency Specializes In: New Technologies, Public Relations

Simon P. Jones *(Mng Dir)*
Ronna Porter *(Dir)*

OPTIMA PUBLIC RELATIONS LLC
PO Box 101134, Anchorage, AK 99510
Tel.: (907) 440-9661
Fax: (504) 889-9898
Web Site: www.optimapublicrelations.com

Agency Specializes In: Advertising, Crisis Communications, Graphic Design, Internet/Web Design, Logo & Package Design, Media Relations, Print, Public Relations, Social Media, T.V.

Tom T. Anderson *(Partner)*
Eugene Harnett *(Dir-Comm)*
Sarah Paulus *(Dir-Design)*

Accounts:
Alaska Pacific University
Alaska Police & Fire Chaplains Ministries
Anchorage CHARR
Burkeshore Marina Inc.
Inlet Keeper
Lime Solar
Mat-Su Farm Bureau
Matanuska Electric Association, Inc.
Midnight Sun Oncology
Northwest Arctic Borough

ORCA COMMUNICATIONS UNLIMITED, LLC.
(d/b/a Orca Communications)
(Private-Parent-Single Location)
4809 E Thistle Landing Dr, Phoenix, AZ 85044
Tel.: (480) 346-4004
E-Mail: info@orcapr.com
Web Site: www.orcacommunications.com

Employees: 11
Year Founded: 2002

Agency Specializes In: Corporate Communications, Media Relations, Public Relations, Radio, Social Media, Strategic Planning/Research, T.V.

Revenue: $1,000,000

Julia Hutton *(Founder & CEO)*
Alice Giannola *(Exec VP)*
Julie Simon *(Sr VP)*
Valery Lodato *(VP)*
Wendy Roberts *(Dir-PR)*
Tana Siebold *(Dir-Creative)*
Suzie Chase Brown *(Acct Exec)*
Lisa Kelly *(Acct Exec)*
Kim Krigsten *(Acct Exec)*
Kate Kukler *(Acct Exec-PR)*

Accounts:
Boxxle
EarHero
Tiny Hands Jewelry

ORSI PUBLIC RELATIONS
1158 Greenacre Ave, Los Angeles, CA 90046
Tel.: (323) 874-4073
Fax: (323) 874-8796
E-Mail: info@orsipr.com
Web Site: www.orsipr.com

Agency Specializes In: Crisis Communications, Event Planning & Marketing, Media Relations, Public Relations, Social Media, Strategic Planning/Research

Janet Orsi *(Founder & Pres)*
Greg Lutchko *(Sr VP)*
Dyann Hawkins *(VP)*
Wanda Moreno *(Office Mgr)*
Racine Diaz *(Acct Exec-PR)*

Accounts:
Hello Kitty
O'Shaughnessey
Terlato Wines

OUTCAST COMMUNICATIONS
123 Townsend St Ste 500, San Francisco, CA 94107
Tel.: (415) 392-8282
Fax: (415) 392-8281
E-Mail: info@outcastpr.com
Web Site: theoutcastagency.com

E-Mail for Key Personnel:
Public Relations: newbusiness@outcastpr.com

Employees: 65
Year Founded: 1997

Agency Specializes In: Business-To-Business, Computers & Software, Corporate Communications, Crisis Communications, High Technology, Information Technology, Media Relations, Media Training, New Technologies, Public Relations, Social Media, Sponsorship, Viral/Buzz/Word of Mouth

Approx. Annual Billings: $8,000,000

Breakdown of Gross Billings by Media: Consulting: $8,000,000

Jenny Dearing *(Partner)*
Elizabeth Mcnichols *(Partner)*
Devon Corvasce *(VP-Media Strategy)*
Meg D'Incecco *(VP-Media Strategy)*
John O'Brien *(VP-Media Strategy)*
Jessica Williams *(VP-Media Strategy)*
Annie Boschetti *(Sr Dir-Bus-HR)*
Andrea Ragni *(Acct Dir)*
Jennifer Zawadzinski *(Dir-Media Strategy)*
Emma Shiflett *(Mgr-Recruiting)*
Kim Ballard *(Coord-Set Decoration)*

Accounts:
Amazon
EMC; Hopkinton, MA Data Storage; 2004
Facebook
Pinterest PR
Ubisoft

OUTHOUSE PR
111 Broadway 11 Fl Ste 1104, New York, NY 10006
Tel.: (212) 349-8543
Fax: (212) 964-4934
E-Mail: info@outhousepr.com
Web Site: www.outhousepr.com

Agency Specializes In: Fashion/Apparel, Public Relations

Jennifer Jones *(Co-Founder & Mng Partner)*

Accounts:
SAINT By Sarah Jane
Tourneau

OUTSIDE PR
207 2nd St, Sausalito, CA 94965
Tel.: (415) 887-9325
Fax: (415) 887-9621
Web Site: www.outsidepr.com

Agency Specializes In: Crisis Communications, Event Planning & Marketing, Public Relations,

Public Relations Firms

Social Media

Gordon Wright *(Pres)*
Jessica Smith *(Brand Mktg Mgr)*
Jenny Radloff *(Sr Acct Mgr)*
Spencer Naar *(Acct Mgr)*
Andrew Ryan *(Acct Exec)*

Accounts:
Allen Sports (Public Relations Agency of Record)
AlterG
Bia Sport (Agency of Record) Media
Bulls Bikes USA (Public Relations Agency of Record)
GU Energy
Hydrapak
King Oscar
Moji
Omegawave
Pearl Izumi
Road ID
The San Francisco Marathon
StreetStrider
Torch Apparel

PAC/WEST COMMUNICATIONS
8600 SW St Helens Dr Ste 100, Wilsonville, OR 97070
Tel.: (503) 685-9400
Fax: (503) 685-9405
Web Site: www.pacwestcom.com

Agency Specializes In: Event Planning & Marketing, Internet/Web Design, Public Relations, Social Media

Paul Phillips *(Co-Owner & Pres)*
Chris West *(Sr VP-Ops)*
Kelly Bantle *(VP)*
Stan Devereux *(VP)*
Ellen Howe *(VP)*
Rashad Henry *(Sr Acct Mgr)*
Laura Probst *(Sr Acct Mgr)*
Alison Attebery *(Acct Mgr)*
Angie Blacker *(Acct Mgr)*

Accounts:
Coalition for a Healthy Oregon

PACE PUBLIC RELATIONS
1350 Ave of the Americas Ste 293, New York, NY 10019
Tel.: (646) 599-9222
E-Mail: info@pacepublicrelations.com
Web Site: www.pacepublicrelations.com

Year Founded: 2010

Agency Specializes In: Internet/Web Design, Media Relations, Media Training, Print, Public Relations, Radio, T.V.

Annie Scranton *(Founder & Pres)*
Susan Scranton *(Dir)*

Accounts:
Dr. Denise Jagroo
Jeanne Kelly
The Security Brief
World Golf Network

PAGE COMMUNICATIONS
4550 Main St Ste 210, Kansas City, MO 64111
Tel.: (816) 531-7243
Web Site: www.pagecomms.com

Agency Specializes In: Brand Development & Integration, Event Planning & Marketing, Public Relations, Social Media

Travis Joyal *(Partner)*
Lee Page *(Principal)*
Sarah Lehman *(Acct Exec-PR)*
Julia Armstrong *(Coord-PR)*
Breanne Frakes *(Coord-PR)*
Lydia Young *(Coord-PR)*

Accounts:
Cooper's Hawk Winery & Restaurant Media, PR
Disney on Ice Media, PR
Feld Entertainment, Inc.
Kansas City Power & Light District
Kansas City Restaurant Week
Legends Outlets Kansas City
Monster Jam Media, PR
Red Door Grill
The Roasterie, Inc.
UnitedHealthcare

PAIGE PR
2519 Palo Pinto Dr, Houston, TX 77080
Tel.: (832) 566-6503
E-Mail: paige@paigepr.com
Web Site: www.paigepr.com

Agency Specializes In: Content, Event Planning & Marketing, Media Relations, Public Relations, Social Media, Strategic Planning/Research

Paige Donnell *(Founder & CEO)*

Accounts:
Acorn International
Associated Credit Union of Texas

PAIGE WOLF MEDIA & PUBLIC RELATIONS
419 S 12th St, Philadelphia, PA 19147
Tel.: (215) 413-3790
Web Site: www.paigewolf.com

Year Founded: 2002

Agency Specializes In: Communications, Event Planning & Marketing, Media Relations, Public Relations, Social Media

Paige Wolf *(Owner)*

Accounts:
Career Wardrobe
CarrierClass Green Infrastructure
Haddonfield Crafts & Fine Art Festival
Juju Salon & Organics
Maya Van Rossum
Mi Casita Spanish Preschool
The Wardrobe Boutique

PALE MORNING MEDIA, LLC
5197 Main St Ste 9, Waitsfield, VT 05673
Tel.: (802) 583-6069
E-Mail: hello@palemorning.com
Web Site: www.palemorningmedia.com

Year Founded: 2001

Agency Specializes In: Event Planning & Marketing, Print, Public Relations, Social Media, Strategic Planning/Research

Drew Simmons *(Founder & Pres)*
Michael Collin *(Dir-Pale Morning Media-East)*
Caitlin Welter *(Sr Acct Mgr)*
Patrick Brown *(Acct Mgr)*
Kara Herlihy *(Acct Mgr)*
Chris Hrenko *(Acct Mgr)*
Anna Mays *(Acct Coord)*

Accounts:
Aquapac
Stormy Kromer Public Relations

PAN COMMUNICATIONS
255 State St, Boston, MA 02109
Tel.: (617) 502-4300
Fax: (978) 474-1903
E-Mail: info@pancomm.com
Web Site: www.pancommunications.com

Employees: 60
Year Founded: 1995

National Agency Associations: COPF-PRSA

Agency Specializes In: Business-To-Business, Children's Market, Communications, Computers & Software, Consumer Goods, Consumer Publications, Corporate Communications, Corporate Identity, Crisis Communications, Digital/Interactive, Direct Response Marketing, E-Commerce, Electronics, Environmental, Event Planning & Marketing, Exhibit/Trade Shows, Fashion/Apparel, Financial, Health Care Services, High Technology, Household Goods, Investor Relations, Luxury Products, Media Relations, Media Training, Mobile Marketing, Newspaper, Newspapers & Magazines, Pharmaceutical, Planning & Consultation, Podcasting, Public Relations, Publicity/Promotions, Real Estate, Recruitment, Retail, Search Engine Optimization, Social Marketing/Nonprofit, Social Media, Strategic Planning/Research, Transportation, Travel & Tourism

Approx. Annual Billings: $5,500,000

Mark C. Nardone *(Principal & Exec VP)*
Darlene Doyle *(VP)*
David Saggio *(VP-PANdigital)*
Jennifer Bonney *(Dir-Creative)*
Tiffany Darmetko *(Dir)*
Nikki Festa *(Dir)*
Michael O'Connell *(Acct Mgr)*
Jodie Wertheim *(Acct Mgr)*
Jenny Gardynski *(Acct Supvr)*
Kristin Flynn *(Sr Acct Exec)*
Danielle Kirsch *(Sr Acct Exec)*
Rebecca Gatesman *(Acct Exec)*
Alyssa Miron *(Acct Exec)*
Alyssa Tyson *(Specialist-Digital Mktg)*

Accounts:
908 Devices
Acquia; Andover, MA
Acsis, Inc.; Marlton, NJ
Ad:Tech Build Out Media, Influencer Relations, Social Channel
Alexander Mann
Arcadia Solutions
Ariba (Agency of Record)
Attivio; Newton, MA Active Intelligence Engine; 2008
Axios Systems; Herndon, VA
Bandwidth Agency of Record
Best Doctors; Boston, MA (Agency of Record)
Beyond.com; King of Prussia, PA; 2007
New-BlazeMeter
Brazilian Footwear
Burns & Levinson; Boston, MA
New-Cambridge Biomarketing
Cambridge Healthtech Institute
Capsule Tech, Inc.
Carbonite Content Development, Digital Media, PR, Strategy
Caserta Concepts; New Canaan, CT
ChoiceStream
CloudBees
CloudSense PR
CODY Systems, Inc.; Pottstown, PA
Conduit Systems; Lincoln, RI
Crowe Paradis Services Corp.
DiCicco, Gulman & Company (Agency of Record)
Drizly Communications, Digital
New-Dyadic
E-Commerce Services

Falcon Social
FLEXcon
New-Flexera
New-Glytec Systems
Harvard Business Publishing
HealthEdge
New-HighGround
HP Hood
hybris Software (North America Public Relations Agency of Record)
IBoard Incorporated; Pennington, NJ
iGATE Corporation
inetwork
Integrate
Keepity
Knoa Software; New York, NY
Kogeto
LoopPay Inc
New-Maestro Health (Public Relations Agency of Record)
Merchant Warehouse; 2007
Mopay
Motricity, Inc.; Bellevue, WA
Nastel Technologies; New York, NY
nfrastructure
Oasys Water; Boston, MA
ONvocal
Outerlink Global Solutions; Wilmington, Mass.
Panzura
PAREXEL International Corporation
Pegasystems (Agency of Record)
Perspecsys (Public Relations Agency of Record) Communications, Digital Media
PicsArt Social Media
Pneuron Corp
Pri-Med
New-Profitect
Qvidian
Radialpoint
Random House Digital
Ruckus Media Group
SDL Content Marketing, Global Public Relations Strategy, Social Media
ShopVisible
Signiant
Solstice Mobile
SUSE
Tahzoo
Terra Technology
Thunderhead
Tiffany & Co
Travelers Insurance
New-Universal Wilde
Veracity Payment Solutions; Atlanta, GA
Wholly Guacamole; Saginaw, TX Campaign: "Check Your Choice"
Yankee Barn Homes

PANTANO & ASSOCIATES L.L.C.

651 Delaware Ave, Buffalo, NY 14202
Tel.: (716) 601-4128
Web Site: www.pantanopr.com

Year Founded: 2009

Agency Specializes In: Crisis Communications, Digital/Interactive, Public Relations

Therese Hickok Fuerst *(VP)*

Accounts:
New-Seneca Nation of Indians

PANTIN/BEBER SILVERSTEIN PUBLIC RELATIONS

89 NE 27th St, Miami, FL 33137
Tel.: (305) 856-9800
Fax: (305) 857-0027
E-Mail: leslie@thinkbsg.com
Web Site: www.thinkbsg.com

E-Mail for Key Personnel:
President: leslie@thinkbsg.com
Public Relations: Sarah@thinkbsg.com

Employees: 13
Year Founded: 1972

Agency Specializes In: Automotive, Bilingual Market, Brand Development & Integration, Broadcast, Business-To-Business, Children's Market, Collateral, Communications, Consulting, Consumer Marketing, Consumer Publications, Event Planning & Marketing, Fashion/Apparel, Government/Political, Health Care Services, Hispanic Market, Integrated Marketing, Investor Relations, Legal Services, Local Marketing, Magazines, Media Relations, Media Training, Medical Products, New Product Development, Pharmaceutical, Promotions, Public Relations, Publicity/Promotions, Radio, Real Estate, Restaurant, Retail, Seniors' Market, Social Media, Sponsorship, Sweepstakes, Travel & Tourism

Approx. Annual Billings: $1,600,000

Breakdown of Gross Billings by Media: Pub. Rels.: $1,600,000

Mitch Shapiro *(Partner & Gen Mgr)*
Bruce Noonan *(Pres-Travel Grp)*
Leslie Pantin, Jr. *(Pres-PR Grp)*
Joe Perz *(Exec VP & Dir-Creative)*
Christine Bucan *(Exec VP-PR)*
Ann Marie Drozd *(VP-Brand Dev)*
Vicki Penn *(Dir-Media)*

Accounts:
Cuba Nostalgia
Great Florida Bank
McDonald's of South Florida
North Broward Hospital District
PGT Custom Windows, Doors, Patio Rooms
Ronald McDonald House Charities

PARADIGM ASSOCIATES

PO Box 364248, San Juan, PR 00936-4248
Tel.: (787) 782-2929
Fax: (787) 774-5722
E-Mail: mail@paradigmpr.com
Web Site: www.paradigmpr.com

E-Mail for Key Personnel:
President: gramis@paradigmpr.com
Creative Dir.: gramis@paradigmpr.com
Media Dir.: titaramirez@paradigmpr.com
Production Mgr.: framis@paradigmpr.com

Employees: 13
Year Founded: 1998

National Agency Associations: AAF

Agency Specializes In: Above-the-Line, Automotive, Below-the-Line, Bilingual Market, Brand Development & Integration, Branded Entertainment, Business-To-Business, Collateral, Consumer Marketing, Corporate Identity, Crisis Communications, Customer Relationship Management, Direct Response Marketing, Direct-to-Consumer, Entertainment, Event Planning & Marketing, Exhibit/Trade Shows, Graphic Design, Health Care Services, Hispanic Market, Hospitality, Integrated Marketing, Logo & Package Design, Luxury Products, Media Buying Services, Media Planning, Package Design, Production (Ad, Film, Broadcast), Production (Print), Promotions, Public Relations, Publicity/Promotions, Real Estate, Restaurant, Retail, Sales Promotion, Sponsorship, Sports Market, Sweepstakes, Teen Market, Travel & Tourism, Viral/Buzz/Word of Mouth

Guillermo J. Ramis *(Pres & CEO)*
Tita Ramirez *(Sr VP)*
Lorena Casado *(Dir-Creative)*
Joseph Lopez *(Dir-Digital Creative)*
Armando Navarro *(Dir-Art)*
Orlando Maldonado *(Mgr-Social Media)*
Yessica Rodriguez *(Sr Acct Exec)*

Accounts:
After Dark Films
Caribbean Cinemas
Costa Caribe
The Document Company
F & R Construction
FOCUS Films
Grupo Cacho
Gutierrer Latimer
IDI Group
Ivan Tort - Villa Del Este
Jose Rodas
Kianvel Development
Lema Developers
Lionsgate Films
Margo Farms
Paramount Pictures/DreamWorks SKG
Premiere Films
Rogue Pictures
Saint John's School
Stella Group
Universal Pictures
Vistalago Inc. (Joe Velez)
The Weinstein Company

PARAMOUNT PUBLIC RELATIONS, INC.

345 N Canal St Ste C202, Chicago, IL 60606
Tel.: (312) 544-4190
E-Mail: info@paramountpr.com
Web Site: www.paramountpr.com

Year Founded: 2003

Agency Specializes In: Event Planning & Marketing, Media Relations, Media Training, Promotions, Public Relations, Social Media

Jessica Prah *(Owner & Principal)*

Accounts:
Big Red Public Relations
Solixir

PARRIS COMMUNICATIONS, INC.

(Private-Parent-Single Location)
4510 Belleview Ste 110, Kansas City, MO 64111
Tel.: (816) 931-8900
Fax: (816) 931-8991
E-Mail: parris@parriscommunications.com
Web Site: www.parriscommunications.com

Employees: 11
Year Founded: 1997

Agency Specializes In: Brand Development & Integration, Crisis Communications, Media Relations, Media Training, Public Relations, Social Media

Revenue: $1,000,000

Roshann Parris *(Pres & CEO)*
Laurie Roberts *(Mng Dir)*
Ryan Holmes *(VP-Community Rels)*
Bob Inderman *(VP)*
George Merritt *(Dir-Pub Policy)*
Kelly Cooper *(Acct Supvr)*

Accounts:
Shawnee Mission Medical Center Public Relations

PASCALE COMMUNICATIONS LLC

430 Devonshire St, Pittsburgh, PA 15213
Tel.: (412) 526-1756
Web Site: www.pascalecommunications.com

Agency Specializes In: Investor Relations, Public

Relations, Social Media

Georgette Pascale *(Founder & CEO)*
Steve Chesterman *(VP)*
Jessica Griffith *(Acct Dir)*
Deb Holliday *(Acct Dir)*
Devon McSorley *(Dir-Bus Dev)*
Allison Potter *(Mgr-Pro Rels)*
Laura Wyant *(Mgr-Digital Media)*
Cassy Dump *(Acct Exec)*
Jamie Hall *(Acct Exec)*

Accounts:
Imprimis Pharmaceuticals
Mederi Therapeutics (Public Relations AOR)
Stretta Therapy

PASSANTINO ANDERSEN
42305 10th St W, Lancaster, CA 93534
Tel.: (661) 538-1100
Web Site: www.passantinoandersen.com

Year Founded: 2007

Agency Specializes In: Brand Development & Integration, Event Planning & Marketing, Media Relations, Promotions, Public Relations

Randy Terrell *(Dir-Pub Affairs)*
Pam Clark *(Office Mgr)*
Dave Saltman *(Sr Acct Exec)*
Chantal Khalilieh *(Acct Exec)*

Accounts:
City of Redlands
Golden Hills Community Services District

PCG ADVISORY GROUP
535 5th Ave 24th Fl, New York, NY 10017
Tel.: (646) 863-6341
E-Mail: info@pcgadvisory.com
Web Site: www.pcgadvisory.com

Year Founded: 2008

Agency Specializes In: Corporate Communications, Digital/Interactive, Media Relations, Public Relations, Social Media, Strategic Planning/Research

Jeff Ramson *(Founder & CEO)*
Gregory Barton *(Mng Dir-Digital Svcs)*
Vivian Cervantes *(Mng Dir-Capital Markets)*
Adam Holdsworth *(Mng Dir-Capital Market Strategies)*
Stephanie Prince *(Mng Dir)*
Kirin Smith *(COO)*
Chuck Harbey *(Mng Dir-Corp Advisory)*
Sean Leous *(Mng Dir-PR)*

Accounts:
Amedica Corporation (Agency of Record)
New-IntelliCell BioSciences (Strategic Communications & Public Relations Agency of Record)
New-IsoRay, Inc (Investor, Public & Digital Communications Agency of Record)
Kirin International Holding, Inc. (US Investor Relations Agency of Record) Corporate Communications, Digital Media, Public Relations, Social Media
Novogen Investor Relations
New-Pivot Pharmaceuticals Inc. (Agency of Record) Digital, Public Relations, Social Media, Strategic
TapImmune Inc. (Agency of Record) Investor Relations, Public Relations, Social Media Relations
New-Youngevity International, Inc (Agency of Record) Corporate Communications Services, Investor Relations

PEAK COMMUNICATORS
403-1155 Robson Street, Vancouver, BC V6E 1B5 Canada
Tel.: (604) 689-5559
Fax: (604) 689-5519
E-Mail: info@peakco.com
Web Site: www.peakco.com

Employees: 10

Agency Specializes In: Communications, Crisis Communications, Event Planning & Marketing, Local Marketing, Media Relations, Media Training, Public Relations, Strategic Planning/Research

Alyn Edwards *(Owner)*
Ross Sullivan *(Partner)*
Shael Gelfand *(VP)*
Charlotte Gilmour *(VP)*
Clare Hamilton-Eddy *(VP)*
Diane Stewart *(Office Mgr)*
Stephanie Orford *(Sr Acct Exec)*
Dawn Tse *(Sr Acct Exec)*

Accounts:
7-Eleven Campaign: "So Long, Winter!"
BC Housing
Chard Developments
City of Trail
Enbridge
Heffel Fine Art Auction House
HSBC Canada
ParkLane Homes
Quattro
Squamish Nation
Telus
Transport Canada
Tri City Group-Paradise Trails

PEARL PR GROUP
311 N Robertson Blvd Ste 688, Beverly Hills, CA 90211
Tel.: (310) 275-3227
E-Mail: info@pearlprgroup.com
Web Site: www.pearlprgroup.com

Year Founded: 2007

Agency Specializes In: Brand Development & Integration, Event Planning & Marketing, Media Relations, Public Relations, Social Media

Lauren Song *(CEO & Partner)*

Accounts:
Lanvin Inc.
NYX Cosmetics

PELOTON SPORTS INC.
3000 Old Alabama Rd Ste 119-348, Alpharetta, GA 30022
Tel.: (678) 362-6228
E-Mail: prinfo@pelotonsports.net
Web Site: www.pelotonsports.net

Year Founded: 1998

Agency Specializes In: Event Planning & Marketing, Media Relations, Public Relations, Social Media, Strategic Planning/Research

Jackie Tyson *(Founder & Pres)*

Accounts:
24 Hours of Booty of Atlanta
Historic Roswell Criterium
Larry H. Miller Tour of Utah
USA Cycling Professional Championships
Uncle Shucks

PENMAN PR, INC.
5114 Balcones Woods Dr 307, Austin, TX 78759
Tel.: (512) 218-0401
E-Mail: penman@penmanpr.com
Web Site: www.penmanpr.com

Employees: 10

Agency Specializes In: Brand Development & Integration, Crisis Communications, International, Media Relations, Newspaper, Product Placement, Real Estate

Patti D. Hill *(Founder & Mng Principal)*
Anna Drake *(Exec Dir)*
Dana Summers *(Exec Dir)*

Accounts:
Aquatic Fitness Swim & Snorkel
The Nova Sleep Center
Procyrion, Inc. Public Relations Agency of Record
QuantumDigital Digital

PEOPLE MAKING GOOD
3 Main St Ste 214, Burlington, VT 05401
Tel.: (802) 863-3929
E-Mail: info@peoplemakinggood.com
Web Site: www.peoplemakinggood.com

Year Founded: 2006

Agency Specializes In: Broadcast, Event Planning & Marketing, Print, Public Relations, Social Media

Nicole Junas Ravlin *(Founder & Partner)*
Phil Tucker *(Acct Dir)*
Claire Storrs *(Acct Supvr)*

Accounts:
Blakes All Natural Foods
Boloco Restaurant Group
Darn Tough Vermont
Duchy Originals
Gibbon Slacklines
Les Trois Petits Cochons (Public Relations Agency of Record) Communications
Northfield Savings Bank Inc.
The Republic of Tea
Small Dog Electronics
Vermont Maple Sugar Makers
Walkers Shortbread, Inc.

PEPPERCOMM
470 Park Ave S 5th Fl, New York, NY 10016
Tel.: (212) 931-6100
Fax: (212) 931-6159
E-Mail: nyc@peppercomm.com
Web Site: www.peppercomm.com

Employees: 80
Year Founded: 1995

National Agency Associations: COPF-PRSA

Agency Specializes In: Automotive, Business-To-Business, Communications, Computers & Software, Consulting, Consumer Goods, Consumer Marketing, Corporate Identity, Crisis Communications, Digital/Interactive, Education, Electronics, Event Planning & Marketing, Financial, Guerilla Marketing, Health Care Services, High Technology, Information Technology, Internet/Web Design, Media Relations, Media Training, New Product Development, Podcasting, Public Relations, Publicity/Promotions, Sponsorship, Sports Market, Strategic Planning/Research, Viral/Buzz/Word of Mouth

Approx. Annual Billings: $13,000,000

Ed Moed *(Co-Founder & CEO)*
Steve Cody *(Co-Founder & Mng Partner)*

Ted Birkhahn *(Pres)*
Maggie O'Neill *(Partner & Mng Dir)*
Erin Howard *(Dir-PR)*
Matt Purdue *(Dir-Content Strategy)*
Nicole Moreo *(Sr Mgr-Res & Analytics)*
Trisha Bruynell *(Acct Supvr)*
Colin Reynolds *(Acct Supvr)*
Joe Checkler *(Specialist-Media & Content)*
Catharine Cody *(Acct Exec)*
Alexandra Gambale *(Acct Exec)*

Accounts:
Astorino
Blucora
BMW of North America Mini USA, PR
Coda Automotive
Datapipe (Agency of Record) Digital Marketing, Integrated Strategic Communications, Media Relations, Social Media, Thought Leadership
Dr. Praeger's Sensible Foods
Duffy & Duffy
Ernst & Young
Fathom
FreshDirect
Gladiator Garageworks
Henkel Corporation
Honeywell
IDG World Expo
Invest Technology Group
J.H. Cohn; 2006
LendingTree Consumer & Financial Communications
Michael C. Fina Brand Awareness, Event Support, Media Relations, Social Media, Strategic Communications Program
Puget Sound Energy
Slipstream
Solar Wall
Solazyme
Steelcase
Suntech
Tasty Bite (Agency of Record) All-Natural Indian Food
T.G.I. Friday's Restaurants Communication Strategies, Public Relations, Social Media, Support Digital, The World Bartender Championship
TNS
TVi Media
Tyco Safety Products
Wikimedia Foundation
Wilbur-Ellis Company

Branches

Peppercom
425 California St Ste 1250, San Francisco, CA 94104
Tel.: (415) 438-3600
Fax: (415) 438-2130
E-Mail: abarlow@peppercom.com
Web Site: peppercomm.com

Employees: 9

National Agency Associations: COPF

Agency Specializes In: Automotive, Communications, Computers & Software, Consumer Goods, Digital/Interactive, Education, Electronics, Entertainment, Environmental, Health Care Services, High Technology, Internet/Web Design, Media Relations, Media Training, Public Relations, Social Marketing/Nonprofit, Viral/Buzz/Word of Mouth

Jackie Kolek *(Partner & Mng Dir)*
Deborah Brown *(Partner & Mng Dir-Strategic Dev)*
Ann Barlow *(Pres-West Coast)*
Michael Dresner *(CEO-Brand Squared Licensing)*
Matt Lester *(Dir-Creative)*
Matt Purdue *(Dir-Content Strategy)*

Accounts:
Foreversafe; 2007
Solazyme; 2008

WalekPeppercomm
(Formerly Walek & Associates)
317 Madison Ave Ste 2300, New York, NY 10017
(See Separate Listing)

PERI MARKETING & PUBLIC RELATIONS, INC.
1777 Larimer St Ste 1202, Denver, CO 80202
Tel.: (303) 298-7374
Fax: (303) 295-7374
Web Site: www.perimarketing.com

Agency Specializes In: Advertising, Brand Development & Integration, Collateral, Event Planning & Marketing, Media Relations, Public Relations

Paula Peri Tiernan *(Founder & Pres)*
Dianna Barrett *(Dir-Creative)*
Holly Lazzeri *(Acct Coord)*

Accounts:
Denver Health Foundation

PERITUS PUBLIC RELATIONS
200 S 5th St, Louisville, KY 40202
Tel.: (502) 585-3919
Fax: (502) 618-5900
Web Site: www.perituspr.com

Employees: 18

Agency Specializes In: Advertising, Below-the-Line, Brand Development & Integration, Business-To-Business, Collateral, Communications, Consulting, Consumer Marketing, Consumer Publications, Crisis Communications, Environmental, Event Planning & Marketing, Exhibit/Trade Shows, Guerilla Marketing, Internet/Web Design, Investor Relations, Legal Services, Logo & Package Design, Market Research, Media Relations, Media Training, New Product Development, Public Relations, Publishing, Real Estate, Strategic Planning/Research

Timothy Mulloy *(CEO)*
Zack Selter *(Sr Designer)*

Accounts:
Almost Family
Arysta Life Science
Colon Cancer Prevention Project
Cricket Wireless
The Gatlinburg Department of Tourism
Louisville Bedding Company
Museum Plaza
New Leash On Life
One View
Second Street Corp. City Block
University Health Care, Inc. Passport Health Plan
University of Louisville Louisville Medical Center Development Corp., University of Louisville Foundation

PERKETT PR, INC.
34 Cohasset Ave, Marshfield, MA 02050
Tel.: (781) 834-5852
Fax: (708) 570-6178
E-Mail: info@perkettpr.com
Web Site: www.perkettpr.com

Employees: 3

Agency Specializes In: Communications, Event Planning & Marketing, Exhibit/Trade Shows, Graphic Design, Investor Relations, Media Relations, Public Relations, Social Marketing/Nonprofit, Viral/Buzz/Word of Mouth

Christine Perkett *(Founder & CEO)*
Vic Miller *(Dir-Digital Production)*

Accounts:
Accuray
Contactual
DesignerPages.com
GiftGirl
Helium
Hitechclub.com
Intranets.com
Juniper Networks
Lotame
Marketing Communications Systems
Marteleron
Salesnet
StreamBase
TeleMessage
TrueAdvantage
Unisphere Networks
WaveMark, Inc.

THE PERRY GROUP
321 S Main St Ste 302, Providence, RI 02903
Tel.: (401) 331-4600
E-Mail: info@perrypublicrelations.com
Web Site: www.perrypublicrelations.com

Agency Specializes In: Crisis Communications, Media Relations, Media Training, Public Relations, Social Media

Gregg Perry *(Pres)*
Siobhan Carroll *(Sr VP)*

Accounts:
Garden City Center

PERRY STREET COMMUNICATIONS
150 W 28th St Ste 1404, New York, NY 10001
Tel.: (212) 741-0014
Fax: (212) 741-0013
Web Site: www.perryst.com

Year Founded: 2006

Agency Specializes In: Crisis Communications, Media Relations, Public Relations

Jon Morgan *(Pres)*
Wendy Tischler *(Sr Mng Dir)*
Jennifer Sanders *(Mng Dir)*

Accounts:
New-Duff & Phelps

PESELMAN PR
165 Chestnut Hill Ave, Boston, MA 02135
Tel.: (617) 669-0290
Web Site: www.peselmanpr.com

Agency Specializes In: Event Planning & Marketing, Media Relations, Media Training, Promotions, Public Relations, Social Media

Rina Peselman *(Owner)*

Accounts:
Hopsters Brew & Boards
Lash L'Amour

THE PHILLIPS GROUP INC
926 Quarrier St, Charleston, WV 25301
Tel.: (304) 345-6046
E-Mail: info@wvtpg.com
Web Site: www.wvtpg.com

Agency Specializes In: Advertising, Content, Graphic Design, Internet/Web Design, Logo & Package Design, Media Relations, Print, Public Relations, Radio, T.V.

Laura Phillips *(Pres)*

Accounts:
Mountaineer Autism Project

PIERCE MATTIE PUBLIC RELATIONS
62 W 45th St Fl 3, New York, NY 10036
Tel.: (212) 243-1431
Fax: (212) 243-7795
E-Mail: joshua@piercemattie.com
Web Site: www.piercemattie.com

Employees: 13

Agency Specializes In: Cosmetics, Fashion/Apparel, Medical Products, Public Relations

Serge Gurin *(Pres & COO)*
Pierce Mattie *(CEO)*
Sonya Hartland *(Mng Partner)*
Joshua Blaylock *(Dir-Bus Dev)*
Roman Iakoubtchik *(Dir-Fin)*
Stephanie Torres *(Sr Acct Exec)*

Accounts:
butter LONDON Nail Care; 2008
David Tishbi Jewelry
Every Man Jack Men's Personal Care Products
Joico Hair Care Products
Ootra

PIERPONT COMMUNICATIONS, INC.
1800 W Loop S Ste 800, Houston, TX 77027-3210
Tel.: (713) 627-2223
Fax: (713) 627-2224
E-Mail: info@piercom.com
Web Site: www.piercom.com

Employees: 20
Year Founded: 1987

Agency Specializes In: Communications, Consumer Marketing, Government/Political, Health Care Services, High Technology, Investor Relations, Media Relations, Public Relations

Approx. Annual Billings: $4,000,000

Philip A. Morabito *(CEO)*
Gary Merkle *(CFO)*
Clint Woods *(COO)*
Sally Ramsay *(Sr VP)*
Bryan Gaskill *(VP-Mktg)*
Mike Gehrig *(VP)*
Dave Stump *(VP-Bus Dev)*
Christopher Wailes *(VP-Media Rels-Natl)*

Accounts:
Elephant Insurance Brand Awareness, Media Relations
Odyssey OneSource
Trinity University

Branch

Pierpont Communications, Inc.
10900-B Stonelake Blvd Ste 110, Austin, TX 78759-6035
Tel.: (512) 448-4950
Fax: (512) 448-9479
E-Mail: info@piercom.com
Web Site: www.piercom.com

Employees: 5

Agency Specializes In: Communications, Consumer Marketing, Government/Political, Health Care Services, High Technology, Investor Relations, Media Relations, Public Relations

Phil Morabito *(Owner)*
Gary Merkle *(CFO)*
Stacy Armijo *(Sr VP & Gen Mgr)*
Mike Gehrig *(VP)*
Lara Zuehlke *(Acct Supvr)*
Danielle Urban *(Sr Acct Exec)*
Michael Miller *(Strategist-Brand-Digital)*

Accounts:
Odyssey OneSource

PILMERPR LLC
184 E 2000 N, Orem, UT 84057
Tel.: (801) 369-7535
Web Site: www.pilmerpr.com

Agency Specializes In: Content, Graphic Design, Media Relations, Public Relations, Social Media

John Pilmer *(CEO)*

Accounts:
Brent Brown Toyota

PILOT COMMUNICATIONS GROUP LLC
30 Green St Ste 2D, Newburyport, MA 1950
Tel.: (617) 201-9200
Web Site: www.pilotcommsgroup.com

Agency Specializes In: Brand Development & Integration, Content, Corporate Identity, Event Planning & Marketing, Internet/Web Design, Logo & Package Design, Market Research, Media Relations, Public Relations, Social Media

Jim Barbagallo *(Founder & CEO)*
Jay Childs *(Dir-Video Svcs)*

Accounts:
KettlePizza
Wenham Museum

PINEAPPLE PUBLIC RELATIONS
3380 Hardee Ave, Atlanta, GA 30341
Tel.: (404) 237-3761
Fax: (770) 454-6607
Web Site: www.pineapple-pr.com

Agency Specializes In: Content, Crisis Communications, Media Relations, Public Relations, Social Media

Deborah Stone *(Founder & Pres)*
Jennifer Nowicki *(Acct Dir)*
Brianna Wagenbrenner *(Acct Mgr)*
Melissa Webb *(Acct Mgr)*
Sarah Bain *(Acct Exec)*

Accounts:
New-Brunswick Islands

PINGER PR AT POWERS
1 W 4th St 5th Fl, Cincinnati, OH 45202-3623
Tel.: (513) 721-5353
Fax: (513) 721-0086
E-Mail: cpowers@powersagency.com
Web Site: www.powersagency.com

E-Mail for Key Personnel:
Public Relations: dlally@powersagency.com

Employees: 15
Year Founded: 1986
National Agency Associations: PRSA

Agency Specializes In: Advertising, Advertising Specialties, Automotive, Brand Development & Integration, Broadcast, Business Publications, Business-To-Business, Cable T.V., Children's Market, Consumer Marketing, Consumer Publications, Corporate Identity, Digital/Interactive, Direct Response Marketing, E-Commerce, Electronic Media, Entertainment, Event Planning & Marketing, Exhibit/Trade Shows, Financial, Graphic Design, Health Care Services, Information Technology, Internet/Web Design, Magazines, Media Buying Services, Medical Products, New Product Development, Newspapers & Magazines, Outdoor, Pharmaceutical, Print, Public Relations, Restaurant, Retail, Strategic Planning/Research, T.V., Telemarketing, Yellow Pages Advertising

Charles W. Powers *(Chm)*

Accounts:
Airport Fast Park
Cincinnati Opera
Frisch's; Cincinnati, OH Big Boy Restaurants; 1997
Golden Corral Buffet & Grill; 2000

PINKSTON GROUP
5270 Shawnee Rd Ste 102, Alexandria, VA 22312
Tel.: (703) 879-1605
E-Mail: info@pinkstongroup.com
Web Site: www.pinkstongroup.com

Agency Specializes In: Crisis Communications, Event Planning & Marketing, Public Relations, Social Media

Christian Pinkston *(Founder & Pres)*
David Fouse *(Partner & Strategist)*
Sean Mccabe *(Partner & Strategist)*
Derek Sarley *(VP)*
Bradford Williamson *(Sr Acct Exec)*

Accounts:
Hillsdale College
Reputation Institute Media Strategy, Public Relations

PINSTRIPE MARKETING
695 Central Ave, Saint Petersburg, FL 33701
Tel.: (727) 214-1555
Web Site: www.pinstripemarketing.com

Year Founded: 1998

Agency Specializes In: Advertising, Brand Development & Integration, Event Planning & Marketing, Internet/Web Design, Media Buying Services, Media Relations, Media Training, Promotions, Public Relations, Social Media

Ginger Reichl *(Pres)*

Accounts:
Cushman & Wakefield, Inc.
McQueen & Siddall LLP
Shriners Hospitals for Children
Tampa Convention Center

PIONEER STRATEGIES
PO Box 1986, Leland, NC 28451
Tel.: (866) 545-5856
Web Site: www.pioneerstrategies.com

Agency Specializes In: Content, Corporate Identity, Graphic Design, Internet/Web Design, Logo & Package Design, Media Relations, Public Relations, Social Media, Strategic Planning/Research

Frank L. Williams *(Founder & Pres)*

Accounts:
Cox Law Firm

PIPELINE PUBLIC RELATIONS & MARKETING
68233 SE 18th ave Ste d, Portland, OR 97202
Tel.: (503) 546-7811
Fax: (503) 546-7915
E-Mail: Tim@pipelineprm.com
Web Site: www.pipelineprm.com

Employees: 1
Year Founded: 2008

Agency Specializes In: Advertising, Market Research, Media Buying Services, Media Planning, Media Relations, Print, Public Relations, Strategic Planning/Research, Trade & Consumer Magazines, Web (Banner Ads, Pop-ups, etc.)

Timm Locke *(Principal)*

Accounts:
Contact Industries

PIPER & GOLD PUBLIC RELATIONS
313 1/2 E Grand River Ave, Lansing, MI 48906
Tel.: (517) 999-0820
E-Mail: info@piperandgold.com
Web Site: www.piperandgold.com

Agency Specializes In: Media Relations, Public Relations, Social Media

Kate Snyder *(Owner & Principal)*

Accounts:
New-Ingham County Land Bank

PIRATE GIRL PR
415 W Vine Ave Ste 1, Knoxville, TN 37902
Tel.: (865) 621-5800
Web Site: www.pirategirlpr.com

Agency Specializes In: Advertising, Brand Development & Integration, Media Buying Services, Media Planning, Print, Public Relations

Jennifer Holder *(Owner)*

Accounts:
Evergreen Services Gentry Griffey Funeral Chapel, Capital Funeral Home & Lindsey Funeral Home
First National Bank
Knoxville Catering
The Shrimp Dock
Susan Dodd, MD PLLC
The Trust Company

PIROZZOLO COMPANY PUBLIC RELATIONS
30 Newbury St Ste 3, Boston, MA 02116
Tel.: (617) 959-4613
Fax: (781) 235-9898
E-Mail: info@pirozzolo.com
Web Site: www.pirozzolo.com

Employees: 5
Year Founded: 1980

Agency Specializes In: Corporate Communications, New Technologies, Public Relations

Dick Pirozzolo *(Founder & Principal)*
Helmut Nollert *(Mng Dir)*
Michael Salius *(Dir-Natl)*

Accounts:
Duke Energy
Morpheus Technologies
Philips International
Rypos, Inc.
Whitesmoke Inc.
Wilmington Trust Company

PISTOL & STAMEN
7811 W Sunset Blvd, Los Angeles, CA 90046
Tel.: (323) 874-2100
E-Mail: info@pistolandstamen.com
Web Site: www.pistolandstamen.com

Agency Specializes In: Brand Development & Integration, Public Relations, Strategic Planning/Research

Denise Weaver *(Founder & Pres)*

Accounts:
New-Adrianna Papell Group

PITCH PRESS
9515 Cresta Dr, Los Angeles, CA 90035
Tel.: (310) 559-8228
E-Mail: admin@pitchpress.com
Web Site: www.pitchpress.com

Year Founded: 2004

Agency Specializes In: Brand Development & Integration, Broadcast, Public Relations, Social Media

Shannon Cavanagh *(Partner)*
Pam Roberts *(Partner)*

Accounts:
Bzees
Naya Shoes

PITCH PUBLIC RELATIONS
PO Box 11027, Chandler, AZ 85248
Tel.: (480) 263-1557
Web Site: www.pitchpublicrelations.com

Year Founded: 2011

Agency Specializes In: Media Training, Public Relations, Social Media, Strategic Planning/Research

Ann Noder *(Pres & CEO)*
Andrea Toch *(VP-PR)*
Jackie Copp *(Sr Acct Mgr)*
Marybeth Grass *(Coord-Media)*

Accounts:
TeetherTops

PIVOT PR
115 E Park Ave Ste 310, Charlotte, NC 28203
Tel.: (704) 774-9271
Web Site: www.pivotpublicrelations.com

Agency Specializes In: Content, Crisis Communications, Event Planning & Marketing, Internet/Web Design, Media Relations, Public Relations, Social Media

Drew Porcello *(Pres & CEO)*
Trisha McGuire *(VP & Client Svcs Dir)*

Accounts:
Charlotte School of Law
Sales Performance International, Inc.
Strategic Management Decisions

PIVOTAL PR
544 S San Vicente Blvd, Los Angeles, CA 90048
Tel.: (323) 933-4646
E-Mail: info@pivotal-pr.com
Web Site: www.pivotal-pr.com

Agency Specializes In: Brand Development & Integration, Public Relations

Jennifer Betts *(Pres)*
R. J. Rousso *(Mng Dir)*
Cate Zovod *(Dir-Global Initiatives & Corp Mktg)*
Johnny Gines *(Jr Acct Exec)*

Accounts:
Hennessy V.S.

PKPR
307 7th Ave Ste 1604, New York, NY 10001
Tel.: (212) 627-8098
Web Site: www.pkpr.com

Year Founded: 2006

Agency Specializes In: Advertising, Digital/Interactive, Event Planning & Marketing, Public Relations, Social Media

Patrick Kowalczyk *(Pres)*
Jenny Chang *(Acct Dir)*
Morghan Kusch *(Acct Coord)*
Mark McArthur *(Acct Coord)*

Accounts:
Advertising Age
Arts Brookfield
Brooklyn CSA+D
Caplow Childrens Prize
Cultural Services of the French Embassy
Dayton Literary Peace Prize
Dumbo Arts Festival
Fractured Atlas
Gawker Media Group
Internet Week New York

PLANA ZUBIZARRETA GROUP
490 Campana Ave, Coral Gables, FL 33156
Tel.: (305) 600-4181
Fax: (305) 600-4182
Web Site: www.zubizarretagroup.com

Year Founded: 2008

Agency Specializes In: Media Relations, Media Training, Print, Public Relations, Social Media, T.V.

Eduardo Plana *(Pres)*
Aymee Y. Zubizarreta *(CEO)*

Accounts:
Pulpo Media

PLANET PR
270 Lafayette St Ste 800, New York, NY 10012
Tel.: (212) 404-4444
Fax: (212) 324-1234
E-Mail: info@planetpr.com
Web Site: www.planetpr.com

Year Founded: 2006

Agency Specializes In: Advertising, Brand Development & Integration, Corporate Communications, Event Planning & Marketing, Media Relations, Public Relations, Social Media

Matthew Rich *(Founder & Principal)*

Accounts:
Steven Assael

PLATINUM PR
114 E German St Ste 200, Shepherdstown, WV

Public Relations Firms

25443
Tel.: (304) 876-8321
E-Mail: info@platinumpr.com
Web Site: www.platinumpr.com

Agency Specializes In: Brand Development & Integration, Collateral, Communications, Corporate Identity, Event Planning & Marketing, Internet/Web Design, Media Relations, Public Relations, Publicity/Promotions

Sandy Sponaugle *(Founder & CEO)*

Accounts:
Charles County Department of Economic Development
Constructing Change Energy Efficiency Homes Tour
Maryland Economic Development Association

PLESSER HOLLAND ASSOCIATES
(Acquired & Absorbed by Kivvit)

PMBC GROUP
345 N Maple Dr Ste 105, Beverly Hills, CA 90210
Tel.: (310) 777-7546
E-Mail: info@pmbcgroup.com
Web Site: www.pmbcgroup.com

Year Founded: 2012

Agency Specializes In: Brand Development & Integration, Corporate Communications, Event Planning & Marketing, Media Relations, Public Relations, Social Media

Ola Danilina *(Founder, Pres & CEO)*
Judy Dixon *(VP)*
Victoria E. Bardsley *(Dir-Bus Dev)*
Maura White *(Dir-PR)*
Lisa Inouye *(Sr Acct Mgr)*
Karen Sorenson *(Sr Acct Mgr)*
Dylan Smith *(Acct Mgr)*
John Yoon *(Acct Mgr)*
Veronica Mendez *(Acct Exec)*

Accounts:
AireLive (Agency of Record) Brand Awareness, Communication, Consumer, Media Relations, Mobile, Social Media, Strategic, Video Sharing
Anomo
Carnivore Club (Agency of Record) Media Relations, Public Relations
ContentChecked Inc (Agency of Record) Consumer, Corporate Communications, Media, SugarChecked, Thought Leadership
Echo Labs (Agency of Record) Biowearable Blood Monitoring Device, Media Relations, Press, Strategic, Thought Leadership
Emogi (Agency of Record) Corporate Communications, Media Relations, Thought Leadership
Farbe Technik (Agency of Record) Media Relations, Strategic, Thought Leadership
New-FortuneBuilders (Public Relations Agency of Record)
Graphiti (Agency of Record) Consumer, Street-Art Inspired Social Media App, Thought Leadership
Hang With Inc
Hilton & Hyland
Ibotta
InviteUp (Agency of Record) Media Relations, Strategic, Thought Leadership
JetMe (Agency of Record) Media, Press, Thought Leadership
New-Linktune (Public Relations Agency of Record)
Locca
New-MaxSold (Public Relations Agency of Record) Brand Awareness
MeetMindful (Public Relations Agency of Record) Brand Awareness, Consumer Press, Media Relations
Momentage
New-NextCore Corporation (Agency of Record) KOOM VR app, NOON VR Headset, Public Relations
New-Onestop Internet (Agency of Record) Brand Awareness, Branding, Public Relations
OwnZones (Agency of Record) Brand Awareness, Consumer Press, Content, Media Relations
New-Peeqsee Brand Awareness
Pipeliner
Rain on Request (Agency of Record) Indiegogo Campaign
Reach (Agency of Record) Media Relations
Rufus Labs (Agency of Record) Media Relations, Rufus Cuff Wrist Communicator, Strategic Thought Leadership
New-Sonavation (Public Relations Agency of Record) Media, Thought Leadership
Tape (Public Relations Agency of Record) Brand Awareness, Media Relations
Tooshlights (Agency of Record) Campaign: "Tooshlights Launch", Media Relations, Social Media Outreach, tooshlights.com
New-Trendy Butler (Agency of Record) Media Awareness
Virtual Piggy Media, Oink Teen Wallet, Strategic Public Relations, Strategic Thought Leadership
Viterbi School of Engineering (Agency of Record) "The Next MacGyver", Media Relations, Strategic, TV

POINT TAKEN COMMUNICATIONS
1600 N Market St, Jacksonville, FL 32206
Tel.: (904) 485-6597
Web Site: www.pointtakenpr.com

Year Founded: 2009

Agency Specializes In: Advertising, Brand Development & Integration, Crisis Communications, Event Planning & Marketing, Media Relations, Outdoor, Public Relations, Radio, Social Media, Strategic Planning/Research

Michelle Guglielmo Gilliam *(Pres)*

Accounts:
Clay County Humane Society Inc

POLISHED PIG MEDIA
PO Box 8961, Roanoke, VA 24014
Tel.: (917) 463-3833
Web Site: www.polishedpigmedia.com

Year Founded: 2012

Agency Specializes In: Broadcast, Content, Crisis Communications, Media Relations, Media Training, Print, Promotions, Public Relations, Social Media

Jennifer Jamison *(Mng Dir)*

Accounts:
Virginia Wine

POLK & COMPANY
1650 Broadway Ste 506, New York, NY 10019
Tel.: (917) 261-3988
E-Mail: contact@polkandco.com
Web Site: www.polkandco.com

Agency Specializes In: Graphic Design, Media Relations, Media Training, Public Relations, Social Media

Matt Polk *(Founder & Pres)*
Joe Lafeir *(CIO & Sr VP)*
Marc Bland *(VP-Diversity & Inclusion-IHS Automotive)*
Joseph Toth *(Sr Product Mgr)*
Benjamin Brown *(Acct Exec-IHS Automotive)*

Accounts:
Roundabout Theatre Company

THE POLLACK PR MARKETING GROUP
1901 Ave of the Stars Ste 1040, Los Angeles, CA 90067
Tel.: (310) 556-4443
Fax: (310) 286-2350
E-Mail: info@ppmgcorp.com
Web Site: www.ppmgcorp.com

Employees: 13
Year Founded: 1985

National Agency Associations: PRSA

Agency Specializes In: Automotive, Aviation & Aerospace, Brand Development & Integration, Business-To-Business, Consulting, Consumer Goods, Consumer Marketing, Corporate Identity, Direct-to-Consumer, E-Commerce, Electronics, Event Planning & Marketing, Exhibit/Trade Shows, Fashion/Apparel, Financial, Food Service, High Technology, Household Goods, Information Technology, Internet/Web Design, Investor Relations, Legal Services, Luxury Products, Market Research, Media Relations, Multimedia, Planning & Consultation, Public Relations, Publicity/Promotions, Restaurant, Retail, Social Marketing/Nonprofit, Strategic Planning/Research, Transportation, Travel & Tourism, Viral/Buzz/Word of Mouth

Stefan Pollack *(Pres)*
Noemi Pollack *(CEO)*
Mike Greece *(Mng Dir)*
Stephanie Goldman *(Sr Acct Mgr)*

Accounts:
Altra Biofuels; Los Angeles, CA Alternative Fuels
American Public Gardens Association Brand Outreach, Public Relations
Axiotron, Inc. Modbook; 2007
The Center for Client Retention Marketing, Public Relations
Docupace Technologies Marketing, Public Relations
Dynamite Data Public Relations
ESI Ergonomic Solutions (Agency of Record) Branding, Public Relations
Fiesta Parade Floats; Irwindale, CA (Agency of Record)
Guidon Performance Solutions Strategic Marketing Communications, Traditional & Social Media
Inclusion Inc. (Agency of Record) Traditional & Social Media Relations
Keller Fay Group Brand Awareness, PR
Koi Design; Santa Monica, CA (Agency of Record)
LeisureLink
Luxe Hotels Community Relations, Media Relations, Public Relations, Social Media Strategy, Website Content & Creation
LuxeYard Brand Awareness, Media Relations
National Notary Association
Netafim USA Market Awareness, Marketing Strategy, PR
Pocket Radar (Agency of Record)
Rain Bird Corp. Consumer Products Div.; Los Angeles, CA
RKF; Los Angeles, CA
RoundTrip; 2008
Santa Monica Convention & Visitors Bureau (Agency of Record)
Scouler & Company Marketing, Public Relations
Stiles Associates Public Relations
United Service Organizations Barbecue for the Troops, Dance for the Troops, Marketing, Media, PR, PSA
U.S. Digital Gaming Digital
Wellbeing Project (Public Relations Agency of Record)
The Writer Consultancy Marketing, Public

Public Relations Firms

Relations

POLLOCK COMMUNICATIONS
665 Broadway, New York, NY 10012
Tel.: (212) 941-4906
Fax: (212) 334-2131
Web Site: www.lpollockpr.com/

Employees: 16
Year Founded: 1991

Agency Specializes In: Event Planning & Marketing, Integrated Marketing, Local Marketing, Media Relations, Media Training, Product Placement, Public Relations, Retail, Strategic Planning/Research

Revenue: $1,700,000

Louise Pollock *(Pres)*
Craig Blakaitis *(VP)*
Valerie Kulbersh *(VP)*
Lara Flanagan *(Sr Acct Exec)*
Korinne Leonardis *(Sr Acct Exec)*
Stephanie Baber *(Asst Acct Exec)*

Accounts:
Ajinomoto Food Ingredients, LLC
American Society for Hypertension
BackJoy
Brassica Protection Products, LLC
Cranberry Institute
Cranberry Marketing Committee
EAS Sports Nutrition
PepsiCo Global Nutrition Group
Prestige Brands Beano, FiberChoice
Purdue Products
Tea Council of the USA, Inc.
USA Rice Federation

THE PONTES GROUP
2048 E Sample Rd, Lighthouse Point, FL 33064
Tel.: (954) 960-6083
Web Site: www.thepontesgroup.com

Agency Specializes In: Brand Development & Integration, Collateral, Event Planning & Marketing, Internet/Web Design, Logo & Package Design, Media Relations, Print, Public Relations, Social Media

Lais Pontes *(Owner & Principal)*

Accounts:
Robert Matthew

POPULAR PRESS MEDIA GROUP
468 N Camden Dr Ste 105, Beverly Hills, CA 90210
Tel.: (310) 860-7774
E-Mail: media@ppmg.fin
Web Site: www.ppmg.info

Agency Specializes In: Brand Development & Integration, Public Relations, Social Media

Michelle Czernin von Chudenitz Morzin *(Founder & CEO)*
Jessica Kill *(Pres)*

Accounts:
New-Jean-Claude Van Damme
New-Justin Daly

PORCH LIGHT PUBLIC RELATIONS
1111 E 54th St Ste 143, Indianapolis, IN 46220
Tel.: (317) 493-1105
E-Mail: contact@porchlightpr.com
Web Site: www.porchlightpr.com

Agency Specializes In: Brand Development & Integration, Content, Event Planning & Marketing, Media Relations, Public Relations, Social Media

Myranda Annakin *(Partner)*
Jennifer Voyles Chan *(Partner)*
Kathleen Thompson *(Partner-Mktg)*

Accounts:
CloudOne
Menchies Frozen Yogurt

PORTER LEVAY & ROSE, INC.
7 Penn Plz Ste 810, New York, NY 10001
Tel.: (212) 564-4700
Fax: (212) 244-3075
E-Mail: info@plrinvest.com
Web Site: www.plrinvest.com

Employees: 12
Year Founded: 1970

Agency Specializes In: Investor Relations, Public Relations

Revenue: $1,600,000

Michael J. Porter *(Pres)*
Lucille Belo *(COO)*
Marlon Nurse *(Sr VP-IR)*
Gloria Crispo *(Coord-Client)*

Accounts:
The Amacore Group, Inc
Premier Biomedical, Inc. Communications Strategies
Provectus

PORTER NOVELLI
7 World Trade Center 250 Greenwich St 36th Fl, New York, NY 10007
Tel.: (212) 601-8000
Fax: (212) 601-8101
Web Site: www.porternovelli.com

Year Founded: 1972

National Agency Associations: COPF-PRSA

Agency Specializes In: Advertising, Bilingual Market, Brand Development & Integration, Business-To-Business, Communications, Computers & Software, Consulting, Consumer Goods, Consumer Marketing, Corporate Communications, Corporate Identity, Crisis Communications, Customer Relationship Management, Digital/Interactive, Direct Response Marketing, E-Commerce, Education, Electronics, Entertainment, Environmental, Event Planning & Marketing, Exhibit/Trade Shows, Fashion/Apparel, Financial, Game Integration, Government/Political, Health Care Services, High Technology, Hispanic Market, Hospitality, Identity Marketing, Information Technology, Integrated Marketing, International, Leisure, Local Marketing, Luxury Products, Market Research, Media Relations, Media Training, Medical Products, Men's Market, Mobile Marketing, Multicultural, Multimedia, New Product Development, New Technologies, Over-50 Market, Pharmaceutical, Podcasting, Public Relations, Publicity/Promotions, Real Estate, Restaurant, Retail, Search Engine Optimization, Seniors' Market, Social Marketing/Nonprofit, Social Media, Sponsorship, Sports Market, Stakeholders, Strategic Planning/Research, Teen Market, Urban Market, Women's Market

Breakdown of Gross Billings by Media: Pub. Rels.: 100%

Angie Schneider *(Pres-Asia Pacific & Partner)*
Rich Cline *(Sr Partner)*
Higinio Martinez Gracia *(Partner)*
Patrick Resk *(Sr Partner & CFO)*
Joseph Russo *(COO)*
Brad MacAfee *(Pres-North America)*
Karen Ovseyevitz *(Pres-Latin America & Sr Partner-Mexico City)*
Sally Ward *(Pres-EMEA)*
Phil Buehler *(Exec VP & Dir-Strategic Plng, Analytics & Res-Global)*
Catherine Fink *(Exec VP-Health & Wellness)*
Mindy Gikas *(Exec VP)*
Doug Elwood *(Sr VP-Global Health & Wellness & Head-Innovation & Engagement)*
Brian McIver *(Sr VP & Head-HP Consumer)*
Adele Myers *(Sr VP & Dir-Creativity)*
Mark Amone *(Sr VP-Fin)*
Jessica Anderson *(Sr VP)*
Tamar Anitai *(Sr VP-Content Strategy-Digital)*
Diana Scott *(Sr VP-Health & Wellness)*
Jacqueline Thompson *(VP & Exec Producer)*
Lori Rodney *(VP)*
Rob Veliz *(VP-Digital)*
Florence Gregeois *(Acct Dir)*
Johnna Graddy *(Sr Mgr-Admin)*
Jenny Hepworth *(Acct Supvr)*

Accounts:
Abundant Forests Alliance
ADT Fire & Security PLC
Amgen
Analog Devices
AstraZeneca
Centers for Medicare & Medicaid Services National Multimedia Education Campaign
Centre for Disease Control
Dow Chemical
Dun & Bradstreet PR, Thought Leadership
Federal Deposit Insurance Corporation
New-Glass Packaging Institute Campaign: "Upgrade to Glass", Digital
GlaxoSmithKline
Hewlett Packard Eprint, Printer
Interbrand
John Theurer Cancer Center (Agency of Record) Social Media, Strategic Planning & Branding, Traditional Media
Johnson & Johnson
McDonald's Restaurants
Merck
Monster.com (Agency of Record)
NetApp Messaging, Strategy
Novartis Pharmaceuticals Corporation
NYCxDESIGN Event Sponsorships, Media Relations, Programming
Ole Smoky Tennessee Distillery Brand Awareness, Media Relations
Penske
Pernod Ricard USA Absolut Vodka
Pfizer, Inc.
Procter & Gamble
Qualcomm
Reckitt Benckiser Airwick, Brand Building, Corporate Communications, Durex, Finish, Media Relations, Public Relations, Resolve, Social Media Programming, Strategic Planning, Woolite, d-CON
SanDisk PR
Shire Pharmaceuticals
T-Mobile USA "Subtitles with Joel McHale", Campaign: "Jump"
Treo Solutions PR
Uncle Ben's Ben's Beginners Cooking Contest
UNICEF Event Planning, Market Visibility, Strategic Communications
Welch's Public Relations

United States

Porter Novelli-Austin
828 W 6th St # 101, Austin, TX 78703-5420
Tel.: (512) 527-9881
Fax: (512) 527-9891

E-Mail: laura.beck@porternovelli.com
Web Site: www.porternovelli.com

Employees: 20
Year Founded: 2000

National Agency Associations: COPF

Agency Specializes In: Business-To-Business, Consumer Publications, Corporate Identity, Event Planning & Marketing, Government/Political, High Technology, Planning & Consultation, Public Relations

Henry Engleka *(Exec VP & Dir-New York Global Health & Wellness)*
Chad Hyett *(Sr VP-Digital)*
Amy Leahing Edwards *(VP-Global Health)*
Kelsey Hammonds *(VP)*
Gennifer Horowitz *(VP)*
Lori Rodney *(VP)*
Arielle Herskovits *(Acct Supvr)*
Kate Northway *(Acct Supvr)*
Suzy An *(Acct Exec)*

Accounts:
Hewlett-Packard
PricewaterhouseCoopers

Orange Palate

250 Greenwich St 36th Fl, New York, NY 10007
Tel.: (212) 601-8000

Gennifer Horowitz *(VP)*

Accounts:
Brooklyn Brewery
Eli Kirshtein
Kelly English
Old 4th Distillery
Sarah Simmons Marketing, Public Relations

Porter Novelli-Bay Area-San Francisco

550 3rd St, San Francisco, CA 94107
Tel.: (415) 975-2200
Fax: (415) 975-2201
E-Mail: bob.wynne@porternovelli.com
Web Site: www.porternovelli.com

Employees: 75
Year Founded: 1988

National Agency Associations: COPF

Agency Specializes In: Business-To-Business, Consumer Marketing, Digital/Interactive, Event Planning & Marketing, Government/Political, Health Care Services, High Technology, Investor Relations, Public Relations, Sponsorship

Dave Black *(Exec VP)*
Keira Anderson *(VP)*
Romina Varriale *(VP-Voce Comm)*
Jessica Kerr *(Acct Mgr)*
Andrew Hussey *(Acct Supvr)*

Accounts:
Hewlett Packard
Wells Fargo

Porter Novelli-Boston

855 Boylston St 5th Fl, Boston, MA 02116-2689
Tel.: (617) 897-8200
Fax: (617) 897-8203
Web Site: www.porternovelli.com

Employees: 35
Year Founded: 1991

National Agency Associations: COPF

Agency Specializes In: Consumer Marketing, Corporate Identity, Government/Political, Health Care Services, High Technology, Public Relations, Sponsorship

Albie Jarvis *(Mng Dir)*
Russell LaMontagne *(Sr VP-Global Health & Wellness)*
Andrew MacLellan *(Sr VP)*
Leonora Fleming *(Acct Exec)*

Porter Novelli-Chicago

200 E Randolph St, Chicago, IL 60601
Tel.: (312) 552-6300
Fax: (312) 856-8807
Web Site: www.porternovelli.com

Employees: 5
Year Founded: 1972

National Agency Associations: COPF

Agency Specializes In: Digital/Interactive, Event Planning & Marketing, Public Relations, Sponsorship, Sports Market, Strategic Planning/Research

Adam Scholder *(Mng Dir)*
Maisha Pearson *(VP)*
Ryan McCormick *(Acct Mgr)*
Nikki Lopez *(Acct Supvr)*

Accounts:
Alzheimer's Association The Alzheimer's Association
CDC
HP
Johnson & Johnson
McDonald's

Porter Novelli-Ft. Lauderdale

950 S Pine Island Rd Ste 1054, Plantation, FL 33324
Tel.: (954) 883-3788
Fax: (954) 727-8439
E-Mail: kovseyevitz@porternovelli.com
Web Site: www.porternovelli.com

Employees: 15
Year Founded: 1996

National Agency Associations: COPF

Agency Specializes In: Children's Market, Consumer Marketing, Digital/Interactive, Event Planning & Marketing, Government/Political, Health Care Services, High Technology, Teen Market

Bill Kolberg *(Partner & Mng Dir-Southern California)*
Erin Osher *(Exec VP & Deputy Mng Dir-New York)*
Mindy Gikas *(Exec VP & Head-North American Talent)*
Dave Black *(Exec VP)*
Brenda Deeley *(Exec VP)*
Darlan Monterisi *(Mng Dir-NY)*
Romina Varriale *(VP)*
Karen Ovseyevitz *(Reg Dir)*
Jessica Kerr *(Acct Mgr)*
Sarah B. Stanley *(Acct Supvr)*
Hailey Thompson *(Acct Supvr)*

Accounts:
Procter & Gamble Tide
UPS Communications

Porter Novelli-Irvine

4 Studebaker, Irvine, CA 92618
Tel.: (949) 583-2600
Fax: (949) 583-2601
Web Site: www.porternovelli.com

Employees: 5
Year Founded: 1975

National Agency Associations: COPF

Agency Specializes In: Consumer Marketing, Corporate Identity, Government/Political, Public Relations

Erin Osher *(Exec VP & Deputy Mng Dir-New York)*
Dave Black *(Exec VP)*
Beverly Durham *(Sr VP)*
Christy Nelson *(Sr VP)*
Darlan Monterisi *(Mng Dir-NY)*
Andrew Hussey *(Acct Supvr)*
Sarah B. Stanley *(Acct Supvr)*
Hailey Thompson *(Acct Supvr)*
Anna Beyder *(Acct Exec)*

Porter Novelli-Los Angeles

10960 Wilshire Blvd Ste 1750, Los Angeles, CA 90024-3715
Tel.: (310) 444-7000
Fax: (310) 444-7004
E-Mail: bkolberg@porternovelli.com
Web Site: www.porternovelli.com

Employees: 20
Year Founded: 1973

National Agency Associations: COPF

Agency Specializes In: Children's Market, Entertainment, Event Planning & Marketing, Food Service, Leisure, Multicultural, Public Relations, Sports Market, Teen Market

Patrick Resk *(Sr Partner & CFO)*
Sally Ward *(Pres-EMEA)*
Fred Shank *(Exec VP & Head-West Coast Consumer Practice)*
Jana Leigh Thomas *(Exec VP)*
Beverly Durham *(Sr VP)*
Chad Hyett *(Sr VP-Digital)*
Sandra Sokoloff *(Sr VP)*
Deanne. Weber *(Sr VP)*
Linda Martin *(Mng Dir-Southern California)*
Gennifer Horowitz *(VP)*
Ashley Blua *(Acct Supvr)*

Accounts:
Almond Board of California
McDonald's Operators' Association of Southern California
Qualcomm

Porter Novelli Public Services

(Formerly Porter Novelli-Washington)
1909 K S NW Ste 400, Washington, DC 20006-1152
Tel.: (202) 973-5800
Fax: (202) 973-5858
E-Mail: jennifer.swint@porternovelli.com
Web Site: www.porternovelli.com

Employees: 120
Year Founded: 1972

National Agency Associations: COPF-PRSA

Agency Specializes In: Business-To-Business, Financial, Government/Political, Public Relations

Mary Christ-Erwin *(Partner & Exec VP)*
Liz Fitzgerald *(Partner & Exec Dir-Creative)*
Jennifer Swint *(Mng Dir)*
Rosemary McGillan *(Exec VP-Health & Social Mktg)*
Sean Smith *(Exec VP)*
Ryan Kuresman *(Sr VP-Pub Affairs & Corp Comm)*
Suzannah Palinkas *(Sr VP)*
Colleen Connors *(VP-HP Bus Partner)*
Natalya Staritskaya *(Project Mgr-Creative)*
Bailey Grover *(Sr Acct Exec-Consumer Mktg)*

Sedale McCall *(Acct Exec)*

Accounts:
Alliance for Potato Research & Education
The Almond Board of California
Bel Brands BabyBel, Laughing Cow
Compassion & Choices Media Relations
Pharmavite (Agency of Record)

Porter Novelli-San Diego
3111 Camino del Rio N Ste 400, San Diego, CA 92108
Tel.: (619) 687-7000
Web Site: www.porternovelli.com

Employees: 2
Year Founded: 1992

National Agency Associations: COPF

Agency Specializes In: Consumer Marketing, Government/Political, Public Relations

Dave Black *(Exec VP)*
Christy Nelson *(Sr VP)*
Sandra Sokoloff *(Sr VP)*
Darlan Monterisi *(Mng Dir-NY)*
Keira Anderson *(VP)*
Tricia Whittemore *(VP & Chief of Staff)*
Jessica Kerr *(Acct Mgr)*
Andrew Hussey *(Acct Supvr)*
Sarah B. Stanley *(Acct Supvr)*
Hailey Thompson *(Acct Supvr)*

Porter Novelli-Seattle
710 2nd Ave Ste 1200, Seattle, WA 98104
Tel.: (206) 727-2880
Fax: (206) 727-3439
E-Mail: angie.schneider@porternovelli.com
Web Site: www.porternovelli.com

Employees: 26
Year Founded: 1997

National Agency Associations: COPF

Agency Specializes In: Consumer Marketing, Government/Political, Health Care Services, High Technology, Public Relations

Gina Lindblad *(VP)*
Patricia Trask *(VP-HR)*
Robert Veliz *(VP-Digital)*
Kristin Fontanilla *(Dir-Lab & Acct Mgr)*
Joe Gurriere *(Acct Mgr)*
Brent Camara *(Acct Supvr)*
Sarah Goehri *(Sr Acct Exec)*
Oliver McIntosh *(Sr Acct Exec)*
Sam Hardy *(Sr Designer)*
Fraser MacPherson *(Acct Coord)*

Accounts:
Hewlett-Packard

Porter Novelli
3500 Lenox Rd Alliance Ctr Ste 1400, Atlanta, GA 30326
Tel.: (404) 995-4500
Fax: (404) 995-4501
E-Mail: brad.macafee@porternovelli.com
Web Site: www.porternovelli.com

Employees: 50
Year Founded: 1997

National Agency Associations: COPF

Agency Specializes In: Business-To-Business, Consumer Marketing, Government/Political, Health Care Services, High Technology, Public Relations, Sponsorship

Brad MacAfee *(Partner & Mng Dir)*
Melissa Taylor *(Deputy Mng Dir & Exec VP)*
Tom Donahue *(Sr VP)*
Ayanna Otite *(Acct Mgr)*
Mark Avera *(Mgr-Social Media)*
Blair Riley *(Sr Acct Exec-Tech)*

Accounts:
Centers for Disease Control & Prevention
Clean Air Campaign
Coalition for Responsible Energy
Georgia's State Road & Tollway Authority State Agency Programs
HP
The National Center for Civil and Human Rights Innovative Cultural Institution
Piedmont Healthcare Digital Strategies, Executive Visibility, Issues Management, Market Research, Media Relations, Physician Marketing, Public Relations, Strategic Planning
Sage Software; Irvine, CA

Voce Communications
298 S Sunnyvale Ave Ste 101, Sunnyvale, CA 94086
(See Separate Listing)

The Americas

Argentina Porter Novelli
Reconquinsta 723 2 FL, Buenos Aires, C1058AAC Argentina
Tel.: (54) 11 5554 7200
Fax: (54) 11 5554 7299
E-Mail: info@porternovelli.com
Web Site: www.porternovelli.com

Employees: 50
Year Founded: 1999

Agency Specializes In: Business-To-Business, Children's Market, Communications, Consumer Marketing, Corporate Identity, Financial, Government/Political, Health Care Services, High Technology, Investor Relations, Public Relations, Sports Market, Teen Market

Aldo Leporati *(Partner & Mng Dir)*
Diego Mendez Canas *(Partner)*
Paola Gemmati *(COO)*
Lucia Guerra *(Acct Dir)*
Carolina Nobile *(Acct Dir-PR & Comm)*
Victoria Lourdes Azar Gonzalez *(Acct Exec)*
Malvina Maria Giunchetti *(Acct Exec)*
Yanina Pezzi *(Acct Exec)*
Josefina Moresco *(Acct Coord)*
Bernadette Mac Dermott *(Project Head)*

Compass Porter Novelli
Diagonal 97 #17-60 Piso 3, Bogota, Colombia
Tel.: (57) 1 635 6074
Fax: (57) 1 255 0498
E-Mail: fernando.gastelbondo@compass.net.co
Web Site: www.porternovelli.com

Employees: 12
Year Founded: 1993

Agency Specializes In: Advertising, Brand Development & Integration, Business-To-Business, Communications, Crisis Communications, Digital/Interactive, Event Planning & Marketing, Financial, Food Service, Government/Political, Graphic Design, High Technology, Investor Relations, Media Relations, Media Training, New Product Development, Planning & Consultation, Public Relations, Publicity/Promotions, Sports Market, Teen Market

Fernando Gastelbondo *(Pres)*

Coordinamos Porter Novelli
Av Colon E4-105 y 9 de Octobre Edificio Solamar Piso 1, Oficina 102, Quito, Ecuador
Tel.: (593) 2 252 6819
Fax: (593) 2 254 3045
E-Mail: info@coordinamos.com

Employees: 12

Agency Specializes In: Public Relations

Rosa Alarcon *(CEO)*

Accounts:
Abbott Laboratorios
Boehringer Ingelheim
GlaxoSmithKline
Goethe-Institut of San jose
Metropolitan Hospital
Mutualista Pichincha
Novartis

Martec Porter Novelli
La Fontaine 36, Chapultepec Polanco, 11560 Mexico, DF Mexico
Tel.: (52) 55 5010 3200
Fax: (52) 55 5010 3201
E-Mail: kovseyevitz@porternovelli.com
Web Site: www.porternovelli.com

Employees: 60
Year Founded: 1993

Agency Specializes In: Advertising, Consumer Marketing, Health Care Services, High Technology, Public Relations

Sandra Kleinburg *(Partner & Mng Dir)*
Karen Ovseyevitz *(Pres-Latin America & Reg Dir)*
Jose Luis Diaz *(Mgr-Customer Svc)*

Accounts:
ADT
AMD
BMW
British Airways
Clorox
Creative Labs
Danone
Genzyme
HP Mexico & Latin America
Henkel
Kingston
Microsoft Latin America
PBBI
Qualcomm
Roche
Trend Micro

Porter Novelli-Toronto
33 Bloor Street East Suite 1450, Toronto, ON M4W 3H1 Canada
Tel.: (416) 423-6605
Fax: (416) 423-5154
Web Site: www.porternovelli.com

Employees: 22
Year Founded: 1993

Agency Specializes In: Consumer Marketing, Health Care Services, High Technology, Pharmaceutical, Planning & Consultation, Public Relations, Teen Market

Eric Tang *(Sr VP)*
Jane Lee Cheung *(Dir-Health & Wellness)*
Melissa Arnold *(Acct Mgr)*
Michael Margiotta *(Acct Mgr)*
Jim Black *(Acct Supvr)*
Janie Mercky *(Acct Supvr)*

Accounts:
Pfizer Canada
Timberland

Porter Novelli
455 Granville St Ste 300, Vancouver, BC V6C 1T1 Canada
Tel.: (604) 602-6401
Fax: (604) 681-0093
E-Mail: mark.nusca@porternovelli.com
Web Site: www.porternovelli.com

Employees: 4
Year Founded: 2000

Agency Specializes In: Consumer Marketing, Government/Political, Health Care Services, High Technology, Public Relations

Janie Mercky *(Acct Supvr)*

Accounts:
Yellowpages Group

Europe/Middle East/Africa

APRA Porter Novelli
111 Georgi S Rakovski Str, Sofia, 1000 Bulgaria
Tel.: (359) 2 981 41 90
Fax: (359) 2 987 8079
E-Mail: alamanov@apraagency.com
Web Site: www.apraagency.com

Employees: 18
Year Founded: 1994

Agency Specializes In: Public Relations

Tomislav Tsolov *(Owner)*
Lubomir Alamanov *(Mng Dir)*
Krassimira Hristoskova *(Acct Mgr)*
Rumena Kazakova *(Media Planner)*

Accounts:
Carlsberg Bulgaria
Coca-Cola Refreshments USA, Inc.
Cosmopolitan
Eko-Elda Bulgaria EAD
Elle
GloBul
Hewlett Packard
Holsten
Nestle Sofia
Pioneer Investments
Tuborg

F&H Porter Novelli
Brabanter Str 4, 80805 Munich, Germany
Tel.: (49) 89 121 750
Fax: (49) 89 121 751 97
E-Mail: info@f-und-h.de
Web Site: www.fundh.de

Employees: 50
Year Founded: 1989

Agency Specializes In: Consumer Marketing, Corporate Identity, Health Care Services, High Technology, Public Relations

Helmut Freiherr von Fircks *(CEO)*
Winfried Pieper *(Dir-Art)*
Martina Ritter *(Dir-Fin & Controlling)*
Rolf Schmitz *(Dir-Creative)*

Accounts:
Analog Devices
BMW Cars
Dow Plastics
Hewlett Packard
Hiscox AG
Logitech
Thyssen Krupp Steel Metals
W.L. Gore & Associates Gore-Tex, Public Relations, Windstopper

Farner Consulting AG
Oberdorfstrasse 28, 8001 Zurich, Switzerland
Tel.: (41) 1 266 6767
Fax: (41) 1 266 6700
E-Mail: info@farner.ch
Web Site: www.farner.ch

Employees: 50
Year Founded: 1951

Agency Specializes In: Public Relations

Roman Geiser *(CEO & Mng Partner)*
Jacqueline B. Moeri *(Partner & COO)*
Daniel Heller *(Partner)*
Roland Oberhauser *(CFO)*
Philipp Skrabal *(Chief Creative Officer)*

FTC
48 Rue Jacques-Dalphin, CH-1227 Carouge, Switzerland
Tel.: (41) 22 348 1411
Fax: (41) 22 348 1456
E-Mail: geva@ftc.ch
Web Site: www.ftc.ch

Employees: 2
Year Founded: 1951

Agency Specializes In: Corporate Communications, Public Relations

Frederic Burnand *(Partner)*
Francois Huguenet *(Partner)*
Pierre-Alain Rattaz *(Partner)*

Gitam Porter Novelli
Gitam House 8 Raul Walenberg St, 69719 Tel Aviv, Israel
Tel.: (972) 3 576 5757
Fax: (972) 3 576 5747
Web Site: www.porternovelli.com

Employees: 16
Year Founded: 1979

Agency Specializes In: Public Relations

Orna Gourell *(Mng Dir)*
Nadav Cohen-Keidar *(Acct Dir)*
Shmuel Dovrat *(Supvr)*

Accounts:
Bank Hapoalim
Israel Cancer Association
Kardan Investments
L'Oreal
Medinol
Nestle Food Services, Purina
Philips
Tirat Zvi
Tnuva Meat
Tnuva Milk
Vitania

IKON Porter Novelli
7 Ethnikis Antistasseos Halandri, Athens, 152 32 Greece
Tel.: (30) 210 68 37670
Fax: (30) 210 68 31 821
Web Site: www.porternovelli.com

Employees: 15
Year Founded: 1994

Agency Specializes In: Public Relations

Elena Savva *(Pres)*
Elia Liataki *(Mng Dir)*
Vasso Kakkasi *(Sr Mgr)*

Accounts:
BMW
Dove
Gillette
HP
LG
Logitech
Pampers
Reebok
SXSW
Tele Atlas

Impact Porter Novelli
Ali Reza Tower 1st Fl 7242, Medina Road, Jeddah, Saudi Arabia
Tel.: (966) 2 651 55 66
Fax: (966) 2 614 30 81
E-Mail: t.walmsley@ipn.ae
Web Site: www.porternovelli.com

Agency Specializes In: Public Relations

Tim Walmsley *(Reg Mng Dir)*

Jop, Ove & Myrthu
Kannikegade 18-1, Arhus, DK-8000 Denmark
Tel.: (45) 86 76 16 20
Fax: (45) 86 76 16 30
E-Mail: post@jom.dk
Web Site: www.jom.dk

Employees: 28
Year Founded: 1989

Agency Specializes In: Public Relations

Anne Hasselholm *(Owner)*
Kim Ruberg *(CEO & Sr Partner)*

Jop, Ove & Myrthu
Aldersrogade 5, Copenhagen, 2100 Denmark
Tel.: (45) 39 27 50 50
Fax: (45) 39 27 50 52
E-Mail: jom@jom.dk
Web Site: www.jom.dk

Employees: 30
Year Founded: 1989

Agency Specializes In: Public Relations

Jess Myrthu *(Owner)*
Lars Joergensen *(Partner & CEO)*
Esben Hostager *(Sr Partner)*

Lynx Porter Novelli AS
Bryggegata 5, 0250 Oslo, Norway
Tel.: (47) 23 13 14 80
Fax: (47) 23 13 14 81
E-Mail: lynx@lynx.no
Web Site: www.lynx.no

Employees: 9
Year Founded: 1985

Agency Specializes In: Consumer Marketing, Corporate Identity, Health Care Services, High Technology, Public Relations

Turid Viker Brathen *(Owner)*
Anne Finstadsveen *(Acct Mgr)*
Ragnhild Dohlen *(Client Dir)*
Lucie Meyer-Landrut *(Client Dir)*

Pagoda Porter Novelli
(Formerly Pagoda PR)
4 Eyre Place, Edinburgh, EH3 5EP United Kingdom
Tel.: (44) 131 556 0770
Fax: (44) 131 558 9463
E-Mail: info@pagodapr.com
Web Site: www.pagodapr.com

Employees: 10

Agency Specializes In: Communications, Government/Political, Media Relations, Strategic Planning/Research

Michael Hirst *(Chm)*
Angela Casey *(Mng Dir)*
Callum Chomczuk *(Acct Dir)*
Sarah McDaid *(Acct Dir)*
Holly Russell *(Acct Dir)*
Lynne Veitch *(Acct Dir)*
Giselle Dye *(Dir)*
Anne McMunn *(Assoc Dir)*
Moray Clark *(Acct Exec)*
Svetlana Hirth *(Acct Exec)*

Accounts:
Alliance Boots
The Crown Estate
Cupar North Consortium
Draw
New-Dundas Castle Public Relations
Electoral Commission
First Scotrail
McCarthy & Stone
Novo Nordisk
Roche Diagnostics
Transport Scotland
New-Unique Venues of Edinburgh Social Media
Waitrose
WSTA

Porter Novelli-London
31 St Petersburgh Pl, London, W2 4LA United Kingdom
Tel.: (44) 20 7853 2222
Fax: (44) 20 7853 2244
E-Mail: jean.wyllie@porternovelli.co.uk
Web Site: www.porternovelli.com

Employees: 75
Year Founded: 1973

Agency Specializes In: Consumer Marketing, Corporate Identity, Health Care Services, High Technology, Public Relations

Paul George *(Partner, Exec VP & Dir-Global Health & Wellness)*
Dave Black *(Partner)*
Sally Ward *(Sr Partner & Pres-EMEA)*
Fenella Grey *(Mng Dir-UK)*
Debbie Spitz *(Bus Dir-HP EMEA)*
Neil Hardman *(Acct Mgr)*

Accounts:
Almond Board of California
Association of Plastic Manufacturers (APME)
British Airways
Cereal Partners
Concerto Software
Eidos Interactive Ltd.
Gillette Group UK
Gillette Venus
GlaxoSmithKline
HP plc
Logitech
Mars Consumer PR, Extra, Wrigley
NHS
Novartis Pharmaceuticals
Novell
Pampers
Sainsbury's Corporate Communications
Shell Chemicals UK
New-ViiV Healthcare Corporate Communication

Porter Novelli-Paris
28 Rue Broca, 75005 Paris, France
Tel.: (33) 1 449 49 797
Fax: (33) 1 449 49 798
Web Site: www.porternovelli.com

Employees: 8
Year Founded: 1998

Agency Specializes In: Advertising, Business-To-Business, Consumer Marketing, Financial, Food Service, Government/Political, Health Care Services, High Technology, Investor Relations, Public Relations, Publicity/Promotions

Accounts:
Analog Devices
Chronopost International
Group Gillette France Braun, Duracell, Gillette, Oral B
Hewlett Packard

Porter Novelli
Av 5 de Outubro 10 2 Esq, 1050-056 Lisbon, Portugal
Tel.: (351) 21 313 61 00
Fax: (351) 21 313 61 01
E-Mail: gelrard@porternovelli.pt
Web Site: www.porternovelli.com

Employees: 16
Year Founded: 1986

Agency Specializes In: Consumer Marketing, Corporate Identity, Health Care Services, High Technology, Public Relations

Mariana Victorino *(Mng Dir)*
Sofia Lages Fernandes *(Dir-Comm)*
Sofia Moreira *(Assoc Dir Bus Dev)*

Accounts:
Imperial Holdings, Inc.
Fujitsu Siemens
Geotur
Pepsi International
Pioneer

Porter Novelli
San Vicente Martir 16, 46002 Valencia, Spain
Tel.: (34) 96 394 39 42
Fax: (34) 96 394 39 41
E-Mail: valencia@porternovelli.es
Web Site: www.porternovelli.com

E-Mail for Key Personnel:
President: juanmas@com-empresarial.com

Employees: 9
Year Founded: 1986

Agency Specializes In: Consumer Marketing, Corporate Identity, Health Care Services, High Technology, Public Relations

Marisa Ortega *(Mng Dir)*
Flora Galera Moreno *(Dir-Comm)*
Bernardo Murgui *(Acct Exec)*

Porter Novelli
Paseo de Gracia 56 ,6, 08037 Barcelona, Spain
Tel.: (34) 93 457 1300
Fax: (34) 93 457 2609
E-Mail: christina.vaoo_llosada@porternovelli.com
Web Site: www.porternovelli.com

Employees: 5
Year Founded: 1986

Agency Specializes In: Consumer Marketing, Corporate Identity, Health Care Services, High Technology, Public Relations

Higinio Martinez Gracia *(Partner)*
Daniel Bargallo *(Mng Dir)*
Gerardo Gonzalez Amago *(Head-Practice & Acct Mgr)*
Palmira Munoz *(Dir-Accts)*
Marta Ubeda-Portugues *(Dir-Big Unit Consumption)*
Anna Guasch Martinez *(Sr Acct Exec)*
Andrea Anguita Toledo *(Sr Acct Exec)*
Natividad Fradejas *(Community Mgr & Acct Exec)*
Eva Toussaint *(Deputy Area Dir-Tech & Comm)*

Accounts:
3M
ADT
AstraZeneca
GTI
JP Morgan
Mcafee
Natra
Pinnacle
SIGRE

Porter Novelli
Amsterdamseweg 204, 1182 HL Amstelveen, Netherlands
Tel.: (31) 20 543 7600
Fax: (31) 20 543 7676
E-Mail: info@porternovelli.nl
Web Site: www.porternovelli.nl

Employees: 35
Year Founded: 1981

Agency Specializes In: Consumer Marketing, Corporate Identity, Health Care Services, High Technology, Public Relations

Monique Botman *(Mng Dir)*
Babette Berg *(Mgr-HR-NL & BE)*
Juriaan Vergouw *(Sr Strategist-Digital)*

Report Porter Novelli-Rome
Via Poli 29, 00187 Rome, Italy
Tel.: (39) 06 699 2 4578
Fax: (39) 06 69 92 5397
Web Site: www.rpn.it

Employees: 6
Year Founded: 1990

Agency Specializes In: Business-To-Business, Consumer Marketing, Financial, Government/Political, Health Care Services, High Technology, Public Relations, Sports Market

Natale Pierluigi Arcuri *(Pres & CEO)*

Accounts:
Atlantia
Cocif
GlaxoSmithKline
Grundig
Hewlett Packard
Linear Assicurazioni
ProLogis
Riccione
Sisvel
SOLTA MEDICAL, INC

Report Porter Novelli
Piazza Grandi 24, 20135 Milan, Italy
Tel.: (39) 02 701 5161

Fax: (39) 02 701 5162 22
E-Mail: info@rpn.it
Web Site: www.rpn.it

Employees: 17
Year Founded: 1990

Agency Specializes In: Public Relations

Natale Pierluigi Arcuri *(Pres & CEO)*
Brunello Angelo *(Chief Client Officer)*
Marianna Tremolada *(Dir-Bus Units)*

Accounts:
ADT
Amgen
Cocif
Expocts
GlaxoSmithKline Consumer Healthcare Products Lactacyd, NiQuitin CQ, Parodontax, Sensodyne, Valda, Verecolene C.M.
Regione Calabria
Riccione Tourism Board
Toyota Europe
Wella Italia

R.I.M. Porter Novelli

36 bld 4 B Novodmitrovskaya st office centre Khrustalny, 127015 Moscow, Russia
Tel.: (7) 495 783 0826
Fax: (7) 495 783 5867
E-Mail: mail@rim-pn.ru
Web Site: www.rim-pn.ru

Employees: 34
Year Founded: 2002

Agency Specializes In: Communications, Corporate Identity, Government/Political, Public Relations

Igor Pisarsky *(Chm)*
Jacob Minevich *(CEO & Partner)*
Tatyana Ruzina *(Partner-Fin & Head-Corp Affairs Practice)*

Accounts:
Avon
CMI Development
Conrad Hotels & Resorts
Dirol Cadbury
EuroChem
European Commission
Horus Capital
Interbrand
Janssen-Cilag
Kommersat Publishing
KrasAir
Logitech
Mirax Group
Planet Fitness
S7 Airlines
Sky Express
Thyssen Krupp Steel
Toyota
Valio

SPEM Communication Group

Gregorciceva ulica 39, 2000 Maribor, Slovenia
Tel.: (386) 2 228 44 30
Fax: (386) 2 252 32 09
E-Mail: info@spem-group.com
Web Site: www.spem-group.com

Employees: 25
Year Founded: 1986

Agency Specializes In: Business-To-Business, Consumer Marketing, Financial, Food Service, Government/Political, Health Care Services, Investor Relations, Public Relations

Suzana Mihelin Ritlop *(Partner)*
Gordana Drecun Mithans *(Gen Mgr)*
Maja Recnik *(Dir-Educational Dept)*

Accounts:
Dravske elektrarne Maribor
Geoplin Plinovodi
HSE
Henkel Slovenija
Luka Koper
NOP Gfk
Nova KBM
Petrol
Premogovnik Velenje
TE Sostanj

Asia Pacific

Bangkok PR Porter Novelli

622 Emporium Tower Fl 22/4, Sukhumvit Rd, Bangkok, 10110 Thailand
Tel.: (66) 2 664 9500
Fax: (66) 2 664 9515
E-Mail: contact@bangkokpr.com
Web Site: www.bangkokpr.com

Employees: 14
Year Founded: 1995

Agency Specializes In: Public Relations

Hasan I. Basar *(Owner)*

Accounts:
Chevron
Coca-Cola Refreshments USA, Inc.
Discovery
GE
Heineken
Honda
Nestle
Pfizer
Procter & Gamble

Bentley Porter Novelli-Shanghai

International Rm 2012 Cloud Nine International Plz, No1018 Changning Road, Shanghai, 200042 China
Tel.: (86) 1058 6969 48
Fax: (86) 21 6327 6001
Web Site: www.porternovelli.com

Employees: 400
Year Founded: 2000

Agency Specializes In: Advertising, Consumer Marketing, Government/Political, Health Care Services, High Technology, Public Relations

John Orme *(Sr Partner & Pres-Shunya Intl PR)*

Focused Communications Co., Ltd.

2-9-1 Nishi Shimbashi, Minato-ku, Tokyo, Japan
Tel.: (81) 3 5157 0033
Fax: (81) 3 5157 0031
E-Mail: info@focused.co.jp
Web Site: www.focused.co.jp

Employees: 20
Year Founded: 2000

Agency Specializes In: Consumer Marketing, Digital/Interactive, Government/Political, Health Care Services, High Technology, Legal Services, Public Relations, Sports Market

Takashi Miura *(Chm)*
Akemi Ichise *(Pres & CEO)*

KorCom Porter Novelli

16F Daewoo Foundation Building 526 Namdaemoon-ro 5-ga, Jung-gu, 100-095 Seoul, Korea (South)
Tel.: (82) 2 6366 1500
Fax: (82) 2 6366 1530
E-Mail: chris@korcom.com
Web Site: www.korcom.com

Employees: 32
Year Founded: 1995

Agency Specializes In: Advertising, Consumer Marketing, Government/Political, Health Care Services, High Technology, Public Relations

Chris Yim *(CEO)*
Erik Cornelius *(VP)*
Kris Yoon *(Sr Acct Dir)*

Accounts:
Benesse Korea
Catholic Medical Center
Haechandle
Korea Highway Corporation
Kyobo Life Insurance
LG Mobile Global PR
W Hotels
Zeniel

Porter Novelli Australia-Melbourne

Level 14 Como Centre 644 Chapel Street, South Yarra, VIC 3141 Australia
Tel.: (61) 3 9289 9555
Fax: (61) 3 9289 9556
E-Mail: pkent@porternovelli.com.au
Web Site: www.porternovelli.com.au

Employees: 20
Year Founded: 1995

Agency Specializes In: Consumer Marketing, Corporate Identity, Health Care Services, High Technology, Public Relations

Mandy Griffiths *(Head-PN Social)*
Arj Ganeshalingam *(Gen Mgr)*
Kirilly Mallard *(Sr Acct Dir)*
Jessica Somers *(Acct Dir)*
Thomas Hann *(Acct Mgr)*
Ashley Mawer *(Acct Mgr)*
Katie Sheppet *(Acct Mgr)*
Kristine Arnott *(Mgr-Social Acct)*
Lauren Neave *(Acct Exec)*

Accounts:
ADA Victoria
Baileys
CSR Smart Sweetener
Disney
Fermiscan
Gillette Australia
Integral Energy
Pharmalink
Visa
VisaEntertainment.com.au

Porter Novelli-Beijing

12A Prime Tower NO22 Chaowai Street, Chaoyang District, Beijing, 100020 China
Tel.: (86) 10 8565 8508
Fax: (86) 10 8565 8899
Web Site: www.porternovelli.com

Year Founded: 1996

Agency Specializes In: Consumer Marketing, Government/Political, Health Care Services, High Technology

John Orme *(Sr Partner & Pres-Shunya Intl PR)*
Moon Hu *(Sr Acct Exec)*
Yuanyuan Liu *(Asst Acct Dir)*

Accounts:
Aston Martin Consumer Engagement, Press, Social Media
Procter & Gamble Campaign: "Sleep Well to be a Dragon"
Reckitt Benckiser 'Normalization', CSR programs, Durex, Social Media Strategy

Porter Novelli New Zealand-Auckland
Zone 23 110/23 Edwin St Mt Eden, PO Box 108 188, Symonds St, Auckland, 1024 New Zealand
Tel.: (64) 9 632 0500
Fax: (64) 9 632 0501
E-Mail: info@porternovelli.co.nz
Web Site: porternovelli.kiwi

Employees: 15
Year Founded: 1992

Agency Specializes In: Public Relations, Publicity/Promotions

Strahan Wallis *(Mng Dir)*
Sarah Williams *(Exec Dir)*
Natasha Gillooly *(Acct Dir)*
Louisa Jones *(Acct Dir)*
Morgan Bailey *(Acct Mgr)*
Kaya Arai *(Sr Acct Exec)*
Lauren Mitchell *(Acct Exec)*

Accounts:
Fonterra
Kapiti Ice Cream
Microsoft
Visa International
Vodafone

Porter Novelli Sydney
Clemenger Building Ground Floor, 118-120 Pacific Highway, Saint Leonards, NSW 2065 Australia
Tel.: (61) 2 8987 2100
Fax: (61) 2 8987 2142
E-Mail: tim.parker@porternovelli.com.au
Web Site: www.porternovelli.com.au

Employees: 30
Year Founded: 1996

Agency Specializes In: Public Relations

Tamsyn Alley *(Mng Dir)*

Accounts:
Frucor
Hutchison Mobiles
Starbucks
Visa

The PRactice Porter Novelli
812 7th Fl Oxford Towers, Airport Rd, Bengaluru, 560 17 India
Tel.: (91) 80 2520 3759
Fax: (91) 80 2520 3759, ext. 35
E-Mail: shane@the-practice.net
Web Site: www.the-practice.net

Employees: 70
Year Founded: 2000

Agency Specializes In: Communications, Event Planning & Marketing, Government/Political, High Technology, Planning & Consultation, Public Relations

Nandita Lakshmanan *(Founder & Chm)*
Shane Jacob *(VP-Digital & Head-Bangalore Ops)*
Abhijit Kaur *(VP-Consumer)*
Geraldine Debrass-Ee *(Head-Client Ops)*
Sameer Khair *(Head-Client Ops)*
Rejoy Leen *(Head-Client Ops)*
Priyanka Pandey *(Head-Client Ops)*
Mitesh Shah *(Head-Client Ops)*
Ritika Kar Sharma *(Head-Client Ops)*
Advait Soman *(Head-Client Ops)*
Walini Dsouza *(Mgr-Accts)*
Toolika Lawrence-Vanbuerle *(Sr Acct Exec)*

Accounts:
Hp India Campaign: "Hp Write&Read"
India Life Hewitt

THE POWELL GROUP
3131 McKinney Ste 402, Dallas, TX 75204
Tel.: (214) 522-6005
Fax: (214) 953-0792
E-Mail: bp@powellgroup.net
Web Site: www.powellgroup.net

Employees: 6

Agency Specializes In: Business-To-Business, Consumer Goods, Public Relations, Retail, Social Marketing/Nonprofit, Sponsorship

Becky Powell-Schwartz *(Founder & CEO)*
Kathleen Stevens *(Mgr-Fin)*

POWER PR
18103 Prairie Ave, Torrance, CA 90504
Tel.: (310) 787-1940
Fax: (310) 787-1970
E-Mail: johne@powerpr.com
Web Site: www.powerpr.com

Employees: 35
Year Founded: 1995

Agency Specializes In: Business-To-Business, Industrial, Public Relations

John W. Elliott *(Founder & Pres)*
Kate Walker *(Partner & Sr VP-Client Svc)*
Heather Metcalfe *(CFO & VP)*

Accounts:
Cilantro Animation Studios
Lasering USA
Off Shore Molds, Inc.
Spiralock

POWERS BRAND COMMUNICATIONS LLC
675 Lancaster Ave Ste 1, Berwyn, PA 19312
Tel.: (610) 644-1022
Web Site: www.powersbc.com

Year Founded: 2012

Agency Specializes In: Content, Corporate Communications, Crisis Communications, Public Relations, Social Media

Vince Powers *(Pres)*
Ann Powers Reilly *(Principal)*

Accounts:
Gute Financial Services
One Global Design
Philanthropy Network Greater Philadelphia

THE PR BOUTIQUE
3000 Weslayan Ste 280, Houston, TX 77027
Tel.: (713) 599-1271
Fax: (713) 599-1281
E-Mail: info@theprboutique.com
Web Site: www.theprboutique.com

Employees: 4
Year Founded: 2005

Agency Specializes In: Public Relations

Gretchen BRICE *(Founder & Partner-Austin)*
Emily Shuffield Hanley *(Sr Acct Exec)*
Charlotte Cameron *(Specialist-Media)*
Lesley Hile *(Acct Exec)*
Rachel Ebersole *(Jr Acct Exec)*
Trevor Thompson *(Jr Acct Exec)*

THE PR CONSULTING GROUP, INC.
(Name Changed to PRCG/Haggerty LLC)

PR/DNA
14503 Aranza Dr, La Mirada, CA 90638
Tel.: (714) 521-4400
Fax: (714) 521-3400
E-Mail: info@prdna.com
Web Site: www.prdna.com

E-Mail for Key Personnel:
President: cpflanzer@prdna.com
Creative Dir.: vsummers@prdna.com
Public Relations: KMason@prdna.com

Employees: 6
Year Founded: 1984

Agency Specializes In: Advertising, Automotive, Business Publications, Business-To-Business, Collateral, Communications, Consulting, Direct Response Marketing, Graphic Design, High Technology, Internet/Web Design, Logo & Package Design, Magazines, Newspaper, Newspapers & Magazines, Public Relations, Publicity/Promotions, Strategic Planning/Research, Trade & Consumer Magazines, Transportation

Breakdown of Gross Billings by Media: Pub. Rels.: 80%; Trade & Consumer Mags.: 20%

Chris Pflanzer *(Pres)*

Accounts:
Advantage
CIE American, Inc.
Ensyc Technologies
Image Arts Foundation
Lavon
Leepers Spare Products
Lexus; 1997
Marriott Residence Inn
Max Moulding
Maxon
Metro
Natural Life
Select University Technologies Inc.
Traveland.com; Los Angeles, CA Travel Agency; 2001
WynStar
Your Life

PR REVOLUTION LLC
355 Eisenhower Pkwy Ste 204, Livingston, NJ 7039
Tel.: (646) 807-4565
Web Site: www.prrevolution.com

Agency Specializes In: Content, Crisis Communications, Digital/Interactive, Event Planning & Marketing, Internet/Web Design, Media Relations, Public Relations, Search Engine Optimization, Social Media, Strategic Planning/Research

Elyse Bender-Segall *(CEO)*

Accounts:
Novus Acquisition & Development Corp

PRAYTELL STRATEGY
1000 Dean St Ste 301, Brooklyn, NY 11238

Tel.: (347) 844-9471
E-Mail: hello@praytellstrategy.com
Web Site: http://www.praytellagency.com/

Year Founded: 2013

Agency Specializes In: Communications, Digital/Interactive, Public Relations, Social Media

Beth Cleveland *(Mng Partner)*
Claudio Taratuta *(Mng Partner)*
Nate Jaffee *(Head-Brand Strategy)*
Jon Chew *(Art Dir)*
Kelly Kaufman *(Dir-Comm)*
Sydney Campos *(Sr Acct Mgr)*
Justin Jahng *(Strategist)*
Maggie Lee *(Strategist)*

Accounts:
Gametime
Kobalt
SnagFilms
SoundCloud

PRCG/HAGGERTY LLC
(Formerly The PR Consulting Group, Inc.)
45 Broadway 31st Fl, New York, NY 10006
Tel.: (212) 683-8100
Fax: (212) 683-9363
E-Mail: mail@prcg.com
Web Site: www.prcg.com

E-Mail for Key Personnel:
President: jhaggerty@prcg.com

Employees: 13
Year Founded: 1982

Agency Specializes In: Consumer Marketing, Public Relations

Approx. Annual Billings: $3,000,000

James F. Haggerty *(Pres & CEO)*
Harvey Englander *(Partner)*
Victoria O'Neill *(Sr Acct Exec)*
Andrea Garcia *(Acct Exec)*
Evelyn Swiderski *(Acct Exec)*

Accounts:
Abbott Laboratories
Barclays Bank
EVA Dimensions
Linear Technology
London School of Economics
Wilshire Blvd. Partners, LLC

Branches

The PR Consulting Group, Inc.-Washington
1101 17th St NW, Washington, DC 20036
Tel.: (212) 683-8100
Fax: (212) 683-9363
E-Mail: mail@prcg.com
Web Site: www.prcg.com

Employees: 22

James F. Haggerty *(Pres & CEO)*
Harvey Englander *(Partner)*
Thom Weidlich *(Mng Dir)*
Victoria O'Neill *(Sr Acct Exec)*
Evelyn Swiderski *(Acct Coord)*

PRECISE COMMUNICATIONS
201 17th St NW Ste 300, Atlanta, GA 30363
Tel.: (678) 538-6475
Fax: (678) 538-6501
E-Mail: info@precisecomm.net
Web Site: www.precisecomm.net

Year Founded: 2002

Agency Specializes In: Brand Development & Integration, Media Relations, Media Training, Public Relations, Social Media

Alexis Davis Smith *(Pres & CEO)*
Janice Lusky Greenspan *(Exec VP-Hispanic Comm)*
Tracey Bowen *(Sr VP)*
Ingrid Vega *(Acct Supvr)*
Will Ayers *(Acct Exec-Digital Strategist)*
Whitney K. Turner *(Acct Exec)*
Greer Johnson *(Acct Coord)*

Accounts:
The Coca-Cola Company
Toyota Industries North America, Inc.

PREFERRED PUBLIC RELATIONS & MARKETING
2630 S Jones Blvd, Las Vegas, NV 89146
Tel.: (702) 254-5704
Fax: (702) 242-1205
Web Site: www.preferredpublicrelations.com

Employees: 20

National Agency Associations: IPREX-PRSA-Women In Communications

Agency Specializes In: Arts, Brand Development & Integration, Consulting, Content, Corporate Communications, Corporate Identity, Crisis Communications, Entertainment, Event Planning & Marketing, Exhibit/Trade Shows, Financial, Food Service, Guerilla Marketing, Market Research, Media Planning, Media Relations, Media Training, Medical Products, Public Relations, Real Estate, Retail, Travel & Tourism

Michele D. Tell-Woodrow *(CEO & Dir-Creative)*
James Woodrow *(COO)*
Mindy Eras *(VP)*
Tana Shivers *(Dir-PR)*
Gina Yager *(Dir-Corp Dev & Special Events)*
Danika Mccauley *(Specialist-PR)*

Accounts:
American Civil Liberties Union of Nevada (Agency of Record) Public Relations
Batali & Bastianich Hospitality Group (Agency of Record) Public Relations
Downtown Grand Hotel & Casino (Public Relations & Promotional Agency of Record)
Grape Street Cafe, Wine Bar & Cellar Public Relations
Jan Rouven
LAKA Manicure Express Media Relations, PR
Morton's The Steakhouse
Peter Max
RT Drapery and Furniture Business Development, Public Relations
Urban Turban
Vivid Vodka
Winder Farms

PREMIER AGENCY
1954 Airport Rd Ste 208, Atlanta, GA 30341
Tel.: (404) 792-3841
Web Site: www.premieragencyinc.com

Year Founded: 2008

Agency Specializes In: Brand Development & Integration, Crisis Communications, Graphic Design, Internet/Web Design, Logo & Package Design, Media Relations, Media Training, Public Relations, Social Media

Mandy Nicholas *(Pres)*
Justin Epstein *(CEO)*
Jeff Corey *(Dir-Creative)*
Natalie Najjar *(Sr Acct Exec)*

Accounts:
ESPN Images
Fit Radio
The Gerber Group Inc
Popeye's Chicken & Biscuits
Porsche Cars North America, Inc.
Starbucks Corporation

PRESCOTT PUBLIC RELATIONS
629 Old Love Point Rd, Stevensville, MD 21666
Tel.: (443) 249-7868
Web Site: www.prescottpr.com

Agency Specializes In: Advertising, Collateral, Content, Corporate Communications, Digital/Interactive, Logo & Package Design, Media Relations, Print, Public Relations, Social Media

Carolyn Cordrey *(Pres)*

Accounts:
Avergan Foundation

PRICHARD COMMUNICATIONS
620 SW 5th Ave Ste 702, Portland, OR 97204
Tel.: (503) 517-2773
Fax: (866) 288-7857
Web Site: www.prichardcommunications.com

Agency Specializes In: Media Relations, Public Relations, Search Engine Optimization, Social Media, Strategic Planning/Research

Mac Prichard *(Founder & Principal)*
Jennie Day-Burget *(VP)*
Anneka Winters *(Mgr-Fin & Office Mgr)*
Jenna Cerruti *(Acct Mgr)*

Accounts:
The Green House Project

PRIORITY PUBLIC RELATIONS
2118 Wilshire Blvd Ste 835, Santa Monica, CA 90403
Tel.: (310) 954-1375
Fax: (661) 964-0344
E-Mail: info@prioritypr.net
Web Site: www.prioritypr.net

Employees: 8
Year Founded: 1990

Agency Specializes In: Broadcast, Cable T.V., Corporate Communications, Entertainment, Event Planning & Marketing, Exhibit/Trade Shows, Media Relations, Promotions, Public Relations, Publicity/Promotions, Social Media

Sandi Straetker *(Owner & Principal)*
Jeff Pryor *(Pres)*
Kristien Brada-Thompson *(Mng Dir & VP)*

Accounts:
2C Media
Alterna TV
Castalia Communications
Merimax, Inc
Rainbow Media
Rainmaker Entertainment; Vancouver, BC
Thunderbird

PRO COMMUNICATIONS
15 W Market St Ste 201, Louisville, KY 40202
Tel.: (502) 562-1969
Web Site: www.prprocom.com

Agency Specializes In: Communications, Crisis

Communications, Event Planning & Marketing, Graphic Design, Logo & Package Design, Public Relations, Social Media

Sarah Provancher *(Pres)*
Polly Moter *(Exec VP)*

Accounts:
New-Signarama Downtown

PRO INK
(Name Changed to Waymaker)

PRODUCTIVITY PR INC.
22801 Ventura Blvd Ste 207, Woodland Hills, CA 91364
Tel.: (818) 223-9046
Fax: (818) 223-9197
Toll Free: (800) 321-4928
Web Site: www.productivitypr.com

Agency Specializes In: Content, Media Relations, Promotions, Public Relations, Social Media

Tracey Rosen *(Pres & CEO)*

Accounts:
Ecovacs Robotics

THE PROFESSIONAL IMAGE INCORPORATED
10 Hughes Ste A200, Irvine, CA 92618
Tel.: (949) 768-1522
Fax: (949) 768-1060
E-Mail: pr@theprofessionalimage.com
Web Site: www.theprofessionalimage.com

Employees: 5
Year Founded: 1988

Agency Specializes In: Collateral, Consulting, Corporate Identity, Internet/Web Design, Logo & Package Design, Magazines, Medical Products, Merchandising, Pharmaceutical

Angela O'Mara *(Pres)*
Giles Raine *(VP)*

PROPHETA COMMUNICATIONS
70 E Tenth St Ste 6P, New York, NY 10003
Tel.: (212) 901-6914
Web Site: propheta.com/

Kevin A. Mercuri *(Founder & Pres)*

Accounts:
Alto Group Holdings Gold Mining Operations
Constellation Asset Advisors, Inc.
Trell Aviation

PROSEK PARTNERS
(Formerly Cubitt Jacobs & Prosek Communications)
1552 Post Rd, Stratford, CT 06824
Tel.: (203) 254-1300
Fax: (203) 254-1330
Web Site: www.prosek.com

Employees: 42

National Agency Associations: COPF

Agency Specializes In: Business-To-Business, Consumer Marketing, Corporate Communications, Education, Financial, Government/Political, Graphic Design, Health Care Services, Industrial, Investor Relations, Public Relations, Publishing

Jennifer Prosek *(Founder & CEO)*
Mark Kollar *(Partner)*
Russell Sherman *(Partner)*
Caroline Harris *(Mng Dir)*
Thomas Rozycki *(Mng Dir)*
Wilson Cleveland *(Sr VP & Exec Producer)*
Vu D. Chung *(VP)*
Amanda Kiely *(Assoc VP)*
Dave Zamba *(Creative Dir)*
Shelby Landesberg *(Dir-Fin)*
Aaron Steinfeld *(Dir-Art)*

Accounts:
Braemar Energy Ventures
GE Corporate Financial Services
The Hartford
OppenheimerFunds (Public Relations Agency of Record) Public Relations
Swiss Re (North American Agency of Record)

Branches

Prosek Partners
(Formerly Cubitt Jacobs & Prosek Communications)
350 5th Ave Ste 3901, New York, NY 10118
Tel.: (212) 279-3115
Fax: (212) 279-3117
Web Site: www.prosek.com

Employees: 30

National Agency Associations: COPF

Jen Prosek *(CEO)*
Russell Sherman *(Partner)*
Josh Passman *(Mng Dir)*
Andrew Waterworth *(Mng Dir)*
Russell Polin *(CFO)*
Hal Bienstock *(Sr VP)*
Josette Robinson *(Sr VP)*
Susan Etkind *(VP & Dir-Editorial)*
Kristina Baldridge *(VP)*
Emily Tracy *(VP)*
Dawn Zinkewich *(VP)*
Frederick Duff Gordon *(Assoc Dir)*
Luke Willoughby *(Specialist-Digital Media)*

Accounts:
GE Financial Services
Hennion & Walsh (Public Relations Agency of Record) Brand Awareness, Content Development, Media Relations, SmartTrust, Social Media, Thought Leadership
Imagine Software Content Creation, Media Relations, Public Relations, Strategic Message Development
Royal Bank of Scotland
Synchrony Financial (Public Relations Agency of Record) Media Relations, Thought Leadership

PROSIO COMMUNICATIONS
1544 Eureka Rd Ste 280, Roseville, CA 95661
Tel.: (916) 251-1280
Fax: (916) 251-1290
E-Mail: info@prosiopr.com
Web Site: www.prosiopr.com

Year Founded: 2013

Agency Specializes In: Advertising, Crisis Communications, Event Planning & Marketing, Media Relations, Public Relations, Social Media

Lori Prosio *(Pres & CEO)*
Christopher Townsend *(Mgr-Bus Ops)*
Alma Murphy *(Acct Supvr)*
Lindsey Nelson *(Acct Exec)*
Linsey Momet *(Asst Acct Exec)*
Daniel Dedoshka *(Acct Coord)*

Accounts:
California Office of Traffic Safety
Danny Oliver Foundation
Sacramento Metropolitan Air Quality Management District

PROSPER STRATEGIES
(Formerly Prosper Public Relations)
1350 N Wells St Ste A311, Chicago, IL 60625
Tel.: (312) 834-3361
E-Mail: hello@prosperstrategies.com
Web Site: www.prosper-strategies.com/

Year Founded: 2012

Agency Specializes In: Event Planning & Marketing, Media Relations, Public Relations, Social Media

Alyssa VandeLeest *(Founder & Pres)*
Julia Markham-Cameron *(Acct Exec)*
Rachel Cali *(Copywriter)*
Brittany Benson *(Assoc Acct Exec)*
Katie Nuckolls *(Assoc Acct Exec)*

Accounts:
Hannah's Bretzel
Positive H2O
Zazoo kids

PROVOCATEUR MEDIA
2340 Pacific Ave, San Francisco, CA 94115
Tel.: (415) 513-5883
E-Mail: info@provocateur-media.com
Web Site: www.provocateur-media.com

Year Founded: 2009

Agency Specializes In: Advertising, Brand Development & Integration, Event Planning & Marketing, Internet/Web Design, Media Training, Public Relations, Social Media

Erin Finnegan *(Strategist-Social Media)*
Mari Tzikas *(Specialist-Mktg & Writing)*

Accounts:
Blackbird Bar
Dadascope
Destination Saratoga
Dress For Success
East Bay Vintners Alliance
LUX SF
Range
Union Square

PRX DIGITAL SILICON VALLEY
(Formerly PRx, Inc.)
991 W Hedding St Ste 201, San Jose, CA 95126
Tel.: (408) 287-1700
Fax: (408) 556-1487
E-Mail: results@prxdigital.com
Web Site: prxdigital.com/

E-Mail for Key Personnel:
President: brenna_bolger@prxinc.com

Employees: 25
Year Founded: 1975

Agency Specializes In: Asian Market, Bilingual Market, Brand Development & Integration, Broadcast, Business-To-Business, Collateral, Communications, Consumer Marketing, Corporate Identity, Digital/Interactive, Direct Response Marketing, E-Commerce, Education, Electronic Media, Entertainment, Environmental, Event Planning & Marketing, Gay & Lesbian Market, Government/Political, Graphic Design, Health Care Services, High Technology, Hispanic Market, Industrial, Information Technology, Internet/Web Design, Logo & Package Design, Medical Products, Newspaper, Newspapers & Magazines, Outdoor, Pharmaceutical, Production, Public Relations, Publicity/Promotions, Radio, Restaurant,

Strategic Planning/Research, T.V., Trade & Consumer Magazines, Travel & Tourism

Approx. Annual Billings: $2,600,000

Breakdown of Gross Billings by Media: Other: $150,000; Production: $450,000; Pub. Rels.: $2,000,000

Brenna Bolger *(Founder & CEO)*
Daniel Garza *(Sr VP)*
Bill Kugler *(Sr VP)*
Douglas P. Walker *(Sr VP-Pub Affairs)*
Lanor Maune *(Dir-Content Mktg)*
Sonja Bree *(Acct Mgr)*
Thuy Nguyen *(Mgr-Acctg)*

Accounts:
Apple Inc.
Blue Cross of California
California Parkinson's Foundation
Cupertino Inn
Cypress Semiconductor
Orchard Supply Hardware
Santa Clara Valley Health & Hospital System
Valley Health Plan
Valley Medical Center Foundation

PUBLIC RELATIONS MARKETING, INC.
30 Walnut Dr, Roslyn, NY 11576-2333
Tel.: (516) 621-3625
Fax: (516) 621-3923

Employees: 5
Year Founded: 1993

Agency Specializes In: Agriculture, Brand Development & Integration, Communications, Consulting, Education, Event Planning & Marketing, Exhibit/Trade Shows, Fashion/Apparel, Financial, Medical Products, Newspaper, Newspapers & Magazines, Planning & Consultation, Print, Public Relations, Publicity/Promotions, Radio, Sales Promotion, Trade & Consumer Magazines

Accounts:
ASAE Services Inc
Building Blocks Day Care Center; Long Island, NY; 1994
Flower Council of Holland; 1993
Golden Era of Baseball Chess Set; Los Angeles, CA; 1997
Great Neck Women's Medical Groups
Market Mentor LLC
Mitsubishi Electric Corporation
Nanostart AG
Universal Wood Product; Searingtown, NY; 2005

PUBLICCITY PR
24300 Southfield Rd Ste 101, Southfield, MI 48075
Tel.: (248) 663-6166
Web Site: www.publiccitypr.net

Year Founded: 2008

Agency Specializes In: Media Relations, Public Relations, Social Media, Strategic Planning/Research

Hope Brown *(Principal-Publicity PR)*
Jason Brown *(Principal)*
Monica Cheick *(Acct Dir)*
Kristin Mullen *(Acct Mgr)*

Accounts:
Barton Malow Company
Life Time Athletic
Medical Weight Loss Clinic

THE PUBLICITY AGENCY
3903 Northdale Blvd Ste 150 W, Tampa, FL 33624
Tel.: (813) 948-7767
E-Mail: info@thepublicityagency.com
Web Site: www.thepublicityagency.com

Agency Specializes In: Crisis Communications, Public Relations, Social Media

Glenn Selig *(Founder & Principal)*

Accounts:
Beauty TV

PUBLICITY MATTERS
75 Whiteladies Road, Clifton, Bristol, BS8 2NT United Kingdom
Tel.: (44) 117 3178206
Fax: (44) 1275 770702
E-Mail: info@publicitymatters.com
Web Site: www.publicitymatters.com

Employees: 8

Agency Specializes In: Public Relations

Rob Cave *(Dir)*

PUDER PUBLIC RELATIONS LLC
26 Broadway Ste 931, New York, NY 10004
Tel.: (212) 558-9400
Web Site: www.puderpr.com

Agency Specializes In: Advertising, Digital/Interactive, Event Planning & Marketing, Media Relations, Media Training, Public Relations, Strategic Planning/Research

Arik Puder *(Founder & Pres)*
Joe Berkofsky *(CEO)*

Accounts:
New-World Jewish Congress

PUGNACIOUS PR
PO Box 318182, San Francisco, CA 94131
Tel.: (415) 501-9784
Web Site: www.pugpr.com

Year Founded: 2013

Agency Specializes In: Advertising, Brand Development & Integration, Crisis Communications, Event Planning & Marketing, Logo & Package Design, Media Relations, Media Training, Public Relations, Social Media, Strategic Planning/Research

Spencer Moore *(Founder & Principal)*
Kevin Plottner *(Dir-Creative)*

Accounts:
Leanlix

PURDUE MARION & ASSOCIATES
3455 Cliff Shadows Pkwy Ste 190, Las Vegas, NV 89129
Tel.: (702) 222-2362
Fax: (702) 222-2386
E-Mail: info@purduemarion.com
Web Site: www.purduemarion.com

Year Founded: 2002

Agency Specializes In: Brand Development & Integration, Crisis Communications, Event Planning & Marketing, Media Relations, Media Training, Public Relations, Social Media, Strategic Planning/Research

Bill Marion *(Partner)*
Lynn Purdue *(Partner)*
Michele Voelkening *(VP)*
Nancy Katz *(Dir-PR)*
Donna Palladino *(Dir-Special Events)*
Gina Thompson *(Dir-Admin)*

Accounts:
Seasons Funeral Planning Services

PURE COMMUNICATIONS, INC.
1015 Ashes Dr Ste 204, Wilmington, NC 28405
Tel.: (910) 509-3970
Web Site: www.purecommunicationsinc.com

Agency Specializes In: Crisis Communications, Digital/Interactive, Graphic Design, Internet/Web Design, Investor Relations, Media Relations, Public Relations, Social Media

Matthew Clawson *(Mng Dir-IR)*
Caton Morris *(VP)*
Krista Sack *(Sr Acct Dir & Strategist-Brand)*
Jill A. Bertotti *(Dir-IR Outreach & Sr Acct Mgr)*
Katie Wilson *(Dir-Media Rels & Acct Mgmt)*
Mike Huckman *(Sr Specialist-Comm)*
Alicia Davis *(Acct Exec)*

Accounts:
Third Rock Ventures

PURPLE PR
35 Great Jones St, New York, NY 10012
Tel.: (212) 858-9888
E-Mail: enquiries@purplepr.com
Web Site: www.purplepr.com

Agency Specializes In: Digital/Interactive, Event Planning & Marketing, Public Relations

Samantha Kain *(Mng Dir)*

Accounts:
New-Frank Ocean

PUSHKIN PUBLIC RELATIONS, LLC
1416 Larimer St Ste 200, Denver, CO 80202
Tel.: (303) 733-3441
Fax: (303) 733-4236
E-Mail: info@pushkinpr.com
Web Site: www.pushkinpr.com

Year Founded: 1997

Agency Specializes In: Crisis Communications, Media Relations, Media Training, Public Relations, Social Media, Strategic Planning/Research

Jon Pushkin *(Owner)*

Accounts:
Colorado Division of Insurance
RK Mechanical, Inc.

QORVIS COMMUNICATIONS
(Acquired by MSLGROUP & Name Changed to Qorvis MSLGROUP)

QORVIS MSLGROUP
(Formerly Qorvis Communications)
1201 Connecticut Ave NW Ste 500, Washington, DC 20036
Tel.: (202) 496-1000
Fax: (202) 496-1300
E-Mail: info@qorvis.com
Web Site: www.qorvis.com

Employees: 100
Year Founded: 2000

Agency Specializes In: Advertising, Communications, Government/Political, Graphic Design, Investor Relations, Public Relations, Sponsorship, Strategic Planning/Research

Michael J. Petruzzello *(Pres & Dir-Pub Affairs-Natl)*
Ron Faucheux *(Partner)*
Gregory Lagana *(Partner)*
Richard Masters *(Partner)*
Esther Thomas Smith *(Partner)*
Joe Chapman *(Mng Dir & VP)*
Jennifer Baskerville *(Mng Dir)*
Elissa Dodge *(Mng Dir)*
Ayal Frank *(Mng Dir)*
Susan Murphy *(Mng Dir)*
Stefan Nagey *(Mng Dir)*
Wyeth Ruthven *(Mng Dir)*
Stanley Collender *(Exec VP)*
D. Archibald Smart *(Exec VP-Social & Digital)*
Sheila McLean *(Sr VP & Dir-North American ECO Network)*
Shereen Soghier *(Sr VP)*
Keith Strubhar *(Sr VP)*
Cassie Elliot *(Mng Dir-Adv & Creative & VP)*
Sol Levine *(Sr Dir)*
Julia Kettle *(Mgr-HR)*
Adam Williams *(Sr Acct Supvr)*
Jennifer Crawford *(Acct Supvr)*
Ben Simmonds *(Acct Supvr-Geopolitical Solutions)*
Nedda Akhonbay *(Acct Exec)*
John Forristal *(Acct Exec)*
Philip Newland *(Acct Exec)*
Monica Khattar *(Asst Acct Exec)*
Julia Schroeder *(Asst Acct Exec)*

Accounts:
AAMCO Campaign: "Trust"
Adobe
Association of International Automobile Manufacturers
Beam Global Spirits & Wine Business & Trade Communications
BGR Consumer Awareness, Media Outreach, Media Relations, Messaging, Research, The Burger Joint
eBay
Embassy of Libya Public Relations
First Horizon Bank
Google
Gov 2.0 Expo
Kingdom of Saudi Arabia
LSU Medical Center Hospitals (pro bono)
Marca Pais Campaign: "MexicoToday"
Mount Vernon Estate and Gardens Campaign: "Website"
National Safety Council Advertising, Creative, Media Relations, MyCarDoesWhat.org, Strategies
Pearson Assessments
Pratt & Whitney
Raytheon
Smithsonian Craft Show
Society for Human Resources Management
The Sugar Association
SunRocket; Vienna, VA
Unitranche Fund LLC
University of Iowa Public Policy Center Creative, MyCarDoesWhat.org, Strategies
The Washington Animal Rescue League Consumer Marketing, Public & Media Relations
YouthAIDS (pro bono)

QUADRANT TWO PUBLIC RELATIONS
7000 JFK Blvd E Ste 25 I, Guttenberg, NJ 07093
Tel.: (646) 234-7196
E-Mail: info@q2pr.com
Web Site: www.q2pr.com

Employees: 7
Year Founded: 1994

Approx. Annual Billings: $850,000

Jose Manuel de Jesus *(Owner & Pres)*

QUINN & CO.
520 8th Ave 21st Fl, New York, NY 10018
Tel.: (212) 868-1900
Fax: (212) 465-0849
Web Site: www.quinn.pr

Employees: 40

National Agency Associations: COPF

Agency Specializes In: Brand Development & Integration, Crisis Communications, Food Service, Media Relations, Media Training, Product Placement, Public Relations, Publicity/Promotions, Real Estate, Sponsorship, Strategic Planning/Research

Florence I. Quinn *(Pres)*
John Frazier *(Exec VP)*
Morgan Painvin *(Sr VP & Deputy Dir)*
Qendresa Bicaj *(VP-HR)*
Sandra Hurtado *(VP)*
Cassandra Small *(VP)*
Alexa Harrison *(Acct Supvr)*
Gina Mazzone *(Sr Acct Exec)*
Lauren Watzich *(Sr Acct Exec)*
Kara McKenna *(Acct Exec)*
Brooke Shaughnessy *(Acct Exec)*

Accounts:
AKA Brand The Algonquin Hotel
Amway Grand Plaza
Flagstone Property Group, LLC (Public Relations Agency of Record)
New Orleans Marriott
Occidental Hotels & Resorts
The Westin New York at Times Square
Wildlife Conservation Society "96 Elephants", Public Relations
Wyndham Rewards

QUINN & HARY MARKETING
(Acquired by Regan Communications Group)

QUINN/BREIN COMMUNICATIONS
403 Madison Ave N Ste 101, Bainbridge Island, WA 98110
Tel.: (206) 842-8922
Fax: (206) 842-8909
E-Mail: ginger@quinnbrein.com
Web Site: www.quinnbrein.com

Employees: 4
Year Founded: 1979

Agency Specializes In: Consumer Marketing, Entertainment, Government/Political, High Technology, Public Relations, Publicity/Promotions, Travel & Tourism

Approx. Annual Billings: $1,000,000

Breakdown of Gross Billings by Media: Newsp.: $50,000; Pub. Rels.: $850,000; Radio: $100,000

Jeff Brein *(Pres)*
Ginger Vaughan *(Client Svcs Dir)*
Elizabeth Scott *(Dir-Market Res)*

Accounts:
Cardinal Logistics
The Grand Ole Opry
Old Farmer's Almanac; Dublin, NH; 1991

QUINN GILLESPIE & ASSOCIATES LLC
1133 Connecticut Ave NW 5th Fl, Washington, DC 20036
Tel.: (202) 457-1110
Fax: (202) 457-1130
E-Mail: jmanley@qga.com
Web Site: qga.com/

Employees: 32
Year Founded: 2000

Agency Specializes In: Government/Political, Planning & Consultation, Public Relations

Kevin Kayes *(Mng Dir)*
John Easton *(VP)*
Jim Manley *(Sr Dir)*
Christopher S. Brown *(Dir-Digital & Social Media Strategy)*
Drew Cole *(Dir-Govt Affairs)*
Michael Diroma *(Counsel & Dir)*
Mike Hussey *(Dir-Fin Svcs & Commerce)*
Sue Garman Kranias *(Dir-Comm Practice)*

Accounts:
ABF Freight Systems, Inc
Association for Information Protection
BNSF Railway
Broadway League
Cayman Finance
Genomatica Inc.
Knights of Columbus
Norwalk Community Health Center
Republic of Macedonia
American Hospital Association
Forest County Potawatomi Community
National Association of Realtors
PricewaterhouseCoopers LLC
Sony Corporation of America
T-Mobile US
Tyson Foods Inc.
Verizon
Verizon Wireless
Zurich Financial Services Corporation

QUIXOTE RESEARCH, MARKETING & PUBLIC RELATIONS
3107 Brassfield Rd, Greensboro, NC 27410
Tel.: (336) 605-0363
Fax: (336) 665-8137
E-Mail: cmattina@quixotegroup.com
Web Site: www.quixotegroup.com

Employees: 12
Year Founded: 1999

Agency Specializes In: Fashion/Apparel, Food Service

Chuck Mattina *(Owner)*
Lisa Kornblum *(Office Mgr)*
Jennifer Whisnant *(Sr Acct Exec)*
Emma Boyette *(Acct Exec)*
Jennifer Ferris *(Acct Exec)*
Renee Harvey *(Asst Acct Exec)*

Accounts:
Acce
CR Home
Detroit Diesel
Mederma
Pulaski
Unifi

R&J PUBLIC RELATIONS
1140 Rte 22 E Ste 200, Bridgewater, NJ 08807
Tel.: (908) 722-5757
Fax: (908) 722-5776
E-Mail: jlonsdorf@randjpr.com
Web Site: www.randjpr.com

Employees: 18
Year Founded: 1986

National Agency Associations: AMA-IABC-NJ Ad Club-PRSA

Agency Specializes In: Corporate Communications, Crisis Communications, Electronics, Health Care Services, Integrated Marketing, Investor Relations, Market Research, Media Planning, Media Relations, Medical Products, Public Relations, Publicity/Promotions, Social Marketing/Nonprofit, Viral/Buzz/Word of Mouth

Approx. Annual Billings: $2,650,000

Breakdown of Gross Billings by Media: Pub. Rels.: 100%

Scott Marioni *(Owner & Exec VP)*
John Lonsdorf *(Pres)*
Kyle Kappmeier *(Acct Dir)*
Tiffany Miller *(Acct Dir)*
John De Bellis *(Dir-Bus Dev)*
Danie Marzigliano *(Office Mgr)*
Tracey Benjamini *(Sr Acct Exec)*
Carlee Pett *(Sr Acct Exec)*
Nicholas Laplaca *(Acct Exec)*

Accounts:
Aerocrine, Inc. NIOX MINO, Public Relations
Amber Sky Home Mortgage Media Relations, PR, Social Media
American Properties Realty, Inc.; Iselin, NJ (Agency of Record)
Audio Bone (Agency of Record)
Berje; Bloomfield, NJ; 2008
BITS Limited; Northport, NY Media Relations, Public Relations, Publicity Campaign
Bogen Imaging
Coffee Bean Direct Brand Awareness, Brand Identity, PR
Cure Auto Insurance (Agency of Record)
Dancker, Sellew & Douglas Branding, Internal & External Communications, PR
Falcon Safety Products Dust-Off
GameChanger Products (Agency of Record) Audio Bone Headphones; 2008
HouseMaster; Bound Brook, NJ Home Inspection Services; 2007
Impact Unlimited
Integrity House
iPEC Media, Strategic PR
IPlay America & Encore Event Center; Freehold, NJ Media Relations, Public Relations
Jersey Artisan Distilling Brand Identity, Communication Strategy, PR
Manfrotto Distribution, Inc Public Relations Agency of Record
Mobelisk Brand Awareness, Brand Identity, PR
National Fire Sprinkler Association; 2006
NJ Fire Sprinkler Advisory Board; North Brunswick, NJ; 2006
NJ PURE (Agency of Record)
Novadebt
Ocean County Sports Medicine Digital Media, Public Relations, Social Media, Website Design
Polaroid Public Relations
Promark International Inc.; Bartlett, IL Cool-Lux, Norman, Photogenic, Public Relations, Smith-Victor
Raritan Bay Medical Center (Agency of Record)
Samsung
Somerset Medical Center; Somerville, NJ Digital Imaging Products, Far Hills Race Meeting, Sleep for Life; 2008
Somfy Systems, Inc.; Dayton, NJ Motors & Control Systems for Awnings, Blinds, Shutters, Public Relations
St. Francis Veterinary Center Public Relations
Torcon Construction Company; 1985
Trutek Corp.; Somerville, NJ (Agency of Record)
United Bank Card Payment & Transaction Processing; 2006
Vetstreet Inc (Public Relations Agency of Record) Brand Diagnostic, Media Relations
The Women's Center For Entrepreneurship Corporation Campaign: "We're Storming Back", Hurricane Sandy Disaster Relief Program, Media Relations, Public Relations, Social Media
Zebra Pen Corp Public Relations Agency of Record

R/P MARKETING PUBLIC RELATIONS
1500 Timberwolf Dr, Holland, OH 43528
Tel.: (419) 241-2221
Web Site: www.r-p.com

Agency Specializes In: Brand Development & Integration, Crisis Communications, Digital/Interactive, Media Relations, Media Training, Print, Public Relations, Radio, Social Media, Strategic Planning/Research

Martha Vetter *(Founder & CEO)*
Susan Cross *(VP-Strategic Comm)*
Allen Mireles *(VP-Client Svcs)*
Christina Carina *(Sr Dir-Strategic Comm)*
Diane Iannucci *(Sr Dir-Media)*
Jessica Lashley *(Sr Dir-Art)*
Andrea Durfey *(Acct Dir)*
Grant Cummings *(Dir-IT & Interactive)*
Valerie Vetter *(Supvr-Traffic)*
Jordan Stoll *(Acct Exec)*
Alex Hall *(Sr Graphic Designer)*
Shannon Minoske *(Planner-Event)*

Accounts:
Libbey, Inc.

RACEPOINT GLOBAL
(Formerly Racepoint Group, Inc.)
53 State St 4th Fl, Boston, MA 02109
Tel.: (617) 624-3200
Fax: (617) 624-4199
E-Mail: agencymarketing@racepointglobal.com
Web Site: racepointglobal.com

Employees: 125
Year Founded: 2003

Agency Specializes In: Health Care Services, High Technology, Public Relations, Publicity/Promotions

Larry Weber *(Chm & CEO)*
Karen Bouchard *(Chief HR Officer & Exec VP-Admin Ops)*
Daniel J. Carter, Jr. *(Mng Dir-North America & Exec VP)*
David Fonkalsrud *(Exec VP & Head-West Coast)*
Matt Bennett *(Sr VP & Head-DC Practice)*
Anne Potts *(Sr VP & Head-Corp Practice)*
John Gonnella *(Sr VP & Grp Dir-Creative)*
Madlene Olander *(Sr VP & Dir-Production Svcs)*
Cathy Pittham *(Mng Dir-Europe)*
Ani Jigarjian *(VP-Global Mktg & Bus Dev)*
Suzy Spillane-Hill *(VP-Media)*
Maureen Miller *(Acct Dir)*
Cassidy Lawson *(Sr Acct Exec)*

Accounts:
ARM
blocher
BlogHer
Cloud9 Analytics
Curaspan
Digital Globe
eHarmony
Evariant
Fanista; 2008
Gamma Medica
GenoSpace
Harmony
Healing for People
HealthEdge
Helicos Biosciences
Intelligent Energy Corporate Affairs, Fuel Cell Technology, Trade & Consumer PR
IST Energy
Jiff Inc.
NuGEN Inc.
Open Source Digital Voting Foundation
PC Helps
Plasma Surgical
Sagentia
ShareFile
SiCortex; 2008
Snapily
Sonus Networks
Spinal Modulation
Stanford Children's Health
taptu
TechSmith
Thermo Fisher Scientific Global PR, Social Media
Thing5
VolitionRx

Branches

Racepoint Global
(Formerly Racepoint Group Asia)
8th Floor The Broadway, 54-62 Lockhart Road, Wanchai, China (Hong Kong)
Tel.: (852) 3111 9988
Fax: (852) 3111 3312
Web Site: www.racepointglobal.com

Agency Specializes In: Public Relations

Andrew Laxton *(Exec VP & Mng Dir-Asia)*
Shijun Ma *(Sr VP)*
Vicky Neill *(VP)*
Xiaonan Wang *(Acct Mgr)*
Shirley Chan *(Sr Acct Exec)*
June Jin *(Sr Acct Exec)*
Edith Y. Chen *(Acct Exec)*
Yuxiao Chen Freyja *(Acct Coord)*
Dan Ma *(Acct Coord)*
Tallulah Song *(Acct Coord)*
Liang Zhao *(Acct Coord)*

Accounts:
Warrior Sports Media, Strategy Development

RAFFETTO HERMAN STRATEGIC COMMUNICATIONS LLC
500 Union St 330, Seattle, WA 98101
Tel.: (206) 264-2400
Web Site: www.rhstrategic.com

Agency Specializes In: Brand Development & Integration, Digital/Interactive, Internet/Web Design, Public Relations, Search Engine Optimization, Social Media

David C. Herman *(Pres)*
John K. Raffetto *(CEO)*
Jeremy Bartram *(VP)*
Jason Poos *(Dir-Mktg)*
Jack Kantelis *(Sr Acct Exec)*
Holly Zuluaga *(Sr Acct Exec)*
Anna Williford *(Acct Exec)*
Landen Zumwalt *(Acct Exec)*

Accounts:
Edifecs
MorphoTrust USA

Branch

Raffetto Herman
1400 Eye St NW 230, Washington, DC 20005
Tel.: (202) 379-0545
E-Mail: info@rhstrategic.com
Web Site: www.rhstrategic.com

Year Founded: 2007

Agency Specializes In: Brand Development & Integration, Digital/Interactive, Public Relations

Jennifer Boone Bemisderfer *(Mng Dir)*
Sarah R. Horowitz *(Sr Acct Exec)*

Accounts:
New-BoldIQ

RAKER GOLDSTEIN & CO.
180 Old Tappan Rd Ste 4 Bldg 3, Old Tappan, NJ 07675
Tel.: (201) 784-1818
Fax: (201) 784-1448
E-Mail: heidi@rakergoldstein.com
Web Site: www.rakergoldstein.com

Employees: 5
Year Founded: 1986

Agency Specializes In: Co-op Advertising, Corporate Identity, Event Planning & Marketing, Media Relations, Public Relations, Strategic Planning/Research

Heidi Raker Goldstein *(Founder & Pres)*
Stuart Goldstein *(Principal)*

Accounts:
Bonefish Grill
Holy Name Hospital
McCormick & Schmick's Seafood Restaurant
Whole Foods Market

RANDALL PR, LLC
4701 SW Admiral Way Ste 308, Seattle, WA 98116
Tel.: (206) 402-4328
Fax: (206) 467-0212
E-Mail: info@randallpr.com
Web Site: www.randallpr.com

Employees: 6
Year Founded: 2001

Agency Specializes In: Public Relations

Approx. Annual Billings: $750,000

Lori Randall *(Owner)*
Colin Baugh *(Acct Exec)*
Ginny Morey *(Copywriter)*

Accounts:
Barrio Restaurant; Seattle, WA; 2008
Cafe Flora; Seattle, WA; 2008
El Gaucho Steakhouse; Portland, OR; Seattle & Tacoma, WA; 2005
Esquin Wine Merchants; Seattle, WA; 2001
Inn at El Gaucho; Seattle, WA Restaurant
Purple Cafe & Wine Bar; Kirkland, WA; Woodinville, WA Restaurant

RANDLE COMMUNICATIONS
925 L St Ste 1275, Sacramento, CA 95814
Tel.: (916) 448-5802
Fax: (916) 448-5872
E-Mail: info@randlecommunications.com
Web Site: www.randlecommunications.com

Year Founded: 2001

Agency Specializes In: Communications, Crisis Communications, Media Relations, Public Relations, Social Media, Strategic Planning/Research

Jeff Randle *(Founder, Pres & CEO)*
Mitch Zak *(Partner)*
Margeaux Cardona *(Mng Dir)*
Kevin Riggs *(Sr VP)*
Ana Helman *(Dir-Strategic Alliances & Partnerships)*
Kellie Randle *(Dir-Special Projects)*
Erin Dunlay *(Acct Mgr)*
Mike Gazda *(Acct Mgr)*
Lindsey Goodwin *(Acct Mgr)*
Paige Bedegrew *(Sr Acct Exec)*

Accounts:
New-Golden State Water Company

RASKY BAERLEIN STRATEGIC COMMUNICATIONS
(Formerly Rasky Baerlein/Prism)
70 Franklin St 3rd Fl, Boston, MA 02110
Tel.: (617) 443-9933
Fax: (617) 443-9944
E-Mail: raskybaerlein@rasky.com
Web Site: www.rasky.com

Employees: 30
Year Founded: 1989

National Agency Associations: COPF

Agency Specializes In: Sponsorship

Joe Baerlein *(Pres)*
George F. Cronin *(Mng Dir)*
Ann Carter *(Principal)*
Bethany Bassett *(Sr VP)*
Justine Griffin *(Sr VP-Crisis Comm & Reputation Mgmt)*
Mark Horan *(Sr VP)*
Christopher Murphy *(Sr VP)*
Kristen Cullen *(Assoc VP)*
Harry-Jacques Pierre *(Assoc VP)*
Zach Stanley *(Assoc VP-Pub Affairs)*
Andy Hoglund *(Sr Acct Exec)*
Dianna Curry *(Acct Exec)*

Accounts:
The American Cancer Society, New England Division
Boston Bruins; 2005
Boston Center for Adult Education Public Relations
Boston Power
Caritas Christi Health Care Public Relations; 2008
EnergyConnect; 2008
Lasell College Public Relations
LoJack Corp.; 2006
MASCOMA
Massachusetts Institute of Technology
MasterCard International
MIT
Museum of Science; 2005
Northeastern
The Screening for Mental Health, Inc.
Valence Technology, Inc (Agency of Record)

RATIONAL 360, INC.
1828 L St NW Ste 640, Washington, DC 20036
Tel.: (202) 470-5337
E-Mail: info@rational360.com
Web Site: www.rational360.com

Agency Specializes In: Advertising, Crisis Communications, Media Buying Services, Public Relations, Strategic Planning/Research

Patrick Dorton *(Mng Partner)*
Peter Barden *(Partner)*
Brian Kaminski *(Partner)*
Don Marshall *(Partner)*
Beth Dozier *(VP)*
Brian Bartlett *(Sr Dir)*
Adelaide Annie Carter *(Dir-Ops)*
Rachelle Grey *(Strategist-Digital)*

Accounts:
Peter G. Peterson Foundation

RAVE COMMUNICATIONS INC
611 Wilson Ste 3B, Pocatello, ID 83201
Tel.: (208) 235-4270
Fax: (208) 235-4286
E-Mail: rave@ravecommunications.com
Web Site: www.ravecommunications.com

Agency Specializes In: Advertising, Digital/Interactive, Industrial, Public Relations

Greg Gunter *(Pres)*
John Wilford *(Mng Dir)*

Accounts:
J.R. Simplot Co Food Processing Services

RAZ PUBLIC RELATIONS
3101 Ocean Pk Blvd Ste 303, Santa Monica, CA 90405
Tel.: (310) 450-1482
Fax: (310) 450-5896
E-Mail: info@razpr.com
Web Site: www.razpr.com

Agency Specializes In: Event Planning & Marketing, Media Relations, Media Training, Public Relations, Social Media

Frances Ratliff *(Sr Acct Supvr)*
Katie Adams *(Acct Supvr)*
Shannon Deoul *(Acct Exec)*

Accounts:
New-Autodesk Media
New-Biscuit Filmworks
New-Shotgun Software
New-Wongdoddy

RBB PUBLIC RELATIONS
355 Alhambra Cir Ste 800, Miami, FL 33134
Tel.: (305) 448-7450
Fax: (305) 448-5027
E-Mail: christine.barney@rbbcommunications.com
Web Site: rbbcommunications.com

Employees: 22
Year Founded: 1975

National Agency Associations: COPF

Agency Specializes In: Digital/Interactive, Exhibit/Trade Shows, Public Relations, Publicity/Promotions, Sponsorship, Travel & Tourism

Tina R. Elmowitz *(Partner & Exec VP)*
Sandra Fine *(VP & Dir-Results Measurement)*
Susan Gilden *(VP)*
Robert C. Gill *(Sr Counsel & VP)*
Jeanine Karp *(VP)*
Abdul Muhammad *(VP-Digital Dev)*
Maite Velez-Couto *(VP)*
Shawn Warmstein *(VP)*
Julie Jimenez *(Acct Dir)*
Rafael Sangiovanni *(Producer-Digital & Social Media)*
Esther Griego *(Mgr-Creative Svcs)*
Kristy Kennedy *(Acct Supvr-Digital)*
Adriana Infante *(Sr Acct Exec)*
Stacy Merrick *(Sr Acct Exec)*
Luisa Yen *(Acct Exec)*
Amelia Gomez *(Acct Coord)*

Accounts:
Activ Doctors Online Media Outreach, Strategic Public Relations Campaign
AMResorts Campaign: "Choose Your Own Escape", Dreams Resorts & Spas, Secrets Resorts & Spas, Sunscape Resorts & Spas; 2008
Apple Leisure Group Media Relations, Public Relations
Arnstein & Lehr Public Relations
Ascendo Resources (Agency of Record)
Baltus Collection (Agency of Record) Brand Management, Media Outreach, Strategic Public Relations

Canyon Ranch Hotel & Spa; Miami Beach, FL (Agency of Record) Boutique Hotel
DubLi.com Marketing, Promotions, Strategic Public Relations
Florida Marlins
Florida Power & Light
Global Keratin
GolTV Consumer & Trade Awareness, PR
Home2 Suites
Homewood Suites Public Relations
Mars, Incorporated M&M's
PriceTravel Marketing, Media Outreach, Promotions Campaign, Strategic Public Relations
Sawgrass Mills (Agency of Record)
Starbucks Corporation
Verizon Wireless
New-VITAS Healthcare Corp. (Agency of Record) Media Relations, Public Relations

R.C. AULETTA & CO.

59 E 54th St, New York, NY 10022-4271
Tel.: (212) 355-0400
Fax: (212) 355-0835
Web Site: www.auletta.com

Employees: 5
Year Founded: 1965

Agency Specializes In: Brand Development & Integration, Broadcast, Business-To-Business, Communications, Consulting, Consumer Marketing, Consumer Publications, Direct Response Marketing, Event Planning & Marketing, Exhibit/Trade Shows, Fashion/Apparel, Financial, Food Service, Health Care Services, High Technology, Legal Services, Leisure, Medical Products, Planning & Consultation, Public Relations, Publicity/Promotions, Real Estate, Recruitment, Restaurant, Retail, Sports Market, Strategic Planning/Research, Travel & Tourism

Richard C. Auletta *(Pres)*
Brian Downey *(VP)*
Jason Solomon *(VP)*

Accounts:
The American Academy of Matrimonial Lawyers
New York Mets
Sterling Stamos

RCW MEDIA GROUP

11500 Tennessee Ave Ste 101, Los Angeles, CA 90064
Tel.: (323) 979-8417
E-Mail: info@rcwmediagroup.com
Web Site: www.rcwmediagroup.com

Agency Specializes In: Brand Development & Integration, Event Planning & Marketing, Public Relations, Strategic Planning/Research

Casandra Walker *(CEO)*
Shelby Stewart *(Jr Acct Mgr)*

Accounts:
Illume Spa

READE COMMUNICATIONS GROUP

850 Waterman Ave, Providence, RI 02915-0039
Mailing Address:
PO Box 15030, Providence, RI 02915
Tel.: (401) 433-7000
Fax: (401) 433-7001
Web Site: www.reade.com

E-Mail for Key Personnel:
President: creade@reade.com

Employees: 35
Year Founded: 1973

Agency Specializes In: Aviation & Aerospace, Business-To-Business, Engineering, High Technology, Industrial, Internet/Web Design, Pharmaceutical, Transportation

Approx. Annual Billings: $1,375,000

Breakdown of Gross Billings by Media: Adv. Specialities: $50,000; Bus. Publs.: $500,000; E-Commerce: $150,000; Foreign: $100,000; Internet Adv.: $500,000; Worldwide Web Sites: $75,000

Charles Reade, Jr. *(Gen Mgr-Sls)*
Karen Ramos *(Sls Mgr-Eastern Reg-Reade Advanced Materials)*
Steven Teixeira *(Coord-Sls)*

Accounts:
Boron, S.B., Ltd.; Chicago, IL Metals
Boy Scouts of America; Irving, TX
F.& A.M.-RI; East Providence, RI Fraternity
Harvard Business School Association-SENE; Providence, RI Alumni Group; 1998
Herreshoff Marine Museum; Bristol, RI America's Cup Hall of Fame
Nano Materials, Inc.; Burrington, RI Nano-Sized Inorganic Materials; 1996
Narragansett Boat Club; Providence, RI Community Service
Providence Preservation Society; Providence, RI Historical Preservations
Reade International Corp.; Riverside, RI Advanced Materials
Reynolds Metals Co.; Richmond, VA
Technical Specialties, Inc.; Bristol, RI Electronics; 1995
ULTRAM International; Denver, CO Nanocrystal Materials
Washington Mills Electro Minerals Corp.; North Grafton, MA High Tech Minerals

Branch

Reade West

(Formerly Reade Communications Group)
1680 O'Malley Dr, Sparks, NV 89501
Mailing Address:
PO Box 12820, Reno, NV 89434
Tel.: (775) 352-1000
Fax: (775) 352-1001
E-Mail: rcg@reade.com
Web Site: www.reade.com

Employees: 4
Year Founded: 1984

Agency Specializes In: Advertising, Automotive, Business-To-Business, Digital/Interactive, E-Commerce, High Technology, Identity Marketing, International, Internet/Web Design, Pharmaceutical, Technical Advertising

Bethany Satterfield *(VP & Reg Mgr-Reade Advanced Materials)*
Charles Reade *(Gen Mgr-Sls)*

RED BANYAN GROUP

1761 W Hillsboro Boulevard Ste 321, Deerfield Beach, FL 33442
Tel.: (954) 379-2115
E-Mail: info@redbanyan.com
Web Site: www.redbanyan.com

Agency Specializes In: Brand Development & Integration, Crisis Communications, Media Relations, Public Relations, Search Engine Optimization, Strategic Planning/Research

Robbin Lubbehusen *(VP)*

Accounts:
New-The Lerman Law Firm

RED ENERGY PUBLIC RELATIONS

100 E Saint Vrain St Ste 205, Colorado Springs, CO 80903
Tel.: (719) 465-3565
E-Mail: contactus@redenergypr.com
Web Site: www.redenergypr.com

Year Founded: 2008

Agency Specializes In: Advertising, Brand Development & Integration, Crisis Communications, Event Planning & Marketing, Exhibit/Trade Shows, Graphic Design, Media Training, Public Relations, Social Media, Strategic Planning/Research

Amy Sufak *(Founder & Pres)*
Vella Murch *(Acct Mgr-Svc)*
Cortney Quintero *(Mgr-Integrated Media)*
Ansley Eskind *(Graphic Designer-Multi-Media)*
Thomas Wright *(Sr Graphic Designer)*
Elena Daly *(Coord-Event)*

Accounts:
Peak Professional Contractors

RED HOUSE COMMUNICATIONS

1908 Sarah St, Pittsburgh, PA 15203
Tel.: (412) 481-7275
E-Mail: gblint@redhousecom.com
Web Site: www.redhousecomm.com

Agency Specializes In: Communications, Public Relations

Gloria Blint *(Pres & CEO)*
Terry McLane *(CFO & Gen Mgr)*
Pete Baird *(Dir-Media)*
Karen Lightell *(Dir-PR)*
Shawn Smith *(Assoc Dir-Creative & Art)*
Cherina Pelissier *(Sr Acct Mgr)*
Grace Calland *(Sr Acct Exec)*

Accounts:
M2M Project

RED JAVELIN COMMUNICATIONS INC

30 Pelham Island Rd, Sudbury, MA 01776
Tel.: (978) 440-8392
Fax: (978) 440-7032
E-Mail: info@redjavelin.com
Web Site: www.redjavelin.com

Agency Specializes In: Brand Development & Integration, Content, Corporate Identity, Crisis Communications, Media Relations, Public Relations, Social Media

Lisa Allocca *(Co-Founder & Principal)*
Dana Harris *(Co-Founder & Principal)*

Accounts:
M-Files

RED JEWELED MEDIA

10207 E Lk Dr, Englewood, CO 80111
Tel.: (303) 815-4043
Toll Free: (888) 552-0735
Web Site: www.redjeweledmedia.com

Year Founded: 2005

Agency Specializes In: Communications, Content, Media Relations, Public Relations, Social Media, T.V.

Jenny Levine Finke *(Founder & CEO)*
Anna Berry *(Specialist-PR)*

RED LIGHT PR
6525 Sunset Blvd 3rd Fl, Hollywood, CA 90028
Tel.: (323) 463-3160
E-Mail: info@redlightpr.com
Web Site: www.redlightpr.com

Year Founded: 2002

Agency Specializes In: Advertising, Digital/Interactive, Event Planning & Marketing, Public Relations, Social Media

Jen Phillips *(Founder & CEO)*
Matt Ambrose *(Dir-Showroom)*
Alexis Newman *(Dir-Fashion)*
Crystal Robles *(Mgr-Showroom)*
Marly Kos *(Acct Exec)*
Alexandria McGaughey *(Acct Exec)*

Accounts:
Lady Lux

RED PR
The Soho Bldg, New York, NY 10012
Tel.: (212) 431-8873
Fax: (212) 431-8906
E-Mail: red@red-pr.com
Web Site: www.red-pr.com

Year Founded: 2000

Agency Specializes In: Brand Development & Integration, Communications, Crisis Communications, Event Planning & Marketing, Graphic Design, Internet/Web Design, Media Relations, Media Training, Public Relations, Social Media

Julia Labaton *(Founder & Pres)*
Charity Guzofski *(VP)*
Courtney Frappier *(Acct Exec)*
Shreya Bhakta *(Acct Coord)*

Accounts:
Andrea DeSimone
Cricket Hair Tools
Gelish Gel-Polish
GROH
New-Louvelle Consumer Public Relations, US Media Relations
Morgan Taylor Professional Nail Lacquer Brand Visibility
Nail Harmony Inc. Brand Awareness, Gelish Soak-Off Gel Polish
Ouidad
Phuse
Preciosa Products
Ramy Beauty Therapy
Zotos Professional AGEbeautiful National PR Campaign, Product Awareness

RED SHOES PR
W6110 Aerotech Dr, Appleton, WI 54914
Tel.: (920) 574-3253
Web Site: www.redshoespr.com

Year Founded: 2008

Agency Specializes In: Content, Crisis Communications, Media Relations, Public Relations, Social Media

Lisa Cruz *(Founder & Pres)*
Vince Gallucci *(CMO)*
Kristina Flores *(VP-Mktg)*
Dian Johnson *(Office Mgr)*
Maria Nelson *(Sr Acct Exec)*
Deniz Cakmak *(Specialist-Creative Media)*
Meagan Hardwick *(Strategist-Client Solutions)*
Sara Montonati *(Strategist-Client Solutions)*

Accounts:
Catalpa Health

RED SKY PUBLIC RELATIONS
404 S 8th Street Suite 400, Boise, ID 83702
Tel.: (208) 953-1299
Fax: (208) 287-2198
Web Site: www.redskypr.com

Year Founded: 2008

Agency Specializes In: Advertising, Communications, Corporate Communications, Media Relations, Public Relations, Social Media, Strategic Planning/Research

Tracy Bresina *(CFO)*
Lynda Bruns *(VP-Client Svc)*
Amanda Watson *(Sr Acct Exec)*
Christina Lenkowski *(Acct Exec)*
Gloria Miller *(Acct Exec)*
Justin Nyquist *(Acct Exec)*
Sara Spencer *(Acct Exec)*
Amber Broeckel *(Acct Coord)*

Accounts:
Idaho STAR Motorcycle Safety Program Vehicle Training Center
Project Athena Foundation Organisation
Sunvalleyharvestfestival Hotels & Restaurants Services
Western States Equipment Agricultural & Industrial Equipment Dealers

REDCHIP COMPANIES, INC.
1017 Maitland Ctr Commons Blvd, Maitland, FL 32751
Fax: (407) 644-0758
Toll Free: (800) 733-2447
E-Mail: chrystina@redchip.com
Web Site: www.redchip.com

Employees: 25

Agency Specializes In: Advertising, Affiliate Marketing, Alternative Advertising, Brand Development & Integration, Business Publications, Business-To-Business, Catalogs, Communications, Consulting, Consumer Publications, Content, Customer Relationship Management, Email, Event Planning & Marketing, Exhibit/Trade Shows, Financial, Graphic Design, Internet/Web Design, Investor Relations, Market Research, Media Buying Services, Media Relations, Multimedia, Newspapers & Magazines, Podcasting, Public Relations, Radio, Sponsorship, Strategic Planning/Research, T.V., Telemarketing

Revenue: $10,000,000

Dave Gentry *(Pres & CEO)*
Jon Cunningham *(VP & Dir-IR)*
Mike Bowdoin *(VP)*
Paul Kuntz *(Dir-Comm)*
Thomas Pfister *(Dir-Res)*
Philip Van De Walker *(Dir-IT)*

Accounts:
ONE Bio, Corp.; Miami, FL Public & Investor Relations

REDPOINT MARKETING PUBLIC RELATIONS INC.
161 Ave of the Americas Ste 1305, New York, NY 10013
Tel.: (212) 229-0119
Fax: (212) 229-0364
E-Mail: info@redpointpr.com
Web Site: www.redpointpr.com

Employees: 15
Year Founded: 2002

Agency Specializes In: Sponsorship

Victoria Feldman de Falco *(Owner)*
Christina Miranda *(Principal)*
Ross Evans *(Dir-Integrated Mktg)*
Gina Dolecki *(Acct Supvr)*
Gina Sisco *(Acct Supvr)*
Elizabeth Carty *(Acct Exec)*
Stephanie Strommer *(Acct Coord)*

Accounts:
Affinia Hotels
Crock-Pot Tools
Cunard Line
Denihan Hospitality Group
Loews Philadelphia Hotel; Philadelphia, PA
Oceania Cruises
Outrigger Hotels & Resorts
Prestige Cruise Holdings (Agency of Record) Media Relations, Oceania Cruises, Regent Seven Seas Cruises, Social Media
Saybrook Point Inn & Spa
Simon Pearce
SYTA Youth Foundation
The Woodstock Inn & Resort

REED PUBLIC RELATIONS
1720 W End Ave Ste 320, Nashville, TN 37203
Tel.: (615) 645-4320
Web Site: www.reedpublicrelations.com

Agency Specializes In: Content, Crisis Communications, Event Planning & Marketing, Media Relations, Media Training, Public Relations, Social Media, Strategic Planning/Research

Lauren Reed *(Pres)*
Katie Adkisson *(Partner & VP-Acct Svcs)*
Beth Neil *(Sr Acct Mgr)*
Raven Brajdic *(Acct Mgr)*
Jennifer Brake *(Acct Mgr)*

Accounts:
New-O'Charley's
New-TBHC Delivers

REEVES LAVERDURE PUBLIC RELATIONS
7820 Glades Rd Ste 275, Boca Raton, FL 33434-4177
Tel.: (561) 483-7040
Fax: (561) 750-6818
E-Mail: dreeves@reevespr.com
Web Site: www.reevespr.com

Employees: 3
Year Founded: 1994

Agency Specializes In: Brand Development & Integration, Crisis Communications, Event Planning & Marketing, Media Relations, Media Training, Public Relations, Publicity/Promotions, Viral/Buzz/Word of Mouth

David Reeves *(Pres)*
Diana Laverdure *(VP)*

Accounts:
Association Financial Services
Bauman Medical Group
Bryason Realty Corporation
CHB Industries
Cutco
James DiGeorgia & Associates
Kadey Krogen
RV Sales of Broward
Shapiro, Blasi, Wasserman & Gora P.A.
Stanton Chase
True World

Public Relations Firms

Walker Design & Construction

REGAN COMMUNICATIONS GROUP
106 Union Wharf, Boston, MA 02109
Tel.: (617) 488-2800
Fax: (617) 488-2830
E-Mail: info@regancomm.com
Web Site: www.regancomm.com

Employees: 30

Agency Specializes In: Direct Response Marketing, Government/Political, Media Buying Services, Public Relations, Sponsorship, Strategic Planning/Research

Alan Eisner *(Pres)*
Paula Gates *(Sr VP & Head-Bus)*
Stacy Wilbur *(Sr VP)*
Scott Mackenzie *(VP)*
Elizabeth Raflowitz *(Dir-Creative Svcs & Acct Supvr)*
Jason Allegrezza *(Mgr-Fin)*
Ira Kantor *(Sr Acct Exec)*
Elizabeth Brabants *(Acct Exec)*
Megan McKay *(Acct Exec)*
Carolyn Rasley *(Acct Exec)*
Katelyn O'Sullivan *(Acct Coord)*

Accounts:
Bank of America
Be Bold, Be Bald!
Besito Mexican Restaurant
Boston Celtics
Boston Park Plaza Hotel
Classic Harbor Line
FitHouse
Friendly's Ice Cream
Legal Sea Foods
Malcolm Baldrige Foundation Marketing, PR
Mintz Levin
Mix 985
Mohegan Sun
New England Center for Homeless Veterans
Ninety Nine
Randolph Engineering, Inc. Brand Awareness, PR
Restaurant City
SBLI
Simon Malls
StairMaster
Sufflok
Weeli Com
Willowbend Real Estate & Country Club; Mashpee, MA Public Relations

Branches

Pierce-Cote Advertising
911 Main St, Osterville, MA 02655-2015
(See Separate Listing)

Quinn & Hary Marketing
PO Box 456, New London, CT 06320
(See Separate Listing)

Regan Communications Group
270 S Central Blvd Ste 200B, Jupiter, FL 33458
Tel.: (561) 935-9953
Web Site: www.regancomm.com

Employees: 50

Agency Specializes In: Consulting, Crisis Communications, Media Relations, Media Training, Public Relations

George K. Regan *(Chm)*
Alan Eisner *(Pres)*
Mariellen Burns *(Chief Strategy Officer)*
Casey Sherman *(Pres-Regan Mktg)*
Lisa Doucet-Albert *(Sr VP)*
Sandrine Sebag *(Sr VP)*
Erin Tracy *(Sr VP-New York City)*
Joanna Roffo *(VP)*
Marci Tyldsley *(VP)*
Kate Barba *(Acct Dir)*

Accounts:
Legal Sea Foods
Suffolk Construction

Regan Communications Group
127 Dorrance St 4th Fl, Providence, RI 02903
Tel.: (401) 351-8855
Fax: (401) 751-3305
E-Mail: gregan@regancomm.com
Web Site: regancomm.com/

Employees: 4

Agency Specializes In: Public Relations

Mariellen Burns *(Chief Strategy Officer)*
Lisa Doucet *(Sr VP)*
Diane E. Mcpherson *(VP & Sr Acct Exec)*
Kate Barba Murphy *(VP)*
Samantha Marsh *(Acct Dir)*

Accounts:
Bank of America
Biogen Idec
Boston Celtics
Boston Magazine
Dunkin Donuts
Equinox
Mohegan Sun
Remax
Twenty-Two Bowen's

REIDY COMMUNICATIONS
447 Manzanita Ave, Corte Madera, CA 94925-1517
Tel.: (415) 891-8300
Fax: (415) 532-2521
E-Mail: info@reidycommunications.com
Web Site: www.reidycommunications.com

Agency Specializes In: Media Relations, Media Training, Public Relations, Strategic Planning/Research

Dan Reidy *(Principal)*
Jen Reidy *(Principal)*
Bronwyn Saglimbeni *(Principal)*

Accounts:
Health Integrated Inc
Interwoven
Neoforma
Onyx Software
Out Systems
Rogue Wave Software, Inc Software Solutions
RPX Corporation
Vitria

THE REILLY GROUP COMMUNICATIONS, INC.
150 N Michigan Ave Ste 2800, Chicago, IL 60601
Tel.: (773) 348-3800
Fax: (773) 348-7119
Web Site: www.reillyconnect.com

Employees: 7
Year Founded: 1997

Agency Specializes In: Public Relations

Susan J. Reilly *(Pres)*
Lydia Bishop *(Acct Supvr)*
Zach Reboletti *(Strategist-Internet Mktg)*
William Richardson *(Specialist-Multi-Media Production)*

Accounts:
Uno Pizzeria and Grill Advertising, Brand Activations, Creative Development, Radio, Television

REINGOLD, INC.
433 E Monroe Ave, Alexandria, VA 22301
Tel.: (202) 333-0400
Web Site: www.reingold.com

Year Founded: 1985

Agency Specializes In: Communications, Digital/Interactive, Internet/Web Design, Media Relations, Public Relations, Social Media, Strategic Planning/Research

Janet Reingold *(Founder)*
Michael Akin *(Pres)*
Kevin Miller *(Partner & Principal)*
Joseph Ney *(Partner & Dir-Creative)*
Jack Benson *(Partner & Bus Mgr)*
Amy Squire Buckley *(Principal)*
Doug Gardner *(VP-Web & Tech)*
Joseph Lamountain *(VP)*
Lynn Schneider-Sullivan *(VP)*
Barbara Wells *(VP)*
Glenn Heitz *(Assoc Dir-Creative)*

Accounts:
The Department of Veterans Affairs

RELEVANCE NEW YORK
150 W 30th St Ste 901, New York, NY 10001
Tel.: (212) 920-7057
E-Mail: hello@relevancenewyork.com
Web Site: www.relevancenewyork.com

Agency Specializes In: Brand Development & Integration, Digital/Interactive, Public Relations, Search Engine Optimization, Social Media, Strategic Planning/Research

Suzanne Rosnowski *(Founder & CEO)*

Accounts:
New-Blue Star Jets
New-Pinkwater Select

RELEVANT PUBLIC RELATIONS, LLC
1535 Richmond Ave, Staten Island, NY 10314
Tel.: (718) 682-1509
E-Mail: info@relevantpr.com
Web Site: www.relevantpr.com

Year Founded: 2009

Agency Specializes In: Brand Development & Integration, Email, Internet/Web Design, Media Relations, Multimedia, Print, Public Relations, Radio, Social Media, T.V.

Barton Horowitz *(Pres)*
Stephannia F. Cleaton *(Dir-National & Media Comm)*

Accounts:
Dr. Victoria Veytsman
Provence Public Relations

REMARKABLE PENDRAGON
(Formerly Pendragon PR)
Imperial Court 2 Exchange Quay, Manchester, M5 3EB United Kingdom
Tel.: (44) 161 359 4100
Fax: (44) 161 288 2880
Web Site: remarkablependragon.co.uk

Amy Hopkinson *(Sr Acct Dir)*
Richard Bowen *(Acct Dir)*
Will Morgan *(Acct Dir)*
Carole Riley *(Acct Dir)*
Rebekah Shepherd *(Acct Dir-Pub Affairs)*
Jamie Gordon *(Dir-Infrastructure & Energy)*
Mike Tamlyn *(Dir-Creative)*
Josh Owens *(Sr Acct Mgr)*
Patrice Henson *(Acct Mgr)*

REMEDY COMMUNICATIONS
6242 Ferris Sq, San Diego, CA 92121
Tel.: (858) 366-4827
E-Mail: info@remedypr.com
Web Site: www.remedypr.com

Year Founded: 2011

Agency Specializes In: Event Planning & Marketing, Media Relations, Public Relations, Social Media

Todd Backus *(Dir-Clients)*

Accounts:
Ridegemont Outfitters Public Relations
SPY Inc

REPUTATION LIGHTHOUSE
(Formerly Caver Public Relations)
14900 Avery Ranch Blvd Ste C 200-307, Austin, TX 78717
Tel.: (512) 832-8588
Fax: (512) 218-8707
E-Mail: info@replighthouse.com
Web Site: www.replighthouse.com

Year Founded: 2003

Agency Specializes In: Corporate Communications, Crisis Communications, Event Planning & Marketing, Media Relations, Promotions, Public Relations, Sponsorship, Strategic Planning/Research

Bonnie Caver *(Pres)*
Russell Caver *(VP-Strategic Plng & Brand)*

RESOLUTE PR
1441 S Carson Ave Ste 200, Tulsa, OK 74119
Tel.: (918) 212-9914
E-Mail: info@resolutepr.com
Web Site: www.resolutepr.com

Agency Specializes In: Advertising, Brand Development & Integration, Event Planning & Marketing, Internet/Web Design, Logo & Package Design, Media Buying Services, Media Relations, Public Relations, Radio, Social Media

Nicole Morgan *(CEO)*
Ally Lightle *(Acct Exec)*

Accounts:
Bios Corporation

RESONANCE PR
6664 E Green Lk Way, Seattle, WA 98103
Tel.: (206) 369-2612
Web Site: www.resonance-pr.com

Agency Specializes In: Brand Development & Integration, Crisis Communications, Exhibit/Trade Shows, Graphic Design, Internet/Web Design, Media Planning, Media Training, Public Relations, Social Media, Strategic Planning/Research

Ralph Fascitelli *(Principal)*
Jamie Markopoulos *(Acct Exec)*

Accounts:
Fierce Inc.
SquareHub
Visible Brands

RESOUND MARKETING
100 Canal Pointe Blvd Ste 204, Princeton, NJ 08540
Tel.: (609) 279-0050
Fax: (877) 505-2258
Toll Free: (877) 505-2258
E-Mail: makesomenoise@resoundmarketing.com
Web Site: www.resoundmarketing.com

Employees: 4
Year Founded: 2003

Agency Specializes In: Public Relations

Kevin McLaughlin *(Principal)*
Marni Bahniuk *(VP)*
Vanessa Giacoppo *(Acct Dir)*
Ashley Willis *(Sr Acct Exec)*
Daniel Capawana *(Acct Exec)*
Marissa Dursin *(Acct Exec)*
Alexis Hankh *(Acct Exec)*
Sara Preto *(Acct Exec)*

Accounts:
Antepo, Inc.
Archi-Tech Systems
Babble
Baby Talk
CampHill Foundation
Connections Cafe
Cool Mom Picks
DIFRwear (Agency of Record) Media
Dipe n' Go (Agency of Record)
FOX News
Good.Co Public Relations
Green Guide
Kiwi
Martha
NBC TODAY show
Parenting
Parents
Real Estate.com
Real Simple
Revelation Generation
Salt Creek Grille
SHL (Agency of Record) Analyst Relations, Media Relations
Smiling Planet (Agency of Record)
THISA (Trusted Healthcare Information Solutions Alliance); 2005
Thrive
Today
TreeHugger
USA Today
XStreamHD

REVOLUTION PUBLIC RELATIONS
2345 SE Ivon St, Portland, OR 97202
Tel.: (503) 380-8292
Fax: (503) 233-1452
E-Mail: rebecca@revolutionpr.com
Web Site: www.revolutionpr.com

Employees: 5

Agency Specializes In: Communications, Public Relations, Strategic Planning/Research

Rebecca Haas *(Principal)*
Jennifer Karkar Ritchie *(Principal)*
Cheryl Cink *(Acct Mgr)*
Angie Malpass *(Acct Mgr)*
Shauna Nuckles *(Acct Exec)*

Accounts:
Art with Heart
Attenex
Backyard Box
Bakon Vodka
Clementine
DepotPoint
Fresh Bistro
kaarsKoker
Noetix
Sleep Country USA
Taco Del Mar

RF BINDER
950 3rd Ave, New York, NY 10022
Tel.: (212) 994-7600
Fax: (212) 994-7541
E-Mail: cynthia.rhea@rfbinder.com
Web Site: www.rfbinder.com

Employees: 80
Year Founded: 2001

Agency Specializes In: Sponsorship

Amy Binder *(CEO)*
Josh Gitelson *(Exec Mng Dir & Head-Boston)*
Atalanta Rafferty *(Exec Mng Dir)*
David Weinstock *(Chief Creative Officer)*
Linda Perry-Lube *(Chief Digital Officer)*
Nicole Carrasco *(Mng Dir-Creative & Production)*
Heath Fradkoff *(Sr Dir)*
Taylor McGrann *(Mgr)*

Accounts:
Ameriprise; 2006
Cargill; 2007
CVS Health; 2010
Dunkin' Donuts; 2005
edX; 2013
German Wine Institute; 2005
Johnson & Johnson; 2003
Talenti Gelato & Sorbetto; 2011

RFPR, INC.
6399 Wilshire Blvd Ste 412, Los Angeles, CA 90048
Tel.: (323) 933-4646
Fax: (323) 933-5229
E-Mail: Rfpr@rf-pr.com
Web Site: www.rf-pr.com

Year Founded: 2002

Agency Specializes In: Brand Development & Integration, Media Planning, Print, Product Placement, Public Relations

Zack Tanck *(Acct Exec)*

Accounts:
Capriotti's
Chocolate Box Cafe
Crustacean Restaurant
Dockers
Ecogear
KPG Solutions Inc
Mercedes-Benz

RHINO PUBLIC RELATIONS
2 Bittersweet Ln, South Hamilton, MA 01982
Tel.: (978) 985-4541
Fax: (978) 560-0617
Web Site: www.rhinopr.com

Year Founded: 2004

Agency Specializes In: Advertising, Brand Development & Integration, Collateral, Logo & Package Design, Media Relations, Media Training, Promotions, Public Relations, Social Media

Susan Shelby *(Pres & CEO)*
Michele Spiewak *(Acct Dir)*

Accounts:
Integrated Interiors, Inc.

RHUMBLINE COMMUNICATIONS

254 Commercial St Ste 105, Portland, ME 04101
Tel.: (207) 450-9943
E-Mail: info@rhumblinecommunications.com
Web Site: rhumblinecom.com

Year Founded: 2011

Agency Specializes In: Advertising, Brand Development & Integration, Internet/Web Design, Public Relations, Social Media

Nicole Jacques *(Owner & Strategist-Mktg)*

Accounts:
Brooklin Boat Yard, Inc.
Front Street Shipyard
Maine Built Boats
Rockport Marine, Inc.
Southport Boats
W-Class Yacht Company

RIALTO COMMUNICATIONS

2003 Western Ave Ste 600, Seattle, WA 98121
Tel.: (206) 599-6099
Fax: (888) 823-6476
E-Mail: info@rialtocommunications.com
Web Site: www.rialtocommunications.com

Year Founded: 2003

Agency Specializes In: Brand Development & Integration, Corporate Identity, Public Relations

Peter B. Summerville *(Founder)*

Accounts:
3DGrid
CHITA
Cortex Medical Management Systems
eSurg.com
HealthKey
iMedica
Pacific Telecom
Stevens Healthcare
T-Mobile US

RICHARDS PARTNERS

8750 N Central Expy Ste 1100, Dallas, TX 75231-6430
Tel.: (214) 891-5700
Fax: (214) 891-5230
E-Mail: ruth_fitzgibbons@richards.com
Web Site: www.richardspartners.com

Employees: 25
Year Founded: 1994

National Agency Associations: 4A's-WOMMA

Agency Specializes In: Advertising, Affluent Market, Bilingual Market, Brand Development & Integration, Broadcast, Business-To-Business, Collateral, Communications, Consulting, Consumer Goods, Consumer Marketing, Corporate Communications, Corporate Identity, Digital/Interactive, Direct Response Marketing, Event Planning & Marketing, Financial, Graphic Design, Health Care Services, Hispanic Market, In-Store Advertising, Integrated Marketing, Investor Relations, Logo & Package Design, Luxury Products, Magazines, Media Relations, Media Training, Newspaper, Newspapers & Magazines, Outdoor, Point of Purchase, Point of Sale, Print, Public Relations, Publicity/Promotions, Real Estate, Restaurant, Retail, Sales Promotion, Social Marketing/Nonprofit, Strategic Planning/Research, Teen Market, Travel & Tourism

Approx. Annual Billings: $10,000,000

Scot Dykema *(CFO)*
Dave Allen *(Principal)*
Scott Crockett *(Principal)*
Ruth Miller Fitzgibbons *(Principal)*
Cort Gorman *(Principal-Brand Media)*
Pete Lempert *(Principal)*
George McCane *(Principal)*
Mary Price *(Principal-Brand Media)*
Kyle Sawai *(Principal)*
Brian Schadt *(Principal)*
Chad Strohl *(Principal-Brand Mgmt)*
Brad Todd *(Principal)*
Rod Ulrich *(Principal)*
Stephanie Vander Linden *(Principal-Brand Mgmt)*
Rob Vangorden *(Principal)*
Rhonda Zahnen *(Principal)*
Sue Batterton *(Grp Head-Creative)*
David Canright *(Grp Head-Creative)*
Gary Gibson *(Grp Head-Creative)*
Tina Johnson *(Grp Head-Creative)*
Tim Tone *(Grp Head-Creative)*
Jeff Armstrong *(Grp Dir-Media)*
Shannon Haydel *(Grp Dir-Media)*
Jaquie Hoyos *(Grp Dir-Media)*
Michael Stagner *(Grp Dir-Media)*
Leslie Tucker *(Grp Dir-Media)*
Mike LaTour *(Sr Dir-Art)*
Matt Butcher *(Brand Dir-Plng)*
Kyle Kelley *(Brand Dir-Creative & Art)*
Dave Snell *(Brand Dir-Plng)*
Emily Taylor *(Brand Dir-Creative & Art)*
Danny Bryan *(Dir-Creative & Writer)*
Steve Grimes *(Dir-Creative & Copywriter)*
Ira Berger *(Dir-Natl Brdcst)*
Sarah Brandon *(Dir-Art)*
Dan Case *(Dir-Art)*
Andy Coulston *(Dir-Art)*
Ron Henderson *(Dir-Creative)*
Lynda Hodge *(Dir-Creative & Art)*
John Keehler *(Dir-Digital Strategy & Emerging Platforms)*
Scott Luther *(Dir-Digital Strategy)*
David Morring *(Dir-Creative)*
Sara Sax *(Dir-Bus Affairs)*
Kristen Scialo *(Dir-Art)*
Dave Stone *(Dir-Art)*
Todd Unruh *(Dir-Digital Strategy)*
Ben Allison *(Brand Mgr)*
Elaine Hirsch *(Brand Mgr)*
Jeffrey Lefkovits *(Brand Mgr)*
Megan Maloney *(Brand Mgr)*
Lucie Prann *(Supvr-Brdcst Negotiating)*
Mallory Rynish *(Supvr-Brand Media)*
Alyssa Waters *(Specialist-Brand Media & Planner-Search Engine)*
Jamie Alvrus *(Strategist-Digital)*
Garrett Bruster *(Strategist-Digital & Social Media)*
Nicholas Daigle *(Strategist-Digital)*
Kylie Kagen *(Strategist-Social)*
Tyler Norton *(Strategist-Social Media)*
Cory O'Brien *(Strategist-Digital)*
Brennen Schlueter *(Strategist-Digital)*
Stephanie Wierwille *(Strategist-Digital)*
Steve Terjeson *(Sr Analyst-Digital)*
Nikki Bayer *(Media Buyer)*
Alexis Crowell *(Copywriter)*
Kayla Dietz *(Media Planner)*
Myia Driscoll *(Planner-Brand)*
Jamie Harms *(Media Planner-Brand)*
Andria Kushan *(Copywriter)*
Samuel Moore *(Planner-Brand)*
Mallorie Rodak *(Planner-Brand)*
Jordan Tatman *(Media Planner-Brand)*
Bonner Voss *(Planner-Brand)*
Connie Andrews *(Coord-Creative & Media)*
Sharron Cole *(Coord-Travel)*
Stuart Hill *(Sr Writer)*

Accounts:
AbitibiBowater (Paper Retriever); Houston, TX Paper Recycling; 2009
Advance Auto Parts
AFI DALLAS International Film Festival
American Heart Association; Dallas, TX
Anderson Erickson Dairy
Behringer Harvard; Addison, TX Real Estate Investments; 2005
Belo Corporation
Buoniconti Fund
CEC Entertainment, Inc. Chuck E Cheese's
Center for BrainHealth; Dallas, TX Scientific Institute for Cutting Edge Brain Research; 2009
Central Dallas Ministries; Dallas, TX Faith Based Non-Profit Organization; 2008
Children's Medical Center; Dallas, TX Not-for-Profit Hospital; 1994
Clarkson Davis; Dallas, TX Management Consulting Service; 2010
Click Here Public Relations; Dallas, TX Digital Affiliate of The Richards Group; 2008
Cooper Aerobics; Dallas, TX Health Facility; 2010
Dallas Children's Chorus: Pro Bono; Dallas, TX
Dallas Citizens Council; Dallas, TX; 1993
Dallas Convention & Visitors Bureau; Dallas, TX; 2005
The Dallas Foundation; Dallas, TX; 1996
Dallas Marathon
Dallas Morning News; Dallas, TX Newspaper; 2005
Dallas White Rock Marathon; Dallas, TX Marathon; 2008
Dixon Ticonderoga; Heathrow, FL Art Supplies; 2005
Donor Bridge; Dallas, TX Non-Profit Database; 2007
Dr Pepper
FCA US LLC
Flexjet
Giant Eagle
Goody's
Honeywell Consumer Product Group; Danbury, CT; 2010
Hyatt Regency
Jason International
Jones Lang LaSalle; Chicago, IL Global Real Estate Services Firm; 2007
Lifeline Skin Care Inc. (Agency of Record)
MD Anderson; Dallas, TX Cancer Treatment Facility; 1998
Nomacorc; Zubulon, NC Manufacturer of Synthetic Wine Closures; 2007
Parkland Hospital; Dallas, TX Non-Profit Hospital
The Patron Spirits Company; Las Vegas, NV Premium Tequila & Spirits
Personal Communication Devices (PCD); Hauppauge, NY Manufacturer of Wireless Devices; 2010
Pilot Pens; Jacksonville, FL Manufacturer of Writing Instruments; 2010
Planned Parenthood; New York, NY Health Service Provider; 2010
Recreation Vehicle Industry Association Go Rving
Reunion Tower
The Salvation Army Public Relations
Sub-Zero/Wolf Appliances; Madison, WI Home Appliances; 2001
ThyssenKrupp Elevator; Frisco, TX Elevator Manufacturer; 2006

RICHESON COMMUNICATIONS LLC

37 N Orange Ave Ste 500, Orlando, FL 32801
Tel.: (407) 616-8108
Web Site: www.prfirmorlando.com

Agency Specializes In: Brand Development & Integration, Event Planning & Marketing, Media Relations, Promotions, Public Relations

Laura Richeson *(Principal)*

Accounts:
Aerosim Flight Academy

RICHMOND PUBLIC RELATIONS
1411 4th Ave Ste 610, Seattle, WA 98101
Tel.: (206) 682-6979
Fax: (206) 682-7062
E-Mail: general@richmondpublicrelations.com
Web Site: www.richmondpr.com

Employees: 15
Year Founded: 1992

Agency Specializes In: Public Relations

Lorne Richmond *(CEO & Partner)*
Elizabeth Richmond *(COO)*
Kimberly French *(Acct Dir)*

Accounts:
CondoCompare, Inc.
Joey's Restaurant
Sencadia
The Sheraton Hotel & Towers
Tom Douglas Restaurant
Tulalip Resort Casino

RIGGS PARTNERS
750 Meeting St, West Columbia, SC 29169
Tel.: (803) 799-5972
Fax: (803) 779-8447
E-Mail: info@riggspartners.com
Web Site: www.riggspartners.com

Employees: 8
Year Founded: 1987

National Agency Associations: Second Wind Limited

Agency Specializes In: Public Relations

Ryon Edwards *(Partner & Designer)*
Tom Barr *(Partner)*
Cathy Monetti *(Partner)*
Kevin Smith *(Partner)*
Kevin Archie *(Art Dir)*
Michael Powelson *(Dir-Creative)*
Katy Miller *(Acct Mgr)*
Jillian Owens *(Specialist-Digital Mktg)*
Alexandra Frazier *(Copywriter)*

Accounts:
Atherton Baptist Homes
Central Carolina Community Foundation
Girl Scouts of South Carolina
Goodwill Industries of Upstate
Protection and Advocacy for People with Disabilities Campaign: "Dennis"
Yesterdays Restaurant

RINCK ADVERTISING
Two Great Falls Plz Unit 8 6th Fl, Auburn, ME 04210
Tel.: (207) 755-9470
Fax: (207) 755-9473
E-Mail: info@rinckadvertising.com
Web Site: www.rinckadvertising.com

Employees: 20

Laura Davis *(Owner)*
Peter Rinck *(CEO)*
Lawrence Rinck *(Chief Inspiration Officer)*
Karly Eretzian *(VP-Creative Svcs)*
Katie Greenlaw *(Dir-PR)*
Sue Schenning *(Dir-Art)*
Vicky Ayer *(Media Planner & Media Buyer)*
Mariah Rinck *(Media Planner)*
Cathy Brezinski *(Coord-Traffic)*

Accounts:
American Beverage Corporation
Amtrak Downeaster
Bluewater Sea Foods
Daily's Cocktails
Dean Foods Company
Dempsey Challenge
Garelick Farms, LLC
The Gorton Group
Green Mountain Coffee Roasters, Inc.
Harvey
Hope & Healing
iParty
Lehigh Valley
Little Hug Fruit Barrels
Maine Cancer Foundation
McDonald's
Norway Savings Bank
Over the Moon
Owner/Operator Association
The Patrick Dempsey Center for Cancer
Tuscan Dairy Farms
University of Southern Maine

RIPLEY PR LLC
200 E Broadway Ave Ste 515, Maryville, TN 37804
Tel.: (865) 977-1973
Web Site: www.ripleypr.com

Year Founded: 2013

Agency Specializes In: Content, Corporate Communications, Event Planning & Marketing, Media Relations, Media Training, Promotions, Public Relations, Social Media, Strategic Planning/Research

Heather Ripley *(Pres & CEO)*
Jonathan Haskell *(Dir-Client Svc)*
Kim Travis *(Specialist-HR & Ops)*
Logan Utsman *(Acct Exec)*
Grayson James *(Jr Acct Mgr)*
Morgan Neal *(Jr Acct Mgr)*

Accounts:
Cherokee Millwright, Inc.

RL PUBLIC RELATIONS + MARKETING
11835 W Olympic Blvd Ste 1155E, Los Angeles, CA 90064
Tel.: (310) 473-4422
Fax: (310) 473-5833
E-Mail: roxana.lissa@rlpublicrelations.com
Web Site: www.rlpublicrelations.com

Agency Specializes In: Public Relations, Sponsorship

Roxana Lissa *(Founder & Pres)*
Mario Flores *(Partner & Mng Dir-Sportive)*
Bob Berry *(CFO)*
Ana Ceron *(Sr Acct Supvr)*
Susana Nunez *(Sr Acct Exec)*
Miguel Lopez *(Acct Exec)*

Accounts:
Delta Air Lines, Inc.
Fresh & Easy Neighborhood Market
Fuji Film
GlaxoSmithKline
MercuryMedia
National Honey Board
Nike
Sea World Parks & Entertainment
Umbral
Yager

Branch

RL Public Relations + Marketing
27 W 24th St Ste 901, New York, NY 10010
Tel.: (212) 206-8668
Fax: (212) 206-8778
E-Mail: melissa.smith@rlpublicrelations.com
Web Site: www.rlpublicrelations.com

Employees: 5

Roxana Lissa *(Founder & Pres)*
Mario Flores *(Partner & Mng Dir-Sportive)*
Victoria Capelli *(VP & Head-New York Office)*

Accounts:
Acineken
Clarins
Delta Air Lines Community Outreach, Hispanic, Hispanic Media, Latin America & Caribbean Flights
Domino's Pizza Hispanic, Marketing, Media & Community Relations, National & Local PR, Strategic Counsel
FujiFilm
Heineken
MercuryMedia
Nike
Sea World Parks & Entertainment
Verizon

RLF COMMUNICATIONS LLC
301 N Elm St, Greensboro, NC 27401
Tel.: (336) 553-1800
Fax: (336) 553-1735
Web Site: www.rlfcommunications.com

Year Founded: 2007

Agency Specializes In: Advertising, Crisis Communications, Graphic Design, Media Relations, Print, Promotions, Public Relations, Social Media

Monty Hagler *(Owner)*
Ron Irons *(VP & Dir-Creative)*
David French *(VP-Client Strategy & Svc)*
Michelle Rash *(VP-Fin & Pro Svcs Brands)*
Amanda Lehmert *(Dir-Fin & Professional Svcs Brands)*
Steffany Reeve *(Dir-Consumer & Lifestyle Brands)*
Carolyn Kuzmin *(Mgr-Comm)*
Marissa Pierre *(Mgr-Comm)*

Accounts:
3C Inc
American Founders Bank
Chesapeake Convention & Visitors Bureau
Chesapeake Economic Development
CNL Financial Group, Inc.
The Greensboro Partnership
MasterShield
Smith Moore LLP
Vestagen Technical Textiles LLC
Woozie

RLM PUBLIC RELATIONS, INC.
260 Madison Ave 8th Fl, New York, NY 10016
Tel.: (212) 741-5106
Fax: (212) 741-5139
E-Mail: info@rlmpr.com
Web Site: www.rlmpr.com

Employees: 25
Year Founded: 1991

Agency Specializes In: Public Relations

Richard Laermer *(Founder & CEO)*

Accounts:
Adbrite
American Bible Society
Anystream
Chegg
ClearOne Communications
Cole Haan
HotChalk
Intellivent Group

Sesame Workshop
Smith & Nephew
SmugMug
Sterling Group
Weathernews Wireless
WhittmanHart

ROARMEDIA
150 Alhambra Cir Ste 725, Coral Gables, FL 33134
Tel.: (305) 403-2080
Fax: (305) 774-9982
E-Mail: info@roarmedia.com
Web Site: www.roarmedia.com

Year Founded: 2005

Agency Specializes In: Automotive, Communications, Internet/Web Design, Media Relations, Paid Searches, Real Estate, Search Engine Optimization, Strategic Planning/Research

Jolie Balido-Hart *(Pres)*
Jacques Hart *(CEO)*
Julia Wakefield *(Sr Acct Supvr)*
Diana Jacome *(Acct Exec-Digital Mktg & Social Media)*
Andrea Phillips-Lopez *(Acct Exec)*

Accounts:
Houses.com

ROBERTSON COMMUNICATIONS CORP.
30211 Avenida de las Banderas 2nd Fl, Rancho Santa Margarita, CA 92688
Tel.: (949) 766-6789
Web Site: www.robertsoncomm.com

Year Founded: 2012

Agency Specializes In: Brand Development & Integration, Public Relations, Social Media

Scott Robertson *(Founder & Pres)*

Accounts:
Moore Benefits, Inc.

ROBIN LEEDY & ASSOCIATES
118 N Bedford Rd Ste 302, Mount Kisco, NY 10549
Tel.: (914) 241-0086
Fax: (914) 242-2061
E-Mail: rrusso@robinleedyassociates.com
Web Site: www.robinleedyassociates.com

Employees: 10
Year Founded: 1986

Agency Specializes In: Health Care Services, Internet/Web Design, Media Relations, Public Relations, Sponsorship

Revenue: $15,000,000

Robin Russo *(Pres)*
Alyson O'Mahoney *(Partner & Exec VP)*
Ashley Hughes *(Acct Exec)*

Accounts:
Cirrus Healthcare Products, LLC EarPlanes
FeverAll
Keri Lotion
Konsyl
Matrixx Initiatives, Inc. Consumer PR, Online Marketing, Social Media, Zicam
Mentholatum Softlips
Oxy Skin Care
Replens
Stopain Cold
VSL#3

ROCKAWAY PR
647 NE 79th St Ste 4, Miami, FL 33138
Tel.: (305) 751-9641
Web Site: www.rockawaypr.com

Year Founded: 2005

Agency Specializes In: Brand Development & Integration, Event Planning & Marketing, Public Relations, Social Media

Alexis Knapp *(Principal)*
Dana Gidney Fetaya *(Acct Dir)*
Terry Zarikian *(Dir-Bus & Dev)*
Christine Procel-Cohen *(Acct Mgr)*
Sandra Molina *(Mgr-Ops)*
Kristin Colville *(Acct Exec)*
Monica Gonzalez *(Acct Coord)*

Accounts:
Margaritaville
Villa Azur

ROCKORANGE
5505 Blue Lagoon Dr 1st Fl, Miami, FL 33126
Tel.: (305) 731-2224
E-Mail: info@rockorange.com
Web Site: www.rockorange.com

Year Founded: 2013

Agency Specializes In: Corporate Communications, Digital/Interactive, Media Relations, Media Training, Promotions, Public Relations

Miguel Piedra *(Principal & Mng Partner)*
Alix Salyers *(Sr VP & Gen Mgr)*
Sergio Claudio *(VP-Digital Innovation & Strategy)*
Paulina Naranjo *(VP-Media Rels)*
David Quinones *(VP-Editorial & Content)*
Ray Munoz *(Sr Dir-Agency Ops)*
Monique N. Gonzalez *(Acct Dir)*
Mahogani Jones *(Dir-New Bus Dev & Mktg Activations)*
Rocio Gonzalez *(Mgr-Editorial)*
Rosanna Castro *(Sr Acct Exec)*
Mari Santana *(Mng Principal)*

Accounts:
AARP
Beto Perez Zumba Fitness
Botran Rums
Cotton Incorporated Cotton's 24 Hour Runway, Public Relations, Strategy
Crescent Moon Records
David Font Design
Driven Brands, Inc.
Estefan Enterprises
Gloria & Emilio Estefan
Gulliver Schools Public Relations
Maaco Franchising, Inc.
Yo Soy Segundo

ROEPKE PUBLIC RELATIONS
800 LaSalle Ave 9th Fl, Minneapolis, MN 55402
Tel.: (612) 677-1717
E-Mail: info@roepkepr.com
Web Site: www.roepkepr.com

Agency Specializes In: Communications, Public Relations

Katherine Roepke *(Pres)*
Natalie Howell *(Sr Mgr-Media Rels)*

Accounts:
Ti Sento Milano Public Relations Counsel
Victory Energy

ROGERS FINN PARTNERS
(Formerly Rogers Ruder Finn)
1875 Century Park E Ste 200, Los Angeles, CA 90067-2504
Tel.: (310) 552-6922
Fax: (310) 552-9052
E-Mail: ron@finnpartners.com
Web Site: www.finnpartners.com/rogers/

Employees: 100
Year Founded: 1978

Agency Specializes In: Automotive, Bilingual Market, Brand Development & Integration, Business-To-Business, Communications, Consumer Marketing, Corporate Identity, E-Commerce, Education, Entertainment, Environmental, Event Planning & Marketing, Fashion/Apparel, Financial, Food Service, Gay & Lesbian Market, Government/Political, Health Care Services, Hispanic Market, Industrial, Investor Relations, Newspaper, Public Relations, Real Estate, Retail, Sponsorship, Strategic Planning/Research, Teen Market, Transportation, Travel & Tourism

Approx. Annual Billings: $11,000,000

Shelly Holmes *(Sr Partner & Exec VP)*
Brenda Lynch *(Sr Partner)*

Accounts:
B/S/H (Bosch & Thermador)
Bandai America
Bosch
The California Endowment
Dole Packaged Foods
Health Net Inc.; 2001
iGo, Inc.; Scottsdale, AZ Public Relations
The Jim Henson Company
Port of Los Angeles Clean Truck Program
University of Denver
Whole Foods Market

ROHATYNSKI-HARLOW PUBLIC RELATIONS LLC
111 N Michigan Ave Ste B, Howell, MI 48843
Tel.: (313) 378-6570
Web Site: www.roharpr.com

Agency Specializes In: Business-To-Business, Crisis Communications, Graphic Design, Media Relations, Multimedia, Public Relations, Strategic Planning/Research

Joe Rohatynski *(Owner)*

Accounts:
New-North American International Auto Show (Public Relations Agency of Record)

ROHER PUBLIC RELATIONS
(Acquired & Absorbed by Feintuch Communications)

ROMANELLI COMMUNICATIONS
2 College St, Clinton, NY 13323
Tel.: (800) 761-3944
E-Mail: info@romanelli.com
Web Site: www.romanelli.com

Agency Specializes In: Brand Development & Integration, Crisis Communications, Digital/Interactive, Logo & Package Design, Print, Public Relations, Radio, Social Media

Joe Romanelli *(Pres)*
Beth Romanelli-Hapanowicz *(VP)*
Josh Clemmons *(Dir-Fin)*
Bernie Freytag *(Dir-Creative)*
Susan Delaney-Ellis *(Mgr-Acctg)*

Accounts:
First Source Federal Credit Union
Good Nature Brewing
Utica Coffee Roasting Company

RON SONNTAG PUBLIC RELATIONS
9406 N 107th St, Milwaukee, WI 53224
Tel.: (414) 354-0200
Fax: (414) 354-5317
Toll Free: (800) 969-0200
E-Mail: ron@rspr.com
Web Site: www.rspr.com

E-Mail for Key Personnel:
President: ron@rspr.com

Employees: 12
Year Founded: 1980

National Agency Associations: PRSA

Agency Specializes In: Advertising, Business-To-Business, Collateral, Communications, Consumer Publications, Corporate Identity, Digital/Interactive, Direct Response Marketing, Event Planning & Marketing, Exhibit/Trade Shows, Internet/Web Design, Logo & Package Design, Multimedia, Planning & Consultation, Print, Public Relations, Publicity/Promotions, Radio, Recruitment, T.V., Telemarketing, Trade & Consumer Magazines, Yellow Pages Advertising

Revenue: $23,000,000

Ron Sonntag *(Chm & CEO)*
Dave Amoroso *(VP)*
Kevin Kosterman *(Dir-Art)*
Cynthia Marsh *(Dir-Editorial Svcs)*
Mark McLaughlin *(Dir-Media Rels)*
Kandi Korth *(Office Mgr)*
Kimberly Greene *(Acct Exec)*
Lindsay Schultz *(Acct Exec)*

RONALD C. SYLVESTER COMMUNICATIONS & PR
998 Montrose Ave, Columbus, OH 43209
Tel.: (514) 314-9216
Web Site: www.ronsylvester.com

Year Founded: 2011

Agency Specializes In: Brand Development & Integration, Collateral, Content, Crisis Communications, Logo & Package Design, Media Planning, Media Relations, Public Relations, Social Media

Ronald C. Sylvester *(Principal)*

Accounts:
Public Performance Partners

ROOP & CO.
3800 Terminal Tower, Cleveland, OH 44113
Tel.: (216) 902-3800
Fax: (216) 902-3800
E-Mail: info@roopco.com
Web Site: www.roopco.com

E-Mail for Key Personnel:
President: jroop@roopco.com
Creative Dir.: ldechant@roopco.com
Public Relations: bkostka@roopco.com

Employees: 9
Year Founded: 1996

National Agency Associations: PRSA

Agency Specializes In: Automotive, Aviation & Aerospace, Brand Development & Integration, Business-To-Business, Collateral, Communications, Consulting, Consumer Marketing, Corporate Communications, Corporate Identity, Event Planning & Marketing, Exhibit/Trade Shows, Financial, Graphic Design, Health Care Services, Industrial, Investor Relations, Legal Services, Logo & Package Design, Media Relations, Medical Products, Multimedia, New Product Development, Newspaper, Outdoor, Print, Production, Public Relations, Publicity/Promotions, Radio, Real Estate, Restaurant, Sales Promotion, Social Media, T.V., Transportation, Travel & Tourism, Viral/Buzz/Word of Mouth

Approx. Annual Billings: $10,000,000

Breakdown of Gross Billings by Media: Bus. Publs.: 5%; Exhibits/Trade Shows: 5%; Graphic Design: 33%; Plng. & Consultation: 10%; Pub. Rels.: 47%

James J. Roop *(Pres)*
Brad Kostka *(Sr VP)*
Lynn Dechant *(Dir-Graphic Design)*
Kathryn Fetheroff *(Asst Acct Exec)*

Accounts:
Alego Health; Cleveland, OH; 2011
Alilyfe Racing
B&F Capital Markets; Cleveland, OH Interest Rate Swaps; 2005
Caliber Jet; Cleveland, OH Fractional Jet Ownership/Usage; 2012
Cell Phone Repair
Cleveland School of Science & Medicine; Cleveland, OH Public High School; 2006
Cleveland Thermal; Cleveland, OH
CM Wealth
Collins & Scanlon PC; Cleveland, OH Law Firm; 1998
The Euclid Chemical Company
Fairport Asset Management
Fiber Reinforced Concrete Association
Fisher & Phillips LLP; Cleveland, OH Legal Services; 2011
Grace Hospital; Cleveland, OH Long Term Acute Care Hospital; 2012
The Hermit Club
HWH Architects, Engineers; Cleveland, OH; 2006
Jacobs Real Estate Services
Key Bank; Cleveland OH Capital Markets, Global Treasury, Institutional Banking
Kirtland Capital Partners; Cleveland, OH
Linsalata Capital Partners
Malachi House
Ohio Aerospace Institute; Berea, OH; 2006
O'Neill Foundation
Republic Steel
RPM International; 1996
Servel
Ticer Technologies
Tremco Commercial Sealants & Waterproofing
Tremco Inc.
Tremco Roofing & Building Maintenance

ROOTED RED CREATIVE
PO Box 43252, Louisville, KY 40253
Tel.: (502) 653-9664
Web Site: www.rootedred.com

Year Founded: 2012

Agency Specializes In: Graphic Design, Internet/Web Design, Media Relations, Public Relations, Social Media

Renee Reithel *(Owner & Pres)*

Accounts:
Big Reach Center of Hope

ROSE COMMUNICATIONS
10601 E Bend Rd, Union, KY 41091-8163
Tel.: (859) 331-0794
Fax: (859) 331-6941
E-Mail: info@rosecommunicate.com
Web Site: www.rosecommunicate.com

Agency Specializes In: Business-To-Business, Communications, Corporate Communications, Crisis Communications, Email, Integrated Marketing, Media Planning, Media Relations, Newspaper, Newspapers & Magazines, Public Relations, Publicity/Promotions

Rosemary Weathers Burnham *(Pres)*

Accounts:
Cincinnati Park Board; Cincinnati, OH
KZF Design; Cincinnati, OH
Partnership for a Drug-Free America; New York, NY
Paul Hemmer Companies
Scripps Howard Foundation; Cincinnati, OH
St. Elizabeth Medical Center
Transit Authority of Northern Kentucky

ROSE COMMUNICATIONS, INC.
80 River St Ste 4C, Hoboken, NJ 07030-5619
Tel.: (201) 656-7178
Fax: (201) 221-8734
E-Mail: rostmann@rosecomm.com
Web Site: www.rosecomm.com

Employees: 7
Year Founded: 2003

Agency Specializes In: Business-To-Business, Collateral, Crisis Communications, Event Planning & Marketing, Exhibit/Trade Shows, Media Planning, Media Relations, Media Training, Public Relations, Strategic Planning/Research, Viral/Buzz/Word of Mouth

Revenue: $1,000,000

Rosemary Ostmann *(Pres & CEO)*
Victoria Grantham *(Mng Dir & Sr VP)*
Tracey Cassidy *(Sr VP & Client Svcs Dir)*
Lisa Trapani *(Sr VP)*
Jennifer Leckstrom *(VP)*
Laurie Petersen *(VP)*
Shwetha Ramani *(Sr Acct Exec)*
Kelsey BaRoss *(Acct Exec)*
Carolyn Lasky *(Acct Exec)*
Stephanie Shaw *(Asst Acct Exec)*

Accounts:
Apex Tool Group (Agency of Record) Social Media Strategy, Traditional Media Relations
BlueRidge Bank
EMM Group
GearWrench
Guardian Industries Corp.
Nucletron; Columbia, MD Media Relations Program, Public Relations

Branch

Rose Communications Inc.
100 N Charles St 15th Fl, Baltimore, MD 21201
Tel.: (410) 245-0094
Fax: (201) 221-8734
E-Mail: ltrapani@rosecomm.com
Web Site: www.rosecomm.com

Employees: 10

Rosemary Ostmann *(Pres & CEO)*
Victoria Grantham *(Mng Dir & Sr VP)*
Tracey Cassidy *(Sr VP & Client Svcs Dir)*
Lisa Trapani *(VP & Dir-Editorial Svcs)*
Jennifer Leckstrom *(Acct Supvr)*
Julie Meyer *(Specialist-Mktg)*

Accounts:
BlueRidge Bank
Bravo Health Insurance; 2008
GearWrench
Kaplan Publishing

THE ROSE GROUP
9925 Jefferson Blvd 2nd Fl, Culver City, CA 90232
Tel.: (310) 280-3710
Fax: (310) 280-3715
E-Mail: info@therosegrp.com
Web Site: therosegrp.strikingly.com

Employees: 5

Agency Specializes In: Public Relations

Elana Weiss-Rose *(Co-Founder)*
Jeff Rose *(Chm)*
Bonnie Lippincott *(COO & VP)*
Paul Rockelmann *(VP-HR)*
Robert Fuller *(Dir-IT)*
Scott Ridgway *(Dir-Ops)*
Paul Trzaska *(Dir-Risk Mgmt & People Svcs)*
Jeffrey Browne *(Mgr-Mktg)*
David Corrigan *(Mgr-IT)*

ROSE+MOSER+ALLYN PUBLIC RELATIONS
7144 E Stetson Dr Ste 400, Scottsdale, AZ 85251
Tel.: (480) 423-1414
Fax: (480) 423-1415
E-Mail: info@rosemoserallynpr.com
Web Site: www.rosemoserallynpr.com

Agency Specializes In: Crisis Communications, Event Planning & Marketing, Government/Political, Public Relations

Jennifer Moser *(Founder & Principal)*

Accounts:
New-Pollack Investments

THE ROSEN GROUP
30 W 26th St Third Fl, New York, NY 10010-2011
Tel.: (212) 255-8455
Fax: (212) 255-8456
E-Mail: thelma@rosengrouppr.com
Web Site: www.rosengrouppr.com

E-Mail for Key Personnel:
President: lori@rosengrouppr.com

Employees: 21
Year Founded: 1984

Agency Specializes In: Public Relations

Approx. Annual Billings: $800,000

Breakdown of Gross Billings by Media: D.M.: $400,000; Pub. Rels.: $280,000; T.V.: $120,000

Lori S. Rosen *(Founder & Pres)*
Diane Stefani *(Exec VP)*
Thelma Rogel *(Mgr)*
Alexandra Pearson *(Sr Acct Exec)*
James Hercher *(Acct Exec)*
Jacob Streiter *(Acct Exec)*
Jaclyn Todisco *(Acct Exec)*

Accounts:
Atlantic Monthly
College Savings Plans Network Section 529
Cooking Light Magazine; 1987
ELDR
Kiplinger's Personal Finance Magazine; Washington, DC Magazine; 1989
Live Well Network
O'Reilly Media
PC Magazine
PCMag Digital Network
SGPTV
Terra USA
WorkPlace Media
World Almanac

Branch

The Rosen Group
1150 Connecticut Ave NW Ste 900, Washington, DC 10036
Tel.: (202) 862-4355
Fax: (215) 623-1986
E-Mail: thelma@rosengrouppr.com
Web Site: www.rosengrouppr.com

Employees: 2

Agency Specializes In: Public Relations

Lori Rosen *(Founder & Pres)*
Diane Stefani *(Exec VP)*
Shawna McGregor *(Sr VP)*
Abby Berman *(VP)*
Thelma Rogel *(Mgr)*
Maggie Beaudouin *(Sr Acct Exec)*
Alexandra Pearson *(Sr Acct Exec)*
Jacob Streiter *(Sr Acct Exec)*
Laura Stevens *(Acct Exec)*

Accounts:
The Atlantic
Brewers Association
Custom Content Council
IFAW
The James Beard Foundation

ROSICA STRATEGIC PUBLIC RELATIONS
95 Rt 17 S Ste 109, Paramus, NJ 07652
Tel.: (201) 843-5600
Fax: (201) 843-5680
E-Mail: pr@rosica.com
Web Site: www.rosica.com

Employees: 15
Year Founded: 1980

Agency Specializes In: Brand Development & Integration, Education, Event Planning & Marketing, Fashion/Apparel, Food Service, New Product Development, Public Relations, Retail, Sports Market, Strategic Planning/Research, Travel & Tourism

Christopher Rosica *(Pres & CEO)*
Kathy Carliner *(Sr VP-Consumer Mktg Div)*
Terese Kelly Greer *(VP-Media Rels)*
Melissa Rubin *(Acct Supvr)*
Maria Habermann *(Sr Acct Exec)*
Kyle Evans *(Acct Coord)*
Marybeth Nibley *(Sr Writer)*

Accounts:
Communities In Schools
Habitat for Humanity
Jamail Larkins
Kaleidoscope of Hope
Kinder Morgan
Makari Skincare
National Computer Systems
Ness Technologies
Nice-Pak
Pfizer; 2008
Salvation Army
United Way
Vcom

ROSLAN & CAMPION PUBLIC RELATIONS
(Formerly Dera, Roslan & Campion Public Relations)
424 W 33rd St, New York, NY 10001
Tel.: (212) 966-4600
Fax: (212) 966-5763
E-Mail: info@rc-pr.com
Web Site: www.rc-pr.com

Employees: 13
Year Founded: 1989

Agency Specializes In: Entertainment, Event Planning & Marketing, Public Relations

Eileen Campion *(Pres)*
Joseph Dera *(CEO)*

Accounts:
Nova
Scripps Networks

ROSS & LAWRENCE PUBLIC RELATIONS
445 Park Ave, New York, NY 10022
Tel.: (212) 308-3333
Fax: (212) 207-8096
E-Mail: kpross@rosslawpr.com
Web Site: www.rosslawpr.com

Employees: 5
Year Founded: 1966

Agency Specializes In: Financial, Legal Services, Public Relations, Real Estate

Guy B. Lawrence *(Mng Dir)*

Accounts:
Freshfield Brukhaus Deringer
W.P. Carey & Company LLC
Watermark Capital Partners, LLC

ROUNTREE GROUP COMMUNICATIONS MANAGEMENT
2550 Northwinds Pkwy, Alpharetta, GA 30009
Tel.: (770) 645-4545
Fax: (770) 645-0147
E-Mail: admin@rountreegroup.com
Web Site: www.rountreegroup.com

Employees: 7
Year Founded: 1985

Agency Specializes In: Automotive, Business Publications, Business-To-Business, Communications, Consumer Marketing, Corporate Communications, Digital/Interactive, Financial, Health Care Services, Hospitality, Local Marketing, Luxury Products, Media Training, Medical Products, Newspaper, Public Relations, Real Estate, Restaurant, Retail, Social Media, Strategic Planning/Research, Teen Market, Tween Market

Don Rountree *(Pres)*
Lisa Hester *(Sr Acct Mgr)*
Krista Beres *(Acct Supvr)*
Leighanne Ferri *(Asst Acct Exec)*

Accounts:
Arbor Terrace
Bright's Creek Golf Glub
Exterior Insulation & Finish Systems B2B
Firebirds Wood Fired Grill Media Relations, Strategy
Fisher & Phillips LLP Agency of Record, B2B
Historic Banning Mills (Agency of Record) Media Relations
Jasper Contractors
Pickron Orthodontic Care Consumer

ROURK PUBLIC RELATIONS

4548 Bob Jones Dr, Virginia Beach, VA 23462
Tel.: (757) 478-0150
Web Site: www.rourkpr.com

Agency Specializes In: Internet/Web Design, Logo & Package Design, Media Relations, Public Relations, Social Media

David Rourk *(Owner)*

Accounts:
Allergy & Asthma Specialists
Gynecology Specialists
IGW Electric
Just Floored Inc
Kitchen Corps Inc
Osen-Hunter
Synergy Medical Center
Winkfield Group

RPR PUBLIC RELATIONS INC.
5951 Wellesley Pk Dr 404, Boca Raton, FL 33433
Tel.: (786) 290-6413
Web Site: www.romanopr.com

Agency Specializes In: Brand Development & Integration, Media Relations, Public Relations, Publicity/Promotions, Social Media

Joe Romano *(Partner)*
Ria Romano *(Partner)*
Jackie Rockefeller *(Mng Dir)*
Adrianna Gambino *(Dir-Tech Clients)*
Marion Louise Ivers *(Dir-Life Sciences)*

Accounts:
Independent Merchant Group
New-MCA Inc (Agency of Record)
Real Time Pain Relief
New-Renesans New York (Agency of Record) Brand Messages, Media Relations, Public Relations, Strategic Communications

RUANE COMMUNICATIONS, INC.
200 S Wacker Dr Ste 3100, Chicago, IL 60606
Tel.: (815) 717-8968
Web Site: www.ruanecommunications.com

Agency Specializes In: Communications, Public Relations, Social Media

John Ruane *(Pres)*

Accounts:
Chicago White Sox Ltd.

RUBENSTEIN ASSOCIATES, INC.
1345 Ave of the Americas Fl 30, New York, NY 10105-0109
Tel.: (212) 843-8000
Fax: (212) 843-9200
E-Mail: info@rubenstein.com
Web Site: www.rubenstein.com

Employees: 200
Year Founded: 1954

Agency Specializes In: Public Relations, Sponsorship

Steven Rubenstein *(Pres & Sr Exec VP)*
Thomas Keaney *(COO)*
Marcia Horowitz *(Sr Exec VP)*
Susan Arons *(Exec VP)*
Amanda Deveaux *(Sr VP)*
Stefan Prelog *(Sr VP)*
Heather Silverberg Resnicoff *(VP)*
Megan Duzi *(Assoc VP)*
Mike Stouber *(Acct Exec)*
Hillary Karsten *(Assoc Acct Exec)*
Kaitlin Esrich *(Acct Coord)*
Sophia Estrada *(Acct Coord)*
Meghan Gumer *(Acct Coord)*
Olivia Hemmerich *(Acct Coord)*
Amalia Safran *(Acct Coord)*
Julia Tomkins *(Acct Coord)*

Accounts:
ABC, Inc.
AECOM
Al Roker Productions
Association for a Better Long Island
Association for a Better New York
Beats Electronics LLC
Beth Israel Medical Center
BMW of North America Auto Shows, BMW I Communications, Golf Initiatives, Marketing Communications
Cathedral of Saint John the Divine
Chrysler Building
City University of New York
Coalition of One Hundred Black Women
Columbia University
Consolidated Edison Company of New York
Countdown Entertainment New Year's Eve Ball Dropping in Times Square
Danielle Steel
EmblemHealth, Inc.
Fleet Week
Fordham University
Grove Street Advisors
Guggenheim Museum
Henry Schein, Inc.
Hunter College
Ideal Properties Group
Intrepid Sea Air Space Museum
The Lefrak Organization
MacAndrews & Forbes Group
Madame Tussaud's NY
Maimonides Medical Center
Metropolitan Opera
Mount Airy Casino Resort
Mount Sinai Hospital
Muriel Siebert & Co.
Museum of Jewish Heritage: A Living Memorial to the Holocaust
New York City Marathon
New York City Police Foundation
New York-Presbyterian Healthcare System; New York, NY
New York Yankees
NY Presbyterian/Weill Cornell Medical Center
One Hundred Black Men, Inc.
Paramount Pictures Corporation
Partnership for New York City
Patsy's Italian Restaurant
Quinnipiac University Poll
Rockefeller Center Christmas Tree Lighting
Rockefeller Center
Rutherford Place
Saint Johns' University
Samson Capital Advisors
Silverstein Properties
Tavistock Restaurant Group
Time Warner Inc.
Tishman Speyer Properties
Tribeca Films
Vornado Realty Trust
Walt Disney Corporation
Wells Real Estate Funds, Inc.; Norcross, GA
Whitney Museum of American Art
Worldwide Pants-Late Show with David Letterman
Yankees Entertainment & Sports Network, LLC; New York

Subsidiary

Rubenstein Public Relations
1345 Ave of the Americas, New York, NY 10105
Tel.: (212) 843-8000
Fax: (212) 843-9200
Web Site: www.rubensteinpr.com/

Employees: 25

Agency Specializes In: Public Relations

Gerry Casanova *(Sr VP & Dir-Client Svcs)*
Lori Traczyk *(Sr VP)*
Kristie Galvani *(VP)*
Laura Salerno *(VP)*
Megan Wilson *(VP)*
Katalin Bergou *(Assoc VP)*
Christian Rizzo *(Assoc VP-Real Estate)*
Michelle Fagan *(Dir-HR)*
Lauren Sachs *(Mgr-Media Rels)*
Olya Moskalenko *(Sr Writer-Bus Dev)*

Accounts:
African Lion & Environmental Research Trust Pro Bono
Altec Lansing (Agency of Record) Media
American Society of Interventional Pain Physicians Pain Management & Minimally-Invasive Techniques
Annual Village Halloween Parade (Agency of Record) Public Relations
The Apple Building Condominium
Apple-Metro, Inc
ARK Development, LLC
Astro Gallery of Gems (Agency of Record)
BiVi Sicilian Vodka (Public Relations Agency of Record) Communications, Media Relations
Bizzi & Partners
Brian Cuban
British Basketball Association Integrated Marketing
Brown Harris Stevens
Butler Burgher Group
Carol Alt
The Centurion
New-Charles Rutenberg, LLC (Agency of Record) Public Relations
Contemporary Art Collection
Continental Properties
The Cutting Room (Agency of Record) Communications Strategy, Media
David Fisher Rotating Tower; 2008
Dr. Suzanne Levine
Fireapps Brand Awareness, Media Coverage
Fundrise
Greencard Creative
GreenHouse Holdings, Inc.; San Diego, CA (Agency of Record)
Halstead Property
HAP Investments Real Estate
The Helmsley Hotel Mindy's Restaurant
Hospitality Holdings
Iconosys, Inc.; Laguna Hills, CA SMS Replier
Ideal Properties Group Real Estate
JMJ Holdings Residential Development
Julius Nasso Media Strategies
Karim Rashid
The Lennon Report (Agency of Record)
Luciano Pavarotti Foundation USA Events, Media Relations, Philanthropic Partnerships
Magnolia Bakery
The Mark Company; San Francisco, CA Marketing, Strategic Planning
MIPIM
Miss Universe Organization
Moon River Studios (Agency of Record)
Mount Airy Casino Resort (Agency of Record)
Nederlander Worldwide Entertainment RENT (Agency of Record)
NeoStem, Inc
NestSeekers International
Philip Stein
Phipps & Co
Pier 59 Studios
Prodigy International
RLTY NYC
Rutherford Place Real Estate
SG Blocks, Inc
Sharon Parker Look Out Cancer... Here I Come
Sheldon Good & Company
Siras Development
Somerset Partners LLC; 2007

South Beach Group; FL Vacation Destination
Tofutti Brands Brand Awareness
US Mortgage Corporation (Agency of Record) Media
US Rare Earths, Inc.
World Business Lenders Brand Awareness, Media Coverage
Zenthea Dental

RUBIN COMMUNICATIONS GROUP
4542 Bonney Rd Ste B, Virginia Beach, VA 23462
Tel.: (757) 456-5212
Fax: (757) 456-5224
Web Site: www.rubincommunications.com

Agency Specializes In: Advertising, Event Planning & Marketing, Graphic Design, Internet/Web Design, Media Buying Services, Media Relations, Media Training, Public Relations, Social Media

Joel Rubin *(CEO)*
Sara Jo Rubin *(COO)*
Danny Rubin *(VP)*
Jessica Bensten *(Creative Dir)*
Ashley H. Martin *(Sr Acct Mgr)*
Rachael Keshishian *(Acct Mgr)*

Accounts:
Achievable Dream Academy
Cintas Corporation
Virginia Dental Association

RUBY MEDIA GROUP
17 State St Ste 4000, New York, NY 10004
Tel.: (914) 220-5871
Web Site: www.rubymediagroup.com

Agency Specializes In: Advertising, Collateral, Content, Graphic Design, Leisure, Media Planning, Media Relations, Promotions, Public Relations, Social Media

Kris Ruby *(Founder & CEO)*

Accounts:
The Crowne Plaza Hotel White Plains

RUDER FINN INC.
301 E 57th St, New York, NY 10022-2900
Tel.: (212) 593-6400
Fax: (212) 593-6397
E-Mail: info@ruderfinn.com
Web Site: www.ruderfinn.com

Employees: 500
Year Founded: 1948

Agency Specializes In: Public Relations, Sponsorship

Approx. Annual Billings: $99,000,000

Dena Merriam *(Vice Chm)*
Kathy Bloomgarden *(CEO)*
Scott Schneider *(Chief Digital Officer)*
Lisa Gabbay *(Pres-Design & Dir-Creative)*
Sarah Anderson *(Exec VP & Head-Consumer Practice-US)*
Jennifer Essen *(Exec VP)*
Anne Glauber *(Exec VP)*
Rachel Spielman *(Exec VP)*
Katy Kelley *(Sr VP-Creative Culture & Global Mktg)*
Emmanuel Tchividjian *(Chief Ethics Officer & Sr VP)*
Meagan Sloan *(Acct Supvr)*
Rachel Bekkerman *(Acct Exec)*
Alexis Bridenbaugh *(Acct Exec)*
Hannah Deixler *(Acct Exec)*
Molly Dobbins *(Acct Exec)*
Stephanie Hyon *(Acct Exec)*

Accounts:
3I
Ad Council
Alliance Data Systems
Bristol-Myers Squibb
Caribou Coffee Public Relations
Cengage Learning Communications, Digital, Global Brand Positioning, Media Relations, Message Development, Thought Leadership
Citi
Council for Responsible Nutrition Foundation Campaign: "Life . . .Supplemented"
Council on Foreign Relations
Girl Scouts
Hotels.com
I-Universe
International Center of Photography
Jamaica Tourist Board
Johnson & Johnson
Keebler
Kellogg
Kenneth Cole Productions Media, Website
King Pharmaceuticals
Kyocera Mita America, Inc.
New-Lafco Enterprise (Public Relations Agency of Record) Content Development, Media Relations, Thought Leadership
MAC AIDS Fund
North Face
Novartis Oncology
Novartis Pharmaceuticals Corporation
Oracle America, Inc.
Ortho-McNeil
Palm, Inc.
PARC (The Palo Alto Research Center)
PepsiCo
Perdue
Pfizer, Inc.
Poetry Foundation
PPR Corporate PR
Quallion
Read Write Think
Schering Plough
Shire
Smithsonian
SONY
TiVo
Tradebeam
Tropicana Hotel & Casino: Las Vegas, NV Bar, Casino, Hotel, Lounges, Media Relations, Promotions, Public Relations, Rebranding, Restaurant, Special Events
Twinings Tea
UNAIDS
U.S. Forest Service Smokey Bear Web Site-Get Your Smokey On Pledge
Verizon Foundation
Vertex Pharmaceuticals
WebPlan
Weight Watchers International, Inc.

Subsidiaries

Arts & Communications Counselors
301 E 57th St, New York, NY 10022-2900
Tel.: (212) 593-6475
Fax: (212) 715-1507
E-Mail: rfnewyork@ruderfinn.com

Employees: 300

Philippa Polskin *(Pres)*
Rachel Shotwell Bauch *(Sr VP)*
Amanda Domizio *(Sr VP)*
Amy Wentz *(Sr VP)*
Kate Lydecker *(VP)*
Maura Klosterman *(Acct Supvr)*
Sarah Brown Mcleod *(Sr Acct Exec)*
Katherine Orsini Slovik *(Acct Exec)*

Finn Partners
301 E 57th St, New York, NY 10022
(See Separate Listing)

RF Binder
950 3rd Ave, New York, NY 10022
(See Separate Listing)

Ruder Finn Healthcare
301 E 57th St, New York, NY 10022-2900
Tel.: (212) 593-6400
Fax: (646) 792-4442
E-Mail: healthcare@ruderfinn.com
Web Site: www.ruderfinn.com

Employees: 400

Mary Conway *(Exec VP & Dir-Healthcare Media)*
Rachel Spielman *(Exec VP)*
Kevin Silverman *(Sr VP & Dir-Healthcare Innovation)*
Beatrice Evangelista *(Sr VP-Healthcare)*
Vilena Katanova Faynberg *(Sr VP)*
Fiona Phillips *(Sr VP)*
Andrea Kurtz *(VP-Consumer Mktg Comm)*
Amanda Taylor *(VP)*
Rachel Zabinski *(VP)*

Accounts:
Affymetrix
Celgene
Johnson & Johnson
Medtronic
Sanofi-Aventis
Schering-Plough
UCB
Vertex

Ruder Finn
220 Montgomery St Ste 269, San Francisco, CA 94104
Tel.: (415) 223-8290
Web Site: www.ruderfinn.com

Agency Specializes In: Advertising, Brand Development & Integration, Digital/Interactive, Media Relations, Public Relations

Dushka Zapata *(Mng Dir-West Coast)*
Lawrence Edmondson *(VP-Ruder Finn & Dir-Tech)*
Scott Beaver *(VP-West)*
Louis Tehan *(VP-Digital Strategy)*
Kaitlyn Belmont *(Acct Supvr)*
Stephanie Auer *(Sr Acct Exec)*
Kristina Breux *(Sr Acct Exec)*
Alexandra Hendricks *(Sr Acct Exec)*
Ashley Paula *(Sr Acct Exec)*

Accounts:
Belkin (Agency of Record) Strategic Communications
The Bodyshop
Bridgelux (Agency of Record) Marketing, Thought Leadership
Cengage Learning Communications, Digital, Global Brand Positioning, Media Relations, Message Development, Thought Leadership
Hytera
Intel Corporation
Macromedia
Mindjet Spigit
Monohm
Seagate Technology
TriNet

U.S. Network:

RF Binder Partners
160 Gould St Ste 115, Needham, MA 02494-2300
Tel.: (781) 455-8250

Fax: (781) 455-8233
E-Mail: nancy.moss@rfbinder.com
Web Site: www.rfbinder.com

Employees: 8

National Agency Associations: COPF

Agency Specializes In: Sponsorship

Josh Gitelson *(Exec Mng Dir)*
Atalanta Rafferty *(Exec Mng Dir)*
Eva Pereira *(Sr Mng Dir)*
Shana Claudio *(Mng Dir)*
Stacy Clougherty *(Mng Dir)*
Stephanie Robinson *(Mng Dir)*
Amy Vittorio *(Mng Dir)*
Amanda Rubin *(Sr Dir)*
Taylor Lavalli *(Acct Dir)*
Etty Lewensztain *(Mgr)*
Jill Metzger *(Mgr)*

Accounts:
Center for Reintegration
Dunkin's Brands
Friends of the High Line
TIAA-CREF

Rogers Finn Partners
(Formerly Rogers Ruder Finn)
1875 Century Park E Ste 200, Los Angeles, CA 90067-2504
(See Separate Listing)

European Network:

Ruder Finn UK, Ltd.
2nd Floor 1 Bedford Street, London, WC2E 9HG United Kingdom
Tel.: (44) 20 7438 3050
Fax: (44) 207 462 8999
E-Mail: mail@ruderfinn.co.uk
Web Site: www.ruderfinn.co.uk

Employees: 35

Nick Leonard *(Mng Dir)*
Alison Denham *(Dir-HR & Ops)*
Emma Morton *(Strategist-Media)*

Accounts:
Creative Skills For Life Bloggers, Digital
Gavi Alliance
Meningitis Research Foundation
Meningitis Trust
Meningitis UK
Novartis
Pfizer
Puressentiel Public Relations
Rosetta Stone Enterprise & Education PR

Asian Network:

Ruder Finn Asia Limited
Room 101 Office Building East Lake Villas 35 Dongzhimenwai Main Street, Dongcheng District, Beijing, 100027 China
Tel.: (86) 10 6462 7321
Fax: (86) 10 6462 7327
E-Mail: info@ruderfinnasia.com
Web Site: www.ruderfinnasia.com

Employees: 80

Paul Yang *(Gen Mgr-Ruder Finn Beijing)*
Cathy Gu *(Acct Dir)*
Peter Li Zhe *(Acct Dir)*
Grace Liang *(Acct Dir)*
Yiyang Wang *(Acct Dir)*
Johanna Hui *(Sr Acct Exec)*
John Mak *(Asst Acct Exec)*
Christine Xiao *(Assoc Acct Dir)*

Accounts:
Boeing Co.
Bosch China Bosch Chassis System Control, Bosch China Corporate, Bosch Diesel System, Bosch Power Tools, Event Organisation, Media Communications, PR, Planning, Strategic Counsel
Cartier China
Cotton Council International
Cotton, Inc.
Hawker Beechcraft Corporation Marketing, Media Relations, PR
Michelin
Mont Blanc China
Tangla Hotels & Resorts
Ullens Centre for Contemporary Art; 2007
Volkswagen Group "push-to-pass engine boost", Audi R8 LMS Cup, Creating Content, GT Asia Series, Media, On-Site Media, Press Releases, Public Relations, Social-Networking, Supporting Materials

Ruder Finn Asia Limited
2nd Floor Block 7 789 Huang Pi Nan Road, Shanghai, 200025 China
Tel.: (86) 21 5383 1188
Fax: (86) 21 6248 3176
Web Site: www.ruderfinnasia.com

Employees: 80

Elan Shou *(Mng Dir-China)*
Tony Dong *(Gen Mgr-Shanghai)*
Grace Liang *(Gen Mgr-Guangzhou)*
Wayne Chen *(Sr Acct Dir)*
Cathy Gu *(Acct Dir)*
Jessica Li *(Acct Dir)*
Ray Ju *(Sr Acct Exec)*
Jackie Wen *(Sr Acct Exec)*

Accounts:
Bang & Olufsen
Belles Montres
Blancpain
Bosch Power Tools
Boucheron
Chateau Margaux
Cotton Inc.
De Beers
De Grisogono PR
Diesel
Emirates Airline Public Relations
Girard-Perregaux
Heifer China Communications, Digital Public Relations
Mead Johnson China
Michelin China Investments Ltd
TOD's
US Cotton Council International Marketing Campaigns, Media Communications, Public Relations

Ruder Finn Asia Limited
1 Coleman Street #08-11 The Adelphi, Singapore, 179803 Singapore
Tel.: (65) 6235 4495
Fax: (65) 6235 7796
E-Mail: sallehm@ruderfinnasia.com
Web Site: www.ruderfinn.com

Employees: 16
Year Founded: 1996

Agency Specializes In: Public Relations

Poh Leng Yu *(Sr VP & Gen Mgr)*
Antoine Monod *(VP)*
Prasanthi Nair *(Acct Exec)*
Jeremy Foo *(Sr Exec-Client)*
Trevor Hawkins *(Sr Counsel)*

Accounts:
Braun Public Relations, Social Media, oCoolTec
Feiyue Media Communications, Media Strategy, Public Relations
GrabTaxi Taxi Booking App
Lexus Media Communications
New-PropertyGuru Communications, Public Relations
Suntec City Mall Communications Strategy, Media Relations

RUNSWITCH PUBLIC RELATIONS
6000 Brownsboro Park Blvd, Louisville, KY 40207
Tel.: (502) 365-9917
E-Mail: info@runswitchpr.com
Web Site: www.runswitchpr.com

Employees: 12
Year Founded: 2012

Agency Specializes In: Advertising, Crisis Communications, Event Planning & Marketing, Logo & Package Design, Media Buying Services, Media Planning, Media Training, Public Relations, Social Media, Strategic Planning/Research

Ready to win? Engage the RunSwitch. They are ready to activate the public relations mechanisms you need to achieve your business, legislative, communications, and marketing goals. They deliver what matters most in business or politics: a winning strategy.

Scott Jennings *(Co-Founder & Partner)*
Gary Gerdemann *(Co-Founder & Principal)*
Rachel Bledsoe *(Acct Dir)*
Kristena Morse *(Acct Dir)*
Lauren Cherry *(Acct Exec)*
Elizabeth Goss Kuhn *(Acct Exec)*
Kelsey Duncan *(Asst Acct Coord)*
Emily Olesh *(Acct Coord)*
Jena Patterson *(Acct Coord)*
Kelsey Shannon *(Asst Acct Coord)*
Sean Southard *(Acct Coord)*

Accounts:
Long John Silver's, LLC

RUSSELL PUBLIC COMMUNICATIONS
4640 E Sunrise Dr Ste 217, Tucson, AZ 85718
Tel.: (520) 232-9840
E-Mail: info@russellpublic.com
Web Site: www.russellpublic.com

Agency Specializes In: Advertising, Event Planning & Marketing, Logo & Package Design, Media Relations, Media Training, Outdoor, Public Relations, Radio, Strategic Planning/Research

Matt Russell *(Pres & CEO)*
Laura Adams-Reese *(Acct Mgr-Hospitality)*
Shelly McGriff *(Mgr-Fin)*

Accounts:
Veria Living

RYAN & RYAN PUBLIC RELATIONS, INC.
90 Conklin St, Farmingdale, NY 11735
Tel.: (516) 293-5700
Fax: (516) 293-5899
Web Site: www.ryanprinc.com

Employees: 5
Year Founded: 1982

Agency Specializes In: Public Relations

Kevin Ryan *(Pres)*
Katherine Ryan *(Sr VP)*

Accounts:
Covanata Energy
Oyster Bay Sewer District
Roosevelt Field Shopping Center; Garden City, NY
Simon Property Group
Trigen Energy Management
Westbury Fire Department
Westbury Water District

S&S PUBLIC RELATIONS, INC.

1 Northfield Plz, Northfield, IL 60093
Tel.: (847) 955-0700
Toll Free: (800) 287-2279
E-Mail: information@sspr.com
Web Site: www.sspr.com

E-Mail for Key Personnel:
President: steve@sspr.com

Employees: 75
Year Founded: 1978

Agency Specializes In: Business Publications, Business-To-Business, E-Commerce, Education, Entertainment, Exhibit/Trade Shows, Financial, Food Service, High Technology, Information Technology, Newspaper, Newspapers & Magazines, Planning & Consultation, Public Relations, T.V., Trade & Consumer Magazines

Approx. Annual Billings: $0

Heather Kelly *(Co-Pres)*
Jill Schmidt *(Co-Pres)*
Mindy Franklin *(Sr VP)*
Molly Antos *(VP)*
Kristin Miller *(VP)*
Steve Fiore *(Acct Dir)*
Stacy Silver *(Sr Acct Mgr)*
Brittany Kelly *(Acct Mgr)*
Lindsey Pugh *(Acct Mgr)*
Krithika Rajaraman *(Sr Acct Exec)*
Lydia Heerwagen *(Acct Exec)*
Andrea Satz *(Acct Exec)*
Sarah Schlief *(Acct Exec)*

Branch

S&S Public Relations, Inc.

120 N Tejon St Ste 201, Colorado Springs, CO 80903
Tel.: (719) 634-1180
Fax: (719) 634-1184
Web Site: sspr.com

Employees: 7

Agency Specializes In: Public Relations

Heather Kelly *(Pres)*
Jen Grenz *(Mng Dir)*
Craig Astler *(VP-Comm Plng)*
Kristin Miller *(VP)*
Lindsey A. Honig *(Sr Acct Exec)*
Taylor Saltzman *(Sr Acct Exec)*
Alexandra Fountain *(Acct Exec)*

Accounts:
iLighter inc
iWave
Lifeway Foods
Nobscot
Patagonia
Soda Club
Sunbelt Software

S. GRONER ASSOCIATES, INC.

100 W Broadway Ste 290, Long Beach, CA 90802
Tel.: (562) 597-0205
Web Site: www.sga-inc.net

Agency Specializes In: Brand Development & Integration, Graphic Design, Internet/Web Design, Media Relations, Public Relations, Strategic Planning/Research

Stephen Groner *(Pres)*

Accounts:
New-Orange County Senior Center
New-Watts Re:Imagined

SAGON-PHIOR

2107 Sawtelle Blvd, West Los Angeles, CA 90025
Tel.: (310) 575-4441
Fax: (310) 575-4995
E-Mail: info@sagon-phior.com
Web Site: www.sagon-phior.com

Employees: 23

Agency Specializes In: Above-the-Line, Advertising, Advertising Specialties, Affiliate Marketing, Affluent Market, African-American Market, Agriculture, Alternative Advertising, Arts, Asian Market, Automotive, Aviation & Aerospace, Below-the-Line, Bilingual Market, Brand Development & Integration, Branded Entertainment, Broadcast, Business Publications, Business-To-Business, Cable T.V., Catalogs, Children's Market, Co-op Advertising, Collateral, College, Commercial Photography, Communications, Computers & Software, Consulting, Consumer Goods, Consumer Marketing, Consumer Publications, Content, Corporate Communications, Corporate Identity, Cosmetics, Crisis Communications, Custom Publishing, Customer Relationship Management, Digital/Interactive, Direct Response Marketing, Direct-to-Consumer, E-Commerce, Education, Electronic Media, Electronics, Email, Engineering, Entertainment, Environmental, Event Planning & Marketing, Exhibit/Trade Shows, Experience Design, Faith Based, Fashion/Apparel, Financial, Food Service, Game Integration, Gay & Lesbian Market, Government/Political, Graphic Design, Guerilla Marketing, Health Care Services, High Technology, Hispanic Market, Hospitality, Household Goods, Identity Marketing, In-Store Advertising, Industrial, Infomercials, Information Technology, Integrated Marketing, International, Internet/Web Design, Investor Relations, Legal Services, Leisure, Local Marketing, Logo & Package Design, Luxury Products, Magazines, Marine, Market Research, Media Buying Services, Media Planning, Media Relations, Media Training, Medical Products, Men's Market, Merchandising, Mobile Marketing, Multicultural, Multimedia, New Product Development, New Technologies, Newspaper, Newspapers & Magazines, Out-of-Home Media, Outdoor, Over-50 Market, Package Design, Paid Searches, Pets , Pharmaceutical, Planning & Consultation, Podcasting, Point of Purchase, Point of Sale, Print, Product Placement, Production, Production (Ad, Film, Broadcast), Production (Print), Promotions, Public Relations, Publicity/Promotions, Publishing, RSS (Really Simple Syndication), Radio, Real Estate, Recruitment, Regional, Restaurant, Retail, Sales Promotion, Search Engine Optimization, Seniors' Market, Shopper Marketing, Social Marketing/Nonprofit, Social Media, South Asian Market, Sponsorship, Sports Market, Stakeholders, Strategic Planning/Research, Sweepstakes, Syndication, T.V., Technical Advertising, Teen Market, Telemarketing, Trade & Consumer Magazines, Transportation, Travel & Tourism, Tween Market, Urban Market, Viral/Buzz/Word of Mouth, Web (Banner Ads, Pop-ups, etc.), Women's Market, Yellow Pages Advertising

Glenn Sagon *(CEO & Partner)*
Rio Phior *(Partner & Chief Creative Officer)*
Rick Rasay *(Mng Dir)*
Bill Fate *(Sr Dir-Creative)*
Mathieu Fischer *(Acct Dir)*
Russell Coon *(Dir-Interactive Media)*
Hillary Ashen *(Sr Graphic Designer)*
Dillon Railey *(Acct Coord)*

Accounts:
American Heart Association
American State Bank
Buckley
Cynvenio Biosystems
Decusoft Software Solutions
DirecTV
F&M Bank
Gelson's Supermarkets
Golden State Medicare Healthcare
Granite Investments
Irvine Company
McCormick Distilling
Microsoft
Nonhuman Rights Project
Organyc Feminine Hygiene Products
Pininfarina
Princess Cruises
Southern California Reproductive Centers
StoneCalibre Private Investments
WaveJet Propulsion Systems
Zero G Colony/Virgin Galactic

Branches

Sagon-Phior

32500 Monterey Dr, Union City, CA 94587
Tel.: (510) 684-2090
Fax: (510) 487-1043
E-Mail: rrasey@sagon-phior.com
Web Site: www.sagon-phior.com

Glenn Sagon *(CEO & Partner)*

Sagon-Phior

5 Georgia Ln, Croton on Hudson, NY 10520
Tel.: (510) 684-2090
Fax: (510) 487-1043
E-Mail: rrasay@sagon-phior.com
Web Site: www.sagon-phior.com

Rick Rasay *(Mng Dir)*

Sagon-Phior

4004 Timberbrook Ct, Arlington, TX 76015
Tel.: (214) 794-7224
Fax: (310) 575-4995
Web Site: www.sagon-phior.com

Year Founded: 1986

Glenn Sagon *(CEO & Partner)*
Rio Phior *(Partner & Chief Creative Officer)*

Accounts:
American Heart Association Fundraising
American Mensa Membership
Cathay Bank Finance
CBS Sports Secret Golf Entertainment TV & App
Irvine Company Real Estate
Kroeger/Gelson's Supermarkets Food & Beverage
Metabolife Health
Microsoft Software
Nissin Foods Food/Packaging
Princess Cruises Cruises
Rodney Strong Estate Vineyards Wine
Valley Presbyterian Hospital Healthcare

SALLY FISCHER PUBLIC RELATIONS

330 W 58th St Ste 509, New York, NY 10019
Tel.: (212) 246-2977
Web Site: www.sallyfischerpr.com

Agency Specializes In: Corporate Communications, Event Planning & Marketing, Media Relations, Public Relations, Social Media

Sally Fischer *(Founder & Pres)*
Virginia Cademartori *(Acct Exec)*

Accounts:
New-The Bauers Hotel
New-Hotel Santavenere
New-Umbra

SALMONBORRE GROUP LTD.
10 E Scranton Ave Ste 302, Lake Bluff, IL 60044
Tel.: (847) 582-1610
E-Mail: info@salmonborre.com
Web Site: www.salmonborre.com

Agency Specializes In: Event Planning & Marketing, Media Relations, Promotions, Public Relations, Social Media, Strategic Planning/Research

Deb Salmon *(Owner)*
Nancy Davies *(VP-Acct Svcs)*

Accounts:
Tomy

SALTERMITCHELL INC.
117 S Gadsden St, Tallahassee, FL 32301
Tel.: (850) 681-3200
Fax: (850) 681-7200
Web Site: www.saltermitchell.com

Agency Specializes In: Crisis Communications, Internet/Web Design, Public Relations, Social Marketing/Nonprofit, Social Media

Peter Mitchell *(Chm & Chief Creative Officer)*
April Salter *(Pres & COO)*
Karen Ong *(Creative Dir)*
Robert Bailey *(Dir-Res)*
Lisa Hall *(Dir-Pub Affairs)*
Christene Jennings *(Dir-Behavior Change Mktg)*
Christina Neuhauser *(Dir-Admin)*
Heidi Otway *(Dir-PR & Social Media)*
Randy Washburn *(Dir-Media)*
Alex Buchholz *(Sr Mgr-Digital)*

Accounts:
Kitson & Partners
Plum Creek
Tampa Bay Estuary Program

SAMANTHA CRAFTON PUBLIC RELATIONS
38 E Serene Ave Ste 314, Las Vegas, NV 89123
Tel.: (847) 502-2001
E-Mail: info@samanthacrafton.com
Web Site: www.samanthacrafton.com

Agency Specializes In: Brand Development & Integration, Event Planning & Marketing, Media Relations, Media Training, Promotions, Public Relations, Social Media

Samantha Crafton *(Founder & CEO)*

Accounts:
Renee Frances Jewelry

SAMMIS & OCHOA
2902 N Flores Ste 1, San Antonio, TX 78212
Tel.: (210) 390-4284
Fax: (210) 399-0767
E-Mail: info@sammisochoa.com
Web Site: www.sammisochoa.com

Year Founded: 2010

Agency Specializes In: Event Planning & Marketing, Media Relations, Public Relations, Social Media, Strategic Planning/Research

Mario Ochoa *(Co-Owner)*
Allie Benson *(Acct Mgr)*
Alyssa Walker *(Acct Mgr)*
Jenny Flores *(Acct Coord)*
Lynnette Montemayor *(Acct Coord)*

Accounts:
Big Red Dog Engineering

SANDBOX STRATEGIES
227 W 29th St Fl 12, New York, NY 10001
Tel.: (212) 213-2451
Web Site: www.sandboxstrat.com

Agency Specializes In: Market Research, Media Planning, Public Relations, Social Media

Corey Wade *(Partner)*
Rob Fleischer *(Partner)*
Bill Linn *(Partner)*
Shaun Norton *(Dir-PR)*
John Mak *(Mgr-Ops)*

Accounts:
New-Activision
New-SteelSeries

SANDRA EVANS & ASSOCIATES
(Formerly & Associates)
3001 Bridgeway Ste K 211, Sausalito, CA 94965
Tel.: (415) 887-9230
E-Mail: sandra@seandassoc.com
Web Site: sandraevansandassociates.com

Year Founded: 2001

Agency Specializes In: Above-the-Line, Advertising, Alternative Advertising, Below-the-Line, Collateral, Communications, Print, Production (Ad, Film, Broadcast), Public Relations

Approx. Annual Billings: $160,000

Sandra Evans *(Founder & Dir-Creative)*
Maryanne Townsend *(Gen Mgr & Controller)*
Katie Lee *(Acct Coord)*
Justina Ngyuen *(Coord-Social Media)*

Accounts:
Black Turtle Lodge; Costa Rica
Bridge Brands Chocolate
Charles Schwab
Clare Computer Solutions
Golden Gate Opera
Grocery Outlet, Inc.
iHear Medical
Kitchen Table Bakers
KMD Architects
McCann Erickson
San Francisco Chocolate Factory
San Mateo Count Event Center
San Mateo County Fair
Soma Beverage Company, LLC
Tommy's Original Margarita Mix, Inc.
Two Leaves & a Bud Tea Company

SANTA CRUZ COMMUNICATIONS INC.
3579 E Foothill Blvd Ste 776, Pasadena, CA 91107
Tel.: (626) 538-4330
Web Site: www.santacruzpr.com

Year Founded: 2001

Agency Specializes In: Event Planning & Marketing, Media Relations, Media Training, Print, Public Relations, Social Media

Claudia Santa Cruz *(Pres)*
Danixa Lopez *(Sr Acct Exec)*

Accounts:
New-Telemundo

SASS PUBLIC RELATIONS INC.
374 Lincoln Ctr, Stockton, CA 95207
Tel.: (209) 957-7277
E-Mail: info@sasspr.com
Web Site: www.sasspr.com

Year Founded: 2006

Agency Specializes In: Advertising, Collateral, Event Planning & Marketing, Graphic Design, Internet/Web Design, Public Relations

Carrie Sass *(Pres)*
Layne Imada *(Creative Dir)*
Janelle Nelson *(Dir-Mktg)*
Debbie Morris *(Coord-Event)*

Accounts:
Flair Boutique

SAVVY INC.
477 Congress St, Portland, ME 04101
Tel.: (207) 482-0637
Fax: (207) 221-1076
Toll Free: (888) 957-4777
E-Mail: info@savvy-inc.com
Web Site: www.savvy-inc.com

Employees: 5
Year Founded: 2000

Agency Specializes In: Consulting, Crisis Communications, Government/Political, Public Relations, Publicity/Promotions

Dennis Bailey *(Pres)*

Accounts:
480 Digital
Apple Inc.
CAP Quality Care
Grid Solar
Head Start Programs
Pike Industries

SAWMILL MARKETING PUBLIC RELATIONS
7 Erwood Ct, Baltimore, MD 21212
Tel.: (410) 372-0827
Web Site: www.sawmillmarketing.com

Agency Specializes In: Crisis Communications, Media Relations, Media Training, Public Relations, Social Media

Susan J. Anthony *(Partner)*
Jeffrey A. Davis *(Partner)*

Accounts:
Capitol Communicator

SAXUM PUBLIC RELATIONS
6305 Waterford Blvd, Oklahoma City, OK 73118
Tel.: (405) 608-0445
Web Site: www.saxum.com

Employees: 14
Year Founded: 2004

National Agency Associations: COPF

Agency Specializes In: Public Relations

Revenue: $1,200,000

Renzi C. Stone *(Chm & CEO)*
Debbie Schramm *(Pres)*
Dan Martel *(Chief Creative Officer & Sr VP)*
Carol Troy *(Sr VP)*
Lindsay Laird *(VP)*
Amy Pyles *(VP-Digital)*
Tosha Lackey *(Controller)*
Lindsay Vidrine *(Acct Dir)*
Houda Elyazgi *(Sr Acct Supvr)*
Lisa Lloyd *(Supvr-Media Rels)*
Conrad Kersten *(Acct Coord)*

Accounts:
New-Hobby Lobby Stores

SBPR CORP.

500 SE 17th St Ste 325, Fort Lauderdale, FL 33316
Tel.: (954) 566-1522
Fax: (954) 566-1524
E-Mail: info@sbprcorp.com
Web Site: www.sbprcorp.com

Employees: 1

Agency Specializes In: Custom Publishing, Media Relations, Product Placement, Public Relations, Publicity/Promotions, Web (Banner Ads, Pop-ups, etc.)

Stephen Bennett *(Pres)*
Patrick Bennett *(Dir-Creative)*
Jorge Rodriguez *(Dir-Audit)*

Accounts:
Gulfstream International Airlines Media Relations, Public Relations, Publicity

SCHMALZ COMMUNICATIONS

84 Nicole Dr, Brick, NJ 08724
Tel.: (732) 785-9317
E-Mail: info@schmalzcommunications.com
Web Site: schmalzcommunications.com/

Agency Specializes In: Event Planning & Marketing, Media Relations, Public Relations

Greg Schmalz *(Pres)*

Accounts:
Independence LED Lighting

SCHMIDT PUBLIC AFFAIRS

917 Prince St, Alexandria, VA 22314
Tel.: (703) 548-0019
Fax: (703) 997-0757
Web Site: www.schmidtpa.com

Agency Specializes In: Brand Development & Integration, Crisis Communications, Digital/Interactive, Event Planning & Marketing, Media Relations, Public Relations, Social Media

John Schmidt *(Principal)*
Emily Adler *(Acct Mgr)*
David Groman *(Acct Exec)*

Accounts:
New-American Kidney Fund
New-Kool Smiles (Agency of Record) Campaign "Smile On"

SCHNEIDER ASSOCIATES

2 Oliver St Ste 402, Boston, MA 02109
Tel.: (617) 536-3300
Fax: (617) 536-3180
E-Mail: launch@schneiderpr.com
Web Site: www.schneiderpr.com

Employees: 23
Year Founded: 1980

National Agency Associations: PRSA

Agency Specializes In: Business-To-Business, Consumer Marketing, Corporate Communications, Crisis Communications, Integrated Marketing, Media Training, Public Relations, Publicity/Promotions, Social Media

Approx. Annual Billings: $3,670,000

Breakdown of Gross Billings by Media: Pub. Rels.: $3,670,000

Phil Pennellatore *(Pres)*
Joan Schneider *(CEO)*
Tom Ryan *(Dir-Mktg)*
Hanna Heycke *(Sr Acct Exec)*
Ariel Ferrante *(Acct Exec-Integrated Design)*
Nicole LeLacheur *(Acct Exec-Integrated Media)*
Lauren Mucci *(Acct Exec)*
Josh Tammaro *(Acct Exec)*
Mariela McAuley *(Acct Coord)*
Victoria Morris *(Acct Coord)*

Accounts:
AAA Southern New England
Atlantic Management
Baskin-Robbins
Baystate Financial
Cassidy Turley FHO
Child & Family Services
Divco West
Ecotech Institute
Hanover Company
Hebrew SeniorLife
John Wm Macy's Cheese Sticks
Massachusetts Institute of Technology
Metropolitan Properties
Mosquito Magnet
National Development
New England College of Business & Finance
New England Confectionery Company
Northeastern University's Custom Executive Education Program
Patriot Construction Services
Penn Foster
Posternak Blankstein & Lund
Rampart Investments
Rockland Trust
Sleep Innovations
Sunstar GUM
University of Pittsburgh's College of Business Administration
UPromise
Virginia College
Westwood Station
Zeo Inc.

SCHUBERT FLINT PUBLIC AFFAIRS

(Name Changed to FSB Core Strategies)

SCHWARTZ MEDIA STRATEGIES

The Offices at Grand Bay Plz 2665 S Bayshore Dr Ste 730, Miami, FL 33133
Tel.: (305) 858-3935
Fax: (305) 858-3925
Web Site: www.schwartz-media.com

Agency Specializes In: Advertising, Crisis Communications, Event Planning & Marketing, Market Research, Media Planning, Media Relations, Public Relations, Strategic Planning/Research

Tadd Schwartz *(Pres)*
Aaron W. Gordon *(Partner)*
Alisha Marks Tischler *(VP)*
Holly Zawyer *(VP)*
Yudi Fernandez *(Acct Dir)*
Katherine Doble *(Dir-Digital Media & Branding)*
Jami Baker *(Sr Acct Exec)*
Julia Bennett *(Sr Acct Exec)*
Jessica Forres *(Sr Acct Exec)*

Accounts:
13th Floor Investments
Apollo Bank
BrickellHouse
Continental Real Estate Companies Real Estate Development Services
Espacio USA
Hospitality Operations Inc.
InterContinental Miami Hotel Media Relations, Social Media, Targeted Marketing Initiatives
J.P. Morgan
Leesfield & Partners P.A. Insurance Services
Lydecker Diaz
Miami Beckham United
Miami Downtown Development Authority (Agency of Record) Digital Media, Marketing, Media relations, Public Relations
Pinnacle Housing Group Media Relations, Social Media, Targeted Marketing Initiatives
Podhurst Orseck P.A. Financial Advisory Services
Resorts World Miami
Skanska USA
Wal-Mart Media Relations, Social Media, Targeted Marketing Initiatives

SCHWARTZ PUBLIC RELATIONS ASSOCIATES, INC.

444 Park Ave S 12th Fl, New York, NY 10016-7321
Tel.: (212) 677-8700
Fax: (212) 254-2507
E-Mail: info@schwartzpr.com
Web Site: www.schwartzpr.com

E-Mail for Key Personnel:
President: barry@schwartzpr.com

Employees: 13
Year Founded: 1961

Agency Specializes In: Brand Development & Integration, Business Publications, Business-To-Business, Children's Market, Communications, Consulting, Consumer Marketing, Consumer Publications, Corporate Identity, Digital/Interactive, Entertainment, Event Planning & Marketing, Exhibit/Trade Shows, Financial, Graphic Design, Information Technology, Internet/Web Design, Investor Relations, Leisure, Magazines, Newspaper, Newspapers & Magazines, Planning & Consultation, Public Relations, Publicity/Promotions, Radio, Strategic Planning/Research, T.V., Teen Market

Approx. Annual Billings: $2,700,000

Breakdown of Gross Billings by Media: Pub. Rels.: 100%

Barry Schwartz *(Pres)*
Steven Wright-Mark *(Exec VP)*

Accounts:
DVD Expo; Los Angeles, CA; 2003
Evident
InterAct Accessories
Monroe Mendelsohn Research; New York, NY; 2005
NanoBusiness Alliance; Chicago, IL; 2002
National Life Group
New Adventures, Inc. Toys; 2005
New York Game Factory ; New York, NY Games; 2004
NewBay Media
TechSmith Corporate PR
Value Added Institute

SCOOTER MEDIA

132 W 6th St, Covington, KY 41011
Tel.: (859) 414-6882
E-Mail: info@scootermediaco.com
Web Site: www.scootermediaco.com

Year Founded: 2012

Agency Specializes In: Event Planning & Marketing, Media Relations, Public Relations, Social Media

Shannan Boyer *(Founder)*
Angel Spyrou Beets *(VP-Client Svcs)*
Bridget Kochersperger *(Mgr-PR)*
Amy Quinn *(Specialist-Social Media)*
Katie Scoville *(Specialist-PR)*

Accounts:
Reach Usa
Whisper Diaper Pail

SCORR MARKETING

2201 Central Ave Ste A, Kearney, NE 68847-5346
Tel.: (308) 237-5567
Fax: (308) 236-8208
E-Mail: scorr@scorrmarketing.com
Web Site: www.scorrmarketing.com

Employees: 30
Year Founded: 2003

Agency Specializes In: Advertising, Agriculture, Business Publications, Business-To-Business, Collateral, Communications, Corporate Communications, Crisis Communications, Email, Event Planning & Marketing, Exhibit/Trade Shows, Guerilla Marketing, Integrated Marketing, Local Marketing, Logo & Package Design, Market Research, Media Buying Services, Media Planning, Media Relations, Media Training, Out-of-Home Media, Print, Promotions, Public Relations, Publicity/Promotions, Search Engine Optimization, Social Marketing/Nonprofit, Social Media, Strategic Planning/Research, Web (Banner Ads, Pop-ups, etc.)

Cinda Orr *(Pres & CEO)*
Ben Rowe *(Chief Creative Officer & Sr VP)*
Lea Studer *(VP-Mktg Comm)*
Robert Jones *(Dir-Copy)*
Brook Pierce *(Dir-Creative Svcs)*
Dallas Darden *(Office Mgr)*
Dee Fuehrer *(Mgr-Trade Show & Event)*
Zach Karl *(Copywriter)*
Sarah Berke *(Coord-Program)*
Holli Kroeker *(Coord-PR & Media)*

Accounts:
Accelerated Vision Marketing
ACR Image Metrix
Cenduit Marketing
New-Cryoport Systems Inc. (Agency of Record) Marketing Strategy
ExecuPharm, Inc. Marketing
Firecrest Clinical (Agency of Record)
Frenova Renal Research
Harlan Contract Research Services Branding, Strategy
LabConnect, LLC Branding
PharmaNet
Princess Posy
Ricerca
Skilled Care Pharmacy (Agency of Record)
TKL Research Inc.
Zyantus (Agency of Record)

SCOTT CIRCLE COMMUNICATIONS, INC.

1900 L St NW Ste 705, Washington, DC 20036
Tel.: (202) 695-8225
E-Mail: info@scottcircle.com
Web Site: www.scottcircle.com

Agency Specializes In: Event Planning & Marketing, Media Relations, Public Relations, Strategic Planning/Research

Laura Gross *(Principal)*
Jeff Shulman *(Principal)*
Sarah Coppersmith *(VP)*
Noa Rabinowitz *(VP-Events)*

Accounts:
Let Freedom Ring 50th Anniversary of the March on Washington

SCOTT PUBLIC RELATIONS

21201 Victory Blvd Ste 270, Canoga Park, CA 91303
Tel.: (818) 610-0270
Fax: (818) 710-1816
E-Mail: inquiry@scottpublicrelations.com
Web Site: www.scottpublicrelations.com

Employees: 12

Agency Specializes In: Health Care Services, Media Relations, Public Relations, Strategic Planning/Research

Joy Scott *(Pres & CEO)*
Bill Colacurcio *(Dir-Programs & Bus Dev-CEU Institute-Natl)*
Deborah Dominguez *(Strategist-Mktg & Branding)*
Lisa Kalustian *(Strategist-Political)*

Accounts:
IPC The Hospitalist Company, Inc
Metagenics, Inc.; San Clemente, CA
One Call Medical, Inc.
The Phoenix Group

SE2

770 Sherman St, Denver, CO 80203
Tel.: (303) 892-9100
Web Site: www.publicpersuasion.com

Agency Specializes In: Advertising, Brand Development & Integration, Digital/Interactive, Public Relations, Radio, T.V.

Eric Sondermann *(Chm)*
Susan Morrisey *(Pres)*
Eric Anderson *(CEO & Principal)*
Brandon Zelasko *(Principal)*
Amy Guttmann *(Dir-Creative)*
Melisa Kotecki Schlote *(Dir-Bus Ops)*

Accounts:
American College of Veterinary Internal Medicine
Colorado Apartment Association
Colorado Department of Human Services
Colorado School of Mines Alumni Association
Donor Alliance

SEEDLING COMMUNICATIONS

PO Box 302199, Austin, TX 78703
Tel.: (512) 215-8977
E-Mail: info@seedling-communications.com
Web Site: www.seedling-communications.com

Year Founded: 2010

Agency Specializes In: Event Planning & Marketing, Public Relations, Social Media

Jennie Whitaker *(Co-Owner)*
Marcus Whitaker *(Co-Owner-Branding & Business Affairs)*
Claire Woll *(Strategist-Comm)*
Casey Creamer *(Designer-Web & Graphic Designer)*

Accounts:
Gary Cash
Head for the Cure

SELIGMAN BRAND STRATEGIES

5080 PGA Blvd Ste 213, Palm Beach Gardens, FL 33418
Tel.: (561) 630-7739
E-Mail: info@sbrandstrategies.com
Web Site: www.sbrandstrategies.com

Agency Specializes In: Advertising, Brand Development & Integration, Collateral, Communications, Graphic Design, Media Relations, Public Relations, Social Media

Alyson Seligman *(Owner & Pres)*
Kimberly Whetsel *(Acct Mgr)*
Heather Lynn Robbins *(Mgr-Accounts & Strategist-Online)*

Accounts:
The City of West Palm Beach
Jupiter Medical Center

SEVAG PUBLIC RELATIONS

107 W Lancaster Ave Ste 202, Wayne, PA 19087
Tel.: (215) 285-1531
Web Site: www.sevagcreative.com

Year Founded: 2010

Agency Specializes In: Brand Development & Integration, Event Planning & Marketing, Graphic Design, Public Relations, Social Media

Kristy Sevag *(Owner)*
Brea Mealey *(Acct Exec)*

Accounts:
Forage American Brasserie

SEVENTWENTY STRATEGIES

1220 19th St NW Ste 300, Washington, DC 20036
Tel.: (202) 962-3955
Fax: (202) 962-0995
E-Mail: info@720strategies.com
Web Site: www.720strategies.com

Agency Specializes In: Branded Entertainment, Digital/Interactive, Media Planning, Public Relations, Social Media

Pam Fielding *(Pres)*
Vlad Cartwright *(Exec VP)*
Kim Sullivan *(Sr VP)*
Christine DiGiovacchino *(Creative Dir)*

Accounts:
New-Bree's Sweet Treats

SEYFERTH & ASSOCIATES INC.

40 Monroe Ctr NW Ste 202, Grand Rapids, MI 49503
Tel.: (616) 776-3511
Fax: (616) 776-3502
Toll Free: (800) 435-9539
E-Mail: info@seyferthpr.com
Web Site: www.seyferthpr.com

E-Mail for Key Personnel:
Media Dir.: zalewski@sstpr.com

Employees: 62
Year Founded: 1984

Agency Specializes In: Brand Development & Integration, Corporate Identity, Event Planning &

Marketing, Exhibit/Trade Shows, Government/Political, Investor Relations, Public Relations, Publicity/Promotions

Ginny M. Seyferth *(Founder & Pres)*
Regina Daukss *(CFO)*
Karen Hogan *(Principal)*
Dan Spaulding *(Principal)*
Tyler Lecceadone *(VP)*
Eileen McNeil *(VP-Community & Pub Affairs)*
Michael Zalewski *(VP)*
Cynthia Domingo *(Acct Supvr)*

Accounts:
Detroit Medical Center
The Henry Ford
Irwin Union Bank
McDonald's Corp.
Taubman
X-Rite

SHAFER COMMUNICATIONS
(Name Changed to Thrive PR)

SHARLA FELDSCHER PUBLIC RELATIONS
325 Cherry St 2nd Fl, Philadelphia, PA 19106
Tel.: (215) 627-0801
Fax: (215) 627-3120
Web Site: www.sf-pr.com

Agency Specializes In: Event Planning & Marketing, Media Relations, Public Relations, Social Media

Sharla Feldscher *(Pres)*
Ellen Weisberg *(Mgr-PR)*
Hope Feldscher Horwitz *(Acct Exec)*

Accounts:
Andrea Green Music
Charitydine
DePue Brothers Band
Eddie Bruce
Enchantment Theatre Company
Erin Dickins
Goldenbergs Peanut Chews
Jacobs Music Company
Japan America Society
Journey Cafe

SHEA COMMUNICATIONS
18 E 41St St, New York, NY 10017
Tel.: (212) 627-5766
Fax: (212) 627-5430
E-Mail: info@sheacommunications.com
Web Site: www.sheacommunications.com

Agency Specializes In: Advertising, Collateral, Event Planning & Marketing, Government/Political, Legal Services, Local Marketing, Planning & Consultation, Real Estate, Strategic Planning/Research

Richard P. Shea *(Pres)*
George C. Shea *(CEO)*

Accounts:
Ethical Culture Fieldston School
Great American Seafood Cook Off
Heiberger & Associates
Japan Sumo Association
Louise Phillips Forbes/Halstead Property Company
Louisiana Seafood Board
Monday Properties
Municipal Art Society
Newman Real Estate Institute
River to River Festival
Robert K. Futterman
Rose Associates
Rosenberg & Estis LLC
White Acre Equities

SHERIDAN PUBLIC RELATIONS LLC
223 4th Ave N, Franklin, TN 37064
Tel.: (615) 472-8879
Web Site: www.sheridanpr.com

Agency Specializes In: Brand Development & Integration, Communications, Crisis Communications, Internet/Web Design, Media Relations, Public Relations, Social Media, Strategic Planning/Research

Jay Sheridan *(Pres)*
Chad Schmidt *(Principal)*
Macey Benton *(Sr Acct Exec)*
Holly Albright *(Sr Acct Exec)*

Accounts:
Kraft Enterprise Systems
Pucketts Boat House

SHERRI JONES PUBLIC RELATIONS
95 W Main St Ste 5-162, Chester, NJ 07930
Tel.: (800) 573-8831
Web Site: www.sherrijonesmba.com/the-publicist/

Year Founded: 2010

Agency Specializes In: Brand Development & Integration, Event Planning & Marketing, Media Relations, Public Relations, Social Media

Sherri Jones *(CEO)*

Accounts:
Industri Designs

SHIFT COMMUNICATIONS
125 5th Ave, New York, NY 10003
Tel.: (646) 756-3700
Fax: (646) 756-3710
Web Site: www.shiftcomm.com

Employees: 7

Agency Specializes In: Corporate Communications, Media Relations, Public Relations, Social Media

Alan Marcus *(Sr VP & Head-NY Office)*
Victoria Boed *(VP-Acct Svcs)*
Chris Penn *(VP-Mktg Tech)*
Karl Scholz *(VP)*
Cathy Summers *(VP-Acct Svcs)*
Matt Trocchio *(VP)*
Reshma Fernandes *(Acct Dir)*
Dave Finn *(Sr Acct Exec)*
Mary McGuire *(Sr Acct Exec)*
Jennifer Modica *(Acct Exec)*

Accounts:
Canadian Club
H&R Block
Hawaii Visitors & Convention Bureau
Lionel Trains
Metromile
Mountainside
Pacific Gas and Electric Company
Socialbakers Media Relations
SOLS
Splash
Suburban Propane
T-Mobile
New-W.C. Bradley Co. Char-Broil, Digital Marketing, Public Relations

SHIFT COMMUNICATIONS LLC
20 Guest St Ste 200, Brighton, MA 02135
Tel.: (617) 779-1800
Fax: (617) 779-1899
E-Mail: jim@shiftcomm.com
Web Site: www.shiftcomm.com

Employees: 50
Year Founded: 2003

Agency Specializes In: Public Relations

Approx. Annual Billings: $10,000,000

Amy Anderson Lyons *(Pres)*
Paula Finestone *(COO)*
Ed Weiler *(Principal)*
Catherine Allen *(Exec VP)*
Amanda Munroe *(VP)*
Christopher Penn *(VP-Mktg Tech)*
Joel Richman *(VP)*
Karl Scholz *(VP)*
Cathy Summers *(VP-Acct Svcs)*
Julie Staadecker *(Acct Dir)*
Jenny Lafortune *(Dir-Art)*
Rebecca Kelley *(Sr Acct Mgr)*
Megan Nemeh *(Acct Mgr)*
Maria Baez *(Sr Acct Exec)*
Kimberly Diesel *(Sr Acct Exec)*
Brian Loschiavo *(Sr Acct Exec)*
Emily Roderick *(Sr Acct Exec)*
Sarah E. Salbu *(Sr Acct Exec)*
Taylor Smith *(Sr Acct Exec-Consumer)*
Stephanie Chan *(Acct Exec)*

Accounts:
ADARA Networks
Ad:Tech (Agency of Record)
AOL
Appia
Appirio
Authoria
Axceler
Beam Global Wine & Spirits, Inc. Public & Media Relations
BearingPoint
Bigcommerce Press
Bing
Canadian Club Public Relations
The Churchill Club
Collective Bias
ConnectEDU
DeKuyper Public Relations
Ektron
Everbank
Fuhu
FutureM
H&R Block Block Talk, Content Strategy, Social Media
Hoover's, Inc. Public Relations
Imogo Mobile Technologies Corp. Public Relations, Social Media
IntelliResponse Company Awareness
Johnson & Johnson
Joss & Main Brand Awareness, Consumer Acquisition
Kaspersky
Lionel Trains Digital Strategy, Social Media
Logitech
MassChallenge
McDonald's Advertising Cooperative Public Relations, Social Media
MedeAnalytics
MetTel Media Relations, Social Media
Mimecast
NeatReceipts
Novell, Inc
Oakley
Overstock.com
Pitney Bowes Business Insight Social Media
Publix
Quantum Corporation
Quiznos; 2010
Rapid7 Campaign: "Go Big or Go Home"
RealNetworks, Inc.; 2007
RSA Security Conference (Agency of Record)
Rubicon Project; Los Angeles, CA
Salesforce.com

Scout
Shimano
Techcrunch DISRUPT (Agency of Record)
Topo Athletic
Toyota Strategic Planning
Travelocity.com
uLocate
Wayfair.com PR
Wells Fargo
Yelp
Yodlee

Branches

SHIFT Communications
275 Sacramento St, San Francisco, CA 94111
(See Separate Listing)

SHIFT Communications
275 Washington St, Boston, MA 02458
Tel.: (617) 779-1800
E-Mail: cwolverton@shiftcomm.com
Web Site: www.shiftcomm.com

Employees: 135
Year Founded: 2003

Agency Specializes In: Public Relations, Sponsorship

Catherine Allen *(Exec VP)*
Cathy Summers *(Sr VP-Acct Svcs)*
Dan Brennan *(VP-Acct Svcs)*
Katie Clark-AlSadder *(VP)*
Amanda Munroe *(VP)*
Annie Perkins *(VP-Consumer & Healthcare)*
Victoria Shaw *(VP-Acct Svcs)*
Peter Buhler *(Dir-Creative)*
Leah Ciappenelli *(Dir-HR)*
Danielle Coe *(Acct Mgr)*

Accounts:
Decision Resources Group
Foxwoods Resort Casino (Public Relations Agency of Record)
Hawaii Visitors & Convention Bureau Social Media Agency of Record
Hood
McDonald's Restaurants
McKesson Healthcare Solutions
Medullan
Orchard Supply Hardware Hardware Stores
Sermo
SharkNinja
T-Mobile Cellular Service
Toyota New England Auto
Wente Family Estates; Livermore, CA Brand Awareness, Double Decker, Offline, Social Media
Whole Foods Market Grocery

Shift Communications
125 5th Ave, New York, NY 10003
(See Separate Listing)

SHORE FIRE MEDIA
32 Court St Ste 1600, Brooklyn, NY 11201
Tel.: (718) 522-7171
Fax: (718) 522-7242
E-Mail: info@shorefire.com
Web Site: www.shorefire.com

Agency Specializes In: Digital/Interactive, Public Relations, Social Media

Marilyn Laverty *(Pres)*
Rebecca Shapiro *(VP)*

Accounts:
New-Emily Kinney Music

SHOTWELL PUBLIC RELATIONS
820 Aptos Ridge Circle, Watsonville, CA 95076
Tel.: (408) 666-9200 (Mobile)
E-Mail: jay@shotwellpr.com
Web Site: www.shotwellpr.com

Agency Specializes In: Brand Development & Integration, Communications, Consumer Marketing, Exhibit/Trade Shows, Graphic Design, Investor Relations, New Product Development, Production, Public Relations, Publicity/Promotions

Jay Shotwell *(Founder)*
Ray Chancellor *(Dir-Creative-ContentX)*
Valerie Foster *(Sr Acct Exec)*

Accounts:
Advanced Recognition Technologies
Aisys Ltd.
AITech International
AITech Micro
ALPS Electric (USA), Inc.
Ampro Computers
Appshop
Atlas Peak Olive Oil
Avatar Peripherals
Bradmark
BTC Corporation
Cemaphore Internet Products & Services
Concept Kitchen
Concurrent Controls, Inc.
Creative Digital Research
CSR
CTX Opto
cyLogistics Telephony, Communications & Wireless Systems
Daewoo/Cordata
DataZONE
DURECT
Emulation Technologies
EUROM FlashWare Solutions
Finland Global Software III
Galil Motion Control
Hewlett Packard
Honeywell Bull Italia
Internet Image
IO Data Device, Inc.
KAO Infosystems
KSI (Korean Software Incubator)
M-Systems FlashDisk Pioneers
Memorex Computer Supplies
Micro-Frame Technologies
Mirapoint
Nav-Tec
NetAPP
OPTi
Ornetix Network Products
PacBell
Pacom International
Pioneer New Media Technologies
Plantronics
Puccini Restaurant Group
RDC Networks
Redwood Mortgage
Rockliffe, Inc.
Sanrad
Scalant Systems
Sceptre Technologies
Shinko Technologies
Siemens
Smart & Friendly
Solar Semiconductor
Solid Data Systems
Tryllian
WebGear
Zedeon, Inc.
ZF Micro Devices

SHOUT PUBLIC RELATIONS
1032 W 18th Ste A-4, Costa Mesa, CA 92627
Tel.: (949) 574-1440
Web Site: www.shoutpr.com

Year Founded: 1997

Agency Specializes In: Advertising, Brand Development & Integration, Event Planning & Marketing, Media Relations, Public Relations, Social Media

Melody Althaus *(Acct Exec)*
Lana Unger *(Acct Exec)*
Elizabeth Wiekamp *(Jr Acct Exec)*

Accounts:
Cozy Orange

SHUMAN & ASSOCIATES INC
120 W 58th St, New York, NY 10019
Tel.: (212) 315-1300
Fax: (212) 757-3005
E-Mail: shumanpr@shumanassociates.net
Web Site: www.shumanassociates.net

Agency Specializes In: Communications, Public Relations, Radio, Strategic Planning/Research, T.V.

Constance Shuman *(Pres)*

Accounts:
Alexander Fiterstein
The All-Star Orchestra
Berliner Philharmoniker
Gilmore Festival
James Conlon
Jennifer Koh
Kirill Gerstein
The Metropolitan Opera
The Minnesota Orchestra
Orchestre de la Suisse Romande
Orpheus Chamber Orchestra
San Francisco Opera
San Francisco Symphony
Shai Wosner
Spoleto Festival USA
Stephen Hough
Tobias Picker
Utah Symphony
Wu Man

SIBRAY PUBLIC RELATIONS
115 White Ave, Beckley, WV 25801
Tel.: (304) 575-7390
E-Mail: contact@sibraypr.com
Web Site: www.sibraypr.com

Agency Specializes In: Content, Internet/Web Design, Media Relations, Public Relations, Search Engine Optimization, Social Media

David Sibray *(Pres)*

Accounts:
Vagabond Kitchen

THE SILVER MAN GROUP INC.
213 W Institute Place Ste 501, Chicago, IL 60610
Tel.: (312) 932-9950
Web Site: www.silvermangroupchicago.com

Agency Specializes In: Media Relations, Public Relations

Beth Silverman *(Pres)*
Elizabeth Neukirch *(VP)*
Rob Walton *(Asst VP)*
Liza Massingberd *(Acct Exec)*
Caitlin Jagodzinski *(Acct Exec)*

Accounts:
New-American Theater Company

New-The Gift Theatre Company

SIMPLY THE BEST PUBLIC RELATIONS
301 Yamato Rd Ste 1240, Boca Raton, FL 33431
Tel.: (954) 261-2149
Web Site: www.simplythebestpublicrelations.com

Agency Specializes In: Advertising, Local Marketing, Public Relations

Adam Goodkin *(Owner)*
Kim Morgan *(Pres)*

Accounts:
Barbara Sanchez Public Relations Agency of Record
Benjamin Mach (Agency of Record) Media
Cheese Culture A whey of Life Cheese Store
Cheri Florance PR
Decolav Household Fruniture Store
Dr. Paul Inselman PR
The English Tap & Beer Garden Cocktails & Other Drinks Bar
ESO Decorative Plumbing (Agency of Record)
Gabi Rose LLC
Green Planet Festival (Agency of Record)
Jennifer Bradley Co. PR
Josef's Table Public Relations
Key College Digital
LA Via Ristorante & Bar (Agency of Record)
L'etoile
Lichi-Zelman Style Interiors PR
Marcello Sport (Agency of Record)
Meatball Room PR
Palm Beach Orthopaedic Institute PR
Salon Sora PR, Social Media
Scanabilities Ventures PR
Silberman Endodontics Public Relations
Simply the Best (Agency of Record) Women's Luxury Fashion Designs
New-South Florida Introductions (Agency of Record) Public Relations, Social Media
Top Shelf Holdings (Agency of Record) Besado Tequila
Wightman Construction PR

SIMPSON COMMUNICATIONS LLC
3031 Warrington Rd, Shaker Heights, OH 44120
Tel.: (216) 991-4297
Web Site: www.simpsoncomm.wordpress.com

Year Founded: 2003

Agency Specializes In: Crisis Communications, Media Relations, Media Training, Public Relations, Social Media, Strategic Planning/Research

Kristen Simpson *(Pres)*
Mike Dilorenzo *(Acct Coord)*

Accounts:
The Automotive Lift Institute
DE-STA-CO PR

SINALA NOIR PUBLIC RELATIONS, LLC.
1330 Ave of the Americas Ste 23A, New York, NY 10019
Tel.: (212) 729-6724
Fax: (212) 729-6824
E-Mail: info@sinalanoir.com
Web Site: www.sinalanoir.com

Agency Specializes In: Advertising, Brand Development & Integration, Digital/Interactive, Entertainment, Event Planning & Marketing, Media Relations, Public Relations, Search Engine Optimization, Social Media, Sponsorship

S. Angelique Mingo *(Brand Mgr)*

Accounts:
Evolution of Curves Media Relations, Online, PR, Social Media
Isla Jewels PR
Native Elianor
Samantha Eng Consumer Awareness, Public Relations, Traditional & Social Media
Y'Sador Creative, Design, Strategic Consulting

SINGER ASSOCIATES INC
47 Kearny St 2nd Fl, San Francisco, CA 94108
Tel.: (415) 227-9700
Fax: (415) 348-8478
E-Mail: info@singersf.com
Web Site: www.singersf.com

Year Founded: 2000

Agency Specializes In: Advertising, Corporate Communications, Crisis Communications, Event Planning & Marketing, Media Buying Services, Media Relations, Media Training, Public Relations, Sponsorship, Strategic Planning/Research

Sam Singer *(Pres)*
Sharon Rollins Singer *(CFO)*
Adam A. Alberti *(Exec VP)*
Jason Barnett *(VP)*
Erin Souza *(Dir-Bus Ops)*
Gina Antonini *(Acct Supvr)*
Mike Aldax *(Sr Acct Exec)*
Alex Doniach *(Sr Acct Exec)*
Jennifer Hoff *(Acct Exec)*

Accounts:
New-City of Milpitas Communications
Recology

SIREN PR LLC
2609 Crooks Rd, Troy, MI 48084
Tel.: (586) 212-4792
Web Site: www.siren-pr.com

Year Founded: 2012

Agency Specializes In: Brand Development & Integration, Crisis Communications, Event Planning & Marketing, Logo & Package Design, Media Relations, Media Training, Public Relations, Social Media, Strategic Planning/Research

Cayce Karpinski *(Acct Exec)*
Meghan Mcalister *(Acct Exec-Beauty Div)*
Allegra Storatz *(Acct Exec-Beauty Div)*

Accounts:
Detroit Bikes

SITRICK & CO.
1840 Century Park E Ste 800, Los Angeles, CA 90067
Tel.: (310) 788-2850
Fax: (310) 788-2855
E-Mail: info@sitrick.com
Web Site: www.sitrick.com

Employees: 50

Michael S. Sitrick *(Chm & CEO)*
Jeffrey Lloyd *(Mng Dir)*
Tom Becker *(Dir-New York Office)*

Accounts:
Alex Rodriguez

SKAI BLUE MEDIA
109 S 13th St Ste 119A, Philadelphia, PA 19107
Tel.: (215) 625-7988
Web Site: www.skaibluemedia.com

Rakia Reynolds *(Pres)*
Christanna Ciabattoni *(Sr Acct Exec)*
Javier Alonzo *(Coord-Creative Comm)*

Accounts:
United By Blue

SKIRT PR
2320 North Damen Ave 2D, Chicago, IL 60647
Tel.: (773) 661-0700
Web Site: www.skirtpr.com

Agency Specializes In: Cosmetics, Fashion/Apparel, Social Media, Women's Market

Lauren Donovan *(Pres)*
Adrienne Eckert Petersen *(CEO)*
Katelyn Lewis *(Dir-Creative & Strategic Dev)*
Isabella Palmer *(Sr Acct Exec)*
Brittany Banion *(Acct Exec)*
Chapin Streitz *(Office Dir)*

Accounts:
Barre Bee Fit
Birchbox
Brides, Bubbles + Bliss
Brideside.com
Carasco Photography
Carats & Cake
Chicago Toy and Game Group
Giftbar.com
Hair Essentials
Indie Lee
Jo Malone London
Lincoln Park Zoo
Lurie Children's Hospital
Paul Stuart
Peruvian Connection
Thompson Chicago
Travel + Leisure
Westfield
WhatRUWearing.net

SLATE COMMUNICATIONS
425 W Mulberry St 201, Fort Collins, CO 80521
Tel.: (970) 797-2015
Fax: (970) 797-4924
E-Mail: info@slatecommunications.com
Web Site: www.slatecommunications.com

Agency Specializes In: Brand Development & Integration, Event Planning & Marketing, Graphic Design, Internet/Web Design, Public Relations, Social Media

Kim Newcomer *(Founder & Principal)*
Ryan Burke *(Founder & Creative Dir)*

Accounts:
New-Alliance for Innovation

SLICE COMMUNICATIONS
1818 Market St 36th Fl, Philadelphia, PA 19103
Tel.: (215) 279-8300
E-Mail: info@slicecommunications.com
Web Site: www.slicecommunications.com

Year Founded: 2008

Agency Specializes In: Public Relations, Social Media

Cassandra Bailey *(Pres & CEO)*
Mason Luvera *(Acct Mgr-PR)*
Darby Rowe *(Acct Mgr-PR)*
Renee Stanzione *(Acct Mgr-PR)*
Jenni Glenn *(Acct Supvr)*
Anthony Stipa *(Acct Supvr-PR)*
Charla Platt-Doble *(Supvr-Ops)*

Accounts:
New-Atlas Bronze Brand Awareness, Media

Relations, Social Media Outreach, Strategic Content Development
BBQ Guru
Be Well Philly
BLT Architects
Bookbinder Specialties
Business Leaders Organized for Catholic Schools
Godshall's Quality Meats
Invisible Sentinel
New-JBGR Retail Brand Awareness, Media Relations, Social Media Outreach, Strategic Content Development
New-National Association for Catering and Events Brand Awareness, Media Relations, Social Media Outreach, Strategic Content Development
Philadelphia Society of Human Resource Management
Saxbys Coffee
New-Sisters of Saint Francis Brand Awareness, Media Relations, Social Media Outreach, Strategic Content Development
Spark Energy
New-StratIS Brand Awareness, Media Relations, Social Media Outreach, Strategic Content Development

SLOANE & COMPANY LLC
(d/b/a Sloane & Company)
7 Times Sq Tower 17th Fl, New York, NY 10036
Tel.: (212) 486-9500
Fax: (212) 486-9094
E-Mail: info@sloanepr.com
Web Site: www.sloanepr.com

Employees: 25
Year Founded: 1998

Agency Specializes In: Communications, Consulting, Exhibit/Trade Shows, Financial, Investor Relations, Public Relations

Revenue: $5,000,000

Elliot Sloane *(CEO)*
Joshua Hochberg *(Mng Dir & Head-IR & Capital Markets)*
Darren Brandt *(Mng Dir)*
Whit Clay *(Mng Dir)*
John Hartz *(Mng Dir)*
Dan Zacchei *(Mng Dir)*
Nevin Reilly *(Sr VP)*

Accounts:
CIENA
EPIX
Green Mountain Coffee Roasters Corporate Public Relations, Strategic Financial
Imax Corporation
New York Life Insurance Company (Public Relations Agency of Record)
Njoy Inc Public Relations
Ryman Hospitality Properties, Inc.
The Street, Inc.
Take Care Health Systems
Tivo, Inc.; Alviso, CA Corporate PR
Vangent, Inc.
Walgreen Co.

SLOWEY MCMANUS COMMUNICATIONS
11 Beacon St Ste 340, Boston, MA 2108
Tel.: (646) 467-7372
Fax: (617) 523-0068
Web Site: www.sloweymcmanus.com

Year Founded: 2006

Agency Specializes In: Collateral, Corporate Communications, Crisis Communications, Internet/Web Design, Media Relations, Media Training, Public Relations, Social Media

Dominic F. Slowey *(Owner & Principal)*
Jeff Roberts *(Mng Partner)*
James McManus *(Principal)*
Katie Kinne *(Acct Dir)*
Megan Thompson *(Sr Acct Exec)*

Accounts:
New-Association for Behavioral Healthcare

SMART CONNECTIONS PR
PO Box 453, Rising Sun, MD 21911
Tel.: (410) 658-8246
E-Mail: info@smartconnectionspr.com
Web Site: www.smartconnectionspr.com

Agency Specializes In: Corporate Communications, Media Relations, Media Training, Public Relations, Search Engine Optimization, Social Media

Joanne Hogue *(Partner)*
Dina Grills Petrosky *(Partner)*
Ira Ruderman *(Partner-Strategic-SEO Svcs)*

Accounts:
Gridstore

SMARTMARK COMMUNICATIONS, LLC
140 Terry Dr Ste 105, Newtown, PA 18940-1896
Tel.: (215) 504-4272
Fax: (215) 504-0872
E-Mail: info@smartmarkusa.com
Web Site: smartmarkglobal.com

Year Founded: 2000

Agency Specializes In: Communications, Public Relations, Strategic Planning/Research

Juliet Shavit *(Pres & CEO)*
Lindsay Ambrose *(Acct Mgr)*
Jenna Shikoff *(Acct Exec)*
Seth Caldwell *(Asst Acct Exec)*

Accounts:
IneoQuest Technologies
NetCracker Technology
Wynntek

SMARTMARKETING COMMUNICATIONS
7836 Hermanson Pl NE, Albuquerque, NM 87110
Tel.: (505) 293-3553
Web Site: www.smartmarketingcommunications.com

Agency Specializes In: Advertising, Graphic Design, Public Relations, Social Media

Lucy Rosen *(Pres)*
Ellen Linnemann *(VP-PR & Client Svcs)*
Kimberly Tatro *(VP-Client Comm)*
Lindsay Doyle *(Dir-Creative Svcs)*

Accounts:
American Association of Nurse Life Care Planners
Ouchies Bandages
Pal-O-Mine

SMITH MARKETING GROUP
1608 W Campbell Ave Ste 196, Campbell, CA 95008
Tel.: (408) 866-5517
Fax: (408) 866-5513
E-Mail: info@smithmarketinggroup.com
Web Site: www.smithmarketinggroup.com

Employees: 10

National Agency Associations: PRSA

Agency Specializes In: Advertising, Advertising Specialties, Alternative Advertising, Brand Development & Integration, Business-To-Business, Collateral, Communications, Consulting, Corporate Identity, Crisis Communications, Custom Publishing, Direct-to-Consumer, Entertainment, Event Planning & Marketing, Graphic Design, Guerilla Marketing, Logo & Package Design, Media Planning, Media Relations, Media Training, Merchandising, Mobile Marketing, Multimedia, Newspapers & Magazines, Planning & Consultation, Print, Production (Ad, Film, Broadcast), Public Relations, Real Estate, Recruitment, Web (Banner Ads, Pop-ups, etc.)

Karen R. Smith *(Pres & CEO)*

Accounts:
Campbell Chamber of Commerce
Campbell European Motors
Hewlett Packard
The Kane Group
Palm Bay Dental Group
Sheridan Enterprises
Silicon Valley Temps
Tech Team 2 Go

SMITH PUBLIC RELATIONS
13600 Marina Pointe Dr Ste 1110, Marina Del Rey, CA 90292
Tel.: (310) 849-5573
Fax: (310) 822-6424
Web Site: www.smithpr.com

Agency Specializes In: Brand Development & Integration, Media Relations, Public Relations, Social Media, Strategic Planning/Research

Steve Smith *(Principal)*

Accounts:
Pacific Shore Holdings Inc (Marketing & Public Relations Agency of Record)

SMOAK PUBLIC RELATIONS
105 N Spring St Ste 111, Greenville, SC 29601
Tel.: (864) 235-8330
Fax: (864) 235-8296
Web Site: www.smoakpr.com

Agency Specializes In: Event Planning & Marketing, Media Relations, Public Relations, Social Media

Katherine Smoak Davis *(Owner)*
Kerry Glenn *(Sr Acct Exec)*
Maddy Varin *(Acct Exec)*
Molly Gunson *(Jr Acct Exec)*

Accounts:
New-Presbyterian College

SNACKBOX LLC
1009 W 6th St Ste 201, Austin, TX 78703
Tel.: (512) 687-6236
Fax: (512) 687-6217
Web Site: www.snackbox.us

Agency Specializes In: Logo & Package Design, Media Relations, Print, Public Relations, Social Media

Eric Oltersdorf *(Principal)*
Jenna Gruhala Oltersdorf *(Principal)*
Natalie Boscia *(Acct Dir-Travel & Tourism)*
Dan McGrath *(Dir)*
Amy Burger *(Sr Specialist-Media)*
Terry Marvin *(Sr Specialist-Media)*
Jeff Salzgeber *(Sr Specialist-Media)*
Maris Callahan *(Specialist-Media-Food & CPG)*
Yahaira Hernandez *(Asst Acct Exec)*
Dana Sotoodeh *(Asst Acct Exec)*
Mark Moseley *(Sr Engr-Software)*

Accounts:
Smoothie King Franchises, Inc.

SOCIALWRX
2100 Grand Ste 301, Kansas City, MO 64110
Tel.: (816) 550-4382
E-Mail: info@socialwrx.com
Web Site: www.socialwrx.com

Agency Specializes In: Brand Development & Integration, Media Relations, Public Relations, Social Media

Jenny Kincaid *(Principal)*

Accounts:
Core Athletic
Hotel Phillips (Public Relations Agency of Record) Brand Awareness, Communications Strategy, Strategic Counsel
MODbath

SOLOMON MCCOWN & COMPANY, INC.
177 Milk St Ste 610, Boston, MA 02109
Tel.: (617) 695-9555
Fax: (617) 695-9505
E-Mail: hsolomon@solomonmccown.com
Web Site: www.solomonmccown.com

Employees: 20
Year Founded: 2003

National Agency Associations: PRSA

Agency Specializes In: Brand Development & Integration, Business-To-Business, Corporate Communications, Corporate Identity, Education, Health Care Services, Legal Services, Public Relations, Real Estate, Restaurant, Retail, Strategic Planning/Research, Travel & Tourism

Approx. Annual Billings: $2,085,000

Ashley McCown *(Owner)*
Helene Solomon *(CEO)*
Jonathan Pappas *(VP)*
T. J. Winick *(VP)*
Michelle Mastrobattista *(Dir-Digital Comm)*

Accounts:
Allston Brighton Community Development Corporation
American Academy of Arts & Sciences
Local Initiatives Support Corporation (LISC)
UMass Memorial Medical Center

SOLOMON TURNER PUBLIC RELATIONS
36 Four Seasons Shopping Ctr Ste 346, Chesterfield, MO 63017
Tel.: (314) 205-0800
Web Site: www.solomonturner.com

Agency Specializes In: Brand Development & Integration, Media Relations, Public Relations

Steve Turner *(Principal)*

Accounts:
New-Northwestern Mutual

SOUTHARD COMMUNICATIONS
515 W 20th St 6th Fl, New York, NY 10011
Tel.: (212) 777-2220
Fax: (212) 993-5811
E-Mail: info.ny@southardinc.com
Web Site: www.southardinc.com

Employees: 15
Year Founded: 1994

Agency Specializes In: Public Relations

Revenue: $3,500,000

Bill Southard *(Pres & CEO)*
Lisa Hanlon *(Sr VP)*
Kelley Devincentis *(VP)*
Scott Goldberg *(VP)*
Brandon Thomas *(Sr Acct Dir)*
Stephania Greendyk *(Sr Acct Exec)*
Aine Byrne *(Acct Exec)*
Alex Studnicky *(Acct Exec)*
Sarah Brokenshire *(Jr Acct Exec)*

Accounts:
American Pool Player's Assoc.
AudibleKids
CB Richard Ellis
New-Choice Collectables
eCarrot
New-Elemental Path
Farah USA
New-The Irish Fairy Door Company
New-iZZi Gadgets Inc
KLC School Partnerships
LeapFrog
Maverix USA
New-Maverix
New-Para'Kito
School Zone Publishing Little Scholar Kids Tablet
New-SleepBelt

SPARK PUBLIC RELATIONS
2 Bryant St Ste 100, San Francisco, CA 94105
Tel.: (415) 962-8200
Fax: (415) 522-0330
E-Mail: info@sparkpr.com
Web Site: www.sparkpr.com

Employees: 28
Year Founded: 1999

Agency Specializes In: Investor Relations, Media Relations, Social Media

Donna Sokolsky *(Co-Founder & Mng Partner)*
Alan Soucy *(CEO & Mng Partner)*
Diane Schreiber *(Mng Dir)*
Toby Trevarthen *(Chief Narrative Officer)*
Stephen Pechdimaldji *(Sr Dir-Sports Tech & Media)*
Amber Conroy *(Sr Acct Dir-Spark PR & Activate)*
Tim Donovan *(Strategist-Narrative)*

Accounts:
Blinkx
Crosslink Capital
Index Ventures
Seedcamp
Skydeck
Sungevity
Verdezyne, Inc.
Ving

SPARKPR
30 W 26th St 4th Fl, New York, NY 10010
Tel.: (646) 833-0308
E-Mail: newyork@sparkpr.com
Web Site: www.sparkpr.com

Agency Specializes In: Content, Digital/Interactive, Internet/Web Design, Media Relations, Public Relations, Social Media

Ruth Sarfaty *(Mng Dir)*
Nicole Bestard *(Mng Dir-Enterprise Practices)*
Faith Paris *(Mng Dir-Consumer-East Coast)*
Tony Telloni *(Gen Mgr)*
Sandra Correa *(Dir-Consumer Lifestyle)*
Kristen Buckley *(Acct Mgr)*
Kyle Sharick *(Mgr-Consumer Media)*
Lee Tawil *(Strategist-Media Rels)*

Accounts:
Steaz (Public Relations Agency of Record)

SPEAKERBOX COMMUNICATIONS
7900 Westpark Dr Ste T410, McLean, VA 22102
Tel.: (703) 287-7800
E-Mail: info@speakerboxpr.com
Web Site: www.speakerboxpr.com

Employees: 20
Year Founded: 1999

Agency Specializes In: High Technology, Media Relations, Public Relations, Strategic Planning/Research

Elizabeth Shea *(Pres & CEO)*
Lisa Throckmorton *(Exec VP)*
Katie Hanusik *(VP)*
Josh Schimel *(Sr Dir)*
Jennifer Edgerly *(Sr Acct Dir)*
Cristina Upston *(Dir-HR)*
Kate Raynovich-Nesbitt *(Acct Mgr)*
Michael Peterson *(Acct Coord)*

Accounts:
HighPoint Global
Intel
Juniper Networks
Red Hat Software Operating System Software
Surety

SPECOPS COMMUNICATIONS, INC.
1201 Bdwy Ste 407, New York, NY 10001
Tel.: (212) 518-7721
E-Mail: info@specopscomm.com
Web Site: www.specopscomm.com

Agency Specializes In: Broadcast, Communications, Content, Corporate Communications, Crisis Communications, Digital/Interactive, Exhibit/Trade Shows, Media Relations, Print, Public Relations

Adam J. Handelsman *(Founder & CEO)*
Mackenzie Mills *(VP & Principal)*
Kirt Rothe *(Sr VP)*
Kayla Inserra *(Acct Supvr)*
Sarah Meyer *(Sr Acct Exec)*
Katie Lambert *(Acct Exec)*

Accounts:
Acacia Research Corporation
Are You Interested
The Grilled Cheese Truck Inc. (Public Relations Agency of Record)
indieFilmFunding.com Media Relations, Public Relations
Mobile Media Summit
Money2020 Digital Outreach, Media
SecureAuth (Public Relations Agency of Record)

SPECTOR & ASSOCIATES, INC.
61 Broadway, New York, NY 10006
Tel.: (212) 943-5858
Fax: (212) 430-3849
E-Mail: info@spectorandassociates.net
Web Site: spectorpr.com

Employees: 18
Year Founded: 1991

Agency Specializes In: Sponsorship

Revenue: $1,600,000

Barry Spector *(Owner)*
Shelley Spector *(Pres)*

Accounts:
AT&T Communications Corp.
Bayer
eCaring Public Relations
Forest Laboratories Inc.
Homewatch CareGivers Marketing, Public Relations
ITT
Logos Technologies Inc.; Arlington, VA Public Affairs, Public Relations
Philips

SPECTRUM

2001 Pennsylvania Ave NW, Washington, DC 20006
Tel.: (202) 955-6222
Fax: (202) 955-0044
E-Mail: info@spectrumscience.com
Web Site: www.spectrumscience.com

Employees: 30

National Agency Associations: COPF-PRSA

Agency Specializes In: Government/Political, Health Care Services, Medical Products, Pharmaceutical, Public Relations

Approx. Annual Billings: $8,500,000

John J. Seng *(Founder, Chm & CEO)*
Jonathan Wilson *(Pres)*
Rosalba Cano *(VP)*
Pamela Lippincott *(VP-Strategy Dev)*
Megan Lustig *(VP)*
Darby Pearson *(VP)*
Amanda Sellers *(VP)*
Lauren Fulk *(Acct Dir)*
Anthony Lafauce *(Dir-Digital Strategy)*
Phyllis Tate *(Dir-Fin)*

Accounts:
Alnylam Pharmaceuticals Biopharmaceuticals
AlterG Rehabilitation Technology
American College of Chest Physicians
Arthur G. James Cancer Hospital
Biogen Idec
DePaul University Athletics
DUSA Pharmaceuticals, Inc; Wilmington, MA
Kennedy Krieger Institute
Maxim Health Systems
Pfizer
Procter & Gamble
Seton Hall University Athletics

SPELLING COMMUNICATIONS

10460 Cheviot Dr, Los Angeles, CA 90064
Tel.: (310) 838-4010
Web Site: www.spellcom.com

Agency Specializes In: Content, Media Relations, Public Relations, Social Media

Dan Spelling *(Owner)*
Brian McWilliams *(VP)*
W. Jason Grimley *(Sr Acct Supvr)*

Accounts:
Level 5 Beverage Company, Inc "Good-for-You", Coffee Boost, Public Relations Agency of Record, The Herbal Collection, Vitamin Creamer, VitaminFIZZ

THE SPI GROUP LLC

165 Passaic Ave Ste 410, Fairfield, NJ 07004
Tel.: (973) 244-9191
Fax: (973) 244-9193
E-Mail: sgoodman@spigroup.com
Web Site: www.spigroup.com

Employees: 16

Year Founded: 1997

National Agency Associations: PRSA

Agency Specializes In: Brand Development & Integration, Business-To-Business, Collateral, Communications, Consulting, Consumer Marketing, Electronic Media, Exhibit/Trade Shows, Graphic Design, Health Care Services, Information Technology, Internet/Web Design, Production, Public Relations, Publicity/Promotions, Real Estate, Sales Promotion, Sweepstakes, Trade & Consumer Magazines

Approx. Annual Billings: $12,000,000 Capitalized

James Koppenal *(Mng Dir)*
Sonali Munjal *(Mng Dir)*
Steve E. Goodman *(Gen Mgr)*
Ollie Hartsfield *(Sr Dir)*
Ellen English *(Dir)*
Tom Gilbert *(Dir)*
Heather Norian *(Dir-Fin & Facilities)*
Michael Dooley *(Sr Mgr)*
Dana Haase *(Sr Mgr)*
Amanda Feliu *(Acct Supvr-Editorial Svcs)*

Accounts:
BOC Group
Caucus Educational Corporation
Coldwell Banker Real Estate Corporation
Consumer Management Systems
Cytec
GE Lighting; Cleveland, OH; 1999
Key Bank
Marsh USA, Inc.
Merck; Whitehouse Station, NJ; 2002
NJ Shares; Ewing, NJ; 1999
Novartis; Switzerland
Pfizer; New York, NY; 1998
Sony

SPIN COMMUNICATIONS

18 E Blithedale Ave Ste 26, Mill Valley, CA 94941
Tel.: (415) 380-8390
Fax: (415) 380-8375
Web Site: www.spinpr.com

Year Founded: 1998

Agency Specializes In: Crisis Communications, Email, Event Planning & Marketing, Media Training, Public Relations, Radio, Strategic Planning/Research, T.V.

DeeDee Taft *(Owner)*
Shelbi Okumura *(Sr Acct Exec)*
Hope Timberlake *(Acct Exec)*

Accounts:
Bay to Breakers
Beijing International Triathlon
Familyevents.com
Hot Rod
Jack London Inn
Motor Trend Auto Shows, LLC
Serramonte Center
Silicon Valley Auto Dealers Association
Strictly Sail Pacific

SPMG MEDIA

385 S Lemon Ave Ste 236, Walnut, CA 91789
Tel.: (888) 841-7779
Web Site: www.spmgmedia.net

Agency Specializes In: Event Planning & Marketing, Media Relations, Public Relations, Social Media

Gina Smith *(Pres)*

Accounts:
ChrystalChyna Marketing, Public Relations
Courageous Woman Brand Marketing Strategy
Custom Business Planning Solutions (Agency of Record) Public Relations
Dr. Shaurice E. Mullins
PraiseWorks, Inc
Telishia Berry Marketing Strategy

SPOTLIGHT MEDIA RELATIONS

244 Fifth Ave Ste B276, New York, NY 10001
Tel.: (212) 489-8774
E-Mail: info@spotlightmediarelations.com
Web Site: www.spotlightmediarelations.com

Agency Specializes In: Event Planning & Marketing, Media Relations, Media Training, Public Relations, Social Media

Jill Budik *(Founder & Pres)*

Accounts:
New-Kristen Levine
New-Limor Suss

THE SPR AGENCY

7201 E Camelback Rd, Scottsdale, AZ 85251
Tel.: (480) 648-1770
E-Mail: info@thespragency.com
Web Site: www.thespragency.com

Year Founded: 2007

Agency Specializes In: Advertising, Content, Public Relations, Search Engine Optimization, Social Media

Al Stevens *(Pres & CEO)*
Christy Stevens *(VP)*
Megann Jakubek *(Asst Acct Exec)*

Accounts:
Corso & Rhude (Agency of Record) Digital Marketing, Public Relations, Social Media, Strategy
Darling Homes Inc
Preston's Steakhouse, North Scottsdale (Agency of Record)
Skin and Cancer Center of Scottsdale (Agency of Record)
Taylor Morrison Phoenix

SPR ATLANTA

1516 Peachtree St NW Ste 400, Atlanta, GA 30309
Tel.: (404) 872-7289
Web Site: www.spratlanta.com

Year Founded: 2002

Agency Specializes In: Brand Development & Integration, Content, Crisis Communications, Internet/Web Design, Media Relations, Media Training, Public Relations, Social Media

Chris Schroder *(Pres)*
Sarah Funderburk *(Partner & Acct Dir)*
Nancy Reynolds *(Acct Dir)*
Susan Greco *(Acct Dir)*
Jan Schroder *(Dir-Editorial)*
Andre Ledgister *(Acct Mgr)*
Emily Tracy *(Acct Mgr)*

Accounts:
HGOR Planners & Landscape Architects
Southeast Mortgage

SPREAD PR

477 Madison Ave Fl 6, New York, NY 10022
Tel.: (212) 696-0006
E-Mail: info@spreadpr.net

Web Site: www.spreadpr.net

Agency Specializes In: Event Planning & Marketing, Media Relations, Promotions, Public Relations

Stephanie Somogyi Miller *(Founder & Pres)*

Accounts:
New-Weitzner Limited

SPRINGBOARD COMMUNICATIONS

17 N Main St, Marlboro, NJ 07746
Tel.: (732) 863-1900
Fax: (732) 863-1915
E-Mail: info@springboardpr.com
Web Site: www.springboardpr.com

Employees: 10
Year Founded: 1995

Agency Specializes In: Event Planning & Marketing, Public Relations

Domenick Cilea *(Pres)*
Greg Casha *(Asst Acct Exec)*
Megan Morreale *(Assoc Acct Exec)*
Courtney Moed *(Acct Coord)*

Accounts:
Advanced Wellness
Alloy Software
ATEN Technology
BUMI
EasyVista
Ericom Software
EtherFAX
Innovi Mobile
Mercedes Distribution Center
MetaWatch
Quickcomm
ReferStar
Synchronoss Technologies
UXC ECLIPSE
Wally World Media

SPRITZ LLC

660 Sacramento St Ste 200, San Francisco, CA 94111
Tel.: (415) 221-2875
E-Mail: info@spritzsf.com
Web Site: www.spritzsf.com

Agency Specializes In: Brand Development & Integration, Digital/Interactive, Event Planning & Marketing, Internet/Web Design, Media Relations, Public Relations, Search Engine Optimization, Social Media

Kaley Gelineau *(Acct Mgr)*

Accounts:
New-Twenty Five Lusk

SPROCKET COMMUNICATIONS

3254 Larimer St, Denver, CO 80205
Tel.: (303) 495-2883
Web Site: www.sprocketcommunications.com

Year Founded: 2006

Agency Specializes In: Communications, Event Planning & Marketing, Media Buying Services, Public Relations, Social Media

Aubrey Cornelius *(Co-Founder)*
Jeff Cornelius *(Co-Founder)*

Accounts:
Atticus Denver
Eon Office
Trelora

SQUIRES PUBLIC RELATIONS

10866 Washington Blvd No 346, Culver City, CA 90232
Tel.: (323) 375-4890
Fax: (310) 693-2628
Web Site: www.squirespr.com

Year Founded: 2007

Agency Specializes In: Event Planning & Marketing, Media Relations, Media Training, Public Relations, Social Media

Accounts:
Go Inspire Go

SS PR

One Northfield Plz Ste 400, Northfield, IL 60093
Tel.: (847) 955-0700
Fax: (847) 955-7720
Toll Free: (800) 287-7720
Web Site: www.sspr.com

Heather Kelly *(Co-Pres)*
Jill Schmidt *(Pres)*
Kristin Miller *(Sr VP)*
Maya Pattison *(Sr VP)*
Craig Astler *(VP-Comm & Plng)*
Mallory Snitker *(VP)*
Steve Fiore *(Acct Dir)*
Alexandra Buchanan *(Acct Supvr)*

Accounts:
GestureTek Inc.
Lifeway Foods
Nobscot
Norlight
Poweron Software

SSA PUBLIC RELATIONS

(Name Changed to InView Communications)

STALWART COMMUNICATIONS

9635 Granite Rdg Dr Ste 330, San Diego, CA 92123
Tel.: (858) 429-7095
E-Mail: info@stalwartcom.com
Web Site: www.stalwartcom.com

Year Founded: 2006

Agency Specializes In: Crisis Communications, Event Planning & Marketing, Media Relations, Media Training, Public Relations, Strategic Planning/Research

David B. Oates *(Pres)*
Elizabeth Ireland *(Sr Program Mgr)*
Alyson Jamison *(Sr Program Mgr)*

Accounts:
Calentix Technologies
Envision Solar International, Inc.
Fitwall
Gap Intelligence
The Glenner Memory Care Centers
Jacob Tyler
LightBridge Hospice
Medsphere Systems Corporation
NoteVault
Redit

STANDING PARTNERSHIP

1610 Des Peres Rd, Saint Louis, MO 63131
Tel.: (314) 469-3500
Fax: (314) 469-3512
Web Site: standingpartnership.com/

Employees: 23
Year Founded: 1991

Agency Specializes In: Advertising, Agriculture, Brand Development & Integration, Business-To-Business, Collateral, Communications, Consulting, Corporate Communications, Corporate Identity, Crisis Communications, Education, Electronic Media, Environmental, Event Planning & Marketing, Financial, Food Service, Government/Political, Health Care Services, Hospitality, Identity Marketing, Industrial, Integrated Marketing, International, Internet/Web Design, Investor Relations, Media Relations, Media Training, New Technologies, Pharmaceutical, Planning & Consultation, Public Relations, RSS (Really Simple Syndication), Recruitment, Search Engine Optimization, Social Marketing/Nonprofit, Sponsorship, Stakeholders, Strategic Planning/Research, Transportation, Travel & Tourism, Viral/Buzz/Word of Mouth

Approx. Annual Billings: $3,000,000

Breakdown of Gross Billings by Media: Pub. Rels.: 100%

Beth Rusert *(Partner & Sr VP)*
Linda Locke *(Sr VP)*
Julie Steininger *(Sr VP)*
Mihaela Grad *(VP)*
Sara Schlenk *(Dir-Ops & Fin)*
Lindsay Auer *(Mgr & Coord-Internship)*
Ashlyn Brewer *(Mgr)*
Nick Sargent *(Mgr)*
Andrea Shea *(Mgr)*

Accounts:
Anheuser Busch
Charlottesville Albermarle Airport
Colliers Turley Martin Tucker
Delaware North Companies; Buffalo, NY
Flexsys
Harrah's St. Louis
LDI Integrated Pharmaceutical Services
Maritz
Monsanto Company
MS Govern
MySci Traveling Science Program; 2005
Partnership for a Drug-Free America
Praxair Distribution, Inc.
Premier Bank
Private Residences at Chase Park Plaza
Ranken Jordan Pediatric Specialty Hospital
Ranken Technical College
Saint Louis Children's Hospital
Saint Louis Mills
St. John's Mercy Medical Center
St. Loius County Economic Council
St. Louis Rams
UniGroup, Inc.
United Van Lines
Virginia High School League
Washington University Science Outreach
World Agricultural Forum

STANTON COMMUNICATIONS, INC.

1150 Connecticut Ave NW Ste 810, Washington, DC 20036
Tel.: (202) 223-4933
Fax: (202) 223-1375
E-Mail: washingtonoffice@stantoncomm.com
Web Site: www.stantoncomm.com

Employees: 40
Year Founded: 1989

National Agency Associations: COPF-PRSA

Agency Specializes In: Business-To-Business, Communications, Consumer Marketing, Education, Electronics, Environmental, Event Planning & Marketing, Financial, Food Service,

Government/Political, Health Care Services, High Technology, Information Technology, Legal Services, Medical Products, Planning & Consultation, Public Relations, Publicity/Promotions, Radio, Retail, Sponsorship, Strategic Planning/Research, Travel & Tourism

Approx. Annual Billings: $1,000,000

Lori Russo *(Pres)*
Peter V. Stanton *(CEO)*
Jeff Urbanchuk *(Acct Mgr)*
Megan Berry *(Mgr-Creative Svcs)*
Elynsey Price *(Acct Exec)*
Elisabeth Wraase *(Acct Exec)*

Accounts:
Al Smith Memorial Foundation Public Affairs
American Nurses Association
American Registry for Internet Numbers
The American Statistical Association Public Relations
The Arc of Delaware County
Asbury Communities Public Relations, Strategic Communications
CareLogistics
Compass Learning
Consumer Electronics Association Brand Building, Consumer Marketing, Media, Strategic Counsel
Corinthian Colleges
Delmarva Power & Light
Dig-It! Games Bloggers, Consumer Press, Trade Media
eInstruction
ELS Educational Services Communication Strategy
Fraunhofer IIS Brand Building, Consumer Marketing, Marketing Communications, Media Relations, Strategic Counsel
New-Madda Fella (Agency of Record)
Maryland Department of Business & Economic Development
MorganFranklin Consulting; 2008
NAMPA
National Association of Professional Background Screeners Crisis Management, Media Relations, PR Counsel, Strategic Planning
Pendrell
Pepco
New-Quad/Graphics
ShelterBox USA Public Relations
Southland Industries
Sprint; 2002
TCF Bank
Vertis Communications
WellDoc BlueStar, Media Relations, Strategic Counsel
WilmerHale
W.L. Gore & Associates; 2002

Branches

Stanton Communications
300 E Lombard St Ste 1440, Baltimore, MD 21202
Tel.: (410) 727-6855
Fax: (410) 727-6156
E-Mail: baltimoreoffice@stantoncomm.com
Web Site: www.stantoncomm.com

Employees: 10
Year Founded: 1992

National Agency Associations: COPF-PRSA

Agency Specializes In: Brand Development & Integration, Business-To-Business, Communications, Consumer Marketing, Corporate Communications, Crisis Communications, Digital/Interactive, Education, Electronics, Environmental, Event Planning & Marketing, Financial, Food Service, Health Care Services, High Technology, Information Technology, Legal Services, Media Planning, Medical Products, Planning & Consultation, Public Relations, Publicity/Promotions, Radio, Travel & Tourism

Lori Russo *(Mng Dir-Mid-Atlantic)*
Amy Bowman *(Acct Mgr)*

Accounts:
Airforwarders Association
Alstom
Atlantic City Electric
CareLogistics
Corinthian Colleges
Delmarva Power
Department of Veterans Affairs
eInstruction
Maryland Department of Business & Economic Development
MorganFranklin
Pendrell Corporation
Pepco
Southland Industries
Sprint
TCF Bank
Vertis Communications
W.L. Gore & Associates

Stanton Communications
400 Madison Ave 14th Fl Ste D, New York, NY 10017
Tel.: (212) 616-3601
Fax: (212) 616-3612
E-Mail: newyorkoffice@stantoncomm.com
Web Site: www.stantoncomm.com

Employees: 15
Year Founded: 1989

National Agency Associations: COPF-PRSA

Agency Specializes In: Brand Development & Integration, Business-To-Business, Communications, Consumer Marketing, Corporate Communications, Crisis Communications, Digital/Interactive, Education, Electronics, Environmental, Event Planning & Marketing, Financial, Food Service, Government/Political, Health Care Services, High Technology, Information Technology, Legal Services, Media Relations, Medical Products, Planning & Consultation, Public Relations, Travel & Tourism

Peter V. Stanton *(Pres & CEO)*
Joseph Contrino *(Acct Exec)*
Cara Greene *(Acct Exec)*

Accounts:
The Arc of Delaware County
Atlantic City Electric
Corinthian Colleges
Delmarva Power
eInstruction
Maryland Department of Business & Economic Development
MorganFranklin
Pendrell Corporation
Pepco
Southland Industries
TCF Bank

STARFISH PUBLIC RELATIONS
1715 Via El Prado Ste 54, Redondo Beach, CA 90277
Tel.: (310) 429-8868
E-Mail: info@starfish-pr.com
Web Site: www.starfish-pr.com

Year Founded: 2002

Agency Specializes In: Digital/Interactive, Media Relations, Public Relations, Social Media

Angela Moore *(Pres)*

Accounts:
AAA Appraisal Management Company
Habitat for Humanity International, Inc.

STC ASSOCIATES
210 5th Ave, New York, NY 10010
Tel.: (212) 725-1900
Fax: (212) 725-1975
E-Mail: newyork@stcassociates.com
Web Site: www.stcassociates.com

E-Mail for Key Personnel:
President: sophie@stcassociates.com
Creative Dir.: laurent@stcassociates.com

Employees: 25
Year Founded: 1992

Agency Specializes In: Advertising, Bilingual Market, Brand Development & Integration, Business-To-Business, Collateral, Communications, Consulting, Consumer Marketing, Corporate Identity, Digital/Interactive, Direct Response Marketing, E-Commerce, Event Planning & Marketing, Exhibit/Trade Shows, Fashion/Apparel, Food Service, Graphic Design, High Technology, Internet/Web Design, Leisure, Logo & Package Design, Print, Production, Public Relations, Publicity/Promotions, Real Estate, Restaurant, Sales Promotion, Strategic Planning/Research, Trade & Consumer Magazines, Travel & Tourism

Approx. Annual Billings: $4,000,000

Breakdown of Gross Billings by Media: Adv. Specialities: 10%; Comml. Photography: 10%; Consulting: 10%; Event Mktg.: 10%; Exhibits/Trade Shows: 10%; Graphic Design: 10%; Internet Adv.: 10%; Point of Sale: 10%; Pub. Rels.: 10%; Worldwide Web Sites: 10%

Sophie Ann Terrisse *(CEO)*
Claire Butkus *(VP-Brand Res & Strategy)*
Keila Taveras-Rodriguez *(Dir-Art & Mgr-Studio)*

Accounts:
AIG
Boswell Group
FRS Health Energy
Global Crossing; New York, NY
Great Spirits Co.; Queens, NY
KDDI America
Switch and Data
Tony Werneke Fine Antiques
VanCleef & Arpels
VSNL International
Weight Watchers
Whitney Museum of American Art
Wild Turkey Bourbon

STEFANUCCI & TURNER
20971 Coastview Ln, Huntington Beach, CA 92648
Tel.: (714) 969-2540
Fax: (714) 908-0381

Employees: 3
Year Founded: 1977

Agency Specializes In: Branded Entertainment, Consulting, Event Planning & Marketing, Integrated Marketing, Public Relations, Sponsorship, Sports Market, Strategic Planning/Research, T.V.

Approx. Annual Billings: $500,000

Brian Turner *(Owner)*

Accounts:
Dana Point Concours d'Elegance; Dana Point, CA Classic Car Show; 1999

Inside F-1 TV Series; 2008
Newport Beach Magazine; Newport Beach, CA; 2009

STEINREICH COMMUNICATIONS
2125 Center Ave, Fort Lee, NJ 07024
Tel.: (201) 498-1600
Fax: (201) 498-1590
E-Mail: info@scompr.com
Web Site: www.scompr.com

Employees: 15
Year Founded: 2002

Agency Specializes In: Consumer Goods, Fashion/Apparel, Financial, Health Care Services, Retail, Social Marketing/Nonprofit, Travel & Tourism

Stan Steinreich *(Grp Pres & CEO)*
Ellyn Small *(Sr VP & Gen Mgr)*
Virginia Montgomery *(VP & Grp Dir-Travel & Tourism)*
Ariella Steinreich *(Dir)*
Priscilla-Marie Ilarraza *(Sr Acct Exec)*

Accounts:
13th Annual Herzliya Conference

STEPHENSON GROUP
37 Hollow Brook Rd, Califon, NJ 07830
Tel.: (908) 439-3660
Fax: (908) 439-3268
E-Mail: newsmakers@stephensongroup.com
Web Site: www.stephensongroup.com

Employees: 42
Year Founded: 1987

Agency Specializes In: Brand Development & Integration, Collateral, Investor Relations, Public Relations, Strategic Planning/Research

Approx. Annual Billings: $4,200,000

Ann Stephenson *(CEO)*
Pam Abrahamsson *(VP-Acct Mgmt)*
Dipka Bhambhani *(VP-Govt Affairs)*
Patricia Jones *(VP-Mktg Comm)*
Lory Torgerson *(Dir-Ops)*

Accounts:
Cisco Systems, Inc.
K/P Corporation
Kane and Associates
Midtown Technologies
Neurologix
SAP
Union Bank of California

Branch

Stephenson Group
1575 Spinnaker Dr Ste 105B-167, Ventura, CA 93001
Tel.: (805) 772-1200
Fax: (805) 830-1600
E-Mail: newsmakers@stephensongroup.com
Web Site: www.stephensongroup.com

Employees: 18

Agency Specializes In: Public Relations

ANN Stephenson *(CEO)*
Lory Torgerson *(Dir-Ops)*

Accounts:
Comcast 8:
The Motley Fool
New York Times

STERLING COMMUNICATIONS
750 University Ave Ste 100, Los Gatos, CA 95032
Tel.: (408) 395-5500
Fax: (408) 395-5533
E-Mail: more@sterlingpr.com
Web Site: www.sterlingpr.com

Employees: 25

Agency Specializes In: Public Relations

Marianne O'Connor *(CEO-Sterling Comm)*
Mark Bonham *(VP)*
Tiffany Bryant *(VP-Ops)*
Kawika Holbrook *(VP)*
Lisa K. Hawes *(Sr Dir-Pub & Media Rels)*
Rosie Brown *(Project Mgr-Creative)*
Wes Warfield *(Project Mgr-Digital Content)*
Ciera Jammal *(Sr Acct Exec)*
Pouneh Lechner *(Sr Acct Exec)*

Accounts:
Actional
AlMetrix
Amber Networks
Attensity
Avolent
IXOS
Knome (Agency of Record)
Mercado
NETGEAR

STERN + ASSOCIATES
(Name Changed to Stern Strategy Group)

STERN STRATEGY GROUP
(Formerly Stern + Associates)
186 Wood Ave S, Iselin, NJ 08830
Tel.: (908) 276-4344
Fax: (908) 276-7007
E-Mail: hello@sternstrategy.com
Web Site: sternstrategy.com/

Employees: 28
Year Founded: 1985

National Agency Associations: PRSA

Agency Specializes In: Business-To-Business, Consulting, Corporate Communications, Corporate Identity, Crisis Communications, Health Care Services, High Technology, Media Relations, Medical Products, Promotions, Public Relations, Social Marketing/Nonprofit

Susan Stern *(Pres)*
Nicole Gagnon *(Sr VP)*
Joan Bosisio *(Grp VP)*
Ned Ward *(Grp VP)*
Tara Baumgarten *(VP)*
Regina Walsweer *(Mgr-HR)*
Tom Healey *(Sr Acct Supvr)*
Whitney Jennings *(Asst Specialist-Sls)*

Accounts:
B. Braun Medical, Inc.; 2007
Ben Heineman; 2008
Bracco Diagnostics Inc.; 2007
Clay Christensen
Convia (Herman Miller); 2006
Farient Advisors; 2009
Greg Unruh; 2009
GS1 US; 2009
Harvard Business Review Brand Awareness, Business Media Relations, Digital, Direct Engagement, Marketing, Media
Henry Chesbrough, PhD
London Business School; 2006
LRN; 2008
MdOnline; 2009
Michael Howe; 2009
Michael Porter
The Mohawk Group Flooring; 2007
Nancy Koehn; 2009
ORC Worldwide; 2007
Prime Resources Group; 2010
The RBL Group
TruePoint

Branch

Stern Strategy Group
(Formerly Stern + Associates)
45 Prospect St, Cambridge, MA 02139
Tel.: (908) 276-4344
Fax: (617) 761-4601
Web Site: sternstrategy.com/

Employees: 20

Agency Specializes In: African-American Market, Brand Development & Integration, Business Publications, Business-To-Business, Communications, Consulting, Consumer Marketing, Consumer Publications, Corporate Communications, Crisis Communications, Education, Electronic Media, Environmental, Financial, Government/Political, Health Care Services, High Technology, Hospitality, Identity Marketing, Industrial, Information Technology, International, Magazines, Media Relations, Media Training, Medical Products, Multicultural, Multimedia, New Technologies, Newspaper, Newspapers & Magazines, Planning & Consultation, Podcasting, Product Placement, Promotions, Public Relations, Publicity/Promotions, Publishing, Radio, Real Estate, Search Engine Optimization, Social Marketing/Nonprofit, Sponsorship, Strategic Planning/Research, T.V., Trade & Consumer Magazines, Travel & Tourism, Viral/Buzz/Word of Mouth

Nicole Gagnon *(Sr VP)*
Jennifer Zottola *(Dir-Editorial)*

Accounts:
AT&T Consumer Products
Fisher & Phillips
Pension Real Estate Association (PREA)

STEVEN DRAKE ASSOCIATES LLC
12912 Two Farm Dr, Silver Spring, MD 20904
Tel.: (301) 680-0585
E-Mail: sdrake@sdrakeassociates.com
Web Site: www.sdrakeassociates.com

Agency Specializes In: Brand Development & Integration, Corporate Communications, Media Relations, Media Training, Public Relations, Social Media

Steve Drake *(Principal)*

Accounts:
Brienzas Academic Advantage
Corinthian Colleges Inc
Easy Rest Adjustable Sleep Systems
Education Industry Association
Greater Silver Spring Chamber of Commerce
Huawei
Infosnap, Inc.

STEWARD MEDIA GROUP
6476 Orchard Lake Rd Ste A, West Bloomfield, MI 48322
Tel.: (248) 973-6070
Fax: (248) 973-6071
E-Mail: info@steward-media.com
Web Site: www.steward-media.com

Agency Specializes In: Event Planning &

Marketing, Public Relations, Social Media

Ryan Jacob Fishman *(VP)*

Accounts:
New-The Alexander & Gabrielle

STIR COMMUNICATIONS
1111 Park Centre Blvd Ste 402, Miami, FL 33169
Tel.: (305) 407-1723
Fax: (305) 407-1729
E-Mail: info@stir-communications.com
Web Site: www.stir-communications.com

Year Founded: 2004

Agency Specializes In: Advertising, Collateral, Event Planning & Marketing, Internet/Web Design, Podcasting, Print, Promotions, Radio, T.V., Web (Banner Ads, Pop-ups, etc.)

Greg Salsburg *(CEO)*
Patricia Ann Micek *(CFO)*
Patricia Micek *(CFO)*
Diedre Krause *(Exec VP)*

THE STORCH-MURPHY GROUP
(Name Changed to Jitsu Public Relations, Inc.)

STRATEGIC COMMUNICATIONS GROUP
1750 Tysons Blvd Ste 1500, McLean, VA 22102
Tel.: (703) 289-5139
E-Mail: pr@gotostrategic.com
Web Site: www.gotostrategic.com

E-Mail for Key Personnel:
President: mhausman@gotostrategic.com

Employees: 15
Year Founded: 1995

Agency Specializes In: Advertising, Brand Development & Integration, Business-To-Business, Collateral, Communications, Consulting, Corporate Identity, Direct Response Marketing, Event Planning & Marketing, Graphic Design, High Technology, Information Technology, Internet/Web Design, Logo & Package Design, Production, Public Relations, Recruitment, Technical Advertising

Marc Hausman *(Founder & CEO)*
Erica Pierson *(Mng Dir)*
Shany Seawright *(Mng Dir)*
Nikki Robinson *(Dir-Fin & Admin)*
Jenna Sindle *(Strategist)*
Eldon Marr *(Analyst-Digital Media)*

Accounts:
Acuity Mobile; 2007
Altron; 2008
Aptara
BearingPoint
British Telecom
Broadsoft
CX Act, Inc. Social Media Campaign
Cyveillance
GlobeRanger
GovDelivery
Inmarsat
Knight Sky Satellite & Wireless Networks; 2007
Merchant Link
Microsoft
Microspace Communications
Monster
Oracle America, Inc.
Solera Networks (Agency of Record)
Spirent Communications
Stanley
TerraGo Technologies
WellDoc Communications
Wireless Matrix
Zebra Technologies Card Printing Solutions; 2008

STRATEGIC OBJECTIVES
184 Front Street E 4th Floor, Toronto, ON M5A 4N3 Canada
Tel.: (416) 366-7735
Fax: (416) 366-2295
E-Mail: contactus@strategicobjectives.com
Web Site: www.strategicobjectives.com

Employees: 40
Year Founded: 1983

Agency Specializes In: Crisis Communications, Digital/Interactive, Media Relations, Public Relations, Social Media, Strategic Planning/Research

Deborah Weinstein *(Co-Founder, Pres & Partner)*
Judy Lewis *(Co-Founder, Partner & Exec VP-Strategic Objectives)*
Victor Anastacio *(CFO)*
Michael Shipticki *(VP)*
Tonisha Bath *(Acct Mgr)*

Accounts:
Build-A-Bear
Carlsberg Canada Belgian Abbey Beer, Carlsberg, Cultural Influence Programs, Grimbergen Dubbel Draught, Kronenbourg, Kronenbourg Blanca, Media Relations, Somersby Cider
New-DMTI Spatial (Public Relations Agency of Record)
Kraft Canada
Kruger Paper Products LP Cashmere, Scotties, SpongeTowels
M&M Meat Shops
Oxford Learning Centre
Pfizer Canada Detrol, Viagra
Pizza Hut Canada
Second Cup (Public Relations Agency of Record)

STRATEGIC VISION LLC
677 Main St, Suwanee, GA 30024
Tel.: (404) 380-1079
E-Mail: info@strategicvision.biz
Web Site: www.strategicvision.biz

Year Founded: 2001

Agency Specializes In: Brand Development & Integration, Crisis Communications, Graphic Design, Media Relations, Public Relations, Social Media

Peter J. Bates *(Pres)*
David Johnson *(CEO)*
Katie Norris *(Acct Exec)*

Accounts:
New-Dr. Keith Kantor
New-Guy Gilchrist
New-Nutritional Addiction Mitigation Eating & Drinking

STRAUSS MARKETING
5757 W Lovers Ln Ste 215, Dallas, TX 75209
Tel.: (214) 352-6700
E-Mail: info@strausspr.com
Web Site: http://www.strausspr.com/

Year Founded: 2000

Agency Specializes In: Brand Development & Integration, Collateral, Crisis Communications, Email, Event Planning & Marketing, Graphic Design, Media Buying Services, Media Training, Public Relations, Social Media

Jenifer Strauss *(Founder)*
Nicki Patel *(Dir-Ops)*
Alexandra Lesiuk *(Mgr-Client)*

Accounts:
Gehan Homes Marketing, PR, Strategy
The Saxton Group

STRAUSS RADIO STRATEGIES, INC.
National Press Bldg Ste 1163 529 14th St NW, Washington, DC 20045
Tel.: (202) 638-0200
Fax: (202) 638-0400
E-Mail: info@straussradio.com
Web Site: www.straussradio.com

Employees: 13

Agency Specializes In: Communications, Consulting, Public Relations, Radio, Sponsorship, Strategic Planning/Research

Richard Strauss *(Pres)*
Howard Davis *(Mng Dir)*
Zach Seidenberg *(Sr Acct Mgr)*
Jeff King *(Acct Mgr & Mgr-Los Angeles)*
Matthew Lawrence *(Sr Acct Exec)*
David Sands *(Sr Acct Exec)*
Mary Elizabeth Elkordy *(Acct Exec)*
Benny Martinez *(Acct Exec)*
Rachael Shackelford *(Acct Exec)*
Martha Serna *(Assoc Acct Exec)*
Lorilee Victorino *(Assoc Acct Exec)*

Accounts:
AARP
Consumer Electronics Association
General Motors
National League of Cities
US Conference of Mayors

Branch

Strauss Radio Strategies, Inc.
262 W 38th St Ste 803, New York, NY 10018
Tel.: (212) 302-1234
Fax: (212) 302-1235
Toll Free: (888) 638-0220
E-Mail: newyork@straussradio.com
Web Site: www.straussradio.com

Employees: 20

Raul Martinez *(Acct Dir)*
Jeff King *(Acct Mgr & Mgr-Los Angeles)*
Marissa Horowitz *(Sr Acct Exec)*
Matt Lawrence *(Sr Acct Exec)*
David Sands *(Sr Acct Exec)*
Justin Goldstein *(Acct Exec)*
Rachael Shackelford *(Acct Exec)*

STUART ROWLANDS PR
7774 Skyhill Dr, Los Angeles, CA 90068
Tel.: (323) 850-1088
Fax: (323) 850-8219
Web Site: www.stuartrowlandspr.com

Agency Specializes In: Crisis Communications, Event Planning & Marketing, Public Relations, Radio, Social Media, T.V.

Stuart Rowlands *(Pres & CEO)*

Accounts:
CXC Simulations
Duke University Marine Laboratory
Lucas Oil Products Inc
MAVTV
UFWC
Wagon Wheel Village

STUNTMAN PUBLIC RELATIONS
285 W Broadway, New York, NY 10013
Tel.: (212) 242-0002
E-Mail: info@stuntmanpr.com
Web Site: www.stuntmanpr.com

Agency Specializes In: Advertising, E-Commerce, Media Relations, Public Relations

Neil Alumkal *(Founder & Pres)*
Tyler Burrow *(Dir-Lifestyle)*
Erika Kuzmicz *(Sr Acct Exec)*

Accounts:
75 Grand
The Bedford
Francois Payard PR
The Frisky
Just Chill
Kanon Organic Vodka
Mellow Mushroom Pizza Bakers
Mexicue Public Relations
Panache Beverages Alibi American Whiskey, PR
Riazul Premium
Talent Maven

STURGES WORD COMMUNICATIONS
810 Baltimore Ave, Kansas City, MO 64105-1718
Tel.: (816) 221-7500
Fax: (816) 221-2174
E-Mail: info@sturgesword.com
Web Site: www.sturgesword.com

Employees: 8
Year Founded: 1995

Agency Specializes In: Advertising, Advertising Specialties, Brand Development & Integration, Business-To-Business, Collateral, Communications, Consulting, Consumer Marketing, Consumer Publications, Corporate Communications, Corporate Identity, Digital/Interactive, E-Commerce, Entertainment, Event Planning & Marketing, Exhibit/Trade Shows, Fashion/Apparel, Financial, Food Service, Gay & Lesbian Market, Graphic Design, Health Care Services, High Technology, In-Store Advertising, Internet/Web Design, Investor Relations, Legal Services, Leisure, Local Marketing, Logo & Package Design, Media Buying Services, New Product Development, Over-50 Market, Planning & Consultation, Public Relations, Real Estate, Recruitment, Restaurant, Retail, Sales Promotion, Seniors' Market, Strategic Planning/Research, Travel & Tourism

Melissa Sturges *(Principal)*
Linda Word *(Principal)*
Jeannie Kee *(Dir-Ops)*
Michelle Cheesman *(Sr Acct Mgr)*
Katie Garcia *(Acct Mgr)*
Liana Rosenbloom *(Acct Exec)*

Accounts:
Cloverland Electric Cooperative
Enterprise Bank & Trust; 2001
Jo Carrol Energy

STYLE HOUSE PR
44 Wall St Ste 703, New York, NY 10005
Tel.: (212) 444-8177
Web Site: www.stylehousepr.com

Year Founded: 2006

Agency Specializes In: Brand Development & Integration, Event Planning & Marketing, Media Training, Public Relations, Social Media

Janna Meyrowitz Turner *(Founder & Pres)*
Jacki Keating *(Acct Exec)*

Accounts:
New-Oasis
New-TULA

SUE PROCKO PUBLIC RELATIONS
5969 Washington Blvd # 2B, Culver City, CA 90232-7324
Tel.: (310) 836-6200
Fax: (323) 653-5013
E-Mail: info@spprinc.com
Web Site: www.spprinc.com

Employees: 12
Year Founded: 1991

Agency Specializes In: Internet/Web Design, Public Relations, Social Media

Sue Procko *(Founder & Pres)*
Ed Peters *(VP)*
Julie Siegel *(Dir-Publicity)*
Tim Williams *(Sr Acct Exec)*
Melinda Giordano *(Coord-Res)*

Accounts:
AVN Media
Overture Films

SUITE PUBLIC RELATIONS
530 7th Ave Mezzanine Fl, New York, NY 10018
Tel.: (646) 504-9566
E-Mail: info@suitepublicrelations.com
Web Site: www.suitepublicrelations.com

Year Founded: 2005

Agency Specializes In: Brand Development & Integration, Collateral, Media Relations, Media Training, Public Relations, Social Media, Strategic Planning/Research

Janelle Langford *(Creative Dir)*

Accounts:
New-Allison Mitchell
New-CASA de MODA
New-Zachary

SUMMERS ADVERTISING
285 W. Shaw, Fresno, CA 92705
Tel.: (559) 222-7100

Pat Summers *(Dir-Mktg & Strategist)*

Accounts:
Ruiz Foods

SUTHERLANDGOLD GROUP
315 Pacific Ave, San Francisco, CA 94133
Tel.: (415) 934-9600
Fax: (800) 886-7452
E-Mail: scott@sutherlandgold.com
Web Site: www.sutherlandgold.com

Employees: 25
Year Founded: 2002

Agency Specializes In: Consulting, High Technology, Information Technology, Media Training, Planning & Consultation, Strategic Planning/Research

Lesley Gold *(Founder & Principal)*
Scott Sutherland *(Founder)*
Melissa Klein *(Sr VP-Media & Content)*
Dana Zemack *(VP-Content Program)*
Mattie Goldman *(Acct Supvr)*
Amanda Purvis *(Sr Acct Exec)*

Accounts:
Blekko
Brash Entertainment
Brightcove
Chegg PR
Lookout
Opensky
Pinger
Velti Media, PR
Wetpaint

SWANK PUBLIC RELATIONS
4223 W Lake St Ste 342, Chicago, IL 60624
Tel.: (773) 982-8124
E-Mail: info@swankpublishing.com
Web Site: www.swankpublishing.com

Agency Specializes In: Brand Development & Integration, Event Planning & Marketing, Public Relations

Briahna Gatlin *(Founder & CEO)*
Terrance Randell *(COO & Coord-Events)*
Jeremy Horn *(Dir-Creative)*
Carol G. Johnson *(Asst Project Mgr)*

Accounts:
I Am Beeware
Marcus Kincy

SWANSON COMMUNICATIONS
1425 K St NW Ste 350, Washington, DC 20005
Tel.: (202) 783-5500
E-Mail: contact@swansonpr.com
Web Site: www.swansonpr.com

Year Founded: 1997

Agency Specializes In: Event Planning & Marketing, Public Relations, Social Media, Strategic Planning/Research, Travel & Tourism

Kelly Swanson *(Founder & Pres)*
Lisa Milner *(VP)*
Sam Jackson *(Acct Exec)*
Andrew Roberts *(Acct Exec)*

Accounts:
Mayweather Promotions

SWISH MARKETING & PR, LLC
PO Box 352752, Columbus, OH 43635
Tel.: (440) 847-9474
Web Site: www.swishmarketingpr.com

Agency Specializes In: Brand Development & Integration, Public Relations, Social Media

Accounts:
Vogue Salon & Spa

SWORDFISH COMMUNICATIONS
5 Stoneleigh Dr, Laurel Springs, NJ 08021
Tel.: (856) 767-7772
Fax: (866) 801-7772
E-Mail: info@swordfishcomm.com
Web Site: www.swordfishcomm.com

Employees: 1

Agency Specializes In: Advertising, Crisis Communications, Exhibit/Trade Shows, Media Relations, Media Training, Public Relations, Radio, Travel & Tourism

Approx. Annual Billings: $2,000,000

Gary Frisch *(Founder)*

Accounts:
Alzheimer's Association

Coatings for Industry Inc.; Souderton, PA Publicity
Gourmet Ads Trade Publicity Campaign
New-Lifespan Care Management, LLC (Public Relations Agency of Record)
McRoskey Mattress Company Public Relations
Street Corner (Agency of Record)
Sumo Heavy Industries; Philadelphia, PA Public Relations Campaign
The Wine Room
Zounds Hearing Community Outreach, Media Relations

SYMPOINT COMMUNICATIONS
21 N Oak Forest Dr, Asheville, NC 28803
Tel.: (503) 567-9677
Fax: (866) 454-7462
E-Mail: info@sympoint.com
Web Site: www.sympoint.com

Employees: 2
Year Founded: 2004

Agency Specializes In: Communications, Corporate Communications, Corporate Identity, Public Relations, Strategic Planning/Research

Peter terHorst *(Co-Founder & Pres)*
Alexandra terHorst *(Owner)*

Accounts:
Crystal River Weaving
Greeson & Fast
The Q Fund

SYNERGIA PARTNERS
1684 Decoto Road Ste 310, Union City, CA 94587
Tel.: (510) 557-5556
E-Mail: contact@synergiapartners.com
Web Site: www.synergiapartners.com

Agency Specializes In: Advertising, Communications, Consulting, Public Relations

Sam Liu *(Dir)*

Accounts:
VIA Technologies

TALLGRASS PUBLIC RELATIONS
4912 Technopolis Dr, Sioux Falls, SD 57106
Tel.: (605) 275-4075
Web Site: www.tallgrasspr.com

Agency Specializes In: Brand Development & Integration, Event Planning & Marketing, Media Relations, Print, Public Relations, Social Media

Karl Post *(CEO)*
Jennifer Fleming *(Pres)*
Lisa Brandli *(Acct Mgr)*
John Lee *(Sr Acct Exec)*
Seth Menacker *(Acct Exec)*

Accounts:
New-Fragmob.com

THE TASC GROUP
153 W 27th St Ste 405, New York, NY 10001
Tel.: (646) 723-4344
Fax: (646) 723-4525
E-Mail: info@thetascgroup.com
Web Site: www.thetascgroup.com

Agency Specializes In: Crisis Communications, Digital/Interactive, Media Relations, Media Training, Public Relations, Social Media

Lawrence Kopp *(Pres)*
Ann Kaiser *(Acct Exec)*

Accounts:
New-United Way of NYC

TAYLOR
350 Fifth Ave Ste 3800, New York, NY 10118
Tel.: (212) 714-1280
Fax: (212) 695-5685
E-Mail: newyork@taylorstrategy.com
Web Site: www.taylorstrategy.com

Employees: 85
Year Founded: 1984

National Agency Associations: COPF

Agency Specializes In: Public Relations, Sponsorship, Sports Market

Approx. Annual Billings: $21,000,000

Breakdown of Gross Billings by Media: Pub. Rels.: $21,000,000

Tony Signore *(CEO & Mng Partner)*
Bryan Harris *(Mng Partner & COO)*
Mark Beal *(Mng Partner)*
Ryan Mucatel *(Mng Partner)*
J. Mark Riggs *(Exec VP)*
Jairo Hoyos *(Sr VP)*
Brianna Kauffman *(Dir-Digital Strategy)*
Matt Fox *(Acct Exec)*

Accounts:
Allstate Insurance
Crown Royal
Diageo Public Relations, Smirnoff
The Gillette Company
Jenny Craig
Johnnie Walker
Jose Cuervo
MasterCard International
Mercedes-Benz Media Relations, Sports Specialty
Nike Jordan, PR
Novartis
Procter & Gamble
Smirnoff
Staples
Tempur Sealy

Branch

Taylor
10150 Mallard Creek Rd Ste 300, Charlotte, NC 28262
Tel.: (704) 548-8556
Fax: (704) 548-0873
E-Mail: charlotte@taylorstrategy.com
Web Site: www.taylorstrategy.com

Employees: 30

National Agency Associations: COPF

Agency Specializes In: Public Relations, Sponsorship

Tony Signore *(CEO & Mng Partner)*
Bryan Harris *(Mng Partner & COO)*
Mark Beal *(Mng Partner)*
John Liporace *(Mng Partner)*
Ryan Mucatel *(Mng Partner)*
Mark Riggs *(Exec VP)*
Zack Smith *(VP-Media & Consumer Engagement)*
Jessie Snider *(VP)*
Gabrielle Jones *(Sr Strategist-Digital)*
Nicole Murphy *(Acct Exec)*

Accounts:
BRP
Crown Royal
DHL
Diageo
Gillette
Master Card
Nestle Purina
Smirnoff
Staples
XBox

TAYLOR JOHNSON
6333 W Howard, Niles, IL 60714
Tel.: (312) 245-0202
Fax: (312) 245-9205
E-Mail: info@taylorjohnson.com
Web Site: www.taylorjohnson.com

Agency Specializes In: Advertising, Brand Development & Integration, Event Planning & Marketing, Internet/Web Design, Media Relations, Public Relations, Social Media

Emily Johnson *(Pres)*
Kim Manning *(VP)*
Pam Kuhn *(Mgr-Fin & Acctg)*
Vanessa Irving *(Sr Acct Exec)*
Julie Liedtke *(Sr Acct Exec)*
Sarah Lyons *(Sr Acct Exec)*
Kelly Shumaker *(Sr Acct Exec)*
Abe Tekippe *(Acct Exec)*

Accounts:
New-1000 South Clark
Amata Office Centers
Blueprint Healthcare Real Estate Advisors
Edge Home
New-The Habitat Company
John Greene Enterprises
Kinzie Real Estate Group
Pangea Real Estate

TBC, INC./PR DIVISION
900 S Wolfe St, Baltimore, MD 21231
Tel.: (410) 347-7500
Fax: (410) 986-1322
E-Mail: ac@tbc.us
Web Site: www.tbc.us

E-Mail for Key Personnel:
Public Relations: bburkhardt@tbc.us

Employees: 7
Year Founded: 1974

National Agency Associations: PRSA

Agency Specializes In: Business-To-Business, Event Planning & Marketing, Government/Political, Health Care Services, Publicity/Promotions, Retail, Sports Market, Travel & Tourism

Approx. Annual Billings: $2,000,000

Howe Burch *(Pres)*
Jason Middleton *(Sr VP & Dir-Creative)*
Casey Rhoads *(VP & Acct Dir)*
Allison Cannavino *(Acct Dir)*
Krista Capurso *(Acct Supvr)*
Laura Jones *(Acct Supvr)*
Lara Franke *(Supvr-PR)*
Anne Wineholt *(Supvr-Media)*
Kerry Weir *(Acct Exec)*
Jean Flors *(Sr Analyst-Digital)*
Beth Williams *(Sr Media Planner)*
Christy Katz *(Sr Media Planner & Buyer)*

Accounts:
DuClaw Brewing
Hair Cuttery
Hollywood Casino Aurora
Hollywood Casino Charlestown
Hollywood Casino Joliet
Hollywood Casino Lawrenceburg
MinuteClinic
Smyth Jewelers

TCGPR
(Formerly The Communications Group, Inc.)
250 Ferrand Dr 4th Fl, Toronto, ON M3C 3G8 Canada
Tel.: (416) 696-9900
Fax: (416) 696-9897
Toll Free: (800) 267-4476
E-Mail: deisenstadt@tcgpr.com
Web Site: www.tcgpr.com

Employees: 8
Year Founded: 1973

Agency Specializes In: Consumer Goods, Event Planning & Marketing, Government/Political, Local Marketing, Media Relations, Public Relations, Real Estate

David Eisenstadt *(Founder & Partner)*
Rhoda Eisenstadt *(Mng Partner)*

Accounts:
Aspen Ridge
Heathwood
L-EAT GROUP PR
Marshall Mattress Public Relations
Ritz-Carlton

TCI-SMITH PUBLICITY
1930 E Marlton Pike Ste I-46, Cherry Hill, NJ 08003
Tel.: (856) 489-8654
Fax: (856) 504-0136
E-Mail: info@smithpublicity.com
Web Site: www.smithpublicity.com

Employees: 10

Sandra Poirier Smith *(Pres)*
Erin MacDonald-Birnbaum *(Dir-Publicity Strategy & Sr Acct Exec)*
Corinne Liccketto *(Dir-Bus Dev)*
Dina Barsky *(Acct Mgr)*
Lynn Coppetelli *(Lynn@smithpublicity.com)*

Accounts:
Arabella Publishing, LLC
Dr. Rossiter
Key Publishing House
Manarin Investment Counsel, Ltd
New Neighborhoods Publishing Company, LLC

TEAGUE COMMUNICATION
28005 Smyth Dr Ste 112, Valencia, CA 91355
Tel.: (661) 297-5292
Fax: (661) 702-9705
E-Mail: info@teaguecommunications.com
Web Site: www.teaguecommunications.com

Employees: 4
Year Founded: 1991

Agency Specializes In: Public Relations

Daryn N. Teague *(Owner)*

Accounts:
Martindale-Hubbell
Mullin Consulting
National Register Publishing
Sinaiko Healthcare Consulting

TEAK MEDIA & COMMUNICATION
840 Summer St Ste 305A, South Boston, MA 2127
Tel.: (617) 269-7171
E-Mail: info@teakmedia.com
Web Site: www.teakmedia.com

Agency Specializes In: Advertising, Crisis Communications, Media Relations, Promotions, Public Relations, Social Media, Strategic Planning/Research

Jackie Herskovitz Russell *(Pres)*
Diana Brown McCloy *(Sr Acct Dir)*
Andrea DIorio *(Dir-Ops & Acct Mgr)*
Katie Stinchon *(Dir-Special Events & Acct Mgr)*
Kirby Franzese *(Mgr-Social Media)*
Deborah Halperin Colbert *(Sr Acct Exec)*
Allison Epstein *(Acct Exec)*

Accounts:
Boston Marathon Jimmy Fund Walk
YMCAs of Greater Boston

TEAM VISION
841 Bishop St Ste 300, Honolulu, HI 96813
Tel.: (808) 536-0416
Fax: (808) 536-1381
E-Mail: info@teamvision.com
Web Site: www.teamvision.com

Employees: 22

Agency Specializes In: Public Relations

Craig Carapelho *(Pres & CEO)*
Kyle Osaki *(Mgr-Production)*
Jessica Pang *(Acct Exec)*
Greg Yoshikane *(Designer-Web)*

Accounts:
Castle & Cooke
Genergraphics
Island of Lana'i
The Kohala Center
Paradise Cove Luau

TECH IMAGE LTD.
1130 W Lake Cook Rd Ste 250, Buffalo Grove, IL 60089
Tel.: (847) 279-0022
Fax: (847) 279-8922
Toll Free: (888) 4-TECH-PR
E-Mail: info@techimage.com
Web Site: www.techimage.com

Employees: 10
Year Founded: 1993

Agency Specializes In: Business-To-Business, E-Commerce, High Technology, Information Technology, Planning & Consultation, Public Relations

Approx. Annual Billings: $25,000,000

Breakdown of Gross Billings by Media: Pub. Rels.: 100%

Daniel M. O'Brien *(Pres)*
Philip Anast *(VP-Acct Svcs)*
Michael A. Monahan *(Dir-Media Rels)*
Donna Gaidamak *(Acct Mgr)*
Andy Ambrosius *(Mgr-Media Rels)*
Beth Campus *(Mgr-Media Rels)*
Marissa Fellows *(Sr Strategist-Digital)*
Meg Avril *(Sr Specialist-Media Rels)*

Accounts:
Allstate Insurance
BladeRoom USA Digital, PR, Social Media Marketing
Cisco Systems, Inc.
Comptia
Forsythe Technology
GlobalSpec; Troy, NY
Gravitant Digital, PR, Social Media Marketing
Infogix Digital, PR, Social Media Marketing
Initiate Systems
International Business Systems Digital, PR, Social Media Marketing
Language Analysis System; Herndon, VA Name Recognition Software
The Marketing Executives Networking Group (Agency of Record)
NEC Display Solutions of America
Omnivex
Robert Bosch Tool Corporation (Public Relations Agency of Record) Content Development, Media Relations, Social Media
Vision Solutions Digital, PR, Social Media Marketing
VMUG Digital, PR, Social Media Marketing

TELLEM GRODY PUBLIC RELATIONS, INC.
30765 Pacific Coast Hwy Ste 243, Malibu, CA 90265
Tel.: (310) 313-3444
Fax: (310) 775-9721
Web Site: www.tellemgrodypr.com

Year Founded: 1994

Agency Specializes In: Crisis Communications, Entertainment, Public Relations

Dan Grody *(Partner)*
John A. Tellem *(Partner)*
Susan M. Tellem *(Sr Partner)*

Accounts:
ALTON BROWN LIVE! The Edible Inevitable Tour
Aurora World Inc.
Blue September
BuildMyBod
California Community Church
California Poison Control System
DrumChannel
The Fresh Beat Band
Guardian Safety Solutions International, Inc.
The Jim Henson Company Pajanimals Live!
Lord of the Dance
Marina Plastic Surgery Associates
Nitro Circus Live
Nurses Lounge PR, Social Media

TERPIN COMMUNICATIONS GROUP
4333 Admiralty Way Ste 200 E Tower, Marina Del Rey, CA 90292
Tel.: (310) 821-6100
Web Site: www.terpin.com

Year Founded: 1990

Agency Specializes In: Public Relations

Jenny Chong *(Acct Exec)*

Accounts:
Augmentum
BitGravity, Inc
Collarity, Inc.
Dave TV
Digital Media Wire, Inc
Marco Polo
Red Herring
Robeks
Tie
Xandros, Inc.

TERRA PUBLIC RELATIONS
65 Mercill Ave Ste 14 C, Jackson, WY 83001
Tel.: (307) 733-8777
Fax: (307) 699-4572
Web Site: www.terrapublicrelations.com

Year Founded: 2008

Agency Specializes In: Corporate Communications, Event Planning & Marketing, Media Relations, Public Relations, Social Media

Alli Noland *(Founder)*
Tara Coyle *(Acct Mgr)*
Keri Jamison *(Acct Mgr)*
Sarah Niklas *(Acct Mgr)*
Brooks Cowles *(Mgr-Accts)*

Accounts:
USA Colab
Wasatch Powder Monkeys
White Sierra (Agency of Record) Media, Public Relations

TEUWEN COMMUNICATIONS
133 W 25th St Ste 4W, New York, NY 10001
Tel.: (212) 244-0622
E-Mail: info@teuwen.com
Web Site: www.teuwen.com

Agency Specializes In: Brand Development & Integration, Event Planning & Marketing, Promotions, Public Relations, Social Media

Geert Teuwen *(Co-Founder & Dir-Creative)*
Stephanie Teuwen *(Pres)*
Louise Jordan *(Acct Dir)*
Marisa Jetter *(Acct Supvr)*
Cassidy Havens *(Acct Exec)*
Alexa Lacey-Varona *(Asst Acct Exec)*

Accounts:
Allegrini
Aquavit
Athenee
Champagne Laurent-Perrier (Agency of Record) Media Relations, Public Relations, Strategic Press Events
Conseil Interprofessionnel du Vin de Bordeaux (Public Relations Agency of Record) Consumer, Media Relations, Press
Elena Walch
Gigondas
GRK Fresh Greek
North Square
The Original Chevre
Vivoli
Wines Of Alsace

TEXT 100 GLOBAL PUBLIC RELATIONS
(Formerly Text 100 Public Relations)
77 Maiden Ln 3rd Fl, San Francisco, CA 94108
Tel.: (415) 593-8400
Fax: (415) 593-8401
E-Mail: info@text100.com
Web Site: www.text100.com

Employees: 55
Year Founded: 1981

National Agency Associations: COPF-PRSA

Agency Specializes In: High Technology, Public Relations, Sponsorship

Approx. Annual Billings: $50,000,000

Breakdown of Gross Billings by Media: Pub. Rels.: $50,000,000

Aedhmar Hynes *(CEO)*
Laurie Eisendrath *(CFO)*
Cecile Missildine *(Exec VP & Reg Dir-Europe, Middle East & Africa)*
Ken Peters *(Exec VP & Reg Dir-North America)*
Sarah Mackenzie *(Exec VP)*

Accounts:
Adobe Systems Inc; San Jose, CA
BlackBerry Global PR
Cisco
IBM
Kroll Ontrack Inc
MTV
Schneider Electric (Agency of Record)
Staples Advantage Business-to-Business, PR
Xerox

United States

Text 100 Boston Corp.
31 Milk St Ste 201, Boston, MA 02109
Tel.: (617) 399-4980
Fax: (617) 723-1045
E-Mail: kenp@text100.com
Web Site: www.text100.com

Employees: 15
Year Founded: 1997

National Agency Associations: COPF

Agency Specializes In: Public Relations

Laurie Eisendrath *(CFO)*
Cecile Missildine *(Exec VP & Reg Dir-Europe, Middle East & Africa)*
Sarah Mackenzie *(Exec VP)*
Ken Peters *(Dir-North America)*

Text 100 New York Corp.
352 Park Ave S 7th Fl, New York, NY 10010
Tel.: (212) 529-4600
Fax: (212) 989-7149
E-Mail: info@text100.com
Web Site: www.text100.com

Employees: 50
Year Founded: 2000

National Agency Associations: COPF

Agency Specializes In: Public Relations

Laurie Eisendrath *(CFO)*
Ken Peters *(Exec VP & Reg Dir-North America)*
Sarah Mackenzie *(Exec VP)*
Jennifer Lynn *(Sr Acct Exec)*
Renatta Siewert *(Sr Acct Exec)*
Kristen Huff *(Acct Exec)*

Accounts:
Adobe
British Airways
Cisco
Citrix
Earthlink
Facebook
FUJIFILM Holdings Corporation
IBM
Lenovo
Paypal

Text 100 Rochester Corp.
4 Commercial St Ste 500, Rochester, NY 14614
Tel.: (585) 697-7723
Fax: (585) 697-7817
E-Mail: erinh@text100.com
Web Site: www.text100.com

Employees: 29
Year Founded: 1997

National Agency Associations: COPF

Agency Specializes In: Public Relations, Sponsorship

Nicole Fachet *(Sr VP)*
Carolina Noguera *(Sr VP)*
Kerry Hall *(VP)*
Erin Humphrey *(VP)*
Jessica Troskosky *(Sr Acct Dir)*
Kristin O'Connell *(Acct Dir)*
Kari Ferini Kees *(Dir-HR-North America)*

Accounts:
Xerox

Germany

Text 100 Munich GmbH
Nymphenburgerstrasse 168, 80634 Munich, Germany
Tel.: (49) 89 99 83 700
Fax: (49) 89 982 888 1
E-Mail: ines.bieger@text100.de
Web Site: www.text100.com

Employees: 24
Year Founded: 1992

Agency Specializes In: Public Relations

Claudia Keller *(Office Mgr)*
David Dieckmann *(Acct Exec)*
Marina Lovric *(Acct Exec)*

Accounts:
IBM
Lenovo
Philips
SanDisk Corp

Italy

Text 100 Milan S.R.L.
Piazza Principessa Clotilde 8, 20121 Milan, Italy
Tel.: (39) 02202021
Fax: (39) 0220404655
E-Mail: text100@text100.it
Web Site: www.text100.com

Employees: 12
Year Founded: 1997

Agency Specializes In: Public Relations

Gennaro Nastri *(Mng Dir)*
Manuela Tuveri *(Sr Acct Dir)*
Luisella Lucchini *(Acct Dir)*
Amelia Marino *(Sr Acct Mgr)*

Accounts:
Airbnb
Amazon Web Services
AOC
eBay
Harman
Lebara
MathWorks
MMD
Quip
Skype
Sony Digital Cinema
TP VIsion
Vodafone
Woox

Spain

Text 100 Madrid S.L.
Plaza de Colon n2 Torre 1, Planta 17, 28046 Madrid, Spain
Tel.: (34) 91 561 94 15
Fax: (34) 91 561 61 25
E-Mail: virginia.huerta@text100.com
Web Site: www.text100.com

Employees: 20
Year Founded: 1997

Agency Specializes In: Public Relations

Virginia Huerta *(Gen Mgr)*

Cesar Pastrana *(Acct Dir)*
Almudena Alameda *(Sr Acct Mgr)*
Ana Reyes *(Acct Mgr)*

Accounts:
Airbnb
Facebook
IBM
Skype
Vodafone
Xerox

Australia

Text 100 Sydney
Level 28 100 Miller St., NSW 2060 Sydney, Australia
Tel.: (61) 2 9956 5733
Fax: (61) 2 9956 5406
E-Mail: info@text100.com
Web Site: www.text100.com

Year Founded: 1998

Agency Specializes In: Public Relations

Karen Coleman *(VP-Integrated Mktg-ANZ)*
Anne Costello *(Reg Dir-APAC)*
Karen Wells *(Reg Dir-APAC)*
Gabrielle Tourelle *(Dir-APAC HR & Global Talent Dev)*

Accounts:
Adobe
Choosi Communications Program
Epsilon
IBM Content
Lenovo
Macquire Telecom
Media Access Australia PR'
Mitsubishi Electric
Optus
Siemens
Symantec
Yahoo 7
New-Zebra Technologies (Asia Pacific Agency of Record) Public Relations

China

Text 100 Hong Kong
Ste 3805 Level 38 Hopewell Center, 183 Queens Rd E, Wanchai, China (Hong Kong)
Tel.: (852) 2821 8694
Fax: (852) 2866 6220
Web Site: www.text100.com

Employees: 7

Agency Specializes In: Public Relations

Jeremy Woolf *(Sr VP & Head-Digital & Social Media Practice-Global)*
Rosemary Merz *(VP)*
Erica Pompen *(VP)*
Colby Jones *(Sr Acct Dir)*
Irene Chua *(Acct Dir)*
Geralynn Wong *(Assoc Dir-Digital Svcs)*
Denise Chan *(Acct Exec)*

Accounts:
Four Seasons Hotels Digital, Email Marketing
QD Vision Build Awareness, Communications
Rakuten Digital Communications, PR
New-Zebra Technologies Public Relations

Text 100 Shanghai
Unit 2005 Ascenda Plz, 333 Tian Yao Qiao Rd, Shanghai, 200030 China
Tel.: (86) 21 6426 3989
Fax: (86) 21 6426 3986
E-Mail: tt.yang@text100.com.cn
Web Site: www.text100.com

Employees: 10

Agency Specializes In: Public Relations

Meiling Yeow *(Sr VP)*
Carrie Hu *(Sr Acct Exec)*
Tina Kan *(Sr Acct Exec)*
Xian Wang *(Acct Coord)*

Accounts:
InMobi Communications Campaigns, Social Media, Strategic Communications
NXG
Rexel Integrated Communications Campaign

Text 100 India Pvt. Ltd.
2nd Fl TDI Centre Plot No.7, near Appolo Hospital, Jasola, New Delhi, 110 025 India
Tel.: (91) 11 406 12000
Fax: (91) 11 406 12052
Web Site: www.text100.com

Employees: 60
Year Founded: 1996

Agency Specializes In: Public Relations

Sunayna Malik *(Sr VP)*
Pooja Parikh *(Dir-HR)*
Ishita Grover *(Sr Acct Mgr)*
Bhawna Sharma Ningthoujam *(Sr Acct Mgr)*
Liza Saha *(Sr Acct Mgr)*
Prerna Kalra *(Assoc Acct Mgr)*
Tanvi Maheshwary *(Acct Mgr)*
Deepshikha Sinha *(Assoc Acct Mgr)*
Aleem Abbasi *(Mgr-Admin)*

Accounts:
Facebook
Virgin Mobile USA, Inc.
Xerox
New-Zebra Technologies Public Relations

Singapore

Text 100 Singapore Pvt. Ltd.
146 Robinson Road, #05-01, Singapore, 068909 Singapore
Tel.: (65) 6603 9000
Fax: (65) 6557 2467
E-Mail: info@text100.com
Web Site: https://www.text100.com/locations/asia-pacific/text100-singapore-office/

Employees: 25
Year Founded: 1998

Agency Specializes In: Experience Design, Public Relations

Marc Ha *(Mng Dir & VP)*
Keeley Benjamin *(Head-ASEAN Digital Brand)*
Mabel Chiang *(Sr Acct Dir)*
Shirley Wong *(Acct Dir)*
Lara D'Souza *(Acct Mgr)*
Suzy Kooy *(Acct Mgr)*
Victoria Lim *(Acct Mgr)*
Irene W. Teoh *(Sr Acct Exec)*
Desmond Wong *(Acct Coord)*

Accounts:
Gartner
iQNECT Integrated Communications, Paid Media, Social Media
Lenovo
New-OMRON Content Marketing, Social Media, Website
Symantec
New-Zebra Technologies Public Relations
Zuji (Agency of Record) Corporate Communications Programme

THINK TANK PR & MARKETING
117 Glen Crossing Rd, Glen Carbon, IL 62034
Tel.: (618) 288-0088
Fax: (618) 288-0088
Web Site: www.thinktankprm.com

Year Founded: 2006

Agency Specializes In: Brand Development & Integration, Event Planning & Marketing, Internet/Web Design, Print, Public Relations, Social Media

Trish Cheatham *(CEO)*
Kevin Zimarik *(Dir-Creative)*
Olivia Hopson *(Mgr-Social Media)*
Rachel Tritsch *(Mgr-Traffic)*
Kerry Musenbrock *(Acct Exec)*
Ben Eversmann *(Sr Graphic Designer)*

Accounts:
Edwardsville Illinois Police Department
Jack Schmitt Chevrolet of Wood River
Madison Mutual Insurance Company
Quit as Desired
Team Med Global Consulting

THINKPR
10 E 23rd St Ste 200, New York, NY 10010
Tel.: (212) 343-3920
Fax: (212) 343-0185
Web Site: www.thinkpublicrelations.com

Agency Specializes In: Brand Development & Integration, Media Relations, Public Relations, Search Engine Optimization, Social Media, Sponsorship

Reshma Patel *(Owner)*
Elaine Drebot Hutchins *(Pres)*
Erin Brunner *(Acct Mgr)*
Aliza Solc *(Sr Acct Exec)*

Accounts:
New-Aulta
New-Vestiaire collective

THINKZILLA
2425 W Loop S Ste 200, Houston, TX 77027
Tel.: (888) 509-1145
Web Site: www.itsthinkzilla.com

Agency Specializes In: Brand Development & Integration, Event Planning & Marketing, Internet/Web Design, Media Relations, Public Relations, Social Media

Velma Trayham *(CEO)*

Accounts:
Alan Powell
Michael Sterling

THIRD STREET MEDIA GROUP
6300 Wilshire Blvd, Los Angeles, CA 90048
Tel.: (323) 651-3200
Web Site: www.thirdstreetmediagroup.com

Agency Specializes In: Corporate Communications, Media Training, Public Relations

Bill Harrison *(Co-Founder & Partner)*
Jacqueline Feldman *(Co-Founder & Partner)*

Accounts:

Popchips (Agency of Record)

THOMAS J. PAYNE MARKET DEVELOPMENT
865 Woodside Way PO Box 281525, San Mateo, CA 94401-1611
Tel.: (650) 340-8311
Fax: (650) 340-8568
E-Mail: info@tjpmd.com
Web Site: www.tjpmd.com

E-Mail for Key Personnel:
President: tpayne@tjpmd.com

Employees: 8
Year Founded: 1986

Agency Specializes In: Agriculture, Communications, Consulting, Food Service, Industrial, New Product Development, Public Relations

Thomas J. Payne *(Owner)*

Accounts:
APEDA; New Delhi, India
California Raisin Marketing Board; Fresno, CA
Cultivated Blueberry Group
Flax Council of Canada; Winnipeg
Freshwater Fish Marketing Corporation of Canada
Industrial Development Corporation
Land O'Lakes International Dairy Division; Honduras
Mozambique, Cashew Industry
National Honey Board; Longmont, CO
North American Blueberry Council
USAID; Washington DC.
Walnut Marketing Board
World Bank; Washington DC
The World Bank; Washington, DC

THOMAS PUBLIC RELATIONS INC
734 Walt Whitman Rd Ste 206, Melville, NY 11747
Tel.: (631) 549-7575
Fax: (631) 549-1128
E-Mail: info@thomaspr.com
Web Site: www.thomas-pr.com

Agency Specializes In: Brand Development & Integration, Crisis Communications, Event Planning & Marketing, Public Relations, Search Engine Optimization, Social Media

Karen Thomas *(Principal)*

Accounts:
Interworks Unlimited Inc
Irvine Mobility
Rocketcases

THOMPSON & BENDER
1192 Pleasantville Rd, Briarcliff Manor, NY 10510
Tel.: (914) 762-1900
Fax: (914) 762-4617
E-Mail: liz@thompson-bender.com
Web Site: www.thompson-bender.com

Employees: 12

Agency Specializes In: Advertising, Print, Production (Print), Public Relations, Publicity/Promotions

Dean Bender *(Pres)*
Jennifer Bannan *(Dir-Adv & Mktg)*
Sarai Bartels *(Dir-Art)*
Mary Cronin *(Dir-Content & Special Projects)*
Jessica Apicella *(Mgr-Mktg & Promos)*
Jerry McKinstry *(Sr Acct Exec)*
Hope Salley *(Sr Acct Exec)*

Accounts:
Community Mutual Savings Bank
Harvest-on-Hudson
Iona College
The Journal News
Provident Bank
Regeneron

THOMPSON & CO. PUBLIC RELATIONS
600 Barrow St, Anchorage, AK 99501
Tel.: (907) 561-4488
Fax: (907) 563-3223
E-Mail: info@thompsonpr.com
Web Site: www.thompsonpr.com/

Employees: 8
Year Founded: 1989

Agency Specializes In: Public Relations, Transportation, Travel & Tourism

Jennifer Thompson *(Pres & CEO)*
Gary Scott *(VP-New & Dir-Media)*
Meghan Aftosmis *(VP-New York)*
Ariel Walsh *(Dir-Ops & Anchorage)*
Bri Gordon *(Sr Acct Exec)*
Abby Cooper *(Acct Exec)*
Stephanie Plieness *(Acct Exec)*
Emily McLaughlin *(Jr Acct Exec)*
Nikkie Viotto *(Jr Acct Exec)*
Sydney Brusewitz *(Acct Coord)*
Emily Kurn *(Acct Coord)*

Accounts:
Alaska Railroad Corporation
Alaska Travel Industry Association
Alaska USA Federal Credit Union
Anchorage Economic Development Corporation
Anchorage Police Department Employees Association
Anchorage Project Access
EpicQuest
GCI (General Communication Inc.)
Icy Strait Point

THOMSON COMMUNICATIONS
100 S Main St Ste 100-J, Middleton, MA 1949
Tel.: (978) 808-7700
Fax: (978) 739-9570
E-Mail: info@thomsoncommunications.com
Web Site: www.thomsoncommunications.com

Agency Specializes In: Content, Event Planning & Marketing, Integrated Marketing, Public Relations, Social Media, Sponsorship

David Thomson *(Principal)*

Accounts:
Northeast Arc

THOUGHT FOR FOOD & SON LLC
186 Shawmut Ave, Marlborough, MA 1752
Tel.: (508) 303-5094
Web Site: www.tffandson.com

Year Founded: 2005

Agency Specializes In: Corporate Identity, Crisis Communications, Event Planning & Marketing, Graphic Design, Internet/Web Design, Logo & Package Design, Media Relations, Public Relations, Social Media, Strategic Planning/Research

Alan A. Casucci *(Mng Dir)*

Accounts:
Dells Maraschino Cherries (Agency of Record) Campaign: "Everything Taste Better with a Dells Maraschino Cherry"
New-Golden Girl Granola (Agency of Record) Design, Public Relations, Social Media
New-Macknight Food Group (Agency of Record) Outreach, Public Relations, Social Media Marketing

THREE GIRLS MEDIA, INC.
700 Sleater Kinney Rd SE Ste B-249, Lacey, WA 98503
Tel.: (408) 218-2391
E-Mail: info@threegirlsmedia.com
Web Site: www.threegirlsmedia.com

Agency Specializes In: Brand Development & Integration, Media Relations, Public Relations, Social Media

Erika Taylor Montgomery *(Founder & CEO)*

Accounts:
New-Lark & Leaf Tea

THRIVE PR
(Formerly Shafer Communications)
6012 Reef Point Ln Ste L, Fort Worth, TX 76135
Tel.: (817) 975-3908
Web Site: www.thrivepublicrelations.com

Year Founded: 2003

Agency Specializes In: Brand Development & Integration, Consulting, Corporate Communications, Corporate Identity, Media Relations, Public Relations, Strategic Planning/Research

Kelly Kirkendoll *(Founder & Pres)*
Laura Kayata *(Dir-Branding & Graphic Design)*
Coleen Spalding *(Mgr-PR & Acct Mgr)*
Jessi Clark *(Mgr-PR & Social Media)*

Accounts:
Access Trips
Bizstarters

TIER ONE PARTNERS
29 Turning Mill Rd, Lexington, MA 02420
Tel.: (781) 861-5249
Fax: (781) 274-0117
E-Mail: info@tieronepr.com
Web Site: www.tieronepr.com

Employees: 18
Year Founded: 2003

Agency Specializes In: Automotive, Brand Development & Integration, Business-To-Business, Communications, Consumer Marketing, Corporate Communications, Corporate Identity, Education, Event Planning & Marketing, Exhibit/Trade Shows, Health Care Services, High Technology, Legal Services, Public Relations, Strategic Planning/Research

Approx. Annual Billings: $1,500,000

Breakdown of Gross Billings by Media: Pub. Rels.: $1,500,000

Jeanne Bock *(Founder & Mng Partner)*
Marian Sly Hughes *(Mng Partner)*
Sue Parente *(Mng Partner)*
Kathleen Wilson *(Mng Partner)*

Accounts:
Aegis Media
Comverse, Inc. (Agency of Record) Communications, Investor Relations Strategy, Public Relations, Social Media, Thought Leadership
Continuum

CP-Desk Positioning/Messaging
CRICO/RMF Strategies (Agency of Record)
DA-Desk (Agency of Record)
Everbridge Social Media
Fluent Public Relation
Formicary Collaboration Group Thought Leadership
Isobar
Jingit Social Media
Kaz Inc.
Koko FitClub
LimoLiner; 2003
Lojack; 2003
Mobiquity Public Relations
Optaros Thought Leadership
Percussion Software
PhoneFusion Business Communications; 2008
Pixily
Ports Direct Positioning/Messaging
ProSential Group Social Media
Springpad Communications Strategy
Trade King
Veson Nautical
Vidergize Public Relation
VirginHealthmiles
Weemba (Agency of Record)
WillowTree Apps Public Relation

TILSON PR
(Formerly Tilson Communications)
1001 Yamato Rd Ste 400, Boca Raton, FL 33431
Tel.: (561) 998-1995
Fax: (561) 998-1790
Toll Free: (888) 397-7878
E-Mail: info@tilsonpr.com
Web Site: www.tilsonpr.com

Employees: 10

Agency Specializes In: Collateral, Email, Event Planning & Marketing, Internet/Web Design, Newspaper, Print, Promotions, Public Relations, Publicity/Promotions, Radio, Sponsorship, Strategic Planning/Research, T.V., Web (Banner Ads, Pop-ups, etc.)

Britt Bradford *(VP)*
Jackie Guzman *(VP)*
Carly Sanders *(Sr Acct Exec)*
Meaghan Edelstein *(Sr Strategist-Social)*
Lauren A. Ricks *(Acct Coord)*
Samantha Gentile *(Coord-PR & Social Media)*

Accounts:
Bonefish Grill PR
Dunkin Donuts
Staples Inc.; 2008
The Venetian Delray Beach Open, Lifestyle, PR, Travel

TK PR
349 Ascot Ridge Ln, Greer, SC 29650
Tel.: (864) 469-7488
E-Mail: taryn@tkpublicrelations.com
Web Site: www.tkpublicrelations.com

Agency Specializes In: Event Planning & Marketing, Media Relations, Public Relations

Laura Moore *(Assoc Dir)*

Accounts:
New-Kids Bowl Free
New-Visit Greenville SC

TOMIC COMMUNICATIONS
3801 Collins Ave, Miami Beach, FL 33140
Tel.: (917) 882-5243
Web Site: www.tomiccommunications.com

Year Founded: 2008

Agency Specializes In: Crisis Communications, Internet/Web Design, Media Training, Public Relations, Social Media

Charlotte Tomic *(Pres)*

Accounts:
IntiMates

TOMMASI PR
11 Bear Hill Rd, Windham, NH 03087
Tel.: (603) 893-5878
Web Site: www.tommasipr.com

Agency Specializes In: Crisis Communications, Event Planning & Marketing, Media Relations, Media Training, Public Relations, Social Media

Anne Tommasi *(Founder & Principal)*

Accounts:
Cosmas Fireboots
Kayland
My Good Dog
Quabaug Corporation
QuaBoing
Vibram FiveFingers

TONY FELICE PR & MARKETING
1027 E Washington St Ste 107, Phoenix, AZ 85034
Tel.: (602) 359-0626
E-Mail: info@tonyfelicepr.com
Web Site: www.tonyfelicepr.com

Year Founded: 2008

Agency Specializes In: Brand Development & Integration, Internet/Web Design, Media Buying Services, Media Training, Public Relations, Social Media

Tony Felice *(Pres & CEO)*
Lisa Wojciechowski *(VP)*
Steven Matzat *(Dir-Bus Dev)*
Tanya Moushi *(Dir-Micro Content)*
Lori Osiecki *(Dir-Creative)*
Tesz Millan *(Copywriter)*

Accounts:
1 Smart Life LLC
Fobie Friends

TOOL GUY PR
1715 Santa Cruz Ave, Menlo Park, CA 94025
Tel.: (650) 327-1641
Fax: (928) 447-1811
E-Mail: kevin@toolguypr.com
Web Site: www.toolguypr.com

Year Founded: 2002

Agency Specializes In: Communications, Content, Media Relations, Public Relations

Kevin Wolf *(Pres)*

Accounts:
Aeroprise
Cloud Sherpas
Integrify
Precise
Verifi
Workstream
Xora Mobile Resource Management Services

TORME LAURICELLA
847 Sansome St, San Francisco, CA 94111
Tel.: (415) 956-1791
Fax: (415) 954-0952
E-Mail: deborah@torme.com
Web Site: www.torme.com

Employees: 13
Year Founded: 1983

National Agency Associations: COPF

Agency Specializes In: Corporate Communications, Corporate Identity, Food Service, Public Relations

Margaret Torme *(Owner)*
Deborah J. Lauricella *(Pres, Head & Dir-Creative)*
Holly Groves *(Office Mgr)*

Accounts:
Petrini's Supermarkets
Safeway

TORRENZANO GROUP
60 E 42nd St Ste 2112, New York, NY 10165-2112
Tel.: (212) 681-1700
Fax: (212) 681-6961
E-Mail: info@torrenzano.com
Web Site: www.torrenzano.com

Employees: 20

Agency Specializes In: Business Publications, Business-To-Business, Corporate Communications, Corporate Identity, Crisis Communications

Edward A. Orgon *(Pres & COO)*
Richard Torrenzano *(CEO)*
Eileen Doherty *(Dir-Consulting)*
Clark S. Judge *(Dir-Consulting)*

Accounts:
Air Products and Chemicals
Argosy Gaming
Baxter
Grant Thornton
Monsanto
Motive Product Group
Nanosphere, Inc.
Radian
WNS

TORRES MULTICULTURAL COMMUNICATIONS
801 E Washington St, Phoenix, AZ 85004
Tel.: (602) 354-3430
E-Mail: info@torresmulticultural.com
Web Site: www.torresmulticultural.com

Agency Specializes In: Collateral, Crisis Communications, Media Planning, Public Relations, Social Media, Strategic Planning/Research

Tania Torres *(Pres & CEO)*

Accounts:
One Arizona

TR CUTLER, INC.
3032 S Oakland Forest Dr Ste 2803, Fort Lauderdale, FL 33309-5684
Tel.: (954) 486-7562
Fax: (954) 739-4602
Toll Free: (888) 902-0300
E-Mail: trcutler@trcutlerinc.com
Web Site: www.trcutlerinc.com

Employees: 43
Year Founded: 1998

Agency Specializes In: Advertising, Alternative Advertising, Automotive, Brand Development &

Integration, Business Publications, Business-To-Business, Communications, Consulting, Consumer Marketing, Consumer Publications, Content, Corporate Communications, Corporate Identity, Cosmetics, Crisis Communications, Customer Relationship Management, Direct Response Marketing, E-Commerce, Electronic Media, Engineering, Event Planning & Marketing, Exhibit/Trade Shows, Food Service, Gay & Lesbian Market, Government/Political, High Technology, Hispanic Market, Identity Marketing, Industrial, Information Technology, International, Internet/Web Design, Magazines, Market Research, New Product Development, New Technologies, Newspaper, Newspapers & Magazines, Planning & Consultation, Print, Public Relations, Publicity/Promotions, Publishing, Regional, Retail, Search Engine Optimization, Sponsorship, Strategic Planning/Research, Technical Advertising, Trade & Consumer Magazines, Travel & Tourism

Approx. Annual Billings: $25,000,000

Breakdown of Gross Billings by Media: Consulting: $19,000,000; D.M.: $1,000,000; Strategic Planning/Research: $5,000,000

Thomas R. Cutler *(Founder)*

Accounts:
AccountingSoftware411 Manufacturing Accounting Software; 2005
Advanced Manufacturing; Canada Manufacturing Media; 2005
American Machinist Machining Media; 2004
Automation Weekly Automation Media; 2004
AutomationMedia; Canada Automation; 2005
Business Excellence Manufacturing Media; 2007
Canadian Management; Canada Management Content; 2005
Canadian Packaging Packaging Media; 2007
Catalyst CAD Technology Manufacturing; 2004
Control Engineering Engineering Media; 2005
Design Product News Manufacturing Design Media; 2007
DestinationCRM CRM Software; 2008
DM Review Distribution Software; 2006
ETO Institute Engineer-to-Order Content; 2004
Focus Marketing Manufacturing Software; 2005
Food & Beverage Journal Food & Beverage Manufacturing Technology'; 2009
Food Engineering Food Manufacturing Software; 2005
Food Quality Food Quality Software; 2005
Industrial 2.0; India Industrial Software; 2004
Industrial Automation Vietnam; Vietnam Industrial Automation Technology Solutions; 2011
Industrial Automation; India Manufacturing Technology; 2009
Industrial Connect; Canada Technology Solutions for the Industrial Sector; 2009
Industrial Distribution Industrial Distribution Software; 2005
Industrial Electronics Today; India Technolgoy Solutions for Industrial Automation; 2011
Industrial Engineer Technology Solutions Impacting Industrial Engineers; 2007
Inside Six Sigma Six Sigma Content; 2007
The Machinist Industrial Content; 2006
Manufacturing & Logistics IT; UK Manufacturing & Logistics Content; 2005
Material Management & Distribution; Canada Material Management & Distribution Content; 2006
MetalForming MetalForming Content; 2005
Moldmaking Technology Moldmaking Technology Content; 2003
Plant Magazine/IT For Industry; Canada Manufacturing Software Content; 2003
Plastics Business Plastics Business Content; 2007
Plastics News Plastics News Content; 2005
Quality Assurance Quality Assurance Software; 2008
Quality Digest Quality Digest Content; 2005
Software Magazine Software Content; 2005
Supply Chain 2.0; India Supply Chain Software; 2008
Times Food Processing Journal; India Food Manufacturing Content; 2007
World Trade Manufacturing in World Trade; 2005

TRACTION PUBLIC RELATIONS
1513 6th St Ste 202, Santa Monica, CA 90401
Tel.: (310) 453-2050
E-Mail: info@tractionpr.com
Web Site: www.tractionpr.com

Employees: 15

Agency Specializes In: Game Integration, Public Relations

David Tractenberg *(Pres)*
Jeremy Roll *(CFO)*
Ben Skerker *(Sr VP)*
Karla Costner *(Dir)*

Accounts:
1C Company
Atomic Games; Raleigh, NC (Agency of Record) Six Days In Fallujah
HP/Compaq
KontrolFreek
Li-Fi, Inc.
Mind Control Software
NexGen
Thrustmaster
Timeplay
Wahoo Studios
Winifred Phillips

TRAINER COMMUNICATIONS
(Name Changed to 10Fold Communications)

TRANSMEDIA GROUP
240 W Palmetto Pk Rd Ste 300, Boca Raton, FL 33432
Tel.: (561) 750-9800
Fax: (561) 750-4660
Web Site: www.transmediagroup.com

Employees: 14
Year Founded: 1981

National Agency Associations: IPRA

Agency Specializes In: Affluent Market, Arts, Bilingual Market, Broadcast, Business Publications, Business-To-Business, Cable T.V., Collateral, Communications, Consulting, Consumer Goods, Consumer Marketing, Consumer Publications, Cosmetics, Crisis Communications, Customer Relationship Management, Direct Response Marketing, Direct-to-Consumer, Education, Electronic Media, Email, Entertainment, Environmental, Event Planning & Marketing, Faith Based, Financial, Food Service, Graphic Design, Guerilla Marketing, Health Care Services, High Technology, Hispanic Market, Hospitality, Infomercials, International, Internet/Web Design, Legal Services, Leisure, Luxury Products, Magazines, Media Relations, Media Training, Medical Products, Men's Market, Multicultural, New Technologies, Newspaper, Newspapers & Magazines, Outdoor, Over-50 Market, Pets , Pharmaceutical, Print, Product Placement, Public Relations, Publicity/Promotions, Radio, Real Estate, Regional, Restaurant, Retail, Seniors' Market, Social Marketing/Nonprofit, T.V., Trade & Consumer Magazines, Travel & Tourism, Urban Market, Viral/Buzz/Word of Mouth, Web (Banner Ads, Pop-ups, etc.), Women's Market

Approx. Annual Billings: $1,000,000

Breakdown of Gross Billings by Media: Other: 10%; Pub. Rels.: 90%

Thomas J. Madden *(Owner)*
Adrienne Mazzone *(Pres)*
Angela Madden *(CFO & VP)*
Lori McQuestion *(VP-PR)*
Cassandra Cardenas *(Creative Dir)*
Bruria Angel *(Dir-US & Israel PR)*
Georgiene Ruocco Laffey *(Dir-Client Rels)*
Carla Pardo *(Dir-Hispanic Media)*

Accounts:
Alexis DeJoria
Anthony Pannozzo MD
Bullying Academy
Child Group Wealth Management; Boca Raton, FL Publicity
DataJack, Inc.
Digital Media Arts College Publicity Program
GL Homes
Greyson International
Knife and Forklift
MA Managed Futures Fund
Madzone Marketing LLC
The Multiple Sclerosis Foundation
Murray Books Publicity, TOOTS Collection, Traditional & Social Media
MyBigMovieBreak.com Public Relations
MyVerifiedPro.com, Inc.
ReasLo Public Relations
RedFin Network, Inc. Public Relations
Simon Sales LLC FamilySignal, Media Relations, Social Media
Spine Revitalizer Publicity
Stand Among Friends; Boca Raton, FL
Stanley Steemer of South Florida
Sun Radio Network
Ticktin Law Group
Uncle Tod Motorsports
Wrap Media Group; Boca Raton, FL Wrapped Rental Vehicle Launch
Zenith Technologies Soniclean

TREBLE PUBLIC RELATIONS
906 E 5th St Ste 105, Austin, TX 78702
Tel.: (512) 485-3016
Web Site: www.treblepr.com

Agency Specializes In: Brand Development & Integration, Media Relations, Public Relations

Rachel Kent *(Acct Exec)*

Accounts:
New-Jahia Solutions

TREVELINO/KELLER
949 W Marietta St NW Ste X106, Atlanta, GA 30318-5275
Tel.: (404) 214-0722
Fax: (404) 214-0729
E-Mail: dtrevelino@trevelinokeller.com
Web Site: www.trevelinokeller.com

Employees: 20
Year Founded: 2003

Genna Keller *(Principal)*
Kira Perdue *(Exec VP)*
Christy Olliff Booth *(Acct Dir)*
Carrie Crabill *(Acct Dir)*
Kelly Galinsky *(Acct Supvr)*
Elisa Graciaa *(Sr Acct Exec)*
Lauren Sullivan Shankman *(Sr Specialist-Media)*
Jason Gilbreth *(Acct Exec)*
Savannah Weeks *(Acct Exec)*
Sarah Bell *(Asst Acct Exec)*
Brittnee Jones *(Asst Acct Exec)*

Accounts:
Atlanta Tech Village Marketing, Public Relations

Bibby Financial Services (North American Agency of Record) Media, Messaging, Public Relations, Social Marketing, Strategy
Bluegiga Public Relations
Boneheads Grilled Fish & Piri Piri Chicken Marketing, PR
Corner Bakery Cafe B2B Public Relations, Marketing Agency of Choice
CustomerCentric Selling Public Relations Strategy
eaHELP, LLC (Public Relations Agency of Record) Media Relations
ExamMed Marketing Strategy, Media Relations, Public Relations, Social Media
FactorTrust Communications Strategy, Marketing, PR
FotoIN Mobile Corporation Public Relations Agency of Record
New-The Gathering Spot (Public Relations & Digital Marketing Agency of Record)
GetOne Rewards Inc Public Relations
Great Parents Academy Marketing Agency of Record, Math Program, Public Relations Agency of Record, Strategy
Great Wraps Public Relations
Innovolt Analyst & Media Relations, Public Relations, Social Media Strategy
Insightpool PR
KidsLink Media Relations, Public Relations, Social Media Strategy, Trade
Savi Provisions Integrated Communications Strategy, Marketing, Rebranding
Shavewise (Agency of Record)
Soupman, Inc. Marketing, Public Relations Agency of Record, Social Media, The Original SoupMan
StoryMark Life StoryMark

TRIPLEPOINT

115 Sansome St Ste 800, San Francisco, CA 94104
Tel.: (415) 955-8500
Fax: (415) 955-8501
E-Mail: info@triplepointpr.com
Web Site: www.triplepointpr.com

Agency Specializes In: Entertainment, Game Integration

Quinn Wageman *(Acct Dir)*
Andrew Jepsen *(Office Mgr)*
Andrew Karl *(Acct Supvr)*
Erin Fan *(Sr Acct Exec)*
Jesse Henning *(Sr Acct Exec)*
Gentry Brown *(Acct Exec)*
Surabhi Srivastava *(Acct Exec)*

Accounts:
Armor Games
Deadline Games
Didmo
Evony
Exit Games
Fantage
GC Developer's Conference
Groove Games
himojo
joymax
Net Devil
Nyko
Red Studios 5
Sega

TRIZCOM, INC.

6818 Southpoint Dr, Dallas, TX 75248
Tel.: (972) 247-1369
Web Site: www.trizcom.com

Year Founded: 2008

Agency Specializes In: Communications, Crisis Communications, Event Planning & Marketing, Media Relations, Media Training, Public Relations, Social Media

Jo Trizila *(Pres & CEO)*
Krista Simmons *(VP & Sr Acct Exec)*
Karen Carrera *(VP)*
Dana Cobb *(Dir-Bus Dev & Sr Acct Exec)*
Jeffrey Cheatham *(Sr Acct Mgr)*
Kim Novino *(Acct Exec)*
Katie Mudd *(Jr Acct Exec)*
Stefanie Lee *(Asst Acct Exec)*

Accounts:
New-Aidan Gray (Agency of Record)
Beatrix Prive
Firearms Legal Protection (Public Relations Agency of Record)
Grenadier Homes
Heroes for Children (Agency of Record)
HipLogiq Social Marketing, SocialCentiv, SocialCompass
Ideal Feet Public Relations
New-Legacy ER & Urgent Care (Public Relations Agency of Record)
North Texas Enterprise Center (Agency of Record)
Revtech (Public Relations Agency of Record)
New-Solis Mammography (Public Relations Agency of Record)
Soulman's Bar-B-Que (Public Relations Agency of Record)
Star Medical Center
New-Transformance, Inc. (Agency of Record) Media Outreach, Public Relations

TROSPER COMMUNICATIONS LLC

2275 Corp Cir Ste 275, Henderson, NV 89074
Tel.: (702) 965-1617
Web Site: www.trospercommunications.com

Year Founded: 2010

Agency Specializes In: Advertising, Brand Development & Integration, Internet/Web Design, Public Relations, Social Media

Elizabeth Trosper *(Principal)*
Frank Fuentes *(Dir-Comm & Social Media)*
Angelina Wyss Gordon *(Specialist-Media Rels-Northern Nevada)*

Accounts:
Ashcraft & Barr LLP
Las Vegas Professional Fire Fighters

TRUE BLUE COMMUNICATIONS

3000 Gulf to Bay Blvd Ste 401, Clearwater, FL 33759
Tel.: (727) 726-3000
Web Site: www.truebluecommunications.com

Year Founded: 2010

Agency Specializes In: Brand Development & Integration, Content, Event Planning & Marketing, Internet/Web Design, Media Training, Public Relations, Search Engine Optimization, Social Media

Noelle Fox *(Pres & Chief Strategist Officer)*
Kasey Coryn *(Acct Exec)*
Christie Ebanks *(Acct Coord)*

Accounts:
New-Give Day Tampa Bay

TRUE POINT COMMUNICATIONS

(Formerly Nunez PR Group)
4890 Alpha Rd Ste 110, Dallas, TX 75244
Tel.: (972) 380-9595
E-Mail: sayhello@truepointagency.com
Web Site: truepointagency.com

Year Founded: 2006

Agency Specializes In: Crisis Communications, Media Relations, Media Training, Public Relations, Social Media, Strategic Planning/Research

Jessica Nunez *(Pres)*
Sohana Kutub *(Sr Acct Exec)*
Tiffany Cunningham *(Acct Exec)*
Calli Gutknecht *(Specialist-Social Media)*
Brittney Magee *(Acct Exec)*
Blair Reich *(Acct Exec)*
Dana Rueda *(Acct Exec)*

Accounts:
Naturalizer

TRYLON SMR

333 7th Ave, New York, NY 10001
Tel.: (212) 863-4199
E-Mail: info@trylonsmr.com
Web Site: www.trylonsmr.com

E-Mail for Key Personnel:
President: lloyd@trylonsmr.com

Employees: 14
Year Founded: 1990

National Agency Associations: COPF-PRSA

Agency Specializes In: Broadcast, Business Publications, Business-To-Business, Cable T.V., Communications, Computers & Software, Consumer Publications, Corporate Communications, Digital/Interactive, E-Commerce, Electronic Media, Electronics, Guerilla Marketing, High Technology, Media Relations, Mobile Marketing, New Technologies, Newspapers & Magazines, Podcasting, Public Relations, Publicity/Promotions, Publishing, RSS (Really Simple Syndication), Radio, Search Engine Optimization, Social Media, T.V., Trade & Consumer Magazines, Viral/Buzz/Word of Mouth

Approx. Annual Billings: $3,000,000

Breakdown of Gross Billings by Media: Pub. Rels.: 100%

Accounts:
Active Response Group; 2008
Adweek
AlmondNet
BET.com
Bloomberg BusinessWeek
BookSwim (Public Relations Agency of Record)
Broadcast Data Systems/Competitive Media Reports
BuyVia Media Relations
CABLEready
Cabletelevision Advertising Association of New York
CNBC
Copyright Clearance Center
Corbis
Countdown Entertainment; 2007
Faith & Values Media
Georgian Partners Media Relations
HBO
HGTV.com
The History Channel
Interoute
ITAC
Lifetime Television
Measurecast
Mediaedge:cia
Men's Health Magazine; 2008
Meredith Corporation BHG.com; 2007
Microsoft
Net Insight
The New York Observer
NewspaperDirect
Peer39 (Agency of Record)
People Capital

Prophet Brand Strategy
RedDot Solutions Enterprise Content Management Software; 2006
Regal Cinemedia Corp.
RSG Media Systems
SecondScreen Networks; New York, NY Media Relations
Showtime
Slate
SNTA - Syndicated Network Television Association
SpaceIL Media Relations
Theorem Public Relations
Thomas Technology Solutions
Times Square BID
TruEffect Media Relations
We Media
The Week Magazine

TSM DESIGN
293 Bridge St Ste 222, Springfield, MA 1103
Tel.: (413) 731-7600
Fax: (413) 730-6689
E-Mail: info@tsmdesign.com
Web Site: www.tsmdesign.com

Agency Specializes In: Advertising, Brand Development & Integration, Collateral, Digital/Interactive, Environmental, Package Design, Radio

Nancy Urbschat *(Principal)*
Janet Bennett *(Dir-Mktg)*
Deborah Walsh *(Dir-Creative)*

Accounts:
Reeds Landing Homeage & Healthcare Services

TTC GROUP
160 Front St, New York, NY 10038
Tel.: (646) 290-6400
E-Mail: info@ttcominc.com
Web Site: www.ttcominc.com

Employees: 10

Agency Specializes In: Public Relations

Revenue: $1,000,000

Victor J. Allgeier *(Partner)*
David Reynolds *(Partner)*
Peter Rice *(Partner)*

Accounts:
Arotech Corporation
EMCORE Corporation
Faro

TUERFF-DAVIS ENVIROMEDIA
1717 W 6th St Ste 400, Austin, TX 78703
Tel.: (512) 476-4368
Fax: (512) 476-4392
E-Mail: careers@enviromedia.com
Web Site: www.enviromedia.com

Employees: 36
Year Founded: 1997

Approx. Annual Billings: $12,000,000

Valerie Davis *(CEO & Principal)*
Tamala Barksdale *(VP)*
Sharon Henry *(Producer-Digital)*
Adam Niederpruem *(Producer-Experiential Mktg)*
Suzie Lopez *(Dir-Media Plng & Buying)*
Malu Faccio *(Mgr-Creative Svcs)*
Melanie Fish Work *(Strategist-PR & Social Media)*
Margot Hake Piper *(Acct Exec)*

Accounts:
Dell, Inc.
Green Mountain Energy Co. Natural Energy; 2004
LCRA
OSU

TUNHEIM PARTNERS
1100 Riverview Tower 8009 34th Ave S, Minneapolis, MN 55425
Tel.: (952) 851-1600
Fax: (952) 851-1610
E-Mail: info@tunheim.com
Web Site: www.tunheim.com

Employees: 30
Year Founded: 1990

National Agency Associations: COPF-PRSA

Agency Specializes In: Communications, Public Relations

Approx. Annual Billings: $4,500,000

Breakdown of Gross Billings by Media: Pub. Rels.: 100%

Kathryn H. Tunheim *(Pres & CEO)*
Pat Milan *(Chief Creative Officer & Exec VP)*
Lindsay Schroeder Treichel *(VP)*
Lou Ann Olson *(Acct Dir)*
Sandi Scott *(Acct Dir)*
Patrick Lilja *(Dir-eStrategy)*
Danielle Pierce *(Acct Exec)*

Accounts:
Target Stores

TURNER PUBLIC RELATIONS
1614 15th St 4th Fl, Denver, CO 80202
Tel.: (303) 333-1402
Fax: (303) 333-4390
E-Mail: info@turnerpr.com
Web Site: www.turnerpr.com

Employees: 10
Year Founded: 2005

Agency Specializes In: Advertising, Print, Production (Print), Public Relations

Angela Berardino *(VP-Travel & Digital)*
Kelsey Comstock *(Sr Dir)*
Deborah Park *(Sr Dir-Travel)*
Campbell Levy *(Dir-Media Rels)*
Alex Aberman *(Sr Mgr-Media)*
Stephanie Mattern *(Mgr & Coord-Culture)*
Caitlin Martz *(Sr Acct Exec)*
Ashley Cox *(Jr Acct Exec)*
Whitt Kelly *(Acct Coord)*

Accounts:
Ariat International PR
Ballast Time Instruments PR
Bermuda Tourism Authority Public Relations, Social Media
Bern Unlimited PR
The Carneros Inn
Emu US Public Relations Agency of Record
Fenix Outdoor
Brunton
Hanwag
Primus
Filson Digital Communications, Marketing, Public Relations
Generator Hostels PR
Gociety
Hyatt Playa Del Carmen
Kappa USA PR
Oliberte Public Relations Agency of Record
Pure Barre (Agency of Record)
Pure Fix Cycles
New-Q&A Residential Hotel
New-Smith Fork Ranch
Utah Office of Tourism Integrated Media Relations, Social Media, Strategic
New-Vidanta
Westgate Park City
New-World Nomads (Agency of Record)

Branch

Turner Public Relations
264 W 40th St Ste 802, New York, NY 10018
Tel.: (212) 889-1700
Fax: (212) 889-1277
E-Mail: info@turnerpr.com
Web Site: www.turnerpr.com

Employees: 25

Agency Specializes In: Outdoor, Public Relations, Real Estate, Travel & Tourism

Mariana DiMartino *(Sr VP-Lifestyle)*
Emma de Vadder *(VP-Tourism)*
Jeff Maldonado *(VP-Digital Comm)*
Kimberly Rodgers *(Sr Acct Supvr)*
Megan Brown *(Sr Acct Supervisor)*
Lauren Ryback *(Sr Acct Exec)*
Samantha Bonizzi *(Acct Exec)*
Kim Gibbs *(Acct Exec)*
Samantha Mittman *(Acct Exec)*
Michelle O'Rourke *(Jr Acct Exec)*

Accounts:
Adam's Rib Ranch
Airwalk
Alternative Apparel PR
Boast USA Cultural Engagement, Event Planning, Product Awareness, Trade Activations
Deckers Sanuk
Hidden Meadow Ranch
Hotel Teatro
JayBird PR
Michael Antonio Footwear
Obermeyer
TOMS Shoes
Waldorf Astoria Park City Media Relations, Strategic Social Media Planning

TWSQUARED LLC
112 Annie St, Orlando, FL 32806
Tel.: (407) 920-0926
Web Site: www.twsquared.com

Agency Specializes In: Brand Development & Integration, Collateral, Crisis Communications, Internet/Web Design, Media Relations, Media Training, Public Relations, Strategic Planning/Research

Lorri Shaban *(Pres)*
Laura Conner *(Acct Mgr)*
Emily Kruse *(Acct Mgr-PR)*
Julie Marshall *(Acct Coord)*

Accounts:
Space Coast Office of Tourism

TYLER BARNETT PUBLIC RELATIONS
8484 Wilshire Blvd Ste 242, Beverly Hills, CA 90211
Tel.: (323) 937-1951
Fax: (323) 659-1903
E-Mail: info@tylerbarnettpr.com
Web Site: www.tylerbarnettpr.com

Employees: 5

Agency Specializes In: Automotive, Brand Development & Integration, Entertainment, Graphic Design, Media Planning, T.V.

Tyler Barnett *(Owner)*
Kaitlyn Bracken *(Sr Acct Exec)*
Travis Culver *(Acct Exec)*

Accounts:
Butler & Associates (Agency of Record) Investigation Services

UGLY DOG MEDIA INC.
1164 E Victoria St, South Bend, IN 46614
Tel.: (574) 344-2056
Web Site: www.uglydogmedia.com

Agency Specializes In: Content, Corporate Communications, Internet/Web Design, Public Relations, Search Engine Optimization, Social Media

Dan Blacharski *(Pres)*

Accounts:
Schoolie.com

UNSER COMMUNICATIONS
9083 Hollow Green Dr, Las Vegas, NV 89129
Tel.: (702) 466-3539
Web Site: www.unsercommunications.com

Agency Specializes In: Brand Development & Integration, Content, Crisis Communications, Market Research, Media Relations, Promotions, Public Relations, Social Media, Strategic Planning/Research

Adam Porsborg *(Founder & CEO)*
Austin Porsborg *(Acct Dir)*

Accounts:
Tease Boutique Salon

UPRAISE MARKETING & PR
111 Maiden Ln Ste 540, San Francisco, CA 94108
Tel.: (415) 397-7600
E-Mail: info@upraisepr.com
Web Site: www.upraisepr.com

Year Founded: 2003

Agency Specializes In: Broadcast, Content, Event Planning & Marketing, Internet/Web Design, Logo & Package Design, Media Relations, Print, Public Relations, Social Media

Tim Johnson *(Pres)*
Cathy Goerz *(Sr VP)*
Ari Brosowsky *(Acct Supvr)*
Victoria Levy *(Sr Acct Exec)*

Accounts:
Vector Resources

UPROAR PR
189 S Orange Ave, Orlando, FL 32801
Tel.: (321) 236-0102
Web Site: www.uproarpr.com

Year Founded: 2011

Agency Specializes In: Brand Development & Integration, Exhibit/Trade Shows, Media Relations, Production, Public Relations, Social Media

Catriona Harris *(Co-Founder & Owner)*
Mike Harris *(Co-Founder & Partner)*
Tory Patrick *(VP)*
Kendall Wayland *(VP-Ops)*
Ashley White *(Acct Dir)*
Lindsey Showalter *(Sr Acct Exec)*
Sydney Hirst *(Asst Acct Exec)*
Lena Oakley *(Asst Acct Exec)*
Catalina Medellin *(Acct Coord)*

Accounts:
3dcart Media
A. Duie Pyle Social Media Strategy
Boxtera
Duo-Gard Strategic Media Relations
FlightScope Marketing, Media Relations
Flossolution Media Relations, Social Media
Front Burner Brands, Inc. Communications, Creative, Media Relations, Public Relations, Social Media, Strategic
New-Fusionetics (Agency of Record)
Green Light Fire Bag Media, Strategy
Hyperice Brand Awareness, Media Outreach, Social Media Strategies, VYPER
Make-A-Wish Foundation of Central and Northern Florida
New-Milestone Sports (Agency of Record)
New-Mio Global (Agency of Record)
Monticello Vineyards
myHealthSphere Brand Awareness, Dooo, Media Outreach, Social Media Strategies
P-Squared Gallery Strategy
Shadowman Sports (Agency of Record) Brand Awareness, Media, Public Relations
ShotTracker
Tessemae's All-Natural Media Relations, Strategic Brand-Building Counsel
ThriftDee PR, Strategic Counsel
Vista Clinical Diagnostics Media Outreach, Press, Public Relations, Social Media Strategies

UPTOWN PR
4861 Magazine St, New Orleans, LA 70115
Tel.: (504) 496-8314
E-Mail: info@uptown-pr.com
Web Site: www.uptown-pr.com

Year Founded: 2011

Agency Specializes In: Brand Development & Integration, Event Planning & Marketing, Media Relations, Public Relations, Social Media

Genevieve J. Douglass *(Founder & Exec Dir)*

Accounts:
Ben Vaughn
Guest Law Firm
The Kupcake Factory
Nola Tiles
RioMar Seafood
Skip N' Whistle
Tallulahs Designs

URIAS COMMUNICATIONS
6617 N Scottsdale Rd Ste103, Scottsdale, AZ 85250
Tel.: (480) 751-5569
Web Site: www.uriascommunications.com

Agency Specializes In: Digital/Interactive, Event Planning & Marketing, Media Buying Services, Media Planning, Public Relations, Radio, T.V.

Lisa Urias *(Pres)*
Jennifer Sanchez *(VP)*
Jesse Palacios *(Creative Dir)*
Christine Kaercher *(Acct Mgr)*
Vanessa Nielsen *(Acct Mgr)*
Marisol Pelaez *(Specialist-PR)*

Accounts:
Arizona Public Service Company

VAN EPEREN & COMPANY
932 Hungerford Dr Ste 32B, Rockville, MD 20850
Tel.: (301) 836-1516
Fax: (301) 581-7272
E-Mail: info@veandco.com
Web Site: veandco.com

Employees: 8

Agency Specializes In: Collateral, Communications, Education, Event Planning & Marketing, Exhibit/Trade Shows, Financial, Government/Political, Health Care Services, Hospitality, Information Technology, Internet/Web Design, Media Relations, Multimedia, Newspaper, Public Relations, Real Estate, Retail, Social Marketing/Nonprofit, T.V.

Karen Addis *(Sr VP)*
Steve Simon *(VP)*
Meghan Carpenter *(Strategist-Website)*

VANDER HOUWEN PUBLIC RELATIONS, INC.
8575 SE 76th Pl, Mercer Island, WA 98040
Tel.: (206) 949-4364
Fax: (206) 236-1715
E-Mail: boyd@vhpr.com
Web Site: www.vhpr.com

Boyd Vander Houwen *(Owner)*
Casey Conroy *(Acct Coord)*

Accounts:
Baker Boyer Bank
City Bank
First Mutual Bank
First Sound Bank
Frontier Bank
GA Creative
Homestead Capital
Pacific Crest Savings Bank
Pacific Northwest Salmon Center

THE VANDIVER GROUP INC.
510 Maryville Ctr Dr Ste 320, Saint Louis, MO 63141
Tel.: (314) 991-4641
Fax: (314) 991-4651
E-Mail: tvg@vandivergroup.com
Web Site: www.vandivergroup.com

Agency Specializes In: Media Relations, Media Training, Public Relations, Social Media

Donna Vandiver *(Pres & CEO)*
Amy Crump *(CFO)*
Andrew Likes *(VP)*
Laura Vandiver *(VP)*

Accounts:
New-Community Service Public Relations Council

VANTAGE PR
(Formerly Vantage Communications)
90 New Montgomery St Ste 1414, San Francisco, CA 94104
Tel.: (415) 984-1970
Fax: (415) 984-1971
E-Mail: info@vantagepr.com
Web Site: vantagepr.com/

Employees: 25
Year Founded: 1990

Agency Specializes In: Brand Development & Integration, Exhibit/Trade Shows, Media Relations, Podcasting, Strategic Planning/Research, Travel & Tourism

Ilene Adler *(Founder & CEO)*
Rob Adler *(Sr VP)*
Katie Blair *(VP)*
Fran Bosecker *(Acct Dir)*
Staci Didner *(Acct Exec)*
Paige Verducci *(Acct Exec)*

Karina Chowdhury *(Acct Coord)*
Rebecca Haynes *(Acct Coord)*

Accounts:
Blue Sky Networks; La Jolla, CA Breaking World Records Without Breaking the Bank
CALMAC
CooTek Media Relations, TouchPal Keyboard
eTelemetry; Annapolis, MD
Florida Venture Forum
Gotootie (Agency of Record) Media
SearchYourCloud
SOMS Technologies
New-Voxbone Public Relations
Xelerated Carrier Ethernet ASSP-Based Chipsets; 2008

VARALLO PUBLIC RELATIONS
640 Spence Ln Ste 122, Nashville, TN 37217
Tel.: (615) 367-5200
Fax: (615) 367-5888
Web Site: www.varallopr.com

Year Founded: 1991

Agency Specializes In: Internet/Web Design, Media Relations, Public Relations, Social Media

Kathleen Varallo *(Acct Exec)*

Accounts:
New-Nashville Lawn & Garden Show

VARCOM SOLUTIONS LLC
12125 Windsor Hall Way, Herndon, VA 20170
Tel.: (571) 434-8466
Fax: (571) 434-8467
Web Site: www.varcom.com

Agency Specializes In: Advertising, Consulting, Media Relations, Outdoor, Public Relations, Sales Promotion

Raul Danny Vargas *(Founder & Pres)*

Accounts:
Congressional Hispanic Leadership Institute Training Services
Core180 Telecom Network Integration Services
Sabianet Marketing Communications, Media Relations, Messaging, Public Relations

VAULT COMMUNICATIONS, INC.
(Formerly FCF Schmidt Public Relations, Inc.)
630 W Germantown Pike Ste 400, Plymouth Meeting, PA 19462
Tel.: (610) 641-0395
Fax: (610) 941-0580
Web Site: www.vaultcommunications.com

Agency Specializes In: Public Relations

Kate Shields *(Pres & Partner)*
Gina Kent *(VP)*
Pamela Caruolo *(Assoc VP)*
Craig Rogers *(Sr Dir-Art)*
Abby Rizen *(Dir-Media Rels)*
Corrinne Upton *(Acct Mgr)*
Allie Artur *(Sr Acct Exec)*
Ariel Vegotsky *(Sr Acct Exec)*
Lauren Nick *(Acct Exec)*
Katy Rambo *(Acct Exec)*
Amanda Michaelson *(Acct Coord)*

Accounts:
Acosta
Bancroft
Cancer Treatment Centers of America
Decision Strategies International
Gwynedd-Mercy University
Rita's Italian Ice (Public Relations Agency of Record) First Day of Spring, Social Media
Saxbys Coffee; Broomall, PA
Sesame Place
Triose
Village of Rosemont, PA (Public Relations Agency of Record)

VEHR COMMUNICATIONS, LLC
700 Walnut St Ste 450, Cincinnati, OH 45202-2011
Tel.: (513) 381-8347
Fax: (513) 381-8348
Toll Free: (877) 381-8347
E-Mail: nvehr@vehrcommunications.com
Web Site: www.vehrcommunications.com

Agency Specializes In: Communications, Corporate Communications, Corporate Identity, Crisis Communications, Digital/Interactive, Event Planning & Marketing, Exhibit/Trade Shows, Government/Political, Internet/Web Design, Investor Relations, Media Relations, Media Training, Newspaper, Public Relations, Viral/Buzz/Word of Mouth

Revenue: $110,000,000

Nick Vehr *(Pres)*
Michael Perry *(VP-Content Strategy)*
Laura Phillips *(VP-Client Svcs)*
Sandy Daugherty *(Office Mgr)*
Destinee Thomas *(Acct Mgr)*
Darcy Little *(Sr Acct Exec)*
Dan Guttridge *(Acct Exec)*
Mindy Kershner *(Acct Exec)*
Molly Ryan *(Acct Coord)*
Sarah Sampson *(Acct Coord)*

Accounts:
3CDC
Cincinnati Union Bethel
City of Cincinnati
Comey & Shepherd
Franklin Savings
GBBN Architects
Government Strategies Group, LLC
Modern Office Methods
Winegardner & Hammons, Inc.

VELOCITAS, INC.
250 NW 23rd St Ste 202, Miami, FL 33127
Tel.: (305) 854-6999
Web Site: www.velocitas.com

Year Founded: 2002

Agency Specializes In: Advertising, Brand Development & Integration, Broadcast, Collateral, Digital/Interactive, Logo & Package Design, Print, Public Relations

Patricia Beitler *(Mng Partner)*

Accounts:
Balaboosta's Bakery
The Bath Club
The CFO Alliance
Clinicare Medical Centers
Cross Country Healthcare, Inc.
HR Solutions, Inc.
Jackson Lewis
Kaptur
Kreative Kontent
Mia Shoes, Inc.
ORT America
The Playroom Gallery
Publix Super Markets, Inc.

VERASONI WORLDWIDE
26 Park St Ste 100, Montclair, NJ 07042
Tel.: (973) 287-6868
Web Site: www.verasoni.com

Year Founded: 2005

Agency Specializes In: Advertising, Crisis Communications, Public Relations, Social Media, Strategic Planning/Research

Abe Kasbo *(CEO)*
Gabriella Ribeiro Truman *(Mng Partner)*
Gina Davison *(Sr VP-Bus Dev & Strategic Partnerships)*
Christine Falco *(Client Svcs Dir)*
Edith Moczarska *(Dir-Creative)*
Sasha Idriss *(Acct Mgr)*

Accounts:
Georgia Pacific Dental
Hixson-Burris Media

VERDE BRAND COMMUNICATIONS
(Formerly Verde PR & Consulting)
120 W Pearl St, Jackson, WY 83001
Tel.: (970) 259-3555
Fax: (970) 259-6999
E-Mail: info@verdepr.com
Web Site: www.verdepr.com

Agency Specializes In: Brand Development & Integration, Communications, Content, Exhibit/Trade Shows, Media Relations, Public Relations

Kristin Carpenter-Ogden *(Founder & CEO)*
Kelly Blake *(Dir-New Bus Dev)*
Tessa Dubois *(Acct Mgr)*
Lars-erik Johnson *(Acct Mgr)*
Liz Millikin *(Acct Mgr-Digital Content & Social Media)*
Sarah Steinwand *(Acct Mgr)*
Lauren Fallert *(Acct Exec)*
Alex Hunt *(Acct Exec)*
Nick Ranno *(Acct Coord-Digital & Social)*
Whitney Coombs *(Key Acct Coord)*
Chris Primavera *(Key Acct Coord)*

Accounts:
AR Devices, LLC (Agency of Record) GogglePal
Bikes Belong Content Solutions Services, Digital Marketing, Green Lane Project, PR, PeopleForBikes.org
Diamondback Bicycles
G-Form Brand Awareness, Strategy
Howler Brothers Brand Messaging
KEEN Inc (Public Relations & Brand Communications Agency of Record)
Pearl Izumi (Public Relations & Brand Communications Agency of Record) Digital Content, Strategy
Reynolds Cycling (Agency of Record)
RinseKit (Agency of Record) Communications Strategy, Outdoor
RockyMounts, Inc Brand Awareness, Strategy
Selk'bag USA (Public Relations Agency of Record)

VERSION 2.0 COMMUNICATIONS
154 Grand St, New York, NY 10013
Tel.: (646) 760-2896
Web Site: www.v2comms.com

Agency Specializes In: Content, Media Relations, Public Relations, Social Media

Elissa Ehrlich *(VP)*
Kristen Leathers *(Sr Acct Exec)*

Accounts:
New-Berklee Institute of Creative Entrepreneurship
New-Joule Unlimited

VISINTINE & RYAN PR

2224 Mason Ln, Manchester, MO 63021-7801
Tel.: (314) 821-8232
Fax: (314) 821-3616
Web Site: www.visintineandryan.com

Agency Specializes In: Public Relations

Priscilla Visintine *(Owner)*
Janet Ryan *(Principal)*

VISION CRITICAL
505 5th Ave 18th Fl, New York, NY 10017
Tel.: (212) 402-8222
Fax: (212) 402-8221
E-Mail: info@visioncritical.com
Web Site: www.visioncritical.com

Agency Specializes In: Communications, Public Relations

Andrew Reid *(Founder, Pres & Chief Product Officer)*
Scott Miller *(CEO)*
Donna de Winter *(CFO)*
Tyler Douglas *(CMO)*
Kobi Ofir *(CTO)*
Mark Bergen *(Exec VP-Sls)*
Jim Cravens *(Exec VP-HR-Global)*
George Skaryak *(Exec VP-Worldwide Sls)*
Ben Hudson *(Dir-Editorial)*
Jenny Smelyanets *(Mgr-PR)*

Accounts:
Deere & Company

VISITECH PR
2000 E 21st Ave, Denver, CO 80205
Tel.: (303) 752-3552
Fax: (303) 752-0822
E-Mail: info@visitechpr.com
Web Site: www.visitechpr.com

Employees: 10
Year Founded: 1998

Agency Specializes In: Education, Event Planning & Marketing, Exhibit/Trade Shows, Financial, Government/Political, Health Care Services, Hospitality, Media Relations, New Technologies, Public Relations, Retail, Strategic Planning/Research, Telemarketing

Lisa Wilson *(Founder & CEO)*
Kendra Westerkamp *(VP)*

Accounts:
American Roamer (Agency of Record) Brand Messaging, MapELEMENTS, Planning, Positioning, Public Relations, Traditional & Social Media
Aurora Networks
Edgeware Partners
Mosaik Solutions

VISTA GROUP
4561 Colorado Blvd, Los Angeles, CA 90039
Tel.: (818) 551-6789
Fax: (818) 840-6880
E-Mail: info@vistagroupusa.com
Web Site: www.vistagroupusa.com

E-Mail for Key Personnel:
President: ericdahlquistsr@vistagroupusa.com
Production Mgr.: karldahlquist@vistagroupusa.com
Public Relations: mariamaniaci@vistagroupusa.com

Employees: 10
Year Founded: 1972

Agency Specializes In: Event Planning & Marketing, Public Relations, T.V.

Approx. Annual Billings: $2,000,000

Karl Dahlquist *(Dir-Ops)*
Carol Schmiederer *(Mgr-Product Placement)*

Accounts:
California Table Grape Commission
Mercedes-Benz; Burbank, CA; 1989

VISTRA COMMUNICATIONS
15436 N Florida Ave Ste 160, Tampa, FL 33613
Tel.: (813) 961-4700
E-Mail: info@consultvistra.com
Web Site: www.consultvistra.com

Agency Specializes In: Brand Development & Integration, Media Relations, Public Relations, Social Media

Brian Butler *(Pres)*
Matt Burnett *(Mgr-Bus)*

Accounts:
New-Integral Energy
New-Paralyzed Veterans of America

VOCE COMMUNICATIONS
298 S Sunnyvale Ave Ste 101, Sunnyvale, CA 94086
Tel.: (408) 738-7840
Fax: (408) 738-7858
E-Mail: info@vocecomm.com
Web Site: vocecommunications.com

Employees: 40
Year Founded: 1999

Agency Specializes In: Communications, Consumer Marketing, Financial, High Technology, Public Relations, Publicity/Promotions, Sponsorship

Richard Cline *(Pres & Head-Global Tech Practice)*
Matt Podboy *(Exec VP)*
Christopher Barger *(Sr VP-Programs-Global)*
Keira Anderson *(VP)*
Mike Gallow *(VP-Ops)*
Stacy Libby *(VP)*
Jeff Urquhart *(VP)*
Romina Varriale *(VP)*
Katie Watson *(VP)*

Accounts:
Citrix Systems, Inc. (Agency of Record) Public Relations
Fujitsu
Ketera
LucidEra
NetApp, Inc.
Network Physics
Peerflix
Sony Computer Entertainment America LLC Campaign: "Recapturing Authenticity"

VOLUME PUBLIC RELATIONS
1745 Shea Center Dr, Highlands Ranch, CO 80129
Tel.: (720) 529-4850
E-Mail: info@volumepr.com
Web Site: www.volumepr.com

Employees: 7
Year Founded: 2001

Elizabeth Edwards *(Founder, Pres & CEO)*
Elizabeth Same *(Asst Acct Exec)*
Emma Hirata *(Acct Coord)*

Accounts:
Big Mo
Corvis
DIGI Tech Systems
IphoneappQuotes.com
KPN Qwest
Mary Jane's Relaxing Soda
Pumpkin Masters
Quiet Light Brokerage Marketing, Messaging, PR
Sony & BMG Entertainment
Tower Cloud (Agency of Record)
The Western Golf Association 2014 BMW Championship

VORTICOM INC
216 E 47th St 28th Fl, New York, NY 10017
Tel.: (212) 532-2208
Web Site: www.vorticom.com

Agency Specializes In: Media Buying Services, Media Relations, Public Relations

Nancy Tamosaitis *(Pres)*
Ron Thompson *(VP)*

Accounts:
American Vanadium Marketing Communications, Media, Public Relations
IBC Advanced Alloys Corp

VOX OPTIMA LLC
505 14th St NW, Albuquerque, NM 87104
Tel.: (866) 499-2947
E-Mail: info@voxoptima.com
Web Site: www.voxoptima.com

Year Founded: 2005

Agency Specializes In: Crisis Communications, Event Planning & Marketing, Media Planning, Media Relations, Media Training, Public Relations, Social Media, Strategic Planning/Research

Merritt Hamilton Allen *(Owner & Exec Dir)*
Mark Osburn *(Sr Dir-Comm)*
Gary Potterfield *(Dir-Comm)*

Accounts:
The National Association of Development Companies (Agency of Record)

VOX PUBLIC RELATIONS
(Formerly The Ulum Group)
1416 Willamette St, Eugene, OR 97401
Tel.: (541) 302-6620
Fax: (541) 302-6622
E-Mail: admin@voxprpa.com
Web Site: www.voxprpa.com

Employees: 10
Year Founded: 1995

Agency Specializes In: Event Planning & Marketing, Government/Political, Media Relations, Public Relations

Patrick Walsh *(CEO-Pub Affairs)*
Amber Williamson *(Dir-PR)*

Accounts:
Chalk Hill Estate Vineyards and Winery
City of Springfield, Oregon
Espwa Fe Viv

VOX SOLID COMMUNICATIONS
1912 S 10th St, Las Vegas, NV 89142
Tel.: (702) 586-2137
Web Site: www.wearevoxsolid.com

Year Founded: 2011

Agency Specializes In: Communications, Public Relations, Social Media

Marina Nicola *(Owner & Partner)*
Krissi Reeves *(Mgr-Social Media)*
Adrianne Offermann *(Specialist-PR & Res)*

Accounts:
Brian James Women's Footwear PR
Downtown Grand Las Vegas Hotel & Casino Public Relations, Social Media
Ferraro's Italian Restaurant & Wine Bar
Madame Tussauds Las Vegas Public Relations, Social Media
Roster

VOXPOP COMMUNICATIONS LLC
PO Box 881, Westminster, MD 21158
Tel.: (443) 487-7164
Web Site: www.vox-pop-communications.com

Year Founded: 2012

Agency Specializes In: Advertising, Brand Development & Integration, Crisis Communications, Event Planning & Marketing, Graphic Design, Logo & Package Design, Outdoor, Print, Promotions, Public Relations

David M. Baker *(Dir-Sls & Mktg)*

Accounts:
Habitat for Humanity of Carroll County

VP+C PARTNERS
13 Crosby St Loft 502, New York, NY 10013
Tel.: (212) 966-3759
E-Mail: info@vpcpartners.com
Web Site: www.vpcpartners.com

Agency Specializes In: Digital/Interactive, Event Planning & Marketing, Public Relations, Social Media, Strategic Planning/Research

Mark Veeder *(Founder & Chief Creative Officer)*
Margaux Caniato *(Chief Brand Officer & Principal)*
Esther Perman *(Principal)*
Meghan Dockendorf *(Acct Mgr)*
Jackie Courlas *(Mgr-Ops)*
Michelle Shen *(Acct Supvr)*
Blaise Foley *(Acct Exec)*
Rachel Hartman *(Acct Exec)*

Accounts:
Crosby St Studios
Davis & Warshow Inc.
Dornbracht USA, Inc.
Forty One Madison
Interface, Inc.
JCPenney
Rocky Mountain
St Charles of NY
Technogel
USAI

VPE PUBLIC RELATIONS
1605 Hope St Ste 250, South Pasadena, CA 91030
Tel.: (626) 403-3200
Fax: (626) 403-1700
Web Site: vpe-pr.com

Employees: 15
Year Founded: 1988

National Agency Associations: COPF

Agency Specializes In: Advertising, Education, Event Planning & Marketing, Media Training, Publicity/Promotions, Sales Promotion, Strategic Planning/Research

Patricia Perez *(Partner)*
Maricela Cueva *(VP)*
Jennifer Gonzalez *(VP)*
Lourdes Rodriguez *(Acct Dir)*
Anna Garcia *(Acct Supvr)*

Accounts:
AbilityFirst
American Academy of Ophthalmology
Building Healthy Communities Eastern Coachella Valley
Disneyland Resort
Edison
Hulu
JustFab Inc.
Latin American Multimedia Corporation Dos y Dos Live Action Bilingual Television Series for Children 2-7 (Agency of Record)
McDonald's Hispanic
Nestle
Valley Presbyterian Hospital

WAGGENER EDSTROM WORLDWIDE, INC.
(Name Changed to WE)

WAGSTAFF WORLDWIDE
(Private-Parent-Single Location)
6725 Sunset Blvd Ste 250, Los Angeles, CA 90028
Tel.: (323) 871-1151
Fax: (323) 871-1171
Web Site: www.wagstaffworldwide.com

Employees: 30
Year Founded: 2000

Agency Specializes In: Communications, Public Relations, Social Media

Revenue: $3,100,000

Mary Wagstaff *(Pres)*
Nadia Al-Amir *(Mng Partner)*
Lisa Hollinger *(VP & Partner-Admin)*
Vanessa Kanegai *(VP)*
Meghan Patke *(VP)*
Kelsey Beniasch *(Exec Dir)*
Gary Knight *(Exec Dir-Admin)*
Linda Smitaman Taylor *(Mgr-HR)*
Ashley Norman *(Sr Acct Supvr-Travel)*
Donna Breitbart *(Acct Exec)*
Megan Buehrer *(Acct Exec)*
Christopher Robin *(Acct Exec-Social Media)*
Elaine Hong *(Acct Coord)*
Jonathan Rosenberg *(Sr Office Mgr)*

Accounts:
Akaryn Hospitality Management Services Public Relations
Plan Check

THE WAKEMAN AGENCY
445 Hamilton Ave Ste 1102, White Plains, NY 10601
Tel.: (212) 500-5953
E-Mail: info@thewakemanagency.com
Web Site: www.thewakemanagency.com

Year Founded: 2003

Agency Specializes In: Communications, Corporate Communications, Event Planning & Marketing, Media Relations, Public Relations

Vanessa Wakeman *(Principal)*
K. Danielle Edwards *(Mgr-Content)*
Tameka Mullins *(Mgr-Social Media)*
Kristen Trojel *(Mgr-Bus Dev)*

Accounts:
SENetwork (Public Relations Agency of Record)

WALEK & ASSOCIATES
(Acquired by Peppercomm & Name Changed to WalekPeppercomm)

WALEKPEPPERCOMM
(Formerly Walek & Associates)
317 Madison Ave Ste 2300, New York, NY 10017
Tel.: (212) 889-4113
Fax: (212) 889-7174
E-Mail: twalek@peppercomm.com
Web Site: www.walekpeppercomm.com/

Employees: 14

Ann Barlow *(Partner & Pres-West Coast)*
Ted Birkhahn *(Partner & Pres-New York Office)*
Deborah Brown *(Partner & Mng Dir-Strategic Dev-New York)*
Jackie Kolek *(Partner & Mng Dir-New York Office)*
Maggie O'Neill *(Partner & Mng Dir-New York Office)*
Thomas Walek *(Pres-Capital Markets & Fin Svcs New York Office)*
Michael Dresner *(CEO-Brand Squared Licensing New York Office)*
Armel Leslie *(Sr Dir-Capital Markets New York Office)*
Sara Whitman *(Sr Dir)*
Matt Lester *(Dir-Creative, Comml & Film)*
Matt Purdue *(Dir-Content Strategy New York Office)*

Accounts:
Abax Global Capital
Custom House Group
Dow Jones Newswires
Everest Capital
First Eagle Investment Management Media Relations
GFI Group Inc.; 2007
The Little Book of Market Wizards
Marinus Capital Advisors
New York Hedge Fund Roundtable
Oppenheimer & Co. Inc
Prologue Capital
Roc Capital Management
Trust Company of America Media Relations, Messaging, Social Media
Venor Capital Management

WALKER SANDS COMMUNICATIONS
121 N Jefferson St, Chicago, IL 60661
Tel.: (312) 267-0066
Fax: (312) 876-1388
Web Site: www.walkersands.com

Year Founded: 2001

National Agency Associations: COPF

Agency Specializes In: Corporate Communications, Crisis Communications, Event Planning & Marketing, Internet/Web Design, Media Training, Public Relations, Search Engine Optimization, Sponsorship

Ken Gaebler *(Founder & Chm)*
Mike Santoro *(Pres)*
Will Kruisbrink *(Partner & Sr Acct Dir)*
Dave Parro *(Partner & Sr Acct Dir)*
John Fairley *(VP-Digital Svcs)*
Andrew Cross *(Sr Acct Dir)*
Daniel Laloggia *(Mgr-Digital Strategy)*

Accounts:
BizBuySell
Corigelan
Dieselpoint
eCoupled

Enterworks (Public Relations Agency of Record) Brand Awareness, Communications, Marketing, News Announcements, Thought Leadership
Evzdrop
Extended Care Information Network
Lanworth
Legacy.Com, Inc
LifeWatch
Ottawa Wireless
SceneTap
SurePayroll

WALL STREET COMMUNICATIONS

1299 E 4500 S, Salt Lake City, UT 84124
Tel.: (801) 266-0077
Fax: (801) 266-0778
E-Mail: info@wallstcom.com
Web Site: www.wallstcom.com

Employees: 25
Year Founded: 1996

Agency Specializes In: Local Marketing, Media Buying Services, Public Relations, Web (Banner Ads, Pop-ups, etc.)

Chris Lesieutre *(Pres)*
Sunny Branson *(Acct Dir)*
Joe Commare *(Acct Dir)*
Lyndsey Albright *(Sr Acct Mgr)*
Joyce Cataldo *(Acct Mgr-PR)*
Elisabetta Fernandez *(Sr Acct Exec)*

Accounts:
Archimedia Technology Content Marketing, Media Relations
BeckTV Content Marketing, Media Relations
BTX
Cobalt Digital (Global Content Marketing Agency of Record)
Compix Media; Irvine, CA
ContentWise Public Relations
Data-Systems International ClientTrack
Dejero Content Marketing, Media Relations, PR
Digigram Global PR, Media Relations
Forbidden Technologies Plc PR
Fx-Motion PR, Remote Camera & Camera Robotics Products, Social Media
HaiVision Systems, Inc.
I-MOVIX Global PR
Linear Acoustic
LiteTouch (Agency of Record) Public Relations, Social Media
Mosart MediaLab Media, Public Relations
NEP Broadcasting PR
Netia
NUGEN Audio Public Relations
Orad
PPC & Perfect Path
Radio-Technische Werkstaetten GmbH & Co KG
Riedel Communications PR
SENSIO Technologies
Society of Motion Picture and Television Engineers Global PR, Media Relations
Vimond Media Solutions Marketing, Public Relations
New-Vogo Content Marketing
New-Vogo (Content Marketing Agency of Record) Communications, Marketing, Public Relations
Wowza Media
Zaxcom

WALSH PUBLIC RELATIONS

305 Knowlton St, Bridgeport, CT 6608
Tel.: (203) 292-6280
E-Mail: info@walshpr.com
Web Site: www.walshpr.com

Year Founded: 1997

Agency Specializes In: Brand Development & Integration, Corporate Communications, Crisis Communications, Logo & Package Design, Promotions, Public Relations, Social Media

Gregory S. Walsh *(Pres)*

Accounts:
New-Tactic USA Inc

WALT & COMPANY

2105 S Bascom Ave Ste 240, Campbell, CA 95008
Tel.: (408) 369-7200
Fax: (408) 369-7201
E-Mail: info@walt.com
Web Site: www.walt.com

E-Mail for Key Personnel:
President: bwalt@walt.com

Employees: 18
Year Founded: 1991

Agency Specializes In: Business Publications, Business-To-Business, Computers & Software, Consumer Marketing, Corporate Identity, Crisis Communications, E-Commerce, Electronics, High Technology, Information Technology, Investor Relations, Media Relations, Media Training, Public Relations, Social Media, Strategic Planning/Research

Approx. Annual Billings: $2,500,000

Breakdown of Gross Billings by Media: Pub. Rels.: 100%

Robert Walt *(Founder & CEO)*
Cyndi Babasa *(Sr VP)*
Merritt Woodward *(Sr VP)*
Jeannie Gustlin *(VP-HR)*
Jane Fainer *(Sr Acct Mgr)*

Accounts:
Actions Semiconductor Co, Ltd. Public Relations
New-Acxiom Corporation (Public Relations & Social Media Agency of Record)
D-Link Systems, Inc. (Agency of Record)
Epson America, Inc. Printers, Projectors, Scanners
Ronald McDonald House at Stanford
Seal Software Public Relation, Social Media
Violin Memory, Inc. (US Public Relations Agency of Record) Strategic Communications

WARD

5959 W Loop S Ste 510, Bellaire, TX 77401
Tel.: (713) 869-0707
Web Site: www.wardcc.com

Agency Specializes In: Brand Development & Integration, Corporate Communications, Corporate Identity, Crisis Communications, Media Relations, Media Training, Public Relations, Search Engine Optimization, Social Media, Strategic Planning/Research

Deborah Ward Buks *(Pres)*
Lynn Hancock *(Sr VP)*
Alisha Wade *(VP)*
Molly LeCronier *(VP)*
Gwen Hambrick *(VP-Admin)*

Accounts:
Greyrock Energy

WARD CREATIVE COMMUNICATIONS, INC.

(Private-Parent-Single Location)
5959 W Loop S Ste 510, Bellaire, TX 77401
Tel.: (713) 869-0707
Web Site: www.wardcc.com

Employees: 12
Year Founded: 1989

Agency Specializes In: Advertising, Brand Development & Integration, Collateral, Corporate Communications, Corporate Identity, Crisis Communications, Media Relations, Media Training, Public Relations, Social Media

Revenue: $1,100,000

Lynn Hancock *(Sr VP)*
Molly Lecronier *(VP & Dir-Energy Practice)*
Gwen Hambrick *(VP-Admin)*
Alisha Wade *(VP)*

Accounts:
Hydrogen Group Communications
International Energy Agency's Gas & Oil Technologies Implementing Agreement Communications
Kraton Polymers
Next Level Urgent Care Communications
North Dakota LNG Communications
Pricelock
VIV Solutions Communications

WARNER COMMUNICATIONS

41 Raymond St, Manchester, MA 01944
Tel.: (978) 526-1960
Fax: (978) 526-8206
E-Mail: office@warnerpr.com
Web Site: www.warnerpr.com

Employees: 7

Carin Warner *(Founder & Pres)*
Dawn Ringel *(Sr VP)*
Erin Vadala *(VP)*
Ariane Doud *(Sr Acct Dir)*
Vashti Brotherhood *(Dir-Creative)*
Amy Watt *(Dir-Creative & Art)*

Accounts:
All Stars Project, Inc. (Agency of Record) Event Promotion Strategy, Thought Leadership, Traditional & Digital Media Relations
Caliper
Cambridge Associates
Confluence
Cumberland Farms
Dancing Deer Baking Company; Boston, MA Campaign: "America's Best Tasting Brownie"
Focus Financial Partners
Gulf Oil, LLP Diesel Fuel, Gas Stations, Heating Oil, Kerosene; 2006
Maguire Associates; Bedford, MA; 2005
Mass Mutual
NineSigma Social & Traditional Media
Olivia's Organics
Omegabright
Outsell; Burlingame, CA; 2005
New-O'verlays Media Relations, Public Relations
Saucony
SeaMarket
Sentinel Benefits
Voltaire
Watson Wyatt Worldwide
WellPet
Wymans

WARSCHAWSKI

1501 Sulgrave Ave Ste 350, Baltimore, MD 21209
Tel.: (410) 367-2700
Fax: (410) 367-2400
E-Mail: info@warschawski.com
Web Site: www.warschawski.com

Employees: 15
Year Founded: 1996

National Agency Associations: PRSA

Agency Specializes In: Advertising, Brand Development & Integration, Business-To-Business, Collateral, Communications, Consulting, Consumer Goods, Consumer Marketing, Corporate Communications, Corporate Identity, Crisis Communications, Digital/Interactive, Direct Response Marketing, Direct-to-Consumer, E-Commerce, Event Planning & Marketing, Fashion/Apparel, Food Service, Government/Political, Integrated Marketing, Internet/Web Design, Investor Relations, Logo & Package Design, Media Relations, Media Training, Outdoor, Product Placement, Promotions, Public Relations, Publicity/Promotions, Retail, Search Engine Optimization, Social Marketing/Nonprofit, Sponsorship, Sports Market, Strategic Planning/Research, Travel & Tourism, Web (Banner Ads, Pop-ups, etc.)

David Warschawski *(CEO)*
Shana Harris *(COO)*
Michele Tomlinson *(Sr Dir)*
Justin Barber *(Dir-Interactive Design)*
Mark Ludwig *(Dir-Design Dev)*
Lauren Scheib *(Dir-Design)*
Allison Beers *(Sr Designer)*

Accounts:
Biologics Consulting Group (Agency of Record) Advertising, Brand Strategy, Public Relations
Chiron Technology Services (Agency of Record) Advertising, Public Relations, Social Media
Concurrent Technologies Corp. (Agency of Record)
Danfoss Marketing Communications Strategy
New-Global Telecom Brokers Strategic Brand Positioning
Icelandic Glacial Natural Spring Water Brand Strategy, Integrated Marketing, Media Relations, Social Media
ImQuest BioSciences Inc. Brand Positioning, Brand Research, Collateral Material, Key Messaging, Website Creation, imquestbio.com
Pixelligent Technologies Strategic Marketing Communications, Website
Pompeian Brand Strategy, Public Relations
Responsive Data Solutions Brand Strategy, Media, Website Redesign
Robert Talbott, Inc. Communications, Marketing, Strategic Brand Positioning
The Topps Company Baseball Cards, Marketing Communications Strategy
Track&Field (US Marketing & Communications Agency of Record) Media Relations, Retail Events, Social Media
Xcel Brands, Inc. Marketing Communications

WATER & WALL GROUP, LLC
41 E 11th St 11th Fl, New York, NY 10003
Tel.: (212) 699-3671
Web Site: www.waterandwallgroup.com

Year Founded: 2012

Agency Specializes In: Brand Development & Integration, Communications, Crisis Communications, Media Relations, Public Relations, Social Media, Strategic Planning/Research

Andrew Healy *(Partner)*
Scott Sunshine *(Partner)*
Matt Kirdahy *(Sr VP)*
Frank Piemonte *(VP)*
Caitlin Byrnes *(Dir-Digital)*
Mark Lavoie *(Sr Acct Exec)*

Accounts:
8of9 Consulting Branding, Media Relations, Messaging, PR, Positioning
HFP Capital Markets
Lear Capital Media Relations, PR, Speaking Engagements
NEPC Branding, Events, Local Community, Media Relations, Messaging, Positioning
Trishield Capital Management Branding, Media Relations, Messaging, PR, Positioning
Wolfe Research Branding, Communications Counsel, Media Relations, Positioning

WATERHOUSE PUBLIC RELATIONS
735 Broad St Ste 1004, Chattanooga, TN 37402
Tel.: (423) 643-4977
Fax: (423) 648-2929
E-Mail: info@waterhousepr.com
Web Site: www.waterhousepr.com

Employees: 10
Year Founded: 1996

Agency Specializes In: Public Relations

Rachel Johnson *(Mgr-Media Svcs)*
Natalie Jenereski *(Strategist-Digital PR)*
Callie Smith *(Coord-Media & Acct Svcs)*

Accounts:
Alexian Brothers of the Southeast
Chattanooga Metropolitan Airport Authority

WATERSHED COMMUNICATIONS
431 NW Flanders St 100, Portland, OR 97209
Tel.: (503) 827-6564
E-Mail: info@watershedcom.com
Web Site: www.watershedcom.com

Year Founded: 1999

Agency Specializes In: Brand Development & Integration, Communications, Media Relations, Public Relations

Lisa Donoughe *(Principal)*
Kristi Koebke *(Dir-Creative)*
Mark Power *(Dir-Pittsburgh)*
Laura Wieking *(Dir-Artisan Foods)*
Leilani Barney *(Acct Mgr-Culinary Activation)*
Sarah Powers *(Brand Strategist)*
Irene Squizzato *(Coord-Accts)*

Accounts:
SoCo Creamery

WAYMAKER
(Formerly Pro Ink)
200 NE 1st St Ste 200, Gainesville, FL 32605
Tel.: (352) 377-8973
Web Site: http://www.thinkwaymaker.com/

Agency Specializes In: Brand Development & Integration, Corporate Communications, Digital/Interactive, Print, Public Relations, Social Media, Strategic Planning/Research

Tracy Bachmann *(Pres)*
Sara Ivines *(Office Mgr & Project Mgr)*
Angela Doughty *(Designer)*

Accounts:
First Magnitude Brewing Company

WCG
(Formerly WeissComm Partners)
60 Francisco St, San Francisco, CA 94133
Tel.: (415) 362-5018
Fax: (415) 362-5019
Web Site: www.wcgworld.com

Agency Specializes In: Corporate Communications, Corporate Identity, Crisis Communications, Integrated Marketing, Media Relations, New Technologies, Pharmaceutical

Aaron Strout *(Pres)*
Lynn Fox *(Mng Dir)*
Michael Walker Hall *(Mng Dir)*
Paul Laland *(Mng Dir)*
David Witt *(Head-Media, Engagement & Consumer Practice-W2O Grp)*
Joe Lin *(Exec Dir-Creative)*
Alysse Esmail *(Sr Mgr-Media & Engagement)*

Accounts:
3M Health Care
3M Worldwide
Anacor Pharmaceuticals
BMC Software Global PR, Media
Genentech
Genomic Health
Iomai Corp.
Metabolex
Novacea
Nuvelo
Oncology Therapeutics Network
Pharmacyclics
Regeneron Pharmaceuticals, Inc.
Topica Pharmaceuticals, Inc.
VIA Pharmaceuticals; 2008

Branch

WCG
(Formerly WeissComm Partners)
114 5th Ave 10th Fl, New York, NY 10011
Tel.: (212) 301-7200
Fax: (212) 867-3249
E-Mail: info@wcgworld.com
Web Site: www.wcgworld.com

Employees: 25
Year Founded: 2006

Agency Specializes In: Health Care Services, Public Relations, Sponsorship

Adam Cohen *(Mng Dir)*
Carissa Caramanis O'Brien *(Dir-Healthcare Social Media & Engagement)*
Jill Simonton *(Mgr-Tech)*

Accounts:
Actelion Pharmaceuticals

WE
(Formerly Waggener Edstrom Worldwide, Inc.)
225 108th Ave NE, Bellevue, WA 98004
Tel.: (425) 638-7000
Fax: (425) 638-7001
Toll Free: (800) 938-8136
E-Mail: talktowe@we-worldwide.com
Web Site: www.we-worldwide.com

Employees: 766
Year Founded: 1983

Agency Specializes In: Brand Development & Integration, Broadcast, Communications, Environmental, Financial, Graphic Design, Health Care Services, High Technology, Internet/Web Design, Media Planning, Media Relations, Media Training, Podcasting, Public Relations, Sponsorship, Viral/Buzz/Word of Mouth, Web (Banner Ads, Pop-ups, etc.)

Approx. Annual Billings: $98,500,000 (Fee Income)

Michael Bigelow *(Chief Admin Officer)*
Kass Sells *(Pres-North America)*
Tiffany Cook *(Exec VP)*
Chris Stamm *(Sr VP & Gen Mgr-Boston)*
Matt Haynes *(Sr VP-Social & Digital Strategies)*
Martin Pearce *(Sr VP-Agency Mktg & Brand)*
Brandon SaNFord *(Acct Dir)*
Jennifer Kelly *(Sr Mgr-Agency & Partner Strategy)*
Kerry Kindinger *(Sr Acct Exec)*
Kelsey Wickman *(Acct Exec)*

Accounts:
AVG Technologies
F5 Networks (Communications Agency of Record)
Microsoft Campaign: "Mission to MARS", Mobile Communications Business
Shire
T-Mobile US
Volvo Automotive
Woodford Reserve Bourbon

Branches

WE
(Formerly Waggener Edstrom GmbH)
Sandstrasse 33, D-80335 Munich, Germany
Tel.: (49) 89 628175 0
Fax: (49) 89 628175 11
E-Mail: beichner@we-worldwide.com
Web Site: www.we-worldwide.de

Employees: 22
Year Founded: 1998

Manuel Huttl *(Gen Mgr-Germany, Switzerland & Austria)*
Annette Mueller *(Assoc Dir)*
Arne Neumeyer *(Sr Acct Mgr)*
Nicole Melzer *(Acct Mgr)*
Esther Altenfeld *(Sr Acct Exec)*
Sibylle Greiser *(Sr Acct Exec)*
Michaela Grandek *(Acct Exec)*
Alena Haage *(Asst Acct Exec)*

Accounts:
Microsoft
Panasonic Public Relations

WE
(Formerly Waggener Edstrom)
8 Rue Royale, 75008 Paris, France
Tel.: (33) 141031659
Fax: (33) 141033091
E-Mail: talktowe@we-worldwide.com
Web Site: www.we-worldwide.com

Year Founded: 1983

Agency Specializes In: Public Relations

Melissa Waggener Zorkin *(Founder, Pres & CEO)*
Corey Kalbfleisch *(CFO)*
Jennifer Granston Foster *(COO)*
Michael Bigelow *(Chief Admin Officer)*
Dawn Beauparlant *(Pres-Tech-North America)*
Julie Allport *(Exec VP)*
Alexandra Moinier *(Acct Mgr)*

Accounts:
Taxibeat

WE
(Formerly Waggener Edstrom)
Tower House Fourth Floor, 10 Southampton Street, London, WC2E 7HA United Kingdom
Tel.: (44) 2076323800
Fax: (44) 2076323801
E-Mail: talktowe@we-worldwide.com
Web Site: www.we-worldwide.co.uk

Year Founded: 1983

Agency Specializes In: Communications, Public Relations, Social Media

Chris Talago *(Exec VP & Gen Mgr-Europe)*
Anna Gray *(VP-Healthcare Practice)*
Laura Gillen *(Assoc Dir)*
Robyn Bemment *(Sr Acct Mgr)*
Annabel Kerr *(Sr Acct Mgr)*
Tom Woods *(Sr Acct Mgr)*
Eleana Stayer *(Acct Mgr)*
Yasmin Hilmi *(Sr Acct Exec)*
Sam Keefe *(Sr Acct Exec)*
David Lang *(Strategist-Digital & Planner)*

Accounts:
Collinson Latitude Global Communications
Digital Shoreditch Communications
Infosecurity Europe Content Creation, Media Relations, Online Community Engagement
Siemens PLM Marketing, Solid Edge, UK Communications
Transversal

WE
(Formerly Waggener Edstrom)
3 Pickering St, #02-50 Mankin Row, China Square Central, Singapore, 048660 Singapore
Tel.: (65) 6303 8466
Fax: (65) 6303 8477
Web Site: www.apac.we-worldwide.com

Matthew Lackie *(Sr VP)*
Carolyn Camoens *(Reg VP-Southeast Asia)*
Shefali Srinivas *(Dir-Healthcare-Asia Pacific)*
Amos Yeo *(Sr Acct Exec)*

Accounts:
Changi Airport Group Digital Communications Strategy, Strategic Counsel
Health Promotion Board Public Relations
Hootsuite (Agency of Record) Marketing, Media Relations
Transitions Optical (Public Relations & Social Media Agency of Record)

WE
(Formerly Waggener Edstrom)
Room 1901-07 19/F Tai Yau Building, Johnston Road, Wan Chai, Hong Kong, China (Hong Kong)
Tel.: (852) 2578 2823
Fax: (852) 2578 2849
Web Site: www.apac.we-worldwide.com

Employees: 30

Matthew Lackie *(Sr VP-Asia Pacific)*
Winnie Lai *(VP-Hong Kong)*
Cathleen Witter *(VP)*
Antoine Calendrier *(Gen Mgr-China)*
Emma Richards *(Gen Mgr)*

Accounts:
7-Eleven
Cole Haan
Dondonya Digital, Event Management
F5 Networks
Hitachi Data Systems
Hong Kong Cyberport Management Company
Kowloon Watch Company Content Creation, Event Management, Media Engagement
New-Magnetic Asia Clockenflap Music & Arts Festival, Content, Media Relations, Public Relations
Samsonite American Tourister, Corporate Communications, Digital, Event Management, PR, Samsonite Black Label, Samsonite Red
Sen-ryo Digital, Social Media
Shire Pharmaceutical
Skype PR
Sony PR, PlayStation, Tablets, Xperia Smartphones
Zuji Hong Kong Travel Business; 2008

WE
(Formerly Waggener Edstrom)
575 Market St, San Francisco, CA 94105
Tel.: (415) 547-7000
Fax: (415) 547-7001
E-Mail: talktowe@we-worldwide.com
Web Site: www.we-worldwide.com

Employees: 20

National Agency Associations: COPF

Agency Specializes In: Public Relations

Katie Huang Shin *(Exec VP)*
Lisa Allen *(Sr VP & Gen Mgr-San Francisco)*
Miranda Duncan *(Sr VP-Healthcare)*
Phil Missimore *(VP)*
Kristin Hampton *(Acct Mgr-Social & Digital Strategy)*
Kristi Lewandowski *(Acct Mgr)*
Jessie Wong *(Acct Mgr)*
Holly Luka *(Sr Acct Exec)*
Amy Sharman *(Sr Acct Exec)*
Stephanie Miceli *(Acct Exec-Healthcare)*
Mallory Richards *(Acct Exec)*

Accounts:
Autonet Mobile PR
AVG Technologies
F5
Honeywell
Limelight Networks, Inc; Tempe,AZ
Lithium Technologies (Communications Agency of Record)
Microsoft
Move PR
Tallie (Public Relations & Communications Agency of Record)
YuMe Thought Leadership

WE
(Formerly Waggener Edstrom)
110 Leroy St 9th Fl, New York, NY 10014
Tel.: (212) 551-4800
Fax: (212) 551-4801
E-Mail: talktowe@we-worldwide.com
Web Site: www.we-worldwide.com

Employees: 25

National Agency Associations: COPF

Alison Yochum *(Partner-HR Bus)*
Caroline Sanderson *(Exec VP)*
Matthew Lackie *(Sr VP-Asia Pacific)*
Aaron Petras *(VP-Agency & Partner Strategy)*
Christopher D. Millward *(Gen Mgr-China)*
Alexis Crofts *(Acct Exec)*
Kate Vorys *(Asst Acct Exec)*

Accounts:
Drambuie Liqueur Co.
HTC
KEF America Brand Promotion, M Series Line of Headphones, X Series Computer Speakers
Mercedes-Benz USA LLC
Microsoft
Samsung
Shire
T-Mobile US
Toshiba
Tupperware
UNCL PR, Sales Strategy
Volvo Cars of North America (Agency of Record) XC90 SUV
William Grant & Sons Inc. Balvenie, Glenfiddich

WE
(Formerly Waggener Edstrom)
3 Centerpointe Dr Ste 300, Lake Oswego, OR 97035
Tel.: (503) 443-7000
Fax: (503) 443-7001
E-Mail: talktowe@we-worldwide.com
Web Site: www.we-worldwide.com

Employees: 300

National Agency Associations: COPF

Agency Specializes In: Public Relations, Sponsorship

Julie Allport *(Exec VP)*
Aimee Corso *(Sr VP & Head-US Healthcare Practice)*
Sarah Marshall *(Acct Dir)*
Jason Love *(Acct Mgr-Microsoft Corp PR)*
Jerry Mischel *(Acct Mgr)*
Kirsten Forsberg *(Mgr-Comm)*
Abigail Espiritu *(Asst Acct Exec)*

Accounts:
Microsoft

WE

(Formerly Waggener Edstrom)
106 E 6th St Ste 750, Austin, TX 78701-3684
Tel.: (512) 527-7000
Fax: (512) 527-7001
E-Mail: talktowe@we-worldwide.com
Web Site: www.we-worldwide.com

Employees: 25

National Agency Associations: COPF

Agency Specializes In: Public Relations

Melissa Waggener Zorkin *(Founder, Pres & CEO)*
Pam Edstrom *(Founder)*
Michael Bigelow *(Chief Admin Officer)*
Hava Jeroslow *(VP-Comm)*
Mindy Nelson *(VP)*
Shannon Roarke *(VP)*
Heather Scott *(VP-Customer Insights)*
Aaron Grabein *(Acct Mgr)*

Accounts:
Austin Technology Council; 2008
Jebsen
Microsoft
Shire
T-Mobile US
Toshiba
Xplore Technologies Corp. Creative Campaigns

WEBER & ASSOCIATES PUBLIC RELATIONS

648 Balmoral Ln, Inverness, IL 60067
Tel.: (847) 705-1802
Fax: (847) 705-0109
E-Mail: cpweber@weberpr.com
Web Site: www.weberpr.com

Employees: 2

Agency Specializes In: Public Relations

Chuck Weber *(Pres)*

Accounts:
Abbott Laboratories
American Academy of Implant Dentistry
American College of Physicians
American Pain Society
American Society of Health-System Pharmacists
Bayer Diagnostics
CTI Molecular Imaging, Inc.
Eli Lilly & Company
International Technidyne Corp.
Ortho-Clinical Diagnostics
Siemens Nuclear Medicine Group

WEBER SHANDWICK

909 3rd Ave, New York, NY 10022
Tel.: (212) 445-8000
Fax: (212) 445-8001
E-Mail: jmurphy@webershandwick.com
Web Site: www.webershandwick.com

Employees: 2,400
Year Founded: 1921

National Agency Associations: 4A's-COPF

Agency Specializes In: African-American Market, Asian Market, Automotive, Aviation & Aerospace, Bilingual Market, Brand Development & Integration, Broadcast, Business-To-Business, Children's Market, College, Communications, Computers & Software, Consulting, Consumer Goods, Consumer Marketing, Corporate Communications, Cosmetics, Crisis Communications, Digital/Interactive, E-Commerce, Electronics, Entertainment, Environmental, Event Planning & Marketing, Fashion/Apparel, Financial, Food Service, Government/Political, Guerilla Marketing, Health Care Services, High Technology, Hispanic Market, Household Goods, Industrial, Information Technology, Integrated Marketing, International, Internet/Web Design, Investor Relations, Leisure, Luxury Products, Media Relations, Media Training, Multicultural, Multimedia, Over-50 Market, Pharmaceutical, Podcasting, Promotions, Public Relations, Publicity/Promotions, Radio, Real Estate, Retail, Seniors' Market, Social Marketing/Nonprofit, Sponsorship, Sports Market, Strategic Planning/Research, Teen Market, Transportation, Travel & Tourism, Viral/Buzz/Word of Mouth, Web (Banner Ads, Pop-ups, etc.), Women's Market

Breakdown of Gross Billings by Media: Pub. Rels.: 100%

Jack Leslie *(Chm)*
Gail Heimann *(Pres)*
Andy Polansky *(CEO)*
Frank Okunak *(COO)*
Lee Noonan *(CTO)*
Abby Gold *(Chief HR Officer)*
Jill Murphy *(Chief Bus Dev Officer)*
Barbara Box *(Pres-New York & Chicago Healthcare)*
Ranny Cooper *(Pres-Pub Affairs)*
Sara Gavin *(Pres-Minneapolis)*
Barb Iverson *(Pres-Fin Svcs)*
Paul Jensen *(Pres-North American Corp Practice)*
Marc Abel *(Exec VP)*
Carol Ballock *(Exec VP-Global Corp Practice)*
Kate Bullinger *(Exec VP-Employee Engagement & Change Mgmt)*
Pete Campisi *(Exec VP)*
Patrick Chaupham *(Exec VP-Creative Tech Strategy)*
Liz Cohen *(Exec VP-Corp Issues)*
Alice Diaz *(Exec VP)*
Cindy Drucker *(Exec VP-Sustainability-Global)*
Joy Farber-Kolo *(Exec VP)*
Allyson Hugley *(Exec VP-Measurement, Analytics & Insights)*
Tara Murphy *(Exec VP-Strategy)*
Kelly Sullivan *(Sr VP & Mgmt Supvr-Global Bus Dev)*
Lisa Chang *(Sr VP-Fin Ops & Digital)*
Lynn Franz *(Sr VP-Strategy)*
Judith Harrison *(Sr VP-Staffing & Diversity & Inclusion)*
Janna Porrevecchio *(Sr VP-Beauty)*
Michael Presson *(Sr VP-Digital)*
Liz Rizzo *(Sr VP-Reputation Res)*
Molly Roenna *(Sr VP-HR)*
Valerie Edmonds *(VP)*
Gillian Kushner *(VP)*
Elizabeth McCarthy *(VP-Employee Engagement & Change Mgmt)*
Andrea Courtney *(Head-Media Rels & Product Reviews)*
Jane Barandes *(Gen Mgr-NY Digital)*
Josh Gilbert *(Exec Dir-Creative-Global Practices)*
Jenna Young *(Exec Dir-Creative)*
Kaileen Connelly *(Acct Dir)*
Kristin Volz *(Dir-Digital)*
Mark Rasmussen *(Assoc Dir-Creative)*
Hamilton Tamayo *(Assoc Dir-Creative)*
Brooke Ackerman *(Acct Supvr-Travel & Lifestyle Practice)*
Ashley Lawless *(Acct Supvr)*
James Richards *(Acct Supvr-Bus Dev)*
Sara Bloomberg *(Sr Acct Exec)*
Kathryn Walsh *(Sr Acct Exec)*
Lane Borgida *(Acct Exec)*
Noelle Caccia *(Acct Exec)*
Jani Crawley *(Acct Exec)*
Sarah Halle *(Acct Exec)*
Lindsay Kaplan *(Acct Exec-Media)*
Ashley Kellam *(Acct Exec)*
Charlotte Otto *(Sr Corp Strategist)*
Alexandra Schrecengost *(Grp Mgr)*

Accounts:
American Airlines Campaign: "I Believe in American"
The Bahamas Ministry of Tourism
Bank of America CSR, Corporate Communications
BBC Worldwide Americas, Inc. BBC World News
Boehringer Ingelheim Corporation
Chobani (Public Relations Agency of Record) Campaign: "#ChotallyAwesome", Campaign: "No Preservatives. No Artificial Flavors", Internal Communications, Social
CVS/Pharmacy
D.O. Ribera del Duero (Agency of Record) Communications Strategy, Consumer Public Relations, Digital, Marketing
D.O. Rueda (Agency of Record) Communications Strategy, Consumer Public Relations, Digital, Marketing
Electrolux Home Products North America
ExxonMobil Lubricants & Specialties
FedEx
Fisher-Price, Inc. (Lead Creative & Public Relations Agency) Campaign: "Share the Joy", Campaign: "The Best Possible Start Begins With Love", Campaign: "Wishes for Baby", Imaginext, Laugh & Learn, Little People
Fontainebleau Miami Beach
General Motors
Honeywell
InterContinental Hotels Group
Jarden Corp ICR, Media
Yankee Candle
Johnson & Johnson
Kohl PR
Mars, Inc; McLean, VA M&M's, Snicker
McCormick & Company Corporate & Consumer Public Relations, Global Media Relations, Thought Leadership
Mexico City Tourism Promotion Fund (North American Public Relations Agency of Record) Branding, Content Development, Media, Social, Strategy
Microsoft EMEA
Microsoft
Milk Processor's Education Program
Mondelez International, Inc. Content Series: "Now We're Newtons", Newtons, Oreo, Public Relations
Motorola Mobility LLC Motorola, Inc.
New-New York Life Insurance Company Consumer Marketing Communications, Public Relations
Ocean Spray Cranberries Inc. B-to-B PR, Ingredient Technology Group
PepsiCo Inc. AMP Energy, Diet Pepsi, Mountain Dew, PR, Pepsi Next, Sierra Mist, SoBe
Pfizer
Royal Caribbean Cruises Ltd.
Samsung Electronics
Sealed Air Corporation (Global Agency of Record) Advertising, Communications, Design Strategies, Digital, Experiential, Marketing, Public Relations, Social Media
Siemens Corp
Siemens
State Farm (Agency of Record)
Technicolor Content Creation
TripAdvisor (Agency of Record) PR
Unilever All, Campaign: "The Adrenalist", Caress,

Hellmann's, Pond's, Q-tips, Sunsilk
United States Army
U.S. Postal Service PR
Yum! Brands

United States

Cassidy & Associates/Weber Shandwick Government Relations

733 10th St NW, Washington, DC 20001
Tel.: (202) 347-0773
Fax: (202) 347-0785
Toll Free: (888) 347-0773
E-Mail: info@cassidy.com
Web Site: www.cassidy.com

Employees: 95
Year Founded: 1975

National Agency Associations: 4A's

Agency Specializes In: Government/Political

Gerald Cassidy *(Founder)*
Kai Anderson *(Co-Chm)*
Barry Rhoads *(Pres)*
Jordan Bernstein *(COO)*
Terry Paul *(Exec VP & Dir-Defense)*
Tom Dennis *(Exec VP)*
Barbara Sutton *(Exec VP)*
Russell J. Thomasson *(Exec VP)*
Dave Belote *(Sr VP)*
Mary Ann Gilleece *(Sr VP)*
Amelia K. Jenkins *(Sr VP)*
Susann Edwards *(VP)*
Andrew Forbes *(VP)*
Michelle Greene *(VP)*

Accounts:
Department of Health and Human Service Americans the Affordable Care Act
Ford Foundation And Independent National Electoral Commission Campaign: "Free and Fair Elections in Nigeria"

Powell Tate-Weber Shandwick

733 Tenth St NW, Washington, DC 20001
Tel.: (202) 383-9700
Fax: (202) 383-0079
E-Mail: rcooper@webershandwick.com
Web Site: www.webershandwick.com

Employees: 100

National Agency Associations: 4A's

Agency Specializes In: Government/Political, Public Relations, Sponsorship

Pam Jenkins *(Pres)*
Cindy Drucker *(Exec VP-Sustainability-Global)*
Joe Farren *(Exec VP)*
Paul Massey *(Exec VP)*
Sally Squires *(Sr VP & Dir-Food, Nutrition & Wellness Comm)*
Dan Drummond *(Sr VP)*
M.P. Gay *(Sr VP)*
David Leavitt *(Sr VP-Digital)*
Karen Oliver *(Sr VP)*
Daniel Pellegrom *(VP-Sustainability & Social Impact)*
Carly Whiteside *(VP)*
Lance Morgan *(Sr Strategist-Comm)*
Adanna Azubuko *(Media Planner & Media Buyer)*

Accounts:
American Cancer Society (Public Relations & Strategic Communications Agency of Record)
District of Columbia Health Benefit Exchange Authority
Pepsico
PoliPulse

Rogers & Cowan

8687 Melrose Ave 7th Fl, Los Angeles, CA 90069
Tel.: (310) 854-8100
Fax: (310) 854-8106
E-Mail: prjobsla@rogersandcowan.com
Web Site: www.rogersandcowan.com

Employees: 85
Year Founded: 1950

Agency Specializes In: Business-To-Business, Cable T.V., Communications, Consumer Marketing, Corporate Identity, Cosmetics, E-Commerce, Entertainment, Event Planning & Marketing, Exhibit/Trade Shows, Fashion/Apparel, Financial, Food Service, Health Care Services, High Technology, Leisure, Magazines, Newspapers & Magazines, Pharmaceutical, Point of Purchase, Point of Sale, Public Relations, Publicity/Promotions, Restaurant, Retail, Sales Promotion, Sponsorship, Sports Market, Strategic Planning/Research, Sweepstakes, Syndication, T.V., Teen Market, Trade & Consumer Magazines, Travel & Tourism

Fran Curtis *(Co-Pres-Entertainment Worldwide)*
Alan Nierob *(Co-Pres-Entertainment Worldwide)*
Richard Davis *(CFO & COO)*
Steve Doctrow *(Exec VP)*
Maureen O'Connor *(Exec VP-Entertainment)*
Sallie Olmsted *(Exec VP)*
Dennis Dembia *(Sr VP)*
Nicole Okoneski *(Assoc VP)*
Natalie Logan *(Acct Supvr)*
Sheryl Tirol *(Acct Exec)*
Amanda Rafter Lencina *(Asst Acct Exec)*

Accounts:
Bahamas International Film Festival
Children's Miracle Network; 2007
New-Coca-Cola
Dylan's Candy Bar (Agency of Record)
Entertainment Industries Council Strategic Marketing
Fiskar Automotive; 2008
GenAudio Inc. (Agency of Record) AstoundSound
The Miami International Film Festival (Agency of Record)
Microsoft
Mondelez International, Inc.
Nitto Tire
Scripps Networks Interactive (Agency of Record) DIY Network, HGTV
Scripps Networks Chinese Food Made Easy, Chuck's Day Off, David Rocco's Dolce Vita, Everyday Exotic, Media Relations, The Cooking Channel (Agency of Record)
Sonos Public Relations
Target Public Relations
TEDMED, LLC.
WebSafety Inc. (Agency of Record)

Rogers & Cowan

919 3rd Ave 18th Fl, New York, NY 10022
Tel.: (310) 854-8100
Fax: (212) 445-8477
E-Mail: inquiries@rogersandcowan.com
Web Site: www.rogersandcowan.com

Employees: 22

National Agency Associations: 4A's

Agency Specializes In: Business-To-Business, Cable T.V., Communications, Consumer Marketing, Corporate Identity, Cosmetics, Entertainment, Event Planning & Marketing, Fashion/Apparel, Leisure, Magazines, Newspapers & Magazines, Point of Purchase, Point of Sale, Public Relations, Publicity/Promotions, Sales Promotion, Strategic Planning/Research, Sweepstakes, Syndication, T.V., Trade & Consumer Magazines, Travel & Tourism

Fran Curtis *(Exec VP)*
Maggie Gallant *(Exec VP)*
John Reilly *(Sr VP-Entertainment & Multicultural Comm)*
Sheila Munguia *(VP-Entertainment & Lifestyle)*
Jenna Hudson *(Acct Dir)*
Cara Hutchison *(Acct Supvr)*
Melissa Koshir *(Acct Supvr)*
Nicole Burgaretta *(Acct Exec)*
Lauren Kenyon *(Acct Exec)*
Vicki Scarfone *(Acct Exec)*

Accounts:
Academy of Interactive Arts & Sciences
The Coca-Cola Company Diet Coke
Colburn School
Dylan's Candy Bar (Agency of Record)
IMAX; 2008
Kohl's
Lindsay Lohan
OK! Magazine; 2006
Phat Fashions (Agency of Record)

Sawmill

(Formerly Sawyer Miller Advertising)
733 10th St NW Ste 500, Washington, DC 20001
Tel.: (202) 585-2932
Fax: (202) 383-0079
Web Site: sawmill.webershandwick.com

Employees: 25

National Agency Associations: 4A's

Agency Specializes In: Public Relations

Timothy C. Ryan *(Gen Mgr)*
Lauren Albrecht *(Acct Supvr)*

Accounts:
Bristol-Myers Squibb
C.V. Starr & Co., Inc.
MasterCard
Merck Serono International SA
Microsoft

Sawmill

(Formerly Sawyer Miller Advertising)
919 3rd Ave, New York, NY 10022
Tel.: (212) 445-8200
Fax: (212) 445-8291
Web Site: sawmill.webershandwick.com

Employees: 200

National Agency Associations: 4A's

Agency Specializes In: Public Relations

Gail Heimann *(Pres & Chief Strategy Officer)*
Paul Jensen *(Pres-North American Corp Practice)*
Matthew Robson *(Sr VP)*
Antoinette Bramlett *(VP)*
Jon Stone *(Dir-Creative)*
Tom Yohe *(Assoc Dir-Creative)*
Daniel Clark *(Acct Exec)*

Accounts:
Colombian Coffee; 2004

Weber Shandwick-Atlanta

1 Buckhead Plz 3060 Peachtree Rd NW Ste 520, Atlanta, GA 30305
Tel.: (404) 266-7555
Fax: (404) 231-1085
Web Site: www.webershandwick.com

Employees: 10
Year Founded: 1987
National Agency Associations: 4A's-COPF

Agency Specializes In: Communications, Public Relations, Sponsorship, Strategic Planning/Research

Frank Okunak *(COO)*
Abby Gold *(Chief HR Officer)*
Laura Schoen *(Chm-Latin America & Pres-Global Healthcare Practice)*
Rob Baskin *(Pres-Atlanta)*
Ranny Cooper *(Pres-Pub Affairs)*
Sara Gavin *(Pres-North America)*
Allyson Hugley *(Pres-Measurement, Analytics & Insights)*
Chris Perry *(Pres-Digital)*
Cathy Calhoun *(Sr VP & Acct Mgmt Dir)*
Ashli Bobo *(Grp Mgr)*

Accounts:
Amerisave Mortgage; 2003
Porter-Cable Corp.

Weber Shandwick-Austin
2009 S Capital of Texas Hwy Ste 300, Austin, TX 78746
Tel.: (512) 794-4700
Fax: (512) 794-6380
E-Mail: gwise@webershandwick.com
Web Site: www.webershandwick.com

Employees: 10
Year Founded: 1998

National Agency Associations: 4A's-COPF

Agency Specializes In: Public Relations

Lara Stott *(Sr VP)*
Sara Ballard *(VP)*
Carrie Lauterstein *(Acct Dir)*
Lauren Munguia *(Acct Supvr)*

Accounts:
American Airlines
Bpex
Electrolux
Horizon

Weber Shandwick-Baltimore
2809 Boston St Ste 8, Baltimore, MD 21224
Tel.: (410) 558-2100
Fax: (410) 558-2188
E-Mail: kokeefe@webershandwick.com
Web Site: www.webershandwick.com

Employees: 35

National Agency Associations: 4A's-COPF

Agency Specializes In: Digital/Interactive, Public Relations

Kevin O'Keefe *(Pres & Gen Mgr-Baltimore)*
Charles Fitzgibbon *(Exec VP)*
Christopher Durban *(Sr VP & Creative Dir)*
Vanessa Wickham-Baker *(Sr VP-Media Svcs)*
Aaron Bickoff *(VP-Digital Project Mgmt & Resource Ops-North America)*
Lindsey Fritz *(Dir-Digital)*
Kaitlin Garvey *(Dir-Digital)*
Adanna Azubuko *(Media Planner & Media Buyer)*
Kara Joyce *(Asst Acct Exec)*

Accounts:
BGE
Centers for Medicare & Medicaid Services Insurance Exchanges Awareness
Honeywell, Inc.
Johns Hopkins University School of Professional Studies in Business & Education; 2004
State of Maryland

Weber Shandwick-Boston/Cambridge
101 Main St 8th Fl, Cambridge, MA 02142
Tel.: (617) 661-7900
Fax: (617) 661-0024
E-Mail: mspring@webershandwick.com
Web Site: www.webershandwick.com

Employees: 100

National Agency Associations: 4A's-COPF

Agency Specializes In: Public Relations, Sponsorship

Micho Spring *(Chm-Global Corp Practice & Pres-New England)*
Peter Mancusi *(Exec VP)*
Tara Murphy *(Exec VP-Strategy)*
Stacey Bernstein *(Sr VP & Dir-US Digital Health)*
Sean Findlen *(Sr VP)*
John Isaf *(Sr VP)*
Sam Mazzarelli *(Acct Dir)*
Danielle Farber *(Dir-Digital & Innovation)*
Sean McNair *(Dir-Digital)*
Ellie Botelho *(Acct Exec)*
Caroline Markey *(Assoc-Digital Health)*

Accounts:
The Allstate Corporation
Electrolux Home Products North America
Maine Lobster Advertising, Digital, Integrated Marketing, Social, Spanning Public Relations
Ocean Spray Cranberries, Inc.
QlikTech International

Weber Shandwick-Chicago
676 N St Clair Ste 1000, Chicago, IL 60611
Tel.: (312) 988-2400
Fax: (312) 988-2363
Web Site: www.webershandwick.com

Employees: 150

National Agency Associations: 4A's-COPF

Agency Specializes In: Public Relations, Sponsorship

Jim Paul *(Mng Dir & Exec Dir-Creative)*
Barbara Box *(Pres-New York & Chicago Healthcare)*
Jerry Gleason *(Exec VP & Dir-Sports Mktg-North America)*
Cori McKeever Ashford *(Sr VP-Chicago Healthcare)*
Matt Collins *(Sr VP)*
Karen Doak *(Sr VP-Digital)*
Julie Ketay *(Sr VP)*
Seth Levine *(Sr VP-Digital Health)*
Molly Roenna *(Sr VP-HR)*
Randa Stephan *(Sr VP-Digital)*
Dan Jividen *(VP & Creative Dir)*
Katrina Greenwood *(VP-Strategy)*
Karianne Wardell *(VP-Digital)*
Kaileen Connelly *(Acct Dir)*
Bryan Brown *(Dir-Project Mgmt)*
Patricia Lee *(Dir-Digital)*
Alana Beseau *(Assoc Dir-Creative)*
Alyssa Bronikowski *(Acct Supvr-Media Rels)*
Mollie Tavel *(Sr Acct Exec)*
Janet Helm *(Strategist-Nutrition-North America)*
Erin Randall *(Acct Exec)*
Ryan Cwiklinski *(Copywriter)*

Accounts:
Big Ten Conference Counsel, Guidance
BPEX
Campbell Soup Company; Camden, NJ Campaign: "Take Back Your 24th Hour", Stamp Out Hunger Food Drive, V8 Fusion, V8 V-Fusion + Energy
Electrolux
Horizon
KFC
McCormick & Company Executive Engagement, Global PR, Grill Mates, Lawry's, McCormick masterbrand, Media Relations, Thought Leadership, Zatarain's; 2007
Pedigree Pet Adoption
Stratasys Media Relations
Unilever
Walgreens Public Relations

Weber Shandwick-Dallas
1717 9th St Ste 1600, Dallas, TX 75201
Tel.: (469) 375-0200
Fax: (972) 868-7671
E-Mail: kluce@webershandwick.com
Web Site: www.webershandwick.com

National Agency Associations: 4A's-COPF

Agency Specializes In: Public Relations, Sponsorship

Neil Nowlin *(Exec VP & Gen Mgr)*
David Nieland *(Exec VP)*
Teisha Van De Kop *(Exec VP)*
Chris Vary *(Exec VP-Digital Program Innovation)*
Dawn Kahle *(Sr VP & Deputy Gen Mgr)*
Alison McMillon *(Sr VP)*
Beth Pedersen *(Dir-Creative)*
Cameron King *(Acct Supvr)*
Yezenia Gonzalez *(Acct Exec)*

Accounts:
American Airlines
BPEX
CSL Biotherapist
Electrolux
Horizon
IndoorDIRECT
Revlimid

Weber Shandwick-Denver
999 18th St Ste 3000, Denver, CO 80202
Tel.: (303) 346-9150
Fax: (303) 526-9514
Web Site: www.webershandwick.com

National Agency Associations: 4A's-COPF

Agency Specializes In: Consumer Goods, Financial, Health Care Services, High Technology, Public Relations

Hugh Williams *(Sr VP)*
Jessica Weidensall *(Dir)*
Kara Tagle *(Acct Supvr)*
Helen Melville *(Sr Acct Exec)*
Casey Westlake *(Sr Acct Exec)*

Accounts:
New-Colorado Education Association (Strategic Communications Agency of Record)

Weber Shandwick-Detroit
360 W Maple, Birmingham, MI 48009
Tel.: (248) 203-8127
Fax: (248) 203-8018
E-Mail: sstein@webershandwick.com
Web Site: www.webershandwick.com

Employees: 25

National Agency Associations: 4A's-COPF

Agency Specializes In: Automotive, Public Relations, Sponsorship

Stan Stein *(Exec VP)*
Janet Tabor *(Sr VP)*
Andy Schueneman *(Gen Mgr-Detroit)*
Cindy Kamerad *(Acct Dir)*
Stacey Rammer *(Mgr-Comm)*
Jeff Wandell *(Sr Acct Exec)*

Accounts:
New-MGM Grand Detroit (Public Relations Agency of Record)

Weber Shandwick-Los Angeles
8687 Melrose Ave 7th Fl, Los Angeles, CA 90069
Tel.: (310) 854-8200
Fax: (310) 854-8201
E-Mail: aazarloza@webershandwick.com
Web Site: www.webershandwick.com

Employees: 28

National Agency Associations: 4A's-COPF

Agency Specializes In: Public Relations, Sponsorship

Josh Rose *(Chief Creative Officer-Multi-Platform Campaigns)*
Leslie Capstraw *(Exec VP & Gen Mgr)*
Alejandro Castro Enciso *(Sr VP & Exec Producer-Digital Creative Grp)*
Mike Hope *(VP)*
Jacqueline Karis *(VP)*
Jose Nerio *(VP-HR-West Reg)*
John Avery *(Exec Dir-Creative)*
Dustin Lawrence *(Acct Exec)*
Anna Romano *(Acct Exec)*

Accounts:
Amdocs Inc; Chesterfield, MO
Budget Blinds
Carl's Jr.
City of Hope; Duarte, CA Marketing, Public Relations, Strategic Communications Program
Electrolux Home Products
General Motors Western Region Campaign: "Drive-Thru Finals with Chevy"
Namco Bandai Games America; 2008

Weber Shandwick-Minneapolis
8000 Norman Ctr Dr Ste 400, Minneapolis, MN 55437
Tel.: (952) 832-5000
Fax: (952) 831-8241
Web Site: www.webershandwick.com

Employees: 150

National Agency Associations: 4A's-COPF

Agency Specializes In: Public Relations

Eric Pehle *(Exec VP & Gen Mgr)*
David Krejci *(Exec VP-Social Media & Digital Comm)*
Nancy Longley *(Exec VP)*
Andy Keith *(Sr VP-Digital Strategy)*
Lida Poletz *(Sr VP)*
Brooke Worden *(Sr VP-Fin Svcs)*
Christy Warner *(VP-Fin Svcs Practice)*
Stephanie Connolly *(Grp Mgr)*
Angie Gassett *(Acct Grp Mgr)*

Accounts:
Amway Corporation Research & Development
BAE Systems (Agency of Record)
Bpex
CSL Bio Therapies
Daily Management Inc
Electrolux
Horizon
The Link Pro Bono
Mall of America
Mentoring Partnership of Minnesota Pro Bono
National Marrow Donor Program "Be the Match Marrowthon"
Revlimid
Stratasys Media Relations
Syngenta Seeds Inc. (Agency of Record)
Taste of the NFL
U.S. Department of Treasury
United States Army

Weber Shandwick-Saint Louis
555 Washington Ave, Saint Louis, MO 63101
Tel.: (314) 436-6565
Fax: (314) 622-6212
Toll Free: (800) 551-5971
E-Mail: mabel@webershandwick.com
Web Site: www.webershandwick.com

Employees: 20

National Agency Associations: 4A's-COPF

Agency Specializes In: Public Relations

Dave Collett *(Exec VP & Gen Mgr)*
Susanne Reimer *(VP)*
Ryan Dampf *(Dir-Art)*
Paul Panday *(Dir-Ecommerce)*
Laura High *(Acct Supvr)*
Sean Hixson *(Acct Supvr)*
Michael Zerman *(Acct Supvr)*
Sam Cosner *(Acct Exec)*
Andrea Raffles *(Acct Exec)*

Accounts:
BPEX
CSL Biotherapies
Hardee's
Horizon
Revlimid

Weber Shandwick-San Francisco
600 Battery St, San Francisco, CA 94111
Tel.: (415) 262-5950
Fax: (415) 262-5982
Web Site: www.webershandwick.com

Employees: 20

National Agency Associations: 4A's-COPF

Agency Specializes In: Public Relations, Sponsorship

Josh Rose *(Chief Creative Officer-Multi-Platform Campaigns)*
Barb Iverson *(Pres-Fin Svcs)*
Paul Jensen *(Pres-North American Corp Practice)*
Ze Schiavoni *(CEO-S2Publicom)*
Leslie Capstraw *(Exec VP & Gen Mgr-Los Angeles)*
Joy Farber-Kolo *(Exec VP & Gen Mgr-New York)*
Michelle Maggs *(Exec VP & Gen Mgr-Seattle)*
Neil Nowlin *(Exec VP & Gen Mgr-Southwest)*
Kathleen Siedlecki *(Exec VP-Sacramento & U.S. Dir-Health Impact)*
Jonathan Carroll *(Sr VP)*
Douglas Myers *(VP-Corp Practice)*
Andy Schueneman *(Gen Mgr-Detroit)*
Jocelyn Shaw *(Sr Acct Exec)*

Accounts:
GlobalLogic
Hitachi
OneRoof Energy Brand Awareness
Taleo (Agency of Record)

Weber Shandwick-Seattle
605 5th Ave S Ste 900, Seattle, WA 98104
Tel.: (425) 452-5400
Fax: (425) 452-5397
E-Mail: csheldon@webershandwick.com
Web Site: www.webershandwick.com

Employees: 50

National Agency Associations: 4A's-COPF

Agency Specializes In: Public Relations

Brooke Shepard *(Exec VP-North America Incite Plng & Exec Dir-Creative-Seattle)*
Rose Berg *(Exec VP-Integrated Healthcare)*
Brenda South *(Exec VP-West Coast Tech Practice)*
Scott Meis *(Sr VP-Digital Content Strategy)*
Michelle Pratt *(Sr Producer-Digital)*
Karissa Sams *(Dir-New Bus & Mktg-Global Tech Practice)*
Matthew Inda *(Strategist-Digital Content)*

Accounts:
Brammo (Agency of Record)
Function(X) Campaign: "Viggle"
LifeWise Health Plan of Washington Integrated Marketing
Microsoft
Samsung
Washington Discover Pass

Weber Shandwick-Sunnyvale
150 Mathilda Pl Ste 302, Sunnyvale, CA 94086
Tel.: (408) 530-8400
Fax: (408) 530-8474
E-Mail: jhammel@webershandwick.com
Web Site: www.webershandwick.com

Employees: 20

National Agency Associations: COPF

Agency Specializes In: Public Relations, Sponsorship

Brad Williams *(Pres-Tech Practice-North America)*
Julianne Whitelaw *(Exec VP & Deputy Gen Mgr)*
Dave Reddy *(Sr VP & Dir-Media)*
Traci Mogil *(Sr VP)*
Heidi Noble Stewart *(Sr VP-Consumer)*
Erin Patton *(VP)*
Smita Rode *(VP)*
Shelby Valdez *(VP)*
Luca Penati *(Gen Mgr-San Francisco & Silicon Valley)*

Accounts:
NETGEAR US Public Relations

Canada

Weber Shandwick
130 Albert St Ste 802, Ottawa, ON K1P 5G4 Canada
Tel.: (613) 230-2220
Fax: (613) 230-3874
E-Mail: tault@webershandwick.com
Web Site: www.webershandwick.com

Employees: 12

Agency Specializes In: Public Relations

Trish Ault *(Exec VP)*
Tara Shields *(VP)*

Accounts:
Home Depot of Canada
Johnson & Johnson
McNeil Consumer Healthcare
Nestle Canada
Novartis Ophthalmics

Weber Shandwick
207 Queen's Quay W Ste 400, Toronto, ON M5J 1A7 Canada
Tel.: (416) 964-6444
Fax: (416) 964-6611
E-Mail: tensor@webershandwick.com
Web Site: www.webershandwick.com

Employees: 40

Agency Specializes In: Public Relations

Greg Power *(Pres/Gen Mgr-Canada)*
Hayes Steinberg *(Exec VP & Exec Dir-Creative)*
Vanessa McDonald *(Exec VP)*
Peter Matheson Gay *(Sr VP & Dir-Creative-Healthcare)*
Sandra D'Ambrosio *(Sr VP)*
Andrew Lane *(Sr VP-Content + Platforms)*
David Akermanis *(VP-Plng)*
Karning Hum *(VP-Media & Creative Strategy)*
Valerie Mendonca *(Sr Acct Dir)*
Ian Roberts *(Sr Acct Dir)*
Jessica Greasley *(Acct Dir)*
Natalie Pavlenko *(Acct Dir)*
Kyle Brown *(Dir-Measurement & Analytics)*
Melissa Adamson *(Acct Mgr)*
Natalie Berardi *(Acct Mgr)*
Jennifer Young *(Office Mgr)*
Michael Kohn *(Acct Coord)*

Accounts:
Johnson & Johnson
McCormick Canada (Digital Agency of Record) Content, Public Relations, Social Media, Social Media Strategy, Video, Website
McDonald's
Rdio
New-Royal Bank of Canada Media Outreach

Belgium

Weber Shandwick
Ave Cortenbergh 100, B 1000 Brussels, Belgium
Tel.: (32) 2 2300775
Fax: (32) 2 894 90 69
E-Mail: info@webershandwick.com
Web Site: webershandwick.be/

Employees: 45

Agency Specializes In: Communications, Public Relations

Monica Vicente Cristina *(Head-Social Impact & Dir-Corp Comm)*
Katie Lazelle *(Acct Dir)*
Erik Lenaers *(Acct Dir)*
Christian Prior *(Acct Dir)*
Steven De Vliegher *(Acct Dir-Corp Affairs)*
Nora Lawton *(Dir-Brand & Consumer PR)*
Karen Verstappen *(Acct Mgr)*

Croatia

Weber Shandwick
Heinzelova 33a, 10 000 Zagreb, Croatia
Tel.: (385) 1 5555 100
Fax: (385) 1 4660 037
E-Mail: edvin-jurin@mccann.hr
Web Site: www.webershandwick.com

Employees: 4
Year Founded: 1998

Agency Specializes In: Health Care Services

Edvin Jurin *(Mng Dir)*

Accounts:
Coca-Cola Refreshments USA, Inc.
Nestle

Cyprus

Action PR Cyprus
Kondilaki 6, PO Box 24676, 1090 Nicosia, Cyprus
Tel.: (357) 2 281 8884
Fax: (357) 2 2 87 3634
E-Mail: action@actionprgroup.com
Web Site: www.actionprgroup.com

Employees: 35
Year Founded: 1971

Agency Specializes In: Communications, Public Relations

Tony Christodoulou *(Founder & Mng Dir-Action Global Comm)*
Michalis Aspris *(CFO)*
Dimitris Ioannides *(Gen Mgr)*
Ria Argyrides *(Acct Mgr)*
Demetra Eleftheriou *(Acct Mgr-PR)*
Amanda Chick *(Client Mgr-Intl)*

Accounts:
Classic Burger Joint Brand Communications, Digital Marketing, Digital Media, Media Relations, Press, Public Relations, Strategic Communications

Czech Republic

Weber Shandwick
Narodni 25, 110 000 Prague, Czech Republic
Tel.: (420) 221 085 360
Fax: (420) 221 085 361
E-Mail: webershandwick@webershandwick.cz
Web Site: www.webershandwick.com

Employees: 12

National Agency Associations: APRA

Agency Specializes In: Public Relations

Vitezslav Horak *(Mng Dir)*
Gabriela Kolarova *(Head-Client Svc)*
Sylva Sulaimanova *(Sr Acct Mgr)*
Lenka Ma Chackova *(Acct Mgr)*
Adele Chvalovsky *(Acct Mgr)*
Klara Vinterova *(Mgr-Ops)*
Michael Kvicerova *(Sr Acct Exec)*
Barbora Umancova *(Sr Acct Exec)*
Martin Moc *(Specialist-Media Relation)*

Accounts:
Budvar
Czech Gas
Nespresso
Puma

Germany

Weber Shandwick
Schonhauser Allee 37 Geb P, 10435 Berlin, Germany
Tel.: (49) 30 20 35 10
Fax: (49) 30 20 35 129
E-Mail: cfischoeder@webershandwick.com
Web Site: www.webershandwick.de

Employees: 12

Agency Specializes In: Public Relations

Leona Malorny *(Head-Client Relationship & Sr Acct Mgr)*
Patrick Klein *(Acct Dir)*
Barbel Hestert-Vecoli *(Dir-Pub Affairs)*
Jan Dirk Kemming *(Dir-Creative Plng)*
Sabine Lorenz *(Assoc Dir-Consumer Mktg)*
Johanna Hille *(Sr Acct Mgr)*
Matthias Wowtscherk *(Sr Acct Mgr)*
Isabella Jasmina El-Shikh *(Acct Mgr)*
Angela Taylor *(Acct Mgr)*
Susann Kobs *(Mgr-Mktg-Germany)*
Frigga Schmidt *(Mgr-HR)*

Weber Shandwick
Seidlstrabe 26, 80335 Munich, Germany
Tel.: (49) 89 38 01 79 0
Fax: (49) 89 38 01 79 22
E-Mail: kontakt@webershandwick.com
Web Site: www.webershandwick.de

Employees: 40

Agency Specializes In: Public Relations

Jan Dirk Kemming *(Chief Creative Officer-Europe)*
Julian Lambertin *(Exec VP-Strategy & Insights-Global)*
Olaf Pempel *(Mng Dir-Consumer Mktg)*
Torsten Rotharmel *(Mng Dir-Healthcare)*
Jan Moller *(Dir-Bus Dev & Strategic Plng)*
Katharina Meyer *(Assoc Dir)*
Susanne Lennartz *(Acct Exec-Consumer Mktg)*

Accounts:
Paramount

Weber Shandwick
Hohenzollernring 79-83, 50672 Cologne, Germany
Tel.: (49) 221 94 99 18 0
Fax: (49) 228 72 27 10
E-Mail: info@webershandwick.com
Web Site: www.webershandwick.de

Employees: 30

Agency Specializes In: Public Relations

Dirk Schroder *(CFO)*
Jan Dirk Kemming *(Chief Creative Officer-Europe)*
Julian Lambertin *(Exec VP-Strategy & Insights-Global)*
Torsten Rotharmel *(Mng Dir-Healthcare)*
Christine Bettinger *(VP-HR)*
Thorsten Dub *(Head-Strategy & Analytics)*
Sabine Lorenz *(Assoc Dir-Consumer Mktg)*
Isabella Jasmina El-Shikh *(Acct Mgr)*

Accounts:
Canon
eBay
Fujitsu Siemens
German Telecom
Microsoft
Opel GM
PayPal
Pfizer
Samsung
Siemens
Texas Instruments DLP

Greece

Action Global Communications
(Formerly Action PR)
49-51 Ypsilantou Str, Kolonaki, 11521 Athens, Greece
Tel.: (30) 210 724 0160
Fax: (30) 210 722 3417
E-Mail: hellasinfo@actionprgroup.com
Web Site: www.actionprgroup.com

Employees: 4

Tony Christodoulou *(Founder & CEO)*
Kathy Christodoulou *(Dir & Mgr-Bus Dev)*
Angela Kiofiri *(Acct Mgr)*
Chris Lazarides *(Mgr-IT)*

Accounts:
Packard Bell
Teuco

Hungary

Weber Shandwick
Montevideo utca 10, 1037 Budapest, Hungary
Tel.: (36) 1 887 8350
Fax: (36) 1 887 8370`
E-Mail: ws@webershandwick.hu
Web Site: www.webershandwick.hu

Employees: 13

Agency Specializes In: Government/Political, Public Relations

Ervin Szucs *(Mng Dir)*

Accounts:
AXA
American Airlines
BPEX
CVS Caremark
Horizon Fuel Cell Technologies
Revlimid

Ireland

Weber Shandwick-FCC
Hambleden House 19-26 Lower Pembroke Street, Dublin, 2 Ireland
Tel.: (353) 6798600
E-Mail: smolloy@webershandwick.com
Web Site: webershandwick.ie/

Employees: 13
Year Founded: 1989

Agency Specializes In: Public Relations

Mary McCarthy *(Mng Dir)*
Siobhan Molloy *(Joint Mng Dir)*

Accounts:
Department of Finance & Personnel Northern Ireland PR

Italy

Weber Shandwick
Via Magazzini Generali, 18, 00154 Rome, Italy
Tel.: (39) 06 8404 341
Fax: (39) 06 840434 1
E-Mail: fgarbagnati@webershandwick.com
Web Site: www.webershandwick.it/

Employees: 12
Year Founded: 1978

Agency Specializes In: Public Relations

Furio Garbagnati *(CEO-Italy)*
Eleonora Pellegrini de Vera *(Exec VP)*
Patrizia Accornero *(Sr VP)*
Cristiana Montani Natalucci *(Acct Dir)*
Valeria Nowak *(Acct Mgr)*
Marta Giglio *(Jr Acct Exec)*

Weber Shandwick
Via Pietrasanta 14, 20141 Milan, Italy
Tel.: (39) 02 573781
Fax: (39) 02 57378402
E-Mail: fgarbagnati@webershandwick.com
Web Site: www.webershandwick.it

Employees: 75
Year Founded: 1976

Agency Specializes In: Public Relations

Furio Garbagnati *(CEO-Italy)*
Giulia Mentore *(Sr VP-Consumer & Digital Comm)*
Novella D'Incecco *(Acct Dir)*
Gaudia Lucchini *(Acct Dir)*
Marika Caputo *(Dir)*
Giacomo Iacovelli *(Assoc Dir)*
Paola Farina *(Acct Mgr)*
Valeria Nowak *(Acct Mgr)*
Valentina Nozza *(Acct Mgr)*
Cristina Gavirati *(Sr Acct Exec)*
Marina Guarino *(Sr Acct Exec)*
Elena Marchi *(Sr Acct Exec)*
Valentina Crovetti *(Jr Acct Exec)*
Marta Giglio *(Jr Acct Exec)*

The Netherlands

Weber Shandwick
Koninginnegracht 23, 2514 AB Hague, Netherlands
Tel.: (31) 70 31 21 070
Fax: (31) 70 364 3770
E-Mail: aboyen@webershandwick.com
Web Site: www.webershandwick.com

Employees: 15

Agency Specializes In: Public Relations

Hafida Abahai *(Mng Dir-Consumer Mktg, Brand PR & Studio)*
Annick Boyen *(Mng Dir-The Netherlands)*
Paul Ten Broeke *(Dir-Creative)*
Badoux Eline *(Acct Mgr-Consumer Mktg)*
Jesarela Florentina *(Office Mgr)*

Accounts:
FDOC
Getty Images
Mastercard
Nespresso
Simmons & Simmons

Portugal

Weber Shandwick-D&E
Av Eng Arantes e Oliveira n 11-2 C, 1900-221 Lisbon, Portugal
Tel.: (351) 21 8410010
Fax: (351) 21 8410039
E-Mail: aperes@dne.pt
Web Site: www.dne.pt

Employees: 20

Agency Specializes In: Public Relations

Antonio Peres *(CEO)*
Rui Silva *(Dir-Comm)*

Slovenia

Pristop Group d.o.o.
Trubarjeva cesta 79, 1000 Ljubljana, Slovenia
Tel.: (386) 1 23 91 200
Fax: (386) 1 23 91 210
E-Mail: pristop@pristop.si
Web Site: www.pristop.si

Employees: 100
Year Founded: 1991

Agency Specializes In: Brand Development & Integration, Communications, Electronic Media, Public Relations

Saso Dimitrievski *(Co-Founder)*
Bojan Jelacin *(Mng Dir)*
Primoz Pusar *(Mng Dir)*
Aljosa Bagola *(Exec Dir-Creative)*
Ula Spindler *(Exec Dir-Quality & Client Svc)*
Robert Bohinec *(Creative Dir)*
Matija Kocbek *(Dir-Art)*
Petra Podgorsek *(Acct Mgr)*
Ales Razpet *(Sr Partner)*

Accounts:
Amnesty International
DARS
Festival of Migrant Film Campaign: "Moby, Bambi, Birds"
Ilirija
Ljubljanske Mlekarne
Mercator
New-Mini Teater
Pliva
POP TV
Posta Slovenije
New-Robert Waltl
Sava Tires
SKB Banka
Sveta Vladar
Vzajemna
New-Zavarovalnica Triglav

South Africa

Gillian Gamsy International
Houghton Pl 51 W St, Houghton, Johannesburg, South Africa
Tel.: (27) 11 728 1363
Fax: (27) 11 728 6613
E-Mail: dlg@ggisa.com
Web Site: www.ggisa.com

Employees: 13
Year Founded: 1983

Agency Specializes In: Public Relations

Gillian Gamsy *(CEO)*
Jennifer Stein *(Mng Dir)*
Khuthalani Khumalo *(Exec Dir)*
Candice Marescia *(Sr Acct Exec)*
Kirsten Wiggill *(Sr Acct Exec)*

Sweden

Prime Public Relations
Slussplan 9, Stockholm, SE-100 64 Sweden
Tel.: (46) 8 503 146 00
Fax: (46) 8 503 146 99
E-Mail: info@primegroup.com
Web Site: www.primegroup.com

Employees: 130

Agency Specializes In: Brand Development & Integration, Crisis Communications, Media Training, Public Relations

Carl Frederik Sammeli *(Founder)*
Peter Lindgren *(Partner & Dir-Creative-Prime)*
Therese Bohlin *(Partner)*
Marcus Wenner *(Head-Plng)*
Tom Beckman *(Exec Dir-Creative)*
Fredrik Olsson *(Dir-Art)*
Jacqueline Arthur *(Acct Mgr & specialist-Media)*
Maria Larsson *(Project Mgr & Planner)*
Karin Schollin *(Key Acct Mgr & Project Mgr)*

Accounts:
Abba Campaign: "Kids Kitchen"
ACO Campaign: "Beauty Share"
Aftonbladet
Alecta Campaign: "Mankind is Shortsighted"
Audi
Civil Rights Defenders Campaign: "Civil Rights Captcha"
Comfort Campaign: "Plumbers without Borders"
Electrolux Vac From The Sea
Fortum
Ikea
Lagerhaus Campaign: "Blog up Stores"

Lulea Business Agency Campaign: "The Node Pole"
Metro International Campaign: "The Metropolitan Mindset"
Mondelez International, Inc. Aladdin Chocolate, Campaign: "Sweet Memory", Marabou
Royal Dramatic Theatre
SCA
Scandic Hotels
Stockholm County Council
Swedish Civil Contingency Agency Campaign: "The Pandora Letter"
Swedish Transport Administration
TeliaSonera Campaign: "No News is Big News"
United Minds

Switzerland

Weber Shandwick
Passage Malbuisson 15, 1211 Geneva, Switzerland
Tel.: (41) 22 879 8500
Fax: (41) 22 879 8510
E-Mail: contactch@webershandwick.com
Web Site: www.webershandwick.com

Employees: 15

Agency Specializes In: Public Relations

Kelley Campau *(VP-Corp Strategy & Media)*
Damini Khosla *(Acct Dir)*
Robin Roothans *(Acct Dir)*
Libby Ducharme *(Sr Acct Exec-Digital)*
Laetitia Tettamanti *(Sr Acct Exec)*

Accounts:
AA
BPEX
CSL Biotherapies
CVS Caremark
Electrolux
Horizon
Nestle Nespresso, Social Media
Revlimid

UK

Weber Shandwick Financial
Fox Court 14 Gray's Inn Road, London, WC1X 8WS United Kingdom
Tel.: (44) 20 7067 0000
Fax: (44) 870 990 5441
Web Site: www.webershandwick.co.uk

Employees: 300

Agency Specializes In: Communications, Financial, Investor Relations

Moray Macdonald *(Mng Dir)*
Colin Byrne *(CEO-UK)*
Joe Phelan *(Exec VP & Head-Intl Comm)*
Rachael Pay *(Mng Dir-Healthcare Europe)*
Stuart Lambert *(Head-Consumer Tech & Dir)*
Tamora Langley *(Deputy Head-Pub Affairs)*
Stephen Finch *(Sr Dir)*
Nick Oborne *(Dir-Capital Markets)*
Kate Sarginson *(Dir)*
Josie Whittle *(Sr Acct Mgr)*
John Lunny *(Acct Mgr)*
Cortney Lusignan *(Acct Mgr)*
Kat Kalinina *(Sr Acct Exec)*
Phee Waterfield *(Sr Acct Exec)*

Accounts:
Agilent
Ashmore Investment Management Ltd.
Asian Citrus Industries
Barclays
Big Yellow Group PLC
Braun
Care UK Plc
Clinton Cards PLC
EDF Energy
Endace Limited
FireOne Group plc
Integrated Asset Management
Mastercard Advisers
MSTV
Opel Meriva
OXFAM
Royal Bank of Scotland
Ultra Electronics
United Biscuits

Weber Shandwick UK
Fox Court 14 Gray's Inn Rd, London, WC1X 8WS United Kingdom
Tel.: (44) 20 7067 0000
Fax: (44) 870 990 5441
E-Mail: cbyrne@webershandwick.com
Web Site: www.webershandwick.co.uk

Employees: 300
Year Founded: 1968

Agency Specializes In: Public Relations

Rachel Friend *(Mng Dir)*
Adam Mack *(Chief Strategy Officer-EMEA & Head-Strategy-Creative Capital)*
Louise Watson *(Chm-Consumer Mktg-EMEA)*
Colin Byrne *(CEO-UK & EMEA)*
Peter Ross *(Exec VP & Mng Dir-Tech-EMEA)*
Ben Burton *(Mng Dir-Corp)*
Mary Whenman *(Mng Dir-Corp Fin & Pub Affairs)*
Al Berry *(Head-Content-Digital)*
Adam Clyne *(Head-Digital-EMEA)*
Nadia Saint *(Head-Digital-EMEA Tech Clients)*
Luke Walker *(Head-Creative)*
Danny Whatmough *(Head-Social-EMEA)*
James Nester *(Exec Creative Dir)*
Wendy Mitchell *(Sr Acct Dir)*
Emma Pointer *(Acct Dir)*
Mark Barber *(Dir-New Bus-UK)*
Elizabeth Gladwin *(Dir-Analytics-UK)*
Dave Morris *(Dir-Change Mgmt-EMEA)*
Andrew Phillips *(Dir-Digital New Bus-EMEA)*
Simon Rothwell *(Dir)*
Andrew Smith *(Assoc Dir)*
Joe Walton *(Assoc Dir)*
Parmita Ghosh *(Sr Strategist-Digital)*

Accounts:
Abbott Laboratories PR, Public Affairs
ByPost.com Public Relations
Colt
Creative Content UK "Education Programme", Consumer PR, Corporate PR, Social PR
New-Dialogue Group (Public Relations Agency of Record) Strategic Communications
Exxon Mobil Corporation
Fireflock.com Crowdfunding, Public Relations
Getty Images Content Marketing, Media Relations
Keep Britain Tidy Strategic Communications
Liverpool Waterfront Raise Awareness
MeetingRooms.com (Public Relations Agency of Record) Content, Global Communications Strategy, Media Relations
Microsoft Mediaroom
Quintiq
SNR Denton Media Outreach, PR
TINT (European Agency of Record) Media Relations, Strategic Communications
Tokyo 2020 Bid Committee Comms PR Strategy
United Nations Volunteers programme Media
New-Vauxhall Motors Social Media, Social Strategy
Westfield B2B, Corporate Communications, Press, Strategic Planning
Whyte & Mackay The Dalmore
Wickes Public Relations

Weber Shandwick
32-38 Linenhall Street, Belfast, BT2 8BG United Kingdom
Tel.: (44) 28 9034 7300
Fax: (44) 28 9076 1012
E-Mail: bboal@webershandwick.com
Web Site: www.webershandwick.co.uk

Employees: 12
Year Founded: 1992

Agency Specializes In: Public Relations

Kelly Genton *(Sr Acct Dir)*
Rosie Ireland *(Acct Dir)*
Catherine Mallaband *(Acct Dir)*
Elaine O'Shaughnessy *(Acct Dir)*
Marta Saez *(Acct Dir)*
Bella Moloney *(Sr Acct Mgr)*
Emma Pointer *(Sr Acct Mgr)*
Josie Whittle *(Sr Acct Mgr)*
John Bowen *(Acct Mgr)*
Benjamin Pfeffer *(Acct Mgr)*
Hem Raheja *(Acct Mgr)*

Accounts:
Down Royal Race Course

Weber Shandwick
58 Queens Rd, Aberdeen, Scotland AB15 4YE United Kingdom
Tel.: (44) 1224 806600
Fax: (44) 1224 208823
E-Mail: jmacdonald@webershandwick.com
Web Site: webershandwick.co.uk/#!/home/

Employees: 7

Agency Specializes In: Public Relations

Andrew Jones *(Sr VP)*
Lindsay Jepp *(Acct Dir)*
Ailsa Nicol *(Sr Acct Mgr)*
Andrew Gill *(Acct Mgr)*
Julie Brander *(Sr Acct Exec)*
Mhairi Greer *(Sr Acct Exec)*

Accounts:
Subsea 7
Talisman Energy

Weber Shandwick
9 York Place, Edinburgh, Scotland EH1 3EB United Kingdom
Tel.: (44) 131 556 6649
Fax: (44) 131 556 6741
E-Mail: hroaa@webershandwick.com
Web Site: www.webershandwick.co.uk

Employees: 25

Agency Specializes In: Public Relations

Moray Macdonald *(Mng Dir)*
Colin Byrne *(CEO-UK & EMEA)*
Stacey Blevins Bridges *(Acct Dir)*
Richard Bright *(Dir)*
Stewart Argo *(Assoc Dir)*
Jenna Ciancia *(Acct Mgr)*
Mhairi Greer *(Sr Acct Exec)*
Nick Hanlon *(Sr Acct Exec)*
Duncan Mckay *(Sr Acct Exec)*
Sarah Ward *(Acct Exec)*

Accounts:
Aldi Consumer Public Relations, Social Media

Weber Shandwick
2 Jordan St Knott Mill, Manchester, M1 54PY United Kingdom

Tel.: (44) 161 238 9400
Fax: (44) 161 228 3076
E-Mail: jleah@webershandwick.com
Web Site: www.webershandwick.co.uk

Employees: 30

Agency Specializes In: Public Relations

Joe Phelan *(Mng Dir, Exec VP & Head-Intl Corp Comm)*
Jo Leah *(Mng Dir)*
Andy Poole *(Deputy Mng Dir)*
Sally Fairclough *(Grp Acct Dir)*
Owen LaBeck *(Dir-Creative)*
Heather Blundell *(Assoc Dir)*
Anna Varley Jones *(Grp Assoc Dir-Consumer Mktg)*
Jessica Wilkinson *(Assoc Dir)*
Gemma Clulow *(Acct Mgr)*
Sarah Roberts *(Acct Mgr)*
Ema Savage *(Office Mgr)*

Accounts:
Advanced Supply Chain Retail Trade
Aldi Wrinklestop.co.uk
Bernard Matthews Ltd. Consumer, Digital, Marketing, Media Strategy
Burnley
Dream Gran Castillo Resort Online, Traditional
Food North Wales Consumer PR
Hancocks PR
Kick4Change
Macdonald Hotels
Manchester Business School
National Trust Wales Porth y Swnt
North West Ambulance Service Creative, Marketing, Patient Transport Service, Public Relations, Radio Advertising, Social Media
Rhug Estate Brand Positioning, PR
Sealed Air
Tourism Partnership North Wales Outdoor
Transline Group Communications, Public Relations
Warburtons Free From
Zip World Integrated Media, Social Media

Argentina

Nueva Comunicacion-Weber Shandwick
Colon 1428 Piso 2 - Dptos A y B, S2000 Rosario, Santa Fe Argentina
Tel.: (54) 341 448 1403
Fax: (54) 341 447 1159
E-Mail: nuevaros@citynet.net.ar
Web Site: www.webershandwick.com

Employees: 20
Year Founded: 1997

Agency Specializes In: Advertising, Communications, Magazines, Media Buying Services, Outdoor, Print, Public Relations, Radio, T.V.

Ivan Damianovich *(Dir Gen-Accts)*
Matteo Goretti *(Dir Gen-Accts)*
Marcela Ibiricu *(Dir Gen-Accts)*
Leyro Luis *(Dir Gen-Accts)*
Gustavo Peralta *(Sr Acct Exec)*
Fernanda Curat *(Acct Exec)*
Eliana Silva *(Acct Exec)*

Brazil

Gaspar & Asociados
Rua Dona Ana Helena de Sales Gusmao, 230, Sao Paulo, 01457-040 Brazil
Tel.: (55) 11 3037 3220
Fax: (55) 11 3812 6284
E-Mail: contato@gaspar.com.br
Web Site: www.gaspar.com.br

Employees: 3

Agency Specializes In: Public Relations

Heloisa Picos *(VP)*

Chile

Extend Comunicaciones-Weber Shandwick
Rosario Norte 555 Piso 12, Las Condes, Santiago, Chile
Tel.: (56) 2 437 77 00
Fax: (56) 2 448 12 36
E-Mail: mvelasco@extend.cl
Web Site: www.extend.cl

Employees: 70

Agency Specializes In: Public Relations

Maria De La Luz Velasco *(Partner & Exec VP)*
Ana Maria Velasco *(Partner & Bus Dir)*
Monica Blanco *(Partner & Dir-Strategic)*
Nora Van Der Schraft *(Partner & Dir-Strategic)*
Isabel Hohlberg *(Partner & Mgr-New Bus)*

Accounts:
Abertis
Andess
Cascal
Corpora Tresmontes
Edelnor
Entel
Entel Internet
Entel PCS
esVAL
General Electric
GM Chile
Sociedad Nacional de Mineria
Sodimac
Verisign

Uruguay

Nueva Comunicacion-Weber Shandwick
Ellauri 1212, 11300 Montevideo, Uruguay
Tel.: (598) 2 707 9956
Fax: (598) 2 707 9957
E-Mail: correo@nuevacomunicacion.com.uy
Web Site: www.webershandwick.com

Employees: 12

Agency Specializes In: Communications, Public Relations

Leticia Pena *(Acct Dir)*
Veronica Garcia Mansilla *(Dir)*

Australia

Weber Shandwick
166 William St, Wooloomooloo, Sydney, NSW 2011 Australia
Tel.: (61) 2 9994 4450
Fax: (61) 2 9994 4025
E-Mail: irumsby@webershandwick.com
Web Site: www.webershandwick.com

Employees: 26

Agency Specializes In: Public Relations

Jacquelynne Willcox *(Exec VP & Head-Corp & Pub Affairs)*
Ava Lawler *(Mng Dir-Australia)*
Lisa Popplewell *(Gen Mgr)*
Linda Kastanias *(Acct Dir)*
Eliza Newton *(Sr Acct Mgr-Pub Affairs & Crisis)*
Kate Fouracre *(Sr Acct Supvr)*
Amanda Porter *(Sr Acct Supvr)*
Kelly Lane *(Acct Supvr)*
Darragh Brennan *(Sr Specialist-Corp Comm)*

Accounts:
AA
BPEX
CSL Biotherapies
Electrolux
Horizon
Kensington PR
Lenovo Social Media Strategy
MasterCard
Revimid
Samsung Consumer Electronics; 2008
Weight Watchers

China

Weber Shandwick
Unit 706 -707 7F China Life Tower, 16 Chaoyangmen Rd Chaoyang, Beijing, 100022 China
Tel.: (86) 10 8580 2022
Fax: (86) 10 8580 4834
E-Mail: dliu@webershandwick.com
Web Site: www.webershandwick.cn

Employees: 100

Agency Specializes In: Public Relations

Charles Shen *(Exec VP)*
Antony Cheng *(Sr VP & Head-Digital & Social Media Comm-China)*
Lydia Lee *(Sr VP & Sr Strategist)*
Jeremy Liu *(Head-Acting Practice & Dir-Healthcare)*
Emma Huang *(Acct Dir)*
Vincent Zhang *(Acct Dir)*
Hellen Shen *(Acct Mgr)*
Palmer Wong *(Acct Mgr)*

Accounts:
Airport City Manchester Investor Relations, Media, Profiling, Road Show
Cofco Wines & Spirits Great Wall Wine, Public Relations
Oral-B Oral Health Awareness
Zippo Brand Image

Weber Shandwick
18/F HuaiHai Plaza, 1045 HuaiHai Zhong Rd, Shanghai, 200031 China
Tel.: (86) 21 2411 0000
Fax: (86) 20 8888 8099
E-Mail: dburns@webershandwick.com
Web Site: www.webershandwick.cn

Agency Specializes In: Public Relations

Darren Burns *(Pres-China)*
Stephanie Yu *(Sr VP-China Healthcare & Corp practice-Shanghai)*
Debbie Chin *(VP-Consumer Practice)*
Shashin Surti *(Acct Dir)*
Wansan Tsai *(Acct Dir)*
Adeline Ong *(Assoc Dir)*
Ivan He *(Acct Mgr)*
Mia Nai Chi Kuo *(Acct Mgr)*
Jie Lin *(Acct Mgr)*

Accounts:
California Walnut Commission Full-Spectrum PR, Offline, Online
Metro Cash & Carry
Montblanc PR
Suntech Power Holdings Co., Ltd. Corporate

Positioning, Global Corporate Communications Strategy, Media Training & Relations, Reputation Management, Strategic Public Relations Counsel

Weber Shandwick
Unit 3301B Guangdong Telecom Plz 18 Zhongshan Er Rd, Yuexiu District, Guangzhou, 510080 China
Tel.: (86) 20-8888 8310
Fax: (86) 20 8327 6157
E-Mail: dburns@webershandwick.com
Web Site: www.webershandwick.cn

Employees: 10

Agency Specializes In: Consulting, Public Relations

Darren Burns *(Pres-China)*
Celine Ng *(Sr Acct Supvr)*

Hong Kong

Weber Shandwick
10/F Oxford House Taikoo Place, 979 King's Rd, Quarry Bay, China (Hong Kong)
Tel.: (852) 2845 1008
Fax: (852) 2868 0224
E-Mail: jfin@webershandwick.com
Web Site: www.webershandwick.com

Employees: 50

Agency Specializes In: Public Relations

Albert Shu *(Mng Dir-Hong Kong & Exec VP-Corp & Fin Svcs Practice)*
Stephan Morgan *(Exec VP & Reg Dir-Asia Pacific)*
Jye Smith *(Sr VP-Digital, Asia Pacific & Head-Strategy & Ops)*
Elizabeth Warr *(Sr VP & Dir)*
Penny Cheung *(VP & Dir-IT Practice)*
Jeremy Cheung *(VP-Consumer Mktg Practice)*

Accounts:
British Consulate-General Hong Kong Campaign : "GREAT", Public Relations
Computer Associates Management Software; 2005
Harvard
Hong Kong University of Science & Technology
Hong Kong Polytechnic University
Moet Hennessy Diageo Baileys, Johnnie Walker, Public Relations, Smirnoff, The Singleton
The Savannah College of Art and Design PR

India

Corporate Voice-Weber Shandwick
No 2561 16th D Main HAL II Stage, Indiranagar, Bengaluru, 560 008 India
Tel.: (91) 80 2525 3891
Fax: (91) 80 525 3887
E-Mail: shiv@corvoshandwick.co.in
Web Site: www.webershandwick.com

Employees: 50

Agency Specializes In: Public Relations

Dilip Yadav *(Mng Dir-Client Svcs)*
Santanu Gogoi *(VP)*
Yasser Alvi *(Acct Dir)*
Reegal Ranjan Jayani *(Acct Dir)*
Saurabh Saggi *(Sr Mgr)*
Kaveri Mandanna *(Sr Acct Mgr)*
Divya Sibal *(Sr Acct Mgr)*
Kavitha Kini *(Acct Mgr)*
Surabi Shetty *(Acct Mgr)*
Shaila Srivastava *(Acct Mgr)*

Accounts:
Goldman Sachs (Indian Public Relations Agency of Record) Communications

Weber Shandwick
(Formerly Corporate Voice-Weber Shandwick)
Vilco Ctr B Wing 4th Fl No 8 Subash Rd, Near Garware House, Vile Parle, Mumbai, 400 057 India
Tel.: (91) 22 4031 1200
Fax: (91) 220 202 2391
Web Site: www.webershandwick.asia

Employees: 50

Agency Specializes In: Public Relations

Valerie Pinto *(CEO)*
Rohan Kanchan *(Mng Dir-Consulting & Strategy-India)*
Shreysi Chandra *(Acct Dir)*

Accounts:
American Airlines
AXA
BPEX
CSL Biotherapies
CVS Caremark
Electrolux
Horizon Fuel Cell Technologies
MasterCard Marketing Communications, Media Relations, Strategy
Revlimid
Wrigley India Boomer, Double Mint, Media Relations, Orbit, PR Strategy, Stakeholder Communication

Weber Shandwick
(Formerly Corporate Voice-Weber Shandwick)
No 212 Second Floor Okhla Industrial Estate, Phase III, New Delhi, 110 020 India
Tel.: (91) 11 4050 1200
Fax: (91) 269 368 36
Web Site: www.webershandwick.com

Employees: 51

Agency Specializes In: Public Relations

Rafi Qadar Khan *(Exec VP)*
Shashikant Someshwar *(Mng Dir-Client Svcs)*
Dilip Yadav *(Mng Dir-Client Svcs)*
Gayathri Sharma *(VP)*
Shankar Ghosh *(Head-Planner)*
Neha Singhvi *(Assoc VP)*
Gunjan Bagga *(Grp Acct Dir)*
Deepti Bhadoria *(Acct Dir)*
Reegal Ranjan Jayani *(Acct Dir)*
Saurabh Saggi *(Sr Mgr)*
Saraswati Mohan *(Sr Acct Mgr)*
Richa Kochhar *(Acct Mgr)*
Rashi Bhatia *(Acct Supvr)*

Accounts:
Hitachi
LG
MSD
Spencer
Whirlpool
Zippo

Indonesia

Weber Shandwick
PT Inpurema Konsultama Gedung BRI II Lt 16, Jl Jend Sudirman Kav 44-46, Jakarta, 10210 Indonesia
Tel.: (62) 21 5290 6550
E-Mail: dsaleh@webershandwick.com
Web Site: www.webershandwick.com

Year Founded: 2003

Agency Specializes In: Public Relations

Tursiana Setyohapsari *(Exec VP)*
Herry Cahyono *(VP)*
Djohansyah Saleh *(Head-Ops-Indonesia)*
Misty Maitimoe *(Gen Mgr-Indonesia)*
Sari Soegondo *(Dir)*
Helina Wulandari *(Office Mgr)*

Accounts:
American Airlines
BPEX
CSL Biotherapies
CVS Caremark
Electrolux
Horizon
Revlimid

Japan

Weber Shandwick
Mita Kokusai Bldg 13th Fl 1-4-28 Mita, Minato-ku, Tokyo, 108-0073 Japan
Tel.: (81) 3 5427 7311
Fax: (81) 3 5427 7310
E-Mail: wswjapan@webershandwick.com
Web Site: www.webershandwick.com

Year Founded: 1959

Agency Specializes In: Public Relations

Gary Conway *(Sr VP)*
Campbell Hanley *(Sr VP)*
Toshiya Takata *(Sr VP)*
Katsuhiro Mitarai *(VP)*
Jeffrey Spivock *(VP-Consumer)*
Rutsuko N. *(Acct Dir)*
Mariko Tyo-Wsw Kusunoki *(Acct Supvr)*
Evelyn Tokuyama *(Sr Acct Exec)*
Erika Akiyama *(Acct Exec)*
Reina Matsushita *(Acct Exec)*

Accounts:
FC Barcelona

South Korea

News Communications
4th Fl Chinyang Bldg, 190-3 Chungjeongno 2-ga, Seodaemun, Seoul, 100-120 Korea (South)
Tel.: (82) 2 319 2112
Fax: (82) 2 771 5053
E-Mail: newscom@newscom.co.kr
Web Site: www.newscom.co.kr

Agency Specializes In: Public Relations

Soo Park *(Pres & Mng Dir)*
Matilda Lee *(Mng Dir)*
Sumi Kim *(Exec Dir)*

Malaysia

Weber Shandwick
4-01 4th Fl Wisma LYL No 12 Jalan 51A/223, 46100 Petaling Jaya, Malaysia
Tel.: (60) 3 7843 3100
Fax: (60) 3 7843 3199
E-Mail: rkhoo@webershandwick.com
Web Site: www.webershandwick.com

Employees: 25
Year Founded: 1994

Agency Specializes In: Public Relations

Rozani Jainudeen *(Mng Dir-Malaysia)*
Blake Hoo *(Acct Dir)*
Ikmal Onn *(Acct Dir)*
Joanna Ooi *(Acct Dir)*
Adli Abdul Karim *(Acct Mgr)*
Kelvin Jude Muthu *(Acct Mgr)*

Philippines

Weber Shandwick
10/F JAKA Bldg 6780 Ayala Ave, Makati City, Manila, 1200 Philippines
Tel.: (63) 2 817 5670
E-Mail: info@webershandwick.com
Web Site: www.webershandwick.com

Employees: 15

Agency Specializes In: Public Relations

Diana Lesaca *(Pres/COO-Philippines)*
Carla Manio *(Acct Dir)*

Accounts:
Unilab Biogesic for Kids

Singapore

Weber Shandwick
40A Orchard Rd, #07-01 The MacDonald House, Singapore, 238838 Singapore
Tel.: (65) 6825 8000
Fax: (65) 6822 8000
E-Mail: bjolly@webershandwick.com
Web Site: www.webershandwick.com

Employees: 50

Agency Specializes In: Public Relations

Margaret Cunico *(Mng Dir)*
Baxter Jolly *(CEO-Asia Pacific)*
Barkha Patel-Zinzuwadia *(Sr VP & Head-Strategy & Reg Client Relationship)*
Sam Ran Boolsambatra *(Sr VP-Healthcare, Govt & Pub Affairs)*
Vanessa Ho-Nikolovski *(Mng Dir-Singapore)*
Jon Wade *(Head-Digital Practice-Asia Pacific)*

Accounts:
AA
BPEX
Changi Airport Group Public Relations
CSL Biotherapies
Electrolux
Horizon
MasterCard
Navteq Digital Map Data
Rolls-Royce PR

WEINBERG HARRIS & ASSOCIATES
623 W 34th St Ste 101-102, Baltimore, MD 21211
Tel.: (410) 243-1333
Fax: (410) 243-1334
Web Site: www.weinbergharris.com

Employees: 12
Year Founded: 1991

Agency Specializes In: Crisis Communications, Event Planning & Marketing, Investor Relations, Media Relations, Media Training, Promotions

Tracey Weinberg *(Pres)*
Gregory Harris *(Partner)*
Roger Mecca *(Dir-Social Media & Media Rels)*
Kate Bowers *(Sr Acct Mgr)*
Nicole Halsey *(Sr Acct Mgr)*
Patricia Mager Wise *(Acct Exec)*
Marina Bucolo *(Asst Acct Exec)*

Accounts:
The Ritz-Carlton Residences

WEINSTEIN PR
4200 Obrist Rd, The Dalles, OR 97058
Tel.: (541) 296-5910
Web Site: www.weinsteinpr.com

Year Founded: 2007

Agency Specializes In: Brand Development & Integration, Logo & Package Design, Media Training, Print, Public Relations, Radio, Social Media, T.V.

Lee Weinstein *(Pres)*
Melinda Weinstein *(VP)*
Julie Beals *(Project Mgr, Copywriter & Editor)*
Laurie Walker *(Project Mgr-Comm)*
Kate Bailey French *(Strategist-Brand, Mktg & PR)*
Aimee Danger *(Designer-UX)*

Accounts:
Chimps Inc
Curt Faus Corporation

WEISS PR INC
1101 E 33rd St Ste C303, Baltimore, MD 21218
Tel.: (443) 451-7144
Fax: (443) 451-7010
E-Mail: info@weisspr.com
Web Site: www.weisspr.com

Agency Specializes In: Brand Development & Integration, Content, Crisis Communications, Email, Graphic Design, Media Relations, Public Relations, Social Media, Strategic Planning/Research

Ray Weiss *(Co-Founder & Pres)*
Jessica Tiller Trzyna *(Co-Founder & Exec VP)*
Matthew Pugh *(VP)*

Accounts:
DDG Influencer Relations, Marketing, Media Relations, Public Relations, Social Media, Strategic Communications Planning
Mind Over Machines Influencer Relations, Marketing, Media relations, Public Relations, Strategic Communications Planning, social Media
OpalStaff
PLDA Interiors
Research Square
SafeMonk
TrainACE
Verne Global
Wynyard Group (U.S. Agency of Record) Influencer Relations, Marketing, Media Relations, Public Relations, Social Media, Strategic Communications Planning

WELLINGTON GROUP
4105 Medical Pkwy Ste 206, Austin, TX 78756
Tel.: (512) 371-8955
Web Site: www.wellingtongrouppr.com

Year Founded: 2007

Agency Specializes In: Brand Development & Integration, Content, Graphic Design, Internet/Web Design, Logo & Package Design, Public Relations, Social Media

Dawn Psaromatis *(Founder & Pres)*
Emily Kealey *(VP)*
Rachel Hoffman *(Acct Exec)*
Megan McCurry *(Acct Exec)*
Michael Wellington *(Strategist)*

Accounts:
Avocare

WEST PUBLIC RELATIONS
739 4th Ave 204, San Diego, CA 92110
Tel.: (619) 501-2756
E-Mail: info@west-pr.com
Web Site: www.west-pr.com

Agency Specializes In: Event Planning & Marketing, Media Relations, Public Relations, Social Media

Krista Lamp *(Dir-West Coast)*

Accounts:
New-Bodyography
New-Electra Bicycle Company
New-Ocean Pearl Spa

WESTWIND COMMUNICATIONS
1310 Maple St, Plymouth, MI 48170
Tel.: (734) 667-2090
Fax: (734) 455-7090
E-Mail: scottlorenz@westwindcos.com
Web Site: www.westwindcos.com

Agency Specializes In: Public Relations

R. Scott Lorenz *(Pres)*

Accounts:
ABC Nightly News
CNN
Good Morning America
The Wall Street Journal

WHAT'S UP PUBLIC RELATIONS
3333 E Florida Ste 35, Denver, CO 80210
Tel.: (406) 579-7909
Web Site: www.whatsuppr.com

Agency Specializes In: Advertising, Brand Development & Integration, Collateral, Corporate Identity, Event Planning & Marketing, Media Planning, Promotions, Public Relations

Beth Cochran *(Founder)*

Accounts:
AFM
BlackRapid Inc (Agency of Record)
Cocoon
Deuter USA Inc.
FITS Sock Co
Gramicci
Hans Saari Memorial Fund
Hero Kits
Krimson Klover (Agency of Record) Public Relations
Nuwa
Outdoor Industry Association

WHITE BEAR PR CORP
(Name Changed to Krakower Poling PR Corp)

WHITEGATE PR
1322 E 14th S 3B, Brooklyn, NY 11230
Tel.: (619) 414-9307
Fax: (858) 605-1673
Web Site: www.whitegatepr.com

Agency Specializes In: Brand Development & Integration, Email, Event Planning & Marketing, Media Relations, Media Training, Public Relations, Publicity/Promotions, Search Engine Optimization, Strategic Planning/Research

Dana Humphrey *(Owner)*

Accounts:
Artists in the Kitchen (Agency of Record) Tour Operating Services
Bark Baby Bark
BH Pet Gear Calm Coat, Marketing Outreach, PR
Carole M. Amber "The Gift of the Ladybug"
Chief Furry Officer Social Media
Chocolate Sauce Books (Agency of Record) Media Relations Programs, Now I Know
Clear Conscience Pet
Cooper's Pack
CoverCouch.com
CritterZone Marketing Outreach
Deja Vu (Agency of Record) Event Marketing Plan, Public Relations Support
Dina L. Wilcox "Why Do I Feel This Way? What Your Feelings Are Trying To Tell You, Book Launch
Dog Fashion
Dr. Catherine Reid, DMV Veterinary Practice
Elegant Linen USA
Evermore Pet Food Inc. Animal Products Mfr
Holistic Touch Therapy
International Cat Association Marketing Outreach
Jeff Magic Dating Advisory Services
Jorge Bendersky (Agency of Record)
K9 Cakery (Agency of Record) Media Relations Programs
K9 Fit Club (Agency of Record)
LE Portfolio (Agency of Record) Marketing, Strategic PR
LMB Designs (Agency of Record)
Lucky Dog Cuisine Inc.
MetroGuest.com (Agency of Record) Online Services
Money.Net
Paranormal Pooch (Agency of Record) Media Relations
ParkingTicket.com Worry Free Parking
Paul Nathan Groomed
Pawz Dog Boots LLC Safespot Locking Leash
Peaceable Kingdom Essentials Media Relations
Pet Wall of Fame
PetCareRx Marketing, Public Relations
PetCraftStore.com
Ruby & Jack's Doggy Shack Local Marketing
Savorian Wines (Agency of Record) Strategic Public Relations
Spa Aura; Hoboken, NJ PR
Spirituality is Sexy (Agency of Record) Media Relations Programs, Spiritually Rich & Sexy
Twigo Pet ID Tag
Wendi Finn A Beginner's Guide to On-line Security

WICKED CREATIVE
6173 S Rainbow, Las Vegas, NV 89118
Tel.: (702) 868-4545
Web Site: www.wickedcreative.com

Year Founded: 2007

Agency Specializes In: Collateral, Crisis Communications, Event Planning & Marketing, Media Training, Public Relations, Social Media, Strategic Planning/Research

Stephanie Wilson *(Pres)*
Lauren Cahlan *(Sr Acct Exec-PR)*
Tyler Krochmal *(Sr Acct Exec)*
Alexa Forshay *(Acct Exec)*
Lisa Green *(Asst Acct Exec)*
Jordan Massanari *(Asst Acct Exec)*
Katie Strickland *(Asst Acct Exec)*
Tara Woodall *(Asst Acct Exec)*
Kaitlin Starcher *(Coord-Internship Program)*

Accounts:
Poppy Den

WIDMEYER COMMUNICATIONS
1129 NW 20th St Ste 200, Washington, DC 20036
Tel.: (202) 667-0901
Fax: (202) 667-0902
Web Site: www.widmeyer.com

Employees: 40

National Agency Associations: COPF

Agency Specializes In: Advertising, Brand Development & Integration, Corporate Communications, Digital/Interactive, Government/Political, Graphic Design, Multimedia, Public Relations, Strategic Planning/Research

Scott Widmeyer *(Founder & Mng Partner)*
Margaret Dunning *(Mng Partner)*
Christine Messina-Boyer *(Partner & Sr VP-Higher Education)*
Jason F. Smith *(Principal)*
Ken Sain *(Sr VP)*
Christina Saull *(VP)*
Andre Witt *(VP-Ops)*
Dan Kaufman *(Sr Partner-PreK-12 Education)*

Accounts:
Adelphi University
The American Energy Innovation Council
American Federation of Teachers
Arizona Board of Regents
Coca-Cola Refreshments USA, Inc.
The College Board
Connecticut College
Foundation for Newark's Future
The Knight Commission on Intercollegiate Athletics
Mayo Clinic Thought Leadership
National Board for Professional Teaching Standards
National Inventors Hall of Fame Foundation
National Vocabulary Championship; 2006
Pfizer
Samuel Curtis Johnson Graduate School of Management Strategic Communications Planning
Shepherd University
Smithsonian American Art Museum
Steelcase Education Solutions Planning, Strategic Communications
The U.S. Consumer Product Safety Commission Campaign: "Pool Safely", Public Education Campaign
U.S. Department of Education's National Math Advisory Panel; 2006
U.S. Department of Health & Human Services Poison Exposure Prevention; 2005
W.K. Kellogg Foundation

Branch

Widmeyer Communications
102 W 38th St 4th Fl, New York, NY 10018
Tel.: (212) 260-3401
Fax: (212) 260-3402
E-Mail: henry.engleka@widmeyer.com
Web Site: www.widmeyer.com

Employees: 25

Agency Specializes In: Advertising, Health Care Services, Pharmaceutical

Scott Widmeyer *(Chm & CEO)*
Marina Stenos *(VP & Dir)*
Marie Gentile *(VP)*
Lydia J. Voles *(VP)*
Jacqui Lipson *(Asst VP)*
Amy Katzel *(Acct Mgr)*
Richard Funess *(Sr Mng Partner)*

Accounts:
Health Research Incorporated
New-U.S. Army Community Management, Digital, Educational Outreach Program, Marketing, Media Relations, Social Media, Strategic Communications

THE WILBERT GROUP
1720 Peachtree St NE, Atlanta, GA 30309
Tel.: (404) 965-5020
E-Mail: info@thewilbertgroup.com
Web Site: www.thewilbertgroup.com

Year Founded: 2009

Agency Specializes In: Communications, Media Relations, Media Training, Public Relations, Social Media

Tony Wilbert *(Pres)*
Caroline Wilbert *(Principal)*
Mark D. Braykovich *(VP)*
Hadley H. Creekmuir *(VP)*
Savannah Duncan *(Acct Exec)*
Liana Moran *(Acct Exec)*
Carolyn Smith *(Acct Exec)*
Stephen Ursery *(Acct Exec)*

Accounts:
Camana Bay
Cooper Carry
Cortland Partners
Franklin Street
FrontDoor Communities
Hubzu
KontrolFreek
Multi Housing Advisors
Renewvia Energy

WILDROCK PUBLIC RELATIONS
4025 Automation Way Ste D4, Fort Collins, CO 80525
Tel.: (970) 449-6870
Web Site: www.wildrockpr.com

Agency Specializes In: Brand Development & Integration, Digital/Interactive, Email, Event Planning & Marketing, Media Relations, Media Training, Promotions, Public Relations, Search Engine Optimization, Social Media

Kristin Golliher *(Founder & CEO)*
Alicia Beard *(Acct Mgr-PR & Mktg)*

Accounts:
Studio Be Salons

WILKINSON FERRARI & COMPANY
1371 E 2100 S Ste 100, Salt Lake City, UT 84105
Tel.: (801) 364-0088
Fax: (801) 364-0072
E-Mail: info@wfandco.com
Web Site: www.wfandco.com

Year Founded: 1993

Agency Specializes In: Advertising, Crisis Communications, Event Planning & Marketing, Government/Political, Graphic Design, Media Buying Services, Media Planning, Media Relations, Media Training, Public Relations

Lindsey Ferrari *(Partner)*
Cindy Gubler *(Partner)*
Brian J. Wilkinson *(Partner)*
Kris McBride *(Acct Mgr)*
Mimi Charles *(Mgr-Pub Involvement)*

Accounts:
Arthur Andersen
BruWest Enterprises
Camco Construction, Inc
Hamlet Homes
HDR Inc.
Holiday Expeditions
Kennecott Land

Metropolitan Water District of Salt Lake & Sandy
Mountainland Association of Governments Long Range Transportation Plan
Rowland Hall
University of Utah Health Sciences
Utah Arts Festival
Utah Department of Transportation
Utah Veterinary Medical Association

WILKINSONSHEIN COMMUNICATIONS
32 S Aberdeen St Ste B, Arlington, VA 22204
Tel.: (703) 907-0010
E-Mail: info@wilkinsonshein.com
Web Site: www.wilkinsonshein.com

Employees: 10
Year Founded: 2003

Agency Specializes In: Business-To-Business, Event Planning & Marketing, Exhibit/Trade Shows, High Technology, Information Technology, Public Relations, Publicity/Promotions, Trade & Consumer Magazines

Leah Wilkinson *(Partner)*
Mary Noyes Joynt *(VP-Strategic Mktg)*
Matthew Swanston *(Dir-Multimedia & Strategist-Social Media)*

Accounts:
Codex Development
DLT Solutions
InfoZen
LGS; 2006
Mintera; 2006
NextPoint Networks, Inc.
NXTcomm; 2007
ObjectVideo
OFC/NFOEC
Opnext, Inc.; NJ; 2004
OSA; 2006
RBN Inc.; San Francisco, CA; 2004
RollStream
Standard Solar
Telus

WILLS & ASSOCIATES
3 Bethesda Metro Ste 700, Bethesda, MD 20814
Tel.: (301) 767-0220
Fax: (240) 465-0733
Web Site: www.wills-pr.com

Agency Specializes In: Public Relations

George Wills *(Owner)*
Brad Wills *(Pres & CEO)*

Accounts:
Actix
Believe Wireless
BoxTone
Cernium
Defywire
Equal Footing Foundation
G.S. Proctor & Associates
Gerretson LLC
Global Wireless Solutions
MedChi

WILSON PUBLIC RELATIONS
(Formerly Tamara Wilson Public Relations)
4111 East Madison St, Seattle, WA 98112
Tel.: (206) 409-6735
Web Site: www.tamarawilson.com

Employees: 10
Year Founded: 1996

John Arthur Wilson *(Pres)*
Emily Eland *(Acct Exec)*
Megan Wenner *(Acct Exec)*

Accounts:
Greek Gods
Healeo
Il Fornaio-Seattle
Ivar's Seafood Bar
Kid Valley Hamburgers & Shakes
Morton's Steak House; Seattle, WA Beef, Cocktails; 2006
New Castle
New Urban Eats
Palomino Restaurants
The Paramount Hotel
Power Play
The Rock Wood-Fired Pizza
Sorrento Hotel
Talking Rain Beverage Company Twist
Terra Vista
Washington State Fruit Commission
Washington Trust Bank

WILT PR
137 E Main St Ste 200, Springfield, OH 45502
Tel.: (937) 688-3878
Fax: (937) 521-1958
Web Site: www.wiltpr.com

Year Founded: 2008

Agency Specializes In: Collateral, Crisis Communications, Event Planning & Marketing, Graphic Design, Internet/Web Design, Media Relations, Public Relations, Social Media, Strategic Planning/Research

Melanie Wilt *(Owner)*
Marin Smith *(Dir-Creative)*
Kristin Davis *(Acct Mgr)*
Dan Toland *(Acct Mgr)*
Emily Bennett *(Mgr-Content)*

Accounts:
AgReliant Genetics LLC
Ohio AgriBusiness Association

WINNING STRATEGIES PUBLIC RELATIONS
550 Broad St Ste 910, Newark, NJ 07102-4517
Tel.: (973) 799-0200
Fax: (973) 799-0210
E-Mail: mcqueeny@winningstrategy.com
Web Site: www.winningstrat.com

Employees: 30
Year Founded: 1997

National Agency Associations: PRSA

Agency Specializes In: Brand Development & Integration, Communications, Corporate Communications, Crisis Communications, Electronic Media, Email, Government/Political, Internet/Web Design, Media Relations, Public Relations, Publicity/Promotions, RSS (Really Simple Syndication), Search Engine Optimization, Social Media, Travel & Tourism, Viral/Buzz/Word of Mouth, Web (Banner Ads, Pop-ups, etc.)

Approx. Annual Billings: $6,668,455

Jim McQueeny *(Chm & Pres)*
Pete McDonough *(Partner)*
Michael A. Estevez *(Exec VP)*
Adam Dvorin *(Dir-Media)*
Noah Lichtman *(Dir)*
Ben Martin *(Dir-Healthcare)*
Suzanne Rowland *(Dir-Digital Strategies)*
Brian Dickerson *(Sr Acct Exec)*
Merrie Snead *(Sr Acct Exec)*
Michael Brennan *(Acct Exec)*

Accounts:
Horizon Blue Cross Blue Shield of New Jersey
Verizon

Branches

Princeton Public Affairs Group, Inc.
160 W State St, Trenton, NJ 08608-1102
Tel.: (609) 396-8838
Fax: (609) 989-7491
E-Mail: ppag@ppag.com
Web Site: www.ppag.com

Agency Specializes In: Government/Political

Norris Clark *(Mng Partner)*
Bradley Brewster *(Partner)*
Dale J. Florio *(Partner)*
Alfred Gaburo *(Partner)*
Lorna D. O'Hara *(Dir-Political Dev-The American Council of Engrg)*

Winning Strategies Washington
409 7th St NW, Washington, DC 20004
Tel.: (202) 589-0800
Fax: (202) 589-1288
E-Mail: info@wswdc.com
Web Site: www.wswdc.com

Employees: 10`

Michael Merola *(Owner)*
Richard Gannon *(Pres & Partner)*
Donna Mullins *(Mng Partner)*
Laura Lay *(Principal & Dir-Grants)*
Robert Zucker *(Principal)*
Alex DelPizzo *(VP)*

WINUK COMMUNICATIONS
25 Brian Ct, Carmel, NY 10512
Tel.: (845) 277-1160
Fax: (845) 277-1168
E-Mail: jay@winukpr.com
Web Site: www.winukpr.com

Year Founded: 1994

Agency Specializes In: Brand Development & Integration, Communications, Crisis Communications, Media Relations, Public Relations, Strategic Planning/Research

Jay S. Winuk *(Pres)*

Accounts:
Alacra, Inc.
Amtrak
Columbia-Presbyterian Medical Center
DestinyUSA
MyGoodDeed
TyRx Pharma Inc.

WIRED ISLAND INTERNATIONAL LLC
146 Seabreeze Cir, Jupiter, FL 33477
Tel.: (408) 876-4418
E-Mail: info@wiredisladnpr.com
Web Site: wiredislandpr.com

Agency Specializes In: Digital/Interactive, Graphic Design, Internet/Web Design, Public Relations, Search Engine Optimization, Social Media

Toni Sottak *(Mng Dir)*

Accounts:
New-The Athena Group Inc

WIRESIDE COMMUNICATIONS
1901 E Franklin St Ste 111, Richmond, VA 23223
Tel.: (804) 612-5393

E-Mail: info@wireside.com
Web Site: www.wireside.com

Year Founded: 2004

Agency Specializes In: Public Relations, Social Media, Strategic Planning/Research

Joya Subudhi *(Founder & Partner)*
Susan Hulcher *(Mgr-Ops)*
Christine Carlson *(Acct Supvr)*
Kristen Ruiz *(Coord-Program)*

Accounts:
NTT America, Inc.

WISE PUBLIC RELATIONS
77 Bleecker St Ste C2-23, New York, NY 10012
Tel.: (212) 777-3235
Web Site: www.wisepublicrelations.com

Year Founded: 2007

Agency Specializes In: Broadcast, Crisis Communications, Media Relations, Public Relations, Search Engine Optimization, Social Media

Harrison Wise *(Founder & Pres)*
Jeff Rutherford *(Partner)*
John McCartney *(Mng Dir-West Coast & VP-Media Rels)*
Tracey Boudine *(VP-Media Rels)*
Robert Zimmerman *(Exec Dir-Strategic Initiatives)*
Michael Lindenberger *(Sr Specialist-Media Rels)*

Accounts:
Adtheorent
Apple Inc. Matt's Pantry
Dynamic Video LLC
Influenster
Infocore Inc
Kiip, Inc.
Legolas Media, Inc.
Liverail
Mediamorph
My6sense
New York Technology Council, Inc.
PPC Associates
Spruce Media
Yieldex

WISER STRATEGIES
836 E Euclid Ave Ste 308, Lexington, KY 40502
Tel.: (859) 269-0123
E-Mail: info@wiserstrategies.com
Web Site: www.wiserstrategies.com

Agency Specializes In: Advertising, Crisis Communications, Event Planning & Marketing, Internet/Web Design, Logo & Package Design, Media Relations, Media Training, Promotions, Public Relations, Social Media

Nancy Wiser *(Pres)*

Accounts:
Rockcastle Regional Hospital

WITECK COMMUNICATIONS
2120 L St NW Ste 850, Washington, DC 20037
Tel.: (202) 887-0500
Fax: (202) 887-5633
E-Mail: info@witeck.com
Web Site: www.witeck.com

Employees: 7
Year Founded: 1993

Agency Specializes In: Advertising, Automotive, Communications, Crisis Communications, Gay & Lesbian Market, Health Care Services, Market Research, Media Relations, Production (Print), Social Marketing/Nonprofit, Sponsorship

Bob Witeck *(Pres)*

Accounts:
American Airlines
Aspen Institute
Bacardi Global Brands
CTIA-The Wireless Association
Disney
Evan Kemp Associates, Inc
GSK Abreva
Interstate Natural Gas Association
Jaguar
LandRover
McGraw-Hill Publishing
MTV Affiliate Sales, Logo
National AIDS Fund
Sunrise Senior Living
Volvo
WalMart
Wells Fargo

THE WOLCOTT COMPANY
6475 E Pacific Coast Hwy 467, Long Beach, CA 90803
Tel.: (213) 200-1563
Web Site: www.thewolcottcompany.com

Year Founded: 2008

Agency Specializes In: Crisis Communications, Media Relations, Media Training, Public Relations

Denis Wolcott *(Pres)*
Elhadj Kabine Kante *(Auditor-Fin)*

Accounts:
UCLA

WOLF-KASTELER
Sunset Media Ctr 6255 Sunset Boulevard ste 1111, Los Angeles, CA 90028
Tel.: (310) 205-0618
Web Site: www.wk-pr.com

Year Founded: 1989

Agency Specializes In: Event Planning & Marketing, Public Relations, T.V.

Samantha R. Hill *(Sr VP)*
Graehme Morphy *(VP)*
Stephanie Kazanjian *(Acct Exec)*

Accounts:
New-Entertainment Industry Foundation

WONACOTT COMMUNICATIONS, LLC
9911 W Pico Blvd, Los Angeles, CA 90035
Tel.: (310) 477-2871
E-Mail: info@wonacottpr.com
Web Site: www.wonacottpr.com

Agency Specializes In: Corporate Communications, Crisis Communications, Digital/Interactive, Integrated Marketing, Media Relations, Product Placement, Public Relations

Jason Wonacott *(Founder & CEO)*
Johner Riehl *(VP & Dir-Creative)*
Andrew Park *(Acct Dir)*
Julie Kim *(Dir-Ops)*
John Iatesta *(Assoc Mgr-PR)*
Alison Farias *(Acct Exec)*

Accounts:
Equity Risk Partners
Fantage.com, Inc. Media Relations, Messaging, Public Relations, Strategy
Meteor Games; 2010
NHN USA
PSYCLOPS
Sanrio Digital
Sleepy Giant
Tethys Solutions
Tritton Technologies Gaming Audio Technology, Public Relations

THE WOODS & CO
59 E 54th St Ste 93, New York, NY 10022
Tel.: (212) 838-1878
E-Mail: info@thewoodsandco.com
Web Site: www.thewoodsandco.com

Year Founded: 2013

Agency Specializes In: Event Planning & Marketing, Internet/Web Design, Media Relations, Public Relations

Susan Woods *(Owner)*
Sheila Hulsey *(VP-Bus Dev)*
Emily Tidswell *(VP)*
Mallory Liebhaber *(Sr Acct Exec)*
Diane Picariello *(Acct Coord)*

Accounts:
2Xu

WORDENGROUP
125 N Cache 2nd Fl, Jackson, WY 83001
Tel.: (307) 734-5335
E-Mail: info@wordenpr.com
Web Site: www.wordenpr.com

Year Founded: 1997

Agency Specializes In: Broadcast, Internet/Web Design, Print, Public Relations, Social Media

Darla Worden *(Principal)*
Amy Stark *(Acct Mgr)*

Accounts:
Landing Resort & Spa
The Sierra Nevada Resort & Spa
Tahoe Resort
Wildlife Expeditions of Teton Science Schools Public Relations
WRJ Design Design

WORDPLAY LLC
1400 W Northwest Hwy Ste 100, Grapevine, TX 76051
Tel.: (817) 756-1233
Web Site: www.wordplaytexas.com

Year Founded: 2000

Agency Specializes In: Advertising, Crisis Communications, Event Planning & Marketing, Media Training, Public Relations, Social Media

Tracy Southers *(Pres)*
Emily Keller *(Acct Exec)*

Accounts:
Keep Grapevine Beautiful
La Margarita Mod Mex

WORDSWORTH COMMUNICATIONS
538 Reading Rd, Cincinnati, OH 45202
Tel.: (513) 271-7222
Web Site: www.wordsworthweb.com

Agency Specializes In: Content, Crisis Communications, Event Planning & Marketing, Public Relations, Social Media

Bridget Castellini *(COO)*
Steve Kissing *(Chief Creative Officer)*
Joe Shields *(Chief Strategic Officer)*
Libby Schreiner *(Acct Exec)*
Owen Serey *(Acct Exec)*
Brianne Kistler *(Asst Acct Exec)*
Klare Williamson *(Asst Acct Exec)*

Accounts:
Verizon Wireless

WORDWRITE COMMUNICATIONS

411 7th Ave Ste 1125, Pittsburgh, PA 15219
Tel.: (412) 246-0340
Fax: (412) 246-0342
E-Mail: info@worldwritepr.com
Web Site: www.wordwritepr.com

Employees: 6
Year Founded: 2002

Agency Specializes In: Business-To-Business, Communications, Consulting, Corporate Communications, Corporate Identity, Crisis Communications, Digital/Interactive, Health Care Services, Investor Relations, Media Training, Public Relations, Publicity/Promotions, Social Marketing/Nonprofit, Social Media, Strategic Planning/Research

Approx. Annual Billings: $800,000

Breakdown of Gross Billings by Media: Pub. Rels.: $900,000

Paul Furiga *(Pres & CEO)*
Brenda Furiga *(CFO & VP)*
Jeremy Church *(VP-Media & Content Strategies)*
Hollie Geitner *(VP-Client Svcs)*
Erin O'Connor *(Sr Acct Exec)*
Rachel Borowski *(Acct Exec)*

Accounts:
Buck Consultants
Family Eye Care
Fragasso Financial Advisors
Kennametal
Koppers Inc Industrial Material Supplier
Light of Life Rescue Mission
MPW Industrial Services (Agency of Record) Media Relations, Strategic Communications, Thought Leadership
Pfizer
Redstone Highlands (Agency of Record)
West Penn Allegheny Health System

WORKHOUSE

133 West 25th St #3W, New York, NY 10001
Tel.: (212) 645-8006
E-Mail: info@workhousepr.com
Web Site: www.workhousepr.com

Employees: 22
Year Founded: 1999

Agency Specializes In: Advertising, Affluent Market, Arts, Brand Development & Integration, Branded Entertainment, Collateral, Communications, Consumer Marketing, Corporate Communications, Corporate Identity, Crisis Communications, Digital/Interactive, Entertainment, Event Planning & Marketing, Fashion/Apparel, Graphic Design, Guerilla Marketing, Identity Marketing, Integrated Marketing, Leisure, Local Marketing, Luxury Products, Media Relations, Media Training, Men's Market, Promotions, Public Relations, Publicity/Promotions, Retail, Social Media, Teen Market, Travel & Tourism, Tween Market, Viral/Buzz/Word of Mouth, Women's Market

Approx. Annual Billings: $5,432,543

Breakdown of Gross Billings by Media: Pub. Rels.: 100%

Adam Nelson *(Owner)*

Accounts:
Amazonas Promotional Campaigns, Public Relations
Amy Laurent
Antojeria La Popular
AvroKO (Agency of Record) Public Relations
B Michael America Public Relations
Copperwood Estate Integrated Promotional Campaigns, Public Relations
Doughboy Bake Shop; New York, NY (Agency of Record) Integrated Promotional Campaigns, Public Relations, Special Events
Genesis Publications Marketing, PR
GoldRun PR
Grupo MYT (Agency of Record) Promotional Campaigns, Public Relations, Special Events
Jung Sik (Agency of Record) Promotional Campaigns, Public Relations, Special Events
Karmaloop Digital Counsel, Marketing, Media, Public Relations, Trade Relations
La Cerveceria (Agency of Record) Integrated Promotional Campaign, Public Relations, Special Events
Lot71; New York, NY (Agency of Record) Promotional Campaigns, Public Relations, Special Events
Luster Integrated Promotional Campaigns, Promotions, Public Relations, Special Events
Mealku; New York, NY Promotional Campaigns, Public Relations, Special Events
Miz Mooz; New York, NY Fashion, Shoes; 2010
Niu Noodle House Promotional Campaigns, Public Relations
Obakki Marketing, Public Relations
The Obakki Foundation Marketing, Public Relations
Omhu; New York, NY Aids for Daily Living, Designer; 2010
Plan B
Simplissimus; New York, NY (Agency of Record) Promotional Campaigns, Public Relations, Special Events
Symbolic Collection PR, Promotional Campaigns, Ronnie Wood Art Exhibit
TEDxEast (Agency of Record) Promotional Campaigns, Public Relations
teNeues Publishing Group;Germany Books; 2010
The Tutu Project Promotional Campaigns, Public Relations, Special Events
Voila 76 Country Kitchen Promotional Campaigns, Public Relations, Special Events
Wantful Promotional Campaigns, Public Relations

WORKMAN GROUP COMMUNICATIONS

118 E 28th St Ste 514, New York, NY 10016
Tel.: (212) 256-0592
E-Mail: info@workmangrp.com
Web Site: www.workmangrp.com

Agency Specializes In: Media Relations, Public Relations, Social Marketing/Nonprofit, Social Media

Pamela Workman *(Founder & CEO)*
Pamela Lipshitz *(VP-PR)*

Accounts:
New-SoundHound

WRAGG & CASAS PUBLIC RELATIONS, INC.

1000 Brickell Ave Ste 730, Miami, FL 33131-3010
Tel.: (305) 372-1234
Fax: (305) 372-8565
E-Mail: info@wraggcasas.com
Web Site: www.wraggcasas.com

Employees: 17
Year Founded: 1991

Agency Specializes In: Brand Development & Integration, Business-To-Business, Communications, Consumer Marketing, Corporate Identity, Event Planning & Marketing, Government/Political, Graphic Design, Internet/Web Design, Public Relations

Ray Casas *(Pres)*
Otis O. Wragg *(Principal)*
Jeanmarie Ferrara *(Exec VP)*
Jeanne Becker *(Sr VP)*
Mery Lewis *(Dir-Creative)*
Tania Longest *(Acct Exec)*
Alexandra Curbelo *(Acct Coord)*
Anabel Mendez *(Acct Coord)*

Accounts:
Akerman Senterfitt
Commerce Bank
Dade Community Foundation
The DJamoos Group
Everest University
Fiduciary Trust International
Florida Power & Light
Gables Water Way
Gunster Yoakley
K. Hovnanian Enterprises
The Melissa Institute
Merrill-Stevens
Merrill-Stevens
Ocean Bank
ONYX Florida/Montenay Power Corp.
Plum Creek Timber Co.
Plum Creek Timber Co.
Podhurst Orseck
Rossman, Baumberger, Reboso & Spier, P.A.
Shutts & Bowen, LLP
Stearns Weaver Miller
United States Sugar Corporation

Branches

Wragg & Casas Public Relations, Inc.

27499 Riverview Ctr Blvd Ste 115, Bonita Springs, FL 34134
Tel.: (239) 444-1724
Fax: (239) 444-1723
Web Site: www.wraggcasas.com

Employees: 3

Agency Specializes In: Public Relations

Ray Casas *(Pres)*
Otis Wragg *(Principal)*
Jeanmarie Ferrara *(Exec VP)*
Gail Rayos *(Mng Dir-Central Florida)*

Wragg & Casas Public Relations, Inc.

121 S Orange Ave Ste 1500, Orlando, FL 32801
Tel.: (407) 244-3685
Fax: (407) 244-3671
E-Mail: info@wraggcasas.com
Web Site: www.wraggcasas.com

Employees: 2

Agency Specializes In: Public Relations

Ray Casas *(Pres)*
Otis Wragg *(Principal)*
Gail Rayos *(Mng Dir-Central Florida)*

Accounts:
American Express Bank, Ltd.
American Red Cross
Colonial Bank

WRITE2MARKET
659 Auburn Ave NE Ste 158, Atlanta, GA 30312
Tel.: (404) 419-6677
Web Site: www.write2market.com

Year Founded: 2006

Agency Specializes In: Communications, Content, Media Relations, Promotions, Public Relations, Social Media

Lisa Calhoun *(Founder & CEO)*
Jean-Luc Vanhulst *(Partner)*
Gary Bevers *(VP-Energy Svcs)*
Paul Snyder *(Dir-Relationship)*
Joe Lloyd *(Acct Mgr)*
T. J. Lane *(Sr Acct Supvr)*
Emily McDougald *(Acct Exec)*

Accounts:
TVTalk

WYATT BRAND
3001 S Lamar 101, Austin, TX 78704
Tel.: (512) 904-9928
E-Mail: info@wyattbrand.com
Web Site: www.wyattbrand.com

Year Founded: 2006

Agency Specializes In: Brand Development & Integration, Communications, Graphic Design, Public Relations, Social Media

David Wyatt *(Co-Founder & Bus Dir)*
Rachel Wyatt *(Co-Founder & Dir-Creative)*
Rachael Craft *(Dir-Art)*
Ryann Malone *(Dir-PR Accts)*
Jennifer Gritti *(Mgr-PR)*
Dasha Rakasovic *(Designer)*
Armando Garcia *(Jr Designer)*

Accounts:
America Martin
Austin Creative Alliance
Austin Dance India
Austin Film Society
Consulate General of Israel
The Devin Fund
H-E-B
House of Torment
The Intergalactic Nemesis
The Invincible Czars
Jessica Postol, LMT
PKW Productions
Sharon Marroquin
Texas Monthly Custom Publishing

XA, THE EXPERIENTIAL AGENCY, INC.
875 N Michigan Ave Ste 2626, Chicago, IL 60610
Tel.: (312) 397-9100
Fax: (312) 573-1313
E-Mail: info@expagency.com
Web Site: www.xapragency.com

Agency Specializes In: Brand Development & Integration, Digital/Interactive, Event Planning & Marketing, Graphic Design, Public Relations, Social Media

Catherine Weiner *(Sr Acct Dir-PR)*
Elizabeth Hamel *(Acct Dir-PR)*
Armon Lewis *(Dir-Bus Dev & Strategic Partnerships)*

Accounts:
Allium
Deca Restaurant & Bar
Food Mafia
Four Seasons Hotel
Jake Melnicks Chicago
Japonais by Morimoto
Joffrey Ballet Chicago
Le Colonial
Ritz-Carlton Chicago
Saks Fifth Avenue
Sola
Sophies
Tanta Chicago
TSG Chicago
Virgin Hotels
William Grant & Sons

XANTHUS COMMUNICATIONS LLC
357 Garfield St, Seattle, WA 98109
Tel.: (206) 284-4122
Web Site: www.xanthuscom.com

Year Founded: 2003

Agency Specializes In: Event Planning & Marketing, Internet/Web Design, Media Relations, Media Training, Public Relations, Strategic Planning/Research

Patricia M. Vaccarino *(Mng Partner)*
Josue Mora *(Brand Mgr)*

Accounts:
Garvey Schubert Barer
TimeXtender Consulting

XENOPHON STRATEGIES
1625 Eye St NW 6th Fl Ste 610, Washington, DC 20006
Tel.: (202) 289-4001
Fax: (202) 777-2030
Web Site: www.xenophonstrategies.com

Employees: 25
Year Founded: 2000

National Agency Associations: COPF

Agency Specializes In: Aviation & Aerospace, Consumer Marketing, Government/Political, Publicity/Promotions

Approx. Annual Billings: $28,000,000

David A. Fuscus *(Pres & CEO)*
Julie Chlopecki *(Partner)*
Bob Brady *(Mng Dir)*
Mark Hazlin *(Sr VP)*
Jennifer June Lay *(VP)*
Will Hubbard *(Acct Coord)*

Accounts:
Air Evac EMS
The Air Transport Association
Airbus Industries of North America
The Church Alliance
Computing Research Association
The Salvation Army
Solebury Township
United States Coast Guard
Williams-Sonoma

Branch

Xenophon Strategies
215 Western Ave Ste A, Petaluma, CA 94952
Tel.: (707) 781-9170
Fax: (707) 781-9182
E-Mail: info@xenophonstrategies.com
Web Site: www.xenophonstrategies.com

Employees: 1

Agency Specializes In: Aviation & Aerospace, Consumer Marketing, Government/Political, Public Relations, Publicity/Promotions, Transportation

David A. Fuscus *(Pres & CEO)*
Julie Chlopecki *(Partner)*
Bob Brady *(Mng Dir)*
Jennifer June Lay *(VP)*
Will Hubbard *(Acct Coord)*
Lexy Karoyli *(Acct Coord)*

Accounts:
Air Transport Association
Airbus Americas
Church Alliance
Computing Research Association
Piedmont Municipal Power Agency
Solebury Township, Pennsylvania
United States Coast Guard
Williams-Sonoma

XPOSURE PR
1191 Appleford Ln, Burlington, ON L7P 3M1 Canada
Tel.: (905) 339-2209
Fax: (905) 339-0099
E-Mail: jane@xposurepr.com
Web Site: www.xposurepr.com

Agency Specializes In: Crisis Communications, Exhibit/Trade Shows, Media Relations, Public Relations

Jane Wilcox *(Owner & Pres)*

Accounts:
The Canadian Institute of Chartered Accountants
CIPS (Canada)
FICPI
Nike 6.0 Action Sports

YAEGER PUBLIC RELATIONS
1020 Warburton Ave, Yonkers, NY 10701
Tel.: (914) 423-7972
Fax: (914) 423-1623
E-Mail: fredyaeger@yaegerpr.com
Web Site: www.yaegerpr.com

Employees: 4

Agency Specializes In: Advertising, Collateral, Corporate Identity, Crisis Communications, Digital/Interactive, Electronic Media, Internet/Web Design, Logo & Package Design, Media Buying Services, Media Planning, Media Relations, Media Training, Print, Publicity/Promotions, T.V.

Fred Yaeger *(Founder & Pres)*

Accounts:
Bronx Museum of the Arts
Community Hospital at Dobbs Ferry
Hudson Valley Hyperbarics
Morris Heights Health Center
New York Eye and Ear Infirmary
United Hospital Fund
Westchester Vein Center

YC MEDIA
231 W 29th St, New York, NY 10001
Tel.: (212) 609-5009
E-Mail: info@ycmedia.com
Web Site: www.ycmedia.com

Year Founded: 2000

Agency Specializes In: Brand Development & Integration, Crisis Communications, Media Relations, Media Training, Public Relations, Social Media, Strategic Planning/Research

Kim Yorio *(Founder & Pres)*
Aimee Bianca *(VP & Dir-Media Rels)*

Accounts:
Mirabeau

YOUNG & ASSOCIATES
1750 Tysons Blvd 4th Fl, McLean, VA 22102
Tel.: (301) 371-6995
E-Mail: info@yapr.com
Web Site: www.yapr.com

Employees: 10
Year Founded: 1982

Agency Specializes In: Event Planning & Marketing, Media Relations, Product Placement, Promotions, Public Relations, Publishing, Search Engine Optimization, Social Marketing/Nonprofit, Strategic Planning/Research, Telemarketing, Travel & Tourism

Jennifer MacLeid Qotb *(Owner & Principal)*
Meggan Manson *(Principal)*
Jennifer Mirabile *(VP)*
Eve Sheridan *(VP)*

Accounts:
In Case of Crisis Strategic PR
Pace Harmon
StartWire
Telmetrics
Wolfe Domain Analyst & Blogger Relations, Media, Public Relations

ZABLE FISHER PUBLIC RELATIONS
7050 W Palmetto Pk Rd 15-637, Boca Raton, FL 33433
Tel.: (561) 445-6075
Web Site: www.zfpr.com

Agency Specializes In: Media Relations, Public Relations, Social Media

Margie Zable Fisher *(Pres)*

Accounts:
New-Stain Rx

ZAG COMMUNICATIONS
4060D Peachtree Rd Ste 534, Atlanta, GA 30319
Tel.: (678) 799-8279
E-Mail: info@zagcommunications.com
Web Site: www.zagcommunications.com

Employees: 5

Agency Specializes In: Corporate Communications, Crisis Communications, Financial, Investor Relations, Local Marketing, Media Planning, Media Relations, New Technologies, Product Placement, Public Relations, Strategic Planning/Research, Travel & Tourism

Zenobia Austin Godschalk *(CEO)*
Laura Armistead *(Strategist-Mktg)*

Accounts:
Cloud Security Alliance
Voke

ZAPWATER COMMUNICATIONS
118 N Peoria St 4th Fl, Chicago, IL 60607-2394
Tel.: (312) 943-0333
Fax: (312) 943-0852
E-Mail: david@zapwater.com
Web Site: www.zapwater.com

Employees: 15
Year Founded: 2004

Agency Specializes In: Communications, Public Relations

Approx. Annual Billings: $500,000

David M. Zapata *(Pres)*
Nora Sarrawi *(Mng Dir & VP)*
Mayra Bacik *(CFO)*
Annie Block *(VP)*
Alana Horinko *(VP)*
Jenn Lake *(VP)*

Accounts:
AC Hotels Chicago Marketing Communications, Media Relations, Social Media
ACME Hotel Company Event Planning, Media Relations, Strategy Development
Bakers Square Events, Media Relations, Promotions
Ball Horticultural Digital Media, Media Relations, Public Relations, Social Media, Strategic Communications
Bella Lounge Bar & Lounge
Dana Hotel & Spa Campaign: "Zombie Takeover"
Del Frisco's Double Eagle Steak House Campaign: "Del Frisco's Steaks Out Chicago"
Downsize Fitness Campaign: "Downsize for Life", Campaign: "Downsizing The Obesity Epidemic"
e+o Food & Drink Campaign: "The Food Buddha Does The Dish"
Entertainment Cruises (Public Relations Agency of Record) Brand Awareness, Media Relations
ErgoSoft Digital Printing
Forum Studio Media Relations, Trade
Funky Junque Media Relations, Social Media
Gilt Campaign: "Chicago's GILTy Pleasure", Event Management, Gilt City, Influencer Relations, PR, Partnership Development, Social Media
GreenLaces
Haberdash for Men Campaign: "The Brand to Follow"
Henry & Belle Digital Strategy, Marketing, Media Relations, Social Media
Jewelers Mutual Insurance Company Brand Awareness, Strategic PR
Perfect Circle Jewelry Insurance Brand Awareness, Consumer PR
JG Custom Design High End Modern Furniture
K. Amato Jewelry; 2007
Kaze Sushi Restaurant
Kendall College Media Relations, Positioning, Public Relations, Strategy
Kiehl's Event Planning, Marketing Strategies, PR, Regional Media Outreach
The Law Offices of Jeffery M. Leving Ltd.
LYFE Kitchen Campaign: "LYFE Begins in Southern California"
NOW Foods Digital, Influencer Relations, Media
Pabst Brewing Co Old Style Beer
Plangraphics, Inc. Satellite Imaging Systems
RA Sushi; 2007
Rayven Inc. Laminations & Coatings
Red Foundry
Room & Board Campaign: "There's No Place Like Home", Event Planning, Marketing, Media Relations, Public Relations, Social Media
Scoop NYC Press Outreach, Social Media
Sebastien Grey
Shrine Haberdashers Media Relations, Social Media
Ted Baker London
Terra Foundation for American Art
Texas de Brazil Churrascaria (Agency of Record)
TheTieBar.com Campaign: "Fit to Be Tied"
New-Thread Experiment Marketing Communications, Media Relations
TieTheKnot.org Campaign: "Tie The Knot for Equality"
Topman Marketing, PR, Social Media
Topshop Campaign: "The British Invade the Windy City"
Uncle Matt's Organic Media Relations, Public Relations
Visit Luxembourg
Weddington Way
Yellowhouse Art Reproduction
Yumz Gourmet Frozen Yogurt Events, Media Relations, Promotions

Branch

Zapwater Communications Inc
11601 Wilshire Blvd Ste 500, Los Angeles, CA 90025
Tel.: (310) 562-4182
Web Site: www.zapwater.com

Agency Specializes In: Content, Digital/Interactive, Event Planning & Marketing, Media Relations, Public Relations, Social Media

Nora Sarrawi *(VP)*

Accounts:
Hollywood & Highland (Public Relations Agency or Record) Digital Content, Media Relations

ZENO GROUP
44 E 30th St, New York, NY 10016
Tel.: (212) 299-8888
Fax: (212) 462-1026
E-Mail: more@zenogroup.com
Web Site: www.zenogroup.com

Employees: 20
Year Founded: 1998

Agency Specializes In: Public Relations, Sponsorship

Barby Siegel *(CEO)*
Thomas Bunn *(Exec VP & Dir-Zeno New York)*
Frank Eliason *(Exec VP-Digital & Customer Experience)*
Jim Goldman *(Exec VP)*
Scott Murphy *(Sr VP)*
Therese Caruso *(Mng Dir-Global Insights & Strategy)*
Mark Shadle *(Mng Dir-Corp Affairs)*
Ame Wadler *(Mng Dir-Health)*
Sarah Rosanova *(VP)*
Greg Tedesco *(VP-Digital Engagement)*
Lindsay Hyman *(Acct Exec)*
Joanna Braeckel *(Corp Sr Acct Exec)*

Accounts:
Arcot Systems; 2007
Astroturf
Canadian Postal Service
Eagle's Flight Strategic Communications
Expion
Export Now Strategic Communications
Four Seasons Hotels & Resorts Corporate & Brand Public Relations, Media Relations, Social Media
Francisco Partners
Hershey Co. Communications, Social
JCJ Architecture Strategic Communications
K2M (Agency of Record)
Kia Motors America Inc.; Irvine, CA Public Relations
Kurion
Lam Research
Life Technologies
Lung Cancer Research Foundation (Agency of Record) Social Media
McAfee
McNeil Consumer Healthcare Online Media, Public Relations, Tylenol
New Medium Enterprises; 2007
North Carolina Beer & Wine Wholesalers Association
North Carolina State University
Oak Investment Partners
OoVoo Brand Awareness
Oracle
Pawngo.com
Pearltrees

Pepperidge Farm
Pfizer
Pizza Hut PR, Social Media, Super Bowl
Quaker
Rail Europe
Redbox
Sears Holdings
Seattle's Best Coffee
Sobieski Vodka (Agency of Record) Marketing, Public Relations
Spin Master Ltd. Public Relations
Sylvan Learning Public Relations, Social Media
Taco Bell
Tech-America
TrustAtlantic Financial Corporation
Tweetsie Railroad
VeriFone
Virtual Health (Agency of Record)
Wargaming America
Williamson-Dickie Dickies (Agency of Record)
WiseWindow Corporate Marketing Communications, Public Relations

Branches

Zeno Group
501 Colorado Blvd Ste 305, Santa Monica, CA 90401
Tel.: (310) 566-2290
Fax: (310) 566-2299
Web Site: www.zenogroup.com

Employees: 20

Agency Specializes In: Public Relations, Sponsorship

Jay Joyer *(Sr VP)*
Leilani Sweeney *(Sr VP)*
John Moore *(VP-Media Strategy)*
Danielle Siemon *(VP)*
Melinda Jenkins *(Sr Acct Supvr)*
Ashley Dolezal *(Sr Acct Exec)*
Liz Fernandez *(Sr Acct Exec)*

Accounts:
The Clorox Company
El Pollo Loco PR
Evolution Fresh
Kia Motors America
Nature's Path Foods, Inc.
Pinkberry

Zeno Group
3222 N St NW 5th Fl, Washington, DC 20007
Tel.: (202) 965-7800
Fax: (202) 298-5988
E-Mail: heather.gartman@zenogroup.com
Web Site: www.zenogroup.com

Employees: 12

Barby K. Siegel *(CEO)*
John Kerr *(Chief Digital Officer-Global)*
Monica Lourenci *(Exec VP-Brazil)*
Steve Earl *(Mng Dir-Europe)*
Cynthia Zamaria *(Mng Dir-Canada)*

Accounts:
Abbott
AT&T Communications Corp.
Discovery Communications
Merck
Pfizer
Pizza Hut

Zeno Group
200 E Randolph St Ste 5230, Chicago, IL 60601
Tel.: (312) 396-9700
Fax: (312) 222-1561
E-Mail: info@zenogroup.com
Web Site: www.zenogroup.com

Employees: 25

Agency Specializes In: Public Relations, Sponsorship

Sabrina Crider *(Exec VP)*
Missy Maher *(Exec VP)*
Hugo Perez *(Exec VP-Global Content & Digital Innovation)*
Tracey Thiele *(Exec VP-Integrated Plng & Digital Engagement)*
Carol Gronlund *(Sr VP-HR)*
Meghann Dowd *(VP)*
Molly Sheehan *(VP)*
Yvonne Schneider *(Acct Dir)*
Liz Risoldi *(Sr Acct Supvr)*
Jaclyn Kohlhagen *(Acct Supvr & Strategist-Digital)*
Danika Kmetz *(Acct Supvr)*
Vusi Moyo *(Acct Supvr-Healthcare)*
Heather Ribeiro *(Acct Supvr)*
John Arango *(Sr Acct Exec)*
Stephanie Kochs *(Sr Acct Exec-Healthcare)*
Maureen Murray *(Sr Acct Exec)*
Anna Tzinares *(Acct Exec)*
Elizabeth Epstein *(Asst Acct Exec)*

Accounts:
Cepia LLC (Agency of Record) Zhu Zhu Pets
Garrett Popcorn Event Execution, Influencer Engagement, Media Outreach, Social Media Strategy
Perfetti Van Melle USA, Inc.
Porter Airlines
The Quaker Oats Company
Scotts Miracle-Gro
Seattle Coffee Company
Starbucks Corporation Seattle's Best Coffee
Turtle Wax, Inc. Campaign: "WaxOnShirtOff", Turtle Wax Ice
Williamson-Dickie Manufacturing Co. Dickies Work Clothes, Williamson-Dickie Manufacturing Co.
World Kitchen Corelle, CorningWare, PR, Pyrex

ZENZI COMMUNICATIONS
646 Valley Ave Ste C, Solana Beach, CA 92075
Tel.: (858) 523-9020
Fax: (858) 523-9670
E-Mail: info@zenzi.com
Web Site: www.zenzi.com

Employees: 12
Year Founded: 2002

Sarah Znerold Hardwick *(Founder & CEO)*
Julie Lyons *(Pres & COO)*
Christina Jesson *(VP-Acct Svcs)*
Hilary McCarthy *(VP)*
Arianne Schumacher *(Acct Dir)*
Graham Hill *(Dir-Res)*
Brooke Joller *(Acct Supvr)*
Hanna Samad *(Acct Supvr)*
Kelsey Loflin *(Acct Exec)*
Tenaya Wickstrand *(Acct Exec)*

Accounts:
Keep a Breast
Parascript Automated Check & Remittance Processing, Forms Processing, Fraud Detection & Prevention, Mail Processing

ZEPPOS & ASSOCIATES, INC.
400 E Mason St Ste 200, Milwaukee, WI 53202-3703
Tel.: (414) 276-6237
Fax: (414) 276-2322
E-Mail: zeppos@zeppos.com
Web Site: www.zeppos.com

Employees: 13
Year Founded: 1994

National Agency Associations: PRSA

Agency Specializes In: Agriculture, Communications, Consulting, Corporate Communications, Crisis Communications, Entertainment, Environmental, Event Planning & Marketing, Financial, Government/Political, Health Care Services, Media Relations, Media Training, Public Relations, Publicity/Promotions, Real Estate, Restaurant, Retail, Sports Market, Strategic Planning/Research, Transportation, Travel & Tourism, Viral/Buzz/Word of Mouth

Approx. Annual Billings: $1,994,081

Adina Zeppos *(Mgr-Fin)*
Lauren Cook *(Acct Exec)*

Accounts:
GE Healthcare
Kennecott Minerals Company
MillerCoors
Pfizer
Quarles & Brady
UFC
Veolia Environmental Services

ZINGPR
2995 Woodside Rd Ste 400, Woodside, CA 94062
Tel.: (650) 369-7784
Web Site: www.zingpr.com

Agency Specializes In: Media Relations, Print, Public Relations, Radio, Social Media, T.V.

Tim Cox *(Founder & Principal)*

Accounts:
Other World Computing

ZLOKOWER COMPANY LLC
333 7th Ave 6th Fl, New York, NY 10001
Tel.: (212) 863-4193
Fax: (212) 863-4141
E-Mail: harry@zlokower.com
Web Site: www.zlokower.com

Employees: 6

Agency Specializes In: Advertising, Collateral, Electronic Media, Entertainment, Financial, Government/Political, Health Care Services, Internet/Web Design, Investor Relations, Print, Real Estate, Social Marketing/Nonprofit

Harry Zlokower *(Pres)*
Gail Horowitz *(Sr VP)*
Dave Closs *(VP)*

Accounts:
BAI Global
Center for Hearing and Communication
East Coast Venture Capital
Equity Now
GemEx Corporation
GeneLink, Inc
Hearts on Fire Diamonds
HMS Associates
Medallion Financial Corp
Townhouse Management Company

ZORCH INTERNATIONAL, INC.
223 W Erie St Ste 3NW, Chicago, IL 60654
Tel.: (312) 254-1060
Fax: (877) 471-0527
E-Mail: newvendorrequests@zorch.com
Web Site: www.zorch.com

Employees: 22

Year Founded: 2002

Agency Specializes In: Brand Development & Integration, Merchandising

Revenue: $24,515,175

Nicole Loftus *(Owner)*

Accounts:
Chase
Citigroup

PERSONNEL INDEX

A

Personnel Index

Allen, Todd, Pres & Exec Dir-Creative -- TODD ALLEN DESIGN, Elkhart, IN, pg. 1149
Alley, Justin, Acct Exec -- MEDIA MIX, Jacksonville, FL, pg. 743
Alley, Maureen, Specialist-PR -- C SQUARED ADVERTISING, Bellevue, WA, pg. 182
Alley, Todd, Dir-Creative -- TKO ADVERTISING, Austin, TX, pg. 1146
Allinson, Rachel, Dir-Creative & Art -- THE MEYOCKS GROUP, West Des Moines, IA, pg. 752
Allocco, Skip, Dir-Creative & Exec Producer -- ROTH PARTNERS LLC, Mamaroneck, NY, pg. 993
Allsop, Nick, Partner-Creative -- TBWA/London, London, United Kingdom, pg. 1124
Allt-Graham, Ed, Acct Dir -- GOODBY, SILVERSTEIN & PARTNERS, INC., San Francisco, CA, pg. 434
Alm, Dave, Assoc Dir-Creative -- BBDO PROXIMITY, Minneapolis, MN, pg. 98
Almeda, Jasmina, Acct Supvr -- Wieden + Kennedy-New York, New York, NY, pg. 1204
Almeida, Greg, Sr VP, Dir-Creative & Copywriter -- MMB, Boston, MA, pg. 767
Almirall, Adam, Acct Exec -- Edelman Brussels, Brussels, Belgium, pg. 1503
Almond, Charlie, Head-Sponsorship PR-Dentsu Aegis Network Sport & Entertainment -- Dentsu Aegis Network Ltd., London, United Kingdom, pg. 299
Alomia, Danitra, Sr Mgr-PR -- REVERB COMMUNICATIONS INC., Twain Harte, CA, pg. 974
Alonso, Ricardo, Art Dir -- Leo Burnett Tailor Made, Sao Paulo, Brazil, pg. 640
Alonzo, Javier, Coord-Creative Comm -- SKAI BLUE MEDIA, Philadelphia, PA, pg. 1650
Alpert, Ashley, Acct Supvr -- GLYNNDEVINS ADVERTISING & MARKETING, Overland Park, KS, pg. 430
Alquicira, Alfredo, Grp Dir-Creative -- Publicis Arredondo de Haro, Mexico, Mexico, pg. 929
Alston, Elliot, Media Planner & Buyer -- M&C SAATCHI PR, New York, NY, pg. 1579
Alston, Karim, Acct Exec -- KINNEY GROUP CREATIVE, New York, NY, pg. 613
Altenbern, Chase, Acct Dir -- COLLECTIVE MEDIA, New York, NY, pg. 1330
Alter, Devon, Acct Supvr -- Fleishman-Hillard Inc., Dallas, TX, pg. 1518
Alter, Jessica, Acct Supvr -- SHARP COMMUNICATIONS, New York, NY, pg. 1036
Althaus, Melody, Acct Exec -- SHOUT PUBLIC RELATIONS, Costa Mesa, CA, pg. 1649
Altinok, Sezay, Sr Creative -- WIEDEN + KENNEDY, INC., Portland, OR, pg. 1202
Altis, Dave, Exec Dir-Creative -- MEERS ADVERTISING, Kansas City, MO, pg. 745
Altmann, Nick, Acct Coord -- Geary Interactive, San Diego, CA, pg. 419
Altmeier, Ann Sophie, Dir-PR -- OMD, Berlin, Germany, pg. 1382
Altomare, Ingrid, Acct Dir-Adv & Digital -- Red Cell, Milan, Italy, pg. 221
Altomare, Ingrid, Acct Dir-Adv & Digital -- Red Cell, Milan, Italy, pg. 1221
Altschuler, Amanda, Acct Supvr-Digital -- 360I, New York, NY, pg. 6
Alush, Ami, Chief Creative Officer -- McCann Erickson, Tel Aviv, Israel, pg. 722
Alvarado, Herbert, Chief Creative Officer -- Publicidad Comercial, La Libertad, El Salvador, pg. 557
Alvarado, Juan, Dir-Digital Creative -- Young & Rubicam Bogota, Bogota, Colombia, pg. 1249
Alvarado, Rudy, Acct Supvr -- KDA Group Inc, Louisville, KY, pg. 206
Alvarado, Victor, Grp Dir-Creative -- Ogilvy & Mather, Mexico, Mexico, pg. 839
Alvarez, Ana Estela, Media Planner -- MEC, Guatemala, Guatemala, pg. 1361
Alvarez, Daniella Cortez, Mgr-PR & Social Media -- FAISS FOLEY WARREN, Las Vegas, NV, pg. 1512
Alvarez, Danny, Assoc Dir-Creative -- DAVID The Agency, Miami, FL, pg. 267
Alvarez, Juan Pablo, Exec Dir-Creative -- Ogilvy & Mather, Bogota, Colombia, pg. 839
Alvarez, Juan Pablo, Gen Dir-Creative -- Ogilvy & Mather, Cali, Colombia, pg. 839
Alvarez, Leandro, Pres & Chief Creative Officer -- TBWA Lisbon, Lisbon, Portugal, pg. 1123
Alvarez, Orlando, Dir-Creative -- Publicidad Comercial, La Libertad, El Salvador, pg. 557
Alvarez-Recio, Emilio, Acct Dir -- THE BRAVO GROUP HQ, Miami, FL, pg. 162
Alvarez-Recio, Emilio, Dir-New Bus -- YOUNG & RUBICAM, New York, NY, pg. 1239
Alves, Rui, Exec Creative Dir -- Y&R Cape Town, Cape Town, South Africa, pg. 1251
Alves, Thiago, Art Dir -- DDB Mozambique, Maputo, Mozambique, pg. 285
Alvey, Courtney, Acct Coord -- BOHLSENPR INC., Indianapolis, IN, pg. 1457
Alvi, Yasser, Acct Dir -- Corporate Voice-Weber Shandwick, Bengaluru, India, pg. 1683
Alwan, Zaid, Assoc Creative Dir & Copywriter -- H&C, Leo Burnett, Beirut, Lebanon, pg. 643
Amabili, Sandro, Acct Dir -- Saatchi & Saatchi, Milan, Italy, pg. 1004
Amador, Victor, Assoc Dir-Creative -- Y&R Miami, Miami, FL, pg. 1248
Aman, Janice, Acct Exec -- MOUNT & NADLER, INC., New York, NY, pg. 1593
Amant, Mark St., Co-Founder & Partner-Creative -- GRENADIER, Boulder, CO, pg. 444
Amato, Allison, Acct Supvr -- CODE AND THEORY, New York, NY, pg. 219
Amato, Dawn, Partner & Chief Creative Officer -- SLIGHTLY MAD, Northport, NY, pg. 1051
Ambler, Jamie, Exec Creative Dir -- THE BRAND UNION, New York, NY, pg. 156
Ambre, Renee, Acct Supvr -- OMA San Francisco, San Francisco, CA, pg. 859
Ambrogi-Yanson, Molly, Mgr-PR & Earned Media -- MERCURYCSC, Bozeman, MT, pg. 747
Ambrose, Jason, Dir-Creative -- 72ANDSUNNY, Playa Vista, CA, pg. 10
Ambrose, Leilah, Assoc Dir-Creative -- Edelman, Toronto, Canada, pg. 1501
Ambrosi, Giulia, Media Planner -- MEC, Verona, Italy, pg. 1359
Ambrosi, Giulia, Media Planner -- MEC, Rome, Italy, pg. 1359
Ambrosi, Giulia, Media Planner -- MEC, Milan, Italy, pg. 1359
Amende, Monte, Dir-Creative -- TDG COMMUNICATIONS, Deadwood, SD, pg. 1134
Amenta, Valentina, Assoc Dir-Creative -- D'Adda, Lorenzini, Vigorelli, BBDO, Milan, Italy, pg. 108
Ames, Yvette, Acct Dir -- BARTON F. GRAF 9000 LLC, New York, NY, pg. 96
Amey, Dawnne, Acct Supvr-Atlanta -- UWG, Dearborn, MI, pg. 1169
Amico, Danielle, Acct Exec-P&G-Venus -- BBDO WORLDWIDE INC., New York, NY, pg. 99
Aminzadeh, Aryan, Creative Dir -- ELEVEN INC., San Francisco, CA, pg. 343
Amir, Ruth, CMO & Dir-New Bus -- SILTANEN & PARTNERS, El Segundo, CA, pg. 1044
Amitai, Keren Bachar, Acct Dir -- Gitam/BBDO, Tel Aviv, Israel, pg. 108
Ammermann, Carrie, Art Dir -- BAKER STREET ADVERTISING, San Francisco, CA, pg. 88
Ammirati, Matthew, Chm-Creative -- Resource/Ammirati, New York, NY, pg. 970
Amodeo, Lou, Assoc Dir-Creative -- RISE INTERACTIVE, Chicago, IL, pg. 983
Amodeo, Silvia, Project Head-Digital & Acct Supvr -- Ogilvy Healthworld Barcelona, Barcelona, Spain, pg. 852
Amodeo, Silvia, Project Head-Digital & Acct Supvr -- Ogilvy Healthworld Madrid, Madrid, Spain, pg. 852
Amorim, Daniel, Acct Dir -- Y&R Sao Paulo, Sao Paulo, Brazil, pg. 1248
Amorim, Fabiana, Acct Dir -- Ogilvy & Mather, Sao Paulo, Brazil, pg. 838
Amorim, Ricardo, Dir-Creative -- AllofUs, London, United Kingdom, pg. 729
Amory, Ryan, Acct Dir -- Ogilvy Cape Town, Cape Town, South Africa, pg. 849
Amos, Stacee, VP & Acct Dir -- THE PARTNERSHIP, Atlanta, GA, pg. 876
Amow, James, Dir-Creative -- Publicis Caribbean, Port of Spain, Trinidad & Tobago, pg. 930
Amsler, Veronica, Acct Dir -- MEC, Miami, FL, pg. 1356
An, Suzy, Acct Exec -- Porter Novelli-Austin, Austin, TX, pg. 1619
Anacker, Steven, Dir-Creative -- PALMER AD AGENCY, San Francisco, CA, pg. 871
Anand, Vartika, Media Planner -- Isobar India, Mumbai, India, pg. 562
Anand, VJ, Exec Dir-Creative -- TBWA Istanbul, Istanbul, Turkey, pg. 1127
Anastasiou, Eleni, Acct Exec -- Ogilvy PR Worldwide, Athens, Greece, pg. 1607
Ancevic, Michael, Mng Partner & Chief Creative Officer -- THE FANTASTICAL, Boston, MA, pg. 368
Andersen, Carol, Pres & Dir-Creative -- KNACK4 DESIGN, INC., Huntington, NY, pg. 615
Andersen, Jamie, Acct Supvr-PR -- LFPR LLC, Irvine, CA, pg. 1575
Andersen, Kristen, Media Planner -- Mullen Lowe, Pittsburgh, PA, pg. 789
Andersen, Kristina, Dir-PR-Sports & Entertainment -- CENTURION STRATEGIES LLC, Tampa, FL, pg. 202
Andersen, Kurt, Acct Exec -- HARRIS, BAIO & MCCULLOUGH INC., Philadelphia, PA, pg. 481
Anderson, Alisa, Project Mgr-Mktg & PR -- PURE BRAND COMMUNICATIONS, LLC, Denver, CO, pg. 938
Anderson, Amy, CFO & Acct Exec -- CAIN & COMPANY, Rockford, IL, pg. 184
Anderson, Anita, Sr VP & Acct Dir -- Doner, El Segundo, CA, pg. 323
Anderson, Anita, Sr VP & Acct Dir -- Doner, El Segundo, CA, pg. 739
Anderson, Anna, Acct Exec-Edelman for Xbox One -- Edelman, Seattle, WA, pg. 1503
Anderson, Ashley Locke, VP & Acct Dir -- Havas Media, Boston, MA, pg. 1340
Anderson, Brent, Exec Creative Dir -- TBWA Chiat Day Los Angeles, Los Angeles, CA, pg. 1114
Anderson, Brent, Exec Dir-Creative -- TBWA Los Angeles, Los Angeles, CA, pg. 1116
Anderson, Brock, Acct Dir -- SECRET WEAPON MARKETING, Santa Monica, CA, pg. 1029
Anderson, Brooke, Assoc Dir-Creative -- Leo Burnett USA, Chicago, IL, pg. 639
Anderson, Bruce, Exec Dir-Creative -- Lowe Bull, Johannesburg, South Africa, pg. 790
Anderson, Cassandra, Dir-Creative -- DDB New York, New York, NY, pg. 275
Anderson, Chuck, Dir-Creative-Design -- HAVAS WORLDWIDE CHICAGO, Chicago, IL, pg. 502
Anderson, Coleman, Acct Exec & Producer-Video -- IMMOTION STUDIOS, Fort Worth, TX, pg. 541
Anderson, Cydni, Acct Exec -- ATOMIC DIRECT, LTD, Portland, OR, pg. 78
Anderson, Daryl, Creative Dir -- CLARK CREATIVE GROUP, Omaha, NE, pg. 213
Anderson, Derek, Assoc Creative Dir -- Publicis Seattle, Seattle, WA, pg. 927
Anderson, Derek, Assoc Creative Dir -- Publicis Seattle, Seattle, WA, pg. 936
Anderson, Doug, Assoc Dir-Creative -- OFF MADISON AVE, Phoenix, AZ, pg. 825
Anderson, Francois, Media Buyer -- HORIZON MEDIA, INC., New York, NY, pg. 1341
Anderson, George, Pres-Creative Svcs -- DEEP FOCUS, Hollywood, CA, pg. 293
Anderson, Greg, Dir-Creative -- VSA PARTNERS, INC., Chicago, IL, pg. 1185
Anderson, Ian, Dir-PR -- BACKBONE MEDIA LLC, Carbondale, CO, pg. 1448
Anderson, J. T., Sr VP & Grp Dir-Creative -- EDELMAN, Chicago, IL, pg. 1500
Anderson, James Todd, Sr VP & Grp Dir-Creative -- Edelman, New York, NY, pg. 1502
Anderson, Jason, Dir-Creative -- Neathawk Dubuque & Packett, Roanoke, VA, pg. 803
Anderson, Jason, Dir-Creative -- NEATHAWK DUBUQUE & PACKETT, Richmond, VA, pg. 803
Anderson, Jeff, Acct Dir -- 360I, New York, NY, pg. 6
Anderson, Jeff, Assoc Creative Dir -- CATALYST MARKETING DESIGN, Fort Wayne, IN, pg. 197
Anderson, Jill, Sr Acct Exec-PR -- SVM PUBLIC RELATIONS & MARKETING COMMUNICATIONS, Providence, RI, pg. 1102
Anderson, JoDee, EVP-PR -- RED7 AGENCY, Charleston, SC, pg. 963
Anderson, Johanna, Acct Supvr -- Wunderman, Irvine, CA, pg. 1230
Anderson, Jon, Editor-Creative -- VIEWPOINT CREATIVE, Newton, MA, pg. 1177
Anderson, Kristen, VP & Acct Dir -- HILL HOLLIDAY/NEW YORK, New York, NY, pg. 515
Anderson, Laura, Acct Exec -- TRACTION FACTORY, Milwaukee,

Personnel Index

COMMUNICATIONS INC., Omaha, NE, pg. 965
Armentano, Ricardo, Gen Dir-Creative -- Ponce Buenos Aires, Buenos Aires, Argentina, pg. 557
Armijo, Chris, Dir-Interactive Creative -- RABBLE + ROUSER INC, Denver, CO, pg. 948
Armour, Justine, Dir-Creative -- WIEDEN + KENNEDY, INC., Portland, OR, pg. 1202
Armstong, Jeff, Assoc Dir-Creative -- SLEIGHT ADVERTISING INC, Omaha, NE, pg. 1051
Armstrong, Athila, Exec Dir-Creative -- Method, San Francisco, CA, pg. 751
Armstrong, Caitlin, Acct Exec-PR -- KONNECT PUBLIC RELATIONS, Los Angeles, CA, pg. 1567
Armstrong, Colonel, Acct Exec -- ADVOCATE DIGITAL MEDIA, Victoria, TX, pg. 35
Armstrong, Emma, Exec VP & Acct Dir-Global -- GREY GROUP, New York, NY, pg. 445
Armstrong, Jennifer, Dir-Creative -- LIQUIDFISH, Oklahoma City, OK, pg. 661
Armstrong, Julia, Coord-PR -- PAGE COMMUNICATIONS, Kansas City, MO, pg. 1612
Armstrong, Robert, Dir-Creative -- SPIRO & ASSOCIATES MARKETING, ADVERTISING & PUBLIC RELATIONS, Fort Myers, FL, pg. 1065
Arnaouty, Osama, Assoc Dir-Creative -- AMA Leo Burnett, Cairo, Egypt, pg. 642
Arndt, Brian, Dir-Creative & Producer -- Paradise Advertising & Marketing-Naples, Naples, FL, pg. 873
Arnesen, Erin, Media Planner -- COLLE+MCVOY, Minneapolis, MN, pg. 221
Arnett, Melanee, Sr Media Planner-Interactive & Media Buyer -- THE LAVIDGE COMPANY, Phoenix, AZ, pg. 632
Arnett, Rebecca, Acct Exec -- GROUP 7EVEN, Valparaiso, IN, pg. 462
Arnold, Clayton, Pres & Dir-Creative -- MARKETING INNOVATIONS, Scottsdale, AZ, pg. 698
Arnold, Dan, Media Buyer -- J. LINCOLN GROUP, The Woodlands, TX, pg. 565
Arnold, Dana, Dir-PR & Social Media -- HIEBING, Madison, WI, pg. 513
Arnold, Dave, Exec Dir-Creative-NY -- PEREIRA & O'DELL, San Francisco, CA, pg. 883
Arnold, Dave, Exec Creative Dir -- Pereira & O'Dell, New York, NY, pg. 883
Arnold, Dustin, Assoc Dir-Creative -- TEAM ONE USA, Los Angeles, CA, pg. 1134
Arnold, Edwina, Specialist-PR -- KUNDELL COMMUNICATIONS, New York, NY, pg. 1569
Arnold, Megan, Acct Coord -- McCormick Company, Johnston, IA, pg. 732
Arnold, Rosie, Deputy Exec Dir-Creative -- BARTLE BOGLE HEGARTY LIMITED, London, United Kingdom, pg. 94
Arnold, Tyler, Strategist-Digital & Acct Exec -- LANDIS COMMUNICATIONS INC., San Francisco, CA, pg. 1571
Arnot, Andrew, VP & Acct Dir -- deutschMedia, New York, NY, pg. 303
Arnot, Tina, Dir-Art -- PMA INC., Palm Springs, CA, pg. 898
Aron, Abi, Grp Head-Creative -- Merkley + Partners/Healthworks, New York, NY, pg. 750
Arora, Mohit, Dir-Unit Creative -- Mullen Lowe Lintas Group, Mumbai, India, pg. 791
Arozian, Matthew, VP-Strategy & Creative Svcs -- ENC MARKETING & COMMUNICATIONS, McLean, VA, pg. 1510
Arredondo, Gaby, Media Buyer -- HELEN THOMPSON MEDIA, San Antonio, TX, pg. 1341
Arrighi, Chris, Coord-Digital Media Creative & Bus -- DEVITO/VERDI, New York, NY, pg. 304
Arrington, Lauren, Acct Exec -- KMR COMMUNICATIONS, New York, NY, pg. 615
Arsenault, Cait, Acct Exec -- DUFFY & SHANLEY, INC., Providence, RI, pg. 331
Arsenault, Kara, Acct Exec -- HAWK MARKETING SERVICES, Moncton, Canada, pg. 503
Arsiray, Ekin, Grp Head-Creative -- Markom/Leo Burnett, Istanbul, Turkey, pg. 646
Artabasy, Chris, Pres & Chief Creative Officer -- ARTAGRAFIK, Atlanta, GA, pg. 73
Arters, Lee, Dir-Creative -- Landor Associates, New York, NY, pg. 625
Arthachinda, Rachel, Media Planner-Digital -- MMGY GLOBAL, Kansas City, MO, pg. 767
Arthur, Priscilla, Acct Dir -- CARMICHAEL LYNCH, Minneapolis, MN, pg. 191
Artiles, Noel, Dir-Creative -- Y&R Latin American Headquarters, Miami, FL, pg. 1240
Artoos, Isabel, Acct Dir -- OgilvyOne Worldwide, Brussels, Belgium, pg. 829
Aruda, Ashley, Acct Supvr-PR & Brand Comm -- CONE COMMUNICATIONS, Boston, MA, pg. 1484
Arvanitakis, Filippos, Exec Dir-Creative -- DigitasLBi, Stockholm, Sweden, pg. 1289
Arvizu, Andy, Acct Exec -- ARVIZU ADVERTISING & PROMOTIONS, Phoenix, AZ, pg. 75
Arzethauser, Viktor, Acct Supvr -- DECK AGENCY, Toronto, Canada, pg. 292
Asai, Hiroyuki, Acct Dir -- Wunderman, Tokyo, Japan, pg. 1233
Asai, Masaya, Dir-Art & Assoc Dir-Creative -- TBWA/Media Arts Lab, Los Angeles, CA, pg. 1116
Asano, Kayako, Dir-PR -- TBWA/Hakuhodo, Tokyo, Japan, pg. 1129
Asante, Anita, Assoc Dir-NEW Bus-NEW YORK -- SELECTNY, New York, NY, pg. 1030
Asch, Jessica, Acct Dir -- BAREFOOT PROXIMITY, Cincinnati, OH, pg. 91
Aschaker, Dana, Acct Exec-Client Svcs -- GMR MARKETING LLC, New Berlin, WI, pg. 1414
Ascherl, Rosemarie, Dir-PR -- SONNHALTER, Berea, OH, pg. 1058
Ascue, Javier, Art Dir -- Y&R Peru, Lima, Peru, pg. 1250
Asendio, Laura, Acct Exec -- DPR GROUP, INC., Germantown, MD, pg. 1497
Ash, Kevin J., Principal & Dir-Creative -- KEVIN J. ASH CREATIVE DESIGN, LLC, Northwood, NH, pg. 609
Ash, Lindsay, Acct Supvr -- Manning Selvage & Lee, Atlanta, GA, pg. 1594
Ashbock, Alyson, Acct Supvr -- R&R PARTNERS, Las Vegas, NV, pg. 945
Ashburn, Kurt, Acct Dir -- MILLER BROOKS, Zionsville, IN, pg. 758
Asher, Larry, Dir-creative & copywriter -- WORKER BEES, INC., Seattle, WA, pg. 1215
Ashley, Michael, Creative Dir -- DigitasLBi, Atlanta, GA, pg. 1290
Ashlock, Jason, Dir-Creative -- McCann Erickson/New York, New York, NY, pg. 714
Ashton, Kim, Acct Dir -- IDEAOLOGY ADVERTISING INC., Marina Del Rey, CA, pg. 534
Ashton, Luke, Dir-Creative-Global -- Cheil Worldwide Inc., Seoul, Korea (South), pg. 474
Ashworth, Jimmy, Exec Dir-Creative -- Neathawk Dubuque & Packett, Roanoke, VA, pg. 803
Ashworth, Jimmy, Exec Dir-Creative -- NEATHAWK DUBUQUE & PACKETT, Richmond, VA, pg. 803
Ashworth, Matt, Exec Dir-Creative -- ARGONAUT INC., San Francisco, CA, pg. 68
Askren, Andy, Partner & Exec Dir-Creative -- GRADY BRITTON, Portland, OR, pg. 437
Aslam, Arshad, Exec Dir-Creative -- Ogilvy & Mather, Karachi, Pakistan, pg. 850
Asmussen, David, Dir-Creative -- J. Walter Thompson Copenhagen, Copenhagen, Denmark, pg. 572
Aspes, Jason, Exec Dir-Creative -- OGILVY & MATHER, New York, NY, pg. 826
Asplund, Chelsea, Acct Exec -- GREENRUBINO, Seattle, WA, pg. 443
Asprea, Suzanne, Assoc Dir-Creative -- PBJS, INC., Seattle, WA, pg. 880
Assi, Akiran, Acct Exec -- TRACYLOCKE, Dallas, TX, pg. 1153
Assohou, Armel, Acct Dir -- McCann Erickson Cameroon, Douala, Cameroon, pg. 718
Assouline, Arnaud, Creative Dir & Copywriter -- BETC Life, Paris, France, pg. 492
Astfalk, Alexis, Acct Exec -- BROWER MILLER & COLE, Irvine, CA, pg. 1463
Astier, Thierry, Exec Dir-Creative -- Grey Paris, Paris, France, pg. 449
Astini, Marcella, Acct Exec -- HAVAS WORLDWIDE CHICAGO, Chicago, IL, pg. 502
Astolpho, Fabio, Creative Dir -- F.biz, Sao Paulo, Brazil, pg. 1223
Asuro, Noreel, Grp Creative Dir -- LEO BURNETT COMPANY LTD., Toronto, Canada, pg. 637
Atalay, Deniz, Acct Supvr -- Y&R Turkey, Istanbul, Turkey, pg. 1247
Atallah, Marc, Art Dir -- CLM BBDO, Boulogne-Billancourt, France, pg. 106
Atassi, Malek, Dir-Creative -- TBWA Raad, Dubai, United Arab Emirates, pg. 1127
Athayde, Edson, CEO & Chief Creative Officer -- FCB Lisbon, Lisbon, Portugal, pg. 374
Athray, Srreram, Sr Dir-Creative -- Ogilvy India, Mumbai, India, pg. 843
Atkatz, Matthew, Exec Dir-Creative -- Sapient Miami/Falls, Miami, FL, pg. 1018
Atkins, Robin, Dir-Creative -- OgilvyOne Business, London, United Kingdom, pg. 837
Atkinson, Anthony, Dir-Creative -- Wieden + Kennedy, London, United Kingdom, pg. 1204
Atkinson, Mark, Partner & Dir-Creative -- Otto, Virginia Beach, VA, pg. 865
Atkinson, Sean, Copywriter -- ZULU ALPHA KILO, Toronto, Canada, pg. 1260
Atlan, Marc, Principal & Dir-Creative -- MARC ATLAN DESIGN, INC., Los Angeles, CA, pg. 691
Atlas, Jordan, Sr VP & Dir-Creative -- Edelman, Los Angeles, CA, pg. 1502
Atoon, Yogev, Acct Supvr -- BBR Saatchi & Saatchi, Ramat Gan, Israel, pg. 1003
Attwater, Simon, Exec Dir-Creative-MENA -- DigitasLBi, London, United Kingdom, pg. 1289
Attwood, Kemp, Partner & Dir-Creative -- AREA 17, Brooklyn, NY, pg. 1282
Atunwa, Ranti, Dir-Creative -- TBWA Concept Unit, Lagos, Nigeria, pg. 1125
Atvara, Daiga, Chief Creative Officer-Digital -- THE UXB, Beverly Hills, CA, pg. 1169
Atwater, Alison, Assoc Dir-Creative -- DUFFEY PETROSKY, Farmington Hills, MI, pg. 331
Au, Chan I., Art Dir -- TBWA Switzerland A.G., Zurich, Switzerland, pg. 1124
Auashria, Katrin, Acct Dir -- DDB Russia, Moscow, Russia, pg. 287
Audette, Ann M., Specialist-PR -- NEOTROPE, Torrance, CA, pg. 1601
Auerbach, Rebecca, Acct Supvr -- Digitas Health, New York, NY, pg. 1289
Aufmann, Alex, Media Planner -- BACKBONE MEDIA LLC, Carbondale, CO, pg. 1448
Auger-Bellemare, Lisanne, Mgr-Print Production -- BLEUBLANCROUGE, Montreal, Canada, pg. 138
Augustine, Dan, Dir-Creative -- EPIC CREATIVE, West Bend, WI, pg. 349
Augustine, Dan, Assoc Dir-Creative -- ZIZZO GROUP MARKETING + PR + NEW MEDIA, INC., Milwaukee, WI, pg. 1258
Augusto, Rafael, Assoc Dir-Creative -- Radius Leo Burnett, Dubai, United Arab Emirates, pg. 646
Auld, Jock, Acct Supvr-Infiniti-Global -- TBWA Hong Kong, Hong Kong, China (Hong Kong), pg. 1128
Ault, George, Assoc Dir-Creative -- ZULU ALPHA KILO, Toronto, Canada, pg. 1260
Aumiller, Denis, Mng Partner & Dir-Creative -- LEHIGH MINING & NAVIGATION, Bethlehem, PA, pg. 635
Aurelius, Tedd, Sr VP, Acct Dir & Dir-One-to-One Engagement -- THE MARTIN AGENCY, Richmond, VA, pg. 702
Aurousseau, Till, Dir-Creative -- Ogilvy & Mather (Eastern Africa) Ltd., Nairobi, Kenya, pg. 848
Austin, Chris, Acct Exec -- IDENTITY MARKETING & PUBLIC RELATIONS, LLC, Bingham Farms, MI, pg. 1548
Austin, Jessica, Acct Exec -- Luckie & Co., San Antonio, TX, pg. 673
Austin, Lauren, Dir-Creative -- MKG, New York, NY, pg. 766
Austin, Tim, Chief Creative Officer -- TPN INC., Dallas, TX, pg. 1431
Austopchuk, Chris, Sr VP & Dir-Creative -- ARCADE CREATIVE GROUP, New York, NY, pg. 66
Austria, Jerome, Exec Dir-Creative -- Deutsch LA, Los Angeles, CA, pg. 302
Autenrieth, Brian, Acct Supvr -- CDMiConnect, New York, NY, pg. 200
Autorino, Joella, Acct Dir & Dir-New media -- STAN ADLER ASSOCIATES, New York, NY, pg. 1073
Avanian, Haik, Head-Creative -- BIG HUMAN, New York, NY, pg. 130
Avantaggio, Chris, Assoc Dir-Creative -- THE VIA AGENCY, Portland, ME, pg. 1175
Avdic, Florian, Sr Planner-Creative -- OgilvyInteractive, Frankfurt, Germany, pg. 832
Avedon, Danielle, VP & Acct Dir -- GREY GROUP, New York, NY, pg. 445
Avery, John, Exec Dir-Creative -- Weber Shandwick-Los Angeles, Los Angeles, CA, pg. 1678
Aveyard, Martin, Sr Dir-Art & Co-Dir-Creative -- TRAPEZE COMMUNICATIONS, Victoria, Canada, pg. 1154
Avila, Jessica Gutierrez, Media Buyer -- MEC, Bogota, Colombia,

B

Personnel Index

Beaton, Lewis, Art Dir -- Leo Burnett, Ltd., London, United Kingdom, pg. 641
Beaty, Anna, Sr Dir-PR -- COHN MARKETING, Denver, CO, pg. 220
Beauchemin, Chris, Acct Supvr -- LMO ADVERTISING, Arlington, VA, pg. 665
Beaucher, Aaron, Partner & Creative Dir -- NEO-PANGEA, LLC, Reading, PA, pg. 805
Beaudin, Abby, Coord-Traffic -- ONE EIGHTEEN ADVERTISING, Los Angeles, CA, pg. 860
Beaulieu, Dominique, Media Planner -- TAM-TAM/TBWA, Montreal, Canada, pg. 1116
Beaupre, Claude, Acct Supvr -- DentsuBos, Toronto, Canada, pg. 299
Beaver, Tommy, Assoc Dir-Creative -- BLUEZOOM, Greensboro, NC, pg. 143
Beavers, Megan, Acct Exec -- Edelman, Atlanta, GA, pg. 1502
Bechely, Joe, Acct Dir -- BRANDMOVERS, Atlanta, GA, pg. 1284
Becher, Irina, Dir-Creative -- Leo Burnett & Target SA, Bucharest, Romania, pg. 644
Beck, Amanda, Acct Exec -- CINCH PR & BRANDING GROUP, San Francisco, CA, pg. 1478
Beck, Jennifer, Acct Supvr -- Ketchum Canada, Toronto, Canada, pg. 1564
Beck, Tyrone, Creative Dir -- Saatchi & Saatchi, Cape Town, South Africa, pg. 1005
Becker, Alvaro, Gen Dir-Creative -- Prolam Y&R S.A., Santiago, Chile, pg. 1249
Becker, Amie, Media Dir -- BROKAW INC., Cleveland, OH, pg. 169
Becker, Cassie, Specialist-PR -- ARCHER MALMO, Memphis, TN, pg. 67
Becker, Christoph, CEO & Chief Creative Officer -- GYRO, New York, NY, pg. 468
Becker, Jack, Partner, Dir-Creative & Strategist-Brand -- ELEMENT ADVERTISING LLC, Asheville, NC, pg. 342
Becker, Josh, Acct Exec & Supvr-Production -- NAARTJIE MULTIMEDIA, Columbus, GA, pg. 799
Becker, Laura, Mgr-Print Production -- Bandy Carroll Hellige Advertising, Indianapolis, IN, pg. 90
Beckerling, Tim, Creative Dir -- MetropolitanRepublic, Johannesburg, South Africa, pg. 1220
Beckert, Caroline, Assoc Dir-Creative -- BBDO China, Beijing, China, pg. 114
Beckett, Alec, Partner-Creative -- NAIL COMMUNICATIONS, Providence, RI, pg. 799
Beckett, Alexis, Dir-Creative -- 140 BBDO, Cape Town, South Africa, pg. 111
Beckett, Alexis, Dir-Creative -- Net#work BBDO, Gauteng, South Africa, pg. 111
Beckett, Anna, Acct Exec -- PBJS, INC., Seattle, WA, pg. 880
Beckett, Nicky, Acct Dir -- OgilvyOne Worldwide Ltd., London, United Kingdom, pg. 837
Beckley, Janet, Coord-Traffic -- LMO ADVERTISING, Arlington, VA, pg. 665
Beckman, Kati, Acct Coord -- 3FOLD COMMUNICATIONS, Sacramento, CA, pg. 7
Beckman, Tom, Exec Dir-Creative -- Prime Public Relations, Stockholm, Sweden, pg. 1680
Beckwith, Charlotte, Acct Supvr -- MRM Worldwide New York, New York, NY, pg. 782
Beckwith, Dan, Exec Creative Dir -- Wieden + Kennedy-New York, New York, NY, pg. 1204
Bedard, Marie, Acct Dir -- FREE FOR ALL MARKETING INC, Toronto, Canada, pg. 403
Bedecarre, Jason, Acct Dir -- GOODBY, SILVERSTEIN & PARTNERS, INC., San Francisco, CA, pg. 434
Bederka, Larry, Acct Exec -- CAIN & COMPANY, Rockford, IL, pg. 184
Bedford, Karlee, Acct Dir -- Taxi 2, Toronto, Canada, pg. 1112
Bedford, Nadine, Acct Supvr-Digital Consumer Mktg -- Edelman, Seattle, WA, pg. 1503
Bedinghaus, Elliott, VP-Creative -- SPARK, Tampa, FL, pg. 1061
Bedoya, Viviana, Acct Dir-Spectacular Holistic Circus -- Circus Communicacion Integrada, Lima, Peru, pg. 641
Bedrossian, Haig, Dir-Creative-NY -- CREATIVE:MINT LLC, San Francisco, CA, pg. 253
Bedway, Tom, Dir-Creative -- BURKHOLDER/FLINT, Columbus, OH, pg. 177
Beebe, Adam, Acct Exec -- ARENA COMMUNICATIONS, Salt Lake City, UT, pg. 68
Beebe, Brittany, Acct Supvr -- PRIMACY, Farmington, CT, pg. 910
Beeby, Thomas, Principal & Exec Dir-Creative -- BEEBY CLARK + MEYLER, Stamford, CT, pg. 122
Beech, Brian, Mng Dir-Havas PR UK -- Havas People Manchester, Manchester, United Kingdom, pg. 497
Beechinor, Mikell, Acct Dir -- LRXD, Denver, CO, pg. 1301
Beechner, Sara, VP-Creative -- ENVIROMEDIA SOCIAL MARKETING, Austin, TX, pg. 349
Beeler, Chuck, Dir & Sr Strategist-PR -- EMA Public Relations Services, Syracuse, NY, pg. 353
Beeler, Chuck, Dir & Sr Strategist-PR -- ERIC MOWER + ASSOCIATES, Syracuse, NY, pg. 353
Beere, Brendan, Acct Dir -- Millward Brown Lansdowne, Dublin, Ireland, pg. 759
Beers, Caroline, Acct Supvr -- BRODEUR PARTNERS, Boston, MA, pg. 1462
Beerson, Danielle, Acct Exec -- Rosetta, San Luis Obispo, CA, pg. 992
Beffa, Pierre, Acct Dir & Assoc Dir -- DDB Paris, Paris, France, pg. 281
Beggin, Vince, Grp Dir-Creative & Brand -- OLSON, Minneapolis, MN, pg. 856
Beggs, Jonathan, Chief Creative Officer -- Saatchi & Saatchi, Cape Town, South Africa, pg. 1005
Behaeghel, Vincent, Dir-Creative-Intl -- BETC Life, Paris, France, pg. 492
Behaeghel, Vincent, Creative Dir -- Havas Worldwide Digital Dusseldorf, Dusseldorf, Germany, pg. 493
Behm, Kelly, Dir-PR Client Strategy -- COHN MARKETING, Denver, CO, pg. 220
Behnen, Paul, Sr VP & Exec Dir-Creative -- TROZZOLO COMMUNICATIONS GROUP, Kansas City, MO, pg. 1159
Behr, Mario, Pres & Dir-Creative -- GREEN DOT ADVERTISING & MARKETING, Miami, FL, pg. 442
Behrendt, Becky, Acct Exec -- RESPONSORY, Brookfield, WI, pg. 972
Beidle, Jennifer, Specialist-PR -- MCGOWAN CRAIN, Saint Louis, MO, pg. 735
Beilock, Ola, Acct Dir -- Ogilvy PR, San Francisco, CA, pg. 1606
Beirne, Ailbhe, Art Dir -- Target McConnells, Dublin, Ireland, pg. 1227
Beke, James, Art Dir -- BBH LA, West Hollywood, CA, pg. 95
Bekerman, Sara, Strategist-Creative -- CODE AND THEORY, New York, NY, pg. 219
Bekhazi, David, Dir-Creative -- Horizon FCB Beirut, Beirut, Lebanon, pg. 375
Bekker, Carla, Art Dir -- M&C Saatchi Abel, Cape Town, South Africa, pg. 678
Bekkering, Herman, Dir-Creative-Natl -- PATTISON OUTDOOR ADVERTISING, Oakville, Canada, pg. 878
Bekkerman, Rachel, Acct Exec -- RUDER FINN INC., New York, NY, pg. 1642
Bekti, Aji, Assoc Dir-Creative -- Ogilvy & Mather, Jakarta, Indonesia, pg. 845
Belcher, Randy, Dir-Creative -- DONER, Southfield, MI, pg. 322
Bele, Frank, Sr VP & Exec Dir-Creative -- PUBLICIS NEW YORK, New York, NY, pg. 935
Belhumeur, Pilar, Partner & Exec Dir-Creative -- GREATER THAN ONE, New York, NY, pg. 441
Belisle, Lindsay, Acct Dir-Intl -- OMD NORTH AMERICA, New York, NY, pg. 1378
Belk, Howard, Co-CEO & Chief Creative Officer -- SIEGEL+GALE, New York, NY, pg. 1041
Belko, Tomas, Dir-Creative -- Mather Communications s.r.o., Prague, Czech Republic, pg. 830
Belko, Tomas, Exec Dir-Creative -- Ogilvy & Mather, Prague, Czech Republic, pg. 830
Bell, Brendan, Acct Dir -- Razorfish Atlanta, Atlanta, GA, pg. 1309
Bell, Gaelen, VP-Social Mktg & PR -- MSI, Chicago, IL, pg. 785
Bell, Hank, Media Planner & Buyer -- LOVE ADVERTISING INC., Houston, TX, pg. 669
Bell, Jeff, Sr Acct Exec-PR -- GLYNNDEVINS ADVERTISING & MARKETING, Overland Park, KS, pg. 430
Bell, Jonathan, Dir-Creative -- D4 Mccann, Guatemala, Guatemala, pg. 721
Bell, Lisa, VP-PR -- 451 MARKETING, Boston, MA, pg. 1436
Bell, Lisa, Owner & Chief Creative Officer -- TIVOLI PARTNERS, Charlotte, NC, pg. 1146
Bell, Lucinda, Acct Exec -- Hill & Knowlton Australia Pty. Ltd., Sydney, Australia, pg. 1545
Bell, Mike, Dir-Creative -- HILE DESIGN LLC, Ann Arbor, MI, pg. 514
Bell, Peter, Creative Dir -- TRACTION FACTORY, Milwaukee, WI, pg. 1153
Bell, Rebekah, Acct Dir -- R&R PARTNERS, Las Vegas, NV, pg. 945
Bell, Scott, Grp Dir-Creative -- DROGA5, New York, NY, pg. 328
Bell, Stephen, Exec Dir-Creative -- Coley Porter Bell, London, United Kingdom, pg. 836
Bell, Stephen, Exec Dir-Creative -- Coley Porter Bell, London, United Kingdom, pg. 1218
Bell, Stephen, VP & Acct Supvr -- Havas Life Metro, Chicago, IL, pg. 487
Bellemare, Jay, Dir-Creative -- PANNOS MARKETING, Bedford, NH, pg. 871
Bellerive, David, VP-Creative & Interactive -- PHOENIX GROUP, Regina, Canada, pg. 889
Belletini, Sergio, VP & Dir-Creative -- FRASER COMMUNICATIONS, Los Angeles, CA, pg. 402
Belling, Noelle, Acct Supvr -- ZAMBEZI, Venice, CA, pg. 1254
Bellini, Giuliano, Dir-Creative -- MRM Worldwide, Milan, Italy, pg. 783
Bellis, Alexandra, Acct Supvr -- GRUPO GALLEGOS, Huntington Beach, CA, pg. 463
Bello, Gerard, Art Dir -- NOTIONIST, Westlake Village, CA, pg. 817
Belloir, Katharine, Acct Supvr -- BALDWIN&, Raleigh, NC, pg. 88
Bellotti, Fernando, Creative Dir -- Leo Burnett Mexico S.A. de C.V., Mexico, Mexico, pg. 640
Bellucci, Mark, Co-Dir-Creative & Copywriter -- GRAHAM & COMPANY ADVERTISING, INC., Melville, NY, pg. 438
Belmont, Dick, VP-Creative Svcs -- THE BCB GROUP, INC., Wallingford, CT, pg. 119
Belmont, Kaitlyn, Acct Supvr -- Ruder Finn, San Francisco, CA, pg. 1642
Belmonte, Gianluca, Assoc Dir-Creative -- FCB Milan, Milan, Italy, pg. 373
Belmore, Chris, Acct Dir -- SAATCHI & SAATCHI, New York, NY, pg. 1000
Belo, Sofia, Acct Dir -- McCann Worldgroup Portugal, Lisbon, Portugal, pg. 726
Belot, Mark, Acct Dir -- ZAMBEZI, Venice, CA, pg. 1254
Belote, Alexis, Media Planner -- OGILVY COMMONHEALTH WORLDWIDE, Parsippany, NJ, pg. 851
Beltran, Maximiliano, Acct Exec -- Del Campo Nazca Saatchi & Saatchi, Buenos Aires, Argentina, pg. 1007
Beltran, Ricardo, Dir-Creative -- Publicis-CB, Bogota, Colombia, pg. 929
Bemfica, Miguel, Dir-Creative-Global -- McCann Worldgroup Johannesburg, Johannesburg, South Africa, pg. 727
Ben Dror, Ori, Acct Exec -- BBR Saatchi & Saatchi, Ramat Gan, Israel, pg. 1003
Ben, Jaison, Assoc Dir-Creative -- FP7, Muscat, Oman, pg. 725
Ben, Jaison, Assoc Dir-Creative -- FP7, Manama, Bahrain, pg. 717
Ben-Shoham, Maayan, Acct Supvr -- Adler, Chomski Grey, Tel Aviv, Israel, pg. 450
Benabib, Donna, Exec Coord-Creative -- YOUNG & RUBICAM, New York, NY, pg. 1239
Benavidez, Rachel, Dir-PR -- CREATIVE CIVILIZATION AN AGUILAR/GIRARD AGENCY, San Antonio, TX, pg. 246
Bench, Becca, Acct Coord -- BLAINE WARREN ADVERTISING LLC, Las Vegas, NV, pg. 135
Bendavid, Matty, Acct Supvr -- JOHN ST., Toronto, Canada, pg. 593
Bender, Dawn, Mgr-Creative Svcs -- GRIGG GRAPHIC SERVICES, INC., Southfield, MI, pg. 460
Bender, Jason, Exec Dir-Creative -- ROCKFISH, Rogers, AR, pg. 1312
Bender, Jesse, Acct Dir -- ALLEBACH COMMUNICATIONS, Souderton, PA, pg. 46
Bender, Matthew, Acct Exec -- RADIUS ADVERTISING, Strongsville, OH, pg. 949
Bender, Sharon, Media Planner & Buyer-Digital -- IONIC MEDIA, Woodland Hills, CA, pg. 559
Benditz, Chad, Specialist-Mktg & PR -- MICROMASS COMMUNICATIONS INC, Cary, NC, pg. 755
Benedetti, Anthony, Acct Dir -- MARTINO FLYNN LLC, Pittsford, NY, pg. 705
Benesa, Gra, Art Dir -- Young & Rubicam Philippines, Manila, Philippines, pg. 1244
Benett, Andrew, CEO-Havas Worldwide & Havas Creative Grp -- HAVAS PR, New York, NY, pg. 1537
Benett, Andrew, CEO-Havas Worldwide & Havas Creative Grp -- Havas PR, New York, NY, pg. 487
Benevides, Vico, Exec Creative Dir -- J. Walter Thompson, Sao Paulo, Brazil, pg. 577
Benford, Trudi, Sr VP & Dir-Creative Svcs -- Greer, Margolis, Mitchell, Burns & Associates (GMMB), Washington, DC, pg. 1518
Benhaim, Melissa, Acct Exec -- CHERYL ANDREWS MARKETING COMMUNICATIONS, Coral Gables, FL, pg. 1477
Benitez, Gabriela, Acct Dir -- KBS+, New York, NY, pg. 604

Personnel Index

Benito, Molly, Mgr-PR -- A.WORDSMITH, Portland, OR, pg. 1447
Benivegna, Marybeth, Sr Creative Dir -- PILOT, New York, NY, pg. 891
Benjamin, Jake, Grp Creative Dir -- THE VIA AGENCY, Portland, ME, pg. 1175
Benjamin, Jay, Chief Creative Officer & Exec VP -- SAATCHI & SAATCHI, New York, NY, pg. 1000
Benjamin, Jay, Chief Creative Officer -- Saatchi & Saatchi New York, New York, NY, pg. 1001
Benjamin, Jessica, Acct Supvr -- Cone Communications LLC, New York, NY, pg. 1484
Benjamin, Kelsey, Acct Exec -- GYK Antler, Boston, MA, pg. 468
Benkaci, Mehdi, Art Dir -- Grey Paris, Paris, France, pg. 449
Benn, Clayton, Sr Acct Exec-Creative Strategy -- GLOW INTERACTIVE, INC., New York, NY, pg. 430
Benner, Phillip, Creative Dir & Copywriter -- Grey Group Germany, Dusseldorf, Germany, pg. 449
Bennett, Brad, VP & Acct Dir -- CAPSTRAT, Raleigh, NC, pg. 1472
Bennett, Colin, Mgr-Traffic -- IDEAS COLLIDE INC., Scottsdale, AZ, pg. 534
Bennett, Dan, Partner & Dir-Creative -- ELEMENT ELEVEN, Nixa, MO, pg. 342
Bennett, Greg, Creative Dir -- B CREATIVE GROUP INC., Baltimore, MD, pg. 84
Bennett, Kevin, Strategist-Acct & Media Buyer -- MEDIACROSS, INC., Saint Louis, MO, pg. 744
Bennett, Lisa, Chief Creative Officer & Partner-Creative -- TM ADVERTISING, Dallas, TX, pg. 1147
Bennett, Myron, Dir-Creative Svcs -- THIRD WAVE DIGITAL, Macon, GA, pg. 1140
Bennett, Nicholas Hayward, Acct Exec -- SCOPPECHIO, Louisville, KY, pg. 1026
Bennett, Pam, Sr Media Planner & Media Buyer -- THE WENDT AGENCY, Great Falls, MT, pg. 1197
Bennett, Patrick, Dir-Creative -- SBPR CORP., Fort Lauderdale, FL, pg. 1646
Bennett, Paul, Acct Exec -- HR ADWORKS LTD., Winnipeg, Canada, pg. 526
Bennett, Susan, Partner & Exec Dir-Creative -- SIMPLE TRUTH COMMUNICATION PARTNERS, Chicago, IL, pg. 1046
Bennett, Tricia, Sr Mgr-PR -- GROUNDFLOOR MEDIA, INC., Denver, CO, pg. 1534
Bennett-Day, Steven, Grp Exec Dir-Creative -- Helia, London, United Kingdom, pg. 498
Bennett-Day, Steven, Grp Exec Dir-Creative -- Helia, London, United Kingdom, pg. 485
Benoit, Genevieve, Acct Coord -- Cohn & Wolfe, Toronto, Canada, pg. 1481
Benourida, Brittany, Acct Exec -- McCann Erickson/New York, New York, NY, pg. 714
Benourida, Brittany, Acct Exec-McCann HumanCare -- McCann Erickson North America, New York, NY, pg. 715
Benscoter, Adam, Acct Supvr -- HABERMAN & ASSOCIATES, INC., Minneapolis, MN, pg. 471
Benson, Kurtis, Editor-Creative -- MARTIN/WILLIAMS ADVERTISING INC., Minneapolis, MN, pg. 704
Benson-Winans, Debby, Sr Producer & Mgr-Office-Cresta Creative -- Cresta West, Los Angeles, CA, pg. 254
Benson-Winans, Deborah, Office Mgr & Sr Producer-Cresta Creative -- CRESTA CREATIVE, Chicago, IL, pg. 253
Bensten, Jessica, Creative Dir -- RUBIN COMMUNICATIONS GROUP, Virginia Beach, VA, pg. 1642
Bentley, Jeff, Dir-Creative -- BLUE C, Costa Mesa, CA, pg. 140
Bentley, Perry Ryan, VP, Sr Dir-Creative, Designer-Web & Graphic Designer -- GRAFITZ GROUP NETWORK, Huntington, WV, pg. 438
Benton, Kelly, Acct Exec -- ADVOCATE DIGITAL MEDIA, Victoria, TX, pg. 35
Benton, Laura, Acct Exec -- BLATTEL COMMUNICATIONS, San Francisco, CA, pg. 137
Benton, Sean, VP, Dir-Creative & Copywriter -- PARTNERS CREATIVE, Missoula, MT, pg. 875
Beraldo, Fabiano, Head-Brdcst Production -- DM9DDB, Sao Paulo, Brazil, pg. 278
Beran, Paul F., Pres, CEO & Dir-Creative -- ADVERTEL, INC., Pittsburgh, PA, pg. 34
Berbari, Alejandro, Sr VP & Dir-Creative -- MARCA MIAMI, Coconut Grove, FL, pg. 692
Berberich, Garrett, Acct Exec -- HIMMELRICH PR, Baltimore, MD, pg. 515
Berckes, Monica, Principal & Dir-New Bus -- DM2 DESIGN CONSULTANCY, Edgewater, NJ, pg. 318
Bercovici, Adam, Acct Exec -- MACLAREN MCCANN CANADA INC., Toronto, Canada, pg. 682
Berdala, Alba, Acct Dir -- McCann Erickson Advertising Ltd., London, United Kingdom, pg. 729
Berenson, Mike, Sr Editor-Creative -- HAMMER CREATIVE, Hollywood, CA, pg. 477
Beres, Krista, Acct Supvr -- ROUNTREE GROUP COMMUNICATIONS MANAGEMENT, Alpharetta, GA, pg. 1640
Berg, Bill, Producer-Brdcst -- DROGA5, New York, NY, pg. 328
Berg, Keith, Acct Exec -- EXCALIBUR EXHIBITS, Houston, TX, pg. 1412
Berg, Mattias, Assoc Dir-Creative -- CP+B, Gothenburg, Sweden, pg. 240
Bergabo, Victor, Art Dir -- Saatchi & Saatchi, Stockholm, Sweden, pg. 1006
Bergan, Gregg, Owner & Chief Creative Officer -- PURE BRAND COMMUNICATIONS, LLC, Denver, CO, pg. 938
Bergas-Coria, Fernando, Acct Exec -- THE SHIPYARD, Columbus, OH, pg. 1038
Bergen, Chris, Acct Dir -- VENABLES, BELL & PARTNERS, San Francisco, CA, pg. 1172
Bergen, Matt, Dir-Interactive Creative -- RISDALL MARKETING GROUP, New Brighton, MN, pg. 982
Berger, Paul, Acct Dir -- OBI CREATIVE, Omaha, NE, pg. 821
Berger, Stephanie, Acct Dir -- /Auditoire, Paris, France, pg. 1118
Bergeron, Jason, Dir-Creative -- DONER, Southfield, MI, pg. 322
Berggard, Goran, Acct Dir -- Havas Worldwide Granath, Stockholm, Sweden, pg. 496
Bergh, Danielle, Acct Dir -- ADJECTIVE & CO, Jacksonville Beach, FL, pg. 28
Bergius, Hanna, Acct Dir -- MediaCom Sverige AB, Stockholm, Sweden, pg. 1370
Berglund, Nicholas, Art Dir -- PETERSON MILLA HOOKS, Minneapolis, MN, pg. 886
Bergman, Hilary, Acct Exec -- ArnoldNYC, New York, NY, pg. 72
Bergman, Robert, Exec Dir-Creative -- M/PAKT, New York, NY, pg. 680
Bergmann, Caitlin, Dir-Content & Creative -- MEDIACOM, New York, NY, pg. 1367
Bergmann, Robyn, Dir-Creative -- Ogilvy Johannesburg (Pty.) Ltd., Johannesburg, South Africa, pg. 849
Bergner, Alicia, Grp Dir-Creative -- MOSAK ADVERTISING & INSIGHTS, Austin, TX, pg. 778
Berkheiser, Anna, Assoc Dir-Creative -- CATCH 24 ADVERTISING & DESIGN, New York, NY, pg. 198
Berkley, Abigail, Acct Exec -- RED LION, Toronto, Canada, pg. 961
Berlamino, Lauren, Acct Dir-Global Brands -- Adrenaline- A Havas Company, New York, NY, pg. 487
Berlamino, Lauren, Acct Dir-Global Brands -- Havas Worldwide-Strat Farm, New York, NY, pg. 490
Berman, Drummond, Grp Head-Creative -- Merkley + Partners/Healthworks, New York, NY, pg. 750
Berman, Drummond, Grp Head-Creative -- MERKLEY+PARTNERS, New York, NY, pg. 750
Berman, Joyce, Acct Coord -- CARYL COMMUNICATIONS, INC., Paramus, NJ, pg. 194
Berman, Ryan, Founder & Chief Creative Officer -- THE I.D.E.A. BRAND, San Diego, CA, pg. 533
Bermejo, Noel, Deputy Exec Dir-Creative -- McCann Erickson (Philippines), Inc., Manila, Philippines, pg. 725
Bermudez, Alejandro, Dir-Creative -- McCann Erickson Corp. (S.A.), Medellin, Colombia, pg. 719
Bermudez, Anna Lopez, Acct Exec -- Edelman, Barcelona, Spain, pg. 1506
Bernal, Maru, Creative Dir -- Lapiz, Chicago, IL, pg. 638
Bernardo, Alessandro, Dir-Creative -- Leo Burnett Tailor Made, Sao Paulo, Brazil, pg. 640
Bernardo, James, Chief Creative Officer -- FCB Manila, Makati, Philippines, pg. 381
Bernardo, Lauren, Acct Dir -- 6DEGREES INTEGRATED COMMUNICATIONS, Toronto, Canada, pg. 10
Bernath, Mark, Exec Creative Dir -- Wieden + Kennedy - Amsterdam, Amsterdam, Netherlands, pg. 1203
Bernath, Mark, Exec Dir-Creative -- WIEDEN + KENNEDY, INC., Portland, OR, pg. 1202
Bernath, Mark, Exec Dir-Creative -- Wieden + Kennedy-New York, New York, NY, pg. 1204
Berney, Richard, Dir-Art & Creative -- 303LOWE, Sydney, Australia, pg. 789
Bernie, T., Dir-PR -- CIRCLE OF ONE MARKETING, Miami, FL, pg. 211
Bernier, Brian, Assoc Dir-Creative -- PJA, Cambridge, MA, pg. 894
Bernier, Jean-Francois, Pres & Dir-Creative -- ALFRED COMMUNICATIONS, Montreal, Canada, pg. 45
Bernstein, Baeu, Dir-Creative -- Publicis Seattle, Seattle, WA, pg. 927
Bernstein, Baeu, Dir-Creative -- Publicis Seattle, Seattle, WA, pg. 936
Bernstein, David, Chief Creative Officer -- THE GATE WORLDWIDE NEW YORK, New York, NY, pg. 417
Bernstein, Ilyssa, Acct Exec -- THE A TEAM, LLC, New York, NY, pg. 1403
Bernstein, Ilyssa, Acct Exec -- The A Team Promotional, Irvine, CA, pg. 1403
Bernstein, Jeremy, Exec VP & Grp Dir-Creative -- deutschMedia, New York, NY, pg. 303
Berrien, Lacey, Mgr-PR -- ALLEN & GERRITSEN, Boston, MA, pg. 46
Berrio, Angela, Media Planner -- Havas Media, Miami, FL, pg. 1340
Berrios, Edwin, Dir-Creative -- DDM ADVERTISING INC, Miami, FL, pg. 290
Berry, Andrea Clarke, Mgr-PR-Cisco Canada -- STRATEGICAMPERSAND INC., Toronto, Canada, pg. 1091
Berry, Anna, Specialist-PR -- RED JEWELED MEDIA, Englewood, CO, pg. 1632
Berry, Courtney, Sr VP & Acct Dir -- GREY GROUP, New York, NY, pg. 445
Berry, Kathleen, Acct Supvr -- S&D MARKETING ADVERTISING, Denver, CO, pg. 999
Berry, Megan, Mgr-Creative Svcs -- STANTON COMMUNICATIONS, INC., Washington, DC, pg. 1654
Berry, Vanessa, Acct Coord -- LIGHTHOUSE MARKETING, East Syracuse, NY, pg. 657
Berryman, Megan, Dir-Creative -- SPRINGBOX, LTD., Austin, TX, pg. 1068
Bersier, Laurine, Acct Exec -- Havas Worldwide Geneva, Geneva, Switzerland, pg. 496
Berstler, Aaron, Grp Acct Dir-Bus PR -- KOHNSTAMM COMMUNICATIONS, Saint Paul, MN, pg. 616
Bertagni, Diego, Assoc Dir-Creative -- DDB Canada, Edmonton, Canada, pg. 273
Bertagni, Diego, Assoc Dir-Creative -- Tribal Worldwide Toronto, Toronto, Canada, pg. 1316
Bertelli, Bruno, Exec Creative Dir -- Publicis Networks, Milan, Italy, pg. 920
Bertelli, Bruno, CEO & Exec Dir-Creative -- Publicis S.R.L., Milan, Italy, pg. 920
Berth, Tom, Dir-Creative -- Publicis, Brussels, Belgium, pg. 1406
Berth, Tom, Creative Dir -- Publicis, Brussels, Belgium, pg. 917
Berthiaume, Cathy, Dir-Creative Svcs -- SABA AGENCY, Bakersfield, CA, pg. 1012
Berthume, Josh, CEO & Dir-Creative -- SWASH LABS, Denton, TX, pg. 1103
Bertino, Fred, Pres & Chief Creative Officer -- MMB, Boston, MA, pg. 767
Berton, Alberto, Art Dir & Copywriter -- Adell Taivas Ogilvy, Vilnius, Lithuania, pg. 833
Bertrand, Victor, Dir-Creative -- FCB CREA, Tegucigalpa, Honduras, pg. 378
Bertschat, Alexander, Art Dir -- Grey Group Germany, Dusseldorf, Germany, pg. 449
Bertz, Traci, Dir-Creative Svcs -- OSBORN & BARR COMMUNICATIONS, Saint Louis, MO, pg. 864
Berzewski, Rebecca, Acct Dir -- TAYLOR WEST ADVERTISING, San Antonio, TX, pg. 1113
Besabe, Bobby, Assoc Dir-Creative-Interactive -- BPG ADVERTISING, Los Angeles, CA, pg. 152
Besagni, Juan Marcos, Creative Dir -- Ogilvy & Mather Argentina, Buenos Aires, Argentina, pg. 837
Beseau, Alana, Assoc Dir-Creative -- Weber Shandwick-Chicago, Chicago, IL, pg. 1677
Besier, Brittany, Media Planner -- DIGITAS HEALTH, Philadelphia, PA, pg. 309
Besseling, Nick, Acct Dir -- HeathWallace Ltd, Reading, United Kingdom, pg. 1227
Bessell, Scott, Dir-Creative -- SONNHALTER, Berea, OH, pg. 1058
Bessire, Jeremy, Dir-Creative Svcs -- DIRECT MARKETING SOLUTIONS, Portland, OR, pg. 311
Bessler, Larry, Chief Creative Officer -- RPM/Las Vegas, Las Vegas, NV, pg. 995
Betcher, Katherine, Dir-Art & Creative -- HANSON WATSON ASSOCIATES, Moline, IL, pg. 479
Betoulaud, Gregoire, Dir-Creative -- Carre Noir, Suresnes, France, pg. 918
Bettencourt, Brian, Sr Dir-Creative -- WATT INTERNATIONAL, INC., Toronto, Canada, pg. 1192

Personnel Index

Personnel Index

Concord, NC, pg. 1187
Campbell, Brad, Dir-Creative -- MARKET CONNECTIONS, Asheville, NC, pg. 695
Campbell, Chad, Sr Art Dir -- AMERICOM MARKETING, Beaumont, TX, pg. 54
Campbell, Chris, Acct Dir -- FALLON WORLDWIDE, Minneapolis, MN, pg. 366
Campbell, Chris, Exec Dir-Creative -- INTERBRAND CORPORATION, New York, NY, pg. 551
Campbell, Cosmo, Chief Creative Officer & Sr VP -- DDB Canada, Toronto, Canada, pg. 274
Campbell, Craig, VP-Mktg & Creative Svcs -- NEIMAN MARCUS ADVERTISING, Dallas, TX, pg. 1271
Campbell, Elizabeth, VP & Acct Dir -- BBDO WORLDWIDE INC., New York, NY, pg. 99
Campbell, Gina, Mgr-Bus Dev & Traffic -- KOCH COMMUNICATIONS, Oklahoma City, OK, pg. 1567
Campbell, James, Dir-Creative -- SWITCH, Saint Louis, MO, pg. 1105
Campbell, Jennifer, VP & Acct Dir -- HOT DISH ADVERTISING, Minneapolis, MN, pg. 524
Campbell, Justin, Dir-Creative -- MODERN CLIMATE, Minneapolis, MN, pg. 770
Campbell, Lindsay, Acct Exec -- CRC MARKETING SOLUTIONS, Eden Prairie, MN, pg. 1410
Campbell, Martha, Project Mgr & Mgr-Traffic -- SUKLE ADVERTISING, INC., Denver, CO, pg. 1097
Campbell, Milo, Creative Dir & Copywriter -- Abbott Mead Vickers BBDO, London, United Kingdom, pg. 112
Campbell, Patrick, Assoc Dir-Creative -- STERLING RICE GROUP, Boulder, CO, pg. 1084
Campbell, Ray, Dir-Creative -- SUPEROXYGEN, INC., Los Angeles, CA, pg. 1100
Campbell, Tom, Dir-Creative -- THIEL DESIGN LLC, Milwaukee, WI, pg. 1138
Campbell, Tommy, Sr VP & Dir-Creative -- BROTHERS & CO., Tulsa, OK, pg. 170
Campbell, Veronika Luquin, Acct Supvr -- MUH-TAY-ZIK HOF-FER, San Francisco, CA, pg. 786
Campbell, Walter, Dir-Creative -- TBWA/UK Group, London, United Kingdom, pg. 1125
Campeau, Jean-Francois, Art Dir -- LUQUIRE GEORGE ANDREWS, INC., Charlotte, NC, pg. 674
Campese, Jeff, Partner & Dir-Creative -- RED ROCKET STUDIOS, Orlando, FL, pg. 962
Campfield, Melanie, Acct Exec -- PBJS, INC., Seattle, WA, pg. 880
Campisto, Claudio, Exec Creative Dir -- DDB Chile, Santiago, Chile, pg. 279
Campolina, Priscilla, Acct Supvr -- DM9DDB, Sao Paulo, Brazil, pg. 278
Campopiano, Javier, Chief Creative Officer -- Conill Advertising, Inc., El Segundo, CA, pg. 230
Campopiano, Javier, Chief Creative Officer -- Del Campo Nazca Saatchi & Saatchi, Buenos Aires, Argentina, pg. 1007
Campopiano, Javier, Chief Creative Officer-Latin America & Multicultural USA -- Saatchi & Saatchi Latin America, Miami, FL, pg. 1000
Campos, Belen Moy, Acct Dir -- Olabuenaga Chemistri, Mexico, Mexico, pg. 929
Campos, Demian, Dir-Creative & Art -- Publicis 67, Caracas, Venezuela, pg. 930
Campos, Giselle, Sr Art Dir -- INNOVISION MARKETING GROUP, San Diego, CA, pg. 548
Campos, Julio, Founder & Exec Dir-Creative -- CAMPOS CREATIVE WORKS, Santa Monica, CA, pg. 188
Campos-Trone, Miquela, Acct Supvr -- THE DIALOG MARKETING GROUP, Austin, TX, pg. 306
Campoverde, Luis, Dir-Creative -- Maruri, Guayaquil, Ecuador, pg. 1596
Canada, Emily, Acct Exec-PR -- The Sells Agency, Inc., Fayetteville, AR, pg. 1031
Canada, Olivia, Assoc Media Buyer -- MASON, INC., Bethany, CT, pg. 707
Canas, Claudia, Assoc Dir-Creative -- GRUPO GALLEGOS, Huntington Beach, CA, pg. 463
Canavan, Mark, Sr VP & Grp Dir-Creative -- McCann Erickson, Birmingham, MI, pg. 715
Canavan, Mark, Sr VP & Grp Dir-Creative -- McCann Worldgroup, San Francisco, CA, pg. 715
Canchola, Serafin, Founder, CEO & Creative Dir -- FUSEBOXWEST, Los Angeles, CA, pg. 410
Candanedo, Idy, Acct Dir -- LOPITO, ILEANA & HOWIE, INC., Guaynabo, PR, pg. 669
Candelario, Yudelka, Acct Supvr -- GREY GROUP, New York, NY, pg. 445
Candelori, Michael, Dir-Creative -- ATS MOBILE, King of Prussia, PA, pg. 1406
Candido, Jeff, Creative Dir -- Leo Burnett USA, Chicago, IL, pg. 639
Candiotti, Fred, Partner & Dir-Creative -- CGT MARKETING LLC, Amityville, NY, pg. 203
Candito, Alessandro, Dir-Art & Supvr-Creative -- Publicis Networks, Milan, Italy, pg. 920
Candito, Alessandro, Dir-Art & Supvr-Creative -- Publicis S.R.L., Milan, Italy, pg. 920
Candler, April, Acct Exec -- FCB GLOBAL, New York, NY, pg. 370
Candor, Rob, Creative Dir -- CARING MARKETING SOLUTIONS, Columbus, OH, pg. 191
Cane, Tony, Dir-Creative -- BLUE OLIVE CONSULTING, Florence, AL, pg. 141
Canga, Nikki, Acct Dir -- FROZEN FIRE, Dallas, TX, pg. 406
Canjura, Rodrigo, Dir-Creative -- Publicidad Comercial, La Libertad, El Salvador, pg. 557
Cannavino, Allison, Acct Dir -- TBC Direct, Inc., Baltimore, MD, pg. 1113
Cannavino, Allison, Acct Dir -- TBC, INC./PR DIVISION, Baltimore, MD, pg. 1659
Canning, Michael, Exec Dir-Creative -- M&C Saatchi, Sydney, Australia, pg. 677
Cannon, Christopher, Assoc Dir-Creative -- BBDO WORLDWIDE INC., New York, NY, pg. 99
Cannon, Sam, Exec Dir-Creative-North America -- Razorfish Chicago, Chicago, IL, pg. 1310
Cannon, Sarah, Acct Exec -- PLANIT, Baltimore, MD, pg. 896
Cannon, William, Dir-Creative -- mcgarrybowen, Chicago, IL, pg. 734
Cannova, Kate, Mgr-Strategic Svcs & Acct Supvr -- CAHG, New York, NY, pg. 184
Cano, Adrian, Creative Dir -- PM PUBLICIDAD, Atlanta, GA, pg. 898
Cano, Oscar, Acct Supvr -- GMR Marketing Spain, Madrid, Spain, pg. 1415
Cano, Roger, Creative Dir -- TBWA Espana, Barcelona, Spain, pg. 1123
Canright, David, Dir-Creative -- THE RICHARDS GROUP, INC., Dallas, TX, pg. 978
Canright, David, Grp Head-Creative -- RICHARDS PARTNERS, Dallas, TX, pg. 1636
Cantau, Stephanie, Acct Dir -- MediaCom Paris, Paris, France, pg. 1369
Cantero, Jorge, Assoc Dir-Creative -- TVGLA, Los Angeles, CA, pg. 1163
Cantillo, Alexis, Acct Exec -- MICHELSEN ADVERTISING, Doral, FL, pg. 754
Cantilo, Joy, Media Planner & Media Buyer -- MEDIA BROKERS INTERNATIONAL, INC., Alpharetta, GA, pg. 1364
Canton, Jorge, Acct Dir -- MEC, Los Angeles, CA, pg. 1356
Cantor, Yoryi, Dir-Creative -- Publicis 67, Caracas, Venezuela, pg. 930
Cantrell, Mary Alice, Mgr-Print Production -- THE CREATIVE OUTHOUSE, Atlanta, GA, pg. 251
Cantrell, Ryan, Jr Acct Exec-PR -- INTEGRATE, Houston, TX, pg. 1551
Cantu, Amy, Acct Coord-Pub Affairs -- KGBTEXAS, San Antonio, TX, pg. 610
Cao, Justin, Art Dir -- TBWA/Vietnam, Ho Chi Minh City, Vietnam, pg. 1131
Cao, Yan, Acct Exec -- Genedigi Group, Beijing, China, pg. 1595
Capalby, Julie, Dir-Creative -- VSA PARTNERS, INC., Chicago, IL, pg. 1185
Capaldo, Luis, Dir-Creative -- DLC Integrated Marketing, Coral Gables, FL, pg. 291
Capanescu, Razvan, Chief Creative Officer & Copywriter -- Leo Burnett & Target SA, Bucharest, Romania, pg. 644
Capawana, Daniel, Acct Exec -- RESOUND MARKETING, Princeton, NJ, pg. 1635
Capcara, Linda, Dir-PR -- KEO MARKETING INC, Phoenix, AZ, pg. 1561
Capel, Brian Charles, Grp Exec Dir-Creative-Jakarta -- Leo Burnett Kreasindo Indonesia, Jakarta, Indonesia, pg. 649
Caperna, Fabrizio, Dir-Creative -- TBWA Roma, Rome, Italy, pg. 1121
Caplan, Chelsea, Acct Coord -- LUQUIRE GEORGE ANDREWS, INC., Charlotte, NC, pg. 674
Caplanis, Mike, Dir-Creative -- LMO ADVERTISING, Arlington, VA, pg. 665
Capobianco, Keith, Assoc Dir-Creative -- George P. Johnson Company, Inc., Boston, MA, pg. 422
Capone, Dominic, Acct Exec -- GIOVATTO ADVERTISING & CONSULTING INC., Paramus, NJ, pg. 426
Caponi, Maria Jose, Acct Dir -- Publicis Impetu, Montevideo, Uruguay, pg. 930
Caporimo, James, Exec Dir-Creative -- Y&R New York, New York, NY, pg. 1240
Caposino, Carol, VP & Dir-Creative Resources -- THE COMPANY OF OTHERS, Houston, TX, pg. 227
Cappello, Elizabeth, Acct Exec-eBay -- TRIAD RETAIL MEDIA, LLC, Saint Petersburg, FL, pg. 1156
Cappiello, Carrie, Acct Exec -- KOROBERI, Chapel Hill, NC, pg. 1567
Capps, Brooke, Strategist-Content & Creative -- SWELLSHARK, New York, NY, pg. 1104
Capps, Mike, Acct Exec -- HOWARD COMMUNICATIONS INC, Elsberry, MO, pg. 1547
Capron, Marlene Cimicato, Dir-PR -- KARLA OTTO, New York, NY, pg. 1558
Capsis, Emily, Media Buyer -- Initiative Melbourne, Melbourne, Australia, pg. 1347
Capurso, Krista, Acct Supvr -- TBC, INC./PR DIVISION, Baltimore, MD, pg. 1659
Caputo, Flora, VP & Exec Dir-Creative -- JACOBS AGENCY, Chicago, IL, pg. 584
Caputo, Gerard, Exec Dir-Creative -- BBH NEW YORK, New York, NY, pg. 118
Capuzzi, Silvia, Mgr-PR-TBWA/Italia Grp -- TBWA Roma, Rome, Italy, pg. 1121
Caraballo, Kristy Huszar, Sr VP & Acct Dir -- Echo Torre Lazur, Mountain Lakes, NJ, pg. 731
Caraker, Dave, Dir-Creative -- IRON CREATIVE COMMUNICATION, San Francisco, CA, pg. 561
Carango, Rich, Pres & Dir-Creative -- SCHUBERT COMMUNICATIONS, INC., Downingtown, PA, pg. 1025
Caraway, Brad, Assoc Dir-Creative -- PRICEWEBER MARKETING COMMUNICATIONS, INC., Louisville, KY, pg. 909
Carbone, Janelle, Acct Dir -- COLLE+MCVOY, Minneapolis, MN, pg. 221
Carbonella, Suzanne, Acct Supvr -- CRONIN & COMPANY, INC., Glastonbury, CT, pg. 255
Carcavilla, Kiko, Creative Dir -- Lowe Porta, Santiago, Chile, pg. 792
Cardelli-Contumelio, Renee, Strategist-Digital Content & PR -- EM MEDIA INC, Steubenville, OH, pg. 345
Cardemil, Francisco, Acct Exec -- Prolam Y&R S.A., Santiago, Chile, pg. 1249
Cardenas, Carlos, Art Dir -- Grey GCG Peru S.A.C., Lima, Peru, pg. 454
Cardenas, Cassandra, Creative Dir -- TRANSMEDIA GROUP, Boca Raton, FL, pg. 1665
Cardenas, Giancarlo, Art Dir -- TBWA Peru, Lima, Peru, pg. 1132
Cardenas, Juan, Creative Dir & Copywriter -- Ogilvy & Mather, Bogota, Colombia, pg. 839
Cardenas, Maria, Assoc Media Buyer -- INSPIRE!, Dallas, TX, pg. 549
Cardillo, Charlie, Pres & Dir-Creative -- UNDERGROUND ADVERTISING, San Francisco, CA, pg. 1166
Cardone, Emilie, Acct Coord -- CREATIVE COMMUNICATION ASSOCIATES, Albany, NY, pg. 246
Cardoso, Camila Paioli, Acct Dir -- Rapp Brazil, Sao Paulo, Brazil, pg. 953
Cardozo, Waldemar, Art Dir -- J. Walter Thompson, Sao Paulo, Brazil, pg. 577
Carducci, Rob, Dir-Creative -- GREY NEW YORK, New York, NY, pg. 446
Cardwell, Paul, Exec Creative Dir -- The Brand Union London, London, United Kingdom, pg. 157
Careless, Jonathan, Grp Dir-Creative -- MACLAREN MCCANN CANADA INC., Toronto, Canada, pg. 682
Carella, Patrick, Creative Dir -- FCB Garfinkel, New York, NY, pg. 371
Carew, Justin, Grp Head-Creative -- Leo Burnett Sydney, Sydney, Australia, pg. 647
Carey, Bruce, Dir-Creative-INSIDE-Los Angeles -- J. WALTER THOMPSON INSIDE, Los Angeles, CA, pg. 580
Carey, Jackie, Media Planner -- ZenithOptimedia, New York, NY, pg. 1398
Carey, Jennifer, Acct Dir -- CAPSTRAT, Raleigh, NC, pg. 1472
Carey, Jennifer, Dir-Creative Dept -- IDENTITY MARKETING & PUBLIC RELATIONS, LLC, Bingham Farms, MI, pg. 1548
Carey, Jim, Dir-Creative -- NORTH, Portland, OR, pg. 813
Carey, Rick, Principal & Dir-Creative -- CONRAD, PHILLIPS & VUTECH, INC., Columbus, OH, pg. 232

Personnel Index

Castellanos, Alexandra, Acct Exec -- Merkley + Partners/Healthworks, New York, NY, pg. 750
Castellanos, Claire, Acct Dir -- Lane Marketing, New York, NY, pg. 1572
Castellanos, Claire, Acct Dir -- LANE PR, Portland, OR, pg. 1571
Castellanos, David, Assoc Dir-Creative -- Deutsch LA, Los Angeles, CA, pg. 302
Castellanos, Rodrigo, Creative Dir & Copywriter -- Punto Ogilvy & Mather, Montevideo, Uruguay, pg. 840
Castelli, Federico, Supvr-Creative -- Wunderman, Milan, Italy, pg. 1233
Castiel, Juliette, Media Planner-Programmatic -- NEO@OGILVY, New York, NY, pg. 805
Castille, Sarah, Acct Exec -- THE BRADFORD GROUP, Nashville, TN, pg. 1459
Castillo, Hugo, VP-Creative & Dir -- ARNOLD WORLDWIDE, Boston, MA, pg. 71
Castillo, Jody, Assoc Dir-Creative -- Campaigns & Grey, Makati, Philippines, pg. 457
Castillo, Mara, Mgr-Creative Resourse & Traffic -- SIXSPEED, Minneapolis, MN, pg. 1048
Castillo, Ron, Sr VP & Dir-Creative -- GREY GROUP, New York, NY, pg. 445
Castle, Clark, Assoc Dir-Creative -- THE MARKETING CENTER OF THE UNIVERSE, New Orleans, LA, pg. 697
Castle, Colleen, Acct Supvr-Siemens & Plenty -- Ogilvy North America, New York, NY, pg. 828
Castle, Dave, Mgr-Traffic -- ADBAY, Casper, WY, pg. 26
Castle, Jeanette, Sr Project Mgr-Creative -- CAPSTRAT, Raleigh, NC, pg. 1472
Castledine, Paul, Partner-Creative & Chief Creative Officer -- Boxer, Birmingham, United Kingdom, pg. 1421
Castledine, Paul, Chief Creative Officer & Partner-Creative -- Boxer Creative, Birmingham, United Kingdom, pg. 1421
Castleton, Henry, Art Dir -- THE RICHARDS GROUP, INC., Dallas, TX, pg. 978
Castner, Sarah, Acct Dir-Global -- CP+B Boulder, Boulder, CO, pg. 240
Castrechini, Lina, Acct Supvr -- Ogilvy Montreal, Montreal, Canada, pg. 829
Castro, Felix, Dir-Creative -- THE WOW FACTOR, INC., Studio City, CA, pg. 1216
Castro, Gabriela, Acct Exec -- DDB Madrid, S.A., Madrid, Spain, pg. 288
Castro, Raul, Chief Creative Officer & Exec VP -- McCann Erickson (Philippines), Inc., Manila, Philippines, pg. 725
Catalano, Christina, Buyer-Brdcst-Natl -- Mindshare, New York, NY, pg. 1336
Catalano, Rob, Exec Creative Dir -- B&P ADVERTISING, Las Vegas, NV, pg. 84
Cataldo, Joyce, Acct Mgr-PR -- WALL STREET COMMUNICATIONS, Salt Lake City, UT, pg. 1672
Catalinac, Kate, Creative Dir -- GOODBY, SILVERSTEIN & PARTNERS, INC., San Francisco, CA, pg. 434
Cates, Laura, Media Planner & Media Buyer -- THE VIMARC GROUP, Louisville, KY, pg. 1177
Cathcart, Anne, Acct Exec -- TWOFIFTEENMCCANN, San Francisco, CA, pg. 1164
Cattaneo, Rana, Acct Supvr -- AKQA, INC., San Francisco, CA, pg. 1280
Catterton, David, Mgr-Creative Svcs -- DEANE/SMITH, Nashville, TN, pg. 1492
Catto, Beth, Acct Dir -- Philip Johnson Associates, San Francisco, CA, pg. 894
Catto, Beth, Acct Dir -- PJA Advertising + Marketing, San Francisco, CA, pg. 894
Caudle, Rosalyn, Acct Coord -- MOMENTUM MARKETING, Charleston, SC, pg. 770
Caufield, Heather, Acct Supvr -- COOPERKATZ & COMPANY, New York, NY, pg. 234
Cauich, Nancy, Specialist-Channel Investment & Media Buyer -- Lopez Negrete Communications West, Inc., Burbank, CA, pg. 669
Caulfield, Ben, Media Planner & Media Buyer -- RED COMMA MEDIA, INC., Madison, WI, pg. 1387
Cauret, Pierre, Art Dir -- BETC Life, Paris, France, pg. 492
Cavallone, Carlo, Exec Dir-Creative -- 72andSunny, Amsterdam, Netherlands, pg. 11
Cavallone, Carlo, Exec Dir-Creative -- 72ANDSUNNY, Playa Vista, CA, pg. 10
Cavanaugh, Jim, Sr VP-New Bus & Grp Acct Dir -- Jack Morton Exhibits, Robbinsville, NJ, pg. 583
Cavanaugh, Mark, Acct Dir -- SMITH, Spokane, WA, pg. 1053
Cavnar, Becky, Acct Coord -- ANGLIN PUBLIC RELATIONS, INC., Oklahoma City, OK, pg. 1444
Cavoli, Eric, Sr VP & Grp Dir-Creative -- CASHMAN & KATZ INTEGRATED COMMUNICATIONS, Glastonbury, CT, pg. 195
Cawley, Ian, Copywriter-Creative -- Doner, London, London, United Kingdom, pg. 323
Cawley, Ian, Copywriter-Creative -- Doner, London, London, United Kingdom, pg. 738
Cayrol, Gaelle, Acct Dir -- FCB Montreal, Montreal, Canada, pg. 372
Cazas, Kyrsten, Acct Exec -- BRUSTMAN CARRINO PUBLIC RELATIONS, Miami, FL, pg. 1464
Cecere, Ashley, Acct Dir -- KING & PARTNERS, LLC, New York, NY, pg. 612
Cecere, Joe, Pres & Chief Creative Officer -- LITTLE & COMPANY, Minneapolis, MN, pg. 662
Cecil, Christopher, Founder & Dir-Creative -- SLANT MEDIA LLC, Charleston, SC, pg. 1051
Cedeno, Manuel, Acct Exec -- CHERYL ANDREWS MARKETING COMMUNICATIONS, Coral Gables, FL, pg. 1477
Cederholm, Peter, Specialist-Online Video & Brdcst -- Initiative Universal Stockholm, Stockholm, Sweden, pg. 1346
Celand, Werner, Dir-Creative -- DDB Tribal Vienna, Vienna, Austria, pg. 277
Celestin, Joelle, VP & Dir-Creative -- VERSO ADVERTISING, INC., New York, NY, pg. 1174
Celing, Don, Mgr-Creative Svcs -- KINZIEGREEN MARKETING GROUP, Wausau, WI, pg. 613
Celis, Lupas, Dir-Creative -- Ogilvy & Mather, Bogota, Colombia, pg. 839
Cella, Joanna, Acct Supvr-Home Decor & Lifestyle -- ALISON BROD PUBLIC RELATIONS, New York, NY, pg. 1442
Cena, Kimberly, Media Planner & Media Buyer -- Maxus, Manila, Philippines, pg. 1354
Centofante, Nick, Media Dir -- VML-New York, New York, NY, pg. 1183
Cerafoli, Sherry, Acct Coord -- MORGAN & MYERS, INC., Waukesha, WI, pg. 774
Cerami, Charles, Acct Exec -- THE ALISON GROUP, North Miami Beach, FL, pg. 1404
Ceraso, Allison, Mng Dir & Chief Creative Officer -- Havas Life Metro, New York, NY, pg. 486
Ceraso, Allison, Co-Mng Dir & Chief Creative Officer -- Havas Life New York, New York, NY, pg. 487
Cerchia, Jennifer, Art Dir -- BBDO Proximity Berlin, Berlin, Germany, pg. 107
Cerdeira, Miguel Angel, Gen Dir-Creative -- Grey Chile, Santiago, Chile, pg. 453
Ceria, Arthur, Founder & Exec Dir-Creative -- CREATIVE FEED, San Francisco, CA, pg. 248
Cermak, Dave, Dir-Creative -- TRUNGALE EGAN + ASSOCIATES, Chicago, IL, pg. 1160
Cernuto, Nicoletta, Creative Dir -- J. Walter Thompson, Rome, Italy, pg. 573
Ceron, Armando, Dir-Creative & Art & Designer -- LEFT FIELD CREATIVE, Saint Louis, MO, pg. 635
Cerri, Martin, Grp Dir-Creative-Hispanic Market Div -- WALTON / ISAACSON, Culver City, CA, pg. 1189
Cerullo, Sam, Art Dir & Grp Creative Dir -- LEO BURNETT COMPANY LTD., Toronto, Canada, pg. 637
Cervantes, Sara, Acct Dir -- TBWA Peru, Lima, Peru, pg. 1132
Cerven, Jozef, Art Dir -- Lowe GGK, Bratislava, Slovakia, pg. 791
Cervera, Tina, Sr Vp & Exec Creative Dir -- VAYNERMEDIA, New York, NY, pg. 1319
Cerwin, Lori, Dir-Creative -- BRANDIMAGE DESGRIPPES & LAGA, Northbrook, IL, pg. 159
Cesano, Paolo, Dir-Creative -- J. Walter Thompson Milan, Milan, Italy, pg. 573
Cesarano, Kristina, Acct Exec -- 15 FINGERS LLC, Buffalo, NY, pg. 2
Cesnick, Megan, Acct Exec -- STRONG, Birmingham, AL, pg. 1092
Cessario, Mike, Assoc Dir-Creative & Copywriter -- HUMANAUT, Chattanooga, TN, pg. 528
Cevalte, Vincent, Acct Dir-Digital -- PROVE AGENCY, Los Angeles, CA, pg. 916
Cha, Sieun, Dir-Creative -- Method, San Francisco, CA, pg. 751
Cha, Sieun, Dir-Creative -- METHOD INC., San Francisco, CA, pg. 751
Chaban, Alexander, Dir-Creative -- Saatchi & Saatchi Brussels, Brussels, Belgium, pg. 1002
Chabot, Jamie, Dir-Creative -- CAPPELLI MILES, Portland, OR, pg. 190
Chacon, Cristina, Acct Supvr -- Almap BBDO, Sao Paulo, Brazil, pg. 102
Chacon, Jhon, Creative Dir -- Ogilvy & Mather, Bogota, Colombia, pg. 839
Chad, Lisa, Acct Dir -- Deutsch New York, New York, NY, pg. 302
Chadwick, George, Pres & Dir-Creative -- VERY, INC., Menlo Park, CA, pg. 1175
Chadwick, Philip, Dir-Creative Svcs -- PACE ADVERTISING, New York, NY, pg. 868
Chaffer, Elliott, VP-Creative -- TROLLBACK + COMPANY, New York, NY, pg. 1159
Chaigneau, Rogier, Art Dir -- DigitasLBi, Stockholm, Sweden, pg. 1289
Chaimoungkalo, Keeratie, Exec Creative Dir -- Leo Burnett, Bangkok, Thailand, pg. 651
Chain, Sarah, Mgr-Mktg & PR -- GAVIN ADVERTISING, York, PA, pg. 418
Chaiparnich, Jessica, Acct Exec -- GREY GROUP, New York, NY, pg. 445
Chaipornkaew, Golf Nuntawat, Exec Dir-Creative-Thailand -- Saatchi & Saatchi, Bangkok, Thailand, pg. 1012
Chakos, Christy, Acct Supvr -- Ogilvy & Mather, Chicago, IL, pg. 828
Chakravarty, Ashish, Creative Dir-Natl -- Contract Advertising (India) Limited, Mumbai, India, pg. 568
Chalekian, George, Dir-Creative -- YELLOW BUS LLC, Santa Cruz, CA, pg. 1238
Chalmers, Corey, Exec Dir-Creative-New Zealand -- Saatchi & Saatchi, Wellington, New Zealand, pg. 1012
Chamberlain, Alexis, Acct Dir-Manifesto Agency -- MANIFEST, Saint Louis, MO, pg. 1301
Chamberlain, Amie, Sr Media Buyer -- THE MORAN GROUP LLC, Baton Rouge, LA, pg. 773
Chamberlain, Dianne, Mgr-Internet Traffic & Acct Coord -- NANCY MARSHALL COMMUNICATIONS, Augusta, ME, pg. 1600
Chamberlain, Gabrielle, Acct Dir-The Americas -- Imagination the Americas, New York, NY, pg. 540
Chamberlain, Gabrielle, Acct Dir -- Imagination (USA) Inc., Dearborn, MI, pg. 540
Chamberlin, Florence, Principal & Dir-Creative -- FLEK, INC., Saint Johnsbury, VT, pg. 392
Chamberlin, Mark, Dir-Mktg & PR -- ARMSTRONG CHAMBERLIN, Haysville, KS, pg. 71
Chambers, Audrey, Acct Dir -- ACROBATANT, Tulsa, OK, pg. 21
Chambers, Brent, Exec Creative Dir -- FCB Auckland, Auckland, New Zealand, pg. 381
Chambers, Clayton, Dir-Creative -- WILLIAMS MEDIA GROUP, Lisbon, IA, pg. 1208
Chambers, J., Assoc Dir-Creative -- RODGERS TOWNSEND, LLC, Saint Louis, MO, pg. 989
Chambers, Jeff, Dir-Creative -- THE CREATIVE DEPARTMENT, Cincinnati, OH, pg. 247
Chambers, Melissa, Acct Exec -- SALES DEVELOPMENT ASSOCIATES, INC., Saint Louis, MO, pg. 1015
Chambers, Nicole, Acct Exec -- Commonwealth, Detroit, MI, pg. 714
Chambers, Todd, VP & Grp Dir-Creative -- BKV, INC., Atlanta, GA, pg. 133
Chamblin, Kirby, Art Dir -- BROCKTON CREATIVE GROUP, Kansas City, MO, pg. 168
Chambliss, Will, Grp Creative Dir -- MCKINNEY, Durham, NC, pg. 736
Chamorro Fajardo, Tito, VP-Creative -- Young & Rubicam Bogota, Bogota, Colombia, pg. 1249
Chamorro, Melisa, Art Dir -- Ogilvy & Mather, Paris, France, pg. 831
Chamrolia, Alka, Assoc Dir-Creative -- GLOBALWORKS, New York, NY, pg. 429
Chan, Adam, Dir-Creative -- BBDO Malaysia, Kuala Lumpur, Malaysia, pg. 116
Chan, Andy, Exec Dir-Creative -- FCB Shanghai, Shanghai, China, pg. 379
Chan, Bill, Creative Dir -- J. Walter Thompson, Shanghai, China, pg. 568
Chan, Bill, Exec Dir-Creative -- Ogilvy & Mather Advertising Beijing, Beijing, China, pg. 841
Chan, Denise, Acct Exec -- Text 100 Hong Kong, Wanchai, China (Hong Kong), pg. 1662
Chan, Emma, Grp Dir-Creative -- Lowe, Quarry Bay, China (Hong Kong), pg. 794
Chan, Jojo, Dir-Creative -- L3 ADVERTISING INC., New York, NY, pg. 621
Chan, Jonathan, Assoc Dir-Creative -- Havas Worldwide Beijing, Beijing, China, pg. 500
Chan, Jonathan, Assoc Dir-Creative -- Havas Worldwide Shanghai, Shanghai, China, pg. 500
Chan, Margaret, Acct Supvr -- Leo Burnett-Hong Kong, Quarry Bay,

Personnel Index

Chickan, Kirill, Creative Dir -- Provid BBDO, Kiev, Ukraine, pg. 112
Chidley, Margie, Dir-Creative -- ELEVEN INC., San Francisco, CA, pg. 343
Chikiamco, Arick, Dir-Creative -- ADCETERA GROUP, Houston, TX, pg. 26
Chikvaidze, Sopho, Acct Dir -- Momentum, Atlanta, GA, pg. 771
Childerhouse, Chris, Dir-Creative -- OGILVY & MATHER, New York, NY, pg. 826
Childerhouse, Chris, Dir-Creative -- Ogilvy New Zealand, Auckland, New Zealand, pg. 846
Childers, Justin, Media Planner & Media Buyer -- HANNA & ASSOCIATES INC., Coeur D'Alene, ID, pg. 478
Childress, Stephen, VP & Grp Dir-Creative -- ERWIN-PENLAND, Greenville, SC, pg. 354
Chilstrom, Lynda, Acct Dir -- GOFF PUBLIC, Saint Paul, MN, pg. 1528
Chilton, Virginia, Media Dir -- BILL HUDSON & ASSOCIATES, INC., ADVERTISING & PUBLIC RELATIONS, Nashville, TN, pg. 132
Chimal, Laura Abril, Art Dir -- Grey Mexico, S.A. de C.V, Mexico, Mexico, pg. 454
Chin, Ashley, Art Dir -- FCB Shanghai, Shanghai, China, pg. 379
Chin-Yu Chou, Bryan, Acct Exec -- TBWA Raad, Dubai, United Arab Emirates, pg. 1127
Ching, Wayne, Dir-Creative -- Ogilvy & Mather (Amsterdam) B.V., Amsterdam, Netherlands, pg. 833
Chiodo, Matt, Acct Dir -- Whybin TBWA, Melbourne, Australia, pg. 1128
Chiopelas, Kirsten, Acct Exec -- NORTON RUBBLE & MERTZ ADVERTISING, Chicago, IL, pg. 816
Chioran, Katie, Acct Exec -- Rosetta, Cleveland, OH, pg. 992
Chiorando, Rick, Principal & Chief Creative Officer -- AUSTIN & WILLIAMS, Hauppauge, NY, pg. 80
Chiromeridou, Amalia, Mgr-New Bus Dev -- Marketway Ltd., Nicosia, Cyprus, pg. 918
Chisholm, Gareth, Dir-Creative -- CREATIVE FEED, San Francisco, CA, pg. 248
Chitwood, Carla, Acct Coord -- CFX INC, Saint Louis, MO, pg. 202
Chitwood, Ken, Partner, Acct Dir & Dir-Media -- SASQUATCH, Portland, OR, pg. 1021
Chiu, Chris, CEO & Chief Creative Officer -- Leo Burnett, Singapore, Singapore, pg. 650
Chiu, James, Exec Dir-Creative-China -- Razorfish Hong Kong, Quarry Bay, China (Hong Kong), pg. 1310
Chiu, Kevin, Grp Dir-Creative -- Saatchi & Saatchi, Beijing, China, pg. 1010
Chiu, Kyle, Creative Dir -- Leo Burnett, Taipei, Taiwan, pg. 651
Cho, Alexander, Acct Exec -- OGILVY & MATHER, New York, NY, pg. 826
Cho, Amy, Dir-Creative -- PARA AGENCY, New York, NY, pg. 872
Cho, Phillip, Dir-Art & Assoc Dir-Creative -- OGILVY & MATHER, New York, NY, pg. 826
Cho, Tae-Ho, Acct Exec -- WPP US, New York, NY, pg. 1223
Cho, Yu Ming, Dir-Creative -- Grey Shanghai, Shanghai, China, pg. 455
Chodel, Peter, Dir-Creative -- Addison Group, London, United Kingdom, pg. 1216
Choe, Annie, Mgr-Creative Svcs -- Alcone Marketing Group, Darien, CT, pg. 1404
Choe, Edmund, Chief Creative Officer-Singapore & Southeast Asia-TBWA/Grp Asia -- TBWA Asia Pacific, Quarry Bay, China (Hong Kong), pg. 1128
Choe, Edmund, Chief Creative Officer-Singapore & Southeast Asia - - TBWA Beijing, Beijing, China, pg. 1128
Choe, Edmund, Chief Creative Officer -- TBWA Hong Kong, Hong Kong, China (Hong Kong), pg. 1128
Choi, Heejeong, Acct Supvr -- TBWA Korea, Seoul, Korea (South), pg. 1131
Choi, Jena, Acct Supvr -- OGILVY & MATHER, New York, NY, pg. 826
Choi, Jung, Sr VP-Creative -- MMI AGENCY, Houston, TX, pg. 768
Choi, Richard, Acct Dir -- PANCOM INTERNATIONAL, INC., Los Angeles, CA, pg. 871
Choi, Sally, Acct Dir -- IW GROUP, INC., West Hollywood, CA, pg. 564
Choi, Sarah, Dir-Creative-Copy -- ADASIA COMMUNICATIONS, INC., Englewood Cliffs, NJ, pg. 26
Cholez, Hugues, Creative Dir -- TBWA Paris, Boulogne-Billancourt, France, pg. 1119
Chomchinda, Shayne, Art Dir -- Saatchi & Saatchi, Bangkok, Thailand, pg. 1012
Chomczuk, Callum, Acct Dir -- Pagoda Porter Novelli, Edinburgh, United Kingdom, pg. 1623
Chong, Calvin, Acct Exec-Asia -- Epsilon International, Singapore, Singapore, pg. 351
Chong, Genevieve, Media Buyer-Brdcst-Natl -- MEDIA STORM LLC, South Norwalk, CT, pg. 1366
Chong, Jenny, Acct Exec -- TERPIN COMMUNICATIONS GROUP, Marina Del Rey, CA, pg. 1660
Chong, Kin, Exec Dir-Creative -- Leo Burnett-Guangzhou, Guangzhou, China, pg. 647
Chong, Richard, Assoc Creative Dir -- McCann Erickson (Malaysia) Sdn. Bhd., Kuala Lumpur, Malaysia, pg. 724
Chonkar, Samir, Head-Creative Function -- Everest Brand Solutions, Mumbai, India, pg. 1242
Choo, Kenny, Reg Dir-Creative-Olay & Safeguard -- Saatchi & Saatchi, Shanghai, China, pg. 1010
Chopek, Meghan, Acct Supvr -- AUDREY NYC, New York, NY, pg. 79
Chopra, Dushyant, Assoc Dir-Creative -- Grey (India) Pvt. Pty. Ltd. (Delhi), Gurgaon, India, pg. 456
Chopra, Geeta, Acct Exec -- THINK SHIFT, Winnipeg, Canada, pg. 1139
Chopra, Ullas, Head-Creative -- Publicis India Communications Pvt. Ltd., Mumbai, India, pg. 932
Chou, Lydia, Mgr-PR & Social Media -- BARNHART, Denver, CO, pg. 93
Chou, Murphy, Chief Creative Officer & Copywriter -- Leo Burnett, Taipei, Taiwan, pg. 651
Choucair, Alexandre, Dir-Creative -- H&C, Leo Burnett, Beirut, Lebanon, pg. 643
Choudhari, Darshan, Head-Creative -- Rediffusion Y&R Pvt. Ltd., Mumbai, India, pg. 1243
Choudhari, Manoj, Dir-Creative -- EGGFIRST, Mumbai, India, pg. 340
Choudhary, Puran, Assoc Dir-Creative -- Leo Burnett India, Mumbai, India, pg. 648
Choudhury, Pereina, Acct Dir -- FAYE CLACK COMMUNICATIONS INC., Toronto, Canada, pg. 1513
Chough, Tim, Specialist-Digital Investment & Media Planner -- Initiative Los Angeles, Los Angeles, CA, pg. 1344
Chouinard, Gilles, Partner & Exec Dir-Creative -- LG2, Montreal, Canada, pg. 656
Choussat, Antoine, Dir-Creative -- TBWA/Media Arts Lab, Los Angeles, CA, pg. 1116
Chow, Kevin, Acct Exec -- Titan Outdoor, Seattle, WA, pg. 1146
Chow, Kevin, Acct Exec -- Titan Worldwide, Boston, MA, pg. 1145
Chow, Stephen, Assoc Dir-Creative-Art -- RPA, Santa Monica, CA, pg. 994
Chow, Tracy, Assoc Dir-Creative -- AGENDA, Hong Kong, China (Hong Kong), pg. 1231
Chow, Tracy, Assoc Dir-Creative -- AGENDA, Hong Kong, China (Hong Kong), pg. 1217
Chow-Kaye, Sharon, Dir-Art & Assoc Dir-Creative -- TWOFIFTEENMCCANN, San Francisco, CA, pg. 1164
Chowdhury, Karina, Acct Coord -- VANTAGE PR, San Francisco, CA, pg. 1668
Chowdhury, Partha, Sr Dir-Creative -- J. Walter Thompson, Mumbai, India, pg. 569
Chrisman, Hallie, VP-PR -- KCD, INC., New York, NY, pg. 1559
Chrisoulaki, Rena, Dir-Creative -- Lowe Athens, Athens, Greece, pg. 793
Christ, Nicole, Media Planner & Buyer-Digital -- ELISCO ADVERTISING, INC., Pittsburgh, PA, pg. 344
Christensen, Aaron, Assoc Dir-Creative -- ERVIN & SMITH, Omaha, NE, pg. 354
Christensen, Abby, Acct Exec -- HANCOCK ADVERTISING GROUP, INC., Midland, TX, pg. 477
Christensen, Abigail, Acct Exec -- HANCOCK ADVERTISING AGENCY, Nacogdoches, TX, pg. 477
Christensen, Erin, Acct Dir -- YOUNG & RUBICAM, New York, NY, pg. 1239
Christensen, Kristie, Acct Supvr -- DNA SEATTLE, Seattle, WA, pg. 319
Christensen, Kristie, Acct Dir -- WONGDOODY, Seattle, WA, pg. 1213
Christensen, Kristie, Acct Dir -- WongDoody, Culver City, CA, pg. 1213
Christensen, Shad, Acct Dir -- MORSEKODE, Minneapolis, MN, pg. 777
Christian, Douglas, Acct Dir -- KBS+, New York, NY, pg. 604
Christian, James, Exec Dir-Creative -- George P. Johnson Company, Inc., Torrance, CA, pg. 422
Christian, Mary, Art Buyer -- SK+G ADVERTISING LLC, Las Vegas, NV, pg. 1049
Christian, Stacy, Acct Dir -- DEUTSER, Houston, TX, pg. 303
Christiansen, Dave, VP & Dir-Creative -- SWANSON RUSSELL ASSOCIATES, Lincoln, NE, pg. 1102
Christiansen, Matt, Creative Dir -- DDB Chicago, Chicago, IL, pg. 274
Christiansen, Richard, Founder & Dir-Creative -- CHANDELIER, New York, NY, pg. 203
Christianson, Lauren, Project Mgr & Acct Exec -- CUNNING COMMUNICATIONS, New York, NY, pg. 260
Christiansson, Carl, Acct Dir -- Mobiento, Stockholm, Sweden, pg. 1287
Christie, Barry, Partner-Creative -- J. Walter Thompson, London, United Kingdom, pg. 575
Christie, Bethany, Acct Exec -- ALICE MARSHALL PUBLIC RELATIONS, New York, NY, pg. 1442
Christmann, Tom, Chief Creative Officer -- DIMASSIMO GOLDSTEIN, New York, NY, pg. 310
Christodoulou, Alex, Art Dir -- FCB Johannesburg, Johannesburg, South Africa, pg. 382
Christon, Alexa, Acct Exec -- SOHO SQUARE, New York, NY, pg. 1057
Christopher, Caitlin, Acct Coord -- WOODRUFF SWEITZER, INC., Columbia, MO, pg. 1214
Christopher, Devin, Acct Exec -- TPN INC., Dallas, TX, pg. 1431
Christopherson, Ashleigh, Acct Exec -- JACOBSON ROST, Milwaukee, WI, pg. 585
Christopherson, Candace, Acct Exec -- KK BOLD, Bismarck, ND, pg. 614
Christophidou, Natalie, Acct Dir -- Action Global Communications, Nicosia, Cyprus, pg. 1531
Christou, Andrew, Chief Creative Officer & Exec VP -- Publicis Seattle, Seattle, WA, pg. 927
Christou, Andrew, Chief Creative Officer & Exec VP -- Publicis Seattle, Seattle, WA, pg. 936
Chrobot, Piotr, Exec Dir-Creative -- Wunderman, Warsaw, Poland, pg. 1234
Chrumka, Robin, Exec VP & Co-Creative Dir -- McCann Erickson, Birmingham, MI, pg. 715
Chrysostomou, Christiana, Acct Dir -- De Le Ma/ McCann Erickson, Nicosia, Cyprus, pg. 719
Chu, Daniel, Global Chief Creative Officer -- Possible Los Angeles, Los Angeles, CA, pg. 1307
Chu, Jonathan, Acct Exec -- Wieden + Kennedy-New York, New York, NY, pg. 1204
Chu, Michael, Dir-Creative -- OgilvyOne, Shanghai, China, pg. 841
Chu, Michael, Dir-Creative -- OgilvyOne Worldwide, Beijing, China, pg. 841
Chu, Polly, Chief Creative Officer -- J. Walter Thompson Beijing, Beijing, China, pg. 568
Chu, Suzie, Dir-Special Events & PR Projects -- BSY ASSOCIATES INC, Holmdel, NJ, pg. 173
Chu, Yen, Creative Dir-Design -- J. WALTER THOMPSON CANADA, Toronto, Canada, pg. 580
Chua, Bobee, Acct Dir -- Saatchi & Saatchi Asia Pacific, Singapore, Singapore, pg. 1012
Chua, Irene, Acct Dir -- Text 100 Hong Kong, Wanchai, China (Hong Kong), pg. 1662
Chua, Xiulu, Art Dir -- Publicis Singapore, Singapore, Singapore, pg. 934
Chuang, Penny, Pres & Dir-Creative -- ADVENTIUM, LLC, New York, NY, pg. 33
Chuasakul, Rojana, Dir-Art & Creative -- J. Walter Thompson, Shanghai, China, pg. 568
Chueng, Winston, Assoc Dir-Creative -- BURRELL, Chicago, IL, pg. 177
Chulick, Samantha, Acct Exec -- LANE PR, Portland, OR, pg. 1571
Chun, Chelsea, Mgr-New Bus Dev -- SWELL, New York, NY, pg. 1104
Chung, Irving, Principal & Acct Dir -- COMMERCE HOUSE, Dallas, TX, pg. 224
Chung, Sam, Chief Creative Officer-China -- WE MARKETING GROUP, Beijing, China, pg. 1276
Chuppe, Tania, Sr Acct Exec-PR -- Fleishman-Hillard Group Ltd., London, United Kingdom, pg. 1519
Churarakpong, Piya, Exec Dir-Creative -- Lowe, Bangkok, Thailand, pg. 794
Church, Brandi, Media Dir -- EDGECORE, Winter Park, FL, pg. 338
Church, John, Dir-Creative -- PRIME ACCESS, New York, NY, pg. 910
Church, Lauren, Acct Exec -- Fahlgren Mortine (Dayton), Beavercreek, OH, pg. 365
Church-McDowall, Colleen, VP & Dir-PR -- Osborn & Barr, Kansas City, MO, pg. 864
Churcher, Jed, Dir-Creative -- J. WALTER THOMPSON CANADA, Toronto, Canada, pg. 580
Churchill, Chris, Assoc Dir-Creative & Copywriter --

CREATIVEONDEMAND, Coconut Grove, FL, pg. 253
Churchill, Dani, Partner & Acct Dir -- HIGH WIDE & HANDSOME, Culver City, CA, pg. 513
Chusid, Robert, Acct Dir -- MILNER BUTCHER MEDIA GROUP, Los Angeles, CA, pg. 1374
Chwirut, Laura, Art Dir -- GLOBAL THINKING, Alexandria, VA, pg. 429
Ciallella, Lauren, Mgr-Creative -- MUNROE CREATIVE PARTNERS, Philadelphia, PA, pg. 796
Ciallella, Lauren, Mgr-Creative -- Munroe Creative Partners, New York, NY, pg. 796
Ciampa, Bethany, Acct Supvr-PR -- MULLEN LOWE GROUP, Boston, MA, pg. 786
Cianciosi, Gary, Media Buyer -- TRUE MEDIA, Columbia, MO, pg. 1393
Cianciosi, Michelangelo, Creative Dir -- DDB S.r.L. Advertising, Milan, Italy, pg. 284
Cianciosi, Michelangelo, Exec Dir-Creative -- Verba S.r.l. Advertising, Milan, Italy, pg. 284
Cianfrone, Bob, Exec Creative Dir -- Deutsch LA, Los Angeles, CA, pg. 302
Cicalini, Barbara, Reg Dir-Creative -- Grey Italia S.p.A, Milan, Italy, pg. 450
Ciccoccioppo, David W., Dir-Creative -- REDROC AUSTIN, Austin, TX, pg. 965
Ciecko, Blair, Dir-PR & Social Media -- CELTIC MARKETING, INC., Niles, IL, pg. 201
Cierco, Nerea, Creative Dir -- DDB Barcelona S.A., Barcelona, Spain, pg. 288
Ciffone, Meghan, Acct Supvr-Target -- Deutsch LA, Los Angeles, CA, pg. 302
Ciffone, Nick, Sr Copywriter -- TBWA Chiat Day Los Angeles, Los Angeles, CA, pg. 1114
Cifuentes, Cesar, Dir-Creative -- TEQUILA Guatemala, Guatemala, Guatemala, pg. 1132
Cignini, Marco, Exec Dir-Creative -- CATCH NEW YORK, New York, NY, pg. 198
Cilli, Darryl, Chief Creative Officer & Principal -- 160OVER90, Philadelphia, PA, pg. 2
Cima, Chris, Dir-Creative -- R/GA, New York, NY, pg. 946
Cimmino, Craig, Grp Dir-Creative -- MCGARRYBOWEN, New York, NY, pg. 733
Cincala, Evan, Acct Exec -- MOTIVATED MARKETING, North Charleston, SC, pg. 779
Cinco, Patrick, Dir-Creative -- RED DOOR INTERACTIVE, INC., San Diego, CA, pg. 960
Cindric, Sandra, Acct Dir -- McCann Erickson, Zagreb, Croatia, pg. 719
Cinque, Erica, Acct Exec -- Erwin Penland, New York, NY, pg. 355
Ciociola, Alex, Acct Dir -- J. WALTER THOMPSON, New York, NY, pg. 565
Cipolla, Nikki, Acct Exec -- ALLEBACH COMMUNICATIONS, Souderton, PA, pg. 46
Cirilli, Dominick, Exec VP & Dir-Creative -- CUMMINS, MACFAIL & NUTRY, INC., Somerville, NJ, pg. 260
Cirillo, Peppe, Dir-Creative -- GreyUnited, Milan, Italy, pg. 450
Cirino, Marcia, Dir-New Bus -- Publicom, Sao Paulo, Brazil, pg. 1531
Cirrito, Vinessa, Acct Exec -- DUREE & COMPANY, Fort Lauderdale, FL, pg. 1499
Ciskowski, Lea, Acct Exec-Social Media -- MESH DESIGN, Baton Rouge, LA, pg. 751
Cisneros, Ashley, Co-Founder & Creative Dir -- CHATTER BUZZ MEDIA, Orlando, FL, pg. 206
Cisneros, Carlos, Dir-Creative -- FCB Mayo, Quito, Ecuador, pg. 378
Cisneros, Eduardo, VP-Creative -- Edelman, Mexico, Mexico, pg. 1505
Citron, Ben, Creative Dir -- VaynerMedia, San Francisco, CA, pg. 1319
Citron, Nicole, Acct Dir -- HALL AND PARTNERS, New York, NY, pg. 475
Cius, Lauren, Assoc Dir-Creative -- SKM GROUP, Depew, NY, pg. 1050
Cizl, Nenad, Art Dir -- Mayer-McCann, Ljubljana, Slovenia, pg. 727
Clack, Matt, Dir-Creative -- IGNITION INTERACTIVE, Los Angeles, CA, pg. 537
Clair, Shaun, Acct Dir -- CATALYST PUBLIC RELATIONS, New York, NY, pg. 197
Clampffer, Gregg, Dir-Creative -- 72andSunny, Amsterdam, Netherlands, pg. 11
Clancy, Simon, Grp Dir-Creative -- Isobar UK, London, United Kingdom, pg. 562
Clapier, Christophe, Creative Dir -- BETC Life, Paris, France, pg. 492
Clapp, Ben, Exec Dir-Creative -- Grey London, London, United Kingdom, pg. 447
Clark, Camielle, Dir-Creative Production -- Edelman, Toronto, Canada, pg. 1501
Clark, Carmen, Acct Supvr -- BROWN COMMUNICATIONS GROUP, Regina, Canada, pg. 170
Clark, Crystal, Acct Dir -- DDB New Zealand Ltd., Auckland, New Zealand, pg. 286
Clark, Daniel, Acct Exec -- Sawmill, New York, NY, pg. 1676
Clark, David, Strategist-Creative & Acct Exec -- TRADEMARK ADVERTISING, Knoxville, TN, pg. 1154
Clark, Frank, Dir-Creative -- SQUARE TOMATO, Seattle, WA, pg. 1069
Clark, Holly, Acct Exec -- AUTOCOM ASSOCIATES, Bloomfield Hills, MI, pg. 81
Clark, Jessi, Mgr-PR & Social Media -- THRIVE PR, Fort Worth, TX, pg. 1663
Clark, Jim, Partner & Creative Dir -- BLIND SOCIETY, Scottsdale, AZ, pg. 138
Clark, Katelyn, Acct Supvr -- C3 - CREATIVE CONSUMER CONCEPTS, Overland Park, KS, pg. 182
Clark, Michele, Dir-Creative -- SELMARQ, Charlotte, NC, pg. 1031
Clark, Moray, Acct Exec -- Pagoda Porter Novelli, Edinburgh, United Kingdom, pg. 1623
Clark, Olivia, Acct Supvr -- DRUMROLL, Austin, TX, pg. 330
Clark, Scott, VP-Creative & Dir -- Deutsch LA, Los Angeles, CA, pg. 302
Clark, Scott, Dir-Creative -- LEGGETT & PLATT INC., Carthage, MO, pg. 1269
Clark, Stephanie, Mgr-Nickelodeon Creative Adv -- NICKELODEON CREATIVE ADVERTISING, New York, NY, pg. 810
Clark, Steve, Acct Dir -- Discovery USA, Chicago, IL, pg. 926
Clark, Todd E., Assoc Dir-Creative -- SKYLINE MEDIA GROUP, Oklahoma City, OK, pg. 1050
Clark, Tom, Art Dir -- KATHODERAY MEDIA INC., Greenville, NY, pg. 603
Clark, Tricia, Sr VP, Head-New Bus & Grp Dir -- GREY SAN FRANCISCO, San Francisco, CA, pg. 458
Clarke, Andy, Exec VP & Exec Dir-Creative -- ARNOLD WORLDWIDE, Boston, MA, pg. 71
Clarke, Chris, Chief Creative Officer-Intl -- DigitasLBi, London, United Kingdom, pg. 1289
Clarke, Christopher, Dir-Creative -- BARTLE BOGLE HEGARTY LIMITED, London, United Kingdom, pg. 94
Clarke, Lawson, VP-Creative & Dir -- HILL HOLLIDAY, Boston, MA, pg. 514
Clarke, Neil, Dir-Creative -- Abbott Mead Vickers BBDO, London, United Kingdom, pg. 112
Clarke, Robyn, Art Dir -- ILLUMINATION ADVERTISING INC., Clearwater, FL, pg. 537
Clarke, Sam, Acct Dir -- PETROL ADVERTISING, Burbank, CA, pg. 887
Clarke, Stephanie, Acct Supvr -- Havas PR, Phoenix, AZ, pg. 1537
Clarke, Will, Sr VP & Exec Dir-Creative -- THE INTEGER GROUP-DALLAS, Dallas, TX, pg. 1416
Clary, Chris, Dir-Creative -- JAFFE & PARTNERS, New York, NY, pg. 585
Claudio, Javier, Assoc Dir-Creative -- Y&R Puerto Rico, Inc., San Juan, PR, pg. 1250
Claverie, Faustin, Exec Dir-Creative -- TBWA Paris, Boulogne-Billancourt, France, pg. 1119
Clavijo, Jimmy, Dir-Creative -- L-AVENUE, San Antonio, TX, pg. 621
Claxton, Christine, Acct Dir -- R/GA, New York, NY, pg. 946
Claxton, John, Grp Dir-Creative -- FCB Chicago, Chicago, IL, pg. 371
Clayton, Hannah, Acct Exec -- JAVELIN MARKETING GROUP, Irving, TX, pg. 588
Clayton, Janice, Acct Dir -- O'KEEFFE & CO., Alexandria, VA, pg. 1610
Clayton, Janice, Acct Dir -- O'Keeffe & Co., Atlanta, GA, pg. 1610
Clayton, Lauren, Acct Exec -- MOREHEAD DOTTS RYBAK, Corpus Christi, TX, pg. 774
Cleary, Meaghan, Acct Dir -- HELLOWORLD, Pleasant Ridge, MI, pg. 509
Cleary, Sharon, Assoc Dir-Creative -- GRUPO GALLEGOS, Huntington Beach, CA, pg. 463
Clelland, Amanda, Creative Dir -- BARTON F. GRAF 9000 LLC, New York, NY, pg. 96
Clemens, Isaac, VP & Acct Dir -- FCB West, San Francisco, CA, pg. 372
Clement, Cameron, VP & Exec Creative Dir -- TWINOAKS, Plano, TX, pg. 1164
Clement, Shelby, Acct Dir -- UNITED MARKETING COMMUNICATIONS, Irving, TX, pg. 1167
Clements, Darren, Acct Exec -- 2020 EXHIBITS, INC., Houston, TX, pg. 3
Clements, Erin, Acct Exec -- MCNEELY, PIGOTT & FOX, Nashville, TN, pg. 1587
Clements, Katie, Assoc Dir-Creative -- CALDWELL VANRIPER, Indianapolis, IN, pg. 184
Clemesha, Ali, Acct Exec -- J. Walter Thompson, Sydney, Australia, pg. 567
Clephane, Scott, Partner & Dir-Creative-Tonic Branding -- TONIC, Dubai, United Arab Emirates, pg. 1150
Clerget, Virginie, Head-New Bus & Strategy -- FCB Paris, Paris, France, pg. 373
Clerk, Andrea, Acct Supvr -- PUROHIT NAVIGATION, Chicago, IL, pg. 939
Clermont, Emmanuelle, Acct Dir -- FutureBrand, Clichy, France, pg. 411
Clermont, Lyne, Acct Dir -- NOLIN BBDO, Montreal, Canada, pg. 812
Cleveland, Hannah, Acct Exec -- WINGARD CREATIVE, Jacksonville, FL, pg. 1209
Clewell, Jason, Assoc Dir-Creative & Interactive -- CONCENTRIC MARKETING, Charlotte, NC, pg. 228
Click, Nancy, Acct Dir -- THE MAYFIELD GROUP, Tallahassee, FL, pg. 1585
Clift, Sarah, Dir-Creative-Intl -- McCann Erickson Advertising Ltd., London, United Kingdom, pg. 729
Climer, Nic, Exec Dir-Creative -- RAPP, New York, NY, pg. 951
Climons, Steve, Founder, Pres & Dir-Creative -- CROSSOVER CREATIVE GROUP, Pinole, CA, pg. 257
Cline, Jennifer, Acct Dir -- PRICEWEBER MARKETING COMMUNICATIONS, INC., Louisville, KY, pg. 909
Clinet, Baptiste, Exec Dir-Creative -- OgilvyHealthcare, Paris, France, pg. 831
Clinkard, Gabriella, Acct Dir -- Buchanan Communications Ltd., London, United Kingdom, pg. 1225
Clinton, John, Chm/CEO-Canada & Head-Creative & Content-North American -- Edelman, Toronto, Canada, pg. 1501
Cloar, Sarah Beth, Acct Supvr -- GYMR PUBLIC RELATIONS, Washington, DC, pg. 1535
Clonts, Mackie, Acct Supvr -- AMELIE COMPANY, Denver, CO, pg. 53
Clormann, Lorenz, Dir-Creative & Art -- Publicis Dialog Zurich, Zurich, Switzerland, pg. 921
Clough, Jeremy, VP-Digital & Dir-Creative -- PIEHEAD PRODUCTIONS LLC, Portsmouth, NH, pg. 890
Cloutier, Lela, Acct Supvr -- COYNE PUBLIC RELATIONS, Parsippany, NJ, pg. 1487
Clutterbuck, William, Vice Chm & Head-Fin Svcs & Litigation PR -- The Maitland Consultancy, London, United Kingdom, pg. 498
Co, Jaclyn, Art Dir -- VML, INC., Kansas City, MO, pg. 1182
Coad, Richard M., Chief Creative Officer-Engagement -- MDB COMMUNICATIONS, INC., Washington, DC, pg. 737
Coamey, Jerry, Sr VP & Grp Dir-Creative -- CAHG, Chicago, IL, pg. 184
Coates, Nick, VP & Dir-Creative Consultancy -- C Space, London, United Kingdom, pg. 314
Coates, Tom, Dir-Creative -- BUTLER, SHINE, STERN & PARTNERS, Sausalito, CA, pg. 179
Coats, David, Principal & Exec Dir-Creative -- KRAUSE ADVERTISING, Dallas, TX, pg. 618
Coats, Todd, Chief Creative Officer -- CAPSTRAT, Raleigh, NC, pg. 1472
Cobb, Tim, Mng Dir & Dir-Creative -- DHX ADVERTISING, INC., Portland, OR, pg. 305
Cobert, Ashley, Acct Exec-PR -- Bader Rutter & Associates, Inc., Lincoln, NE, pg. 86
Cobos, Horacio, Exec Dir-Creative -- REVEL, Dallas, TX, pg. 974
Cobos, Horacio, Exec Dir-Creative -- REVEL UNITED, Dallas, TX, pg. 974
Coburn, Jeff, Sr VP & Dir-Creative Strategy -- Momentum, Saint Louis, MO, pg. 771
Coburn, Rachel, Media Buyer -- Zenith Media, Chicago, IL, pg. 1397
Cocca, Toniann, Acct Coord -- JACK NADEL INTERNATIONAL, Westport, CT, pg. 1418
Cocchiere, Scott, Dir-Creative Relevance -- Emanate, New York, NY, pg. 1562
Cocchiola, Lynn, Acct Exec -- MOUNT & NADLER, INC., New York, NY, pg. 1593
Cochran, Steve, Exec Dir-Creative -- Colenso BBDO, Auckland, New Zealand, pg. 116

Personnel Index

Cochran, Taylor, Acct Exec -- INFINITEE COMMUNICATIONS, INC., Atlanta, GA, pg. 545
Cocito, Beto, Exec Dir-Creative -- DDB Argentina, Buenos Aires, Argentina, pg. 276
Cocke, Tom, Sr VP & Grp Dir-Creative -- THE BUNTIN GROUP, Nashville, TN, pg. 175
Cockerham, Kristin Schellinger, Acct Exec -- LANDIS COMMUNICATIONS INC., San Francisco, CA, pg. 1571
Cockrel, Warren, Dir-Creative & Copywriter -- HEAT, San Francisco, CA, pg. 507
Cockrell, Phil, Creative Dir -- DLKW Lowe, London, United Kingdom, pg. 789
Coco, Mary, Assoc Dir-Creative -- GREY GROUP, New York, NY, pg. 445
Codesido, Enrique, Exec Dir-Creative -- J. Walter Thompson, Mexico, Mexico, pg. 578
Codling, John, Creative Dir -- J. WALTER THOMPSON, New York, NY, pg. 565
Cody, Catharine, Acct Exec -- PEPPERCOMM, New York, NY, pg. 1614
Coego, Erick, Dir-Creative & Art -- GMG ADVERTISING, Miami, FL, pg. 431
Coelho, Andre, Dir-Creative -- DDB Mozambique, Maputo, Mozambique, pg. 285
Coelho, John, Acct Dir -- TEAM ONE USA, Los Angeles, CA, pg. 1134
Coelho, Jorge, Creative Dir -- Ogilvy & Mather Portugal, Lisbon, Portugal, pg. 834
Coelho, Luis, Dir-Creative -- Wunderman, Lisbon, Portugal, pg. 1234
Coelho, Paulo, Exec Creative Dir -- Ogilvy & Mather, Sao Paulo, Brazil, pg. 838
Coello, Ericka, Acct Exec -- Ogilvy & Mather, Sao Paulo, Brazil, pg. 838
Coello, Ivan, Dir-Creative -- Norlop J. Walter Thompson, Guayaquil, Ecuador, pg. 578
Coen, Taylor, Acct Exec -- AVALON COMMUNICATIONS, Austin, TX, pg. 1447
Coffey, Megan, Chief Creative Officer -- SPRINGBOX, LTD., Austin, TX, pg. 1068
Coggin, Clark, Creative Dir -- CAMPAIGN CONNECTIONS, Raleigh, NC, pg. 1472
Coghill, Annie, Dir-PR Svcs -- AMELIE COMPANY, Denver, CO, pg. 53
Cogswell, Mckinzie A., Sr Acct Exec-PR -- FAISS FOLEY WARREN, Las Vegas, NV, pg. 1512
Cohen, Adam, Sr VP & Dir-Creative -- CAPSTRAT, Raleigh, NC, pg. 1472
Cohen, Adam, Mng Partner & Dir-Creative -- CONCENTRIC PHARMA ADVERTISING, New York, NY, pg. 228
Cohen, Alyssa, Media Planner & Buyer -- R&R Partners, El Segundo, CA, pg. 945
Cohen, Christopher, Art Dir -- Spike/DDB, Brooklyn, NY, pg. 276
Cohen, Dan, Sr VP & Creative Dir -- PUBLICIS USA, New York, NY, pg. 935
Cohen, Dana, Dir-Creative -- Jupiter Drawing Room, Rivonia, South Africa, pg. 1251
Cohen, Dana, Dir-Creative -- Jupiter Drawing Room, Rivonia, South Africa, pg. 1220
Cohen, Dave, Exec Dir-Creative -- GREY GROUP, New York, NY, pg. 445
Cohen, Edmond, Dir-Creative -- NEWKIRK COMMUNICATIONS, INC., Philadelphia, PA, pg. 807
Cohen, Eli, Assoc Dir-Creative -- BEMIS BALKIND, Los Angeles, CA, pg. 123
Cohen, Emily, Media Planner -- TIERNEY COMMUNICATIONS, Philadelphia, PA, pg. 1143
Cohen, Fern, Sr VP & Dir-Creative -- Y&R New York, New York, NY, pg. 1240
Cohen, Fern, Sr VP & Dir-Creative -- YOUNG & RUBICAM, New York, NY, pg. 1239
Cohen, Martha, Acct Supvr -- CREATE DIGITAL, Glen Allen, VA, pg. 1286
Cohen, Merav, Acct Dir -- DAVID & GOLIATH, El Segundo, CA, pg. 267
Cohen, Nick, Exec Creative Dir -- MAD DOGS & ENGLISHMEN, Oakland, CA, pg. 684
Cohen, Ramiro Rodriguez, Exec Creative Dir -- BBDO Argentina, Buenos Aires, Argentina, pg. 102
Cohen, Roy, Dir-Creative -- Blue Hive, London, United Kingdom, pg. 1217
Cohen, Ryan, Acct Supvr, Media Planner & Buyer -- MILLER ADVERTISING AGENCY INC., New York, NY, pg. 757
Cohen-Keidar, Nadav, Acct Dir -- Gitam Porter Novelli, Tel Aviv, Israel, pg. 1622
Coie, James, VP & Dir-Creative -- Deutsch New York, New York, NY, pg. 302
Coiffard, Rene, Assoc-Creative -- BROWNING ADVERTISING LLC, New Providence, NJ, pg. 170
Coil, Kenny, Dir-Creative -- HYPE GROUP LLC, Saint Petersburg, FL, pg. 530
Coimbra, Bobby, Pres & Dir-Creative -- Ogilvy & Mather, Caracas, Venezuela, pg. 840
Cojocaru, Ion, Art Dir -- Saatchi & Saatchi, Dubai, United Arab Emirates, pg. 1006
Colalillo, Allison, Acct Supvr -- High Road Communications, Toronto, Canada, pg. 1519
Colar, Ben, Assoc Dir-Creative -- ARCHER MALMO, Memphis, TN, pg. 67
Colbert, Kacie, Acct Exec -- MLB ADVANCED MEDIA, L.P., New York, NY, pg. 1303
Colburn, Bill, VP-Creative Svcs -- DIXON SCHWABL ADVERTISING, Victor, NY, pg. 317
Colburn, Sandra, Acct Exec -- Agency59 Response, Toronto, Canada, pg. 39
Coldefy-Lefort, Cecile, Acct Dir-Digital -- /EXCEL, Paris, France, pg. 1119
Cole, Andy, Acct Exec -- DEVENEY COMMUNICATIONS, New Orleans, LA, pg. 1493
Cole, Chris, Creative Dir -- LEO BURNETT WORLDWIDE, INC., Chicago, IL, pg. 637
Cole, Christopher, Sr VP & Dir-Creative -- Leo Burnett USA, Chicago, IL, pg. 639
Cole, Danielle, Acct Coord -- BAM STRATEGY, Montreal, Canada, pg. 89
Cole, Glenn, Chief Creative Officer -- 72ANDSUNNY, Playa Vista, CA, pg. 10
Cole, Jackie, Acct Supvr -- THE STONE AGENCY, Raleigh, NC, pg. 1088
Cole, Jeff, Sr Producer-Creative & Digital Media -- IDEA HALL, Costa Mesa, CA, pg. 534
Cole, Jeff, VP & Dir-Creative -- THREE ATLANTA, Atlanta, GA, pg. 1141
Cole, Kim, Media Buyer -- KRE8 MEDIA INC, Winter Park, FL, pg. 618
Cole, Marty, Sr Dir-Creative -- PBJS, Chicago, IL, pg. 880
Cole, Mike, Acct Dir -- MOTIVE, Denver, CO, pg. 780
Cole, Tim, Dir-Creative -- MCGARRAH JESSEE, Austin, TX, pg. 733
Cole, Ward, Assoc Dir-Creative-Digital -- THE GLOVER PARK GROUP, Washington, DC, pg. 429
Cole, Ward, Assoc Dir-Creative-Ketchum Digital -- Ketchum, Washington, DC, pg. 1562
Coleman, Kristin, Acct Dir -- NOVITA COMMUNICATIONS, New York, NY, pg. 817
Coleman, Lauren, Art Dir -- GCG MARKETING, Fort Worth, TX, pg. 419
Coleman, Rachel, Acct Exec -- Fleishman-Hillard Inc., Chicago, IL, pg. 1517
Coleman, Ryan, Assoc Dir-Creative -- LUQUIRE GEORGE ANDREWS, INC., Charlotte, NC, pg. 674
Coleman, Valerie, Acct Dir -- NCOMPASS INTERNATIONAL, West Hollywood, CA, pg. 802
Colhouer, Lori, Acct Supvr -- ZILLNER MARKETING COMMUNICATIONS, Lenexa, KS, pg. 1256
Coliban, Mihai, Dir-Creative -- BBDO Moscow, Moscow, Russia, pg. 110
Colinet, Fritz, Exec Dir-Creative -- RETNA MEDIA INC., Houston, TX, pg. 974
Coll, Steve, Exec Dir-Creative -- Havas Worldwide Sydney, Sydney, Australia, pg. 500
Coll-Dimayo, Arlene, Acct Exec-B2B Mktg -- FORTYTWOEIGHTYNINE, Rockford, IL, pg. 398
Collantes, Sebastian, Dir-Creative -- Lowe Porta, Santiago, Chile, pg. 792
Collette, Sarah-Emily, Media Buyer -- Havas Media, Toronto, Canada, pg. 1340
Collignon, Rob, Dir-Creative -- KBS+, New York, NY, pg. 604
Collins, Andy, Dir-Creative -- LATORRA, PAUL & MCCANN, Syracuse, NY, pg. 629
Collins, Brian, CEO & Dir-Creative -- COLLINS:, New York, NY, pg. 222
Collins, David, Principal & Dir-Creative -- GRAFIK MARKETING COMMUNICATIONS, Alexandria, VA, pg. 438
Collins, Hannah, Acct Exec & Copywriter -- PARADIGM MARKETING & CREATIVE, Memphis, TN, pg. 872
Collins, Jaclyn, Acct Dir -- IMAGEMAKERS INC., Wamego, KS, pg. 538
Collins, Jennifer, Dir-New Bus -- PEAK CREATIVE MEDIA, Denver, CO, pg. 880
Collins, Jimmy, VP & Creative Dir -- Erwin Penland, New York, NY, pg. 355
Collins, Karl, Media Planner -- WIEDEN + KENNEDY, INC., Portland, OR, pg. 1202
Collins, Lauren, Acct Exec -- Hacker Agency, Seattle, WA, pg. 554
Collins, Lauren, Acct Exec -- Hacker Agency, Seattle, WA, pg. 370
Collins, Matt, Dir-Creative -- PK NETWORK COMMUNICATIONS, New York, NY, pg. 894
Collins, Paul, Exec Creative Dir -- DigitasLBi, Stockholm, Sweden, pg. 1289
Collins, Sydni, Media Planner & Media Buyer -- CAPSTRAT, Raleigh, NC, pg. 1472
Collins, Tom, Assoc Dir-Creative -- ERIC MOWER + ASSOCIATES, Syracuse, NY, pg. 353
Collinson, Sarah, Acct Dir -- ANOMALY, New York, NY, pg. 60
Collyer, Phil, Sr VP & Head-Creative -- JACK MORTON WORLDWIDE, Boston, MA, pg. 582
Colna, Jill, VP-PR -- SVM PUBLIC RELATIONS & MARKETING COMMUNICATIONS, Providence, RI, pg. 1102
Colon, Aida, Acct Dir -- Pages BBDO, Santo Domingo, Dominican Republic, pg. 103
Colovin, Stewart, Exec VP-Creative & Brand Strategy -- MMG, Bradenton, FL, pg. 767
Colovin, Stewart, Exec VP-Creative & Brand Strategy -- MMGY GLOBAL, Kansas City, MO, pg. 767
Colpaert, Didier, Dir-Creative -- Carre Noir, Suresnes, France, pg. 918
Colton, Christopher, Dir-Creative -- GSD&M, Austin, TX, pg. 464
Colville, Kristin, Acct Exec -- ROCKAWAY PR, Miami, FL, pg. 1638
Colvin, Alan, Principal & Dir-Creative -- CUE INC, Minneapolis, MN, pg. 259
Colvin, Spencer, Acct Exec -- Lapiz, Chicago, IL, pg. 638
Colvin, Tony, Acct Exec -- VaynerMedia, San Francisco, CA, pg. 1319
Comand, Cristian, Deputy Dir-Creative-Art -- Y&R Italia, srl, Milan, Italy, pg. 1245
Comas, Christina, Acct Exec -- ARCHER MALMO, Memphis, TN, pg. 67
Comas, Jordi, Dir-Creative Content -- Tiempo BBDO, Barcelona, Spain, pg. 111
Combs, Amanda, Acct Exec -- NORTHWEST STRATEGIES, Anchorage, AK, pg. 1604
Combs, Josh, Creative Dir -- FALLON WORLDWIDE, Minneapolis, MN, pg. 366
Combs, Scott, VP & Dir-Creative -- McCann Worldgroup, San Francisco, CA, pg. 715
Combuechen, Andreas, Chm, CEO & Chief Creative Officer -- Atmosphere Proximity, New York, NY, pg. 99
Comeaux, Cali, Coord-Traffic -- BBR CREATIVE, Lafayette, LA, pg. 118
Comer, Kevin, Partner-Creative -- AMPLE, LLC, Cincinnati, OH, pg. 56
Comer, Marjorie, Acct Mgr-PR -- AXIA PUBLIC RELATIONS, Jacksonville, FL, pg. 83
Comitis, John, Dir-Creative -- VBAT, Amsterdam, Netherlands, pg. 1223
Command, Lauren, Acct Coord-Programmatic Media -- AMNET GROUP, New York, NY, pg. 1324
Commare, Joe, Acct Dir -- WALL STREET COMMUNICATIONS, Salt Lake City, UT, pg. 1672
Commerford, Jonathan, Grp Head-Creative & Copywriter -- J. Walter Thompson Cape Town, Cape Town, South Africa, pg. 566
Compton, Brett, VP & Creative Dir -- RED CLAY INTERACTIVE, Buford, GA, pg. 1311
Comstock, Rebecca, Acct Exec -- Padilla/CRT, Richmond, VA, pg. 869
Comte-Liniere, Jean-baptiste, Exec Dir-Creative -- Publicis Shanghai, Shanghai, China, pg. 931
Conachan, Mark, Dir-Creative -- MYJIVE INC, Charlotte, NC, pg. 798
Conant, Teresa, Supvr-Brdcst -- NORBELLA INC., Boston, MA, pg. 1377
Concejo, Jacobo, Dir-Creative-Global -- BBDO PROXIMITY, Minneapolis, MN, pg. 98
Conciatore, Matthew, Mng Partner & Dir-Creative -- IMPULSE CONCEPT GROUP, Norwalk, CT, pg. 542
Conda, Kathryn M., Acct Exec -- ANNE KLEIN COMMUNICATIONS GROUP, LLC, Mount Laurel, NJ, pg. 1444
Conde, Vanessa, Dir-Mktg & New Bus Dev -- LGD COMMUNICATIONS, INC., Miami, FL, pg. 656
Condon, Alison, Acct Supvr -- RAPP, New York, NY, pg. 951

Personnel Index

Personnel Index

Wynnewood, PA, pg. 244

Cramp, Matt, Exec Dir-Creative -- ARNOLD WORLDWIDE, Boston, MA, pg. 71

Cramsie, Nicole, Media Buyer-Integrated -- ZIMMERMAN ADVERTISING, Fort Lauderdale, FL, pg. 1256

Cramsie, Nicole, Media Buyer-Integrated -- THE ZIMMERMAN AGENCY LLC, Tallahassee, FL, pg. 1257

Crane, Jenna, Acct Supvr -- SQ1, Dallas, TX, pg. 1068

Crane, Karen, Exec Dir-Creative Talent -- 360I, New York, NY, pg. 6

Craner, Nate, Dir-Creative -- THE INTEGER GROUP - DENVER, Lakewood, CO, pg. 1416

Craven, Jerry, Sr VP-Creative Svcs -- UPSHOT, Chicago, IL, pg. 1168

Craven, Mick, Deputy Dir-Creative -- McCann-Erickson Communications House Ltd , Macclesfield, Prestbury, United Kingdom, pg. 730

Craw, Adam, Acct Dir -- CARMICHAEL LYNCH, Minneapolis, MN, pg. 191

Crawford, Andrew, Acct Exec -- TEAM ONE USA, Los Angeles, CA, pg. 1134

Crawford, Brooke Baumer, Acct Dir -- GRIFFIN COMMUNICATIONS GROUP, Seabrook, TX, pg. 459

Crawford, Craig, Grp Dir-Creative -- TEAM ONE USA, Los Angeles, CA, pg. 1134

Crawford, Erin, Co-Founder & Dir-Creative -- ONTOGENY ADVERTISING & DESIGN LLC, Mosinee, WI, pg. 862

Crawford, Jennifer, Acct Supvr -- QORVIS MSLGROUP, Washington, DC, pg. 1628

Crawford, Linda, Mgr-Media & Creative Svcs -- LASPATA DECARO, New York, NY, pg. 627

Crawford, Steve, Exec Dir-Creative -- Rapp Melbourne, Richmond, Australia, pg. 954

Crawford, Taylor, Acct Supvr -- THE ARCHER GROUP, Wilmington, DE, pg. 67

Crawley, Amanda, Acct Exec -- M&C Saatchi Abel, Cape Town, South Africa, pg. 678

Crawley, Jani, Acct Exec -- WEBER SHANDWICK, New York, NY, pg. 1675

Crawley, Jessica, Media Buyer & Coord -- ROBINSON & ASSOCIATES INC, Tupelo, MS, pg. 988

Creally, Justin, Co-Founder & Strategist-Creative -- NORTH STRATEGIC, Toronto, Canada, pg. 1604

Creamer, Scott, Founder & Dir-Creative -- SCREAMER CO., Austin, TX, pg. 1028

Credeur, Raymond, Creative Dir -- THE GRAHAM GROUP, Lafayette, LA, pg. 438

Credle, Susan, Assoc Creative Dir -- CHANDELIER, New York, NY, pg. 203

Credle, Susan, Chief Creative Officer -- LEO BURNETT WORLDWIDE, INC., Chicago, IL, pg. 637

Creedon, Laura, Acct Dir -- PILOT PMR, Toronto, Canada, pg. 1425

Creet, Simon, Chief Creative Officer & VP -- THE HIVE, Toronto, Canada, pg. 517

Crenshaw, Dorothy, CEO & Dir-Creative -- CRENSHAW COMMUNICATIONS, New York, NY, pg. 1488

Crespi, Lorenzo, Creative Dir -- Havas Worldwide Digital Milan, Milan, Italy, pg. 494

Crespo, Joaquim, Dir-Creative -- Vinizius/Y&R, Barcelona, Spain, pg. 1246

Crespo, Joaquim, Dir-Creative -- Young & Rubicam, S.L., Madrid, Spain, pg. 1246

Cressman, Krista, Acct Dir -- LG2, Montreal, Canada, pg. 656

Criddle, Leanna, Acct Exec -- YOUNG & RUBICAM, New York, NY, pg. 1239

Crifasi, Jack, Dir-Creative -- LEO BURNETT DETROIT, INC., Troy, MI, pg. 637

Crilley, Lauren, Acct Dir -- R&R Partners, El Segundo, CA, pg. 945

Crimi-Lamanna, Nancy, VP & Dir-Creative -- FCB Toronto, Toronto, Canada, pg. 372

Crisafi, Carol, Acct Exec -- BRISTOL PUBLIC RELATIONS, INC., Coral Gables, FL, pg. 1461

Crist, Nancy, Specialist-PR & Writer -- J.W. MORTON & ASSOCIATES, Cedar Rapids, IA, pg. 600

Crivello, Samantha, Acct Exec -- BROGAN TENNYSON GROUP, INC., Dayton, NJ, pg. 168

Crobeddu, Jane, Acct Exec -- Ogilvy Public Relations, Paris, France, pg. 1607

Croce, Andrew, Dir-Creative -- VIUS, Philadelphia, PA, pg. 1319

Croce, Colette, Acct Dir -- QUATTRO DIRECT LLC, Berwyn, PA, pg. 942

Croci, Dan, Dir-Creative Svcs -- BLUESPIRE MARKETING, West Hartford, CT, pg. 143

Crockett, Shaun, Dir-Creative -- AdFarm, Kansas City, MO, pg. 28

Crockett, Stephanie, Partner & Acct Dir -- ERIC MOWER + ASSOCIATES, Syracuse, NY, pg. 353

Crofoot, Nick, Assoc Dir-Creative -- BARKLEY, Kansas City, MO, pg. 92

Croft, Dan, Dir-Creative-Web Svcs -- LMD AGENCY, Laurel, MD, pg. 665

Crofts, Alexis, Acct Exec -- WE, New York, NY, pg. 1674

Croker, Neil, Creative Dir -- Publicis Life Brands Resolute, London, United Kingdom, pg. 934

Crompton, William, Mgr-Media & Creative Svcs -- LASPATA DECARO, New York, NY, pg. 627

Cronin, Colleen, Acct Supvr -- SPAWN IDEAS, Anchorage, AK, pg. 1063

Cronin, Dawn, Acct Dir -- Havas People Birmingham, Birmingham, United Kingdom, pg. 497

Cronin, Jeff, Sr Acct Mgr-PR -- DDCWORKS, Conshohocken, PA, pg. 290

Cronin, Mike, VP & Assoc Dir-Creative -- KRUSKOPF & COMPANY, INC., Minneapolis, MN, pg. 619

Cronk, Nick, Acct Dir -- TAXI Vancouver, Vancouver, Canada, pg. 1112

Cronwright, Cuanan, Assoc Dir-Creative & Copywriter -- Publicis Johannesburg Pty. Ltd., Sandton, South Africa, pg. 924

Crook, Lucie, Acct Dir -- TBWA\PW, London, United Kingdom, pg. 1125

Crosby, Jennifer, Acct Dir-Integrated Plng -- ZenithOptimedia Canada Inc., Toronto, Canada, pg. 1398

Croshaw, Jeff, Acct Exec -- THE GEARY COMPANY, Las Vegas, NV, pg. 419

Cross, James, Grp Head-Creative -- McCann Erickson Worldwide, London, United Kingdom, pg. 730

Cross, Jennifer, VP & Acct Dir -- Mullen Lowe, Winston Salem, NC, pg. 788

Cross, Jeremy, Assoc Dir-Creative -- RAZORFISH NEW YORK, New York, NY, pg. 1309

Cross, Muriel, Acct Coord -- BOHLSENPR INC., Indianapolis, IN, pg. 1457

Cross, Robin, Specialist-Acct Exec & Social Media -- INSIDER MEDIA MANAGEMENT, Boca Raton, FL, pg. 1551

Croteau, Samantha, Acct Coord -- CONVENTURES, INC., Boston, MA, pg. 1485

Crow, Claudia, Dir-Creative -- Talk PR, London, United Kingdom, pg. 679

Crowley, Caitlin, Acct Supvr -- Fleishman-Hillard Inc., Atlanta, GA, pg. 1517

Crowley, Ned, Chief Creative Officer -- mcgarrybowen, Chicago, IL, pg. 734

Crowther, Zoe, Dir-Mktg & New Bus -- Leo Burnett, Ltd., London, United Kingdom, pg. 641

Cruickshank, Brittany, Sr Acct Coord -- DEVENEY COMMUNICATIONS, New Orleans, LA, pg. 1493

Crump, Jordan, Sr Specialist-PR -- ARCHER MALMO, Memphis, TN, pg. 67

Crumpton, Megan, Acct Exec-Sls -- FORCE MARKETING LLC, Atlanta, GA, pg. 397

Cruse, Brian, Acct Dir -- HEILBRICE, Irvine, CA, pg. 507

Crutchfield, Michael, Dir-North America Design & Creative -- Saatchi & Saatchi, Lake Oswego, OR, pg. 1002

Cruthirds, Jason, Dir-Creative -- DOGWOOD PRODUCTIONS, INC., Mobile, AL, pg. 321

Cruz, Andrea, Acct Supvr -- MCGARRAH JESSEE, Austin, TX, pg. 733

Cruz, Bob, Assoc Creative Dir -- J. Walter Thompson, Makati, Philippines, pg. 571

Cruz, Carlo, Art Dir -- Leo Burnett Manila, Makati, Philippines, pg. 650

Cruz, Diego, Dir-Creative-MAYO Digital -- FCB Mayo, Santiago, Chile, pg. 377

Cruz, Ivan, Head-Creative -- WINTR, Seattle, WA, pg. 1211

Cruz, Jeff, Assoc Partner & Exec Dir-Creative -- VSA Partners, Inc., Minneapolis, MN, pg. 1185

Cruz, Neel Roy, Exec Creative Dir -- Orchard Advertising, Bengaluru, India, pg. 649

Cruz-Letelier, Carolina, Acct Dir -- MUH-TAY-ZIK HOF-FER, San Francisco, CA, pg. 786

Crymes, Clay, Assoc Dir-Creative -- THE MARS AGENCY, Southfield, MI, pg. 701

Csolak, Ryan James, Pres & Dir-Creative & Accounts -- RYAN JAMES AGENCY, Hamilton Square, NJ, pg. 999

Csovari, Nora, Art Dir -- DDB Budapest, Budapest, Hungary, pg. 283

Cubano, Erika, Acct Exec -- PACE ADVERTISING, New York, NY, pg. 868

Cubel, Eduard, Art Dir -- McCann Erickson S.A., Madrid, Spain, pg. 727

Cubillos, Ruben, Dir-Creative & Designer -- A BIG CHIHUAHUA, INC., San Antonio, TX, pg. 13

Cuccinello, David, Copywriter -- GREY NEW YORK, New York, NY, pg. 446

Cudiamat, Jana, Acct Exec -- Pereira & O'Dell, New York, NY, pg. 883

Cue, Alex, Dir-Creative Svcs -- EDGECORE, Winter Park, FL, pg. 338

Cuellar, Silver, Assoc Dir-Creative -- VAN WINKLE & ASSOCIATES, Atlanta, GA, pg. 1171

Cuerbo, Augustine, Chief Creative Officer & Exec VP -- Media Resources/Boston, Reading, MA, pg. 1366

Cuervo, Rebecca, Media Buyer -- ANTHONY BARADAT & ASSOCIATES, Miami, FL, pg. 62

Cuesta, Santiago, Creative Dir -- DDB Latin America, Miami, FL, pg. 275

Cueto, Jaime, Chief Creative Officer -- TBWA/Colombia Suiza de Publicidad Ltda, Bogota, Colombia, pg. 1132

Cuevas, Daniela, Partner & Dir-Creative -- THE SPARK GROUP, New York, NY, pg. 1314

Cui, Dana, Acct Supvr -- TWOFIFTEENMCCANN, San Francisco, CA, pg. 1164

Cuison, J P, Assoc Creative Dir & Dir-Art -- Publicis JimenezBasic, Makati, Philippines, pg. 934

Cuker, Aaron, CEO & Chief Creative Officer -- CUKER, Solana Beach, CA, pg. 259

Culbertson, David, Chief Creative Officer & Sr VP -- MELT, Atlanta, GA, pg. 746

Culic, Dan, Acct Dir -- RETHINK, Vancouver, Canada, pg. 973

Cullen, Steve, Dir-Design & Creative -- CREATURE, Seattle, WA, pg. 253

Culley, Beth, Sr VP & Acct Dir -- GREY GROUP, New York, NY, pg. 445

Cullinan, Dana, Creative Dir -- Jupiter Drawing Room, Rivonia, South Africa, pg. 1251

Cullinan, Dana, Creative Dir -- Jupiter Drawing Room, Rivonia, South Africa, pg. 1220

Cullinan, Jessica, Media Planner -- Optimedia-Dallas, Plano, TX, pg. 1382

Cullinan, Jessica, Media Planner -- Optimedia-Seattle, Seattle, WA, pg. 1383

Cullinan, Thomas, Partner-Creative -- Jupiter Drawing Room, Rivonia, South Africa, pg. 1251

Cullinan, Thomas, Partner-Creative -- Jupiter Drawing Room, Rivonia, South Africa, pg. 1220

Cullipher, David, Pres & Dir-Creative -- SABERTOOTH INTERACTIVE, Venice, CA, pg. 1313

Culp, Brian, Assoc Dir-Creative -- mcgarrybowen, Chicago, IL, pg. 734

Culp, Emily, Media Planner -- MARTIN/WILLIAMS ADVERTISING INC., Minneapolis, MN, pg. 704

Culpepper, Chip, Owner & Chief Creative Officer -- MANGAN HOLCOMB PARTNERS, Little Rock, AR, pg. 689

Culver, David, VP-PR -- BTC MARKETING, Wayne, PA, pg. 173

Culver, Travis, Acct Exec -- TYLER BARNETT PUBLIC RELATIONS, Beverly Hills, CA, pg. 1667

Cumbo, Melanie, Acct Dir -- Nurun France, Boulogne-Billancourt, France, pg. 925

Cummings, Bryan, Chief Creative Officer -- THE GARRIGAN LYMAN GROUP, INC, Seattle, WA, pg. 415

Cummings, Joey, Founder, CEO, Chief Creative Officer & Chief Strategic Officer -- THE JOEY COMPANY, Brooklyn, NY, pg. 593

Cummings, Joy, Acct Coord -- STRONG, Birmingham, AL, pg. 1092

Cummings, Neil, Dir-Creative -- WOLFF OLINS, London, United Kingdom, pg. 1212

Cunningham, Gary, Exec Grp Dir-Integrated Creative Services -- AFG&, New York, NY, pg. 36

Cunningham, Geoff, Jr., Dir-Creative -- MICROARTS, Greenland, NH, pg. 755

Cunningham, Jennifer, Acct Dir -- CUNDARI INTEGRATED ADVERTISING, Toronto, Canada, pg. 260

Cunningham, Kenneth, Acct Exec -- PointRoll Inc., New York, NY, pg. 901

Cunningham, Kimberly, Acct Exec -- MEADSDURKET, San Diego, CA, pg. 740

Cunningham, Kimmy, Acct Supvr -- BARTON F. GRAF 9000 LLC, New York, NY, pg. 96

Cunningham, Margaret, Sr Dir-Creative -- CUNNINGHAM GROUP, Montgomery, AL, pg. 260

Cunningham, Megan, Acct Exec -- GEAR COMMUNICATIONS, Stoneham, MA, pg. 1526

D

Personnel Index

Del, Sabrina, Acct Dir -- TUXEDO AGENCY, Montreal, Canada, pg. 1163
Delach, Mike, Art Dir & Designer -- DUNN&CO, Tampa, FL, pg. 333
Delahays, Marie, Acct Dir -- ZenithOptimedia, Levallois-Perret, France, pg. 1399
Delaine, Marie-Astrid, Acct Dir -- The Brand Union Paris, Paris, France, pg. 158
Delaney, Kathy, Chief Creative Officer-Global-Publicis Healthcare Comm Group -- Publicis Touchpoint Solutions, Yardley, PA, pg. 935
Delaney, Kathy, Chief Creative Officer -- SAATCHI & SAATCHI WELLNESS, New York, NY, pg. 1012
Delaney, Kristofer, VP & Creative Dir -- Erwin Penland, New York, NY, pg. 355
Delaney, Nicole, Acct Dir -- PARADISE ADVERTISING & MARKETING, Saint Petersburg, FL, pg. 873
Delaney, Nicole, Acct Dir -- Paradise Advertising & Marketing-Naples, Naples, FL, pg. 873
DelaOsa, Daniella, Sr Acct Coord-PR -- THE ZIMMERMAN AGENCY LLC, Tallahassee, FL, pg. 1257
Delaplane, Mitch, Dir-Creative -- GOLIN, Chicago, IL, pg. 1529
Delatorre, Jennifer, Mgr-Traffic -- REALWORLD MARKETING, Scottsdale, AZ, pg. 958
Delehag, Henrik, Dir-Creative -- CP+B, London, United Kingdom, pg. 240
DeLeon, Ken, Pres & Dir-Creative -- DELEON GROUP, LLC, Staten Island, NY, pg. 294
Delgadillo, Jimena, Acct Dir -- Ogilvy & Mather, Mexico, Mexico, pg. 839
Delgado, Alex, Dir-Creative -- AR MEDIA, New York, NY, pg. 65
Delgado, Daisy, Acct Dir -- YOUNG & RUBICAM, New York, NY, pg. 1239
Delgado, Diana, Acct Exec -- THE CONROY MARTINEZ GROUP, Coral Gables, FL, pg. 232
Delgado, Rene, Assoc Dir-Creative -- Leo Burnett USA, Chicago, IL, pg. 639
Delgado, Roberto, Dir-Creative -- McCann Erickson (Peru) Publicidad S.A., Lima, Peru, pg. 725
Delger, Tim, Dir-Art & Assoc Dir-Creative -- BOHAN, Nashville, TN, pg. 146
Delichte, Jason, VP & Exec Dir-Creative -- CRITICAL MASS INC., Calgary, Canada, pg. 255
Dello Stritto, Mark D., Founder & Dir-Creative -- LOADED CREATIVE LLC, Bellefonte, PA, pg. 666
DelMonte, Danielle, Acct Exec -- E3 COMMUNICATIONS, Buffalo, NY, pg. 1499
DeLong, Charles, Dir-Creative -- THE ZIMMERMAN AGENCY LLC, Tallahassee, FL, pg. 1257
DeLong, Kathryn, Acct Exec -- FRENCH/WEST/VAUGHAN, INC., Raleigh, NC, pg. 404
Delorenzo, Katie, Acct Exec -- MCKEE WALLWORK & COMPANY, Albuquerque, NM, pg. 735
Delp, Liz, Assoc Dir-Creative -- GREY NEW YORK, New York, NY, pg. 446
DelPurgatorio, Danny, Dir-Creative -- VITAMIN PICTURES, Chicago, IL, pg. 1180
Delsol, Bob, Exec Dir-Creative -- ZLRIGNITION, Des Moines, IA, pg. 1258
Deltour, Adrien, Dir-New Bus -- The Brand Union Paris, Paris, France, pg. 158
Deluna, Ruben, Dir-Creative -- FREE RANGE STUDIOS, Washington, DC, pg. 403
Demarchi, Dave, Client Dir, Assoc Dir-Creative & Copywriter -- SUMMERFIELD ADVERTISING INC., Columbus, OH, pg. 1098
DeMarco, Tony, CEO & Dir-Creative -- SIGNATURE COMMUNICATIONS, Philadelphia, PA, pg. 1043
DeMars, Rob, Chief Creative Officer -- MARKETING ARCHITECTS, INC., Minnetonka, MN, pg. 696
Demas, Dana, Assoc Dir-Creative -- ISOBAR, New York, NY, pg. 561
Demas, Dana, Assoc Dir-Creative -- ISOBAR US, Boston, MA, pg. 561
Dembo, Janna, Acct Dir -- SPN Ogilvy Communications Agency, Moscow, Russia, pg. 834
Demby, Ashley, Acct Dir -- BRASCO DESIGN + MARKETING, Raleigh, NC, pg. 162
Demchinskaya, Anastacia, Acct Dir -- Lowe Adventa, Moscow, Russia, pg. 790
Demeersman, Nicolas, Creative Dir -- CLM BBDO, Boulogne-Billancourt, France, pg. 106
Demetis, Stamatina, Media Planner-Digital -- ZENITH MEDIA SERVICES, New York, NY, pg. 1396
Demetriades, Alexandra, Acct Exec -- KETCHUM, New York, NY, pg. 1561
Demetrius, Bob, Partner & Sr Dir-Creative -- LSHD ADVERTISING INC., Chicopee, MA, pg. 672
Demilio, Chavo, Exec Dir-Creative -- McCann Erickson, Buenos Aires, Argentina, pg. 716
Demko, Lyubov, Mgr-New Bus -- Lowe Adventa, Moscow, Russia, pg. 790
Denardi, Kate, Acct Coord -- O'KEEFFE & CO., Alexandria, VA, pg. 1610
Denberg, Josh, Partner & Dir-Creative -- DIVISION OF LABOR, Sausalito, CA, pg. 316
Denekas, Steven, Exec Dir-Creative -- INSTRUMENT, Portland, OR, pg. 550
Deng, Bo, Dir-Creative -- Ogilvy & Mather Asia/Pacific, Central, China (Hong Kong), pg. 842
Deng, Rebecca, Acct Dir -- TDW+CO, Seattle, WA, pg. 1134
Denham, Christine, Acct Supvr -- COYNE PUBLIC RELATIONS, Parsippany, NJ, pg. 1487
Denholm, Alex, Exec Dir-Creative -- GLUTTONY NEW YORK, New York, NY, pg. 430
Denis, Vladyslava, Dir-Creative-JWT Ukraine -- JWT, Kiev, Ukraine, pg. 1220
Denise, Angela, Creative Dir -- KBS+, New York, NY, pg. 604
Denison, Adam, Acct Supvr -- METHOD COMMUNICATIONS, Salt Lake City, UT, pg. 1589
Deniz, Elvan, Art Dir -- McCann Erickson WorldGroup Turkey, Istanbul, Turkey, pg. 729
Denney, Bess, Acct Dir -- LEVLANE ADVERTISING/PR/INTERACTIVE, Philadelphia, PA, pg. 654
Denney, Kelly, Mgr-Traffic -- HADFIELD COMMUNICATIONS, Houston, TX, pg. 471
Dennis, Maria, Acct Exec -- SOURCELINK, Itasca, IL, pg. 1059
Dennison, Ashley, Acct Dir -- REPUTATION PARTNERS, Chicago, IL, pg. 969
Denniston, Guy, Creative Dir -- Y&R, Auckland, New Zealand, pg. 1223
Denniston, Guy, Creative Dir -- Y&R, Auckland, New Zealand, pg. 1233
Denser, Flavia, Acct Dir -- SapientNitro iThink, Sao Paulo, Brazil, pg. 1020
Densmore, Eric, VP & Acct Dir -- ABELSON-TAYLOR, INC., Chicago, IL, pg. 16
Densmore, Jim, Assoc Dir-Creative -- ARKETI GROUP, Atlanta, GA, pg. 69
Dent, Amanda, Assoc Dir-Creative & Copywriter -- ARCHER MALMO, Memphis, TN, pg. 67
Dent, Rich, Acct Dir-Mgmt -- DOUBLEPOSITIVE MARKETING GROUP, INC., Baltimore, MD, pg. 326
Denyak, Iryna, Acct Dir -- Adventa Lowe, Kiev, Ukraine, pg. 789
Deo, Siddharth, Grp Dir-Creative -- TBWA India, New Delhi, India, pg. 1129
Deon, Diego, Gen Dir-Creative -- FCB CREA, San Salvador, El Salvador, pg. 378
Deordio, Cameron, Acct Coord -- BREAKAWAY COMMUNICATIONS LLC, New York, NY, pg. 1460
Deoul, Shannon, Acct Exec -- RAZ PUBLIC RELATIONS, Santa Monica, CA, pg. 1631
DePalma, Brielle, Acct Supvr -- AGENCYRX, New York, NY, pg. 39
Depasquale, Anthony, Sr VP-Creative Content Production-Television/Video -- ICR, Norwalk, CT, pg. 532
DePinto, Gina, Acct Dir -- WESTBOUND COMMUNICATIONS, INC., Orange, CA, pg. 1198
Deppe, Tod, VP-Creative -- OIA MARKETING COMMUNICATIONS, Dayton, OH, pg. 854
der Heul, Jeena van, Art Dir -- Ubachswisbrun J. Walter Thompson, Amsterdam, Netherlands, pg. 574
Derby, Andrea, VP & Acct Dir -- BBDO Atlanta, Atlanta, GA, pg. 100
Dergachev, Ivan, Assoc Dir-Creative -- Leo Burnett Moscow, Moscow, Russia, pg. 645
DerHovsepian, Sandy, Assoc Dir-Creative & Writer -- CRAMER-KRASSELT, Chicago, IL, pg. 242
Deri, Henrietta, Acct Dir & Planner -- TBWA Budapest, Budapest, Hungary, pg. 1120
Derkach, Kaitlin, Acct Dir -- THE PROMOTION FACTORY, New York, NY, pg. 913
Dermer, Adam, Acct Coord -- A&C AGENCY, Toronto, Canada, pg. 1438
Derogee, Natascha, Acct Exec -- Hollander en Van der Mey/MS&L, Voorburg, Netherlands, pg. 1595
Derouault, Thomas, Exec Dir-Creative -- HAVAS, Puteaux, France, pg. 484
Derouault, Thomas, Dir-Creative -- Havas 360-Annecy, Annecy-le-Vieux, France, pg. 493
Derouault, Thomas, Dir-Creative -- Havas 360 Rennes, Rennes, France, pg. 493
Derouault, Thomas, Exec Dir-Creative -- Havas Digital, Puteaux, France, pg. 486
Derrick, Dave, Assoc Dir-Creative -- LEO BURNETT WORLDWIDE, INC., Chicago, IL, pg. 637
Derrick, Mike, Dir-Creative -- THE ADCOM GROUP, Cleveland, OH, pg. 27
Dery, Paul, Exec Dir-Creative -- R/GA, New York, NY, pg. 946
Desai, Swapna, Acct Dir -- MARTIN/WILLIAMS ADVERTISING INC., Minneapolis, MN, pg. 704
Desanti, Yvonne, Dir-Creative -- Havas Worldwide-Strat Farm, New York, NY, pg. 490
Desantis, Anna, Mgr-Traffic -- BREEN SMITH ADVERTISING, Atlanta, GA, pg. 163
DeSantis, Anna, Mgr-Traffic -- BREENSMITH ADVERTISING, Atlanta, GA, pg. 163
Desatnik, Penny, Acct Supvr -- BLATTEL COMMUNICATIONS, San Francisco, CA, pg. 137
Desautel, Brian, Dir-Creative -- THE BUDDY GROUP, Irvine, CA, pg. 174
Desautel, Sara, Acct Dir -- DH, Spokane, WA, pg. 305
Deschamps, Eric, Dir-Creative -- BOZ Paris, Paris, France, pg. 918
Deschamps, Olivia, Acct Dir-Global -- MediaCom Paris, Paris, France, pg. 1369
Descollonges, Justine, Principal & Dir-Creative -- HDSF, San Francisco, CA, pg. 505
DeSena, Brian, Acct Exec -- NATIONAL PROMOTIONS & ADVERTISING INC., Los Angeles, CA, pg. 801
Desfretier, Pierre, Creative Dir-Digital -- Edelman, Hong Kong, China (Hong Kong), pg. 1506
Deshler, Kevin, Acct Exec -- THE LACEK GROUP, Minneapolis, MN, pg. 622
Desikan, Raghu, Dir-Creative -- OGILVY HEALTHWORLD, New York, NY, pg. 852
Desilva, Anna, Acct Supvr -- BBDO WORLDWIDE INC., New York, NY, pg. 99
DeSilva, Sue, VP & Creative Dir -- MULLEN LOWE GROUP, Boston, MA, pg. 786
DeSimone, Rich, Dir-Creative -- THE EGC GROUP, Melville, NY, pg. 339
Desira, Nicholas, Grp Head-Creative -- BADJAR Ogilvy, Melbourne, Australia, pg. 840
Desmazieres, Marc, Dir-Creative -- Hakuhodo France S.A., Paris, France, pg. 475
Desmidt, Kristen, Dir-PR -- DAIGLE CREATIVE, Jacksonville, FL, pg. 263
Desmond, Courtney, Media Planner-Integrated -- CONNELLY PARTNERS, Boston, MA, pg. 231
Desogus, Matteo, Art Dir & Graphic Designer -- TBWA Roma, Rome, Italy, pg. 1121
Desrosiers, Christian, VP & Dir-Creative -- J. Walter Thompson Canada, Montreal, Canada, pg. 566
Desrousseaux, Richard, Exec Dir-Creative -- BETC Life, Paris, France, pg. 492
Determann, Julie, Acct Supvr -- THE WEINSTEIN ORGANIZATION, INC., Chicago, IL, pg. 1195
Detwiler, Bryan, Acct Supvr -- IOSTUDIO, Nashville, TN, pg. 560
Dev, Sangita, Dir-Creative -- Ogilvy & Mather, Hyderabad, India, pg. 843
Dev, Sangita, Dir-Creative -- Ogilvy & Mather, Bengaluru, India, pg. 842
Devenney, Alasdair, Acct Dir -- Havas People Glasgow, Glasgow, United Kingdom, pg. 497
Devenney, Alasdair, Acct Dir -- Havas People London, London, United Kingdom, pg. 497
Devereaux, Joanna, Acct Supvr -- Moroch, Saint Louis, MO, pg. 775
Devers, Wade, Mng Partner & Exec Dir-Creative -- ARNOLD WORLDWIDE, Boston, MA, pg. 71
Devgun, Rohit, Dir-Creative -- McCann Erickson India, Mumbai, India, pg. 721
Devgun, Rohit, Dir-Creative -- McCann Erickson India, New Delhi, India, pg. 722
Devin, Machel, Acct Supvr -- STRUCK, Salt Lake City, UT, pg. 1093
Devine, Samantha, Acct Supvr -- OGILVY & MATHER, New York, NY, pg. 826
DeVito, Chris, Partner & Dir-Creative -- DEVITO GROUP, New York, NY, pg. 304
DeVito, Sal, Dir-Creative -- DEVITO/VERDI, New York, NY, pg. 304

Personnel Index

Dosmann, Greg, Grp Assoc Dir-Creative -- MICROMASS COMMUNICATIONS INC, Cary, NC, pg. 755
Doss, Gabby, Acct Exec -- PENNEBAKER, Houston, TX, pg. 882
Dotson, Aaron, Co-Founder & Creative Dir -- ELEVATION ADVERTISING LLC, Richmond, VA, pg. 343
Dotterer, Holly, Acct Supvr -- CAROLYN GRISKO & ASSOCIATES INC., Chicago, IL, pg. 1473
Douaihy, Collette, Sr VP & Grp Dir-Creative -- DIGITAS HEALTH, Philadelphia, PA, pg. 309
Doubal, Rob, Co-Pres & Co-Chief Creative Officer -- McCann Erickson Advertising Ltd., London, United Kingdom, pg. 729
Dougherty, Dan, Assoc Dir-Creative -- TM ADVERTISING, Dallas, TX, pg. 1147
Dougherty, Heather, Acct Dir -- THE KARMA AGENCY, Philadelphia, PA, pg. 1558
Dougherty, Jen, Assoc Dir-Creative -- LIVEAREALABS, Seattle, WA, pg. 663
Dougherty, Jennyfer Butzen, Media Planner & Sr Acct Exec -- LKH&S, Chicago, IL, pg. 664
Doughty, Scott C, Exec VP & Dir-Creative -- DJ-LA LLC, Los Angeles, CA, pg. 317
Douglas, Cole, Acct Coord -- APEX PUBLIC RELATIONS, Toronto, Canada, pg. 1445
Douglas, Jamie, Acct Exec -- Fleishman-Hillard Inc., Marina Del Rey, CA, pg. 1517
Douglas, Kate, Acct Dir -- McCann Erickson Advertising Ltd., London, United Kingdom, pg. 729
Douglas, Tillman, Jr., Acct Dir -- THE PARTNERSHIP, Atlanta, GA, pg. 876
Dousova, Katerina, Mgr-PR -- Pleon Impact, Prague, Czech Republic, pg. 105
Dover, Jodie, Acct Exec -- CENTRO LLC, Chicago, IL, pg. 1285
Dow, Bill, VP & Dir-Creative -- CRAMER-KRASSELT, Chicago, IL, pg. 242
Dow, Leigh, VP-PR -- LANETERRALEVER, Phoenix, AZ, pg. 625
Dowdeswell, Ryan, Assoc Dir-Creative -- PHOENIX GROUP, Regina, Canada, pg. 889
Dowdy, Brandon, Acct Supvr -- AGENCY ENTOURAGE LLC, Dallas, TX, pg. 38
Dowell, Laurie, Specialist-Creative Mktg -- JACK NADEL, INC., Los Angeles, CA, pg. 1418
Dowerah, Sameera, Dir-Creative -- Orchard Advertising, Bengaluru, India, pg. 649
Dowling, Mike, VP-Creative Svcs -- PAULSEN MARKETING COMMUNICATIONS, INC., Sioux Falls, SD, pg. 879
Down, Lex, Creative Dir -- Grey London, London, United Kingdom, pg. 447
Downes, Hannah, Acct Dir -- FCB Auckland, Auckland, New Zealand, pg. 381
Downey, Judy, Acct Exec -- NEWBERRY PUBLIC RELATIONS & MARKETING INC, East Providence, RI, pg. 1602
Downey, Kerry Shea, Dir-Creative -- THE FANTASTICAL, Boston, MA, pg. 368
Downs, Jenny, Acct Exec -- THE JOHNSON GROUP, Chattanooga, TN, pg. 594
Downs, Joshua, Dir-Creative -- FORMATIVE, Seattle, WA, pg. 397
Downs, Tim, Exec Creative Dir -- MARTINO FLYNN LLC, Pittsford, NY, pg. 705
Doyle, Chelsea, Acct Exec -- Alcone Marketing Group, San Francisco, CA, pg. 1404
Doyle, Chrissy, Acct Exec -- WORLDLINK MEDIA, Los Angeles, CA, pg. 1215
Doyle, Dale, Exec Dir-Creative -- Landor Associates, Cincinnati, OH, pg. 625
Doyle, Darcy, VP & Dir-Creative -- HOFFMAN AND PARTNERS, Braintree, MA, pg. 520
Doyle, Kayla, Media Planner -- Mullen Lowe, Detroit, MI, pg. 788
Doyle, Kelly, Acct Supvr-PR -- CORBIN-HILLMAN COMMUNICATIONS, New York, NY, pg. 1486
Doyle, Lindsay, Dir-Creative Svcs -- SMARTMARKETING COMMUNICATIONS, Albuquerque, NM, pg. 1651
Doyle, Matthew, Exec VP-Brdcst Production -- GYK Antler, Boston, MA, pg. 468
Doyle, Taylor, Acct Supvr -- SAATCHI & SAATCHI, New York, NY, pg. 1000
Draddy, Anne, Acct Dir -- COHN & WOLFE, New York, NY, pg. 1480
Drago, Alessandro, Creative Dir -- Critical Mass Inc., Toronto, Canada, pg. 255
Drago, Cris, Dir-PR -- PARADISE ADVERTISING & MARKETING, Saint Petersburg, FL, pg. 873
Drake, Bill, Sr VP & Dir-Creative -- HOFFMAN AND PARTNERS, Braintree, MA, pg. 520
Drake, Emily, Art Dir -- Saatchi & Saatchi, Auckland, New Zealand, pg. 1011
Drake, Haley, Acct Supvr -- 88/BRAND PARTNERS, Chicago, IL, pg. 12
Drake, Kristina, Coord-PR -- CHATTER BUZZ MEDIA, Orlando, FL, pg. 206
Drakulich, Rachel, Acct Exec -- EDELMAN, Chicago, IL, pg. 1500
Dransfield, Emily, Mgr-Creative Svcs -- FREE RANGE STUDIOS, Washington, DC, pg. 403
Drape, Emily, Acct Exec -- TROZZOLO COMMUNICATIONS GROUP, Kansas City, MO, pg. 1159
Draughon, Roman, Dir-Creative -- DUFOUR ADVERTISING, Sheboygan, WI, pg. 332
Drayer, David, Assoc Dir-Creative -- PUBLICIS NEW YORK, New York, NY, pg. 935
Drazen, Zoe, Acct Coord -- HUB STRATEGY AND COMMUNICATION, San Francisco, CA, pg. 526
Dreifuss, Ruby, Media Planner -- Young & Rubicam Wellington, Wellington, New Zealand, pg. 1242
Dreistadt, Jason, Dir-Creative & Ops -- INFINITY CONCEPTS, Export, PA, pg. 545
Drennon, Allison, Acct Exec -- THE SELLS AGENCY, INC., Little Rock, AR, pg. 1031
Drennon, Allison, Acct Exec -- The Sells Agency, Inc., Fayetteville, AR, pg. 1031
Dressler, Stephanie, VP-PR & Digital Strategy -- DUKAS PUBLIC RELATIONS, INC., New York, NY, pg. 1498
Drever, Cecilia, Acct Dir -- Corporacion / J. Walter Thompson, Montevideo, Uruguay, pg. 579
Drew, Tom, Dir-Creative -- BARTLE BOGLE HEGARTY LIMITED, London, United Kingdom, pg. 94
Drewes, Melanie, Acct Coord -- WEST ADVERTISING, Alameda, CA, pg. 1197
Dreyer, Yadelle, Acct Supvr -- MOSAIC MULTICULTURAL, Phoenix, AZ, pg. 778
Driggers, Amanda, Acct Dir -- FIREHOUSE, INC., Dallas, TX, pg. 1412
Driggers, Avery, Acct Exec -- THE BRADFORD GROUP, Nashville, TN, pg. 1459
Driscoll, James, VP & Dir-Creative Tech -- CONCENTRIC PHARMA ADVERTISING, New York, NY, pg. 228
Drob, Aimee, Acct Exec -- ROBERTS + LANGER DDB, New York, NY, pg. 987
Drobova, Elena, Dir-Creative -- RDA INTERNATIONAL, New York, NY, pg. 956
Dropkin, Meredith, Sr Acct Supvr-PR -- ERIC MOWER + ASSOCIATES, Syracuse, NY, pg. 353
Drossman, Neil, Dir-Creative -- NEEDLEMAN DROSSMAN & PARTNERS, New York, NY, pg. 803
Drouet, Jessica, Sr Acct Exec-PR -- BEBER SILVERSTEIN GROUP, Miami, FL, pg. 121
Droy, Brad, Pres & Dir-Creative -- DROY ADVERTISING, Denver, CO, pg. 330
Drozd, Mark, Partner & Exec Dir-Creative -- SIMPLE TRUTH COMMUNICATION PARTNERS, Chicago, IL, pg. 1046
Drozdowska, Gosia, Sr Dir-Art & Dir-Creative -- FCB Warsaw, Warsaw, Poland, pg. 374
Drozdowska, Magdalena, Deputy Creative Dir -- DDB Warsaw, Warsaw, Poland, pg. 287
Drummer, Alan, Dir-Creative-Content -- NAVAJO COMPANY, Milpitas, CA, pg. 802
Drummond, Ashley, Acct Exec -- MASS MEDIA MARKETING, Augusta, GA, pg. 708
Drummond, Gavin, Co-Creative Dir -- Ogilvy Montreal, Montreal, Canada, pg. 829
Drummond, Keith, Assoc Dir-Creative -- Forward, London, United Kingdom, pg. 1227
Drust, Stefan, CEO & Exec Dir-Creative -- FUSE INTERACTIVE, Laguna Beach, CA, pg. 410
Dryer, Jeff, Assoc Dir-Creative -- CP+B, Coconut Grove, FL, pg. 239
Drzadinski, Carrie, Acct Supvr -- RED BROWN KLE, Milwaukee, WI, pg. 959
Dsouza, Valerian, Dir-Creative -- TBWA India Corporate, New Delhi, India, pg. 1129
Du Toit, Dallas, Exec Dir-Creative -- Gloo Design Agency, Cape Town, South Africa, pg. 848
Du Toit, Mel, Dir-Creative -- TBWA Singapore, Singapore, Singapore, pg. 1130
Du, Mark, Acct Dir -- Millward Brown China, Shanghai, China, pg. 759
Duarte, Mitchell, Dir-Creative -- 10TH DEGREE, Lake Forest, CA, pg. 1279
Dube, Clay, Acct Dir-Natl -- SMAK, Vancouver, Canada, pg. 1052
Dube, Madeleine, Media Planner -- Initiative Toronto, Toronto, Canada, pg. 1345
Dubin, Chelsea, Acct Exec -- RED TETTEMER O'CONNELL & PARTNERS, Philadelphia, PA, pg. 963
Dubois, Alice, Acct Dir -- 451 MARKETING, Boston, MA, pg. 1436
Dubois, David, Art Dir -- THE PITCH AGENCY, Culver City, CA, pg. 893
Dubon, Yuliana, Acct Exec -- ECO Y&R, S.A, Guatemala, Guatemala, pg. 1250
Dubrick, Mike, Assoc Dir-Creative -- RETHINK, Vancouver, Canada, pg. 973
Dubrovsky, Alex, Assoc Dir-Creative -- SPACE150, Minneapolis, MN, pg. 1061
Dubs, Bill, Partner-Creative -- DUBS & DASH, Guelph, Canada, pg. 331
Dubs, Jake, Assoc Dir-Creative & Writer -- PEREIRA & O'DELL, San Francisco, CA, pg. 883
Dubs, Jake, Assoc Dir-Creative -- Pereira & O'Dell, New York, NY, pg. 883
Dubsky, Annie, Acct Dir -- EXPONENT PR, Minneapolis, MN, pg. 1512
Duccoli, Sebastin, Creative Dir -- Del Campo Nazca Saatchi & Saatchi, Buenos Aires, Argentina, pg. 1007
Duchene, Delphine, Acct Dir -- The Marketing Store, Levallois-Perret, France, pg. 1421
Duchon, Scott, Partner & Chief Creative Officer -- TWOFIFTEENMCCANN, San Francisco, CA, pg. 1164
Duder, Emily, Acct Dir -- SapientNitro, Singapore, Singapore, pg. 1020
Dudley, Danielle, Sr VP & Reg Mgr-Brdcst -- Team Detroit, Dearborn, MI, pg. 1222
Dudley, Oliver, Grp Dir-Creative -- MCGARRYBOWEN, New York, NY, pg. 733
Dueck, Joshua, Strategist-Media & Media Buyer -- TAMM + KIT, Toronto, Canada, pg. 1108
Duer, Cathy, Media Planner & Media Buyer -- HANNA & ASSOCIATES INC., Coeur D'Alene, ID, pg. 478
Duffy, John, Dir-Creative -- MERKLEY+PARTNERS, New York, NY, pg. 750
Duffy, Kevin, Pres & Chief Creative Officer -- STRAIGHT NORTH, LLC., Downers Grove, IL, pg. 1089
Duffy, Ryan, Dir-Creative & Copywriter -- PULSE MARKETING & ADVERTISING LLC, Leawood, KS, pg. 937
Dufour, Mathieu, Art Dir -- LG2, Montreal, Canada, pg. 656
DuFour, Taylor, Acct Exec -- HAVAS WORLDWIDE CHICAGO, Chicago, IL, pg. 502
Duft, Ward, Dir-Creative -- STOLTZ MARKETING GROUP, Boise, ID, pg. 1087
Dugish, Justin, Acct Exec -- NELSON ADVERTISING SOLUTIONS, Sonoma, CA, pg. 1271
Dugow, Len, Pres & Chief Creative Officer -- LGD COMMUNICATIONS, INC., Miami, FL, pg. 656
Duhalde, Tomas, Dir-Art & Creative -- THE COMMUNITY, Miami, FL, pg. 227
Duignan, Conor, Producer-Brdcst -- GOODBY, SILVERSTEIN & PARTNERS, INC., San Francisco, CA, pg. 434
Duke, Dustin, Exec Dir-Creative -- Havas PR, New York, NY, pg. 487
Duke, Dustin, Exec Dir-Creative -- HAVAS WORLDWIDE, New York, NY, pg. 488
Dula, Michael, Chief Creative Officer -- BRANDINGBUSINESS, Irvine, CA, pg. 159
Dulce, Santiago, Dir-Creative-Brazil -- J. Walter Thompson, Sao Paulo, Brazil, pg. 577
Dulla, Lindsey, Assoc Media Buyer -- SPARK COMMUNICATIONS, Chicago, IL, pg. 1389
Duman, Mike, Partner & Co-Dir-Creative -- SKAR ADVERTISING, Omaha, NE, pg. 1049
Dumitrescu, Alexandru, Exec Dir-Creative -- McCann Erickson Romania, Bucharest, Romania, pg. 726
Dump, Cassy, Acct Exec -- PASCALE COMMUNICATIONS LLC, Pittsburgh, PA, pg. 1613
Duncan, Greg, Acct Exec -- BLUE HERON COMMUNICATIONS, Norman, OK, pg. 1456
Duncan, Jane, Acct Supvr -- LUQUIRE GEORGE ANDREWS, INC., Charlotte, NC, pg. 674
Duncan, Kelsey, Asst Acct Coord -- RUNSWITCH PUBLIC RELATIONS, Louisville, KY, pg. 1643
Duncan, Marquis, Media Planner -- CP+B, Coconut Grove, FL, pg. 239
Duncan, Mike, CEO & Dir-Creative -- SAGE ISLAND, Wilmington, NC, pg. 1014
Duncan, Robert, Owner & Exec Dir-Creative -- DUNCAN CHANNON, San Francisco, CA, pg. 332

Duncan, Savannah, Acct Exec -- THE WILBERT GROUP, Atlanta, GA, pg. 1685
Duncan, Steve, Acct Dir -- DCI-West, Aurora, CO, pg. 304
Duncan, Steve, Acct Dir -- DEVELOPMENT COUNSELLORS INTERNATIONAL, LTD., New York, NY, pg. 304
Dundina, Natalia, Creative Dir -- Leo Burnett Kiev, Kiev, Ukraine, pg. 646
Dundore, Bruce, Dir-Creative-North America -- SPARK44, Culver City, CA, pg. 1062
Dungate, Scott, Dir-Creative -- Wieden + Kennedy, London, United Kingdom, pg. 1204
Dunkak, Geoff, VP-Creative Svcs -- BUSINESS-TO-BUSINESS MARKETING COMMUNICATIONS, Raleigh, NC, pg. 178
Dunkley, Steve, Partner & Chief Creative Officer -- LUQUIRE GEORGE ANDREWS, INC., Charlotte, NC, pg. 674
Dunlap, Lillian, Acct Dir -- LEWIS PR, Boston, MA, pg. 1575
Dunlap, Susanne, Assoc Dir-Creative -- QUINN FABLE ADVERTISING, New York, NY, pg. 944
Dunlea, Caroline, Acct Dir -- bcg2, Auckland, New Zealand, pg. 1217
Dunlop, Patty, Dir-Creative Svcs -- Razorfish San Francisco, San Francisco, CA, pg. 1310
Dunlop, Trent, Acct Dir -- MCGARRYBOWEN, New York, NY, pg. 733
Dunn, Allison, Media Buyer -- THE GLENN GROUP, Reno, NV, pg. 427
Dunn, Claire, Acct Exec -- GCG MARKETING, Fort Worth, TX, pg. 419
Dunn, Ian, Dir-Creative -- THE VIA AGENCY, Portland, ME, pg. 1175
Dunn, Jennifer, Dir-PR -- CONVERSA, Tampa, FL, pg. 1486
Dunn, Kaila, Assoc Dir-Creative -- ARC WORLDWIDE, Chicago, IL, pg. 1405
Dunn, Libby, Acct Supvr -- HEAT, San Francisco, CA, pg. 507
Dunn, Michael, Dir-Creative -- BFG COMMUNICATIONS, Bluffton, SC, pg. 128
Dunn, Mike, Acct Exec -- PERFORMANCE MARKETING, West Des Moines, IA, pg. 884
Dunn, Mike, Mgr-Print Production -- YOUNG & RUBICAM, New York, NY, pg. 1239
Dunn, Ryan, Exec Dir-Creative -- CHRLX, New York, NY, pg. 210
Dunn, Troy, Pres & Chief Creative Officer -- DUNN&CO, Tampa, FL, pg. 333
Dunn-Blough, Marie, Pres & Chief Creative Officer -- REDHYPE, Greenville, SC, pg. 965
Dunton, Becky, Acct Dir -- NELSON SCHMIDT, Milwaukee, WI, pg. 804
Dupont, Christelle, Acct Supvr -- MEDIALINE PR, Dallas, TX, pg. 1588
Dupont, Stephen, VP-PR & Content Mktg -- POCKET HERCULES, Minneapolis, MN, pg. 899
Dupre, Lesley, Acct Mgr & Specialist-PR -- THE BALCOM AGENCY, Fort Worth, TX, pg. 88
Dupre, Lisa, Dir-Creative & Art -- Young & Rubicam NZ Ltd., Auckland, New Zealand, pg. 1242
Duque, Carolina, Acct Exec -- Lowe SSP3, Bogota, Colombia, pg. 793
Duque, Jaime, Exec Dir-Creative-LOWE & SSP3 -- Lowe SSP3, Bogota, Colombia, pg. 793
Duque, Lina, Acct Exec-LATAM & Caribbean Markets -- THE ALISON GROUP, North Miami Beach, FL, pg. 1404
Duran, Alex, Acct Exec -- ADSERVICES INC., Hollywood, FL, pg. 32
Duran, Federico, Creative Dir -- Conill Advertising, Inc., El Segundo, CA, pg. 230
Durand, Marjo, Acct Dir -- RETHINK, Vancouver, Canada, pg. 973
Durant, Tripp, VP & Acct Dir -- LUCKIE & COMPANY, Birmingham, AL, pg. 672
Durban, Christopher, Sr VP & Creative Dir -- Weber Shandwick-Baltimore, Baltimore, MD, pg. 1677
Durfey, Andrea, Acct Dir -- R/P MARKETING PUBLIC RELATIONS, Holland, OH, pg. 1630
Durham, Charlene, Sr Acct Supvr-PR -- CRONIN & COMPANY, INC., Glastonbury, CT, pg. 255
Durham, Jeff, Creative Dir -- DW ADVERTISING, Bloomfield, CT, pg. 333
Durkin, Rebecca, Assoc Dir-Creative -- Padilla/CRT, Richmond, VA, pg. 869
Durr, Lindsay, Acct Dir -- 360 PUBLIC RELATIONS LLC, Boston, MA, pg. 1436
Durrett, Jake, Coord-Creative -- GERSHONI, San Francisco, CA, pg. 423
Durrieu, Juan, Creative Dir -- Quorum Nazca Saatchi & Saatchi, Lima, Peru, pg. 1009
Dursin, Marissa, Acct Exec -- RESOUND MARKETING, Princeton, NJ, pg. 1635
Dusman, Michael, Acct Supvr -- VICTORS & SPOILS, Boulder, CO, pg. 1176
Dutkowsky, Anna, Acct Exec -- CINDY RICCIO COMMUNICATIONS, INC., New York, NY, pg. 1478
Dutt, Surjo, Creative Dir -- Sapient Corporation Private Limited, Gurgaon, India, pg. 1019
Dutta, Nobin, Controller-Creative -- Ogilvy & Mather, Hyderabad, India, pg. 843
Duttlinger, Andy, Art Dir -- GYRO DENVER, Denver, CO, pg. 470
Dutton, Greg, Partner & Exec Dir-Creative -- WINGNUT ADVERTISING, Minneapolis, MN, pg. 1210
Dutton, Sian, Acct Exec -- Havas People Birmingham, Birmingham, United Kingdom, pg. 497
DuVal, Stephanie, Acct Exec -- Helia, Glen Allen, VA, pg. 490
Duvall, Dylan, Coord-Brdcst -- Media Experts, Montreal, Canada, pg. 1365
Dveirin, Ben, Assoc Dir-Creative -- RIESTER, Phoenix, AZ, pg. 980
Dveirin, Ben, Assoc Dir-Creative -- RIESTER ROBB, El Segundo, CA, pg. 980
Dwiggins, Sara, Acct Supvr -- THE INTEGER GROUP - DENVER, Lakewood, CO, pg. 1416
Dwyer, Amanda, Acct Supvr -- Erwin Penland, New York, NY, pg. 355
Dwyer, Amanda Sims, Acct Dir -- AKQA, Inc., Portland, OR, pg. 1281
Dwyer, Lorraine, Head-Lifestyle PR & Dir -- Wilson Hartnell (WH), Dublin, Ireland, pg. 1607
Dye, Dave, Head-Art & Creative Dir -- J. Walter Thompson, London, United Kingdom, pg. 575
Dye, Karen, Dir-PR -- DEMOSS, Atlanta, GA, pg. 1493
Dyer, Kristine, VP & Acct Dir-Media -- OGILVY COMMONHEALTH INSIGHTS & ANALYTICS, Parsippany, NJ, pg. 1271
Dykstra, Julie, Acct Supvr -- LEO BURNETT WORLDWIDE, INC., Chicago, IL, pg. 637
Dykstra, Steve, Acct Exec -- KRUEGER COMMUNICATIONS, Venice, CA, pg. 619
Dykta, Brenna, Acct Supvr -- STRATEGIC, New York, NY, pg. 1090
Dynes, Brooke, Dir-Traffic & Fin -- MESH DESIGN, Baton Rouge, LA, pg. 751
Dyrhaug, John, Dir-Creative -- SCALES ADVERTISING, Saint Paul, MN, pg. 1023

E

Ea, Sia, Sr Dir-Creative -- ANSIBLE MOBILE, New York, NY, pg. 60
Eade, Alice, Acct Mgr-PR -- FCB Auckland, Auckland, New Zealand, pg. 381
Eagan, Alicia, Acct Supvr -- Edelman, Sacramento, CA, pg. 1501
Eagan, Roy, Acct Exec -- PROOF ADVERTISING, Austin, TX, pg. 913
Eagle, Jim, Dir-Creative -- THE ALTUS AGENCY, Philadelphia, PA, pg. 52
Eagle, Ron, Sr VP-PR -- R&R PARTNERS, Las Vegas, NV, pg. 945
Eagleston, Paul, Dir-Creative -- FUEL MARKETING, Salt Lake City, UT, pg. 407
Eagleton, Jenna, Acct Exec-Subway Restaurants -- NL PARTNERS, Portland, ME, pg. 810
Eagleton, Nick, Dir-Creative-UK -- The Partners, London, United Kingdom, pg. 1221
Eakin, Jordan, Assoc Creative Dir -- MCKINNEY, Durham, NC, pg. 736
Earle, Drex, COO & Dir-Creative -- BOUNCE MARKETING AND EVENTS, LLC, Austin, TX, pg. 1407
Earley, Megan, Acct Exec -- The Bravo Group, Chicago, IL, pg. 162
Earley, Megan, Acct Exec -- BRAVO GROUP INC., Harrisburg, PA, pg. 1459
Earls, Kristen, Acct Dir -- WIT MEDIA, New York, NY, pg. 1211
Early, Kristina, Media Planner & Media Buyer -- BRIGGS & CALDWELL, Houston, TX, pg. 165
Early, Molly, Acct Exec -- DEVINE + PARTNERS, Philadelphia, PA, pg. 1494
East, Tiffany, VP-PR -- THE GLENN GROUP, Reno, NV, pg. 427
Eastburn, Eileen, Acct Dir -- CHANDELIER, New York, NY, pg. 203
Easterlin, Maggie, Acct Supvr -- Stratacomm, Inc., Novi, MI, pg. 1518
Eastman, David, Dir-Creative & Copywriter -- THE RICHARDS GROUP, INC., Dallas, TX, pg. 978
Easton, Darren, VP & Dir-Creative -- THE CYPHERS AGENCY, INC., Annapolis, MD, pg. 262
Eatherton, Megan, Media Planner -- GSD&M Chicago, Chicago, IL, pg. 465
Eaton, Andrew, Dir-Creative -- R/GA, New York, NY, pg. 946
Eaton, Meredith L., Acct Dir -- MARCH COMMUNICATIONS, Boston, MA, pg. 1582
Ebanks, Christie, Acct Coord -- TRUE BLUE COMMUNICATIONS, Clearwater, FL, pg. 1666
Ebel, Blake, Founder & Chief Creative Officer -- FEAR NOT AGENCY, Denver, CO, pg. 383
Ebert, Kirsten, Strategist-PR & Digital Media -- STYLE ADVERTISING, Birmingham, AL, pg. 1094
Ebner, Renee, Head-Community & Acct Exec -- FRONTIER STRATEGIES LLC, Ridgeland, MS, pg. 1523
Echenoz, Dave, Mgr-Print Production -- DNA SEATTLE, Seattle, WA, pg. 319
Echevarria, Marco, Owner & Dir-Creative -- BURN CREATIVE, Carlisle, PA, pg. 177
Echols, Courtney, Acct Exec -- FATHOM COMMUNICATIONS, New York, NY, pg. 369
Ecke, Shannon, Sr Designer-Creative -- BLIND SOCIETY, Scottsdale, AZ, pg. 138
Ecker, Brittany, Acct Dir -- SQ1, Dallas, TX, pg. 1068
Ecker, Brittany, Acct Supvr -- SQUARE ONE MARKETING, West Hartford, CT, pg. 1069
Eckford, Mandy, Acct Dir-Consulting -- VICTORS & SPOILS, Boulder, CO, pg. 1176
Eckman, Jon, Grp Dir-Creative -- HAVAS WORLDWIDE CHICAGO, Chicago, IL, pg. 502
Eckols, Bruce, Dir-Creative & Art -- CAPPELLI MILES, Portland, OR, pg. 190
Eckstein, Axel, Exec Dir-Creative -- Spillmann/Felser/Leo Burnett, Zurich, Switzerland, pg. 645
Eddy, Nelson, Mng Partner-Creative -- DYE, VAN MOL & LAWRENCE, Nashville, TN, pg. 333
Eddy, Sam, Acct Dir -- The Marketing Store, London, United Kingdom, pg. 1421
Edelstein, Pamela, Mgr-PR & Social Media -- OWENS, HARKEY & ASSOCIATES, LLC, Phoenix, AZ, pg. 867
Edgar, Alan, Exec Dir-Creative -- TBWA Hunt Lascaris (Durban), Durban, South Africa, pg. 1126
Edge, Devin, Assoc Media Buyer -- HORIZON MEDIA, INC., New York, NY, pg. 1341
Edgerton, David, Assoc Dir-Creative & Acct Mgr -- JONES ADVERTISING, Seattle, WA, pg. 596
Edghill, Winston, Dir-Media & Creative Svcs -- SOJE/Lonsdale Communications Inc./Y&R, Christ Church, Barbados, pg. 1248
Edmeades, Chris, Acct Dir -- J. Walter Thompson Canada, Montreal, Canada, pg. 566
Edmonds, Jill, Acct Dir -- MARKETEL, Montreal, Canada, pg. 695
Edmondson, Dee Dee, Sr Acct Exec-PR -- RDW Group, Inc., Worcester, MA, pg. 956
Edmunds, Maggie, Acct Coord -- BACKBONE MEDIA LLC, Carbondale, CO, pg. 1448
Edu, Michelle, Art Dir -- BBDO Guerrero, Makati, Philippines, pg. 117
Edwards, Clark, Dir-Creative -- Abbott Mead Vickers BBDO, London, United Kingdom, pg. 112
Edwards, Geoff, Co-Founder & Chief Creative Officer -- DOJO, San Francisco, CA, pg. 321
Edwards, Greg, Dir-Creative & Copywriter -- MARC USA, Pittsburgh, PA, pg. 691
Edwards, Justin, Dir-Creative -- WEDNESDAY NEW YORK, New York, NY, pg. 1194
Edwards, Kinney, Exec Dir-Creative -- TRIBAL WORLDWIDE, New York, NY, pg. 1316
Edwards, Kinney, Exec Dir-Creative -- Tribal Worldwide Chicago, Chicago, IL, pg. 1316
Edwards, Mary, Acct Dir -- QUATTRO DIRECT LLC, Berwyn, PA, pg. 942
Edwards, Rory, Acct Dir -- madano partnership, London, United Kingdom, pg. 1601
Edwards, Scott, Exec Dir-Creative -- INNIS MAGGIORE GROUP, INC., Canton, OH, pg. 547
Edwards, Scott, Creative Dir-Asia -- The Marketing Store, Quarry Bay, China (Hong Kong), pg. 1421
Edwards, Thomas, Art Dir -- TROLLBACK + COMPANY, New York, NY, pg. 1159
Edwards, Will, Assoc Dir-Creative -- J. Walter Thompson, Sydney, Australia, pg. 567
Effman, Richard, Dir-Creative -- THE CAUSEWAY AGENCY, Westport, CT, pg. 198
Efird, Hayley, Art Dir -- BBDO Atlanta, Atlanta, GA, pg. 100

Personnel Index

Personnel Index

F

Fadule, Sarah, Media Planner -- TIERNEY COMMUNICATIONS, Philadelphia, PA, pg. 1143
Fagan, Cynthia, Acct Exec -- Q STRATEGIES, Chattanooga, TN, pg. 940
Fagan, Jake, Acct Coord -- LEWIS COMMUNICATIONS, Birmingham, AL, pg. 655
Fagelbaum, Ashley, Acct Supvr -- PULSAR ADVERTISING, INC., Beverly Hills, CA, pg. 936
Fagerburg, Brent, Assoc Dir-Creative -- EDELMAN, Chicago, IL, pg. 1500
Fagerstrom, Jerker, Partner & Exec Creative Dir -- DTDigital, Sydney, Australia, pg. 1218
Faicol, Mark, Acct Exec -- REBEL INDUSTRIES, Los Angeles, CA, pg. 958
Faircloth, Carley, Sr VP & Acct Dir -- Jack Morton Worldwide, New York, NY, pg. 584
Faith, Sarah, Acct Dir -- CONE COMMUNICATIONS, Boston, MA, pg. 1484
Falco, Carie, Creative Dir -- LORRAINE GREGORY COMMUNICATIONS, Farmingdale, NY, pg. 669
Falen, Steve, VP & Dir-Creative -- PARTNERS CREATIVE, Missoula, MT, pg. 875
Falk, Matthew, Exec VP & Dir-Creative -- FALK HARRISON, Saint Louis, MO, pg. 366
Falkner, Maureen, Sr Acct Exec-PR & Social -- Cramer-Krasselt, Milwaukee, WI, pg. 243
Falkow, Mike, Dir-Creative -- MERITUS MEDIA, Altadena, CA, pg. 1589
Fall, Dan, Media Buyer -- FALL ADVERTISING, Santee, CA, pg. 366
Falla, Catherine, Acct Supvr -- Publicis JimenezBasic, Makati, Philippines, pg. 934
Faller, Chrissy, Dir-PR -- REESE, Reading, PA, pg. 966
Fallert, Lauren, Acct Exec -- VERDE BRAND COMMUNICATIONS, Jackson, WY, pg. 1669
Fallon, Doug, Dir-Creative -- GREY NEW YORK, New York, NY, pg. 446
Fallon, Matt, Acct Dir -- MMB, Boston, MA, pg. 767
Fallone, Michael, Principal & Dir-Creative -- ID29, Troy, NY, pg. 532
Falter, Cory, Chief Creative Officer -- LURE AGENCY, La Mesa, CA, pg. 674
Faltman, Magnus, Dir-Creative -- FCB Faltman & Malmen, Stockholm, Sweden, pg. 375
Falusi, Corinna, Chief Creative Officer -- OGILVY & MATHER, New York, NY, pg. 826
Falusi, Corinna, Chief Creative Officer & Sr Partner-Ogilvy & Mather New York -- Ogilvy & Mather New York, New York, NY, pg. 827
Falvay, Laszlo, Dir-Creative -- Y&R Budapest, Budapest, Hungary, pg. 1248
Familetti, Elyse, Acct Exec -- WIT MEDIA, New York, NY, pg. 1211
Famularcano, Paulo, Assoc Dir-Creative -- Publicis JimenezBasic, Makati, Philippines, pg. 934
Fan, Adams, Exec Dir-Creative -- DDB China - Shanghai, Shanghai, China, pg. 279
Fan, Edwardth, Acct Dir -- OgilvyOne Worldwide, Taipei, Taiwan, pg. 847
Fancett, Matt, Acct Supvr -- CAMPBELL MARKETING & COMMUNICATIONS, Dearborn, MI, pg. 188
Fang, Kai, Exec Dir-Creative -- Ogilvy Public Relations Worldwide, Washington, DC, pg. 1606
Fannon, Fred, Dir-Creative -- McCann Worldgroup Portugal, Lisbon, Portugal, pg. 726
Fant, Ben, Principal & Dir-Creative -- FARMHOUSE, Memphis, TN, pg. 368
Fantich, Eric, Dir-Creative -- FANTICH MEDIA GROUP, McAllen, TX, pg. 368
Fantine, Pete, VP-Bus Analytics & Acct Dir -- SBC ADVERTISING, Columbus, OH, pg. 1023
Farabaugh, Michelle, Acct Exec -- BONEAU/BRYAN-BROWN, New York, NY, pg. 1458
Farago, Tamas, Dir-Creative -- J. Walter Thompson Budapest, Budapest, Hungary, pg. 573
Farano, Liz, VP-Mktg & Dir-Creative -- DOUGLAS MARKETING GROUP, LLC, Detroit, MI, pg. 326
Faraut, Billy, Dir-Creative -- J. WALTER THOMPSON, New York, NY, pg. 565
Farber, Josh, Acct Dir -- OPTIMUM SPORTS, New York, NY, pg. 863
Farber, Micky, Sr VP-Acct Svcs & Direct Mktg -- SKM GROUP, Depew, NY, pg. 1050
Farella, Chris, Assoc Dir-Creative & Sr Writer-Creative -- HAWK MARKETING SERVICES, Moncton, Canada, pg. 503
Farhadi, Jason, Acct Exec-PR -- THE MCDONNELL GROUP INC., Roswell, GA, pg. 1586
Farhang, Omid, Chief Creative Officer -- Momentum, Atlanta, GA, pg. 771
Farhang, Omid, Chief Creative Officer-North America -- MOMENTUM WORLDWIDE, New York, NY, pg. 770
Faria, Andrea, Media Buyer -- TABER CREATIVE GROUP, Roseville, CA, pg. 1106
Faria, Serena, Acct Supvr -- CAMBRIDGE BIOMARKETING, Cambridge, MA, pg. 186
Faria, Sylvia Navas, Acct Dir -- J. Walter Thompson, Caracas, Venezuela, pg. 579
Farias, Alison, Acct Exec -- WONACOTT COMMUNICATIONS, LLC, Los Angeles, CA, pg. 1687
Farias, Amy, Acct Dir -- TBWA Chiat Day New York, New York, NY, pg. 1115
Farid, Mohsen, Acct Dir-Adv Discipline -- MEMAC Ogilvy, Cairo, Egypt, pg. 848
Farin, Nicole, Acct Coord -- R/WEST, Portland, OR, pg. 947
Farina, Rachel, Acct Exec -- ELLINGSEN BRADY ADVERTISING (EBA), Milwaukee, WI, pg. 345
Farina, Zico, Dir-Creative -- DM9DDB, Sao Paulo, Brazil, pg. 278
Farinella, David, Dir-Creative -- FARINELLA, Oakland, CA, pg. 368
Fariz, Ahmad, Assoc Dir-Creative -- M&C Saatchi, Kuala Lumpur, Malaysia, pg. 678
Farkas, Maribeth, Acct Supvr -- CAPONIGRO MARKETING GROUP, LLC, Southfield, MI, pg. 189
Farkas, Maribeth, Acct Supvr -- CAPONIGRO PUBLIC RELATIONS, INC., Southfield, MI, pg. 1472
Farley, Brian, Acct Exec -- COYNE PUBLIC RELATIONS, Parsippany, NJ, pg. 1487
Farley, Greg, Exec Creative Dir -- Y&R New York, New York, NY, pg. 1240
Farley, Gregory, Exec Creative Dir -- YOUNG & RUBICAM, New York, NY, pg. 1239
Farmer, Chad, Pres & Exec Dir-Creative -- LAMBESIS, INC., La Jolla, CA, pg. 624
Farmer, Justin, Assoc Dir-Creative -- MMGY GLOBAL, Kansas City, MO, pg. 767
Farmer, Ryan, Dir-Interactive Creative -- MAD GENIUS, Ridgeland, MS, pg. 684
Farr, Annie, Media Buyer -- 22squared Inc., Tampa, FL, pg. 4
Farr, Mike, Exec Dir-Creative -- Wieden + Kennedy - Amsterdam, Amsterdam, Netherlands, pg. 1203
Farra, Caroline, Creative Dir -- H&C, Leo Burnett, Beirut, Lebanon, pg. 643
Farrell, Sean, Dir-Art -- GOODBY, SILVERSTEIN & PARTNERS, INC., San Francisco, CA, pg. 434
Farrington, Kim, Acct Supvr -- BLUE SKY COMMUNICATIONS, New York, NY, pg. 142
Farrington, Olly, Dir-Art & Creative & Copywriter -- Saatchi & Saatchi London, London, United Kingdom, pg. 1007
Farrish, Ryan, Acct Exec -- UNDERTONE, New York, NY, pg. 1166
Farrugia, Sarah, VP & Acct Supvr -- AGENCYRX, New York, NY, pg. 39
Farthing, Doug, Partner & Chief Creative Officer -- INSIGHT CREATIVE GROUP, Oklahoma City, OK, pg. 549
Fasoli, Carlo Maria, Exec Creative Dir -- Razorfish Milan, Milan, Italy, pg. 1309
Fassett, Wayne, Dir-Creative & Writer -- GSW WORLDWIDE, Westerville, OH, pg. 465
Fate, Bill, Sr Dir-Creative -- SAGON-PHIOR, West Los Angeles, CA, pg. 1644
Fattah, Layla Safwat, Acct Dir -- BPG Group, Dubai, United Arab Emirates, pg. 1218
Fattizzi, Kristen, Acct Exec -- THE BRANDMAN AGENCY, New York, NY, pg. 159
Fattizzi, Kristen, Acct Exec -- The Brandman Agency Inc., Beverly Hills, CA, pg. 159
Fatula, April, Acct Exec-PR -- GHIDOTTI COMMUNICATIONS, Little Rock, AR, pg. 1527
Faulkenberry, Kevyn, VP & Exec Dir-Creative -- Dalton Agency Atlanta, Atlanta, GA, pg. 264
Faulkner, Ivette Marques, VP-PR -- THE ZIMMERMAN AGENCY LLC, Tallahassee, FL, pg. 1257
Faulkner, James, Principal & Dir-Creative -- SODAPOP MEDIA LLC, Lewisville, TX, pg. 1057
Faulkner, Joyce, Sr VP & Acct Dir-New Bus -- FITZGERALD MEDIA, Atlanta, GA, pg. 1335
Faulkner, Joyce, Sr VP & Acct Dir-New Bus -- FITZGERALD+CO, Atlanta, GA, pg. 391
Faulkner, Sean, Acct Exec -- ABC CREATIVE GROUP, Syracuse, NY, pg. 16
Faure, Jessica, Acct Exec-Pub Affairs -- Hill + Knowlton Strategies, Brussels, Belgium, pg. 1542
Faust, Joyclyn, Sr Dir-Buying & Mgr-Brdcst & Convergence -- HARMELIN MEDIA, Bala Cynwyd, PA, pg. 1338
Faust, Russ, VP-Creative Svcs -- THE ST. GREGORY GROUP, INC., Cincinnati, OH, pg. 1071
Faux, Kate, Acct Dir -- BARTON F. GRAF 9000 LLC, New York, NY, pg. 96
Favat, Pete, Chief Creative Officer -- DEUTSCH, INC., New York, NY, pg. 301
Fawcett, Gary, Dir-Creative -- TBWA/Manchester, Manchester, United Kingdom, pg. 1125
Fay, Sean K., CEO & Dir-Creative -- ENVISION RESPONSE INC., Seattle, WA, pg. 349
Fayad, Mazen, Exec Dir-Creative -- J. Walter Thompson, Daiya, Kuwait, pg. 576
Fayad, Paul, Dir-Creative -- Impact BBDO, Dubai, United Arab Emirates, pg. 112
Faye, Cecilie, Chief Creative Officer & Mng Dir -- Maxus, Oslo, Norway, pg. 1354
Fazio, Pete, Art Dir -- GOLD DOG COMMUNICATIONS, Falls Church, VA, pg. 433
Fazzari, Ammiel, Dir-Creative -- Del Campo Nazca Saatchi & Saatchi, Buenos Aires, Argentina, pg. 1007
Fdez, Dani Garcia, Sr Dir-Creative & Art -- SCPF, Barcelona, Spain, pg. 1222
Fead, Kelley, Partner, Exec VP, Head-Brand Practice & Dir-Creative -- SLACK AND COMPANY, Chicago, IL, pg. 1051
Feath, Deb, Assoc Dir-Art & Creative -- Echo Torre Lazur, Mountain Lakes, NJ, pg. 731
Febbraio, Monique, Acct Exec -- LITZKY PUBLIC RELATIONS, Hoboken, NJ, pg. 1577
Fecteau, Jimmy, Dir-Creative -- NURUN INC., Montreal, Canada, pg. 819
Feddern, John, Acct Dir -- WAHLSTROM GROUP, Norwalk, CT, pg. 1186
Federico, David, Sr VP & Dir-Creative -- LEO BURNETT COMPANY LTD., Toronto, Canada, pg. 637
Federico, Paul, Dir-Creative -- PRINCETON PARTNERS, INC., Princeton, NJ, pg. 911
Fedorenko, Tatiana, Creative Dir -- Leo Burnett Kiev, Kiev, Ukraine, pg. 646
Fedorov, Alexey, Creative Dir -- BBDO Moscow, Moscow, Russia, pg. 110
Fedorzyn, Liz, Sr Art Dir -- PRIMARY DESIGN INC, Haverhill, MA, pg. 910
Fedullo, Charles, Dir-PR -- NORTHWEST STRATEGIES, Anchorage, AK, pg. 1604
Fee, Meaghan, Acct Exec -- ANOMALY, New York, NY, pg. 60
Feehery, Pat, Creative Dir -- CP+B Boulder, Boulder, CO, pg. 240
Feeley, Michelle, Acct Dir -- DROGA5, New York, NY, pg. 328
Feeney, Anne Catherine, Acct Dir -- CP+B, Coconut Grove, FL, pg. 239
Feese, Martina, Copywriter-Creative -- LTC Advertising Lagos, Lagos, Nigeria, pg. 566
Feger, Debbie, VP & Dir-Creative Art -- MEDERGY HEALTHGROUP INC., Yardley, PA, pg. 741
Fehr, Josh, Exec Dir-Creative -- Camp Pacific, Vancouver, Canada, pg. 1286
Fei, Wei, Chief Creative Officer-Greater China -- FCB Shanghai, Shanghai, China, pg. 379
Feigen, Craig, Dir-Creative -- Commonwealth, Detroit, MI, pg. 714
Feigin, Irene, Dir-Media-Brdcst -- MEDIA BROKERS INTERNATIONAL, INC., Alpharetta, GA, pg. 1364
Feigley, Stuart, Partner & Dir-Creative -- WRIGHT FEIGLEY COMMUNICATIONS, Baton Rouge, LA, pg. 1228
Feijo, Fabiano, Exec Creative Dir -- MCCANN ERICKSON WORLDWIDE, New York, NY, pg. 713
Feinberg, Bob, Dir-Creative-Direct Mktg -- STEPHAN PARTNERS, INC., New York, NY, pg. 1083
Feinberg, Steve, Chief Creative Officer -- THE SEIDEN GROUP, New York, NY, pg. 1030
Feirman, Jason, Acct Dir & Brand Strategist -- MESH DESIGN, Baton Rouge, LA, pg. 751
Fejzoski, Laura, Acct Exec -- WYSE, Cleveland, OH, pg. 1235
Feldman, Ale, Art Dir -- BBR Saatchi & Saatchi, Ramat Gan, Israel, pg. 1003
Feldman, Gena, Acct Exec -- UNDERTONE, New York, NY, pg. 1166
Feldman, Larry, Specialist-PR -- YS AND PARTNERS, INC., Newport Beach, CA, pg. 1252
Feldman, Nina, Media Buyer-TV, Radio & Digital -- TCAA, Cincinnati, OH, pg. 1133

Foo, Ezra, Head-Creative -- Havas Worldwide Kuala Lumpur, Petaling Jaya, Malaysia, pg. 501
Foo, Sharon, Sr VP & Acct Dir -- Jack Morton Worldwide, New York, NY, pg. 584
Foong, Aaron, Acct Dir -- Tribal Worldwide Malaysia, Petaling Jaya, Malaysia, pg. 1317
Forbes, Erin, Media Buyer -- HOCKING MEDIA GROUP INC., Troy, MI, pg. 1341
Forbes, Fredna Lynn, Dir-Creative -- MASS MEDIA MARKETING, Augusta, GA, pg. 708
Forbes, Jamie, Acct Exec -- CRUCIAL INTERACTIVE INC., Toronto, Canada, pg. 258
Forbes, Kate, Media Planner & Media Buyer -- Media Works Charlotte, Huntersville, NC, pg. 1367
Force, Mike, Assoc Dir-Creative -- HARVEST CREATIVE, Memphis, TN, pg. 483
Ford, Dan, Creative Dir -- ADMO, INC., Saint Louis, MO, pg. 30
Ford, Ellis, Acct Exec -- MRM London, London, United Kingdom, pg. 783
Ford, Ismael, Assoc Dir-Creative -- ETA ADVERTISING, Long Beach, CA, pg. 357
Ford, Kathleen, Mgr-Production & Sr Designer-Creative -- AD WORKSHOP, Lake Placid, NY, pg. 23
Ford, Kerry, VP & Grp Dir-PR -- STERN ADVERTISING, INC., Cleveland, OH, pg. 1085
Ford, Mark, Creative Dir -- 3HEADED MONSTER, Dallas, TX, pg. 7
Ford, Ralph, Acct Dir -- WORLD MARKETING HOLDINGS, LLC, Milwaukee, WI, pg. 1215
Ford, Ryan, Chief Creative Officer & Exec VP -- CASHMERE AGENCY, Los Angeles, CA, pg. 195
Ford, Shannon, Acct Exec -- OPTIMUM SPORTS, New York, NY, pg. 863
Ford, Tara, Creative Dir -- Whybin TBWA, Melbourne, Australia, pg. 1128
Ford-Glencross, Kristin, Acct Dir -- STRATACOMM, LLC, Washington, DC, pg. 1090
Fordham, Kathy, Acct Dir -- EVOK ADVERTISING, Heathrow, FL, pg. 360
Foreman, Kevin, Creative Dir-Digital -- MOROCH PARTNERS, Dallas, TX, pg. 774
Forero, John Raul, VP-Creative -- Ogilvy & Mather, Cali, Colombia, pg. 839
Forkheim, Kirsten, Acct Coord -- CREATIVE CIVILIZATION AN AGUILAR/GIRARD AGENCY, San Antonio, TX, pg. 246
Forman, Abby, Acct Exec -- Access Communications, New York, NY, pg. 19
Formosa, Sarah, Acct Dir-Global -- MediaCom Paris, Paris, France, pg. 1369
Forras, Laszlo, Head-Creative Svcs -- Wunderman, Budapest, Hungary, pg. 1233
Forrest, Jenn, Acct Dir -- PLAY Communication, Surry Hills, Australia, pg. 1337
Forrest, Judy E., Mgr-Fin, Media Planner-Print & Buyer -- MARTIN ADVERTISING, Anderson, SC, pg. 702
Forrester, Ian C., Acct Exec -- ARC WORLDWIDE, Chicago, IL, pg. 1405
Forrester, Maddie, Acct Supvr -- IDFIVE, Baltimore, MD, pg. 536
Forristal, John, Acct Exec -- QORVIS MSLGROUP, Washington, DC, pg. 1628
Forsey, Craig, Assoc Dir-Creative -- THE MARKETING DEPARTMENT, London, Canada, pg. 697
Forshay, Alexa, Acct Exec -- WICKED CREATIVE, Las Vegas, NV, pg. 1685
Forslund, Kathy, Exec VP & Acct Exec -- Hellman, Saint Paul, MN, pg. 509
Forsyth, Paul, VP & Dir-Creative -- Doner, Cleveland, OH, pg. 323
Forsyth, Paul, VP & Dir-Creative -- Doner, Cleveland, OH, pg. 740
Forsyth, September, Media Buyer -- STARCOM MEDIAVEST GROUP, Chicago, IL, pg. 1074
Forsythe, Brad, Pres & Exec Dir-Creative -- FORSYTHE & BUTLER CO., INC., Houston, TX, pg. 398
Fortier-Jordan, Camille, Acct Dir -- FCB Montreal, Montreal, Canada, pg. 372
Fortin, Vincent, Partner & Acct Dir -- REPUBLIK PUBLICITE + DESIGN INC., Montreal, Canada, pg. 969
Fortin-Laurin, Vincent, Partner & Acct Dir -- REPUBLIK PUBLICITE + DESIGN INC., Montreal, Canada, pg. 969
Fortuna, Brianne, Mgr-PR & Promos -- MAMMOTH ADVERTISING LLC, Brooklyn, NY, pg. 688
Fortunate, Ann Marie, Acct Supvr -- FRANCO PUBLIC RELATIONS GROUP, Detroit, MI, pg. 1523
Foster, Emily, Program Mgr & Mgr-Traffic -- THE IN-HOUSE AGENCY, INC., Morristown, NJ, pg. 543
Foster, Eric, Dir-Creative -- BEDFORD ADVERTISING INC., Carrollton, TX, pg. 122
Foster, Jenn, Acct Dir -- THE FANTASTICAL, Boston, MA, pg. 368
Foster, Meghan, Mgr-Traffic -- ERIC ROB & ISAAC, Little Rock, AR, pg. 354
Foster, Michael, Acct Exec -- BARBER MARTIN AGENCY, Richmond, VA, pg. 91
Foth, Mike, Acct Dir-Svcs -- RON FOTH ADVERTISING, Columbus, OH, pg. 990
Foth, Ron , Jr., Sr VP-Creative -- RON FOTH ADVERTISING, Columbus, OH, pg. 990
Foucaud, Benjamin, Creative Dir -- McCann Erickson Paris, Clichy, France, pg. 720
Foulatier, Julien, Dir-Creative -- J. Walter Thompson France, Neuilly-sur-Seine, France, pg. 573
Foulkes, Paul, Sr VP & Exec Dir-Creative -- MULLEN LOWE GROUP, Boston, MA, pg. 786
Foulks, Patrick, Media Planner & Buyer-Digital -- PERISCOPE, Minneapolis, MN, pg. 884
Foulques, Luisa, Media Planner -- Havas Media, Miami, FL, pg. 1340
Fountain, Alexandra, Acct Exec -- S&S Public Relations, Inc., Colorado Springs, CO, pg. 1644
Fournier, Stephane, Assoc Dir-Creative -- Tribal Worldwide Vancouver, Vancouver, Canada, pg. 1316
Foust, Travis, Media Buyer -- PINEAPPLE ADVERTISING, Tulsa, OK, pg. 892
Foust, Uriaha, Dir-Creative -- MILLER BROOKS, Zionsville, IN, pg. 758
Fowler, David, Sr Partner & Exec Dir-Creative -- OGILVY & MATHER, New York, NY, pg. 826
Fowler, Sara, Acct Supvr -- Doremus (San Francisco), San Francisco, CA, pg. 324
Fowles, Anna, VP-Creative & Production Svcs -- NORTHERN LIGHTS DIRECT, Chicago, IL, pg. 815
Fowles, Eric, CEO & Dir-Creative -- VOLTAGE LTD, Louisville, CO, pg. 1184
Fox, Doreen, Sr Partner & Dir-Creative -- OGILVY & MATHER, New York, NY, pg. 826
Fox, Doug, VP & Acct Supvr -- Havas Life Metro, Chicago, IL, pg. 487
Fox, Hayley, Media Planner & Media Buyer -- CROSSMEDIA, New York, NY, pg. 1331
Fox, Hilary, Acct Supvr -- Sanders/Wingo, Austin, TX, pg. 1017
Fox, Hilary, Acct Supvr -- SANDERS/WINGO ADVERTISING, INC., El Paso, TX, pg. 1016
Fox, Jessica, Mgr-PR -- FKQ ADVERTISING + MARKETING, Clearwater, FL, pg. 391
Fox, Ken, Principal & Exec Dir-Creative -- 50,000FEET, INC., Chicago, IL, pg. 9
Fox, Kevin, Exec VP & Exec Dir-Creative -- GSW WORLDWIDE, Westerville, OH, pg. 465
Fox, Kristin, Sr Acct Exec -- WALLACE & COMPANY, Dulles, VA, pg. 1188
Fox, Lyndsey, Acct Supvr -- THE VIA AGENCY, Portland, ME, pg. 1175
Fox, Matt, Acct Exec -- TAYLOR, New York, NY, pg. 1659
Fox, Patti, Acct Supvr-Fin -- THE MARTIN AGENCY, Richmond, VA, pg. 702
Foye, Jon, Art Dir -- MJW Hakuhodo, Sydney, Australia, pg. 475
Fozman, Mike, Partner & Dir-Creative -- ROSBERG FOZMAN ROLANDELLI ADVERTISING, Jacksonville, FL, pg. 991
Fradejas, Natividad, Community Mgr & Acct Exec -- Porter Novelli, Barcelona, Spain, pg. 1623
Fragapane, Federica, Acct Dir -- Publicis Networks, Milan, Italy, pg. 920
Fragata, Pedro, Acct Dir -- Almap BBDO, Sao Paulo, Brazil, pg. 102
Fraire, Peter, Pres, COO & Creative Dir -- MITHOFF BURTON PARTNERS, El Paso, TX, pg. 764
Frakes, Breanne, Coord-PR -- PAGE COMMUNICATIONS, Kansas City, MO, pg. 1612
Frampton, Shauna, Acct Dir -- JESSON + COMPANY COMMUNICATIONS INC., Toronto, Canada, pg. 1555
France, Kelly, Acct Dir -- BREWLIFE, San Francisco, CA, pg. 164
Francis, Andrea, Sr Media Planner & Media Buyer -- DIXON SCHWABL ADVERTISING, Victor, NY, pg. 317
Francis, Dalyn, Acct Exec -- NIGHT AGENCY, New York, NY, pg. 1305
Francis, David, CEO & Dir-Creative -- SHOREPOINT COMMUNICATIONS, LLC, Lakewood, NJ, pg. 1039
Francis, Jessica, Acct Dir -- M&C Saatchi, Santa Monica, CA, pg. 676
Francis, Michael, Dir-Creative -- LIVEAREALABS, Seattle, WA, pg. 663
Francis, Nick, Dir-Creative-Casual Films -- THEFRAMEWORKS, Troy, MI, pg. 1138
Francklyn, Sally, Acct Exec -- DENNY INK, Jackson, WY, pg. 1493
Franco, Angelina, Acct Exec -- COYNE PUBLIC RELATIONS, Parsippany, NJ, pg. 1487
Franco, Bitan, Exec Dir-Creative -- Publicis, Madrid, Spain, pg. 921
Franco, Fernando, Art Dir -- Saltiveri Ogilvy & Mather, Guayaquil, Ecuador, pg. 839
Franco, Fernando, Art Dir & Creative Dir -- Saltiveri Ogilvy & Mather Guayaquil, Quito, Ecuador, pg. 839
Franco, Wilson, Dir-Creative -- Norlop J. Walter Thompson, Guayaquil, Ecuador, pg. 578
Francois, Troy, Dir-Art & Assoc Dir-Creative -- BRANDMOVERS, Atlanta, GA, pg. 1284
Frandsen, Laura, Partner & Acct Supvr -- CADE & ASSOCIATES ADVERTISING, INC., Tallahassee, FL, pg. 183
Frangie, Chelsea, Creative -- Impact BBDO, Dubai, United Arab Emirates, pg. 112
Frank, Erica, Acct Dir -- MARCH COMMUNICATIONS, Boston, MA, pg. 1582
Frank, Gerry, Chief Creative Officer -- FRANK STRATEGIC MARKETING, Columbia, MD, pg. 401
Frank, Heidi, Acct Supvr -- PUBLICIS HEALTHCARE COMMUNICATIONS GROUP, New York, NY, pg. 934
Frank, Jonas, Art Dir -- Saatchi & Saatchi, Stockholm, Sweden, pg. 1006
Frank, Martin, Exec Dir-Creative -- ZOOM Advertising, Cape Town, South Africa, pg. 850
Frank, Megan, Owner & Exec VP-Creative -- CFX INC, Saint Louis, MO, pg. 202
Franke, Lara, Supvr-PR -- TBC Direct, Inc., Baltimore, MD, pg. 1113
Franke, Lara, Supvr-PR -- TBC, INC./PR DIVISION, Baltimore, MD, pg. 1659
Frankel, Ryan, Pres & Dir-Creative -- FRANKEL MEDIA GROUP, Newberry, FL, pg. 401
Franklin, Curtis, Dir-Creative -- KENNEDY COMMUNICATIONS, Vancouver, WA, pg. 609
Franks, Julia, Dir-New Bus -- Saatchi & Saatchi EMEA Region Headquarters, London, United Kingdom, pg. 1007
Fransen, Erica, Acct Dir -- POP, Seattle, WA, pg. 903
Franz, Jennifer, Acct Exec -- MEDIA SOLUTIONS, Sacramento, CA, pg. 1366
Frappier, Courtney, Acct Exec -- RED PR, New York, NY, pg. 1633
Fraser, Bruce, Dir-Creative -- ELEVATOR STRATEGY, ADVERTISING & DESIGN, Vancouver, Canada, pg. 343
Fraser, Keisey, Acct Exec -- MANHATTAN MARKETING ENSEMBLE, New York, NY, pg. 689
Fraser, Maurus, Dir-Creative -- WINKREATIVE, Toronto, Canada, pg. 1210
Fraser, Patrick, Head-PR -- McCann Erickson Bristol, Bristol, United Kingdom, pg. 730
Fraser, Paul, Dir-Creative -- DDB Sydney Pty. Ltd., Ultimo, Australia, pg. 277
Fraser, Tyler, Creative Dir -- TRADEMARK PRODUCTIONS, Royal Oak, MI, pg. 1154
Fratesi, Anne Lauren, Acct Exec-Social Media -- THE RAMEY AGENCY LLC, Jackson, MS, pg. 951
Fraticelli, Damian, Dir-Creative -- HIGH WIDE & HANDSOME, Culver City, CA, pg. 513
Frattura, Nicole, Media Planner -- MULLEN LOWE GROUP, Boston, MA, pg. 786
Frauen, Sierra, Media Planner & Media Buyer -- SKAR ADVERTISING, Omaha, NE, pg. 1049
Frawley, Jim, Acct Dir-Strategic Svcs -- ADAMS & KNIGHT, INC., Avon, CT, pg. 24
Frazier, Carrie Crawford, VP & Acct Dir -- SCOPPECHIO, Louisville, KY, pg. 1026
Frazier, Meredith, Partner & Acct Dir -- BIGFISH COMMUNICATIONS, Brookline, MA, pg. 1454
Freda, Thomas, Acct Exec-Met-Rx & Pure Protein -- OCTAGON, Norwalk, CT, pg. 823
Frederick, Andrea, Acct Dir -- PAPPAS GROUP, Arlington, VA, pg. 872
Fredette, David, Assoc Dir-Creative -- HAVAS WORLDWIDE, New York, NY, pg. 488
Fredheim, Sophie, Acct Dir -- Grey London, London, United Kingdom, pg. 447
Free, Shane, Sr Editor-Creative -- HAMMER CREATIVE, Hollywood, CA, pg. 477
Freedman, Bianca, Acct Dir-Digital-Corp Practice -- Edelman, Toronto, Canada, pg. 1501

Personnel Index

Freedman, Kara, Acct Exec -- HEMSWORTH COMMUNICATIONS, Davie, FL, pg. 1538
Freeman, Allison, Acct Supvr -- TRUE MEDIA, Columbia, MO, pg. 1393
Freeman, Andrew, Acct Exec -- BOND PUBLIC RELATIONS & BRAND STRATEGY, New Orleans, LA, pg. 1458
Freeman, Charles, Dir-Creative -- REDHEAD COMPANIES, Ellicott City, MD, pg. 964
Freeman, Chris, Dir-Creative -- VIP MARKETING & ADVERTISING, North Charleston, SC, pg. 1178
Freeman, Jason, Acct Exec -- FCB Toronto, Toronto, Canada, pg. 372
Freeman, Julie, Exec VP & Mng Dir-PR -- MMGY Global, New York, NY, pg. 768
Freeman, Liz, Acct Supvr -- Edelman, Seattle, WA, pg. 1503
Freeman, Roddy, Media Planner -- ADVERTISING FOR GOOD, Atlanta, GA, pg. 34
Freer, Ming, Acct Dir -- KGLOBAL, Washington, DC, pg. 610
Freer, Phillip, Dir-Creative -- FRCH DESIGN WORLDWIDE, Cincinnati, OH, pg. 402
Freese, Jurgen, Art Dir -- M&C Saatchi Abel, Cape Town, South Africa, pg. 678
Freezman, Ali, Acct Exec -- SEER INTERACTIVE, Philadelphia, PA, pg. 1030
Fregoso, Riccardo, Exec Dir-Creative -- McCann Erickson Paris, Clichy, France, pg. 720
Freid, Mark, Pres-Creative & Dir-Strategic -- THINK CREATIVE INC., Orlando, FL, pg. 1139
Freiler, Megan, Acct Exec -- LAFORCE & STEVENS, New York, NY, pg. 1570
Freitag, Craig, Exec VP-Creative -- CKR INTERACTIVE, Campbell, CA, pg. 212
Freitag, Wayne A., VP & Dir-Creative -- FORREST & BLAKE INC., Mountainside, NJ, pg. 398
Frej, David, Chief Creative Officer & VP -- OTHERWISE INC, Chicago, IL, pg. 865
French, Erin, Acct Exec -- FRENCH CREATIVE GROUP, Monroe, LA, pg. 404
French, Kate Bailey, Strategist-Brand, Mktg & PR -- WEINSTEIN PR, The Dalles, OR, pg. 1684
French, Kimberly, Acct Dir -- RICHMOND PUBLIC RELATIONS, Seattle, WA, pg. 1637
French, Mary, Acct Dir -- ROUNDHOUSE, Portland, OR, pg. 994
French, Rebekkah, Dir-Creative -- SPECK COMMUNICATIONS, Dallas, TX, pg. 1063
Fresen, Max, Sr VP-Creative & Experience Design -- DIGITASLBI, Boston, MA, pg. 1288
Frew, John H., Pres-Hamilton PR -- HAMILTON PUBLIC RELATIONS, New York, NY, pg. 1535
Frey, Mike, Creative Dir -- ETA ADVERTISING, Long Beach, CA, pg. 357
Frey, Noelle, Acct Supvr -- VERTICAL MARKETING NETWORK LLC, Tustin, CA, pg. 1432
Frey, Robyn, VP & Dir-Creative -- BOLCHALK FREY MARKETING, ADVERTISING & PUBLIC RELATIONS, Tucson, AZ, pg. 146
Freyder, Mike, Creative Dir -- THE MORAN GROUP LLC, Baton Rouge, LA, pg. 773
Freyja, Yuxiao Chen, Acct Coord -- Racepoint Global, Wanchai, China (Hong Kong), pg. 1630
Freytag, Bernie, Dir-Creative -- ROMANELLI COMMUNICATIONS, Clinton, NY, pg. 1638
Freytez, Gustavo, VP-Creative Svcs -- Ogilvy & Mather, Caracas, Venezuela, pg. 840
Frias, Maria Dolores, Acct Exec -- Hill & Knowlton de Argentina, Buenos Aires, Argentina, pg. 1542
Fric, Lobke, Acct Dir -- Wunderman, Boulogne-Billancourt, France, pg. 1232
Fridman, Derek, Grp Dir-Creative -- HUGE, Brooklyn, NY, pg. 526
Friedberg, Samantha, Acct Supvr -- R/GA, New York, NY, pg. 946
Friedel, Cyndi, Acct Exec-Online -- GOLDSTEIN GROUP COMMUNICATIONS, Solon, OH, pg. 434
Friedman, Francine, Assoc Dir-Creative -- PBJS, INC., Seattle, WA, pg. 880
Friedman, Leigh, Dir-Creative Svcs -- GO!, Atlanta, GA, pg. 315
Friedman, Michelle, Acct Dir -- BOARDROOM COMMUNICATIONS INC., Fort Lauderdale, FL, pg. 1457
Friedman, Michelle, Acct Dir -- THE MARINO ORGANIZATION, INC., New York, NY, pg. 694
Friedman, Mitch, Dir-Creative -- THE POINT GROUP, Dallas, TX, pg. 899
Friedman, Nathan, Reg Mng Dir-Ogilvy PR West -- Ogilvy PR, Culver City, CA, pg. 1606
Friedman, Scott, Creative Dir -- DAVID & GOLIATH, El Segundo, CA, pg. 267
Friedrich, Ashley, Acct Supvr -- 22SQUARED, Atlanta, GA, pg. 4
Fries, Daniel, Principal & Dir-Creative-Live-Action -- LEROY + CLARKSON, New York, NY, pg. 652
Fries, Kurt, Exec Dir-Creative -- mcgarrybowen, Chicago, IL, pg. 734
Frinculescu, Dan, Grp Creative Dir -- Publicis, Bucharest, Romania, pg. 921
Fris, Pavel, Creative Dir & Copywriter -- Havas Worldwide Prague, Prague, Czech Republic, pg. 492
Frisbie, Kevin, Acct Exec -- MGA COMMUNICATIONS, INC., Denver, CO, pg. 1590
Frisch, Aaron, Dir-Creative -- Y&R New York, New York, NY, pg. 1240
Frisch, Gary, Dir-PR & Head-Comm Strategy -- ADAMUS MEDIA, Williamstown, NJ, pg. 25
Frischkorn, Rebekah, Acct Exec -- ANTITHESIS ADVERTISING, Rochester, NY, pg. 62
Frisina, Ralph, VP & Dir-Creative -- WINSTANLEY PARTNERS, Lenox, MA, pg. 1210
Frittaion, Giulio, Art Dir -- Saatchi & Saatchi, Milan, Italy, pg. 1004
Frizzell, Michael, Assoc Creative Dir -- THREE ATLANTA, Atlanta, GA, pg. 1141
Frobel, Karen, Specialist-Print Production -- RIGER ADVERTISING AGENCY, INC., Binghamton, NY, pg. 981
Froedge, Robert, Dir-Creative -- Lewis Communications, Nashville, TN, pg. 656
Frontoni, Corrado, Dir-Art & Deputy Dir-Creative -- Y&R Roma srl, Rome, Italy, pg. 1246
Frost, Karen, VP & Dir-Creative -- NOBLE, Springfield, MO, pg. 811
Frost, Kelsey, Acct Exec -- FRANKEL MEDIA GROUP, Newberry, FL, pg. 401
Frost, Kim, Acct Dir -- POSSIBLE NEW YORK, New York, NY, pg. 1307
Frost, Matthaus, Assoc Dir-Creative -- FCB Toronto, Toronto, Canada, pg. 372
Frost, Michelle, Acct Coord -- DECIBEL BLUE, Tempe, AZ, pg. 292
Frost, Robert, Exec Dir-Creative -- J. WALTER THOMPSON, New York, NY, pg. 565
Frost, Susan, VP-Mktg & Creative Svcs -- PHASE 3 MARKETING & COMMUNICATIONS, Atlanta, GA, pg. 887
Frota, Antonio, Acct Dir-Brazil -- AMG WORLDWIDE, Miami, FL, pg. 55
Froy, Tiffany, Acct Supvr -- RPM/Las Vegas, Las Vegas, NV, pg. 995
Frusciante, Tony, Assoc Dir-Creative -- MULLEN LOWE GROUP, Boston, MA, pg. 786
Fu, Barbara, Co-Exec Dir-Creative-Hong Kong -- J. Walter Thompson, Quarry Bay, China (Hong Kong), pg. 568
Fu, Caroline, Acct Dir -- Fleishman-Hillard Link Ltd., Beijing, China, pg. 1521
Fuente Portela, Maria Laura, Acct Coord -- MEC, Buenos Aires, Argentina, pg. 1361
Fuentes, Javier, Dir-Creative -- 360I, New York, NY, pg. 6
Fugate, Bob, Assoc Dir-Creative & Copywriter -- ZELLER MARKETING & DESIGN, East Dundee, IL, pg. 1255
Fujii, Scott, Sr VP-Print Production & Studio Svcs -- UPSHOT, Chicago, IL, pg. 1168
Fujimoto, Pam, Exec Dir-Creative -- WongDoody, Culver City, CA, pg. 1213
Fujimoto, Shannon, Media Planner & Buyer-Adv -- ANTHOLOGY MARKETING GROUP, Honolulu, HI, pg. 1445
Fuks, Romina, Acct Dir -- Y&R Peru, Lima, Peru, pg. 1250
Fukumoto, Christine, Media Buyer -- MEC, Toronto, Canada, pg. 1357
Fulcher, Chuck, Owner & Dir-Creative -- LODESTONE ADVERTISING, Great Falls, MT, pg. 666
Fulchini, Alyssa, Acct Exec -- UNDERTONE, New York, NY, pg. 1166
Fulena, Dana, Acct Supvr -- Ogilvy & Mather, Chicago, IL, pg. 828
Fulford, Charles, Grp Dir-Creative -- HUGE, Brooklyn, NY, pg. 526
Fulk, Lauren, Acct Dir -- SPECTRUM, Washington, DC, pg. 1653
Fulkerson, Gary, Principal & Dir-Creative Svcs -- DVA ADVERTISING, Bend, OR, pg. 333
Fulks, Kerri, Mgr-PR Ops & Acct Dir -- HCK2 PARTNERS, Addison, TX, pg. 504
Fuller, Donna, Acct Exec -- JKR ADVERTISING & MARKETING, Orlando, FL, pg. 591
Fuller, Kate, Brand Mgr-New Bus -- THE RICHARDS GROUP, INC., Dallas, TX, pg. 978
Fuller, Misty, Acct Supvr -- ADFERO GROUP, Washington, DC, pg. 28
Fulmer, Ashley, Sr Acct Exec-PR -- BIG COMMUNICATIONS, INC., Birmingham, AL, pg. 130
Fulmer, Kelley, Media Planner -- TRACYLOCKE, Dallas, TX, pg. 1153
Fulsher, Megan, Jr Art Dir-Creative -- CELTIC, INC., Brookfield, WI, pg. 201
Fund, Ari, Acct Supvr -- AR NEW YORK, New York, NY, pg. 66
Funderburk, Sarah, Partner & Acct Dir -- SPR ATLANTA, Atlanta, GA, pg. 1653
Fung, Frankie, Grp Creative Dir -- J. Walter Thompson, Quarry Bay, China (Hong Kong), pg. 568
Fung, Monica, Acct Dir -- AGENDA, Hong Kong, China (Hong Kong), pg. 1231
Fung, Monica, Acct Dir -- AGENDA, Hong Kong, China (Hong Kong), pg. 1217
Fung, Selina, Media Planner -- OMD Hong Kong, Hong Kong, China (Hong Kong), pg. 1381
Fung, Toby, Acct Exec -- Maxx Marketing Ltd., Kowloon, China (Hong Kong), pg. 841
Funke, Erich, Dir-Creative -- Saatchi & Saatchi Los Angeles, Torrance, CA, pg. 1001
Funkhouser, David, Owner & Dir-Creative -- FUNKHAUS, Los Angeles, CA, pg. 409
Funston, Jeff, Owner & Dir-Creative -- BRAVADA CONSUMER COMMUNICATIONS INC., Waterloo, Canada, pg. 162
Furman, Chere, Sr VP & Dir-Creative Support Svcs -- MULLEN LOWE GROUP, Boston, MA, pg. 786
Furman, Matt, Acct Exec -- HEILBRICE, Irvine, CA, pg. 507
Furtado, Robert, Acct Dir -- PILOT PMR, Toronto, Canada, pg. 1425
Furukawa, Yuya, Exec Dir-Creative -- DENTSU INC., Tokyo, Japan, pg. 297
Fusari, Saulo, Acct Dir -- Wunderman, Sao Paulo, Brazil, pg. 1231
Fusco, Frank, Dir-Creative -- SAATCHI & SAATCHI, New York, NY, pg. 1000
Fusco, Liz, Assoc Dir-Creative & Content -- BROWN BAG MARKETING, Atlanta, GA, pg. 170
Fuset, Carol, Acct Dir -- PSM S.A., Madrid, Spain, pg. 41
Futcher, Guy, Dir-Creative -- Leo Burnett Sydney, Sydney, Australia, pg. 647
Futterman, Lauren, Media Buyer-Natl TV & HorizonAdvanced -- HORIZON MEDIA, INC., New York, NY, pg. 1341

G

Ga, Naoki, Assoc Dir-Creative -- WIEDEN + KENNEDY, INC., Portland, OR, pg. 1202
Gabany, Peter, Pres & Dir-Creative -- LIMELIGHT ADVERTISING & DESIGN, Port Hope, Canada, pg. 658
Gabbard, Mary, Mgr-Traffic -- LABOV ADVERTISING, MARKETING AND TRAINING, Fort Wayne, IN, pg. 622
Gabbay, Lisa, Pres-Design & Dir-Creative -- RUDER FINN INC., New York, NY, pg. 1642
Gabel, Jeffery, Mng Partner & Chief Creative Officer -- PARTNERS+NAPIER, Rochester, NY, pg. 875
Gabor, Torday, Dir-Creative -- TBWA Budapest, Budapest, Hungary, pg. 1120
Gabriel, Pat, Dir-Creative -- GCG MARKETING, Fort Worth, TX, pg. 419
Gabrielli, Carlota, Acct Dir -- Savaglio TBWA, Buenos Aires, Argentina, pg. 1131
Gachou, Abel, Acct Exec -- GREY NEW YORK, New York, NY, pg. 446
Gadala-Maria, Camila, Acct Exec -- PINTA, New York, NY, pg. 892
Gadaleta, Amanda, Acct Exec -- PINTA, New York, NY, pg. 892
Gadhallah, Khaled, Founder, Partner & Chief Creative Officer -- TONIC, Dubai, United Arab Emirates, pg. 1150
Gadomska, Dagmara, Acct Dir -- Publicis Sp. z.o.o., Warsaw, Poland, pg. 921
Gadoua, Alexandre, Sr Creative Dir -- TANK, Montreal, Canada, pg. 1109
Gadtke, Chealsea, Media Buyer -- CLARITY COVERDALE FURY ADVERTISING, INC., Minneapolis, MN, pg. 213
Gaede, Fred, Chief Creative Officer -- BOOMM! MARKETING & COMMUNICATIONS, La Grange, IL, pg. 148
Gaedtke, Rob, VP-Creative Svcs -- KPS3 MARKETING, Reno, NV, pg. 617
Gagliano, Pietro, Partner & Dir-Creative -- SECRET LOCATION, Toronto, Canada, pg. 1029
Gagne, Katelyn, Acct Exec -- YELLOW BUS LLC, Santa Cruz, CA, pg. 1238
Gagnon, Louis, Dir-Creative -- PAPRIKA COMMUNICATIONS, Montreal, Canada, pg. 872

Gagnon, Nate, Assoc Dir-Creative -- MUH-TAY-ZIK HOF-FER, San Francisco, CA, pg. 786
Gagnon, Olivier, Acct Coord -- Cohn & Wolfe, Toronto, Canada, pg. 1481
Gahan, Dawn, Mgr-Traffic -- UNBOUNDARY, INC., Atlanta, GA, pg. 1166
Gahan, Sheila, Head-Corp & Dir -- Wilson Hartnell (WH), Dublin, Ireland, pg. 1607
Gahlaut, Ajay, Exec Creative Dir -- Ogilvy, New Delhi, India, pg. 844
Gainer, Lei, Dir-PR -- LHWH ADVERTISING & PUBLIC RELATIONS, Myrtle Beach, SC, pg. 656
Gaines, Michelle, Media Buyer -- MATRIX MEDIA SERVICES, INC., Columbus, OH, pg. 1353
Gainsford, Kirk, Exec Dir-Creative -- Lowe Bull, Johannesburg, South Africa, pg. 790
Gaiser, Dana, Acct Exec -- The Lippin Group, New York, NY, pg. 1577
Gaitan, Luis, Gen Creative Dir -- J. Walter Thompson, Mexico, Mexico, pg. 578
Gaither, Paul, Acct Dir -- TANIS COMMUNICATIONS, Mountain View, CA, pg. 1109
Gajjar, Bhavik, Assoc Dir-Creative -- OgilvyOne Worldwide, Toronto, Canada, pg. 829
Galacz, Karolina, Deputy Dir-Creative -- Y&R Budapest, Budapest, Hungary, pg. 1248
Galacz, Karolina, Deputy Dir-Creative -- YOUNG & RUBICAM, New York, NY, pg. 1239
Galafti, Franceska, Dir-Creative -- OgilvyOne Worldwide, Athens, Greece, pg. 833
Galante, John, VP-Television Programming & Dev-New Bus Dev & Strategist -- BOZEKEN, LLC, Wayne, PA, pg. 152
Galassini, Valerie, Acct Exec -- MOTION PR, Chicago, IL, pg. 1592
Galasso, Casey, Acct Coord -- CORNERSTONE COMMUNICATIONS, New York, NY, pg. 1487
Galbreath, Jonathan, Founder & Dir-Creative -- THE ARLAND GROUP, Saint Louis, MO, pg. 70
Gale, Joey, Acct Coord -- FLYNN WRIGHT, Des Moines, IA, pg. 395
Gale, Sarah, Acct Coord -- JDCOMMUNICATIONS INC, Canton, MA, pg. 589
Galeano, Francis, Graphic Designer & Designer-Creative -- Mass Publicidad S.R.L., Asuncion, Paraguay, pg. 641
Galeoto, Paige, Dir-Creative -- ESTIPONA GROUP, Reno, NV, pg. 356
Galiana, Guillermo Barbera, Acct Supvr -- Starcom, Barcelona, Spain, pg. 1079
Galiano, Felipe, Assoc Dir-Creative -- Razorfish GmbH, Frankfurt, Germany, pg. 1310
Galindo, Sergio, Art Dir -- Havas Worldwide Mexico, Mexico, Mexico, pg. 499
Galinsky, Kelly, Acct Supvr -- TREVELINO/KELLER, Atlanta, GA, pg. 1665
Gall, Andrew, Assoc Dir-Creative -- COPACINO + FUJIKADO, LLC, Seattle, WA, pg. 234
Gallagher, Katie, Acct Dir -- OCEAN MEDIA INC., Huntington Beach, CA, pg. 1377
Gallagher, Mike, Dir-Creative -- HAGER SHARP INC., Washington, DC, pg. 1535
Gallaher, Devin, Acct Dir -- DDB VANCOUVER, Vancouver, Canada, pg. 273
Gallaty, Amber, VP-Consumer PR -- BRAND ACTION TEAM, LLC, Avon, CT, pg. 155
Gallea, Elizabeth, Acct Exec -- JAY ADVERTISING, INC., Rochester, NY, pg. 588
Gallego, Gonzalo, Art Dir -- Y&R New York, New York, NY, pg. 1240
Gallego, Theresa, Acct Coord-Digital -- L7 CREATIVE, Carlsbad, CA, pg. 621
Gallego, Tom, Chief Creative Officer -- L7 CREATIVE, Carlsbad, CA, pg. 621
Gallegos, Jacob, Exec Creative Dir -- HIGHER GROUND CREATIVE AGENCY, Las Vegas, NV, pg. 513
Gallet, Mari, Pres & Dir-New Bus Strategies -- OUTOFTHEBLUE ADVERTISING, Miami, FL, pg. 866
Galli, Lia, Acct Exec -- MEDIA MIX, Jacksonville, FL, pg. 743
Galli, Roberto, Media Planner-Intl -- ZenithOptimedia, Milan, Italy, pg. 1399
Galligan, Sherry, Supvr-Brdcst-Mars Adv -- THE MARS AGENCY, Southfield, MI, pg. 701
Galligos, Dave, Sr VP & Exec Dir-Creative -- Ogilvy & Mather, Culver City, CA, pg. 828
Gallimore, Megan, Assoc Dir-Creative -- ALLEN & GERRITSEN, Boston, MA, pg. 46
Gallion, Cheyenne, Assoc Creative Dir -- GSD&M, Austin, TX, pg. 464
Gallione, Jeanne, Media Planner -- OGILVY COMMONHEALTH WORLDWIDE, Parsippany, NJ, pg. 851
Gallmann, Michael, Art Dir -- Advico Y&R AG, Zurich, Switzerland, pg. 1246
Gallo, Julian, Assoc Dir-Creative -- TRISECT, LLC, Chicago, IL, pg. 1158
Galloway, Beth, Sr VP & Acct Dir -- GREY GROUP, New York, NY, pg. 445
Galloway, Claudine, Acct Supvr -- HABERMAN & ASSOCIATES, INC., Minneapolis, MN, pg. 471
Galloway, Jon, Dir-Creative -- CREATIVE CANNON, Amarillo, TX, pg. 246
Galloway, Kelly, Acct Dir -- KRAUSE ADVERTISING, Dallas, TX, pg. 618
Galmes, Peter, Dir-Creative -- DDB Sydney Pty. Ltd., Ultimo, Australia, pg. 277
Galvan, Mauricio, Partner & Chief Creative Officer -- D EXPOSITO & PARTNERS, LLC, New York, NY, pg. 262
Galvao, Marcelo, Dir-Creative -- CREAXION CORPORATION, Atlanta, GA, pg. 253
Galvez, Lee, Creative Dir -- Ogilvy & Mather, Mexico, Mexico, pg. 839
Galvez, Toni, Acct Exec -- AD CLUB, Modesto, CA, pg. 1324
Galvin, Timothy W., VP & Acct Dir -- Team Detroit, Dearborn, MI, pg. 1222
Gama, Alejandro, Dir-Creative -- Ogilvy & Mather, Mexico, Mexico, pg. 839
Gambale, Alexandra, Acct Exec -- PEPPERCOMM, New York, NY, pg. 1614
Gamble, Jeffry, Chief Creative Officer -- mcgarrybowen, Shanghai, China, pg. 734
Gamble, Max, Creative Dir -- PLAN A ADVERTISING, Wilmington, NC, pg. 896
Gambrell, Ryan, Acct Exec -- Dalton Agency Atlanta, Atlanta, GA, pg. 264
Gamer, Richard, Dir-Creative -- MASON, INC., Bethany, CT, pg. 707
Gammill, Christal, Acct Dir -- Publicis Dialog Boise, Boise, ID, pg. 927
Gammill, Christal, Acct Dir -- Publicis Dialog Boise, Boise, ID, pg. 936
Ganci, Kristen, Jr Dir-Interactive Art -- CRONIN & COMPANY, INC., Glastonbury, CT, pg. 255
Gandarillas, Martin, Acct Dir -- Havas Worldwide Mexico, Mexico, Mexico, pg. 499
Gandhi, Radhika, Acct Dir -- Publicis-Graphics, Dubai, United Arab Emirates, pg. 924
Gangitano, Kate, Acct Dir -- Starcom Melbourne, Melbourne, Australia, pg. 1079
Gangotena, Diego, Copywriter-Creative -- Maruri, Guayaquil, Ecuador, pg. 1596
Gannaway, Liz, Acct Dir-Fin -- THE COMPANY OF OTHERS, Houston, TX, pg. 227
Gannon Yant, Molly, Acct Dir -- PLAN B (THE AGENCY ALTERNATIVE), Chicago, IL, pg. 896
Gano, Carinna, Acct Coord -- BRIDGE GLOBAL STRATEGIES LLC, New York, NY, pg. 1461
Gans, Sandy, Dir-Creative Svcs -- BOARDROOM COMMUNICATIONS INC., Fort Lauderdale, FL, pg. 1457
Ganser, Matt, Dir-Creative -- VSA PARTNERS, INC., Chicago, IL, pg. 1185
Ganser, Stephan, Exec Dir-Creative-Munich -- Publicis Pixelpark, Munich, Germany, pg. 919
Ganshert, Kyle, Acct Dir -- COLUMN FIVE, Newport Beach, CA, pg. 223
Ganswindt, Rebecca, Supvr-New Bus -- McCann Erickson/New York, New York, NY, pg. 714
Ganther, Brian, Grp Dir-Creative -- BVK, Milwaukee, WI, pg. 179
Gantt, Brad, VP-Creative -- PHELPS, Santa Monica, CA, pg. 888
Ganz, Solomon, Acct Dir -- PUBLICIS NEW YORK, New York, NY, pg. 935
Ganzer, Bruce, VP-Creative -- STRATEGIC AMERICA, West Des Moines, IA, pg. 1090
Gapinske, Lisa, Acct Exec -- MMB, Boston, MA, pg. 767
Garaventi, Jim, Founder, Partner & Dir-Creative -- MECHANICA, Newburyport, MA, pg. 741
Garavito, Carlos, VP & Dir-Creative -- The Marketing Store, Toronto, Canada, pg. 1421
Garay, Jonathan, Assoc Dir-Creative -- GLOBALHUE, Southfield, MI, pg. 429
Garbarz, Michelle, Media Buyer -- MALLOF, ABRUZINO & NASH MARKETING, Carol Stream, IL, pg. 688
Garber, Ari, Dir-Creative -- RED TETTEMER O'CONNELL & PARTNERS, Philadelphia, PA, pg. 963
Garber, Israel, Grp Exec Dir-Creative & Mng Dir -- Havas PR, New York, NY, pg. 487
Garbowski, Jennifer, Dir-New Bus -- K2 KRUPP KOMMUNICATIONS, INC, New York, NY, pg. 1558
Garbutt, Chris, Pres-Global Creative & Chief Creative Officer -- TBWA/WORLDWIDE, New York, NY, pg. 1114
Garbutt, Rachel, Coord-New Bus & Mktg -- MediaCom Vancouver, Vancouver, Canada, pg. 1369
Garcia Amaya, Fabiola Andrea, Acct Dir-Digital -- McCann Erickson Corp. S.A., Bogota, Colombia, pg. 719
Garcia, Alejandro, Art Dir -- Publicis Arredondo de Haro, Mexico, Mexico, pg. 929
Garcia, Andrea, Acct Exec -- PRCG/HAGGERTY LLC, New York, NY, pg. 1626
Garcia, Anna, Acct Supvr -- VPE PUBLIC RELATIONS, South Pasadena, CA, pg. 1671
Garcia, Armando, Grp Dir-Creative -- ZUBI ADVERTISING SERVICES, INC., Coral Gables, FL, pg. 1259
Garcia, Ashlee, Acct Exec -- COHEN COMMUNICATIONS, Fresno, CA, pg. 219
Garcia, Chad, VP & Dir-Creative-Studio -- Zimmerman Advertising, New York, NY, pg. 1257
Garcia, Christina, Acct Supvr -- VaynerMedia, San Francisco, CA, pg. 1319
Garcia, Clarisa, Media Planner -- MUNN RABOT LLC, New York, NY, pg. 795
Garcia, Crystal, Media Planner & Media Buyer -- MARTIN RETAIL GROUP/MARTIN ADVERTISING, Birmingham, AL, pg. 704
Garcia, Dennis, Assoc Dir-Creative -- AD PARTNERS INC., Tampa, FL, pg. 23
Garcia, Eric F., Owner & Dir-Creative -- EFG CREATIVE INC., Albuquerque, NM, pg. 339
Garcia, Federico, Dir-Creative -- Ogilvy & Mather Japan K.K., Tokyo, Japan, pg. 845
Garcia, Francine, Dir-Print Production -- BERNSTEIN-REIN ADVERTISING, INC., Kansas City, MO, pg. 126
Garcia, Franz, Gen Dir-Creative -- Y&R Damaris, C. Por A., Santo Domingo, Dominican Republic, pg. 1250
Garcia, Javier Menasalvas, Acct Dir -- PSM S.A., Madrid, Spain, pg. 41
Garcia, Jillian, Acct Exec -- FORCE MARKETING LLC, Atlanta, GA, pg. 397
Garcia, Josie, Media Planner-Digital-Walt Disney Studios -- OMD Los Angeles, Los Angeles, CA, pg. 1379
Garcia, Josie, Media Planner-Digital-Walt Disney Studios -- OMD WORLDWIDE, New York, NY, pg. 1380
Garcia, Miguel, Grp Creative Dir -- WALTON / ISAACSON, Culver City, CA, pg. 1189
Garcia, Paco, Dir-Creative -- J. Walter Thompson, Madrid, Spain, pg. 575
Garcia, Patricia Carceller, Media Planner-Online & Planner-Strategic -- Zenith Media, Madrid, Spain, pg. 1400
Garcia, Rosario, Acct Supvr -- Publicis, Madrid, Spain, pg. 921
Garcia, Tom, Dir-Creative -- Leo Burnett Belgium, Brussels, Belgium, pg. 642
Garcia, Yirayah, Assoc Dir-Creative -- UWG, Dearborn, MI, pg. 1169
Garcia, Yvi, Partner & Dir-Creative -- PG CREATIVE, Miami, FL, pg. 887
Gard, Beth, Acct Supvr -- LOTUS823, Tinton Falls, NJ, pg. 1578
Gard, William, Acct Exec -- MRM Worldwide, Birmingham, MI, pg. 783
Gardiner, Chris, Assoc Dir-Creative -- SANDSTROM PARTNERS, Portland, OR, pg. 1313
Gardiner, Daryl, Assoc Dir-Creative -- DDB VANCOUVER, Vancouver, Canada, pg. 273
Gardiner, Mat, Acct Dir -- iCrossing, Inc., Brighton, United Kingdom, pg. 1296
Gardiner, Ryan, Acct Supvr -- McKinney New York, New York, NY, pg. 736
Gardiner, Shannon, VP & Acct Supvr -- GKV COMMUNICATIONS, Baltimore, MD, pg. 427
Gardini, Joanna, Media Buyer-Direct Response -- ACTIVE INTERNATIONAL, Pearl River, NY, pg. 1323
Gardner, April, Dir-Creative Strategy -- ARGUS, Boston, MA, pg. 69
Gardner, Dan, Co-Founder & Dir-Creative-UX -- CODE AND THEORY, New York, NY, pg. 219
Gardner, Joanna, Acct Supvr -- ELA (EVERYTHINGLA), Irvine, CA, pg. 342
Gardner, Joshua, Acct Dir -- SYMMETRI MARKETING GROUP,

Personnel Index

Personnel Index

Personnel Index

Gonzaga, Justin, Acct Supvr -- TWOFIFTEENMCCANN, San Francisco, CA, pg. 1164
Gonzales, Mannie, III, Designer-Web & Creative -- IGNITE DESIGN AND ADVERTISING, INC., Rancho Cucamonga, CA, pg. 536
Gonzales, Matt, Assoc Dir-Creative -- WELL DONE MARKETING, Indianapolis, IN, pg. 1196
Gonzales, Mona, Acct Dir -- PEREIRA & O'DELL, San Francisco, CA, pg. 883
Gonzales, Veronica, Acct Dir -- MediaCom Vancouver, Vancouver, Canada, pg. 1369
Gonzalez, Abel, Dir-Creative -- BARU ADVERTISING, Los Angeles, CA, pg. 96
Gonzalez, Alberto, Founder, Pres & Exec Dir-Creative -- PULSAR ADVERTISING, INC., Beverly Hills, CA, pg. 936
Gonzalez, Alex, Co-Founder & Exec Dir-Creative -- AR NEW YORK, New York, NY, pg. 66
Gonzalez, Aracely, Acct Exec -- BOUNCE MARKETING AND EVENTS, LLC, Austin, TX, pg. 1407
Gonzalez, Daniel, Creative Dir -- McCann Erickson Corp. S.A., Bogota, Colombia, pg. 719
Gonzalez, Danny, Dir-Creative -- GOODBY, SILVERSTEIN & PARTNERS, INC., San Francisco, CA, pg. 434
Gonzalez, Diossy, Acct Supvr-Client Engagement -- RAZORFISH NEW YORK, New York, NY, pg. 1309
Gonzalez, Emiliano, Exec Dir-Creative -- Circus Communicacion Integrada, Lima, Peru, pg. 641
Gonzalez, Emiliano, Exec Dir-Creative-Circus Grey -- Grey GCG Peru S.A.C., Lima, Peru, pg. 454
Gonzalez, Francisco, Creative Dir -- J. Walter Thompson, Panama, Panama, pg. 578
Gonzalez, Guillermo, Dir-Creative -- Publicis-CB, Bogota, Colombia, pg. 929
Gonzalez, Henry, VP & Acct Dir -- CP+B, Coconut Grove, FL, pg. 239
Gonzalez, Jaime, Acct Dir -- Ogilvy & Mather, Mexico, Mexico, pg. 839
Gonzalez, Kathy, Media Buyer -- CORNERSTONE ADVERTISING & DESIGN, Beaumont, TX, pg. 236
Gonzalez, Lauren, Acct Exec -- Munroe Creative Partners, New York, NY, pg. 796
Gonzalez, Luis, Exec Dir-Creative -- LOPEZ NEGRETE COMMUNICATIONS, INC., Houston, TX, pg. 668
Gonzalez, Marcie, Assoc Dir-Creative -- INTEGRATED MARKETING WORKS, Newport Beach, CA, pg. 1417
Gonzalez, Mario, Acct Exec -- THE LIPPIN GROUP, Los Angeles, CA, pg. 1577
Gonzalez, Maura, Acct Dir -- KOVEL/FULLER, Culver City, CA, pg. 617
Gonzalez, Melanie, Acct Supvr-Global -- DDB Chicago, Chicago, IL, pg. 274
Gonzalez, Melissa, Acct Exec -- SK+G ADVERTISING LLC, Las Vegas, NV, pg. 1049
Gonzalez, Michael, Pres & Dir-Creative -- EL CREATIVE, INC., Dallas, TX, pg. 342
Gonzalez, Monica, Acct Coord -- ROCKAWAY PR, Miami, FL, pg. 1638
Gonzalez, Monique N., Acct Dir -- ROCKORANGE, Miami, FL, pg. 1638
Gonzalez, Paola, Acct Dir -- Havas Worldwide Mexico, Mexico, Mexico, pg. 499
Gonzalez, Vasty, Acct Supvr -- CONILL ADVERTISING, INC., Miami, FL, pg. 230
Gonzalez, Vicky, VP & Dir-Print Production -- Erwin Penland, New York, NY, pg. 355
Gonzalez, Victor, Dir-New Bus -- EL CREATIVE, INC., Dallas, TX, pg. 342
Gonzalez, Yezenia, Acct Exec -- Weber Shandwick-Dallas, Dallas, TX, pg. 1677
Gonzalez-Herba, Javier, Exec Dir-Creative -- TIPPIT & MOO ADVERTISING, Houston, TX, pg. 1145
Good, Alli, Acct Supvr -- LIPPE TAYLOR, New York, NY, pg. 1576
Goodale, Todd, Dir-Creative -- OGILVY & MATHER, New York, NY, pg. 826
Goode, Patricia, Acct Exec-Digital -- SK+G ADVERTISING LLC, Las Vegas, NV, pg. 1049
Gooden, Kate, Sr Producer-Brdcst -- Saatchi & Saatchi Australia, Sydney, Australia, pg. 1010
Goodhue, Tracy, Mgr-Traffic & Production -- The Boner Group, Inc./Ann K. Savage, Leesburg, VA, pg. 129
Gooding, Megan, Acct Supvr -- ANSON-STONER INC., Winter Park, FL, pg. 61
Goodman, Alyssa, Acct Exec-PR -- DENMARK ADVERTISING & PUBLIC RELATIONS, Atlanta, GA, pg. 296
Goodman, Carolyn, Pres & Dir-Creative -- TARGET MARKETING, Rockland, ME, pg. 1431
Goodman, Dan, Dir-New Bus Ops -- YOUNG & RUBICAM, New York, NY, pg. 1239
Goodman, Erin, Media Buyer -- RED CROW MARKETING INC., Springfield, MO, pg. 959
Goodman, Gillian, Assoc Dir-Creative -- HIRSHORN ZUCKERMAN DESIGN GROUP, Rockville, MD, pg. 516
Goodman, Jae, Chief Creative Officer & Co-Head-CAA Mktg -- CREATIVE ARTISTS AGENCY, Los Angeles, CA, pg. 245
Goodman, Michael, Media Dir -- DIGITAS HEALTH, Philadelphia, PA, pg. 309
Goodman, Richie, Acct Supvr -- Fleishman-Hillard Inc., Charlotte, NC, pg. 1517
Goodness, Terri, Dir-Creative -- THE GOODNESS COMPANY, Wisconsin Rapids, WI, pg. 435
Goodnow, Jeff, Dir-Brdcst Production -- RAPP, New York, NY, pg. 951
Goodrich, Tom, Assoc Dir-Creative -- THE INTEGER GROUP - DENVER, Lakewood, CO, pg. 1416
Goodson, Ashley, Acct Exec -- Cossette, Chicago, IL, pg. 237
Goodwin, Erica, Strategist-Creative -- ISTRATEGYLABS, Washington, DC, pg. 563
Goodwin, Mark, Dir-Creative -- M&C SAATCHI PLC, London, United Kingdom, pg. 675
Goodwin, Zach, Dir-Creative -- ISTRATEGYLABS, Washington, DC, pg. 563
Goodyear, Kristine, Sr Acct Mgr-PR -- WALKER MARKETING, INC., Concord, NC, pg. 1187
Goosmann, Tom, Chief Creative Officer -- TRUE NORTH INTERACTIVE, San Francisco, CA, pg. 1318
Goran, Jill, Sr VP & Dir-Creative -- Brierley & Partners, Sherman Oaks, CA, pg. 1227
Goran, Jill, Sr VP & Grp Dir-Creative -- Brierley & Partners, London, United Kingdom, pg. 165
Goran, Jill, Sr VP & Grp Dir-Creative -- BRIERLEY & PARTNERS, Plano, TX, pg. 164
Goran, Jill, Sr VP & Grp Dir-Creative -- Brierley & Partners, London, United Kingdom, pg. 1227
Goran, Jill, Sr VP & Dir-Creative -- Brierley & Partners, Sherman Oaks, CA, pg. 165
Gordee, Bradley, Assoc Dir-Creative -- RPM ADVERTISING, Chicago, IL, pg. 995
Gordon, Dave, Assoc Dir-Creative -- Pereira & O'Dell, New York, NY, pg. 883
Gordon, Grant, Pres & Dir-Creative -- KEY GORDON COMMUNICATIONS, Toronto, Canada, pg. 609
Gordon, Jeff, Principal & Dir-Creative -- JD GORDON CREATIVE LABS, Sioux City, IA, pg. 589
Gordon, Kevin, Acct Dir -- MEC, Dublin, Ireland, pg. 1359
Gordon, Kim, Principal & Acct Dir -- JD GORDON CREATIVE LABS, Sioux City, IA, pg. 589
Gordon, Lisa, Sr VP-PR -- HJMT COMMUNICATIONS, LLC, Melville, NY, pg. 517
Gordon, Michelle, Acct Exec & Specialist-Social Media -- STREAM COMPANIES, Malvern, PA, pg. 1091
Gordon, Nick, Head-Creative -- FCB Kuala Lumpur, Kuala Lumpur, Malaysia, pg. 381
Gordon, Sid, Dir-Creative -- Rapp London, London, United Kingdom, pg. 952
Gordon, Tim, Grp Dir-Creative -- DROGA5, New York, NY, pg. 328
Gordon-Rogers, Gav, Dir-Creative -- MRY, London, United Kingdom, pg. 785
Gore, Sarah, Acct Supvr -- PUBLICIS NEW YORK, New York, NY, pg. 935
Gore, Shari, Media Dir -- SANDIA ADVERTISING, Colorado Springs, CO, pg. 1017
Gorelick, Sara, Acct Dir -- COLANGELO & PARTNERS PUBLIC RELATIONS, New York, NY, pg. 1483
Goren, Gil, Dir-Creative -- Yehoshua TBWA, Tel Aviv, Israel, pg. 1126
Gorges, Sophia, Acct Dir -- Edelman Frankfurt, Frankfurt am Main, Germany, pg. 1504
Gorman, Jon, Assoc Dir-Creative -- Buck NY, New York, NY, pg. 173
Gorodetski, David, Co-Founder, COO & Exec Dir-Creative -- SAGE COMMUNICATIONS, McLean, VA, pg. 1013
Gorsek, Kim, Acct Exec -- BRIGHTON AGENCY, INC., Saint Louis, MO, pg. 166
Gorska, Kamila, Acct Dir-Central Europe -- Saatchi & Saatchi, Warsaw, Poland, pg. 1005
Gorski, Kayla, Acct Dir -- Mullen Lowe, Pittsburgh, PA, pg. 789
Gorson, Sophie, Acct Exec -- DEFYMEDIA, New York, NY, pg. 1287
Goskeson, Dustin, Media Planner & Media Buyer -- HELEN THOMPSON MEDIA, San Antonio, TX, pg. 1341
Goslin, Liz, Assoc Media Buyer -- Mindshare, New York, NY, pg. 1336
Gosling, Andrew, Dir-Creative Svcs -- TBWA/London, London, United Kingdom, pg. 1124
Gosling, Andrew, Head-Creative Svcs -- TBWA/UK Group, London, United Kingdom, pg. 1125
Gosnar, Brian, VP & Exec Producer-Brdcst -- HILL HOLLIDAY, Boston, MA, pg. 514
Goss, Amos, Exec Creative Dir -- THE VIA AGENCY, Portland, ME, pg. 1175
Goss, Ben, Acct Dir -- TRO, Isleworth, United Kingdom, pg. 316
Gosselin, Martin, Partner & VP-Creative -- Ogilvy Montreal, Montreal, Canada, pg. 829
Goswami, Varun, Exec Dir-Creative -- Grey (India) Pvt. Pty. Ltd. (Delhi), Gurgaon, India, pg. 456
Gotbatkin, Kira, Art Dir -- GREY NEW YORK, New York, NY, pg. 446
Gothold, Jon, Exec Dir-Creative & Partner -- AMUSEMENT PARK, Santa Ana, CA, pg. 56
Goto, Naoko, Acct Dir -- Dentsu Y&R Japan, Tokyo, Japan, pg. 1241
Gottesman, Marc, VP & Grp Dir-Creative -- Digitas Health Boston, Boston, MA, pg. 1288
Gottlieb, Chloe, Sr VP & Exec Dir-Creative-New York -- R/GA, Austin, TX, pg. 947
Gottlieb, Chloe, Sr VP & Exec Dir-Creative-New York -- R/GA, New York, NY, pg. 946
Gotz, Chris, Exec Dir-Creative -- Ogilvy Cape Town, Cape Town, South Africa, pg. 849
Gotz, Chris, Exec Dir-Creative -- OgilvyInteractive, Cape Town, South Africa, pg. 849
Gotz, Chris, Exec Dir-Creative -- OgilvyOne Worldwide-Cape Town, Cape Town, South Africa, pg. 850
Gouaux, Allison, Acct Exec -- BEUERMAN MILLER FITZGERALD, INC., New Orleans, LA, pg. 127
Goudey, Katie, Acct Supvr -- Cone Communications LLC, New York, NY, pg. 1484
Gouin, Kathy, Sr VP & Acct Dir -- G.W. HOFFMAN MARKETING & COMMUNICATIONS, Darien, CT, pg. 1415
Gould, Andy, Exec Dir-Creative -- VML, Kalamazoo, MI, pg. 1319
Goulding, Erin, Acct Exec -- LEVERAGE PR, Austin, TX, pg. 1574
Goulette, Andrea, Acct Supvr -- Commonwealth, Detroit, MI, pg. 714
Gourevitch, Hannah, Acct Dir -- Wieden + Kennedy, London, United Kingdom, pg. 1204
Gourki, Kiumars, Dir-Creative -- DARLING, New York, NY, pg. 266
Gowland, Marc, Exec VP & Exec Creative Dir-Tech -- Deutsch LA, Los Angeles, CA, pg. 302
Gowland-Smith, Jarrod, Head-Brdcst & Digital -- Active International Ltd., London, United Kingdom, pg. 1324
Grable, Megan, VP-Creative & Strategy -- BULLDOG DRUMMOND, INC., San Diego, CA, pg. 174
Grabosky, Herman, Acct Dir -- M8 AGENCY, Miami, FL, pg. 681
Grabowski, Alison, Acct Exec -- PUSHTWENTYTWO, Pontiac, MI, pg. 940
Graby, Hope, Dir-PR & Mgr-Client -- SCHEFFEY INC, Lancaster, PA, pg. 1024
Graccioli, Sebastian, Dir-Creative -- Grey Argentina, Buenos Aires, Argentina, pg. 453
Grace, Brad, Assoc Dir-Creative -- SPEAK, Hillsboro, OR, pg. 1063
Grace, Russ, Exec Producer-Video-Brdcst -- MOB MEDIA, Foothill Ranch, CA, pg. 768
Grady, Kaitlynn, Acct Exec -- MEDIASOURCE, Columbus, OH, pg. 1588
Graf, Caroline, Acct Exec -- AGENCE BRAQUE, Montreal, Canada, pg. 37
Graf, Karen, VP & Acct Dir -- Havas Media, Boston, MA, pg. 1340
Graff, Jason, Exec Dir-Creative -- PUBLICIS NEW YORK, New York, NY, pg. 935
Graham, Alasdair, Creative Dir -- Havas Worldwide London, London, United Kingdom, pg. 498
Graham, Bill, Assoc Dir-Creative -- KBS+, New York, NY, pg. 604
Graham, Doug, Co-Pres & Chief Creative Officer -- BIGBUZZ MARKETING GROUP, Melville, NY, pg. 132
Graham, Emily, Media Planner -- OMD NORTH AMERICA, New York, NY, pg. 1378
Graham, Jamie, Media Buyer-Spark PHD -- PHD New Zealand, Auckland, New Zealand, pg. 1385
Graham, Jason, Head-Copy & Creative Grp-London -- Mars Y&R, London, United Kingdom, pg. 1247

Personnel Index

Graham, Kristin, Assoc Dir-Creative -- GOODBY, SILVERSTEIN & PARTNERS, INC., San Francisco, CA, pg. 434

Graham, Maggie May, Acct Supvr -- EDELMAN, Chicago, IL, pg. 1500

Graham, Mark, Acct Dir -- JOHN ST., Toronto, Canada, pg. 593

Graham, Steven S., Dir-PR -- GODFREY ADVERTISING, Lancaster, PA, pg. 432

Graham, Travis, Partner & Dir-Creative -- TACO TRUCK CREATIVE, Carlsbad, CA, pg. 1106

Grais, Ian, Founder & Creative Dir-Natl -- RETHINK, Vancouver, Canada, pg. 973

Grall, Ellen, Acct Exec -- QUIET LIGHT COMMUNICATIONS, Rockford, IL, pg. 943

Grams, Colleen, Acct Dir -- Bader Rutter & Associates, Inc., Lincoln, NE, pg. 86

Granberg, Lisa, Dir-Art & Creative -- DDB Stockholm, Stockholm, Sweden, pg. 289

Grandal, Victoria, Coord-New Bus -- ON IDEAS, INC., Jacksonville, FL, pg. 859

Grandek, Michaela, Acct Exec -- WE, Munich, Germany, pg. 1674

Granderson, Danielle, Acct Supvr -- GREY GROUP, New York, NY, pg. 445

Grandy, John, Dir-Creative Svcs -- THE BOSTON GROUP, Boston, MA, pg. 150

Graner, Alan, Chief Creative Officer -- DALY-SWARTZ PUBLIC RELATIONS, Lake Forest, CA, pg. 1490

Granger, Tony, Chief Creative Officer-Global -- Armstrong Y&R, Lusaka, Zambia, pg. 1252

Granger, Tony, Chief Creative Officer-Global -- Young & Rubicam Brands, San Francisco, San Francisco, CA, pg. 1241

Grannis, Greg, Exec Dir-Creative -- CATALYST MARKETING COMPANY, Fresno, CA, pg. 197

Granowicz, Stephanie, Acct Coord -- KILLIAN BRANDING, Chicago, IL, pg. 611

Grant, Ali, Dir-PR & Talent -- BE SOCIAL PUBLIC RELATIONS LLC, Solana Beach, CA, pg. 1450

Grant, Cindi, VP & Dir-Brdcst -- ID Media-Chicago, Chicago, IL, pg. 1344

Grant, Hayley, Acct Supvr -- CONCEPT FARM, New York, NY, pg. 229

Grant, Susan, Acct Dir -- DDB Canada, Edmonton, Canada, pg. 273

Grant, Susan, Acct Dir -- Tribal Worldwide Toronto, Toronto, Canada, pg. 1316

Grantham, Greg, Assoc Dir-Creative & Copywriter -- BLUE SKY AGENCY, Atlanta, GA, pg. 142

Granzow, Gwen, VP, Principal & Dir-Creative -- DESIGN NORTH, INC., Racine, WI, pg. 1411

Grassa, Marta, Acct Supvr -- McCann Erickson S.A., Madrid, Spain, pg. 727

Gratacos, Lucille, Acct Supvr -- Lapiz, Chicago, IL, pg. 638

Grau, Rodrigo, VP-Creative -- DAVID, Sao Paulo, Brazil, pg. 267

Graulty, Bill, Acct Supvr -- MINTZ & HOKE COMMUNICATIONS GROUP, Avon, CT, pg. 763

Gravel, Joaquin, Head-Creative & Dir-Art -- HUXLEY QUAYLE VON BISMARK, INC., Toronto, Canada, pg. 529

Graves, Chris, Chief Creative Officer -- TEAM ONE USA, Los Angeles, CA, pg. 1134

Gravina, J. P., Dir-Art & Assoc Dir-Creative -- BBDO Toronto, Toronto, Canada, pg. 101

Gravolet, Ben, VP-Creative & Strategy -- TOUCHPOINTS MARKETING, LLC, Gretna, LA, pg. 1152

Gray, Andrea Still, Acct Dir -- JPA HEALTH COMMUNICATIONS, Washington, DC, pg. 597

Gray, Genevieve, Acct Exec -- GREY NEW YORK, New York, NY, pg. 446

Gray, Glenn, Dir-PR -- BUFFALO BRAND INVIGORATION GROUP, Vienna, VA, pg. 1464

Gray, Gordon, Acct Dir -- DAVID & GOLIATH, El Segundo, CA, pg. 267

Gray, Jay, Art Dir-Digital -- Leo Burnett Sydney, Sydney, Australia, pg. 647

Gray, Karen M., Assoc Dir-Creative -- PARTNERSHIP OF PACKER, OESTERLING & SMITH (PPO&S), Harrisburg, PA, pg. 876

Gray, Mel, Assoc Strategist-Creative -- DigitasLBi, Chicago, IL, pg. 1290

Gray, Michael J., Pres & Dir-Creative -- G&G ADVERTISING, INC., Billings, MT, pg. 412

Gray, Rachel, Acct Supvr -- HABERMAN & ASSOCIATES, INC., Minneapolis, MN, pg. 471

Gray, Richard, Dir-Creative -- ZIMMERMAN ADVERTISING, Fort Lauderdale, FL, pg. 1256

Grayson, Chris, Art Dir -- RED OLIVE, Sandy, UT, pg. 1311

Grayson, Jonathan, Acct Exec -- Vitro NY, New York, NY, pg. 1180

Grayum, Julie, Acct Dir-PR & Social Media -- LOPEZ NEGRETE COMMUNICATIONS, INC., Houston, TX, pg. 668

Grayum, Julie Jameson, Acct Dir-PR & Social Media -- Lopez Negrete Communications West, Inc., Burbank, CA, pg. 669

Greaney, Brendan, Dir-Creative -- George Patterson Y&R, Canberra, Australia, pg. 1219

Greaney, Brendan, Dir-Creative -- George Patterson Y&R, Fortitude Valley, Australia, pg. 1219

Greasley, Jessica, Acct Dir -- Weber Shandwick, Toronto, Canada, pg. 1678

Greason, Zac, Art Dir -- VML, INC., Kansas City, MO, pg. 1182

Grebe, Rodrigo, Art Dir -- Prolam Y&R S.A., Santiago, Chile, pg. 1249

Greco, Steve, VP-Creative Svcs -- DON JAGODA ASSOCIATES, INC., Melville, NY, pg. 1411

Greco, Susan, Acct Dir -- SPR ATLANTA, Atlanta, GA, pg. 1653

Greco, Tom, Creative Dir -- TAXI, Toronto, Canada, pg. 1111

Green, Alastair, Exec Dir-Creative -- TEAM ONE USA, Los Angeles, CA, pg. 1134

Green, Amanda, Acct Dir -- TBWA Whybin Limited, Auckland, New Zealand, pg. 1130

Green, Cameron, CEO & Dir-Creative -- GREENRUBINO, Seattle, WA, pg. 443

Green, Cassandra, Acct Dir-Jaguar & Land Rover -- THE IMAGINATION GROUP, London, United Kingdom, pg. 540

Green, Cynthia, Media Buyer -- GREMILLION & POU, Shreveport, LA, pg. 444

Green, Dennis, Creative Dir -- FAHRENHEIT CREATIVE, Okemos, MI, pg. 365

Green, Derek, Exec Dir-Creative -- Ogilvy Sydney, Saint Leonards, Australia, pg. 840

Green, Jeff, VP & Acct Supvr -- MICHAEL A. BURNS & ASSOCIATES, INC., Dallas, TX, pg. 1590

Green, Josh, Dir-Creative -- Octagon, London, United Kingdom, pg. 824

Green, Katja, Acct Dir -- Saatchi & Saatchi, Auckland, New Zealand, pg. 1011

Green, Marvin, Acct Exec & Specialist-Social Media -- YELLO ADVERTISING, Los Angeles, CA, pg. 1238

Green, Shawanda, Acct Dir -- YOUNG & RUBICAM, New York, NY, pg. 1239

Green, Sheila, VP-PR -- THE CASTLE GROUP, Boston, MA, pg. 1474

Green, Tim, Exec Dir-Creative -- Havas Worldwide Australia, North Sydney, Australia, pg. 499

Green, Vikki, Owner & Dir-Creative -- SANDLOT STUDIOS, Phoenix, AZ, pg. 1017

Greenaway, Andy, Exec Dir-Creative-Asia & Pac -- SAPIENTNITRO USA, INC., New York, NY, pg. 1019

Greenberg, Courtney, Acct Supvr -- DKC Los Angeles, Los Angeles, CA, pg. 1495

Greenberg, Gary, Exec VP & Chief Creative Officer -- Allen & Gerritsen, Harrisburg, PA, pg. 47

Greenberg, Gary, Exec VP & Creative Dir -- ALLEN & GERRITSEN, Boston, MA, pg. 46

Greenberg, Janet, VP & Head-Creative Svcs-NYC -- Jack Morton Worldwide, Detroit, MI, pg. 583

Greenberg, Lisa, Sr VP, Dir-Creative & Head-Art -- LEO BURNETT COMPANY LTD., Toronto, Canada, pg. 637

Greenberg, Paige, Acct Exec -- INFLUENT50, Washington, DC, pg. 545

Greenblatt, Melanie, Acct Exec -- McCann Erickson North America, New York, NY, pg. 715

Greenblatt, Nikolas, Dir-Creative, Publr & Strategist-Digital -- 2ONE5 CREATIVE INC, Philadelphia, PA, pg. 5

Greene, Adair, Media Planner -- Razorfish Philadelphia, Philadelphia, PA, pg. 1310

Greene, Cara, Acct Exec -- Stanton Communications, New York, NY, pg. 1655

Greene, Donna L., VP & Acct Dir -- SPM MARKETING & COMMUNICATIONS, La Grange, IL, pg. 1066

Greene, Kimberly, Acct Exec -- RON SONNTAG PUBLIC RELATIONS, Milwaukee, WI, pg. 1639

Greene, Linda, Dir-Creative -- CHILLINGWORTH/RADDING INC., New York, NY, pg. 209

Greenfield, Jennifer, Dir-Art & Creative -- VISION CREATIVE GROUP, INC., Cedar Knolls, NJ, pg. 1178

Greenhalgh, Tim, Chm & Chief Creative Officer -- FITCH, London, United Kingdom, pg. 390

Greenhalgh, Tim, Chief Creative Officer -- Fitch, Scottsdale, AZ, pg. 390

Greenhalgh, Tim, Chm & Chief Creative Officer -- Fitch:London, London, United Kingdom, pg. 390

Greenheck, Abigail, Acct Dir -- BEEHIVE PR, Saint Paul, MN, pg. 1451

Greenlaw, Katie, Dir-PR -- RINCK ADVERTISING, Auburn, ME, pg. 1637

Greenlaw, Liam, Dir-Creative -- WASSERMAN & PARTNERS ADVERTISING INC., Vancouver, Canada, pg. 1191

Greenspan, Josh, Dir-Creative -- HAVAS WORLDWIDE, New York, NY, pg. 488

Greenspan, Kathy, Owner & Dir-Strategic & Creative -- THE POMERANTZ AGENCY LLC, Annapolis, MD, pg. 903

Greenspun, Mark, Founder & Dir-Creative -- ADWORKS, INC., Washington, DC, pg. 36

Greenstein, Bari, Project Mgr-Global New Bus -- Havas Worldwide-Strat Farm, New York, NY, pg. 490

Greenwald, Dan, Founder & Dir-Creative -- WHITE RHINO PRODUCTIONS, INC., Burlington, MA, pg. 1200

Greenwald, Katie, Acct Mgr-PR -- HITCHCOCK FLEMING & ASSOCIATES, INC., Akron, OH, pg. 516

Greenwood, Alisa, Dir-Mktg & Creative Svcs -- COMPASS MARKETING, Annapolis, MD, pg. 228

Greenwood, Eddy, Exec Dir-Creative -- J. Walter Thompson GmbH, Frankfurt am Main, Germany, pg. 573

Greer, Kristen, Acct Exec -- FREE AGENTS MARKETING, Glen Allen, VA, pg. 403

Greer, Morgan, Media Planner -- Optimedia-Indianapolis, Indianapolis, IN, pg. 1383

Greer, Tara, Exec VP & Exec Dir-Creative-Platforms -- Deutsch LA, Los Angeles, CA, pg. 302

Greeves, Shane, Exec Dir-Creative-Global -- FUTUREBRAND, New York, NY, pg. 410

Greeves, Shane, Exec Dir-Creative-Global -- FutureBrand, London, United Kingdom, pg. 410

Grefen, Jens, Dir-Creative-Germany -- Interbrand, Hamburg, Germany, pg. 858

Gregeois, Florence, Acct Dir -- PORTER NOVELLI, New York, NY, pg. 1619

Gregor, Christina, Acct Supvr -- HAVAS FORMULA, El Segundo, CA, pg. 1537

Gregor, Jean-Pierre, Dir-Integrated Creative -- Saatchi & Saatchi, Frankfurt am Main, Germany, pg. 1003

Gregorachi, Paulo, Vice-Chm & Chief Creative Officer -- McCann Erickson Publicidade Ltda., Rio de Janeiro, Brazil, pg. 717

Gregorio, Megan, Acct Exec -- BLANC & OTUS PUBLIC RELATIONS, San Francisco, CA, pg. 1455

Gregory, Chase, Acct Exec -- RED MOON MARKETING, Charlotte, NC, pg. 961

Gregory, Hannah Brazee, Founder & Chief Creative Officer -- SHOESTRING, Gardiner, ME, pg. 1039

Gregory, Lauren, Acct Supvr -- DRIVEN SOLUTIONS INC., Ferndale, MI, pg. 328

Greif, Arel, Media Buyer -- Mindshare, New York, NY, pg. 1336

Grelik, Debra, Acct Dir -- Wunderman, Toronto, Canada, pg. 1231

Grelli, Luca, Exec Dir-Creative -- Saatchi & Saatchi Fallon Tokyo, Tokyo, Japan, pg. 367

Grelli, Luca, Exec Dir-Creative -- Saatchi & Saatchi Fallon Tokyo, Tokyo, Japan, pg. 1011

Grendus, Cathy, Acct Dir -- DDB Canada, Toronto, Canada, pg. 274

Grenville, Tanya, Acct Supvr -- J. WALTER THOMPSON CANADA, Toronto, Canada, pg. 580

Gresehover, Ehren, Co-Founder & Dir-Creative -- STELLAR ENGINE, Brooklyn, NY, pg. 1083

Grether, Daniel, Grp Dir-Creative -- Saatchi & Saatchi, Frankfurt am Main, Germany, pg. 1003

Gretz, Mal, Acct Exec -- AKQA, INC., San Francisco, CA, pg. 1280

Greve, Mel, Sr VP & Dir-Brdcst -- KELLY SCOTT MADISON, Chicago, IL, pg. 1349

Grey, Charlotte, Acct Dir -- Saatchi & Saatchi, Johannesburg, South Africa, pg. 1006

Grice, Caroline, Acct Coord -- THIRD DEGREE ADVERTISING, Oklahoma City, OK, pg. 1140

Grice, Jeremy, Assoc Partner & Assoc Dir-Creative -- SPRING ADVERTISING, Vancouver, Canada, pg. 1067

Grice, Mike, Principal & Chief Creative Officer -- KEYSTONE MARKETING, Winston Salem, NC, pg. 610

Grider, Jon, Dir-Creative -- NONBOX, Hales Corners, WI, pg. 813

Grieco, Katie, Acct Exec-PR -- MGH, INC., Owings Mills, MD, pg. 752

Griego, Esther, Mgr-Creative Svcs -- RBB PUBLIC RELATIONS, Miami, FL, pg. 1631

Grieve, Alex, Exec Dir-Creative -- Abbott Mead Vickers BBDO, London, United Kingdom, pg. 112

Grieves, Mark, Dir-Creative -- FAHLGREN MORTINE, Columbus,

Personnel Index

H

Hall, Ken, Dir-Creative & Digital -- RENEGADE COMMUNICATIONS, Hunt Valley, MD, pg. 968
Hall, Libby, Creative Dir -- VML, INC., Kansas City, MO, pg. 1182
Hall, Peter, Art Dir -- Arena BLM, London, United Kingdom, pg. 485
Hall, Tom, Principal-Creative -- MSI Advertising, Chicago, IL, pg. 786
Hall, Tony, Head-Print Production -- Whybin TBWA, Melbourne, Australia, pg. 1128
Hall, Will, Exec Dir-Creative -- RAIN, Portsmouth, NH, pg. 950
Hall, Yvonne, Assoc Dir-Creative -- Saatchi & Saatchi, Johannesburg, South Africa, pg. 1006
Hallahan, Devin, Acct Exec -- GIGUNDA GROUP, INC., Manchester, NH, pg. 425
Halle, Sarah, Acct Exec -- WEBER SHANDWICK, New York, NY, pg. 1675
Hallen, Kathy, Assoc Dir-Creative -- THE BOSWORTH GROUP, Charleston, SC, pg. 150
Hallett, Alison, Acct Dir -- SHEEPSCOT CREATIVE, Portland, OR, pg. 1037
Halley, Lauren, Acct Exec -- SAESHE ADVERTISING, Los Angeles, CA, pg. 1013
Halliday, John, Dir-Creative -- VENTURE COMMUNICATIONS LTD., Calgary, Canada, pg. 1173
Hallman, Kimberly, Dir-PR -- 160OVER90, Philadelphia, PA, pg. 2
Hallock, Matthew, Pres & Dir-Creative -- THE VOICE, Fairfield, CT, pg. 1184
Halloran, John, Dir-Creative Svcs -- MACY + ASSOCIATES INC., Los Angeles, CA, pg. 683
Halloran, John, Dir-Creative Svcs -- Macy + Associates Inc., San Francisco, CA, pg. 683
Hallsten, Magnus, Dir-Creative -- Monterosa, Stockholm, Sweden, pg. 95
Halpin, Lindsey, Acct Dir -- MGH, INC., Owings Mills, MD, pg. 752
Hamali, Lina, Copywriter-Creative -- De Le Ma/ McCann Erickson, Nicosia, Cyprus, pg. 719
Hamamci, Asli, Sr VP & Acct Dir-Global -- PHD New York, New York, NY, pg. 1384
Hamamoto, Margaret, Acct Supvr -- RILEY HAYES ADVERTISING, Minneapolis, MN, pg. 981
Haman, Sarah, Acct Supvr -- GREY GROUP, New York, NY, pg. 445
Hamblock, Diana, Art Dir -- QUIET LIGHT COMMUNICATIONS, Rockford, IL, pg. 943
Hamburg, Steve, Chief Creative Officer -- CALCIUM, Philadelphia, PA, pg. 184
Hamdalla, Ahmed, Assoc Dir-Creative -- Impact BBDO, Cairo, Egypt, pg. 106
Hamel, Elizabeth, Acct Dir-PR -- XA, THE EXPERIENTIAL AGENCY, INC., Chicago, IL, pg. 1689
Hamelinck, Peter, Exec Dir-Creative -- Y&R Amsterdam B.V., Amsterdam, Netherlands, pg. 1246
Hamidi, Jamal, Exec Dir-Creative -- Edelman, Sydney, Australia, pg. 1505
Hamidi, Madjid, Acct Supvr -- CUNDARI INTEGRATED ADVERTISING, Toronto, Canada, pg. 260
Hamilton, Ashleigh, Art Buyer & Producer-TV, Radio & Print -- Y&R Cape Town, Cape Town, South Africa, pg. 1251
Hamilton, Barbara, Dir-Creative-Global -- RED FUSE COMMUNICATIONS, INC., New York, NY, pg. 960
Hamilton, Davina, Acct Exec -- CAMPBELL EWALD, Detroit, MI, pg. 187
Hamilton, Douglas, Assoc Dir-Creative & Copywriter -- BBH Singapore, Singapore, Singapore, pg. 95
Hamilton, Jennifer, Acct Supvr -- Hill + Knowlton Strategies, Tampa, FL, pg. 1540
Hamilton, Latoya, Acct Dir -- TMP Worldwide/Advertising & Communications, Glendale, CA, pg. 1148
Hamilton, Latoya, Acct Dir -- TMP Worldwide/Advertising & Communications, New Albany, IN, pg. 1148
Hamilton, Liz, Acct Mgr-PR -- ARCHER MALMO, Memphis, TN, pg. 67
Hamilton, Nichole, Acct Exec -- FLEISHMAN-HILLARD INC., Saint Louis, MO, pg. 1515
Hamilton, Wendi, Producer-Brdcst -- Juniper Park/TBWA, Toronto, Canada, pg. 1116
Hamilton-Sustad, Barbara, Acct Dir -- NEMER FIEGER, Minneapolis, MN, pg. 804
Hamlin, Julie, Dir-PR -- BURKHOLDER/FLINT, Columbus, OH, pg. 177
Hamlin, Natalie, Acct Exec -- JMPR, INC., Woodland Hills, CA, pg. 1556
Hamling, Tom, Grp Dir-Creative -- GSD&M, Austin, TX, pg. 464
Hamm, Dusky, Mgr-Creative -- KOCH COMMUNICATIONS, Oklahoma City, OK, pg. 1567
Hamm, Jon, Chief Creative Officer-Global -- GEOMETRY GLOBAL, New York, NY, pg. 421
Hammelman, Bobby, Acct Exec -- Edelman, New York, NY, pg. 1502
Hammer, Alison, Creative Dir -- MARC USA, Pittsburgh, PA, pg. 691
Hammerquist, Fred, Founder & Dir-Creative -- HAMMERQUIST STUDIOS, Seattle, WA, pg. 477
Hammes, Gwen, VP & Acct Dir -- DDB Chicago, Chicago, IL, pg. 274
Hammett, Elyse, VP-PR-Corp & Lifestyle -- PHASE 3 MARKETING & COMMUNICATIONS, Atlanta, GA, pg. 887
Hammill, Kristin, VP & Acct Dir -- HAVAS MEDIA, New York, NY, pg. 1338
Hammill, Patrick, Acct Dir -- Havas Life, Toronto, Canada, pg. 487
Hammond, Kevin, Dir-Creative -- 20NINE DESIGN STUDIOS LLC, Conshohocken, PA, pg. 3
Hammond, Steve, Exec Dir-Creative -- H2R AGENCY, Loveland, CO, pg. 471
Hampe, Gina, Acct Dir -- FOODMIX MARKETING COMMUNICATIONS, Elmhurst, IL, pg. 396
Hampton, Andrea Brady, Dir-PR -- NEW WEST LLC, Louisville, KY, pg. 807
Hampton, Brandon, Assoc Dir-Creative -- Moxie Interactive Inc., Pittsburgh, PA, pg. 1304
Hampton, Damion, Acct Dir -- Halesway, Andover, United Kingdom, pg. 383
Hampton, Tyler, Dir-Creative -- VENABLES, BELL & PARTNERS, San Francisco, CA, pg. 1172
Hamza, Khaled, Mgr-Creative Svcs -- FP7, Dubai, United Arab Emirates, pg. 729
Han, Tiffany, Media Planner & Buyer-Digital -- PROOF ADVERTISING, Austin, TX, pg. 913
Hanchett, Alison Avezzie, Art Dir -- SIR ISAAC, Salem, MA, pg. 1047
Hancock, Leslie, Media Buyer -- ADRENALIN, INC, Denver, CO, pg. 31
Hancock, Nicola, Brand Strategist, Media Planner & Buyer -- REVOLVE, Bedford, Canada, pg. 975
Hancock, Rupert, Dir-Creative -- Ogilvy Sydney, Saint Leonards, Australia, pg. 840
Handerhan, Megan, Media Buyer-Mediahub -- Mullen Lowe, Winston Salem, NC, pg. 788
Handley, Calum, Exec Dir-Creative -- MXM, Culver City, CA, pg. 798
Handley, Calum, Exec Dir-Creative -- MXM MOBILE, New York, NY, pg. 798
Handlos, Linda, Acct Exec -- RIZEN CREATIVE, Boise, ID, pg. 984
Handlos, Oliver, Co-Creative Dir-Activation & PR -- GREY NEW YORK, New York, NY, pg. 446
Hanford, Diana, Acct Dir -- PIERSON GRANT PUBLIC RELATIONS, Fort Lauderdale, FL, pg. 891
Hang, Sherry, Dir-Mktg & Creative Svcs -- YECK BROTHERS COMPANY, Dayton, OH, pg. 1237
Hankh, Alexis, Acct Exec -- RESOUND MARKETING, Princeton, NJ, pg. 1635
Hanks, Skeet, Assoc Dir-Creative -- ENTREPRENEUR ADVERTISING GROUP, Kansas City, MO, pg. 349
Hanley, Laurie, Coord-PR -- AHA CREATIVE STRATEGIES INC., Gibsons, Canada, pg. 1441
Hanlon, Christopher, Founder & Dir-Creative -- HANLON CREATIVE, Kulpsville, PA, pg. 478
Hanna, Amy, Acct Dir -- MANHATTAN MARKETING ENSEMBLE, New York, NY, pg. 689
Hanna, Shelley, VP & Exec Dir-Creative -- Grey Healthcare Group, Kansas City, MO, pg. 423
Hannaway, Sean, Assoc Creative Dir -- Leo Burnett USA, Chicago, IL, pg. 639
Hanneken, Dave, Exec Dir-Creative -- JIGSAW LLC, Milwaukee, WI, pg. 591
Hannigan, Elizabeth, Acct Dir -- Havas Media, Boston, MA, pg. 1340
Hannon, Nancy, Exec VP & Exec Dir-Creative -- Leo Burnett USA, Chicago, IL, pg. 639
Hanrahan, Magen, Sr VP & Media Dir -- STARCOM MEDIAVEST GROUP, Chicago, IL, pg. 1074
Hanratty, Darcie, Acct Coord-Traffic & Print Media Buying -- SMITH, PHILLIPS & DI PIETRO, Yakima, WA, pg. 1054
Hansa, John, Exec VP & Dir-Creative -- LEO BURNETT WORLDWIDE, INC., Chicago, IL, pg. 637
Hansen, Amy, Dir-PR & Client Svcs -- SEROKA, Waukesha, WI, pg. 1033
Hansen, Claus, Creative Dir -- CP+B Boulder, Boulder, CO, pg. 240
Hansen, Corey, Mgr-Content, Acct Exec & Coord-Mktg -- THE DONALDSON GROUP, Weatogue, CT, pg. 322
Hansen, Hans, Co-Founder & Exec Dir-Creative -- SOLVE, Minneapolis, MN, pg. 1058
Hansen, Jesper, Dir-Creative & Art, Copywriter -- Uncle Grey A/S, Arhus, Denmark, pg. 448
Hansen, Lucy, Creative Dir -- HANGAR 30 INC, Denver, CO, pg. 477
Hansen, Spencer, Art Dir -- DROGA5, New York, NY, pg. 328
Hansen, Susan, Acct Supvr -- VML, Kalamazoo, MI, pg. 1319
Hansen, Wendy, Assoc Creative Dir -- MITHUN, Minneapolis, MN, pg. 765
Hanson, Brittney, Specialist-Digital PR & Social Media -- Flint Interactive, Duluth, MN, pg. 394
Hanson, Ellie Gorlin, Acct Supvr -- Finn Partners, Jerusalem, Israel, pg. 387
Hanson, Joey, Acct Supvr -- RPA, Santa Monica, CA, pg. 994
Hanson, Lee, Assoc Dir-Creative -- COLLE+MCVOY, Minneapolis, MN, pg. 221
Hanson, Scott, Acct Exec-Digital -- RHYTHMONE, Burlington, MA, pg. 977
Hanus, Malin, Dir-Creative -- Poke, London, United Kingdom, pg. 922
Hanzlicek, Jakub, Dir-Creative -- Publicis, Prague, Czech Republic, pg. 918
Hao, Rocky, Head-Creative -- Leo Burnett Shanghai Advertising Co., Ltd., Shanghai, China, pg. 648
Hao, Shum Qi, Art Dir -- DDB, Singapore, Singapore, pg. 288
Hara, Elyse, Acct Exec -- Fathom Communications, Chicago, IL, pg. 370
Hara, Elyse, Acct Exec -- FATHOM COMMUNICATIONS, New York, NY, pg. 369
Hara, Miriam, Chief Creative Officer -- 3H COMMUNICATIONS INC., Oakville, Canada, pg. 7
Harap, Lisa, Acct Dir -- DDB New York, New York, NY, pg. 275
Harari, Sandi, Sr VP & Dir-Creative -- BARKER/DZP, New York, NY, pg. 92
Harbeck, Jan, Mng Dir-Creative -- BBDO Proximity Berlin, Berlin, Germany, pg. 107
Harbison, Emily, Media Planner -- MOXIE INTERACTIVE INC., Atlanta, GA, pg. 1303
Hardatt, Devina, Acct Supvr -- ZULU ALPHA KILO, Toronto, Canada, pg. 1260
Harder, Heather, Acct Exec-Pub Affairs -- CAPSTRAT, Raleigh, NC, pg. 1472
Hardie, Candice, Acct Exec -- OgilvyOne, San Francisco, CA, pg. 829
Hardin, Drew, Acct Coord -- FRONTIER STRATEGIES LLC, Ridgeland, MS, pg. 1523
Harding, Dana, Dir-Creative -- D.L. MEDIA INC., Nixa, MO, pg. 317
Harding, Jeff, Creative Dir -- KAMP GRIZZLY, Portland, OR, pg. 601
Harding-Aimer, Julie, Acct Dir -- Blaze Advertising, Kent Town, Australia, pg. 1217
Harding-Aimer, Julie, Acct Dir -- Blaze Advertising, Kent Town, Australia, pg. 1147
Hardison, Lucas, Mgr-Creative -- ELITE SEM, New York, NY, pg. 1333
Hardwick, Laura, Designer-Creative -- WASHINGTON MEDIA GROUP, Washington, DC, pg. 1191
Hardy, Aly, VP & Acct Dir -- RTC, Washington, DC, pg. 1240
Hardy, D. J., Acct Dir -- EXPOSURE, New York, NY, pg. 362
Hardy, Penny, Partner & Dir-Creative -- PS, New York, NY, pg. 916
Hare, Lisa, Supvr-Creative -- MARTINO FLYNN LLC, Pittsford, NY, pg. 705
Hariharan, Ramakrishnan, Dir-Creative & Copywriter -- Ogilvy India, Mumbai, India, pg. 843
Harjani, Menka, Acct Dir-Intl -- TBWA Europe, Boulogne-Billancourt, France, pg. 1119
Harkness, Stuart, Co-Exec Creative Dir -- 72andSunny, Amsterdam, Netherlands, pg. 11
Harleman, Rachael, Acct Supvr -- BRIAN COMMUNICATIONS, Bryn Mawr, PA, pg. 1460
Harman, Amy, Acct Supvr -- FAHLGREN MORTINE, Columbus, OH, pg. 364
Harman, Elissa, Sr VP & Exec Creative Dir-Content -- Liquid Thread, New York, NY, pg. 1076
Harmon, Heidi, Acct Coord -- BOHLSENPR INC., Indianapolis, IN, pg. 1457
Harmon, Lauren, Acct Supvr -- RED212, Cincinnati, OH, pg. 963
Harmon, Tad, Principal & Dir-Creative -- 206 INC., Seattle, WA, pg.

Personnel Index

Personnel Index

I

Personnel Index

J

Personnel Index

Personnel Index

Cleveland, OH, pg. 73
Jones, Kevin, Exec Dir-Creative -- CP+B LA, Santa Monica, CA, pg. 241
Jones, Kimberly, Acct Dir -- SPEAKEASY DIGITAL MARKETING, Dallas, TX, pg. 1063
Jones, Laura, Acct Supvr -- TBC Direct, Inc., Baltimore, MD, pg. 1113
Jones, Laura, Acct Supvr -- TBC, INC./PR DIVISION, Baltimore, MD, pg. 1659
Jones, Louisa, Acct Dir -- Porter Novelli New Zealand-Auckland, Auckland, New Zealand, pg. 1625
Jones, Madison, Acct Exec -- KONNECT PUBLIC RELATIONS, Los Angeles, CA, pg. 1567
Jones, Mahogani, Dir-New Bus Dev & Mktg Activations -- ROCKORANGE, Miami, FL, pg. 1638
Jones, Marc, Acct Exec -- Initiative Los Angeles, Los Angeles, CA, pg. 1344
Jones, Maree, Specialist-PR & Social Media -- LUCKIE & COMPANY, Birmingham, AL, pg. 672
Jones, Mark, Pres & Dir-Creative -- JONES ADVERTISING, Seattle, WA, pg. 596
Jones, Mark, Sr Art Dir -- Whybin TBWA, Melbourne, Australia, pg. 1128
Jones, Mike, Assoc Dir-Creative -- DSP+P, Toronto, Canada, pg. 330
Jones, Paula, Acct Exec -- THE BRADFORD GROUP, Nashville, TN, pg. 1459
Jones, Rachael, Owner & Media Dir -- SCREEN STRATEGIES MEDIA, Fairfax, VA, pg. 1028
Jones, Regina H., Acct Supvr -- THE CARTER MALONE GROUP LLC, Memphis, TN, pg. 194
Jones, Robert, Acct Dir -- SPOTCO, New York, NY, pg. 1067
Jones, Stef, Partner-Creative -- BIG AL'S CREATIVE EMPORIUM, London, United Kingdom, pg. 129
Jones, Steve, Creative Dir -- Abbott Mead Vickers BBDO, London, United Kingdom, pg. 112
Jones, Steve, Art Dir -- DW ADVERTISING, Bloomfield, CT, pg. 333
Jones, Terry, VP & Dir-Creative -- Carol H. Williams Advertising, Chicago, IL, pg. 192
Jones, Tessa, Dir-Traffic -- BIEMEDIA, Denver, CO, pg. 129
Jones, Tim, Dir-Creative -- CORNETT INTEGRATED MARKETING SOLUTIONS, Lexington, KY, pg. 236
Jones, Tony, Dir-Creative -- MRM Worldwide New York, New York, NY, pg. 782
Jones, Troy, Dir-Creative -- RED RAG & BULL, Denver, CO, pg. 962
Jones-Pittier, Rachel, Acct Supvr -- KOHNSTAMM COMMUNICATIONS, Saint Paul, MN, pg. 616
Jonk, Danielle, Acct Dir -- TBWA Designers Company, Amsterdam, Netherlands, pg. 1122
Jordan, Andrew, Media Planner -- Ackerman McQueen, Inc., Dallas, TX, pg. 20
Jordan, Ann, Partner & Dir-Creative -- UNIT PARTNERS, San Francisco, CA, pg. 1167
Jordan, Eric, Pres & Chief Creative Officer -- 2ADVANCED STUDIOS, LLC., Aliso Viejo, CA, pg. 5
Jordan, Jessica, Art Dir -- IBEL AGENCY, Columbus, OH, pg. 531
Jordan, Louise, Acct Dir -- TEUWEN COMMUNICATIONS, New York, NY, pg. 1661
Jordan, Michael, CEO & Dir-Creative -- 31 LENGTHS LLC, New York, NY, pg. 6
Jordan, Nathan, Dir-Creative -- MARKET CONNECTIONS, Asheville, NC, pg. 695
Jordan, Paul, Exec Creative Dir -- mcgarrybowen, London, United Kingdom, pg. 734
Jordan, Ryan, VP-Creative & Dir -- IMRE, New York, NY, pg. 543
Jordan, Ryan, VP & Creative Dir -- IMRE, Baltimore, MD, pg. 542
Jordan, Tre, Acct Exec -- Y&R New York, New York, NY, pg. 1240
Jorgensen, Karen, Pres & Chief Creative Officer -- KALEIDOSCOPE, New York, NY, pg. 601
Jorgensen, Lars, Exec Creative Dir -- ANOMALY, New York, NY, pg. 60
Jorgge, Mariel, Acct Exec -- Biedermann Publicidad S.A., Asuncion, Paraguay, pg. 725
Josendale, Jessica, Acct Supvr -- EVB, Oakland, CA, pg. 359
Joseph, Jully, Acct Coord -- JAVELIN MARKETING GROUP, Irving, TX, pg. 588
Joseph, Mridula, Controller-Creative -- Ogilvy & Mather India, Chennai, India, pg. 842
Joseph, Mridula, Controller-Creative -- Ogilvy India, Mumbai, India, pg. 843
Joshi, Kashyap, Sr Dir-Creative -- J. Walter Thompson, Mumbai, India, pg. 569
Joshi, Makarand, Dir-Creative -- Ogilvy India, Mumbai, India, pg. 843
Joshi, Prasoon, CEO, Chief Creative Officer & Chm-Asia Pacific -- McCann Erickson India, Mumbai, India, pg. 721
Joshpe, Kent, Co-Owner & Dir-Creative -- ANTITHESIS ADVERTISING, Rochester, NY, pg. 62
Joshua, Ronjini M., Owner & Acct Dir -- THE SILVER TELEGRAM, Long Beach, CA, pg. 1044
Joubert, David, Exec Dir-Creative-Sydney -- George Patterson Y&R, Sydney, Australia, pg. 1219
Joubert, David, Exec Dir-Creative -- George Patterson Y&R, Canberra, Australia, pg. 1219
Joubert, David, Exec Dir-Creative -- Young & Rubicam Australia/New Zealand, Sydney, Australia, pg. 1242
Jourdain, Vaness, Media Buyer-Web -- Cossette Communication-Marketing (Montreal) Inc., Montreal, Canada, pg. 238
Jourdan, Raymond, Acct Supvr -- ROBINSON & ASSOCIATES INC, Tupelo, MS, pg. 988
Joyce, Kayla, Acct Exec -- BRAND ACTION TEAM, LLC, Avon, CT, pg. 155
Joyce, Mary Kate, Acct Supvr-PR -- GATESMAN+DAVE, Pittsburgh, PA, pg. 417
Joyce, Thayer, Acct Dir -- Y&R New York, New York, NY, pg. 1240
Joyner, Jeff, Dir-Creative -- SEROKA, Waukesha, WI, pg. 1033
Jreish, Sharbel, Art Dir -- Impact BBDO, Beirut, Lebanon, pg. 108
Juarbe, Michelle, Acct Exec -- Nobox Marketing Group, Inc., Guaynabo, PR, pg. 812
Judd, Natalie, Acct Exec -- RILEY HAYES ADVERTISING, Minneapolis, MN, pg. 981
Judd, Peter, Partner & Dir-Creative -- HUB STRATEGY AND COMMUNICATION, San Francisco, CA, pg. 526
Juenger, Jacki, Acct Supvr -- THE MARTIN AGENCY, Richmond, VA, pg. 702
Juggan, Phoebe, Acct Supvr -- HILL HOLLIDAY/NEW YORK, New York, NY, pg. 515
Juhasz, Eva, Grp Head-Creative -- DDB Budapest, Budapest, Hungary, pg. 283
Julson, Lynette, Media Planner & Media Buyer -- ODNEY, Bismarck, ND, pg. 824
Junadi, Idran, Acct Dir -- The Hoffman Agency, Singapore, Singapore, pg. 1546
Juncker, Jill, Acct Supvr -- CALISE PARTNERS INC., Dallas, TX, pg. 185
Jundi, Udai Al, Mgr-Traffic -- J. Walter Thompson, Damascus, Syria, pg. 577
Jung, Billie, VP-Creative -- ES ADVERTISING, Los Angeles, CA, pg. 355
Jung, Calvin, Founder, Owner & Grp Dir-Creative -- CREATIVE:MINT LLC, San Francisco, CA, pg. 253
Jungerberg, Nat, Acct Supvr -- COLLE+MCVOY, Minneapolis, MN, pg. 221
Jungles, Brad, Dir-Creative -- BARKLEYREI, Pittsburgh, PA, pg. 93
Jungmann, Phil, VP-Creative & Dir -- Energy BBDO, Chicago, IL, pg. 100
Juniot, Marcio, Dir-Creative -- Leo Burnett Tailor Made, Sao Paulo, Brazil, pg. 640
Junius, Megan, Pres & Creative Dir -- PETER HILL DESIGN, Minneapolis, MN, pg. 886
Junker, Alexis, Media Buyer -- ADPERIO, Denver, CO, pg. 1280
Jurek, Jenny, Media Planner -- HAWORTH MARKETING & MEDIA COMPANY, Minneapolis, MN, pg. 1340
Jurentkuff, JD, Dir-Creative -- TBWA/Media Arts Lab, Los Angeles, CA, pg. 1116
Jurisic, Stephen, Partner & Co-Exec Creative Dir -- JOHN ST., Toronto, Canada, pg. 593
Justice, Jim, Acct Supvr -- 1 TRICK PONY, Hammonton, NJ, pg. 1
Justice, Mel, Media Buyer -- HOUSER & HENNESSEE, Bridgeport, MI, pg. 524
Justin, Weng, Acct Dir -- Wunderman, Shanghai, China, pg. 1231
Justin, Weng, Acct Dir -- Wunderman Beijing, Beijing, China, pg. 1231
Juwita, Lintang Indah, Acct Exec -- Prisma Public Relations, Jakarta, Indonesia, pg. 1463

K

Kabbani, Mohamed, Assoc Dir-Creative -- J. Walter Thompson, Beirut, Lebanon, pg. 577
Kabra, Ujjwal, Dir-Creative -- Mullen Lowe Lintas Group, Mumbai, India, pg. 791
Kacenka, Peter, Exec Dir-Creative -- Wiktor/Leo Burnett, s.r.o., Bratislava, Slovakia, pg. 645
Kaczyk, Meg, Dir-Creative -- CMD, Portland, OR, pg. 217
Kadam, Satyajeet, Dir-Creative -- DDB Mudra Group, Mumbai, India, pg. 283
Kadavy, Troy, Creative Dir -- 92 WEST, Omaha, NE, pg. 13
Kaddoum, Shady, Assoc Dir-Creative -- Saatchi & Saatchi, Beirut, Lebanon, pg. 1004
Kadne, Manasi, Sr Creative Dir -- Ogilvy India, Mumbai, India, pg. 843
Kafadar, Engin, Sr Dir-Creative-Geometry Global & Istanbul -- Grey Istanbul, Istanbul, Turkey, pg. 452
Kagarakis, Alexis, Acct Coord -- PERRY COMMUNICATIONS GROUP, INC., Sacramento, CA, pg. 885
Kager, Karen, Mgr-Production & Traffic -- BHW1 ADVERTISING, Spokane, WA, pg. 129
Kahagalle, Chagali, Acct Supvr -- OGILVY HEALTHWORLD-TORONTO, Toronto, Canada, pg. 853
Kahana, Jake, Dir-Creative & Design -- MATTER UNLIMITED LLC, New York, NY, pg. 710
Kahl, Les, Mng Partner-US & Dir-Creative -- AdFarm, Fargo, ND, pg. 28
Kahl, Les, Mng Partner-US & Dir-Creative -- AdFarm, Kansas City, MO, pg. 28
Kahl, Matilda, Art Dir -- Saatchi & Saatchi New York, New York, NY, pg. 1001
Kahle, Brian, Partner & Dir-Creative Svcs -- ADVENTIVE MARKETING, INC., Arlington Heights, IL, pg. 33
Kahn, Casey, Acct Dir -- BECCA PR, New York, NY, pg. 1450
Kahn, Edward, Acct Dir -- GRAHAM OLESON, Colorado Springs, CO, pg. 439
Kaier, Scott, Acct Dir -- SMAK STRATEGIES, Boulder, CO, pg. 1052
Kaihoi, Jessica, Assoc Dir-Creative -- OgilvyOne Worldwide, Chicago, IL, pg. 828
Kaiman, Joel, Acct Supvr -- TJM COMMUNICATIONS, Oviedo, FL, pg. 1146
Kaiman, Natalie, Acct Supvr -- 6DEGREES INTEGRATED COMMUNICATIONS, Toronto, Canada, pg. 10
Kaiser, Ann, Acct Exec -- THE TASC GROUP, New York, NY, pg. 1659
Kaiser, Barbara, Acct Exec -- MRM London, London, United Kingdom, pg. 783
Kaiser, Katie, Acct Supvr -- RHEA + KAISER, Naperville, IL, pg. 976
Kaiser, Matt, Assoc Dir-Creative -- Connelly Partners Travel, Boston, MA, pg. 231
Kaka, Kaka Ling, Dir-Creative -- Havas Worldwide Beijing, Beijing, China, pg. 500
Kaka, Kaka Ling, Dir-Creative -- Havas Worldwide Shanghai, Shanghai, China, pg. 500
Kakomanolis, Elias, Dir-Creative Ops-NY -- MCKINNEY, Durham, NC, pg. 736
Kalaji, Ronda, Acct Exec -- THE LIPPIN GROUP, Los Angeles, CA, pg. 1577
Kalathara, Tony, Assoc Creative Dir -- DAVID The Agency, Miami, FL, pg. 267
Kalchev, Alexander, Exec Creative Dir -- DDB Paris, Paris, France, pg. 281
Kalia, Peggy, Acct Supvr -- EPOCH 5 PUBLIC RELATIONS, Huntington, NY, pg. 1511
Kalimbet, Anna, Dir-Creative & Art -- DARE, London, United Kingdom, pg. 1286
Kalina, Jenna, Acct Coord -- Summit Group, Itasca, IL, pg. 1099
Kalina, Ron, Assoc Dir-Creative-Design -- HARRIS, BAIO & MCCULLOUGH INC., Philadelphia, PA, pg. 481
Kalinauskiene, Violeta, Acct Dir -- J. Walter Thompson Lithuania San Vilnius, Vilnius, Lithuania, pg. 574
Kaliser, Christy, Acct Exec -- TIC TOC, Dallas, TX, pg. 1142
Kalish, Ellie, Acct Exec -- TOTAL PROMOTIONS, Highland Park, IL, pg. 1431
Kalita, Mriganka, Grp Head-Creative -- BPG Group, Dubai, United Arab Emirates, pg. 1218
Kalliches, Joanna, Dir-Creative -- Merkley + Partners/Healthworks, New York, NY, pg. 750
Kalmanovitz, Andrea, Dir-PR -- DECIBEL BLUE, Tempe, AZ, pg. 292
Kaloff, Constantin, Exec Dir-Creative-Global -- FCB Hamburg, Hamburg, Germany, pg. 373
Kalule, Britny, Acct Exec -- DITTOE PUBLIC RELATIONS, INC., Indianapolis, IN, pg. 1495
Kalusevic, Sonja, Acct Exec -- Ovation Advertising, Belgrade, Serbia, pg. 110
Kaluzny, Norbert, Acct Dir -- ZenithOptimedia, Warsaw, Poland, pg. 1399
Kam, Nathan, Pres-PR Grp-Anthology Mktg Grp -- MCNEIL WILSON

Personnel Index

L

INC., Irving, TX, pg. 1486
Landres-Schnur, Adam, Acct Supvr -- ACCESS COMMUNICATIONS, San Francisco, CA, pg. 18
Landries, Sara, Media Buyer -- DRM PARTNERS, INC., Hoboken, NJ, pg. 1332
Landsberg, Steve, Founder, Partner & Chief Creative Officer -- GROK, New York, NY, pg. 461
Lane, John, Chief Strategy Officer & Sr VP-Creative -- CENTERLINE DIGITAL, Raleigh, NC, pg. 1285
Lane, Keith, Chief Creative Officer -- KEITH LANE CREATIVE GROUP, Salem, MA, pg. 606
Lane, Kelly, Acct Supvr -- Weber Shandwick, Sydney, Australia, pg. 1682
Lane, Kelynn, Acct Mgr & Media Planner -- LION DIGITAL MEDIA, Mountlake Terrace, WA, pg. 1301
Lang, Graham, Chief Creative Officer -- Y&R Cape Town, Cape Town, South Africa, pg. 1251
Lang, Graham, Chief Creative Officer -- Y&R Johannesburg, Wendywood, South Africa, pg. 1251
Lang, Jonathan, Exec Dir-Creative -- J. Walter Thompson, Rivonia, South Africa, pg. 567
Lang, Jonathan, Exec Dir-Creative -- J. Walter Thompson Cape Town, Cape Town, South Africa, pg. 566
Lang, Kate, Acct Dir -- Clemenger BBDO Melbourne, Melbourne, Australia, pg. 114
Lang, Kristine, Acct Dir -- KENNA, Mississauga, Canada, pg. 608
Lang, Michel, Dir-Creative -- SANDBOX, Toronto, Canada, pg. 1016
Lang, Morgan, Acct Exec -- SWEENEY, Wilmington, NC, pg. 1103
Lang, William, Assoc Dir-Creative -- CGT MARKETING LLC, Amityville, NY, pg. 203
Lange, Chris, Co-Founder & Co-Chm-Creative -- MONO, Minneapolis, MN, pg. 771
Lange, Jennifer, Acct Supvr -- 360I, New York, NY, pg. 6
Lange, Jody, Dir-Creative -- Proof Integrated Communications, New York, NY, pg. 1227
Lange, Jody, Dir-Creative -- Proof Integrated Communications, New York, NY, pg. 914
Lange, Nick, Dir-Creative -- NURTURE DIGITAL, Culver City, CA, pg. 819
Langenberg, Will, Acct Exec -- BBDO WORLDWIDE INC., New York, NY, pg. 99
Langenkamp, Alyson, Acct Supvr -- GLYNNDEVINS ADVERTISING & MARKETING, Overland Park, KS, pg. 430
Langer, Andy, Chief Creative Officer -- ROBERTS + LANGER DDB, New York, NY, pg. 987
Langerman, Elliot, Creative Dir -- AREA 23, New York, NY, pg. 68
Langevad, Hans-Henrik, Dir-Creative -- LoweFriends AS, Copenhagen, Denmark, pg. 795
Langford, Janelle, Creative Dir -- SUITE PUBLIC RELATIONS, New York, NY, pg. 1658
Langford, Tim, Exec Dir-Creative -- IMAGINUITY INTERACTIVE, INC., Dallas, TX, pg. 1298
Langham, Michael, Dir-Creative Svcs -- POLARIS RECRUITMENT COMMUNICATIONS, Miamisburg, OH, pg. 902
Langhans, Eva, Acct Dir -- Razorfish Germany, Berlin, Germany, pg. 1310
Langhauser, Courtney, Acct Dir -- Digitas Health London, London, United Kingdom, pg. 1288
Langkjaer, Morten, Dir-Creative -- DENMARK ADVERTISING & PUBLIC RELATIONS, Atlanta, GA, pg. 296
Langley, Simon, Exec Dir-Creative-Sydney -- J. Walter Thompson, Sydney, Australia, pg. 567
Langsfeld, Benjamin, Assoc Dir-Creative -- Buck NY, New York, NY, pg. 173
Langston-Wood, Melissa, Assoc Dir-Creative -- Deutsch LA, Los Angeles, CA, pg. 302
Lanham, Kipp, Acct Exec -- MEDIA & COMMUNICATIONS STRATEGIES INC., Washington, DC, pg. 1588
Lanier, Hailey, Acct Exec -- FLACKABLE LLC, Wyomissing, PA, pg. 1515
Lanier, Phillip, Exec Dir-Creative -- ESWSTORYLAB, Chicago, IL, pg. 357
Lanio, Court, Acct Supvr -- Ogilvy & Mather, Culver City, CA, pg. 828
Lankford, Rachael, Acct Dir -- THE HONEY AGENCY, Sacramento, CA, pg. 522
Lannuzzi, Lucho, Acct Dir -- Punto Ogilvy & Mather, Montevideo, Uruguay, pg. 840
Lanphier, Derek, Dir-Creative Dev -- SIGNET INTERACTIVE LLC, Houston, TX, pg. 1044
Lansbury, Jim, Principal & Chief Creative Officer -- RP3 AGENCY, Bethesda, MD, pg. 994
Lansche, Hunter, Assoc Dir-Creative -- DOVETAIL, Saint Louis, MO, pg. 326
Lansford, Maura, Acct Exec -- SOAR COMMUNICATIONS, Salt Lake City, UT, pg. 1056
Lanza, Jack, Dir-Creative -- APCO WORLDWIDE, Washington, DC, pg. 63
Lanzi, Diego, Creative Dir -- BBDO Guatemala, Guatemala, Guatemala, pg. 103
Laparra, Erick, Dir-Creative -- Tribu DDB El Salvador, San Salvador, El Salvador, pg. 280
Lapenas, Gintas, Partner & Sr Dir-Creative -- Lukrecija BBDO, Vilnius, Lithuania, pg. 109
Lapine, Jacqueline, Dir-PR & Social -- ARRAS KEATHLEY AGENCY, Cleveland, OH, pg. 73
Laplaca, Nicholas, Acct Exec -- R&J PUBLIC RELATIONS, Bridgewater, NJ, pg. 1629
Larach, Carolina, Acct Dir -- FCB Mayo, Santiago, Chile, pg. 377
Largo, Ty, Principal & Creative Dir -- AWE COLLECTIVE, Scottsdale, AZ, pg. 1447
Larios, Arnaldo, Acct Exec -- MARION INTEGRATED MARKETING, Houston, TX, pg. 694
LaRiviere, Travis, Dir-Creative -- TLG MARKETING, Long Beach, CA, pg. 1146
Lark, Corey, Acct Supvr-Digital -- THE MARKETING ARM, Dallas, TX, pg. 696
Larkins, Leslie, Media Planner & Buyer -- Asher Agency, Inc., Charleston, WV, pg. 76
Laroche, Madison, Acct Dir -- Cohn & Wolfe Austin, Austin, TX, pg. 1481
Larouche, Jean-Francois, CEO & Dir-Creative -- JFLAROUCHE ADVERTISING AGENCY, Quebec, Canada, pg. 590
Larratt-Smith, Geordie, Acct Supvr -- MCCANN ERICKSON WORLDWIDE, New York, NY, pg. 713
Larrinaga, Naroa Marcos, Acct Dir -- Millward Brown Spain, Madrid, Spain, pg. 760
Larroquet, Nicolas, Dir-Creative -- Santo Buenos Aires, Buenos Aires, Argentina, pg. 1222
Larsen, Aileen, VP & Assoc Dir-Brdcst -- PHD New York, New York, NY, pg. 1384
Larsen, Beth, Acct Dir -- Wunderman, Copenhagen, Denmark, pg. 1232
Larsen, Glenn, Dir-Creative -- THE GEARY COMPANY, Las Vegas, NV, pg. 419
Larson, Craig, Media Planner-Interactive -- HELIX EDUCATION, Salt Lake City, UT, pg. 508
Larson, Kraig, Founder, Partner & Chief Creative Officer -- CICERON, INC., Minneapolis, MN, pg. 1285
Larson, Laura, Creative Dir -- THE PUBLIC RELATIONS & MARKETING GROUP, Patchogue, NY, pg. 917
Larson, Sarah, VP-PR -- FURIA RUBEL COMMUNICATIONS, Doylestown, PA, pg. 1525
Larson, Scott, Exec Dir-Creative -- Razorfish Seattle, Seattle, WA, pg. 1310
Larue, Lance, Creative Dir -- AMERICOM MARKETING, Beaumont, TX, pg. 54
LaRue, Lee Anne, Media Buyer-Brdcst-Natl -- Mindshare, New York, NY, pg. 1336
LaRue, Scott, Acct Exec -- PLANIT, Baltimore, MD, pg. 896
LaSalle, Courtney, Acct Exec -- GKV COMMUNICATIONS, Baltimore, MD, pg. 427
Lascault, Remi, Art Dir -- Leo Burnett, Paris, France, pg. 642
Lash, Amy, Acct Supvr -- 5W Public Relations, Los Angeles, CA, pg. 1438
Lasheen, Tarek, Dir-PR -- MEMAC Ogilvy, Cairo, Egypt, pg. 848
Lashua, Chelsea, Acct Coord -- CHEMISTRY, San Diego, CA, pg. 1477
Lasker, Sarah, Coord-Traffic -- ABELSON-TAYLOR, INC., Chicago, IL, pg. 16
Lasky, Carolyn, Acct Exec -- ROSE COMMUNICATIONS, INC., Hoboken, NJ, pg. 1639
Lasota, Chad, Assoc Dir-Creative -- Alcone Marketing Group, San Francisco, CA, pg. 1404
LaSota, Chad, Assoc Dir-Creative -- ALCONE MARKETING GROUP, Irvine, CA, pg. 1403
Lasota, Chad, Assoc Dir-Creative -- Alcone Marketing Group, Darien, CT, pg. 1404
Lasselin, Marion, Acct Exec -- Gyro Paris, Paris, France, pg. 469
Lasser, Jimm, Dir-Creative -- Wieden + Kennedy-New York, New York, NY, pg. 1204
Lasso, Begona, Acct Dir -- Teran TBWA, Mexico, Mexico, pg. 1132
Latchaw, John, Acct Exec -- DEVINE + PARTNERS, Philadelphia, PA, pg. 1494
Latorre, Amber, Media Planner-Digital-NBCU Digital -- MAXUS GLOBAL, New York, NY, pg. 1353
Latreille, William, III, Acct Mgr & Coord-Traffic -- LATREILLE ADVERTISING & TALENT INC, Fenton, MI, pg. 629
Lattin, Brooke, Acct Exec -- PERISCOPE, Minneapolis, MN, pg. 884
Lau, Adam, Creative Dir -- THE BARBARIAN GROUP, New York, NY, pg. 90
Lau, Doris, Acct Exec -- YOUNG & RUBICAM, New York, NY, pg. 1239
Lau, Frankie, Acct Coord -- Cohn & Wolfe impactasia, Central, China (Hong Kong), pg. 1482
Lau, Katie, Acct Exec -- AOR, INC., Denver, CO, pg. 63
Lau, Takho, Exec Dir-Creative -- Leo Burnett-Guangzhou, Guangzhou, China, pg. 647
Lau, Takho, Exec Dir-Creative -- Leo Burnett Shanghai Advertising Co., Ltd., Shanghai, China, pg. 648
Laudanska, Maja, Acct Dir-Digital -- BBDO, Warsaw, Poland, pg. 109
Laudicina, Chiara, Acct Exec -- Fleishman-Hillard Italy, Milan, Italy, pg. 1520
Lauer, Alejandra, Acct Coord -- FSB CORE STRATEGIES, Sacramento, CA, pg. 1524
Laufer, Kayla, Acct Exec-Volkswagen -- Deutsch LA, Los Angeles, CA, pg. 302
Laura, Poggio, Mgr-PR & Comm -- Burson-Marsteller S.r.l., Milan, Italy, pg. 1468
Laura, Poggio, Mgr-PR & Comm -- Marsteller, Milan, Italy, pg. 1468
Laurentino, Andre, Exec Creative Dir-Global -- Ogilvy & Mather EMEA, London, United Kingdom, pg. 836
Lauri, Steve, Pres & Dir-Creative -- THE ENGINE ROOM, Aliso Viejo, CA, pg. 348
Lauria, Gustavo, Chief Creative Officer & Mng Partner -- CommongroundMGS, New York, NY, pg. 225
Lauricella, Deborah J., Pres, Head & Dir-Creative -- TORME LAURICELLA, San Francisco, CA, pg. 1664
Laursen, Nicolet, Art Dir -- CLM MARKETING & ADVERTISING, Boise, ID, pg. 216
Lauten, Matthias, Acct Dir -- Razorfish GmbH, Frankfurt, Germany, pg. 1310
Lauterstein, Carrie, Acct Dir -- Weber Shandwick-Austin, Austin, TX, pg. 1677
Lautier, Nicolas, Dir-Creative -- Ogilvy & Mather, Paris, France, pg. 831
Lavalli, Taylor, Acct Dir -- RF Binder Partners, Needham, MA, pg. 1642
Lavery, Jeff, Acct Supvr-PR -- SVM PUBLIC RELATIONS & MARKETING COMMUNICATIONS, Providence, RI, pg. 1102
Lavi, Daniella, Media Buyer-Natl Television -- PALISADES MEDIA GROUP, INC., Santa Monica, CA, pg. 1383
Lavin, Jon, Exec Creative Dir -- McCann Erickson S.A., Madrid, Spain, pg. 727
Lavin, Kourtney, Media Buyer-Local Audio -- HORIZON MEDIA, INC., New York, NY, pg. 1341
Lavoie, Joe, Art Dir -- ADVENTURE, Minneapolis, MN, pg. 34
Law, Amy, Assoc Dir-Creative -- SWIRL ADVERTISING, San Francisco, CA, pg. 1104
Law, C. Blair, III, Acct Coord -- 16W MARKETING, LLC, Rutherford, NJ, pg. 3
Law, Marc, VP & Assoc Dir-Creative-Art -- THE CEMENTWORKS, LLC, New York, NY, pg. 201
Lawal, Elizabeth, Media Buyer -- RPM/Las Vegas, Las Vegas, NV, pg. 995
Lawall, Tara, Assoc Dir-Creative -- DROGA5, New York, NY, pg. 328
Lawes, Jason, Dir-Creative -- M&C SAATCHI PLC, London, United Kingdom, pg. 675
Lawler, Brooke, Acct Dir -- MIDNIGHT OIL CREATIVE, Burbank, CA, pg. 755
Lawless, Ashley, Acct Supvr -- WEBER SHANDWICK, New York, NY, pg. 1675
Lawless, Sharon, Dir-Print Production -- SMITH & JONES, Troy, NY, pg. 1053
Lawley, Brad, Dir-Creative -- FIREFLY CREATIVE, INC., Atlanta, GA, pg. 388
Lawlor, Joanna, Acct Dir -- Arnold KLP, London, United Kingdom, pg. 72
Lawrence, Dale, Mgr-Print Production -- Arc South Africa, Cape Town, South Africa, pg. 924
Lawrence, Dustin, Acct Exec -- Weber Shandwick-Los Angeles, Los Angeles, CA, pg. 1678
Lawrence, Jennifer, Acct Exec -- JKR ADVERTISING & MARKETING, Orlando, FL, pg. 591
Lawrence, Jennifer, VP & Acct Dir -- PLANET CENTRAL, Huntersville, NC, pg. 896

Personnel Index

pg. 328
Long, Stacey, Designer-Creative -- SANDIA ADVERTISING, Colorado Springs, CO, pg. 1017
Longest, Tania, Acct Exec -- WRAGG & CASAS PUBLIC RELATIONS, INC., Miami, FL, pg. 1688
Longhin, Ellie, Acct Dir -- PHD Toronto, Toronto, Canada, pg. 1385
Longmire, Ahlilah, Dir-PR -- CANOPY BRAND GROUP, New York, NY, pg. 189
Longoni, Stefano, Dir-Creative -- Red Cell, Milan, Italy, pg. 221
Longoni, Stefano, Dir-Creative -- Red Cell, Milan, Italy, pg. 1221
Longoria, Ray, Dir-Creative -- GSD&M, Austin, TX, pg. 464
Lonn, Andreas, Partner & Dir-Creative -- ANR BBDO, Gothenburg, Sweden, pg. 111
Lontok, Evelyn Capistrano, Acct Dir -- 160OVER90, Philadelphia, PA, pg. 2
Loo, Daniel, Art Dir & Copywriter -- McCann Erickson (Malaysia) Sdn. Bhd., Kuala Lumpur, Malaysia, pg. 724
Loockx, Tom, Exec Dir-Creative -- Havas Worldwide Brussels, Brussels, Belgium, pg. 491
Loockx, Tom, Exec Dir-Creative -- Havas Worldwide Digital Brussels, Brussels, Belgium, pg. 491
Looney, Amy, Acct Dir -- HAVIT ADVERTISING, LLC, Washington, DC, pg. 502
Looney, Tama, Acct Dir -- FISHBOWL MARKETING, Alexandria, VA, pg. 1413
LoParco, Melissa, VP & Dir-PR -- CATALYST MARKETING COMMUNICATIONS INC., Stamford, CT, pg. 197
Lopaty, Shelby, Acct Supvr -- KONNECT PUBLIC RELATIONS, Los Angeles, CA, pg. 1567
Loper, Jennifer, Acct Dir -- C3 - CREATIVE CONSUMER CONCEPTS, Overland Park, KS, pg. 182
Lopes, Ines, Acct Dir -- Havas Worldwide Digital Portugal, Lisbon, Portugal, pg. 495
Lopes, Katherine, Acct Coord -- RP3 AGENCY, Bethesda, MD, pg. 994
Lopez, Adam, Dir-Creative -- ARROWHEAD ADVERTISING, Peoria, AZ, pg. 73
Lopez, Adriana, Acct Supvr-Digital & Social -- THE AXIS AGENCY, Los Angeles, CA, pg. 83
Lopez, Andrew, Acct Dir -- THE PITCH AGENCY, Culver City, CA, pg. 893
Lopez, Angela Prieto, Acct Exec -- Edelman, Madrid, Spain, pg. 1505
Lopez, Belinda, Acct Exec-Adv -- JOBELEPHANT.COM INC., San Diego, CA, pg. 592
Lopez, Ben, Dir-Creative -- BRAVE PEOPLE, Tampa, FL, pg. 162
Lopez, Dale, Art Dir & Exec Dir-Creative -- BBDO Guerrero, Makati, Philippines, pg. 117
Lopez, Delci, Acct Dir-Intl -- Publicitas USA, New York, NY, pg. 1428
Lopez, Eva, Acct Exec -- NOYD COMMUNICATIONS INC, Manhattan Beach, CA, pg. 1604
Lopez, Eyra, Assoc Dir-Creative -- THE COOPER GROUP, New York, NY, pg. 233
Lopez, Fran, Dir-Creative -- TBWA Espana, Madrid, Spain, pg. 1123
Lopez, Gabe, Founder & Dir-Creative -- BRAVE PEOPLE, Tampa, FL, pg. 162
Lopez, Jissette, Acct Supvr-Res -- Ogilvy North America, New York, NY, pg. 828
Lopez, Joseph, Dir-Digital Creative -- PARADIGM ASSOCIATES, San Juan, PR, pg. 1613
Lopez, Justin, Media Planner -- XACTA ADVERTISING, Lake Charles, LA, pg. 1236
Lopez, Kiki, Mgr-Production & Traffic -- ESPARZA ADVERTISING, Albuquerque, NM, pg. 356
Lopez, Maruchi, Acct Dir -- LOPITO, ILEANA & HOWIE, INC., Guaynabo, PR, pg. 669
Lopez, May, Media Planner & Buyer -- JEKYLL AND HYDE, Redford, MI, pg. 589
Lopez, Miguel, Acct Exec -- RL PUBLIC RELATIONS + MARKETING, Los Angeles, CA, pg. 1637
Lopez, Nikki, Acct Supvr -- Porter Novelli-Chicago, Chicago, IL, pg. 1620
Lopez, Paula, Dir-Creative -- DDB Madrid, S.A., Madrid, Spain, pg. 288
Lopez, Ray, Creative Dir -- Havas Worldwide Mexico, Mexico, Mexico, pg. 499
Lopez, Romina, Acct Dir -- VIVA PARTNERSHIP, Miami, FL, pg. 1181
Lopez, Ron, Dir-Creative -- R&R PARTNERS, Las Vegas, NV, pg. 945
Lopez, Salvador, Acct Dir -- MEC, Mexico, Mexico, pg. 1362
Lopresti, Vincent, Principal & Dir-Creative -- COMMERCE HOUSE, Dallas, TX, pg. 224
Lopriore, Lou, Partner & Co-Dir-Creative-Art -- LOBO & PETROCINE, INC., Melville, NY, pg. 666
Lorber, Abby, Acct Supvr -- Energy BBDO, Chicago, IL, pg. 100
Lord, Morgan, Media Planner -- CLM MARKETING & ADVERTISING, Boise, ID, pg. 216
Lord, Tom, Dir-Creative -- OLSON, Minneapolis, MN, pg. 856
Lorenzetti, Ilaria, Acct Supvr -- Saatchi & Saatchi, Rome, Italy, pg. 1004
Lorenzetti, Ilaria, Acct Supvr -- Saatchi & Saatchi, Milan, Italy, pg. 1004
Lorenzini, Luca, Dir-Creative-Global -- SAATCHI & SAATCHI, New York, NY, pg. 1000
Lorenzini, Luca, Dir-Creative-Global -- Saatchi & Saatchi New York, New York, NY, pg. 1001
Lorenzo, Annelise, Acct Exec -- DAVID & GOLIATH, El Segundo, CA, pg. 267
Lorenzo, Lixaida, Creative Dir -- MISTRESS, Santa Monica, CA, pg. 764
Lorenzo, Nicky, Assoc Dir-Creative & Copywriter -- OGILVY & MATHER, New York, NY, pg. 826
Lorie, Yvonne, Pres-SWAY PR -- CommongroundMGS, Miami, FL, pg. 224
Lorusso, Pamela, VP & Dir-Creative -- FORT GROUP, Ridgefield Park, NJ, pg. 398
Lorusso, Pamela, VP & Dir-Creative -- FORT INTEGRATED MARKETING GROUP, Ridgefield Park, NJ, pg. 398
LoRusso, Vincenzo, Exec Creative Dir -- VENABLES, BELL & PARTNERS, San Francisco, CA, pg. 1172
Loscher, Bill, Dir-Creative -- EVERETT STUDIOS, Armonk, NY, pg. 359
Loseby, Richard, Grp Head-Creative -- Ogilvy New Zealand, Auckland, New Zealand, pg. 846
Lostracco, Sarah, Acct Dir -- MACLAREN MCCANN CANADA INC., Toronto, Canada, pg. 682
Lotterman, Deborah, Chief Creative Officer -- LEHMANMILLET, Boston, MA, pg. 636
Lotz, Regner, Dir-Creative -- Saatchi & Saatchi, Copenhagen, Denmark, pg. 1002
Lotze, Simon, Assoc Dir-Creative -- Ogilvy & Mather EMEA, London, United Kingdom, pg. 836
Lou, Alice, Acct Dir -- NFUSION GROUP, Austin, TX, pg. 809
Loughman, Beth, Acct Supvr -- Energy BBDO, Chicago, IL, pg. 100
Lougovtsov, Alex, Acct Exec -- LINX COMMUNICATIONS CORP., Smithtown, NY, pg. 659
Louie, Steven, Dir-Creative -- FLIGHTPATH INC, New York, NY, pg. 393
Louie, Wen, Grp Dir-Creative -- wwwins Isobar, Shanghai, China, pg. 562
Louis, Charisse, Pres & Creative Dir -- CHARENE CREATIVE, Aurora, OH, pg. 204
Louis, Cyril, Dir-Creative -- Razorfish UK, London, United Kingdom, pg. 1311
Lourenco, Marcelo, Dir-Creative -- FUEL AGENCY, INC., Oakland, CA, pg. 407
Lourenco, Rui, Chief Creative Officer-Havas Worldwide Digital Portugal -- Havas Experience Lisbon, Lisbon, Portugal, pg. 495
Lourenco, Rui, Chief Creative Officer -- Havas Worldwide Digital Portugal, Lisbon, Portugal, pg. 495
Louw, Cara, Acct Dir-PR -- Epic MSLGROUP, Johannesburg, South Africa, pg. 1595
Loux, Terri, Dir-Creative Ops -- MRM MCCANN, New York, NY, pg. 782
Love, Amanda, Acct Supvr-Medical Education -- OGILVY COMMONHEALTH WORLDWIDE, Parsippany, NJ, pg. 851
Love, Craig, Exec Creative Dir -- STRAWBERRYFROG, New York, NY, pg. 1091
Love, Craig, Reg Creative Dir -- Y&R Hong Kong, North Point, China (Hong Kong), pg. 1241
Love, DeNeatra, Acct Supvr-Commonwealth & McCann -- McCann Erickson North America, New York, NY, pg. 715
Love, Jason, Acct Mgr-Microsoft Corp PR -- WE, Lake Oswego, OR, pg. 1674
Love, Richard B., Partner & Dir-Creative -- LOVE COMMUNICATIONS, Salt Lake City, UT, pg. 670
Lovegrove, Michael, Chief Creative Officer -- TracyLocke, Wilton, CT, pg. 1154
Lovegrove, Michael, Pres & Chief Creative Officer -- TRACYLOCKE, Dallas, TX, pg. 1153
Lovejoy, Ben, Creative Dir -- ATOMIC20, Boulder, CO, pg. 78
Loveless, Vivian Calzada, Acct Exec -- GIBBONS/PECK MARKETING COMMUNICATION, Greenville, SC, pg. 424
Lovell, Larry, Mgmt Supvr-PR -- PETER MAYER ADVERTISING, INC., New Orleans, LA, pg. 886
Lovett, Trey, Acct Dir -- CREATIVE HEADS ADVERTISING, INC., Austin, TX, pg. 248
Loving, Lisa, Acct Exec -- THE MARTIN AGENCY, Richmond, VA, pg. 702
Lovingood, Sarah, Media Buyer -- THE BRANDON AGENCY, Myrtle Beach, SC, pg. 160
Lovitz, Alan, VP & Acct Dir -- BUYER ADVERTISING, INC., Newton, MA, pg. 179
Lovric, Marina, Acct Exec -- Text 100 Munich GmbH, Munich, Germany, pg. 1661
Low, Andrew, Exec Dir-Creative -- Leo Burnett Malaysia, Kuala Lumpur, Malaysia, pg. 650
Low, Auston, Art Dir & Designer -- BBDO Malaysia, Kuala Lumpur, Malaysia, pg. 116
Low, Jack, Sr Partner & Dir-Creative -- OGILVY & MATHER, New York, NY, pg. 826
Low, Matt, VP & Assoc Dir-Creative -- CROWLEY WEBB, Buffalo, NY, pg. 257
Low, Neritta, Acct Exec -- The Hoffman Agency, Singapore, Singapore, pg. 1546
Low, Selwyn, Grp Head-Creative -- J. Walter Thompson Singapore, Singapore, Singapore, pg. 571
Low, Swee Chen, Head-Creative & Gen Mgr -- Publicis Guangzhou, Guangzhou, China, pg. 931
Lowe, Alyssa Alexandra, Acct Exec -- HOCKING MEDIA GROUP INC., Troy, MI, pg. 1341
Lowe, Bryn, Acct Exec -- LEOPARD, Denver, CO, pg. 651
Lowe, Jarrod, Creative Dir -- J. Walter Thompson, Sydney, Australia, pg. 567
Lowe, Keith, Jr Art Dir -- SHEPHERD, Jacksonville, FL, pg. 1037
Lowe, Meredith, Acct Exec -- Edelman, New York, NY, pg. 1502
Lowenthal, Noah, VP & Grp Dir-Creative -- ABELSON-TAYLOR, INC., Chicago, IL, pg. 16
Lowery, Nathan, Dir-Creative -- LIPOF ADVERTISING, Plantation, FL, pg. 660
Lowrey, Ronald, Media Buyer -- J. LINCOLN GROUP, The Woodlands, TX, pg. 565
Lowry, Robin, Dir-CGI Creative -- Burrows Shenfield, Brentwood, United Kingdom, pg. 1234
Lowy, Jenna, Art Dir -- MERKLEY+PARTNERS, New York, NY, pg. 750
Loy, Ken, Dir-Creative -- E-B DISPLAY CO., INC., Massillon, OH, pg. 334
Lozano, Carlos, Art Dir -- RUSTY GEORGE CREATIVE, Tacoma, WA, pg. 998
Lu, Jiankai, Dir-Creative -- Ogilvy & Mather Advertising Beijing, Beijing, China, pg. 841
Lu, Jiankai, Dir-Creative -- Ogilvy & Mather Asia/Pacific, Central, China (Hong Kong), pg. 842
Lu, Ricky, Dir-Creative -- GREY NEW YORK, New York, NY, pg. 446
Lubars, David, Chm & Chief Creative Officer -- BBDO NORTH AMERICA, New York, NY, pg. 98
Lubarsky, Caleb, Acct Dir -- YOUNG & RUBICAM, New York, NY, pg. 1239
Lubart, Gabrielle, Acct Exec -- PointRoll Inc., New York, NY, pg. 901
Lubenow, Lindsey, Media Planner -- AIR INTEGRATED, Phoenix, AZ, pg. 41
Lublin, Petter, Dir-Art & Creative -- Lowe Brindfors, Stockholm, Sweden, pg. 790
Lubow, Arthur D., Pres & Creative Dir -- A.D. LUBOW, LLC, New York, NY, pg. 22
Luby, Colleen, Acct Exec -- CATALYST MARKETING COMMUNICATIONS INC., Stamford, CT, pg. 197
Lucas, Brianne, Acct Dir -- PLACE CREATIVE COMPANY, Burlington, VT, pg. 895
Lucas, Jamie, Acct Dir -- SQUIRES & COMPANY, Dallas, TX, pg. 1070
Lucas, Jan, Dir-Creative -- M&C Saatchi, Berlin, Germany, pg. 677
Lucas, Jason, Exec VP & Exec Dir-Creative -- Publicis Seattle, Seattle, WA, pg. 927
Lucas, Jason, Exec VP & Exec Dir-Creative -- Publicis Seattle, Seattle, WA, pg. 936
Lucchini, Gaudia, Acct Dir -- Weber Shandwick, Milan, Italy, pg. 1680
Lucchini, Luisella, Acct Dir -- Text 100 Milan S.R.L., Milan, Italy, pg. 1661
Lucci, Tiago, Dir-Creative -- SapientNitro iThink, Sao Paulo, Brazil, pg. 1020
Lucero, Lindsey, Acct Dir -- DDB San Francisco, San Francisco, CA, pg. 276

M

Personnel Index

Personnel Index

Personnel Index

Personnel Index

Kingdom, pg. 72
Moore, Josh, Exec Dir-Creative -- Y&R, Auckland, New Zealand, pg. 1223
Moore, Josh, Exec Dir-Creative -- Y&R, Auckland, New Zealand, pg. 1233
Moore, Josh, Exec Dir-Creative -- Young & Rubicam NZ Ltd., Auckland, New Zealand, pg. 1242
Moore, Kristina, Mgr-PR & Mktg -- 15 MINUTES, INC., Conshohocken, PA, pg. 2
Moore, Lisa, Acct Exec & Specialist-SEO -- LKF MARKETING, Kalamazoo, MI, pg. 664
Moore, M. Ryan, Dir-Creative -- SPARK44, Culver City, CA, pg. 1062
Moore, Mark, Acct Exec -- GRIFFIN COMMUNICATIONS, INC., Towson, MD, pg. 459
Moore, Matt, Dir-Creative -- BARTON F. GRAF 9000 LLC, New York, NY, pg. 96
Moore, Megan, Acct Exec -- NORTHWEST STRATEGIES, Anchorage, AK, pg. 1604
Moore, Ryan, Acct Supvr-Gatorade-Global -- TBWA Chiat Day Los Angeles, Los Angeles, CA, pg. 1114
Moore, Sarah, Acct Exec -- THE MILLERSCHIN GROUP, Auburn Hills, MI, pg. 1591
Moore, Steve, Acct Exec -- CULTIVATOR ADVERTISING & DESIGN, Denver, CO, pg. 259
Moore, Thomas, Acct Dir -- HCK2 PARTNERS, Addison, TX, pg. 504
Moore, Traci, Dir-Creative -- FALK HARRISON, Saint Louis, MO, pg. 366
Moquim, Sarah, Dir-Creative -- J. Walter Thompson, Karachi, Pakistan, pg. 571
Mora, Daniel A., Dir-Art & Creative -- Sancho BBDO, Bogota, Colombia, pg. 103
Moraes, Fernanda, Acct Dir -- Rapp Brazil, Sao Paulo, Brazil, pg. 953
Morales, Angicel, Acct Supvr -- Sapient, New York, NY, pg. 1019
Morales, Dan, Creative Dir -- J. WALTER THOMPSON, New York, NY, pg. 565
Morales, Edwina, Media Planner -- OPTIMEDIA INTERNATIONAL US INC., New York, NY, pg. 1382
Morales, Gabriela, Acct Dir -- BBDO Mexico, Mexico, Mexico, pg. 104
Morales, Iris, Acct Coord -- BOC PARTNERS, Middlesex, NJ, pg. 145
Morales, Nestor, Dir-Creative -- DDB Worldwide Colombia, S.A., Cali, Colombia, pg. 280
Moran, Aiden, Head-Creative Ops -- Proximity Worldwide & London, London, United Kingdom, pg. 113
Moran, Ashley, Acct Mgr-PR & Content Mktg -- WRAY WARD MARKETING COMMUNICATIONS, Charlotte, NC, pg. 1228
Moran, Kyle, Acct Exec -- DANARI MEDIA, Sherman Oaks, CA, pg. 1286
Moran, Liana, Acct Exec -- THE WILBERT GROUP, Atlanta, GA, pg. 1685
Moran, Paul, Dir-Creative -- Grey London, London, United Kingdom, pg. 447
Moran, Tom, Exec Dir-Creative -- POP, Seattle, WA, pg. 903
Morano, Adrian, Dir-Creative -- Maruri, Guayaquil, Ecuador, pg. 1596
Moranville, David, Partner & Chief Creative Officer -- Davis Elen Advertising, Arlington, VA, pg. 270
Moranville, David, Partner & Chief Creative Officer -- Davis-Elen Advertising, Inc., Portland, OR, pg. 270
Moranville, David, Partner & Chief Creative Officer -- DAVIS ELEN ADVERTISING, INC., Los Angeles, CA, pg. 270
Moraud, Patrice, Dir-Creative -- TBWA/Compact, Toulouse, France, pg. 1119
Morauw, Nastasya, Dir-PR -- FRANK PR, New York, NY, pg. 1523
Morba, Heather, Acct Exec -- WIEDEN + KENNEDY, INC., Portland, OR, pg. 1202
Moreau, Whitney, Acct Exec -- NANCY MARSHALL COMMUNICATIONS, Augusta, ME, pg. 1600
Morehart, Emily, Specialist-PR & Copywriter -- INSIGHT CREATIVE INC., Green Bay, WI, pg. 549
Moreira Costa, Renato F., Acct Dir -- RappDigital Brazil, Sao Paulo, Brazil, pg. 953
Moreira, A. Chris, Exec Dir-Creative -- Saatchi & Saatchi New York, New York, NY, pg. 1001
Moreira, Andre, Head-Art & Dir-Creative-Global -- Havas Worldwide London, London, United Kingdom, pg. 498
Moreland, Matthew, Dir-Creative -- BARTLE BOGLE HEGARTY LIMITED, London, United Kingdom, pg. 94
Morelle, Keka, Dir-Creative -- DDB Brazil, Sao Paulo, Brazil, pg. 278
Morelli, Joe, Acct Exec -- Wieden + Kennedy-New York, New York, NY, pg. 1204
Moreno, Andres, Dir-Creative -- Arnold Madrid, Madrid, Spain, pg. 72
Moreno, Carlos, Chief Creative Officer -- Cossette Communications, Halifax, Canada, pg. 237
Moreno, Facundo Gonzalez, Acct Exec -- MEC, Buenos Aires, Argentina, pg. 1361
Moreno, Miguel, Brand Dir-Creative -- RICHARDS/LERMA, Dallas, TX, pg. 979
Moreno, Miguel Angel, Dir-Creative -- TBWA/Colombia Suiza de Publicidad Ltda, Bogota, Colombia, pg. 1132
Moreno, Yker, Assoc Dir-Creative -- BUCK LA, Los Angeles, CA, pg. 173
Moresco, Josefina, Acct Coord -- Argentina Porter Novelli, Buenos Aires, Argentina, pg. 1621
Morey, Tyler, Acct Exec -- RISDALL MARKETING GROUP, New Brighton, MN, pg. 982
Morgan, Alistair, Dir-Creative -- Lowe Bull, Johannesburg, South Africa, pg. 790
Morgan, Carey, Acct Dir -- SPECK COMMUNICATIONS, Dallas, TX, pg. 1063
Morgan, Clark, Grp Dir-Creative -- Huge, Los Angeles, CA, pg. 527
Morgan, Jack, Media Planner-Digital & Buyer -- Havas People Birmingham, Birmingham, United Kingdom, pg. 497
Morgan, Jay, Creative Dir-Digital Grp -- J. Walter Thompson, Sydney, Australia, pg. 567
Morgan, Julian, Acct Exec -- Agency59 Response, Toronto, Canada, pg. 39
Morgan, Richard, Art Dir -- DigitasLBi, London, United Kingdom, pg. 1289
Morgan, Will, Acct Dir -- REMARKABLE PENDRAGON, Manchester, United Kingdom, pg. 1634
Morgulis, Shlomo, Acct Exec -- BECKERMAN PUBLIC RELATIONS, Hackensack, NJ, pg. 1451
Mori, Renzo, Dir-Creative -- Gramma FCB, Santa Cruz, Bolivia, pg. 377
Mori, Yuki, Acct Supvr -- MRM Worldwide, Tokyo, Japan, pg. 784
Morillo, Sito, Exec Dir-Creative -- Publicis, Madrid, Spain, pg. 921
Morilo, Francisco, Media Planner-Digital & Buyer -- HISPANIC GROUP, Miami, FL, pg. 516
Morin, Frederic, Acct Dir -- AGENCY59, Toronto, Canada, pg. 39
Moriuchi, Kenji, Art Dir -- Saatchi & Saatchi Fallon Tokyo, Tokyo, Japan, pg. 367
Moriuchi, Kenji, Art Dir -- Saatchi & Saatchi Fallon Tokyo, Tokyo, Japan, pg. 1011
Mork, Angela, Dir-Content & Acct Supvr -- LEPOIDEVIN MARKETING, Brookfield, WI, pg. 651
Morley, Susie, Art Buyer -- Fallon London, London, United Kingdom, pg. 366
Moro, Monica, Chief Creative Officer -- McCann Erickson S.A., Madrid, Spain, pg. 727
Morr, Tom, Acct Supvr -- KAHN MEDIA INC, Reseda, CA, pg. 1418
Morra, Tim, Exec Dir-Creative -- JADI COMMUNICATIONS, Laguna Beach, CA, pg. 585
Morring, David, Dir-Creative -- THE RICHARDS GROUP, INC., Dallas, TX, pg. 978
Morring, David, Dir-Creative -- RICHARDS PARTNERS, Dallas, TX, pg. 1636
Morris, Brett, Chief Creative Officer -- FCB Johannesburg, Johannesburg, South Africa, pg. 382
Morris, Bryan, Sr Dir-Creative -- WATT INTERNATIONAL, INC., Toronto, Canada, pg. 1192
Morris, Carrie, Assoc Dir-Creative -- FAHLGREN MORTINE, Columbus, OH, pg. 364
Morris, Dawn, Assoc Dir-Creative -- Sawtooth Health, Woodbridge, NJ, pg. 1022
Morris, Gemma, Acct Dir & Producer -- The Brooklyn Brothers, London, United Kingdom, pg. 169
Morris, Haydn, Exec Dir-Creative -- MCGARRYBOWEN, New York, NY, pg. 733
Morris, Jeff, Dir-Creative -- BORSHOFF, Indianapolis, IN, pg. 149
Morris, Matthew, Co-Dir-Creative -- MORRIS & CASALE INC., Thousand Oaks, CA, pg. 776
Morris, Minnie Escudero, Acct Supvr & Coord-Hispanic Mktg -- Bitner/Hennessy PR, Orlando, FL, pg. 1454
Morris, Nicole, Media Planner -- KRT MARKETING, Lafayette, CA, pg. 619
Morris, Sarah, Media Planner & Media Buyer -- COSSETTE INC., Quebec, Canada, pg. 237
Morris, Simon, Art Dir -- TBWA/London, London, United Kingdom, pg. 1124
Morris, Suzanne, Mng Partner & Head-Creative -- SAGEFROG MARKETING GROUP, LLC, Doylestown, PA, pg. 1014
Morris, Victoria, Acct Coord -- SCHNEIDER ASSOCIATES, Boston, MA, pg. 1646
Morrison, Christina, Acct Dir -- DC3, New York, NY, pg. 273
Morrison, Emily, Acct Supvr -- GMR MARKETING LLC, New Berlin, WI, pg. 1414
Morrison, Emily, Acct Exec -- ZENO Group, London, United Kingdom, pg. 1503
Morrison, James, Acct Dir -- ID29, Troy, NY, pg. 532
Morrison, Jay, Assoc Dir-Creative -- MITHUN, Minneapolis, MN, pg. 765
Morrison, Jeff, Acct Dir -- GWA/GREGORY WELTEROTH ADVERTISING, Montoursville, PA, pg. 468
Morrison, Rachael, Acct Coord -- BOLT PUBLIC RELATIONS, Irvine, CA, pg. 1458
Morrissey, Danielle, Acct Supvr -- MULLEN LOWE GROUP, Boston, MA, pg. 786
Morrow, Stephanie, Acct Coord -- MYRIAD TRAVEL MARKETING, Manhattan Beach, CA, pg. 798
Morrow-Voelker, Kathy, Co-Dir-Creative -- STIEGLER, WELLS, BRUNSWICK & ROTH, INC., Bethlehem, PA, pg. 1086
Morse, Alicia, Acct Coord -- CONVENTURES, INC., Boston, MA, pg. 1485
Morse, Kristena, Acct Dir -- RUNSWITCH PUBLIC RELATIONS, Louisville, KY, pg. 1643
Morse, Rebecca, VP-Creative -- VREELAND MARKETING & DESIGN, Yarmouth, ME, pg. 1185
Mortensen, Dean, Grp Head-Creative -- George Patterson Y&R, Sydney, Australia, pg. 1219
Mortensen, Gerald, Founder & Dir-Creative -- FLAPJACK CREATIVE, Madison, WI, pg. 392
Mortimer, Matt, Assoc Dir-Creative -- Leo Burnett USA, Chicago, IL, pg. 639
Morton, Ben, Acct Exec -- CENTRO LLC, Chicago, IL, pg. 1285
Morton, Courtney, Sr Counsel-PR -- BRANDHIVE, Salt Lake City, UT, pg. 158
Morton, Kevin, Acct Exec -- Wunderman, Irvine, CA, pg. 1230
Morton, Rosalie, Acct Supvr -- Padilla/CRT, Richmond, VA, pg. 869
Morvant, Zach, Dir-Creative-Copy -- IRON CREATIVE COMMUNICATION, San Francisco, CA, pg. 561
Morvil, Jeff, Pres & Dir-Creative -- MORVIL ADVERTISING & DESIGN GROUP, Wilmington, NC, pg. 778
Moscardini, Arianna, Acct Exec -- Ogilvy & Mather S.p.A., Milan, Italy, pg. 1608
Moscatello, Mariel, Supvr-Brdcst-Natl -- INITIATIVE, New York, NY, pg. 1344
Moser, Taylor, Media Planner -- DIGITAS HEALTH, Philadelphia, PA, pg. 309
Moses, Jeremy, Dir-Creative -- UNITED LANDMARK ASSOCIATES, INC., Tampa, FL, pg. 1167
Mosgofian, Becky, Specialist-PR -- BARNETT COX & ASSOCIATES, San Luis Obispo, CA, pg. 93
Moshapalo, Kabelo, Exec Dir-Creative -- TEQUILA Durban Marketing Services, Durban, South Africa, pg. 1126
Mosher, Aaron, Grp Dir-Creative -- 360i, New York, NY, pg. 6
Mosher, Ian, Dir-Creative -- BOYDEN & YOUNGBLUTT ADVERTISING & MARKETING, Fort Wayne, IN, pg. 151
Moskal, Mark, Co-Founder & Exec Dir-Creative -- LIVEAREALABS, Seattle, WA, pg. 663
Moss, Chet, Exec VP & Dir-Creative -- ICC, Parsippany, NJ, pg. 531
Moss, David, Acct Exec -- DATAXU, INC., Boston, MA, pg. 1331
Moss, Matt, Acct Dir -- SHOTWELL DIGITAL, Los Angeles, CA, pg. 1039
Moss, Michele, Sr VP & Dir-Creative -- OGILVY COMMONHEALTH WELLNESS MARKETING, Parsippany, NJ, pg. 851
Moss, Sarah, Art Dir -- BREAKAWAY, Boston, MA, pg. 163
Moss, Veronica, Acct Supvr -- PETER MAYER ADVERTISING, INC., New Orleans, LA, pg. 886
Mosterio, Joao, Dir-Creative -- DDB Brazil, Sao Paulo, Brazil, pg. 278
Mostoles, Carlo, Chief Creative Officer & VP -- Kinetic, Makati, Philippines, pg. 1350
Mota, Judite, Exec Dir-Creative & Copywriter -- Y&R Portugal, Lisbon, Portugal, pg. 1246
Motacek, Martin, Dir-Creative -- Wiktor/Leo Burnett, s.r.o., Bratislava, Slovakia, pg. 645
Moten, Brittany, Media Planner & Media Buyer -- HAVAS MEDIA, New York, NY, pg. 1338
Moten, Tiffany, Acct Exec -- Momentum, Chicago, IL, pg. 771
Motlong, Craig, Exec Dir-Creative -- SUPER GENIUS LLC, Chicago,

N

O

Personnel Index

Personnel Index

Panepinto, Jackie, VP & Sr Mgr-Traffic -- PUBLICIS USA, New York, NY, pg. 935
Pang, Jessica, Acct Exec -- TEAM VISION, Honolulu, HI, pg. 1660
Pang, Rebecca, Sr Acct Supvr-PR -- ANTHOLOGY MARKETING GROUP, Honolulu, HI, pg. 1445
Pang, Will, Assoc Dir-Creative -- BRUSHFIRE, INC., Cedar Knolls, NJ, pg. 172
Panichpairoj, Wasawad, Art Dir -- TBWA Thailand, Bangkok, Thailand, pg. 1131
Panko, Dustin, Dir-Creative -- PHOENIX GROUP, Regina, Canada, pg. 889
Pankow, Jenna, Acct Exec -- BRIGHTLINE ITV, New York, NY, pg. 166
Pannell, Audrey, Dir-PR & Social Media -- STYLE ADVERTISING, Birmingham, AL, pg. 1094
Pannese, Luca, Dir-Creative-Global -- SAATCHI & SAATCHI, New York, NY, pg. 1000
Panteleev, Mikhail, Dir-Creative -- Lowe Adventa, Moscow, Russia, pg. 790
Pantelic, Alison, Acct Dir -- HEALTH SCIENCE COMMUNICATIONS, New York, NY, pg. 505
Pantigoso, Flavio, Exec Dir-Creative -- FCB Mayo, Lima, Peru, pg. 379
Pantin, Leslie, Pres-PR Grp -- BEBER SILVERSTEIN GROUP, Miami, FL, pg. 121
Pantin, Leslie, Jr., Pres-PR Grp -- PANTIN/BEBER SILVERSTEIN PUBLIC RELATIONS, Miami, FL, pg. 1613
Pantland, Charles, Creative Dir -- TBWA Hunt Lascaris (Johannesburg), Johannesburg, South Africa, pg. 1126
Pantzerhielm, Fredrik, Acct Dir -- ANR BBDO, Stockholm, Sweden, pg. 111
Paolantonio, Mary, Acct Mgr & Media Buyer -- INTEGRATE, Houston, TX, pg. 1551
Paonessa, Jay, Dir-Creative -- MACLYN GROUP, Lisle, IL, pg. 683
Papadopoulos, Katie, Acct Dir -- DQMPR, New York, NY, pg. 1497
Papanikolaou, Theodosis, Exec Dir-Creative -- BBDO Athens, Athens, Greece, pg. 107
Papas, Katina, Acct Exec -- YUME, Redwood City, CA, pg. 1253
Papazis, Alexandra, Acct Supvr -- MARINA MAHER COMMUNICATIONS, New York, NY, pg. 1582
Pape, Chris, Exec Dir-Creative -- GENUINE INTERACTIVE, Boston, MA, pg. 421
Papini, Barbara, Acct Dir -- Fleishman-Hillard Italy, Milan, Italy, pg. 1520
Papp, Heather, Sr Media Planner & Media Buyer -- MEDIA BUYING SERVICES, INC., Phoenix, AZ, pg. 1364
Pappanduros, Ken, VP, Dir-Creative & Copywriter -- RPA, Santa Monica, CA, pg. 994
Pappas, Gina, Dir-New Media & Sr Specialist-PR -- ALBERS COMMUNICATIONS GROUP, Bellevue, NE, pg. 1442
Pappaterra, Kristen, Coord-PR -- EBERLY & COLLARD PUBLIC RELATIONS, Atlanta, GA, pg. 1500
Paprocki, Joe, Owner & Dir-Creative -- PAPROCKI & CO., Atlanta, GA, pg. 872
Papworth, Kim, Sr Dir-Creative -- Wieden + Kennedy, London, United Kingdom, pg. 1204
Paquette, Joelle, Mgr-PR & Comm -- SID LEE, Amsterdam, Netherlands, pg. 1040
Paquette, Joelle, Mgr-PR & Comm -- SID LEE, Paris, France, pg. 1040
Paquette, Katy, Acct Dir -- DERSE INC., Milwaukee, WI, pg. 300
Parab, Mahesh, Sr Dir-Creative -- Ogilvy & Mather, Bengaluru, India, pg. 842
Parab, Mahesh, Sr Dir-Creative -- Ogilvy India, Mumbai, India, pg. 843
Paradis, Sylvain, Art Dir -- BETC Life, Paris, France, pg. 492
Paradise, Liz, Exec Dir-Creative -- MCKINNEY, Durham, NC, pg. 736
Pardiansyah, Fanny, Grp Head-Creative & Copywriter -- Lowe, Jakarta, Indonesia, pg. 794
Pardiwalla, Priya, VP & Exec Dir-Creative -- J. Walter Thompson, Mumbai, India, pg. 569
Parente, Fran, VP & Dir-Creative -- DANIELS & ROBERTS, INC., Boynton Beach, FL, pg. 265
Parenti, Joni, Dir-Creative -- HEILBRICE, Irvine, CA, pg. 507
Parenti, Lisa, Assoc Dir-Creative -- MARTINO FLYNN LLC, Pittsford, NY, pg. 705
Parham, Edward, VP-PR -- RUECKERT ADVERTISING, Albany, NY, pg. 996
Parham, Jamaal, Creative Dir -- AKA NYC, New York, NY, pg. 43
Pari, Cesare, Sr VP & Dir-Creative -- SGW, Montville, NJ, pg. 1035
Parinnayok, Chotika, Art Dir -- Saatchi & Saatchi, Bangkok, Thailand, pg. 1012
Paris, Angela, Assoc Dir-Creative -- LEO BURNETT WORLDWIDE, INC., Chicago, IL, pg. 637
Paris, Brittany, Acct Supvr -- BROWN BAG MARKETING, Atlanta, GA, pg. 170
Park, Andrew, Acct Dir -- WONACOTT COMMUNICATIONS, LLC, Los Angeles, CA, pg. 1687
Park, Bill, Acct Exec -- CBC ADVERTISING, Saco, ME, pg. 199
Park, Hannah, Acct Exec -- GREY GROUP, New York, NY, pg. 445
Park, Hannah, Acct Exec -- YOUNG & RUBICAM, New York, NY, pg. 1239
Park, Rich, Dir-Creative -- WILLIAMS WHITTLE ASSOCIATES, INC., Alexandria, VA, pg. 1208
Park, Scott, Principal & Dir-Creative -- SPARK MEDIA, Macon, GA, pg. 1061
Park, Ted, Partner & Dir-Creative -- ADCREASIANS, INC., Los Angeles, CA, pg. 27
Park, Woong Hyun, Exec Dir-Creative -- TBWA Korea, Seoul, Korea (South), pg. 1131
Parke, Jennifer, Exec Dir-Creative -- TINY REBELLION, Santa Monica, CA, pg. 1145
Parker, Adrienne, Principal & Dir-Creative -- PARKER AVENUE, San Mateo, CA, pg. 874
Parker, Becky, Acct Coord -- KCD PUBLIC RELATIONS, San Diego, CA, pg. 1559
Parker, Cheryl, Acct Supvr -- EVOK ADVERTISING, Heathrow, FL, pg. 360
Parker, Chloe, Media Buyer-Spark PHD -- PHD New Zealand, Auckland, New Zealand, pg. 1385
Parker, Chris, Partner-Creative -- INTERPLANETARY, New York, NY, pg. 554
Parker, Clifton, Dir-Creative & Photography Art -- ELLEV LLC, Myrtle Beach, SC, pg. 345
Parker, Kris, Acct Dir-Natl -- DIGILANT, Boston, MA, pg. 307
Parker, Lee, Acct Exec -- EVOLVE, INC., Greenville, NC, pg. 360
Parker, Meg, Acct Dir -- HOLLYWOOD PUBLIC RELATIONS, Scituate, MA, pg. 1546
Parker, Richard, Founder, Pres & Dir-Creative -- CREATIVE DIRECTION, INC., Indianapolis, IN, pg. 247
Parker, Russell, Acct Dir -- Moroch, San Antonio, TX, pg. 776
Parker, Susan, Assoc Dir-Creative -- BREWLIFE, San Francisco, CA, pg. 164
Parker, Todd Rone, Assoc Dir-Creative & Art -- BBDO WORLDWIDE INC., New York, NY, pg. 99
Parkes, Martin, Dir-Creative -- McCann Erickson, Birmingham, MI, pg. 715
Parkes, Stacey, Assoc Creative Dir -- ROBERTS + LANGER DDB, New York, NY, pg. 987
Parkin, Fiona, Dir-Creative -- CLM BBDO, Boulogne-Billancourt, France, pg. 106
Parkowski, Alex, Acct Supvr -- AB+C, Wilmington, DE, pg. 15
Parks, Angela, Dir-Creative & Graphic Designer -- HIP ADVERTISING, Springfield, IL, pg. 515
Parks, Bruce, Sr VP & Dir-Creative -- Ackerman McQueen, Inc., Tulsa, OK, pg. 20
Parks, Bruce, Sr VP & Dir-Creative -- ACKERMAN MCQUEEN, INC., Oklahoma City, OK, pg. 20
Parks, Cheryl, Mgr-Print Production -- ON IDEAS, INC., Jacksonville, FL, pg. 859
Parks, Karen, Dir-Creative Svcs -- SIGNATURE ADVERTISING, Memphis, TN, pg. 1043
Parks, Melissa, Sr Media Planner -- NV ADVERTISING, Tampa, FL, pg. 819
Parmekar, Lars, Acct Dir -- AIMIA, Minneapolis, MN, pg. 41
Parnell, David, Acct Exec -- Signature Graphics, Porter, IN, pg. 315
Parolin, Paul, Assoc Dir-Creative -- THE HIVE, Toronto, Canada, pg. 517
Parr, Kimberly, Dir-PR -- LATORRA, PAUL & MCCANN, Syracuse, NY, pg. 629
Parr, Richard, CEO & Creative Dir -- EXECUTIONISTS, Marina Del Rey, CA, pg. 1293
Parra, Fernando, Dir-Creative-Coca-Cola -- Ogilvy & Mather, Cali, Colombia, pg. 839
Parrelli, Melissa, Acct Exec -- HOLLYWOOD PUBLIC RELATIONS, Scituate, MA, pg. 1546
Parretti, Carla, Acct Dir -- Ogilvy & Mather, Sao Paulo, Brazil, pg. 838
Parris, Melinda, Acct Dir -- Tribal Worldwide Melbourne, Richmond, Australia, pg. 1317
Parrish, Lance, Dir-Creative -- GREY GROUP, New York, NY, pg. 445
Parrish, Lance, Creative Dir -- GREY NEW YORK, New York, NY, pg. 446
Parrott, Doug, Exec VP-PR & Gen Mgr-Omaha -- Bailey Lauerman, Lincoln, NE, pg. 87
Parrotta, Angela, Art Dir -- GLOBAL THINKING, Alexandria, VA, pg. 429
Parry, Jim, Dir-Creative-Adv -- STEPHAN PARTNERS, INC., New York, NY, pg. 1083
Parry, Matt, Sr Mgr-Content-PR -- EMA Public Relations Services, Syracuse, NY, pg. 353
Parseghian, Stacia, Acct Dir -- DAVID & GOLIATH, El Segundo, CA, pg. 267
Parsell, Tara, Specialist-PR -- BELLE COMMUNICATIONS, Columbus, OH, pg. 1451
Parsons, Abby, Acct Exec -- TDA_BOULDER, Boulder, CO, pg. 1133
Parsons, Robin, Dir-Creative -- SCRIBBLERS' CLUB, Kitchener, Canada, pg. 1028
Parsons, Sharron, Acct Dir -- BIMM COMMUNICATIONS GROUP, Toronto, Canada, pg. 133
Parsons, Steven, Acct Supvr -- MCCANN WORLDGROUP, New York, NY, pg. 731
Parsonson, Troy, Acct Dir -- Publicis UK, London, United Kingdom, pg. 923
Partika, Sebastien, Art Dir -- Wieden + Kennedy - Amsterdam, Amsterdam, Netherlands, pg. 1203
Parvez, Masud, Acct Dir -- Grey Bangladesh Ltd., Dhaka, Bangladesh, pg. 455
Paschall, Wade, Partner & Dir-Creative -- GRENADIER, Boulder, CO, pg. 444
Pasco, Marc, Acct Dir -- CAMPBELL MARKETING & COMMUNICATIONS, Dearborn, MI, pg. 188
Pascoe, Karyn, Exec VP & Grp Dir-Creative -- deutschMedia, New York, NY, pg. 303
Pascual, D. Erica, Acct Dir -- HALL AND PARTNERS, New York, NY, pg. 475
Pascual, David, Art Dir -- TAPSA, Madrid, Spain, pg. 1224
Pasini, Alex, Partner & Dir-Creative -- SID LEE, Amsterdam, Netherlands, pg. 1040
Paskill, Jim, Principal & Dir-Creative -- PASKILL STAPLETON & LORD, Glenside, PA, pg. 877
Paskill, Jim, Principal & Dir-Creative -- Paskill Stapleton & Lord, Springfield, MA, pg. 877
Pasotti, Nick, Acct Supvr -- TRENDYMINDS INC, Indianapolis, IN, pg. 1156
Pasquali, Andre, VP-Creative -- Rapp Brazil, Sao Paulo, Brazil, pg. 953
Pasqualucci, Angela, Exec VP & Acct Dir-BAL Worldwide -- PUBLICIS USA, New York, NY, pg. 935
Passananti, Jessica, Acct Exec -- GRIFFIN INTEGRATED COMMUNICATIONS, New York, NY, pg. 1534
Passos, Diego, Acct Dir -- Y&R Sao Paulo, Sao Paulo, Brazil, pg. 1248
Pastir, Chris, Dir-Creative -- FRED AGENCY, Atlanta, GA, pg. 402
Pastor, Lisa, Acct Coord -- MARCH COMMUNICATIONS, Boston, MA, pg. 1582
Pastore, Tom, Creative Dir -- BERLIN CAMERON UNITED, New York, NY, pg. 125
Pastrana, Cesar, Acct Dir -- Text 100 Madrid S.L., Madrid, Spain, pg. 1661
Patch, Jeffrey, Exec Dir-Creative -- RDW GROUP INC., Providence, RI, pg. 956
Patel, Antra, Dir-Creative -- TONIC, Dubai, United Arab Emirates, pg. 1150
Patel, Bhumieka, Acct Supvr -- TWOFIFTEENMCCANN, San Francisco, CA, pg. 1164
Patel, Dhruva, Media Buyer -- HILL HOLLIDAY, Boston, MA, pg. 514
Patel, Hema, Acct Dir -- Saatchi & Saatchi, Dubai, United Arab Emirates, pg. 1006
Patel, Jayshri, Acct Exec -- Ketchum, Washington, DC, pg. 1562
Patel, Mitul, Art Dir -- BBH Mumbai, Mumbai, India, pg. 96
Patel, Nisha, Acct Mgr-PR -- CRAWFORD STRATEGY, Greenville, SC, pg. 245
Patell, Rayomand J., Exec Dir-Creative -- Havas Worldwide Mumbai, Mumbai, India, pg. 502
Paterson, Paul, Acct Supvr-Traditional & Digital Strategy -- PHD Canada, Toronto, Canada, pg. 1386
Paterson, Paul, Acct Supvr-Traditional & Digital Strategy -- PHD Toronto, Toronto, Canada, pg. 1385
Pathak, Neha, Head-PR-India -- Sapient Corporation Private Limited, Gurgaon, India, pg. 1019
Pathare, Sanket, Dir-Creative -- Rediffusion Y&R Pvt. Ltd., Mumbai, India, pg. 1243
Patil, Makarand, Dir-Creative -- TD&A DDB, Sharjah, United Arab

Personnel Index

Praspaliauskas, Remigijus, Art Dir -- DDB Argentina, Buenos Aires, Argentina, pg. 276
Prassinas, Stacia, Media Buyer -- DEVANEY & ASSOCIATES, Towson, MD, pg. 303
Prat, Leo, Dir-Creative -- The Community, Buenos Aires, Argentina, pg. 227
Prat, Leo, Dir-Creative -- THE COMMUNITY, Miami, FL, pg. 227
Prato, Paul, Dir-Creative -- PP+K, Tampa, FL, pg. 907
Prats, Shum, Dir-Creative -- RABBLE + ROUSER INC, Denver, CO, pg. 948
Pratt, Ashley, Acct Exec -- TBWA Chiat Day Los Angeles, Los Angeles, CA, pg. 1114
Pratt, Carly, Acct Dir -- DDB New Zealand Ltd., Auckland, New Zealand, pg. 286
Pratt, Corky, Dir-Studio Creative -- PureRED Creative, Atlanta, GA, pg. 939
Pratt, Steve, Acct Exec -- BRENER, ZWIKEL & ASSOCIATES, INC., Reseda, CA, pg. 1460
Pratt, Whitney, Assoc Dir-Creative -- FRANKLIN STREET MARKETING, Richmond, VA, pg. 402
Prefontaine, Diane, VP & Supvr-Brdcst -- CWMEDIA, Jamison, PA, pg. 261
Prego, Vinicius, Art Dir -- Ogilvy & Mather, Sao Paulo, Brazil, pg. 838
Pregont, Christy, Creative Dir -- MOVEMENT STRATEGY, Boulder, CO, pg. 780
Prehar, Jem, Acct Dir -- J. Walter Thompson Australia, Richmond, Australia, pg. 567
Prejean, Kevin, Owner & Dir-Creative -- PREJEAN CREATIVE, INC., Lafayette, LA, pg. 908
Prejean, Sarah, Acct Supvr -- CURRENT LIFESTYLE MARKETING, Chicago, IL, pg. 1490
Premchund, Sharon, Acct Dir -- MetropolitanRepublic, Johannesburg, South Africa, pg. 1220
Prenoveau, Kevin, Acct Dir -- HMH-Charlotte N.C., Charlotte, NC, pg. 519
Prentice, Brian, Dir-Creative -- PADILLA/CRT, Minneapolis, MN, pg. 869
Prentiss, Lauren, Strategist-Creative -- CAPTAINS OF INDUSTRY, Boston, MA, pg. 190
Prescott, Kate, Acct Supvr -- Ogilvy North America, New York, NY, pg. 828
Presicci, Laura, VP & Dir-Creative -- PALIO+IGNITE, Saratoga Springs, NY, pg. 871
Press, Darren, Dir-Creative & Mktg & Copywriter -- MAY SKY, INC., Stanfordville, NY, pg. 712
Press, Samantha, Acct Exec -- MAKE ME SOCIAL, Saint Augustine, FL, pg. 687
Pressly, Amanda, Acct Supvr -- NURUN/ANT FARM INTERACTIVE, Atlanta, GA, pg. 819
Pressman, Nadav, Exec Creative Dir -- BBR Saatchi & Saatchi, Ramat Gan, Israel, pg. 1003
Prest, George, VP & Exec Creative Dir-Global Unilever -- R/GA London, London, United Kingdom, pg. 946
Preston, Andy, Art Dir -- Havas Worldwide London, London, United Kingdom, pg. 498
Preston, Chris, Principal, Exec VP & Dir-Creative -- PRESTON KELLY, Minneapolis, MN, pg. 908
Preston, Stephanie, Acct Exec -- CONNECTIONS ADVERTISING & MARKETING, Lexington, KY, pg. 230
Prestopino, Domenico, Art Dir -- DDB S.r.L. Advertising, Milan, Italy, pg. 284
Preto, Sara, Acct Exec -- RESOUND MARKETING, Princeton, NJ, pg. 1635
Pretorius, Neill, Dir-Creative -- Gloo Design Agency, Cape Town, South Africa, pg. 848
Prettyman, Paige, Acct Dir -- George Patterson Y&R, Melbourne, Australia, pg. 1219
Prevost, Robert, Dir-Brand Strategy & PR -- NERLAND CO, Minneapolis, MN, pg. 805
Prexta, Boris, Dir-Creative -- Mayer/McCann-Erickson s.r.o., Bratislava, Slovakia, pg. 727
Price, Andrew, Global Chief Creative Officer -- FACTORY DESIGN LABS, Denver, CO, pg. 364
Price, Ann Marie, Acct Exec -- SCATENA DANIELS COMMUNICATIONS INC., San Diego, CA, pg. 1023
Price, Dave, Exec Creative Dir -- McCann-Erickson Communications House Ltd , Macclesfield, Prestbury, United Kingdom, pg. 730
Price, Elynsey, Acct Exec -- STANTON COMMUNICATIONS, INC., Washington, DC, pg. 1654
Price, Emily, Acct Exec -- DEEPLOCAL INC., Pittsburgh, PA, pg. 293
Price, Larry, Dir-Creative -- VISION CREATIVE GROUP, INC., Cedar Knolls, NJ, pg. 1178
Price, Lauren, Acct Supvr-Digital -- Fleishman-Hillard Inc., New York, NY, pg. 1517
Price, Leanne, Media Buyer-Digital -- GOODWAY GROUP, Jenkintown, PA, pg. 1335
Price, Rebecca, Acct Supvr -- MSLGROUP, New York, NY, pg. 1593
Price, Risa, Dir-Client Svcs & New Bus Dev -- ELITE MARKETING GROUP, New Hyde Park, NY, pg. 1412
Price, Rob, Founder & Dir-Creative -- ELEVEN INC., San Francisco, CA, pg. 343
Price, Tyler, Dir-Creative -- RELEVANT 24, Boston, MA, pg. 967
Prideaux, David, Exec Dir-Creative -- Publicis UK, London, United Kingdom, pg. 923
Priest, Brian, Sr VP-Creative -- UPSHOT, Chicago, IL, pg. 1168
Prieto, Estefania, Acct Exec -- Grey Argentina, Buenos Aires, Argentina, pg. 453
Prieto, Natalia, Acct Exec -- CREATIVE CIVILIZATION AN AGUILAR/GIRARD AGENCY, San Antonio, TX, pg. 246
Prigent, Dominic, Acct Dir -- BOB, Montreal, Canada, pg. 144
Prihadi, Didot, Assoc Dir-Creative -- DDB Indonesia, Jakarta, Indonesia, pg. 284
Primack, Laura, VP-Culture & Creative Svcs -- AVATARLABS, Encino, CA, pg. 81
Primm, Ronald J., Chm & Dir-Creative -- THE PRIMM COMPANY, Norfolk, VA, pg. 910
Prince, Jennifer, Sr VP & Dir-Brdcst-Natl -- HILL HOLLIDAY/NEW YORK, New York, NY, pg. 515
Prince, Josh, Chief Creative Officer -- CDM West, Los Angeles, CA, pg. 200
Prindle, Mark, Acct Supvr -- Fusion Public Relations, Inc., Los Angeles, CA, pg. 1525
Pringle, Nicholas, Grp Dir-Creative -- GREY GROUP, New York, NY, pg. 445
Pringle, Stacy, Acct Supvr -- PHD Toronto, Toronto, Canada, pg. 1385
Prior, Audrey, Media Planner -- THE FOOD GROUP, New York, NY, pg. 396
Prior, Christian, Acct Dir -- Weber Shandwick, Brussels, Belgium, pg. 1679
Pritchett, Barbara, Acct Exec -- BOHAN, Nashville, TN, pg. 146
Pritchett, Scott, Art Dir -- 303LOWE, Sydney, Australia, pg. 789
Pritzker, Billie, Acct Exec -- DDB Chicago, Chicago, IL, pg. 274
Pritzl, Lisa, Dir-Process Mgmt & Art Dir -- PROPHIT MARKETING, Green Bay, WI, pg. 915
Prochaska, Laura, Acct Supvr -- THE MX GROUP, Burr Ridge, IL, pg. 797
Proctor, Briana, Media Buyer -- EISENBERG, VITAL & RYZE ADVERTISING, Manchester, NH, pg. 341
Proctor, Julia, Acct Supvr -- Archer Malmo, Austin, TX, pg. 67
Prokop, Lukas, Acct Dir -- DDB Prague, Prague, Czech Republic, pg. 280
Prokos, Helen, Grp Dir-Creative -- PUBLICIS HAWKEYE, Dallas, TX, pg. 1308
Prompicharn, Rit, Exec Dir-Creative -- TBWA Thailand, Bangkok, Thailand, pg. 1131
Propach, Jan, Dir-Creative -- Tribal Worldwide, Dusseldorf, Germany, pg. 282
Prophet, Addison, Acct Exec -- PLANET CENTRAL, Huntersville, NC, pg. 896
Prospero, Nicholas, Acct Exec -- MANSFIELD INC., Toronto, Canada, pg. 690
Protheroe, Emily, Acct Exec -- Titan, Philadelphia, PA, pg. 1145
Proud, Mark, Dir-Creative -- STEP ONE CREATIVE, Oswego, NY, pg. 1083
Prough, Kyle, Dir-Creative -- SWIRE, Glendora, CA, pg. 1274
Prouty, Courtney, Acct Exec -- MASS MEDIA MARKETING, Augusta, GA, pg. 708
Provence, Lauren, Acct Exec -- THE SILVER TELEGRAM, Long Beach, CA, pg. 1044
Provenzano, Rachel, Acct Supvr -- Ketchum, Chicago, IL, pg. 1563
Proxmire, Brocky, Acct Exec -- Summit Group, Itasca, IL, pg. 1099
Pruden, Ricci, Acct Supvr -- Davis-Elen Advertising, Inc., Portland, OR, pg. 270
Pruett, Jennifer, Mgr-PR -- HDE, LLC., Phoenix, AZ, pg. 505
Pruett, Matt, Grp Dir-Creative -- OLSON, Minneapolis, MN, pg. 856
Pruzincova, Dora, Dir-Creative -- Y&R Praha, s.r.o., Prague, Czech Republic, pg. 1248
Przybylski, Joe, Dir-Interactive Creative -- ESWSTORYLAB, Chicago, IL, pg. 357
Pschirer, Michael, Acct Exec-Print Procurement -- TAG WORLDWIDE, New York, NY, pg. 1107
Pucci, John, Chief Creative Officer -- HAWTHORNE DIRECT INC., Fairfield, IA, pg. 503
Puch, Koko, Mgr-Print Production -- Del Campo Nazca Saatchi & Saatchi, Buenos Aires, Argentina, pg. 1007
Puckett, Jeff, Acct Exec -- BLUE HERON COMMUNICATIONS, Norman, OK, pg. 1456
Puckett, Michael, Chief Creative Officer -- ADVANTAGE COMMUNICATIONS, INC., Little Rock, AR, pg. 33
Puckett, Tom, Sr Dir-Creative -- THOMAS PUCKETT ADVERTISING, Las Vegas, NV, pg. 1141
Puddephatt, Caroline, Acct Exec-PR -- GHIDOTTI COMMUNICATIONS, Little Rock, AR, pg. 1527
Puder, Jessica, Acct Supvr -- ERWIN-PENLAND, Greenville, SC, pg. 354
Puebla, Chacho, Partner & Chief Creative Officer -- Lola Madrid, Madrid, Spain, pg. 556
Puffer, Brian, Acct Dir -- TRENDYMINDS INC, Indianapolis, IN, pg. 1156
Pugh, Margaret, Dir-PR -- SOLEMENE & ASSOCIATES, Dallas, TX, pg. 1057
Pugh, Michelle, Acct Exec -- ERIC ROB & ISAAC, Little Rock, AR, pg. 354
Pugliese, LouAnn, Acct Supvr -- IMPRESSIONS-A.B.A. INDUSTRIES, INC., Mineola, NY, pg. 542
Pugliese, Rita, Acct Dir -- IntraMed Communications Milan, Milan, Italy, pg. 1096
Pugliese, Veronica, Acct Dir -- J. Walter Thompson, Mexico, Mexico, pg. 578
Puglionisi, John, Co-Founder & VP-Creative -- GRAFICAGROUP, Morristown, NJ, pg. 437
Puglionisi, John, Co-Founder, VP & Dir-Creative -- GRAFICAINTER.ACTIVE, LTD., Chester, NJ, pg. 438
Puglise, Ang, Art Dir -- LEO BURNETT WORLDWIDE, INC., Chicago, IL, pg. 637
Puglisi-Barley, Joanna, Mgr-PR -- THE SIMON GROUP, INC., Sellersville, PA, pg. 1045
Puhalj, Marino, Exec Dir-Creative -- VML, Kalamazoo, MI, pg. 1319
Puig, Carles, Dir-Creative -- Grey Chile, Santiago, Chile, pg. 453
Pujals, Lisa, Dir-Creative -- BOUCHARD MCELROY COMMUNICATIONS GROUP INC., Roseville, CA, pg. 150
Pujols, Betsy, Acct Exec -- 3A/WORLDWIDE, Miami, FL, pg. 1436
Pulaski, Kristin, Acct Exec -- PUBLICIS NEW YORK, New York, NY, pg. 935
Pulchin, Howard, Dir-Creative Strategy & Community-Global -- APCO Worldwide, New York, NY, pg. 64
Puleo, John, Media Planner-Integrated -- ZIMMERMAN ADVERTISING, Fort Lauderdale, FL, pg. 1256
Pulman, Celeste, Acct Dir-Oreo -- 360i, New York, NY, pg. 6
Pultar, Liv, Acct Dir -- Blaze Advertising, Sydney, Australia, pg. 1217
Pultar, Liv, Acct Dir -- Blaze Advertising, Kent Town, Australia, pg. 1217
Pultar, Liv, Acct Dir -- Blaze Advertising, Kent Town, Australia, pg. 1147
Pumfery, Aaron, Art Dir -- EDGE PARTNERSHIPS, Lansing, MI, pg. 338
Pundsack, Jodie, Co-Founder & Strategist-Creative -- GASLIGHT CREATIVE, Saint Cloud, MN, pg. 416
Puopolo, Kristin, Acct Exec -- BOATHOUSE GROUP INC., Waltham, MA, pg. 144
Purcell, Benjamin, Media Buyer-Long Form -- ICON MEDIA DIRECT, Van Nuys, CA, pg. 1343
Purdin, Bill, Pres-Adv Agency & Dir-Creative -- LEGEND INC., Marblehead, MA, pg. 635
Purdy, Jessica, Acct Supvr -- KERN, Woodland Hills, CA, pg. 609
Puricelli, Emily, Assoc Dir-Creative -- CHECKMARK COMMUNICATIONS, Saint Louis, MO, pg. 1265
Purnell, Brady, Media Planner -- SULLIVAN BRANDING, Memphis, TN, pg. 1097
Purnell, Brady, Media Buyer -- Sullivan Branding LLC, Nashville, TN, pg. 1097
Purtill, Tara, Acct Exec -- MODCO GROUP, New York, NY, pg. 769
Puszczykowski, Crys, Acct Supvr -- OLSON, Minneapolis, MN, pg. 856
Putini, Anelene, Acct Exec -- Leo Burnett Tailor Made, Sao Paulo, Brazil, pg. 640
Putnam, Jennifer, Chief Creative Officer -- ALLEN & GERRITSEN, Boston, MA, pg. 46
Puttagio, Marissa, Dir-Creative -- EVENTIGE MEDIA GROUP, New York, NY, pg. 359
Putti, Julian, Assoc Dir-Creative -- McCann Erickson, Birmingham, MI, pg. 715
Py, Jean-Laurent, Creative Dir -- McCann Erickson Advertising Ltd.,

Personnel Index

Personnel Index

Personnel Index

S

Personnel Index

Personnel Index

Suh, Jai, Dir-Creative-Brand Mktg & Adv Strategies -- CREATIVE MEDIA ALLIANCE, Seattle, WA, pg. 251
Suhanjaya, Agung P., Dir-Creative -- Matari Advertising, Jakarta, Indonesia, pg. 1243
Suhr, Jay, Chief Creative Officer & Sr VP -- T3 (THE THINK TANK), Austin, TX, pg. 1106
Sule, Tunde, Creative Dir -- DDB Casers, Lagos, Nigeria, pg. 286
Sulewski, Tanya, Acct Dir -- FutureBrand, Melbourne, Australia, pg. 411
Sullentrup, Greg, Dir-Creative Svcs -- Momentum, Saint Louis, MO, pg. 771
Sullivan, Bob, Chief Creative Officer & Exec VP -- FERRARA & COMPANY, Princeton, NJ, pg. 385
Sullivan, Brian, Media Buyer -- MAXUS GLOBAL, New York, NY, pg. 1353
Sullivan, Dave, Dir-Creative -- Publicis UK, London, United Kingdom, pg. 923
Sullivan, Dawn, Strategist-PR -- HB/Eric Mower + Associates, Newton, MA, pg. 354
Sullivan, Kate, Assoc Dir-Creative -- LEO BURNETT WORLDWIDE, INC., Chicago, IL, pg. 637
Sullivan, Kelly, Acct Exec -- MARKETING DIRECTIONS, INC., Cleveland, OH, pg. 697
Sullivan, Kevin, Acct Exec -- MILLENNIAL MEDIA INC., Baltimore, MD, pg. 756
Sullivan, Matt, Creative Dir -- MARC USA CHICAGO, Chicago, IL, pg. 691
Sullivan, Meg, Acct Supvr -- CDMiConnect, New York, NY, pg. 200
Sullivan, Mike, Grp Dir-Creative -- DDB New York, New York, NY, pg. 275
Sullivan, Pamela E., Pres & Dir-Creative -- SULLIVAN CREATIVE SERVICES, LTD., Concord, NH, pg. 1097
Sullivan, Patrick, VP & Acct Dir -- Zimmerman Advertising, Oakbrook Terrace, IL, pg. 1257
Sullivan, Rich , Jr., Pres & Exec Dir-Creative -- RSQ, Mobile, AL, pg. 996
Sullivan, Ry, Acct Exec -- Edelman, Tokyo, Japan, pg. 1504
Sullivan, Samantha, Acct Exec -- Summit Group, Atlanta, GA, pg. 1099
Sullivan, Seth, Creative Dir -- 131DIGITAL, Pawleys Island, SC, pg. 2
Sullivan, Shannon, VP & Acct Dir -- M/C/C, Dallas, TX, pg. 679
Sullivan, Shannon, VP & Acct Dir -- MC COMMUNICATIONS, Dallas, TX, pg. 713
Sullivan, Tom, Sr VP & Grp Dir-Creative -- McCann Erickson/New York, New York, NY, pg. 714
Sulzer, Eric, Dir-Creative -- McCann Erickson / SP, Sao Paulo, Brazil, pg. 718
Sulzer, Michelle, Creative Dir -- KILROY COMMUNICATIONS, Tampa, FL, pg. 1566
Sumal, Kirandeep, Acct Supvr -- PROTAGONIST LLC, New York, NY, pg. 915
Suman, Javed Akter, Dir-Creative -- Grey Bangladesh Ltd., Dhaka, Bangladesh, pg. 455
Sumedi, Din, Chief Creative Officer -- Lowe, Jakarta, Indonesia, pg. 794
Sumedi, Din, Chief Creative Officer -- Ogilvy & Mather, Jakarta, Indonesia, pg. 845
Summerer, Kristian, Principal & Dir-Creative -- MACHINERY, Philadelphia, PA, pg. 681
Summers, Lynn, Acct Exec -- Rethink, Toronto, Canada, pg. 973
Sumners, Kristian, Sr Dir-Creative -- M5 NEW HAMPSHIRE, Manchester, NH, pg. 680
Sun, Angela, Acct Supvr -- SAPIENTNITRO USA, INC., New York, NY, pg. 1019
Sun, Kate, Acct Dir -- Grey Shanghai, Shanghai, China, pg. 455
Sundaram, Latha, Acct Dir-Global -- OMD Chicago, Chicago, IL, pg. 1379
Sundby, Joe, Founder & Exec Dir-Creative -- ROUNDHOUSE, Portland, OR, pg. 994
Sundell, Mike, Pres & Dir-Creative -- CHARACTER & KLATCH, BRAND DEVELOPMENT, ADVERTISING AND DESIGN, Toronto, Canada, pg. 204
Sundermeyer, Max, Acct Exec-Environmental Sciences Practice -- PADILLA/CRT, Minneapolis, MN, pg. 869
Sunil, V., Exec Dir-Creative -- Wieden + Kennedy India, New Delhi, India, pg. 1205
Sunol, Alvar, Co-Pres & Chief Creative Officer -- ALMA, Coconut Grove, FL, pg. 50
Supple, Jack, Chief Creative Officer -- POCKET HERCULES, Minneapolis, MN, pg. 899
Sura, Carolyn, Exec VP & Dir-Brdcst -- LOCKARD & WECHSLER, Irvington, NY, pg. 666
Suraiya, Harshik, Grp Head-Creative -- Ogilvy India, Mumbai, India, pg. 843
Surattanasathitkul, Yuwarat, Art Dir -- TBWA Thailand, Bangkok, Thailand, pg. 1131
Surgeon, Aoife, Acct Dir -- Havas Worldwide Dublin, Dublin, Ireland, pg. 494
Suri, Prateek, Grp Head-Creative -- Contract Advertising (India) Limited, Mumbai, India, pg. 568
Suria, Jorge, Pres & Dir-Creative -- HOOAH LLC., Winter Park, FL, pg. 522
Surowiec, Joanna, Acct Exec -- LSHD ADVERTISING INC., Chicopee, MA, pg. 672
Surrett, Elizabeth, Acct Supvr -- Mullen Lowe, Winston Salem, NC, pg. 788
Surrett, Jessica, Mgr-Creative Svcs -- THE JONES AGENCY, Palm Springs, CA, pg. 596
Surrey, Chris, Exec Dir-Creative -- GlobalHue, New York, NY, pg. 429
Surti, Shashin, Acct Dir -- Weber Shandwick, Shanghai, China, pg. 1682
Surufka, Greg, VP-Creative & Dir -- HEINZEROTH MARKETING GROUP, Rockford, IL, pg. 508
Suskin, Andrew, Media Planner & Buyer-Digital -- Havas Media, Boston, MA, pg. 1340
Sutanto, Dhani, Dir-Creative -- Spinifex Group, Alexandria, Australia, pg. 913
Sutcliffe, Mike, Exec Dir-Creative-Asia Pacific -- DigitasLBi, Quarry Bay, Hong Kong, pg. 1289
Suter, Devon, Exec VP & Exec Dir-Creative -- Dalton Agency Atlanta, Atlanta, GA, pg. 264
Sutherland, Erica, Dir-PR & Media Buyer -- COXRASMUSSEN & CROSS MARKETING & ADVERTISING, INC., Eureka, CA, pg. 239
Sutherland, Mike, Dir-Creative -- Abbott Mead Vickers BBDO, London, United Kingdom, pg. 112
Sutherland, Ross, Dir-Creative -- ROTH PARTNERS LLC, Mamaroneck, NY, pg. 993
Sutherland, Sean, Acct Exec -- FRANK STRATEGIC MARKETING, Columbia, MD, pg. 401
Sutomo, Budi, Dir-Creative -- MALONEY STRATEGIC COMMUNICATIONS, Dallas, TX, pg. 688
Sutter, Joe, Chief Creative Officer -- GMR MARKETING LLC, New Berlin, WI, pg. 1414
Sutterfield, Jenna, Asst Mgr-Traffic -- SWANSON RUSSELL ASSOCIATES, Lincoln, NE, pg. 1102
Sutton, Jamie, Art Dir -- CUNNINGHAM GROUP, Montgomery, AL, pg. 260
Sutton, Matt, Acct Dir -- Fahlgren Mortine (Dayton), Beavercreek, OH, pg. 365
Sutton, Michael, Art Dir -- LEO BURNETT WORLDWIDE, INC., Chicago, IL, pg. 637
Suzuki, Katsuhiko, Dir-Creative & Art -- HAKUHODO INCORPORATED, Tokyo, Japan, pg. 473
Svendsen, Kindra, Strategist-PR & Digital Mktg -- SPEAK CREATIVE, Memphis, TN, pg. 1314
Sverdlin, Leon, Dir-Creative -- Mark BBDO, Prague, Czech Republic, pg. 105
Svitekova, Dina, Mgr-PR -- Pleon Impact, Prague, Czech Republic, pg. 105
Swago, Lauren, Art Dir -- FCB Chicago, Chicago, IL, pg. 371
Swainey, Mike, Acct Dir -- FACTION MEDIA, Denver, CO, pg. 363
Swan, Greg, VP-PR & Emerging Media -- SPACE150, Minneapolis, MN, pg. 1061
Swan, Robert, VP & Exec Dir-Creative -- BRANDIMAGE DESGRIPPES & LAGA, Northbrook, IL, pg. 159
Swaney, Rachel, Acct Exec -- ANVIL MEDIA, INC., Portland, OR, pg. 1325
Swanker, Aaron, Co-Founder & Dir-Creative -- FLIGHT PATH CREATIVE, Traverse City, MI, pg. 393
Swanner, Jessica, Acct Exec -- CAPSTRAT, Raleigh, NC, pg. 1472
Swanson, Jim, Partner-Creative -- PERFORMANCE MARKETING, West Des Moines, IA, pg. 884
Swanson, Matt, Grp Dir-Creative -- Doner, El Segundo, CA, pg. 323
Swanson, Matt, Grp Dir-Creative -- Doner, El Segundo, CA, pg. 739
Swartz, Dave, Dir-Creative -- CP+B, Coconut Grove, FL, pg. 239
Swartz, Julie, Acct Dir-Mgmt -- ALBERS COMMUNICATIONS GROUP, Bellevue, NE, pg. 1442
Swasey, Courtenay, Assoc Dir-Brdcst-Natl -- OMD NORTH AMERICA, New York, NY, pg. 1378
Swearingen, Dave, Dir-Creative -- BLACKTOP CREATIVE, Kansas City, MO, pg. 135
Sweatman, Mackie, Acct Supvr -- AMELIE COMPANY, Denver, CO, pg. 53
Sweeney, Bryan, Exec VP & Dir-Creative Production -- HILL HOLLIDAY, Boston, MA, pg. 514
Sweeney, Carrie, Acct Dir -- DUFFEY PETROSKY, Farmington Hills, MI, pg. 331
Sweeney, Karin, Acct Supvr -- FCB HEALTH, New York, NY, pg. 383
Sweeney, Rita, Acct Dir -- THRESHOLD INTERACTIVE, Marina Del Rey, CA, pg. 1142
Sweet, Eric, Pres & Chief Creative Officer -- SCRIBBLERS' CLUB, Kitchener, Canada, pg. 1028
Sweet, Patti, Acct Dir -- iCrossing, Inc., Brighton, United Kingdom, pg. 1296
Sweitzer, Elizabeth, Acct Exec -- RDW Group, Inc., Worcester, MA, pg. 956
Swenson, Tim, Acct Exec -- D.TRIO, Minneapolis, MN, pg. 331
Sweredoski, Melissa, Mgr-PR -- KIP HUNTER MARKETING, Fort Lauderdale, FL, pg. 613
Swernoff, Robyn, Acct Supvr & Specialist-Event & Experiential Mktg -- BVK DIRECT, Colleyville, TX, pg. 181
Sweterlitsch, Haydn, Global Chief Creative Officer -- Hacker Agency, Seattle, WA, pg. 554
Sweterlitsch, Haydn, Global Chief Creative Officer -- Hacker Agency, Seattle, WA, pg. 370
Swetnam, Hal, Sr Strategist-Creative -- GRAFIK MARKETING COMMUNICATIONS, Alexandria, VA, pg. 438
Swiderski, Evelyn, Acct Coord -- The PR Consulting Group, Inc.-Washington, Washington, DC, pg. 1626
Swiderski, Evelyn, Acct Exec -- PRCG/HAGGERTY LLC, New York, NY, pg. 1626
Swietlik, Chris, Acct Exec -- C BLOHM & ASSOCIATES INC, Monona, WI, pg. 1471
Swinburne, Matt, Dir-Creative -- MCCANN ERICKSON WORLDWIDE, New York, NY, pg. 713
Swinburne, Matt, Creative Dir -- MCCANN WORLDGROUP, New York, NY, pg. 731
Swingle, Juli, VP & Acct Dir-Social CRM -- INNOCEAN USA, Huntington Beach, CA, pg. 547
Swisher, John, Chief Creative Officer -- RONIN ADVERTISING GROUP, Coral Gables, FL, pg. 991
Switzer, Amy, Acct Dir -- GMR Entertainment, New York, NY, pg. 949
Swoboda, Dan, Dir-Creative Svcs -- ANDERSON PARTNERS, Omaha, NE, pg. 59
Swoish, Erica, Acct Exec -- FRANCO PUBLIC RELATIONS GROUP, Detroit, MI, pg. 1523
Sworn, Simon, Dir-Creative -- J. Walter Thompson, London, United Kingdom, pg. 575
Syberg-Olsen, Matt, VP & Dir-Creative -- J. WALTER THOMPSON CANADA, Toronto, Canada, pg. 580
Syed, Nizamuddin, Mgr-Events & Traffic -- Publicis-Graphics, Riyadh, Saudi Arabia, pg. 924
Sygar, Dan, VP & Assoc Dir-Creative -- PERICH ADVERTISING + DESIGN, Ann Arbor, MI, pg. 884
Sykora, Jim, Dir-Creative -- THE WOLF AGENCY, Dallas, TX, pg. 1212
Sylver, Phil, Creative Dir -- EXTREME GROUP, Toronto, Canada, pg. 1293
Sylver, Phil, Creative Dir -- Extreme Group, Halifax, Canada, pg. 1293
Sylves, Jamie, Assoc Dir-PR & Social Media -- SMITH BROTHERS AGENCY, LP, Pittsburgh, PA, pg. 1054
Syring, Sharyl, Media Planner -- ESROCK PARTNERS, Orland Park, IL, pg. 356
Sytsma, Daniel, Partner & Dir-Creative -- ACHTUNG, Amsterdam, Netherlands, pg. 1279
Szafranski, Michelle, Acct Exec -- CRONIN & COMPANY, INC., Glastonbury, CT, pg. 255
Szalay, Kate, Producer-Brdcst -- BRANDTAILERS, Irvine, CA, pg. 161
Szczepanik, Mark, Dir-Creative -- THE ADCOM GROUP, Cleveland, OH, pg. 27
Szczuka, Gina, Acct Supvr -- THE ARCHER GROUP, Wilmington, DE, pg. 67
Szimonisz, Greg, Acct Dir -- SPINX INC., Los Angeles, CA, pg. 1314
Szkambara, Larysa, Coord-Traffic -- IntraMed Educational Group, New York, NY, pg. 1096
Szopinski, Corey, VP & Dir-Creative Technical-Physical Computing -- CP+B, Coconut Grove, FL, pg. 239

T

Ta, Keith, Exec Dir-Creative-Southeast Asia -- Wunderman,

Personnel Index

Tlapek, Rich, Grp Dir-Creative -- SACRED COW, Austin, TX, pg. 1013
Toal, Keelin, Acct Exec & Coord-Traffic -- MOJO LAB, Spokane, WA, pg. 770
Tobin, Andrew, Dir-Creative -- NSG/SWAT, New York, NY, pg. 818
Tobler, Asja, Producer-Brdcst, Print & Brand Strategy -- OISHII CREATIVE, Los Angeles, CA, pg. 854
Tocchi, Rossana, Dir-Creative -- TBWA Roma, Rome, Italy, pg. 1121
Toch, Andrea, VP-PR -- PITCH PUBLIC RELATIONS, Chandler, AZ, pg. 1617
Todai, Amin, Pres & Chief Creative Officer -- ONEMETHOD INC, Toronto, Canada, pg. 861
Todd, Andy, Partner-Creative -- Proximity Worldwide & London, London, United Kingdom, pg. 113
Todd, Darbi Lou, Acct Exec -- MELT, Atlanta, GA, pg. 746
Todd, Hugh, Creative Dir -- Leo Burnett, Ltd., London, United Kingdom, pg. 641
Todd, Ian, Dir-Creative -- BRYAN MILLS IRADESSO CORP., Toronto, Canada, pg. 173
Todenhagen, Amy, Dir-Creative & Interaction Design -- THE BARBARIAN GROUP, New York, NY, pg. 90
Todisco, Jaclyn, Acct Exec -- THE ROSEN GROUP, New York, NY, pg. 1640
Todman, Caroline, Acct Dir-Out of Home -- C2C MEDIA, LLC, New York, NY, pg. 1328
Todoroff, Jenna, Mgr-Digital Comm & Acct Exec -- COMMON GROUND PUBLIC RELATIONS, Chesterfield, MO, pg. 1483
Toemtechatpong, Supachai, Creative Dir -- J. Walter Thompson Thailand, Bangkok, Thailand, pg. 572
Toepper, Eric, Media Buyer-Local -- STARCOM MEDIAVEST GROUP, Chicago, IL, pg. 1074
Toerner, Erin, Acct Supvr -- TBWA/Media Arts Lab, Los Angeles, CA, pg. 1116
Togneri, Joe, Head-Brdcst Production -- Wieden + Kennedy - Amsterdam, Amsterdam, Netherlands, pg. 1203
Toh, Jamie, Art Dir -- McCann Healthcare Melbourne, Melbourne, Australia, pg. 716
Toher, Joni, Principal & Creative Dir -- THIRDEYE DESIGN, Newburyport, MA, pg. 1140
Tokuno, Yuki, Art Dir -- TBWA/Hakuhodo, Tokyo, Japan, pg. 1129
Tol, Joris, Creative Dir -- DDB Amsterdam, Amstelveen, Netherlands, pg. 286
Tolias, Vangelis, Dir-Creative-Bold Ogilvy Athens -- OgilvyOne Worldwide, Athens, Greece, pg. 833
Tolkin, Danielle, Acct Exec -- BURNSGROUP, New York, NY, pg. 177
Toll, Jeff, Dir-Creative -- BKWLD, Sacramento, CA, pg. 1454
Tollefson, Liv, Acct Supvr & Sr Strategist-Media -- LINNIHAN FOY ADVERTISING, Minneapolis, MN, pg. 659
Tolley, Geoff, Chief Creative Officer -- CHEMISTRY COMMUNICATIONS INC., Pittsburgh, PA, pg. 207
Tolley, Joe, Dir-Art & Assoc Dir-Creative -- LUQUIRE GEORGE ANDREWS, INC., Charlotte, NC, pg. 674
Tolmos, Charlie, Creative Dir -- Y&R Peru, Lima, Peru, pg. 1250
Tolnas, Roxanne, Acct Dir -- DNA SEATTLE, Seattle, WA, pg. 319
Tolsa, Marina, Assoc Dir-Creative -- McCann Worldgroup (Singapore) Pte Ltd, Singapore, Singapore, pg. 727
Tom, Helen, VP-Creative Ops -- TMP Worldwide/Advertising & Communications, Toronto, Canada, pg. 1148
Tomek, Cindy, Assoc Dir-Creative -- MARC USA CHICAGO, Chicago, IL, pg. 691
Tomek, Lindsay, Acct Dir-Global -- FCB/RED, Chicago, IL, pg. 372
Tomkins, Julia, Acct Coord -- RUBENSTEIN ASSOCIATES, INC., New York, NY, pg. 1641
Tomlinson, Becky, Acct Dir -- GWP BRAND ENGINEERING, Toronto, Canada, pg. 468
Tomlinson, Brenda, Dir-PR -- MCDANIELS MARKETING COMMUNICATIONS, Pekin, IL, pg. 732
Tomson, Kiersten, Dir-New Bus Dev & Media Strategies -- MAVEN COMMUNICATIONS LLC, Philadelphia, PA, pg. 711
Tone, Tim, Grp Head-Creative -- RICHARDS PARTNERS, Dallas, TX, pg. 1636
Tong, Annie, Head-Brdcst -- DDB Worldwide Ltd., Hong Kong, China (Hong Kong), pg. 283
Tong, Jennifer, Acct Supvr -- LEVICK, Washington, DC, pg. 1574
Tong, Richard, Dir-Creative-Integrated Design -- Saatchi & Saatchi, Guangzhou, China, pg. 1010
Tong, William, Acct Dir -- SMA NYC, New York, NY, pg. 1052
Tonnarelli, Cristiano, Exec Dir-Creative -- TONIC, Dubai, United Arab Emirates, pg. 1150
Toofer, Mike, Dir-New Bus -- MISTRESS, Santa Monica, CA, pg. 764
Toorenaar, Jaap, Dir-Creative -- ARA Groep, Rotterdam, Netherlands, pg. 1121
Topiel, Jennifer, Acct Supvr -- DDR PUBLIC RELATIONS, Pleasantville, NY, pg. 1492
Torbay, Chris, Dir-Creative -- YIELD BRANDING, Toronto, Canada, pg. 1238
Tornell, Carlos, Dir-Creative -- GRUPO GALLEGOS, Huntington Beach, CA, pg. 463
Toro, Alyssa D'Arienzo, Sr Partner & Chief Creative Officer -- CONNELLY PARTNERS, Boston, MA, pg. 231
Toro, Joaquin, Art Dir -- Prolam Y&R S.A., Santiago, Chile, pg. 1249
Toro, Sabatini, Creative Dir -- THE EVIL GENIUS GROUP INC, New York, NY, pg. 1511
Toro, Winifred, Acct Dir -- ARTEAGA & ARTEAGA, San Juan, PR, pg. 74
Torok, Frank, Acct Exec -- DDB New York, New York, NY, pg. 275
Torrance, Gavin, Assoc Dir-Creative -- DARE, London, United Kingdom, pg. 1286
Torreano, Alan, Exec VP & Dir-Creative -- LATINOLANDIA USA, Irvine, CA, pg. 628
Torrecillas, Marta, Acct Dir -- McCann Erickson S.A., Barcelona, Spain, pg. 728
Torres Cornejo, Tonatiuh, Art Dir -- Publicis Arredondo de Haro, Mexico, Mexico, pg. 929
Torres, Beatriz, Acct Dir -- Havas Worldwide Mexico, Mexico, Mexico, pg. 499
Torres, Blair, Acct Dir -- FIREHOUSE, INC., Dallas, TX, pg. 1412
Torres, Hector L., Dir-New Bus -- THE GROUP ADVERTISING, Orlando, FL, pg. 462
Torres, Kathleen, Dir-Brdcst -- MOROCH PARTNERS, Dallas, TX, pg. 774
Torres, Vanessa, Mgr-Print Production -- GREY PUERTO RICO, San Juan, PR, pg. 458
Torriani, Antonio, Art Dir -- CP+B, Coconut Grove, FL, pg. 239
Tortolero, Bernardo, Dir-Creative -- J. Walter Thompson, Caracas, Venezuela, pg. 579
Toscana, Agostino, Exec Dir-Creative -- Saatchi & Saatchi, Rome, Italy, pg. 1004
Toscana, Agostino, Exec Dir-Creative -- Saatchi & Saatchi Healthcare, Milan, Italy, pg. 1004
Toscano, Melinda, Acct Dir -- Joule, New York, NY, pg. 1350
Toth, Alicia, Dir-Creative Resources -- THE ROXBURGH AGENCY INC, Costa Mesa, CA, pg. 994
Toth, Jackie, Acct Exec -- ESB ADVERTISING, Springfield, VA, pg. 355
Toth, Jim, Partner & Exec Dir-Creative -- VSA PARTNERS, INC., Chicago, IL, pg. 1185
Toth, Julia, Dir-Creative -- J. Walter Thompson Inside, Atlanta, GA, pg. 580
Toth, Krisztian, CEO & Chief Creative Officer -- Possible, Budapest, Hungary, pg. 1308
Toth, Mike, Pres & Chief Creative Officer -- TOTH BRAND & IMAGING, New York, NY, pg. 1152
Totsky, Matt, Assoc Dir-Creative -- REAL INTEGRATED, Bloomfield Hills, MI, pg. 957
Toulouse, Chelle, Acct Exec -- Deutsch LA, Los Angeles, CA, pg. 302
Tous, Joa, Assoc Dir-Creative -- NOBOX MARKETING GROUP, INC., Miami, FL, pg. 812
Tovar, Maria, Acct Dir -- Sancho BBDO, Bogota, Colombia, pg. 103
Towns, Lauren, Acct Exec -- FRENCH/WEST/VAUGHAN, INC., Raleigh, NC, pg. 404
Townsend, Andrew J., Principal & Dir-Creative -- KRACOE SZYKULA & TOWNSEND INC., Troy, MI, pg. 617
Townsend, Berri, Dir-Creative -- CLAPP COMMUNICATIONS, Baltimore, MD, pg. 213
Townsend, Brian, Head-New Bus Dev -- GOCONVERGENCE, Orlando, FL, pg. 432
Toyama, Stan, Exec Dir-Creative -- IW Group, San Francisco, CA, pg. 564
Traazil, Leon, Acct Dir -- J. Walter Thompson Singapore, Singapore, Singapore, pg. 571
Trabert, Ken, Dir-Creative -- 15 FINGERS LLC, Buffalo, NY, pg. 2
Trace, Jim, Dir-Brdcst & Video Comm -- NATIONAL HOT ROD ASSOCIATION, Glendora, CA, pg. 1270
Trace, Lauren, Sr Acct Dir -- M&C Saatchi, Sydney, Australia, pg. 677
Tracey, Kim, VP & Acct Dir -- BARKER/DZP, New York, NY, pg. 92
Tracey, Sean, Dir-Creative & Brand Strategist -- SEAN TRACEY ASSOCIATES, Portsmouth, NH, pg. 1029
Tracy, Michael, Acct Supvr -- MARTINO FLYNN LLC, Pittsford, NY, pg. 705
Tracy, Xin Zheng, Media Planner-Digital-Team P&G -- MediaCom Japan, Tokyo, Japan, pg. 1373
Trad, Bruno, Art Dir -- DM9DDB, Sao Paulo, Brazil, pg. 278
Traflet, Laura, Acct Exec -- DDB New York, New York, NY, pg. 275
Trahan-Miller, Cherise, Partner & Dir-Creative -- ASHAY MEDIA GROUP, Brooklyn, NY, pg. 76
Trahar, John, Founder & Dir-Creative -- GREATEST COMMON FACTORY, Austin, TX, pg. 442
Trammel, Wes, Dir-Creative -- STYLE ADVERTISING, Birmingham, AL, pg. 1094
Tramontana, Jessica, Acct Exec -- MARTIN WAYMIRE, Lansing, MI, pg. 704
Tran, Chau, Acct Dir -- Lowe, Ho Chi Minh City, Vietnam, pg. 794
Tran, Deborah, Acct Exec -- Ogilvy Sydney, Saint Leonards, Australia, pg. 840
Tran, Laure-Elise, Acct Supvr -- Nurun France, Boulogne-Billancourt, France, pg. 925
Trapp, Justin, Assoc Dir-Creative -- UWG, Dearborn, MI, pg. 1169
Traquino, Ricardo, Supvr-Creative -- DDB Mozambique, Maputo, Mozambique, pg. 285
Trask, Linda, Office Mgr & Media Buyer -- 802 CREATIVE PARTNERS, INC., Montpelier, VT, pg. 12
Trauring, Jeff, Acct Dir -- KOHNSTAMM COMMUNICATIONS, Saint Paul, MN, pg. 616
Traver, Eric, Acct Supvr-Engagement -- Fleishman-Hillard Inc., New York, NY, pg. 1517
Traverso, Mark, VP-New Bus & Sls -- LIGHTHOUSE LIST COMPANY, Pompano Beach, FL, pg. 657
Traykova, Reneta, Acct Exec -- McCann Erickson Sofia, Sofia, Bulgaria, pg. 718
Treacy, Maria, Acct Supvr -- CURLEY COMPANY INC, Washington, DC, pg. 1489
Treacy, Susan, Exec VP & Exec Dir-Creative -- FCB Chicago, Chicago, IL, pg. 371
Treadaway, John, Head-Future Creative -- THE BECKET AGENCY, Charleston, SC, pg. 1451
Trecate, Cristina, Acct Coord -- LOTUS823, Tinton Falls, NJ, pg. 1578
Treinen, Lauren, Acct Exec -- NICKELODEON CREATIVE ADVERTISING, New York, NY, pg. 810
Trejo, Alan, Acct Supvr -- FCB Mexico City, Mexico, Mexico, pg. 378
Trejos, Lisseth, Acct Dir -- J. Walter Thompson, Bogota, Colombia, pg. 578
Treleven, Todd, Dir-Creative & Art -- PUROHIT NAVIGATION, Chicago, IL, pg. 939
Tremblay, Louis-Phillipe, Exec VP & Sr Dir-Creative -- BBDO Atlanta, Atlanta, GA, pg. 100
Trent, Carrie, Acct Dir -- MERCURY LABS, Saint Louis, MO, pg. 1588
Trent, Rob, Dir-Creative -- 72ANDSUNNY, Playa Vista, CA, pg. 10
Trepal, Judy, Co-Founder, Dir-Creative & Principal -- ETHOS MARKETING & DESIGN, Westbrook, ME, pg. 358
Trepanier, Jason, Dir-Creative -- DOUGLAS MARKETING GROUP, LLC, Detroit, MI, pg. 326
Tresidder, Melissa, Art Dir -- PRESTON KELLY, Minneapolis, MN, pg. 908
Tresler, Malachi, Dir-Creative Svcs -- Axxis Advertising LLC, Tampa, FL, pg. 83
Tressel, Peter, VP & Dir-Creative & Digital -- PRESTON KELLY, Minneapolis, MN, pg. 908
Tressler, Claudia Rodriguez, Partner & Chief Creative Officer -- BROAD STREET, New York, NY, pg. 167
Trevino, Marcela, Acct Dir -- DDB Mexico, Mexico, Mexico, pg. 285
Trew, Caitlin, Project Mgr & Acct Exec -- I2 MARKETING INC, Asheville, NC, pg. 531
Trexler, Clark, Dir-Creative -- MARKETSHARE PLUS, INC., Fort Wayne, IN, pg. 700
Tribe, Norm, Partner & Dir-Creative & Digital -- GEARSHIFT ADVERTISING, Costa Mesa, CA, pg. 419
Trierweiler, Spencer, Dir-Creative -- MOTIVE, Denver, CO, pg. 780
Triggs, Alex, Acct Exec -- Vibrant Media Ltd., London, United Kingdom, pg. 1176
Trigidou, Matina, Acct Dir -- Bold Ogilvy Greece, Athens, Greece, pg. 832
Trigueros, Camila, Acct Exec -- Publicidad Comercial, La Libertad, El Salvador, pg. 557
Trimino, Anthony, Chief Creative Officer & Principal -- TRAFFIK, Irvine, CA, pg. 1154
Trimino, Julian, Dir-Creative -- TRAFFIK, Irvine, CA, pg. 1154

Trinanes, John, Sr VP & Exec Dir-Creative -- George P. Johnson Company, Inc., Boston, MA, pg. 422
Trinidad, Megan, Dir-Creative -- R/GA, New York, NY, pg. 946
Trinneer, Matt, Dir-Creative -- PIVOT+LEVY, Seattle, WA, pg. 894
Tripi, Julie, VP & Acct Supvr -- AGENCYRX, New York, NY, pg. 39
Tripi, Mike, Art Dir -- FOURTH IDEA, Buffalo, NY, pg. 400
Tripodi, John, Creative Dir -- NEPTUNE ADVERTISING, Ocala, FL, pg. 805
Tripodi, Kevin, Sr Partner & Dir-Creative -- ERIC MOWER + ASSOCIATES, Syracuse, NY, pg. 353
Tripoli, Marcelo, Chief Creative Officer-Latam Reg -- SapientNitro iThink, Sao Paulo, Brazil, pg. 1020
Tripp, Hannah, Acct Exec -- COHN MARKETING, Denver, CO, pg. 220
Trisadikun, Sompat, Exec Dir-Creative -- Leo Burnett, Bangkok, Thailand, pg. 651
Tritsch, Rachel, Mgr-Traffic -- THINK TANK PR & MARKETING, Glen Carbon, IL, pg. 1662
Trivelato, Marcelo, Acct Supvr -- DDB Brazil, Sao Paulo, Brazil, pg. 278
Trocchio, Olivia, Acct Coord -- AMNET GROUP, New York, NY, pg. 1324
Troedsson, Erik, Acct Supvr -- Razorfish San Francisco, San Francisco, CA, pg. 1310
Trogdon, Emily, Dir-PR -- MOMENTUM MARKETING, Charleston, SC, pg. 770
Trollback, Jakob, Pres & Dir-Creative -- TROLLBACK + COMPANY, New York, NY, pg. 1159
Troncone, Bill, Pres & Dir-Creative -- TRONCONE + PARTNERS, Walden, NY, pg. 1159
Troncoso, Tommy, VP & Assoc Dir-Creative -- PUBLICIS NEW YORK, New York, NY, pg. 935
Trondsen, Marte Aagesen, Mgr-Brdcst -- Maxus, Oslo, Norway, pg. 1354
Tronolone, Natalie, Acct Exec -- CROWLEY WEBB, Buffalo, NY, pg. 257
Tronquini, Ricardo, Dir-Creative -- DM9DDB, Sao Paulo, Brazil, pg. 278
Tropp, Harry, Media Dir -- POSNER MILLER ADVERTISING, New York, NY, pg. 904
Trott, Ryan, Media Buyer -- MEDIA WORKS, LTD., Baltimore, MD, pg. 1367
Troust, Deanna, VP-Creative Svcs -- VANGUARDCOMM, East Brunswick, NJ, pg. 1171
Troutman, Lainie, Mgr-Print Production -- TBC INC., Baltimore, MD, pg. 1113
Troutman, Scott, Dir-Creative -- DOE-ANDERSON, Louisville, KY, pg. 320
Trouton, Ronnie, Dir-Creative -- DDFH&B Advertising Ltd., Dublin, Ireland, pg. 573
Trovato, Vince, Creative Dir -- AVC MEDIA GROUP, Woodbury, NJ, pg. 82
Trowell, Jim, Dir-Creative -- THE JOEY COMPANY, Brooklyn, NY, pg. 593
Troy, Shannon, Acct Exec -- Myriad Travel Marketing, New York, NY, pg. 798
Trueba, Isabel, Acct Exec -- BEBER SILVERSTEIN GROUP, Miami, FL, pg. 121
Trueland, Meaghan, Acct Coord -- SDI MARKETING, Toronto, Canada, pg. 1028
Trujillo-Kalianis, Shelly, Media Buyer-Brdcst -- BAKER STREET ADVERTISING, San Francisco, CA, pg. 88
Trump, Joe Van, Dir-Creative -- Leo Burnett Sydney, Sydney, Australia, pg. 647
Truong, Duyen, VP-PR -- SAGE COMMUNICATIONS, McLean, VA, pg. 1013
Trybus, Mary, Dir-Creative -- Jack Morton Worldwide, Detroit, MI, pg. 583
Tsai, Wansan, Acct Dir -- Weber Shandwick, Shanghai, China, pg. 1682
Tsami, Anastasia, Dir-Creative & Copywriter -- Telia & Pavla BBDO, Nicosia, Cyprus, pg. 105
Tsandes, Ted, Exec VP & Exec Dir-Creative-West Reg -- McCann Erickson/Salt Lake City, Salt Lake City, UT, pg. 715
Tsang, Charlie, Acct Exec -- Ogilvy & Mather Advertising, Central, China (Hong Kong), pg. 842
Tsang, Kato, Assoc Dir-Creative -- H&C, Leo Burnett, Beirut, Lebanon, pg. 643
Tsao, Brian, Acct Dir -- PMK*BNC, Los Angeles, CA, pg. 557
Tseng, Richard, Assoc Dir-Creative -- Rapp Los Angeles, El Segundo, CA, pg. 952
Tso, Chuck, Dir-Creative & Art -- McCann Erickson/New York, New York, NY, pg. 714
Tsui, Samantha, Acct Exec -- BECKER COMMUNICATIONS, Honolulu, HI, pg. 1450
Tsujioka, Terry, Acct Exec & Copywriter -- RIPLEY-WOODBURY MARKETING COMMUNICATIONS, INC., Huntington Beach, CA, pg. 981
Tubekis, Carolyn, Art Dir -- HAVAS WORLDWIDE CHICAGO, Chicago, IL, pg. 502
Tubekis, Ted, Acct Exec -- RhythmOne, New York, NY, pg. 977
Tubtimtong, Santi, Creative Dir -- Leo Burnett, Bangkok, Thailand, pg. 651
Tucay, Christi, Acct Dir -- TDA_BOULDER, Boulder, CO, pg. 1133
Tucci, Mark, Owner & Dir-Creative -- TUCCI CREATIVE INC, Tucson, AZ, pg. 1161
Tucciarone, Kristen, Media Planner -- US International Media, New York, NY, pg. 1395
Tuck, Megan, Acct Supvr -- BlissPR, Chicago, IL, pg. 139
Tucker, Angus, Partner & Co-Exec Creative Dir -- JOHN ST., Toronto, Canada, pg. 593
Tucker, Ashley, Acct Supvr -- INTEGRATE, Houston, TX, pg. 1551
Tucker, James, Dir-Creative -- SAATCHI & SAATCHI, New York, NY, pg. 1000
Tucker, Jennifer, Acct Coord -- BULLDOG CREATIVE SERVICES, Huntington, WV, pg. 174
Tucker, Lisa, Acct Dir -- Wirestone, Fort Collins, CO, pg. 1211
Tucker, Michael, Dir-Creative -- DOREMUS, New York, NY, pg. 324
Tucker, Michelle, Grp Dir-Creative-Ragu -- HAVAS WORLDWIDE CHICAGO, Chicago, IL, pg. 502
Tucker, Phil, Acct Dir -- PEOPLE MAKING GOOD, Burlington, VT, pg. 1614
Tucker, Sean, Assoc Dir-Creative -- STATION FOUR, Jacksonville, FL, pg. 1081
Tudico, Rico, Acct Supvr -- DDB Canada, Toronto, Canada, pg. 274
Tudor, Claire, Acct Supvr -- GSD&M, Austin, TX, pg. 464
Tuisk, Erkki, Acct Dir -- DDB Estonia Ltd., Tallinn, Estonia, pg. 280
Tujunen, Vesa, Exec Dir-Creative -- TBWA PHS, Helsinki, Finland, pg. 1118
Tun, Lina, Dir-Creative -- Hakuhodo Hong Kong Ltd., North Point, China (Hong Kong), pg. 474
Tunick, Amy, Pres-GREY Activation & PR -- GREY GROUP, New York, NY, pg. 445
Tunno, Stefano, Art Dir -- McCann Erickson Italiana S.p.A., Rome, Italy, pg. 732
Tunno, Stefano, Art Dir -- McCann Erickson Italiana S.p.A., Rome, Italy, pg. 723
Tupper, Dave, Dir-Creative -- HUGE, Brooklyn, NY, pg. 526
Turcios, Ricardo, Exec Dir-Creative -- Havas Worldwide Bangkok, Bangkok, Thailand, pg. 501
Turgeon, Kim, Mgr-Production & Acct Coord -- MAIER ADVERTISING, INC., Farmington, CT, pg. 687
Turgeon, Lauren, Mgr-Events & Sponsorship & Acct Coord -- MOMENTUM MARKETING, Charleston, SC, pg. 770
Turgeon, Marie-Claude, Acct Dir -- Havas Life, Toronto, Canada, pg. 487
Turier, David, Acct Dir -- Fleishman-Hillard, Brussels, Belgium, pg. 1520
Turk, Aaron, Head-Digital Creative -- Colenso BBDO, Auckland, New Zealand, pg. 116
Turk, Barnett, Dir-Creative -- PURDIE ROGERS, INC., Seattle, WA, pg. 938
Turkin, Evgeny, Dir-Creative & Art -- MEDIA STORM LLC, South Norwalk, CT, pg. 1366
Turlej, Melissa, Acct Dir-Digital -- Edelman, Toronto, Canada, pg. 1501
Turley, Janet, Acct Supvr-PR -- Grey Healthcare Group, Kansas City, MO, pg. 423
Turner, Chris, Sr Partner, Head-Creative Integration & Grp Dir-Creative -- Ogilvy & Mather, Chicago, IL, pg. 828
Turner, Christian, Acct Supvr -- WYSE, Cleveland, OH, pg. 1235
Turner, Clay, Mng Dir, Exec VP & Dir-Creative -- Ackerman McQueen, Inc., Colorado Springs, CO, pg. 20
Turner, Courtney, Acct Coord -- ADVERTISING SAVANTS, INC., Saint Louis, MO, pg. 34
Turner, Crandall, Acct Exec -- LUQUIRE GEORGE ANDREWS, INC., Charlotte, NC, pg. 674
Turner, Gareth, Acct Exec-Energy Practice -- madano partnership, London, United Kingdom, pg. 1601
Turner, Jeanne, Mgr-PR -- QUIET LIGHT COMMUNICATIONS, Rockford, IL, pg. 943
Turner, Libby, Acct Dir -- ROOM 214, INC., Boulder, CO, pg. 991
Turner, Nic, Acct Exec -- Saatchi & Saatchi, Auckland, New Zealand, pg. 1011
Turner, Nick, Exec Dir-Creative-Intl -- Razorfish UK, London, United Kingdom, pg. 1311
Turner, Ron, Dir-Creative -- SOUTH COMPANY, Aiken, SC, pg. 1060
Turner, Russ, Sr VP, Dir-Creative & Acct Supvr -- FALL ADVERTISING, Santee, CA, pg. 366
Turner, Sam, Dir-Creative -- MILLER-REID, INC., Chattanooga, TN, pg. 758
Turner, Sarah, Dir-Art & Creative -- E.W. BULLOCK ASSOCIATES, Pensacola, FL, pg. 361
Turner, Stuart, Dir-Creative -- Havas Worldwide Australia, North Sydney, Australia, pg. 499
Turner, Stuart, Creative Dir -- Havas Worldwide Sydney, Sydney, Australia, pg. 500
Turner, Todd, Dir-Corp Creative -- Adams Outdoor Advertising, Ladson, SC, pg. 25
Turner, Whitney K., Acct Exec -- PRECISE COMMUNICATIONS, Atlanta, GA, pg. 1626
Turon, Marek, Mgr-PR -- Ogilvy & Mather, Brno, Czech Republic, pg. 830
Turpin-Lawlor, Katie, Dir-New Bus Dev -- FALLON MEDICA LLC, Tinton Falls, NJ, pg. 366
Turquet, Etienne, Exec Dir-Creative -- BETC Life, Paris, France, pg. 492
Turrini, Geneva, Acct Coord -- SPAWN IDEAS, Anchorage, AK, pg. 1063
Turski, Ireneusz, Acct Dir -- Grey Group Poland, Warsaw, Poland, pg. 451
Turski, Ireneusz, Acct Dir -- Grey Worldwide Warsaw, Warsaw, Poland, pg. 1482
Tursky, Paul, Acct Dir -- ABELSON-TAYLOR, INC., Chicago, IL, pg. 16
Turton, Penny, Media Planner -- MINTZ & HOKE COMMUNICATIONS GROUP, Avon, CT, pg. 763
Tutssel, Mark, Chief Creative Officer-Worldwide -- Leo Burnett Tailor Made, New York, NY, pg. 639
Tutssel, Mark, Chief Creative Officer-Global -- LEO BURNETT WORLDWIDE, INC., Chicago, IL, pg. 637
Tutunnik, Tatiana, Dir-Creative -- Young & Rubicam FMS, Moscow, Russia, pg. 1248
Tuzel, Joanna, Media Planner -- Merkley + Partners/Healthworks, New York, NY, pg. 750
Tviet, Mary, Dir-Interactive Creative -- PRICE & PARTNERS, INC., Atlanta, GA, pg. 909
Tvrdik, Jonathan, VP & Exec Dir-Creative -- PHENOMBLUE, Omaha, NE, pg. 888
Twigg, Jeremy, Acct Dir -- Fleishman-Hillard, Vancouver, Canada, pg. 1519
Twining, Stephanie, Acct Supvr -- Fleishman-Hillard Inc., San Diego, CA, pg. 1516
Tyler, Laura, Acct Exec -- LHWH ADVERTISING & PUBLIC RELATIONS, Myrtle Beach, SC, pg. 656
Tyrell, Brandon, Acct Supvr -- KRUSKOPF & COMPANY, INC., Minneapolis, MN, pg. 619
Tyson, Joy, Acct Mgr-PR & Social Media -- THE CALIBER GROUP, Tucson, AZ, pg. 185
Tzempelikos, Panagiotis, Dir-Creative -- Lowe Athens, Athens, Greece, pg. 793
Tzinares, Anna, Acct Exec -- Zeno Group, Chicago, IL, pg. 1691

U

Ucedo, Favio, Chief Creative Officer -- WING, New York, NY, pg. 1209
Uden, Becky, Acct Dir -- SAY Media, Inc., San Francisco, CA, pg. 1222
Ueland, Eivind, Sr VP & Dir-Creative -- ALLEN & GERRITSEN, Boston, MA, pg. 46
Uemura, Keiichi, Dir-Creative -- I&S BBDO Inc., Tokyo, Japan, pg. 115
Uffelman, Caroline, Acct Exec -- DDB New York, New York, NY, pg. 275
Ullah, Neiki, Acct Supvr-Strategy -- VaynerMedia, Sherman Oaks, CA, pg. 1319
Ullakko, Jari, Creative Dir -- SEK & Grey, Helsinki, Finland, pg. 449
Ullman, Lynn, VP & Creative Dir -- UPBRAND COLLABORATIVE, Saint Louis, MO, pg. 1168
Ulloa, Cristian, Exec Creative Dir -- DDB Chile, Santiago, Chile, pg. 279
Ulloa, Melissa, Assoc Dir-Creative -- AREA 23, New York, NY, pg. 68
Ulmer, Hannah, Media Buyer -- VEST ADVERTISING, Louisville, KY, pg. 1175
Umbach, Mark, Acct Dir -- MWWPR, East Rutherford, NJ, pg. 1598

V

W

Walters, Sarah Ann, Acct Dir -- THE KARMA AGENCY, Philadelphia, PA, pg. 1558
Walters, Victoria, Media Planner -- BLUE CHIP MARKETING WORLDWIDE, Northbrook, IL, pg. 140
Walthall, Corey, Coord-PR -- CLYNE MEDIA INC., Nashville, TN, pg. 217
Walton, Jordan, Acct Exec -- M5 NEW HAMPSHIRE, Manchester, NH, pg. 680
Walton, Matt, Dir-Creative -- ANOMALY, New York, NY, pg. 60
Walton, Valencia, Acct Exec -- Signal Outdoor Advertising, Stamford, CT, pg. 1043
Walton-Sealy, Natalie, Acct Exec -- GHA/DDB, Saint Michael, Barbados, pg. 278
Walz, Stephen, Media Planner -- EBAY ENTERPRISE, King of Prussia, PA, pg. 1292
Wampold, Morgan, Acct Exec -- THE EHRHARDT GROUP, New Orleans, LA, pg. 1508
Wan, Wallace, Assoc Dir-Creative -- DDB Worldwide Ltd., Hong Kong, China (Hong Kong), pg. 283
Wanamaker, Beth, Acct Exec -- NEVINS & ASSOCIATES, Towson, MD, pg. 1602
Wanczyk, Steve, Acct Supvr -- BRAITHWAITE COMMUNICATIONS, Philadelphia, PA, pg. 1459
Wang, Daqing, Exec Partner-Creative -- OgilvyOne, Shanghai, China, pg. 841
Wang, Ivan, Dir-Creative -- DDB Guoan Communications Beijing Co., Ltd., Beijing, China, pg. 279
Wang, Jane, Acct Dir -- THE HOFFMAN AGENCY, San Jose, CA, pg. 1545
Wang, Jonathan, CEO & Dir-Creative -- EAT SLEEP WORK, El Segundo, CA, pg. 336
Wang, Josephine, Acct Dir -- Fleishman-Hillard Link Ltd., Beijing, China, pg. 1521
Wang, Linna, Acct Exec -- Fleishman-Hillard Link Ltd., Beijing, China, pg. 1521
Wang, Michelle, Mgr-Creative Svcs -- HAVAS HEALTH, New York, NY, pg. 486
Wang, Stephanie, Acct Exec -- M&C Saatchi, Shanghai, China, pg. 678
Wang, Tuan Pu, Exec Dir-Creative -- ADMERASIA, INC., New York, NY, pg. 30
Wang, Xia, Art Dir -- Publicis Shanghai, Shanghai, China, pg. 931
Wang, Xian, Acct Coord -- Text 100 Shanghai, Shanghai, China, pg. 1662
Wang, Yali, Dir-Creative -- ETHNICOM GROUP, Bala Cynwyd, PA, pg. 357
Wang, Yiyang, Acct Dir -- Ruder Finn Asia Limited, Beijing, China, pg. 1643
Wangbickler, Mike, Acct Exec -- BALZAC COMMUNICATIONS, Napa, CA, pg. 89
Waradkar, Nikhil, Team Head-Creative-Art -- McCann Erickson India, Mumbai, India, pg. 721
Waraksa, Rosemarie, Acct Supvr -- Laughlin/Constable New York, New York, NY, pg. 630
Ward, Heather, Acct Exec -- HILL HOLLIDAY, Boston, MA, pg. 514
Ward, Josh, Mgr-Creative & Acct Exec -- BLUE HERON COMMUNICATIONS, Norman, OK, pg. 1456
Ward, Lauren, Acct Supvr -- MCNEELY, PIGOTT & FOX, Nashville, TN, pg. 1587
Ward, Lori, Acct Exec -- MARCHEX, INC., Seattle, WA, pg. 692
Ward, Matt, Creative Dir -- BARNHART, Denver, CO, pg. 93
Ward, Michael, VP & Assoc Dir-Creative-Copy -- FLASHPOINT MEDICA, LLC, New York, NY, pg. 392
Ward, Michael, Partner & Dir-Creative -- ROCKET SCIENCE, Larkspur, CA, pg. 989
Ward, Mike, VP, Dir-Creative & Writer -- LEO BURNETT WORLDWIDE, INC., Chicago, IL, pg. 637
Ward, Sarah, Acct Exec -- Weber Shandwick, Edinburgh, United Kingdom, pg. 1681
Ward, Stephanie, Supvr-Brdcst -- Moroch, Houston, TX, pg. 776
Warden, Ben, VP & Acct Dir -- GREY SAN FRANCISCO, San Francisco, CA, pg. 458
Warden, Lori, Acct Exec-PR -- PARTNERS CREATIVE, Missoula, MT, pg. 875
Wardlaw, Jane, Grp Acct Dir -- FCB Auckland, Auckland, New Zealand, pg. 381
Wardwell, Joani, Dir-PR-Global -- WIEDEN + KENNEDY, INC., Portland, OR, pg. 1202
Wark, Ed, Principal-PR -- COLOUR, Halifax, Canada, pg. 223
Warnecke, Steve, Dir-New Bus Dev -- NEWTON MEDIA, Chesapeake, VA, pg. 1376
Warner, Alexandra, Acct Exec -- CAMBRIDGE BIOMARKETING, Cambridge, MA, pg. 186
Warner, Carl, Grp Head-Creative -- THE RICHARDS GROUP, INC., Dallas, TX, pg. 978
Warner, Kallana, VP & Acct Dir -- HAVAS MEDIA, New York, NY, pg. 1338
Warner, Paul, Exec Dir-Creative -- MetropolitanRepublic, Johannesburg, South Africa, pg. 1220
Warren, Katey, Specialist-PR & Social Media -- LITTLE DOG AGENCY INC., Mount Pleasant, SC, pg. 662
Warshaw, Alyson, Chief Creative Officer -- LAUNDRY SERVICE, New York, NY, pg. 631
Warthen, Brad, Dir-Comm & PR -- ADCO, Columbia, SC, pg. 26
Washburn, Tim, Mng Partner & Exec Dir-Creative -- NOMADIC AGENCY, Scottsdale, AZ, pg. 813
Washington, Larry, Exec Dir-Creative -- LAWLER BALLARD VAN DURAND, Birmingham, AL, pg. 632
Washington, Lourdes, Acct Dir -- ACENTO ADVERTISING, INC., Santa Monica, CA, pg. 19
Washington, Shannon, Sr Dir-Creative -- INVNT, New York, NY, pg. 559
Wasil, Alex, Acct Mgr & Media Planner -- The Boner Group, Inc./Ann K. Savage, Leesburg, VA, pg. 129
Wasilewski, Mike, Founder, Partner & Dir-Creative -- FRANK COLLECTIVE, Brooklyn, NY, pg. 401
Wasko, Eva Marie, Acct Exec -- Cohn & Wolfe, Los Angeles, CA, pg. 1482
Wasserman, Berk, VP & Creative Dir -- BARKLEY, Kansas City, MO, pg. 92
Wasserman, Berk, VP & Dir-Creative -- BARKLEY PUBLIC RELATIONS, Kansas City, MO, pg. 1449
Wasserman, Dave, Creative Dir -- J. WALTER THOMPSON, New York, NY, pg. 565
Wasserman, Scott, Acct Exec -- THE MARCUS GROUP, INC., Little Falls, NJ, pg. 693
Wassom, Jeremiah, Assoc Creative Dir -- Deutsch LA, Los Angeles, CA, pg. 302
Wasson, Dana, Acct Exec -- THE BARBAULD AGENCY, Valparaiso, IN, pg. 91
Waszkelewicz, Brett, Partner & Creative Dir -- WONDERSAUCE LLC, New York, NY, pg. 1320
Waterman, Seth, Acct Supvr -- DDB Canada, Edmonton, Canada, pg. 273
Waters, Deanna, Acct Dir -- EXCLAIM LLC, Seattle, WA, pg. 361
Waters, Laura, Acct Supvr -- TWO BY FOUR, Chicago, IL, pg. 1164
Waters, Maggie, Sr Mgr-PR -- HALEY MIRANDA GROUP, Culver City, CA, pg. 1415
Waters, Terri, Mgr-PR -- STUDIO D MARKETING COMMUNICATIONS, Saint Louis, MO, pg. 1094
Watford, Margaret, Acct Coord -- SULLIVAN BRANDING, Memphis, TN, pg. 1097
Watkins, Gabe, VP-Creative, Brand & Campaigns -- RED INTERACTIVE AGENCY, Santa Monica, CA, pg. 1311
Watkins, Zach, Creative Dir & Copywriter -- DLKW Lowe, London, United Kingdom, pg. 789
Watkinson, Brian, Acct Exec -- CBC ADVERTISING, Saco, ME, pg. 199
Watson, Andrew, VP & Dir-Creative -- THE MARTIN AGENCY, Richmond, VA, pg. 702
Watson, Betsy, Dir-PR & Copywriter-Mktg -- I2 MARKETING INC, Asheville, NC, pg. 531
Watson, Cat, Acct Exec -- CURIOSITY ADVERTISING, Cincinnati, OH, pg. 260
Watson, Darren, Exec Creative Dir -- Fitch Design Pvt. Ltd., Singapore, Singapore, pg. 391
Watson, Dave, Dir-Creative Design-North America -- TAXI Calgary, Calgary, Canada, pg. 1112
Watson, David, Dir-Creative -- THE MERIDIAN GROUP, Virginia Beach, VA, pg. 748
Watson, Devon, Acct Dir-Digital Adv -- TMP WORLDWIDE ADVERTISING & COMMUNICATIONS, LLC, New York, NY, pg. 1147
Watson, Emma, Acct Exec -- M&C Saatchi Sport & Entertainment, London, United Kingdom, pg. 677
Watson, Heather, Acct Dir-Yellow Shoes Creative Grp -- DISNEY'S YELLOW SHOES CREATIVE GROUP/WALT DISNEY PARKS & RESORTS, Lake Buena Vista, FL, pg. 1266
Watson, Kerry Anne, Pres-PR -- THE ZIMMERMAN AGENCY LLC, Tallahassee, FL, pg. 1257
Watson, Laurie, Pres & Dir-Creative -- MERLIN EDGE INC., Calgary, Canada, pg. 750
Watson, Mark, Dir-Creative -- WONGDOODY, Seattle, WA, pg. 1213
Watson, Mike, Art Dir -- Ogilvy & Mather, Ltd., London, United Kingdom, pg. 836
Watson, Mike, Dir-Creative -- Possible London, London, United Kingdom, pg. 1307
Watson, Ollie, Art Dir & Creative Dir -- WIEDEN + KENNEDY, INC., Portland, OR, pg. 1202
Watson, Phil, Dir-Creative-Digital, Direct & Brand Activation -- 303LOWE, Sydney, Australia, pg. 789
Watson, Ralph, Chief Creative Officer-Boulder & VP -- CP+B Boulder, Boulder, CO, pg. 240
Watson, Scott, Chief Creative Officer & Exec VP -- OGILVY COMMONHEALTH WORLDWIDE, Parsippany, NJ, pg. 851
Watt, Amy, Dir-Creative & Art -- WARNER COMMUNICATIONS, Manchester, MA, pg. 1672
Watters, Johnny, Dir-Creative -- Ogilvy & Mather EMEA, London, United Kingdom, pg. 836
Watters, Kirk, Acct Exec -- Signal Outdoor Advertising, Stamford, CT, pg. 1043
Watts, Brent, Exec Dir-Creative -- STRUCK, Salt Lake City, UT, pg. 1093
Watts, Dan, Dir-Creative -- Fallon London, London, United Kingdom, pg. 366
Watts, Emily, Acct Supvr -- HORNERCOM, Harleysville, PA, pg. 524
Watts, Jillian, Sr Acct Exec-Hospitality PR -- 451 MARKETING, Boston, MA, pg. 1436
Wax, Judi, Exec VP & Dir-PR -- LUQUIRE GEORGE ANDREWS, INC., Charlotte, NC, pg. 674
Waymire, Alex, Media Buyer -- CAYENNE CREATIVE, Birmingham, AL, pg. 199
Wayner, Pete, Acct Exec-PR -- DIXON SCHWABL ADVERTISING, Victor, NY, pg. 317
Weadick, Skye, Acct Dir -- ATOMIC DIRECT, LTD, Portland, OR, pg. 78
Weaver, Bonnie, VP & Acct Supvr -- AUGUST, LANG & HUSAK, INC., Bethesda, MD, pg. 79
Weaver, David, Exec VP-Creative & Strategy -- BARKLEY, Kansas City, MO, pg. 92
Weaver, Don, Exec Dir-Creative -- PLAN B (THE AGENCY ALTERNATIVE), Chicago, IL, pg. 896
Weaver, Kareth, Assoc Dir-Lifestyle & Mktg PR -- Hill+Knowlton Strategies B.V., Amsterdam, Netherlands, pg. 1543
Weaver, Lois, Sr VP & Dir-Creative -- MICHAEL A. BURNS & ASSOCIATES, INC., Dallas, TX, pg. 1590
Weaver, Michael, Dir-Creative -- GROUP46, Bluffton, SC, pg. 462
Weaver, Nathan, Media Buyer -- Zenith Media, Denver, CO, pg. 1397
Weaver, Sarah, Acct Coord -- NVS DESIGN INC., Indianapolis, IN, pg. 819
Weaver, Whitney, Acct Coord -- HOCKING MEDIA GROUP INC., Troy, MI, pg. 1341
Webb, Ashley, Acct Exec -- REVIVEHEALTH, Nashville, TN, pg. 975
Webb, Elizabeth, Media Buyer -- Totalcom, Inc., Huntsville, AL, pg. 1151
Webb, Eric, Dir-Creative -- DRINKCAFFEINE, Madison, CT, pg. 1291
Webb, Frances, Dir-Creative -- 360I, New York, NY, pg. 6
Webb, Jamie, Acct Dir -- Saatchi Masius, London, United Kingdom, pg. 1007
Webb, Mary, Exec VP & Exec Dir-Creative -- Havas Edge Portland, Portland, OR, pg. 488
Webb, Shane, Dir-Creative -- THE MERIDIAN GROUP, Virginia Beach, VA, pg. 748
Webb, Simon, Exec Dir-Creative-Global -- HeathWallace Ltd, Reading, United Kingdom, pg. 1227
Webber, Heleena, Acct Dir & Dir-Content -- ZGM, Calgary, Canada, pg. 1256
Webber, Shannon, Acct Dir -- ATLAS MARKETING, Sewickley, PA, pg. 78
Webdell, Michael, Dir-Creative -- AMERICAN MASS MEDIA, Chicago, IL, pg. 54
Weber, Dan, Dir-Creative -- Team Detroit, Dearborn, MI, pg. 1222
Weber, Dave, Dir-Creative -- RIEGNER & ASSOCIATES, INC., Southfield, MI, pg. 980
Weber, Donna, Media Buyer -- THE GRAHAM GROUP, Lafayette, LA, pg. 438
Weber, Emily, Acct Exec -- BLUE CHIP MARKETING WORLDWIDE, Northbrook, IL, pg. 140
Weber, Emily, Acct Dir -- WALLWORK CURRY MCKENNA, Charlestown, MA, pg. 1188
Weber, Germano, Art Dir -- Publicis Brasil Communicao, Sao Paulo, Brazil, pg. 929
Weber, Grant, Assoc Dir-Creative -- Ogilvy & Mather, Chicago, IL, pg. 828
Weber, Jeffrey, Art Dir -- TEAM EPIPHANY, New York, NY, pg.

Personnel Index

Wexler, Mitchell, Acct Dir -- Story Worldwide, Seattle, WA, pg. 1089
Weymouth, Sydney, Acct Exec -- JH COMMUNICATIONS LLC, Providence, RI, pg. 591
Whaites, Chris, Dir-Creative -- HEARTBEAT DIGITAL, New York, NY, pg. 506
Whalen, Maggie, VP & Exec Dir-Creative -- SIMANTEL, Saint Louis, MO, pg. 1045
Wharton, Ian, Grp Creative Dir -- AKQA, Inc., London, United Kingdom, pg. 1281
Wharton, Paul, VP-Creative -- LARSEN, Minneapolis, MN, pg. 627
Whatley, Anne Marie, Acct Exec -- Luckie & Company, Duluth, GA, pg. 673
Wheat, Lee, Pres & Exec Dir-Creative -- WHOLE WHEAT CREATIVE, Houston, TX, pg. 1201
Wheat, Russ, Acct Supvr -- BHW1 ADVERTISING, Spokane, WA, pg. 129
Wheeler, Ben, Media Buyer -- HORIZON MEDIA, INC., New York, NY, pg. 1341
Wheeler, Bria, Acct Exec -- BBR CREATIVE, Lafayette, LA, pg. 118
Wheeler, Holly, Acct Dir -- TOTH BRAND IMAGING, Cambridge, MA, pg. 1152
Wheeler, Kate, Acct Dir-Johnson & Johnson -- J. WALTER THOMPSON, New York, NY, pg. 565
Whelan, Jim, Acct Dir -- Clear Ideas Ltd., Richmond, United Kingdom, pg. 676
Whelehan, Gina, Media Buyer-Local Brdcst & Specialist-Market -- The Martin Agency Media, Richmond, VA, pg. 703
Whidden, Hailey, Acct Coord -- SOCIAL DISTILLERY, Austin, TX, pg. 1056
Whipkey, Sarah, Creative Dir & Copywriter -- JUNE ADVERTISING, Omaha, NE, pg. 600
Whipple, Bethany, Acct Dir -- Havas Media, Chicago, IL, pg. 1340
Whipple, Bethany, Acct Dir -- HAVAS WORLDWIDE CHICAGO, Chicago, IL, pg. 502
Whitcomb, Elizabeth, Acct Exec -- Grey Healthcare Group, Kansas City, MO, pg. 423
White, Ashley, Acct Dir -- UPROAR PR, Orlando, FL, pg. 1668
White, Brad, Mng Dir & Chief Creative Officer -- LUCKIE & COMPANY, Birmingham, AL, pg. 672
White, Brad, Mng Dir & Chief Creative Officer -- Luckie & Co., San Antonio, TX, pg. 673
White, Brad, Chief Creative Officer -- Luckie & Company, Duluth, GA, pg. 673
White, Brian, Dir-Creative -- TRILION STUDIOS, Lawrence, KS, pg. 1276
White, Charlotte, Acct Exec -- OMD New Zealand/Auckland, Auckland, New Zealand, pg. 1381
White, Cindy, CEO & Dir-Creative -- PARKERWHITE INC., Cardiff By The Sea, CA, pg. 875
White, Clint, Pres & Creative Dir -- WIT MEDIA, New York, NY, pg. 1211
White, Daniel, Acct Exec -- GETO & DEMILLY, INC., New York, NY, pg. 1527
White, Gemma, Acct Exec -- Johnson King Public Relations, London, United Kingdom, pg. 387
White, Hannah, Acct Exec -- ELIZABETH CHRISTIAN PUBLIC RELATIONS, Austin, TX, pg. 1509
White, Jack K., Mgr-Brdcst Production -- OTEY WHITE & ASSOCIATES, Baton Rouge, LA, pg. 865
White, Jen, Exec Creative Dir -- GLYNNDEVINS ADVERTISING & MARKETING, Overland Park, KS, pg. 430
White, Karen L., Dir-Creative -- TIPTON COMMUNICATIONS, Newark, DE, pg. 1145
White, Kristine, Acct Exec -- PERFORMANCE MARKETING, West Des Moines, IA, pg. 884
White, Lynda, Acct Exec -- BLOHM CREATIVE PARTNERS, East Lansing, MI, pg. 139
White, Mary, Media Buyer -- MARCUS THOMAS LLC, Cleveland, OH, pg. 693
White, Maura, Dir-PR -- PMBC GROUP, Beverly Hills, CA, pg. 1618
White, Melissa, Acct Supvr -- NEWMARK ADVERTISING, INC., Encino, CA, pg. 808
White, Robert, VP & Dir-Creative -- OPFER COMMUNICATIONS INC., Springfield, MO, pg. 863
White, Sam, Acct Supvr -- GREY GROUP, New York, NY, pg. 445
White, Shannon, Acct Exec -- BOLT PUBLIC RELATIONS, Irvine, CA, pg. 1458
White, Spencer, Grp Head-Creative -- LIDA, London, United Kingdom, pg. 676
Whitehouse, Geoff, Head-PR & Analyst Rels -- Sapient Limited, London, United Kingdom, pg. 1019
Whiteley, Kate Turner, VP-PR -- KIRVIN DOAK COMMUNICATIONS, Las Vegas, NV, pg. 1567
Whiteside, Tony, Dir-Creative -- OGILVY & MATHER, New York, NY, pg. 826
Whiting, Josh, Creative Dir -- NEWFIRE MEDIA, North Augusta, SC, pg. 807
Whitlock, Amanda, Acct Exec -- CLEARPOINT AGENCY, Encinitas, CA, pg. 1479
Whitney, Scott, Principal & Creative Dir -- HEADFIRST CREATIVE, Chapel Hill, NC, pg. 505
Whittier, Steve, Dir-Digital & Integrated Creative -- SELECTNY, New York, NY, pg. 1030
Whittle, Jennifer, Acct Supvr -- THE LAVIDGE COMPANY, Phoenix, AZ, pg. 632
Whitworth, Sarah, Acct Supvr -- Greer, Margolis, Mitchell, Burns & Associates (GMMB), Washington, DC, pg. 1518
Whybin, Scott, Chm & Reg Exec Dir-Creative-Australia & New Zealand -- Whybin TBWA, Sydney, Australia, pg. 1127
Whybin, Scott, Chm & Reg Exec Dir-Creative-Australia & New Zealand -- Whybin TBWA, Melbourne, Australia, pg. 1128
Whyte, David, Media Planner -- QUARRY INTEGRATED COMMUNICATIONS, Saint Jacobs, Canada, pg. 942
Whyte, Maureen, Media Buyer -- JL MEDIA, INC., Union, NJ, pg. 1348
Wibowo, Ivan Hady, Exec Dir-Creative -- J. Walter Thompson, Jakarta, Indonesia, pg. 570
Wickham, Alyssa, Acct Coord -- HEMSWORTH COMMUNICATIONS, Davie, FL, pg. 1538
Wickman, Charley, Exec VP & Exec Dir-Creative -- Leo Burnett USA, Chicago, IL, pg. 639
Wickman, Charley, Exec VP & Exec Dir-Creative -- LEO BURNETT WORLDWIDE, INC., Chicago, IL, pg. 637
Wickman, Kelsey, Acct Exec -- WE, Bellevue, WA, pg. 1673
Wickman, Sarah, Acct Supvr -- AMP AGENCY (ALLOY MARKETING & PROMOTION), Boston, MA, pg. 1405
Wicks, David, Chief Creative Officer -- SIX POINT CREATIVE WORKS, Springfield, MA, pg. 1047
Wicks, Libby, Acct Supvr -- ANOMALY, New York, NY, pg. 60
Wicks, Simone, Mgr-Creative Svcs -- SYNDCTD, Los Angeles, CA, pg. 1105
Wickstrand, Tenaya, Acct Exec -- ZENZI COMMUNICATIONS, Solana Beach, CA, pg. 1691
Wico, Antoniette, Sr VP & Acct Dir -- Leo Burnett USA, Chicago, IL, pg. 639
Widegren, James, Co-Founder & Exec Dir-Creative -- YOUR MAJESTY, New York, NY, pg. 1252
Wider, Joe, Assoc Dir-Creative & Copywriter -- THE ALISON GROUP, Charlotte, NC, pg. 45
Widerschein, Neil, Partner & Chief Creative Officer -- SBC ADVERTISING, Columbus, OH, pg. 1023
Widjaja, Marco, Dir-Creative -- Publicis Indonesia, Jakarta, Indonesia, pg. 933
Widjaya, Olivia, Acct Dir -- R/GA, New York, NY, pg. 946
Widodo, Yuwono, Dir-Creative -- Ogilvy & Mather, Jakarta, Indonesia, pg. 845
Wiechmann, Scott, Sr Dir-Creative -- LAWRENCE & SCHILLER, INC., Sioux Falls, SD, pg. 632
Wiedemann, Alecia, Acct Supvr -- UMARKETING, New York, NY, pg. 1165
Wiederin, Alex, Dir-Creative -- BUERO NEW YORK, New York, NY, pg. 174
Wielopolski, Liam, Exec Dir-Creative -- DDB South Africa, Johannesburg, South Africa, pg. 288
Wiener, Jonathan, Dir-New Bus Dev -- ACTIVE INTERNATIONAL, Pearl River, NY, pg. 1323
Wiener, Michele, Copywriter-Digital & Creative -- Teran TBWA, Mexico, Mexico, pg. 1132
Wienke, Jennifer, Mgr-Production & Traffic -- Chernoff Newman, Mount Pleasant, SC, pg. 208
Wienke, Mike, Dir-Creative -- MOOSYLVANIA MARKETING, Saint Louis, MO, pg. 773
Wienke, Steve, Dir-Creative -- PHOENIX CREATIVE CO., Saint Louis, MO, pg. 1424
Wiens, Kari, Acct Supvr -- GYRO DENVER, Denver, CO, pg. 470
Wiesner, Nick, Dir-Creative -- AVENUE MARKETING & COMMUNICATIONS, Chicago, IL, pg. 82
Wiganowske, Doug, Assoc Dir-Creative -- CATCH NEW YORK, New York, NY, pg. 198
Wigger, Kris, Project Mgr & Acct Exec -- TWENTY FOUR SEVEN, INC., Portland, OR, pg. 1163
Wiggers, Betsy, Art Dir -- KEEGAN ASSOCIATES, Cortland, NY, pg. 605
Wight, Stephanie, Acct Exec -- GYMR PUBLIC RELATIONS, Washington, DC, pg. 1535
Wignall, Brad, VP-Creative Svcs -- CMD, Portland, OR, pg. 217
Wikoff, Greg, VP & Assoc Dir-Creative -- FCB Garfinkel, New York, NY, pg. 371
Wilbanks, Lydia Caffery, VP-Mktg & New Bus -- COOKERLY PUBLIC RELATIONS, Atlanta, GA, pg. 1486
Wilburn, Jamie, Coord-PR -- LHWH ADVERTISING & PUBLIC RELATIONS, Myrtle Beach, SC, pg. 656
Wilcox, Bart, Assoc Dir-Creative & Copywriter -- SULLIVAN HIGDON & SINK INCORPORATED, Wichita, KS, pg. 1097
Wilcox, Jack, Dir-Creative -- LEE BRANDING, Minneapolis, MN, pg. 634
Wilcox, Matt, Dir-Creative & Copywriter -- ESCAPE POD, Chicago, IL, pg. 355
Wildasin, Keith, Sr Dir-Creative Strategy -- BPG ADVERTISING, Los Angeles, CA, pg. 152
Wildasinn, Cari, Acct Supvr -- Fahlgren Mortine (Dayton), Beavercreek, OH, pg. 365
Wilde, Paul, Acct Dir -- DLKW Lowe, London, United Kingdom, pg. 789
Wilden, Carly, Media Buyer-Direct Mktg -- HORIZON MEDIA, INC., New York, NY, pg. 1341
Wildenhaus, Mark, Dir-Creative -- STUDIO CENTER, Virginia Beach, VA, pg. 1093
Wilder, Annette, Acct Dir -- HORNALL ANDERSON, Seattle, WA, pg. 523
Wilder, Brad, Co-Founder & Dir-Creative -- GLYPHIX ADVERTISING, West Hills, CA, pg. 430
Wilder, Everett, Principal & Grp Dir-Creative -- FIREHOUSE, INC., Dallas, TX, pg. 1412
Wildermuth, Joan, Exec VP & Grp Creative Dir -- JUICE PHARMA WORLDWIDE, New York, NY, pg. 599
Wilds, Nathan, Dir-Creative -- CLEARRIVER COMMUNICATIONS GROUP, Midland, MI, pg. 215
Wildsmith, Tessa, Media Buyer -- TENNESSEE PRESS SERVICE, INC, Knoxville, TN, pg. 1392
Wiles, Ford, Chief Creative Officer -- BIG COMMUNICATIONS, INC., Birmingham, AL, pg. 130
Wilesmith, Margaret, Pres & Dir-Creative -- WILESMITH ADVERTISING & DESIGN, West Palm Beach, FL, pg. 1207
Wiley, Greg, Sr VP & Dir-Creative Dev -- SWANSON RUSSELL ASSOCIATES, Lincoln, NE, pg. 1102
Wilgar, Trish, Acct Dir -- TWIN ADVERTISING, Pittsford, NY, pg. 1164
Wilhelm, Chris, VP & Creative Dir -- QUEUE CREATIVE MARKETING GROUP LLC, Chicago, IL, pg. 943
Wilkerson, Jourdan, Acct Supvr -- SQ1, Dallas, TX, pg. 1068
Wilkes, Nancy, Dir-PR -- PLATYPUS ADVERTISING + DESIGN, Pewaukee, WI, pg. 897
Wilkie, Rob, Dir-Creative -- PUSH22, Pontiac, MI, pg. 940
Wilkie, Rob, Dir-Creative -- PUSHTWENTYTWO, Pontiac, MI, pg. 940
Wilking, Joan, Dir-Creative -- DOERR ASSOCIATES, Winchester, MA, pg. 1496
Wilkins, Scott, Media Buyer -- ERWIN-PENLAND, Greenville, SC, pg. 354
Wilkinson, Dylan, Creative Dir -- CRAVE WIN MARKETING, Beaumont, TX, pg. 244
Wilkinson, Jack, Acct Dir -- FIREVINE INC., Edwardsburg, MI, pg. 388
Wilkinson, John, Acct Dir -- RUSS REID COMPANY, INC., Pasadena, CA, pg. 997
Wilkinson, Phyllis, Acct Exec -- QUINLAN MARKETING COMMUNICATIONS, Carmel, IN, pg. 944
Wilkof, Ronit, Acct Supvr -- Millward Brown, New York, NY, pg. 761
Wilks, Lauren, Acct Coord-PR -- CREATIVE CIVILIZATION AN AGUILAR/GIRARD AGENCY, San Antonio, TX, pg. 246
Willain, Anais, Acct Exec -- Edelman Brussels, Brussels, Belgium, pg. 1503
Willenberg, Rich, Dir-New Bus Dev -- Campbell Marketing & Communications, Torrance, CA, pg. 188
Willett, Danielle, VP & Acct Dir -- BBDO Atlanta, Atlanta, GA, pg. 100
Williams, Angle, Acct Dir -- JNA ADVERTISING, Overland Park, KS, pg. 592
Williams, Anne, Acct Dir -- INTREPID, Salt Lake City, UT, pg. 1552
Williams, Barb, Exec Dir-Creative -- TrackDDB, Toronto, Canada, pg. 952
Williams, Beth, Sr Media Planner -- TBC, INC./PR DIVISION, Baltimore, MD, pg. 1659
Williams, Brian, Deputy Exec Dir-Creative -- The Martin Agency, London, United Kingdom, pg. 704
Williams, Brittany, Acct Exec -- THE LAVIDGE COMPANY, Phoenix,

Personnel Index

X

Y

Personnel Index

Yoder, Melissa, Acct Supvr -- WELL DONE MARKETING, Indianapolis, IN, pg. 1196
Yohan, Tasha, Acct Exec -- GOODMAN PUBLIC RELATIONS, Fort Lauderdale, FL, pg. 1532
Yohe, Tom, Assoc Dir-Creative -- Sawmill, New York, NY, pg. 1676
Yokota, Shoji, Acct Dir -- McCann Erickson Japan Inc., Tokyo, Japan, pg. 723
Yong, Kera, Acct Exec -- BATES/LEE ADVERTISING, Costa Mesa, CA, pg. 97
Yong, May Ling, Assoc Dir-Creative -- Publicis (Malaysia) Sdn. Bhd., Petaling Jaya, Malaysia, pg. 934
Yontz, Robin, VP & Dir-Creative -- TRONE BRAND ENERGY, INC., High Point, NC, pg. 1159
Yoon, John, Acct Exec -- THE SILVER TELEGRAM, Long Beach, CA, pg. 1044
Yore, Patrick, Owner & Chief Creative Officer -- BRAINBLAZE ADVERTISING & DESIGN, Fairfax, CA, pg. 153
York, Ben, Art Dir -- IMAGEMAKERS INC., Wamego, KS, pg. 538
York, Cody, Acct Supvr -- 160OVER90, Philadelphia, PA, pg. 2
York, Kevin, Principal & Dir-Creative -- ART4ORM INC, Portland, OR, pg. 73
Yoshida, Pat, Acct Dir -- HIGH-TOUCH COMMUNICATIONS INC., Montreal, Canada, pg. 513
Yoshikawa, Kazuhi, Art Dir -- Wieden + Kennedy Japan, Tokyo, Japan, pg. 1205
Yoshishige, Takei, Creative Dir -- Saatchi & Saatchi Fallon Tokyo, Tokyo, Japan, pg. 367
Yoshishige, Takei, Creative Dir -- Saatchi & Saatchi Fallon Tokyo, Tokyo, Japan, pg. 1011
You, Ji, Acct Dir-DICK'S Sporting Goods-P&G -- ANOMALY, New York, NY, pg. 60
You, Michelle, Acct Dir -- Hill & Knowlton Hong Kong Ltd., Quarry Bay, China (Hong Kong), pg. 1544
Younes, Josephine, Dir-Art & Assoc Dir-Creative -- FP7, Dubai, United Arab Emirates, pg. 729
Young, Abby, Media Planner & Media Buyer -- Cramer-Krasselt, Milwaukee, WI, pg. 243
Young, Amber, Acct Dir -- COLLE+MCVOY, Minneapolis, MN, pg. 221
Young, Ayala, Acct Exec -- Finn Partners, Jerusalem, Israel, pg. 387
Young, Bart, CEO & Dir-Creative -- YOUNG COMPANY, Laguna Beach, CA, pg. 1252
Young, Carmin, Media Buyer -- VAN WINKLE & ASSOCIATES, Atlanta, GA, pg. 1171
Young, Dan, Assoc Creative Dir -- DDB New York, New York, NY, pg. 275
Young, Diane Galante, Acct Dir -- Sullivan Higdon & Sink Incorporated, Kansas City, MO, pg. 1098
Young, Emmakate, Acct Dir -- J. Walter Thompson U.S.A., Inc., Coral Gables, FL, pg. 581
Young, Evan, VP & Dir-Creative -- Discovery USA, Chicago, IL, pg. 926
Young, Ian, Dir-Creative& Copywriter -- CREATIVE LIFT INC., San Francisco, CA, pg. 249
Young, Jenna, Exec Dir-Creative -- WEBER SHANDWICK, New York, NY, pg. 1675
Young, Lindsey, Acct Exec -- BIZCOM ASSOCIATES, Addison, TX, pg. 133
Young, Lydia, Coord-PR -- PAGE COMMUNICATIONS, Kansas City, MO, pg. 1612
Young, Natalie, Acct Dir -- Ogilvy & Mather, Ltd., London, United Kingdom, pg. 836
Young, Rohan, Exec Creative Dir -- TBWA Raad, Dubai, United Arab Emirates, pg. 1127
Young, Sandy, Acct Supvr -- JWALCHER COMMUNICATIONS, San Diego, CA, pg. 600
Young, Scott, Exec VP & Dir-Creative -- EVANSHARDY & YOUNG, INC., Santa Barbara, CA, pg. 358
Young, Sean, Exec VP & Head-New Bus-Global -- UM NY, New York, NY, pg. 1393
Young, Tracy, Co-Founder & Acct Dir -- PYPER YOUNG, Saint Petersburg, FL, pg. 940
Youngblood, Mariah, Media Planner -- CRAMER-KRASSELT, Chicago, IL, pg. 242
Younker, Andy, Producer-Brdcst -- THE RICHARDS GROUP, INC., Dallas, TX, pg. 978
Yourkiewicz, Leon, Assoc Dir-Creative -- SBC ADVERTISING, Columbus, OH, pg. 1023
Yousif, Noor, Acct Exec -- IPG MEDIABRANDS, New York, NY, pg. 560
Yu, Arnold, Acct Exec -- Ogilvy & Mather Advertising, Central, China (Hong Kong), pg. 842
Yu, Caprice, Exec Creative Dir -- McCann Erickson/New York, New York, NY, pg. 714
Yu, Christina, Exec VP -- RED URBAN, Toronto, Canada, pg. 963
Yu, Paul, Dir-Creative -- DDB Worldwide Ltd., Hong Kong, China (Hong Kong), pg. 283
Yuchun, Kit, Exec Creative Dir -- McCann Erickson Guangming Ltd., Guangzhou, China, pg. 718
Yue, Chee Guan, Exec Dir-Creative -- Grey Beijing, Beijing, China, pg. 455
Yuki, Nobu, Principal & Exec Dir-Creative -- YS AND PARTNERS, INC., Newport Beach, CA, pg. 1252
Yuki, Yoshinabu, Pres, CEO & Dir-Creative -- YS AND PARTNERS, INC., Newport Beach, CA, pg. 1252
Yun, Sun, Dir-Interactive Creative -- GRAFIK MARKETING COMMUNICATIONS, Alexandria, VA, pg. 438
Yunov, Eugeny, Dir-Creative -- Primary Saatchi & Saatchi, Minsk, Belarus, pg. 1002
Yusay, Kyla, Acct Coord-Svcs -- EIGHT HORSES, Irvine, CA, pg. 340
Yuskoff, Claudia, Supvr-Mgmt & Social Media Creative Content -- Conill Advertising, Inc., El Segundo, CA, pg. 230
Yuskoff, Claudia, Supvr-Mgmt & Social Media Creative Content -- CONILL ADVERTISING, INC., Miami, FL, pg. 230
Yuzbasioglu, Figen, Copywriter-Creative -- C-Section, Istanbul, Turkey, pg. 1247
Yznaga, Ralph, Exec Dir-Creative -- MOSAK ADVERTISING & INSIGHTS, Austin, TX, pg. 778

Z

Zabala, Carmela, Creative Dir -- CONVERSA, Tampa, FL, pg. 1486
Zaborowski, Russ, Assoc Dir-Creative -- Success Advertising, Parsippany, NJ, pg. 1095
Zaborowski, Russ, Assoc Dir-Creative -- Success Communications Group, San Diego, CA, pg. 1095
Zaborowski, Russ, Assoc Creative Dir -- SUCCESS COMMUNICATIONS GROUP, Parsippany, NJ, pg. 1095
Zacaroli, Scott, Grp Dir-Creative -- MERKLEY+PARTNERS, New York, NY, pg. 750
Zadkovic, Ivana Balog, Acct Dir -- McCann Erickson, Zagreb, Croatia, pg. 719
Zafirova, Mina, Media Planner -- ZenithOptimedia, Sofia, Bulgaria, pg. 1398
Zagales, Fernando, Dir-Creative -- The Community, Buenos Aires, Argentina, pg. 227
Zahr, Munah, Exec Dir-Creative -- Radius Leo Burnett, Dubai, United Arab Emirates, pg. 646
Zaidi, Zehra, Exec Dir-Creative -- Ogilvy & Mather, Karachi, Pakistan, pg. 850
Zaitzev, Vlada, Acct Exec & Jr Producer -- NOLIN BBDO, Montreal, Canada, pg. 812
Zajfert, Iza, Acct Dir -- Digital One, Lodz, Poland, pg. 495
Zakhar, Adam, Acct Exec -- BILLBOARD EXPRESS, INC., Rancho Santa Margarita, CA, pg. 1326
Zakhary, Nancy, Assoc Mng Dir-PR -- BRAINERD COMMUNICATORS, INC., New York, NY, pg. 153
Zakovich, Ken, Dir-Creative -- Flint Interactive, Duluth, MN, pg. 394
Zalaznick, Jessica, Assoc Creative Dir-Copy -- MCGARRYBOWEN, New York, NY, pg. 733
Zaldivar, Claire, Dir-Brdcst -- ZUBI ADVERTISING SERVICES, INC., Coral Gables, FL, pg. 1259
Zale, Emily, Acct Supvr -- OGILVY & MATHER, New York, NY, pg. 826
Zaluski, Henry, Assoc Dir-Creative -- SCOTT THORNLEY + COMPANY, Toronto, Canada, pg. 1027
Zamansky, Natalie, Acct Supvr -- MARTIN/WILLIAMS ADVERTISING INC., Minneapolis, MN, pg. 704
Zamba, Dave, Creative Dir -- PROSEK PARTNERS, Stratford, CT, pg. 1627
Zambetti, A. J., Dir-Creative -- MASLOW LUMIA BARTORILLO ADVERTISING, Wilkes Barre, PA, pg. 707
Zamboni, Luca, Dir-Creative -- J. Walter Thompson Milan, Milan, Italy, pg. 573
Zambujo, Marina, Acct Supvr -- TBWA Lisbon, Lisbon, Portugal, pg. 1123
Zamiar, Alex, Assoc Dir-Creative -- DDB New York, New York, NY, pg. 275
Zamorano, Gabriela, Dir-PR & Event Plng -- VSBROOKS, Coral Gables, FL, pg. 1185
Zamudio, Andres, Dir-Creative -- PACO COMMUNICATIONS, INC, Chicago, IL, pg. 868
Zander, Holly, Mgr-PR & Media -- LEOPOLD KETEL & PARTNERS, Portland, OR, pg. 651
Zane, Melissa, VP & Dir-Creative Svcs -- GODFREY ADVERTISING, Lancaster, PA, pg. 432
Zanini, Sebastien, Exec Dir-Creative -- Gyro Paris, Paris, France, pg. 469
Zansky, Mandi, Assoc Dir-Creative -- Jack Morton Worldwide, New York, NY, pg. 584
Zanto, Andy, Assoc Dir-Creative -- SPAWN IDEAS, Anchorage, AK, pg. 1063
Zanvit, Margherita, Acct Dir-Digital -- M&C Saatchi Milan, Milan, Italy, pg. 676
Zapanta, Nico, Art Dir -- Leo Burnett Manila, Makati, Philippines, pg. 650
Zaparyniuk, Chelsea, Acct Exec -- LPI COMMUNICATIONS GROUP INC., Calgary, Canada, pg. 671
Zapata, Chantel, Sr Dir-Art & Dir-Creative -- FLY COMMUNICATIONS, New York, NY, pg. 394
Zapata, Paloma, Media Planner & Buyer -- BLEU MARKETING SOLUTIONS, INC., San Francisco, CA, pg. 138
Zapata, Thiara M., Dir-Studio & Creative -- Allied Advertising, Public Relations, New York, NY, pg. 48
Zappi, Elena, Media Planner -- ZenithOptimedia, Milan, Italy, pg. 1399
Zaragoza, Diego, Dir-Creative -- DPZ-Duailibi, Petit, Zaragoza, Propaganda S.A., Sao Paulo, Brazil, pg. 19
Zaragoza, Diego, Dir-Creative -- DPZ-Duailibi, Petit, Zaragoza, Propaganda S.A., Sao Paulo, Brazil, pg. 928
Zaretsky, Marni, Acct Exec -- Manning Selvage & Lee, Toronto, Canada, pg. 1594
Zarr, Gary, Co-Founder & Partner-Strategic Mktg PR Reputation & Crisis Mgmt -- PHIL & CO., New York, NY, pg. 888
Zarrillo, Vito, Grp Dir-Creative -- GYRO, New York, NY, pg. 468
Zars, Paige, Acct Exec -- JohnsonRauhoff Marketing Communications, Benton Harbor, MI, pg. 595
Zasa, Jay, Sr VP & Exec Dir-Creative-Campaigns -- R/GA, New York, NY, pg. 946
Zast, Jon, Exec Dir-Creative-New York -- J. WALTER THOMPSON, New York, NY, pg. 565
Zavala, Adriana, Acct Exec -- Leo Burnett USA, Chicago, IL, pg. 639
Zavala, Bryan, Coord-Traffic -- THE JAMES AGENCY, Scottsdale, AZ, pg. 586
Zavarce, Xiomara, Acct Exec -- MARKETLOGIC, Miami, FL, pg. 1422
Zawadowski, Cass, Dir-Creative-Global Braun Acct -- BBDO Dusseldorf, Dusseldorf, Germany, pg. 106
Zdenek, Jessica, Acct Dir -- MULLEN LOWE GROUP, Boston, MA, pg. 786
Zdobylak, Mary, Mgr-Traffic -- RED7E, Louisville, KY, pg. 964
Zefferino, Massimo, Dir-Creative-Bus Dev-Big Cheese -- ZFACTOR COMMUNICATIONS INC., Waterloo, Canada, pg. 1256
Zeigler, Susan, Sr Media Planner & Media Buyer -- PUSH, Orlando, FL, pg. 939
Zeiler, Bianca, Dir-Creative Strategy -- RONIN ADVERTISING GROUP, Coral Gables, FL, pg. 991
Zein, Ali, Reg Dir-Creative -- Impact BBDO, Beirut, Lebanon, pg. 108
Zeineddine, Jenni, Acct Exec -- MCCABE PROMOTIONAL ADVERTISING, London, Canada, pg. 1422
Zeiner, Becky, Media Buyer -- MEDIA PARTNERS, INC., Wichita, KS, pg. 743
Zeiris, Victor, Assoc Dir-Creative & Writer-Beauty Grp -- PUBLICIS USA, New York, NY, pg. 935
Zeiser, Katie, Acct Supvr -- ACCESS COMMUNICATIONS, San Francisco, CA, pg. 18
Zeitz, Allyson, Acct Exec-Programmatic Sls -- DATAXU, INC., Boston, MA, pg. 1331
Zeko, Mike, Founder, Mng Partner & Dir-Creative -- BOZEKEN, LLC, Wayne, PA, pg. 152
Zelenko, Alexander, Dir-Digital Creative -- Havas Worldwide Kiev, Kiev, Ukraine, pg. 497
Zelinsky, Glen, Media Buyer -- HR ADWORKS LTD., Winnipeg, Canada, pg. 526
Zeller, Tim, Chief Creative Officer & Mng Partner -- RECESS CREATIVE LLC, Cleveland, OH, pg. 959
Zelley, Matthew, Grp Dir-Creative -- Campbell Ewald San Antonio, San Antonio, TX, pg. 555
Zellmann, Caitlin, Sr Buyer-Brdcst -- HAWORTH MARKETING & MEDIA COMPANY, Minneapolis, MN, pg. 1340
Zellmer, Stefani, Partner & Dir-Creative -- ZELLMER MCCONNELL ADVERTISING, Austin, TX, pg. 1255
Zellner, Jeff, Dir-Creative -- MEDIALINKS ADVERTISING, Findlay, OH, pg. 744
Zello, John, Creative Dir -- MP AGENCY, LLC, Scottsdale, AZ, pg. 781

Personnel Index

Zeltser, Julia Vakser, Co-Founder & Dir-Creative -- HYPERAKT, Brooklyn, NY, pg. 530
Zeng, Qiang, Sr Dir-Creative -- Lowe Profero China, Shanghai, China, pg. 791
Zenk, Becky, Acct Dir -- SIXSPEED, Minneapolis, MN, pg. 1048
Zenobi, Peter, Sr VP & Acct Dir-Integrated -- GREY NEW YORK, New York, NY, pg. 446
Zentil, Jaimes, Creative Dir -- Cossette B2B, Toronto, Canada, pg. 238
Zepeda, Robert, Principal & Dir-Creative -- EL CREATIVE, INC., Dallas, TX, pg. 342
Zepp, Jeanne, Dir-PR -- DPR GROUP, INC., Germantown, MD, pg. 1497
Zer-Aviv, Or, Acct Supvr -- McCann Erickson, Tel Aviv, Israel, pg. 722
Zerman, Michael, Acct Supvr -- Weber Shandwick-Saint Louis, Saint Louis, MO, pg. 1678
Zernholt, Olga, Acct Exec -- NIKI JONES AGENCY, Port Jervis, NY, pg. 810
Zerouali, Akim, Art Dir -- Y&R Paris, Boulogne, France, pg. 1245
Zettel, Kelly, Grp Creative Dir & Copywriter -- LEO BURNETT COMPANY LTD., Toronto, Canada, pg. 637
Zhang, Angel, Acct Dir -- THE BROOKLYN BROTHERS, New York, NY, pg. 169
Zhang, Cathy, Acct Dir -- Hill & Knowlton Hong Kong Ltd., Quarry Bay, China (Hong Kong), pg. 1544
Zhang, Rong, VP & Acct Dir -- GREY GROUP, New York, NY, pg. 445
Zhang, Vincent, Acct Dir -- Weber Shandwick, Beijing, China, pg. 1682
Zhang, Yusong, Dir-Art & Assoc Dir-Creative -- COSSETTE INC., Quebec, Canada, pg. 237
Zhao, Devin, Sr Creative Dir -- wwwins Isobar, Shanghai, China, pg. 562
Zhao, Liang, Acct Coord -- Racepoint Global, Wanchai, China (Hong Kong), pg. 1630
Zhao, Zoe, Art Dir -- Publicis Shanghai, Shanghai, China, pg. 931
Zheng, Cindy, Media Planner-Strategy -- ZenithOptimedia, New York, NY, pg. 1398
Zheng, Li, Creative Dir -- DDB China - Shanghai, Shanghai, China, pg. 279
Zhong, Tam Jian, Grp Head-Creative -- Leo Burnett Malaysia, Kuala Lumpur, Malaysia, pg. 650
Zhou, Joe, Sr Dir-Creative -- TBWA Greater China, Beijing, China, pg. 1128
Zhou, Joe, Sr Dir-Creative -- TBWA Shanghai, Shanghai, China, pg. 1128
Zhu, Kevin, Grp Dir-Creative -- Wunderman, Guangzhou, China, pg. 1232
Zhuang, Bamboo, Dir-Creative -- Ogilvy & Mather (China) Ltd., Shanghai, China, pg. 841
Ziarko, Joey, Acct Dir & Acct Supvr -- MCGARRYBOWEN, New York, NY, pg. 733
Ziems, Melanie, Acct Exec-PR -- DESIGN AT WORK, Houston, TX, pg. 300
Zientowski, Karla, Acct Supvr -- Ogilvy & Mather, Culver City, CA, pg. 828
Zier, Kevin, VP, Head-Creative Integration, Dir-Creative & Copywriter -- LEO BURNETT WORLDWIDE, INC., Chicago, IL, pg. 637
Zierenberg, Jennifer, Assoc Dir-Creative -- DE LA CRUZ & ASSOCIATES, Guaynabo, PR, pg. 291
Zierler, Keri, Assoc Creative Dir -- DIGITAL KITCHEN, Seattle, WA, pg. 308
Zigarelli, Merrilee, Dir-New Bus Dev -- CUMMINS, MACFAIL & NUTRY, INC., Somerville, NJ, pg. 260
Zilincar, Jenna, Owner & Creative Dir -- M STUDIO, Asbury Park, NY, pg. 680
Zilioli, Marco, Art Dir -- MCCANN WORLDGROUP S.R.L, Milan, Italy, pg. 732
Zillo, Ashley, Acct Supvr -- Moroch, Albuquerque, NM, pg. 775
Zillo, Ashley, Acct Supvr -- Moroch, Parkersburg, WV, pg. 776
Zillo, Ashley, Acct Supvr -- Moroch, Raleigh, NC, pg. 775
Zimarik, Kevin, Dir-Creative -- THINK TANK PR & MARKETING, Glen Carbon, IL, pg. 1662
Zimmer, Laura, Acct Supvr -- LEO BURNETT WORLDWIDE, INC., Chicago, IL, pg. 637
Zimmerman, Andrea, Acct Dir -- LITTLE & COMPANY, Minneapolis, MN, pg. 662
Zimmerman, Debbie, Sr VP & Acct Dir -- Davis Elen Advertising, Arlington, VA, pg. 270
Zimmerman, Debbie, Sr VP & Acct Dir -- Davis Elen Advertising Inc, Tukwila, WA, pg. 271
Zimmerman, Debbie, Sr VP & Acct Dir -- DAVIS ELEN ADVERTISING, INC., Los Angeles, CA, pg. 270
Zimmerman, Debbie, Sr VP & Acct Dir -- Davis Elen Advertising, Inc., Solana Beach, CA, pg. 271
Zimney, Tony, Dir-Creative -- MUH-TAY-ZIK HOF-FER, San Francisco, CA, pg. 786
Zinny, Luis Sanchez, Dir-Creative -- Leo Burnett Inc., Sucursal Argentina, Buenos Aires, Argentina, pg. 640
Zinoviev, Sergii, Dir-Creative -- Provid BBDO, Kiev, Ukraine, pg. 112
Ziolo, Agata, Acct Dir -- TBWA Group Poland, Warsaw, Poland, pg. 1122
Zivanovic, Sacha, Acct Dir -- ANOMALY, New York, NY, pg. 60
Zivkovic, Mina, Acct Exec -- BLUE C, Costa Mesa, CA, pg. 140
Ziwei, Tan, Art Dir -- Grey Singapore, Singapore, Singapore, pg. 458
Zizila, Nicole, Dir-Creative -- Resource/Ammirati, New York, NY, pg. 970
Zizila, Steven, Dir-Creative -- Resource/Ammirati, New York, NY, pg. 970
Zobitz, Jocelyn L., Acct Supvr -- HAVIT ADVERTISING, LLC, Washington, DC, pg. 502
Zolla, Donna, Acct Dir -- SUCCESS COMMUNICATIONS GROUP, Parsippany, NJ, pg. 1095
Zonta, Marko, Principal & Dir-Creative -- ZYNC COMMUNICATIONS INC., Toronto, Canada, pg. 1260
Zorn, David, Dir-Creative -- TBWA/Media Arts Lab, Los Angeles, CA, pg. 1116
Zota, Manolo, Dir-Creative -- CommongroundMGS, Miami, FL, pg. 224
Zouag, Frederic, Art Dir -- VVL BBDO, Brussels, Belgium, pg. 105
Zub, Sandra A., Grp Dir-Creative -- CHECKMARK COMMUNICATIONS, Saint Louis, MO, pg. 1265
Zubarik, Sarah, Coord-Social Media, PR, Direct Mail & Radio Promos -- IMAGE MAKERS ADVERTISING INC, Waukesha, WI, pg. 538
Zuber, Marina, Acct Dir -- DDB New York, New York, NY, pg. 275
Zubieta, Sabrina, Media Buyer -- Horizon Media, Inc., Los Angeles, CA, pg. 1342
Zucker, Nina, Dir-PR -- K2 COMMUNICATIONS, Doylestown, PA, pg. 601
Zuckerkorn, Beth, VP-Creative Svcs -- GOODMAN PUBLIC RELATIONS, Fort Lauderdale, FL, pg. 1532
Zuckerman, Karen, Founder, Pres & Chief Creative Officer -- HIRSHORN ZUCKERMAN DESIGN GROUP, Rockville, MD, pg. 516
Zuehlke, Lara, Acct Supvr -- Pierpont Communications, Inc., Austin, TX, pg. 1616
Zuercher, Greg, Acct Supvr -- NEATHAWK DUBUQUE & PACKETT, Richmond, VA, pg. 803
Zuerker, Elisabeth, Acct Supvr -- THE DEALEY GROUP, Dallas, TX, pg. 291
Zuk, Hannah, Acct Exec -- GO BIG MARKETING, Orlando, FL, pg. 431
Zukowski, Stan, VP-Creative Svcs -- ALTITUDE MARKETING, Emmaus, PA, pg. 51
Zulu, Tina, Founder & Chief Creative Officer -- ZULU CREATIVE, Houston, TX, pg. 1260
Zuluaga, Alicia, Producer-Brdcst & Content -- OGILVY & MATHER, New York, NY, pg. 826
Zumba, Mary Elizabeth, Acct Supvr -- SAPIENTNITRO USA, INC., New York, NY, pg. 1019
Zumwalt, Landen, Acct Exec -- RAFFETTO HERMAN STRATEGIC COMMUNICATIONS LLC, Seattle, WA, pg. 1630
Zung, Kevin, Exec Creative Dir -- Publicis Brasil Communicao, Sao Paulo, Brazil, pg. 929
Zuniga, Enrique, Dir-Creative -- TBWA Frederick, Santiago, Chile, pg. 1131
Zuniga, German, Gen Dir-Creative -- Young & Rubicam Bogota, Bogota, Colombia, pg. 1249
Zuniga, Veronica, Acct Supvr -- Zubi Advertising Services, Inc., Brea, CA, pg. 1259
Zupancic, Tamara, Mgr-Creative Mktg -- DONLEY COMMUNICATIONS, New York, NY, pg. 1496
Zuzelski, Lauren, Acct Dir -- BROGAN & PARTNERS CONVERGENCE MARKETING, Birmingham, MI, pg. 168
Zweifel, Sarah, Acct Exec -- RED BROWN KLE, Milwaukee, WI, pg. 959
Zweigle, Casey, Acct Coord -- MANGOS, Malvern, PA, pg. 689
Zwieg, Laura, Specialist-New Bus -- Spong, Minneapolis, MN, pg. 192
Zwirlein, Rachel, Acct Supvr -- COLLE+MCVOY, Minneapolis, MN, pg. 221
Zwoyer, Ashley, Media Planner -- ZenithOptimedia, San Francisco, CA, pg. 1397
Zydzik, Michael, Dir-Creative -- FUSIONFARM, Cedar Rapids, IA, pg. 410
Zywicki, Ron, VP-Creative Svcs -- DAVID JAMES GROUP, Oakbrook Terrace, IL, pg. 268

AGENCY RESPONSIBILITIES INDEX

Account Coordinator

Abela-Froese, Jessica, Account Coordinator --BOB'S YOUR UNCLE, Toronto, Canada, pg. 145
Aguiar, Aryana, Account Coordinator --OSTER & ASSOCIATES, INC., San Diego, CA, pg. 865
Aigen, Alexander, Account Coordinator --French/West/Vaughan, Inc., New York, NY, pg. 405
Akao, Rafael Ryuiti, Account Coordinator --The Jeffrey Group Brazil, Sao Paulo, Brazil, pg. 1555
Altmann, Nick, Account Coordinator --Geary Interactive, San Diego, CA, pg. 419
Alvey, Courtney, Account Coordinator --BOHLSENPR INC., Indianapolis, IN, pg. 1457
Annie, Bria, Account Coordinator --HORNERCOM, Harleysville, PA, pg. 524
Aponte, Sami, Account Coordinator --TARA, INK., Miami Beach, FL, pg. 1109
Arnold, Megan, Account Coordinator --McCormick Company, Johnston, IA, pg. 732
Aviles, Jorge, Account Coordinator --TDW+CO, Seattle, WA, pg. 1134
Ayers, Emily, Account Coordinator --UNION, Charlotte, NC, pg. 1318
Babakitis, Lilly, Account Coordinator --LUCID AGENCY, Tempe, AZ, pg. 672
Baker, Shannon, Account Coordinator --ALLEBACH COMMUNICATIONS, Souderton, PA, pg. 46
Banegas, Esther, Account Coordinator --NEW WEST LLC, Louisville, KY, pg. 807
Banner, Samantha, Account Coordinator --S3, Boonton, NJ, pg. 999
Bargenquast, Jessica, Account Coordinator --ARROWHEAD ADVERTISING, Peoria, AZ, pg. 73
Barnett, Christel, Account Coordinator --O2IDEAS, INC., Birmingham, AL, pg. 820
Bastin, Shelby, Account Coordinator --THE CARSON GROUP, Houston, TX, pg. 193
Baumann, Katie, Account Coordinator --COPACINO + FUJIKADO, LLC, Seattle, WA, pg. 234
Beaman, Holly, Account Coordinator --ARROWHEAD ADVERTISING, Peoria, AZ, pg. 73
Beckman, Kati, Account Coordinator --3FOLD COMMUNICATIONS, Sacramento, CA, pg. 7
Bench, Becca, Account Coordinator --BLAINE WARREN ADVERTISING LLC, Las Vegas, NV, pg. 135
Benoit, Genevieve, Account Coordinator --Cohn & Wolfe, Toronto, Canada, pg. 1481
Berman, Joyce, Account Coordinator --CARYL COMMUNICATIONS, INC., Paramus, NJ, pg. 194
Berry, Vanessa, Account Coordinator --LIGHTHOUSE MARKETING, East Syracuse, NY, pg. 657
Bhakta, Shreya, Account Coordinator --RED PR, New York, NY, pg. 1633
Bingham, Austin, Account Coordinator --Sanders/Wingo, Austin, TX, pg. 1017
Biter, Jennifer, Account Coordinator --EISBRENNER PUBLIC RELATIONS, Royal Oak, MI, pg. 1509
Blackmer, Melissa, Account Coordinator --RCP MARKETING, Muskegon, MI, pg. 956
Blake, Samantha, Account Coordinator --ARCHER MALMO, Memphis, TN, pg. 67
Blome, Jennifer, Account Coordinator --ARCHER MALMO, Memphis, TN, pg. 67
Bobman, Rachael, Account Coordinator --DANA AGENCY, Miami, FL, pg. 1491
Botti, Evelyn, Account Coordinator --Muchnik, Alurralde, Jasper & Assoc./MS&L, Buenos Aires, Argentina, pg. 1597
Boulton, Katelyn, Account Coordinator --SORENSON ADVERTISING, Saint George, UT, pg. 1059
Boye, Rachel, Account Coordinator --AMNET GROUP, New York, NY, pg. 1324
Brady, Kristin, Account Coordinator --AVID MARKETING GROUP, Rocky Hill, CT, pg. 1406
Brist, Kaylee, Account Coordinator --HOT DISH ADVERTISING, Minneapolis, MN, pg. 524
Broadbent, Emily, Account Coordinator --GBRITT P.R. & MARKETING, South Portland, ME, pg. 1526
Broeckel, Amber, Account Coordinator --RED SKY PUBLIC RELATIONS, Boise, ID, pg. 1633
Bronstein, Lara, Account Coordinator --BRAVE PUBLIC RELATIONS, Atlanta, GA, pg. 1459
Brounstein, Kim, Account Coordinator --JS2 COMMUNICATIONS, Los Angeles, CA, pg. 598
Brown, Lauren, Account Coordinator --AMNET GROUP, New York, NY, pg. 1324
Brueck, Emily, Account Coordinator --ARCHER MALMO, Memphis, TN, pg. 67
Brusewitz, Sydney, Account Coordinator --THOMPSON & CO. PUBLIC RELATIONS, Anchorage, AK, pg. 1663
Bullard, Sharon, Account Coordinator --HOWERTON+WHITE, Wichita, KS, pg. 525
Bush, Sarah, Account Coordinator --BENEDICT ADVERTISING, Daytona Beach, FL, pg. 124
Butterman, Matt, Account Coordinator --O2 SPORTS MEDIA, San Francisco, CA, pg. 1604
Campagna, Tiana, Account Coordinator --THE ABBI AGENCY, Reno, NV, pg. 1438
Cantu, Amy, Account Coordinator --KGBTEXAS, San Antonio, TX, pg. 610
Caplan, Chelsea, Account Coordinator --LUQUIRE GEORGE ANDREWS, INC., Charlotte, NC, pg. 674
Cardone, Emilie, Account Coordinator --CREATIVE COMMUNICATION ASSOCIATES, Albany, NY, pg. 246
Carpenter, Erin, Account Coordinator --CINCH PR & BRANDING GROUP, San Francisco, CA, pg. 1478
Caudle, Rosalyn, Account Coordinator --MOMENTUM MARKETING, Charleston, SC, pg. 770
Cavnar, Becky, Account Coordinator --ANGLIN PUBLIC RELATIONS, INC., Oklahoma City, OK, pg. 1444
Cerafoli, Sherry, Account Coordinator --MORGAN & MYERS, INC., Waukesha, WI, pg. 774
Chamberlain, Dianne, Account Coordinator --NANCY MARSHALL COMMUNICATIONS, Augusta, ME, pg. 1600
Chapple, Hannah, Account Coordinator --COLOUR, Halifax, Canada, pg. 223
Chavez, Diego A., Account Coordinator --SAESHE ADVERTISING, Los Angeles, CA, pg. 1013
Chia, Darren, Account Coordinator --RUSSO PARTNERS LLC, New York, NY, pg. 998
Chitwood, Carla, Account Coordinator --CFX INC, Saint Louis, MO, pg. 202
Chowdhury, Karina, Account Coordinator --VANTAGE PR, San Francisco, CA, pg. 1668
Christopher, Caitlin, Account Coordinator --WOODRUFF SWEITZER, INC., Columbia, MO, pg. 1214
Cocca, Toniann, Account Coordinator --JACK NADEL INTERNATIONAL, Westport, CT, pg. 1418
Cole, Danielle, Account Coordinator --BAM STRATEGY, Montreal, Canada, pg. 89
Command, Lauren, Account Coordinator --AMNET GROUP, New York, NY, pg. 1324
Cone, Adriana, Account Coordinator --BEYOND FIFTEEN COMMUNICATIONS, INC., Irvine, CA, pg. 1453
Conley, Kaylee, Account Coordinator --LER PUBLIC RELATIONS, New York, NY, pg. 1573
Conner, Kim, Account Coordinator --ROI MEDIA, Tulsa, OK, pg. 1388
Connors, Caitlin, Account Coordinator --FUEL PARTNERSHIPS, Boca Raton, FL, pg. 407
Connors, Emily, Account Coordinator --HIEBING, Madison, WI, pg. 513
Conroy, Casey, Account Coordinator --VANDER HOUWEN PUBLIC RELATIONS, INC., Mercer Island, WA, pg. 1668
Conway, Catherine, Account Coordinator --DALTON AGENCY JACKSONVILLE, Jacksonville, FL, pg. 264
Cook, Simone, Account Coordinator --SONSHINE COMMUNICATIONS, North Miami Beach, FL, pg. 1058
Copeland, Lexi, Account Coordinator --ER MARKETING, Kansas City, MO, pg. 352
Costello, Kristen, Account Coordinator --FORREST & BLAKE INC., Mountainside, NJ, pg. 398
Cote-Bruneau, Nicolas, Account Coordinator --FCB Montreal, Montreal, Canada, pg. 372
Cox, Brianne, Account Coordinator --RUMBLETREE, North Hampton, NH, pg. 997
Cross, Muriel, Account Coordinator --BOHLSENPR INC., Indianapolis, IN, pg. 1457
Croteau, Samantha, Account Coordinator --CONVENTURES, INC., Boston, MA, pg. 1485
Cruickshank, Brittany, Account Coordinator --DEVENEY COMMUNICATIONS, New Orleans, LA, pg. 1493
Cummings, Joy, Account Coordinator --STRONG, Birmingham, AL, pg. 1092
Cunningham, Monica, Account Coordinator --STRADEGY ADVERTISING, Louisville, KY, pg. 1089
Curbelo, Alexandra, Account Coordinator --WRAGG & CASAS PUBLIC RELATIONS, INC., Miami, FL, pg. 1688
Curry, Kayla, Account Coordinator --AARS & WELLS, INC., Dallas, TX, pg. 14
Da Silva, Julianna, Account Coordinator --HL GROUP, New York, NY, pg. 517
DAdamo, Stephanie, Account Coordinator --DQMPR, New York, NY, pg. 1497
Dagenhart, Brittany, Account Coordinator --WALKER MARKETING, INC., Concord, NC, pg. 1187
Daily, Alyson, Account Coordinator --AHA COMMUNICATIONS, Austin, TX, pg. 40
Dale, Savana, Account Coordinator --STRATEGIC AMERICA, West Des Moines, IA, pg. 1090
Dammen, Jessica, Account Coordinator --AdFarm, Fargo, ND, pg. 28
De Dios, Mike, Account Coordinator --GREENSTRIPE MEDIA, INC., Newport Beach, CA, pg. 1335
Dedoshka, Daniel, Account Coordinator --PROSIO COMMUNICATIONS, Roseville, CA, pg. 1627
deFreese, Amanda, Account Coordinator --MARQUETTE GROUP, Peoria, IL, pg. 701
Denardi, Kate, Account Coordinator --O'KEEFFE & CO., Alexandria, VA, pg. 1610
Deordio, Cameron, Account Coordinator --BREAKAWAY COMMUNICATIONS LLC, New York, NY, pg. 1460
Dermer, Adam, Account Coordinator --A&C AGENCY, Toronto, Canada, pg. 1438
Dilorenzo, Mike, Account Coordinator --SIMPSON COMMUNICATIONS LLC, Shaker Heights, OH, pg. 1650

Responsibilities Index

Account Director

Responsibilities Index

Responsibilities Index

Responsibilities Index

Gangitano, Kate, Account Director --Starcom Melbourne, Melbourne, Australia, pg. 1079
Gannaway, Liz, Account Director --THE COMPANY OF OTHERS, Houston, TX, pg. 227
Gannon Yant, Molly, Account Director --PLAN B (THE AGENCY ALTERNATIVE), Chicago, IL, pg. 896
Ganshert, Kyle, Account Director --COLUMN FIVE, Newport Beach, CA, pg. 223
Ganz, Solomon, Account Director --PUBLICIS NEW YORK, New York, NY, pg. 935
Garcia Amaya, Fabiola Andrea, Account Director --McCann Erickson Corp. S.A., Bogota, Colombia, pg. 719
Garcia, Javier Menasalvas, Account Director --PSM S.A., Madrid, Spain, pg. 41
Gardiner, Mat, Account Director --iCrossing, Inc., Brighton, United Kingdom, pg. 1296
Gardner, Joshua, Account Director --SYMMETRI MARKETING GROUP, LLC, Chicago, IL, pg. 1105
Gardner, Sydney, Account Director --JZPR, Santa Barbara, CA, pg. 1557
Garizio, Steve, Account Director --Harte-Hanks, Inc., Deerfield Beach, FL, pg. 482
Garlick, Frankie, Account Director --TBWA/London, London, United Kingdom, pg. 1124
Garson, Hardish, Account Director --THINK MINT MEDIA, North Vancouver, Canada, pg. 1139
Garvey, Keith, Account Director --COLANGELO, Darien, CT, pg. 220
Garzon, Beatriz, Account Director --Grey: REP, Bogota, Colombia, pg. 453
Gasna, Ragne, Account Director --DDB Estonia Ltd., Tallinn, Estonia, pg. 280
Gatinel, Marielle, Account Director --Lowe Strateus, Paris, France, pg. 793
Gautier, Charlotte, Account Director --Reputation, Copenhagen, Denmark, pg. 918
Gay, Amity, Account Director --Grayling, San Francisco, CA, pg. 1533
Gee, Dianne, Account Director --Saatchi & Saatchi Los Angeles, Torrance, CA, pg. 1001
Geiger, Bruce, Account Director --LEAP STRATEGIC MARKETING, LLC, Waukesha, WI, pg. 634
Geipel, Jay, Account Director --DUDNYK HEALTHCARE GROUP, Horsham, PA, pg. 331
Gelfman, Lauren, Account Director --THE TERRI & SANDY SOLUTION, New York, NY, pg. 1136
Gellman, Marc, Account Director --JOHANNES LEONARDO, New York, NY, pg. 1299
Gen, Samantha, Account Director --DDB New York, New York, NY, pg. 275
George, Geralyn, Account Director --THE MARS AGENCY, Southfield, MI, pg. 701
George, Katie, Account Director --LEO BURNETT WORLDWIDE, INC., Chicago, IL, pg. 637
Georghiou, Helena, Account Director --FCB Inferno, London, United Kingdom, pg. 375
Gergely, Daniel, Account Director --The Community, Buenos Aires, Argentina, pg. 227
Gerth, Josh, Account Director --BRUNSWICK MEDIA SERVICES LLC, New Brunswick, NJ, pg. 172
Ghanem, Rasha, Account Director --ASDA'A Burson - Marsteller, Dubai, United Arab Emirates, pg. 1469
Ghorayeb, Ghaled, Account Director --Saatchi & Saatchi, Dubai, United Arab Emirates, pg. 1006
Ghosh, Shagorika, Account Director --IW GROUP, INC., West Hollywood, CA, pg. 564
Giacon, Felipe, Account Director --J. Walter Thompson, Sao Paulo, Brazil, pg. 577
Giacoppo, Vanessa, Account Director --RESOUND MARKETING, Princeton, NJ, pg. 1635
Gianfaldoni, Giulia, Account Director --TBWA Italia, Milan, Italy, pg. 1121
Gibson, Leigh, Account Director --INTREPID, Salt Lake City, UT, pg. 1552
Giese, Melissa, Account Director --CONVENTURES, INC., Boston, MA, pg. 1485
Gilchrist, Elizabeth, Account Director --GREY NEW YORK, New York, NY, pg. 446
Gill, Rachel, Account Director --FCB West, San Francisco, CA, pg. 372
Gillooly, Natasha, Account Director --Porter Novelli New Zealand-Auckland, Auckland, New Zealand, pg. 1625
Giordano Dimakopoulos, Emily, Account Director --GREY GROUP, New York, NY, pg. 445
Giordano, Jennifer, Account Director --BLEU MARKETING SOLUTIONS, INC., San Francisco, CA, pg. 138
Giss, Kevin, Account Director --FACTORY PR, New York, NY, pg. 364
Giverson, Carrie, Account Director --ONE7 COMMUNICATIONS, Henderson, NV, pg. 1611
Glaus, Diane, Account Director --Moroch, Saint Louis, MO, pg. 775
Glidewell, Chad, Account Director --Octagon, Atlanta, GA, pg. 823
Glunz, Kristin, Account Director --SCHAFER CONDON CARTER, Chicago, IL, pg. 1024
Golden, Joan, Account Director --HILL HOLLIDAY, Boston, MA, pg. 514
Goldman, Elissa, Account Director --The Martin Agency-NY, New York, NY, pg. 703
Goldman, Shelby, Account Director --BULLFROG & BAUM, New York, NY, pg. 174
Goldner, Ali, Account Director --OLSON, Minneapolis, MN, pg. 856
Goldstein, Jenna, Account Director --ZenithOptimedia, New York, NY, pg. 1398
Goldstein, Kim, Account Director --HAVAS MEDIA, New York, NY, pg. 1338
Goldstein, Lesley, Account Director --6DEGREES INTEGRATED COMMUNICATIONS, Toronto, Canada, pg. 10
Gollamudi, Snigdha, Account Director --GREY GROUP, New York, NY, pg. 445
Gomes, Gabi, Account Director --ZYNC COMMUNICATIONS INC., Toronto, Canada, pg. 1260
Gomez, Cristian, Account Director --Prolam Y&R S.A., Santiago, Chile, pg. 1249
Gomez, Enrique, Account Director --FCB Mayo, Bogota, Colombia, pg. 377
Gonsior, Jenny, Account Director --ANSIRA, Saint Louis, MO, pg. 61
Gonzales, Mona, Account Director --PEREIRA & O'DELL, San Francisco, CA, pg. 883
Gonzales, Veronica, Account Director --MediaCom Vancouver, Vancouver, Canada, pg. 1369
Gonzalez, Henry, Account Director --CP+B, Coconut Grove, FL, pg. 239
Gonzalez, Jaime, Account Director --Ogilvy & Mather, Mexico, Mexico, pg. 839
Gonzalez, Maura, Account Director --KOVEL/FULLER, Culver City, CA, pg. 617
Gonzalez, Monique N., Account Director --ROCKORANGE, Miami, FL, pg. 1638
Gonzalez, Paola, Account Director --Havas Worldwide Mexico, Mexico, Mexico, pg. 499
Gordon, Kevin, Account Director --MEC, Dublin, Ireland, pg. 1359
Gordon, Kim, Account Director --JD GORDON CREATIVE LABS, Sioux City, IA, pg. 589
Gorelick, Sara, Account Director --COLANGELO & PARTNERS PUBLIC RELATIONS, New York, NY, pg. 1483
Gorges, Sophia, Account Director --Edelman Frankfurt, Frankfurt am Main, Germany, pg. 1504
Gorska, Kamila, Account Director --Saatchi & Saatchi, Warsaw, Poland, pg. 1005
Gorski, Kayla, Account Director --Mullen Lowe, Pittsburgh, PA, pg. 789
Goss, Ben, Account Director --TRO, Isleworth, United Kingdom, pg. 316
Goto, Naoko, Account Director --Dentsu Y&R Japan, Tokyo, Japan, pg. 1241
Gouin, Kathy, Account Director --G.W. HOFFMAN MARKETING & COMMUNICATIONS, Darien, CT, pg. 1415
Gourevitch, Hannah, Account Director --Wieden + Kennedy, London, United Kingdom, pg. 1204
Grabosky, Herman, Account Director --M8 AGENCY, Miami, FL, pg. 681
Graf, Karen, Account Director --Havas Media, Boston, MA, pg. 1340
Graham, Mark, Account Director --JOHN ST., Toronto, Canada, pg. 593
Grams, Colleen, Account Director --Bader Rutter & Associates, Inc., Lincoln, NE, pg. 86
Grant, Susan, Account Director --DDB Canada, Edmonton, Canada, pg. 273
Grant, Susan, Account Director --Tribal Worldwide Toronto, Toronto, Canada, pg. 1316
Gray, Andrea Still, Account Director --JPA HEALTH COMMUNICATIONS, Washington, DC, pg. 597
Gray, Gordon, Account Director --DAVID & GOLIATH, El Segundo, CA, pg. 267
Grayum, Julie, Account Director --LOPEZ NEGRETE COMMUNICATIONS, INC., Houston, TX, pg. 668
Grayum, Julie Jameson, Account Director --Lopez Negrete Communications West, Inc., Burbank, CA, pg. 669
Greasley, Jessica, Account Director --Weber Shandwick, Toronto, Canada, pg. 1678
Greco, Susan, Account Director --SPR ATLANTA, Atlanta, GA, pg. 1653
Green, Amanda, Account Director --TBWA Whybin Limited, Auckland, New Zealand, pg. 1130
Green, Cassandra, Account Director --THE IMAGINATION GROUP, London, United Kingdom, pg. 540
Green, Katja, Account Director --Saatchi & Saatchi, Auckland, New Zealand, pg. 1011
Green, Shawanda, Account Director --YOUNG & RUBICAM, New York, NY, pg. 1239
Greene, Donna L., Account Director --SPM MARKETING & COMMUNICATIONS, La Grange, IL, pg. 1066
Greenheck, Abigail, Account Director --BEEHIVE PR, Saint Paul, MN, pg. 1451
Gregeois, Florence, Account Director --PORTER NOVELLI, New York, NY, pg. 1619
Grelik, Debra, Account Director --Wunderman, Toronto, Canada, pg. 1231
Grendus, Cathy, Account Director --DDB Canada, Toronto, Canada, pg. 274
Grey, Charlotte, Account Director --Saatchi & Saatchi, Johannesburg, South Africa, pg. 1006
Griffin, Daniel, Account Director --ALLING HENNING & ASSOCIATES, Vancouver, WA, pg. 49
Griffin, Jenny, Account Director --LUCKIE & COMPANY, Birmingham, AL, pg. 672
Griffith, Brendan, Account Director --REPUTATION PARTNERS, Chicago, IL, pg. 969
Griffith, Jessica, Account Director --PASCALE COMMUNICATIONS LLC, Pittsburgh, PA, pg. 1613
Griffith, Patti, Account Director --MEREDITH XCELERATED MARKETING, Arlington, VA, pg. 1302
Griffiths, Beth, Account Director --Luminous Experiential MSLGROUP, Causeway Bay, China (Hong Kong), pg. 931
Griffiths, Jason, Account Director --KENNA, Mississauga, Canada, pg. 608
Griotto, Paolo, Account Director --Leo Burnett Co. S.r.l., Turin, Italy, pg. 643
Groener, Lisa, Account Director --GLYNNDEVINS ADVERTISING & MARKETING, Overland Park, KS, pg. 430
Grome, David, Account Director --BUTLER/TILL, Rochester, NY, pg. 1327
Groppo, Peggy, Account Director --PJA Advertising + Marketing, San Francisco, CA, pg. 894
Grotenfelt, Vilja, Account Director --OMD Finland Oy, Helsinki, Finland, pg. 1381
Grove, Joseph, Account Director --BISIG IMPACT GROUP, Louisville, KY, pg. 133
Gruen, Meredith, Account Director --TEAM ONE USA, Los Angeles, CA, pg. 1134
Gruninger, Emily, Account Director --SCHUPP COMPANY, INC., Saint Louis, MO, pg. 1025
Grymek, Jerry, Account Director --LMA, Toronto, Canada, pg. 665
Gu, Ada, Account Director --Fleishman-Hillard Guangzhou, Guangzhou, China, pg. 1520
Gu, Ada, Account Director --Fleishman-Hillard Link, Ltd., Shanghai, China, pg. 1521
Gu, Cathy, Account Director --Ruder Finn Asia Limited, Shanghai, China, pg. 1643
Gu, Cathy, Account Director --Ruder Finn Asia Limited, Beijing, China, pg. 1643
Guerin, Kate, Account Director --Edelman South Africa, Randburg, South Africa, pg. 1507
Guerin, Noelle, Account Director --CERCONE BROWN CURTIS, Boston, MA, pg. 202
Guerra, Lucia, Account Director --Argentina Porter Novelli, Buenos Aires, Argentina, pg. 1621
Guerrero, Yasmin, Account Director --BVK/MEKA, Miami, FL, pg. 180
Guffanti, Jimena, Account Director --Edelman, Buenos Aires, Argentina, pg. 1507
Guiang, Christine, Account Director --AVREA FOSTER, Dallas, TX, pg. 82
Guo, Vivian, Account Director --Ogilvy & Mather Advertising Beijing, Beijing, China, pg. 841
Gurr, Claire, Account Director --ZENO Group, London, United Kingdom, pg. 1503
Guryn, Gosia, Account Director --BBDO, Warsaw, Poland, pg. 109
Gustafsson, Maria, Account Director --Initiative Universal Stockholm, Stockholm, Sweden, pg. 1346

Responsibilities Index

Responsibilities Index

Responsibilities Index

Responsibilities Index

Account Executive

TX, pg. 300
Alganaraz, Camila, Account Executive --Punto Ogilvy & Mather, Montevideo, Uruguay, pg. 840
Ali, Yara, Account Executive --FP7 Cairo, Cairo, Egypt, pg. 719
Aliaga, Hazel, Account Executive --SPARK44, Culver City, CA, pg. 1062
Allan, Caroline, Account Executive --FAHLGREN MORTINE, Columbus, OH, pg. 364
Allan, Caroline, Account Executive --Fahlgren Mortine (Dayton), Beavercreek, OH, pg. 365
Allen, Kelly, Account Executive --Q STRATEGIES, Chattanooga, TN, pg. 940
Alley, Justin, Account Executive --MEDIA MIX, Jacksonville, FL, pg. 743
Almirall, Adam, Account Executive --Edelman Brussels, Brussels, Belgium, pg. 1503
Alston, Karim, Account Executive --KINNEY GROUP CREATIVE, New York, NY, pg. 613
Althaus, Melody, Account Executive --SHOUT PUBLIC RELATIONS, Costa Mesa, CA, pg. 1649
Aman, Janice, Account Executive --MOUNT & NADLER, INC., New York, NY, pg. 1593
Amico, Danielle, Account Executive --BBDO WORLDWIDE INC., New York, NY, pg. 99
An, Suzy, Account Executive --Porter Novelli-Austin, Austin, TX, pg. 1619
Anastasiou, Eleni, Account Executive --Ogilvy PR Worldwide, Athens, Greece, pg. 1607
Andersen, Kurt, Account Executive --HARRIS, BAIO & MCCULLOUGH INC., Philadelphia, PA, pg. 481
Anderson, Amy, Account Executive --CAIN & COMPANY, Rockford, IL, pg. 184
Anderson, Anna, Account Executive --Edelman, Seattle, WA, pg. 1503
Anderson, Coleman, Account Executive --IMMOTION STUDIOS, Fort Worth, TX, pg. 541
Anderson, Cydni, Account Executive --ATOMIC DIRECT, LTD, Portland, OR, pg. 78
Anderson, Laura, Account Executive --TRACTION FACTORY, Milwaukee, WI, pg. 1153
Anderson, Natalie, Account Executive --ANTHEMIC AGENCY, Los Angeles, CA, pg. 62
Anderson, Sarah, Account Executive --SVM PUBLIC RELATIONS & MARKETING COMMUNICATIONS, Providence, RI, pg. 1102
Andrew, Jan, Account Executive --THE HENDRA AGENCY INC., Brooklyn, NY, pg. 1538
Andrews, Charlene, Account Executive --BAUSERMAN GROUP, Reno, NV, pg. 97
Anich, Peter, Account Executive --BULLY PULPIT INTERACTIVE, Washington, DC, pg. 174
Anistranski, John, Account Executive --DEUTSCH, INC., New York, NY, pg. 301
Ansell, Kirstie, Account Executive --INFINITY CONCEPTS, Export, PA, pg. 545
Anthony, Michael, Account Executive --ADFARM, Calgary, Canada, pg. 28
Antig, Agustina, Account Executive --Rapp Argentina, Buenos Aires, Argentina, pg. 953
Aranda, Michael, Account Executive --THE TRUTH AGENCY, Santa Ana, CA, pg. 1160
Araya, Cesar, Account Executive --BBDO Chile, Santiago, Chile, pg. 102
Arbuckle, Harriet, Account Executive --Rapp New Zealand, Auckland, New Zealand, pg. 954
Archibald, Nicholas, Account Executive --STAPLEGUN, Oklahoma City, OK, pg. 1073
Arentsen, Amanda, Account Executive --MASSMEDIA CORPORATE COMMUNICATIONS, Henderson, NV, pg. 708
Armstrong, Caitlin, Account Executive --KONNECT PUBLIC RELATIONS, Los Angeles, CA, pg. 1567
Armstrong, Colonel, Account Executive --ADVOCATE DIGITAL MEDIA, Victoria, TX, pg. 35
Arnett, Rebecca, Account Executive --GROUP 7EVEN, Valparaiso, IN, pg. 462
Arnold, Tyler, Account Executive --LANDIS COMMUNICATIONS INC., San Francisco, CA, pg. 1571
Arrington, Lauren, Account Executive --KMR COMMUNICATIONS, New York, NY, pg. 615
Arsenault, Cait, Account Executive --DUFFY & SHANLEY, INC., Providence, RI, pg. 331
Arsenault, Kara, Account Executive --HAWK MARKETING SERVICES, Moncton, Canada, pg. 503
Arvizu, Andy, Account Executive --ARVIZU ADVERTISING & PROMOTIONS, Phoenix, AZ, pg. 75
Aschaker, Dana, Account Executive --GMR MARKETING LLC, New Berlin, WI, pg. 1414
Asendio, Laura, Account Executive --DPR GROUP, INC., Germantown, MD, pg. 1497
Asplund, Chelsea, Account Executive --GREENRUBINO, Seattle, WA, pg. 443
Assi, Akiran, Account Executive --TRACYLOCKE, Dallas, TX, pg. 1153
Astfalk, Alexis, Account Executive --BROWER MILLER & COLE, Irvine, CA, pg. 1463
Astini, Marcella, Account Executive --HAVAS WORLDWIDE CHICAGO, Chicago, IL, pg. 502
Austin, Chris, Account Executive --IDENTITY MARKETING & PUBLIC RELATIONS, LLC, Bingham Farms, MI, pg. 1548
Austin, Jessica, Account Executive --Luckie & Co., San Antonio, TX, pg. 673
Aviv, Ron, Account Executive --UNDERTONE, New York, NY, pg. 1166
Avrasin, Pola, Account Executive --COLANGELO & PARTNERS PUBLIC RELATIONS, New York, NY, pg. 1483
Ayers, Will, Account Executive --PRECISE COMMUNICATIONS, Atlanta, GA, pg. 1626
Azar Gonzalez, Victoria Lourdes, Account Executive --Argentina Porter Novelli, Buenos Aires, Argentina, pg. 1621
Azark, Matt, Account Executive --ADMARKETPLACE, New York, NY, pg. 29
Aziz, Lauren, Account Executive --GREY GROUP, New York, NY, pg. 445
Azizi, Souhila Mohammed, Account Executive --FP7 McCann Algeria, Algiers, Algeria, pg. 716
Babcock, Jillian, Account Executive --YOUNG & RUBICAM, New York, NY, pg. 1239
Baer, Gwen, Account Executive --COHN & WOLFE, New York, NY, pg. 1480
Bailey, Natalie, Account Executive --MOXLEY CARMICHAEL, Knoxville, TN, pg. 781
Bailey, Tyler, Account Executive --COOKSEY COMMUNICATIONS, INC., Irving, TX, pg. 1486
Bain, Sarah, Account Executive --PINEAPPLE PUBLIC RELATIONS, Atlanta, GA, pg. 1616
Baio, Chris, Account Executive --WHITEMYER ADVERTISING, INC., Zoar, OH, pg. 1200
Bair, Emilie, Account Executive --ESB ADVERTISING, Springfield, VA, pg. 355
Baker, Lauren, Account Executive --Ogilvy Cape Town, Cape Town, South Africa, pg. 849
Baker, Maggie, Account Executive --FLYNN WRIGHT, Des Moines, IA, pg. 395
Baker-Cliff, Holly, Account Executive --Wieden + Kennedy, London, United Kingdom, pg. 1204
Baldasarre, Katherine, Account Executive --BML PUBLIC RELATIONS, Montclair, NJ, pg. 1457
Ball, Gavin, Account Executive --AGENCY59, Toronto, Canada, pg. 39
Ball, Greg, Account Executive --BRENER, ZWIKEL & ASSOCIATES, INC., Reseda, CA, pg. 1460
Ballinger, Molly, Account Executive --HIP ADVERTISING, Springfield, IL, pg. 515
Balmer, Megan, Account Executive --SPENCER ADVERTISING AND MARKETING, Mountville, PA, pg. 1064
Balzo, Lisa, Account Executive --Allied Integrated Marketing, Scottsdale, AZ, pg. 48
Banion, Brittany, Account Executive --SKIRT PR, Chicago, IL, pg. 1650
Banks, Kylie, Account Executive --KONNECT PUBLIC RELATIONS, Los Angeles, CA, pg. 1567
Baray, Andrea, Account Executive --WHEELER ADVERTISING, Arlington, TX, pg. 1199
Barbanell, Priscilla, Account Executive --JOHNSON GRAY ADVERTISING, Irvine, CA, pg. 594
Barbeisch, Victoria, Account Executive --ZONE 5, Albany, NY, pg. 1258
Barberena, Gunther, Account Executive --OMD NORTH AMERICA, New York, NY, pg. 1378
Barbi, Martina, Account Executive --Leo Burnett Rome, Rome, Italy, pg. 643
Bardo, Elisabeth, Account Executive --KRAUSE ADVERTISING, Dallas, TX, pg. 618
Bare, Wade, Account Executive --MeringCarson, Encinitas, CA, pg. 748
Barendse, Alison, Account Executive --TEAM ONE USA, Los Angeles, CA, pg. 1134
Barger, Jim, Account Executive --MEDIALINKS ADVERTISING, Findlay, OH, pg. 744
Barnes, Kate, Account Executive --Clemenger BBDO Melbourne, Melbourne, Australia, pg. 114
BaRoss, Kelsey, Account Executive --ROSE COMMUNICATIONS, INC., Hoboken, NJ, pg. 1639
Barrera, Paula, Account Executive --FCB Mayo, Quito, Ecuador, pg. 378
Barrett, Kelly, Account Executive --FUSE INTERACTIVE, Laguna Beach, CA, pg. 410
Barretta, Joli, Account Executive --BRAND33, Torrance, CA, pg. 158
Barron, Laura, Account Executive --PROTERRA ADVERTISING, Addison, TX, pg. 915
Barry, Megan, Account Executive --IDEA HALL, Costa Mesa, CA, pg. 534
Bartron, Adie, Account Executive --OLIVER RUSSELL, Boise, ID, pg. 855
Basler, Leslie, Account Executive --CLAPP COMMUNICATIONS, Baltimore, MD, pg. 213
Bass, Samantha, Account Executive --ESB ADVERTISING, Springfield, VA, pg. 355
Basso, Jose, Account Executive --GMG ADVERTISING, Miami, FL, pg. 431
Bates, Ann, Account Executive --BRAVE PUBLIC RELATIONS, Atlanta, GA, pg. 1459
Batto, Gabby, Account Executive --DRIVEN PUBLIC RELATIONS, Temecula, CA, pg. 1498
Bauer, Paul, Account Executive --LINKMEDIA 360, Independence, OH, pg. 659
Baugh, Colin, Account Executive --RANDALL PR, LLC, Seattle, WA, pg. 1631
Bean, Keena, Account Executive --FIRMANI & ASSOCIATES, Seattle, WA, pg. 388
Bear, Bridget, Account Executive --EG INTEGRATED, Omaha, NE, pg. 339
Beard, Michael, Account Executive --BADJAR Ogilvy, Melbourne, Australia, pg. 840
Beas, Yadira, Account Executive --PERRY COMMUNICATIONS GROUP, INC., Sacramento, CA, pg. 885
Beavers, Megan, Account Executive --Edelman, Atlanta, GA, pg. 1502
Beck, Amanda, Account Executive --CINCH PR & BRANDING GROUP, San Francisco, CA, pg. 1478
Becker, Josh, Account Executive --NAARTJIE MULTIMEDIA, Columbus, GA, pg. 799
Beckett, Anna, Account Executive --PBJS, INC., Seattle, WA, pg. 880
Bederka, Larry, Account Executive --CAIN & COMPANY, Rockford, IL, pg. 184
Beebe, Adam, Account Executive --ARENA COMMUNICATIONS, Salt Lake City, UT, pg. 68
Beerson, Danielle, Account Executive --Rosetta, San Luis Obispo, CA, pg. 992
Behrendt, Becky, Account Executive --RESPONSORY, Brookfield, WI, pg. 972
Bekkerman, Rachel, Account Executive --RUDER FINN INC., New York, NY, pg. 1642
Bell, Lucinda, Account Executive --Hill & Knowlton Australia Pty. Ltd., Sydney, Australia, pg. 1545
Beltran, Maximiliano, Account Executive --Del Campo Nazca Saatchi & Saatchi, Buenos Aires, Argentina, pg. 1007
Ben Dror, Ori, Account Executive --BBR Saatchi & Saatchi, Ramat Gan, Israel, pg. 1003
Bender, Matthew, Account Executive --RADIUS ADVERTISING, Strongsville, OH, pg. 949
Benhaim, Melissa, Account Executive --CHERYL ANDREWS MARKETING COMMUNICATIONS, Coral Gables, FL, pg. 1477
Benjamin, Kelsey, Account Executive --GYK Antler, Boston, MA, pg. 468
Bennett, Nicholas Hayward, Account Executive --SCOPPECHIO, Louisville, KY, pg. 1026
Bennett, Paul, Account Executive --HR ADWORKS LTD., Winnipeg, Canada, pg. 526
Benourida, Brittany, Account Executive --McCann Erickson/New York, New York, NY, pg. 714
Benourida, Brittany, Account Executive --McCann Erickson North America, New York, NY, pg. 715
Benton, Kelly, Account Executive --ADVOCATE DIGITAL MEDIA, Victoria, TX, pg. 35
Benton, Laura, Account Executive --BLATTEL COMMUNICATIONS, San Francisco, CA, pg. 137
Berberich, Garrett, Account Executive --HIMMELRICH PR, Baltimore, MD, pg. 515
Bercovici, Adam, Account Executive --MACLAREN MCCANN CANADA INC., Toronto, Canada, pg. 682

Responsibilities Index

Responsibilities Index

Responsibilities Index

Responsibilities Index

Responsibilities Index

Responsibilities Index

Responsibilities Index

Ward, Josh, Account Executive --BLUE HERON COMMUNICATIONS, Norman, OK, pg. 1456
Ward, Lori, Account Executive --MARCHEX, INC., Seattle, WA, pg. 692
Ward, Sarah, Account Executive --Weber Shandwick, Edinburgh, United Kingdom, pg. 1681
Warden, Lori, Account Executive --PARTNERS CREATIVE, Missoula, MT, pg. 875
Warner, Alexandra, Account Executive --CAMBRIDGE BIOMARKETING, Cambridge, MA, pg. 186
Wasko, Eva Marie, Account Executive --Cohn & Wolfe, Los Angeles, CA, pg. 1482
Wasserman, Scott, Account Executive --THE MARCUS GROUP, INC., Little Falls, NJ, pg. 693
Wasson, Dana, Account Executive --THE BARBAULD AGENCY, Valparaiso, IN, pg. 91
Watkinson, Brian, Account Executive --CBC ADVERTISING, Saco, ME, pg. 199
Watson, Cat, Account Executive --CURIOSITY ADVERTISING, Cincinnati, OH, pg. 260
Watson, Emma, Account Executive --M&C Saatchi Sport & Entertainment, London, United Kingdom, pg. 677
Watters, Kirk, Account Executive --Signal Outdoor Advertising, Stamford, CT, pg. 1043
Wayner, Pete, Account Executive --DIXON SCHWABL ADVERTISING, Victor, NY, pg. 317
Webb, Ashley, Account Executive --REVIVEHEALTH, Nashville, TN, pg. 975
Weber, Emily, Account Executive --BLUE CHIP MARKETING WORLDWIDE, Northbrook, IL, pg. 140
Weber, Jordan, Account Executive --BUXTON COMMUNICATIONS, Portland, ME, pg. 179
Weber, Kate, Account Executive --TPN INC., Dallas, TX, pg. 1431
Wechsler, Brittany, Account Executive --M18 PUBLIC RELATIONS, New York, NY, pg. 1580
Weddingfeld, Kristin, Account Executive --LANGDON FLYNN COMMUNICATIONS, Las Vegas, NV, pg. 1572
Weeks, Savannah, Account Executive --TREVELINO/KELLER, Atlanta, GA, pg. 1665
Weinberg, Brett, Account Executive --VECTOR MEDIA, New York, NY, pg. 1172
Weinberg, Jay, Account Executive --ALL-WAYS ADVERTISING COMPANY, Bloomfield, NJ, pg. 1404
Weir, Kerry, Account Executive --TBC Direct, Inc., Baltimore, MD, pg. 1113
Weir, Kerry, Account Executive --TBC, INC./PR DIVISION, Baltimore, MD, pg. 1659
Welburn, Brian, Account Executive --Carol H. Williams Advertising, Chicago, IL, pg. 192
Welke, Libby, Account Executive --Ogilvy & Mather, Chicago, IL, pg. 828
Wells, Lisa M., Account Executive --SPAR, INCORPORATED, New Orleans, LA, pg. 1061
Welsh, Kristin, Account Executive --ALLYN MEDIA, Dallas, TX, pg. 50
Wenner, Megan, Account Executive --WILSON PUBLIC RELATIONS, Seattle, WA, pg. 1686
Wenzel, Lauren, Account Executive --GATESMAN+DAVE, Pittsburgh, PA, pg. 417
West, Tyler, Account Executive --EROI, INC., Portland, OR, pg. 354
Westley, Jorie, Account Executive --Edelman, San Mateo, CA, pg. 1501
Westling, Lauren, Account Executive --RISDALL MARKETING GROUP, New Brighton, MN, pg. 982
Weymouth, Sydney, Account Executive --JH COMMUNICATIONS LLC, Providence, RI, pg. 591
Whatley, Anne Marie, Account Executive --Luckie & Company, Duluth, GA, pg. 673
Wheeler, Bria, Account Executive --BBR CREATIVE, Lafayette, LA, pg. 118
Whitcomb, Elizabeth, Account Executive --Grey Healthcare Group, Kansas City, MO, pg. 423
White, Charlotte, Account Executive --OMD New Zealand/Auckland, Auckland, New Zealand, pg. 1381
White, Daniel, Account Executive --GETO & DEMILLY, INC., New York, NY, pg. 1527
White, Gemma, Account Executive --Johnson King Public Relations, London, United Kingdom, pg. 387
White, Hannah, Account Executive --ELIZABETH CHRISTIAN PUBLIC RELATIONS, Austin, TX, pg. 1509
White, Kristine, Account Executive --PERFORMANCE MARKETING, West Des Moines, IA, pg. 884
White, Lynda, Account Executive --BLOHM CREATIVE PARTNERS, East Lansing, MI, pg. 139
White, Shannon, Account Executive --BOLT PUBLIC RELATIONS, Irvine, CA, pg. 1458
Whitlock, Amanda, Account Executive --CLEARPOINT AGENCY, Encinitas, CA, pg. 1479
Wickman, Kelsey, Account Executive --WE, Bellevue, WA, pg. 1673
Wickstrand, Tenaya, Account Executive --ZENZI COMMUNICATIONS, Solana Beach, CA, pg. 1691
Wigger, Kris, Account Executive --TWENTY FOUR SEVEN, INC., Portland, OR, pg. 1163
Wight, Stephanie, Account Executive --GYMR PUBLIC RELATIONS, Washington, DC, pg. 1535
Wilkinson, Phyllis, Account Executive --QUINLAN MARKETING COMMUNICATIONS, Carmel, IN, pg. 944
Willain, Anais, Account Executive --Edelman Brussels, Brussels, Belgium, pg. 1503
Williams, Brittany, Account Executive --THE LAVIDGE COMPANY, Phoenix, AZ, pg. 632
Williams, Grace, Account Executive --BLASTMEDIA, Fishers, IN, pg. 1455
Williams, Jason, Account Executive --5METACOM, Carmel, IN, pg. 10
Williams, Tor, Account Executive --MRM London, London, United Kingdom, pg. 783
Williams, Union, Account Executive --PIVOT MARKETING, Indianapolis, IN, pg. 894
Williams, Wenona, Account Executive --BODDEN PARTNERS, New York, NY, pg. 145
Williamson, Suzi, Account Executive --Leo Burnett Melbourne, Melbourne, Australia, pg. 647
Williford, Anna, Account Executive --RAFFETTO HERMAN STRATEGIC COMMUNICATIONS LLC, Seattle, WA, pg. 1630
Wilson, Becca, Account Executive --LEO BURNETT WORLDWIDE, INC., Chicago, IL, pg. 637
Wilson, Emma, Account Executive --MARLO MARKETING COMMUNICATIONS, Boston, MA, pg. 1583
Wilson, Humphrey, Account Executive --THE NULMAN GROUP, Flemington, NJ, pg. 819
Wilson, Jamie, Account Executive --HOWARD MILLER ASSOCIATES, INC., Lancaster, PA, pg. 525
Wilson, Kim, Account Executive --DW ADVERTISING, Bloomfield, CT, pg. 333
Wing, Elizabeth, Account Executive --COMCAST SPOTLIGHT, Fort Wayne, IN, pg. 224
Wingate, Michelle, Account Executive --MMI PUBLIC RELATIONS, Cary, NC, pg. 1591
Wininger, Amanda, Account Executive --eci san francisco, San Francisco, CA, pg. 314
Winn, Lauren, Account Executive --MYRIAD TRAVEL MARKETING, Manhattan Beach, CA, pg. 798
Winter, Danielle, Account Executive --Rosetta, New York, NY, pg. 992
Winther, Haley, Account Executive --Erwin Penland, New York, NY, pg. 355
Wise, Patricia Mager, Account Executive --WEINBERG HARRIS & ASSOCIATES, Baltimore, MD, pg. 1684
Wittenberg, Caroline, Account Executive --STIR ADVERTISING & INTEGRATED MARKETING, Milwaukee, WI, pg. 1087
Wiznitzer, Dan, Account Executive --HIMMELRICH PR, Baltimore, MD, pg. 515
Woit, Claire, Account Executive --PADILLA/CRT, Minneapolis, MN, pg. 869
Wojcehowicz, Lisa, Account Executive --GLYNNDEVINS ADVERTISING & MARKETING, Overland Park, KS, pg. 430
Wolden, Alexandra, Account Executive --DELTA MEDIA, INC., Miami, FL, pg. 295
Wolf, Beth, Account Executive --OMNIBUS ADVERTISING, Arlington Heights, IL, pg. 857
Wolf, Lorin, Account Executive --ORANGE BARREL, Grove City, OH, pg. 863
Wolfrom, Angie, Account Executive --NICKELODEON CREATIVE ADVERTISING, New York, NY, pg. 810
Wood, Aaron, Account Executive --AH&M MARKETING COMMUNICATIONS, Pittsfield, MA, pg. 40
Wood, Dawn, Account Executive --GRAHAM OLESON, Colorado Springs, CO, pg. 439
Wood, Justin, Account Executive --A. BROWN-OLMSTEAD ASSOCIATES, Atlanta, GA, pg. 13
Wood, Kennan, Account Executive --TPN INC., Dallas, TX, pg. 1431
Woods, Carrie, Account Executive --OPTIMEDIA INTERNATIONAL US INC., New York, NY, pg. 1382
Wraase, Elisabeth, Account Executive --STANTON COMMUNICATIONS, INC., Washington, DC, pg. 1654
Wrenn, Rebecca, Account Executive --SWEENEY, Cleveland, OH, pg. 1103
Wright, Kathleen Chandler, Account Executive --G7 ENTERTAINMENT MARKETING, La Vergne, TN, pg. 412
Wright, Mikala, Account Executive --ANTHONYBARNUM, Austin, TX, pg. 1445
Wrubleski, Beth, Account Executive --ISA ADVERTISING, New York, NY, pg. 561
Wurz, Emily, Account Executive --BUNTIN OUT-OF-HOME MEDIA, Nashville, TN, pg. 1327
Wyker, T., Account Executive --MILLER ADVERTISING, Harrison, NY, pg. 757
Yamahira, Yuko, Account Executive --Edelman, Tokyo, Japan, pg. 1504
Yancey, Brittany, Account Executive --TRENDYMINDS INC, Indianapolis, IN, pg. 1156
Yanes, Desiree, Account Executive --PUBLICIS NEW YORK, New York, NY, pg. 935
Yang, Sasa, Account Executive --Wieden + Kennedy, Shanghai, China, pg. 1205
Yanoshak, Erica, Account Executive --DMW WORLDWIDE LLC, Chesterbrook, PA, pg. 319
Yarnell, Jamie, Account Executive --Moroch, Metairie, LA, pg. 775
Yeh, Chan Yun, Account Executive --Ogilvy Public Relations Taiwan, Taipei, Taiwan, pg. 1609
Yen, Luisa, Account Executive --RBB PUBLIC RELATIONS, Miami, FL, pg. 1631
Yip, Liz, Account Executive --Ketchum ICON Singapore, Singapore, Singapore, pg. 1563
Yohan, Tasha, Account Executive --GOODMAN PUBLIC RELATIONS, Fort Lauderdale, FL, pg. 1532
Yong, Kera, Account Executive --BATES/LEE ADVERTISING, Costa Mesa, CA, pg. 97
Yoon, John, Account Executive --THE SILVER TELEGRAM, Long Beach, CA, pg. 1044
Young, Ayala, Account Executive --Finn Partners, Jerusalem, Israel, pg. 387
Young, Lindsey, Account Executive --BIZCOM ASSOCIATES, Addison, TX, pg. 133
Yousif, Noor, Account Executive --IPG MEDIABRANDS, New York, NY, pg. 560
Yu, Arnold, Account Executive --Ogilvy & Mather Advertising, Central, China (Hong Kong), pg. 842
Zaitzev, Vlada, Account Executive --NOLIN BBDO, Montreal, Canada, pg. 812
Zakhar, Adam, Account Executive --BILLBOARD EXPRESS, INC., Rancho Santa Margarita, CA, pg. 1326
Zaparyniuk, Chelsea, Account Executive --LPI COMMUNICATIONS GROUP INC., Calgary, Canada, pg. 671
Zaretsky, Marni, Account Executive --Manning Selvage & Lee, Toronto, Canada, pg. 1594
Zars, Paige, Account Executive --JohnsonRauhoff Marketing Communications, Benton Harbor, MI, pg. 595
Zavala, Adriana, Account Executive --Leo Burnett USA, Chicago, IL, pg. 639
Zavarce, Xiomara, Account Executive --MARKETLOGIC, Miami, FL, pg. 1422
Zeineddine, Jenni, Account Executive --MCCABE PROMOTIONAL ADVERTISING, London, Canada, pg. 1422
Zeitz, Allyson, Account Executive --DATAXU, INC., Boston, MA, pg. 1331
Zernholt, Olga, Account Executive --NIKI JONES AGENCY, Port Jervis, NY, pg. 810
Ziems, Melanie, Account Executive --DESIGN AT WORK, Houston, TX, pg. 300
Zivkovic, Mina, Account Executive --BLUE C, Costa Mesa, CA, pg. 140
Zuk, Hannah, Account Executive --GO BIG MARKETING, Orlando, FL, pg. 431
Zumwalt, Landen, Account Executive --RAFFETTO HERMAN STRATEGIC COMMUNICATIONS LLC, Seattle, WA, pg. 1630
Zweifel, Sarah, Account Executive --RED BROWN KLE, Milwaukee, WI, pg. 959

Account Supervisor

Abeles, Melissa, Account Supervisor --OMG Los Angeles, Los Angeles, CA, pg. 859
Ackerman, Brooke, Account Supervisor --WEBER SHANDWICK, New York, NY, pg. 1675
Ackerman, Mark, Account Supervisor --ACKERMAN MCQUEEN, INC., Oklahoma City, OK, pg. 20
Adachi, Kohei, Account Supervisor --Wieden + Kennedy Japan,

Responsibilities Index

Art Buyer

Art Director

Responsibilities Index

Broadcast Production

Wong, Shukmei, Broadcast Production --HORIZON MEDIA, INC., New York, NY, pg. 1341
Woodus, Bradley, Broadcast Production --DARE, London, United Kingdom, pg. 1286
Yi, Sun, Broadcast Production --COPACINO + FUJIKADO, LLC, Seattle, WA, pg. 234
Younker, Andy, Broadcast Production --THE RICHARDS GROUP, INC., Dallas, TX, pg. 978
Zaldivar, Claire, Broadcast Production --ZUBI ADVERTISING SERVICES, INC., Coral Gables, FL, pg. 1259
Zellmann, Caitlin, Broadcast Production --HAWORTH MARKETING & MEDIA COMPANY, Minneapolis, MN, pg. 1340
Zuluaga, Alicia, Broadcast Production --OGILVY & MATHER, New York, NY, pg. 826

Chief Creative Officer

Abesamis, Badong, Chief Creative Officer --Young & Rubicam Philippines, Manila, Philippines, pg. 1244
Adkins, Doug, Chief Creative Officer --HUNT ADKINS, Minneapolis, MN, pg. 528
Adkins, Fred, Chief Creative Officer --FRED AGENCY, Atlanta, GA, pg. 402
Aksenov, Alexander, Chief Creative Officer --GLOBAL ADVERTISING STRATEGIES, New York, NY, pg. 428
Aleman, Ileana, Chief Creative Officer --BVK/MEKA, Miami, FL, pg. 180
Alexander, Joe, Chief Creative Officer --THE MARTIN AGENCY, Richmond, VA, pg. 702
Alexander, Joe, Chief Creative Officer --The Martin Agency-NY, New York, NY, pg. 703
Alkadhi, Bashar, Chief Creative Officer --ASDA'A Burson - Marsteller, Dubai, United Arab Emirates, pg. 1469
Allebach, Jamie, Chief Creative Officer --ALLEBACH COMMUNICATIONS, Souderton, PA, pg. 46
Alush, Ami, Chief Creative Officer --McCann Erickson, Tel Aviv, Israel, pg. 722
Alvarado, Herbert, Chief Creative Officer --Publicidad Comercial, La Libertad, El Salvador, pg. 557
Alvarez, Leandro, Chief Creative Officer --TBWA Lisbon, Lisbon, Portugal, pg. 1123
Amato, Dawn, Chief Creative Officer --SLIGHTLY MAD, Northport, NY, pg. 1051
Ancevic, Michael, Chief Creative Officer --THE FANTASTICAL, Boston, MA, pg. 368
Andersson, Nils, Chief Creative Officer --TBWA Greater China, Beijing, China, pg. 1128
Appleby, Jennifer O., Chief Creative Officer --WRAY WARD MARKETING COMMUNICATIONS, Charlotte, NC, pg. 1228
Artabasy, Chris, Chief Creative Officer --ARTAGRAFIK, Atlanta, GA, pg. 73
Athayde, Edson, Chief Creative Officer --FCB Lisbon, Lisbon, Portugal, pg. 374
Atvara, Daiga, Chief Creative Officer --THE UXB, Beverly Hills, CA, pg. 1169
Austin, Tim, Chief Creative Officer --TPN INC., Dallas, TX, pg. 1431
Bacino, Brian, Chief Creative Officer --BAKER STREET ADVERTISING, San Francisco, CA, pg. 88
Backaus, Gary, Chief Creative Officer --ARCHER MALMO, Memphis, TN, pg. 67
Bae, Charles, Chief Creative Officer --ROKKAN, New York, NY, pg. 990
Baiocco, Rob, Chief Creative Officer --THE BAM CONNECTION, Brooklyn, NY, pg. 89
Baird, Rob, Chief Creative Officer --PREACHER, Austin, TX, pg. 908
Baka, Jeremy, Chief Creative Officer --Cohn & Wolfe, London, United Kingdom, pg. 1481
Barlow, Toby, Chief Creative Officer --Team Detroit, Dearborn, MI, pg. 1222
Barnum, David, Chief Creative Officer --WASABI RABBIT INC, New York, NY, pg. 1191
Baroin, Vincent, Chief Creative Officer --Interbrand, London, United Kingdom, pg. 551
Barrett, Russell, Chief Creative Officer --BBH Mumbai, Mumbai, India, pg. 96
Batista, Dave, Chief Creative Officer --BEAM INTERACTIVE, Boston, MA, pg. 1283
Batten, Matt, Chief Creative Officer --Wunderman, London, United Kingdom, pg. 1235
Batten, Matt, Chief Creative Officer --Wunderman Interactive, London, United Kingdom, pg. 1234
Baudenbacher, Beat, Chief Creative Officer --LOYALKASPAR, New York, NY, pg. 671
Bauman, Christian, Chief Creative Officer --H4B Chelsea, New York, NY, pg. 487
Baxter, Mat, Chief Creative Officer --IPG MEDIABRANDS, New York, NY, pg. 560
Beaman, Darin, Chief Creative Officer --OIC, Pasadena, CA, pg. 854
Beard, Tony, Chief Creative Officer --PRICEWEBER MARKETING COMMUNICATIONS, INC., Louisville, KY, pg. 909
Becker, Christoph, Chief Creative Officer --GYRO, New York, NY, pg. 468
Beggs, Jonathan, Chief Creative Officer --Saatchi & Saatchi, Cape Town, South Africa, pg. 1005
Belk, Howard, Chief Creative Officer --SIEGEL+GALE, New York, NY, pg. 1041
Bell, Lisa, Chief Creative Officer --TIVOLI PARTNERS, Charlotte, NC, pg. 1146
Benjamin, Jay, Chief Creative Officer --SAATCHI & SAATCHI, New York, NY, pg. 1000
Benjamin, Jay, Chief Creative Officer --Saatchi & Saatchi New York, New York, NY, pg. 1001
Bennett, Lisa, Chief Creative Officer --TM ADVERTISING, Dallas, TX, pg. 1147
Bergan, Gregg, Chief Creative Officer --PURE BRAND COMMUNICATIONS, LLC, Denver, CO, pg. 938
Berman, Ryan, Chief Creative Officer --THE I.D.E.A. BRAND, San Diego, CA, pg. 533
Bernardo, James, Chief Creative Officer --FCB Manila, Makati, Philippines, pg. 381
Bernstein, David, Chief Creative Officer --THE GATE WORLDWIDE NEW YORK, New York, NY, pg. 417
Bertino, Fred, Chief Creative Officer --MMB, Boston, MA, pg. 767
Bessler, Larry, Chief Creative Officer --RPM/Las Vegas, Las Vegas, NV, pg. 995
Bevilaqua, Adrianna, Chief Creative Officer --M. BOOTH & ASSOCIATES, New York, NY, pg. 679
Bhattacharyya, Sandipan, Chief Creative Officer --Grey (India) Pvt. Ltd., Mumbai, India, pg. 456
Biancoli, Bill, Chief Creative Officer --McCann Erickson Deutschland, Frankfurt am Main, Germany, pg. 720
Bird, Andy, Chief Creative Officer --PUBLICIS USA, New York, NY, pg. 935
Bjorkman, Lincoln, Chief Creative Officer --WUNDERMAN, New York, NY, pg. 1229
Bjorkman, Lincoln, Chief Creative Officer --Wunderman Interactive, Chicago, IL, pg. 1229
Blose, Alan, Chief Creative Officer --THE FRANK AGENCY INC, Overland Park, KS, pg. 400
Bolin, Scott, Chief Creative Officer --BOLIN MARKETING, Minneapolis, MN, pg. 147
Bonelli, Fabian, Chief Creative Officer --Publicis 67, Caracas, Venezuela, pg. 930
Bongiovanni, Brad, Chief Creative Officer --ROCKIT SCIENCE AGENCY, Baton Rouge, LA, pg. 989
Bonis, Joseph, Chief Creative Officer --O'SULLIVAN COMMUNICATIONS, Acton, MA, pg. 865
Bonner, Daniel, Chief Creative Officer --Razorfish UK, London, United Kingdom, pg. 1311
Boudreau, Wil, Chief Creative Officer --BBDO Atlanta, Atlanta, GA, pg. 100
Bowen, Gordon, Chief Creative Officer --MCGARRYBOWEN, New York, NY, pg. 733
Brabender, John, Chief Creative Officer --BRABENDERCOX, Leesburg, VA, pg. 152
Brady, Conor, Chief Creative Officer --Critical Mass Inc., New York, NY, pg. 255
Brady, Conor, Chief Creative Officer --Critical Mass Inc., London, United Kingdom, pg. 255
Braun, Ken, Chief Creative Officer --LOUNGE LIZARD WORLDWIDE, Patchogue, NY, pg. 669
Brocker, Jennifer, Chief Creative Officer --STEPHENS & ASSOCIATES ADVERTISING, INC., Overland Park, KS, pg. 1084
Brothers, Jim, Chief Creative Officer --VOYAGE LLC, Orlando, FL, pg. 1185
Brourman, Paul, Chief Creative Officer --SPONGE, LLC, Chicago, IL, pg. 1066
Brown, Keisha, Chief Creative Officer --LAGRANT COMMUNICATIONS, Los Angeles, CA, pg. 622
Brown, Ronnie, Chief Creative Officer --Doremus (United Kingdom), London, United Kingdom, pg. 325
Bryan, Sean, Chief Creative Officer --McCann Erickson/New York, New York, NY, pg. 714
Bull, Matthew, Chief Creative Officer --MCGARRYBOWEN, New York, NY, pg. 733
Buonaguidi, Dave, Chief Creative Officer --CP+B, London, United Kingdom, pg. 240
Butler, Stephen, Chief Creative Officer --TBWA California, Los Angeles, CA, pg. 1114
Butler, Stephen, Chief Creative Officer --TBWA Chiat Day Los Angeles, Los Angeles, CA, pg. 1114
Byrne, Mike, Chief Creative Officer --Anomaly, Toronto, Canada, pg. 60
Byrne, Mike, Chief Creative Officer --Anomaly, Toronto, Canada, pg. 738
Caguin, Mike, Chief Creative Officer --COLLE+MCVOY, Minneapolis, MN, pg. 221
Caguin, Mike, Chief Creative Officer --EXPONENT PR, Minneapolis, MN, pg. 1512
Camp, Roger, Chief Creative Officer --CAMP + KING, San Francisco, CA, pg. 187
Campbell, Cosmo, Chief Creative Officer --DDB Canada, Toronto, Canada, pg. 274
Campopiano, Javier, Chief Creative Officer --Conill Advertising, Inc., El Segundo, CA, pg. 230
Campopiano, Javier, Chief Creative Officer --Del Campo Nazca Saatchi & Saatchi, Buenos Aires, Argentina, pg. 1007
Campopiano, Javier, Chief Creative Officer --Saatchi & Saatchi Latin America, Miami, FL, pg. 1000
Capanescu, Razvan, Chief Creative Officer --Leo Burnett & Target SA, Bucharest, Romania, pg. 644
Carley, Brian, Chief Creative Officer --ROKKAN, New York, NY, pg. 990
Carpenter, Reyan, Chief Creative Officer --CAPITOL MARKETING GROUP, INC., Fairfax, VA, pg. 189
Carter, David, Chief Creative Officer --MITHUN, Minneapolis, MN, pg. 765
Case, Bob, Chief Creative Officer --THE LAVIDGE COMPANY, Phoenix, AZ, pg. 632
Caserta, Joseph, Chief Creative Officer --DSC (DILEONARDO SIANO CASERTA) ADVERTISING, Philadelphia, PA, pg. 330
Cassese, Marco, Chief Creative Officer --Acento Advertising, Chicago, IL, pg. 20
Cassese, Marco, Chief Creative Officer --ACENTO ADVERTISING, INC., Santa Monica, CA, pg. 19
Castledine, Paul, Chief Creative Officer --Boxer, Birmingham, United Kingdom, pg. 1421
Castledine, Paul, Chief Creative Officer --Boxer Creative, Birmingham, United Kingdom, pg. 1421
Castro, Raul, Chief Creative Officer --McCann Erickson (Philippines), Inc., Manila, Philippines, pg. 725
Cecere, Joe, Chief Creative Officer --LITTLE & COMPANY, Minneapolis, MN, pg. 662
Ceraso, Allison, Chief Creative Officer --Havas Life Metro, New York, NY, pg. 486
Ceraso, Allison, Chief Creative Officer --Havas Life New York, New York, NY, pg. 487
Charles, Allan, Chief Creative Officer --TBC INC., Baltimore, MD, pg. 1113
Charlton, Peter, Chief Creative Officer --RICOCHET PARTNERS, INC., Portland, OR, pg. 980
Cheong, Eugene, Chief Creative Officer --Ogilvy & Mather Advertising, Singapore, Singapore, pg. 846
Cherry, Robert, Chief Creative Officer --SEED STRATEGY, INC., Crestview Hills, KY, pg. 1030
Chiorando, Rick, Chief Creative Officer --AUSTIN & WILLIAMS, Hauppauge, NY, pg. 80
Chiu, Chris, Chief Creative Officer --Leo Burnett, Singapore, Singapore, pg. 650
Choe, Edmund, Chief Creative Officer --TBWA Asia Pacific, Quarry Bay, China (Hong Kong), pg. 1128
Choe, Edmund, Chief Creative Officer --TBWA Beijing, Beijing, China, pg. 1128
Choe, Edmund, Chief Creative Officer --TBWA Hong Kong, Hong Kong, China (Hong Kong), pg. 1128
Chou, Murphy, Chief Creative Officer --Leo Burnett, Taipei, Taiwan, pg. 651
Christmann, Tom, Chief Creative Officer --DIMASSIMO GOLDSTEIN, New York, NY, pg. 310
Christou, Andrew, Chief Creative Officer --Publicis Seattle, Seattle, WA, pg. 927
Christou, Andrew, Chief Creative Officer --Publicis Seattle, Seattle, WA, pg. 936
Chu, Daniel, Chief Creative Officer --Possible Los Angeles, Los Angeles, CA, pg. 1307
Chu, Polly, Chief Creative Officer --J. Walter Thompson Beijing, Beijing, China, pg. 568
Chung, Sam, Chief Creative Officer --WE MARKETING GROUP,

Responsibilities Index

Responsibilities Index

WORLDWIDE, Cincinnati, OH, pg. 402
Leduc, Michele, Chief Creative Officer --ZIP COMMUNICATION INC, Montreal, Canada, pg. 1258
Lee, Owen, Chief Creative Officer --FCB Inferno, London, United Kingdom, pg. 375
Lee, Ruth, Chief Creative Officer --DDB Worldwide Ltd., Hong Kong, China (Hong Kong), pg. 283
Legorburu, Gaston, Chief Creative Officer --Sapient Atlanta, Atlanta, GA, pg. 1018
Legorburu, Gaston, Chief Creative Officer --Sapient Chicago, Chicago, IL, pg. 1018
Legorburu, Gaston, Chief Creative Officer --Sapient Corporation, Miami, FL, pg. 1018
Legorburu, Gaston, Chief Creative Officer --SAPIENT CORPORATION, Boston, MA, pg. 1017
Legorburu, Gaston, Chief Creative Officer --Sapient Houston, Houston, TX, pg. 1018
Legorburu, Gaston, Chief Creative Officer --Sapient Securities Corporation, Boston, MA, pg. 1019
Legorburu, Gaston, Chief Creative Officer --SAPIENTNITRO USA, INC., New York, NY, pg. 1019
Lemme, Michael, Chief Creative Officer --DUNCAN CHANNON, San Francisco, CA, pg. 332
Leonard, Nils, Chief Creative Officer --Grey London, London, United Kingdom, pg. 447
Lesniewicz, Terrence, Chief Creative Officer --LESNIEWICZ ASSOCIATES LLC, Perrysburg, OH, pg. 652
Lev, Bruce, Chief Creative Officer --LEVLANE ADVERTISING/PR/INTERACTIVE, Philadelphia, PA, pg. 654
Lev, Bruce, Chief Creative Officer --LevLane Advertising/PR/Interactive-Florida, Boynton Beach, FL, pg. 654
Levine, Andrew T., Chief Creative Officer --DEVELOPMENT COUNSELLORS INTERNATIONAL, LTD., New York, NY, pg. 304
Levy, Rich, Chief Creative Officer --FCB HEALTH, New York, NY, pg. 383
Lewis, Kyle, Chief Creative Officer --THE MORRISON AGENCY, Atlanta, GA, pg. 776
Lieman, Todd, Chief Creative Officer --SKADADDLE MEDIA, Sausalito, CA, pg. 1049
Lieppe, Matt, Chief Creative Officer --PROOF INTEGRATED COMMUNICATIONS, Washington, DC, pg. 914
Lieu, Alex, Chief Creative Officer --42 ENTERTAINMENT, LLC, Burbank, CA, pg. 8
Lima, Claudio, Chief Creative Officer --Y&R Latin American Headquarters, Miami, FL, pg. 1240
Lima, Claudio, Chief Creative Officer --Y&R Miami, Miami, FL, pg. 1248
Lipton, Pierre, Chief Creative Officer --360I, New York, NY, pg. 6
Lira, Joaquin, Chief Creative Officer --M8 AGENCY, Miami, FL, pg. 681
Littlejohn, David, Chief Creative Officer --HUMANAUT, Chattanooga, TN, pg. 528
Litzinger, Matthew, Chief Creative Officer --RED LION, Toronto, Canada, pg. 961
Long, Brian, Chief Creative Officer --RESPONSE MARKETING GROUP LLC, Richmond, VA, pg. 971
Lotterman, Deborah, Chief Creative Officer --LEHMANMILLET, Boston, MA, pg. 636
Lourenco, Rui, Chief Creative Officer --Havas Experience Lisbon, Lisbon, Portugal, pg. 495
Lourenco, Rui, Chief Creative Officer --Havas Worldwide Digital Portugal, Lisbon, Portugal, pg. 495
Lovegrove, Michael, Chief Creative Officer --TracyLocke, Wilton, CT, pg. 1154
Lovegrove, Michael, Chief Creative Officer --TRACYLOCKE, Dallas, TX, pg. 1153
Lubars, David, Chief Creative Officer --BBDO NORTH AMERICA, New York, NY, pg. 98
MacKellar, Ian, Chief Creative Officer --Ogilvy & Mather, Toronto, Canada, pg. 829
MacKellar, Ian, Chief Creative Officer --OgilvyOne Worldwide, Toronto, Canada, pg. 829
Mackler, Jonathan, Chief Creative Officer --KBS+, New York, NY, pg. 604
Madill, Alan, Chief Creative Officer --Juniper Park/TBWA, Toronto, Canada, pg. 1116
Mahimkar, Chandan, Chief Creative Officer --Saatchi & Saatchi Direct, Bengaluru, India, pg. 1011
Malak, Tarik, Chief Creative Officer --SWELL, New York, NY, pg. 1104
Mandelbaum, Jaime, Chief Creative Officer --Y&R Praha, s.r.o., Prague, Czech Republic, pg. 1248
Mangada, Melvin M., Chief Creative Officer --TBWA Santiago Mangada Puno, Manila, Philippines, pg. 1130
Manggunio, Victor, Chief Creative Officer --Leo Burnett Shanghai Advertising Co., Ltd., Shanghai, China, pg. 648
Marcionetti, Peter, Chief Creative Officer --DUFFY & SHANLEY, INC., Providence, RI, pg. 331
Marco, Harvey, Chief Creative Officer --THE GARAGE TEAM MAZDA, Costa Mesa, CA, pg. 414
Mariotti, Beatrice, Chief Creative Officer --Carre Noir Turino, Turin, Italy, pg. 920
Martel, Dan, Chief Creative Officer --SAXUM PUBLIC RELATIONS, Oklahoma City, OK, pg. 1645
Martinez, Raul, Chief Creative Officer --AR NEW YORK, New York, NY, pg. 66
Mastromatteo, Giuseppe, Chief Creative Officer --Ogilvy & Mather, Milan, Italy, pg. 833
Mastromatteo, Giuseppe, Chief Creative Officer --Ogilvy & Mather, Rome, Italy, pg. 833
Matsui, Miki, Chief Creative Officer --TBWA/Hakuhodo, Tokyo, Japan, pg. 1129
Maxham, John, Chief Creative Officer --DDB Chicago, Chicago, IL, pg. 274
Mayer, Josh, Chief Creative Officer --PETER MAYER ADVERTISING, INC., New Orleans, LA, pg. 886
McBride, Chuck, Chief Creative Officer --CUTWATER, San Francisco, CA, pg. 261
McCormack, Joe, Chief Creative Officer --DOREMUS, New York, NY, pg. 324
McCormick, Lance, Chief Creative Officer --JNA ADVERTISING, Overland Park, KS, pg. 592
McCormick, Michael, Chief Creative Officer --RODGERS TOWNSEND, LLC, Saint Louis, MO, pg. 989
McCracken, Todd, Chief Creative Officer --Ogilvy & Mather (Vietnam) Ltd., Ho Chi Minh City, Vietnam, pg. 848
McGoldrick, Jack, Chief Creative Officer --MCGOLDRICK MARKETING, Medford, MA, pg. 735
McInnes, Gavin, Chief Creative Officer --ROOSTER, New York, NY, pg. 991
McKee, Chris, Chief Creative Officer --THE GEPPETTO GROUP, New York, NY, pg. 423
McKeon, Kevin, Chief Creative Officer --OLSON, Minneapolis, MN, pg. 856
Mckinnis, Jim, Chief Creative Officer --SPLASH MEDIA GROUP, Addison, TX, pg. 1065
McMillan, Dorothy, Chief Creative Officer --BOB'S YOUR UNCLE, Toronto, Canada, pg. 145
McMillan, Mike, Chief Creative Officer --INTROWORKS, INC., Minnetonka, MN, pg. 558
McNeill, Nick, Chief Creative Officer --FUEL, Myrtle Beach, SC, pg. 406
McNellis, Michael, Chief Creative Officer --BARU ADVERTISING, Los Angeles, CA, pg. 96
McShane, Kevin, Chief Creative Officer --OMNICOM GROUP INC., New York, NY, pg. 857
McVey, Jon, Chief Creative Officer --Possible, Seattle, WA, pg. 1230
McVey, Jon, Chief Creative Officer --Possible, Seattle, WA, pg. 1221
Melentin, Artur, Chief Creative Officer --GRAVITY MEDIA, New York, NY, pg. 440
Mercurio, John, Chief Creative Officer --AGENCYSACKS, New York, NY, pg. 39
Messina, Mario G., Chief Creative Officer --MGM GOLD COMMUNICATIONS, New York, NY, pg. 753
Metelenis, Michael, Chief Creative Officer --Centron, New York, NY, pg. 506
Meyer, John, Chief Creative Officer --INNERSPIN MARKETING, Los Angeles, CA, pg. 547
Mietelski, Steve, Chief Creative Officer --THE FANTASTICAL, Boston, MA, pg. 368
Milan, Pat, Chief Creative Officer --TUNHEIM PARTNERS, Minneapolis, MN, pg. 1667
Millman, Ken, Chief Creative Officer --SPIKE ADVERTISING INC., Burlington, VT, pg. 1064
Millstein, Jacqueline, Chief Creative Officer --RITTA, Englewood, NJ, pg. 984
Milner, Duncan, Chief Creative Officer --TBWA/Media Arts Lab, Los Angeles, CA, pg. 1116
Milner, Duncan, Chief Creative Officer --TBWA/WORLDWIDE, New York, NY, pg. 1114
Missen, Barclay, Chief Creative Officer --GA HEALTHCARE COMMUNICATION, Chicago, IL, pg. 413
Mitchell, Peter, Chief Creative Officer --SALTERMITCHELL INC., Tallahassee, FL, pg. 1645
Monello, Mike, Chief Creative Officer --CAMPFIRE, New York, NY, pg. 188
Monroe, Kipp, Chief Creative Officer --WHITE & PARTNERS, Herndon, VA, pg. 1199
Monteiro, Joanna, Chief Creative Officer --FCB Sao Paulo, Sao Paulo, Brazil, pg. 377
Moranville, David, Chief Creative Officer --Davis Elen Advertising, Arlington, VA, pg. 270
Moranville, David, Chief Creative Officer --Davis-Elen Advertising, Inc., Portland, OR, pg. 270
Moranville, David, Chief Creative Officer --DAVIS ELEN ADVERTISING, INC., Los Angeles, CA, pg. 270
Moreno, Carlos, Chief Creative Officer --Cossette Communications, Halifax, Canada, pg. 237
Moro, Monica, Chief Creative Officer --McCann Erickson S.A., Madrid, Spain, pg. 727
Morris, Brett, Chief Creative Officer --FCB Johannesburg, Johannesburg, South Africa, pg. 382
Mostoles, Carlo, Chief Creative Officer --Kinetic, Makati, Philippines, pg. 1350
Moudry, Tom, Chief Creative Officer --MARTIN/WILLIAMS ADVERTISING INC., Minneapolis, MN, pg. 704
Mouzannar, Bechara, Chief Creative Officer --H&C, Leo Burnett, Beirut, Lebanon, pg. 643
Mouzannar, Bechara, Chief Creative Officer --Leo Burnett Warsaw SP.Z.O.O., Warsaw, Poland, pg. 644
Mouzannar, Bechara, Chief Creative Officer --Radius Leo Burnett, Dubai, United Arab Emirates, pg. 646
Mouzannar, Bechara, Chief Creative Officer --Targets/Leo Burnett, Riyadh, Saudi Arabia, pg. 645
Moya, Jorge R., Chief Creative Officer --COMMONGROUNDMGS, Chicago, IL, pg. 224
Moya, Jorge R., Chief Creative Officer --CommongroundMGS, Miami, FL, pg. 224
Mroueh, Zak, Chief Creative Officer --ZULU ALPHA KILO, Toronto, Canada, pg. 1260
Muccino, Alfredo, Chief Creative Officer --LIQUID AGENCY, INC., San Jose, CA, pg. 661
Muniz, Christopher, Chief Creative Officer --DIVISION ADVERTISING & DESIGN, Houston, TX, pg. 316
Murphy, Thomas, Chief Creative Officer --McCann Erickson/New York, New York, NY, pg. 714
Murphy, Tom, Chief Creative Officer --MCCANN ERICKSON WORLDWIDE, New York, NY, pg. 713
Musmanno, Anthony, Chief Creative Officer --THE IDEA MILL, Pittsburgh, PA, pg. 534
Muthucumaru, Kishan, Chief Creative Officer --BEMIS BALKIND, Los Angeles, CA, pg. 123
Naja, Ramsey, Chief Creative Officer --J. Walter Thompson Cairo, Cairo, Egypt, pg. 576
Nathanson, David, Chief Creative Officer --Zimmerman Advertising, Oakbrook Terrace, IL, pg. 1257
Nathanson, David, Chief Creative Officer --Zimmerman Advertising, New York, NY, pg. 1257
Neary, Jack, Chief Creative Officer --M2 Universal Communications Management, Toronto, Canada, pg. 715
Neill, Evelyn, Chief Creative Officer --DOREMUS, New York, NY, pg. 324
Nel-lo, Enric, Chief Creative Officer --Grey Madrid, Madrid, Spain, pg. 452
Nelson, Erik, Chief Creative Officer --UPROAR, Seattle, WA, pg. 1168
Ng, Ronald, Chief Creative Officer --DigitasLBi, New York, NY, pg. 1290
Ng, Tian It, Chief Creative Officer --DDB Guoan Communications Beijing Co., Ltd., Beijing, China, pg. 279
Nichols, Chris, Chief Creative Officer --NL PARTNERS, Portland, ME, pg. 810
Nikolay, Megvelidze, Chief Creative Officer --BBDO Moscow, Moscow, Russia, pg. 110
Nisson, Bob, Chief Creative Officer --JAY ADVERTISING, INC., Rochester, NY, pg. 588
Nordin, Bill, Chief Creative Officer --SURDELL & PARTNERS, LLC, Omaha, NE, pg. 1101
Nunziato, John, Chief Creative Officer --LITTLE BIG BRANDS, White Plains, NY, pg. 662
Nuss, Mark, Chief Creative Officer --THE ADCOM GROUP, Cleveland, OH, pg. 27
O'Keefe, Kelly, Chief Creative Officer --Padilla/CRT, Richmond, VA, pg. 869
Oakley, David, Chief Creative Officer --BOONEOAKLEY, Charlotte, NC, pg. 148
Oberman, Mike, Chief Creative Officer --FUSION IDEA LAB, Chicago, IL, pg. 410
Obregon, Ish, Chief Creative Officer --OISHII CREATIVE, Los Angeles, CA, pg. 854

Creative

Responsibilities Index

Responsibilities Index

Responsibilities Index

Responsibilities Index

Responsibilities Index

Responsibilities Index

Jorgensen, Lars, Creative --ANOMALY, New York, NY, pg. 60
Joseph, Mridula, Creative --Ogilvy & Mather India, Chennai, India, pg. 842
Joseph, Mridula, Creative --Ogilvy India, Mumbai, India, pg. 843
Joshi, Kashyap, Creative --J. Walter Thompson, Mumbai, India, pg. 569
Joshi, Makarand, Creative --Ogilvy India, Mumbai, India, pg. 843
Joshpe, Kent, Creative --ANTITHESIS ADVERTISING, Rochester, NY, pg. 62
Joubert, David, Creative --George Patterson Y&R, Sydney, Australia, pg. 1219
Joubert, David, Creative --George Patterson Y&R, Canberra, Australia, pg. 1219
Joubert, David, Creative --Young & Rubicam Australia/New Zealand, Sydney, Australia, pg. 1242
Joyner, Jeff, Creative --SEROKA, Waukesha, WI, pg. 1033
Judd, Peter, Creative --HUB STRATEGY AND COMMUNICATION, San Francisco, CA, pg. 526
Juhasz, Eva, Creative --DDB Budapest, Budapest, Hungary, pg. 283
Jung, Billie, Creative --ES ADVERTISING, Los Angeles, CA, pg. 355
Jung, Calvin, Creative --CREATIVE:MINT LLC, San Francisco, CA, pg. 253
Jungles, Brad, Creative --BARKLEYREI, Pittsburgh, PA, pg. 93
Jungmann, Phil, Creative --Energy BBDO, Chicago, IL, pg. 100
Juniot, Marcio, Creative --Leo Burnett Tailor Made, Sao Paulo, Brazil, pg. 640
Jurentkuff, JD, Creative --TBWA/Media Arts Lab, Los Angeles, CA, pg. 1116
Jurisic, Stephen, Creative --JOHN ST., Toronto, Canada, pg. 593
Kabbani, Mohamed, Creative --J. Walter Thompson, Beirut, Lebanon, pg. 577
Kabra, Ujjwal, Creative --Mullen Lowe Lintas Group, Mumbai, India, pg. 791
Kacenka, Peter, Creative --Wiktor/Leo Burnett, s.r.o., Bratislava, Slovakia, pg. 645
Kaczyk, Meg, Creative --CMD, Portland, OR, pg. 217
Kadam, Satyajeet, Creative --DDB Mudra Group, Mumbai, India, pg. 283
Kaddoum, Shady, Creative --Saatchi & Saatchi, Beirut, Lebanon, pg. 1004
Kafadar, Engin, Creative --Grey Istanbul, Istanbul, Turkey, pg. 452
Kahana, Jake, Creative --MATTER UNLIMITED LLC, New York, NY, pg. 710
Kahl, Les, Creative --AdFarm, Fargo, ND, pg. 28
Kahl, Les, Creative --AdFarm, Kansas City, MO, pg. 28
Kahle, Brian, Creative --ADVENTIVE MARKETING, INC., Arlington Heights, IL, pg. 33
Kaihoi, Jessica, Creative --OgilvyOne Worldwide, Chicago, IL, pg. 828
Kaiser, Matt, Creative --Connelly Partners Travel, Boston, MA, pg. 231
Kaka, Kaka Ling, Creative --Havas Worldwide Beijing, Beijing, China, pg. 500
Kaka, Kaka Ling, Creative --Havas Worldwide Shanghai, Shanghai, China, pg. 500
Kakomanolis, Elias, Creative --MCKINNEY, Durham, NC, pg. 736
Kalchev, Alexander, Creative --DDB Paris, Paris, France, pg. 281
Kalimbet, Anna, Creative --DARE, London, United Kingdom, pg. 1286
Kalina, Ron, Creative --HARRIS, BAIO & MCCULLOUGH INC., Philadelphia, PA, pg. 481
Kalita, Mriganka, Creative --BPG Group, Dubai, United Arab Emirates, pg. 1218
Kalliches, Joanna, Creative --Merkley + Partners/Healthworks, New York, NY, pg. 750
Kaloff, Constantin, Creative --FCB Hamburg, Hamburg, Germany, pg. 373
Kamei, Nick, Creative --WALTON / ISAACSON, Culver City, CA, pg. 1189
Kammien, Craig, Creative --SWITCH, Saint Louis, MO, pg. 1105
Kamp, Bill, Creative --BURKHEAD BRAND GROUP, Cary, NC, pg. 176
Kamran, Nadia, Creative --DDB New York, New York, NY, pg. 275
Kamzelas, Paul, Creative --BBH NEW YORK, New York, NY, pg. 118
Kanarek, Monica Noce, Creative --PUROHIT NAVIGATION, Chicago, IL, pg. 939
Kandarian, Israel, Creative --SET CREATIVE, New York, NY, pg. 1034
Kane, Christina, Creative --THE MARS AGENCY, Southfield, MI, pg. 701
Kang, Elizabeth, Creative --GODA ADVERTISING, Inverness, IL, pg. 432
Kang, Gab-Soo, Creative --FCB Seoul, Seoul, Korea (South), pg. 380
Kanofsky, Thomas, Creative --Saatchi & Saatchi, Frankfurt am Main, Germany, pg. 1003
Kanzer, Adam, Creative --McCann Erickson/New York, New York, NY, pg. 714
Kapadia, Harsh, Creative --VML-New York, New York, NY, pg. 1183
Kapec, Charles, Creative --NAS RECRUITMENT INNOVATION, Cleveland, OH, pg. 800
Kaplan, Nick, Creative --BARTON F. GRAF 9000 LLC, New York, NY, pg. 96
Kapoor, Puneet, Creative --McCann Erickson India, Mumbai, India, pg. 721
Karakasoglu, Zeynep, Creative --TBWA Istanbul, Istanbul, Turkey, pg. 1127
Karanikolas, Kostas, Creative --Saatchi & Saatchi, Lake Oswego, OR, pg. 1002
Karanikolas, Kostas, Creative --Saatchi & Saatchi London, London, United Kingdom, pg. 1007
Karasyk, Erik, Creative --HUSH, Brooklyn, NY, pg. 1295
Karatas, Mark, Creative --J. Walter Thompson GmbH, Frankfurt am Main, Germany, pg. 573
Karelson, Tina, Creative --Risdall Public Relations, New Brighton, MN, pg. 983
Karena, Anna, Creative --Wunderman, Sydney, Australia, pg. 1230
Karir, Anand, Creative --DDB Mudra Group, Mumbai, India, pg. 283
Karkhanis, Ashutosh, Creative --Saatchi & Saatchi, Mumbai, India, pg. 1011
Karlen, Kacy, Creative --CAPTAINS OF INDUSTRY, Boston, MA, pg. 190
Karlsson, Jens, Creative --YOUR MAJESTY, New York, NY, pg. 1252
Karlsson, Linus, Creative --Commonwealth, Detroit, MI, pg. 714
Karmakar, Kainaz, Creative --Ogilvy India, Mumbai, India, pg. 843
Karnowsky, Debbie, Creative --MARICICH BRAND COMMUNICATIONS, Irvine, CA, pg. 693
Karstad, David, Creative --FRANK CREATIVE INC, Portland, OR, pg. 401
Kartha, Malini, Creative --CAMP + KING, San Francisco, CA, pg. 187
Katalinic, Tony, Creative --Leo Burnett USA, Chicago, IL, pg. 639
Katalinic, Tony, Creative --LEO BURNETT WORLDWIDE, INC., Chicago, IL, pg. 637
Kathriarachchi, Athula, Creative --Leo Burnett Solutions Inc., Colombo, Sri Lanka, pg. 650
Katona, Diti, Creative --CONCRETE DESIGN COMMUNICATIONS INC, Toronto, Canada, pg. 229
Kaufman, Sandy, Creative --COLUMBIAD, New York, NY, pg. 1265
Kaufmann, Deborah, Creative --BIG APPLE CIRCUS, Brooklyn, NY, pg. 1264
Kause, Tony, Creative --GLOBALHUE, Southfield, MI, pg. 429
Kavanagh, Simon, Creative --Rapp London, London, United Kingdom, pg. 952
Kavander, Tim, Creative --Publicis Dialog Boise, Boise, ID, pg. 927
Kavander, Tim, Creative --Publicis Dialog Boise, Boise, ID, pg. 936
Kavander, Tim, Creative --Publicis Toronto, Toronto, Canada, pg. 926
Kawasaki, Kohei, Creative --J. Walter Thompson Japan, Tokyo, Japan, pg. 570
Kaya, Erkan, Creative --Y&R Turkey, Istanbul, Turkey, pg. 1247
Kayal, Brad, Creative --BARRETTSF, San Francisco, CA, pg. 94
Kayuk, Erika, Creative --Commonwealth, Detroit, MI, pg. 714
Kaza, Paul, Creative --HAGAN ASSOCIATES, South Burlington, VT, pg. 472
Kazarinoff, Elyse, Creative --Landor Associates, New York, NY, pg. 625
Keamy, Paula, Creative --M&C Saatchi, Sydney, Australia, pg. 677
Kearney, Peter, Creative --Erwin Penland, New York, NY, pg. 355
Kearse, John, Creative --ARNOLD WORLDWIDE, Boston, MA, pg. 71
Kearse, John, Creative --MULLEN LOWE GROUP, Boston, MA, pg. 786
Keasler, Sam, Creative --RED DELUXE BRAND DEVELOPMENT, Memphis, TN, pg. 959
Keathley, Tom, Creative --ARRAS KEATHLEY AGENCY, Cleveland, OH, pg. 73
Keating, Katie, Creative --FANCY LLC, New York, NY, pg. 367
Keeler, Laura, Creative --DigitasLBi, Chicago, IL, pg. 1290
Keene, Margaret, Creative --Mullen Lowe, Winston Salem, NC, pg. 788
Keene, Margaret, Creative --Mullen Lowe, El Segundo, CA, pg. 788
Keenleyside, Tim, Creative --FINGERPRINT COMMUNICATIONS, Toronto, Canada, pg. 1334
Keeven, Jason, Creative --BRIGHTON AGENCY, INC., Saint Louis, MO, pg. 166
Keff, Darren, Creative --Leo Burnett, Ltd., London, United Kingdom, pg. 641
Keil, Thomas, Creative --McCann Erickson Deutschland, Frankfurt am Main, Germany, pg. 720
Keith, Brian, Creative --EL CREATIVE, INC., Dallas, TX, pg. 342
Keith, Richard, Creative --G.W. HOFFMAN MARKETING & COMMUNICATIONS, Darien, CT, pg. 1415
Kelderhouse, Aaron, Creative --B2C ENTERPRISES, Roanoke, VA, pg. 85
Kell, Josh, Creative --SWITCH, Saint Louis, MO, pg. 1105
Kell, Ronnie, Creative --BENCHMARK USA, Mission Viejo, CA, pg. 1407
Kellam, Shep, Creative --TM ADVERTISING, Dallas, TX, pg. 1147
Keller, Denise, Creative --HUGHES & STUART, INC., Greenwood Village, CO, pg. 527
Keller, Kurt, Creative --PHIRE GROUP, Ann Arbor, MI, pg. 889
Kelley, Jeff, Creative --MESS, Chicago, IL, pg. 1302
Kelley, Katy, Creative --RUDER FINN INC., New York, NY, pg. 1642
Kelley, Kyle, Creative --RICHARDS PARTNERS, Dallas, TX, pg. 1636
Kelley, Shawn, Creative --HMH-Charlotte N.C., Charlotte, NC, pg. 519
Kelliher, Linda, Creative --KELLIHER SAMETS VOLK, Burlington, VT, pg. 607
Kellogg, Ryan, Creative --HUGE, Brooklyn, NY, pg. 526
Kelly, Buffy McCoy, Creative --TATTOO PROJECTS, Charlotte, NC, pg. 1111
Kelly, Emmy Lou, Creative --LIPPE TAYLOR, New York, NY, pg. 1576
Kelly, James, Creative --KETCHUM, New York, NY, pg. 1561
Kelly, Niall, Creative --JOHN ST., Toronto, Canada, pg. 593
Kelly, Shawn, Creative --BANDUJO ADVERTISING & DESIGN, New York, NY, pg. 89
Kelly, Tom, Creative --BRAND CONTENT, Boston, MA, pg. 155
Kelly, Troy, Creative --Ackerman McQueen, Inc., Dallas, TX, pg. 20
Kemble, John, Creative --Dudnyk, San Francisco, CA, pg. 331
Kemble, John, Creative --DUDNYK HEALTHCARE GROUP, Horsham, PA, pg. 331
Kemerer, Lisa, Creative --MOTUM B2B, Toronto, Canada, pg. 780
Kemming, Jan Dirk, Creative --Weber Shandwick, Berlin, Germany, pg. 1679
Kemp, Marcus, Creative --FREE ENTERPRISE LLC, New York, NY, pg. 403
Kempf, R. Craig, Creative --CK COMMUNICATIONS, INC. (CKC), Melbourne, FL, pg. 212
Kenefick, Jim, Creative --DEVINE COMMUNICATIONS, Saint Petersburg, FL, pg. 304
Kenger, Dan, Creative --GIN LANE MEDIA, New York, NY, pg. 426
Kennedy, Heath, Creative --BROTHERS & CO., Tulsa, OK, pg. 170
Kennedy, Kurt, Creative --KENNEDY COMMUNICATIONS, Vancouver, WA, pg. 609
Kennedy, Meredith, Creative --THE CDM GROUP, New York, NY, pg. 200
Kenney, Tom, Creative --PP+K, Tampa, FL, pg. 907
Kent, Kevin, Creative --METROPOLIS ADVERTISING, Orlando, FL, pg. 752
Keogh, Ant, Creative --Clemenger BBDO Melbourne, Melbourne, Australia, pg. 114
Keong, Tan Chee, Creative --BBDO Malaysia, Kuala Lumpur, Malaysia, pg. 116
Keong, Tan Chee, Creative --Ogilvy & Mather Advertising, Kuala Lumpur, Malaysia, pg. 845
Keown, Roisin, Creative --DDFH&B Advertising Ltd., Dublin, Ireland, pg. 573
Kerekes, Danièl, Creative --LEVY MG, Pittsburgh, PA, pg. 655
Kern, Michael, Creative --WELIKESMALL, INC, Salt Lake City, UT, pg. 1196
Kerr, Graham, Creative --Maher Bird Associates, London, United Kingdom, pg. 1124
Kerr, Haydn, Creative --DDB New Zealand Ltd., Auckland, New Zealand, pg. 286
Kerr, Marney, Creative --ORGANIC, INC., San Francisco, CA, pg. 1306

Responsibilities Index

Maani, Marzuki, Creative --M&C Saatchi, Kuala Lumpur, Malaysia, pg. 678
Macadam, Angus, Creative --mcgarrybowen, London, United Kingdom, pg. 734
MacAloon, Grant, Creative --Leo Burnett Sydney, Sydney, Australia, pg. 647
Macaluso, Tom, Creative --ANSON-STONER INC., Winter Park, FL, pg. 61
MacArthur, Jonathan, Creative --THE PARTNERSHIP, Atlanta, GA, pg. 876
Macbeth, Jim, Creative --BERLINE, Royal Oak, MI, pg. 125
Macdonald, Kelsey, Creative --Havas Life, Toronto, Canada, pg. 487
Macdonald, Matt, Creative --BBDO Atlanta, Atlanta, GA, pg. 100
MacDougall, Don, Creative --SULLIVAN BRANDING, Memphis, TN, pg. 1097
Maceachern, Jeff, Creative --TAXI, Toronto, Canada, pg. 1111
MacEachern, Jeff, Creative --Taxi 2, Toronto, Canada, pg. 1112
Maceachern, Jeff, Creative --TAXI Calgary, Calgary, Canada, pg. 1112
Macgadie, Colin, Creative --BDG architecture+design, London, United Kingdom, pg. 1217
Machado, Diego, Creative --AKQA, INC., San Francisco, CA, pg. 1280
Machado, Felipe, Creative --DEUTSCH, INC., New York, NY, pg. 301
Machak, Joel, Creative --Crosby Marketing Communications, Bethesda, MD, pg. 256
Machin, Rich, Creative --SHEEHY & ASSOCIATES, Louisville, KY, pg. 1037
Mack, Adam, Creative --Weber Shandwick UK, London, United Kingdom, pg. 1681
Macken, Jan, Creative --TBWA Brussels, Brussels, Belgium, pg. 1117
Macken, Jan, Creative --TBWA Group, Brussels, Belgium, pg. 1117
Mackinnon, Angus, Creative --Poke, London, United Kingdom, pg. 922
Maclay, Sam, Creative --3 ADVERTISING, Albuquerque, NM, pg. 5
Maclay, Sam, Creative --3B ADVERTISING, LLC, Clive, IA, pg. 7
MacMillin, Andy, Creative --PUSH, Orlando, FL, pg. 939
Macomber, Patrick, Creative --160OVER90, Philadelphia, PA, pg. 2
Madariaga, Miguel, Creative --SCPF, Barcelona, Spain, pg. 1222
Madcharo, Karl, Creative --COLLE+MCVOY, Minneapolis, MN, pg. 221
Madden, Carla, Creative --FCB West, San Francisco, CA, pg. 372
Madden, Christian, Creative --MULLEN LOWE GROUP, Boston, MA, pg. 786
Maddox, David, Creative --ARCHER MALMO, Memphis, TN, pg. 67
Maddox, Michael, Creative --VISUAL PRINT GROUP & DESIGN, Fort Oglethorpe, GA, pg. 1179
Madruga, Luis, Creative --Publicis Arredondo de Haro, Mexico, Mexico, pg. 929
Magestro, Mike, Creative --MINDSPIKE DESIGN LLC, Milwaukee, WI, pg. 762
Maggipinto, Donata, Creative --AISLE ROCKET STUDIOS, Chattanooga, TN, pg. 42
Magila, Marlene, Creative --PACIFIC COMMUNICATIONS, Costa Mesa, CA, pg. 868
Magnason, Sigtryggur, Creative --The Icelandic Ad Agency, Reykjavik, Iceland, pg. 108
Magnuson, Brett, Creative --MAGNUSON DESIGN, Boise, ID, pg. 687
Magro, Nacho, Creative --Bassat, Ogilvy & Mather Comunicacion, Barcelona, Spain, pg. 1608
Magro, Nacho, Creative --Bassat, Ogilvy & Mather Comunicacion, Barcelona, Spain, pg. 834
Maguire, Joe, Creative --SWANSON RUSSELL ASSOCIATES, Lincoln, NE, pg. 1102
Mahajan, Jaideep, Creative --Rediffusion Y&R Pvt. Ltd., Gurgaon, India, pg. 1243
Mahan, Richard, Creative --DAILEY & ASSOCIATES, West Hollywood, CA, pg. 263
Mahoney, Tim, Creative --Commonwealth, Detroit, MI, pg. 714
Maier, Chris, Creative --50,000FEET, INC., Chicago, IL, pg. 9
Maier, Renee, Creative --TUREC ADVERTISING ASSOCIATES, INC., Saint Louis, MO, pg. 1162
Mainoli, Flavio, Creative --J. Walter Thompson Milan, Milan, Italy, pg. 573
Maiolo, Dominick, Creative --LEO BURNETT WORLDWIDE, INC., Chicago, IL, pg. 637
Maite, Carrillo, Creative --McCann Erickson S.A., Barcelona, Spain, pg. 728
Majee, Partha, Creative --DDB Mudra Group, Mumbai, India, pg. 283
Major, Robb, Creative --Charles Ryan Associates, Richmond, VA, pg. 205
Major, T. Scott, Creative --MONO, Minneapolis, MN, pg. 771
Majumder, Neel, Creative --DM9DDB, Sao Paulo, Brazil, pg. 278
Majumder, Neel, Creative --TBWA ISC Malaysia, Kuala Lumpur, Malaysia, pg. 1130
Majumder, Neel, Creative --Y&R Paris, Boulogne, France, pg. 1245
Maki, Jeff, Creative --GSD&M, Austin, TX, pg. 464
Makowski, John, Creative --HARVEY & DAUGHTERS, INC./ H&D BRANDING, Sparks, MD, pg. 483
Maktal, Mesh, Creative --THE JOEY COMPANY, Brooklyn, NY, pg. 593
Malagon, Javier, Creative --TBWA Chiat Day Los Angeles, Los Angeles, CA, pg. 1114
Malden, Ronnie, Creative --J. Walter Thompson, Rivonia, South Africa, pg. 567
Maldini, Maria, Creative --GRUPO GALLEGOS, Huntington Beach, CA, pg. 463
Malhoit, Todd, Creative --PUSH22, Pontiac, MI, pg. 940
Malloy, Mark, Creative --EMI STRATEGIC MARKETING, INC., Boston, MA, pg. 1412
Malone, Mike, Creative --THE RICHARDS GROUP, INC., Dallas, TX, pg. 978
Maloney, Suzanne, Creative --Ketchum, San Francisco, CA, pg. 1562
Maloy, Kurt, Creative --CELTIC MARKETING, INC., Niles, IL, pg. 201
Maly, Dave, Creative --Possible Cincinnati, Cincinnati, OH, pg. 1307
Malyon, Ed, Creative --THE PARTNERSHIP, Atlanta, GA, pg. 876
Mambro, Jamie, Creative --MMB, Boston, MA, pg. 767
Man, Jeffrey, Creative --PHOENIX MEDIA GROUP INC., New York, NY, pg. 890
Manchester, Kris, Creative --SID LEE, Montreal, Canada, pg. 1040
Mancuso, Brad, Creative --GREY GROUP, New York, NY, pg. 445
Mandelbaum, Juan, Creative --GEOVISION, Watertown, MA, pg. 423
Mandy, Freddy, Creative --MOTHER LTD., London, United Kingdom, pg. 779
Mangali, Erick, Creative --Deutsch LA, Los Angeles, CA, pg. 302
Mani, Rajesh, Creative --BBH Mumbai, Mumbai, India, pg. 96
Manion, Mark, Creative --H&L Partners, Saint Louis, MO, pg. 470
Manion, Mark, Creative --H&L PARTNERS, San Francisco, CA, pg. 470
Manion, Thomas, Creative --Jack Morton Worldwide, Melbourne, Australia, pg. 583
Manion, Tom, Creative --Jack Morton Worldwide, San Francisco, CA, pg. 583
Manklow, Kevin, Creative --SCRATCH, Toronto, Canada, pg. 1028
Manmohan, Vidya, Creative --Grey Group Middle East Network, Dubai, United Arab Emirates, pg. 452
Mann, Irene, Creative --DMW WORLDWIDE LLC, Chesterbrook, PA, pg. 319
Mann, Luanne, Creative --FECHTOR ADVERTISING LLC, Columbus, OH, pg. 383
Mannan, Aman, Creative --Leo Burnett India, Mumbai, India, pg. 648
Manne, Rob, Creative --Edelman, Toronto, Canada, pg. 1501
Mannes, Peter, Creative --CMT CREATIVE MARKETING TEAM, Houston, TX, pg. 218
Manning, Christer, Creative --FOUNDRY 9 LLC, New York, NY, pg. 399
Manning, Jonathan, Creative --RED THE AGENCY, Edmonton, Canada, pg. 963
Mannion, Julie, Creative --KCD, INC., New York, NY, pg. 1559
Mannschreck, Mark, Creative --TVA MEDIA GROUP, INC., Studio City, CA, pg. 1318
Manny, Michael, Creative --HARLO INTERACTIVE INC., Portland, OR, pg. 480
Manohar, Ketan, Creative --MOXIE SOZO, Boulder, CO, pg. 780
Mansfield, Abby, Creative --HCB HEALTH, Austin, TX, pg. 504
Mansfield, Robert, Creative --THE MAAC GROUP, Lexington, MA, pg. 681
Manuel, Mike, Creative --EVENTIGE MEDIA GROUP, New York, NY, pg. 359
Manuyakorn, Chalit, Creative --BBDO Bangkok, Bangkok, Thailand, pg. 117
Manzella, Keith, Creative --EASTWEST MARKETING GROUP, New York, NY, pg. 336
Manzione, Tom, Creative --THE TOPSPIN GROUP, Princeton, NJ, pg. 1151
Marais, Werner, Creative --Y&R Cape Town, Cape Town, South Africa, pg. 1251
Maravilla, Patrick, Creative --EVB, Oakland, CA, pg. 359
Marcato, Antonio, Creative --CP+B LA, Santa Monica, CA, pg. 241
Marceau, Bill, Creative --GSD&M, Austin, TX, pg. 464
Marceau, Bill, Creative --GSD&M Chicago, Chicago, IL, pg. 465
Marchand, Louis Hugo, Creative --Cossette Communication-Marketing, Quebec, Canada, pg. 238
Marchand, Louis-Hugo, Creative --COSSETTE INC., Quebec, Canada, pg. 237
Marchini, Thomas, Creative --CASON NIGHTINGALE CREATIVE COMMUNICATIONS, New York, NY, pg. 195
Marder, Alicia Dotter, Creative --RPA, Santa Monica, CA, pg. 994
Maree, Daniel, Creative --DEVRIES GLOBAL, New York, NY, pg. 1494
Marguccio, Tom, Creative --Success Advertising, Parsippany, NJ, pg. 1095
Marguccio, Tom, Creative --SUCCESS COMMUNICATIONS GROUP, Parsippany, NJ, pg. 1095
Marholin, Hleb, Creative --WATSON DESIGN GROUP, Los Angeles, CA, pg. 1320
Mariappan, Preethi, Creative --Razorfish Germany, Berlin, Germany, pg. 1310
Marin, Tony, Creative --VML, Kalamazoo, MI, pg. 1319
Marino, Daniel, Creative --RAKA, Portsmouth, NH, pg. 950
Marino, Marco, Creative --BLACKJET INC, Toronto, Canada, pg. 134
Mariotti, Beatrice, Creative --Carre Noir Tokyo, Tokyo, Japan, pg. 934
Mariutto, Pam, Creative --BROADHEAD, Minneapolis, MN, pg. 168
Markham, Nick, Creative --GLASS & MARKER, Oakland, CA, pg. 427
Markley, Amy, Creative --TOM, DICK & HARRY CREATIVE, Chicago, IL, pg. 1149
Markley, Natasha, Creative --THE BROOKLYN BROTHERS, New York, NY, pg. 169
Markovic, Slobodan, Creative --MRM MCCANN, New York, NY, pg. 782
Marks, Jason, Creative --Partners+Napier, New York, NY, pg. 876
Markus, Craig, Creative --Cramer-Krasselt, New York, NY, pg. 243
Marlo, Michele, Creative --ADVANCED MARKETING STRATEGIES, San Diego, CA, pg. 33
Marlow, Jay, Creative --Grey London, London, United Kingdom, pg. 447
Marques, Ricardo, Creative --J. Walter Thompson, Sao Paulo, Brazil, pg. 577
Marrazza, Nick, Creative --CRAMER-KRASSELT, Chicago, IL, pg. 242
Marrocco, Ludovic, Creative --J. WALTER THOMPSON, New York, NY, pg. 565
Marrone, Daniele, Creative --Leo Burnett Rome, Rome, Italy, pg. 643
Marsen, Jay, Creative --Pereira & O'Dell, New York, NY, pg. 883
Marshall, Lana, Creative --SOCIAL DISTILLERY, Austin, TX, pg. 1056
Marshall, Robert, Creative --GHA/DDB, Saint Michael, Barbados, pg. 278
Martell, Chelsea, Creative --QUESTUS, San Francisco, CA, pg. 943
Martell, Dorn, Creative --TINSLEY ADVERTISING, Miami, FL, pg. 1144
Martin, Daniel, Creative --TAPSA, Madrid, Spain, pg. 1224
Martin, David, Creative --HYPHEN COMMUNICATIONS, Vancouver, Canada, pg. 531
Martin, Dean, Creative --CUNDARI INTEGRATED ADVERTISING, Toronto, Canada, pg. 260
Martin, Jason, Creative --LUCKIE & COMPANY, Birmingham, AL, pg. 672
Martin, Jeff, Creative --EPIC MARKETING, Draper, UT, pg. 350
Martin, Lance, Creative --UNION, Toronto, Canada, pg. 1166
Martin, Lori, Creative --THE ST. GREGORY GROUP, INC., Cincinnati, OH, pg. 1071
Martin, Melanie Laurence, Creative --Hill + Knowlton Strategies, Houston, TX, pg. 1541
Martin, Mike, Creative --Ogilvy Johannesburg (Pty.) Ltd., Johannesburg, South Africa, pg. 849
Martin, Nuno, Creative --Grey Madrid, Madrid, Spain, pg. 452
Martin, Phil, Creative --Abbott Mead Vickers BBDO, London, United Kingdom, pg. 112

Responsibilities Index

Responsibilities Index

410
Zywicki, Ron, Creative --DAVID JAMES GROUP, Oakbrook Terrace, IL, pg. 268

Creative Director

Abramovitz, Bill, Creative Director --Ideopia Medical Marketing, Cincinnati, OH, pg. 535
Abudi, Sigal, Creative Director --McCann Erickson, Tel Aviv, Israel, pg. 722
Acosta, Roger, Creative Director --TBWA/Colombia Suiza de Publicidad Ltda, Bogota, Colombia, pg. 1132
Adams, Bill, Creative Director --POTTS MARKETING GROUP LLC, Anniston, AL, pg. 905
Aikens, Kyle, Creative Director --CREATIVE MULTIMEDIA SOLUTIONS LLC, Washington Crossing, PA, pg. 1286
Ainsley, Craig, Creative Director --Anomaly, London, United Kingdom, pg. 60
Ainsley, Craig, Creative Director --Anomaly, London, United Kingdom, pg. 738
Akay, Emrah, Creative Director --Markom/Leo Burnett, Istanbul, Turkey, pg. 646
Al-Asady, Zaid, Creative Director --Deutsch LA, Los Angeles, CA, pg. 302
Al-Samarraie, Dominic, Creative Director --THE RICHARDS GROUP, INC., Dallas, TX, pg. 978
Alam, Shafiq, Creative Director --Impact BBDO, Jeddah, Saudi Arabia, pg. 110
Albores, Peter, Creative Director --BBH LA, West Hollywood, CA, pg. 95
Alder, Bart, Creative Director --ALDER ASSOCIATES, Richmond, VA, pg. 45
Alija, Carlos, Creative Director --Wieden + Kennedy, London, United Kingdom, pg. 1204
Allen, Bill, Creative Director --TETHER, INC., Seattle, WA, pg. 1137
Aminzadeh, Aryan, Creative Director --ELEVEN INC., San Francisco, CA, pg. 343
Anderson, Daryl, Creative Director --CLARK CREATIVE GROUP, Omaha, NE, pg. 213
Anderson, Miles, Creative Director --HORICH HECTOR LEBOW, Hunt Valley, MD, pg. 522
Anderson, Perrin, Creative Director --RPA, Santa Monica, CA, pg. 994
Anderson, Rachel, Creative Director --454 CREATIVE, Orange, CA, pg. 9
Anderson, Ryan, Creative Director --FLUID ADVERTISING, Bountiful, UT, pg. 394
Antoniadis, Alexandros, Creative Director --Grey Group Germany, Dusseldorf, Germany, pg. 449
Aramini, Steven, Creative Director --BAUSERMAN GROUP, Reno, NV, pg. 97
Ariely, Amir, Creative Director --BBR Saatchi & Saatchi, Ramat Gan, Israel, pg. 1003
Ashley, Michael, Creative Director --DigitasLBi, Atlanta, GA, pg. 1290
Assouline, Arnaud, Creative Director --BETC Life, Paris, France, pg. 492
Astolpho, Fabio, Creative Director --F.biz, Sao Paulo, Brazil, pg. 1223
Awasano, Jennifer, Creative Director --DigitasLBi, New York, NY, pg. 1290
Ayce, Kaan, Creative Director --McCann Erickson WorldGroup Turkey, Istanbul, Turkey, pg. 729
Ayrault, Terry, Creative Director --J.R. THOMPSON CO., Farmington Hills, MI, pg. 597
Ayres, Colin, Creative Director --PISTON AGENCY, San Diego, CA, pg. 893
Baeza, Gonzalo, Creative Director --Lowe Porta, Santiago, Chile, pg. 792
Bailey, Steve, Creative Director --SPITBALL LLC, Red Bank, NJ, pg. 1065
Baldwin, David, Creative Director --BALDWIN&, Raleigh, NC, pg. 88
Ball, Robert, Creative Director --The Partners, London, United Kingdom, pg. 1221
Bancud, Elmer, Creative Director --ASTERIX GROUP, San Francisco, CA, pg. 77
Barbush, J, Creative Director --RPA, Santa Monica, CA, pg. 994
Barissever, Selmi, Creative Director --Havas Worldwide Digital Milan, Milan, Italy, pg. 494
Barker, Steve, Creative Director --BARKER & CHRISTOL ADVERTISING, Murfreesboro, TN, pg. 92
Barreras, Alex, Creative Director --PINTA USA LLC, Miami Beach, FL, pg. 892
Barrett, Steve, Creative Director --TETHER, INC., Seattle, WA, pg. 1137
Barrow, Jake, Creative Director --George Patterson Y&R, Melbourne, Australia, pg. 1219
Barry, Mike, Creative Director --Ogilvy Sydney, Saint Leonards, Australia, pg. 840
Battiston, Eduardo, Creative Director --Leo Burnett Tailor Made, Sao Paulo, Brazil, pg. 640
Bayett, Kelly, Creative Director --LUQUIRE GEORGE ANDREWS, INC., Charlotte, NC, pg. 674
Bayett, Kelly, Creative Director --TBWA Chiat Day Los Angeles, Los Angeles, CA, pg. 1114
Baylinson, Lisa, Creative Director --SUASION COMMUNICATIONS GROUP, Somers Point, NJ, pg. 1094
Beaucher, Aaron, Creative Director --NEO-PANGEA, LLC, Reading, PA, pg. 805
Beck, Tyrone, Creative Director --Saatchi & Saatchi, Cape Town, South Africa, pg. 1005
Beckerling, Tim, Creative Director --MetropolitanRepublic, Johannesburg, South Africa, pg. 1220
Behaeghel, Vincent, Creative Director --Havas Worldwide Digital Dusseldorf, Dusseldorf, Germany, pg. 493
Belko, Tomas, Creative Director --Mather Communications s.r.o., Prague, Czech Republic, pg. 830
Bell, Peter, Creative Director --TRACTION FACTORY, Milwaukee, WI, pg. 1153
Bellotti, Fernando, Creative Director --Leo Burnett Mexico S.A. de C.V., Mexico, Mexico, pg. 640
Benivegna, Marybeth, Creative Director --PILOT, New York, NY, pg. 891
Benner, Phillip, Creative Director --Grey Group Germany, Dusseldorf, Germany, pg. 449
Bennett, Greg, Creative Director --B CREATIVE GROUP INC., Baltimore, MD, pg. 84
Bensten, Jessica, Creative Director --RUBIN COMMUNICATIONS GROUP, Virginia Beach, VA, pg. 1642
Bernal, Maru, Creative Director --Lapiz, Chicago, IL, pg. 638
Berth, Tom, Creative Director --Publicis, Brussels, Belgium, pg. 917
Besagni, Juan Marcos, Creative Director --Ogilvy & Mather Argentina, Buenos Aires, Argentina, pg. 837
Bhambhani, Vivek, Creative Director --McCann Erickson India, Mumbai, India, pg. 721
Bianchini, Diana, Creative Director --DI MODA PUBLIC RELATIONS, Beverly Hills, CA, pg. 1494
Bielby, Matt, Creative Director --TAXI Vancouver, Vancouver, Canada, pg. 1112
Bircher, Christian, Creative Director --Spillmann/Felser/Leo Burnett, Zurich, Switzerland, pg. 645
Bisi, Robert, Creative Director --THE COMMUNITY, Miami, FL, pg. 227
Blair, Chris, Creative Director --MAGNETIC IMAGE INC., Evansville, IN, pg. 686
Bloom, Joel, Creative Director --Atmosphere Proximity, New York, NY, pg. 99
Blumberg, Sagi, Creative Director --Gitam/BBDO, Tel Aviv, Israel, pg. 108
Boccardi, Paolo, Creative Director --MCCANN WORLDGROUP S.R.L, Milan, Italy, pg. 732
Bodet, Florian, Creative Director --Ogilvy & Mather, Paris, France, pg. 831
Bogard, Tabitha, Creative Director --MASONBARONET, Dallas, TX, pg. 707
Bogle, Iain, Creative Director --BLOHM CREATIVE PARTNERS, East Lansing, MI, pg. 139
Bohinec, Robert, Creative Director --Pristop Group d.o.o., Ljubljana, Slovenia, pg. 1680
Bois, Todd Allen, Creative Director --MUH-TAY-ZIK HOF-FER, San Francisco, CA, pg. 786
boland, Nicole, Creative Director --VIRGEN ADVERTISING, CORP., Las Vegas, NV, pg. 1178
Bonds, Sam, Creative Director --SANDERS/WINGO ADVERTISING, INC., El Paso, TX, pg. 1016
Bonequi, Israel, Creative Director --ZENERGY COMMUNICATIONS, New York, NY, pg. 1255
Borde, Manuel, Creative Director --TBWA Raad, Dubai, United Arab Emirates, pg. 1127
Bossin, Jeff, Creative Director --Deutsch LA, Los Angeles, CA, pg. 302
Bostoen, Jeroen, Creative Director --TBWA Brussels, Brussels, Belgium, pg. 1117
Bowers, Bryan, Creative Director --BLUEZOOM, Greensboro, NC, pg. 143
Bozkurt, Ozan Can, Creative Director --Medina/Turgul DDB, Beyoglu, Turkey, pg. 289
Braccia, Nick, Creative Director --CAMPFIRE, New York, NY, pg. 188
Bradley, Randy, Creative Director --JORDAN ASSOCIATES, Oklahoma City, OK, pg. 597
Braga, Federico, Creative Director --Saltiveri Ogilvy & Mather, Guayaquil, Ecuador, pg. 839
Braga, Federico, Creative Director --Saltiveri Ogilvy & Mather Guayaquil, Quito, Ecuador, pg. 839
Brannon, Matt, Creative Director --GRAVITY DIGITAL, Conroe, TX, pg. 440
Brenes, Leane, Creative Director --BRENESCO LLC, New York, NY, pg. 163
Breshears, Jason, Creative Director --J. LINCOLN GROUP, The Woodlands, TX, pg. 565
Bright, Will, Creative Director --J. WALTER THOMPSON, New York, NY, pg. 565
Brink, Matthew, Creative Director --Ireland/Davenport, Sandton, South Africa, pg. 1220
Brinkhus, Dave, Creative Director --TRIGHTON INTERACTIVE, Ocoee, FL, pg. 1318
Brittain, Michael, Creative Director --IGNITION INTERACTIVE, Los Angeles, CA, pg. 537
Brock, Tayte, Creative Director --BENNET GROUP, Honolulu, HI, pg. 1452
Brockhoff, Libby, Creative Director --ODYSSEUS ARMS, San Francisco, CA, pg. 825
Broomfield, Rod, Creative Director --OgilvyOne Worldwide Ltd., London, United Kingdom, pg. 837
Brown, Rob, Creative Director --McCann Erickson Advertising Ltd., London, United Kingdom, pg. 729
Brumbley, Kyle, Creative Director --MEDIA MIX, Jacksonville, FL, pg. 743
Brunelle, Tim, Creative Director --BBDO PROXIMITY, Minneapolis, MN, pg. 98
Brusnighan, Todd, Creative Director --mcgarrybowen, Chicago, IL, pg. 734
Bruzzesi, Marcelo, Creative Director --Leo Burnett Tailor Made, Sao Paulo, Brazil, pg. 640
Bryan, Jesse, Creative Director --BELIEF LLC, Seattle, WA, pg. 123
Buchanan, Victoria, Creative Director --Tribal Worldwide London, London, United Kingdom, pg. 1317
Burke, Jim, Creative Director --BURKE ADVERTISING LLC, Bedford, NH, pg. 176
Burke, Ryan, Creative Director --SLATE COMMUNICATIONS, Fort Collins, CO, pg. 1650
Burnay, Tom, Creative Director --BIG AL'S CREATIVE EMPORIUM, London, United Kingdom, pg. 129
Burrin, Joseph, Creative Director --Wieden + Kennedy - Amsterdam, Amsterdam, Netherlands, pg. 1203
Bush, Gerard, Creative Director --BUSH RENZ, Miami, FL, pg. 178
Bystrov, Will, Creative Director --MUSTACHE AGENCY, New York, NY, pg. 796
Byun, Peter, Creative Director --PANCOM INTERNATIONAL, INC., Los Angeles, CA, pg. 871
Cain, Melissa, Creative Director --McCann Erickson Advertising Ltd., London, United Kingdom, pg. 729
Calabrese, Tom, Creative Director --PEARL BRANDS, Fort Myers, FL, pg. 881
Cambiano, Lucas, Creative Director --Ponce Buenos Aires, Buenos Aires, Argentina, pg. 557
Campbell, Milo, Creative Director --Abbott Mead Vickers BBDO, London, United Kingdom, pg. 112
Canchola, Serafin, Creative Director --FUSEBOXWEST, Los Angeles, CA, pg. 410
Candido, Jeff, Creative Director --Leo Burnett USA, Chicago, IL, pg. 639
Candor, Rob, Creative Director --CARING MARKETING SOLUTIONS, Columbus, OH, pg. 191
Cano, Adrian, Creative Director --PM PUBLICIDAD, Atlanta, GA, pg. 898
Cano, Roger, Creative Director --TBWA Espana, Barcelona, Spain, pg. 1123
Carcavilla, Kiko, Creative Director --Lowe Porta, Santiago, Chile, pg. 792
Cardenas, Cassandra, Creative Director --TRANSMEDIA GROUP, Boca Raton, FL, pg. 1665
Cardenas, Juan, Creative Director --Ogilvy & Mather, Bogota, Colombia, pg. 839
Carella, Patrick, Creative Director --FCB Garfinkel, New York, NY, pg. 371
Carlton, Rory, Creative Director --ARKETI GROUP, Atlanta, GA, pg. 69

Responsibilities Index

Responsibilities Index

Responsibilities Index

Direct Marketing/Direct Response

Media Buyer

Media Director

Media Planner

New Business Contact

Print Production

Public Relations

Traffic